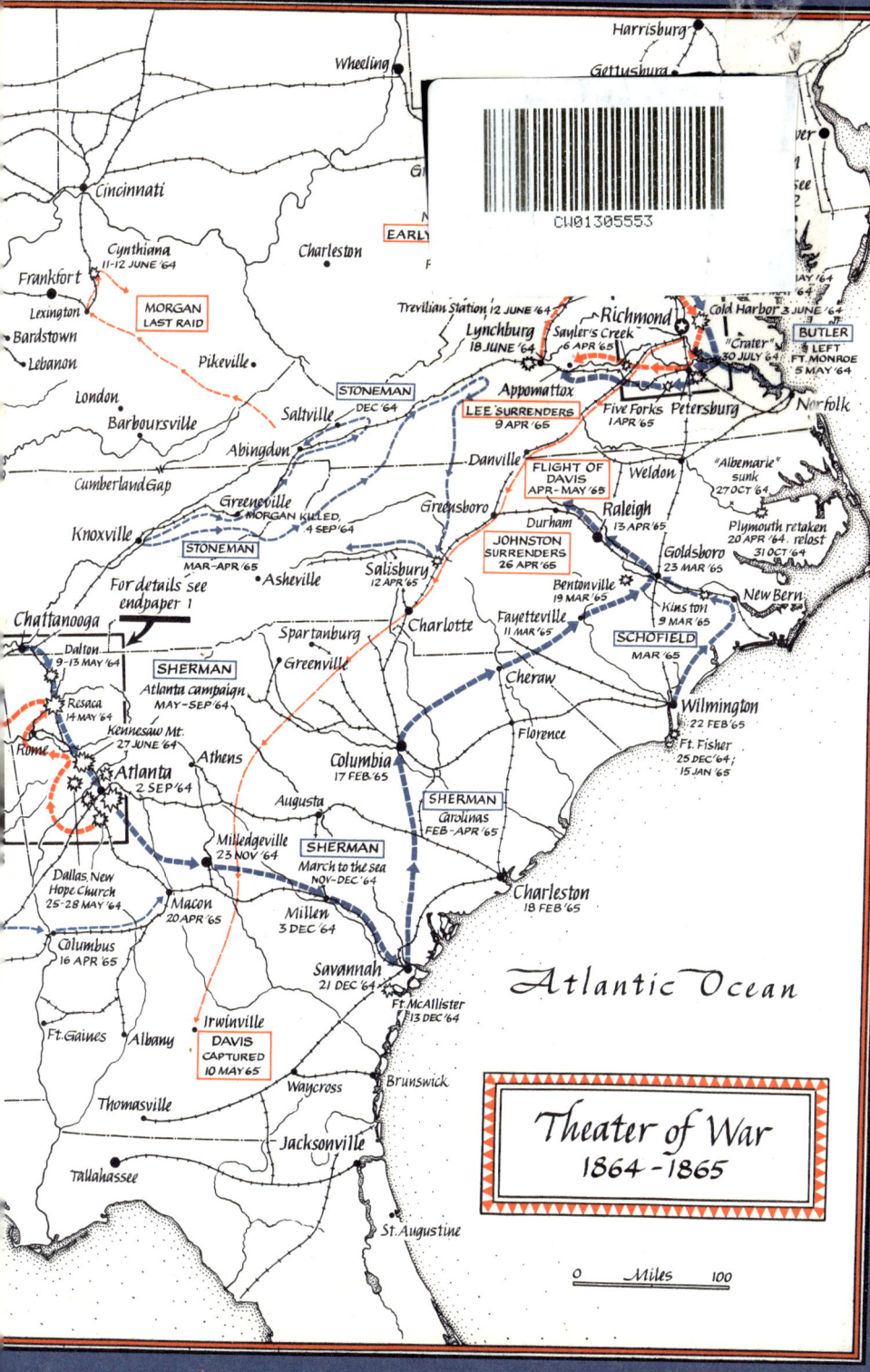

The Civil War
A Narrative

ALL THESE WERE HONOURED IN THEIR GENERATIONS

AND WERE THE GLORY OF THEIR TIMES

THERE BE OF THEM

THAT HAVE LEFT A NAME BEHIND THEM

THAT THEIR PRAISES MIGHT BE REPORTED

AND SOME THERE BE WHICH HAVE NO MEMORIAL

WHO ARE PERISHED AS THOUGH THEY HAD NEVER BEEN

AND ARE BECOME AS THOUGH THEY HAD NEVER BEEN BORN

AND THEIR CHILDREN AFTER THEM

BUT THESE WERE MERCIFUL MEN

WHOSE RIGHTEOUSNESS HATH NOT BEEN FORGOTTEN

WITH THEIR SEED SHALL CONTINUALLY REMAIN

A GOOD INHERITANCE

AND THEIR CHILDREN ARE WITHIN THE COVENANT

THEIR SEED STANDETH FAST

AND THEIR CHILDREN FOR THEIR SAKES

THEIR SEED SHALL REMAIN FOR EVER

AND THEIR GLORY SHALL NOT BE BLOTTED OUT

THEIR BODIES ARE BURIED IN PEACE

BUT THEIR NAME LIVETH FOR EVERMORE

Ecclesiasticus xliv

THE Civil War

A Narrative

---   ★ ★ ★   ---

RED RIVER *to* APPOMATTOX

---   ★ ★ ★   ---

By SHELBY FOOTE

RANDOM HOUSE · NEW YORK

2011 Modern Library Edition

Copyright © 1974 and copyright renewed 2002 by Shelby Foote

All rights reserved.

Published in the United States by Modern Library, an imprint of
The Random House Publishing Group, a division of
Random House, Inc., New York.

MODERN LIBRARY and the TORCHBEARER Design are
registered trademarks of Random House, Inc.

This work was originally published in hardcover in 1974 by
Random House, an imprint of The Random House Publishing Group,
a division of Random House, Inc.

ISBN 978-0-679-64370-8

Printed in China on acid-free paper

www.modernlibrary.com

2 4 6 8 9 7 5 3 1

Case and box photographs: Library of Congress

CONTENTS

★ ✗ ☆

I

1. Another Grand Design   3
2. The Forty Days   146
3. Red Clay Minuet   318

II

4. War Is Cruelty ...   427
5. You Cannot Refine It   627

III

6. A Tightening Noose   735
7. Victory, and Defeat   802
8. Lucifer in Starlight   957

LIST OF MAPS, BIBLIOGRAPHICAL NOTE, AND INDEX   1061

☆ I ☆

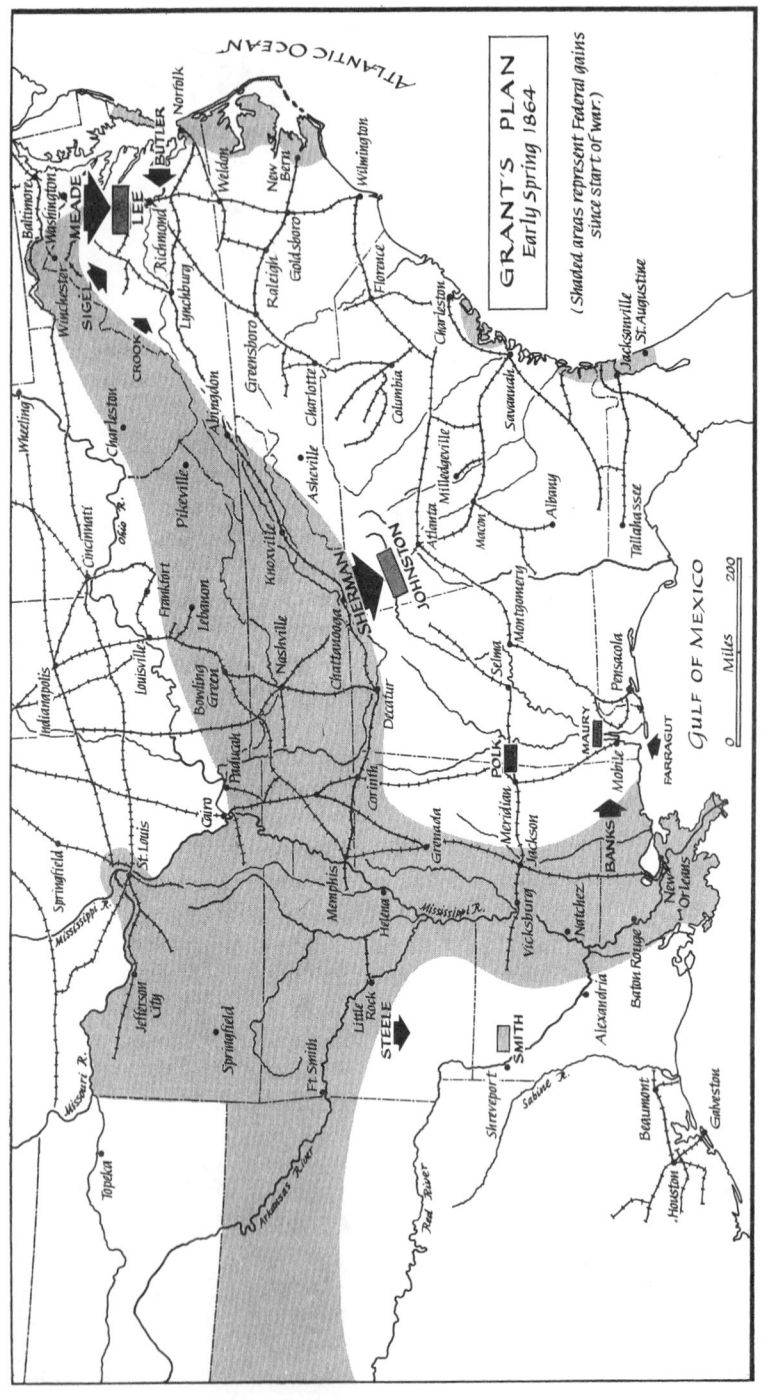

CHAPTER

× 1 ×

Another Grand Design

★ ✗ ☆

LATE AFTERNOON OF A RAW, GUSTY DAY in early spring — March 8, a Tuesday, 1864 — the desk clerk at Willard's Hotel, two blocks down Pennsylvania Avenue from the White House, glanced up to find an officer accompanied by a boy of thirteen facing him across the polished oak of the registration counter and inquiring whether he could get a room. "A short, round-shouldered man in a very tarnished major general's uniform," he seemed to a bystanding witness to have "no gait, no station, no manner," to present instead, with his ill-fitting jacket cut full in the skirt and his high-crowned hat set level on his head, a somewhat threadbare, if not quite down-at-heels, conglomerate impression of "rough, light-brown whiskers, a blue eye, and rather a scrubby look withal . . . as if he was out of office and on half pay, with nothing to do but hang round the entry of Willard's, cigar in mouth." Discerning so much of this as he considered worth his time, together perhaps with the bystander's added observation that the applicant had "rather the look of a man who did, or once did, take a little too much to drink," the clerk was no more awed by the stranger's rank than he was attracted by his aspect. This was, after all, the best known hostelry in Washington. There had been by now close to five hundred Union generals, and of these the great majority, particularly among those who possessed what was defined as "station," had checked in and out of Willard's in the past three wartime years. In the course of its recent and rapid growth, under the management of a pair of Vermont brothers who gave it their name along with their concern, it had swallowed whole, together with much other adjacent real estate, a former Presbyterian church; the President-elect himself had stayed here through the ten days preceding his inauguration, making of its Parlor 6 a "little White House," and it was here, one dawn two years ago in one of its upper rooms, that Julia Ward Howe had written her "Battle Hymn of the Republic," the anthem for the crusade the new President had begun to design as soon as he took office. Still, bright or tarnished, stars were stars; a certain respect was owed, if not to the man who wore them, then in any case to the rank they signified; the clerk replied at last that he would give him what he had, a small top-floor room, if that would do. It would, the other said, and when the register was given its practiced half-circle twirl he signed without delay. The desk clerk turned it back again, still maintaining the accustomed, condescending air he was about to lose in shock when he read what the weathered applicant had written: "U.S. Grant & Son — Galena, Illinois."

Whereupon (for such was the aura that had gathered about the name "Unconditional Surrender" Grant, hero of Donelson, conqueror of Vicksburg, deliverer of Chattanooga) there was an abrupt transformation, not only in the attitude of the clerk, whose eyes seemed to start from his head at the sight of the signature and who struck the bell with a force that brought on the double all the bellboys within earshot, but also in that of the idlers, the loungers roundabout the lobby, who soon learned the cause of the commotion in the vicinity of the desk. It was as if the prayers of the curious had been answered after the flesh. Here before them, in the person of this undistinguished-looking officer — forty-one years of age, five feet eight inches tall, and weighing just under a hundred and forty pounds in his scuffed boots and shabby clothes — was the man who, in the course of the past twenty-five months of a war in which the news had mostly been unwelcome from the Federal point of view, had captured two rebel armies, entire, and chased a third clean out of sight beyond the roll of the southern horizon. Now that he made a second visual assessment, more deliberate and above all more informed than the first, the bystander who formerly had seen only an "ordinary, scrubby-looking man, with a slightly seedy look," perceived that there was more to him than had been apparent before the authentication that came with the fixing of the name. The "blue eye" became "a clear blue eye," and the once stolid-seeming face took on "a look of resolution, as if he could not be trifled with."

Such, then, was the effect of the gathered aura. And yet there was a good deal more to it than fame, past or present. There was also anticipation, and of a particular national form. Just last week, on Leap Year Day, the President had signed a congressional act reviving the grade of lieutenant general, and Grant had been summoned east to receive in person his promotion, together with command of all the armies of the Union, which he was expected to lead at last to final victory over the forces that had threatened its destruction. Forgotten now was the small top-floor room his modesty had been willing to accept. Instead, the clerk obsequiously tendered the distinguished guest "the best in the house": meaning Parlor 6, where Abraham Lincoln himself had held court in the days preceding his inauguration, less than one week more than three years ago today.

Grant accepted this as he had the other, with neither eagerness nor protest, which caused a second witness to remark upon "his shy but manly bearing." Still another even saw virtue in the dead-level way he wore his hat. "He neither puts it on behind his ears, nor draws it over his eyes; much less does he cock it on one side, but sets it straight and very hard on his head." A fourth believed he detected something else beneath the general's "rough dignity" of surface. "He habitually wears an expression as if he had determined to drive his head through a brick wall, and was about to do it." Just now though, here in the close atmosphere of the lobby of Willard's — which a disgruntled Englishman complained was compounded, in about equal parts, of "heat, noise, dust, smoke, and expectoration" — what he mainly seemed to desire was an absence of fanfare.

But that was not to be. For a week now the town talk had been of his imminent arrival, and now that the talkers had him within actual reach they intended to make the most of him. Returning downstairs presently for dinner in the main dining room, and holding his son Fred by the hand as if for mutual reassurance, he managed to get as far as his table and even to order the meal before he was recognized by a gentleman from New Orleans who came over for a handshake. Then, as before, all hope of privacy ended. Word of his presence "spread from table to table," according to one who was there; "people got up and craned their necks in an anxious endeavor to see 'the coming man.'" This reached a climax when one of the watchers, unable to contain his enthusiasm, mounted a chair and called — prematurely, for the promotion had not yet been conferred — for "Three cheers for Lieutenant General Grant!" These were given "in the most tremendous manner" and were followed by a pounding that made the glasses and silverware dance on the tables, "in the midst of which General Grant, looking very much astonished and perhaps annoyed, rose to his feet, awkwardly rubbed his mustache with his napkin, bowed, and resumed his seat." For a time, good sense prevailed; "the general was allowed to eat in peace." But when he rose again and began to make his way out, once more with his son in tow, a Pennsylvania congressman took him in hand and began a round of introductions. "This was his first levee," the witness added; after which his retreat through the crowded lobby and up the staircase to his rooms was characterized by "most unsoldierly blushing."

Hard as this was on a man who valued his privacy and was discomfited by adulation, before the night was over he would find himself at storm center of an even worse ordeal. Word of his arrival having spread, he found on his return to Parlor 6 a special invitation to come by the White House, presumably for a conference with the Commander in Chief, whom he had never met although they both were from Illinois and were by now the two most famous men in the country.

If he had known that the President's weekly receptions were held on Tuesday evenings he would perhaps have postponed his call, but by the time he completed the short walk up the avenue to the gates of the executive mansion it was too late. He found himself being ushered up the steps, through the foyer, down a corridor, and finally into the brightly lighted East Room, where the reception was in full swing. The crowd, enlarged beyond the norm tonight by the news that he would be there, fell silent as he entered, then parted before him to disclose at the far end of the room the tall form of Abraham Lincoln, who watched him approach, then put out a long arm for a handshake. "I'm glad to see you, General," he said.

The crowd resumed its "stir and buzz"; there was a spattering of applause and even "a cheer or two," which struck Navy Secretary Gideon Welles as "rowdy and unseemly." Lincoln turned Grant over to Secretary of State William H. Seward for presentation to Mrs Lincoln, who took his arm for a turn round the room while her husband followed at a distance, apparently much amused by the general's reaction to being placed thus on display before a crowd that soon began to get somewhat out of hand, surging toward him, men and women alike, for a close-up look and a possible exchange of greetings. Grant "blushed like a schoolgirl," sweating heavily from embarrassment and the exertion of shaking the hands of those who managed to get nearest in the jam. "Stand up so we can all have a look at you!" someone cried from the rim of the crowd, and he obliged by stepping onto a red plush sofa, looking out over the mass of upturned faces whose eyes fairly shone with delight at being part of an authentic historical tableau. "It was the only real mob I ever saw in the White House," a journalist later wrote, describing how "people were caught up and whirled in the torrent which swept through the great East Room. Ladies suffered dire disaster in the crush and confusion; their laces were torn and crinolines mashed, and many got up on sofas, chairs, and tables to be out of harm's way or to get a better view of the spectacle.... For once at least the President of the United States was not the chief figure in the picture. The little, scared-looking man who stood on a crimson-covered sofa was the idol of the hour."

Rescued from this predicament — or, as the newsman put it, "smuggled out by friendly hands" — Grant presently found himself closeted in a smaller chamber, which in time he would learn to identify as the Blue Room, with the President and the Secretary of War, Edwin M. Stanton. Lincoln informed him that he would be given his lieutenant general's commission at a ceremony here next day and would be expected to reply to a short speech, "only four sentences in all, which I will read from my manuscript as an example which you may follow ... as you are perhaps not so much accustomed to public speaking as I am." For guidance in preparing his reply, he gave him a copy of what he himself would say, together with two suggestions for remarks which he hoped the general would incorporate in his response: first, something that would "prevent or obviate any jealousy" on the part of the generals about to come under his command, and second, something that would put him "on as good terms as possible with the Army of the Potomac," to which he was a stranger. "If you see any objection to doing this," Lincoln added as a final sign of consideration for a man about to be cast in an unfamiliar role, "be under no restraint whatever in expressing that objection to the Secretary of War."

Grant expressed no objection, but as he returned to the hotel after midnight for his first sleep in Washington he was perhaps regretful that he had ever left the West, where life was at once less pushy and more informal, and convinced no doubt of the wisdom of his resolution to go back there at the first opportunity.

Returning next day to the White House for the ceremony that would correspond to a laying-on of hands, he brought with him his chief of staff and fellow townsman, Brigadier General John Rawlins, who had come east with him from Nashville in response to the presidential summons, and the thirteen-year-old Fred. Promptly at 1 o'clock, as scheduled, the Galena trio was shown into the presence of the President, the seven members of his Cabinet, his private secretary John Nicolay, and Major General Henry W. Halleck, the present general-in-chief, over whose head the man they had gathered to honor was about to be advanced. Facing Grant, Lincoln handed him the official document and read the speech of which he had given him a copy the night before. "General Grant: The nation's appreciation of what you have done and its reliance upon you for what remains to do in the existing great struggle are now presented with this commission, constituting you lieutenant general in the Army of the United States. With this high honor devolves upon you also a corresponding responsibility. As the country herein trusts you, so under God it will sustain you. I scarcely need to add that with what I here speak for the nation goes my own hearty personal concurrence." Brief as this was, Grant's response was briefer by seven words. He took from his coat pocket a half-sheet of notepaper covered with a hasty lead-pencil scrawl. Either the light was poor or else he had trouble reading his own writing. In any case he read it badly. "Mr President," he replied, groping and hesitant as he strained to decipher the words: "I accept this commission with gratitude for the high honor conferred. With the aid of the noble armies that have fought on so many fields, it will be my earnest endeavor not to disappoint your expectations. I feel the full weight of the responsibilities now devolving on me and know that if they are met it will be due to those armies, and above all to the favor of that Providence which leads both nations and men."

The surprise in this, to anyone aware of the Blue Room exchange the night before, was that the general had not incorporated either of the remarks the President recommended for inclusion in his acceptance speech. Nicolay, for one, thought that Grant, in an attempt to establish an independence none of his predecessors had enjoyed, had decided it would be wise to begin his career as general-in-chief by disregarding any suggestions from above. Lincoln himself, on the other hand, seemed not to notice the omission which his secretary considered, if not a downright act of insubordination, then in any case a snub.

Once the congratulations were over, the two leaders had a short talk that began with Grant asking what special service was required of him. The taking of Richmond, Lincoln said, adding wryly that the generals who had been told this in the past "had not been fortunate in their efforts in that direction." Did Grant think he could do it? Grant replied that he could if he had the troops, whereupon Lincoln assured him that he would have them. That ended their first strategy conference, such as it was, and Nicolay observed that nothing was said as to the route or method to be employed, the jump-off date, or the amount of time the operation would require. All Grant said was that he could take Richmond if he had the troops, and Lincoln had been willing to let it go at that; after which the general took his leave. He was going down to Virginia today, specifically to Brandy Station, headquarters of the Army of the Potomac, for a consultation with its commander as a prelude to the planning of his over-all campaign.

One thing remained to be done before he got aboard the train. No truly recognizable photograph had been made of him since the early days of the war, when his beard reached the middle buttons on his blouse, and he had agreed — perhaps without considering that he thus would lose the near-anonymity he had enjoyed among strangers up to now — to an appointment that would remedy the lack. Accompanied by Stanton, who proposed to go to the station to see him off, he rode from the White House, down Pennsylvania Avenue, to the intersection of Seventh Street, where the carriage stopped in front of Mathew Brady's Portrait Gallery. The photographer was waiting anxiously, and wasted no time in getting the general upstairs into what he called his "operating room," where he had four of his big cameras ready for action. It was past 4 o'clock by now and the light was failing; so while Grant took his place in a chair on which the cameras, their lenses two full feet in length and just under half a foot in diameter, were trained like a battery of siege guns, Brady sent an assistant up on the roof to draw back the shade from the skylight directly overhead. To his horror, the fellow stumbled, both feet crashing through the glass to let fall a shower of jagged shards around the general below. "It was a miracle that some of the pieces didn't strike him," the photographer later said. "And if one had, it would have been the end of Grant; for that glass was two inches thick." Still more surprising, in its way, was the general's reaction. He glanced up casually, with "a barely perceptible quiver of the nostril," then as casually back down, and that was all. This seemed to Brady "the most remarkable display of nerve I ever witnessed."

It was otherwise with Stanton, who appeared unstrung: not only for Grant's sake, as it turned out, but also for his own, though none of the splinters had landed anywhere near him. Grasping the photographer by the arm, he pulled him aside and sputtered excitedly, "Not a word about this, Brady, not a word! You must never breathe a word of what happened here today.... It would be impossible to convince the people that this was not an attempt at assassination!"

The train made good time from Alexandria, chuffing through Manassas and Warrenton Junction, on to Brandy, a distance of just under sixty miles; Grant arrived in a driving rain, soon after nightfall, to find that the Army of the Potomac, whatever its shortcomings in other respects — there was scarcely a place-name on the landscape that did not mark the scene of one or more of its defeats — knew how to greet a visitor in style. A regiment of Zouaves, snappy in red fezzes and baggy trousers, was drawn up to give him a salute on his arrival, despite the rain, and a headquarters band, happily unaware that Grant was tone-deaf — he once remarked that he only knew two tunes in all: "One was Yankee Doodle. The other wasn't" — played vigorous music by way of welcome as the army commander, Major General George G. Meade, emerged from his tent for a salute and a handshake. He and Grant, six years his junior and eight years behind him at West Point, had not met since the Mexican War, sixteen years ago, when they were lieutenants.

Tall and dour, professorial in appearance, with a hook nose, a gray-shot beard, glinting spectacles, and heavy pouches under his eyes, Meade was one of the problems that would have to be dealt with before other, larger problems could be tackled. Specifically, the question was whether to keep him where he was, a prima donna commander of a prima donna army, or remove him. His trouble, aside from a hair-trigger temper that kept his staff on edge and caused associates to refer to him, behind his back, as "a damned old goggle-eyed snapping turtle," was that he lacked the quality which Grant not only personified himself but also prized highest in a subordinate: the killer instinct. At Gettysburg eight months ago, after less than a week in command, Meade had defeated and driven the rebel invaders from his native Pennsylvania, but then, with his foe at bay on the near bank of a flooded, bridgeless river, had flinched from delivering the coup de grâce which Lincoln, for one, was convinced would have ended the war. Instead, the Confederates, low on ammunition and bled down to not much more than half their strength, had withdrawn unmolested across the rain-swollen Potomac to take up a new defensive position behind the Rapidan, where they still were. Meade had crossed in late November, with the intention of coming to grips with them in the wintry south-bank thickets, but then at the last minute had held his hand; had returned, in fact, ingloriously to the north bank, and ever since had seemed content to settle for the stalemate that resulted, despite practically unremitting prodding from the press and the politicians in his rear. Just last week he had been grilled by Congress's radical-dominated Joint Committee on the Conduct of the War, whose members for the most part, in admiration of his politics and his bluster, favored recalling Major General Joseph Hooker to the post he had lost to Meade on the eve of Gettysburg. Much bitterness had ensued between the Pennsylvanian and his critics; "My enemies," he called them in a letter this week to a kinsman, maintaining that they consisted "of certain politicians who wish me removed to restore Hooker; then of certain subordinates, whose military reputations are involved in the destruction of mine; finally, [of] a class of vultures who in Hooker's day preyed upon the army, and who sigh for a return of those glorious days."

This was accurate enough, as far as it went, but it seemed to Grant — as, indeed, it must have done to even a casual observer — that the trouble lay deeper, in the ranks of the army itself. Partly the reason was boredom, a lack of employment in the craft for which its members had been trained. "A winter in tents is monotonous," one officer complained. "Card playing, horse racing, and kindred amusements become stale when made a steady occupation." Moreover, Grant would have agreed with an assessment later made by a young West Pointer, a newcomer like himself to the eastern theater, that the trouble with the Army of the Potomac, predating both Meade and Hooker, was its "lack of springy formation and audacious, self-reliant initiative. This organic weakness was entirely due to not having had in its youth skillfully aggressive leadership. Its early commanders had dissipated war's best elixir by training it into a life of caution, and the evil of that schooling it had shown on more than one occasion."

Before coming down to Brandy, Grant had rather inclined to the belief that the removal of Meade was a prerequisite to correction of this state of mind in the army he commanded. But once the round of greetings and introductions had ended and the corps and division commanders had retired for the night, leaving the two men alone for a private conference, Meade showed Grant a side of himself that proved not only attractive but disarming. He began by saying that he supposed Grant would want to replace him with some general who had served with him before and was therefore familiar with his way of doing things: Major General William T. Sherman, for example, who had been Grant's mainstay in practically all of his campaigns to date. If so, Meade declared, he hoped there would be no hesitation on his account, since (as Grant paraphrased it afterwards) "the work before us was of such vast importance to the whole nation that the feeling or wishes of no one person should stand in the way of selecting the right men for all positions. For himself, he would serve to the best of his ability wherever placed." Grant was impressed. The offer, he said, gave him "even a more favorable opinion of Meade than did his great victory at Gettysburg," and he assured him, then and there, that he had "no thought of substituting anyone for him," least of all Sherman, who "could not be spared from the West." Now it was Meade who was impressed, and he said as much the following day in a letter to his wife. "I was much pleased with Grant," he wrote, "and most agreeably disappointed in his evidence of mind and character. You may rest assured he is not an ordinary man."

Mutual admiration on the part of the two leaders might be a good and healthy thing for all concerned, but the troops themselves, having paid in blood for the blasting of a number of overblown reputations in the drawn-out course of the war, were unconvinced and noncommittal. While this latest addition to the doleful list of their commanders was on his way eastward, they had engaged in some rather idle speculation as to his professional ability, and it did not seem to them that the mere addition of a third star to each of his shoulders would necessarily increase his military worth.

"Who's this Grant that's made a lieutenant general?"

"He's the hero of Vicksburg."

"Well, Vicksburg wasn't much of a fight. The rebs were out of rations and they had to surrender or starve. They had nothing but dead mules and dogs to eat, as I understand."

About the best thing they could say for him was that he was unlikely to be any worse than John Pope, who had also brought a western reputation east, only to lose it at Bull Run. "He cannot be weaker or more inefficient," a jaundiced New York veteran declared, "than the generals who have wasted the lives of our comrades during the past three years." For one thing, Grant was likely to find a good deal less room between bullets here in Virginia than he had found in the region of his fame. "If he's a fighter," another hard-case infantryman put it, "he can find all the fighting he wants." Then he arrived and some of them got a look at him. What they saw was scarcely reassuring.

"Well, what do you think?" one asked a friend, who replied thoughtfully, having studied the firm-set mouth and the level glance of the clear blue eyes:

"He looks as if he meant it."

Nodding agreement, the first allowed that they would find out for themselves before too long. Meanwhile he was willing to defer judgment, except as to looks. "He's a little 'un," he said.

Talk of Vicksburg brought on the inevitable comparison of western and eastern Confederates, with particular reference to the presence here in the Old Dominion of General Robert E. Lee, the South's first soldier. Grant could never have penned up Lee, as he had done John Pemberton, thereby forcing his surrender by starvation; Lee, they said, "would have broken out some way and foraged around for supplies." Thus the men. And Rawlins, as he moved among the officers on Meade's staff, found a similar respect for the southern commander, as if they took almost as great a pride in having opposed "Mars Robert" as the Virginian's tattered veterans took in serving under him. "Well, you never met Bobby Lee and his boys," they replied when Grant's chief of staff presumed to speak of victories in the West. "It would be quite different if you had." As for the campaign about to open here in the East, they seemed to expect nothing more than another version of the old story: advance and retreat, Grant or no Grant. They listened rather impatiently while Rawlins spoke of past successes, off on the far margin of the map. "That may be," they said. "But, mind you, Bobby Lee is just over the Rapidan."

In any case, whatever opinions had been formed or deferred, the new chieftain and his major eastern army had at least had a look at each other, and next morning, after a second conference at which both past and future campaigns in Virginia were discussed, Grant returned to the station and got aboard the train for Washington. Last night he had received a presidential telegram extending an invitation from Mrs Lincoln for him and Meade "to dine with us Saturday evening," and he had replied by wire that they were pleased to accept. Overnight, however, he changed his mind. Today was Friday, March 11, and he would be leaving at once for the West — but only for a visit of a week or ten days, in order to confer with Sherman and other commanders there; after which, despite his previous resolution to avoid the political snares so thickly strewn about the eastern theater, he would be returning here to stay. Paradoxically, now that he had seen them at first hand, it was just those snares that determined his decision. "When I got to Washington and saw the situation," he later explained, "it was plain that here was the point for the commanding general to be. No one else could, probably, resist the pressure that would be brought to bear upon him to desist from his own plans and pursue others."

Not that the adulation and the invasions of his privacy did not continue to go against his grain. They did indeed. Closeted that afternoon with the President at the White House, he complained that the past three days, in Washington and at Brandy, had been "rather the warmest campaign I have witnessed during the war." Lincoln could sympathize with this, but he was disappointed that the general would not stay on through tomorrow night for the banquet planned in his honor. "We can't excuse you," he protested. "Mrs Lincoln's dinner without you would be *Hamlet* with Hamlet left out." But Grant was firm. "I appreciate the honor Mrs Lincoln would do me," he said, "but time is very important now. And really, Mr Lincoln," he added frankly, "I have had enough of this show business."

He left that evening on a westbound train, with stops for inspection at several points along the way, and reached Nashville in time to keep a St Patrick's Day appointment with Sherman, whose troops were advanced beyond Chattanooga, into northwest Georgia, to confront the main western Confederate army under General Joseph E. Johnston, around Dalton. They traveled together by rail to Cincinnati, the voluble red-head, "tall, angular, and spare, as if his superabundant energy had consumed his flesh" — so an acquaintance saw him at the time — and the new lieutenant general, who had once been described as "a man who could be silent in several languages" and who now seemed doubly reticent by contrast with his talkative companion. In the Ohio city they left the cars and checked into a hotel for privacy and room to spread their maps. There they worked on a preliminary draft of the over-all campaign which Sherman defined long afterwards: "He was to go for Lee and I was to go for Joe Johnston. That was his plan."

That was what it basically was. That was what it came to, in the end. At the outset, however, the plan — which might better have been defined, at this stage, as a plan for a plan — was a good deal more complicated, involving a great many other forces that were thrown, or were intended to be thrown, into action against the South. Grant had under him more than half a million combat soldiers, "present for duty, equipped," about half of them in the ranks of six field armies, three in the East and three in the West, while the other half were scattered about the country in nineteen various departments, from New England to New Mexico and beyond. His notion was to pry as many as possible of the latter out of their garrisons, transfer them to the mobile forces in the field, and bring the resultant mass to bear in "a simultaneous movement all along the line." Long ago in Mexico, during a lull in the war, he had written home to the girl he later married: "If we have to fight, I would like to do it all at once and then make friends." Apparently he felt even more this way about it now that the enemy were his fellow countrymen. In any case, the plan as he evolved it seemed to indicate as much.

"From an early period of the rebellion," he said afterward, looking back, "I had been impressed with the idea that active and continuous operations of all the troops that could be brought into the field, regardless of season and weather, were necessary to a speedy termination of the war." The trouble from the outset, east and west, was that the Federal armies had "acted independently and without concert, like a balky team, no two ever pulling together, enabling the enemy to use to great advantage his interior lines of communication." It was this that had made possible several of the greatest Confederate triumphs, from First Bull Run to Chickamauga, where reinforcements from other rebel departments and even other theaters had tipped the tactical scale against the

Union. "I determined to stop this," Grant declared. Moreover, convinced as he was "that no peace could be had that would be stable and conducive to the happiness of the people, both North and South, until the military power of the rebellion was entirely broken," he held fast to his old guideline; he would work toward Unconditional Surrender. He had it very much in mind to destroy not only the means of resistance by his adversaries, but also the will. The Confederacy was not only to be defeated, it was to be defeated utterly, and not only in the field, where the battles were fought, but also on the home front, where the goods of war were produced. "War is cruelty," Sherman had said four months ago, in response to a southern matron's complaint that his men appeared hardhanded on occasion. "There is no use trying to reform it. The crueler it is, the sooner it will be over." Grant felt much the same way about the matter, and here at the start, in formulating his plan for achieving what he called "a speedy termination," he was determined to be guided by two principles of action: 1) "to use the greatest number of troops practicable," and 2) "to hammer continuously against the armed force of the enemy and his resources, until by mere attrition, if in no other way, there should be nothing left to him but an equal submission with the loyal section of our common country to the Constitution and the laws of the land."

To achieve the first of these, the concentration of fighting men on the actual firing line, he proposed that most of the troops now scattered along the Atlantic coast, in Florida, Georgia, and the Carolinas, be brought to Virginia for a convergent attack on Richmond and the army posted northward in its defense. All down the littoral, various forces of various sizes were attempting to make their way toward various objectives, few if any of them vital to Grant's main purpose. Accordingly, he prepared orders for abandoning all such efforts south of the James, along with as much of the region so far occupied as was not clearly needed to maintain or strengthen the naval blockade. The same would apply in the West, along the Mississippi River from New Orleans to Cairo, where the men thus gained were to be employed in a similar convergence upon Atlanta and the forces likewise posted in its defense. As for the troops held deep in the national rear, serving mainly by their numbers to justify the lofty rank of political or discredited generals assigned to duty there, Grant proposed to abolish some of these commands by merging superfluous departments, thus freeing the men for duty at the front. As for the generals themselves, useless as most of them were for combat purposes, he favored their outright dismissal, which would open the way for just that many promotions in the field. Though this last was rather a ticklish business, verging as it did on the political, he thought it altogether worth a try because of the added opportunities it would afford him to reward the ablest and bravest of his subordinate commanders, even before the fighting got under way, and thus incite the rest to follow their example. By such methods (though little came of the last; out of more than a hundred generals Grant recommended for removal, Lincoln let no more than a handful go, mindful as he had to be of the danger of making influential enemies with the presidential election less than nine months off) he would reduce the ratio of garrison to combat troops from one-to-one to one-to-two, which in itself was a considerable accomplishment, one that no previous general-in-chief, from Winfield Scott through George McClellan to Henry Halleck, had conceived to be possible even as a goal.

As for his method of employing that continuous hammering which he believed was the surest if not the only way to bring the South to her knees, the key would be found in orders presently issued to the commanders involved: "So far as practicable all the armies are to move together, and toward one common center." This was to be applied in two stages. West and East, there would be separate but simultaneous convergences upon respective goals, Atlanta and Richmond, by all the mobile forces within each theater; after which, the first to be successful in accomplishing that preliminary task — the reduction of the assigned objective, along with the defeat of the rebel army charged with its defense — would turn east or west, as the case might be, to join the other and thus be in on the kill, the "speedy termination" for which Grant had conceived his grand design. It was for this, the western half of it at least, that he had come to Tennessee to confer with Sherman, his successor in command of the largest of the three main armies in this and the enormous adjoining theater beyond the Mississippi.

There the commanders of the Departments of the Gulf and Arkansas, Major Generals Nathaniel P. Banks and Frederick Steele, were engaged in the opening phase of a campaign of which Grant disapproved and which they themselves had undertaken reluctantly on orders from Lincoln, issued through Halleck before Grant was given over-all command. Advancing on Shreveport by way of Red River, which would afford them gunboat support, they were charged with the invasion and conquest of East Texas, not because there was much of strategic importance there, but because of certain machinations by the French in Mexico, which Lincoln thought it best to block by the occupation of Texas, thus to prevent a possible link-up between the forces of Napoleon III and those of the Confederacy, with which that monarch was believed to be sympathetic. Grant opposed the plan, not because of its international implications, of which he knew little and understood less, but because of its interference with, or in any case its nonfurtherance of, his design for ending the rebellion by concentrating "the greatest number of troops practicable" against its military and manufacturing centers. None of these was in the Lone Star State, so far at least as he could see, or for that matter anywhere else in the Transmississippi, which he preferred to leave to the incidental attention of Steele alone, while

Banks moved eastward, across the Mississippi, to play a truly vital role in the drama now being cast. Yet here he was, not only moving in the opposite direction, but taking with him no less than 10,000 of Sherman's best soldiers, temporarily assigned by Halleck to assist him in seizing the Texas barrens. Grant found this close to intolerable, and though he could not directly countermand an order issued by authority of the Commander in Chief, he could at least set a limit to the extent of the penetration and, above all, to the amount of time allowed for the execution of the order, and thus ensure that Sherman would get his veterans back in time for the opening of the offensive in northwest Georgia. Accordingly, two days before Sherman joined him in Nashville on March 17, he wrote to Banks informing him that, while he regarded "the success of your present move as of great importance in reducing the number of troops necessary for protecting the navigation of the Mississippi River," he wanted him to "commence no move for the further acquisition of territory" beyond Shreveport, which, he emphasized, "should be taken as soon as possible," so that, leaving Steele to hold what had been won, he himself could return with his command to New Orleans in time for the eastward movement Grant had in mind for him to undertake in conjunction with Sherman's advance on Atlanta. Above all, Banks was told, if it appeared that Shreveport could not be taken before the end of April, he was to return Sherman's 10,000 veterans by the middle of that month, "even if it leads to the abandonment of the main object of your expedition."

Sherman's own instructions, as stated afterward by Grant in his final report, were quite simple and to the point. He was "to move against Johnston's army, to break it up, and go into the interior of the enemy's country as far as he could, inflicting all the damage he could upon their war resources." For the launching of this drive on the Confederate heartland — admittedly a large order — the Ohioan would have the largest army in the country, even without the troops regrettably detached to Banks across the way. It included, in fact, three separate armies combined into one, each of them under a major general. First, and largest, there was George Thomas's Army of the Cumberland, badly whipped six months ago at Chickamauga, under Major General William S. Rosecrans, but reinforced since by three divisions from Meade for the Chattanooga breakout under Thomas, which had thrown General Braxton Bragg back on Dalton and caused his replacement by Joe Johnston. Next there was the Army of the Tennessee, veterans of Donelson and Shiloh under Grant, of Vicksburg and Missionary Ridge under Sherman, now under James B. McPherson, who had been promoted to fill the vacancy created by Sherman's advancement to head the whole. Finally there was the Army of the Ohio, youngest and smallest of the three, takers of Knoxville and survivors of the siege that followed under Major General Ambrose Burnside, who was succeeded now by

John M. Schofield, lately transferred from guerilla-torn Missouri. Made up in all of twenty infantry and four cavalry divisions, these three armies comprised the Military Division of the Mississippi under Sherman, redoubtable "Uncle Billy" to the 120,000 often rowdy western veterans on its rolls. This was considerably better than twice the number reported to be with Johnston around Dalton, but the defenders had a reserve force of perhaps as many as 20,000 under Lieutenant General Leonidas Polk at Demopolis, Alabama, and Meridian, Mississippi, in position to be hastened by rail either to Mobile or Atlanta, whichever came under pressure in the offensive the North was expected to open before long.

That was where Banks came in; that was why Grant had been so insistent that the Massachusetts general finish up the Red River operation without delay, in order to get his army back to New Orleans for an eastward march with 35,000 soldiers against Mobile, which would also be attacked from the water side by Rear Admiral David G. Farragut, whose Gulf squadron would be strengthened by the addition of several of the ironclads now on station outside Charleston, where the naval attack had stalled and which, in any case, was no longer on the agenda of targets to be hit. This double danger to Mobile would draw Polk's reserve force southward from Meridian and Demopolis, away from Atlanta and any assistance it might otherwise have rendered Johnston in resisting Sherman's steamroller drive on Dalton and points south. Later, when Banks and Sherman had achieved their primary goals, the reduction of Mobile and Atlanta, they would combine at the latter place for a farther penetration, eastward to the Atlantic and Lee's rear, if Lee was still a factor in the struggle by that time. "All I would now add," Grant told Banks in a follow-up letter sent two weeks after the first, "is that you commence the concentration of your forces at once. Preserve a profound secrecy of what you intend doing, and start at the earliest possible moment."

Such, then, was the nature of the offensive Grant intended to launch in the West, with Sherman bearing the main tactical burden. Similarly in the East, in accordance with his general plan "to concentrate all the force possible against the Confederate armies in the field," he planned for Meade to move in a similar manner, similarly assisted by a diversionary attack on the enemy rear. But he wanted it made clear from the start that this was to be something more than just another "On to Richmond" drive, at least so far as Meade himself was concerned. "Lee's army will be your objective point," his instructions read. "Wherever Lee goes, there you will go also."

If past experience showed anything, it clearly showed that in Virginia almost anything could happen. Moreover, with Lee in opposition, that *anything* was likely to be disastrous from the Federal point of view. Four of the five offensives so far launched against him — those by McClellan, by Pope, by Burnside, by Hooker — had broken in blood and ended in headlong blue retreat, while the fifth — Meade's own, the previous fall — had managed nothing better than a stalemate; which last, in the light of Grant's views on the need for unrelenting pressure, was barely preferable to defeat. Numerical odds had favored the Union to small avail in those encounters, including Hooker's three-to-one advantage, yet that was a poor argument against continuing to make them as long as possible. Just now, as a result of the westward detachments in September, the Army of the Potomac was down to fewer than one hundred thousand men. By way of lengthening the odds, Grant proposed to bring unemployed Ambrose Burnside back east to head a corps of four newly raised divisions which would rendezvous at Annapolis, thus puzzling the enemy as to their eventual use, down the coast or in Virginia proper, until the time came for the Rapidan crossing, when they would move in support of the Army of the Potomac, raising its strength to beyond 120,000 effectives, distributed among fifteen infantry and three cavalry divisions.

Such assurance as this gave was by no means certain. Lee was foxy. No mere numerical advantage had served to fix him in position for slaughter in the past. But Grant had other provisions in mind for securing that result, involving the use of the other two eastern armies. In the West, the three mobile forces had three separate primary assignments: going for Johnston, taking Mobile, riding herd on Transmississippi rebels. In the East, all three were to have the same objective from the start.

Posted in defense of West Virginia and the Maryland-Pennsylvania frontier, the smallest of these three armies was commanded by Major General Franz Sigel; "I fights mit Sigel" was the proud boast of thousands of soldiers, German-born like himself, who had been drawn to the colors by his example. This force was not available for use elsewhere, since its left lay squarely athwart the northern entrance to the Shenandoah Valley, that classic avenue of Confederate invasion exploited so brilliantly two years ago by Stonewall Jackson, who had used it to play on Lincoln's fears, thereby contributing largely to the frustration of McClellan's drive on Richmond at a time when the van of his army could hear the hours struck by the city's public clocks. To Grant, however, the fact that Sigel's 26,000 troops were not considered withdrawable, lest another rebel general use the Valley approach to serve him as Stonewall had served Little Mac, did not mean that this force was not usable as part of the drive on the Virginia capital and the gray army charged with its defense. It seemed to him, rather, that a movement up the Valley by a major portion of Sigel's command would serve even better than an immobile guard, posted across its northern entrance — or exit — to deny it to the enemy as a channel of invasion. Elaborating on this, he directed that the advance was to be in two columns, one under Brigadier General George Crook, who would march west of the

Alleghenies for a rapid descent on the Virginia & Tennessee Railroad, along which vital supply line he would move eastward, tearing up track as he went, then north for a meeting near Staunton with Sigel himself, who would have led the other column directly up the Valley. There they would combine for a strike at Lee's flank while Meade engaged his front; or if by then Lee had fallen back on Richmond, as expected, they would join in the pursuit, by way of the Virginia Central — another vital supply line — to the gates of the city and beyond.

So much for the task assigned the second of the three Union armies in Virginia. The third, being larger, had a correspondingly larger assignment, with graver dangers and quite the highest prize of all awaiting the prompt fulfillment of its task.

One reason Grant expected Lee to fall back on Richmond in short order, before Sigel had time to get in position on his flank, was that he intended to oblige him to do so by launching a back-door attack on the capital, from across the James, at the same time Meade was effecting a crossing of the Rapidan, sixty-odd miles to the north. The commander of this third force would be Major General Benjamin F. Butler, who had won a reputation for deftness, along with the nickname "Spoons," in the course of his highly profitable occupation of New Orleans, all of last year and most of the year before. Much as Sigel had been commissioned to attract German-born patriots to the colors, Butler had been made a general to prove to Democrats — at whose Charleston convention in 1860 he had voted fifty-seven consecutive times to nominate Jefferson Davis for President of the United States — that the war was not exclusively a Republican affair; Grant did not select, he inherited him, political abilities and all. For the work at hand, the former Bay State senator would have some 35,000 effectives of all arms, about half of them to be brought up from Florida and South Carolina by the commander of the Department of the South, Major General Quincy A. Gillmore, while the other half would be drawn from Butler's own Department of Virginia and North Carolina. He was to have naval support in moving up the James from his initial base at Fortress Monroe, as well as for the landing at City Point. That would put him within easy reach of Petersburg, the southside railroad center only twenty miles from his true objective, Richmond, which he was then to seize by means of a sudden lunge across the river. Or if Lee had managed a quick fall-back in such strength as to prevent a crossing at that point, Butler, having severed the city's rail connections with the granaries to the south, would combine with Meade and Sigel, upstream or down, for the resultant siege of the capital and its eventual surrender.

If all went as intended in the three-way squeeze he had designed to achieve Lee's encompassment, Grant himself would be there to receive the gray commander's sword at the surrender ceremony. For by now he had decided not only that he would return to the East for the duration of the war, so as to be able to interpose between the Washington politicians and the strategy they might attempt to subvert, but also that the most effective position from which to do this would be in close proximity to the headquarters of the Army of the Potomac. There were, indeed — in addition to the most obvious one, that being in the field would remove him from the constricting atmosphere of the District of Columbia and the disconcerting stares of over-curious civilians, in and out of government — several reasons for the decision: not the least of which was that Meade, in command of much the largest of the three armies in Virginia and charged with much the heaviest burden in the fighting, was outranked not only by Butler and Sigel, whose armies were assigned less arduous tasks, but also by Burnside, whose corps would move in his support and had to be more or less subject to his orders if he was to avoid delays that might prove disastrous. Although the problem could be ignored in the easier-going West — there Thomas, for instance, outranked Sherman, and McPherson was junior to several other major generals in all three armies — Easterners were notoriously touchy about such matters, and if a command crisis arose from the striking of personality sparks on the question of rank, Grant wanted to be there to settle it in person, as only he could do. If this resulted in some discomfort for Meade, whose style might be cramped and whose glory would no doubt be dimmed by the presence of a superior constantly peering over his shoulder and nudging his elbow, this was regrettable, but not nearly as much so, certainly, as various other unfortunate things that might happen without Grant there.

Besides, there was still another reason, perhaps of more importance than all the rest combined. For all its bleeding and dying these past three years, on a scale no other single army could approach, the paper-collar Army of the Potomac had precious few real victories to its credit. It had, in fact, in its confrontations with the adversary now awaiting its advance into the thickets on the south bank of the river it was about to cross, a well-founded and long-nurtured tradition of defeat. The correction for this, Grant believed, was the development of self-confidence, which seemed to him an outgrowth of aggressiveness, an eagerness to come to grips with the enemy and a habit of thinking of wounds it would inflict rather than of wounds it was likely to suffer. So far, this outlook had been characteristic not of eastern but of western armies; Grant hoped to effect, in person, a transference of this spirit which he had done so much to create in the past. Twenty months ago, it was true, John Pope had come east "to infuse a little western energy" into the flaccid ranks of the accident-prone divisions that came under his command in the short-lived Army of Virginia. Unfortunately, he had only contrived to lengthen by one (or two or three, if Cedar Mountain and Chantilly were included) the list of spectacular defeats;

his troops had wound up cowering in the Washington defenses — what was left of them after the thrashing Lee had administered, flank and rear. But Grant, despite this lamentable example, had much the same victory formula in mind. The difference was that he backed it up, as Pope had been unable to do, with an over-all plan, on a national scale, that embodied the spirit of the offensive.

Sherman, for one, believed he would succeed, although the severely compressed and beleaguered Confederacy still amounted, as Grant said, to "an empire in extent." He expected victory, not only because of the plan they had developed in part between them in the Cincinnati hotel room, but also because he believed that the struggle had entered a new phase, one that for the first time favored the forces of the Union, which at last had come of age, in a military sense, while those of the South were sliding past their prime. Or so at any rate it seemed to Sherman. "It was not until after both Gettysburg and Vicksburg that the war professionally began," he later declared. "Then our men had learned in the dearest school on earth the simple lesson of war... and it was then that we as professional soldiers could rightly be held to a just responsibility." Heartened by the prospect, he expressed his confidence to Grant before they parted: he to return to Nashville, the headquarters of his new command, and his friend and superior to Washington for a time, riding eastward past crowds that turned out to cheer him at every station along the way.

Nor was there any slackening of the adulation at the end of the line. "General Grant is all the rage," Sherman heard from his senator brother John the following week. "He is subjected to the disgusting but dangerous process of being lionized. He is followed by crowds, and is cheered everywhere." The senator was worried about the effect all this might have on the man at whom it was directed. "While he must despise the fickle fools who run after him, he, like most others, may be spoiled by this excess of flattery. He may be so elated as to forget the uncertain tenure upon which he holds and stakes his really well-earned laurels." Sherman, though he was pleased to note that his brother added: "He is plain and modest, and so far bears himself well," was quick to jump to his friend's defense, wherein he coupled praise with an admonition. "Grant is as good a leader as we can find," he replied. "He has honesty, simplicity of character, singleness of purpose, and no hope or claim to usurp civil power. His character, more than his genius, will reconcile armies and attach the people. Let him alone. Don't disgust him by flattery or importunity. Let him alone."

Let him alone, either then or later, was the one thing almost no one in Washington seemed willing to do; except Lincoln, who assured Grant that he intended to do just that, at least in a military sense. "The particulars of your plan I neither know nor seek to know," he was to tell him presently, on the eve of commitment, and even at their first interview, before the general left for Tennessee, he had told him (according to Grant's recollection of the exchange, years later) "that he had never professed to be a military man or to know how campaigns should be conducted... but that procrastination on the part of commanders and the pressure from the people at the North and Congress, which was always with him, forced him to issue his series of 'Military Orders' — one, two, three, etc. He did not know but they were all wrong, and did know that some of them were. All he wanted or had ever wanted was someone who would take the responsibility and act, and call on him for all the assistance needed."

Welcome though this was to hear, Grant was no doubt aware that the President had said similar things to previous commanders (John C. Frémont, for example, whom he told: "I have given you carte blanche. You must use your own judgment, and do the best you can." Or McClellan, who quoted his assurances after Antietam: "General, you have saved the country. You must remain in command and carry us through to the end. I pledge myself to stand between you and harm") only to jerk the rug from under their feet a short time later, when their backs were turned; Lincoln had never been one to keep a promise any longer than he believed the good of the country was involved. However, in this case he supplemented his private with public remarks to the same effect. "Grant is the first *general* I have had," he was reported to be saying. "I am glad to find a man who can go ahead without me." To a friend who doubted that Grant should be given so free a rein, he replied: "Do you hire a man to do your work and then do it yourself?" To another, who remarked that he was looking well these days, he responded with an analogy. "Oh, yes, I feel better," he laughed, "for now I'm like the man who was blown up on a steamboat and said, on coming down, 'It makes no difference to me; I'm only a passenger.'"

Partly Lincoln's ebullience was the result of having learned, if not the particulars, then at any rate certain features of Grant's plan. Of its details, an intimate said later that they "were communicated only to Grant's most important or most trusted subordinates" — Meade, Butler, and Sigel, of course, along with Sherman and Banks. "To no others, except to members of his personal staff, did Grant impart a knowledge of his plans; and, even among these, there were some with whom he was reticent." The President and the Secretary of War were both excluded, though he was willing to discuss with them the principle to be applied in bringing "the greatest number of troops practicable" to bear against the forces in rebellion; for example, that the units charged with the occupation of captured territory and the prevention of rebel incursions into the North "could perform this service just as well by advancing as by remaining still, and by advancing they would compel the enemy to keep detachments to hold them back, or else lay his own territory open to invasion." Lincoln saw the point at once, having urged it often in the past, although with small success. "Those not skinning can hold a leg," he said. Grant, as the son of a tanner, knew that this had reference to hog-killing time in the West, where all hands were given a share in the work even though there were not enough skinning-knives to go round. He liked the expression so well, in fact, that he passed it along to Sherman the following week in a letter explaining Sigel's share in the Virginia campaign: "If Sigel can't skin himself he can hold a leg while someone else skins."

By that time he was in the field, where he enjoyed greater privacy in working on his plan for the distribution of knives to be used in flaying the South alive. Having returned to Washington on March 23, he established headquarters three days later at Culpeper, six miles beyond Brandy Station on the Orange & Alexandria Railroad, about midway between the Rappahannock and the Rapidan. This was the week of the vernal equinox; tomorrow was Easter Sunday. Yet a fifteen-inch snow had fallen that Tuesday and the land was still locked in the grip of winter, as if to mock the hope expressed to Sherman that the armies could launch their separate but concentric attacks by April 25. To the west, in plain view, the Blue Ridge Mountains bore on their peaks and slopes deep drifts of snow, which Grant had been told by old-timers hereabouts would have to have melted away before he could be sure that bad weather had gone for good and the roads would support his moving trains and guns. Down here on the flat at least its whiteness served to hide the scars inflicted by commanders North and South, who, as one observer remarked, "had led their armies up and down these fields and made the landscape desolate." Roundabout Culpeper, he added, "not a house nor a fence, not a tree was to be seen for miles, where once all had been cultivated farmland or richly wooded country. Here and there, a stack of chimneys or a broken cistern marked the site of a former homestead, but every other landmark had been destroyed. The very hills were stripped of their forest panoply, and a man could hardly recognize the haunts familiar to him in his childhood."

Although at present much of this was mercifully blanketed from sight, the worst of the scars no snow could hide, for they existed in men's minds and signified afflictions of the spirit, afflictions Grant would have to overcome before he could instill into the Army of the Potomac the self-confidence and aggressiveness which he considered prerequisite to the successful prosecution of its offensive against an adversary famed throughout the world as the embodiment of the qualities said to be lacking on the near side of the river that ran between the armies. Discouraging to his hopes for the inculcation of the spirit of the offensive, the very landmarks scattered about this fought-over section of Virginia served as doleful reminders of what such plans had come to in the past. Westward beyond the snow-clad Blue Ridge lay the Shenandoah Valley, where Banks and Frémont had been sorely drubbed and utterly confused, and northeastward, leading down this way, ran the course of the Buckland Races, in which the cavalry had been chased and taunted. Cedar Mountain loomed dead ahead; there Sigel, thrown forward by bristly Pope, had come a cropper, as Pope himself had done only three weeks later, emulating the woeful example of Irvin McDowell on the plains of Manassas, where the rebels feasted on his stores, forty miles back up the railroad. Downriver about half that distance, Burnside had suffered the throbbing pain and numbing indignity of the Fredericksburg blood-bath and the Mud March; while close at hand, just over the Rapidan, brooded the Wilderness, where Hooker had come to grief in a May riot of smoke-choked greenery and Meade had nearly done the same, inching forward through the ice-cramped woods a scant four months ago, except that he pulled back in time to avoid destruction. All these were painful memories to the veterans who had survived them and passed them on to recruits as a tradition of defeat — a tradition which Grant was seeking now, if not to erase (for it could never be erased; it was too much a part of history, kept alive in the pride of the butternut scarecrows over the river) then at any rate to overcome by locking it firmly in the past and replacing it with one of victory.

In working thus at his plans for bringing that tradition into existence, here and elsewhere, he was assisted greatly by a command arrangement allowed for in the War Department order appointing him general-in-chief in place of Halleck, who was relieved "at his own request" and made chief of staff, an office created to provide a channel of communication between Grant and his nineteen department heads, particularly in administrative matters. The work would be heavy for Old Brains, the glory slight; Hooker, who had feuded with him throughout his eastern tenure, sneered that his situation was like that of a man who married with the understanding that he would not sleep with his wife. But Halleck thereby freed Grant from the need for attending to a great many routine distractions. Instead of being snowed under by paperwork, the lieutenant general could give his full attention to strategic planning, and this he did. From time to time he would return to Washington for an overnight stay — primarily, it would seem, to visit Mrs Grant, who had joined him in Cincinnati for the ride back east — but mainly he kept to his desk in the field, poring over maps and blueing the air of his Culpeper headquarters with cigar smoke, much as he had done a year ago in the former ladies' cabin of the *Magnolia*, where he planned the campaign that took Vicksburg.

✗ 2 ✗

Of all these several component segments, each designed to contribute to Grant's over-all pattern for victory on a national scale, the first to go awry was the preliminary one — preliminary, that is, in the sense that it would have to be wound up before the more valid thrust at Mobile could begin — involving Banks and Steele in the far-off Transmississippi, hundreds of miles from the two vital centers around which would swirl the fighting that would determine the outcome of the war. It was the first because it had already begun to falter before Grant was in a position to exercise control. Moreover, once he was in such a position, as general-in-chief, his attempts along that line only served to increase the frustration which both subordinates, proceeding as it were against their hearts, had been feeling all along. Not that it mattered all that much, whatever he did or did not do, for the seeds of defeat had been planted in the conception. By then the only cure would have been to abandon the crop entirely; which would not do, since Lincoln himself, with a fretful sidelong glance at France's latter-day Napoleon, had had a hand in the sowing.

Promptly after the midsummer fall of Port Hudson opened the Mississippi to Union trade throughout its length, Halleck had taken the conquest of Texas as his prime concern in the western theater. It seemed to him the logical next step. Besides, he had always liked to keep things tidy in his rear, and every success achieved under his direction had been followed by a pause for just that purpose. After Donelson, after Corinth, after Vicksburg, he had dismembered the victorious blue force, dispersing its parts on various lateral or rearward assignments, with much attendant loss of momentum. Consequently, although it was here that the North had scored all but a handful of its triumphs in the field, the war in the West had consisted largely of starts and stops, with the result that a considerable portion of the Federal effort had been expended in overcoming prime inertia at the start of each campaign. And so it was to be in the present case, if Old Brains had his way. With the President's unquestioning approval — which, as usual, tended to make him rather imperious in manner and altogether intolerant of objections — Halleck had been urging the conquest of Texas on Banks, who had been opposed in the main to such a venture, so far at least as it involved his own participation. A former Massachusetts governor and Speaker of the national House of Representatives, he was, like most political appointees, concerned with building a military reputation on which to base his postwar bid for further political advancement. He had in fact his eye on the White House, and he preferred a more spectacular assignment, one nearer the center of the stage and attended with less risk, or in any case no more risk than seemed commensurate with the prize, which in his opinion this did not; Texas was undeniably vast, but it was also comparatively empty. He favored Mobile as a fitting objective by these standards, and had been saying so ever since the surrender of Port Hudson first gave him the feel of laurels on his brow. Halleck had stuck to Texas, however, and Halleck as general-in-chief had had his way.

Texas it was, although there still was considerable disagreement as to the best approach to the goal, aside from a general conviction that it could not be due west across the Sabine and the barrens, where, as one of Banks's staff remarked, there was "no water in the summer and fall, and plenty of water but no road in the winter and spring." Halleck favored an ascent of Red River, to Shreveport and beyond, which would allow for gunboat support and rapid transportation of supplies; but this had some of the same disadvantages as the direct crosscountry route, the Red being low on water all through fall and winter. While waiting for the spring rise, without which the river was unnavigable above Alexandria, barely one third of the distance up to Shreveport, Banks tried his hand at a third approach, the mounting of amphibious assaults against various points along the Lone Star coast. The first of these, at Sabine Pass in September, was bloodily repulsed; the navy lost two gunboats and their crews before admitting it could put no troops ashore at that point. So Banks revised his plan by reversing it, end for end. He managed an unsuspected landing near the mouth of the Rio Grande, occupied Brownsville unopposed, and began to work his way back east by way of Aransas Pass and Matagorda Bay. There he stopped. So far he had encountered no resistance, but just ahead lay Galveston, with Sabine Pass beyond, both of them scenes of past defeats which he would not risk repeating. All he had got for his pains was a couple of dusty border towns and several bedraggled miles of beach, amounting to little more in fact than a few pinpricks along one leathery flank of the Texas elephant. By now it was nearly spring, however, and time for him to get back onto what Halleck, in rather testy dispatches, had kept assuring him was the true path of conquest: up the Red, which soon was due for the annual rise that would convert it into an artery of invasion.

By now, too, as a result of closer inspection of the prize, Banks had somewhat revised his opinion as to the worth of the proposed campaign. Mobile was still what he ached for, but Mobile would have to wait. Meantime, a successful ascent of the Red, as a means of achieving the subjugation of East Texas, would not only add a feather to his military cap; it would also, by affording him and his army valuable training in the conduct of combined operations, serve as excellent preparation for better and more difficult things to come. Besides, study disclosed immediate advantages he had overlooked before. In addition to providing a bulwark against the machinations of the French in Mexico,

Another Grand Design

the occupation of Shreveport would yield political as well as strategic fruits. First there was Lincoln's so-called Ten Percent plan, whereby a state would be permitted to return to the national fold as soon as ten percent of its voters affirmed their loyalty to the Union and its laws. With Shreveport firmly in Federal hands, Confederate threats would no longer deter the citizens of West Louisiana and South Arkansas from taking the oath required; Louisiana and Arkansas, grateful to the Administration which had granted them readmission, would cast their votes in the November election, thereby winning for the general who had made such action possible the gratitude of the man who, four years later, would exert a powerful influence in the choice of his successor. There, indeed, was a prize worth grasping. Moreover, the aforementioned strategic fruits of such a campaign had been greatly enlarged in the course of the fall and winter, occasioned by Steele's advance on Little Rock in September, which extended the Federal occupation down to the Arkansas River, bisecting the state along a line from Fort Smith to Napoleon, and posed a threat to Confederate installations farther south. Ordnance works at Camden and Arkadelphia had been shifted to Tyler and Marshall, Texas, where they now were back in production, as were others newly established at Houston and San Antonio. Cut off from the industrial East by the fall of Vicksburg, still-insurgent Transmississippians had striven in earnest to develop their own resources. Factories at Tyler, Houston, and Austin, together with one at Washington, Arkansas, were delivering 10,000 pairs of shoes a month to rebel quartermasters, and inmates of the Texas penitentiary at Huntsville were turning out more than a million yards of cotton and woolen cloth every month, to be made into gray or butternut uniforms for distribution to die-hard fighters in all three states of the region. Shreveport itself had become an industrial complex quite beyond anyone's dream a year ago, with foundries, shops, and laboratories for the production of guns and ammunition, without which not even the doughtiest grayback would constitute the semblance of a threat. If Banks could lay hands on Shreveport, then move on into the Lone Star vastness just beyond, the harvest would be heavy, both in matériel and glory. By late January, having considered all this, and more, he was so far in agreement with Halleck that he wired him: "The occupation of Shreveport will be to the country west of the Mississippi what that of Chattanooga is to the east. And as soon as this can be accomplished," he added, his enthusiasm waxing as he wrote, "the country west of Shreveport will be in condition for a movement into Texas."

Another persuasive factor there was, which in time would be reckoned the most influential of them all, though less perhaps on Banks himself than on various others, in and out of the army and navy, about to be involved in the campaign. This was cotton. Banks was intrigued by the notion that the proposed invasion not only could be carried out on a self-supporting basis, financially speaking, but could result in profits that would cover other, less lucrative efforts, such as the ones about to be launched through the ravaged counties of northern Virginia and across the red-clay hills and gullies of North Georgia. What was more, he backed his calculations with experience. On his march up Bayou Teche to Alexandria, in April of the year before, he had seized an estimated $5,000,000 in contraband goods, including lumber, sugar and salt, cattle and livestock, and cotton to the amount of 5000 bales. This last represented nearly half the value of the spoils — and would represent even more today, with the price in Boston soaring rapidly toward two dollars a pound in greenbacks. Yet those 5000 bales collected along the Teche were scarcely more than a dab compared to the number awaiting seizure in plantation sheds along the Red and in the Texas hinterland; Banks predicted that the campaign would produce between 200,000 and 300,000 bales. Even the lower of these two figures, at a conservative estimate of $500 a bale, would bulge the Treasury with no less than a hundred million dollars, which by itself would be enough to run the whole war for two months. Nor was that all. In addition to this direct financial gain, he would also put back into operation the spindles lying idle in the mills of his native state, where he had got his start as a bobbin boy and where the voters would someday turn out in hordes to express their thanks for all he had done for them and the nation in their time of trial. It was no wonder his enthusiasm rose with every closer look at the political, strategic, and financial possibilities of a campaign he formerly had thought not worth his time.

Perhaps the most persuasive factor of all, so far at least as Banks was concerned, was that he secured Halleck's approval of a plan, worked out between them, that assured the coöperation not only of Steele, who would move south from Little Rock to the vicinity of Shreveport with 15,000 troops, but also of Sherman, who was to send 10,000 of his veterans to Alexandria for a combination with the 20,000 Banks himself would bring to that point by repeating last year's profitable march up the Teche. Including a marine brigade and the crews of twenty-odd warships under Rear Admiral David D. Porter, which were to serve as escort for the transports bringing Sherman's men from Vicksburg and thenceforth as an integral part of the command in its ascent of the Red, this would give Banks a total strength of just under 50,000; which he believed was sufficient, in itself, to guarantee success in the campaign. His opponent, General Edmund Kirby Smith, commanding that vast, five-state Transmississippi region already beginning to be known as "Kirby-Smithdom," had not much more than half that many soldiers in all of Arkansas, Louisiana, Texas, and the Indian Territory combined. Such opposition as Smith might be able to offer the veteran 45,000-man blue army and its hard-hitting 210-gun fleet, Banks was not unjustified in believing, would only serve to swell the glory involved in the inevitable outcome.

Sherman himself was inclined to agree with this assessment, though he was aware (as Banks perhaps was not, having had little time for theoretic study) of Napoleon's dictum that the most difficult of all maneuvers was the combination of widely divided columns, regardless of their over-all numerical superiority, on a field of battle already occupied by an enemy who thus would be free, throughout the interim preceding their convergence, to strike at one or another of the approaching columns. His only regret, the red-haired general said when he came down to New Orleans in early March to confer with Banks about his share in the campaign, was that Grant had forbidden him to go along. He stayed two days, working out the arrangements for his troops to be at Alexandria in time for a meeting with Banks's column on the 17th — the same day, as it turned out, that he would meet with Grant in Nashville, though he did not know that yet — then steamed back upriver to Vicksburg, declining his host's invitation to stay over for the inauguration on March 5 of the recently elected Union-loyal governor of Louisiana, one Michael Hahn, a Bavaria-born lawyer and sugar planter who had opposed secession from the start. Despite the delay it would entail, Banks apparently felt obliged to remain for the ceremony — which was quite elaborate, one item on the program being a rendition of the "Anvil Chorus" in Lafayette Square by no less than a thousand singers, accompanied by all the bands of the army, while church bells pealed and cannon were fired in unison by electrical devices — then at last, after managing to get through another two weeks of attending to additional political and administrative matters, got aboard a steamboat for a fast ride up the Mississippi and the Red for the meeting at Alexandria with Sherman's men and his own, whose ascent of the Teche had been delayed by heavy going on roads made nearly bottomless by rain. Before leaving he had written to Halleck of the public reaction to the inaugural celebration, thousand-tongued chorus, electrically fired cannon, and all. "It is impossible to describe it with truth," he wrote. In the future, much the same thing would be said of the campaign he was about to give the benefit of his personal supervision.

It was March 24 by the time he reached Alexandria, one week late. Even so, he got there ahead of the men in his five divisions, who did not complete their slog up the Teche until next day. Plastered with mud and eight days behind schedule, they did not let the hard and tardy march depress their spirits, which were high. "The *soldier* is a queer fellow," a reporter who accompanied them wrote; "he is not at all like other white men. Tired, dusty, cold or hungry — no matter, he is always jolly. I find him, under the most adverse circumstances, shouting, singing, skylarking. There is no care or tire in him." Banks, for all the dignity he was careful to preserve, shared this skylark attitude when he arrived, and with good cause. The time spent waiting for him to show had been put to splendid use by Sherman's veterans, who had arrived on time, with one considerable victory already to their credit and another scored before the Massachusetts general joined them.

Three divisions under Brigadier General A. J. Smith, a Pennsylvania-born West Pointer, they had left Vicksburg on March 10 and gone ashore two days later at Simsport, just up the Atchafalaya from its confluence with the Red. While Porter's twenty-two heavily gunned warships — thirteen of them ironclads, accompanied by some forty transports and quartermaster boats — returned to the Red for a frontal attack on Fort De Russy, a once-abandoned but now reoccupied Confederate strongpoint about halfway up to Alexandria, the infantry crossed a lush, bayou-mazed prairie called Avoyelles to come upon the fortification from the rear. Such few rebels as they saw en route were quick to scamper out of reach, having no apparent stomach for a fight. By late afternoon of March 14 the bluecoats were in position for a mass assault, not only hearing the roar of Porter's guns, which showed that he too was in place on schedule, but also receiving a few of his heavy shells that overshot the fort. Just before sundown, at a cost of only 38 killed and wounded, they stormed and took it, along with its ten guns and its garrison of 300 bitter, shell-dazed men, who, according to a newsman with the attackers, "screamed in demoniac tones, even after our banners flaunted from their bastions and ramparts." This done, the victors got back aboard their transports for the thirty-mile ride to Alexandria: all, that is, but the men of one division, who stayed behind to raze the fort by tearing out and burning its wooden beams and leveling the earthworks, after which they gave it the finishing touch by blowing up the powder magazine.

They had received excellent schooling in such work under Sherman, especially on the recent expedition to Meridian, where, in Sherman's words, they had cut "a swath of desolation fifty miles broad across the State of Mississippi which the present generation will not forget." In such work they used sledges and crowbars more than rifles, and though it involved much vigorous exercise, it was not only a fine way of relaxing from the rigors of the Vicksburg siege, it was also a good deal safer, since their efforts were mainly directed against civilians. Moreover, this particular division had a commander, Brigadier General T. Kilby Smith, whose views along these lines coincided more or less with their own. "The inhabitants hereabouts are pretty tolerably frightened," the thirty-three-year-old former lawyer was presently to write home to his mother in Ohio. "Our western troops are tired of shilly shally, and this year they will deal their blows very heavily. Past kindnesses and forbearance has not been appreciated or understood; frequently ridiculed. The people now will be terribly scourged." Presumably such words had been passed down as well as out, for private residences had begun to burn in Simsport almost as soon as the transports ran out their gangplanks for the troops to go ashore, and their progress across the lovely Avoyelles Prairie was marked by the ruins of burnt-out houses, some with nothing to show they had been there except an unsupported chimney; "Sherman Monuments," these were called. Arcadians of the region, a gentle people with a heritage of freedom, many of whom had been pro-Union up to now, were indeed "terribly scourged." The pattern was set for the campaign, so far at least as the western troops — "Sherman's gorillas," they dubbed themselves — were concerned. Next would come the turn of the inhabitants of the piny uplands beyond Alexandria, although a correspondent of the St Louis *Republican* was already predicting that unless such practices were discouraged there was a danger of "our whole noble army degenerating into a band of cutthroats and robbers."

By way of proving their skill as fighters as well as burners, six regiments of gorilla-guerillas, accompanied by a brigade of Banks's cavalry that rode in ahead of his infantry, pressed on above Alexandria to Henderson's Hill, twenty miles up Bayou Rapides, on a forced reconnaissance which reached a climax on the night of March 21 with a surprise attack, through rain and hail and darkness, that captured a whole regiment of rebel cavalry, some 250 men and mounts, together with all four guns of a battery also caught off guard by the assault. Returning to base three days later, they paraded their captives before Banks, who had just arrived and was delighted to find that they had not wasted the time spent waiting for him and the rest of the five divisions they were supposed to reinforce. When these wound up their march next day, March 25, he had concentrated under his immediate command by far the most impressive display of military strength ever seen in the Transmississippi, on land or water. With ninety pieces of field artillery and considerably better than twice that number of heavier guns afloat, he had 30,000 effectives on hand, practically all of them seasoned campaigners, and was about to move up the Red for a conjunction near Shreveport with half that many more under Steele, who he now learned had left Little Rock two days ago, marching south-southwest toward the same objective. The outlook was auspicious, especially in light of the fact that his troops had already proved their superiority, first at Fort De Russy and again at Henderson's Hill, over such forces of the enemy as they had managed to trick or cower into remaining within their reach. But then next day, as he was about to order a resumption of the march, a high-ranking courier arrived with Grant's eleven-day-old letter of instructions from Nashville, written while waiting for Sherman to join him there.

This could not but give Banks pause, stipulating as it did that if he did not feel certain of taking Shreveport by the end of April he was to return A. J. Smith's command to Sherman by the middle of that month "for movements east of the Mississippi." Discouraging as this was in part — for it not only fixed him with a tighter schedule than he had felt obliged to follow when he set out, it also threatened him with the imminent loss of the three best divisions in his army — Banks took heart at something else the letter said. If the expedition was successful, he was to leave the holding of Shreveport and the line of the Red to Steele, while he himself returned to New Orleans for an advance on Mobile as part of the new general-in-chief's design for a spring offensive in the central theater. This was the assignment he had coveted all along, and though he was aware of the danger of being over-hasty in military matters, this went far toward reconciling him to the step-up in the tempo of his march. With Mobile to follow, more or less as a reward for past successes, he wanted this Red River business over and done with as soon as possible. Accordingly, he put his cavalry in motion that same day and followed it two days later with his infantry, while A. J. Smith's men got back aboard their transports to accompany the fleet. The immediate objective was Grand Ecore, sixty miles upstream or roughly half the total distance. His plan was to move rapidly to that point and to Natchitoches, four miles south of Grand Ecore and the river, after which would come the leap at Shreveport that would wind up the campaign.

Banks himself did not leave Alexandria until after April 1, having remained behind to supervise an election on that date, by such voters as had taken the loyalty oath, of delegates to a state convention whose task it would be to draw up a new constitution tying Louisiana more firmly to the Union. Meanwhile the troops had been making excellent progress, encountering nothing more than scattered resistance that was easily brushed aside. By the time of the April Fool election, both Natchitoches and Grand Ecore had been occupied by leading elements of the respective columns, one advancing by land, the other by water. This meant that the campaign was back on schedule, despite the delay at the start. So far all was well, except perhaps that the lack of opposition had resulted in a dwindling of public concern outside the immediate area of operations. "It is a remarkable fact," the New Orleans correspondent of the New York *Tribune* declared on April 2, "that this Red River expedition is not followed by that anxious interest and solicitude which has heretofore attended similar army movements. The success of our troops is looked upon as a matter of course, and the cotton speculators are the only people I can find who are nicely weighing probabilities and chances in connection with the expedition."

If anxious interest and solicitude were what he was seeking, he could have found them not only in the New Orleans cotton exchange but also up Red River, aboard the flagship of the fleet. Porter had already lost one of his prized vessels, the veteran *Conestoga,* sunk March 8 in a collision on the Mississippi while returning from Vicksburg with a heavy load of ammunition that took her to the bottom in four minutes. She was the eighth major warship the admiral had lost in the past sixteen months, and two of these had been captured and turned against him, at least for a time. What was worse, it had begun to seem to him that if he continued to go along with Banks he would be in danger of losing a great many more, not so much through enemy action — he had never been one to flinch from combat — as through an act of nature; or, rather, a non-act. The annual rise of the Red, which usually began around New Year's, had not thus far materialized. Perhaps it was merely late this year; but twice before, in 1846 and 1855, it had not occurred at all. That was a nine-year interval, and now that another nine years had elapsed, there were indications that if Porter got his boats above the mile-long falls and rapids at Alexandria, he might not be able to get them down again. If the river, instead of rising, took a drop, he would be left with the agonizing choice of blowing them up or having them fall into rebel hands, which would mean nothing less than the undoing of all the navy had accomplished in these past two years of war on the western waters. That was unthinkable, but he had boasted so often that he could take his fleet "wherever the sand was damp," the admiral now found it impossible to renege on his promise to stay with the army to the end of its upstream trek. After three days of tugging and bumping — during which time the river, to his alarm, began to dwindle, then rose slightly — he got his largest ironclad, *Eastport,* over the falls; after which he followed with a dozen lighter-draft gunboats and twenty transports laden with troops. "The water is quite a muddy red and looks anything but inviting," a sailor wrote in his diary as the column began its winding crawl to Grand Ecore. "The transports from the head belch out three bellowing whistles which is caught up by the next, and sometimes two or three vie in a euphonious concert much resembling the bellowing of cattle at the smell of blood."

So far, except for the considerable slaughter of pigs and chickens encountered on the march, the smell of blood had been little more than a figurative expression. Moreover, if Banks could judge by indications, the Confederates were either content to have it remain so, or else they were incapable of having it otherwise, knowing only too well that most of the blood that would be spilled would be their own. In any case, the one thing they had not done was fight, and as he boarded his headquarters boat at Alexandria for an upstream ride on the evening of April 2 — a nattily dressed man in his vigorous prime, two years short of fifty, wearing highly polished boots and chinking spurs, a light-blue overcoat, buckskin gauntlets elbow-high, a bell-crowned hat, and a neatly groomed mustache and brief imperial — he got off a dispatch to

Halleck expressing his confidence in "an immediate and successful issue" of the campaign, the end of which he believed was in plain view.

"Our troops now occupy Natchitoches," he informed Old Brains, "and we hope to be in Shreveport by the 10th of April. I do not fear concentration of the enemy at that point. My fear is that they may not be willing to meet us."

In the course of the past three years Lincoln had read other such dispatches, and all too often they had turned out to be prologues to disaster. Reading this one, when in time it reached Washington, he frowned and shook his head in disapproval.

"I am sorry to see this tone of confidence," he said. "The next news we shall hear from there will be of a defeat."

A defeat was what the Confederates had very much in mind for the invaders: especially Major General Richard Taylor, Kirby Smith's West Louisiana commander, who had crossed swords with Banks before, first in the Shenandoah Valley, two years ago, and then along the Teche the previous year. Tactically, the second of these confrontations had not been as brilliant as the first, in which Taylor, serving as one of Stonewall Jackson's ablest lieutenants, had helped to strip the former Bay State politician of so many well-stocked wagons that he had been nicknamed "Commissary" Banks; but the aptness of this nom-de-guerre had been redemonstrated last summer, west of New Orleans, when Taylor's surprise descent on Banks's forward supply base at Brashear City, yielding an estimated $2,000,000 in ordnance and other stores, helped immeasurably to equip the army he had been raising for the defense of his home state ever since his transfer from Virginia. A son of Zachary Taylor and brother of Jefferson Davis's first wife, now just past his thirty-eighth birthday, he was described by one of his soldiers as "a quiet, unassuming little fellow, but noisy on retreats, with a tendency to cuss mules and wagons which stall on the road."

This tendency had been given a free rein for the past three weeks, in the course of which he had been obliged to fall back nearly two hundred miles before an adversary he was convinced he could whip, if he could only manage to meet him on anything approaching equal terms. But there was the rub. With fewer than 7000 troops in the path of better than four times that number backed by the guns of the Union fleet, he had no choice except to continue his retreat, hard though it was to suffer without retaliation the vandalism of A. J. Smith's gorillas, not to mention such professional indignities as Fort De Russy and the loss of most of his cavalry at Henderson's Hill. His consolation was that he was falling back toward reinforcements, which Kirby Smith kept assuring him were on the way from Arkansas and Texas. However — as might have been expected of a young man who had served his war apprenticeship under the bloody-minded and highly time-conscious Stonewall — he chafed at the delay. On the last day of March, with his troops in motion for a concentration forty miles northwest of Natchitoches and less than half that distance from the Texas border, he sent an irate dispatch informing the department commander that his patience was near the snapping point. "Had I conceived for an instant that such astonishing delay would ensue before reinforcements reached me," he told Smith, "I would have fought a battle even against the heavy odds. It would have been better to lose the state after a defeat than to surrender it without a fight. The fairest and richest portion of the Confederacy is now a waste. Louisiana may well know her destiny. Her children are exiles; her labor system is destroyed. Expecting every hour to receive the promised reinforcements, I did not feel justified in hazarding a general engagement with my little army. I shall never cease to regret my error."

"Hydrocephalus at Shreveport produced atrophy elsewhere," he afterwards protested, complaining acidly that while his superior "displayed much ardor in the establishment of bureaux, and on a scale proportioned rather to the extent of his territory than to the smallness of his force," Smith neglected the more vital task of resisting blue aggression in the field. In thus indulging his fondness for classical allusion, while at the same time venting his spleen, Yale man Taylor was not altogether fair to a West-Point-trained commander who by now had spent a hectic year being responsible for a region the size of western Europe, much of it trackless and practically none of it self-sustaining, at any rate in a military sense, at the time he assumed his manifold duties. Not the least of these was the establishment of those bureaus of supply and communication scorned by Taylor but made altogether necessary by the loss, within four months of Smith's arrival, of all practical connection with the more prosperous half of his country lying east of the Mississippi. In short, he had been involved in a year-long strategic and logistic nightmare. If at times he seemed to vacillate in the face of danger, that was to a large extent because of the scantiness of his resources, both in manpower and equipment, in contrast to those of an adversary whose own were apparently limitless and who could move against him, more or less at will, by land and water. Missouri had been lost before he got there. Then had come the subtraction of the northern half of Arkansas, suffered while pinprick lodgments were being made along the lower coast of Texas. Now it turned out that all this had been by way of preparation for a simultaneous advance by two blue columns under Steele and Banks, converging respectively from the north and east upon his headquarters at Shreveport and containing between them more veteran troops than he had in his entire five-state department, including guerillas and recruits. If he was jumpy it was small wonder, no matter how resentful Richard Taylor might feel at being obliged to backtrack, across the width of his beloved home state, before the menace of a force four times his own.

Warned early of the double-pronged threat to his headquarters and supply base — the fall of which would mean the loss, not only of Louisiana and what remained of Arkansas, but also of much that lay beyond — Smith decided to meet the nearer and larger danger first: meaning Banks. He would hit him with all the strength he could muster, then turn and do the same to Steele when he came up. Accordingly, he alerted his Texas commander, Major General John B. Magruder, to prepare his entire force, garrisons excluded, for a march to support Taylor. In Arkansas, Lieutenant General Theophilus Holmes was given similar instructions, except that he was to retain his cavalry for use against Steele's column, slowing it down as best he could until such time as Taylor had disposed of Banks and was free to come in turn to his assistance. These alerting orders were issued in late February, before either enemy force had been assembled. In early March, though neither Federal column had yet set out, Magruder was told to put his men in motion. They amounted in all to some 2500 horsemen, combined in a division under Brigadier General Thomas Green, and left Magruder with only about the same number for the defense of all of Texas: a situation the Virginian considered not unlike the one he had faced two years ago, on the York-James peninsula, when he found himself standing with one brigade in the path of McClellan's huge blue juggernaut. Meanwhile Holmes, whose deafness was only one of the symptoms of his superannuation, had been relieved at his own request and succeeded by Major General Sterling Price, his second in command; Price was told to put his alerted troops — two small divisions of infantry under Brigadier General T. J. Churchill, with a combined strength of 4500 effectives — on the march for Shreveport. These were the reinforcements Taylor had been expecting all the time he was fading back across the width of Louisiana, protesting hotly at their nonarrival.

Green's progress was necessarily slow across the barrens and the Sabine, but Churchill's was impeded by Smith himself. By now the Transmississippi chieftain had begun to suspect that he had hoisted himself onto the horns of a dilemma: as indeed he had, since he thought he had. Having attended boldly to the threat posed by Banks, he feared that he had erred in leaving Price too little strength to hinder Steele, who might be able to descend on Shreveport before Taylor could dispose of Banks and come to its defense. Taking council of his fears, which were enlarged by information that Steele had set out from Little Rock on March 23, Smith held Churchill for a time at headquarters, so as to be able to use him in either direction, north or south, depending on whether the need was greater in Arkansas or Louisiana, then finally, in response to Taylor's increasingly strident dispatches, ordered Churchill to move south to Keatchie, a hamlet roughly midway between Shreveport and Taylor's latest point of concentration, just southeast of Mansfield. He had known what to do, but he had been so hesitant to do it that he had wound up not knowing what to do after all.

Dick Taylor had not helped with his hard-breathing threats to gamble everything on a single long-odds strike, provoked by desperation and congenital impatience. "When Green joins me, I repeat," he notified headquarters, "I shall fight a battle for Louisiana, be the forces of the enemy what they may." Horrified, Smith urged caution. "A general engagement should not be risked without hopes of success," he warned, reminding his impetuous lieutenant that rashness "would be fatal to the whole cause and to the department. Our role must be a defensive policy." Moreover, such resolution as he had managed so far to maintain, regarding his plan for meeting the two-pronged Federal menace, was grievously shaken by Taylor's expressed opinion that Steele, a "bold, ardent, vigorous" professional, might constitute a graver danger, despite his reported disparity in numbers, than the amateur Banks, who was "cold, timid, [and] easily foiled." Smith continued to waver under the suspicion that he had chosen the wrong man to tackle first. Finally on April 5, alarmed by news that Steele was making rapid progress, and in fact had completed nearly half his southward march by crossing the Little Missouri River the day before, he decided to ride down to Mansfield for a conference with Taylor. His intention was to revise his plan by reversing it. He would concentrate everything first against Steele, rather than in front of Banks, even if this meant standing a siege at Shreveport or retreating into Texas, where — it now occurred to him, as a further persuasive argument for postponing the showdown — a defeat would be more disastrous for the invaders.

Taylor was dismayed by his chief's vacillation. Asked for his advice three days ago he had been quick to give it. "Action, prompt, vigorous action, is required," he replied. "While we are deliberating the enemy is marching. King James lost three kingdoms for a mass. We may lose three states without a battle." He still felt that way about it, and he said so, face to face with Smith at Mansfield on the morning of April 6. Smith heard him out, a mild-mannered Floridian just under forty, outwardly unperturbed by the short-tempered Taylor, but left that afternoon to return to his headquarters, still gripped inwardly by indecision. Taylor, though he had been reinforced that day by Green, whose arrival raised his strength to 9000 effectives, still had been given no definite instructions. Churchill's 4500 were at Keatchie, twenty miles away, but when or whether they would be released to him he did not know. All Smith had said was that he would inform him as soon as he made up his mind — the one thing he seemed incapable of doing. Taylor apparently decided, then and there, that if anything was going to be done in this direction he would have to accomplish it on his own. And that was what he did, beginning the following day, except that he had considerable help from his opponent, who presented him with a tactical opportunity he did not feel he could neglect, with or without the approval of his superior, forty miles away in Shreveport.

Banks came on boldly, still exuding confidence as he prepared at Natchitoches and Grand Écore for the final stage of his ascent of the Red. Alexandria lay sixty miles behind him, Shreveport only sixty miles ahead. The first half of this 120-mile stretch had been covered in five days of easy marching, and he planned to cover the second half in less.

Such frets as he had encountered up to now came not from the rebels, who he was convinced wanted no part of a hand-to-hand encounter, but from internal complications. For one thing, smallpox had broken out in the Marine Brigade, with the result that it was returned to Vicksburg and Kilby Smith's division took over the pleasant duty of "escorting" — that is, riding with — the fleet. The loss of these 3000 marines, who had not been included in his original calculations anyhow, was largely offset by the arrival of the 1500-man Corps d'Afrique, composed of Negro volunteers who had proved their combat worth to doubters at Port Hudson the year before.

Another complication was not so easily dismissed, however, for it had to do with money: meaning cotton. Banks had been getting very little of this because of Porter, who had been getting a great deal of it indeed — all, in fact, that came within his 210-gun reach. Unlike the army, which seized and turned over rebel cotton to the government as contraband of war, the navy defined cotton as subject to seizure more or less as if it was an authentic high-seas prize, the proceeds of which were to be divided among the officers and crew of the vessel that confiscated it, the only stipulation being that the bales had to have been the property of the Confederate government. Very little of it was, of course, but that did not cramp Porter or his sailors. They simply stenciled "C.S.A." on each captured bale, then drew a line through the still-wet letters and stenciled "U.S.N." below. When an army colonel remarked that the result signified "Cotton Stealing Association of the United States Navy," the admiral laughed as loud as anyone, if not louder, in proportion to his lion's share of the proceeds as commander of the fleet. This would not have been so bad, in itself; Banks, though punctiliously honest, had grown more or less accustomed to such practices by others, in the service as in politics. The trouble was that the upriver planters, hearing of Porter's activities below, began to burn their cotton rather than have it fall into his hands. By the time the civilian speculators, who had accompanied the army from New Orleans and were prepared to pay the going backwoods price for the hoarded staple, arrived in the wake of the gunboats, bearing trade permits signed by Chase and even Lincoln, there was nothing left for them to buy, either cheap or dear, for resale to the hungry mills of New England. Moreover, they directed their resentment less at Porter, who after all was doing nothing they would not have done in his place, than at Banks, who they believed had lured them up this winding rust-colored river only to dash their hopes by failing to deliver even a fraction of what he had encouraged them to expect. By the time they reached Alexandria it was evident there was nothing to be gained by going farther; Banks made it official by ordering their return. They had no choice except to obey, but they were bitter as only men could be who had been wounded in their wallets. "When General Banks sent them all back to Alexandria, without their sheaves," a staff officer later wrote, "they returned to New Orleans furious against him and mouthing calumnies."

It was of course no good thing, militarily or politically, for a man to have such enemies in his rear, but at least he was rid of a frock-coated clan who, he complained, had "harassed the soul out of me." And though they would be quick to fix the blame on him in case of a mishap, let alone an outright failure, Banks was more confident than ever that nothing of the kind was going to happen. It was not going to happen because there would be no tactical occasion for it to happen; Taylor simply would not risk a probable defeat. After reviewing his troops at Natchitoches on April 4 — a frequent practice which always brought him pleasure and tended to enlarge his self-respect — the former Bay State governor said as much in a letter to his wife. "The enemy retreats before us," he informed her, "and will not fight a battle this side of Shreveport if then."

When two days later — April 6: the second anniversary of Shiloh — he set out on the final leg of his advance, his route and order of march demonstrated, even more forcefully than his letters to Halleck and Mrs Banks had done, the extent of his conviction that the rebels would not dare to stand and fight before he reached his goal. At Grand Ecore the land and water columns diverged for the first time in the campaign, the former taking an inland road that curved west, then northwest, through the villages of Pleasant Hill and Mansfield, and finally northeast, back toward the Red, for a meeting with the fleet abreast of Springfield Landing, roughly two thirds of the way to Shreveport, which they then would capture by a joint attack. Banks chose this route either because he did not know there was a road along the river (there was, and a good one) or else because he thought the inland road, leading as it did through piny highlands, would make for better progress. If this last was what he had in mind, he was mistaken in that too. According to one of the marchers, a heavy rain soon made the single narrow road "more like a broad, deep, red-colored ditch than anything else." Heavy-footed, sometimes ankle-deep in mire, they cursed him as they slogged: particularly A. J. Smith's Westerners, who by now had acquired a scathing contempt for the former Massachusetts politician and the men of his five divisions, mainly Easterners from New York and New England. Paper-collar dudes, they called them, and referred with grins to the general himself, whose lack of military training and acumen was common gossip around their campfires, as "Napoleon P. Banks" or, even more scornfully, "Mr Banks."

Nor was the poor condition of the road itself the worst of the disadvantages an inland march involved. Beyond Natchitoches, in addition to being deprived of the support of Porter's heavy guns, the westering column would encounter few streams or wells, which would make for thirsty going, and little or nothing in the way of food or feed. One look at the sparsely settled region back from the river convinced a newsman that "such a thing as subsisting an army in a country like this could only be achieved when men and horses can be induced to live on pine trees and resin." Fortunately — at least from the subsistence point of view — Banks had brought along a great many wagons, no fewer in fact than a thousand, which assured that his soldiers would suffer no shortage of bacon or hardtack or coffee while crossing the barrens, although Smith's gorillas, whom Sherman had accustomed to traveling light, were so unappreciative as to sneer that they were loaded with iron bedsteads, feather bolsters, and other such creature comforts for the city-bred dandies under his command. That was of course false, or in any case a gross exaggeration, but it was altogether true that those thousand wagons and their teams did at once decrease the speed and greatly increase the length of the column: the more so because of the way they were distributed along it, with an eye for accessibility rather than for delivering or receiving an attack. Up front was a division of cavalry, followed by its train of 300 wagons. Next came the three remaining infantry divisions (the fourth had been left on guard at Alexandria, charged with unloading and reloading supply boats in order to get them over the low-water falls and rapids) of the two corps that had slogged up the Teche under Major General William B. Franklin, top man in the West Point class of 1843, in which he had finished twenty places above his classmate U. S. Grant, and a veteran of hard fighting in Virginia. Close behind them came their train of 700 wagons, with the Corps d'Afrique as escort. A. J. Smith's two remaining divisions (the third, Kilby Smith's, was taking it easy aboard transports, ascending Red River with the fleet) brought up the rear. However, so slow was the progress, so wretched the road, and so strung-out the column by the accordion action of all those interspersed mules and wagons, it was not until the following morning that Smith's jeering veterans lurched into motion out of Grand Ecore. By then the column measured no less than twenty miles from head to tail: a hard day's march under better conditions, by far, than here prevailed.

That was April 7, and before it was over Banks had cause to

suspect that he had erred in his estimate of the enemy's intention. Three miles beyond Pleasant Hill by midafternoon of this second day out, the cavalry encountered mounted graybacks who, for once, did not scamper at the threat of contact. Instead, to the dismay of the Federal horsemen, they set spur to their mounts, some half a dozen regiments or more, and charged with a wild Texas yell. The bluecoats broke, then rallied on their reserves; whereupon the rebels fell back, as before. That was about all there was to it; but the cavalry commander, Brigadier General Albert Lee, a thirty-year-old former Kansas lawyer, began to reflect intently on the disadvantages of his situation, particularly with regard to those 300 wagons directly in his rear, between him and the nearest infantry support. Several times already he had asked Franklin to let him shift his train back down the column, combining it with the infantry's, but Franklin had declined; let the cavalry look after its own train, he said. Now that the rebs were showing signs of fight, Lee made the same request again, with a further plea for infantry reinforcements, and received the same reply to both requests. In fact, when the young cavalryman tried to make camp near sunset, six miles beyond Pleasant Hill, Franklin sent word for him to push on four miles farther, train and all, so that the infantry would have plenty of room to clear the town next morning. Lee obeyed, though with increased misgivings, and was brought to a halt at nightfall, just short of his objective, Carroll's Mill, where he found gray riders once more drawn up in a strong position directly across his front, midway between Pleasant Hill and Mansfield.

Depressed by the notion of what was likely to result if he was struck by superior numbers on the march next day, he repeated his plea for reinforcements to Colonel John S. Clark, one of Banks's aides, who came forward that night to see how things were going. The colonel, agreeing that things were not going well, or in any case that the danger Lee foresaw was possible, rode back to present the cavalryman's request to Franklin in person, only to have him refuse it as flatly as before. So Clark returned to Pleasant Hill, where headquarters had been established that afternoon, for a conference with the army commander. Banks agreed that caution was in order, overruled Franklin, and directed him to send a brigade of infantry to reinforce the cavalry by daybreak. Franklin did so, though it went against his grain, and when Lee started forward next morning at sunrise he was pleased to find the rebel horsemen once more fading back from contact after each long-range exchange of shots, apparently intimidated by the steely glint of bayonets down the column, which signified that the front-riding cavalry now had close-up infantry support.

This continued for half a dozen miles: quick spatters of small-arms fire, followed by sudden gray withdrawals. It was hard for Lee to tell whether the Johnnies were really afraid of him or only pretending to be, in order to lure him on. Then the head of the column emerged from the dense pine woods to find itself on the rim of a large clearing, half a mile deep and half again as wide, with a broad, low hill in the center, on whose crest he saw a line of butternut skirmishers. He halted, brought his infantry to the front, and sent them forward, textbook style. The gray pickets gave ground before the massed advance, but when Lee rode up to the crest of the hill down whose opposite slope the rebs had scrambled for safety, he found his worst fears realized. There below him, in the woods along the far edge of the clearing, stretched a Confederate line of battle: not merely cavalry now, he saw, but infantry too, in heavy files, with artillery mixed in.

It was Taylor, and it was here, within twenty miles of the Texas border — only that bit short of having retreated across the entire width of his home state, leaving its people to the by no means tender mercy of the self-styled "gorillas" in his wake — that he was determined to make his stand. Last night, on his own initiative, he had sent Churchill word to march at dawn from Keatchie, twenty miles away; after which (but no sooner than the sun was four hours high, lest there be time for his order to be countermanded) he got off a note to Kirby Smith at Shreveport, saying laconically of Banks: "I consider this as favorable a point to engage him at as any other."

Sabine Crossroads, the place was called, three miles short of Mansfield, where four roads forked. One led east, allowing the Federals a chance to effect an early junction with their fleet; another branched northwest to Keatchie, which would place them in the path of the reinforcements moving toward him; while the other two ran generally north along parallel routes, giving the invaders a straight shot at Shreveport. Once they were where those four roads came together, free to choose whichever fit their fancy, Taylor's hope of blocking them would be gone, along with his chance to catch them out from under the umbrella protection of their heavy naval guns, strung out on a narrow, ditchlike road in a single, wagon-choked column. Moreover, in considering the tactical opportunity Banks was thus affording him, he had more in mind than a mere defensive stand, whatever numerical odds he might encounter. Like his old mentor in the Shenandoah Valley, he hoped to inflict what Stonewall had sometimes called "a speedy blow" or, more often, "a terrible wound."

Accordingly, while Tom Green and his Texans continued the harassment they had begun in earnest three miles this side of Pleasant Hill, Taylor chose his field of fight and began to make his preparations, including the summoning of the two infantry divisions then at Keatchie. The two already with him, under Major General J. G. Walker and Brigadier General Alfred Mouton, were ordered to return at first light, from Mansfield back to Sabine Crossroads, where they would take position along the near edge of the clearing, respectively on the right and left of the road that crossed the low hill just ahead. Cavalry

Another Grand Design [43]

under Brigadier Generals Hamilton Bee and James Major would guard the flanks, and a four-gun battery, posted astride the road, would stiffen the center. In Mansfield itself, by way of further preparation, private houses were selected and put in order for use as hospitals, and surplus wagons were sent rearward to clear the streets. Taylor was leaving as little as possible to chance, though he was also prepared to seize upon anything chance offered in the way of tactical opportunities; Green's troopers, for example, the most experienced and dependable body of men in his command, were to be employed wherever they seemed likely to prove most useful in that regard when they arrived. This force of 9000 infantry, cavalry, and artillery would be increased to 13,500 when Churchill got there, and though Taylor would not enjoy a numerical superiority even then — there were 20,000 blue effectives in the twenty-mile-long column toiling toward him — he intended to make up for that with the sheer fury of his attack, which he would design to make the most of his intimate knowledge of the ground, having chosen it with just that aim in mind. Nor was terrain the only advantage on which he based his belief that he would win when it came to shooting. "My confidence of success in the impending engagement was inspired by accurate knowledge of the Federal movements," he later wrote, adding that he was encouraged as well by previous acquaintance with "the character of their commander, General Banks, whose measure had been taken in the Virginia campaigns of 1862 and since."

By midmorning, April 8, he had established the line of battle the blue cavalry commander found confronting him when he topped the hill at midday. Young Lee sent back at once for additional reinforcements, meantime getting his batteries into positions from which to probe the gray defenses. A long-range artillery duel ensued, in the course of which Banks arrived in person for a look at the situation. He was undismayed. In fact, this was precisely what he had said he wanted on the day he set out from Grand Ecore: "The main force of the enemy was at last accounts in the vicinity of Mansfield, on the stage road between Natchitoches and Shreveport, and the major general commanding desires to force him to give battle, if possible, before he can concentrate behind the fortifications of Shreveport or effect a retreat westerly into Texas." Warned now by Lee that, in his opinion, "we must fall back immediately, or we must be heavily reinforced," Banks told him to hold what he had; he himself would "hurry up the infantry." That took time, partly because the cavalry train had two or three miles of the road blocked, but about 3.30 the other brigade of Franklin's lead division arrived to join the first. Hard on its heels came a courier with instructions for Lee to advance immediately on Mansfield. Shocked — for the town was three miles beyond the enemy line of battle, and he estimated that the rebels "must have some 15,000 or 20,000 men there; four or five times as many as I had" — the young cavalryman rode in search of Banks, who confirmed the validity of the order. Paraphrasing his protest, Lee said later: "I told him we could not advance ten minutes without a general engagement, in which we would be most gloriously flogged, and I did not want to do it." Given pause by this, although he was unwilling to abandon the attack, the army commander at any rate agreed to postpone it until another division of Franklin's infantry arrived, and he sent a staffer back to see that it was hurried forward with a minimum of delay.

Dick Taylor had bided his time up to now, but only by the hardest. Though he affected the unbuttoned, rather languid combat style of his father, Old Rough-and-Ready, sitting his horse with one leg thrown across the pommel of his saddle while casually smoking a cigar, he was anxious to force the issue. At one point, around 2 o'clock, when he believed he saw bluecoats massing for an attack on his left, he shifted one of Walker's brigades to Mouton and one of Bee's regiments to Major, but aside from this he did little except watch for an opening that would justify going over to the offensive before Churchill arrived from Keatchie. Meantime the Union buildup continued, although toward no apparent climax; Banks seemed unwilling to throw the punch that would invite the counterblow Taylor was eager to deliver. Finally, just after 4 o'clock, with a scant three hours of daylight still remaining, he decided to wait no longer. Mouton, on the strengthened left, was told to go forward.

He did so, promptly: "like a cyclone," one blue defender later said, while another described the charging graybacks as "infuriated demons." Mouton was among the first to fall, thirty-five years old, a West-Point-trained Shiloh veteran, son of the Creole governor who had helped to vote Louisiana out of the Union. His senior brigadier, Camille Armand Jules Marie, Prince de Polignac — "Polecat" to his Louisianians and Texans, who were unable to pronounce the royal name of the young Crimea veteran with the dapper beard and spike mustache — took over and pressed the uphill charge. His unleashed soldiers struck and broke the Federal right, routing two of the regiments there, and turned three captured guns on the fugitives as they fled. Taylor, observing the success of this while it was still in midcareer, sent word for Walker and Bee to go in, too: which they did, with similar results on the right, while Green threw his Texans into the melee on the left, exploiting on horseback the confusion Mouton and Polignac had begun on foot. All down the line, as the gray chargers emerged from the pine woods into the clearing to strike at both ends of the confused blue line, the high-throated rebel yell rang out.

Some on the opposite side did what they could to stay the rout. "Try to think you're dead and buried," a Massachusetts colonel told his men, "and you will have no fear." Either they did not try it at all, or else they tried and found it did not work; in any case, they ran and kept on running. Apparently it was the abruptness of the assault that made it so demoralizing, and this applied as much to those in the rear as to those up front. "Suddenly," a journalist on Banks's staff would recall, "there was a rush, a shout, the crashing of trees, the breaking down of rails, the rush and scamper of men. It was as sudden as though a thunderbolt had fallen among us, and set the pines on fire. I turned to my companion to inquire the reason of this extraordinary proceeding, but before he had the chance to reply, we found ourselves swallowed up, as it were, in a hissing, seething, bubbling whirlpool of agitated men." Franklin was among them by then, having brought his second division up the hill in time for it to join the rout and add to the lengthening casualty list, which would include some 1500 captives and about half that many killed and wounded. One of these last was Franklin himself, who was struck by a bullet in the shin and lost his horse, then took off rearward on a borrowed mount to brace his third division for the shock about to come. Banks too was intimately involved in the confusion, and like Franklin he did what he could, which was not much. Removing his hat for easy recognition, he shouted to the skulkers running past him on the road: "Form a line here! I know you will not desert me." He knew wrong. "Hoo!" they cried, and kept running. So he drew his sword and waved it about; but that worked no better. By then the fleeing troops had become what one of them afterwards called "a disorganized mob of screaming, sobbing, hysterical, pale, terror-stricken men."

Taylor was intent on completing his triumph by pressing the pursuit. Near sundown there was an interruption by a courier who arrived from Shreveport with a letter Kirby Smith had written that morning, urging caution. "A general engagement now could not be given with our full force," he advised. "Reinforcements are moving up — not very large, it is true. . . . Let me know as soon as you are convinced that a general advance is being made and I will come to the front." Taylor scanned it hastily, then looked up smiling. "Too late, sir," he said. "The battle is won." However, he took time to get off a dispatch announcing the victory to his chief, so far as it had been accomplished up to now. "Will report again at the close of the action," he ended the message. "Churchill's troops were not up in time to take part [but] will be fresh in the morning. I shall push the enemy to the utmost."

He did not wait for morning; Jackson-style, he made full use of the hour of daylight still remaining, though the going was as rough for him as it was for the retreating Federals. Panicky teamsters, unable to turn around on the narrow road, had unhitched their mules for a mounted getaway and left the wagons behind as a barricade against pursuit, their bare tongues extended at all angles to trip the unwary. One result of this was the denial of the road to such guns as had avoided capture up to then; Taylor took no less than twenty of them in all, along with ten times as many wagons, some with and some without their teams, but all loaded. Meantime Franklin was putting his third division, which was as large as the other two combined, into a stout defensive position along a ridge just back from a creek in a ravine about four miles from Sabine Crossroads. The pursuers came up raggedly, attacked piecemeal in the dusk, and were repulsed. Taylor knew it was time to call a halt, but not quite yet if his men were to have water for the night; so he contented himself with driving the blue pickets back to their ridge and taking possession of the creek in the ravine. There he stopped, intending to renew the pressure in the morning, and the firing died away in the darkness, giving place to a silence broken only by the wounded crying for water and by the scavengers, back up the road, reveling on the good things found in the captured Yankee train.

As one of his own generals had predicted at the outset, to his face, Banks had been "most gloriously flogged." Out of 12,000 Federals engaged, 2235 had been killed, wounded, or captured, while Taylor, with 9000, had lost less than half as many. Nor was that the worst of it, by any means. In addition to twenty guns and two hundred wagons, Banks had also lost time — the one thing he could least afford to lose if he was to occupy Shreveport and get Sherman's soldiers back to him on schedule. And to make matters worse, caught as he was without water for his parched troops on the ridge, he must lose still more time by retreating still farther to reach another stream and another stout position in which to defend himself from the blood-thirsty graybacks, whom he could hear feasting on their spoils, back up the road, and who obviously intended to have another go at him tomorrow, probably at daylight. Even if he could stay here all night without water, it was doubtful whether A. J. Smith's two divisions, camped a dozen miles away at Pleasant Hill, could arrive in time for a share in the defense. A council of war advised the obvious, and the withdrawal got under way at 10 o'clock. By midnight all the survivors were on the march in a bedraggled column made up largely of stragglers blown loose from their commands, "men without hats or coats, men without guns or accoutrements, cavalrymen without horses and artillerymen without cannon, wounded men bleeding and crying at every step, men begrimed with smoke and powder, all in a state of fear and frenzy."

One among them saw them so, yet supposed in his extreme distress that Banks was the most dejected man of all. He had left Grand Ecore expecting to be in Shreveport within four days, yet here he was, marching in the opposite direction into the dawn of that fourth day. As he rode among his trudging men it must have begun to occur to him that a great deal more than the van of his army had been wrecked at Sabine Crossroads. Any general who could not capture Shreveport with the odds as much in his favor as these had been was not likely to be given the chance to take Mobile. And without that feather in his cap, his chances of occupying the White House were considerably diminished, if not abolished, especially when he recalled the scapegoat hunt that invariably followed every failure such as the one in which he was now involved. Who that scapegoat was likely to be, he knew only too well; perhaps he even had time to regret the cotton speculators he had sent back to New Orleans "without their sheaves," and who were there now, "mouthing calumnies." He was indeed dejected by the time he drew near Pleasant Hill, having failed to spot a good defensive position anywhere along the road, though it may well have improved his outlook to find A. J. Smith's hard fighters already disposed for battle and looking determined. "If it comes to the worst," an Iowa colonel had told his troops when he called them out at 2 o'clock that morning to give them news of the defeat a dozen miles away, "I ask of you to show yourselves to be men."

They showed that, and more, when Taylor came up eleven hours later, hard on the trail of the dejected bluecoats he had whipped the day before, and after a two-hour rest halt, required by Churchill's road-worn Arkansans and Missourians, flung his reinforced victors forward with orders for them to "rely on the bayonet, as we had neither time nor ammunition to waste."

This was bravely said, but it was far from easily done. Taking heart from the stalwart look of Sherman's veterans, Banks had spent the morning hours preparing to defend the low, open, house-dotted plateau known felicitously as Pleasant Hill. During this time, according to a newsman, the area "had the appearance of a parade ground on a holiday, regiments marching to the right, regiments marching to the left, batteries being moved and shifted." Near the center of all this activity, in the yard of a house affording a panoramic view of the line thus being drawn, the journalist observed "a small cluster of gentlemen to whom all this phantasmagoria had the meaning of life and death, and power, and fame." It was Banks, surrounded by his chief lieutenants. He wore his light blue overcoat buttoned high against the April chill, and he passed the time "strolling up and down, occasionally conversing with a member of his staff or returning the salute of a passing subaltern." Franklin was there, limping on his wounded leg, his manner calm except for an occasional nervous tug at his whiskers, and so were A. J. Smith, sunlight glinting on his spectacles, and Brigadier General Charles P. Stone, who, after six months of confinement in army prisons and nine of unemployment, had been militarily resurrected by Banks as his chief of staff, thus giving the West Pointer a chance to dispel the cloud of suspicion that had gathered about his head and caused his arrest following Ball's Bluff, where he was accused of having treasonably exposed his men to slaughter. Not yet forty, "a quiet, retiring man who is regarded, by the few that know him, as one of the finest soldiers of our time," Stone sat on a rail fence, smoking cigarettes — a modern touch; cigarettes would continue to be rare and exotic until well into the following decade — and seemed to the reporter "more interested in the puffs of smoke that curled around him than in the noise and bustle that filled the air."

Gradually the noise and bustle died away as the various outfits settled down in their assigned positions and the day wore on and grew warmer. The genial cluster of uniformed gentlemen began to seem to the newsman "a rather tedious party," and apparently they themselves were of much the same opinion. Having done all they could in the way of preparation, the gold braid wearers had nothing to do now but wait, and while they did so they milled about rather aimlessly; "group after group formed and melted away," the reporter noted, "and re-formed and discussed the battle of the evening before, and the latest news and gossip of New Orleans, and wondered when another mail would come."

Whatever tedium his lieutenants might be experiencing, Banks had felt his confidence rise steadily with the sun. By noon, when the generals broke for lunch, he had convinced himself there would be no serious fighting today, and afterward, digesting the excellent meal while the sun swung past the overhead and began its long decline, he took such heart that he began to think of recovering the initiative and thereby repairing the damage his reputation had suffered yesterday. Surely Grant and Lincoln would forgive him for being a little behind schedule if he emerged from these piny highlands with a substantial victory in his grasp. He would go back over to the offensive; he would redeem his failure; he would salvage his career. Though his train was already well on its way to Grand Ecore — what was left of it, at any rate — he made up his mind to resume the advance on Shreveport, and he got off a message saying as much to Porter. "I intend to return this evening on the same road with General Franklin's and General A. J. Smith's commands," he informed the admiral. Today was Saturday, and he added that he expected "to be in communication with the transports of General Kilby Smith and the gunboats at Springfield Landing on Sunday evening or Monday forenoon."

Once more he was wrong in a prediction, but this time it was not for lack of a tactical success. Aware that the Federals were braced for an attack from straight ahead, Taylor took his time about deploying for an end-on strike by Churchill, designed to crumple and roll up the Union left while Walker held in front; Green meantime would probe and feint at the enemy right, working his way around it in order to cut off the expected blue retreat to Grand Ecore, and Polignac would be in reserve, since his division had suffered two thirds of the casualties yesterday, though he would of course be committed when the time was ripe. It was close to 5 o'clock before Churchill, having roused his men from their two-hour rest, had marched them into position in the woods due west of the unsuspecting Federal left.

He then went forward with much of the fury Mouton had shown the day before, provoking similar consternation in the Union ranks. To one defender, "the air seemed all alive with the sounds of various projectiles." These ranged, he said, "from the spiteful, cat-like spit of the buckshot, the *pouf* of the old-fashioned musket ball and the *pee-ee-zing* of the minie bullet, to the roar of the ordinary shell and the *whoot-er whoot-er* of the Whitworth 'mortar-pestle'; while the shrieks of wounded men and horses and the yells of the apparently victorious rebels added to the uproar." Back up the Mansfield road, Green and Walker chimed in with their guns, contributing new tones to the concert, and now that the assailed enemy flank had begun to crumble, they put their troops in motion, mounted and dismounted, against the right and center. Churchill kept up the pressure, gathering prisoners by the score as Franklin's unstrung men fled eastward across the open ground of the plateau. Determined to make up for having missed it, the Arkansans and Missourians were intent on restaging yesterday's blue rout, about which they had heard so much since their arrival from Keatchie the night before, in time to share in the pursuit but not the glory.

A. J. Smith's two divisions had not been at Sabine Crossroads either, but they too were very much in the thick of things at Pleasant Hill: as Churchill's elated attackers soon found out. Smith had seen the flank give way, the graybacks whooping in pursuit of Franklin's rattled soldiers, who by now were in flight through the village behind their line, and had sent a reserve brigade in that direction on the double, soon following it with other units which he pulled out of his portion of the line to meet the graver threat. Attempting a wide left wheel, which would enable them to assault the Federal center from the rear and in mass, the cheering rebels at the extremity of the pivot were caught end-on by the advancing blue brigade, freezing the cheers in their throats and bringing them to a huddled, stumbling halt. They wavered, lashed by sheets of fire, and then gave way, not in a single rush but in fragments, as regiment after regiment came unhinged. They made one stand, in a heavy growth of cane along a creekbank they had passed on their way in, but Smith's Westerners came after them with a roar, delivering point-blank volleys and finally closing with clubbed muskets; whereupon the gray withdrawal, already touched with panic, degenerated abruptly into a rout. Now it was the Federals doing the whooping and the crowing, and the Confederates doing the running, as the counterattack grew into a grand right wheel, pivoting irresistibly on the retaken village of Pleasant Hill, so recently overrun by gray attackers.

Taylor saw and tried to forestall the sudden reverse, but Walker had just been carried from the field with a bullet in his groin, Green was intent on maneuvering to cut off the expected blue retreat, and Polignac could not come up through the gathering dusk in time for anything more than a try at discouraging the exultant pursuit. This he managed to do, holding a line two miles from the scene of the break, while the other three divisions fell back another four miles to the nearest water. The battle was over and Taylor had lost it, along with three guns abandoned when his flankers were themselves outflanked and thrown into sudden retreat. With some 12,500 men engaged, the Confederates had suffered a total of 1626 casualties, while the Federals, with about the same number on the field, had lost 1369. Though it was by no means as great as yesterday's, when fortune had smiled on the other side and blood had flowed more freely, Banks knew whom to thank for this disparity, along with much else. When the firing stopped and the rebels had passed out of sight in the pines and darkness, he rode over to A. J. Smith and took him gratefully by the hand. "God bless you, General," he said. "You have saved the army."

Tremendously set up by the sudden conversion of near-certain defeat to absolute victory, he was more anxious than ever to get back on the track to Shreveport, and he not only said as much to Smith while shaking his hand; he also sent a message instructing Albert Lee, who was riding escort, to turn the wagon train around and come back to Pleasant Hill. However, when he returned to headquarters to confer with Franklin and two of his brigadiers, William H. Emory and William Dwight — both had commanded divisions under Banks for more than a year, and both had always given him dependable advice — he found all three West Pointers opposed to resuming the offensive, especially in the precipitous manner he proposed. Franklin and Emory favored an eastward march across Bayou Pierre to Blair's Landing on the Red, there to reunite with Kilby Smith, secure a safe supply line, and regain the protection of the fleet, whereas Dwight urged a return to Grand Ecore for the same purpose. This last was much the safest course, and Banks, his enthusiasm quenched by this dash of cold water from the high-ranking trio of professionals, decided to adopt it. Orders went out for an immediate resumption of the retreat.

When word of this reached A. J. Smith he went at once to protest what seemed to him a loss of backbone. Banks refused to reconsider his decision, citing his lack of supplies, his loss in the past two days of just over 3600 men, and the advice of all his other generals. Smith then asked for time at least to bury his dead and finish gathering up his wounded, but Banks declined that too. Furious, the bespectacled Pennsylvanian, his gray-streaked whiskers bristling with indignation, went to Franklin, whom he found enjoying a cup of coffee, and proposed that, as second in command, he put Banks in arrest and take charge of the army for a rapid advance on Shreveport. Franklin stirred and sipped his coffee, nursed his injured shin, and said quietly: "Smith, don't you know this is mutiny?" That ended the protest, if not the anger. In the small hours after midnight, leaving their non-walking wounded behind — the train had left that morning with all the wagons: including through some mixup, those containing the army's medical supplies — the weary bluecoats formed ranks and slogged away from the scene of their victory, down the road to Grand Ecore.

Ten miles in the opposite direction, up the Mansfield road at Carroll's Mill, Taylor was wakened from his badly needed sleep at 10 o'clock that night by Kirby Smith, who had learned of the Sabine Crossroads fight at 4 o'clock that morning and left Shreveport at once to join his army in the field, only to find at the end of his sixty-mile horseback ride that still a second unauthorized battle had been fought. What was worse, even though this one had been lost, Taylor seemed intent on provoking a third — with any number of others to follow, so long as his blood was up and anything blue remained within his reach. It was more or less clear to Smith by now that if the Louisianian was left to his own devices he would use up the army entirely, leaving him nothing with which to defend his Transmississippi headquarters and supply base from an amphibious assault by Porter, whose gunboats and gorilla-laden transports were at Loggy Bayou, within pouncing distance of Shreveport, and/or an overland attack by Steele, whose troops had crossed the Little Missouri five days ago, brushing Price's horsemen casually aside, and by now might well be closer to their goal than its supposed defenders were at Carroll's Mill. Informed of this, Taylor increased his chief's dismay by proposing to ignore that double threat in order to keep the heat on Banks; both Porter and Steele would withdraw of their own accord, he argued, as soon as they learned that the main Federal column had pulled back. Smith would not hear of taking such a risk, even though Taylor kept insisting that, with Banks on the run and Porter likely to be stranded by low water, "we had but to strike vigorously to capture or destroy both." Finally the department commander ended the discussion with a peremptory order for the infantry to take up the march for Shreveport the following day. If the danger there was as slight as Taylor claimed, he could return and try his hand at the destruction he had in mind downriver.

The result next morning was a rather unusual tactical situation wherein two armies, having met and fought, retreated in opposite directions from the field for which they had presumably been contending. It was made even more unusual, perhaps, by the fact that the victors were unhappier than the losers, and this was especially true of the two commanders. Disgruntled though Taylor was at having been overruled by his superior, Banks was put through the worse ordeal of being sneered at by his military inferiors, all the way down to the privates in the ranks. Taking their cue from Franklin, who avoided such blame as came his way by letting it be known that he would never have recommended a withdrawal if the army had had a competent general at its head, even regimental commanders looked askance at Banks as he rode by them, doubling the column. The men themselves did more than exchange sly glances. Angry because some four hundred of their wounded comrades had been left behind to be nursed and imprisoned by the rebels, they began the march in a mutinous frame of mind, muttering imprecations. But presently the company clowns took over. After the manner of all soldiers everywhere, in all ages, they began to ridicule their plight and mock at the man who had caused it, inventing new words for old songs which they chanted as they slogged. For example, in remembrance of Bull Run:

> *In eighteen hundred and sixty-one*
> *We all skedaddled to Washington.*
> *In eighteen hundred and sixty-four*
> *We all skedaddled to Grand Ecore.*
> *Napoleon P. Banks!*

This last — "Napoleon P. Banks!" — was shouted for good measure as the general rode past, and recurred as a refrain in all the parodies they sang. Nor were such high jinks limited, as before, to A. J. Smith's irreverent gorillas. Banks's own men, whom he had commanded at Port Hudson and through the easy-living months in New Orleans, took up the songs and bawled them as he passed along the roadside, trailing a kite tail of smirking officers from his staff.

Fortunately, they had nothing worse to contend with, in the way of opposition on the march, than butternut cavalry which mainly limited its attention to stragglers until near the end of the second day, April 11, when it made a cut-and-slash attack that drove the rear brigade into Grand Ecore on the run. Once there, their prime concern was to protect themselves from the vengeful Taylor, who was reported to be hard on their heels with 25,000 effectives. They themselves would not have that many on hand until Franklin's fourth division came up the Red from Alexandria and A. J. Smith's third division returned from Loggy Bayou with the fleet, whose heavy guns they presently heard booming in the distance, apparently involved in some kind of trouble far upstream. Meantime they kept busy constructing a semicircular line of intrenchments around the landward side of the high-sited village on its bluff. They worked hard and well, incorporating the trunks and tops of large trees which they felled for use as breastworks and abatis. Not only did they require no urging from their officers in this work; they kept at it after they were told that they could stop.

"You don't need any protection. We can whip them easily here," Franklin chided a detail of diggers as he rode on a tour of inspection.

But they remembered Sabine Crossroads and the hilltop they had lost to a savage rebel charge: the result, they now believed, of having trusted their security to generals like this one. They kept digging.

"We have been defeated once," a spokesman replied, leaning on his shovel, "and we think we will look out for ourselves."

In point of fact they were by no means in such danger as they feared. Far from closing on their heels, Taylor's four divisions of infantry were fifty muddy miles away at Mansfield, marched there against his wishes in order to have them within supporting distance of Shreveport. And even when it turned out that the withdrawal had been unnecessary because his prediction was fulfilled — Steele veered from his southwest course on April 12 for an eastward strike at Camden, which would put him as far from Shreveport as he had been when he crossed the Little Missouri a week ago, and Porter not only ventured no farther up the Red, he was even now bumping his way downstream in an effort to rejoin Banks — Taylor constituted no real threat to the Federals intrenched at Grand Ecore, even though he was free at last to move against them, since he had by then a good deal less than one fourth the number of soldiers his adversary believed he was about to use in an all-out assault on the blufftop citadel. Convinced by captured dispatches that Banks would soon be obliged to withdraw if he was to get Sherman's troops across the Mississippi within the little time remaining, Kirby Smith believed there would be small profit in pursuing him through a region exhausted of supplies. Instead, he decided to go in person after Steele, who was still a threat, and for this purpose he took from Taylor not only Churchill's Arkansans and Missourians, who had been lent to help in stopping Banks, but also Walker's Texans, who would now return the favor by helping to stop Steele. That left the Louisiana commander with barely 5000 men in all: Polignac's infantry, bled down to fewer than 2000 effectives, and Green's cavalry, which numbered only a little above 3000, including a small brigade that had just arrived. In any case, however few they were, on April 14 he started them southward for Grand Ecore, where the bluecoats had obligingly penned themselves up, as if in a stockyard, awaiting slaughter.

Taylor himself went up to Shreveport next day, on the outside chance that he could persuade his chief to countermand the orders which he believed would deprive him of a golden opportunity. "Should the remainder of Banks' army escape me I shall deserve to wear a fool's cap for a helmet," he had said the week before, but now that his force had been reduced by more than half he was less confident of the outcome: especially when he learned that Tom Green, while attempting to add to the problems of the Union fleet in its withdrawal down the still-falling Red, had been killed two days ago in an exchange of fire with the gunboats at Blair's Landing, twenty miles above Grand Ecore. A veteran of the Texas war for independence, the Mexican War, the horrendous New Mexico expedition of early 1862, and the retaking of Galveston, the fifty-year-old Hero of Valverde had been Taylor's most dependable lieutenant in last year's fighting on the Teche and the Atchafalaya, as well as in the campaign still in progress down the Red. His loss was nearly as heavy a blow as the loss of the three divisions about to set out for Arkansas, and caused Taylor to redouble his efforts to have them returned while there was still a chance to overtake and destroy the invaders of Louisiana, afloat and ashore. But Kirby Smith was not to be dissuaded; Steele was the major danger now, and he intended to go after him in strength. "Should you move below and Steele's small column push on and accomplish what Banks has failed in, and destroy our shops at Jefferson and Marshall," he told Taylor, "we will not only be disgraced, but irreparably deprived of our means and resources."

Accordingly, he left Shreveport on April 16, taking Walker and Churchill with him. Taylor stayed on for two more days, arranging for the shipment of supplies, and then set out on the 19th to join what he called "my little force near Grand Ecore." He was still hopeful that the Federals could be bagged, despite the disparity in numbers, and he counted on using deception to that end. Compelled, as he said, "to eke out the lion's skin with the fox's hide," he had instructed his unit commanders to keep Banks on edge, and deceived as to their strength, "by sending drummers to beat calls, lighting campfires, blowing bugles, and rolling empty wagons over fence rails."

All this they had done, and more, with such effect that when Taylor dismounted near Grand Ecore on the evening of April 21, ending his ninety-mile ride, he found that the Federals had begun to pull out of the place that afternoon. The head of their column was already beyond Natchitoches, slogging south in an apparent attempt to take up a safer position at Alexandria, if not to get away entirely. Determined not to permit this, Taylor set about planning how to intercept the retiring bluecoats and, if possible, bring them to battle, although they outnumbered him five to one, exclusive of their heavily gunned flotilla. Their march was down the narrow "island" lying between Cane River and the Red, and it was his hope to force them into a strung-out halt that would give him a chance to go to work on them piecemeal. With this in mind, he sent Bee's brigade of cavalry on a fast ride south to Monett's Ferry, forty miles away at the far end of the island, with instructions to block the crossing of the Cane at that point, so that the rest of his troops could be thrown upon some vulnerable segment of the blue column stalled between there and Natchitoches. This was an ambitious undertaking for some 5000 men opposed by 25,000, but Taylor undertook it gladly, anticipating the Cannae he had been seeking all along.

Banks anticipated much the same thing, and moved rapidly to avoid it if he could. He was by now, as a result of the strain of the past ten days, about as edgy as even Taylor could have wished, and this edginess had been provoked by more than the various nerve-jangling ruses those "22,000 to 25,000" graybacks had been practicing in the woods beyond his semicircular line. For one, there was a growing sense of failure. He still had spasms and flickers of hope, during which he planned to go back over to the offensive, but these grew fewer and weaker as the days wore on, until finally they stopped. For another, he had found waiting for him at Grand Ecore a message from Sherman, notifying him that his lease on A. J. Smith's three divisions had expired and ordering their immediate return. This could be ignored or countermanded because of the exigencies of the situation, which plainly would permit no such detachment; but a few days later, on April 18, he received from Grant a follow-up letter of instructions that had for him, in his present hemmed-in state, a sound of hollow mockery not so easily dismissed. Written at the end of March, it set forth in some detail the procedure he was to follow, once Shreveport had been taken, in moving without delay against Mobile. "You cannot start too soon," the letter ended. "All I would now add is that you commence the concentration of your force at once. Preserve a profound secrecy of what you intend doing, and start at the earliest possible moment."

That was perhaps the cruelest blow; Grant had written as if in fervid haste, lest time be wasted between the fall of Shreveport, apparently expected momentarily, and the arrival of his letter urging Banks to be quick in taking the road to glory, which led from Shreveport to the White House, by way of Mobile, Atlanta, and Richmond. Contrasting what was with what might have been — for the road's only entrance, for him, was Shreveport, and he could not get there to take it — the former Bay State governor was correspondingly depressed. He relieved his spleen to some degree, however, with a pair of summary dismissals. One was of Stone, his chief of staff (Stone took no further part in the war, though afterwards he served the Khedive of Egypt in the same capacity for thirteen years, with the rank of lieutenant general, and then returned to act as chief engineer in the construction of the pedestal for the Statue of Liberty); Banks let him go because he found him "very weak," and the same might have been said of young Albert Lee, whom he relieved of duty as cavalry commander and sent back to New Orleans, although not without regret. He testified later that Lee had been "active, willing, and brave," if not skillful, and had "suffered, more or less unjustly, as all of us did, for being connected with that affair."

Such administrative corrections had little effect on a tactical situation which seemed to be growing increasingly grim as the rebels out in the brush continued to beat drums, build a myriad of campfires, blow bugles, and bring up what sounded like thousands of wagonloads of supplies and ammunition. For what purpose all this was being done Banks could only guess, but with every passing hour he was brought closer to the inevitable conclusion that if he could not go forward, as was obviously the case, then he would do well not to postpone going back. This applied most of all to Porter's gunboats, for the river was still falling: was already down, in fact, to half the seven-foot depth required to float them over the double falls at Alexandria. The thing to do was get back there as soon as possible, before the river took another perverse drop, for a close-up look at what was reported to be an impossible situation. So the admiral advised, although the temptation was strong to remain where he was, under the friendly bluff at Grand Ecore, his recent trip to Loggy Bayou having given him all too graphic a preview of what to expect in the course of his return to the Mississippi, down those more than three hundred winding miles of the Red. "It is easy to die here, and there are many ways of doing it," a sailor diarist had observed en route. In addition to the more or less normal dangers involved in descending a swift and crooked river at the speed required to maintain steerage — staved-in bows, unshipped rudders, broken wheels, and punctured hulls, all brought on by collisions with other boats, with underwater snags, with the iron-hard red clay bottom — there were the rebels to contend with, fast-firing marksmen who shot at passing or stalled vessels from hidden positions along both banks. At Blair's Landing, for example, where Tom Green was killed by a blast of canister, the fleet was exposed to what one veteran skipper called "the heaviest and most concentrated fire of musketry I have ever witnessed." As a result of this and other such nightmare encounters at places with names like Campti and Coushatta Chute, the thirty-boat flotilla got back from its ten-day upstream excursion sadly altered in appearance: especially the vessels loaded with Kilby Smith's gorillas, to which the butternut riflemen and cannoneers had given their particular attention. "The sides of some of the transports are half shot away," a soldier noted in his diary on April 15, after watching them come in, "and their smokestacks look like huge pepper boxes."

Porter recommended an immediate return to Alexandria, but Banks was not quite ready to make so frank an admission of defeat. That took him another four days, two of which he used to compose a letter to Grant, explaining that his retrograde movement from Mansfield had been due more to a shortage of water and the nonarrival of Steele than to resistance by the enemy — though he added, rather ingeniously, that the stubborn quality of the latter had proved the campaign to be "of greater importance than was generally anticipated at its commencement," and asked therefore that he be allowed to continue it beyond schedule, but only a bit, since "immediate success, with a concentration of our forces, is within our reach." Knowing Grant's low tolerance for failure, however skillfully disguised, he did not have much hope that his request would be granted, and he had even less hope, in case it was, that he would be continued in command. At the end of the four days (April 19: the day Taylor set out on his ninety-mile ride from Shreveport) Banks issued orders for a withdrawal to Alexandria. It got underway two days later, after A. J. Smith moved out and occupied Natchitoches, from which point he would cover the retreat by protecting the flanks of the column as it passed, then follow to serve as rear guard on the long march down the "island" between the two rivers, Cane and Red.

Whatever shortcomings the invaders had shown in the past forty days, they demonstrated conclusively, in the course of the next two, that their ability to cover ground at a fairly dazzling rate of speed not only had not been impaired, but in fact had been considerably improved by the events of the past two weeks. The march began at 5 o'clock in the afternoon, and by the time the tail of the column left Grand Ecore at 3 o'clock next morning, April 22, the men at the head were twenty miles away, taking their first rest while waiting for the others to close up. Before nightfall, the entire command had cleared Cloutierville, thirty-two miles from the starting point. Not even then was the blistering pace relaxed; Banks had learned that the rebels intended to contest his crossing of the Cane at Monett's Ferry, another dozen miles southeast, and he pressed on, determined to get off this jungly island and past the last natural obstacle between him and Alexandria, where he would recover the protection of the fleet and his army could once more break out its shovels and throw up dirt between itself and the danger of assault.

So far, its performance had been highly commendable from the logistics point of view; nor had it permitted haste to interfere unduly with the exercise of its various other talents. A. J. Smith's irrepressible campaigners, while holding off pursuers with one hand, so to speak, still found time for more than their usual quota of vandalism and destruction with the other. Grand Ecore had gone up in flames at the outset, along with the surplus goods the army left behind; then Natchitoches, whose old-world French and Spanish charm had been admired by many of its blue-clad visitors, was put to the torch as a farewell gesture. Gray cavalry came up in time to turn fire-fighters and save the latter place, as well as Cloutierville the following day, far down the island. But Smith's troops made up for this double disappointment with the amount of damage they inflicted on barns and houses along the road between the two, including even the cabins of the Negroes who turned out to welcome them. "At night the burning buildings mark our pathway," a marcher recorded. "As far as the eye can reach, we see in front new fires breaking out, and in the rear the dying embers tell the tale of war."

Close in their rear with Polignac, while his cavalry harassed their flanks and rode hard to get into position in their front, Taylor was finding it "difficult to restrain one's inclination to punish the ruffians engaged in this work." He meant that the prisoners were a temptation in that regard — blue-clad stragglers picked up along the roadside, blown and blistered or drunk on looted whiskey, unable to hold the pace Banks was setting them in his eagerness to attain the safety Alexandria would afford — but there was also the temptation for the pursuers to strike before the tactical iron was hot. Too quick a blow, delivered before the Federals had been brought to a disjointed halt on unfavorable terrain, would merely hasten their march and inflict only superficial damage, not to mention that it would be likely to disclose the smallness of Taylor's command; whereas if he waited till their path was blocked he might be able to bag the lot by tricking them (much as Bedford Forrest had tricked Abel Streight, about this time last year in Alabama) into surrendering to the "superior force" Banks believed was breathing down his neck. However, the Lousianian soon had cause to regret that he had stayed his hand, forgoing a leaner in hope of a fatter prize. Brigadier General Richard Arnold, Lee's replacement as chief of the Union cavalry — a thirty-six-year-old West Pointer, son of a former governor of Rhode Island and descendant of a distinguished New England family that included the notorious Benedict — had come upon Bee's dismounted brigade in a stout defensive position overlooking, from the opposite bank, the approaches to the Cane at Monett's Ferry. Instead of attempting the suicidal attack Bee expected, head-on down the road, Arnold located an upstream crossing for the infantry to use while he kept up a show of force in front and probed industriously below, as if in search of another crossing a couple of miles downriver, to attract Bee's attention in that direction.

It was neatly done. Emory's division, coming up at the head of the Federal main body on the morning of April 23, crossed the river two miles above the ferry and struck in force at the upstream rebel flank, while a second arriving division added its weight to the frontal demonstration and the downstream feint. This last was so well carried out, indeed, that Bee — a Charleston-born adoptive Texan whose younger brother had given T. J. Jackson his nom-de-guerre at First Manassas, but who himself had been a desk soldier until the present campaign — believed he was swamped on the right as well as the left, though in fact he had managed to inflict rather heavy casualties on the attackers from upstream. "The critical moment had come," he later reported; "the position turned on both flanks and a large force close in front ready to spring on the center." He counted himself fortunate to get away — "in good order at a walk," he noted — with a loss of "about 50 men and 1 artillery wagon . . . while the enemy lost full 400 killed and wounded," and he complained that, with fewer than 2000 men in all, he had been expected to block the path of "an army of 25,000 marching at their leisure on the main road to Alexandria." Yet that was exactly what had been expected of him, and Taylor was no more inclined to be charitable in such cases than was the man Bee's brother had caused to be nicknamed Stonewall. The fact remained that Banks had made his getaway, avoiding the destruction planned for him, and Bee had let the escape hatch be slammed ajar with a loss to himself of only "about 50 men and 1 artillery wagon." Nor was the disparity of losses any mitigation of the offense. "He displayed great personal gallantry, but no generalship," Taylor said of the South Carolinian, and ordered his removal from command.

Into the clear at last, though greatly relieved to be out of a jungle whose gloom seemed made for ambuscades, Banks did not slacken the pace for his foot-sore troops. He was still not half way to his goal, and he covered the last fifty miles with something of the hard-breathing urgency of a long-distance runner entering the stretch and catching sight of the tape drawn taut across the finish line, ready to be breasted. All through what was left of that day and the next, molested by nothing worse than small clusters of Confederate horse taking pot shots at the column from off in the pines, he kept going hard and fast, his over-all casualties now increased to about 4000, more than half of them captured or missing in battle and on the march. On the third day, April 25 — the fifth since he left Grand Ecore — the lead division slogged into Alexandria, followed next day by the others. There they promptly got to work with their shovels, heaving dirt, despite the recovered protection of Porter's fleet: what was left of it, at any rate, after an equally strenuous five days of fighting rebels and the river.

The admiral had suffered woes beyond a landman's comprehension, including the loss of his finest ironclad, the 700-ton *Eastport*. Sunk by a torpedo eight miles below Grand Ecore, she was patched and raised with the help of two pump boats hastily summoned upriver, and continued on her way — only to ground again in the shallow water forty miles below. Porter unshipped her four 9-inch guns, along with her other four 50- and 100-pounder Dahlgren and Parrott rifles, loading them onto a flat behind the light-draft gunboat *Cricket*, and thus got her afloat; at least for a time. She had only gone a few more miles, bumping bottom as she went, when she ran full tilt into a pile of snags, and there she stuck and settled. After three days' work by her crew and skipper, Lieutenant Commander Ledyard Phelps, who could not bear to lose "the pride of the western waters," Porter, having observed that such efforts to haul her off only made her stick the harder, gave orders for her destruction. A ton and a half of powder was distributed about her machinery and hold. When the electrical detonator failed to work, Phelps himself, in accordance with the tradition requiring the captain to be the last to abandon ship, applied a "slow match," then went over the side and into a waiting launch. The match was almost not slow enough, however. When the *Eastport* blew, Phelps was only a short way off and barely avoided being crushed by one of the dory-sized fragments from the 280-foot iron hull that came hurtling down and raised huge red geysers all around the launch.

Porter had a double reason for ordering the ironclad's destruction. One was that further delay seemed likely to cost him not only the *Eastport* — which, in point of fact, had been Confederate at the outset, captured uncompleted up the Tennessee River near the Mississippi town that gave her her name, just after the fall of Fort Henry in early 1862 — but his other boats as well. While the attempted salvage work was in progress, enemy marksmen were gathering on both hostile banks of the river and adding to his discomfort by sniping at the flotilla. Small-arms fire, though deadly enough, was only part of the danger; for presently, emboldened by the absence of the infantry escort now on the march with Banks, they brought up batteries of horse artillery and opened fire from masked positions. So intense and accurate was this, Porter lost one of his unarmored pump boats that afternoon and the other the following morning, together with all but five of about 175 Negroes, mostly fieldhands taken aboard from surrounding plantations, who were scalded to death by steam from a punctured boiler. The gunboats *Juliet* and *Fort Hindman* lost 22 men between them in the course of the downstream run, along with their stacks and most of their upper works. Hardest hit of all, though, was the *Cricket*, now serving as the flagship. Rounding a bend, she came upon a rebel battery cleverly sited atop a bluff, and took 38 hits within the five minutes she was exposed to its plunging fire. Out of her crew of fifty, 31 were casualties, including a dozen killed. "Every shot [went] through and through us, clearing all our decks in a moment," according to the admiral, who had to take the wheel himself when he ran up to the pilot house and found the helmsman badly wounded.

This was the firing the soldiers heard at the end of their long march from Grand Ecore, and when Porter reached Alexandria next morning, April 27, he saw at close range the validity of his other reason for having abandoned the deep-draft ironclad far upstream: which was that, even if he had managed to get her this far down, he would not have been able to get her one mile farther. The Red had dwindled by now to a depth of three feet four inches over the falls — two inches less than half the draft of his heavier gunboats — and there still was no sign that the river was going to rise at all this spring, if indeed it ever stopped falling. In fact, it was becoming more evident every day that the fate of the *Eastport* was likely to be the fate of every warship in the fleet; that is, if they were to be kept out of enemy hands. And now there was added to the admiral's woes, as if this last was not enough, the apprehension that he was about to be left on his own by the army. Banks came aboard the badly shot-up *Cricket* with a ten-day-old letter just arrived from the general-in-chief, peremptorily ordering him to desist from any activity that might cause him to be "detained one day after the 1st of May in commencing your movement east of the Mississippi." Today was Wednesday; May Day was Sunday, barely four days off. "No matter what you may have in contemplation," Grant had added by way of emphasis, "commence your concentration, to be followed without delay by your advance on Mobile."

Knowing how eager the Massachusetts general was to engage in the very campaign Grant's letter not only authorized but *ordered* him to undertake at once, Porter had a nightmare vision of the fleet — or anyhow the dozen vessels trapped above the falls — being left stranded high and dry, unprotected from heavy-caliber snipers or highly explosive underwater devices, its fate restricted to a choice between capture and self-destruction. If the former was unthinkable, involving as it well might do the loss of all the navy had won in the past two years on western rivers, the latter choice was only a bit less so, since either would mean professional ruin for the admiral himself. Partly his apprehension was based on his contempt for Banks, which encouraged him to think the worst of the one-time politician, especially in regard to his feeling any obligation to a man who he knew despised him, who was of a rival and often high-handed branch of the service, and whom he could protect only by disregarding a direct order from a superior famed for sternness in such matters.

But in this the admiral did the general wrong. Banks quickly made it clear that he had no more intention of abandoning the navy here at Alexandria than he had had at Grand Ecore the week before, and for much the same reasons. One was that it was not his way, no matter what Porter might think of him, to desert an associate in distress. Another was that he still had nearly a hundred downriver miles to go before he would be out of the Red River country, and he wanted naval protection all the way. Still another, which would require the navy's continued support even more, was that he had not completely given up the notion that he could retrieve his reputation in the region where he had lost it. Whether he would get that chance depended on Grant's reply to the letter sent ten days ago from Grand Ecore, suggesting a return to the recently abandoned upriver offensive, provided he could secure "a concentration of our forces." That meant Steele, who was long since overdue, but about whose progress Banks knew little except for a disconcerting rumor that the Arkansas commander had turned aside from his southwest march on Shreveport for an eastward lunge at Camden, 165 air-line miles due north of Alexandria and almost twice that far by the few roads.

Meantime, while waiting to hear again from Grant and finally from Steele, Banks and Porter — despite their mutual distaste for striking, even figuratively, so intimate an attitude — put their heads together in an attempt to solve the apparently insoluble problem of how to get armored gunboats, drawing seven feet of water, down a still-falling river whose rocky bottom was in places only three feet four inches below its russet surface.

★ ★ ★

Steele had been at Camden, just as Kirby Smith had been informed and Banks had chanced to hear. In fact, he had been there for the past twelve days, penned up like his supposed partner at Grand Ecore, behind intrenchments. But he was there no longer. He had pulled out during the small hours of this same April 27 — headed not for the Red, as Banks expected and Smith intended to prevent, but back toward Little Rock, the headquarters he had left five weeks ago today. In the course of the first three of these he had crossed the Saline, the Ouachita, the Little Missouri, then the Ouachita once more, along with a number of lesser streams in a region as wet as the upper Red was dry; now he was hard on the march for the Saline again, fifty air-line miles to the north, hoping to put that river between him and his pursuers, a superior force dead bent on his destruction, and thus bring an end to what a Saint Louis newsman would presently call "a campaign of forty days in which nothing has been gained but defeat, hard blows, and poor fare."

Although he seemed on the face of it to have done even worse than Banks — who, in all conscience, had done poorly enough by almost any standards, not excluding Pleasant Hill, which amounted to little more than a pause in his flight before inferior numbers — it could at least be said of Steele, by way of extenuation, that he had never had a moment's belief that anything good was going to come of an undertaking he had protested being involved in from the start. Unlike the former Massachusetts governor, whose inveterate optimism was inclined to feed on straws, he had not been lured by cotton or dazzled by stars in a political firmament which for him did not exist. Yet he had certain other disadvantages. For one, while Banks merely believed he was outnumbered, Steele actually was outnumbered, at any rate in the final stage, when Kirby Smith came after him with all but a handful of the infantry Dick Taylor had used to drive the larger Federal column pell-mell down the Red, ironclads and all. The Arkansas commander's losses, though so far only half as great as those in Louisiana, stood a dismal chance of being considerably greater in the end. Banks had lost some 4000 men to date, but at least he had found sanctuary within the Alexandria intrenchments: whereas Steele, in northward flight for Little Rock with hordes of exultant graybacks hot on his trail across the hundred miles of intervening hinterland, was in grievous danger of losing about three times that many, the only limit being that that was all he had. Still, for whatever consolation it was worth, the outcome could scarcely be direr than he had predicted in response to Halleck's original suggestion that he move on Shreveport in coöperation with Banks's ascent of the Red. He could only do so, he wired back, "against my own judgment and that of the best-informed people here. The roads are most if not quite impracticable; the country is destitute of provision." Moreover, he added, if he marched south the butternut guerillas were likely to hold carnival in North Arkansas and Southwest Missouri, with predictable results. "If they should form in my rear in considerable force I should be obliged to fall back to save my depots, &c." He thought it best not to go at all, in any case not in earnest. A feint at Arkadelphia or

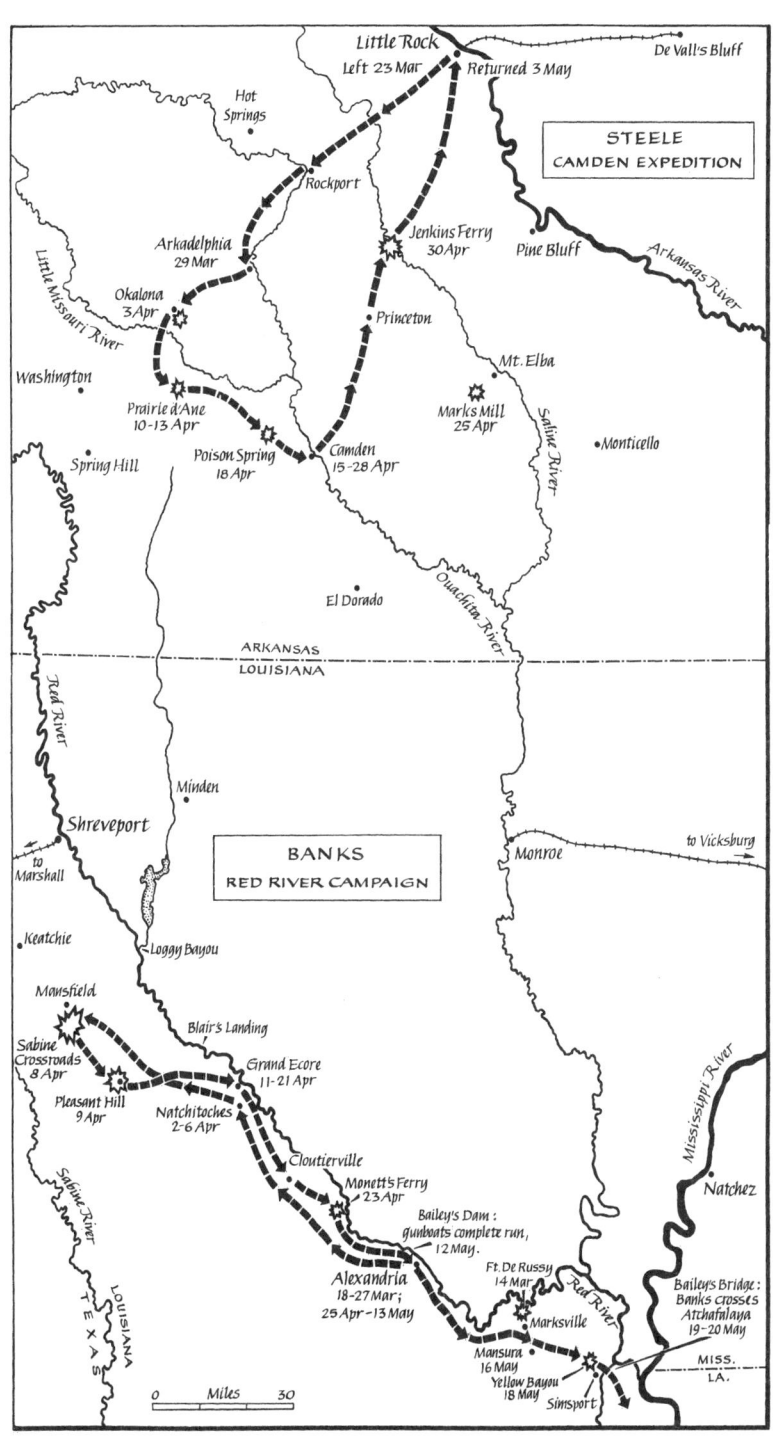

Hot Springs was the most he could recommend as a means of discouraging a rebel concentration against Banks, and having said as much — this was March 12, ten days past the time Old Brains had wanted him to set out southward — he remained at Little Rock, awaiting a reply. It came within three days, but not from Washington and not from Halleck. A brief telegram signed *U. S. Grant Lieutenant General* arrived from Nashville on March 15: "Move your force in full coöperation with General N. P. Banks' attack on Shreveport. A mere demonstration will not be sufficient."

That was that. Grant might or might not approve of this Transmississippi undertaking, conceived before his appointment as director of the nation's military effort, but it was clear he wanted it over and done with in the shortest possible time, and it was equally clear that to achieve this he intended to employ his accustomed method of bringing everything available to bear: including Steele. Accordingly, the Arkansas commander wasted no more energy on appeals which might have influenced Halleck but would obviously — as he knew from past experience, first as a classmate at West Point, then as a division commander in the Vicksburg campaign — do nothing but anger the new general-in-chief and probably bring on his own dismissal. Rather, he spent the next eight days preparing to move (an election of delegates to a constitutional convention, requiring the presence of his troops as poll watchers to protect the reconverted "loyal" ten percent of the state's voters from as many of the irreconcilable ninety percent as were not already in the field with Price, had been held the day before, March 14, with predictably satisfactory results) and then on March 23, midway through Holy Week, he set out.

Originally he had intended to proceed due south down the Ouachita, by way of Monroe, for a meeting with Banks at Alexandria. By now, though, it was too late for that; Alexandria had been taken, and he would scarcely be helping Banks by making him wait for him that far down the Red. So he chose instead to march southwest, through Arkadelphia and Washington to reach the upper Red, which he would then descend for a combination, near Shreveport, with the amphibious column moving northwest up that river toward that goal. An epicure and a sportsman, a breeder and racer of horses, forty-five years old, high-voiced and dandified in dress — "a velvet-collared esthete," one observer called him — Fred Steele was rumored by his enemies to live in the style of an Oriental prince, surrounded by silk-clad servants and pedigreed lapdogs, although this alleged limp-wristed aspect was considerably at odds with a lifetime habit of blasphemy, a full if silky beard, and a combat infantry record going back to the Mexican War, in which he had won two brevets for gallantry as an officer of the line. He had under him, for service in the campaign now beginning, some 14,000 effectives of all arms. Of these, a column including a little more than half — 5000 infantry and artillery, 3000 cavalry — left Little Rock under his immediate supervision, while another containing 4000 — the so-called Frontier Division, in occupation of Indian territory — marched from Fort Smith under Brigadier General John M. Thayer, who had orders to join the main body at Arkadelphia by April 1. A third force of about 2000, mostly cavalry and therefore highly mobile, was based on Pine Bluff, with instructions to divert attention in that direction, away from the column on the march to the southwest, and keep a close watch on the rebel garrison at Camden, one of the places where Sterling Price had had his headquarters since his loss of all the northern portion of the state in the fall of the previous year.

A warm-up march of nine miles on the first day flexed muscles used but scantly during months of easy duty. But next morning — Holy Thursday, and the weather remained clear — the men turned out of their blankets in the chill pre-dawn to find themselves involved in the full panoply of war. "Bugles rang out as we had never heard them before," an Iowa soldier would recall. "If an enemy had been in hearing distance, he must have thought we were at least a hundred thousand men, to raise such a wide-spread din." On the near bank of the Saline River by nightfall, still with no evidence that a single rebel was within earshot, they were informed that they would be on half-rations for the balance of the march. Digesting this as best they could, they woke to find it raining, which made for a hard Good Friday on soft roads. The same was true the next day and the next, Easter Sunday, when they crossed the Ouachita. The going was slow, especially across the frequent bottoms, which had to be corduroyed to get the wagons through. They did not reach Arkadelphia until March 29, having covered only seventy miles in a solid week of marching.

The worst of it, though, was that there was no sign at the rendezvous of the column from Fort Smith, and no word of its whereabouts came back from scouts sent out to find it. A three-day wait, while welcome as a rest, reduced the dwindling supply of food and forage in the trains, and still there was no message from Thayer, whose division was known to have left Fort Smith two days before the main body left Little Rock. The earth might have swallowed him up: or the rebels, none of whom seemed to be lurking in this direction. On April 1, after three days of marking time and further depleting his supplies, Steele decided he could wait no longer. He ordered the southwest march resumed down the old military road that led to Washington, thirty miles beyond the Little Missouri, which lay twenty-five miles ahead. On that day — April Fools' — the marchers encountered their first opposition, in the form of slashing attacks by mounted graybacks who struck them flank and rear.

They encountered only cavalry because that was all Price had to send against them. His two small divisions of infantry, summoned to

Louisiana to help Taylor go for Banks, had reached Kirby Smith at Shreveport on the day Steele set out from Little Rock with the same goal in mind; so that, however much this might benefit him tactically by reducing the type and number of troops he would encounter on his march through Arkansas, the Federal commander had no sooner gotten started than he failed in his main purpose, which was to keep the Transmississippi Confederates from ganging up on Banks. In any case, having accomplished this much without the firing of a shot, Price was left with only five brigades of cavalry, some 5000 effectives in all, badly scattered about the state. Two of these, combined in a division under Brigadier General James Fagan, were stationed east of the Saline to counter a possible Union advance from Pine Bluff, while two of the remaining three were posted at Camden, on the lower Ouachita, and the third was just west of Washington, on the upper Red. These three were under Brigadier General John S. Marmaduke and contained about 3200 troopers, veterans of many fights and raids, particularly those in Brigadier General J. O. Shelby's brigade, hard-bitten Missourians who asked for nothing better than a chance to come to grips with the bluecoats on the march. Two more brigades were said to be on the way from Indian Territory under Brigadier General Samuel B. Maxey, freed by Thayer's withdrawal to Fort Smith for his share in the Arkansas offensive, but Price had no way of knowing when they would arrive. "Retard the enemy's advance," Smith urged him in an Easter dispatch. "Operate on their communications if practicable. Time is everything with us." This aggressiveness was somewhat modified, however, by a warning not unlike the ones that were stretching Taylor's patience thin at the same time: "Do not risk a general action unless with advantage to yourself. You fall back toward reinforcements." Accordingly, Price held Fagan where he was, shielding Camden from attack by the bristly Pine Bluff garrison, and turned Marmaduke loose on Steele with instructions to deal as roughly with him as the disparity in numbers would allow. Marmaduke ordered a concentration of two brigades in the path of the Federal advance, intending to give ground as slowly as conditions would permit, while the third brigade — Jo Shelby's — set out on a circuitous march to get into position to harass the flanks and rear of the enemy slogging through Arkadelphia. Which Shelby did: beginning with the slashing attack he launched on All Fools' Day against just those tender parts of the blue column.

Steele came on, skirmishing front and rear, still not knowing what had become of Thayer or whether his division still existed. Sizeable clashes at Hollywood, a few miles out of Arkadelphia, and then next day at Spoonville and Antoine, along Terre Noir Creek, cost him more in time than they did in men. Time was what he could least afford, however, obliged as he was to balance his consumption of rations against his dwindling supply, already reduced by about three fourths though he was still a good deal short of halfway to his goal. On April 3, while the head of the column moved into the valley of the Little Missouri, diverging from the Washington road to secure a crossing at Elkin's Ferry, off to the south, Marmaduke launched a concerted attack on the main body, back at Okolona. Steele had to call a halt to fight him off, losing still more time and consuming still more rations. At this rate, he perceived, he was never going to make it; Shreveport might as well have been on the Gulf of Mexico or the back side of the moon. Still he pressed on, and next day, having secured a bridgehead at the ferry, he began to cross the river, still under attack from several directions. Then on April 6, with most of his men across, word came from Thayer. He had been delayed by poor roads; he had had to change his route; he would arrive from Hot Springs in a day or two or three. Steele cursed, shrill-voiced and blasphemous, and kept his troops at work corduroying the soggy bottoms for the passage of his and Thayer's trains. Finally, on April 9 — one day short of three weeks on the march — the Frontier Division came up and began to cross the Little Missouri. For Steele and his men, marking time on the south bank, the meeting with the frontiersmen was a let-down. "While we lay here," one recorded in disgust, "the long-looked-for and much-talked-of reinforcement of 'Thayer's command' arrived, from Fort Smith. A nondescript style of reinforcement it was too, numbering almost every kind of soldier, including Indians, and accompanied by multitudinous vehicles, of all descriptions, which had been picked up along the roads."

Worst of all, from Steele's point of view, though the buggies and carriages and buckboards were heavily loaded with plunder, they had little in them in the way of food. What Thayer had mainly brought him was another 4000 mouths to feed, reducing still further any chance Steele had of getting to Shreveport before he starved. There was nothing for it, he decided, but to send back word to department headquarters for a train to be made up and dispatched to him at once, "using, if necessary, every wagon and mule at Little Rock," with a thirty-day supply of "one-half rations of hard bread, one-quarter rations of bacon, and full rations of salt and coffee for 15,000 men." Whether he could survive in the barrens surrounding Elkin's Ferry until the supplies arrived, and whether they had any chance of getting through the rebel-infested region he had just traversed with so much fret, Steele did not know. Nor did he intend to find out, on either count. "Leaving here," he informed his adjutant in Little Rock, thereby giving the destination for the train, "I shall proceed directly to Camden with the whole force."

Nothing Confederate was any longer there to dispute its seizure; Price had evaluated Camden and joined Marmaduke two days ago, bringing Fagan's two brigades along to get in on the action. That raised the total to half a dozen gray brigades, one of Maxey's having ridden in the day before from Indian Territory, so that Price now had about half as many troops as Steele and Thayer, who had 12,000 between them. The Virginia-born former Missouri governor, white-haired in his middle fifties and weighing close to three hundred pounds, mild-mannered despite his imposing bulk and much beloved by his soldiers — although he and they had won no solid victory since Wilson's Creek and Lexington, back in the early days of the war in his home state — had intended to use all six brigades to contest a crossing at Elkin's Ferry; but when he arrived to find the Federals established in their bridgehead he revised his plan to take advantage of a line of shallow earthworks already dug along the near side of the Prairie d'Ane, a gently rolling stretch of meadowland affording his horsemen an excellent field for maneuver, five to ten miles back from the river and about midway between Arkadelphia and Spring Hill. The latter place he now thought was Steele's immediate objective, and the earthworks blocked the way there.

Preliminary skirmishing continued through April 8 and 9 (Banks had left Natchitoches two days before, and while Thayer was crossing the Little Missouri the Louisiana commander was falling back from Sabine Crossroads and Pleasant Hill) and then on April 10 Steele moved against Price across the undulating prairie. All morning and into the late afternoon (while Banks was intrenching feverishly at Grand Ecore and Tom Green was riding toward Blair's Landing, where he would encounter Porter and the naval gun that killed him) the skirmishing continued, gradually building almost to battle proportions — including a noisy exchange of long-range artillery fire which accomplished little except to demoralize a pet bear named Postlewait, the mascot of a rebel battery — until it faded and died away. The following day was much the same, long blue lines of skirmishers moving forward only to recede, and so was the next. On April 13 Maxey's other brigade arrived, Choctaw riders led by Colonel Tandy Walker, eager to use their scalping knives on Thayer's men, who had been despoiling their homes for the past year out in the Territory. But that was not to be: at least not yet. Under cover of these impressive demonstrations, it soon developed, Steele had been preparing, not for a mass assault, but for a withdrawal, a tangential march due east to Camden, forty miles away.

It was neatly done, and in the course of it Steele's soldiers gave a good account of themselves. Left holding the bag on the Prairie d'Ane, Price sent Marmaduke on a cross-country ride to block the road ahead, while Fagan and Maxey set out to overtake the bluecoats who had camped the night before on Terre Rouge Creek, well to the east. Both gray forces were able to get in position for their work, front and rear, but neither had the strength to carry it out. Thayer, whose division served as rear guard, managed to hold off his attackers through a two-day running fight, and German-born Brigadier General Frederich Salomon, commanding the advance division, repulsed Marmaduke in a hotly contested two-hour engagement, fourteen miles from Camden, on the morning of April 15. Just before dark of that same day Steele's lead brigade marched into the town, followed that night and next morning by all the others. While the Federals got to work improving the Confederate-dug intrenchments, semicircular in design and anchored at both ends to the Ouachita, above and below, Price came up and made a leisurely investment of the place. Steele was besieged: besieged by greatly inferior numbers: *self*-besieged, so to speak. Rare as this was in military annals, the situation was not unlike the one that obtained at the same time at Grand Ecore, 125 air-line miles to the south, with the difference that Steele had only a two-to-one advantage, while Banks had better than twice that.

Another difference, far more stringent and constricting, was that the Louisiana Federals had a fleet to bring supplies up the river they were based on, whereas those in Arkansas had to depend on foraging expeditions, highly vulnerable to ambush and assault by the enemy waiting just outside their lines for just such opportunities. Steele had managed to get his wagons through, but there was little in them that was edible. "Our supplies were nearly exhausted, and so was the country," he wrote Halleck on April 17, explaining his perpendicular divergence. "We were obliged to forage from five to fifteen miles on either side of the road to keep our stock alive." The same was true at Camden, however, and next day he received a double shock, half of which provided a graphic demonstration of the risk attendant on venturing outside his fortifications, although the only alternative was starvation. Fifteen miles out the Washington road there was a settlement with an ominous name: Poison Spring. Returning from a successful hunt for food in that direction, a train of 198 heavily loaded wagons, escorted by a mixed command of 1100 infantry, cavalry, and artillery with four guns, was jumped by Marmaduke and Maxey, who had better than 3000 troops between them. The slaughter was heavy, the rebel success almost complete. All four guns were taken, together with 170 of the wagons and their teams, the rest being burned. According to one of the captors, the train was "laden with corn, bacon, stolen bed quilts, women's and children's clothing, hogs, geese, and all the *et ceteras* of unscrupulous plunder." This helped to explain the heavy losses of the escort, nearly one third of whom were killed or captured by the infuriated attackers: particularly by Tandy Walker's Choctaws, who whooped with delight at finding the 1st Kansas (Colored) to their front. This was one of Thayer's outfits, well known for its ransack activities in the past, and the troopers unsheathed their knives for bloody work. According to the regimental commander, the high death rate among his casualties, 117 out of 182, was due to the fact that a number of the wounded were "murdered on the spot" by the vengeful red men. Confederate losses totaled 115, many of them only slightly hurt. The Federals lost 301, mostly killed or missing, plus all their guns and wagons.

By the time the survivors came stumbling back from Poison Spring that afternoon, Steele had been profoundly shaken by the other half of the double shock to his nervous system. It had been given him by a scout sent out the week before to get some news of Banks. Returning with word that the Louisiana commander had been thrown into reverse, first at Sabine Crossroads and then again at Pleasant Hill, the messenger reported that he had left him at Grand Ecore, three days back, though where he might be now he did not know. Steele was quick to perceive the dangers of noncoöperation, now that they were directed at himself. If his supposed partner were to pull out, every rebel in the Transmississippi would be free to concentrate against Camden and its hungry garrison, with results no doubt as grisly as those at Poison Spring this morning. He thought this over for four days, wincing at the prospect — which was in fact more likely than he yet knew; Banks left Grand Ecore on the third of these days, beginning another withdrawal, this time to Alexandria, another ninety miles downriver — and then appealed to his superiors not to allow him to be swamped and slaughtered because an adjoining commander lost his army or his nerve. "Although I believe we can beat Price," he protested, "I do not expect to meet successfully the whole force which Kirby Smith could send against me, if Banks should let him go."

Next day, April 23, he heard at last from Banks himself, who proposed, in a dispatch written a week ago at Grand Ecore, before he decided to withdraw farther down the river, that Steele march south at once to join him on the Red for a resumption of the advance upriver. "If you can join us on this line," Banks told him, "I am confident we can move to Shreveport without material delay, and that we shall have an opportunity of destroying the only organized rebel army west of the Mississippi."

Steele wanted no part of such an operation, and frankly said as much that same day in his reply. "Owing to contingencies," he wrote, "it is impossible for me to say definitely that I will join you at any point on Red River within a given time." Among the contingencies, he was careful to say, was Price's army, which was not only highly "organized," whatever Banks might imply to the contrary, but had recently been "very much encouraged by an order of General E. K. Smith, detailing his success against your command." He wished Banks well in whatever he might undertake of an offensive nature down in Louisiana, but as for himself, he had his hands full where he was; "I desire to coöperate with you in the best manner possible, at the same time covering Arkansas until Shreveport shall be ours." Moreover, he informed the man he held responsible for a large part of the woes he now saw looming, "We have been receiving yesterday and today rumors of reinforcements sent by Kirby Smith to Price at this point, and of a contemplated attack. It is said that 8000 infantry have arrived." Interrupted by the jar of guns, he set his pen aside to look into the cause of the disturbance, then took it up again with something of the perverse satisfaction of a prophet watching his gloomiest fears materialize in fact. "They have just opened upon my outposts with artillery," he continued. "This may be to get as near our lines as possible tonight, preparatory to a general attack tomorrow morning."

He was wrong about the attack next morning. Rather than a prelude to assault, the boom of guns was part of a design to frighten him into retreat. But he was altogether right about the rebel reinforcements and his adversary's intention to make bloody use of them. Kirby Smith had arrived three days ago from Shreveport, accompanied by three divisions of infantry flushed with pride for their recent victory over Banks, and he had it in mind to bag the Camden garrison entirely: in which case, he said later, "the prize would have been the Arkansas Valley and the fortifications of Little Rock," to be used in turn, quite possibly, as a base from which to recover the offensive in Missouri. Before this ambitious program for reversing the tide of war could be placed in execution, however, Steele would have to be disposed of, and Smith had no intention of trying to do so by attacking him in his intrenchments, either at Camden or at Little Rock. He preferred to catch him out in the open, between the two, after frightening or forcing him into attempting a retreat across the intervening barrens, where the blue column could be intercepted and cut to pieces by the now superior gray force. The infantry-artillery demonstration of April 23 having resulted only in causing the Federals to button themselves more tightly in their works, Smith intensified his efforts to smoke them out by disrupting their supply lines, particularly those beyond the Ouachita, which Price had not felt strong enough to threaten up to now. Accordingly, while the Camden demonstration was in progress, Fagan crossed the river at Eldorado Landing, twenty miles downstream, with instructions to use his division, reinforced to a strength of more than 3000 by the addition of Shelby's brigade, to strike at logistical targets along the Saline and the Arkansas, as well as along the roads that ran between and across them, from Little Rock and Pine Bluff, down to Camden. The result was not long in coming, and when it came it was as decisive, on a larger scale, as the rout at Poison Spring.

Crossing the Ouachita on the morning of April 24, Fagan was informed by Shelby's scouts, who had ridden ahead, that a large train, heavily guarded, had left Camden two days ago, sent by Steele to Pine Bluff for supplies. Determined to intercept the Federals before they got across the Saline at Mount Elba, he led his troopers on a forced march of forty-five miles to halt at midnight near Marks Mill, where the road he had taken from Eldorado Landing joined the one connecting Camden and Pine Bluff, five miles short of the river. He was pleased to learn that the blue train, delayed by muddy going on cut-up roads, had made camp at nightfall on the near side of Moro Bottom, a few miles to the west, and he was also pleased to hear that the prize was quite as plump as he had hoped: 240 government wagons, together with a number of other vehicles belonging to "cotton speculators, refugees, sutlers, and other army followers," escorted by three regiments of infantry, one of cavalry, and a six-gun battery — in effect, a reinforced brigade, whose strength of 1440 effectives was less than half his own. Anticipating a larger reward than Marmaduke and Maxey had won at Poison Spring, a week ago tomorrow, Fagan instructed Shelby to use his Missourians to block the road between Marks Mill and Mount Elba, thus to prevent an escape across the Saline, and posted his other brigades near Marks Mill itself, with orders to assail the flank and rear of the slow-grinding column as soon as it came up next morning.

It came up shortly after dawn and the action went as planned, except for a more determined resistance by the Iowa, Ohio, and Indiana infantrymen than had been expected. Alarmed by the sudden attack, they panicked, then rallied and counterattacked. Fagan used his superior numbers with skill, however, and after about four hours of hard fighting, some of it hand to hand — especially when Shelby came back and forced the issue; "I determined to charge them first, last, and all the time," he later reported — the blue regiments surrendered one by one, in different quarters of the field. "Less than 150 of the brigade escaped from the conflict," the Federal commander admitted, "the balance, including the wounded, being made prisoners." Himself among them, these totaled 1300, excluding the civilian hangers-on, whose captured vehicles brought the haul to more than 300 wagons, together with their teams. All were taken, along with the six guns and the four regimental standards, and Fagan, whose own loss of more than 300 killed and wounded testified to the savagery of the fighting, rode off northward, mindful of Kirby Smith's instructions for him to maneuver in the region between Camden and Little Rock, not only in order to continue his depredations, but also in order to be in position to intercept the retreat of Steele, which was expected any day now.

Even so, it came sooner than either side had anticipated before hearing of Fagan's coup. Informed of the disaster that night by the handful of fugitives who made it back to Camden from Marks Mill, Steele called an immediate council of war to ponder what had better be done to meet this latest crisis. The choice seemed limited to starvation, surrender, or flight. Without exception, his chief subordinates — Salomon, Thayer, and Brigadier General Eugene Carr, his cavalry commander — advised the last, and after a day of feverish preparations, including the destruction of such goods as there was no room for in the depleted train, issued what scant rations were left to his alerted troops, which in some cases consisted of two crackers of hardtack and half a pint of cornmeal, together with a warning that this was likely to be all they would get until they had covered a considerable portion of the hundred-mile trek to Little Rock. All day (while Porter was blowing up the *Eastport* and Banks was getting resettled in Alexandria, which the tail of his column had reached that morning) they worked from dawn to dark to complete their preparations for departure, loading wagons, rolling packs, destroying unneeded equipment with a minimum of noise and smoke, lest the rebels in their camps across the way become aware that they were leaving. By way of adding to the deception, and thereby lengthening the head start, drums beat a noisy tattoo at 8 o'clock, followed an hour later by taps, which was sounded on a far-carrying bass drum. Meantime the loaded wagons were rolling slowly across the Ouachita on the pontoon bridge. By midnight all were over and the infantry followed, breaking step to muffle the hollow sound of their crossing. In the small hours of April 27, with Camden lying silent and empty behind them, dark except for a few scattered lamps left burning to encourage the illusion that the army was still there, the engineers silently took up the bridge, knowing that it would be needed when and if they reached the Saline, then hurried after the column, which had been halted several miles beyond the river to give the troops some rest for the ordeal that lay ahead.

Back at Camden, the Confederates did not discover until well after sunrise that they were besieging an empty town. It was midmorning before they marched in, and even then the infantry could not take out after the departed garrison until some way was found for them to cross the bridgeless Ouachita. While Marmaduke's troopers were swimming their mounts across, and Maxey's were preparing for an unexpected return to Indian Territory in response to a report of a threatened invasion from Missouri — Kirby Smith made them a speech of thanks for their Arkansas service before they set out on their long ride home — Price began the construction of a "floating bridge," to be used in ferrying Churchill's and Walker's three divisions over the swollen river. Building and then using the raft, which had a limited capacity, was an all-afternoon, all-night affair; it was daylight, April 28, before the pursuit began in earnest. As a result of the loss of Maxey and the recent detachment of Fagan, who had done excellent work at Marks Mill but now was somewhere off to the north and west, unaware that Camden had been evacuated or that a race to the death was in progress in his rear, Smith was down to about 10,000 effectives. Although this amounted to nothing like the preponderance he might have enjoyed, he pressed them hard in the wake of the fleeing Federals — whose trail was marked by abandoned equipment, including personal effects, foundered mules, and wagons buried axle-deep in mud — knowing only too well that if he did not overtake them before they crossed the Saline he might as well give up hope of coming to grips with them anywhere short of Little Rock; which meant, in effect, that he would not be able to come to grips with them at all, since there they would have the advantage of intrenchments and could summon reinforcements from other departments roundabout.

Steele was down to roughly the same number of troops as Smith, having suffered 2000 casualties in the past month without inflicting half as many. What was worse, his men had been on short rations all this time, which tended to make them trembly in the legs and short on endurance. However, he had not only gained them a full day's head start in the race for the Arkansas capital, he had also managed to coax or prod them into making good time on the way there. Shortly after noon on this second day out of Camden, the head of the column reached the town of Princeton, in whose streets his rear guard bivouacked that night, two thirds of the distance to the Saline, which in turn was halfway to his goal. He had chosen this nearly barren route to Little Rock, rather than the more accustomed one through Pine Bluff, in order to avoid the Moro swamps, where the train that fell to Fagan had been so grievously delayed; but presently, as rain began to patter on the marchers and the road, he began to doubt that he had chosen wisely. The mud deepened, slowing the pace of his soldiers as they slogged along in the ankle-twisting ruts of the wagons up ahead, and the rain came down harder every hour. Before nightfall, rebel troopers — Marmaduke's amphibious horsemen — were shooting and slashing at the bedraggled tail of the column. By that time, though, the van had reached the Saline at Jenkins Ferry, and the engineers were getting their pontoons launched and linked and floored, while other details worked at corduroying the two-mile long approach across the bottoms giving down upon the river, beyond which there stretched another just as long and just as mean. Such labor was too heavy for troops in their condition, faint for sleep as well as food. While they strained at cutting and placing timbers, Steele's chief engineer afterwards reported, "wagons settled to the axles and mules floundered about without a resting place for their feet." After dark, he added, the work continued by the light of fires, and "every exertion [was] made to push the impedimenta across before daylight, it being evident that the enemy was in force in our rear. But we failed. The rain came down in torrents, putting out many of the fires, the men became exhausted, and both they and the animals sank down in the mud and mire, wherever they were, to seek a few hours' repose."

It was here, in this "sea of mud," as the engineer called it, that fleers and pursuers — blue and gray, though both would be dun before the thing was over — fought the Battle of Jenkins Ferry, a miry nightmare of confusion and fatigue. This last applied as much to one side as the other; for if the Confederates had no foundered mules and shipwrecked wagons to haul along or strain at, they had to make a faster march, with fewer halts, in order to overcome the substantial Union lead. North of Princeton by nightfall, they took a four-hour rest, then moved out again at midnight. By 7.30 next morning, April 30, the lead brigade had come up to where Marmaduke's dismounted troopers were skirmishing with blue infantry posted astride the road leading down to the ferry, two miles in its rear. Price committed his troops as fast as they arrived, first Churchill's own and then its companion division, led by Brigadier General Mosby Parsons. They made little headway, for the Federals were crouched behind stout log breastworks, in a position whose access was restricted on the left and right by Toxie Creek and an impenetrable swamp. Moreover, this narrow, alley-like approach not only afforded the charging infantry no cover, it was for the most part slathered over with a spongy, knee-deep layer of mud and brim-full pools of standing water. Their only protection was a blanket of fog, thickened presently by gunsmoke, which lay so heavily over the field that marksmen had to stoop to take aim under it or else do their shooting blind. In point of fact, however, this was more of an advantage for the defenders, who were already lying low, than it was for the attackers toiling heavy-footed toward them through the mire. Besides, fog stopped no bullets: as the rebels soon found out, encountering fire that was no less murderous for being blind. They fell back, abandoning three guns in the process, and failed to recover them when Price, after giving the blown attackers time to catch their breath, ordered the assault renewed.

Kirby Smith was on the field by then, coming up with Walker, who insisted on remaining with his men despite his unhealed Louisiana wound, suffered three weeks ago today at Pleasant Hill. Committed just after Churchill and Parsons were thrown back the second time, his Texans attacked with such fury and persistence that all three of their brigade commanders were wounded, two of them mortally. But they did no better, in the end, than the Arkansans and Missourians had done before them. The bluecoats were unshaken behind their breastworks, apparently ready to welcome another attempt to budge them, although the Confederates were not disposed to try it, having lost no fewer than 1000 casualties in the effort, as compared to about 700 for the defenders, including stragglers who had fallen by the wayside on the three-day march from Camden. It was past noon; the last Federal wagon had passed over the river an hour ago, escorted by the cavalry, and now the infantry followed, unmolested by the former owners of the three captured guns they took along. Once on the far side of the Saline, they cut the bridge loose from the south bank and set it afire, partly because they had no further use for it, having no more rivers to cross, and partly because their mules were too weary to haul it. Bridgeless, the rebels could do nothing but let them go, even if they had been of a mind to stop them; which they no longer were, having tried.

Fagan came up soon afterward from over near Arkadelphia, where he had gone for supplies after proceeding north, then west and south, from the scene of his coup five days ago at Marks Mill, less than thirty miles downstream from the battle fought today. Though he made good time on his thirty-four-mile ride from the Ouachita to the Saline, which began at dawn when he learned that Steele was on the march for Little Rock by way of Jenkins Ferry, he not only arrived too late for his 3000 troopers to have a share in the fighting, he was also on the wrong side of the river for them to undertake pursuit. Kirby Smith saw in his failure to intercept and impede the Federals one of the might-have-beens of the war, saying later that if Fagan had "thrown himself on the enemy's front on his march from Camden, Steele would have been brought to battle and his command utterly destroyed long before he reached the Saline." Dismissing this, however, as "one of those accidents which are likely to befall the best of officers," the even-tempered Floridian was more inclined to count his gains than to bemoan lost opportunities. He had, after all, frustrated both Union attempts to seize his Shreveport base and drive him from his department, and though Banks at Alexandria was still to be reckoned with as a menace, the Arkansas column was no longer even the semblance of a threat, at least for the present, to the region it had set out forty days ago to conquer. At a cost to himself of about 2000 casualties, a good portion of whom had already returned to his ranks, Smith had inflicted nearly 3000, two thirds of them killed or captured and therefore permanent subtractions. Losing three guns he had taken ten, all told, in a campaign that had cost the invaders 635 wagons surrendered or destroyed, according to the Federal quartermaster's own report, along with no less than 2500 mules. The list of captured matériel was long, including weapons of all types, complete with ammunition, not to mention sutler goods, rare medical supplies, and enough horses to mount a brigade of cavalry. But the major gain, as Smith himself declared, was that he had "succeeded in driving Steele from the valley of the Ouachita ... and left myself free to move my entire force to the support of Taylor."

That was clearly the next order of business. With one prong of the two-pronged Union offensive — Steele — now definitely snapped off, it was time to attend to the other — Banks — already severely bent. After giving the divisions of Churchill, Parsons, and Walker two days of badly needed rest, Smith issued orders on May 3 for them to return at once to Camden and proceed from there "by the most direct route to Louisiana."

Steele's men returned on the same day to Little Rock near exhaustion, having found the going even more arduous on the north side of the Saline than on the south. Partly this was because they were one day hungrier and one battle wearier, but it was also because the mud was deeper and timber scarce. As a result of this shortage of corduroy material, they had a much harder time trying to keep the wagons rolling. When one stuck beyond redemption, as many did, it was burned to keep it from falling into rebel hands, and when teams grew too weak to be led, as many did, they were set free: all of which added greatly to the army's loss of equipment and supplies. From dawn of May Day to 4 a.m. the next, out of the soggy bottoms at last, the infantry slogged in a daze that was intensified that night by the lurid flicker of roadside fires the cavalry had kindled to light their way through the darkness. "A strange, wild time," one marcher was to term it, recalling that hardtack sold for two dollars a cracker, while in one instance two were swapped for a silver watch. Late the second afternoon a shout went up from the head of the column, announcing that a train had come out from the capital with provisions. They made camp for the night, wolfing their rations before turning in, and were off again at sunrise. When the fortifications of Little Rock came into sight, around midmorning of May 3, they halted to dress their tattered ranks and thus present as decent an appearance as they could manage, then proceeded into town, giving a prominent place in the column to the three captured guns that were all they had to show, in the way of trophies, for their forty-two days of campaigning.

"The Camden Expedition," Steele called the unhappy affair, as if Shreveport had never been part of his calculations. But the men themselves, being rather in agreement with the Saint Louis journalist that all they had gained for their pains was "defeat, hard blows, and poor fare," were not deceived. They had failed to reach their assigned objective, whatever their silky-whiskered commander might claim to the contrary, and they knew only too well what the failure had cost them: not to mention what it might cost Banks, who seemed likely to lose a great deal more, now that Steele had left the rebels free to shift their full attention to matters in Louisiana.

★ ★ ★

All would now depend on speed in that direction: speed for the three divisions on the way to Taylor, speed for him in bringing them to bear, and speed for Banks and Porter in solving, before that happened, the problem of how to get ten gunboats, some of which drew seven feet of water, down and past a mile-long stretch of river less than half that deep. It was in that sense a race, with the odds very much in favor of the Confederates. So far at least as the concentration went, they had only to do in Louisiana what they had just finished doing in

Arkansas; whereas the Federals were confronted with a problem that seemed, on the face of it, insoluble. Yet by now, before they even knew that Steele had backtracked and a race was therefore on, the blue commanders had found a way to win it. Or in any case they had found a man who believed he knew a way to win it, if they would only let him try.

On April 29 — while Marmaduke was closing on Steele near Jenkins Ferry and opening the action that would swell to battle proportions tomorrow morning — Lieutenant Colonel Joseph Bailey, Franklin's chief of engineers, came to Banks with a plan for raising the level of the river by installing, above Alexandria, a system of wing dams that would constrict and thereby deepen the channel leading down to and over the falls. A former Northwest lumberman, thirty-nine years old this week, he had used such methods to get logs down sluggish Wisconsin streams, and he was convinced they would work here, too, on a larger scale and for a larger purpose. "I wish I was as sure of heaven as I am that I can save the fleet," he said. Banks needed little persuading, not only because he was desperate enough by now to try almost anything, but also because the young engineer had demonstrated his ability along those lines the previous summer at Port Hudson, where he had salvaged, by damming a shallow creek to float them free, a pair of transports the rebels had left lying on their sides in the mud. The general took him that evening to present his plan to Porter. Contemplating the loss of his gunboats and the wreck of his career, the admiral was in an unaccustomed state of dejection; "This fatal campaign has upset everything," he had recently complained to Wells in a dispatch designed to prepare the Secretary for darker ones to follow. His first reaction to Bailey's proposal was to scoff at it. "If damning would get the fleet off, we would have been afloat long ago," he broke in, brightening a bit at this evidence that his sense of humor, such as it was, was still in working order. When it was explained to him further that the navy would have little to do but stand by and watch the army sweat and strain, he declared that he was willing on those terms. Accordingly, Banks issued orders on the last day of April for the thing to be tried, and Bailey, given 3000 soldiers to use as he saw fit in getting it done, put them to work without delay on May Day morning.

His plan was to construct above the lower falls, where the Red was 758 feet wide, a pair of wing dams, each extending about three hundred feet out into the river, then sink high-sided barges filled with brick across the remaining gap. The north bank dam was to be formed of large trees laid with the current, their branches interlocked and their trunks cross-tied with heavy timbers on the downstream side; while the one on the south bank, where trees were scarce, would consist of huge cribs, pushed out and sunk and anchored in place with rubble of all kinds. Most of the left-bank work was done by a Maine regiment of highly skilled axmen and loggers, the rest being left to three regiments of New Yorkers, experienced in tearing down old buildings — one was the military academy of which Sherman had been superintendent just before the war — for bricks and stone, to be used to hold the sunken cribs and barges in position against the force of the nine-knot current. They worked day and night, under a broiling sun and by the light of bonfires, much of the time up to their necks in the swift, rust-colored water.

At the outset they provoked more jeers than cheers from the sailors and off-duty soldiers looking on, but as the ends of the two dams drew closer together, day by day and hour by hour, interest mounted and skepticism lessened among the spectators on the gunboats and both banks, who now began to tell each other that Bailey's notion might just be practicable, after all. The sailors, especially those aboard the "teakettles," as the ironclads were called, were pleased to be afforded this diversion, now that rising temperatures had added physical discomfort to their boredom. "During the day," an officer recorded, "the iron on the decks would get so hot that the hand could barely rest upon it. At night, sleep was impossible. The decks were kept wetted down, and the men lay on them, getting, toward the morning hours when the hulls had cooled down, such sleep as could be secured." Nor were excursions ashore of much help in this regard, involving, as they sometimes did, another form of torture which southern women, then and later, were adept at inflicting. "Saw quite a number of ladies from Pine Village opposite Alexandria," a sailor wrote in his diary after one such visit. "Two in particular were out on display promenade, one of whom had a beautiful black squirrel which ran all over her, up her dress sleeves and under her lace cape into her bosom, with a familiarity that made me envy the little favorite and sent a thrill that did not feel very bad through all the little veins in my body."

Still, being bored or titillated, painful though they were in their different ways, was better than getting shot at: as a good many soldiers and sailors could testify from experience while the dams were being built. If Taylor lacked the strength to interfere with the work going on behind the Federal intrenchments, he could at least make life hectic for the troops who manned them, and he could do considerably worse to those who ventured outside them, on foot or afloat. On the day Bailey started construction, the transport *Emma* was captured at David's Ferry, thirty miles below Alexandria, her captain and crew looking on as prisoners while the rebels burned her. Three days later another, the *City Belle*, was served in much the same fashion a few miles farther down, this time with a 700-man Ohio regiment aboard. More than a third of the soldiers were captured — 276 by Taylor's count — while the rest went over the side, escaped ashore, and eventually made their way back through the lines. Next day, May 5, saw the gravest loss of all. The transport *Warner*, escorted by the gunboats *Covington* and *Signal* while taking another regiment of Ohioans downriver to begin their reënlistment furloughs, came under fire from a masked battery as she rounded a bend near the mouth of Dunn's Bayou. Disabled by an unlucky shot in her rudder, she spun with the current, absorbing heavy punishment from riflemen posted along the high south bank, and when the two warships tried to come to her assistance by bringing their seventeen guns to bear on the rebel four, they were given the same treatment in short order. *Covington*, hulled repeatedly, went aground and was set afire by her skipper, who got away into the woods with 32 of his crew of 74, leaving the rest to the mercy of the gray marksmen who by then were at work on *Signal*. They cut her up so badly that the captain, prevented from destroying her by the fact that there was no time for removing the wounded, struck his colors and surrendered his 54 survivors, together with some 125 killed and wounded left strewn about the decks of the *Warner* when she and they were abandoned by her crew and their fellow soldiers. That brought the total for the past five days to better than 600 amphibious Federals killed or captured, together with three transports and two gunboats, at a cost to the Confederates of little more than the ammunition they expended. Worst of all, from the point of view of the soldiers and sailors cooped up in Alexandria or marooned above the falls, the Red was emphatically closed to Union shipping. They had to subsist on what they had, which by now was very little, or starve; or leave.

Along with everyone else in blue, Banks preferred the last of these three alternatives, although it appeared about as unlikely as the first. At this stage, the choice seemed narrowed to the second — starvation — which was scarcely a choice at all. As of May Day, he computed that he could subsist his army for three weeks on half-rations out of what he had on hand. That might or might not be enough, depending on whether the work begun on the dams that day could be completed within that span, but there seemed little doubt, at best, that he would lose his train for lack of animals to haul the wagons. Forage was so short already that Taylor was complaining, and exulting, that the horses he captured were little more than skeletons. Pitiable as they were, he intended to be still harder on them in the immediate future, as a means of being harder on the men who rode or drove them. On May 7, after claiming that his downstream successes near Dunn's Bayou had converted the lower Red, formerly a broad Federal highway of invasion, into "a *mare clausum*," he reported to Kirby Smith: "Forage and subsistence of every kind have been removed beyond the enemy's reach. Rigid orders are given to destroy everything useful that can fall into his hands. We will play the game the Russians played in the retreat from Moscow."

So he intended, gazing all the while back over his shoulder for some sign of the approach of the troops from Arkansas, without whom he lacked the strength to come to earnest grips with the beleaguered Unionists. All he could do was pray that they would arrive before the bluecoats started the downstream march that would increase the distance his reinforcements would have to cover before they could be brought to bear.

In point of fact, the race was closer than he knew. Faith had replaced skepticism in the attitude of the watchers at the dam site. "Before God, what won't the Yankees do next!" a gray-haired contraband cried in amazement at his first sight of the week-old work in progress, now rapidly nearing completion. Crews of the largest of the ten warships above the falls, having caught the spirit of the workers in the water, were busy lightening their vessels by stripping off side armor, which they dumped in a five-fathom hole upstream to keep it out of rebel hands, and unloading such heavy materials as commandeered cotton, anchors, chains, ammunition, and most of the guns, which — all but eleven old 32-pounders, spiked and sunk, like the iron plating, to forestall salvage — were to be carted below on wagons for reloading in deep water beyond the falls. By the following day, May 8, the river had risen enough to allow three of the lighter-draft boats, the tinclad *Fort Hindman* and the broad-bottomed monitors *Osage* and *Neosho*, to pass the upper falls and take station just above the dam, awaiting the further rise that would enable them to make their run. That would not take long, apparently, for now that the dam was finished and the rubble-laden barges sunk to plug the gap between the wings, the river was rising so swiftly that it deepened more than a foot between sunset and midnight, increasing the midstream depth to a full six feet. Another foot would do it, the engineers said. As the depth increased, however, so did the speed of the current and the resultant pressure on the dam, which mounted in ratio to both. Banks, for one, began to fear that the whole affair would be swept away in short order. Arriving for an inspection by the light of bonfires late that night, he sent Porter a message expressing hope that the flotilla would be ready to move down at a moment's notice, since it seemed to him unlikely that the dam, already trembling under the weight of all that water, could survive past dawn.

He was wrong by about one hour. It held all night, then blew at 5.30 next morning when two of the barges shifted, first tentatively, then with a rush, and went with the boom and froth of current through the re-created gap.

Porter was on the scene. He had paid Banks's warning no mind last evening, but now that its validity was being demonstrated so cataclysmically, he reacted in a hurry by leaping astride a horse for a fast ride upstream to order the boats above the upper falls to start their run before the water, rushing Niagara-like between the unplugged wings of the dam, fell too low for them to try it. All but *Lexington*, the oldest vessel with the fleet — one of the three original "timberclads," she was a veteran of practically all the river fights since Belmont, where Grant got his start, and had harassed the Confederates trying to get some sleep in the captured Federal camps after the first day's fight at Shiloh — were unready for action of any kind, moored to bank with their steam down and all but their anchor watches taking it easy about the decks. *Lexington* got under way at once, passing scantly over the rocks of the upper falls, and headed straight for the 66-foot opening between the two remaining barges. The admiral, one of the thousands of soldiers and sailors who lined both banks of the Red to watch her go, later reported her progress and the reaction, afloat and ashore: "She entered the gap with a full head of steam on, pitched down the roaring current, made two or three spasmodic rolls, hung for a moment on the rocks below, and then was swept into deep water by the current and rounded to, safely into the bank. Thirty thousand voices rose in one deafening cheer, and universal joy seemed to pervade the face of every man present."

Encouraged by *Lexington*'s example, the skippers of the three boats that had crossed the upper falls the previous day decided to try their hand at completing the run before the mass of water drained away and left them stranded in the shallows of the rapids. *Neosho* led off, advancing bravely under a full head of steam. At the last minute, however, just as she was about to enter the gorge, the pilot lost his nerve and signaled for the engine to be stopped. It was, but not the monitor herself. She went with the sucking rush of the current, out of control; her low hull plunged from sight beneath the spume as she went into the gap, careening through at an angle so steep it was nearly a dive, and struck bottom with an iron clang, loud against the bated silence on both banks; then reappeared at last below, taking cheers from the watchers and water through the hole the stones had punched along her keel. This last was slight and soon repaired — a small price to pay for deliverance from a month's captivity, not to mention the risk of self-destruction or surrender. The other two warships, *Osage* and *Hindman*, made it through in a more conservative style, with less excitement for the troops on shore but also with less damage to themselves. Four boats were now below the double falls, assured of freedom and continuing careers in their old allegiance. But the remaining six were trapped as completely as before, the water having fallen too low for them to cross the upper falls by the time they got up steam enough to risk the run.

Banks was more or less unstrung by the fulfillment of his prediction that the dam was about to go. He foresaw indefinite postponement of the departure which just last night had seemed so near, and he was correspondingly cast down, having seen the effects of starvation only too clearly last summer at Port Hudson when the scarecrow garrison lined up for surrender. "We have exhausted the country," he told Porter that afternoon, "and with the march that is before us it will be perilous to remain more than another day."

The admiral, perhaps because he had put less faith in the dam as a means of deliverance, reacted less despairingly to the mishap. After all, he had saved four of his boats already — four less than he had feared he well might lose — and he believed he could save the other half dozen as well, if the army would only stand fast until the dam could be replugged. But there was the rub. Banks, in his depression, was giving what seemed to Porter signs that he was about to pull out, bag and baggage, workers and all, and leave the stranded warships to the mercy of butternut marksmen who had demonstrated at Dunn's Bayou, four days ago, their skill at naval demolition when there was no army standing by to hold them off. On May 11, when Banks displayed further jumpiness by sending a staff officer to complain that the navy seemed unmindful of the need for utmost haste, Porter did what he could to calm him down. "Now, General," he replied soothingly, "I really see nothing that should make us despond. You have a fine army, and I shall have a strong fleet of gunboats to drive away an inferior force in our front." Up to now, he artfully pointed out, the press had been highly critical of the conduct of the campaign; but think what a glorious finish the salvation of the flotilla would afford the journalists for the stories yet to be filed. And having thus appealed to the former governor's political sensibilities, the admiral closed with an exhortation designed to stiffen his resolution. "I hope, Sir, you will not let anything divert you from the attempt to get these vessels all through safely, even if we have to stay here and eat mule meat."

No blue-clad soldier or sailor had yet been reduced to such a diet; nor would one be here, though Banks was quick to reply that he had no intention of leaving the navy in the lurch. The reason again was Bailey, who once more solved a difficult engineering problem in short order. Instead of attempting to plug the swift-running gap between the still-intact wings of the dam just above the lower falls, he decided instead to construct another at the upper falls, similar to the first, and thus not try any longer to sustain the weight of all that water with one dam. It was done with such dispatch, his thousand-man detail being thoroughly experienced in such work by now, that within three days — that is, before sunset of the day Porter urged Banks to stand by him "even if we have to stay here and eat mule meat" — three more vessels completed their runs down the mile-long rapids and over the two sets of falls. These were the veteran Eads gunboats *Mound City*, *Pittsburg*, and *Carondolet*. Next day, May 12, the remaining three — the armored steamer *Chillicothe*, the fourth Eads gunboat *Louisville*, and finally the third monitor *Ozark*, successor to the *Eastport* as the pride of the river fleet — did the same. The admiral and his precious warships were delivered, thanks to Bailey, to whom he presented, as a personal gift, a $700 sword. The engineer also received, as tokens of appreciation, a $1600 silver vase from the navy, a vote of thanks from Congress, and in time a two-step promotion to brigadier general. None of this was a whit too much, according to Porter, who said of the former Wisconsin logger in his report: "Words are inadequate to express the admiration I feel for the abilities of Lieutenant Colonel Bailey. This is without doubt the best engineering feat ever performed. Under the best circumstances a private company would not have completed this work under one year, and to an ordinary mind the whole thing would have appeared an utter impossibility."

He might have added that his own mind seemed to fit in that category, since he had prejudged the attempt in just that way. But for the present, steaming down the lower Red, where the going was deep and easy because of backwater from the swollen Mississippi, he was altogether occupied with savoring his freedom, his narrow delivery from ruin. "I am clear of my troubles," he wrote home to his mother that week, though he was not so far clear of them that he forgot to add: "I have had a hard and anxious time of it."

So had Banks had a hard and anxious time of it, and so was he still, along with the slogging troops under his command. Leaving Alexandria on May 13, the day after Porter completed his run, they had another sixty hostile miles to cover before they would return to their starting point, Simsport on the Atchafalaya, where Sherman's men had opened the campaign, just one day more than two full months ago. In point of fact, except as a location on the map, the town no longer existed; A. J. Smith's gorillas had burned it at the outset. And now, looking back over their shoulders as they set out, they had a similar satisfaction — similar not only to Simsport, but also to Grand Ecore, three weeks ago, as well as to a number of lesser hamlets in their path, before and since — of seeing Alexandria aflame. It burned briskly under a long, wind-tattered plume of greasy smoke, while over the levee and down by the bank of the river, as one Federal would recall, "thousands of people, mostly women, children, and old men, were wringing their hands as they stood by the little piles of what was left of all their worldly possessions." They had been driven there by the sudden press of heat from a score of fires that quickly merged after starting simultaneously with the help of a mixture of turpentine and camphene, which the soldiers slopped on houses and stores with mops and brooms. Experience had greatly improved their incendiary technique. "Hurrah, boys! This looks like war!" Smith shouted by way of encouragement as he rode through the streets, rounding up his men for departure.

They had their usual assignment as rear guard, the post of honor on retreat, while the Easterners took the lead. Banks rode with the more congenial troops up front, commanded now by Emory; Franklin, after recommending that his chief engineer's proposal for saving the fleet be tried, had left on May Day, still fretted by his shin wound, which seemed to require more skilled attention than the Transmississippi doctors were able to furnish, and by disgust and bitterness at having been prominently connected with still another large-scale defeat. Banks of course had that fret too, without the red-badge distraction of a physical injury, but he felt better, all in all, than he had done at any time in the past horrendous month. For one thing, the salvation of the flotilla had given journalists the upbeat ending Porter had dangled as bait for prolonging the army's stay in Alexandria, and for another his casualties had been replaced, before the end of April, by reinforcements who arrived from Pass Cavallo, Texas, under Major General John A. McClernand, resurrected from his Grant-enforced retirement in Springfield, Illinois, and put in command of the lower Texas coast by his old friend and fellow townsman Abraham Lincoln. That brought the army's total strength to 31,000 effectives up the Red, more than Banks had had directly under him so far in the campaign. Even though there was no compensation for the loss of twenty guns, two hundred wagons, and something over a thousand mules, this added strength brought added confidence; which, aside from military skill, had been the thing most lacking at headquarters since the crossroads confrontation short of Mansfield, five weeks ago today. Moreover, there was the relief of having the end at last in sight, whatever disappointments had occurred along the way, and of discovering that Taylor, for all his bluster in the course of the Alexandria siege, seemed considerably less a menace now that the cooped-up bluecoats were out in the open, inviting the attack he formerly had seemed anxious but now seemed strangely reluctant to deliver.

At any rate that appeared to be the case throughout the first three days of the march downriver. Crossing the Choctaw Bayou swamps on the second day out of smouldering Alexandria, the Federals occupied Marksville on the evening of the third. That was May 15; they had covered forty miles by then, molested by nothing worse than grayback cavalry, which failed in its attempts to get at the wagons drawn by scarecrow mules, and were a good two thirds of their way to the sanctuary a crossing of the Atchafalaya would afford them. Banks tempered his optimism, however, by reminding himself that the tactical situation resembled the one that had obtained, or had seemed to obtain, on the march from Natchitoches to within three miles of Mansfield, where it ended in disarray. The resemblance was altogether too close for comfort, let alone for premature self-congratulation; Taylor might well be planning a repeat of that performance at another crossroads, somewhere up ahead. And sure enough, advancing next morning across the Avoyelles Prairie, five miles south of Marksville, Banks found the Confederates disposed in force athwart his path, much as they had been at Sabine Crossroads, except that here the terrain was open and gave him a sobering view of what he faced. Their line of battle extending east and west of the village of Mansura, they had thirty-odd pieces of artillery — more than half of them had been his own, up to the time of the previous confrontation just short of Mansfield, which this one so uncomfortably resembled — unlimbered and ready to take him under fire as soon as he ventured within range. Their numbers in infantry and cavalry were hard to estimate, masked as their center was by the town, but Banks did not decline the challenge. He shook out his skirmishers, put his own guns in position — as many of the remaining seventy, in any case, as he could find room for on the three-mile width of prairie — formed his infantry for attack with cavalry posted neatly on both flanks, and then went forward, blue flags rippling in the breeze.

The result, as the troops began to move and the guns to growl, was enough to make observers in both armies, each of which had a full view of the other, catch their breath in admiration. Advancing across the lush and level prairie — "smooth as a billiard table," Taylor was to say of it in his report — the Union host was "resplendent in steel and brass," according to one of its members, a Connecticut infantryman who afterward tried his hand at a word sketch of the scene, including "miles of lines and columns; the cavalry gliding over the ground in the distance with a delicate, nimble lightness of innumerable twinkling feet; a few batteries enveloped in smoke and incessantly thundering, others dashing swiftly to salient positions; division and corps commanders with their staff officers clustering about them, watching through their glasses the hostile army; couriers riding swiftly from wing to wing; everywhere the beautiful silken flags; and the scene ever changing with the involutions and evolutions of the vast host." It was, in short, that seldom-encountered thing, picture-book war — which it also resembled, as events developed, in its paucity of bloodshed. Though the armies remained in approximate confrontation for four hours, the action was practically limited to artillery exchanges, since neither commander seemed willing to venture within point-blank range of the other's guns. When at last Banks brought A. J. Smith's Westerners forward for an attack on the rebel left, Taylor withdrew in that direction, south and west, and the Federals resumed their march to the south and east, through Mansura, then on to Bayou de Glaise, on whose banks they stopped for the night. Next day, May 17, after skirmishing warmly with enemy horsemen on both sides of Moreauville, they pushed on to Yellow Bayou, within five miles of Simsport and the Atchafalaya, which would shield them from further pursuit once they were across it.

If Banks had known the extent of the odds in his favor, he not only would have been less surprised at the sidelong rebel withdrawal from Mansura, he would also have been considerably less concerned for the safety of his army, which in fact enjoyed a five-to-one numerical advantage over the force attempting to waylay and impede it. Taylor fairly ached for some sign of the three divisions on the march from Arkansas; to no avail. "Like 'Sister Ann' from her watch tower," he was to write, "day after day we strained our eyes to see the dust of our approaching comrades.... Vain, indeed, were our hopes. The commander of the 'Trans-Mississippi Department' had the power to destroy the last hope of the Confederate cause, and exercised it with all the success of Bazaine at Metz. 'The affairs of mice and men aft gang aglee,' from sheer stupidity and pig-headed obstinacy." And lest his meaning be clouded by his fondness for religious and historical allusions and poetic misquotations, he made the charge specific and identified by name the man he held responsible for his woes: "From first to last, General Kirby Smith seemed determined to throw a protecting shield around the Federal army and fleet."

This bitterness would grow; would in time become obsessive. But for the present the Louisiana general directed most of his attention to a search for some way, despite the odds, to inflict more vengeful damage on the spoilers of his homeland before they fled beyond his reach. The side-step at Mansura, allowing them to press on south and east, had been as necessary as it was painful; for if Taylor was to preserve his little army for future use, he could not afford to take on the blue host without a tactical advantage totally lacking on the open prairie. Then next day he received, as if from Providence, what he believed might be the chance for which he prayed. Pushing on through Moreauville, the Federal main body reached Yellow Bayou only to learn from its scouts, who had ridden ahead, that backwater from the Mississippi had swollen the Atchafalaya to a width too great for spanning by all the pontoons the engineers had on hand. Without a bridge, the crossing would be at best a slow affair, involving the use of transports as ferries. Penned up with its back to the river, as it had been at Grand Ecore and Alexandria, the blue mass would grow more vulnerable as it shrank, regiment by regiment, until at last a gray assault could be launched against the remnant — perhaps with the help, by then, of the slow-moving troops from Arkansas — extracting payment in blood for the vandalism of the past nine weeks. Taylor brightened at the prospect, and next morning, May 18, moved his infantry up to join his cavalry on Yellow Bayou, intending to advance from there and establish a semi-circular, close-up line of intrenchments from which to observe the dwindling Union army, held under siege amid the ashes of what had once been Simsport.

Looking out across the unbridgeable 600-yard expanse of the Atchafalaya, a swollen barrier to the safety his army could only attain by reaching the far side, Banks foresaw an outcome all too similar to the one his adversary was moving to effect. Still, his despair was not so deep as to keep him from doing all he could to ward it off. When he was informed, around midmorning, that Taylor had moved up to

Yellow Bayou, close in his rear, he instructed A. J. Smith to countermarch and drive him back. Smith returned to the Bayou, crossed three brigades, and pitched without delay into the rebel skirmish line, throwing it back on the main body, which then attacked and drove him back in turn. It went that way for a couple of hours, first one side gaining ground and then the other — each had about 5000 men engaged — until at last the underbrush caught fire and both withdrew in opposite directions, choked and scorched, from the crackling barricade of smoke and flame. That ended the action. Unresolved and indecisive as it was, Smith's gorillas once more had proved their worth as fighters as well as burners, losing about 350 to inflict a total of 608 casualties on Taylor.

Nothing daunted, the Louisianian prepared to return to the offensive next day, May 19. But that was not to be. The back-and-forth engagement on the west side of Yellow Bayou turned out to be the last of the campaign — for the simple reason that presently no blue-clad troops remained within his reach. Banks by then had bridged the unbridgeable Atchafalaya.

Once more the *deus ex machina* was Joe Bailey. Handed the problem by Banks, the engineering colonel promptly solved it by mooring all the available riverboats and transports side by side across the near-half-mile width of the stream, like oversized pontoons, and bolting them together with timbers which then served as stringers for planks laid crosswise on them to form a roadbed. Soon after midday, though the varying heights of the boats on which it rested gave it something of the crazy, up-and-down aspect of a roller coaster, Banks had the bridge he needed to reach the sanctuary beyond the river. The wagon train began to cross at once, followed that night by the guns and ambulances; next morning, May 20, the troops themselves were marched across and the makeshift bridge dismantled in their rear. Two days later — a solid month past the time when they had been scheduled to rejoin Sherman in far-off Georgia — Smith's three divisions filed back aboard their transports and set out for Vicksburg. Banks meantime was as full of praise for Bailey, here on the Atchafalaya, as Porter had been the week before, back up the Red. "This work was not of the same magnitude, but was as important to the army as the dam at Alexandria was to the navy," he said of the improvised bridge in his final report, and repeated his recommendation that the former logger be promoted to brigadier as a reward for his resourcefulness under pressure.

Another upbeat flourish had been provided, but so had additions been made to the list of casualties — more than fifteen hundred of them, all told, since the return to Alexandria in late April. Army losses for the campaign now stood at 5245 killed, wounded, and missing, and to this were added some three hundred naval casualties, suffered in the course of the subtraction from the flotilla of an ironclad, two tinclads, three transports, a pair of pump boats, and 28 guns of various calibers, captured or spiked and abandoned up the Red. This Federal total of about 5500 exceeded by well over a thousand the Confederate total of 4275. Losses in matériel were of course even more disproportionate, not only because the rebels had lost much less in battle, but also because they had had a great deal less to lose: aside, that is, from civilian property, the destruction of which, if included, would doubtless swing the balance the other way. But perhaps the greatest contrast lay in what a member of Banks's official family called "the great and bitter crop of quarrels" raised in the northern ranks by what he referred to as "this unhappy campaign." If on the Confederate side there were arguments in the scramble to divide the glory, on the Union side there were hotter ones involved in the distribution of the blame. Looking back over the events of the past seventy days, the staffer noted that feelings had been severely ruffled and several lofty reputations quite undone. "Franklin quitted the department in disgust," he recalled; "Stone was replaced by Dwight as chief of staff, and Lee as chief of cavalry by Arnold; A. J. Smith departed more in anger than in sorrow; while between the admiral and the general commanding, recriminations were exchanged in language well up to the limits of 'parliamentary' privilege."

Now still another illustrious name was added to the list: Banks's own. Not that he was relieved outright or shunted into obscurity, as so many others had been in the doleful course of the past six weeks. This was an election year, and too much rode on the outcome for the authorities to risk alienating a man with as many votes as the one-time Speaker of the House controlled. Lincoln and Halleck put their heads together and came up with the answer. Major General Edward R. S. Canby, a forty-six-year-old Kentucky-born West Pointer, had come east after the New Mexico campaign of 1862, in which he had managed to save the Far West for the Union, and had since been involved in administrative matters, including the reëstablishment of law and order in New York after the draft riots of 1863. In all these positions his outstanding characteristic had been his prudence, a rare quality nowadays in the Transmississippi; Lincoln and Halleck, with Grant's concurrence — Canby had been another of his classmates at the Point — decided to send him there to supply it, not as Banks's replacement, but rather as his superior, by placing him in charge of the newly created "Military Division of West Mississippi," which stretched from Missouri to the Gulf and from Florida to Texas. Banks's unquestioned abilities as an administrator, honest amid corruption, were thus preserved for the government's use, along with his political support, while his military ineptness was set aside by depriving him of any further independence — or, as it turned out, service — in the field.

Canby was waiting for him with the necessary papers at Simsport, and accompanied him on the final leg of the retreat, another hundred miles downriver to Donaldsonville, where the campaign formally ended on May 26, seventy-five days after its start and more than a month beyond its scheduled finish. An Iowa soldier wrote in his diary that Banks looked "dejected and worn" at that stage, and small wonder. More had ended and more had been lost, for him, than the campaign. The former governor, whose reduction of Port Hudson had opened the Mississippi to northern trade throughout its length, was now the mere desk-bound head of a subdepartment in an organization commanded by a man almost two years his junior in age and three full years behind him in date of rank. That came hard, but that was by no means the worst of it for Banks, who was taunted not only by the thought of what he had lost but also by the thought of what he had failed to gain. Mobile might someday be attacked and taken, but not by him, and along with much else that had gone with the winds of war — including all those hundreds of thousands of bales of cotton, which were to have put the national effort on a pay-as-you-go basis, but which instead had tainted it with scandal — were his hopes for the highest political office. All that had ended up the Red. He not only had been defeated by his enemies up that river, he had been oversloughed by his superiors on his return: "a fit sequel," the Saint Louis *Republican* asserted, "to a scheme conceived in politics and brought forth in iniquity."

If contention was less widespread on the Confederate side, where there was more credit than blame to be divided, such contention as there was only flared the higher on that account. Taylor's distress in reaction to his fear that the Federals were going to escape — the result, he claimed, of "sheer stupidity and pig-headed obstinacy" on the part of the high command at Shreveport — was mild compared to the frustration he felt when the bluecoats did in fact improvise an Atchafalaya crossing before the arrival of the Arkansas reinforcements enabled him to exact the retribution he felt they owed. Though his pride in his outnumbered army was as boundless as his contempt for the invaders ("Long will the accursed race remember the great river of Texas and Louisiana," he said of the latter in a congratulatory order he issued to his troops on May 23. "The characteristic hue of its turbid waters has a darker tinge from the liberal admixture of Yankee blood. The cruel alligator and the ravenous garfish wax fat on rich food, and our native vulture holds high revelry over many a festering corpse") his wrath had mounted with each passing day of the unimpeded blue retreat. Moving up to Yellow Bayou five days ago, he had taken time to communicate his chagrin at having been obliged to step aside, just when he had the vandals within his grasp, for lack of strength to stand his ground at Mansura. "I feel bitterly about this," he protested in a dispatch to Kirby Smith's adjutant, "because my army has been robbed of the just measure of its glory and the country of the most brilliant and complete success of the war."

The further it receded into the past, the more "brilliant and complete" that missed victory became. Indeed, within a week or so, Taylor had come to believe that his superior's military ineptness, which had obliged him to forgo a certain triumph, might well have cost the South its one best chance to win its independence. What was more, he said as much to Kirby Smith himself on June 5, in a letter combining indignation and despair. "In truth," he wrote, quite as if he had a corner on that rare commodity, "the campaign as a whole has been a hideous failure. The fruits of Mansfield have turned to dust and ashes. Louisiana, from Natchitoches to the Gulf, is a howling wilderness and her people are starving. Arkansas is probably as great a sufferer. In both States abolition conventions are sitting to overthrow their system of labor. The remains of Banks' army have already gone to join Grant or Sherman, and may turn the scale against our overmatched brethren in Virginia and Georgia." What made the hot-tempered Louisianian angriest was the contrast between this and the situation that might have obtained if his chief had not rejected his advice on how to go about disposing of the invaders, which he was certain would have led to their destruction and the reversal of the tide of war. "The roads to Saint Louis and New Orleans should now be open to us. Your strategy has riveted the fetters on both." The more he wrote — and he wrote at length, including a full critique of the campaign, with emphasis on the mismanagement of events beyond his reach, both here and in Arkansas — the angrier he grew: until finally, as he drew to a close, his wrath approached incandescence. "The same regard for duty which led me to throw myself between you and popular indignation, and quietly take the blame for your errors," he wound up, "compels me to tell you the truth, however objectionable to you. The grave errors you have committed in the recent campaign may be repeated if the unhappy consequences are not kept before you. After the desire to serve my country, I have none more ardent than to be relieved from longer serving under your command."

Thus Taylor, whose rage had made him as blind to the virtues of others as he was perceptive of their faults. To refer to the just-ended campaign as "a hideous failure," simply because it had not yielded all that he had hoped for, was to overlook its fruits, which in fact were far from slight. Inflicting more than 8000 casualties on Steele and Banks, at a cost to Price and Taylor of 6500, Smith had captured or caused the destruction of 57 pieces of artillery, nearly half of them naval, along with about a thousand wagons, most of them loaded with valuable supplies, and more than 3500 mules and horses. This was a considerable tactical haul, by almost any standards, and yet the strategic gains were even greater. Despite the hot-tempered Louisianian's claim to the contrary, the campaign had cost Sherman the use of 10,000 veterans in North Georgia; which meant that he moved with that many fewer against Joe Johnston, while Johnston's own army was enlarged by nearly twice that number because the upset of Banks' schedule had ruled out an early movement against Mobile, leaving Polk free to shift from Demopolis toward Dalton with some 20,000 troops who otherwise would have been drawn in the opposite direction by the threat to coastal Alabama. The greatest effect of the campaign up Red River thus was felt in northern Georgia, where a net difference of 30,000 men was registered in favor of the defenders of Atlanta. If the South was going to lose the war, then this would no doubt prolong the conflict. On the other hand, this might just narrow the long odds enough for the South to win it.

That of course remained to be seen. In the meantime, there was nothing Kirby Smith could do, despite his disinclination in such matters, but act on Taylor's insubordinate letter. Appointing Walker as his successor, he ordered him to Natchitoches, there to await instructions from their superiors, and forwarded the correspondence to Richmond with a covering letter to his friend the President. The good of the service required that he or Taylor be removed from command, the mild-mannered Floridian declared, adding that if Davis thought it best — as he well might do; Smith freely acknowledged the Louisianian's "merits as a soldier" — "I will willingly, with no feeling of envy or abatement of interest in the service of my country, turn over my arduous duties and responsibilities to a successor."

It made a sorry end, this falling-out by the victors, after all the glory that had been garnered up the Red and on the Saline; Dick Taylor was afterwards far from proud of his conduct in the quarrel, and set it down as the result of overwork and nervous strain. For the present, though, he was not unhappy to be reunited with his wife and children in Natchitoches, the lovely old French-Spanish town he recently had saved from Sherman's burners, there to await the judgment of his presidential brother-in-law.

※ 3 ※

Davis had troubles enough by then, and differences enough to attempt to compose, without the added problem of trying to heal this latest split between two of his friends, one of whom was among the nation's ranking field commanders, responsible for the conduct of affairs in the largest of all its military departments, while the other was his first wife's younger brother. Down in Georgia, for example, on March 10 — the day A. J. Smith's gorillas left Vicksburg, beginning the ten-week campaign that would take them up and down Red River, and the day before Grant left Washington for the meeting with Sherman in Nashville, where they would begin to plan the campaign designed to bring Georgia to its knees and the Confederacy to extinction — Governor Joseph E.

Brown addressed the state legislature, which he had called into special session to hear some things he had to say on the subject of the war. What he had to say, in essence, was that the war had been a failure. This was not only because it was now to be waged on his doorstep, so to speak, but also because, as he saw it, the authorities in Richmond had abandoned the principles embodied in the Declaration of Independence, including "all self-government and the sovereignty of the States."

Brown's solution, as set forth in his address, was for the Confederacy to dissolve itself into its components, thus calling a halt to discord and bloodshed: after which, in an atmosphere of peace and fellowship, a convention of northern and southern governors would assemble at Baltimore or Memphis, Montreal or the Bermuda Islands, and each state, North as well as South, would "determine for herself what shall be her future connection, and who her future allies." In other words, he would stop and start anew, this time without taking so many wrong turnings in the pursuit of happiness along the path that led to independence. Brown was careful, in the course of his speech, not to propose that Georgia rejoin the Union. That would have amounted to outright treason. He proposed, rather, that the Union rejoin Georgia, and he favored "negotiation" as the means of achieving this end. "In a crisis like the present," he maintained, "Statesmanship is ever more important than Generalship. Generals can never stop a war, though it may last twenty years till one has been able to conquer the other. Statesmen terminate wars by negotiation."

Praised for its acumen or condemned as disloyal, the address pleased some of its hearers and outraged others, depending largely on their predilections. Politically, an observer remarked, "Georgia was rent asunder." Among the governor's firmest supporters, though he was not in Milledgeville to hear him, was Alexander H. Stephens, Vice President of the Confederacy. Stephens not only gave the speech his full approval — as well he might; "I advised it from stem to stern," he admitted privately — but arrived in person six days later from Liberty Hall, his estate at nearby Crawfordville, to reinforce it with one of his own, twice as long and twice as bitter, in which he lashed out at the national authorities for their betrayal of the secessionist cause by adopting conscription and suspending the writ of habeas corpus. "Better, in my judgment," he declared, "that Richmond should fall and that the enemy's armies should sweep our whole country from the Potomac to the Gulf than that our people should submissively yield to one of these edicts." A small, pale-faced man with burning eyes and a shrill voice, weighing less than a hundred pounds in the voluminous overcoat he wore against the chill he felt in all but the hottest weather, he spoke for three full hours, in the course of which he sustained at several points a critic's charge that his alarm "had long ago vaulted into the hysterical." Where personal freedom was concerned Stephens rejected all arguments as to expediency. "Away with the idea of getting our independence first, and looking after liberty afterward!" he cried. "Our liberties, once lost, may be lost forever." If he had to be ruled by a despot, he said darkly, he preferred that it be a northern one, and he closed on a dramatic note, quite as if he expected to be clapped in arrest by government agents as soon as he came down off the rostrum. "I do not know that I shall ever address you again, or see you again," he told the legislators filling the chamber, row on row, from wall to wall. "As for myself," he added by way of farewell — though he knew, as Patrick Henry had not known before him, that the authority he assailed would not dare call him to account — "give me liberty as secured in the Constitution, amongst which is the sovereignty of Georgia, or give me death!"

He proceeded not to the dungeon he had seemed to predict, but back to Liberty Hall, where he continued to fulminate, in letters and interviews, against the government of which he was nominally a part and the man whose place he would take in case of death or the impeachment he appeared to recommend. Reproached by a constituent for having "allowed your antipathy to Davis to mislead your judgment," Stephens denied that he harbored any such enmity in his bosom. "I have regarded him as a man of good intentions," he replied, "weak and vacillating, petulant, peevish, obstinate but not firm." Having gone so far, however, he then revoked the disclaimer by adding: "Am now beginning to doubt his good intentions." Meantime, back in Milledgeville, Brown's managers were steering through the legislature a double set of resolutions introduced by Little Aleck's younger brother Linton, one condemning the Richmond authorities for having overridden the Constitution, the other defining Georgia's terms for peace as a return, North and South, to the "principles of 1776." This took three days; the governor had to threaten to hold the legislators in special session "indefinitely" in order to ram the resolutions through; then on March 19 they passed them and were permitted to adjourn. Brown had his and the Vice President's addresses printed in full, together with Linton Stephens's resolutions, and distributed copies to all the Georgia soldiers in the armies of Lee and Johnston.

Stephens and Brown were two of the more unpleasant facts of Confederate life that had to be faced in Richmond by officials trying to get on with a long-odds war amid runaway inflation and spreading disaffection. Others were nearer at hand. In North Carolina, for example — that "vale of humility," a native called the state, "nestled between two humps of pride," Virginia and South Carolina — the yearning for peace had grown in ratio to a general disenchantment with "glory," of which the war, according to Governor Zebulon Vance, had afforded the Old North State too meager a share. Less bitter than Joe Brown — of whom a fellow Georgian was saying this spring,

"Wherever you meet a growling, complaining, sore-headed man, hostile to the government and denunciatory of its measures and policy, or a croaking, despondent dyspeptic who sees no hope for the country, but, whipped himself, is trying to make everybody else feel as badly as himself, you will invariably find a friend, admirer, and defender of Governor Brown" — Vance was an unrelenting critic of the ways things were done or left undone at Richmond, and his correspondence was heavy with complaints, made directly to the President, that Carolinians were constantly being slighted in the distribution of promotions and appointments. Late in March, Davis lost patience and sought to break off the exchange, protesting that Vance had "so far infringed the proprieties of official intercourse as to preclude the possibility of reply. In order that I may not again be subjected to the necessity of making so unpleasant a remark, I must beg that a correspondence so unprofitable in its character, and which was not initiated by me, may here end, and that your future communications be restricted to such matters as may require official action." But Vance, a self-made man from old Buncombe County, had long since learned the political value of persistence; he was not so easily restrained. Scarcely a mail arrived from Raleigh that did not include a protest by the governor that some worthy Tarheel had been snubbed or overlooked in the passing out of favors, military as well as civil. Davis could only read and sigh, thankful at least that Vance kept his distance, even though it was not so great as the distance Brown and Stephens kept.

That was by no means the case with Edward A. Pollard, who was not only very much at hand as associate editor of the Richmond *Examiner*, but also took the trouble to let the authorities know it daily. He often seemed to despise the Confederacy to its roots, and seldom relaxed in his efforts to impale its chief executive on what was agreed to be the sharpest pen in the journalistic South. Invective was his specialty, and when he got on his favorite subject — Jefferson Davis — he sometimes raised this specialty to an art. "Serene upon the frigid heights of infallible egotism," the Kentucky-born Mississippian was "affable, kind, and subservient to his enemies" but "haughty, austere, and unbending to his friends," and though he assumed "the superior dignity of a satrap," he was in fact, behind the rigid mask, "an amalgam of malice and mediocrity." Future historians of various persuasions were to take their cue from this carving-up of a man on his wrong side; it was small wonder that Pollard, who spoke with the gadfly rancor of Thersites, found many who nodded in gleeful agreement as they read his jabs and jibes. They read him, in this fourth and gloomiest spring of a war they had begun to believe they could not win, to find relief from a frustration which grew, like his own, in ratio to the dwindling of their hopes.

Thoroughly familiar with the American proclivity for blaming national woes on the national leader, Davis had engaged in the practice too often himself not to expect it to be turned against him. He viewed it as an occupational hazard, one that more or less went with his job, and he spoke of it as a man might speak of any natural phenomenon — gravity, say, or atmospheric pressure — which could not be abolished simply because it bore within it the seeds of possible disaster. "Opposition in any form can only disturb me inasmuch as it may endanger the public welfare," he had said. Moreover, no one could sympathize more with the people who felt this fourth-spring frustration, for no one was in a position to know as well how soundly based the feeling was. Such blame as he attached to men like Stephens and Brown and Pollard was not for entertaining, but rather for giving vent to their defeatist conclusions, since by so doing they betrayed their high positions, converting them to rostrums for the spreading of despair, and did indeed "endanger the public welfare." As for the frustration itself, Davis not only sympathized with, he shared it. However much he might condemn those who gave way under pressure, he knew only too well how great that pressure was: especially for those who saw the problem, as he did, from within. Wherever he looked he perceived that the Confederacy's efforts to "conquer a peace" were doomed to failure. And this applied most obviously to the three most obvious fields for aggressive endeavor, whereby the South might attempt to force its will upon its mortal adversary: 1) by entering upon negotiations with representatives from the North to obtain acceptable peace terms, 2) by mounting and sustaining a military offensive which would end with the imposition of such terms, or 3) by securing the foreign recognition and assistance which would afford the moral and physical strength now lacking to achieve the other two.

As for the first of these, Davis had pointed out the difficulty, if not the impossibility, of pursuing this line of endeavor three months ago in response to a letter from Governor Vance, in which the Carolinian urged that attempts be made to negotiate with the enemy, not only because such an expression of willingness on the part of the South to stop shooting and start talking would "convince the humblest of our citizens... that the government is tender of their lives and happiness, and would not prolong their sufferings unnecessarily one moment," but also because the rejection by the North of such an offer would "tend greatly to strengthen and intensify the war feeling [of our people] and will rally all classes to a more cordial support of the government." Davis replied that while such results were highly desirable, "insuperable objections" stood in the way of their being achieved. One was that, by the simple northern device of refusing to confer with "rebel" envoys, all such offers — except to the extent that they were "received as proof that we are ready for submission" — had been rejected out of hand. He himself had seldom neglected an opportunity, in his public addresses and messages to Congress, to inform the enemy and the world that "All we ask is to be let alone." Nothing had come of this, in or out of official channels, and it was becoming increasingly clear that to continue such efforts was "to invite insult and contumely, and to subject ourselves to indignity, without the slightest chance of being listened to."

Suppose, though, that they did somehow manage to break through the barrier of silence. What would that do, Davis asked, but confront them with another barrier, still more "insuperable" than the first? "It is with Lincoln alone that we could confer," he reminded Vance, "and his own partisans at the North avow unequivocally that his purpose in his message and proclamation [of Amnesty and Reconstruction] was to shut out all hope that he would *ever* treat with us, on *any* terms." The northern President himself had made this clear and certain, according to Davis. "Have we not been apprised by that despot that we can only expect his gracious pardon by emancipating all our slaves, swearing obedience to him and his proclamation, and becoming in point of fact the slaves of our own Negroes?" In the light of this, he asked further, "can there be in North Carolina one citizen so fallen beneath the dignity of his ancestors as to accept or enter into conference on the basis of these terms? That there are a few traitors in the state who would be willing to betray their fellow citizens to such a degraded condition, in hope of being rewarded for their treachery by an escape from the common doom, may be true. But I do not believe that the vilest wretch would accept such terms for himself."

Having gone so far — for the letter was a long one, written in the days before he sought to break off corresponding with the Tarheel governor — Davis then proceeded to the inevitable conclusion that peace, if it was to come at all, would have to be won by force of arms. "To obtain the sole terms to which you or I could listen," he told Vance, "this struggle must continue until the enemy is beaten out of his vain confidence in our subjugation. Then and not till then will it be possible to treat of peace."

That brought him to the second, and much the bloodiest, of his three aggressive choices: the launching of an offensive that would not stop short of the table across which peace terms would be dictated to an enemy obliged to accept them as a condition of survival in defeat. Pleasant though this was to contemplate as a fitting end to slaughter and privation, it amounted to little more than an exercise in the realm of fantasy. If three blood-drenched years of war, and three aborted invasions of the North, had taught anything, they had taught that, however the conflict was going to end, it was not going to end this way. Davis, for one, never stopped hoping that it might, and even now was urging a course of action on Joe Johnston, down in Georgia, designed to bring about just such a closing scene. That the general declined to march all-out against the Union center was not surprising; Johnston had always bridled at cut-and-slash urgings or suggestions, and in this case, outnumbered and outgunned as he was, he protested with ample cause. Nor was he the only one to demonstrate reluctance. "Our role must be a defensive policy," Kirby Smith was warning his impetuous lieutenants out in the Transmississippi; while nearer at hand, and weightiest by far in that regard, the nation's ranking field commander was tendering much the same advice to his superior in Richmond. The most aggressive of all the Confederate military chieftains — indeed, one of the most aggressive soldiers of all time, of whom a subordinate had declared, quite accurately, on the occasion of his appointment to head the Virginia army, just under two years ago: "His name might be Audacity. He will take more chances, and take them quicker, than any other general in this country, North or South" — R. E. Lee had taken care, well before the occasion could arise, to forestall even the suggestion that he attempt another large-scale offensive when the present "mud truce" ended in the East. Back in early February, in response to a presidential request for counsel, he said flatly: "We are not in a condition, and never have been, in my opinion, to invade the enemy's country with a prospect of permanent benefit."

There Davis had it. For though Lee added characteristically that he hoped, by a limited show of force, to "alarm and embarrass [the enemy] to some extent, and thus prevent his undertaking anything of magnitude against us," this was no real modification of his implied opinion that past efforts to end the war on northern soil — his own two, which had broken in blood along Sharpsburg ridge and across the stony fields of Gettysburg, as well as Bragg's, which had gone into reverse at Perryville — had been errors of judgment, serving, if for nothing else, to demonstrate the folly of any attempt at repetition of them. Such a statement, from such a source, was practically irrefutable, especially since it was echoed by the commanders of the other two major theaters, Smith and Johnston. The war, if it was to be won at all by southern arms, would have to be won on southern ground.

Third and last of these choices, the securing of foreign recognition and assistance, had long been the cherished hope of Confederate statesmen: especially Davis, who had uttered scarcely a public word through the first twenty months of the war that did not look toward intervention by one or another of the European powers. However, as time wore on it became clearer that nothing was going to come of such efforts and expectations — Russia had been pro-Union from the start, and France, whatever her true desires might be, could not act without England, where the Liberals in power took their cue from voters who were predominantly anti-slavery and therefore, in accordance with Lincoln's persuasions, anti-Confederate — the southern President, smarting under the snubs his unacknowledged envoys suffered, grew increasingly petulant and less guarded in his reaction. Fifteen months ago, addressing his home-state legislature on the first of his western journeys to revive confidence and bolster morale, he lost patience for the first time in public. " 'Put not your trust in princes,' " he advised, "and rest not your hopes on foreign nations. This war is ours; we must fight it out ourselves." The applause this drew, plus the growing conviction that nothing any Confederate said or did had any effect whatever on the outcome in Europe, encouraged further remarks along this line. Nor was his reaction limited to remarks. In June of 1863, with Lee on the march for Gettysburg and Vicksburg soon to fall, the exequatur of the British consul at Richmond was revoked. The presence of such consuls had long been irksome, not only because they sought to interfere in such matters as the conscription of British nationals and the collection of British debts, but also because they were accredited to a foreign power, the United States, rather than to the country in which they operated, the Confederate States, whose very existence their government denied except as a "belligerent." The strain increased. In August, James M. Mason, the still unreceived ambassador to England, was told to consider his mission at an end, and before the following month was out he gave up his London residence and removed the diplomatic archives to Paris. In October the final strings were cut. Declaring their continued presence at Charleston, Savannah, and Mobile "an unwarranted assumption of jurisdiction," as well as "an offensive encroachment," Davis expelled all British consular agents from the South.

In Paris, Mason found the position of his fellow ambassador, John Slidell, highly enviable at first glance. Fluent in New Orleans French, the urbane Louisianian had practically free — though, alas, unofficial — access to Napoleon and Eugénie, both of whom were sympathetic to his cause; or so they kept assuring him, although nothing tangible in the way of help had so far proceeded from their concern. In many ways, the situation in Paris was more frustrating than the one in London, where Mason's non-reception at least had not built up hopes that came to nothing every time. By now, as a result of such recurrent disappointments, Slidell had become convinced that he was being led along for some purpose he could not fathom, but which he suspected would be of little benefit, in the end, either to him personally or to the government he represented. Disenchanted with the postcard Emperor, he was turning bitter in his attitude toward his job. "I find it very difficult to keep my temper amidst all this double dealing," he informed his friend and chief, Secretary of State Judah P. Benjamin. In point of fact, his experiences at court seemed to have jaundiced him entirely, for he added, by way of general observation: "This is a rascally world, and it is most hard to say who can be trusted."

What it came down to, in the end as in the beginning, whether Slidell was right or wrong about Napoleon and his motives, was that France could not act without England. And now, as the war moved into its fourth critical spring, Davis could not resist lodging a protest which, in effect, burned the last bridge that might have led to a rapprochement with that all-important power. The trouble stemmed from British acceptance of evidence supplied by U.S. Ambassador Charles Francis Adams that certain warships under construction by the Lairds of Liverpool, ostensibly for the Viceroy of Egypt, were in fact to be sold to the Confederacy, which intended to use these powerful steam rams to shatter the Union blockade. "It would be superfluous in me to point out to your lordship that this is war," Adams informed Foreign Secretary Lord John Russell. It was indeed superfluous, since Russell, already alarmed by Seward's tail-twisting threats along that line, had previously taken steps to prevent delivery of the vessels by detaining them. That was in September, six months ago, and as if this was not enough to placate Seward there arrived in Richmond on April 1 — not through regular diplomatic channels, but by special courier under a flag of truce, as between belligerents — a message for Jefferson Davis from Lord Richard Lyons, the British minister in Washington, containing an extract from a dispatch lately sent by Russell protesting "against the efforts of the authorities of the so-called Confederate States to build war vessels within Her Majesty's dominions to be employed against the Government of the United States."

Davis bristled. Hard as this governmental decision was to take — for the matter was still in litigation in the British courts, and he hoped for a favorable outcome there — the phrase "so-called" cut deeper, adding insult to injury as it did. Never one to accept a slight, let alone a snub, the Mississippian summoned his secretary and dictated a third-person reply. "The President desires me to say to your Lordship, that ... it would be inconsistent with the dignity of the position he fills, as Chief Magistrate of a nation comprising a population of more than twelve millions, occupying a territory many times larger than the United Kingdom ... to allow the attempt of Earl Russell to ignore the actual existence of the Confederate States, and to contumeliously style them 'so-called,' to pass without a protest and a remonstrance. The President, therefore, does protest and remonstrate against this studied insult, and he instructs me to say that in future any document in which it may be repeated will be returned unanswered and unnoticed." Lyons had not used diplomatic channels for delivery of his message; Davis, stung in his national pride, did not use diplomacy at all in his response. Warming as he dictated, he termed British neutrality "a cover for treacherous, malignant hostility," and closed with an icy pretense of indifference. "As for the specious arguments on the subject of the rams . . . while those questions are still before the highest legal tribunal of the kingdom . . . the President himself will not condescend to notice them." The signature read, "Burton N. Harrison, Private Secretary."

Such satisfaction as Davis got from thus berating the Foreign

Secretary for his government's "persistent persecution of the Confederate States at the beck and bidding of officers of the United States" was small recompense for the knowledge that the South, engaged in what its people liked to think of as the Second American Revolution, would have no help from Europe in its struggle for independence. And what made this especially bitter to accept was a general historical agreement that in the original Revolution, with the Colonists in much the same position the Confederates were in now — unable, on the face of it, either to enforce or to negotiate a peace — such help had made the difference between victory and defeat. "This war is ours; we must fight it out ourselves," Davis had warned, by way of prelude to a year of hard reverses, and though the words were bravely spoken and loudly applauded at the time, there was sadness in the afterthought of what they meant in terms of the lengthening odds against success or even survival. Militarily, the handwriting on the wall was all too clear. In late November, within five months of the staggering midsummer news from Gettysburg and Vicksburg that Lee's army had been crippled and Pemberton's abolished, Bragg's army was flung bodily off Lookout Mountain and Missionary Ridge, impregnable though both positions had been said to be, and harried southward into Georgia. With these defeats in mind, it was no wonder that every Sunday at Saint Paul's in Richmond — the obvious goal of the huge offensive the North was about to launch as a follow-up of its triumphs, east and west, over the three main armies on which the Confederacy had depended for existence — the congregation recited the Litany with special fervor when it reached the words, "From battle and murder, and from sudden death, good Lord, deliver us."

The good Lord might, at that. For though military logic showed that the South could not win an offensive war, fought beyond the Potomac or the Ohio, there was still a chance that it could win a defensive one, fought on its own territory. It could win, in short, because the North could lose. In his letter to Vance, defining the conditions for peace under "the sole terms to which you or I could listen," Davis had not simply declared that the enemy must be beaten, period. He had said that the enemy must be "beaten out of his vain confidence in our subjugation," which was quite another thing. What he was saying was that for the North, committed by necessity to achieving an unconditional surrender, to settle for anything less than total conquest would amount to giving the South the victory by default. Lincoln knew this as well as Davis did, of course, and was not likely to coöperate in the dismemberment he had pledged himself to prevent. Yet the whole say-so would not be Lincoln's. Beyond the looming figure of the northern leader were the northern soldiers, and behind them were the northern people. If either became discouraged enough, soldiers or civilians, the war would end on terms not only acceptable but welcome to the South. The problem was how to get at them, beyond the loom of their leader, in order to influence their outlook and their choice. Davis saw cause for hope in both directions — tactical on one hand, political on the other — if certain requirements could be met.

Paradoxically, the tactical hope resulted from past Confederate defeats. Davis saw in every loss of mere territory — Nashville and Middle Tennessee, New Orleans, even Vicksburg and the Mississippi and the amputation of all that lay beyond — a corresponding gain, not only because what had been lost no longer required a dispersal of the country's limited strength for its protection, but also because the resultant contraction allowed a more compact defense of what remained. What remained now was the heartland, an 800-mile-wide triangle roughly defined by lines connecting Richmond, Savannah, and Mobile. Agriculturally and industrially, as well as geographically, this was the irreducible hard core of the nation, containing within it the resources and facilities to support a war of infinite length and intensity, so long as it and its people's will to fight remained intact. How long that would have to be, not in theory but in fact, depended on the validity of the companion political hope, according to which it would only be until November — specifically, the first Tuesday after the first Monday in that month — or, at worst, until early the following March — specifically, Inauguration Day. For this was a presidential election year in the North. The northern people, restrained by an iron hand these past three years, would finally have the chance to speak their minds on the question of war or peace, and the southern leader did not doubt that if his tactical hope was fulfilled — if no great Union victory, worth the agony to the army and the sorrow on the home front, was scored within that eight-month span by the blue drive on the heartland — his political hope would be fulfilled in turn. Weary of profitless bloodshed, the northern people would vote to end the war by turning Lincoln out of office and replacing him with a man who preferred to see half the nation depart in peace, as the saying went, rather than to continue the aimless destruction the two halves would have been visiting on each other for nearly three years. That was the prospect Davis had referred to, four months ago, when he declared in his State of the Nation address, opening the fourth session of Congress: "We now know that the only reliable hope for peace is in the vigor of our resistance, while the cessation of hostility [on the part of our adversaries] is only to be expected from the pressure of their necessities."

In brief, the problem between now and November was how to add to the North's war weariness, already believed to be substantial in certain regions where Copperheads were rampant, without at the same time increasing the South's disconsolation beyond the point of no return. This might or might not be possible, in light of the long odds, but in any case the prerequisite was that the northern people were to be denied the tonic of a large-scale victory within the triangular confines of the secessionist heartland — especially a tonic of the spirit-lifting kind that had come with the celebration of such victories as Vicksburg and Missionary Ridge, which had seemed to show beyond denial that a blue army could rout or capture a gray one as the result of a confrontation wherein Federal generalship was up to the standard set by the Confederates in the first two years of the war. Moreover, the general who had designed and directed both of those triumphs was now in over-all command of the Union forces, presumably chafing for the mud truce to end so he could get his armies headed south. Given the conditions that obtained in regard to numbers and equipment, plus the lightweight boxer's need for yielding ground in order to stay free to bob and weave and thus avoid a slugging match with his heavyweight opponent, there were bound to be southern losses and northern gains in the months immediately ahead; but that was not in itself a ruinous concession by the South, provided the losses and gains could be kept respectively minor and high-priced. In fact, such losses would serve admirably to drive home to the North the point that the prize was by no means worth the effort. The object was to make each gain so costly in blood and tears that the expense would be clearly disproportionate to the profit — if not in the judgment of the Federal high command, whose political or professional survival depended on continuing the conflict, then at any rate in the minds of those who would be casting their ballots in November, many of whom had an intensely personal interest in the casualty lists, future as well as past, and who might therefore be persuaded that their survival, unlike their leaders', depended on bringing the conflict to a close. Thus the South would be waging war not only on its own terrain (an advantage from which it had profited largely in the past) but also in the minds of northern voters who would be going to the polls, under what Davis termed "the pressure of their necessities" some seven months from now, to register a decision as to whether sustaining Lincoln's resolution that the rebels not be allowed to depart in peace was worth the continuing loss of their blue-clad sons and brothers and nephews and grandsons down in Georgia and Virginia.

Time and time alone would provide the answer to the question of survival; Patrick Henry's "liberty or death" applied quite literally to Confederate hopes and fears, which had between them no middle ground a man could stand on, patriot or traitor. Give or take a week or two, depending on the weather, the six months that would follow the end of large-scale inactivity in Georgia and Virginia, where the major forces lay mud-bound in their camps, would decide the issue, since Lincoln's appeal on that all-important Tuesday in November was likely to be in ratio to the progress of his soldiers in the field. Meantime, though, while the outsized armies on both sides took their ease and prepared as best they could for the shock to come, lesser forces had not been idle, east or west. And for the most part, when the military balance sheet was struck, the result of these out-of-season confrontations was encouraging to the hopes of the South for continuing its resistance to the superior weight the North could bring to bear.

Of these several upbeat Confederate successes — for though it was by far the most remote (Shreveport and Richmond were a thousand air-line miles apart; communication between them was necessarily slow and at best uncertain) it was not only the largest in numbers engaged, it was also achieved against the longest odds — the most encouraging was Kirby Smith's frustration of the double-pronged offensive designed by the Federals for completion of their conquest of the Transmississippi. All through the last half of March and the first half of April, the news from Louisiana and Arkansas had been gloomy; Banks and Steele appeared unstoppable in their respective penetrations, across the width and down the length of those two states, with Texas obviously next on the inexorable blue list. Then came word of Mansfield and Pleasant Hill, of Prairie d'Ane and Poison Spring; Steele and Banks were in full retreat from Price and Taylor, and Porter's dreaded ironclads were in flight from probable capture or destruction, bumping their bottoms as they scurried down the Red. It was incredible, and Camden and Jenkins Ferry, like Mansura and Yellow Bayou, only added to the glory and the uplift when news of them reached Richmond across those thousand embattled air-line miles. Other successes had preceded this, and others were to follow. Down in Florida, for example, an all-out Union effort to return that scantly defended state to its old allegiance, in accordance with Lincoln's recent proclamation, had been thrown into sudden reverse by Brigadier General Joseph Finegan's decisive late-February victory at Olustee, which drove the disarrayed invaders all the way back to the banks of the Saint Johns River. About the same time, westward in Mississippi, Sherman was slogging practically unopposed from Vicksburg to Meridian, where he was to be joined by a heavy cavalry column from Memphis for a hundred-mile extension of the march to Selma, a major industrial center whose destruction would do much to weaken the South's ability to sustain its armies in the field. This went by the board, however, when he learned that no cavalry column was any longer moving toward him; Nathan Bedford Forrest, lately promoted to major general with authority to raise a cavalry force of his own in the region the blue troopers would traverse, had whipped them soundly at Okolona, despite their two-to-one numerical advantage, and sent them staggering back to Memphis, part afoot and the rest on mounts so winded that two thirds of them were presently judged unfit for service. Sherman, left marking time, had to be content with wrecking what he held. "Meridian, with its depots, storehouses, arsenals, hospitals, offices, hotels, and cantonments, no longer exists," he reported as his wreckers, having done their worst, fell in for the march back to Vicksburg. But Selma still existed, together with all that Sherman listed and still more — including its vital cannon foundry, which, thanks to Forrest and his green command, continued to forge the heavy-caliber guns that would tear the ranks of other columns of invasion in other quarters of the South. Similarly the following week, as March came in, a raid by 3500 horsemen under Brigadier General Judson Kilpatrick, intended to achieve the liberation of an equal number of prisoners held in Richmond, was turned back at the city limits by old men and boys, home guardsmen serving worn-out artillery pieces long since replaced by new ones, captured or manufactured, in the batteries with Lee on the Rapidan. Soon regular graybacks arrived from there, overtaking the raiders who had slipped past them two nights ago, and harried the survivors into the Union lines, well down the York-James peninsula. Like March itself, Kilpatrick (called "Kill Cavalry" now) had come in like a lion and gone out like a lamb, and Richmonders were proud of their scratch resistance in the emergency that prevailed until the regulars came up.

Olustee and Okolona, like the improvised action that marked the limit of Kilpatrick's penetration, were primarily defensive victories, counterpunches landed solidly in response to Federal leads. But now, between mid-March and mid-April, there followed two exploits that were even more encouraging to Confederate hopes, though admittedly on a limited scale, because they proved that the South could still defy the lengthening odds by mounting and being successful in offensive operations. One was eastern, necessarily amphibious since it occurred in the region giving down upon the North Carolina sounds, while the other was western, staged throughout the length of the critical geographical corridor that lay between the Tennessee River and the Mississippi and extended all the way north to Kentucky's upper border, the Ohio, whose waters no uniformed Confederate had gazed upon since John Morgan's troopers crossed it, ten months ago, on the ill-fated raid from which the colorful brigadier himself had returned only by breaking out of prison.

Forrest, in command of what he called "the Cavalry Department of West Tennessee and North Mississippi," had never stopped thinking of this river-bound, 100-mile-wide, 200-mile-long stretch of land as belonging to him, particularly as a recruiting area, although all of it lay well beyond the Union lines and had done so in fact for nearly two years now. For him, as for most of his men — North Mississippians, West Tennesseans, and Kentuckians — the region was home, and he and they looked forward to returning there, if only on a visit. Indeed, he had already done so twice since it passed into northern hands, once at the beginning and once at the end of the year just past, and now he was going back for the third time. Accordingly, after disposing of Sherman's troopers by chasing them pell-mell into Memphis, he reorganized his own, grown to a strength of about 5000 and seasoned by their recent victory, into two divisions, commanded by Brigadier Generals Abraham Buford and James R. Chalmers, and set out northward with one of them — Buford's — on March 15 from his headquarters at Columbus, Mississippi. There were, he said, some 3000 recruits still available in West Tennessee, and he intended to have them, along with much else that was there in the way of horses and equipment which now were U.S. Army property.

The alarm went out at once to Federal garrisons in all three states bordering the Mississippi south of the Ohio; Forrest was much feared, his unorthodox methods and slashing attacks, often delivered in utter disregard of the odds and the tactics manuals, having led one blue opponent to protest that he was "constantly doing the unexpected at all times and places." Nor did all the complaints have their origin beyond the enemy lines. Some Southerners had their objections, too, although these were primarily social. A former Memphis alderman and planter, a self-made millionaire before the war, the forty-two-year-old Forrest had not only been "in trade"; the trade had been in slaves. And though some Southerners might fight for the peculiar institution, or send their sons to fight for its preservation, they would not willingly associate with others who made, or once had made, a living from it. "The dog's dead," a young Mississippi aristocrat wrote in his diary this winter. "Finally we are under N. Bedford Forrest. . . . I must express my distaste to being commanded by a man having no pretension to gentility — a negro trader, gambler — an ambitious man, careless of the lives of his men so long as preferment be *en prospectu*. Forrest may be, and no doubt is, the best cavalry officer in the West, but I object to a tyrannical, hotheaded vulgarian's commanding me."

In Jackson, Tennessee, on March 20 — presumably with the disgruntled young grandee in tow — Forrest sent word for Chalmers to take up the march, feinting at Memphis en route to add to the confusion in his rear, and detached a regiment to move against Union City, up in the northwest corner of the state. This was the 7th Tennessee Cavalry, Confederate, and by coincidence the town was garrisoned by the 7th Tennessee Cavalry, Union, whose surrender was accomplished in short order four days later, March 24, by a pretense of overwhelming strength, including the use of wheeled logs in place of guns (actually, there were fewer troops outside than there were inside, while the outer 7th had no guns at all) and a blood-curdling note, sent forward under a flag of truce, which ended: "If you persist in defense, you must take the consequences. N. B. Forrest, Major General, Commanding." The Union colonel decided not to persist. Instead he surrendered his 481 men, together with 300 horses and a quantity of arms and stores — all, as the colonel who had signed the general's name declared, "almost without the loss of blood or the smell of powder." Sending his prisoners south, where Chalmers was bristling as if on the verge of clattering into

Memphis, he rode hard to catch up with the main column, which Forrest had led northward through Trenton two days ago, then across the Kentucky line near Fulton, to descend on Paducah in the early afternoon of the following day, March 25, having covered the final muddy hundred miles in fifty hours.

Paducah, strategically located at the confluence of the Tennessee and the Ohio, was an important Union supply base, and it was supplies the general was after, not the garrison, which retired posthaste into a stoutly fortified earthwork supported by two gunboats patrolling the river in its rear. While sending in his usual demand for an unconditional surrender — "If you surrender you shall be treated as prisoners of war, but if I have to storm your works you may expect no quarter" — Forrest put his troopers to work on the unprotected depot, gleaning what he later reported to be "a large amount of clothing, several hundred horses, and a large lot of medical stores," along with about fifty prisoners who had not made it into the fort before the gates were shut. Inside, the blue commander declined to capitulate despite continued threats and demonstrations, including one all-out attack that was launched by a Kentucky regiment whose colonel, a native of Paducah, disobeyed restraining orders, apparently in an excess of pride and joy at being home again, and led a charge in which he and some two dozen of his men were killed or wounded. These were the only Confederate casualties, although the town itself was badly damaged by shells thrown into it from the gunboats and the fort. At midnight, having gathered up everything portable and destroyed much that was not — a government steamboat found in dry dock, for example, and a number of bales of precious cotton awaiting shipment on the landing — Forrest withdrew in the direction from which he had appeared, eight hours before. At Mayfield, a dozen miles southwest, he halted to give his captives a head start south and to furlough his three Kentucky regiments, with instructions to go to their nearby homes for a week, there to secure new clothes and mounts, at the end of which time they would reassemble at Trenton, fifty miles south of the Tennessee line. This they did, on schedule and to a man, many of them accompanied by recruits, fellow Kentuckians anxious for service under "the Wizard of the Saddle," as Forrest was beginning to be called.

He was by then in Jackson, planning another strike before he ended what was afterward referred to as his "occupation" of West Tennessee. His losses so far, including those of Chalmers, who had been skirmishing much of the time near Memphis, amounted to 15 killed and 42 wounded, as compared to Federal losses of 79 killed, 102 wounded, and 612 captured. This was a clear gain, but there was more. While planning a sudden enlargement of these figures, he did not neglect the normal intelligence-gathering duties of cavalry on the prowl. In fact, from his vantage point well within the enemy lines — even as Grant was at work on the details in Washington, Cincinnati, Culpeper, and elsewhere — Forrest not only saw through the latest Union "grand design" for the conquest of the South, he also recommended a method by which he believed it could be frustrated, if not shattered, at least in the western theater. "I am of the opinion," he wrote Joe Johnston on April 6, "that everything available is being concentrated against General Lee and yourself. Am also of opinion that if all the cavalry in this and your own department could be moved against Nashville that the enemy's communication could be broken up." What would come of this plea that he be turned loose on Sherman's life line remained to be seen. For the present, however, he had a lesser blow in mind, one that he had mentioned two days earlier in a report to Polk, whereby he intended to mount and equip his growing number of recruits: "There is a Federal force of 500 or 600 at Fort Pillow which I shall attend to in a day or two, as they have horses and supplies which we need."

Fort Pillow, established originally by the Confederates atop a bluff overlooking the Mississippi forty miles above Memphis, had been in enemy hands for nearly two years, ever since the evacuation of Corinth following Shiloh, and was garrisoned by a force of about 550. Half were Negroes, former slaves who had volunteered for service in the army that freed them in the course of its occupation of the plantations they had worked on, while the other half were Union-loyal whites; "Tennessee Tories" and "Homemade Yankees," their since-departed neighbors, many of whom now rode with Forrest, contemptuously styled the latter. This was the place and these were the men Forrest had said he would "attend to," and accordingly, by way of creating a diversion, he sent Buford with one brigade to menace Columbus and ride back into Paducah, where newspapers were boasting that he had overlooked 140 fine government horses kept hidden in an old rolling mill throughout the recent raid. Buford's instructions were to get those horses and, in the process, draw the enemy's attention northward, away from Pillow, which would be attacked by his other brigade and one from Chalmers, who was told to come along and take command of both — 1500 men in all — for the march, which got under way on April 10, and the investment, which began at daylight two days later. Northward, on the Mississippi and the Ohio, Buford carried out his assignment to the letter, detaching a couple of companies to menace Columbus while he rode with the main body into Paducah at noon on April 14. There, as before, the defenders fell back to their fortified position, and the raiders gathered up the horses they had missed three weeks ago. Returning south across the Tennessee line next day, they found that Chalmers too had carried out his assignment to the letter: so zealously so, in fact, that he and his men and Forrest, who was in over-all command, were already being widely accused of having committed *the* atrocity of the war. "The Fort Pillow Massacre," it was called, then and thereafter, in the North.

Arriving at dawn of April 12 Chalmers had the fort invested by the time Forrest came up at midmorning and took over. Pillow's original trace, some two miles long and an average 600 yards in depth, had been reduced to about half that by the Confederates before their evacuation, and now the Federals had contracted it still farther into a single earthwork, 125 yards in length, perched on the lip of the bluff and surrounded on three sides by a ditch six feet deep and twelve feet wide. Parapets four feet thick at the top and eight feet tall added greatly to the sense of security when the defenders were driven in from their outer line of rifle pits, although they presently found a drawback to this massiveness which the attackers were quick to exploit. "The width or thickness of the works across the top," a rebel captain afterwards explained, "prevented the garrison from firing down on us, as it could only be done by mounting and exposing themselves to the unerring fire of our sharpshooters, posted behind stumps and logs on all the neighboring hills." Their six guns were similarly disadvantaged, since the cannoneers could not depress them enough to fire at the attackers at close range. "So far as safety was concerned," the captain summed up, "we were as well fortified as they were; the only difference was that they were on one side and we were on the other of the same fortification." In partial compensation, the Federals had a gunboat in support, which flung a total of 282 rounds of shell, shrapnel, and canister at the dodging graybacks in the course of the fight. Also, there was the reassuring thought of what half a dozen double-shotted guns could do in the way of execution if any mass of rebels tried to scale those high dirt walls and poke their heads above that flat-topped parapet.

Forrest was thinking of that too, of course, but he did not let it deter him any more than he did the loss of three horses shot from under him in the course of the five hours he spent maneuvering for a closer hug and waiting for the arrival of his ammunition train to refill the nearly empty cartridge boxes of his rapid-firing troopers. Shortly after 3 o'clock the train arrived, and the general sent forward under a flag of truce his usual grisly ultimatum. "Should my demand be refused," the note closed, "I cannot be responsible for the fate of your command." By way of reply, the Union commander requested "one hour for consultation with my officers and the officers of the gunboat." But Forrest by now had spotted a steamer "apparently crowded with troops" approaching, as well as "the smoke of three other boats ascending the river." Believing that the Federals were stalling for time in which to gain reinforcements and additional naval support, he replied that he would give them twenty minutes and no more; "If at the expiration of that time the fort is not surrendered, I shall assault it." Either because he considered this a bluff, or else because he believed an assault was bound to fail — his soldiers, white and black, apparently were of the same conviction, for they had been taunting the rebels gleefully and profanely from the parapets throughout the cease-fire that attended the exchange — the Union commander replied succinctly, "I will not surrender." Forrest had no sooner read the note than he turned to his bugler and had him sound the charge.

The assault was brief and furious, practically bloodless up to a point, and proceeded according to plan. While the sharpshooters back on the hillsides kept up a harassing fire that skimmed the parapet, the first wave of attackers rushed forward, leaped into the slippery six-foot ditch, and crouched in the mud at the bottom, presenting their backs to the men of the second wave, who thus were able to use them as stepping-blocks to gain the narrow ledge between the ditch and the embankment just beyond, then lean down and hoist their first-wave comrades up beside them. It was as neatly done as if it had been rehearsed for weeks, and in all this time not a shot had been fired except from the hillsides and around on the flanks, where Forrest had other marksmen at work on the gunboat. "Shoot at everything blue betwixt wind and water," he had told them: with the result that the vessel, which had closed to canister range, kept its ports tight shut to protect its gunners and took no part in attempting a repulse. By now the attackers were all on the narrow ledge, holding their unfired weapons at the ready and keeping their heads well down while the hillside snipers continued to kick dirt on the parapet, across whose width, although the graybacks were only a few feet away, flattened against the opposite side of the earthwork, no member of the garrison could fire without exposing two thirds of his body to instant perforation. At a signal, the sharpshooters held their fire and the men on the ledge went up and over the embankment, emptying their pistols and rifles into the blue mass of defenders, who fought briefly against panic, then broke rearward for a race to the landing at the foot of the bluff, where they had been told that the gunboat, in the unlikely event of a rebel breakthrough, would cover their withdrawal by pumping grape and canister into the ranks of their pursuers.

It did not work out that way, not only because the gunboat was shut up turtle-tight and took no part in the action, but also because the graybacks were too close on their heels for the naval gunners to have been able to fire without hitting their own men, even if they had tried. Flailed from the rear by heavy downhill volleys, the running bluecoats next were struck in the flanks by the troopers who had been shooting at the gunboat. Some kept going, right on into the river, where a number drowned and the swimmers became targets for marksmen on the bluff. Others, dropping their guns in terror, ran back toward the Confederates with their hands up, and of these some were spared as prisoners, while others were shot down in the act of surrender. "No quarter! No quarter!" was being shouted at several points, and this was thought by some to be at Forrest's command, since he had predicted and even threatened that what was happening would happen. But the fact was, he had done and was doing all he could to end it, having ordered the firing stopped as soon as he saw his troopers swarm into the fort, even though its flag was still flying and a good part of the garrison was still trying to get away. He and others managed to put an end to the killing and sort out the captives, wounded and unwounded. Out of a total Federal force of 557, no less than 63 percent had been killed or wounded, and of these about two thirds — 221, or forty percent of the whole — had been killed. Forrest himself lost 14 killed and 86 wounded. Before nightfall, having seen to the burial of the dead by the survivors, he gathered up his spoils, including the six pieces of artillery, and moved off with 226 prisoners, twenty of whom were men so lightly wounded they could walk. Next morning he sent his adjutant, accompanied by a captured Union captain, back to signal another gunboat — which had resumed the shelling of the woods around the fort, unaware that there was no longer anything Confederate there to shoot at, only Federals — to put in, under a flag of truce, and take the more seriously wounded aboard for treatment downriver in Memphis. That ended the Fort Pillow operation.

But not the talk, the cultivated reaction which quickly mounted to a pitch of outraged intensity unsurpassed until "the Rape of Belgium" fifty years later, when propaganda methods were much improved by wider and faster means of disseminating "eyewitness" accounts of such "atrocities," true or false. Within six days a congressional committee — strictly speaking, a subcommittee of the feared and ruthless Joint Committee on the Conduct of the War — left Washington for Tennessee, having been appointed to gather "testimony in regard to the massacre at Fort Pillow," and within another three days was taking depositions from survivors, along with other interested parties, which resulted in a voluminous printed report that the rebels had engaged in "indiscriminate slaughter" of men, women, and children, white and black, and afterwards had not only set barracks and tents afire, roasting the wounded in their beds, but had also "buried some of the living with the dead," despite their piteous cries for mercy while dirt was being shoveled on their faces. "Many other instances of equally atrocious cruelty might be enumerated," the report concluded, "but your committee feels compelled to refrain from giving here more of the heart-sickening details." Southerners might protest that the document was "a tissue of lies from end to end," as indeed it largely was, but they could scarcely argue with the casualty figures, which indicated strongly that unnecessary killing had occurred, although it was in fact the opposite of "indiscriminate." For example, of the 262 Negro members of the garrison, only 58 — just over twenty percent — were marched away as prisoners; while of the 295 whites, 168 — just under sixty percent — were taken. The rest were either dead or in no shape for walking. Here was discrimination with a vengeance, as well as support for a Confederate sergeant's testimony, given in a letter written home within a week of the affair, describing how "the poor, deluded negroes would run up to our men, fall upon their knees and with uplifted hands scream for mercy, but were ordered to their feet and then shot down." This was not to say that Forrest himself had not done all he could, first to prevent and then to end the unnecessary bloodshed. He had, and perhaps the strongest evidence of his forbearance came not from his friends but from his enemies of the highest rank. Within three days of the fall of the fort, when news of the "massacre" reached Washington, Lincoln told Stanton to investigate without delay "the alleged butchery of our troops." Stanton passed the word to Grant, who wired Sherman that same day: "If our men have been murdered after capture, retaliation must be resorted to promptly." Sherman undertook the investigation, as ordered, but made no such recommendation: proof in itself that none was justified, since no one doubted that otherwise, with Sherman in charge, retaliation would have been as prompt as even Grant could have desired.

As for Forrest, his mind was soon on other things, including the removal of his spoils and a stepped-up enforcement of the conscription laws throughout West Tennessee. His recruiting methods were as rigorous as they were thorough. "Sweep the country, bringing in every man between the ages of eighteen and forty-five," he told his agents. "Take no excuse, neither allow conscripts to go home for clothes or anything else; their friends can send them." Haste was required, for before he got back to Jackson, two days after Pillow fell, he received a dispatch from Polk directing him to return promptly to Okolona, where his two divisions would combine with those under Major General Stephen D. Lee, Polk's chief of cavalry in the Department of Mississippi, Alabama, and East Louisiana, to meet an anticipated raid-in-force from Middle Tennessee, southward through Decatur, Alabama. Forrest replied that the order would of course be complied with, though in his opinion "no such raid will be made from Decatur or any point west of there." Events were to prove him right in this, but even if such a raid had been intended he believed that the best way to turn it back was by striking deep in its rear. He still had his eye on Sherman's life line. He wanted to hit it, and he wanted to hit it hard. This time, however, he presented his views not only to Polk and Johnston, who seemed unwilling or unable to act on them, but also to Jefferson Davis, addressing him directly. Stephen Lee had about 7000 cavalry, and he himself was approaching that strength by now. "With our forces united," he wrote Davis on April 15, "a move could be made into Middle Tennessee and Kentucky which would create a diversion of the enemy's forces and enable us to break up his plans." It was Sherman he meant — specifically, the long rail supply line reaching down from Louisville on the Ohio, through Nashville on the Cumberland, to Chattanooga on the Tennessee. That was a lot of track, and Forrest had long since shown what he could do to a railroad when he turned his troopers loose on one in earnest. Moreover, he assured the Commander in Chief lest the plan be considered an impractical hare-brained escapade like the one on which John Morgan had come to grief last summer, "such an expedition, managed with prudence and executed with rapidity, can be safely made."

Whatever merit there was in the proposal, for the present at least the authorities in Richmond were more interested in a project closer at hand, involving an attempt to recover the North Carolina coastal region, which got under way in earnest that same week, two days after Forrest wrote his letter. A Tarheel brigade under a native North Carolinian, Brigadier General Robert Hoke, had been detached from the Army of Northern Virginia to undertake the job in coöperation with an ironclad ram that had been under construction for the past year in a cornfield at Edwards Ferry, two thirds of the way up the Roanoke River to Weldon. General Braxton Bragg, assigned as the President's chief military adviser after his removal from command of the Army of Tennessee, had conceived the plan, secured the troops, and worked out the details, beginning with an amphibious assault on Plymouth at the point where the Roanoke flowed into Albemarle Sound. Occupied for more than two years by the Federals, who had fortified it stoutly, the town would have to be attacked by water as well as by land, since otherwise the heavy guns of the Union fleet, on station in support of the place, would drive the attackers out about as soon as they got in. Bragg had much confidence in Hoke, who was given large discretion after a detailed briefing on this opening phase of the campaign — a veteran, though not yet twenty-seven, he had fought with distinction in all the major eastern engagements from Big Bethel through Chancellorsville, where he was severely wounded — as well as in the ironclad successor to the *Virginia* and the *Arkansas,* both of glorious memory.

Christened *Albemarle,* she was launched from the riverside cornfield in which she had been built, mostly by local carpenters and blacksmiths, and set off downstream on the day she was commissioned, April 17, en route to her maiden engagement. Sheathed in two layers of two-inch iron and mounting a pair of 6.4-inch Brooke rifles pivoted fore and aft to fire through alternate portholes, she was just over 150 feet in length, 34 feet in the beam, and drew 9 feet of water. Because of the numerous twists and turns in the river this far up — which, incidentally, had served to protect her from interference by Federal gunboats during her construction — she set out stern-foremost, dragging a heavy chain from her bow to steer by. Fitters were still at work on her armor and machinery, and portable forges were brought along for emergency repairs. They soon were needed, first when the main driveshaft wrenched loose from its coupling, late that night, and next when the rudderhead broke off, early the following morning. Three miles from Plymouth the second night, and ten hours behind schedule because of time-out for repairs, she was stopped by reports that the river ahead was obstructed by hulks which the enemy, hearing rumors that the *Albemarle* was approaching completion, had sunk in the channel to tear out her bottom in case she ventured down. Aboard as a volunteer aide to her skipper, Commander James W. Cooke — another Tarheel and a veteran of more than thirty years in the old navy — was her builder, Gilbert Elliott, a native of nearby Elizabeth City, where he had learned his craft in his grandfather's shipyard. Elliott set out in the darkness in a small boat with a pilot and two men, taking a long pole for soundings, and presently returned to report that, thanks to the unusually high stage of the river this spring, "it was practicable to pass the obstructions provided the boat was kept in the middle of the stream."

Cooke by then had turned the ram around and cleared for action. He had no contact with Hoke ashore, but on being informed that a sporadic attack had been in progress against Plymouth most of the day and up until 9 o'clock that night, when the skirmishers withdrew — presumably because of the nonarrival of the *Albemarle*, without whose help the town could not be held under the frown of a quartet of gunboats just inside the mouth of the river — he weighed anchor and stood down to engage. It was close to 4 o'clock in the morning, April 19, when he passed safely over the sunken hulks, taking a few harmless heavy-caliber shots from the fort as he went by, and came in sight of the four Union warships. Warned of his approach, they were prepared to receive him. The two largest, *Miami* and *Southfield* — big, double-ended side-wheel steamers of a novel design, with rudders fore and aft for quick reversals — were lashed together, but not too tightly, in accordance with a plan to catch the *Albemarle* between them, thus making her useless as a ram, while they tossed explosives down her stack. Cooke avoided this by steering close to the south bank, then turning hard aport as he drew nearly abreast of the shackled gunboats, presenting his long, tapered bow to the nearer of the two. Both opened on him with solids at close range, bringing as many of their dozen guns into play as could be brought to bear, but with no more effect than if the shots had been tennis balls, except that they left spoon-shaped dents in the armor when they bounced. Closing fast, with the force of the current added to her thrust, the ironclad put her snout ten feet into *Southfield*'s flank, penetrating all the way to her fireroom, but then had trouble withdrawing it from so deep a wound. The two hung joined, the ram taking water into her forward port because of the weight of the rapidly sinking gunboat: seeing which, the captain of the *Miami* ran to one of his 9-inch Dahlgrens, depressed it quickly, and fired three explosive shells pointblank at the rebel monster. All three shattered against the iron casemate, a scant twenty feet away. Pieces of the third, which was fired with a short fuse, flew back from the target and knocked down most of the gun crew, including the captain, who lay dead with the jagged fragments stuck deep in his chest and face.

Albemarle's captain was backing his engines hard to free the ram of the weight on her bow, but by the time he managed to do so, the *Miami* — called the "Miasma" by her crew, who had found duty aboard her boring up to now — cut loose from the sinking *Southfield* and ran with all her speed for open water. Followed out into Albemarle Sound by the other two gunboats, which had observed the action at long range, she wanted no more of a fight with an adversary impervious to shot and shell alike. Cooke attempted a brief pursuit, then broke off when he saw that it was fruitless, mainly because his engines were getting almost no draft through his badly shot-up smokestack, and turned back to give his full attention to the fort. Now it was the Federals' turn to learn what it was like to try to hold the place while under attack from the river as well as the land.

They found it hard indeed. Delaying only long enough to patch up his riddled stack and get in touch with the Confederates ashore, Cooke steamed back past Plymouth that afternoon and opened on the fort in conjunction with Hoke, whose batteries were skillfully disposed for converging fire and whose infantry returned to within small-arms range of the Federal ramparts. The result was altogether harrowing for the defenders, caught thus as it were between the devil and the deep blue sea, the landward attackers and the *Albemarle*, both of which kept up the pressure until well after sunset and resumed it at daylight with even greater fury. "This terrible fire had to be endured without reply, as no man could live at the guns," the fort's commander was to report. "The breast-height was struck by solid shot on every side, fragments of shell sought almost every interior angle of the work, the whole extent of the parapet was swept by musketry, and men were killed and wounded even on the banquette slope.... This condition of affairs could not be long endured without a reckless sacrifice of life; no relief could be expected, and in compliance with the earnest desire of every officer I consented to hoist a white flag, and at 10 a.m. of April 20 I had the mortification of surrendering my post to the enemy with all it contained." This included 2834 soldiers, thirty guns, and a large haul of supplies, all secured at a cost to the attackers of less than 300 casualties, only one of whom was naval, a seaman hit by a pistol ball while the *Albemarle* had her snout in the sinking *Southfield*. "Heaven has crowned our efforts with success," a presidential aide-observer wired Davis, who replied directly to Hoke: "Accept my thanks and congratulations for the brilliant success which has attended your attack and capture of Plymouth. You are promoted to be a major general from that date."

Young Hoke was the hero of the hour, together with Cooke and the *Albemarle*, all down the eastern seaboard, and Bragg — though his basic planning went unnoticed amid the general praise for Hoke and Cooke — was hard at work, now that the ram had reversed the naval advantage, projecting exploits of a similar nature for the immediate future.

It was this the Federals feared. Unable to get an ironclad through any of the shallow inlets into Pamlico Sound, and with no time left in which to build one there, they saw no way to stop the apparently invulnerable, new-hatched monster before it returned the whole region to Confederate control. "The ram will probably come down to Roanoke Island, Washington, and New Bern," the district commander, Major General John J. Peck, informed his department chief, Ben Butler, on the day Plymouth fell. "Unless we are immediately and heavily reinforced, both by the army and navy, North Carolina is inevitably lost." Butler shared the alarm, although belatedly. Two months earlier, when the navy had asked him to send troops up the Roanoke to destroy the rebel vessel on its stocks, he had replied: "I don't believe in the ironclad," and even now, in passing on to Halleck the news that the fort had been reduced in part by the guns of the nonexistent warship, he declined to accept a fraction of the blame, which he declared was all the navy's for having left the garrison's water flank exposed. "Perhaps this is intended as a diversion," he ended blandly. "Any instructions?"

In point of fact, New Bern was next on the *Albemarle*'s list, once she finished off the gunboats skittishly awaiting her emergence into the Sound from which she took her name, and Hoke was told to prepare for this, rather than for an early return to the Army of Northern Virginia, despite that army's commander's pleas that he and his brigade were needed to help meet the attack that was soon to be launched across the Rapidan. Whatever disappointment this might involve for Lee, outnumbered two to one by the bluecoats on the north side of the river, Plymouth made a fine addition to the list of late winter and early spring victories which the President was compiling for inclusion in the message he was preparing for delivery to Congress when it convened next week in Richmond.

"Recent events of the war are highly creditable to our troops," he wrote, "exhibiting energy and vigilance combined with the habitual gallantry which they have taught us to expect on all occasions. We have been cheered by important and valuable successes in Florida, northern Mississippi, western Tennessee and Kentucky, western Louisiana, and eastern North Carolina, reflecting the highest honor on the skill and conduct of our commanders and on the incomparable soldiers whom it is their privilege to lead. . . . The armies in northern Georgia and in northern Virginia," he added, by way of compensation for the fact that there had been no such recent, gloom-dispelling triumphs in either of those regions, "still oppose with unshaken front a formidable barrier to the progress of the invader, and our generals, armies, and people are animated by cheerful confidence."

So he would say, and so Congress would be pleased to hear. But there were things he left unmentioned because to air them — involving, as they did, plans untried and expectations unfulfilled — would serve to deepen, rather than relieve, the nation's gloom regarding one of the two main armies on which it depended for survival. Davis's disappointment was not in Lee, who was fairly immobilized by the fact that a solid third of the Army of Northern Virginia had been detached for the past seven months; it was in Johnston, who had been given command of the Army of Tennessee with the understanding, at least on the part of the Richmond authorities, that he would go over to the offensive in an attempt to recover East and Middle Tennessee, lost by his predecessor in the course of the bloody, erratic, year-long retreat from Murfreesboro to Dalton. "You are desired to have all things in readiness at the earliest practicable moment for the movement indicated," the transplanted Virginian was reminded in early March. "The season is at hand and the time seems propitious."

Plans for such an offensive were quite explicit. Union forces now preparing at Chattanooga and Knoxville for a spring advance were dependent on uninterrupted communication with Nashville; if this supply line could be severed, both would be obliged to abandon what they held, with much attendant disruption of their plans. In line with this, Richmond's proposal was that Johnston be reinforced by Polk for a shift northeast to Kingston, forty miles west of Knoxville, where he would be joined by two divisions under Lieutenant General James Longstreet, detached from Lee and wintering near Greeneville, for an advance across the Tennessee River with a combined strength of more than 70,000 men. By such a move, the authorities assured him, "Knoxville [would be] isolated and Chattanooga threatened, with barely a possibility for the enemy to unite. Should he not then offer you battle outside of his entrenched lines, a rapid move across the mountains from Kingston to Sparta (a very practicable and easy route) would place you with a formidable army in a country full of resources, where it is supposed, with a good supply of ammunition, you may be entirely self-sustaining, and it is confidently believed that such a move would necessitate the withdrawal of the enemy to the line of the Cumberland." Bragg was the author of these suggestions, and he wrote from experience. In essence, they called for a repetition of the movement he himself had made soon after he assumed command of the army in the summer of 1862, whereby the western seat of war was shifted, practically overnight and practically without bloodshed, from Mississippi to North Georgia and from there all the way north to Kentucky. The Federals then had been obliged to give up, at least for a season, their designs on Chattanooga, and Bragg was of the opinion that if Johnston would only profit by his example the same results could be obtained in regard to their designs on Atlanta — provided, of course, that he advanced before his adversaries did. "To accomplish this," he was re-reminded in mid-March, "it is proposed that you move as soon as your means and force can be collected."

Johnston had many objections to the plan. Time had probably run out; he lacked supplies, as well as the mules and wagons needed to haul them; the Federals, in greatly superior numbers, would combine and jump him as soon as he got started, obliging him to fight at a disadvantage and with nothing to do, in case of defeat, but scatter his troops in the mountains. What he preferred, he told Bragg on March 18, was to stand where he was, letting the bluecoats crack their skulls against his works, then follow them up when they retreated. Meantime, he urged, the proffered reinforcements under Longstreet should be sent to him at Dalton for a share in the defensive battle, rather than have them wait in idleness to join him on the march. Bragg's reply, three days later, was curt and stiff: "Your dispatch . . . does not indicate an acceptance of the plan proposed. The troops can only be drawn from other points for an advance. Upon your decision of that point further action must depend." Alarmed at this evidence that he would not be reinforced on his own terms, Johnston was quick to assert that he had been misunderstood. "I expressly accept taking offensive," he wired back. "Only differ with you as to details. I assume that the enemy will be prepared for an advance before we are and will make it to our advantage. Therefore, I propose as necessary both for offensive and defensive to assemble our troops here immediately. Other preparations for advance are going on."

For two weeks there was no reply to this. The answer, when it came on April 7, was in a dispatch addressed not to Johnston but to Longstreet, who was told to prepare his two divisions for an immediate return to Virginia. Johnston was depressed by this lack of confidence, and outraged by reports that he had declined to move against the enemy. "I learn that it is given out," he wrote to a senator friend whose son was on his staff, "that it has been proposed to me to take the offensive with a large army & that I refused. Don't believe any such story." Besides, he said, after outlining his objections to the plan he had rejected, Lee's army, not his, was the one that should have been ordered to advance. "It would have been much easier to take the offensive (excuse such frequent use of that expression) in Va. than here," he wrote, basing his statement on the erroneous double claim that Lee's army was not only larger than his but also had a smaller blue army to its front. However, he was not greatly surprised at the way things had gone. The authorities in Richmond — Davis himself, Secretary of War James A. Seddon, and now Bragg, his erstwhile friend — had about as low an opinion of him, apparently, as he had of them;

which was low indeed. His consolation was in his men. "If this army thought of me and felt toward me as some of our high civil functionaries do," he closed his letter, "it would be necessary for me to leave the military service. But thank heaven, it is my true friend."

It was true the army was his friend; no general on either side, not even R. E. Lee or George McClellan, had more affection from the soldiers he commanded. "He was loved, respected, admired; yea, almost worshipped by his troops," a Tennessee veteran was to say. Richmond had taken this quality into account in sending him to Dalton to repair the shattered morale of an army which had recently been thrown off Missionary Ridge and chased southward into Georgia by the opponent it faced there now. And in this he had succeeded. "He restored the soldier's pride; he brought the manhood back to the private's bosom," the same veteran declared. The drawback, according to those who had advised against his appointment, was that he was too defensive-minded for the tactical part of his assignment. He had only assumed the offensive once in the whole course of the war, and that had been at Seven Pines, which might well seem to him the exception that proved the unwisdom of attacking, since all it had got him was the wound that had cost him the command he most preferred, now held by Lee, and a subsequent transfer to the less congenial West. Those who had opposed his appointment in December, on grounds that he would never go forward as intended, were quick to point out now in April that their prediction had been fulfilled. In fact, they said, if he continued to follow his accustomed pattern of behavior, he would be likely to fall back from Dalton at the first bristly gesture by the Federals in his front. Davis and Seddon, who had favored his appointment — primarily, it was true, because no one could think of another candidate for the job — were obliged to admit the strength of this, as evidence of what to expect, and so was Bragg after his exchanges with the general, by letter and wire, throughout the latter part of February and the first two thirds of March. It was then, on the heels of this admission by Davis and Seddon and Bragg, that the summons went to Longstreet for a quick return to Lee. They had given up on Johnston, who would neither go forward nor refuse to go forward, and who they knew from past experience (in northern Virginia, down on the York-James peninsula, outside beleaguered Vicksburg, and back in the piny woods of Mississippi) would wind up doing exactly as he pleased in any case. He always had. He always would. The only decision left was whether to keep him — and the fact was, they had no one to put in his place. So they kept him. And in keeping him, however regretfully, they committed the Army of Tennessee to the defensive and gave up all hope for a slash at the Union center as a means of disrupting at the outset the latest Grand Design for their subjugation.

Lee was committed to the defensive, too, though not by inclination or from choice. "At present my hands are tied," he confessed in a mid-April letter to Bragg. "If I was able to move ... the enemy might be driven from the Rappahannock and obliged to look to the safety of his own capital instead of the assault upon ours." As it was, he added, writing from the stripped region about Orange where his infantry was camped, "I cannot even draw to me the cavalry or artillery of the army, and the season has arrived when I may be attacked any day."

It was a question of subsistence for mounts and men. Scarcely a tree in the district wore its bark below the point to which a horse could lift its mouth, and few of the few animals on hand were fit for rigorous service; "Fully one half of them were incapable of getting up a gallop," a cavalry officer complained, "a trembling trot being their fastest gait." Conditions were nearly as bad for the leaned-down soldiers. Though Davis himself had managed to get hold of 90,000 pounds of meat for shipment to the Rapidan during a critical, near-starvation period that winter, this did not go far with troops whose usual daily ration comprised four ounces of bacon or salt pork, often rancid, and a scant pint of rough-ground corn meal. Sprouting grass was a help to the horses this rainy April, but hunger was still a condition of existence for the men. This pained Lee, who did not like to add to other people's troubles by recounting his own, into making a formal complaint to the President, coupled with the strongest warning he had given at any time in the twenty-two months since he assumed command: "My anxiety on the subject of provisions for the army is so great that I cannot refrain from expressing it to Your Excellency. I cannot see how we can operate with our present supplies. Any derangement in their arrival or disaster to the railroad would render it impossible for me to keep the army together, and might force a retreat into North Carolina."

That too was in mid-April — April 12 — one week after he had alerted the army to prepare for a Union crossing, any day now, of the river to its front. On that same April 5, having pored over information received from scouts, northern papers, and citizens beyond the Rapidan, he gave Davis his estimate of the situation. "The movements and reports of the enemy may be intended to mislead us, and should therefore be carefully observed," he wrote. "But all the information that reaches me goes to strengthen the belief that Genl Grant is preparing to move against Richmond." This was as far as he went at the time; he said nothing of his new opponent's probable route (or routes) or schedule. Three days later, however, he wrote of receiving two more reports from reliable scouts, in which "the general impression was that the great battle would take place on the Rapidan, and that the Federal army would advance as soon as the weather is settled." Continuing to study all the evidence he could gather — including much, of course, that was false or merely worthless — he arrived within another week at a considerably more detailed estimate, and he passed this too along to

Davis, saying: "We shall have to glean troops from every quarter to oppose the apparent combination of the enemy."

He expected three attacks, all to be delivered simultaneously from three directions: 1) a main assault across the Rapidan, more or less against his front, 2) a diversionary advance up the Shenandoah Valley, off his western flank, and 3) a rear attack, up the James, to menace Richmond from the east and south. To meet this last, he proposed that General P. G. T. Beauregard be shifted from his present command at Charleston, which Lee believed was no longer on the list of Union objectives, and brought to Petersburg or Weldon to take charge of the defense of southside Richmond. The Valley threat he would leave for the time being to Major General John C. Breckinridge, who had a small command in the Department of Southwest Virginia. As for the main effort, the blue lunge across the Rapidan, he kept that as the continuing exclusive concern of the Army of Northern Virginia. Recent news that Longstreet would soon be coming back with two of his three divisions, after seven months in Georgia and Tennessee, made Lee yearn for a return to the old days and the old method of dealing with such a threat as he faced now. "If Richmond could be held secure against the attack from the east," he told the President on April 15, "I would propose that I draw Longstreet to me and move right against the enemy on the Rappahannock. Should God give us a crowning victory there, all their plans would be dissipated, and their troops now collecting on the waters of the Chesapeake would be recalled to the defense of Washington." Having said as much, however, he returned to such realities as the scarcity of food for his men and horses, then closed on a note of ominous regret: "But to make this move I must have provisions and forage. I am not yet able to call to me the cavalry or artillery. If I am obliged to retire from this line, either by a flank movement of the enemy or the want of supplies, great injury will befall us."

On April 18 he ordered all surplus baggage sent to the rear, a sort of ultimate alert well understood by the troops to mean that fighting might begin at any time. Still Grant did not move. Lee's impatience mounted during the following week — in the course of which Breckinridge was warned to brace for action in the Valley and Beauregard, in compliance with orders from Richmond, reached Weldon to assume command of the region between the James and Cape Fear rivers — though he acknowledged that the gain was worth the strain, if only because the half-starved horses thus were allowed more time to graze in peace on the new-sprung grass. "The advance of the Army of the Potomac seems to be delayed for some reason," he wrote Davis on April 25. "It appears to be prepared for movement, but is probably waiting for its coöperative columns." He closed with an invitation for the President to visit the army, "if the enemy remains quiet and the weather favorable," by way of affording himself a diversion from the daily grind in Richmond. Davis declined, under pressure of business; Congress would convene next week, for one thing. But four days later Lee enjoyed a diversion of his own.

Longstreet's two divisions had arrived at last from Tennessee and were in camp around Gordonsville, nine miles south of army headquarters at Orange. Lee did not know whether Meade would cross the Rapidan on his left or right, taking John Pope's intended route down the Orange & Alexandria Railroad or Joe Hooker's through the Wilderness. He rather thought (and certainly hoped) it would be the latter, but since he lacked solid evidence to that effect he kept Longstreet's hard-hitting veterans off to his left rear, in case the bluecoats came that way. On April 29 he rode down to review them for the first time in nearly eight months, which was how long it had been since they left the Old Dominion to supply Bragg's Sunday punch at Chickamauga. They were turned out in their ragged best, leather patched, metal polished, their shot-torn regimental colors newly stitched with the names of unfamiliar western battles, and when Lee drew rein before them, removing his hat in salute, the color bearers shook their flags like mad and the troops responded with an all-out rebel yell that reverberated from all the surrounding hills, causing the gray-haired general's eyes to brim with tears. "The effect was as of a military sacrament," an artillerist later wrote. Lee wept, another veteran explained, because "he felt that we were again to do his bidding." Deep Southerners or Westerners to a man — South Carolinians and Georgians, Alabamians and Mississippians, Arkansans and Texans — there was not a Virginian among them, and yet it was as if they had come home. A First Corps chaplain riding with the staff turned to a colonel as the yell went up and Lee sat there astride his gray horse Traveller, uncovered in salute, and asked: "Does it not make the general proud to see how these men love him?" The colonel shook his head. "Not proud," he said. "It awes him."

Awed or proud — no doubt with something of both, despite the staffer's protest — Lee felt his impatience mount still faster next day, back at Orange, when he got word that a four-division corps under Ambrose Burnside, formerly encamped at Annapolis and thought to be intended for service down the coast, had passed through Centerville two days ago and had by now reached Rappahannock Station, from which position it could move in direct support of the Army of the Potomac. Perhaps it was for this that Grant had been waiting to put his three-pronged war machine in motion. As for Meade, Lee informed Davis on this final day in April, "Our scouts report that the engineer troops, pontoon trains, and all the cavalry of Meade's army have been advanced south of the Rappahannock.... Everything indicates a concentrated attack on this front." His faith was in God and in the "incomparable infantry" of the Army of Northern Virginia, but now as he awaited the onslaught of the blue juggernaut whose numbers were roughly twice his own, he displayed more urgency of manner than those closest to him had ever seen him show on his own ground. Evidence of an early assault continued to accumulate, and still the Federal tents remained unstruck beyond the Rapidan. Lee's aggressive instinct, held in check by hard necessity, broke its bounds at last. "Colonel," he told a member of his staff, "we have got to whip them; we must whip them!" Apparently that was the high point of his impatience, for having said as much he paused, then added with a smile of amused relief: "It has already made me better to think of it."

Lee's confidence was based on past performance, against odds as long and sometimes longer, and Davis too drew reassurance from that source, having just completed his third full year of playing Hezekiah to Lincoln's Sennacherib. Whatever frets he had about developments out in Georgia, here in the Old Dominion at least the Confederacy had won for itself the military admiration of the world. Six blue comanders, in all their majesty and might — Irvin McDowell and George McClellan, John Pope and Ambrose Burnside, Joseph Hooker and George Meade — had mounted half a dozen well-sustained offensives, each designed to achieve the reduction of Richmond in short order, and all six had been turned back in various states of disarray. Now there was Grant, who seemed to many only a seventh name to be added to the list of discomfited eastern opponents. "If I mistake not," a young officer on Lee's staff wrote home on hearing of the elevation of this latest transfer from an inferior western school, "[Grant] will shortly come to grief if he attempts to repeat the tactics in Virginia which proved so successful in Mississippi." There were dissenters: Longstreet, for example, who had been Grant's friend at the Academy and a groomsman at his wedding — and who had fought, moreover, in a theater where Grant was in command. "We must make up our minds to get into line of battle and to stay there," Old Peter had told his visitors at Gordonsville the day before, "for that man will fight us every day and every hour till the end of the war." But for the most part there was general agreement that what had been done six times before (four of them, and the last four at that, more or less on this same Rapidan-Rappahannock line) could be done again by Lee, whose army was a rapier in his hand. If Grant was a fighter, as Longstreet said, there would be nothing unusual in that. One of the worst-defeated of the six had been known as "Fighting Joe," and the one who had been given the soundest drubbing of them all — the "miscreant" Pope — had also arrived with western laurels on his brow and a reputation for coming to savage grips with whatever tried to stand in his path of conquest.

Besides, what was called for now was not necessarily the outright defeat or even repulse of the invaders, east or west. What was called for, Davis could remind himself, was a six-month holding action which

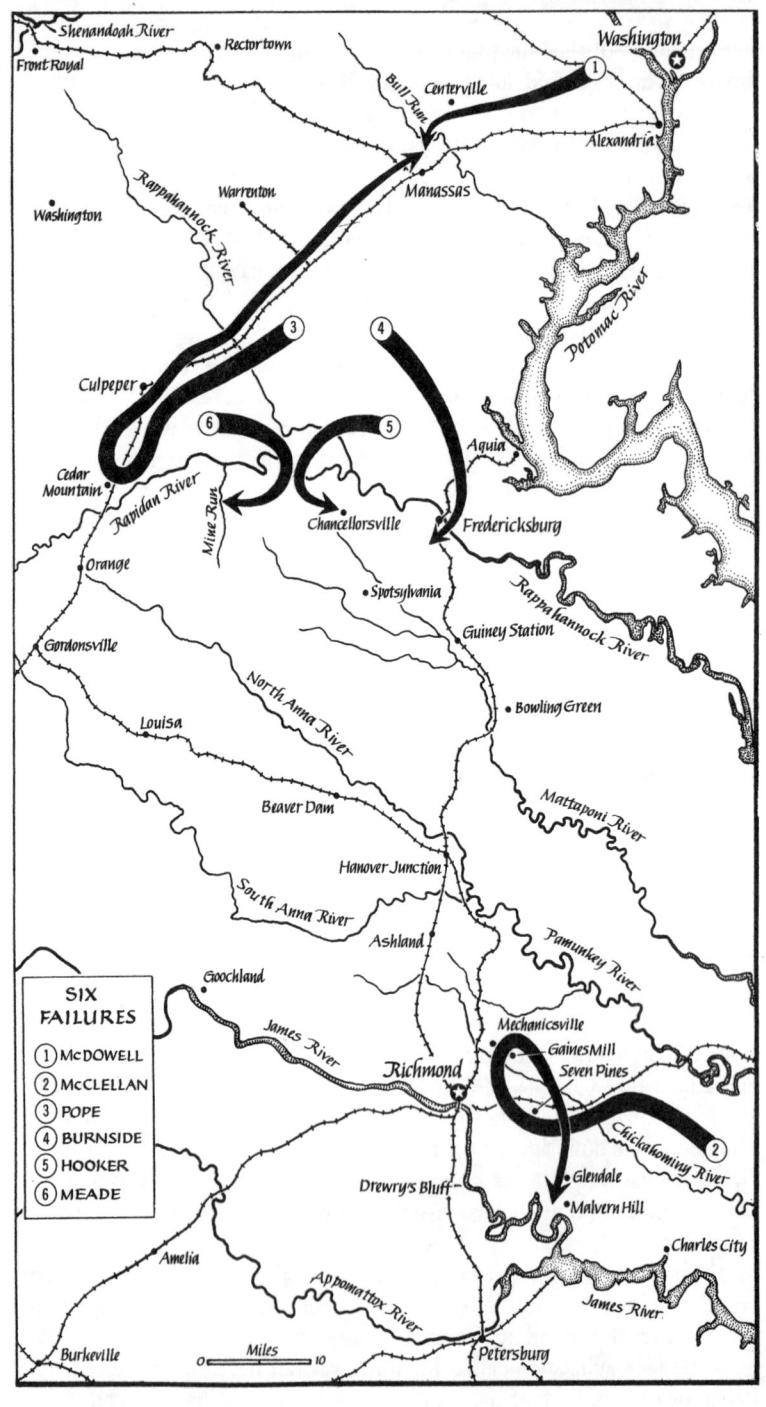

would allow them no appreciable gain except at a price that would be regarded as prohibitive, in money and blood, by voters who would be making their early-November choice between peace and war. In light of this, a head-down fighter like Grant might serve the South's purpose far better than would an over-all commander who was inclined to count his casualties and take counsel of his fears. Not that Davis abandoned all hope for a repetition of what had happened in the past to opponents who had come in roaring and gone out bleating; he hoped for it profoundly, and not without cause. Don Carlos Buell and William S. Rosecrans were western examples to match the six discomfited in Virginia, and Sherman had shown himself to have many of the qualities that made Grant an ideal opponent at this juncture. In some ways, now that the notion of an offensive against the Union center had been abandoned as a gambit, Joe Johnston seemed an excellent choice as a foil for the red-haired Ohioan, whose impulsiveness might expose him to the kind of damage his government could least afford on the eve of its quadrennial election. By way of further encouragement, Davis had only to consider more recent successes, scored east and west by Kirby Smith, Finegan, Forrest, and Hoke, for proof that the South could still stand up to combinations designed for its destruction, and could also carry the war to the enemy when the opportunity came. Just as Banks and Steele had been driven back across the Atchafalaya and the Saline — not only against the numerical odds, but also, as it were, against the tactics manuals — so might Sherman and Grant be driven back across the Tennessee and the Rappahannock. Like many brave men, before and since, Davis had found that when a difficulty amounted to an impossibility, the best course to pursue was one that did not take the impossibility into account. That was what he had meant all along when he said, "I cultivate hope and patience, and trust to the blunders of our enemy and the gallantry of our troops for ultimate success."

For the most part this attitude was shared by the people of Richmond. In fact, among the party-goers and the well-to-do — they had to be that; a dollar in gold was worth more than thirty in Confederate paper, while calico and coffee were $10 a yard and pound, eggs $2 a dozen, and cornfield beans were selling at $60 a bushel — there had never been a social season as lively as the one now drawing to a close. "Starvation parties" were all the rage, along with charades and taffy pulls, although they seemed to one diarist to have a quality of desperation about them, as if the guests were aware that these revels, honoring "Major This, or Colonel That, or Captain T'other," would be the last. In February Lincoln had issued a draft call for 500,000 men — more than the Confederacy could muster in all its camps between the Rappahannock and the Rio Grande — and then in March had upped the ante by calling for "200,000 more." All the South could do, by way of response, was lower and raise the conscription age limits to seventeen and fifty, robbing thus the cradle and the grave, as some complained, or as Davis put it, in regard to the half-grown boys about to be drafted and thrown into the line, "grinding the seed corn of the nation." Meanwhile U. S. Grant, "a bull-headed Suvarov," was poised on the semicircular horizon, about to lurch into motion from three directions, and in Richmond, his known goal, the revelry continued. "There seems to be for the first time," the diarist noted, "a resolute determination to enjoy the brief hour, and never look beyond the day."

Elsewhere about the country it was apparently much the same; a young man just back from Mobile reported that he had attended sixteen weddings and twenty-seven teas within the brief span of his visit. He did not add that he had found the gayety forced in that direction, but to a Richmond belle, looking back a decade later on this fourth and liveliest of the capital's wartime springs, the underlying sense of doom had been altogether inescapable. "In all our parties and pleasurings," she would recall, "there seemed to lurk a foreshadowing, as in the Greek plays where the gloomy end is ever kept in sight."

※ 4 ※

Grant was angered throughout April by increasingly glum reports of developments out in the Transmississippi, which in effect snapped off one prong of his spiky offensive before it could even be launched. "Banks, by his failure," he complained to Halleck, "has absorbed 10,000 veteran troops that should now be with Sherman, and 30,000 of his own that should have been moving toward Mobile; and this without accomplishing any good result." Nor was that the worst of it. Even more exasperating, from a somewhat different point of view, was the knowledge that Johnston now would not only have no worries about his rear and his supply lines to the Gulf, but would also be able to summon to the defense of North Georgia reinforcements who otherwise would have been occupied with the defense of South Alabama. Banks and Steele, as co-directors of the Louisiana-Arkansas fiasco, had disarranged the Grand Design at the outset; or as a friend of Grant's, after repeating his complaint that "30,000 men were rendered useless during six of the most important months of the military year," was to put it in a later appraisal of the situation, "The great combination of campaigns was inaugurated with disaster."

By way of insuring against such blunders here in the East, Grant contented himself with sending explicit and detailed instructions to Franz Sigel, who had received a military education in his native Germany, regarding the projected movement up the Shenandoah Valley and down the Virginia Central Railroad. But he went in person, soon after his return from Tennessee, to confer with the altogether nonprofessional Ben Butler, whom he had never met and with whom he had had no correspondence as to his share in the three-pronged convergence on Lee and Richmond. Arriving on April 1 at Fortress Monroe, the Massachusetts general's headquarters at the tip of the York-James peninsula, he decided that a good way to size up the former Bay State politician would be to invite his views on the part he thought he ought to play in the campaign scheduled to open within four weeks. Butler promptly gave them, and Grant was pleased, as he said later, to find that "they were very much such as I intended to direct"; that is, an amphibious movement up James River for a landing at City Point, eight miles northeast of Petersburg, the hub of Virginia's life-sustaining rail connections with the Carolinas and Georgia, and a fast northward march of twenty miles for a knock at the back door of the Confederate capital while Meade, so to speak, was climbing the front steps and Sigel was coming in through the side yard. This augured well. Still, gratifying as it was to find his military judgment confirmed in advance by the man who was charged with carrying out this portion of the plan it had produced, Grant did not neglect to give Butler, before he got back aboard the boat next morning for the return up Chesapeake Bay, written instructions as to what would be expected of him when jump-off time came round. "When you are notified to move," he told him, "take City Point with as much force as possible. Fortify, or rather intrench, at once, and concentrate all your troops for the field there as rapidly as you can." He added that, though "from City Point directions cannot be given at this time for your future movements," Butler was to bear in mind "that Richmond is to be your objective point, and that there is to be coöperation between your force and the Army of the Potomac."

The latter, being charged with the main effort, was of course Grant's main concern, and when he returned to Culpeper next day he found it in the throes of an unwelcome top-to-bottom reorganization. Designed to achieve the double purpose of tightening the chain of command and of weeding out certain generals who had proved themselves incompetent or unlucky, the shakeup involved the consolidation of a number of large units. Indeed, there was no unit above the size of a brigade that was unaffected by the change. Two of the five corps were broken up and distributed among the remaining three, while the same was done with four of the fifteen infantry divisions, leaving eleven. The result was painful to men in outfits which thus were abolished or in any case lost their identity in the shuffle. Cast among strangers they felt rejected, disowned, orphaned. They felt resentful at having been cannibalized, stung in their unit pride that theirs had been the organizations selected for such a fate, and they voiced their resentment to all who would listen. "The enemies of our country have, in times past, assailed [this division] in vain," one dispossessed commander protested, "and now it dissolves by action of our own friends." Although the recommendation had been made by Meade before Grant left Tennessee, the soldiers put the blame on the new general-in-chief, since the order of approval came down from Washington just two weeks after his arrival. By way of registering their complaint, at the first large-scale review Grant held after his return from Fortress Monroe in early April the men of one absorbed outfit wore their old corps badge on the crown of their caps, as usual, and — as he could see as soon as they swung past him — pinned the new one to the seat of their trousers.

He took no apparent offense at this, having other, more pressing matters on his mind. One was numbers. However well the chain of command was tightened, however ruthlessly high-ranking incompetents were purged, the army would be able to do little effective fighting, especially of the steam-roller kind Grant favored, unless its ranks were full and reserves were ample. And there was the rub. As spring advanced, the army moved closer to the time when it might lose the very cream of its membership, the men who had come forward on hearing that Sumter had been fired on, back in the pre-draft spring of 1861, and had learned since then, in what Sherman termed "the dearest school on earth," what it meant and what it took to be a soldier. Such veterans, survivors of many a hard-fought field, were scarcely replaceable. They were in fact not only the backbone, they were the body of the army, constituting roughly half the total combat force. Now their three-year enlistments were about to expire, and if they did not reënlist the army was apt to melt away, like the snow on the crest of the Blue Ridge, along with the volunteer organizations whose rolls they filled. Nor was this true only of the Army of the Potomac. Of the 956 volunteer infantry regiments in all the armies of the Union, 455 — nearly half — were scheduled to leave the service before the end of summer, while of the 158 volunteer batteries of artillery, 81 — more than half — would presently be free to head for home: unless, that is, enough of their members reënlisted to justify continuing their existence. By way of encouraging such commitments, the government offered certain inducements designed to make a combined appeal to greed and pride. These included, in the former category, a $400 bounty (to be increased by the amount his home town and county, or rather the civilians who had remained there for whatever reasons, were willing to put up) and a thirty-day furlough. As for pride, a man who reënlisted was to be classified as a "volunteer veteran" and was authorized to wear on his sleeve a special identifying chevron, a certificate of undeniable cold-blood valor. To these was added, as an appeal to *unit* pride, the guarantee that any regiment in which as many as three fourths of the troops "shipped over" would retain its numerical designation and its organizational status.

This last was perhaps the most effective of the lot: especially when regimental commanders, anxious to hold their outfits together as a prerequisite for holding onto their rank, carried the process down to the company level, where a man's deepest loyalties lay. Any company that attained its quota was encouraged to parade through the regimental camps, fifes shrieking and drums throbbing, while onlookers cheered and tossed their caps. Such enthusiasm was contagious, and the pressure grew heavier on holdouts in ratio to the nearness of the goal, until at last reluctance amounted to disloyalty, not only to comrades already committed, who stood in danger of being scattered among strangers, but also to the regiment, which would die a shameful death without its quota of reënlisted volunteers. "So you see I am sold again," one such wrote home, explaining that he had been swept off his feet by a fervor as strong as the spirit that makes a man be "born again" at a church revival. Not that the bounty and the prospect of a trip home, sporting the just-earned chevron, were not attractive. They were indeed, and especially together; $400, a tempted veteran pointed out, "seemed to be about the right amount for spending-money while on a furlough." Besides, regional supplements often raised the sum to more than a thousand dollars: a respectable nest egg, and enough for the down payment on a farm or a small business, once the fighting ended. Until then, after three years of life in the service, home was likely to be no great fun anyhow, except on a visit — and even that had its limitations, according to some who had been there and found that it fell considerably short of their expectations. "I almost wish myself back in the army," a furloughed soldier, barely a week after his departure, wrote to a comrade still in camp. "Everything seems to be so lonesome here. There is nothing going on that is new." In any case, as a result of these several attractions and persuasions, by mid-April no less that 136,000 veterans had signed on for another three years or the duration of the war.

Most of these were in the West, where the troops expected an early victory and were determined to be in on the kill; "fierce-fighting western men," one of their generals called them, "in for work and in for the war." In the Army of the Potomac the result was less spectacular; 26,767 veterans reënlisted — about half as many as signed up for another three years under Sherman, and also about half as many as were up for discharge. This meant that about the same number would soon be going home, dropped as emphatically from the army roster as if each man had stopped a rebel bullet. They would have to be replaced, and mainly this would be done by the conscripts and substitutes who now were arriving as a result of Lincoln's February call. Whatever they meant to Grant and Meade, for whom they were merely numbers on a fatted strength report, to the men they joined they were a mixed blessing at best. At worst, they were considerably less. "Such another depraved, vice-hardened and desperate set of human beings never before disgraced an army," an outraged New Englander complained. Partly this was the result of rising wages, which made enlistment a greater sacrifice than ever, and partly it was because the outsized bounties had created a new breed of soldier: the bounty jumper. "Thieves, pickpockets, and vagabonds would enlist," a later observer remarked, "take whatever bounty was paid in cash, desert when opportunity offered, change their names, go to another district or state, reënlist, collect another bounty, desert again, and go on playing the same trick until they were caught." One nimble New Yorker confessed to having made thirty-two such "jumps" before he wound up in the Albany penitentiary, while another New England veteran recorded that no less than half the recruits in his regiment received in one large draft had so quickly forgotten their assumed names, on the trip down to the Rappahannock, that they could not answer roll call when they got there. What was more, the delivery system was far from efficient. Out of a shipment of 625 recruits intended for a distinguished New Hampshire regiment, 137 deserted en route and another 118 managed to do the same within a week of their arrival — 36 to the rear, 82 into the Confederate lines — leaving a residue of 370, who were either the most patriotic or else the least resourceful of the lot. Across the way, on the south bank of the Rapidan, rebel pickets put up a placard: "Headquarters, 5th New Hampshire Volunteers. RECRUITS WANTED." In much the same vein, they sent over a mock-formal message inquiring when they could expect to receive the regimental colors.

Something else this latest influx of draftees brought into the Rappahannock camps that was more disturbing than the rising desertion rate. Though few in numbers, compared to the men already there, the newcomers effected a disproportionate influence on certain aspects of soldier life. "They never tired of relating the mysterious uses to which a 'jimmy' could be put by a man of nerve," a startled veteran would recall, "and how easy it was to crack a bank or filch a purse." Such talents did not go unexercised, so far at least as the limited field allowed; nothing anyone owned was safe that was not nailed down, and there were more ways than one to skin a cat or fleece a sheep. With all that crisp new bounty money injected into the economy, gambling increased hugely and so did the stakes. According to one awed observer, "Thousands of dollars would change hands in one day's playing, and there were many ugly fights engaged in, caused by their cheating each other at cards." Outraged by what he called "this business of filling up a decent regiment with the outscourings of humanity," another veteran infantryman recorded that "the more we thought of it, the more discontented we became. We longed for a quiet night, and when day came we longed to be away from these ruffians." The result was a necessary tightening of restrictions, in and out of drill hours and applicable to all. That came hard. "No pleasure or privilege for the boys in camp any more," a volunteer lamented, "for the hard lines and severe military discipline apply with a rigidness never before applied." Old-timers yearned for a return to the easy-going life they once had groused about, and they blamed its loss, illogically or not, on Grant, whom they saw as a newcomer like all those unwelcome others, though in fact the change had begun before he had any notion, let alone intention, of coming east to assume command of all the armies.

More logically — quite accurately, in fact — they put the blame on him for another change which was going to have an even more baleful effect on the lives of thousands of men now in his charge. In mid-April, in a further attempt to lengthen his numerical advantage over the forces in rebellion, Grant put an official end to the three-year-old practice of exchanging Federal and Confederate prisoners of war. Whatever its shortcomings from a humanitarian point of view, militarily the decision was a sound one. Not only did a man-for-man exchange favor the side on which a man was a larger fraction of the whole, but in this case there was also the added dividend that, in ending such a disadvantageous arrangement, the Union would be burdening its food-poor adversary with a mounting number of hungry mouths to feed. Just how much prolonged misery this was likely to cause, Grant's own troops knew only too well, either from having been captured in the days when they could be exchanged, or from awareness of what the daily food allowance consisted in the camps across the river. It was hard enough on the rebels, whose stomachs had long since shrunk to fit their rations, but for men accustomed to eating all they could hold ("Our men are generally overloaded, fed, and clad," their chief quartermaster was protesting even now, "which detracts from their marching capacity and induces straggling") such deprivation would amount to downright torture. Moreover, the prospect was further clouded by the knowledge that it had been devised by their own commander, the same man they accused of having foisted the detested reorganization upon them, as well as of having polluted their camps with rowdy gangs of thugs.

One further thing Grant did, however, that went far toward making up for the unpopularity of those other changes that followed hard on his arrival. This was to reach into the back areas of the war, especially into the fortifications around the capital, and pluck thousands of easy-living soldiers from their cushy jobs for reassignment to duty in the field. Individually and in groups, stripped of their plumes and fire-gilt buttons, they came down to the Rappahannock in a somewhat bewildered condition, if not in a state of downright shock, and the troops already there were glad to welcome them with cheers and jeers. The warmest welcome went to regiments of heavy artillery, prised out of their snug barracks, issued Springfields, and converted overnight into congeries of unblooded rifle companies; "Heavy Infantry," the veterans called them, or just "Heavies." The shocking thing about such regiments, aside from their greenness, was their size. Popular with volunteers in search of easy duty and security from wounds, several of them had as many as 1800 men apiece. "What division is this?" a Massachusetts soldier asked when one of them marched in, his own regiment being down to 207 effectives at the time. Other conversions were applauded about as lustily. Parade-ground cavalry units, for example, were suddenly unhorsed, handed muskets in place of carbines, and told that they would henceforth go afoot. "Where are your horses?" a heavy infantryman inquired of a dismounted cavalry outfit that came slogging into camp soon after his own regiment arrived. "Gone to fetch your heavy guns," one of the former troopers snapped. Teamsters too were subject to such abrupt indignity, and many of them were similarly converted and accoutered, as a result of an order reducing transportation to one wagon per brigade. "You needn't laugh at me," a transmuted teamster called to a braying mule in a passing train. "You may be in the ranks yourself before Grant gets through with the army."

In point of fact, now that they had time to look him over and examine the results of some of the changes he introduced, the men had begun to see that, whatever else he might do, in or out of combat, he clearly meant business, and they found they liked the notion of this. Some high-ranking officers, particularly the starch-collared regulars among them, might have doubts about the new general-in-chief (an old-line colonel of artillery, for instance, wrote home that he found him "stumpy, unmilitary, slouchy and western-looking; very ordinary, in fact") but the troops themselves, according to an enlisted diarist, would "look with awe at Grant's silent figure" whenever he rode out on inspection, which was often. They liked his reticence, his disregard of mere trappings, his eye for the essential. He was seldom cheered, except by greenhorn outfits trying to make points, but he seemed not to care or even notice. "Grant wants soldiers, not yawpers," a veteran observed approvingly. What was more, his success in prising the heavies out of the Washington fortifications was good evidence that he had the confidence of the authorities there — something most of his predecessors had lacked, to their discomfort and the resultant discomfort of the army in their charge. This was seen as an excellent sign, as well as a source of present satisfaction. There was also a solidity about him that was welcome after service under a series of commanders who had shown a tendency, and sometimes more than a tendency, to fly asunder under pressure. A New Englander put it simplest: "We all felt at last that *the boss* had arrived." Grant returned the compliment in kind. "The Army of the Potomac is in splendid condition and evidently feels like whipping somebody," he informed Halleck on April 26, one month after establishing headquarters at Culpeper: adding, "I feel much better with this command than I did before seeing it."

He had good cause to feel so, even though by now he was already one day past the date he had set for the simultaneous jump-off, east and west. Numerically, as a result of those various recruitment stratagems in the army and on the home front, he was in better shape than anyone had dared to hope, particularly on the Rappahannock. After Burnside shifted his corps into position for closeup support of Meade, Grant had 122,146 infantry, cavalry, and artillery effectives on hand for the main-effort crossing of the Rapidan. This figure included only the troops who were "present for duty, equipped"; another 24,602 were on extra duty, sick, or in arrest, bringing the total to just under 147,000. Even at the lower figure, and leaving Butler and Sigel out of account, he had about twice as many effectives as Lee, who had 61,953 of all arms. In Georgia, moreover, the ratio was roughly the same. Sherman had 119,898, including men on reënlistment furloughs, while Johnston had 63,949, including Polk, who would be free to join him once the pressure was on and the Union strategy was disclosed. Just when that would be, east and west, depended in part on the method by which this pressure was to be applied; that is, on the tactical details of the strategy Grant and Sherman had worked out between them, six weeks ago, in the Cincinnati hotel room. Grant was willing to leave the working out of such details to his red-haired friend, as far as they were to be applied in the West. In the East, however, he had made the matter his prime concern ever since he had set up headquarters in the field.

From Culpeper, there in the toppled V of the rivers, and from the peak of nearby Stony Mountain, where an observation post had been established for surveillance of the landscape roundabout, he could give the problem informed attention. South of the V, disposed on a front of nearly twenty miles along the right bank of the river, from Mine Run upstream to Rapidan Station and beyond, Lee and his army lay in wait under cover of intrenchments they had spent the past six months improving. The problem was how to get at him: or, more precisely, how to get around him and then at him, since a frontal assault, across the river and against those earthworks, would amount to downright folly, if not suicide en masse. Once the blue army was on his flank or in his rear, however, with nothing substantial between itself and Richmond, Lee would be obliged to come out of his works for the showdown battle Meade had been told to seek. This being so, the question was reduced to whether to move around his right flank or his left, east or west of that twenty-mile line of intrenchments. Much could be said for the latter course. The country was more open in that direction, affording the attackers plenty of room for bringing all of their superior force to bear, and there was also the prospect of gobbling up what was left of the Orange & Alexandria Railroad, down to Gordonsville, and then moving onto the Virginia Central, converting them into a supply line leading back to the Potomac, while denying their use to the defenders. All this was good, so far as it went, but there were two considerable drawbacks. One was that the rebels would wreck the railroad as they withdrew, requiring the pursuers to rebuild it and then keep it rebuilt despite attempts by regular and irregular grayback cavalry to re-wreck it. To guard against this would require the crippling detachment of fighting men from the front to the rear in ever-increasing numbers, all the way back to the Rappahannock, since even a temporary break might prove disastrous, dependent as the army would be on that single line for everything it needed, including food for 56,500 horses and mules and better than twice that many soldiers. The other drawback was that a movement around Lee's west flank would uncover the direct approach to Washington. In some ways this was a greater disadvantage than the other; Lincoln was notoriously touchy in regard to the safety of his capital, and every commander who had neglected to remember this had found himself in trouble as a result. So far, since the advent of the new general-in-chief, the President had maintained a hands-off attitude toward all things military, for which Grant was altogether thankful, but that attitude might not extend to the point of seeing Washington endangered, even in theory, especially now that the surrounding fortifications had been stripped of their outsized regiments. Between them, these two drawbacks — one having to do with supply difficulties, the other having to do with Lincoln — fairly well ruled out a movement around the Confederate left. Grant shifted his attention to the region beyond Lee's right: more specifically, to the country between Mine Run and the confluence of the rivers, fifteen miles east of Stony Mountain and about ten miles this side of Fredericksburg.

That way, the march would be shorter, Washington would be covered from dead ahead, and the supply problem would be solved by ready access to navigable streams on the outer flank, affording rapid, all-weather connection with well-stocked depots in the rear and requiring no more than minimal protection. Here too there was a drawback, however, one that was personally familiar to every soldier who had served for as long as half a year in the eastern theater. The Wilderness, it was called: a forbidding region, some dozen miles wide and eight miles deep, which the army would enter as soon as it crossed that stretch of the Rapidan immediately east of Lee's right flank, a leafy tangle extending from just beyond Mine Run to just beyond Chancellorsville. Joe Hooker, for one, could testify to the pitfalls hidden in that jungle of stunted oak and pine, and so could the present commander of the army that had come to grief in its depths, chief among them being that the force on the defensive had the advantage of silent concealment — an advantage the butternut veterans had used so well, five months ago, that Meade still considered himself lucky to have got back out of there alive. Conversely, the blue army's main advantage, its preponderance in men and guns, would scarcely matter if it was brought to battle there; numbers counted for little in those thickets, except to increase the claustrophobia and the panic that came from being shot at from close quarters by a foe you could not see, and artillery had to fire blind or not at all. As a drawback, this could hardly be overrated; but Grant believed he saw a way to avoid it. The answer was speed. If the troops moved fast enough, and began their march after nightfall screened the crossing from the rebel lookout station on Clark's Mountain across the way, they could get through the Wilderness and gain the open country just beyond it, where there was plenty of room for maneuver, before Lee had time to interfere. Moreover, this belief was founded on experience. Both Meade and Hooker, who had crossed by the same fords Grant intended to use now — Ely's and Germanna — had spent two full days on the far side of the river before they came to grips with anything substantial, and in both cases, what was more, they had done so as part of their plans: Meade by moving directly against the enemy at Mine Run, Hooker by calling a halt at Chancellorsville and inviting the enemy to attack him. Grant had no intention of doing either of these things. He intended to bull right through, covering those eight vine-choked miles in the shortest possible time — certainly less than two full days — and thus be out in the open, where Lee would have nothing better than a choice between attacking or being attacked. Either would suit Grant's purpose admirably, once he had his troops on ground where their superior numbers and equipment could be brought to bear and thus decide the issue in accordance with the odds.

By way of assuring speed on the projected march, or in any case a touch of the hard-driving ruthlessness that would be needed to obtain it, he had already made one important change in the makeup of the arm of the service that would lead the way across the Rapidan and down the roads beyond. In conference with Lincoln and Halleck, soon after his return from Tennessee and before he established headquarters in the field, he had expressed his dissatisfaction with cavalry operations in the eastern theater. What was needed, he said, was "a thorough leader." Various candidates for the post were mentioned and discarded, until Halleck came up with the answer. "How would Sheridan do?" he asked. This was Major General Philip H. Sheridan, then in command of an infantry division under Thomas near Chattanooga. His only experience with cavalry had been a five-week term as colonel of a Michigan regiment after Shiloh, nearly two years ago, and he had not only never served in Virginia, he had never even been over the ground in peacetime, so great was his dislike of all things southern. But Grant thought he would do just fine in command of the eastern army's three divisions of 13,000 troopers. "The very man I want," he said, and Sheridan was sent for. He arrived in early April, checked into Willard's, and went at once to the White House, much as Grant had done the month before. The interview was marred, however, when the President brought up the familiar jest: "Who ever saw a dead cavalryman?" Sheridan was not amused. If he had his way, there were going to be a great many dead cavalrymen lying around, Union as well as Confederate. Back at Willard's with friends, he said as much, and more. "I'm going to take the cavalry away from the bobtailed brigadier generals," he vowed. "They must do without their escorts. I intend to make the cavalry an arm of the service."

He was different, and he brought something different and hard into the army he now joined. "Smash 'em up, smash 'em up!" he would say as he toured the camps, smacking his palm with his fist for emphasis, and then ride off on his big hard-galloping horse, a bullet-headed little man with close-cropped hair and a black mustache and imperial, bandy-legged, long in the arms, all Irish but with a Mongol look to his face and form, as if something had gone strangely wrong somewhere down the line in Ireland. Just turned thirty-three, he was five feet five inches tall and he weighed 115 pounds with his spurs on; "one of those long-armed fellows with short legs," Lincoln remarked of him, "that can scratch his shins without having to stoop over." Mounted, he looked about as tall and burly as the next man, so that when he got down from his horse his slightness came as a shock. "The officer you brought on from the West is rather a little fellow to handle your cavalry," someone observed at headquarters, soon after Sheridan reported for duty. Grant took a pull at his cigar, perhaps remembering Missionary Ridge. "You'll find him big enough for the purpose before we get through with him," he said. And in point of fact, the undersized, Ohio-raised West Pointer held much the same views on war as his chief, who was Ohio born and had finished West Point ten years earlier, also standing about two thirds of the way down in his class. Those views, complementing Sheridan's even more succinct "Smash 'em up, smash 'em up!" could be stated quite briefly, a staff physician found out about this time. They were sitting around, idle after a hard day's work, and the doctor asked the general-in-chief for a definition of the art of war. Grant turned the matter over in his mind — no doubt preparing to quote Jomini or some other highly regarded authority, his listeners thought — and then replied, as if in confirmation of what his friend Longstreet was telling Lee's staff about now, across the way: "Find out where your enemy is. Get at him as soon as you can, and strike him as hard as you can. And keep moving on."

That was to be the method, and by now he had also arrived at the date on which it would begin to be applied. April 27 — the day after he told Halleck, "I feel much better with this command" — was his forty-second birthday; a year ago today, at Hard Times, Louisiana, he had braced his western army for the crossing of the greatest river of them all, the Mississippi, and the opening of the final stage in the campaign that took Vicksburg. It was therefore a fitting day for fixing the date for what would be the greatest jump-off of them all, east or west, east *and* west. Burnside by now was in motion from Annapolis, charged with replacing Meade's troops on guard along the railroad between Manassas and the Rappahannock, and Meade was free to concentrate his whole force in the V of the two rivers. Today was Wednesday. Allowing a full week for the completion of all this, together with final preparations for crossing the Rapidan at designated fords, Grant set the date for Wednesday next: May 4. Notice of this was sent at once to Meade and Burnside, as well as to Sigel and Butler, at Winchester and Fort Monroe, and to Sherman in North Georgia, who would pass the word to subordinates already poised for the leap at Dalton. This was nine days later than the tentative date Grant had set in early April, but he saw in the delay a double gain. Not only would it afford more time for preparation, which should help to eliminate oversights and confusion; it would also allow the Wilderness roads just that much additional time to dry, an important factor in consideration of the need for speed in getting out of that briery snare in the shortest possible time.

As for getting out of Washington — also a highly desirable thing, from a personal point of view — Grant had done that, for good, the previous Sunday. Except for the chance they gave him to be with his wife, his brief visits there had brought him little pleasure and much strain. The public adulation had increased, and with it the discomfort, including a flood of letters requesting his autograph (he had found a way to cut down on these, however; "I don't get as many as I did when I answered them," he said dryly) and a great deal of staring whenever he ventured out, which he seldom did unless it was unavoidable, as it was for example in getting from the station to Willard's and back. Observing his "peculiar aloofness," a protective garment he wore against the stares, one witness remarked that "he walked through a crowd as though solitary." On his last morning there, having taken breakfast in the hotel dining room before leaving to catch the train for Virginia, he was spotted by a reporter as he came out into the lobby. "He gets over the ground queerly," the journalist informed a friend that night. "He does not march, nor quite walk, but pitches along as if the next step would bring him on his nose. But his face looks firm and hard, and his eye is clear and resolute, and he is certainly natural, and clear of all appearance of self-consciousness." On the theory that this might be his last chance for some time, the reporter presumed to intercept him with a question: "I suppose, General, you don't mean to breakfast again until the war is over?" — "Not here I don't," Grant said, and went on out.

Nothing he had said or written, in conference or in correspondence with Lincoln or Halleck or anyone else, had given any estimate as to how much time the campaign about to open would require before it achieved what he called "the first great object," which was "to get possession of Lee's army." His preliminary instructions to Meade, for instance — "Lee's army will be your objective point.

Wherever Lee goes, there you will go also" — had been dated April 9; but whether the result so much desired would be attained within a year, or more, or considerably less, or not at all, remained to be seen. No one was more concerned with the specific timing than Lincoln, who would face a fight for survival in November, a fight he had good cause to believe he would lose unless the voters' confidence was lifted within the next six months by a substantial military accomplishment, rather than lowered by the lack of one to compensate for the lengthening casualty lists. And yet, despite the anxiety and strain — so well had he learned his lesson in the course of having shared in the planning, and often in the prosecution, of half a dozen failed offensives here in the East in the past three bloody years — he maintained his hands-off attitude, even to the extent of not asking his new general-in-chief for an informal guess at the schedule, east or west. It was as if, having tried interference to the limit of his ability, he now was determined to try abstention to the same extent. He had learned patience, and something more; he had learned submission. "I attempt no compliment to my own sagacity," he recently had told a Kentucky friend in a letter he knew would be published. "I claim not to have controlled events, but confess plainly that events have controlled me."

In line with this, as if to underscore his hands-off intention while at the same time giving assurance of continuing support, he sent Grant a farewell note on the last day of April, four days before the big offensive was to begin.

> Lieutenant General Grant:
>   Not expecting to see you again before the spring campaign opens, I wish to express in this way my entire satisfaction with what you have done up to this time, so far as I understand it. The particulars of your plan I neither know nor seek to know. You are vigilant and self-reliant; and, pleased with this, I wish not to obtrude any constraints or restraints upon you. While I am very anxious that any great disaster or capture of our men in great numbers shall be avoided, I know these points are less likely to escape your attention than they would be mine. If there is anything wanting which is within my power to give, do not fail to let me know it. And now, with a brave army and a just cause, may God sustain you.
>   Yours very truly,
>   A. LINCOLN.

Next day — May Day — Grant "acknowledged with pride" the President's "very kind letter" as soon as it reached him at Culpeper. "It will be my earnest endeavor that you and the country shall not be disappointed," he wrote, and added, by way of returning the compliments paid him: "Since the promotion which placed me in command of all the armies, and in view of the great responsibility and importance of success, I have been astonished at the readiness with which everything asked for has been yielded, without even an explanation being asked. Should my success be less than I desire and expect, the least I can say is, the fault is not with you."

And having said as much he turned his attention back to matters at hand. Two nights from now, in the small hours of Wednesday morning, the army would be moving down to the river for a crossing.

★ ★ ★

Braced as best he could manage for the blow he knew was coming, though he did not know just when or where it would land, Jefferson Davis had cause to be grateful for the apparent delay beyond the final day of April, which arrived without bringing word to Richmond that the Union drive had opened from any direction, east or west. Not only did this afford him time for additional preparations, such as getting a few more soldiers up to Lee or down to Beauregard; it also seemed to mean that he and his country would emerge unscathed from what had been in the past, for them, the cruelest month. Although he was by no means superstitious, the pattern was too plain to be denied. In April of 1861 the war itself had begun when Lincoln maneuvered him into opening fire on Sumter. Next year it had brought the death of his friend and idol, Albert Sidney Johnston, together with defeat in the half-won battle of Shiloh. Last year, in that same unlucky month, Grant and Hooker had launched the two offensives that cost the Confederacy the knee-buckling double loss of Vicksburg and Stonewall Jackson. However, this fourth April seemed about to be proved the exception to the rule. Militarily, so far as actual contact was concerned, the news from all three major theaters — from Louisiana and Arkansas, out in the Transmississippi, from Fort Pillow in the West, and from Plymouth, here in the East — had been nothing but good all month. If Davis, on the last morning in April, having walked the four blocks from the White House to his office adjoining Capitol Square and found no unduly woeful dispatch on his desk, paused to congratulate himself and his country on their delivery from the jinx, it would not have been without apparent justification. Yet he would have been wrong, horribly wrong. Before the day was over he would be struck the heaviest personal blow of the war: just such a blow as his adversary Lincoln had been struck, twenty-six months ago, in that other White House up in Washington.

He worked all morning, partly on administrative matters, which critics saw as consuming a disproportionate share of his time, and partly on intelligence reports — they made for difficult sifting, since different commanders predicted different objectives for the overdue Union offensive, generally in hair-raising proximity to their headquarters — then broke for lunch, which his wife brought on a tray from home to tempt his meager appetite. Before the dishes could be set in front of him, however, a house servant came running with news that Joe, their five-year-old, third of the four children who ranged in age from nine to three, had fallen from a high rear balcony onto the brick-paved courtyard thirty feet below. They hurried there to find him unconscious. Both legs were broken and his skull was fractured, apparently the result of having climbed a plank some carpenters had left resting against the balustrade when they quit for the noonday meal. He died soon after his mother reached him, and the house was filled with the screams of his Irish nurse, hysterical with sorrow and guilt from having let him out of her sight. His brother Jeff, two years older, had been the one to find him lying crumpled on the bricks. "I have said all the prayers I know how," he told a neighbor who came upon him kneeling there beside his dying brother, "but God will not wake Joe."

Under the first shock of her loss, the emotional impact of which was all the greater because she was seven months pregnant, Varina Davis was nearly as bad off as the nurse. But the most heartbreaking sight of all, Burton Harrison thought, was the father's "terrible self-control," which denied him the relief of tears. Little Joe had been his favorite, the child on whom he had "set his hope," according to his wife. Each night the boy had said his prayers at his father's knee, and often he had come in the early morning to be taken up into the big bed. Davis retired to his White House study, determined to go on with his work as an antidote to thinking of these things, and Mrs Davis joined him there as soon as she recovered from her initial shock. Presently a courier arrived with a dispatch from Lee. Davis took it, stared at it for a long minute, then turned to his wife with a stricken expression on his face. "Did you tell me what was in it?" he asked. Grief had paralyzed his mind, she saw, and her husband realized this too when he tried to compose his answer. "I must have this day with my little son," he cried, and moved blindly out of the room and up the stairs. Visitors heard him up there in the bedroom, pacing back and forth and saying over and over as he did so: "Not mine, O Lord, but thine." Meantime the boy was laid out in a casket, also in one of the upper rooms. His nurse lay flat on the floor alongside him, keening, while across the hall the father paced and paced the night away. "Not mine, O Lord, but thine," he kept saying, distracted by his grief.

All night the mourners came and went, cabinet members, high-ranking army and navy officers, dignitaries in town for the convening of Congress two days later, and yet the tall gray stucco house had an aspect of desolation, at once eerie and garish. Every room was brightly lighted, gas jets flaring, and the windows stood open on all three stories, their curtains moving in and out as the night breeze rose and fell. Next afternoon — May Day: Sunday — the funeral procession wound its way up the steep flank of Oregon Hill to Hollywood Cemetery, where many illustrious Confederates lay buried. Although Joe had been too young for school, having just turned five in April, more than a thousand schoolchildren followed the hearse, each bearing a sprig of evergreen or a spray of early flowers which they let fall on the hillside plot as they filed past. Standing by the open grave, Davis and his wife were a study in contrast. Heavy with the child she would bear in June, she wore black, including a veil, and her tall figure drooped beneath the burden of her grief, while her husband, twenty years her senior at fifty-five, yet lithe of form and erect as one of the monuments stark against the sky behind him, wore his accustomed suit of homespun gray. Down below, the swollen James purled and foamed around its rocks and islands, and now for the first time, as they watched him stand uncovered in the sunlight beside the grave of the son on whom he had set his hope, people saw that Davis, acquainted increasingly with sorrow in his private as in his public life, had begun to look his age and more. The words "vibrant" and "boyish," so often used by journalists and others to describe their impression of him, no longer applied. Streaks of gray were in his hair, unnoticed until now, and the blind left eye looked blinder in this light.

There was no evidence of this, however, in his message of greeting to the newly elected Second Congress when it convened the following day on Capitol Hill. Though the words were read by the clerk, in accordance with custom, their tone of quiet reliance and not-so-quiet defiance was altogether characteristic of their author. "When our independence, by the valor and fortitude of our people, shall have been won against all the hostile influences combined against us, and can no longer be ignored by open foes or professed neutrals, this war will have left with its proud memories a record of many wrongs which it may not misbecome us to forgive, [as well as] some for which we may not properly forbear from demanding redress. In the meantime, it is enough for us to know that every avenue of negotiation is closed against us, that our enemy is making renewed and strenuous efforts for our destruction, and that the sole resource for us, as a people secure in the justice of our cause and holding our liberties to be more precious than all other earthly possessions, is to combine and apply every available element of power for their defense and preservation." By way of proof that such a course of action could be effective against the odds, he was pleased to review the triumphs scored in all three major theaters since the previous Congress adjourned: after which he passed at once to the expected peroration, assuring his hearers that, just as they were on God's side, so was God on theirs. "Let us then, while resolute in devoting all our energies to securing the realization of the bright auspices which encourage us, not forget that our humble and most grateful thanks are due to Him without whose guidance and protecting care all human efforts are of no avail, and to whose interposition are due the manifold successes with which we have been cheered."

Just over sixty air-line miles northwest of the chamber in which the clerk droned through the presidential message, Lee was meeting with his chief infantry lieutenants atop Clark's Mountain, immediately northeast of the point where the railroad crossed the Rapidan north of Orange. He had called them together, his three corps and eight division commanders, to make certain that each had a good inclusive look at the terrain for which they would be fighting as soon as Grant made the move that Lee by now was convinced he had in mind. Not that most of them had not fought there before; they had, except for Longstreet and his two subordinates, who had missed both Chancellorsville and Mine Run; but the panoramic view from here, some six or seven hundred feet above the low-lying country roundabout, presented all the advantages of a living map unrolled at their feet for their inspection and instruction, and as such — lovely, even breath-taking in its sweep and grandeur, a never-ending carpet with all the vivid greens of advancing spring commingled in its texture — would serve, as nothing else could do, to fix the over-all character of the landscape in their minds.

For the most part — though their youth was disguised, in all but two heavily mustached cases, by beards in a variety of styles, from full-shovel to Vandyke — they were men in their prime, early-middle-aged at worst. Longstreet was forty-three, and the other two corps commanders, Lieutenant Generals Richard S. Ewell and A. P. Hill, were respectively four years older and five years younger, while the division commanders averaged barely forty, including one who was forty-eight; "Old Allegheny," he was called, as if he vied in ancientness with the mountains beyond the Blue Ridge. Aside from him, Lee at fifty-seven was ten years older than any other general on the hilltop, and like Davis, despite the vigor of his movements, the quick brown eyes in his high-colored face, and the stalwart resolution of his bearing, he had begun to show his age. His hair, which had gone from brown to iron gray in the first year of the war, was now quite white along his temples, and the same was true of his beard, which he wore clipped somewhat closer now than formerly, as if in preparation for long-term fighting. The past winter had been a hard one for him, racking his body with frequent attacks that were diagnosed as lumbago, and though his health improved with warming weather, the opening months of spring had been even harder to endure, not only because they brought much rain, which tended to oppress him, but also because it galled his aggressive nature to be obliged to wait, as he fretfully complained, "on the time and place of the enemy's choosing" for battle. Just over twenty months ago, after less than three months in command of the newly-assembled army with which he had whipped McClellan back from the outskirts of

Richmond, he had stood on this same mountaintop and watched Pope's blue host file northward out of the trap he had laid for it there in the V of the rivers, and he had said to Longstreet then: "General, we little thought that the enemy would turn his back upon us thus early in the campaign." It was different now. Grant he knew would move, not north across the Rappahannock, but south across the Rapidan, and all Lee could do was prepare to meet him with whatever skill and savagery were required to drive him back: which, in part, was why he had brought his ranking subordinates up here for a detailed look at the terrain on which he planned to do just that. Believing as he did that an outnumbered army should be light on its feet and supple in the hands of its commander, his custom was to give his lieutenants a great deal of latitude in combat, and he wanted to make certain that they were equipped, geographically at least, to exercise with judgment the initiative he encouraged them to seize whenever they were on their own — as, in fact, every unit commander, gray or blue, was likely to be in that tangled country down below, especially in the thickets that lay like pale green smoke over that portion called the Wilderness, stretching eastward beyond Mine Run.

The Rapidan flowed to their right, practically at their feet as they stood looking north toward Culpeper, the hilltop town ten miles away, where A. P. Hill had been born and raised and where Grant now had his headquarters. Another ten miles farther on, hazy in the distance, the dark green line of the Rappahannock crooked southeast to its junction with the nearer river, twenty miles due east of the domed crest of Clark's Mountain, and then on out of sight toward Fredericksburg, still another ten miles beyond the roll of the horizon. All this lay before and below the assembled Confederates, who could also see the conical tents and white-topped wagons clustered and scattered in and about the camps Meade's army had pitched in the arms of the stream-bound V whose open end was crossed by the twin threads of the railroad glinting silver in the sunlight. There was a good deal of activity in those camps today, as indeed there had been the day before, a Sunday, but the generals on the mountain gave their closest attention to the gray-green expanse of the Wilderness, particularly its northern rim, as defined by the meandering Rapidan; Hooker and Meade had both crossed there in launching the two most recent Union offensives, and Lee believed that Grant would do the same, even to the extent of using the same fords, Ely's and Germanna, four and ten miles respectively from the junction of the rivers. He not only believed it, he said it. Apparently that was another reason he had brought his lieutenants up here: to say it and to show them as he spoke. Suddenly, without preamble or explanation, he raised one gauntleted hand and pointed specifically at the six-mile stretch of the Rapidan that flowed between the two points where the Federals twice had thrown their pontoon bridges in preparation for all-out assaults on the Army of Northern Virginia. "Grant will cross by one of these fords," he said.

Deliberately spoken, the words had the sound of a divination, now and even more so in the future, when they were fulfilled and his hearers passed them down as an instance of Lee's ability to read an opponent's mind. However, though this faculty was real enough on the face of it, having been demonstrated repeatedly in most of his campaigns, it was based on nothing occult or extrasensory, as many of his admirers liked to claim, but rather on a careful analysis of such information as came to hand in the normal course of events — from enemy newspapers closely scanned, from scouts and spies and friendly civilians who made it through the Yankee lines, from loquacious deserters and tight-mouthed prisoners tripped by skillful interrogation — plus a highly developed intelligence procedure, by which he was able not only to put himself in the other man's position, but also to *become* that man, so to speak, in making a choice among the opportunities the situation seemed to afford him for accomplishing the destruction of the Army of Northern Virginia. Like other artists in other lines of endeavor, Lee produced by hard labor, midnight oil, and infinite pains what seemed possible only by uncluttered inspiration. Quite the opposite of uncanny, his method was in fact so canny that it frequently produced results which only an apparent wizard could achieve. The Clark's Mountain prediction was a case in point. Lee had spent a major part of his time for the past two months — ever since Grant's arrival and elevation, in early March — at work on the problem of just what his new adversary was going to do, and for the past two weeks — ever since April 18, when he ordered all surplus baggage sent to the rear — he had given the matter his practically undivided attention: with the result that, after a process of selection and rejection much like Grant's across the way, he had come up with what he believed was the answer. Grant would cross the Rapidan by Ely's Ford or Germanna Ford, and having done so he either would turn west for an attack on the Confederate right flank, as Meade had done in November, or else he would do as Hooker had intended to do, a year ago this week, and maneuver for a battle in the open, where he could bring his superior numbers to bear. Which of these two courses the Federal commander meant to adopt once he was across the river did not really matter to Lee, since he did not intend to give him a chance to do either. Lee's plan was to let him cross, then hit him there in the Wilderness with everything he had, taking advantage of every equalizing impediment the terrain afforded, in order to whip him as thoroughly as possible in the shortest possible time, and thus drive him, badly cut up, back across the Rapidan. He did not say all this today, however. He merely said that Grant would cross by one of those fords on the rim of the Wilderness, and then he mounted Traveller and led the way back down the mountain.

Nor did he act, just yet, on the contingent decision he had reached. Only today, in fact, he had instructed Longstreet to shift one of his two divisions northwest of Gordonsville, in order to have it in a better position to meet the challenge Grant would pose if he attempted a move around the Confederate left, in the opposite direction from the one predicted. Lacking definite confirmation of what was after all no more than a theoretical opinion, an educated guess, Lee could not commit his army to a large-scale counteraction of a movement which there was even an outside chance the enemy might not make; he had to leave a sizeable margin for error, including total error. That night, however, the signal station on Clark's Mountain reported observing moving lights in the Federal camps, and next morning — May 3: Tuesday — there were reports of heavy clouds of dust, stirred up by columns marching here and there, and smoke in unusual volume, as if the bluecoats were engaged in the last-minute destruction of camp equipment and personal belongings for which they would have no use when they moved out.

All day this heightened activity continued, past sundown and into the night. Presently the signalmen blinked a message to army headquarters that long columns of troops were passing in front of campfires down there on the far bank of the Rapidan. Headquarters responded with a question: Was the movement west or east, upstream in Hill's direction on the left or downstream in Ewell's direction on the right? The signal station was in visual communication with both corps commanders, as well as with Lee, but it could find no answer to the question. All that could be seen across the way was the winking of campfires as files of men passed in front of them. There was no way of telling, from this, whether the troops were moving upstream or down, to the left or to the right. By now it was close to midnight; May 4 would be dawning within five hours. Lee decided to act at last on yesterday's prediction, and sent word accordingly for the signalmen to flash a message to the corps on the right, down toward Mine Run: "General Ewell, have your command ready to move at daylight."

CHAPTER 2

The Forty Days

★ ✗ ☆

GRANT CAME AS LEE HAD SAID HE WOULD, only more so, crossing the Rapidan not merely by "one of those fords," Ely's or Germanna, but by both — and, presently, by still another for good measure. Sheridan's new-shod cavalry led the way, splashing across the shallows in the darkness soon after midnight, May 4, and while the engineers got to work in the waist-deep water, throwing a pair of wood and canvas pontoon bridges at each of the two fords, the troopers established bridgeheads on the enemy side of the river at both points and sent out patrols to explore the narrow, jungle-flanked, moonless roads tunneling southward through the Wilderness. Near the head of one column the horsemen got to talking as they felt their way toward Chancellorsville, a name depressing to the spirits of any Federal who had been there with Joe Hooker just a year ago this week. One of the group, anticipating a quick pink-yellow stab of flame and a humming, bone-thwacking bullet from every shadow up ahead, remarked uneasily that he had never supposed "the army went hunting around in the night for Johnnies in this way."

"We're stealing a march on old man Lee," a veteran explained.

They thought this over, remembering the loom of Clark's Mountain and the rebel lookout station on its peak, and before long someone put the thought into words. "Lee will miss us in the morning."

"Yes, and then watch out," another veteran declared. "He'll come tearing down this way ready for a fight."

Though all agreed that this would certainly be in character, Lee did no such thing: at least not yet. Morning came and the crossing progressed smoothly in their rear, including the installation of still a fifth bridge at Culpeper Mine Ford, two miles above Ely's, to speed the passage of the army train, the laggard, highly vulnerable element to which all the others, mounted or afoot, had to conform for its protection on the march. Slow-creaking and heavily loaded with ten days' subsistence for nearly 150,000 men and ten days' grain for better than 56,000 mules and horses (strung out along a single road, if any such had been available, this monster train would have covered the sixty-odd miles from the Rapidan to Richmond without a break from head to tail) the wagons passed over the two lower fords in the wake of Major General Winfield S. Hancock's II Corps, the largest of Meade's three, which crossed at Ely's in the darkness and began to make camp at Chancellorsville, five miles from the river, before noon. The brevity of the march was necessary if the combat units were to provide continuous protection for the road-jammed train, but the men, slogging along under packs about as heavy-laden as the wagons in their rear, were thankful for the early halt; they carried, as directed in the carefully worded order, "50 rounds of ammunition upon the person, three days' full rations in their haversacks, [and] three days' bread and short rations in their knapsacks." At Germanna, meantime, Major General Gouverneur K. Warren's V Corps crossed and marched six miles southeast to Wilderness Tavern, near the intersection of the Germanna Plank Road and the Orange-Fredericksburg Turnpike, where it made camp in the early afternoon, five miles west of Hancock, leaving room behind for Major General John Sedgwick's VI Corps to bed down beside the road, between the tavern and the river, well before sundown. Grant was pleased, when he reached the upper ford about midday and clattered over with his staff, to note that the passage of the Rapidan was being accomplished in excellent order, strictly according to schedule, and without a suggestion of enemy interference. "This I regarded as a great success," he later reported, because "it removed from my mind the most serious apprehensions I had entertained, that of crossing the river in the face of an active, large, well-appointed, and ably-commanded army."

Gratified by the evidence that he had indeed stolen a march on old man Lee, he got off a wire at 1.15 to Burnside at Rappahannock Station, instructing him to bring his IX Corps down to Germanna without delay. Another went to Halleck, back in Washington: "The crossing of the Rapidan effected. Forty-eight hours now will demonstrate whether the enemy intends giving battle this side of Richmond. Telegraph Butler that we have crossed." This done, he rode on a short distance and established headquarters beside the road, near a deserted house whose front porch afforded him and his military family a shaded, airy position from which to observe his soldiers on the march. He was dressed uncharacteristically in full regimentals, including his sword and sash and even a pair of brown cotton-thread gloves, three stars glinting impressively on each shoulder of his best frock coat. What was more, his manner was as expansive as his trappings — a reaction, apparently, to his sudden release from concern that he might be attacked with his army astride the river. As he sat there smoking and swapping remarks with his associates, a newspaper correspondent approached and asked the question not even

Lincoln had put to him in the past two months. How long was it going to take him to reach Richmond?

Grant not only expressed no resentment at the reporter's inquisitive presumption; he even answered him. "I will agree to be there in about four days," he said, to the astonishment of the newsman and his staff. Then he added: "That is, if General Lee becomes a party to the agreement. But if he objects, the trip will undoubtedly be prolonged."

Laughter increased the pervasive feeling of well-being and relief, and orders soon were distributed for tomorrow's march, which had been prepared beforehand for release if all went well: as, indeed, all had. One change there was, however, occasioned by a report that Sheridan received that afternoon. Chagrined at encountering none of Major General J. E. B. Stuart's highly touted butternut troopers in the course of his probe of the Wilderness south of the two fords, he learned that this was because they were assembled near Fredericksburg for a grand review next day at Hamilton's Crossing, a dozen miles to the east, and he asked permission to take two of his three divisions in that direction at first light in order to get among them, smash them up, and thus abolish at the outset of the campaign one of the problems that would have to be solved before its finish. Grant was willing, and so was Meade, though more reluctantly, being hidebound in his notion as to the primary duty of cavalry on a march through enemy country. In any case, the army would still have one of its mounted divisions for such work, and that seemed ample, especially if tomorrow's advance required no more of the blue outriders than today's had done. For one thing, since the train would not complete its crossing of the Rapidan before late tomorrow afternoon, and would thus require that the three infantry corps hold back and keep well closed up for its protection, the marches were to be about as brief. Hancock would move south and west, first to Todd's Tavern and then to Shady Grove Church, down on the Catharpin Road, extending his right toward Parker's Store on the Orange Plank Road, which was to be Warren's stopping point. Warren in turn would extend his right toward Wilderness Tavern, his present position astride the Orange Turnpike, which Sedgwick would occupy tomorrow, leaving one division on guard at Germanna Ford until Burnside's lead division arrived. Despite their brevity (Hancock had nine miles to cover, Warren and Sedgwick barely half that) all marches were to begin at 5 o'clock promptly, which was sunup. Upon reaching their designated objectives, Wilderness Tavern, Parker's Store, and Shady Grove Church — each commanding a major road coming in from the west, where Lee presumably still was unless he had already taken alarm and fallen back southward — all units were to prepare at once for getting under way as promptly the following day, Friday the 6th, which would take them out of the Wilderness and into the open country beyond, in position for coming to grips with the Confederates on terrain that would favor the army superior in numbers.

Forty-eight hours would tell the story, Grant had informed Halleck early that afternoon, and all the indications were that the story would have an ending that was happy from the Federal point of view. Careful planning seemed to have paid off handsomely. Not only were his "most serious apprehensions" — that he would be jumped while astride the Rapidan — behind him, but his second greatest worry — that he would have to fight in the blind tangle of the Wilderness — was all but behind him, too. "Enemy moving infantry and trains toward Verdiersville," the signal station on Stony Mountain informed him at 3 p.m. "Two brigades gone from this front. Camps on Clark's Mountain breaking up. Battery still in position behind Dr Morton's house, and infantry pickets on the river." That had far more the sound of preparations for a withdrawal than for an attack, and there seemed to be little of urgency in the Confederate reaction, such as it was. Grant could turn in for a good night's sleep in a much less fretful state of mind than the one in which he had lain down the night before, while poised for the crossing which now was complete except for a couple of thousand more wagons and Burnside's corps, whose arrival would give him a combat strength of 122,000 effectives on the rebel side of the river: an army which, arrayed for battle, two ranks deep, with one third of its units held rearward in reserve, would extend for twenty-five miles from flank to flank. That was roughly twice as many troops as Lee could muster of all arms. Grant was not only willing, he was altogether anxious to take him on at the earliest possible moment, preferably out in the open, where he could bring his superior ordnance to bear, or if not there then here in this green maze of vines and briers and stunted oaks and pines, if the opportunity offered and that was what it came to. He turned in early and apparently slept well.

That was not the case with a good many of the men who were bivouacked in this haunted woodland by his orders. Unlike him, they had been here before, and the memory was painful. In the fields around Wilderness Tavern, it was afterwards recalled — including the one just east of the deserted, ramshackle tavern itself, where Stonewall Jackson's maimed left arm was buried — there was little or no singing round the campfires, the usual pastime after a not-too-hard day's march, and there was even a tendency to avoid the accustomed small talk. This was due, one soldier declared, to "a sense of ominous dread which many of us found it almost impossible to shake off." There was, in fact, much about the present situation that was remindful of the one a year ago, when all ranks had engaged in a carnival of self-congratulation on the results of careful planning and stout marching; "The rebel army is now the legitimate property of the Army of the Potomac," Hooker had announced on that other May Day, just before he came to grief, suffering better than 17,000 casualties before he managed to scurry out of this scrub oak jungle and back across the Rappahannock, beyond the reach of a gray army barely one third the size of his own. Grant, they knew, was no such spouter, but they remembered Fighting Joe and other even more unpleasant things, such as brush fires set by bursting shells, in which men with broken backs and bullet-shattered legs had been roasted alive before the stretcher bearers could get at them. Even recruits could see the danger. "These woods will surely be burned if we fight here," one said when they first called a halt that afternoon.

Over near Chancellorsville, where the whippoorwills began calling plaintively soon after sunset, now as then, the mood was much the same. The fighting had been heaviest around here last year, and there still were many signs of it, including skeletons in rotted blue, washed partly out of their shallow graves by the rains of the past winter. No one but the devil himself would choose such ground for a field of battle, veterans said; the devil and old man Lee. In an artillery park near the ruin of the Chancellor mansion, which had burned to its brick foundations on the second day of conflict, a visiting infantryman looked glumly at a weathered skull that stared back with empty sockets, grinning a lipless grin. He prodded it with his boot, then turned to his comrades — saying "you" and "you," not "we" and "us," for every soldier is superstitious about foretelling his own death, having seen such words come true too many times — and delivered himself of a prediction. "This is what you are all coming to," he told them, "and some of you will start toward it tomorrow."

In point of fact, the conversion of the blue invaders into skeletons was just the kind of grisly work Lee had in mind, and he was moving toward it, even now, with everything he had. Grant had taken care, in his assignment of objectives for the following day, to see that each of the three main roads coming in from the west would be covered by a corps of infantry; for though logic and the evidence, such as it was, tended to indicate that his adversary was in the process of falling back to a strong defensive position athwart his path — probably on the banks of the North Anna, twenty miles to the south — there was a chance that the old fox might mass his troops for an attack, down one or another of those roads, in an attempt to strike while the Union army was strung out in the Wilderness. The truth was, Lee was coming by all three, a corps on each.

Ewell, alerted the night before, would march eastward on the Orange Turnpike, nearest the river, while Hill took the Orange Plank Road, which paralleled the turnpike at a distance that varied from one to three miles until the two converged, just short of Chancellorsville, twenty-five miles away; Longstreet, down around Gordonsville, had a greater distance to travel and would make a later start, having to call in his troops from the far-left positions they had been obliged to hold until Grant was committed to the upstream movement with all his force. Ewell, with three divisions, began his march at 9 o'clock. Hill reached Orange before noon, left one division there to guard the nearby Rapidan crossings, and had his other two in motion on the plank road shortly afterwards, the army commander riding with him near the head of the column. Since the troops on the turnpike had a three-hour head start and a straighter route, Ewell was told to regulate his speed by that of Hill. Longstreet then was notified by courier to set out with his two divisions, crossing the North Anna by Brock's Bridge, due east of Gordonsville, then turning north to strike the Catharpin Road at Richard's Shop, from which point his march would parallel those of the other two corps, on his left between him and the Rapidan. Lee's plan, though he announced no details yet, was to get within reach of the Federals as soon as possible, bring them to a Wilderness-hampered halt with Hill and Ewell, then launch an all-out hip-and-thigh assault with all three corps, as soon as Longstreet came up on the right.

Ewell stopped for the night at Locust Grove, a couple of miles into the Wilderness beyond Mine Run. Clustered about their skillet wagons for supper, the men of his three divisions had no such reaction to their surroundings as the men of Warren's four divisions were experiencing around Wilderness Tavern, five miles up the pike, or those of Hancock's four at Chancellorsville, another five miles east. Outnumbered as usual on the eve of contact, and having fought here against odds as long and longer, the butternut veterans understood that the cramped, leaf-screened terrain would work to their advantage, now as before, and their bivouacs hummed with banter and small talk as they bedded down, after ravening their rations, to rest for the shock they knew was likely to come tomorrow. Five miles southwest on the plank road, and still five miles short of the western limits of the Wilderness, it was much the same with the men of Hill's two divisions, rolled in their blankets and sleeping under the stars. At sundown he had called a halt at Verdiersville, eleven miles beyond Orange and nine from Parker's Store; "My Dearsville," Hill's troops dubbed the hamlet. Here Lee had had his headquarters during the Mine Run confrontation last November, and his tent was pitched, tonight as then, in a field beside the road. Soon there began to come to its flap a series of couriers bearing dispatches from all quarters of Virginia — dispatches which in turn bore out, to the letter, predictions he had been making for the past month as to the nature of the offensive the Federals now had launched.

Of these, the most alarming came from the President himself. A blue force, estimated at 30,000 of all arms and said to be commanded by Ben Butler, was unloading from transports at City Point and Bermuda Hundred, on the south bank of the James less than twenty miles from

Richmond, in position to break its vital rail connections with Petersburg and points south, if not indeed to come swarming across its bridges and into its streets in a matter of hours, since the capital had scarcely one tenth that many troops for its defense. "With these facts and your previous knowledge," Davis wired, demonstrating his accustomed calmness under pressure, as well as his abiding trust in Lee, "you can estimate the condition of things here, and decide how far your own movements should be influenced thereby." Lee's decision was not to allow his movements to be influenced at all by this development. He would continue to concentrate on meeting the threat to his immediate front, he informed Davis, and leave Butler to Beauregard, who had been ordered to proceed at once from Weldon to confront the southside invaders with such troops as he could muster in his newly formed department. Lee's reaction to a second grievous danger, reported from out in the Shendandoah Valley, was much the same. Warned that a force of undetermined strength under Sigel had begun an advance up the Valley in conjunction with another movement west of the Alleghenies, he replied with a wire instructing Breckinridge to assume "general direction of affairs" beyond the Blue Ridge. "I trust you will drive the enemy back," he told him. This done, he put both dangers — one to his rear, the other to his flank, and both to his lines of supply and communication — out of his mind, at least for the present, in order to give his undivided attention to the problem at hand: specifically, how best to deal with Meade's blue host, which had crossed the Rapidan bent on his destruction, but which was camped for the present across his front in the green toils of the Wilderness.

That the Federals had called at least a temporary halt, instead of pressing ahead on a night march to escape those toils and oblige him to race southward for a meeting in the open, was welcome news indeed, received in a series of messages Jeb Stuart kept sending to Verdiersville from shortly after dark until near midnight, when he apparently decided that the time had come to give his short-winded animals some rest. Abandoning his plans for the Hamilton's Crossing review next day, the cavalry leader was bringing his spruced-up troopers westward along the southern fringes of the Wilderness in order to get in position by morning on the right front of the army, there to protect its open flank and reconnoiter the enemy advance when it resumed. That too was welcome news, ensuring a continuous stream of intelligence, such as only cavalry could gather, and providing a resilient cushion against shock. Welcome, too, was a late-evening dispatch from Longstreet informing headquarters that he had crossed Brock's Bridge and would camp there tonight, on the near bank of the North Anna; he expected to reach Richard's Shop by noon tomorrow, nine miles from Shady Grove Church and twelve from Todd's Tavern. This meant that he most likely would be able to move into his assigned position, up the Catharpin Road, by nightfall, in plenty of time for launching the all-hands attack at first light Friday, after

The Forty Days [153]

Ewell and Hill made contact tomorrow and set the bluecoats up for the assault designed to drive them back across the river they had crossed today. Accordingly, Lee had his adjutant notify Ewell that he was to move out early in the morning, continuing his march up the turnpike in order to menace the Union flank if Grant kept heading south. If he veered east, toward Fredericksburg, Ewell was to pursue him and fall upon his rear; or if he turned this way, Ewell was to take up a strong defensive position and hold him there in the tangled brush until Hill and Longstreet came up on the right, at which point they would all three go over to the offensive in accordance with Lee's plan. In any case, the adjutant added, "the General's desire is to bring him to battle as soon now as possible."

At breakfast next morning between dawn and sunup Lee was in excellent spirits, refreshed by four or five hours of sleep and encouraged by a follow-up message, just in from Stuart, that the three Federal corps had in fact spent the whole night in their Wilderness camps. He expressed his satisfaction at this evidence that all was working as he hoped, as well as at information that a brigade of Ewell's, detached for guard duty at Hanover Junction, would be rejoining no later than tomorrow. Together with last-minute piecemeal reinforcements sent from Richmond during the past week, this would give him an over-all strength of nearly 65,000 men in his eight divisions of infantry and three of cavalry. Four brigades were still detached (Hoke's, in North Carolina, and three with Major General George E. Pickett, comprising Longstreet's third division, still convalescing in southside Virginia from its brief, horrific experience on the third day at Gettysburg, ten months back) but Lee regretted this less than he might have done except for a miscalculation that contributed to the boldness of his plan for the annihilation or quick repulse of the enemy in the thickets up ahead. He estimated the combined strength of Meade and Burnside at not more than 75,000 men, and therefore assumed — quite erroneously, since the Federals, with considerably better than half again that many troops, had in fact almost twice the number Lee could muster — that he was about to fight against the shortest odds he had faced at any time since he assumed command of the Army of Northern Virginia, two victory-crowded years ago next month. Rising from breakfast he mounted Traveller and gave A. P. Hill the word to resume his march up the plank road, first across the "Poison Fields," as the leached-out mining region west of the Wilderness was called, and then into the briery hug of the jungle where he intended to come to grips with the invaders who, Stuart reported, seemed unaware of his presence on their flank.

Beyond the moldering six-months-old intrenchments around the headwaters of Mine Run, a couple of miles out of Verdiersville, this unawareness ended with a spatter of fire from a detachment of Union cavalry armed with seven-shot carbines. They were few in number, apparently, and easily driven back (Stuart had arrived by now, resplendent in his red-lined cape, to attend to this by fanning his horsemen out on the right and front) but word was certainly on the way to Grant that graybacks were approaching Parker's Store in strength. Moreover, a staff officer arrived from Ewell about this time to report that he had sighted heavy columns of bluecoats crossing the Wilderness Tavern intersection, two miles ahead on the Germanna Plank Road, perpendicular to the turnpike. It stood to reason that if Ewell could see the enemy, so could the enemy see him; Grant would be forewarned in that direction, too. Lee repeated his instructions that the Second Corps, continuing to regulate its march by that of the Third, was to move on and make contact, but added that he preferred not to "bring on a general engagement" until Longstreet came up. Hill was deep in the Wilderness by then, out of touch with Ewell as a result of a widening divergence, beyond Verdiersville, of the plank road from the turnpike, which was

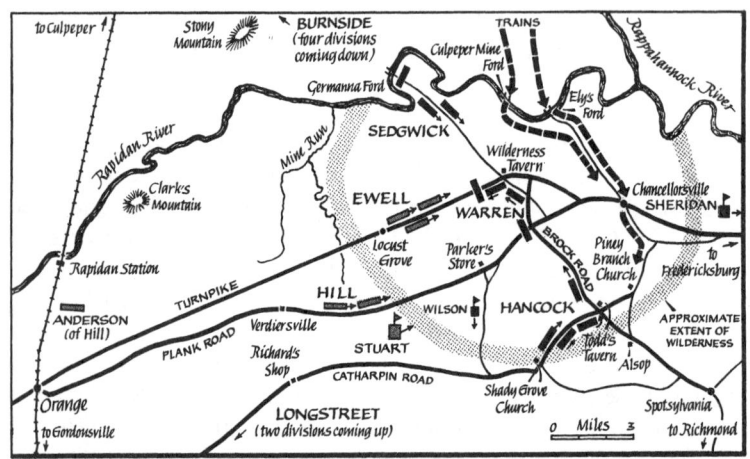

almost three miles away by the time he reached Parker's Store at noon. At this point, still riding near the head of Hill's two-division column, Lee heard a rising clatter of rifle fire from the left front. Obviously there was fighting on the turnpike, and from the sound of it, filtered through three miles of brush and branches, the engagement was indeed "general," mounting to a quick crescendo like the rapid tearing of canvas, though it lacked the deeper, rumbling tones artillery gave a battle at that distance.

Mindful of Lee's admonition not to "bring on a general engagement," Ewell had deployed his lead division when he got within a couple of miles of the Union-held crossroad, then brought up the second for close support on both sides of the pike, warning the two commanders — Major Generals Edward Johnson and Robert Rodes, who at forty-eight and thirty-five were the oldest and youngest infantry division commanders in the army — "not to allow themselves to become involved, but to fall back slowly if pressed." So he later reported, but the words had little application when the time came, as it did all too soon: especially for the men of Johnson's lead brigade, Virginians under Brigadier General John M. Jones, who caught the initial and overwhelming impact of a whole blue division that came hurtling at them, as if out of nowhere, through brush and vines that limited vision to less than sixty feet in any direction. Caught thus, they found it as impossible to "fall back slowly" as they had to avoid becoming "involved." Losing Jones, who was killed by an early volley from the dense wave of attackers, they broke and fled, spreading panic through the ranks of an Alabama brigade Rodes had posted in their rear. Ewell, so close to the front that the attack exploded practically in his face, whirled his horse and raced back to bring help from his third division, Major General Jubal Early's, which had kept to the road in order to come up fast in an emergency such as the one that was now at hand. In the lead was Brigadier General John B. Gordon's brigade, Georgians who had a reputation for aggressiveness on short notice.

"General Gordon!" Ewell cried, his dragoon mustache bristling and his prominent eyes bulging as he checked his mount with a hard pull on the reins, "the day depends on you!"

"These men will save it, sir," Gordon replied, partly for the benefit of the troops themselves, who had come crowding up, as was their custom at such times, to hear what the brass had to say.

Going at once from march to attack formation, he advanced one regiment unsupported in a countercharge straight up the pike, while the rest deployed to go in on the right. On the left, two of Johnson's three intact brigades reacted by clawing their way through the brush toward the sound of firing, and Rodes's four did likewise, including the Alabamians who had been rattled by the flight of the Virginians through their ranks. As suddenly as it had risen, the tide of battle turned, and for the former attackers, overlapped on both flanks and savagely assailed from dead ahead by the screaming Georgians, the outcome was even more disastrous. Now it was their turn to backtrack, losing heavily in the process — though not as heavily as two other blue divisions, coming up in sequence on the left and groping blindly for the flank they had been told to support but could not find. Struck before they could form for attack or defense, they were driven eastward in confusion, suffering grievously in killed and wounded and losing several hundred prisoners, many of whom fled unknowingly into the rebel lines, bereft of all sense of direction in that maze of vines and brambles. It was, as one veteran said, a conflict "no man saw or could see"; "A battle of invisibles with invisibles," another called it. "As for fighting," a third declared, "it was simply bushwhacking on a grand scale, in brush where all formation beyond that of regiments or companies was soon lost and where such a thing as a consistent line of battle on either side was impossible."

The pattern of Wilderness fighting had been set, and one of its principal elements was panic, which came easily and spread rapidly on terrain that had all the claustral qualities of a landscape in a nightmare, with a variety of background sounds that ranged from a foreboding silence, so dense that a man was likely to jump six feet at the snap of a twig, to a veritable cataract of noise, referred to by a participant as "the most terrific musketry firing ever heard on the American continent."

Ewell, still mindful of Lee's admonition, did not pursue beyond the point at which the fight had opened, just under two miles west of the crossroad. It was 3 o'clock by now, and he could tell himself, quite truthfully, that he had done all that was asked of him and more, inflicting much heavier casualties than he suffered and fixing the enemy there in the tangled depths of the Wilderness. He put his men to work intrenching a line that extended about a mile to the left and a mile to the right of the turnpike, and after hauling off two guns he had captured in the course of his counterattack, he settled down to wait for tomorrow, when Longstreet would be up and the army would go over to the offensive. Fighting continued on a lesser scale all afternoon and into the evening, and though he lost two more brigade commanders — Brigadier Generals Leroy Stafford of Louisiana and John Pegram of Virginia, the former mortally wounded and the latter shot in the leg — Ewell had no doubt that he would be able to hold his newly fortified position, no matter what the Yankees sent against him.

There was no such assurance down on the plank road, three miles south, where a separate battle swelled to a sudden and furious climax at about the time the disjointed contest on the pike began to wane. For Hill, whose two divisions were struck by a much heavier and far better coördinated attack than the one that had been launched against Ewell's three, there was no waning; there was hard, stand-up fighting from the moment of earnest contact, around 4 o'clock, until darkness and exhaustion persuaded the troops of both sides to rest on their arms, where they then were, for a resumption at first light tomorrow of a struggle that had been touch-and-go for the past four hours. His two divisions, commanded by Major Generals Henry Heth and Cadmus Wilcox, had continued their march beyond Parker's Store to within a mile of the Brock Road, on which the Union infantry was known to be moving south, when stiffened resistance brought the head of the gray column to a halt. Heth formed for battle astride the road, and Lee — taking over for Hill, who was sick today, as he had been at Gettysburg — set up headquarters in a roadside clearing near the farmhouse of a widow named Tapp. He had no sooner dismounted to confer with Stuart and Hill, who had stayed with his men despite his disability, than a platoon of blue-clad skirmishers walked into the clearing from behind a stand of pines in its northeast corner, rifles at the ready. Apparently as startled as the high-ranking Confederates were by the sudden confrontation, the Federals faded back into the pines instead of opening fire or advancing to make the capture that would have changed the course of the war. However thankful Lee was for this deliverance from the hands of the bluecoats, their presence served to emphasize the dangerous possibility of an enemy plunge, whether on purpose or by accident, into the heavily wooded gap which the divergence of the two routes had created between Hill, down here on the plank road, and Ewell, whose battle was still in full swing on the turnpike. Accordingly, Lee sent word for Wilcox to extend Hill's left by moving his division northward into the brush beyond the clearing, thus to forestall a penetration of the gap, while Heth resumed his eastward advance to develop the strength of the blue force in his front. Though he still intended to withhold delivery of his main effort until Longstreet was on hand, the southern commander's hope was that Heth would be able to carry the Brock Road intersection, less than a mile away, as an effective means of bringing the Union army to a severed, panicky halt in the very depths of the Wilderness, half a dozen miles from open ground in any direction.

It was now past 3 o'clock. A note went at once to Heth asking whether, in his judgment, he could seize the intersection without bringing on a "general engagement." Heth replied that the enemy seemed to be there in strength; he could not tell how much an attack would spread the action, but he was willing to give the thing a try if that was what was wanted. While Lee was turning this over in his mind, back at the Widow Tapp's, a sudden uproar from the immediate front — louder, even, than the one that had exploded in Ewell's face, four hours ago — informed him that the decision had been taken out of his hands. Unsupported by Wilcox, who had moved off to the left, Heth was under heavy, all-out assault from dead ahead.

Both attacks — the one against Ewell, up on the turnpike, and the present one down the plank road against Hill — were the result of a deliberate decision by Grant, whose self-confidence and natural combativeness had not been lessened by the enlargement of his responsibilities and who was determined, moreover, not to yield the tactical initiative to an opponent with a reputation for making the most of it on all occasions. If this meant the abandonment of his original intention to get into, through, and out of the Wilderness in the shortest possible time, then that just had to be. His primary talent had always been instinctive, highly improvisatorial at its best, and though there was little about him that could be described as Napoleonic, he trusted, like Napoleon, in his star. The overriding fact, as Grant saw it, was that the rebels were there in the tangled brush, somewhere off to the west, and he was determined to hit them. He was determined, in Sheridan's phrase, to smash them up at every opportunity.

Meade began it, quite on his own. Shortly after 7 o'clock that morning, by which time the leading elements of all three corps had been two hours on the march, he was notified by Warren that the commander of his rear division, preparing to head south from Wilderness Tavern, had sighted a heavy butternut column moving toward him on the turnpike, two or three miles west of the Germanna Plank Road intersection. Reacting fast, Meade ordered Warren to bring his other three divisions back to their starting point and advance his whole corps down the pike, in order to confront and, if possible, destroy the rebel force. He believed that it amounted to no more than a division, "left here to fool us," he told Warren, "while they concentrate and prepare a position toward the North Anna," and he saw in the situation an opportunity to effect a considerable subtraction from Lee's army before coming to earnest grips with the rest of it in the open country to the south. With time to spare and the train still grinding slowly down the crowded roads to the east, he could afford a brief delay, especially one that held the promise of so rich a prize. In any case, with his exterior flank so threatened by a force of undetermined strength, he believed the decision was tactically sound; for, as he told Grant in a note informing him of the order for Warren to countermarch and attack, "until this movement of the enemy is developed, the march of the corps must be suspended."

Arriving shortly afterward for a meeting near the tavern, in whose yard Meade was conferring with Warren, Grant not only indorsed his chief lieutenant's aggressive reaction to the news that there were rebels on his flank; he also enlarged upon it, in a characteristic manner, with words that applied not only here but elsewhere. "If any opportunity presents itself for pitching into a part of Lee's army," he told him, "do so without giving time for disposition." In accordance with this policy — which might be described as: "Hit now. Worry later" — when word was brought that another gray force had been spotted marching eastward on the plank road, down around Parker's Store, Hancock too was given orders to backtrack. Instead of continuing down the Catharpin Road to Shady Grove Church, his previous objective, he would turn right when he reached Todd's Tavern and take the Brock Road north to its intersection with the road on which this second rebel column was advancing. Similarly, now that the plot had thickened, Sedgwick was told to send one division to join Warren's turnpike attack and another down the Brock Road to the intersection Hancock had been assigned to cover. His third division would remain on guard at Germanna Ford until Burnside's arrival, expected by midday, when it too would come down and get in on the action — whichever, if either, fight was still in progress by that time — leaving Burnside's four divisions as an available reserve, to be on call if they were needed. Thus Grant, though he still had no specific information as to the size or composition of either rebel column approaching his open flank, was determined to strike them both with everything he had.

While couriers went pounding off to deliver these several messages, Grant and Meade rode a short way down the pike, a bit under half a mile beyond a boggy little stream called Wilderness Run, and turned off into the southwest quadrant of the Germanna Plank Road intersection, where there was a meadow adjoined by a farmhouse belonging to a family named Lacy. Headquarters tents were being pitched there, in accordance with the change in plans, and the two generals dismounted and climbed a knoll on the far side of the field. Grant took a seat on a convenient stump, lighted another of the twenty cigars he distributed among the various pockets of his uniform at the start of every day, and sat calmly, an imperturbable figure wreathed in tobacco smoke, waiting for the attack to be launched beyond the heavy screen of brush at the rim of the clearing. Time dragged, the sun edging slowly toward meridian, and presently he took a penknife out of his trouser pocket, picked up a stick, and started to whittle. Snagged by the blade, the fingertips of his thread gloves began to fray, until at last they were ruined. He took them off, unbuttoned his coat because of the increasing heat, and resumed his whittling. At noon, or a little after, a sudden clatter of stepped-up rifle fire announced that the action had finally opened about one mile down the turnpike.

At first it was difficult to tell how the thing was going. The clatter moved westward, diminished briefly, as if it had paused for breath, then swelled louder than ever and rolled back east for another pause: after which a similar uproar came from the left front, subsided, and then was repeated. Along the limited horizon, west and southwest, the trees began leaking smoke along a line that seemed to conform in general to the one from which the initial attack had been launched an hour ago. All that was clear, so far, was that little or nothing had been gained, although it was fairly certain by now that there were a good many more graybacks out there in the brush than Meade had supposed at the outset. Grant kept whittling.

Presently details filtered rearward, brought to the Lacy meadow by dispatch bearers on lathered horses. Complying with Grant's instructions, relayed by Meade, that he was to give no "time for disposition," Warren had told Brigadier General Charles Griffin, the commander of what had been his rear but now was his lead division, not to wait for word from the heads of the three divisions assigned to support him on the flanks — Brigadier General Horatio G. Wright of Sedgwick's corps, on the march down from Germanna to go in on his right, and Brigadier Generals James S. Wadsworth and Samuel W. Crawford of his own corps, who were countermarching to come up on his left — but to pitch right into the Confederates, hard and fast, as soon as he got his troops in line astride the pike, trusting that the others would be there in time to furnish whatever assistance he might need. That was what he did; but he did so, as it turned out, unsupported in the crisis that resulted. Wright did not arrive for a full two hours, having gotten lost in the woods about as soon as he left the road, and Wadsworth and Crawford only came up in time to get badly mauled themselves, floundering around in the brush as if they were involved in a gigantic and altogether murderous game of blindman's bluff: as indeed they were — particularly Wadsworth, a Hudson River grandee who, at fifty-six, was nine years older than any other division commander in the army. Just now he was feeling the weight of all those years. Trying to navigate by compass in that leafy sea of green, he got badly turned around and drifted northward so that his naked left was exposed to a sudden descent by Gordon's screaming Georgians, who tore into it so savagely that the whole division fell back in disorder, the men crying "Flanked! We're flanked!" as they ran. Crawford caught it even worse from the rallied Alabamians when he came up, groping blind after he lost touch with the navigating Wadsworth. A former army surgeon who had been on duty at Fort Sumter when it fell, he was thirty-four, the next-to-youngest of Meade's division commanders, but he looked considerably older after three years of combat, including a bad wound taken at Antietam. "A tall, chesty, glowering man, with heavy eyes, a big nose, and bushy whiskers," he habitually wore what one of his soldiers described as "a turn-out-the-guard expression." His expression just now, however, was one of outrage. His division had once been Meade's own, made up entirely of Pennsylvanians, and Crawford was outraged at the heavy and useless losses he had suffered, including one veteran regiment captured practically intact when it fled in the wrong direction and found itself surrounded by grinning rebel scarecrows when it stumbled to a halt.

Unquestionably though, to judge by individual reaction, the most outraged man on the field today was Griffin. A hard-case West Pointer and a veteran of the Mexican War at thirty-eight, he was much admired by his men, including a brigade of regulars who had followed him through a lot of fighting over the past two years. An old line artilleryman, he was especially furious at the loss of a section of guns which had to be abandoned down the turnpike when his flanks were overlapped and his troops fell back to avoid being swamped by no less than seven Confederate brigades. The blame, as he saw it, lay with the commanders who had failed to come up on his left and right, and as soon as he managed to stabilize the line his three brigades had fallen back to, he got on his horse and galloped off to protest to Meade in person. Crossing the headquarters meadow, he dismounted and stalked up the knoll at the far side, fuming and cursing as he came. Meade heard him out and did what he could to soothe him, although with small success.

The air was full of God-damns. Finally, relieved by at least having vented his spleen, Griffin went back down the knoll, remounted his horse, and rode off to rejoin his division on the firing line. Grant, who had stopped whittling for the first time while the tirade was in progress, got up from his stump and walked over to Meade. He had not quite caught Griffin's name, but he had never been one to put up with out-of-channels insubordination, even in the easier-going West. "Who is this General Gregg?" he asked. "You ought to put him under arrest." Meade, whose extreme irascibility was masked today by an unaccustomed calm, turned to Grant with the same gentleness he had shown the angry brigadier. "His name's Griffin, not Gregg," he said, "and that's only his way of talking." In grizzled contrast to his younger chief, and towering a full head above him, Meade leaned forward as he spoke and buttoned up Grant's coat for him, as if in concern that he might catch cold after being overheated. Grant went back to his stump and his whittling.

By then it was close to 3 o'clock. Off to the south, although the sound of it did not get through until Warren's had died down, the second battle had been shaping up for the past hour. All that was there at the start was Brigadier General George W. Getty's division of Sedgwick's corps, which had come down from Germanna before midday to take over from a hard-pressed regiment of cavalry the task of delaying the progress of the second Confederate force, in position astride the plank road about half a mile from the Brock Road intersection, while Hancock came up from Todd's Tavern on a march that was much impeded by V Corps artillery, which had halted to await developments. Hancock arrived at 2 o'clock, riding at the head of his four-division column, and when Getty informed him that the graybacks to his front were commanded by the ever-aggressive A. P. Hill and that he might have to fall back at any moment under increasing pressure from such a savage fighter, thus uncovering the crossroad whose loss would cut the army in two and expose its train to capture or destruction, Hancock ignored Grant's instructions to forgo time-consuming preparations and instead put his troops to work improvising crude log breastworks along the road in rear of the position, north and south of the plank road intersection, thus to provide them with something on which to rally in case they were repulsed. Peremptory orders for an immediate advance put an end to this at about 3.30. Leaving Brigadier Generals Francis Barlow's and John Gibbon's divisions posted well down the Brock Road to guard against an attack from the southwest — he had been warned that Longstreet's corps was on the march, somewhere off in that direction, though it was not expected to arrive until tomorrow — Hancock put Major General David Birney's and Brigadier General Gershom Mott's divisions in line on the right and left of Getty's and sent them forward with orders to drive the enemy back on

Parker's Store, three miles from the vital crossroad in their rear, and thus abolish, for once and for all, this threat to the safe passage of the army through the Wilderness, together with its train. It was just past 4 o'clock by then, and on second thought, by way of giving more weight to the blow, he had Gibbon send two of his three brigades to stiffen the center of the attack which had now begun to roll.

It did not roll far, even though at this stage all that blocked the path of these 25,000 attackers was a single gray division with fewer than 7500 in its ranks. Advancing through the tangled brush, the Federals delivered blind volleys of musketry that lopped the saplings at breast height, all across their front, and made it nearly impossible, so heavy and continuous was the fire, for any standing defender to survive. The trouble was that scarcely a Confederate was standing.

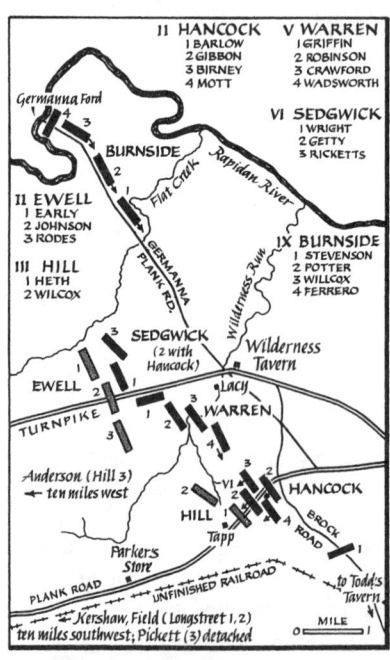

While waiting for a reply to his offer to go forward, if that was what Lee wanted, Heth — like Hancock, who was similarly engaged at the same time, half a mile away on the Brock Road — had had his men dig in and lie low along the slight, densely wooded ridge on which they had halted when the blue resistance stiffened. Prone beneath solid-seeming sheets of lead that slashed the leaves and clipped the breast-high branches, the troops along the ridge replied with volleys of their own. Not only were these as heavy as the ones the front-rank Federals were throwing; they were also a good deal more deadly. Caught thus, erect and unprotected by anything more substantial than smoke and foliage, the attackers suffered cruelly from a foe they could not see. Mott's division, bogged shoetop-deep in a swamp on the left, directly in front of the ridge, broke and ran from that first decimating fire, as did other outfits all along the line. Whole companies, whole regiments fell back in shock and panic, some of them all the way to the log defenses they had built an hour ago. There they were met, individually and collectively, with a curt demand from provost guards with leveled bayonets: "Show blood!" Those who could not show it were hoicked back into line alongside the troops who had not bolted, who were still in position, up there in

The Forty Days

the bullet-whipped brush, firing blind — "by earsight," it was called — in the general direction of the rebels lying prone in comparative safety on their ridge, pumping volley after horrendous volley into the blue mass down in the boggy swale to their immediate front.

Hancock, a hard hitter, never hit harder than he did here in the Wilderness today, despite confounding difficulties of terrain far better suited for defense (once the shock of surprise had been dispelled) than for attack. A second assault was mounted and delivered, then a third and a fourth, all with the disadvantage of trying to maintain alignment, as well as a precarious sense of direction, while attacking veterans who had only to lie low and fire as rapidly as they could load their overheated rifles. Up at army headquarters, where there was full awareness of the importance of keeping the Brock Road clear for travel, Meade had Warren send Wadsworth's division south, across the mile-wide gap between him and Hancock, with instructions to strike the left flank of the rebels, fixed in position by headlong pressure from the front. Hancock meantime was doing all he could to increase that pressure, having added two of Barlow's four brigades to the struggle. This gave him close to 30,000 men in his attack force, even after the deduction of casualties, which were heavy and getting heavier by the minute, including Brigadier General Alexander Hays, a lifelong friend of Grant's and one of the heroes of Gettysburg, killed at the head of his brigade in Birney's division. However, Lee by then had recalled Wilcox from his attempt to link up with Ewell and close the gap across the center. He came back fast and went in hard, supporting Heth just as his flank was about to crumble. This doubled the number of defenders and reduced the odds from three- to two-to-one. Even so, the issue could not have remained much longer in doubt, except that gathering darkness finally ended the contest. It dwindled by common consent, then flared up momentarily as Wadsworth finally arrived in the twilight after thrashing around in the brush on a three-hour search for the battle raging furiously one mile to the south. When he came up, in position at last to wreck the interior rebel flank, Lee had no reserves to throw in his path except a single Alabama battalion of 125 men, detailed to guard the host of prisoners who had been streaming rearward ever since the fight began. The Alabamians formed a widespread skirmish line, leaving the prisoners to the care of a handful of wounded, and went in yelling for all they were worth, quite as if they had an army at their backs. Wadsworth stumbled to a halt, apparently convinced that his jungle-foundered soldiers were about to be swamped by superior numbers, and hastily took up a stout defensive position on Hancock's right as night came down.

While both sides turned to attend to such of their wounded as they could reach — lucky ones, these, compared to others caught between the lines, calling for help that could not come because the slightest movement drew instant volleys from troops made panicky by fear of a night attack at such close quarters, or trapped by fires that sprang up and spread rapidly when the night breeze rose and fanned the sparks in the dry leaves to flames — Grant went to his headquarters tent in the Lacy meadow to study reports of what had happened today and to make plans for what he wanted to happen tomorrow. He would, of course, continue the offensive on both fronts, though his best chance for a breakthrough seemed to lie with Hancock, who reported that he would have made one today if darkness had not ended the battle an hour too soon. Sedgwick, joined late in the day by his third division under Brigadier General James B. Ricketts, would remain in position on the right of the northern sector, with Warren, minus Wadsworth, on the left. These five divisions had attacked again near sunset, but with no greater success than before; Ewell, buttoned up tight in his intrenchments, would not budge. Tomorrow's attack in this sector would be made primarily to prevent him from sending reinforcements down to Hill, who was to be hit with everything Hancock could lay hands on: his own four divisions, plus one from each of the other three corps, including Burnside's, which had been arriving all afternoon, too late for today's fight but in plenty of time for tomorrow's. In addition to sending one division to Hancock, Burnside would leave another on guard at Germanna Ford and march the other two down the Germanna Plank Road tonight, turning off, south of the turnpike intersection, to move west through the woods for a plunge into the gap between Warren's left and Hancock's right and a drive against Hill's interior flank, which he would assail by turning south again, as soon as he was well into the gap between the two Confederate corps. Such was Grant's victory formula, compounded tonight for application tomorrow.

Jump-off time, he said, would be at first light, 4 o'clock. Sedgwick and Warren, with five divisions, would attack and pin down Ewell, while Hancock and Burnside, with nine divisions, were overrunning Hill — and Longstreet too, if he arrived by then and was put into that portion of the line. All that was known just now was that he was on the march, somewhere off to the south and west; Hancock was warned to be on the lookout for him on the far left, in case Lee tried something foxy in that direction, though Grant was as usual a good deal more intent on what he had in mind to do to the enemy than he was on what the enemy might or might not do to him. Meade was in full agreement with these orders, as indeed he had been with all orders from the start, except that he suggested that the jump-off be advanced an hour to sunrise, 5 o'clock, so that the troops commanders would have a little daylight time in which to get their men in line for the assault. Grant considered this briefly, then agreed, and the two turned in, along with their staffs, to get some sleep for the hard day coming up.

. . .

Lee too was planning an offensive for tomorrow, and he intended, moreover, to launch it in the same region Grant had chosen as the scene of his main effort: in the vicinity of the plank road intersection. This involved a revision, not of purpose — the Virginian had counted, all along, on going over to the offensive as soon as his whole army was at hand — but of method. Formerly Longstreet had been told to proceed up the Catharpin Road to Todd's Tavern, a position from which he could turn the Union left, but the daylong need for closing the tactically dangerous gap between Hill and Ewell now provoked a change of plans, whereby Old Peter would shift from the Catharpin to the Plank Road and come up, not on Hill's right, but in his rear; Little Powell then could sidle northward to connect with Ewell, thus abolishing the gap, while Longstreet took over his position and prepared to launch, with his own two divisions and Hill's third, a dawn attack designed to crumple Grant's left flank, roll it up, and in conjunction with Hill and Ewell, who would advance in turn against the Federals to their front, fling the blue invaders back across the Rapidan. Accordingly, around 7 o'clock, while Hill's battle was still raging and the outcome was in doubt, Lee sent Longstreet word of the change in objectives, together with a guide to insure against going astray on the cross-country night march he would have to make in order to get from one road to the other. A message went at the same time to Major General Richard Anderson, commander of Hill's third division, which had moved from Orange to Verdiersville today, instructing him to continue his march up the plank road beyond Parker's Store tonight, in order to be with Longstreet in plenty of time for the attack at first light tomorrow.

Heth and Wilcox — who could testify to the all-too-probable truth of Hancock's claim, across the way, that another hour of daylight would have given him the breakthrough he had been seeking — were pleased to learn from Hill that Longstreet and Anderson would be up tonight to relieve their fought-out men. Whether Lee had revised his previous estimate of the enemy strength or not, Little Powell was convinced that his 15,000 veterans had taken on upwards of 40,000 bluecoats in the Wilderness today, and he had little patience with the concern of his two division commanders about the tangled condition of their lines, which had come so close to buckling under repeated assaults that, in the words of one witness, "they were like a worm fence, at every angle." Heth went to Hill and told him flatly: "A skirmish line could drive my division and Wilcox's, situated as we now are." He proposed that a new line be drawn, just in rear of their present disordered position, for them to fall back on before morning, when, as he predicted, "we shall certainly be attacked." Little Powell would not hear of this, partly because such a move would have meant abandoning many of the wounded and also because it would rob his soldiers of their hard-earned rest. "Longstreet will be up in a few hours," he said. "He will form in your front.... The men have been marching and fighting all day and are tired. I don't wish them disturbed." Heth went back to his troops, but soon returned with Wilcox, who joined him in the proposal that both divisions be withdrawn to a new line. Hill repeated that he wanted the men to get their sleep between now and midnight, when Longstreet was expected. They went away, but Heth, whose heart was heavy with foreboding, came back for still a third time to renew the argument. This vexed Hill, whose own sleep was being interrupted now. "Damn it, Heth," he said angrily, "I don't want to hear any more about it. The men shall not be disturbed." Heth retired for good this time, though it was already after midnight and Longstreet was obviously behind schedule. 1 o'clock, 2 o'clock, 3 o'clock passed, and still there was no news that Old Peter was approaching. Not long before dawn, the two division commanders sent for a battalion of corps engineers to come forward with picks and shovels in a belated attempt to complete the neglected intrenchments before they were overrun by the blue attackers Heth was convinced would come with the sun, if not sooner.

Back at the Tapp farm, Lee had known since 10 o'clock that the First Corps would not be up till daylight at the earliest. The young cavalry officer who had ridden down to the Catharpin Road with instructions for the change in routes, Major Henry McClellan of Stuart's staff, had also been charged with giving Longstreet's lead division verbal orders to press on without delay, thereby assuring an early arrival in Hill's rear. He left about 7 and returned three hours later, highly indignant, to report to Lee that the commander of that division, Major General Charles W. Field, a West Pointer and a stickler for regulations — he had lately been promoted and appointed to his post, having served in Richmond as superintendent of the Bureau of Conscription since the loss of a leg at Second Manassas, twenty months ago — flatly declined to accept from a stray cavalryman possibly garbled verbal orders that were in contradiction to the ones he had received from his corps commander, which were that he was to rest his men at Richard's Shop until 1 o'clock in the morning. Then and not until then, he said stiffly, would the march be resumed. This meant that Old Peter's leading elements could scarcely arrive before sunup, since the distance from Richard's Shop was about a dozen miles, two or three of them over rugged terrain, across fields, through woods, and by roundabout lanes connecting the two main roads; but Lee seemed oddly unperturbed. When McClellan offered to ride back with written orders which Field would have no choice except to obey, the Virginian declined with a shake of his gray head. "No, Major," he said calmly. "It is now past 10 o'clock, and by the time you could return to General Field and he could put his division in motion, it would be 1 o'clock. At that hour he will move."

Lee returned to his tent for more paper work, including an 11 o'clock dispatch informing the Secretary of War of what had occurred since Grant's crossing of the Rapidan the day before — "By the blessing of God," he wrote of today's hard fight, "we maintained our position against every effort until night, when the contest closed" — then turned in for another four or five hours of sleep before rising to face what might well be disaster.

He did not mention the possibility of disaster or its cause, either to Seddon in Richmond or to Hill, whose troops were sleeping helter-skelter in the brush, in whatever random positions they had occupied when darkness ended the fighting and they fell asleep on their arms, many of them too weary to eat the scant rations sent up later in the evening. Perhaps, like Little Powell, Lee reasoned that rest would do more for them than would fretting about a situation they could do but little to repair in the few hours of darkness that remained. In any case, he left them and their commander undisturbed until dawn began to filter through the thickets and a popping of rifles, like individual handclaps, warned that another day of battle had begun: May 6. Exposed by daylight to this picket fire, the engineers dropped their picks and shovels, which they had had small chance to use, and scuttled rearward. Within an hour, sharply at 5 o'clock as the sun was rising, this intermittent racket merged and grew in abrupt intensity to a steady clatter, described by one observer as "the noise of a boy running with a stick pressed against a paling fence, faster and faster until it swelled into a continuous rattling roar." The Federals were attacking in greater strength than yesterday, along and down both sides of the plank road, and after a brief resistance the two Confederate divisions did just what Heth had said they would do. They broke. Though they did not scatter in panic or drop their rifles, still they made for the rear, more or less in a body, some among them firing as they went. "The men seemed to fall back upon a deliberate conviction that it was impossible to hold the ground and, of course, foolish to attempt it," one among them later wrote by way of explanation, adding rather philosophically: "It was mortifying, but it was only what every veteran has experienced."

Up on Ewell's front the dug-in troops held firm under assault, but Sedgwick and Warren were accomplishing all that was asked of them by keeping him from sending reinforcements down to the far end of the line. Such flaw as there was in the execution of Grant's plan was in the center. Burnside, ordered to penetrate the rebel gap and descend on Hill's interior flank, had gotten himself and his two divisions lost as soon as he left the road last night and struck out through the brush; he was somewhere rearward now, behind the space between Warren and Hancock, disoriented and wandering in circles while the conflict raged, first to his right, then his left, sometimes front and sometimes rear. Hancock was furious at this dereliction. Shouting to be heard above the din on the plank road, he told one of Meade's staff officers that if those missing 10,000 men could be added to the pressure being exerted, "we could smash A. P. Hill all to pieces!" In point of fact, he seemed well on the way to doing it anyhow. Except for the troops with Barlow, whose division had been reunited down the Brock Road to guard against a possible flank attack, he had all the men assigned to the main effort massed and in motion, flushing graybacks as they went. Forty years old, "a tall, soldierly man with light brown hair and a military jaw," he had what the staffer described as "the massive features and the heavy folds round the eye that often mark a man of ability." Elated by the propitious opening of that portion of the battle in his charge, he made a handsome figure on horseback, and his elation grew as the attack continued. Just ahead was the Tapp clearing, and beyond it the white tops of wagons parked in the Confederate rear. "We are driving them, sir!" Hancock called proudly to the staff man. "Tell General Meade we are driving them most beautifully."

Lee was there in the clearing, doing all he could to stiffen what little was left of Hill's resistance, and so had Longstreet himself been there, momentarily at least, when the blue assault was launched. He came riding up just before sunrise, a mile or two in advance of his column, the head of which had reached Parker's Store by then, and Hill's chief of staff crossed the Tapp farmyard to welcome him as he turned off the road. "Ah, General, we have been looking for you since 12 o'clock last night. We expect to be attacked at any moment, and are not in any shape to resist." Unaccustomed to being reproached by unstrung colonels, however valid their anxiety, Old Peter looked sternly down at him. "My troops are not up," he said. "I've ridden ahead — " At this point the sudden clatter of Hancock's attack erupted out in the brush, and Longstreet, without waiting to learn more of what had happened, whirled his horse and galloped back to hurry his two divisions forward. So Lee at least knew that the First Corps would soon be up. His problem, after sending his adjutant to order the wagon train prepared for withdrawal, was to hang on till these reinforcements got there, probably within the hour, to shore up Hill's fast-crumbling line. Presently, though, this began to look like more than he could manage; Wilcox and Heth, overlapped on both flanks, gave ground rapidly before a solid mass of attackers, and skulkers began to drift rearward across the clearing, singly and in groups, some of them turning to fire from time to time at their pursuers, while others seemed only intent on escape. Their number increased, until finally Lee saw a whole brigade in full retreat. Moreover, this was not just any brigade; it was Brigadier General Samuel McGowan's brigade of South Carolinians, Wilcox's best and one of the finest in the army.

"My God, General McGowan!" Lee exclaimed from horseback,

breasting the flood of fugitives. "Is this splendid brigade of yours running like a flock of geese?"

"General, these men are not whipped," McGowan answered, stung in his pride by this public rebuke. "They only want a place to form and they will fight as well as they ever did."

But there was the rub. All that was left by now for them to form on was a battalion of Third Corps artillery, four batteries under twenty-eight-year-old Lieutenant Colonel William Poague, lined up along the west side of the clearing which afforded one of the Wilderness's few real fields of fire. The cannoneers stood to their loaded pieces, waiting for Hill's infantry to fall back far enough to give them a chance to shoot at the bluecoats in pursuit. However, there was no time for this; Poague, with Lee's approval, had his guns open at what was already point-blank range, shaving the heads of the Confederate retreaters in order to throw their anti-personnel rounds into the enemy ranks. This took quick effect, particularly near the road, where the Federals tended to bunch up. Flailed by double-shotted grape and canister, they paused and began to look for cover: seeing which, the cannoneers stepped up their rate of fire. Lee remained mounted alongside Poague, who kept his men at their work — "getting the starch out of our shirts," they called it — without infantry support. This could not continue long before they would be overrun, but meantime they were making the most of it. Smoke from the guns drifted back, sparkling in the early-morning sunlight, and presently Lee saw through its rearward swirls a cluster of men running toward him, carrying their rifles at the ready and shouldering Hill's fugitives aside.

"Who are you, my boys?" he cried as they came up in rear of the line of bucking guns.

"Texas boys!" they yelled, gathering now in larger numbers, and Lee knew them: Hood's Texans, his old-time shock troops, now under Brigadier General John Gregg — the lead brigade of Field's division. Longstreet was up at last.

"Hurrah for Texas!" Lee shouted. He took off his wide-brimmed hat and waved it. "Hurrah for Texas!"

No one had ever seen him act this way before, either on or off the field of battle. And presently, when the guns ceased their fuming and the Texans started forward, they saw something else they had never seen: something that froze the cheers in their throats and brought them to a halt. When Gregg gave the order, "Attention, Texas Brigade! The eyes of General Lee are upon you. Forward... march!" Lee rose in his stirrups and lifted his hat. "Texans always move them," he declared. They cheered as they stepped out between the guns. "I would charge hell itself for that old man," a veteran said fervently. Then they saw the one thing that could stop them. Lee had spurred Traveller forward on their heels; he intended to go in with them, across the field and after the bluecoats in the brush. They slacked their pace and left off cheering. "Lee to the rear!" began to be heard along the line, and some of them addressed him directly: "Go back, General Lee, go back. We won't go unless you go back." He was among them now, flushed with excitement, his eyes fixed on the woods ahead. They stopped, and when an attempt by Gregg to head him off had no effect, a sergeant reached out and took hold of Traveller's rein, bringing the animal to a halt. "Lee to the rear! Lee to the rear!" the men were shouting. But his blood was up; he did not seem to hear them, or even to know that he and they were no longer in motion. At this point a staff colonel intervened. "General, you've been looking for General Longstreet. There he is, over yonder." Lee looked and saw, at the far end of the field, the man he called his war horse. For the first time since he cleared the line of guns he seemed to become aware that he was involved in something larger than a charge. Responding to the colonel's suggestion, he turned Traveller's head and rode in that direction. On the way he passed in rear of Brigadier General Evander Law's Alabama brigade, about to move out on the left. "What troops are these?" he asked, and on being told he called to them: "God bless the Alabamians!" They went forward with a whoop, alongside the Texans, who were whooping too. "I thought him at that moment the grandest specimen of manhood I ever beheld," one among them later wrote. "He looked as though he ought to have been, and was, the monarch of the world."

Longstreet yielded to no man in his admiration for Lee, yet his admiration never amounted to idolatry, especially if idolatry included a willingness to put up with tactical interference. Seeing him thus "off his balance," he later wrote, he informed him with jocular bluntness, as soon as he came up, "that his line would be recovered in an hour if he would permit me to handle the troops, but if my services were not needed I would like to ride to some place of safety, as it was not quite comfortable where we were." Lee complied by retiring westward a short distance with his staff officers, who no doubt were glad to get him out of there, and Old Peter kept his word, here and on the opposite side of the plank road as well.

There his other division had been put in line by its commander, Brigadier General Joseph Kershaw, whose Georgians, South Carolinians, and Mississippians hooted cruelly when Heth's badly shaken troops fell back through their ranks. "Do you belong to Lee's army?" they jeered, seeing their old comrades thus for the first time in eight months. "You don't look like the men we left here. You're worse than Bragg's men!" Taking over, they stalled Hancock's advance on this side of the road, while Field was doing the same across the way. Then the two divisions went forward together against the Federals, who were wearier and a good deal more disorganized than they had known until they were brought to a halt, first by Poague's four rapid-firing batteries and then by 10,000 newly committed rebels whose appearance was as sudden as if they had dropped out of the sky. Still, the going was rough for the First Corps, most of whose members had never fought in the region west of Fredericksburg before. Some brigades lost heavily, including the Texans, who went in boasting that they had "put General Lee under arrest and sent him to the rear." A captured private from the brigade expressed its collective opinion when his captors asked him what he thought of this Battle of the Wilderness. "Battle be damned," he said hotly. "It aint no battle, it's a worse riot than Chickamauga! At Chickamauga there was at least a rear, but here there aint neither front nor rear. It's all a damned mess! And our two armies aint nothing but howling mobs."

Before 10 o'clock, despite the various impediments of terrain and the refusal by most of Hancock's men to panic under pressure, Longstreet fulfilled his promise to recover the line that had begun to be lost at sunrise. Halting there, within half a mile of the Brock Road, he proceeded to consolidate the position, reinforced presently by Anderson, whose division arrived while the First Corps was advancing and moved up in its support. Hill meantime had rallied his other two divisions and swung them northward, in accordance with Lee's orders, to plug the gap that had yawned since yesterday between him and Ewell. Finding it unexploited by the Federals, whose own gap had been enlarged by Longstreet — Law's whooping Alabamians had struck and scattered Wadsworth's ill-starred division on Hancock's right, driving the remnant west and north, all the way to the Lacy meadow, and Burnside was still on his circuitous tour of the brush — Hill's men, willingly and hurriedly, did what they had failed to do the night before. They intrenched. Lee's line was now a continuous one, reasonably compact, and he had all his troops on hand at last, including Ewell's detached brigade, which arrived at midmorning from Hanover. The time had come for him to go over to the all-out offensive he had planned to launch as soon as he managed to bring Grant to a standstill in the thickets — as he now had done.

"There was a lull all along the line," a regimental commander later said of this period during which reconnaissance parties went out and came back and last-minute instructions were delivered: adding, "It was the ominous silence that precedes the tornado."

Tactically, Grant was in far worse shape than he or anyone else in the Lacy meadow seemed to know. In addition to the unmanned gap across his center, he had both flanks in the air. No blue army had ever remained long in any such attitude, here in Virginia, without suffering grievously at the hands of Lee for having been so neglectful or inept; Hooker, for example, had left only one flank open, but his discomfiture had been complete. Now the same treatment might well be in store for Grant, on practically that same ground just one year later.

Headquarters had been more or less in a turmoil for the past two hours, ever since Hancock's attack went into reverse. First, there was the matter of Burnside's nonarrival, which not only reduced the intended strength of the main effort but also left it unsupported on the right, exposing Wadsworth to the catastrophe that ensued. In point of fact, after all that had happened yesterday, the aging New Yorker — a brigadier since shortly after First Bull Run, military governor of the District of Columbia during the tenure of McClellan, whom he had helped to frustrate, and an unsuccessful candidate for governor of his home state on the Republican ticket in '62, the year of the Democratic sweep — had seemed to suspect from the start that today would be no better. He was feeling his years, and he told an aide he thought perhaps he ought to turn the command of his division over to someone else and go to the rear. As it was, however, he stayed and managed, today as yesterday, to lose his sense of direction in the course of the attack and came crowding down on the units to his left, creating a jam on the near side of the plank road and thereby adding to the effectiveness of Poague's fire from the Tapp farmyard, as well as to the confusion that prevailed when Law assailed his unprotected right. One of his three brigades disintegrated without more ado, and Wadsworth, in an attempt to keep the other two from doing likewise, appealed to them from horseback to stand firm; whereupon he was hit in the back of the head and fell to the ground with a bullet in his brain. His troops ran off and left him, pursued by the rebels, who gathered him up and took him back to one of their aid stations. (He died there two days later, having been stared at by a great many of his enemies, who came for a look at a man reputed to possess "more wealth than the treasury of the Confederate government." Rich men were not unusual in the armies of the South, where the West Point tradition was strong in leading families and no $300 commutation fee could secure exemption from conscription, but were rarely encountered on the other side, particularly on the firing line.) Meantime the fallen general's troops continued their flight all the way to the Lacy meadow, as if they expected to find sanctuary there with Grant, who sat on his accustomed stump atop the knoll, still whittling, still wreathed in cigar smoke. Headquarters was alarmed by their sudden appearance, even though they did not seem to be pursued, and presently, when long-range shots began to fall in the vicinity, an anxious staffer, fearful that the meadow was about to be overrun, suggested that it would be prudent to shift the command post rearward. Grant stopped whittling. "It strikes me it would be better to order up some artillery and defend the present location," he said quietly. This was done, although there was nothing the gunners could see in the way of targets, and Hancock bolstered what remained of Wadsworth's division by sending reinforcements over from the left.

On the right, Sedgwick and Warren had suffered heavy losses in carrying out their instructions to keep attacking Ewell's intrenchments and thus prevent his sending reinforcements down to Hill. This they had done, and in doing it they had kept him on the defensive. But if they assumed from this that he would remain so, or that Sedgwick's outer flank was secure because it was covered by Flat Creek, they would be disabused before nightfall; Gordon, whose brigade was on the left, was trying even now to get permission from his superiors to turn the Federal flank, which he insisted was wide open to such a maneuver, having scouted it himself. So far, Ewell and Early had declined to let him try it, being convinced that Burnside's corps was posted rearward in support. Obviously, Sedgwick's immunity from attack, based as it was on this misconception by Gordon's superiors, was going to last no longer than Burnside remained unaccounted for in the Union order of battle. Once he found his way up to the firing line and was identified, Ewell and Early would have to abandon their objection to Gordon's proposal and unleash him, with results that were likely to be spectacular if Sedgwick's dispositions were as faulty as the Georgian claimed to have seen with his own eyes.

Just now, however — for Burnside, having spent the past five hours out of pocket, was to spend another three in the same fashion, lost to friend and foe alike, before he managed to get where he belonged — the gravest danger was on the opposite flank, which was also exposed to being turned or struck end-on. This was due to a combination of misconceptions, based on erroneous information from headquarters. Hancock had kept Barlow in position down the Brock Road all this time, yesterday and today, in expectation that Longstreet would arrive from that direction. Instead he had come up the plank road, converting Hill's near rout into a counteroffensive; but Hancock still held Barlow where he was, outside the action, because only two of Old Peter's divisions, Field's and Kershaw's, had so far been identified. The third, Pickett's — reported to have been with Longstreet at Gordonsville, though in fact it was south of Richmond — might be maneuvering for an attack up the Brock Road, perhaps in conjunction with Anderson's division of Hill's corps, which had also not yet been accounted for. So Barlow was kept where he was, a mile and a half from the plank road intersection, to guard against a tangential strike by these 10,000 missing rebels. Meantime, evidence had accumulated to support the belief that they were already at hand, including one frantic eyewitness report that they were advancing in mass up the Brock Road. This was a case of mistaken identity; the advancing mass turned out to be a herd of Federal convalescents, marching from

Chancellorsville to rejoin the army by Hancock's roundabout route. No sooner was this mistake discovered, however, than heavy firing was heard from down around Todd's Tavern, where the Brock and Catharpin roads intersected, less than three miles from Barlow's outpost on the Union left. The assumption was that the cavalry must have encountered Pickett's column, coming up from the Catharpin Road, and was doing what it could to hold him off while Barlow got ready to receive him. This was partly correct and partly wrong. It was cavalry, right enough, but that was all it was. The blue troopers were shooting, not at Pickett (who was perhaps of greater service to his country here today, though he was not within sixty miles of the battle, than he had been ten months ago at Gettysburg, leading the charge that would be known forever after by his name) but at Stuart. Sheridan had served Grant poorly yesterday by plunging eastward, with two thirds of the army's cavalry, into the vacuum Stuart had left around Fredericksburg when he moved westward to take position on Lee's right. Still intent on closing with the graybacks, more for the purpose of destroying them than of finding out what was happening in their rear, Sheridan's horsemen made such a racket with their rapid-firing carbines that Barlow thought a large-scale action was in progress, though in fact it was nothing more than an unprofitable skirmish, which did not result in the slightest penetration of the cavalry screen Stuart kept tightly drawn to prevent his adversary from catching even a glimpse of the preparations now being made for attack, four miles northwest. As it was, Barlow was so impressed by the uproar down around Todd's Tavern that he called urgently for reinforcements to help him meet what he was convinced was coming, and Hancock obliged by sending him two brigades from the main body, which by then was back on the line it had left at sunrise.

Hancock had his hands full where he was, holding Longstreet west of the Brock Road, immediately north and south of the plank road intersection. For better than five hours now, advancing and retreating, the fighting had been as heavy as any he had ever seen, and so too had his casualties and the expenditure of ammunition. Drummer boys were pressed into unfamiliar service as stretcher bearers, and when they got to the rear with their anguished burdens, the stretchers were loaded with boxes of cartridges for the return to the firing line, so that, as one reporter wrote, "the struggle shall not cease for want of ball and powder." Involved as he was in the direction of all this, blinded by thickets and appealed to simultaneously from the left and right — Barlow was convinced that he was about to be hit by Pickett, and Wadsworth's division, adjacent to the unmanned gap across the army's center, had just come apart at the seams — Hancock was apparently too busy to notice that the contraction of his front in the vicinity of the crossroad, resulting from his losses and the withdrawal

The Forty Days

of four brigades to meet the reported dangers on the far left and the right, had widened to about a mile the brush-choked interval between the main body and Barlow's outpost position down the road. Consequently, though he was reasonably well protected against a flank attack by Pickett, who wasn't there, he was not protected at all from one by Longstreet, who was. His immediate left — as Gordon was saying of Sedgwick's right, four miles away — was wide open to either a turning movement or an end-on strike.

Then came the lull, a half-hour breathing space. Hancock spent it shoring up his line against an expected renewal of Longstreet's frontal effort to drive him back from the vital crossroad. Atop the knoll in the Lacy meadow, Grant, with a hole in his center and both flanks in the air, continued to whittle. Then, around 11 o'clock, the storm broke. Within minutes of the opening shots, according to Meade's chief of staff, the uproar of the rebel attack "approached the sublime."

"Longstreet, always grand in battle, never shone as he did here," a First Corps artillerist said of the general in his conduct of this morning's fighting on the right. Within three hours of his arrival he introduced tactics into a battle which, up to then, had been little more than a twenty-hour slugging match, with first one side then the other surging forward through the brush, only to fall back when momentum was lost and the enemy took his turn at going over to the offensive. All attacks had been frontal except for chance encounters, when some confused unit — a regiment or a brigade or, as in Wadsworth's case, a division — got turned around, usually in the course of an advance through blinding thickets, and exposed a naked flank to being torn. Now Old Peter, who was always at his calmest when the conflict roared its loudest, undertook to serve a Federal corps, reinforced to a strength of seven divisions, in that same tearing fashion.

Lee had ordered the army's chief engineer, Major General Martin L. Smith, to report to Longstreet at about the time the Federals began to yield the ground they had won from Hill. Sent out to reconnoiter the Union left, Smith — a forty-four-year-old New-York-born West Pointer whose most distinguished service to his adopted country up to now had been at Vicksburg, where he not only laid out and supervised the construction of its hilly defenses, but also commanded one of the divisions that manned them under siege — returned at 10 o'clock to report that he had found Hancock's flank wide open to attack from within the mile-wide gap that yawned between his main body and Barlow's outpost. Moreover, an unfinished and unmapped railroad, work on which had been abandoned when the war began, afforded an ideal covered approach to that vulnerable point; troops could be massed in the brush-screened cut, just where the roadbed made a turn southeast, perpendicular to the unguarded flank a briery quarter mile away.

Old Peter's eyes lighted up at the news, but he was no more inclined to be precipitate here than he had been at Second Manassas when a similar opportunity arose. He summoned his young chief of staff, Lieutenant Colonel G. Moxley Sorrel, instructed him to take charge of a force made up of three brigades, one from each of the three divisions at hand, and conduct them to the designated point for the attack. Knowing how likely such maneuvers were to become disorganized under the influence of exuberance, he stressed the need for careful preparation. "Form a good line," he told him, "and then move, your right pushed forward and turning as much as possible to the left." Characteristically, before sending him on his way, he added in true First Corps style: "Hit hard when you start, but don't start until you have everything ready."

Sorrel assembled the three brigades, headed by Brigadier Generals William Wofford, G. T. Anderson, and William Mahone, respectively from Kershaw's, Field's, and Richard Anderson's divisions, and just as he was about to move out, Colonel John M. Stone of Heth's division, in position on Longstreet's left, requested permission to add the weight of his Mississippi brigade to the blow about to be struck. Hill and Heth were willing, and that made four brigades from as many divisions, a pair each from two corps, not one of them under a professional soldier and all in charge of a young staff officer who never before had commanded troops in action. Sorrel was a former bank clerk, twenty-six years old, intensely ambitious and strikingly handsome, a Georgian like his chief, though of French not Dutch extraction. As he set out, leading this force of about 5000 into the railway cut, then eastward through its leafy tunnel to the bend where they would mass for the attack, he knew that his great hour had come and he was determined to make the most of it, for his own and his country's sake. Old Peter, who had a great affection for him dating back to First Manassas, watched him disappear in the woods, then settled back to wait for the uproar that would signal the launching of the flank assault. He kept his remaining eleven brigades in position astride the plank road, maintaining frontal contact and preparing to increase the pressure when the time came. Already he was planning a larger turning movement to follow the one about to start. Once Hancock's line had been rolled up, the fronts of the other two Confederate corps would be uncovered in rapid sequence; Hill's two divisions would join the grand left wheel, and Ewell's three would drive straight ahead, cutting the Federals off from the fords by which they had crossed the Rapidan. Obliged to fall back on Fredericksburg, Grant's army would be cut to pieces, train and all, as it jammed the narrow Wilderness trails and scattered in the brush. Anticipation made the wait seem long, though in fact it was quite brief. At 11 o'clock, within half an hour of his setting out, Sorrel's attack exploded on the Union left and began to roll northward, clattering across the right front of the Confederate position. Longstreet ordered his main body forward simultaneously to exploit and enlarge the panic already evident in the enemy ranks.

The end-on blow was as successful as even Sorrel had dared to hope it would be. Struck without preamble by a horde of rapid-firing rebels who came screaming through what up to then had been a curtain of peaceful green, the first blue unit — a brigade that had just been withdrawn from the line to catch its breath while the lull was on — disintegrated on contact, its members taking off in all directions to escape the sudden onslaught, and though others reacted differently, having at least had a semblance of warning that something horrendous was headed in their direction from the left, the result was much the same in the end, as unit after unit, finding itself under simultaneous fire from the front and flank, sought to achieve a similar deliverance from fury. Consternation in such cases was followed by a strangely deliberate acceptance of the military facts of life, the difference being that they reacted, not as individuals, but as a group seeking safety in numbers. A man from one of Gibbon's brigades reported that the first he knew of a flank attack was when he saw troops from Mott's division, on his left, trudging rearward in a body. At first, so deliberate was their step, so oddly sullen their expression, he could not make out what was happening. "[They] did not seem to me demoralized in manner," he declared, "nor did they present the appearance of soldiers moving under orders, but rather of a throng of armed men returning dissatisfied from a muster." The best explanation another observer could give was that "a large number of troops were about to leave the service," and apparently they were doing all they could to leave it alive. One thing at least was clear to a staff officer who watched them slogging rearward, oblivious to pleas and threats alike. "They had fought all they meant to fight for the present," he said, "and there was an end to it." Hancock himself put it simplest, in a statement years later to Longstreet: "You rolled me up like a wet blanket."

Elation on the Confederate side was correspondingly great, and it too was a sort of mass reaction. Here, the cheering troops perceived as soon as the flank attack began to roll, was another Chancellorsville in the making. Moreover, they were aware of the highly encouraging difference that, instead of launching their turning movement with a scant two hours of daylight left for its exploitation, as Jackson's men had done, they now had a substantial eight or nine such hours: enough, surely, to complete the destruction already under way. Not that they wasted time, simply because so much of it was available; Sorrel had carried out his orders with speed and precision. Wofford and Mahone were abreast in front, respectively on the left and right, supported by G. T. Anderson and Stone, whose added pressure shattered what little resistance was encountered or by-passed in the course of the advance.

Within less than an hour they had driven northward all the way to the plank road; some of Wofford's Georgians, in fact, plunged eagerly across it, intent on the chase, though Mahone's Virginians called a halt at that point, in accordance with instructions. When Sorrel rode up he found the plank road unobstructed all the way to its intersection with the Brock Road, where the displaced and rattled Federals were taking shelter behind the breastworks Hancock had had them build the day before. From the opposite direction he saw Longstreet and his staff riding toward him on the plank road, accompanied by several unit commanders to whom the burly lieutenant general was apparently giving directions for the follow-up assault. They made up a sizeable cavalcade, and Sorrel could see from their manner, their gestures and expressions as they rode, that they shared the exuberance he was feeling at the success of his first experience as a leader of men in battle.

Their high spirits were voiced by Brigadier General Micah Jenkins, the twenty-eight-year-old commander of a brigade in Field's division, who had just been informed that his troops would play a major role in the follow-up attack. "I am happy," the young South Carolina aristocrat told Longstreet, excited by the prospect of enlarging the gains already made. "I have felt despair for the cause for some months, but now I am relieved, and feel assured that we will put the enemy back across the Rapidan before night." When Sorrel came up Jenkins embraced and congratulated him warmly. "We will smash them now," he said.

Old Peter thought so, too. Engineer Smith had returned from a second reconnaissance of the Union left to report that a second turning movement, designed to flank the rallying bluecoats out of their breastworks along the Brock Road, was altogether as feasible as the first. Just then, however, as the cavalcade continued its ride east to within musket range of the Brock Road intersection, there was a sudden spatter of fire from the woods to the right front; some of Mahone's men were shooting at some of Wofford's, having mistaken them for Federals when they came hurrying back across the plank road to take their proper place in line. Aggressive as always, Longstreet whirled his horse in that direction, apparently intending to stop the undisciplined firing. Others followed his example — including Joe Kershaw, who had ridden forward to confer with Wofford on the condition of his detached brigade — and were met by a heavier volley from the Virginians in the woods. Four men were hit: a courier and a staff captain, both of whom were killed instantly, Micah Jenkins, who died a few hours later with a bullet in his brain, and Longstreet. "Friends! They are *friends!*" Kershaw shouted in a voice that rang above the clatter and the groans, and almost at once Mahone's veterans ceased firing and hurried out of the woods to express their regret for what had happened.

The Forty Days

By then solicitous hands were helping the wounded lieutenant general to dismount. Hit solidly by a bullet that passed through the base of his neck and lodged in his right shoulder, he had been lifted straight up by the impact and had come down hard, his right arm hanging useless, though he managed to stay in the saddle, bleeding heavily, until his companions were there to ease him to the ground, the upper part of his body propped against the trunk of a roadside tree. Exultation turned to dismay as word spread rapidly through the Wilderness that Old Peter had been hit. All down the line, men's thoughts were more than ever of Chancellorsville, but with the bitter irony of remembering that Jackson too had been shot by his own soldiers, less than four miles up the road through these same woods, at the climax of a successful flank attack. As for Longstreet, his thoughts were neither on the past nor on the present, despite his pain. His concern was for the immediate future, the follow-up assault that would complete his victory. Field being the ranking division commander present in the corps, Longstreet blew the bloody foam from his mouth to say to Sorrel: "Tell General Field to take command, and move forward with the whole force and gain the Brock Road." Soon his staff physician was there to tend his wounds, and when Lee arrived he told him, in such detail as his shaken vocal cords allowed, of his plan for turning the Federals out of their new position. By now a stretcher had been brought. He was lifted onto it, his hat placed over his face to shield his eyes, and carried back down the plank road to a waiting ambulance. On the way, when he heard troops by the roadside saying, "He is dead. They are only telling us he is wounded," he raised his hat from his face with his usable hand. The answering cheers, he declared long afterward, served to ease his pain somewhat on the jolting rearward journey.

A wandering artillery major, on a fruitless search for a decent gun position, came up just as the ambulance moved off. Later he wrote of what he saw and felt. Members of the general's staff, "literally bowed down with grief," were all around the vehicle; "One, I remember, stood upon the rear step of the ambulance, seeming to desire to be as near him as possible. All of them were in tears." The doctor had said that Longstreet's wounds were not necessarily fatal, but they recalled that the prognosis had been even more favorable in Jackson's case right up to the day he died, a year ago next week. Though he had never really liked Old Peter, the artillerist wanted to see for himself what his condition was. For one thing, the procession's resemblance to a funeral cortege lent credence to a rumor that the general was dead. "I rode up to the ambulance and looked in. They had taken off Longstreet's hat and coat and boots. The blood had paled out of his face and its somewhat gross aspect was gone. I noticed how white and dome-like his great forehead looked and, with scarcely less reverent admiration, how spotless white his socks and his fine gauze undervest, save where the black red gore from his breast and shoulder had stained it. While I gazed at his massive frame, lying so still except when it rocked inertly with the lurch of the vehicle, his eyelids frayed apart till I could see a delicate line of blue between them, and then he very quietly moved his unwounded arm and, with his thumb and two fingers, carefully lifted the saturated undershirt from his chest, holding it up a moment, and heaved a deep sigh. He is not dead, I said to myself, and he is calm and entirely master of the situation. He is both greater and more attractive than I have heretofore thought him."

Back up the road, at the scene of the wounding, Field was doing what he could to carry out his orders to "take command, and move forward." But this was by no means as easy a task as Longstreet seemed to think. Other disruptive accidents, like the one that had just cost the corps its chief, were apt to follow if the main body, still in line astride the plank road, and Sorrel's flankers, drawn up facing it, were left to fight with their fronts at right angles. Lee ordered a postponement of the follow-up assault until the lines were readjusted. This was done, although the process was a slow one. Not only was the confusion greater than had been thought, it had also been increased by the loss of Jenkins and Old Peter. Four mortal hours, from noon to 4 o'clock, were required to get the troops untangled and into satisfactory positions for attack, and when they went forward at 4.15 they found that Hancock, too, had made good use of the time afforded for adjustments. He had strengthened his breastworks, brought up reinforcements, and posted a secondary line in support of the first. Worst of all (or best, depending on the point of view) he had shored up and realigned

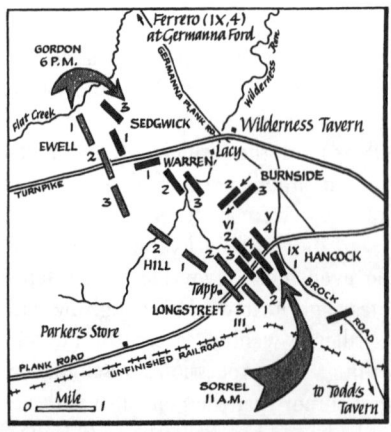

his outer flank, which the attackers found no longer dangling in the air. At a couple of points the Confederates achieved a penetration — one, where the log breastworks caught fire, forcing the defenders to abandon them, and Jenkins's Carolinians came leaping through the flames, intent on avenging the fall of their young brigadier — but in both cases supporting troops came up and restored the line by driving them out again: proof, if any such was needed, that seven divisions, snug behind breastworks and with both flanks secure (Burnside had come up at last, midway through the four-hour lull, and gone into position on Hancock's right) were not to be driven, or even budged, by three divisions attacking head-on through bullet-flailed brush. An hour of such fighting was quite enough to show that nothing more was going to be accomplished here. It was time — indeed, almost past time — to look elsewhere: meaning in Ewell's direction, up on the opposite flank.

All day, though he had had no chance to go in person, Lee had been sending messages to the Second Corps, urging an offensive in that quarter to relieve the pressure on the First or, if that was impracticable, the detachment of reinforcements to strengthen the offensive on the right. Invariably Ewell had replied that he could do neither. There was no fit opening for an attack; he needed all his troops to maintain his position astride the turnpike. When Lee arrived at 5.30 asking, "Cannot something be done on this flank?" Ewell said again that he believed it would be unwise to assault the Federals in their intrenchments, and he was supported in this by Early, who was at corps headquarters when Lee rode up. Gordon was also there, intending to renew his daylong plea that he be unleashed, and when his two superiors finished protesting that there was nothing to be done, he presumed to appeal to the army commander himself for permission to strike at the enemy flank, which he insisted had been wide open to attack for more than eight hours now. Ewell and Early repeated their objections, based on the conviction that Burnside was posted in Sedgwick's rear to forestall such a move. Lee, who knew that Burnside was in front of Hill, wasted no more time on reproaches, although, as Gordon later wrote, "his silence and grim looks . . . revealed his thoughts almost as plainly as words could have done." He simply ordered the attack to be made at once.

It was launched at straight-up 6 o'clock, and within the limitations of the little daylight time remaining — sunset came at 6.50 and darkness followed quickly in the thickets of the Wilderness — it was altogether as successful as Gordon, for the past nine hours, had been telling Ewell and Early it would be. With the support of the brigade that had arrived that morning from Hanover, North Carolinians under twenty-seven-year-old Brigadier General Robert D. Johnston, the Georgians struck and scattered Ricketts's unwary flank brigade and captured its commander, Brigadier General Truman Seymour. Seymour had led a division in the ill-starred Florida campaign, and after being whipped at Olustee had returned to Virginia to head a brigade whose members were known in both armies as "Milroy's weary boys," a description applied two years ago, after Stonewall Jackson gave them the run-around in the Shenandoah Valley, and confirmed last year when Ewell encountered them near Winchester on his way to Gettysburg. Weary or not, they broke badly again today and spread panic through the rest of the division, as well as through part of Wright's division, which was next in line and which also had a brigade commander scooped up by the rebels in the confusion. This was Brigadier General Alexander Shaler, a Connecticut-born New Yorker whose capture was especially welcome because he had recently been in charge of the prison for Confederate officers on Johnson's Island in Sandusky Bay, where winters were cold and blankets few; now he would get a taste of prison life from the inside, looking out, instead of from the outside, looking in. Seymour and Shaler, for all their lofty rank, were only two among some 600 Federals taken captive in the attack, while about as many more were killed or wounded, bringing Sedgwick's total loss to well over a thousand in one hour. Gordon himself lost only about fifty in the course of what his men referred to, ever afterwards, as their "finest frolic." The blue right flank was "rolled up" for more than a mile before dusk put an end to the advance and obliged the Georgians and Carolinians, who by then had plunged all the way to the Germanna Plank Road, to pull back with their prisoners, their booty from the overrun camps, and their conviction that an earlier attack, in Gordon's word's, "would have resulted in a decided disaster to the whole right wing of General Grant's army, if not in its entire disorganization."

Lee was inclined to think so, too, especially if the attack on this flank, against Sedgwick, had been delivered at the same time as Longstreet's against Hancock, on the other; in which case the indications were that Grant would have been overwhelmed and routed, not merely discomfited and bled down another one percent. An earlier visit to the left by the army commander would no doubt have resulted in an earlier attack, but Lee had come as soon as he felt he could leave the critical right, where the contest had been touch-and-go since sunrise. The trouble was that he could not be everywhere at once, despite the need for him to do just that. Although this impossible need had grown more pressing ever since the death of Stonewall Jackson, today it had become downright acute. Longstreet's departure left his corps in the hands of a newly promoted major general who had been with it less than three months, none of the time in combat, and whose deskbound year in Richmond seemed to have made him utterly inflexible at a time when flexibility was among the highest virtues. Hill's failing health, worse today than yesterday, and likely to be still worse tomorrow, obviously required him to take a sick leave that would deprive the army, however briefly, of the most aggressive of its corps commanders. It was harder, even, to think of Lee without A. P. Hill than it was to think of him without Longstreet, for Hill had never been detached. As for Ewell, although by ordinary standards he had done well today and yesterday, holding his own against the odds, he seemed incapable of doing one whit more than was required by specific orders; Ewell in the Wilderness, unable to bring himself to unleash Gordon despite repeated pleas from headquarters that *some*thing be attempted in that direction, was disturbingly like Ewell at Gettysburg, where his indecisiveness had cost the army its one best chance for a quick victory in what, instead, turned out to be a bloody three-day battle that ended in retreat.... All this might well have been heavy on Lee's mind as he rode southward, three miles through the twilight, to the Tapp farm. He was faced, at this most critical juncture, with a crisis of command: a crisis that would have to be resolved if the Army of Northern Virginia — at the close of only the second day of fighting, in what promised to be the longest and grimmest of its campaigns — was to survive the continuing confrontation, here in the depths of the Wilderness, with an enemy force roughly twice its size, superbly equipped, and still in possession of the main artery leading southeast, through the thickets and beyond into open country, where the tactical odds would lengthen and the capital itself would be in danger of being taken, either by sudden assault or inexorable maneuver.

All around him, as he dismounted in front of his tent in the Tapp farmyard, was confusion. East and north, out in the jungle where the battle had raged for two incredibly savage days, the moans of the wounded, blue and gray, were heightened to screams of terror when a brisk wind sprang up, shortly after dark, and fanned random smouldering embers into flames that spread faster through the underbrush than an injured man could crawl. Dead pines, their sap long dried to rosin, burned like twenty-foot torches, and the low clouds took on an eerie yellow cast, as if they reflected the glow from molten sulphur on the floor of hell. The roar of wind-whipped flames through crackling brush was punctuated from time to time by a clatter resembling the sudden clash of pickets, as groups of disabled men from both sides, huddled together against a common danger, were engulfed by the inferno and the paper-wrapped charges in their pockets or cartridge boxes caught fire and exploded. While stretcher bearers and volunteers did what they could to rescue all the wounded they could reach, others along the Confederate line of battle — including those Third Corps veterans who had thought they were too tired for such exertion the night before — worked hard to strengthen their defenses for a renewal of the contest at first light tomorrow. They expected it, and so did their commander. Less soundly beaten, tactically, and with no greater losses, Hooker had pulled back across the river. But neither Lee nor his soldiers thought it likely that Grant would do what Fighting Joe had done; at least not yet. Judging their new opponent by his western reputation, as well as by his aggressive performance over the past two days, they believed he would stay and fight.

Next to a retreat, which he did not expect, Lee preferred a Federal attack, and that was what he had his men prepare for. If Grant was to be beaten further, to and beyond the point at which he would have no choice except to pull back across the river, it would have to come as the result of a bloody, morale-shattering repulse. In any case, the next move was up to the invader. Today's abortive follow-up assault by the First Corps, launched after the long delay occasioned in part by the fall of its commander, had shown only too clearly that the Confederates, whatever their successes when they caught the enemy off balance, lacked the strength to drive an opponent who was not only twice their size but was also braced for the shock in well-prepared intrenchments — and there could be no doubt that the Federals were as hard at work on their defenses, left and right and center, as the graybacks were on their side of the line. Obliged as he was, now that all chances for surprise had been exhausted, to rule out a resumption of the offensive by his badly outnumbered army, Lee's decision not to attack amounted to a surrender of the initiative. This was a dangerous procedure against an adversary as nimble as Grant had shown himself to be in the campaign that brought Vicksburg under siege, but Lee had no choice. His hope, as he turned in for the night, was that Grant, despite his freedom to maneuver, would continue to forget his Vicksburg method and hold instead to the pattern of headlong assault he had followed so far in Virginia. That might lead to his repulse, and another repulse, if decisive enough, might lead to his destruction. The alternative for Lee, who had no such freedom to maneuver, was stalemate and defeat.

This second day of battle in the Wilderness had been Grant's hardest since the opening day at Shiloh, where his army and his reputation had also been threatened with destruction. Here as there, however — so long, at least, as the fighting was in progress — he bore the strain unruffled and "gave his orders calmly and coherently," one witness noted, "without any external sign of undue tension or agitation." Internally, a brief sequel was to show, he was a good deal more upset than he appeared, but outwardly, as he continued to sit on his stump atop the knoll in the Lacy meadow, smoking and whittling the critical hours away, he seemed altogether imperturbable. When word came, shortly before noon, that Hancock's flank had been turned and the left half of his army was in imminent danger of being routed, his reaction was to send more troops in that direction, together with additional supplies of ammunition, followed at 3 o'clock by orders for a counterattack to be launched at 6 to recover the lost ground and assure the holding of the Brock Road leading south. As it turned out, Hancock was himself assaulted a second time, nearly two hours before that, and had to use up so much of the ammunition in repelling the attack that not enough was left for compliance with the order. Besides, Grant by then was faced with an even graver crisis on his right. Sedgwick too had been flanked and was being routed, he was told, by a rebel force that had penetrated all the way to the Germanna Plank Road, cutting the army off from its nearest escape hatch back across the Rapidan.

Meade was a steadying influence, in this case as in others. "Nonsense," he snorted when a pair of flustered staffers came riding in from the crumpled flank after sundown to report that all was lost in that direction, including all hope of deliverance from the trap the rebels had sprung on Sedgwick and were about to enlarge in order to snap up everything in blue. "Nonsense! If they have broken our lines they can do nothing more tonight." He had confidence in John Sedgwick, the least excitable of his corps commanders, and he showed it by sending reinforcements from the center to help shore up the tottered right. Grant approved, of course, and had an even stronger reaction to an officer of higher rank who came crying that this second flank assault meant the end of the northern army unless it found some way to get out from under the blow about to fall. "This is a crisis that cannot be looked upon too seriously," he declared. "I know Lee's methods well by past experience. He will throw his whole army between us and the Rapidan, and cut us off completely from our communications." Grant was not a curser, but his patience had run out. He got up from the stump, took the cigar out of his mouth, and turned on this latest in the series of prophets of doom and idolators of his opponent. "Oh, I am heartily tired of hearing about what *Lee* is going to do," he said testily. "Some of you always seem to think he is suddenly going to turn a double somersault and land in our rear and on both our flanks at the same time. Go back to your command and try to think what we are going to do ourselves, instead of what *Lee* is going to do."

Further reports of havoc on the right were received with the same firmness, the same quick rejection of all notions of defeat, although — as Rawlins told a friend who rode over to headquarters to see him later that evening — "the coming of officer after officer with additional details soon made it apparent that the general was confronted by the greatest crisis in his life." By nightfall, however, Meade's assessment was confirmed; Sedgwick established a new and stronger line, half a mile south and east of the one he had lost to Gordon's flankers, who withdrew in the twilight from their position astride the road leading back to Germanna Ford. Then, and not until then, did the general-in-chief show the full effect of the strain he had been under, all this day and most of the day before. He broke. Yet even this was done with a degree of circumspection and detachment highly characteristic of the man. Not only was his personal collapse resisted until after the damage to both flanks had been repaired and the tactical danger had passed; it also occurred in the privacy of his quarters, rather than in the presence of his staff or gossip-hungry visitors. "When all proper measures had been taken," Rawlins confided, "Grant went into his tent, threw himself face downward on his cot, and gave way to the greatest emotion." He wept, and though the chief of staff, who followed him into the tent, declared that he had "never before seen him so deeply moved" and that "nothing could be more certain than that he was stirred to the very depths of his soul," he also observed that Grant gave way to the strain "without uttering any word of doubt or discouragement." Another witness, a captain attached to Meade's headquarters — Charles F. Adams, Jr, son and namesake of the ambassador — put it stronger. "I never saw a man so agitated in my life," he said.

However violent the breakdown, the giving way to hysteria at this point, it appeared that Grant wept more from the relief of tension (after all, both flanks were well shored up by then) than out of continuing desperation. In any case it was soon over. When Rawlins's friend, Brigadier General James H. Wilson — a friend of Grant's as well, formerly a member of his military family and recently appointed by him to command one of Sheridan's cavalry divisions — reached headquarters about 9 o'clock, less than an hour after the collapse Rawlins presently described, he found the general "surrounded by his staff in a state of perfect composure," as if nothing at all had happened. And in fact nothing had: nothing that mattered, anyhow. Unlike Hooker, who broke inside as a result of similar frustrations, Grant broke outside, and then only in the privacy of his tent. He cracked, but the crack healed so quickly that it had no effect whatever on the military situation, then or later. Whereas Hooker had reacted by falling back across the river, such a course was no more in Grant's mind now than it had been that morning, before sunup, when he was accosted by a journalist who was about to leave for Washington to file a story on the first day's fighting. Asked if he had any message for the authorities there, Grant, whose usual procedure was to hold off sending word of his progress in battle until the news was good, thought it over briefly, then replied: "If you see the President, tell him, from me, that, whatever happens, there will be no turning back."

Late that evening another journalist, New York *Herald* correspondent Sylvanus Cadwallader, was reassured to find that Grant still felt that way about the matter, despite the tactical disappointments of the day just past. Seated on opposite sides of a smouldering headquarters campfire, these two — the reporter because he was too depressed for sleep, and the general, he presumed, for the same reason — were the last to turn in for the night. Formerly of the Chicago *Times*, Cadwallader had been with Grant for nearly two years now, through the greatest of his triumphs, as well as through a two-day drunk up the Yazoo last summer, and for the first time, here in the Wilderness tonight, he began, as he said afterward, "to question the grounds of my faith in him. . . . We had waged two days of murderous battle, and had but little to show for it. Judged by comparative losses, it had been disastrous to the Union cause. We had been compelled by General Lee to fight him on a field of his own choosing, with the certainty of losing at least two men to his one, until he could be dislodged and driven from his vantage ground. [Yet] we had gained scarcely a rod of the battlefield at the close of the two days' contest." He wondered, as a result of this disconsolate review of the situation, whether he had followed Grant all this long way, through the conquest of Vicksburg and the deliverance of Chattanooga, only "to record his defeat and overthrow" when he came up against Lee in the Virginia thickets. Musing thus beside the dying embers of the campfire, he looked across its low glow at the lieutenant general, who seemed to be musing too. "His hat was drawn down over his face, the high collar of an old blue army overcoat turned up above his ears, one leg crossed over the other knee, eyes on the ashes in front." Only the fitful crossing and recrossing of his legs indicated that he was not asleep, and Cadwallader supposed that the general's thoughts were as gloomy as his own — until at last Grant spoke and disabused him of the notion. He began what the reporter termed "a pleasant chatty conversation upon indifferent subjects," none of which had anything to do with the fighting today or yesterday. As he got up from his chair to go to bed, however, he spoke briefly of "the sharp work General Lee had been giving us for a couple of days," then turned and went into his tent to get some sleep. That was all. But now that Cadwallader realized that the general had not been sharing them, he found that all his gloomy thoughts were gone. Grant opposed by Lee in Virginia, he perceived, was the same Grant he had known in Mississippi and Tennessee, where Pemberton and Bragg had been defeated. "It was the grandest mental sunburst of my life," he declared years later, looking back on the effect this abrupt realization had had on his state of mind from that time forward. "I had suddenly emerged from the slough of despond, to the solid bedrock of unwavering faith."

In the course of the next twenty hours or so — May 7 now, a Saturday — the whole army experienced a like sequence of reactions, from utter doubt to mental sunburst. Reconnaissance parties, working their way along and across the charred, smoky corridors last night's fires had left, found the rebels "fidgety and quick to shoot" but content, it seemed, to stay tightly buttoned up in the breastworks they had built or improved since yesterday. Lee preferred receiving to delivering an attack, and Grant apparently felt the same, since he issued no orders directing that one be made. For this the troops were duly thankful, especially those who had had a close-up look at the enemy lines, but they were also puzzled. The Federal choice seemed limited to attack or retreat, and they had not thought that Grant, despite the drubbing he had received these past two days, would give up quite this early. Still, word soon came that the pontoon bridges had been taken up at Germanna and relaid at Ely's Ford to hasten the passage of the ambulance train with the wounded, who were to be sent by rail to Washington. This meant that a withdrawal of the army, whether by that route or through Fredericksburg, would have to proceed by way of Chancellorsville, the hub where roads from the south and west converged to continue north and east. Swiftly now the conviction grew that everything blue would be headed in that direction after sundown. Sure enough, such guns as had found positions for direct support of the infantry — including those on the knoll in the Lacy meadow — were limbered and started rearward that afternoon, obviously to avoid jamming the roads that night, and in this the men saw confirmation of their worst judgments and suspicions. Grant, for all his western bulldog reputation, was merely another Pope, another Hooker, at best another Meade. They had been through this before; they recognized the signs. "Most of us thought it was another Chancellorsville," a Massachusetts infantryman would remember, while a Pennsylvania cavalryman recorded that his comrades used a homlier term to describe the predicted movement. They called it "another skedaddle."

If the Chancellorsville parallel was obvious — both battles had been waged in the same thicket, so to speak, between the same two armies, at the same time of year, and against the same Confederate commander — it was also, at this stage, disturbingly apt. By every tactical standard, although the earlier contest was often held up as a model of Federal ineptitude, the second was even worse-fought than the first. Hooker had had one flank turned; Grant had both. Hooker had achieved at least a measure of surprise in the opening stage of his campaign; Grant achieved none. Indeed, the latter had been surprised himself, while on a march designed to avoid battle on the very ground where this one raged for two horrendous days, not only without profit to the invaders, but also at a cost so disproportionate that it emphasized the wisdom of his original intention to avoid a confrontation on this terrain. Moreover, it was in the three-way assessment of casualties, Hooker's and Lee's, along with his own, that the comparison became least flattering. Grant lost 17,666 killed and wounded, captured and missing — about four hundred more than Hooker — while Lee, whose victory a year ago had cost him nearly 13,000 casualties, was losing a scant 7800, considerably fewer than half the number he inflicted. Here the comparison tended to break down, however, because for anything like comparable losses, North and South, it was necessary to go back to Fredericksburg, the most one-sided of all the large-scale Confederate triumphs. In plain fact, up to the point of obliging Grant to throw in the sponge and pull back across the river, Lee had never beaten an adversary so soundly as he had beaten this one in the course of the past two days.

What it all boiled down to was that Grant was whipped, and soundly whipped, if he would only admit it by retreating: which in turn was only a way of saying that he had not been whipped at all. "Whatever happens, there will be no turning back," he had said, and he would hold to that. The midafternoon displacement of the guns deployed along the Union line of battle was in preparation for a march, just as the troops assumed, but not in the direction they supposed. No more willing to accept a stalemate than he was to accept defeat, he would shift his ground, and in doing so he would hold to the offensive; he would move, not north toward Washington, but south toward Richmond, obliging Lee to conform if he was to protect the capital in his rear. Grant thus clung to the initiative Lee surrendered when he had exhausted all his chances for surprise. Now it was Grant's turn to try again for a surprise, and he planned accordingly.

The objective was Spotsylvania Courthouse, less than a dozen miles down the Brock Road from the turnpike intersection. With an early start, to be made as soon as darkness screened the movement from the rebels in their works across the way, it was not too much to expect that the leading elements would be in position there by dawn, plying shovels and swinging axes in the construction of fortifications which Lee, when he caught up at last, would be obliged to storm, even if the storming meant the destruction of his army, because they would stand between him and the capital whose protection was his prime concern. Warren would have the lead and would go all the way tonight, marching down the Brock Road across the rear of Hancock, who would fall in behind, once Warren had passed, and stop at Todd's Tavern, where he would guard the rear and slow the progress of the rebels if they attempted to follow by this route. Sedgwick would move east on the turnpike to Chancellorsville, then south by the road past Piney Branch Church to its junction with the Brock Road at Alsop, between Todd's Tavern and Spotsylvania, close in Warren's rear and also within supporting distance of Hancock. Burnside would follow Sedgwick after taking the plank road to Chancellorsville, but would call a halt at Piney Branch Church to protect the trains and the reserve artillery, which were to assemble at that point. Sheridan's troopers would probe the darkness in advance of both columns, and he was directed to patrol the western flank in strength, in order "to keep the corps commanders advised in time of the approach of the enemy." Warren and Sedgwick would move out at 8.30, Hancock and Burnside as soon thereafter as the roads were clear. The emphasis was on silence and speed, both highly desirable factors in a maneuver designed to outfox old man Lee.

Meade issued the march order at 3 o'clock, in compliance with earlier instructions from Grant, and when the guns pulled out soon afterward, taking a five-hour lead to clear the roads for the infantry that night, the troops along the line of battle drew their conclusions and went on exchanging occasional long-range shots with the graybacks while awaiting their turn to join what they were convinced was a retreat. Soon after dark the expected orders came; Warren's and Sedgwick's veterans slung their packs, fell in quietly on the Brock Road and the turnpike, and set out. To the surprise of the V Corps men, the march was south, in rear of Hancock's portion of the line. At first they thought that this was done to get them onto the plank road, leading east to Chancellorsville, but when they slogged past the intersection they knew that what they were headed for was not the Rapidan or the Rappahannock, but another battle somewhere south, beyond the unsuspecting rebel flank. Formerly glum, the column now began to buzz with talk. Packs were lighter; the step quickened; spirits rose with the growing realization that they were stealing another march on old man Lee. Then came cheers, as a group on horseback — "Give way, give way to the right," one of the riders kept calling to the soldiers on the road — doubled the column at a fast walk, equipment jingling. In the lead was Grant, a vague, stoop-shouldered figure, undersized-looking on Cincinnati, the largest of his mounts; the other horsemen were his staff. Cincinnati pranced and sidled, tossing his head at the sudden cheering, and the general, who had his hands full getting the big animal quieted down, told his companions to pass the word for the cheers to stop, lest they give the movement away to the Confederates sleeping behind their breastworks in the woods half a mile to the west. The cheering stopped, but not the buzz of excitement, the elation men felt at seeing their commander take the lead in an advance they had supposed was a retreat. They stepped out smartly; Todd's Tavern was just ahead, a little beyond the midway point on the march to Spotsylvania.

Up on the turnpike, where Sedgwick's troops were marching, the glad reaction was delayed until the head of the column had covered the gloomy half dozen miles to Chancellorsville. "The men seemed aged," a cannoneer noted as he watched them slog past a roadside artillery park. Weary from two days of savage fighting and two nights of practically no sleep, dejected by the notion that they were adding still another to the long list of retreats the army had made in the past three years, they plodded heavy-footed and heavy-hearted, scuffing their shoes in the dust on the pike leading eastward. Beyond Chancellorsville, just ahead, the road forked. A turn to the left, which they expected, meant recrossing the river at Ely's Ford, probably to undergo another reorganization under another new commander who would lead them, in the fullness of time, into another battle that would end in another retreat; that was the all-too-familiar pattern, so endless in repetition that at times it seemed a full account of the army's activities in the Old Dominion could be spanned in four short words, "Bull Run: da capo." But now a murmur, swelling rapidly to a chatter, began to move back down the column from its head, and presently each man could see for himself that the turn, beyond the ruins of the Chancellor mansion, had been to the right. They were headed south, not north; they were advancing, not retreating; Grant was giving them another go at Lee. And though on sober second thought a man might be of at least two minds about this, as a welcome or a dread thing to be facing, the immediate reaction was elation. There were cheers and even a few tossed caps, and long afterwards men were to say that, for them, this had been the high point of the war.

"Our spirits rose," one among them would recall. "We marched free. The men begin to sing.... That night we were happy."

※ 2 ※

Lee was marching too, by then, having divined once more his adversary's intention. That morning, after riding the length of his Wilderness line and finding it strangely quiet — in contrast, that is, to the fury of the past two days, when better than 25,000 men had been shot or captured, blue and gray, along that four-mile stretch of tangled woodland — he drew rein on the far left to talk with Gordon, who supposed from Grant's lack of aggressiveness that he was about to retreat. "Grant is not going to retreat," Lee told him. "He will move his army to Spotsylvania." Surprised, the Georgian asked if there was any evidence that the Federals were moving in that direction. "Not at all, not at all," Lee said as he turned Traveller's head to ride back down the line. "But that is the next point at which the armies will meet. Spotsylvania is now General Grant's best strategic point."

There was, as he said, no indication that Grant was moving, but there was at least negative evidence that when he did move — as obviously he would have to do, in lieu of assaulting the Wilderness intrenchments, before he used up the supplies in his train — it would not be back across the Rapidan; Ewell had sent word, shortly after sunup, that the Federals were dismantling their pontoon bridges at Germanna, and though Ely's Ford was still available it seemed unlikely that they would give up either if they intended to retire to the north bank. That left Fredericksburg as a possible escape route, and in fact there were reports from cavalry scouts that wagon traffic was heavy in that direction. But there was also a report from Stuart, waiting for Lee when he got back to the Widow Tapp's, that the Union cavalry had returned to Todd's Tavern this morning, in strength enough to drive the Confederate horsemen out and hold the place against all efforts to retake it. Todd's Tavern was down the Brock Road, midway between Grant's present position and Spotsylvania, which lay in the angle between the Richmond, Fredericksburg & Potomac and the Virginia Central railroads and offered an excellent approach to Hanover Junction, where the two lines crossed en route to Richmond from the north and west, both of them vital to the subsistence of Lee's army. Spotsylvania then, as Lee told Gordon, was his adversary's "best strategic point," if what he wanted was either to steal the lead in a race for Richmond or to take up a stout defensive position which Lee would be obliged to attack, whatever the tactical disadvantages, not only because it would sever his lines of supply, but also because it lay between him and the capital whose protection was his primary concern.

As evidence, this was far from conclusive, but it was persuasive enough to cause him to summon Brigadier General William N. Pendleton, the fifty-four-year-old former Episcopal rector who served as his chief of artillery, and instruct him to begin at once the cutting of a road through the woods, due south from the army's right flank on the Orange Plank Road, down to Shady Grove Church on the Catharpin Road — the midpoint for Lee, as Todd's Tavern, which was also on the Catharpin Road, was for Grant — to be used as soon as the first hard evidence reached headquarters that his opponent had taken, or was about to take, the first step in the race for Spotsylvania. The new road, if it was finished in time, would shorten the march by doing away with the need to backtrack down the plank road to Parker's Store before turning south; but this was small comfort alongside the knowledge that Grant even then would have a shorter route, a better road to travel all the way, and the advantage of deciding when the race would begin or whether, indeed, it would be run at all.

Another, and possibly greater, disadvantage lay in the fact that the lead corps on the march would be the First, since its position was on the right and therefore closest to the objective. Normally — as in the case of the movement into the Wilderness earlier this week — one or both of the other two corps, composed for the most part of Jackson's famed "foot cavalry," sought out the foe or rounded his flank to set him up for the Sunday punch methodical Old Peter would deliver when he came up in turn. Moreover, the corps was now to be commanded by a general, forty-two-year-old Richard Anderson, whose reputation had never been one for dash or fire and whose performance over the past year under Hill had been undistinguished at best, while at worst it had been a good deal less than that. At Gettysburg, for example, the kindest thing that could be said of the easy-going South Carolinian's lack of aggressiveness was that it had been due to sloth. His earlier record, made in the days when he commanded first a brigade and then a division under Longstreet, had been better, and this was Lee's main reason, together with the consideration that he was the senior major general with the army, for giving the post to him instead of Early, whom Lee otherwise preferred. A former member of the corps, which Early was not — Field was of recent appointment and Kershaw was still a brigadier — Anderson would be welcomed back by the officers and men of the two divisions he would command, while his Third Corps division would pass into the capable hands of Mahone, the army's senior brigadier. Yet this was perhaps the greatest of all gambles, the appointment of genial, uninspired Dick Anderson to replace his most dependable lieutenant at a time when dash and fire, both of which were conspicuous by their absence from his record, seemed likely to be the decisive factors in a contest that would begin at any moment and had Richmond for the prize. The fact that Lee was more or less obliged to take that gamble was one measure of the extent to which attrition was wearing down the army in his charge.

That afternoon he saw that still another such change was in the offing. Riding his line for the second time that day, he stopped off at Third Corps headquarters, which had been set up in a deserted house about midway between the plank road and the turnpike, and found A. P. Hill looking paler and sicker than ever. Though red-bearded Little Powell was unwilling to relinquish command at this critical juncture, it was evident that he soon would be obliged to do so. This meant that, once more — with Anderson transferred and Heth and Wilcox insufficiently seasoned — a temporary successor would have to be found outside a corps whose regular chief was incapacitated. In this case, however, the problem was simplified by having been faced beforehand, although in another connection; Jubal Early, runner-up as a candidate for command of the First Corps, would be brought in from the Second to lead the Third, at least until Hill recovered from the ailment he would not yet admit was grave enough to require him to step down. One dividend of this arrangement, similar to the one that had given Anderson's division to Mahone, was that Early's division could pass to Gordon, for whom Lee felt a growing admiration because of his performance yesterday. Lee's conversation with Little Powell was interrupted about 4 o'clock by a staff colonel who came down from the attic of the house, where he had established an observation post by ripping some shingles from the roof, to report on something he had seen with the aid of a powerful marine glass trained on what he believed was Grant's headquarters, a bit under two miles across the way. A number of heavy guns, held in reserve there all through the fighting, had just pulled out and headed south down the Brock Road, toward the Confederate right.

Though Grant's dead were still thickly strewn in the woods in front of his line, along with a few surviving wounded, and though none of the blue infantry had yet shown any sign of preparing for a shift, Lee took this limited artillery displacement as the first step in the race for Spotsylvania, which lay in the direction the guns had gone. Accordingly, he returned at once to the Tapp farm and issued orders for Anderson to march that night, taking Pendleton's just-cut southward trace through the woods to Shady Grove Church, then eastward across the Po River to Spotsylvania, which he was to hold against all comers: provided, of course, that he got there first. The new corps commander's instructions were for him to withdraw his two divisions from their present lines as soon as darkness masked the movement from the enemy, then give the troops a few hours' rest and sleep before setting out, at 3 o'clock in the morning, on the race for the objective a dozen miles away. Ewell and Hill were told to follow, in that order, as soon as they judged that the situation in their front would justify withdrawal.

In accordance with these instructions, Anderson pulled back about 9 o'clock, but finding no suitable rest area in the immediate rear — fires had sprung up again in the smouldering brush, fanned alive, as on the past two nights, by the early evening breeze — he set out at once, down Pendleton's trace, with the intention of making a bivouac farther south, outside the smoky battle zone, in which the men could get some rest between then and 3 a.m., the designated hour for the start of the march. He had not gone far, however, before he abandoned the notion of making any considerable halt at all. For one thing, there simply was no usable stopping place this side of Shady Grove, down along the fringes of the Wilderness, and for another the condition of the newly built "road," stump-pocked and cluttered with fallen trunks and limbs, was so miserable that the rate of march along it in the dark could scarcely be much better than a mile-an-hour crawl. He perceived that if he was to win the race for Spotsylvania he would need every minute of the four or five hours he would gain by keeping moving instead of halting in accordance with Lee's order; so he kept moving. Eager to do well on his first assignment as a corps commander, Anderson here rendered Lee and the Confederacy the greatest service of his career.

Jeb Stuart too had one of his great days, perhaps his finest, although the action promised little of the glory he had chased in former times. His three cavalry divisions, under Major Generals Wade Hampton, Fitzhugh Lee, and W. H. F. Lee — the first was a wealthy South Carolina planter-sportsman, fifteen years older at forty-six than his cinnamon-bearded chief, while the second and third, Virginians both, were respectively the commanding general's twenty-eight-year-old nephew and twenty-seven-year-old son — were scattered about the landscape to undertake the double task of protecting the Confederate march and impeding that of the Federals. There were six brigades, two in each division. Stuart assigned half of these to accompany the gray column, shielding its flank and clearing its front, while the other three moved out ahead to block and bedevil the bluecoats who were slogging southeast on a parallel route, a couple of densely wooded miles away. Brigadier General Thomas Rosser, detached from Hampton, led his brigade directly to Spotsylvania, under instructions to hold the place, if possible, until Anderson arrived. Fitz Lee meantime turned northwest, up the Brock Road, to give his full attention to the Federals moving down it: two brigades of mounted men opposing a four-division corps

The Forty Days

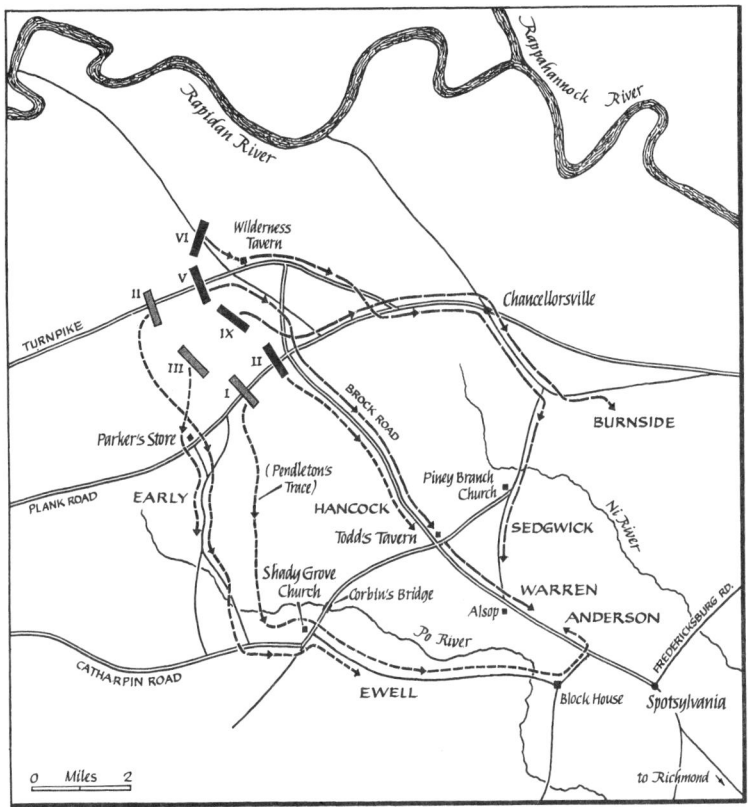

of infantry preceded by a cavalry division half again larger than his own. Near Todd's Tavern he put his troopers to work in the darkness, felling trees to obstruct the road as they withdrew. This gave the blue marchers almost as hard a time as their opponents were having on the crude trace across the way, and presently they had an added problem the Confederates did not have. When daylight began to filter through the thickets, the graybacks began to take potshots at the head and flanks of the Federal column, bringing it to a stumbling halt from time to time while details moved cautiously forward to flush the rebel marksmen out of their ambuscades. This continued, down past Alsop, to within two miles of Spotsylvania. There at last, beyond the fringes of the Wilderness and on comparatively open ground where he could bring his horse artillery into play, Fitz Lee had his dismounted men pile fence rails for a barricade and get down behind it, there in the dust of the road and the grass of the adjoining fields, for a last-ditch fight while couriers set out to bring Anderson cross-country to join in the defense. So far it had been cavalry against cavalry, and Fitz had managed to hold his own, despite the Union advantage of numbers and rapid-fire weapons. Sooner or later, however, the blue troopers would be replaced by infantry, brought forward Grant-style in a solid mass to overlap and overrun his flimsy breastwork. Unless Anderson came up fast and first, there would be nothing substantial between the Federals and Spotsylvania; Grant would have won the race whose prize was Richmond.

The sun by then was an hour high, and Anderson's two divisions, having covered nine miles on their all-night march out of the Wilderness, were ending an hour-long breakfast halt in the open fields, half a mile short of the Po and within about three miles of their objective. Sustained and heartened by the meal, such as it was — a frizzled chunk of fatty bacon, a piece of hardtack warmed and softened in the grease, and a cup of "coffee" boiled from roasted peanuts: poor fare, by any ordinary standards, but quite as much as they were accustomed to (and considerably more, in any case, than Warren's road-worn men received across the way) — the troops resumed their eastward march across the Po. Kershaw's division had the lead. About halfway to Spotsylvania, as he drew near a peculiar roadside dwelling built of squared logs and referred to locally as the Block House, he was met by a cavalry courier urging speed in the final heat of the race; Fitz Lee needed help, and he needed it quick. Fortified by the meager Sunday breakfast, the two front brigades quickened their step and hurried a mile northward, across the fields, to where the dismounted troopers were making their last-ditch stand on the Brock Road. "Run for our rail piles!" a cavalryman shouted as the men of the leading regiment came up. "The Federal infantry will reach them first if you don't run!"

They did run, and barely made it. Crouching behind the hastily improvised works, they opened fire on the advancing bluecoats at a range of sixty yards and blasted them back, at least for the moment. Thanks to Lee and Anderson, as well as to Stuart and Fitzhugh Lee — not to mention their own stout legs — they had won the race, although by a margin of less than a minute.

Whether it would stay won was another matter. Apparently not; for while the Federal infantry, recovering from the shock of having encountered more than cavalry in defense of the stacked rails, was massing for a heavier assault, Stuart sent word that Rosser's brigade had been driven out of Spotsylvania by a division of blue troopers who came surging down the road from Fredericksburg. Calm despite this evidence that the race had been lost after all, Anderson rerouted Kershaw's other two brigades, instructing them to proceed at once to the courthouse and fling the Federals out before they had time to intrench or bring in reinforcements. Field's division was coming up by now, and Anderson got the men into line on Kershaw's left, just in time to repulse a second and much heavier attack, which otherwise would have turned his western flank. No sooner had this been done than word came from the south that the blue horsemen had withdrawn from Spotsylvania of their own accord, apparently in the belief that they were escaping from a trap. Anderson at once summoned Kershaw's two detached brigades to rejoin him, leaving the defense of the town to Stuart, who by now had brought Fitz Lee down to help Rosser prevent a return by the rapid-firing Federals, in case they got their nerve back. Kershaw's men came hurrying up the Brock Road in time to extend his right and share in the repulse of a still heavier third assault by the Union infantry. This time, though they were punished even more cruelly in the course of their advance across the open fields and down the road, the bluecoats did not scatter or fall back as far as they had done before; they took up a semi-circular position, just beyond easy rifle range of the defenders, and began to intrench.

This last was something the Confederates had been doing all along. Familiar enough with Grant's method by now to expect that at least one more all-out attack would be made on their line before the Union commander would be satisfied that it could not be shattered, they worked with picks and shovels and axes, bayonets and frying pans, tin cups and anything else that came to hand, improving and extending the fence-rail "works" they had inherited from Fitz Lee. By the time the sun swung past the overhead and the third assault had been repulsed, the artillery-studded defenses, extending about one mile west and half a mile east of the Brock Road, roughly a mile and a half from Spotsylvania, had grown as formidable as if they had been occupied for days. Across the way, however, in the woods and fields beyond the line the Federals were at work on, more blue troops were coming up and massing south of Alsop, obviously in preparation for a fourth assault, to be launched with greater numbers and on a broader front. Anderson's two divisions had fought Warren's four to a standstill, but now that Sedgwick's three were being added to the weight that Grant could bring to bear, the odds seemed overwhelming. About 2.30 the commanding general arrived, having ridden across the Po ahead of Ewell, whose corps by now was passing Shady Grove Church, a good two hours from the field of fight. Informed of the situation, Lee sent word for Ewell to hasten his march. This was no easy thing to ask of men who were trudging wearily through heat that was more like June than May, but fortunately the weather seemed to be having an even more lethargic effect on the Federals, who, unlike Ewell, had been marching all the previous night. It was 5 o'clock before they completed their leaden-legged dispositions and started forward. By then, Ewell's lead division had arrived and gone into position on Anderson's right, in time to block the attack on that flank and assist in driving the bluecoats back upon their works. It was smartly done, and that ended the fighting for the day.

Lee turned in early, rounding out a busy, fateful Sunday. Rising at 3 o'clock next morning — May 9; just one week ago today, although it seemed a great deal longer, he had stood on Clark's Mountain, extended a gauntleted hand, and told his assembled generals: "Grant will cross by one of those fords" — he wired the President of his success in frustrating the designs of the Army of the Potomac by winning the race for Spotsylvania: "We have succeeded so far in keeping on the front flank of that army, and impeding its progress, without a general engagement, which I will not bring on unless a favorable opportunity offers, or as a last resort. Every attack made upon us has been repelled and considerable damage done to the enemy." He expected the attacks to be renewed today, but he had little doubt of being able to withstand them, so long as the Federals held to the headlong methods they had favored on three of the past four days. A. P. Hill's corps, under Early — Hill had broken down at last, too sick to mount a horse, though he insisted on riding along in an ambulance in order to be with his men — was on the march even now, under instructions to come up on Ewell's right. With his army united and intrenched, dispositions complete and both flanks snug, Lee feared nothing the blue force could do, at least on this front, and he said as much in the telegram this morning. "With the blessing of God," he told Davis, "I trust we shall be able to prevent General Grant from reaching Richmond."

On the Union side, the trouble the leading elements had encountered in losing the race for Spotsylvania was compounded, in about equal parts, of weariness and Sheridan. Or perhaps it just came down to a prevalent loss of temper; weariness made tempers short, and Sheridan's was short enough already. In any case, after the elation that came with finding they were advancing, not retreating, the troops settled down to an ill-regulated march — stop and go, but mostly stop — that soon became what one of Sedgwick's men described as "a medley of phantasmagoria." Down on the Brock Road, tunneling southeast through the blackness, Warren's dust-choked marchers had it worse, for though the total distance was less, their progress was jerkier, mainly because of the cavalry up front, which seemed not only to have no definite notion of where it was going, but also to be in no hurry whatever to get there. One delay of about an hour, for example, was occasioned by an all-out fistfight between two cavalry regiments, one composed of veterans who effected a forcible exchange of their run-down horses for the well-groomed mounts of the other, made up of recruits who were not so green as to take such treatment without protest, even though the protest accomplished nothing except a prolongation of the delay. All this was short of Todd's Tavern, the midpoint of the march, where the real jam-up began.

Sheridan, like Stuart except that he began the campaign with 13,000 sabers, as compared to the Confederate 8500, had three divisions in his charge. One of these, James Wilson's, he ordered to move roundabout by the Fredericksburg road to Spotsylvania, while the other two,

The Forty Days

under Brigadier Generals Alfred Torbert and David Gregg, moved out in front of Warren's infantry to block the crossings of the Po before the rebels got there. So he intended. As all too often happened, however, someone failed to get the word — in this case, two someones: Gregg and Torbert. Reaching Todd's Tavern around midnight, Meade and his escort found the infantry column stalled and the crossroad jammed with Gregg's troopers, held up in turn by Torbert's, who were waiting for orders on the road beyond. Neither had been told what to do, and neither was doing anything at all. Meade got them moving by telling Gregg to proceed down the Catharpin Road toward Corbin's Bridge, where he would cover the wooded approaches from Parker's Store, and Torbert (or rather his senior brigadier, Wesley Merritt; Torbert was sick tonight) to remain on the Brock Road, clearing the way to Spotsylvania for the infantry and sending one brigade to the Block House, where it would stand in the path of any rebels on the march from Shady Grove. After issuing these instructions Meade sent word of them to Sheridan, wherever he might be, and rode back to get Warren on the move again. By now it was past 1 a.m. and the going was even slower than before. Up ahead, in the woods beyond the tavern, Merritt's troopers found the narrow road obstructed and enemy horsemen taking shots at them, out of the darkness, when they dismounted by lantern light to drag the just-felled timber from their path. This got worse as the march continued, especially for the infantry, with sudden starts and stops, races to close the resultant gaps, and long waits for the column to lurch into motion, segment by jangled segment. The first glimmers of daylight, so fervently hoped for in the gloom, only made things worse by improving the marksmanship of the snipers in the brush. Just before sunup Sheridan himself came pounding onto the scene on his big black horse. Fuming at Meade's highhanded "interference," which seemed to him to have exposed the cavalry to piecemeal destruction by scattering it about the countryside, he sent word for Wilson to withdraw at once from Spotsylvania, lest he be trapped there without adequate support when the rebel infantry arrived. Meantime the dismounted graybacks continued to snipe at the head of the column, toppling riders from their saddles. Beyond Alsop, within two miles of the courthouse — where, for all he knew, Wilson was being cut to pieces by superior numbers before he could pull out — Sheridan was galled even more by having to call on Warren's infantry to come forward with their bayonets and pry Fitz Lee's stubborn troopers out of their fence-rail barricade, which had proved too formidable for Merritt's frazzled cavalry to storm.

Chafed by the delays and aggravations, Warren was determined, now that Sheridan had his horsemen out of the way, to settle the issue before the defenders had time to strengthen their position on the low ridge just ahead, barely a mile and a half from the objective of his disjointed nightlong march. He told Brigadier General John C. Robinson, whose division had the lead, to attack as fast as his men could make it down the road. Weary, outdone, and unfed as they were, wobbly on their legs for lack of sleep, this wasn't very fast; but it was fast enough, as the thing developed, to accomplish their destruction in short order.

Robinson, a large, hairy New Yorker with an outsized beard and shaggy brows, a crusty manner, and a solid reputation earned in practically all of the major eastern battles, was at forty-seven Wadsworth's successor as the oldest division commander in the army. He studied the terrain, peering briefly out across a shallow valley, scarped along its bottom and lightly timbered, then up the gentle slope on its far side to where the graybacks crouched behind the fence rails they had stacked along the thickly wooded crest, about a quarter mile away. The scene had a certain bucolic charm, particularly by contrast with the smothering hug of the Wilderness, but Robinson found the situation tactically unpromising and he said as much to Warren, asking for time to bring up his three strung-out brigades and mass them before launching the assault. Warren said no, there was nothing across the way but dismounted cavalry; go in now, with the brigade at hand, and go in hard. This Robinson did, as hard at least as his winded men could manage after crossing the gullied valley and wheezing up the incline, only to have the rebel line explode in their faces, a scant sixty yards away. In quality and volume — a sudden, heavy bank of flame-stabbed smoke, jetting up and out, and a rattling clatter much too loud for carbines — the fire left no doubt that the line was occupied, not by cavalry, as the attackers had been informed when they set out, but by infantry who met them with massed volleys and blasted them back down the slope, a good deal faster than they had climbed it on their way to the explosion.

Nor was that the worst of the affair. By now the second brigade, four regiments of Maryland troops whose enlistments were to expire before the month was out, had come up and begun its descent into the valley, coincident with the arrival of Anderson's corps artillery on the ridge ahead. Startled to find the first wave of attackers in retreat from momentary contact with the rebels, the second was caught and churned up fearfully by a deluge of projectiles. The Marylanders broke, scrambling rearward in a race with the comrades they had intended to support. Dismayed and angered, Robinson hurried forward to rally them in person, but went down with a bullet through one knee. His third brigade fared no better, being struck in the flank and scattered by a savage counterattack, launched about as soon as it came up. This brought the casualty total to just under 1200 killed and wounded in less than an hour, while as many more were fugitives and stragglers, captured or otherwise unaccounted for. Robinson's knee wound cost him his leg, which was taken off that night. He was out of the war for keeps. And so, as another result of this brief engagement, was his division. It was disbanded next day, the remnants of its three cut-up brigades being distributed among the other divisions of the corps. Demoralized or not, these reinforcements were badly needed by all three, for they had suffered cruelly in the wake of Robinson's fiasco; Anderson's second division had arrived by then to strengthen the rebel line against the Federals, who were committed division by division, as fast as they came up, and division by division were repulsed. By the time Meade arrived, around midday, Warren had done his worst. He had to admit that he could not get over or around the Confederate intrenchments with what was left of his corps. Meade told him to hold what he had, then summoned Sedgwick from his reserve position, north of Alsop, to add the weight of his three divisions to the attack.

This took time — five hours, in all; Sedgwick's men were weary too — but the interim was livened, at any rate for the gossip-hungry clerks and staff, by a personality clash. Sheridan dropped by army headquarters, still fuming about last night's "interference," and Meade, losing his famous temper at last, retorted hotly that the cavalry had been doing less than had been expected of it ever since the campaign opened. That the charge was true did not make it any more acceptable to Sheridan, who replied, bristling, that he considered the remark a calculated insult. Meade recovered his balance for a moment. "I didn't mean that," he said earnestly, placing one hand on the cavalryman's shoulder in a conciliatory gesture. Sheridan stepped back out of reach ("All the Hotspur in his nature was aroused," a staff observer later wrote) and continued his protest. If the cavalry had done less than had been hoped for, he declared, it was not his fault, but Meade's; Meade had countermanded his orders, interfered with his tactical dispositions, and worst of all had kept his troopers hobbled by assigning them such unprofitable and distractive tasks as guarding the slow-plodding trains and providing escorts for the brass. If results were what Meade wanted, he should let the cavalry function as it was meant to function — on its own, as a compact hard-hitting body. Give him a free rein, Sheridan said, and he would tackle Jeb Stuart on his own ground, deep in the Confederate rear, and whip him out of his boots. The argument continued, both men getting madder by the minute, until Meade at last decided there was only one way to resolve their differences. He went to Grant.

Three days ago, the general-in-chief's reaction to a similar confrontation had been decisive. "You ought to put him under arrest," he had said of the riled-up Griffin. Today though, having heard Meade out, he seemed more amused than angered: especially by the bandy-legged cavalryman's reported claim that he would whip Jeb Stuart out of his boots if Meade would only turn him loose. "Did Sheridan say that?" he asked. Meade nodded. "Well," Grant said, "he generally knows what he's talking about. Let him start right out and do it."

Meade, having thus been taught the difference between eastern and western insubordination, returned to his own headquarters and issued the order; Sheridan would take off next morning, with all three of his divisions, on a maneuver designed to provoke Stuart into hand-to-hand combat by threatening the capital in his rear. Meantime Sedgwick was coming up. By 5 o'clock he had his three divisions in line alongside what was left of Warren's four, and all seven went forward, more or less together, in a final attempt to turn the day's disjointed fighting into a Union victory by taking possession of Spotsylvania, a mile and a half beyond the rebel works. It failed, as the earlier attacks had failed, because Lee again managed to get enough of his veterans — in this case, Ewell's lead division — up to the critical point in time to prevent a breakthrough. His losses had been light today, while Meade's had been comparatively heavy. "The ground was new to everyone, and the troops were tired," Meade's chief of staff explained.

For Grant, who smoked as he watched the sunset repulse, the day had been a grievous disappointment. Not only had he failed to pass Lee's front, but the resultant tactical situation in which he now found himself seemed to favor the defensive at least as much as had been the case in the one he abandoned, just last night, in the belief that it offered him little or no chance to achieve the Cannae he was seeking. Moreover, though he said that he left the Wilderness because he saw no profit in assaulting the works Lee's men had thrown up in the brush, the fortifications here were even more formidable, laid out on dominant ground between unfordable rivers, and getting stronger by the hour. Still smoking, he looked out across the shallow valley where so many of Warren's men had fallen — tousled rag-doll shapes becoming indistinguishable as the daylight faded into dusk — then turned, as imperturbable as ever, and rode back to his tent, there to make a study of the situation, based on such information as had been gathered.

Today's reconnaissance (for that was all it came to, in the end) had been costly, and next morning it grew more so, although nothing so patently wasteful as a repetition of yesterday's headlong approach to the problem was attempted. While Hancock and Burnside were on the march, summoned to come up on the right and left, Warren and Sedgwick limited their activities to improving their intrenchments and making a cautious investigation of the Confederate position. Restricted in scope by the absence of the cavalry, which had taken off soon after sunrise to challenge Stuart, this last was a gingerly business at best. Rebel marksmen, equipped with imported Whitworth rifles mounting telescopic sights, were quick to draw a bead on anything blue that moved, especially if it had a glint of brass about the shoulders. Moreover, in addition to this lack of respect for rank, they seemed to have none for the supposed reduction of accuracy by distance, with the result that there was a good deal of ducking and dodging on the Union side, even though the range was sometimes as great as half a mile. This not only interfered with work, it was also thought to be

The Forty Days

detrimental to discipline and morale. John Sedgwick looked at it that way, for one, and reproved his troops for flinching from a danger so remote. "What? Men dodging this way for single bullets?" he exclaimed when he saw one outfit react in such a manner to a far-off sniper. "What will you do when they open fire along the whole line? I am ashamed of you. They couldn't hit an elephant at this distance." The soldiers wanted to believe him, partly because they admired him so — "Uncle John," they called him with affection — but the flesh, being thus exposed, was weak; they continued to flinch at the crack of the sharpshooter's rifle, even though it was a good 800 yards away, and at the quick, unnerving whiplash of near misses, which seemed to part the hair of every man at once. "I'm ashamed of you, dodging that way," Sedgwick said again, laughing, and repeated: "They couldn't hit an elephant at this distance." Next time the glass-sighted Whitworth cracked, a couple of minutes later, Sedgwick's chief of staff was startled to see the fifty-year-old general stiffen, as if in profound surprise, and slowly turn his head to show blood spurting from a half-inch hole just under his left eye. He pitched forward, taking the unbraced colonel down with him, and though the doctors did what they could to help, they could not staunch or even slow the steady spurt of blood from the neat new hole beside his cheekbone. He smiled strangely, as if to acknowledge the dark humor of what had turned out to be his last remark, and did not speak again. Within a few minutes he was dead.

Sudden as it was, his death was a knee-buckling shock to the men of his corps, who had made him the best-loved general in the army. Besides, when corps commanders started toppling, alive one minute and dead the next, struck down as if by a bolt of blue-sky lightning, who was safe? All down the line, from brigadiers to privates, spirits were heavy with intimations of mortality. Sorrowfully, the staff carried his body back to army headquarters and laid it in a bower of evergreens beside the road, there to receive the salute of passing troops till nightfall, when he began the journey north to Cornwall Hollow, his home in the Connecticut Berkshires. Nor was the grieving limited to those who had served under him, or even under the same flag today; R. E. Lee, across the way, was saddened by this final news of his old friend. Meade wept, and Grant himself was stunned when he heard that Sedgwick had been hit. "Is he really dead?" he asked. Later, after characterizing the fallen general as one who "was never at fault when serious work was to be done," he told his staff that Sedgwick's loss was worse for him than the loss of a whole division. For the present, though, he found it hard to accept the fact that he was gone. "Is he really dead?" he asked again.

One fact was clear, in any case, and this was that a great many men of various ranks, now alive, were likely to be dead before long if they were ordered to overrun the intrenchments to their front. Formidable as these works had seemed at sundown, they were downright awesome this morning after an unmolested night of labor by the troops who manned them. Studded with guns at critical points throughout its convex three-mile length, Lee's Spotsylvania line was constructed, Meade's chief of staff declared, "in a manner unknown to European warfare, and, indeed, in a manner new to warfare in this country." Actually, it was not so much the novelty of the individual engineering techniques that made this log-and-dirt barrier so forbidding; it was the combination of them into a single construction of interlocking parts, the canny use of natural features of the terrain, and the speed with which the butternut veterans, familiar by now with the fury of Grant's assaults, had accomplished their intricate task. Traverses zigzagged to provide cover against enfilade fire from artillery, and head logs, chocked a few inches above the hard-packed spoil on the enemy side of the trench, afforded riflemen a protected slit through which they could take unruffled aim at whatever came their way. Where there were woods in front of the line, the trees were slashed to deny concealment for two hundred yards or more, and wherever the ground was open or insufficiently obstructed, timber barricades called abatis were installed within easy rifle range, bristling with sharpened sticks to entangle or slow the attackers while the defenders, more or less at their leisure, picked them off. For Grant, the prospect was altogether grim. To assault seemed suicidal, and yet to do nothing was militarily unsound, since a stalemate under such circumstances might well allow Lee to detach troops for operations against Butler or Sigel, back near Richmond or out in the Shenandoah Valley. On the other hand, to maneuver him out of position again by swinging wide around one of his flanks would amount to nothing more than a postponement of the inevitable showdown, which in that case would occur in closer proximity to his capital and would probably result in his being reinforced by units from the garrison charged with its ultimate defense. Grant pondered these three alternatives, unwelcome as they were, until about midday, when Burnside, coming up on the left, provided information which suggested a fourth alternative, more acceptable than the others. While making his far-out eastern swing across Ni River, the ruff-whiskered general reported, he had encountered Confederate infantry, and though he had not had much trouble driving them off, it seemed to him that they might be the leading element of a detached force of considerable strength, engaged in a deep penetration of the Federal left rear for a strike at the army's Fredericksburg supply base.

Burnside could scarcely be classed as a skilled assessor of enemy intentions, but in the absence of Sheridan's cavalry, which might otherwise have been sent out to confirm or refute the validity of the report, Grant accepted the information at face value, partly on grounds that such a move would be altogether in character for Lee. By now, after

The Forty Days

the buffeting he had taken in the course of the past five days, the old fox must be groping rather desperately in his bag of tricks for some such table-turning maneuver as the one he had devised, under similar circumstances, when he sent Jackson wide around Pope's flank for a strike at the supply base in his rear, compelling that hapless commander to abandon his position in short order. Grant's reaction was equally characteristic, and quite different. Instead of allowing concern for his base to deflect him from his purpose, he saw in this supposed development a chance to strike from an unexpected direction while his opponent's attention was distracted and his army was divided. Hancock, who had come up on the right, was instructed to detach one division, as a possible reinforcement for Burnside, and proceed westward with the other three for an upstream crossing of the Po. A fast march down the opposite bank — first south, to reach the road from Shady Grove, then eastward along it to the bridge one mile west of the Block House — would put him in position for a second crossing, well below the point where the rebel flank was anchored, and a sudden descent on Lee's left rear. At worst, this should bring the Confederates out of their intrenchments by obliging them to turn and meet the unexpected threat; while at best, assailed as they would be from two directions, north and south, it would result in their destruction. In any case that was the plan, devised in reaction to Burnside's report, and Grant considered it well worth a try, especially since the ablest of his surviving corps commanders was charged with its execution.

Hancock crossed upstream that afternoon, putting in three pontoon bridges, and encountered only sporadic opposition from butternut horsemen on the prowl. Even so, he had not reached the Shady Grove Road, leading eastward to the downstream point where he was to make the crossing that would land him in Lee's rear, before darkness obliged all three divisions to call a halt in the woods on the south bank. An early start next morning — Tuesday, May 10 — brought the head of the column within easy reach of Blockhouse Bridge by sunup. To Hancock's surprise, there on the opposite bank, fortifications had been thrown up overnight and were occupied in considerable strength, bristling with guns trained expectantly on the bridge and its approaches. Once more, with the help of his hard-working cavalry, Lee had forestalled a maneuver designed to discomfit or destroy him; Hancock could only regret that he had not waited until this morning to make his upstream crossing, in which case he would not have afforded the rebels a full night to work on their plans for his reception. Not much given to spilt-milk thinking, he devised an alternate crossing, half a mile downriver, and got one division in motion at once, intending to follow with the other two, when a courier arrived from Meade with instructions for a quick return by two of his divisions to their former position in line on the right of Warren. He himself was to come back with them, the message directed, to take charge of his and Warren's corps for an all-out frontal attack on the Confederate intrenchments at 5 o'clock that afternoon.... Hancock scarcely knew what to make of this sudden change of plans. By now, one brigade of the advance division was across the river; he had only to follow with the other two divisions and Lee's flank would be turned; instead of which, apparently, Meade intended to revert to a direct assault, Fredericksburg style, on fortifications that were admittedly the most formidable ever constructed by an army in the field. Still, orders were orders, comprehensible or not. Recalling the crossed brigade, lest it be gobbled up in the bridgehead it was holding, he left his lead division behind, with instructions to continue what had now become no more than a demonstration, and set out at once with the other two to recross the Po by the three bridges they had installed with such high hopes the day before.

Back on the main front, to which Hancock was returning, Grant had ordered the change in plans as a result of Lee's failure to sustain Burnside's assessment that he had detached a major portion of his army for a strike at the Union supply base. In point of fact, what the IX Corps had encountered on its approach march, down across the Ni the day before, had not been infantry at all, but more of Stuart's ubiquitous cavalry, dismounted as skirmishers to delay the Federal concentration; Burnside had simply been mistaken, here as elsewhere in his career, and Grant decided that if Lee had not divided his army, it would be unwise for him to divide his own, particularly if this involved detaching Hancock, his most dependable lieutenant, who would be needed to help meet whatever crisis Lee had it in mind to precipitate, not in theory but in fact. Accordingly, he had had Meade summon Hancock back to his former position alongside Warren, who had also contributed to the decision by informing his superiors that, despite his failure yesterday, he believed he could score a breakthrough today if he was properly supported. It was true, the attack would be made against what seemed to be the most impregnable part of the rebel line, but when Warren declared that he had examined it carefully and believed it could be broken, Grant was altogether willing to give him the chance to prove his claim. Hancock would come up on his right, and Sedgwick's corps was already posted on his left; at 5 o'clock they would all go forward together, and if Warren's judgment proved sound, Lee's defenses would be pierced, his position overrun, and his army shattered. Richmond then would be Grant's for the taking, which in turn would mean that the war was approximately over, all but the incidental task of picking up the pieces.

It did not work out that way for a variety of reasons. Like Sheridan two days ago, Warren was anxious to accomplish something solid that would cancel his poor showing up to now, and this apparently

The Forty Days

made him oversanguine in his assessment of the chances for a breakthrough, as well as overeager to get started. Faulty judgment thus laid the groundwork for a failure which impatience served to enlarge. Around 3.30, with Sedgwick's corps alerted on his left and one of Hancock's divisions back in position on his right, he decided that to wait another hour and a half for jump-off time, as scheduled, would be to risk losing the opportunity he believed he saw. Or perhaps he acted out of knowledge that Hancock, when he came up on the right, would take command by virtue of his rank. In any case he appealed to Grant, through Meade, for permission to attack at once. Always ready to encourage aggressiveness, Grant was willing, and Warren — who had put on his dress uniform that morning, evidently for the purpose of making a good appearance on what he hoped would be his finest day since Gettysburg — went forward, around 4 o'clock; into chaos. Exposed in the slashings and snagged by the abatis, his troops were badly cut up, their ranks thrown into disorder by artillery and rifle fire from the flanks and dead ahead. Some among the bravest pressed on to within point-blank range of the rebel works, and a few even made it to the crest of the parapet. But that was all; there was no penetration anywhere along the line. Warren kept trying, only to have the process repeated. He was deeply discouraged at seeing his hopes break in blood on the rim of the intrenchments, even though Grant and Meade were not: not so deeply, at any rate, that it caused them to discontinue the effort to score a breakthrough here today. When Hancock arrived soon after 5 o'clock with his other division, back at last from his overnight excursion on the far side of the Po, he was ordered to resume the attack at 6.30, taking charge of all the troops on the right, his own and Warren's.

Elsewhere along the concave Union line, north and northwest of Spotsylvania, results had been no better up to now. Posted astride the Fredericksburg Road to block the movement Lee failed to make, Burnside had scarcely been engaged; his only consequential loss today was the commander of his lead division, Brigadier General T. G. Stevenson, a young Bostonian of high promise, who was killed instantly, much as Sedgwick had been the day before, by a long-range sniper. Sedgwick's corps, headed now by Horatio Wright, who was also a Connecticut-born professional, had made no more of a dent in the enemy defenses than Warren's corps had done, but a close-up look at the rebel works had given one brigade commander a notion of how to go about making a good deal more than a dent.

This was Colonel Emory Upton, a twenty-four-year-old New Yorker who had graduated from West Point less than a month after Sumter and since then, aside from a brief, unhappy period as a drill instructor of volunteers, had served with distinction in all the army's battles, winning five promotions along the way. Strong on theory, as well as action, Upton returned from a personal examination of the Confederate fortifications to report to his division chief, Wright's successor Brigadier General David Russell, that he believed he knew a way to score a breakthrough in short order. His notion was that the troops should attack on a narrow front, four lines deep, without pausing to fire until a limited penetration had been achieved; whereupon the first line would fan out left and right to widen the breach and the second would plunge straight ahead to deepen it, supported by the third and fourth, which would form the reserve and be called upon, as needed, in any or all of the three directions. Russell liked the plan and took Upton to see the corps commander, who liked it too. In fact, Wright liked it so well that he not only gave the young colonel twelve regiments to use in the attack, but also arranged to have a full division standing by to exploit whatever success was gained. Speed and precision being the main elements, together with a clear distribution of duties, Upton took the dozen unit commanders forward to the line of departure, along the edge of a dense belt of pines 200 yards from the rebel works, and indicated to each of them just what was expected of him. The point selected for assault was about midway down the western face of a salient which Ewell's corps had occupied to deny the Federals possession of some high ground where they might otherwise have posted batteries to enfilade this central portion of Lee's line, the two wings of which slanted sharply back from the salient or "angle," as it was called. Rebel guns were thick in there, thicker than anywhere else along the line, but it was Upton's plan to get among them fast and overwhelm the crews before they had much chance to use them. Having explained all this to the individual leaders, and shown them their objectives on the map and on the ground, he told them to bring their regiments forward, one at a time to avoid attracting attention to the buildup, and post them under cover for the assault, which was set for 6 o'clock, one hour before sunset and two before dark.

  At ten minutes past the appointed time, having waited for the prearranged bombardment to die down, Upton gave the signal and the column started forward with a cheer, three regiments in each of its four lines. Almost at once the rebel guns took up the challenge, blasting away at the mass of bluecoats running toward them across the field, but despite the delay involved in breaking through the tangled abatis, set up about midway between the woods and the intrenchments, men of all three leading regiments were mounting the parapet within five minutes of the jump-off. These first arrivers were shot or bayonetted or clubbed back — Upton later reported that at this stage the defenders "absolutely refused to yield the ground" — but as others came up, the weight of numbers began to tell. Presently there was hand-to-hand fighting in the trenches, which broke off when the second wave of attackers arrived and the badly outweighed Confederates turned and ran for their secondary defenses, just under 200 yards in their rear. Many did not make it, being captured or shot down. Meantime the first Federal line had fanned out left and right, widening the gap, and the reserves were surging forward to support the second in its continued penetration. So far, everything had worked precisely as Upton had planned; the rebel line was broken. Whether the break would be extended, or even remain — Confederate reinforcements were coming in fast by then from other parts of the salient — depended now on the division Wright had given the assignment of exploiting just such a success as had been gained.

This was not one of his own divisions, but the one that had been detached from Hancock when he crossed the Po the day before. Originally intended for support of the IX Corps, it had been attached to Wright when the threat to Burnside turned out to be nonexistent, and Wright had given its commander, Gershom Mott, instructions to support Upton by advancing simultaneously on the apex of the "angle," thus to divert the attention of the defenders away from the main effort, midway down the western face of the salient; after which he was to move fast to consolidate, and if possible enlarge, whatever gains had been scored in that direction. As it turned out, he was only too successful, both for his own sake and for Upton's, in carrying out the first half of this assignment. Forming his two brigades in full view of the objective, half a mile away, Mott did such a thorough job of attracting the attention of the rebels (particularly the gunners, who had crowded into that narrow space no fewer than 22 pieces of artillery with which to take him under fire across half a mile of open ground) that his division was knocked to pieces within minutes. Already badly shaken by their Wilderness experience, the troops milled about briefly under this pounding, some of them attempting ineffectively to return the fire with their outranged rifles, then scuttled backward in confusion, seeking cover and concealment. Staff officers, sent out to search for them that evening, found them deep in the rearward woods, huddled in groups about their regimental flags and boiling coffee to help them recover from the shock. Like Robinson's division, which had gone out of existence as a result of its misadventure two days ago, Mott's too would presently be abolished, the remnant of its two brigades being assigned three days afterward to another division in Hancock's corps.

But that was later. A more immediate consequence of the rout was that Upton's breakthrough went for nothing, not only because he was left without support, but also because the defenders now were free to concentrate all their attention and strength on healing the breach. This they were quick to do, obliging Upton to fight his way out of the rebel lines with much of the fervor and urgency he had displayed while fighting his way in. Darkness, gathering fast after sundown, was a help in the disengagement; all twelve regiments made it back to their own lines, having suffered about one thousand casualties. That was also about the number they inflicted, mostly in the form of prisoners taken in the initial rush and escorted into the Federal lines before the counterattack obliged their captors to follow in their wake. Far on the right, Hancock's attack, deferred till sunset, was repulsed at about the same time, as decisively as Warren's had been earlier, and Burnside continued his pointless vigil on the left. Night came down as the fighting ended. Men sat around campfires and discussed the events of the day, which provoked much blame of Mott and praise for Upton. Across the way, notes faint in the distance and filtered through the trees, a Confederate band lent an eerie touch to the scene by playing "Nearer, My God, to Thee," but this was offset to some extent, or anyhow balanced, when a Union band responded with the "Dead March" from *Saul*.

One of Upton's warmest admirers was the general-in-chief, who rewarded him with a battlefield promotion — subject, of course, to Washington approval — "for gallant and meritorious services." Much encouraged by the young colonel's tactical contribution, which he saw as the key to Lee's undoing if the maneuver could be repeated on a larger scale and properly supported, Grant was in high spirits. A headquarters orderly saw him talking to Meade about the prospect that night with unaccustomed animation, puffing rapidly on a cigar. "A brigade today," he was saying; "we'll try a corps tomorrow."

Thinking it over he realized however that tomorrow would be too soon. One trouble with today's attack was that it had been launched with not enough daylight left for its full exploitation; dawn would be a much better time in that regard, and the preceding darkness would help to conceal the massing of large bodies of troops within charging distance of the rebel works. So Grant, having ruled out tomorrow, decided that the assault would be delivered at first light on the following day, May 12 — which would also give him plenty of time for briefing all commanders, high and low, and an unhurried movement of units, large and small, into their designated jump-off areas. Given the method, the tactical execution was fairly obvious. Hancock would be shifted from the far right to the center, where he would be in charge of the main effort, and he would make it with his whole corps, against the very point that Mott had failed to hit today, the apex of the "angle," the military theory being that the tip of a salient was hard to defend because fire from the lines slanting back from that forward point could not converge on a force advancing from dead ahead. It was true, this theory had not applied too well on that same ground today; Mott had been wrecked before he got within reach of the objective. But Hancock's assault would be delivered Upton-style, without pauses for alignment or for firing, and if it worked as well for him as it had worked for Upton, his men would be up to the enemy works, and

The Forty Days

maybe over them, before the defenders had time to offer much resistance. Moreover this attack, unlike the one today, would be heavily supported. Burnside, off on the left, would move up close tomorrow night and launch a simultaneous assault next morning against the salient's eastern face, while Wright and Warren kept up the pressure on the right and the far right. Further details could be worked out next day, when the formal order was drawn up. In any case, after Upton's demonstration late today, a Tuesday, Grant had little doubt that Lee's defenses would be breached on Thursday and that careful planning would see to it that the breach was enlarged to victory proportions. He went to bed in a better frame of mind than he had done on any of the other five nights since May 4, when his army completed its crossing of the Rapidan unopposed.

That his mood was still the same on Wednesday, hopeful and determined, was demonstrated shortly after breakfast by his response to a request from a distinguished visitor, U. S. Representative Elihu B. Washburne of Illinois, that he give him some word of encouragement to take back to Washington with him. Grant's congressional guardian angel from the outset of the war, Washburne had spent the past week at headquarters, where, incongruous in somber civilian broadcloth amid the panoply of the staff, he had been something of a puzzle to the troops; they could not figure who or what he was, until a wit explained that the general, with his usual concern for the eventualities, had brought his private undertaker along on the campaign. Now that he was returning to his duties at the capital, the congressman told Grant as they stood outside the latter's tent to say goodbye, it might be a good idea to relieve the anxiety of the President and the Secretary of War by sending them some word on the progress of the fighting here in Virginia. "I know they would be greatly gratified," Washburne said, "if I could carry a message from you giving what encouragement you can as to the situation." Grant looked doubtful. He was aware that anything of the kind would be released to the public, and he did not want to be hurt, as others before him had been hurt, by the boomerang effect of overoptimistic statements. Pleased though he was with his progress so far, he replied, he knew that the road ahead was a long one and he was therefore "anxious not to say anything just now that might hold out false hopes to the people." He hesitated, then added: "However, I will write a letter to Halleck, as I generally communicate through him, giving the general situation, and you can take it with you." He stepped inside the tent, sat down at his field desk, and after heading a sheet of paper, "Near Spottsylvania C. H., May 11, 1864 — 8.30 a.m.," scribbled a couple of hundred words, puffing away at his cigar as he wrote. "We have now ended our sixth day of very hard fighting," he informed Halleck. "The result up to this time is much in our favor. But our losses have been heavy, as well as those of the enemy.... I am now sending back to Belle Plain all my wagons for a fresh supply of provisions and ammunition, and purpose to fight it out on this line if it takes all summer.... I am satisfied the enemy are very shaky, and are only kept up to the mark by the greatest exertions on the part of their officers and by keeping them intrenched in every position they take."

When he finished he had a clerk make a fair copy, which he then signed and folded and gave to Washburne, along with a farewell handshake, before returning to work on his plans for tomorrow's dawn assault. Staff officers read the retained draft of the letter, one afterwards recalled, without finding in it anything unusual or "epigrammatic" until a few days later, when the New York papers reached camp with excerpts from it splashed across their front pages in large headlines — particularly a phrase or sentence which someone, either the copyist here or another at the far end, polished up a bit: "I propose to fight it out on this line if it takes all summer." That caught the attention of the editors, and through them the public, with a force unequaled by anything Grant had said or written since the Unconditional Surrender note at Donelson, more than two years ago. "I propose to move immediately upon your works" had passed into history as a watchword signifying Federal determination to press for total victory over the forces in rebellion, and so too, now, did "I propose to fight it out on this line if it takes all summer."

Grant's assessment of the Confederates as "very shaky" indicated that he had not really believed it would take "all summer" to settle the issue at hand that Wednesday morning, north of Spotsylvania. By mid-afternoon — coincident with a sudden change in the weather, brought on by a light drizzle of rain that dropped the temperature from the unseasonable high it had been holding for the past few days — the field order for tomorrow's attack was being distributed to the commanders of all four corps. Already in close proximity to the enemy along their respective portions of the line, Warren and Wright would remain more or less where they were, and Burnside had only a limited adjustment to make. It was otherwise with Hancock, who had to shift three of his divisions into position with the fourth, Mott's, which by now, although considerably diminished and dejected, had been reassembled just in rear of the area where it had begun its ill-fated advance the day before. The division he had left beyond the Po when he returned with the other two, in accordance with orders from Meade, had also recrossed the river after a clash with a rebel force Lee sent over from his right, and in this rear-guard action the division had had to leave behind a gun that, in the haste of the withdrawal, got wedged so tightly between two trees that it could not be freed. Hancock took this hard, the more so because it was the only piece of artillery the II Corps had ever lost in battle, and he was determined to get full revenge tomorrow.

Just now, though, he had his hands full getting his troops into position for the attack at first light, which the almanac said would come at 4 a.m. The march began at dusk, along a narrow road soon churned to mud by a pelting rain that seemed to be getting harder by the hour. It was midnight before the head of the column reached the jump-off area and the four divisions, three of them wet and cold from their rainy march, started forming in the dripping woods. This too was a difficult business, for more reasons than the unpleasantness of the weather or the loss of sleep and lack of food. Here on reconnaissance earlier that day, unable to see far or clearly through the steely curtain of rain, Hancock had tried to get Mott's disheartened men to drive the enemy pickets back so he could get a look at the objective; but little or nothing came of the attempt — they had too vivid a memory of what those 22 guns up there had done to them the day before — with the result that his examination of the apex of the "angle," along with most of the intervening ground across which he would charge, had practically been limited to what he could learn from the map. And so it was tonight, in the rain and darkness. The best Hancock could do was give his division commanders a compass bearing, derived from the map by drawing a line connecting a house in their rear with a house in the approximate center of the rebel salient, and tell them to move in that direction when they received his order to advance.

Four o'clock came, but not daylight; the almanac had not taken the rain or fog into account. Finally at 4.30, though there still was scarcely a glimmer of light from what the compass showed to be the east, word came for the lead division to go forward, followed closely by the other three.

Fearing the worst as they stumbled forward through fog so dense that it held back the dawn, Hancock and his soldiers were in better luck than they had any way of knowing. For one thing, those 22 guns assigned to defend the apex of the salient up ahead, which they expected to start roaring at any moment, tearing their close-packed ranks with shot and shell within seconds of hearing a picket give the alarm, were by no means the threat they had been two days ago, when they all but demolished one of these four divisions attempting this same thing on this same ground. They were in fact no threat at all. They were not there. They had been withdrawn the night before, as the result of an overdue error by Lee, whose intelligence machinery, after a week of smooth if not uncanny functioning, had finally slipped a cog.

Reports of activity beyond the Union lines had been coming in from various sources all the previous afternoon. A lookout perched in the belfry of a Spotsylvania church, which commanded a view of the roads in rear of the enemy left, informed headquarters of what seemed to be a large-scale withdrawal in that direction, and this was confirmed between 4 and 5 o'clock by two messages from Lee's cavalryman son, whose division — left behind by Stuart when he took out after Sheridan, two days ago, with three of his six brigades — was probing for information in that direction. Heavy trains were in motion for Fredericksburg, young Lee declared, and Federal wounded were being taken across the Rappahannock in large numbers to Belle Plain, eight miles beyond on the Potomac. "There is evidently a general move going on," he notified his father. Here as in the Wilderness, the southern commander was alert to the danger of having his opponent steal a march on him, and here as there he was prepared to react on the basis of information less than conclusive or even substantial. Such activity in Grant's left rear could mean that, having found the Spotsylvania confrontation unprofitable and restrictive, he had one of two strategic shifts in mind: 1) a limited retreat to Fredericksburg, where he would consolidate his forces and better cover his supply line for a subsequent advance by land or water, or 2) another swing around the Confederate right, to interpose his army between Lee and Richmond. From Lee's point of view, though a similar endeavor had failed four days ago, the latter was the more dangerous maneuver, one that he simply could not afford to have succeed. In this case, however, he believed from the evidence that what Grant was about to attempt was a withdrawal to the Rappahannock line, and he wanted to prevent this — or, more strictly speaking, take advantage of it — almost as much as he did the other. In conversation with two of his generals about an hour before sundown he told why.

It began as a discussion of Grant's worth as a tactician. Lee was visiting Harry Heth's headquarters, on the far right near the courthouse, as was A. P. Hill, up and about but still not well enough to return to duty, when a staff officer happened to remark that, in slaughtering his troops by assaulting earthworks, the Union commander was little better than a butcher. Lee did not agree. "I think General Grant has managed his affairs remarkably well up to the present time," he said quietly. Then he turned to Heth and told him what he had come for. "My opinion is the enemy are preparing to retreat tonight to Fredericksburg. I wish you to have everything in readiness to pull out at a moment's notice, but do not disturb your artillery till you commence moving. We must attack those people if they retreat."

Hill spoke up, pale but impetuous as always. "General Lee, let them continue to attack our breastworks. We can stand that very well."

The talk was then of casualties, and though no one knew the actual number of the fallen on either side (Grant in fact had lost about 7000 men by now in front of Spotsylvania, while Lee was losing barely one third that many) all expressed their satisfaction with the present position, which they were convinced they could maintain longer than the Federals could afford to keep assaulting it. Lee rose to go; "We must attack those people if they retreat," he had declared, and in parting he explained what he meant by that. "This army cannot stand a siege," he said. "We must end this business on the battlefield, not in a fortified place."

From there he rode in the rain to the center, where Ewell had disposed his three divisions to defend the salient, one along its eastern face and the apex, another along its western face, where Upton had scored an abortive breakthrough yesterday, and the third in reserve, posted rearward under instructions to move quickly in support of any stricken point along the inverted U of the intrenched perimeter. Dubbed the "Mule Shoe" by its defenders in description of its shape, the position was a little under a mile in depth and about two thirds as wide, heavily wooded for the most part and crisscrossed by a few narrow, winding roads. Because of this last, which would make removal of the guns a difficult business in the dark and the deepening mud, Lee told Ewell to get the batteries that were posted in the forward portion of the salient withdrawn before nightfall, in order to avoid delaying pursuit of the Federals when word arrived that their retreat was under way. It was close to sunset now, and while Ewell got to work on this Lee rode to First Corps headquarters on the left. After giving Anderson the instructions he had earlier given Heth — to be ready to pull out at a moment's notice, but to leave his artillery in position until then — the gray commander returned to his tent to get what sleep he could between then and 3.30, his usual rising time at this critical stage of the campaign.

Within the salient, as night wore on and the rain came down harder, a feeling of uneasiness, which began with the departure of the guns, pervaded the bivouacs and trenches. At first it was vague — "a nameless something in the air," one soldier was to call it, looking back — but after midnight it grew less so, particularly for the men who held the "toe" of the shoe-shaped line and were closest to the enemy position. A sort of rumble, slow but steady, came from the saturated darkness out in front; some likened it to the muffled thunder of a waterfall, others to the grinding of a powerful machine. Veterans who heard it, over and under the pelting of the rain, identified it as the sound of troops in motion by the thousands. Either a retreat was under way, as Lee had said, or else a heavy attack was in the making. If it was the latter, there was difficulty in telling whether the enemy was moving to the left or right, for a strike at Anderson or Early, or massing for another assault on the Mule Shoe. One of Edward Johnson's brigade commanders, Brigadier General George H. Steuart, a Maryland-born West Pointer, went out to his picket line for a closer investigation. He had not listened long before he decided that the Federals not only were preparing an attack, but were aiming it at him. His next thought was of the gun pits standing empty along his portion of the works, and he went at once to Johnson to urge the prompt return of his artillery, parked since sundown back near Spotsylvania. Old Allegheny passed the request to

Ewell, who approved it. All 22 of the withdrawn guns would be back in position by 2 o'clock, he said.

When the appointed time had come, but not the guns, Steuart's anxiety mounted. After waiting another hour he went again to Johnson, who had a staff officer make the round of the brigades with orders for the troops to turn out and check the condition of their rifles, while another rode back to inform Ewell that the artillery had not arrived as promised. All this time, that muffled grinding sound continued in the outer darkness. Shortly before 4.30, just as the fog began to lift a bit, Johnson was relieved to learn that the missing guns were returning up the road from the base of the salient. Before they came in sight, however, the sound out front in the paling darkness rose in volume and intensity, drawing nearer, until it became the unmistakable tramp of a marching host. From a distance of about 300 yards a mighty cheer went up — the deep-chested roar of charging Federals, as distinguished from the high-throated scream that was known as the rebel yell — and heavy masses of blue infantry, close-packed and a-bristle with bayonets glinting steely in the dawn, broke through the fog directly in front of the apex of the salient. Alerted, the Confederates rose and gave the attackers point-blank volleys. In some cases the fire was effective, while in others it was not, depending on whether unit commanders had acted on the warning to have their men draw the dampened charges from their rifles and reload. Not that it mattered tactically; for whether their losses were high or low, the various elements of the dense blue mass surged up and over the parapet, into the trenches. Johnson, who was sometimes called "Old Clubby" because of the stout hickory stick he used as a cane to favor the leg he had been shot in, two years back, limped about amid the confusion and implored his troops to keep fighting, despite the odds; the guns would soon be up to settle the issue, he told them, and for a moment it seemed to be true. The lead battery unlimbered, there in the toe of the Mule Shoe, and managed to get off one round each from two of the pieces. But that was all. "Stop firing that gun!" the cannoneers heard someone shout as they prepared to reload, and looked around to find scores of rifles leveled at them by hard-eyed Federals who had broken the gray line. They raised their hands. Others were less fortunate, taking fire from all directions before they knew the place had been overrun. "Where shall I point the gun?" a rattled corporal asked a badly wounded lieutenant. "At the Yankees," he replied with his last breath. But the two rounds already gotten off were all that were fired before all but two of the 22 guns were surrendered, most of them still in limber on the road.

Lee was breakfasting by lantern light when the rapid-fire clatter erupted in the Mule Shoe to inform him that the enemy, far from retreating, was launching an assault upon his center, which he had stripped of guns the night before. From the volume of sound he knew the attack was a heavy one, and presently, when he mounted Traveller to ride in that direction, he saw at first hand that, so far at least, it had also been successful. Fugitives fled past him, streaming rearward, with and without their weapons. "Hold on!" he cried, removing his hat so they would know him. "Your comrades need your services. Stop, men!" Some stopped and some kept running past him with a wild look in their eyes. "Shame on you men; shame on you!" he called after them in his deep voice. "Go back to your regiments." As he drew near the base of the salient he met an officer from Edward Johnson's staff riding to bring him word of what had happened up ahead. Pouring in through a quick break just east of the apex, which was held by Stonewall Jackson's old Manassas brigade, the Federals had fanned out rapidly, left and right, to come upon the adjoining brigades from the flank and rear. Johnson himself had been taken, after being surrounded and very nearly shot because he would not stop hobbling about, brandishing his hickory club and calling for his troops to rally, even though a whole company of bluecoats had their rifles trained on him. Steuart too was a prisoner, along with a number of his soldiers, and the Stonewall Brigade had surrendered practically en masse when the enemy came up in its rear and blocked the possibility of escape. In all, no less than half of Johnson's 5000-man division had been shot or captured in the first half hour of fighting, along with twenty guns and well over half of the regimental flags.

That was the worst of it. On the credit side, Lee was presently to learn, Rodes's division, by "refusing" its flank adjoining the break at the apex, was holding fast to the western face of the salient, and Wilcox had managed to do the same on the right, where Early's line joined Ewell's, even though an attack of nearly equal strength had been made against that point by Burnside at about the same time Hancock struck. This meant that, up to now at any rate, the breakthrough was laterally contained. Whether it could also be contained in depth was another matter, and it was to this that Lee gave his immediate attention. "Ride with me to General Gordon," he told the orphaned staff man, and continued to spur Traveller toward the open end of the Mule Shoe, where Gordon's division had been posted with instructions to support Rodes or Johnson in such a crisis as the one at hand.

Gordon had already begun to meet the situation by sending one of his three brigades forward on a wide front, the men deployed as skirmishers to blunt the Federal penetration, and was preparing to counterattack with the other two, his own Georgians and Pegram's Virginians, when Lee rode up. "What do you want me to do, General?" Gordon asked. Lee wanted him to do just what he was doing, and said so, knowing only too well that unless the Union drive was stopped his army would be cut in half. Gordon saluted and returned to the work at hand. However, as he was about to give the signal to go forward he looked back and saw that Lee, faced with a crisis as grave as the one six days ago in the Wilderness, was responding in the same fashion here at Spotsylvania. Still with his hat off, he had ridden to a position near the center of the line, between the two brigades, with the obvious intention of taking part in the charge. Horrified — for he knew how great the danger was, even here near the base of the salient, having just had his coat twitched by a stray bullet out of the woods he was about to enter — the young brigadier wheeled his horse and rode back to confront his gray-haired chief. "General Lee, this is no place for you," he told him. "Go back, General; we will drive them back." Soldiers from both brigades began to gather about the two horsemen for a better view, and Gordon spoke louder, wanting them to reinforce his plea. "These men are Virginians and Georgians. They have never failed you. They never will. Will you, boys?" The answer was prompt and vociferous. "No! No!" "General Lee to the rear; Lee to the rear!" "We'll drive them back for you, General!" Lee kept looking straight ahead, apparently determined not to be put off, until a tall Virginia sergeant took the matter into his own hands by grabbing Traveller's rein, jerking his head around, and leading him rearward through the cheering ranks.

Behind him Lee heard Gordon's voice ring out above the roar of battle, which grew louder as the breakthrough deepened: "Forward! Guide right!" And while the Virginians and Georgians crashed into the woods to come to grips with the attackers, as they had promised they would do, the southern commander resumed his higher duties. Of these, the most immediate was to find some means of strengthening the counterattack now being launched, and in this connection his first thought was of the fugitives, the troops blown loose from their units when the forward part of the salient went. "Collect together the men of Johnson's division and report to General Gordon," he told the orphaned staffer. That would help, though probably not enough. He thought then of Mahone's division, detached from Early two days ago to meet the threat from across the Po at Blockhouse Bridge, and sent word for Mahone to leave one brigade in the newly dug intrenchments there, protecting his flank, and move at once with the other three to reinforce Gordon's effort to restore the integrity of his broken center.

In point of fact Gordon was already doing remarkably well on his own, first by stemming, then by reversing the flow of the blue flood down the salient. His success in this unequal contest — in effect, a matching of three brigades against four divisions — was due in part to the fury of his assault, inspired by Lee, and in part to the assistance given by the hard-core remnant of Johnson's division, as well as by the troops from the adjoining divisions of Rodes and Wilcox, whose interior flanks hooked onto the wings of his line as he advanced. All this helped; but perhaps the greatest help came from the Federals themselves, who by then were in no condition, tactically or otherwise, to offer sustained resistance to what Gordon threw at them. Boiling over the works and onto unfamiliar ground, a maze of trenches and traverses, thickly wooded in spots and cluttered with prisoners and debris, they scarcely knew which way to turn in order to make the most of the breakthrough they had scored with such comparative ease and speed. The impetus at this point came mainly from the rear, as more and more of Hancock's men continued to pour into the salient; eventually there were close to 20,000 of them in an area less than half a mile square, with such resultant jumbling of their ranks that what had been meant to be a smoothly functioning military formation quickly degenerated into a close-packed mob, some of whose members were so tightly wedged against their fellows that, like muscle-bound athletes, they could not lift their arms to use their weapons. It was at this discordant stage that Gordon struck, and the effect of his fire on the men in that hampered mass of blue was appalling. A bullet could scarcely miss its mark, or if it did it struck another quite as vital. Turning to breast the pressure from the rear, where there was little knowledge of what was going on up front, they broke as best they could, a stumbling herd, and fled back up the salient to gain the protection of the intrenchments they had crossed on their way in. Gordon's troops came after them, screaming and firing as they ran.

Down the eastern face of the salient, the critical point being near its base, where Ewell's line joined Early's, Burnside had attacked at about the same time Hancock did; but there was less confusion here, on both sides, for the simple reason that there had been no penetration. Recoiling, the three blue divisions — made up of greener, less determined men than the veterans under Meade — found what cover they could, within range of the rebel works, and contented themselves with firing at whatever showed above the parapet. This gave Wilcox so little trouble that he was free to assist in Gordon's counterattack, thus helping to keep Hancock off his flank. Across the way, down the western face of the salient, Rodes was able to do the same, for the even simpler reason that he had not been hit at all; not yet. But then at 6 o'clock, with Hancock's attackers tamped firmly back into the toe of the Mule Shoe, Wright struck. He came up hard, with everything he had, against that portion of Rodes's front where Upton had scored the original breakthrough, two days back. Rodes managed to prevent a repetition of that archetypical success, though only by the hardest. Much of the fighting was hand-to-hand, across the works, but Wright's attack, like Hancock's, was muscle-bound, hampered by its bulk; he too had close to 20,000 men and he was mindful of Grant's concern that he bring the weight of every one of them to bear. Rodes kept his badly outnumbered division in position, but he knew that the line might go with a rush at any moment under all that pressure. Accordingly, he sent word to Lee that if he was to prevent a second breakthrough — potentially even more dangerous than the first, since it would put the attackers in rear of practically every Confederate in the salient — he must have reinforcements, and have them quick.

They were already on the way from Blockhouse Bridge. Sent for earlier to strengthen Gordon's counterattack, the three brigades from Mahone's division could be used instead to shore up Rodes; provided of course that they came up in time. Impatient at their nonarrival, Lee rode westward in rear of Anderson's position — which had not been attacked, so far, but was under fire from Warren's long-range artillery — to meet them and save time by redirecting their march to the hardpressed west face of the salient, where the Federals were hammering at the works. Presently he came upon the lead brigade, Carnot Posey's Mississippians, now under Brigadier General Nathaniel Harris, a thirty-year-old former Vicksburg lawyer. Lee rode alongside Harris, giving instructions, and the Union gunners, spotting the column in brisk motion across the way, lengthened their ranges to bring it under fire. They concentrated mainly on the horsemen at its head, with the result that Lee had to give all his attention to Traveller, who began to rear wildly amid a flurry of plunging shot and bursting shell. Lee kept his seat, doing what he could to calm the animal, but Traveller kept rearing. It was well he did; for as he went back on his hind legs, boxing the air with his forehoofs, a solid shot, which otherwise would have killed or maimed both horse and rider, passed directly under his belly. Horrified, the Mississippians began to yell: "Go back, General! Go back! For God's sake, go back!" They tried to get between him and the exploding shells, urging him to hurry out of range, but Lee was in no more of a mind to retire from this fourth Lee-to-the-rear tableau than he had been to quit the other three. His blood was up, now as before; anxiety was on him. At last he said, "If you will promise me to drive those people from our works, I will go back." The soldiers cheered and, while Lee watched admiringly, took up the march at a faster rate, joining Rodes in time to prevent a breakthrough which one of his brigadiers had just warned him was only minutes away.

Now, however, this second phase of the contest, which ended with the approximate restoration of Lee's line, merged into the third, a struggle even fiercer than the two that had gone before. Tamped back into the toe of the Mule Shoe, Hancock's troops found cover by recrossing the log parapet and taking shelter behind it. There they stayed and there they fought, sometimes at arm's length, much as Wright's men were doing on their right, down the western face of the salient, where the region of Upton's abortive penetration acquired a new name: The Bloody Angle. The term had been used before, in other battles elsewhere in the war, but there was no doubt forever after, at least on the part of those who fought there, that here was where the appellation best applied. It soon became apparent to both sides that what they were involved in now was not only fiercer than what had gone before, today, but was in fact more horrendous than what had gone before, ever. This was grimmer than the Wilderness — a way of saying that it was worse than anything at all — not so much in bloodshed, although blood was shed in plenty, as in concentrated terror. These were the red hours of the conflict, hours no man who survived them would forget, even in his sleep, forever after. Fighting thus at arm's length across that parapet, they were caught up in a waking nightmare, although they were mercifully spared the knowledge, at the outset, that it was to last for another sixteen unrelenting hours. "All day long it was one continuous assault," a Pennsylvanian would recall. But in truth it was as much a defense as it was an attack, on either side, and the two were simultaneous. Neither victory nor defeat was any longer a factor in the struggle. Men simply fought to keep on fighting, and not so much on instinct as on pure adrenalin. Slaughter became an end in itself, unrelated to issues or objectives, as if it had nothing whatever to do with the war. Troops were killed by thrusts and stabs through chinks in the log barricade, while others were harpooned by bayonetted rifles flung javelin-style across it. Sometimes in this extremity even the instinct for self-preservation went by the board. From point to point, some wrought-up soldier would leap up on the parapet and fire down into the opposite mass of blue or gray, then continue this with loaded rifles passed up by comrades until he was shot down and another wrought-up soldier took his place. Rain fell, slacked, fell again in sheets, drenching the fighters and turning the floor of their slaughter pen to slime. Down in the trenches, dead and wounded men were trampled out of sight in the blood-splotched mud by those who staggered up to take their posts along the works, until they too were dropped or forced to retire because their weapons became so powder-fouled from rapid firing that they could not be loaded to fire again. High though the casualties were along this portion of the line, they would have been much higher if there had been time or room for taking aim. As it was, the largely unaimed fire — particularly heavy from the Federal side, where men were stacked up twenty deep in places — passed over the heads of the Confederates to destroy a whole grove of trees within the salient;

some, including an oak nearly two feet in diameter, were actually felled by the chipping bullets, which, to the amazement of a Vermont brigadier, continued their work until the fallen trunks and limbs "were cut to pieces and whipped into basket-stuff." One of Wright's officers, fighting in the Bloody Angle, tried afterwards to sum up what he had lived through. "I never expect to be believed when I tell of what I saw of the horrors of Spotsylvania," he wrote, "because I should be loath to believe it myself were the cases reversed."

Warren's infantry moved out at last, shortly after 9 o'clock, in a full-scale assault on the Confederate left, but this was broken up so effectively by Anderson's artillery and massed small-arms fire that not a Federal reached the works along this portion of the line. Severely hurt, the attackers recoiled and did not venture out again, permitting Lee to detach a brigade from each of the two First Corps divisions as reinforcements for Ewell in the Mule Shoe. They were sorely needed. It was noon by then and men were falling there from nervous exhaustion as well as from wounds. Veterans who had survived the worst this war afforded, up to now, went through the motions of combat after the manner of blank-faced automatons, as if what they were involved in had driven them beyond madness into imbecility; they fought by the numbers, unrecognizant of comrades in the ultimate loneliness of a horror as profoundly isolating in its effect as bone pain, nausea, or prolonged orgasm, their vacant eyes unlighted by anger or even dulled by fear. There were exceptions. One man, for example, stopped fighting to plunder an abandoned knapsack, and finding clean clothes in it, stripped off his butternut rags to exchange them for the laundered finery, underwear and all, then returned cheerfully to the grisly work at hand, apparently refreshed. But for the most part they had that look, well known to experienced officers of the line, of troops whose numbness under pressure might give way at any moment to utter panic, an abrupt collapse of all resistance. Unit commanders began to send word to superiors that the men were near their limits of endurance, but the answer was always the same: Hold on longer, a little longer, until a new line of intrenchments, under construction across the base of the salient by Martin Smith's engineers, could be completed to provide shelter for the troops when they withdrew. So they kept fighting, albeit mechanically, up in the blood-drenched toe of the Mule Shoe and down its western shank, and Hancock and Wright kept battering, although they too had most of the same problems with regard to keeping their larger masses of men involved in the meat-grinder action along those two portions of the line.

Sunset, twilight, and the following darkness brought no slackening of the struggle; 9 o'clock came, then 10, and then 11; "Not yet" was still the answer to urgent requests for permission to retire to the line being drawn across the gorge of the salient, half a mile in rear of the apex which had been under bloody contention for the past eighteen hours. Finally, at midnight, word arrived and was passed along the zigzag curve of trenches — defined against the moonless blackness by the wink and glare of muzzle flashes, fitful stabs of pinkish yellow stitching their pattern back and forth across the parapet — for a piecemeal disengagement to begin. Unit by unit, so stealthily that they were not detected, the weary graybacks stumbled rearward through the bullet-tattered woods to where the new line had been dug. It was close to dawn before the last of them completed their somnambulistic withdrawal and took up their position in the works near the Brock Road. Daybreak showed the abandoned salient held only by corpses, the sodden trenches yawning empty save for these and other shattered remnants of the all-day battle. Still hugging the outward face of the log barricade, the Federals did not cross it even now that the defenders had departed, and the Confederates were glad that this was so. Exhausted, out of contact at last, blue and gray alike slept on their arms in the mud where they lay, oblivious to the pelting rain. Lee had preserved the integrity of his position, but at a cruel cost, having had nearly 3000 of his hard-core veterans captured and a somewhat larger number killed or wounded. Grant had lost as many, if not more; 6820 was the subsequent Federal count for this one day, a figure almost as great as the total for the three preceding days, when the Confederates lost fewer than one third as many. The gray army, fighting for the most part behind intrenchments, had managed to maintain its one-for-two ratio of casualties suffered and inflicted since the start of the campaign. But that was by no means the whole story of comparable attrition, which, as it applied to the men of highest rank on the two rosters, was just the other way around. Eight days of combat had cost the Army of Northern Virginia better than one third of its corps, division, and brigade commanders — 20 out of 57, killed or captured or severely wounded — while its adversary was losing barely half as many, 10 out of 69. And presently word arrived that still another Confederate general was to be added to the doleful list, one whose loss might prove the hardest to bear of them all, since his absence in the past had left the army and its famed commander groping blind.

Soon after the blue assault was launched, on the morning of May 12, Lee received a telegram informing him of the mishap, which had occurred within ten miles of Richmond the afternoon before. "Gentlemen, we have very bad news," he announced to a group around him; "General Stuart has been mortally wounded. A most valuable and able officer — " He paused, as if in search of further words for a formal statement, but then gave up and merely added in a shaken voice: "He never brought me a piece of false information." His sorrow was commensurate with his personal affection for, and his military debt to, the stricken horseman. Still, throughout the long day's fight at Spotsylvania, he kept hoping that somehow Jeb would pull through this crisis, as he had escaped so many other dangers over the past three years. Late that night, however, shortly before the withdrawal to the line still under construction across the base of the embattled salient, a second message came; Stuart was gone. Lee put his hands over his face to conceal his emotion. Presently he retired to his tent to master his grief, and when one of the dead cavalryman's staff officers arrived to tell him of Jeb's last minutes, back in Richmond, he remarked: "I can scarcely think of him without weeping."

★ ★ ★

Directed by Grant, through Meade, to "cut loose from the Army of the Potomac, pass around Lee's army, and attack his cavalry and communications," Sheridan was determined not only to make the most of the opportunity, which came his way as a result of the high-tempered clash at headquarters earlier that same Sunday, May 8, but also to do so in a style that was in keeping with his claim that, left to the devices he had been urging all along, he could whip Jeb Stuart out of his boots. "We are going out to fight Stuart's cavalry in consequence of a suggestion from me," he told his three division commanders that evening, and he added, by way of emphasizing the highly personal nature of the challenge as he saw it: "In view of my recent representations to General Meade I shall expect nothing but success."

His method of assuring this was demonstrated at first light next morning, back near Fredericksburg, when the march began down the Telegraph Road, the main-traveled artery to Richmond. Riding four abreast, accompanied by all 32 of their guns and such forage and ordnance wagons as were needed, the 12,000 blue troopers comprised a column thirteen miles in length. They moved not at a run or trot, and not by separate, converging routes — both of which had been standard procedure on raids in the past — but at a walk and in a single inspissated column, compact as a fist clenched for striking on short notice. Not much concerned with deception, and even less with speed, Sheridan's dependence was on power, the ability of his three combined divisions to ride through or over whatever got in their path. Previous raiders had sought to avoid the fast-moving rebel horsemen, lest they be delayed or thwarted in their attempt to reach their assigned objectives; but Sheridan's objective, so to speak, was just such a confrontation. He defined the raid as "a challenge to Stuart for a cavalry duel behind Lee's lines, in his own country," and the more there were of the gray riders when the showdown was at hand, the better he would like it, since that would mean there were more to be "smashed up." His confidence was in numbers and the superiority of his horses and equipment: as was shown within an hour of the outset, when the head of the column ran into brisk fire from an enemy outpost line and stopped to ponder the situation. Little Phil, as his troopers had taken to calling him, came riding up and asked what was the matter. Skirmishers, he was told — apparently in strength. "Cavalry or infantry?" he demanded, and on being informed that they were cavalry, barked impatiently: "Keep moving, boys. We're going on through. There isn't cavalry enough in all the Southern Confederacy to stop us."

Southward the march led down across the Ni, the Po, the Ta, and around the mazy sources of the Mat — four streams that combined to contribute their waters and their names to the Mattaponi — until, well in the rear of Lee's far right, the column turned off the Telegraph Road and headed southwest for Chilesburg and the North Anna, three miles beyond which lay Beaver Dam Station, Lee's advance supply base on the Virginia Central Railroad. Stores of all kinds were collected there, drawn from the Carolinas and the Shenandoah Valley; Sheridan planned to "go through" them in the course of his move on Stuart and the Confederate capital itself, which he would approach by the front door, if it came within his reach, while Ben Butler's infantry was knocking at the back. Torbert's division, still under Wesley Merritt, had the lead, followed by Gregg and Wilson. Progress was steady all day long, mainly because Sheridan refused to be distracted, whether by threats or the rumor of threats, which were frequent, front and rear. When a rebel brigade launched an attack on his rear guard south of the Ta, for example, he simply detached one of Gregg's brigades as a reinforcement and kept the main body moving at the deliberate pace he had set at the start, on the far side of the Ni. Just before dusk the North Anna came in sight; Merritt crossed with his three brigades while the other two divisions went into camp on the near bank. Before long, the sky was aglow in the direction Merritt had moved and the night breeze was fragrant with the aroma of burning bacon, wafted northward all the way from Beaver Dam.

Much of the burning — close to a million rations of meat and better than half a million of bread, along with Lee's entire reserve of medical stores — had been done by the depot guards themselves, who fired the sheds to keep their contents out of the hands of the raiders. First on the scene was the brigade of twenty-four-year-old Brigadier General George A. Custer, Michiganders as skilled in wrecking as they were in fighting. They added more than a hundred railway cars to the conflagration, as well as two locomotives — one fourth of all the Virginia Central had in operation at the time — and for lagniappe freed 378 Union soldiers, captured in the Wilderness and en route to prison camps. After the excitement of all this, the horsemen bedded down for a few hours' sleep by the fitful light of the fading embers of the station, and were roused before dawn to get to work on the railroad track. Ten miles in all were torn up, together with the telegraph wires and poles that ran beside it, before the whooping troopers fell back into column to resume their march. Like their comrades on the north bank, they were well rested despite their overnight carnival of destruction, having slept in one large bivouac that required few sentinels, rather than in scattered groups requiring many. Reconsolidated, the three divisions proceeded again at an energy-saving walk, a road-wide dusty blue serpent more than a dozen miles long and crawling inexorably south. So leisurely, so unperturbed was this horseback saunter through the springtime greenness of Virginia — except of course for those engaged in the rear-guard fret of fending off the rebels snapping persistently at their heels — that the raiders had to remind themselves from time to time that they were deep in enemy country, out for blood.

By late afternoon (Tuesday, May 10: Upton was massing for his abortive penetration of Ewell's works, thirty air-line miles due north) the head of the column reached Ground Squirrel Bridge on the South Anna, and there in the grassy fields beside the river, well over halfway to Richmond, Sheridan called a halt for the night. He might have kept on; today's march had been a good deal shorter than yesterday's and there were still a couple of daylight hours left; but this was an excellent place to feed and water his mounts and rest his men. Besides, he not only was in no hurry, he also reasoned that Stuart by now, as he said later, was "urging his horses to the death so as to get in between Richmond and our column," and he preferred it so.

He wanted Jeb to win the race, since only in that way would it end in the confrontation he was seeking.

Stuart had accepted the gambit and was proceeding much as Sheridan supposed: with one exception. Unlike his opponent, who had stripped the Federal army of practically every horseman he could lay hands on, the southern cavalry commander had resisted the temptation to jump this latest adversary with everything he had, and instead of leaving Lee to grope as blind as Grant was going to be for the next week or two, had taken up the pursuit with only three of his six brigades, some 4500 sabers opposing 12,000 engaged in what might turn out to be an attempt to seize the scantly defended capital already menaced by Butler's army from the far side of the James. One factor in this decision to forgo a better chance at personal laurels was that he could not know, until the Yankees cleared Beaver Dam on the morning of the second day, whether their intention was to keep on riding south for Richmond or turn north for a strike at Spotslyvania from the rear, in which case Lee of course would need all the help he could get, especially from his cavalry. As a result of this limiting decision, made at the outset, Stuart knew as well as Sheridan did that, in light of the numerical odds prevailing, the confrontation could have only one result if it was head-on; Sheridan — whose three well-mounted divisions were equipped with rapid-fire carbines, whereas the three gray brigades

The Forty Days

were armed with single-shot muzzle loaders and mounted on crowbait horses — would ride right over him. Stuart's solution, in considering this dilemma, was not to avoid the confrontation, despite the likelihood that it would be disastrous on those terms, but rather to arrange for it to be something other than head-on and to get what assistance he could from the Richmond garrison, scant as it was, when the march of the two columns intersected in the vicinity of the threatened capital.

Whatever he lacked in comparative strength — even at the outset of the raid, before his underfed, short-winded horses started breaking down from the strain of the chase — there was at least no diminution of his accustomed vigilance and vigor. Pressing close in rear of the outsized blue formation with one of Fitz Lee's brigades, he sent for Fitz and his other brigade, as well as Brigadier General James B.

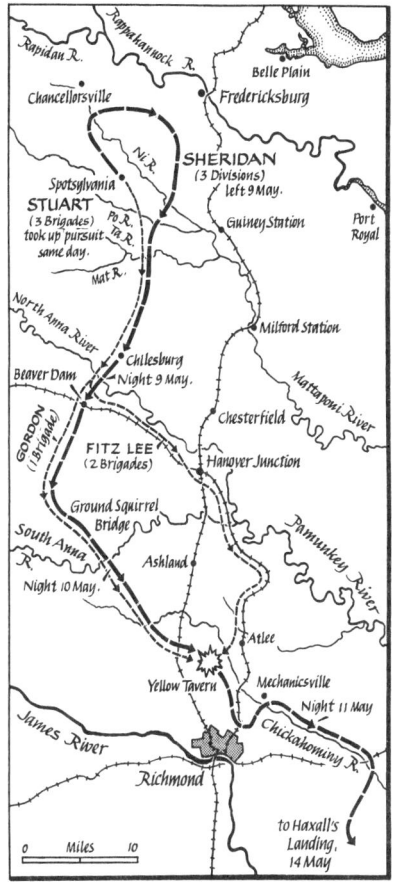

Gordon's brigade of W. H. F. Lee's division, and with these three took up the pursuit in earnest, first down the Telegraph Road, then southeast to the North Anna, beyond which, as night came down, he saw to his distress the spreading reflection of the flames at Beaver Dam, where a three-week supply of food went up in smoke while the men for whom it had been intended went hungry in the Spotsylvania woods. In just one day, by this one blow, Sheridan had accomplished more than any of his predecessors had managed to do in the past three years. What was worse, with Richmond not much farther south than he had come already, he seemed likely to accomplish a great deal more, unless Stuart found some way to check or divert him. Up to now, the grayjackets had been limited to attacks on the Union rear, since to have doubled the blue column for a strike at its head would have left the raiders free to turn for an unmolested dash against the rear of Lee's intrenchments. By next morning, though, with all the enemy horsemen over the North Anna, proceeding south past the charred base they had destroyed the night before, Stuart was free at least of that restriction; he could give his full attention to covering Richmond, since that now seemed without much doubt to be the Federal objective. Accordingly, he told Gordon to keep his brigade of North Carolinians close on the tail of the blue column, impeding it all he could, while Fitz Lee and his two Virginia brigades, under Brigadier Generals Lunsford Lomax and Williams Wickham, rode east along the Virginia Central to regain the Telegraph Road, just this side of Hanover Junction, and hurry down it to take up a position in which to intercept the raiders before they got to Richmond. A message went to Braxton Bragg, informing him of the danger to the capital in his charge. Stuart hoped to be reinforced from the city's garrison in time for the confrontation on its outskirts, but if Sheridan brushed past him, he told Bragg, "I will certainly move in his rear and do what I can."

So much for intention; execution, he knew, would be a larger order. However, before setting out to catch up with Fitz, Jeb took advantage of an opportunity Sheridan had unwittingly given him to call on his wife Flora and their two children, who were visiting on a plantation near Beaver Dam Station, thought until yesterday to be a place of safety from the Yankees. She came out to meet him on the front steps of the house, and though he did not take the time to dismount, he at least had the satisfaction of leaning down from the saddle to kiss her hello and goodbye before continuing on his way. The parting had a somber effect on the normally jovial cavalier. So many goodbyes by so many soldiers had turned out to be last goodbyes in the course of the past three years, and today was the anniversary, moreover, of the death of his great and good friend Stonewall Jackson. Stuart rode in silence for a time before he spoke to his only companion, a staff major, on a theme he seldom touched. He did not expect to survive the war, he said, and he did not want to live anyhow if the South went down in defeat.

Sheridan's calculation that his adversary would be "urging his horses to the death so as to get in between Richmond and our column" was nearly confirmed quite literally that night. Tireless himself, Jeb was not inclined to have much patience with tiredness in others. "We must substitute *esprit* for numbers," he had declared in the early days of the war, adding in partial explanation, not only of his exuberant foxhunt manner, but also for the gaudy uniform — red-lined cape, bright yellow sash, black ostrich plume, and golden spurs — he wore with such flamboyance, on and off the field of battle: "I strive to inculcate in my men the spirit of the chase." Overtaking Fitz Lee soon after dark near Hanover Junction, he learned from Gordon, who sent a courier cross country, that the Federals had made an early halt that afternoon at Ground Squirrel Bridge on the South Anna. This was within twenty miles of Richmond, five miles closer than Stuart himself was at the time;

Jeb was all for pushing ahead on an all-night march, until Fitz persuaded him that unless he stopped to feed and rest his weary mounts he would arrive with no more than a handful of troopers, the remainder having been left behind to clutter the road with broken-down horses. Stuart relented, on condition that Fitz would have his men back in the saddle by 1 a.m., but rode on himself for another few miles before he lay down by the roadside to get a little sleep. Up and off again before the dawn of May 11 — unaware, of course, that this was to be his last day in the field — he crossed the South Anna at sunrise and passed the farm where he had bivouacked, one month less than two years ago tomorrow night, on the eve of his first "ride around McClellan," the exploit that had made his name a household word. Nearing Ashland, four miles south on the Richmond, Fredericksburg & Potomac, he found that a brigade of raiders, detached from the main column, had struck the place the night before, burning a locomotive and a train of cars, along with several government warehouses, while tearing up six miles of track. Stuart quickened his pace at this evidence of what might be in store for Richmond, fifteen miles away, unless he managed to head the marauders off or force them into retreat by pitching into their rear while they were attacking the works that ringed the city. Today as yesterday, however, a staff officer who rode with him found him inclined to speak of personal rather than of military matters. "He was more quiet than usual, softer and more communicative," the staffer observed, believing, as he later wrote, that Jeb somehow felt "the shadow of the near future already upon him."

Informed by another courier from Gordon that the Federal main body had resumed its march from Ground Squirrel Bridge this morning on the Mountain Road from Louisa, Jeb found his problem as to the choice of an interceptive position more or less solved before he got there. Less than half a mile below the junction of the Mountain and Telegraph roads, which came together to form Brook Turnpike, a macadamized thoroughfare running the last six miles into Richmond, was an abandoned stagecoach inn called Yellow Tavern, paintless now, made derelict by progress, and set amid rolling, sparsely wooded fields of grass and grain. Stuart arrived at 8 o'clock, ahead of his troops, and after sending word to Bragg that he had won the race, proceeded at once to plan his dispositions. Sporadic firing up the Mountain Road confirmed that Gordon still was snapping terrierlike at the heels of the Union column, as instructed, and gave warning that Fitz Lee not only had no time to spare in getting ready to receive it, but also could expect no reinforcements from Bragg on such brief notice. Stuart's decision was to compromise between taking up a frontal and a flank position, since the former would invite the powerful enemy force to run right over him, while the latter would afford him little more than a chance to pepper the blue troopers as they galloped past him, bound for Richmond. He had Fitz put Wickham on the right, one mile north of Yellow Tavern, facing south into the V of the converging roads, and Lomax on the left, his left advanced so that the two brigades came together at an angle, presenting a concave front which allowed a concentration of fire upon whatever moved against them down the western arm of the V. By 10 o'clock these dispositions were completed; Stuart had his men in line, dismounted except for a single regiment, the 1st Virginia, which he held in reserve to be hurried wherever it was needed most. Within another hour the enemy too had come up and was massing for attack.

This was approximately what Sheridan had been wanting all along, and now that he had it he took care to make the most of it. Richmond lay just ahead, the prize of prizes, but he was in no hurry; Richmond would still be there tonight and tomorrow, whereas Stuart, with his reputation for hairbreadth extractions, might skedaddle. From noon until about 2 o'clock he reconnoitered the Confederate position, probing here and there to test its strength, then settled down in earnest, using one brigade to hold off Gordon in his rear, two more to block the turnpike escape route, and the remaining four against Fitz Lee, whom he outnumbered two-to-one in men and three-to-one in guns. For another two hours the fight was hot, sometimes hand to hand at critical points. By 4 o'clock Sheridan had found what he believed was the key to Lee's undoing, and orders went for Merritt to press the issue on the right, crumpling Lomax to fling him back on Wickham, after which the whole line would move forward to exploit the resultant confusion. Merritt passed the order on to Custer, who promptly attacked with two regiments mounted and the other two on foot as skirmishers, striking hard for the left of the rebel line just north of Yellow Tavern.

Stuart was there, having sensed the point of greatest danger from his command post near the center. A conspicuous target in his silk-lined cape and nodding plume, he laughed at an aide's protest that he was exposing himself unnecessarily. "I don't reckon there is any danger," he replied. For three years this had apparently been true for him, although his clothes had been slit repeatedly by twittering bullets and he once had half of his mustache clipped off by a stray round. Moreover, he was encouraged by a dispatch from Bragg expressing the opinion that he could hold the Richmond works with his 4000 local defense troops and the help of three brigades of regulars he had ordered to join him from the far side of the James, provided the raiders could be delayed long enough for these reinforcements to make it across the river. Jeb figured there had been time for that already, and once again was proudly conscious of having carried out a difficult assignment, though he was determined to gain still more by way of allowing a margin for error. Arriving on the far left as the two Michigan regiments thundered past in a charge on a section of guns just up the line, he drew his big nine-shot LeMatt revolver and fired at the blue horsemen going by. They took the guns, scattering the cannoneers, but soon came tumbling back, some mounted and some unhorsed by a counterattack from the 1st Virginia, which Fitz Lee threw at them. Stuart had ridden forward to a fence, putting his horse's head across it between two of his butternut soldiers in order to get as close as possible to the bluecoats coming back. "Steady, men, steady!" he shouted, still firing his silver-chased pistol at the enemy beyond the fence. "Give it to them!" Instead, it was they who gave it to him: one of them anyhow. A dismounted private, trotting past with his revolver drawn — John A. Huff of the 5th Michigan, who had served a two-year hitch in a sharpshooter outfit, winning a prize as the best marksman in his regiment, then returned home and reënlisted under Custer, apparently out of boredom, though at forty-five he was old for that branch of the service — took time to fire, almost casually in passing, at the red-bearded officer thirty feet away. Jeb's head dropped suddenly forward, so that his plumed hat fell off, and he clapped one hand to his right side. "General, are you hit?" one of the men alongside him cried as the blue trooper ran off down the fence line, pistol smoking from the fire of that one unlucky shot. "I'm afraid I am," Stuart replied calmly when the question was asked again. "But don't worry, boys," he told the distressed soldiers gathering rapidly around him; "Fitz will do as well for you as I have done."

They got him off his horse and did what they could to make him comfortable while waiting for an ambulance. Fitz Lee came riding fast when he heard of the wound, but Jeb sent him back at once to take charge of the field. "Go ahead, Fitz, old fellow," he said. "I know you'll do what is right." Then the ambulance came and they lifted him into it, obviously in pain. Just as it started rearward a portion of the line gave way and a number of flustered gray troopers made off across the field. "Go back!" Stuart called after them, sitting up in his indignation despite the wrench to his hurt side. "Go back and do your duty, as I have done mine, and our country will be safe. Go back, go back!" Then he added, though in different words, what he had told the staff major yesterday about not wanting to survive the South's defeat: "I'd rather die than be whipped!" Presently a surgeon and other members of his staff overtook the mule-drawn ambulance and stopped it, out of range of the Federals, for an examination of the wound. While his blood-stained sash was being removed and his bullet-torn jacket opened, Stuart turned to Lieutenant Walter Hullihen, a staff favorite, and addressed him by his nickname: "Honeybun, how do I look in the face?" Hullihen lied — for his chief was clearly in shock and getting weaker by the minute. "You are looking all right, General," he replied. "You will be all right." Jeb mused on the words, as if in doubt, knowing only too well what lay in store for a gut-shot man. "Well, I don't know how this will turn out," he said at last, "but if it is God's will that I shall die I am ready."

By now the doctor had completed his examination and ordered the ambulance to move on. He believed there was little chance for the general's survival, but he wanted to get him to Richmond, and expert medical attention, as soon as possible. An eighteen-year-old private followed the vehicle for a time on horseback, looking in under the hood at the anguished Stuart until it picked up speed and pulled away. "The last thing I saw of him," the boy trooper later wrote, "he was lying flat on his back in the ambulance, the mules running at a terrific pace, and he was being jolted most unmercifully. He opened his eyes and looked at me, and shook his head from side to side as much as to say, 'It's all over with me.' He had folded arms and a look of resignation."

Fitz Lee by then had restored his line, and Sheridan, after prodding it here and there for another hour, decided the time had come to move on after all. Shadows were lengthening fast; moreover he had intercepted a rebel dispatch urging Bragg to send substantial reinforcements. So he broke off what he called "this obstinate contest" north of Yellow Tavern, and pushed on down Brook Turnpike, through the outer works of Richmond, to within earshot of the alarm bells tolling frantically in the gathering darkness. This was the route Kilpatrick had taken ten weeks ago, only to call a halt when he came under fire from the fortifications, and Little Phil had a similar reaction when he drew near the intermediate line of defense, three miles from Capitol Square. "It is possible that I might have captured the city of Richmond by assault," he would report to Meade, "but the want of knowledge of your operations and those of General Butler, and the facility with which the enemy could throw in troops, made me abandon the attempt." His personal inclination was to plunge on down the pike, over the earthworks and into the streets of the town, though he knew he lacked the strength to stay there long; "the greatest temptation of my life," he later called the prospect, looking back. "I should have been the hero of the hour. I could have gone in and burned and killed right and left. But I had learned this thing: that our men knew what they were about.... They would have followed me, but they would have known as well as I that the sacrifice was for no permanent advantage."

Forbearance came hard, but he soon had other matters on his mind. Withdrawal, under present circumstances, called for perhaps more daring, and certainly more skill, then did staying where he was or going in. Gordon was still clawing at his rear on Brook Turnpike, and Fitz Lee was somewhere off in the darkness, hovering on his flank; Bragg, for all he knew, had summoned any number of reinforcements from beyond the James, and presently the confusion was compounded by a howling wind- and rainstorm (the one that was giving Hancock so much trouble, out on its fringes, on the night march into position for his dawn assault on the toe of Ewell's Mule Shoe) so severe that the steeple of old St John's Church, on the opposite side of Richmond, was blown away. Sheridan turned eastward, headed for Meadow Bridge on the Chickahominy, which he intended to cross at that point, putting the river between him and his pursuers, and then recross, well downstream, to find sanctuary within Butler's lines, as had been prearranged, at Haxall's Landing on the James. In addition to the rain-lashed darkness, which made any sense of direction hard to maintain, the march was complicated by the presence of land mines in his path; "torpedoes," they were called, buried artillery projectiles equipped with trip wires, and the first one encountered killed a number of horses and wounded several men. Sheridan had an answer to that, however. Bringing a couple of dozen prisoners forward to the head of the column, he made them "get down on their knees, feel for the wires in the darkness, follow them up and unearth the shells." Despite the delay he reached Meadow Bridge at daylight: only to find that the rebels had set it afire the night before to prevent his getaway. At the same time he discovered this, Bragg's infantry came up in his rear and Fitz Lee's vengeance-minded troopers descended whooping on his flank.

He faced Wilson and Gregg about to meet the double challenge, and gave Merritt the task of repairing the bridge for a crossing. Fortunately, last night's rain had put the fire out before the stringers and ties burned through; a new floor could be improvised from fence rails. While these were being collected and put in place, the two divisions fighting rearward gave a good account of themselves, having acquired by now some of the foxhunt jauntiness formerly limited to their gray-clad adversaries. For example, when instructed by Sheridan to "hold your position at all hazards while I arrange to withdraw the corps to the north side of the river," James Wilson made a jocular reply. "Our hair is badly entangled in [the enemy's] fingers and our nose firmly inserted in his mouth. We shall, therefore, hold on here till something breaks." Nothing broke; not in the blue ranks anyhow, though James Gordon was mortally wounded on the other side, shot from his horse while leading a charge by his brigade. Merritt finished his repair work in short order and the three divisions withdrew, without heavy losses, to camp for the night down the left bank of the Chickahominy, near the old Gaines Mill battlefield. Proceeding by easy marches they rode past other scenes from the Seven Days, including Malvern Hill, to Haxall's Landing, which they reached on May 14. The raid was over, all but the return, and Sheridan was greatly pleased with the results, not only because of the specific damage accomplished at Beaver Dam and Ashland, but also because of other damage, no less grave for being more difficult to assess. At a cost of 625 killed and wounded and missing, he had freed nearly 400 Union prisoners and brought them with him into Butler's lines, along with some 300 captive rebels. How many of the enemy he had killed or wounded in the course of the raid he could not say, but he knew at least of one whose loss to Lee and the Confederacy was well-nigh immeasurable. The killing of Jeb Stuart at Yellow Tavern, he declared, "inflicted a blow from which entire recovery was impossible."

After three days' rest with Butler he was off to rejoin Grant. The northward march was uneventful except for a rather spectacular demonstration, staged while crossing the high railroad bridge over Pamunkey River, of the indestructibility of the army pack mule. Falling from a height of thirty feet, one of these creatures — watched in amazement by a regiment of troopers whose colonel recorded the incident in his memoirs — "turned a somersault, struck an abutment, disappeared under water, came up, and swam ashore without disturbing his pack." On May 24 the three divisions rejoined the army they had left, two weeks and one day ago, near Spotsylvania.

Stuart by then had been eleven days in his grave, not far from the church that lost its steeple in the windstorm on the night he arrived from Yellow Tavern. After six mortal hours of being jounced on rutted country roads because the ambulance had to take a roundabout route to avoid the raiders on the turnpike, he reached his wife's sister's house on Grace Street at 11 o'clock that evening, and there, attended by four of Richmond's leading physicians through another twenty hours of suffering, he made what was called "a good death" — a matter of considerable importance in those days, from the historical as well as the religious point of view. After sending word of his condition to his wife at Beaver Dam, in hope that she and the children would reach him before the end, he gave instructions for the disposition of his few belongings, including his spurs and various horses. "My sword I leave to my son," the impromptu will concluded. The night was a hard one, with stretches of delirium, but toward morning he seemed to improve; an aide reported him "calm and composed, in the full possession of his mind." Shortly after sunrise on May 12, when the rumble of guns was heard from the north, he asked what it meant, and on being told that part of the capital garrison had gone out to work with the cavalry in an attempt to trap the raiders at Meadow Bridge: "God grant that they may be successful," he said fervently, then turned his head aside and returned with a sigh to the matter at hand: "But I must be prepared for another world." Later that morning the President arrived to sit briefly at his bedside. "General, how do you feel?" he asked, taking the cavalryman's hand. "Easy; but willing to die," Jeb said, "if God and my country think I have fulfilled my destiny and done my duty."

Davis could scarcely believe the thirty-one-year-old Virginian was near death; he seemed, he said afterward, "so calm, and physically so strong." But one of the doctors, seeing the Chief Executive out, told him there was no chance for Stuart's recovery. The bullet had pierced his abdomen, causing heavy internal bleeding, and probably his liver and stomach as well; "mortification" — peritonitis — had set in, and he was

The Forty Days

not likely to see another dawn. That afternoon Jeb himself was told as much. "Can I last the night?" he asked, realizing that his wife might not arrive before tomorrow because of the damage to the railroad north of Richmond, and received the doctor's answer: "I'm afraid the end is near." Stuart nodded. "I am resigned, if it be God's will," he said. "I would like to see my wife. But God's will be done." Near sunset he asked a clergyman to lead in the singing of "Rock of Ages," and it was painful to see the effort he made to join the slow chorus of the hymn. "I am going fast now, I am resigned; God's will be done," he murmured. That was shortly after 7 o'clock, and within another half hour he was dead.

Flora Stuart and the children did not arrive until four hours later, but were with him in plenty of time for the funeral next day at St James Church and the burial in Hollywood Cemetery. There was no military escort; the home guard was in the field and Lee could spare no soldiers from the Spotsylvania line. Davis and Bragg were there, along with other government dignitaries, but Fitz Lee's troopers were still out after Sheridan, down the Peninsula. Such were the last rites for the man John Sedgwick, dead himself for four days now, had called "the greatest cavalry officer ever foaled in America."

"His achievements form a conspicuous part of the history of this army, with which his name and services will be forever associated," Lee was presently to declare in a general order mourning the fallen Jeb. This was the hardest loss he had had to bear since the death of Jackson, and coupled as it was with the disablement of Longstreet, the indisposition of A. P. Hill, and the increasing evidence that one-legged Ewell would never fulfill the expectations which had attended his appointment as Stonewall's successor, there was cause for despair in the Confederate army, near exhaustion from its twenty-hour struggle for the Mule Shoe. Fortunately, as if in respectful observation of Stuart's funeral fifty miles away in Richmond, the following day was one of rest. For the next two days, and into a third, rain fell steadily — "as if Heaven were trying to wash up the blood as fast as the civilized barbarians were spilling it," a South Carolina sergeant of artillery observed. Such killing as there was was mostly done at long range, by cannoneers and snipers on both sides. There was little actual fighting, only a lumbering shift by the Union army, east and south. Lee conformed to cover Spotsylvania, extending his right southward, beyond the courthouse, to the crossing of the Po. The blue maneuver seemed quite purposeless, not at all like Grant; Lee was puzzled. Unable to make out what the Federals were up to, if anything, he remarked sadly to a companion: "Ah, Major, if my poor friend Stuart were here I should know all about what those people are doing."

Grant was not as quiescent as he seemed; anyhow he hadn't meant to be. During the day of rest from his exertions of May 12 he considered what to do to break the stalemate his headlong efforts had produced. A move around Lee's left would draw the old fox into open country, but in the absence of Sheridan's troopers Grant would be at a disadvantage, maneuvering blind against a foe who still had half his cavalry on hand. His decision, then, was to strike the enemy right by shifting Warren from his own right to his left on a night march that would end in a surprise attack at first light, May 14; Wright would follow to extend the envelopment which, if successful, would turn Lee out of his Spotsylvania works and expose him to destruction when he retreated. Orders to effect this were issued before the day of rest was over; but all that came of them was lumbering confusion and the loss of many tempers. Floundering through roadless mud, rain-whipped underbrush, and swollen creeks, the V Corps did not reach its jump-off position on the Fredericksburg Road until 6 a.m., two hours behind schedule, and had to spend the rest of the day collecting the thousands of mud-caked stragglers left exhausted in its wake. The attack had to be called off, and instead there followed another day of rest.

This time it was Wright who had a notion. The Confederates having conformed to the Union movement by shifting Anderson to their right, Wright suggested that a sudden reversal of last night's march — left to right, instead of right to left — would provide a capital opportunity for a breakthrough on the rebel left, which had been thinned to furnish troops for the extension of the line down to Snell's Bridge on the Po. Grant liked and enlarged the plan to include Hancock, setting dawn of May 18 as the time of attack. Reoccupying the abandoned Mule Shoe in the darkness of the preceding night, Hancock and Wright were to assault the new works across its base, while Burnside made a diversionary effort on their left and Warren stood by to join them once the fortifications were overrun. That gave two full days for getting ready; Grant wanted the thing done right, despite the mud. Moreover, on the first of these two days the rain left off, letting the roads begin to dry, and the second — May 17 — hastened the drying process with a sun as hot as summer. Everything went smoothly and on schedule: up to the point at which the six divisions moved into the Mule Shoe in the darkness, under instructions to take up positions for the 4 a.m. assault. So much time was spent occupying and moving through the first and second lines of the original intrenchments, undefended though they were, that it was 8 o'clock before the troops were in position to make the surprise attack that should have been launched four hours ago, at the first blush of dawn.

It would not have been a surprise in any case, even if the attackers had stayed on schedule. Rebel cavalry scouts, undistracted by the blue troopers taking their rest at Haxall's Landing, and lookouts in the Spotsylvania belfry, surveying the Union rear with glasses, had reported the countermovement yesterday. That left only the question of just where on the left the blow was going to land, and this in turn was answered by Ewell's outpost pickets, who came back in the night to announce that the assault would be delivered from the Mule Shoe. At first the defenders could not credit their luck; this must be a feint, designed to cover the main effort elsewhere. An artillery major, whose battalion had lost eight of its twelve guns in the dawn assault six days ago, reported later that he and his cannoneers "could not believe a serious attempt would be made to assail such a line as Ewell had, in open day, at such a distance," but he added that "when it was found that a real assault was to be made, it was welcomed by the Confederates as a chance to pay off old scores." Pay them off they did, and with a vengeance, from the muzzles of 29 guns commanding the gorge of the abandoned salient and the shell-ripped woods beyond, first with round shot, then with case and canister as the Federals pressed forward "in successive lines, apparently several brigades deep, well aligned and steady, without bands, but with flags flying, a most magnificent and thrilling sight, covering Ewell's whole front as far as could be seen." The conclusion was foregone, but the gunners made the most of their opportunity while it lasted. Double-timing over the mangled corpses of the fallen, the attackers managed to reach the abatis at scattered points, only to find the fire unendurable at that range. They fell back with heavy losses and the worst wounds of the campaign, and when they reëntered the woods they had emerged from such a short time back, the guns fell silent, not out of mercy, but simply to save ammunition in case the attack was resumed. It was not. "We found the enemy so strongly intrenched," Meade admitted in a letter to his wife, "that even Grant thought it useless to knock our heads against a brick wall, and directed a suspension." By 10 o'clock the one-sided carnage was over, and nowhere along the line had the opposing infantry come to grips. "This attack fairly illustrates the immense power of artillery well handled," Ewell's chief of artillery said proudly.

Perhaps by now, if not earlier, Grant had learned the error of his statement to Halleck, a week ago today: "I am satisfied the enemy are very shaky." By now perhaps he also had discovered the basis for what had seemed to him the overexaltation of Lee by many high-ranking Federals, who had not agreed with their new general-in-chief that the Virginian would be likely to fall back in haste from the Rapidan when he found the blue army on his flank. "Lee is not retreating," Colonel Theodore Lyman of Meade's staff wrote home that night. "He is a brave and skillful soldier and will fight while he has a division or a day's rations left." As for the troops who served the gray commander, wretchedly fed and clad though they were, Lyman considered them anything but shaky. "These rebels are not half starved," he added. "A more sinewy, tawny, formidable-looking set of men could not be. In education they are certainly inferior to our native-born people, but they are usually very quick-witted, and they know enough to handle weapons with terrible effect. Their great characteristic is their stoical manliness. They never beg or whimper or complain, but look you straight in the face with as little animosity as if they had never heard a gun fired." Indeed, at this stage of the contest, there was a good deal more disaffection in the Union than there was in the Confederate ranks. "We fought here. We charged there. We accomplished nothing," a blue artillerist complained, while a disgruntled infantryman protested specifically, in the wake of this second Mule Shoe fiasco, that the army was being mishandled from the top. The Wilderness had been "a soldier's battle," he said, in which no one could see what he was doing anyhow. "The enlisted men did not expect much generalship to be shown. All they expected was to have battle-torn portions of the line fed with fresh troops. There was no chance for a display of military talent." But that was not the case at Spotsylvania, he went on. "Here the Confederates are strongly intrenched, and it was the duty of our generals to know the strength of the works before they launched the army against them." He was bitter, and the bitterness was spreading: not without cause. There was a saying in the army, "A man likes to get the worth of his life if he gives it," and the survivors here could not see that their fallen comrades, shot down in close-packed masses flung off-schedule against impregnable intrenchments, had gotten the smallest fraction of the worth of theirs.

Whatever else he saw (or failed to see; he was admittedly not much given to engaging in hindsighted introspection) Grant saw clearly enough that something else he had said in the week-old letter to Halleck was going to have to be revised, despite the wide publicity it had received in the newspaper version: "I propose to fight it out on this line if it takes all summer." Stalemate was little better than defeat, in his opinion, and yet — having assaulted headlong twice, without appreciable success, and tried in vain to turn both enemy flanks — that seemed the best he could do in this location. Ten May days were a long way short of "all summer," yet they sufficed to show that he had nothing to gain from continuing the contest on "this line." So he decided, quite simply, to abandon it: not, of course, by retreating (retreat never entered his mind) but by shifting his weight once more with a wide swing around Lee's right, in the hope once more that he would catch him napping. Still without his cavalry to serve as a screen for the movement and keep him informed of his adversary's reaction — although it was true Sheridan had failed him in both offices before — he decided to try a different method of achieving Lee's destruction. He would mousetrap him.

Hancock was to be the bait. Grant's plan, as set forth in orders issued next morning, May 19, was for the II Corps to march that night to the Richmond, Fredericksburg & Potomac Railroad, six miles east, then down it on the far side of the Mattaponi River to Milford Station, well beyond Lee's flank and deep in his right rear. Lee could be expected to try to overtake and destroy Hancock, and this would mean that he would be exposed to the same treatment by Grant, who would give Hancock about a twenty-mile head start before moving out with the other three corps for a leap at the gray army whose attention would be fixed on the bright lure dangling off its flank, beyond the Mattaponi. That was the plan, and there was about it a certain poetic justice, since it was a fairly faithful reproduction of what Lee himself had done to Pope on the plains of Manassas — except that he had lacked the strength to follow it through to the Cannae he was seeking, whereas Grant did not, having just received about half of the more than 30,000 reinforcements sent from Washington over a ten-day period starting four days ago. By way of preparation for the move, he shifted Burnside around to the far left on May 18, returned Wright to his former position alongside Warren, and placed Hancock in reserve beyond the Ni, ready to take off promptly the following night on the march designed to lure Lee out of his Spotsylvania intrenchments and into open country, where he would be exposed to slaughter.

First, though, there was a delay involving bloodshed. On the day whose close was scheduled to see Hancock set out eastward, Lee lashed out at the denuded Federal right.

Alert to the possibility that Grant might steal a march on him, the Confederate commander, on receiving word that morning that the Federals had resumed their ponderous sidle to his right, ordered Ewell, who held the left, to test the validity of the report by making a demonstration to his front. Though he was down to about 6000 effectives — considerably less than half his infantry strength two weeks ago, when he opened the fight in the Wilderness — Ewell, feeling perky as a result of his easy repulse of yesterday's assault, asked if he might avoid the risk of a costly frontal attack, in case the Yankees were still there, by conducting a flank operation. Lee was willing, and Ewell took off shortly after noon on a reconnaissance in force around the end of the empty-looking — and, as it turned out, empty — Union works. Accompanied by Hampton's two brigades of cavalry, he carried only six of his guns along because of the spongy condition of the roads, and even these he sent back when he reached the Ni, about 3 o'clock, and found the mud too deep for them to make it over, although Hampton managed to get his four lighter pieces across by doubling the teams. So far, Old Bald Head had encountered nothing blue; but presently, he reported, less than a mile beyond the river, on his own in what had been the Federal right rear, "I came upon the enemy prepared to meet me."

What he "came upon" was Warren's flank division, posted beyond the Ni as a covering force for Hancock, whose corps was getting ready to take off eastward after sundown. Responding to orders from headquarters to reinforce Warren instead, Hancock sent his largest division first — a new one, just arrived the day before from Washington, under Brigadier General Robert Tyler — and followed with Birney's three bled-down brigades. Tyler had been a heavy artilleryman until recently, and so had all his men, except that, unlike him, they had seen no combat up to now. Their reception by the Army of the Potomac was unkind, to say the least. In addition to the usual taunts — "Why, dearest, did you leave your earthworks behind you?" — they were greeted by the veterans, who were returning from their botched and bloody assault down the Mule Shoe, with a gruesome demonstration of what was likely to happen to infantry in battle. "This is what you'll catch up yonder," the wounded told them, displaying shattered arms and other injuries Ewell's batteries had inflicted at close range. One roadside group had a mangled corpse which they kept covered with a blanket until one of the oversized greenhorn regiments drew abreast, and then they would uncover it with a flourish. The heavies had been singing as they marched, perhaps to keep their courage up, but they fell silent under the impact of this confrontation with what was left of a man who had been where they were headed. As it happened, the attack was suspended before they were committed. That was yesterday, however. This was today, and they were about to discover at first hand what combat meant.

Ewell, having found what he came looking for — or, to put the case more critically, having blundered into what he had been in search of — would have been glad to withdraw without bloodshed, but the bluecoats gave him no choice except to fight, not only at a numerical disadvantage, but also without guns to take up the challenge from the many turned against him. The resultant two-hour struggle, which began about 5.30, might well have completed the destruction of Lee's Second Corps if Wade Hampton had not managed to post his rapid-firing battery of horse artillery where it could hold the enemy off while Ewell fell back across the Ni and returned under cover of darkness to his intrenchments, minus another 900 of his men. The Federals lost a good deal more — 1535 killed or wounded or missing, most of them Tyler's — but at least they could claim a victory, having remained in control of the field and taken no less than 472 prisoners. A larger gain was the admission of the heavies to full membership in the army that had greeted them with jeers the day before. They had made up in staunchness, even veterans agreed, for what they lacked in skill. "Well, they got a little mixed and didn't fight very tactically," one of their officers replied to a question from a correspondent, "but they fought confounded plucky."

This last was good news for Grant, who was going to have to depend increasingly on such replacements in the weeks ahead. Three days ago, on May 16, with 12,000 of his cavalry away, his strength was down to 56,124 effectives — less than half the number he had mustered when he crossed the Rapidan, twelve days before. About 35,000 of the absent were battle casualties, lost in the Wilderness and here at Spotsylvania. Another 4000-odd had fallen sick and been sent to Washington hospitals to recover or to die. The rest, a substantial 14,000, were deserters or men whose enlistments had expired, members of the first of the thirty-six regiments scheduled for discharge when their time was up in May and June. There was, therefore, much encouragement for Grant in this May 19 evidence that he could count on the heavies, as well as on the newly drafted troops among them, for staunchness during the critical period in which they learned their bloody trade and became, in their turn, veterans more or less like the men who had jeered at them on their arrival but now would jeer no more. In any case, he depended on them to lend their weight to whatever blows he decided to throw, and he did not let his heavy losses for the past two weeks, on and off the field of battle, deter him from his purpose, which was to whip the rebel army in the process of maneuvering it back on Richmond. Today's affair amounted to no more than an interruption, a twenty-four-hour delay. He would move out tomorrow night, as planned: with one exception, one revision prompted by Ewell's sortie across the Ni that afternoon, which apparently served to remind Grant just how bloody-minded Bobby Lee could be. Instead of sending Hancock well in advance of the other three corps, to be dangled as bait on the east bank of the Mattaponi, he decided to move at a much closer interval, lest the bait be gobbled before the rest of the army came up in support. Accordingly, orders were sent, not only to Hancock, but also to Warren, Wright, and Burnside, that the march to Milford Station would begin tomorrow night, May 20, and would be conducted with all possible secrecy — in the hope, once more, of stealing a march on old man Lee.

But no amount of secrecy could hide what Lee already knew as a result of Ewell's rather heavy-handed investigation of the Union dispositions in his front. Grant had stripped his right for another shift in the opposite direction, and Lee prepared for another interception, alerting all three of his corps commanders to be ready to march at the tap of a drum. Despite such precaution, the enemy would of course move first; yet Lee had little fear that he would lose the pending race, whenever it began. He had chosen Hanover Junction as his point of concentration just beyond the North Anna, at the crossing of the two critical rail lines back to Richmond. From there he believed he would be able to parry any thrust the Federals were likely to attempt, and this time — unlike the last, in the sprint for Spotsylvania — he would have the advantage of the interior route of march, traveling the chord of the arc his adversary's movement would necessarily describe. His confidence, in this as in much else, was based on the events of the past two weeks; especially on a comparison of losses. Though he did not know the precise figures, even for his own army, let alone Grant's — the latter had suffered a total of 36,065 casualties (17,666 in the Wilderness, 18,399 at Spotsylvania) while Lee was losing barely half as many (just under 8000 in the Wilderness, just over 10,000 at Spotsylvania) — he knew that Grant's were disproportionately heavy. No opponent, so far, had been able to sustain such losses without removal from command or frustration of his plans by Washington; nor, he hoped, would this one, despite his known tenacity and his reported unconcern for costs. Lee's confidence was in himself and in his men. "With the blessing of God, I trust we shall be able to prevent General Grant from reaching Richmond," he had told the President ten days ago, and that trust had been confirmed. Moreover, though it was true the contemplated shift to Hanover Junction would mean giving up half the region between his present position and the capital in his rear, the line of the North Anna was one of great natural strength, highly dangerous for an army attempting to cross it, as Grant's would do, in the face of determined resistance. Besides, he was presently to remind Davis, "[Grant's] difficulties will be increased as he advances, and ours diminished."

One reason for this — in addition, that is, to the advantageous lengthening and shortening of their respective lines of supply and communication, vulnerable to attack by raiders and tedious to maintain — was that Lee would be moving toward the first reinforcements he had been able to count on, or even contemplate with any real degree of hope, since the opening of Grant's triple-pronged offensive. The reason he could count on them now was that two of the Federal prongs had, in effect, been snapped off short in the course of the past week. Breckinridge, out in the Shenandoah Valley, and Beauregard, on the far side of the James, had scored tactical successes which served not only to neutralize or abolish the separate threats from those directions by Franz Sigel and Ben Butler, but also to convert at least a part of each of those two outnumbered and hard-pressed Confederate forces into reserves, available for rapid shipment by rail to the Army of Northern Virginia from the south and west; which, incidentally, was still another reason for Lee's choice of Hanover Junction, where the two lines met and crossed from Richmond and the Valley, as his point of concentration after leaving Spotsylvania. By May 20, with the evidence getting heavier by the hour that the Federals in his immediate front were about to begin their march around his right, Lee called on both victorious commanders — Breckinridge by orders wired directly, since he was already under his command, and Beauregard by means of an urgent request to the War Department — to hasten the departure for Hanover Junction of every soldier they could spare from those two fronts.

It was well that he specified haste, for the signs of Grant's imminent departure continued to multiply all day. By nightfall Lee was so convinced that the Federals were about to march that he decided to begin his own next morning. Accordingly, he sent instructions for Ewell, whose corps would peel off from the left in order to lead the movement south, to start at daylight unless he saw an opening for a strike at the

The Forty Days [243]

enemy rear. Old Bald Head, finding no such opportunity, stepped off at 4 a.m. May 21 — a scant six hours, events would show, after Hancock started out across the way.

✗ 3 ✗

Sigel's offensive, like his chief's, was subdivided into three columns of penetration, each with a different preliminary objective to be attained before all three combined for a linkup with Grant's main body in front of Richmond. His own main body, consisting of about 8000 of all arms, would march the length of the Shenandoah Valley, from Winchester to Staunton, where he would strike the Virginia Central Railroad. Crook meantime, with roughly the same number, would move west of the Valley, southward in two columns, one of about 6000 infantry under his personal direction, the other of about 2000 cavalry under Brigadier General W. W. Averell, against the Virginia & Tennessee. Crook's objective was Dublin Station and the nearby railway bridge across New River, Averell's the salt works and lead mines at Saltville and Wytheville, a day's ride west of Dublin: from which point the two would proceed east along the Virginia & Tennessee to Salem, tearing up track as they went, and then turn north, through Lexington, for a hookup with Sigel at Staunton and, subsequently, with Meade somewhere east or southeast along the Virginia Central, which was to be given the same hardhanded treatment as the reunited 16,000 moved along it to be in on the kill when Lee was brought to bay.

Crook's being the more lucrative assignment, at least in the opening stage of the campaign — salt and lead were rare necessities in the Confederacy, and the intended double blow at Saltville and Wytheville would go far toward making them rarer — Sigel started first, on April 30, hoping to draw attention and troops away from the region beyond the Alleghenies. It worked. By the time Crook's infantry set out from Gauley Bridge on May 2, beginning the rugged trek from the Kanawha, southward up the left bank of New River to Dublin Station, a roundabout distance of more than a hundred miles, the rebel department commander was busy stripping Southwest Virginia of its few defenders in order to get them aboard trains for rapid shipment to Staunton and a fast march northward, down the turnpike, to challenge Sigel's bid for control of the wheat-rich Shenandoah Valley. Within another three days, when Averell's mounted column began its parallel march on May 5 from Logan Courthouse, fifty miles southwest of Gauley Bridge, the Confederate shift was well under way. Crook made good time, considering the nature of the terrain. At Shannon's Bridge by sunset of May 8, only seven miles from Dublin, he learned that a rebel force was lying in wait for him two miles ahead on a wooded spur of Cloyd's Mountain.

A fork-bearded West Pointer, Ohio born and thirty-five years old, a veteran of Antietam and Chickamauga, he rode ahead next morning to look the position over — and found it strong. "They may whip us," he said as he lowered his binoculars, "but I guess not."

He guessed right. The Confederate force of about 3000, part militia and home guards, commanded by Brigadier General Albert Jenkins, a former Charleston lawyer in what was now called West Virginia, was routed by a charge in which one of Crook's brigade commanders, Colonel Rutherford B. Hayes, made a showing that stood him in good stead when he ran for President twelve years later. Jenkins was wounded and taken, along with two of his three guns and many rifles dropped by his green troops when they fled; Union surgeons removed his mangled arm and gave him such care as they had time for, but he died the following week, thirty-three years old and still a captive. His losses at Cloyd's Mountain numbered 538, the Federals' 643. Crook, overcome by excitement and exhaustion — he had hurried about the contested field with his waterproof boots full of water from crossing a creek — fell to the ground in a faint as soon as he saw that the battle was won, but revived in time, attended by his staff, to order an immediate advance on Dublin and the Virginia & Tennessee Railroad, five miles ahead. Arriving before dark, he put his men to work firing and wrecking the depot installations, along with a large accumulation of military stores, and set out at first light next morning, May 10, to destroy the 400-foot wooden railway bridge across New River, eight miles east. By midday it was burning briskly, and soon afterwards it collapsed with a great hiss of steam into the river. "A fine scene it was," Hayes noted in his diary.

Having thus carried out his preliminary assignment — marching and fighting and wrecking, all three boldly and with skill — Crook now had only to wait for Averell to join him and continue the movement as planned, east along the railroad to Salem, then north through Lexington for the meeting with Sigel at Staunton. Yet he did neither. He not only declined to wait for the cavalry column, he also declined to press on eastward in accordance with his orders. Instead he decided to return at once to West Virginia: specifically to Meadow Bluff, on the Greenbrier River near Lewisburg, where he could draw supplies from Gauley Bridge, his starting point some fifty miles northwest. His reason, as he gave it two weeks later in his report, was that "I saw [at the Dublin telegraph office] dispatches from Richmond stating that General Grant had been repulsed and was retreating, which determined me to move to Lewisburg as rapidly as possible." Isolated as he was, and accepting the rebel claim at face value, he feared that Lee would send troops west by rail from Orange to cut him off and up, and under pressure of this fear he bolted for the fastness of the mountains. Not even the arrival of outriders from Averell, bringing word that the troopers had found

The Forty Days [245]

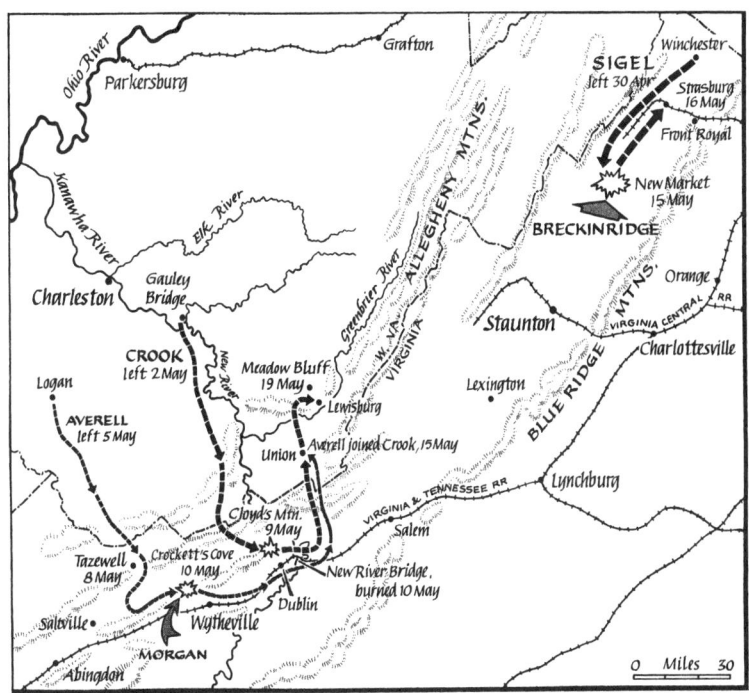

Saltville too well guarded for attack but that the column was moving on Wytheville even now, deterred Crook from making as quick a getaway as he could manage. He simply replied that Averell was to do his best to carry out the instructions he himself had just discarded, and took off northward, well beyond New River, which he crossed upstream and down. He made good time. It was five days later, May 15, before the cavalry overtook him at Union, eight miles beyond the West Virginia line.

Averell had a harrowing tale to tell: one that was unrelieved, moreover, by any such tactical victory as Cloyd's Mountain or any such gaudy feat as the demolition of New River Bridge. He had raided in this direction before, with conspicuous success, including the burning of Salem in December, but that had been done against next to no opposition. This time there was not only a considerable force in opposition — as he was told when he reached Tazewell on May 8, just this side of the state line — it was also commanded by John Morgan, who was known to be hungry for revenge for the indignities he had suffered in the Ohio Penitentiary during the four months preceding his year-end breakout. Now he was back in the field at last, having been rejoined by about 750 of his "terrible men," survivors of the disastrous July raid through Indiana and Ohio, and was posted at Abingdon to work with local units in defense of a department including portions of Southwest

Virginia and East Tennessee. At Tazewell Averell learned that the famed Kentuckian had shifted his headquarters and his troops to Saltville when he got word that a blue column was headed that way. What his strength was Averell did not know; he estimated it at 4500, better than twice his own. Consequently, he decided to forgo the scheduled destruction of the salt works, vital though they were to the Confederacy's efforts to feed its armies, and to strike instead directly at Wytheville and the lead mines, leaving Morgan holding the bag at Saltville. He feinted in that direction on May 9, then swung east, riding hard to give the rebels the slip. He thought he had succeeded until, approaching Wytheville the following afternoon, he found Morgan drawn up to meet him at a place called Crockett's Cove.

The position was admirably suited for defense, but that was not what Morgan had in mind. Fuming because the approach of the enemy column had delayed a projected return to his native Bluegrass, he charged and struck and kept on charging and striking the rattled Federals, who thus were afforded no chance to discover that they were not outnumbered. "My men fought magnificently, driving them from hill to hill," he wrote his wife that night. "It was certainly the greatest sight I ever witnessed to see a handful of men driving such masses before them. Averell fought his men elegantly, tried time and time again to get them to charge, but our boys gave them no time to form." This was Morgan's first engagement since the late-November jailbreak and he made the most of it until darkness ended the running fight, four miles east of Wytheville. He turned back then for Abingdon, to resume his plans for another "ride" into Kentucky, and Averell, minus 114 of his troopers, limped eastward to Dublin and beyond, where the railroad bridge had toppled hissing into New River that afternoon. Informed by his outriders that Crook had shied off into the mountains, he forded the river and tore up another ten miles of track and culverts before turning north to overtake his chief at Union on May 15. Hungry because supplies were low, and lashed by heavy rains, the reunited column spent two days getting over the swollen Greenbrier, then trudged upstream to Meadow Bluff, May 19, on the verge of exhaustion.

Crook's infantry had been seventeen days on the march from Gauley Bridge, the last eight without a regular issue of rations, and had crossed seventeen mountain ranges, each a bit steeper, it seemed, than the one before. They had accomplished little, aside from incidental damage to the railroad and the destruction of the New River bridge, but Crook was reassured to learn at Meadow Bluff that his superior, the major general commanding the department, had accomplished even less in the Shenandoah Valley. In fact, it now developed, the wide-swinging western column had been quite right not to press on east and north to Staunton, as instructed, since Sigel had covered barely half the distance from Winchester to that point, marching deliberately up the Valley

The Forty Days

Pike, before he was obliged to turn and flee back down it, pursued by the victors of the battle that had defined the limit of his penetration.

It was Breckinridge's doing, and he did it on his own. Hearing from Lee in early May, while the Army of Northern Virginia was on its way to the confrontation with Grant in the thickets south of the Rapidan, that he was to assume "general direction of affairs" beyond the Blue Ridge, the former U.S. Vice President, electoral runner-up to Lincoln in the presidential race of 1860, continued his efforts to collect all movable troops in Southwest Virginia for a meeting with Sigel in the Valley. "I trust you will drive the enemy back," Lee had told him, and the tall, handsome Kentuckian, forty-three years old, with lustrous eyes, a ponderous brow, and the drooped mustache of a Sicilian brigand, was determined to do just that. Accordingly, he left the defense of the western reaches of his department to Jenkins and Morgan, scant though their resources would be in event of an attack, and set out for Staunton at once, by rail, with two veteran brigades of infantry totaling just under 2500 men. North of there, and hard at work observing and impeding Federal progress south of Winchester, was Brigadier General John D. Imboden, whose 1500 cavalry were all that would stand in Sigel's path until Breckinridge arrived. The Kentuckian reached Staunton on May 12 and set off promptly down the turnpike for New Market, forty miles away, where Imboden was skirmishing with advance elements of the blue main body, still a dozen miles to the north. Including these butternut troopers, Breckinridge would go into battle with close to 5000 of all arms: a figure he attained by mustering all the militia roundabout — 750 at the most — and by summoning from Lexington the cadet corps of the Virginia Military Institute, 247 strong, all under conscription age and commanded by one of their professors, who later recalled that although Breckinridge said he hoped to keep these fifteen-, sixteen-, and seventeen-year-olds in reserve through the bloodiest part of the fighting (thus to avoid what Jefferson Davis had referred to as "grinding the seed corn of the nation") he added in all honesty that, "should occasion require it, he would use them very freely."

Occasion was likely to require it. Pleased that he had succeeded in drawing the rebels north and east, away from the now vulnerable installations in Southwest Virginia, Sigel was intent on completing his preliminary assignment by winning control of the Shenandoah Valley before the wheat in its fields was ripe for grinding into flour to feed Lee's army. This would entail whipping the gray force gathering to meet him, and he marched south with that welcome task in mind, anticipating his first victory since Pea Ridge, out in Arkansas more than two years ago, for which he had been made a major general. All the battles he had been involved in since that time, however slightly, had been defeats — Second Bull Run and Fredericksburg were examples — with the result that his demonstrations of military competence had been limited to the conduct of retreats. A book soldier, academy-trained in his native Germany, which he had fled in his mid-twenties after serving as Minister of War in the revolution of 1848, he was anxious to win the glory he had prepared for, though he did not let ambition make him rash. Advancing from Winchester, up the turnpike that led ninety miles to Staunton, he moved with skill and proper deliberation. There were mishaps, such as the loss of 464 men in a cavalry regiment surprised and captured by Imboden while on outpost duty beyond Front Royal, May 11, but Sigel knew how to accept such incidental reverses without distraction, even though this one, combined with the need for detaching troops to guard his lengthening supply line, reduced his combat strength to roughly 6500 of all arms. Past Strasburg by then, he kept his mind on the job ahead and continued his march up the pike to Mount Jackson, terminus of the Manassas Gap Railroad, on May 14. This was only seven miles from New Market, occupation of which would give him control of the single road across Massanutton Mountain and thus secure his left flank practically all the rest of the way to Staunton. He had sent his cavalry ahead to seize the crossing of the north fork of the Shenandoah River, two miles south of Mount Jackson, and when they arrived that afternoon they were taken under fire by a rebel battery posted on a height just over a mile beyond the bridge. They settled down to a brisk artillery exchange, preparing to force a crossing, but Sigel — perhaps recalling what had happened three days ago, when nearly 500 other troopers had been gobbled up near Front Royal — sent word that he preferred to wait until the infantry came up next morning, when all arms would combine to do the thing in style.

Breckinridge was within earshot of the cannonade. Just arrived from Staunton with his two brigades, plus the VMI cadets, he was taking a late afternoon dinner with Imboden at Lacy Springs, a dozen miles to the south, and when he heard the guns begin to rumble he told the cavalryman to return at once to New Market, hold the crossing of the North Fork till dark if possible, then fall back to a position just this side of the town, where he would join him before daybreak. Imboden, with Sigel's coöperation, carried out these instructions to the letter. Awakened at dawn by the arrival of the infantry — Sunday, May 15 — he assisted in getting the troops in line for what was intended to be a defensive battle. But when sunrise gave a clear view of the field, Breckinridge studied it carefully through his glasses and changed his mind. Sigel's men had crossed the river at first light to take up a position astride the turnpike north of town, and the Kentuckian apparently liked the looks of what he saw. "We can attack and whip them here," he said. "I'll do it."

And did. While the Confederates were adjusting their dispositions for attack, the guns on both sides — 28 of them Union, opposed by half as many firing north — began exchanging long-range shots across the rooftops of the town. This continued for an hour, at the end of which the gray line started forward, one brigade on the right, the other on the left, with a regiment of dismounted cavalry between them on the pike, supported by the cadets whose spruce uniforms had resulted in their being greeted with cat-calls by veterans on the march; "Katydids," they called them. Imboden struck first with a horseback charge through some woods on the right, and the infantry went forward through the town, cheered by citizens who came running out to meet them. On the far side, they scattered the blue pickets, then went for the main line. Sigel disengaged skillfully and fell back half a mile, disposing his troops on high ground to the left and right of a hillock on which a six-gun battery was slamming rapid-fire shots into the ranks of the advancing rebels. Spotting this as the key to the position, Breckinridge ordered the dismounted troopers to charge and take it, supported by the cadets; which they did, though only by the hardest, not only because of heavy fire from the well-served artillery, but also because of a gully to their front, less than two hundred yards from the fuming line of guns and floored with what turned out to be calf-deep mud. Moreover, as the movement progressed, it was the troopers who were in support. Lighter, more agile, and above all more ardent, the cadets made better time across the soft-bottomed depression, and though they were hit repeatedly with point-blank canister, they soon were among the cannoneers, having suffered better than twenty percent casualties in the charge: 8 killed and 46 wounded. Slathered with clay and stained by smoke, many of them barefoot, having lost their shoes and socks in the mud of the gully, the survivors were scarcely recognizable as yesterday's dapper Katydids. But they carried the position. "A wild yell went up," Imboden would remember, "when a cadet mounted a caisson and waved the Institute flag in triumph over it."

Sigel was in his element. Lean-faced and eager, not yet forty, his lank hair brushed dramatically back to bring out his sharp features and brief chin beard, he maintained an icy, steel-eyed posture under fire, but betrayed his inner excitement by snapping his fingers disdainfully at shellbursts as he rode about, barking orders at his staff. Unfortunately, he barked them in German, which resulted in some confusion: as, for example, when he directed that two companies of a West Virginia regiment move up to protect the six-gun battery under attack by the cadets. "To my surprise," he later protested, "there was no disposition to advance. In fact, in spite of entreaties and reproaches, the men could not be moved an inch!" And when the rest of the gray line surged forward to take advantage of the respite gained by the boy soldiers, there was nothing Sigel could do but attempt another displacement, and this he did, as skillfully as he had performed the first, though at a considerably higher cost. By now he was back on the knoll from which the rebel horse artillery had challenged his crossing of the river yesterday, four miles north of town. He held on there, through a lull occasioned by the need for refilling the cartridge boxes of the attackers, and when they came on again he fell back across the North Fork, burning the bridge behind him. Secure from pursuit, at least for the present, he intended to stand his ground despite heavy losses (831 killed and wounded and missing, as compared to the enemy's 577) but decided a better course would be to retire to Mount Jackson, where he could rest and refit before resuming his interrupted southward march. He got there around 7 o'clock that evening, took up a stout position, and remained in it about two hours before concluding that the wisest course, after all, would be to return to Strasburg, another twenty miles back down the pike. A night march got him there the following afternoon, and after one more trifling readjustment — rearward across Cedar Creek next morning, May 17, to make camp on the heights he had left a week ago — he finished his long withdrawal from the unfortunate field of New Market and began making incisive preparations for a return.

But that was not to be; not for Sigel at any rate. Stymied at Spotsylvania, Grant was growing impatient at having heard nothing of or from his director of operations beyond the Blue Ridge. "Cannot General Sigel go up Shenandoah Valley to Staunton?" he wired Halleck, who replied that, far from advancing, Sigel was "already in full retreat. ... If you expect anything from him you will be mistaken," Halleck added. "He will do nothing but run. He never did anything else." Grant was furious: about as much so as he was with Banks, whose Red River fiasco came to an end that same week. Four days later, on May 21, Franz Sigel was relieved of his over-all command.

Lee on the other hand was delighted with his lieutenant's conduct of affairs in that direction, and was quick to express his gratitude. "I offer you the thanks of this army for the victory over General Sigel," he wired Breckinridge on the morning after the battle. "Press him down the Valley, and if practicable follow him into Maryland." This last was in line with the suggestion he had made to Stonewall Jackson, two years ago today, at the outset of the campaign that had frightened the Washington authorities into withholding troops from McClellan's drive on Richmond, and he hoped that it might have the same effect on Grant's more energetic effort. In any event, New Market had saved the wheat crop in what was called "the bread basket of Virginia," and even if Breckinridge lacked the strength to undertake a crossing of the Potomac, it at least freed a portion of his command to reinforce the army north of Richmond. Lee, in a follow-up telegram that same day, left the decision to the general on the scene. "If you can follow Sigel into Maryland, you will do more good than by joining us," he wired. "[But] if you cannot, and your command is not otherwise needed in the Valley or in your department, I desire you to prepare to join me."

Breckinridge answered next morning that he preferred the latter course. He would move, he said, with 2500 men. Anticipating the shift from Spotsylvania, Lee replied: "Proceed with infantry to Hanover Junction by railroad. Cavalry, if available, can march."

★ ★ ★

That was on May 17, the day when news of a greater victory, together with the promise of much heavier reinforcements, was relayed to Lee from Beauregard, twelve days into a campaign that began with every prospect of a Union triumph, south of the James, and ended quite the other way around. Indeed, nothing could better illustrate the abruptness with which fortune's frown and smile were interchangeable than the contrast between the elation of Richmond's citizens on that date and the gloom that had descended on May 5, when they learned from downstream lookouts that an amphibious column ten miles long, containing no less than two hundred enemy vessels, was steaming up the river that laved the city's doorstep. Loaded at Yorktown the day before — while Grant was crossing the Rapidan — the armada had rounded the tip of the York-James peninsula in the night, and now, with the morning sun glinting brilliant on the water — and Grant and Lee locked in savage combat, eighty miles to the north — it was proceeding up the broad, shining reaches of the James.

Five ironclads led the way and other warships were interspersed along the line of transports, a motley array of converted ferries, tugs and coasters, barges and canal boats, whose decks were blue with 30,000 soldiers, all proud to be playing a role in what seemed to one of them "some grand national pageant." What was more, they had a commander who knew how to supply the epitomizing gesture. Riding in the lead, Ben Butler brought his headquarters boat about, struck a pose on the hurricane deck, and steamed back down the line. As he sped past each transport, past the soldiers gaping from its rail, he swung his hat in a wide vertical arc toward the west and lurched his bulky torso in that direction, indicating their upstream goal and emphasizing his belief that nothing could stop them from reaching it in short order. Unaware that within two weeks he and they were to wind up caged — or, as his superior was to put it, "corked" — they cheered him wildly from ship after ship as he went by, then cheered again, even more wildly, as he turned and churned back up the line, still waving his hat and lunging his body toward Richmond.

After dropping one division off at City Point, within nine miles of Petersburg, the flotilla proceeded north, past the adjoining mouth of the Appomattox River, and debarked the other five divisions at Bermuda Hundred, a plantation landing eighteen crow-flight miles from the rebel capital. Ashore, as afloat, the gesticulating Butler rode with the van, and close up he was even stranger-looking than he had been when viewed across the water; "the strangest sight on a horse you ever saw," one witness thought, attempting a word portrait of the former Massachusetts senator who shared with Banks, though he was more than a year his junior at forty-five, the distinction of being the U.S. Army's ranking active major general. "With his head set immediately on a stout, shapeless body, his very squinting eyes, and a set of legs and arms that look as if made for somebody else and hastily glued to him by mistake, he presents a combination of Victor Emmanuel, Aesop, and Richard III, which is very confusing to the mind. Add to this a horse with a kind of rapid, ambling trot that shakes about the arms, legs, etc. till you don't feel quite sure whether it is a centaur or what it is, and you have a picture of this celebrated General."

Despite the neckless, bloated look, the oddly assorted members, and the disconcerting squint of his mismatched eyes, Butler was all business here today. Mindful of Grant's injunction that he was to "use every exertion to secure footing as far up the south side of the river as you can, and as soon as you can," he landed the bulk of his army just short of the first of the half dozen looping bends or "curls" of the James,

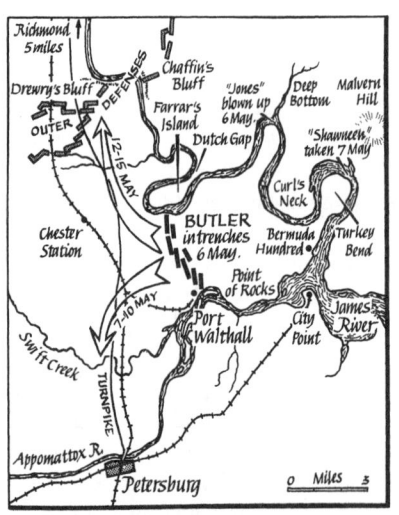

where the Confederates had heavy-caliber guns sited high on the steep bluffs to discourage efforts to approach the city by water, and next morning he began to comply with another item in his instructions: "Fortify, or rather intrench, at once, and concentrate all your troops for the field there as rapidly as you can." Five miles west of Bermuda Hundred, between Farrar's Island and Port Walthall, the James and the Appomattox were less than four miles apart. By intrenching this line he would be safe from a frontal attack, while the rivers secured his flanks and rear. It was true, the Bermuda debarkation required a crossing of the Appomattox to reach either City Point or Petersburg, but this was better, Butler reasoned — bearing in mind Grant's double-barreled admonition "that Richmond is to be your objective point, and that there is to be coöperation between your force and the Army of the Potomac" — than having to cross it in order to reach the fattest and probably best-defended prize of all. By sundown of May 6, his first full day ashore, he not only had completed the preliminary intrenchment of the line connecting the bends of the two rivers, he also had sent a brigade of infantry another two or three miles west to look into the possibility of cutting the railroad between Petersburg and Richmond, which in turn afforded the rebel defenders their only rail connection with the Carolinas and the reinforcements they no doubt were calling for, even now, in their distress at his appearance on their doorstep.

Encouraged by a report from the brigadier who conducted the reconnaissance (he had run into spirited resistance on the turnpike, half a mile short of the railroad, but nothing that could not be brushed aside, he thought, by a more substantial force) Butler decided next morning to go for the railroad in strength, then turn southward down it to knock out Petersburg and thus assure that his rear would be unmolested when he swung north to deal with Richmond. While the others kept busy with axes and spades, improving the earthworks protecting their base from attack, four of the fourteen brigades in the two corps, each of which had three divisions, moved out to attend to this preamble to the main effort: three from Gillmore and one from Major General W. F. Smith, whose third division had debarked at City Point and was still there, despite his protest that it "might as well have been back in Fort Monroe." The march was along the spur track from Port Walthall, and their initial objective was its junction with the trunk line, three miles west. As they approached it around midday, a spatter of fire from the skirmishers out front informed them that the junction — grandly styled Port Walthall Junction, though all it contained was a run-down depot and a couple of dilapidated shacks — was defended. The four brigades came up in turn to add their weight to the pressure being exerted, but the rebels either were there in heavy numbers or else they were determined not to yield, whatever the odds. This continued for two hours, in the course of which the Federals managed to overlap one gray flank and tear up about a quarter mile of track on the main line. But that was all. At 4 o'clock, having suffered 289 casualties, Butler decided to pull back behind his fortifications and return in greater strength tomorrow; or, as it turned out, the day after.

Both good and bad news awaited him, back on Bermuda Neck. The bad was from the navy, which had sent a squadron out the day before to investigate an account by a runaway slave that the Confederates had torpedoes planted thickly in the James, especially in the vicinity of Deep Bottom, a dozen miles up the winding river from Bermuda Hundred. It was all too true: as the crew of the big double-ender *Commodore Jones* found out, about 2 o'clock that afternoon. A 2000-pound torpedo, sunk there some months ago and connected by wires to galvanic batteries on the bank, "exploded directly under the ship with terrible effect, causing her destruction instantly." So her captain later reported from a bed in the Norfolk Naval Hospital. Another witness, less disconcerted because he was less involved, being aboard another gunboat, went into more detail. "It seemed as if the bottom of the river was torn up and blown through the vessel itself," he wrote. "The *Jones* was lifted almost entirely clear of the water, and she burst in the air like an exploding firecracker. She was in small pieces when she struck the water again." For days, bodies and parts of bodies floated up and were fished out of the James; the death toll was finally put at 69. Just now, though, the problem of how to keep the same thing from happening over and over again was solved by the capture of two men caught lurking in the brush where the batteries were cached. They had triggered the explosion, and what was more they had helped to plant other such charges up ahead. They refused to talk, however, until one of them was placed in the bow of the lead vessel and the squadron continued its upstream probe: whereupon, in the words of an interrogator, he "signified his willingness to tell all."

That more or less solved the problem of torpedoes (in any case, of the ones already planted; future sowings were of course another matter) but next day, about the time the four brigades began their skirmish down the spur track from Port Walthall, the navy was given a violent reminder that older dangers, familiar to sailors long before anyone thought of exploding powder under water, still threatened the existence of the fleet. U.S.S. *Shawneen,* a 180-ton sidewheel gunboat on patrol at Turkey Bend, dropped anchor under the loom of Malvern Hill to give her crew time out for the midday meal, only to have it interrupted when a masked battery and four companies of Confederate infantry opened fire from the north bank, peppering the decks with bullets and puncturing the steam drum. While most of the crew went over the side to keep from being scalded, *Shawneen*'s captain ordered her colors struck to save the lives of the injured still aboard. Ceasing fire, the rebel colonel in command sent out a boat to remove survivors and blow the vessel up; "which was effectively done," he reported, "consigning all to the wind and waves."

Such was the bad news — bad for Butler because it meant that the navy, having lost two ships in as many days, was likely to be reluctant to give him the slam-bang close support he would want when he moved against or beyond the high-sited batteries on Chaffin's and Drewry's bluffs, fortified works flanking the last tortuous upstream bend of the river below Richmond, both of them integral parts of the hard-shell outer defenses he would have to pierce if he was to put the hug on the rebel capital. The good news came from his cavalry, two brigades combined in a 3000-man division under Brigadier General August Kautz, a thirty-six-year-old German-born West Pointer. Off on his own while the rest of the army was steaming up the James, Kautz rode due west out of Suffolk on May 5 for a strike at the Petersburg & Weldon Railroad, damage to which would go far toward delaying the arrival of enemy reinforcements from the Carolinas. Encountering little opposition he did his work in a slashing style: first at Stony Creek on May 7, where he burned the hundred-foot railway bridge twenty miles south of Petersburg, and then next day at the Nottoway River, another five

The Forty Days

miles down the line, where he put the torch to a second bridge, twice as long, before turning north to rejoin the army two days later at City Point. Encouraged by news of the first of these two burnings, which reached him on May 8, Butler spent that day in camp, secure behind his Bermuda Neck intrenchments, putting the final touches to his plans for a movement against Petersburg next morning, much heavier than the one that had taken him only as far as Port Walthall Junction the day before.

This time he got a solid half of his infantry in motion, 14,000 in all. Smith, on the left, again ran into fire as he approached the Junction and called on Gillmore, who had advanced by then to Chester Station unopposed, to come down and join the fight. Gillmore did, although regretfully, having just begun to rip up track and tear down telegraph wire along the turnpike. But when the two corps began to maneuver in accordance with a scheme for bagging the force at the Junction, the graybacks slipped from between them and scuttled south. Pursuing, the Federals found the Confederate main body dug in behind unfordable Swift Creek, three miles north of Petersburg, which in turn lay beyond the unfordable Appomattox. When Butler came up to observe their fruitless exchange of long-range shots with the enemy on the far side of the creek, Gillmore and Smith informed him that Petersburg couldn't be taken from this direction. The thing to do, they said, was return at once to Bermuda Neck and lay a pontoon bridge across the Appomattox at Point of Rocks, which would permit an attack on Petersburg from the east. Fuming at this after-the-fact advice from the two professionals, Butler replied testily that he had no intention of building a bridge for West Pointers to retreat across as soon as things got sticky, and Smith later declared that he found this remark "of such a character as to check voluntary advice during the remainder of the campaign."

Tempers got no better overnight. Contemplating the situation next morning, with the uncrossable creek still before him, Butler decided that Petersburg was of little importance anyhow, now that Kautz had burned two bridges on the railroad in its rear. Accordingly, he ordered everyone back to Bermuda Neck, there to regroup for an advance to be made on Richmond as soon as he got his plans worked out. They returned the following day, May 11, filing in through gaps in the intrenchments around noon, and Butler retired to his tent to think things over for a while.

If he was bitter, so were his lieutenants, contrasting what had been so boldly projected with what had been so timidly and erratically performed. In Smith's opinion, based on what he had seen in the past six unprofitable days, the army commander was "as helpless as a child on the field of battle and as visionary as an opium eater in council." Butler returned the compliment in kind, including Gillmore in the indictment. Both generals, he said, "agreed upon but one thing and that was how they could thwart and interfere with me," while, to make matters worse, neither of them "really desired that the other should succeed." Feeling his reputation threatened (in the North, that is; in the South he was already known as "Beast" Butler, hanger of patriots, insulter of women) he had written to Stanton two nights ago, from the near bank of Swift Creek, reviewing his progress to date and placing it in the best possible light, even though this involved a rather ingenuous reinterpretation of his share in Grant's over-all design for the crushing of Lee and the taking of Richmond.

"We can hold out against the whole of Lee's army," he informed the Secretary, and he added for good measure: "General Grant will not be troubled with any further reinforcements to Lee from Beauregard's force."

Lee of course had no intention of attacking Butler, who was not even in his department, and though it was true he wanted reinforcements from any source whatever, he certainly expected none from the general opposing the southside threat, since, at the outset at least, that unfortunate commander — George Pickett, of Gettysburg fame — had practically no troops to fight with, let alone detach. He had, in all, fewer than 750 of all arms to stand in the path of the 30,000 Federals debarking at Bermuda Hundred and City Point, nine miles respectively from Drewry's Bluff and his district headquarters at Petersburg, whose garrisons were included in the total that showed him facing odds of forty-to-one or longer. Beauregard, sixty-five miles to the south at Weldon, which he had reached two weeks ago to assume command of the newly created Department of North Carolina and Southern Virginia, replied to an urgent summons from Richmond on May 5 that he was "indisposed," too ill to take the field. Three brigades were en route from his old command at Charleston; he would do his utmost to speed them northward, so long at least as the railroad stayed in operation, and would come up in person as soon as he felt well enough to travel. In the meantime, though, he left it to Pickett to improvise as best he could a defense against the host ascending the James.

Pickett himself was not even supposed to be there, having received orders the day before to proceed by rail to Hanover Junction and there await the arrival of his four brigades — two of which were now with Hoke in the movement against New Bern, down the coast, while the other two were with Major General Robert Ransom, charged with defending Richmond north of the James — for a reunion with Lee's army, then on its way eastward into the Wilderness to challenge Grant's advance. The long-haired Virginian looked forward to returning to duty under Longstreet, whose guidance he had missed these past eight months on detached service. Warned of the landings downriver today, however, he stayed to meet the threat to the near vacuum between the James and the Appomattox, although he was to regret profoundly, in the course of the next five days, that he had not caught an earlier northbound train. Those five days, May 5–10, were an unrelenting nightmare, illuminated from time to time by flashes of incredible luck which then were seen to have served perversely, not to resolve, but rather to prolong the strain on his jangled nerves. Fortunately, two regiments from the first of the three promised brigades from Charleston reached Petersburg on the morning of May 6, and Pickett got these 600 Carolinians up the turnpike in time to delay the advance of the brigade Butler sent probing for the railroad. They managed this, though only by the hardest, and just as they were about to be overrun they were reinforced by a brigade sent down from Richmond: Tennesseans who had arrived that morning under Brigadier General Bushrod Johnson, the first of two western outfits summoned east to replace Pickett's two brigades in the capital defenses. Johnson was a heavy hitter, as he had shown by spearheading the Chickamauga breakthrough, and his attack drove the reconnoitering Federals back on the line of intrenchments constructed that day across Bermuda Neck. Pickett told Johnson to dig in along the pike, and then — reinforced by the rest of the Charleston brigade, which came up after midnight to lift his strength to about 3000 — settled down to wait, as best his tormented nerves would permit, for what tomorrow was going to bring.

What tomorrow brought was Butler's four-brigade attack, 6000 strong, and news that Kautz had burned the bridge over Stony Creek, cutting off hope for the early arrival of more troops from the south. One reinforcement Pickett did receive, however, and this was Major General D. H. Hill, famed for a ferocity in battle rivaling that of his late brother-in-law Stonewall Jackson. His caustic tongue having cost him lofty posts in both of the Confederacy's main armies — together with a promotion to lieutenant general, withdrawn when he fell out with Bragg after Chickamauga — Hill had offered his services to Beauregard as an aide-de-camp, and Beauregard sent him at once to Petersburg to see if Pickett thought he could be of any help. Pickett did indeed think so, and put the rank-waiving North Carolinian in charge of the two brigades in position up the turnpike. Hill handled them so skillfully in the action today around Port Walthall Junction, losing 184 to inflict 289 casualties on a force twice the size of his own, that Butler pulled back, more or less baffled, and spent what was left of that day and all of the next, May 8, brooding behind his Bermuda Neck intrenchments.

Greatly relieved by this turn of events, Pickett experienced a mixed reaction to news that Hoke's projected attack on New Bern had been a failure, due to the nonarrival of the *Albemarle*, which had retired up the Roanoke River on May 5 after a three-hour fight with seven Union gunboats in the Sound from which the ironclad took her name. She had inflicted severe damage on her challengers and suffered little herself, except to her riddled stack, but the engagement had proved her so unwieldy that her skipper decided there was no hope of steaming down into Pamlico Sound to repeat at New Bern the victory she had helped to win two weeks ago at Plymouth. This meant that, without the support of the ram, Hoke's scheduled attack had to be called off: which in turn freed him and his five brigades, including the two from Pickett, for use elsewhere. Nowhere were they needed worse than at Petersburg, and Pickett was pleased to learn that they were to join him there by rail from Goldsboro — though when they would arrive was even more doubtful now than it had been the day before, word having just come in that Kautz had burned a second railway bridge, this one across the Nottoway, twice the length of the first and therefore likely to require about twice the time to replace.

Offsetting this last, there was good news from above. While Hill was making his fight for the Junction, the second western brigade reached Richmond — Alabamians under Brigadier General Archibald Gracie, another Chickamauga hero — and was sent across the James by Ransom, who not only followed in person but also brought along Pickett's other pair of brigades and posted all three in the works around Drewry's Bluff, bracing them for a stand in case the Federals turned in that direction. This addition of 4500 troops, combined with Pickett's remnant and the two brigades with Hill, increased the strength of the southside force to about 8000, roughly one third the number Butler had on Bermuda Neck. Pickett was greatly encouraged by this reduction of the odds — and so, apparently, was Beauregard, who wired from Weldon on May 8: "The water has improved my health." Whether the cause was the water or the buildup (not to mention the strangely hesitant performance by Pickett's opponent, who seemed to be groping his way piecemeal toward eventual destruction) the Louisiana general announced that he soon would be well enough to come to Petersburg and lift the awesome burden of responsibility from the district commander's shoulders.

By then Butler had ended his spell of brooding, and next morning he came on again, this time with half his army, only to pull up short on the north bank of Swift Creek, whose presence he seemed not to have suspected until now. Beauregard arrived the following day, May 10, in time to watch the baffled Army of the James — so Butler styled it — fade back once more from approximate contact and set out rearward to find sanctuary within its fortifications. Coming fast behind him on the railroad were seven veteran brigades of infantry, Hoke's five from Goldsboro and two more from Charleston. All reached Petersburg by nightfall, having marched across the five-mile gap between the Nottoway and Stony Creek, where they got aboard waiting cars for the last twenty miles of their ride. Pickett's five days were up at last, and rather as if the strain had been what kept him rigid, after all, he collapsed and took to his bed with a nervous exhaustion vaguely diagnosed as "fever." To replace him, Beauregard summoned Major General W. H. C. Whiting from Wilmington, and turned at once to the task of organizing the twelve brigades now south of the James into four divisions. Their combined strength was just under 20,000: enough, he thought, to deal with Ben Butler for once and for all by going over to the offensive, provided of course that the Beast could be lured from behind his intrenchments and out from between the two rivers protecting his flanks.

Butler complied, two days later, by moving northward against the works around Drewry's Bluff, apparently having decided to go for Richmond after all. Beauregard had anticipated this by sending Hoke with seven brigades to join Ransom, and now he prepared to follow and take command in person, leaving Whiting to hold Petersburg with the other two brigades of infantry, plus one of cavalry just come up from North Carolina. Arriving at 3 a.m. May 14, after taking a roundabout route to avoid capture, he found that the Federals had driven the defenders from some of the outworks, south and west of Drewry's, and now were consolidating their gains, obviously in preparation for an all-out assault that would open the way to Richmond. The high-spirited Creole, with his big sad bloodhound eyes and his hair brushed forward in lovelocks over his temples, did not quail before this menace; he welcomed it as a chance to catch Butler off balance and drop him with a counterpunch.

Though it came at a rather awkward time, Ransom having detached two brigades two days ago to help fend off Sheridan, whose troopers had broken through the outer defenses north of the capital, Beauregard had a plan involving Grand Strategy which he hoped would provide him with all the soldiers needed to dispose of the threat to Richmond, not only from the south, but from the north as well: not only of Butler, that is, but also of Grant. For three years now the Hero of Sumter had specialized in providing on short notice various blueprints for total victory, simple in concept, large in scale, and characterized by daring. This one was no exception. In essence, the plan was for Lee to fall back on the capital, avoiding all but rear-guard actions in the process, then send Beauregard 10,000 of his veterans, together with Ransom's two detached brigades, as reinforcements to be used in cutting Butler off from his base and accomplishing his destruction; after which, Old Bory subsequently explained, "I would then move to attack Grant on his left flank and rear, while Lee attacked him in front." He added that he not only "felt sure of defeating Grant," but was convinced that such a stroke would "probably open the way to Washington, where we might dictate *Peace! !*"

Thus Beauregard — at 3 o'clock in the morning. Wasting no time by putting the plan on paper, he outlined it verbally for a colonel on his staff and sent him at once to Richmond with instructions to pass it on without delay to the Commander in Chief. Davis was unavailable at that hour, but Bragg was not. Having heard the proposal, he dressed and rode to Drewry's for a conference with its author. Old Bory was waiting, and launched into a fervent plea for action. "Bragg," he said, "circumstances have thrown the fate of the Confederacy in your hands and mine. Let us play our parts boldly and fearlessly. Issue those orders and I'll carry them out to the best of my ability. I'll guarantee success!" Though noncommittal, the grim-faced military adviser listened to further details of the plan and returned to the capital, having promised to lay the facts before the President as soon as possible. This he did: along with his objections, which were stringent.

Not only did the scheme ignore the loss of the Shenandoah Valley and the Virginia Central Railroad, he declared, but "the retreat of General Lee, a distance of sixty miles, from the immediate front of a superior force with no less than 8000 of the enemy's cavalry between him and the Chickahominy ... at least endangered the safety of his army if it did not involve its destruction." Moreover, he said, such a concentration of troops beyond the James was quite unnecessary; Beauregard already had a force "ample for the purpose of crushing that under Butler, if promptly and vigorously used." Davis agreed that the plan was neither practical not requisite, and in courtesy to the Louisiana general, as well as out of concern for his touchy pride, he rode to Drewry's Bluff to tell him so in person, in the gentlest possible terms.

Beauregard's spirits drooped; but only momentarily. They rebounded at the President's assurance that Ransom's two brigades, having wound up their pursuit of Sheridan, would be ordered back across the James for a share in the attack, and Old Bory, savoring the prospect of belaboring the Beast who had tyrannized New Orleans, set to work devising a plan for assailing him, first frontally, to put him in a state of shock, and then on the flanks and rear, so that, being "thus environed by three walls of fire, [Butler] could have no resource against substantial capture or destruction, except in an attempt at partial and hazardous escape westward, away from his base, trains, or supplies." To accomplish this consummation, his first intention was to assemble all twelve infantry brigades at Drewry's for the assault, but then he decided that, instead of waiting for the troops to arrive from Petersburg by a roundabout march to avoid the Federals on the turnpike, he would have Whiting move up to Port Walthall Junction and pitch into their rear when he heard the guns announce the opening of the attack on their front by the other ten brigades, four each under Hoke and Ransom and two in a reserve division under Brigadier General Alfred Colquitt, who commanded one of the three brigades from Charleston. Notifying

The Forty Days

Whiting by messenger and the other three division chiefs in person, he set dawn of May 16 as the jump-off hour.

That gave them a full day to get ready, if Butler would only coöperate by remaining where he was. He did just that, though more from ineptness than by design; an attack planned for that day had to be called off when it turned out that he had provided so well for the defense of his newly won position that there were no troops left for the offensive. Butler was not greatly disturbed by this development, apparently having become inured to the fact that fumbling brought delay. For one thing, he had done well these past three days — especially by contrast with the preceding seven — and had encountered only token opposition in occupying the outworks around Drewry's. So had his cavalry, which he unleashed again when he left Bermuda Neck; Kautz had struck the Richmond & Danville two days ago, wrecking switches and culverts, and by now was astride the Southside line, tearing up sections of track. Back on the James, moreover, though the river was too shallow for the ironclads to proceed beyond City Point, the navy had been persuaded to lend a hand by pushing a few lighter-draft gunboats up to Chaffin's for a duel with the batteries on that bluff. All this should give the rebels plenty to fret about for the next day or two, Butler reasoned; by which time he would be ready to hit them in earnest.

His two corps commanders, while considering themselves honor-barred from tendering any more "voluntary advice," were by no means as confident that the Confederates would be willing to abide a waiting game. Smith, in fact — called "Baldy" from his cadet days when his hair began to thin, though he protested unavailingly nowadays that he still had more of it than did many who addressed him by this unwanted sobriquet — was so disturbed by what he took to be signs of a pending assault on his position that he spent a good part of May 15, a Sunday, scavenging rebel telegraph wire along the turnpike and stringing it from stumps and bushes across his front, low to the ground to trip the unwary; "a devilish contrivance none but a Yankee could devise," Richmond papers were presently to say of this innovation which Burnside had found useful in his defense of Knoxville six months before. Smith hoped it would serve as well here on Butler's right, though he ran out of wire before he reached his flank brigade, nearest the James. He and Gillmore each had two divisions on line; his third was still at City Point, completely out of things, and one of Gillmore's was posted in reserve, back down the pike. The night was dark, soggy with intermittent rain and a heavy fog that seemed to thicken with Monday's dawn, providing a curtain through which — true to Baldy's uncommunicated prediction — the graybacks came screaming and shooting and, as it turned out, tripping over the low-strung wire across much of the Federal right front, where the blow first fell.

Along those hampered portions of the line, Smith was to say, the attackers were "slaughtered like partridges." But unfortunately, as the next phase of the fight would show, there was no wire in front of Gillmore's two divisions on the left; nor was there any in front of the brigade on the far right, where Beauregard was intent on unhinging the Union line, severing its connection with the river, and setting it up for the envelopment designed, as he said, "to separate Butler from his base and capture his whole army, if possible." Struck and scattered, the flank brigade lost five stands of colors and more than 400 prisoners, including its commander, and though the adjoining brigades and Smith's other division stood fast behind their wire, inflicting heavy casualties on Ransom, Gillmore's divisions gave ground rapidly before an advance by Hoke, also losing one of their brigade commanders, along with a good many lesser captives and five guns. Confusion followed on both sides, due to the fog and the disjointed condition of the lines. Beauregard threw Colquitt in to plug the gap that developed between Hoke and Ransom, and Gillmore got his reserve division up in time to stiffen the resistance his troops were able to offer after falling back. By 10 o'clock, after five hours of fighting, the battle had reached the pendulous climax Old Bory intended for Whiting to resolve when he came up in the Union rear, as scheduled, to administer with his two brigades the rap that would shatter the blue mass into westward-fleeing fragments, ready to be gathered up by the brigade of saber-swinging troopers he was bringing with him, up the railroad from the Junction. Two hours ago, a lull in the fighting had allowed the sound of firing to come through from the south. It grew, then died away, which was taken to mean that Whiting had met with slight resistance and would soon be up. Since then, nothing had been heard from him, though Beauregard sent out couriers to find him somewhere down the pike, all bearing the same message: "Press on and press over everything in your front, and the day will be complete."

None of the couriers found him, for the simple yet scarcely credible reason that he was not there to be found. Not only was he not advancing, as ordered, from Port Walthall Junction; he had fallen back in a state of near collapse at the first threat of opposition, despite the protests of subordinates and Harvey Hill, who had reverted to his role of volunteer aide. A brilliant engineer, whose talent had made Wilmington's Fort Fisher the Confederacy's stoutest bastion and who had attained at West Point the highest scholastic average any cadet had ever scored, the forty-year-old Mississippian was cursed with an imagination that conjured up lurid pictures of all the bloody consequences incaution might bring on. Intelligence could be a liability when it took this form in a military man, and Chase Whiting was a case in point for the argument that a touch of stolidity, even stupidity, might be a useful component in the makeup of a field commander. In any event, wrought-up as he was from the strain of the past two lonely days at Petersburg, which he was convinced was about to be attacked by the superior blue force at City Point, he went into something resembling a trance when he encountered sporadic resistance on the turnpike beyond Swift Creek, and ordered a precipitate return to the south bank. Dismayed, the two brigade chiefs had no choice except to obey, and Hill, though he retired from Whiting's presence in disgust, later defended him from rumors that he had been drunk or under the influence of narcotics. Whiting himself had a simpler explanation, which he gave after the return to Petersburg that evening. Berated by the two brigadiers, who could not restrain their anger at having been denied a share in the battle today, he turned the command over to Hill, "deeming that harmony of action was to be preferred to any personal consideration, and feeling at the time — as, indeed, I had felt for twenty-four hours — physically unfit for action."

Up at Drewry's, the truth as to what was happening below lay well outside the realm of speculation. Expecting Whiting to appear at any moment on the far side of the field, Beauregard abstained from attempting a costly frontal assault, which might or might not be successful, to accomplish what he believed could be done at next to no cost by pressure from the rear. Jefferson Davis, who could seldom resist attending a battle whose guns were roaring within earshot, rode down from Richmond to share in the mystery and the waiting. "Ah, at last!" he said with a smile, shortly before 2 o'clock, when a burst of firing was heard from the direction of Whiting's supposed advance. It died away and did not recur, however, and Beauregard regretfully concluded that it had been produced by a cavalry skirmish, not by an infantry attack. After another two hours of fruitless waiting and increased resistance, the Creole general would report, "I reluctantly abandoned so much of my plan as contemplated more than a vigorous pursuit of Butler and driving him to his fortified base.... I therefore put the army in position for the night, and sent instructions to Whiting to join our right at the railroad in the morning."

As it turned out, no "driving" was needed; Butler drove himself. Badly confused by the events of the day — he had lost 4160 killed, wounded, or missing, including two brigade commanders and 1386 other prisoners, as compared to Beauregard's total of 2506 in those three categories — he ordered a nighttime withdrawal to Bermuda Neck. "The troops having been on incessant duty for five days, three of which were in a rainstorm," he informed Washington, quite as if no battle had been fought, "I retired at leisure to within my own lines." Once back there, within the sheltering arms of the two rivers, he busied himself with strengthening his three-mile line of intrenchments, followed by the victorious Confederates, who came up next morning and began digging a three-mile line of their own, studded with guns confronting those in the Union works. Thus, after two weeks of fitful confusion, in the course of which the Federals suffered just under 6000 casualties to inflict about half as many, a stalemate was achieved; Beauregard could not get onto Bermuda Neck, but neither could Butler get off it. The Beast was caged.

Richmonders exulted in the thought of cock-eyed Butler snarling behind bars, but Grant employed a different simile to describe the outcome of his well-laid plan for obliging Lee to fall back, in haste and probable disarray, to protect the threatened capital in his rear. Angered by the news from Bermuda Hundred, which reached him hard on the heels of equally woeful accounts of what had happened to Banks and Sigel, up the Red and at New Market, he borrowed a phrase from a staff engineer whom he sent to look into the tactical situation beyond the James. Butler's army, he presently reported, "was as completely shut off from further operations directly against Richmond as if it had been in a bottle strongly corked."

As for Beauregard the corker, though he was proud of his victory and its outcome, he was by no means content. "We could and should have done more," he said. "We could and should have captured Butler's entire army." Believing that this could still be done, he returned to his former proposal that he and Lee collaborate in disposing of the enemies before them, except that this time he reversed the order of their destruction. "The crisis demands prompt and decisive action," he notified Bragg on the night of May 18, outlining a plan whereby he would detach 15,000 troops for a flank attack on Grant while Lee pulled back to the Chickahominy. Once Grant was whipped, then Lee would reinforce Beauregard for attending to Butler in much the same fashion. Admittedly the odds were long, but Old Bory considered the prize well worth the gamble, especially by contrast with what was likely to result from not trying at all. "Without such concentration," he declared, "nothing decisive can be effected, and the picture presented is one of ultimate starvation."

Davis agreed that the future seemed bleak, but he could not see that Beauregard's plan, which reached his desk the following morning, was one that would make it rosy. All the previous objections still obtained, particularly the danger to Lee in falling back before a superior blue army reported to be receiving heavy reinforcements almost daily, while he himself got none, and it was to this problem that Davis gave his attention in returning the rejected plan to Bragg. "If 15,000 men can be spared for the flank movement," he noted, "certainly 10,000 may be sent to reinforce General Lee." This was not at all what Old Bory had had in mind, since it denied him anything more than a subservient role in Richmond's further deliverance from peril. He protested for all he was worth, and not entirely without success. Not 10,000, but 6000 were ordered detached that day, May 20, from the force that manned the intrenchments confronting and corking the bluecoats on Bermuda Neck. Pickett's four brigades, plus one of the three sent up from Charleston in the course of the past week — all five had been scheduled to do so anyhow, before Butler's appearance up the James — left next day to join or rejoin the Army of Northern Virginia.

✗ 4 ✗

Lee never liked the notion of abandoning any part of the Old Dominion to its foes, but in this case, setting out from Spotsylvania on May 21 to intercept another crablike Union sidle around his right, he not only was moving toward 8500 reinforcements, he also believed he was about to avail himself of his best chance, so far, to "end this business on the battlefield, not in a fortified place." With the two armies in motion, on more or less parallel routes, almost anything could happen, and he was exhilarated, as always, by the prospect. Best of all, though, he looked forward to the confrontation likely to follow on the line of the North Anna, a couple of miles this side of Hanover Junction, where the troops from Breckinridge and Beauregard had been told to join him in time to strengthen the attack he hoped to launch while Grant was astride the deep-banked river. Moreover, with his army holding the inside track, there was little of the strain there had been two weeks ago in the breakneck race for Spotsylvania; Ewell, whose corps had been withdrawn across the Po at dawn, had barely 25 miles to go on the main-traveled Telegraph Road, while Hancock, whose starting point was the north bank of the Ni, had 34 roundabout miles to cover, by inferior roads and without the customary mass of rapid-firing blue troopers to clear and screen his front. This meant that Lee could avoid exhausting his men on the march and still have plenty of time, at its end, for preparing the ground on which he would stand to deliver the blow he had in mind.

Ewell set off down the Telegraph Road at noon, Anderson four hours later. While Lee waited beside the Po, preparing to follow, A. P. Hill reported himself fit for duty. Despite his pallor, which seemed to deny his claim of recovery, Lee at once restored him to command, with instructions to hold his corps in position till well after nightfall unless the last of the departing Federals pulled out before that time, and sent Early ahead to resume charge of his division under Ewell. He himself left at 8 o'clock that evening. "Come, gentlemen," he told his staff, and turned Traveller's head southward in the twilight.

Two thirds of the way to Hanover Junction, having ridden past Anderson's marchers under the flooding light of a full moon, he took a two-hour rest beside Polecat Creek — which contributed its waters, but fortunately not its name, to the Mattaponi — and reached the North Anna soon after 8 o'clock next morning, about the same time the head of Ewell's column passed over and began filing into position along the south bank, covering Chesterfield Bridge, by which it had crossed, and the railroad span half a mile below, both of which were also protected by bridgeheads set up on the other side. When Anderson arrived at noon, his two divisions extended the line a mile and a half upstream to Ox Ford, the only point along this stretch of river where the right bank was higher than the left. Army headquarters was established in the southwest quadrant of the crossing of the Virginia Central and the Richmond, Fredericksburg & Potomac; Grant was reported to be marching down the latter. Breckinridge was waiting at Hanover Junction with his two brigades, as ordered, and was given a position in line between Anderson and Ewell. Pickett's division was also there (but not its ringleted commander, who was still convalescing from the strain he had been under, south of the James); Lee assigned it temporarily to Hill, who would arrive tomorrow to extend the line a couple of miles beyond Ox Ford, in case the bluecoats tried a flanking movement from that direction when they came up. For the present, Lee required no digging to be done, partly because he did not know for sure that Grant would attempt a crossing here when he found the graybacks once more in his path, intrenched or not, and also because he wanted to give his soldiers the leisure to enjoy their first full day out of contact with the enemy since the meeting engagement in the Wilderness, seventeen bloody days ago.

Hill arrived the following morning, May 23, coming in from the west shortly before the midday appearance of the Federals from the north. His approach was by the Virginia Central, since he had crossed the North Anna near Beaver Dam by a longer westerly route to guard the wagon train, and Lee had him rest his three divisions, with Pickett's as a fourth, under cover of some woods around Anderson Station, three miles short of Hanover Junction. While the last of his men were

The Forty Days [267]

filing in to drop their packs in the shade of the trees, the first enemy columns came into sight beyond the river, heavy blue streams flowing sluggishly down the Telegraph Road and the tracks of the R.F.&P. Greeted by guns emplaced on high ground overlooking Ox Ford, they paused, then resumed their flow as the Union batteries took up the challenge. Short of the ford and the two bridgeheads, they stopped again and engaged the outpost rebels in the kind of long-range firefight known to veterans as a "squabble." Lee was watching with suppressed excitement, foreseeing his chance at another Fredericksburg if Grant would only continue to do as he so much hoped he would, when news arrived from the far left that another Union column was about to force a crossing beyond Jericho Mills, three or four miles above. Hill was available to counter such an upstream threat, but Lee decided to look into it in person before disturbing Little Powell's road-worn troops. Still weary from his all-night ride two nights ago, and feeling the first twinges of an intestinal disorder, he went in a borrowed carriage to the point that was said to be menaced and studied carefully with his binoculars some bluecoats in a skirt of woods across the river. He took his time, then turned at last to a courier he had brought along. "Go back and tell A. P. Hill to leave his men in camp," he said. "This is nothing but a feint. The enemy is preparing to cross below."

He was both right and wrong in this assessment: right in a lesser, wrong in a larger sense: as he discovered when he got back to headquarters, late that afternoon, and heard the uproar of a sizeable engagement on the far left, in the upstream region he had just returned from. Warren had his whole corps there and by 4.30 had completed a crossing of the river, not at the point where Lee had reconnoitered, but at nearby Jericho Mills — which was in fact "below," as Lee had predicted, but a good deal less so than he apparently had expected. Learning that the Federals had crossed and were advancing southward through the woods in unknown strength, Hill sent Wilcox up to meet them and Heth to follow in support if needed. The action opened briskly, on a promising note. Wilcox, by the luck of the draw, struck Wadsworth's depleted division, now under Brigadier General Lysander Cutler, and drove it back in panic on the other two divisions. At this point, however, things began to go badly for the attackers, who seemed to have forgotten, in the course of more than two weeks of defensive combat, how to function on the offensive. Confused by their quick success, they fought disjointedly when they moved forward to complete the Union rout. Struck in turn, they backpedaled and fell into confusion, glad to make their escape under cover of the woods and a furious rainstorm that broke over them at sundown to end the fighting before Heth arrived to join it. They had lost 642 men in the engagement, veterans who would be sorely missed in battles still to come, and had gained nothing more than the infliction of an equal number of casualties on an enemy who could far better afford the loss.

In any case, here was the first definite indication that Grant intended to attack Lee where he was, rather than continue his march downriver in search of an uncontested crossing, and presently there was another such indication, quite as definite, near the opposite end of the line. Under cover of the rainstorm that ended the Jericho Mills affair at sunset, Hancock launched a sudden two-brigade assault on the Chesterfield bridgehead, which was taken so quickly that the defenders not only had no time to fire the wooden structure in their rear, but also lost more than a hundred of their number killed or captured before they could scramble back across.

This was a small price to pay for the disclosure that the Federals were preparing to attack both Confederate wings tomorrow, above and below Ox Ford. On the off chance that it might be a ruse, employed by Grant to screen another sidle, Lee alerted Anderson to be ready for a downstream march next morning. At the same time, though — before turning in for such badly needed sleep as his cramped bowels would permit — he began devising a trap, the design for which was based on personal reconnaissance of the ground and careful study of the map, for Grant's reception if that general acted on the larger probability that he would hold to the plan whose beginnings had just been disclosed, upstream and down, for a widespread double attack on the gray army fanned out along the south bank of the river to his front.

That was just what the northern commander had in mind, and his confidence that he could bring it off, following up the double attack with a double envelopment, was shared by all around and under him, from major generals down to drummer boys and teamsters. Leaving Spotsylvania on May 21, however, after sixteen unrelenting, unavailing days of combat (waged at an average cost of 2300 casualties a day, as compared to Lee's 1100) the blue marchers had been discouraged by this second tacit admission that, despite their advantage in numbers and equipment and supplies, whenever the tactical situation was reduced to a direct confrontation, face to face, it was they and not their ragged, underfed adversaries who broke off the contest and shifted ground for another try, with the same disheartening result.

"Now what is the reason that we cannot walk straight through them with our far superior numbers?" a Michigan soldier asked, and after ruling out individual skill as a factor in the equation — "We fight as good as they" — came up with two possible answers: "They must understand the country better, or there is a screw loose somewhere in the machinery of our army."

Presently though, moving southeast, then south, and then south-southwest through a region so far untouched by war, with well-tended crops along the road and plenty of fence rails available for campfires at the end of each day's march, they perceived once more that the shift was not only sideways but forward. It was Lee, not Grant, who was yielding ground, and sooner or later — sooner, at this rate, for the march to the North Anna was better than twice the length of the one two weeks ago, out of the Wilderness — the southern commander would have none left to yield. Then would come the showdown, the last battle: which, after all, was the only one that counted in the long run, the only one they really had to win to win the war. And steadily, as this conviction grew, so did their confidence in themselves and the man who led them. A Massachusetts regiment, having crossed the Mattaponi on the morning of May 23, was slogging down the railroad, past a siding, and saw Grant, in his now tarnished uniform, perched on a flatcar gnawing a ham bone. When the New Englanders gave him a cheer he responded with a casual wave of the bone, which he then went back to. They liked that in him. It seemed to them that this singleness of purpose, this refusal to be distracted, was as characteristic of his way of fighting as it was of his way of eating. He was giving Lee the kind of attention he gave the ham bone, and it seemed to them that the result might be the same, just ahead on the North Anna — or if not there, then somewhere else this side of Richmond, where Lee would finally run out of space for backing up.

Grant believed the showdown would come here; anyhow he acted on that premise when he came within sight of the river around midday. Warren having taken the lead by turning south at Guiney Station, eight miles short of Milford, he sent him upstream to Jericho Mills and kept Hancock, who followed close behind, marching straight ahead to confront the rebels defending Chesterfield Bridge and the railroad span below. He had hoped that Lee would venture after him for an all-out scrap in the open country south and east of the Mattaponi, but since the old fox had declined the challenge there was nothing for Grant to do, as he saw it, but go for Lee where he now was. As for turning back, he had just finished making this practically impossible by closing down his Belle Plain base on the Potomac, severing all connection with that river except by sea, and opening another at nearby Port Royal on the Rappahannock. If Lee eluded him here on the North Anna he was prepared to leapfrog his base southward again when he took up the pursuit, thus keeping his supply line short and easily defended. But he did not intend to be eluded; he intended to fix the rebel army where it was by striking both of its flanks at once and moving around them to gain its rear; in which case, disadvantaged though the defenders would be, as to position as well as numbers, Lee would have no choice except to fight the showdown battle his adversary was seeking.

Soon after sunset Grant was pleased to learn that all was going well upstream and down. Warren, having crossed unmolested at

Jericho Mills, had repulsed a savage attempt by A. P. Hill to drive him back across the river. He was intrenching now, as a precaution, and would press on south and east tomorrow, to strike and turn the rebel left. Hancock too was ready for full offensive action, having seized the approaches to Chesterfield Bridge by driving off or capturing the hundred or so graybacks attempting to hold it. He would cross at first light, under instructions to serve the enemy right in much the same fashion. Burnside and Wright would be up by then, and they too would have a share in the attack, Burnside by crossing at Ox Ford to exert pressure against the center, thereby helping to fix the defenders in position, and Wright by crossing in Warren's wake to extend his right and make certain that rebel flank was overlapped and overwhelmed.

Such were the orders, and Grant turned in for a good night's sleep, with high hopes for tomorrow. These were encouraged, first thing next morning, May 24, by reports from the left and right. Hancock crossed dry-shod, unopposed, as did Wright upstream at Jericho Mills, following Warren, who encountered only token opposition when he proceeded southeast down the Virginia Central Railroad and the south bank of the river. While Burnside moved into position for a lunge across Ox Ford, good news came from Sheridan that he would be rejoining today, winding up his fifteen-day excursion down to Richmond and the James; Grant was pleased to have him back, along with his 11,000-odd troopers, presumably to undertake the welcome task of gathering up Lee's fugitives at the climax of the movement now in progress. Meantime, awaiting developments across the way, the general-in-chief attended to certain administrative and strategic details, the first of which was the incorporation of the IX Corps into the Army of the Potomac, thus ending the arrangement whereby Burnside, out of deference to his rank, had been kept awkwardly independent of Meade so far in the campaign.

Two other matters he also attended to in the course of the day, both having to do with rectifying, as best he could, the recent setbacks his diversionary efforts had suffered out in the Shenandoah Valley and down on Bermuda Neck. Sigel's successor, Major General David Hunter, was given specific instructions to accomplish all that Sigel had failed to do, and more; that is, to march up the Valley to Staunton, proceed across the Blue Ridge to Charlottesville, and continue from there southwest to Lynchburg, living off the country all the way. As for Butler, though there was no serious thought of removing him from command despite his ineptness, Grant now viewed his bottled army as a reservoir from which idle soldiers could be drawn for active service with the army still in motion under Meade. Accordingly, he was ordered to load a solid half of his infantry aboard transports — under Baldy Smith, whom Grant admired — for immediate shipment, down the James and up the York, to the Army of the Potomac. These 15,000 added reinforcements might or might not be useful, depending on what came of the maneuver now in progress across the North Anna.

Reports from there were beginning to be mixed and somewhat puzzling, not so much because of what was happening, but rather because of so much that was not. First off, finding Ox Ford covered by massed batteries frowning down from the high ground just across the way, Burnside felt obliged to state that any attempt to force a crossing at that point would result in nothing better than a bloodying of the water. Grant saw for himself that this was all too true, and accordingly changed the ruff-whiskered general's orders to avoid a profitless repulse. Leaving one division to keep up a demonstration against the ford, which in fact would serve his purpose about as well, Burnside was told to send his other two divisions — his fourth was still detached, guarding supply trains — upstream and down, to strengthen the attacks on the rebel left and right. But there was where the puzzlement came in. Neither Hancock nor Warren, who by now had been joined by Wright, had met with even a fraction of the resistance they had expected to encounter in the course of their advance. Enemy pickets did little more than fire and fall back at the slightest pressure, they reported. Except for the presence of these few graybacks, together with those in plain view on the high ground opposite Ox Ford, Lee's army might have vanished into quicksand. They found this strange, and proceeded with caution, scarcely knowing what to expect.

All Grant could do, under the circumstances, was approve the caution and advise a continuation of the advance, southeast from the right and southwest from the left. Sooner or later, he felt certain, Hancock and Warren would come upon the rebels lurking somewhere between them, over there, and grind them up as if between two millstones.

Lee rose early, despite a difficult night, and rode again in the borrowed carriage to visit A. P. Hill near Anderson Station. There he learned the details of yesterday's botched attack on Warren, made piecemeal by a single gray division, when a concerted blow by all the available four would have taken full advantage of the original blue confusion to wreck a solid quarter of Grant's army. Contrasting what might have been with what now was — Warren smashed, with Warren advancing southeast through the woods — Lee turned on Little Powell. "Why did you not do as Jackson would have done," he fumed: "thrown your whole force upon those people and driven them back?"

Red-bearded Little Powell had fallen out rather spectacularly, at one time or another, with every other superior he had ever had, including Longstreet and the general whose spirit was being invoked; but he held onto his temper now, rebuked though he was in the presence of his staff, and accepted from Lee, without protest, what he would never have taken from any other man. For one thing, he was aware of the justice of the charge, and for another he could see that Lee was not himself. Unaccustomed to illness, the gray commander had lost his balance under pressure of his intestinal complaint, and lashed out at Little Powell in an attempt to relieve the strain.

None of this was evident, however, when he moved on to the question of how to deal with the advancing Federals. This had to do with the preparation of the topographical trap he had devised the night before; Ewell and Anderson were already at work on their share of it on the right and in the center, down the railroad east of Hanover Junction and along the river in the vicinity of Ox Ford.

The North Anna was no more defensible here at close range than the Rappahannock had been at Fredericksburg, for the same reason that the opposite bank, being higher, permitted the superior Union batteries to dominate the position — all, that is, but a brief stretch of the south bank overlooking Ox Ford and extending about half a mile below. Here the Confederate batteries had the advantage, and here Lee found the answer to his problem: not of how to prevent a crossing, which was practically impossible anywhere else along the line, but of how to deal with the Federals once they were on his side of the river. He would hold this stretch of high ground with half of Anderson's corps, strongly

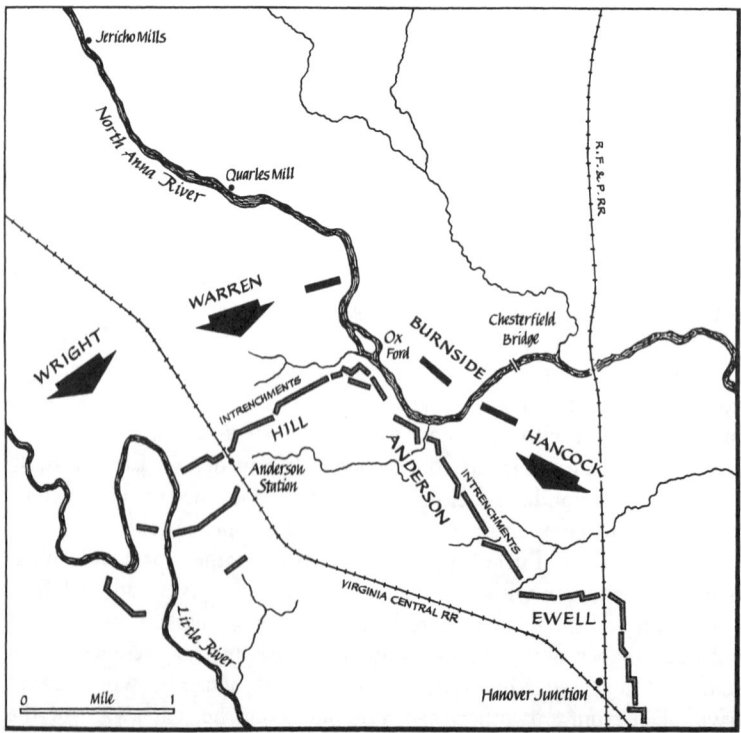

supported by artillery, and pull the other half, along with all of Ewell's, back on a line running southeast to Hanover Junction, just east of which there was swampy ground to cover this new right flank. Similarly, Hill would occupy a line extending southwest from Ox Ford to a convenient northward loop of Little River, just west of Anderson Station. Intrenched throughout its five-mile length, this inverted V, its apex to the north and both flanks securely anchored, would provide compact protection for Lee's army, either wing of which could be reinforced at a moment's notice from the other. Best of all, though, it not only afforded superb facilities for defense; it also gave him an excellent springboard for attack. By stripping one arm of the V to a minimum needed for holding off the enemy on that side, he could mass his troops along the other arm for an attack on that isolated wing of the blue army: *which* wing did not matter, since either would have to cross the river twice in order to reinforce the other, and would therefore not be likely to arrive in time to do anything more than share in the disaster. Here was something for Grant to ponder, when and if he saw it. But the hope was that he wouldn't see it until it blew up in his face.

Leaving Hill to get started on the intrenchment of the western arm, Lee rode back to his headquarters to await developments that would determine which Union wing he would assault. Ewell and Anderson, with Breckinridge still between them, were hard at work, the former having been reinforced by the fifth of the five brigades sent up from Richmond. So skillful were the men by now at this labor, which they formerly had despised as unfit for a white man to perform, that by midday formidable earthworks, complete with slashings and abatis, had risen where none had been six hours before. This augured well for the springing of the trap, once the bluecoats came within snapping distance of its jaws. While Lee waited, however, his intestinal complaint grew worse, and though he tried to attend to administrative matters as a distraction, they only served to heighten his irascibility. The result was fairly predictable. "I have just told the old man he is not fit to command this army!" a flustered aide protested as he emerged from the tent where he had been given a dressing-down by Lee.

Before long it was obvious that the charge, though highly irreverent, was true. Even the general himself had to admit it by taking to his cot, betrayed by his entrails on the verge of the crisis he hoped to resolve by defeating, with a single well-planned attack, the foe who had maneuvered him rearward across forty miles of his beloved Virginia in the past twenty days. If Lee could not deliver the blow, then no one could. It was too late to send for Beauregard, and none of his three ranking lieutenants — one-legged Ewell, who was also nearing physical collapse, or sickly Hill, who had shown only the day before that he was in no condition for larger duties, or lackluster Anderson, who had been less than three weeks in command of anything more than a division — seemed capable of exploiting the present opportunity, which would vanish as soon as the Federals spotted the danger and reacted, either by intrenching or by pulling back across the river for a crossing farther down, beyond reach of the trap that had been installed for their undoing. Time was passing all too fast, and the chance, once gone, might never recur. Lee on his cot broke out vehemently against this deprivation of the victory he felt slipping from his grasp.

"We must strike them a blow," he kept saying. "We must never let them pass us again. We must strike them a blow!"

Betrayed from within, he raged against fate — and rightly; for before the day was over his worst fears were realized. Hancock, nudging down from his crossing at Chesterfield Bridge, and Warren and Wright, skirmishing fitfully all the way from Jericho Mills, came at last upon what the old gray fox had devised for their destruction. Not only were the works about as formidable as the ones they had assaulted with little success at Spotsylvania, but the rebels were still at work with picks and shovels, adding traverses at critical points to avoid exposure to enfilade fire. Moreover, the blue generals were not long in perceiving that such fortifications might have an offensive as well as a defensive use. They took a good hard look and went into a frenzy of digging, east and west, throwing up intrenchments of their own against the attack they believed might come at any moment from either arm of Lee's inverted V. And while they dug they sent headquarters word of the situation, best described years later by Evander Law, commander of one of the three Alabama brigades in the works ahead: "Grant found himself in what may be called a military dilemma. He had cut his army in two by running it upon the point of a wedge. He could not break the point, which rested upon the river, and the attempt to force it out of place by striking on its sides must of necessity be made without much concert of action between the two wings of his army, neither of which could reinforce the other without crossing the river twice; while his opponent could readily transfer his troops, as needed, from one wing to the other, across the narrow space between them."

This was no more apparent to Law, then or later, than it presently was to Grant, who quickly sent down orders canceling the attack. It was apparent, too, that as soon as a withdrawal could be effected without heavy losses, the thing to do was get back out of there. Meantime, the digging progressed and dirt continued to fly. Fortunately the graybacks seemed content with such long-range killing as their snipers and artillery could manage, but this did little to relieve the feeling on the Union side that they had once more been outgeneraled. This was their twentieth day of contact, and the showdown was no closer within their reach than at the outset. Dejection was taking its toll, along with the profitless wear and tear of the past three weeks. "The men in the ranks did not look as they did when they entered the Wilderness," one among them would recall. "Their uniforms were now torn, ragged, and stained with mud; the men had grown thin and haggard. The experience of those twenty days seemed to have added twenty years to their age."

All night they stayed there, and all next day and the following night, still digging, while Grant pondered the situation. He had never liked the notion of backing away from any predicament, most of which he had found would resolve themselves if he held on long enough for the enemy's troubles, whether he knew what they were or not, to be enlarged by time and idleness to unbearable proportions; in which case, he had also found, it was his adversary who got jumpy and pulled back, leaving the field to him. That was not likely to happen here, although Lee's headquarters had been shifted three miles down the R.F.& P. from Hanover Junction, on his doctor's orders to provide a more restful atmosphere for the still ailing general. Fretful and regretful though he was that his well-laid trap had gone unsprung, Lee looked now to the future and the chance to devise another that would not fail. "If I can get one more pull at him," he said of Grant this morning, "I will defeat him."

But that was not likely to happen here either. On May 26, their second day of confronting the Confederates with a divided army, the Federals put on the kind of show that generally preceded a withdrawal and a shift. There were demonstrations along the river and both arms of the fortified V, together with an upstream probe by a full division of cavalry, as if for a crossing in that direction: a likely course for Grant to follow, Lee believed, since it would keep him on the direct route to Richmond and at the same time deprive Lee of the use of the Virginia Central, his only rail connection with the Shenandoah Valley, which not only provided most of the food his army ate but was also his classic route for a counteroffensive designed to frighten the Washington authorities out of their military wits, as he had done twice already to bring about the calling-off or the recall of invasions by Hooker and McClellan, last year and the year before. Though he preferred a downstream Union sidle, which he hoped would eventually put Grant in much the same position as the one that had brought Little Mac to grief two years ago, astride "the confounded Chickahominy," Lee followed his usual intelligence procedure of assuming that his adversary would do what he himself would have done in his place. For that reason, as well as the evidence of the cavalry demonstration, he thought the shift would be upstream, for a crossing beyond his left.

He was wrong: as he found out next morning, in plenty of time to rectify his error with a rapid southward march, still on the chord of the arc the Federals were traveling. Grant had pulled back under cover of darkness and set off down — not up — the North Anna, which combined with the South Anna, five miles southeast of Hanover Junction, to become the Pamunkey. The Pamunkey in turn combined with the Mattaponi to become the York, another forty miles below, but Grant marched only about one third of this distance down the left bank for a crossing at Hanovertown, which put him within fifteen miles of Richmond, ten miles closer than he had been on the North Anna. That was not his only reason for preferring to repeat his accustomed sidle to the left, around Lee's right; he would also be keeping in close touch with his supply base, leapfrogging it south once more as he moved in that direction. As for leaving the Virginia Central in Confederate control, he counted on Hunter to conquer the Valley, now that Breckinridge had departed, and thereby deny its use to Lee even as a source of supplies, let alone as a possible avenue of invasion. Besides, he saw the outcome of this latest confrontation not as a repulse — which in fact it was, with far-reaching effects, despite its comparative bloodlessness (he had suffered only 1973 casualties, and Lee less than half that number) — but rather as conclusive proof that the opposing army had lost its fabled sting. If the rebels would not fight him there on the North Anna, with all the advantage they had secured through Lee's admitted engineering skill, they apparently were in no condition to fight him anywhere at all. Knowing nothing of Lee's debility, he assigned its results to the deterioration of the force his adversary commanded.

"Lee's army is really whipped," he informed Halleck on the day he set out down the Pamunkey. "The prisoners we now take show it, and the action of his army shows it unmistakably. A battle with them outside of intrenchments cannot be had. Our men feel that they have gained the *morale* over the enemy, and attack him with confidence. I may be mistaken," he summed up, "but I feel that our success over Lee's army is already assured."

Grant's march was in two columns, of two corps each, along the left bank of the Pamunkey; Warren and Burnside crossed at Hanovertown, Wright and Hancock four miles short of there. Preceded by Sheridan's troopers, who had little to do on the way down but brush off prowling scouts, all four corps passed over on pontoon bridges between noon and midnight, May 28, and though they were delayed by a rackety seven-hour cavalry fight near Haw's Shop, three miles beyond the river, by nightfall of the following day the whole army had pushed south and west to Totopotomoy Creek, which had its beginnings above Atlee, a station on the Virginia Central about midway between the James and the South Anna, and flowed sluggishly eastward a dozen miles to join the Pamunkey just below Hanovertown. Weary

The Forty Days

from better than forty miles of marching — southeast for two days, then southwest for another — the Federals approached the marsh-fringed creek at last, within ten miles of Richmond, only to find Lee drawn up to meet them on the opposite bank, guns emplaced and all three corps arrayed for battle.

He had been there two days waiting for Grant to make a commitment. Before sundown of May 27, whose dawn showed the enemy gone from the North Anna, he had covered the eighteen miles from Hanover Junction to Atlee, where he took up a position from which he could block a variety of approaches by the wide-ranging bluecoats, either around the headwaters of the Totopotomoy, which would put them back astride the vital railroad north of Richmond, or down across the creek for a five-mile sprint to the Chickahominy and a quick descent on the capital only four miles beyond. Still obliged by his intestinal disorder to continue using the borrowed carriage, he rode in the lead with Ewell's corps — but not with its commander, who made the trip in an ambulance, racked by the same malady that afflicted Lee. Ewell was so much worse next day that he had to yield his place to Early and accept a sick leave of indefinite length; which meant that the army now had two of its three corps, four of its nine infantry divisions, and sixteen of its thirty-five original brigades under men who had not led them at the start of the campaign. Warned that elements of the Union host were across the Pamunkey at Hanovertown, Lee sent Hampton and Fitzhugh Lee to Haw's Shop to discover whether the crossing included infantry — and, if so, where it was headed. Unless he knew that, he could not move out to meet the invaders, lest they slip around one of his flanks for a lunge at Richmond from the north or the northeast.

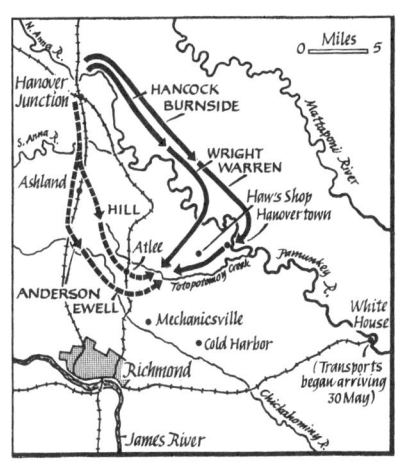

The result was the largest cavalry engagement since Brandy Station, just under a year ago. After seven hours of savage combat, mounted and dismounted, with heavy losses on both sides — especially in a green South Carolina brigade whose troopers arrived in time for a share in a fight that converted the survivors into veterans overnight — Fitz and Hampton were obliged to give ground, but not before they had driven Sheridan's horsemen back on their supports and taken prisoners from both the V and VI Corps, which gave Lee at least half the information he was seeking. Grant's infantry was indeed over the

Pamunkey, already beyond Haw's Shop, and next day it began working its way south and west along the north bank of the Totopotomoy, still without disclosing whether it intended to cross or round the creek.

Fixed in position east of Atlee until he knew the answer, the southern commander by now had received 10,000 reinforcements. This amounted to about half his losses so far in the campaign: whereas Grant had received some 40,000, roughly the number he had lost in battle. Such disproportionate attrition could have but one result, and Lee implied as much that afternoon to Jefferson Davis, who rode out from the capital to see him for the first time since the opening of the Federal offensive. Further reinforcements would have to come from south of the James, of course, and the President was doubtful that any could be spared from there; Beauregard had been protesting all week that his force — which he had regrouped into two divisions, under Robert Hoke and Bushrod Johnson, and which he kept reminding the Commander in Chief was all that kept Butler's still-bottled army from making a sudden breakout and a dash for the back door of Richmond — had been bled down to, maybe past, the danger point. Davis made it fairly clear, before he left, that the question of detaching more troops from beyond the James would depend to a large extent on the judgment of the commander of that department. That evening Beauregard himself appeared at Atlee for a conference, the upshot of which was that, while he sympathized with Lee in all his troubles, he could not see that they were any larger than his own. As for evidence advanced by Lee that Butler was sending men to Grant, the dapper Creole admitted that perhaps 4000 had left Bermuda Hundred aboard transports in the past few days, but he stressed the claim that a substantial 24,000 still remained to pop the cork he was trying to hold in place with only half as many troops. "My force is so small at present," he had told Davis earlier today, "that to divide it for the purpose of reinforcing Lee would jeopardize the safety of the part left to guard my lines, and would greatly endanger Richmond itself." The most he would agree to was a further study of the situation on his front, and with that he departed to return there, leaving Lee no better off, even in prospect, than he had been when the rather baffling conference began.

Next morning, May 30, Grant pressed down closer along the Totopotomoy, massing opposite Anderson in the center and overlapping Early on the right; Hill, on the left, had only cavalry in his front. That seemed to rule out the Virginia Central as the enemy objective, and presently this view was strengthened by reports that two of the four blue corps had crossed downstream and were taking up a position on the near bank, facing west. Lee believed he saw now what the Federals were up to, and also how to head them off: "After fortifying this line they will probably make another move by their left flank over toward the Chickahominy. This is just a repetition of their former movements. It can only be arrested by striking at once at that part of their force which has crossed the Totopotomoy."

These words were included in a message instructing Anderson to support Early, whose corps, being on that flank, would lead the attack designed to discourage this latest sidle around the Confederate right to gain the Old Church Road, which led down across Beaver Dam Creek to Mechanicsville, where the Seven Days had opened in flame and blood. But even if he was successful in dealing with the immediate threat to Richmond from this line, Lee saw a larger danger looming. Beyond the Chickahominy lay the James, where McClellan had found sanctuary after the holocaust of Malvern Hill. Fortunately, the Washington authorities had not seen fit to sustain him in his position on the north bank of that river, nor to approve his proposal that he cross it for a movement against Richmond from the south, astride its lines of supply from Georgia and the Carolinas. Grant was no Little Mac, however, and the high command might well have learned a lesson from what had followed its failure to sustain his predecessor. In speaking to Early, who was preparing to attack at midday, Lee did not say, as he had said to Anderson, that the Federal threat must be "arrested"; he said, rather, that the Federals themselves must be destroyed. Otherwise the contest would come down to what he wanted to avoid, the loss of all freedom to maneuver.

"We must destroy this army of Grant's before he gets to James River," he told Early. "If he gets there it will become a siege, and then it will be a mere question of time."

Unfortunately, Early came closer to wrecking his newly inherited corps than he did to destroying even a portion of Grant's army. Repeating Hill's error at Jericho Mills, he attacked with one division and failed to bring the other two up promptly to exploit the initial success. Counterattacked from Bethesda Church, his objective on the Old Church Road, he barely managed to hold his ground, and Anderson only arrived in time for a share in the defensive action. Lee rebuked neither of them for the botched performance, in part because they were busy intrenching their new line, which at least forestalled an advance down the ridge between Beaver Dam and Totopotomoy creeks, and in part because of a report that reached him about the time it became apparent that the attack had failed — a report so alarming in its implications that it took precedence over his other dire concerns. Grant's new supply base was at White House Landing, fifteen miles down the Pamunkey from Hanovertown; Lee now received word that substantial reinforcements, identified as Smith's whole corps from Butler's army, were unloading there from transports which had left Bermuda

Hundred yesterday for an overnight trip down the James and up the York.

Grievous though it was to learn that he soon would be facing still a fifth blue corps with his embattled three, the danger here was more than numerical. From his debarkation point at White House, Smith was free to march due west, unhindered, to a position beyond Grant's left (to Cold Harbor, for example, a vital crossroads three miles southeast of Bethesda Church, where the Union line was anchored south of the Totopotomoy after standing firm against Early's mismanaged assault) and thus extend it beyond the reach of Lee's already thin-stretched right for a rapid swing around that flank and a leap across the Chickahominy. Convinced that this was what Grant had in mind, because it was what he would have attempted in his place, Lee first did what he could to meet the threat with what he had on hand in that direction: meaning cavalry. He sent Fitz Lee instructions to take up a position at Cold Harbor and hang on there until he was reinforced, hopefully by morning.

As things now stood, such reinforcements could not come from Hill or Anderson or Early, whose withdrawal from any part of the line would open the way for Grant to move on Atlee or Mechanicsville. They could come from only one source, beyond the James, and Lee had no time to spare for going through regular channels to procure them. Abandoning protocol he telegraphed an urgent request directly to Beauregard for every man he could spare, and when the Creole replied at sunset that the War Department would have to decide "when and what troops to order from here," Lee appealed by wire to the President in Richmond: "General Beauregard says the Department must determine what troops to send.... The result of this delay will be disaster. Butler's troops (Smith's corps) will be with Grant tomorrow. Hoke's division, at least, should be with me by light tomorrow."

It was unlike Lee to use the unequivocal word "disaster," and because it was unlike him it got immediate results. Davis promptly instructed Bragg to send Beauregard a peremptory order detaching Hoke's division for shipment by rail to Lee without delay, and before midnight Lee was informed that every effort was being made to get Hoke and his four brigades north of the Chickahominy by morning.

Once more it was as if Lee had sat in on his adversary's councils or even paid him a visit inside his head. Dissatisfied with the Totopotomoy confrontation (as well he might be; it had cost him another 2013 killed and wounded and missing, first at Haw's Shop and then along the mazy fringes of the creek, with no gain except the infliction of about an equal number of casualties) Grant by now had decided to try another sidle: a brief one, this time, aimed at just the crossroad Lee predicted he would head for.

The Forty Days

The choice of Cold Harbor was natural enough. It was there — well clear of the toils of the Totopotomoy, but not quite into those of the treacherous Chickahominy — that the roads from Bethesda Church and White House Landing came together, enabling him to extend his left for a meeting with Baldy Smith, whose corps was debarking fifteen miles due east. Depending more on celerity than surprise, which seemed to be unobtainable here in Virginia anyhow, Grant counted on a rapid concentration at that point for a concerted drive up the left bank of the Chickahominy, one that would strike the assembling rebels before they got set to resist it and would pen them up for capture or destruction with their backs to Powhite Creek, less than two miles west, or Beaver Dam Creek, another three miles upstream; after which he would cross the river with all five corps, either below Mechanicsville or beyond at Meadow Bridge, for a quick descent on Richmond. Accordingly, while Lee was instructing his nephew Fitz to hold Cold Harbor against all comers, Grant sent word for Sheridan to seize and hang onto that vital hub until Wright, crossing in rear of Hancock on the Totopotomoy and then in rear of Burnside and Warren at Bethesda Church, arrived for a meeting with Smith at the end of his march from White House. The result next day, May 31, was another all-out cavalry engagement.

This too was a nearly all-day fight, with no infantry involved on either side till after sunset. Beauregard's bridling reaction to Lee's request for troops had delayed Hoke's departure so effectively that his lead brigade did not unload at Meadow Bridge until near midday, and consequently did not complete its eight-mile hike down the north bank of the Chickahominy until dusk was gathering on the scene of Fitz Lee's long-drawn-out defense of the crossroad his uncle had asked him to hold. As for the Federals, there was no infantry in the attacking columns even then. Concerned with keeping his withdrawal secret in order to give him a decent head start in the shift to the southeast, Grant instructed Wright to wait for nightfall before he set out on a march that was necessarily roundabout, through Haw's Shop, since there was no direct road available down across the Totopotomoy; he would arrive tomorrow morning at the soonest. Smith's delay was for other reasons, mostly involving slip-ups on Grant's staff. His original orders, issued when he embarked two days ago at Bermuda Hundred, called for a march from White House, up the south bank of the Pamunkey to New Castle, and from there to a position supporting the main effort on the Totopotomoy. Since then, Grant's plans had changed, but not Smith's orders, which were forgotten in all the flurry of preparation for the latest sidle. Completing his White House debarkation by midafternoon, May 31, Smith struck out northwestward, at a tangent to his intended route due west. Though he called a halt that night near Old Church, two miles short of his assigned objective, to send a wire requesting clarification from headquarters — it seemed to him he was moving into a military vacuum — the reply came back, after some delay, that his orders stood: he was to continue his march to New Castle. This he did, getting farther and farther at every step from the scene of the daylong engagement, now six miles in his left rear, which Sheridan had had to fight alone.

Little Phil frequently preferred it thus, so long at least as what opposed him was cavalry on its own. That was the case here, but he found it difficult to budge or even get at the graybacks, who declined to fight him in the smash-up style he favored. Instead, when he came within a mile of the crossroads about midday, with Torbert's three brigades — Torbert himself, up from his sickbed, had returned to duty the week before — he discovered Fitz Lee's two brigades dismounted and crouched behind fence-rail breastworks, which gave them the advantage of taking aim from an unjogged platform, with little exposure to the rapid-firing weapons of the horsemen galloping toward them. In their rear was Cold Harbor, a name of British derivation signifying an inn that afforded overnight lodging without hot food, adopted here because of the settlement's main feature, a frame tavern set in a triangular grove of trees at the intersection of five roads coming in from all round the compass. Charges by Merritt and Custer were repulsed before they could be pressed home, and as the afternoon wore on it became evident that standard cavalry tactics would not serve; Sheridan had Torbert dismount his men and work them forward, troop by troop, while their fellows provided covering fire to make the defenders keep their heads down. Swarming over the dusty fields and through the brush, pumping lead from their stubby carbines, the blue troopers in their tight-fitting trousers, bobtail jackets, and short-billed kepis looked to one observer "as though they had been especially equipped for crawling through knotholes."

It was a slow and costly business, involving much risk and a good many wounds. Giving up on Baldy Smith after a patrol returned from a fruitless eastward search for some sign of his 15,000-man corps, Sheridan sent for Gregg to come down from Bethesda Church and add his two brigades to the effort being exerted, but the sun was down behind the trees along Powhite Creek by the time the courier rode off with the summons. As it turned out, such reinforcements as reached the field before full dark were Confederate, and infantry at that.

Hard-pressed by the agile blue troopers, who were about within range for a mass charge through the gathering dusk, Fitz Lee's men looked over their shoulders and, seeing Hoke's lead brigade moving toward them up the road past the triangular grove of trees, decided the time had come to fall back on these overdue supports. They did so, only to find that the startled foot soldiers fell back too. Hot and tired from their dusty trek down the Chickahominy, and softened by two weeks of inactivity in the southside trenches, they joined what they took to be

The Forty Days

— and what now became — a general retreat, to and through Cold Harbor; which their pursuers seized and occupied, rounding up some fifty laggard graybacks in the process. Sheridan's elation over his sudden victory was modified considerably, however, when he learned from these captives that three more brigades of infantry would soon be up to join the one he had scattered. He decided, despite the arrival of Gregg's division hard on the heels of the rout, that his wisest course would be to pull back from the tavern crossroads before he was overrun. "I do not feel able to hold this place," he notified Meade as the withdrawal got under way. "With the heavy odds against me here, I do not think it prudent to hold on."

Meade thought otherwise, and so did Grant, in view of the sidle now in progress and the intended concentration there; Cold Harbor was to be reoccupied and "held at all hazards," they replied. Little Phil reversed his march, disposed his two divisions about the southwest quadrant of the crossroads, and had the dismounted troopers get to work in the darkness, throwing up temporary breastworks to provide them with cover for meeting the attack he expected would come with the dawn, if not sooner.

It would come with the dawn, and the odds would be even heavier than Sheridan had feared when he pulled back, saying, "I do not think it prudent to hold on." Lee was about to go over to the offensive. What was more, in preparation for bloodier work to follow, he intended to begin with the retaking of the ground the troopers stood on.

Far from being discouraged by his nephew's report that the crossroads had been seized by Sheridan, he saw in this development confirmation of his suspicion that Grant had another sidle in progress, that Cold Harbor was his intended point of concentration, and that so far he had nothing there but cavalry; which meant that his infantry was still in motion in that direction, strung out on roads converging from the north and east, and might therefore be defeated in detail as it came up — provided, of course, that Lee could get there first with a force substantial enough to inflict the damage he had in mind. He thought he could. Hoke's division was assembling there already, and this was only a fraction of what had become available now that Grant had tipped his hand. Formerly fixed in position east of Atlee by the danger that the Federals would round the headwaters of the Totopotomoy to turn his left, Lee was now free to draw troops from there for use on the opposite flank. His choice was Anderson, whose strength was up to three divisions for the first time in the campaign, Pickett having rejoined him on the march from Hanover Junction. Both the Third and the Second corps had had their turns at offensive action, Hill eight days ago on the North Anna and Early here at Bethesda Church the day before, and both had failed. Now the First — Old Peter's dependables, who had rolled up the blue flank in the Wilderness and won the hairbreadth race for Spotsylvania — would have its turn. Anderson was told to pull back from his position on the Totopotomoy, leaving Little Powell to fill the gap, and make a night march down below Cold Harbor to join Hoke, who was placed under his command for the attack, first on Sheridan, to get possession of the crossroads shortly after dawn, and then on the other Union columns as they arrived from the east and north.

Though he still had not recovered sufficiently from his illness to resume direction of tactical operations, Lee advanced his headquarters to Shady Grove Church, a couple of miles southeast of Atlee Station, to be at least that much nearer the scene of tomorrow's action. Two years ago this evening, riding back from the confused field of Seven Pines — less than ten miles from where he would camp tonight — he had been informed by the President that he would replace the fallen Johnston, and next day he had assumed command of the Army of Northern Virginia. As he retired to his tent in the churchyard tonight to sleep out the final hours of this bloodiest May in American history, he had cause for hope that he would celebrate tomorrow's anniversary with an offensive victory as glorious as the one he had begun to plan on that night two years ago, when McClellan's vast blue host hovered within even easier reach of Richmond than Grant's did now.

There was no occasion for any such celebration on the hot first day of June, only a sorry repetition of the ineptness which had led Grant to believe that the fight had gone out of Lee's army. Anderson moved promptly enough, pulling Kershaw's division out of line in plenty of time for the march across Early's rear and into position on Hoke's left before daylight. His notion was to knock Sheridan back from the crossroads with a dawn attack by these two divisions, then continue the operation when the other two arrived. But a notion was all it remained. Kershaw went forward on schedule, giving his old brigade the lead, and that was when the trouble began and the offensive ended. Colonel Lawrence Keitt, a forty-year-old former congressman, had brought his green but handsomely uniformed regiment up from South Carolina the week before, and by virtue of his seniority over the other colonels took command of the brigade. Long on rank but short on combat experience, he went into his first attack in the gallant style of 1861, leading the way on a spirited gray charger; only to be killed by the first rattling clatter of semiautomatic fire from the two divisions of cavalry in the breastworks just ahead.

That was what had been expected by seasoned observers, who saw in Keitt's display only "inexperience and want of self control," but the reaction among his troops, recently uprooted from two years of languid garrison life in their home state, was something else. When they saw the colonel get toppled from his saddle — transformed, in the wink

The Forty Days

of an eye, from a saber-waving cynosure into a mangled corpse — they broke for the rear in what a dismayed artillerist called "the most abject rout ever committed by men in Confederate uniform." Nor was that the worst of the shame. "Some were so scared they could not run, but groveled on the ground trying to burrow into the earth." Veteran regiments on their flanks were obliged to give way too; the advance dissolved in panic, unredeemed by Hoke, who had not moved at all. First the brigade and then the division as a whole pulled out of range of the fast-firing Union carbines. Kershaw got the fallback stopped and even attempted to mount another attack, but it went no better. By the time Pickett and Field came up to form on Kershaw's left, around midmorning, so had Wright arrived with his three divisions in relief of Sheridan, who retired with pride from the defense of what he called "our little works."

They did not stay little long; Wright's men got busy with picks and shovels, deepening and extending them north and south to cover the western approaches to Cold Harbor. Smith's wandering corps slogged wearily into position alongside Wright that afternoon, reaching up to connect with Warren, whose four divisions occupied two miles of line below the Old Church Road, beyond which Burnside anchored the northern flank to the south bank of the Totopotomoy. That left only Hancock's corps and Sheridan's third division north of the creek; Grant sent word for Hancock to withdraw at nightfall for a march to the far left, where Torbert and Gregg were patrolling a boggy two-mile extension of the line down to the Chickahominy. He was instructed to come up in time to take part in a dawn assault that would be launched by all five corps.

Grant's decision to make such an attack was arrived at by a process of elimination. This was coffin corner; another sidle would involve him in the toils of the Chickahominy, and even if he cleared them intact he would find himself confronted, when he swung back west, by Richmond's permanent defenses. He would, in short, be mounting a siege, which at this stage he wanted as little as Lee did, since it represented the stalemate he had avoided from the start. His decision, then, despite the shocks and throes of the past four weeks — the stunning repulse in the green riot of the Wilderness and the unrelieved horror of Spotsylvania, which together had cost him a solid third of the infantry that crossed the Rapidan, and the close call on the North Anna, where incaution had nearly cost him the other two thirds, along with his reinforcements — was to attack the old fox where he was, or anyhow where he would be tomorrow morning. If this was coffin corner for Grant, it was something worse for Lee, whose back was to the wall of his capital and who would have neither time nor space for recovery if even a limited breakthrough could be scored. Grant kept his mind on that agreeable possibility, and when Meade suggested that something might be done with what was left of today, by way of improving tomorrow's chances, he was altogether willing.

Meade proposed a preliminary effort, restricted to the southern half of his present line, to give Wright and Smith a closer hug on the rebel works along their front and better jump-off positions from which to launch their share of the all-out dawn assault. That was how it came about that Anderson, whose four divisions were busy intrenching three miles of line, north and south of a road leading due east to Cold Harbor, was struck by a six-division attack, shortly after 5 o'clock, which not only disposed of any vestigial intention to resume his boggled offensive, but also came close to driving him from his uncompleted works. Pickett and Field held firm under pressure, but a break quickly developed between Hoke's left, where a brigade gave way in panic, and Kershaw's right. Anderson detached a brigade from Pickett to heal the breach, and by sunset the line was approximately restored. Yet the fact remained that, at a moderate price in casualties — moderate, that is, as such things went in this campaign: about 1000 for Smith, 1200 for Wright — Meade had secured the jump-off positions he wanted for tomorrow. Anderson's losses had been light, consisting mainly of stragglers captured when Hoke's left gave way, but he saw only too clearly what might come of this. "Reinforcements are necessary to enable us to hold this position," he notified Lee that night.

This message, conveying Anderson's doubts that he could hold the ground he had been ordered to advance from, put a dispiriting end to an anniversary which had dawned with high hopes that it would close with the celebration of an offensive victory. For the third time in nine days, a corps commander had shown himself incapable of mounting a sustained attack, even under favorable circumstances.

One thing common to all three attempts, in addition to failure, was that neither Lee nor his "poor Stuart" had taken part in them first hand. Jeb of course was gone for good, three weeks in his grave, and Lee was still in no condition for personal conduct of operations in the field; but that did not mean that the ailing general would not keep to his task of devising plans for the frustration of the invaders of his country and his state. Foiled in his efforts to go over to the offensive, he would continue to improvise a defensive in which, so far, he had managed to inflict casualties in ratio to the odds he faced at the opening of the campaign. In this connection he had already moved to meet Anderson's needs before they were expressed, ordering Breckinridge to take up a position on Hoke's right tonight, and now he followed through with instructions that would add Hill's three divisions to the line tomorrow, one on the left of Early and two on the right beyond Breckinridge, tying those flanks respectively to the Totopotomoy and the Chickahominy. All this would take time, however — first for marching, then for digging — and Grant was bristling aggressively all along the seven miles of Confederate front when the sun came up on the second day of June.

Fortunately, despite the flurry, there was no attack; Lee had plenty of time to look to the extension and improvement of his line. Mounting Traveller for the first time in ten days, he rode down to Mechanicsville, where he found Breckinridge and his two brigades enjoying a leisurely breakfast, midway through their march to the far right. He got the distinguished Kentuckian back on the road again and then resumed his ride, eastward past Walnut Grove Church to his new headquarters beyond Gaines Mill, a mile and a half due west of Unionheld Cold Harbor and about the same distance northwest of the scene of his first victory, scored two years ago this month, when Hood and Law broke Fitz-John Porter's line on Turkey Hill, now also Unionheld. Mindful of the importance of that feature of the terrain, Lee had Breckinridge go forward, about 3 o'clock that afternoon, and with the assistance of one of Hill's divisions, which had just come up, drive a brigade of bluecoats off its slopes, thus affording his artillery a position from which to dominate the Chickahominy bottoms on the right. Simultaneously on the left, Early's corps and Hill's remaining division felt out the Federal installations above Old Church Road, on toward the Totopotomoy, and after brushing aside a sizeable body of skirmishers, who yielded stubbornly, confronted the main enemy works northwest and north of Bethesda Church.

While these two adjustments were being made at opposite ends of the long line, a heavy rain began to fall, first in big individual drops, pocking the dust like buckshot scattered broadcast, and then in a steady downpour that turned the dust to mud. The discomfort was minor on both sides, compared to the relief from heat and glare and the distraction from waiting to receive or deliver the attack both knew was soon to be made, if not today then certainly tomorrow.

Rain often had a depressing effect on Lee, perhaps because it reminded him of the drenched fiasco his first campaign had been, out in western Virginia in the fall of 1861; but not now; now he valued it as a factor that would make for muddy going when the Federals moved against him. Back at his headquarters, near the ruins of Dr William Gaines's once imposing four-story gristmill on Powhite Creek — Sheridan's troopers had burned it when they passed this way two weeks ago, returning from the raid that killed Jeb Stuart — the southern commander kept to his tent, still queasy from his ten-day illness, reading the day's reports while rain drummed on the canvas overhead. He had done all he could to get all the troops he could muster into line. "Send to the field hospitals," he had told his chief lieutenants in a circular issued the last day of May, "and have every man capable of performing the duties of a soldier returned to his command." Such efforts, combined with those of Davis, who had summoned reinforcements from as far away as Florida in the course of the past two weeks, had brought his strength back up to nearly 60,000. Grant had about 110,000 across the way, but Lee feared the odds no more here than he had done elsewhere. In fact he feared them less; for, thanks to Grant's forbearance today — whatever its cause — he had had plenty of time to dispose his army as he chose. Having done so, he was content to leave the rest to God and the steady valor of his troops, whose defensive skill had by now become instinctive.

This last applied in particular to the use they made of terrain within their interlocking sectors. Whether the ground was flat or hilly, bare or wooded, firm or boggy — and it was all those things from point to various point along the line from Pole Green Church to Grapevine Bridge — they never used it more skillfully than here. Occupying their assigned positions with a view to affording themselves only so much protection as would not interfere with the delivery of a maximum of firepower, they flowed onto and into the landscape as if in response to a natural law, like water seeking its own level. The result, once they were settled in, was by no means as imposing as the fortifications they had thrown up three weeks ago at Spotsylvania or last week on the North Anna. But that too was part of the design. No such works were needed here and they knew it, having installed them with concern that they not appear so formidable as to discourage all hope of success in the minds of the Federal planners across the way. Crouched in the dripping blackness after sundown, with both flanks securely anchored on rising streams and Richmond scarcely ten miles in their rear, the defenders asked for nothing better, in the way of reward for their craftsmanship and labor, than that their adversaries would advance into the meshed and overlapping fields of fire they had established, unit by unit, along their seven miles of front.

They were about to get their wish. Indeed, they would have gotten it at dawn today — ten hours before they completed their concentration and were in any condition to receive it — except that Hancock's three divisions had not arrived on the Union left until about 6.30, two hours late and in no shape for fighting, tired and hungry as they were from their grueling all-night march. Grant accepted the delay as unavoidable, and rescheduled the attack for 5 o'clock that afternoon. That would do about as well, he seemed to think. But then, as the jump-off hour drew near, the rebs went into action on both flanks, seizing Turkey Hill and driving the outpost skirmishers back on their works above Bethesda Church. This called for some changes in the stand-by orders, and Grant, still unruffled, postponed the attack once more until 4.30 next morning. After all, all he wanted was a breakthrough, almost anywhere along those six or seven miles of enemy line; he could see that a hot supper and a good night's rest would add to the strength and steadiness of the men when they went forward.

The Forty Days [289]

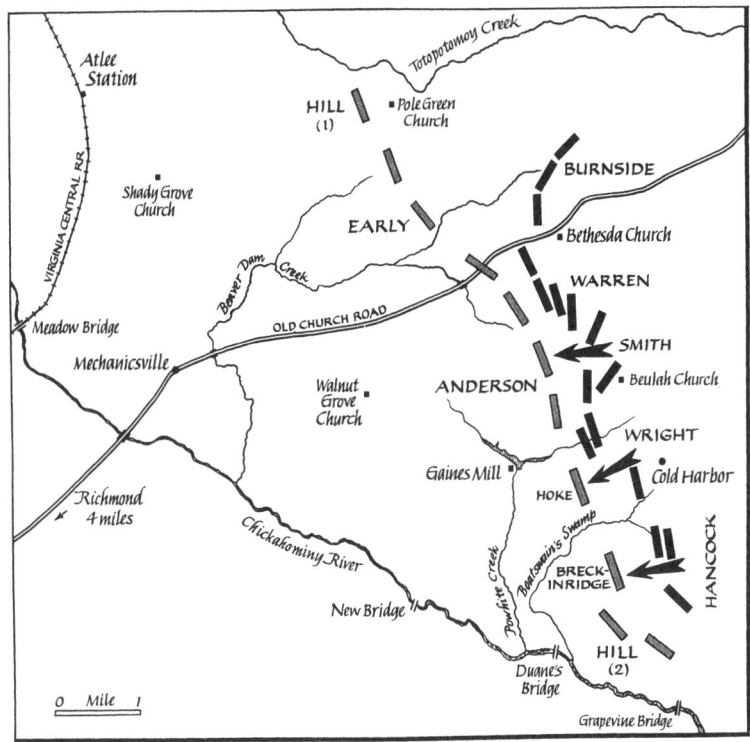

Aside from a general directive that the main effort would be made by the three corps on the left, where the opposing works were close together as a result of yesterday's preliminary effort, tactics seemed to have gone by the board, at least on the upper levels of command. Neither Grant nor Meade, or for that matter any member of their two staffs, had reconnoitered any part of the Confederate position; nor had either of them organized the attack itself in any considerable detail, including the establishment of such lateral communications as might be needed to assure coöperation between units. Apparently they assumed that all such incidental problems had been covered by a sentence in Meade's circular postponing the late-afternoon attack till dawn: "Corps commanders will employ the interim in making examinations of the ground on their front and perfecting the arrangements for the assault." New as he was to procedure in the Army of the Potomac, Baldy Smith — "aghast," he later wrote, "at the reception of such an order, which proved conclusively the utter absence of any military plan" — sent a note to Wright, who was on his left, "asking him to let me know what was to be his plan of attack, that I might conform to it, and thus have two corps acting in unison." Wright's reply was simply that he was "going to pitch in": which left Smith as much in the dark as before, and even more aghast. Grant, in short, was proceeding here at Cold Harbor as if he subscribed quite literally to the words he had written Halleck from the North Anna, a week ago today: "I feel that our success over Lee's army is already assured."

Up on the line, that was by no means the feeling prevalent among the troops who were charged with carrying out the orders contrived to bring about the result expected at headquarters. Unlike their rearward superiors, they had been uncomfortably close to the rebel works all day and knew only too well what was likely to come of any effort to assault them, let alone such a slipshod one as this. Their reaction was observed by Lieutenant Colonel Horace Porter, a young West Pointer, formerly an aide to McClellan and now serving Grant in the same capacity. Passing through the camps that rainy evening, he later wrote, "I noticed that many of the soldiers had taken off their coats and seemed to be engaged in sewing up rents in them." He thought this strange, at such a time, but when he looked closer he "found that the men were calmly writing their names and home addresses on slips of paper and pinning them on the backs of their coats, so that their bodies might be recognized and their fate made known to their families at home."

Some went even further in their gloom. A blood-stained diary, salvaged from the pocket of a dead man later picked up on the field, had this grisly final entry: "June 3. Cold Harbor. I was killed."

They came with the dawn and they came pounding, three blue corps with better than 60,000 effectives, striking for three points along the center and right center of the rebel line, which had fewer men defending its whole length than now were assaulting half of it. Advancing with a deep-throated roar — "Huzzah! Huzzah!" a Confederate thought they were yelling — the attackers saw black slouch hats sprout abruptly from the empty-looking trenches up ahead, and then the works broke into flame. A heavy bank of smoke rolled out, alive with muzzle flashes, and the air was suddenly full of screaming lead. "It seemed more like a volcanic blast than a battle," one Federal later said, "and was just about as destructive."

Dire as their expectations had been the night before, they perceived now for the first time the profoundly intricate nature of the deadfall Lee had devised for their undoing. Never before, in this or perhaps in any other war, had so large a body of troops been exposed to such a concentration of firepower; "It had the fury of the Wilderness musketry, with the thunders of the Gettysburg artillery superadded," an awed cannoneer observed from his point of vantage in the Union rear. And now, too, the committed victims saw the inadequacy of Grant's preparation in calling for a three-pronged assault, directed against three vague and widely spaced objectives. Smith on the right

The Forty Days

was enfiladed from his outer flank, as was Hancock on the left, and Wright, advancing between them with a gap on either side, found both of his flanks exposed at once to an even crueler flailing. What was worse, the closer the attackers got to the concave rebel line, the more this crossfire was intensified and the more likely an individual was to be chosen as a simultaneous target by several marksmen in the works ahead. "I could see the dust fog out of a man's clothing in two or three places where as many balls would strike him at the same moment," a defender was to say.

Under such conditions, losses tended to occur in ratio to the success of various units in closing the range. Barlow's division for example, leading Hancock's charge against Lee's right, struck a lightly defended stretch of boggy ground in Breckinridge's front and plunged on through to the main line, which buckled under sudden pressure from the cheering bluecoats. Barlow, not yet thirty — "attired in a flannel checked shirt, a threadbare pair of trousers, and an old blue kepi," he looked to a staff observer "like a highly independent mounted newsboy" — was elated to think he had scored the breakthrough Grant had called for. But his elation was short-lived. Attached to one of Hill's divisions on the adjoining slope of Turkey Hill, Joseph Finegan, who had arrived that week with two Florida battalions and been put in charge of a scratch brigade, counterattacked without waiting to be prompted and quickly restored the line, demonstrating here in Virginia the savagery he had shown at Olustee, three months ago in his home state. Barlow's men were ousted, losing heavily in the process, and it was much the same with others up the line. Though nowhere else was there a penetration, even a temporary one, wherever the range became point-blank the attack dissolved in horror; the attackers huddled together, like sheep caught in a hailstorm, and milled about distractedly in search of what little cover the terrain afforded. "They halted and began to dodge, lie down, and recoil," a watching grayback would remember, while another noted that "the dead and dying lay in front of the Confederate line in triangles, of which the apexes were the bravest men who came nearest to the breastworks under that withering, deadly fire."

The attack, now broken, had lasted just eight minutes. So brief was its duration, and so abrupt its finish, that some among the defenders had trouble crediting the fact that it had ended, while others could scarcely believe it had begun; not in earnest, at any rate. One of Hoke's brigadiers, whose troops were holding a portion of the objective assigned to Wright, square in the center of the three-corps Federal effort, afterwards testified that he "was not aware at any time of any serious assault having been given."

Part of the reason for this was the lightness of Confederate losses, especially as compared to those inflicted, although these last were not known to have been anything like as heavy as they were until the smoke began to clear. An Alabama colonel, whose regiment had three men killed and five wounded, peered out through rifts in the drifting smoke along his front, where Smith had attacked with close-packed ranks, and saw to his amazement that "the dead covered more than five acres of ground about as thickly as they could be laid." Eventually the doleful tally showed that while Lee was losing something under 1500, killed and wounded in the course of the day, Grant lost better than 7000, most of them in the course of those first eight minutes.

The attack had ended, but neither by Grant's intention nor with his consent. No sooner had the Union effort slackened than orders came for it to be renewed, and when Wright protested that he could accomplish nothing unless Hancock and Smith moved forward to protect his flanks, he was informed that they had filed the same complaint about his lack of progress in the center, which left them equally exposed. Faced with this dilemma, headquarters instructed each of the corps commanders to go forward on his own, without regard for what the others might be doing.

Up on the line, such instructions had a quality of madness, and a colonel on Wright's staff did not hesitate to say so. "To move that army farther, except by regular approaches," he declared, "was a simple and absolute impossibility, known to be such by every officer and man of the three corps engaged." Here too was a dilemma, and here too a simple answer was forthcoming. When the order to resume the attack was repeated, unit commanders responded in the same fashion by having their troops step up their rate of fire from the positions where they lay.

It went on like that all morning. Dodging shells and bullets, which continued to fall abundantly, dispatch bearers crept forward with instructions for the assault to be renewed. The firing, most of it skyward, would swell up and then subside, until another messenger arrived with another order and the process was repeated, the men lying prone and digging in, as best they could in such cramped positions, to provide themselves with a little cover between blind volleys. Finally, an order headed 1.30 came down to all three corps, eight minutes less than nine hours after it had been placed in execution: "For the present all further offensive operations will be suspended."

Over near Gaines Mill, with occasional long-range Federal projectiles landing in the clearing where his headquarters tent was pitched, Lee had spent an anxious half hour awaiting the return of couriers sent to bring him word of the outcome of the rackety assault, which opened full-voiced on the right, down near the Chickahominy, and roared quickly to a sustained climax, northward to the Totopotomoy. For all he knew, the Union infantry might get there first to announce a breakthrough half a mile east of the shell-pocked meadow overlooking the ruined mill. Mercifully, though, the wait was brief. Shortly after sunrise the couriers began returning on lathered horses, and their reports varied only in degrees of exultation. "Tell General Lee it is the same all along my front," A. P. Hill had said, pointing to where the limits of the enemy advance were marked by windrows of the dead and dying. Confederate losses were low; incredibly low, it seemed. Hoke, as an extreme example, reported that so far, though the ground directly in front of his intrenchments was literally blue with fallen attackers, he had not lost a single man in his division. In Anderson's corps, Law was hit in the head by a stray bullet that was to take him away from his brigade for good, and Breckinridge, after ending Barlow's costly short-term penetration, was badly shaken up when his horse, struck by a solid shot, collapsed between his knees. No other high-ranking defender received so much as a scratch or a bruise throughout the length of the gray line. By midmorning, with the close-up Union effort reduced to blind volleys of musketry fired prone in response to orders for a resumption of the attack, it was clear that Lee had won what a staff colonel was to call "perhaps the easiest victory ever granted to Confederate arms by the folly of Federal commanders."

Back in Richmond, although fighting had raged even closer to the city throughout five of the Seven Days, two years ago, citizens had been jolted awake that morning by the loudest firing they had ever heard. Windows rattled with the coming of dawn and kept on rattling past midday, one apprehensive listener declared, "as if whole divisions were firing at a word of command."

No one could say, at that range, who was getting the worst and who the best of it. Before noon, as a result, distinguished visitors began arriving at Lee's headquarters in search of firsthand information. Among them was Postmaster General John H. Reagan, who brought two lawyer friends along to help find out how the battle was going. Lee told them it was going well, up to now at least, and when they wondered if the artillery wasn't unusually active here today, the general said it was, but he added, with a gesture toward the contending lines, where the drumfire of a hundred thousand rifles sounded to Reagan like the tearing of a sheet: "It is that that kills men."

What reserves did he have on hand, they asked, in case Grant managed a breakthrough at some point along his front?

"Not a regiment," Lee replied, "and that has been my condition ever since the fighting commenced on the Rappahannock. If I shorten my lines to provide a reserve, he will turn me. If I weaken my lines to provide a reserve, he will break them."

Thinking this over, the three civilians decided it was time to leave, and in the course of their ride back to the capital they met the President coming out. Today was his fifty-sixth birthday. He had spent the morning, despite the magnetic clatter of the batteries at Cold Harbor, with his three children and his wife, who was soon to be delivered of their sixth; but after lunch, unable any longer to resist the pull of guns that had been roaring for nine hours, he called for his horse and set out on the nine-mile ride to army headquarters. There he found the situation much as it had been described in a 1 o'clock dispatch ("So far every attack has been repulsed," Lee wired) except that by now the Federals had abandoned all pretense of resuming the assault. The staff atmosphere, there in the clearing above Gaines Mill, was one of elation over a victory in the making, if not in fact over one already achieved. Returning to Richmond soon after dark, Davis was pleased to read a message Seddon had just received from Lee in summary of the daylong battle, which now had ended with his army intact and Grant's considerably diminished. "Our loss today has been small," the general wrote, "and our success, under the blessing of God, all that we could expect."

Beyond the lines where Lee's men rested from their exertions, and beyond the intervening space where the dead had begun to spoil in the heat and the wounded cried for help that did not come, the repulsed survivors brooded on the outcome of a solid month of fighting. This was the thirtieth day since the two armies first made contact in the Wilderness, and Union losses were swelling toward an average of 2000 men a day. Some days it was less, some days more, and some days — this one, for example — it was far more, usually as the result of a high-level miscalculation or downright blunder. Even Grant was infected by the gloom into which his troops were plunged by today's addition to the list of headlong tactical failures. "I regret this assault more than any one I ever ordered," he told his staff that evening. Uncharacteristic as it was, the remark made for a certain awkwardness in the group, as if he had sought to relieve his anguish with a scream. "Subsequently the matter was seldom referred to in a conversation," a junior staffer was to state.

Others were less reticent. "I think Grant has had his eyes opened," Meade wrote home, not without a measure of grim satisfaction, "and is willing to admit now that Virginia and Lee's army is not Tennessee and Bragg's army."

According to some observers, such an admission was a necessity if the campaign was to continue. James Wilson, riding over for a visit, found that several members of Grant's official family, including Rawlins, "feared that the policy of direct and continuous attack, if persisted in, would ultimately so decimate and discourage the rank and file that they could not be induced to face the enemy at all. Certain it is," the cavalryman added, "that the 'smash-'em-up' policy was abandoned about that time and was never again favored at headquarters." This would indeed be welcome news, if it was true, but just now the army was in no shape to take much note of anything except its weariness and depletion. A line colonel, stunned and grimy from not having had a full night's sleep or a change of clothes since May 5, found himself in no condition to write more than a few bleak lines in a family letter. "I can only tell my wife I am alive and well," he said; "I am too stupid for any use."

In the past month the Army of the Potomac, under Grant, had lost no less than half as many men as it had lost in the previous three years under McDowell, McClellan, Pope, Burnside, Hooker, and Meade on his own. Death had become a commonplace, though learning to live with it produced a cumulative strain. High-strung Gouverneur Warren, whose four bled-down divisions had fewer troops in them by now than Wright's or Hancock's three, broke out tonight in sudden expostulation to a friend: "For thirty days it has been one funeral procession past me, and it has been too much!" Criticism was mounting, not only against Grant, who had planned — or, strictly speaking, failed to plan — today's attack, but also against those immediately below him on the military ladder. "I am disgusted with the generalship displayed," young Emory Upton wrote his sister on the morning after the battle. "Our men have, in many cases, been foolishly and wantonly slaughtered." Next day, continuing the letter, he went further in fixing the blame. "Our loss was very heavy, and to no purpose. . . . Some of our corps commanders are not fit to be corporals. Lazy and indolent, they will not even ride along their lines; yet, without hesitancy, they will order us to attack the enemy, no matter what their position or numbers. Twenty thousand of our killed and wounded should today be in our ranks."

Horror was added to bitterness by the suffering of the wounded, still trapped between the lines, and the pervasive stench of the dead, still unburied after two sultry nights and the better part of a third day under the fierce June sun. "A deserter says Grant intends to *stink* Lee out of his position, if nothing else will suffice," a Richmond diarist noted, but a Federal staff colonel had a different explanation: "An impression prevails in the popular mind, and with some reason perhaps, that a commander who sends a flag of truce asking permission to bury his dead and bring in his wounded has lost the field of battle. Hence the resistance upon our part to ask a flag of truce."

No more willing to give that impression here in Virginia than he had been a year ago in Mississippi, following the repulse of his two assaults on the Vicksburg fortifications, the Union general held off doing anything to relieve either the stench or the drawn-out agony of his fallen soldiers until the afternoon of June 5, and even then he could not bring himself to make a forthright request for the necessary Confederate acquiescence. "It is reported to me," he then wrote Lee, "that there are wounded men, probably of both armies, now lying exposed and suffering between the lines." His suggestion was that each side be permitted to send out unarmed litter bearers to take up its casualties when no action was in progress, and he closed by saying that "any other method equally fair to both parties you may propose for meeting the end desired will be accepted by me." But Lee, who had no wounded out there, was not letting his adversary off that easy. "I fear that such an arrangement will lead to misunderstanding and difficulty," he replied. "I propose therefore, instead, that when either party desires to remove their dead or wounded a flag of truce be sent, as is customary. It will always afford me pleasure to comply with such a request as far as circumstances will permit."

Thus admonished, Grant took another night to think the matter over — a night in which the cries of the injured, who now had been three days without water or relief from pain, sank to a mewling — and tried a somewhat different tack, as if he were yielding, not without magnanimity, to an urgent plea from a disadvantaged opponent. "Your communication of yesterday is received," he wrote. "I will send immediately, as you propose, to collect the dead and wounded between the lines of the two armies, and will also instruct that you be allowed to do the same." Not so, Lee answered for a second time, and after expressing "regret to find that I did not make myself understood in my communication," proceeded to make it clear that if what Grant wanted was a cease-fire he would have to come right out and ask for it, not informally, as between two men with a common problem, but "by a flag of truce in the usual way." Grant put on as good a face as he could manage in winding up this curious exchange. "The knowledge that wounded men are now suffering from want of attention," he responded, "compels me to ask a suspension of hostilities for sufficient time to collect them in; say two hours."

By the time Lee's formal consent came back across the lines, however, the sun was down on the fourth day of exposure for the wounded and even the mewling had reached an end. Going out next morning, June 7, search parties found only two men alive out of all the Federal thousands who had fallen in the June 3 assault; the rest had either died or made it back under fire, alone or retrieved by comrades in the darkness. At the end of the truce — which had to be extended to give the burial details time to roll up the long blue carpet of festering corpses — Grant fired a parting verbal shot in concluding his white-flag skirmish with Lee: "Regretting that all my efforts for alleviating the sufferings of wounded men left upon the battlefield have been rendered nugatory, I remain, &c., U. S. Grant, Lieutenant General."

Lee made no reply to this, no doubt feeling that none was called for, and not even the northern commander's own troops were taken in by a blame-shifting pretense which did little more than show their chief at his worst. They could discount the Copperhead charge that he was a butcher, "a bull-headed Suvarov," since his methods so far had at least kept the rebels on the defensive while his own army moved forward more than sixty air-line miles. But this was something else, this sacrifice of brave men for no apparent purpose except to salve his rankled pride. Worst of all, they saw in the agony of their comrades, left to die amid the corpses on a field already lost, a preview of much agony to come, when they themselves would be left to whimper through days of pain

The Forty Days

while their leader composed notes in defense of conduct which, so far as they could see, had been indefensible from the start.

There was that, and there was the heat and thirst, the burning sun, the crowded trenches, and always the snipers, deadly at close range. "I hated sharpshooters, both Confederate and Union," a blue artillerist would recall, "and I was always glad to see them killed." Because of them, rations and ammunition had to be lugged forward along shallow parallels that followed a roundabout zigzag course and wore a man down to feeling like some unholy cross between a pack mule and a snake. "In some instances," another observer wrote, "where regiments whose terms of service had expired were ordered home, they had to leave the field crawling on hands and knees through trenches to the rear." That was a crowning indignity, that a man had to crouch to leave the war, at a time when he wanted to crow and shout, and that even then he might be killed on his way out. Devoured by lice and redbugs, which held carnival in the filthy rags they wore for clothes and burrowed into flesh that had not been washed for more than a month, the men turned snappish, not only among themselves but toward their officers as well. Tempers flared as the conviction grew that they were doing no earthly good in their present position, yet they saw no way to change it without abandoning their drive on Richmond, a scant ten miles away. At a cost of more than 50,000 casualties, Grant had landed them in coffin corner — and it did not help to recall, as a few surviving veterans could do, that McClellan had attained more or less the same position, two years ago, at practically no cost at all.

One who could remember that was Meade, the "damned old goggle-eyed snapping turtle" who had contributed a minor miracle to the campaign by holding onto his famous hair-trigger temper through a month of tribulations and frustrations. But now, in the wake of Cold Harbor, he lost it: lost it, moreover, in much the spectacular manner which those who knew him best had been expecting all along.

Baldy Smith was the first to see it coming. Two days after the triple-pronged assault was shattered, and with thousands of his soldiers lying dead or dying in front of his works, Meade paid Smith a routine visit, in the course of which the Vermonter asked him bluntly how he "came to give such an order for battle as that of the 2d." According to Baldy, Meade's reply was "that he had worked out every plan for every move from the crossing of the Rapidan onward, that the papers were full of the doings of *Grant's* army, and that he was tired of it and was determined to let General Grant plan his own battles." The result, once Grant had been left to his own devices, was the compounded misery out there between the lines. Smith saw from this reaction what was coming of the buildup of resentment, and two days later it came.

While the burial details were at work out front at last, Meade glanced through a hometown newspaper, a five-day-old copy of the

Philadelphia *Inquirer,* and his eye was caught by a paragraph that referred to him as being "entitled to great credit for the magnificent movements of the army since we left Brandy, for they have been directed by him. In battle he puts troops in action and controls their movements; in a word, he commands the army. General Grant is here only because he deems the present campaign the vital one of the war, and wishes to decide on the spot all questions that would be referred to him as general-in-chief." This was gratifying enough, but then the Pennsylvanian moved on to the following paragraph, the one that brought on the foreseen explosion. "History will record, but newspapers cannot, that on one eventful night during the present campaign Grant's presence saved the army, and the nation too; not that General Meade was on the point of committing a blunder unwittingly, but his devotion to his country made him loth to risk her last army on what he deemed a chance. Grant assumed the responsibility, and we are still on to Richmond."

Meade reacted fast. Though the piece was unsigned, he had the *Inquirer* correspondent — one Edward Crapsey — brought to his tent, confronted him with the article, and when the reporter admitted that he had written it, demanded to know the source of his remarks. Crapsey rather lamely cited "the talk of the camp," to the effect that after the second day of battle in the Wilderness, with both flanks turned and his center battered, only Grant had wanted to keep moving south. Enraged by the repetition of this "base and wicked lie," Meade placed the offender in arrest and had his adjutant draw up a general order directing that he "be put without the lines [of the army] and not permitted to return." The provost marshal was charged with the execution of the order next morning, June 8, and he carried it out in style. Wearing on his breast and back large placards lettered LIBELER OF THE PRESS, Crapsey was mounted face-rearward on a mule and paraded through the camps to the accompaniment of the "Rogue's March," after which he was less ceremoniously expelled. "The commanding general trusts that this example will deter others from committing like offenses," Meade's order read, "and he takes this occasion to notify the representatives of the public press that ... he will not hesitate to punish with the utmost rigor all [such] instances."

Whatever he might have "trusted," the outcome was that Meade now had two wars on his hands, one with the rebels in his front, the other with "the representatives of the public press" in his immediate rear. Making his way to Washington, Crapsey recounted his woes to newspaper friends, who were unanimous in condemning the general for thus "wreaking his personal vengeance on an obscure friendless civilian." What was more, their publishers backed them up; Meade, one said, was "as leprous with moral cowardice as the brute that kicks a helpless cripple on the street, or beats his wife at home." By way of retaliation for what they called "this elaborate insult," they agreed that his name would never be mentioned in dispatches except in connection with a defeat, and they held to this for the next six months or more, with the result that another casualty was added to the long Cold Harbor list, a victim of journalistic strangulation.

Eleven months ago, the Gettysburg victor had been seen as a sure winner in some future presidential election; but not now. Now and for the rest of the year, a reporter noted privately, "Meade was quite as much unknown, by any correspondence from the army, as any dead hero of antiquity."

★ ★ ★

Meade had his woes, but so it seemed did everyone around him, high or low, in the wake of a battle whose decisive action was over in eight holocaustic minutes. Not only had it been lost, and quickly lost; it had been lost, the losers now perceived, before it began. Despite the distraction of wounds that smarted all the more from having been self-inflicted, so to speak, this made for a certain amount of bitter introspection at all levels, including the top. A colonel on Lee's staff, coupling quotes from Grant and Hamlet — admittedly an improbable combination — remarked that the Union commander's resolution "to fight it out on this line if it takes all summer" seemed, at this stage, to be "sicklied o'er with the pale cast of thought."

It was in fact, all quips aside, a time for taking stock. Beyond the knowledge that attrition was a knife that cut both ways, Grant had accepted from the outset, as a condition of the tournament, the probability that the knife would slice deeper into the ranks of the attacker; but how much deeper he hadn't known, till now. For twenty-nine days he had been losing about two men to Lee's one, and if this was hard, it was at any rate in proportion to the size of the two armies. Then came the thirtieth day, Cold Harbor, and his loss was five to one, a figure made even more doleful by the prospect that future losses were likely to be as painfully disproportionate if he tried the same thing again in this same region. Lodged as he was in coffin corner, it was no wonder if the cast of his thought was sicklied o'er, along with the thoughts of those around him, staff or line; Rawlins and Upton, for example. Moreover, the effect of that month of losses was cumulative, like the expenses of a spender on a spree, and during the lull which now ensued the bill came due. Halleck sent him what amounted to a declaration of bankruptcy, or in any case a warning that his credit was about to be cut off. On June 7, while the burial details were at work and Meade was berating Crapsey in his tent, Old Brains served notice from Washington that the bottom of the manpower barrel was in sight: "I inclose a list of troops forwarded from this department to the Army of the Potomac since the campaign opened — 48,265 men. I shall send you a few regiments more, when all resources will be exhausted till another draft is made."

These were hard lines, coming as they did at this disappointing juncture in the campaign. Just as the addition of Smith's 15,000 from the Army of the James had not made up for the number who departed from Meade's army because their enlistments had expired or they had broken down physically under the thirty-day strain, so too was Halleck's figure, even with the inclusion of those "few regiments more," considerably short of the number who had been shot or captured in the course of the month-long drive from the Rapidan to the Chickahominy. This would make for restrictions, which in turn seemed likely to require a change in style. Up to the present, Grant had been living as it were on interest, replacing his fallen veterans with conscripts, but from now until another of Lincoln's "calls" had been responded to, and the drafted troops approximately trained for use in the field, he would be living on principal. Formerly replaceable on short notice, a man hit now would be simply one man less, a flat subtraction from the dwindling mass. The law of diminishing utility thus obtained, and though Grant no doubt would find it cramping, if not prohibitive in its effect on his previous method of sailing headlong into whatever got in his path, it afforded in any case a gleam of hope for those around and under him. Some members of his staff had expressed the fear that any attempt to repeat the army's latest effort, here between the Totopotomoy and the Chickahominy, would render it unfit for future use. Now they could stop worrying; at least about that. Grant had no intention of provoking another Cold Harbor and they knew it, not only because they had heard him express regret that he had tried such a thing in the first place, but also because they knew that he could no longer afford it, even if he changed his mind.

One possible source of reinforcements was the remnant of Butler's army, still tightly corked in its bottle on the far side of the James and doing no earthly good except for keeping Beauregard's even smaller remnant from joining Lee. However, as a result of his casualties during the corking operation and the subsequent detachment of Smith, the cock-eyed general was down to about 10,000 men, scarcely enough to warrant the trouble of getting them on and off transports and certainly not enough to make any significant change in the situation north of the Chickahominy. Besides, Grant's mind was turning now toward a use for them in the region where they were. He still thought his plan for a diversionary effort south of the James had been a good one; aside, that is, from the designation of Butler as the man to carry it out. If a real soldier, a professional rather than an all-thumbs amateur, had been in over-all command — Baldy Smith, for example — Richmond might not have fallen by now, but at least it would have been cut off from Georgia and the Carolinas by the occupation of the Petersburg rail hub, and its citizens would be tightening their belts another notch or two to relieve far greater pangs of hunger than they were feeling with their supply lines open to the south. Grant's notion was to reinforce Butler for a

The Forty Days

breakout from Bermuda Neck, due west to Walthall Junction, or a sidle across the Appomattox for a quick descent on Petersburg. Smith's corps would go, he and his men being familiar with the southside terrain, and possibly a corps or two from Meade. In fact, the more Grant thought about it, there in the stench and dust around Cold Harbor, the more he was persuaded that the thing to do was send Meade's whole army, not only to assure the success of the operation beyond the James, but also to resolve what was fast becoming a stalemate, here on the north bank of the Chickahominy, and remove the troops from the scene of their most disheartening repulse.

Halleck was against it before he even learned the details. He preferred the slower but less risky investment of the Confederate capital from the north, which would not expose the army to the danger of being caught astride the James and would have the added virtue of covering Washington if Lee reverted to his practice of disrupting Union strategy with a strike across the Potomac. But Grant had had quite enough of maneuvering in that region.

"My idea from the start has been to beat Lee's army, if possible, north of Richmond," he admitted in a letter to the chief of staff on June 5, the day he opened negotiations for the burial of his dead, but he saw now that "without a greater sacrifice of human life than I am willing to make, all cannot be accomplished that I had designed." Then he told just what it was he had in mind. "I will continue to hold substantially to the ground now occupied by the Army of the Potomac, taking advantage of any favorable circumstance that may present itself, until the cavalry can be sent to destroy the Virginia Central Railroad from about Beaver Dam for some 25 or 30 miles west. When this is effected, I will move the army to the south side of James River." Cut off from supplies from the north and south, Lee would have no choice except to stay inside his capital and starve, abandon it to his foe, or come out and fight for it in the open. Grant had no doubt about the outcome if his adversary, as seemed likely from past usage, chose the third of these alternatives and tried to stage another Seven Days. "The feeling of the two armies now seems to be that the rebels can protect themselves only by strong intrenchments," he closed his letter, "while our army is not only confident of protecting itself without intrenchments, but can beat and drive the enemy whenever and wherever he can be found without this protection."

Then suddenly things began to happen fast. He learned that night that while he had been writing to Halleck, outlining his plan without committing himself to a schedule, Sigel's successor David Hunter had scored a victory out in the Shenandoah Valley that would shorten considerably the time Grant had thought he would have to devote to smashing Richmond's northwestern supply line. Disdaining the combinations his predecessor had favored — and which, it could be seen now, had contributed to the failure of that segment of the grand design for Lee's defeat — Hunter had simply notified Crook and Averell that he was heading south, up the Valley pike, and that they were to join him as soon as they could make it across the Alleghenies from their camp on the Greenbrier River. He set out from Cedar Creek on May 26, five days after taking command of the troops whipped at New Market the week before, and at the end of a ten-day hike up the turnpike, which he interrupted from time to time to demolish a gristmill, burn a barn, or drive off butternut horsemen trying to scout the column at long range, he reached the village of Piedmont, eleven miles short of Staunton, and found the rebels drawn up in his path, guns booming. Attacking forthwith he wrecked and scattered what turned out to be three scratch brigades, all that were left to defend the region after Breckinridge departed. His reward, gained at a cost of less than 500 killed and wounded, included more than 1000 prisoners, a solid fifth of the force that had opposed him; the body of Brigadier General William E. Jones, abandoned on the field by the fugitives he had commanded until he was shot; and Staunton. Hunter occupied the town next day, his two divisions marching unopposed down streets no blue-clad troops had trod before. Two days later, on June 8, having torn up the railroad west of town as they approached, Crook and Averell arrived from West Virginia to assist in the consumption and destruction of commissary and ordnance stores collected at Staunton for shipment to Lee's army. With his strength thus doubled to 18,000, Hunter promptly took up the march for Lynchburg, another important depot of supplies, located where the Virginia & Tennessee Railroad branched east to form the Southside and the Orange & Alexandria; after which he intended to strike northeast for Charlottesville, where he would get back astride the Virginia Central and move down it to join Grant near Richmond, twisting rails and burning crossties as he went.

Again he was moving toward reinforcements, this time of the doughtiest kind. Grant had no sooner learned of Hunter's coup at Piedmont than he decided to proceed at once with the opening phase of the plan he had outlined that day for Halleck. He sent for Sheridan and gave him orders to take off at dawn of June 7, westward around Lee's north flank, for a link-up with Hunter near Charlottesville; he was to lend the help of his hard-handed troopers in wrecking the Virginia Central on his way back and, if necessary, fight off any graybacks, mounted or dismounted, who might try to interfere. In this connection Grant conferred next day with Meade, explaining the ticklish necessity of keeping enough pressure on Lee to discourage him from sending any part of his army against Sheridan or Hunter, yet not so much pressure that Lee would fall back to the permanent fortifications in his rear, whose strength might also permit such a detachment of troops for the protection of the vital rail supply route from the Shenandoah Valley. (This

The Forty Days

was also why Grant, in addition to his habitual disinclination in such matters, had not wanted to risk encouraging his opponent by making a forthright request for permission to bury his dead and bring in the wounded suffering in his front.) At the same time, Meade was instructed to start work on a second line of intrenchments, just in rear of his present works, stout enough to be held by a skeleton force if Lee attacked while the army was in the early stages of its withdrawal across the Chickahominy, down beyond White Oak Swamp, to and across the James.

One thing more Grant did while Sheridan was preparing to take off next morning, and that was to call in two of his aides, Horace Porter and another young lieutenant colonel, Cyrus Comstock, who was also a West Pointer and a trained engineer. Both were familiar with the region to be traversed, having served under McClellan in the course of that general's "change of base" two years ago, and Grant had a double mission for them: one as carriers of instructions for Butler at Bermuda Hundred, the other as selectors of a site for what promised to be the longest pontoon bridge in American military history. "Explain the contemplated movement fully to General Butler," he told them, "and see that the necessary precautions are made by him to render his position secure against any attack from Lee's forces while the Army of the Potomac is making its movement." That was their first assignment, and the second, involving engineering skill, followed close behind. "You will then select the best point on the river for the crossing."

They left, and the following day — with Sheridan's troopers gone before dawn, the burial squads at their grisly task out front, and Meade in a snit over Crapsey's piece in the *Inquirer* — Grant got to work, while awaiting the outcome of his preliminary arrangements, on logistic details of the projected shift. He did so, however, over the continuing objections of the chief of staff. Halleck had been against a southside campaign two years ago, when McClellan pled so fervently for permission to undertake what Grant was about to do, and he still was as much opposed as ever, believing that such a maneuver was practically an invitation for Lee to cross the Potomac. The old fox had already crossed it twice without success, it was true, but the third time might prove to be the charm that won him Washington, especially now that Grant, having stripped its forts of soldiers, proposed to leave it strategically uncovered.

Old Brains continued thus to take counsel of his fears; but not Grant, whose mind was quite made up. "We can defend Washington best," he informed Halleck, putting an end to discussion of the matter, "by keeping Lee so occupied that he cannot detach enough troops to capture it. I shall prepare at once to move across James River."

Grant being Grant, and Halleck having long since lost the veto, that was that. The Union commander was soon to find, however, that his effort to keep Lee so occupied with the close-up defense of Richmond that he would not feel able to send any considerable part of his outnumbered force against Hunter or Sheridan had failed. Learning on June 6 of Jones's defeat at Piedmont and Hunter's rapid occupation of Staunton, Lee sent at once for Breckinridge and informed him that he and his two brigades would be leaving next morning for Lynchburg to prevent the capture of that important railroad junction by the bluecoats they had whipped three weeks ago under Sigel, a hundred miles to the north. Instructed to combine his 2100 veterans with the Piedmont fugitives for this purpose, the Kentuckian left on schedule, determined to repeat his New Market triumph, although he would be facing longer odds and was personally in a near-invalid condition as a result of having his horse collapse on him four days ago.

With Grant likely to resume his hammering at any moment, here at Cold Harbor or elsewhere along a semicircular arc from Atlee Station down to Chaffin's Bluff — all within ten miles of Capitol Square — even so minor a reduction in strength as this detachment of two brigades was a risky business for Lee, no matter how urgent the need. Yet before the day was over he was warned of another threat which called for a second detachment, larger and more critical than the first. Sheridan, he learned from outpost scouts, had taken off before dawn with two of his divisions, about the same time Breckinridge left Richmond, headed west by rail for Lynchburg. The bandy-legged cavalryman's march was north, across the Pamunkey; he made camp that night on the near bank of the Mattaponi, and next morning — June 8 — he was reported moving west. Lee reasoned that the blue horsemen intended to effect a junction with Hunter on this or the far side of the Blue Ridge, somewhere along the Virginia Central, which they would obstruct while waiting for him to join them for the return march. If Sheridan was to be thwarted it would have to be done by a force as mobile as his own, and though Lee found it hard to deprive himself of a single trooper at a time when his adversary was no doubt contemplating another sidle, he sent Hampton orders to set out next morning, with his own and Fitzhugh Lee's divisions, to intercept the raiders before they reached either Hunter or the railroad.

Yet this too, as it turned out, was a day that brought unwelcome news of the need for still another reduction of the outnumbered army in its trenches near Cold Harbor. Crook and Averell, Lee was informed, had joined Hunter that morning in Staunton, doubling his strength beyond anything Breckinridge, with less than a third as many troops — including the Piedmont fugitives, once he managed to round them up — could be expected to confront, much less defeat. Obviously he would have to be reinforced; but how? Then came the notion Halleck was even now warning Grant that his proposed maneuver would invite from Lee, who had a way of making a virtue of necessity. Hunter's strength was

The Forty Days

put at 20,000, and it was clear that if he was to be stopped it would have to be done by two or three divisions, available only — if at all — from the Confederate main body. Such a decrease in the force confronting Grant, merely for the sake of blocking Hunter, seemed little short of suicidal. But how would it be if a sizeable detachment could be used offensively, as a means not only of reclaiming the Shenandoah Valley and covering the supply lines leading to it, but also of threatening Washington by crossing the Potomac? Twice before, a dispersion of force, made in the face of odds as long or longer, had relieved the pressure on Richmond by playing on the fears of the Union high command. McClellan and Hooker had been recalled to protect the menaced capital in their rear; so might Grant be summoned back to meet a similar threat. Impossible though it seemed at this fitful juncture, such a maneuver was never really out of Lee's mind, and it was especially attractive now that rumors had begun to fly that Grant was designing a shift to the James, perhaps for a link-up with Butler on the other side. "If he gets there it will become a siege," Lee had told Early the week before, "and then it will be a mere question of time."

Hampton had no sooner taken off next morning, riding the chord of Sheridan's arc to intercept him, than an alarm from beyond the James lent credence to the rumor that the Federals were preparing a new effort in that direction, or in any case an improved resumption of the old one. Butler, crossing a portion of his command from Bermuda Neck by a pontoon bridge he had thrown across the Appomattox near Port Walthall, launched a dawn attack on the Petersburg intrenchments, four miles south. Beauregard, down to fewer than 8000 troops by now, managed to contain and repulse this cavalry-infantry assault because of the strength of the works and the valiance of the men who occupied them, mostly under- and over-aged members of a militia battalion, reinforced for the crisis by volunteers from the city hospital and the county jail. In the resultant "Battle of the Patients and the Penitents," as it came to be called, these inexperienced defenders — inspired by a local Negro band whose vigorous playing gave the attackers the impression that the works were heavily manned — held their own long enough for gray-jacket cavalry to arrive from the main line, beyond the Appomattox, and drive the bluecoats off. It was over by midafternoon, a near thing at best, and Beauregard, though proud of what had been achieved, warned that he could not be expected to repeat the performance unless the troops he had sent Lee were restored to him. Moreover, he told the War Department, they had better be returned at once, since in his opinion today's attack presaged a much larger one soon to come.

"This movement must be a reconnaissance connected with Grant's future operations," he wired Bragg while the fight was still in progress, and presently he added, by way of emphasizing the risk: "Without the troops sent to General Lee I will have to elect between abandoning lines on Bermuda Neck and those of Petersburg. Please give me the views of the Government on the subject."

Presented thus with a choice between losing Richmond to assault or by starvation, Bragg could only reply that the mercurial Creole was to do what he could to hold both positions, while he himself conferred with Davis, who authorized the return of Gracie's brigade from the capital defenses, and with Lee, who agreed to alert Hoke's division for a crossing at Drewry's in case another southside attack developed. Mainly, though, the Virginian saw this abortive maneuver of Butler's as a feint, designed to distract his attention from more serious threats presented by more dependable Union commanders on the north side of the James: by Meade, who might even now be bracing his army for another all-out lunge, here at Cold Harbor or elsewhere along the Richmond-hugging arc: by Hunter, who was evidently about to resume his march from Staunton, with either Lynchburg or Charlottesville as his intermediate goal, preparatory to a combination with Meade: or by Sheridan, who was in motion between the other two, probably with the intention of descending on the Virginia Central before linking up with Hunter for a return march that would complete the destruction of that vital supply line. Despite a rather superfluous warning from the President, who added his voice to Bragg's — "The indications are that Grant, despairing of a direct attack, is now seeking to embarrass you by flank movements" — Lee could not see that the thing to do, at this critical juncture, was weaken his army below the present danger point for the sake of relieving Beauregard's fears as to what Butler might or might not be up to, down on the far side of the James. Until Grant's intentions became clearer, and until he could see what came of the two detachments already made — Breckinridge, two days ago, and Hampton just this morning — Lee preferred to hold what he had, and hope that others, elsewhere, would measure up to his expectations.

Wade Hampton, whose assignment to lead the two-division column in pursuit of Sheridan was the nearest Lee had come to designating a successor to the fallen Stuart, was intent on fulfilling his share of the army commander's hopes, not so much because of a desire for fame or an ache for glory — "I pray for peace," he would presently say in a letter to his sister, having won the coveted post by demonstrating his fitness for it in the current operation; "I would not give peace for all the military glory of Bonaparte" — as because of a habitual determination to accomplish what was required of him, in this as in other phases of a life of privileged responsibility. He wore no plume, no red-lined cape, and a minimum of braid, preferring a flat-brimmed brown felt hat and a plain gray jacket of civilian cut. His manner, while friendly, was grave, and though he was perhaps the richest man in the South, his spurs were brass, not gold. A Virginia trooper noted another difference between the Caro-

The Forty Days

linian and his predecessor as chief of cavalry, which was that, whereas Jeb had "sometimes seemed to have a delight in trying to discharge his mission with the smallest possible number of men, Hampton believed in superiority of force and exerted himself to concentrate all the men he could at the point of contact."

Superiority of force would not be possible short of the point of contact in this case; for though both mounted columns were composed of two divisions containing a total of five brigades, Sheridan had 8000 troopers, compared to Hampton's 5000, and four batteries of horse artillery opposing three. One advantage the gray riders had, however, and this was that they traveled lighter, with fewer impediments to slow them down. The Federals had a train of 125 supply wagons and ambulances, as well as a herd of beef to butcher on the march, while all the Confederates had was an issue of three-day rations, consisting of half a pound of bacon and a pound and a half of hardtack, carried on the person, along with a sack of horse corn slung from the pommel of each saddle. Another advantage, although no one could be sure of it beforehand, was that Lee had been right about Sheridan's objective; Hampton had a much shorter distance to travel, northwest from Atlee, across the South Anna, in order to get there first. This he did, despite the blue column's two-day head start in setting out on its roundabout route from Cold Harbor, first north across the Pamunkey, then west through Chilesburg, up the left bank of the North Anna for a crossing short of Gordonsville and a quick descent, as ordered, on the Virginia Central between that place and Louisa Courthouse, a dozen miles down the track. Shortly after sunrise, June 11, within about three miles of his objective at the outset of his fifth day on the go, Sheridan ran into fire from rebel skirmishers, who, he now found, had arrived the previous evening and had rested from their two-day ride within earshot of the bugles that called his troopers to horse this morning.

Hampton was not only there, he was attacking in accordance with plans made the night before, after learning that he had won the race for the stretch of railroad Sheridan had in mind to wreck. His own division, with three brigades, was to advance northeast from Trevilian Station, eight miles short of Gordonsville and half that distance above Louisa, where Fitz Lee, having bivouacked his two brigades nearby, was to set out north at daybreak for a convergence upon Sheridan's camp, five miles away. Each division had a convenient road to move on, and Hampton at least was unhindered on the approach march. Hearing firing off to the east, which he took to be Fitz brushing pickets from his path, he sent his lead brigade forward, dismounted, and made contact with the Federals, driving them rapidly back on their supports, who resisted stubbornly even when hit by a second brigade. Hampton withheld full commitment, waiting for Lee to come up and strike the defenders flank and rear. At this point, however, a sudden clatter from the south informed him that his own rear had been struck. By what, and how, he did not wait to learn. Disengaging with all possible speed, and pursued now by the enemy he had driven, he withdrew to find a host of blue marauders laying claim to his headquarters and the 800 horses left behind when he dismounted his lead brigade for the sunrise attack. He attacked again, this time rearward, and what had been a battle became a melee.

The marauders were members of Custer's brigade, one of Torbert's three. While the other two were holding fast under pressure from Hampton, Gregg's division had got the jump on Fitz and driven him back toward Louisa, enabling the Michiganders to slip between the converging gray columns for a penetration deep into Hampton's rear, near Trevilian. Yet they had no sooner begun to gather the fruits of their boldness — the 800 riderless horses, several ordnance wagons, and a couple of guns being held there in reserve — than they were hit, simultaneously from the north and east, by three hornet-mad rebel brigades, two of them Hampton's and one Lee's. Custer not only had to abandon what he had won; he also lost much that he brought with him, including a considerable number of troopers shot or captured, his headquarters wagon containing all his records and spare clothes, and his Negro cook Eliza, known to the soldiers as "the Queen of Sheba" because she usually rode in a dilapidated family carriage the yellow-haired general had commandeered for her professional use and comfort. Shaken, he fell back to the station and held on grimly against the odds, while Torbert fought his way down with the other two brigades and Gregg continued to slug it out with Fitz. The result was about as bewildering to one side as to the other, and was to be even more confusing to future students attempting to reconcile conflicting reports of the action. The Confederates at last pulled back, Hampton toward Gordonsville and Lee in the opposite direction. Sheridan did not pursue, west or east, but contented himself with holding the four miles of track between Trevilian and Louisa. It was a gloomy night for the Federals, especially those in Custer's brigade, which had lost heavily today; but their dejection was relieved, just before sunup, by the reappearance of the Queen of Sheba, grinning broadly and lugging along the gaudy young general's personal valise, which she had managed to bring with her when she stole out of the rebel lines and into her own.

Sheridan was far from pleased with the development of events. After a night of fitful sleep, with graybacks hovering east and west — about to be joined, for all he knew, by reinforcements from both directions, infantry by rail and cavalry on horseback — he put Gregg to work with sledges and crowbars on the four-mile stretch of track and prepared to enlarge his present limits of destruction, first by driving Hampton back on Gordonsville, eight miles northwest, and then by thrusting him aside to clear the way for the scheduled meeting with

Hunter, another twenty miles up the line at Charlottesville. It was past noon, however, before he got Torbert deployed for action; by which time Fitz Lee had joined Hampton, coming roundabout from Louisa, and the two divisions were dug in just above Trevilian, blocking both the Virginia Central and the turnpike leading west. Repeated and costly dismounted assaults failed to budge the rebels, snug in their works, and after nightfall, Gregg having done all the damage he could to the railroad within the cramped limits of the Federal occupation, Sheridan decided to abandon both his position and his mission.

Under cover of darkness he withdrew across the North Anna and took up the return march, retracing the route that had brought him to the unhappy confrontation at Trevilian. He pulled back, he said, because his supplies and munitions were low and there was no word from Hunter, either at Charlottesville or elsewhere, as to their intended combination. In any case, having spent four days on the march out, he took nine to make it back to White House Landing, his ambulances overloaded with wounded and his horses distressed at being reduced to a diet of bearded wheat. Meantime, the limited damage Gregg had done the railroad was repaired so promptly by work gangs that Virginia Central trains were back on schedule before Sheridan reached the Pamunkey and recrossed it under the protection of gunboats whose heavy-caliber frown kept the still-hovering butternut cavalry at bay. Hampton had lost nearly 1100 men in the course of the raid; Sheridan reckoned his own loss at about 800, though a more accurate revision put the figure at 1516, considerably better than twice the number he had lost on the Richmond raid the month before.

R. E. Lee of course was pleased to learn that Little Phil had been disposed of as a threat to his main supply route from the Shenandoah Valley: so pleased, indeed, that he at last named Hampton, rather than his nephew Fitz, as his new chief of cavalry. But word of Sheridan's repulse came in the wake of news of a fateful development, out beyond the Blue Ridge, which not only presented a more substantial menace to the newly delivered supply line, but also served notice that, even if the railroad escaped seizure, there would be little in the way of supplies available for shipment from the region, either to Richmond or to any other point in the shrinking Confederacy. The news was that David Hunter, his strength doubled by the arrival of Crook two days before, had resumed his march up the Valley on June 10. Leaving Breckinridge holding the bag at Rockfish Gap, where the Virginia Central passed through the mountains east of Staunton — the Kentuckian had shifted there from Lynchburg to block the western approach to Charlottesville, which he thought was next on the Union list — Hunter struck out south, not east, and by noon of the day the cavalry battle opened near Trevilian Station, eighty air-line miles away, reached Lexington and took under fire, from across North River, the crenelated turrets and ramparts of V.M.I., whose cadets had shared in the defeat of his predecessor four weeks ago. Marching in, flags flying, he completed his work of destruction, next day and the day after, by putting the torch to what was left of the Institute and turning his soldiers loose on the town to plunder a number of private homes and the library of Washington College. For good measure, after a visit to Stonewall Jackson's grave — perhaps to make certain the famed rebel had not come bursting out of it in his wrath — Hunter ordered the residence of Former Governor John Letcher burned, as he later reported, in retaliation for its absent owner's having issued "a violent and inflammatory proclamation... inciting the population of the country to rise and wage guerrilla warfare on my troops."

Such hard-handedness toward civilians was remindful of John Pope, of whom Lee had said: "He ought to be suppressed," and then had proceeded to do just that by dividing his army, confronted near Richmond by a superior force, and sending part of it north and west, under the one-time V.M.I. professor now buried in outraged Lexington, against the fire-breathing secondary invader attempting a descent on his left flank and rear. Close though the resemblance was between the situations then and now, there were also differences, none of them advantageous from the Confederate point of view. One was that Jackson, Lee's right arm, was no longer available to carry out the suppression, and another was the present depleted condition of the Army of Northern Virginia, which had lost in the past forty days a solid forty percent of the strength it had enjoyed at the beginning of the campaign. Its casualties totaled about 27,000, and though it had inflicted a precisely tabulated 54,929 — a number greater than all its original infantry and artillery combined — the forty percent figure, unlike Grant's forty-five percent, applied at the higher levels of rank as well as at the lower. Of the 58 general officers in command of troops on the eve of conflict, back in early May, no less than 23 had fallen in battle, eight of them killed, thirteen gravely wounded, and two captured. Nor was the distribution of these casualties, high and low, by any means even throughout the three corps. Hardest hit of all was the Second: just the one Lee had in mind to detach, since it contained, as a nucleus, the survivors of Jackson's old Army of the Valley and was therefore more familiar than the others with the region Hunter was laying waste. Not only had the corps commander been replaced, but so had the leaders of two of the three divisions, while of the twelve original brigade commanders only one remained at his post, two having been promoted and the other nine shot or captured. At Spotsylvania the corps had lost the equivalent of a full division, and this contributed largely to the reduction, by half, of its outset strength of just over 17,000. There now were barely 8000 infantry in its ranks, distributed through three divisions with only three brigades in each, all but one under leaders new to their responsibilities.

These were drawbacks not to be ignored in reaching a decision; but neither was the need for dealing promptly with Hunter to be passed over. From his current position at Lexington he would no doubt cross the Blue Ridge, marching southeast against Lynchburg or northeast against Charlottesville. One would be about as bad as the other, so far as Richmond was concerned, and there was also the possibility that the wide-ranging Hunter might move against them both, in that order. At Lynchburg, just under a hundred miles due west of the captial, he would be in a position to wreck not only the Southside Railroad but also the James River Canal, both vital to the subsistence of Richmond's citizens and its armies, while at Charlottesville he would be back astride the Virginia Central, which he would destroy, with or without Sheridan's help, on the march to join Grant or come down on Lee's flank. Reduced to those terms, the problem solved itself, insofar at least as they applied to reaching a decision. Like Pope, Hunter would have to be "suppressed," or anyhow stopped and, if possible, driven back. Lee's mind was quite made up. Moreover, there was the persuasive chance that in moving against the despoilers of Lexington he would be killing two birds with one stone. If, after disposing of the bluecoats out in the Valley, the gray column then moved down it, to and across the Potomac to threaten Washington from the rear, still larger benefits might accrue. There was small chance, at this late stage, that Grant's whole force would be recalled — as McClellan's had been — from the gates of Richmond, but it was altogether possible that he would be required to detach part of it for the closeup defense of his capital; or else, in desperation to avoid that, he might be provoked into launching another ill-considered Cold Harbor assault, there or elsewhere, in an attempt to settle the issue overnight. In either event, Lee reasoned, his adversary would be reduced enough for the Army of Northern Virginia to launch an all-out assault of its own: hopefully one that would be as productive as the Seven Days offensive, but in any case one that would be conducted with all the fighting skill his soldiers had acquired in their many victories since that grim beginning under his command.

His decision reached — June 12, a Sunday; the horseback fight was into its second day at Trevilian Station, and Hunter was putting the torch to Governor Letcher's house in Lexington — Lee sent for Jubal Early to talk over with him the nature of his mission. Tall despite an arthritic stoop, a bachelor at forty-seven, dour of face, with a scraggly beard and a habit of profanity, this fellow Virginian and West Pointer was admittedly no Stonewall; but who was? No other corps commander since the fall of Longstreet had done any better on the offensive, and though this was surely the faintest of praise — since, conversely, it could also be said that none had done any worse — the only really black mark against him was his failure, in conjunction with Ewell on the second day in the Wilderness, to take prompt advantage of Gordon's report that Sedgwick's flank was open to attack. No such opportunities must be missed if he was to succeed against the odds that lay before him, first in the Valley and then beyond the Potomac. Tactful as always, Lee made this clear in giving Early verbal instructions for setting out next morning, before daylight, with all three of his divisions and two battalions of artillery. Following as it did the detachment of Breckinridge, with whom he would combine to cover Charlottesville and Lynchburg, Early's departure would deprive Lee of nearly a fourth of his infantry; yet, even with the inclusion of the Piedmont fugitives, the gray force would not be up to Hunter's present strength. Victory would have to be won by superior generalship, by celerity, stealth, and an absolute dedication to the offensive: in short, by the application of principles dear to the commander of the erstwhile Army of the Valley, which was now to be resurrected under Early.

In written orders, sent that night while the Second Corps veterans were preparing feverishly and happily to be gone with the dawn, these hopes were repeated, together with specific instructions for the march. It would be northwest, like Hampton's four days earlier, for a link-up with Breckinridge near Rockfish Gap and a quick descent on Hunter before he reached Lynchburg. After that, if all went well, would come the northward march against a new old adversary, Abraham Lincoln — and, through Lincoln and his fears, against U. S. Grant, who presumably would still be knocking at the gates of Richmond, a hundred miles away.

Grant might still be knocking when the time came, but if so it would be at the back gate, not the front. Under cover of the darkness that would obscure Early's departure, north and west, the Army of the Potomac had begun its withdrawal, east and south, from its works around Cold Harbor for the crossing of the James. Moreover, if all went as intended, here and elsewhere, the issue would have been settled — so far, as least, as Richmond was concerned — well before any rebel detachment, of whatever size, had time to reach the Potomac, much less cross it to threaten Washington. With Sheridan astride the Virginia Central and Hunter about to wreck both the Southside Railroad and the James River Canal at Lynchburg (Grant did not know that Sheridan was being driven off that evening, any more than he knew that Lee was sending Early next morning to do the same to Hunter) Federal seizure of the Petersburg rail hub would cut all but one of the gray capital's major supply lines, the Richmond & Danville, which had only been extended down to Greensboro, North Carolina, the month before. No single route, let alone one as limited as this, could supply the city's needs, including subsistence for its defenders; Lee, more than ever, would be obliged to evacuate his capital or come out from behind his intrenchments for a fight in the open, and Grant did not believe that the Confederacy could survive what would follow the adoption of either course.

He had bided his time, anticipating solutions, and when they came he moved swiftly. When the two aides, Porter and Comstock, returned from their reconnaissance that Sunday morning to report that they had found a good site for the pontoon bridge across the James, ten miles downriver from City Point and just beyond Charles City Courthouse, he evidenced some measure of the strain he had been under this past week. "While listening to our report," Porter would recall, "Grant showed the only nervousness he ever manifested in my presence. After smoking his cigar vigorously for some minutes, he removed it from his mouth, put it on the table, and allowed it to go out; then relighted it, gave a few puffs, and laid it aside again. We could hardly get the words out of our mouths fast enough to suit him, and the numerous questions he asked were uttered with much greater rapidity than usual." This was a different Grant from the stolid, twig-whittling commander of the past six weeks. It was, as the next few days would show, the Grant of the Vicksburg campaign, fast on the march, sudden in striking, and above all quick to improvise amid rapidly developing events. "At the close of the interview," Porter wrote, still amazed years later at the transformation in his chief, "he informed us that he would begin the movement that night."

It began, in point of fact, that afternoon, when Grant and Meade and their two staffs proceeded down the north bank of the Chickahominy, past Dispatch Station on the defunct York River Railroad, to make camp for the night beside a clump of catalpa trees in the yard of a farmhouse near Long Bridge, where two of the five corps were to cross the river, ten miles downstream from the present Union left. The bridge was out, but Wilson's cavalry splashed across the shallows, just after sundown, and got to work throwing a pontoon span to be used by Warren, who began his march in the twilight and was over the river by midnight. Hancock and Wright meantime fell back to the newly dug second line, under orders to hold it at all costs, in case Lee got wind of the withdrawal and launched a night attack. Smith and Burnside simultaneously marched rearward from their positions on the right, the latter turning south beyond the railroad for a crossing of the Chickahominy at Jones Bridge, five miles below Long Bridge, and Smith continuing east to White House Landing, where transports were waiting to give his troops a fast, restful trip down the York and up the James to Bermuda Hundred. Satisfied that Lee had no overnight interference in mind, Hancock and Wright pulled out after midnight to follow Warren and Burnside, respectively, over Long and Jones bridges. Once across, three of the four corps would march hard for Charles City and the James, but Warren was instructed to turn west and take up a defensive position near Riddell's Shop in support of Wilson's troopers, who would

patrol the region between White Oak Swamp and Malvern Hill in case Lee, having missed his chance tonight, tried to strike tomorrow at the blue army in motion across his front. Like Wright and Hancock earlier, once he was convinced that Lee had been outfoxed, Warren would take up the march for Charles City and the crossing of the James.

Intricate as these various interdependent movements were, they had been worked out in accordance with the required logistics of allotted time and road space. All went smoothly. Despite the heat of the night and the choking dust stirred up by more than a hundred thousand pairs of shoes, the men stepped out smartly in the darkness, glad to be leaving a dismal field where they had buried so many comrades after so much purposeless suffering. Occupied as they had been with improving their intrenchments, right up to the hour they got orders to withdraw, they took it as an excellent sign that their departure had been preceded by no rumor that a shift was being considered, since what came as a surprise to them was likely to be even more of one to the johnnies across the way, including Old Man Lee. "It was not now the custom," one veteran observed approvingly, "to inform the rank and file, and the newspapers and the enemy, of intended movements." He and others like him in those several widespread dusty columns could remember another nighttime withdrawal from that same field, just two weeks short of two full years ago, and though Cold Harbor was in itself an even more horrendous experience than Gaines Mill, the feeling now was different, and altogether better. Now as then the march was south, away from the scene of a defeat; but they felt now — as they had not done then, while trudging some of these same James-bound roads — that they were moving toward a victory, even Victory itself.

Grant thought so, too, and on sounder ground, knowing, as they did not, what he had devised for the undoing of the rebels on the far side of the river. Smith, whose corps was familiar with the terrain down there, would arrive first, being steam-propelled, and after going ashore at Bermuda Hundred would repeat the maneuver Butler had rehearsed four days ago, across the Appomattox, when his Petersburg reconnaissance-in-strength was stalled by green militia, convicts, convalescents, and Negro bandsmen. That was not likely to happen this time, for three reasons. One was that Baldy would be in charge of the advance, not the nonprofessional Butler, and Grant had already explained to his fellow West Pointer the importance of striking hard and fast. Another was that this attack would not only be made in much greater strength than the other, but would also be launched with the advantage of knowing the layout of the Petersburg defenses. The third reason was that, if there was any delay in the quick reduction of the place, Hancock — whose three divisions, in the lead on the march from Cold Harbor, would be ferried across the James to save time while the 2100-foot pontoon bridge was being assembled — would soon be down to add the weight of the hardest-hitting corps in Meade's army to the pressure Smith was exerting. As for the others, Burnside, Warren, and Wright would be arriving in that order behind Hancock and could be used as then seemed best: probably for a breakout westward from Bermuda Neck, dislodging Beauregard's cork, and a turning movement against Drewry's Bluff, which would block the path of any reinforcements Lee might try to send to Petersburg when he found what Grant had been up to all this time.

Members of the two staffs — Grant's and Meade's — shared the sanguine expectations of their chiefs, at least to the extent that they were privy to the plan, and their confidence grew as the day wore on and they rode south, doubling the columns of guns and men on the dusty roads. All the signs were that the army had indeed stolen a march on Lee, whose cavalry, unable to penetrate Wilson's screen below the Chickahominy, could give him no inkling of what was in progress east of Riddell's Shop, near which Warren's four divisions remained in position without firing a shot all afternoon, so effectively did the blue troopers perform, and then resumed their roundabout hike for the James. By that time the head of Hancock's column had come within sight of the broad, shining river, its choppy little waves as bright as polished hatchets in the sunlight.

Transports and gunboats were riding at anchor, all with steam up for the crossing, and army engineers were at work assembling their pontoons for the nearly half-mile span by which the other three corps would cross, tomorrow and the next day. An officer on Meade's staff observed Hancock's troops slogging down to Wilcox Landing just before sunset, hot and tired from their thirty-mile overnight march, their faded, sweat-splotched uniforms in tatters from forty days of combat, and was struck by the thought that, so far as these hard-bitten veterans were concerned, "the more they serve, the less they look like soldiers and the more they resemble day laborers who have bought second-hand military clothes." Then he watched them react with suspicion and puzzled dislike, much as he himself had done earlier, to their first sight of the neatly turned-out sailors and the engineers in uniforms of dark unweathered blue, until at last they saw, as he had seen, what it was that was so wrong about these strangers. They were clean — clean as visitors from some dirtless planet — and Grant's men, after six weeks on the go, shooting and being shot at, with neither the water nor the time for bathing, had become mistrustful of anyone not as grimy as themselves.

Yet despite the grime and the suspicion that went with it, despite the added weariness and the fret that over the past six weeks they had suffered three separate 18,000-man subtractions from their ranks — first in the Wilderness, then at Spotsylvania, and last on the North Anna, Totopotomoy Creek, and the Chickahominy — their spirits were even higher near the end of the Jamesward trek than at the outset: not only from being on the move again, away from the stench and snipers at Cold Harbor, but also because they could see what had begun to come of this latest sidle. Though they knew nothing of what lay ahead, on the far side of the shining river, they trusted Grant to make the most of the fact that they had given Lee the slip the night before and stolen a march on him today.

They had indeed done both those things, and were now in a position to do more. The first Lee had known of their departure was at sunup — two hours after Early withdrew his three divisions and set out for the Shenandoah Valley — when messengers reached headquarters, back near Gaines Mill, with reports that the Yankees were gone from their works around Cold Harbor. Advancing scouts uncovered a second line of intrenchments, newly dug and intricately fashioned as if for permanent occupation, but these too were deserted, as were the woods and fields a mile and more beyond. June 13, which was to have been the fortieth day of contact for the two armies, turned out to be a day of practically no contact at all; Grant was gone, vanished with his blue-clad throng, perhaps toward the lower stretches of the Chickahominy, more likely to a new base on the James from which to mount a new advance on Richmond, either by crossing the river for a back-door attack or else by moving up its near bank for an all-out assault on the capital fortifications.

Whichever it was, Lee warned the government of this latest threat and moved to meet it, shifting south to put what was left of his army in position below White Oak Swamp, where he would block the eastern approaches to the city and also be closer to Drewry's for a crossing in case the blow was aimed at Beauregard. While his son's two thin-spread cavalry brigades — all that were left since Hampton and Fitz Lee took out after Sheridan four days ago — probed unsuccessfully at rapid-firing masses of Federal horsemen coming down the Long Bridge Road toward Riddell's Shop, he posted Hill's corps in their support, athwart the field of the Seven Days fight at Glendale, and Anderson's off to the right, reaching down to Malvern Hill, which the cavalry then occupied as a post of observation, although nothing of much interest could be seen from there except a good deal of apparently purposeless activity by Union gunboats at Deep Bottom, down below. Lee's ranks were so gravely thinned by Early's departure that he might have been expected to recall him while there still was time; but when the President inquired that afternoon whether this might not be the wisest course, Lee replied, rather laconically, that he did not think so. At the end of the Forty Days, as at the beginning, he remained the gambler he had always been, the believer that the weaker force must take the longer chances.

"I do not know that the necessity for his presence today is greater than it was yesterday," he said of Early. "His troops would make us more secure here, but success in the Valley would relieve our difficulties that at present press heavily upon us."

Those first four words, "I do not know," were the crux of the matter. All the prisoners taken so far today had been cavalry, which left him with nothing but guesses as to the whereabouts of the Union infantry and artillery, all hundred thousand of them. Most likely they were in motion for the James, but whether Grant intended for them to cross it or advance up the north bank Lee could not tell; nor could he act, for fear of being decoyed out of position, until he secured more or less definite information as to which course his adversary had taken or would take. Either way, the defense of Richmond had come down to a siege, the thing he had tried hardest to avoid. "This army cannot stand a siege," he had told Little Powell a month ago, just as Beauregard, one week later, had warned Bragg: "The picture presented is one of ultimate starvation."

CHAPTER

3

Red Clay Minuet

★ ✗ ☆

AIR-LINE, THE HUNDRED-MILE DISTANCE from Chattanooga to Atlanta was the same as that from Washington to Richmond, and so were the respective sizes of the armies, which in each paired case gave the Union commander a roughly two-to-one numerical advantage. But there for the most part the resemblance stopped. Meade and Sherman (or for that matter Grant and Sherman, since that was what it came to) were as different from each other as were Lee and Johnston, two very different men indeed, and so too — despite the fact that down in Georgia, as in Virginia, the rivers mainly ran athwart the projected lines of advance and retreat — was the terrain, flat or gently rolling in the East, but mountainous in the West and therefore eminently defensible, at any rate in theory, although few of the place-names strewn about the map had been connected with much bloodshed since the era when settlers ousted the aborigines. In point of fact, harking back to those massacre days, Sherman had something similar in mind for the Confederates to his front, military and civilian. "If the North design to conquer the South," he had written home two years ago, "we must begin at Kentucky and reconquer the country from there as we did from the Indians."

Now that he faced completion of that massive undertaking, he was in what he liked to call "high feather." Instructed by Grant "to move against Johnston's army, break it up, and get into the interior of the enemy's country as far as you can, inflicting all the damage you can against their war resources," the red-haired Ohioan, by way of showing how well he understood his task, replied in paraphrase: "I am to knock Jos. Johnston, and to do as much damage to the resources of the enemy as possible."

By way of help in carrying out this project he would have an advantage, a man-made facility available neither to his flintlock-carrying predecessors nor to his cohorts in the East: namely, a rapid-transit all-weather supply line in the form of a railroad, the Western & Atlantic, running all the way to Atlanta — provided, of course, he could put and keep it in shape while nudging Johnston backward; for the rebels would surely wreck it in their wake, and almost as surely would strike at it with cavalry in his rear as he advanced. With this in mind, he made the training of rail repair gangs an integral part of his preparations, including daily workouts as rigorous and precise as the drill required of gun crews, and elevated gandy dancers to a combat status as high as that of riflemen or cannoneers. The same precaution was taken with regard to the much longer line extending rearward from Chattanooga, up through Middle Tennessee and across Kentucky to Louisville, his main supply base on the Ohio. Practically all of this more than three hundred miles of highly frangible track was subject to strikes by grayback troopers from adjoining departments, hard-handed horsemen schooled in destruction by John Morgan and Bedford Forrest, and though Sherman planned to keep these slashers occupied by making adjunctive trouble for them in their own back yards, he also hoped to forestall or reduce the delays that were likely to attend such depredations, in case the raiders broke out anyhow, by turning Nashville into what an amazed staff brigadier presently described as "one vast storehouse — warehouses covering city blocks, one a quarter of a mile long; stables by the ten and twenty acres, repair shops by the fieldful." Also of help in reducing the supply problem would be a certain amount of belt-tightening by the troops, whose divisional trains, in accordance with Sherman's orders, would carry only "five days' bacon, twenty days' bread, and thirty days' salt, sugar, and coffee; nothing else but arms and ammunition." The main thing, as the commanding general saw it, was to keep moving: and this applied as much to rearward personnel as it did to the men up front. "I'm going to move on Joe Johnston the day Grant telegraphs me he is going to hit Bobby Lee," he told a quartermaster officer. "And if you don't have my army supplied, and keep it supplied, we'll eat your mules up, sir; eat your mules up!" Having passed before through un-fought-over regions of the South — recently, for example, on a march across the midriff of Mississippi, from Vicksburg to Meridian and back — he was aware of another resource which he did not intend to neglect. "Georgia has a million of inhabitants," he wrote Grant. "If they can live, we should not starve."

Thus Sherman; a violent-talking man whose bite at times measured up to his bark, and whose commitment was to total war. "I believe in fighting in a double sense," he said this spring, "first to gain physical results and next to inspire respect on which to build up our nation's power." Tecumseh or "Cump" to his family, he was Uncle Billy to his soldiers, one of whom called him "the most American-looking man I ever saw; tall and lank, not very erect, with hair like thatch, which he rubs up with his hands, a rusty beard trimmed close, a wrinkled face, sharp, prominent red nose, small, bright eyes, coarse red hands; black felt hat slouched over the eyes, dirty dickey with the points wilted down, black old-fashioned stock, brown field officer's coat with high collar and no shoulder straps, muddy trowsers and one spur. He carries his hands in his pockets, is very awkward in his gait and motions, talks continually and with immense rapidity." Such intensity often brought on a reaction in observers, including this one. "At his departure I felt it a relief, and experienced almost an exhaustion after the excitement of his vigorous presence."

All this, moreover, was by way of diversion, a spare-time release of superabundant energy from an organism described by another associate as "boiling over with ideas, crammed full of feeling, discussing every subject and pronouncing on all." His main concern for the past two months, as Grant's western heir, had been how to get at or around Johnston's army, posted thirty miles southeast of Chattanooga for the past five months, in occupation of Dalton and the wide, hilly valley of the Oostanaula, which extended southward forty-odd miles to the Etowah and southwestward about the same distance to Rome, where the two rivers combined to form the Coosa. The immediate tactical problem was Rocky Face Ridge, a steep, knife-edge bastion twenty miles long, rimming the upper valley on the west to cover Dalton and the railroad, which after piercing the ridge at Mill Creek Gap, one third of the way down, ran south and east for another hundred miles, through Resaca and Kingston, Allatoona and Marietta, on across the Chattahoochee to Atlanta, Johnston's base and Sherman's goal in the campaign about to open, here in North Georgia, in conjunction with Meade's plunge across the Rapidan, six hundred crow-flight miles to the northeast. Unlike Meade — thanks to Banks, holed up by now in Alexandria after his defeat at Sabine Crossroads — Sherman would not have the supposed advantage of diversionary attacks on the enemy flank or rear by troops from other departments, such as Sigel and Butler had been told to make. Whatever was going to be accomplished in the way of driving or maneuvering Johnston from his position along that ridge would have to be done by the men on hand. And though it was true that at present the Federals enjoyed a better than two-to-one numerical advantage (Johnston had just under 45,000 of all arms, with 138 guns, while Sherman had just over 110,000, with 254) the prospect was anything but pleasing. For one thing — thanks again to Banks, who was in no position to discourage, let alone interfere with, anything the Confederates might take it in mind to do on this side of the Mississippi River — Johnston had another 19,000 effectives and 50 guns, down in Alabama under Polk, presumably ready to join him at the first sign of danger, whereas Sherman could only look forward to receiving about 10,000 due back next month from reenlistment furloughs. That still would leave him roughly a two-to-one advantage, but this by no means

Red Clay Minuet

assured victory in assailing a position such as the one the rebels occupied, just ahead on Rocky Face Ridge.

Johnston, while successfully resisting Richmond's efforts to nudge him forward across the Tennessee, had spent the past four months preparing to resist the pending Union effort to prod him backward across the Chattahoochee. His two infantry corps, commanded by Lieutenant Generals William J. Hardee and John Bell Hood, each with about 20,000 men, were disposed along the northern half of the ridge, charged with giving particular attention to defending Mill Creek Gap, four miles northwest of Dalton, and Dug Gap, a second notch in the knife edge, five miles south. From the north end of this fortified position, Major General Joseph Wheeler's 5000 cavalry extended the line eastward to give warning in case the Federals tried to descend on Dalton by rounding the upper end of the ridge for a southward strike down the Oostanaula valley, where the ground was far less rugged and less easy to defend.

Sherman had no intention of moving in that direction, however, since to do so would uncover his base at Chattanooga: which brought him, regrettably, back to the dilemma of having to challenge the rebs in their apparently unassailable position, dead ahead on Rocky Face Ridge, securely intrenched and with high-sited guns ready-laid to blast the life out of whatever moved against them, in whatever strength. Moreover, as if nature had not done enough for him already, Johnston's engineers had lengthened the odds against the attackers by clogging the culverts of the railway ramp on the near side of the ridge, thus converting Mill Creek into an artificial lake across the rear of the gap that bore its name. Natives had a grislier designation; Buzzard Roost, they called the desolate notch through which the railroad wound its way. But Sherman, when at last he got a look at the rocky, high-walled gorge, catching glints of sunlight on the guns emplaced for its defense, pronounced it nothing less than "the terrible door of death," a term which would apply about as well to Dug Gap, just below.

George Thomas, who had felt out the gray defenses back in February, as a diversion intended to discourage Johnston from sending reinforcements to Polk while Sherman marched on Meridian, came up with the suggestion that, while McPherson and Schofield took over the position he now held in front of Ringgold, confronting the Rocky Face intrenchments, he take his four-corps Army of the Cumberland down the west side of the ridge to its far end, then press on eastward through unguarded Snake Creek Gap for a descent on the railroad near Resaca, fifteen miles in Johnston's rear. At best, this would expose the Confederates to a mauling when they fell back to protect their life line, as they would be obliged to do; while at worst, even if they somehow managed to avoid encirclement, it would turn them out of their all-but-impregnable position between Chattanooga and Dalton and thus convert the present stalemate, which favored the defenders, into a war of maneuver, which would favor the side with the greater number of troops and guns. Sherman, though the result his lieutenant promised was all he hoped for, rejected the proposal for two reasons. Thomas's command, twice the size of McPherson's and Schofield's combined, comprised a solid two thirds of the Federal total; secrecy would surely be lost in withdrawing so large a force and moving it such a distance, first across the enemy's front, then round his flank — and without secrecy, Sherman was convinced, it would be dangerous in the extreme to divide his army in the presence of so wily an adversary as the distinguished Virginian he faced. That was the first reason. The second was Thomas himself, the plodding, imperturbable Rock of Chickamauga. His specialty was staunchness, not celerity, the quality most needed in the movement he proposed.

But then, having dismissed the project as impractical when examined from that angle, Sherman shifted his point of view and experienced a surge of joy not unlike that of a poet revising the rejected draft of a poem he now perceives will become the jewel of his collection. Celerity, presumed to be lacking in Thomas, was McPherson's hallmark, and the size of his command — just under 25,000, as compared to Thomas's more than 70,000 — seemed about right for the job. Moreover, there would be no need for a withdrawal from the immediate presence of a vigilant opponent; McPherson's two corps, not yet on line, could march south from Chattanooga, under cover of Taylor's Ridge, then swing east through Ship's Gap and Villanow to make a sudden descent on Resaca, by way of Snake Creek Gap, for the cutting of Johnston's life line before the Virginian even knew he was threatened from that direction, his attention having been focused all the while on Thomas, active in his front, and on Schofield, who would feint with his 13,000-man Army of the Ohio against the opposite flank, which lay in the path of his march down the railroad from Knoxville. Thus Sherman set the pattern for the campaign about to open in North Georgia, a pattern that would utilize Thomas's outsized command — which contained more infantry and cavalry than all of Johnston's army, including the troops in Alabama under Polk — as the holding force, fixing the enemy in place, while McPherson and Schofield probed or rounded his flank or flanks to prise or chevy him out of position and expose him to being assailed on the march, or in any case to being struck before he had time to do much digging, anywhere between Dalton and Atlanta.

Sherman was delighted at the prospect, now that it loomed, and he also took a chauvinistic pleasure in the fact that such an arrangement gave the stellar role to McPherson, his favorite as well as Grant's, and the Army of the Tennessee, which had been his own and, up till Vicksburg, Grant's. Grant would approve, he knew when he wrote him of the plan, and as soon as that approval came down he passed the word to his three lieutenants. They would be in position no later than May 3, troops alerted for the jump-off next day, coincidental with Meade's crossing of the Rapidan.

And so it was. Detraining on schedule at Cleveland, where the East Tennessee & Georgia, coming down from Knoxville, branched to connect with Chattanooga and Dalton, both just under thirty miles away, Schofield prepared to march his army — in reality a corps, with three divisions of infantry and one of cavalry — southward along the left fork of the railroad to Red Clay, the state-line hamlet from which he was to launch his disconcerting strike at Johnston's right, down the valley east of Rocky Face. Thomas was poised beyond Ringgold, prepared to confront the defenders on the ridge and hold them in position there by pressing hard against Buzzard Roost and Dug Gap, threatening a breakthrough at both places. McPherson meantime had moved down to Lee & Gordon's Mill, at the south end of Chickamauga battlefield, which gave him a twelve-mile leg on the roundabout march to Resaca and the Oostanaula crossing. On May 4, in accordance with orders, all three began their separate movements designed to "knock Jos. Johnston." Sherman rode with Thomas in the center, but his hopes were with McPherson; "my whiplash," he called the Army of the Tennessee.

Despite the setbacks the rebels had suffered East and West in the past year, hard fighting lay ahead and Sherman knew it. "No amount of poverty or adversity seems to shake their faith," he marveled; "niggers gone, wealth and luxury gone, money worthless, starvation in view... yet I see no sign of let up — some few deserters, plenty tired of war, but the masses determined to fight it out." What they needed was more violent persuasion, he believed, and he was prepared to give it in full measure. "All that has gone before is mere skirmishing," he wrote his wife on setting forth.

Mere skirmishing was all it came to in the course of the next two days — the horrendous span of the Wilderness conflict, up in Virginia, where Lee and Meade lost better than 25,000 men between them — while Thomas felt his way forward along the Western & Atlantic and Schofield trudged down the other railroad to Red Clay, which took its name from the salmon-colored soil, powdery in dry weather and a torment to the nostrils of men on the march, but quick to turn as slippery as grease, newcomers would soon discover, under the influence of even the briefest shower.

There was no hurry at this stage of the game, both commanders having been told to give McPherson plenty of time on his roundabout march. On the third day out, the Cumberlanders ran into their first substantial opposition at Tunnel Hill, where the railroad went underground before emerging for its plunge through the gap in the ridge, two miles beyond. The rebs had set up a fortified outpost here, and

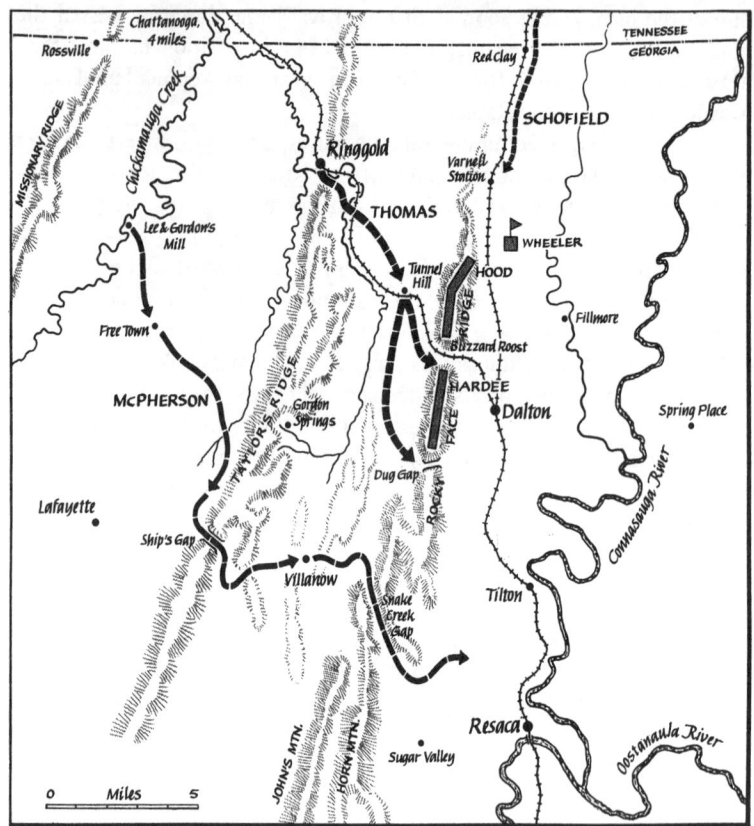

Thomas had to attack with a whole corps next day, May 7, in order to drive them back on their main line, dug in along the steep west slope of Rocky Face Ridge, above Buzzard Roost and below it down to Dug Gap, five miles south. While this success — so complete, indeed, that the Confederate rear guard had no time to damage the tunnel before retreating — was being followed up, preparatory to coming to grips in earnest with the defenders on their ridge, Schofield crossed the Georgia line and pressed on for Varnell Station, his initial objective, a little less than midway between Red Clay and Dalton. Harassed by small bodies of gray horsemen, he moved slowly, that day and the next, and then on May 9 detached a brigade of cavalry to brush these gadflies from his path. It was a mistake. Wheeler's troopers, fading back, drew the blue riders out of contact with the main body, then turned and, with a sudden, unexpected slash, killed or captured some 150 of them, including the colonel in command, and drove the remainder headlong from the field.

Sherman was no more upset by this than he was by Thomas's lack of progress on the near side of the intervening ridge. Three full-scale assaults the day before, and another five today — mainly against Mill Creek Gap, but also against Dug Gap, down the line — had met with failure in varying degrees. Two of the uphill attacks, in fact, had managed to put blue troops on the actual crest, within clear sight of Dalton, but they stayed there no longer than it took the defenders to counterattack and drive them back downhill. If anything, this was better than he had expected them to do: especially after his first hard look at what he described as "the terrible door of death that Johnston had prepared for them in the Buzzard Roost." Thomas and Schofield were charged with attracting and holding the attention of the rebels in their respective fronts, and this they had surely done. Sherman's main concern and hopes were still with McPherson, far off beyond the mountains to the south. What one observer called his "electric alertness," while following the progress of the fighting down the railroad below Ringgold, was probably due more to anxiety about his protégé, from whom he had heard nothing in the past three days, than it was to any expectation of victory in Thomas's contest on Rocky Face or Schofield's around Varnell Station, half a dozen miles across the way. Believing strongly in McPherson's military judgment and acumen, he had given him full discretion in conducting the movement designed to outfox Johnston; but he knew only too well that in war few things were certain, least of all the safety of a column deep in the enemy rear, no matter how capably led.

Then all, or nearly all, his worries vanished, giving way to jubilation and high feather. Taking an early supper near Tunnel Hill late that afternoon, May 9, he was delighted to receive a courier bearing McPherson's first dispatch, written that morning when he emerged from Snake Creek Gap after rounding the far end of Rocky Face Ridge. He was within five miles of Resaca, he reported, and pressing on, with nothing to contest his progress but a scattered handful of butternut horsemen, flushed out of the brush on the west side of the gap. Sherman boiled over with elation at the news, for it meant that by now McPherson's guns most likely had destroyed the bridges across the Oostanaula, thereby cutting the Confederates at Dalton off from all supplies and reinforcements south of that critical point; in which case they would have no choice except to turn and flee, and when they did he would come down hard and heavy on their rear, while McPherson stood firm in their front, astride the railroad.

Exultant, he banged the table so emphatically with his fist that the supper dishes did a rattling dance. "I've got Joe Johnston dead!" he cried.

He very nearly did; very nearly; except that Johnston, taking alarm at the first sign of his advance, had moved to forestall him without even suspecting what he was up to, out there beyond the screening ridges to the west and south. The bluecoats had no sooner stirred from their camps, May 4, than the southern commander renewed his plea to Richmond for reinforcements from Polk, even if they amounted to no more than a single division. "I urge you to send [these troops] at once to Rome, and put them at my disposal till the enemy can be met," he wired Bragg. Bragg replied, promptly for once, with orders for Polk to do as Johnston asked. Moreover, Jefferson Davis (in still another instance of that "presidential interference" with which his critics often charged him) enlarged the order by telegraphing instructions for his friend the bishop-general to go along in person and take with him not only the one requested division, but also "any other available force at your command." Polk had three divisions of infantry and one of cavalry, a total of 19,000 men. His decision was to hold none of them back except a garrison of about 2000 for Selma. After getting the first division on the road to Rome, where boxcars were being collected to speed this advance contingent down the branch line, east to Kingston, then northward up the Western & Atlantic to join Johnston around Dalton, he prepared to follow with the rest next day for a share in the task of keeping the Yankees out of Atlanta and the heartland.

That was how it came about that Sherman's "whiplash" lost its sting. For while Polk was en route from Demopolis — first by rail, through Selma and Talladega, to Blue Mountain, the end of the line, and then on foot the rest of the way, seventy rugged miles cross-country to Rome — a brigade of about 2000 men under Brigadier General James Cantey was summoned from Mobile to join him there and thus complete what would constitute a third corps for the Army of Tennessee, roughly equal in strength to each of the other two. Traveling all the way by rail, through Montgomery and Atlanta, Cantey reached Rome on May 5, but was shifted two days later to Resaca, clearing the way for Polk's arrival, placing him closer to Dalton in case he was needed sooner, and incidentally doubling the strength of the small garrison in the intrenchments Johnston had had constructed there to cover the critical Oostanaula crossing. Two mornings later, on May 9, after pausing only long enough to send the message that would cause Sherman to set the supper dishes dancing, McPherson pressed on across Sugar Valley, still driving the handful of butternut cavalry before him, and at midday, within a mile of Resaca, came under heavy infantry fire from a line of intrenchments, anchored on the south to the Oostanaula and curving west and north of the town.

There were only about 4000 Confederates in the works; but McPherson did not know that, and in any case this was about 4000 more than he expected. He felt out the defenses, found them stout, and decided that under the circumstances, unsupported as he was, deep in the rear of an enemy twice his size, his wisest course was to exercise the discretion his orders afforded him and return to Snake Creek Gap, where his 25,000 would be safe from attack by whatever forces Johnston had sent or was sending to meet this no-longer-secret threat to the rebel life line. He was back in the gap by nightfall, and there, with both flanks covered, his front intrenched, and his rear out of reach of the enemy east of the ridge, he lay coiled in compact security — like a snake, ready to strike, or a whip laid away in a cubbyhole, unused.

When Johnston learned that evening of the sudden appearance of bluecoats in his rear he reacted by ordering Hood to move at once with three divisions, one from his own and two from Hardee's corps, to help Cantey meet any renewal of the threat. Hood did so, but when he reconnoitered west of Resaca next afternoon and reported McPherson still immured in Snake Creek Gap, Johnston interpreted the movement as a feint designed to draw his attention away from the main Union effort to turn or overrun the northern half of Rocky Face Ridge. Accordingly, he told Hood to come back to his former position but to drop Hardee's two divisions off at Tilton, a station on the railroad between Dalton and Resaca, from which they could move swiftly to meet a crisis in either direction. Meantime Hardee, stripped of half his corps, had been puzzled by the relative inactivity of Thomas, who, after three days of obstinate hammering, had finally slackened his effort to break through the two gaps. "I am only uneasy about my right," the Georgia-born West Pointer said, "and won't be uneasy about that when Hood returns." All the same, finding himself "unable to decide what the Yankees are endeavoring to accomplish," he began to suspect that they were up to something not in Johnston's calculations.

And so, by now, did Johnston himself. Polk had reached Rome today with his lead division and was sending it on to Resaca ahead of the others, which were close behind. This gave Johnston considerably more security at both places, but still he wondered at the easing of the pressure against one end of the ridge while McPherson took up a position off the other end. He began to suspect that Sherman might be moving more than McPherson, perhaps in the same direction and even farther, for a crossing of the river deep in his rear. Next morning, May 11, he gave Wheeler orders to send some horsemen around the north end of Rocky Face, if possible, for a probe at the flank of the Federals in position there. "Try to ascertain where their left rests," he told him, "and whether they are in motion toward the Oostanaula."

Altogether aware of Sherman's advantage, that with close to twice the number of troops he could apply immobilizing pressure in front while rounding or striking one or both Confederate flanks, Johnston had to count on luck as well as skill in maneuvering his opponent into committing some tactical gaffe that would expose the superior blue army, or anyhow some vital portion of it, to destruction. Such an opportunity, if it came, could scarcely occur except while that army was in motion, and for this reason — plus the fact that it had always been his style, his inclination, even back in the Old Dominion, around Manassas or down on the York-James peninsula — the Virginian was prepared from the outset to relinquish almost any position, no matter how strong, if by so doing he could encourage his adversary, on taking up the pursuit, to commit the blunder that might lead to his undoing. The odds against this were long, he knew, but so were the odds he faced. Moreover, he would be falling back toward reinforcements, even if they amounted to no more than Governor Brown's kid-glove militia, and would be shortening his supply line while the enemy's grew longer and more vulnerable. He also took encouragement from the belief that Sherman — who, after all, had been relieved of duty, back in the first year of the war, under suspicion of insanity — was high-strung, erratic in the extreme, and reported to be enamored of long-chance experiments, both tactical and strategic. These were qualities much to be desired in an opponent at this juncture. The trouble was that Johnston himself, with far less margin for error, had to rely on subordinates quite as erratic and a good deal more temperamental. "If I were President," he confided to a friend soon after taking over the faction-riddled Army of Tennessee, which had just been driven from Missionary Ridge after eighteen months under Braxton Bragg, "I'd distribute the generals of this army over the Confederacy."

In point of fact, that was precisely what R. E. Lee had been doing with some of those subordinates who failed or displeased or failed to please him in the course of the past two years; but Johnston, less in harmony with the authorities in Richmond, mainly had to make do with what he had. Fortunately, this wholesale condemnation did not include the leaders immediately below him on the military ladder. Highly dependable if not brilliant in the discharge of their duties, Polk and Hardee had been corps commanders ever since Shiloh, and Hood, though young and new to both his post and the army — he was thirty-two and had been made a lieutenant general at the time of his transfer from Longstreet, just three months ago, whereas Polk and Hardee, fifty-eight and thirty-eight respectively, had held that rank ever since it was created in the fall of '62 — was a fighter any chief would be glad to have at his disposal when victory swung in the balance and an extra measure of savagery was called for.

While he thus was counting his blessings and woes — and incidentally, such was the diminution of blue pressure against the gaps, admonishing some impetuous artillerists on Rocky Face Ridge for firing at targets not worth their ammunition — he sent word for Polk to proceed at once from Rome to Resaca, where he would assume command "and make the proper dispositions to defend the passage of the river and our communications." Johnston also took the occasion to suggest "the immediate movement of Forrest [who had been left behind for the defense of North Mississippi] into Middle Tennessee." Quite as desirous of cutting Sherman's life line as Sherman was of cutting his, he added that he was "fully persuaded" that Forrest, rested by now from his raid on Paducah and the reduction of Fort Pillow, "would meet no force there that could resist him." What might come of this he did not know; such a decision, involving the abandonment of a portion of the President's home state to Yankee depredations, was up to Richmond. But as evidence accumulated in Dalton that some kind of movement was in progress on the other side of Rocky Face, Johnston took the precaution of shifting another of Hardee's divisions south of Dug Gap, to a position with a road in its rear leading down into Sugar Valley. Late in the day Wheeler returned from his probe of the Union left with confirmation of the wisdom of such precautions. Beyond the ridge, the Federals were "moving everything" to their right, though whether they were massing near Dug Gap for a renewal of their try for a breakthrough there, or were heading for Snake Creek Gap to join McPherson for an attack on Resaca, or had it in mind to slog on past both gateways for a crossing of the Oostanaula farther down, no one could say. In any case Johnston saw that if it turned out to be either of the last two choices he could not long remain where he now was; he would certainly have to fall back no later than tomorrow. The question was whether he would end his withdrawal on this or the far side of the river fifteen miles in his rear.

That evening he was encouraged by a visit and some welcome news from Polk, who had encountered Hood at Resaca and returned with him to Dalton for a conference with their chief. The good news was that his second division had reached Rome today, was already on its way by rail to join the first in the Resaca intrenchments, and would soon be followed by the other two, expected at Rome tomorrow. Johnston shook his old friend warmly by the hand; they had been cadets together at West Point thirty-five years ago. "How can I thank you?" he said with feeling. "I asked for a division, but you have come yourself and brought me your army."

Polk flushed with pleasure at the praise, and after the council of war had ended, around midnight, took part in another exchange which gave him even greater pleasure than the first. On the train ride up to Dalton, Hood had confided that he wished to be baptized and received into the Church, and now that army business was out of the way the churchman was glad to oblige. Episcopal Bishop of Louisiana for twenty years before the war, he often remarked that he looked forward to returning to his priestly calling as soon as the fighting was over and independence had been won. Meantime he seldom neglected a chance, such as this, to work for the salvation of any soul. The two repaired to the young general's quarters, accompanied by members of their staffs, and there by candlelight Polk performed the baptismal rites, using a tin washpan for a font. Then came the confirmation. Because of the mutilations Hood had suffered at Chickamauga and Gettysburg, where he had lost a leg and the use of one arm, the bishop absolved the candidate from kneeling, as was customary, suggesting instead that he remain seated for the ceremony. But Hood would have none of this. If he could not kneel, and he could not, he would stand. And thus it was that, leaning on his crutches, the big tawny-bearded Kentuckian was received into the fold. "Defend, O Lord, this thy child with thy heavenly grace," the bishop intoned, his hand upon the bowed head before him, "that he may continue thine forever, and daily increase in thy Holy Spirit more and more, until he come unto thy everlasting kingdom."

Despite the lateness of the hour, Polk returned that night to Resaca, charged with holding the place on his own until such time as the rest of the now three-corps army joined him. He was unlikely to be alone for long, however; Johnston's mind was about made up. Next morning, as evidence of a full-scale Union sidle continued to mount, he decided to evacuate Dalton — or, more accurately, to complete the evacuation, since nearly half of his army, exclusive of Polk, was already south of the town in any case — as soon as the night was dark enough to mask his withdrawal from the covering ridge.

He would do so, what was more, with small regret. "The position had little to recommend it," he afterwards explained. "At Dalton the Federal army, even if beaten, would have had a secure place of refuge at Chattanooga, while our only place of safety was Atlanta, a hundred miles off with three rivers intervening.... I therefore decided to remain on the defensive." His mind, it would seem from this subsequent outline of his strategic intentions, was already on the third of those three rivers. "Fighting under cover," he went on, "we would have trifling losses compared with those inflicted. Moreover, due to its lengthening lines the numerical superiority of the Federal army would be reduced daily so that we might hope to cope with it on equal terms beyond the Chattahoochee, where defeat would be its destruction."

This did not mean that he did not hope to inflict a defeat on the enemy in the course of his hundred-mile withdrawal. He did hope for it, despite the odds, either as the result of breaking the railroad deep in Sherman's rear, which would oblige the blue host to retire, or else as the result of catching his adversary in a tactical blunder that would expose him to piecemeal destruction somewhere down the line: maybe even within the next couple of days near Resaca, Johnston's intended first stop, on the near bank of the Oostanaula, first of the three rivers in his rear.

That was his destination now, and by sunrise next morning — Friday the 13th — not a Confederate was left on the northern half of Rocky Face Ridge or in Dalton itself. Johnston was off on what an opposing general called "one of his clean retreats."

Sherman by now was on the verge of completing the movement that prompted Johnston's pull-out. Vexed by the news that his protégé had flinched from pressing the attack that was to have crowned his roundabout march to the outskirts of Resaca — news that hit all the harder by arriving close on the heels of the first report that the objective was practically within McPherson's grasp — the northern commander felt terribly let down. "Such an opportunity does not occur twice in a single life," he lamented, although he was quick to admit that his fellow Ohioan had been "perfectly justified" by his discretionary orders. "I regret beyond measure that you did not break the railroad, however little," he replied next morning, "but I suppose it was impossible."

He rather suspected that he should have used a larger force on the flanking operation, as Thomas originally suggested, and he planned to follow through by doing so now, all out. Leaving one corps of infantry and a cavalry division to continue the demonstration in front of "the terrible door of death," thereby covering Chattanooga and holding the Confederate main body in position around Dalton, he would march the rest of Thomas's army and all of Schofield's down the valley west of Rocky Face Ridge, on around its lower end, to join McPherson for a massive lunge at Resaca, the railroad that ran through it, and the vital river crossing in its rear. Johnston then would be cut off from his base, with no choice except to scatter or give battle: which in either case, as Sherman saw it, would result in his defeat. There was of course an outside chance that Johnston, who would have the advantage of moving a shorter distance over superior roads, might fall rapidly back on Resaca, while the rest of the blue army was en route, and turn on the force holed up in Snake Creek Gap; but that had been considered and taken care of, more or less, beforehand. "Should he attack you," Sherman told McPherson at the close of the dispatch informing him of his measureless regret and his new plan, "fight him to the last and I will get to you."

This was a good deal easier said, and planned, than done. Close to 70,000 troops had to be disengaged from contact with an enemy mainly on high ground, which made secrecy all the more difficult to maintain, and put in motion on narrow, meandering roads. A day was needed to get ready, then better than two more for the march. It was late afternoon of the fourth day, Friday the 13th, before the three commands were consolidated and put into attack formations, west of Resaca, for the contemplated lunge. By then the sun was too far down for anything more than a bit of preliminary skirmishing, including a crossroads cavalry clash in which Judson Kilpatrick and Joe Wheeler — West Pointers both, the former four months into and the latter four months short of his twenty-eighth year — took each other's measure. Kilpatrick was unhorsed by a stray bullet on this unlucky day, and though friendly troopers managed to lug him off the field before the graybacks could get at him, he would be out of action for some weeks.

Regrettable as this was, the loss of time on the cramped approach march down the valley was even more so. McPherson, Thomas, and Schofield were on hand and in line of battle by sundown, within gun range of the rebel works, but Johnston was there ahead of them with all three of his corps, Hood and Hardee having completed their retrograde movement from Dalton before noon. Increased in strength by nearly one third with the addition of Polk's corps to their army, they occupied skillfully laid-out intrenchments that ran in a long convex line from the Oostanaula, downstream from Resaca on their left, to the near bank of a tributary river, the Connasauga, on their right beyond the railroad north of town.

Sherman was neither daunted nor discouraged by his loss of the race for Resaca; Johnston was there, inviting attack with his back to the river, and the redhead planned to oblige him. "I will press him all that is possible," he wired Halleck. "Weather fine and troops in fine order. All is working well." Informed that Grant had emerged from the Wilderness and now was mauling Lee at Spotsylvania, he added, still in the pep-talk vein: "Let us keep the ball rolling."

It rolled, but only a short distance in the course of the daylong fight; Johnston's engineers had given him all he asked in the way of protection for his men. McPherson, on the right — goaded no doubt by Sherman's reproach when they met in Snake Creek Gap the day before: "Well, Mac, you missed the opportunity of your life" — scored what little gain there was by driving Polk's forward elements from some high ground west of the town. Elsewhere along the four-mile curve of the rebel works, the ball either stopped or rebounded. Thomas made no headway in the center, and Schofield took a beating on the left, beyond the railroad, when the Confederates in his front launched a sudden attack that drove him back nearly half a mile as the day ended. This came about as the result of Johnston's calculation that McPherson's success against his left, down near the Oostanaula, must mean that Sherman was concentrating most of his strength in that direction. Accordingly, while Bishop Polk, informally clad in an old hunting shirt and a slouch hat, stiffened his resistance to limit the enemy gains in his front, and Hardee continued to stand fast in the center, wearing by contrast a new dove-gray uniform with fire-gilt buttons and a white cravat, Johnston sent word for Hood to test the Union left for the weakness he suspected. This Hood did, with good results which might have been much better if darkness had not put an end to his pursuit.

Johnston, highly pleased, ordered a renewal of the attack at first light next morning.

He had been in excellent spirits all that day, riding from point to point along the line, at his jaunty best "in a light or mole colored hat, with a black feather in it." A Tennessee private, seeing him thus, recalled the scene years later. A small man, neatly turned out and genial in manner, fluffy white side-whiskers framing the wedge-shaped face with its trim mustache and grizzled chin beard — "like the pictures you see hung upon the walls," the veteran was to write — Johnston sat his horse, head cocked to catch the swell of gunfire, left and right and center, where Polk and Hood and Hardee were defending the works his foresight had provided. Scattered whoops of recognition prompted the rest of the troops in the passing column of Tennesseans, "and the very ground seems to shake with cheers. Old Joe smiles as blandly as a modest maid, raises his hat in acknowledgement, makes a polite bow, and rides toward the firing."

This brightened outlook persisted into the night, but darkened progressively in reaction to the arrival, in all too rapid sequence, of three unwelcome intelligence reports. While visiting Hood on the right he learned that the Union corps left at Dalton had completed its march down the railroad this evening to reinforce Schofield, and riding westward to confer with Polk he found McPherson had brought artillery onto the high ground lost today, with the result that long-range shells were able to reach both the railway and turnpike bridges close in his rear. Endangering as it did his line of retreat, this gave him pause indeed. He instructed his staff engineer to throw a pontoon bridge a mile above the permanent spans, beyond reach of the Yankee guns, and start at once to build a road leading down to it on the near bank and away from it on the other. Sensitive as always to such threats to his flanks or rear, he countermanded Hood's instructions for tomorrow and told him to return instead to the position from which he had launched his attack this afternoon. Presently, with the arrival of the third unwelcome bit of news, he had cause for greater alarm and even greater caution. Cavalry scouts reported that enemy units of considerable strength had crossed the Oostanaula several miles downstream, where a deep eastward bend of the river brought them within easy reach of the Western & Atlantic. Johnston reacted swiftly to this threat to the railroad and his line of retreat by ordering the immediate detachment of Major General W. H. T. Walker's division from Hardee for a night march to the reported point of crossing, there to contest any further advance by the Federals while the rest of the army prepared for a quick withdrawal across the river, either to reinforce Walker or outstrip the blue column which by then might have overwhelmed him.

Morning brought a renewal of Federal pressure all along the line, quite as if there had been no reduction for a sidle. Johnston held his ground, awaiting developments, and shortly after noon received a dispatch from Walker informing him that the report of a downstream crossing was untrue. By then the pressure against Resaca had somewhat diminished, and Johnston decided to go back to his plan for a renewal of the attack by Hood, who promptly returned to the position he had won the day before. A battery, pushed well to the front to support the jump-off, opened prematurely and was replied to so effectively, by infantry and counterbattery fire, that the cannoneers had to abandon all four guns, left mute and unattended between the lines. This did not augur well for the success of Hood's assault, but as he was about to go forward in all-out earnest, a message came from the army commander, once more canceling the attack and instructing the three lieutenant generals to attend a council of war that evening at his headquarters.

There they learned the reason for this second change of plans. A follow-up dispatch from Walker reported the bluecoats over the downstream Oostanaula after all, and Johnston had decided to give up Resaca. The council had not been called for a discussion of his decision, but rather for the assignment of routes on the march to meet this threat to the army's life line; Polk and Hardee would use the turnpike and railway spans, despite the danger of long-range interdictory fire, and Hood the new-laid pontoon bridge.

All went as planned, or nearly so, including heavy volleys of musketry by front-line units at midnight to cover the withdrawal of iron-tired artillery and supply vehicles. Rear guards took up the pontoons and loaded them onto wagons for use in crossing other rivers, farther south, and the railroad bridge was set afire to burn till it fell hissing into the Oostanaula. Through some administrative oversight — not unlike the one at Tunnel Hill a week ago, which left the railway tunnel unobstructed — in the last-minute confusion, as dawn was breaking, the turnpike bridge was overlooked and left standing, fit for use by the pursuers. All that was really lost in the way of army property, however, was the four-gun Confederate battery abandoned between Hood's and Schofield's lines that afternoon. This came hard for the young Kentucky-born West Pointer, who had a great deal of pride in such matters (in time he would take it even harder, since they turned out to be the only guns Johnston lost in the whole course of the campaign) but who consoled himself, as best he could, by pointing out "that they were four old iron pieces, not worth the sacrifice of the life of even one man."

Sherman pressed on after the retiring Confederates, hoping to catch up with them before they had time to develop still another stout position in which to receive him, and continued simultaneously two flanking operations he had set in motion two days ago, both involving only cavalry at the outset. Kilpatrick's division, minus its wounded leader, had been sent five miles downriver on May 14 to install a pair of pontoon bridges at Lay's Ferry, and Sherman had followed this up yesterday by detaching Brigadier General Thomas Sweeny's infantry division from McPherson to march down and cross the river at that point, along with Kilpatrick's troopers, in order to menace Johnston's rear; which Sweeny had done with such success that the graybacks were now in full retreat. At the same time, a wider, deeper, and potentially even more profitable thrust was launched by sending another of Thomas's mounted divisions, under Brigadier General Kenner Garrard, far down the right bank of the Oostanaula to threaten and if possible enter Rome, wrecking its factories and iron works and taking over the branch-line railroad leading east along the north bank of the Etowah to Kingston, on the Western & Atlantic, better than twenty miles below Resaca. Now that Johnston was falling back, Sherman decided to beef up this deeper probe by sending Brigadier General Jefferson C. Davis's division of Cumberlanders to follow the cavalry and take part in the raid on Rome and the eastward strike at Kingston.

The red-haired commander was leaving no card unplayed in his eagerness to come to grips with his skittish opponent, and he scoffed at the notion, advanced by several members of his staff, that Johnston was falling back quite willingly, in accordance with a plan to draw his pursuers southward to their destruction. "Had he remained in Dalton another hour, it would have been his total defeat," Sherman insisted, "and he only evacuated Resaca because his safety demanded it." As for the disappointment some critics expressed at his failure, so far, to bring the wily Virginian to all-or-nothing battle — particularly before Polk arrived from Alabama, in the interim between Dalton and Resaca, to shorten the long numerical odds — he countered that, while he shared the regret that he had not managed to do this, he also saw a clear advantage in the way the campaign had developed up to now. "Of course I was disappointed not to have crippled his army more at that particular stage of the game," he later wrote; "but, as it resulted, these rapid successes gave us the initiative, and the usual impulse of a conquering army."

Determined to make the most of that conquering impulse, he devised a pursuit combining speed with other tactical advantages. While Thomas struck out down the railroad, hard in the wake of the fleeing enemy, McPherson was instructed to proceed at once to Lay's Ferry for a crossing that would place him well to the right on the march south, in position to make another rapid flanking movement as soon as the rebels called a halt or were brought to one by pressure against their rear, and Schofield was told to do the same in the opposite direction, crossing upstream from Resaca at Field's Ferry for a march well to the east, in case it developed that the enemy right was the flank that should be turned. This not only increased the celerity of the pursuit by not funneling all the Federal troops down one crowded road; it also assured that when the time came for fighting, all three component armies would be ready for action in their accustomed roles, Thomas's as the holding force and McPherson's and Schofield's as flankers. Moreover, to bring all three into better numerical balance and lessen the traffic on the turnpike, Sherman detached Hooker's three divisions from Thomas and sent them off to the left with Scho-

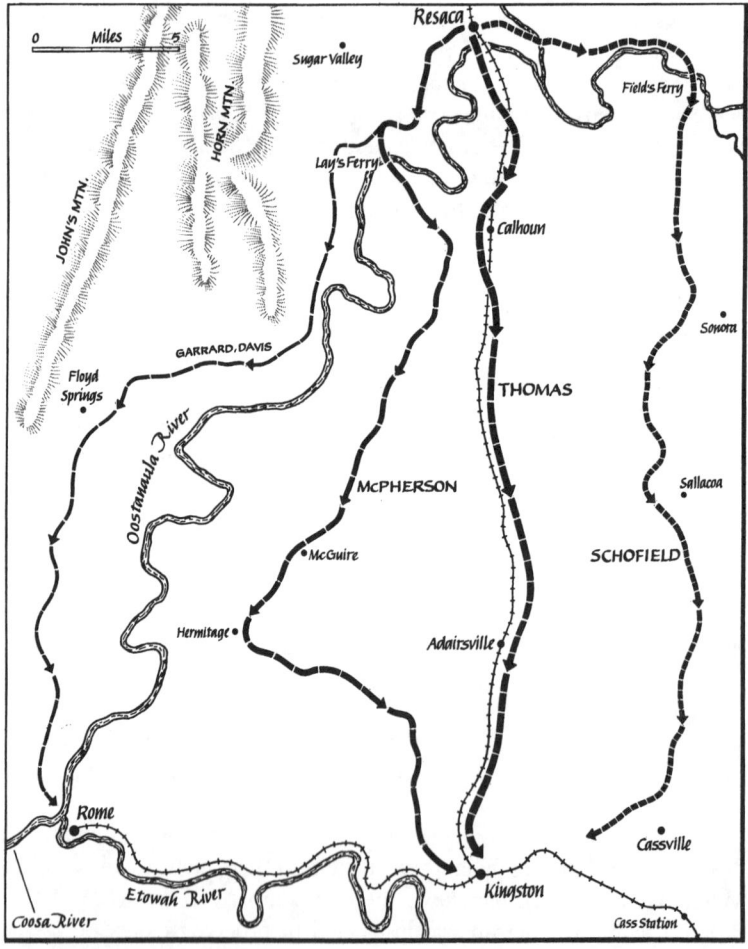

field, whose strength thus was raised to more than 30,000 while Thomas's was reduced to about 40,000, three other divisions, including two of cavalry, having already been detached for the raid on Rome, still in progress down the Oostanaula, and the preliminary crossing at Lay's Ferry, where Sweeny's division rejoined McPherson, together with

Kilpatrick's troopers, who fanned out frontward to provide a screen for the column west of the railroad.

The first day's march, May 16, ended at Calhoun, where Sherman thought it likely that Johnston would make a stand, six miles down the track from Resaca, but before he could call in either of the lateral columns, which were also over the river by then, the Confederate rear guard pulled out southward in the darkness, headed apparently for Adairsville, ten miles down the line. There was heavier skirmishing there next day near sundown, but dawn of May 18 showed the graybacks gone again. Schofield by now was in the vicinity of Sallacoa and McPherson at McGuire, hamlets respectively half a dozen miles east and west of Adairsville; Sherman, riding with Thomas in the center, held to this spread-eagle formation as he took up the march for Kingston, another ten miles down the Western & Atlantic. He felt certain that Johnston would dig in there, on the near bank of the Etowah, and he wanted to get at him before he had much chance to get set for the shock.

Spirits were high in all three columns of pursuit, not only because the rebs were on the run, having been turned out of two practically impregnable positions in less than two weeks, but also because well-drilled rail repair gangs — helped considerably, it was true, by the enemy's rattled negligence in failing to obstruct the tunnel short of Buzzard Roost — had functioned with such efficiency that even the troops out front, in the process of covering better than half the distance from Chattanooga to Atlanta, had scarcely missed a meal along the way. "The rapidity with which the badly broken railroad was repaired seemed miraculous," Major General O. O. Howard, one of Thomas's corps commanders, later noted. "We had hardly left Dalton before trains with ammunition and other supplies arrived. While our skirmishing was going on at Calhoun, the locomotive whistle sounded in Resaca. The telegraphers were nearly as rapid: the lines were in order to Adairsville on the morning of the 18th. While we were breaking up the state arsenal at Adairsville, caring for the wounded, and bringing in Confederate prisoners, word was telegraphed from Resaca that bacon, hard bread, and coffee were already there at our service."

All this had been accomplished, moreover, at a cost of fewer than 4000 casualties, and not only was this figure much lower than had been anticipated, it was also — despite the supposed high price entailed in attacking prepared defenses — not much larger than the enemy total, which included a number of lightly wounded men who had to be left behind and thus became permanent losses, as captives, whereas a Union soldier, left behind under similar circumstances, could be patched up and returned to duty, sometimes overnight. It was no wonder then, with success achieved at so low a cost and without the sacrifice of creature comforts, that spirits were high and the outcome of the expected Kingston confrontation seemed foregone. What was more, as the three main widespread columns prepared for a convergence at that point — forty air-line miles from Tunnel Hill, scene of the opening clash eleven days ago — word came that a prize even more valuable than the state arsenal at Adairsville had fallen into the hands of the invaders. That same morning, May 18, Rome fell undefended to Davis and Garrard, who soon would be working their way east along the branch-line railroad to rejoin the Army of the Cumberland.

Rome with its factories and iron works, so important to the rebel cause, was a strategic plum worth giving thanks for, but tactically the railroad was a prize worth even more, since practically all of Johnston's reinforcements had reached him by that route. Now it was closed, except to Federal use, and Sherman — still with Thomas, who was engaged in what Howard called "a running skirmish" down the Western & Atlantic with troops from Hardee's corps, which apparently had been given the rear-guard post of honor on the Confederate retreat — had 100,000 effectives converging as fast as their legs could carry them toward Kingston, where reports indicated that Johnston had at last been brought to bay with his back to the Etowah River.

For once, by dint of hard marching on rural roads and steady pressure on the rebel rear, execution matched conception; the convergence would be effected by midday tomorrow, May 19, on schedule and with each of the three component armies in its assigned position for the final thrust, Schofield left, McPherson right, and Thomas center. The trouble was that Sherman, for all the speed and precision of his approach, was converging on a vacuum. Johnston was not at Kingston; he was at Cassville, five miles east, preparing to spring an ambush that would eliminate, or at any rate badly mangle, a solid third of the blue force whose commander had at last afforded him the opportunity he had been awaiting ever since the campaign opened, two weeks and better than forty miles ago.

Leaving Resaca, two days back, he had intended to make a stand at Calhoun, provided he could find a suitable position — athwart a rather narrow valley, say, which would afford protection for his flanks and thus oblige the Federals to come at him head-on, their numerical advantage canceled by the limited width of front — but when reconnaissance revealed none he moved on that night, hoping to find what he was seeking near Adairsville the following day, May 17. He did not. He did, however, receive a telegraphic dispatch and some cavalry reports which together had the double effect of lifting his spirits and enabling him to arrive at a plan for stopping the blue army in its tracks. Stephen Lee, left in charge of the adjoining department when Polk departed for Georgia, responded to Johnston's week-old request by announcing that Forrest, with 3500 picked horsemen and two batteries of artillery, would set out within three days for an attack on Sherman's lines of supply and communication up in Middle Tennessee. This was welcome news, indeed, and Johnston called a council of war that evening to pass it on to his corps commanders, along with their respective assignments for carrying out his table-turning plan.

Intelligence reports from Wheeler made it clear that Sherman's pursuit was in three columns, widely spaced, and now that Johnston had decided to continue his march toward the Etowah, he saw in this a rare opportunity to deal with one of those isolated segments before it could call on either of the other two for help. From Adairsville, railroad and turnpike ran due south to Kingston; Hardee would continue on that route, skirmishing as he went, to draw Thomas after him and encourage the impression that he was guarding the rear of the other two corps as they moved ahead of him, down the tracks and pike, for a stand at Kingston. But that was by no means to be the case. Polk and Hood would march instead by a road leading east of south to Cassville, a village about two miles on this side of the Western & Atlantic, which swung due east at Kingston, five miles west. The advantage was that Schofield, reinforced to 30,000, would pass near there on his way to the convergence Sherman would surely order when he became convinced that the graybacks intended to call a halt at Kingston. With Thomas five miles off, McPherson perhaps ten, and Hardee in position to delay their eastward advance along the railroad, Hood and Polk should have ample time to dispose of Schofield before the other two could reach him. With any luck, all three gray corps could then combine to take on Thomas and strike at McPherson when he came up in turn. Dealt with piecemeal, all three Union armies might be destroyed in short order, or anyhow crippled and brought to a stumbling halt; which would serve about as well, since they soon would get the news that Forrest had severed their life line, up in Tennessee. That would leave them no choice except starvation or retreat. Either way, the campaign would be over and the world once more would stand amazed at still another Confederate triumph against overwhelming odds.

Eager though they were to take up their divergent marches, which were to end with a long-deferred return to the offensive, all three corps commanders went with their chief to his tent, where Polk donned his surplice and stood in front of an improvised altar, preparing to fulfill a request Mrs Johnston had made in a letter written two days ago. She wanted the bishop to do for her husband what he had done for Hood the week before; "lead my soldier nearer to God. General Johnston has never been baptised. It is the dearest wish of my heart that he should be, and that you should perform the ceremony." Once more with candlelight glinting on the brass and gold lace of the uniforms of candidate and witnesses, the rite of baptism was performed, after which the group dispersed to prepare for the execution of the plan designed to reverse the tide of war in North Georgia.

Hardee took up his march, southward down the railroad, and with the dawn resumed his "running skirmish" with Thomas, who continued to press hard upon his rear. Meantime the other two corps set out on the road for Cassville, Hood in front with orders to occupy a position tonight from which to strike at the left of Schofield's column next morning, while Polk attacked the front; Hardee would join them from Kingston, later in the day, so that all three could then turn on Thomas and McPherson, simultaneously or in sequence, when they came up in response to Schofield's cries for help. Unwelcome news from Stephen Lee reached Johnston in the course of the approach march, to the effect that a heavy enemy movement out of Memphis had obliged him to postpone Forrest's raid on Sherman's life line. Offsetting this somewhat, however, there was a report from Richmond that the Federals had acknowledged the so-far loss of 45,000 men in Virginia, thirty-one of them generals, and this gave rise to the airing of a theory by some members of Johnston's staff that Sherman's intention was to maneuver his adversary south of the Etowah, then call a halt and hurry reinforcements to the bled-down Army of the Potomac. Johnston put no stock in such talk; he remained intent on the prospect of giving Sherman so much trouble, on this side of the Etowah, that he soon would be seeking assistance, not sending it either to Meade or to Banks, whose fight at Yellow Bayou today was the last on his costly, disheartened retreat down Red River.

Nightfall found the divided Confederate army in position: Hardee at Kingston, prepared to turn east, and Hood and Polk at Cassville, their ambush laid. Johnston's spirits were as high as Sherman's across the way, and on far sounder grounds. Some measure of the Virginian's confidence and martial elation came through in a general order he composed that night and had read at the head of each regiment next morning, May 19:

> Soldiers of the Army of Tennessee:
> You have displayed the highest qualities of the soldier—firmness in combat, patience under toil. By your courage and skill you have repulsed every assault of the enemy. By marches by day and marches by night you have defeated every attempt upon your communications. Your communications are secured. You will now turn and march to meet his advancing columns. Fully confiding in the conduct of the officers, the courage of the soldiers, I lead you to battle. We may confidently trust that the Almighty Father will still reward the patriots' toils and the patriots' banners. Cheered by the success of our brothers in Virginia and beyond the Mississippi, our efforts

will equal theirs. Strengthened by His support, these efforts will be crowned with the like glories.

J. E. JOHNSTON,
General.

Despite the weariness resulting from three days and four nights of marches broken only by rearward skirmishes and fitful snatches of roadside sleep — not to mention the cumulative depression that went with having abandoned better than forty miles of highly defensible terrain without so much as a single fight that attained the dignity of a fullscale battle — the reaction on all levels to the reading of this order, from regimental commanders down to drummer boys, was quite as ecstatic as even its author could have wished.

Among those officers who were better informed on current events, mainly through having read such newspapers as were available in camp and on the march, there lately had been growing an anxiety that the good effect of the news from Louisiana and Virginia, which had raised the price of gold on the New York market to 210, would be impaired by the apparently irreversible retreat of the Confederates in North Georgia. Now though, with the word that they were going over to the offensive, their anxiety was relieved and their hope soared, anticipating a still greater drop in the pocketbook barometer that best measured northern greed and fears. As for the men in the ranks, though their faith in Old Joe had never wavered, their spirits took an even higher bounce as they stood and heard the order read to them this morning. "I never saw troops happier or more certain of success," one private would recall. "A sort of grand halo illuminated every soldier's face.... We were going to whip and rout the Yankees."

Johnston apparently shared this conviction that the Yankees would be whipped and routed: especially as it applied to Schofield, who was reported to be advancing heedlessly into the trap about to be sprung northwest of Cassville. At 10.20, hearing from Hardee that Thomas was moving in strength on Kingston and soon would be too heavily committed to effect a rapid disengagement, he sent his chief of staff, Brigadier General W. W. Mackall — who had served Bragg, his West Point classmate, in the same capacity — to tell Polk and Hood "to make quick work" of their combined lunge at Schofield, so that they would be ready to turn without delay on Thomas, when he came up in Hardee's wake, for the second phase of the Confederate offensive. With accustomed caution, Johnston added to Hood's instructions a warning that, in launching his flank attack, he was not to undertake "too wide a movement," lest he lose contact with Polk on his left, which not only might leave Schofield an escape hatch, but also would delay the consolidation of all three corps for the follow-up strike at Thomas and McPherson.

Such a warning was altogether superfluous, the staffer found when he encountered Hood near Cassville. Not only had the Kentuckian moved out before Mackall got there; by now he was moving back again, feverishly preparing to take up a defensive position in which to resist attack by a blue column reported to be advancing on a road in his right rear, skirmishers deployed and guns booming.

Mackall sent word of this surprise development to Johnston, who flatly declined to credit the report. "It can't be," he said. He did not believe the Federals were there because none of Polk's cavalry had encountered them this morning while reconnoitering in that direction. (In point of fact, they had not been there earlier this morning, and it was entirely accidental that they were there at all. A nomadic fragment from Major General Daniel Butterfield's division, Hooker's corps, they had missed a turning, lost their way, and wound up deep in Hood's right rear, some five miles east of their comrades trudging south on the far side of Cassville.) All the same, though Johnston did not believe in their existence — then, any more than he did ten years later, when he declared: "The report upon which General Hood acted was manifestly untrue" — he took no chances. Having rejected the evidence, he proceeded to act upon it. "If that's so," he said, examining the situation on a map, "General Hood will have to fall back at once."

Accordingly, when Mackall presently returned, he sent him riding again to Polk and Hood with orders canceling their attack. Once more, as had been its custom for the past two weeks, the army would take up a stout defensive position and there await developments: meaning Sherman.

Johnston quickly found what he was seeking along a wooded ridge immediately southeast of Cassville, overlooking the town and the "broad, open, elevated valley" in which it lay. Hood and Polk fell back to there, followed prudently by Schofield, who by now had notified Sherman of the snare he had so narrowly avoided, and Hardee came up that afternoon to take position on their left, closely pursued by Thomas and McPherson, the latter having closed the gap between him and the Cumberlanders in the course of the daylong skirmish, first north, then east of Kingston. Before sundown the guns of both armies were banging away at each other, arching their shots above the hill-cradled streets and rooftops of the village. Despite the dismay of the townspeople at this harrowing turn of events ("Consternation of citizens," a staff lieutenant jotted in his diary; "many flee, leaving all; some take away few effects, some remain between hostile fires") Johnston was greatly pleased with his new position, later referring to it as "the best I saw occupied during the war."

Polk and Hood did not agree with this assessment, and they said as much that evening when they came to headquarters for the council of war to which they had been summoned. Protesting that Union batteries enfiladed that portion of the ridge where their lines joined, they liked the position so little, in fact, that both wanted to leave it at the earliest possible moment. The army had no choice, they said, except to schedule a dawn attack, on the chance of beating Sherman to the punch, or else to fall back tonight across the Etowah. Johnston did not want to do either: certainly not attack the reunited Federals with no better promise of success than the tactical situation seemed to him to afford. Hardee, who arrived at this point in the discussion, sided altogether with his chief, hoping like him that Sherman would oblige them tomorrow by exposing his superior numbers to severe and sudden curtailment by advancing them head-on across that broad, open valley to challenge the defenders on the wooded ridge.

Johnston ended by deciding to retreat. He did so, he explained later, not because he agreed with Hood and Polk that the position had its drawbacks, but "in the belief that the confidence of the commanders of two of the three corps of the army, of their inability to resist the enemy, would inevitably be communicated to their troops, and produce that inability."

The fall-back to the Etowah that night, though Sherman made no attempt to interfere, was by far the most disruptive of the campaign. "All hurried off without regard to order," the young staff diarist recorded. "Reach Cartersville before day, troops come in after day. General Johnston comes up — all hurried over bridges; great confusion caused by mixing trains and by trains which crossed first parking at river's edge and others winding around wrong roads."

Much of the mixup was a manifestation of the army's chagrin at the two-step disappointment it had suffered, first in the cancellation of the attack, which came hard on the heels of the reading of Old Joe's "I lead you to battle" address — "I could not restrain my tears when I found we could not strike," Mackall confessed in a home letter — and then in the directive, which came down that night, for a resumption of the southward march. "Change of line not understood but thought all right," the diarist put it, "but night retreat after issuing general order impaired confidence; great alarm in country round. Troops think no stand to be made north of Chattahoochee, where supply train is sent." Civilians north and immediately south of the Etowah reacted to their abandonment much as the people of Cassville had done the day before, milling about like ants in an upset ant hill. Johnston put the blame, or anyhow most of it, on Hood, and so did members of his staff, including the diarist, who wrote: "One lieutenant general talks about attack and not giving ground, publicly, and quietly urges retreat."

By way of consolation for its woes, the disgruntled army could see for itself the strength of its new position near Allatoona, four miles down the Western & Atlantic from the river. Here, beginning the day of their arrival, May 20, Johnston had his soldiers throw up breastworks commanding the deep, narrow gorge through which the railroad snaked its way, his flanks protected, left and right, by Pumpkin Vine and Allatoona creeks. Fifteen miles to the south, his new supply base was Marietta, just beyond Kennesaw Mountain, about midway between the Etowah and the Chattahoochee, last of the three main rivers between Chattanooga and Atlanta.

Allatoona Pass, as the gorge through this spur of the Appalachians was called, was a still more "terrible door of death" than Buzzard Roost had been, some sixty miles to the north. Paradoxically, though, it was precisely in this abundance of natural strength that the strategic weakness of the position lay. Sherman would be even less apt to call for a main effort here than he had been at Rocky Face Ridge. His solution, now as then, would most likely be to try another sidle — and there was always the danger that, sooner or later, one or another of these complicated flank maneuvers would succeed in accomplishing its purpose of placing the superior blue army squarely between the Confederates and Atlanta; in which case Johnston would have no choice except to attack the Federals where they were, intrenched and waiting, or scatter into the surrounding hills. Either course would mean the loss not only of the campaign (meaning Atlanta) but also of the army, whether by destruction or disintegration, the difference being that one would be somewhat less sudden than the other. All Johnston could do, in the way of attempting to forestall such a calamity, was alert Wheeler to be on the lookout for the first sign of another sidle, up or down the Etowah. He felt sure that one was pending, but he could not move to thwart it until he knew its direction, right or left.

One other thing he could attempt, however, and that was to protect himself from his detractors, in some measure at least, by putting his performance in the best possible light for his Richmond superiors, with emphasis on his desire for coming to grips with his pursuer. Since this latest retreat had no doubt set his critics' teeth on edge, he no sooner crossed the Etowah than he got off a wire to the President explaining the cancellation of the "general attack" he had ordered yesterday: "While the officer charged with the lead was advancing he was deceived by a false report that a heavy column of the enemy had turned our right and was close upon him, and took a defensive position. When the mistake was discovered it was too late to resume the movement." Despite this disappointment, which had obliged him to continue the withdrawal, he pointed out that he had "kept near [Sherman] to prevent his detaching to Virginia, as you directed, and have repulsed every attack he has made."

Next day, May 21, the army having spent the night improving its position near Allatoona, still with no sign of what the Federals were up to, he followed through with another message along similar lines. "In the last six days the enemy has pressed us back to this point, thirty-two miles," he conceded, but he assured Davis that, all this time, "I have earnestly sought an opportunity to strike." The trouble was that Sherman, by constantly extending his right as he moved down the railroad, had obliged the defenders to give ground no less constantly, and then, "by fortifying the moment he halted," had also "made an assault upon his superior forces too hazardous." Without committing himself to anything specific — as, indeed, he could scarcely be expected to do, under the circumstances outlined here — Johnston wanted the Commander in Chief to know that he was in full agreement as to the need for going over to the offensive at the earliest possible moment. Meantime, despite the discouragements generally involved in making a lengthy retrograde movement, he was pleased to report that the slightness of his losses from straggling or desertion showed that the army was in good shape for such exertions as he might presently require.

The answer came not from Davis — not just yet — but from Bragg, who combined good news with bad and wound up with a flourish that seemed to indicate that the Georgia commander perhaps had oversold his case. Another brigade of infantry from Mobile and a regiment of South Carolina cavalry were on their way to join him, but these were the last the government would be sending.

"From the high condition in which your army is reported," the message ended, "we confidently rely on a brilliant success."

★ ★ ★

Johnston's concern, lest the very strength of his Allatoona position deprive him of the quick defensive victory he felt certain he would score if his adversary could only be persuaded to attack him there, was better founded than he knew. Two decades back, as a young artillery lieutenant on detached duty at Marietta with the inspector general, Sherman "rode or walked, exploring creeks, valleys, hills" in the surrounding region, while his less energetic comrades "spent their leisure Sundays reading novels, card-playing, or sleeping." Now this seemingly useless pastime stood him in good stead. "Twenty years later the thing that helped me to win battles in Georgia was my perfect knowledge of the country. I knew more of Georgia than the rebels did." In the course of his rambles, sketch pad in hand, he had spent several days investigating some Indian mounds on the south bank of the Etowah, just north of the gorge where Johnston was intrenched, and "I therefore knew that the Allatoona Pass was very strong, would be hard to force, and resolved not even to attempt it, but to turn the position."

First, though, he would call a halt, a brief time-out from war; the combat troops would take a welcome three-day rest ("to replenish and fit up," he explained to Halleck) while Colonel W. W. Wright and his 2000 nimble rail repairmen, having rebuilt the Resaca bridge in jig time, put the Western & Atlantic back in operation down to Kingston.

"The dead were buried, the sick and wounded were made more comfortable, and everybody got his mail and wrote letters," one appreciative officer would recall. Then on May 23, with twenty days' rations in his wagons, Sherman was ready to cut loose from the railroad and strike out cross-country with everything he had.

His preliminary objective on this all-out flanking operation was Dallas, a road-hub settlement just under twenty miles west of Marietta and about the same distance southwest of Allatoona, where Johnston would be left holding the bag unless he pulled back in time to meet this massive threat to his new supply base, fifteen miles down the track in his rear. As usual, Thomas would take the direct central route, south from Kingston through Euharlee and Stilesboro, while Schofield marched on his left, by way of Burnt Hickory, and McPherson swung well to the right, through Van Wert, to approach Dallas from the west. The march would be a rigorous one, Sherman knew from previous exploration, "as the country was very obscure, mostly in a state of nature, densely wooded and with few roads." It might take longer than he

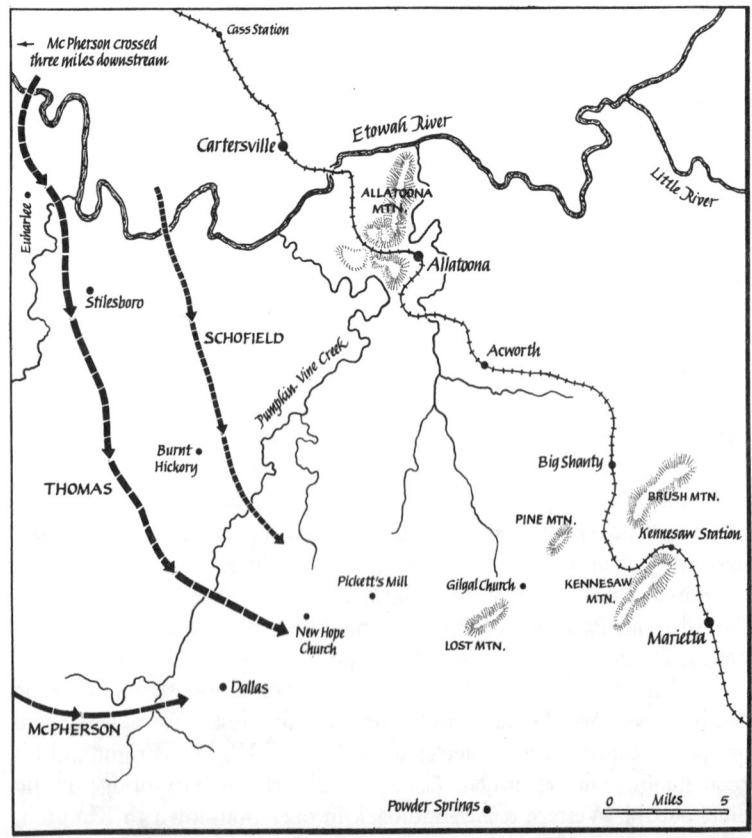

planned: in which case, he told Halleck, his twenty-day rations could be stretched to thirty. But he was not inclined to worry much as he set out from Kingston, riding with Thomas across the Etowah; "the Rubicon of Georgia," he called that river in a dispatch sent just after he gave the jump-off signal. "We are now all in motion like a vast hive of bees," he declared, fairly buzzing with pleasure at being once more on the go, "and expect to swarm along the Chattahoochee in five days."

So he said. But when Schofield captured a lone gray rider at Burnt Hickory next day and found on him a dispatch which showed Johnston already reacting to this latest turning movement, Sherman not only knew that secrecy had gone by the board, along with all hope for a substantial head start in the projected five-day sprint for the Chattahoochee; he also perceived that "it accordingly became necessary to use great caution, lest some of the minor columns should fall into ambush," as Schofield had so nearly done, four days ago, near Cassville.

Caution was indeed called for, he found out the following morning, May 25, when Thomas pressed down in advance of the other two armies for a crossing of Pumpkin Vine Creek. Hooker had the lead, driving butternut cavalry pickets over a bridge which they set on fire just as the first of his three divisions came in sight. He doused the flames, double-timed across, and continued his pursuit of the skittery horsemen. Four miles northeast of Dallas, near a Methodist meeting-house called New Hope Church, he came under fire from a mass of rebel infantry whose march he had apparently interrupted. With soldierly instinct, and as if determined to justify his nom de guerre, Fighting Joe shook out a line of skirmishers and attacked with his lead division, commanded by Brigadier General John W. Geary, a six-foot six-inch Pennsylvanian who had been San Francisco's first mayor and a territorial governor of Kansas. A colonel in the Mexican War before he was thirty, he now was forty-four and had seen much fighting, East and West, including Chancellorsville and Gettysburg, Wauhatchie and Chattanooga, but in none of these had he and his men found harder work than was required of them in the next three hours around New Hope Church, which the attackers ever afterwards referred to as the "Hell Hole."

What Geary struck, and promptly rebounded from, was Hood. His corps had been last of the three to leave Allatoona the day before, when Johnston, warned by Wheeler that Sherman was off on another sidle, marched southwest up the near bank of Pumpkin Vine Creek to intercept him around Dallas. Hardee was there now, with Polk in position on his right to connect with Hood near New Hope Church; so that what Hooker had encountered was not a mere segment of Johnston's army on the march, as he first thought, but the entire right wing of that army, already beginning to scratch out intrenchments in expectation of his arrival hard on the heels of the cavalry pickets fading back before him through what Sherman called "the obscurity of the ambushed country." Undaunted by the truth, which he began to suspect as soon as Geary was flung back, Hooker brought up his other two divisions, led by Butterfield and Brigadier General Alpheus Williams, massed them on a front no wider than Geary had spanned alone, and sent them forward, closely packed, against the rebel center. As a result, Major General Alexander P. Stewart's division caught the brunt of the all-out blue attack, some 20,000 strong. Known to his soldiers as "Old Straight," the nickname he had acquired while teaching mathematics at West Point and at Cumberland University in his home state of Tennessee, Stewart was forty-two and a veteran of all the army's battles, a strict disciplinarian much admired by his men, who gave him today all he asked of them, and more: especially the artillerists, whose guns were advantageously sited to exact a heavy toll from the charging bluecoats. Hooker's three divisions could make no headway against this one, despite two hours of trying without pause. Hood's other two divisions, under Major Generals Thomas Hindman and Carter Stevenson, had little to do on the left and right of the sector being assaulted, but when Johnston himself, alarmed by the desperate nature of the struggle, sent to ask Stewart if he needed reinforcements, the Tennessean replied calmly: "My own troops will hold the position."

Still another hour of such fighting remained, and it was this third hour, even more than the previous two, that prompted the Hell Hole description of the scene. Thunder rumbled and lightning crackled from a huge black cloud that gathered above the crossroad, dwarfing the boom of guns and the flicker of muzzle flashes, then loosed its torrential burden with all the abruptness of a water-filled bag split open, drenching men already wet with sweat from heat and exertion, whether prone behind log barricades or scrambling through bullet- and rain-whipped brush. "No more persistent attack or determined resistance was anywhere made," Stewart was to report with impartial praise. Thunderstorm and fighting came to a simultaneous end as the cloud blew off and the sun went down in a glory of red and purple beyond Dallas and the mountains to the west. Hooker put his casualties at 1665 killed or wounded, but the Confederates, knowing his reputation for understating his own losses while overestimating those of his opponent, were convinced the figure was much too low, since they themselves, fighting mostly behind cover, had lost nearly half that many in the course of the three-hour contest.

Darkness made the going hard for the rest of Thomas's army, coming up in the center, as well as for the other two, closing in on the left and right. "All was hurry and confusion," a Kentucky Federal recorded in his diary, "nearly everyone swearing at the top of his voice." Sherman would later recall that he "slept on the ground, without cover, alongside of a log, [and] got little sleep," but Schofield had worse luck. Swept off his horse by a low-hanging branch while combing the moonless woods in search of Sherman's bivouac, he was hurt by the fall and would be out of action for several days; leadership of his Army of the Ohio passed temporarily to Brigadier General Jacob Cox, the senior division commander. McPherson made it nearly to Dallas by daylight, coming in from the west to find Hardee securely intrenched there, as were Polk and Hood to the northeast.

Sherman probed cautiously at the five-mile rebel line, all that day and part of the next, but found no weakness he considered would justify attack. Accordingly, by midmorning of the second day of unproductive probing, May 27, he decided to turn Johnston's right with a strike at Pickett's Mill, two miles beyond the Hell Hole Hooker had failed to take two days ago. This time Howard drew the assignment, and presently all three of his divisions were in position, massed for assault in case there was serious opposition.

There was indeed, and "serious" was by no means too strong a description of what he was about to encounter in the way of resistance. Suspecting that the Federals would attempt some such maneuver, Johnston the day before had instructed Hardee to shift one of his divisions from the far left to a position beyond Hood's right: specifically, to Pickett's Mill. It was Howard's ill fortune — as it had been Sherman's, on Missionary Ridge six months ago, and Hooker's, two days later at Ringgold Gap — that the division posted in his path was Major General Patrick Cleburne's, by common agreement the best in Johnston's army. Before emigrating to become a lawyer in Helena, Arkansas, Irish-born Cleburne had done a three-year hitch in Her Majesty's 41st Regiment of Foot, an experience that stood the former corporal in good stead when it came to training his division of Arkansans, Texans, Mississippians, and Tennesseans. Except under specific orders, which sometimes had to be repeated, he and his men had never given up a piece of ground assigned to their defense; nor did they do so here today at Pickett's Mill. One-armed Howard gave the lead to his fellow West Pointer, Brigadier General Thomas Wood — whose abrupt, inadvertent withdrawal under orders at Chickamauga had created the "chasm" through which Longstreet plunged to defeat Rosecrans. Wood had his division in place by early afternoon, formed six ranks deep for an end-on strike at the rebel flank, wherever it might be. He moved out, floundered about for a couple of hours in the heavy brush, then paused for some badly needed rest, having sighted the newly turned earth of fresh intrenchments through the trees. It was 4.30 by the time he got his three brigades in motion again, still in a compact formation of two lines each, and what turned out to be a three-hour fight, with an equally horrendous nighttime epilogue added for good measure, began almost at once.

His repulse was as complete as it was sudden. Ahead through the trees, as the close-packed blue infantry came on, the head-logs of the newly dug rebel intrenchments seemed to burst into flame, and a long, low cloud of smoke boiled up and out, billowing as it grew, lighted from within by the pinkish yellow blink and stab of muzzle flashes; Cleburne's emphasis on rapid-fire marksmanship in training produced a clatter as continuous as the uproar in a 5000-man boiler factory and an incidence of casualties that matched the stepped-up rate of fire. Wood's division fell apart, transformed abruptly from a compact mass into huddled clusters groping for cover in such low ground as the field afforded. "Under these circumstances," Howard reported, "it became evident that the assault had failed." He brought up reinforcements from Major General John M. Palmer's adjoining corps, as well as from Schofield's army, which was posted in reserve here on the Union left, and did what he could "to bring off the wounded and to prevent a successful sally of the enemy from his works." Darkness helped in both these efforts, but not much. At 10 o'clock, in a rare night action, Cleburne threw Brigadier General Hiram Granbury's Texas brigade into a charge that swept through a ravine where a number of fugitives from the attack had taken refuge, capturing all that were left alive when it was over. Howard's losses in Wood's division alone were 1457 killed, wounded, or captured. Cleburne's were 448, although Howard thought them higher in advancing a claim that "the enemy suffered immensely in the action, and regarded it as the severest attack made during this eventful campaign."

Now it was Johnston's turn to try his hand at what Sherman had been attempting all along. Reasoning that if his adversary was thus extending his left he might also have weakened his right, the Virginian told Hardee to test the Federal defenses around Dallas next morning. Hardee did, passing the word for Major General William Bate to make a probing attack with his division. Bate's repulse, though not as bloody, was as complete as Wood's had been the day before, at the far end of the line. He lost close to 400 men, half of them from the dwindling "Orphan" brigade of Kentuckians under Brigadier General Joseph Lewis, successor to Mrs Lincoln's brother-in-law, Ben Hardin Helm, who had fallen at Chickamauga.

All Bate got for his pains was the knowledge that McPherson was still around Dallas, apparently in undiminished strength — although the fact was he had been under orders to pull out for a march beyond New Hope Church and was about to leave when the rebel attack exploded against his works. Having fought it off, with fewer than half the casualties he inflicted, he notified Sherman and held his ground, awaiting instructions.

Meantime Johnston convened a council of war, at which Hood proposed that his corps be shifted eastward, beyond Cleburne, for an attack on the Union left, to be taken up in sequence by the other two corps with strikes at the right and center. Johnston liked the plan and issued the necessary orders, stipulating that Polk and Hardee would go forward when they heard Hood's artillery begin to roar. They waited past dawn and through sunup, May 29, poised for assault, heads cocked to catch the boom of guns that did not come. What came instead, around midmorning, was a note from Hood informing Johnston that he had found a newly arrived blue division intrenched in his path, perpendicular to the line he had scouted the day before. Finding it "inexpedient" to advance under these conditions, he had halted and now awaited new instructions. Johnston promptly canceled the offensive, directing instead that the army give all its attention to improving its defenses.

McPherson, Thomas, and Schofield were doing the same across the way, each on his own initiative, with the result that both lines grew more formidable than any seen so far in the campaign. Quick to improvise intrenchments — "The rebs must carry their breastworks with them," Federals were saying, marveling at the speed with which their adversaries could establish field fortifications, while the Confederates returned the compliment by remarking that "Sherman's men march with a rifle in one hand and a spade in the other" — blue and gray alike had become adept at the art of making any position well-nigh impregnable within a couple of days. While some troops hastily scratched and scooped out a ditch with bayonets and wooden shovels, canteen halves and fingers, others felled trees to provide timber for the dirt-and-log revetment, atop which a head log would rest on poles extending rearward across the trench to keep it from falling on the defenders in case it was struck by a shell while they were firing through the slit along its bottom between the skid poles. Other trees out front were cut so that their tops fell toward the enemy, their interlaced branches providing an entanglement to discourage assault, and if there was time for more methodical work, sharpened stakes were set in holes bored in logs and these too were placed to delay or impale attackers; *chevaux-de-frise* was the engineers' term for these spiky devices, which Westerners on both sides called "sheep racks." Whatever their name, they were cruelly effective and contributed largely to the invulnerability of the occupants of the trenches, taking it easy under the shade of blankets laid over the works to shield them from the sun. Taking it easy, that is, in a relative sense; for the snipers were sharp-eyed, quick to shoot from dawn to dusk, and the pickets on both sides were fearfully trigger-happy from dusk to dawn; Thomas alone was expending 200,000 rounds of small-arms ammunition daily.

May now ended, and as June came in, two days after Bate's repulse by McPherson helped to offset the subtractions Hooker and Howard had undergone in their assaults on Stewart and Cleburne, both commanders could take a backward look at what the four-week "running skirmish," uninterrupted by anything approaching either the dignity or the carnage of a full-scale battle, had cost them. Sherman's loss throughout the month of May was 9299, including nearly two thousand killed and missing; Johnston's, less precisely tabulated, was about 8500, three thousand of them captured or otherwise missing, left behind on his retrograde movement from Dalton to Dallas. Not even the larger of the two was a shudder-provoking figure at this stage of the war — particularly in comparison with the one being registered simultaneously in Virginia, where Meade was losing men at the rate of 2000 a day and would lose three times that many tomorrow, within less than twenty minutes, at Cold Harbor — but Sherman was getting edgy, all the same, over his inability to come to grips with his opponent on any terms except those that would clearly involve self-slaughter.

This he declined, around New Hope Church, as he had done before, wherever the Confederates called a halt to invite attack on their intrenchments. Instead, he continued to extend his left flank eastward toward the Western & Atlantic, obliging Johnston to conform by extending his right to keep him from slipping past it.

He was eager to get back astride the railroad, since two of his mounted divisions — Garrard's, which had rejoined from Rome, and another led by Major General George Stoneman, former chief of cavalry in the Army of the Potomac, under Hooker, now filling that position in Schofield's Army of the Ohio — had seized lightly held Allatoona Pass that morning, June 1, clearing the way for Sherman's rail repair gangs to extend his all-weather supply line across the Etowah, down to Acworth and beyond. Though Acworth was within ten miles of New Hope Church, the going would be rough, not only because of the rugged nature of the terrain and the probable interference of the rebels, but also because on the day Allatoona fell the rain began to fall as well: no brief tumultuous spring thunderstorm, such as had drenched the Hell Hole fighters, stopping about as abruptly as it started, but rather the slow, steady, apparently endless downpour of a dripping Georgia June. "Rain! Rain!! Rain!!!" an entry in a soggy diary read a few days later. This was as much of a strain on the spirits of men as it was on the backs and legs of mules who lugged ration and ammunition wagons through soupy troughs of wet red clay that once had passed for roads. "These were the hardest times the army experienced," Howard was to say, looking back. "It rained continuously for seventeen days; the roads, becoming as broad as the fields, were a series of quagmires." Mosquitoes stung and thrived, along with something new that bit and burrowed: redbugs, *Eutrombicula alfreddugesi* — chiggers. "Chigres are big, and red as blood," an Illinois private wrote. "They will crawl through any cloth and bite worse than fleas, and poison the flesh very badly. Many of the boys anoint their bodies with bacon rines which chigres can't go. Salt water bathing would cure them but salt is too scarce to use on human flesh."

Salt was not the only scarcity. Cut loose from their bountiful rail supply line, and with little chance to forage on their own, the troops had to live mainly on hardtack and bacon. Men began to come down with the symptoms of scurvy, "black-mouthed, loose-toothed fellows" who went on the roam in search of wild onions or anything green and fit to eat, though with small success in this barren, up-and-down backwoods region, miles off the main track. It was, as Howard said, a difficult time for everyone concerned, including Sherman.

Then on the night of June 4, the sounds of withdrawal muffled by the drumming of the rain, Johnston gave him the slip again. Morning showed the Confederates gone, and though some of his soldiers cheered "the nocturnal departure of the rebellious gentlemen," Sherman himself was far from pleased: especially when he received reports of their new position, which seemed, on the face of it, about as strong as any they had occupied in the past four weeks. Hardee held the left, on Lost Mountain and at Gilgal Church, Polk the center, from Pine Mountain to the Western & Atlantic, six miles below Acworth, and Hood the right, across the railroad, along the base of Brush Mountain. Cavalry covered and extended the flanks, Wheeler eastward, beyond Hood, and Brigadier General William H. Jackson's division, which had come with Polk from Alabama, westward beyond Hardee. Kennesaw Mountain, a commanding height, was two miles in the rear, handy in case another fallback was required, and Marietta about the same distance beyond its crest, which was less than twenty air-line miles from the heart of Atlanta.

By the following day, June 6, the three Union armies were again in confrontation with their foe, Thomas in the center, Schofield on the right, and McPherson on the left, astride the railroad at Big Shanty, a little more than midway between Allatoona and Marietta. Three days later Major General Francis P. Blair, Junior — brother of Lincoln's Postmaster General and a close friend of Sherman's — rejoined McPherson, bringing the 10,000 men of his corps back from their reënlistment furloughs and, incidentally, more than making up for the combat losses in all three armies up to now. By June 11 the hard-working railroad crews had the track repaired all the way to Big Shanty, and the troops, back on full rations and fairly well rested from their recent excursion through the wilds, felt much better.

"If we get to Atlanta in a week, all right," one veteran wrote home. "If it takes two months you won't hear this army grumbling."

Sherman was inclined to be less patient at this point. Though he was pleased that his latest sidle had accomplished its main purpose by obliging the rebels to give up impregnable Allatoona Pass, he was disappointed that it had not taken him all the way to the Chattahoochee (as he had predicted it would do, within five days) instead of fifteen rugged miles short of that river, with Johnston dug in across his front and able to look down his throat, so to speak, from the high ground up ahead. Obviously, if the graybacks were to be dislodged at something less than an altogether grievous price in casualties, this called for another sidle. Yet Sherman did not much like the notion of setting out on still another roundabout march away from the railroad: mainly, no doubt, because the last one had cost him more than he had planned for, both in morale and blood. In fact, before he crossed the Etowah and started his swing around Dallas, his losses had actually been lower than his adversary's, but now, as a result of the repulses he had suffered at New Hope Church and Pickett's Mill, they were nearly a thousand higher. Moreover, it seemed to him that his practice of avoiding pitched battle, wherever the terrain appeared unfavorable, had tended to make his soldiers unaggressive, timid in the face of possible ambush, and flinchy when confronted by intrenchments. Schofield, recovered by now from his horseback fall the week before, accounted for the reaction somewhat differently, seeing the nonprofessional volunteers and draftees as men who brought to army life, and to war itself, the practicality they had learned as civilians with the need for earning a living in the peacetime world outside. "The veteran American soldier fights very much as he has been accustomed to work his farm or run his sawmill," the young West Pointer declared. "He wants to see a fair prospect that it is going to pay."

That might be; Sherman yielded to no man in his admiration for and his understanding of the western volunteer. Still it seemed to him that all three armies were in danger of losing their fighting edge, if indeed they had not already lost it, and he put most of the blame on their commanders. Even McPherson, protégé or not, had begun to receive tart messages complaining of his slowness on the march. As for Schofield, he had come a long way from measuring up to expectations, and Sherman did not hesitate to say so. But Thomas, who had direct charge of two thirds of all the Federals in North Georgia, was the main object of the redhead's impatience and downright scorn.

"My chief source of trouble is with the Army of the Cumberland," Sherman informed Grant by telegraph this week. "A fresh furrow in a plowed field will stop the whole column and all begin to intrench. I have again and again tried to impress on Thomas that we must assail and not defend; we are on the offensive, and yet it seems that the whole Army of the Cumberland is so habituated to be[ing] on the defensive that from its commander down to its lowest private I cannot get it out of their heads."

He turned snappish in reaction to the delays and disadvantages involved in fighting what he called "a big Indian war" against an opponent whose army remained elusively intact and who, as Sherman complained in a letter to his brother in Washington, could "fight or fall back, as he pleases. The future is uncertain," he wound up gloomily, "but I will do all that is possible."

Aside from another unwanted sidle on muddy roads, not much seemed possible just now except to keep up the pressure, dead ahead, in hope that something would give. Nothing did. Johnston had contracted, somewhat retired, and thereby strengthened his line of defense, pulling Hardee in around Gilgal Church and Hood behind Noonday Creek, astride the railroad; Lost and Brush mountains were left to the protection of the cavalry, and Polk reinforced the center, on call to help cover not only the Western & Atlantic but also the wagon roads between Acworth and Marietta.

For outpost and observation purposes, a brigade from Bate's division remained on Pine Mountain, occupying what had become a salient when the line was readjusted in its rear. Called Pine Top by the natives, it was not so much a mountain as it was an overgrown hill, detached from the others roundabout and bristled atop with pine trees. Steepest on its northern face, it afforded a fine view of all three Federal armies and thus was well worth holding onto; Johnston had posted two batteries on its crest to help defend it, including one from South Carolina commanded by Lieutenant René Beauregard, the Creole general's son. Hardee was apprehensive, however, that both troops and guns were too far in advance of the main position for support to reach them before they were gobbled up by a sudden blue assault, and he asked his chief to go with him next morning, June 14, to judge in person the risk to which the salient was exposed.

Johnston agreed and the two set out on horseback as arranged, accompanied by their staffs and also by Polk, who wanted to come along for a look at the country from the hilltop. The rain had slackened and a cool breeze made the ride and the climb up the south slope a pleasant interlude, although Johnston had not gone far before he agreed that Hardee's fears were well founded; he told him to withdraw Bate's brigade and the two batteries after nightfall. Reaching the crest, however, he decided to avail himself of this last chance to study the enemy position from Pine Top, despite a warning that a battery of rifled Parrott guns, about half a mile in front, had been firing with deadly accuracy all morning at anyone who exposed himself to view. Sure enough, the three generals had no sooner mounted the parapet and begun adjusting their binoculars than they were greeted by a bursting shell.

Sherman himself, riding out on a line inspection down below, had seen them, although without personal recognition at that range, and had taken offense at their presumption. "How saucy they are," he said, and he turned to Howard, who held this portion of the front, and told him to have one of his batteries throw a few shots in their direction to "make 'em take cover." He rode on, and Howard passed the word to Battery I, 1st Ohio Light Artillery, whose commander, Captain Hubert Dilger, had already acted on the order before it reached him.

Dilger was something of a character, well known throughout the army, partly because of the way he dressed, immaculate in a white shirt with rolled sleeves, highly polished top boots, and doeskin trousers — hence the nickname "Leatherbreeches" — and partly because of his habit of taking his guns so close to the front in battle that one general had proposed to equip them with bayonets. On leave from the Prussian army, in which he was also an artillerist, he had been visiting New York in 1861 and had joined the Army of the Potomac, fighting in all its battles through Gettysburg before coming west with Hooker to join the Army of the Cumberland. Perhaps because he spoke with a heavy German accent, he trained his crews to respond to hand claps, rather than voice commands, and had won such admiration as an expert, famed for the rapidity and precision of his fire, that he was allowed to function largely on his own, roving about as a sort of free lance and posting his battery wherever he judged it could do the most good. Today he was within half a mile of Pine Top, and when he saw the cluster of saucy Confederates mount the parapet on its crest he ran forward to one of his rifled Parrotts, sighted it carefully, then stepped back. "Shust teeckle them fellers," he told the cannoneer on the lanyard, and clapped his hands.

That was the first shot, a near miss. Johnston gave the order to disperse, and all three generals and their staffs had begun to do so when a second projectile landed even closer.

Hardee and Johnston moved briskly, heading for shelter behind the crest of the hill, but Polk, a portly figure apparently mindful of his dignity, walked off slowly by himself, hands clasped behind his back as if in deep thought. Just then the third shell came shrieking; Dilger had been quick to find the range. It struck the churchly warrior squarely in the side, passing through his left arm and his body and his right arm before emerging to explode against a tree. Johnston and Hardee turned and hurried back through other shell-bursts to kneel beside the quivering corpse of the bishop general. "My dear, dear friend," Hardee groaned, tears falling. Johnston too was weeping as he laid his hand upon the dead man's head. "We have lost much," he said, and presently added: "I would rather anything but this."

An ambulance, summoned by wigwag from the Pine Top signal station, brought Polk's mangled remains down off the mountain that afternoon, followed that night, in accordance with Johnston's evacuation order, by the men of the two batteries and the infantry brigade, who filed down in a long column not unlike a funeral cortege. Indeed, the whole army mourned the fifty-eight-year-old bishop's passing; he had been with it from the outset, before Shiloh, and at one time or another had commanded nearly every soldier in its ranks. There were, of course, those who doubted that his clerical qualities justified his elevation to the leadership of a corps. "Thus died a gentleman and a high Church dignitary," one of his division commanders wrote. "As a soldier he was more theoretical than practical." Though there was truth in this, it overlooked the contribution he made to the army's moral tone, which was one of the factors that enabled it to survive hardships, defeats, retreats, and Bragg. Northerners might express outrage that a man of the cloth, West Point graduate or not, should take up the sword of rebellion; Southerners took his action as strong evidence that the Lord was on their side, and they on His. That was part of what Jefferson Davis meant when he later referred to his old friend's death as "an irrepairable loss" and said that the country had sustained no heavier blow since the fall of Sidney Johnston and Stonewall Jackson.

One service Polk's maiming performed, at any rate, and that was to break up the pattern of Sherman's incipient depression. He had small use for the clergy anyhow, as a class, let alone this one who had joined in the current unholy attempt to dissolve the finest government the world had ever known, and when the news reached his headquarters at Big Shanty that afternoon — Federal signalmen decoded a wigwag appeal from atop Pine Mountain: "Send an ambulance for General Polk's body" — he took it as a sign that things were going better than he had thought. Sure enough, morning showed the enemy gone from the troublesome salient opposite his center. The rain had resumed its drumming on his tent, still further increasing the depth of the mud on all the roads, but Sherman did not let that keep his rising spirits from taking another mercurial jump. Ordering Thomas to close the gap in front while McPherson and Schofield stepped up the pressure on the flanks, he rode out to see it done and returned much pleased with the events of the past two days. Though he was careful, then and down the years, to deny the rumor that it was he, not Leatherbreeches Dilger, who had laid with his own hands the gun that sniped the militant churchman off of Pine Top, he was delighted with the result produced on this fortieth day of his campaign to "knock Jos. Johnston."

"We killed Bishop Polk yesterday," he wired Halleck, once more in high feather, "and made good progress today."

※ 2 ※

Not that, in his revived ebullience, he had dismissed all fear for what he called "that single stem of railroad 473 miles long," back through Nashville and Bowling Green, hurdling rivers and burrowing under mountains to reach his base on the Ohio; "Taxed [as it was] to its utmost to supply our daily wants," Sherman said flatly that without it "the Atlanta campaign was an impossibility." It was as much on his mind as ever, along with the two famed raiders who threatened its unbroken operation. "Thus far we have been well supplied, and I hope it will continue," he wrote his wife this week from Big Shanty, "though

I expect to hear every day of Forrest breaking into Tennessee from some quarter. John Morgan is in Kentucky, but I attach little importance to him or his raid. Forrest is a more dangerous man."

Even as he wrote, events were proving him right in both assessments. Morgan, after his victory at Crockett's Cove in the second week of May, reverted to his plan for a return to his homeland, which had been interrupted by the need for keeping Averell away from the salt works and lead mines in the Department of Southwest Virginia. His application for permission to make the raid had been turned down by the Richmond authorities, on the grounds that he was needed where he was, but he did not let that stop him now any more than he had done ten months ago, when he set out on the "ride" that landed him in the Ohio Penitentiary. Besides, having just learned that Brigadier General Stephen Burbridge, Union commander of the District of Kentucky, and a subordinate, Brigadier General Edward Hobson, were even then assembling troops in separate camps for a march across the Cumberlands to visit on Saltville and Wytheville the destruction Averell had failed to accomplish, Morgan believed he now had a more persuasive argument in favor of a quick return to the Bluegrass. Their combined forces were better than twice the size of his own, which amounted to fewer than 3000 men, and he was convinced that the only way to stop them was to distract them before they got started. "This information has determined me to move at once into the State of Kentucky," he informed the War Department on the last day of the month, "and thus divert the plans of the enemy by initiating a movement within his lines."

Forestalling another refusal, he set out that same day. By the time the message reached Richmond, two days later — "A most unfortunate withdrawal of forces from an important position at a very critical moment," Bragg indorsed it, and Seddon added: "Unfortunately, I see no remedy for this movement now" — Morgan was through Pound Gap and back on the soil of his native state.

That was June 2. It took him another five days to complete the rugged 150-mile trek across the mountains to within sight of the Bluegrass, and then on the morning of June 8 he approached the town of Mount Sterling, a day's ride west of Lexington. His strength was 2700 men, less than a third of them veterans from his old command, while another third were unmounted recruits for whom he hoped to find horses and equipment in the stock-rich country up ahead. A beginning was made at Mount Sterling, which he surrounded and captured, along with 380 Federals posted there to guard a large accumulation of supplies, including some badly needed boots.

While the prisoners were being paroled and Morgan was preparing to move on, looters began to break into shops, plunder homes, and even rough up citizens to relieve them of watches and wallets. "It was a general robbery," one merchant later protested, and though officers did what they could to stop the pillage, the undisciplined recruits, many of whom had spent the past two years avoiding conscription and stealing to make a living while on the run, were so far beyond control that some even drew pistols on women to rob them of their jewelry — an outrage the blood-thirstiest guerilla in Missouri had not perpetrated up to now. Confederates had mostly been greeted joyously on previous raids through this section of Kentucky, of which Morgan himself was a boasted product, but they were not likely to be welcome in the future, if indeed there was to be a future for them. A sort of climax was reached when a group of townspeople called indignantly on Morgan to show him an order, issued over the name of one of his brigade commanders, demanding immediate delivery of all the money in the local bank, under penalty of having "every house in the place" put to the torch; $72,000 in gold and greenbacks had been handed over. Morgan paled and turned to the colonel in question, who pronounced the signature a forgery and asked who had presented it. A light-haired officer with a blond beard and a German accent, he was told. Surgeon R. R. Goode answered that description, but when he was sent for he did not appear. He was missing — and remained so, though afterwards he was rumored to be living high in his native Germany.

Morgan could afford no time for an investigation, however desirable one was to clear his name, and set out without further delay for Lexington, his home town just over thirty miles away, leaving the foot-sore, horseless troopers behind to complete the distribution and destruction of the captured stores before taking up the march to join him.

Only about half of them ever did, the rest being killed or captured as the result of a miscalculation. "There will be nothing in the state to retard our progress except a few scattered provost guards," Morgan had predicted on setting out, and this opinion had been bolstered by reports from scouts that the heavy Union column under Burbridge, unaware of what was in progress across the way, had begun its eastward march toward the Cumberlands just before the Confederates emerged from them, headed west. Morgan's announced purpose was to oblige the blue invaders to turn back, but he had not thought they would react with anything like the speed they did. When Burbridge learned at Prestonburg that his adversary had passed him en route, by way of Pound Gap to the south, he not only countermarched promptly; he did so with such celerity that he was on the outskirts of Mount Sterling before daylight, June 9, and launched a dawn attack that caught the scantly picketed gray recruits so completely by surprise that many of them, still groggy from their excesses of the previous day and night, were shot before they could struggle out of their blankets. The survivors — about 450 of the original 800 — managed to fall back through the town and down the road to the west, thankful that the Federals were too worn by their hard return march to pursue.

Morgan was halfway to Lexington when he found out what had happened, and though his first reaction was to turn back and counterattack with his whole command, on second thought (Burbridge had about twice as many men, well supported by artillery, and Morgan had been able to bring no guns across the mountains) he decided to wait for what was left of the horseless brigade to join him, then continue on to his home town. He approached it that night, made camp astride the pike, and rode in next morning to find, along with much else in the way of supplies and equipment, enough horses in its several government stables to mount all of his still-dismounted men and replace the animals broken down by the long march from Virginia.

Despite this valid military gain, June 10 was another stain on the reputation the raid had been designed, in part, to burnish. "Though the stay of Morgan's command in Lexington was brief, embracing but a few hours," the local paper reported next day, "he made good use of his time — as many empty shelves and pockets will testify." Once more looters took over, and this time veterans joined the pillage. Another bank was robbed, though more forthrightly than the one two days ago; the celebrants simply put a pistol to the cashier's head and made him open the vault, from which they took $10,000. Several buildings were set afire and whiskey stores were stripped, with the result that a good many troopers, too drunk to stay on a horse, had to be loaded into wagons for the ride to Cynthiana, thirty miles northeast. Morgan had learned there were supplies and a 500-man garrison there, and he was determined to have or destroy them both.

He marched by way of Georgetown to arrive next day, demanding surrender. This was declined, at first, but then accepted after a house-to-house fight in which, Morgan informed Richmond, "I was forced to burn a large portion of the town." Before he could enjoy the fruits of victory, lookouts spotted a blue column, 1200 strong, approaching from the east. It was Hobson; he too had turned back, well short of the Virginia line, on hearing from Burbridge that the raiders were in his rear. Headed for Lexington, he marched hard for Cynthiana when he saw the smoke and heard the firing. As it turned out, he was marching to join the surrender. Morgan threw two brigades directly at him and circled around to gain his rear with the other. This being done, Hobson was left with no choice except to be slaughtered or lay down his arms. He chose the latter course; which was doubly sweet for Morgan, Hobson having been widely praised for his share in the capture, near Buffington on the north bank of the Ohio River last July, of about half of Morgan's "terrible men," including the raider's second in command and two of his brothers, whom he later joined in prison as a felon. Now with Hobson himself a captive the tables were turned.

Proud of this latest exploit — as well he might be; he now had more prisoners than troopers — Morgan refused to be alarmed when scouts rode in at nightfall to report that Burbridge, having learned of his appearance at Cynthiana, was on the way from Mount Sterling with close to 5000 men. That was three times the strength of the Confederates, who were down to about 1400, half their original force, as a result of casualties, stragglers, and detachments sent out to mislead the numerous Union garrisons roundabout. Even more serious, perhaps, was a shortage of cartridges for the Enfield rifles his raiders favored so much that they declined to exchange them for captured Springfields, even though there was plenty of ammunition for the latter. But Morgan's mind was quite made up. Determined to give his weary men a good night's rest, he announced to his brigade commanders that he would meet the bluecoats next morning on ground of his own choosing, two miles south of town, and whip them as he had whipped Hobson today, whatever the odds. When one colonel protested that Burbridge was too strong to be fought without full cartridge boxes, the Alabama-born Kentuckian replied curtly: "It is my order that you hold your position at all hazard. We can whip him with empty guns."

Preceding another victory, the words would have had a defiant, martial ring, fit for the books and altogether in keeping with his earlier career; but followed as they were by a defeat, they took on the sound not of bravery, but of bravado. Burbridge attacked at dawn, June 12, and though Morgan was prevented from employing his accustomed flanking tactics by the need for putting all his men in line, he managed to stem the assault successfully until the shout, "Out of ammunition!" came from the right and was taken up next by the center, then the left. "Our whole command was soon forced back into the streets of the town, routed and demoralized," one raider would recall. "The confusion was indescribable.... There was much shooting, swearing, and yelling. Some from sheer mortification were crying."

Morgan did what he could to accomplish an orderly withdrawal, but what was left of his force by now had been split in two, with the halves presently blasted into fragments, some men fleeing southwest across the Sinking River to Leesburg, others northeast to Augusta. Many, caught on foot, surrendered; others were shot down. Not over half escaped, including their leader. "While falling back on the town," the same trooper wrote, "I saw General Morgan, on his step-trotting roan, going toward the Augusta road. He was skimming along at an easy pace, looking up at our broken lines and — softly whistling. I was glad to see him getting away, for had he been captured he would doubtless have fared badly."

He fared badly enough as it was. Back in Virginia before the month was out — minus half his troopers, even after all the stragglers had come in by various routes across the mountains, and considerably better than half his reputation — he put the raid in the best light he could manage in composing his report, stressing the frustration of Burbridge's expedition against the salt works and lead mines, the capture and parole of almost as many soldiers as he took with him, the procurement of nearly a thousand horses for men afoot and the exchange of roughly the same number of broken-down mounts for fresh ones, the destruction of "about 2,000,000$ worth of U.S. Govt. property," and the disruption of Federal recruitment in central and eastern Kentucky. All this was much; but it was not enough, in the minds of his Richmond superiors, to offset his unauthorized departure in the first place, the misbehavior of his raiders wherever they went, and his second-day defeats at Mount Sterling and Cynthiana. Moreover, he now faced all his old problems, with only about half as many troops, and the confirmed displeasure, if not the downright enmity, of the Confederate War Department. It was fairly clear, in any case, that John Morgan had taken his last "ride," that his beloved home state had seen its last of him and his terrible men.

Sherman was pleased, but hardly surprised, by Morgan's failure. Indeed, aside from having work crews standing by to make quick repairs in case the Kentuckian broke through to damage the railroad below Louisville, he feared him so little that he had scarcely planned for his coming beyond warning local commanders to be on the lookout. The other raider was another matter. After telling his wife, "Forrest is a more dangerous man," the red-haired Ohioan added: "I am in hopes that an expedition sent out from Memphis about the first of June will give him full employment."

It certainly should have done at least that, preceded as it was by a top-to-bottom shakeup of department personnel, beginning with Major General Stephen Hurlbut, commander of the District of West Tennessee. A Shiloh veteran and prewar Republican politician, Hurlbut had high-placed friends — Lincoln himself had made him a brigadier within a month of Sumter — but Sherman, far from satisfied with the "marked timidity" of his attempts to keep Forrest out of the region this past year, replaced him, less than a week after the fall of Fort Pillow, with Major General Cadwallader C. Washburn, who also had lofty Washington connections, including his brother Elihu, Grant's congressional guardian angel. Washburn had shown aggressiveness at Vicksburg, and Sherman chose him for that quality, which he encouraged by sending him a new chief of cavalry who shared it, Brigadier General Samuel D. Sturgis.

Seasoned by combat in Missouri as well as in Virginia (where he had contributed at least one famous quotation to the annals of this war: "I don't care for John Pope one pinch of owl dung") Sturgis had graduated from West Point alongside Stonewall Jackson and George McClellan. That he was more akin militarily to the former than to the latter was demonstrated by the manner in which he took hold on arrival in late April. Forrest by then was returning to North Mississippi from his raid to the Ohio; Sturgis pursued him as far as Ripley, seventy-five miles southeast of Memphis, before turning back for lack of subsistence for his 6400-man column. "I regret very much that I could not have the pleasure of bringing you his hair," he wrote Sherman on his return to Tennessee, "but he is too great a plunderer to fight anything like an equal force, and we have to be satisfied with driving him from the state. He may turn on your communications... I rather think he will, but see no way to prevent it from this point and with this force."

In part — the remark about Forrest's hair, for example — this had a true aggressive ring, confirming the choice of Sturgis for the post he filled, but Sherman did not enjoy being told there was no way to keep the raider off his life line. His Georgia campaign had opened by then, and the farther he got from his starting point (Dalton to Resaca; across the Oostanaula to Kingston; then finally over the Etowah for the roundhouse swing through Dallas) the more vital that supply line became, and the more exposed it was to depredation. Concerned lest Forrest give Washburn the slip, he wired orders for the West Tennessee commander to launch "a threatening movement from Memphis," southeast into Mississippi, to prevent Forrest "from swinging over against my communications" in North Georgia or Middle Tennessee. Sturgis was to have charge of the expedition, but Washburn himself saw to the preparations, taking two full weeks to make certain nothing was omitted that might be needed, either in men or supplies or equipment. "The force sent out was in complete order," he later reported, "and consisted of some of our best troops. They were ordered to go in the lightest possible marching order, and to take only wagons for commissary stores and ammunition. They had a supply for twenty days. I saw to it personally that they lacked nothing to insure a successful campaign. The number of troops deemed necessary by General Sherman, as he telegraphed me, was 6000, but I sent 8000."

He sent in fact 8300: three brigades of infantry, totaling 5000, under Colonel William L. McMillen, the senior field officer in the district, and two of cavalry, totaling 3300, led by Brigadier General Benjamin Grierson, who had come into prominence a year ago with the 600-mile raid that distracted Vicksburg's defenders while Grant was beginning the final phase of the campaign that accomplished its surrender. In over-all charge of the two divisions, Sturgis also had 22 guns, of various calibers, and 250 wagons loaded with the twenty-day supply of food and ammunition. Grierson's troopers were equipped with repeating carbines of the latest model, which would give them a big advantage in firepower over their butternut opponents, and part at least of McMillen's command was armed with a zeal beyond the normal, one of his brigades being made up of Negro soldiers who had taken an oath to avenge Fort Pillow by showing Forrest's troops no quarter. "In case of an action in which they are successful," Hurlbut had stated on the eve of his departure, "it will be nearly impracticable to restrain them from retaliation." Now they and their white comrades, mounted and afoot, were on the march toward a confrontation with the man from whom they had sworn to exact vengeance.

They left Memphis on June 1, and as they set out from Collierville next day the rain began to fall, drenching men and horses and drowning fields and roads, much as it was doing 300 miles away in Georgia. Here, as there, the result was slow going, especially for the wagons lurching hub-deep through the mud. Five days of slogging about seven miles a day brought the marchers as far as Salem, a North Mississippi hamlet whose only historical distinction was that it had been Bedford Forrest's boyhood home. A disencumbered flying column of 400 troopers was detached there for a forty-mile ride due east to strike the Mobile & Ohio at Rienzi, a dozen miles below Corinth, in hopes that breaking the railroad at that point would delay the concentration, somewhere down the line, of the Confederates who no doubt by now had begun to gather in the path of the main column. Another three days of heavy-footed plodding, through June 8, covered another twenty miles of the nearly bottomless road to Ripley, where Sturgis had turned back from his pursuit of the plunderer a month ago.

Discouraged by the slowness of his march, as well as by the thought of all those graybacks probably gathering up ahead, he was inclined toward doing the same thing tomorrow, and that night he held a conference with his division commanders to get their views on the matter. Grierson felt much as his chief did. Delay had most likely enabled the rebs "to concentrate an overwhelming force against us," and he was impressed as well by "the utter hopelessness of saving our train or artillery in case of defeat." McMillen, on the other hand, declared that he "would rather go on and meet the enemy, even if we should be whipped, than to return again to Memphis without having met them." The key word here was *again*, Sturgis having turned back at this same point the month before. He thought it over and decided, on balance, that "it would be ruinous on all sides" — not least, it would seem, to the aggressive reputation that had won him his present post — "to return again without first meeting the enemy."

"Under these circumstances, and with a sad foreboding of the consequences," he afterwards summed up, "I determined to move forward, keeping my force as compact as possible and ready for action at all times."

His fears were better founded than he knew, although he was completely wrong about the odds he thought he faced. The Confederates were indeed preparing to oppose him, but it could scarcely be with an "overwhelming force," since the number of men available to the defenders was barely more than half as many as were in the blue column toiling toward them through the rain. On the day Sturgis left Memphis, June 1, Forrest had left Tupelo with 2200 troopers and six guns, bound at last for Middle Tennessee and a descent on Sherman's life line below Nashville. He was in North Alabama on June 3, preparing to cross the Tennessee River, when an urgent message from Stephen Lee summoned him back to meet Sturgis's newly developed threat to the department Lee had inherited from Polk. Forrest returned to Tupelo on June 5, the day the Federals reached his boyhood home fifty miles northwest. Uncertain whether they were headed for Corinth or Tupelo — the 400-man flying column, detached that day for the strike at Rienzi, contributed to the confusion — Lee told Forrest to dispose his men along the M. & O. between those two towns, ready to move in either direction, while he himself did what he could to get hold of more troops to help ward off the 8300-man blow, wherever it might land. His notion was that, if the enemy moved southward, the cavalry should retire toward Okolona, about twenty miles below Tupelo, in order to protect the Black Prairie region just beyond, where most of the subsistence for his department was grown and processed, and also to draw Sturgis as far as possible from his base of supplies and place of refuge in Memphis before giving him battle with whatever reinforcements had been rounded up by then. Lee made it clear before they parted, however, that Forrest was left to his own devices as to what should be done in the meantime, and Forrest took full advantage of the discretion thus allowed him.

He had at the time some 4300 troopers within reach: 2800 in Colonel Tyree Bell's brigade, which was part of Abraham Buford's division, and about 750 in each of two small brigades under Colonels Hylan Lyon and Edmund Rucker. While waiting for Sturgis to show his hand, Forrest spent the next two days posting these commands in accordance with Lee's instructions to cover both Tupelo and Corinth. Bell, with considerably better than half the available force, was sent to Rienzi, which he reached in time to drive off the 400 detached bluecoats before they did any serious damage to the railroad. Rucker and Lyon, with 1500 between them, moved to Booneville, nine miles south of Rienzi, accompanied by Captain John Morton's two four-gun batteries, all the artillery on hand. Forrest was there on June 8 when he received word that Sturgis was at Ripley, twenty miles away, and when he learned next morning that the mud-slathered Union column was continuing southeast, there was no longer any doubt that it was headed not for Corinth but for Tupelo, twelve miles below Guntown, a station on the M. & O. at the end of the road down which Sturgis was marching. A brigade remnant of 500 men under Colonel William A. Johnson arrived that day from Alabama, raising Forrest's strength to 4800. That was all he was likely to have for several days, but he figured it was enough for what he had in mind. He told Johnson to rest his troopers near Baldwyn, twenty miles down the track from Booneville, having decided to hit Sturgis, and hit him hard, before he got to Guntown.

In fact, he had already chosen his field of fight, twenty miles from Ripley and six miles short of the railroad — a timber-laced low plateau where the Ripley-Guntown road, on which the Federals were moving southeast, was intersected at nearly right angles by one from Booneville that ran southwest to Pontotoc — and when he learned that evening that Sturgis had called an overnight halt at Stubbs Farm, nine miles from the intended point of contact, his plan was complete. Orders went out to all units that night, June 9, and the march began before dawn next morning. Forrest led the way with his hundred-man escort company and Lyon's small Kentucky brigade; Rucker and Bell were to follow, along with Morton's guns, and Johnson would come in from the east. The result, that day, was the battle variously celebrated as Guntown, Tishomingo Creek, or Brice's Crossroads.

The enemy had close to a two-to-one advantage in men, as well as nearly three times as many guns, but Forrest believed that boldness and the nature of the terrain, which he knew well, would make up for the numerical odds he faced. "I know they greatly outnumber the troops I have at hand," he told Rucker, who rode with him in advance of his brigade, "but the road along which they will march is narrow and muddy; they will make slow progress. The country is densely wooded and the undergrowth so heavy that when we strike them they will not know how few men we have."

His companion might have pointed out, but did not, that the road they themselves were on — called the Wire Road because in early days, before the railroad, the telegraph line to New Orleans had run along it — was as muddy and as narrow as the one across the way. Moreover, all the Federals were within nine miles of the objective, while aside from Johnson's 500 Alabamians, seven miles away at Baldwyn, all the Confederates had twice as far to go or farther; Lyon, Rucker, and Morton had eighteen miles to cover, and Bell just over twenty-five. Forrest had thought of that as well, however, and here too he saw compensating factors, not only in the marching ability of his troopers, but also in the contrasting effect of the weather on their blue-clad adversaries. The rain had stopped and the rising sun gave promise that the day would be a scorcher.

"Their cavalry will move out ahead of their infantry," he explained, "and should reach the crossroads three hours in advance. We can whip their cavalry in that time. As soon as the fight opens they will send back to have the infantry hurried in. It is going to be hot as hell, and coming on the run for five or six miles, their infantry will be so tired out we will ride right over them."

Aside from the temperature estimate, which was open to question in the absence of any thermometer readings from hell, Rucker was to discover that this was practically a blow-by-blow account of what would follow; but the general quickly returned to present matters. "I want everything to move up as soon as possible," he said. "I will go ahead with Lyon and the escort and open the fight."

Sturgis rose at Stubbs Farm in a better frame of mind, encouraged by the letup of the rain and the prospect that a couple of days of mid-June heat would bake the roads dry, down through Tupelo and beyond. The flying column had returned from Rienzi the night before, and though their mounts were badly jaded the 400 troopers were doubly welcome as replacements for about the same number of "sick and worn-out men" he started back toward Memphis this morning in forty of the wagons his two divisions had eaten empty in the past nine days. These ailing bluecoats would miss a signal experience this hot June 10 at Brice's Crossroads, nine miles down the Guntown road, but their commander — round-faced and rather plump, Pennsylvania-born and a former Indian fighter, with a thick shock of curly hair, a trim mustache, and an abbreviated chin beard, he would be forty-two years old tomorrow: Forrest's age — did not know that, yet. All he knew, for the present, was "that it was impossible to gain any accurate or reliable information of the enemy and that it behooved us to move and act constantly as though in his presence."

This last, however, was precisely what he failed to do. Despite his previous resolution "to move forward, keeping my force as compact as possible and ready for action at all times," compassion for his weary foot soldiers led him to give them an extra couple of hours in camp to dry their clothes and get themselves in order for another hard day's march. Grierson and his troopers rode off for Guntown at 5.30 but McMillen's lead brigade did not set out till 7 o'clock, thus giving Forrest a full measure of the time he estimated he would need to "whip their cavalry" before the infantry "hurried up."

His plan, whose execution today would advance his growing reputation as "the Wizard of the Saddle," was for a battle in three stages: 1) holding attack, 2) main effort, and 3) pursuit. But Sturgis, riding with McMillen at the head of the infantry column, knew nothing of this — not even that Forrest was nearby — until shortly after 10 o'clock, when a courier from Grierson came pounding back with news that the cavalry was hotly engaged, some five miles down the road, with a superior hostile force; he had, he said, "an advantageous position," and could hold it "if the infantry was brought up promptly." Leaving orders for McMillen to proceed "as rapidly as possible without distressing the troops," Sturgis galloped ahead to examine the situation at first hand.

It did not look at all good from the rear, where a nearly mile-long causeway across a stretch of flooded bottomland led to and from a narrow bridge over Tishomingo Creek; "artillery and ambulances and led horses jammed the road," he observed, and when he reached Brice's about noon, another mile and a half toward Guntown, he found the cavalry hard pressed, fighting dismounted amid "considerable confusion." One brigade commander declared flatly that he "would have to fall back unless he received some support," while the other, according to Sturgis, was "almost demanding to be relieved." Grierson was more stalwart. Though the rebels were there "in large numbers, with double lines of skirmishers and heavy supports," he was proud to report that he and his rapid-firing troopers had "succeeded in holding our own and repulsing with great slaughter three distinct and desperate charges." The sun by now was past the overhead. How much longer he could hang on he did not say, but it could scarcely be for long unless he was reinforced, heavily and soon, by men from the infantry column toiling toward him through the mud and heat. Sturgis reacted promptly. With no further mention of concern about "distressing the troops," he sent word for McMillen to hurry his three brigades forward and save the day. "Make all haste," he told him, and followed this with a second urgent message: "Lose no time in coming up."

Grierson was wrong in almost everything he said, and Sturgis was fatally wrong in accepting his estimate of the situation. Those three "desperate charges," for example, had simply been feints, made by Forrest — a great believer in what he called "bulge" — to disguise the fact that his troopers, dismounted and fed piecemeal into the brush-screened line as soon as they came up, were badly outnumbered by those in the two blue brigades, who overlapped him on both flanks and had six pieces of horse artillery in action, unopposed, and four more in reserve. He opened the fight, as he had said he would do, by attacking with Lyon astride the Wire Road, then put Rucker and Johnson in on the left and right, when they arrived, for a second and a third attack to keep the Federals off balance while waiting for Morton's guns and the rest of his command to complete their marches from Booneville and Rienzi. "Tell Bell to move up fast and fetch all he's got," he told a staff major, who rode back to deliver the message.

It was just past 1 o'clock when this last and largest of his brigades came onto the field, close behind Morton; by which time, true to his schedule, Forrest had the enemy cavalry whipped.

Convinced, as he said then and later, that he had been "overwhelmed by numbers," Grierson was asking to have his division taken out of line, "as it was exhausted and well-nigh out of ammunition" for its rapid-firing carbines. McMillen rode up to the crossroads at that point, in advance of his lead brigade, and was dismayed to find that "everything was going to the devil as fast as it possibly could." Like Sturgis earlier, he threw caution to the winds. Though many of his troops had already collapsed from heat exhaustion on the hurried approach march, and though all were blown and in great distress from the savage midday, mid-June Mississippi sun, he sent peremptory orders for his two front brigades to come up on the double quick and restore the crumbling cavalry line before the rebels overran it.

They were hurrying to destruction, and hurrying needlessly at that; for just as they came into position, every bit as "tired out" as Forrest had predicted, a lull fell over the crossroad. It was brief, however, and lasted only long enough for the Confederate commander, now that all his troops were on the field, to mount and launch his first real assault of the day. Giving direction of the three brigades on the right to Buford, a Kentucky-born West Pointer two years his senior in age, he went in person to confer with Bell, whose newly arrived brigade comprised the left. This done, he came back to the right, checking his line along the way. In shirtsleeves because of the heat, with his coat laid over the pommel of his saddle, he "looked the very God of War," one soldier would remember, and as he rode among them on his big sorrel horse, saber in hand, he spoke to the dismounted troopers lying about for some rest in the blackjack thickets. "Get up, men," he told them. "I have ordered Bell to charge on the left. When you hear his guns, and the bugle sounds, every man must charge, and we will give them hell." Other things he said, then and later, went unrecorded. "I notice some writers on Forrest say he seldom cursed," one watcher was to recall. "Well, the fellow who writes that way was not where the 7th Tennessee was that day.... He would curse, then praise and then threaten to shoot us himself, if we were so afraid the Yankees might hit us."

Drawing rein at Morton's position, Forrest told him to double-shot four of his guns with canister and join the charge when the bugle sounded, then keep pace with the front rank as it advanced. Afterwards, the young artillerist, who had celebrated his twenty-first birthday on the field of Chickamauga, told his chief: "You scared me pretty badly when you pushed me up so close to their infantry and left me without protection. I was afraid they might take my guns." Forrest laughed. "Well, artillery is made to be captured," he said, "and I wanted to see them take yours."

But that was after the third stage ended, two days later; now the second, the main effort, was just beginning, and there was a grim struggle, much of it hand to hand, before the contest reached the climactic point at which Forrest judged the time had come to go all-out. Returning to the left, where he believed the resistance would be stiffest, he put an end to the thirty-minute lull by starting Bell's advance up the Guntown road. McMillen's second brigade was posted there, sturdy men from Indiana, Illinois, and Minnesota who, winded though they were from their sprint to reach the field, not only broke the gray attack but launched one of their own, throwing the Tennesseans into such confusion that Forrest had to dismount his escort troopers and lead them into the breach, firing pistols, to stop what had the makings of disaster. Over on the right, Buford too was finding the enemy stubborn, and had all he could do to keep up the pressure along his front. Finally, though, the pressure told. Orders came from Forrest — who fought this, as he did all his battles, "by ear" — that the time had come to "hit 'em on the ee-end." It was past 4 o'clock by now, and simultaneous attacks, around the flanks and into the rear of the Union left and right, made the whole blue line waver and cave in, first slowly, then with a rush.

"The retreat or rout began," in Forrest's words, or as Sturgis put it: "Order gave way to confusion and confusion to panic.... Everywhere the army now drifted toward the rear, and was soon altogether beyond control."

Fleeing past the two-story Brice house at the crossroads, the fugitives sought shelter back up the road they had run down, four hours ago, to reach the battle that now was lost. But conditions there were in some ways worse than those in what had been the front: especially along the causeway through the Tishomingo bottoms and on the railless bridge across the creek, the narrow spout of the funnel-shaped host of panicked men, who, as Sturgis said, "came crowding in like an avalanche from the battlefield." Morton's batteries had the range, and their execution was increased by the addition of four Federal guns, captured with their ammunition. Presently a wagon overturned on the high bridge and others quickly piled up behind it, creating what a retreating colonel described as "one indiscriminate mass of artillery, caissons, ambulances, and broken, disordered troops." Some escaped by leaping into the creek, swollen neck-deep by the rains, and wading to the opposite bank. But there was no safety there either. Though Sturgis had hoped to form a new line on the far side of the stream, the rebels were crossing so close in his rear that every attempt to make a stand only brought on a new stampede. The only thing that slowed the whooping graybacks was the sight of abandoned wagons, loaded with what one hungry pursuer called "fresh, crisp hardtack and nice, thin side bacon." They would pause for plunder, wolf it down, and then come on for more.

This continued, well past sundown, to within three miles of last night's bivouac, where there was another and still worse stretch of miry road across one of the headwater prongs of the Hatchie River. It was night now and the going was hard, one officer noted, "in consequence of abandoned vehicles, drowned and dying horses and mules, and the depth of the mud." Despairing of getting what was left of his shipwrecked train through this morass, Sturgis went on to Stubbs Farm, where he was approached before midnight by Colonel Edward Bouton, whose Negro brigade had served as train guard during the battle and had therefore suffered less than the other two infantry commands had done.

"General, for God's sake don't let us give up so," he exclaimed.

But Sturgis, quite unstrung, was at his wit's end. "What can we do?" he said, not really asking.

Bouton wanted ammunition with which to hold Forrest in check, on the far side of the bottoms, while the remaining guns and wagons were being snaked across to more solid ground beyond. Sturgis was too far in despair, however, to consider this or any other proposal involving resistance. Besides, he had no ammunition to give.

"For God's sake," he broke out, distraught by the events of this longest day in his life and the prospect of a sad birthday tomorrow, "if Mr Forrest will let me alone, I will let him alone! You have done all you could, and more than was expected.... Now all you can do is to save yourselves."

Mr Forrest, as Sturgis so respectfully styled the man he had said a month ago was "too great a plunderer to fight anything like an equal force," had no intention of letting him alone so long as there was profit to be gained from pressing the chase. Heaving the wreckage off the Tishomingo bridge and into the creek, along with the dead and dying animals, he continued to crowd the rear of the retreating bluecoats. "Keep the skeer on 'em," he told his troopers, remounted now, and they did just that, past sunset and on into twilight and full night. "[Sturgis] attempted the destruction of his wagons, loaded with ammunition and bacon," Forrest would report, "but so closely was he pursued that many of them were saved without injury, although the road was lighted for some distance." Furious at this incendiary treatment of property he considered his already, he came upon a group of his soldiers who had paused, still mounted, to watch the flames. "Don't you see the damned Yankees are burning my wagons?" he roared. "Get off your horses and throw the burning beds off." Much toasted hardtack and broiled bacon was saved that way, until finally, some time after 8 o'clock, "It being dark and my men and horses requiring rest" — they did indeed, having been on the go, marching and fighting, for better than sixteen hours — "I threw out an advance to follow slowly and cautiously after the enemy, and ordered the command to halt, feed, and rest."

By 1 a.m. he had his troopers back in the saddle and hard on the equipment-littered trail. Within two hours they reached the Hatchie bottoms, where they came upon the richest haul of all. Despite Bouton's plea, Sturgis had ordered everything movable to proceed that night to Stubbs Farm and beyond, abandoning what was left of his train, all his non-walking wounded, and another 14 guns, all that remained of the original 22 except for four small mountain howitzers that had seen no action anyhow. This brought Forrest's total acquisition to 18 guns, 176 wagons, 1500 rifles, 300,000 rounds of small-arms ammunition, and much else. He himself lost nothing, and though he had 492 killed and wounded in the battle — a figure larger in proportion than the 617 casualties he inflicted — his capture of more than 1600 men on the retreat brought the Federal loss to 2240, nearly five times his own. Many of the enemy, especially from Bouton's brigade, which had the misfortune to bring up the rear and suffered heavily in the process, were picked up here in the Hatchie bottoms. A Tennessee sergeant later recalled the scene. "Somewhere between midnight and day, we came to a wide slough or creek bottom; it was miry and truly the slough of despair and despond to the Yanks. Their artillery and wagons which had heretofore escaped capture were now bogged down and had to be abandoned. This slough was near kneedeep in mud and water, with logs lying here and there. On top of every log were Yanks perched as close as they could be, for there were more Yanks than logs." They put him in mind "of chickens at roost," he said, but added: "We who were in front were ordered to pay no attention to prisoners. Those in the rear would look after that."

Four miles short of Ripley at dawn, the pursuers came upon a rear-guard remnant, which Forrest said "made only a feeble and ineffectual resistance." He drove its members back on the town, where they were reinforced and rallied briefly, only to scatter when attacked. "From this place," Forrest's report continued, "the enemy offered no organized resistance, but retreated in the most complete disorder, throwing away guns, clothing, and everything calculated to impede his flight." Beyond Ripley he left the direct pursuit to Buford and swung onto a roundabout adjoining road with Bell's brigade, intending to cut the Federals off at Salem. But that was a miscalculation. Buford pressed them so hard the interception failed; the blue column cleared the hamlet before Forrest got there around sundown. He called off the chase at that point and turned back to scour the woods and brush for fugitives, gather up his spoils, and give his men and mounts some rest from their famous victory, which would be studied down the years, in war colleges here and abroad, as an example of what a numerically inferior force could accomplish once it got what its commander called "the bulge" on an opponent, even one twice its size.

There was no rest, though, for Sturgis and his men, who continued to flee in their ignorance that they were no longer pursued except by rumors of graybacks hovering on their flank. "On we went, and ever on," a weary colonel was to write, "marching all that day and all that interminable [second] night. Until half past ten the next morning, when we reached Collierville and the railroad, reinforcements and supplies, we marched, marched, marched, without rest, without sleep, without food." At any rate they made excellent time. The march down had taken more than a week, but the one back took only a night and a day and a night. In Collierville that morning (June 12; Morgan's troopers were scattering from Cynthiana, 300 miles northeastward in Kentucky) the wait for the train that would take them on to the outskirts of Memphis, seventeen miles away, was in some ways even harder than the 90-mile forced march had been. Relieved of a measure of their fright, they now knew in their bones how tired they were and how thoroughly they had been whipped. An Ohio regimental commander reported that, in the course of their wait beside the railroad track, his troops "became so stiffened as to require assistance to enable them to walk. Some of them, too foot-sore to stand upon their feet, crawled upon their hands and knees to the cars."

Sturgis's hurts were mainly professional, being inflicted on his career. Back in Memphis, amid rumors that he had been drunk on the field — a conclusion apparently reached by way of the premise that no sober man could be so roundly trounced — he put the disaster in the best light he could manage. Winding up his official report with "regret that I find myself called upon to record a defeat," he added: "Yet there is some consolation in knowing that the army fought nobly while it did fight, and only yielded to overwhelming numbers." Just over 8000 troops had been thrown into a rout and driven headlong for nearly a hundred miles by just under 5000, but he persisted in claiming (and even believing, so persuasive were Forrest's tactics) that the odds had been the other way around, and longer. "The strength of the enemy is variously estimated by my most intelligent officers at from 15,000 to 20,000 men."

So he said; but vainly, so far as concerned the salvation of his career. For him, the war ended at Brice's Crossroads. Despite the board's finding no substance in the charge that he had been drunk, either in battle or on the birthday retreat, Sturgis spent the rest of the conflict on the sidelines, awaiting orders that did not come. Disconsolate as he was, he only shared what those who had served under him were feeling. Though in time their aching muscles would find relief and their wounds would heal, the inward scars of their drubbing would remain. "It is the fate of war that one or the other side should suffer defeat," a cavalry major who survived the battle was to write, more than twenty years later. "But here there was more. The men were cowed, and there pressed upon them a sense of bitter humiliation, which rankles after nearly a quarter of a century has passed."

Sherman was disappointed, of course, but he was also inclined to give Sturgis credit for having achieved his "chief object," which had been "to hold Forrest there [in Mississippi] and keep him off our [rail] road." There was truth in a participating colonel's observation that the expedition had been "sent out as a tub to Forrest's whale," and though the price turned out to be high, both in men and equipment, it was by no means exorbitant, considering the alternative. Learning that the raider had been in North Alabama, poised for a strike across the Tennessee River before Sturgis lured him back, the red-haired Ohioan wired the district commander instructions designed to discourage a return: "You may send notice to Florence that if Forrest invades Tennessee from that direction, the town will be burned, and if it occurs you will remove the inhabitants north of the Ohio River, and burn the town" — adding, as if by afterthought: "and Tuscumbia also."

He would send both places up in smoke, along with much else, if it would help to keep "that devil Forrest" off his life line. But that was only an interim deterrent. He had it in mind to follow through, as soon as possible, with a second expedition into northern Mississippi, stronger and better led, to profit by the shortcomings of the first. "Forrest is the very devil," he declared, "and I think has got some of our troops under cower." He proposed to correct this in short order. A. J. Smith's three divisions were on their way back from service up Red River with Banks, hard-handed veterans whose commanders had been closely observed by Sherman in the course of the fighting last year around Vicksburg. He had intended either to bring them to Georgia as reinforcements or else to send them against Mobile; but now, he notified Washington, he had what he considered a better, or in any case a more urgent, use for them. "I will order them to make up a force and go out and follow Forrest to the death, if it costs 10,000 lives and breaks the Treasury. There will never be peace in Tennessee till Forrest is dead."

★ ★ ★

Up in Washington, news of Morgan's defeat was about as welcome as that of Forrest's victory was irksome, although neither of these side shows of the main event provided much more than a brief diversion from the prevalent fret over Grant and Sherman — what their progress against Lee and Johnston meant, if anything, and above all what it was costing them in casualties per mile. These two, between them, would win or lose, if not the war, then in any event the election in November; which perhaps was the same thing. The Democrats would convene in August to nominate a candidate who would run on the issue of ending the conflict by declaring peace, whatever accommodations might be required by their late fellow countrymen down South, and it was generally agreed that the Republicans could not survive a prolongation of the bloody three-year stalemate through the five months between now and the election.

Lincoln had declared himself "only a passenger" on the juggernaut of war, but his hand was still on the tiller of the ship of state and he intended to keep it there if he could. Public attention was mainly fixed on the fighting in Virginia, where the casualties had been awesome from the start, and he tried to offset the civilian reaction by stressing his admiration for Grant's refusal to be distracted by the bloodshed and by recommending that his listeners do likewise. "I think, without knowing the particulars of the plans of General Grant, that what has been accomplished is of more importance than at first appears," he told a crowd that came to serenade him on hearing that the Army of the Potomac had resumed its southward march after two days of cataclysmic battle in the Wilderness. "I believe I know — and am especially grateful to know — that General Grant has not been jostled in his purposes, that he has made all his points, and today he is on his line as he purposed before he moved.... I commend you to keep yourselves in the same tranquil mood that is characteristic of that brave and loyal man."

Tranquillity was easier to prescribe than to attain. Hemmed in as he was by cares from all directions, including the importunities of incessant office seekers — "Too many pigs for the tits," he said wryly — Lincoln found the sight of the wounded, returning in their thousands from where he had sent them to get hit, a heavy burden on his spirit. "Look yonder at those poor fellows," he said one day when a long line of ambulances creaked past his halted carriage. "I cannot bear it. This suffering, this loss of life is dreadful." It was during this dark time that a White House visitor watched him pace the dawn-gray corridors in his nightshirt and long wrapper, hands clasped behind his back, head bent low, and with black rings under his eyes from loss of sleep.

By no means all the strain was of a purely military nature. While it was true that some events which normally would have awakened a sharp sense of national loss were muted by the uproar of the guns — the death of Nathaniel Hawthorne, for example, was barely noted amid the excitement over Grant's shift from Spotsylvania to the North Anna — others were so closely tied to the conflict that they stood out in stark relief against its glare. One was the so-called Gold Hoax, perpetrated on May 18, the day before Hawthorne died, by Joseph Howard, the journalist who three years ago had written of Lincoln's furtive passage through Baltimore in a "Scotch cap and long military cloak" to avoid assassination on the way to his inauguration. At 4 a.m. that morning Howard distributed anonymously to all the New York papers a bogus proclamation, complete with the forged signature of the President, fixing May 26 "as a day of fasting, humiliation and prayer," and calling for an additional draft of 400,000 men required by "the situation in Virginia, the disaster at Red River, the delay at Charleston, and the general state of the country."

Defeat, it seemed from the doleful tone of the document, was just around the corner. Only two papers, the *New York World* and the *Journal of Commerce,* were on the street with the story before the forgery was detected; bulletins of denial promptly quashed its effect on the gold market, defeating the scheme. With Lincoln's approval, Stanton moved swiftly in reprisal, padlocking the offices of both papers and clapping their editors into military arrest, along with Howard, who was soon sniffed out. Within three days the editors were released and their papers resumed publication; even Howard was freed within about three months, on the plea that he was "the only spotted child of a large family" and had been guilty of nothing worse than "the hope of making some *money.*" No real harm was done, except to increase the public's impression of Stanton — and, inferentially, his chief — as a tyrant, an enemy of free speech and the press. One witness declared, however, that the affair "angered Lincoln more than almost any other occurrence of the war period." His ire was aroused in part by the fact that the country's reaction to the bogus proclamation obliged him to defer issuing an order he had prepared only the day before, calling, in far less doleful words, for the draft of 300,000 additional troops.

They were likely to be needed sooner, not later, at the rate men were falling in Grant's attempt to overrun Lee and Sherman's to outflank Johnston. And on top of these losses, before the month was out, there occurred a hemispheric provocation that seemed likely to bring on a second war, this one with a foreign power: France. Following up his occupation of Mexico City a year ago, purportedly to collect a national debt, Napoleon III landed his puppet Maximilian, whom he had persuaded to assume the title of Emperor of Mexico, at Vera Cruz, May 28; the Austrian archduke and his wife Charlotte were on their way to the capital, where they would reign over an empire designed to stand, with the help of still more French soldiers than the 35,000 already sent, as a bulwark against Anglo-Saxon expansion in Central and South America. This continued defiance of the Monroe Doctrine was hard for Lincoln to abide, but not so hard that he did not manage to do so, deferring action until he could afford to give it his full attention, preferably with a reunited country at his back; "One war at a time" was as much his policy now as it had been on the occasion of his near confrontation with England over the *Trent* affair, more than two years ago.

Besides, a domestic concern of a far more urgent nature than any posed by the latter day Napoleon — specifically, the double-barreled problem of getting renominated and reëlected — was hard upon him at the time. Three days after Maximilian stepped ashore at Vera Cruz, the radicals of Lincoln's own party, aware that they lacked the strength to dominate the regular Republican convention at Baltimore on June 7, called a convention of their own in Cleveland on May 31, one week earlier, and by acclamation nominated John C. Frémont as their candidate for President in the November election.

For some time Jacobinic disaffection had been growing, especially among New England abolitionists and German-born extremists in Missouri, who resented Lincoln's "manifest tendency toward temporary expedients," and complained bitterly that he had "*words* for the ultras and *acts* for the more conservative." Now their opposition had taken this form; they were out in the open, determined to bring him down. Frémont, the party's first presidential candidate in 1856 — he had polled a respectable 1,300,000 votes, as compared to James Buchanan's 1,800,000 — accepted the nomination "with a view to prevent the misfortune of [Lincoln's] reëlection," which he said "would be fatal to the country." Glad to be back in the public eye, after nearly two years of promoting railroads in New York State, the Pathfinder looked forward to a vigorous campaign. The trouble was that his most influential backers had to avoid giving him open support, for fear of committing political suicide, and this had been evident at the convention in Ohio, which one critic described as a "magnificent fizzle," attended mainly by "disappointed contractors, sore-head governors, and Copperheads."

Thousands had been expected, but only about four hundred showed up. Informed of this, Lincoln reached for the Bible on his desk, thumbed briefly through I Samuel until he found what he was seeking, then read it out: *And every one that was in distress, and every one that was in debt, and every one that was discontented, gathered themselves unto him; and he became a captain over them: and there were with him about four hundred men.*

A joke had its uses, particularly as therapy for a spirit as gloomy by nature as this one, but the million-odd votes Frémont might poll in November were no laughing matter. Before then, there would probably be ways to lure the Jacobins back into the fold. Some piece of radical legislation hanging fire in Congress for lack of Executive pressure, say, could be put through; or the scalp of some Administration stalwart they had singled out as an enemy could be yielded up. Meantime, however, the thing to do, if possible, was to solidify what was left of the party and broaden its base to attract outsiders, meaning those hard-war Democrats who would be repelled by the peace plank their leaders were sure to include in the platform at their Chicago convention in late August, nearly three months after the Republicans gathered next week in Baltimore.

Lincoln of course did not attend, despite the proximity to Washington; nor did David Davis, his manager at the convention four years ago and now a Supreme Court justice. Not since Andrew Jackson's reëlection, thirty-two years ago, had any man been chosen to serve a second term as President, although several had tried and failed to get renominated and Van Buren had even succeeded, only to be defeated at the polls. But Davis foresaw no difficulty requiring his considerable talent for maneuver, so far as the place at the top of the ticket was concerned, and he was right; there was no real opposition, only some wistful talk about "the salutary one-term principle," and no trouble. On the first ballot, Missouri's delegates rocked the boat a bit by casting their 22 votes for Grant, but switched when all the other 484 went to Lincoln, whose nomination thus was made unanimous. This done, the convention was free to turn to the business of solidification and broadening; which could be done, at least in part — so it was hoped — by the selection of the right man to replace Vice President Hannibal Hamlin, who not only lacked luster but also had sided with the radicals on most of the whipsaw issues before Congress.

A beginning had been made in this regard, first by changing the name of the party to National Union, which helped to reduce the onus of sectionalism, and then by adopting a platform that had, as one observer put it, "a radical flavor but no Radical planks." Appealing for unity in continuing the national effort to put down the rebellion, it called for the extirpation of slavery as the root cause of the war, promised to visit upon all rebels and traitors "the punishment due to their crimes," thanked soldiers and civilians alike for their sacrifices over the past three years, and wound up by favoring the encouragement of immigration and the construction of a transcontinental railroad. Now came the vice-presidential nomination, and though Lincoln kept aloof from the contest, not wanting to anger the friends of disappointed candidates — "Convention must judge for itself," he indorsed a letter requesting a statement of his wishes as to the contest for second place on the ticket — he had confidants on the scene, including his secretary Nicolay and Henry J. Raymond, editor of the friendly *New York Times* and chairman of the platform committee. When Raymond saw to it that the name of Andrew Johnson, former senator and now military governor of Tennessee, was presented at a critical juncture, scarcely anyone failed to see that here was the best possible way of strengthening the ticket by giving simultaneous recognition to the claims of loyal men from the South, especially the border states, as well as to War Democrats all across the land. Johnson was both, and with an outburst of enthusiasm so vociferous that one delegate later testified that he "involuntarily looked up to see if the roof were lifted," his nomination too was made unanimous.

Lincoln learned informally of the outcome that afternoon, when he happened to walk over to the War Department and was congratulated as he entered the telegraph office. "What! Am I renominated?" he exclaimed, smiling, and when the operator showed him a confirming telegram his first thought was of his wife: "Send it over to the Madam. She will be more interested than I am."

He perhaps wanted to brace her for things to come, and they were not long in coming. Next day the *New York World*, back on the streets after being shut down for its unwitting share in the Gold Hoax three weeks ago, served notice that this was to be the bitterest of campaigns. Commenting on the nominations of Lincoln and Johnson — who like his running mate was a self-made man, having started out as a tailor before he studied law and entered politics — the *World* clucked its tongue over the come-down the national tone had suffered with the selection by the opposition party of this ungracious pair of candidates for the two most honored posts in all the land. "The age of statesmen is gone," the lead editorial lamented; "the age of rail-splitters and tailors, of buffoons, boors, and fanatics, has succeeded.... In a crisis of the most appalling magnitude, requiring statesmanship of the highest order, the country is asked to consider the claims of two ignorant, boorish, third-rate backwoods lawyers, for the highest situations in the government. Such nominations, in such a conjecture, are an insult to the common-sense of the people. God save the Republic!"

Lincoln hoped God would, but he was modest in his judgment of why he had been chosen to compete again for the task of serving as God's chief helper in the search for that salvation. "I do not allow myself to suppose that [the delegates] have concluded to decide that I am either the greatest or best man in America," he replied to formal congratulations which presently followed, "but rather they have concluded it is not best to swap horses while crossing the river, and have further concluded that I am not so poor a horse that they might not make a botch of it in trying to swap."

Renomination was only the first, and much the lower, of the two formal hurdles to be cleared if he was to retain his post. The second was reëlection, and that would be a far more difficult matter, requiring not only a great deal of skill in maneuvering his way along the thorny path of politics — skill, that is, such as he had just shown while skimming the first hurdle — but also a great deal of ability on the part of his hand-picked commanders in the field. In short, they would have to convince the public that he and they could win the war; otherwise, neither he nor the war would continue. Up to now, whatever admiration he might express for their refusal to be "jostled," their progress had been made at a price the voters were likely to find excessive, particularly if they were obliged to continue paying it over the course of the next five months. Even as the delegates converged on Baltimore, Grant was engaged in the grisly and belated task of burying his dead at Cold Harbor — a position McClellan had reached two years ago, the opposition press was pointing out, with the loss of less than a tenth as many soldiers — and Sherman, after his fruitless roundhouse swing through Dallas, was just getting back astride the railroad at Big Shanty, having also suffered checks about as abrupt, though not as bloody, along the way at New Hope Church and Pickett's Mill. As a result, in his continuing attempt to bolster national morale, Lincoln was reduced to the necessity of making what he could of such minor victories as Cynthiana, which at least disposed of John Morgan for a season, more or less.

That was on the Sunday ending the week of the Republican convention, and one week later there occurred another side-show triumph which more or less disposed of another Confederate raider; one even more famous, or infamous, than Morgan.

★ ★ ★

Sunday, June 12; U.S.S. *Kearsarge,* a thousand-ton sloop named for one of New Hampshire's rugged mountains, was anchored off the Dutch coast, in the mouth of the River Scheldt near Flushing, when her skipper, Captain John A. Winslow, received word from his government's minister in Paris that the Confederate cruiser *Alabama,* which had eluded him throughout a year-long search of European waters, had steamed into Cherbourg the day before to discharge prisoners, take on coal, and perhaps refit. If he hurried, the telegram said, she might still be there when he arrived.

Winslow hurried. Firing a gun to recall his men on shore, he had the *Kearsarge* under weigh within two hours. Two days later he entered Cherbourg harbor, three hundred miles to the west, and there "lying at anchor in the roads" was the rebel vessel, just as he had prayed she would be. He stopped engines and lay to, looking her over and being in turn looked over; which done, he left to assume a position in the English Channel, beyond the three-mile limit required by international law, for intercepting her when she ventured out. He took precautions against a sudden night attack, knowing the enemy to be tricky, but his principal fear was that the raider might slip past him in the dark and thus avoid the fate he had in mind for her.

He need not have worried on that score, he discovered next day when the American vice consul sent him a message just received from the skipper of the *Alabama:* "My intention is to fight the *Kearsarge* as soon as I can make the necessary arrangements. I hope these will not detain me more than until tomorrow evening, or after the morrow morning at furthest. I beg she will not depart before I am ready to go out.... I have the honor to be, respectfully, your obedient servant, *R. Semmes*, Captain."

Winslow made no reply to this except to maintain station beyond the breakwater; which, after all, was answer enough, and spared him moreover the loss of dignity involved in exchanging cards, as it were, with a "pirate" who by now had captured, burned, or ransomed 83 U.S. merchant vessels, worth more than five million dollars, and sunk the heavier gunboat *Hatteras* in short order. Raphael Semmes, for his part, gave all his attention to trimming ship, drilling his gun crews, and otherwise preparing to meet the challenge extended by the *Kearsarge* when she steamed into the harbor, looked him over from stem to stern, then turned with the same cool insolence and steamed back out again to await his response, if any, to the insult. "The combat will no doubt be contested and obstinate," he wrote in his journal that night, "but the two ships are so evenly matched that I do not feel at liberty to decline it. God defend the right, and have mercy upon the souls of those who fall, as many of us must."

Fame aside — for Winslow had none whatever, and the *Kearsarge* had never been within gunshot of a foe; whereas Semmes and the *Alabama* were better known around the world than any other sailor or vessel afloat — the two warships and their captains were indeed quite evenly matched. Messmates for a time in the Mexican War, both men were southern-born, the Confederate in Maryland, Winslow farther south in North Carolina; Semmes was fifty-five, his opponent less than two years younger, and both had close to forty years of naval service, having received appointments as midshipmen in their middle teens. Alike as they were in their histories up to the outbreak of the current war, they were altogether different in looks. Winslow, going blind in his right eye, was rather heavy-set and balding, with a compensating ruff of gray-shot whiskers round his jaw, while Semmes was tall and slender, with a full head of hair, a tuft of beard at his lower lip, and a fantastical mustache twisted to needle points beyond the outline of his face; "Old Beeswax," his men called him.

Conversely, it was not in their histories, which were about as mutually different as could be, but in their physical attributes that the two ships were alike. Both were three-masted and steam-propelled, just over two hundred feet in length and a thousand tons in weight. *Kearsarge* had a complement of 163, *Alabama* about a dozen less. The Federal carried seven guns, the Confederate eight — though this implied advantage was deceptive, mainly because of a pair of 11-inch Dahlgrens mounted on pivots along the center line of the *Kearsarge*, which, combined with the 32-pounders on each flank, enabled her to throw a 365-pound broadside, port or starboard. *Alabama*'s heaviest guns were an 8-inch smoothbore and a 7-inch Blakely rifle, also pivot-mounted, so that, in combination with three 32-pounders on each flank, her broadside came to 264 pounds, a hundred less than her adversary's. Two other disadvantages she had, both possibly dire. One was the state of her ammunition, which had not been replenished since she was commissioned, nearly two years ago; percussion caps had lately been failing to explode the shells, whose powder had been weakened by exposure to various climates on most of the seven seas. The other disadvantage had to do with the vessel's maneuverability and speed. Entering Cherbourg harbor, Semmes declared, she was like "the weary foxhound, limping back after a long chase, footsore and longing for quiet and repose." He had intended to put her in dry dock and give all aboard a two-month holiday; her bottom, badly fouled, needed scraping and recoppering, and her boilers had begun to leak at the seams. *Kearsarge*, on the other hand, though nine months older, had been refitted only three months ago and was in trim shape for the contest. Semmes, however, had confidence in his crew, which he affectionately referred to as "a precious set of rascals," his Blakely rifle, which not only had more range but also provided greater accuracy than did Winslow's outsized Dahlgrens, and his luck, which had never failed him yet.

Concern for this last but by no means least of the things in which he put his trust caused him to defer the promised action three days beyond the "morrow morning at furthest" he had fixed in his Wednesday note begging Winslow not to depart. He wanted to fight on Sunday, considering that his lucky day. It was a Sunday when he ran the *Sumter*, his first raider, past the Union gauntlet below New Orleans, out of the mouth of the Mississippi and into the Gulf of Mexico to begin his career as the scourge of Yankee commerce; a Sunday off the Azores, back in August '62, when he christened the *Alabama*, and a Sunday when he sank the *Hatteras*, as well as many of the other prizes he had taken in the course of the past three years.

His crew found the waiting hard, being anxious for the duel and the shore leave that would follow, but Semmes and his officers kept them busy. They cleaned and oiled the guns and other weapons, including cutlasses and pikes, sorted powder and shot from the magazines and laid them out in relays, took down the light spars, disposed of top hamper, and stoppered the standing rigging. They polished brasswork and holystoned the decks as for a ball, and while they worked they roared out a chantey a British seaman composed for the occasion:

> *We're homeward bound, homeward bound,*
> *And soon shall stand on English ground.*
> *But ere that English land we see*
> *We first must fight the Kearsargee!*

Such work continued through Saturday, June 18, when Semmes, aware that "the issue of combat is always uncertain," put ashore four sacks containing 4700 gold sovereigns, the ransom bonds of ten ships he had released for lack of space for their crews aboard the *Alabama*, and the large collection of chronometers taken from his victims, which he periodically wound by way of keeping tally or counting coup. After notifying the port authorities that he would be steaming out next morning, he went ashore for Mass, then came back and turned in early as an example for his officers and men, who did so too, despite many invitations to dine that night in Cherbourg with admirers.

Sunday dawned bright and nearly cloudless, cool for June, with a calm sea and a mild westerly breeze to clear the battle smoke away. After a leisurely breakfast, the crew weighed anchor at 9.45 and headed out, cheered by crowds along the mole and in the upper windows of houses affording a view of the Channel and the *Kearsarge*, still on station beyond the breakwater. News of the impending duel had been in all the papers for the past three days and excursion trains had brought so many spectators from Paris and other cities that there was no room left in the hotels; many sportsmen-excursionists had slept on the docks, as if at the entrance to a stadium on the night before a game between archrivals. They fluttered handkerchiefs and cheered, some waving small Confederate flags hawked by vendors along with spyglasses and camp stools. "Vivent les Confederates!" they cried, looking down at the trim and polished raider, all of whose sailors were dressed in their Sunday best except the gun crews, who were stripped to the waist, like athletes indeed, and stood about on decks that had been sanded to keep them from slipping in their blood when the contest opened. "Vivent les Confederates!" the crowd shrilled, flourishing its home-team pennants triumphantly when the *Kearsarge*, seeing the *Alabama* emerge from around the western end of the breakwater, turned suddenly and steamed away northeastward, as if in unpremeditated flight.

Semmes knew better: knew, indeed, that this maneuver signified that his adversary meant to give him the fight-to-a-finish he was seeking. Engaged in reading the Sunday service when a yardarm watchman sang out the warning, "She's coming out and she's headed straight for us!" Winslow closed the prayer book, ordered the drum to beat to quarters, and brought his ship about in a run for bluer water, his intention being to lure the rebel well beyond the three-mile limit, inside which she could take sanctuary in case she was disabled. This applied as well to the *Kearsarge*, of course, but Winslow was thinking of punishment he would inflict, rather than of damage he might suffer; his aim was not just to cripple, but to kill.

The warning had been given at 10.20; at 10.40, some seven miles out, he once more came about and bore down on the *Alabama*, just over two miles away, wanting to bring his two big Dahlgrens within range of his adversary.

Semmes held his course, closing fast. Resplendent in a new gray uniform, long-skirted and with a triple row of bright brass buttons down the breast, epaulets and polished sword making three fierce glints of sunlight, he had had all hands piped aft as soon as he cleared the breakwater, then mounted a gun carriage to deliver his first speech since setting out from the Azores. "Officers and seamen of the *Alabama!*" he declaimed, pale but calm behind the fantastical mustache whose spike-tips quivered as he spoke. "You have, at length, another opportunity of meeting the enemy — the first that has been presented to you since you sank the *Hatteras*.... The name of your ship has become a household word wherever civilization extends. Shall that name be tarnished by defeat? The thing is impossible! Remember that you are in the English Channel, the theater of so much of the naval glory of our race, and that the eyes of all Europe are at this moment upon you. The flag that floats over you is that of a young Republic who bids defiance to her enemies, whenever and wherever found; show the world that you know how to uphold it. Go to your quarters!" Having said as much, he set the example, while the crew still cheered, by taking station on the horseblock abreast the mizzenmast, a vantage point from which he could see and be seen by the enemy throughout the fight to come.

Watch in hand, he waited until there was barely a mile between the two ships bearing down on each other, then at 10.57 turned to his executive, Lieutenant John Kell, a six-foot two-inch Georgian who, like himself, was a veteran of the old navy: "Are you ready, Mr Kell?" Kell said he was. "Then you may open fire at once, sir."

The Blakely roared. Its 100-pound shell raised a sudden geyser, well short of the target, and was followed within two minutes by another, which, overcorrected, went screaming through the Federal's rigging. By now the other guns had joined, but their shots too were high, fired without proper calculation of the reduction of space between the rapidly closing vessels. Not until the range was down to half a mile did Winslow return fire, sheering to bring his starboard battery to bear. All the shots fell short, but Semmes had to port his helm sharply to keep from being raked astern. He succeeded, though at the cost of having *Kearsarge* close the range. As the Confederate swung back to starboard, Winslow followed suit and the two warships began to describe a circle, steaming clockwise around a common center and firing at each other across the half-mile diameter.

Alabama drew first blood with a shell that exploded on the Union quarterdeck and knocked out three of the after Dahlgren's crew. Then came what Semmes had prayed for, ashore at church last night. A shell from the Blakely struck and lodged itself in the sternpost of the *Kearsarge*. But as he watched through his telescope, awaiting the explosion that would signal the end of the enemy vessel — "Splendid! Splendid!" he exclaimed from his perch on the horseblock — the long moment passed with no sign of smoke or flame in that vital spot. The projectile, a dud, accomplished nothing except to make the helmsman's job a little harder by binding the rudder, which was already set to starboard anyhow. *Alabama*'s gunners kept hard at it, firing fast while straining for another, luckier hit.

Winslow's gunnery was methodical by contrast, and a good deal more effective; he would get off a total of 173 shots in the course of the engagement, only about half as many as Semmes, but the accuracy in both cases, a tally of hits and misses would show, was in inverse ratio to the rate of fire. As the two sloops continued their wheeling fight, churning along in one another's wake, a three-knot current bore them westward so that they described a series of overlapping circles, each a little tighter than the one before, with the result that the range was constantly shortened, from half a mile on the first circle, down to little more than a quarter-mile on the seventh, which turned out to be the last.

From the outset, once the blue crews got on target, the damage inflicted by the 11-inchers was prodigious; *Alabama* was repeatedly hit and hulled by the 135½-pound shells aimed at her waterline by the Dahlgrens, in accordance with Winslow's orders, while the 32-pounders swept her decks. The combined effect was devastating: as for example when a projectile breached the 8-inch smoothbore's port, disemboweling the first man it struck, then plunging on to mangle eighteen others when it blew. Survivors and replacements cleared away the wounded and heaved the corpses overboard, but resumption of fire had to wait for a shovel to be used to scrape up the slippery gobs of flesh and splinters of bone; only then, with the deck re-sanded, could the crew secure a proper footing for its work. Meantime, Semmes had seen the most discouraging thing he had encountered since the shot lodged in the enemy sternpost failed to explode. Observing that shells of all sizes were bouncing ineffectively off the Federal's sides, like so many tennis balls, he told Kell to switch to solids for better penetration. Yet these too either splintered or rebounded, and it was not until after the battle that he found out that the cause lay in anything more than the weakened condition of his powder. *Kearsarge* was armored along her midriff with 120 fathoms of sheet chain, suspended from her scuppers to below her waterline, bolted down and boxed out of sight with one-inch planking. Indignant at the belated disclosure that his adversary was "iron-clad," Semmes protested that this violation of the code duello had produced an unfair fight. "It was the same thing as if two men were to go out and fight a duel, and one of them, unknown to the other, were to put on a suit of mail under his outer garment."

However true or false the analogy — and Old Beeswax, one of the trickiest skippers ever to prowl the sea lanes, was scarcely in a position to protest the use of a stratagem that had been common in all navies ever since Farragut employed it, more than two years ago, to run past the forts below New Orleans — the *Alabama,* with all her timbers aquiver from the pounding being inflicted by the *Kearsarge,* was clearly nearing the end of her career. Semmes, nicked in the right hand by a fragment of shell as the raider went into her seventh circle, had a quartermaster bind up the wound and rig a sling, never leaving his perch on the horseblock. From there he could see better than anyone the damage being done his ship and the ineffectiveness of his return fire. This seventh circle must be the last. The only course left was to attempt a run for safety. Accordingly, he told the exec: "Mr Kell, as soon as our head points to the French coast in our circuit of action, shift your guns to port and make all sail for the coast."

Kell tried, but Winslow quickly interposed the *Kearsarge,* slamming in shots from dead ahead and at a shorter range than ever. At this point the *Alabama*'s chief engineer came topside to report that his fires were being flooded by rising water from holes the Dahlgrens were blasting in the hull. "Go below, Mr Kell," Semmes said grimly, "and see how long the ship can float."

The Georgian went, and on his way through the wardroom saw a sight he would never forget. Assistant Surgeon David Llewellyn, a Briton and the only non-Southerner among the two dozen officers aboard, stood poised alongside where his operating table and patient had been until an 11-inch solid crashed through the adjoining bulkhead, snatching table, wounded seaman, and all his instruments from under the ministering hand of the doctor, who stood there, abruptly alone, with a dazed expression of horror and disbelief. Kell continued down to the engine room, where he saw through the steam from her drowned fires that the ship could scarcely remain afloat another ten minutes. He picked his way back up, through the wreckage and past the still-dazed surgeon, to report to the captain that the *Alabama*'s ordeal was nearly over.

"Then sir," Semmes replied, "cease firing, shorten sail, and haul down the colors. It will never do in this nineteenth century for us to go down, and the decks covered with our gallant wounded."

Across the water, less than 500 yards away, Winslow saw the rebel flag come down, but being, as he later explained, "uncertain whether Captain Semmes was using some ruse," called out to his gun crews: "He's playing a trick on us. Give him another broadside." They did just that, adding to the carnage on *Alabama*'s bloody, ripped-up decks with every gun that could be brought to bear; whereupon a white flag was run up from the stern. "Cease firing!" Winslow cried at last.

Through his telescope he observed on board the sinking raider a pantomime that called up within him, in rapid sequence, mixed emotions of pity, mistrust, sympathy, and resentment. Settling fast, with only a thread of smoke from her riddled stack, the *Alabama* had lost headway; Semmes, though still on his horseblock, obviously had given the order to abandon ship. While some of the crew milled about in confusion, engaging Winslow's pity by their plight — which, after all, might have been his own if the 100-pound shell lodged in his sternpost had not turned out to be a dud — others aroused his mistrust by piling into a dinghy and shoving off, apparently in an attempt to avoid capture. This was disproved, however, when the dinghy made for the *Kearsarge* and he saw, when it came within hailing distance, that it was filled with wounded men, including a master's mate who shouted up a request that boats be sent to rescue survivors gone over the side and thrashing about in the water.

Winslow had only two boats not smashed in the course of the fight, but he ordered them lowered without further delay and gave permission, moreover, for the rebel dinghy to be used as well, once the wounded had been unloaded. Obviously, though, these three small boats would not hold all the men in the water; so he called through his speaking trumpet to a nearby English pleasure yacht whose owner had sailed out of Cherbourg that morning for a closeup view of the duel: "For God's sake, do what you can to save them!" The yacht responded promptly, and as she did so Winslow turned his telescope back to the final scene of the tableau being enacted on *Alabama*'s canted deck.

The rebel skipper by now had descended from his perch, and he and another officer, a large, heavily bearded man — John Kell — began to undress for their leap into the Channel. The big man stripped to his underwear, but Semmes, apparently mindful of his dignity, retained his trousers and waistcoat. He seemed to part reluctantly with his sword. After unbuckling it rather awkwardly with his unhurt left hand, he held it above his head for a long moment, flashing brightly in the noonday sunlight, before he did the thing that brought Winslow's resentment to a boil. He flung it whirling and glinting into the sea, thereby making impossible the ceremony of handing it over to his vanquisher. Winslow could scarcely expect him to bring it along while he swam one-handed across four hundred yards of choppy water to the *Kearsarge* to surrender, but it seemed to the Federal captain that his adversary took a spiteful pleasure in this gesture which deprived him of a customary right.

Semmes followed Kell and his sword into the Channel, and the two men struck out as best they could, the former clutching a life preserver, the latter a wooden grating, to avoid the suction that might pull them under when the *Alabama* sank. She was filling fast now, air gurgling, hissing, chuckling under her punctured decks while the sea poured in through rents in her hull. Her stern awash, her prow was lifting, and suddenly it rose higher as her guns, still hot from battle, tore loose from their lashings and slid aft. The breeze freshening, she recovered a little headway with her sails, and as she moved she left behind her a broad ribbon of flotsam, broken spars and bodies, bits of tackle and other gear. Fifty yards off, Semmes turned to watch her die. Backward she went, beginning her long downward slide, anchors swinging wildly in the air below her bow; the main-topmast, split by a solid in the fight, went by the board when she paused, nearly vertical; then she was gone, the Channel boiling greenly for a time to mark the place where she had been.

It was 12.24, just under ninety minutes since she fired her first shot at the *Kearsarge*. For all his grief, Semmes was glad in at least one sense that she was on the forty-fathom bottom with his sword. "A noble Roman once stabbed his daughter, rather than she should be polluted by the foul embrace of a tyrant," he later wrote. "It was with a similar feeling that Kell and I saw the *Alabama* go down. We had buried her as we had christened her, and she was safe from the polluting touch of the hated Yankee!"

By now the trim British yacht *Deerhound* — whose captain-owner John Lancaster, a wealthy industrialist on vacation with his family, had had her built up the Clyde by the Lairds two years ago, at the same time they were at work on the sloop that became the *Alabama* — was within reach of the crewmen bobbing amid the whitecaps. She lowered her boats and began fishing them out, including Semmes and Kell and Marine Lieutenant Beckett Howell (Varina Davis's younger brother) but not Dr Llewellyn; a nonswimmer, he had drowned. Forty-two men were saved in all by the *Deerhound* in response to Winslow's plea; another dozen by the captains of two French pilot boats, who needed no urging; while seventy more were taken and made captive aboard the *Kearsarge*. Semmes himself might have been among these last except for Kell's quick thinking. Exhausted, the Confederate skipper was laid "as if dead" on the sternsheets of one of *Deerhound*'s boats when the *Kearsarge* cutter came alongside. "Have you seen Captain Semmes?" a blue-clad officer asked sharply. Kell, who had put on a *Deerhound* crewman's cap and taken an oar to complete the disguise, had a ready answer. "Captain Semmes is drowned," he said, to the Federal's apparent satisfaction. Aboard the yacht, after the shipwrecked men had been given hot coffee and shots of rum to counter the chill and exhaustion, Lancaster put the question: "Where shall I land you?" This time it was Semmes who had the answer that meant salvation. "I am now under English colors," he said, "and the sooner you put me, with my officers and men, on English soil the better."

Well before nightfall the *Deerhound* put in at Southampton, where, news of the battle having preceded them, Semmes and his men were given a welcome as hearty as if they had won; "A set of first-rate fellows," the London *Times* pronounced them. As soon as he had rested from his ordeal, the Maryland-born Alabamian used the gold left at Cherbourg to pay off the survivors and send allotments to the nearest kin of the nine men killed in action and twelve drowned. He was banqueted by admirers, including officers of the Royal Navy, who united to present him with an elegant, gold-mounted sword, engraved along the blade to signify that it was a replacement for the one he had flung into the Channel after his "engagement off Cherbourg with a chain-plated ship of superior power, armament, and crew." However, when Confederate officials tendered him a new command with which to continue the record begun aboard the *Sumter*, he declined, needing time to absorb the shock of his "impossible" defeat. Though he was promoted to rear admiral and eventually made his way, via Cuba and Mexico, back to the Confederacy (none of whose ports the *Alabama* ever touched) he had done all he would do afloat. Other raiders would continue to strike at Yankee shipping around the globe, but not Raphael Semmes. "I considered my career upon the high seas closed by the loss of my ship," he later explained.

As for Winslow, he too was being lionized by now as the man who had abolished in single combat the myth that the *Alabama* was invincible. After clearing his decks and assembling the crew for thanksgiving prayers — which helped to ease his dudgeon at having seen the British yachtsman make off with his prize of prizes, Semmes — he steamed into Cherbourg, flags aflutter from every mast of the *Kearsarge*, and was promptly surrounded by boatloads of people out to greet the ship whose victorious crew had somehow been transformed into the home team.

Her casualties were limited to the three men hit early in the duel, one of whom died a few days later; *Alabama*'s came to 43, just under half of them drowned or killed in action. Once he had paroled his prisoners and patched up superficial damage, Winslow went to Paris to consult a specialist about his failing eye, only to learn that he had waited too long for treatment to be of any use. A victory banquet, tendered by patriotic fellow countrymen in the French capital, helped to dispel the medical gloom of the occasion, and a letter from Gideon Welles was even more effective in that regard. "I congratulate you," the Secretary wrote, "on your good fortune in meeting the *Alabama*, which had so long avoided the fastest ships and some of the most vigilant and intelligent officers of the service, and for the ability displayed in the contest you have the thanks of the Department.... The battle was so brief, the victory so decisive, and the comparative results so striking that the country will be reminded of the brilliant actions of our infant Navy, which have been repeated and illustrated in the engagement."

Presently this was followed, upon the President's recommendation, by a vote of thanks from Congress and a promotion to date from June 19. Commodore Winslow returned to the United States by the end of the year, and while the *Kearsarge* was being refitted in the Boston Navy Yard carpenters removed a section of her sternpost, still with the 100-pound dud embedded in the oak, and boxed it for shipment to

Washington, the Commander in Chief having expressed a desire to see for himself what a close call the ship and all aboard had had on that famous Sunday, six miles out in the English Channel, when she sank the *Alabama*.

Lincoln was indeed glad to learn that the most famed of rebel raiders had been struck from the list of woes to be endured until the war had run its course. Lately, though, he had begun to perceive that while striving to keep up national morale he would also have to deal with national impatience, which mounted with every indication, true or false, that the end might not be far off. Earlier that week, on June 14 — the day Bishop Polk was cannon-sniped on Pine Top and Grant began crossing the James — he had confessed to a friendly newsman that the country's tendency to "expect too much at once" was, for him, a matter of considerable private anxiety: "I wish, when you write or speak to people, you would do all you can to correct the impression that the war in Virginia will end right off and victoriously.... As God is my judge, I shall be satisfied if we are over with the fight in Virginia within a year. I hope we shall be 'happily disappointed,' as the saying is; but I am afraid not. I am afraid not."

This was something new, this concern lest the public, in its ebullience, demand an end to the war before it was won, and Lincoln bore down to counteract it two days later, nine days after his renomination, when he went to attend and address a sanitary fair in Philadelphia. "It is a pertinent question often asked in the mind privately, and from one to the other: When is the war to end? Surely I feel as deep an interest in this question as anyone can, but I do not wish to name a day, or month, or a year when it is to end. I do not wish to run any risk of seeing the time come, without our being ready for the end, and for fear of disappointment because the time had come and not the end. We accepted this war for an object, a worthy object, and the war will end when that object is attained. Under God, I hope it never will until that time."

Cheers went up at this, and he pressed on to warn his hearers that the approach of victory might call for more, not fewer sacrifices. "If I shall discover that General Grant and the noble officers and men under him can be greatly facilitated in their work by a sudden pouring forward of men and assistance, will you give them to me?"

"Yes! Yes!" the crowd roared, catching fire.

"Then I say, stand ready," Lincoln told the upturned faces about the rostrum, as well as those that would be downturned over tomorrow's newspapers all across the land, "for I am watching for the chance."

✗ 3 ✗

Now that Johnston had relinquished Pine Top, retiring down its rearward slope with the corpse of Bishop Polk, Sherman followed close on his heels, determined to keep up the pressure which, so far, had gained him eighty of the critical hundred air-line miles between Chattanooga and Atlanta, his base and his objective. He did so with caution, however, being confronted on the left and right by the loom of Brush and Lost mountains, both occupied by butternut marksmen who asked nothing more, in the way of compensation for their pains, than one quick glimpse down their rifle barrels at blue-clad soldiers moving toward them, within range and without cover. "We cannot risk the heavy loss of an assault at this distance from our base," the red-haired Ohioan had wired Halleck on the day before Polk's mangling. But on June 16, two days after that event, he changed his mind and began to consider trying what he had said he could not risk. "I am now inclined to feign on both flanks and assault the center," he told Old Brains. "It may cost us dear, but in results would surpass any attempt to pass around."

Presently, though, he changed his mind again — or, more strictly speaking, had it changed for him by Johnston, who gave him the slip the following night with another of his "clean retreats." This one was not so much an outright withdrawal, however, as it was a rectification, an adjustment whereby the foxy Confederate not only shortened his rather extended line but also shored up the sagging center Sherman had planned to assault. Turning loose of the high ground on his flanks, he fell back to Kennesaw Mountain, two miles in rear of the abandoned Pine Top salient. Polk's corps — temporarily under Major General W. W. Loring, the senior division commander — was posted there, dug in along its northern face, with Hood on the right, astride the Western & Atlantic, and Hardee on the left, denying the Federals access to Marietta by blocking the roads coming in from Dallas and Burnt Hickory. Johnston's line, which had been concave after he gave up Pine Top, was now convex, and its center, which had been its weakest element when Sherman contemplated launching a headlong strike, was now its stoutest part. In point of fact, the graybacks had occupied no stronger position in the course of their six-week retreat.

"Kennesaw Mountain is, I should think, about 700 feet high," an Illinois major wrote home in reaction to his first sight of this forbidding piece of geography reared up in the army's path, "and consists of two points or peaks, separated by a narrow gorge running across the top. The mountain itself is entirely separated from all mountain ranges, and swells up like a great bulb from the plain." Sherman too was impressed and given pause by what he called "the bold and striking twin mountain." Rebel signalmen were at work on its two bulbous peaks, both of which were "crowned with batteries," while "the spurs were alive with men busy felling trees, digging pits, and preparing for the grand struggle impending." As he stood and looked, awe gave way to determination. "The scene was enchanting; too beautiful to be disturbed by the harsh clamor of war," he was to say, years later; "but the Chattahoochee lay beyond, and I had to reach it."

He had to reach it; but how? In an attempt to find some easier means than a headlong assault, which seemed foredoomed, he brought up his guns and began to pound away at the fortified slopes of the mountain, hoping to fix the enemy in position there while he probed both flanks of the rebel line in search of a way around it, one that would enable him to menace the railroad in Johnston's rear and thus provoke him into abandoning his present all-but-impregnable position, as he had done so many others in the course of his long retreat, rather than risk a fight whose loss would mean the severance of his supply line. The result was a series of skirmishes, some of which attained the dignity of engagements, first at Gilgal Church, where the graybacks fought a holding action to cover their withdrawal, and then along Mud and Nose (or Noyes) creeks, both of which had to be crossed if Sherman was to turn the rebel left for a strike at Marietta, Johnston's base, two miles back of Kennesaw, or at Smyrna Station, another four miles down the railroad. While Schofield, reinforced by Hooker, was doing all he could in that direction, McPherson, strengthened by Blair's return the week before, was feeling out the Confederate right, but with little success, being under the guns and surveillance of the enemy on the taller of Kennesaw's two peaks. Thomas meantime kept up the pressure dead ahead, firing so many rounds from his massed batteries — he had 130 guns in all: half a dozen more than McPherson and Schofield combined — that his soldiers, watching the bombardment from dug-in positions on the flat, began to tell each other that Uncle Billy was determined to take the double-crested mountain in their front, or else "fill it full of old iron."

For three days this continued, neither Thomas nor McPherson achieving much with their pounding and probing, and then on June 22, having proceeded well to the south around Kennesaw's western flank, Schofield too was brought to a sudden halt.

It happened at a place called Culp's (or Kolb's) Farm, four miles southwest of Marietta on the road from Powder Springs, and it came about because Johnston, in reaction to Sherman's continuing effort to reach around his left, had issued instructions the night before for Hood, whose intrenchments on the right would be occupied temporarily by Wheeler's dismounted troopers, to march at daylight across the rear of Kennesaw and go into position beyond Hardee on the far left, south of the mountain's western flank, in order to block the Federal turning movement. Hood did this, and more. Within a mile of his objective by midday, he encountered troops from Schofield's corps advancing up the Powder Springs Road, and with soldierly instinct, but without taking time for reconnaissance, attacked at once.

Assuming he had the flankers outflanked, he figured that a prompt assault would "roll them up," drive them back with heavy casualties, and abolish this threat to Johnston's lifeline. The result was heavy casualties, all right, though not for Schofield, who had taken the precaution of having his and Hooker's men dig in while awaiting reports from patrols sent out to find the best route up the valley of Olley's Creek for a strike at the Western & Atlantic above Smyrna, three miles across the way. Hood drove these forward elements rapidly back, giving chase with the two divisions on hand, but at Culp's Farm the pursuers came unexpectedly upon the enemy main body, stoutly intrenched, and were bloodily repulsed. A second assault, launched near sundown, only added to the carnage; Stevenson's division alone lost more than 800 men, and Hindman's brought the total to better than 1000. Schofield and Hooker, whose soldiers did their fighting behind earthworks for a change, suffered less than a third that many casualties in breaking the two attacks. Then at nightfall, while the graybacks dug in too along the line where the fighting stopped, Schofield and Hood sent word to their superiors at Big Shanty and Marietta of what had happened.

Johnston's anger at this loss of a thousand badly needed veterans, once more as a result of Hood's impetuosity, was exceeded by Sherman's when he received an out-of-channels dispatch that evening from Hooker, proudly reporting that he had "repulsed two heavy attacks" and calling urgently for reinforcements before he was overrun. "Three entire corps are in front of us," he added by way of lending weight to his proud cry for help. "Hooker must be mistaken; Johnston's army has only three corps," Sherman noted in passing the message along to Thomas, who, knowing only too well that Hardee and Loring were still in position to his and McPherson's front, replied rather mildly: "I look upon this as something of a stampede." Sherman agreed and next morning, still miffed, rode down to Culp's Farm in a pouring rain to tell Fighting Joe he wanted no more of his boasts and misrepresentations. In reaction, Hooker went into a month-long pout; or, as his superior later put it, "From that time he began to sulk."

This would have its consequences for all concerned; but the fact was, Sherman's anger had its source in something far more irksome than Hooker's inability to avoid exaggeration. Daylight showed the graybacks intrenched across Schofield's front. This meant that the army had gone as far as it could go in that direction without turning loose of its supply line, already under threat from rebel horsemen, and the drowned condition of the roads precluded any movement on them so long as the rain continued.

Confronted thus with the probability of a stalemate — which was not only undesirable on its own account, here in Georgia, but might also give Richmond the chance to reinforce Lee's hard-pressed Virginia army from Johnston's, biding its time north of the Chattahoochee — Sherman reverted to his notion, expressed a week ago, "to feign on both flanks and assault the center." The trouble was that the center now was Kennesaw Mountain, and Kennesaw seemed unassailable. But there, perhaps, was just the factor that might augur best; an attacker would greatly increase his chance for success by striking where the blow was least expected. Besides, continued probes by McPherson today showed that Loring's corps had been extended eastward to include a portion of the works abandoned yesterday by Hood when he set out westward to counter Schofield's flanking threat. That march, with its extension of the Confederate left while Loring spread out to cover the right, stretched Johnston's line to a width of about eight miles, exclusive of the cavalry on his flanks. It must be quite thin somewhere, and that somewhere was likely to be dead ahead on Kennesaw, whose frown alone was enough to discourage assault. So Sherman reasoned, at any rate, in his search for some way to avoid a stalemate. Moreover, he explained afterwards, he conferred with his three army commanders, "and we all agreed that we could not with prudence stretch out any more, and therefore there was no alternative but to attack 'fortified lines,' a thing carefully avoided up to that time."

Such a change in tactics, abruptly sprung, would also serve to increase the element of surprise, which figured largely in Sherman's calculations. But the outlook remained grim, if not downright awesome. "The whole country is one vast fort," he informed Halleck on June 23. "Johnston must have full fifty miles of connected trenches, with abatis and finished batteries.... Our lines are now in close contact and the fighting incessant, with a good deal of artillery. As fast as we gain one position, the enemy has another all ready."

These were minor adjustments, permitting no more than a closer look at the honeycombed slopes of the mountain up ahead, and a closer look only magnified the original impression of impregnability. One-armed Howard, studying the rebel line from a position well to the front, pronounced it "stronger in artificial contrivances and natural features than the cemetery at Gettysburg," which he had helped to hold despite Lee's all-out efforts to oust him. But Sherman refused to be distracted, let alone dissuaded. Determined, as he had told Grant the week before, to "inspire motion into a large, ponderous and slow, by habit, army," he believed that his soldiers, weary of roundabout marches that never quite managed to bring the enemy to bay, needed the stimulus the pending assault would provide, even if most of the blood that was shed turned out to be their own — and he was concerned, as well, lest Johnston's habitual caution, which had led him to give up so many stout positions in the course of the past seven weeks, should be replaced by a conviction that the Federals would never attack him once he was snugly intrenched. Both of these things counted heavily in the redhead's calculations, as did the promise of all that would be gained if the attack was anything like as successful as the one up Missionary Ridge, seven months ago, by many of these same men against many of these same opponents, with the difference that there had been no unfordable Chattahoochee in the rebel rear on that occasion.

Other factors there were, too, no less persuasive because Sherman himself — defined by Walt Whitman as "a bit of stern open air made up in the image of a man" — was perhaps not even aware of their influence on him. For one, the Union army in Virginia was not only doing most of the bleeding in the double-pronged offensive, it was also getting most of the headlines, and despite his dislike of journalists, and indeed of the press in general, he could see that his troops would be heartened by a more equitable distribution of praise, such as the overrunning of Kennesaw would secure. Moreover, back in Nashville and Chattanooga, while preparing for the campaign, he had learned that certain observers snidely characterized him as "not a fighting general." He dismissed the charge without exactly denying it, saying: "Fighting is the least part of a general's work. The battle will fight itself." Still, the imputation rankled, containing as it did some grains of truth, and he welcomed the opportunity, now at hand, to refute it for once and for all. On June 24 he issued a special field order directing his army commanders to "make full reconnaissances and preparations to attack the enemy in force on the 27th instant, at 8 a.m. precisely."

That left two full days for getting set; Sherman, having decided to be rash, had also decided to go about it methodically, even meticulously, so as to minimize the cost if the breakthrough failed. For one thing, he would limit the weight of his assault to less than a fifth of the troops on hand, and for another, despite its regrettable but inevitable detraction from the element of surprise, the jump-off would be preceded by an hour-long bombardment from every gun that could be brought to bear on the critical objectives. Of these there were two, main and secondary, neither of them, properly speaking, on the mountain that would give the battle its name, although the secondary effort, assigned to McPherson, would be made against — and, if successful, across — the gently rolling southwest slope of the lower of the two peaks, called Little Kennesaw to distinguish it from Big Kennesaw, the taller and more massive portion of the mountain to the east, overlooking the slow curve of the Western & Atlantic on that flank. This attack would be launched astride the Burnt Hickory Road, simultaneously with Thomas's main effort, along and to the right of the Dallas Road, one mile south; both commanders would assault with two divisions, their others standing by to exploit whatever progress was achieved. Schofield and Hooker would feint on the far right, Garrard's cavalry on the left, all at the same prearranged hour, hard on the heels of the softening-up artillery bombardment, so as to prevent Johnston from knowing which part of his line to reinforce from any other, or from his reserves if he had them, before it was swamped. "At the time of the general attack," the special order ended, foreseeing a happy outcome to the rashness so meticulously prescribed, "the skirmishers at the base of Kennesaw will take advantage of it to gain, if possible, the summit and hold it. Each attacking column will endeavor to break a single point of the enemy's line, and make a secure lodgment beyond, and be prepared for following it up toward Marietta and the railroad in case of success."

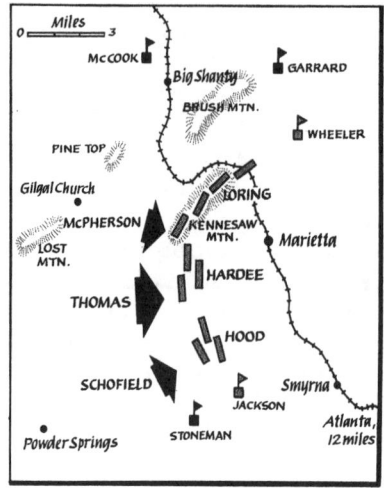

Throughout that two-day interim, although few along the eight-mile curve of intrenchments knew what they were waiting or getting set for — "All commanders will maintain reserve and secrecy even from their staff officers," the field order had cautioned — fire fights, picket clashes, and sudden cannonades would break into flame from point to point, then subside into sputters and die away, sporadic, inconclusive, and productive of little more than speculation. Whether off on the flanks or crouched near the critical center, men listened and wondered, unable to find a pattern to the action. The crash of guns would come from somewhere up or down the line, an Indiana soldier would recall, "then the hurrahing, sometimes the shrill, boyish rebel yell, sometimes the loud, full-voiced, deep-toned, far-sounding chorus of northern men; then again the roar of cannon, the rattle of musketry and the awful suspense to the listeners. If, as the noise grew feebler, we caught the welcome cheer, answering shouts ran along. But if the far-off rebel yell told of our comrades' repulse, the silence could be felt."

Across the way, within the horseshoe curve of works containing Kennesaw and Marietta, the reaction was much the same, but in reverse. No one there could discern a pattern either, including the men of Major Generals Samuel French's and Benjamin Cheatham's divisions

Red Clay Minuet [397]

of Loring's and Hardee's corps, respectively astride the Burnt Hickory and Dallas roads, up which the two Union assaults were to be delivered on Monday morning, June 27, one week past the summer solstice.

The rain left off on Sunday and the sun came up in a cloudless sky next morning at 4.40 to begin its work of drying the red clay roads, the sodden fields and breathless woods. By the time it was three hours high the day was hot and steamy with the promise of much greater heat to come. Twenty minutes later, precisely at 8 o'clock and without preamble, 200-odd Union cannon roared into action, pounding away at the rebel line on the mountainside and across the flats beyond. Crouched in their pits and ditches, jarred and shaken about by the sudden hurtle of metal exploding over and around them, the defenders marveled at the volume and intensity of the fire, which was to them still another manifestation of Yankee ingenuity and wealth. "Hell has broke loose in Georgia, sure enough!" one grayback shouted amid shellbursts, and as the bombardment continued, sustained by an apparently inexhaustible supply of ammunition, they began to snatch down the blankets pegged for shade across the open tops of their trenches, preparing for what they knew would come when the guns let up. Finally, close to 9 o'clock, the uproar reached a spasmodic end; the cannoneers stepped back from their pieces, panting, and the blue infantry started forward in two clotted masses, about a mile apart, to assail the Confederate center.

For a time they advanced in relative security, protected by the intervening woods and the butternut pickets trotting back to join their comrades along the main line of resistance. Then the attackers emerged into brilliant sunlight, silhouetted against the bright green backdrop of trees, and the rebel headlogs seemed to burst spontaneously into flame along their bottoms, all up and down that portion of the line. Sam French, whose left-flank division of Loring's corps was challenged first on Little Kennesaw's lower slopes, said later that the rattle and flash of musketry, combined with the deep-voiced boom of guns whose crews had held their fire till now, produced "a roar as constant as Niagara and as sharp as the crash of thunder with lightning in the eye."

Such was the fury of the sound that accompanied McPherson's attack, launched astride the Burnt Hickory Road by Brigadier General Morgan Smith, whose division was reinforced for the effort by a brigade from another division in Major General John A. Logan's corps. Sound and fury were all it came to, however, in the end. In the course of their plunge across a rocky, brush-choked gully, unexpectedly encountered in rear of the line abandoned by the gray pickets, 563 of the 4000 attackers fell before they could get to grips with the defenders intrenched on the far side. At one point "within about thirty feet of the enemy's main line," Smith reported, they came close; but there, receiving the full blast of massed rifles, they "staggered and sought cover as best they could behind logs and rocks." Stalled ("It was almost sure death to take your face out of the dust," one prone Federal declared, while another expressed a somewhat less gloomy view of the consequences, saying: "It was only necessary to expose a hand to procure a furlough") they were no longer much of a threat to French, who turned his high-sited batteries a quarter circle to the left and added the weight of the metal to Hardee's resistance, a mile away, astride and beyond the Dallas Road.

There Thomas was making a sturdier bid for a breakthrough, and Cheatham's division had all it could do to keep from being overrun by nearly twice as many Federals as French had had to deal with. "They seemed to walk up and take death as coolly as if they were automatic or wooden men," one defender was to say of these troops from two divisions under Jeff Davis and Brigadier General John Newton, respectively of Palmer's and Howard's corps.

Two of Cheatham's four brigades were posted where Hardee's line bent sharply to the south, creating a somewhat isolated salient, and it was here at the hinge, known thereafter as the Dead Angle, that Thomas struck. "The least flicker on our part would have been sure death to all," a Tennessee private who helped to hold it later declared. "We could not be reinforced on account of our position, and we had to stand up to the rack, fodder or no fodder." They did stand up, inflicting in the process — with the help of French's guns and Cleburne, whose marksmen brought their rifles to bear from up the line — a total of 654 casualties on Newton and 824 on Davis, both of whom notified their superiors that they hoped they could hang on where they were, if that was what was wanted, but that there was no further hope of carrying the position. Howard put it strongest, some time later, looking back. "Our losses in this assault were heavy indeed," he wrote, "and our gain was nothing. We realized now, as never before, the futility of direct assault upon intrenched lines already well prepared and well manned." Thomas agreed, sending word around 11 o'clock for those who could fall back to do so at once, while those who could not were to dig in where they were and wait for darkness.

The sudden resultant drop in the intensity of the fighting came none too soon for the defenders of the Angle, one of whom was to testify that he fired no less than 120 rounds in the course of the repulse. "My gun became so hot that frequently the powder would flash before I could ram home the ball," he said, adding: "When the Yankees fell back and the firing ceased, I never saw so many broken down and exhausted men in my life. I was sick as a horse, and as wet with blood and sweat as I could be, and many of our men were vomiting with excessive fatigue, overexhaustion, and sunstroke; our tongues were parched and cracked for water, and our faces blackened with powder and smoke, and our dead and wounded were piled indiscriminately in the trenches."

Cheatham's loss came to 195, French's to 186; between them, they had shot down 2041 of the 12,000 Federals thrown against their works. Other losses, elsewhere in Loring's and Hardee's corps, as well as in Hood's, which had been skirmishing with Schofield all the while, brought the Confederate total to 552. Sherman put his at 2500 — a figure Johnston vowed was a good deal less than half the true one — but later revised it upward to "about 3000."

Even so, and despite the shock of the sudden double repulse, he had been willing to drive it still higher at the time. From Signal Hill, his command post on the left, he could see that McPherson had shot his wad, and word had come from Schofield that little could be done on the far right. That left Thomas, the Rock of Chickamauga. He too had been checked, losing two of his best brigade commanders in the process, but he might be willing to try again for a repetition of what he had achieved on Missionary Ridge despite conditions even more unfavorable. "McPherson and Schofield are at a deadlock," Sherman wired him at 1.30. "Do you think you can carry any part of the enemy's line today? ... I will order the assault if you think you can succeed at any point." Thomas replied: "We have already lost heavily today without gaining any material advantage. One or two more such assaults would use up this army."

He recommended a change to siege methods, the digging of saps for a guarded approach. But Sherman, wanting no part of such a time-consuming business, preferred to maneuver the rebels out of position, as before. Encouraged by the let-up of the rain and the fast-drying condition of the roads, he telegraphed Thomas that evening: "Are you willing to risk [a] move on Fulton, cutting loose from our railroad?" Fulton was two miles beyond Smyrna Station, within three miles of the Chattahoochee and about ten miles in Johnston's rear; Sherman proposed to move by the right flank "with the whole army." Thomas considered the venture highly risky, exposing as it would the Union life line to Confederate seizure while the wheeling movement was in progress; but in any case, he replied before turning in for the night, "I think it decidedly better than butting against breastworks twelve feet thick and strongly abatised."

While waiting for the roads to finish drying Sherman worked on plans for his newest sidle and, eventually, on securing a truce for the burial of the unfortunates who had fallen in the double-pronged repulse. Undaunted — at least on paper — he took the offensive in defending his decision to strike at the rebel center, even though all it had got him was a lengthened casualty list. "The assault I made was no mistake; I had to do it," he wired Halleck, explaining that after nearly eight weeks of gingerly skirmishing, all the time conforming to a pattern about as precise as if he and Johnston were partners in a classic minuet, Federals and Confederates alike "had settled down into the conviction that the assault of lines formed no part of my game." Now that both sides knew better, having seen the dance pattern broken as if with a meat ax, he expected to find his adversary "much more cautious." That was his gain, as he saw it, and he continued to pursue this line of consolation. "Failure as it was, and for which I assume the entire responsibility," he would assert in his formal report of the lost battle, "I yet claim it produced good fruit, as it demonstrated to General Johnston that I would assault, and that boldly."

Earlier, while smoke still hung about the field and the wounded mewled for help between the lines, he had reminded Thomas: "Our loss is small compared with some of those in the East. It should not in the least discourage us. At times assaults are necessary and inevitable." However, his most forthright statement with regard to losses was reserved for his wife, to whom he wrote two days after the Kennesaw repulse. " I begin to regard the death and mangling of a couple of thousand men as a small affair, a kind of morning dash," he told her, adding: "It may be well that we become hardened. . . . The worst of the war is not yet begun."

That might well be, though there could be no denying that for a considerable number of his soldiers — young and old, recruits and veterans alike — the best was over, along with the worst. Their interment was a grisly thing to watch. "I get sick now when I happen to think about it," a Confederate wrote years later, remembering the June 30 burial armistice that was asked and granted "not for any respect either army had for the dead, but to get rid of the sickening stench." Although three days of festering midsummer Georgia heat had made the handling of the corpses a repugnant task, he recalled that Yankee ingenuity once more had measured up to the occasion. "Long and deep trenches were dug, and hooks made from bayonets crooked for the purpose, and all the dead were dragged and thrown pell mell into these trenches. Nothing was allowed to be taken off the dead, and finely dressed officers, with gold watch chains dangling over their vests, were thrown into the ditches. During the whole day both armies were hard at work, burying the Federal dead."

Thus June ended, bringing with it another pause for a backward look at the casualty count in each of the two armies. In both cases these were lower than they had been the month before, and they were similar in another way as well. Just as New Hope Church and Pickett's Mill, engagements fought near the bottom of the previous calendar leaf, had reversed the May tally, raising Sherman's losses above Johnston's, which had been higher than his opponent's before the clashes around Dallas, so now did Kennesaw Mountain reverse the count for June, which had been lower for the Union up till then. Sherman's loss for the past month was 7500, Johnston's around 6000. This brought their respective totals for the whole campaign to just under 17,000 and just over 14,000. Roughly speaking, to put it another way, one out of every four Confederates had been shot or captured, as compared to one out of seven Federals.

In time, when the guns had cooled and approximate figures from both sides became available in books, Sherman would take great pride in this reversal of the anticipated ratio of losses between attacker and defender (as well he might: especially in reviewing a campaign fought on ground as unfavorable to the offensive as North Georgia was, against an adversary he admired as much as he did Joe Johnston) but just now there was the war to get on with, the wheeling movement he had designed to flank the rebels off their impregnable mountain and back across the only remaining river between them and his goal, Atlanta. By July 1 the roads were baked about hard enough for marching; the sidle began next day.

Garrard's dismounted troopers replaced the infantry in the trenches astride the Western & Atlantic, blocking a possible track-breaking sortie by the graybacks on that flank, and McPherson set out across Thomas's rear to join Schofield for a lunge around Hood's left the following day. If successful, this would not only sever Johnston's life line, it would also oblige him to fight without the protection of intrenchments when he fell back, through Marietta and Smyrna, to where the flankers would be waiting around Fulton, three miles short of the Chattahoochee and better than 50,000 strong. McPherson thus was given a chance to redeem his Resaca performance by repeating it without flaws, although Sherman's expectations were by no means as great as they had been eight weeks ago, some eighty miles back up the railroad. Warned by lookouts high on Kennesaw, which afforded a panoramic view of the country for miles and miles around, Johnston would probably choose to give up his present position rather than risk the consequences of fighting simultaneously front and rear, with a force about as large as his own in each direction. Anticipating this reaction the night before, Sherman told Garrard and Thomas to advance their pickets at daylight, July 3, and determine whether the Kennesaw trenches were occupied or abandoned; whether Johnston had chosen to stand his ground, despite the menace to his life line, or fall back, as he had always done in the face of such a threat.

On Signal Hill before dawn next morning, while the skirmishers were groping their way forward through the brush, Sherman waited impatiently for the light to grow enough to permit the use of a large telescope he had had mounted on a tripod and trained on the double-humped bulk of Kennesaw, looming blacker than the starless sky beyond it. Presently the sun broke clear and he saw, through the high-powered glass, "some of our pickets crawling up the hill cautiously. Soon they stood upon the very top, and I could see their movements as they ran along the crest."

Not a shot had been fired; the works were empty; the rebels had pulled out southward in the night.

The red-haired Ohioan caught fire at the notion that now they were out in the open, somewhere between the abandoned mountain and the river ten miles in its rear — his for the taking, so to speak, if he could overhaul them with his superior numbers before they reached whatever sanctuary their commander had it in mind to fortify. "In a minute I roused my staff, and started them off with orders in every direction for a pursuit by every possible road, hoping to catch Johnston in the confusion of retreat, especially at the crossing of the Chattahoochee River." Thomas could be depended on to descend at once on Marietta, but what was needed most just now, if the pursuers were to overcome whatever head start the Confederates might have gained, was cavalry. Sherman told Garrard to get his three brigades remounted and ride hard to bring the enemy to bay, short of the Chattahoochee, while McPherson and Schofield caught up to close in for the kill.

Events moved fast now, but not fast enough for Sherman. Without waiting for Garrard, he rode ahead with a small escort, around the eastern flank of the mountain and on into Marietta, nestled in its rear. He got there by 8.30 and was pleased to find that, although the graybacks had made a clean getaway with all their stores and had torn up several miles of railroad to the south, Thomas already had soldiers in the town. As the minutes ticked off, however, and no troopers appeared, his impatience mounted. "Where's Gar'd?" he began to storm. "Where's Gar'd? Where in hell's Gar'd?" Finally the cavalryman — a fellow Ohioan, seven years his junior in age and eleven years behind him at West Point — arrived, explaining that it had taken time to bring his horses forward and get his men into column on the road. Dissatisfied to find still more time being wasted on excuses, Sherman yelled at him: "Get out of here quick!" Garrard was flustered. Transferred from the East on the eve of the present campaign, he was not yet accustomed to being addressed in this manner. "What shall I do?" he asked, and his red-haired chief barked angrily: "Don't make a damned bit of difference so you get out of here and go for the rebs."

Despite such urgency it was midafternoon before contact was reëstablished near Smyrna, five miles down the line, and reconnaissance used up the daylight needed for mounting an assault. Fortified in advance for ready occupation, its flanks protected east and west by Rottenwood and Nickajack creeks, the rebel position astride the railroad, midway between Marietta and the river crossing five miles in its rear, obviously called for caution if the Federals were to avoid blundering into a bloody repulse. Sherman was convinced, however, that his adversary had occupied it only in hope of delaying the blue pursuit, and he said as much in a message to Thomas near sundown: "The more I reflect the more I know Johnston's halt is to save time to cross his material and men. No general, such as he, would invite battle with the Chattahoochee behind him.... I know you appreciate the situation. We will never have such a chance again, and I want you to impress on Hooker, Howard, and Palmer the importance of the most intense energy of attack tonight and in the morning.... Press with vehemence at any cost of life and material. Every inch of line should be felt and the moment there is a give, pursuit should be made."

But there was no give, and no pursuit. In fact there was no attack. Vehemence yielded to prudence next morning — July 4: the first anniversary of Vicksburg's fall, Lee's retreat from Gettysburg, and Holmes's drubbing at Helena — when Sherman found the works in his front still a-bristle with bayonets and Johnston apparently desirous of nothing so much as he was of a blue assault that would permit a repetition of what had happened on the slopes of Little Kennesaw a week ago today.

On second thought, the Ohioan cancelled his sundown instructions to Thomas, which had called for "the most intense energy of action," and reverted instead to his time-tested method of attempting to maneuver, rather than knock, the graybacks out of fortifications established in his path. While the Cumberlanders kept up a noisy demonstration in front, banging away with all their guns as if in celebration of the Fourth, McPherson set out on another of his whiplash marches, down the near bank of Nickajack Creek, to threaten the Confederate left rear. Darkness fell before his troops were in position, and the following sunrise proved Sherman right after all. The Smyrna works yawned empty; the rebs once more had stolen away in the night. Eager as ever to catch them amid the confusion that always attended a river crossing, the northern commander took off fast, making excellent time on a march of about three miles; which ended unexpectedly, within two miles of the Chattahoochee, when he came upon Johnston, just beyond Vining Station, in occupation of what Sherman frankly called "the best line of field intrenchments I have ever seen."

Looking back on the experience, years later — mindful no doubt of what he had said, two nights before, about his adversary's unwillingness to "invite battle with the Chattahoochee behind him" — he expanded the compliment: "No officer or soldier who ever served under me will question the generalship of Joseph E. Johnston. His retreats were timely, in good order, and he left nothing behind."

One exhilarating gain there was at any rate, available from the crest of a hill inclosed by a loop of the railroad as it approached the Chattahoochee beyond Vining's. "Mine eyes have beheld the promised land," an Illinois major wrote home to his wife. "The 'domes and minarets and spires' of Atlanta are glittering in the sunlight before us, only eight miles distant." Sherman and Thomas were both on the hilltop for a Pisgah view of the prize beyond the river, and though the

Union-loyal Virginian took it calmly, as always — to look at his deep-set eyes and massive brow, a newsman declared, "made one feel as if he were gazing into the mouth of a cannon; and the cannon said nothing" — the volatile Ohioan, as usual, let his exhilaration show. "Stepping nervously about, his eyes sparkling and his face aglow, casting a single glance at Atlanta, another at the river, and a dozen at the surrounding valley," he seemed to the major to be studying the rebel dispositions in order to "see where he could best cross the river, how best he could flank them."

Clearly this would take some doing: Johnston once more had chosen well. Faced with the problem of defending a stream whose low south bank was dominated by high ground on the side which a crossing would leave in enemy control, he had intrenched in advance a six-mile line along the north bank, above and below the critical railroad span. With this and five other bridges at his back — a pair for each of his three corps — he could withdraw quickly in case of a breakthrough, left or right, or counterattack without delay if the Federals were repulsed. His wagons were already over the river, parked in safety beyond a secondary line of south-bank works, preconstructed for instant occupation if needed, and so was his cavalry, posted upstream and down to guard against probes in either direction. Sherman, after a look at these canny dispositions from the Vining's hilltop, wired Halleck that he would have to "study the case a little" before proceeding. He foresaw delays and he wanted Washington braced for the disappointment they would bring.

"I am now far ahead of my railroad and telegraph, and want them to catch up," he explained; "[I] may be here some days. Atlanta is in plain view, nine miles distant.... The extent of the enemy's parallels already taken is wonderful, and much of the same sort confronts us yet, and is seen beyond the Chattahoochee."

Still, he was not long in deciding that he "could easily practice on that ground to better advantage our former tactics of intrenching a moiety in [Johnston's] front, and with the rest of our army cross the river [above or below] and threaten either his rear or the city of Atlanta itself." Accordingly, while repair gangs were hard at work restoring the railroad down to Vining's, he confronted the north-bank rebel *tête-du-pont* (as he called it) with the forces of Thomas and McPherson, posted Schofield rearward in reserve, under instructions to be ready to march at a moment's notice, and sent a division of cavalry in each direction, upstream and down, in search of a likely point or points for crossing.

Stoneman, who led the downriver column, found all the bridges destroyed and their sites covered by horse artillery on the opposite bank. Although Garrard, who rode all the way to Roswell, nearly twenty miles above, had no better luck with regard to bridges, in other respects he was fortunate indeed. Roswell was a manufacturing center; or it had been, anyhow, until Garrard's troopers put in a hard day's work with sledges and torches, wrecking and burning. One problem there was, of a somewhat diplomatic nature, but not for long. He came upon a cotton mill running full tilt, still turning out gray cloth for the rebel armies; a French flag flew above it and the Gallic owner claimed immunity from damage or interference on the grounds that he was not only not a Confederate but was of foreign allegiance. Feeling rather beyond his depth in international waters, the cavalryman referred the claim to Sherman, who reacted with predictable indignation. "Such nonsense cannot deceive me," he wired Halleck, a specialist in such matters. "I take it a neutral is no better than one of our own citizens." And to Garrard went instructions to proceed against the foreign-owned mill as he had done against the others. As for the Frenchman himself, Sherman was specific as to how he might be dealt with. "Should you, under the impulse of natural anger, natural at contemplating such perfidy, hang the wretch," he told Garrard, "I approve the act beforehand."

But there was neither a hanging nor another burning; Garrard let the Frenchman go and tore down his mill to provide material for rebuilding the nearby bridge, destroyed the week before. This took three days, which allowed plenty of time for one of McPherson's corps to arrive for a crossing on July 10, dry-shod and without rebel opposition, Schofield having crossed two days earlier, about midway between Roswell and the Confederate right at Pace's Ferry, and driven the butternut vedettes away from their picket posts on the south bank. Sherman thus had been quick to solve the Chattahoochee problem, and Johnston's stand with his back to the river was correspondingly brief. Much of the credit went to Stoneman, whose downriver excursion had drawn the enemy's attention in that direction, but most of it went to Schofield, who showed for the first time in the campaign what he could accomplish when left to his own devices.

Ordered to carry out an upstream crossing, the New-York-born West Pointer — he had been a schoolteacher and a surveyor on the western plains by the time he was seventeen, and even now, though balding fast, was two years less than twice that age — arrived at daylight, July 8, reconnoitered briefly, and decided to cross where Soap Creek emptied into the river, seven miles below Roswell, the opposite bank being held at that point by a light force of gray cavalry, apparently not over-vigilant and equipped with only one gun. Silently he brought up his batteries, screened by brush along the north bank, and loaded infantry assault teams into pontoon floats launched well back from the creek mouth. "At the appointed time," he later reported, "the artillery was pushed quickly into position and opened fire, a line of battle advanced, rapidly firing, to the river bank, while the batteaux, loaded with men, were pulled down the creek and across the river.... The astonished rebels fired a single shot from their single gun, delivered a few random discharges of musketry, and fled, leaving their piece of artillery in our possession. The crossing was secured without the loss of a man." By dawn of July 9, the pontoon bridge having been installed the night before, "two divisions occupied a secure tête-de-pont a mile in depth, giving ample room for the *debouché* of the whole army."

Johnston reacted to Schofield's upstream crossing as expected, and with all his accustomed stealth and skill. Destroying or dismantling the six bridges in his wake — and, incidentally, provoking Sherman's one uncomplimentary postwar comment on the quality of his generalship throughout the long campaign: "I have always thought Johnston neglected his opportunity there, for he had lain comparatively idle while we got control of both banks of the river above him" — he withdrew his main body across the Chattahoochee that night, and after temporarily occupying the south-bank works, prepared in advance for just such an emergency, continued the pull-back the following day, July 10, to a line in rear of Peachtree Creek, apparently prompted by concern that if he took up a position any closer to the river the Federals might cut in behind him and seize the city. In any case he now was less than five miles from the heart of Atlanta.

Grateful though Sherman was for this development, which meant that he would be able to cross this last of North Georgia's three broad rivers without a battle that had seemed likely to prove costly both in casualties and time, he once more found himself confronted with the problem that had loomed with every major gain: What now? — meaning *how?* Should he swing left or right, upstream or down, for the accustomed flanking effort, or bull straight ahead for an end-all strike at an opponent whose back was at last to the gates of the city in his charge, with little room for maneuver unless he chose to give it up without a fight?

While the red-haired general pondered and pored over maps and reports, his troops moved up to the unguarded Chattahoochee, anticipating their first leisurely bath in ten weeks. Admiration for their commander had grown with every tactical leap or sidestep, and now it reached a climax in which almost anything seemed possible. "Charley," one dusty infantry man told a comrade as they approached this last natural barrier and saw smoke rising from the buildings along its banks, "I believe Sherman has set the river on fire." Nor was the wonder limited to wearers of the blue. A butternut prisoner, conducted rearward past exuberant Federals in their tens of thousands, was so impressed by their multitude that he said to his captors: "Sherman ought to get on a high hill and command, 'Attention! Kingdoms by the right wheel!'" The general, in point of fact, was squatting naked in the

Red Clay Minuet

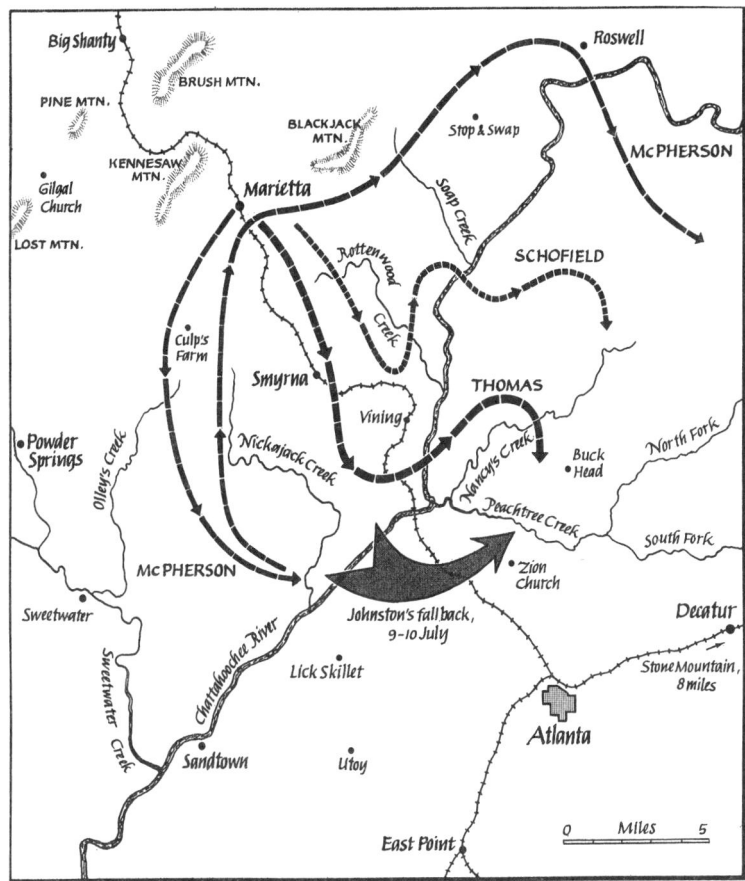

Chattahoochee at the time, discussing the temperature of the water with a teamster who admired him from the bank, while all around them other soldiers lolled neck deep in the river, soaking away the grime of more than a hundred red-clay miles of marching and fighting and the caked sweat of seventy days of exertion and fear, or else whooped and splashed in pure delight at having nothing else to do.

But not for long. After the brief time-out for his dip in the Chattahoochee, Sherman returned to his maps and reports, designing the next, and he hoped final, move in the campaign to whip Joe Johnston and take Atlanta. With the two-weeks-old repulse at Kennesaw fresh in mind, he quickly rejected the notion of mounting an all-out frontal attack on the Confederates dug in behind Peachtree Creek — attractive though that would be as a slam-bang finish, if successful — and reverted instead to his accustomed practice of operating on or around one of the enemy flanks.

Mostly, before, he had moved by his right, in a series of mirror images, so to speak, of Grant's leftward sidles in Virginia; but in this case the choice was by no means simple. It was true, a downstream crossing would not only give him ground that favored the offensive (the south-bank creeks, below, ran into the Chattahoochee at right angles, affording Johnston no perpendicular ridges to defend but many to cross in changing position to meet the challenge, while permitting Sherman to advance on the city by moving up the ravines, unhindered in front and sheltered on the flanks); it would also place him in rear of his objective from the outset, within easy striking distance of the railroads leading southwest through Montgomery to Mobile and southeast through Macon to Savannah, without which Atlanta could not long survive a siege. An upstream crossing, on the other hand, would give the advantage of terrain to the defenders; for there the creeks ran more or less parallel to the Chattahoochee, presenting Sherman with ridges to cross while advancing and Johnston with ravines to shelter his army while shifting to meet the threat. Geography clearly favored a downriver flanking operation. Yet there was a good deal more to the problem than geography per se. For one thing, there was the risk of exposing the all-important Union supply line to depredations, and this would be a far greater danger if the crossing was made below the railroad bridge. Just above there, after receiving the waters of Peachtree Creek, the Chattahoochee swerved northward (on the map, that is; the flow, of course, was south) and ran alongside the Western & Atlantic all the way beyond Vining Station, the newly established Federal railhead and supply dump, which would be within easy reach not only of rebel cavalry but also of rebel infantry, launched across the nearby river on a track-breaking sortie that could scarcely be blocked if most of the blue army moved below. This gave Sherman pause, as well it might, and so did something else. Recent dispatches from Grant indicated that their previous concern, lest Johnston reinforce Lee for a blow at Meade, was now reversed; Lee's current problem, Grant explained, was not how he could get more troops, but rather how he could feed the ones he had, and under such circumstances it was not unlikely that he might detach a sizeable portion of them for service in far-off Georgia, just as he had done the year before, on the eve of Chickamauga. If he did so, they would come by rail: specifically, by way of Augusta on the Georgia Railroad, the one line into Atlanta that would not be threatened, let alone broken, if Sherman crossed downriver to close in on the city from the west.

Thus to define the problem was to solve it, so far at least as the choice of directions was concerned: Sherman decided to break the pattern of his campaign and move by the left, crossing the river well upstream for a preliminary strike at the Georgia Railroad. Schofield in fact had already begun the movement three days ago, when his improvised amphibious assault teams emerged from the mouth of

Red Clay Minuet [409]

Soap Creek to surprise the rebel pickets across the way, and Sherman had followed through by sending one of McPherson's corps to join Garrard at Roswell, seven miles beyond Schofield. On July 13, having reached a firm decision the night before, he continued the buildup by ordering McPherson to take his second corps upriver and reinforce the first, leaving the third in position on Thomas's right to maintain the downstream feint until Stoneman got back from the ride designed to mislead Johnston still further into thinking that the Federals were about to cross below.

"All is well," Sherman wired Halleck next day. "I have now accumulated stores at Allatoona and Marietta, both fortified and garrisoned points. Have also three places at which to cross the Chattahoochee in our possession, and only await General Stoneman's return from a trip down the river, to cross the army in force and move on Atlanta."

Stoneman got back the following night and McPherson's third corps set out for Roswell next morning, July 15. Reunited, the whiplash Army of the Tennessee would thus be on the rim of what Sherman described as "a general right wheel," designed to roll down on the city from the north and east, with Schofield about midway out the twelve-mile radius and Thomas holding the hub, or pivot, to confront and fix the Confederate main body in position for the crunch. McPherson would cross the river and march south to strike the railroad near Stone Mountain, six miles east of Decatur, Schofield's preliminary objective, about the same distance east of Atlanta. The two commands would then advance westward in tandem along the right-of-way, tearing up track as they went, and link up with Thomas for the final push that would assail Johnston along his front, outflank him on his right, and drive him back through the streets of the city in his rear.

"Each army will form a unit and connect with its neighbor by a line of pickets," the warning order read. "Should the enemy assume the offensive at any point, which is not expected until we reach below Peachtree Creek, the neighboring army will at once assist the one attacked.... A week's work after crossing the Chattahoochee should determine the first object aimed at, viz, the possession of the [Georgia Rail]road east of Decatur, or of Atlanta itself."

July 17 was the jump-off date, a Sunday, and everything went as ordered for all three armies involved in the grand wheel. Crossing with Schofield in the center, Sherman grew concerned, as usual, about what was happening out of sight: particularly in Thomas's direction, where the going was likely to be slow. "Feel down strong to Peach Tree and see what is there," he urged the Virginian. "A vigorous demonstration should be made, and caution your commanders not to exhibit any of the signs of a halt or pause." Next morning he rode over to check on the progress of the Cumberlanders, and found them crossing Nancy's

Creek on schedule to descend on Buckhead, a crossroads hamlet where Thomas would set up headquarters before sundown, within a mile of Peachtree Creek and its intrenched defenders.

"I am fully aware of the necessity of making the most of time," Sherman wired Halleck, "and shall keep things moving." Accordingly, he kept prodding Thomas: "I would like you to get to Buckhead early today and then to feel down strong on Atlanta," meantime fretting about McPherson's progress on the far left: "I want that railroad as quick as possible and the weather seems too good to be wasted."

Informed after nightfall that both Schofield and McPherson had reached their objectives and would begin their wrecking marches westward along the railroad at daybreak, Sherman exulted: as well he might, having accomplished within two days what he had predicted would require "a week's work after crossing the Chattahoochee." He had control of the Georgia Railroad from Stone Mountain through Decatur, and now, secure against reinforcements sped from Virginia by Lee, he was out to take Atlanta by bringing his combinations to bear on its outflanked defenders. The question was whether Johnston would stand, as he had done at Kennesaw, or skedaddle, as he had done everywhere else in the course of the seventy-seven-day campaign.

Riding out to confer on the matter with Thomas next morning, July 19, the red-haired Ohioan encountered an answer of sorts in a copy of yesterday's newspaper, brought out of the semi-beleaguered city by a spy. Johnston, it seemed, would neither stand nor skedaddle. "At this critical moment," Sherman later put it, looking back, "the Confederate Government rendered us most valuable service."

※ 4 ※

In Atlanta, all this time, there had been growing consternation as Sherman's "worse than vandal hordes" bore down on the city, preceded by a stream of refugees in wagons and on foot, mostly old men and boys, below or beyond the conscription limits of seventeen and fifty-two, and "yellow-faced women and their daughters in long-slatted sun-bonnets and faded calico," who had fled their upcountry farms and hamlets at the approach of the blue outriders. City parks were no longer parks; they bloomed instead with gray-white clusters of hospital tents, where the reek of disinfectants competed with the morbid stench of gangrene, and both combined to rival the predominant smell of horses. Trains chuffed into the station, day and night, loaded with sick and wounded soldiers, many of them dying, many dead before they got there. "Embalming: Free from Odor of Infection," signs proclaimed, soliciting business, and Bohnefield's Coffin Shop on Luckie Street had more orders than it could fill. "Give us this day our daily bread," the Second Baptist minister had taken as his text the previous Sunday, when news came that Marietta had been abandoned in still another retreat. And before the dawn of another sabbath, so quickly did things move at this late stage of the campaign, word arrived that the gray army had retired across the Chattahoochee, burning in its rear the bridges spanning the last natural barrier between Atlanta and destruction. "Stay a few days longer," a member of Hardee's staff advised a family he joined in town that afternoon for Sunday dinner. "I think we will hold this place at least a week."

They did not take the colonel's advice, but left next morning, scrambling with others like themselves for places on a southbound train. Places were hard to get now, for the military had commandeered most of the cars for removal of the wounded, along with all government stores and the vital machinery taken from outlying mills and factories, a salvage project assigned by Johnston to a high-ranking volunteer aide, Major General Mansfield Lovell, who presumably was experienced in such matters, having given up New Orleans two years back. Atlanta had not expected to share the fate of the Crescent City, but as the fighting grew nearer, week by week, the possibility seemed less and less remote, until finally even diehards had to admit that it had developed into a probability. Loyal admirers of Old Joe — including an editor who maintained, even now, that his reputation had "grown with every backward step" — were hard put to defend the general from charges that he intended to give up the city without a fight. For the most part, he retained the confidence and above all the devotion of his soldiers, but there were those who questioned his Fabian strategy, which they saw as leading only to one end: especially after he turned loose of Kennesaw and fell back to the Chattahoochee.

"There was not an officer or man in this Army who ever dreamed of Johnston falling back this far," a young artillery lieutenant, whose home in Atlanta was then only seven miles in his rear, wrote his mother from the north bank of that river, "or ever doubted he would attack when the proper time came. But I think he has been woefully outgeneraled and has made a losing bargain."

Official concern had been growing proportionately as the Union forces closed down on Atlanta. "This place is to the Confederacy as important as the heart is to the body. We must hold it," Joe Brown wrote Jefferson Davis in late June, appealing for strategic diversions and substantial reinforcements to help Johnston avert what seemed certain to happen without them. The governor was in touch with other prominent men throughout the South, and he urged them to use their influence on the President to this end.

His chief hope was in a fellow Georgian, Senator Benjamin Hill, who occupied the unusual position of being the friend of both Davis and Johnston, a relationship they could scarcely be said to enjoy in reference to each other. Brown's hope was that Hill could serve as a go-between, if not to bring the two leaders together, then in any case to improve communications — particularly at the far end of the line, where Brown believed the messages were having the greater difficulty in getting through. He suggested that the senator write at once to the Commander in Chief, urging a more sympathetic response to the general's pleas now that the crisis was at hand. Hill said he would do better than that; "Time is too precious and letters are too inadequate"; he would go to Richmond and talk with Davis face to face. First, though, he thought it best to confer with Johnston for a clearer understanding of the hopes and plans he then would pass along. Accordingly, he rode up to the general's headquarters at Marietta next morning, July 1, and had what he later called a "free conversation" along these lines with the Virginian.

Reviewing the situation, Johnston declared that his principal aim, up to now, had been to defeat Sherman by obliging him to attack Confederate intrenchments, but after the limited effort which had been so decisively repulsed, four days ago at Kennesaw, he doubted that his adversary could be persuaded to try the thing again. As for himself, he certainly had no intention of wasting his outnumbered veterans in any such attempt. All he could do with his present force, he said, was block the direct path to Atlanta, thus delaying another Union advance until such time as Sherman again compelled his retreat by "ditching round his flank." Aside from the long-odds chance that the enemy mass would expose itself to piecemeal destruction by dividing into segments he could leap at, one by one, he saw but a single hope for reversing the blue tide, which even then was lapping the flanks of Kennesaw and would otherwise in time no doubt roll down to the Chattahoochee and beyond. This was that 5000 cavalry be thrown without delay against Sherman's life line up in Tennessee, either by Forrest or John Morgan; in which case, Johnston said, the Federals would have to accept battle on his terms — that is, attack him in his intrenchments — or else retreat to avoid starvation. Asked why he did not use his own cavalry for such a profitable venture, the general replied that all his horsemen were needed where they were. Observing that "I must go to Richmond, and Morgan must go from Virginia or Forrest from Mississippi, and this will take some time," Hill expressed some doubt whether either body of gray cavalry could reach the Federal rear before the Federals reached Atlanta. "How long can you hold Sherman north of the Chattahoochee River?" he pointedly asked Johnston, who replied somewhat evasively that the bluecoats had covered less than a dozen southward miles in the past month, shifting their ground from around New Hope Church to Kennesaw Mountain, where they had made no progress at all in the past two weeks; Hill could figure for himself, the general said, how long it would take them to reach the river at this rate.

Hill calculated, accordingly, that the Confederates could remain north of the Chattahoochee "at least fifty-four days, and perhaps sixty."

Johnston assented, but not Hood, who though present throughout the interview had held his peace till now. He disagreed, saying: "Mr Hill, when we leave our present line, we will, in my judgment, cross the Chattahoochee River very rapidly." Johnston turned on the tall blond Texan, who was twenty-four years his junior in age, as well as in length of service. "What makes you think that?" he asked, and Hood replied: "Because this line of Kennesaw is the strongest line we can get in this country. If we surrender this to Sherman he can reconnoiter from its summit the whole country between here and Atlanta, and there is no such line of defense in the distance." Johnston demurred. "I differ with your conclusion," he said. "I admit this is a strong line of defense, but I have two more strong lines between this and the river, from which I can hold Sherman a long time."

Hill took his leave, pleased to learn that two more stout positions had been prepared for the army to defend before it retired across the Chattahoochee, some fifty-four to sixty days in the future, according to his Johnston-approved calculations, or in any case "a long time" from now. Delayed by personal matters, he took a train for Virginia before the end of the following week, passing en route a group of public men proceeding by rail on a mission similar to his own, except that the two were headed in opposite directions toward diametric goals. Hill was going from Atlanta to Richmond in hope of impressing Johnston's views on Davis, while they were going from Richmond to Atlanta in hope of impressing Davis's views on Johnston. Congressmen all, they had been delegated by their colleagues, as friends of the general, to warn him that his conduct of the Georgia campaign was under heavy attack in the capital and to urge him to disarm these rearward critics by taking aggressive action against the enemy in his front.

Reaching Atlanta on the evening of July 8 they proceeded next morning to army headquarters for a conference with Johnston, who by then had fallen back through Smyrna, the first of his two stout positions south of Kennesaw, to his bridgehead on the north bank of the Chattahoochee, which was his second. The Virginian received them graciously, heard them out, and replied, alas, as if they had been dispatched for irksome purposes by the President himself: "You may tell Mr Davis that it would be folly for me under the circumstances to risk a decisive engagement. My plan is to draw Sherman further and further from his base in the hope of weakening him and by cutting his army in two. That is my only hope of defeating him."

There was silence at this until one delegate, a Missourian, remarked that what was required, both for the country's sake and the general's own, was for him to strike the Yankees "a crushing blow," and then went on — tactlessly, but apparently in hope of jogging

Johnston into action — to say that lately he had heard the President quoted to the effect that "if he were in your place he could whip Sherman now." The general was jogged into action, all right, but not of the kind intended. He bridled and did not try to hide his scorn.

"Yes," he said icily, "I know Mr Davis thinks he can do a great many things other men would hesitate to attempt. For instance, he tried to do what God failed to do. He tried to make a soldier of Braxton Bragg, and you know the result. It couldn't be done."

This might have wound up the matter then and there, to no one's satisfaction, but a courier arrived at that point with news of a development to which Johnston's response provided the conference with an upbeat ending. Schofield had effected a south-bank lodgment yesterday, seven miles upriver, the courier reported, and this morning he had continued the crossing with what appeared to be most, if not all, of his command.... If the general's visitors expected him to react with dismay to this information that he had been flanked, they were agreeably disappointed. Pointing out that Sherman had thus divided his army, north and south of the deep-running Chattahoochee, Johnston declared that the time at last had come to strike and "whip him in detail."

The delegates returned to Atlanta expecting to hear before nightfall the roar of guns that would signal the launching of the attack. It did not come, either then or the following morning, July 10, when all that broke the sabbath stillness was the peal of church bells, summoning the city's dwindling population to pray for a deliverance which Johnston himself seemed less and less willing to attempt.

Bells were tolling that Sunday morning in Richmond, too, when Benjamin Hill stepped off the train from Georgia. He went straight to his hotel and stayed there only long enough to wash up before going to the White House for the appointment he had secured by wiring ahead. Having, as he said, "repelled the idea that any influence with the President was needed, if the facts were as General Johnston reported them," the senator was convinced that all the situation required was for him to relay the general's requests to Davis; "I did not doubt he would act promptly."

He was ushered without delay into the Chief Executive's residential office, and as he advanced across the white rug that was said to provoke temerity in the breasts of men who called in unscraped boots, the Mississippian rose to greet him with a geniality that matched the Virginia general's own, nine days ago in Marietta. Davis heard him out, his smile fading when Hill spoke of Morgan and Forrest as presumably lying more or less idle in Southwest Virginia and North Mississippi. As for Morgan, he replied, it was true that he was where Johnston said he was, having just returned, sadly depleted, from just such an expedition as Johnston recommended, whipped and in no condition for anything more than an attempt to pull his few survivors together for operations necessarily weeks in the future. Forrest too was unavailable, Davis said, although for different reasons. Having disposed of Sturgis at Brice's Crossroads in mid-June, he now was engaged in opposing a 15,000-man Union force that had left Memphis two weeks ago under A. J. Smith, bound either for Georgia to reinforce Sherman, in front or in rear of Atlanta, or for Mobile in conjunction with an even larger blue column reported to be on the march from New Orleans under Canby; he not only could not be spared for the proposed raid into Middle Tennessee, but his superior, Polk's successor Stephen Lee, was protesting hotly — as Johnston had only recently been informed — that he needed "his troops now with Johnston more than the latter can need Forrest."

Hill's hopes, which had been so high on the ride east, declined rapidly while he listened to this double-barreled refutation of the "facts" behind them. But presently they took an even sharper drop when Davis paused and asked: "How long did you understand General Johnston to say he could hold Sherman north of the Chattahoochee River?" Fifty-four to sixty days, the senator replied; whereupon Davis took up and read to him a telegraphic dispatch received just before his arrival. It was from Johnston and it announced that, a part of Sherman's army having crossed upriver two days ago, several miles beyond his right, he had begun his withdrawal across the Chattahoochee last night and completed it this morning.... Hill retired in some confusion, which was increased next day when the Secretary of War called on him "to reduce my interview with General Johnston to writing, for the use of the Cabinet."

He perceived now that his trip to Richmond, designed to help the Atlanta commander, had resulted instead in furnishing the general's Confederate foes with ammunition they could use in urging his removal from command. Three days later, after taking a still closer look at the attitude of those in high positions at the capital, he wired Johnston by way of warning: "You must do the work with your present force. For God's sake do it."

Just as the pressure had been greater, so now was Johnston's time even shorter than Hill knew — unless, that is, the general was somehow able to follow his friend's advice and "do the work." Atlanta, with its rolling mill and foundries, its munition plants and factories, its vital rail connections and vast store of military supplies, was the combined workshop and warehouse of the Confederate West, and as Sherman closed down upon it, Davis later wrote, the threat of its loss "produced intense anxiety far and wide. From many quarters, including such as had most urged his assignment, came delegations, petitions, and letters," insisting that the present army commander be replaced by one who would fight to save the city, not abandon it to the fate which Johnston seemed to consider unavoidable without outside help. "The clamor for his removal commenced immediately after it became known that the army had fallen back from Dalton," Davis added, "and it gathered volume with each remove toward Atlanta."

Nowhere was this clamor more vociferous than at meetings of the cabinet, not one of whose six members was by now in favor of keeping the Virginia general at his Georgia post. Some had advised against sending him there in the first place: including the Secretary of State, who afterwards told why. "From a close observation of his career," the shrewd-minded Benjamin declared, "I became persuaded that his nervous dread of losing a battle would prevent at all times his ability to cope with an enemy of nearly equal strength, and that opportunities would thus constantly be lost which under other commanders would open a plain path to victory." Still, those who had opposed his selection were not nearly so strident in their demands for his removal, at this stage, as were those who had been his supporters at the outset. The Secretary of War, for example, explained that, having made "a great mistake" seven months ago, "he desired to do all he could, even at this late date, to atone for it."

Davis resisted — now as in the case of that other Johnston, two and a half years ago, after Donelson and on the eve of Shiloh — both the public and the private clamor for the general's removal; Seddon later revealed that though "the whole Cabinet concurred in advising and even urging" the change, the President moved toward a decision "slowly and not without much hesitation, misgiving and, even to the last, reluctance." His concern was for Atlanta, for what it contained and for what it represented, not only in the minds of his own people, but also in the minds of the people of the North, who would be voting in November whether to sustain their present hard-war leader or replace him with one who might be willing, in the name of peace, to let the South depart in independence. A military professional, Davis knew only too well, as he put the case, "how serious it was to change commanders in the presence of the enemy," and he told Senator Hill flatly, in the course of their Sunday conference at the White House, that he "would not do it if he could have any assurance that General Johnston would not surrender Atlanta without a battle."

In this connection, he had sent his chief military adviser, Braxton Bragg, to determine at first hand, if possible, what the intentions of the western commander were. Bragg had left the previous day, July 9, but before he reached Atlanta — a three-day trip, as it turned out — the War Department received from Johnston himself, on July 11, a telegram which seemed to some to answer only too clearly the question as to the city's impending fate: "I strongly recommend the distribution of the U.S. prisoners, now at Andersonville, immediately."

Andersonville, a prisoner-of-war camp for enlisted personnel, established that spring near Americus, Georgia, and already badly crowded as a result of the northern decision to discontinue the exchange of prisoners, was more than a hundred miles due south of Atlanta. That distance, combined with the use of the word "immediately," gave occasion for alarm. For though Davis knew that what mainly caused Johnston to recommend the camp's evacuation was fear that Sherman, finding it within present cavalry range, might send out a flying column to liberate its 30,000 Federal captives — and thus create, as if by a sowing of dragon teeth, a ferocious new blue army deep in the Confederate rear — still, following hard as it did on the heels of news that Atlanta's defenders had retired in haste across the Chattahoochee, the telegram was an alarming indication of the direction in which Johnston's mind had turned now that Sherman was about to leap the last natural barrier in his path. For the first time since the clamor for the Virginian's removal began, two months ago, Davis agreed that his relief seemed necessary, and he said as much next day in a cipher telegram asking R. E. Lee's advice in choosing a successor: "General Johnston has failed and there are strong indications that he will abandon Atlanta.... It seems necessary to remove him at once. Who should succeed him? What think you of Hood for the position?"

Lee replied, also by wire and in cipher: "I regret the fact stated. It is a bad time to relieve the commander of an army situated as that of Tenne. We may lose Atlanta and the army too. Hood is a bold fighter. I am doubtful as to other qualities necessary." That evening he expanded these words of caution and regret in a follow-up letter. "It is a grievous thing," he said of the impending change. "Still if necessary it ought to be done. I know nothing of the necessity. I had hoped that Johnston was strong enough to deliver battle." As for the choice of his former star brigade and division chief as his old friend's successor out in Georgia, second thoughts had not diminished his reservations. "Hood is a good commander, very industrious on the battlefield, careless off, and I have had no opportunity of judging his action when the whole responsibility rested upon him. I have a high opinion of his gallantry, earnestness, and zeal." Further than this Lee would not go, either in praise or detraction, but he added suggestively: "General Hardee has more experience in managing an army. May God give you wisdom to decide in this momentous matter."

A series of telegrams and letters from Bragg, who reached Atlanta next morning, July 13, confirmed the need for early action, either by Johnston or the government. "Indications seem to favor an entire evacuation of this place," he wired Davis on arrival, and followed with a second gloomy message a few hours later, still without having ridden out to the general's headquarters in the field: "Our army is sadly depleted, and now reports 10,000 less than the return of the 10th June. I find but little encouraging." Two days later he was able to report more fully on conditions, having paid two calls on Johnston in the meantime. "He has not sought my advice, and it was not volunteered," Bragg wired. "I cannot learn that he has any more plan for the future than he has had in the past. It is expected that he will await the enemy on a line some three miles from here, and the impression prevails that he is now more inclined to fight.... The morale of our army is still reported good."

In a letter sent by courier to Richmond that same day he went more fully into this and other matters bearing on the issue. Johnston's apparent intention, now as always, Bragg declared, was to "await the enemy's approach and be governed, as heretofore, by the development in our front." What was likely to follow could be predicted by reviewing what had happened under similar circumstances at Dalton, Resaca, Cassville, and Marietta — or, indeed, by observing what had happened in and around Atlanta just this week; "All valuable stores and machinery have been removed, and most of the citizens able to go have left with their effects.... Position, numbers, and morale are now with the enemy." Which said, Bragg moved on to the problem of choosing a successor to the general who had brought the army to this pass. Hardee had disqualified himself, not only because he had declined the post seven months ago (and thereby brought on Johnston) but also because he had "generally favored the retiring policy" of his chief. Alexander Stewart, who had been promoted to lieutenant general and given command of Polk's corps on the retreat to the Chattahoochee, was too green for larger duties yet, despite the commendable savagery he had displayed at New Hope Church. That left Hood, who had "been in favor of giving battle" all the way from Dalton and who, in fact — aside, that is, from the peculiar circumstances that prevailed at Cassville — had done just that whenever he was on his own. By way of evidence that this was so, Bragg included a letter he had received from the young Texan the day before, expressing regret that the army had "failed to give battle to the enemy many miles north of our present position."

"If any change is made," Bragg concluded, "Lieutenant General Hood would give unlimited satisfaction." Then, as if aware of the misgiving Lee had expressed three days ago, he added: "Do not understand me as proposing him as a man of genius, or a great general, but as far better in the present emergency than any one we have available."

Davis agreed that Hood was the man for the post, if its present occupant had to be replaced, but he would not act without giving Johnston one last chance to commit himself to a fight to save Atlanta, in which case he would keep him where he was. Accordingly, in a wire next day, July 16, he put the case to the general in no uncertain terms: "I wish to hear from you as to present situation, and your plan of operations so specifically as will enable me to anticipate events."

Johnston felt no more alarm at this than he had done at Hill's

"For God's sake do it" telegram, received the day before. Busy with tactical matters, he did not take the time or trouble to outline for the Commander in Chief what he afterwards claimed was his plan for the overthrow of the blue host in his front: which — as he would set it forth some ten years later, after the guns had cooled but not the controversy — was to engage the enemy "on terms of advantage" while they were divided by Peachtree Creek. If this did not work he planned to hold the intrenchments overlooking the creek with 5000 state militia, lately sent him by Governor Brown, "and leisurely fall back with the Confederate troops into the town and, when the Federal army approached, march out with the three corps against one of its flanks." If this was successful, the bluecoats would be driven back against the unfordable Chattahoochee and cut to pieces before they could recross; if not, "the Confederate army had a near and secure place of refuge in Atlanta, which it could hold forever, and so win the campaign." So he later said — "forever" — but not now. Now he merely responded, as before, that he would have to be governed by circumstances; circumstances which it was clear would be of Sherman's making. "As the enemy has double our number, we must be on the defensive," he replied to Davis's request for specific information. "My plan of operations must, therefore, depend on that of the enemy. It is mainly to watch for an opportunity to fight to advantage. We are trying to put Atlanta in condition to hold it for a day or two by the Georgia militia, that army movements may be freer and wider."

On the defensive. A day or two. The Georgia militia. Freer and wider movements.... Johnston would later maintain that just as he was about to deliver the blow that would "win the campaign," and which he had had in mind all along, his sword was wrenched from his grasp by the Richmond authorities; but the fact was, he signed his own warrant of dismissal when he put his hand to this telegram declaring, more clearly than anything else it said, that he had no plan involving a battle to save Atlanta.

Word came next morning — July 17, another Sunday — that Sherman's whole army was over the Chattahoochee, apparently engaged in an outsized turning movement designed to close down on the city from the north and east. After nightfall Johnston was at his headquarters three miles out the Marietta Road, conferring with his chief engineer about work on the Atlanta fortifications, when a message for him from Adjutant General Samuel Cooper clicked off the telegraph receiver:

> Lieutenant General J. B. Hood has been commissioned to the temporary rank of General under the late law of Congress. I am directed by the Secretary of War to inform you that as you have failed to arrest the advance of the enemy to the vicinity of Atlanta,

far in the interior of Georgia, and express no confidence that you can defeat or repel him, you are hereby relieved from the command of the Army and Department of Tennessee, which you will immediately turn over to General Hood.

Old Joe spent most of the rest of the night in the throes of composition, preparing first a farewell address, in which he expressed his affection for the troops who had served under him, and then a response to his superiors, in which he managed to vent a measure of the resentment aroused by the backhand slap they had taken at him in the order for his removal. "I cannot leave this noble army," he told its members, "without expressing my admiration of the high military qualities it has displayed. A long and arduous campaign has made conspicuous every soldierly virtue, endurance of toil, obedience to orders, brilliant courage. The enemy has never attacked but to be repulsed and severely punished. You, soldiers, have never argued but from your courage, and never counted your foes. No longer your leader, I will still watch your career, and will rejoice in your victories. To one and all I offer assurances of my friendship, and bid an affectionate farewell."

The other document was briefer, if no less emotional under its surface of ice. "Your dispatch of yesterday received and obeyed," it began, and passed at once to a refutation of the charges made in the dismissal order: "Sherman's army is much stronger compared with that of Tennessee than Grant's compared with that of Northern Virginia. Yet the enemy has been compelled to advance much more slowly to the vicinity of Atlanta than to that of Richmond and Petersburg, and has penetrated deeper into Virginia than into Georgia." Then at the end came the stinger. "Confident language by a military commander is not usually regarded as evidence of competency. J. E. Johnston."

Hood too got little if any sleep after he received at 11 p.m. the War Department telegram which, he said, "so astounded and overwhelmed" him that he "remained in deep thought throughout the night." He had in fact much to ponder, including a follow-up wire from Seddon: "You are charged with a great trust. You will, I know, test to the utmost your capacities to discharge it. Be wary no less than bold. . . . God be with you." His appointment was plainly an endorsement of the aggressive views he had been propounding all the way south from the Tennessee line, and he was clearly expected to translate them into action. But he perceived that to do so here on the flat terrain south of the Chattahoochee, with his back to the gates of the city in his care, was a far more difficult undertaking than it would have been in the rugged country Johnston had traversed in the course of his long retreat from Dalton. "We may lose Atlanta and the army too," Lee had warned Davis five days ago, and though Hood had not seen the message, he was altogether aware of the danger pointed out — as well as of his own shortcomings, which Lee had by no means listed in full.

For one, there was his youth. He had just last month turned thirty-three, the crucifixion age, which made him not only younger than any of his infantry corps or division commanders, but also a solid ten years younger than the average among them. Then too there was his physical condition; Gettysburg had cost him the use of his left arm, paralyzed by a fragment of bursting shell as he charged the Devil's Den, and at Chickamauga his right leg had been amputated so close to the hip that from then on he had to be strapped in the saddle to ride a horse. Worst of all, though, was the timing of the change now ordered by the War Department. Sherman's final lunge at Atlanta was in full career, and only Johnston knew what plans had been made, if any, to meet and survive the shock. Certainly Hood knew nothing of them, except as they applied to the disposition of his corps on the Confederate right, astride the Georgia Railroad. Emerging at last from the brown study into which the telegram had plunged him, the blond, Kentucky-born Texan came out of his tent before dawn, mounted his horse with the help of an orderly, and set out for Johnston's headquarters near the far end of the line.

On the way there, about sunrise, he encountered Stewart on the way there too. Old Straight, who had led a division under Hood until his recent promotion to head the corps that had been temporarily under Loring, was also disturbed by the untimely change. He proposed that they unite with Hardee "in an effort to prevail on General Johnston to withhold the order and retain command of the army until the impending battle has been fought." Hood readily agreed, and they rode on together.

At headquarters, where a candle flickered atop a barrel with the telegram beside it, Johnston received them courteously, but when Hood appealed to him to "pocket that dispatch, leave me in command of my corps, and fight the battle for Atlanta," the Virginian would have no part of such an irregular procedure. He was off the hook and he intended to stay off. "Gentlemen, I am a soldier," he said. "A soldier's first duty is to obey." So that was that.

Or perhaps not. Hardee having arrived by now, the three lieutenant generals dispatched a joint telegram to the President requesting that he postpone the transfer of command "until the fate of Atlanta is decided."

Davis's answer was not long in coming, and it was a flat No: "A change of commanders, under existing circumstances, was regarded as so objectionable that I only accepted it as the alternative of continuing a policy which had proved so disastrous.... The order has been executed, and I cannot suspend it without making the case worse than it was before the order was issued."

Hood made one last try, returning to plead a second time, "for the good of the country," that Johnston "pocket the correspondence" and remain in command, "as Sherman was at the very gates of the city." Old Joe again declined: whereupon Hood launched into a personal appeal, referring to "the great embarrassment of the position in which I had been placed." Not only was he in the dark as to such plans as had been made for meeting the enemy now bearing down on Atlanta and its defenders, he did not even know where the other two corps of the army were posted. "With all the earnestness of which man is capable," Hood later wrote, "I besought him, if he would under no circumstances retain command and fight the battle for Atlanta, to at least remain with me and give me the benefit of his counsel whilst I determined the issue." Touched at last, and "with tears of emotion gathering in his eyes," Johnston assured his young successor that, after a necessary ride into Atlanta, he would return that evening and help him all he could. So he said. According to Hood, however, "he not only failed to comply with his promise, but, without a word of explanation or apology, left that evening for Macon, Georgia."

There was some fear, according to a number of observers, that the men in the ranks "would throw down their muskets and quit" when they learned of the transfer of command: not so much from distrust of Hood, who at this stage was little more than a damaged figurehead to most of them, as because of their "love for and confidence in Johnston," who many said "had been grievously wronged" by his superiors in Richmond. "A universal gloom seemed cast over the army," a lieutenant on Hood's own staff declared, and a Tennessee private — a veteran who remembered Bragg and the aftermath of Missionary Ridge — later told why the news was received with so much sorrow and resentment: "Old Joe Johnston had taken command of the Army of Tennessee when it was crushed and broken, at a time when no other man on earth could have united it. He found it in rags and tatters, hungry and broken-hearted, the morale of the men gone, their manhood vanished to the winds, their pride a thing of the past. Through his instrumentality and skillful manipulation, all these had been restored.... Farewell, old fellow!" he cried, breaking into an apostrophe of remembered grief as he approached the end of this "saddest chapter" of the war; "We privates loved you because you made us love ourselves."

Not all who felt that way about the Virginia general had to say goodbye from such a distance, either of time or space. Between the reading of his farewell address that Monday morning and his actual departure for Macon that afternoon, several units passed his headquarters on their way up to the lines on Peachtree Creek, and thereby got the chance to demonstrate their affection in his presence. A Georgia regiment happened to march out the Marietta Road, for example, and the colonel left a record of how he and his men reacted to what they thought would be their last look at their former commander, who came out of the house and stood by the gate to watch them pass. "We lifted our hats. There was no cheering. We simply passed silently, our heads uncovered. Some of the officers broke ranks and grasped his hand, as the tears poured down their cheeks."

Higher up the ladder of rank, the reaction was scarcely less emotional. Hardee, upset at having someone more than a year his junior in grade promoted over his head, promptly asked to be relieved, complaining that the President — who in the end persuaded him to withdraw his application for a transfer — was "attempting to create the impression that in declining the command [six months ago] at Dalton, I declined it for all future time." He doubted Hood's ability to fill the position to which he had been elevated, and others felt, as one of them put it, that the appointment was an "egregious blunder." Sam French called at headquarters that evening to assure the new commander of his full coöperation, but did not fail to add, with his usual forthrightness, that he regretted the change. "Although he took my hand and thanked me," he later said of Hood, "I was ever afterwards impressed with the belief that he never forgave me for what I said." Still others, aware of the reason behind the shift, foresaw hard fighting and had mixed opinions concerning the fate of Atlanta, as well as their own. Undoubtedly, Hood being Hood, they were about to go over to the offensive; Pat Cleburne, for one, believed that this was likely to take them far — in miles, at any rate. "We are going to carry the war to Africa," he predicted, "but I fear we will not be as successful as Scipio was."

Across the way, on the far side of Peachtree Creek and eastward out the Georgia Railroad, the reaction among Federals of rank was not dissimilar, so far as expectation of a step-up in the scale of fighting went, when it became known next day that the Confederates, in Lincoln's current campaign phrase, had "swapped horses in midstream."

McPherson and Schofield had been West Point classmates of Hood's, standing first and seventh respectively in a class of fifty-two, while he stood forty-fourth — ten places below even Sheridan, who had been held back a year for misconduct. Schofield in fact had been his roommate, and by coaching him in mathematics, which gave the Kentucky cadet a great deal of trouble, had managed to keep his military career from ending in academic failure and dismissal. "I came very near thinking once or twice that perhaps I had made a mistake," the Illinois general would remark in later years, though for the present he simply warned his chief: "He'll hit you like hell, now, before you know it." McPherson agreed, and so did Thomas, under whom Hood had served five years ago in Texas. But perhaps the most convincing testimony as to this new opponent's boldness came from a Union-loyal fellow Kentuckian who had watched him play old-army poker. "I seed Hood bet $2500," this witness declared, "with nary a pair in his hand."

Warned from all sides that his adversary was "bold even to rashness, and courageous in the extreme," Sherman took the precaution of advising his unit commanders to keep their troops "always prepared for battle in any shape."

Not that he regretted the predicted shift in rebel tactics. His casualties would undoubtedly mount, but there was plenty of room for taking up the slack that was evident from a comparison of Union losses, east and west. In the eleven weeks of his campaign against Johnston and Atlanta, he had lost fewer men than Meade had lost in the two-day Wilderness battle that opened his drive on Lee and Richmond. Besides, as Sherman saw it, the heavier the casualties were — provided, of course, that they could be kept in ratio, Federal and Confederate — the sooner the fighting would end with him in occupation of his goal. That was what he meant, in part, when he wrote home the following week: "I confess I was pleased at the change."

CHAPTER

4

War Is Cruelty ...

★ ✗ ☆

EASTWARD, WITH LEE AT LAST OUT-FOXED, the blue tide ran swift and steady, apparently inexorable as it surged toward the gates of the capital close in his rear. But then, at the full, the outlying Richmond bulwarks held; Beauregard, as he had been wont to do from the outset — first at Sumter, three years back, then again two years ago at Corinth, and once more last year in Charleston harbor — made the most of still another "finest hour" by holding Petersburg against the longest odds ever faced by a major commander on either side in this lengthening, long-odds war.

Grant's crossing of James River went like clockwork, and the clock itself was enormous. Preceded in the withdrawal by Baldy Smith, whose corps took ship at White House Landing on June 13 for the roundabout journey to rejoin Butler at Bermuda Hundred, Hancock reached Wilcox Landing by noon of the following day, completing a thirty-mile hike from Cold Harbor to the north bank of the James, and began at once the ferrying operation that would put his corps on Windmill Point, across the way, by dawn of June 15. While he crossed, the engineers got to work on the pontoon bridge, two miles downriver, by which the other three corps of the Army of the Potomac were to march in order to reinforce Smith and Hancock in their convergence on Petersburg, the rail hub whose loss, combined with the loss of the Virginia Central — Hunter and Sheridan were presumed to be moving down that critical Shendandoah Valley supply line even now — would mean that Richmond's defenders, north as well as south of the James, would have to abandon the city for lack of subsistence, or else choose between starvation and surrender. In high spirits at the prospect, Grant was delighted to recover the mobility that had characterized the opening of the final phase of his Vicksburg campaign, which the current operation so much resembled. Now as then, he was crossing a river miles downstream from his objective in order to sever its lines of supply and come upon it from the rear. Whether it crumpled under a sudden assault, as he intended, or crumbled under a siege, which he hoped to avoid, the result would be the same; Richmond was doomed, if he could only achieve here in Virginia the concert of action he had enjoyed last year in Mississippi.

By way of ensuring that this would obtain, he did not tarry long on the north bank of the James, which he reached on the morning of June 14 to find the head of Hancock's column arriving and the engineers already hard at work corduroying approaches to the bridge the pontoniers would presently throw across the nearly half-mile width of river to Windmill Point. Instead, wanting to make certain that Butler understood his part in the double-pronged maneuver, Grant got aboard a steamer for a fast ride up to Bermuda Hundred and a conference with the cock-eyed general. Butler not only understood; he was putting the final touches to the preliminary details, laying a pontoon bridge near Broadway Landing, where Smith would cross the Appomattox tonight for a quick descent on Petersburg next morning, and preparing to sink five stone-laden vessels in the channel of the James at Trent's Reach, within cannon range of his bottled-up right, to block the descent below that point of rebel gunboats which might otherwise make a suicidal attempt to disrupt the main crossing, some thirty winding miles downstream. Satisfied that no hitch was likely to develop in this direction, either from neglect or misconception, Grant prepared to return to Wilcox Landing for a follow-up meeting with Meade, but before he left he got off a wire to Halleck, who had opposed the movement from the outset in the belief that the scattered segments of both armies, Meade's and Butler's, would be exposed to piecemeal destruction by Lee while it was in progress. "Our forces will commence crossing the James today," Grant informed him. "The enemy show no signs yet of having brought troops to the south side of Richmond. I will have Petersburg secured, if possible, before they get there in much force. Our movement from Cold Harbor to the James River has been made with great celerity and so far without loss or accident."

The answer came next morning, not from Old Brains, who was not to be dissuaded from taking counsel of his fears, but from the highest authority of all:

> Have just read your dispatch of 1 p.m. yesterday. I begin to see it. You will succeed. God bless you all.
>
> A. LINCOLN

By that time Smith was over the Appomattox and moving directly on Petersburg, whose outer defenses lay within six miles of Broadway Landing. He had 16,000 men in his three infantry divisions, including one that joined him from City Point at daybreak — a Negro outfit under Brigadier General Edward Hincks, which had been left behind when the rest of the corps shifted northside for a share in the Cold Harbor

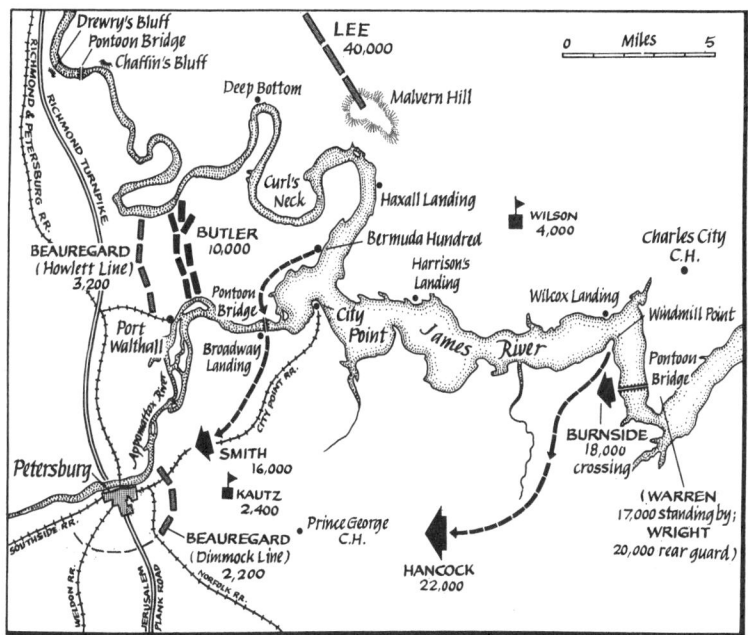

nightmare — plus Kautz's 2400 wide-ranging troopers, over toward the City Point Railroad, where they covered the exposed southeast flank of the column on the march. Four miles from the river, after receiving long-range shots from rebel vedettes who scampered when threatened, the marchers came upon a fast-firing section of artillery posted atop an outlying hill with butternut infantry in support. Hincks, on the left, sent his unblooded soldiers forward at a run. One gun got away, but they took the other, along with its crew, and staged a jubilation around the captured piece, elated at having made the most of a chance to discredit the doubts that had denied them a role in the heavy fighting two weeks ago. Baldy too was delighted, despite the delay, as he got the celebrants back into column, left and right, and resumed the march; for this was the route by which he believed Petersburg could have been taken in the first place, back in early May, and he had said as much, repeatedly though without avail, to Butler at the time. Another mile down the road, however, he came upon a sobering view, spirit-chilling despite the noonday heat, and called a halt for study and deployment.

What he saw, dead ahead down the tracks of the railroad, might well have given anyone pause, let alone a man who had just returned from playing a leading role in Grant's (and Lee's) Cold Harbor demonstration of what could happen to troops, whatever their numerical advantage, who delivered a hair-trigger all-out attack on a prepared position, however scantly it might be defended. Moreover, this one had been under construction and improvement not for two days, as had been the case beyond the Chickahominy, but for nearly two years, ever since August 1862, when Richmond's defenders learned that McClellan had wanted to make just such a southside thrust, as a sequel to *his* Peninsular "change of base," only to be overruled by Halleck, who had favored the maneuver no more then, when he had the veto, than he did now that he lacked any final say-so in the matter. Called the "Dimmock Line" for Captain Charles H. Dimmock, the engineer who laid them out, the Petersburg fortifications were ten miles in length, a half oval tied at its ends to the Appomattox above and below the town, and contained in all some 55 redans, square forts bristling with batteries and connected by six-foot breastworks, twenty feet thick at the base and rimmed by a continuous ditch, another six feet deep and fifteen wide. In front of this dusty moat, trees had been felled, their branches sharpened and interlaced to discourage attackers, and on beyond a line of rifle pits for skirmishers, who could fall back through narrow gaps in the abatis, the ground had been cleared for half a mile to afford the defenders an unobstructed field of fire that would have to be crossed, naked to whatever lead might fly, by whatever moved against them. Confronting the eastward bulge of this bristly, hard-shelled oval, Smith gulped and then got down to figuring how to crack it. First there was reconnoitering to be done; a risky business, and he did much of it himself, drawing sniper fire whenever he ventured out of the woods in which he concealed his three divisions while he searched for some apparently nonexistent weak point to assault.

Despite a superfluity of guns frowning from all those embrasures, there seemed to be a scarcity of infantry in the connecting works. Accordingly, he decided to try for a breakthrough with a succession of reinforced skirmish lines, strong enough to overwhelm the defenders when they came to grips, yet not so thickly massed as to suffer unbearable losses in the course of their naked advance across the slashings. All this took time, however. It was past 4 o'clock when Smith wound up his reconnaissance and completed the formulation of his plan. Aware that the defenders were in telegraphic contact with Richmond, from which reinforcements could be rushed by rail — the track distance was only twenty-three miles — he set 5 o'clock as the jump-off hour for a coördinated attack by elements from all three divisions, with every piece of Federal artillery firing its fastest to keep the heads of the defenders down while his troops were making their half-mile sprint from the woods, where they now were masked, to the long slow curve of breastworks in their front.

It was then that the first organic hitch developed. Unaware that an attack was pending (for the simple reason that no one had thought to inform him) the corps artillery chief had just sent all the horses off for water; which meant that there could be no support fire for the attackers until the teams returned to haul the guns into position along the western fringe of the woods. Angered, Baldy delayed the jump-off until 7. While he and his 18,000 waited, and the sun drew near the landline, word came that Hancock, after a similar hitch on Windmill Point this morning, was on the way but would not arrive till after dark. For a moment Smith considered another postponement; Hancock's was the largest corps in Meade's army, and the notion of more than doubling the Petersburg attack force to 40,000 was attractive. But the thought of Confederate reinforcements, perhaps racing southward in untold thousands even now, jam-packed into and onto every railway car available in this section of Virginia — plus the companion thought that Hancock outranked him and might therefore hog the glory — provoked a rejection of any further delay. The revised order stood, and at 7 o'clock the blue skirmishers stepped from the woods, supported by fire from the just-arrived guns, and started forward to where friendly shells were bursting over and around the rebel fortifications, half a mile ahead.

Once more Hincks and his green black troops showed the veterans how to do the thing in style. Swarming over the cleared ground and into the red after-glory of the sunset, they pursued the grayback skirmishers through the tangled abatis, across the ditch, and up and over the breastworks just beyond. Formidable as they had been to the eye, the fortifications collapsed at a touch; no less than seven of the individual bastions fell within the hour, five of them to the jubilant Negro soldiers, who took twelve of the sixteen captured guns and better than half of the 300 prisoners. Astride and south of the railroad, the blue attackers occupied more than a mile of intrenchments, and Hincks, elated at the ease with which his men had bashed in the eastern nose of the rebel oval, wanted to continue the drive right into the streets of Petersburg, asking only that the other two divisions support him in the effort. Smith demurred. It was night now, crowding 9 o'clock, and his mind was on Lee, who was reported to have detached a considerable portion of his army for a crossing of the James that afternoon; they had probably arrived by now, in which case the Federals might be counterattacked at any moment by superior numbers of hornet-mad Confederate veterans. The thing to do, he told Hincks, was brace for the shock and prepare to hold the captured works until Hancock arrived to even or perhaps reverse the odds. Then they would see.

Hancock arrived something over an hour later; two of his three divisions, he said, were a mile behind him on the road from Prince George Courthouse. This had been a trying day for him and his dusty marchers, beginning at dawn, when he received orders to wait on Windmill Point for 60,000 rations supposedly on the way from Butler. He had no use for them, having brought his own, but he waited as ordered until 10.30 and then set out without them. That was the cause of the first delay, a matter of some five hours. The second, equally wasteful of time, was caused by an inadequate map, which misled him badly — with the result that the distance to Petersburg by the direct route, sixteen miles, was nearly doubled by the various countermarches he was obliged to make when he found that the roads on the ground ran in different directions from those inked on paper — and faulty instructions, which identified as his destination a point that later turned out to lie within the enemy lines. "I spent the best hours of the day," he would complain in his report, "marching by an incorrect map in search of a designated position which, as described, was not in existence."

Nor was that the worst of the oversights and errors that developed in the course of this long hot June 15, from which so much had been expected and of which some ten critical hours thus were thrown away. Approaching Prince George Courthouse about sunset, Hancock met a courier from Baldy Smith, who gave him a dispatch headed 4 p.m. and including the words: "If the II Corps can come up in time to make an assault tonight after dark, in the vicinity of Norfolk & Petersburg Railroad, I think we can be successful." This was the first he had heard that he and his 22,000 were intended to have any part in today's action; no one on Grant's staff had thought to tell Meade, who could scarcely be expected to pass along orders he himself had not received. Hancock hastened his march and rode ahead to join Smith at about 10.30, two miles east of Petersburg, only to find that the Vermonter had changed his mind about a night attack. He requested, rather, that Hancock relieve Hincks's troops — whether as a restful reward for all they had done today, or out of a continuing mistrust of their fighting qualities, he did not say — in occupation of the solid mile of rebel works they had taken when they charged into the sunset.

It was done, though Hincks continued to insist that he could march into Petersburg if his chief would only unleash and support him. Hancock rather agreed, though he declined to assume command, being unfamiliar with the ground and partly incapacitated by his Gettysburg wound, which had reopened under the strain of the fretful march. Smith — suffering too, as he said, "from the effects of bad water, and malaria brought from Cold Harbor" — was willing, even glad, to bide his time; his mind was still on all those probable grayback reinforcements coming down from Richmond in multi-thousand-man relays. The 40,000 Federals on hand would be about doubled tomorrow by the arrival of Burnside, who was over the James by now, and Warren, who had just begun to cross. Wilson and Wright would bring the total to roughly 100,000 the following morning; which would surely be enough for practically anything, Smith figured, especially since they had only to expand the gains already made today.

"Unless I misapprehend the topography," he wired Butler before turning in at midnight, "I hold the key to Petersburg."

Beauregard agreed that Baldy held the key. What was more, he also agreed with Hincks that the key was in the lock, that all the bluecoats had to do at this point was give the thing a turn and the gate would swing ajar. "Petersburg was clearly at the mercy of the Federal commander, who had all but captured it," he said later, looking back on that time of strain and near despair.

He had in all, this June 15, some 5400 troops in his department: 3200 with Bushrod Johnson, corking the bottle in which Butler was confined on Bermuda Hundred, and 2200 with Brigadier General Henry A. Wise at Petersburg. The rest — Hoke's division and the brigades of Ransom and Gracie; about 9000 in all — were beyond the James, detached to Lee or posted in the Richmond fortifications. Wise, it was true, had held his own last week in the "Battle of the Patients and the Penitents," which turned back a similar southside thrust, but the Creole identified this recent probe by Butler as no more than "a reconnaissance connected with Grant's future operations." Heavier blows were being prepared by a sterner commander, and he had been doing all he could for the past five days to persuade the War Department to return the rest of his little army to him before they landed. Smith had no sooner been spotted moving in transports up the James the day before, June 14, than Beauregard redoubled his efforts, insisting, now that the crisis he had predicted was at hand, that Hoke and the others be sent without delay. Next morning — today — with Smith bearing ponderously down on him from Broadway Landing and his detached units still unreleased by Richmond, he warned Bragg that even when these were returned, as he was at last assured they would be, he probably would have to choose which of his two critical southside positions to abandon, the Howlett Line above the Appomattox or the Dimmock Line below, if he was to scrape together enough defenders to make a fight for the other. While Wise shifted his few troops into the eastern nose of the intrenchments ringing Petersburg, thus to confront the enemy approaching down the City Point Railroad, Beauregard put the case bluntly in a wire to Richmond: "We must now elect between lines of Bermuda Hundred and Petersburg. We can not hold both. Please answer at once." Evading the question, Bragg merely replied that Hoke was on the way and should be used to the best advantage. Old Bory lost patience entirely. "I did not ask your advice with regard to the movement of troops," he wired back, "but wished to know preference between Petersburg and lines across Bermuda Hundred Neck, for my guidance, as I fear my present force may prove unequal to hold both."

Bragg made no reply at all to this, and while Wise and his 2200, outnumbered eight-to-one by the blue host assembling in front of their works, made enough of a false show of strength to delay through the long afternoon an assault that could scarcely fail, the Creole general fumed and fretted.

Smith's sunset attack was about as successful as had been expected, though fortunately it was not pressed home; Hoke came up in time to assist in work on the secondary defenses, to which Wise and his survivors had fallen back when more than a mile of the main line caved in. Beauregard's strength was now about 8000 for the close-up defense of the town, but this growth was inconsiderable in the light of information that a second Federal column, as large as the first, was approaching from Prince George Courthouse. Dawn would no doubt bring a repetition of the sunset assault, which was sure to be as crumpling since it could be made with twice the strength. Alone in the darkness, ignored by his superiors, and convinced that Wise and Hoke were about to be swamped unless they could be reinforced, the southside commander, who had joined them by then from his headquarters north of the Appomattox, notified Richmond that he had decided to risk uncorking Butler so as to reinforce Petersburg, even though this was likely to mean the loss of its vital rail and telegraph connections with the capital beyond the James. "I shall order Johnson to this point," he wired Bragg. "General Lee must look to the defenses of Drewry's Bluff and Bermuda Hundred, if practicable."

Notified of this development two hours past midnight, Lee reacted promptly. He had suspected from the outset that Grant would do as he had done; "I think the enemy must be preparing to move south of James River," he warned Davis at noon on June 14, before the first blue soldier crossed to Windmill Point. Still, that did not mean that he could act on the supposition. Responsible for the security of Richmond, he had his two remaining corps disposed along a north-south line from White Oak Swamp to Malvern Hill, where he covered the direct approach to the capital twelve miles in his rear, and he could not abandon or even weaken this line until he was certain that the Federals did not intend to come this way. Information that Smith was back at Bermuda Hundred, and then that he had crossed the Appomattox for an attack on Petersburg, was no real indication of what *Meade* would do; Smith was only returning to the command from which he had been detached two weeks ago. Nor was the report that a corps from the Army of the Potomac was on the march beyond the James conclusive evidence of what Grant had in mind for the rest of that army. Butler had reinforced Meade for the northside strike at Lee: so might Meade be reinforcing Butler for the southside strike at Beauregard — who, in point of fact, had yet to identify or take prisoners from any unit except Smith's; all he had really said, so far, was that he had an awesome number of bluecoats in his front, and that was by no means an unusual claim for any general to make, let alone the histrionic Creole.

However, when Lee was wakened at 2 o'clock in the morning to learn that the Howlett Line had been stripped of all but a skeleton force of skirmishers ("Cannot these lines be occupied by your troops?" Beauregard inquired. "The safety of our communications requires it") he no longer had any choice about what to do if he was to save the capital in his rear. A breakout by Butler, westward from Bermuda Hundred, would give the Federals control of the one railroad leading north from Petersburg, and that would have the same effect as if the three railroads leading south had been cut; Richmond would totter, for lack of food, and fall. Accordingly, Lee had Pickett's division on the march by 3 a.m. and told Anderson to follow promptly with one of his other two divisions, Field's, and direct the action against Butler, who almost certainly would have overrun the Howlett Line by the time he got there. Moreover, leaving instructions for A. P. Hill to continue shielding Richmond from a northside attack by Meade — whose army, even with one corps detached, was still better than twice as large as the Army of Northern Virginia, depleted by Early's departure three days ago — Lee struck his tent at Riddell's Shop, while it still was dark, and mounted Traveller for the headquarters shift to Chaffin's Bluff, where Anderson's troops would cross by a pontoon bridge to recover the critical southside works Beauregard had abandoned the night before.

Sure enough, when Lee reached Chaffin's around 9.30 this June 16 and crossed the James behind Pickett, just ahead of Field, the nearby popping of rifles and the distant rumble of guns informed him, simultaneously, that Butler had indeed overrun the scantly manned Bermuda works, whose northern anchor was six miles downriver, and that Beauregard was fighting to hang onto Petersburg, a dozen miles to the south. Presently word came from Anderson that Butler's uncorked troops had advanced westward to Port Walthall Junction, where they were tearing up track and digging in to prevent the movement of reinforcements beyond that point, either by rail or turnpike. Lee replied that they must be driven off, and by nightfall they were, though only as far as the abandoned Howlett Line, which they held in reverse, firing west. All this time, Beauregard's guns had kept growling and messages from him ranged in tone from urgent to laconic, beginning with a cry for help — to which Lee replied, pointedly, that he could not strip the north bank of the James without evidence that more than one of Meade's corps had crossed — and winding up proudly, yet rather mild withal: "We may have force sufficient to hold Petersburg." In response to queries about Grant, whose whereabouts might indicate his intentions, Old Bory could only say at the end of the long day's fight: "No satisfactory information yet received of Grant's crossing James River. Hancock's and Smith's corps are however in our front."

Lee already knew this last. What he did not know, because Beauregard did not know it to pass it along to him, was that Burnside had been in front of Petersburg since midmorning (in fact, his was the corps responsible for such limited gains as the Federals made today) and that Warren was arriving even then, bringing the blue total to more than 75,000, with still another 25,000 on the way. Wilson, who had served Grant well in Sheridan's absence with the other two mounted divisions, was riding hard through the twilight from Windmill Point, and Wright would finish crossing the pontoon bridge by midnight with the final elements of Meade's army. Beauregard, whose strength had been raised in the course of the day to just over 14,000 by the arrival of Johnson from Bermuda Hundred and Ransom and Gracie from Richmond, might find the odds he had faced yesterday and today stretched unbearably tomorrow, despite the various oversights and hitches that had disrupted the Union effort south of the James for the past two days.

In all that time, hamstrung by conflicting orders and inadequate maps — and rendered cautious, moreover, by remembrance of Cold Harbor, fought two weeks ago tomorrow — the attackers had not managed to bring their preponderance of numbers to bear in a single concerted assault on the cracked and creaking Dimmock Line. Yet Grant, for one, was not inclined to be critical at this juncture. As he prepared for bed tonight in his tent at City Point, where he had transferred his headquarters the day before, he said with a smile, sitting half undressed on the edge of his cot: "I think it is pretty well, to get across a great river and come up here and attack Lee in the rear before he is ready for us."

So he said, and so it was; "pretty well," indeed. But June 17, even though all of Meade's army was over the James before it dawned and had been committed to some kind of action before it ended, turned out to be little different. Today, as yesterday, the pressure built numerically beyond what should have been the rebel breaking point — better than 80,000 opposed by fewer than 15,000 — yet was never brought decisively to bear. From the outset, things again went wrong: beginning with Warren, who came up the previous night. Instructed to extend the left beyond the Jerusalem Plank Road for a sunrise attack up that well-defined thoroughfare, he encountered skirmishers on the approach march and turned astride the Norfolk Railroad to drive them back, thus missing a chance (which neither he nor his superiors knew existed) to strike beyond the occupied portion of the Dimmock Line. If this had not happened, if Warren had brushed the skirmishers aside and continued his march as instructed, Beauregard later said, "I would have been compelled to evacuate Petersburg without much resistance." As it was, the conflict here at the south end of the line amounted to little more than an all-day long-range demonstration.

Northward along the center, where Burnside's and Hancock's corps were posted, the fighting was a good deal bloodier, although not much more productive in the end. One of Burnside's divisions started things off by seizing a critical hill, yet could not exploit the advantage because he failed to alert his other two divisions to move up quickly in support. The Confederates had time to shore up their crumbling defenses, both here and just to the north where Hancock's three divisions were

War Is Cruelty ... [437]

lying idle; Hancock having been obliged by his reopened wound to turn the command over to Birney — a good man, but no Hancock — they too had failed to get the word, with the result that they were about as much out of things as were Wright's three divisions, one of which was used to bolster the fought-out Smith, inactive on the right, while the other two were sent in response to Butler's urgent plea for reinforcements to keep Lee from driving him back into the bottle he had popped out of yesterday. Wright went, but failed to arrive in time to do anything more than join the Bermuda Hundred soldiers in captivity. By midafternoon, Pickett and Field had retaken the Howlett Line from end to end; Butler was recorked, this time for good, and still more troops were reported to be on the march from Lee's position east of Richmond.

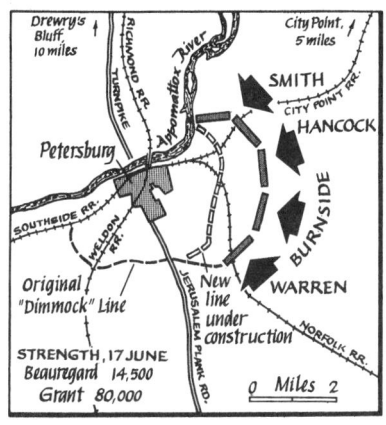

If they got there, if Petersburg was heavily reinforced, the Army of the Potomac would simply have exchanged one stalemate for another, twice the distance from the rebel capital and on the far side of a major river. There still was time to avoid this, however. None of Lee's veterans was yet across the Appomattox, and most of them were still beyond the James. With the railroad severed at Walthall Junction, even the closest were unlikely to reach the field by first light tomorrow; which left plenty of time for delivering the coördinated attack the Federals had been trying for all along, without success.

Happily, near sunset, at least a portion of the army recovered a measure of its old élan. Burnside and Birney, suddenly meshing gears, surged forward to seize another mile of works along the enemy center, together with a dozen guns and about 500 prisoners. A savage counterattack (by Gracie's brigade, it later developed, though at the time the force had seemed considerably larger) forestalled any rapid enlargement of the breakthrough, either in width or depth. Dusk deepened into darkness, and though the moon, only two nights short of the full, soon came out to flood the landscape with its golden light, Meade — 'ike Smith before him, two dusks ago — declined to follow through by continuing the advance. Instead, he issued orders for a mass assault to be launched all along the line at the first wink of dawn.

Beauregard said afterwards that at this point, with his center pierced and Petersburg once more up for grabs, it seemed to him that "the last hour of the Confederacy had arrived." In fact, he had been expecting his patched-up line to crack all day, and he had begun at noon the laying out of a new defensive position, the better part of a mile in rear of the present one, to fall back on when the time came. He had no engineers, and indeed no reserves of any kind for digging; all he could do was mark the proposed line with white stakes, easily seen at night, and hope the old intrenchments would hold long enough for darkness to cover the withdrawal of his soldiers, who would do the digging when they got there. The old works, or what was left of them, did hold; or anyhow they nearly did, and Gracie's desperate counterattack delayed a farther blue advance until nightfall stopped the fighting. Old Bory ordered campfires lighted all along the front and sentinels posted well forward; then at midnight, behind this curtain of light and the fitful spatter of picket fire, the rest of his weary men fell back through the moon-drenched gloom to the site of their new line, which they then began to dig, using bayonets and tin cans for tools and getting what little sleep they could between shifts.

At 12.40 a.m. their commander got off his final dispatch of the day to Lee. "All quiet at present. I expect renewal of attack in morning. My troops are becoming much exhausted. Without immediate and strong reinforcements results may be unfavorable. Prisoners report Grant on the field with his whole army."

Lee now had a definite statement, the first in five days, not only that Meade's army was no longer in his front, but also that it was in Beauregard's, and he reacted accordingly. In point of fact, he had begun to act on this premise in response to a dispatch written six hours earlier, in which the southside commander informed him that increasing pressure along his "already much extended lines" would compel him to retire to a shorter line, midway between his original works and the vital rail hub in his rear. "This I shall hold as long as practicable," he added, "but without reinforcements I may have to evacuate the city very shortly." Petersburg's fate was Richmond's; Lee moved, as he had done two nights ago when the Creole stripped the Howlett Line, to forestall disaster — or anyhow to be in a better position to forestall it — by ordering Anderson's third division to proceed to Bermuda Neck and A. P. Hill to cross the James at Chaffin's Bluff and await instructions for a march in either direction, back north or farther south down the Petersburg Turnpike, depending on developments.

So much he had done already, and now that Beauregard's 12.40 message was at hand, stating flatly that Grant was "on the field with his whole army," he followed through by telling Anderson to send his third division on to Petersburg at once and follow with the second. A. P. Hill would go as well, leaving one of his three divisions north of the Appomattox in case Richmond came under attack. This last seemed highly unlikely, however; for a report came in, about this time, that cavalry had ridden down the Peninsula the previous afternoon, as far as Wilcox Landing, and found that all four of Meade's corps had crossed to Windmill Point in the course of the past three days. Beauregard's information, gathered from prisoners, thus was confirmed beyond all doubt. It was now past 3.30 in the morning, June 18; Lee's whole army, except for one division left holding the Howlett Line against Butler — and of course Early, who made contact with Hunter at Lynchburg that same day — would be on the march for Petersburg within the hour.

Two staff officers arrived just then from beyond the Appomattox, sent by their chief to lend verbal weight to his written pleas for help. "Unless reinforcements are sent before forty-eight hours," one of them told Lee he had heard Old Bory declare, "God Almighty alone can save Petersburg and Richmond." Normally, Lee did not approve of such talk; it seemed to him tinged with irreverence. But this was no normal time. "I hope God Almighty will," he said.

For the first time since the crossing of the James, Meade's army gave him on schedule all he asked for. In line before dawn, the troops went forward before sunrise, under orders to take the Confederate works "at all costs." They took them, in fact, at practically no cost at all; for they were deserted, covered only by a handful of pickets who got off a shot or two, then scampered rearward or surrendered.

The result was about as disruptive to the attackers, however, as if they had met the stiffest kind of resistance. First, there was the confusion of calling a halt in the abandoned trenches, which had to be occupied for defense against a tricky counterstroke, and then there followed the testy business of groping about to locate the vanished rebels. All this took time. It was midmorning before they found them, nearly a mile to the west, and presently they had cause to wish they hadn't. Beauregard had established a new and shorter line, due south from the Appomattox to a connection with the old works beyond the Jerusalem Plank Road, and was dug in all along it, guns clustered thicker than ever. A noon assault, spearheaded by Birney, was bloodily repulsed: so bloodily and decisively, indeed, that old-timers among the survivors — who had encountered this kind of fire only too often throughout six weeks of crablike sidling from the Rapidan to the Chickahominy — sent back word that Old Bory had been reinforced: by Lee.

It was true. Anderson's lead division had arrived at 7.30 and the second marched in two hours later, followed at 11 o'clock by Lee himself, who rode out to confer with Beauregard, now second-in-command, his lonely ordeal ended. As fast as the lean, dusty marchers came up they were put into line alongside the nearly fought-out defenders, some of whom tried to raise a feeble cheer of welcome, while others wept from exhaustion at the sudden release from tension. They were pleased to hear that A. P. Hill would also be up by nightfall to reduce the all-but-unbearable odds to the accustomed two-to-one, but as far as they were concerned the situation was stabilized already; they had considered their line unbreakable from the time the first of the First Corps veterans arrived to slide their rifles across the newly dug earth of the parapets and sight down them in the direction from which the Yankees would have to come when they attacked.

Across the way, the men who would be expected to do the coming flatly agreed. Remembering one Cold Harbor, they saw here the makings of another, and they wanted no part of it. The result, after the costly noon repulse, was a breakdown of the command system, so complete that Meade got hopping mad and retired, in effect, from any further participation in the effort. "I find it useless to appoint an hour to effect coöperation.... What additional orders to attack you require I cannot imagine," he complained in a message sent to all corps commanders. His solution, if it could be called such, was for them "to attack at all hazards and without reference to each other."

Under these circumstances, the army was spared another Cold Harbor only because its members, for the most part, declined to obey such orders as would have brought on a restaging of that fiasco. Hancock's troops had come up in high spirits, three days ago; "We knew that we had outmarched Lee's veterans and that our reward was at hand," one would recall. These expectations had died since then, however, along with a great many of the men who shared them. "Are you going to charge those works?" a cannoneer asked as a column of infantry passed his battery, headed for the front, and was told by a foot soldier: "No, we are not going to charge. We are going to run toward the Confederate earthworks and then we are going to run back. We have had enough of assaulting earthworks."

As the afternoon wore on, many declined to do even that much. Around 4 o'clock, for example, Birney massed a brigade for an all-out attack on the rebel center. He formed the troops in four lines, the front two made up of half a dozen veteran units, the rear two of a pair of outsized heavy-artillery regiments, 1st Massachusetts and 1st Maine. All four lines were under instructions to remain prone until the order came to rise and charge; but when it was given, the men in the front ranks continued to hug the ground, paying no attention to the shouts and exhortations of their saber-waving officers. They looked back and saw that the rear-rank heavies had risen and were preparing to go forward. "Lay down, you damn fools! You can't take them works!" they cried over their shoulders. For all their greenness, the Bay State troops knew sound advice when they heard it. They lay back down. But the Maine men were rugged. They stepped through and over the prone ranks of veterans and moved at the double against the enemy intrenchments, which broke into flame at their approach. None of them made it up to the clattering rebel line, and few of them made it back to their own. Of the 850 who went forward, 632 fell in less than half an hour. That was just over 74 percent, the severest loss suffered in a single engagement by any Union regiment in the whole course of the war.

This could not continue, nor did it. Before sunset Meade wired Grant that he believed nothing more could be accomplished here today. "Our men are tired," he informed his chief, "and the attacks have not been made with the vigor and force which characterized our fighting in the Wilderness; if they had been," he added, "I think we should have been more successful." Grant — who had maintained a curious hands-off attitude throughout the southside contest, even as he watched his well-laid plan being frustrated by inept staff work and the bone-deep disconsolation of the troops — invoked no ifs and leveled no reproaches. Declaring that he was "perfectly satisfied that all has been done that could be done," he agreed that the time had come to call a halt. "Now we will rest the men," he said, "and use the spade for their protection until a new vein can be struck."

A new vein might be struck, in time, but not by the old army, which had suffered a further subtraction of 11,386 killed, wounded, or captured from its ranks since it crossed the James. That brought the grand total of Grant's losses, including Butler's, to nearly 75,000 men — more than Lee and Beauregard had had in both their armies at the start of the campaign. Of these, a precisely tabulated 66,315 were from the five corps under Meade (including Smith's, such time as it was with him) and that was only part of the basis for the statement by its historian, William Swinton, that at this juncture "the Army of the Potomac, shaken in its structure, its valor quenched in blood, and thousands of its ablest officers killed and wounded, was the Army of the Potomac no more."

Much the same thing could be said of the army in the Petersburg intrenchments. Though its valor was by no means "quenched," it was no longer the Army of Northern Virginia in the old aggressive sense, ready to lash out at the first glimpse of a chance to strike an unwary adversary; nor would it see again that part of the Old Dominion where its proudest victories had been won and from which it took its name. When Lee arrived that morning, hard on the heels of one corps and a few hours in advance of the other, Beauregard was in such a state of elation ("He was at last where I had, for the past three days, so anxiously hoped to see him," the Creole later wrote) that he proposed an all-out attack on the Union flank and rear, as soon as A. P. Hill came up. Lee rejected the notion out of hand, in the conviction that his troops were far too weary for any such exertion and that Hill's corps would be needed to extend the present line westward to cover the two remaining railroads, the Weldon and the Southside, upon which Richmond — and perhaps, for that matter, the Confederacy itself — depended for survival. He did not add, as he might have done, that he foresaw the need for conserving, not expending in futile counterstrokes, the life of every soldier he could muster if he was to maintain, through the months ahead, the stalemate he had achieved at the price of his old mobility. "We must destroy this army of Grant's before he gets to James River," he had told Early three weeks ago, in the course of the shift from the Totopotomoy. "If he gets there it will become a siege, and then it will be a mere question of time." It was not that yet; Richmond was not under direct pressure, north of the James, and Petersburg was no more than semi-beleaguered; but that too, he knew, was only a "question of time."

Grant agreed, knowing that the length of time in question would depend on the rate of his success in reaching around Lee's right for control of the two railroads in his rear. First, though, there was the need for making the hastily occupied Federal line secure against dislodgment. The following day, June 19, was a Sunday (it was also the summer solstice; *Kearsarge* and *Alabama* were engaged off Cherbourg, firing at each other across the narrowing circles they described in the choppy waters of the Channel, and Sherman was maneuvering, down in Georgia, for ground from which to launch his Kennesaw assault); Meade's troops kept busy constructing bombproofs and hauling up heavy guns and mortars that would make life edgy, not only for the grayback soldiers just across the way, but also for the civilians in Petersburg, whose downtown streets were so little distance away that the blue gun crews could hear its public clocks strike the hours when all but the pickets of both armies were rolled in blankets. Grant had it in mind, however, to try one more sudden lunge — a two-corps strike beyond the Jerusalem Plank Road — before settling down to "gradual approaches."

Warning orders went out Monday to Wright, whose three divisions would be reunited by bringing the detached two from Bermuda Hundred, and to Birney, whose corps would pull back out of line for the westward march, and on Tuesday, June 21, the movement got under way. Simultaneously, while still waiting for Sheridan to return from his failure to link up with Hunter near the Blue Ridge, Wilson, reinforced by Kautz, was sent on a wide-ranging strike at both the Petersburg & Weldon and the Southside railroads, with instructions to rip up sizeable stretches of both before returning. Grant had settled down at his City Point headquarters that afternoon to await the outcome of this double effort by half of Meade's infantry and all of the cavalry on hand, when "there appeared very suddenly before us," a staff colonel wrote his wife, "a long, lank-looking personage, dressed all in black and looking very much like a boss undertaker."

It was Lincoln. After sending his "I begin to see it" telegram to Grant on the 15th, he had gone up to Philadelphia for his speech next day at the Sanitary Fair; after which he returned to Washington, fidgeted through another three days while the Petersburg struggle mounted to climax, and finally, this morning, boarded a steamer for a cruise down the Potomac and a first-hand look at the war up the James. "I just thought I would jump aboard a boat and come down and see you," he said, after shaking hands all round. "I don't expect I can do any good, and in fact I'm afraid I may do harm, but I'll just put myself under your orders and if you find me doing anything wrong just send me right away."

Grant replied, not altogether jokingly, that he would do that, and the group settled down for talk. By way of reassurance as to the outcome of the campaign, which now had entered a new phase — one that opened with his army twice as far from the rebel capital as it had been the week before — the general took occasion to remark that his present course was certain to lead to victory. "You will never hear of me farther from Richmond than now, till I have taken it," he declared. "I am just as sure of going into Richmond as I am of any future event. It may take a long summer day, as they say in the rebel papers, but I will do it."

Lincoln was glad to hear that; but he had been watching the casualty lists, along with the public reaction they provoked. "I cannot pretend to advise," he said, somewhat hesitantly, "but I do sincerely hope that all may be accomplished with as little bloodshed as possible."

Aside from this, which was as close to an admonition as he came, he kept the conversation light. "The old fellow remained with us till the next day, and told stories all the time," the staff colonel informed his wife, adding: "On the whole he behaved very well."

One feature of the holiday was a horseback visit to Hincks's division, where news of Lincoln's coming gathered around him a throng of black soldiers ("grinning from ear to ear," the staffer wrote, "and displaying an amount of ivory terrible to behold") anxious for a chance to touch the Great Emancipator or his horse in passing. Tears in his eyes, he took off his hat in salute to them, and his voice broke when he thanked them for their cheers. This done, he rode back to City Point for the night, then reboarded the steamer next morning for an extension of his trip upriver to pay a courtesy call on Ben Butler, whose views on politics were as helpful, in their way, as were Grant's on army matters. He returned to Washington overnight, refreshed in spirit and apparently reinforced in the determination he had expressed a week ago at the Sanitary Fair: "We accepted this war for an object, a worthy object, and the war will end when that object is attained. Under God, I hope it never will until that time."

Helpful though the two-day outing was for Lincoln, by way of providing relaxation and lifting his morale, the events of that brief span around Petersburg had an altogether different effect on Grant, or at any rate on the troops involved in his intended probe around Lee's right. After moving up, as ordered, on the night of June 21, Wright and Birney (Hancock was still incapacitated, sloughing fragments of bone from the reopened wound in his thigh) lost contact as they advanced next morning through the woods just west of the Jerusalem Plank Road, under instructions to extend the Federal left to the Weldon Railroad. Suddenly, without warning, both were struck from within the gap created by their loss of contact. Lee had unleashed A. P. Hill, who attacked with his old fire and savagery, using one division to hold Wright's three in check while mauling Birney's three with the other two. The result was not only a repulse; it was also a humiliation. Though his loss in killed and wounded was comparatively light, no fewer than 1700 of Birney's men — including those in a six-gun battery of field artillery, who then stood by and watched their former weapons being used against their former comrades — surrendered rather than risk their lives in what he called "this most unfortunate and disgraceful affair." Hardest hit of all was Gibbon's division, which had crossed the Rapidan seven weeks ago with 6799 men and had suffered, including heavy reinforcements, a total of 7970 casualties, forty of them regimental commanders. Such losses, Gibbon declared in his formal report, "show why it is that troops, which at the commencement of the campaign were equal to almost any undertaking, became toward the end of it unfit for almost any."

Wilson, after a heartening beginning, fared even worse than the infantry in the end. Reinforced by Kautz to a strength of about 5000 horsemen and twelve guns, he struck and wrecked a section of the Weldon Railroad above Reams Station, nine miles south of Petersburg, then plunged on to administer the same treatment to the Southside and the Richmond & Danville, which crossed at Burkeville, fifty miles to the west. Near the Staunton River, eighty miles southwest of Petersburg, with close to sixty miles of track ripped up on the three roads, he turned and started back for his own lines, having been informed that they would have been extended by then to the Petersburg & Weldon. On the way there, he was harried by ever-increasing numbers of gray cavalry, and when he approached Reams Station he found it held, not by Wright or Birney, who he had been told would be there, but by A. P. Hill. Moreover, the mounted rebels, pressing him by now from all directions, turned out to be members of Hampton's other two divisions, returned ahead of Sheridan from the fight at Trevilian Station. Outnumbered and all but surrounded, Wilson set fire to his wagons, spiked his artillery, and fled southward in considerable disorder to the Nottoway River, which he succeeded in putting between him and his pursuers for a getaway east and north. He had accomplished most of what he was sent out to do, but at a cruel cost, including 1500 of his troopers killed or captured, his entire train burned, and all twelve of his guns abandoned.

Grant had the news of these two near fiascos to absorb, and simultaneously there came word of still a third, one hundred air-line miles to the west, potentially far graver than anything that had happened close at hand. Wright and Birney at least had extended the Federal left beyond the Jerusalem Road, and Wilson and Kautz had played at least temporary havoc with no less than three of Lee's critical rail supply lines. But David Hunter, aside from his easy victory two weeks ago at Piedmont and a good deal of incidental burning of civilian property since, accomplished little more, in the end, than the creation of just such a military vacuum as Lee specialized in filling.

Descending on Lynchburg late in the day, June 17, Hunter found Breckinridge drawn up to meet him with less than half as many troops. He paused overnight, preparing to stage another Piedmont in the morning, only to find, when it broke, that Jubal Early had arrived by rail from Charlottesville to even the odds with three veteran divisions: whereupon Hunter (for lack of ammunition, he later explained) went over to the defensive and fell back that night, under cover of darkness, to the shelter of the Blue Ridge. Early came on after him, and Hunter decided that, under the circumstances, his best course would be to return to West Virginia without delay. For three days Early pursued him, with small profit, then gave it up and on June 22 — while A. P. Hill was mauling Birney, south of Petersburg — marched for Staunton and the head of the Shenandoah Valley, that classic route for Confederate invasion which Lee had used so effectively in the past to play on Halleck's and Lincoln's fears.

These last were likely to be enlarged just now, and not without cause. With Hunter removed from all tactical calculations, nothing blue stood between Early and the Potomac, and with the capital defenses stripped of their garrisons to provide reinforcements and replacements for Meade, little remained with which to contest a gray advance from the Potomac into Washington itself. Lincoln had come up the James this week for a first-hand look at the war, but now it began to appear that he needed only to have waited a few days in the White House for the war to come to him.

So much was possible; Halleck's worst fears as to the consequences of the southside shift for the failed assault might now be proved only too valid. But Grant was not given to intensive speculation on possible future disasters; he preferred to meet them when they came, having long since discovered that few of them ever did. Instead, in writing to Old Brains on June 23 he stressed his need for still more soldiers, as a way of forestalling requests (or, in Lincoln's case, orders) for detachments northward from those he had on hand. "The siege of Richmond bids fair to be tedious," he informed him, "and in consequence of the very extended lines we must have, a much larger force will be necessary than would be required in ordinary sieges against the same force that now opposes us." Two days later, in passing along the news that Hunter was indeed in full retreat, he added that Sheridan had at last returned, though with his horses too worn down to be of any help to Wilson, who was fighting his way back east against lengthening odds. "I shall try to give the army a few days' rest, which they now stand much in need of," Grant concluded, rather blandly.

★ ★ ★

After frightening Hunter's 18,000 away from Lynchburg, westward beyond the Blue Ridge, and enjoying a day's rest from the three-day Allegheny chase that followed, the 14,000 Confederates took up the march for Staunton via Lexington, where on June 25 part of the column filed past Stonewall Jackson's grave, heads uncovered, arms reversed, bands intoning a dirge with muted horns and muffled drums. This salute to the fallen hero was altogether fitting as an invocation of the spirit it was hoped would guide the resurrected Army of the Valley through the campaign about to be undertaken by his old Second Corps, now led by Jubal Early. "Strike as quick as you can," Lee had telegraphed a week ago, as soon as he learned that Meade's whole army was south of the James, "and, if circumstances authorize, carry out the original plan, or move upon Petersburg without delay."

The original plan, explained to Early on the eve of his departure from Cold Harbor, June 13, was for him to follow the slash at Hunter with a fast march down the Valley, then cross the Potomac near Harpers Ferry and head east and south, through western Maryland, for a menacing descent on the Federal capital itself. Lee's hope was that this would produce one of two highly desirable results. Either it would alarm Lincoln into ordering heavy detachments northward from the Army of the Potomac, which might give Richmond's defenders a chance to lash out at the weakened attackers and drive them back from the city's gates, or else it would provoke Grant into staging a desperate assault, Cold Harbor style, that would serve even better to bleed him down for being disposed of by the counterattack that would follow his repulse. Given his choice, Early stuck to the original plan. After driving Hunter beyond the mountains, which removed him from all immediate tactical calculations, the gray pursuers rested briefly, then passed for the last time in review by their great captain's grave in battered Lexington and continued on to Staunton, where their hike down the Valley Turnpike would begin.

Early got there next day, ahead of his troops, and reorganized the 10,000 foot soldiers into two corps while awaiting their arrival. By assigning Gordon's division to Breckinridge, who coupled it with his own, he gave the former Vice President a post befitting his dignity and put thirty-five-year-old Robert Rodes — a native of Lynchburg, which he had just helped to save from Hunter's firebrands, and a graduate and one-time professor at V.M.I., whose scorched ruins he viewed sadly, and no doubt angrily as well, after marching his veterans past that other V.M.I. professor's grave — in charge of the remaining corps, composed of his own and Dodson Ramseur's divisions; Ramseur, a North Carolinian, promoted to major general the day after his twenty-seventh birthday early this month, was the youngest West Pointer to achieve that rank in Lee's army. The remaining 4000 effectives were cavalry and artillery, and these too were included in the shakeup designed to promote efficiency in battle and on the march. Robert Ransom, sent from Richmond for the purpose, was given command of the three mounted brigades ("buttermilk rangers," Early disaffectionately styled these horsemen, riled by their failure to bring Hunter to bay the week before) along with instructions to infuse some badly needed discipline into their ranks. As for the long arm, it was not so much reshuffled as it was stripped by weeding out the less serviceable guns and using only the best of teams to draw the surviving forty, supplemented by ten lighter pieces the cavalry would bring along. Recalling his predecessor Ewell's dictum, "The road to glory cannot be followed with much baggage," Early stipulated that one four-horse "skillet wagon" would have to suffice for transporting the cooking utensils for each 500 men, and he even warned that "regimental and company officers must carry for themselves such underclothing as they need for the present expedition." One major problem remained unsolved: a lack of shoes for half the army. This would not matter greatly in Virginia, but experience had shown that barefoot men suffered cruelly on the stony Maryland roads. Assured by the Quartermaster General that a shipment of shoes would overtake him before he crossed the Potomac, Early put the column in motion at first light June 28. Already beyond New Market two days later, some fifty miles down the turnpike, he informed Lee that his troops were "in fine condition and spirits, their health greatly improved.... If you can continue to threaten Grant," he added, "I hope to be able to do something for your relief and the success of our cause shortly. I shall lose no time."

True to his word, he reached Winchester on July 2, the Gettysburg anniversary, and there divided his army, sending one corps north, through Martinsburg, and the other east toward Harpers Ferry, where they were to converge two days later; Franz Sigel was at the former place with a force of about 5,000, while the latter contained a garrison roughly half that size, and Early wanted them both, if possible, together with all their equipment and supplies. It was not possible. Sigel — who by now had been dubbed "The Flying Dutchman" — was too nimble for him, scuttling eastward to join the Ferry garrison before the rebel

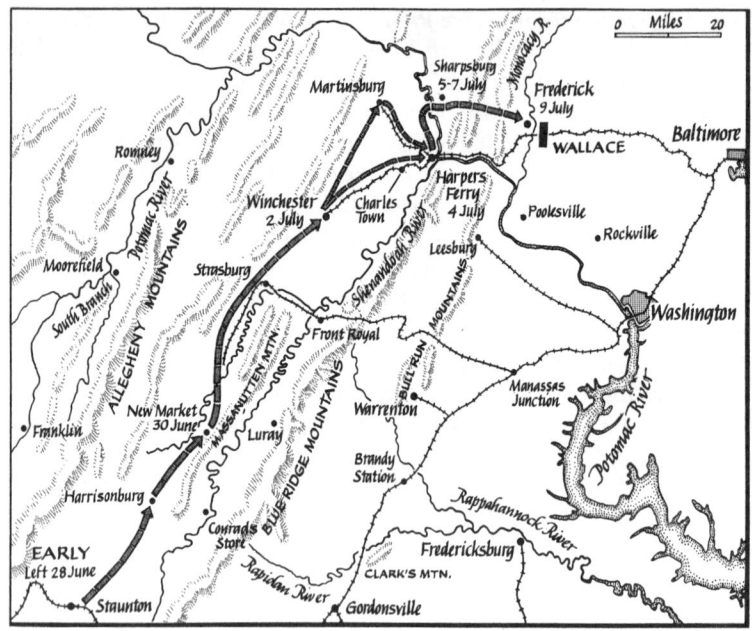

jaws could close and then taking sanctuary on Maryland Heights, which Early found too stout for storming when he came up on Independence Day. While one brigade maneuvered on Bolivar Heights to keep up the scare across the way, the rest of the Valley army settled down to feasting on the good things the Federals had left behind, here and at Martinsburg as well. Two days were spent preparing to cross the Potomac at Boteler's Ford, just upstream near Shepherdstown, and distributing the shipment of shoes that arrived on schedule from Richmond. On July 6 the crossing began in earnest; a third gray invasion was under way. No bands played "My Maryland," as before, but there was a chance for some of the veterans to revisit Sharpsburg, where they had fought McClellan, two Septembers back, from dawn to dusk along Antietam Creek. On they trudged, across South Mountain on July 8, breaking in their new shoes, and entered Frederick next morning in brilliant sunlight. East and southeast, beyond the glittering Monocacy River, the highway forked toward Baltimore and Washington, their goal.

Certain adjunctive matters had been or were being attended to by the time the infantry cleared Frederick. Coincident with the Potomac crossing, Imboden's cavalry had been sent westward, out the Baltimore & Ohio, to wreck a considerable stretch of that line and thus prevent a rapid return by Hunter's numerically superior force from beyond the Alleghenies, and simultaneously, by way of securing reparation for Hunter's recent excesses in the Old Dominion, a second mounted brigade, under Brigadier General John McCausland — another V.M.I.

graduate and professor — was sent to Hagerstown with instructions to exact an assessment of $200,000, cash down, under penalty of otherwise having the torch put to its business district. En route, McCausland somehow dropped a digit, and the Hagerstown merchants, knowing a bargain when they saw one, were prompt in their payment of $20,000 for deliverance from the flames. No such arithmetical error was made at Frederick, where McCausland rejoined in time to see the full $200,000 demanded and paid in retaliation for what had been done, four weeks ago in Lexington, to Washington College and his alma mater. No sooner had he returned than the third brigade of horsemen, under Colonel Bradley Johnson, was detached. Hearing from Lee, in a sealed dispatch brought north by his son Robert, that a combined operation by naval elements and undercover agents was planned for the liberation of 17,000 Confederate prisoners at Point Lookout, down Chesapeake Bay at the mouth of the Potomac, Early sent for Johnson — a native of Frederick, familiar with the region to be traversed — and told him to take his troopers eastward, cut telegraph wires and burn railroad bridges north and south of Baltimore in order to prevent the flow of information and reinforcements through that city when the gray main body closed on Washington, and then be at or near Point Lookout on the night of July 12, in time to assist in setting free what would amount to a full new corps for the Army of Northern Virginia. If things worked out just right, for them and for Early, the uncaged veterans might even return south armed with weapons taken from various arsenals, ordnance shops, and armories in the Federal capital, just over forty miles from Frederick, at the end of a two-day march down the broad turnpike.

Two days, that is, provided there was no delay en route: a battle, say, or even a sizeable skirmish, anything that would oblige a major portion of the army to deploy, engage, and then get back into march formation on the pike — always a time-consuming business, even for veterans such as these. And sure enough, Early had no sooner ridden southeast out of Frederick, down the spur track of the B. & O. toward its junction with the main line near the Monocacy, than he saw, drawn up to meet him on the far side of the river, with bridgeheads occupied to defend the crossings — the railroad itself and the two macadamized turnpikes, upstream and down — a considerable enemy force, perhaps as large as his own, with sunlight glinting from the polished tubes of guns emplaced from point to point along the line. Its disposition looked professional (which might signify that Grant had hurried reinforcements north from the Army of the Potomac, under orders from Lincoln to cover the threatened capital) but Early's first task, in any case, was to find out how to come to grips with this new blue assemblage and thereby learn its identity and size, preferably without a costly assault on one of the bridgeheads. McCausland promptly gave him the answer by plunging across a shallow ford, half a mile to the right of the Washington road, and launching a dismounted charge that overran a Federal battery. Counterattacked in force, the troopers withdrew, remounted, and splashed back across the river. Though they were unable to hold the guns they had seized, they brought with them something far more valuable: the key to the enemy's undoing. So Early thought at any rate.

By now it was noon, and he wasted no time in fitting the key to the lock. Rodes and Ramseur would feint respectively down the Baltimore pike and the railroad, while the main effort was being made downstream by Gordon, who would cross by the newly discovered ford for a flank assault, with Breckinridge in support. "No buttermilk rangers after you now, damn you!" Old Jube had shouted three weeks ago at Lynchburg, shaking his fist at the bluecoats as they backpedaled under pressure from his infantry, just off the cars from Charlottesville. He repeated this gesture today on the Monocacy, confident that victory was within his grasp whether the troops across the way were veterans, up from Petersburg, or hundred-day militia, hastily assembled from roundabout the Yankee capital and dropped in his path as a tub to the invading rebel whale.

They were both, but mostly they were veterans detached from the Army of the Potomac three days ago, on July 6, just as Early began crossing into Maryland. Warned by Halleck that Hunter had skittered westward, off the tactical margin of the map, and that Sigel too had removed his troops from contention with the 20,000 to 30,000 Confederates reported to be about to descend on Washington — which had nothing to defend it but militia, and not much of that — Grant loaded Ricketts' 4700-man VI Corps division onto transports bound for Baltimore, along with some 3000 of Sheridan's troopers, dismounted by the breakdown of their horses on the recent grueling raids beyond Burkeville and Louisa. Three days later, with Early across South Mountain and Washington approaching a state of panic, if not of siege, he not only followed through by ordering Wright to steam north in the wake of Ricketts with his other two divisions; he also informed Old Brains that he would be sending the XIX Corps, whose leading elements were due about now at Fortress Monroe, en route from New Orleans and the fiasco up Red River. This last came hard, badly needed as these far-western reinforcements were as a transfusion for Meade's bled-down army, straining to keep up the pressure south of the James. Yet Grant was willing to do even more, if need be, to meet the rapidly developing crisis north of the Potomac.

"If the President thinks it advisable that I should go to Washington in person," he wired Halleck that evening from City Point, while the last of Wright's men were filing aboard transports for the trip up Chesapeake Bay, "I can start in an hour after receiving notice, leaving everything here on the defensive."

Meantime Ricketts had landed at Baltimore, headquarters of Major

General Lew Wallace's Middle Department, including Maryland, Delaware, and the Eastern Shore of Virginia. Wallace was not there, however. He had left two days ago, on July 5, after learning that the rebels were at Harpers Ferry in considerable strength, their outriders already on the loose in western Maryland as an indication of where they would be headed next. A former Illinois lawyer, now thirty-seven years old, he had been at the time of Shiloh the youngest major general in the Union army, but his showing there had soured Grant on him; the brilliant future predicted for him was blighted; he was shifted, in time, to this quiet backwater of the war. Quiet, that is, until an estimated 30,000 graybacks appeared this week on the banks of the Potomac, with nothing substantially blue between them and the national capital. Wallace said later that when he pondered the consequences of such a move by Early, "they grouped themselves into a kind of horrible schedule." If Washington fell, even temporarily, he foresaw the torch being put in rapid sequence to the Navy Yard, the Treasury, and the Quartermaster Depot, whose six acres of warehouses were stocked with $11,000,000 in equipment and supplies; "the war must halt, if not stop for good and all." Accordingly, having decided to meet the danger near the rim of his department — though at considerable personal risk, for while he knew that Halleck was keeping tabs on him for Grant, watching sharply for some infraction that would justify dismissal, he could not inform his superiors of what he was about to do, since he was convinced that they would forbid it as too risky — he got aboard a train for Monocacy Junction, where the roads from nearby Frederick branched toward Baltimore and Washington. There he would assemble whatever troops he could lay hands on, from all quarters, and thus cover, from that one position, the approaches to both cities: not so much in hope of winning the resultant battle, he afterwards explained, as in hope of slowing the rebel advance by fighting the battle at all. Whatever the outcome, the delaying action on the Monocacy would perhaps afford the authorities time to brace for the approaching shock, not only by assembling all the available militia from roundabout states, but also by summoning from Grant, down in Virginia, a substantial number of battle-seasoned veterans to throw in the path of the invaders.

Sure enough, after managing to scrape together in two days, July 6–7, a piecemeal force of 2300 of all arms, he learned that this last had in fact been done, or at least was in the process of being done. Troops from the Army of the Potomac were debarking at Baltimore even then, hard-handed men in weathered blue who had taken the measure of Lee's touted veterans down the country and were no doubt willing and able to do the same up here. Greatly encouraged, Wallace sent for Ricketts to bring his division to Monocacy Junction without delay, leaving Sheridan's unhorsed troopers — more than a third of whom lacked arms as well as mounts — to man the Baltimore or Washington defenses, and thereby help, perhaps, to reduce the civilian panic reported to be swelling in both places. Ricketts arrived by rail next day, and none too soon; Early came over South Mountain that afternoon, July 8, and on into Frederick next morning. By noon he had his army moving by all the available roads down to the Monocacy, where Wallace had disposed his now 7000-man force to contest a crossing, posting Ricketts on the left, astride the Washington pike, where he figured the rebels would launch their main attack.

He figured right, but not right enough to forestall an end-on blow that soon resulted in a rout. Gordon struck from beyond the capital pike, not astride it, coming up from the ford downstream for an attack that Ricketts saw would roll up his line unless he effected a rapid change of front. He tried and nearly succeeded in getting his soldiers parallel to the turnpike, facing south, before they were hit. They gave ground, uncovering the unburnable iron railroad bridge for a crossing by Ramseur, who together with Breckinridge added the pressure that ended all resistance on this flank. Rickett's two brigades, or what was left of them by now — the second, made up of veterans long known as "Milroy's weary boys," had been through this kind of thing before — scrambled northward for the Baltimore road, the designated avenue of retreat, and there lost all semblance of order in their haste to get out of range of the whooping rebels, one of whom afterwards called this hot little Battle of the Monocacy "the most exciting time I witnessed during the war."

By 4 o'clock it was over, and though Wallace (with 1880 casualties, including more than a thousand captured or otherwise missing, as compared to fewer than 700 killed or wounded on the other side) managed to piece together a rear guard not far east of the lost field, there was no real pursuit; Early did not want to be encumbered with more prisoners than he had already taken, more or less against his will. Nor did he want to move eastward, in the direction of Baltimore. His route was southeast, down the Washington pike, which Gordon's attack had cleared for his use in continuing the march begun that morning out of Frederick.

In any case he knew now, from interrogating captives with the canted VI Corps cross on the flat tops of their caps, that troops had arrived from the Army of the Potomac, and though he had whipped them rather easily — as well he might have expected to do, with the odds at two-to-one — he knew only too well that others were probably on the way, if indeed they were not already on hand in the capital defenses. If this was a source of satisfaction, knowing that he had fulfilled a considerable measure of Lee's purpose by obliging Grant to reduce the pressure on Petersburg and Richmond, it also recommended caution. Additional blue detachments might have arrived or be arriving from down the country in such numbers that his small army, cut off from the few available fords across the Potomac as he advanced, would be swamped and abolished. As it was, he had only to turn southwest, down the B. & O. to Point of Rocks, for a crossing that would gain him the security of the Virginia Piedmont, after which he could move south or west, unmolested, for a return to Lee or the Shenandoah Valley. Either course had its attractions, but Early dwelt on neither. He would move as he had intended from the outset, against Washington itself, and deal with events as they developed, knowing from past service under Jackson that audacity often brought its own rewards. Today was too far gone for resumption of the march, but he passed the word for his men to bed down for a good night's rest, here on the field where they had fought today, and be ready to move at "early dawn."

Sunday, July 10, was hot and dusty. By noon, the cumulative effect of all those twenty-mile hikes since the army left Staunton twelve days ago had begun to tell. Straggling increased as the day wore on, until finally the head of the column went into bivouac short of Rockville, just over twenty miles from the Monocacy and less than ten from the District of Columbia. Rear elements did not come up till after midnight, barely three hours before Early, hopeful of storming the Washington defenses before sundown, ordered the march resumed in the predawn darkness. Aware that he might be engaged in a race with reinforcements on the way there, he could afford to show his weary men no mercy, though he sought to encourage them, as he doubled the column on his lathered horse, with promises of rest and a high feast when the prize was won. Beyond Rockville, he had McCausland's troopers hold to the main pike for a feint along the Tenallytown approaches, while the infantry forked left for Silver Spring, half a dozen miles from the heart of the city by way of the main-traveled Seventh Street Road.

Heat and dust continued to take their toll; "Our division was stretched out almost like skirmishers," one of Gordon's veterans, tottering white-faced with fatigue near the tail of the column, would recall. Then, close to 1 o'clock, the heavy, ground-thumping boom-bam-*boom* of loud explosions — guns: siege guns! — carried back from the front, where the head of the column had come within range of the outlying capital works.

Early rode fast toward the sound of firing, beyond the District line, and drew rein in time to watch his advance cavalry elements dismount and fan out to confront a large earthwork on rising ground to the right of the road, two miles below Silver Spring. Identified on the map as Fort Stevens, a major installation, it lay just over a thousand yards away, and when he studied it through his binoculars he saw a few figures on the parapet; by no means enough, it seemed to him, to indicate that the work was heavily, even adequately, manned. He had won his race with Grant. All he had to do, apparently, was bring up his men and put them in attack formation, then move forward and take it, along with much that lay beyond, including the Capitol itself, whose new dome he could see plainly in the distance, six miles south of where he stood.

Just now, though, his troops were in no condition for even the slightest exertion, whatever prize gleamed on the horizon. Diminished by cavalry detachments, by their losses in battle two days ago, and by stragglers who had fallen out of the column yesterday and today, they scarcely totaled 10,000 now, and of these no more than a third were fit for offensive action without a rest. All the same, he told Rodes, whose division was in the lead, to see what he could accomplish along those lines, and while Rodes did his best — which wasn't much; his men were leaden-legged, short of wind and spitting cotton — Early continued to study the objective just ahead. Beyond it, around 1.30, he saw a long low cloud of dust approaching from the rear, up the Seventh Street Road. Reinforcements, most likely; but how many? and what kind? Then he spotted them in his glass, the ones at the head of the fast-stepping column at any rate, and saw that they were dressed not in linen dusters and high-crowned hats, after the manner of home guardsmen or militia, but in the weathered blue tunics and kepis he had last encountered two days ago, when he found Ricketts' VI Corps veterans drawn up to meet him on the Monocacy.

Veterans they were, all right, and VI Corps veterans at that; Wright and the first of his other two divisions, the second relay of reinforcements ordered north from the Army of the Potomac, had begun debarking at the Sixth Street docks a little after noon and were summoned at once to the point of danger, out the Seventh Street Road. Grant himself might be on the way by now, moreover, for Lincoln — under increasing pressure as the rebel column, having knocked Wallace out of its path, drew closer to Washington hour by hour — had responded approvingly to the general's offer to come up and take charge "in person," adding that it might be well if he brought still more of his soldiers along with him. "What I think," he told Grant, "is that you should provide to retain your hold where you are, certainly, and bring the rest with you personally and make a vigorous effort to destroy the enemy's force in this vicinity. I think there is really a fair chance to do this if the movement is prompt." In other words, hurry. But then, mindful once more of his resolution not to interfere in military matters, even with the graybacks practically at the gate, he closed by saying: "This is what I think, upon your suggestion, and it is not an order."

If he was jarred momentarily from his purpose — and, after all, the notion was Grant's in the first place; Lincoln merely concurred —

it was small wonder, what with Hunter fled beyond recall up the Kanawah, Sigel holed up at Harpers Ferry, out of touch since July 4, and Washington panicked by rumors of Armageddon. Wallace, falling back down the Baltimore pike from his sudden drubbing on July 9, reported that Early had hit him with 20,000 of all arms, and though this was 10,000 fewer than Sigel had reported before the wire went dead in his direction, it still was 10,000 more than had been mustered, including War Department clerks and green militia, to man the capital defenses. Sheridan's dismounted troopers arrived about that time, a rather straggly lot who did less to bolster confidence here than their removal from Baltimore had done to provoke resentment there. When a group of that city's leading citizens telegraphed Lincoln that Sunday evening, July 10, protesting that they had been abandoned to their fate, he did what he could to reassure them. "Let us be vigilant, but keep cool," he replied. "I hope neither Baltimore nor Washington will be taken."

They remained disgruntled, wanting something more substantial. By next morning things looked better, however, at least in their direction. Returning with Ricketts, Wallace assured them that Early was headed for Washington, not Baltimore just yet. And even in the capital there was encouraging news to balance against reports that the rebel column had cleared Rockville soon after sunrise; Wright was expected hourly from Virginia with his other two divisions, and an advance detachment of 600 troops was already on hand from the XIX Corps, fine-looking men with skin tanned to mahogany by the Louisiana sun. Even Henry Halleck — who, according to an associate, had spent the past week "in a perfect maze, bewildered, without intelligent decision or self-reliance" — recovered his spirits enough to reply with acid humor to a telegram from an unattached brigadier at the Fifth Avenue Hotel, New York City, offering his services in the crisis now at hand. "We have five times as many generals here as we want," Old Brains informed him, "but are greatly in need of privates. Anyone volunteering in that capacity will be thankfully received." Then at noon the transports arrived at the Sixth Street docks (near which the Navy had a warship berthed with steam up, ready to whisk the President downriver in case the city fell); Wright's lead division came ashore and marched smartly through the heart of town to meet Early, who was reported to be approaching by way of Silver Spring. Presently the boom of guns from that direction made it clear how close the race had been, and was.

Lincoln, having ridden down to the docks to greet them from his carriage, also rode out the Seventh Street Road to watch them reinforce Fort Stevens; he may have been one of the figures — surely, if so, the tallest — Early saw etched against the sky when he focussed his binoculars on the parapet of the works just over a thousand yards ahead. Watching the dusty blue stream of veterans flow into position in the course of the next hour, Old Jube — or "Jubilee," as soldiers often styled him — knew there could be no successful assault by his weary men today. A good night's rest might make a difference, though, depending on how heavily the defenses had been reinforced by morning, either here or elsewhere along the thirty-seven miles of interconnected redans, forts, and palisades ringing the city and bristling with heavy guns at every point. What remained of daylight could be used for reconnaissance (and was; "Examination showed what might have been expected," Early would report, "that every application of science and unlimited means had been used to render the fortifications around Washington as strong as possible") but the thing to do now, he saw, was put the troops into bivouac, then feed and get them bedded down, while he and his chief lieutenants planned for tomorrow. He and they had come too far, and Lee had risked too much, he felt, for the Army of the Valley to retire from the gates of the enemy capital without testing to see how stoutly they were hung.

Accordingly, he turned his horse and rode back toward Silver Spring, where his staff had set up headquarters, just beyond the District line, in the handsome country house of Francis P. Blair, who had decamped to avoid an awkward meeting with one-time friends among the invaders. A member of Andrew Jackson's "kitchen cabinet" and an adviser to most of the Presidents since, Old Man Blair had two sons in high Union places: Montgomery, Lincoln's Postmaster General, whose own home was only a short walk up the road, and Frank Junior, the former Missouri congressman, now a corps commander with Sherman.

Guards had been posted to protect the property; especially the wine cellar, which contributed to the festive spirit that opened the council of war with recollections by Breckinridge, as the toasts went round, of the good times he had had here in the days when he was Vice President under Buchanan. Someone remarked that tomorrow might give him the chance to revisit other scenes of former glory, such as the U.S. Senate, where he had presided until Lincoln's inauguration and then had sat as a member until he left, eight months later, to throw in with other Confederate-minded Kentuckians for secession. This brought up the question Early had called his lieutenants together to consider: Was an attack on Washington tomorrow worth the risk? Time was short and getting shorter; Hunter and Sigel could be expected to come up from the rear, eventually, and Grant was known to have sent what seemed to be most of a corps already. Doubtless other reinforcements were on the way, from other directions, and though the prize itself was the richest of all — perhaps even yielding foreign recognition, at long last, not to mention supplying the final straw that might break the Federal home-front camel's back — was it worth the risk of losing one fourth of Lee's army in the effort?

Early considered, with the help of his four division commanders, and decided that it was. He would launch an assault at dawn, he told them, "unless some information should be received before that time showing its impracticability."

Such information was not long in coming. The council of war had scarcely ended when a courier arrived from Bradley Johnson, whose brigade was still on its way to Point Lookout. After wrecking railroad bridges and tearing down telegraph lines around Baltimore he had sent scouts into the city to confer with Confederate agents, and from these he learned that not one but *two* Federal corps, the VI and the XIX, were steaming up Chesapeake Bay and the Potomac to bolster the Washington defenses. In the light of this intelligence that tomorrow might find him outnumbered better than two to one by the bluecoats in the capital intrenchments, Early countermanded his orders for a dawn assault. This came hard. Just thirty days ago tomorrow he had received instructions from Lee to attempt what he was on the verge of doing. Now though — as a result, he perceived, of the victory Wallace had obliged him to win on the Monocacy, at the cost of a twenty-hour delay — it began to appear that the verge was as close as he was likely to get. Daylight would give him the chance to reconnoiter the Union works and thus determine the weight of this new unwelcome information, but he could see already that an attack was probably beyond his means and a good deal worse than risky.

Dawn broke, July 12, over a Washington in some ways even more distraught than it had been the morning before, with the rebels bearing down on its undermanned defenses. Overnight the shortage had been considerably repaired; Wright's third division followed the second out the Seventh Street Road at dusk, and soon after dark the first of the two XIX Corps divisions landed. But as these 20,000 stalwarts arrived to join about the same number of militiamen, galvanized clerks, and dismounted cavalry in the outworks, so did a host of rumors, given unlimited opportunity for expansion by the fact that the city was cut off from all communication northward, either by rail or wire, newspapers or telegrams, speech or letters. Known secessionists did not trouble to mask broad smiles, implying that they knew secrets they weren't sharing. One that leaked out by hearsay was that Lee had given Meade the slip, down around Richmond, and was crossing the Potomac, close at hand, with an army of 100,000 firebrands yelling for vengeance for what had been done, these past three years, in the way of destruction to their homeland.

Lincoln rose early, despite a warning from Stanton that an assassination plot was afoot, and rode with Seward to visit several of the fortifications out on the rim of town, believing that the sight of him and the Secretary of State, unfled and on hand to face the crisis unperturbed, would help to reduce the panic in the streets through which their carriage passed. His main hope, now that he knew Grant would not be coming — "I think, on reflection, it would have a bad effect for me to leave here," the general had replied from City Point to the suggestion that he come north without delay — was in Horatio Wright, who had helped to drive these same gray veterans southward, down in Virginia, throughout the forty days of battle in May and June. Lincoln's belief was that the Connecticut general, now that he had the means, could do the same up here.

Wright rather thought so too. Taking Early's failure to attack this morning as a sign that the rebels were preparing to withdraw, probably after nightfall, he wanted to hit them before they got away unscathed. In particular he wanted to drive off their skirmishers, who had crept to within rifle range of Fort Stevens and were sniping at whatever showed above the parapet. However, when he requested permission, first of the fort commander and then of the district commander, Major Generals Alexander McCook and C. C. Augur — both of whom outranked him, although neither had seen any action for nearly a year, having been retired from field service as a result of their poor showings, respectively, at Chickamauga and Port Hudson — they declined, saying that they did not "consider it advisable to make any advance until our lines are better established."

By midafternoon this objection no longer applied; McCook, bearded in his command post deep in the bowels of the fort, agreed at last to permit a sortie by units from one of the VI Corps divisions. Wright started topside for a last-minute study of the terrain, and as he stepped out of the underground office he nearly bumped into Abraham Lincoln, who had returned from a cabinet meeting at the White House to continue his tour of the fortifications. Informed of what was about to be done, he expressed approval, and when the general asked, rather casually, whether he would care to take a look at the field — "without for a moment supposing he would accept," Wright later explained — Lincoln replied that he would indeed. Six feet four, conspicuous in his frock coat and a stovepipe hat that added another eight inches to his height, he presently stood on the parapet, gazing intently at puffs of smoke from the rifles of snipers across the way. Horrified, wishing fervently that he could revoke his thoughtless invitation, Wright tried to persuade the President to retire; but Lincoln seemed not to hear him amid the twittering bullets, one of which struck and dropped an officer within three feet of him. From down below, a young staff captain — twenty-three-year-old Oliver Wendell Holmes, Junior, whose combat experience had long since taught him to take shelter whenever possible under fire — looked up at the lanky top-hatted civilian and called out to him, without recognition: "Get down, you damn fool, before you get shot!"

This got through. Lincoln not only heard and reacted with amusement to the irreverent admonition, he also obeyed it by climbing down and taking a seat in the shade, his back to the parapet, safe at last from the bullets that continued to twang and nicker overhead.

Relieved of the worst of his concerns, Wright turned now to the interrupted business of clearing his front. Deployment of the brigade assigned the task required more time than had been thought, however, with the result that it was close to 6 o'clock before the signal could be given to move out. The firing swelled, and Lincoln, popping up from time to time to peer over the parapet, had his first look at men reeling and falling in combat and being brought past him on stretchers, groaning or screaming from pain, leaking blood and calling on God or Mamma, in shock and out of fear. Presently the racket stepped up tremendously, and the brigade commander sent back for reinforcements, explaining that he had encountered, beyond the retiring screen of pickets, a full-fledged rebel line of battle. Supporting regiments moved up in the twilight and the attack resumed, though with small success against stiffened resistance. Gunflashes winked and twinkled along the slope ahead until about 10 o'clock, when they diminished fitfully and finally died away. The cost to Wright had been 280 killed and wounded in what one of his veterans called "a pretty and well-conducted little fight."

Across the way, the Confederates considered it something worse: especially at the outset, when it erupted in the midst of their preparations to depart. Early had needed no more than a cursory look at the enemy works that morning to confirm last night's report that they would be substantially reinforced by dawn. Permanently canceling the deferred assault, he ordered skirmishers deployed along a line that stretched for a mile to the left and a mile to the right of the Seventh Street Road to confront Forts Reno, Stevens, and De Russy, while behind this he had Rodes and Gordon form their divisions, in case the Federals tried a sortie, and sent word for McCausland to keep up the feint on the far right, astride the Georgetown pike. Here they would stay, bristling as if about to strike, until night came down to cover the withdrawal, back through Silver Spring to Rockville, then due west for a recrossing of the Potomac. Fortunately, the Yankees seemed content to remain within their works, and Early, having learned that the amphibious raid on Point Lookout had been called off because the prison authorities had been warned of it, had time to send a courier after Johnson, whose horsemen were beyond Baltimore by then, instructing him to turn back for the Confederate lines by whatever route seemed best now that the capture of Washington was no longer a part of the invasion plan. Preparations for the retirement were complete — were, in fact, about to be placed in execution — when Wright's attack exploded northward from Fort Stevens, flinging butternut skirmishers back on the main body, which then was struck by the rapid-firing Federals coming up in apparently endless numbers through the gathering dusk. The thing had the look of an all-out battle that would hold the Army of the Valley in position for slaughter tomorrow by preventing it from taking up its planned retreat tonight. Major Kyd Douglas, formerly of Jackson's staff and now of Early's, said quite frankly that he thought "we were gone up."

Presently though, to everyone's relief, the fireworks sputtered into darkness; the field grew still, except for the occasional jarring explosion of a shell from one of the outsized siege guns in the forts, and Early, resuming his preparations for withdrawal, summoned to headquarters Breckinridge and Gordon, whose divisions would respectively head and tail the column, for last-minute orders on the conduct of the march. They arrived to find him instructing Douglas to take charge of a rear-guard detail of 200 men and with them hold the present position until midnight, at which time he too was to pull out for Rockville: provided, of course, the bluecoats had not gotten wind of what was up, beforehand, and obliterated him. When the handsome young Marylander left to assume this forlorn assignment, Early called after him, apparently in an attempt to lift his spirits: "Major, we haven't taken Washington, but we've scared Abe Lincoln like hell!"

Douglas stopped and turned. "Yes, General," he said, as if to set the record straight, "but this afternoon when that Yankee line moved out against us, I think some other people were scared blue as hell's brimstone."

"How about that, General?" Breckinridge broke in, smiling broadly beneath his broad mustache.

"That's true. But it won't appear in history," Early replied, thereby assuring the exchange a place in all the accounts that were to follow down the years.

It turned out there were no further losses, even for the rear-guard handful under Douglas, who took up the march on schedule without a parting shot being fired in his direction. He saw, as he went past it after midnight, that except for the depletion of its wine cellar and linen closets — all the bedclothes had been ripped into strips for bandages — Old Man Blair's mansion had suffered no damage from the occupation, but that his son Montgomery's house, just up the road, had been reduced to bricks and ashes by some vengeance-minded incendiary. Although the act perhaps was justified by Hunter's burning of Former Governor Letcher's home the month before, Early's regret that this had been done was increased when he learned that Bradley Johnson, off on his own, had also indulged in retaliation by setting fire to Governor A. W. Bradford's house near Baltimore. Such exactions, he knew, were unlikely to encourage pro-Confederate feelings, either here in Maryland or elsewhere. In any case, dawn of July 13 — thirty days, to the hour, since the re-created Army of the Valley pulled out of Cold Harbor, bound for Lynchburg and points north — found the column slogging through Rockville, where it turned left for Poolesville and the Potomac. At White's Ford by midnight, just upstream from Ball's Bluff and thirty miles from its starting point on the outskirts of Washington, the army crossed the river in good order next morning, still unmolested, to make camp near Leesburg for a much needed two-day rest; after which it shifted west, July 16, beyond the Blue Ridge. Back once more in the Lower Valley, within an easy day's march of Harpers Ferry, Early began preparing for further adventures designed to disrupt the plans of the Union high command.

This recent thirty-day excursion had accomplished a great deal in that direction, as well as much else of a positive nature, including the recovery of the grain-rich Shenandoah region from Hunter and Sigel, just in time for the harvesting of its richest crop in years, and the return from beyond the Potomac with a large supply of commandeered horses and cattle, not to mention $220,000 in greenbacks for the hard-up Treasury and close to a thousand prisoners, most of them captured on the Monocacy, the one full-scale battle of the campaign. In fact, aside from his two main hopes — and hopes were all they were — that he could occupy Washington, even for a day, and that he could provoke Grant into making a suicidal assault on Lee's intrenchments, Early had accomplished everything that could have been expected of him. Best of all, he had obliged Grant to ease the pressure on Petersburg by sending large detachments north, and still had managed, despite the smallness of his force, if not to reverse the tide of the war, then anyhow to strike fear in the hearts of the citizens of Washington and Baltimore, both of which saw gray-clad infantry at closer range than any Federal had come, so far, to Richmond. This was much; yet there was more. For in the process Early had won the admiration not only of his fellow countrymen, whose spirits were lifted by the raid, but also of foreign observers, who still might somehow determine the outcome of this apparently otherwise endless conflict.

"The Confederacy is more formidable than ever," the London *Times* remarked when news of this latest rebel exploit crossed the ocean the following week. And closer at hand, on July 12 — even as Early and his veterans bristled along the rim of the northern capital, quite as if they were about to assail and overrun the ramparts in a screaming rush — the *New York World* asked its readers: "Who shall revive the withered hopes that bloomed on the opening of Grant's campaign?"

★ ★ ★

Who indeed. The task was Lincoln's, as the national leader, but evidence piled higher every day that it would be his no longer than early March, when the outcome of the presidential election, less than four months off, was confirmed on the steps of the lately threatened Capitol. Despite setbacks, such as Cold Harbor, Petersburg, and this recent gray eruption on the near bank of the Potomac, he was convinced that he had found in U. S. Grant the man to win the war. But that was somewhat beside the point, which was whether or not the people could be persuaded, between now and November, to believe it, too — and whether or not, believing it, they would agree that the prize was worth the additional blood, the additional money, the additional drawn-out anguish it was clearly going to cost. They, like Grant, would have to "face the arithmetic," and keep on facing it, to the indeterminate end.

One of the things that made this difficult was that the arithmetic kept changing, not only in the lengthening casualty lists, but also in the value fluctuations of what men carried in their wallets, a region where their threshold of pain was notoriously low. Gold opened the year at 152 on the New York market. By April it had risen to 175, by mid-June to 197, and by the end of that month to an astronomical 250. Reassurances from money men that the dollar was "settling down" brought the wry response that it was "settling down out of sight." Sure enough, on July 11, as Early descended on Washington, gold soared to 285, reducing the value of the paper dollar to forty cents. Moreover, Lincoln faced this crisis without the help of the man who had advised him in such matters from the outset: Salmon Chase.

In late June, with the office of assistant treasurer of New York about to be vacated, the Secretary recommended a successor unacceptable to Senator Edwin D. Morgan of that state, who suggested three alternates for the post. "It will really oblige me if you will make a choice among these three," Lincoln wrote Chase, explaining the political ramifications of a tiff with Morgan at this time. Chase then requested a personal interview, which Lincoln refused "because the difficulty does not, in the main part, lie within the range of a conversation between you and me." In reaction to this snub, the Secretary went home and, as was his custom in such matters, "endeavored to seek God in prayer." So he wrote in his diary that night, adding: "Oh, for more faith and clearer sight! How stable is the City of God! How disordered the City of Man!" Mulling it over he reached a decision. His resignation was on the presidential desk next morning. "I shall regard it as a real relief if you think proper to accept it," he declared in a covering letter.

Lincoln read this fourth of the Ohioan's petulant resignations, and accepted it forthwith. "Of all I have said in commendation of your ability and fidelity, I have nothing to unsay," he replied, "and yet you and I have reached a point of mutual embarrassment in our official relationship which it seems cannot be overcome or longer sustained consistently with the public service." Ohio's Governor John Brough, who happened to be in town, went to the White House in an attempt to "close the breach," as he had done in one of the other instances of a threatened resignation, only to find that he could perform no such healing service here today. "You doctored the business up once," Lincoln told him, "but on the whole, Brough, I reckon you had better let it alone this time." Chase departed, still in something of a state of shock from the unexpected thunderclap, and retired to think things over, for a time, in the hills of his native New Hampshire.

A replacement was not far to seek. Next morning, July 1, when William Pitt Fessenden of Maine, chairman of the Senate Finance Committee, called on the President to recommend someone else for the Treasury post, Lincoln smiled and informed him that his nomination had just been sent for approval by his colleagues on the Hill. Fessenden's dismay was plain. "You must withdraw it. I cannot accept," he protested. His health was poor; Congress was to adjourn tomorrow, and he looked forward to a vacation away from the heat and bustle of the capital. "If you decline, you must do it in open day," Lincoln told him, "for I shall not recall the nomination." Fessenden hurried over to the Senate in an attempt to block the move, only to find that he had been unanimously confirmed in about one minute. Regretfully, with congratulations pouring in from all quarters — even Chase's — he agreed to serve, at least through the adjournment. A soft-money man like his predecessor, he was sworn in on July 5, and it was observed that no appointment by the President, except perhaps the elevation of Grant four months before, had met with such widespread approval by the public and the press. "Men went about with smiling faces at the news," one paper noted.

Lincoln himself was not smiling by then. His trouble with Chase — whom he described as a man "never perfectly happy unless he is thoroughly miserable, and able to make everyone else just as uncomfortable as he is" — had been personal; Chase irked him and he got rid of him. But on the day after Fessenden's appointment he found himself in an even more irksome predicament, one that was susceptible to no such resolution because the men involved were not subject to dismissal; not by him, at any rate. On the morning of July 2, last day of the congressional session that was scheduled to adjourn at noon, Lincoln sat in the President's room at the Capitol, signing last-minute bills, including one that repealed the Fugitive Slave Law and another that struck the $300 commutation clause from the Draft Act. Both of these he signed gladly, along with others, but as he did so there was thrust upon him the so-called Wade-Davis bill, passed two months ago by the House and by the Senate within the hour. He set it aside to go on with the rest, and when an interested observer asked if he intended to sign it, he replied that the bill was "a matter of too much importance to be swallowed in that way."

He found it hard, in fact, to swallow the bill in any way at all, since what it represented was an attempt by Congress — more specifically, by the radicals in his party — to establish the premise that the legislative, not the executive, branch of government had the right and duty to define the terms for readmission to the Union by states now claiming to have left it; in other words, to set the tone of Reconstruction. Sponsored by Benjamin Wade in the Senate and Henry Winter Davis in the House, the bill proceeded from Senator Charles Sumner's thesis that secession, though of course not legally valid, nonetheless amounted to "State suicide," and it set forth certain requirements that would have to be met before the resurrected corpse could be readmitted to the family it had disgraced by putting a bullet through its head. Lincoln had done much the same thing in his Proclamation of Amnesty and Reconstruction, back in December, but this new bill, designed not so much to pave as to bar the path to reunion, was considerably more stringent. Where he had required that ten percent of the qualified voters take a loyalty oath, the Wade-Davis measure required a majority. In addition, all persons who had held state or Confederate offices, or who had voluntarily borne arms against the United States, were forbidden to vote for or serve as delegates to state constitutional conventions; the rebel debt was to be repudiated, and slavery outlawed, in each instance. Moreover, this was no more than a precedent-setting first step; harsher requirements would come later, once the bill had established the fact that Congress, not the President, was the rightful agency to handle all matters pertaining to reconstruction of the South. Sumner and Zachariah Chandler in the Senate, Thaddeus Stevens and George W. Julian in the House — Jacobins all and accomplished haters, out for vengeance at any price — were strong in their support of the measure and were instrumental in ramming it through on this final day of the session.

Gideon Welles saw clearly enough what they were after, and put what he saw in his diary. "In getting up this law, it was as much an object of Mr. Henry Winter Davis and some others to pull down the Administration as to reconstruct the Union. I think they had the former more directly in view than the latter." Lincoln thought so, too, and was determined to keep it from happening, if he could only find a way to do so without bringing on the bitterest kind of fight inside his party.

The fact was, he had already found what he perceived might be the beginning of a way when he set the bill aside to go on signing others. Zachariah Chandler, who had asked him whether he intended to endorse it and had then been told that it was "too important to be swallowed in that way," warned him sternly, in reference to the pending election: "If it is vetoed, it will damage us fearfully in the Northwest. The important point is the one prohibiting slavery in the reconstructed states." "That is the point on which I doubt the authority of Congress to act." "It is no more than you have done yourself." "I conceive that I may, in an emergency, do things on military grounds which cannot be done constitutionally by Congress," Lincoln replied, and Chandler stalked out, deeply chagrined.

His chagrin, and that of his fellow radicals, was converted to pure rage the following week — July 8; Early was crossing South Mountain to descend on Frederick — when Lincoln, having declined either to sign or to veto the bill, issued a public proclamation defending his action (or nonaction) on grounds that, while he was "fully satisfied" with some portions of the bill, he was "unprepared" to give his approval of certain others. "What an infamous proclamation!" Thaddeus Stevens protested. "The idea of pocketing a bill and then issuing a proclamation as to how far he will conform to it!"

By means of the "pocket veto," as the maneuver came to be called, Lincoln managed to avoid, at least for a season, being removed from all connection with setting the guidelines for Reconstruction; but he had not managed to avoid a fight. Indeed, according to proponents of the bill now lodged in limbo, he had precipitated one. Convinced, as one of them declared, that his proposed course was "timid and almost pro-slavery," they took up the challenge of his proclamation, which they defined as "a grave Executive usurpation," and responded in more than kind, early the following month in the New York *Tribune*, with what became known as the Wade-Davis Manifesto. Seeking "to check the encroachments of the Executive on the authority of Congress, and to require it to confine itself to its proper sphere," bluff Ben Wade and vehement Henry Davis charged that "a more studied outrage on the legislative authority of the people has never been perpetrated," and they warned that Lincoln "must understand that our support is of a cause and not of a man," especially not of a man who would connive to procure electoral votes at the cost of his country's welfare.

All this the manifesto set forth, along with much else of a highly personal nature from the pens of these Republican leaders, just three months before the presidential election. Lincoln declined to read or discuss it, not wanting to be provoked any worse than he was already, but he remarked in this connection: "To be wounded in the house of one's friends is perhaps the most grievous affliction that can befall a man."

Horace Greeley, editor of the paper in which the radical manifesto made its appearance, had been involved for the past month in an affair that added to Lincoln's difficulties in presenting himself as a man of war who longed for peace. Hearing privately in early July that Confederate emissaries were waiting on the Canadian side of Niagara Falls with full authority to arrange an armistice, Greeley referred the matter to the President and urged in a long, high-strung letter that he seize the opportunity this presented to end the fighting. "Confederates everywhere [are] for peace. So much is beyond doubt," he declared. "And therefore I venture to remind you that our bleeding, bankrupt, almost dying country also longs for peace — shudders at the prospect of fresh conscription, of further wholesale devastations, and of new rivers of human blood." Placed thus in the position of having to investigate this reported gleam of sunlight (which he suspected would prove to be moonshine) Lincoln was prompt with an answer. "If you can find any person anywhere professing to have any proposition of Jefferson Davis in writing, for peace, embracing the restoration of the Union and the abandonment of slavery, whatever else it embraces, say to him he may come to me with you." The editor, aware of the risk of ridicule, had not counted on being personally involved. He responded with a protest that the rebel agents "would decline to exhibit their credentials to me, much more to open their budget and give me their best terms." Lincoln replied: "I was not expecting you to send me a letter, but to bring me a man, or men." He also told Greeley, in a message carried by John Hay, who was to accompany him on the mission, "I not only intend a sincere effort for peace, but I intend that you shall be a personal witness that it is made."

Being thus coerced, Greeley went with Hay to Niagara, where he discovered, amid the thunder and through the mist, what Lincoln had suspected from the start: that the "emissaries" not only had no authority to negotiate, either with him or with anyone else, but seemed to be in Canada for the purpose of influencing, by the rejection of their empty overtures, the upcoming elections in the North. He retreated hastily, though not in time to prevent a rash of Copperhead rumors that the President, through him, had scorned to entertain decent proposals for ending the bloodshed. Lincoln wanted to offset the effect of this by publishing his and Greeley's correspondence, omitting of course the editor's references to "our bleeding, bankrupt, almost dying country," as well as his gloomy prediction of a Democratic victory in November. Greeley said no; he would consent to no suppression; either print their exchange in full or not at all. Obliged thereby to let the matter drop, Lincoln explained to his cabinet that it was better to withhold the letters, and abide the damaging propaganda, than "to subject the country to the consequences of their discouraging and injurious parts."

Simultaneously, in the opposite direction — down in Richmond itself — another peace feeler was in progress, put forth by Federal emissaries who had no more official sanction than their Confederate counterparts in Canada. Still, Lincoln had better hopes for this one, not so much because he believed that it would end the conflict, but rather, as he remarked, because he felt that it would "show the country I didn't fight shy of Greeley's Niagara business without a reason." What he wanted was for the northern public to become acquainted with Jefferson Davis's terms for an armistice, which he was sure would prove unacceptable to many voters who had been lured, in the absence of specifics, by the siren song of orators claiming that peace could be his for the asking, practically without rebel strings. Moreover, he got what he wanted, and he got it expressed in words as strong and specific as any he himself might have chosen for his purpose.

Colonel James F. Jaquess, a Methodist minister who had raised and led a regiment of Illinois volunteers, had become so increasingly shocked by the sight of fellow Christians killing each other wholesale — especially at Chickamauga, where he lost more than two hundred of his officers and men — that he obtained an extended leave of absence to see what he could do, on his own, to prepare the groundwork for negotiations. He had no success until he was joined in the effort by J. R. Gilmore, who enjoyed important Washington connections. A New York businessman, Gilmore had traveled widely in the South before the war, writing of his experiences under the pen name Edmund Kirke, and he managed to secure Lincoln's approval of an unofficial visit to Richmond by Jaquess and himself, under a flag of truce, for the purpose of talking with southern leaders about the possibility of arriving at terms that might lead to a formal armistice. On Saturday, July 16, the two men were conducted past one of Ben Butler's outposts and were met between the lines by Judge Robert Ould, head of the Confederate commission for prisoner exchange. By nightfall they were lodged in the Spotswood Hotel, in the heart of the rebel capital, Jaquess wearing a long linen duster over his blue uniform. Next morning, amid the pealing of church bells, they conferred with Judah Benjamin, who promised to arrange a meeting for them that evening, here in his State Department office, with the President himself. They returned at the appointed time, and there — as Gilmore later described the encounter — at the table, alongside the plump and smiling Benjamin, "sat a spare, thin-featured man with iron-gray hair and beard, and a clear, gray eye full of life and vigor." Jefferson Davis rose and extended his hand. "I am glad to see you, gentlemen," he said. "You are very welcome to Richmond."

Although he neither mentioned the fact nor showed the strain it cost him, he had not been able to receive them earlier this Sunday because of the lengthy cabinet meeting that had resulted in the dismissal telegram Joe Johnston was reading now, on the outskirts of Atlanta. "His face was emaciated, and much wrinkled," Gilmore observed from across the table, "but his features were good, especially his eyes, though one of them bore a scar, apparently made by some sharp instrument. He wore a suit of grayish brown, evidently of foreign manufacture.... His manners were simple, easy and quite fascinating, and he threw an indescribable charm into his voice."

Jaquess opened the interview by saying that he had sought it in the hope that Davis, wanting peace as much as he did, might suggest some way to stop the fighting. "In a very simple way," the Mississippian replied. "Withdraw your armies from our territory, and peace will come of itself." When the colonel remarked that Lincoln's recent Proclamation of Amnesty perhaps afforded a basis for proceeding, Davis cut him short. "Amnesty, Sir, applies to criminals. We have commited no crime." Gilmore suggested that both sides lay down their arms, then let the issue be decided by a popular referendum. But Davis, thinking no doubt of the North's more than twenty millions and the South's less than ten, was having no part of that either. "That the *majority* shall decide it, you mean. We seceded to rid ourselves of the rule of the majority, and this would subject us to it again." It seemed to Gilmore that the dispute narrowed down to "Union or Disunion," and the Confederate President agreed, though he added that he preferred the terms "Independence or Subjugation." Despairing of semantics and the profitless exchange of opposite views that had brought on the war in the first place, the New Yorker made an appeal on personal grounds. "Can you, Mr Davis, as a Christian man, leave untried any means that may lead to peace?" Davis shook his head. "No, I cannot," he replied. "I desire peace as much as you do; I deplore bloodshed as much as you do." He spoke with fervor, but seemed to choose his words with care. "I tried in all my power to avert this war. I saw it coming, and for twelve years I worked night and day to prevent it, but I could not. And now it must go on till the last man of this generation falls in his tracks, and his children seize his musket and fight his battle, *unless you acknowledge our right to self-government....* We are fighting for Independence — and that, or extermination, we will have."

Additional matters were discussed or mentioned, including the military situation, which Davis saw as favorable to the South, and slavery, which he maintained was never "an essential element" in the contest, "only a means of bringing other conflicting elements to an earlier culmination." But always the talk came back to that one prerequisite. Whether it was called Self-Government or Disunion, all future discussion between the two parties would have to proceed from that beginning if there was to be any hope of ending the carnage they both deplored. The Confederate leader made this clear as he rose to see his visitors to the door, shook their hands, and spoke his final words. "Say to Mr Lincoln, from me, that I shall at any time be pleased to receive proposals for peace on the basis of our Independence. It will be useless to approach me with any other."

Whatever sadness he felt on hearing this evidence that the war was unlikely to end through negotiation, Lincoln perceived that the closing message, along with much that preceded it, would serve quite well to further his other purpose, which was to demonstrate his adversary's intransigence in the face of an earnest search for peace. He asked Gilmore, who had stopped by Washington on his return journey from Richmond, what he proposed to do with the transcript he had made of the interview. "Put a beginning and an end to it, Sir, on my way home," the New Yorker said, "and hand it to the *Tribune*." Lincoln demurred. He had had enough of Horace Greeley for a while. "Can't you get it into the *Atlantic Monthly*? It would have less of a partisan look there." Gilmore was sure he could; but first, by way of counteracting what Lincoln called "Greeley's Niagara business," it was decided to release a shorter version in the Boston *Evening Transcript* the following week, while the full *Atlantic* text was being set in type and proofed for review by Lincoln. "Don't let it appear till I return the proof," he cautioned. "Some day all this will come out, but just now we must use discretion." The *Transcript* piece appeared July 22, followed a month later by the one in the *Atlantic*, from which the President had deleted a few hundred words mainly having to do with terms he had found acceptable off the record. Both received much attention, especially the longer version. Indeed, so widely was it reprinted, at home and abroad, that another distinguished contributor — Oliver Wendell Holmes, whose son had lately cursed Lincoln off the parapet at Fort Stevens — soon told Gilmore that it had attracted more readers than any magazine article ever written.

Meantime (as always) Lincoln had kept busy with other problems, military as well as political. Often they overlapped, as in the case of facing up to the need for replacing the troops whose fall or discharge left gaps in the ranks of the two main armies: especially Meade's, which had a lower reënlistment quotient and had been further reduced, moreover, by detachments northward to shield Washington from attack by Early, still hovering nearby. On Sunday, July 17, while Jaquess and Gilmore talked in Richmond with Jefferson Davis — who had just put a message on the wire to Atlanta that presaged a step-up in the fighting there — Lincoln telegraphed Grant: "In your dispatch of yesterday to General Sherman I find the following, to wit: 'I shall make a desperate effort to get a position here which will hold the enemy without the necessity of so many men.' Pressed as we are by lapse of time, I am glad to hear you say this; and yet I do hope you may find a way that the effort shall not be desperate in the sense of a great loss of life." He sent this by way of preparation for a proclamation, issued next day, calling for 500,000 volunteers and ordering a draft to take place immediately after September 5 for any unfilled quotas.

This must surely be the last before November, he was saying, although there were already those who believed, despite the recent removal of the $300 exemption clause, that the results would not suffice even for the present. "We are not now receiving one half as many [troops] as we are discharging," Halleck complained to Grant the following day. "Volunteering has virtually ceased, and I do not anticipate much from the President's new call, which has the disadvantage of again postponing the draft for fifty days. Unless our government and people will come square up to the adoption of an efficient and thorough draft, we cannot supply the waste of our army."

Coming square up was easily said, but it left out factors that could not be ignored, including the reaction to this latest call for volunteers, which was seen as a velvet glove encasing the iron hand of a new draft. "Only half a million more! Oh that is nothing," one angry Wisconsin editor fumed, and followed through by saying: "Continue this Administration in power and we can all go to war, Canada, or to hell before 1868."

Now that the year moved into the dog days, with the fall elections looming just beyond, there was need for caution, if not in the military, then certainly in the political arena. Yet even caution might not serve, so portentous were the signs that a defeat was in the making. Frémont was something of a joke as an opponent, though not as a siphon for drawing off the Radical votes that would be needed if Lincoln was to prevail against the Democrats, who were scheduled to convene in Chicago in late August to adopt a platform and select a candidate for November. The platform would be strong for peace, and the candidate, it was believed, would be George McClellan: a formidable combination, one that might well snare both the anti-war and the soldier vote, not to mention the votes of the disaffected, likely to go to almost any rival of the present national leader. Indeed, the prospect so thoroughly alarmed a number of members of the Republican hierarchy that a secret call went out for a convention to meet in Cincinnati in September "to consider the state of the nation and to concentrate the Union strength on some one candidate who commands the confidence of the country, even by a new nomination if necessary."

For the present this was circulated privately, with the intention of bringing it out in the open when the time was ripe. In point of fact, however, the time seemed ripe enough already, to judge by the immediate response. Dissatisfaction with Lincoln had grown by now to include even close friends: Orville Browning, for example, who confessed he had long suspected that his fellow Illinoisan could not measure up to the task required. "I thought he might get through, as many a boy has got through college, without disgrace; but I fear he is a failure." Others agreeing were the eminent lawyer David Dudley Field, whose brother Lincoln had recently appointed to the Supreme Court, and

Schuyler Colfax, Speaker of the House. Chase expressed interest in the supersession, of course, and Ben Butler lent encouragement from down on Bermuda Hundred. Henry Davis was vehemently for it, but Wade and Sumner remained aloof for the time being, the former because he preferred to wait till after the Democratic convention, the latter because he thought it would make less trouble for the party if they gave Lincoln a chance to withdraw voluntarily. Many prominent editors favored the maneuver, including Parke Godwin of the New York *Evening Post* and Whitelaw Reid of the *Cincinnati Gazette*. But the most vociferous of them all was Horace Greeley, whose expression was cherubic but whose spirit had lately been strained beyond forbearance. "Mr Lincoln is already beaten," he declared. "He cannot be elected. And we must have another ticket to save us from overthrow."

Lincoln knew little or nothing yet of this plan by his friends and associates for a midstream swap, but he saw as clearly as they did that the drift was toward defeat and was likely to remain so unless some way could be found, between now and November, to turn the tide. A military victory would help, even one on a fairly modest scale — the more modest the better, in fact, so far as bloodshed was concerned — just so it encouraged the belief that things were looking up for one or another of the armies. But that was mainly up to Grant, locked in a stalemate below Richmond, and Sherman, apparently no better off in front of Atlanta. The other possibility was politics, Lincoln's field, and he was prepared to do all he could in that direction. His native Kentucky would be the first state to hold an election since his nomination; August 1 was the balloting date, and though only some county offices and an appellate judgeship were at stake, the contest was certain to be regarded as a bellwether for the rest, which were to follow in September. Consequently, he took off the gloves for this one. Declaring martial law, he suspended the writ of habeas corpus on July 5, continued the suspension through election day, and gave a free rein to Stephen Burbridge, who, having recently disposed of John Morgan at Cynthiana, proposed to move in a similar aggressive manner against all foes of the Administration throughout his Department of Kentucky. As a result, prominent Democrats were arrested wholesale for "disloyalty," and the name of their candidate for the judgeship was ordered stricken from the ballot on the same vague charge, obliging the survivors to make a last-minute substitute nomination for the post. Lincoln awaited the outcome with much interest, only to find on August 1 that all his pains had gone for nothing. The Democratic candidates swept the state.

There would be other contests; Maine, for instance, was coming up next, to be followed by Vermont. Although the snub just given him in his native state did not augur well for the result, he had no intention of doing anything less than his best to win in all of them, with the help of whatever devices he thought might help and despite the clamor of his critics, left and right, in his own party or the other. "The pilots on our western rivers steer from point to point, as they call it," he told a caller one of these days, "setting the course of the boat no farther than they can see. And that is all I propose to do in the great problems that are before us." One such point now was Atlanta; or anyhow it seemed to him it might be. Events that followed hard on the rebel change of commanders there had brought the fighting to a pitch of intensity, throughout the last two weeks in July, that matched the savagery of the struggle here in the East before it subsided into stalemate. The same thing might happen there — for that seemed to be the pattern: alternate fury and exhaustion — but Lincoln kept peering in that direction, seeking a point to steer by in his effort to land the boat in his charge before it split and sank.

✗ 2 ✗

"The appointment has but one meaning," the Richmond *Examiner* declared on July 19, in reference to Johnston's supersession down in Georgia the day before, "and that is to give battle to the foe." Because John Bell Hood, in contrast to his predecessor, was "young, dashing, and lucky," the rival *Whig* informed its readers that same day, "the army and the people all have confidence in his ability and inclination to fight, and will look to him to drive back Sherman and save Atlanta." Thus the two papers were in agreement on the matter, not only with each other, but also, for once, with the new western leader's red-haired adversary, who rarely subscribed to any journalist's opinion, North or South. "I inferred that the change of commanders meant fight," Sherman remarked after conferring with subordinates who had known Hood in the days before the war. But he added, in contrast to the inference the two Confederate editors drew, five hundred miles away: "This was just what we wanted, viz., to fight in open ground, on anything like equal terms, instead of being forced to run up against prepared intrenchments."

He was about to get what he said he wanted. Hood — whose recent association with Johnston, he later explained, had made him "a still more ardent advocate of the Lee and Jackson school" — needed only one full day at his post before he resolved to go over to the offensive. By then, moreover, though he had had to spend a good part of the time discovering where his own troops were, he not only had decided to lash out at the encircling Federal host; he also had determined just when and where and how he would do so, with a minimal adjustment of the lines now held by his three corps. Accordingly, on the evening of July 19, he summoned Hardee and Stewart to headquarters along with Ben Cheatham, his temporary successor as corps commander, and gave them face-to-face instructions for an attack to be launched soon after midday tomorrow in order to take advantage of an opportunity Sherman was affording them, apparently out of overweening contempt or unconcern, to accomplish his piecemeal destruction. In the execution of what he termed "a general right wheel" from the near bank of the Chattahoochee, with Thomas inching the pivot forward across Peachtree Creek to close down on Atlanta from the north, and McPherson and Schofield swinging wide to come in from the east along the Georgia Railroad, the Ohioan had in effect divided his army and developed a better than two-mile gap between the inner edges of its widespread wings. It was Hood's intention, expressed in detail at his first council of war tonight on the outskirts of the city in his charge, not to plunge into but rather to preserve this gap, and thus keep the two blue wings divided while he crushed them in furious sequence, left and right.

Cheatham, with the help of Wheeler's troopers and some 5000 Georgia militia, would confront McPherson and Schofield from his present intrenchments east of Atlanta, taking care to mass artillery on his left and thus prevent the bluecoats in front from crossing the gap between them and Thomas, who meantime would be receiving the full attention of the other two corps. The Union-loyal Virginian's infantry strength was just above 50,000 — about the number Hood had in all — but the intention was to catch him half over Peachtree Creek, which he had begun to bridge today, and hit him before he could intrench or bring up reinforcements. Hardee on the right and Stewart on the left, disposed along a jump-off line roughly four miles north of the city, were to attack in echelon, east to west, each holding a division in reserve for immediate exploitation of any advantage that developed, "the effort to be to drive the enemy back to the creek, and then toward the river, into the narrow space formed by the river and creek." Once Thomas had been tamped into that watery pocket and ground up, the two gray corps would shift rapidly eastward to assist Cheatham in mangling Schofield and McPherson, with Wheeler's free-swinging horsemen standing by to carry out the roundup that would follow. Hood explained all this to his chief lieutenants "by direct interrogatory," having long since learned "that no measure is more important, upon the eve of battle, than to make certain in the presence of commanders that each thoroughly comprehends his orders."

His concern in this regard was not unfounded. Remembering, as he must have done, the Army of Tennessee's latest — and indeed, under Johnston, only — contemplated full-scale offensive at Cassville two months ago today, midway down the doleful road from Tunnel Hill to Atlanta, Hood knew only too well the dangers that lurked in tactical iotas. Nothing had come of the Cassville design, largely because of his own reaction to finding a misplaced blue column approaching his flank,

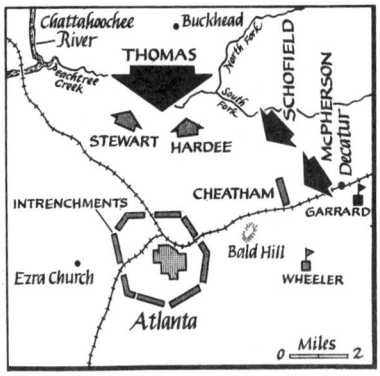

and presently on July 20, with all his troops in position and the 1 o'clock jump-off hour at hand, there were signs that a repetition was in the making. Cheatham sent word before noon that he would have to shift his line southward to keep McPherson from overlapping his right, beyond the railroad. Hood could only approve, and issue simultaneous instructions for Hardee and Stewart to conform by sidestepping half a division-front to their right, thus to prevent too wide an interval from developing between them and Cheatham, through which Schofield might plunge when he came up alongside McPherson. Hardee then had a difficult choice to make. Sidestepping as ordered, he found the interval wider than Hood had supposed, which left him with the decision whether to continue the sidling movement, at the cost of delaying his jump-off, or go forward on schedule — it was 1 o'clock by now — with a mile-wide gap yawning empty on his right. He chose the former course, Stewart conforming on his left, and thus delayed the attack for better than two hours. Shortly after 3 o'clock he sent three of his four divisions plunging northward into the valley of Peachtree Creek.

George Thomas was there, in strength and largely braced. Though the attack achieved the desired surprise, those extra two hours had given him time, not only to get nearly all of his combat elements over the creek, but also to get started on the construction of intrenchments. Hardee struck them and rebounded as if from contact with a red-hot stove, followed by Stewart, who drove harder against the enemy right with no better luck. The Federals either stood firm or hurried reinforcements to shore up threatened portions of their line. Moreover, in the unexpected emergency, Thomas abandoned his accustomed role of Old Slow Trot. Urging his guns forward to "relieve the hitch," he used the point of his sword on the rumps of laggard battery horses, then crossed the stream to direct in person the close-up defense of the bridgehead. An Indiana officer judged the progress of the fighting by the way Old Tom fiddled with his short, thick, gray-shot whiskers. "When satisfied he smoothes them down; when troubled he works them all out of shape." They were badly tousled now, and presently, when he saw the attackers falling back from the blast of fire that met them, he moved even further out of character in the opposite direction. "Hurrah!" he shouted, and took off his hat and slammed it on the ground in pure exuberance. "His whiskers were soon in good shape again," the Hoosier captain noted.

They might have been worse ruffled shortly thereafter; Hardee was about to throw Cleburne's reserve division into the melee, and in fact had just summoned him forward, when an urgent dispatch from Hood directed that troops be sent at once to the far right, where Cheatham's flank was under heavy pressure from McPherson. Cleburne arrived after nightfall, in time to confront a piece of high, cleared ground known as Bald Hill, two miles east of Atlanta and a mile south of the Georgia Railroad; Wheeler's dismounted troopers, after being pushed back all morning, had managed to hang on there through most of the afternoon. Northward, the battle raged along Peachtree Creek, but with decreasing fury, until about 6 o'clock, when it sputtered out. At a cost of 2500 casualties suffered, and 1600 inflicted, Hood's plan for crushing first Thomas, then the other two Union armies, had failed because the Rock of Chickamauga declined, as usual, to be budged or flustered. The southern commander had only praise for Cheatham and Wheeler, who fought hard all day against long odds, and especially for Stewart, who, though his losses were close to two thirds of the Confederate total, "carried out his instructions to the letter." He put the blame for his lack of success on Hardee — his former senior, known since Shiloh as Old Reliable — whose corps, "although composed of the best troops in the army, virtually accomplished nothing" and in fact, as a comparison of casualties would show, "did nothing more than skirmish with the enemy."

So Hood would report afterwards, when he got around to distributing blame for the failure of his first offensive action; the Battle of Peachtree Creek, it was called, or "Hood's First Sortie." But that did not keep him from choosing Hardee to deliver the main effort, two days later, in what would be referred to as "Hood's Second Sortie" or the Battle of Atlanta.

While Cleburne struggled the following day to prevent a blue advance past Bald Hill — the fighting on this third anniversary of First Manassas, he said, was "the bitterest" of his life — Wheeler moved still farther to the right, another mile beyond the railroad, to forestall another Federal flanking effort. What he found instead was an invitation for just such a movement by the Confederate defenders. McPherson, apparently with his full attention drawn to the day-long contest with Cleburne, had his left flank "in the air," unprotected by cavalry and wide open to assault. Informed of the situation early that morning, Hood grasped eagerly at this chance to turn the tables on the attackers. It was one of the chief regrets of his career that he had missed Chancellorsville, having been on detached service with Longstreet around

Suffolk while the Lee-Jackson masterpiece was being forged in the smoky, vine-choked Wilderness a hundred miles away. Now here was a God-given once-in-a-lifetime opportunity to stage a Chancellorsville of his own, down in the piny woods of Georgia, within a scant five days of his appointment to command the hard-luck Army of Tennessee.

In preparation for exploiting this advantage — and also because both ends of his present line were gravely threatened, Thomas having begun to build up pressure against the left about as heavy as McPherson had been exerting on the right — Hood directed that all three corps begin a withdrawal at nightfall to the works rimming the city in their rear, already laid out by Johnston the month before. These were to be held by Stewart and Cheatham, on the north and east, while Hardee marched south, then southeast, six miles down the McDonough Road to Cobb's Mill, where he would turn northeast and continue for the same distance up the Fayetteville Road to the Widow Parker's farm, south of the railroad about midway between Atlanta and Decatur. This would put his four divisions (including Cleburne's, which would join him on his way through town) in position for an all-out assault on McPherson's left rear. Though the route was as circuitous and long as Stonewall's flanking march had been, fourteen months ago in Virginia, an early start this evening should enable Old Reliable to launch a dawn attack, and a dawn attack would give him a full day in which to accomplish McPherson's destruction, whereas Jackson had had only the few hours between sunset and dusk to serve Hooker in that fashion. Moreover, by way of increasing the blue confusion and distress, Wheeler's troopers, after serving as guides and outriders for the infantry column, would continue eastward to Decatur for a strike at McPherson's wagon train, known to be parked in the town square with all his reserve supplies and munitions. Hood explained further that once the flank attack got rolling he would send Cheatham forward to assail McPherson's front and keep Schofield from sending reinforcements to the hardpressed Union left, while Stewart, around to the north, engaged Thomas for the same purpose. Now, as before the Peachtree venture, he assembled a council of war to make certain that each of his lieutenants understood exactly what was required of him, and why. This was all the more advisable here, because of the greater complexity of what he was asking them to do. "To transfer after dark our entire line from the immediate presence of the enemy to another line around Atlanta, and to throw Hardee, the same night, en-

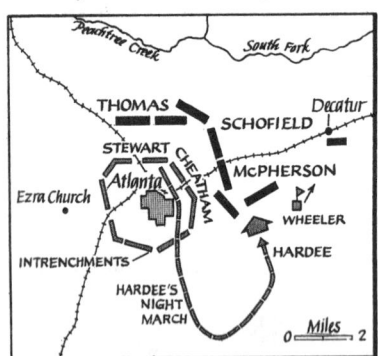

tirely to the rear and flank of McPherson — as Jackson was thrown, in a similar movement, at Chancellorsville and Second Manassas — and to initiate the offensive at daylight, required no small effort on the part of the men and officers. I hoped, however, that the assault would result not only in a general battle, but in a signal victory to our arms."

Such hope was furthered by the secrecy and speed of the nighttime withdrawal to Atlanta's "inner line," which Stewart and Cheatham then began improving with picks and shovels while Hardee set out on his march around the Federal south flank. Almost at once the first hitch developed. Two miles to the east, confronting the enemy on Bald Hill, Cleburne had trouble breaking contact without giving away the movement or inviting an attack; it was crowding midnight before Hardee solved the problem by instructing him to leave his skirmishers in position and fall in behind W. H. T. Walker's men, marking time in rear of the other two divisions under Bate and George Maney, Cheatham's senior brigadier. Cleburne managed this by 1 a.m. of the projected day of battle — Friday, July 22 — but it was 3 o'clock in the morning before the final elements of the corps filed out of the unoccupied intrenchments south of town.

That was the first delay. Another was caused by the weariness of the marchers, still unrested from Wednesday's bloody work and Thursday's fitful skirmishing under the burning summer sun. Strung out on the single, narrow road, which had to be cleared from time to time when Wheeler's dusty horsemen clattered up or down it, the head of the column did not reach Cobb's Mill until dawn, the supposed jump-off hour. Disgruntled, Hardee turned northeast for the Widow Parker's, another half dozen miles up the troop-choked road. It was close to noon by the time he got there, evidently unsuspected by the enemy in the woods across the way, and 12.30 before the corps was formed for assault, Maney and Cleburne on the left, astride the Flat Shoals Road, which ran northwest past Bald Hill, where McPherson's flank was anchored — Cleburne thus had nearly come full circle — and Walker and Bate on the right, on opposite sides of Sugar Creek, which also led northwest, directly into McPherson's rear. Old Reliable could take pride in being just where he was meant to be, in position to duplicate Jackson's famous end-on strike at Hooker, but he was also uncomfortably aware that he was more than six hours behind schedule.

This made him testy: as anyone near him could see in these final minutes before he gave the order to go forward. When Wheeler sent word that a sizeable column of blue troopers had passed this way a while ago, apparently headed southward on a raid, and requested permission to take out after them, Hardee was quick to say no; "We must attack, as we arranged, with all our force." So Wheeler, disappointed at being denied the chance to cross sabers with the intruders, set out eastward for Decatur and McPherson's unsuspecting and perhaps unguarded wagon train. Then Walker came to headquarters to report that he had discovered in his immediate front a giant brier patch, which he asked to be allowed to skirt when he advanced, despite the probable derangement of his line and the loss of still more time. Normally courteous, Hardee was emphatic in refusal. "No, sir!" he said roughly, not bothering to disguise his anger. "This movement has been delayed too long already. Go and obey my orders!"

Walker, a year younger at forty-seven than his chief, who had finished a year behind him at West Point—a veteran of the Seminole and Mexican wars, heavily bearded, with stern eyes, he was one of three West Pointers among the eight Confederate generals named Walker—then demonstrated a difficulty commanders risked with high-strung subordinates in this war, particularly on the southern side. He took offense at his fellow Georgian's tone, and he said as much to an aide who rode with him on the way back to his division. "Major, did you hear that?" he asked, fuming. The staffer admitted he had; "General Hardee forgot himself," he suggested. Walker was not to be put off, however. "I shall make him remember this insult. If I survive this battle, he shall answer me for it." Just then an officer from Hardee's staff overtook them with the corps commander's regrets for "his hasty and discourteous language" and assurance that he would have "come in person to apologize, but that his presence was required elsewhere, and would do so at the first opportunity." So the envoy informed Walker, whose companion remarked soothingly, after they had ridden on: "Now that makes it all right." But Walker's blood was up. He was by no means satisfied. "No, it does not," he said hotly. "He must answer me for this."

As it turned out, no one on this earth was going to answer to W. H. T. Walker for anything. Ordered forward shortly thereafter, he and his three brigades clawed their way through the brier patch, hearing Maney's and Cleburne's attack explode on the left as it struck McPherson's flank, and then emerged from a stand of pines into what was to have been the Union rear, only to find a nearly mile-long triple line of bluecoats confronting them on ground that had been empty when it was reconnoitered, half an hour before. Walker had little chance to react to this discovery, however, for as he and his men emerged from the trees, sunlight glinting on his drawn saber and their rifles, a Federal picket took careful aim and shot him off his horse.

Hood, who had waited and watched impatiently for the past six hours in a high-sited observation post on the outskirts of Atlanta, was dismayed by what he saw no more than a mile away across the treetops. Plunging northwest, on the far left of the Confederate assault, Maney overlapped the Union flank and had to swing hard right as he went past it, which threw his division head-on against the enemy intrenchments facing west. This caused Hood to assume — and later charge — that

Hardee's attack had been launched, not into the rear of the blue left flank, as directed, but against its front, with predictable results; Maney rebounded, then lunged forward again, and again rebounded. Beyond him, out of sight from Hood's lookout tower, Cleburne was doing better, having struck the Federals endwise, and was driving them headlong up the Flat Shoals Road, which ran just in rear of their works below Bald Hill. Still farther to the east, however, Bate and Walker's successor, Brigadier General Hugh Mercer, were having the hardest time of all. In this direction, the element of surprise was with the defenders, whose presence was as unexpected, here on the right, as the appearance of the attackers had been at the opposite end of the line.

Advancing westward yesterday and this morning, under instructions "not to extend any farther to the left" beyond the railroad, lest his troops be spread too thin, McPherson's front had contracted so much that he could detach one of his three corps, led by Major General Grenville M. Dodge, to carry out an order from Sherman to "destroy every rail and tie of the railroad, from Decatur up to your skirmish line." Dodge completed this assignment before midday and was moving up to take a position in support of Blair, whose corps was on the left, when he learned that a heavy force of graybacks was approaching from the southeast, up both banks of Sugar Creek. Under the circumstances, all he had to do was halt and face his two divisions to the left, still in march formation on an east-west road, to establish the triple line of defense whose existence Walker and Bate had not suspected until they emerged from the screen of pines and found it bristling in their front. If they had come up half an hour earlier they would have stepped into a military vacuum, with little or nothing between them and the rear of Blair and Logan, whose corps was on Blair's right, connecting McPherson and Schofield. Now, instead, Walker was dead and Bate and Mercer were involved in a desperate fight that stopped them in their tracks, much as Maney had been stopped on the left, under different circumstances. Thus, of the four gray divisions involved in the attack from which so much had been expected, only Cleburne's was performing as intended. Yet he and his fellow Arkansans made the most of their advantage, including the killing of the commander of the Army of the Tennessee.

McPherson was not with his troops when Hardee's attack exploded on his flank. He was up in rear of Schofield's left, just over half a mile north of the railroad, conferring with Sherman in the yard of a two-story frame house that had been taken over for general headquarters, about midway of the line confronting Atlanta from the east. What he wanted was permission to open fire with a battery of long-range 32-pounders on a foundry whose tall smokestack he could see beyond the rebel works from a gun position he had selected and already had under construction on Bald Hill — or Leggett's Hill, as it was called on the Federal side, for Brigadier General Mortimer Leggett, whose division of Blair's corps occupied it. McPherson's notion was that if he could "knock down that foundry," along with other buildings inside Atlanta, he would hasten the fall of the city. Moreover, he had personal reasons for wanting to accomplish this in the shortest possible time, since what he was counting on, in the way of reward, was a leave of absence that would permit him to go to Baltimore and marry a young lady to whom he had been engaged since his last leave, just after the fall of Vicksburg. He had tried his best to get away in March and April, but Sherman had been unwilling, protesting that there was too much to be done before the drive through Georgia opened in early May. So the thirty-five-year-old Ohioan had had to bide his time; though only by the hardest. Just last week he had asked his friend Schofield when he supposed his prayers would be answered. "After the capture of Atlanta, I guess," Schofield replied, and McPherson had taken that as his preliminary objective, immediately preceding the real objective, which was Baltimore and a union that had little to do with the one he and more than a hundred thousand others would die fighting to preserve.

Sherman readily assented to the shelling of the city, and ordered it to begin as soon as the guns were in position. His first impression, on finding the rebel trenches empty in his front this morning, had been that Hood had evacuated Atlanta overnight; but that had lasted only until he relocated the enemy in occupation of the city's inner line, as bristly as ever, if not more so, and now he took the occasion of McPherson's midday visit to show him, on the headquarters map, his plan for shifting all three armies around to the west for the purpose of cutting Hood's remaining rail connections with Macon and Mobile, which would surely bring on the fall of Atlanta if the proposed bombardment failed. It was by then around 12.30, and as they talked, bent over the map, the sound of conflict suddenly swelled to a roar: particularly southward, where things had been quiet all morning. Sherman whipped out his pocket compass, trained it by earshot, and "became satisfied that the firing was too far to our left rear to be explained by known facts." McPherson quickly called for his horse and rode off to investigate, trailed by members of his staff. Sherman stood and watched him go, curly bearded, six feet tall, with lights of laughter often twinkling in his eyes; "a very handsome man in every way," according to his chief, who thought of his fellow Ohioan as something more than a protégé or younger brother. He thought of him in fact as a successor — and not only to himself, as he would tell another friend that night. "I expected something to happen to Grant and me; either the rebels or the newspapers would kill us both, and I looked to McPherson as the man to follow us and finish the war."

From a ridge in rear of the road on which Dodge had been marching until he stopped and faced his two divisions left to meet the assault by Bate and Walker, McPherson could see that the situation here was less desperate than he had feared; Dodge was plainly holding his own, although the boom of guns from the east gave warning that a brigade he had posted at Decatur to guard the train in the cavalry's absence was also under attack. Sending the available members of his staff in both directions, with instructions for all units to stand firm at whatever cost, the army commander turned his attention westward to Blair's position, where the threat seemed gravest.

In point of fact it was graver than he knew. Cleburne by now had driven Blair's flank division back on Leggett, whose troops were fighting to hold the hill that bore his name, and numbers of enemy skirmishers had already worked their way around in its rear to seize the wooded ground between there and Dodge's position. That was how it happened that McPherson, who had sent away all of his staff except an orderly, encountered graybacks while trotting along a road that led across to Leggett's Hill. Indeed, he was practically on top of one group of Confederates before he suspected they were there. An Arkansas captain, raising his sword as a signal for the two riders to surrender, was surprised by the young general's response ("He checked his horse slightly, raised his hat as politely as if he were saluting a lady, wheeled his horse's head directly to the right, and dashed off to the rear in a full gallop") but not for long. "Shoot him," the gray-clad officer told a corporal standing by, and the corporal did.

McPherson was bent over his mount's withers to keep from being swept from the saddle by the drooping limbs of trees along the road. He fell heavily to the ground, struck low in the back by a bullet that ranged upward through or near his heart. His companion, unhorsed and momentarily stunned by a low-hanging branch, recovered consciousness to find the general lying beside him, clutching his breast in pain, and the butternut soldiers hurrying toward them. He bent over him and asked if he was hurt. "Oh, orderly, I am," McPherson said, and with that he put his face in the dust of the road, quivered briefly, and died. The orderly felt himself being snatched back and up by his revolver belt; "Git to the rear, you Yankee son of a bitch," he heard the rebel who had grabbed him say. Then the captain got there and stood looking down at the polished boots and buff gauntlets, the ornate sash about the waist, and the stars of a major general on both dead shoulders. "Who is this lying here?" he asked. The orderly had trouble answering. Sudden grief had constricted his throat and tears stood in his eyes. "Sir, it is General McPherson," he said. "You have killed the best man in our army."

Sherman's grief was as great, and a good deal more effusive. "I yield to no one but yourself the right to exceed me in lamentations for our dead hero," he presently wrote the Baltimore fiancée. "Though the cannon booms now, and the angry rattle of musketry tells me that

I also will likely pay the same penalty, yet while life lasts I will delight in the memory of that bright particular star which has gone before to prepare the way for us more hardened sinners who must struggle to the end."

But that was later, when he could spare the time. Just now he responded to the news that McPherson's horse had come riderless out of the woods in back of Leggett's Hill by ordering John Logan, the senior corps commander, to take charge of the army and counterattack at once to recover the ground on which his chief might be lying wounded. Logan did so, and within the hour McPherson's body was brought to headquarters in an ambulance. Someone wrenched a door off its hinges and propped it on two chairs for a catafalque, and Sherman went on directing the battle from the room where his fellow Ohioan was laid out. Already he had sent a brigade from Schofield to support the one Dodge had defending Decatur from Wheeler's attack, but aside from this he sent no reinforcements to help resist the assault on his left flank and rear. "I purposely allowed the Army of the Tennessee to fight this battle almost unaided," he later explained, partly because he wanted to leave to McPherson's veterans the honor of avenging his fall, and also because he believed that "if any assistance were rendered by either of the other armies, the Army of the Tennessee would be jealous."

His confidence in his old army — it had also once been Grant's, and had yet to come out loser when the smoke of battle cleared — was justified largely today because of Logan, who exercised his new command in style. Dubbed "Black Jack" by his soldiers, the former Illinois politician knew how to translate stump oratory into rousing military terms. Clutching his flop-brim hat in one hand so that his long raven hair streamed behind him in the wind, he spurred from point to embattled point and bellowed: "Will you hold this line with me? Will you hold this line?" The veterans showed they would. "Black Jack! Black Jack!" they chanted as they beat off attacks that soon were coming from all directions: particularly on Leggett's Hill, which Hood by now had ordered Cheatham to assault from the west while Cleburne kept up pressure from the south and east. Brigadier General Manning Force's brigade, menaced front and rear, was obliged at times to fight on alternate sides of its breastworks. At one critical point he called for a flag, and a young lieutenant, assuming from the look of things that the time had come to surrender, began a frantic search for a white handkerchief or shirt. "Damn you, sir!" Force shouted. "I don't want a flag of truce; I want the *American* flag!" Shot in the face shortly thereafter, he lost the use of his voice and fell back on conducting the hilltop defense with gestures, which were no less flamboyant and seemed to work as well. The hill was held, though at a cost of ten guns — including the four McPherson had planned to use against Atlanta at long range — fifteen stands of colors, and better than a thousand prisoners, mostly from Blair's other division under Brigadier General Giles A. Smith (one of an even dozen Federal generals with that name, including one who spelled it Smyth) which had given way at the outset, badly rattled by Cleburne's unexpected flank-and-rear assault.

Although there were no other outright surprises, the issue continued to swing in doubt from time to time and place to place. Sherman watched with interest from his headquarters on the central ridge, and when Cheatham scored a breakthrough around 4 o'clock, just north of the railroad, he had Schofield mass the fire of several batteries to help restore Logan's punctured right. Word came then from Decatur that the two brigades of infantry had managed to keep Wheeler's troopers out of the town square, where the train was parked, and from Dodge that he was confident of holding against weakening attacks on the left rear. Mercurial as always, despite the tears that trickled into his stub red beard whenever he thought of McPherson laid out on his improvised bier inside the house, Sherman was in high spirits as a result of these reports, which reached him as he paced about the yard and watched the progress of the fighting in all directions. Presently the headquarters came under long-range fire, obliging him and his attendants to take cover in an adjoining grove of trees. Sheltered behind one of these, he noticed a terrified soldier crouched nearby in back of another, moaning: "Lord, Lord, if I once get home," and: "Oh, I'll be killed!" Sherman grinned and picked up a handful of stones, which he then began to toss in that direction. Every pebble that struck the tree brought a howl or a groan from behind it. "That's hard firing, my man," he called to the unstrung soldier, who replied without opening his tight-shut eyes: "Hard? It's fearful! I think thirty shells have hit this tree while I was here." The fire subsided, and the general stepped into the open. "It's all over now; come out," he told the man, who emerged trembling. When he saw who had been taunting him, he took off running through the woods, pursued by the sound of Sherman's laughter.

From end to end, the Federal line was held or restored, except where Smith's unfortunates had been driven back across the lower slopes of Leggett's Hill, and though the fighting was sometimes hand-to-hand and desperate, on past sundown into twilight, there was by then no doubt that Hood's Second Sortie — aside, that is, from the capture of a dozen guns and an assortment of Union colors — had been no less a failure than his First, two days ago. It was, however, considerably more expensive; for this time the Confederate leader held almost nothing back, including the Georgia militia, which he used in a fruitless attack on Schofield that had no effect on the battle except to swell the list of southern casualties. In the end, Hood's loss was around 8000 killed, wounded, and missing, as compared to Sherman's 3700.

All next day the contending armies remained in position, licking their wounds, until Hardee withdrew unimpeded the following night into the Atlanta works. Saddened by the loss of Walker, who had called at headquarters on the eve of battle to assure him of his understanding and support, as well as by the news about McPherson — "No soldier fell in the enemy's ranks whose death caused me equal regret," he later said of his West Point friend and classmate — Hood was profoundly disappointed by the failure of his two sorties to accomplish the end for which they had been designed; but he was by no means so discouraged that he did not intend to attempt a third, if his adversary presented him with still another opportunity. He knew only too well how close he had come, except for the unlucky appearance of Dodge's corps in exactly the wrong place at the wrong time, to wrecking the encircling Union host entirely.

Frank Blair, for one, concurred in this belief. Hood's flanking movement, he afterwards declared, "was a very bold and a very brilliant one, and was very near being successful. The position taken up accidentally by [Dodge's] corps prevented the full force of the blow from falling where it was intended to fall. If my command had been driven from its position at the time that [Logan's] corps was forced back from its intrenchments, there must have been a general rout of all the troops of the Army of the Tennessee ... and, possibly, the panic might have been communicated to the balance of the army."

Sherman was not much given to speculation on the might-have-beens of combat, and in any case he no more agreed with this assessment than he did with subsequent criticism that, in leaving Schofield and Thomas standing comparatively idle on the sidelines while Logan battled for survival, he had missed a prime chance to break Atlanta's inner line, weakened as it was by the withdrawal of a major portion of its defenders for the attack on his south flank. What he mainly concluded, once the smoke had cleared, was that in staging two all-out sorties in as many days — both of them not only unsuccessful but also highly expensive in energy, blood, and ingenuity — Hood had shot his wad. And from this Sherman concluded further that he was unlikely to be molested in his execution of the maneuver he had described to McPherson at their final interview; that is, "to withdraw from the left flank and add to the right," thereby shifting his whole force counterclockwise, around to the west of the city, in order to probe for its rail supply lines to the south.

First, though, there was the problem of finding a permanent replacement for his fallen star, McPherson. On the face of it, Logan having performed spectacularly under worse than trying conditions, the solution should have been simple. But it turned out to be extremely complicated, involving the exacerbation of some tender feelings and, in the end, nothing less than the reorganization of the command structure of two of the three armies in his charge.

Thomas came promptly to headquarters to advise against keeping

Logan at his temporary post. Although there was bad blood between them, dating back to Chattanooga, basically his objection was that Black Jack, like all the other corps and division leaders in the Army of the Tennessee — not one of them was a West Pointer, whereas two thirds of his own and half of Schofield's were Academy graduates — was a nonprofessional. "He is brave enough and a good officer," the Virginian admitted, "but if he had an army I am afraid he would edge over on both sides and annoy Schofield and me. Even as a corps commander he is given to edging out beyond his jurisdiction." Sherman agreed in principle that volunteers from civilian life, especially politicians, "looked to personal fame and glory as auxiliary and secondary to their political ambition.... I wanted to succeed in taking Atlanta," he later explained, "and needed commanders who were purely and technically soldiers, men who would obey orders and execute them promptly and on time." That ruled out Logan, along with Blair. Who then? he asked Thomas, who replied: "You cannot do better than put Howard in command of that army." Sherman protested that this would make Logan "terribly mad" and might also create "a rumpus among those volunteers," but then agreed. One-armed and two years younger even than McPherson, O. O. Howard, West Point '54, a Maine-born recent eastern import to the western theater, was then announced as the new commander of the army that had once been Sherman's own.

Returned to his corps, Logan managed to live with the burning aroused in his breast by this disappointment. But the same could not be said for Old Tom's ranking corps commander, the altogether professional Joe Hooker. Outraged at having been passed over in favor of the man he largely blamed for his defeat at Chancellorsville, Fighting Joe characterized the action as "an insult to my rank and services" and submitted at once a request to be relieved of his present duties. Thomas "approved and *heartily* recommended" acceptance of this application, which Sherman was quick to grant, remarking incidentally that the former commander of the Army of the Potomac had not even been considered for the post that now was Howard's, since "we on the spot did not rate his fighting qualities as high as he did." Hooker departed for an inactive assignment in the Northern Department, where he spent the rest of the war, further embittered by the news that his successor was Major General Henry W. Slocum, another enemy, who had been sent to Vicksburg on the eve of the present campaign to avoid personality clashes between them. Pending Slocum's arrival from Mississippi, Alpheus Williams would lead the corps as senior division commander, much as Major General David S. Stanley had succeeded to the command of Howard's corps, though on a permanent basis.

By July 25, within five days of the Peachtree crossing, when work on it began, the railroad bridge over the Chattahoochee — 760 feet long and 90 high — was completed and track relaid to a forward base immediately in Thomas's rear. Sherman, his supplies replenished and generals reshuffled, was ready within another two days to begin the counterclockwise western slide designed to bring on the fall of Atlanta by severing its rail connection with the world outside. Already this had been accomplished up to the final step; for of the four lines in and out of the city all but one had been seized or wrecked by now, beginning with the Western & Atlantic, down which the Federals had been moving ever since they chevied Johnston out of Dalton. Then Schofield and McPherson had put the Georgia Railroad out of commission by dismantling it as they moved westward from Stone Mountain and Decatur. Of the remaining two — the Atlanta & West Point and the Macon & Western, which shared the same track until they branched southwest and southeast at East Point, five miles south of the city — the former, connecting with Montgomery and Mobile, had been severely damaged the week before by Major General Lovell Rousseau, who raided southward through Alabama with 2500 troopers, practically unopposed, and tore up close to thirty miles of the line between Montgomery and Opelika, where it branched northeast for West Point and Atlanta. That left only the Macon road, connecting eastward with Savannah, for Hood's use in supplying his army and for Sherman to destroy. He began his large-scale semicircular maneuver to accomplish this on July 27, ordering Howard to swing north, then west — in rear of Schofield and Thomas, who would follow him in turn — for a southward march down the near bank of the Chattahoochee, which would serve as an artery for supplies, to descend as soon as possible on that one railroad still in operation out of a place that once had boasted of being "the turntable of the Confederacy."

Simultaneously, by way of putting two strings to his bow, he turned 10,000 horsemen loose on the same objective in an all-out double strike around both rebel flanks. Brigadier General Edward McCook, his division reinforced to a strength of 3500 by the addition of a brigade from Rousseau — who, it was hoped, had established the model for the current operation, over in Alabama the week before — would ride down the north bank of the Chattahoochee for a crossing at Campbelltown, under orders to proceed eastward and hit the Macon & Western at or below Jonesboro, just under twenty miles on the far side of Atlanta. This was also the goal of the second mounted column, 6500 strong, which would set out from Decatur under Stoneman, who had Garrard's division attached to his own for a southward lunge around the enemy right. Both columns were to start on July 27, the day the infantry slide began; Sherman expected them back within three days at the most. But when Stoneman asked permission to press on, once the railroad had been wrecked, to Macon and Andersonville for the purpose of freeing the prisoners held in their thousands at both places, he readily agreed to this hundred-mile extension of the raid, on condition that Garrard head back as soon as the Macon road was smashed, to work with McCook in covering the infantry's left wheel around Atlanta. The redhead's hopes were high, but not for long: mainly because of Joe Wheeler, who, though outnumbered three-to-two by the blue troopers, did not neglect this opportunity to deal with them in detail.

Right and left, at Campbelltown and Decatur, both of them closer to Jonesboro than they were to each other at the outset, the two columns took off on schedule, though not altogether in the manner Sherman intended. Stoneman's mind was fixed so firmly on his ultimate goal — Andersonville and its 30,000 inmates, whose liberation would be nothing less than the top cavalry exploit of the war — that he no longer had any discernible interest in the limited purpose for which the two-pronged strike had been conceived. Accordingly, without notifying anyone above him, he sent Garrard's 4300 troopers pounding due south to draw off the enemy horsemen while he and his 2200 rode east for Covington, which Garrard had raided five days ago during the Battle of Atlanta. In this he was successful; he reached Covington undetected and turned south, down the east bank of the Ocmulgee River, for Macon, the first of his two prison-camp objectives. Garrard meantime had been no less successful in carrying out his part of the revised design, which was to attract the attention of the rebels in his direction. On Snapfinger Creek that afternoon, barely ten miles out of Decatur, he ran into mounted graybacks whose number increased so rapidly overnight that at Flatrock Bridge next morning, another five miles down the road, he had to turn and ride hard, back to Decatur, to keep from losing everything he had. His nimbleness kept down his losses; yet even so these would have been much heavier if Wheeler, about to give chase with eight brigades — just over 6000 sabers in all — had not received word that McCook had crossed the Chattahoochee, en route for the Macon & Western, and that Stoneman was beyond the Ocmulgee, apparently headed for Macon itself. The Georgia-born Alabamian, two months short of his twenty-eighth birthday, left one brigade to keep up the pressure on Garrard and turned with the other seven to meet these rearward threats, sending three brigades to deal with Stoneman while he himself set out with the rest to intercept McCook.

As it turned out, the interception came after, not before, McCook struck the railroad at Lovejoy Station, seven miles beyond Jonesboro. He got there four hours ahead of Wheeler, which gave him time to burn the depot, tear up a mile and a half of track, and destroy a sizeable wagon train, along with its 800 mules, before the graybacks arrived to drive him off and pursue him all the way to the Chattahoochee. Overtaken at Newnan, due west on the West Point road, McCook lost 950 troopers killed and captured, along with his pack train and two guns, between there and the river, which he crossed to safety on July 30, reduced in strength by nearly a third and much the worse for wear.

By that time Stoneman had reached the outskirts of Macon, only to find it defended by local militia. While he engaged in a long-range duel across the Ocmulgee with these part-time soldiers, hoping to cover his search for a downstream ford, the three brigades sent after him by Wheeler came up in his rear. He tried for a getaway, back the way he had come, then found himself involved in a running fight that ended next day near Hillsboro, twenty-five miles to the north, when he was all but surrounded at a place called Sunshine Church. He chose one brigade to make a stand and told the other two to escape as best they could; which they did, while he and his chosen 700 were being overrun and rounded up. One of the two surviving brigades made it back to Decatur two days later, but the other, unable to turn west because of the swarm of rebels on that flank, was wrecked at Jug Tavern on August 3, thirty miles north of Covington. Stoneman and his captured fellow officers were in Macon by then, locked up with the unfortunates they had set out to liberate, and the enlisted men were in much the same position, though considerably worse off so far as the creature comforts were concerned, sixty miles to the southwest at Andersonville.

"On the whole," Sherman reported to Washington in one of the prize understatements of the war, "the cavalry raid is not deemed a success."

In plain fact, aside from McCook's fortuitous interception of the 800-mule train — the break in the track at Lovejoy's, for example, amounted to nothing worse than a two-day inconvenience, after which the Macon & Western was back in use from end to end — the raid not only failed to achieve its purpose, it was also a good deal harder on the raiders than on the raided. Sherman's true assessment was shown by what he did, on the return of his badly cut up horsemen, rather than by what he wrote in his report. Garrard's division, which had suffered least, was dismounted and used to occupy the intrenchments Schofield vacated when he began his swing around the city in Howard's wake, and the other two were reorganized, after a period of sorely needed rest and refitment, into units roughly half their former size. Not that Sherman expected much from them, offensively speaking, in the critical days ahead. "I now became satisfied," he said later, "that cavalry could not, or would not, make a sufficient lodgment on the railroad below Atlanta, and that nothing would suffice but for us to reach it with the main army."

But that turned out to be about as difficult an undertaking as the one assigned to Stoneman and McCook. For one thing — against all his expectations, which were founded on the belief that Hood by now had shot his wad — he had no sooner begun his counterclockwise wheel, shifting Howard around in rear of Schofield and Thomas to a position west of the city so that his right could be extended to reach the vital railway junction at East Point, than he was confronted with still a third sortie by his Confederate opponent, quite as savage as the other two.

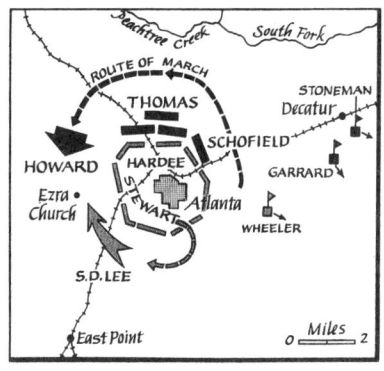

All had gone well on the first day, July 27; Howard pulled out undetered and took up the march, first north, then west along the near bank of Peachtree Creek. Riding south next morning in rear of Logan, whose corps was in the lead, Sherman and the new army commander came under fire from a masked battery as they approached the Lickskillet Road, which ran due east into Atlanta, three miles off. Howard did not like the look of things, and said so. "General Hood will attack me here," he told his companion, who scoffed at the notion: "I guess not. He will hardly try it again." But Howard remained persuaded that he was about to be struck, explaining later that he based his conviction on previous acquaintance with the man who would do the striking; "I said that I had known Hood at West Point, and that he was indomitable."

Indomitable. Presented thus with a third chance to destroy an isolated portion of the enemy host, Hood had designed still another combined assault, once more after the manner of Lee and Jackson, to forestall this massive probe around his left. His old corps, now under Stephen D. Lee — the South Carolinian had been promoted to lieutenant general and brought from Alabama to take over from Cheatham — would march out the Lickskillet Road on the morning of July 28 to occupy a position from which it could block Howard's extension of the Union right and set him up for a flank attack by Stewart, who would bring his corps out the Sandtown Road that evening, a mile in Lee's rear, to circle the head of the stalled blue column and strike from the southwest at Howard's unguarded outer flank next morning. Hardee, reduced to three divisions, each of which received a brigade from the fallen Walker's broken-up division, would hold Atlanta's inner line against whatever pressure Schofield and Thomas might exert. Lee, who had assumed command only the day before, moved as ordered, determined to prove his mettle in this first test at his new post — two months short of his thirty-first birthday, he was six years younger than anyone else of his rank in the whole Confederacy — but found himself involved by midday, three miles out the Lickskillet Road, near a rural chapel known as Ezra Church, in a furious meeting engagement that left him no time for digging in or even getting set. So instead he took the offensive with all three of his divisions.

They were not enough: not nearly enough, as the thing developed. Howard, who was only two years older than Lee and no less anxious to prove his mettle, having also assumed command the day before, had foreseen the attack (or anyhow forefelt it, despite Sherman's scoff) and though there was no time for intrenching, once he had called a halt he had his lead corps throw up a rudimentary breastwork of logs and rails; so that when Lee's men charged — "with a terrifying yell," the one-armed commander would recall — they were "met steadily and repulsed." They fell back, then charged again, with the same result. Busily strengthening their improvised works between attacks, Logan's four divisions stood their ground, reinforced in the course of the struggle by others from Dodge and Blair, while Sherman rode back and alerted Thomas to be ready to send more. These last were unneeded, even though Hood by then had abandoned his plan for a double envelopment and instead told Stewart to go at once out the Lickskillet Road to Lee's assistance. Stewart added the weight of one division to the contest before sundown, without appreciable effect. "Each attack was less vigorous and had less chance than the one before it," a Union veteran was to note.

Alarmed by reports coming in all afternoon from west of Atlanta, Hood had Hardee turn his corps over to Cheatham, who had returned to his division, and proceed without delay to Ezra Church to take charge of the other two. Old Reliable arrived to find that the battle had sputtered out, and made no effort to revive it. Lee and Stewart between them had lost some 2500 killed and wounded — about the same number that had fallen along Peachtree Creek eight days ago — as compared to Howard's loss of a scant 700. Nor was that the worst of it, according to Hardee, who afterwards declared: "No action of the campaign probably did so much to demoralize and dishearten the troops engaged in it."

Sherman knew now that he had been wrong, these past five days, in thinking that Hood had shot his wad in the Battle of Atlanta. He would have been considerably closer to the truth, however, if he had reverted to this belief on the night that followed the Battle of Ezra Church. Moreover, there were Confederates in the still smoky woods, out beyond Howard's unbroken lines, who would have agreed with him; almost.

"Say, Johnny," one of Logan's soldiers called across the breastworks, into the outer darkness. "How many of you are there left?"

"Oh, about enough for another killing," some butternut replied.

This attitude on both sides, now that another month drew to a close, was reflected in their respective casualty lists. Including his cavalry subtractions, which were heavy, Sherman had lost in July about 8000 killed, wounded, and missing — roughly the number that fell in June, and better than a thousand fewer than fell in May. The over-all Federal total, from the outset back at Tunnel Hill, came to just under 25,000.

Hood, on the other hand, had suffered 13,000 casualties in the course of his three sorties, which brought the Confederate total, including Johnston's, to 27,500. That was about the number Lee had lost during the same three-month span in Virginia, whereas Sherman had lost considerably fewer than half as many as Meade. Grant could well be proud of his western lieutenant, if and when he got around to comparing the cost, in men per mile, of the campaigns in Georgia and the Old Dominion, West and East.

Still, there was a good deal more to war than mere killing and maiming. "Lee's army will be your objective point," he had instructed Meade before the jump-off, only to have the eastern offensive wind up in a stalemate, a digging contest outside Petersburg. Similarly, he had told Sherman to "move against Johnston's army," and the red-haired Ohioan had done just that — so long as the army was Johnston's. But now that it was Hood's, and had come out swinging, a change set in: particularly after Ezra Church, the third of Hood's three roaring sorties. Lopsided as that victory had been for Sherman, it served warning that, in reaching for the railroad in his adversary's rear, his infantry might do no better than his cavalry had done, and indeed might suffer as severely in the process.

Inching southward all the following week he found rebel intrenchments bristling in his path. On August 5, having brought Schofield around in the wake of Howard, he reinforced him with a corps from Thomas and ordered the drive on the railroad resumed. Schofield tried, the following morning, but was soon involved in the toils of Utoy Creek and suffered a bloody repulse. It was then that the change in Sherman — or, rather, in his definition of his goal — became complete. Formerly the Gate City had been no more than the anvil on which he intended to hammer the insurgent force to pieces. Now it became the end-all objective of his campaign. He would simply pound the anvil.

"I do not deem it prudent to extend any more to the right," he wired Halleck next day, "but will push forward daily by parallels, and make the inside of Atlanta too hot to be endured."

In line with McPherson's proposal at their farewell interview, he sent to Chattanooga for siege guns and began a long-range shelling of the city, firing over the heads of its defenders and into its business and residential districts. "Most of the people are gone; it is now simply a big fort," he informed his wife that week, and while this was by no means true at the time, it became increasingly the case with every passing day of the bombardment. "I can give you no idea of the excitement in Atlanta," a southern correspondent wrote. "Everybody seems to be hurrying off, especially the women. Wagons loaded with household furniture and everything else that can be packed upon them crowd every street, and women old and young and children innumerable are hurrying to and fro. Every train of cars is loaded to its utmost capacity.

The excitement beats everything I ever saw, and I hope I may never witness such again." Presently, though the destruction of property was great and the shelling continued day and night, the citizens learned to take shelter in underground bombproofs, as at Vicksburg the year before, and Hood said later that he never heard "one word from their lips expressive of dissatisfaction or willingness to surrender." Sherman's reaction was to step up the rate of fire. "We can pick out almost any house in town," he boasted to Halleck. He was by nature "too impatient for a siege," he added, but "One thing is certain. Whether we get inside of Atlanta or not, it will be a used-up community when we are done with it."

His troops shared his ebullience, if not his impatience, finding much to admire in this notion of bloodless engagement at long range. "There goes the Atlanta Express!" they cheered as the big shells took off at fifteen-minute intervals over their and the rebel trenches. When one of the outsized guns developed the habit of dropping its projectiles short, they turned and shouted rearward through cupped hands: "Take her away! She slobbers at the mouth." Sherman moved among them, a reporter noted, with "no symptoms of heavy cares — his nose high, thin, and planted with a curve as vehement as the curl of a Malay cutlass — tall, slender, his quick movements denoting good muscle added to absolute leanness, not thinness." Uncle Billy, they called him, with an affection no blue-clad soldiers had shown for a commander, West or East, since Little Mac's departure from the war. What was more, unlike McClellan, he shared their life as well as their rations, though a staffer recorded that he was mostly "too busy to eat much. He ate hardtack, sweet potatoes, bacon, black coffee off a rough table, sitting on a cracker box, wearing a gray flannel shirt, a faded old blue blouse, and trousers he had worn since long before Chattanooga. He talked and smoked cigars incessantly, giving orders, dictating telegrams, bright and chipper."

Partly this was exuberance. Partly it was fret, which he often expressed or covered in such a manner. Either way, it was deadly: as was shown in a message he sent Howard, August 10, amid the roar of long-range guns. "Let us destroy Atlanta," he said, "and make it a desolation."

★ ★ ★

Sherman's ebullience was heightened by news that arrived next day, roundabout from Washington, of a great naval victory scored the week before by Farragut down in Mobile Bay. Long the target of various plans that had come to nothing until now — including Grant's, which went badly awry up the Red that spring with the near destruction of Banks's army and Porter's fleet — this last of the South's major Gulf of Mexico ports, second only to Wilmington as a haven for blockade runners, had been uppermost in Farragut's mind ever since the fall of New Orleans, more than two years ago. He then solicited the Department for permission to steam booming into the bay before its defenses could be strengthened, only to be told that he and his sea-going vessels would continue to prowl the Mississippi until the big river was open from source to mouth. By the time this was accomplished, a year later at Port Hudson, both the admiral and his flagship *Hartford* were sorely in need of rest and repairs. However urgent its priority, the reduction of Mobile would have to await their return, respectively, from Hastings-on-Hudson, the Tennessee-born sailor's adoptive home, and the Brooklyn Navy Yard.

A Christmas visit to New York City was disrupted by an intelligence report that reached him amid the splendors of the Astor House, confirming his worst fears. Not only had Mobile's defenders greatly strengthened the forts guarding the entrance to the harbor; refugees now declared that they also were building a monster ironclad up the Alabama River, more formidable in armament and armor than any warship since the *Merrimac*. Farragut knew, from a study of what the latter had done in Hampton Roads before the *Monitor*'s arrival — as well as from his own experience, near Vicksburg, when the *Arkansas* steamed murderously through the blue flotilla — just what damage one such vessel could do to any number of wooden ships. The answer, he saw, was to get back down there fast and, if possible, go up the river and destroy her before she was ready to engage; or else acquire some ironclads of his own, able to fight her on a give-and-take basis. In any case, after four months of rest and relaxation, he was galvanized into action. He went straight to Brooklyn and served notice that he expected the workmen to have the *Hartford* ready for sea by the evening of January 3. She was, and he dropped anchor at Pensacola two weeks later.

Off Mobile next day, January 18, he learned at first hand, not only that the rebel ironclad existed, as rumored, but also that she was now in the mouth of Dog River, up at the head of the bay. C.S.S. *Tennessee* was her name, and Admiral Franklin Buchanan, former commander of the *Merrimac-Virginia* and ranking man in the Confederate navy, was in charge; "Old Buck," Farragut called him, though at sixty-four Buchanan was only a year his senior and in fact had five years less service, having waited till he was fifteen to become a midshipman, which Farragut had done at the age of nine. Informed of a rumor that the ram was about to come down and attack the nine blockaders on station outside the bay, the Federal admiral braced his captains for the shock, and though he had small personal use for the new-fangled weapons ("If a shell strikes the side of the *Hartford*," he explained, "it goes clean through. Unless somebody happens to be directly in the path, there is no damage excepting a couple of easily plugged holes. But when a shell makes its way into one of those damned tea-kettles, it can't get out again") he submitted an urgent request for at least a pair of monitors. "If I had them," he told Washington, "I should not hesitate to become the assailant instead of awaiting the attack."

Actually, though she had just completed the 150-mile downriver run from Selma, where she was built, there was little danger that the *Tennessee* would steam out into the Gulf. At this point, indeed, there was doubt that she could even make it into the bay, since she drew fourteen feet of water and the depth over Dog River Bar was barely ten. Ingenuity, plus three months of hard labor, solved the problem by installing "camels" — large floats attached to the hull below the water line — which lifted her enough to clear the bar with a good tide. By mid-May she was in Mobile Bay, and Farragut got his first distant glimpse of her from a gunboat cruising Mississippi Sound; "a formidable-looking thing," he pronounced her, though to one of his lieutenants "she looked like a great turtle."

More than 200 feet in length and just under 50 in the beam, she wore six-inch armor, backed by two solid feet of oak and pine, and carried six hard-hitting 6.4- and 7-inch Brooke rifles, one forward and one aft, mounted on pivots to fire through alternative ports, and two in each broadside. Her captain was Commander J. D. Johnston, an Alabama regular who had spent the past two years on duty in the bay, and her skeleton crew was filled out with volunteers from a Tennessee infantry regiment, inexperienced as sailors but proud to serve aboard a vessel named for their native state. Two drawbacks she had, both grave. One was that her engines, salvaged from a river steamboat, gave her a top speed of only six knots, which detracted from her maneuverability and greatly reduced her effectiveness as a ram. The other was that her steering chains led over, rather than under, her armored rear deck, and thus would be exposed to enemy fire. However, she also had one awesome feature new to warfare, described by her designer as "a hot water attachment to her boilers for repelling boarders, throwing one stream forward of the casemate and one abaft." What was more, with Buchanan directing events, there was every likelihood that the device would be brought into play; for he was a proud, determined man, with a fondness for close-quarter fighting and no stomach for avoiding dares.

"Everybody has taken it into their heads that one ship can whip a dozen," he wrote a friend while the ironclad was being readied for action, "and if the trial is not made, we who are in her are damned for life; consequently, the trial must be made. So goes the world."

Mobile's reliance was by no means all on the iron ram, however. In addition to three small paddle-wheel gunboats that completed the gray squadron — *Morgan* and *Gaines*, with six guns each, and *Selma* with four, all unarmored except for strips of plate around their boilers — three dry-land installations guarded the two entrances down at the far end of the thirty-mile-long bay. The first and least of these, Fort Powell, a six-gun earthwork on speck-sized Tower Island, a mile off Cedar Point, covered the approach from Mississippi Sound, off to the west, through Grant's Pass. Another was Fort Gaines, a pentagonal structure on the eastern tip of Dauphin Island, crowned with sixteen guns that commanded the western half of the main entrance, three miles wide, between there and Mobile Point, a long narrow spit of sand at whose extremity — the site of old Fort Bowyer, whose smoothbores had repelled the British fifty years ago — Fort Morgan, the stoutest and most elaborate of the three defensive works, reared its mass of dark red brick. This too was a five-sided structure, double-tiered and mounting no less than forty heavy guns in barbette and casemates, together with seven more in an exterior water battery on the beach in front of its northwest curtain. Both entrances had been narrowed by rebel contrivance, the one from the Sound by driving pilings from Cedar Point to Tower Island and from the northern end of Dauphin Island to within about half a mile of Fort Powell, the one from the Gulf by sinking others southeastward from Fort Gaines to within a mile of Mobile Point, while just in rear of the remaining gap a triple line of mines (called "torpedoes") had been strewn and anchored, barely out of sight below the surface, to within about two hundred yards of the western tip of the spit of land across the way. The eastern limit of this deadly underwater field was marked by a red buoy, fixed there for the guidance of blockade runners whose pilots could avoid sudden destruction by keeping to the right of it and steaming directly under the high-sited guns of Fort Morgan, almost within pistol range of those in the water battery on the beach.

Farragut planned to take that route, mainly because there seemed to be no other. Grant's Pass was too shallow for all but the lightest of his vessels, which would be no match for the iron ram once they entered the bay, and the combination of piles and mines denied him the use of any part of the main Gulf channel except that scant, gun-dominated 200-yard stretch just off the tip of Mobile Point. He was willing to take his chances there, as he had done in similar runs past Forts Jackson and St Philip and the towering bluffs at Vicksburg and Port Hudson, yet he did not enjoy the notion of getting inside the bay with the forts alive in his rear, his wooden ships crippled, and the *Tennessee* likely to pound or butt them into flotsam. Contemplating this, he saw more clearly than ever the need for ironclads of his own, and though four of these had been promised him by now, two from the Atlantic squadron and two from the Mississippi, none had arrived by the time the squat metallic rebel monster steamed down the bay and dropped anchor behind Fort Morgan on May 20, intending either to await the entrance of the Union fleet or else run out and smash it in the Gulf. Farragut stormed at the delay, his patience stretched thin by the nonarrival of the monitors.

"I am tired of watching Buchanan," he wrote home in June, "and

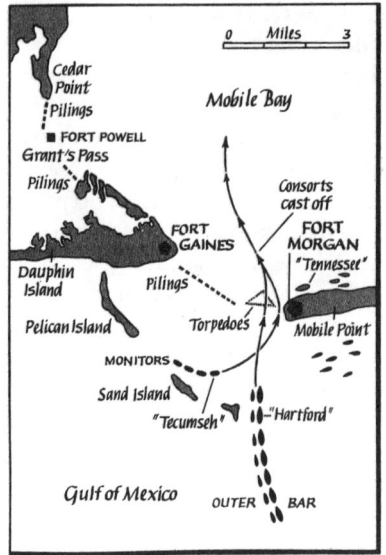

wish from the bottom of my heart that Buck would come out and try his hand upon us. The question has to be settled, iron versus wood, and there never was a better chance.... We are today ready to try anything that comes along, be it wood or iron, in reasonable quantities."

His plan was for the monitors to lead the way, holding to the right of the red buoy and providing an iron screen for the wooden ships as the two columns made their parallel runs past Fort Morgan, then going on to engage the ram in an all-out fight inside the bay, with such help as the multi-gunned sloops could provide. He would more or less ignore Fort Gaines while steaming in, not only because it was more than two miles off, but also because he planned to distract the attention of its gunners by having the army make a landing on the other end of Dauphin Island, then move east to invest the work from the landward side; after which Morgan would be served in the same fashion. But here too was a rub. The army, like the monitors, though promised, did not come. First there was Banks's drawn-out involvement up the Red, then a delay while Canby got the survivors back to New Orleans and in shape for the march to Mobile — which finally was cancelled when Grant was obliged to summon all but a handful to Virginia in late June, as replacements for Meade's heavy casualties. Canby visited the fleet in early July and agreed to send Major General Gordon Granger with 2000 men in transports, admittedly a small force but quite as large as he felt he could afford.

Farragut had to be satisfied, and in any case his impatience was mainly with the monitors, which still had not arrived. By way of diversion from the heat and boredom, both of which were oppressive, he rehearsed the run past Fort Morgan, and the fight that was to follow inside the bay, on a wardroom table grooved with the points of the compass, maneuvering little boat-shaped wooden blocks carved for him by the *Hartford*'s carpenter. Meanwhile, Buchanan's inactivity puzzled and irked him more and more. "Now is the time," he declared in mid-July. "The sea is as calm as possible and everything propitious.... Still he remains behind the fort, and I suppose it will be the old story over again. If he won't visit me, I will have to visit him. I am all ready as soon as the soldiers arrive to stop up the back door of each fort."

He was not, of course, "all ready," nor would he be so until the monitors were on hand, the *Albemarle* having redemonstrated in April and May, at Plymouth and in the North Carolina Sound from which she took her name, what was likely to happen to his wooden ships if he had no ironclads of his own to stand between them and the *Tennessee*. Then on July 20 the first of the promised four arrived from the Atlantic coast; *Manhattan* she was called, wearing ten inches of armor on her revolving turret, which carried two 15-inch guns. Ten days later the *Chickasaw* put in from New Orleans, double turreted with a pair of 11-inch guns in each, followed next day by her sister ship *Winnebago*. All were on hand by August 1 except the *Tecumseh*, en route from the Atlantic in the wake of her twin *Manhattan*. Farragut found the waiting even harder now that it was about to end; he improved the time by instructing his skippers in their duties, using the tabletop wooden blocks to show just where he expected their ships to be put in all eventualities. Meantime, as he had been doing for the past ten days, he continued to send out nightly boat crews, under cover of darkness and with muffled oars, to grapple for or sink as many as possible of the torpedoes anchored between the end of the line of pilings southeast of Dauphin Island and the red buoy just off Mobile Point. A number were so removed or destroyed, and the admiral was pleased to learn that many were found to be duds, their firing mechanisms having long been exposed to the corrosive effect of salt water.

Granger's 2000 soldiers arrived on August 2. They were taken around into Mississippi Sound the following night for a landing on the west end of Dauphin Island, and from there began working their way through heavy sand toward the back door of Fort Gaines. *Tecumseh* still had not appeared, but Farragut now was committed. "I can lose no more days," he declared. "I must go in day after tomorrow morning at daylight or a little later. It is a bad time, but when you do not take fortune at her offer you must take her as you can find her." Despite a heavy squall that evening, the grapplers went about their work in the mine field, undetected, and early next morning, August 4, the admiral took his fleet captains aboard the tender *Cowslip* for a closer look at the objective, cruising under the lee of Sand Island where the three monitors were anchored, ready to move out. Returning he went to his cabin, took out pen and paper, and composed a provisional farewell. "My dearest Wife: I write and leave this letter for you. I am going into Mobile Bay in the morning, if God is my leader, as I hope He is, and in Him I place my trust. . . . The Army landed last night, and are in full view of us this morning. The *Tecumseh* has not yet arrived."

Just then she did, steaming in from Pensacola to take position at the head of the iron column on the far side of Sand Island. The Union line of battle was complete. Asked at bedtime if he would consent to giving the men a glass of grog to nerve them up for the fight next morning, Farragut replied: "No, sir. I never found that I needed rum to enable me to do my duty. I will order two cups of good coffee to each man at 2 o'clock, and at 8 o'clock I will pipe all hands to breakfast in Mobile Bay."

Fog delayed the forming of the line past daybreak, the prearranged time for the start of the run, but a dawn breeze cleared the mist away by sunup, which came at 5.30 this Friday morning, August 5. As the four monitors began their movement eastward off the lee shore of Sand Island, in preparation for turning north beyond the line of pilings and the mine field — at which point the wooden column of seven heavy ships, each with a gunboat lashed to its port side for reserve power in case its boilers or engines were knocked out, would come up in their left rear for the dash past Mobile Point and the brick pentagon looming huge and black against the sunrise — Farragut was pleased to see that fortune had given him the two things he prayed for: a westerly wind to blow the smoke of battle away from the fleet and toward the fort, and a flood tide that would carry any pair of vessels on into the bay, even if both were disabled. Captain James Alden's 2000-ton 24-gun *Brooklyn* led the way, given the honor because she was equipped with chase guns and an antitorpedo device called a cowcatcher. Then came Flag Captain Percival Drayton's *Hartford* with the admiral aboard, followed by the remaining five, *Richmond, Lackawanna, Monongahela, Ossipee,* and *Oneida,* each with its gunboat consort attached to the flank away from the fort and otherwise readied for action in accordance with instructions issued as far back as mid-July: "Strip your vessels and prepare for the conflict. Send down all superfluous spars and rigging. Trice up or remove the whiskers. Put up the splinter nets on the starboard side, and barricade the wheel and steersmen with sails and hammocks. Lay chains or sandbags on the deck over the machinery to resist a plunging fire. Hang the sheet chains over the side, or make any other arrangements for security that your ingenuity may suggest." As a result, according to a Confederate who studied the uncluttered ships from Mobile Point, "They appeared like prize fighters ready for the ring."

Buchanan, aboard the *Tennessee,* got word that they were coming at 5.45, shortly after they started his way. He hurried on deck in his drawers for a look at the Yankee vessels, iron and wood, and while he dressed passed orders for the ram and its three attendant gunboats to move westward and take up a position athwart the main channel, just in rear of the inner line of torpedoes, for crossing the Union T if the enemy warships — eighteen of them, mounting 199 guns, as compared to his own four with 22 — passed Fort Morgan in an attempt to enter the bay. Balding, clean-shaven like Farragut, with bright blue eyes and a hawk nose, the Marylander assembled the *Tennessee*'s officers and crew on her gun deck and made them a speech that managed to be at once brief and rambling. "Now, men, the enemy is coming, and I want you to do your duty," he began, and ended: "You shall not have it said when you leave this vessel that you were not near enough to the enemy, for I will meet them, and you can fight them alongside of their own ships. And if I fall, lay me on the side and go on with the fight."

Farragut came on deliberately in accordance with his plan, the flagship crossing the outer bar at 6.10 while the iron column up ahead was making its turn north into the channel. Ten minutes later the lead monitor *Tecumseh* fired the opening shot, a 15-inch shell packed with sixty pounds of powder and half a bushel of cylindrical flathead bolts. It burst squarely over the fort, which did not reply until shortly after 7 o'clock, when the range to *Brooklyn,* leading the wooden column, had been closed to about a mile. Morgan's heaviest weapon was a 10-inch Columbiad, throwing a projectile less than half the weight of the one from *Tecumseh,* but the effect was altogether memorable for a young surgeon on the *Lackawanna,* midway down the line of high-masted vessels. "It is a curious sight to catch a single shot from so heavy a piece of ordnance," he later wrote. "First you see the puff of white smoke upon the distant ramparts, and then you see the shot coming, looking exactly as if some gigantic hand has thrown in play a ball toward you. By the time it is half way, you get the boom of the report, and then the howl of the missile, which apparently grows so rapidly in size that every green hand on board who can see it is certain that it will hit him between the eyes. Then, as it goes past with a shriek like a thousand devils, the inclination to do reverence is so strong that it is almost impossible to resist it."

Now the action became general, and by 7.30 the leading sloops, closing fast on the sluggish monitors, had their broadsides bearing fairly on the fort, whose gun crews were distracted by flying masonry, clouds of brickdust, and an avalanche of shells. Then two things happened, one in each of the tandem columns, for which Farragut had not planned while rehearsing the operation on the table in his cabin. Directly ahead of the flagship, *Brooklyn* had to slow to keep from overtaking the rear monitor *Chickasaw.* Presently, to the consternation of all astern, Alden stopped and began making signals: "The monitors are right ahead. We cannot go on without passing them. What shall we do?" While Farragut was testily replying, "Go ahead!" — and the guns of the fort and water battery, less than half a mile away, were stepping up their fire — Commander Tunis Craven of the *Tecumseh,* at the head of the iron column, reacted to a similar crisis in quite a different way, though it too involved a departure from instructions. Approaching the red buoy that marked the eastern limit of the mine field, he saw the breakers off Mobile Point, just off his starboard bow, and said to his pilot, out of fear of running aground: "It is impossible that the admiral means us to go inside that buoy." He ordered a hard turn to port, which carried the *Tecumseh* to the left, not right, of the red marker. But not for long. A sudden, horrendous explosion against her bottom, square amidships — whether of one or more torpedoes was later disputed — shook and stopped the iron vessel, set her lurching from side to side, and sent water pouring down her turret as she wallowed in the waves.

All aboard her must have known the hurt was mortal, though no one guessed how short her agony would be. Craven and his pilot, for example, standing face to face at the foot of the ladder that led to the only escape hatch, staged a brief, courtly debate.

"Go ahead, Captain."

"After you, Pilot."

So they said; "But there was nothing after me," the pilot later testified. As he put his foot on the top rung of the ladder, *Tecumseh* and her captain dropped from under him.

Through a sight slit in the turret of *Manhattan*, next in line, an engineer watched the lead monitor vanish almost too abruptly for belief. "Her stern lifted high in the air with the propeller still revolving, and the ship pitched out of sight like an arrow twanged from the bow." With her went all but a score of her 114-man crew, including four who swam to Mobile Point and were taken captive, while the others who managed to wriggle out before she hit bottom were picked up by a boat from the *Hartford*'s consort, *Metacomet*.

Farragut sent the boat, though the fact was he had problems enough on his hands by then, including the apparent likelihood that such rescue work was about to be required in his own direction. *Brooklyn*'s untimely halt, practically under Morgan's guns, had thrown the wooden column into confusion; for when she stopped her bow yawed off to starboard, subtracting her broadside from the pounding the fort was taking, and what was worse she lay nearly athwart the channel, blocking the path of the other ships. Nor was that the end of the trouble she and her captain made. Alarmed by the sudden dive of the *Tecumseh* ("Sunk by a torpedo! Assassination in its worst form!" he would protest in his report) Alden spotted, just under his vessel's prow, "a row of suspicious-looking buoys" which he took to be floats attached to mines. He reacted by ordering *Brooklyn*'s engines reversed, and this brought her bearing down, stern foremost, on the *Hartford*. Farragut, who had climbed the mainmast rigging as far as the futtock shrouds for a view above the smoke — he was tied there with a rope passed round his body by a sailor, sent aloft by Drayton, lest a collision or a chance shot bring him crashing to the deck some twenty feet below — angrily hailed the approaching sloop, demanding to know the cause for such behavior, and got the reply: "Torpedoes ahead."

Like the *Brooklyn*, which took 59 hits in the course of the fight, *Hartford* was absorbing cruel punishment from the guns on Mobile Point: particularly from those in the water battery, whose fire was point-blank and deadly. Men were falling fast, their mangled bodies placed in a row on one side of the deck, while the wounded were sent below in numbers too great for the surgeons to handle. A rifled solid tore a gunner's head off; another took both legs off a sailor who threw up his arms as he fell, only to have them carried away by still another. Farragut looked back down the line, where the rest of his stalled vessels were being served in much the same fashion, and saw that it would not do. He either had to go forward or turn back. In his extremity, he said later, he called on God: "Shall I go on?" and received the answer from a commanding voice inside his head: "Go on." *Brooklyn* blocked the channel on the right, so he asked the pilot, directly above him in the maintop, whether there was enough water for the *Hartford* to pass her on the left. The pilot said there was, and the admiral, exultant, shouted down to Drayton on the quarterdeck: "I will take the lead!" Signaling "close order" to the ships astern, he had the *Metacomet* back her engines and the flagship go all forward. This turned her westward, clear of *Brooklyn*, which she passed as she moved out. Someone called up a reminder of Alden's warning, but Farragut, lashed to the rigging high above the smoke of battle, with Mobile Bay in full view before him, had no time or mind for caution. "Damn the torpedoes!" he cried. "Full speed ahead!"

Ahead he went, followed by the others, west of where the *Brooklyn* lay until she rejoined the column — and west, too, of the red buoy marking the eastern limit of the mine field. Though Farragut had been encouraged by the work of his nighttime grapplers, who not only had removed a considerable number of mines in the course of the past two weeks, but also reported a high percentage of duds among them, *Tecumseh* had just given an only-too-graphic demonstration of what might await him and all his warships, iron or wood, as a result of this sudden departure from his plan to avoid the doom-infested stretch of water the *Hartford* now was crossing. And sure enough, while she steamed ahead with all the speed her engines could provide, the men on deck — and, even worse, the ones cooped up below — could hear the knock and scrape of torpedo cases against her hull and the snap of primers designed to ignite the charges that would blast her to the bottom. None did, either under the *Hartford* or any of the vessels in her wake, but the passage of Morgan became progressively more difficult as the lead sloops steamed out of range and left the tail of the column, along with the slow-moving monitors, to the less-divided attention of the cannoneers in the fort and on the beach. *Oneida*, which brought up the rear, took a 7-inch shell in the starboard boiler, scalding her firemen with escaping steam, and another that burst in the cabin, cutting both wheel ropes. Powerless and out of control, she too made it past, tugged along by her consort, only to emerge upon a scene of even worse destruction, just inside the bay.

Buchanan had succeeded in his design to cross the Union T; with the result that when Farragut ended his sprint across the mine field he found the *Tennessee* and the three rebel gunboats drawn up to receive him in line ahead, presenting their broadsides to the approaching column, whose return fire was limited to the vessels in the lead, and even these could bring only their bow guns into play. *Hartford*'s was promptly knocked out by a shot from *Selma*, smallest of the three, and this was followed by another that passed through the chain armor on the flagship's starboard bow, killing ten men, wounding five, and hurling bodies, or parts of bodies, aft and onto the decks of the *Metacomet*, lashed alongside. Farragut kept coming, with *Brooklyn* and *Richmond* close astern, and managed to avoid an attempt by Buchanan to ram and sink him, meantime bringing his big Dahlgrens to bear on the gunboats, one of which then retired lamely toward Fort Morgan, taking water through a hole punched in her hull. This was the *Gaines*; she was out of the fight, and presently so were the others, *Morgan* and *Selma*; for *Hartford* and *Richmond* cast off their consorts to engage them and they fled. *Metacomet* led the chase, yawing twice to fire her bow gun, but then stopped firing to concentrate on speed. While *Morgan* made it to safety under the lee of Mobile Point, *Selma* kept running eastward across the shallows beyond the channel, still pursued despite the *Metacomet*'s deeper draft. Out on the bow of the northern vessel, a leadsman was already calling one foot less than the ship drew, but her captain, feeling the soft ooze of the bottom under her keel, refused to abandon the chase. "Call the man in," he told his exec. "He is only intimidating me with his soundings."

Persistence paid. Overtaken, *Selma* lost eight killed and seven wounded before she hauled down her flag. Westward, the *Gaines* burned briskly, set afire by her crew, who escaped in boats as she sank in shallow water. Only *Morgan* survived, anchored under the frown of the fort's guns to wait for nightfall, when she would steal around the margin of the bay to gain the greater safety of Mobile, inside Dog River Bar.

Left to fight alone, Buchanan steamed after the *Hartford* for a time, still hoping to ram and sink her, despite the agility she had shown in avoiding his first attempt, but soon perceived that her speed made the chase a waste of effort; whereupon he turned back and made for the other half-dozen sloops, advancing in closer order. *Tennessee* passed down the line of high-walled wooden men-of-war, mauling and being mauled. Two shots went through and through the *Brooklyn*, increasing her toll of killed and wounded to 54, but another pair flew high to miss the *Richmond*. Both ships delivered point-blank broadsides that had no effect whatever on the armored vessel as she bore down on *Lackawanna*, next in line, and *Monongahela*, which she struck a glancing blow, then swung round to send two shells crashing into the *Ossipee*. That left *Oneida*, whose bad luck now turned good, at least for the moment.

War Is Cruelty . . . [503]

Aboard the ram, defective primers spared the crippled ship a pounding; then one gun fired a delayed shot that cost the northern skipper an arm and the use of his 11-inch after pivot, which was raked. *Tennessee* turned hard aport in time to meet the three surviving monitors, just arriving, and exchanged volleys in passing that did no harm on either side. Then she proceeded to Fort Morgan and pulled up, out of range on the far side of the channel.

Farragut dropped anchor four miles inside the bay, and the rest of the blue flotilla, wood and iron, steamed up to join him, their crews already at work clearing away debris and swabbing the blood from decks, while belowdecks surgeons continued to ply their scalpels and cooks got busy in the galleys. It was 8.35; he was only a bit over half an hour behind schedule on last night's promise to "pipe all hands to breakfast in Mobile Bay" by 8 o'clock. All the same, despite the general elation at having completed another spectacular run past formidable works, rivaling those below New Orleans and at Vicksburg and Port Hudson, there was also a tempering sorrow over the loss of the *Tecumseh* and considerable apprehension, as well, from the fact that the murderous rebel iron ram was still afloat across the way.

Drayton promptly expressed this reservation to the admiral, who by now had come down from the flagship's rigging and stood on the poop. "What we have done has been well done, sir," he told him. "But it all counts for nothing so long as the *Tennessee* is there under the guns of Morgan." Farragut nodded. "I know it," he said, "and as soon as the people have had their breakfasts I am going for her."

As it turned out, there was no need for that, and no time for breakfast. At 8.50, fifteen minutes after *Hartford* anchored, there was a startled cry from aloft. "The ram is coming!" So she was, and presently those on deck saw her steaming directly for the fleet, apparently too impatient to wait for a fight in which she would have the help of the guns ashore. Farragut prepared for battle, remarking as he did so: "I did not think Old Buck was such a fool."

Fool or not, throughout the pause Buchanan had been unwilling to admit the fight was over, whatever the odds and no matter how far he had to go from Fort Morgan to renew it. Instrumental in the founding of the academy at Annapolis, he had served as its first superintendent and thought too highly of naval tradition to accept even tacit defeat while his ship remained in any condition to engage the enemy. "If he won't visit me, I will have to visit him," his adversary had remarked three weeks ago, and Buchanan felt much the same about the matter now as he gazed across three miles of water at the Yankee warships riding at anchor in the bay — *his* bay — quite as if there was no longer any question of their right to be there. Gazing, he drew the corners of his mouth down in a frown of disapproval, then turned to the *Tennessee*'s captain. "Follow them up, Johnston. We can't let them off that way." With that, the ram started forward: one six-gun vessel against a total of seventeen, three of them wearing armor heavier than her own, mounting 157 guns, practically all of them larger than any weapon in her casemate. That Buchanan was in no mood for advice was demonstrated, however, when one of his officers tried to call his attention to the odds. "Now I am in the humor, I will have it out," he said, and that was that. The ram continued on her way.

The monitors having proved unwieldy, Farragut's main reliance was on his wooden sloops, particularly the *Monongahela* and the *Lackawanna*, which were equipped with iron prows for ramming. Their orders were to run the ram down, while the others pitched in to do her whatever damage they could manage with their guns. Accordingly, when the *Tennessee* came within range about 9.20, making hard for the flagship, *Monongahela* moved ahead at full speed and struck her amidships, a heavy blow that had no effect at all on the rebel vessel but cost the sloop her iron beak, torn off along with her cutwater. *Lackawanna* rammed in turn, with the result that an eight-foot section of her stem was crushed above and below the waterline. *Tennessee* lurched but held her course, and the two flagships collided nearly head on. "The port bow of the *Hartford* met the port bow of the ram," an officer aboard the Federal vessel later wrote, "and the ships grated against each other as they passed. The *Hartford* poured her whole port broadside against the ram, but the solid shot merely dented the side and bounded into the air. The ram tried to return the salute, but owing to defective primers only one gun was discharged. This sent a shell through the berth-deck, killing five men and wounding eight. The muzzle of the gun was so close to the *Hartford* that the powder blackened her side."

When the two ships parted Farragut jumped to the port quarter rail and held to the mizzen rigging while he leaned out to assess the damage, which was by no means as great as he had feared. Finding the perch to his liking he remained there, lashed to the rigging by friendly hands for the second time that day, and called for Drayton to give the *Tennessee* another thump as soon as possible. As the *Hartford* came about, however, she was struck on the starboard flank by the *Lackawanna*, which was also trying to get in position, crushing her planking on that side and upsetting one of the Dahlgrens. "Save the admiral! Save the admiral!" the cry went up, for it was thought at first that the flagship was sinking, so great was the confusion on her decks. Farragut untied himself, leaped down, and crossed to the starboard mizzen rigging, where he again leaned out to inspect the damage, which though severe did not extend to within two feet of the water. Again he ordered full speed ahead, only to find the *Lakawanna* once more looming on his starboard quarter. At this, one witness later said, "the admiral became a trifle excited." Forgetting that he had given the offending ship instructions to lead the ram attack, he turned to the communications officer on the bridge.

"Can you say 'For God's sake' by signal?"

"Yes, sir."

"Then say to the *Lackawanna*, 'For God's sake, get out of our way and anchor.'"

By now the ironclad had become the target for every ship that could get in position to give her a shot or a shove, including the double-turreted *Chickasaw*, which "hung close under our stern," the *Tennessee*'s pilot afterwards declared, "firing the two 11-inch guns in her forward turret like pocket pistols." Such punishment began to tell. Her flagstaff went and then her stack, giving the ram what one attacker called "a particularly shorn, stubby look" and greatly reducing the draft to her fires. Her steam went down, and then, as a sort of climax to her disablement, the monitor hard astern succeeded in cutting her rudder chain, exposed on the afterdeck, so that she would no longer mind her helm. Still she kept up the fight, exploiting her one advantage, which was that she could fire in any direction, surrounded as she was, without fear of hitting a friend or missing a foe. Presently, though, this too was reduced by shots that jammed half of her gunport shutters against the shield, thereby removing them from use. When this happened to the stern port, Buchanan sent for a machinist to unjam it, and while the man was at work on the cramped bolt, an 11-inch shell from the *Chickasaw* exploded against the edge of the cover just above him. "His remains had to be taken up with a shovel, placed in a bucket, and thrown overboard," a shipmate would recall. One of the steel splinters that flew inside the casemate struck Buchanan, breaking his left leg below the knee. "Well, Johnston," he said to the *Tennessee*'s captain as he was taken up to be carried down to the berth deck, "they've got me. You'll have to look out for her now. This is your fight, you know."

Johnston did what he could to sustain the contest with the rudderless, nearly steamless vessel, blind in most of her ports and taking heavy-caliber punches from two big sloops on each quarter and the monitor astern. Finally he went below and reported the situation to Buchanan. "Do the best you can, sir," the admiral told him, teeth gritted against the pain from the compound fracture of his leg, "and when all is done, surrender." Returning topside, the Alabamian found the battle going even worse. Unable to maneuver, the ram could not bring a single gun to bear on her tormentors; moreover, Johnston afterwards reported, "Shots were fairly raining upon the after end of the shield, which was now so thoroughly shattered that in a few moments it would have fallen and exposed the gun deck to a raking fire of shell and grape." He lowered the *Tennessee*'s ensign, in token of her capitulation, and when this did not slacken the encircling fire — it had been shot down before, then raised again on the handle of a rammer staff poked through the overhead grille of the smoky casemate — "I then decided, although with an almost bursting heart, to hoist the white flag."

At 10 o'clock the firing stopped, and presently Farragut sent an officer to demand the wounded admiral's sword, which then was handed over. *Tennessee*'s loss of two men killed and nine wounded brought the Confederate total for all four ships to 12 killed and 20 wounded. Union losses were 172 killed, more than half in the *Tecumseh*, and 170 wounded. Their respective totals, 32 and 342, were thus about in ratio of the strength of the two fleets, though in addition 243 rebel sailors were captured aboard *Selma* and the ironclad.

"The Almighty has smiled upon me once more. I am in Mobile Bay," Farragut wrote his wife that night, adding: "It was a hard fight, but Buck met his fate manfully. After we passed the forts, he came up in the ram to attack me. I made at him and ran him down, making all the others do the same. We butted and shot at him until he surrendered."

Westward across the bay, as he wrote, there was a burst of flame and a loud explosion off Cedar Point. The garrison of Fort Powell, taken under bombardment from the rear that afternoon by one of the big-gunned monitors at a range of 400 yards, had evacuated the place under cover of darkness and set a slow match to the magazine. Next morning the fleet dropped down and began shelling the eastern end of Dauphin Island, where Fort Gaines was under pressure from the landward side by Granger and his soldiers. This continued past nightfall, and the fort's commander asked for terms the following day, August 7. Told they were unconditional, he accepted and promptly surrendered his 818 men, together with all guns and stores. That left Fort Morgan; a much tougher proposition, as it turned out.

While the troops were being taken aboard transports for the shift to Mobile Point and a similar rear approach to the fortifications there, Farragut submitted under a flag of truce a note signed by himself and Granger, demanding the unconditional surrender of Fort Morgan "to prevent the unnecessary sacrifice of human life which must follow the opening of our batteries." The reply was brief and negative. "Sirs: I am prepared to sacrifice life, and will only surrender when I have no means of defense.... Respectfully, etc. *R. L. Page*, Brigadier General."

Approaching fifty-seven, Richard Page was a Virginian, a forty-year veteran of the Union and Confederate navies, who had transferred to the army five months ago when he assumed command of the outer defenses of Mobile Bay. His beard was white, his manner fiery; "Old Ramrod" and "Bombast Page" were two of his prewar nicknames, and if he bore a resemblance to R. E. Lee (both were born in 1807) it was no wonder. His mother had been Lee's father's sister.

Farragut's run past Morgan had come as a shock to its defenders, who fired close to 500 shots at the slow-moving Yankee column. "I do

War Is Cruelty ... [507]

not see how I failed to sink the *Hartford*," Page said ruefully, shaking his head as the smoke cleared; "I do not see how I failed to sink her." Fort Powell's evacuation and the unresistant capitulation of Fort Gaines, neither of which had been done with his permission, angered and made him all the more determined to resist to the utmost the amphibious seige that got under way on August 9, shortly after he rejected unconditional surrender. Granger's men had been put ashore that morning on the bay side of Mobile Point, just over a mile to the east of the fort, and by nightfall — after they had performed the back-breaking labor of hauling guns and ammunition through shin-deep sand, which one of them said was "hot enough during the day for roasting potatoes" — took the east curtain and ramparts under fire with their batteries, while the sloops and ironclads, including the captured *Tennessee*, poured in shells and hotshot from the bay and Gulf. The fort shook under this combined pounding, but Page was no more of a mind to surrender now than he had been when he first declined the combined demand at midday.

For two weeks this continued, and throughout that time the pressure grew. Daily the troops drew closer on the landward side, increasing the number of weapons they brought to bear until at last there were 25 guns and 16 heavy mortars, their discharges echoed by those from the ships beyond and on both sides of the point. The climax came on August 22, when 3000 rounds were flung at the fort in the course of a twelve-hour bombardment, under whose cover the blue infantry extended its parallels to within reach of the glacis. All but two of the fort's guns were silenced and the citadel was burning; sharpshooters drew beads on anything that showed above the ramparts, and 80,000 pounds of powder had to be removed from the magazine and flooded, so close were the flames. Practically all that remained by now was wreckage and scorched debris. At 5 o'clock next morning two last shots were fired by the defenders, and one hour later the white flag went up. Farragut sent Drayton to arrange the formal surrender, which took place that afternoon amid the rubble. He had Buchanan's sword for a trophy, but he did not get Page's. The general and all his officers, displaying what Farragut called "childish spitefulness," had broken or thrown away their side arms just before the ceremony.

The admiral did get another 546 prisoners, however, which brought the total to better than 1700 on land and water — and he did get Mobile Bay, which after all was what he had come for. Blockade running might continue on the Atlantic coast, where Wilmington and Charleston still held out, but it was ended on the Gulf except for the sealed-off region west of the Mississippi, which in any case lay outside the constricting Anaconda coils. Mobile itself, thirty miles away at the head of the bay, was no part of Farragut's objective. Except as a port, it contributed little to the South's defense, and it was a port no longer. Moreover, Canby not only lacked the strength to expel the town's defenders; he could not have afforded to garrison it afterwards, so urgent were the calls for replacements for the men who had fallen in Georgia and, above all, in Virginia.

Best of all the immediate gains obtained from the naval battle, though, was the elation that followed, throughout the North, the announcement of the first substantial victory that had been scored, East or West, in the three months since the opening of Grant's spring offensive. Lincoln and his political supporters were pleased above all, perhaps, with the lift it seemed to give his chances for survival in the presidential contest, which by then was less than three months off.

As usual, there was bad news with the good, and in this case the bad was double-barreled, concerning as it did a pair of highly spectacular reverses, one afloat and one ashore. In Washington on August 12, while the celebration of Farragut's week-old triumph over the *Tennessee* was still in progress at the Navy Department — word had come belatedly by wire from Ben Butler, who read of the bay battle in a Richmond paper smuggled through his Bermuda Hundred lines the day before — the telegraph line from coastal New Jersey began to chatter about a mysterious rebel cruiser at work off Sandy Hook. Yesterday she had taken seven prizes, and today she was adding six more to her list, which would reach a total of thirty U.S. merchant vessels within the week. It was as if the *Alabama*, eight weeks in her watery grave outside Cherbourg, had been raised, pumped out, and sped across the Atlantic to lay about her in a manner even more destructive than when she was in her prime. Quickly, all the available Federal warships within reach were ordered out to find and sink her at all costs. But who, or what, was she? Where had she come from? Who was her captain?

She was the *Tallahassee*, a former blockade runner, built up the Thames the year before and purchased that summer by the Confederates, who converted her into a raider by installing three guns and sent her out from Wilmington under Commander John T. Wood, a onetime Annapolis instructor, grandson of Zachary Taylor, aide to Jefferson Davis, and participant in a number of naval exploits, including the *Merrimac-Monitor* fight, New Bern, and the retaking of Plymouth. Setting out on the night of August 6 he showed the blockaders a clean pair of heels; for that was the ship's main virtue, speed. Twin stacked, with a 100-horsepower engine driving each of her two screws, she was 220 feet in length and only 24 in the beam, a combination that gave her a top speed of seventeen knots and had enabled her, on her shakedown cruise, to make the Dover-Calais crossing in seventy-seven minutes. Five mornings later, 500 miles up the Atlantic coast, *Tallahassee* encountered her first prize, the schooner *Sarah Boyce*, and before the day was over she ran down six more Union merchant vessels, ransoming the last to put all prisoners ashore. That was Thursday, August 11; "Pirate off Sandy Hook capturing and burning," the commandant of the Brooklyn Navy Yard wired Washington. Friday, off Long Island, she took six prizes, Saturday two, and Sunday — as if by way of resting on the Sabbath — one. By now she was cruising the New England coast, and on Monday she took six ships, Tuesday five, and Wednesday three, rounding out a week that netted her thirty prizes, all burned or scuttled except seven that were ransomed to clear her crowded decks of captured passengers and crews. On August 18, running low on coal, she put into the neutral port of Halifax to refuel.

Under instructions from the Queen, and over ardent protests from the American consul, the Nova Scotia authorities gave Wood twenty-four hours to fill his bunkers, and when this did not suffice they granted him a twelve-hour extension. *Tallahassee* steamed out the following night in time to avoid half a dozen enemy warships that arrived next day, the vanguard of a fleet of thirteen ordered to Halifax as soon as the consul telegraphed word of the raider's presence in the harbor. She headed straight for Wilmington, taking so little chance on running out of coal that she only paused to seize one prize along the way, and arrived on the night of August 26 to speed and shoot her way through the blockade flotilla and drop anchor up the Cape Fear River, whose entrance was guarded by Fort Fisher. Her twenty-day cruise had cost the enemy 31 merchant vessels and had given Wood's fellow countrymen some welcome news to offset the bad from Mobile Bay, where Fort Morgan had fallen three days ago. They took pride in the fact that "this extemporaneous man-of-war," as Jefferson Davis called the *Tallahassee*, had "lit up the New England coast with her captures," and they could tell themselves, as well, that no matter what misfortunes befell their regular navy, outnumbered as it invariably was in combat, their irregular navy (so to speak) had won them the admiration of the world and was rapidly scouring the seas of Yankee shipping.

That was the first Federal reverse. The second, which occurred simultaneously ashore, was quite as spectacular and, if anything, even more "irregular" — as was often the case in operations involving Bedford Forrest. He had been given a free rein to conduct the defense of North Mississippi by Major General Dabney Maury, who succeeded to command of the Department of Alabama, Mississippi, and East Louisiana in late July, when Stephen Lee left to join Hood at Atlanta. "We must do the best we can with the little we have," Maury wrote from Meridian in early August, "and it is with no small satisfaction I reflect that of all the commanders of the Confederacy you are accustomed to accomplish the very greatest results with small means when left to your own untrammeled judgment. Upon that judgment I now rely."

Forrest took him at his word. "All that can be done shall be done," he replied, adding that since he lacked "the force to risk a general engagement" in resisting the next blue incursion, he would "resort to all other means." Other means, in this case, included a raid on Memphis, the enemy's main base, under occupation for better than two years. Tactically, such a strike would be likely to disrupt the plans of the Federals for extending their conquest deep into Mississippi. Moreover, Forrest himself — a former alderman — would not only derive considerable personal satisfaction from returning to his home town, which no Confederate had entered, except as a spy or prisoner, since its fall in June of 1862; he would also be exacting vengeance for a battle fought the month before, near Tupelo, which was as close to a defeat as he had come so far in his career. Lee had been in command of the field, one week before his departure for Atlanta, but the memory rankled and Forrest was anxious to wipe it out or anyhow counterbalance it.

Hard on the heels of Brice's Crossroads in mid-June, when he received orders from Sherman "to make up a force and go out and follow Forrest to the death, if it costs 10,000 lives and breaks the Treasury," C. C. Washburn, the Memphis commander, assigned the task to A. J. Smith, reinforcing two of his divisions, just returned from their excursion up and down Red River, with Bouton's brigade of Negro infantry and Grierson's cavalry division, both of them recent graduates of the hard-knocks school the Wizard of the Saddle was conducting for his would-be conquerers down in Mississippi. On July 5 this column of 14,200 effectives, mounted and afoot, supported by six batteries of artillery and supplied with twenty days of rations — "a force ample to whip anything this side of Georgia," Washburn declared — set out southward from La Grange, fifty miles east of Memphis. Sherman's orders by then had been expanded; Smith and his gorilla-guerillas, who had polished their hard-handed skills in Louisiana under Banks, were to "pursue Forrest on foot, devastating the land over which he passed or may pass, and make him and the people of Tennessee and Mississippi realize that, although [he is] a bold, daring, and successful leader, he will bring ruin and misery on any country where he may pause or tarry. If we do not punish Forrest and the people now," the red-haired Ohioan wound up, "the whole effect of our past conquests will be lost."

Three days out, and just over fifty miles down the road, Smith showed that he took this admonition to heart by burning much of the town of Ripley, including the courthouse, two churches, the Odd Fellows Hall, and a number of homes. Next day, July 9, still mindful of his instructions to "punish Forrest and the people," he pressed on across the Tallahatchie and through New Albany, trailed by a swath of desolation ten miles wide.

Ahead lay Pontotoc, and beyond it Okolona, where Sooy Smith had come to grief five months before, checked almost as disastrously as Sturgis had been at nearby Brice's Crossroads, a month ago tomorrow. So far, only token opposition to the current march had developed, but at

Pontotoc, which he cleared on July 11, this new Smith began to encounter stiffer resistance. Butternut troopers hung on the flanks of the column, as if to slow it down before it made contact with whatever was waiting to receive it up ahead, perhaps at Okolona. Smith would never know; for at dawn on July 13, well short of any ambush being laid for him there or south of there, he abruptly changed direction and struck out instead for Tupelo, fifteen miles to the east on the Mobile & Ohio, "his column well closed up, his wagon train well protected, and his flanks covered in an admirable manner."

So Forrest's scouts informed him at Okolona, where he was waiting — it was his forty-third birthday — for both Smith and Stephen Lee, who was on the way with 2000 troops and had ordered him not to commit his present force of about 6000 until these reinforcements got there to reduce the odds. Arriving from the south to find that the blue column had veered east, Lee took charge of pressing the pursuit. His urgency was based on reports from Dabney Maury, at Mobile, that Canby was preparing to march from New Orleans and attack the city from the landward side; Lee wanted Smith dealt with quickly so that the men he had brought to reinforce Forrest could be sent to Maury. "As soon as I fight I can send him 2000, possibly 3000," he explained in a dispatch to Bragg, though he added that this depended on whether the Mississippi invaders did or did not "succeed in delaying the battle." Smith was capable and canny, halting from time to time to beat off rearward threats while Grierson's horsemen rode on into Tupelo and began tearing up track above and below the town. All day the Federal infantry marched, then called a halt soon after nightfall at Harrisburg, two miles west of Tupelo, which had grown with the railroad and swallowed the older settlement as a suburb. Forrest came up presently in the darkness and "discovered the enemy strongly posted and prepared to give battle the next day."

Smith was at bay, and though his position was a stout one, nearly two miles long and skillfully laid out — flanks refused, rear well covered by cavalry, the line itself strengthened with fence rails, logs, timbers from torn-down houses, and bales of cotton — Forrest counted this a happy ending to an otherwise disappointing birthday. "One thing is certain," he told Lee; "the enemy cannot remain long where he is. He must come out, and when he does, all I ask or wish is to be turned loose with my command." No matter which way Smith headed when he emerged fretful and hungry, Forrest said, "I will be on all sides of him, attacking day and night. He shall not cook a meal or have a night's sleep, and I will wear his army to a frazzle before he gets out of the country."

Lee could see the beauty of that; but he had Mobile and Canby on his mind, together with the promises he had made to Bragg and Maury, and did not feel that he could afford the time it would take to deal with the penned-up bluecoats in this manner. There were better that 14,000 of them, veterans to a man, and though he had only about 8000 troops on hand he issued orders for an all-out assault next morning. Forrest would take the right and he the left. Together they would storm the Union works, making up for the disparity in numbers by the suddenness and ardor of their charge.

Ardor there was, and suddenness too, but these turned out to be the qualities that robbed Lee of what little chance he had for success in the first place. July 14 dawned hot and still, and the troops on line were vexed by delays in bringing several late-arriving units into position for the attack. Around 7.30, a Kentucky brigade near the center jumped the gun and started forward ahead of the others, who followed piecemeal, left and right, with the result that what was to have been a single, determined effort, all along the line, broke down from the outset into a series of individual lunges. Smith's veterans, snug behind their improvised breastworks, blasted each rebel unit as it advanced. "It was all gallantry and useless sacrifice," one Confederate was to say. To Smith, the disjointed attack "seemed to be a foot race to see who should reach us first. They were allowed to approach, yelling and howling like Comanches, to within canister range.... They would come forward and fall back, rally and forward again, with the like result. Their determination may be seen from the fact that their dead were found within thirty yards of our batteries." None got any closer, and after two hours of this Lee called a halt. He had lost 1326 killed and wounded and missing, Smith barely half that many, 674.

Skirmishing resumed next morning, but so fitfully and cautiously that it seemed to invite a counterattack. Smith instead clung fast to his position. He did, that is, until midday, when he was informed that much of the food in his train had spoiled in the Mississippi heat, leaving only one day's rations fit to eat, and that his reserve supply of artillery ammunition was down to about a hundred rounds per gun: whereupon he decided to withdraw northward, back in the direction he had set out from ten days ago, even though this meant leaving his more grievously wounded men behind in Tupelo. There followed the curious spectacle of a superior force retreating from a field on which it had inflicted nearly twice as many casualties as it suffered and being harassed on the march by a loser reduced to less than half the strength of the victor it was pursuing. In any case, after setting fire to what was left of Harrisburg, the Federals not only withdrew in good order and made excellent time on the dusty roads; they also succeeded, when they made camp at sunset on Town Creek, five miles north, in beating off a rebel attack and inflicting on Bedford Forrest, whom Lee had put in charge of the pursuit — and whom Smith had been told to "follow to the death" — his third serious gunshot wound of the war. The bullet struck him in the foot (the base of his right big toe, to be explicit) causing him so much

War Is Cruelty... [513]

pain that he had to relinquish the command, temporarily at least, and retire to a dressing station.

Smith kept going, unaware of this highly fortunate development, back through New Albany and across the Tallahatchie. Midway between there and La Grange he encountered a supply train sent to meet him. He kept going, despite this relief, and returned to his starting point on July 21, after sixteen round-trip days of marching and fighting. "I bring back everything in good order; nothing lost," he informed Washburn, who found the message so welcome a contrast to those received from other generals sent out after Forrest that he passed it along with pride to Sherman.

Far from proud, Sherman was downright critical, especially of the resultant fact that Forrest had been left to his own devices, which might well include a raid into Middle Tennessee and a strike against the blue supply lines running down into North Georgia. Engaged at the time in the Battle of Atlanta, Sherman replied that Smith was "to pursue and continue to follow Forrest. He must keep after him till recalled.... It is of vital importance that Forrest does not go to Tennessee." Smith returned to Memphis on July 23, miffed at this unappreciative reaction to his campaign, and began at once to prepare for a second outing, one that he hoped to improve beyond reproach.

This time the invasion column would number 18,000 of all arms, one quarter larger than before, and he would proceed by a different rout — down the Mississippi Central, which he would repair as he advanced, thus solving the problem of supplies whose lack had obliged his recent withdrawal in mid-career. By August 2 the railroad was in running order down to the Tallahatchie, and Washburn notified Sherman that Smith's reorganized command, which he assured him could "whip the combined force of the enemy this side of Georgia and east of the Mississippi," would set out "as soon as possible.... Forrest's forces were near Okolona a week since," he added, saving the best news for last; "Chalmers in command. Forrest [has] not been able to resume command by reason of wound in fight with Smith. I have a report today that he died of lockjaw some days ago."

It was true that Chalmers was in nominal command, but not that Forrest was dead, either of lockjaw or of any other ailment, although a look at him was enough to show how the rumor got started. Troubled by a siege of boils even before he was wounded, "sick-looking, thin as a rail, cheekbones that stuck out like they were trying to come through the skin, skin so yellow it looked greenish, eyes blazing" — one witness saw him thus at Tupelo that week — he rode about the camps in a buggy, his injured foot propped on a rack atop the dashboard, waiting impatiently for it to heal enough for him to mount a horse and resume command of his two divisions. They were all that were left him now, about 5000 horsemen, after his casualties at Harrisburg and the departure of Stephen Lee, first for Mobile (where the reinforcements he took with him turned out not to be needed, Grant having ruled out Canby's attack by diverting his troops to Virginia) and then for Atlanta, to join Hood. Partly, too, Forrest's haggard appearance was a result of the recent bloody repulse he had suffered in the assault on Smith. Even though he had advised against the attack, and was thereby absolved from blame for its failure, he was unaccustomed to sharing in a defeat and he burned with resentment over the useless loss of a thousand of his men, just at a time when they seemed likely to be needed most. Smith, he knew, was refitting in Memphis and would soon be returning to North Mississippi, stronger than before and with a better knowledge of the pitfalls. Sure enough, by early August the new blue column of 18,000 effectives had moved out to Grand Junction and begun its advance down the Mississippi Central to Holly Springs, a day's march from the Tallahatchie. "We knew we couldn't fight General Smith's big fine army," a butternut artillery lieutenant would recall, "and we knew that we couldn't get any reinforcements anywhere, and we boys speculated about what Old Bedford was going to do."

Old Bedford wondered too, for a time. At first he thought Smith's movement down the railroad was a feint, designed to "draw my forces west and give him the start toward the prairies." Back in command — and in the saddle, though he only used one stirrup — he sent Chalmers's division over to cover the Mississippi Central, but kept Buford's around Okolona to oppose what he believed would be the main blue effort. He soon learned better. On August 8 Smith moved in strength from Holly Springs and forced a crossing of the Tallahatchie, sending his cavalry ahead next day to occupy Oxford, twelve miles down the line. Forrest wired Chalmers to "contest every inch of ground," and set out at once for Oxford with Buford's division. Grierson fell back when he learned of this on August 10, and Smith remained at the river crossing, constructing a bridge to ensure the rapid delivery of supplies when he continued his march south. It was then, in this driest season of the Mississippi year, that the rain began to fall. It fell and kept falling for a week, marking what became known thereafter in these parts as "the wet August."

Both sides were nearly immobilized by the deepening mud and washouts, but they sparred as best they could, in slow motion, and planned for the time ahead. On August 18, though the weather still was rainy, Smith began inching southward; muddy or not, he had made up his mind to move, however slowly.

So by then had Forrest. At 5 o'clock that afternoon he assembled on the courthouse square at Oxford, after a rigorous "weeding out of sick men and sore-back and lame horses," close to 2000 troopers from two brigades and Morton's four-gun battery. In pelting rain and under a sky already dark with low-hanging clouds, the head of the column took up the march westward; Chalmers, left behind with the remaining 3000, had been told to put up such a show of resistance to the advancing Federals, who outnumbered him six to one, that Smith would not suspect for at least two days that nearly half of Forrest's command had left his front and was moving off to the west — in preparation for turning north around his flank, some were saying up and down the long gray column. "It got abroad in camp that we were going to Memphis," one rider later wrote. "That looked radical, but pleased us."

They knew they were right next morning, after a night march of twenty-five miles across swollen creeks and up and down long slippery hills, when they reached Panola and crossed the Tallahatchie, taking the route of the Mississippi & Tennessee Railroad, which ran north some sixty bee-line miles to Memphis. Four separate invasions they had repulsed in the past six months, three by pitched battle, one by sheer bluff, and now they were out to try their hand at turning back the fifth with a strike at the enemy's main base, close to a hundred miles in his rear. Radical, indeed. But Forrest knew what he would find when he got there; home-town operatives had kept him well informed. Washburn, under repeated urgings from Sherman to strengthen Smith to his utmost, had stripped the city's defense force to a minimum, and Fort Pickering, whose blufftop guns bore on the river and the city, but not on its landward approaches, offered little in the way of deterrent to an operation of this kind; Forrest did not intend to stay there any longer than it took his raiders to spread confusion among the defenders and alarm them into recalling Smith, who by now was skirmishing with Chalmers around Oxford, unaware that the man he was charged with following "to the death" had already rounded his flank and was about to set off an explosion deep in his rear.

Twenty miles the butternut column made that day, north from Panola to Senatobia, lighter by about two hundred troopers whose mounts had broken down before they reached the Tallahatchie and turned back, along with all but two of Morton's guns, whose teams were increased to ten horses each to haul them. The rain had stopped, as if on signal from the Wizard. All day the sun beamed down on roads and fields, but only enough, after eight days of saturation, to change the mud from slippery to sticky.

One mile north of Senatobia, which he cleared at first light, August 20, Forrest came upon Hickahala Creek, swollen to a width of sixty feet between its flooded banks; a formidable obstacle, but one for which he had planned by sending ahead a detachment to select a crossing point and chop down two trees on each bank, properly spaced, the stumps to be used for the support of a pair of cables woven from muscadine vines, which grew to unusual size and in great profusion in the bottoms. By the time the main body came up, the suspension cables had been stretched and were supported in midstream by an abandoned flatboat, which in turn was buoyed up by bundles of poles lashed to its sides. All that remained was for the span to be floored, and this was done with planks the troopers had ripped from gins and cabins on the approach march. In all, the crossing took less than an hour; but six miles north lay the Coldwater River, twice as wide. That took three, the work party having hurried ahead to construct another such grapevine bridge with the skill acquired while improvising the first. The heaviest loads it had to bear were the two guns, which were rolled across by hand, and several wagons loaded with unshucked corn for the horses, which were unloaded, trundled empty over the swaying rig, and then reloaded on the opposite bank. Forrest set the example by carrying the first armload, limping across on his injured foot, much to the admiration and amusement of his soldiers. "I never saw a command more like it was out for a holiday," one later wrote, while the general himself was to say: "I had to continually caution the men to keep quiet. They were making a regular corn shucking out of it."

Many of them, like him, were on their way home for the first time in years, and it was hard to contain the exuberance they were feeling at the prospect. Eight miles beyond the Coldwater by dark, Forrest called a rest halt at Hernando, where he had spent most of his young manhood, twenty-five miles from downtown Memphis. Near midnight the column pushed on, reduced to about 1500 sabers (so called, though for the most part they preferred shotguns and navy sixes) by the breakdown of another 200-odd horses, and stopped at 3 a.m. just short of the city limits, there to receive final instructions for the work ahead — work that was based on detailed information smuggled out by spies. One detachment under the general's brother, Captain William Forrest, would lead the way over Cane Creek Bridge and ride straight for the Gayoso House on Main Street, where Washburn's predecessor Stephen Hurlbut was quartered while awaiting reassignment; two other detachments, one of them under another brother, Lieutenant Colonel Jesse Forrest, would proceed similarly to capture Brigadier General R. P. Buckland, commander of the garrison, and Washburn himself, both of whom were living with their staffs in commandeered private residences. Two major generals and a brigadier would make a splendid haul and Forrest intended to have them, along with much else in the way of spoils assigned to still other detachments. Half an hour before dawn of this foggy Sunday morning, August 21, the head of the column entered the sleeping city whose papers had carried yesterday a special order from the department commander, prohibiting all "crying or selling of newspapers on Sunday between the hours of 9 a.m. and 5 p.m.," the better to preserve the peace and dignity of the Sabbath.

In some ways, the raid — the penetration itself — was anticlimactic. For example, all three Federal generals escaped capture, one because he slept elsewhere that night (just *where* became the subject of much scurrilous conjecture) and the other two because they were alerted in time to make a dash for safety under Fort Pickering's 97 guns, which Forrest had no intention of storming. Buckland woke to a hammering, a spattering of gunfire some blocks off, and leaned out of his upstairs bedroom window to find a sentry knocking at the locked door of the house. He called down, still half asleep, to ask what was the matter.

"General, they are after you."

"Who are after me?"

"The rebels," he was told.

He had time to dress before hurrying to the fort. Not so Washburn, who had to make a run for it in his nightshirt through back alleys; so sudden was the appearance of the raiders at his gate, he barely had time to leave by the rear door as they entered by the front. By way of consolation, Jesse Forrest captured two of his staff officers, along with his dress uniform and accouterments. Bill Forrest got even less when he clattered up Main Street to the Gayoso and, without pausing to dismount, rode his horse through the hotel doorway and into the lobby; Hurlbut, as aforesaid, had slept elsewhere and had only to lie low, wherever he was, to avoid capture. This he did, and survived to deliver himself of the best-remembered comment anyone made on either side in reference to the raid. "They removed me from command because I couldn't keep Forrest out of West Tennessee," he declared afterwards, "and now Washburn can't keep him out of his own bedroom."

By then enough blue units had rallied to bring on a number of vicious little skirmishes and fire-fights, resulting in a total of 35 Confederates and 80 Federals being killed or wounded, in addition to 116 defenders captured — many of them officers, rounded up in their night clothes at the Gayoso and elsewhere — along with some 200 horses. All this time, surprise reunions were in progress around town, despite the fact that recognition was not always easy: as, for example, in the case of a young raider who hailed his mother and sister from the gate of the family home, only to find that they had trouble identifying a tattered mud-spattered veteran as the boy they had kissed goodbye when he left three years ago, neatly turned out in well-pressed clothes for a war that would soon be won. At 9 o'clock, satisfied that he had created enough disturbance to produce the effect he wanted, Forrest had the recall sounded and began the prearranged withdrawal. Beyond Cane Creek he paused to return, under a flag of truce, Washburn's uniform, which his brother Jesse proudly displayed as a trophy of the raid. (Whatever deficiencies he might show in other respects, Washburn knew how to return a courtesy. Some weeks later he sent Forrest, also under a flag of truce, a fine gray uniform made to measure by the cavalryman's own prewar Memphis tailor.) The column then took up the southward march, clearing Hernando that afternoon to ride back across the Tallahatchie and into Panola, late the following day. "If the enemy is falling back, pursue them hard," Forrest instructed Chalmers in a message taken cross-country by a courier who found him just below Oxford, still resisting Smith's advance.

That admonition — "pursue them hard" — was presently translated into action. Smith had entered Oxford that morning, but had no sooner done so than he began to backpedal in response to the news, brought forward under armed escort, that Forrest had raided Memphis the day before. Withdrawing, the Federals set fire to the courthouse, along with other public buildings and a number of private residences. "Where once stood a handsome little country town," an Illinois correspondent wrote, "now only remain the blackened skeletons of houses, and smouldering ruins." Smith's retrograde movement was hastened by a follow-up report next day, August 23, that the raiders were returning to Memphis for a second and heavier strike. The report was false (Forrest was still at Panola, a hard two-day march to the south, resting his troopers from their 150-mile excursion through the Mississippi bottoms) but was almost as disruptive, in its effect, as if it had been true. Alarm bells rang; regulars and militiamen turned out — "eager for the fray," one of the latter said — and Washburn asked the naval commander to have a gunboat steam downriver, below Fort Pickering, to shell the southern approaches to the city. This was done, but with no more than pyrotechnical effect, since the raiders were only there by rumor, not in fact. "The whole town was stampeded," Washburn's inspector general declared, calling the reaction "the most disgraceful affair I have ever seen." This too had its influence. Within another two days no part of A. J. Smith's command remained below the Tallahatchie, and so closely did Chalmers press him, in accordance with Forrest's instructions, that he soon abandoned close to a hundred miles of telegraph wire along the route from the river-crossing, all the way back to the outskirts of Memphis.

Washburn put the best possible interpretation on the outcome of the visit paid him by the raiders. "The whole Expedition was barren of spoils," he wrote his congressman brother Elihu. "They were in so great a hurry to get away that they carried off hardly anything. I lost two fine horses, which is about the biggest loss of anybody." So did Sherman tend to look on the bright side of the event. "If you get the chance," he wired Washburn on August 24, the day after the big stampede, "send word to Forrest that I admire his dash but not his judgment. The oftener he runs his head against Memphis the better."

There was much in that; Forrest's activities, these past four months, had been limited to North Mississippi and the southwest corner of Tennessee, with the result that he had been kept off Sherman's all-important supply line throughout this critical span. But it also rather missed the point that, with Memphis under cower and afflicted with a bad case of the shakes, the Wizard now was free to ride in practically any direction he or his superiors might choose: including Middle Tennessee, a region that nurtured a vital part of that supply line. The question was whether there was time enough, even if he were given his head at last, for Forrest's movement to be of much help to Hood in besieged Atlanta.

Encouraged by Wheeler's recent victories over Stoneman and McCook, which he believed more or less disposed of the blue cavalry as a threat, Hood by then had thrown his own cavalry deep into the Union rear in North Georgia and East Tennessee, hoping, as he explained in a wire requesting the President's approval, that by severing Sherman's life line he would provoke him into rashness or oblige him to retreat. Davis readily concurred, having urged such a strike on Johnston, without success, from the outset to the time of his removal. He replied that he shared Hood's hope that this would "compel the enemy to attack you in position," but added, rather pointedly, and in a tone not unlike Lincoln's when cautioning Grant, down near Richmond the month before, on the heels of repulses even more costly than Hood had just suffered around Atlanta: "The loss consequent upon attacking him in his intrenchments requires you to avoid that if practicable."

Wheeler set out on August 10, taking with him some 4500 effectives from his eight brigades and leaving about the same number behind, including William Jackson's three-brigade division, to patrol and protect Hood's flanks and rear while he was gone. His itinerary for the following week, northward along the Western & Atlantic, resembled a synopsis, in reverse, of the Johnston-Sherman contest back in May. Marietta, Cassville, Calhoun, Resaca: all were hit on a five-day ride that saw the destruction of some thirty miles of track and the rebuilt bridge across the Etowah. On August 14, after detaching one brigade to escort his prisoners and captured livestock back to Atlanta, he began a two-day demonstration against Dalton, then continued north, around and beyond Chattanooga, to Loudon. He intended to cross the Tennessee River there, but found it in flood and had to continue upstream nearly to Knoxville, where he detached two more brigades to wreck the railway bridge at Strawberry Plains, then turned southwest, beyond the Holston and the Clinch, to descend on the Nashville & Chattanooga Railroad, which he broke in several places before he recrossed the Tennessee at Tuscumbia, Alabama, on September 10, his twenty-eighth birthday. At a total cost of 150 casualties on this month-long raid, in the course of which he "averaged 25 miles a day [and] swam or forded 27 rivers," Wheeler reported the seizure of "1000 horses and mules, 200 wagons, 600 prisoners, and 1700 head of beef cattle," and claimed that his command had "captured, killed, or wounded three times the greatest effective strength it has ever been able to carry into action."

As an exploit, even after allowing for the exaggeration common to most cavalry reports, this was much. In other respects, however, it amounted to little more than a prime example of how events could transform a tactical triumph into a strategic cipher. Although Wheeler accomplished practically everything he was sent out to do, and on a grander scale than had been intended, the only real effect of the raid was not on Sherman — whose work gangs were about as quick to repair damage to the railroads as the gray troopers had been to inflict it — but on Hood, who was deprived thereby of half his cavalry during the critical final stage of the contest for Atlanta; which, in point of fact, had ended before Wheeler recrossed the Tennessee. One further result of the raid, also negative, was that Hood at last was convinced, as he said later, "that no sufficiently effective number of cavalry could be assembled in the Confederacy to interrupt the enemy's line of supplies to an extent to compel him to retreat."

Sherman was no more provoked into rashness than he was into retreat, but Wheeler's absence did encourage him, despite the recent failure of such efforts, to venture still another cavalry strike at the Macon & Western, Hood's only remaining rail connection, whose rupture would oblige him to evacuate Atlanta for lack of supplies. Another persuasive factor was Judson Kilpatrick. Back in the saddle after a ten-week convalescence from the wound he had taken at Resaca, he seemed to Sherman just the man to lead the raid. Unlike Garrard — who, in Sherman's words, would flinch if he spotted "a horseman in the distance with a spyglass" — Little Kil had a reputation as a fighter, and though in the present instance he was advised "not to fight but to work," only boldness would assure success. Reinforced by two brigades from Garrard, the bandy-legged New Jerseyite took his division southeast out of Sandtown on the night of August 18, under instructions to "break up the Macon [rail]road about Jonesboro," twenty miles below Atlanta. He got there late the following day, unimpeded, and began at once to carry out Sherman's orders, passed on by Schofield: "Tell Kilpatrick he cannot tear up too much track nor twist too much iron. It may save this army the necessity of making a long, hazardous flank march."

First he set fire to the depot, then turned his attention to the road itself. But before he had ripped up more than a couple of miles of track he was attacked from the rear by a brigade of Texans from Jackson's division. Kilpatrick pressed on south, pursued by this and Jackson's other two brigades, but ran into infantry intrenched near Lovejoy Station and veered east, then north to reënter his own lines at Decatur. That was on August 22, and he proudly reported that he had done enough damage to Hood's life line to remove it from use for the next ten days. Sherman was delighted: but only overnight. Next morning, heavy-laden supply trains came puffing into Atlanta over tracks he had been assured were demolished. Told "not to fight but to work," Kilpatrick apparently had not done much of either, or else the rebel crews were as adept at repairs as their Union counterparts north of the city. In any case, Sherman said later, "I became more than ever convinced that cavalry could not or would not work hard enough to disable a railroad properly, and therefore resolved at once to proceed to the execution of my original plan."

This was the massive counterclockwise slide, the "grand left wheel around Atlanta," which he had designed to bring on the fall of the city by transferring all but one of his seven infantry corps around to the south, astride its only rail connection with the outside world. Interrupted at Ezra Church in late July, the maneuver had been resumed only to stall again in the toils of Utoy Creek in early August. Since then, Sherman had sought by continuous long-range shelling, if not to convert the Gate City into "a desolation," as he had proposed two weeks ago, then in any case to reduce it to "a used-up community," and in this he had succeeded to a considerable extent, though not at a rate that matched his impatience, which was quickened by the spirit-lifting news of Farragut's triumph down in Mobile Bay. Now — Kilpatrick having failed, in Wheeler's absence, to spare him "the necessity of making a long, hazardous flank march" — he was ready to resume his ponderous shift. Leaving Slocum's corps (formerly Hooker's) north of Atlanta, securely intrenched in a position from which to observe the reaction there and also protect the railway bridge across the Chattahoochee, he pulled all three armies rearward out the Sandtown Road on August 26 and started them south the following day in three wide-sweeping arcs, Howard and Schofield on the left and right, Thomas as usual in the center. Their respective objectives, all on the Macon Railroad, were Rough & Ready Station, four miles below East Point; Jonesboro, ten miles farther down the line; and a point about midway between the two. Thomas and Howard took off first, having longer routes to travel, and reached the inactive West Point Railroad next day at Red Oak and Fairburn, where

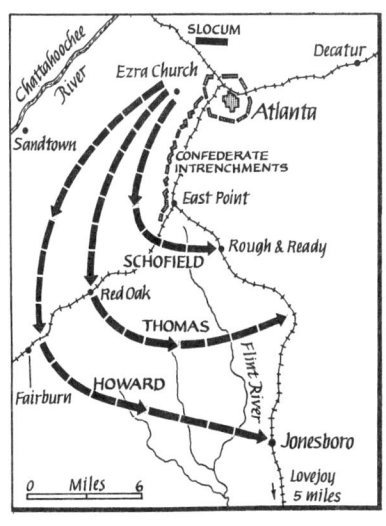

they were to swing east. Then Schofield set out on his march, which was shorter but was presumably much riskier, since he would be a good deal closer to the rebels massed in and around Atlanta. As it turned out, however, he met with no more resistance than Howard and Thomas had done in the course of their wider sweeps; which was practically none at all. Welcome as this nonintervention was, Sherman also found it strange, particularly in contrast to his opponent's previous violent reaction to any attempt to move across his front or round his flank.

Hood's reaction, or nonaction, was stranger than any Federal supposed, being founded on a total misconception of what his adversary was up to. Not that his error had been illogically arrived at; it had not; but the logic, such as it was, was based insubstantially on hope. Suddenly, on August 26, after weeks of intensive shelling, the bombardment of Atlanta stopped as abruptly as a dropped watch, and when patrols went out at midday to investigate this unexpected silence — which somehow was even heavier with tension than the diurnal uproar that preceded it — they found the Union trenches empty and skirmishers posted rear-guard-fashion along and on both sides of the road leading west to Sandtown and the Chattahoochee. Apparently a mass movement was in progress in that direction. Only on the north side of the city, in position to defend the indispensable railroad crossing and forward base, were the old works still occupied in strength. Hood's spirits took a leap at the news; for the brigade detached by Wheeler the week before, up near Calhoun, had returned that morning with its haul of prisoners and cattle and a first-hand account of the extensive damage so far done to the Western & Atlantic, including the burning of the vital span across the Etowah. Wheeler himself, according to a report just in, was beyond Chattanooga with the rest of his command, preparing by now to cross the Tennessee River and descend on the blue supply line below Nashville. All this was bound to have its effect; Sherman must already be hurting for lack of food and ammunition. Indeed, there was testimony on hand that this was so. Six days ago, a woman whose home was inside Schofield's lines had appealed to one of his division commanders for rations, only to be refused. "No," she was told; "I would like to draw, myself. I have been living on short rations for seven days, and now that your people have torn up our railroad and stolen our beef cattle, we must live a damned sight shorter." On such evidence as this, and out of his own sore need for a near miracle, Hood based his conclusion that Sherman, threatened with the specter of starvation by Wheeler's disruption of his life line, was in full retreat across the Chattahoochee with all of his corps but one, left temporarily in position north of the city to cover the withdrawal by rail of what remained of his sorely depleted stockpile of provisions.

Orders went out for Jackson to bring his overworked troopers in from the flanks and take up the pursuit toward Sandtown. Jackson did, beginning next day, but reported that the bluecoats seemed to him to be regrouping, not retreating. Hood rejected this assessment, preferring to believe that his cavalry simply lacked the strength to penetrate the Federal rear guard. So near the end of his military tether that he had nothing to fall back on but delusion, he held his three corps in the Atlanta intrenchments, which had been extended down to East Point, awaiting developments.

They were not long in coming. Sherman had Howard and Thomas spend a day astride the West Point Railroad, "breaking it up thoroughly," as he said, lest the rebels someday try to put it back in commission. His veterans were highly skilled at such work by now, and he later described how they went about it. "The track was heaved up in sections the length of a regiment, then separated rail by rail; bonfires were made of the ties and of fence rails on which the rails were heated, carried to trees or telegraph poles, wrapped around and left to cool." Not content with converting the rails into scrap iron — "Sherman neckties," the twisted loops were called — he then proceeded against the roadbed itself. "To be still more certain, we filled up many deep cuts with trees, brush, and earth, and commingled with them loaded shells, so arranged that they would explode on an attempt to haul out the bushes. The explosion of one such shell would have demoralized a gang of negroes, and thus would have prevented even the attempt to clear the road." Next morning, August 30, he started both armies east toward the headwaters of Flint River, which flowed south between the two converging railroads, the one he had just undone in his rear and the one ahead, whose loss would undo Hood.

Elated at the prospect of achieving this objective, he accompanied Thomas on the march, and as they approached the Flint that afternoon — still without encountering serious opposition, though the Macon road lay only a scant two miles beyond the river — he exulted to the Virginian riding beside him: "I have Atlanta as certainly as if it were in my hand!"

Hood by now had begun to emerge from his wishful three-day dream. Reports that Union infantry had appeared in strength on the West Point road the day before, above and below Fairburn and Red Oak, obliged him to concede that part at least of Sherman's host was headed for something other than the Chattahoochee River, and when follow-up dispatches informed him this morning that the same blue wrecking force was moving eastward, in the direction of the Macon road, he knew he had to act. All surplus goods were ordered packed for shipment out of the nearly beleaguered city, by whatever routes might be available when the time came, and Hardee was told to shift to Rough & Ready, bracing his corps for the defense of the rail supply line, there or farther down, while Lee moved out to take his place at East Point, under instructions to be ready for a march in either direction, southward to reinforce Hardee or back north to assist Stewart in the close-up defense of Atlanta, depending on which turned out to need him worst. Old Straight remained in the works that rimmed the city, not only because of Slocum's hovering menace, but also because Hood had revised — indeed, reversed — his estimate of the enemy's intentions. It seemed to him that Sherman was trying to draw him out of Atlanta with a strike at his supply line, say by half the Federal force, so that when he moved to meet this threat, the other half, concealed till then near the Chattahoochee, could swoop down and take the city. Hood's job, as he assessed it, was to avoid being lured out in such numbers that Atlanta would fall in their absence, its scantly manned intrenchments overrun, and yet at the same time to prevent the seizure or destruction of the Macon Railroad, whose loss would require him to give up the city for lack of subsistence.

Caught thus between the blue devil and the deep blue sea, Hood saw no choice, now that he had been shaken out of the dream that transformed his red-haired opponent from a destroyer into a deliverer, except to try to meet these separate dangers as they developed. All in all, outnumbered as he was, the situation was pretty much as Sherman was describing it to Thomas even now, a dozen-odd miles to the south: "I have Atlanta as certainly as if it were in my hand." What had the earmarks of a frothy boast — of a kind all too common in a war whose multi-thumbed commanders were often in need of reassurance, even if they had to express it themselves — was in fact merely a tactical assessment, somewhat florid but still a good deal more accurate than most.

Or maybe not. When Hood heard from Hardee, around midday, that the blue march seemed to be aimed at both Rough & Ready and Jonesboro, ten miles apart, he saw once more a chance to strike the enemy in detail. And having perceived this he was no less willing to undertake it than he had been three times before, in as many costly sorties. Now as then he improvised a slashing assault designed to subject a major portion of the Union host to destruction. His plan — refined to deal with a later, more specific report that Logan's corps had crossed the Flint that afternoon and gone into camp within cannon range of Jonesboro, supported only by Kilpatrick's horsemen, while the other two corps of the Army of the Tennessee remained on the west bank of the stream — was for Hardee to fall upon this exposed segment early next morning and "drive the enemy, at all hazards, into Flint River, in their rear." Moreover, when the rest of Howard's troops attempted to come to Logan's assistance they could be whipped in detail with help from Lee, whose corps would set out down the railroad from East Point at the same time Hardee's moved from Rough & Ready on a night march that would put them in position for attack at first light, August 31. To make certain that his plan was understood, Hood wired both generals to leave their senior division commanders in charge of the march to Jonesboro and report to him in Atlanta, by rail, for the usual face-to-face instructions, which experience had shown were even more necessary than he had thought when he first took charge of the Army of Tennessee.

In Atlanta that night, at the council of war preceding this Fourth Sortie, Hood expanded his plan to include a follow-up attack September 1. After sharing in tomorrow's assault, which would drive the Federals away from the Macon road and back across the Flint, Lee was to return to Rough & Ready Station, where he would be joined by Stewart for an advance next morning, down the west bank of the river, that would strike the flank of the crippled bluecoats, held in position overnight by Hardee, and thus complete their destruction. This was in some ways less risky and in others riskier than Hood knew, believing as he did that only Howard's army was south of the city, which thus would be scantly protected from an assault by Thomas and Schofield. For that reason, Hood took what he believed was the post of gravest responsibility: Atlanta, whose defenses would be manned, through this critical time, only by Jackson's dismounted troopers and units of the Georgia militia. It was late when the council broke up and Hardee, who was put in charge of the attack, boarded a switch engine for a fast ride to Jonesboro. He arrived before dawn, expecting to find his and Lee's corps being posted for the assault at daybreak. Neither was there; nor could he find anyone who could tell him where they were — Lee's, which that general must have rejoined by now, or his own, which had set out southward from Rough & Ready the night before.

Howard remained all morning in what he called a "saucy position," content to reinforce Logan's corps, intrenched on the east bank of the Flint, with a single division from Dodge, who was away recuperating from being struck on the forehead by a bullet the week before. He expected to be attacked by a rebel force that seemed to be gathering in Jonesboro, less than a mile across the way; that was why he kept most of his troops out of sight on the west side of the river, hoping, now that Logan's men had had plenty of time to strengthen their intrenchments, that the graybacks would come to him, rather than wait for him to storm their works along the railroad. But when nothing had come of this by the time the sun swung past the overhead, he decided he would have to prod them. He told Logan to move out at 3 o'clock. At 2.45, just as Black Jack's veterans were preparing to leave their trenches, long lines of butternut infantry came surging out of Jonesboro in far greater numbers than Howard had expected while trying to provoke them into making an attack.

Hardee was even tardier in launching Hood's Fourth Sortie than he had been in either of the other two committed to his charge, the first having opened two hours behind schedule, the second nearly seven, and this one more than nine. Yet here again the blame was hard to fix. Cleburne, left in corps command when Old Reliable went to Atlanta the night before, had found enemy units blocking his line of march and had had to detour widely around them, which delayed his arrival in Jonesboro until an hour after sunrise; while Lee, whose longer route was even worse obstructed, did not come up till well past noon. As a result, it was 2 o'clock before Hardee could get the two road-worn corps into jump-off positions and issue orders for the attack. These were for Cleburne to turn the enemy's right and for Lee to move against their front as soon as he heard Cleburne's batteries open. Such a signal had often failed in the past, and now it did so here. Mistaking the clatter of skirmishers' rifles for the roar of battle, Lee started forward on his own and thus exposed his corps to the concentrated fire of the whole Union line, with demoralizing results. Cleburne then moved out, driving Kilpatrick's troopers promptly across the Flint, but found Logan's works too stoutly held for him to effect a lodgment without assistance. Hardee urged Lee to renew his stalled advance, only to be told that it was impossible; Howard was bringing reserves across the river to menace the shaken right. In reaction, Hardee called off the attack and ordered both Cleburne and Lee to take up defensive positions, saying later: "I now consider this a fortunate circumstance, for success against such odds could at best have only been partial and bloody, while defeat would have [meant] almost inevitable destruction to the army."

That ended the brief, disjointed Battle of Jonesboro; or half ended it, depending on what Howard would do now. Lee and Cleburne had suffered more than 1700 casualties between them, Logan and Kilpatrick less than a fourth as many, and these were the totals for this last day of August, as it turned out, since Howard did not press the issue. Late that night, in response to Hood's repeated summons, Hardee detached Lee's three divisions for the return march north, tomorrow's scheduled follow-up offensive down the west bank of the Flint having been ruled out by the failure of today's attempt to set up Howard for the kill.

What Hood now wanted Lee for, though, was to help Stewart hold Atlanta against the assault he expected Sherman to make next morning with the other two Federal armies, which he still thought were lurking northwest of the city. He presently learned better. Soon after dark, reports came in that bluecoats were across the Macon road in strength at Rough & Ready, as well as at several other points between there and Jonesboro. Lee not only confirmed this when he reached East Point at daylight, having managed to slip between the enemy columns in the darkness; he also identified them as belonging to Schofield and Thomas. This was a shock, and its meaning was all too clear. Atlanta was doomed. The only remaining question, now that Sherman had the bulk of his command astride the city's last rail supply line, squarely between Hardee and the other two corps, was whether the Army of

Tennessee was doomed as well. Hood and his staff got to work at once on plans for the evacuation of Atlanta and the reunion, if possible, of his divided army, so that it could be saved to fight another day.

Such a reunion was not going to include Hardee's third of that army if Sherman had his way. Primarily he had undertaken this six-corps grand left wheel as a railroad-wrecking expedition, designed to bring on the fall of Atlanta by severing its life line, but now that he saw in Hardee's isolation an opportunity to annihilate him, he extended its scope to achieve just that. Both Schofield and Thomas were told to move on Jonesboro without delay, there to combine their three corps with Howard's three — a total of more than 60,000, excluding cavalry — for an assault on Hardee's 12,500, still licking the wounds they had suffered in their repulse the day before. While this convergence was in progress Howard put the rest of Dodge's corps across the Flint, where Logan confronted the rebels in their works, and sent Blair to cut the railroad south of town and stand in the path of any escape in that direction. Noon came and went, this hot September 1, still with no word from Thomas or Schofield, who were to attack the Confederates on their right while Howard clamped them in position from the front. Sherman fumed at the delay, knowing the graybacks were hard at work improving their intrenchments, and kept fuming right up to 3 o'clock, when the first of Slow Trot Thomas's two corps arrived, formerly John Palmer's but now under Jeff C. Davis, Palmer having departed in a huff after a squabble with Schofield, who he claimed had mishandled his troops in the Utoy Creek fiasco. The other Cumberland corps, David Stanley's, was nowhere in sight, and in fact did not turn up till after sundown, having got lost on its cross-country march, and Schofield moved so slowly from Rough & Ready, tearing up track as he went, that he arrived even later than Stanley. Combined with the detachment of Blair to close the southward escape hatch, the nonappearance of these two corps reduced the size of the attacking force by half. But that still left Sherman with considerably better than twice the number he faced, and he also enjoyed the advantage of having Davis come down unexpectedly on the enemy right, which was bent back across the railroad north of town.

Davis was a driver, a hard-mannered regular who had come up through the ranks, thirty-six years old, with wavy hair and a bushy chin-beard, a long thin nose and the pale, flat eyes of a killer; which he was. Still a brigadier despite his lofty post and a war record dating back to Sumter, he had been denied promotion for the past two years because of the scandal attending his pistol slaying of Bull Nelson in Kentucky, long ago in '62, and he welcomed such assignments as this present one at Jonesboro, seeing in them opportunities to demonstrate a worth beyond the grade at which he had been stopped in his climb up the military ladder. He put his men in line astride the railroad — three divisions, containing as many troops as Hardee had in all — and sent them roaring down against the rebel flank at 4 o'clock. Cleburne's division was posted there, in trenches Lee had occupied the day before. Repulsed, Davis dropped back, regrouped quickly, and then came on again in a mass assault that went up and over the barricade to land in the midst of Brigadier General Dan Govan's veteran Arkansas brigade. Two batteries were overrun and Govan himself captured, along with more than half his men. "They're rolling them up like a sheet of paper!" Sherman cried, watching from an observation post on Howard's front.

But Granbury's Texans were next in line, and there the rolling stopped. Cleburne shored up his redrawn flank, massing fire on the lost salient, and Davis had all he could do to hold what he had won. Unwilling to risk a frontal assault by Howard, Sherman saw that what he needed now was added pressure on the weakened enemy right by Stanley, who was supposed to be coming up in rear of Davis. Angrily he turned to Thomas, demanding to know where Stanley was, and the heavy-set Virginian, who already had sent courier after courier in search of the errant corps, not only rode off in person to join the hunt, but also did so in a manner that later caused his red-haired superior to remark that this was "the only time during the campaign I can recall seeing General Thomas urge his horse into a gallop." Even so, the sun had set by the time Stanley turned up, and night fell before he could put his three divisions in attack formation. Darkness ended this second day of the Battle of Jonesboro, which cost Sherman 1275 casualties, mostly from Davis's corps, and Hardee just under 1000, two thirds of them captured in the assault that cracked his flank.

Disgruntled, Sherman bedded down, hopeful that tomorrow, with Schofield up alongside Stanley, he would complete the fate he planned for Hardee. He had trouble sleeping, he would recall, and soon after midnight, to add to his fret, "there arose toward Atlanta sounds of shells exploding, and other sounds like that of musketry." This was disturbing; Hood might well be doing to Slocum what he himself intended to do to Hardee. Yesterday he had instructed Thomas to have Slocum "feel forward to Atlanta, as boldly as he can," adding: "Assure him that we will fully occupy the attention of the rebel army outside of Atlanta." This last he had failed to do, except in part, and it seemed to him likely, from those rumblings twenty miles to the north, that he had thereby exposed Slocum to destruction by two thirds of Hood's command. Other listeners about the campfire disagreed, interpreting the muffled clatter as something other than battle, and Sherman decided to settle the issue by visiting a nearby farmhouse, where he had seen lights burning earlier in the evening. Shouts brought the farmer out into the yard in his nightshirt. Had he lived here long? He had. Had he heard such rumblings before? Indeed he had. That was the way it sounded when there was heavy fighting up around Atlanta.

War Is Cruelty . . . [529]

The noise faded, then died away; which might have an even more gruesome meaning. Sherman returned to his campfire, still unable to sleep. Then at 4 o'clock it rose again, with the thump and crump and muttering finality of a massive coup de grâce. Again it died, this time for good. Dawn came, and with the dawn a new enigma. Thomas and Schofield moved as ordered, the latter on the left to sweep across the rebel rear — "We want to destroy the enemy," Sherman told them, anxious to be done with the work at hand — but found that Hardee had departed under cover of darkness and the distractive far-off rumblings from the north. Sherman took up the pursuit, southward down the railroad, still wondering what had happened deep in his rear. This was the hundred and twentieth day of the campaign, and while he was at Jonesboro another month had slipped into the past, costing him 7000 casualties and his adversary 7500: a total to date of 31,500 Federals and 35,000 Confederates, rough figures later precisely tabulated at 31,687 and 34,979 respectively. Close to 20,000 of the latter had been suffered by Hood in the nearly seven weeks since he took over from Johnston, while Sherman had lost just under 15,000 in that span.

Presently, as the six blue corps toiled southward down the railroad in search of Hardee's three vanished divisions, Schofield sent word that he took last night's drumfire rumblings from the direction of Atlanta to be the sound of Hood blowing up his unremovable stores, in preparation for evacuation. Two hours later, at 10.25, he followed this with a report that a Negro had just come into his lines declaring that the rebs were departing the city "in great confusion and disorder." Unconvinced, still troubled about "whether General Slocum had felt forward and become engaged in a real battle," Sherman kept up his pursuit of Hardee until he came upon him near Lovejoy Station, six miles down the line, his corps posted in newly dug intrenchments "as well constructed and as strong as if these Confederates had a week to prepare them." Such was his assessment after a tentative 4 o'clock probe was savagely repulsed. "I do not wish to waste lives by an assault," he warned Howard, explaining more fully to Thomas: "Until we hear from Atlanta the exact truth, I do not care about your pushing your men against breastworks." Still fretted by doubts about Slocum, he maintained his position of cautious observation through sunset into darkness. "Nothing positive from Atlanta," he informed Schofield within half an hour of midnight, "and that bothers me."

Finally, between then and sunup, September 3, a courier arrived with a dispatch from Slocum, who was not only safe but was safe inside Atlanta. Alerted by last night's racket, just across the way — it turned out to be the explosion of 81 carloads of ammunition, together with five locomotives, blown up in relays when they were found to be cut off from escape by the loss of the Macon road — he had felt his way forward at daylight to the city limits, where the commander of his lead division encountered a delegation of civilians. "Sir," their leader said with a formal bow. His name, it developed, was James M. Calhoun, and that was strangely fitting, even though no kinship connected him with the South Carolina original, John C. "The fortunes of war have placed the city of Atlanta in your hands. As mayor of the city I ask protection for noncombatants and private property." Slocum telegraphed the news to Washington: "General Sherman has taken Atlanta," and passed the word to his chief, approaching Lovejoy by then, that Hood had begun his withdrawal at 5 p.m. the day before, southward down the McDonough Road and well to the east of the Macon & Western, down which Howard and Thomas and Schofield were marching.

This meant that Hood had crossed their front and flank with Stewart and Lee and the Georgia militia, last night and yesterday, and by now had reunited his army in the intrenchments hard ahead at Lovejoy Station. Wise by hindsight, Sherman began to see that he had erred in going for Hardee, snug in his Jonesboro works, when he might have struck for the larger and more vulnerable prize in retreat on the McDonough Road beyond. Moreover, if he had been unable to pound the graybacks to pieces while he had them on the Atlanta anvil, there seemed little chance for success in such an effort now that they were free to maneuver as they chose. Such at last was the price he paid for having redefined his objective, not as the Army of Tennessee — "Break it up," Grant had charged him at the outset, before Dalton — but rather as the city that army had been tied to, until now.

In any case, he had it, and he was ready and anxious to take possession in person. "Atlanta is ours, and fairly won," he wired Halleck. "I shall not push much farther in this raid, but in a day or so will move to Atlanta and give my men some rest."

※ 3 ※

Slocum's wire, received in Washington on the night of the day it was sent — "General Sherman has taken Atlanta" — ended a hot-weather span of anxiety even sorer than those that followed the two Bull Runs, back in the first two summers of the war. The prospect of stalemate, at this late stage, brought on a despondency as deep as outright defeat had done in those earlier times, when the national spirit displayed a resilience it had lost in the course of a summer that not only was bloody beyond all past imagining, but also saw Early within plain view of the Capitol dome and Democrats across the land anticipating a November sweep. Farragut's coup, down in Mobile Bay, provided no more than a glimmer of light, perfunctorily discerned before it guttered out in the gloom invoked by Sherman's reproduction, on the outskirts of Atlanta, of Grant's failure to take Richmond when he reached it the month before. Both wound up, apparently stalled, some twenty miles beyond their respective objectives, and by the end of August it had begun to appear that neither of them, having overshot the mark, was going to get back where he had been headed at the outset.

Nowhere, East or West or in between, was the disenchantment so complete as it was on the outskirts of Petersburg by then. Partly this was because of the high price paid to get there (Meade's casualties, exclusive of Butler's, were more than twice as heavy as Sherman's, though the latter had traveled nearly twice as far by his zigzag route) and partly too because, time and again, the public's and the army's expectations had been lifted only to be dashed, more often than not amid charges of incredible blundering, all up and down the weak-linked chain of command. A case in point, supplementing the fiasco that attended the original attack from across the James, was an operation that came to be called "The Crater," which occurred in late July and marked a new high (or low) for mismanagement at or near the top, surpassing even Cold Harbor in that regard, if not in bloodshed.

Early that month, after the failure of his probe for the Weldon Railroad in late June, Grant asked Meade how he felt about undertaking a new offensive against Lee's center or around his flank. Faced as he was with the loss of Wright, whose corps was being detached just then to counter Early's drive on Washington, Meade replied that he was doubtful about the result of either a flank or a frontal effort, citing "the facility with which the enemy can interpose to check an onward movement." However, lest his chief suppose that he was altogether without aggressive instincts or intentions — which, in point of fact, he very nearly was by now — Meade did let fall that he had in progress a work designed to permit a thrust, not through or around, but *under* the Confederate intrenchments. Burnside was digging a mine.

The proposal had come from a regimental commander, Lieutenant Colonel Henry Pleasants, whose 48th Pennsylvania was made up largely of volunteers from the anthracite fields of Schuylkill County, one of whom he happened to hear remark, while peering through a firing slit at a rebel bastion some 150 uphill yards across the way: "We could blow that damned fort out of existence if we could run a mine shaft under it." Formerly a civil engineer engaged in railroad tunneling, Pleasants liked the notion and took a sketch of it to his division commander, Brigadier General Robert Potter, who passed it along to corps. Burnside told Pleasants to start digging, then went himself to Meade for approval and assistance. He got Meade's nod, apparently because the work at least would keep some bored men busy for a time, but not his help, his staff having advised that the project was impractical from the engineering point of view. No such tunnel could exceed 400 feet in length, the experts said, that being the limit at which fresh air could be provided without ventilation shafts, and this one was projected to extend for more than 500 feet from the gallery entrance to the powder chamber at its end.

Pleasants had been hard at work since June 25, the day Burnside told him to start burrowing into the steep west bank of an abandoned railway cut, directly in rear of his picket line and well hidden from enemy lookouts. By assigning his men to shifts so that the digging went forward round the clock, he managed to complete the tunnel within a month — though his miners later claimed they could have done the job in less than half that time, if they had been given the proper tools. Not that Pleasants hadn't done his best in that regard. Denied any issue of special implements, such as picks, he contrived his own with the help of regimental blacksmiths, converted hardtack boxes into barrows for moving dirt, took over a wrecked sawmill to cut timbers and planks for shoring up the gallery walls and roof, and even borrowed a theodolite, all the way from Washington, when Meade's engineers declined to lend him one of theirs. Technical problems he solved in much the same improvisatory fashion, including some which these same close-fisted experts defined as prohibitive; ventilation, for example. Just inside the entrance he installed an airtight canvas door and beneath it ran a square wooden pipe along the floor of the shaft to the diggers at the end, extending it as they progressed. A fireplace near the sealed door sent heated air up its brush-masked chimney, creating a draft that drew the stale air from the far end of the tunnel and pulled in fresh air through the pipe, whose mouth was beyond the door. Working in the comparative comfort of a gallery five feet high, four feet wide at the bottom and two feet at the top — they had sweated and strained and wheezed and shivered through longer hours, with considerably less headroom and under far worse breathing conditions, back home in the Pennsylvania coal fields — the miners completed 511 feet of shaft by July 17.

This put them directly under the rebel outwork, whose defenders they could hear walking about, twenty feet above their heads, apparently unmindful of the malevolent, mole-like activity some half-dozen yards below the ground they stood on. Next day the soldier miners began digging laterally, right and left, to provide a powder chamber, 75 feet long, under the enemy bastion and the trenches on both flanks. By July 23 the pick and shovel work was done. After a four-day rest, Pleasants brought in 320 kegs of black powder, weighing 25 pounds each, and distributed this gritty four-ton mass among eight connected magazines, sandbagged to direct the explosion upward. When his requisition for insulated wire and a galvanic battery did not come through, he got hold of two fifty-foot fuzes, spliced them together, then secured one end to the monster charge and ran the other back down the gallery as far as it would reach; after which he replaced the earth of the final forty feet of tunnel, firmly tamped to provide a certain backstop.

That was on July 28. All that remained was to put a match to the fuze, and get out before the boom.

Next afternoon, with the mine scheduled to be exploded early the following morning, Burnside assembled his division commanders to give them last-minute instructions for the assault that was to be launched through the resultant gap in the rebel works. Of these there were four, though only three of their divisions had done front-line duty so far in the campaign; the fourth, led by Brigadier General Edward Ferrero, was composed of two all-Negro brigades whose service up to now had been confined to guarding trains and rearward installations, largely because of the continuing supposition — despite conflicting evidence, West and East — that black men simply were not up to combat. "Is not a Negro as good as a white man to stop a bullet?" someone asked Sherman about this time, over in Georgia. "Yes; and a sandbag is better," he replied. Like many eastern generals he believed that former slaves had their uses in war, but not as soldiers. Burnside felt otherwise, and what was more he backed up his contention by directing that Ferrero's division, which was not only the freshest but was also by now the largest of the four, would lead tomorrow's predawn charge. By way of preparation, he had had the two brigades spend the past week rehearsing the attack until every member knew just what he was to do, and how; that is, rush promptly forward, as soon as the mine was sprung, and expand the gap so that the other three divisions, coming up behind, could move unopposed across the Jerusalem Plank Road and onto the high ground immediately in rear of the blasted enemy intrenchments, which would give them a clear shot at Petersburg itself.

He was in high spirits, partly because the digging had gone so well and partly because Meade and Grant, catching a measure of his enthusiasm as the tunnel neared completion, had expanded the operation. Not only were Warren's and Baldy Smith's corps ordered to stand by for a share in exploiting the breakthrough — which was to be given close-up support by no less than 144 field pieces, mortars, and siege guns: more artillery, pound for pound, than had been massed by either side at Gettysburg — but Grant also sent Hancock's corps, along with two of Sheridan's divisions, to create a diversion, and if possible score an accompanying breakthrough, on the far side of the James. Hancock, who had returned to duty the week before, found the Confederates heavily reinforced in front of Richmond: as did Sheridan, who was worsted in a four-hour fight with Hampton on the day the fuze was laid to Pleasants's mine. Still, the feint served its purpose by drawing large numbers of graybacks away from the intended scene of the main effort, about midway down the five-mile rebel line below the Appomattox. Intelligence reported that five of Lee's eight infantry divisions were now at Bermuda Hundred or north of the James, leaving Beauregard with only three divisions, some 18,000 men in all, for the defense of the Petersburg rail hub. Moreover, there still was time for Hancock to return tomorrow — the day of Burnside's last-minute council of war — to lend still greater weight to the assault that would accompany the blasting of the undermanned enemy works before daylight next morning.

Burnside was happily passing this latest news along to his lieutenants when he was interrupted by a courier from army headquarters, bearing a message that had an effect not unlike the one expected, across the way, when the mine was sprung tomorrow. It contained an order from Meade, approved by Grant, for the assault to be spearheaded not by Ferrero's well-rehearsed Negroes, but by one of the white divisions. This change, which landed like a bomb in the council chamber, was provoked by racism; racism in reverse. "If we put the colored troops in front and [the attack] should prove a failure," Grant would testify at the subsequent investigation, "it would then be said, and very properly, that we were shoving those people ahead to get killed because we did not care anything about them."

Stunned, Burnside tried to get the order rescinded, only to be told that it would stand; Meade was not about to give his Abolitionist critics this chance to bring him down with charges that he had exposed black recruits to slaughter in the forefront of a long-shot operation. By now the scheduled assault was less than twelve hours off, all but four of them hours of darkness, and the ruff-whiskered general, too shaken to decide which of his three unrehearsed white divisions should take the lead, had their commanders draw straws for the assignment. It fell to Brigadier General James H. Ledlie, a former heavy artilleryman, least experienced of the three. Potter and Brigadier General Orlando Willcox would attack in turn, behind Ledlie; Ferrero would bring up the rear.

As they departed to alert their troops, Burnside could find consolation only in reports that the Confederates — two South Carolina regiments, posted in support of the four-gun battery poised above the sealed-off powder chamber — seemed to have abandoned their former suspicion that they were about to be blown skyward. For a time last week they had tried countermining, without success, and when the underground digging stopped, July 23, so did their attempts at intersection. Apparently they too had experts who advised them that such a tunnel was impracticable; with the result that when the sound of picks and shovels stopped, down below, they decided that the Yanks had given up, probably after a disastrous cave-in or mounting losses from asphyxiation.

Eventually the troops were brought up in the darkness, groping their way over unfamiliar terrain to take up assigned positions for the jump-off: Ledlie's division out front, just in back of the ridge where the pickets were dug in, Potter's and Willcox's along the slope of the railway cut, and Ferrero's along its bottom, aggrieved at having been shunted to the rear. Elsewhere along the Union line the other corps stood by, including Hancock's, which had returned from its demonstration beyond the James. Shortly after 3 o'clock Pleasants entered the tunnel to light the fuze. The guns and mortars were laid, ammunition stacked and cannoneers at the ready, lanyards taut. Burnside had his watch out, observing the creep of its hands toward 3.30, the specified time for the springing of the mine. 3.30 finally came; but not the explosion. Half an hour went by, and still the night was black, unsplit by flame. Another half hour ticked past, bringing the first gray hint of dawn to the rearward sky, and though Pleasants had accepted his mine-boss sergeant's offer to go back into the tunnel and investigate the delay, there still was no blast. Grant, losing patience, considered telling Burnside to forget the explosion and get on with his 15,000-man assault. Daylight grew, much faster now, and the flat eastern rim of earth was tinted rose, anticipating the bulge of the rising sun, by the time the sergeant and a lieutenant who had volunteered to join him — Harry Reese and Jacob Douty were their names — found that the fuze had burned out at the splice. They cut and relit it and scrambled for the tunnel entrance, a long 150 yards away, emerging just before 4.44, when the 8000-pound charge, twenty feet below the rebel works, erupted.

"A slight tremor of the earth for a second, then the rocking as of an earthquake," an awed captain would recall, "and, with a tremendous blast which rent the sleeping hills beyond, a vast column of earth and smoke shoots upward to a great height, its dark sides flashing out sparks of fire, hangs poised for a moment in mid-air, and then, hurtling down with a roaring sound, showers of stones, broken timbers and blackened human limbs, subsides — the gloomy pall of darkening smoke flushing to an angry crimson as it floats away to meet the morning sun." Another watcher of that burgeoning man-made cloud of dust and turmoil, a brigadier with Hancock, left an impression he never suspected would be repeated at the dawn of a far deadlier age of warfare, just over eighty years away: "Without form or shape, full of red flames and carried on a bed of lightning flashes, it mounted toward heaven with a detonation of thunder [and] spread out like an immense mushroom whose stem seemed to be of fire and its head of smoke."

Added to the uproar was the simultaneous crash of many cannon, fired by tense gunners as soon as they saw the ground begin to heave from the overdue explosion. Ledlie's men, caught thus between two shock waves, looked out and saw the rising mass of earth, torn from the hillside hard ahead, mount up and up until it seemed to hover directly above them, its topmost reaches glittering in the full light of the not-yet-risen sun. As the huge cluster started down, they recovered at least in part from their shock and reacted by breaking in panic for the rear. This was not too serious; their officers got them back in line within ten minutes and started them forward before the dust and smoke had cleared.

But what happened next was serious indeed. In his dismay over the last-minute change in orders, Burnside had neglected to have the defensive tangle of obstacles cleared from in front of the parapets, with the result that the attack formation was broken up as soon as the troops set out. Instead of advancing on a broad front, as intended — a brigade in width, with the second brigade coming up in close support — they went forward through a hastily improvised ten-foot passway that not only delayed their start but also confined them to a meager file of wary individuals who advanced a scant one hundred yards, then stopped in awe of what they saw before them. Where the Confederate fort had stood there now was a monstrous crater, sixty feet across and nearly two hundred feet wide, ranging in depth from ten to thirty feet. All was silent down there on its rubbled floor except for the thin cries of the wounded — who, together with the killed, turned out to number 278 — mangled by the blast and buried to various depths by the debris.

As Ledlie's soldiers stood and gazed at this lurid moonscape, strewn with clods that ranged in size up to that of a small house, they not only forgot their instructions to fan out right and left in order to widen the breakthrough for the follow-up attack; they even forgot to keep moving. At last they did move, but not far. For more than a month their fighting had been confined to rifle pits and trenches, and now here at their feet was the biggest rifle pit in all the world. They leaped into it and busied themselves with helping the Carolinian survivors, many of whom, though badly dazed, had interesting things to say when they were uprooted and revived. Ledlie might have gotten his division back in motion by exhortation or example, but he was not available just now. He was immured in a bombproof well behind the lines, swigging away at a bottle of rum he had cadged from a staff surgeon. It later developed that this had been his custom all along, in times of strain. In any case, there he remained throughout what was to have been a fast-moving go-for-broke assault on Petersburg, by way of the gap Henry Pleasants had blown in the rebel line.

That gap was already larger than any Federal knew. When the mine was sprung, the reaction of the graybacks right and left of the hoisted battery was the same as that of the intended attackers across the way. They too bolted rearward, panicked by the fury of the blast, and thus broadened the unmanned portion of their line to about 400 yards. What was more, it remained so for some time. The second and third blue waves rolled forward, paused in turn on the near rim of the crater, much as the first had done, and then, like it, swept down in search of cover amid the rubble at the bottom. By then, most of the bolted Confederates had returned to their posts on the flanks of the excavation, and Beauregard was bringing up reinforcements, along with all the artillery he could lay hands on.

They arrived, men and guns, at about the time Burnside's fourth wave started forward. Loosed at last (but without Ferrero; he had joined Ledlie in the bombproof, nearly a quarter-mile away) the Negro soldiers advanced in good order. "We looks like men a-marching on, We looks like men of war," they sang as they came up in the wake of the other three divisions, which were scarcely to be seen, having vanished quite literally into the earth. Disdaining the crater, they swung around it, in accordance with the maneuver they had rehearsed, and drove for the high ground beyond. However, now that the defenders had rallied and been reinforced, they not only failed to get there; they also lost a solid third of their number in the attempt — 1327 out of just under 4000. "Unsupported, subjected to a galling fire from batteries on the flanks, and from infantry fire in front and partly on the flank," a witness later wrote, "they broke up in disorder and fell back to the crater."

Conditions there were not much better. In some ways they were worse. Presently they were much worse in every way. More than 10,000 men, crowded hip to hip in a steep-walled pen less than a quarter-acre in extent, presented the gray cannoneers with a compact target they did not neglect. Counterbattery work by the massed Union guns was excellent, but the surviving rebel pieces, including hard-to-locate mortars, still delivered what one occupant of the crater termed "as heavy a fire of canister as was ever poured continuously upon a single objective point." The result was bedlam, a Bedlam in flames, and this got worse as the enemy infantry grew bolder, inching closer to the rim of the pit, where marksmanship would be about as superfluous as if the shots were directed into a barrel of paralyzed fish. Anticipating this, some bluecoats chose to run the gauntlet back to their own lines, while others preferred to remain and risk the prospect: which was soon at hand. Around 9.30, with Grant's disgusted approval, Meade had cancelled the follow-up attack and told Burnside to withdraw his corps.

But that was easier said than carried out. Burnside by then had fallen into a state of euphoric despair, much as he had done at Fredericksburg twenty months ago, under similar circumstances, and delayed transmission of the order till after midday, apparently in hope of some miraculous deliverance. Shortly after noon, two brigades from Mahone's division — they had slipped away from Warren's front unseen — gained the lip of the crater, where they added rapid-fire rifle volleys to the horror down below, then followed up with a bayonet charge that shattered what little remained of blue resistance. Hundreds surrendered, thousands fled, more hundreds fell, and the so-called Battle of the Crater was soon over. It had cost Burnside 3828 men, nearly half of them captured or missing, and losses elsewhere along Meade's line raised the Union total above 4000 for the day; Confederate casualties, mostly wounded, came to about one third that number. By nightfall, all that remained as evidence of this latest bizarre attempt to break Lee's line was a raw scar, about midway down its length below the Appomattox, which in time would green over and loose its jagged look, but would never really heal.

Nor would a new bitterness Southerners felt as a result of this affair. Not only had they been blown up while sleeping — "a mean trick," they declared — but for the first time, here in the Old Dominion, black soldiers had been thrown into the thick of a large-scale fight. That was something far worse than a trick; that was infamy, to Lee's men's way of thinking. And for this they cursed their enemy in cold blood. "Eyes gleamed, teeth clenched," a nurse who tended Mahone's wounded would recall, "as they showed me the locks of their muskets, to which blood and hair still clung, when, after firing, without waiting to reload, they had clenched the barrels and fought hand to hand." Privately — like the troopers who stormed Fort Pillow, out in the wilder West — they admitted to having bayoneted men in the act of surrender, and they were by no means ashamed of the act, considering their view of the provocation. It was noted that from this time forward there were no informal truces in the vicinity of the Crater. Sniping was venomous and continuous, dawn to dusk, along that portion of the line.

Ledlie (but not Ferrero, who was somehow overlooked in the caterwaul that followed) presently departed, condemned by a Court of Inquiry for his part in the mismanagement of what Grant pronounced "the saddest affair I have witnessed in this war." Burnside left even sooner, hard on the heels of a violent argument with Meade, an exchange of recriminations which a staff observer said "went far toward confirming one's belief in the wealth and flexibility of the English language as a medium of personal dispute." Meade wanted the ruff-whiskered general court martialed for incompetence, but Grant, preferring a quieter procedure, sent him home on leave. "He will never return whilst *I* am here," Meade fumed.

Nor did he. Resigning from the service, Ambrose Everett Burnside, forty years old, returned to his business pursuits in Rhode Island, where he not only prospered but also recovered the geniality he had lost in the course of a military career that required him to occupy positions he himself had testified he was unqualified to fill. In time he went into politics, serving three terms as governor, and would die well into his second term as a U.S. senator, twenty years after the war began.

Tactically speaking, Lee no doubt regretted Burnside's departure. He would miss him, much as he missed McClellan, now in retirement, and John Pope and Joe Hooker, who had been shunted to outlying regions where their ineptitudes would be less costly to the cause they served. This was not to say that mistakes came cheap from those commanders who remained near the violent center. Meade's losses for July, swollen by the botched attempt to score an explosive breakthrough near its end, totaled 6367, and he had scarcely an inch of ground to show for their subtraction. Yet Lee could take small comfort in the knowledge that his own were barely half that. In contrast to his custom in the old aggressive days, when a battle was generally followed by a Federal retreat, he now not only derived no positive gain for his losses; he was also far less able to replace them, so near was the Confederacy to the bottom of its manpower barrel. "There is the chill of murder about the casualties of this month," one of his brigadiers reported from the Petersburg intrenchments. Even such one-sided triumphs as the Crater were getting beyond his means, and much the same thing could be said of Early's recent foray to the gates of Washington, which, for all its success in frightening the authorities there, had failed to lure the Army of the Potomac into staging another Cold Harbor south of the James.

That was what Lee had wanted, and even expected. "It is so repugnant to Grant's principles and practice to send troops from him," he wrote Davis, "that I had hoped before resorting to it he would have preferred attacking me." Instead, Grant had detached two corps whose partial arrival discouraged Early from storming the capital defenses and obliged him to fall back across the Potomac. After a brief rest at Leesburg, in defiance of the superior blue force charged with pressing his pursuit, Old Jube returned to the lower Shenandoah Valley and continued to maneuver between Winchester and Harpers Ferry, Jackson style, as if about to move on Washington again. Before his adversaries managed to combine against him — they were drawn from four separate departments, with desk-bound Halleck more or less in charge by telegraph — he lashed out at George Crook near Kernstown, July 24, and after inflicting close to 1200 casualties, drove him all the way north across the Potomac. Following this, in specific retaliation for Hunter's burning of the homes of three prominent Virginians, Early sent two brigades of cavalry under John McCausland to Chambersburg, Pennsylvania, to demand of its merchants, under penalty of its destruction, $100,000 in gold or a cool half-million in greenbacks. When they refused, McCausland evacuated the 3000 inhabitants and set fire to the business district. That was on July 30, the day of the Crater, and by midnight two thirds of the town was in ashes, another casualty of a war that was growing harsher by the month.

Lee's acute concern for Early — whose foot-loose corps, though badly outnumbered, not only continued to disrupt the plans of the Union high command by bristling aggressively on both banks of the Potomac just upstream from Washington, but also served through this critical stretch of time as a covering force for the grain-rich Shenandoah region and the Virginia Central Railroad — was increased on August 4, five days after the Crater, by reports that Grant was loading another large detachment of troops aboard transports at City Point. "I fear that this force is intended to operate against General Early," Lee told Davis, "and when added to that already opposed to him, may be more than he can manage. Their object may be to drive him out of the Valley and complete the devastation they [had] commenced when they were ejected from it." In point of fact, next to provoking his adversary into making a headlong assault on his intrenchments, there was nothing Lee wanted more than just such a weakening of the pressure against them. However, there were limits beyond which a precarious balance would be lost; Early's defeat would mean the loss, as well, of the Shenandoah Valley and the Virginia Central, both necessary for the survival of the rest of the army, immobilized at Petersburg and Richmond. Lee conferred next day with the President and reached the conclusion that, whatever the risk to his thinly held works beyond the James, he would have to strengthen Early. Accordingly, on August 6 he ordered Richard Anderson to leave at once, with Kershaw's division of infantry and Fitz Lee's of cavalry, for Culpeper, where he would be in a position either to speed back to Richmond by rail, in case of an emergency there, or else to fall on the flank and rear of the Federals, just beyond the Blue Ridge, in case they advanced up the Valley.

As usual, Lee was right about Grant's intentions, though in this case they were more drastic than he knew. Not only did the Federal commander plan to "complete the destruction" begun by Hunter before Early drove him off; he already had directed that this was to be accomplished by a process of omnivorous consumption. When Early fell back in turn from Washington in mid-July, Grant told Halleck to see to it that he was pursued by "veterans, militiamen, men on horseback, and everything that can be got to follow," with specific instructions to "eat out Virginia clean and clear as far as they go, so that crows flying over it for the balance of this season will have to carry their own provender with them."

Nothing much had come of that, so far. The crows waxed fat on the Valley harvest, deep in Early's rear, while Halleck, convinced that all his doubts about Grant's movements since Cold Harbor had been confirmed by the events of the past month, fumbled his way through a pretense of directing the "pursuit" from his desk in Washington. "*Entre nous,*" he wrote Sherman on July 16, "I fear Grant has made a fatal mistake in putting himself south of James River. He cannot now reach Richmond without taking Petersburg, which is strongly fortified, crossing the Appomattox, and recrossing the James. Moreover, by placing his army south of Richmond he opens the capital and the whole North to rebel raids. Lee can at any time detach 30,000 to 40,000 men without our knowing it till we are actually threatened. I hope we may yet have full success, but I find that many of Grant's general officers think the campaign already a failure." Old Brains was determined to play no active role in what he saw as a discredited operation, and Grant soon found there was little he himself could do from an even greater distance. One answer might be for him to go up the Potomac and take charge of the stalled pursuit, but the fact was he had problems enough on his hands at Petersburg just then, including Meade's immovability, Burnside's mine, and the presence of Ben Butler, who by virtue of his rank would assume command of all the forces south of the James if Grant went up the country.

Unable to get Butler transferred (though he tried — only to find that this was no time to risk offending a prominent hard-war Democrat who might retaliate by taking the stump against the Administration) Grant turned on his one-time favorite Baldy Smith, who by now, mainly because of what Rawlins called "his disposition to scatter the seeds of discontent throughout the army," had become as much of a thorn in Grant's side as he had been in his cock-eyed superior's all along. On July 19 he was relieved and Major General Edward Ord, in temporary command at Baltimore, was brought down to take charge of his three divisions. Similarly, when the dust of the Crater settled, Burnside was superseded by his long-time chief of staff, Major General John G. Parke. Both of these new corps commanders — Ord was forty-five, a West Pointer like Parke, who was thirty-six — had fought under Grant at Vicksburg, and he was pleased to have them with him, here in front of Petersburg, to help conduct another siege.

None of this improved conditions northwest of Washington, however, and on the last day of July, with the ashes of Chambersburg still warm in that direction, Grant went down the James to Fortress Monroe for a conference with Lincoln about the situation Early had created up the Potomac.

For weeks he had favored merging the separate departments around the capital under a single field commander, though when he suggested his classmate William Franklin for the post — Franklin was conveniently at hand in Philadelphia, home on leave from Louisiana — he was told that the Pennsylvanian "would not give satisfaction," apparently because of his old association with McClellan, which still rankled in certain congressional minds. Rebuffed, Grant then considered giving Meade the job, with Hancock as his successor in command of the Army of the Potomac, but then thought better of it and decided that David Hunter, with his demonstrated talent for destruction, was perhaps the best man for the assignment after all. By the time he got to Fort Monroe on July 31, however, he had changed his mind again, and with the President's concurrence announced his decision next day in a telegram to Halleck: "I want Sheridan put in command of all the troops in the field, with instructions to put himself south of the enemy and follow him to the death."

Back in Washington, Lincoln saw the order two days later, and though he already had approved the policy announced, he was so taken with the message that he felt called upon to wire its author his congratulations — together with a warning. "This, I think, is exactly right as to how our forces should move," he replied, "but please look over the dispatches you may have received from here, even since you made that order, and discover, if you can, [whether] there is any idea in the head of anyone here of 'putting our army south of the enemy' or of 'following him to the death' in any direction. I repeat to you it will neither be done nor attempted unless you watch it every day and hour and force it."

This last was sound advice, and Grant reacted promptly despite his previous reluctance to leave the scene of his main effort. Delaying only long enough to compose a carefully worded note for Butler — "In my absence remain on the defensive," he told him, adding: "Please communicate with me by telegraph if anything occurs where you may wish my orders" — he was on his way down the James within two hours of reading Lincoln's message. In Washington next morning he visited neither the White House nor the War Department, but went instead to the railway station and caught a train for Monocacy Junction, where Hunter had gathered the better part of the 32,500-man force supposed to be in hot pursuit of Early. Grant arrived on August 5 to find him in a state of shock, brought on by having been harassed for more than a month by the rebels and his superiors, who had confused him with conflicting orders and unstrung his nerves with alarmist and misleading information. In any case, his jangled state facilitated the process of removal. Displaying what Grant later called "a patriotism none too common in the army," Hunter readily agreed not only to stand aside for Sheridan, whom he outranked, but also to step down for Crook, who took over his three divisions when he presently departed for more congenial duty in the capital.

Sheridan arrived on August 6, in time for a brief interview with Grant, who also gave him a letter of instructions. Two of his three cavalry divisions had been ordered up from Petersburg, and these, combined with the troops on hand, the Harpers Ferry garrison, and the rest of Emory's corps en route from Louisiana, would give him a total of just over 48,000 effectives: enough, Grant thought, to enable him to handle Jubal Early and any other problem likely to arise as he pressed south toward a reunion with Meade near Richmond, wrecking as he went. He would have to take preliminary time, of course, to acquaint himself with his new duties in an unfamiliar region, as well as to restore some tone to Hunter's winded, footsore men, now under Crook, and to Wright's disgruntled veterans, who had little patience with the mismanagement they had recently undergone. But Grant made it clear — despite protests from Stanton and Halleck, being registered in Washington even now, that the thirty-three-year-old cavalryman was too young for the command of three full corps of infantry — that he looked forward to hearing great things from this direction before long, when Sheridan began to carry out what was set forth in his instructions. "In pushing up the Shenandoah Valley, as it is expected you will have to do first or last," the letter read, "it is desirable that nothing should be left to invite the enemy to return. Take all provisions, forage, and stock wanted for the use of your command. Such as cannot be consumed, destroy.... Bear in mind, the object is to drive the enemy south, and to do this you want to keep him always in sight. Be guided in your course by the course he takes."

The interview was brief because Grant was in a hurry to get back down the coast before Lee reached into his bag of tricks and dangled something disastrously attractive in front of Butler's nose. Returning to Washington, he boarded the dispatch steamer that had brought him up Chesapeake Bay four days ago, and stepped ashore at City Point before sunrise, August 9.

His haste came close to costing him his life before the morning ended. Around noon he was sitting in front of his headquarters tent, which was pitched in the yard of a high-sited mansion overlooking the wharves and warehouses of the ordnance supply depot he had established near the confluence of the James and the Appomattox, when suddenly there was the roar of an explosion louder than anything heard in the region since the springing of Pleasants's mine, ten days back. "Such a rain of shot, shell, bullets, pieces of wood, iron bars and bolts, chains and missiles of every kind was never before witnessed. It was terrible — awful — terrific," a staffer wrote home. Grant agreed. "Every part of the yard used as my headquarters is filled with splinters and fragments of shell," he telegraphed Halleck before the smoke had cleared.

By then it was known that an ammunition barge had exploded, along with an undeterminable number of the 20,000 artillery projectiles on its deck and in its hold, though whether by accident or by sabotage was difficult to say, all aboard having died in the blast, which scattered parts of their bodies over a quarter-mile radius and flung more substantial chunks of wreckage twice that far. A canal boat moored alongside, for example, was loaded with cavalry saddles that went flying in every direction, one startled observer said, "like so many big-winged bats." These were nearly as deadly in their flight as the unexploded shells, and contributed to the loss of 43 dead and 126 injured along the docks, while others, killed or wounded on the periphery — including a head-quarters orderly and three members of Grant's staff — nearly doubled both those figures. "The total number killed will never be known," an investigator admitted, though he guessed at "over 200," and it was not until the war ended that the cause of the disaster was established by the discovery of a report by a rebel agent named John Maxwell.

He had stolen through the Union lines the night before, bringing with him a "horological torpedo," as he called the device, a candle box packed with twelve pounds of black powder, a percussion cap, and a clockwork mechanism to set it off. Reaching City Point at daybreak — about the same time Grant arrived — he went down to the wharves to watch for a chance to plant his bomb. It came when he saw the captain of a low-riding ammunition vessel step ashore, apparently intent on business: whereupon the agent set the timer, sealed the box, and delivered it to a member of the crew, with a request from the skipper to "put it down below" till he returned. "The man took it without question," Maxwell declared, "while I went off a little distance." His luck held; for though, as he said, he was "terribly shocked by the explosion," which soon followed, he not only was uninjured by falling debris, he also made it back in safety to the Confederate lines, having accomplished overnight, with a dozen pounds of powder, more damage, both in lives and property, than the Federals had done ten days ago with four tons of the stuff, after a solid month of digging.

Fearful though the damage was — estimates ran to $2,000,000 and beyond — wrecked equipment could be repaired and lost supplies replaced. More alarming, in a different way, was an intelligence report, just in, that Lee had detached Anderson's entire First Corps three days ago, along with Fitz Lee's cavalry, to reinforce Early out in the Valley. If true (which it was not, except in part; Anderson had been detached, but only with Kershaw's, not all three of his infantry divisions) this would give Early close to 40,000 soldiers, veterans to a man; enough, in short, to enable him to overrun Sheridan's disaffected conglomeration for a second crossing of the Potomac, this time with better than twice the strength of the one that had wound up at the gates of Washington last month. As things stood now, Lincoln might or might not survive the November election, but with 40,000 graybacks on the outskirts of the capital, let alone inside it, there was little doubt which way the votes would go. And as the votes went, so went Grant — a hard-war man, unlikely to survive the inauguration of a soft-war President. Promptly he got off a warning to Little Phil that his adversary was being reinforced to an extent that would "put him nearer on an equality with you in numbers than I want to see." What was called for, under the circumstances, was caution: particularly on the part of a young general less than a week in command, whose total strategy up to now could be summarized in his watchword, "Smash 'em up!"

Caution he recommended; caution he got. Sheridan had begun an advance from Halltown, near Harpers Ferry, and had pressed on through Winchester, almost to Strasburg — just beyond which, after cannily fading back, Early had taken up a strong position at Fisher's Hill, inviting attack — when word came on August 14, via Washington, that Anderson was on the way from Richmond, if indeed he had not come up already, with reinforcements that would enable Early to go over to the offensive with close to twice his estimated present strength of better than 20,000 veterans. Little Phil, experiencing for the first time the loneliness of independent command, reacted with a discretion unsuspected in his makeup until now. "I should like very much to have your advice," he wrote Grant, rather plaintively, as he began a withdrawal that presently saw him back at Halltown, within comforting range of the big guns at Harpers Ferry.

Early too returned to his starting point in the Lower Valley, skirmishing with such enemy units as he could persuade to venture beyond reach of the heavy batteries in their rear, and resumed his harassment of the Baltimore & Ohio, threatening all the while to recross the Potomac for another march on the Yankee capital. He had 16,500 men, including detached cavalry, and when Kershaw and Fitz Lee joined him the total came to 23,000: about half the number his adversary enjoyed while backing away from a confrontation. The result was a scathing contempt which Old Jube did not bother to conceal, remarking then and later that Sheridan was not only "without enterprise" but also "possessed an excessive caution which amounted to timidity." As the stand-off continued, on through August and beyond, Early's confidence grew to overconfident proportions. "If it was his policy to produce the impression that he was too weak to fight me, he did not succeed," he said of Little Phil, "but if it was to convince me that he was not an energetic commander, his strategy was a complete success."

Grant meantime had not been long in finding that only one of Anderson's divisions had left the Richmond-Petersburg front; yet he still thought it best for Sheridan to delay his drive up the Valley until pressure from Meade obliged Lee to recall the reinforcements now with Early. Accordingly, he began at once to exert that pressure, first on one bank of the James, pulling the few Confederate reserves in that direction, then the other. Hancock, with his own and one of Butler's corps, plus the remaining cavalry division, was ordered to repeat the northside maneuver he had attempted on the eve of the Crater. This began on August 14, the day Sheridan started to backtrack, and continued on the morrow, but with heavier casualties than before and even less success. Attacking at Deep Bottom Run with hopes of turning the Chaffin's Bluff defenses, Hancock found veterans, not reserves, in occupation of Richmond's outer works, and suffered a repulse. A renewal of the assault next day, just up the line, brought similar results until he called it off, confessing in his report that his men had not behaved well in the affair. His losses were just under 3000, more than three times Lee's, but Grant had him remain in position to distract his opponent's attention from a second offensive, off at the far end of the line.

Warren had the assignment, which was basically to repeat the late-June effort to get astride the Weldon Railroad a couple of miles southwest of where the present Union left overlapped the Jerusalem Plank Road. This time he succeeded. Moving with four divisions on the morning of August 18 he struck the railroad at Globe Tavern, four miles south of Petersburg, and quickly dispossessed the single brigade of cavalry posted in defense of the place while most of the gray infantry

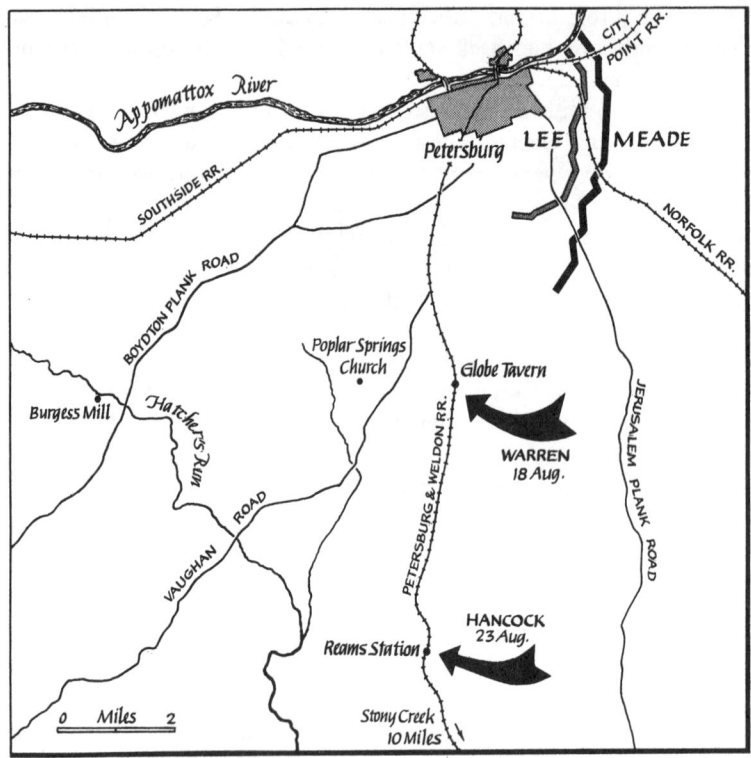

confronted Hancock on the far side of the James. Elated by their success, the attackers pushed north from the tavern, but soon found that holding the road was a good deal harder than breaking it had been. Beauregard counterattacked that afternoon, using such troops as he could scrape together, then more savagely next morning, when A. P. Hill came down with two of his divisions. Warren lost 2700 of his 16,000 men, captured in mass when two brigades were caught off balance in poorly aligned intrenchments, but managed to recover the ground by sundown. That night he fell back to a better position, just over a mile down the line, where he was reinforced for two more days of fighting before the Confederates were willing to admit that they could not dislodge him. His casualties for all four days came to 4500, while the rebel loss was only 1600 — plus of course the Weldon Railroad; or anyhow the final stretch of track. Lee at once put teamsters to work hauling supplies in wagons by a roundabout route from the new terminus at Stony Creek, twenty miles below Petersburg and about half that distance beyond the limits of Federal destruction.

Grant was determined to lengthen this mule-drawn interval, if only to keep up the pressure he hoped would bring Anderson back from the Valley, and when Hancock recrossed the James on August 21 —

the day Lee gave up trying to drive Warren off the railroad — he received orders to proceed south with two of his divisions, plus Gregg's troopers, for a follow-up strike at the vital supply line near Reams Station, about five miles below Globe Tavern and ten above Stony Creek. He reached his objective on August 23, and by the close of the following day had torn up three miles of track beyond it. That night, while resting his wreckers for an extension of their work tomorrow, he learned that A. P. Hill was moving in his direction. Arriving at noon, Little Powell drove in the blue cavalry so fast that the infantry had little time to get set. The main blow fell on three New York regiments, green troops lately assigned to Gibbon's division, some of whom fled, while most surrendered, and to Hancock's further outrage a reserve brigade, ordered into the resultant gap, "could neither be made to go forward nor fire." Before darkness ended the fighting, better than 2000 men here and elsewhere along the Union line chose prison over combat. Two more divisions were on the way as reinforcements, but Hancock decided not to wait for them and instead pulled out that night. He had lost 2750 killed or wounded or missing, along with nine guns, a dozen battle flags, and well over 3000 rifles abandoned on the field. Hill's loss was 720.

This came hard for Hancock — "Hancock the Superb," newsmen had called him ever since the Seven Days; *Hancock*, who had broken Pickett's Charge, stood firm amid the chaos of the Wilderness, and cracked the Bloody Angle at Spotsylvania — as well as for his veteran lieutenants, especially John Gibbon, former commander of the Iron Brigade, whose division had been considered one of the best in the whole army until it was bled down to skeleton proportions and then fleshed out with skulkers finally netted by the draft. Ashamed and angered, Gibbon submitted his resignation, then was persuaded to withdraw it, though he presently left both his division and the corps: the hard-driving II Corps, which had taken more than forty enemy colors before it lost one of its own, and then abandoned or surrendered twelve of these in a single day at Reams Station, August 25. After that, even Grant was obliged to admit that its three divisions were unfit for use on the offensive, now and for some time to come, and Hancock's adjutant later said of his chief's reaction to the blow: "The agony of that day never passed from that proud soldier, who for the first time, in spite of superhuman exertions and reckless exposure on his part, saw his lines broken and his guns taken."

Back at Petersburg next day, Hill was pleased but not correspondingly elated, having done this sort of thing many times before, under happier circumstances. Moreover, it was much the same for Lee, who saw deeper into the matter. A month ago, in a letter to one of his sons, he had said of Grant, with a touch of aspersion: "His talent and strategy consists in accumulating overwhelming numbers." Now he was faced with the product of that blunt, inelegant strategy — that "talent" — which included not only the loss of the final stretch of the Weldon Railroad, but also the necessity for extending his undermanned Petersburg works another two miles westward to match the resultant Federal extension beyond Globe Tavern.

Of the two problems thus posed for him, the first might seem more irksome at the moment, coming as it did at a time when the army's reserve supply of corn was near exhaustion; but the second was potentially the graver. For while there were other railroads to bring grain from coastal Georgia and the Carolinas — the Southside line, on this bank of the Appomattox, and the Richmond & Danville, coming down from beyond the James for an intersection at Burkeville — the accustomed influx of recruits from those and other regions had dwindled to a trickle. Lee could scarcely replace his losses, let alone avoid the thinning of a line already stretched just short of snapping. "Without some increase of our strength," he warned Seddon, even as Hill was moving against Hancock, "I cannot see how we are to escape the natural military consequences of the enemy's numerical superiority." Ten days later he reviewed the situation in a letter to the President, stressing "the importance of immediate and vigorous measures to increase the strength of our armies.... The necessity is now great," he said, "and will soon be augmented by the results of the coming draft in the United States. As matters now stand, we have no troops disposable to meet movements of the enemy or to strike where opportunity presents, without taking them from the trenches and exposing some important point. The enemy's position enables him to move his troops to the right or left without our knowledge, until he has reached the point at which he aims, and we are then compelled to hurry our men to meet him, incurring the risk of being too late to check his progress and the additional risk of the advantage he may derive from their absence. This was fully illustrated in the late demonstration north of James River, which called troops from our lines here, who if present might have prevented the occupation of the Weldon Railroad."

Across the way, at City Point, admonitions flowed in the opposite direction. Halleck warned Grant in mid-August that draft riots were likely to occur at any time in New York and Pennsylvania, as well as in Indiana and Kentucky: in which case he would be called upon, as Meade had been last summer, to furnish troops to put them down. Anticipating such troubles between now and the election in November, Old Brains suggested it might be well for the army to avoid commitment to any operation it could not discontinue on short notice. "Are not the appearances such that we ought to take in sail and prepare the ship for a storm?" he asked.

Grant thought not, and said so. Such police work should be left for the various governors to handle with militia, which should be called out now for the purpose. "If we are to draw troops from the field to keep the loyal states in harness," he declared, "it will prove difficult to suppress the rebellion in the disloyal states." Besides, he added, to ease the pressure on Lee at Petersburg and Richmond would be to allow him to reinforce Hood at Atlanta, just as he had reinforced Bragg at Chickamauga a year ago this month, and that "would insure the defeat of Sherman." In short, Grant had no intention of relaxing his effort on either bank of the James, whatever civilian troubles might develop up the country in his rear.

Lincoln read this reply on August 17 and promptly telegraphed approval. "I have seen your dispatch expressing your unwillingness to break your hold where you are. Neither am I willing. Hold on with a bulldog grip, and chew and choke as much as possible."

Scanning the words at his headquarters overlooking City Point, Grant laughed aloud — a thing he seldom did — and when staffers came over to see what had amused him so, passed them the message to read. "The President has more nerve than any of his advisers," he said.

Nerve was one thing, hope another, and Lincoln was fast running out of that: not so much because of the current military situation — though in point of fact this was glum enough, on the face of it, with Meade and Sherman apparently stalled outside Petersburg and Atlanta, Forrest rampant in Memphis, and the *Tallahassee* about to light up the New England coast with burning merchantmen — as in regard to his own political survival, which was seen on all sides as unlikely, especially in view of what had happened this month in his native Kentucky despite some highly irregular efforts to forestall defeat for a party that soon was still worse split by the Wade-Davis Manifesto. Six days after his chew-and-choke message to Grant, and six days before the Democrats were scheduled to convene in Chicago to nominate his November opponent — a time, he would say, "when as yet we had no adversary, and seemed to have no friends" — Lincoln sat in his office reading the morning mail. Thurlow Weed, an expert on such matters, recently had informed him that his reëlection was impossible, the electorate being "wild for peace." Now there came a letter from Henry J. Raymond, editor of the friendly *New York Times* and chairman of the Republican National Executive Committee, who said much the same thing.

"I feel compelled to drop you a line," he wrote, "concerning the political condition of the country as it strikes me. I am in active correspondence with your staunchest friends in every state, and from them all I hear but one report. The tide is setting strongly against us." Oliver Morton, Simon Cameron, and Elihu Washburne had respectively warned the New Yorker that Indiana, Pennsylvania, and Illinois were probably lost by now. Moreover, he told Lincoln, he was convinced that his own state "would go 50,000 against us tomorrow. And so of the rest. Nothing but the most resolute action on the part of the government and its friends can save the country from falling into hostile hands.... In some way or other the suspicion is widely diffused that we can have peace with Union if we would. It is idle to reason with this belief — still more idle to denounce it. It can only be expelled by some authoritative act, at once bold enough to fix attention and distinct enough to defy incredulity and challenge respect."

What Raymond had in mind was another peace commission, armed with terms whose rejection by Richmond would "unite the North as nothing since the firing on Fort Sumter has hitherto done." Lincoln knew only too well how little was apt to come of this, having tried it twice in the past month, and was correspondingly depressed. If this was all that could save the election he was whipped already. Sadly he took a sheet of paper from his desk and composed a memorandum.

> Executive Mansion
> Washington, Aug. 23, 1864
> This morning, as for some days past, it seems exceedingly probable that this Administration will not be reëlected. Then it will be my duty to so coöperate with the President-elect as to save the Union between the election and the inauguration; as he will have secured his election on such ground that he cannot possibly save it afterwards.
> A. LINCOLN

He folded the sheet, glued it shut, and took it with him to the midday cabinet meeting, where, without so much as a hint as to the subject covered, he had each member sign it on the back, in blind attestation to whatever it might contain — a strange procedure but a necessary precaution, since to tell them what was in the memorandum would be to risk increasing the odds against his reëlection by having it spread all over Washington, by sundown, that he himself had predicted his defeat. "In this peculiar fashion," his two secretaries later explained, "he pledged himself and the Administration" (so far, at least, as the pledge was binding: which was mainly on himself, since he alone knew the words behind the seal) "to accept loyally the anticipated verdict of the people against him, and to do their utmost to save the Union in the brief remainder of his term of office."

Not that he did not intend to do all he could, despite the odds, in the eleven weeks between now and the day the issue would be settled. Treading softly where he felt he must, and firmly where he didn't, he attended to such iotas as recommending in advance to field commanders that Indiana soldiers, who were required by law to be present to cast their ballots, be given furloughs in October to go home and offset the pacifist vote in their state election, considered important as a forecast of what to expect across the nation in November and as an influence on those whose main concern was that their choice be a winner. Besides, he foresaw trouble for his opponents once they came out in the open, where he had spent the past four years, a target for whatever mud was flung. The old Democratic rift, which had made him President in the first place, was even wider than it had been four years ago, except that now the burning issue was the war itself, not just slavery, which many said had caused it, and Lincoln expected the rift to widen further when a platform was adopted and a candidate named to stand on it. The front runner was Major General George B. McClellan, who was expected to attract the soldier vote, although numbers of Democrats were saying they would accept no candidate "with the smell of war on his garments." Either way, as Lincoln saw the outcome, platform and man were likely to be mismatched, with the result that half the opposition would be disappointed with one or the other, perhaps to the extent of bolting or abstaining when Election Day came round. "They must nominate a Peace Democrat on a war platform, or a War Democrat on a peace platform," he told a friend who left that weekend for the convention in his home state, "and I personally can't say I care much which they do."

He was right. Convening in Chicago on August 29, in a new pine Wigwam like the one set up for the Republicans in 1860, the Democrats heard New York's Governor Horatio Seymour establish the tone in a keynote speech delivered on taking the gavel as permanent chairman. "The Administration cannot save the Union. We can. Mr Lincoln views many things above the Union. We put the Union first of all. He thinks a proclamation more than peace. We think the blood of our people more precious than edicts of the President." After this, the assembly got down to adopting a platform framed in part by Clement L. Vallandigham, the nation's leading Copperhead and chairman of the Resolutions Committee, who had returned last year from presidential banishment, first beyond the rebel lines, then back by way of Canada, to run unsuccessfully for governor of Ohio. The former congressman's hand was most apparent in the peace plank, which resolved: "That this convention does explicitly declare, as the sense of the American people, that after four years of failure to restore the Union by the experiment of war ... justice, humanity, liberty, and the public welfare demand that immediate efforts be made for a cessation of hostilities, with a view to an ultimate convention of the States, or other peaceable means, to the end that at the earliest practicable moment peace may be restored on the basis of the Federal Union of the States."

The stress here, as in Seymour's keynote speech, was on achieving peace through restoration of the Union, not "at any price," as was claimed by hostile critics. Vallandigham had emphasized this on the eve of the convention, saying: "Whoever charges that I want to stop this war in order that there may be Southern independence charges that which is false, and lies in his teeth, and lies in his throat!" But presently the nominee himself lent strength to the charge by repudiating the plank in question. It was McClellan, as expected; he was chosen by acclaim on the first ballot, with Congressman George H. Pendleton of Ohio, long an advocate of negotiated peace, as his running mate. Ten days after his nomination — a delay that prompted a Republican wit to remark in the interim that Little Mac was "about as slow in getting up on the platform as he was in taking Richmond" — he tendered the notification committee his letter of acceptance. "I could not look in the face of my gallant comrades of the army and navy who have survived so many bloody battles," he declared, "and tell them that their labors and the sacrifices of so many of our slain and wounded brethren have been in vain, that we had abandoned that Union for which we have so often periled our lives. A vast majority of our people, whether in the army and navy or at home, would, as I would, hail with unbounded joy the permanent restoration of peace, on the basis of the Union under the Constitution, without the effusion of another drop of blood. But no peace can be permanent without Union."

Thus McClellan sought to deal with the dilemma Lincoln had foreseen, and wound up infuriating the faction that admired what he rejected: as Lincoln also had foreseen. But that was not as important by then as it had seemed the week before, when the charge that the "experiment of war" had been a failure, East and West, was one that could perhaps be contested but could scarcely be refuted in the face of evidence from practically every front. Aside from Farragut's coup in Mobile Bay — seen now as rather a one-man show, with the credit all his own — incredible casualties had produced only stalemates or reverses, whether out in North Mississippi, down around Richmond and Atlanta, or up in the Shenandoah Valley. United in their anticipation of victory at the polls in November, whatever internal troubles racked the party, the Democrats adjourned on August 31, having wound up their business in jig time. Then two days later fate intervened, or seemed to. Slocum's wire reached Washington on September 2, followed next day by Sherman's own: "Atlanta is ours, and fairly won."

Church bells rang across the land as they had not rung since the fall of Vicksburg, fourteen months ago. "Sherman and Farragut have knocked the bottom out of the Chicago platform," Seward exulted, and Lincoln promptly tendered "national thanks" to the general and the admiral, issuing at the same time a Proclamation of Thanksgiving and Prayer, to be offered in all churches the following Sunday, for "the glorious achievements" of the army and the navy at Atlanta and in Mobile Bay. Grant too rejoiced, and telegraphed Sherman next day: "In honor of your great victory, I have ordered a salute to be fired with *shotted* guns from every battery bearing upon the enemy." Within earshot of that cannonade, the editor of the Richmond *Examiner* spoke of "disaster at Atlanta in the very nick of time when a victory alone could save the party of Lincoln from irretrievable ruin.... It will obscure the prospect of peace, late so bright. It will also diffuse gloom over the South."

Gladdened by congratulations from all sides, including some from political associates who he knew had been about to desert what they had thought was a sinking ship, Lincoln enjoyed the taste of victory so well that it made him hungry for still more. "Sheridan and Early are facing each other at a deadlock," he wired Grant on September 12. "Could we not pick up a regiment here and there, to the number of say ten thousand men, and quietly but suddenly concentrate them at Sheridan's camp and enable him to make a strike? This is but a suggestion." A suggestion was enough. Grant replied next day that he had been intending for a week "to see Sheridan and arrange what was necessary to enable him to start Early out of the Valley. It seems to me it can successfully be done." Content to have Meade in charge while he was gone — Butler was conveniently on leave — he set out the following day on his second trip up the Potomac in six weeks. Once more without stopping in Washington, he reached Sheridan's headquarters near Harpers Ferry on September 16.

"That's Grant," a veteran sergeant told a comrade, pointing him out. "I hate to see that old cuss around. When that old cuss is around there's sure to be a big fight on hand."

This applied even more to the present visit than to most, since Grant had in his pocket a plan for a campaign to drive Early all the way to Richmond, destroying first the Shenandoah Valley and then the Virginia Central Railroad in his wake. However, he was not long in finding that Little Phil had plans of his own which he was anxious to place in execution, having received from a spy in Winchester, just that morning, word that the time was ripe for an advance. A Quaker schoolteacher, Rebecca Wright by name, had smuggled out a note, wrapped in tinfoil and cached in the mouth of a Negro messenger, informing him that Anderson had left the Valley two days ago, with Kershaw's division and three batteries of artillery, recalled by Lee to help meet the stepped-up pressure from Meade on both sides of the James. What was more, Early — encouraged, as Lee had been in withdrawing the reinforcements, by his opponent's apparent quiescence under cover of the guns on Bolivar Heights for the past month — had posted three of his four infantry divisions in scattered positions above Winchester, toward the Potomac, to promote the fear that he was about to take the offensive with many more troops than the 18,000 or so which Sheridan now knew were all he had. Sheridan's plan was to use his field force of 40,000 not merely to drive Early from the Valley but to annihilate him by attacking his lone division at Winchester, then moving over or around it to cut off the escape of the rest up the Valley Turnpike.

Grant heard the ebullient young general out, and finding him "so clear and so positive in his views, and so confident of success," said nothing about the plan that remained in his pocket. Instead — today was Friday — he asked if the whole blue force could be ready to move by Tuesday. Sheridan replied that, subject to Grant's approval, he intended to take up the march before daybreak Monday, September 19. Grant thought this over, then nodded and issued his briefest order of the war: "Go in."

He left next morning, and though he still avoided Washington he managed a side excursion to Burlington, New Jersey, where his wife had taken a house after coming East. That night and part of Sunday he spent with her and the children, then returned to City Point on Monday, hoping for news of the Valley offensive, which had been scheduled to open that morning. Delayed by breakdowns, Sheridan's wire did not arrive till the following day, but when it did it more than justified the buildup of suspense. Headed "Winchester, 7.30 p.m." — itself a confirmation of success — the telegram read: "I have the honor to report that I attacked the forces of General Early on the Berryville pike at the crossing of Opequon Creek, and after a most stubborn and sanguinary engagement, which lasted from early in the morning until 5 o'clock in the evening, completely defeated him." There followed a list of their losses, including "2500 prisoners, five pieces of artillery, nine army flags, and most of their wounded," but a companion message, written in greater heat by his chief of staff, better caught the public's fancy, being quoted in all the papers: "We have just sent them whirling through Winchester, and we are after them tomorrow. This army behaved splendidly."

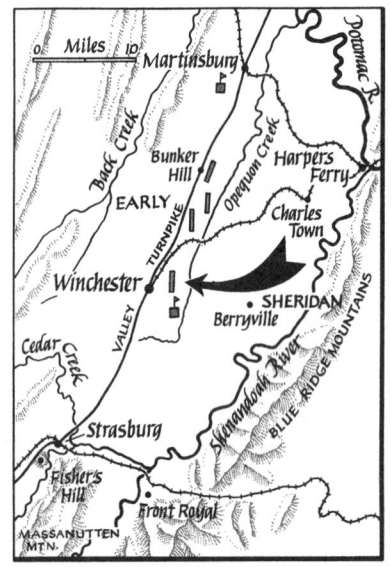

Actually, there had been a good deal more to it than that. For one thing, Sheridan's loss was considerably heavier than Early's — just over 5000 killed, wounded, or missing, as compared to just under 4000 — and for another, despite his achievement of surprise at the outset, he had come close to getting whipped before he got rolling. On the approach march, against orders, Wright brought his corps train along, old-army style, which so clogged the Berryville Pike in his rear that Emory was unable to cross Opequon Creek in time to join the dawn assault on Ramseur's division and Fitz Lee's troopers, posted three miles east of

Winchester. Ramseur alternately held his position and withdrew slowly, in good order, and thus not only gave Early time to call in his other three infantry divisions, six to ten miles north of town, but also enabled him to launch a counterattack by Gordon and Rodes when Emory came up around midmorning, led onto the field by Sheridan himself, who, in a rage at the delay, had ordered Wright's wagons flung into ditches to clear the pike. Here fell Robert Rodes, the tall blond Virginia-born Alabamian who had led Jackson's flank attack at Chancellorsville, thirty-five years old and a veteran of all the army's major battles, from First Manassas on. Shot from his horse while directing the charge into the breach between Emory and Wright, he did not live to see it healed by the latter's reserves when they arrived. Emory, badly shaken — he had finished at West Point in 1831, the year Sheridan was born — had to be reinforced by Crook, whose two divisions had been intended for use in a flanking effort to block the path of a Confederate escape. Still, as the fight continued the weight of numbers told. Early, with some 14,000 men on hand, gave ground steadily all afternoon, under pressure from Sheridan's 38,000, and finally, about 5 o'clock, fell back through the streets of the town and retreated up the Valley Turnpike, which Fitz Lee's horsemen managed to keep open although Fitz himself had had to retire from the conflict, pinked in the thigh by a stray bullet. The battle — called Third Winchester by the defenders and Opequon Creek by the attackers — was over. Early did not stop till he reached Fisher's Hill, beyond Strasburg, twenty miles to the south, where Sheridan had ended his advance the month before, preceding his withdrawal to Harpers Ferry.

Grant's response next day was threefold. Wiring Stanton a recommendation that Sheridan be rewarded with a promotion to regular-army brigadier (which was promptly conferred) he also ordered the firing of a hundred-gun celebration salute in front of Richmond, just as he had done two weeks ago in Sherman's honor, and telegraphed Sheridan his congratulations for "your great victory," adding: "If practicable, push your success and make all you can of it."

Sheridan — whose 5018 casualties, though more than a thousand heavier than Early's 3921, had cost him only an eighth of his command, whereas Early had lost a solid fourth — intended to do just that. Late next day, with a force that was now three times the size of the one he was pursuing, he called a halt near Strasburg, advancing two corps across Cedar Creek and holding the third in reserve while he went forward to study the rebel position, two miles beyond the town. He found it quite as formidable as it had been six weeks ago, when he had declined to test its strength.

Massanutton Mountain, looming dead ahead between the sun-glinted forks of the Shenandoah, divided the Valley into two smaller valleys: Luray on the left, beyond Front Royal, and what remained of the main valley on the right, narrowed at this point to a width of about four miles between the North Fork of the Shenandoah River and Little North Mountain, a spur of the Alleghenies. His flanks anchored east and west on the river and the mountain, Early also enjoyed the advantage of high ground overlooking a boggy stream called Tumbling Run, which the Federals would have to cross, under fire from massed artillery and small arms, if they were to attack him from the front. Down to fewer than 10,000 effectives as a result of his battle losses and the need for detaching two of Fitz Lee's three brigades to hold the midway notch in Massanutton (lest Sheridan send part of his superior force up the Luray Valley for a crossing there to get astride the turnpike at New Market, twenty miles in the Confederate rear) Early had to dismount troops from his other cavalry division, under Lunsford Lomax — most of whom had arrived too late for yesterday's fight, having been involved in railroad wrecking around Martinsburg, some fifty miles to the north — to man the western extension of his four-mile line to the lower slopes of Little North Mountain. Although the Winchester defeat had gone far toward disabusing him of the notion that his opponent "possessed an excessive caution which amounted to timidity," he had confidence in the natural strength of his position on Fisher's Hill, as well as in the veterans who held it, and believed that the bluecoats had little choice except to come at him head-on, in which case they were sure to be repulsed.

He was mistaken: grievously mistaken, as it turned out. Sheridan intended to approach him only in part from the front, using Wright's three and Emory's two divisions to fix him in place while Crook's two, kept hidden in reserve, made a flanking march, under cover of Little North Mountain, for a surprise descent on the Confederate left — where Early, expecting an assault on his right center, had posted his least dependable troops. All next day this misconception was encouraged by the sight of heavy blue columns filing through Strasburg, down toward Tumbling Run. Moreover, here as at Winchester two days ago, Little Phil intended to do more than merely whip or wreck his adversary; he planned to bag him entirely, and with this in mind he detached two of his three cavalry divisions, under Torbert, for a fast ride up Luray Valley and across Massanutton Mountain, through the midway notch in its knife-edge crest, to get control of the Valley Turnpike at New Market and thus prevent the escape of such gray fugitives as managed to slip through the net he would fling over Fisher's Hill tomorrow.

Crook set out before dawn, September 22, marching with flags and guidons trailed to keep them from being spotted by butternut lookouts while he rounded the wooded upper slopes of Little North Mountain, beyond the rebel left. Wright and Emory began their frontal demonstration after sunup, banging away with all their guns and bristling along Tumbling Run, as if about to splash across at any moment. This was a drawn-out business, continuing well past midday, since Crook's West Virginians — so-called because that was where they had done most of their fighting until now, though in fact they were in large part from Ohio, with a sprinkling of Pennsylvanians and New Yorkers thrown in to leaven or "easternize" the lump — had a long hard way to travel, much of it uphill. Finally at 4 o'clock, twelve hours after they set out, they struck.

"Flanked! Outflanked!" the cry went up on Early's left as the dismounted horsemen he had scorned from the outset, calling them buttermilk rangers and worse, fled before the onslaught of Crook, whose two divisions came whooping down the mountainside to strike them flank and rear. Eastward along Fisher's Hill, where the defenders had begun to remark that Sheridan must have lost his nerve and called off the attack he had been threatening all day, the confusion spread when Wright's corps joined the melee, advancing division by division across Tumbling Run as the gray line crumbled unit by unit from the shattered left. Fearful of being trapped in the angle between river and run, they too bolted, leaving the teamless cannoneers to slow the blue advance while they themselves took off, first down the rearward slope, then southward up the turnpike.

"Forward! Forward everything!" Sheridan yelled, coursing the field on his black charger and gesturing with his flat-topped hat for emphasis. "Don't stop! Go on!" he shouted as his infantry overran and captured twelve of the guns on Fisher's Hill.

Anticipating "results still more pregnant," he counted on Averell, whose division he presently launched in pursuit of the rebels fleeing through the twilight, to complete the Cannae he had had in mind when he sent Torbert with two divisions up the Luray Valley for a crossing of Massanutton to cut off Early's retreat at New Market. Alas, both cavalry generals failed him utterly in the crunch. Torbert came upon Fitz Lee's two brigades, posted in defense of a narrow gorge twelve miles beyond Front Royal, and decided there was nothing to be gained from being reckless. He withdrew without attempting a dislodgment. Sheridan was "astonished and chagrined" when he heard of this next morning. But his anger at Torbert was mild compared to what came over him when he learned that Averell had put his troopers into bivouac the night before to spare them the risk of attacking Early's rear guard in the darkness. Enraged, Little Phil fired off a message informing the cavalryman that he expected "resolution and actual fighting, with necessary casualties, before you retire. There must be no more backing and filling," he fumed, and when Averell did no better today, despite this blistering, he relieved him of command and sent him forthwith back to West Virginia, "there to await orders from these headquarters or higher authority."

By that time Early had cleared New Market, and though Sheridan kept up the pursuit beyond Harrisonburg, where the graybacks turned off eastward around the head of Massanutton to find shelter near one of the Blue Ridge passes a dozen miles southeast of Staunton, he had to be content with what he had won at Fisher's Hill and picked up along the turnpike afterwards. This included four additional guns, which brought the total to sixteen, and more than a thousand prisoners. Early's over-all loss, in the battle and on the retreat, was about 1400 killed, wounded, and missing; Sheridan's came to 528.

Gratifying as the comparison was, another was even more so. When Sheridan took over Hunter's frazzled command at Monocacy eight weeks ago, the rebs were bristling along the upper Potomac, as if their descent on Washington the month before had been no more than a rehearsal for a heavier blow. Now they were a hundred miles from that river, and it seemed doubtful they would ever return to its banks, so complete had been his triumph this past week, first near Winchester and then, three days later, at Fisher's Hill. "Better still," Grant replied to his protégé's announcement of the second of these victories, "it wipes out much of the stain upon our arms by previous disasters in that locality. May your good work continue is now the prayer of all loyal men."

Exultation flared among Lincoln supporters, whose number had grown considerably in the course of the three-week September span that opened with news of Atlanta's fall and closed with this pair of Shenandoah victories to balance the tally East and West. The candidate himself was in "a more gleeful humor," friends testified after visits to the White House. "Jordan has been a hard road to travel," he told one caller, "but I feel now that, notwithstanding the enemies I have made and the faults I have committed, I'll be dumped on the right side of that stream."

Abrupt though it was, he had cause for this change in mood from gloom to glee. Within two weeks of his August 23 pledge-prediction, countersigned blindly by the cabinet as a prelude to defeat, the news from Sherman down in Georgia produced a scurry by disaffected Jacobins to get back aboard the bandwagon: especially after the mid-September elections in Maine and Vermont showed the party not only holding its own, contrary to pre-Atlanta expectations, but also registering a slight gain. These straws in the wind grew more substantial with the announcement of Sheridan's triumphal march up the Valley. Salmon Chase paid his respects at the White House, then left to take the stump in Ohio, Vallandigham's stamping ground, while Horace Greeley, privately declaring that he intended to "fight like a savage in this campaign — I hate McClellan," he explained — announced that the *Tribune* would "henceforth fly the banner of Abraham Lincoln for President." Even Ben Wade and Henry Davis, whose early-August manifesto had sought to check what they called his "encroachments," took to the stump, like Chase, in support of the very monster they had spent the past two months attacking, though they maintained a measure of consistency by spending so much of their time excoriating the Democratic nominee that they had little left for praise in the other direction. "To save the nation," Wade told a colleague in explanation of his support for a leader he despised, "I am doing all for *him* that I could possibly do for a better man."

Meantime Lincoln, no doubt as amused as he was gratified by these political somersaults, did not neglect the particulars incident to victory and available to the candidate in office. Patronage and contracts were awarded to those who could do most for the party, and a binding promise went to James Gordon Bennett that he would be appointed Minister to France in exchange for his support in the New York *Herald*. There remained the thorny problem of Frémont, whose continuation in the race threatened to siphon off a critical number of die-hard radical voters. These had long been calling for the removal of Montgomery Blair, whose presence in the cabinet they considered an affront, and though Lincoln, aware that his compliance would be interpreted as an act of desperation, had resisted their demand for the Postmaster General's removal, now that Atlanta had turned the tide he felt willing to be persuaded: provided, that is, he got something commensurate in exchange.

The something in this case was Frémont's withdrawal, and he got it without having to drop the pretense of unwillingness he had kept up all along. "The President was most reluctant to come to terms, *but came*," Zachariah Chandler informed his wife after serving as go-between in the bargain. On September 22 — by coincidence, the day Sheridan hustled Early off Fisher's Hill — Frémont renounced his candidacy. "The union of the Republican Party has become a paramount necessity," he explained in his announcement of withdrawal, but he added, by way of a backhand lick in parting: "In respect to Mr Lincoln I continue to hold exactly the sentiments contained in my letter of acceptance. I consider that his administration has been politically, militarily, and financially a failure, and that its necessary continuance is a cause of regret for the country."

Blair's head rolled next day. "My dear Sir," Lincoln wrote him: "You have generously said to me more than once that whenever your resignation could be a relief to me it was at my disposal. The time has come." There followed compliments and thanks, if not regrets. Blair saw clearly enough that he was in fact "a peace offering to Frémont and his friends." The thought rankled. "The President has, I think, given himself, and me too, an unnecessary mortification in this matter," he wrote his wife before clearing out his desk, "but then I am not the best judge and I am sure he acts from the best motives." A good party man, like all the Blairs, he soon was out wooing voters for the chief who had let him go when bargain time came round.

While this high-level politicking was in progress up the country, Grant tried another pendulum strike at opposite ends of Lee's line, first north then south of the James. Encouraged by news from the Valley, which seemed to show what determination could accomplish, he was also provoked by a mid-September coup the rebel cavalry scored at his expense. On Coggins Point, six miles downriver from his headquarters, a large herd of cattle awaited slaughter for Meade's army; or so it was thought until a rustling operation, dubbed "Hampton's Cattle Raid," caused the beef to wind up in stomachs unaccustomed to such fare. Hampton set out with three brigades on a wide swing around the Union left, September 14, and reached his objective before dawn two days later. Two brigades fought a holding action, hard in the Federal rear, while the third rounded up the animals on Coggins Point; then all three turned drovers and rode back into their own lines next day with just over 300 prisoners and just under 2500 beeves, at a cost of fewer than 60 casualties. Lee's veterans were feasting on Yankee beef by the time Grant returned from his Harpers Ferry conference with Sheridan to find that in his absence, and to his outrage, the graybacks had foraged profitably half a dozen miles in rear of City Point. Determined to avenge this indignity — and aware, as well, that the year was about to move into the final month before the national election, still without the main eastern army having chalked up a gain to compare with those scored recently in Georgia and the nearby Shenandoah Valley — he told Meade to proceed with another of those sequential right-left strikes, such as he had attempted twice in the past month, designed to throw Lee off balance and overrun at least a portion of his works.

Both times before, the initial attack north of the James had been made by Hancock, but his corps by now was practically *hors de combat* as a result of these and other efforts there and elsewhere. So this time the assignment went to Butler. Presumably refreshed by his recent leave, the Massachusetts general drew up a plan whereby 20,000 men from Kautz's cavalry and the two corps of infantry under Ord and David Birney — successors to the disgruntled and departed Baldy Smith and Quincy Gillmore — crossed the river on the night of September 28 for a double-pronged assault on Forts Harrison and Gilmer, works that were part of Richmond's outer line, down near the James, and covered Lee's critical Chaffin's Bluff defenses. Ord, coming up on schedule through a heavy morning fog, launched an all-out attack which quickly overran the first of these, a mile beyond the river, along with its surprised and meager garrison, though at the cost of a crippling wound that caused him to be carried off the field. Alerted by the racket, just over a mile away, the defenders of Fort Gilmer were ready when Birney struck. Repulsed, he drew back and struck again, with help from Ord, only to find that the place had been reinforced from Richmond, where the tocsin still was sounding. Grant arrived that afternoon to order still a third assault, which was also unsuccessful, and the effort here was abandoned in favor of bracing Fort Harrison against Lee's expected attempt to retake it. This came next day, September 30, when two gray divisions and part of a third, 10,000 men in all, came over from Petersburg under Richard Anderson to make three desperate attacks, all of which failed. Butler's loss for the two days was 3327 of all arms. Lee's was about 2000; plus the fort.

This last was no great deprivation. Lee promptly drew a retrenchment in rear of Fort Harrison, still beyond small-arms range of Chaffin's Bluff, that resulted in a stronger line than the one laid out before. Still, Ben Butler had provided northern journalists with an item fit for crowing over, and best of all — potentially at least — Lee once more had been decoyed into stripping that portion of his defenses where the main blue effort was about to land, off beyond the far end of the long curve of intrenchments south of the James.

Warren and Parke, with two divisions each and Gregg's cavalry in support, set out westward from Globe Tavern while Butler's assault on the forts was in progress. Their mission was to cut, and if possible hold, both the Boydton Plank Road and the Southside Railroad, the two remaining arteries whose severance would bring on the collapse of Petersburg. They were stopped next day along Vaughan Road, less than halfway to the first of these objectives, by Hampton, who skirmished with Warren's column at Poplar Springs Church. Moving west to meet the threat with two divisions from the Petersburg defenses — already weakened by the detachment of Anderson for the attempt to retake Fort Harrison that same day — A. P. Hill encountered Parke at nearby Peebles Farm. Badly shot up, Parke managed to hang on until Warren sent reinforcements to help him hold his ground along Squirrel Level Road, where both corps dug in at nightfall. That was the limit of their lateral advance, and it cost them 2889 casualties, all told, as compared to about 900 for Hill and Hampton. With scarcely a pause for rest, the Federals got busy with picks and shovels, constructing a line of intrenchments from their new position, back east to Globe Tavern, two miles away on the Weldon Railroad. Lee, of course, was obliged to conform, extending once more the length of line his dwindling army had to cover to keep its flank from being turned.

By ordinary standards, Grant's gain in this third of his pendulum strikes at the Richmond-Petersburg defenses — a rather useless rebel earthwork, one mile north of the James, plus a brief stretch of country road, two miles beyond the previous western limit of his line — was incommensurate with his loss of just over 6000 men, a solid half of them captives already on their way to finish out the struggle in Deep

South prison camps, as compared to just under 3000 for Lee, most of them wounded and soon to return to the gray ranks. But with the presidential contest barely five weeks off, this was no ordinary juncture. Ordinary standards did not apply. What did apply was that Lincoln supporters now had something they could point to, down around the Confederate seat of government itself, which seemed to indicate, along with recent developments in Atlanta and the Shenandoah Valley, that the war was by no means the failure it had been pronounced by the opposition in Chicago, five weeks back.

In recognition of this, Democrats lately had shifted their emphasis from the conduct to the nature of the war; "The Constitution as it is, the Union as it was," was now their cry. How effective this would prove was not yet known, for all its satisfying ring. But the evidence from Pennsylvania, Ohio, and Indiana, all of which held their state and congressional elections on October 11, was far from encouraging to those who were out of power and wanted in. With help from Sherman, who at Lincoln's urging not only granted furloughs wholesale to members of the twenty-nine Hoosier regiments in his army down in Georgia, but also sent John A. Logan and Frank Blair with them on electioneering duty, all three states registered gains for the Union ticket, both in Congress and at home.

"There is not, now, the slightest uncertainty about the reëlection of Mr Lincoln. The only question is, by what popular and what electoral majority?" Chase had told a friend in Ohio the week before, and once the ballots were tallied in these three states — all considered spheres of Copperhead influence — *Harper's Weekly* was quick to agree with the former Treasury head's assessment: "The October elections show that unless all human foresight fails, the election of Abraham Lincoln and Andrew Johnson is assured."

Neither of these nominees campaigned openly, any more than McClellan or Pendleton did, but their supporters around the country — men of various and sometimes awesome talents, such as the stout-lunged New Orleans orator, who "when he got fairly warmed up," one listener declared, "spoke so loud it was quite impossible to hear him" — more than made up for this traditional inactivity, which was designed to match the dignity of offices too lofty to be sought. Behind the scenes, other friends were active, too; especially those on the Union executive committee, responsible for funding the campaign. Cabinet members were assessed $250 each for the party coffers, and a levy of five percent was taken from the salaries of underlings in the War, Treasury, and Post Office departments. Gideon Welles alone refused to go along with this, pronouncing the collectors "a set of harpies and adventurers [who] pocket a large portion of the money extorted," and though workers in the Brooklyn Navy Yard "walked the plank in scores" for demonstrating support or sympathy for the opposition, Welles was by no means as active in this regard as Edwin Stanton, who at a swoop fired thirty War Department clerks for the same cause, including one whose sole offense was that he let it be known he had placed a bet on Little Mac. Such methods had produced excellent results in the recent state elections, held four weeks, to the day, before the national finale, scheduled for November 8, when still better returns were not only hoped for but expected, as the result of yet a third Sheridan-Early confrontation, providentially staged within three weeks of that all-important first Tuesday following the first Monday in November.

After Fisher's Hill, Sheridan's progress southward up the Valley — described by a VI Corps veteran as "a grand triumphal pursuit of a routed enemy" — ended at Mount Crawford, beyond the loom of Massanutton, where he gave his three infantry corps some rest while the cavalry raided Staunton and Waynesboro, a day's march ahead on the Virginia Central. Grant wanted the whole force, horse and foot, to move in that direction and down that railroad for a junction with Meade, wrecking Lee's northside supply lines as it went. "Keep on," he wired, "and your good work will cause the fall of Richmond." But Sheridan, with Hunter's unhappy example before him — not to mention that of bluff John Pope, who had tried such a movement two years ago, only to wind up riding herd on Indians out in Minnesota — replied that, even though Early had been eliminated as a deterrent, this was "impracticable with my present means of transportation.... I think that the best policy will be to let the burning of the crops in the Valley be the end of this campaign, and let some of this army go elsewhere." Lured by the notion of bringing Wright's hard-hitting corps back down the coast to Petersburg, Grant agreed that Sheridan would do well to make a return march down the Valley, scorching and smashing left and right to ensure that this classic "avenue of invasion" would no longer furnish subsistence even for those who lived there, let alone for Lee's army around Richmond. "Carry off stock of all descriptions, and negroes, so as to prevent further planting," he reminded Little Phil, elaborating on previous instructions. "If this war is to last another year we want the Shenandoah Valley to remain a barren waste."

He knew his man. Beginning the countermarch October 6, Sheridan reported the following night from Woodstock, forty miles away, that he had "destroyed over 2000 barns filled with wheat, hay, and farming implements; over 70 mills filled with flour and wheat; have driven in front of the army over 4000 head of stock, and have killed and issued to the troops not less than 3000 sheep.... Tomorrow I will continue the destruction of wheat, forage, &c. down to Fisher's Hill. When this is completed the Valley, from Winchester up to Staunton,

92 miles, will have but little in it for man or beast." Others attested to his proficiency in destruction, which continued round the clock. "The atmosphere, from horizon to horizon, has been black with the smoke of a hundred conflagrations," a correspondent wrote, "and at night a gleam brighter and more lurid than sunset has shot from every verge.... The completeness of the devastation is awful. Hundreds of nearly starving people are going north. Our trains are crowded with them. They line the wayside. Hundreds more are coming." They had little choice, a staff captain noted, having been "left so stripped of food that I cannot imagine how they escaped starvation."

To hurt the people, the land itself was hurt, and the resultant exodus was both heavy and long-lasting. A full year later, an English traveler found the Valley standing empty as a moor.

By now, although Early was being careful to maintain a respectful distance with his twice-defeated, twice-diminished infantry, butternut cavalry was snapping at the heels of the blue column, and Sheridan took this as continuing evidence of the timidity his own cavalry had shown, just over two weeks ago, after Fisher's Hill. Approaching that place from the opposite direction, October 9, he gave Torbert a specific order: "Either whip the enemy or get whipped yourself," then climbed nearby Round Hill for a panoramic view of the result. It was not long in coming. After crossing Tom's Brook, five miles short of Strasburg, Torbert had Merritt and Custer whirl their divisions around and charge the two pressing close in their rear under Lomax and Tom Rosser, who had recently arrived from Richmond with his brigade. Startled, the gray troopers stood for a time, exchanging saber slashes till their flanks gave way, then panicked and fled southward up the pike, pursued by the whooping Federals, who captured eleven of the dozen rebel guns in the course of a ten-mile chase to Woodstock and beyond, along with some 300 graybacks on fagged horses. "The Woodstock Races," the victors dubbed the affair, taking their cue from the Buckland Races, staged at Custer's expense by Jeb Stuart, a year ago this month, on the far side of the Blue Ridge. His temper cooled, his spirits lifted, Sheridan passed through Strasburg and crossed Cedar Creek next morning to put Crook's and Emory's corps in bivouac on the high ground, while Wright prepared his three divisions for an eastward march through Ashby's Gap, as agreed upon beforehand, to rejoin Grant at Petersburg.

They set out two days later, on October 12: only hours, as it developed, before Early reappeared on Fisher's Hill, five miles to the south. He had been reinforced from Richmond, not only by Rosser's cavalry brigade, but also by Kershaw's infantry division, which had been with him last month until it was recalled by Lee on the eve of the Federal strike at Winchester. Aware of these acquisitions, Sheridan was not disturbed, knowing as he did that they barely lifted Early's strength to half his own. If Old Jubal was in search of a third drubbing, he would be happy to oblige him when the time came.

All the same, he recalled the three VI Corps divisions from Ashby's Gap next day, deferring their departure until the situation cleared, and set about making his Cedar Creek position secure against attack while he determined his next move. Amid these labors, which included preparations for a horseback raid to break up the railroad around Charlottesville, he was summoned to Washington by Halleck for a strategy conference, October 16. He left that morning to catch a train at Front Royal, and when he got there he was handed a telegram from Wright, whom he had left in command on Cedar Creek, quoting a message just intercepted from a rebel signal station on Massanutton Mountain: "Be ready to move as soon as my forces join you, and we will crush Sheridan." The signature was *Longstreet*; which was news in itself, if the message was valid. Little Phil considered it "a ruse," however, designed to frighten him out of the Valley, and he declined to be frightened. Besides, he had confidence in Wright, who assured him: "I shall hold on here until the enemy's movements are developed, and shall only fear an attack on my right, which I shall make every preparation for guarding against and resisting." Aside from calling off the Charlottesville raid, Sheridan did not change his plans. Boarding the train for Washington, he advised Wright: "Look well to your ground and be well prepared. Get up everything that can be spared," he added, and promised to return within two days, "if not sooner."

He was right in assuming the intercepted dispatch was a plant, and right as well about its purpose. But he was altogether wrong if he thought his twice-whipped adversary did not intend to try something far more drastic if the invoked ghost of Old Peter failed to frighten him away. In point of fact, so thoroughly had the bluecoats scorched the country in his rear, Early believed he had no choice except "to move back for want of provisions and forage, or attack the enemy in his position with the hope of driving him from it." Another reason, despite his usual crusty disregard for the opinions of others in or out of the army, was that he had a reputation to retrieve; "To General Sheridan, care of General Early," cynics had chalked on the tubes of guns sent from Richmond to replace the 21 pieces he had lost in battle this past month, exclusive of the eleven abandoned by the cavalry last week in its panicky flight from Tom's Brook to Woodstock. Admittedly, with the blue force nearly twice his size, securely in position on high ground, its front covered by a boggy creek and one flank anchored on the Shenandoah, the odds against a successful assault were long. But his predecessor Jackson, in command of these same troops, had taught him how far audacity could go toward evening such odds, and Lee himself, in a letter that followed the sending of reinforcements, had just told him: "I have weakened myself very much to strengthen you. It was done with the expectation of enabling you to gain such success that you could return the troops if not rejoin me yourself. I know you have endeavored to gain that success, and believe you have done all in your power to assure it. You must not be discouraged, but continue to try. I rely upon your judgment and ability, and the hearty coöperation of your officers and men still to secure it. With your united force it can be accomplished."

Sustained and appealed to thus, Early was "determined to attack." But how, against such odds, could he do so with any real hope of success? Crippled as he was by arthritis, which aged him beyond his not quite forty-eight years and prohibited mountain climbing, he sent John Gordon, his senior division commander since the fall of Rodes, and Major Jedediah Hotchkiss, a staff cartographer inherited from Jackson, atop Massanutton to study the enemy position, which lay spread out below them, facing southwest along Cedar Creek. Crook's two divisions were nearest, on the Federal left, then Emory's two, beyond the turnpike, and finally Wright's three, on the distant right, where most of the blue cavalry was posted, obviously in expectation that if an attack was made it would come from that direction. Hotchkiss had discovered and recommended the route for the movement around Hooker's flank at Chancellorsville, but what he and Gordon saw from their high perch this bright fall morning, October 18, was an opportunity for an end-on strike that might outdo even Stonewall's masterpiece. A night march around the steep north face of Massanutton,

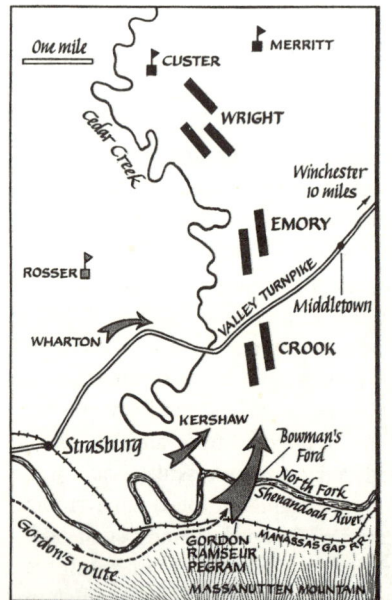

following a crossing of the Shenandoah near Fisher's Hill, would permit a recrossing of the river beyond its confluence with Cedar Creek, and this in turn would place the flanking column in direct confrontation with the unsuspecting Union left, which could be assaulted at first light in preparation for further assaults on Emory and Wright, once Crook's position had been overrun. Gordon, in fact, was so confident of success that when he came down off the mountain to urge the adoption of the plan, he offered to take all responsibility for any failure that occurred.

Early had never been one to avoid responsibility, nor did

he delay approval of the plan. He would march tonight and strike at dawn, he announced at a council of war called that afternoon. Gordon would be in charge of the turning column made up of his own and the divisions of Ramseur and Rodes, the latter now commanded by its senior brigadier John Pegram, recently recovered from the leg wound he had taken in the Wilderness. Kershaw would move through Strasburg, also under cover of darkness, and attack on the right of the Valley pike, crossing lower Cedar Creek to join the flanking effort as soon as he heard Gordon open fire, and Brigadier General Gabriel Wharton — successor to Breckinridge, who had been recalled to eastern Virginia on the eve of Fisher's Hill — would advance along and to the left of the turnpike, accompanied by Rosser's troopers, to menace and fix the Federals in position on the far side of the creek while the massed Second Corps, with Kershaw's help, struck their flank and drove them north across his front. Rosser then would take up the pursuit, as would Lomax, whose horsemen were to come upon the field by a roundabout march through Front Royal in order to cut off the blue retreat this side of Winchester, fifteen miles beyond Middletown, which was close in the Union rear. The plan was elaborate, involving a convergence by three columns, but it seemed pat enough to Early and his lieutenants, who went straight from the meeting to prepare for the various night marches designed to yield revenge for the two defeats they had recently suffered, here in the Valley from which their army took its name. The first of these — Third Winchester — had occurred exactly a month ago tomorrow, and this made them and their butternut veterans all the more eager to get started on the observance of that anniversary.

Aided by the light of a moon only three nights past the full, Gordon's column set out shortly after dark, the men of all three divisions having left their cooking utensils and even their canteens behind to avoid any give-away clink of unnecessary metal, and was in position in the shadows close to Bowman's Ford before daybreak, half a mile beyond the confluence of Cedar Creek and the river, prepared to splash across on signal. Similarly, accompanied by Early and his staff, as well as by most of the army's guns, Kershaw moved undetected around Strasburg to the near bank of the creek, across which he could see low-burnt campfires glowing in the darkness. Wharton followed, turning off to the left of the macadamized pike, preceded by Rosser, whose troopers rode at a walk to muffle the sound of hoofbeats on the stony ground. At 4.30, after an hour's wait on the creekbank, Early told Kershaw to go ahead and cross. He did, and while he was getting his men back into column on the other side, the boom of Rosser's horse artillery came from well upstream, along with the rattling clatter of picket fire nearby on the right, where Gordon was fording the Shenandoah just off the unalerted Union flank. The surprise was complete, if not quite overwhelming at the outset. "As we emerged from a thicket into the open," one of Kershaw's South Carolinians later wrote, "we could see the enemy in great commotion. But soon the works were filled with half-dressed troops, and they opened a galling fire upon us."

Kershaw charged, and as he did so, racing uphill through the spreading dawn, Gordon struck the left rear of the hastily formed blue line, which promptly broke. Elated (for these were Crook's men, the so-called West Virginians who had flanked them unceremoniously off Fisher's Hill four weeks ago) the Confederates surged forward on a broad front across the turnpike, pursuing and taking prisoners by the hundreds. With only a bit more time for getting set, Emory's corps fared little better, its unbraced ranks plowed by shells from rebel batteries massed on a hill beyond the creek. Fugitives from the four routed divisions fled northward through Wright's camps, in rear of which his Potomac veterans were falling in for battle. By now the sun was rising, alternately bright and pale as drifts of smoke blew past it, and the graybacks — joined at this stage by Wharton, who had been left with nothing in his front — came on yelling as they drove Wright's troops northeast across the open fields, first to a second and then to still a third position nearly two miles in rear of Middletown, where Jackson had captured Banks's wagon train in May of '62. This seemed to some a comparable achievement, while others went further afield in search of a parallel triumph. "The sun of Middletown! The sun of Middletown!" Early kept exclaiming, as if to say he had found his Austerlitz.

It was now past 9 o'clock, and he was delighted that within a scant four hours he had driven seven infantry divisions from the field with only five of his own, taking in the process more than 1300 prisoners, 18 guns, and an uncounted number of flags.

He was delighted; but he was also satisfied, it seemed. "Well, Gordon, this is glory enough for one day," he declared on meeting the Georgian near the front soon afterward. They stood looking across the fields at the Yankees reduced to stick men in the distance. "This is the 19th," he went on. "Precisely one month ago today we were going in the opposite direction." Gordon too was happy, but his thoughts were on the immediate future, not the past. "It is very well so far, General," he replied, "but we have one more blow to strike, and then there will not be left an organized company of infantry in Sheridan's army." His chief demurred. "No use in that. They will all go, directly." The Georgian was doubtful, and said so, indicating the bluecoats on the horizon. "This is the VI Corps, General. It will not go unless we drive it from the field." Once more Early shook his head. "Yes, it will go directly," he insisted as he continued to wait for the whipped Federals to withdraw.

War Is Cruelty ...

Gordon said no more just then, but he later wrote: "My heart went into my boots." He was remembering "that fatal halt on the first day at Gettysburg," as well as Old Jube's daylong refusal, back in May, to let him strike Grant's unguarded flank in the Wilderness, which he believed had cost the Army of Northern Virginia the greatest of all its victories.

His heart might have sunk still deeper if he had known what was happening, across the way, while he and his chief stood talking. Sheridan had just arrived and was reassembling his scattered army for an all-out counterattack. True to his promise to return from the capital in two days, "if not sooner," he had slept last night in Winchester and had heard the guns of Cedar Creek, some fifteen miles away, while still in bed this morning. Dismissing the cannonade as "irregular and fitful" — most likely a reconnaissance-in-force by one of Wright's brigades — he tried to get back to sleep, without success. At breakfast, the guns still were muttering in the distance, faint but insistent, and he ordered his staff and cavalry escort to saddle up without delay. On the way out of town, he noticed "many women at the doors and windows of the houses, who kept shaking their skirts at us and who were otherwise markedly insolent in their demeanor." It occurred to him that they "were in rapture over some good news," mysteriously received, "while I as yet was utterly in ignorance of the actual situation." What was more, the sound of firing seemed to be moving to meet him; an ominous development. But it was not until he crossed Mill Creek, beyond Kernstown, and reached the crest of a low hill on the far side, that he and his staff and escort saw their worst fears confirmed by "the appalling spectacle of a panic-stricken army."

His first notion was to rally what was left of his command, here if not still farther back toward Winchester, for a last-ditch stand against the rebel force, which might or might not include Longstreet and his famed First Corps. With this in mind, Little Phil ordered his staff and escort to form a straggler line along the crest of the hill: all, that is, except two aides and a score of troopers, who would proceed with him toward Cedar Creek to find out what had happened.

In the course of the twelve-mile ride — "Sheridan's Ride," it came to be called — his purpose changed. Partly this was because of his aggressive nature, which reasserted itself, and partly it was the result of encountering groups of men along the roadside boiling coffee. That did not seem to indicate demoralization; nor did the cheers they gave when they saw him coming up the turnpike. "As he galloped on," one of the two aides later wrote, "his features gradually grew set, as though carved in stone, and the same dull red glint I had seen in his piercing black eyes when, on other occasions, the battle was going against us, was there now." Grimness then gave way to animation. He began to lift his little flat-topped hat in jaunty salute, rather as if in congratulation for a victory, despite the contradictory evidence. "The army's whipped!" an unstrung infantry colonel informed him, only to be told: "You are, but the army isn't." He put the spurs to Rienzi — an undersized, bandy-legged man, perched high on the pounding big black horse he had named for the town in Mississippi where he acquired him two years ago — and called out to the retreaters, "About face, boys! We are going back to our camps. We are going to lick them out of their boots!" He kept saying that, shouting the words at the upturned faces along the pike. "We are going to get a twist on those fellows. We are going to lick them out of their boots!"

And did just that: but not with the haste his breakneck manner had implied. Arriving about 10.30 he found Crook's corps disintegrated and Emory's not much better off, though most of it at least was still on hand. Wright's, however, was holding firm in its third position, a couple of miles northwest of Middletown, its line extended southeast across the turnpike by Merritt's and Custer's horsemen. Sheridan got to work at once, concentrating on getting Emory's troops, together with a trickle of retreaters who were returning in response to the exhortations he had shouted as he passed them on the pike, regrouped to support Wright in his resistance to the expected third assault by Early's whooping graybacks. Nor was he unmindful, even at this stage, of the fruits a sudden counterstroke might yield. "Tell General Emory if they attack him again to go after them, and to follow them up, and to sock it to them, and to give them the devil. We'll have all those camps and cannon back again." Emory got the message, and reacted with a sort of fervid resignation. "We might as well whip them today," he said. "If we don't, we shall have to do it tomorrow. Sheridan will get it out of us sometime."

Noon came and went, then 1 o'clock, then 2, and Little Phil continued to withhold his hand: as did Early, across the way.

At 3 o'clock, having at last persuaded his chief to let him undertake a limited attack, Gordon probed the Federal position beyond Middletown, but was easily repulsed. Still Sheridan held back, his numbers growing rapidly as more and more blue fugitives returned from their flight down the turnpike. Finally, after interrogating prisoners to make certain Longstreet was not there, he gave orders for a general advance at 4 o'clock. At first, though their ranks were thinned by looters prowling the Yankee camps in search of food and booty, the graybacks refused to budge. But then one of Emory's brigades found a weak spot in the rebel line, and before it could be reinforced Custer struck with his whole division, launching an all-out mounted charge that sundered the Confederate force and sent the two parts reeling back on Cedar Creek. "Run! Go after them!" Sheridan cried. "We've got the God-damnedest twist on them you ever saw!"

Early did what he could; which, at that stage, wasn't much. For the past four hours — hearing nothing from Lomax, whose roundabout march with half the cavalry later turned out to have been blocked near Front Royal by Torbert's third division — he had watched the steady buildup across the way, aware that this, combined with the rearward leakage from his idle ranks, restored the odds to about what they had been at daybreak, when he enjoyed the lost advantage of surprise. Increasingly apprehensive, he withdrew his captured guns beyond Cedar Creek for quick removal in a crisis, and started his nearly two thousand prisoners on their long trek south to Staunton. All this time, the vaunted "sun of Middletown" was declining, and the nearer it drew to the peaks of the Alleghenies the clearer he saw that the Federals not only had no intention of quitting their third position, in which they had little trouble fending off a belated feeling-out by Gordon, but were in fact preparing to launch a massive counterstroke. When it came, as it did at straight-up 4 o'clock, Early managed to withstand the pressure, left and center, until Emory drove a wedge between two of Gordon's brigades, opening a gap into which Custer flung his rapid-firing troopers; whereupon the Georgian's veterans, foreseeing disaster, began a scurry for the crossings in their rear. Rapidly the panic spread to the divisions of Kershaw and Ramseur, next in line. Dodson Ramseur — a major general at twenty-seven, the youngest West Point graduate to attain that rank in the Confederate army — tried his best to stay the rout, appealing from horseback to his men, but took a bullet through both lungs and was left to die in enemy hands next day, near Sheridan's reclaimed Belle Grove headquarters, where he fell.

By then there would be no uncaptured rebels within twenty miles; Sheridan, having spared his hand until he felt that victory was clearly within reach, exploited the break for all he was worth. "It took less time to drive the enemy from the field than it had for them to take it," according to Merritt, whose division clashed with Rosser's and overran the Confederate far left. Early pulled in Wharton and Pegram to brace the center, under assault from the VI Corps, but only succeeded in delaying Wright's advance. Rearward, meantime, a flying column of Union cavalry wrecked the bridge at Spangler's Mill, just west of Strasburg, with the result that the three miles of turnpike between there and the crossing at Cedar Creek were crowded with artillery and vehicles of all kinds, trapped and at the mercy of the pursuers. Little Phil thus recovered all the guns lost that morning, together with 25 of his adversary's, which enabled him to report that he had taken no less than 43 pieces at one swoop, though he neglected to mention that 18 of them were his own, recaptured in the confusion of the gray retreat.

Early fell back to Fisher's Hill in the twilight, intending to make a stand there in the morning, but soon saw that it would not do. Though his casualties were only a bit over half as heavy as Sheridan's this day —

2910, as compared to 5665 — his army, routed for the third time in thirty days, was in no condition for further resistance to an enemy twice its size. He took up the march for New Market before daylight, fighting off Custer's and Merritt's horsemen, who snapped at his heels all the way. Summing it up afterwards, Old Jube remarked sadly: "The Yankees got whipped. We got scared."

No explanation could shield him now, however, from the blame about to be heaped upon his head by his own people; blame that outweighed the praise that had come his way, three months ago, when he hovered defiantly on the outskirts of the northern capital. Indeed, the brightness of that midsummer exploit only served to deepen, by contrast, the shadows that gathered in this dark autumn of the Confederacy, which some were already saying would be its last. In the past thirty days Early had fought three full-scale battles, and all three had turned out to be full-scale routs. It mattered little to his critics that he had obliged Grant to lessen the pressure on Lee by detaching a veteran corps from Meade and rerouting another, on its way by sea to reinforce him, in order to meet Jubal's threat, first on the far and then on the near side of the Potomac. Nor did it matter that in the course of his follow-up campaign in the Valley, where he was outnumbered roughly three-to-one from start to finish, he inflicted a total of 16,592 casualties on his adversary — the equivalent of still another blue corps, by Sheridan's own count, and about as many combat troops as he himself had been able to scrape together for any one of those several confrontations — at a cost of less than 10,000 of his own. What mattered in the public's estimation was that, here on the field of Stonewall Jackson's glory, Early had been whipped three times running, each time more soundly than before. Tart of tongue, intolerant of the shortcomings of others since the outset of the war, the former Commonwealth's Attorney of Franklin County now found himself accused of ineptness, inefficiency, incompetence, even drunkenness and cowardice, in the journals and in public and private talk, here in his native Virginia as well as elsewhere in the South.

It was otherwise for Sheridan, whose praises now were being sung throughout the North. "With great pleasure," Lincoln wrote him, three days after Cedar Creek, "I tender to you and your brave army the thanks of the nation and my own personal admiration and gratitude for the month's operations in the Shenandoah Valley, and especially for the splendid work of October 19." The following evening, shortly before midnight, he was awakened by Assistant Secretary of War Charles A. Dana, who had just arrived from Washington to present him with the most prized of all rewards: his commission as a major general in the regular army, together with a commendation from the Adjutant General's office citing him "for the personal gallantry, military skill, and just confidence in the courage and patriotism of his troops . . .

whereby, under the blessing of Providence, his routed army was reorganized, a great national disaster averted, and a brilliant victory achieved." Riding through the camps with Little Phil next morning, October 25, Dana thought he had never seen a general so popular with all ranks: not even Sherman or Pap Thomas — maybe not even McClellan in his heyday.

Grant by then was ready to try still another of his pendulum swings at Lee. After ordering a second hundred-gun salute fired with shotted guns in honor of his protégé's third victory in the Valley, he wrote his wife: "I hope we will have one here before a great while to celebrate," and put his staff to work at once on plans for the heaviest strike, so far, at the Richmond-Petersburg defenses. Butler would feint north of the James, with the same number as before, but this time the lunge around the enemy right would be made by no less than 43,000 troops from Hancock, Warren, and Parke, on the theory that what two corps had failed to achieve, just under a month ago, might be accomplished now by three.

On October 27, with Butler already over the river, demonstrating for all he was worth at Fair Oaks, the companion blow was launched. As a further diversion, Parke was to hit the western end of the gray line, just east of Hatcher's Run, while Hancock and Warren swung wide around that stream to cross the Boydton Plank Road and then press north to get astride the Southside Railroad. Alas, no part of this flanking effort went well, and most parts went very badly indeed. Parke encountered stiff resistance and was stalled, and though Hancock made it to his initial objective on schedule, he had to stop and wait for Warren, who was delayed by difficult terrain. While Hancock waited Hill and Hampton struck him flank and front, attacking with about half of the 23,000 effectives Lee had kept south of the river, and forced him to withdraw that night, nearly out of ammunition and altogether out of patience. Meantime Warren turned east, under orders from Grant to help Parke envelop the Hatcher's Run defenses, but was unable to cross the creek; so he too withdrew. None of the three corps in this direction, Parke's or Hancock's or Warren's, had carried out its part of a plan whose only tangible result was the loss of 1758 men — plus the confirmation of Hancock's resolution to seek duty elsewhere; which he would do the following month, suffering as much from recent damage to his pride as from the continuing discomfort of his Gettysburg wound. North of the James, where Lee was not deceived by his gyrations around Fair Oaks, Butler lost 1103 killed, wounded, and missing, as compared to a Confederate loss of 451 there and perhaps twice that number in the opposite direction, along the Boydton Road and Hatcher's Run.

All lines remained the same, north and south of the river, as both armies prepared to go into winter quarters. No more discouraged by this latest failure than he had been by those others outside Petersburg and Richmond, Grant maintained what Lincoln called his "bulldog grip," prepared to "chew and choke" as long as need be. He could fail practically any number of times, and only needed to succeed but once. "I will work this thing out all right yet," he told his wife in a home letter.

In any case, this late-October affair down around Richmond went practically unnoticed by a public still absorbed in the recent Shenandoah drama, finding it restorative of the romantic, picture-book aspect so long missing from the war. "The nation rings with praises of Phil Sheridan," the Chicago *Tribune* noted, three days after the famous ride that saved the day at Cedar Creek and prompted black Rienzi's master to change his name to Winchester in commemoration of the exploit. Various poets tried their hand at the subject, including Herman Melville, but the one who caught the public's fancy best was T. Buchanan Read in a ballad titled "Sheridan's Ride."

> *Hurrah! Hurrah for Sher-i-dan!*
> *Hurrah! Hurrah for horse and man!*

its refrain went. Availing himself of a poetic license which the general he praised sometimes employed in his reports, Read doubled the distance of the gallop, eliminated all stops along the way, and had Rienzi himself announce the nick-of-time arrival to the troops:

> *"I have brought you Sheridan, all the way*
> *From Winchester, down to save the day."*

Widely read and recited, the piece made a fine recruiting and electioneering appeal, especially when delivered by professionals such as James E. Murdoch, a retired actor and celebrated "reader," whose declamation of the poem at a theater in Cincinnati on November 1, just one week before the presidential contest was to be settled at the polls, threw the crowd into a frenzy of approval for the war and for the men who fought and ran it.

※ 4 ※

Elsewhere — not only in the embattled heartland of the South, but also in places as far afield as Kansas, Vermont, and Brazil — both sides undertook desperate measures, throughout the critical two-month span that opened with the fall of Atlanta, in attempts to influence militarily the early-November political decision that perhaps would begin to end the war itself, come Inauguration Day. For example:

Aside from an abortive Union gunboat probe down White River in late June, which was turned back at Clarendon before the flotilla could enter the Arkansas to help patrol that line of Federal occupation, there had been no significant clash of arms in the Transmississippi since Frederick Steele retired from Camden in late April and Banks and Porter abandoned in May their effort to ascend the Red. Since then, Kirby Smith had seemed content to rest on his laurels, clinging precariously to what was left of Texas, Louisiana, Arkansas, and the Indian Territory — "Kirby-Smithdom," this vast but empty stretch of the continent was called — and resisted all efforts by Richmond and homesick subordinates to persuade him to go over to the offensive, either toward New Orleans or Saint Louis. Discontent to have so many good troops standing idle, even against such odds as here obtained, the authorities instructed him in mid-July to prepare Richard Taylor's corps, along with "such other infantry as can be spared," for a prompt movement across the Mississippi to assist in the defense of Atlanta and Mobile. Smith passed the order to Taylor, who had been sulking in Natchitoches for the past six weeks, his hurt feelings, if not his animosity toward his chief, somewhat relieved by a promotion to lieutenant general as a reward for his repulse of Banks. Eager to shake the dust of Kirby-Smithdom from his feet, Taylor looked into the possibility of a crossing, either by ferries or by the employment of what would have been the longest pontoon bridge in history, but replied in the end that it couldn't be done, since the Federals, getting wind of the project, had stationed ironclads at twelve-mile intervals all the way from Vicksburg past the mouth of the Red, with gunboats on constant patrol between them, day and night. "A bird, if dressed in Confederate gray, would find it difficult to fly across the river," a reconnoitering cavalryman declared.

Regretfully, for he was as anxious to get rid of Taylor as Taylor was to be quits with him, Smith informed his superiors in Virginia that the shift could not be made. By then the year had moved into August, and Richmond's answer solved at least a part of his problem by dusting the gadfly Taylor off his back. Stephen Lee having been sent to Georgia to head a corps under Hood, the Kentucky-born Louisianian (and presidential brother-in-law) was ordered to replace him in command of the Department of Alabama, Mississippi, and Eastern Louisiana, temporarily under Maury at Mobile. On a moonless night, within a week of receiving the order on August 22, Taylor crossed the river in a dugout canoe, swimming his mare alongside, and set out eastward for his new headquarters in Meridian. Before he reached it, Smith — or, more specifically, Sterling Price — had placed an alternate plan in execution, back in the Transmississipi, by launching 12,000 horsemen northward into Missouri.

Originally designed to draw attention away from the downriver crossing, the operation was now to be undertaken for its own sake: first against St Louis, where government warehouses bulged with the goods of war, then westward along the near bank of the Missouri River to the capital, Jefferson City — whose occupation, however brief, would refurbish the somewhat tarnished star representing the state on the Confederate battle flag — then finally back south "through Kansas and the Indian Territory, sweeping that country of its mules, horses, cattle, and military supplies." So Price was told by Smith in his instructions for the raid, which was also to serve the double-barreled purpose of discouraging the departure of still more bluecoats to lengthen the odds against Hood and Lee, east of the Mississippi, and of attracting recruits to the gray column as it swept through regions whose voters were about to get their chance, as the case was being put to them in the campaign already under way, to "throw off the yoke of oppression." Mounted on Bucephalus, a warhorse as gray as its rider and stockily built to withstand his two hundred and ninety dead-weight pounds, Old Pap left Camden on August 28 and was joined next day at Princeton by the divisions of Marmaduke and Fagan, who rode with him across the Arkansas River at Dardanelle on September 2, midway between Little Rock and Fort Smith, neither of whose blue garrisons ventured out to challenge the invaders. At Pocahontas on the 13th, up near the Missouri line, Jo Shelby added his division to the column, now 12,000 strong, with fourteen guns, though only about two thirds of the troopers were adequately armed — a deficiency Price intended to repair when he encountered opposition. On September 19, the day before his fifty-fifth birthday, he crossed into his home state, headed for Ironton, eighty miles to the north, terminus of the railroad running south out of St Louis, another eighty miles away. At nearby Pilot Knob there was a Union fort, Fort Davidson, with a garrison of about one thousand men and seven guns, and he had chosen this as his first prize of the campaign, to be followed by those other, larger prizes, north and west.

Assembling his three divisions at Fredericktown on the 25th — a day's ride east of Pilot Knob, which he intended to move against tomorrow — he received news from St Louis that was both good and bad, from different points of view. Department Commander William Rosecrans, on learning in early September that the graybacks had crossed the Arkansas in strength, wired Halleck a request that A. J. Smith's two veteran divisions, then aboard transports at Cairo on their way to rejoin Sherman after service up the Red and in North Mississippi, be sent instead to help defend Missouri against this new incursion. Old Brains complied by ordering Smith upriver at once to "operate against Price & Co." This meant that one purpose of the raid had been achieved before the first blow landed; Price not only had discouraged the sending of more troops east across the Mississippi, he had even provoked a drain in the opposite direction, though at the cost of lengthening the odds against fulfilling his other objectives, including the strike at goods-rich St Louis, whose defenses now were manned by Smith's 8000 gorilla-guerillas, in addition to its regular complement. In any case, after sending a brigade to rip up track on the railroad above Ironton and thus prevent the sudden arrival of reinforcements, he completed his plans for the reduction of Fort Davidson, twenty miles west of Fredericktown, and had it invested by nightfall the following day. He badly wanted its thousand-man garrison and their arms: especially those seven guns, whose addition would increase by half the firepower of the artillery he had brought along for blasting a path through his beloved Missouri.

Brigadier General Thomas Ewing, commander of the District of St Louis — Sherman's brother-in-law and author, too, of last year's infamous Order 11, which emptied Missouri's western counties of civilians in an attempt to ferret out guerillas whose bloody work grew bloodier in reaction to the hardships thus imposed on their women and children — had come down to the fort on an inspection trip, only to have the railroad cut in his rear, and decided not to abandon the place under threat from ten times the number he had for its defense. Accordingly, when a rebel delegation came forward under a flag of truce that night, demanding surrender, he sent it back with a defiant challenge, and when the demand was repeated a few hours later he did the same thing, adding that he would fire on the next white flag that approached his works. These were extremely stout, heptagonal in shape, with earthen walls nine feet tall and ten feet thick, surrounded by a dry moat as deep as the walls were high. Next day, September 27, they were tested in a furious six-hour fight that cost the attackers 1500 casualties, half again more than the total number of defenders, who lost 200. Falling back at dark, Old Pap's troopers began the construction of scaling ladders to use when they renewed the assault at dawn, and Ewing, knowing the fort could not hold out past then — and that he himself, as the author of Order 11, was unlikely to survive capture — assembled a council of war to decide whether to surrender or risk attempting a getaway. The vote was for the latter; which succeeded. Under cover of darkness the blue garrison built a drawbridge, draped it with canvas to muffle the sound of boots and hoofs, and withdrew undetected through a gap in the gray lines, leaving behind a slow fuze laid to the powder magazine. Slogging along in a column of twos, Ewing and his 800 survivors were well out the road to Rolla, seventy miles northwest, when the magazine blew with a great eruption of flame that gave the investors their first hint the fort was empty.

Marmaduke and Shelby, furious over their losses and fairly itching to fit Ewing for a noose, wanted to take out after him at once, but their fellow Missourian Price, already regretting a fruitless three-day interlude which had deprived him of more than a tenth of his command and netted him nothing but rubble and spiked guns, was unwilling to use up still more time on a project that he suspected had already cost him whatever chance there had been for surprising Rosecrans in St Louis.

Sure enough, after following the Iron Mountain Railroad to within thirty miles of the city, he found its garrison reinforced to a strength reportedly greater than his own. So he turned west, as planned — though he had not intended to do so empty-handed — up the south bank of the Missouri, wrecking bridges and culverts along the Pacific Railroad as he proceeded, first across the Gasconade River and then the Osage, which he cleared on October 6 to put his raiders within easy reach of Jefferson City.

But this too was untakable, he decided upon learning that its defenses were manned by bluecoats drawn from beyond the river despite a flurry of apprehension caused there the week before by a ruthless attack on Centralia, fifty miles north of the capital, by a force of about 200 butternut guerillas under William Anderson, who bore and lived up to the nickname "Bloody Bill." A former lieutenant in William C. Quantrill's gang, of Lawrence and Fort Baxter fame, he had quarreled with his chief in Texas and returned to his old stomping ground, near the Missouri-Kansas border, along with other disaffected members of the band, including George Todd and David Pool, as well as Frank James and his seventeen-year-old brother Jesse. Clattering into Centralia at midday, September 27 — the day of the Fort Davidson assault, one hundred and fifty miles southeast at Pilot Knob — they held up a stagecoach and an arriving train, killed two dozen unarmed soldiers aboard on furlough, along with two civilians who tried to hide valuables in their boots, and left hurriedly, with $3000 in greenbacks from the express car, when three troops of Union cavalry unexpectedly appeared and gave chase. Three miles out of town, the guerillas turned on their pursuers, who numbered 147, and shot dead or cut the throats of all but 23 who managed to escape on fast horses. "From this time forward I ask no quarter and give none," Anderson had announced on the square in Centralia, and then proceeded to prove he meant it, first in town and then out on the prairie.

Price's decision to forgo a strike at Jefferson City, the main political objective of his raid, was based on more than information that the capital had been reinforced, not only from beyond the Missouri, but also from scattered posts on this side of the river, including Springfield and Rolla. He learned too, while skirmishing on the outskirts after crossing the Moreau, that Rosecrans, supposedly left holding the bag in St. Louis, had sent Smith's 8000 infantry westward in his wake, along with 7000 troopers under Major General Alfred Pleasonton, who had served the better part of a year as cavalry commander in the Army of the Potomac until Grant replaced him with Sheridan, back in March, and sent him west to share Old Rosy's exile. Price was aware that any prolonged attempt to break through the capital defenses was likely to be interrupted by the arrival of Pleasonton and Smith, now toiling along the demolished Pacific Railroad with a combined strength greater than his own. Moreover, scouts coming in from the Kansas border, a hundred and forty miles in the opposite direction, reported that more than 20,000 regulars and militia were being assembled there for his reception by the department commander, Major General Samuel R. Curtis, his old Pea Ridge adversary. The thing to do, he reasoned, was get there fast, before Curtis got organized or Smith and Pleasonton came up in his rear to make the fight for Kansas City a two-front affair. Accordingly, he turned his back on the state capitol, plainly visible on its hill beyond the treetops, and continued his march another forty miles upriver to Boonville, which he reached October 9. Riding due west for Lexington, sixty-odd miles away — the scene of his one unassisted victory, back in the first September of the war, hard on the heels of the triumph he had shared with Ben McCulloch at Wilson's

Creek — he put Marmaduke's division in the lead and had Shelby strike out left and right at Sedalia and Glasgow, both of which were taken on the 15th, together with their garrisons, while Fagan covered the rear, on the lookout for Pleasonton's horsemen, who were known to have reached Jefferson City four days ago. Four days later at Waverly, his home town on the south bank of the Missouri, twenty miles short of Lexington, Shelby encountered a force of Coloradans and Kansans under Major General James Blunt, brought in from the plains by Curtis and sent forward to delay the approach of the raiders. Here were fired the opening shots of what turned out to be a week-long running skirmish, covering more than a hundred miles of the border region, with several pauses for full-scale engagements along the way.

Shelby drove Blunt back through Lexington, October 20, and on across the Little Blue next day, fighting house-to-house through Independence to the Big Blue, just beyond. Curtis had established a line of works along the opposite bank, manned by 4000 regulars and an equal number of Kansas militia, some 16,000 of whom had come forward in the current emergency, though only about one fourth of them were willing to cross into Missouri, the remainder having called a halt at the state line, half a dozen miles to the west. His plan was to hang on there, securely intrenched, till Pleasonton came up in Price's rear, then go over to the offensive, east and west, against the graybacks trapped between the Big and Little Blues. It did not work out quite that way: partly because of the timid militia, skulking rearward on home ground, but mainly because of black-plumed Jo Shelby. While Marmaduke and Fagan took the bluecoats under fire from across the river on the morning of the 22d, Shelby splashed his three brigades across an upstream ford to flank the defenders out of their works and throw them into retreat on Westport, immediately south of Kansas City and within two miles of the state line. As a result, when Pleasonton arrived that night he found Curtis's intrenchments bristling in his path, occupied by the butternut invaders he had been trailing ever since he left St Louis, three weeks back.

Confronted east and west by forces that totaled three times his own, Old Pap took stock and pondered his next move. Staffers advised that this be south without delay, while the long road home lay open for a withdrawal in good order. But he was urged by Shelby, whose blood was up, to take advantage of a position which, though not without obvious dangers, fairly glittered with Napoleonic possibilities. Using one division to hold Pleasonton in check on the far side of the Big Blue, he could move with the other two against Curtis at nearby Westport, then turn, having disposed of the Kansan and his green militia, to crush Pleasonton and thus cap the raid with a stunning double victory; after which, according to Shelby, he could proceed at his leisure, rounding up Federal garrisons and Confederate recruits, as intended from the outset, on the final leg of his march back across the Arkansas. Price liked the notion, partly for its own glittering sake, partly because of the chance it gave him to put a gainful end to a campaign that so far had profited his country and his reputation next to nothing. Accordingly, after lodging Marmaduke's two brigades in the Union intrenchments overlooking the Big Blue, he ordered Fagan and Shelby to prepare their six for the attack on Curtis, whose troops were deployed along Brush Creek below Westport, at daybreak tomorrow, October 23.

Pleasonton, having posted his four brigades for a dawn assault on the former Union works across the river west of town, spent the night in Independence. A graduate of West Point and the hard-knocks school of combat in the East — including Brandy Station, where he had taken Jeb Stuart's measure on the eve of Gettysburg — he intended to do to Price tomorrow what Price had done to Curtis today; that is, dispossess him of those works. Even though no blue infantry was at hand (A. J. Smith's two divisions had turned south at Lexington, under orders from Rosecrans to head off a rebel swerve in that direction, and thus were removed from all possible contact with the raiders, now or later) the forty-year-old cavalryman was satisfied he could do the job on his own, and with this in mind had his cannoneers keep heaving shells across the Blue to discourage the intrenched defenders from getting much sleep till after midnight, a scant five hours before he planned to strike them.

By that time Curtis was planning to strike them too, despite his mistrust of the balky militia that comprised about four fifths of his command. Persuaded by Blunt — as Price had been by Shelby — that a victory was within his reach if he would only grasp it, the fifty-nine-year-old department head reversed his previous decision to fall back on Fort Leavenworth, twenty-five miles north on the Missouri, and agreed instead, under pressure from Blunt and others at a council of war in the Gillis House that night in Kansas City, to go over to the offensive in the morning. Down along Brush Creek all this while, his green recruits were kept awake by the boom of Pleasonton's guns on the far side of the river and by the nerve-jarring crump of shells on the near bank, close in their rear. "I'd rather hear the baby cry," one married volunteer remarked. Presently the guns left off, but he continued to fret, confiding in a friend that he expected to be killed in tomorrow's contest, and found small comfort in assurances that the future life was superior to this one. "Well, I don't know about that," he said, still worried.

His chances for survival were better than he knew. Next day's battle, though numerically the largest ever fought in the Transmississippi — out of 40,000 Federals and Confederates on the field, close to 30,000 were engaged, as compared to just under 27,000 at Pea Ridge, the next largest, and only about half that many at Wilson's Creek —

was neither as hotly contested nor as bloody as both sides had expected when they lay down to sleep the night before. Fagan and Shelby went forward as ordered, shortly after daybreak, and threw Curtis's greenhorns into skittery retreat, much as Shelby had predicted and Curtis, who watched the action through a spyglass from the roof of a convenient farmhouse, had feared. But not for long. Thrown back on Westport and the Kansas line, the militiamen and regulars, outnumbering the attackers better than two to one, not only rallied and held their own against renewed assaults by the yelling graybacks, but even, in response to a horseback appeal from their commander, who came down off his roof to ride among them, began massing for a counterattack to recover the lost ground along the creek. Whereupon, in this moment of crisis — it was now about midmorning — Price was informed that Pleasonton had broken Marmaduke's line on the near bank of the Big Blue and was approaching his right rear, threatening to come between the raiders and their train, parked southward on the road he had been persuaded not to take the night before.

Enraged to find the dawn attack deferred to await his arrival from Independence, Pleasonton had begun his day with on-the-spot dismissals of two brigade commanders — "You're an ambulance soldier and belong in the rear," he told one of the brigadiers, shaking a cowhide whip in his face quite as if he meant to use it — and peremptory orders for their successors to throw everything they had against Byram's Ford, a strongly defended crossing on the rebel right. He did this on the theory that the enemy would least expect a major effort there, and the result was all he hoped for. When the dismounted horsemen splashed across the ford, through the abatis on the opposite bank, then up and over the intrenchments on the ridge beyond, he followed with a third brigade to deepen and widen the breakthrough, while the fourth came on behind. Marmaduke's rattled defenders, turned suddenly out of their works by twice their number, fled rearward across the prairie that stretched to the Kansas line, unobstructed except by the trees along Brush Creek, where Price's effort against Curtis was in crisis.

Pleasonton reined in his horse to watch them flee, and as he did he stabbed the air with one hand, pointing at the sticklike figures, running or wavering, near and far. "Rebels! Rebels! Rebels!" he shouted at his troopers, who had stopped, much as he himself had done, to watch this flight across the rolling tableland. "Fire! Fire, you damned asses!" he kept shouting.

There was not much time for that, however. Faced with the threat of annihilation on the open prairie, Price disengaged Fagan, pulled him back alongside Marmaduke's reassembled fugitives, and used them both to cover the withdrawal of his train, southward down the road on which it had been parked for ready accessibility or a sudden getaway. Shelby — as was only fair, since he was the one who had talked his chief into this predicament in the first place — was charged with stalling the blue pursuit, at least until the wagons and guns and the other two divisions, remounted to make the best possible time, escaped the closing jaws of the trap and got a decent head start down the road to Little Santa Fe, a dozen miles below on the Kansas border. Hemmed in as he was on three sides (and grievously outnumbered; Curtis and Pleasonton had just over 20,000 infantry and cavalry engaged from first to last — less than three quarters of their total force — while Price had only about 9000 — all that he had arms for) this was no easy task; but Shelby managed it in style, cutting his way out with a mounted charge in the final stage, near sunset, to join the gray column grinding its way south in the darkness. Too ponderous for even heavy-hocked Bucephalus to bear his weight for long, Price rode in a carriage on the retreat, depressed by the knowledge that Westport — sometimes disproportionately referred to as "the Gettysburg of the Transmississippi," though in point of fact it was fought for no real purpose and settled nothing — had merely added another repulse to his long list of reverses, east and west of the Mississippi River. Fortunately it was not a costly one, however. Neither commander filed a casualty report, but their losses seem not to have reached a thousand men on either side.

A heavier defeat, with heavier losses, came two days later, fifty miles beyond Little Santa Fe, soon after the raiders crossed the Marais des Cygnes, which flowed eastward into Missouri and the Osage. They had made good time, marching day and night through wet and blustery weather, but Pleasonton and Curtis dogged their heels, eager to close in for the kill. Swinging west to take advantage of better roads leading south beyond the Kansas line, Price halted Marmaduke on the far bank of the tributary river — mostly referred to hereabouts as the Mary Dayson — in hope of delaying his pursuers at that point. This the Missouri West Pointer did, briefly at least, and then fell back to a similar position on Mine Creek, three miles below, where Fagan had been deployed to support the rear-guard effort with ten of the column's fourteen pieces of artillery. Here on that same morning, October 25, occurred the first and last full-scale engagement between regulars, Federal and Confederate, to be fought on Kansas soil. The first Price knew of its outcome was when he saw troops from both divisions come stumbling toward him in disorder, pursued by whooping bluecoats, mounted and afoot. All ten guns were lost in the rout, along with close to a thousand prisoners, including Marmaduke himself, Brigadier General William Cabell — Old Pap's only other West Pointer, in charge of one of Fagan's Arkansas brigades — and four colonels. Hit in the arm and thrown from his horse, Marmaduke was taken single-handedly by James Dunlavy, an Iowa private, who marched his muddy, dejected captive directly to army headquarters. "How much longer have you to serve?" the department commander asked. Told, "Eight months, sir," Curtis turned to his adjutant: "Give Private Dunlavy a furlough for eight months." The Iowa soldier left for home next day, taking with him the long-haired rebel general's saber for a souvenir of the war that was now behind him, and Marmaduke and Cabell were soon on their way to northern prison camps, the war behind them too.

Once more Price called Shelby back to contest a further advance by the exultant Federals, who were delayed in following up their victory by an argument that broke out between Curtis and Pleasonton as to whether the latter's prisoners were to be sent to Leavenworth or St Louis and thus be credited to Curtis or to Rosecrans. While Shelby fought successive rear-guard actions on the Little Osage and the Marmiton, Price reassembled the other two divisions and pressed on south with the train. Beyond the Little Osage the road forked, one branch leading to Fort Scott, six miles south across the Marmiton, the other back southeast into Missouri. Formerly the fort had been on Old Pap's list of trophies to be picked up on this final leg of the raid, but now he had neither the time nor the strength to move against it. After pausing to lighten the train by burning some 400 wagons, together with the excess artillery ammunition — excess because only one four-gun battery remained — he took the left-hand fork and set out on a forced march of just over sixty miles to Carthage, down near the southwest corner of his home state. Although most of the blue pursuers stopped for food and a night's sleep at Fort Scott, and though Shelby managed to keep the rest from overtaking the train and its escort, still the night-long day-long night-long trek, ending at Carthage on the morning of the 27th, was an experience not soon forgotten by those who made it. "I don't know that a longer march graces history; a fatal day for horse flesh," one weary raider noted in his journal at its close.

Price rewarded their efforts with a full day's rest, then resumed the march next morning, hoping to reach and cross the Arkansas River, still more than a hundred miles away, without having to stop for another time- and man-killing fight for survival. His hope was not fulfilled. At Newtonia that afternoon, twenty-odd miles beyond Carthage, the Federals came up in his rear and obliged him to turn and form ranks for a battle no one knew was to be the last ever fought between regular forces west of the Mississippi. Back at Fort Scott two days ago, the Kansas militia and two of the Missouri cavalry brigades had retired from the chase — as had Pleasonton himself, after falling sick — but Curtis, with his regulars and Blunt's plainsmen still on hand, as well as Pleasonton's other two brigades, was determined to overtake the still-outnumbered raiders before they escaped. Here at Newtonia he got his chance; along with cause to regret it. Spotting dust clouds south of town, Blunt thought Price was attempting a getaway and galloped hard around his flank to cut him off, only to be cut off himself by Shelby, who handled him roughly until other blue units broke through to cover his withdrawal. The fighting sputtered out at sundown, with little or no advantage on either side, and Price took up his march southward, unpursued, while Curtis waited for Blunt to lick his wounds. "I must be permitted to say that I consider him the best cavalry officer I ever saw," Old Pap wrote gratefully of Shelby in his report of the campaign: an opinion echoed and enlarged upon by Pleasonton years later, when he said flatly that the Missourian was "the best cavalry general of the South."

Curtis rested briefly, then proceeded, no longer in direct pursuit of Price, who veered southwest beyond Newtonia, but rather by a shorter route, due south across the Arkansas line, in hope of intercepting the raiders when they swung back east to recross the Arkansas River between Fort Smith and Little Rock; probably at Dardanelle, he figured, where they had crossed on their way north eight weeks ago. Hurrying from Pea Ridge to the relief of Fayetteville, which was reported under attack by a detachment from the rebel main body at Cane Hill, just under twenty miles southwest, the Kansan supposed that his cut-off tactics had succeeded. When he reached Fayetteville on November 4, however, he not only found the attackers gone, he also learned that his adversary was moving en masse in the opposite direction, away from the trap contrived for his destruction. Reduced by casualties and desertions, badly worn by a thousand miles of marching, and even lower in spirits than he was on food and ammunition — which was low indeed — Price was in no condition to risk another heavy engagement, and to avoid one he had decided not to attempt a march east of Fort Smith, whose garrison would be added to the force that would surely intercept him before he made it across the river in that direction. Instead, he would move on west, toward Tahlequah in the Indian Territory, for an upstream crossing of the Arkansas twenty-odd miles beyond the border. Curtis followed as far as a north-bank settlement called Webber's Falls, November 8, only to find that the raiders, assisted by friendly Choctaws, had destroyed all the available boats on reaching the south bank the day before. So he pronounced the campaign at an end, fired a 24-gun salute in celebration, the booms reverberating hollowly across the empty plains, and turned back toward Kansas, glad to be done with an opponent who, as he declared in closing his report, had "entered Missouri feasting and furnishing his troops on the rich products and abundant spoils of the Missouri Valley, but crossed the Arkansas destitute, disarmed, disorganized, and avoiding starvation by eating raw corn and slippery-elm bark."

Worse things were said of Price by his own soldiers in the course of their detour through the wintry territorial wilds. "God damn Old Pap!" was among the milder exclamations on the march, and afterwards there was to be a formal inquiry into charges of "glaring mismanagement and distressing mental and physical military incapacity." One trooper wrote that his unit subsisted for four days on parched acorns, while another told how he and his comrades butchered and devoured a fat pony along the way. A cold wind cut through their rags, freezing the water in their canteens, and coyotes laughed from the darkness beyond their campfires, a terrifying sound to men too weak from hunger or dysentery to keep up with the column. Even so, hundreds fell out in the course of this last long stage of the raid, south through Indian country, down across the Red into Texas, and finally back east to Laynesport, Arkansas, which they reached on December 2, still a hundred miles west of Camden, which Price had left just over three months ago. Though he put the case as best he could in his report — "I marched 1434 miles; fought 43 battles and skirmishes; captured and paroled over 3000 Federal officers and men . . . [and] do not think I go beyond the truth when I state that I destroyed in the late expedition to Missouri property to the amount of $10,000,000 in value" — his claim that his own losses totaled fewer than a thousand men, in and out of combat, scarcely tallied with the fact that he returned with only 6000, including recruits, or barely half the number who had ridden northward with him in September.

Whatever the true figures were, in men or money, and however great the disruption had been along the Missouri River and the Kansas border, this last campaign in the Transmississippi had no more effect on the outcome of the national conflict than did a much smaller, briefer effort made at the same time, up near the Canadian border, against St Albans, a Vermont town of about 5000 souls. This too was a raid designed to bring home to voters remote from the cockpit of war — Westport and St Albans were both just under a thousand miles from Charleston — some first-hand notion of the hardships involved in a struggle they were about to decide whether to continue or conclude: with the difference that the New England blow was struck primarily at what was reputed to be a New Englander's tenderest spot, his wallet.

First Lieutenant Bennett Young, a twenty-one-year-old Kentuckian who had ridden with Morgan, reconnoitered St Albans on a visit from Canada, fifteen miles away, and returned on the evening of October 18 with twenty followers, most of them escaped or exchanged prisoners like himself. Arriving in twos and threes to avoid suspicion, they checked into various hotels and boarding houses, then assembled at 3 o'clock the following afternoon in the town square, where they removed their overcoats to reveal that each wore a gray uniform and a pair of navy sixes. At first, when Young announced that the place was under formal occupation and ordered all inhabitants to gather in the square, the townspeople thought they were being treated to some kind of joke or masquerade, but when the raiders began discharging pistols in the direction of those who were slow to obey the lieutenant's order, they knew better. Meantime, three-man details proceeded to the three banks and gathered up all the cash on hand, though not before outraged citizens began to shoot at them from second-story windows. In the skirmish that ensued, one townsman was killed, three invaders were wounded, and several buildings around the square were set aflame with four-ounce bottles of Greek fire, brought along to be flung as incendiary grenades.

Back in Canada not long after nightfall, once more in civilian dress, Young and his men counted the take from this farthest north of all Confederate army operations. It came to just over $200,000; none of which ever found its way to Richmond, as originally intended, being used instead to finance other disruptions in other Federal regions that had not felt the hand of war till now.

Afloat as ashore, throughout this critical span of politics and war, there were desperate acts by desperate men intent on winning a reputation before it was too late. Commander Napoleon Collins, for example, a fifty-year-old Pennsylvanian with thirty years of arduous but undistinguished service, learned while coaling at Santa Cruz de Tenerife in mid-September that the rebel cruiser *Florida* had been there for the same purpose the month before; reports attending her departure, August 4, were that her next intended port of call was Bahia, just around the eastern hump of South America, some 1500 nautical miles away. His orders, as captain of the U.S.S. *Wachusett* — a sister ship of the *Kearsarge* — were to intercept and sink her, much as Winslow had sunk the *Alabama* three months ago off Cherbourg, and he wasted no time in clearing the Canaries for Brazil. Arriving in early October he did not find the prize he sought in Bahia harbor; nor, despite her six-week head start and her reputed greater speed, had she been there. Apparently the Santa Cruz report was false, or else she had been terribly busy on the way. Then two days later, shortly after dark, October 4, a trim, low-lying sloop of war put into All Saints Bay, and when Collins dispatched a longboat to look her over he found to his delight that the report had been true after all. The twin-stacked handsome vessel, riding at anchor no more than a long stone's throw off his starboard flank, was indeed the *Florida*, one of the first and now the last of the famed Confederate raiders that had practically driven Federal shipping from the Atlantic.

Since her escape from Mobile Bay in January of the previous year, *Florida* had burned or ransomed 37 prizes, and to these could be added 23 more, taken by merchantmen she had captured and converted into privateers, thereby raising her total to within half a dozen of the *Alabama*'s record 66. Most of the time she had been in Commander John Maffitt's charge, but since the beginning of the current year, Maffitt having fallen ill, she had been under her present skipper, Lieutenant

Charles M. Morris. Her most recent prize was taken a week ago, and Collins had it very much in mind to see that she took no more. Employing Winslow's tactics, he sent Morris next day, through the U.S. consul at Bahia, a formal invitation to a duel outside the three-mile limit. But Morris not only declined the challenge, he even declined to receive the message, addressed as it was to "the sloop *Florida*," quite as if he and his ship were nationless. He would leave when he saw fit, he said, having been granted an extension of the two-day layover allowed by international law, and would be pleased to engage the *Wachusett* if he chanced to meet her on the open sea. Collins absorbed the failure of this appeal to "honor," which had worked so well for Winslow against Semmes, then fell back on a secondary plan, rasher than the first and having nothing whatever to do with honor. Tomorrow night would be the *Florida*'s third in Bahia harbor, and he was determined, regardless of the security guaranteed by her presence in a neutral port, that it would be her last.

Suspecting nothing, Morris coöperated fully in the execution of the plan now being laid for his undoing. He had had the shot withdrawn from his guns, as required by law before entering the harbor, and assured the port authorities — who seemed disturbed by the thought of what he (not Collins, with whose government their own had long-standing diplomatic relations) might do in the present edgy situation — that he would commit no hostile act, in violation of their neutrality, against the enemy vessel anchored off his flank. This done, he let his steam go down, hauled his fires, and gave the port and starboard watches turnabout shore leave while off duty. On the night of October 6 he went ashore himself, with several of his officers, to attend the opera and get a good night's sleep in a hotel, leaving his first lieutenant aboard in charge of half the crew. Long before dawn next morning he was awakened by the concierge, who informed him that his ship was under attack by the *Wachusett* in the harbor down below.

Collins had planned carefully and with all the boldness his given name implied. Slipping his cables in the deadest hour of night, he backed quietly to give himself space in which to pick up speed for a ram that would send the raider to the bottom, then paused to build up a full head of steam before starting his run on the stroke of 3 o'clock. His intention was to bear straight down on the sitting vessel and thus inflict a wound that would leave her smashed beyond repair; but *Wachusett* went a bit off course and struck instead a glancing blow that crushed the bulwarks along the rebel's starboard quarter and carried away her mizzenmast and main yard. Convinced that he had inflicted mortal damage, Collins was backing out to let his adversary sink, when there was a spatter of small arms fire from the wreckage on her deck. He replied in kind and added the boom of two big Dahlgrens for emphasis, later saying:

"The *Florida* fired first." As he withdrew, however, he saw that the raider was by no means as badly hurt as he had thought. Accordingly, he changed his plan in mid-career and decided to take her alive. Guns reloaded, he stopped engines at a range of one hundred yards and called out a demand for the sloop's immediate surrender before he blew her out of the water.

Aboard the crippled *Florida*, with no steam in her boilers, no shot in her guns, and only a leave-blown skeleton crew on hand, the lieutenant left in charge had little choice except to yield, though he did so under protest at this hostile action in a neutral port. Collins promptly attached a hawser to the captive vessel and proceeded to tow her out to sea, fired on ineffectively by the guns of a harbor fort and pursued by a Brazilian corvette which he soon outdistanced. Morris arrived from the hotel in time to see the two sloops leave the bay in this tandem fashion, *Wachusett* in front and his own battered *Florida* in ignominious tow, and though he too protested this "barbarous and piratical act," they were by then beyond recall on the high seas, bound for Norfolk.

After a stopover in the West Indies, Napoleon Collins brought the two warships into Hampton Roads on November 12, both under their own power. There he received a welcome as enthusiastic as the one that had greeted his former squadron commander, Captain Charles Wilkes — also at one time skipper of the *Wachusett* — following his removal, three years ago, of Mason and Slidell from the British steamer *Trent*. Seward, on learning of what had happened in Bahia harbor, was only too aware that the two cases were uncomfortably similar, except that this was an even more flagrant violation of international law. Like the two Confederate envoys, the *Florida* was likely to prove an elephant on the State Department's hands, and he began to regret that Collins had not sunk her outright instead of bringing her in, since there could be little doubt that the courts would order her returned intact to the neutral port where he had seized her. "I wish she was at the bottom of the sea," the Secretary was afterwards reported to have remarked in discussing the affair with David Porter, recently transferred from duty on the Mississippi to command the North Atlantic Blockading Squadron. "Do you mean it?" Porter asked, and Seward replied: "I do, from my soul." The admiral returned to his headquarters in Hampton Roads and ordered the captive sloop moved to Newport News and anchored, as an act of poetic justice, near the spot where the *Merrimac* had sunk the *Cumberland*. In the course of the shift, the raider collided with a transport, losing her jibboom and figurehead and being severely raked along one side. She began leaking rather badly, and though her pumps were put to work, suddenly and mysteriously in the early-morning hours of November 28 she foundered and went to the bottom, nine fathoms down. Or maybe not so mysteriously after all; Porter subsequently confided that he had put an engineer aboard with orders to "open her sea cock before midnight, and do not leave that engine room until the water is up to your chin."

This might or might not account for her loss (for with Porter as an unsupported witness, no set of facts was ever certain) but in any case Seward's task in responding to the formal Brazilian protest, which arrived next month, was greatly simplified. "You have justly expected that the President would disavow and regret the proceedings at Bahia," he replied, adding that the captain of the *Wachusett* would be suspended from duty and court-martialed. As for the rebel sloop, there could be no question of returning her, due to "an unforeseen accident which casts no responsibility upon the United States." All the same, a U.S. gunboat was to put into All Saints Bay on the Emperor's birthday, two years later, and fire a 21-gun salute as the *amende honorable* for this offense against the peace and dignity of Brazil. Collins himself was tried within six months, as Seward promised, and despite his plea that "the capture of the *Florida* was for the public good," was sentenced to be dismissed from the service. Gideon Welles, much pleased with the commander's response to a situation that had worked out well in the end, promptly set the verdict aside, restored the Pennsylvanian to duty, and afterwards promoted him to captain. Like Charles Wilkes, he would be a rear admiral before he died, a decade later.

Welles's pleasure was considerably diminished, however, by reports that followed hard on the heels of Collins's exploit, indicating that this was by no means the end of rebel depredations against Federal shipping on the sea lanes of the world. By coincidence, on October 8 — the day after the *Florida* was taken under tow in Bahia harbor — the Clyde-built steamer *Sea King*, a fast sailer with a lifting screw, an iron frame, and six-inch planking of East India teak, left London bound for Madeira, which she reached ten days later to rendezvous with a Liverpool-based tender bearing guns and ammunition and James I. Waddell, a forty-year-old former U.S. Navy lieutenant who had gone over to the Confederacy, with equal rank in its infant navy, when his native North Carolina left the Union. He took over at once as captain of the *Sea King*, supervised the transfer and installation of her armament, formally commissioned her as the C.S.S. *Shenandoah*, and set out two days later, October 20, on a cruise designed to continue the *Alabama-Florida* tradition. In point of fact, his mission was to extend that tradition into regions where his country's flag had never flown. Like the raid on St Albans, staged the day before he left Madeira, and the recent 31-prize sortie by the *Tallahassee*, to Halifax and back, *Shenandoah*'s maiden effort was designed as a blow at the pocketbooks of New England, although Waddell had no intention of sailing her anywhere near that rocky shore. "The enemy's distant whaling grounds have not been visited by us," Secretary Mallory had noted in an August letter of instructions. "This commerce constitutes one of his reliable sources of national wealth no less than one of his best schools for seamen, and we must strike it, if possible."

Nothing in the new captain's orders precluded the taking of prizes en route to the field of his prime endeavor. He took six — two brigs, two barks, a schooner, and a clipper — between the day he left Madeira and November 12, the day the captive *Florida* steamed into Hampton Roads. Three more he took — another schooner and two barks, bringing the total to nine in as many weeks — in the course of a stormy year-end voyage around the Cape of Good Hope to Hobson's Bay, Australia, where the *Shenandoah* stopped to refit before setting out again, northward through the Sea of Japan and into the North Pacific, to take up a position for intercepting Yankee whaling fleets bound for Oahu with the product of their labors in the Arctic Ocean and the Bering Sea. A whaler filled with sperm oil, Waddell had been told, would give a lovely light when set afire.

Cruisers were and would remain a high-seas problem, mainly viewed through a murk of inaccurate reports. But there were other problems the Union navy considered far more pressing, especially through this critical season of decision, because they were closer to home and the November voters. One was blockade-runners; or, more strictly speaking, the discontent they fostered. Although by now only three out of four were getting through the cordon off the Carolina coast, as compared to twice that ratio two years back, there was general agreement that they could never really be stopped until their remaining ports were sealed from the landward side. Meantime, sleek and sneaky, they kept weary captains and their crews on station in all weathers, remote from combat and promotion and contributing for the most part nothing but their boredom to a war they felt could be quickly won if only they were free to bring their guns to bear where they would count. Another problem was rebel ironclads, built and building, which threatened not only to upset plans for future amphibious gains, but also to undo gains already made.

A prime example of this last, now that the *Merrimac-Virginia*, the *Arkansas*, and the *Tennessee* had been disposed of, was the achievement of the *Albemarle* in reclaiming the region around the Sound whose name she bore. Since mid-April, when she retook Plymouth and blocked ascent of the Roanoke toward Petersburg and Richmond, a stalemate advantageous to the Confederacy had obtained there, and though the commander of the half-dozen Federal vessels lying off the mouth of the river had devised a number of highly imaginative plans for her discomfort — including one that involved the use of stretchers for lugging hundred-pound torpedoes across the intervening swamps, to be planted and exploded alongside the Plymouth dock where she was moored —

none had worked, so vigilant were the graybacks in protecting this one weapon whose loss would mean the loss of everything within range of her hard-hitting rifles, all up and down the river she patrolled. Not since early May, when she tried it and came uncomfortably close to being sunk or captured for her pains, had the ironclad ventured out to engage the fleet, but neither could the Union ships invite destruction by steaming up to engage her at close quarters within the confines of that narrow stream. It was clear, however, that something had to be done about her before long: for there were reports that two more rams were under construction up the river, one of them in the very cornfield where she herself had taken shape. One *Albemarle* was fearful enough to contemplate, even from a respectful distance. A flotilla of three, churning down into the Sound, was quite unthinkable.

The answer came from Lieutenant William B. Cushing, who presented two plans for getting rid of the iron menace. One involved the use of India-rubber boats, to be packed across the swamps to within easy reach of the objective, then inflated for use by a hundred-man assault force that would board the ram under cover of darkness, overpower her crew, and take her down to join the fleet at the mouth of the river, eight miles off. Plan Two, also a night operation, called for the boarding party to move all the way by water in a pair of light-draft steamers, each armed with a bow howitzer and a long spar tipped with a torpedo, to be used to sink the rebel warship if the attempt to seize her failed. He submitted his proposal in July, and when the Hampton Roads authorities chose the second plan and passed it on to Washington — where Welles approved it too, though with misgivings, since it seemed likely to cost the service one of its most promising young officers, not to mention the volunteers he proposed to take along — he left at once for New York, his home state, to purchase "suitable vessels" for the undertaking up the Roanoke.

No one who knew or knew of Cushing, and he was well known by now on both sides of the line, would have been surprised, once they learned that he was the author of the plan, at the amount of risk and verve its execution would require. Wisconsin-born, the son of a widowed schoolteacher, and not yet twenty-two — the age at which his brother Alonzo had died on Cemetery Ridge the year before, a West Pointer commanding one of the badly shot-up batteries that helped turn Pickett's Charge — he already had won four official commendations for similar exploits he had devised and carried out in the course of the past three years. Perhaps this was compensatory daring; he had been at Annapolis until midway through his senior year in 1861, when he was permitted to resign and thus avoid dismissal for unruly conduct and a lack of what the authorities called "aptitude for the naval service." He volunteered as an acting master's mate, in reaction to Sumter, and was restored to the rank of midshipman within six months. "Where there is danger in the battle, there will I be," he informed a kinsman at the time, "for I will gain a name in this war." By now he had done so, and had won promotion to lieutenant, first junior, then senior grade, as well as those four commendations signed by Welles. None of this was enough; he wanted more; nothing less, indeed, than the highest of all military honors. "Cousin George," he wrote as he left New York in mid-October to keep his appointment with the *Albemarle* near Plymouth, "I am going to have a vote of thanks from Congress, or six feet of pine box by the next time you hear from me."

He had secured two open launches originally built for picket duty, screw-propelled vessels thirty feet long and narrow in the beam, of shallow draft and with low-pressure engines for quiet running, his notion being that one could stand by to provide covering fire and to pick up survivors if the other was sunk in the assault. As it turned out, this duplication was useful much sooner than he had expected; for one was lost in a Chesapeake storm on the way down, and he decided to go ahead with a single boat rather than wait for a replacement. Steaming in through Hatteras Inlet — whose bar no Union monitor could cross to ascend the Roanoke and engage the homemade iron ram — he joined the fleet riding at anchor fifty miles up Albemarle Sound. Two days he spent reconnoitering and drilling his volunteer crew, including fourteen men in the launch with him and another twelve in a towed cutter, the latter group to be used to silence rebel lookouts posted aboard the wreck of the *Southfield*, sunk in April a mile downstream from the dock where the *Albemarle* was moored. Soon after moonset, October 26, Cushing began his eight-mile run, the cutter in tow, only to be challenged just beyond the mouth of the river by Federal pickets who nearly opened fire when they heard the launch approaching. He turned back, warned by this apparent mishap that the expedition would have failed, and next day had a carpenter box-in the engine to muffle its sound, then set out again the following night, having added a tarpaulin to reduce the noise still more.

This time all went well on the run upriver. A rainstorm afforded such good additional cover that the launch chugged past the grounded *Southfield* undetected, thus enabling Cushing to keep the cutter with him in hope of using its dozen occupants to help overpower the crew of the ram when he went aboard. But that was not to be. Challenged by a sentry as he drew within hailing distance of the wharf, he changed his plan in mid-career; "Ahead fast!" he called out, and cast the cutter loose with orders to return downriver and deal with the pickets on the *Southfield*. As he approached the ram, a signal fire blazed up ashore and he saw by its light that the ironclad was surrounded by a pen of logs chained in position to shield her from just such an attack as he was about to make. Hailed by a sailor on her deck, he replied with a shot from his howitzer and ran within pistol range for a better look at the problem. The logs were placed too far out for him to reach the ram with the torpedo attached to the tip of its fourteen-foot spar, although closer inspection showed that they perhaps were slimy enough for the launch to slide onto or even over them if it struck hard, at a direct angle. (Getting off or out was of course another matter, but that was no part of the plan as he had revised it.) He came about, under heavy fire from the enemy ship and shore, and picked up speed for the attempt. The launch struck and mounted and slithered across the encircling pen of logs, and Cushing found himself looking into the muzzle of one of the big rifles on the *Albemarle*, which he later described as looming before him like a "dark mountain of iron."

Then came the hardest part. To control and produce the explosion he had three lines tied to his wrists: one to raise or lower the long spar goose-necked to the bow of the launch, another to arm the torpedo by dropping it into a vertical position, and a third to activate the firing mechanism. All three required the coolness and precision of a surgeon performing a delicate operation, since too sudden a pull on any one of the lines would result in a malfunction. In this case, moreover, the surgeon was grievously distracted, having lost the tail of his coat to a blast of buckshot and the sole of one shoe to a bullet. Working as calmly under fire as he had done while rehearsing the performance in the quiet of his quarters, Cushing maneuvered the spar and swung the torpedo under the overhang of the ram's iron deck to probe for a vital spot before he released the firing pin. As he did so, the big rifle boomed, ten feet ahead, and hurled its charge of grape across the bow and into the stern of the stranded launch, which then was swamped by the descent of a mass of water raised by the explosion, nearly strangling all aboard. "Abandon ship!" the lieutenant cried, removing his shoes and shucking off his coat to go over the side.

The river was cold, its surface lashed by fire from the shore and the now rapidly sinking ram, whose captain would later testify that the hole blown in her hull was "big enough to drive a wagon through." Cushing struck out for the opposite bank, intent on escape, and as he did, heard one of his crew, close behind him, give "a great gurgling yell" as he went down. Ceasing fire, the Confederates came out in boats to look for survivors; Cushing heard them call his name, but continued to go with the current, paddling hard to keep afloat until he made it to shallow water, half a mile below. Exhausted, he lay in the mud till daylight, then crept ashore to take cover in the swamp. Later he found an unguarded bateau, and at nightfall began a stealthy trip downstream.

"Ship ahoy! Send a boat!" the crew of a Union patrol ship heard someone call from the darkness of the mouth of the river before dawn. An armed detail sent to investigate presently returned with Cushing and the news that he had sunk the *Albemarle*. Cheers went up, as did rockets, fired to inform the other ships of the triumph scored two nights ago, and before long the weary lieutenant, who had been reported lost with all his crew, was sipping brandy in the captain's cabin. A few days later he was with Porter at Hampton Roads. "I have the honor to report, sir, that the rebel ironclad is at the bottom of the Roanoke River."

By then Plymouth, untenable without the protection of the ram, was back in Federal hands, having been evacuated after its works were taken under bombardment by the fleet on October 31. Upriver, the two unfinished ironclads were burned in their stocks when the whole region passed from rebel occupation. Cushing was promptly rewarded with a promotion to lieutenant commander, along with the thanks of Congress, upon Lincoln's recommendation, for having displayed what Porter called "heroic enterprise seldom equaled and never excelled." Much was expected of him in his future career, and he gave every sign of fulfilling those expectations. Before he was thirty, six years after the conflict ended, he would become the youngest full commander in the U.S. Navy. But that was as far as he went. He died at the age of thirty-two in a government asylum for the insane, thereby provoking much discussion as to whether heroism and madness, like genius and tuberculosis, were related — and, if so, had insanity been at the root of his exploits? or had the strain of performing them, or even of having performed them, been more than a sane man could bear? In any case Farragut himself, in a subsequent conversation with Welles, stated flatly that "young Cushing was the hero of the war."

Westward to the Mississippi and north to the Ohio, Confederates did what they could to offset the loss of Atlanta by harassing the supply lines that sustained its Federal occupation. John Morgan was not one of these, for two sufficient reasons. One was that his command had by no means recovered from its unauthorized early-summer excursion into Kentucky, which had cost him half of his "terrible men," along with at least as great a portion of what remained of a reputation already diminished by the collapse of his Ohio raid the year before. The other was that he was dead — shot down in a less-than-minor skirmish on September 4, two days after Atlanta fell and nine months short of his fortieth birthday.

Informed that a blue column had set out from Knoxville for a strike at Saltville and the Southwest Virginia lead mines, he left Abingdon on September 1 and two days later reached Greeneville, Tennessee, where he prepared to confront the raiders when they emerged from Bull's Gap tomorrow or the next day. Down to about 2000 men, he deployed them fanwise to the west, covering three of the four roads in that direction, and retired for the night in the finest house in town, which as usual meant that its owner had Confederate sympathies. Greeneville, like many such places in East Tennessee, was a town with divided loyalties; Longstreet had wintered here, awaiting orders to rejoin Lee, and Andrew Johnson had been its mayor in the course of his rise from tailor to Lincoln's running mate in the campaign now in progress. Around sunup, after a rainy night, Morgan was wakened this Sunday morning by rifle fire, spattering in the streets below his bedroom window, and by a staff captain who brought word that the Union advance guard had arrived by the untended road. He pulled on his trousers and boots and went out by a rear door in an attempt to reach the stable and his horse, but was cut off and had to turn back, taking shelter in a scuppernong arbor that screened the walkway from the house.

"That's him! That's Morgan, over there among the grape vines!" a woman called from across the street to the soldiers pressing their search for the raider.

"Don't shoot; I surrender," Morgan cried.

"Surrender and be God damned — I know you," a blue trooper replied as he raised and fired his carbine at a range of twenty feet.

"Oh God," Morgan groaned, shot through the breast, and collapsed among the rain-wet vines, too soon dead to hear what followed.

"I've killed the damned horse thief!" the trooper shouted, and he and his friends tore down an intervening fence in their haste to get at Morgan's body, which they threw across a horse for a jubilant parade around the town before they flung it, stripped to a pair of drawers, into a muddy roadside ditch. Two captured members of the general's staff were allowed to wash and dress the corpse in the house where he had slept the night before, and others, returning after the enemy withdrew, reclaimed the body and sent it back to Abingdon, where his widow — the former Mattie Ready, pregnant with the daughter he would never see — had it removed to a vault in Richmond, to await the time when it could be returned in peace to the Bluegrass region he had loved and raided. That was the end of John Hunt Morgan.

It was otherwise with Forrest. Not only was he still very much alive, he now also had a department commander who would use him for something more than repelling Memphis-based raids into North Mississippi; would use him, indeed, on raids of his own against Sherman's life line up in Middle Tennessee. One of Richard Taylor's first acts, on assuming command at Meridian in early September, was to notify his presidential brother-in-law of this intention, while summoning the cavalryman to headquarters for instructions. Davis approved, and Forrest arrived by rail on September 5, "a tall, stalwart man, with grayish hair, mild countenance, and slow and homely of speech."

Taylor saw him thus for the first time, two weeks after his Memphis strike — three days after Atlanta fell and the day after Morgan died — though he knew him, of course, by reputation: nothing in which had prepared him for the Wizard's initial reaction to the news that he was to be sent at last "to worry Sherman's communications north of the

Tennessee River." Forrest responded more with caution than with elation, inquiring about the route prescribed, the problem of subsistence, his possible lines of retreat in case of a check, and much else of that nature. "I began to think he had no stomach for the work," Taylor later wrote. But this was in fact his introduction to the Forrest method; for presently, he noted, "having isolated the chances of success from causes of failure with the care of a chemist experimenting in his laboratory," the Tennessean rose and brought the conference to an end with an abrupt transformation of manner. "In a dozen sharp sentences he told his wants, said he would leave a staff officer to bring up his supplies, asked for an engine to take him back north to meet his troops, informed me he would march with the dawn, and hoped to give an account of himself in Tennessee."

That was how Taylor would recall the parting, but here again he misconstrued the method. Far from marching "with the dawn," Forrest took ten days to get ready before he set out from below Tupelo with everything in order, plans all laid and instructions clearly understood by subordinates charged with carrying them out. Chief among these was Abraham Buford, in command of his own two brigades and one from Chalmers, who would remain behind to patrol the region around Memphis. Eight guns rolled with the column, which left on September 16 with just over 3500 effectives, anticipating a meeting near the Tennessee River with nearly a thousand Alabama troopers under William Johnson, who had shown his mettle at Brice's Crossroads back in June. At Tuscumbia on the 20th Forrest also met someone he had not expected: Joe Wheeler. The diminutive Georgian was recrossing the river to wind up his long raid through East and Middle Tennessee, begun on August 10. Although the destruction he had wrought was about as extensive as he claimed to Hood, he neglected to add that Sherman's road gangs had repaired the damage about as fast as it was inflicted, often appearing on the scene before the twisted rails were cool. Moreover, there was something else the young West Pointer did not include in his report, and this was the condition of his command. Grievously diminished (for he tallied only his combat losses, which were barely a twentieth of the total suffered in the course of his six-week ride from Atlanta, up to Strawberry Plains near Knoxville, then back into North Alabama) the survivors were scarecrow examples of what could happen to troopers off on their own behind enemy lines. Originally 4500 strong — the number Forrest would have when Johnson joined tomorrow — they now counted fewer than 2000. A good many of the missing were stragglers whose mounts had broken down, and Forrest wrote Taylor that night, amid preparations for crossing the river next day: "I hope to be instrumental in gathering them up."

Fording his horsemen and floating his guns and wagons across on flatboats, he camped the following night on the north bank of the river, five miles west of Florence, which he passed through next morning,

September 22, on the way to his main objective, the Tennessee & Alabama Railroad, just over forty miles to the east. One of Sherman's two main supply lines, running from Nashville through Columbia and Pulaski to Decatur, where it joined the Memphis & Charleston to connect with Chattanooga and Atlanta, its nearest point was Athens, and that was where Forrest was headed. He got there after sunset on the 23d to begin his investment of the town and its adjoining fort, a ditched and palisaded work a quarter-mile in circumference, occupied by a force of 600 infantry and considered impregnable to assault: as indeed perhaps it was, although no one would ever know. Soon after daybreak John Morton opened fire with his eight guns, "casting almost every shell inside the works," according to the garrison commander. Before long, Forrest halted fire to send in a white-flag note demanding "immediate and unconditional surrender." The Federal declined, but then unwisely consented to a parley, in the course of which Forrest pulled his customary trick of exposing troops and guns in triplicate, thereby convincing his adversary that he was besieged by a host of 15,000 of all arms, with no less than two dozen cannon. Capitulation came in time for the graybacks to give their full attention to a relief column that arrived from Decatur to take part in a brief skirmish before joining the surrender. Reduction of two nearby railway blockhouses raised the day's bag to 1300 prisoners, two pieces of artillery, 300 horses, and a mountain of supplies and equipment, including two locomotives captured with their cars in Athens. Forrest put the torch to the stores and installations, issued the horses to those of his men who needed them, smashed the rolling stock, and sent the prisoners back through Florence for removal south. Then he took up the march northward along the railroad, wrecking as he went.

Halfway to the Tennessee line next morning, September 25, he came upon the Sulphur Branch railway trestle, 72 feet high and 300 long, guarded by a double-casemated blockhouse at each end and a large fortress-stockade with a garrison of about one thousand men. Surrender declined, Morton opened fire and kept it up for two cruel hours, slamming in 800 rounds that left the fort's interior "perforated with shell, and the dead lying thick along the works." So Forrest would report, adding that a repeated demand for surrender was promptly accepted. This time the yield was 973 bluecoats, two more guns, another 300 horses, and a quantity of stores. Again he sent his prisoners rearward, together with the captured guns and four of his own, so greatly had the bombardment reduced his supply of artillery ammunition, and after setting fire to the two blockhouses, the buildings in the fort, and the long trestle they had been designed to shield, rode on north to the Elk River, which he reached next day, about midway between Athens and Pulaski. Here too there was a blockhouse at each end of a bridge even longer than the trestle at Sulphur Branch; but they were unmanned, abandoned by a commander who had heard from below how little protection they afforded, either to the installations they overlooked or to the garrisons they contained. Forrest burned them, along with the Elk River span, and pushed on to Richland Creek, seven miles beyond the Tennessee line and the same distance from Pulaski. Here there was a 200-foot-long truss bridge, stoutly built to take the weight of heavy-laden supply trains. The raiders crossed and sent it up in flames.

Now the character of the expedition changed. "Enemy concentrating heavily against me," Forrest notified Taylor the following night, September 27, from the vicinity of Pulaski. Touched where he was tender, Sherman had reacted hard and fast, sending George Thomas himself from Atlanta with two divisions to take charge in Middle Tennessee, with instructions for "the whole resources" of the region, including Kentucky and North Alabama, to be "turned against Forrest ... until he is disposed of." Other divisions were on the way by rail and river from Memphis and Chattanooga, and Rosecrans had been urged to return A. J. Smith's gorillas from Missouri. As a result, fully 30,000 reinforcements were converging by now from all directions upon Pulaski, where Lovell Rousseau, arriving from Nashville to meet the threat, already had more men in its fortifications than were in the gray column on its outskirts. "Press Forrest to the death," Thomas wired ahead, "keeping your troops well in hand and holding them to the work. I do not think that we shall ever have a better chance than this."

The chance was not as good as the blue Virginian thought: not yet at any rate. Though he kept his Pulaski defenders "well in hand," Rousseau found the raiders gone from his front next morning. Forrest had built up his campfires the night before, and leaving them burning had pulled out. Having done what he could, at least for the present, to cripple the Tennessee & Alabama, he now was moving toward that other, more vital supply line, the Nashville & Chattanooga, fifty miles to the east. He was obliged, however, to do it no more than superficial damage, learning from scouts when he got beyond Fayetteville on the 29th that the Chattanooga road was heavily protected by reinforcements hurried up it from Georgia and down it from Kentucky. He contented himself with detaching a fifty-man detail to tear up wires and track around Tullahoma, then confused the regathering Federals still more by splitting his force in two. Buford turned south with his division and Morton's four remaining guns, under orders to return to the Tennessee River by way of Huntsville, which he was to capture if possible, and tear up track on the Memphis & Charleston, between there and Decatur, before re-crossing. Forrest himself, with the other two brigades, turned northwest through Lewisburg, then north across Duck River, passing near his Chapel Hill birthplace on the last day of September to descend once more, at high noon of the following day, on the already hard-hit Tennessee & Alabama near Spring Hill, ten miles north of Columbia and about

four times that distance above Pulaski, which he had left four days ago.

He turned south, ripping up track, capturing three more blockhouses — mainly by bluff, since Buford had the guns — firing bridges, and smashing culverts all the way to Columbia, which he bypassed on October 2 to avoid the delay of a gunless fight with the bluecoats in its works. The time had come to get out, and Forrest, as one of his troopers said, was "pretty good on a git." Taking off southwest away from what remained of the Tennessee & Alabama, he moved by country roads through Lawrenceburg, where he camped on the night of the 3d, and crossed the Alabama line the next day to return to Florence on October 5, one day less than two weeks after he left it. Buford was there ahead of him, having found Huntsville too stoutly garrisoned to be taken, and though the Tennessee was swollen past fording he had managed to get his men and guns across in relays on three rickety ferries, swimming the horses alongside. Now it was Forrest's turn.

A slow and risky business, with the enemy reported close astern, the piecemeal crossing took two full days, and was only accomplished, a veteran would recall, with "considerable disregard of the third commandment." Fretted and tired, the general was in the last boat to leave. While helping to pole against the swift-running current he noticed a lieutenant standing in the bow and taking no part in the work. "Why don't you take hold of an oar or pole and help get this boat across?" The lieutenant replied that, as an officer, he did not feel "called on to do that kind of work" while private soldiers were available to perform it. Astounded by this implied reproach — for he himself was as hard at work as anyone aboard — Forrest slapped the young man sprawling into the river, then held out the long pole and hauled him back over the gunwale, saying: "Now, damn you, get hold of the oars and go to work! If I knock you out of the boat again I'll let you drown." Another passenger observed that the douched lieutenant "made an excellent hand for the balance of the trip."

In the two weeks spent south of Nashville, within the great bend of the Tennessee, Forrest had captured 2360 of the enemy and killed or wounded an estimated thousand more, at a cost to himself of 340 casualties, only 47 of whom were killed. He had destroyed eleven blockhouses, together with the extensive trestles and bridges they were meant

War Is Cruelty ...   [601]

to guard, and had taken seven U.S. guns, 800 horses, and more than 2000 rifles, all of which he brought out with him, in addition to fifty captured wagons loaded with spoils too valuable for burning. Best of all, he had wrecked the Tennessee & Alabama so thoroughly that even the skilled blue work crews would need six full weeks to put it back in operation. Indeed, Taylor was so encouraged by this Middle Tennessee expedition that he promptly authorized another, to be aimed this time at Johnsonville, terminus of the newly extended Nashville & Northwestern Railroad, by which supplies, unloaded from steamboats and barges on the Tennessee, were sent to Sherman by way of Nashville, seventy-five miles due east. A blow at this riverport depot, whose yards and warehouses were crowded with stores awaiting transfer, would go far toward increasing the Union supply problem down in Georgia, and Forrest spent only a week resting and refitting his weary troopers, summoning Chalmers to join him en route, and adding a pair of long-range Parrotts to Morton's two batteries, before he took off again for Johnsonville, a hundred miles north of Corinth, to which he had returned on October 9.

Much was expected of this follow-up strike, even though the first — successful as it had been, within its geographic limitations — had failed to achieve its major purpose, which was to make Sherman turn loose of Atlanta for lack of subsistence for his army of occupation. Not only did the red-haired Ohioan by then have ample stockpiles of supplies, he also had the scarcely interrupted use of the Nashville & Chattanooga line, having repaired within twelve hours the limited damage inflicted near Tullahoma by the fifty-man detail Forrest had detached when he turned north beyond Fayetteville. If the raid had been made a month or six weeks earlier, while the Federals were fighting outside Atlanta, opposed by an aggressive foe and with both overworked railroads barely able to meet their daily subsistence needs, the result might have been different. Even so, Forrest with only 4500 troopers had managed to disrupt Sherman's supply arrangements, as well as the troop dispositions in his rear, and had brought him to the exasperated conclusion, expressed to Grant on October 9, that it would be "a physical impossibility to protect the roads, now that Hood, Forrest, Wheeler, and the whole batch of devils are turned loose without home or habitation."

※ 5 ※

First there had been the fret of verbal contention. Drawing back from Jonesboro, as he said, "to enjoy a short period of rest and to think well over the next step required in the progress of events," Sherman announced on September 8 that "the city of Atlanta, being exclusively required for warlike purposes, will at once be evacuated by all except the armies of the United States." He foresaw charges of inhumanity, perhaps from friends as well as foes, but he was determined neither to feed the citizens nor to "see them starve under our eyes.... If the people raise a howl against my barbarity or cruelty," he told Halleck, "I will answer that war is war and not popularity-seeking."

Sure enough, when Mayor Calhoun protested that the suffering of the sick and aged, turned out homeless with winter coming on, would be "appalling and heart-rending," Sherman replied that while he gave "full credit to your statement of the distress that will be occasioned," he would not revoke his orders for immediate resettlement. "They were not designed to meet the humanities of the case, but to prepare for the future struggle.... You cannot qualify war in harsher terms than I will. War is cruelty, and you cannot refine it.... You might as well appeal against the thunder storm as against these terrible hardships of war.... Now you must go," he said in closing, "and take with you your old and feeble, feed and nurse them, and build for them, in more quiet places, proper habitations to shield them against the weather until the mad passions of men cool down and allow the Union and peace once more to settle over your old homes at Atlanta. Yours in haste."

Hood attacked as usual, head down and full tilt, in response to a suggestion for a truce to permit the removal southward, through the lines, of the unhappy remnant of the city's population. He had, he said, no choice except to accede, but he added: "Permit me to say that the unprecedented measure you propose transcends, in studied and ingenious cruelty, all acts ever brought to my attention in the dark history of war. In the name of God and humanity, I protest."

"In the name of common sense," Sherman fired back, "I ask you not to appeal to a just God in such a sacrilegious manner. You who, in the midst of peace and prosperity, have plunged a nation into war — dark and cruel war — who dared and badgered us to battle, insulted our flag, seized our arsenals and forts." There followed an arm-long list of Confederate outrages, ending: "Talk thus to the marines, but not to me, who have seen these things.... If we must be enemies, let us be men and fight it out as we propose to do, and not deal in such hypocritical appeals to God and humanity. God will judge us in due time, and he will pronounce whether it be more humane to fight with a town full of women and the families of a brave people at our backs, or to remove them to places of safety among their own friends."

For two more days, though both agreed that "this discussion by two soldiers is out of place and profitless," the exchange continued, breathy but bloodless, before a ten-day truce was agreed on and the exodus began. Union troops escorted the refugees, with such clothes and bedding as they could carry, as far as Rough & Ready, where Hood's men took them in charge and saw them south across the fifteen-mile railroad gap to Lovejoy Station, within the rebel lines. Sherman was glad to see them go, and truth to tell had rather enjoyed the preceding altercation, which he saw as a sort of literary exercise, beneficial to his spleen, and in which he was convinced he had once more gotten the best of his opponent. But in other respects, having little or nothing to do with verbal fencing, he was far less satisfied, and a good deal more perturbed.

On September 8, the day he ordered Calhoun and his people to depart, he also issued a congratulatory order proclaiming to his soldiers that their capture of Atlanta "completed the grand task which has been assigned us by our Government." This was untrue. Welcome as the fall of the city was at this critical time — he was convinced, for one thing, that it assured Lincoln's reëlection, and for another he could present it, quite literally, to his troops as a crowning reward for four solid months of combat — his real objective, agreed on beforehand and identified by Grant in specific instructions, was the Army of Tennessee; he had been told to "break it up," and Atlanta had been intended merely to serve as the anvil upon which the rebel force was to be fixed and pounded till it shattered. That had been, and was, his true "grand task." Not only was Hood's army still in existence, it was relatively intact, containing close to 35,000 effectives, even with Wheeler gone for the past month; whereas Sherman's own, though twice as strong as Hood's at the time of occupation, started dwindling from the wholesale loss of veterans whose three-year enlistments ran out about the time the truce began. Subtractions from the top were even heavier in proportion. Schofield had to return for a time to Knoxville to attend to neglected administrative matters in his department, and Dodge, wounded soon after he received a promotion to major general, took off on sick leave, never to return; his corps was broken up to help fill the gaps in Howard's other two, whose commanders, Logan and Blair — "political soldiers," Sherman scornfully styled them — had been given leaves of absence to stump for Lincoln in their critical home states. Presently even George Thomas was gone, along with two of his nine infantry divisions, sent back to Tennessee when the news came down that Forrest was on the rampage there, scooping up rear-guard detachments and providing the rail repair gangs with more work than they could handle in a hurry.

Various possibilities obtained, even so, including a march on Macon, Selma, or Mobile; but what the army needed most just now was rest and refitment, a brief period in which to digest its gains and shake its diminished self together, while its leader pondered in tranquillity his next move. Fortified Atlanta seemed an excellent place for this, although the situation afforded little room for error. "I've got my wedge pretty deep," Sherman remarked in this connection, "and must look out I don't get my fingers pinched." One drawback was that the interlude surrendered the initiative to Hood, who had shown in the past that he would be quick to grasp it, however stunned his troops might be as a result of their recent failures, including the loss of the city in their charge. Wheeler's damage to the supply line running back to Chattanooga had long since been repaired, but it seemed likely that his chief would strike there again, this time in heavier force; perhaps, indeed, with all he had.

This was in fact what Hood intended, if only because he felt he had no other choice. Determined to do *some*thing, yet lacking the strength to mount a siege or risk another large-scale confrontation on the outskirts of Atlanta, he had begun to prepare for a rearward strike while exchanging verbal shafts with his opponent inside the city. First he asked Richmond for reinforcements, and was told: "Every effort [has been] made to bring forward reserves, militia, and detailed men for the purpose.... No other resource remains." This denial had been expected, but it was promptly followed by another that had not. By gubernatorial proclamation on September 10, one week after Atlanta's fall, Joe Brown withdrew the Georgia militia beyond Confederate reach, granting blanket furloughs for his "pets," as they were called, "to return to their homes and look for a time after other important interests," by which he meant the tending of their farms. Discouraged but not dissuaded by this lengthening of the numerical odds, Hood held to his plan for a move northward, requesting of the government that the 30,000 Andersonville inmates, ninety miles in his rear, be transferred beyond reach of the Federals in his front and thus permit him to shift his base from Lovejoy Station, on the Macon & Western, to Palmetto on the Atlanta & West Point; that is, from south of the city to southwest. This, he explained in outlining his proposed campaign, would open the way for him to recross the Chattahoochee, west of Marietta, for a descent on the blue supply line north of the river. Sherman most likely would follow to protect his communications, leaving a strong garrison to hold Atlanta; in which event Hood would be able to fight him with a far better chance of winning than if he tried to engage him hereabouts, with the odds at two-to-one. If, on the other hand, Sherman responded to the shift by moving against Augusta, Mobile, or some other point to the east or south, Hood would return and attack his rear. In any case, whatever risk was involved in his proposal, he was convinced that this was the time to act, since "Sherman is weaker now than he will be in the future, and I as strong as I can expect to be."

Richmond, approving this conditional raid-in-force, ordered the transfer of all able-bodied prisoners from Andersonville, near Americus, to stockades down in Florida. This began on September 21, by which time Hood had completed his twenty-mile shift due west to Palmetto, about the same distance southwest of Atlanta, and had his subordinates hard at work on preparations for the march north around Sherman's flank. They were still at it, four days later — September 25, a rainy Sunday that turned the red dust of their camps to mire — when Jefferson Davis arrived for a council of war.

He came for other purposes as well, including the need — even direr now than at the time of his other western trips, in early winter and late fall of the past two years, when Bragg had been the general in trouble — "to arouse all classes to united and desperate resistance." Outwardly at least, Davis himself never quailed or wavered under adversity, Stephen Mallory would testify after working close to him throughout the war. "He could listen to the announcement of defeat while expecting victory, or to a foreign dispatch destructive to hopes widely cherished, or to whispers that old friends were becoming cold or hostile, without exhibiting the slightest evidence of feeling beyond a change of color. Under such circumstances, his language temperate and bland, his voice calm and gentle, and his whole person at rest, he presented rather the appearance of a man, wearied and worn by care and labor, listening to something he knew all about, than of one receiving ruinous disclosures." But this reaction was by no means characteristic of the high-strung people, in or out of uniform, to and for whom he was responsible as Commander in Chief and Chief Executive: and it was especially uncharacteristic now that the Federal penetration of the heartland had regional leaders of the caliber of Brown and Aleck Stephens crying havoc and talking of calling the dogs of war to kennel. Leaving Richmond five days ago, the day after Early's defeat at Winchester provided a companion setback in the eastern theater, Davis remarked to a friend: "The first effect of disaster is always to spread a deeper gloom than is due to the occasion." Then he set out for Georgia, as he had done twice before, in an attempt to dispel or at any rate lighten the gloom that had gathered and deepened there since the fall of Atlanta, three weeks back.

Army morale was a linked concern. Addressing himself to this on the day of his arrival at Palmetto, he attempted to lift the spirits of the troops with a speech delivered extemporaneously to Cheatham's Tennesseans, who flocked to meet him at the station. "Be of good cheer," he told them, "for within a short while your faces will be turned homeward and your feet pressing the soil of Tennessee."

Shouts of approval greeted this extension of the plan Hood had proposed; but other responses had a different tone. "Johnston! Give us Johnston!" Davis heard men cry or mutter from the ranks, and though he made no reply to this, it pointed up another problem he had come west to examine at first hand — the question of possible changes in the structure of command. Hardee, for example, had recently repeated his request for a transfer that would free him from further service under Hood, who blamed him for the collapse of two of his three Atlanta sorties, as well as for his failure to whip the enemy at Jonesboro, which had brought on the fall of the city. So Hood said, at any rate, wiring Richmond: "It is of the utmost importance that Hardee should be relieved at once. He commands the best troops in this army. I must have another commander." One or the other clearly had to go. Now at Palmetto, in tandem interviews, Davis heard the two generals out, recriminations abounding, and arrived at a decision that pleased them both: Hood by replacing Hardee with Cheatham, his senior division commander, and Hardee by ordering him to proceed at once to Charleston, where he would head the Department of South Carolina, Georgia, and Florida.

That was Beauregard's old bailiwick, and he was there even now, conducting a rather superfluous inspection of the coastal defenses. But there would be no overlapping of duties when Hardee arrived, since Davis planned for the Creole to be gone by then, summoned west as the solution to another command problem in the Army of Tennessee, this one at the very top. In mid-September, just before he left Richmond, he had received from Samuel French, who led a division in Stewart's corps, a private communication reminiscent of the famous round-robin letter that reached him after Chickamauga. This one was signed only by French, though it was written, he said, at the request of several high-ranking friends "in regard to a feeling of depression more or less apparent in parts of this army." His suggestion — or theirs, for the tone of the letter was strangely indirect — was that the President "send one or two intelligent officers here to visit the different divisions and brigades to ascertain if that spirit of confidence so necessary for success has or has not been impaired within the past month or two." Hood was not mentioned by name or position, as Bragg had been in the earlier document, but he was clearly responsible for conditions in a command which he had assumed "within the past month or two" and from which, the letter implied, he ought to be removed. This, combined with the public outcry over the loss of Atlanta, was part of what prompted the President's visit, and even before he set out he had arrived at a tentative solution to the problem by inviting Beauregard to go along. Old Bory was down in Charleston at the time, and Davis could not wait for him. He did, however, ask R. E. Lee to find out whether the Louisianian would be willing to return to duty in the West. Frustrated by subservience to Lee for the three months since Petersburg came under formal siege, Beauregard replied that he would "obey with alacrity" any such order for a transfer, and Davis wired from Palmetto for the Creole to meet him in Augusta on his way back in early October.

Beauregard, receiving the summons, assumed that he was about to return, as Hood's successor, to command of the army that had been taken from him more than two years ago, after Shiloh and the evacuation of Corinth. In this he was mistaken: though not entirely. Davis had it in mind to put him in charge not only of Hood's but also of Taylor's department, the whole to be known as the Military Division of the West, containing all of Alabama and Mississippi, together with major parts of Georgia and Louisiana and most of Tennessee. Assigned primarily in an advisory capacity, he would exercise direct control of troops only when he was actually with them — and only then, in Davis's words, "whenever in your judgment the interests of your command render it expedient." This was the position in which Johnston had fretted so fearfully last year; "a political device," a later observer was to term its creation, "designed to silence the critics of Hood, satisfy the friends of Beauregard, and save face for the Administration." That was accurate enough, as far as it went, but for Davis the arrangement had two other pragmatic virtues. One was that Hood's accustomed rashness might be tempered, if not controlled, by the presence of an experienced superior close at hand, and the other was that there was no room left for Joe Johnston, whose return Davis was convinced would result in a retreat down the length of the Florida peninsula. In any case, Beauregard was highly acceptable to the generals Davis talked with at Palmetto, including Hood, and he was determined to offer him the post when they met in Augusta the following week.

Mainly, though, the presidential visit was concerned with the strategy Hood had evolved for drawing the blue army north by striking at its supply line beyond the Chattahoochee, where he would take up a strong defensive position inviting a disadvantageous attack. Now in discussion this was expanded and improved. If Sherman appeared too strong even then, or if Hood, as Davis put it, "should not find the spirit of his army such as to justify him in offering battle" at that point, he was to fall back down the Coosa River and through the mountains to Gadsden, Alabama, where he would establish a new base, supplied by the railroad from Selma to Blue Mountain, and there "fight a conclusive battle" on terrain even more advantageous to the defender; Sherman, drawn far from his own base back in Georgia, might then be annihilated. If, on the other hand, the Ohioan declined battle on those terms and returned to Atlanta, Hood would follow, and when Sherman, his supply line cut, moved from there, Hood would still pursue: either northward, across the Tennessee — which would undo the Federal gains of the past four months and open the way for a Confederate march on Nashville — or south or east, through Selma or Montgomery to the Gulf or through Macon or Augusta to the Atlantic, in which case the Union rear could be assaulted. That was the expanded plan, designed to cover all contingencies, as Hood and the Commander in Chief developed it over the course of the three-day visit. Then on the evening of September 27 Davis took his leave.

In Macon next morning, at a benefit for the impoverished Atlanta refugees, he took up the spirit-lifting task he had begun at Palmetto when he told the Tennessee soldiers their faces would soon turn homeward. "What though misfortune has befallen our arms from Decatur to Jonesboro," he declared, "our cause is not lost. Sherman cannot keep up his long line of communications; retreat sooner or later he must. And when that day comes, the fate that befell the army of the French Empire in its retreat from Moscow will be re-enacted. Our cavalry and our people will harass and destroy his army, as did the Cossacks that of Napoleon, and the Yankee general, like him, will escape with only a bodyguard...."

"Let no one despond," he said in closing, and repeated the words the following day in Montgomery, speaking at the Capitol where he had been inaugurated forty-three months ago. "There be some men," he told the Alabamians, in support of his advice against despondence, "who when they look at the sun can only see a speck upon it. I am of a more sanguine temperament perhaps, but I have striven to behold our affairs with a cool and candid temperance of heart, and, applying to them the most rigid test, am more confident the longer I behold the progress of the war.... We should marvel and thank God for the great achievements which have crowned our efforts."

Closeted that night with Richard Taylor, who had transferred his headquarters from Meridian to Selma, he was glad to learn the particulars of Forrest's current raid into Middle Tennessee, but disappointed to be told that any hopes he retained for securing reinforcements from beyond the Mississippi were quite groundless, not only because the situation there would not permit it, but also because of the gunboats Taylor had had to dodge, even at night in a small boat, when he returned. Davis was able to counter this with news that Hood had begun today a crossing of the Chattahoochee near Campbelltown, twenty miles southwest of Atlanta, for his strike at the Federal life line. Taylor was pleased to hear it, remarking that the maneuver would no doubt "cripple [Sherman] for a time and delay his projected movements." Whatever enthusiasm surged up in him on hearing of this new offensive was certainly well contained. Moreover: "At the same time," he later wrote of the exchange, "I did not disguise my conviction that the best we could hope for was to protract the struggle until spring. It was for statesmen, not soldiers, to deal with the future."

This was chilling in its implications, coming as it did from a friend and kinsman whose opinion he respected and whose experience covered all three major theaters of the war, but Davis refused to be daunted; like Nelson off Copenhagen, putting the telescope to his blind eye, he declined to see these specks upon the Confederate sun. The two men parted to meet no more in the course of a conflict Taylor believed was drawing to a close, and Davis resumed his journey eastward from Montgomery next day, joined en route by Hardee for the scheduled meeting with Beauregard in Augusta on October 2, the President's second Sunday away from Richmond. Old Bory's spirits took a drop when he learned that he was to occupy an advisory rather than a fighting post, but they soon revived at the prospect of conferring with Hood on plans for reversing the western tide of battle. In the end, he was as pleased as

Hardee was with his new assignment, and both generals sat on the rostrum with their chief the following day at a patriotic rally. "We must beat Sherman; we must march into Tennessee," Davis told the Augustans. "There we will draw from 20,000 to 30,000 to our standard, and, so strengthened, we must push the enemy back to the banks of the Ohio and thus give the peace party of the North an accretion no puny editorial can give." Such was the high point of his last speech in Georgia, and having made it he presented the two generals to the crowd. Beauregard, who had fired the first gun of the war, was cheered for saying that he "hoped to live to fire the last," and Hardee, a native son, drew loud applause when he reported that Hood had recently told him "he intended to lay his claws upon the state road in rear of Sherman, and, having once fixed them there, it was not his intention to let them loose their hold."

Next day, October 4 — by which time the three speakers had reached or were moving toward their separate destinations: Beauregard west, Hardee east, and Davis north to the South Carolina capital — Hood had carried out at least the first part of this program. Completing his crossing of the Chattahoochee before September ended, he struck the Western & Atlantic at Big Shanty and Acworth, capturing their garrisons, and now was on the march for Allatoona, the principal Union supply base near the Etowah. Best of all, Sherman had taken the bait and was hurrying northward from Atlanta with most of his army, apparently eager for the showdown battle this gray maneuver had been fashioned to provoke. While the opening stage of the raid was in progress, and even as Hood's troops were tearing up some nine miles of track around Big Shanty, Davis delivered in Columbia the last in his current series of addresses designed to lift the spirits of a citizenry depressed by the events of the past two months.

"South Carolina has struggled nobly in the war, and suffered many sacrifices," he declared, beginning as usual with praise for the people of the state in which he spoke. "But if there be any who feel that our cause is in danger, that final success may not crown our efforts, that we are not stronger today than when we began this struggle, that we are not able to continue the supplies to our armies and our people, let all such read a contradiction in the smiling face of our land and in the teeming evidences of plenty which everywhere greet the eye. Let them go to those places where brave men are standing in front of the foe, and there receive the assurance that we shall have final success and that every man who does not live to see his country free will see a freeman's grave." He himself was on his way back from such a visit, and he had been reassured by what he saw. "I have just returned from that army from which we have had the saddest accounts — the Army of Tennessee — and I am able to bear you words of good cheer. That army has increased in strength since the fall of Atlanta. It has risen in tone; its march is onward, its face looking to the front. So far as I am able to judge, General Hood's strategy has been good and his conduct has been gallant. His eye is now fixed upon a point far beyond that where he was assailed by the enemy. He hopes soon to have his hand upon Sherman's line of communications, and to fix it where he can hold it. And if but a half — nay, one fourth — of the men to whom the service has a right will give him their strength, I see no chance for Sherman to escape from a defeat or a disgraceful retreat. I therefore hope, in view of all the contingencies of the war, that within thirty days that army which has so boastfully taken up its winter quarters in the heart of the Confederacy will be in search of a crossing of the Tennessee River." Having claimed as much, he pressed on and claimed more. "I believe it is in the power of the men of the Confederacy to plant our banners on the banks of the Ohio, where we shall say to the Yankee: 'Be quiet, or we shall teach you another lesson.'"

So he said, bowing low to the applause that followed, and after a day's rest — badly needed, since two weeks of travel on the buckled strap-iron of a variety of railroads amounted to a form of torture rivaling the rack — ended his fifteen-day absence from Richmond on the morning of October 6. The warm bright pleasant weather of Virginia's early fall belied the strain its capital was under; Fort Harrison had toppled just one week ago, creating a dent in the city's defenses north of the James, and the fight next day at Peebles Farm, though tactically a victory, had obliged Lee to extend his already thin-stretched Petersburg lines another two miles west. For Davis, however, any day that brought him back to his family was an occasion for rejoicing. And rejoice he did: especially over its newest member, three-month-old Varina Anne. Born in late June, while the guns were roaring on Kennesaw and Jubal Early was heading north from Lynchburg, she would in time be referred to as the "Daughter of the Confederacy," but to her father she was "Winnie," already his pet name for her mother, or "Pie-Cake," which her sister and brothers presently shortened to "Pie." He was glad to be back with her and the others, Maggie, Little Jeff, Billy, and his wife, who was pleased, despite her distress at the wear he showed, to hear how well the trip had gone in regard to his efforts to lift the flagging morale of the people with predictions of great success for Hood — whose troops were moving northward even now — and "defeat or a disgraceful retreat" for Sherman.

Grant, for one, disagreed with this assessment of the situation in North Georgia. Informed of Davis's late-September prediction that the fate that crumpled Napoleon in Russia now awaited Sherman outside Atlanta, he thought it over briefly, then inquired: "Who is to furnish the snow for this Moscow retreat?"

Afterwards, Sherman took this one step further, professing to have been delighted that the rebel leader's "vainglorious boasts" had in

War Is Cruelty . . . [611]

effect presented "the full key to his future designs" to those whom they were intended to undo; "To be forewarned was to be forearmed," he explained. But that was written later, when he seemed to have taken what he called "full advantage of the occasion." Davis in fact had said very little more in his recent impromptu speeches, including his proposal "to plant our banners on the banks of the Ohio," than he (and, indeed, many other Confederate spokesmen) had expressed on previous tours undertaken to lift spirits that had sagged under the burden of defeat. As for Hood's reported promise to "lay his claws" on the railroad north of Atlanta, they were already fixed there by the time Sherman heard from his spies or read in the papers of what Davis or Hardee was supposed to have said — days after Hood's whole army was across the Chattahoochee in his rear. Besides, the red-haired Ohioan was far too busy by then, attempting to deal with this newly developed threat to his life line, to conjecture much about what Hood might or might not have in mind as a next step.

Leaving Slocum's corps to hold Atlanta, he began recrossing the Chattahoochee with the other five — some 65,000 of all arms, exclusive of the two divisions sent back to Tennessee with Thomas the week before — when he discovered on October 3 that Hood, after crossing in force near Campbelltown, was moving north through Powder Springs, apparently with the intention of getting astride the Western & Atlantic somewhere around or beyond Marietta. Sherman rushed a division from Howard north by rail, under Brigadier General John M. Corse, to cover Rome in case the graybacks veered in that direction, but by the time he got the last of his men over the river next day he learned that the rebs had taken Big Shanty and Acworth, along with their garrisons, and had torn up nine miles of track on their way to seize his main supply base at Allatoona, which they would reach tomorrow. He got a message through for Corse to shift his troops by rail from Rome to Allatoona, reinforcing its defenders, and to hang on there till the rest of the army joined him.

Corse complied, but only by the hardest. When Sherman climbed Kennesaw next morning, October 5, he could see the Confederate main body encamped to the west around Lost Mountain, his own men at work repairing the railroad past Big Shanty, just ahead, and gunsmoke lazing up from Allatoona Pass, a dozen air-line miles to the north, where Corse was making his fight. Hood had detached Stewart's corps for the Acworth strike, and Stewart, before heading back to rejoin Hood last night, had in turn detached French's division to extend the destruction to the Etowah. "General Sherman says hold fast; we are coming," the Kennesaw signal station wigwagged Allatoona over the heads of the attackers. Corse — a twenty-nine-year-old Iowan who had spent two years at West Point before returning home to study law and run for public office, only to lose the election and enter the army, as was said, "to relieve the pain of political defeat" — had arrived, although with less than half of his division, in time to receive a white-flag note in which French allowed him five minutes "to avoid a needless effusion of blood" by surrendering unconditionally. He declined, replying: "We are prepared for the 'needless effusion of blood' whenever it is agreeable to you." The engagement that followed was as savage as might have been expected from this exchange. Corse had just under 2000 men, French just over 3000, and their respective losses were 706 and 799 killed, wounded, or captured. After two of the three redoubts had fallen, Corse withdrew his survivors to the third, near the head of the pass, and kept up the resistance, despite a painful face wound and the loss of more than a third of his command. By 4 o'clock, having intercepted wigwag messages that help was on the way from the 60,000 Federals in his rear, French decided to pull out before darkness and Sherman overtook him. Corse was exultant: so much so that when Sherman, still on Kennesaw, inquired by flag as to his condition the following day, he signaled back: "I am short a cheekbone and an ear, but am able to whip all hell yet."

Such was the stuff of which legends were made, including this one of the so-called Battle of Allatoona Pass. "Hold the fort, for I am coming," journalists quoted Sherman as having wigwagged from the top of Kennesaw, and that became the title of P. P. Bliss's revival hymn, inspired by the resolute valor Corse and his chief had shown in defending a position of such great natural strength that the latter had chosen not to risk an attack when he found it looming across his southward path in May. French, moreover, got clean away, long before any blue relief arrived, and when Sherman encountered the high-strung young Iowa brigadier a few days later he was surprised to find on his cheek only a small bandage, removal of which revealed no more than a scratch where the bullet had nicked him in passing, and no apparent damage to the ear he had claimed was lost. Sherman laughed. "Corse, they came damned near missing you, didn't they?" he said.

He laughed, yet the fact was he found small occasion for humor in the present situation. Hood withdrew his reunited army westward beyond Lost Mountain to New Hope Church and Dallas. There he stopped, or anyhow paused. Sherman, however, had no intention of reentering that tangled wasteland, even though this meant leaving the initiative to an adversary who had just shown that he would use it to full advantage and now seemed about to do as much again. Sure enough, when the sun came up on October 7 the graybacks had disappeared. Wiring Slocum that they had "gone off south," Sherman warned that they might be doubling back for a surprise attack on Atlanta, and when he discovered later in the day that they were actually headed north, he charged that Hood was an eccentric: "I cannot guess his movements as

I could those of Johnston, who was a sensible man and only did sensible things."

Delayed by an all-day rain next day, he did not reach Allatoona until October 9, when he heard from scouts that the butternut column was on the march for Rome. But that was not true either, it turned out. Crossing the Coosa River west of Rome, then moving fast up the right bank of the Oostanaula, Hood struck Resaca on October 12 and wrecked a dozen miles of railroad between there and Dalton, where he captured the thousand-man garrison next day and then ripped up another five miles of track on his way to Tunnel Hill, where the contest for North Georgia had begun five months ago. When Sherman moved against him from Rome and Kingston, he fell back through Snake Creek Gap to a position near LaFayette, some twenty miles south of where Bragg and Rosecrans had clashed about this time last year at Chickamauga, and there took up a defensive stance, both flanks stoutly anchored and a clear field of fire to his front. Sherman came on after him from Resaca, reaching LaFayette on October 17. By the time he got his troops arrayed for battle, however, Hood was gone again — vanished westward, across the Alabama line, into even more rugged terrain where Sherman would be obliged to risk defeat a long way from his base. Exasperated, the red-head complained bitterly that everything his adversary had done for the past three weeks was "inexplicable by any common-sense theory." Recalling Jefferson Davis's boast of Hood's intentions: "Damn him," he said testily of the latter. "If he will go to the Ohio River I will give him rations.... Let him go north. My business is down South."

Whether this last was to be the case or not was strictly up to the general-in-chief, and that was the main cause of Sherman's irritability through this difficult and uncertain time, even more than the loss of much of the railroad in his rear. The railroad could be rebuilt — would in fact be back in use within ten days — but Hood's evident ability to smash it, more or less at will, might have an adverse influence on the decision Grant had been pondering for the past month, ever since Sherman first made it clear what he meant when he said that his business was "down South."

Back in early May, at the start of his campaign to "knock Jos. Johnston," a staffer had asked what he planned to do at its end; "Salt water," he replied, flicking the ash from his cigar. Mobile and the Gulf had been what he meant, but thanks to Farragut there was not much left in that direction worth the march. He now had a different body of water in mind, rimming a different coast. In brief, his proposal — first made on September 20, while the refugee truce was still in effect below Atlanta — was that the navy secure and provision a base for him on the Atlantic seaboard — probably Savannah, since that was the closest port — and his army would "sweep the whole state of Georgia" on its way there. Such a march, he told Grant, would be "more than fatal to the possibility of Southern independence. They may stand the fall of Richmond, but not of all Georgia," he declared, and added a jocular, upbeat flourish to close his plea: "If you can whip Lee and I can march to the Atlantic, I think Uncle Abe will give us a twenty days' leave of absence to see the young folks."

Grant had doubts. With its attention fixed on Wilmington, the last major port still open to blockade runners, the navy would not willingly divert its strength to a secondary target more than two hundred miles down the coast; besides which, the mounting of such an effort would take months, and previous attempts against Charleston had shown there was little assurance of success, even if every ironclad in the fleet was employed in the attack. His main objection, however, was the continued existence of Hood's army. Speaking in Georgia, Alabama, and South Carolina, hard on the heels of Sherman's proposal, Jefferson Davis announced plans for a northward campaign that might well succeed if Sherman marched eastward and thus removed from Hood's path the one force that could stop him. Grant said as much, opposing the expedition on both counts, but Sherman replied that he did not really need for the navy to take Savannah before he got there; all he wanted was for supply ships to be standing by, ready to steam in after he reduced the city from the landward side. As for Hood, Thomas was on the way to Nashville even now with two divisions which he would combine with troops already there and others on the way; "Why will it not do to leave Tennessee to the forces which Thomas has, and the reserves soon to come to Nashville, and for me to destroy Atlanta and march across Georgia to Savannah or Charleston, breaking roads and doing irreparable damage? We cannot remain on the defensive."

That was written October 1. By the time the message reached City Point, Forrest had rampaged through Middle Tennessee, smashing installations within thirty miles of Nashville, and Hood was across the Chattahoochee, ripping up track on the Western & Atlantic thirty miles north of Atlanta. Grant saw these strikes as confirmation of his objection to Sherman's departure, but Sherman took them as proof of his contention that he was wasting time by remaining where he was; that it was, in fact, as he insisted on October 9, "a physical impossibility to protect the roads, now that Hood, Forrest, Wheeler, and the whole batch of devils are turned loose.... By attempting to hold the roads, we will lose a thousand men each month and will gain no result." Having said as much, he returned to his plea that he himself be "turned loose" to make for the coast. This time, noting that he had some 8000 head of cattle on hand, as well as 3,000,000 rations of bread, and expected to find "plenty of forage in the interior of the state," he went into logistical details of the expedition. "I propose that we break up the railroad from Chattanooga forward, and that we strike out with our wagons for Milledgeville, Millen, and Savannah. Until we can repopulate Georgia, it is useless for us to occupy it; but the utter destruction of its roads, houses, and people will cripple their military resources.... I can make this march, and make Georgia howl!"

Hood by then had retired westward, but soon he was on the go again, about to throw another punch at the railroad forty miles farther north. Even before it landed, Sherman predicted that it would be successful and renewed his appeal to be spared the patchwork soldiering that would follow, urging Grant to let him "send back all my wounded and unserviceable men, and with my effective army move through Georgia, smashing things to the sea. Hood may turn into Tennessee and Kentucky," he admitted, "but I believe he will be forced to follow me." In any case, Thomas could handle him, he said, and best of all, "instead of being on the defensive, I will be on the offensive. Instead of my guessing at what he means to do, he will have to guess at my plans. The difference in war would be fully 25 percent.... Answer quick, as I know we will not have the telegraph long."

Grant's reply next day, October 12 — the day Hood landed astride the railroad at Resaca — was encouraging. "On reflection I think better of your proposition," he wired back. "It will be much better to go south than to be forced to come north." He suggested that the move be made with "every wagon, horse, mule, and hoof of stock, as well as the Negroes," and that plenty of spare weapons be taken along to "put them in the hands of Negro men," who could serve as otherwise unobtainable reinforcements on the march. All the same, his approval was only tentative, not final, and Sherman continued to fume, irked in front by Hood and from the rear by Grant.

The former got away westward again, through Snake Creek and Ship's gaps, to a position just below LaFayette, which he abandoned at the approach of the blue army, and fell back down the valley of the Chattooga River, across the Alabama line. "It was clear to me that he had no intention to meet us in open battle," Sherman later wrote, "and the lightness and celerity of his army convinced me that I could not possibly catch him on a stern-chase." Angry at being drawn in the direction he least wanted to go — and resentful, above all, at the mounting proof of his error in having turned back to Atlanta, when the city fell to Slocum in his rear, instead of pressing after Hood to achieve the true purpose of his campaign — the red-head called a halt at Gaylesville, thirty miles short of Gadsden, and there continued to fret and fume as October wore away, still with no definite go-ahead from the general-in-chief. Evidence of his snappishness appeared in a telegram he sent a cavalry brigadier, posted at Calhoun on rear-guard duty, when he heard that a sniper had taken pot shots at cars along the newly repaired Western & Atlantic: "Cannot you send over about Fairmont and Adairsville, burn ten or twelve houses of known secessionists, kill a few at random, and let them know that it will be repeated every time a train is fired on from Resaca to Kingston?"

Across the way at Gadsden, while Sherman thus was breathing fire and threatening random slaughter, Hood's troubles were not so much with his superior, Beauregard, as they were with his subordinates, who he felt had let him down. Drawn up for combat near LaFayette the week before, he had "expected that a forward movement of one hundred miles would reinspirit the officers and men to a degree to impart to them confidence, enthusiasm, and hope of victory," but when he took a vote at a council of war, assembled on the eve of what he intended as an all-out effort to whip Sherman, "the opinion was unanimous that although the army was much improved in spirit, it was not in a condition to risk battle against the numbers reported." Disappointed, he withdrew down the Chattooga Valley and the Coosa River to Gadsden for a meeting on October 21 with Beauregard, who had formally assumed command of the new Military Division of the West only four days ago. To the Creole's great surprise, Hood presented for his approval a broad-scale plan, conceived en route, for "marching into Tennessee, with a hope to establish our line eventually in Kentucky."

'Broad-scale' was perhaps not word enough; spread-eagle was more like it. But knowing as he did that time was on the side of the Union — that delay would enable Thomas to complete his buildup in Tennessee and combine with Sherman to corner and crush the fugitive gray army, wherever it might turn — Hood was determined to extend and enlarge the flea-bite offensive by which he had managed, ever since he left Palmetto three weeks back, to keep his adversaries edgy and off-balance. A northward march, into or past the mouth of the Federal lion, was admittedly a risky undertaking, but he was of the Lee-Jackson school, whose primary tenet was that the smaller force must take the longest chances, and moreover he had before him the example of Bragg, who by just such a maneuver after the fall of Corinth, two years ago, had reversed the gloomy situation in this same theater by dispersing the superior enemy combinations then being assembled to bring on his destruction.

His plan, he said, was to cross the Tennessee River at Guntersville, which would place him within reach of Sherman's single-strand rail supply line in the delicate Stevenson-Bridgeport area, and move promptly on Nashville, smashing Thomas's scattered detachments on the way. Possessed of the Tennessee capital, he would resupply his army from its stores, thicken his ranks with volunteers drawn to his banner, and move on through Kentucky to the Ohio, where he would be in a position to threaten Cincinnati and receive still more recruits from the Bluegrass. If Sherman followed, as expected, Hood would then be strong enough to whip him; after which he would either send reinforcements to beleaguered Richmond or else take his whole command across the Cumberlands to come up in rear of the blue host outside Petersburg. Or if Sherman did not follow, but instead took off southward for the Gulf or eastward for the Atlantic, Hood explained that he would move by the interior lines for an attack on Grant "at least two weeks before he, Sherman, could render him assistance." Such a shift, he said, winding up in a blaze of glory, "would defeat Grant and allow General Lee, in command of our combined armies, to march upon Washington or turn upon and annihilate Sherman."

Old Bory was amazed, partly by the bold sweep of the plan, which seemed to him as practicable as it was entrancing, and partly by the shock of recognition, occasioned by its resemblance to the half-dozen or so which he himself had submitted to friends and superiors over the course of the past three years, invariably without their being adopted. One difference was that he had always insisted on heavy reinforcement at the outset, whereas Hood proposed to strike with what he had. If this seemed rash, Beauregard could see that it might well be a virtue in the present crisis, not only because no reinforcements were available, but also because it would save time, and time was of the essence in a situation depending largely on how rapidly the invaders moved — especially against Thomas, who must not be given a chance to pull his scattered forces together for the protection of the capital in his care. In any case, approval was little more than a formality; Hood had informed the government two days ago that he intended to cross the Tennessee, and only yesterday had wired ahead to Richard Taylor, whose department he had entered for the crossing: "I will move tomorrow for Guntersville." Beauregard did not withhold his blessing, though after much discussion he insisted that Wheeler's cavalry, which had rejoined the army near Rome ten days ago, be left behind to operate against Sherman's communications and attack his rear if he set out south or east, through otherwise undefended regions between Atlanta and the Gulf or the Atlantic. Hood readily agreed to this subtraction when the Creole added that Forrest would join him on the march, replacing Wheeler, as soon as he and his troopers returned from their current raid on Johnsonville; which, incidentally, would add to the Federal confusion Hood hoped to provoke when he moved on Nashville.

Word went out to the camps that the shift northward would begin at daylight, and their commander later recalled that the news was greeted with "that genuine Confederate shout so familiar to every Southern soldier." By this he meant the rebel yell, the loudest of which no doubt came from the bivouacs of the Tennesseans. Davis had told them four weeks ago that their feet would soon be pressing native soil, and now they whooped with delight at finding the promise about to be kept.

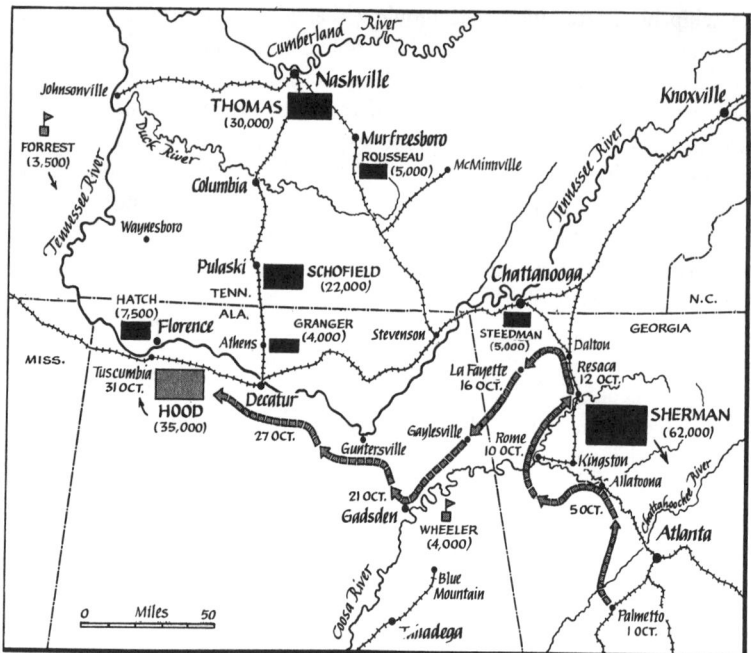

It was kept, although by no means as promptly as they and Beauregard expected when they parted at Gadsden next morning. Guntersville, thirty-odd miles northwest, turned out to be crowded with bluecoats, and Hood decided to veer west for a crossing at Decatur, just over forty miles downriver. However, when he drew close to there on October 26, after four days on the march, he found that it, like Guntersville, was too stoutly garrisoned to be stormed without heavier losses than he felt he could afford; so he pressed on for Courtland, twenty miles beyond Decatur, which he bypassed the following day. It was not until then that Beauregard, who had been off making supply arrangements and was miffed at not having been informed of the change in route, caught up with the column some fifty miles west of its original objective. He was aggrieved not only because the detour had ruled out the disruptive strike at Stevenson, now clearly beyond range of the butternut marchers, but also because of the loss of time, which Sherman and Thomas would surely use to their advantage. He had said from the start that celerity was Hood's best hope for success in this long-odds undertaking; yet five whole days had already been spent in search of a crossing that still had not been reached. Nor was that the worst of it. Informed by his engineers that they did not have enough pontoons to bridge the rain-swollen Tennessee at Courtland, Hood decided to push on and use the partly demolished railway span at Tuscumbia, another twenty-five miles downstream and well over eighty from Guntersville, where he had intended to ford the river a week ago. At Tuscumbia on the last day of October, he further alarmed his superior by announcing that he lacked sufficient provisions for the march that would follow the crossing, as well as shoes for his men and the horses in Jackson's two slim brigades, which were all the cavalry he would have until Forrest returned from Johnsonville, more than a hundred miles downriver to the north.

Taylor had unwelcome news for them in that regard as well. Unmindful of the need for haste, he had waited till Hood drew near Decatur on the 26th to send a courier summoning Forrest, who had left five days ago, and even then had told him to complete his mission before heading back. Hood took this, then and later, as evidence that he had done well to shift his infantry westward in search of a crossing, since this reduced the gap between it and the cavalry he was obliged to wait for anyhow. Moreover, while he marked time at Tuscumbia, doing what he could to repair his supply deficiencies and giving his men some well-earned rest through the first fine days of November, word came back that the delay had perhaps been worth the vexation after all, adding as it did a highly colorful chapter to the legend surrounding the Wizard of the Saddle.

After reaching the Tennessee River near the Kentucky line on October 28, thirty miles north of Johnsonville, Forrest converted a portion of his 3500 troopers into literal horse marines and put them aboard two Union vessels, the gunboat *Undine* and the transport *Venus*, which he captured by posting batteries at both ends of a five-mile stretch of river to prevent their escape when he took them under fire with other guns along the bank. For three days, November 1–3, while this improvised two-boat navy molested traffic and drew attention northward, he led his horsemen south, up the west bank of the swollen Tennessee, to carry out the devastation that was the purpose of his raid. Well before midday November 4, after losing the *Venus* in an engagement with two gunboats and burning the eight-gun *Undine* to prevent her recapture, the two divisions were directly opposite Johnsonville, masked from view by trees and brush. While Morton was sneaking his guns into position, under orders to open fire at 2 o'clock, Forrest examined with his binoculars the unsuspecting target on the far side of the half-mile-wide river. Three gunboats, eleven transports, and eighteen barges were moored at the wharves, aswarm with workers unloading stores, and beyond them, spread out around a stockade fortress on high ground, warehouses bulged with supplies and acres of open storage were piled ten feet high with goods of every description, covered with tarpaulins to protect them from the weather. Two freight trains were being made up for the run to Nashville, just under eighty miles away, and neither the soldiers at work nor the officers scattered among them seemed aware that they were in any more danger now than they had been at any time since the base — named for the military governor who was Lincoln's running mate in the election only four days off — was put in operation, six months back.

Promptly at 2 o'clock they found out better. Morton having synchronized the watches of his chiefs of section, all ten pieces went off with an enormous bang that seemed to come from a single heavy cannon. For nearly an hour, after this introductory clap of thunder out of a cloudless sky, their fire was concentrated on the gunboats, the most dangerous enemy weapon, and when these were abandoned by their crews, who left them to burn and sink with the transports and barges they had been ordered to protect, the rebel artillerists shifted their attention to the landward installations, including the hilltop fortress whose unpracticed cannoneers replied wildly, blinded by smoke from riverside sheds and warehouses that had been set afire by sparks from the burning wharves and exploding vessels down below. Soon all those acres of high-piled stores were a mass of flames, and the exultant rebel gunners chose individual targets of opportunity, neglected until now. Perhaps the most spectacular of these was a warehouse on high ground, which, when struck and set afire, turned out to be stocked with several hundred barrels of whiskey that burst from the heat and sent a crackling blue-flame river of bourbon pouring down the hillside. Tantalized by the combined aroma of burnt liquor, roasting coffee beans, and frizzled bacon, wafted to them through a reek of gunsmoke, Morton's hungry veterans howled with delight and regret as they kept heaving shells into the holocaust they had created across the way. Forrest himself took a hand in the fun, directing the fire of one piece. "Elevate the breech of that gun a little lower!" he shouted, and the crew had little trouble understanding this unorthodox correction of the range. Within two hours all of Johnsonville was ablaze, resulting in a scene that "beggared description," according to one Federal who confined himself to the comment that it was "awfully sublime."

It was also awfully expensive. The base commander later put his loss at $2,200,000, taking the burned-out steamers and barges into account, but not the three sunken gunboats — four, including the *Undine*, subtracted during the naval phase of the raid, along with three more transports and three barges, mounting a total of 32 guns. Forrest's estimate of $6,700,000 included all of these, and probably came closer to the truth. His own loss, over-all, was two men killed and nine wounded, plus two guns lost when the *Venus* was recaptured. Retiring southward by the glare of flames still visible when he made camp six miles away, he encountered in the course of the next few days a series of couriers from Beauregard, all bearing orders for him to report at once to Hood, who was waiting at Tuscumbia for the outriders he would need on his march north. Forrest did what he could to hurry, but the going was slow through the muddy Tennessee bottoms, especially for the artillery. Even with sixteen horses to each piece, spelled by oxen impressed from farms adjoining the worst stretches along the way, he could see that he would need more than a week to reach Hood in Northwest Alabama.

Beauregard's distress at this development was matched by opposite reactions up the Coosa and beyond the Tennessee. Not only did the delay give Thomas added time to prepare for the blow Hood's drawn-out march had warned him was about to land; it also prompted Sherman to send still more reinforcements to Nashville, even while putting the final touches to his plan for making Georgia howl by slogging roughshod across it to the sea.

Grant by now had assented unconditionally to the expedition, though not until he recovered from a last-minute fit of qualms brought on by the news that Hood was headed north. Sherman at Gaylesville had not known that the gray army had left Gadsden, thirty miles away, until it turned up near Decatur, ninety miles to the west, on October 26. His reaction, once Hood's departure had ruled out a confrontation near the Alabama-Georgia line, was to send Stanley's corps to strengthen Thomas, and when he learned that Hood was still in motion westward, apparently intending to force a crossing at Tuscumbia, he also detached Schofield's one-corps Army of the Ohio and directed that A. J. Smith's divisions return at once from Missouri to join in the defense of Middle Tennessee. Between them, Stanley, Schofield, and Smith had close to 40,000 men, and these, added to those already on hand — including more than half of Sherman's cavalry, sent back earlier; sizeable garrisons at Murfreesboro, Chattanooga, Athens, and Florence; and recruits coming down from Kentucky and Ohio, in response to Forrest's early-October penetration of the region below Nashville — would give Thomas about twice as many troops as Hood could bring against him. Surely that was ample, even though most of them were badly scattered, others were green, and some had not arrived. Best of all, however, from Sherman's point of view, this new arrangement provided a massive antidote for dealing with Grant's reawakened fears as to what might happen if Old Pap was left to face the invasion threat alone. "Do you not think it advisable, now that Hood has gone so far north, to entirely ruin him before starting on your proposed campaign?" Grant inquired on November 1, and added, rather more firmly: "If you see a chance of destroying Hood's army, attend to that first, and make your other move secondary."

This, of all things, was the one Sherman wanted least to hear, and in his reply he marshaled his previous arguments in redoubled opposition. "No single army can catch Hood," he declared, "and I am convinced that the best results will follow from our defeating Jeff. Davis's cherished plan of making me leave Georgia by maneuvering." Edgy and apprehensive, fearing a negative reaction, he followed this with a second, more emphatic plea, before there was time for an answer to the first. "If I turn back, the whole effect of my campaign will be lost. By my movements I have thrown Beauregard (Hood) well to the west, and Thomas will have ample time and sufficient troops to hold him.... I am clearly of opinion that the best results will follow my contemplated movement through Georgia."

To his great relief, Grant wired back on November 2 that he was finally persuaded that Thomas would "be able to take care of Hood and destroy him." Moreover, he added, echoing his lieutenant's words in closing, "I really do not see that you can withdraw from where you are to follow Hood without giving up all we have gained in territory. I say, then, go as you propose."

Here at last was the go-ahead Sherman had been seeking all along, and now that he had it he moved fast, as if in fear that it might be revoked. Trains that had been shuttling between Chattanooga and Atlanta for the past two months, heavy-laden coming down and empty going back, now made their runs the other way around, returning all but the supplies he would take along in wagons when he set out for the sea with his four remaining corps, two from what was left of the Army of the Cumberland, under Slocum, and two from his old Army of the Tennessee, under Howard. They numbered better than 60,000 of all arms, including a single division of cavalry under Kilpatrick. He saw this mainly as an infantry operation, much like the one against Meridian last year, and had ordered the rest of his troopers back to Nashville for reorganization under James Wilson, who had recently been promoted to major general and sent by Grant to see what he could do about the poor showing western horsemen had been making ever since the start of the campaign. Sherman might have taken him along, a welcome addition on a march into the unknown, except that Thomas would most likely need him worse. Besides, he said, "I know that Kilpatrick is a hell of a damned fool, but I want just that sort of a man to command my cavalry on this expedition."

In "high feather," as he nearly always was when he was busy, he reëstablished headquarters at Kingston, the main-line railroad junction on the Etowah east of Rome, and there, with trains grinding north and rattling south at all hours of the day and night, supervised the final runs before the Western & Atlantic was closed down and its several depot garrisons withdrawn to become part of Major General J. B. Steedman's command at Chattanooga, on call for service under Thomas against Hood. His own army seemed to Sherman in splendid condition, fattened by veterans returning from thirty-day reënlistment furloughs, yet trimmed for hard use by evacuating all who were judged by surgeons not to be in shape for the 300-mile cross-Georgia march. On Sunday, November 6, he took time out to compose a farewell letter to Grant, a general statement of his intention, as he put it, "to act in such a manner against the material resources of the South as utterly to negative Davis' boasted threat." While he wrote, paymasters were active in all the camps, seeing to it that the soldiers would be in an appreciative frame of mind to support the Administration in the election two days off. "If we can march a well-appointed army right through his territory, it is a demonstration to the world, foreign and domestic, that we have a power which Davis cannot resist. This may not be war, but rather statesmanship. Nevertheless it is overwhelming to my mind that there are thousands of people abroad and in the South who reason thus: If the North can march an army right through the South, it is proof positive that the North can prevail."

He would set out, he told his chief, hard on the heels of Lincoln's reëlection — "which is assured" — and would thereby have the advantage of the confusion, not to say consternation, that event would provoke in the breasts of secessionists whose heartland he would be despoiling. What he would do after he reached Savannah he would decide when he got there and got back in touch with City Point. Meantime, he said, "I will not attempt to send couriers back, but trust to the Richmond papers to keep you well advised."

Grant — observing with hard-won equanimity the unusual spectacle of the two main western armies, blue and gray, already more than two hundred miles apart, about to take off in opposite directions — replied next day: "Great good luck go with you. I believe you will be eminently successful, and at worst can only make a march less fruitful than is hoped for."

★ ★ ★

In Richmond that same day, November 7 — election eve beyond the Potomac — Congress was welcomed back into session by a message from the Chief Executive, who had continued in Virginia the efforts made on his Georgia trip to lift spirits depressed by the outcome of the Hood-Sherman contest for Atlanta. Indeed, Davis went further here today in his denial that the South could be defeated, no matter what calamities attended her resistance to the force that would deny her independence.

After speaking of "the delusion fondly cherished [by the enemy] that the capture of Atlanta and Richmond would, if effected, end the war by the overthrow of our government and the submission of our people," he said flatly: "If the campaign against Richmond had resulted in success instead of failure, if the valor of [Lee's] army, under the leadership of its accomplished commander, had resisted in vain the overwhelming masses which were, on the contrary, decisively repulsed — if we had been compelled to evacuate Richmond as well as Atlanta — the Confederacy would have remained as erect and defiant as ever. Nothing could have been changed in the purpose of its government, in the indomitable valor of its troops, or in the unquenchable spirit of its people. The baffled and disappointed foe would in vain have scanned the reports of your proceedings, at some new legislative seat, for any indication that progress had been made in his gigantic task of conquering a free people." And having said as much he said still more in that regard. "There are no vital points on the preservation of which the continued existence of the Confederacy depends. There is no military success of the enemy which can accomplish its destruction. Not the fall of Richmond, nor Wilmington, nor Charleston, nor Savannah, nor Mobile, nor of all combined, can save the enemy from the constant and exhaustive drain of blood and treasure which must continue until he shall discover that no peace is attainable unless based on the recognition of our indefeasible rights."

He spoke at length of other matters, including foreign relations and finances — neither of them a pleasant subject for any Confederate — and referred, near the end, to the unlikelihood of being able to treat for peace with enemy leaders "until the delusion of their ability to conquer us is dispelled." Only then did he expect to encounter "that willingness to negotiate which is now confined to our side." Meantime, he told the assembled representatives, the South's one recourse lay in self-reliance. "Let us, then, resolutely continue to devote our united and unimpaired energies to the defense of our homes, our lives, and our liberties. This is the true path to peace. Let us tread it with confidence in the assured result."

Nowhere in the course of the long message did he mention tomorrow's election in the North, although the outcome was no less vital in the South — where still more battles would be fought if the hard-war Union party won — than it was throughout the region where the ballots would be cast. For one thing, any favorable reference to McClellan by Jefferson Davis would cost the Pennsylvanian votes he could ill afford now that Atlanta's fall and Frémont's withdrawal had transformed him, practically overnight, from odds-on favorite to underdog in the presidential race. In point of fact, much of the suspense had gone out of the contest, it being generally conceded by all but the most partisan of Democrats, caught up in the hypnotic fury of the campaign, that Little Mac had only the slimmest of chances.

Lincoln himself seemed gravely doubtful the following evening, however, when he crossed the White House grounds, soggy from a daylong wintry rain, to a side door of the War Department and climbed the stairs to the telegraph office, where returns were beginning to come in from around the country. These showed him leading in Massachusetts and Indiana, as well as in Baltimore and Philadelphia, and the trend continued despite some other dispatches that had McClellan ahead in Delaware and New Jersey. By midnight, though the storm delayed results from distant states, it was fairly clear that the turbulent campagin would end in Lincoln's reëlection.

Earlier he had said, "It is strange that I, who am not a vindictive man, should always, except once, have been before the people in canvasses marked by great bitterness. When I came to Congress it was a quiet time, but always, except that, the contests in which I have been prominent have been marked with great rancor." Now he lapsed into a darkly reminiscent mood, telling of that other election night, four years ago in Springfield, and a strange experience he had when he came home, utterly worn out, to rest for a time on a horsehair sofa in the parlor before going up to bed. Across the room, he saw himself reflected in a mirror hung on the wall above a bureau, almost at full length, murky, and with two faces, one nearly superimposed upon the other. Perplexed, somewhat alarmed, he got up to study the illusion at close range, only to have it vanish. When he lay down again it reappeared, plainer than before, and he could see that one face was paler than the other. Again he rose; again the double image disappeared. Later he told his wife about the phenomenon, and almost at once had cause — for both their sakes — to wish he hadn't. She took it as a sign, she said, that he would be reëlected four years later, but that the pallor of the second face indicated that he would not live through the second term.

The gloom this cast was presently dispelled by further reports that put all of New England and most of the Middle West firmly in his column. Around 2 o'clock, word came that serenaders, complete with a band, had assembled on the White House lawn to celebrate a victory whose incidentals would not be known for days. These would show that, out of some four million votes cast this Tuesday, Lincoln received 2,203,831 — just over 55 percent — as compared to his opponent's 1,797,019. Including those of Nevada, whose admission to the Union had been hurried through, eight days ago, so that its three votes could tip the scales if needed, he would receive 212 electoral votes and McClellan only the 21 from Delaware, New Jersey, and Kentucky. Yet the contest had been a good deal closer than these figures indicated. Connecticut, for example, was carried by a mere 2000 votes and New York by fewer than 7000, both as a result of military ballots, which went overwhelmingly for Lincoln, here as elsewhere. Without these two states, plus four others whose soldier voters swung the balance — Pennsylvania, Illinois, Maryland, and Indiana — he would have lost the election. Moreover, even in victory there were disappointments. New York City and Detroit went Democratic by majorities that ran close to three to one, and McClellan not only won the President's native state, Kentucky, he also carried Sangamon County, Illinois, and all the counties on its border. Lincoln could say to his serenaders before turning in that night, "I give thanks to the Almighty for this evidence of the people's resolution to stand by free government and the rights of humanity," but there was also the sobering realization, which would come with the full returns, that only five percent less than half the voters in the nation had opposed with their ballots his continuance as their leader.

Still, regardless of its outcome, he found consolation in two aspects of the bitter political struggle through which the country had just passed, and he mentioned both, two nights later, in responding to another group of serenaders. One was that the contest, for all "its incidental and undesirable strife," had demonstrated to the world "that a people's government can sustain a national election in the midst of a great civil war." This was much, but the other aspect was more complex, involving as it did the providence of an example distant generations could look back on when they came to be tested in their turn. "The strife of the election is but human nature practically applied to the facts of the case," he told the upturned faces on the lawn below the window from which he spoke. "What has occurred in this case must ever recur in similar cases. Human nature will not change. In any future great national trial, compared with the men of this, we shall have as weak and as strong, as silly and as wise, as bad and as good. Let us therefore study the incidents of this, as philosophy to learn wisdom from, and none of them as wrongs to be revenged."

Even so, a cruel paradox obtained. McClellan the loser was soon off on a European tour, a vacation that would keep him out of the country for six months, whereas Lincoln now more than ever, despite the stimulus of victory at the polls, could repeat what he had said two years before, in another time of trial: "I am like the starling in Sterne's story. 'I can't get out.' "

He had this to live with, as well as the memory of that double-image reflection in the mirror back in Springfield: both of which no doubt contributed, along with much else, to the nighttime restlessness a member of the White House guard observed as he walked the long second-story corridor, to and fro, past the door of the bedroom where the President lay sleeping. "I could hear his deep breathing," the sentry would recall. "Sometimes, after a day of unusual anxiety, I have heard him moan in his sleep. It gave me a curious sensation. While the expression of Mr Lincoln's face was always sad when he was quiet, it gave one the assurance of calm. He never seemed to doubt the wisdom of an action when he had once decided on it. And so when he was in a way defenseless in his sleep, it made me feel the pity that would almost have been an impertinence when he was awake. I would stand there and listen until a sort of panic stole over me. If he felt the weight of things so heavily, how much worse the situation of the country must be than any of us realized! At last I would walk softly away, feeling as if I had been listening at a keyhole."

You Cannot Refine It

INDIAN SUMMER HAD COME TO VIRGINIA while Northerners were going to the polls, muting with its smoky haze the vivid yellow vivid scarlet flare of maples and dogwoods on the Peninsula and down along the sunlit reaches of the James, where close to a hundred thousand blue-clad soldiers, in camps and trenches curving past the mouth of the Appomattox, celebrated or shook their heads at the news that they and more than half the men back home had voted to sustain a war that lacked only a winter of being four years old. Across the way, in the rebel works, the reaction was less mixed — and less intense. Partly this was because of distractions, including hunger and the likelihood of being hoisted by a mine or overrun; partly it proceeded from a sense of contrast between the present molelike state of existence and the old free-swinging foot cavalry days when the Army of Northern Virginia ranged the region from which it took its name but now would range no more.

"We thought we had before seen men with the marks of hard service upon them," an artillery major was to write, recalling his impression of the scarecrow infantry his battalion had been ordered to support on arriving from beyond the river back in June, "but the appearance of this division made us realize for the first time what our comrades in the hottest Petersburg lines were undergoing. We were shocked at the condition, the complexion, the expression of the men ... even the field officers. Indeed, we could scarcely realize that the unwashed, uncombed, unfed, and almost unclad creatures were officers of rank and reputation in the army." Thus he had reacted and reflected in early summer. Now in November he knew that he too looked like that, if not more so, with an added five hard months of wear and tear.

Richmond and Petersburg, semi-beleaguered at opposite ends of the line, were barely twenty crow-flight miles apart, but the intrenchments covering and connecting them had stretched by now to nearly twice that length. From White Oak Swamp on the far left, due east of the capital, these outer works (as distinguished from the 'inner' works, two miles in their rear) ran nine miles south, in a shielding curve, to Chaffin's Bluff on the James; there they crossed and continued for four gun-studded miles along the river's dominant right bank to a westward loop where the Howlett Line — Beauregard's cork in Butler's bottle — began its five-mile run across Bermuda Neck to the Appomattox, then jogged another four miles south, up the left bank of that stream, to connect with the trenches covering Petersburg at such close range that its citizens had grown adept at dodging Yankee shells. The first four miles of these trans-Appomattox installations — disfigured about midway by the red yawn of the Crater — defined the limits of the original blue assault as far south as the Jerusalem Plank Road, where both sides had thrown up imposing and opposing fortifications. Officially dubbed Forts Sedgwick and Mahone, but known respectively by their occupants as Fort Hell and Fort Damnation, these were designed to serve as south-flank anchors, back in June, for the two systems winding northward out of sight. Since that time, however, as a result of Grant's four all-out pendulum strikes (staged one a month, July through October, and costing him some 25,000 casualties, all told, as compared to Lee's 10,000) the gray line had been extended nine miles to the west and southwest, covering the Boydton Plank Road down to Hatcher's Run. All these segments brought the Confederate total to thirty-five miles of earthworks, not including cavalry extensions reaching up to the Chickahominy on the left and down past Burgess Mill to Gravelly Run on the right. Lee's basic problem, with only about half as many troops as he opposed, was that his line was not only longer, it was also more continuous than Grant's, who, having no national capital or indispensable railroad junction close in his rear, had less to fear from a breakthrough at any given point.

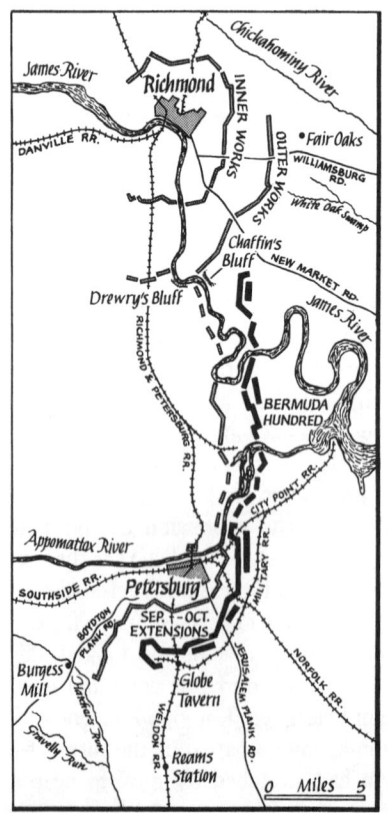

Another problem was food; or rather the lack of it. Badly as Lee needed men — and the need was so stringent he could not give his Jewish soldiers a day out of the trenches for Rosh Hashana or Yom Kippur — he saw no way of feeding substantial reinforcements even if they had been available, which they were not. As it was, he barely managed to sustain the troops on hand by reducing their daily ration to a pint of cornmeal, baked into pones when there was time, and an ounce or two of bacon. Moreover, with the Shenandoah Valley put to the torch and only two rail lines open to Georgia and the Carolinas — the Southside out of Petersburg, the Danville out of Richmond — there was little hope that the fare could be improved, despite the fact that the trench-bound men were losing weight and strength at an alarming rate. They looked fit enough, to a casual eye, but would "pant and grow faint" at the slightest exertion, a staffer noted. "General, I'm hongry," some would reply when Lee rode out and asked them how they were. All through this grim time, a veteran would say, "I thanked God I had a backbone for my stomach to lean up against."

Others remarked that the quality of such food as they received was even lower than its quantity; which was low indeed. The meal was unbolted, generally with much of the cob ground in, and alive with weevils. But the bacon remained longest in their memories and nightmares. Nassau bacon, it was called, though one memorialist was to testify that "Nausea with a capital would have been better. It came through the blockade, and we believed it was made from the hog of the tropics and cured in the brine of the ocean. More likely it was discarded ship's pork, or 'salt junk.'... It was a peculiarly scaly color, spotted like a half-well case of smallpox, full of rancid odor, and utterly devoid of grease. When hung up it would double its length. It could not be eaten raw, and imparted a stinking smell when boiled. It had one redeeming quality: elasticity. You could put a piece in your mouth and chew it for a long time, and the longer you chewed it the bigger it got. Then, by a desperate effort, you would gulp it down. Out of sight, out of mind."

Nor was the outer man, in his butternut rags, any better served than the inner. Shoes, for example, had always been a scarce requisition item, and now that the once bounteous yield of well-shod Union corpses had diminished as a dividend of battle, the shortage was acute. Even so, and with cold weather coming on, many soldiers preferred going barefoot to wearing the "pitiable specimens" of footgear issued by the government as a substitute for shoes. "Generally made of green, or at best half-cured leather," one who suffered from them later wrote, "they soon took to roaming. After a week's wear, the heel would be on one side, at an angle to the foot, and the vamp in turn would try to do duty as a sole.... While hot and dry, they would shrink like parchment, and when wet they just slopped all over your feet."

Crippling as this was, other shortages cramped the army's style still more. Chief among these, despite the sacrifice of most of the South's stills, was the scarcity of copper, indispensable in the manufacture of percussion caps, without which not a shot could be fired. Riflemen in the critical outer pits were limited to eighteen caps a day, while their Federal counterparts across the way complained of bruised shoulders from being required to expend no less than a hundred rounds in the same span. Other metals not only were less rare, they also could be salvaged from incoming projectiles, much as boots and overcoats had been scavenged from incoming infantry, back in the days of mobile warfare. "As an inducement to collecting scrap iron for our cannon foundries," a line officer would recall, "furloughs were offered, a day for so many pounds collected. Thus, gathering fragments of shells became an active industry among the troops. So keen was their quest that sometimes they would start toward the point where a mortar shell fell, even before it exploded." Similarly, the loose dirt of the parapets was periodically sifted for spent lead, but only under cover of darkness, when snipers were inactive. Twice each day, an hour before dawn and half an hour before dusk, every regiment mounted the fire step along its portion of the trenches and remained there, on the alert, until full daylight spread or night came down. Between times, round the clock, half the men kept watch, while the other half slept or rested on their arms, ready to assist in repelling an attack whenever their on-duty comrades sounded the alarm.

Outnumbered and outgunned, ill-clad, ill-shod, and invariably hungry, running after fragments of shell as they once had run after rabbits — except that now they were not in direct pursuit of food, for there was none at the scene of the chase, but rather of the chance to win a day out of the trenches, on the roam where a few mouthfuls could be scrounged from roadside gardens ("They stole more from us than the Yankees did; poor things," a farmwife was to say long afterwards) — Lee's veterans fought less by now for a cause than they did for a tradition. And if, in the past six months, this had become a tradition not so much of victory as of undefeat, it had nonetheless been strengthened by the recent overland campaign and now was being sustained by the current stalemate, which was all that Grant's hundred thousand casualties had earned him in this latest On-to-Richmond effort, launched in May. Mainly, though, Lee's veterans fought for Lee, or at any rate for the pride they felt when they watched him ride among them. He had "a fearless look of self-possession, without a trace of arrogance," a Tarheel captain noted, and though a fellow Virginian observed that "he had aged somewhat in appearance," it was also evident that he "had rather gained than lost in physical vigor, from the severe life he had led. His hair had grown gray, but his face had the ruddy hue of health and his eyes were as clear and bright as ever."

Partly this appearance of well-being derived from the extended spell of golden weather, which continued through November into December; Lee had always been responsive to climatic fluctuations, good and bad, even before the onset of what doctors called his rheumatism. A staff cavalryman, however, looking back on this hale, autumnal time — when the general, as he said, "seldom, if ever, exhibited the least trace of anxiety, but was firm, hopeful, and encouraged those around him in the belief that he was still confident of success" — believed he saw deeper into the matter. "It must have been the sense of having done his whole duty, and expended upon the cause every energy of his being, which enabled him to meet the approaching catastrophe with a calmness which seemed to those around him almost sublime."

Perceptive as this was by hindsight, there were other, more evident causes for the confidence he displayed. One was the return of Longstreet in mid-October, on the day of Early's defeat at Cedar Creek. His right arm partly paralyzed by the effects of his Wilderness wound, Old Peter had learned to write with his left hand, and he gladly accepted full responsibility for the defense of that part of the line above the James, where he soon demonstrated that he had lost none of his cool, hard-handed skill in conducting a battle. Lee's wisdom in leaving the fighting there to his "old war horse" was confirmed within eight days of the Georgian's return to duty; no northside drive on Richmond was ever so easily shattered, at such low cost to the defenders, as the one that made up part of Grant's fourth and final pendulum strike, October 27. What was more, the confidence this inspired was enlarged by Hill's and Hampton's canny resistance along Hatcher's Run, where three Federal corps were turned back in confusion the following day, after suffering even heavier losses than had been inflicted on the other two corps, at the far end of the line.

Small wonder, then, that Lee gave an impression of vigor and well-being as he rode north or south, through the flare and haze of Indian Summer, to inspect his nearly forty miles of unbroken line from the Chickahominy down past Burgess Mill. Even Grant, who was slow to learn negative lessons, had apparently been convinced by this latest failure that he would never take the Confederate capital by storm, and this estimate was strengthened in mid-November by the recall of Kershaw's division from Early to join Longstreet, whose reunited First Corps now occupied all the defenses north of the Appomattox, including those across Bermuda Neck. A. P. Hill's Third Corps held the Petersburg intrenchments, supported by Hampton's cavalry on the right, and a new Fourth Corps was improvised by combining the divisions of Hoke and Bushrod Johnson (but only on paper; Hoke remained north and Johnson south of the James) to provide a command for Richard Anderson, commensurate with his rank, after Old Peter's return. With Dick Ewell in charge of the reserves in Richmond, on call for manning the city's inner works, Lee felt that his army was not only back under his immediate control — aside, that is, from Early's three Second Corps divisions, still licking their wounds out on the near rim of the Shenandoah Valley — but also, in the light of its performance against four all-out assaults in as many months by twice its numbers, that it had recovered a considerable measure of the responsive, agile quality that made it like a rapier in his hand.

Still, for all its delicate balance and true temper, the rapier had become an exclusively defensive weapon, swift in parry and effective in occasional riposte, but not employed for months now to deliver a bold, original thrust or slash, as in the days when Lee's aggressive use of it, whether to pink or maim, had dazzled admirers all over the world. Moreover, he knew that in time, without proper care or refurbishment, the fine-honed instrument would wear out (or the fencer would, which came to the same thing) under the constant hammering of the Union broadsword, any one of whose strokes would end the duel if his arm wearied and let it past. "Without some increase of strength," he had warned Seddon more than two months ago, "I cannot see how we can escape the natural military consequences of the enemy's numerical superiority." Nothing much had come of this, nor of a follow-up protest to Bragg one month later: "I get no additions. The men coming in do not supply the vacancies caused by sickness, desertions, and other casualties." Now in November he appealed to the President himself. "Grant will get every man he can. . . . Unless we obtain a reasonable approximation to his force I fear a great calamity will befall us."

Nothing came of that either; Davis could only reply, as he had done to similar pleas from Hood, "No other resource remains." And now that Lincoln's reëlection had dashed Confederate hopes for an early end to the war by negotiation, Lee saw clearly enough that all his skilled resistance had really gained him, north and south of the James, was time — time with which, lacking substantial reinforcements, he could do little except continue to resist; until time ran out, as it finally must, and broke the vicious, tightening circle. His belief that Grant was at last convinced of the folly involved in prolonging a series of bungled attempts to overrun him was encouraged, if not confirmed, when November drew to a close without a major assault having been launched against any part of his works from start to finish, the first such month since the siege began. But he also knew this did not mean there would be a let-up in Grant's efforts to accomplish by attrition what he had failed to achieve by overwhelming force. Expecting renewed strikes at his overworked supply lines, west and south of Petersburg and Richmond, Lee told Davis in early December: "All we want to resist them is men."

Subsequently, looking back on his close association as the general's

You Cannot Refine It

aide, a staff colonel declared that the two- or three-week span from late November into December was "the most anxious period of Grant's entire military career." Although Horace Porter, who made the statement, had not shared his chief's times of trial out West — after Donelson, when Halleck tried to sack him: after Shiloh, when Sherman persuaded him not to quit the service in dejection: after Vicksburg, when he spent a fretful month watching his army be dismembered, while he hobbled about on crutches from his New Orleans horseback fall — the young West Pointer had practical as well as psychological grounds for his contention that this latest tribulation was the hardest. Those previous afflictions of the spirit had followed significant battlefield successes, two of them even resulting in rebel surrenders, whereas this one came at a time when the best Grant could claim, at any rate for the army under his hand, was a stalemate achieved at a cost in casualties roughly twice as great as the number he inflicted. Victory was a future, not a present thing, as in two of those other three cases, and its nearness — within his reach, as he believed, but not within his grasp, as Lee had shown — was one source of his frustration. Another, which raised this reaction to the pitch of true anxiety, was a growing apprehension that things might go dreadfully awry in Tennessee (or, what was worse, Kentucky) on the very eve of triumph in Virginia. He had never been one to take counsel of his fears, but there were plenty of veteran officers around — including Porter, who had served on McClellan's staff — to remind him that Little Mac once had stood about where he was standing now, close enough to hear the tocsin clang in Richmond, and yet had wound up confronting a Maryland invasion fifty miles northwest of his own capital, which lay more than a hundred miles in rear of Harrison's Landing, just across the way from City Point.

First there was the unavoidable admission that the headlong approach, which by now had cost Meade and Butler some 36,000 casualties between them — 11,000 in the initial June assault, plus 25,000 since — provided no quick solution to the Petersburg dilemma. That came hard for Grant, who seldom acknowledged failure, especially in large-scale undertakings, and in fact declined to do so now; except tacitly, by desisting. Hancock did it for him, though, in a ceremony staged at his headquarters on November 26, when he bid farewell to the once-proud II Corps. Ostensibly, he was returning to Washington under War Department orders to recruit and organize a new I Corps of reënlisted veterans for service in the spring. Nothing was to come of that, however. Nor was there much validity in the claim that he was leaving because of his unhealed Gettysburg wound. The real damage was to his soldier's pride, which had suffered cruelly in the series of dispiriting reverses he and his troops had undergone in the course of the past five months, north of the James and south of the Appomattox. His departure was a measure of the extent to which Grant's breakthrough concept had broken down in the fire of Lee's resistance, and it was clear that the men of the three divisions Hancock left behind would need a great deal of rest and recuperation before they were fit for any such use by his successor, Major General A. A. Humphreys, a fellow Pennsylvanian and West Pointer, who had served as Meade's chief of staff for the past year and was fifty-four years old.

Sharpest of the stings involved in the stalling of Grant's offensive was the fact that he could almost never get his orders carried out as he intended; Baldy Smith had been the first, after the passage of the James, but he was by no means the last offender in this regard. "Three different times has Richmond or Petersburg been virutally in his hands," a military visitor wrote home about this time, "and by some inexcusable neglect or slowness each time his plans were ruined and the opportunity lost. How Grant stands it I do not see." Moreover, there seemed to be no cure for this condition: not even the removal of Baldy and Burnside, along with such lesser lights as Ledlie and Ferrero. These, after all, were only four among the many — including Butler, who could not be dealt with in that fashion, though he was at times, because of his lofty rank and large command, a greater trial than all the rest combined.

Just now, for example, he was at work on a plan for cracking Wilmington's seaward defenses, obviously a top-priority assignment, not only because it would close the South's last major port and thus increase Lee's problem of subsistence, but also because it would divert attention, as well as possible rebel reinforcements, away from Sherman's destination on the Georgia coast, 250 miles below. Yet Butler kept delaying the start of the movement, which he was to make with two of his divisions and the support of David Porter's fleet, by thinking up ways to ensure that the amphibious assault would be brief and successful, without too great a cost in ships and men. His latest notion was to pack an expendable ocean-going steamer with 350 tons of powder and run it under the walls of Fort Fisher, which would be reduced to rubble by the timed explosion, leaving the attackers little to do but move in and take over when the smoke cleared. Grant liked the plan and approved it, though he did not like or approve of the delays. He kept prodding the cock-eyed general, urging him to be off before the Carolinians got word of what was in store for them; but Butler, still "as visionary as an opium eater in council," refused to be hurried, insisting that a close attention to details provided the only guarantee of success. Then on November 27 — the day after Hancock's farewell ceremony — an enemy agent came close to solving Grant's problem by removing the former Bay State politician not only from his command but from the earth.

Butler and Porter were conferring aboard the former's headquarters steamer *Greyhound*, a short distance up the James from Bermuda Landing, "when suddenly an explosion forward startled us, and in a moment large volumes of smoke poured out of the engine room." So Porter later described the mishap, which fortunately was no worse because the explosion set off no others and the flames were soon extinguished, but he marveled at an ingenuity rivaling his companion's in such matters. What was thought at first to have been a boiler accident turned out to have been caused by a "coal torpedo," a blackened piece of cast iron, machined to resemble a lump of coal and loaded with ten pounds of powder, which the rebel agent had somehow placed in the steamer's bunker and a stoker had shoveled into the furnace. "In devices for blowing up vessels the Confederates were far ahead of us, putting Yankee ingenuity to shame," the admiral declared.

Three days later, on the last day of November, Grant learned that part of the Wilmington garrison was being withdrawn to intercept Sherman at Augusta, Georgia, on the theory that he would pass that way en route to Charleston. Not only was this no immediate threat to Sherman, whose true destination was almost a hundred miles farther down the coast, it also simplified Butler's task by reducing, at least for the present, the resistance he would encounter when he struck Wilmington's defenses. Informed of this, the Massachusetts general replied that he was delighted; he would proceed as soon as his floating bomb was ready for use, a further delay having been required by his notion of altering the steamer's lines to make her resemble a blockade runner, which he figured would cause the rebel cannoneers to cheer her, rather than shoot at her, right up to the moment she blew. Grant could see the humor in this, but he was losing patience. Aware that the Confederates would soon have the choice of returning to Wilmington or ganging up on Sherman, he told Butler on December 4 to start for North Carolina at once, "with or without your powder boat." But that did not work either. For ten more days the squint-eyed Butler, unruffled by his superior's apprehensions or his own near brush with death aboard the *Greyhound,* continued to balk and tinker before he got his two divisions onto transports at Hampton Roads and headed down the coast.

Grant's concern for Sherman's welfare, even his survival, off on his own and due to pop up any day now, more than four hundred miles down the seaboard — a ready target for whatever combination of forces the rebels were able to throw in that direction — was real enough, but it was by no means as grievous a source of anxiety as were several others, over which — at least in theory, since he was in direct communication with the subordinates in charge — he could exercise some measure of control. For one thing, as he had told Stanton at the outset, seeking to reassure the Secretary as to the degree of risk involved in cutting loose from Atlanta for the march through Georgia to the coast, "Such an army as Sherman has (and with such a commander) is hard to corner or capture." For another, his over-all design for the

Confederacy's defeat by strangulation did not hinge on the outcome of the current maneuver by his red-haired friend, whose success could shorten but whose defeat would not lengthen the war by so much as a day. Besides, his reliance on Sherman and Sherman's army — once his own — was unmatched by any such feeling of confidence in George Thomas and the scratch collection of recruits, dismounted cavalrymen, and culled veterans Old Tom had been attempting to put together in Middle Tennessee ever since Sherman set out for the sea, leaving Hood and Hood's hard-hitting army alive in his rear, poised for a strike at the critical Union center.

There was the rub. The Rock of Chickamauga was superb on the defensive, and at Chattanooga he had shown what he could do in an assault on a fixed position. But how would Old Slow Trot perform in a fluid situation requiring him to deal with an enemy in motion around his flank? So far the signs were unpromising, and that was the chief source of Grant's anxiety: that Hood would bypass Nashville, where Thomas was intrenched, and cross the Cumberland River unmolested, perhaps on a march all the way to the Ohio. If that happened, all Grant's well-laid plans might come undone in a sudden reversal of the tide of war. Even the siege of Richmond might have to be lifted, in order to furnish troops for the protection of Kentucky, and Sherman's march through Georgia might as well have occurred in a vacuum, ending as it would in nothing more than a long ride north aboard transports, then west by rail to resume the contest with his old adversary in a region two hundred miles in rear of the one through which he had fought his way in May and June.

Lincoln saw it, too, and abandoned for the time, at least by proxy, his hands-off policy with regard to military operations. "The President feels solicitous about the disposition of General Thomas to lay in fortifications for an indefinite period," Stanton wired on December 2. "This looks like the McClellan and Rosecrans strategy of do nothing and let the rebels raid the country. The President wishes you to consider the matter."

Grant did consider the matter and stepped up the pressure, warning Thomas that he would "suffer incalculable injury . . . if Hood is not speedily disposed of. Put forth therefore every possible exertion to gain this end," he told him, but with no more success than he was having at the same time in getting Butler on the go for Wilmington. Stanton returned to the charge, protesting that the Virginian seemed "unwilling to attack because it is hazardous — as if war was anything but hazardous," he sneered — which drew from Grant the admission that, for all of Thomas's reputed bulldog qualities, "I fear he is too cautious to take the initiative." All the same, he tried again, this time with a direct order: "Attack Hood at once and wait no longer. . . . There is great danger of delay resulting in a campaign back to the Ohio River."

This was clear enough, but it only caused the Tennessee commander to shift his ground under prodding from the rear. He had been on the verge of launching an all-out attack, he replied, but "a terrible storm of freezing rain has come on today, which will make it impossible for our men to fight to any advantage."

Thwarted thus at every turn in his efforts to get Butler and Thomas moving, stalled on the outskirts of Richmond by a resistance so discouraging that it had just cost Meade the best of his corps commanders, deprived of any reliable information as to Sherman's progress or misfortune in the Georgia hinterland, and harried as he was beginning to be by superiors who had been altogether forbearing up till now, Grant was determined to do what he personally could at City Point, through this "most anxious period," if only by way of relieving the strain that came with finding how much there was that he could not do elsewhere. One thing he could do, despite his recent abandonment of headlong tactics against Petersburg's intrenchments, was keep up the pressure on its overtaxed supply lines. That would not only add to Lee's subsistence problem, in direct ratio to the degree of success achieved; it would also prevent the old fox from sending reinforcements to Tennessee or Georgia, as he had done the year before, in the absence of such pressure. Accordingly, Grant planned another strike at the Weldon Railroad, this time down near the Carolina line, its purpose being to lengthen the twenty-mile wagon haul the rebels now were obliged to make from Stony Creek, the terminus of the road since August, when Hancock wrecked it that far south. The assignment went to Warren, whose three divisions would be reinforced by one from Humphreys, and Gregg's troopers would go along to screen the march.

First, though, Grant decided to lengthen the numerical odds against his adversary by returning Wright's long-absent corps from the Shenandoah Valley, where all it had been doing for the past six weeks was assist Sheridan in the destruction being visited on that much-fought-over region, once the classic avenue for invasions that played on northern fears, but now not even a source of grain or cattle, practically all of which had been put to the torch or gone under the Union knife. Wright's leading elements began unloading from transports at City Point on December 4; three days later Warren set out on his march to strike the Petersburg & Weldon at the crossing of the Meherrin River, twenty miles beyond Stony Creek.

When Lee discovered that Wright was en route from the Valley to rejoin Meade, he countered by ordering Early to send back two of his divisions, Gordon's and Ramseur's, the latter now under its senior brigadier, John Pegram. Neither arrived in time to help fend off Warren's threat to the railroad, which began on December 7, but the southern commander, gambling on his belief that Grant would attempt no more frontal assaults this year, risked pulling most of Hill's corps out of the Petersburg works to undertake, along with Hampton's cavalry, an interception of what he thought was a drive on Weldon. Next day, however, the weather turned intensely cold. Pelted by sleet, the butternut marchers shivered in their rags, and many fell out of the slow-moving column after slogging barefoot over miles of frozen ground. When those who managed to keep going reached the railroad below Stony Creek, December 9, they found sixteen miles of track ripped up, piles of ties still smoking, heat-twisted rails warm to the touch, and the Federals gone, turned back by home-guard batteries at Hicksford, firing at them from just beyond the Meherrin, as well as by the miserable weather and the near exhaustion of their three-day rations. Hampton overtook and slashed at the flanks of the blue column trudging north, but only managed to kill or capture about a hundred stragglers; the rest got away into their own lines the following day. If there was some criticism of Hill for not having engaged the marauders before they escaped, there was also a feeling of relief that they had not inflicted heavier damage on the already crippled supply line, whose railhead now was forty miles south of Petersburg's hungry defenders.

Winter came with mid-December vengeance, and though the advantage had to be weighed against the suffering of his thinly clad men in the trenches astride the James, Lee knew that the Federals too, for all their sturdy boots, snug overcoats, and rations that warmed them inside as well as out, would be restricted by ice and mud and frozen rain if they continued their efforts to move around his flanks. Moreover, the rough weather afforded him one last chance — however slight, in comparison with what Wright's return brought Grant — to increase the number of troops he could post along his thirty-odd miles of line between White Oak Swamp and Hatcher's Run. When he got word that a six-inch snow had clogged the roads in the upper Valley, he told Early to send the third of his divisions to Richmond in the wake of the other two (which had just arrived) but to remain out there himself, as district commander, with a force reduced to Wharton's undersized infantry division and Rosser's two slim cavalry brigades, in necessarily long-range observation of Sheridan's continuing depredations. Presently the old Second Corps, down to a skeleton strength of fewer than 9000 effectives — the result of its six-month excursion down and up the Valley and its brief side trip to the outskirts of Washington and back — was again an integral, on-hand part of the Army of Northern Virginia.

Lee named Gordon acting corps commander, the first nonprofessional to occupy so high a post. This was an indication of what inroads attrition had made at the upper levels, as was the fact that two of the three divisions were similarly led by their senior brigadiers. Clement Evans, a former Georgia lawyer like his chief, succeeded Gordon, and Bryan Grimes, once a North Carolina planter, had taken over from the fallen Rodes. Only Pegram, a Virginia-born West Pointer, had seen military service before the war. And of the four, including the major general in charge of all three divisions, only Grimes had reached his middle thirties. He was thirty-six; Gordon and Pegram were thirty-two, and Evans was thirty-one.

Glad as Lee was at the reassembling of his army, however shrunken it might be at all its levels, he was also saddened by the knowledge that this had been accomplished at the price of abandoning hope of going over to the offensive. Not since Chancellorsville and the death of Jackson, close to twenty months ago, had he won the kind of brilliant, large-scale victory that brought him and his lean, caterwauling veterans the admiration of the world, and now that the Valley was irretrievably lost, along with Stonewall, his recall of the Second Corps to join the others huddled in the trenches around Petersburg and Richmond set the seal on his admission, however tacit, that the war, however much or little of it was left to fight, was for him and them no longer a pursuit of glory on the road to national independence, but rather a grim struggle for survival, which would take them down a quite different road to the same goal — if they could reach its end. Yet here was where a paradox came in. While Grant reacted to the prospect of ultimate victory by growing jumpy at the thought of having the prize snatched from him just as it seemed about to come within his grasp, Lee faced the ultimate prospect of defeat with "a fearless look of self-possession" and "a calmness which seemed to those around him almost sublime."

Or perhaps there was no paradox in that. Perhaps the two reactions were quite natural, considering the two quite different kinds of strain imposed on these two quite different kinds of men. In some ways, since nothing worse could happen to him than what seemed foreordained, Lee's was the easier role to play. Expectation braced him for the shocks: even the loss, before the month was out, of more than a tenth of the force he had been at such pains to assemble for Richmond's protection in mid-December. Warned that Wilmington was about to be hit, three hundred miles down the coast, he was obliged to send Hoke's division to its defense — a detachment that cost him the equivalent of a solid two thirds of all he had gained by the return of Early's survivors from the Valley. His year-end strength, including 5358 reservists under Ewell, came to 57,134. Across the way, Meade had 83,846 and Butler 40,452: a total of 124,278 for Grant.

Outnumbered two to one, the gaps in their ranks only partly chinked with conscripts, the defenders saw clearly enough that time, which they were being told was on their side, could only lengthen the odds against survival. Good men had fallen and were falling every day, picked off by snipers or dropped by mortars in a roughly man-for-man exchange that worked to the considerable disadvantage of the smaller force, not only because its proportionate loss was twice as heavy on that basis, but also because the replacements being scraped from the bottom of the Confederate barrel did not "supply the vacancies," as Lee had complained to Bragg three months before. Moreover, some who fell could scarcely have been replaced in the best of times: Rodes and Ramseur, for example, or John Gregg and Archibald Gracie, both of whom had won distinction at Chickamauga. Gregg was cut down at the head of his Texas brigade, in a skirmish east of Richmond in October, and Gracie was killed in early December by a shell that burst over a normally quiet stretch of Petersburg intrenchments while he was training a telescope on the works across the way. Such losses, suffered without the compensating stimulus of victory, came hard for the survivors, whose spirits drooped as their numbers dwindled. "Living cannot be called a fever here," a butternut artillerist declared, "but rather a long catalepsy." Desertions rose with the rising proportion of conscripts, many of them netted after years of avoiding the draft, and even the stalwarts who stood by their banners looked forward to furling them — whatever arrangements might have to be made to bring that end about.

"As we lay there watching the bright stars," one veteran lieutenant was to say, "many a soldier asked himself the question: What is this all about? Why is it that 200,000 men of one blood and one tongue, believing as one man in the fatherhood of God and the universal brotherhood of man, should in the nineteenth century of the Christian era be thus armed with all the improved appliances of modern warfare and seeking one another's lives? We could settle our differences by compromising, and all be at home in ten days."

�֍ 2 ✶

Early morning, November 16; Sherman sat his horse on Bald Hill, where the worst of the fighting had raged in July, and looked down on the copse where McPherson had fallen, shot through the back while opposing the second of Hood's three all-out sorties. "Behind us lay Atlanta, smouldering and in ruins," he would recall, "the black smoke rising high in air and hanging like a pall over the ruined city. Away off in the distance, on the McDonough Road, was the rear of Howard's column, the gun barrels glistening in the sun, the white-topped wagons stretching away to the south, and right before us the XIV Corps [of Slocum's column] marching steadily and rapidly, with a cheery look and swinging pace that made light of the thousand miles that lay between us and Richmond."

Leading elements of both columns having stepped off the day before, east and southeast down the railroads, Atlanta had been set afire last night, partly by rear-guard arsonists, who stole away from, then rejoined their units passing through, and partly by design, in accordance with orders that nothing be left intact that might be of use to the rebs when they returned. In any case, the results were spectacular. "All the pictures and verbal descriptions of hell I have ever seen never gave me half so vivid an idea of it as did this flame-wrapped city tonight," a staff major wrote in his journal after dodging sparks and debris from explosions as he picked his way through the streets. Dawn showed more than a third of the town in ashes, with smoke still rising thick and slow from the longer-lasting fires. While Sherman watched from his hilltop, a mile beyond the eastward bend of Hood's abandoned fortifications, a band in the blue column below struck up the John Brown song, and presently the marchers joined in, roaring the words as they slogged along. "Never before or since have I heard the chorus of 'Glory, glory, hallelujah!' done with more spirit or in better harmony of time and place," their red-haired commander was to say.

He twitched his horse's head to the east and came down off the hill, trailed by his staff. "Uncle Billy," a weathered veteran hailed him near the bottom, "I guess Grant is waiting for us at Richmond!" Sherman grinned and rode on, doubling the column. "Atlanta was soon lost behind the screen of trees, and became a thing of the past. Around it clings many a thought of desperate battle, of hope and fear, that now seem like the memory of a dream.... I have never seen the place since."

Orders governing the expedition had been issued the week before, to afford all ranks plenty of time for study before moving out. They made no mention of route or destination, being mainly concerned with logistics and rules of conduct for the 62,000 participants, just over 5000 of whom were cavalry, under Kilpatrick, and just under 2000 were artillery, with 64 guns. Each of the four infantry corps — two in each of two "wings," both of which were equipped with 900-foot collapsible pontoon bridges transported in special trains — would move by a separate road, where practicable, and be independent for supplies. "The army will forage liberally on the country during the march," Sherman directed, though he specified that the foraging was to be done only by authorized personnel; "Soldiers must not enter the dwellings of inhabitants or commit any trespass." He hoped to keep nonmilitary damage to a minimum, but he made it clear that if guerillas or other civilians attempted to interfere with his progress, say by damaging bridges or obstructing roads, "then army commanders should order and enforce a devastation more or less relentless, according to the measure of such hostility." Privately, he expanded this admonition and directed that word of it be spread wherever the army went, in hopes that it would be carried ahead by the rebel grapevine, if not by the rebel papers. "If the enemy burn forage and corn in our route," he said, "houses, barns, and cotton gins must also be burned to keep them company."

Every man carried forty rounds of small-arms ammunition on his person, and another 200 followed in the wagons, along with a twenty-day supply of hardtack and coffee. Only a five-day reserve of grain went along for the horses, but he figured that was enough to get them clear of the clean-picked region around Atlanta; "I knew that within that time we would reach a country well stocked with corn, which had been gathered and stored in cribs, seemingly for our use, by Governor Brown's militia." The same went for foodstuffs for the men. Pigs and turkeys squealed and gobbled in farmyards all along the 300 miles of unspoiled hinterland his veterans would traverse, and sweet potatoes were waiting to be roasted in the ashes of a thousand campfires every night of the three or four weeks he expected it would take him to reach Savannah, where the navy would be standing by with supply ships.

That the march was made in two divergent columns, each about 30,000 strong and with half the guns, served a triple purpose: first, to avoid the crowding and delays that would result from trying to move all four corps along a single route: second, to broaden not only the foraging area but also the swath of destruction, which thus would be twice as horrendous: and third, to confuse and mislead the enemy as to Sherman's objective or objectives, on the Atlantic and on the way there. Howard's right wing, made up of his two-corps Army of the Tennessee — Blair was back from his electioneering duties, but Major General Peter Osterhaus, Logan's senior division commander, had charge of the XV Corps in the continued absence of his chief, who remained North after stumping for Lincoln — tramped south down the Macon & Western, as if bound for Macon, while Slocum's left wing, containing the corps under Davis and Williams — formerly part of Thomas's Army of the Cumberland, now styled the Army of Georgia — followed the line of the

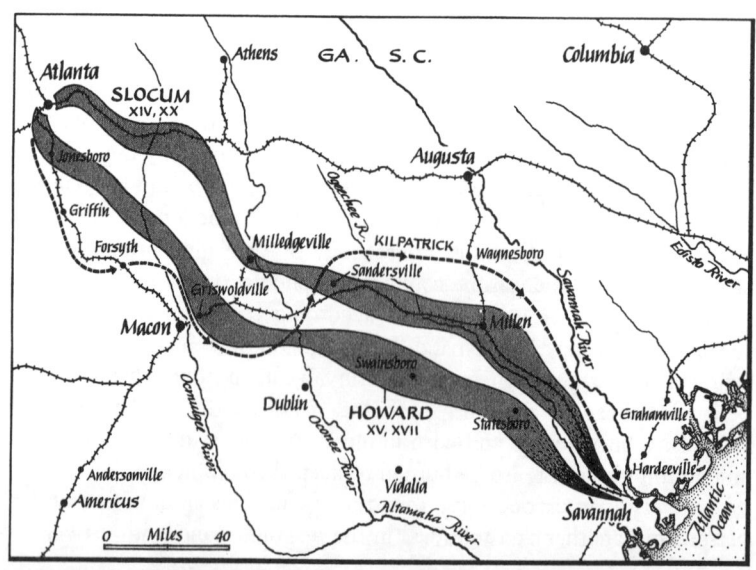

Georgia Railroad, which ran due east to Augusta. By now, most likely, the Confederates must be rushing all available reserves to the defense of both population centers. At any rate that was what Sherman hoped they would do; for he intended to move through neither, but rather through Milledgeville, the state capital, which lay between them.

This began to be fairly obvious to the right-wing marchers on their second day out of Atlanta, when Howard veered southeast from Jonesboro, leaving Kilpatrick to keep up the feint down the railroad nearly to Forsyth, twenty miles short of Macon, where he too turned off to rejoin the infantry column beyond the bypassed town. Slocum continued eastward from Atlanta for three days, ripping up track as he went, and then on the fourth — by which time the two wings were close to fifty miles apart — turned south along the near bank of the Oconee River toward Milledgeville, some forty miles downstream. "God has put a ring in Sherman's nose and is leading him to destruction," a Richmond clergyman had remarked when the widespread march began. But now, as a result of conflicting reports by his adversaries, which in turn were the result of careful planning on his part, scarcely anyone but God and the farmers whose crops he was consuming as he progressed knew where he was.

If the march had its rigors, mainly proceeding from the great distance to be covered and the occasional hard work of bridging creeks and corduroying roads, it also had its attendant compensations derived from the fatness of the land and the skylark attitude of the men fanned out across it in two columns, foraging along a front that varied from thirty to sixty miles in width. "This is probably the most gigantic pleasure excursion ever planned," one of Howard's veterans declared after swinging eastward on the second day out of Atlanta. "It already beats everything I ever saw soldiering, and promises to prove much richer yet." Expectations were as high, and as amply rewarded, in the column to the north. Riding with Slocum past Stone Mountain that same day, Sherman pulled off on the side of the road to review the passing troops and found them unneglectful of such opportunities as had come their way. One marcher who drew his attention had a ham slung from his rifle, a jug of molasses cradled under one arm, and a big piece of honeycomb clutched in the other hand, from which he was eating as he slogged along. Catching the general's eye, he quoted him *sotto voce* to a comrade as they swung past: "Forage liberally on the country."

Sherman afterwards told how he "reproved the man, explaining that foraging must be limited to the regular parties properly detailed," but he was not long in showing that despoilment had a place in his calculations, quite as much as it did in theirs. Four days later, after turning south toward Milledgeville just short of the Oconee, he came upon a well-stocked plantation which he happened to learn belonged to Major General Howell Cobb. A leading secessionist and one-time speaker of the U.S. House and Treasury Secretary under Buchanan, Cobb had been appointed by Joe Brown to command the state reserves in the present crisis; in which capacity — though it turned out there were no "reserves" for him to command — he had been exhorting his fellow Georgians to resist the blue invasion by the destruction of everything edible in its path. "Of course, we confiscated his property," Sherman would recall, "and found it rich in corn, beans, peanuts, and sorghum molasses.... I sent back word to General Davis to explain whose plantation it was, and instructed him to spare nothing. That night huge bonfires consumed the fence rails, kept our soldiers warm, and the teamsters and men, as well as the slaves, carried off an immense quantity of corn and provisions of all sorts."

His aim, he said, in thus enforcing "a devastation more or less relentless," was to convince the planters roundabout "that it is in their interest not to impede our movements." Simultaneously, however, this conclusion was discouraged by the activities of his foragers — "bummers," they were called, and called themselves, although the term had been one of opprobrium at the start — who worked along the fringes of the march, sometimes as "regular parties properly detailed," sometimes not. Isolated plantation owners, mostly wives and mothers whose sons and husbands were with Hood or Lee in Tennessee or Virginia, buried their silver and jewels on hearing of Sherman's approach, and the search for these provided fun, as well as the possibility of profit, for the blue-clad visitors. Out would come the ramrods for a vigorous probing of lawns and flowerbeds. "It was comical to see a group of these red-bearded, barefooted, ragged veterans punching the unoffending earth in an apparently idiotic but certainly most energetic way," an officer who observed them was to write. "A woman standing upon the porch of a house, watching their proceedings, instantly became an object of suspicion, and she was watched until some movement betrayed a place of concealment. Fresh earth thrown up, a bed of flowers just set out, the slightest indication of a change in appearance or position, all attracted the gaze of these military agriculturists. If they 'struck a vein' a spade was instantly put in requisition and the coveted wealth was speedily unearthed. It was all fair spoil of war, and the search made one of the excitements of the march." Other diversions included the shooting of bloodhounds, hated for their use in tracking runaway slaves and convicts through the swamps. Sometimes, by way of a joke, the definition was expanded to cover less offensive breeds. For example, when a poodle's mistress appealed for her lap dog to be spared, the soldier who had caught up the pet and was bearing it off to execution replied: "Madam, our orders are to kill every bloodhound." "But this is not a bloodhound!" she protested, only to be told: "Well, madam, we cannot tell what it will grow into if we leave it behind."

If there was a core of cruelty to such humor, it was precisely in such cruelty that the humor had its source. In time Sherman would concede that "many acts of pillage, robbery, and violence were committed by these parties of foragers." He had also "heard of jewelry taken from women and the plunder of articles that never reached our commissary," though he insisted that such depredations were "exceptional and incidental." In any case, whatever factors contributed to the total, he would report at the end of the march across Georgia that the damage inflicted came to no less than $100,000,000: "at least twenty millions of which has inured to our advantage, and the remainder is simple waste and destruction. This may seem a hard species of warfare," he declared, "but it brings the sad realities of war home to those who have been directly or indirectly instrumental in involving us in its attendant calamities." Such, after all, was one of the main purposes of the expedition, and if, in its course, southern women had been subjected to certain discourtesies in their homes, there was a measure of justice in that as well, since they were among the fiercest proponents of a war that might have ended by now except for their insistence that it be fought to the last ditch. Many of the soldiers believed as much, at any rate. "You urge young men to the battlefield where men are being killed by the thousands, while you stay home and sing *The Bonnie Blue Flag*," an Ohio colonel heard one of his troopers lecture a resentful housewife, "but you set up a howl when you see the Yankees down here getting your chickens. Many of your young men have told us they are tired of war, and would quit, but you women would shame them and drive them back." This applied only to white women, of course. Black ones were far more sympathetic to the invaders, especially on visits to their roadside bivouacs at night. "And they didn't charge us a cent," one grateful infantryman recorded.

So far, except for skittery detachments of butternut cavalry, not so much opposing as observing Kilpatrick's movement down the Macon & Western, neither Union column had encountered any organized resistance. One reason for this, in addition to their confusion as to Sherman's whereabouts or goal, was that the Confederates had little or nothing with which to confront him except Wheeler's 3500 scattered horsemen and an overload of brass. Within a week of his departure from Atlanta, both Hardee and Richard Taylor were at Macon, ordered there from Charleston and Selma by Beauregard — who himself was on the way from North Alabama — to confer with the Governor and his two chief military advisers, Howell Cobb and Major General G. W. Smith. Of these four high-ranking commanders, only the last brought any troops along, and all he had was 3000 Georgia militia summoned back into service by Brown to help meet the impending crisis. Learning that the blue infantry had left the railroad at Jonesboro, Hardee decided that Milledgeville, not Macon, was Howard's intermediary objective on a march that would continue southeast, through Millen to Savannah, and that Slocum would most likely push on eastward, through Augusta, to reach Charleston. He therefore advised that the militia be shifted northward to stand in Slocum's path, while he himself returned by rail to Savannah to prepare for its defense. Brown approving, the four makeshift brigades — so called, though none was much larger than a standard regiment — were ordered to set out at once, commanded by a militia brigadier named P. J. Phillips; Smith remained behind to make arrangements for supplies. That was on November 22, the day Sherman had one of Slocum's divisions clean out Cobb's plantation, ten miles north of Milledgeville, and that was how it came about that a brigade from one of Howard's divisions, ten miles east of Macon, fought that afternoon the only sizeable infantry action of the campaign between Atlanta and the Atlantic.

Aside from the high rate of casualties on one side, in contrast to the low rate on the other, there was little to distinguish the engagement from other such exercises in futility, staged for the most part in the early, picture-book days of the war, when blue and gray were green alike. Howard had bypassed Macon the day before, quarter-circling it clockwise from the north, and today, while Brown and the four generals were conferring, had posted a rear guard beyond Griswoldville, nine miles out the Central Georgia Railroad, which he crossed at that point on his way toward the Oconee for a crossing about midway between Milledgeville and Dublin. This rear guard, a single brigade from the tail division of Osterhaus's corps, had taken position along the crest of a hill one mile east of the station, its flanks protected by swampy ground and with open fields in front. So far, there had been no threat except from rebel troopers, who were easily kept off, but late that afternoon the 1500 defenders saw a heavy column of infantry moving toward them through the town. To their surprise, the marchers formed for attack and came straight at them across the stubble of the fields, displaying what one Federal called "more courage than discretion." With accustomed ease, the XV Corps veterans leveled their rifles and blasted the attackers back, only to see them reassemble and come on again, in much the same style and with similar results. Three times they charged uphill in close formation, and three times they were blown rearward by heavy volleys from the breastworks on the crest; until at last they gave it up and limped away, back through Griswoldville, toward Macon. Whooping, the victors moved out into the field to gather up the booty. Soon, however, the cheers froze in their throats at the sight of what lay before them in the stubble. They saw for the first time, to their horror, that they had been fighting mostly old men and young boys, who lay about in attitudes of death and agony — more than 600 of them in all, as compared to their own loss of 62.

"I was never so affected at the sight of dead and wounded before," an Illinois infantryman afterwards wrote home. "I hope we will never have to shoot at such men again. They knew nothing at all about fighting and I think their officers knew as little." A comrade, reacting not only to this but also to the pillage he had seen and shared in, put his thoughts in stronger words. "There is no God in war," he fumed. "It is merciless, cruel, vindictive, un-Christian, savage, relentless. It is all that devils could wish for."

Slocum's lead corps entered Milledgeville that same afternoon, twenty miles northeast of this scene of innocent valor, and the other arrived the following morning, accompanied by Sherman, who slept that night in the mansion vacated two days ago by Joe Brown, the fifth Confederate governor to be routed from his bed or desk by the approach of blue invaders. Unlike Nashville, Baton Rouge, Jackson, and Little Rock, all firmly in the Federal grip, the Georgia capital underwent only a temporary occupation; Slocum crossed the Oconee next morning, November 24, slogging eastward along the Central Georgia through Sandersville, toward Millen, while Howard took up a parallel route, some twenty miles to the south, toward Swainsboro. Brief as it was, the Milledgeville layover had been welcome, not only as a chance to get some rest after hiking the hundred miles from Atlanta, but also as a diversion from the workaday grind of converting more than sixty miles of railroad into a trail of twisted iron. Ebullient young officers, under the influence of what Sherman called "the spirit of mischief," assembled in the abandoned Hall of Representatives, and there, after a rousing debate, repealed the ordinance of secession and appointed committees to call forthwith on Governor Brown and President Davis for the purpose of landing official kicks on their official rumps. While this parliamentary business was in progress, soldiers ransacked the State House and amused themselves by heaving out of its windows all the books and papers they could find. A New Englander on Osterhaus's staff took private exception to such conduct, which seemed to him to go beyond a line that could not be crossed without a loss, if not of honor, then anyhow of due propriety. "I don't object to stealing horses, mules, niggers, and all such little things," he recorded in his journal, "but I will not engage in plundering and destroying public libraries."

Sherman, wearing low-quarter shoes and only one spur — "a general without boots," an admirer marveled — rode with Slocum, as before, except that Kilpatrick had been shifted from the right wing to provide cover for the flank that would be threatened if Richmond sent reinforcements from Virginia or the Carolinas. Apparently there were none of these; but there was something far more shocking, the red-haired Ohioan discovered when he came upon a division toiling across muddy fields because a young lieutenant had just had a foot blown off by an eight-inch shell that had been fuzed with matches and planted in the road. "This was not war, but murder," Sherman later wrote, "and it made me very angry. I immediately ordered a lot of rebel prisoners to be brought from the provost guard, armed with picks and spades, and made them march in close order along the road, so as to explode their own torpedoes or to discover and dig them up. They begged hard, but I reiterated the order, and could hardly help laughing at their stepping so gingerly along the road, where it was supposed sunken torpedoes might explode at each step."

There was no more trouble with torpedoes on the march after that; nor, indeed, from any other source. "No enemy opposed us," Sherman noted, "and we could only occasionally hear the faint reverberation of a gun to our left rear, where we knew that Kilpatrick was skirmishing with Wheeler's cavalry." In point of fact, though the scheduled rate of march had been reduced from fifteen to ten miles a day, thus assuring an unhurried and therefore thorough job of destruction across a front that varied in width from thirty to fifty miles, there was so little for Howard's wing to do that Blair's corps was summoned north to get in on the demolition of the Central Georgia. Up ahead was Millen, an important railroad junction on the far side of the Ogeechee, where a branch line ran north to Augusta to connect in turn with Wilmington and Richmond; Sherman sent word for Kilpatrick to take the lead and try his hand at effecting a "most complete and perfect break" in the installations there. "Let it be more devilish than can be dreamed of," he told the man he had called "a hell of a damned fool." Meantime both infantry wings kept slogging eastward unmolested, twisting iron and burning as they went. He was pleased to see that his "general orders of devastation" were being heeded by the Georgians in his path. Evidently the grapevine was in operation; "The people did not destroy food, for they saw clearly that it would be ruin to themselves."

At Millen, a hundred miles beyond Milledgeville and Macon, he paused for another one-day rest, two thirds of the way to his goal. Then he was off again, with his two now unequal wings on opposite banks of the Ogeechee, on the final lap of his march to the sea. It was early December now, and here on the left, beyond the river, marchers observed a change in the manner of the citizens whose crops they were despoiling; a change not so much in their attitude toward the invaders, as toward their neighbors across the Savannah River and toward the war itself. "All I ask is that when you get to South Carolina you will treat them the same way," one farmer said, and was echoed by another: "Why don't you go over to South Carolina and serve them this way? They started it." Sherman was encouraged by such talk. At the outset he had retained the option of switching his objective — including a tangential sprint for Pensacola, down on the Gulf — in case he encountered serious resistance. But no such shift was even considered, since there had been no resistance worth the name, either from regulars or guerillas. "Pierce the shell of the Confederacy and it's all hollow inside!" he exulted as he set out from Millen for Savannah, less than a hundred miles to the southeast.

One trouble there was, of increasing concern, despite his efforts to guard against it from the start. In the course of the march now approaching its end, an estimated 25,000 blacks of both sexes and all ages joined the various infantry columns at one time or another, and though at least three fourths of these turned back, either from weariness or homesickness, a considerable number managed to tag along, a growing encumbrance. Sherman tried to discourage this by explaining to their spokesmen — gray-haired preachers, for the most part — that he "wanted the slaves to remain where they were, and not load us down with useless mouths which would eat up the food needed for our fighting men." They nodded agreement, but continued to throng in the wake of each blue column, preferring instant liberty to the promise of eventual freedom, once the war was over. Beyond the Ogeechee the problem became acute, or seemed about to, not only because the land was less fruitful toward the seaboard, but also because of reports that Bragg had reached Augusta with reinforcements; Sherman decided to rid himself, in one way or another, of what might prove a military embarrassment in the event of a clash on that congested flank. He had not followed Grant's suggestion that he recruit able-bodied slaves as reinforcements, in part because he lacked missionary zeal and in part because he considered this a practice that would lead to future ills, both for the army and the country. "The South deserves all she has got from her injustice to the Negro," he would presently tell Halleck, "but that is no reason why we should go to the other extreme." In any case, he was determined to do what he could to disencumber his threatened left of these "useless mouths."

At Ebenezer Creek, which lay between the Ogeechee and the Savannah, about two thirds of the way from Millen to the coast, he found his chance — or, more strictly speaking, had it found for him, and acted upon, by one of his chief lieutenants. Davis's corps brought up the rear of Slocum's wing, and as soon as the last of his infantry cleared the unfordable stream he had his engineers hurriedly take up the pontoon bridge, leaving the refugees who were tailing the column stranded on the opposite bank. Whatever glee Davis and his soldiers felt at the success of this stratagem, which accomplished in short order all that weeks of exhortation and admonition had failed to achieve, was changed to sudden dismay when they saw what followed, first across the way and then in Ebenezer Creek itself. Wailing to find their march toward freedom halted thus in midstride and themselves abandoned to the mercy of Confederate horsemen, who soon would be upon them, the Negroes hesitated briefly, impacted by the surge of pressure from the rear, then stampeded with a rush into the icy water, old and young alike, men and women and children, swimmers and nonswimmers, determined not to be left behind by the deliverers they supposed had come to lead them out of bondage. Many drowned, despite the efforts of the engineers, who, horrified by the sight of the disaster their action had brought on, waded into the muddy creek to rescue as many of the unfortunates as they could reach. "As soon as the character of the unthinking rush and panic was seen," a Federal observer wrote, "all was done that could be done to save them from the water; but the loss of life was still great enough to prove that there were many ignorant, simple souls to whom it was literally preferable to die freemen rather than to live slaves."

In far-off City Point and Washington, all this time, nothing was known except at second hand — and rebel hand, at that — of what had occurred between the western army's high-spirited departure from Atlanta, three weeks back, and the tragic crossing of Ebenezer Creek, within thirty miles of Savannah. Mindful of its commander's plan to alter his route if serious opposition loomed, Grant drew an analogy that was apt: "Sherman's army is now somewhat in the condition of a ground-mole when he disappears under a lawn. You can here and there trace his track, but you are not quite certain where he will come out until you see his head." The President used much the same metaphor when John Sherman came to the White House to ask if there was any news of his brother down in Georgia. Lincoln replied that there was no word of the general's whereabouts or even his destination. "I know the hole he went in at, but I can't tell you the hole he will come out of."

In his December message that week he told Congress, "The most remarkable feature of the military operations of the year is General Sherman's attempted march of three hundred miles directly through the insurgent region. It tends to show a great increase of our relative strength that our General-in-Chief should feel able to confront and hold in check every active force of the enemy, and yet to detach a well-appointed large army to move on such an expedition." In the original draft, a sentence followed: "We must conclude that he feels our cause could, if need be, survive the loss of the whole detached force, while by the risk he takes a chance for the great advantages which would follow success." But this was dropped from the delivered text, on the grounds that it might be thought to show a lack of concern for the lives of 60,000 soldiers being risked on a long-odds gamble, hundreds of miles from the possibility of assistance. No one who was near Lincoln during this critical period would have made that error: least of all a friend who attended a reception at which the Chief Executive stood shaking hands with guests as they arrived. He seemed preoccupied, strangely perfunctory in his greetings, and the friend, refusing to be shuttled along like the others, stood his ground until the tall, sad-faced man emerged from his abstracted mood with a smile of recognition. "How do you do? How do you do?" he said warmly. "Excuse me for not noting you. I was thinking of a man down South."

Understandable as this was at that remove, events were soon to show that such concern had been unwarranted. By now Lincoln's "man down South" was approaching the goal of his trans-Georgia expedition, and those who were with him exulted in the damage they had inflicted and avoided. From first to last, barely two percent of their number, including the wounded, were judged unfit for duty in the course of a nearly four-week march that saw more than two hundred miles of railroad "utterly abolished" and the Confederacy riven. "The destruction could hardly have been worse," a veteran declared, "if Atlanta had been a volcano in eruption and the molten lava had flowed in a stream sixty miles wide and five times as long." Mostly they were young men, even those of highest rank; the twenty commanders of armies, corps, and divisions averaged forty years of age, while the volunteers from civilian life outnumbered the West Pointers, twelve to eight. Close to half their 218 regiments were from Ohio and Illinois, and all but 33 of the rest were from other western states. Their exuberance undiminished by strain or combat — aside, that is, from some momentary sadness after Griswoldville — the marchers treated the whole campaign, one soldier commentator said, as "a vast holiday frolic" and livened their nights, when they might have been sleeping, with occasional sham battles in which the principal weapon was lighted pine knots, flung whirling through the darkness with an effect as gaudy as anything seen in contests whose losses ran into the thousands. Cheering, they closed down upon Savannah's outer defenses on December 9 and 10.

Chief among these was Fort McAllister, a dozen miles to the south, on the right bank of the Ogeechee just above Ossabaw Sound. Sherman decided to reduce it first, thus clearing the way for the navy to steam upriver — if in fact the ships were waiting off the coast, as prearranged — before he moved against the city proper.

The navy was there all right, he discovered when he climbed to the roof of a rice mill, December 13, for a view of the fort and, beyond it, the blue waters of the sound; Howard had set up a signal station atop the mill to study the terrain and report on the progress of the attack by Brigadier General William Hazen's division. This had been Sherman's old Shiloh outfit, and concern for the survivors of those days — when Hazen, a thirty-year-old West Pointer, commanded an Ohio regiment — increased his impatience at finding the assault delayed far into the afternoon. However, while he waited and chafed, a lookout peering eastward spotted what Sherman later described as "a faint cloud of smoke and an object gliding, as it were, along the horizon above the tops of the sedge toward the sea, which little by little grew till it was pronounced to be the smokestack of a steamer." Soon, as the ship drew closer, the watchers identified the U.S. flag at her peak and a signalman asking in wigwag from her deck: "Who are you?" "General Sherman," the answer went back, and when this was followed by another question: "Is Fort McAllister taken?" Sherman replied: "Not yet, but it will be in a minute."

And it was, very nearly within that span. Hazen's division swarmed out of the woods, across flats that had been thickly sown with torpedoes, through the abatis, over the palisade, and into the fort itself, where, as Sherman watched from his distant perch on the rice mill roof, "the smoke cleared away and the parapets were blue with our men, who fired their muskets in the air and shouted so that we actually heard them, or felt that we did." The attack had lasted barely fifteen minutes; Hazen lost 134 killed and wounded, many of them victims of exploding torpedoes, and inflicted 48 casualties on the 250-man garrison, the rest of whom were captured along with fifteen guns. "It's my old division; I knew they'd do it!" Sherman crowed, and had an aide get off a message to Slocum at the far end of the line. "Dear General. Take a good big drink, a long breath, and then yell like the devil. The fort was carried at 4.30 p.m."

That night the ship steamed in through Ossabaw Sound and up the Ogeechee River unopposed. Others followed, next day and the next, bringing 600,000 rations and, best of all -- for, as Sherman said, "This prompt receipt of letters had an excellent effect, making us feel that home was near" — the mail that had been piling up for the troops ever since they left Atlanta, four weeks, to the day, before the fall of Fort McAllister.

There was also news, both good and bad, of recent developments in Virginia and Tennessee, as well as of an effort, less than thirty miles from Savannah, to break the railroad between there and Charleston. That had been two weeks ago, on the last day of November, and practically everything about the operation was unsatisfactory from the Union point of view. From his headquarters up the South Carolina coast at Hilton Head, Major General John G. Foster, successor to Quincy Gillmore as commander of the Department of the South, sent a 5500-man force inland to get astride the railroad near Grahamville Station and thus prevent the Confederates from opposing Sherman with reinforcements sent by rail, in advance of his arrival, from points along the seaboard between there and Richmond. As luck would have it — rebel luck, that is — G. W. Smith reached Savannah that same day with the Georgia militia; Joe Brown's Pets had come roundabout through Albany and Thomasville after their savage treatment, eight days ago, by Howard's rear guard east of Macon. Down to about 1400 effectives as a result of that and other mishaps, they were sent by Hardee to meet Foster's threat to the Charleston & Savannah. Meet it they did, and with such élan, although the odds were as heavy against them here as they had been in their favor back at Griswoldville, that they not only wiped out the stain of that encounter, they also reversed the ratio of casualties suffered. Encountering the invaders at Honey Hill, three miles south of Grahamville, they took up a position confronting a swamp-bound causeway, flung them back, frustrated a flank attack by setting fire to a field of broomsedge, and finally drove them out of range of the railroad, much as had been done two years ago at nearby Pocotaligo, where a similar blue force attempted the same maneuver with no better luck. Smith's loss was 8 killed, 42 wounded. The Federals lost 755, including 88 killed, 623 wounded, and 44 missing.

The newly arrived Westerners professed no great surprise at this defeat, having come to expect such ineptness from their allies in the paper-collar East, even against militia they themselves had trounced so roundly such a short time before. Besides, for all his success in keeping the railroad open northward, Hardee still had fewer than 15,000 inexperienced troops for the defense of Savannah against four times that number of hardened veterans. As for Sherman, he was far more interested in developments back in Middle Tennessee, where part of Thomas's scratch command had already fought one battle, more or less against his wishes, and seemed about to have to fight another, despite his apparent reluctance to do anything but sit tight. In a two-week-old letter, delivered to his red-haired friend at Fort McAllister by the navy, Grant sounded rather put out by the Tennessee situation and the way Old Pap was meeting it, but he expressed no discontent with his own lack of progress around Petersburg and Richmond. In fact, he was looking forward to a shipboard holiday. "After all becomes quiet, and the roads become so bad up here that there is likely to be a week or two when nothing can be done, I will run down the coast to see you," he wrote, adding the happy afterthought: "If you desire it, I will ask Mrs. Sherman to go with me."

Perhaps in part because even those who had wives back home could expect no such reunion by special delivery, most of this had little interest for soldiers who had just completed what was being hailed as one of the great marches of all time. By and large, their feeling was that now that they had reached the East the war would soon be over; but even this they were willing to leave to Uncle Billy, knowing that he would use them to that end when the time was right. They were more concerned with their own letters, reading and rereading them while improving their investment of Savannah and waiting for the siege guns their commander had requisitioned to reduce not only the city's defenses but also their own losses when the hour came for launching the assault. Except for coffee, which ran low at last, not even the delivery of those 600,000 rations provided much of a diversion. The fact was they had never eaten better than they had done for the past month, and Sherman even now was informing Grant that, after setting out from Atlanta with a herd of 5000 cattle and feeding beef to all who wanted it along the way, he had wound up on the coast with twice as many cows as when he started. For some time now a steady diet of sweet potatoes, corn, and pork had palled on northern palates. What they mainly looked forward to, throughout the final week of the march, was oysters, and now that they had reached salt water they had all of them they wanted. Just outside Savannah, over toward Ossabaw Sound, one soldier recorded a sample menu in a letter home: "Oyster soup, oysters on the half shell, roast goose, fried oysters, rice, raisins, and roast oysters."

Hood at last issued orders for the march north from the Tennessee River on November 16, the day Sherman drew rein on Bald Hill, two hundred air-line miles to the southeast, for a farewell look at smouldering Atlanta. Now as before, however — although Forrest, the ostensible cause of the army's marking time ever since it reached the northwest corner of Alabama in late October, had returned from his Johnsonville raid two days ago — there were further delays, occasioned by last-minute supply arrangements and a fierce storm that grew still worse throughout the next four days, converting the rain to sleet and the roads to hub-deep troughs of icy mud. But Hood would wait no longer. Just last week, in a message so characteristic that it was practically superfluous, he had told Jefferson Davis: "You may rely upon my striking the enemy whenever a suitable opportunity presents itself, and that I will spare no effort to make that opportunity." On November 20, a Sunday, he set out, and by the following morning — three weeks, to the day, since his arrival in Tuscumbia, just across the river — the last of his troops filed out of Florence, bound for Nashville and, it might be, the Ohio.

Preceded by Forrest, whose 6000 horsemen swept the front and covered the right flank, the march was in three columns, a three-division corps of just over 10,000 men in each: Stewart by way of Lawrenceburg, Cheatham by way of Waynesboro, thirty miles to the west, and Lee by way of country roads between. All three would converge on Mount Pleasant, seventy miles away by the nearest route, and move together — 38,000 strong, including the three cavalry divisions and the artillery with 108 guns — to Columbia, twelve miles northeast on Duck River, whose crossings at that point were the objective in this first stage of the advance through Middle Tennessee. Hood's purpose was to interpose his army between Thomas, who had been gathering troops at Nashville for the past month, and Schofield, posted eighty miles south at Pulaski with his own and Stanley's corps, detached by Sherman before he set out from Atlanta. Schofield had roughly 30,000 of all arms, Thomas about the same number, and if Hood got between them, in control of the Duck crossings with a force superior to either, he could deal with them individually, in whatever order he chose, and thus score a crowning double victory that would give him the Tennessee capital, together with all its stores, and clear the way for his drive to the Ohio; which in turn — or so ran the dream unfolded for Beauregard, now departed — would provoke the recall of Sherman, at the end of his race through the Georgia vacuum to the sea, and perhaps free Hood to work the deliverance of Richmond by crossing the Cumberlands into Virginia to rejoin his beleaguered hero, R. E. Lee.

Despite the unseasonably bitter weather, which alternately froze the roads iron hard, with ankle-twisting ruts, or thawed them into quagmires that made every step a wrenching effort, the butternut veterans clocked good time on their march beyond the Tennessee line. Indeed, so successful was Forrest in driving Brigadier General Edward Hatch's reinforced cavalry division "from one position to another," thereby preventing any penetration of the screen, that Stewart's corps reached Lawrenceburg, more than halfway to Columbia, before Schofield, twenty miles due east at Pulaski, even knew that Hood was not only on the way around his flank but was also not much farther by now than he himself was from Duck River, which he would have to cross if he was to avoid being cut off from Nashville and the other half of the army Thomas had spent the past month assembling for the defense of Middle Tennessee. That was on the night of November 22; Schofield began his withdrawal at first light next morning, prodding his five divisions, 62 guns, and 800 wagons northward up the turnpike. He knew he was involved in a race whose stakes were life or death, and thanks to a faster, somewhat shorter track he won it handily by getting his lead division to Columbia on the 24th, in time to keep the fast-riding rebel troopers from seizing either of the two bridges across the Duck. Moreover, he had his entire force dug in along the outskirts of the south-bank town, guns emplaced, when Hood's infantry arrived from Mount Pleasant on the 26th and took up a position, that day and the next, confronting the newly erected breastworks anchored right and left on the river above and below.

Hood was not discouraged by this loss of a long-odds race in which some of his troops covered more than a hundred miles on inferior roads while Schofield's did less than thirty-five on the turnpike. Nor was he provoked into launching a headlong assault, which in fact was no longer practicable — let alone judicious — by the morning of November 28, when he discovered that his one-time West Point roommate and mathematics coach had withdrawn in the night to the north bank, destroying the two bridges over the river now in his front. What Hood had in mind instead, his lieutenants found when they reported as ordered to his headquarters beside the Pulaski pike that afternoon, was a flanking movement similar to the one he had just attempted, except that this time the odds were by no means long and he once more enjoyed the confidence that came with employing the tactics he had so much admired in Virginia, back in the days when he had both of his legs and the vigorous use of both his arms. As he saw it, later describing the frame of mind that led to the formulation of his plan, "The situation presented an occasion for one of those interesting and beautiful moves upon the chessboard of war, to perform which I had often desired an opportunity.... I had beheld with admiration the noble deeds and grand results achieved by the immortal Jackson in similar maneuvers; I had seen his corps made equal to ten times its number by a sudden attack on the enemy's rear, and I hoped in this instance to be able to profit by the teachings of my illustrious countryman."

The plan itself was as simple as it was bold. James Wilson having joined Schofield beyond the Duck with another 4000 horsemen, Forrest would cross the river today, ten miles upstream at Huey's Mill, and drive the blue cavalry northward, away from possible interference with Hood's infantry, which would cross at dawn at Davis Ford, three miles above the town. Cheatham would lead, his corps being posted on the right, and Stewart would follow, reinforced by one of Lee's divisions. Each would take along a single battery, for emergencies, and leave the rest of the guns behind — an even hundred, as it turned out — for use by Lee, who would demonstrate with them and his two remaining divisions in order to fix the Federals in position on the opposite bank of the river, while the bulk of the superior gray army moved around their left and into their rear at Spring Hill, a dozen miles up the turnpike from Columbia and about the same distance from Franklin, whose seizure would give the flankers control of the Harpeth River crossings, less than twenty miles from Nashville. In other words, another race would start at dawn, and this one too would be a matter of life or death for Schofield, though Hood did not intend for him to know — any more than he had known before — that a contest was in progress until it was at least half over; by which time, in contrast to the previous maneuver, there would be little he could do except look for a roundabout avenue of escape. At that point Hood would be free either to turn on his former roommate or, having eliminated him as a factor by holding the rail and turnpike bridges across the Harpeth, plunge straight ahead for the Tennessee capital without delay. He seemed to favor the latter course just now, for he spoke that night, soon after the council of war broke up and the participants went out into the falling snow to alert their commands for tomorrow's march, of "calling for volunteers to storm the key of the works about the city." Next morning, while Cheatham's men were moving through the predawn darkness toward the pontoons thrown for them at Davis Ford the night before, he made this even more emphatic. "The enemy must give me a fight," he told a friend — Chaplain-Doctor, later Bishop, Charles Quintard — "or I'll be in Nashville before tomorrow night."

Mindful of the failure of a similar maneuver four months ago, which brought on the lost Battle of Atlanta, he went along this time in person, as he had not done before, riding with Cheatham near the head of the flanking column to see for himself that his Jacksonian plan was

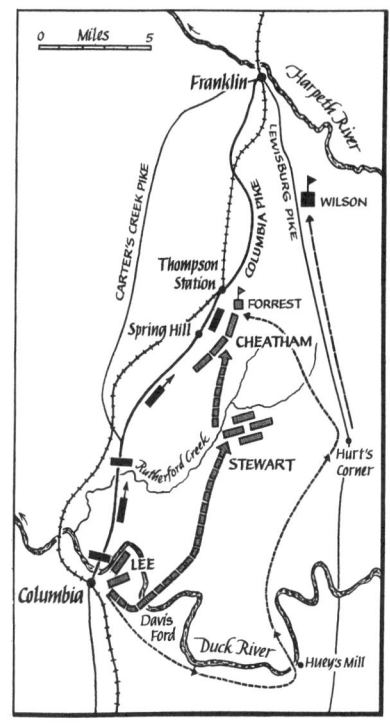

carried out as he intended. The result, throughout the opening phase, was all he could have hoped for. Both the crossing and the march north beyond the river, parallel to the turnpike three miles west, were unimpeded, thanks to Schofield's apparent lack of vigilance and to Forrest, whose three divisions clashed with Wilson's two at Hurt's Corner around midday, six miles out, and drove them headlong up the Lewisburg Pike toward Franklin; Forrest detached a brigade to keep up the pressure on the fleeing bluecoats and turned northwest with the rest of his troopers, as ordered, for a strike at Spring Hill in advance of the infantry. Moving up, Hood halted Stewart's reinforced corps at Rutherford Creek — presumably to protect his rear in case Schofield took alarm and moved against him from Columbia, though the steady booming of Lee's one hundred guns beyond the Duck gave assurance that the two Union corps were still in position on the north bank, unmindful of the fact that Hood had all his cavalry and all but two of his nine infantry divisions on their flank or in their rear. Elated, he told Cheatham, as he rode with him beyond the creek to within three miles of Spring Hill, to commit his lead division without delay, alongside Forrest's horsemen, and follow with the other two as soon as they came up. Meantime, Hood himself rode back to check on Stewart, whose four divisions could also be committed if they were needed; which seemed unlikely.

By then it was just after 3 o'clock. Behind him, over toward the turnpike in the direction of Spring Hill, a spatter of gunfire presumably announced that Forrest even now was overriding such resistance as the blue garrison could offer, surprised as its few members must be, midway between Columbia and Franklin, to find a host of graybacks bearing down on the little country town a dozen miles in Schofield's rear.

But that was by no means the case: mainly due to the vigilance of James Wilson. Though he lacked the time needed to whip Thomas's defeat-prone horsemen into any shape for standing up even briefly to a superior force of veterans under the Wizard of the Saddle, the young Illinois-born West Pointer had not forgotten the primary cavalry assignment of furnishing his chief with information. In fact he had sent a warning the night before, when, impressed by Forrest's aggressiveness, he notified headquarters that a heavy Confederate movement seemed to be in progress across the Duck, ten miles upstream. Schofield telegraphed word of this to Nashville, and Thomas promptly ordered a further withdrawal to Franklin. Accordingly, while Hood's infantry was passing unobserved over Davis Ford, Schofield started his 800 wagons and most of his guns up the turnpike with a train guard of two divisions under David Stanley, who was told to drop one of them off at Rutherford Creek, to secure the crossing there, and proceed with the other to Spring Hill, which he would cover for the rest of the army, soon to follow. By midmorning Stanley had cleared the creek, about one third of the distance between Columbia and Spring Hill, and learning as he drew near the latter place that rebel troopers were approaching in strength — it was by now past 2 o'clock — he double-timed Brigadier General George Wagner's division into position, just east of the town and the pike, in time to help the two-regiment garrison ward off an all-out mounted attack.

It was a near thing, and a bloody one as well, according to a Wisconsin infantryman who watched the charge get broken up, for the most part by artillery. "You could see a rebel's head falling off his horse on one side and his body on the other, and the horse running and nickering and looking for its rider. Others you could see fall off with their feet caught in the stirrup, and the horse dragging and trampling them, dead or alive. Others, the horse would get shot and the rider tumble head over heels, or maybe get caught by the horse falling on him."

Having repulsed the rebel troopers, who returned piecemeal to probe warily at his defenses, Stanley — Howard's successor as IV Corps commander, thirty-six years old, an Ohio-born West Pointer and peacetime Indian fighter, chief of cavalry under Rosecrans during the last campaign in this region, back in the summer of '63 — proceeded to align his force of just over 5000 for the protection of Spring Hill. Resolute as he was in making his preparations for defense, he was fortunate not to have his resolution strained by awareness that this might have to be attempted against twice that number of gray infantry now crossing Rutherford Creek with Cheatham, less than three miles southeast across the fields, and an even larger number close in their rear with Stewart. In any case, he parked the train between the turnpike and the railroad, west of town, and unlimbered his 34 guns in close support of Wagner's three brigades, disposed along a convex line to the east, both flanks withdrawn to touch the pike above and below. Here, under cover of breastworks hastily improvised by dismantling snake-rail fences, they settled down to their task of keeping Schofield's escape route open in their rear. Around 4 o'clock, half an hour before sundown, the first concerted assault struck their right, driving the flank brigade from its fence-rail works and back on its support, three batteries massed on the southern outskirts of the town for just such an emergency as was now upon them. These eighteen pieces roared and plowed the ranks of the attackers, who stumbled rearward in confusion, having no guns of their own. In the red light of the setting sun, when Stanley saw that their regimental flags bore the full-moon device of Cleburne's division — by common consent, Federal and Confederate, the hardest-hitting in Hood's army — he warned Wagner to brace his men for their return, probably with substantial reinforcements.

They did return, their number doubled by the arrival of another gray division; but little or nothing came of this menace in the end. After milling about in the twilight, apparently with the intention of launching a swamping assault, they paused for a time, as if bemused, and then — incredibly, for they presently were joined by still a third division — went into bivouac, more or less where they were, their cookfires twinkling in the frosty outer darkness, just beyond easy musket range of Spring Hill and the turnpike close in rear of the makeshift breastworks Stanley had feared were about to be rushed and overrun. Meantime Schofield put two more divisions in motion north, leaving one at Columbia to discourage Lee from crossing the Duck, and another at Rutherford Creek, where it had been posted that morning. By midnight the first two had cleared Spring Hill, subjected to nothing worse along the way than sporadic fire from the roadside and the loss of a few stragglers, although there was a clash with some late-roaming butternut troopers at Thompson Station, three miles up the pike. These were soon brushed aside, and the two divisions that followed close behind, from Rutherford Creek and Columbia, encountered even less trouble. As a result, Wagner's division, which formerly had led the march but now brought up the rear, was able to follow the unmolested train and guns out of Spring Hill before dawn. By that time the lead division was at Franklin and had secured the crossings of the Harpeth, within twenty miles of heavily-fortified Nashville.

Just what had happened, out in the cookfire-twinkling darkness beyond the now abandoned Union breastworks east of Spring Hill and the turnpike, was not too hard to establish from such reports as were later made, both on and off the record. *Why* it happened was far more difficult to determine, though many tried in the course of the heated controversy that followed down the years. Still, whatever their persuasion as to a rightful distribution of the guilt — of which, in all conscience, there was enough to go around — a Texas lieutenant in Cleburne's division, after noting that Hood, Cheatham, "and others in high places have said a good deal in trying to fix the blame for this disgraceful failure," arrived at an assessment with which few could disagree: "The most charitable explanation is that the gods of war injected confusion into the heads of our leaders."

After Cleburne's 18-gun repulse he was joined by Bate, who came up on his left. Just as they were about to go forward together, shortly after sunset — Forrest had pulled back for lack of ammunition, the supply train having been left with Lee to disencumber the flanking column — an order came from Cheatham for the attack to be delayed until the third division arrived under Major General John C. Brown, who would give the signal to advance as soon as he got in position on Cleburne's right. Brown came up about 5.30, but finding his own right overlapped by the blue defenders, informed Cheatham that any advance by him "must meet with inevitable disaster." While he waited, obliging Cleburne and Bate to wait as well, Cheatham reported the problem to Hood, who authorized a suspension of the gunless night attack until Stewart arrived from Rutherford Creek. Stewart did not get there at all, however, having been misguided up a country road that paralleled the turnpike. Only his fourth division, detached from Stephen Lee, under Edward Johnson — Old Clubby, captured six months ago in the Spotsylvania Mule Shoe, had recently been exchanged and transferred West — was stopped in time to move into position on the left of Bate, adjoining the turnpike south of town. Stewart by then had received permission to put his other three divisions into bivouac where they were, two miles to the north and well back from the pike. By that time, practically everyone else — Cleburne and Bate and Brown and all their men, stalled on the verge of their twilight assault — had begun to bed down, too: including Hood, who had spent a long day strapped in the saddle, with considerable irritation to the stump of the leg he had lost at Chickamauga. He was close to exhaustion, and there still had been no report that Schofield had begun a rearward movement. In fact, Lee's guns were still growling beyond Duck River, strong evidence that the Federals were still on its north bank, when Hood retired for the night. Before he did so, he told Cheatham (as Cheatham later testified) that he "had concluded to wait until the morning, and directed me to hold my command in readiness to attack at daylight."

Not quite everyone was sleeping, he discovered when a barefoot private came to his farmhouse headquarters some time after midnight to report that he had seen Union infantry in motion on the turnpike in large numbers. Hood roused himself and told his adjutant to send Cheatham orders "to advance a line of skirmishers and confuse the enemy by firing into his columns." Cheatham passed the word to Johnson, whose division was nearby, but when the Virginian reconnoitered westward, two miles south of Spring Hill, he found the road lying empty in the moonlight, with nothing moving on it in either direction. Most likely he had encountered a gap between segments of the blue army on the march; in any case, like Hood and Cheatham before him, he too returned to the warmth of his blankets while Schofield's troops continued to slog north along the turnpike, just beyond earshot of the rebels sleeping eastward in the fields. Not all the marchers made it. "We were actually so close to the pike," a butternut lieutenant later wrote, "that many Federal soldiers came out to our fires to light their pipes and were captured." Not even all of these were gathered up, however. For example, two Confederates were munching cornbread beside a low fire when a man strolled up; "What troops are you?" he asked, and on being told, "Cleburne's division," turned and walked off in the darkness. "Say, wasn't that a Yank? Let's go get him," one grayback said, only to have his companion reply: "Ah, let him go. If you're looking for Yankees go down the pike and get all you want."

Amid all this confusion, high and low, one thing at least was clear with the dawn of the last day in November. Schofield had gotten clean away, undeterred after darkness fell, except for a brief clash at Thompson Station with one of Forrest's divisions which had managed to capture a meager supply of ammunition. If Hood was saddened by this Spring Hill fiasco — "The best move in my career as a soldier," he said later, "I was thus destined to behold come to naught" — he was also furious, mainly with Cheatham, but also with almost everyone in sight, including the ragged, barefoot men themselves. In his anger he renewed the charge that Joe Johnston had spoiled them for use in the offensive. "The discovery that the army, after a forward march of 180 miles, was still, seemingly, unwilling to accept battle unless under the protection of breastworks, caused me to experience grave concern. In my inmost heart I questioned whether or not I would ever succeed in eradicating this evil."

This he would say long afterward, not stopping then, any more than now, to consider what he asked of them in designing still another of those swift Jacksonian movements that had worked so well two years ago in Virginia; whereas the fact was, not even Lee's army was

"Lee's army" any longer; let alone Hood's. All the same, he believed he saw a corrective for the fault. If a flanking maneuver was beyond the army's capacity, perhaps a headlong assault was not only within its means but might also provide a cure for its lamentable habit of flinching at Yankee breastworks and depending so much on its own. In any case he was determined now to give the thing a disciplinary try — and he said as much, years later, looking back. "I hereupon decided, before the enemy would be able to reach his stronghold at Nashville, to make that same afternoon another and final effort to overtake and rout him, and drive him into the Harpeth River at Franklin."

※ 3 ※

So he said, anticipating vengeance. But when the Army of Tennessee set out from its camps around Spring Hill that morning — three fourths of it, at any rate; Stephen Lee was marching from Columbia, a dozen miles to the south, with his other two divisions and the artillery and trains — its commander, nearly beside himself with rage at last night's bungling, seemed "wrathy as a rattlesnake" to one of his subordinates, who were themselves engaged in a hot-tempered flurry of charges and countercharges as a result of Schofield's escape from the trap so carefully laid for his destruction. Down in the ranks, where mutual recrimination afforded less relief, the soldiers "felt chagrined and mortified," one afterwards remarked, "at the occurrence of the preceding day."

Yet this soon passed, at least as the dominant reaction, partly because of the weather, which had faired. "The weather was clear and beautiful," another infantryman wrote; "the cool air was warmed by the bright sunshine, and our forces were in fine condition." By way of added encouragement, the band from a Louisiana brigade, reported to be the army's best, fell out beside the turnpike and cut loose with a few rollicking numbers to cheer the marchers tramping past. "Each man felt a pride in wiping out the stain," the first soldier would recall, while the second added: "Their spirits were animated by encouraging orders from General Hood, who held out to them the prospect that at any moment he might call on them to deal the enemy a decisive blow."

This was as he had done before, on the march north from Florence, and the spirit now was much as it had been then, when the promise was that the Federals were about to be outflanked. For the Tennesseans the campaign was literally a homecoming, but for all the army's veterans it was a glad return to fields of anticipated glory, when they and the war were young and hopes were high. Once more patriot-volunteers of a Second American Revolution, many of them barefoot in the snow, as their forebears had been at Valley Forge, they were hailed along the way as returned deliverers, fulfillers of the faded dream that victory waited on the banks of the Ohio, which was once again their goal. Gladdest of all these scenes of welcome had been the march from Mount Pleasant to Columbia, a region of old families whose mansions lined the pike and whose place of worship — tiny, high-roofed St John's Church, ivy-clad and Gothic, where Bishop-General Polk had preached and his Episcopal kinsmen had their graves amid flowers and shrubbery fresh and green in bleak November — had so impressed Pat Cleburne, for one, that he checked his horse in passing and remarked that it was "almost worth dying for, to be buried in such a beautiful spot." Impromptu receptions and serenades greeted the returning heroes, and prayers of thanksgiving were offered in this and other churches along the way, especially in Pulaski and Columbia, where the Yankees had been thrown into retreat by the gray army's passage round their flank. Spring Hill too had been delivered, though at a heavy cost in Confederate mortification, which soon was transmuted into determination that the bluecoats, having escaped their pursuers twice, would not manage it still a third time unscathed. Accordingly, the seven gray divisions stepped out smartly up the Franklin Turnpike, preceded by Forrest's troopers. Hood was pleased, he later said, to find his army "metamorphosed, as it were, in one night.... The feeling existed which sometimes induces men who have long been wedded to but one policy to look beyond the sphere of their own convictions, and, at least, be willing to make trial of another course of action." In other words, they now seemed ready to charge breastworks, if need be, and he was prepared to take them up on that.

Stewart led the march today, having overshot the mark the night before, and Cheatham followed, accompanied by Johnson's division from Lee's corps, which was three hours in the rear. A dozen miles to the north by 2 o'clock, the vanguard approached Winstead Hill, three miles short of Franklin. On its crest, astride the turnpike, a Union brigade was posted with a battery, apparently under instructions to delay the gray pursuit; but Hood, unwilling to waste time on a preliminary skirmish — perhaps designed by Schofield to give the rest of his army a chance to get away unharmed — swung Stewart's three divisions to the right, along Henpeck Lane, and kept the other four marching straight on up the pike. To avoid being outflanked, the bluecoats limbered their guns and fell back out of sight beyond the rim of the slope up which the head of Cheatham's column now was toiling. When the Tennesseans topped the rise they gave a roaring cheer at the sight of the Harpeth Valley spread before them, with the town of Franklin nestled in a northeastward bend of the river and the Federals intrenched in a bulging curve along its southern and western outskirts. Beyond the crest, on the forward slope of Winstead Hill, Hood turned off to the left of the road, and while his staff got busy setting up a command post, the one-legged general dismounted — painfully, as always, with the help of an orderly who passed him his crutches once he was afoot — and there, in the shade of an isolated linn tree, removed his binoculars from their case for a careful study of the position his adversary had chosen for making a stand.

Schofield had been there since dawn, nine hours ago, and by now had completed the organization of an all-round defense of his Franklin bridgehead, on the off chance that the Confederates would attempt to interfere with the crossing or the follow-up sprint for the Tennessee capital, eighteen miles away. He would have been well on his way there already, safely over the river and hard on the march up the Nashville Pike, except that when he arrived with his two lead divisions, under Jacob Cox and Brigadier General Thomas Ruger, he found that the turnpike bridge had been wrecked by the rising Harpeth and Thomas had failed to send the pontoons he had so urgently requested, two days ago at Columbia, after burning his own for lack of transportation. Placing Cox in charge, he told him to have the two XXIII Corps divisions dig in astride the Columbia Pike, his own on the left and Ruger's on the right, half a mile south of the town in their rear, while awaiting the arrival of the three IV Corps divisions, still on the march from Rutherford Creek and Spring Hill. By the time Stanley got there with Thomas Wood's and Brigadier General Nathan Kimball's divisions, around midmorning, the engineers had floored the railroad bridge with planks ripped from nearby houses and the wagon train had started crossing. Schofield ordered Kimball to dig in on a line to the right of Ruger, extending the works northward so that they touched the river below as well as above the town, and passed Wood's division, along with most of Stanley's artillery, across the clattering, newly-planked railway span to take position on the high far bank of the Harpeth, overlooking Franklin and the fields lying south of the long curve of intrenchments thrown up by the other three divisions. That way, Wood could move fast to assist Wilson's horsemen in dealing with rebel flankers on that side of the river, upstream or down, and Cox was braced for confronting a headlong assault, if that was what developed.

This last seemed highly unlikely, however, since Hood — with two of his nine divisions far in the rear, together with all but eight of his guns — had fewer than 30,000 troops on hand, including cavalry, while Schofield had well above that number — 34,000 of all arms — stoutly intrenched for the most part and supported by 60-odd guns, nearly all of them able to pound anything that tried to cross the two-mile-deep plain that lay between the bristling outskirts of Franklin and the foot of Winstead Hill. Moreover, that deadly stretch of ground was not only about as level as a tabletop, it was also unobstructed. Originally there had been a small grove of locusts in front of Ruger's part of the line, but these had been felled for use as headlogs and abatis. Similarly, on the left, a thick-set hedge of Osage orange had been thinned to clear a field of fire for Cox, leaving only enough of the growth to provide a thorny palisade. There was one obstacle out front: two brigades from Wagner's division, intrenched in an advance position, half a mile down and astride the Columbia Pike, with instructions to remain in observation there unless Hood, when he came up, "showed a disposition to advance in force," in which case they were to retire within the lines and serve as a reserve for the three divisions now in their rear. Otherwise, one defender said, there was "not so much as a mullein stalk" to obstruct the aim of the infantry in the trenches or the cannoneers in emplacements they had selected and dug at their leisure, not yet knowing there could be little or no counterbattery fire, even if the rebels were so foolish as to provoke battle on a field so disadvantageous to them.

Wagner had arrived at noon with the last of the five divisions, weary from yesterday's Spring Hill fight, the all-night vigil behind his fence-rail breastworks, and this morning's hurried march as rear guard of the army. Leaving one brigade on Winstead Hill to serve as a lookout force, he put the other two in position as instructed, half a mile in front of the main line, and set them digging. While they dug, the rest of the troops, snug in their completed works, did what they could to make up for their loss of sleep on last night's march. From across the river, at high-sited Fort Granger — a bastioned earthwork, constructed more than a year ago for the protection of the two critical bridges over the Harpeth — Schofield looked south, beyond the bulge of his semicircular line, and saw the brigade Wagner had left on lookout withdraw in good order down the hill and up the turnpike. He knew from this that the rebels must be close behind, for the brigade commander was Colonel Emerson Opdycke, a thirty-four-year-old Ohioan with a fiery reputation earned in most of the theater's major battles, from Shiloh, where he had been a captain, to Resaca, where he had been badly wounded, back in May, but recovered in time to lead the charge up Kennesaw six weeks later. Sure enough, soon after Opdycke's displacement, the first graybacks appeared on Winstead Hill. They gathered faster and began to flow, rather like lava, in heavy columns down the forward slope and around the east flank of the hill. Schofield watched with mounting excitement. It was now about 3 o'clock; all but the last of his 700 wagons had clattered across the railroad bridge and he had just issued orders for the rest of his men and guns to follow at 6 o'clock, shortly after dark, unless Hood attacked before sunset; which Schofield did not believe he would do, once he had seen what lay before him there along the northern margin of that naked plain.

He was mistaken. Three miles away, under the linn tree on the hillside to the south, Hood completed his study of the Federal dispositions, lowered his glasses, and announced to the subordinates who by now had clustered round him: "We will make the fight."

When he explained what he meant by "make the fight" — an all-out frontal assault, within the hour — consternation followed hard upon doubt by his lieutenants that they had heard aright. They too had looked out over the proposed arena, and could scarcely believe their ears. Attack? here? headlong and practically gunless, against a foe not only superior in numbers but also intrenched on chosen ground and backed by the frown of more than sixty pieces of artillery? ... For a time, only too aware of their commander's repeated scornful charge that they invariably flinched at Yankee breastworks, they held their tongues. Then Ben Cheatham broke the silence. "I do not like the looks of this fight," he said. "The enemy has an excellent position and is well fortified." Leaning on his crutches, his blond beard glinting in the sunlight, Hood replied that he preferred to strike the Federals here, where they had had only a short time to organize their defenses, rather than at Nashville, "where they have been strengthening themselves for three years."

Cheatham protested no more, having been reproached quite enough for one day. But Bedford Forrest — who was familiar with the region, including the location of usable fords over the Harpeth well this side of the enemy position, and who moreover had Hood's respect for his aggressive instincts — spoke out in support of his fellow Tennessean's assessment of the situation, though with a different application. He favored an attack, yet not a frontal one. "Give me one strong division of infantry with my cavalry," he urged, "and within two hours I can flank the Federals from their works." Hood afterwards reported that "the nature of the position was such as to render it inexpedient to attempt any further flanking movement." Just now, however, he expressed doubt that, for all their apparent confidence, the bluecoats would "stand strong pressure from the front. The show of force they are making is a feint in order to hold me back from a more vigorous pursuit."

This put an end to such unasked-for opposition as had been voiced. Hood's fame had begun when he broke Fitz-John Porter's center at Gaines Mill, back in Virginia thirty months ago, and he intended to do the same to Schofield here today. His final order, dismissing the informal council of war, was explicit as to how this was to be accomplished: "Drive the enemy from his position into the river at all hazards."

Stewart, who had rounded Winstead Hill on the approach march, would attack on the right, up the railroad and the Lewisburg Pike, which ran northwest along the near bank of the Harpeth; Loring's division was on that flank of the corps front, French's on the other, over toward the Columbia Pike, and Major General Edward Walthall's was posted astride the railroad in the center. Cleburne and Brown, of Cheatham's corps, would advance due north up both sides of the Columbia Pike, Cleburne on the right, adjoining French, with Bate on Brown's left, extending the line westward to the Carter's Creek Pike, which ran northeast. All three turnpikes converged on the outskirts of Franklin, half a mile in rear of the southward bulge of the Union works; Hood assumed that this configuration would serve to compact the mass, like a hand clenched gradually into a fist, by the time the attackers reached and struck the main blue line. Johnson's division remained in reserve behind the center, for rapid exploitation of any breakthrough right or left, and Forrest's horsemen would go forward on the flanks, near the river in both directions. At 3.45, one hour before sundown, Stewart and Cheatham sent word that their lines were formed and they were ready.

Hood could see them in panorama from his command post, the two corps in an attack formation well over a mile in width, their star-crossed flags hanging limp in the windless air of this last day in November, which was also to be the last in the lives of many who were about to follow those tattered symbols across the fields now in their front: six divisions, twenty brigades, just over one hundred regiments, containing in all some 18,000 infantry, with another 3500 in the four reserve brigades. Promptly Hood's order came down from Winstead Hill for them to go forward, and they did, stepping out as smartly as if they were passing in review; "a grand sight, such as would make a lifelong impression on the mind of any man who could see such a resistless, well-conducted charge," a Federal officer discerned from his post near the blue center, just under two miles across the way. "For the moment we were spellbound with admiration, although we knew that in a few brief moments, as soon as they reached firing distance, all that orderly grandeur would be changed to bleeding, writhing confusion."

It did not work out quite that way just yet. Opdycke, when he retired from the crest of Winstead Hill, had not stopped alongside the other two brigades of Wagner's division, intrenched half a mile in front of the main works, but continued his withdrawal up the turnpike to the designated reserve position in rear of a one-story brick residence owned by a family named Carter, less than a hundred yards inside the lines. Wagner had set up headquarters in a grove of trees beside the pike and just beyond the house, anticipating the arrival of the rest of his troops as soon as the gray host, now gathering two miles to the south, showed what his orders termed "a disposition to advance." Apparently he doubted that Hood would do so at all, after studying the field, or else he believed the preparations would take a lot more time than they actually did. In any case, the mass advance was well under way before the Ohio-born former Hoosier politician, whose view in that direction was blocked by the house and trees, even knew that it had begun. As a result, the two colonels left in charge out front not only delayed their withdrawal, they also chose to stand fast in their shallow works long enough to get off a couple of short-range volleys before retiring. This was to cost Wagner his command within the week, but it cost the men of those two brigades a great deal more today.

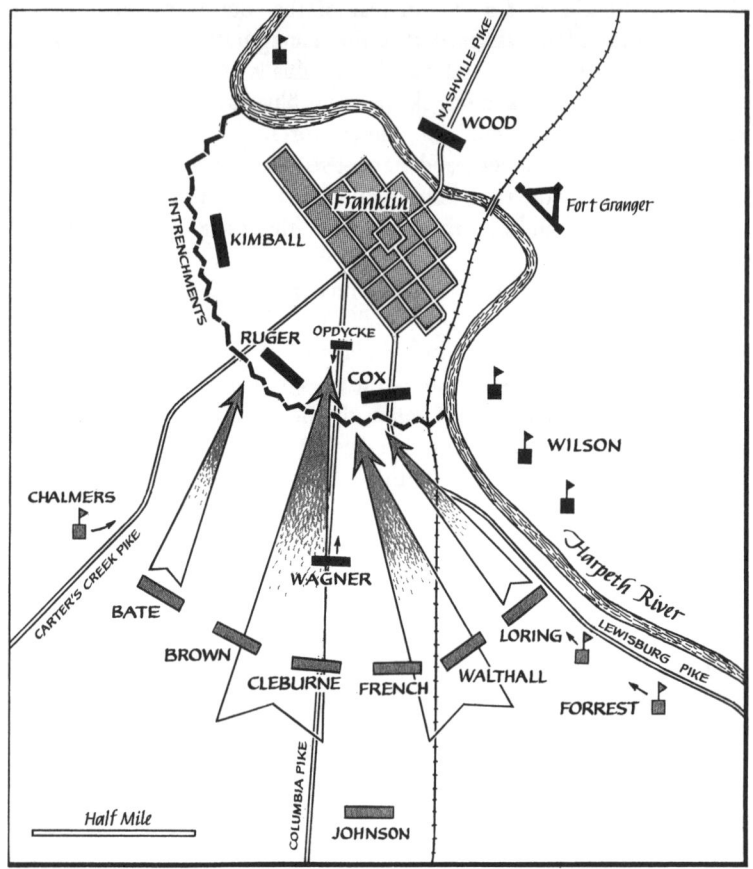

The gray line advanced steadily, preceded by scampering rabbits and whirring coveys of quail, flushed from the brush by the approach of close to 20,000 pairs of tramping feet. When they got within range, the outpost Federals gave them a rattling fusillade that served to check them for a moment; but not for long. Absorbing the shock, the men under Cleburne and Brown — old rivals, from the days when the latter's division was under Cheatham — came on with a rush and a yell, directly against the front and around the flanks of the two unfortunate brigades, both of which gave way in a sudden bolt for the security of the intrenchments half a mile in their rear. Too late; "Let's go into the works with them!" the attackers cried, and pressed the pursuit up the turnpike, clubbing and shooting the terrified bluecoats as they fled. "It seemed bullets never before hissed with such diabolical venom," a Union captain was to say, recalling too that the cries of the wounded, left to the mercy of the screaming graybacks when they fell, "had a pathetic note of despair I had never heard before." More than 700 were captured, hurt or unhurt, and the main-line defenders, dead ahead, were kept from firing at the pursuers by fear of hitting their comrades in the lead. A staff colonel observed, however, that there was little time for thought at this critical juncture. "The triumphant Confederates, now more like a wild, howling mob than an organized army, swept on to the very works, with hardly a check from any quarter. So fierce was the rush that a number of the fleeing soldiers — officers and men — dropped exhausted into the ditch, and lay there while the terrific contest raged over their heads." Of these, the captain who had outrun the hissing bullets noted, "some were found [afterwards] with their thumbs chewed to a pulp. Their agony had been so great that they had stuck their thumbs in their mouths and bit on them to keep from bleating like calves."

That was the kind of battle it was, first for one side, then the other, combining the grisliest features of Pickett's Charge and Spotsylvania's Bloody Angle. Because they had sprinted the last half mile, and had a shorter distance to cover in reaching the southward bulge of the enemy line, Cleburne's and Brown's divisions struck and penetrated the Federal works before the units on their left or right came up to add weight to the effort. In close pursuit of the two fugitive brigades, they not only broke through along the turnpike, they also widened the gap by knocking a regiment loose from the intrenchments on each side and seized four guns still loaded with canister, which they turned on the enemy but could not fire because the battery horses had bolted with the primers in the ammunition chests. Suddenly then it was too late; the blue reserves were upon them, advancing through the smoke with bayonets flashing, and they were too blown from their race up the pike, too confused by their abrupt success, to stand long under the pounding of most of the two dozen guns Cox and Ruger had posted along this part of the line. They yielded sullenly, under savage attack from Opdycke, who had brought his brigade on the run from north of the Carter house, and fell back to find cover in front of the works they had crossed when they broke through. There they stayed, exchanging point-blank fire with the bluecoats on the other side of the ditch.

Stewart by then had come up on the right, where French made contact with Cleburne, but the other two divisions were roughly handled in their attempt to get to grips with the Union left. Approaching a deep railroad cut near the northward bend of the Harpeth, they found it under plunging fire from the guns massed in Fort Granger, and when they changed front to move around this trap they were struck on the flank by other batteries masked on the east bank of the river. Forrest drove these last away by sending Jackson's division across a nearby ford, but Wilson met this threat to Schofield's rear by throwing the rebel troopers back on the crossing and holding them there, under pressure from three times their number. Walthall and Loring meantime had rounded the railway cut and clawed their way through the Osage hedge, only to find themselves confronting an intrenched brigade equipped with repeating rifles that seemed to one observer "to blaze out a continuous sheet of destruction." Here the attackers had all they could do to hang on where they were, though some among them continued to try for a breakthrough: Brigadier General John Adams, for example, who was killed while attempting a mounted leap over the enemy works and whose body was found next morning alongside his horse, dead too, with its forefeet over the Federal palisade. Another of Loring's three brigade commanders, Brigadier General T. M. Scott, was gravely wounded, as was Brigadier General William Quarles of Walthall's division; both were out of the war for good, and in Quarles's brigade, so heavy was the toll of successive commanders, there presently was no surviving officer above the rank of captain. French's division, fighting near the center, also lost two of its three brigade leaders — Colonel William Witherspoon, killed outright, and Brigadier General Francis Cockrell, severely wounded — bringing Stewart's loss to five of the nine brigade commanders in his corps, along with more than half of the colonels and majors who began the attack at the head of his nearly fifty regiments.

Cheatham's losses were heavier still, though they were comparatively light in Bate's division, which only had one of its three brigades engaged when it struck the enemy trenches at an angle; the other two drifted northward to mingle with Chalmers' horsemen beyond the Carter's Creek Pike, where they remained in observation, dodging long-range shots from guns on the Union right. Cleburne and Brown, however, still holding the works astride the Columbia Turnpike in the center, more than made up for any shortage of bloodshed on the Confederate left. The sun by now was behind the rim of Winstead Hill, and in point of fact, so far as its outcome was concerned, the battle was over: had been over, at least in that respect, ever since Opdycke's furious counterassault stopped and shattered the initial penetration. All that remained was additional killing and maiming, which continued well into the night. "I never saw the dead lay near so thick. I saw them upon each other, dead and ghastly in the powder-dimmed starlight," Opdycke would report. Brown himself was out of the action, badly crippled by a shell, and so were all four of his brigadiers, beginning with G. W. Gordon, who had been captured in the side yard of the Carter house just as the breakthrough was turned back. John C. Carter, who succeeded Brown in command of the division, was mortally wounded shortly afterwards (he would die within ten days) and States Rights Gist and Otho Strahl were killed in the close-quarters struggle that ensued. "Boys, this will be short but desperate," Strahl had told his Tennesseans as they prepared to charge; which was half right. After the repulse he stood in the Federal ditch, passing loaded rifles up to the men on top, and when one of them asked if it might not be wise to withdraw, he replied: "Keep on firing." Then he fell.

The resultant desperation, unrelieved by the saving grace of brevity, was quite as bad as he had predicted for Brown's division, but the strain was even worse for the Arkansans, Mississippians, Alabamians, and Texans next in line, heightened as it was by dread uncertainty as to the fate of their commander. "I never saw men put in such a terrible position as Cleburne's division was," an opposing bluecoat was to say. "The wonder is that any of them escaped death or capture." All too many of them did not; Hiram Granbury had been killed at the head of his Texas brigade in the first assault, and fourteen of the twenty regimental commanders were to fall before the conflict slacked and died away. Meantime a disheartening rumor spread through the ranks that Cleburne was missing — Irish Pat Cleburne, of whom it was said: "Men seemed to be afraid to *be* afraid where he was." He had last been seen going forward in the attack, dismounted because two horses had been shot from under him in the course of the advance. "If we are to die, let us die like men," he told a subordinate, speaking with the brogue that came on him at such times and thickened as the excitement rose. When his second horse was killed by a shot from a cannon, he went ahead on foot through the smoke and din, waving his cap. The hope of his veterans, who idolized him, was that he had been wounded for the third time in the war, or even captured; but this hope collapsed next morning, when his body was found beside the Columbia Pike just short of the enemy works. A single bullet had gone through his heart. His boots had been stolen, along with his sword and watch and everything else of value on him. He was buried first near Franklin, then in St John's churchyard, whose beauty he had admired on the march to his last fight, and finally, years later, back in Arkansas on a ridge overlooking Helena, his home town. His epitaph, as well as that of his division, was pronounced by his old corps commander, William Hardee, who wrote when he learned of his death: "Where this division defended, no odds broke its line; where it attacked, no numbers resisted its onslaught, save only once; and there is the grave of Cleburne."

High on his hillside two miles to the south, Hood knew even less about the progress of the battle than did the troops involved in the moiling, flame-stabbed confusion down below; which was little indeed. He had seen Cleburne and Brown go storming into the Union center, hard on the heels of Wagner's unfortunates, but what happened next was blanketed in smoke that hung heavy in the windless air and thickened as the firing mounted to a sustained crescendo. At 7 o'clock, an hour after full darkness cloaked the field, he committed his reserve division, and though Old Clubby's men attacked with desperation, stumbling over Cheatham's dead and wounded in the gloom, they only succeeded in adding Brigadier General Arthur Manigault's name to the list of a dozen brigade and division commanders who had fallen in the past three hours, as well as nine more regimental commanders, bringing the total to fifty-four; roughly half the number present. Of the twelve generals lost to the army here today, six were dead or dying, one was captured, and three of the remaining five were out of the war for good, while the other two, Brown and Cockrell, would not return for months. Down in the ranks, moreover, this dreadful ratio was approximated; 6252 Confederate veterans were casualties, including 1750 killed in action — as many as had died on either side in the two days of Shiloh or under McClellan throughout the Seven Days: more than had died under Rosecrans at Stones River, under Burnside at Fredericksburg, or under Hood himself in any of his three Atlanta sorties: almost as many, indeed, as Grant had had killed outright when he assaulted at Cold Harbor with three times as many men. Hood had wrecked his army, top to bottom, and the army knew it; or soon would. In the judgment of a Tennessee private who survived the wrecking, he had done so in the manner of a clumsy blacksmith, thinking "he would strike while the iron was hot, and while it could be hammered into shape.... But he was like the fellow who took a piece of iron to the shop, intending to make him an ax. After working for some time, and failing, he concluded he would make him a wedge, and, failing in this, said: 'I'll make a skeow.' So he heats the iron red-hot and drops it in the slack tub, and it went s-k-e-o-w, bubble, bubble, s-k-e-o-w, bust."

Hood did not know this yet, however — and would not have been likely to admit it if he had; Howard's word 'indomitable' still fit. He watched unseeing while the battle continued to rage with the same fury, even though all the combatants had to aim at now was the flash of each other's weapons. "Time after time they came up to the very works," a Union colonel afterwards said of the attackers, "but they never crossed them except as prisoners." Around 9 o'clock the uproar slacked. "Don't shoot, Yanks; for God Amighty's sake, don't shoot!" defenders heard pinned-down rebels implore from the smoky darkness just beyond their parapets. Within two more hours the contest sputtered into silence. Stephen Lee was up by then with his other two divisions and the army's guns, and Hood ordered the attack renewed at daybreak, preceded this time by a hundred-round bombardment. The batteries opened at first light, as directed, then ceased fire when word came back that there was nothing in the works ahead but Federal dead and wounded. Schofield had departed in the night.

That was really all the northern commander had wanted from the outset: a chance to get away, if Hood would only let him. Soon after his arrival the previous morning, on finding the turnpike bridge washed out and no pontoons on hand, he wired Nashville for instructions, and was told to defend the Harpeth crossing unless such an effort would require him "to risk too much." He responded: "I am satisfied that I have heretofore run too much risk in trying to hold Hood in check.... Possibly I may be able to hold him here, but do not expect to be able to do so long." Thomas, busy gathering troops to man the capital defenses, then put a limit to his request, in hope that this would serve to stiffen his lieutenant's resistance to the scarcely deterred advance of the rebel column up through Middle Tennessee. "Do you think you can hold Hood at Franklin for three days longer? Answer, giving your views," he wired, and Schofield replied: "I do not believe I can." In point of fact, both question and answer by then were academic. He had already ordered a nighttime withdrawal and Hood had just appeared on Winstead Hill. "I think he can effect a crossing tomorrow, in spite of all my efforts," Schofield added, "and probably tonight, if he attempts it. A worse position than this for an inferior force can hardly be found. ... I have no doubt Forrest will be in my rear tomorrow, or doing some greater mischief. It appears to me that I ought to take position at Brentwood at once."

Nevertheless — having no choice — he stayed and fought, and won. His casualties totaled 2326, about one third the number he inflicted, and of these more than half were from Wagner's division: just under a thousand killed or captured in the two-brigade rearward sprint up the pike and just over two hundred killed and wounded in the other brigade, when Opdycke saved the day with a counterassault that cost him five of his seven regimental commanders but netted him 394 prisoners and nine Confederate flags. Except for David Stanley, who took a bullet through the nape of his neck and had to be lugged off the field at the height of the melee, no Federal above the rank of colonel was on the list of casualties when Schofield evacuated Franklin between 11 o'clock and midnight, leaving his dead and his nonwalking wounded behind as he crossed the river and set fire to the planked-over bridge in his rear. The blue column reached Brentwood by daylight, halfway to Nashville, and by noon all five divisions were safe in the capital works, alongside the others Thomas had been assembling all this time.

Hood sent Forrest to snap at the heels of the retreating victors, but deferred pursuit by his infantry now in occupation of the field. "Today spent in burying the dead, caring for the wounded, and reorganizing the remains of our corps," a diarist on Cheatham's staff recorded. Never before had even these veterans looked on horror so compacted. In places, hard against the abandoned works, the slain lay in windrows, seven deep; so thick, indeed, that often there was no room for those on top to touch the ground. One of Strahl's four successors was so tightly wedged by corpses, it was noted, that "when he at last received the fatal shot, he did not wholly fall, but was found stiffened in death and partly upright, seeming still to command the ghastly line of his comrades lying beneath the parapet." Blue and gray, in a ratio of about one to five, the wounded soon filled all the houses in the town, as well as every room in the courthouse, schools, and churches. Meantime the burial details were at work, digging long shallow ditches into which the perforated ragdoll shapes were tossed and covered over with the spoil. Federals and Confederates were lodged in separate trenches, and the even greater disparity in their numbers — roughly one to eight — imparted a hollow sound to Hood's congratulatory order, read at the head of what was left of each regiment that afternoon. "While we lament the fall of many gallant officers and brave men," its final sentence ran, "we have shown to our countrymen that we can carry any position occupied by our enemy."

Perhaps the battle did show that; perhaps it also settled in Hood's mind, at last, the question of whether the Army of Tennessee would charge breastworks. But, if so, the demonstration had been made at so high a cost that, when it was over, the army was in no condition, either in body or in spirit, to repeat it. Paradoxically, in refuting the disparagement, the troops who fell confirmed it for the future. Nor was the horror limited to those who had been actively involved; Franklin's citizens now knew, almost as well as did the few survivors among the men they had sent away three years ago, the suffering that ensued once the issue swung to war. This was especially true of the Carter family, an old man and his two daughters who took shelter in their cellar, just in rear of the initial breakthrough point, while the fighting raged outside and overhead. Emerging next morning from their night of terror, they found the body of their son and brother, Captain Tod Carter of Brown's division, Cheatham's corps, lying almost on the doorstep he had come home to when he died.

Nothing daunted — though his 7500 casualties over the past week, including more than 6000 the day before, had reduced his infantry strength to a scant 22,000 — Hood took up the march north that afternoon. Lee's corps was in the lead, only one of its three divisions having been exposed to the Franklin holocaust, and Stewart and Cheatham followed in that order, so severely bled down at all levels that Brown's division, for example, was under a colonel who had never commanded anything larger than a regiment, while several brigades in both these corps were led by officers with even less experience. Hood might have turned back and taken up a defensive position along Duck River, as Bragg had done two years ago under similar circumstances, or even along the Tennessee, which he had left ten days before. That would doubtless have been the most prudent course to follow, especially since one main purpose of the campaign — to provoke a countermarch by Sherman down in Georgia — had clearly failed already; the Ohioan was more than halfway to the Atlantic Ocean by now, and apparently had not given so much as a backward glance at the threat to Thomas, far in his rear. But it was not in the Kentucky-born Texan's nature to take counsel of his fears, if indeed he felt them in the first place, and prudence was by no means an integral part of his makeup. His concern was with quite different factors. One was time, which was running out, and the other was honor. "In truth," he said afterwards, "our army was in that condition which rendered it more judicious the men should face a decisive issue rather than retreat — in other words, rather than renounce the honor of their cause without having made a last and manful effort to lift up the sinking fortunes of the Confederacy. I therefore determined to move upon Nashville."

Moving upon it was no great task; Forrest's troopers by now had called a halt in sight of the Capitol tower and within plain view of the long curve of earthworks behind which Schofield had already taken shelter by the time the gray infantry forded the Harpeth. What Hood would do once he got there was a different matter, however, involving a choice between two highly unpromising alternatives. The first, to launch an immediate all-out assault, was rejected out of hand. No one wanted another Franklin, not even John Bell Hood, and Nashville — similarly cradled in the northward bend of a still wider river, with far stouter intrenchments ready-dug across its face — was Franklin magnified. Besides, after yesterday's grim Confederate subtractions, Schofield alone had more troops than Hood could bring against the place, and Thomas most likely had as many more gathered inside it, raising the numerical odds against the attacker to two, maybe three, to one. Assault was out. Yet so, Hood saw, was the alternative of crossing the Cumberland above or below, as originally envisioned, for a march to the Ohio. This would land him in Thomas's rear, true enough, but so would it put Thomas in Hood's own rear, undiminished and able to summon reinforcements from all over the North, while Hood himself, under the circumstances which now obtained, would scarcely be able to add a single recruit to the rolls of his Franklin-ravaged command. "In the absence of the prestige of complete victory," he later explained in answer to those who had urged the adoption of such a course, "I felt convinced that the Tennesseans and Kentuckians would not join our forces, since we had failed in the first instance to defeat the Federal army and capture Nashville."

Having rejected the notion of retiring southward as an admission of defeat, and having decided to forgo his previous intention of assaulting or bypassing Nashville, which he saw now as an invitation to disaster, he then — either in ignorance or defiance of Napoleon's definition of the passive defensive as "a form of deferred suicide" — settled on a plan that combined, simultaneously or in sequence, the worst features of all three of these dismissed or postponed alternatives. He would march to the outskirts of the Tennessee capital, intrench his army in direct confrontation with the outsized garrison lodged there, and await the inevitable attack, "which, if handsomely repulsed, might afford us an opportunity to follow up our advantage on the spot and enter the city on the heels of our enemy." So he said, apparently remembering the ease with which his troops had followed Wagner's into the Franklin works, but apparently not considering what had happened to them as soon as they achieved the penetration. In any case that was his plan, as he evolved it after the long march north and the frustrations he had encountered, first at Tuscumbia and Florence, where he waited three weeks before setting out, and then at Columbia, Spring Hill, and Franklin, where he not only failed to destroy a sizeable part of his opponent's army, but also came close to destroying his own. Still the old dream held for Hood: perhaps because he had no other to fall back on. "Should [Thomas] attack me in position," he subsequently reported, "I felt that I could defeat him and thus gain possession of Nashville with abundant supplies.... Having possession of the state, we should have gained largely in recruits and could at an early date have moved forward to the Ohio, which would have frustrated the plans of the enemy, as developed in his campaign toward the Atlantic coast." There was that, and there was still the pressure of knowing that this might well be the last chance, either for him or for the Confederacy itself. What better way was there to go down, or out, than in a blaze of glory? He seemed to ask that, later adding: "The troops would, I believed, return better satisfied even after defeat if, in grasping at the last straw, they felt that a brave and vigorous effort had been made to save the country from disaster."

So he went on, making camp that night at Brentwood, and pulled up in front of Nashville the following day, December 2. Lee took position astride the Franklin Pike, with Stewart and Cheatham respectively on his left and right, directly confronting the Union works, which extended northeast and northwest, as far as the eye could follow, from the bend of the river below to the bend above. Disposed along high ground in a ten-mile arc, some three miles from the marble Capitol in plain view on its hill in the heart of town, these required no more than a cursory look to confirm the claim that Nashville, along with Washington and Richmond, was among the three most heavily fortified cities in the land.

That was one part of Hood's problem, and almost at once another became apparent. "The entire line of the army will curve forward from General Lee's center," he directed on arrival, "so that General Cheatham's right may come as near the Cumberland as possible above Nashville, and General Stewart's left as near the Cumberland as possible below Nashville. Each position will be strengthened as soon as taken, and extended as fast as strengthened." But when the three corps settled in, plying spades and picks, it developed that the widest front they could cover with any measure of security was four miles — a good deal less than half the distance required if the line was to stretch to the near bank of the Cumberland in both directions; whereas in fact it did not reach the river in either direction, but left a vacancy of two miles beyond

Cheatham's outer flank and four beyond Stewart's. Of the eight turnpikes converging spokelike on the capital hub to cross by the single bridge in its rear, four were covered and four remained uncovered, two on the left and two on the right, except by cavalry patrols. Both Confederate flanks thus were exposed to possible turning movements by the greatly superior force in the works ahead.

Hood had little fear of such a threat, however; at least for now. Familiar with his adversary's ponderous manner and lethargic nature, not only over the past six months of confrontation, stalemate, and maneuver, but also from old army days before the war — one had been a lieutenant, the other a major in Sidney Johnston's Texas-based 2d Cavalry — he counted on having as much time as he needed to prepare and improve his position in front of the Tennessee capital. Indeed, so confident was he of this, despite the long numerical odds, that he risked a further reduction of force, as great as the one he had suffered at Franklin, for the sake of a sideline operation which seemed to offer a chance to make up for the prize he had failed to grasp at Spring Hill, where a sizeable part of the blue host now confronting him slipped through his fingers. Now another isolated segment, though only about one fourth as large, had come within his reach — provided, that is, he was willing to do a little stretching; which he was. When Hood set out from Florence to outflank Schofield at Pulaski, ten days back, Thomas had pulled Granger's 4000 troops out of the region below Athens, directly across the Tennessee River from Decatur, and combined them with Rousseau's 5000 at Murfreesboro, thirty-odd miles down the Chattanooga & Nashville from his capital headquarters, in case the gray invasion column veered west to approach or bypass him from that direction. These 9000 bluecoats were still there, and Hood had a mind to gather them up, or at any rate smash the railroad between there and Nashville, before Thomas called them in. Accordingly, while still on the approach march, he detached Bate, whose division had suffered least of the seven engaged at Franklin, and sent him crosscountry, reinforced by a brigade from each of the other two corps, for a strike at Murfreesboro and its garrison. Forrest meantime, on Hood's arrival at Nashville, would move down the Chattanooga Railroad with two of his divisions, breaking it up as he went, for a combined attack which he would direct by virtue of his rank.

Although the maneuver served its purpose of keeping Rousseau and Granger from reinforcing Thomas, it failed to achieve the larger design for bagging them entirely. Forrest left with Buford's and Jackson's divisions as soon as Hood came up, and after three days of reducing blockhouses, burning bridges, and wrecking several miles of track, combined with Bate on December 5, some ten miles north of the objective. Next day's reconnaissance disclosed that Murfreesboro was almost as stoutly fortified as Nashville; Fortress Rosecrans, mounting

57 guns and enclosing 200 acres of the field where Bragg had come to grief two years ago this month, was practically unassailable; especially with 9000 defenders on hand to resist the 6500 graybacks moving against it, mounted and afoot. Forrest called a halt and decided instead to lure the garrison out for a fight in the open. In this he was partly successful the following day, December 7, when a 3500-man Union column staged a sally. He posted his infantry in the path of the attackers, with orders to stand firm while he brought his cavalry down on their flank. Everything went as planned, up to the critical moment when Bate's division — spooked no doubt by remembrance of Franklin, where its performance had been less than standard, eight days back — gave way in a panic, unspringing the trap. Forrest rode among the rattled soldiers, appealing to them to stand and fight, then cursing them for refusing to do so. He stood in the stirrups, eyes blazing, face gone red with rage, and began to lay about him with the flat of his saber, whacking the backs of the fleeing troops; to small avail. Ignoring the Wizard as best they could, the retreaters scuttled rearward beyond his grasp, even when he seized a color-bearer's flag, whose staff afforded a longer reach, and swung it bludgeonlike until at last, perceiving that this was equally ineffective, he flung it from him in disgust. "Right comical, if it hadn't been so serious," one veteran was to say.

Fortunately, the Federals did not press the issue, having just been recalled by Rousseau, and Bate was summoned back to Nashville two days later by Hood, who sent another brigade from Cheatham's corps to replace the three that left. Down to about 4500 of all arms — half the number inside the works — Forrest had to be content with bristling to discourage sorties that might have swamped him. This he did with such success that within another two days he felt justified in sending Buford to Andrew Jackson's Hermitage, ten miles northeast of Nashville, with instructions to picket a nearby stretch of the Cumberland and thereby prevent the arrival of reinforcements by that route. Next day, December 12, with the enemy still tightly buttoned up in Fortress Rosecrans, he had the infantry begin completing the destruction of the railroad back to La Vergne, just under twenty miles away. Thus, by the employment of barely half as many troops, Hood was able to prevent an additional 9000 effectives from joining the Nashville garrison: though whether this was wise or not, under the circumstances, was quite another matter. For one thing, even longer odds obtained in the vicinity of the Tennessee capital, where he remained in confrontation with Thomas, and for another, in the showdown battle which now was imminent, it seemed likely to cost him the use of two sorely-needed cavalry divisions, together with the help of their commander, whose talents would be missed.

Reduced as he was, by casualties and detachments, to a strength of less than 24,000 of all arms, it was no wonder one apprehensive infantryman remarked that the Confederate main line of resistance, which stretched and crooked for four miles under the frown of long-range Union guns in permanent fortifications, looked "more like the skirmish line of an investing army than of that army itself." To make matters worse, there had not been time for the completion of such outlying installations as had been planned to strengthen the flanks of the position: particularly on the left, where three redoubts were under construction beyond the Hillsboro Pike, the western limit of Hood's line, to blunt the force of an attack from that direction, whether end-on or oblique. Work on these began, but on the night of December 8, after a spell of deceptively mild weather, the mercury dropped to nearly twenty degrees below freezing and a cold rain quickly turned to sleet and fine-grained snow. By morning, all the trees wore glittering cut-glass armor, each twig sheathed in ice, and the earth was frozen iron hard, unpierceable even with a knife, let alone a shovel. Work stopped, perforce, and the soldiers huddled in unfinished trenches, shivering in their rags. For four days this continued. Then on the fifth — December 13, the winter solstice; Sherman had reached Savannah by now, completing his march across Georgia's midriff, and would capture Fort McAllister before sundown — a thaw set in, relieving the rigid misery in which the besiegers had been locked, but bringing with it troubles of a different kind. The army floundered in Napoleon's "fifth element," unable to move forward, back, or sideways in a Sargasso Sea of mud; all transportation stalled, guns and wagons bellied axle deep, even on main-traveled roads, and no supplies arrived to relieve shortages that had developed during the four-day storm.

It was midway through this doleful immobilized span, with his men and horses frozen or stuck in their tracks by alternate ice and mud, that Hood apparently first became aware, in the fullest sense, of the peril to which he had exposed his troops when he took up his present position in point-blank confrontation with Thomas, whose army was not only superbly equipped and entrenched, but was also better than twice the size of his own. Earlier, when Forrest departed for Murfreesboro with the other two cavalry divisions, Chalmers had been obliged to send one of his two brigades to patrol the region between Cheatham's right and the river, and when he reported that this reduced his strength too much for him to be able to perform that duty adequately on the left, where the distance was twice as great, Hood detached a brigade of infantry from Stewart and posted it beyond the Harding Pike, about midway between his western flank and the river below Nashville. This was not much help, really, for the unit chosen — Brigadier General Matthew Ector's brigade of French's division, now under its senior colonel while Ector recovered from the loss of a leg at Atlanta — was down to fewer than 700 effectives as a result of its heavy casualties at Franklin. Clearly enough, Chalmers' horsemen had more than they could handle in both directions, especially the left, and Hood's alarm was intensified when the ice storm halted work on the outlying redoubts he had ordered installed to provide at least a measure of security for that vulnerable flank.

On December 8, the day the freeze set in, he issued a circular order calling for "regular and frequent roll calls ... as a preventive of straggling." He used the term as a euphemism for desertion, which had become a growing problem. Of 296 dismounted troopers reassigned to the infantry, all but 42 protested the indignity by departing without leave: a loss that far outweighed the total of 164 recruits who had joined Hood since he entered Tennessee. All too conscious of the odds he faced, the crippled leader of a crippled army implored Beauregard to forward any stray units he could lay hands on, and even appealed to the War Department to order Kirby Smith to send "two or more divisions" from the Transmississippi. This was a forlorn hope if ever there was one, and Seddon was prompt to tell him so. Besides, even if all the reinforcements he requested had been started in his direction without delay, it was altogether unlikely that they could arrive — even from North Alabama, let alone elsewhere — in time to help him meet the crisis now at hand. Two days later, midway through the ice storm, a follow-up circular warned that it was "highly probable that we will fight a battle before the close of the present year." Corps commanders were told to look to their defenses and line of retreat; Lee, who had the center, was cautioned to "select all good points in rear of his right and left flanks, and fortify them with strong self-supporting detached works, so that, should it become necessary to withdraw either of the corps now upon his flanks, the flank thus becoming the right or left flank of the army may be in condition to be easily defended." Furthermore, so important did Hood consider resumption of work on the outlying strongholds, all three lieutenant generals were urged to supervise their construction in person, "not leaving them either to subordinate commanders or engineer officers."

He did what he could, ice-bound as he was, and three days later, while the thaw converted the sleet to slush and the frozen earth to slime, word came that Thomas had crossed his cavalry from Edgefield, over the Cumberland, to Nashville. He was massing behind his works there, spies reported, for an all-out attack on the Confederate left, where dirty and fair weather had combined to prevent completion of the vital redoubts. Hood warned Stewart to "give Chalmers such assistance as you think necessary, keeping in communication." Next day, December 14, with the roads beginning to dry a bit, corps commanders were able to begin complying with orders to "send all their wagons, except artillery, ordnance, and ambulances, to the vicinity of Brentwood," five miles in their rear. At the same time, previous instructions regarding the hoarding of ammunition — in limited supply because of the transportation breakdown — still applied: "Not a cartridge of any kind will be burned until further orders, unless the enemy should advance upon us."

※ 4 ※

Thomas intended to do just that: advance: but he was determined not to do so, despite prods and threats from his Washington and City Point superiors, until he felt that his army was in condition to accomplish the annihilation Hood had been inviting ever since he took up his present position, in front of the Tennessee capital, two weeks back. Numerically, the blue force assembled to oppose him had reached that stage before the end of the first week; Thomas by then had gathered 71,842 soldiers under his command, "present for duty, equipped." Of these, 9000 were at Murfreesboro and about the same number were garrison troops, two thirds of them posted at Nashville and the other third at such outlying points as Johnsonville and Chattanooga, whose complements had been stripped to skeleton proportions. The rest — some 54,000 of all arms — were available as a striking force, and that was the use their commander had in mind to make of them as soon as he judged the time was ripe. A. J. Smith's 12,000 arrived by transport from Missouri while the battle raged at Franklin, and next morning Schofield marched in with his own 10,000 and Stanley's 14,000 survivors, now under Wood. Steedman came by rail from Chattanooga, that day and the next, with 6000 more, including a number of veterans who had returned from reenlistment furloughs too late to march with Sherman to the sea. Finally there was the cavalry, 12,000 strong, though more than a third lacked horses and the others were badly frazzled after a week of contesting Hood's advance from Duck River to the Harpeth and beyond.

This necessity for resting and refitting his weary troopers, while trying to find mounts for the 4000 Wilson had had to leave behind when he rode out to join Schofield at Columbia, was the principal cause of delay, at least at the outset. In response to a pair of wires from Grant, December 2, urging him to "move out of Nashville with all your army and force the enemy to retire or fight upon ground of your own choosing," Thomas stressed his need for "a cavalry force sufficient to contend with Forrest," who had "at least 12,000" veteran horsemen. That was close to twice the Wizard's actual strength, and roughly six times the number he left with Hood when he departed for Murfreesboro next morning; but Thomas accepted the estimate as a figure to be matched, or at any rate approximated, before he undertook Hood's destruction. His main problem, even with all of Kentucky at his back, was the procurement of remounts, which were in short supply after more than three years of a war that had been about as hard on horses as it was on men, and broke them down at an even faster rate. Some measure of his difficulty was shown by the response George D. Prentice, the Union-loyal editor of the Louisville *Courier,* received when he complained to Military Governor Andrew Johnson about the use to which the army had put a $5000 investment he had made in cotton down in Nashville. The bales had been commandeered for installation as part of the capital fortifications; he wanted them back, he wrote Johnson, with something less expensive put in their place. But there was nothing the Vice President-elect could do for him in the matter, having himself just had a fine team of carriage horses seized for conversion to cavalry mounts. Others suffered similar deprivations, including a traveling circus, whose bareback riders were left poised in mid-air, so to speak, and the city's streetcar line, which had to suspend operations throughout the crisis for lack of mules to draw its cars. All within reach, of whatever crowbait description, were sent across the Cumberland to Edgefield, where Wilson was reorganizing and getting his troopers in shape for their share in the deferred offensive against the rebels intrenched southward, in plain view from Capitol Hill and the high-sited forts that rimmed the city in that direction.

All this required time, however, and time was the one thing his superiors did not consider he, or they, could afford at the present critical juncture; especially Grant. Halleck kept warning Thomas that their chief was losing patience, but the Virginian's files contained by then a sheaf of dispatches that made only too clear the City Point general's feelings in that regard. "You will now suffer incalculable injury upon your railroads if Hood is not speedily disposed of. Put forth, therefore, every possible exertion." "Hood should be attacked where he is. Time strengthens him, in all probability, as much as it does you." "Attack Hood at once, and wait no longer for a remount of your cavalry. There is great danger of delay resulting in a campaign back to the Ohio River." "Why not attack at once? By all means avoid the contingency of a foot race to see which, you or Hood, can beat to the Ohio." Thus Grant fumed through the first week of the Tennessee stalemate. Thomas's replies, over that same span — in which he spoke of his "crippled condition" and promised to move out, first, "in a few days," then within "less than a week," and finally by December 7, "if I can perfect my arrangements" — only goaded his chief into greater exasperation. Moreover, Halleck by now was warning that continued inaction might lead to his removal. Thomas replied that he regretted Grant's "dissatisfaction at my delay in attacking the enemy. I feel conscious that I have done everything in my power. . . . If he should order me to be relieved I will submit without a murmur." That was on December 9, and he closed with a weather report that seemed to him to rule out, at least for the present, any further talk of an advance. "A terrible storm of freezing rain has come on since daylight, which will render an attack impossible until it breaks."

He also passed news of this to Grant. "I had nearly completed my preparations to attack the enemy tomorrow morning, but a terrible storm of freezing rain has come on today, which will make it impossible for our men to fight to any advantage. I am, therefore, compelled to wait for the storm to break and make the attempt immediately after." And he added: "Major General Halleck informs me that you are very much dissatisfied with my delay in attacking. I can only say I have done all in my power to prepare, and if you should deem it necessary to relieve me I shall submit without a murmur." Alas, the reply he received that night was, if anything, even more chill and grudging than the others. "I have as much confidence in your conducting a battle rightly as I have in any other officer," Grant informed the Rock of Chickamauga, "but it has seemed to me that you have been slow, and I have had no explanation of affairs to convince me otherwise.... I telegraphed to suspend the order relieving you until we should hear further. I hope most sincerely that there will be no necessity for repeating the order, and that the facts will show that you have been right all the time."

Thomas was hard put to comprehend how Grant, five hundred miles away in front of Richmond — stalemated himself, not for a week but for the past six months — could presume to say what was practicable for a conglomerate army, so hastily and recently assembled under a man who was a stranger to more than half its members. However, his chief of staff, Brigadier General William Whipple, an old-line West Pointer, had a theory that someone hereabouts was "using the wires to undermine his commander" in Washington or City Point or both. At first he suspected Andrew Johnson, but on being informed that the governor was too brusque and aboveboard for such tactics, he shifted to Schofield as a likelier candidate for the Judas role. Sure enough, a prowling staffer picked up at the telegraph office the original of a recent message from the New Yorker to Grant: "Many officers here are of the opinion that General Thomas is certainly slow in his movements." Thomas read it with considerable surprise, then turned to James Steedman, who was with him at the time. "Steedman, can it be possible that Schofield would send such a telegram?" Steedman, whose share in the glory of Chickamauga had been second only to his chief's, replied that he must surely be familiar with his own general's writing. Thomas put on his glasses and examined the message carefully. "Yes, it is General Schofield's handwriting," he admitted, and asked, puzzled: "Why does he send such telegrams?" Steedman smiled at the Virginian's guileless nature, uncorrupted by twenty-four years of exposure to army politics. "General Thomas," he presently asked, "who is next in command to you in case of removal?" Thomas hung fire for a moment. "Oh, I see," he said at last, and shook his head at what he saw.

In point of fact, there was more behind Grant's exasperation, and a good deal more had come of it, than Thomas or anyone else in Tennessee had any way of knowing. Prodded by Stanton, who translated Lincoln's trepidation into sneers at "the McClellan and Rosecrans strategy of do nothing and let the rebels raid the country," Grant said later, in confirmation of earlier testimony by his aide: "I was never so anxious during the war as at that time." Indeed, under pressure of this anxiety, he lost his accustomed military balance. His fret, of course, was not only for Slow Trot Thomas, out in Nashville; it was also for Sherman, who had not yet emerged from his trans-Georgia tunnel, and for Butler, who continued to resist being hurried down the coast to Wilmington. Worst of all, he saw the possibility of the war being turned around just at the moment when he believed it was practically won. "If I had been in Hood's place," he afterwards declared, "I would have gone to Louisville and on north until I came to Chicago." Taking counsel of his fears, he had told Halleck on December 8: "If Thomas has not struck yet, he ought to be ordered to hand over the command to Schofield." Old Brains replied that if this was what Grant wanted he would have to issue orders to that effect. "The responsibility, however, will be yours, as no one here, so far as I am informed, wishes General Thomas's removal." Grant drew back: "I would not say relieve him until I hear further from him." But there was no let-up in the telegraphic goading. "If you delay attack longer," he wired the Virginian on December 11, three days into the ice storm, "the mortifying spectacle will be witnessed of a rebel army moving for the Ohio River, and you will be forced to act, accepting such weather as you find. . . . Delay no longer for weather or reinforcements."

Thomas's reply, delivered the following morning — "I will obey the order as promptly as possible, however much I may regret it, as the attack will have to be made under every disadvantage. The whole country is covered with a perfect sheet of ice and sleet, and it is with difficulty the troops are able to move about on level ground" — exhausted what little patience Grant had left. "As promptly as possible" was far from a commitment, and the rest of the message seemed to imply that the blame for any failure, when and if the attack was launched, could not properly be placed on a commander who had done his best to resist untimely orders. Grant reacted by concluding that the hour was at hand for a change in Middle Tennessee commanders.

As it happened, John A. Logan was visiting City Point headquarters at the time, on leave from his corps, which had reached the outskirts of Savannah two days ago; he was still celebrating the national election, which he had helped the Administration win, and he still was trying to digest the disappointment he felt at not having been appointed to succeed McPherson as permanent head of the Army of the Tennessee. George Thomas had been instrumental in keeping him from receiving that reward, so there was a certain poetic justice in what Grant now had in mind; which was to make Logan the Virginian's own successor. He told him so next day, December 13, when he gave him a written order to that effect, along with verbal instructions to proceed at once by rail to Nashville, going by way of Washington and Louisville. If by the time he reached the latter place Thomas had attacked, Logan was to remain there and get in touch with Grant by telegraph. Otherwise he would proceed to Nashville and take over, as directed in the order.

Logan had no sooner left than Grant began to fret anew. Black Jack was unquestionably a fighter; indeed, that was why he had been chosen; plus, of course, the fact that he was handy at the time. But perhaps, as Sherman had indicated by passing him over for Howard after the Battle of Atlanta, he lacked other qualities indispensable in the commander of an army and a department; in which case personal supervision was required. That day, that night, and most of the day that followed — December 14; Ben Butler had finally departed for Wilmington and the powder-boat explosion he believed would abolish Fort Fisher — Grant pondered his way to a decision he reached by sundown. "I am unexpectedly called away," he told Meade in a last-minute note, and got aboard a fast packet for Washington, where he expected to catch the first train west. Arriving next morning he read a telegram Thomas had sent Halleck the night before: "The ice having melted away today, the enemy will be attacked tomorrow morning." Grant decided the best thing to do was suspend his journey and await the outcome, which he would learn from Logan at Louisville or Nashville, or from Thomas himself, before the day was over.

Accordingly, he checked into Willard's to wait in comfort; but not for long. Presently there was word from Halleck that Old Slow Trot had advanced as promised, with conspicuous success, although the battle was still in progress. "Well, I guess we won't go to Nashville," Grant remarked, passing the message to an aide, and then composed for Thomas an order so characteristic that it scarcely needed a signature: "Push the enemy and give him no rest until he is entirely destroyed. ... Do not stop for trains or supplies, but take them from the country as the enemy has done. Much is now expected."

Much was expected. In downtown Nashville, five days ago, the Virginian had said more or less the same thing to his chief subordinates when they assembled in his quarters at the St Cloud Hotel on December 10, midway through the ice storm, to receive preliminary instructions for the attack they would launch as soon as the rebel-occupied hills to the south unfroze enough for climbing. Close to twenty miles of intricate Federal intrenchments stretched from bend to bend of the Cumberland, including seven that ran in a secondary line a mile behind the first-line right and center, manned by the 8000 garrison and service troops under Chief Quartermaster J. L. Donaldson, a fifty-year-old West Pointer who had been awarded the brevet rank of brigadier. When the jump-off came, these would move forward and take over the works in their front, simultaneously guarding against a counterstroke and freeing well over half the 54,000 combat soldiers now arrayed in a long arc, east to west, under Steedman, Schofield, Wood, A. J. Smith, and Wilson, for the assault and the pursuit that was to follow the dislodgment. First off, Steedman would feint against the enemy right, drawing Hood's attention away from the main effort, which would then be made against his left by Smith and Wood in a grand left wheel, with Wilson's troopers shielding the outer flank and Schofield's two divisions waiting in reserve to be committed in either direction. Thus, with Donaldson's and Steedman's men employed on the defensive and the remaining 48,000 available for offensive use against barely half their number, Thomas had been able to plan something more than the usual massing of troops for a breakthrough at a single point. Instead, his line of battle would be of practically equal strength throughout its length as it swung forward gatelike, south and southeast, inexorably crunching whatever it encountered. In this way, once a thaw set in, the ponderous Virginian intended not only to defeat Hood, there on the ground where he stood, but also to destroy him in the process.

West Pointers all, except the battle-tested Steedman, the six lieutenants gave full approval to the plan, although Schofield expressed some disappointment at the comparatively minor role assigned his corps in the attack. He had nothing to say, however, regarding another matter that came up when Thomas told of the pressure being exerted on him to advance before he judged his cavalry was ready or the ground was fit for maneuver. Speaking first, as was customary for the junior at such councils, Wilson quickly protested any suggestion of a commitment until the ice had melted from the pikes and hillsides. "If I were occupying such an intrenched line as Hood's with my dismounted cavalrymen, each armed with nothing more formidable than a basket of brickbats," he declared, "I would agree to defeat the whole Confederate army if it should advance to the attack under such circumstances." Four of the other five generals (Donaldson and Smith, fifty and forty-nine respectively, were older than their chief, while Steedman and Wood, at forty-seven and forty-one, were younger) were similarly outspoken on the subject of untimely haste, and Schofield, who was thirty-three, concurred at least to the extent of keeping silent. With that, the conference adjourned; whereupon Thomas, after asking Wilson to remain behind — ostensibly for further instructions, but actually to thank him for his exuberant support — confided sadly: "Wilson, the Washington authorities treat me as if I was a boy." Thus, for the first and only time, the stolid Virginian, reported to be as ponderous of mind as he was of body, demonstrated some measure of the resentment he felt at being prodded and lectured by Grant and Halleck, neither of whom was within five hundred miles of the scene of the action they kept insisting was overdue. Having said as much, even if only in confidence to a subordinate barely three months past his twenty-seventh birthday, he seemed to experience a certain lift of spirits. "If they will just let me alone, I will show them what we can do. I am sure my plan of operations is correct, and that we shall lick the enemy if only he stays to receive our attack."

There was little to fear on the last count, however, since the condition of the roads precluded a Confederate withdrawal quite as much as it did a Federal advance. Thomas received confirmation of this when, two days later — in partial compliance with Grant's telegraphic order the day before: "Delay no longer for weather or reinforcements" — he had Wilson begin the movement of his troopers across the river from Edgefield. Rough-shod though they were for surer footing, a considerable number of horses slipped and fell on the icy bridge and cobbled streets, injuring their riders as well as themselves in the course of the crossing by the four divisions to take position in rear of A. J. Smith on the far right. "The Yankees brought their weather as well as their army with them," Nashvillians were saying, watching men and mounts topple and thrash about on the sleety pavement, with much attendant damage to knees and dispositions. Thomas was watching, too, as the freeze continued into its fourth day. An aide told how the thick-set army commander, glumly stroking his gray-shot whiskers and brooding under his massive overhang of brow, "would sometimes sit by the window for an hour or more, not speaking a word, gazing steadily out upon the forbidding prospect, as if he were trying to will the storm away."

He seemed to have succeeded the following day, December 13, when a warm rain began melting the sleet that rimed the hills and caked the hollows. Indeed, he seemed to have known he would succeed; for only last night he had passed out written orders for the attack, explaining that it would be launched as soon as a thaw provided footing for the troops. Each man was to be issued three days' rations and sixty rounds of ammunition, while supply and ordnance wagons were to be fully loaded and double-teamed, ready to roll at a moment's notice. Next morning the sun came out, glittering on what little ice remained, and even began to dry the roads a bit. At 3 o'clock that afternoon Thomas reassembled the corps commanders in his quarters and discussed with them the details of his plan. By way of revision, Steedman was told to convert his feint into a real attack, if he found reason to believe one would succeed, and Schofield was placated with assurance that his veterans were only being required to stay their hand for delivery of the knockout blow, which would be landed as soon as the enemy had been set up for the kill. Reveille would sound at 4 a.m. in all the camps, allowing time for the designated units to breakfast and be poised for the jump-off two hours later, at first light; "or as soon thereafter as practicable," the orders read.

That night, having sent a wire to Halleck announcing tomorrow's long-deferred attack, Thomas left a call at the St Cloud desk for 5 o'clock, and when it came — an hour before dawn, two hours before sunrise, December 15 — went down to the lobby, checked out, and after handing his packed suitcase to an orderly mounted his horse for the three-mile ride to the front: specifically to Lawrence Hill, a high salient jutting out from the left of Wood's position in the center. This was to be the pivot for the "grand left wheel," and it also would afford him a clear view of most of the field, including Montgomery Hill, a somewhat lower eminence directly opposite, where the rebels had established a matching salient less than half a mile away.

It would have afforded a view, that is, except for the fog that rose from the warming earth to hold back the dawn and obscure the sun when it came up beyond Steedman's position, an hour past the time originally scheduled for the attack to open there. Still another hour went by before the first shots broke the cotton-wrapped stillness on the left; but Thomas did not fret at the delay. He was convinced there would be time enough, despite the brevity of mid-December daylight, to accomplish all he had in mind. Besides, he did not need to see the field to know it, having studied it carefully in the past from this same observation post, as well as on maps in the small-hours quiet of his room. Four of the eight main thoroughfares, radiating spokelike from the city in his rear, were open or scantly obstructed; the Lebanon and Murfreesboro turnpikes on the left, the Charlotte and Harding turnpikes on the right, were available for use by the superior blue force in moving out to strike the flanks of Hood's four-mile line of intrenchments, which covered the other four main-traveled roads, the Nolensville Pike on his right, the Hillsboro Pike on his left, and the Franklin and Granny White pikes between, running nearly due south in his rear. If Thomas could sweep wide around the rebel flank to seize and hold the latter two, meantime pinning his adversary in position on the hills confronting the Union fortifications, he could then, with better than twice as many troops and something over three times as many guns, destroy him at his leisure. That was just what he intended to do, once the delays were overcome and the crunch got under way.

It seemed however, at least for a time, that there would be no end to the delays, caused first by the fog, which held up the advance on the left till 8 o'clock, two hours behind schedule, and then by the initial attack there, which stalled almost as soon as it got started. Cheatham's corps, posted on Rains Hill, beside the Nolensville Pike, and on to a steep-banked railway cut beyond, held firm against repeated assaults by Steedman's three brigades, each about the size of a Con-

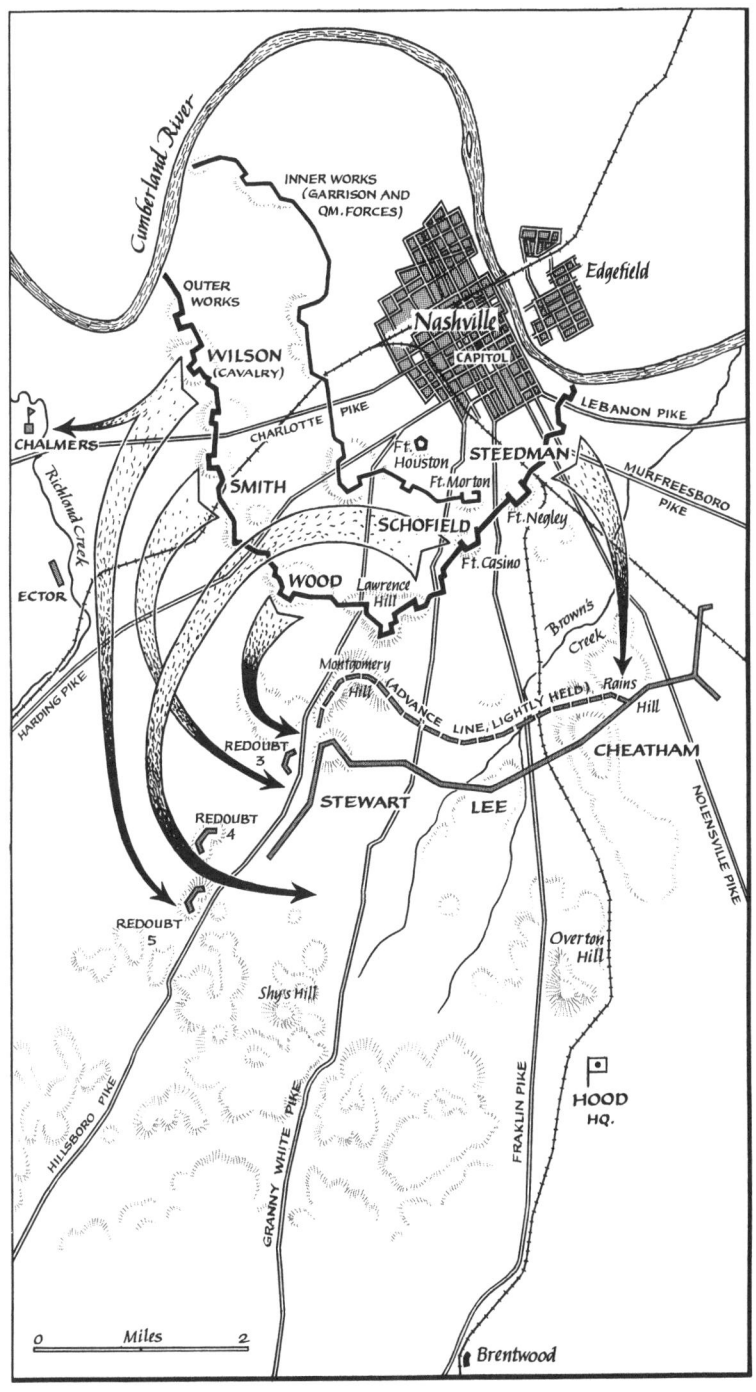

federate division. Two were composed of Negro troops, the first to be committed offensively in the western theater since the bloody repulse at Port Hudson, nearly twenty months ago — and the outcome here was much the same, as it turned out. Crossing Brown's Creek, whose banks were shoe-top deep in mud, they encountered the remnant of Granbury's Texas brigade of Cleburne's division, well dug in but numbering fewer than 500 survivors, and were badly cut up in a crossfire. They fell back "in a rather disorderly manner," one regimental commander admitted; then came on again. This continued, with much the same result, for two hours. Thomas, watching from his command post now that the mist had thinned and drifted off in tendrils, was not discouraged by the failure to gain ground with what had been intended as a feint in any case. Steedman apparently had not drawn Hood's reserves eastward to meet the threat, but at least he was keeping Cheatham occupied with only about an equal number of men — which helped to stretch the odds at the opposite end of the line, where the main effort was to be exerted. Hopefully, Thomas looked in that direction: only to find that, on the right as on the left, a snag had delayed the execution of his well-laid plan.

Beyond Wood's right, in rear of Smith and beyond his right in turn, Wilson's troopers awaited the signal to advance. A third of them, still without horses, would fight dismounted — supplementary infantry, so to speak — while the other 9000, armed to a man with the new seven-shot carbine repeater, comprised a highly mobile strike force. But Thomas no sooner ordered them forward, around 8.30, than the horsemen found both turnpikes blocked by one of Smith's divisions, which he was unexpectedly shifting eastward, across their front, for a closer link with Wood. For more than an hour Wilson fumed and fretted, champing at the bit until at last the slow-trudging foot soldiers cleared his path and let him get on with his task of rimming the "grand wheel." It was close to 10 o'clock by the time he moved out the Harding and Charlotte pikes to take position in Smith's front and on his outer flank.

The last wisps of fog had burned away by then, and well in rear of the advancing columns, along and behind the lofty fortress-studded double curve of intrenchments, spectators crowded the hilltops for a panoramic view of the show about to open on the right. Three years ago, before the occupation that followed hard on the fall of Donelson to Grant, Nashville had had a population of less than 30,000. Now it had better than three times that many residents: "nearly all of whom" — despite this triplicate influx of outsiders — "were in sympathy with the Confederacy," a Federal general observed. When he looked back and saw them clustered wherever the view was best, anticipating carnage, it crossed his mind that any applause that might come from those high-perched galleries was unlikely to be for him or the blue-clad men he rode among. "All the hills in our rear were black with human beings watching the battle, but silent. No army on the continent ever played on any field to so large and so sullen an audience."

What followed was still preliminary, for a time at any rate. Wilson and Smith, with a combined strength of 24,000 sabers and bayonets in their seven divisions, had small trouble driving Rucker's and Ector's outpost brigades — respectively from Chalmers' and French's divisions, and containing fewer than 2000 men between them, mounted and afoot — down the two pikes and over Richland Creek, where they could offer little or no resistance to the massive wheeling movement soon in progress across their front. By noon, so smoothly did the maneuver work once it got under way, the two blue corps were beyond the Harding Pike, confronting the mile-long extension of Hood's left down the Hillsboro Pike from the angle where his line bent sharply south in rear of Montgomery Hill. A low stone wall afforded cover for the division of graybacks crouched behind it on the east side of the road, and three unfinished redoubts bristled with guns on the side toward the Federals, who were massing to continue their advance across the remaining stretch of muddy, stump-pocked fields. Half the daylight had been used in getting set for the big push designed to bring on Hood's destruction. Now the other half remained for its execution.

Moreover, Thomas had another 24,000 standing by under Wood and Schofield, whose five divisions made up the other half of his right-wing strike force, awaiting orders to double the weight of the mass about to be thrown against Hood's left. These were the men who had stood fast at Franklin, and Wood, who had succeeded there to command of the army's largest corps when Stanley took a bullet through the neck, wanted nothing so much as he did an opportunity to wipe out the stain that had marred his record ever since he complied with instructions to "close up on Reynolds" at Chickamauga, thereby creating the gap through which Longstreet's troops had plunged. Still a brigadier, despite the mettle he had proved at Missionary Ridge and Lovejoy Station, he wanted above all a chance to show what he could do on his own. And here at Nashville he got it, just past noon, when word came down for him to execute his share of the grand wheel. All morning he had stood on Lawrence Hill, the pivotal center, obliged to contribute nothing more to the battle than long-range artillery fire, while Steedman and Wilson and Smith moved out, flags aflutter, on the left and on the right. Now that his turn had come, he was determined to make the most of it by storming the enemy works on Montgomery Hill, just opposite his command post.

This was by no means as difficult an undertaking as it appeared to be from where he stood. Five days ago, screened by the blinding fall of sleet, Hood had had Stewart withdraw his main line half a mile rearward, from the brow to the reverse slope of Montgomery Hill, leaving no more than a skeleton crew to man the works established on his arrival, two weeks back. Old Straight had only two full divisions on hand there anyhow, since one of French's three brigades was Ector's, on outpost duty two miles west, and another had been detached to guard the mouth of Duck River, lest Union gunboats penetrate the region in Hood's rear. French himself, a victim of failing eyesight, had departed just that morning, leaving only his third brigade, under Brigadier General Claudius Sears, posted between Walthall's division on the left and Loring's on the right. Stewart thus had barely 4800 men in the path of the 48,000 earmarked by Thomas for the execution of his grand left wheel.

Shortly after 12.30 Loring's pickets looked out from the all-but-abandoned trenches along the crest of the hill, midway between the two main lines of battle, and saw Wood's infantry coming toward them, out of the intervening valley and up the hillside. "The sharp rattle of fifty-caliber rifles sound[ed] like a canebrake on fire," one of the handful of defenders was to say. He and his fellows gave the advancing throng a couple of volleys, then scuttled rearward. Wood, peering intently from his command post on the far side of the valley, was impressed by what he saw. "When the grand array of troops began to move forward in unison," he would write in his report, "the pageant was magnificently grand and imposing. Far as the eye could reach, the lines and masses of blue, over which the national emblem flaunted proudly, moved forward in such perfect order that the heart of the patriot might easily draw from it the happy presage of the coming glorious victory." What pleased him most, apparently, was the progress made by the lead brigade of his old division, now under Brigadier General Samuel Beatty. Recalling its surge up the hillside in advance of all the rest, he waxed Homeric. "At the command, as sweeps the stiff gale over the ocean, driving every object before it, so swept the brigade up the wooded slope, over the enemy's intrenchments; and the hill was won."

What was won in fact was the crest of the hill and a line of empty trenches, not the new main line resistance, half a mile beyond, which held firm under the follow-up attack. Hood, having avoided being drawn off balance by the secondary effort against his right, saw clearly enough his adversary's true over-all intention, and on hearing from Stewart that his portion of the line — the critical left, already menaced by masses of bluecoats, north and west — was "stretched to its utmost tension," did what he could to reduce the lengthening odds in that direction. Stephen Lee, whose corps had scarcely fired a shot from its central position, was told to send Johnson's division to bolster the left, and similar orders went to Cheatham, who was having little trouble containing Steedman's effort on the right, to send Bate's division there as well. Whether they would arrive in time was another matter; Wood's assault had no sooner been launched against Stewart's front than Smith and Wilson resumed their combined advance upon his flank. Hard on the heels of this, moreover, Thomas passed the word for Schofield to join in the attack, bringing the total right-wheel commitment to just under 50,000 of all arms. That was better than twice the number Hood had on hand in his entire command, and roughly ten times as many as Stewart would have in his depleted corps until reinforcements reached him.

One unit had arrived by then as a reinforcement, albeit a small one: Ector's 700-man brigade, which came in from the west around 11 o'clock, after being driven back across Richland Creek by Smith and Wilson. Appealed to by the occupants of one of the redoubts short of the Hillsboro Pike, who urged them to join in its defense, the winded veterans replied: "It can't be done. There's a whole army in your front," and kept going, taking position on the left of Walthall, whose three brigades were strung out behind the stone wall running south along the far side of the pike. Such words were far from encouraging to the troops in the three redoubts, each of which was built on rising ground and contained a four-gun battery, manned by fifty cannoneers and supported by about twice that number of infantry lodged in shallow trenches alongside the uncompleted breastworks. These miniature garrisons had been told to hold out "at all hazards," and they were determined to do so, knowing they were all that stood between Hood's unshored left flank and the Federals who soon were massing to the west and northwest after completing the first stage of their grand wheel. Between noon and 1 o'clock, while Wood's attack exploded northward beyond the loom of Montgomery Hill, Wilson and Smith opened fire with their rifled batteries at a range of just under half a mile. The defenders replied as best they could with their dozen smoothbores, but hoarded their energy and ammunition for the close-up work that would follow when the dark blue mass, already in attack formation and biding its time through the bombardment, moved against them.

As it turned out, these three redoubts, numbered 3 and 4 and 5 — 1 and 2 lay northward, east of the pike, where Stewart's line bent south — held up the next stage of the wheeling movement, here on the Federal right, even longer than fog had delayed the jump-off on the left. For close to an hour the Union gunners made things hot for the clustered graybacks, who could do little more than hug their shell-jarred works and wait their turn. This came around 1.30 when the iron rain let up and the multiwaved assault rolled within range of their 12-pounders. Flailed ragged along its near edge by double-shotted canister, the blue flood paused in front of Redoubts 3 and 4, but not for long in front of Redoubt 5, which was unsupported on its outer flank, three quarters of a mile beyond the end of Walthall's line. Wilson's rapid-firing troopers, charging dismounted — somewhat awkwardly, it was true, for no one had thought to tell them to leave their low-slung cavalry sabers behind — rushed past it on the left and right and swamped it from the rear. They had no sooner done so, though, than they received a high-angle salvo from Redoubt 4, next up the line, where Captain Charles Lumsden's Alabama battery was supported by a hundred Alabama infantry. Lumsden, a V.M.I. graduate and one-time commandant of cadets at the University of Alabama, had already notified Stewart that he and his men, with a combined strength of 148, were likely to be swept away in short order, once the enemy pressed the issue. Old Straight's reply: "Hold on as long as you can," was followed to the letter. Firing front and flank with their brass Napoleons and rifles, the Alabamians held fast against the menace of a dozen regiments from Smith and four from Wilson. In the end, nearly three hours past the opening of the preliminary bombardment, the attackers came tumbling between the fuming guns, bayonets flashing, carbines a-clatter. "Take care of yourselves, boys!" Lumsden called out, and the survivors trotted back to the main line, half a mile rearward, prepared to join in its defense against the final stage of the blue assault.

Two of Johnson's brigades had arrived by then from Lee's corps in the center, and Old Clubby was on the way with the other two, while Bate hurried westward from the far right, sent by Cheatham on orders from Hood to help shore up the hard-pressed left. Even if both divisions arrived in time, however, they would do little to reduce the odds; Schofield had come up, across the way, and was taking position on Smith's right to overlap Stewart's extension of his line down the Hillsboro Pike. It was now past 3 o'clock. While the Federal batteries displaced forward, beyond fallen Redoubt 4, to try their hand at knocking down the stone fence Walthall's men were crouched behind, Smith's left division, commanded by Brigadier General John McArthur, advanced upon and captured Redoubt 3. Taken promptly under fire by Redoubt 2, across the pike, McArthur — a Scotch-born former blacksmith who had prospered as the proprietor of a Chicago ironworks and had served with bristly distinction in most of the western campaigns — stormed and took the companion work as well, turning its guns on nearby Redoubt 1, already under heavy pressure from two of Wood's divisions.

If this went, all went: Stewart knew that, and so did Wood, who had ordered two six-gun batteries advanced to bring converging, almost point-blank fire to bear on the angle where Sears's brigade was posted, hinge-like, between Walthall and Loring. Then at 4 o'clock, after a good half hour's pounding by these dozen guns, Wood told Brigadier General Washington Elliott — Wagner's replacement after Franklin — to assault the rebel salient with his division "at all costs." At 4.30, angered by the delay, which Elliott claimed was needed to give Smith's corps time to come up on his right, Wood passed the word for Kimball to make the strike instead. Kimball did so, promptly and with what his superior later called "the most exalted enthusiasm." As his troops entered the works from the northeast, followed closely by the tardy Elliott's, McArthur's flank brigade came storming in from the west to assist in the reduction, together with the capture of four guns, four stands of colors, and "numerous prisoners."

Mainly these last were laggards or members of the forlorn hope, left behind to cover the withdrawal of the main body of defenders. Stewart, foreseeing disaster — both on his left, which was considerably overlapped by Schofield, and in his center, where the hinge was about to buckle under pressure from Wood and Smith — had just ordered a pull-back to a new position shielding the vital Granny White Pike, a mile in rear of the line that now was crumbling along the Hillsboro Pike and the near slope of Montgomery Hill. Despite the panic in certain units, what followed between sunset at 4.45 and full darkness, one hour later, was not a rout. Johnson's two advance brigades, posted in extension of Walthall's left before the fall of Redoubt 4, came unglued when the Federals charged them, and Ector's brigade was cut off from the rest of Stewart's corps, northward beyond the gap their flight created. Elsewhere, though, Walthall's and Loring's veterans responded in good order to instructions for disengagement. Up in the critical angle, under assault from two directions, Sears managed to pull most of his men out, avoiding capture, but as they fell back he turned to study the lost post with his binoculars and was struck in the right leg by a well-aimed solid, perhaps from one of his abandoned guns. He fell heavily, then was hustled off to an aid station, where surgeons removed his mangled leg that night. Meantime Stewart, reinforced at last by Bate and Johnson's other two brigades, got his two divisions realigned in a southward prolongation of Lee's unshaken left, helped by the jubilant confusion of the Federals, who were about as disorganized by their sudden twilight victory as his own troops were by their defeat.

Hood was there, too, intent on shoring up this battered third of his army. He had lost 16 guns today, along with some 2200 soldiers, more than half of them made prisoner in the collapse of his left wing, the rest killed or wounded here and on the right, which had stood firm. Meeting Ector's peripatetic brigade as it fell back from its second cut-off position, across the Hillsboro Pike from Redoubt 5, he spoke briefly to the men and led them nearly a mile eastward to a hill that loomed just short of the Granny White Pike. Four of the six regiments were one-time Texas cavalry outfits, long since dismounted for lack of horses and down to about a hundred men apiece.

"Texans," he said, "I want you to hold this hill regardless of what transpires around you."

They looked at the hill, then back at Hood, and nodded. "We'll do it, General," they told him.

★ ★ ★

Union and Confederate, the lines ran helter-skelter in the dusk. Still on Lawrence Hill, Thomas watched his army's campfires blossom where rebel fires had burned the night before. Except for unexpected delays — caused first by the fog, then by Smith's last-minute adjustment of his front, which held up the start of the grand wheel, and finally by the prolonged resistance of the flimsy enemy redoubts west of the Hillsboro Pike — he was convinced he would have achieved the Cannae he had planned for, and expected, until darkness caught up with the attackers before they could complete the massive turning movement he had designed to cut off Hood's retreat. In any case, not being much given to dwelling on regrets, he perceived that the best course now was for all units to bivouac where they were, in preparation for taking up their unfinished work tomorrow, well rested from the day-long exertions that had put them where they were tonight, practically within reach of the only two unseized turnpikes leading south. Just how far they would have to go, before the battle was resumed, would depend on what progress Hood's beaten troops could make on the muddy roads toward Franklin and the Harpeth — if, indeed, they were in any condition to move at all — before daylight and better than 50,000 Federals overtook them.

Returning to Nashville for a good night's sleep in a proper bed, Thomas got off to Halleck at 9 o'clock a telegram that somehow managed to be at once both ponderous and exuberant. "I attacked the enemy's left this morning and drove it from the river, below the city, very nearly to the Franklin Pike, a distance [of] about eight miles.... The troops behaved splendidly, all taking their share in assaulting and carrying the enemy's breastworks. I shall attack the enemy again tomorrow, if he stands to fight, and, if he retreats during the night, will pursue him, throwing a heavy cavalry force in his rear, to destroy his trains, if possible." A reply from Edwin Stanton himself, sent three hours later, hailed "the brilliant achievements of this day" as "the harbinger of a decisive victory that will crown you and your army with honor and do much toward closing the war. We shall give you a hundred guns in the morning." From Grant there came two wires, sent fifteen minutes apart, between 11.30 and midnight. "Much is now expected," the first ended, and the second had rather the nature of an afterthought — a brief correction of, if not quite an apology for, a lapse in manners. "I congratulate you and the army under your command for today's operations, and feel a conviction that tomorrow will add more fruits to your victory."

Closer at hand, there were those who did not share this conviction. Receiving after dark Thomas's order, "which was in substance to pursue the retreating enemy next morning," Schofield took alarm at the thought that such evident overconfidence, in addition to costing the army its half-won victory, might also expose it to defeat. He had supplied the crowning blow today, coming in hard around the crumpled rebel left at sunset, but he was by no means convinced that what had been delivered was a knockout punch, as his superior seemed to think. In fact he did not believe for a minute that Hood was in retreat. For all he knew, his former roommate was even then planning a first-light strike at one of the Union flanks: most likely his own, though both were more or less exposed. "He'll hit you like hell, now, before you know it," he had warned Sherman when Hood first took over, down around Atlanta five months ago, and it seemed to him, from the order just received, that Thomas needed reminding of that danger. Accordingly, he called for his horse and rode through the darkness to headquarters, back in Nashville, where he found the Virginian about to retire for the night. "You don't know Hood," he protested earnestly. "He'll be right there, ready to fight you in the morning."

Thomas knew Hood a good deal better than Schofield seemed to think; but even so this warning gave him pause. And having paused he acted in revision of his plans. Previously he had alerted his cavalry for a fast ride south at the first glimmer of the coming day, his purpose being to cut the retreating graybacks off, or anyhow bring them to a halt before they crossed the Harpeth, and thus expose them to slaughter without the protection of that river barrier, which might oblige the blue pursuers to fight a second Franklin, in reverse. Now instead he sent word for Wilson to "remain in your present position until it is satisfactorily known whether the enemy will fight or retreat." That would help cover his right, where the troopers had drawn rein at nightfall, and by way of further insurance he had A. J. Smith send one of his three divisions to reinforce Schofield on that flank, in case Hood really was planning the dawn assault his one-time roommate feared. This done, Thomas at last turned in for the good night's sleep he had prescribed for his whole army.

There was little or no rest, however, for the gray-clad troops across the way: not because they were on the march, as Thomas had presumed, but because they were digging — digging in. Schofield was right, at least in part: Hood had chosen to stay and fight, if only on the defensive. The crumpling of his left today, while the other two thirds of his army stood firm, had by no means convinced him that the enemy host, for all its heavy numerical advantage, was capable of driving him headlong from the field: whereas a Federal repulse, here at the capital gates, might still afford him an opening for the counterstroke on which his hopes were pinned. Moreover, the position he retired to, just under two miles south, was so much stronger than the first — especially in man-saving compactness, though it covered only two of the eight converging turnpikes — that the wonder was he had not occupied it at the outset, when he came within sight of Nashville, two weeks ago tomorrow.

Despite the confusion attending the sunset collapse of his defenses along the Hillsboro Pike and across Montgomery Hill, the nighttime withdrawal to this new line was accomplished in good order. Lee's corps, which had scarcely been engaged today except for part of Johnson's division, simply fell back two miles down the Franklin Pike to Overton Hill, east of the road, where the new right flank was anchored. The left was just over two miles away, beyond the Granny White Pike, and its main salient was the hill on which Hood had posted Ector's brigade at twilight (Shy's Hill, it would afterwards be called for young Lieutenant Colonel William Shy, who would die on its crown tomorrow at the head of his Tennessee regiment); Cheatham, whose losses had also been light today, occupied this critical height, his flank bent south around its western slope. In the center, disposed along a range of hills between the outer two, Stewart's diminished corps took position and began to prepare for the resumption of the battle, as the others were doing on the right and left, by scraping out shallow trenches and using the spoil to pile up breastworks along that low range lying midway between Brentwood, less than four miles south, and the Nashville fortifications. Like Ector's Texans, who by now had been joined by Bate's division on its arrival from the right, they were determined to give Hood all he asked of them, though they had trouble understanding why he did so with two turnpikes leading unobstructed to the crossing of the Harpeth, barely a dozen miles in their rear.

Dawn found them settled in, weary from their all-night toil but confident, as one division commander said, that their improvised works were "impervious to ordinary shots." Extraordinary shots presumably would have to be taken as they came, but at any rate Chalmers had combined his two brigades in Cheatham's rear, where his troopers were in position to help fend off a repetition of yesterday's overlapping assault upon that flank. Still, for all his determination not to be hustled into disorderly retreat, Hood knew the odds he faced and was quite aware of what they might portend. Accordingly, he ordered all wagons to proceed at first light to the Harpeth, clearing the narrow gorges in his rear, and soon afterwards, at 8 o'clock, sent warning notes to all three corps commanders, specifying that "should any disaster happen to us today," Lee would hold fast on the Franklin Pike, until Stewart had moved down it, and Cheatham would take the Granny White Pike, his withdrawal covered by Chalmers. Minor adjustments were made in the line, which was only half as long as the one the day before, but most of the morning was spent in idle waiting by the graybacks for the shock that would come when Thomas resumed his effort to destroy them where they stood.

The slowness of the Federals in getting back to grips with their opponents was due to the scattered condition of the army when it bedded down the night before. On the right, Wilson and Schofield

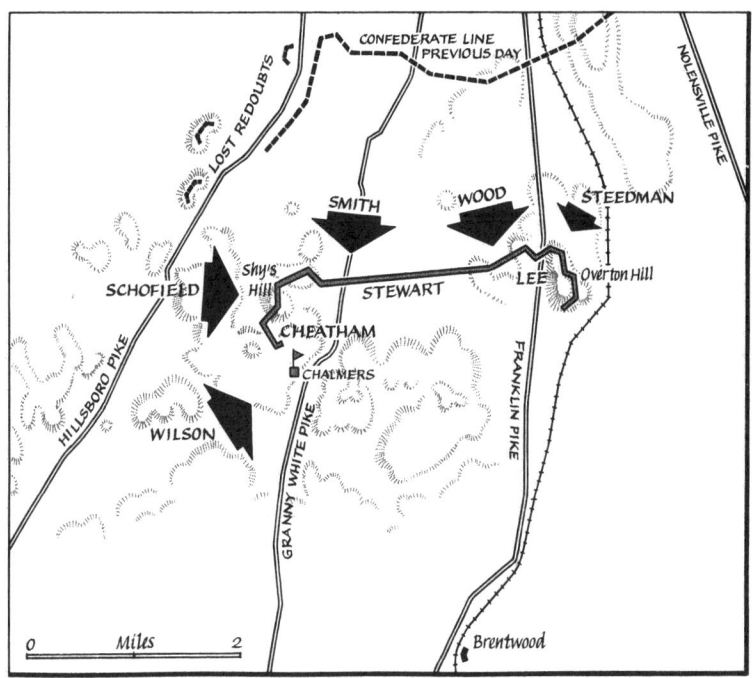

were in reasonable proximity to Cheatham on Shy's Hill, and so presently, on the left, was Steedman in relation to Lee, whose skirmishers he encountered as he approached Overton Hill, east of the Franklin Pike, around midmorning. It was in the center, in particular the right center, that the worst delays occurred; Smith and Wood were at right angles to each other, and neither knew, when the day began, whether the rebels had pulled out in the night, or, if not, what position Hood had chosen for another stand. By the time they found out, and got their troops aligned for the confrontation, noon had come and action had opened on the left. This was as it had been the day before, except that at no stage of the planning was Steedman's effort, reinforced by one of Wood's divisions, intended as a feint. His orders called for the Confederates to be "vigorously pressed and unceasingly harrassed," for if Hood's right could be turned and "his line of retreat along the Franklin Pike and the valley leading to Brentwood commanded effectually," Thomas would succeed today in bringing off the Cannae he had intended yesterday. The result, here on the Union left, was the bloodiest fighting of the two-day battle.

Two of Lee's divisions, under Major Generals Henry Clayton and Carter Stevenson, not only had scarcely been engaged the day before, they had not even taken part in the assault at Franklin, and their conduct here today, astride the Franklin Pike and on the crest of Overton

Hill, gave some notion of what Hood's whole army might have accomplished at the gates of Nashville, just over two weeks later, if it had been spared the late-November holocaust that cost it 6000 of its best men, including Pat Cleburne and a dozen other brigade and division commanders. At full strength, both in numbers and morale, these five brigades — reinforced by a sixth from Johnson, whose division was on their left, adjoining Stewart's corps in the center — stood off, between noon and 3 o'clock, a series of combined attacks by Wood and Steedman, whose persistence cost them dearly. Suffering little themselves, despite massed incoming artillery fire that Wood pronounced "uncommonly fine" and one defender said "was the most furious I ever witnessed," they inflicted such heavy punishment on the attackers that finally, after three hours of surging up and stumbling down the muddy slopes of the hill on the far Confederate right, the blue flood receded. Steedman's losses were especially cruel. One unit, the 13th U.S. Colored Infantry, suffered 221 casualties in all, the greatest regimental loss on either side. "After the repulse," Wood later reported, "our soldiers, white and colored, lay indiscriminately near the enemy works at the outer edge of the abatis."

When this attack first opened, threatening to turn his right and cut the Franklin Pike, Hood ordered Cheatham to send three of the four brigades from the division on his left — formerly Cleburne's, now under its senior brigadier, James A. Smith — to reinforce the opposite flank. As it turned out, this was a serious mistake. Lee not only needed no help, but by the time Smith's men reached him, around 3.30, the attack had been suspended. Worse, there wasn't time enough for them to return to their former position below Shy's Hill, which they had no sooner left than they were sorely missed. Stewart had been watching in both directions from his command post in the center, east of the Granny White Pike, and had seen trouble coming: not on the right, though the Overton Hill assault was even then approaching its climax, but on the left, where the situation was uncomfortably similar to the one he himself had faced the day before, when his had been the corps on that flank. "Should Bate fall back," he said in a hastily-written 2 o'clock note to Walthall, whose division adjoined Bate's on Cheatham's right, "keep your left connected with him, falling back from your left toward right and forming a new flank line extending to hills in rear."

There was more to this than a generally shared mistrust of Bate, whose three brigades had not done well in recent operations. All morning, though none of the five blue infantry divisions arrayed in a nearly semicircular line confronting Shy's Hill from the north and west had so far come to grips with the defenders, Wilson, fighting with two divisions dismounted while the other two ranged wide, had been pressing Chalmers' horsemen back on their supports. By noon, as a result, the Granny White Pike was firmly in Union possession to the south, no longer a possible rebel escape route, and Cheatham's left was bent in the shape of a fishhook. Hood pulled Ector's troops back from the crest of the hill to help Smith's remaining brigade hold off Wilson's attackers, whose repeaters gave them a firepower out of proportion to their already superior numbers. This caused Bate to have to extend his line still farther westward in taking over the works Ector's men had occupied, and worst of all, now that the rapid-firing blue troopers had pushed within carbine range, this part of the line was taking close-up fire not only from its front and flank but also from its rear. "The Yankee bullets and shells were coming from all directions, passing one another in the air," a butternut private would recall.

By 3 o'clock, when the blue attack finally sputtered out on the Confederate right, a good part of the night-built breastworks on Shy's Hill had been flattened or knocked apart — small wonder; one of Schofield's batteries, for example, pumped 560 rounds into the hill before the day was over — by well-aimed shots from artillery massed north and west and south. A cold rain had begun at midday, and the defenders could do little, under the fall of icy water and hot metal, but hug the earth and hope for a let-up that did not come, either of raindrops or of shells. It was more or less clear to everyone here, as it was to Stewart in the center, that the position now being pounded by close to a hundred guns could not be held much longer than it took the commanders of the three Union corps — one in its front, one on its flank, one in its rear — to stage the concerted push the situation called for.

Thomas, though he still declined to be hurried in his conduct of the battle — not even by a midday wire from the Commander in Chief, in which, after tendering "the nation's thanks for your good work of yesterday," Lincoln ended on a sterner note, as if on cue from Grant: "You made a magnificent beginning. A grand consummation is within your easy reach. Do not let it slip" — saw clearly enough what was called for, and was moving even now to bring it off. About the time the Overton Hill attack subsided he set out from his Franklin Pike command post and rode westward through the pelting rain in rear of the extension of Wood's line, on beyond the Granny White Pike, where A. J. Smith had his two remaining divisions in position, and then around the southward curve of front to Schofield's headquarters, due west of Shy's Hill. Wilson was there, remonstrating against Schofield's delay in giving the prearranged signal he and Smith had agreed would launch the converging assault by all three corps. The cavalryman had sent a series of couriers urging action for the past two hours, ever since he gained the rebel rear, and now at last — within an hour of sunset — had come in person to protest, although with small effect; Schofield wanted another division from Smith before advancing, on grounds that to attack high-sited intrenchments without a greater advantage in numbers than he now enjoyed would be to risk paying more in blood for the hill than it was worth. Thomas heard him out, then said dryly: "The battle must be fought, if men *are* killed." He looked across the northwest slope of the fuming hill, where it seemed to him that McArthur, adjusting his line for a closer take-off, was about to slip the leash. "General Smith is attacking without waiting for you," he told Schofield. "Please advance your entire line."

Here at last was a direct order; Schofield had no choice but to obey. He did so, in fact, so promptly that Wilson, riding happily south to rejoin his troopers in rear of the blue-clamped rebel left, did not get back in time to direct their share of the three-sided push that drove the defenders from Shy's Hill. So sudden indeed was the gray collapse that Hood himself, watching from horseback in rear of his left center, said later that he could scarcely credit what he saw. "Our forces up to that moment had repulsed the Federals at every point, and were waving their colors in defiance, crying out to the enemy, 'Come on, come on.'" With the crisis weathered on his right and sunset barely an hour away, he planned to withdraw after nightfall for a dawn assault on the Union right, which he believed was exposed to being turned and shattered. Alas, it was his own flank that was shattered as he watched. "I beheld for the first and only time" — he had not been on Missionary Ridge with Bragg, just over a year ago — "a Confederate army abandon the field in confusion."

Old Straight had seen disaster coming two hours before, and it came as he had warned. Assailed by Smith and Schofield on both sides of the angle, all the while taking fire from Wilson's dismounted horsemen in their rear, Bate's three brigades gave back from their enfiladed works, fought briefly, and then for the most part fled, although some units — the Tennesseans under twenty-five-year-old William Shy, for instance, whose fall gave the lost hill its future name — resisted till they were overrun. By that time, the attack had widened and the panic had infected Stewart's corps, along with the rest of Cheatham's; "The breach once made, the lines lifted from either side as far as I could see," Bate would report. All three of his brigade commanders were captured, and so was Edward Johnson when the break extended beyond the center, under pressure from Smith and Wood, and spread to his division on Lee's left. Everywhere to the west of there, eastward across the rear of what had been the Confederate left and center, butternut veterans were in headlong flight for the Franklin Pike, the one remaining avenue of escape. They wanted to live: perhaps to fight another day, but certainly not here.

"It was more like a scene in a spectacular drama than a real incident in war," a colonel on Thomas's staff would note. "The hillside in front, still green, dotted with boys in blue swarming up the slope, the dark background of high hills beyond, the lowering clouds, the waving flags, the smoke rising slowly through the leafless treetops and drifting across the valleys, the wonderful outburst of musketry, the ecstatic cheers, the multitude racing for life down into the valley below — so exciting was it all that the lookers-on instinctively clapped their hands as at a brilliant and successful transformation scene; as indeed it was. For in those few moments an army was changed into a mob, and the whole structure of the rebellion in the Southwest, with all its possibilities, was utterly overthrown."

But that was to overstate the case, if not in regard to the eventualities, then at any rate in regard to the present dissolution of Hood's army. On Overton Hill, in the final moments before the opposite flank gave way, Stephen Lee observed that his troops were "in fine spirits and confident of success," congratulating themselves on their recent repulse of Wood and Steedman. Then out of nowhere came the collapse, first of Cheatham's corps, then Stewart's, and the blue attack rolled eastward to engulf them; Johnson's division wavered and broke, its commander taken, and Stevenson's, next in line, seemed about to follow. East of the Franklin Pike, in rear of Clayton's division, Lee spurred his horse westward, taking the fences on both sides of the turnpike, and drew rein amid the confusion behind his center, crowded now with graybacks who had bolted. He leaned down and snatched a stand of colors from a fugitive color bearer, then brandished it from horseback as he rode among the panicked veterans, shouting hoarsely at them: "Rally, men, rally! For God's sake, rally! This is the place for brave men to die!"

Some few stopped, then more. "The effect was electrical," one among them was to write. "They gathered in little knots of four or five, and he soon had around him three or four other stands of colors." They were not many, but they were enough, as it turned out, to cause the attackers — confused as much by their abrupt success today as they had been at the same late hour the day before — to hesitate before moving forward again through the smoky, rain-screened dusk that followed hard upon sunset. By that time Clayton, unmolested on the right, had managed to withdraw his division from Overton Hill and form it in some woods astride the Franklin Pike, half a mile below. When Lee fell back to there, the same observer noted, "he was joined by a few pieces of artillery and a little drummer boy who beat the long roll in perfect time." Stevenson's fugitives rallied too, in response to this steady drumming, and together the two divisions comprised a rear guard that kept open, well into darkness, the one escape route still available to the army.

This was of course no help to the men already rounded up in their thousands on the field of battle, including Johnson — he had just been exchanged in October, five months after his previous capture at Spotsylvania — and all three of Bate's brigade commanders, Brigadier Generals Henry Jackson and T. B. Smith and Major Jacob Lash. Old Clubby, still crippled from the leg wound he had suffered at McDowell, two and a half years ago, was taken while trying to limp away from his shattered line, and it was much the same with Jackson, a forty-four-year-old former Georgia lawyer-politician, who found the rearward going slow because of the mud that weighted down his boots. He had stopped, and was trying to get them off with the help of an aide, when a blue-clad corporal and three privates came upon him by the roadside.

"You're a general," the corporal said accusatively, spotting the wreathed stars on his prisoner's collar.

"That is my rank," Jackson admitted.

"Captured a general, by God!" the Federal whooped. He took off his flat-topped forage cap and swung it round and round his head. "I'll carry you to Nashville myself."

Smith and Lash on the other hand were taken on Shy's Hill itself, along with most of their men, when their lines were overrun. Imprisoned, Lash would not receive the promotion he had earned by surviving his superiors, but Smith's was a crueler fate. A graduate of the Nashville Military Institute and a veteran of all the western battles, he had risen from second lieutenant, over the years, to become at twenty-six the army's youngest brigadier; which perhaps, since his youth and slim good looks implied a certain jauntiness in happier times, had something to do with what presently happened to him. While being conducted unarmed to the Union rear he was slashed three times across the head with a saber by the colonel of the Ohio regiment that had captured him, splitting his skull and exposing so much of his mangled brain that the surgeon who examined his wounds pronounced them fatal. He did not die, however. He survived a northern prison camp to return to his native state when the conflict was over, then lived for nearly another sixty years before he died at last in the Tennessee Hospital for the Insane, where he spent the last forty-seven of his eighty-five years, a victim of the damage inflicted by the Ohio colonel. This was another face of war, by no means unfamiliar on either side, but one unseen when the talk was all of glory.

It was not the face Thomas saw when, completing a sunset ride from the far right, he urged his horse up Overton Hill, which had just been cleared, and looked out over the field where his troops were hoicking long columns of butternut captives to the rear. He lifted his hat in salute to the victors in the twilight down below, exclaiming as he did so: "Oh, what a grand army I have! God bless each member of it."

Such hilltop crowing was uncharacteristic of the Rock of Chickamauga, however well it might suit him in his new role as the Sledge of Nashville, but in any case both salute and blessing were deserved. His army captured here today an additional 3300 prisoners, bringing its two-day haul, as a subsequent head-count would show, to 4462 rebels of all ranks. Moreover, another 37 pieces of artillery were taken, which made 53 in all, one more than R. E. Lee had captured throughout the Seven Days to set the previous battle record. Thomas's loss in killed, wounded, and missing, though twice heavier today than yesterday, barely raised his overall total above three thousand: 3061. Hood lost only half as many killed and wounded as he had done the day before, but his scant loss in those two categories — roughly 1500 for both days, or less than half the number his adversary suffered — only showed how readily his soldiers had surrendered under pressure, thereby lifting his loss to nearly 6000 casualties, almost twice as many as he inflicted. Thomas of course did not yet know these comparative figures. All he knew was that he had won decisively, more so tactically perhaps than any general in any large-scale battle in this war, and that was the cause of his exuberance on Overton Hill and afterwards, when he came down off the height and rode forward in the gathering darkness.

Normally mild of speech and manner, practically never profane or boastful, he continued to be quite unlike himself tonight: as was shown when he spotted his young cavalry commander riding back up the Granny White Pike to meet him. He recalled what he had told him in private on the eve of battle, and he greeted him now, the other would note, "with all the vehemence of an old dragoon" and in a voice that could be heard throughout this quarter of the rain-swept field. "Dang it to hell, Wilson!" he roared, "didn't I tell you we could lick 'em? Didn't I tell you we could lick 'em?"

Southward, the disorderly gray retreat continued. Lee's rear guard task was eased by having only Wood's corps to contend with; Steedman had stopped, apparently from exhaustion, and Smith and Schofield had been halted to prevent confusion when their two corps came together at right angles on Shy's Hill. Below there, Wilson's remounted troopers were opposed by Ector's surviving handful of infantry and Rucker's cavalry brigade, assigned by Chalmers to keep the bluecoats off the Franklin Pike, which was clogged with fugitives all the way to Brentwood. Rucker managed it, with the help of Ector's veterans and the rain and darkness, though at the cost of being captured — the fourth brigade commander in the past two hours — when he was shot from his horse in a hand-to-hand saber duel with two opponents. Lee meantime withdrew in good order, two miles beyond Brentwood to Hollow Tree Gap, where he set up a new rear-guard line by midnight, six miles short of Franklin and the Harpeth.

In this way, from sunset well into darkness, when they finally desisted, the Federals were kept from interfering with the retreat of the army they had routed. But neither could that army's own leaders interfere with its rearward movement, though they tried. "It was like trying to stop the current of Duck River with a fish net," one grayback was to say. Not even Ben Cheatham, for all the fondness his men had for him, could prevail on them to pause for longer that he could fix them with his eye. He would get one stopped, and then when he turned to appeal to another, the first would duck beneath the general's horse and continue on his way. Even so, he had better luck than did some younger staffers who tried their hand. One such, hailing a mud-spattered infantryman headed rearward down the turnpike, ordered him to face about and meet the foe. "You go to hell — I've been there," the man replied, and kept on trudging southward in the rain. None among them had any way of knowing that the war's last great battle had been fought. All they knew was they wanted no more of it; not for now, at any rate.

Hood was no better at organizing a rally short of Brentwood than the least of his subordinates had been. He tried for a time, then gave it up and went with the flow. A bandaged Tennessee private who had seen and pitied him earlier, just before the break — "How feeble and decrepit he looked, with an arm in a sling and a crutch in the other hand, trying to guide and control his horse" — felt even sorrier for him tonight when, seeking him out to secure "a wounded furlough," he came upon the one-legged general near Hollow Tree Gap, alone in his headquarters tent beside the Franklin Pike, "much agitated and affected" by the events of the past six hours "and crying like his heart would break." His left arm dangling useless at his side, he ran the fingers of his right hand through his hair in a distracted gesture as the tears ran down his cheeks into his beard, golden in the light of the lantern on the table by his chair. Unabashed — after the manner of Confederates of all ranks, who respected their superiors in large part for the respect they knew they would receive in turn if they approached them — the bullet-nicked private entered, asked for, and received his furlough paper, then went back out into the darkness and the rain, leaving Hood to resume his weeping if he chose. "I pitied him, poor fellow," the Tennessean wrote long afterward, remembering the scene. "I always loved and honored him, and will ever revere and cherish his memory.... As a soldier, he was brave, good, noble, and gallant, and fought with the ferociousness of the wounded tiger, and with the everlasting grit of the bulldog; but as a general he was a failure in every particular."

For all its harshness, Franklin and Nashville had confirmed and reconfirmed this assessment, so far at least as most of the Kentucky-born Texan's critics were concerned, before it was made: not only because he fought them with so little tactical skill, offensive or defensive, but also because he fought them at all. Within a span of just over two weeks, these two battles had cost him 12,000 casualties — better than twice the number he inflicted — and in the end produced a rout as complete as the one a year ago on Missionary Ridge. Pat Cleburne had saved Bragg's retreat then with his defense of Ringgold Gap, and though the Arkansan now was in his grave in St John's churchyard, Stephen Lee performed a similar service for Hood next morning at Hollow Tree Gap, which he held under pressure from Wilson and Wood while the rest of the graybacks crossed the Harpeth. Outflanked, he followed, burning the bridge in his wake, and took up a covering position on Winstead Hill, three miles south of Franklin, where Hood had had his command post for the attack that cost him the flower of his army. Today's defense only cost him Lee, who was wounded there and had to turn his corps over to Stevenson when he fell back that evening to take up a new position near Spring Hill, another place of doleful memory.

By the following morning, December 18, Cheatham had reassembled enough of his corps to assume the duty of patrolling rain-swollen Rutherford Creek, which the pursuers could not cross, once the turnpike bridge was burned, until their pontoon train arrived. The resultant two-day respite from immediate blue pressure (for the train, having been missent toward Murfreesboro by a clerical error, then recalled, was obliged to creak and groan its way by a roundabout route over roads hub-deep in mud) was heartening to the graybacks plodding down the Columbia Pike. But the best of all news, especially for Chalmers' drooping horsemen, was the arrival last night of one of the four detached brigades of cavalry, followed today by another, which brought word that Forrest himself would soon be along with the other two. Sure enough, he rode in that night. Ordered by Hood to fall back from Murfreesboro through Shelbyville to Pulaski, he had decided instead to rejoin by a shorter route, through Triune, and had done so: much to his superior's relief. Hood's plan had been to call a halt along Duck River and winter in its lush valley, much as Bragg had done two years ago, but he saw now there could be no rest for his ground-down command short of the broader Tennessee, another seventy miles to the south. Accordingly, having begun his withdrawal across the Duck, he was all the more pleased by Forrest's early return, since it meant that the Wizard and his veteran troopers, lately conspicuous by their absence, would be there to hold off the Federals while the rest of the army went on with its dangerous task of crossing a major river in the presence of a foe not only superior in numbers, warmly clad, and amply fed, but also flushed with victory and clearly bent on completing the destruction begun three days ago at the gates of Nashville.

In taking over this rear-guard assignment — for which he had about 3000 cavalry whose mounts were still in condition for hard duty, plus 2000 infantry under Walthall, roughly a fourth of them barefoot and all of them hungry, cold in their cotton tatters, and close to exhaustion from two days of battle and two of unrelieved retreat — Forrest combined his usual inventiveness with a highly practical application of the means at hand, however slight. Part of the problem was the weather, which changed next day from bad to worse. Alternate blasts of sleet and rain deepened the mud, stalled the supply train, and covered the roads and fields with a crust of ice that crunched and shattered under foot and made walking a torture for ill-shod men and horses. He solved the immobilized wagon dilemma by leaving half of them parked along the pike and using their teams to double those in the other half, which then proceeded. Because of the drawn-out Federal delay, first in clearing brim-full Rutherford Creek and then the more formidable Duck, four miles beyond, there was time for the doubled teams to haul the first relay far to the south and then return for the second before the pursuers bridged and crossed both streams. As for the infantry crippled for lack of shoes, Forrest solved that problem by commandeering empty wagons in which the barefoot troops could ride until they were called on to jump down and hobble back to their places in the firing line. "Not a man was brought in contact with him who did not feel strengthened and invigorated," one among them was to say of the general who thus converted shoeless cripples into horse-drawn infantry.

Not until the night of December 21, with their pontoons up and thrown at last, did the first Federals cross Duck River to begin next day at Warfield Station, three miles beyond Columbia, a week-long running fight that proceeded south across the frozen landscape in the earliest and coldest winter Tennesseans had known for years. Outflanked, Forrest fell back, skirmishing as he went, and at nightfall took up a new position at Lynnville, twelve miles down the line. Here he staged a surprise attack the following morning, using Walthall's men to block the pike while his troopers slashed at the Union flanks, then retired on the run before his pursuers recovered from the shock, bringing off a captured gun which he employed next day in a brisk Christmas Eve action on Richland Creek, eight miles north of Pulaski, where Buford suffered a leg wound to become the twenty-first Confederate brigade, division, or corps commander shot or captured in the course of the campaign. By then the main body, unmolested since Forrest took over the duty of guarding its rear, was well beyond the Alabama line, approaching the Tennessee River, and next day the head of the column pulled up on the near bank opposite Bainbridge, just below Muscle Shoals. It was Christmas, though scarcely a merry one, and a Sunday: five weeks, to the day, since Hood left Florence, four miles downstream, on the expedition that by now had cost him close to 20,000 veterans killed, wounded, or missing in and out of battle, including one lieutenant general, three major generals, and an even dozen brigadiers, together with five brigade commanders of lesser rank. Of these, moreover, only two — Lee and Buford — were alive, uncaptured, and had wounds that would permit an early return to the army that had set out for Middle Tennessee in such high spirits, five weeks back, with twice as many troops and guns as were now in its straggled ranks.

Forrest too was over the Alabama line by then, holding Wilson off while the gray main body bridged the river with the pontoons he had saved by doubling their teams. Gunboats, sent roundabout by Thomas from the Cumberland and the Ohio, tried their hand at shelling the rickety span, but were driven off by Stewart's artillery and Rear Admiral Samuel P. Lee's fear of getting stranded if he ventured within range of the white water at the foot of Muscle Shoals. Hood finished crossing on December 27; Forrest's cavalry followed, and Walthall's forlorn hope got over without further loss on the 28th, cutting the bridge loose from the northern bank. Thomas — whose own pontoons were still on the Duck, seventy miles away, and whose infantry had not cleared Pulaski — declared the pursuit at an end next day. Hood's army, he said, "had become a disheartened and disorganized rabble of half-naked and barefooted men, who sought every opportunity to fall out by the wayside and desert their cause to put an end to their sufferings. The rear guard, however, was undaunted and firm," he added, "and did its work bravely to the last."

Schofield was more generous in his estimate of the defeated army's fighting qualities, especially as he had observed them during the long-odds Battle of Nashville, where fewer than 25,000 graybacks held out for two days against better than 50,000 bluecoats massed for the most part of their flank. "I doubt if any soldiers in the world ever needed so much cumulative evidence to convince them they were beaten," he declared. This was not to say they weren't thoroughly convinced in the end. They were indeed, and they showed it through both stages of the long retreat: first, as one said, while "making tracks for the Tennessee River at a quickstep known to Confederate tactics as 'double distance on half rations,'" and then on the follow-up march beyond, after Hood decided his troops were no more in condition for a stand on the Tennessee than they had been when they crossed the Duck the week before. By way of reinforcing this assessment, Thomas would list in his report a total of 13,189 prisoners and 72 pieces of artillery captured on and off the field of battle in the course of the forty days between Hood's setting out, November 20, and his own calling of an end to the campaign, December 29. Moreover, weary as they were from their 120-mile trek over icy roads in the past two weeks, the butternut marchers themselves agreed that the better part of valor, at least for now, would be to find some place of refuge farther south, if any such existed. "Aint we in a hell of a fix?" one ragged Tennessean groaned as he picked himself up, slathered with mud from a fall on the slippery pike. "Aint we in a hell of a fix: a one-eyed President, a one-legged general, and a one-horse Confederacy!"

Their goal, they learned as they slogged west across North Alabama toward the Mississippi line, was Tupelo. There, just thirty months ago this week, Braxton Bragg had taken over from Beauregard after the retreat from Corinth, and there he had given them the name they made famous, the Army of Tennessee, first in Kentucky, then back again in Middle and East Tennessee and Georgia. Bragg's tenure had ended soon after Missionary Ridge, and so would Hood's after Nashville, a comparable rout; there was little doubt of that, either in or out of the army. "The citizens seemed to shrink and hide from us as we approached them," a soldier would recall, and the reaction of his comrades was shown in a song they sang as they trudged into Mississippi and the New Year. The tune was the banjo-twanging "Yellow Rose of Texas," but the words had been changed to match their regret, if not their scorn, for the quality of leadership that had cost them Pat Cleburne and so many others they had loved and followed down the years.

> *So now I'm marching southward,*
> *My heart is full of woe;*
> *I'm going back to Georgia*
> *To see my Uncle Joe.*
> *You may talk about your Beauregard*
> *And sing of General Lee,*
> *But the gallant Hood of Texas*
> *Played hell in Tennessee.*

✕ 5 ✕

Back at City Point after breaking off his intended western trip, Grant had the familiar hundred-gun victory salute fired twice in celebration of the Nashville triumph. "You have the congratulations of the public for the energy with which you are pushing Hood," he wired Thomas on December 22, adding: "If you succeed in destroying Hood's army, there will be but one army left to the so-called Confederacy capable of doing us harm. I will take care of that and try to draw the sting from it, so that in the spring we shall have easy sailing." He sounded happy. One week later, however, on learning that Hood's fugitives had crossed the Tennessee and Thomas had ordered his erstwhile pursuers into winter quarters to "recuperate for the spring campaign," Grant's petulance returned. "I have no idea of keeping idle troops in any place," he telegraphed Halleck, who passed the word to Thomas on the last day of the year: "General Grant does not intend that your army shall go into winter quarters. It must be ready for active operations in the field."

Grant's fear, throughout the two weeks leading up to the thunderous two-day conflict out in Tennessee, had been that Old Tom's balkiness would allow the rebels to prolong the war by scoring a central breakthrough all the way to the Ohio, thereby disrupting the combinations he had devised for their destruction. Yet this fear had no sooner been dispelled, along with the smoke from the mid-December battle, than another took its place; namely, that this same "sluggishness," as he called it during the two weeks following the clash at the gates of Nashville, would delay the over-all victory which now at last seemed practically within his grasp, not only because of the drubbing given Hood, whose survival hung in the balance until he crossed the Tennessee River, but also because of other successes registered elsewhere, at the same time, along and behind the butternut line stretching west from the Atlantic. A sizeable budget of good news reached City Point while Thomas was failing to overtake his defeated adversary, and every item in it only served to whet Grant's appetite for more. That had always been his way, but it was even more the case now that he saw the end he had worked so hard for in plain view, just up the road.

Chief among these simultaneous achievements was the occupation of Savannah, eleven days after Sherman's arrival before it at the end of his march from Atlanta. Having stormed and taken Fort McAllister on December 13, which enabled the waiting supply ships to steam up the Ogeechee, he proceeded with a leisurely investment — or near investment — of the city just over a dozen miles away. Within four days he had progressed so far with his preparations that he thought it only fair to give the defenders a chance to avoid bloodshed by surrendering. He was "prepared to grant liberal terms to the inhabitants and garrison," he said in a message sent across the lines; "but should I be forced to resort to assault, or to the slower and surer process of starvation, I shall then feel justified in resorting to the harshest measures, and shall make little effort to restrain my army, burning to avenge the national wrong which they attach to Savannah and other large cities which have been so prominent in dragging our country into civil war." The rebel commander replied in kind, declining to surrender, and in closing dealt in measured terms with Sherman's closing threat. "I have hitherto conducted the military operations intrusted to my direction in strict accordance with the rules of civilized warfare, and I should deeply regret the adoption of any course by you that may force me to deviate from them in the future. I have the honor to be, very respectively, your obedient servant, *W. J. Hardee*, Lieutenant General."

Hardee, with barely 15,000 regulars and militia — two thirds of them lodged in the city's defenses, the rest posted rearward across the Savannah River to cover his only escape route, still menaced by Foster near Honey Hill — had appealed to Richmond for reinforcements to help him resist the 60,000 newly arrived bluecoats closing in from the east and south. Davis conferred with Lee at Petersburg, then replied on December 17 — the day of Sherman's threat to unleash his burning veterans on Savannah when it fell — that none were available; he could only advise the Georgian to "provide for the safety of your communications and make the dispositions needful for the preservation of your army." This authorized the evacuation Beauregard had been urging from his headquarters in Charleston, a hundred miles up the coast. With a bridgeless river at his back and no pontoons on hand, that seemed about as difficult as staying to fight against six-to-one odds, but Old Reliable found the answer in the employment of some thirty 80-foot rice flats, lashed together endwise, then planked over to provide a three-section island-hopping span from the Georgia to the Carolina bank. It was finished too late for use on the night of December 19, as intended, so a circular was issued for the withdrawal to begin soon after dark next evening — by coincidence, the fourth anniversary of South Carolina's secession from the Union — preceded by daylong fire from all the guns, which would not only discourage enemy interference but would also reduce the amount of surplus ammunition to be destroyed, along with the unmovable heavy pieces, when the cannoneers fell back. Wagons and caissons would cross the river first, together with the light artillery, and the men themselves would follow, filing silently out of their trenches after moonset. "Though compelled to evacuate the city, there is no part of my military life to which I look back with so much satisfaction," Hardee was to say. And the fact was he had cause for pride. The operation went as planned from start to finish, despite some mixups and much sadness, especially for long-time members of the garrison, who thus were obliged to turn their backs on what had been their home for the past three years. "The constant tread of the troops and the rumblings of the artillery as they poured over those long floating bridges was a sad sound," one retreater would presently recall, "and by the glare of the large fires at the east of the bridge it seemed like an immense funeral procession stealing out of the city in the dead of night."

Sherman was not there for the formal occupation next morning, having gone up the coast to confer with Foster about bringing in more troops from Hilton Head to block the road to Charleston; the road over which, as it developed, Hardee marched to safety while the conference was in progress. When the Ohioan returned the following day, December 22 — chagrined if not abashed by the escape of 10,000 rebels he had thought were his for the taking — he found his army in possession of Savannah and quartermaster details busy tallying the spoils. These were considerable, including more than 200 heavy guns and something over 30,000 bales of cotton, negotiable on the world market at the highest prices ever known. Most of the guns had been spiked, but the rich haul of cotton was intact, not only because there had been no time or means to remove it, but also because, as Hardee explained to his superiors, it was "distributed throughout the city in cellars, garrets and warehouses, where it could not have been burnt without destroying the city." A U.S. Treasury agent was already on hand from Hilton Head, reckoning up the profit to the government, and when the red-haired commander bristled at him, as was his custom when he encountered money men, the agent turned his wrath aside with a suggestion that the general send a message, first by ship to Fort Monroe and then by wire to the White House, announcing the fall of Savannah as a Christmas present for Lincoln. "The President particularly enjoys such pleasantry," he pointed out. Sherman considered this a capital notion, and at once got off the following telegram, composed before the tally was complete.

> To his Excellency President Lincoln,
> Washington, D.C.
>
> I beg to present you, as a Christmas gift, the city of Savannah, with 150 heavy guns and plenty of ammunition; also about 25,000 bales of cotton.
>
> W. T. Sherman
> *Major General.*

He was, as usual, in high spirits after a colorful exploit — and this, which reached its climax with the taking of Savannah and would afterwards find its anthem in the rollicksome "Marching Through Georgia," had been the most colorful of all. Partly because of that scarehead aspect, lurid in its reproduction in the memory of participants, as well as in the imagination of watchers on the home front, the march achieved a significance beyond its considerable military value, and though the risk had turned out slight (103 killed, 428 wounded, 278 captured or otherwise missing: barely more, in all, than one percent of the force involved) even Sherman was somewhat awed in retrospect. "Like a man who has walked a narrow plank," he wrote his wife, "I look back and wonder if I really did it." In effect, after seven months of grinding combat at close quarters, he and his bummers had broken out of the apparent stalemate, East and West, to inject a new spirit of exuberance into the war. You could see the feeling reflected in the northern papers brought to headquarters by the navy, first up the Ogeechee, then the Savannah. "Tecumseh the Great," editors called him now, who had formerly judged him insane, and there was a report of a bill introduced in Congress to promote him to lieutenant general so that he and Grant could divide control of the armies of the Union. His reaction to this was similar to his reaction four months ago, at the time of the Democratic convention in Chicago, when there was talk of nominating him for President. "Some fool seems to have used my name," he wrote Halleck from his position in front of besieged Atlanta. "If forced to choose between the penitentiary and the White House... I would say the penitentiary, thank you." So it was now in regard to this latest proposal to elevate him. "I will accept no commission that would tend to create a rivalry with Grant," he informed his senator brother. "I want him to hold what he has earned and got. I have all the rank I want." As if to emphasize this conviction, he presently remarked to a prying inquirer, in a tone at once jocular and forthright: "Grant is a great general. I know him well. He stood by me when I was crazy and I stood by him when he was drunk. And now, sir, we stand by each other always."

In point of fact, the general-in-chief was standing by him now, even to the extent of deferring to his military judgment: and that, too, was part of the cause for his red-haired exuberance. He had just made Georgia howl. Now he was about to make the Carolinas shriek.

Originally — that is, in orders he found waiting for him when he reached the coast — Grant had intended for Sherman and his Westerners to proceed by water "with all dispatch" to Virginia, where they would help Meade and Butler "close out Lee." He was to establish and fortify a base near Savannah, garrison it with all his cavalry and artillery, together with enough infantry to protect them and "so threaten the interior that the militia of the South will have to be kept at home," then get the rest aboard transports for a fast ride north to the Old Dominion. "Select yourself the officer to leave in command, but you I want in person," Grant told him, adding: "Unless you see objections to this plan which I cannot see, use every vessel going to you for the purpose of transportation."

Sherman did have objections, despite the compliment implied in this invitation to be in on the kill of the old gray fox at Petersburg, and was prompt to express them. He much preferred a march by land to a boatride up the coast for the reunion, he replied, partly because of the damage he could inflict en route and the effect he believed an extension of his trans-Georgia swath would have on the outcome of the war. Besides, there was a certain poetic justice here involved. "We can punish South Carolina as she deserves, and as thousands of people in Georgia hoped we would do. I do sincerely believe that the whole United States, North and South, would rejoice to have this army turned loose on South Carolina, to devastate that state in the manner we have done in Georgia." He was convinced moreover, he said in closing, that the overland approach "would have a direct and immediate bearing upon the campaign in Virginia," and he went into more detail about this in a letter to Halleck, invoking his support. "I attach more importance to these deep incursions into the enemy's country," he declared, "because this war differs from European wars in this particular: We are not only fighting hostile armies, but a hostile people, and must make old and young, rich and poor, feel the hard hand of war, as well as their organized armies. I know that this recent movement of mine through Georgia has had a wonderful effect in this respect. Thousands who have been deceived by their lying newspapers to believe that we were being whipped all the time now realize the truth, and have no appetite for a repetition of the same experience." In short, he told Old Brains, "I think the time has come when we should attempt the boldest moves, and my experience is that they are easier of execution than more timid ones.... Our campaign of the last month, as well as every step I take from this point northward, is as much a direct attack upon Lee's army as though we were operating within the sound of his artillery."

To his surprised delight, Grant readily agreed: so readily, indeed, that it turned out he had done so even before his friend's objections reached him. In a letter written from Washington on the same date as Sherman's own — December 18: he was about to return to City Point: Fort McAllister had fallen five days ago, and Savannah itself would be taken in three more — the general-in-chief sent his congratulations "on the successful termination of your campaign" from Atlanta to the Atlantic. "I never had a doubt of the result," he said, though he "would not have intrusted the expedition to any other living commander." Then he added a few sentences that made Sherman's ears prick up. "I did think the best thing to do was to bring the greater part of your army here, and wipe out Lee. [But] the turn affairs now seem to be taking has shaken me in that opinion. I doubt whether you may not accomplish more toward that result where you are than if brought here, especially as I am informed, since my arrival in the city, that it would take about two months to get you here with all the other calls there are for ocean transportation. I want to get your views about what ought to be done, and what can be done.... My own opinion is that Lee is averse to going out of Virginia, and if the cause of the South is lost he wants Richmond to be the last place surrendered. If he has such views, it may be well to indulge him until we get everything else in our hands.... I subscribe myself, more than ever, if possible, your friend."

This reached Sherman on Christmas Eve, three days after the occupation of Savannah, and lifted his spirits even higher. Here, in effect, was the go-ahead he had sought for himself and his bummers, whom he described as being "in splendid flesh and condition." Promptly that same evening he replied to Grant at City Point, expressing his pleasure at the change in orders; "for I feared that the transportation by sea would very much disturb the unity and morale of my army, now so perfect.... In about ten days I expect to be ready to sally forth again. I feel no doubt whatever as to our future plans. I have thought them over so long and well that they appear as clear as daylight."

Chief among those "other calls ... for ocean transportation" were the ones that had secured for the Butler-Porter expedition, whose mission was the reduction of Fort Fisher, the largest number of naval vessels ever assembled under the American flag. Packed with 6500 troops in two divisions, Butler's transports cleared Hampton Roads on December 13, and five days later joined Porter's fleet of 57 ironclads, frigates, and gunboats at Beaufort, North Carolina, ninety miles up the coast from their objective. Next morning, December 19, they arrived off Wilmington to find bad weather making up and the surf too rough for a landing. This obliged the transports to return to Beaufort for shelter, but the warships remained on station, riding out the storm while the admiral studied the rebel stronghold through his telescope. Unlike prewar forts, which mostly were of masonry construction, this one had walls of sand, piled nine feet high and twenty-five thick, designed to withstand by absorption the fire of the heaviest guns afloat, and was laid out with two faces, one looking seaward, close to 2000 yards long, and the other about one third that length, looking northward up the narrow sand peninsula, formerly called Federal Point but renamed Confederate Point by the secessionists when they began work on the place in 1861. Defended by a total of 47 guns and mortars, including a battery posted atop a sixty-foot mound thrown up at the south end of the seaward face to provide for delivering plunging fire if the enemy ventured close, the fort seemed all but impossible to reduce by regular methods; nor could the ships run past it, as had been done at New Orleans and Mobile, since that would merely cram them into Cape Fear River, sitting ducks for the rebel cannoneers, who would only have to reverse their guns to blow the intruders out of the water. Porter however had in mind a highly irregular method in which by now he placed great faith. This was the ingenious Butler's powder ship, brought along in tow from Norfolk and primed at Beaufort for the cataclysmic explosion the squint-eyed general claimed would abolish Fort Fisher between two ticks of his watch.

Porter was inclined to agree, though less emphatically, having made a close inspection of the floating bomb. She was, or had been, the U.S.S. *Louisiana,* an overaged iron gunboat of close to three hundred tons, stripped of her battery and part of her deckhouse to lighten her draft and make her resemble a blockade runner. In a canvas-roofed framework built amidships, as well as in her bunkers and on her berth deck — all above the water line, for maximum shock effect — 215 tons of powder had been stored and fuzed with three clockwork devices, regulated to fire simultaneously an hour and a half after they were activated. The plan was for a skeleton crew to run the vessel in close to shore, anchor her as near as her eight-foot draft would allow to the seaward face of the fort on the beach, set the timing mechanisms, then pull hard away in a boat to an escort steamer that would take them well offshore to await the explosion; after which the fleet, poised twelve miles out for safety from the blast, would close in and subject what was left of the place to a heavy-caliber pounding, while troops were being landed two miles up the peninsula to close in from the north. Some said the result of setting off that much powder — which, after all, was more than fifty times the amount used near Petersburg, five months ago, to create the still-yawning Crater — would be the utter destruction of everything on or adjoining Federal or Confederate Point. Others — mainly demolition "experts," who as usual were skeptical of anything they themselves had not conceived — discounted such predictions, maintaining that the shock would probably be no worse than mild. "I take a mean between the two," Porter declared judiciously, "and think the effect of the explosion will be simply very severe, stunning men at a distance of three or four hundred yards, demoralizing them completely, and making them unable to stand for any length of time a fire from the ship. I think that the concussion will tumble magazines that are built on framework, and that the famous Mound will be among the things that were, and the guns buried beneath the ruins. I think that houses in Wilmington [eighteen miles away] will tumble to the ground and much demoralize the people, and I think if the rebels fight after the explosion they have more in them than I gave them credit for."

In the fort meantime, during what turned out to be a three-day blow, the garrison prepared to resist the attack it had known was coming ever since the huge assembly of Union warships bulged over the curve of the eastern horizon. Determined to hold ajar what he termed "the last gateway between the Confederate States and the outside world," Fort Fisher's commander, Colonel William Lamb, had at first had only just over 500 men for its defense, half the regular complement having been sent to oppose Sherman down in Georgia. Blockade runners kept coming and going all this time, however, under cover of the storm, and on December 21 — when four of the swift vessels made outward runs after nightfall, all successful in slipping through the cordon of blockaders off the coast — some 400 North Carolina militia showed up, followed two days later by 450 Junior Reserves, sixteen to eighteen years of age. This total of 1371 effectives, most of them green and a third of them boys, were all Lamb would have until the arrival of Hoke's division, which had begun leaving Richmond two days ago, detached by Lee in the emergency, but was delayed by its necessarily roundabout rail route through Danville, Greensboro, and Raleigh.

The gale subsided on the day the Junior Reserves marched in, December 23, and though the wind remained brisk all afternoon, the night that followed was clear and cold. Despite the heightened visibility, which greatly lengthened the odds against blockade runners, the fast steamer *Little Hattie*, completing her second run that month, made it in through the mouth of the Cape Fear River, shortly before midnight, and soon was tied up at the dock in Wilmington, unloading the valuable war goods she had exchanged in Nassau a week ago for her outbound cargo of cotton.

Although no one aboard knew it, she had overtaken and passed the *Louisiana* coming in, and the signals flashed from Fort Fisher in response to those from the *Hattie* were of great help to the skeleton crew on the powder ship, groping its way through the darkness toward the beach. Encouraged by improvement in the weather, Porter had ordered the doomed vessel in at 11 o'clock that night, and had also sent word to Beaufort for the transports to return at once for the landing next day. Lightless and silent, the *Louisiana* dropped anchor 250 yards offshore, just north of the fort, and her skipper, Commander A. C. Rhind — told by the admiral, "You may lose your life in this adventure, but the risk is worth the running.... The names of those connected with the expedition will be famous for all time to come" — started all three clockwork fuzes ticking at precisely twelve minutes short of midnight. Finally, before abandoning ship, he set fire to half a cord of pine knots piled in the after cabin on instructions from Porter, who had little faith in mechanical devices; after which Rhind and his handful of volunteers rowed in a small boat to the escort steamer waiting nearby to take them (hopefully) out of range of the explosion, due by then within about an hour. Now there was nothing left to do but wait.

Twelve miles out, crews of the nearly sixty warships watched and waited too, training all available glasses on the starlit stretch of beach in front of the rebel earthwork. Started at 11.48, the ticking fuzes should do their job at 1.18 in what by now was the morning of Christmas Eve; or so the watchers thought, until the critical moment came and went and there was no eruption. By then, however, the pinpoint of light from Rhind's fire in the after cabin had grown to a flickering glow, and Porter felt certain all 215 tons of powder would go as soon as the flames reached the nearest keg. He was right, of course, though the wait was hard. 1.30: 1.35: 1.40: then it came — a huge instantaneous bloom of light, so quickly smothered in dust and smoke you could almost doubt you'd seen it. Just under one minute later the sound arrived; a low, heavy boom, a *New York Times* reporter was to say, "not unlike that produced by the discharge of a 100-pounder." Moreover, there seemed to be no accompanying shock wave, only the one deep cough or rumble, and a colleague aboard the press boat saw a gigantic cloud of thick black smoke appear on the landward horizon, sharply defined against the stars and the clear sky. "As it rose rapidly in the air, and came swiftly toward us on the wings of the wind," he later wrote, "[it] presented a most remarkable appearance, assuming the shape of a monstrous waterspout, its tapering base seemingly resting on the sea. In a very few minutes it passed us, filling the atmosphere with its sulphurous odor, as if a spirit from the infernal regions had swept by us."

If this was anticlimactic — which in fact was to put the measure of Porter's disappointment rather mildly — what followed, over the course of the next two days, was even more so. Subsequent testimony would show that, while there were those who claimed to have felt the shock as far away as Beaufort, the monster explosion had done the fort no damage whatever, producing no more than a gentle rocking motion, as if the earth had twitched briefly in its sleep. A sentinel on duty at the time made a guess to the man who relieved him that one of the Yankee ships offshore had blown her boiler. Many in the garrison, veterans and greenhorns alike, said later that they had not been awakened by the blast, though this was denied by one of the boy soldiers, captured next day in an outlying battery. "It was terrible," he said. "It woke up nearly everybody in the fort." Daylight showed no remaining vestige of the *Louisiana*, but Fort Fisher was unchanged, its flag rippling untattered in the breeze. Only in one respect did Butler's experiment work, even approximately, and that was in the disguise he had contrived for the vanished powder vessel. Lamb recorded in his diary that morning: "A blockader got aground near the fort, set fire to herself, and blew up."

Porter spent the morning absorbing the shock of failure, then steamed in at noon to begin the heaviest naval bombardment of the war to date. Capable of firing 115 shells a minute, his 627 guns heaved an estimated 10,000 heavy-caliber rounds at Fort Fisher in the course of the next five hours, to which the fort replied with 622, though neither seriously impaired the fighting efficiency of the other. Ashore, two guns were dismounted, one man killed, 22 injured, and most of the living quarters flattened, while the fleet lost 83 dead and wounded, more than half of them mangled by the explosion of five new hundred-pounder Parrotts on five of the sloops and frigates. Near sunset, Butler finally showed up with a few transports. The rest would soon be along, he said: much to Porter's disgust, for the day by then was too far gone for a landing. Disgruntled, the admiral signaled a cease fire.

As the ships withdrew, guns cooling, the fort boomed out a single defiant shot, the last. "Our Heavenly Father has protected my garrison this day," Lamb wrote in his diary that night, "and I feel that He will sustain us in defending our homes from the invader."

By 10.30 next morning — Christmas Day and a Sunday — the fleet was back on station, lobbing still more thousands of outsized projectiles into the sand fort. Three hours later, three miles up the way, just over 2000 soldiers were put ashore under Major General Godfrey Weitzel, second in command to Butler, who observed the landing from his flagship, a sea-going tug which he kept steaming back and forth in front of the beach while the troops were moving southward down it, capturing a one-gun outwork when they got within a mile of Fort Fisher's landward face. Porter maintained a methodical fire — mainly to make the defenders keep their heads down, since he believed he had done all necessary damage to their works the day before. Reports from Weitzel, however, showed that this was far from true. Approaching the fort, his men received volleys of canister full in their faces, and it soon developed that the final hundred yards of ground was planted thickly with torpedoes wired to detonator switches which rebel lookouts could throw whenever they judged an explosion would be most effective. Moreover, prisoners taken on the approach march bragged that Hoke's division, 6000 strong, was expected to arrive at any minute on the road from Wilmington, hard in the Federal rear. Butler weighed the evidence, along with signs that the rising wind would soon make it impossible for boats to return through the booming surf, and promptly ordered a withdrawal by all ashore. "In view of the threatening aspect of the weather," he signaled Porter when two thirds of Weitzel's men had been reloaded — the other third, some 700 wet and cold unfortunates for whom this holy day was anything but merry, were stranded when the breakers grew too rough for taking them off — "I caused the troops with their prisoners to re-embark." Seeing, as he said, "nothing further that can be done by the land forces," he announced: "I shall therefore sail for Hampton Roads as soon as the transport fleet can be got in order."

Fairly beside himself with rage at this unceremonious abandonment of the supposedly joint effort, Porter kept up a nightlong interdictory fire to protect "those poor devils of soldiers," whose rifles he could hear popping on the beach. Next afternoon, when the wind changed direction, he managed to get them off, thereby limiting the army's loss to one man drowned and 15 wounded — a total clearly indicative of something less than an all-out try for the fort's reduction. Butler by then was on his way to Norfolk, however, and the admiral had no choice except to retire as well, though only as far as Beaufort, withdrawing his ships a few at a time, that night and the following morning, so that Fort Fisher's defenders would not be able to claim a mass repulse.

Nevertheless: "This morning, December 27, the foiled and frightened enemy left our shore," Lamb wired Wilmington, where Hoke's veterans were at last unloading from their long train ride. The garrison had in fact had a harder time than Porter knew, losing 70 men in the second day's bombardment, which, though less intense, had been far more accurate than the first. "Never since the foundation of the world was there such a fire," a Confederate lieutenant testified. "The whole interior of the fort... was one 11-inch shell bursting. You can now inspect the works and walk on nothing but iron." Lamb began repairing the damage without delay, knowing only too well that the Yankees would soon return, perhaps next time with an army commander willing to press the issue beyond pistol range of the sand walls.

That was just what Porter had in mind now that his fleet was reassembled at Beaufort, replenishing its stores and ammunition. Moreover, he could see at least one good proceeding from the abortive Yuletide expedition. "If this temporary failure succeeds in sending General Butler into private life, it is not to be regretted," he wrote

Welles, "for it cost only a certain amount of shells, which I expend in a month's target practice anyhow."

Grant was of the same opinion in regard to the need for a change when the effort against Fort Fisher was renewed, as he certainly intended it to be. "The Wilmington expedition has proven a gross and culpable failure," he informed Lincoln on December 28, adding: "Who is to blame I hope will be known." A wire to Porter, two days later, indicated that he had already decided on a cure. "Please hold on where you are for a few days," he requested, "and I will endeavor to be back again with an increased force and without the former commander."

His concern was based on a number of developments. First, because it had been determined that Sherman would march north through the Carolinas, Grant saw Wilmington as an ideal place of refuge, easily provisioned and protected by the navy, in case the rebels somehow managed to gang up on his red-haired friend. Second, he believed that a full report on the recent fiasco would provide him with excellent grounds for getting rid of Ben Butler, whose political heft was unlikely to stand him in nearly as good stead with the Administration now that the election had been won. Third — and no one who knew Grant would think it least — he was no more inclined than ever to accept a setback; especially now, when so many welcome reports were clicking off the wire at City Point from all directions, indicating that the end of the struggle was by no means as far off as it had seemed a short while back.

One of the most welcome of these came from George Stoneman, exchanged since his late-July capture down in Georgia and recently given command of all the cavalry in Northeast Tennessee. Anxious to retrieve his reputation, he set out from Knoxville on December 10 with 5500 troopers in an attempt to reach and wreck the salt and lead mines in Southwest Virginia, so long the object of raids that had come to nothing up to now. Beyond Kingsport, three days later, he brushed aside the remnant of Morgan's once-terrible men, still grieved by the loss of their leader three months before, and pressed on through Bristol, across the state line to Abingdon, where he drove off a small force of graybacks posted in observation by Breckinridge, whose main body, down to a strength of about 1200, was at Saltville, less than twenty miles ahead. Stoneman bypassed him for a lunge at Marion, twelve miles up the Virginia & Tennessee Railroad, obliging Breckinridge to back-pedal in an effort to save the vital lead works there and at Wytheville. This he did, by means of a fast march and a daylong skirmish on December 18; but while the fighting was in progress Stoneman sent half his horsemen back to undefended Saltville, with instructions to get started on the wreckage that was the true purpose of the expedition. Reuniting his raiders there next day, after giving Breckinridge the slip, he spent another two days completing the destruction of the salt works, then withdrew on December 21. Back in Knoxville by the end of the year, he could report complete success. Salt had been scarce in the Old Dominion for two years. Now it would be practically nonexistent, leaving the suppliers of Lee's army with no means of preserving what little meat they could lay hands on for shipment by rail or wagon to the hungry men in the trenches outside Petersburg and Richmond.

Sheridan too had not been idle during this period of stepped-up Federal activity, coincident with Thomas's pursuit of Hood and Sherman's occupation of Savannah. While the greater part of his army continued its impoverishment of the people in the Shenandoah region by the destruction of their property and goods — a scourging process he defined as "letting them know there is a God in Israel" — he launched a two-pronged strike, by three divisions of cavalry, at military targets beyond the rim of his immediate depredations. Torbert, with 5500 horsemen in two divisions, would aim for Gordonsville and the Virginia Central, east of the Blue Ridge, while Custer diverted attention from this main effort by taking his 2500-man division south up the Valley Pike for a raid on Staunton, which if successful could be continued to Lynchburg and the Orange & Alexandria. Both left their camps around Winchester on December 19, Torbert riding through Chester Gap next morning to cross the Rapidan two days later at Liberty Mills. Apparently Custer had decoyed Early's troopers westward from their position near Rockfish Gap, just east of Staunton, for there was no sign of them as the blue column approached Gordonsville after dark. There was, however, a barricade thrown up by local defenders to block a narrow pass within three miles of town, and Torbert chose to wait for daylight, December 23, before deciding whether to storm or outflank it. Alas, he then found it would be unwise to attempt either. Warned of his approach, Lee had detached a pair of veteran brigades from Longstreet, north of the James, and hurried them by rail to Gordonsville the night before. "After becoming fully satisfied of the presence of infantry," Torbert afterwards reported, "I concluded it was useless to make a further attempt to break the Central Railroad." Instead, he withdrew and made a roundabout return march, through Madison Courthouse and Warrenton, to Winchester on December 28.

Custer by then had been back five days, having done only too good a job of attracting Early's attention. In camp the second night, nine miles from Harrisonburg, he was attacked before reveille, December 21, by Rosser's cavalry division, which Early had sent to intercept him a day's march short of Staunton. Driven headlong, Custer kept going northward down the pike, abandoning the raid, and returned to his starting point next day. Between them, he and Torbert had lost about 150 killed or wounded or captured, exclusive of some 230 of Custer's men severely frostbitten during their fast rides out and back. He would have stayed and fought, he informed Sheridan — he would never be flat whipped till Little Big Horn, twelve years later — except for a shortage of rations and "my unprepared state to take charge of a large body of wounded, particularly under the inclement state of the weather. In addition," he said, straight-faced, "I was convinced that if it was decided to return, the sooner my return was accomplished the better it would be for my command."

Grant was not inclined to censure anyone involved: least of all Sheridan, who had exercised his aggressive proclivities in weather most generals would have considered fit for nothing but sitting around campfires, toasting their toes and swapping yarns. Moreover, hard as the two-pronged raid had been on Union horseflesh, not to mention the blue riders' frost-nipped hands and feet and noses — 258 of Torbert's mounts had broken down completely in the course of his ten-day outing — it had no doubt been even harder on the scantly clad Confederates and their crowbait nags, which would be that much worse off when spring unfroze the roads and northern troopers came pounding down them, rapid-fire carbines at the ready. That too was a gain, perhaps comparable in its future effect to Stoneman's descent on Saltville, and the two together fit nicely into the year-end victory pattern whose larger pieces were supplied by Thomas and Sherman, in Tennessee and Georgia, as well as by Pleasonton and Curtis out in the Transmississippi, where the last of Price's fugitive survivors came limping into Laynesport this week, in time for a far-from-Merry Christmas.

Now that all these pieces were coming together into a pattern, West and East, even those who had cried out loudest against Grant as "a bull-headed Suvarov" — a commander who relied on strength, and strength alone, to make up for his lack of military talent — could see the effects of the plan he had devised nine months ago, before launching the synchronized offensive that had re-split the South and was now about to go to work on the sundered halves.

With mounting excitement, though not without occasional stretches of doubt and fret at the lack of progress in front or back of Richmond, Atlanta, and Nashville, Lincoln had watched the pattern emerge with increasing clarity, until he saw at last in these year-end triumphs the fruits of the hands-off policy he had followed in all but the times of greatest strain. Sherman's wire — "I beg to present you, as a Christmas gift, the city of Savannah" — reached Washington on Christmas Eve, and the President released it for publication Christmas morning, pleased to share this gift with the whole country. Next day, when John Logan called at the White House, back from Louisville and on his way down the coast to resume command of his XV Corps, Lincoln gave him a letter for delivery to Sherman, expressing his thanks for the timely gift and restating his intention not to interfere with the actions or decisions of commanders in the field.

"When you were about leaving Atlanta for the Atlantic coast, I was anxious, if not fearful," he admitted, "but feeling that you were the better judge, and remembering that 'nothing risked, nothing gained,' I did not interfere. Now, the undertaking being a success, the honor is all yours; for I believe none of us went further than to acquiesce. And taking the work of General Thomas into the count, as it should be taken, it is indeed a great success. Not only does it afford the obvious and immediate military advantage, but in showing to the world that your army could be divided, putting the stronger part to an important new service, and yet leaving enough to vanquish the old opposing force of the whole — Hood's army — it brings those who sat in darkness to see a great light. But what next? I suppose it will be safer if I leave General Grant and yourself to decide."

Other duties, more clerkly in nature, had continued to require his attention as Commander in Chief throughout this final month of the year. One was the approval of a general order, December 2, removing Rosecrans from command of the Department of the Missouri and replacing him with Grenville Dodge, who had recovered by then from the head wound he had suffered near Atlanta in mid-August. Old Rosy had enjoyed no more success than his predecessors had done in reconciling the various "loyal" factions in that guerilla-torn region, and now he was gone from the war for good. Another departure, under happier circumstances, was made by Farragut, who left Mobile Bay aboard the *Hartford* about that same time, and dropped anchor December 13 in the Brooklyn Navy Yard. Like his flagship, soon to go into dry dock, the old man was in need of repairs, having declined command of the Fort Fisher expedition on a plea of failing health. "My flag [was] hauled down at sunset," he informed Welles a week later. As it turned out, he and the *Hartford* ended their war service together, though there was no end to the honors that came his way. Two days later, on December 22, Congress passed a bill creating the rank of vice admiral, and Lincoln promptly conferred it on the Tennessee-born sailor, who thus became the nation's first to hold that rank, just as he had been its first rear admiral. To crown his good with creature comforts, a group of New York merchants got up and presented to him, on the last day of the year, a gift of $50,000 in government bonds. "The citizens of New York can offer no tribute equal to your claims on their gratitude and affection," an accompanying letter read. "Their earnest desire is to receive you as one of their number, and to be permitted, as fellow citizens, to share in the renown you will bring to the Metropolitan City."

Two other events of a more or less military nature, widely separated in space but provoking simultaneous reactions, engaged the attention of the public and the President at this time. One was a late-

November attempt by a group of eight Confederate agents, operating out of Canada, to terrorize New York City by setting fire to a score of hotels with four-ounce bottles of Greek Fire, similar to those used at St Albans the month before. In the early evening of November 25, nineteen fires were started within a single hour, but they burned with nothing like the anticipated fury, apparently because the supposedly sympathetic local chemist had concocted a weak mixture, either to lengthen his profit or, as one agent later said, to "put up a job on us after it was found that we could not be dissuaded from our purpose." In any case, firemen doused the flames rather easily, except at Barnum's Museum, a target of opportunity, where bales of hay for the animals blazed spectacularly for a time. All the arsonists escaped save one, who was picked up afterwards in Michigan, trying to make it back to Toronto, and returned to Fort Lafayette for execution in the spring. Though the damage was minor, as it turned out, the possibilities were frightening enough. Federal authorities could see in the conspiracy a forecast of what might be expected in the months ahead, when the rebels grew still more desperate over increasing signs that their war could not be won on the field of battle.

The other semi-military event occurred four days later in the Colorado Territory, 1500 miles away. Indians throughout much of the West had been on the rampage for the past three years, seeing in the white man's preoccupation with his tribal war back East an opportunity for the red man to return to his old free life, roving the plains and prairies, and perhaps exact, as he did so, a measure of bloody satisfaction for the loss of his land in exchange for promises no sooner made than broken. When John Pope took over in Minnesota two years ago, hard on the heels of his Bull Run defeat, he put down one such uprising by the Santee Sioux, in which more than 400 soldiers and settlers had been killed, and had the survivors arraigned before a drumhead court that sentenced 303 of them to die for murder, rape, and arson. Reviewing the sentences, despite a warning from the governor that the people of Minnesota would take "private revenge" if there was any interference on his part, Lincoln cut the list to 38 of "the more guilty and influential of the culprits." Hanged at Mankato on the day after Christmas, 1862, wearing paint and feathers and singing their death song with the ropes about their necks, these 38 still comprised the largest mass execution the country had ever staged. Now two years later, farther west in Colorado, there was another — a good deal less formal, lacking even a scaffold, let alone a trial, but larger and far bloodier — in which the President had no chance to interfere, since it was over before he had any way of knowing it was in progress.

Colonel John M. Chivington, a former Methodist preacher and a veteran of the New Mexico campaign, rode out of Denver in mid-November with 600 Colorado Volunteers, raised for the sole purpose, as he said, of killing Indians "whenever and wherever found." The pickings were rather slim until he reached Fort Lyon, sixty miles from the Kansas border, and learned that 600 Cheyennes and Arapahoes were camped on Sand Creek, forty miles northeast. They had gathered there the month before, after a parley with the governor, and had been promised security by the fort commander on their word, truthful or not, that they had taken no part in recent depredations elsewhere in the territory. Chivington did not believe them, but it would not have mattered if he had. "I have come to kill Indians," he announced on arrival, "and believe it is right and honorable to use any means under God's heaven to kill Indians." Asked if this included women, he replied that it did. And children? "Nits make lice," he said.

He left Fort Lyon early the following evening, November 28, reinforced by a hundred troopers from the garrison, on a wintry all-night ride that brought the 700-man column and its four mountain howitzers within reach of the objective before dawn. Two thirds of them squaws and children — most of the braves of fighting age were off hunting buffalo, several miles to the east — the Indians lay sleeping in their lodges, pitched in a bend of the creek at their back. They knew nothing of the attack until it burst upon them, aimed first at the herd of ponies to make certain there would be no horseback escape in the confusion soon to follow. It did follow, and the slaughter was indiscriminate. The soldiers closed in from three sides of the camp, pressing toward the center where the terrified people gathered under a large American flag that flew from the lodgepole of a Cheyenne chief, Black Kettle, who had received it earlier that year, as a token of friendship and protection, from the Commissioner of Indian Affairs. He displayed it now, along with a white flag raised amid the smoke of the attack. Both were ignored. "It may perhaps be unnecessary for me to state that I captured no prisoners," Chivington would report. He claimed between four and five hundred killed, all warriors; but that was exaggeration. A body count showed 28 men dead, including three chiefs, and 105 women and children. The attackers lost 9 killed and 38 wounded, most of them hit in the crossfire. By way of retaliation, or perhaps out of sheer exuberance, the soldiers moved among the dead and dying with their knives, lifting scalps and removing private parts to display as trophies of the raid. Then they pulled out. Behind them, the surviving Indians scattered on the plains, some to die of their wounds and exposure, others to spend what remained of their lives killing white men.

This too — the Sand Creek Massacre — was part of America's Civil War, and as such, like so much else involved, would have its repercussions down the years. For one thing, Chivington's coup discredited every Cheyenne or Arapahoe chief (and, for that matter, every Sioux or Kiowa or Comanche) who had spoken for peace with the white man: including Black Kettle, who, in addition to the bright-striped flag, had been given a medal by Lincoln himself for his efforts in that direction. Moreover, when the buffalo-hunting braves returned and saw the mutilations practiced by the soldiers on their people — fathers and sons, mothers and daughters, wives and sisters — they swore to serve their enemy in the same fashion when the tables were turned, as they soon would be, in the wake of a hundred skirmishes and ambuscades. Nor was that the only emulation. There were those in and out of the region who approved of Chivington's tactics as the best, if not indeed the only, solution to the problem of clearing the way for the settlers and the railroads: Sheridan, for example, who took them as a guide, some four years later, in pursuing a policy summed up in the dictum: "The only good Indian is a dead Indian."

News of these and other late-November developments found Lincoln hard at work on the year-end message his secretary would deliver at a joint meeting of the House and Senate on December 6, the day after Congress began its second session. Otherwise, much of the month that followed his reëlection — the first ever won by a free-state President — was spent in putting his political house in order. In addition to paying off, as best he could with the limited number of posts at his disposal, the debts he had contracted in the course of the campaign, this meant a clearing up of administrative business that had hung fire while the outcome was in doubt, including the retirement and replacement of a long-time cabinet member, as well as the appointment of a new Chief Justice.

The cabinet member was Attorney General Edward Bates, a septuagenarian old-line Democrat of a type still fairly common in Washington, but getting rarer year by year as the new breed of office-holders settled in. For some time now the Missourian had been feeling out of step with the society around him, out of place among his radical cohorts, and out of touch with the leader who had summoned him here, four years ago, to play a role he found increasingly distasteful. Decrying the "pestilent doctrines" of the ultras, right and left, and complaining in a letter to a friend of "how, in times like these, the minds of men are made dizzy and their imaginations are wrought up to a frenzy by the whirl of events," Bates believed he saw the cause of the disruption: "When the public cauldron is heated into violent ebulition, it is sure to throw up from the bottom some of its dirtiest dregs, which, but for the heat and agitation, would have lain embedded in congenial filth in the lowest stratum of society. But once boiled up to the top they expand into foam and froth, [and] dance frantically before the gaping crowd, often concealing for a time the whole surface of the agitated mass." He was disillusioned, he was disillusioned and bitter; he was, in short, a casualty of this war. He had to go, and on December 1, the election safely over, he went. Lincoln found a replacement in another Border State lawyer-politician, James Speed of Kentucky. Now only

Seward and Welles remained of the original cabinet slate drawn up in Springfield.

Another source of disappointment for Bates, now on his way home to Missouri, was Lincoln's rejection of his application to succeed Roger Taney as Chief Justice, and it was no great consolation that others with the same ambition — Montgomery Blair and Edwin Stanton, for two — were similarly passed over in favor of still a fourth one-time cabinet member: Salmon Chase. The eighty-seven-year-old Taney — appointed as John Marshall's successor by Andrew Jackson in 1836, nine Presidents ago — died in mid-October, following a long illness. Hated as he was by abolitionists for his Dred Scott decision, and scorned by most liberals for several others since, when he fell sick and seemed about to pass from the scene ahead of James Buchanan, Ben Wade prayed hard that he would live long enough for Lincoln to name his successor. As a result, the Marylander not only survived Buchanan's term, he seemed likely to outlast Lincoln's. "Damned if I didn't overdo it," Wade exclaimed. Then in October, perhaps in answer to supplementary prayers sent up on the eve of what might be a victory for McClellan, the old man died. Chase was the party favorite for the vacant seat at the head of the Court, his views being sound on such issues as emancipation, summary arrests, and a number of controversial financial measures he had adopted as Treasury chief; but Lincoln took his time about naming a replacement. The election was less than four weeks off, and delay ensured Chase's continued fervent support — as well as Blair's. Moreover, here was one last chance to watch the Ohioan squirm, a prospect Lincoln had always enjoyed as retribution for unsuccessful backstairs politics. "I know meaner things about Mr Chase than any of these men can tell me," he remarked after talking to callers who objected to the appointment on personal grounds. One day his secretary brought in a letter from Chase. "What is it about?" Lincoln asked, having no time just then to read it. "Simply a kind and friendly letter," Nicolay replied. Lincoln smiled and made a brief gesture of dismissal, saying: "File it with his other recommendations." All the same, and with the uncertain hope (in vain, as it turned out) that this would cure at last the gnawing of the presidential grub in Chase's bosom, he sent to the Senate on December 6, four weeks after election, his nomination of "Salmon P. Chase of Ohio, to be Chief Justice of the Supreme Court of the United States vice Roger B. Taney, deceased." He wrote it out in his own hand, signing his name in full, as he only did for the most important documents, and the Senate confirmed the appointment promptly, without discussion or previous reference to committee.

On that same day, the President's fourth December message was read to the assembled Congress. Primarily a report on foreign relations and the national welfare, about which it went into considerable diplomatic and financial details furnished by Seward and Fessenden, the text made little mention of the war being fought in the field, except to state that "our arms have steadily advanced." But in it Lincoln spoke beyond the heads of his immediate listeners — albeit through the voice of Nicolay, who delivered it for him at the joint session — to the people of the South, much as he had done at his inauguration, just under four years ago, when he addressed them as "my dissatisfied countrymen." Now he had reason to believe that their dissatisfaction extended in quite a different direction, and he bore down on that, first by demonstrating statistically the emptiness of all hope for a Federal collapse or let-up. Pointing to the heavy vote in the recent election, state by northern state, as proof "that we have more men now than we had when the war began; that we are not exhausted, nor in process of exhaustion; that we are gaining strength, and may, if need be, maintain the contest indefinitely," he declared flatly that the national resources, in materials as in manpower, "are unexhausted, and, as we believe, inexhaustible." So, too, was the resolution of the northern people "unchanged, and, as we believe, unchangeable," to an extent that altogether ruled out a negotiated settlement. Previously he had avoided public reference to Jefferson Davis, making it his policy to pretend that the Mississippian was invisible at best. Now this changed. He spoke openly of his adversary, though still not by name, referring to him rather as "the insurgent leader," and pronounced him unapproachable except on his own inadmissable terms. "He would accept nothing short of severance of the Union," Lincoln pointed out: "precisely what we will not and cannot give. His declarations to this effect are explicit and oft repeated. He does not attempt to deceive us. He affords us no excuse to deceive ourselves.... Between him and us the issue is distinct, simple, and inflexible. It is an issue which can only be tried by war, and decided by victory. If we yield, we are beaten; if the Southern people fail him, he is beaten. Either way, it would be the victory and defeat following war." This did not mean, however, that those who followed Davis could not accept what he rejected. "Some of them, we know, already desire peace and reunion," Lincoln said. "The number of such may increase. They can, at any moment, have peace simply by laying down their arms and submitting to the national authority under the Constitution. After so much, the government could not, if it would, maintain war against them."

He spoke in this connection of "pardons and remissions of forfeiture," these being things within his right to grant, but he added frankly that there was much else "beyond the Executive power to adjust," including "the admission of members into Congress, and whatever might require the appropriation of money." Nor did he sugar his offer, or advice, with any concession on other matters: least of all on the slavery issue. Not only would the Emancipation Proclamation stand, he also urged in the course of his message the adoption of a proposed amendment to the Constitution abolishing slavery throughout the United States. It had nearly passed in the last session, and would surely pass in the next, whose Republican majority had been increased by last month's election; "And as it is to so go, at all events, may we not agree that the sooner the better?" Above all, he wanted to speak clearly, both to his friends and to his present foes, and he did so in a final one-sentence paragraph addressed to those beyond the wide-flung line of battle: "In stating a single condition of peace, I mean simply to say that the war will cease on the part of the government whenever it shall have ceased on the part of those who began it."

All this he said, or Nicolay said for him, on December 6. The next ten days were crowded with good news: first from Georgia, where Sherman reached the coast at last, so little worn by his long march that he scarcely paused before he stormed Fort McAllister to make contact with the navy waiting off the mouth of the Ogeechee: then from Middle Tennessee, where Thomas crushed Hood's left, in front of Nashville, and flung him into full retreat with the loss of more than fifty guns. Lincoln responded by tightening the screws. In late November the War Department had done its part by lowering the minimum standard height for recruits to "five feet, instead of five feet three as heretofore." Now the Commander in Chief followed through, December 19 — Sherman by then had closed in on Savannah, which Hardee would evacuate next day — by issuing another of his by now familiar calls for "300,000 more," this time presumably including men who were not much taller than the Springfields they would shoulder. Privately, moreover, Stanton assured Grant that still another 200,000 troops would be called up in March if those netted by the current proclamation did not suffice to "close out Lee."

Success, as usual, fostered impatience and evoked a sense of urgency: especially in Lincoln, who had read with pleasure a message Grant sent Sherman after the fall of Atlanta, just under four months ago: "We want to keep the enemy pressed to the end of the war. If we give him no peace whilst the war lasts, the end cannot be distant." Sherman then had marched to the sea, eastward across the Confederate heartland, and after taking Savannah, bloodlessly though at the cost of having its garrison escape, obtained approval for a follow-up march north through the Carolinas. He was preparing for it now. "I do not think I can employ better strategy than I have hitherto done," he wrote Halleck on the last day of the year: "namely, make a good ready and then move rapidly to my objective, avoiding a battle at points where I would be encumbered by my wounded, but striking boldly and quickly when my objective is reached." Lincoln liked the sound of that, much as he had enjoyed Grant's hustling tone in the Atlanta dispatch. But when Stanton set out the following week, on a trip down the coast to confer with the red-haired commander, it occurred to the impatient President that if the Westerners were to come up hard and fast to join in putting the final squeeze on Lee, there had perhaps not been enough stress on the advantage of an early start. Accordingly, he got off a reminding wire to that effect. "While General Sherman's 'get a good ready' is appreciated, and is not to be overlooked," he told the Secretary, "*Time*, now that the enemy is wavering, is more important than ever."

His advice to the southern people, tendered in the December message to Congress, had been more grim than conciliatory; they need only reject their "insurgent leader ... by laying down their arms," and he would do what he could for them in the way of "pardons and remissions." Since then, however, the news from Nashville and Savannah had encouraged him to believe that the hour was near when they would no longer have any choice in the matter, if only he could provoke in his generals the sense of urgency he was convinced would end the rebellion in short order, and he said as much in the wire that followed Stanton down the coast. Now that their adversary was "on the downhill, and somewhat confused," he wanted the Secretary to impress on Sherman the importance of "keeping him going."

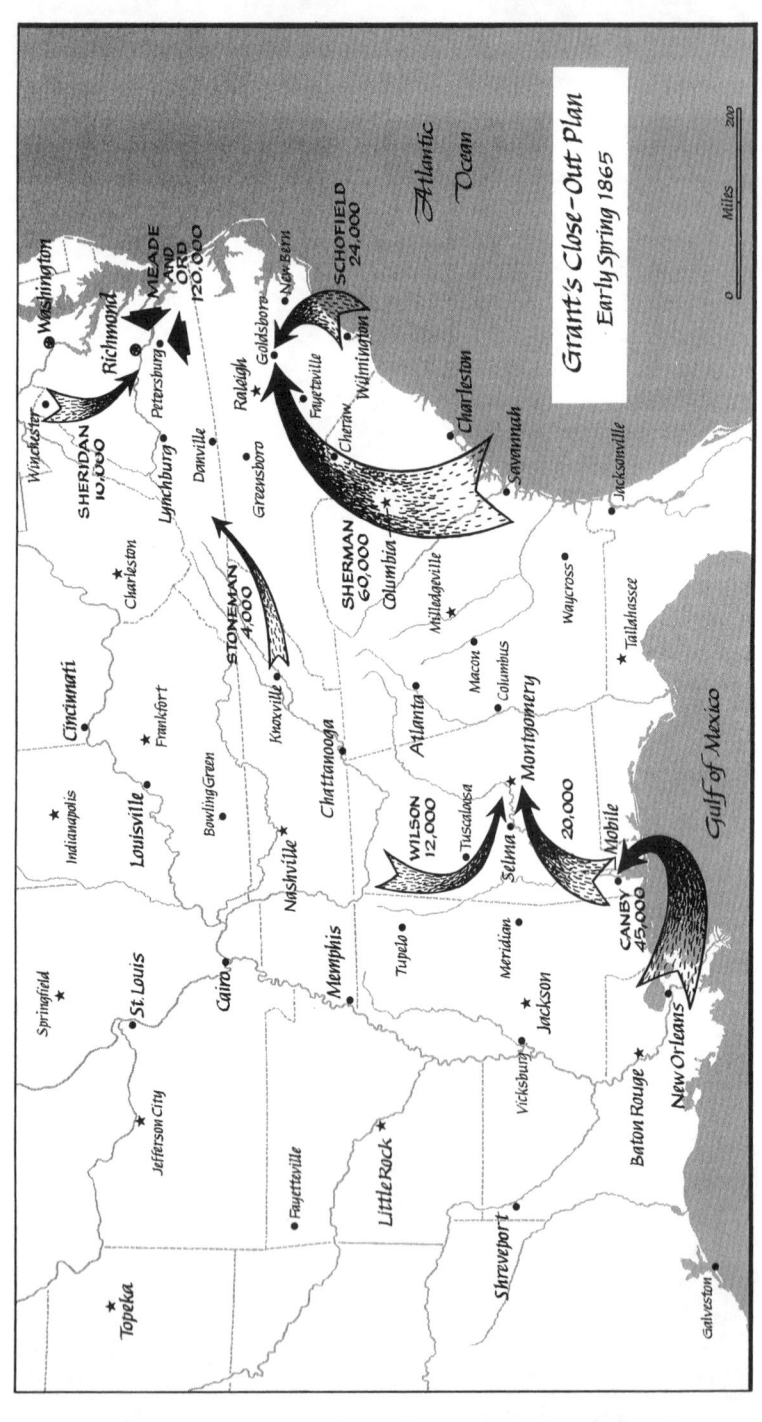

CHAPTER 6

A Tightening Noose

★ ✗ ☆

TECUMSEH SHERMAN SHEATHED HIS CLAWS for the occupation of Savannah. Not only did he retain the city's elected officials at their posts, conducting business more or less as usual; he even allowed Episcopal ministers to omit from their services the traditional prayer for God to "behold and bless" the President of the United States. "Jeff Davis and the devil both need it," he remarked, implying that Abraham Lincoln didn't. Meantime he kept a restraining hand on the veterans he had described, on the eve of their arrival, as "burning to avenge the national wrong." Geary's division garrisoned the town — milder-mannered Easterners for the most part, whose commander, exercising talents he had developed as mayor of San Francisco a decade back, tempered discipline with compassion. He hauled in firewood to warm the hearths and hearts of citizens, reopened markets for the sale of farm goods, and encouraged public meetings at which, in time, a vote of thanks was tendered "the noble Geary" and a resolution was adopted urging Governor Brown to call a state convention for peace discussions. Savannah's people knew that this was basically Sherman's doing, and all in all the consensus was that the red-haired conqueror, whose coming they had so greatly feared while he drew nearer mile by smoky mile, had been maligned by editors whose views were printed in regions he had not visited, so far. If not benign, he proved at any rate forbearing, and certainly not the apocalyptic monster they had been told to expect before he landed in their midst.

He himself was rather amused, seeing in all this a parallel to the behavior in far-off Natchez, well over two years ago, of propertied Confederates who found in coöperation a hope for the preservation, if not of their treasured way of life, then in any case of their fine old homes: an inducement altogether lacking, incidentally, in such new-rich towns as Vicksburg and Atlanta, whose defiance was characterized as an outgrowth of their war-boom attitude. He could chuckle over that, referring to Savannah's mayor, Dr Richard D. Arnold, as "completely 'subjugated.'" But there was little of amusement in the reaction of those editors who had warned of his savage nature. "A dangerous bait to deaden the spirit of resistance in other places," the Richmond *Examiner* said of this pretended mildness down the coast, and the rival *Dispatch* was even more specific that same day, January 7, in exposing the duplicity being practiced. "Sherman seems to have changed his character as completely as the serpent changes his skin with the approach of spring," the Virginia editor observed, and then discerned a likeness in the general to an animal just as sneaky in its way, but considerably more voracious: "His repose, however, is the repose of the tiger. Let him taste blood once more and he will be as brutal as ever."

In point of fact, there were sounder grounds for this suppositional metaphor than anyone had any way of knowing without access to certain letters the Ohioan was sending and receiving through this period of rest and preparation. "Should you capture Charleston," Halleck wrote on learning that the Carolina march had been approved, "I hope that by *some accident* the place may be destroyed, and if a little salt should be sown upon its site it may prevent the growth of future crops of nullification and secession." Sherman's plan was not to move on Charleston, "a mere desolated wreck... hardly worth the time it would take to starve it out," but rather to feint simultaneously at that point and Augusta, respectively on the right and left of his true line of march, and strike instead at Columbia, the capital between. However, he told Halleck, "I will bear in mind your hint as to Charleston, and do not think 'salt' will be necessary. When I move, the XV Corps" — Logan's: the Illinois soldier-politician returned to duty January 8, bringing Lincoln's congratulatory thank-you note along — "will be on the right of the right wing, and their position will naturally bring them into Charleston first.... If you have watched the history of that corps, you will have remarked that they generally do their work pretty well."

Nor was that the worst of it, by far. For all the alarm rebel editors felt on contemplating the repose of the tiger in coastal Georgia, they would have been a great deal more disturbed, and with equal justification, if they had known what was in store for them throughout the rest of their country east of the Mississippi. Sherman's march to scourge the Carolinas on his way to gain Lee's rear, while altogether the heftiest, was by no means the only move Grant planned to make on the thousand-mile-wide chessboard he pored over in his tent at City Point. The time had come to close out the Confederacy entirely, he believed, and he proceeded accordingly. He did so, moreover, not without a measure of personal satisfaction, although this was incidental to his larger purpose. Benjamin Prentiss, John McClernand, Don Carlos Buell, William Rosecrans, all had incurred his displeasure in the course of his rise to the top of the military heap — with the result that, shelved or snubbed into retirement, they were all four out of the war. And so too now, to all effect, was George Thomas: or soon would be, so far at least as a share in the final victory was concerned. Idle since its mid-December triumph over Hood, his army was quite the largest force available for carrying out the peripheral work Grant had in mind, but the general-in-chief had no intention of exposing himself to another nerve-wracking span of trying to prod Old Slow Trot into motion. Instead he proposed to do to the Virginian, in the wake of the botched pursuit that followed Nashville, what Halleck had done to Grant himself after Shiloh and Vicksburg; to wit, dismember him. This he would do by dispersing his troops — some 46,000 of them, all told — leaving Thomas with barely a third of his present command to garrison Middle and East Tennessee and northern Alabama: a thankless assignment, unlikely to call for much fighting, if any, unless Lee somehow managed to get away westward, in which case Thomas would be expected to stand in his path while Meade and Sherman came up in his rear to accomplish his destruction.

Schofield was the first to be subtracted. In early January, expecting Fort Fisher to fall under renewed pressure from Porter and units already on the way back there from the Army of the James, Grant ordered the XXIII Corps detached from Thomas and hurried north and east, by boat and rail, to a point near Washington. There Schofield would put his 14,000 men aboard transports for a trip down the coast and a share in the follow-up drive on Wilmington, which then would be converted from a haven for blockade-runners to an intermediary refuge and supply base for Sherman, in case he ran into trouble slogging north. Otherwise, reinforced to a strength of 24,000 by troops from Foster and the Army of the James, Schofield was to move up the North Carolina littoral to occupied New Bern, where he would turn inland for a meeting with Sherman at Goldsboro, and from there the two columns would go on together — better than 80,000 strong — for the rest of the march, by way of Raleigh, into Virginia. Meade by then would have been joined by Sheridan from the Shenandoah Valley, and Grant would have well over 200,000 seasoned fighting men around Petersburg and Richmond: surely enough, and more than enough, as he put it, to "wipe out Lee." However, by way of encouraging further confusion in the region to be traversed, he also instructed Thomas to send Stoneman and 4000 troopers pounding eastward from Knoxville into North Carolina, where they would serve to distract the state's defenders while Sherman and Schofield were moving northward through it near the coast. This done, Stoneman too would cross into Virginia, where he would not only rip up Lee's supply lines west of Lynchburg, but would also perhaps be in position, when the time came, to get in on the kill.

That so much concerted havoc was about to be visited on the Carolinas and the Old Dominion did not mean that the Deep South was to be neglected or spared. No; Grant had plans for its disruption, too. In addition to Schofield's corps, shifted eastward in mid-January, he also ordered A. J. Smith's detached, along with a division of cavalry under Brigadier General Joseph Knipe, and sent by steamer down the Mississippi to New Orleans, where Edward Canby had gathered the survivors of last year's expedition up and down Red River. Smith's 16,000 veterans, most of whom had also had a share in that unfortunate adventure, would lift Canby's available strike force to a strength of 45,000 of all arms: enough, Grant thought, for him to undertake the long-deferred reduction of Mobile, which continued defiant, behind its outlying fortifications, despite the loss of its Bay and access to the Gulf. Moreover, that was only to be the first step in the campaign Grant proposed. Once the city fell (if not before; haste was to be the governing factor) Canby would move with a flying column of 20,000, mainly composed of Smith's free-swinging gorilla-guerillas, north and east into the heart of Alabama. Specifically he would proceed against Selma, the principal center for the production of munitions in that part of the country, where he would make contact — much as Sherman was to do with Schofield, six hundred miles to the northeast — with still another detachment from Thomas's fast-dwindling army up in Tennessee. In the weeks that followed the pursuit of Hood from Nashville, James Wilson had continued to mount, arm, and train incoming cavalry units at so rapid a rate that by the end of January he had no less than 22,000 troopers under his command. Knipe took 5000 of these to New Orleans with Smith, and Wilson presently was instructed to strike southward with 12,000 of the rest, sturdily mounted and armed to a man with repeaters that gave them more firepower than a corps of infantry. Forrest would no doubt attempt to interfere, as he had done before in such cases; Grant was willing to leave it to Wilson whether to avoid or run right over him, which he should be able to do rather easily, considering his advantage in numbers and equipment. In any case, his immediate objective would be Selma, where he would combine with Canby's flying column, after wrecking the manufactory installations there, to continue the heartland penetration eastward: first to Montgomery, the Confederacy's original capital, and then across the Georgia line to Columbus and Macon, all three of which had been spared till now the iron hand of war.

Such then was Grant's close-out plan. As he saw it, the Confederacy was already whipped and clinging groggily to the ring ropes; all that remained was for him to land what boxers called a one-two punch, delivered in rapid sequence to belly and jaw, except that this was to be thrown with both hands simultaneously. In broad outline, the design resembled the one he had worked out nearly a year ago, on taking command of all the armies of the Union, but this time he was not obliged to include any unwanted elements, such as the Red River venture, or any unwanted subordinates, such as Banks. For example, aside from maintaining garrisons within it to preserve the status quo, and gunboats on patrol along its watery flank to keep it cut off from all contact eastward, the Transmississippi had no share in his calculations; either it would wither on its own, from sheer neglect or folly such as Price's recent raid, or else he would attend to it in a similar undistracted fashion when the time came. Not only would this affordable neglect represent a considerable savings in troops who could be used where they were wanted, but the fact was he now had more of them than he had had when he began his forward movement, back in May. Despite heavy losses incurred in the past nine months — 100,000 in eastern Virginia alone, and about that number elsewhere — his total combat force, East and West, had grown to better than 600,000 effectives, exclusive of reserves amounting to half as many more; whereas the enemy's had dwindled to barely 160,000 of all arms. That too was part of his calculations, and part of his hope for an early end to the conflict which by now had cost the country — the two countries, Confederates insisted — close to a million casualties, on and off the field of battle, North and South.

Nowhere in all this was there any mention of an assignment for Ben Butler, and the reason was quite simple. He was no longer around. Grant had fired him; or at any rate — now that the election was safely over — had persuaded Lincoln to fire him. The one-time Democratic senator was out of the war for good.

Fort Fisher had been the final straw. Though Grant said nothing of the ineffectual powder-boat explosion or even of the precipitate withdrawal, when he had determined the facts in the case he wrote to Stanton requesting the Massachusetts general's removal. "I do this with reluctance," he declared, "but the good of the service requires it. In my absence General Butler necessarily commands, and there is a lack of confidence felt in his military ability, making him an unsafe commander for a large army. His administration of the affairs in his department is also objectionable." This was put aboard a fast packet at City Point on January 5, and when Grant found out next morning that Stanton was on his way to Savannah to visit Sherman, he followed it up with a telegram directly to the Commander in Chief. "I wrote a letter to the Secretary of War, which was mailed yesterday, asking to have General Butler removed from command. Learning that the Secretary left Washington yesterday, I telegraph asking you that prompt action may be taken in the matter."

Lincoln's response was prompt indeed. General Order Number 1, issued "by direction of the President of the United States," arrived by wire the following day. "Maj. Gen. B. F. Butler is relieved from command of the Department of North Carolina and Virginia.... [He] will repair to Lowell, Mass., and report by letter to the Adjutant General of the Army."

Grant passed the word to Butler next morning, January 8, and named Ord the new commander of the Army of the James, some 8000 of whose members had embarked — or reëmbarked for the most part, having only just returned from the fiasco down the coast — at Bermuda Hundred four days ago, under Brigadier General Alfred Terry, for another go at Fort Fisher. Butler, however, did not "repair to Lowell" as ordered; at least not yet. He went instead to Washington, where political connections assured him a sympathetic hearing before the Joint Congressional Committee on the Conduct of the War, which assembled just under ten days later to hear his complaint of unjust treatment by the Administration and its three-starred creature down at City Point. Grant had left the charges vague, presumably on grounds that they would be harder to refute that way, but Butler at once got down to specifics. He had been relieved, he said, for his failure to take Fort Fisher, and he brought along charts and duplicates of reports by subordinates to prove that he had been right to call off the attack in midcareer, not only because Porter had failed to give him adequate support, but also because a close-up study of the thick-walled fort and its outlying torpedo fields had shown it to be impregnable in the first place, both to naval bombardment and to infantry assault. While he spoke, referring assiduously to the documents at hand, a hubbub rose outside the room — cheers in the street, the muffled crump of shotless guns discharging a salute, and newsboys crying, "Extra! Extra! Read all about it!" Fort Fisher, it seemed, had fallen. "Impossible!" Butler protested, clutching his papers. "It's a mistake, Sir." But it turned out to be more than possible; it was a fact, confirmed by dispatches on hand from Porter. Laughter rippled, then roared through the room. After a moment of shock adjustment, the cock-eyed general joined in as heartily as anyone. Adjournment followed, and as the members and spectators began filing out, still laughing, Butler raised his hand and called pontifically for silence. "Thank God for victory," he intoned.

In time, the committee not only voted unanimously to exonerate the former Bay State senator — referred to affectionately by a colleague as "the smartest damned rascal that ever lived" — from all blame in connection with the failure of the earlier expedition; its members also commended him for having had the nerve, the presence of mind under pressure, to call off the assault at the last minute, thereby saving many lives. Such action, they ruled, "was clearly justified by the facts then known," including Porter's ragged gunnery, which had done little damage to the fort, and his inadequate support of the troops ashore. Not that their judgment affected either officer's future war career; Butler had none, and the admiral even now was receiving congratulations for his share in one of the best-conducted operations of the war, by land or sea or both.

Terry and his 8000 — Butler's force, plus two brigades of Negro troops for added heft — reached Beaufort on schedule, January 8, for the rendezvous with Porter and his sixty warships. Delayed there by another three-day blow, they planned carefully for this second amphibious strike at Fort Fisher, then set out down the coast and dropped anchor before nightfall, January 12, within sight of the objective. Porter was altogether pleased with his new partner, whom he pronounced "my beau ideal of a soldier and a general," adding: "Our coöperation has been most cordial." Partly this was the result of Grant's instructions, which were for Terry to get along harmoniously with his sea-going associate, and partly it was because of Terry's natural tact and training, in and out of the army, where, as the phrase went, he had "found a home." A thirty-seven-year-old former clerk of the New Haven County superior court, admitted to the Connecticut bar while still at Yale, he had fought as a militia colonel at First Bull Run and then stayed on to pick up much experience in coastal operations, including the expedition against Port Royal, the reduction of Fort Pulaski, and the siege of Battery Wagner, after which he was made a brigadier and put in charge of a division in the Army of the James. Now that he had command of a provisional corps, with a promotion to major general in the works, he was determined to justify the added star by disproving Butler's contention that Fort Fisher could not be taken by assault. Once ashore, he told Porter, he intended to stay there until Confederate Point was Federal Point again, by right of exclusive occupation, and blockade runners would no longer find a haven up Cape Fear River for the discharge of their cargoes.

Just how important those cargoes were to continued resistance by the rebels was shown by the fact that R. E. Lee himself had sent word to the fort commander, William Lamb, that he could not subsist his army without the supplies brought in there. More specifically, a government report of goods run into Wilmington and Charleston during the last nine weeks of the year — practically all into the North Carolina port, for Charleston was tightly blockaded — amounted to "8,632,000 pounds of meat, 1,507,000 pounds of lead, 1,933,000 pounds of saltpeter, 546,000 pairs of shoes, 316,000 pairs of blankets, 520,000 pounds of coffee, 69,000 rifles, 97 packages of revolvers, 2639 packages of medicine, 43 cannon," and much else. Lamb was back down to a garrison of 800 men, the Junior Reservists having departed, and though he had appealed to both the district and department commanders, W. H. C. Whiting and Braxton Bragg, no reinforcements had arrived by the time the outsized Union armada returned and dropped anchor, just out of range of his biggest guns, on the evening of January 12.

Two hours before dawn, Porter opened the action by committing all five ironclads at short range, his object being to provoke the defenders into disclosing the location of their guns by muzzle flashes. It worked, and he followed this up after sunrise by bringing the rest of his 627 pieces to bear on targets the lookouts had spotted. The result, according to one Confederate crouched beneath this deluge of better than a hundred shells a minute, was "beyond description. No language can describe that terrific bombardment." Moreover, the fire was not only heavy; it was highly accurate. Butler's complaint that the navy's gunnery had been ragged throughout the previous attempt was in large part true, and Porter, amid his denials, had taken pains to correct it. For one thing, his marksmen then had fired at the rebel flag, high on its staff above the fort, so that many of their shots plunged harmlessly into the river beyond the narrow sand peninsula. This time, he cautioned in his preliminary directive, "the object is to lodge the shell in the parapets, and tear away the traverses under which the bombproofs are located. A shell now and then exploding over a gun en barbette may have good effect, but there is nothing like lodging the shell before it explodes.... Commanders are directed to strictly enjoin their officers and men never to fire at the flag or pole, but to pick out the guns; the stray shots will knock the flagstaff down." And so it was. He saw through the smoke and flying debris that his instructions were being followed to the letter. One by one, sometimes two by two, rebel pieces winked out and fell silent in the boil of dust and flame. "Traverses began to disappear," he would report, "and the southern angle of Fort Fisher commenced to look very dilapidated."

Since 8 o'clock that morning, four hours into the bombardment, Terry had been landing troops on the stretch of beach Weitzel had selected in December. By 3 o'clock all 8000 were ashore. This time, in addition to the accustomed "forty rounds," each man carried three days' rations on his person, backed by a six-day reserve of hard bread and a 300,000-round bulk supply of rifle ammunition. He had come to stay, and he emphasized this by digging a stout defensive line across the peninsula, facing north in case Hoke's division, known to be camped this side of Wilmington, tried an attack from that direction. Out on the water all this time the fleet kept up its smothering fire on the fort two miles below. Porter was clearly having the better of the exchange, yet a number of his ships had taken cruel punishment; *Canonicus*, for example, a monitor from the James River squadron, took 36 hits in the course of the day, and though none of them pierced her armor she was badly cut up about her deck and wore out several relays of gunners, stunned by the jar of solids against their turret and unnerved by the ping and spatter of bullets aimed at their sight-slits by sharpshooters in the fort. Porter cared little or nothing for any of this, however. He kept banging away past sunset, using every gun that could be brought to bear, and only retired his wooden vessels after twilight. Even so, he held the ironclads on station all night long, with instructions to continue lobbing their 11- and 15-inch shells into the shoreward darkness and thus discourage the rebel repair crews from doing much about the damage the place had suffered from the unrelenting daylong pounding, much of it heavy caliber and most of it point-blank.

Friday the 13th had indeed been an unlucky day for Lamb and the fort in his charge. More than a hundred of its defenders had fallen, and less than half the guns on its seaward face were still in operation. Despite his pleas, no reinforcements had come downriver: only the district commander and his staff, who arrived at the height of the bombardment. Whiting had come unglued at Petersburg last spring, victim of a too vivid imagination, but he seemed resolute now, even jaunty, in contrast to the gloomy news he brought. "Lamb, my boy," he announced as he entered the works, "I have come to share your fate. You and your garrison are to be sacrificed." Startled, the young colonel replied: "Don't say so, General. We shall certainly whip the enemy again." But the Mississippian explained that when he left Wilmington that morning, the department commander — Bragg had returned by now from his failed attempt to intercept Sherman down in Georgia — "was hastily removing his stores and ammunition, and was looking for a place to fall back upon." In other words, so far as the survival of Fort Fisher was concerned, Hoke and his 6000 veterans might as well have remained with Lee in Virginia; Bragg was unlikely to order them within range of Porter's big-gunned warships for a fight with the superior force Terry had landed and intrenched just north of the doomed fort. Lamb hoped against hope that Whiting was wrong in this assessment, yet as the day wore on he came more and more to see that, under the rain of all that metal, there was little he could do about it, even in the way of repairing damages. Nightfall brought a slackening though by no means a cessation of the fire. Still at work beyond the surf, the five ironclads bowled their big projectiles "along the parapets, scattering shrapnel in the darkness" with such effect, Lamb said later, that "we could scarcely gather up and bury our dead without fresh casualties."

Dawn brought a resumption of the full-scale bombardment, with all the Federal warships back on station. In the December effort Porter had fired 20,271 projectiles weighing 1,275,000 pounds. This time, having called for a more deliberate rate of fire, he would expend several hundred fewer rounds — 19,682 all told — but greater reliance on his heavier weapons resulted in a total weight of 1,652,638 pounds, a new record for the amount of metal thrown in a single naval engagement. Lamb's casualties rose above two hundred before this second day was over, and though some 700 North Carolina soldiers and a detachment of 50 sailors arrived to lift the strength of the garrison to about 1550 — minus, of course, the sick and wounded and the dead — there was little the defenders could do but huddle in their bombproofs, awaiting word from lookouts that the land assault was under way, at which point they were to turn out and contest it, hand-to-hand if necessary.

It did not come today, as Lamb expected, but it would tomorrow. Porter and Terry met that evening aboard the flagship *Malvern*, and while the ironclads kept up their nightlong harassment, holding the rebel gunners in their burrows, the two commanders planned the timing for next day's climax to their joint effort. The fleet would resume its all-out pounding of the objective until 3 o'clock, then suddenly cease fire for the assault, which would be made by two separate columns driving down opposite sides of the peninsula, thus avoiding the field of torpedoes north of the fort. On the river flank, half of Terry's troops would attack the land face near its western end, leaving the other 4000 to hold the intrenchments against a possible attempt by Hoke to interfere at this critical moment. Simultaneously, a 2000-man all-navy column, recruited piecemeal from most of the vessels of the fleet — 1600 sailors, armed with cutlasses and revolvers, and 400 marines armed with rifles — would advance down the beach to strike the northeast salient of the fort, where the land and seaward faces joined. Both forces were to press the issue until Fort Fisher was secured.

Sunday, January 15, went much as Porter and Terry had planned it aboard the *Malvern*. A calm sea, after two days of intensive target practice, so improved the fleet's marksmanship that by noon only one gun remained in service on the seaward face and none at all on the other, whose palisade was swept away by the longitudinal fire. Around 2 o'clock a steamer put in at the wharf in rear and began unloading a brigade of South Carolinians sent downriver by Bragg in response to Whiting's telegraphic pleas. Only about a third of them made it ashore, however, before the boat was driven off by a storm of shells from the warships on the far side of the fort. These 350, exposed without preamble to this holocaust of screaming metal, barely replaced the casualties Lamb had suffered over the past three days, and by the time he got them into bombproofs, he said later, "they were out of breath, disorganized, and more or less demoralized." Just then a lookout shouted, "Colonel, the enemy are about to charge!" A heavy blue column was working its way down the beach, apparently with the intention of gaining a close-up position from which to launch an assault. While Lamb called out the garrison to meet the threat, Whiting got off a frantic wire to Bragg: "Enemy on the beach in front of us in very heavy force. ... Attack! Attack! It is all I can say and all you can do." By now the time was straight-up 3 o'clock, and the roar of guns hushed abruptly beyond the surf. There was a moment of eerie stillness, broken in turn by all the steam whistles of the fleet, shrieking and moaning in concert. Lamb wondered at this, then realized they were sounding the charge for the troops ashore. "A soul-stirring signal," he called it, "both to besiegers and besieged."

Cutlasses flashing in the wintry sunlight, the bluejackets made their dash along the beach, only to be stopped within 300 yards of the objective by well-aimed volleys of musketry. There they held on for a time, their losses mounting while they dug frantically in the loose sand for cover, then turned, despite the pleas of their officers — who "in their anxiety to be the first into the fort," a wounded ensign later said, "had advanced to the heads of the columns, leaving no one to steady the men behind" — and fled back up the low-tide-widened beach. One who did what he could to stop them was William Cushing, recently promoted for having sunk the *Albemarle*. He was weeping over the loss of a friend, shot down along with some 300 others in the course of the attack, and swearing at the retreaters in his frustration; to no avail. "We witnessed what we had never seen before," Lamb would report, "a disorderly rout of American sailors and marines."

Exultant, he looked down the line of blasted works and saw, to his dismay, three Federal battle flags atop the ramparts near its western end. Concealed by trees and brush along the river, the army column had made its way up close to the fortifications undetected, then mounted them in a rush.

Whiting too had seen the enemy flags, and while Lamb prepared to follow with the rest of the main body, which had repulsed and been distracted by the attack on this end of the land face, the Mississippian led a countercharge against the other. He retook one of two lost gun chambers, but was wounded twice in quick succession. By the time Lamb arrived with reinforcements, the general had been carried rearward on a stretcher and a fierce struggle was raging for possession of the connecting traverse. With the penetration thus contained (though only by the hardest; "The contestants were savagely firing into each other's faces, and in some cases clubbing their guns, being too close to load and fire") the attackers seemed to falter; Lamb believed that if he could hold on until nightfall he would be able to drive them out. Just then, however, the fleet steamed back into action, shelling the Confederates massed in rear of the lost segment of their line. The result, combined with all that had gone before, was "indescribably horrible," he said. "Great cannon were broken in two, and over their ruins were lying the dead; others were partly buried in graves dug by the shells which had slain them." Up near the occupied portion of the works, where the warships could not intervene for fear of hitting their own men, the fighting continued at close quarters. "If there has ever been a longer or more stubborn hand-to-hand encounter," Lamb declared, "I have failed to meet with it in history."

Knocked sprawling by a bullet in the hip, he was put in a cot alongside Whiting's in the hospital bombproof. Outside, the fighting and shelling continued past sundown, on into darkness. At 8 o'clock an aide reported the land face lost from end to end; the contest now was for the interior, and he suggested that further resistance would be a useless sacrifice of life. Lamb replied that so long as he lived he would never surrender. Whiting approved. "Lamb," he assured him from the adjoining cot, "when you die I will assume command, and I will not surrender the fort."

By now, however, Terry had four brigades inside the place. They did their work well, as indeed they had done from the outset, pressing the defenders southward down the sea face, traverse by traverse, until there was nothing left to fall back on. At 10 o'clock that night the flag came down. Something over 500 men had fallen in its defense, and now the survivors were prisoners, including Lamb and Whiting. (The former would survive his wound and a doleful stretch as a captive in Fort Columbus, New York Harbor, but Chase Whiting would die there in March, after nearly eight weeks of suffering from his wounds, complaining bitterly all the while of Bragg's failure to support the beleaguered garrison during a three-day resistance "unparalleled in the history of the war.") Terry lost 955 killed and wounded, Porter 386, ashore and afloat. "If hell is what it is said to be," a weary sailor wrote home next day, "then the interior of Fort Fisher is a fair comparison. Here and there you see great heaps of human beings laying just as they fell, one upon the other. Some groaning piteously, and asking for water. Others whose mortal career is over, still grasping the weapon they used to so good an effect in life."

For all the compacted horror of the scene, and despite the even steeper price the victors paid in blood for its creation, nothing deterred the gaudy all-night celebration that followed the announcement of surrender. "Cheer after cheer came from the fort," a Federal officer would recall, "and was answered by the ships with cheers, rockets, lights of all colors, ringing of bells, steam whistles, and all sorts of unearthly noises." To a watching sailor, "The rockets seemed to shoot higher and sparkle more brilliantly than usual," and even the shrieking whistles, whose shrillness had always hurt his ears, "seemed to discourse a sweet melody." Ashore, the informal distribution of whiskey found among the captured medical stores livened the rout for the jubilant soldiers, sailors, and marines, for whom the end of the fighting meant the end of discipline. Fort Fisher had been a hard go, and officers tended to overlook excesses, including the rapid-fire discharge of revolvers and a good deal of rowdy prowling after souvenirs in the wreckage. In the end, this resulted in tragedy. Guards had been posted at the entrances of some thirty underground powder magazines, but somehow the largest of these — a 20 by 60 foot chamber, roofed over with 18 feet of sand piled in a flat-topped mound sodded with grass to keep the rain from washing it away — was missed. Apparently no one suspected there were between six and seven tons of powder under the springy turf: certainly not the wearier members of a New York regiment, who found it too inviting a bed to be resisted this mild January night, and certainly not two drunken seamen who entered the magazine with lighted torches, shortly after dawn, in

A Tightening Noose [747]

search of loot. The resultant explosion added 104 killed and wounded and missing to the Union casualty list, which thus was increased to just under 1500, or roughly three times the number the garrison suffered before it surrendered.

Confederates might find grim satisfaction in such a mishap, just as they did when news arrived that off Charleston this same day, 150 miles to the south, the monitor *Patapsco* struck a torpedo while searching for obstructions in the harbor channel. She went down fast, with the loss of more than half her crew of just over a hundred. Porter, however, was no more inclined to be daunted by this than he was by the explosion of the powder magazine. "Our success is so great that we should not complain," he informed Welles in the dispatch that broke up Butler's hearing before the Joint Committee. "Men, it seems, must die that this Union may live.... We regret our companions in arms and shed a tear over their remains, but if these rebels should succeed we would have nothing left us and our lives would be spent in terror and sorrow."

Fort Fisher's fall confirmed Butler's. Whatever his friends on the Washington committee might say as to his perspicacious conduct during the earlier attempt, he was gone for good. And so too now, to all effect, was Samuel Curtis; not at Grant's urging, but his own. Promoted to major general as a reward for his Pea Ridge victory nearly three years ago, he was disappointed to find little attention being paid to his recent Westport achievement or the rigorous follow-up southward, down the length of Missouri, into Arkansas and the Indian Territory. Apparently neither the newspapers nor the War Department had space or time for anything but Sherman's triumphal march across Georgia to the sea. Taken aback by this imbalance Curtis fell into a fit of pique. "Sherman's success was glorious," he wrote privately to his brother in early January, "but in justice to myself not equal to my pursuit of Price, in that I had a less force against a larger, won several victories, and had to go as far *through a desolate country*." Thinking it over, and finding it rankled, he applied to the War Department to be spared the strain of another campaign, and his request was promptly granted. Before the month was out he was transferred to command of the Department of the Northwest, with headquarters at Milwaukee, well removed from any possible clash of arms. Nor was there a commander appointed in his stead. As if to suggest that Curtis's role had been superfluous in the first place, Dodge's adjoining Department of the Missouri was simply enlarged to include Kansas and the Nebraska and Utah territories.

But this too went largely unnoticed. A peripheral shift having little to do with the close-out maneuver everyone could see was in the making on the seaboard, such a subtraction had no more bearing on the central issue than, say, the death of seventy-one-year-old Edward Everett, whose two-hour oration had preceded Lincoln's two-minute speech at Gettysburg just over a year ago. By now, with the end conceivably in sight, men looked beyond the cease-fire to insist with a new fervor that the victory be put to proper use. Slavery returned as the burning issue it had been at the outset.

Everett died on January 15, amid a congressional furor over the proposed adoption of a constitutional amendment — the first in more than sixty years — forbidding the existence of slavery "within the United States or any place subject to their jurisdiction." The Senate had approved it nine months earlier, but House proponents then had failed to secure the two-thirds vote required. Lincoln in his December message urged reconsideration during the present session, on grounds that approval would surely follow the seating of newly elected Republicans at the next. "As it is to so go, at all events, may we not agree that the sooner the better?" He asked that, yet he also did a good deal more than ask. He set out to get the necessary votes, mainly by logrolling. One opposed Democrat was promised a government job for his brother in New York; another was assured support in holding onto his contested seat; while a third, hired by a railroad to fight off adverse legislation, was guaranteed the threat would not mature. These three came over more or less gladly, and eight others, firmer in their resistance or more fearful of the home reaction to an outright shift, were similarly bargained into agreeing to abstain. Finally, on the last day of January — as soon as the Administration was reasonably certain of the outcome — House Speaker Schuyler Colfax put the resolution to a vote. Members and spectators alike followed the tally with mounting excitement. It came out 119 aye, 56 nay; passing thus with three switched votes to spare. Colfax's announcement of the result, according to the usually staid *Congressional Globe*, was greeted with an outburst of emotion. "The members on the Republican side of the House instantly sprang to their feet, and, regardless of parliamentary rules, applauded with cheers and clapping of hands. The example was followed by male spectators in the galleries, who waved their hats and cheered long and loud, while the ladies, hundreds of whom were present, rose in their seats and waved their handkerchiefs, participating in adding to the general excitement and intense interest of the scene. This lasted for several minutes."

Outside the chamber it lasted considerably longer. Three batteries of regular artillery, loaded and ready when the time came, began firing a hundred-gun salute from Capitol Hill, and men embraced on the streets in celebration. In addition to the realization that a goal had been reached, there was the feeling that a new road had been taken, even though by no means all were pleased to travel it, not being satisfied that they wanted to go where it led. All twelve amendments up to now, including the last in 1804, had dealt exclusively with governmental powers and functions; that is, they were "constitutional" in the strictest sense.

But this one — lucky or unlucky Thirteen — went beyond that to effect reform in an area recently considered outside the scope of the Constitution, overriding protests that no combination of parties to that contract, however sizeable their majority, could alter it to outlaw a domestic institution that existed before it was written. Pendleton of Ohio, McClellan's running mate in November, voiced his party's opposition in the debate leading up to the roll call. "Neither three-fourths of the states, nor all the states save one, can abolish slavery in that dissenting state," he told the House, "because it lies within the domain reserved entirely to each state for itself, and upon it the other states cannot enter." Such was the States Rights position, many of whose principal supporters had departed, just four years ago this month, to set up on their own. Then came the vote, and States Rights went by the board. Moreover, any last-ditch hope that the Supreme Court might overturn the measure was abandoned when it was noted, not only that five of the nine members — including Salmon Chase — were present for the vote, but also that their judicial gravity scarcely masked their satisfaction at the outcome.

Ironically, this Thirteenth Amendment abolished slavery, rather than assuring its continuance, as a direct result of secession. Six weeks before Sumter, both the Senate and the House had passed by a two-thirds vote a proposed Thirteenth Amendment stating flatly that Congress could never be given "the power to abolish or interfere within any State with the domestic institutions thereof, including that of persons held to labor or service by the laws of said State." Buchanan signed it on the eve of Lincoln's inauguration, but the measure was forgotten when the issue swung to war. On the other hand, if the departed Southerners had remained in Washington they and their northern friends, whose influence would have been for peace, could almost certainly have secured the requisite three-fourths ratification by their respective states. Charles Sumner, well aware of this, wasted no time in consolidating the victory he had worked so hard to win. He appeared before the Supreme Court next day, February 1, to move that a fellow lawyer, John S. Rock of Boston, be admitted to practice before it. Embraced by the Chief Justice, who had prepared his colleagues, the motion carried. Here indeed was a change; for Rock was a Negro, the first of his race to address that high tribunal, which less than a decade ago had denied that Dred Scott, a non-citizen, even had the right to be represented there.

Elated, a crowd with a brass band trooped onto the White House lawn that night and shouted for the President, who came out on a balcony to take the music and greet the serenaders. "Speech! Speech!" they called up, and he obliged them. He praised Congress's action yesterday as "the fitting if not indispensable adjunct to the consummation of the great game we are playing," and emphasized that his aim all along had been to root out this basic cause of national disturbance —

slavery — against the day when the states would be reunited. The Emancipation Proclamation had been issued with that in mind, he said, even though it freed only those slaves who came within the reach of blue-clad soldiers. Moreover, once the war had ended, it might be held invalid by the courts, leaving much of the evil uncorrected and still a subject for contention. "But this amendment is a King's cure for all the evils. It winds the whole thing up." Applauded, Lincoln paused and then remarked in closing that he could not but congratulate all present — himself, the country, and the world — "upon this great moral victory."

The victory claim was valid on other grounds as well, but only within problematical limitations. Ratification, once it came, would give the nation all that he maintained. Yet the dimensions of the victory depended altogether on the dimensions of the country when the amendment was adopted, and this in turn depended — more or less as had been the case, over the past two years, in the application of the Emancipation Proclamation — on the progress, between now and then, of Union arms. In short, it depended on whether Grant's close-out plan succeeded. Sherman's part was the critical one, at least in the early stages, and by coincidence he set out in earnest, this same February 1, on his march north through the Carolinas to gain Lee's rear.

Although he was thus some four weeks behind the schedule he had set for himself when he wrote Grant on Christmas Eve that he expected to start north "in about ten days," the delay was unavoidable. Heavy winter rains had swollen creeks and swamps along his projected route of march, while ice on the Potomac — their staging area, once they arrived from Nashville — prevented Schofield's men from steaming downriver aboard transports on their way to Wilmington. This last did not disturb the red-haired general, any more than had Butler's failure to clear the way by reducing Fort Fisher. "Fizzle; great fizzle!" he snorted when he heard of that yuletide fiasco. "I shall have to go up there and do that job myself. Eat 'em up as I go, and take 'em backside." In this connection he requested Dahlgren to keep up the scare along the South Carolina coast, maneuvering his warships as if to cover a series of landings by Foster, whose troops would go along. That would confuse the rebels throughout Sherman's period of preparation at Savannah. Later, when his march had pulled the defenders inland and cut the seaports off from reinforcements and supplies, such feints could be converted to actual landings, probably against nothing worse than token opposition, and possibly not even that. "I will shake the tree," he told Foster, "and you must be quick to pick up the apples."

He was feeling good, despite the delay, and he showed it. Pride in all his men had done was matched by pride in their conduct throughout the present span of comparative repose: as was demonstrated in a letter informing Grant that, "notwithstanding the habits begotten during our rather vandalic march," the behavior of his soldiers in Savannah had "excited the wonder and admiration of all." Not even a four-day visit by Stanton, January 11–15 — ostensibly for reasons of health, but actually to explore his fellow Ohioan's position on the Negro question — upset Sherman's feeling of well-being. He fancied he had set the Secretary straight as to his views on "Inevitable Sambo," alarming though they were to abolitionists up in Washington. "The South deserves all she has got for her injustice to the negro," he wrote Halleck at the time, "but that is no reason why we should go to the other extreme." Stanton heard him say such things, and seemed not to disapprove. As for the restoration of states now claiming to have departed from the Union, Sherman told Georgians who called on him in the course of the Secretary's visit: "My own opinion is that no negotiations are necessary, nor commissioners, nor conventions, nor anything of the kind.... Georgia is not out of the Union, and therefore talk of 'reconstruction' appears to me inappropriate." Meantime he kept busy, doing all he could to "make a good ready" for the expedition north. Dahlgren's loss of the *Patapsco* outside Charleston, along with 64 of her crew, was more than offset by the news that Porter and Terry had taken Fort Fisher that same day, preparing the way for Schofield, who wrote that he would be off down the coast as soon as the Potomac ice broke up. January was more than half gone by now, and Sherman stepped up the pace of his preparations.

His march would be due north in two columns, enabling him to feint simultaneously at Charleston and Augusta, on the right and left, while aiming in fact at Columbia, between and beyond them. North of the South Carolina capital he would feint again, this time at Chester and Charlotte, then turn east-northeast, through Cheraw and Fayetteville, for Goldsboro — chosen because two rail lines ran from there to Wilmington and New Bern, up which Schofield would be marching with supplies from those two ports. Refitted and reinforced to a strength of better than 80,000 Sherman then could drive on Raleigh, the North Carolina capital, en route to Petersburg and the combination with Meade. Now as before, Slocum would lead the two-corps left wing, Howard the two-corps right, while Kilpatrick's horsemen shielded the western flank. This time, though, they would stay closer together, cutting a narrower swath for readier mutual support, since an attack was considered far likelier here than in Georgia, where the outcome had been less obviously disastrous to the Confederate high command. "If Lee is a soldier of genius," the red-head explained to his staff, "he will seek to transfer his army from Richmond to Raleigh or Columbia. If he is a man simply of detail, he will remain where he is and his speedy defeat is sure. But I have little fear that he will be able to move; Grant holds him in a vise of iron."

In point of fact, so far as interference was concerned, there was

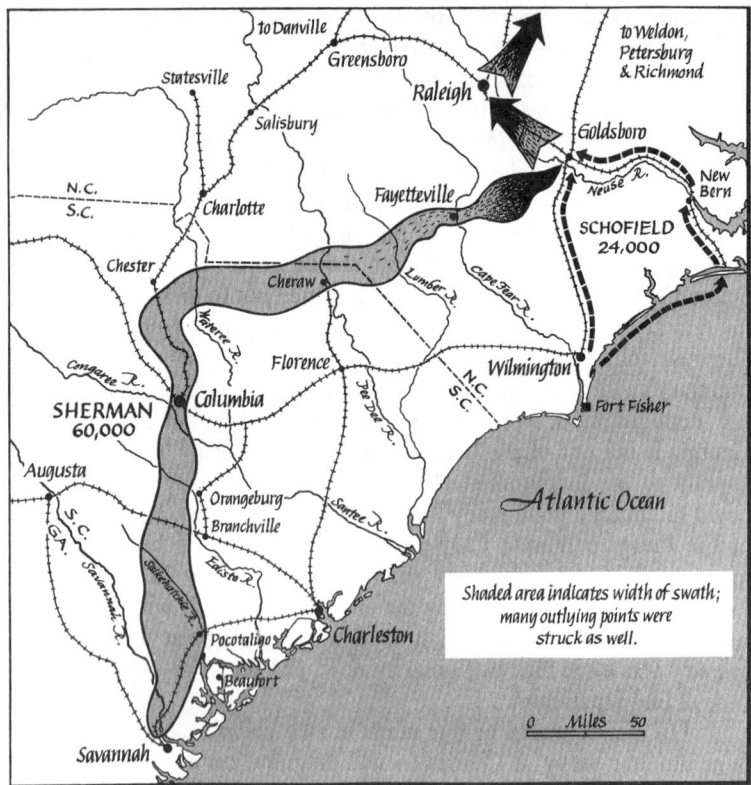

more to fear from rebel terrain than there was from rebel armies. Not only would the Carolinas march — 425 miles, all told, from Savannah to Goldsboro — be nearly half again longer than the one from Atlanta to the sea; the difference in natural obstacles he would encounter, both in kind and number, made the earlier expedition appear in retrospect as something of a lark, a holiday outing in pleasant weather, through a region of rich crops, ripe for harvest, and livestock waiting only to be rounded up and butchered. Here the crops had already been gathered, such as they were, and the cattle were few and scrubby at best, having little to graze on but muck and palmetto. Moreover, luck had exposed him to almost no rain on his way through Georgia, and it would not have mattered a lot in any case; whereas he would be marching now in the dead of winter, the rainiest in years, and it mattered a great deal. Many rivers lay ahead, all reportedly brim full. After the Savannah, there would be the Salkehatchie and the Edisto, the Congaree and the Wateree, the Pee Dee and the Lumber, the Cape Fear and finally the Neuse, all nine of them major streams, with creeks and bayous webbing the swampy ground between, wet with all the rain that had fallen and was falling between the seaboard and the near slopes of the Appalachians. Yet here too Sherman could prepare for trouble, much as he had done when he drilled repair crews for work on the railroads north of Atlanta and Chattanooga. Michigan lumbermen and rail-splitters from Indiana and Illinois were organized into a pioneer corps, 6600 strong, armed with axes for cutting, splitting, and laying saplings flat-side-down to corduroy roads for the 2500 wagons and 600 ambulances rolling northward in the wake of his 60,000 marchers. He did not intend to get bogged down, nor did he intend to be slowed down in avoiding it: in token of which he had already selected a rangy half-thoroughbred bay named Old Sam to serve as his accustomed mount on the campaign. Sam, a staff major noted ominously, was "a horribly fast-walking horse."

Beginning the feint, Sherman sent Howard's wing by boat to Beaufort, forty miles up the coast beyond Port Royal Sound, with instructions to move inland and occupy Pocotaligo, on the railroad about midway between Savannah and Charleston. By January 20 this had been done, and Slocum began slogging in the opposite direction, thirty miles up the drowned west bank of the Savannah River to Sister's Ferry, as if about to close upon Augusta. Unrelenting rain made the march a roundabout nine-day affair, with much discomfort for the troops. For them, however, as for their chief, "city life had become dull and tame, and we were anxious to get into the pine woods again." Moreover, they were sustained by anticipation of another kind. Ahead lay South Carolina, and they had been promised a free hand in visiting upon her the destruction she deserved for having led the Confederate exodus from the Union. "Here is where treason began, and by God here is where it shall end," they vowed, pleased with their role as avenging instruments and eager to put into sterner practice the talents they had acquired on the march through Georgia, accounts of which had reached and frightened the people in their new path northward. Sherman approved of the fear aroused. "This was a power, and I intended to utilize it," he said later, explaining: "My aim then was to whip the rebels, to humble their pride, to follow them to their inmost recesses, and make them fear and dread us. 'Fear of the Lord is the beginning of wisdom.'"

Already there were signs that the two-pronged feint was working in both directions. Augusta was in ferment over Slocum's approach, and in Charleston, menaced from the landward side by Howard and by Dahlgren from the sea, clerks were busy packing and shipping official records and historical mementos to Columbia for safe-keeping, never suspecting that the inland capital was not only high on Sherman's list of prime objectives, but was also to be dealt with as harshly as Atlanta had been served two months ago. "I look upon Columbia as quite as bad as Charleston," he wrote Halleck while cooling his army's heels in Savannah, "and I doubt if we shall spare the public buildings there as we did in Milledgeville." What was more, subordinates from private to major general took this prediction a step further when the march began in earnest, February 1. Blair and Logan cleared Pocotaligo and Davis and Williams crossed the Savannah in force that day. On the far left, at Sister's Ferry, Kilpatrick's troopers led the way, hoofs drumming on the planks of a pontoon bridge thrown there the day before. Soldiers of a Michigan infantry regiment, waiting their turn to cross, had heard that the bandy-legged cavalry commander had instructed his men to fill their saddlebags with matches for the work ahead, and now they believed it; for as he rode out onto the bridge he called back over his shoulder, "There'll be damned little for you infantrymen to destroy after I've passed through that hell-hole of secession!"

Here indeed was an end to what the Richmond editor termed "the repose of the tiger," in the course of which Sherman had told Old Brains: "The truth is the whole army is burning with an insatiable desire to wreak vengeance upon South Carolina. I almost tremble for her fate, but feel that she deserves all that seems in store for her."

※ 2 ※

A proposal that the women of the South cut off their hair for sale in Europe, thereby bringing an estimated 40,000,000-dollar windfall to the cause, had gained widespread approval by the turn of the year, despite some protests — chiefly from men, who viewed the suggested disfigurement with less favor than did their wives and sweethearts — that the project was impractical. After the fall of Fort Fisher, however, the Confederacy's last port east of the Mississippi was no longer open to blockade runners, coming or going, and the plan was abandoned. Even if the women sheared their heads there was no way now for the bulky cargo to be shipped, either to Europe or anywhere else; or if it could somehow be gotten out — from Charleston, say, in a sudden dash by a high-speed flotilla — the odds were even longer against a return with whatever the money would buy in the way of necessities, all of which were running low and lower now that the war was about to enter its fifth spring. Like so many other proposals, farfetched but by no means impossible if they had been adopted sooner, this one came too late.

Another was a return to the suggestion advanced informally by Pat Cleburne the previous winter, soon after Missionary Ridge, that the South free its slaves and enlist them in its armies. Hastily suppressed at the time as "revolting to Southern sentiment, Southern pride, and Southern honor," the proposition seemed far less "monstrous" now than it had a year ago, when Grant was not at the gates of Richmond and Sherman had not made his march through Georgia. Seddon, for one, had been for it ever since the fall of Atlanta, except that he believed emancipation should follow, not precede, a term of military service. In early January, Governor William Smith — "Extra Billy" to Old

Dominion voters — proposed that Virginia and the other states, not the central government, carry out the plan for black recruitment. Appealed to, R. E. Lee replied that he favored such a measure. "We must decide whether slavery shall be extinguished by our enemies and the slaves used against us, or use them ourselves at the risk of the effects which may be produced upon our social institutions. My own opinion is that we should employ them without delay. I believe that with proper regulation they can be made efficient soldiers." This was powerful support. If Lee wanted Negro troops, a once-oppugnant Richmond editor wrote soon afterward, "by all means let him have them." Westward, Richard Taylor agreed. In Mobile, when he congratulated a group of impressed slaves on their skill in building fortifications, their leader told him: "If you will give us guns we will fight for these works, too. We would rather fight for our own white folks than for strangers." Down in South Carolina, however, Mary Boykin Chesnut had her doubts. "Freeing Negroes is the latest Confederate Government craze," the mistress of Mulberry Plantation wrote in her diary. "We are a little slow about it; that is all.... I remember when Mr Chesnut spoke to his Negroes about it, his head men were keen to go in the army, to be free and get a bounty after the war. Now they say coolly that they don't want freedom if they have to fight for it. That means they are pretty sure of having it anyway."

Opinions differed: not so much along economic lines, as might have been expected — large slave-holders versus the slaveless majority of small farmers, merchants, and wage earners — but rather as a result of opposition from die-hard political leaders who contended that no government, state or central, whatever its desperation under the threat of imminent extinction, had the right to interfere in matters involving social institutions: especially slavery, which Aleck Stephens had called the "cornerstone" of the Confederacy, insisting that it made the nation's citizens truly free, presumably to establish a universal white aristocracy, by keeping the Negro in the inferior position God and nature intended for him to occupy down through time. As a result, after intense discussion, Virginia's General Assembly voted to permit the arming of slaves but included no provision for their emancipation, either before or after military service. Little or nothing came of that, as Mrs Chesnut had foreseen, but even less seemed likely to proceed from a similar bill introduced in the Confederate House and Senate in early February, only to run into virulent Impossiblist opposition. Despite Lee's earlier warning "that whatever measures are to be adopted should be adopted at once. Every day's delay increases the difficulty. Much time will be required to organize and discipline the men, and action may be deferred until too late," debate dragged on, week in, week out, as the legislators wrangled. Meanwhile, Federal enlistment teams kept busy in the wake of blue advances, signing up and swearing in black volunteers, many of them substitutes to help fill the draft quotas of northern states. In the end, of the nearly 180,000 Negroes who served in the Union ranks — 20,000 more than the "aggregate present" in all the armies of the South on New Year's Day — 134,111 were recruited in states that had stars in the Confederate battle flag, and the latter figure in turn was several thousand greater than the total of 125,994 gray-clad soldiers "present for duty" that same day; when the North had 959,460 and 620,924 in those respective categories.

It was by no means as great, however, as the total of 198,494 listed that day as absent from Confederate ranks. Moreover, this invisible army of the missing grew with every passing week, its membership swollen even by veterans from the Army of Northern Virginia, whose morale was said to be high despite short rations and the bone-numbing chill of the Petersburg trenches. Adversity had given them a pinched and scarecrow look, hard to connect with the caterwauling victors of so many long-odds battles in the past. A Connecticut soldier, peering through a Fort Hell sight-slit one cold morning to watch a detail of them straggle out to relieve their picket line, wrote home that he "could not help comparing them with so many women with cloaks, shawls, double-bustles and hoops, as they had thrown over their shoulders blankets and tents which flapped in the wind." Many by now had reached their limit of endurance; they came over into the Union lines in increasing numbers, especially from units posted where the rival works were close together and a quick sprint meant an end to shivering misery and hunger. A New England private told how he and his comrades would speculate each day on how many were likely to come in that night, depending on the darkness of the moon. "The boys talk about the Johnnies as at home we talk about suckers and eels. The boys will look around in the evening and guess that there will be a good run of Johnnies." Lee of course felt the drain, and knew only too well what the consequences must be if it continued. Before the end of January he warned Davis that if Grant was appreciably reinforced, either by Thomas from the west or by Sherman from the south — or, for that matter, by Lincoln from the north — "I do not see how in the present position he can be prevented from enveloping Richmond."

If in Virginia a sort of numbness obtained because of the military stalemate and the long-term deprivation of troops confined to earthworks, something approaching chaos prevailed at this time in the Carolinas while the various commanders — Bragg at Wilmington, Hardee at Charleston, G. W. Smith at Augusta, who between them mustered fewer than 25,000 effectives, including militia — engaged in a flurry of guesses as to where Sherman would strike next, and when, and how best to go about parrying the thrust, outnumbered and divided as they were. Yet the region in which conditions were by far the worst in regard to the physical state and morale of its defenders, even though there was no immediate enemy pressure on them, was Northeast Mississippi: specifically in the vicinity of Tupelo, where the Army of Tennessee made camp at last, January 8–10, on returning from its disastrous five-week excursion into the state from which it took its name. Its strength was down to 17,700 infantry and artillery, barely half the number answering roll-call when the long files set out north in mid-November. Most of the foot soldiers had no shoes, having worn them out on the icy roads, and an equal proportion of batteries had no guns; 72 pieces had been lost, along with a score of brigade and division commanders. Edward Walthall, whose division had shared with Forrest's horsemen the rear-guard duty that saved what remained of the army in the course of its ten-day retreat across the Tennessee, ended his official report on a sad and bitter note: "The remnant of my command, after this campaign of unprecedented peril and hardship, reduced by battles and exposure, worn and weary with its travel and its toil, numbered less when it reached its rest near Tupelo than one of its brigades had done eight months before."

Aside from a raft of scarehead accounts in northern papers, which told of a great conflict outside Nashville, of rebel prisoners taken in their thousands, and of victory salutes being fired in celebration all across the North, the authorities in Richmond heard nothing of what had occurred until more than two weeks after the battle, when a wire Hood sent on Christmas Day, via Corinth, reached the War Department on January 3. Headed Bainbridge, Alabama, it merely informed Seddon: "I am laying a pontoon here to cross the Tennessee River." That was all it said. But another, addressed to Beauregard at Montgomery, repeated this jot of information, then added: "Please come to Tuscumbia or Bainbridge."

The Creole was already on his way in that direction, not from Montgomery but from Charleston, whose defenses he had been attempting to bolster against expected pressure from occupied Savannah. His purpose in returning West was two-fold: first, to see for himself the condition of Hood's army, widely rumored to be dire, and second to draw troops from it, if possible, to help resist Sherman's pending drive through the Carolinas. He set out on the last day of the year, armed with authority from Davis to replace Hood with Richard Taylor if in his judgment a change in commanders was required. At Macon, three days later, he received two dispatches from Hood, both encouraging. One was nearly three weeks old, having been sent from Spring Hill on December 17, the morrow of the two-day fight at the gates of the Tennessee capital. In it Hood admitted the loss of "fifty pieces of artillery, with several ordnance wagons," but added flatly: "Our loss in killed and wounded is very small." The other message, dated January 3 and wired from Corinth, was quite as welcome. "The army has recrossed the Tennessee River without material loss since the battle in front of Nashville. It will be assembled in a few days in the vicinity of Tupelo, to be supplied with shoes and clothing, and to obtain forage for the animals." A few days later, still pressing westward by a roundabout route on the crippled railroads, Beauregard received a more detailed report, dated January 9, in which Hood not only repeated his claim that his loss in killed and wounded had been light, but also declared that few were missing from other causes. "Our exact loss in prisoners I have not been able to ascertain," he wrote, "but do not think it great."

Considerably reassured by what he had heard from Hood in the course of his balky two-week ride from Charleston, the Louisianan reached Tupelo on January 15 to find his worst fears confirmed by his first sight of the Army of Tennessee in the two months since he parted from it at Tuscumbia, about to set out in balmy weather on a march designed to carry the war to the Ohio. Now only about 15,000 infantry were on hand, huddled miserably in their camps, and of these fewer than half had shoes or blankets to help them withstand the coldest winter the Deep South had known for years. In shock from the sudden fall of the scales from his eyes, Beauregard saw in their faces the horror of Franklin and in their bearing the ravage of the long retreat that followed their rout on the near bank of the Cumberland. He looked at the tattered, shattered ranks, the shot-torn flags and gunless batteries, and could scarcely recognize what he himself had once commanded. "If not, in the strictest sense of the word, a disorganized mob," he later wrote, "it was no longer an army." Rage at Hood for having misled him so grievously these past three weeks, in slanted and delayed reports, gave way in part to sadness when he realized that the distortion had proceeded, not so much from deception, as from embarrassment; not so much from confusion, even, as from shame. Still, it was clear enough that the Kentucky-born Texan had to go, and the sooner the better for all concerned. Hood in fact had already spared him the unpleasant ritual of demanding his resignation. "I respectfully request to be relieved from the command of this army," he had wired Seddon two days ago, and by now the Secretary's answer was on the way: "Your request is complied with. . . . Report to the War Department in Richmond."

Beauregard now had seen for himself the all-too-wretched condition of the main western force, and this seemed on the face of it to preclude action on the second purpose of his trip — the reinforcement of Bragg and Hardee for the defense of the Carolinas against Sherman. "An attempt to move Hood's army at this time would complete its destruction," Dick Taylor wired Davis from Meridian as he prepared to set out for Tupelo to assume command of what one of its members described as "the shattered debris of an army." Old Bory was inclined to agree: the more so because he found it necessary to grant immediate furloughs to some 3500 of the worse broken-down troops, while another 4000 had to be sent to Mobile to help meet what the local commander said was an all-out threat from Canby in New Orleans. Taylor replaced Hood on January 23, and Forrest next day was put in charge of the Department of Mississippi, East Louisiana, and West Tennessee, which he would defend with his three cavalry divisions, now detached. Returning stragglers by then had brought the army's total strength to 18,742 of all arms, including the furloughed men and those on their way to Mobile, whose deduction left only about 11,000 so-called effectives. Not only was this fewer, in all, than the number Beauregard had hoped to send East, but the bedraggled state of this remnant was such that both he and Taylor doubted whether the troops could survive the move from Tupelo to the Carolinas, even if the crippled railroads could manage to get them there before Sherman took up, or indeed completed, his northward drive on Richmond.

Both generals were mistaken, at least in regard to the first of these assessments. Like so many others down the years, they underestimated the toughness of this most resilient of Confederate armies, whose ability to survive mistreatment and defeat was rivaled only by the Army of the Potomac. Even as Taylor assumed command, Stephen Lee's corps — now under Stevenson, pending Lee's recovery from the wound he had suffered on the retreat — was loading aboard the cars, 3078 strong, for its eastern journey over the bucking strap-iron and rotted crossties of a dozen railroads. Despite the Creole's telegraphed protest that "to divide this small army at this juncture to reinforce General Hardee would expose to capture Mobile, Demopolis, Selma, Montgomery, and all the rich valley of the Alabama River," the War Department would neither cancel nor delay the transfer. Cheatham's corps left two days later, and part of Stewart's followed before the month was out. Taylor thus lost practically his whole army within a week of taking over from Hood. Including Forrest's troopers, the furloughed men, the strengthened Mobile garrison, and detachments scattered at random from the Mississippi River to the Georgia line, he retained in all perhaps as many as 30,000 troops for use against greatly superior possible combinations by Thomas, Canby, Washburn, and others. Few as that was, it still was better than five times the number headed east with Beauregard, who was recalled simultaneously to organize and take charge of the defense of the Carolinas.

He reached Augusta on February 1, the day Sherman set out in earnest from Savannah. That was well in advance of the first relay of reinforcements from the Army of Tennessee, who had a more circuitous route to follow. Cheatham's men, for example, after leaving Tupelo on foot, trudged to West Point, where they boarded the cars for Meridian, then changed for Selma and a steamboat ride from there to Montgomery, after which they went by rail again to Columbus, Georgia. From Columbus they marched through Macon and Milledgeville to Mayfield, where they took the cars for Augusta — ten days after Beauregard passed that way — then marched again to Newberry, South Carolina, for a reunion with Stevenson's corps, which had preceded them by a no less roundabout route. Presently, sixty miles across the state, Mrs Chesnut watched them pass through the streets of Camden. In proof of their unquenchable spirit they were singing as they swung along, and the sound of it nearly broke her heart, combined as it was with the thought of all they had been through in the grim three years since Donelson. "So sad and so stirring," she wrote in her diary at nearby Mulberry that night. "I sat down as women have done before and wept. Oh, the bitterness of such weeping! There they go, the gay and gallant few, the last flower of Southern manhood. They march with as airy a tread as if they still believed the world was all on their side, and that there were no Yankee bullets for the unwary."

She had seen their former commander some weeks before, at the end of January, when Hood stopped off in Columbia on his way to Richmond. He no more considered his war career at an end now than he had done after losing a leg at Chickamauga. "I wish to cross the Mississippi River to bring to your aid 25,000 troops," he wired his friend the President on leaving Tupelo. "I know this can be accomplished, and earnestly desire this chance to do you so much good service. Will explain my plan on arrival." Breaking his journey at the South Carolina capital — which no one yet suspected lay in Sherman's path — he visited the family of Brigadier General John S. Preston, whose daughter Sally he was engaged to marry and whose son Willie had been killed fighting under him at Atlanta. "He can stand well enough without his crutch," Mrs Chesnut observed, "but he does very slow walking. How plainly he spoke out those dreadful words, 'My defeat and discomfiture. My army destroyed. My losses.' He said he had nobody to blame but himself."

She found him changed, remote, profoundly grieved, and so did Sally's younger brother Jack, who took her aside to ask: "Did you notice how he stared in the fire, and the livid spots which came out on his face, and the huge drops of perspiration that stood out on his forehead?"

"Yes, he is going over some bitter hours," Mrs Chesnut said. "He sees Willie Preston with his heart shot out. He feels the panic at Nashville, and its shame."

"And the dead on the battlefield at Franklin," Jack agreed. "That agony in his face comes again and again. I can't keep him out of those absent fits.... When he looks in the fire and forgets me, and seems going through in his own mind the torture of the damned, I get up and come out as I did just now."

In and around Richmond — where Hood was headed with a scheme no more farfetched, and considerably less expensive, than the one that put him in motion for the Ohio, ten weeks back — R. E. Lee and his troops had just endured their worst hunger crisis of the war to date. Heavy January rains washed out trestles on the Piedmont Railroad, completed last year as a link between Danville and the western Carolinas, and floods at the same time cut off supplies from the upper valley of the James, obliging the army to fall back on its meager food reserve. Within two days Commissary General Lucius Northrop's storehouses were as empty as the men's bellies. Lee's anger flared. "If some change is not made and the commissary department reorganized," he protested to Seddon, "I apprehend dire results. The physical strength of the men, if their courage survives, must fail under this treatment." Davis saw the letter and added his endorsement: "This is too sad to be patiently considered, and cannot have occurred without criminal neglect or gross incapacity." In early February he followed through by replacing the detested Northrop with Colonel Isaac St John, who had performed near miracles in charge of the Nitre and Mining Corps. Promoted to brigadier, St John reorganized the system for delivering supplies from outlying regions and instigated a plan whereby a local farmer undertook to ration an individual soldier for six months: all of which helped to some degree, though not enough. Hunger, even starvation, was a specter that stalked the camps of the Army of Northern Virginia.

Lee fretted and sometimes fumed. "Unless the men and animals can be subsisted," he informed the government, "the army cannot be kept together, and our present lines must be abandoned. Nor can it be moved to any other position where it can operate to advantage without provisions to enable it to move in a body." The implications were clear. There could be but one end for an army that could neither remain where it was nor shift its ground. "Everything, in my opinion, has depended and still depends upon the disposition and feelings of the people. Their representatives can best decide how they will respond to the demands which the public safety requires." Invited to Richmond for a meeting with Virginia congressmen, he told them of his army's plight and repeated what he had said in his report. They replied with professions of loyalty and devotion, expressing a willingness to make any sacrifice required; but that was as far as it went. They had nothing to propose, either to Lee or anyone else, as to what the sacrifice might be. That night after supper, which he took in town with his eldest son Custis, a major general serving under Ewell in the capital defenses, Lee paced up and down the room, gravely troubled. Suddenly he stopped and faced his son, who was seated reading a newspaper by the fire. "Well, Mr Custis," he said angrily, "I have been up to see the Congress and they do not seem able to do anything except eat peanuts and chew tobacco, while my army is starving. I told them the condition my men were in, and that something must be done at once, but I can't get them to do anything." He fell silent, resumed his pacing, then came back. "Mr Custis, when this war began I was opposed to it, bitterly opposed to it, and I told these people that unless every man should do his whole duty, they would repent it. And now" — he paused — "they will repent."

Hunger distressed him, but so did the dwindling number of the hungry. His strength was below 50,000 mainly because of recent detachments which left him with barely more than a man per yard of his long line, including Ewell's reserve militia and the three divisions of troopers, most of whom were posted a hard day's ride or more away, where forage was available for their mounts. Following Hoke's departure for Wilmington, Lee declined a request from the War Department that he send Bushrod Johnson's division as well. "It will necessitate the abandonment of Richmond," he told Davis, who deferred as usual to his judgment in such matters. In early January, however, with Sherman in occupation of Savannah and Governor Andrew G. Magrath calling urgently for troops to reinforce Hardee, Lee sent him a veteran South Carolina brigade from Kershaw's division of Longstreet's corps. That was little enough, considering the risk, not only to Charleston but also to his own rear, if Sherman marched northward unchecked for a link-up with Grant at Petersburg. Still, it was all he felt he could afford, at any rate until Wade Hampton approached him soon afterward with a proposal that Calbraith Butler's troopers be sent to South Carolina for what remained of the winter, leaving their horses behind and procuring new ones for the harassment of the invader once they reached their native state. Lee scarcely enjoyed the notion of losing a solid third of his cavalry, even temporarily, but he saw in this at least a partial solution to the growing remount problem. Accordingly, on January 19 — his fifty-eighth birthday — after a conference with the President, he authorized the horseless departure of Butler's division by rail for the Palmetto State, "with the understanding that it is to return to me in the spring in time for the opening of the campaign." Moreover, having thought the matter through ("If Charleston falls, Richmond follows," Magrath had written; "Richmond may fall and Charleston be saved, but Richmond cannot be saved if Charleston falls") he ordered Hampton himself to go along, explaining to Davis that the South Carolina grandee, badly needed as he was at his Virginia post, would "be of service in mounting his men and arousing the spirit and strength of the State and otherwise do good."

With his chief of cavalry gone far south, along with a third of his veteran troopers — gone for good, events would show, though he did not know that yet — Lee could find small solace elsewhere, least of all in any hope of distracting the host that hemmed him in at Petersburg and Richmond. Off in the opposite direction, conditions were tactically even worse for Jubal Early out on the fringes of the Shenandoah Valley. Discredited and unhappy, down in strength to a scratch collection of infantry under Wharton, called by courtesy a division though it numbered barely a thousand men, and two slim brigades of cavalry under Rosser, he could only observe from a distance Sheridan's continued depredations, which consisted by now of little more than a stirring of dead coals. In mid-January, however, Rosser struck with 300 horsemen across the Alleghenies at Beverly, West Virginia, a supply depot guarded by two Ohio regiments, one of infantry, one of cavalry. At scant cost to himself, he killed or wounded 30 of the enemy and captured 580, along with a considerable haul of rations. Welcome as these last were to his hungry troopers, the raid was no more than a reminder of the days when Jeb Stuart had done such things, not so much to obtain a square meal as to justify his plume. George Crook, the outraged commander of the blue department, secured the dismissal of a pair of lieutenant colonels, heads of the two regiments, "in order that worthy officers may fill their places, which they have proved themselves incompetent to hold," but otherwise the Federals suffered nothing they could not easily abide: certainly not Sheridan, who was chafing beyond the mountains for a return to the main theater. He soon would receive and execute the summons, despite Old Jube, who was charged with trying to hold him where he was.

Meantime Grant did not relax for a moment his close-up hug on Lee's thirty-odd miles of line from the Williamsburg Road to Hatcher's Run. Though he had attempted no movement that might bring him to grips with his opponent since the early-December strike down the Weldon Railroad, no day passed without its long-range casualties and the guns were never silent; not even at night, when the spark-trickling fuzes of mortar bombs described their gaudy parabolas above the rebel earthworks. Boredom provoked strange responses, as when some outdone soldier on either side would leap atop the parapet and defy the marksmen on the other. But a more common phenomenon was the "good run of Johnnies" who came over — "rejoining the Union," they called it — while, across the way, one grayback complained that "the enemy drank coffee, ate fat, fresh beef and good bread, and drank quantities of whiskey, as their roarings at night testified." Reactions varied, up and down the trenches. "There are a good many of us who believe this shooting match had been carried on long enough," one Maryland Confederate declared. "A government that has run out of rations can't expect to do much more fighting and to keep on in a reckless and wanton expenditure of human life. Our rations are all the way from a pint to a quart of cornmeal a day, and occasionally a piece of bacon large enough to grease your palate." On the other hand, a North Carolinian regretted to hear that people back home were in despair over the loss of Fort Fisher. "If some of them could come up here and catch the good spirits of the soldiers," he wrote his family, "I think they would feel better."

Lee himself was a military realist, and as such he had said nine months ago, a month before Grant maneuvered him into immobility south of the James, that a seige could only end in defeat for his penned-up army. He had also shown, however, that as a fighter he was perhaps most dangerous when cornered. Long odds encouraged his fondness for long chances, and not even the present gloom was deep enough to suppress an occasional flash of his old aggressive outlook. "Cheer up, General," a Virginia representative told him on the Richmond visit; "we have done a good work for you today. The legislature has passed a bill to raise an additional 15,000 men for you." Lee did not seem heartened by the news. "Passing resolutions is kindly meant," he replied with a bow, "but getting the men is another matter." He paused, and in that moment his eye brightened. "Yet if I had 15,000 fresh troops, things would look very different," he said. Hope died hard in Lee, whose resolution was shared by those around him. "My faith in this old Army is unshaken," a young staff colonel wrote his sweetheart at the time, adding: "Like a brave old lion brought to bay at last, it is determined to resist to the death and, if die it must, to die game. But we have not quite made up our minds to die, and if God will help us we shall yet prove equal to the emergency."

In essence, that was the view Jefferson Davis applied to the whole Confederacy. He had never embraced the notion that, without allies, the South could win an offensive war against the North; but this was not to say that her people could not confirm her independence for all time, provided they stood firm in the conviction that sustained their forebears in the original Revolution. What had worked for that other infant nation would work for this one. Moreover, once its enemy came to understand that defeat did not necessarily mean submission, that nothing much short of annihilation could translate conquest into victory, a nation willing to "die game" was unlikely to have to die at all. That had been at the root of his November claim that "not the fall of Richmond, nor Wilmington, nor Charleston, nor Savannah, nor Mobile, nor of all combined, can save the enemy from the constant and exhaustive drain of blood and treasure which must continue until he shall discover that no peace is attainable unless based on the recognition of our indefeasible rights." Since then, Savannah had fallen, and Wilmington and Charleston were directly threatened, as Mobile had been for the past six months and Richmond had been from the outset. Yet even here there was comfort for those who saw as Davis and Lee's young colonel did. As the odds lengthened, the margin for choice narrowed; the grimmer the prospect, the readier the people would be to accept their leader's view that resolution meant survival; or so he believed at any rate. After all, the only alternative was surrender, and he considered them no more ready for that than he was, now or ever.

Throughout January, while Sherman reposed in Savannah, letters and telegrams with the familiar signature *Jeff'n Davis* went out to Beauregard, Taylor, Bragg, and Hardee, as well as to the governors of North and South Carolina, Georgia, Alabama, and Mississippi, urging mutual support in the present crisis and vigorous preparation for the day when the tiger unsheathed his claws and started north. Not even Kirby Smith, remote and all but inaccessible, was overlooked as a possible source of borrowed strength. "Under these circumstances," Davis wrote him, stressing the massive Federal shift of troops from west to east, "I think it advisable that you should be charged with military operations on both banks of the Mississippi, and that you should endeavor as promptly as possible to cross that river with as large a force as may be prudently withdrawn." Nothing was likely to come of this; nor did it; yet when Hood showed up the following month, big with his plan for recruiting volunteers in his adoptive Texas, Davis gladly approved the mission and sent him on his Quixotic way, reduced to his previous rank of lieutenant general. Another defeated hero who returned at the same time, Raphael Semmes, was also welcomed and employed. Crossing the Atlantic in late October, four months after he fought and lost the famous channel duel off Cherbourg, he landed at Matamoros, Mexico, then worked his way on a wide swing east from Brownsville to his home in Mobile, where he rested before pushing on to Richmond, saddened by the devastation he saw had been visited on the land since his departure in the summer of '61. Promoted to rear admiral, he was given command of the James River squadron, though Davis in turn was saddened by his inability to award the former captain of the *Alabama* with anything more substantial than three small ironclads and five wooden gunboats, which collectively were no match for a single enemy monitor and in fact could do little more than support the forts and batteries charged with guarding the water approach to the capital in their rear.

Intent as he was on gathering and bracing his scattered and diminished armies for the shock of an eastern Armageddon, Davis had the still harder concomitant task of preparing the nation at large for survival after the defeat made probable by the odds. He too was a military realist, in his way, and as such he knew that, far more important than the loss of any battle — even one on such a promised cataclysmic scale as this — was the possible loss of the will to fight by those behind the lines. There was where wars were ultimately won or lost, and already there were signs that this will, though yet unbroken, was about to crumble. "It is not unwillingness to oppose the enemy," Governor Magrath informed him from threatened South Carolina, "but a chilling apprehension of the futility of doing so which affects the people." Just so: and Davis took as his chief responsibility, as the people's leader, the task of replacing this chill with the warmth of resolution. Whatever the odds, whatever the losses, he believed that so long as they had that, to anything like the degree that he possessed it, their desperate bid for membership in the family of nations could never be annulled.

His need to rally the public behind him had never been more

acute, but neither had it ever been more stringently opposed by his political adversaries, who saw in the current dilemma a fulfillment of all the woes they had predicted from the outset if Congress continued to let him have his way on such issues as conscription and the periodic suspension of the writ of habeas corpus, in violation of the rights not only of the states but also of individuals. Under the press of circumstance, Davis by now had gone beyond such preconceptions. "If the Confederacy falls," he told one congressman in a fruitless effort to bring him over, "there should be written on its tombstone, *Died of a Theory*."

That might be; still, the hard-line States Righters could not see it. Desist from such wicked practices, they were saying, and volunteers would flock again to the colors in numbers sufficient to fling the invader back across the Mason-Dixon line. Yet here was the Chief Executive, clearly seeking to move toward the arming of the slaves, with emancipation to follow as the worst of all possible violations of the rights they held dearest. "What did we go to war for, if not to protect our property?" R. M. T. Hunter wanted to know. A Virginian, he was president pro tempore of the Senate and one of its largest slave-holders, known privately to favor a return to the Union on terms likely to be gentler now than after the South's defeat, which the present crisis had convinced him was inevitable. Some colleagues agreed, while others believed the war could still be won if the Commander in Chief only had men around him who knew how to go about it. In mid-January, accordingly, Speaker of the House Thomas Bocock, after conferring with other Virginia members of that body, informed the President that his state desired a complete change in the Cabinet, all but Treasury Secretary George A. Trenholm, who had succeeded his fellow South Carolinian Christopher Memminger in July; otherwise they would put through a vote of censure that might bring the Government down. Davis had no intention of yielding to this unconstitutional threat, but the maneuver was partly successful anyhow, paradoxically costing him — and them — the only remaining member of his official family from the Old Dominion. Affronted by this slur from representatives of his native state, and wearied by two years and two months of almost constant tribulation, James Seddon promptly submitted his resignation and declined to withdraw it, only consenting to remain through the end of the month and thus give his successor, Kentuckian John C. Breckinridge, time to clear up matters in his Department of Southwest Virginia before coming to Richmond to take over as the Confederacy's fifth Secretary of War.

Under pressure, men responded in accordance with their lights. Some were convinced the time had come for one-man rule, not by Davis but by Lee, the one leader they believed could "guide the country through its present crisis." This went up in smoke, however, when Representative William C. Rives, a fellow Virginian and chairman of the

Committee on Foreign Affairs, went to the general with the proposal carefully worded to lessen the shock. Lee reacted as he might have done if presented with a gift-wrapped rattlesnake. Not only did he consider this man-on-horseback scheme a reflection on his loyalty as a soldier and a citizen, he also sent back word by Rives "that if the President could not save the country, no one could." Others were busy on their own. One-time U.S. Supreme Court Justice John A. Campbell of Alabama, for example, having failed to stave off war by his negotiations with Seward over Sumter, four years back, was in correspondence with a former associate, Supreme Court Justice Samuel Nelson of New York, "proposing to visit him [in Washington] and confer," a confidant noted, "with a view to ascertaining whether there is any way of putting an end to the war and suggesting conference, if Judge Nelson thinks it may lead to any good result, to be held by Judge Campbell with Mr Stanton or one or two other leading men." Supporters of Joe Johnston also stepped up their clamor for his reinstatement at this time, partly as a way of striking at the Administration, while some among them favored more drastic methods. "One solution which I have heard suggested," a War Department official confided in his diary, "is an entire change of the Executive by the resignation of the President and Vice President. This would make Hunter, as president of the Senate, the President, would really make Lee commander-in-chief, and would go far to restore lost confidence."

Davis was spared at least one measure of exacerbation through this period by the absence of his long-time stump opponent Henry Stuart Foote, who had defeated him in a Mississippi race for governor ten years before the war, but now represented a Tennessee district in Congress, where he fulminated alternately against the Yankees and the government. Arrested in early January while trying to cross the Potomac, he announced that he had been on his way to Washington to sue for peace and deliver his people from despotism. On his release, a vote to expel him from the House having failed for lack of a two-thirds majority, he struck out again. This time he made it all the way to Canada, only to find that no Federal authority would treat with him: whereupon he sailed for London, and there issued a manifesto calling on his constituents to secede from the Confederacy and again find freedom in the Union.

Good riddance, friends of the President said. But such relief as his departure brought was more than offset by the simultaneous reappearance of Alexander Stephens, who reacted in just the opposite way to a gloom as deep as Foote's. Instead of entering, he emerged from exile to lead a headlong attack on the Administration, not only for its failure to check Sherman's march through his beloved Georgia, but also for all its previous sins of omission and commission. Resuming his vice-presidential chore of presiding over the Senate, he arrived in time to cast the deciding vote restoring habeas corpus, then moved on to deliver a ringing speech in which he arraigned the government for incompetence, slack judgment, and despotic arrogance at all levels. The war having failed, he called for the removal of Davis or, short of impeachment, the opening of direct negotiations for peace with Washington, ignoring the Executive entirely, since there could be no end to the fighting so long as the present leader remained in control of the nation's destiny. Thus Stephens, whom Davis in friendlier days had referred to as "the little pale star from Georgia," and the Richmond *Examiner* took up the cry in its January 17 issue, urging the assembly of a convention to abolish the Constitution and remove the Chief Executive from office, both in preparation for a return to principles long since betrayed by those in whom the people, to their current dismay, had placed their trust.

On that same day Virginia's General Assembly passed and sent to the President a resolution calling for the appointment of R. E. Lee as commander of all the Confederate armies, on grounds that this would promote their efficiency, reanimate their spirit, and "inspire increased confidence in the final success of our arms." Though Davis saw the request as an attempt to infringe on his constitutional designation as Commander in Chief, he handled the matter tactfully in a letter to Lee, asking whether he wished to undertake this larger duty "while retaining command of the Army of Northern Virginia." Lee promptly replied that he did not. "If I had the ability I would not have the time.... I am willing to undertake any service to which you think proper to assign me, but I do not wish you to be misled as to the extent of my capacity." This was written on January 19, but Davis had known so well what Lee would say that he had not waited for an answer. His letter of response to the Assembly had gone out the day before. Thanking the members for their suggestion, as well as for "the uncalculating, unhesitating spirit with which Virginia has, from the moment when she first drew the sword, consecrated the blood of her children and all her natural resources to the achievement of the object of our struggle," he assured them "that whenever it shall be found practicable by General Lee to assume command of all the Armies of the Confederate States, without withdrawing from the direct command of the Army of Northern Virginia, I will deem it promotive of the public interest to place him in such command, and will be happy to know that by so doing I am responding to [your] expressed desire."

That more or less took care of that; or should have, except that the issue would not die. While the Virginians were framing their request, the Confederate Senate — by a 14–2 vote, January 16 — passed a resolution not only favoring Lee's elevation to general-in-chief, but also proposing that Beauregard take charge in South Carolina and that Johnston be restored to command of the Army of Tennessee. Varina Davis was indignant at this attempt to clip her husband's presidential wings. "If I were he," she told one cornered senator, "I would die or be hung before I would submit to the humiliation that Congress intended him." Davis himself had no intention of complying with the resolution, which landed on his desk a few days later. For one thing, he had just disposed of the Lee question, at least to his and the general's satisfaction, and Beauregard was already slated to assume the recommended post on his return from Mississippi, where he was busy turning Hood's army over to Richard Taylor. As for Johnston, Davis was presently engaged in composing a 5000-word survey of that other Virginian's war career from First Manassas to Peachtree Creek, a thorny indictment rounded off with a brief summation: "My opinion of General Johnston's unfitness for command has ripened slowly and against my inclination into a conviction so settled that it would be impossible for me again to feel confidence in him as the commander of an army in the field." Moreover, the lengthy document would close with a final cutting answer to those critics who sought to curtail the Chief Executive's military prerogatives. "The power to assign generals to appropriate duties is a function of the trust confided in me by my countrymen. That trust I have ever been ready to resign at my country's call; but, while I hold it, nothing shall induce me to shrink from its responsibilities or to violate the obligations it imposes."

He would not bow to the three-count resolution. However, now that Lee's deferential reply to the recent feeler had been received, he saw a chance for a compromise that would cost him nothing, either in principle or in practical application, yet would serve to placate his congressional foes, at least in part, and would also, as the Virginia members put it, "inspire increased confidence in the final success of our arms." Accordingly, on January 26 he gladly signed, apparently with no thought of the predicted veto, an act that had passed both houses three days ago, providing for the appointment of a Confederate general-in-chief. Congress of course had Lee in mind, and on the last day of the month Davis recommended his appointment, which the Senate quickly approved. Lee's response, addressed to Adjutant General Samuel Cooper, was something of a snub to the politicians who had worked for his elevation. "I am indebted alone to the kindness of His Excellency the President for my nomination to this high and arduous office," he declared, and a final sentence indicated how little he was likely to assert his independence at the post: "As I have received no instructions as to my duties, I do not know what he desires for me to undertake." To Davis himself, soon afterward, Lee expressed his thanks for "your indulgence and kind consideration.... I must beg you to continue these same feelings to me in the future and allow me to refer to you at all times for counsel and advice. I cannot otherwise hope to be of service to you or the country. If I can relieve you from a portion of the constant labor and anxiety which now presses upon you, and maintain a harmonious action between the great armies, I shall be more than compensated for the addition to my present burdens." This was no more and no less than Davis had expected. Not to be outdone in graciousness, he replied: "The honor designed to be bestowed has been so fully won, that the fact of conferring it can add nothing to your fame."

Greeted with enthusiasm, Lee's appointment encouraged many waverers to hope that his genius, which had transformed near-certain defeat into triumph in Virginia two and one half years ago, would now work a like miracle on a larger scale; the man who had saved beleaguered Richmond from McClellan, flinging him back in confusion, first on his gunboats and then on his own capital, would save the beleaguered Confederacy from Grant. But Davis knew only too well that the confirmed defeatists — men like Hunter, Campbell, and Stephens — were not converted by this stroke, which after all was of the pen and not the sword. They were for peace, peace *now*, and would not believe that anyone, even Robert E. Lee, could do anything more than stave off defeat and thus make the terms for surrender that much stiffer when it came. Above all, they and the Impossiblists, who wanted him removed for other reasons, mainly having to do with his overriding of States Rights, believed that Davis would never consent to the mildest compromise the Union authorities might offer, not only because of his known conviction that the loss of the war meant the loss of honor, but also because of his personal situation as the leader of a failed rebellion. "We'll hang Jeff Davis on a sour apple tree!" blue-clad troops were singing now, to the tune of *John Brown's Body*, and Republican politicians were saying much the same thing, in words as harsh and even more specific, from stumps all over the North, to wild applause.

Davis knew this, and knew as well that he had to find some way to answer and, if possible, discredit his domestic critics before he could unite the nation to meet the impending crisis. But how? He watched and waited. Then it came: from Lincoln, of all people — or, more specifically, Old Man Blair.

Blair, that long-time adviser to all the Presidents back through Jackson, wanted to add one more to his list in the person of Jefferson Davis, who had been his friend for more than twenty years, but was now beyond his reach. Or perhaps not. Approaching seventy-four, the distinguished Marylander hoped to crown a life of public service with a trip to Richmond for the purpose of persuading Davis to treat for peace and thereby end the war. In mid-December, shortly after Sherman reached the coast, Blair went to Lincoln and asked permission to make the trip. "Come to me after Savannah falls," the President told him; which he did, and on December 28 was handed a card inscribed, "Allow the bearer, F. P. Blair, Senr. to pass our lines, go South and return. A. Lincoln."

He left at once, and on December 30 sent Davis two letters from Grant's headquarters at City Point. One was brief, requesting admission to the Confederacy to search for some title papers missing since Jubal Early's July visit to his home in Silver Spring. The other, considerably longer, remarked that the first would serve as a cover for his true purpose, which was to "unbosom my heart frankly and without reserve" on matters regarding the "state of affairs of our country." He was "wholly unaccredited," he said, but he hoped to offer certain "suggestions" he believed would be of interest.

There were delays. Davis recognized another peace feeler, and though he did not expect to find anything advantageous in the exchange under present circumstances, he knew that a refusal to see the Washington emissary was apt to bring still heavier charges of intransigence on his head. Besides, his wife encouraged the visit for old times' sake. In the end he wrote the elder statesman to come on, and Blair did. Lodged unregistered at the Spotswood on January 12, he came that evening to the White House, where Mrs Davis met him with a hug.

Alone with Davis in the presidential study, he elaborated on what he had meant by "suggestions." In brief, his plan was for the North and South to observe a cessation of hostilities for such time as it might take to drive the French and their puppet Maximilian out of Mexico, possibly with none other than Jefferson Davis in command of the joint expeditionary force; after which the two former combatants, flushed with victory from their common vindication of the Monroe Doctrine, could sit down and discuss their various differences in calm and dignity. Davis did not think highly of the plan, mainly because it sounded to him like one of Seward's brainstorms, concocted for some devious purpose. Blair replied that the crafty New Yorker had had and would have no part in the matter. "The transaction is a military transaction, and depends entirely on the Commander in Chief." Whatever Seward's shortcomings, which admittedly were many, Lincoln was altogether trustworthy, Blair declared. Davis said he was glad to hear it. In point of fact, he added, he was willing now, and always had been, to enter into negotiations for ending the war by this or any other honorable method, and in demonstration of his sincerity he drafted a letter for Blair to take back and show Lincoln. "Notwithstanding the rejection of our former offers," the letter read in closing, "I would, if you could promise that a commission, minister, or other agent would be received, appoint one immediately, and renew the effort to enter into a conference with a view to secure peace to the two countries."

Back in Washington, Blair had a second interview with Lincoln on January 18. After giving him Davis's letter to read he reported that he had seen a number of prominent Confederates in the southern capital, many of them friends of long standing, and had found them for the most part despondent about the outcome of the war. Lincoln appeared more interested in this last than in the letter, which seemed to him to promise little in the way of progress, but in the end gave Blair a letter of his own, in indirect answer to the one from Davis. "You may say to him that I have constantly been, am now, and shall continue, ready to receive any agent whom he, or any other influential person now resisting the national authority, may informally send to me with the view of securing peace to the people of our one common country."

There in the final words of the paired notes — "the two countries": "our one common country" — the impasse was defined and, paradoxically, the maneuvering began in earnest: not so much between the two leaders, though there was of course that element in what followed, as between them and their respective home-front adversaries. Blair went back to Richmond four days later, then returned, his part complete, and newspapers North and South began to speculate frantically on what might come of the old man's go-between travels back and forth. Southern journalists accused Davis of near treason for having entertained a "foreign enemy" in the White House, while those who were for peace at almost any price expressed fears that he had rejected an offer to end the war on generous terms. Conversely, up in Washington, the Jacobins set up a hue and cry that Lincoln was about to stop the fighting just short of the point where they could begin to exact the vengeance they saw as their due from the rebellion. Each of the two Presidents thus had much to fret him while playing their game of high-stakes international poker, and they functioned in different styles: different not only from each other, but also different each from what he had been before. During this diplomatic interlude, Lincoln and Davis — fox and hedgehog — swapped roles. Lincoln remained prickly and unyielding, almost stolid, though always willing to engage on his own terms as he defined them. It was Davis who was foxy, secretive and shifty, quick to snap.

He began by inviting the Vice President to a consultation — their first since the government moved to Richmond, nearly four years ago — at which he showed him Lincoln's letter, reviewed its background, and requested an opinion. Stephens replied that he thought the matter should be pursued, "at least so far as to obtain if possible a conference upon the subject." Asked for recommendations on the makeup of the proposed commission, he suggested the Chief Executive as the most effective member, then added the names of several men who were known to be as strong for peace as he was, including John A. Campbell, the former Supreme Court Justice, now Assistant Secretary of War. Davis thanked him for his time and trouble, and next day, January 25, summoned the chosen three to his office. They were Campbell, Robert Hunter — who presided over the Senate, as president pro tem, in the Vice President's frequent absences — and Stephens himself. The frail Georgian protested but was overruled, and all three were handed their instructions: "In conformity with the letter of Mr Lincoln, of which the foregoing is a copy, you are requested to proceed to Washington City for an informal conference with him upon the issues involved in the existing war, and for the purpose of securing peace to the two countries."

There again were the critical words, "two countries." Judah Benjamin in the original draft had written, "for conference with him upon the subject to which it relates," but Davis had made the revision, not wanting to leave the trio of known "submissionists" any leeway when they reached the conference table. He knew well enough how little was likely to come of the effort with this stipulation attached, though he did not go into that at present. He merely informed the commissioners that they would set out four days from now, on Sunday the 29th, passing beyond the farthest Petersburg outworks under a flag of truce, presumably bound for Washington and a talk with Lincoln about the chances of ending the war without more bloodshed.

※ 3 ※

And so it was. Due east of Petersburg on that designated Sunday, near the frost-rimed scar of the Crater, a white flag appeared on the rebel parapet and a messenger came over with a letter addressed to Lieutenant General U. S. Grant. Word spread up and down the opposing lines that something was up; something important, from the look of things — something that maybe had to do with peace.

As it turned out, there was plenty of time for speculation. Grant was down the coast, looking over the Wilmington defenses with Schofield, who was to move against them as soon as his transports could descend the ice-jammed Potomac. By the time a fast packet got the flag-of-truce message to Fort Fisher, and word came back that the applicants were to be admitted and lodged at headquarters pending Grant's return, two days had passed. Then at last, on the final afternoon in January, a carriage bearing the three would-be commissioners came rolling out the Jerusalem Plank Road, which was lined with gray-clad soldiers and civilians, and on to an opening in the works, which were crowded left and right, as far as the eye could follow — northward to the Appomattox and south toward Fort Hell and Fort Damnation — with spectators who jammed the parapets for a look at what some were saying meant an end to all the killing. Across the way, the Union works were crowded too, and when the carriage turned and began to jolt eastward over the shell-pocked ground between the trenches, a roar of approval went up from opposite sides of the line of battle. "Our men cheered loudly," Meade would write his wife that night, "and the soldiers on both sides cried out lustily, 'Peace! Peace!'" Blue and gray alike, west and east of that no-man's land the carriage rocked across, spokes twinkling in the sunlight, men swung their hats and hollered for all they were worth. "Cheer upon cheer was given," a Federal artillerist would recall, "extending for some distance to the right and left of the lines, each side trying to cheer the loudest. 'Peace on the brain' appeared now to have spread like a contagion. Officers of all grades, from lieutenants to major generals, were to be seen flying in all directions to catch a glimpse of the gentlemen who were apparently to bring peace so unexpectedly."

Grant had returned by then, and though he saw to it that the three Confederates were made comfortable on a headquarters steamer tied up at the City Point wharf, he was careful not to discuss their mission with them. Which was just as well, since he received next morning a wire from the Commander in Chief, warning against any slackening of vigilance or effort on his part. "Let nothing which is transpiring change, hinder, or delay your military movements or plans," Lincoln told him, and Grant replied: "There will be no armistice in consequence of the presence of Mr Stephens and others within our lines. The troops are kept in readiness to move at the shortest notice if occasion should justify it." That afternoon Major Thomas Eckert, who normally had charge of the War Department telegraph office in Washington, arrived with instructions from the President to interview the proposed commissioners. Seward was on his way to Fort Monroe, and Eckert was to send them there to talk with him, provided they would state in writing that they had come for the purpose Lincoln had specified; that is, "with a view of securing peace to the people of our one common country."

Eckert saw them that evening. One look at their instructions quickly convinced him the main condition was unmet. At 9.30 he wired Washington, "I notified them that they could not proceed."

That seemed to be that; another peace effort no sooner launched than sunk. Lincoln inclined to that view next morning, February 2, when he received a somewhat puzzled telegram Seward had sent last night from Fort Monroe: "Richmond party not here." Eckert's followed, explaining the holdup. Lincoln was about to recall them both, ending the mission, when Stanton came in with a message just off the wire from Grant, a long and earnest plea that negotiations go forward despite Eckert's disapproval. In it, the general seemed to have come under the influence of the contagion that infected his soldiers, two days ago, while they watched the rebel carriage approach their lines. He had had a letter from and a brief talk with two of the Confederates, following Eckert's refusal to let them proceed, and he had been favorably impressed. "I will state confidentially, but not officially to become a matter of record," he wired Stanton, "that I am convinced, upon conversation with Messrs Stephens and Hunter, that their intentions are good and their desire sincere to restore peace and union.... I fear now their going back without any expression from anyone in authority will have a bad influence." He himself did not feel free to treat with them, of course; "I am sorry however that Mr Lincoln cannot have an interview with the two named in this dispatch, if not all three now within our lines. Their letter to me was all the President's instructions contemplated to secure their safe conduct if they had used the same language to Major Eckert."

For Lincoln, this put a different face on the matter. He got off two wires at once. One was to Seward, instructing him to remain where he was. The other was to Grant. "Say to the gentlemen I will meet them personally at Fortress Monroe as soon as I can get there."

He left within the hour, not even taking time to notify his secretary or any remaining member of his cabinet, and by nightfall was with Seward aboard the steamer *River Queen*, riding at anchor under the guns of Fort Monroe. The rebel commissioners were on a nearby vessel, also anchored in Hampton Roads; Seward had not seen them yet, and Lincoln sent word that he would receive them next morning in the *Queen*'s saloon. His instructions to the Secretary of State had been brief and to the point, listing three "indispensable" conditions for peace. One was "restoration of the national authority throughout all the states"; another was that there be no "receding" on the slavery question; while the third provided for "no cessation of hostilities short of the end of the war, and the disbanding of all forces hostile to the government." Lincoln considered himself bound by these terms as well, and had no intention of yielding on any of them, whatever else he might agree to.

The Confederates were punctual, coming aboard shortly after breakfast Friday morning, February 3. Handshakes and an exchange of amenities, as between old friends, preceded any serious discussion. "Governor, how is the Capitol? Is it finished?" Hunter asked. Seward described the new dome and the big brass door, much to the interest of the visitors, all three of whom had spent a good part of their lives in Washington, Campbell as a High Court justice, Hunter as a senator, and Stephens as a nine-term congressman. Lincoln was particularly drawn to the last of these, having admired him when they served together in the House at the time of the Mexican War, which they both opposed. "A little, slim, pale-faced, consumptive man," he called him then, writing home that his fellow Whig had "just concluded the very best speech of an hour's length I ever heard." Stephens, though still pale-faced, seemed to have put on a great deal of weight in the past few years; that is until he took off a voluminous floor-length overcoat fashioned from blanket-thick cloth, a long wool muffler, and several shawls wound round and round his waist and chest against the cold. Then it was clear that he had not added an ounce of flesh to his ninety-four pounds of skin and bones. "Never have I seen so small a nubbin come out of so much husk," Lincoln said with a smile as they shook hands.

That too helped to break the ice, and when the five took seats in the saloon, conversing still of minor things, the Union President and Confederate Vice President spoke of their days as colleagues, sixteen years ago. There had been a welcome harmony between the states and sections then, Stephens remarked, and followed with a question that went to the heart of the matter up for discussion: "Mr President, is there no way of putting an end to the present trouble?" Lincoln responded in kind, echoing the closing words of his recent message to Congress. "There is but one way," he said, "and that is for those who are resisting the laws of the Union to cease that resistance." Although this was plain enough, so far as it went, Stephens wanted to take it further. "But is there no other question," he persisted, "that might divert the attention of both parties for a time?" Lincoln saw that the Georgian was referring to the Mexico scheme, about which he himself had known nothing until Blair's return from Richmond, and declared that it had been proposed without the least authority from him. "The restoration of the Union is a *sine qua non* with me," he said; anything that was to follow had to follow that. Stephens took this to mean that a Confederate pledge for reunion must precede such action, and maintained that it was unneeded. "A settlement of the Mexican question in this way would necessarily lead to a peaceful settlement of our own." But that was not what Lincoln had meant — as he now made clear. He would make no agreement of any kind, he said, until the question of reunion was disposed of once and for all. That had to come first, if only because he could never agree to bargain with men in arms against the government in his care. Hunter, who had preceded Benjamin as Secretary of State and prided himself on a wide knowledge of international precedents, remarked at this point that Charles I of England had dealt with his domestic foes in just that way. Lincoln looked askance at the Virginian, then replied: "Upon questions of history I must refer you to Mr Seward, for he is posted in such things. My only distinct recollection of the matter is that Charles lost his head."

Hunter subsided, at least for a time, and the talk moved on to other concerns. Campbell, ever the jurist, wanted to know what the northern authorities had in mind to do, when and if the Union was restored, about southern representation in Congress, the two Virginias, and wartime confiscation of property, including slaves. Lincoln and Seward, between them, dealt with the problems one by one. Congress of course would rule on its own as to who would be admitted to a seat in either house. West Virginia was and would remain a separate state. As for compensation, both considered it likely that Congress would be lenient in its handling of property claims once the war fever cooled down, and Lincoln added that he would employ Executive clemency where he could, though he had no intention of revoking the Emancipation Proclamation, which was still to be tested in the courts. At this point Seward broke the news of the Thirteenth Amendment, approved while the commissioners were entering Grant's lines three days ago, and Lincoln remarked that he still favored some form of compensation by the government for the resultant loss in slaves — provided, of course, that Congress would go along, upon ratification, and vote the money for payment to former owners; which seemed unlikely, considering the present reported mood and makeup of that body.

All this came as a considerable shock to the three rebel listeners, but the shock was mild compared to what followed when Hunter, having recovered a measure of his aplomb, expressed their reaction in a question designed to demonstrate just how brutally intransigent such terms were. "Mr President, if we understand you correctly, you think that we of the Confederacy have committed treason; that we are traitors to your government; that we have forfeited our rights, and are proper subjects for the hangman. Is that not about what your words imply?" There was a pause while they waited for Lincoln's answer, and presently he gave it. "Yes," he said. "You have stated the proposition better than I did. That is about the size of it."

That remained about the size of it throughout the four-hour exchange in the *River Queen* saloon. He was unyielding, and though he told a couple of tension-easing stories — causing Hunter to observe with a wry smile, "Well, Mr Lincoln, we have about concluded that we shall not be hanged as long as you are President: if we behave ourselves" — the most he offered was a promise to use Executive clemency when the time came, so far at least as Congress would allow it. The Confederates, bound as they were by their own leader's "two countries" stipulation, could offer quite literally nothing at all, and so the conference wound down to a close.

Amid the flurry of parting handshakes, Lincoln said earnestly: "Well, Stephens, there has been nothing we could do for our country. Is there anything I can do for you personally?" Little Aleck, once more immured within his bulky overcoat and wrappers, shook his head. "Nothing," he said. But then he had a thought. "Unless you can send me my nephew who has been for twenty months a prisoner on Johnson's Island." Lincoln brightened at the chance. "I'll be glad to do it. Let me have his name." He wrote the name in a notebook, and that was how it came about that Lieutenant John A. Stephens, captured at Vicksburg in mid-'63, was removed from his Lake Erie island prison camp and brought to Washington the following week for a meeting with the President at the White House. Lincoln gave him a pass through the Union lines and a photograph of himself as well, saying of the latter: "You had better take that along. It is considered quite a curiosity down your way, I believe."

Young Stephens and the photograph were about all the South got out of the shipboard conference in Hampton Roads, except for an appended gift from the Secretary of State. Reaching their own steamer the commissioners looked back and saw a rowboat coming after them, its only occupant a Negro oarsman. He brought them a basket of champagne and a note with Seward's compliments. As they waved their handkerchiefs in acknowledgment and thanks, they saw the genial New Yorker standing on the deck of the *Queen,* a bosun's trumpet held to his mouth. "Keep the champagne," they heard him call to them across the water, "but return the Negro."

Stephens, Hunter, and Campbell spent another night tied up to the wharf at City Point, and then next day recrossed the Petersburg lines, their mission ended. "Today they returned to Richmond," Meade wrote his wife that evening, "but what was the result of their visit no one knows. At the present moment, 8 p.m., the artillery on our lines is in full blast, clearly proving that at this moment there is no peace."

★ ★ ★

A basket of wine, supplemented in time by a homesick Georgia lieutenant bearing a photograph of Lincoln, seemed a small return for the four-day effort by the three commissioners, who came back in something resembling a state of shock from having learned that negotiations were to follow, not precede, capitulation. Davis, however, was far from disappointed at the outcome. His double-barreled purpose — to discredit the submissionists and unite the country behind him by having them elicit the northern leader's terms for peace — had been fulfilled even beyond a prediction made in the local *Enquirer* while the conference was in progress down the James. "We think it likely to do much good," the editor wrote, "for our people to understand in an authoritative manner from men like Vice President Stephens, Senator Hunter, and Judge Campbell the exact degree of degradation to which the enemy would reduce us by reconstruction. We believe that the so-called mission of these gentlemen will teach our people that the terms of the enemy are nothing less than unconditional surrender." Now that this had been borne out, Davis used much the same words in a note attached to a formal report of the proceedings, submitted to Congress on the Monday after the Saturday the three envoys reappeared in Richmond: "The enemy refused to enter into negotiations with the Confederate States, or with any of them separately, or to give to our people any other terms or guaranties than those which the conqueror may grant, or to permit us to have [peace] on any other basis than our unconditional submission to their rule."

Wasting no time, he struck while the propaganda iron was hot. Amid the rush of indignation at the news from Hampton Roads, Virginia's redoubtable Extra Billy called a meeting at Metropolitan Hall that same evening, February 6, to afford the public a chance to adopt resolutions condemning the treatment its representatives had received three days ago, on board the *River Queen,* at the hands of the northern leader and his chief lieutenant. Robert Hunter was one of the speakers. "If anything was wanted to stir the blood," he informed the close-packed gathering, "it was furnished when we were told that the United States could not consent to entertain any proposition coming from us as a people. Lincoln might have offered *some*thing.... No treaty, no stipulation, no agreement, either with the Confederate States jointly or with them separately: what was this but unconditional submission to the mercy of the conquerors?"

The crowd rumbled its resentment, subsiding only to be aroused by other exhortations, then presently stirred with a different kind of excitement as a slim figure in worn gray homespun entered from Franklin Street, paused in the doorway, and started down the aisle. It was Davis. Governor Smith greeted the unexpected visitor warmly and escorted him to the platform, where he stood beside the lectern and looked out over the cheering throng. "A smile of strange sweetness came to his lips," one witness later wrote, "as if the welcome assured him that, decried as he was by the newspapers and pursued by the clamor of politicians, he had still a place in the hearts of his countrymen."

When the applause died down at last he launched into an hour-long oration which all who heard it agreed was the finest he ever delivered. Even Pollard of the *Examiner,* his bitterest critic south of the Potomac, noting "the shifting lights on the feeble, stricken face," declared afterwards that he had never "been so much moved by the power of words spoken for the same space of time." Others had a similar reaction, but no one outside the hall would ever know; Davis spoke from no text, not even notes, and the absence of a shorthand reporter caused this "appeal of surpassing eloquence" to be lost to all beyond range of his voice that night. Hearing and watching him, Pollard experienced "a strange pity, a strange doubt, that this 'old man eloquent' was the weak and unfit President" he had spent the past three years attacking. "Mr Davis frequently paused in his delivery; his broken health admonished him that he was attempting too much; but frequent cries of 'Go on' impelled him to speak at a length which he had not at first proposed.... He spoke with an even, tuneful flow of words, spare of gestures; his dilated form and a voice the lowest notes of which were distinctly audible, and which anon rose as a sound of a trumpet, were yet sufficient to convey the strongest emotions and to lift the hearts of his hearers to the level of his grand discourse."

Apparently the speech was in part a repetition of those he had made last fall, en route through Georgia and the Carolinas, in an attempt to whip up the flagging spirits of a people distressed by the loss of Atlanta. Now, as then, he praised the common soldier, decried the profiteer, and expressed the conviction that if half the absent troops would return to the ranks no force on earth could defeat the armies of the South. In any case, with or without these shirkers, he predicted that if the people would stand firm, the Confederacy would "compel the Yankees, in less than twelve months, to petition us for peace on our own terms." The darker the hour, the greater the honor for having survived it — and, above all, the deeper the discouragement of the enemy for his failure to bring a disadvantaged nation to its knees. As it was, he had nothing but scorn for those who spoke of surrender: especially now that Lincoln had unmasked himself at Hampton Roads, revealing the true nature of his plans for the postwar subjugation of all who had opposed him and his Jacobin cohorts in the North. The alternative to continued resistance was unthinkable. Not only did he prefer death "sooner than we should ever be united again" with such a foe; "What shall we say of the disgrace beneath which we should be buried if we surrender with an army in the field more numerous than that with which Napoleon achieved the glory of France — an army standing among its homesteads?" All this he said, and more, in response to enthusiastic urgings from the crowd, before he reached the ringing peroration. "Let us then unite our hands and hearts; lock our shields together, and we may well believe that before another summer solstice falls upon us, it will be the enemy who will be asking us for conferences and occasions in which to make known *our* demands."

There followed a series of patriotic rallies featuring speakers who took their cue from this lead-off address by the President in Metropolitan Hall. Three days later, at the African Church — requisitioned for the occasion because of its vast capacity — Hunter once more described how Lincoln had "turned from propositions of peace with cold insolence," and told his indignant listeners: "I will not attempt to draw a picture of subjugation. It would require a pencil dipped in blood." Benjamin, the next man up, came forward with his accustomed smile. "Hope beams in every countenance," he said. "We know in our hearts that this people must conquer its freedom or die." He brought up the touchy subject of arming the slaves, calling on Virginia to set the example by furnishing 20,000 black recruits within the next twenty days, and was pleased to find that the subject was not so touchy after all. The outsized crowd approved with scarcely a murmur of dissent. Davis spoke too, though briefly, again predicting a Confederate victory by the end of summer, then left the rostrum to other dignitaries who continued the daylong oratory into the evening. Judge Campbell, unstrung by his recent visit beyond the enemy lines, was not among them; nor was Stephens, who — though he was present, as Campbell was not —

was too disheartened to join the chorus of affirmation. Like all the rest, he was swept along by the President's address, which he praised for its "loftiness of sentiment and rare form of expression," as well as for the "magnetic influence in its delivery."

Even so, looking back on it later, he pronounced it "little short of demention." Asked by Davis after the meeting what his plans were, he replied that he intended "to go home and remain there." He would "neither make any speech, nor even make known to the public in any way of the general condition of affairs, but quietly abide the issue of fortune." Discredited, outmaneuvered, he threw in the sponge at last. He left Richmond next day, returning to Liberty Hall, his home near Crawfordville — a deserter, like some hundred thousand others — and there remained, in what he termed "perfect retirement," for the balance of the war.

Such defection was rather the exception through this time, even among the Vice President's fellow Georgians who lately had been exposed to the wrath or whim of Sherman's bummers. Howell Cobb, whose plantation had been gutted on specific orders from the red-haired destroyer himself, spoke fervently in Macon that same week, calling on the people to unite behind their government, which he said could never be conquered if they held firm. "Put me in my grave," he cried, "but never put on me the garments of a Submissionist!" Benjamin Hill followed Stephens back to their native state, but for a different purpose. Addressing crowds in Columbus, Forsyth, and La Grange, he declared that the Confederacy still had half a million men of military age, together with plenty of food and munitions; all it lacked was the will to win. "If we are conquered, subjugated, disgraced, ruined," the senator asserted with a figurative sidelong glance at Joe Brown in Milledgeville and Little Aleck in nearby Liberty Hall, "it will be the work of those enemies among us [who] will accomplish that work by destroying the faith of our people in their government." Robert Toombs, the fieriest Georgian of them all, emerged from his Achilles sulk to assume the guise of Nestor in reaction to the news from Hampton Roads. All that was needed was resolution, a recovery of the verve that had prevailed in the days when he himself was in the field, he told a wrought-up audience in Augusta. "We have resources enough to whip *forty* Yankee nations," he thundered, "if we could call back the spirit of our departed heroes." Similarly, in North Carolina, even so confirmed an obstructionist as Zeb Vance came over when he learned of Lincoln's "terms" for acceptance of the South's surrender. In response, the governor issued a mid-February proclamation calling for all Tarheels to "assemble in primary meetings in every county in the State, and let the whole world, and especially our enemies, see how a free people can meet a proposition for their absolute submission.... Great God! Is there a man in all this honorable, high spirited, and noble Commonwealth so steeped in every conceivable meanness, so blackened with all the guilt of treason, or so damned with all the leprosy of cowardice as to say: 'Yes, we will submit to this'... whilst there yet remains half a million men amongst us able to resist?... Should we willfully throw down an organized government, disband our still powerful armies, and invite all these fearful consequences upon our country, we would live to have our children curse our gray hairs for fastening our dishonor upon them."

Editors formerly critical of practically everything Davis did or stood for, especially during the twenty months since Gettysburg and the fall of Vicksburg, now swung abruptly to full support of his administration, as if in admission of their share in reducing public morale to so low a point that Lincoln felt he could afford to spurn all overtures for peace except on terms amounting to unconditional surrender. Formerly gloomy, they turned hopeful, claiming to find much that was encouraging in the current military situation. "Nil Desperandum," writing in the *Enquirer*, pointed out that less of the Confederacy was actually occupied by the enemy now than there had been two years ago; Sherman had marched through it, true enough, but had not garrisoned or held what he traversed, except for Savannah, where he had been obliged to stop and catch his breath. What was more, he had not really whipped anyone en route, according to the Georgia humorist Charles H. Smith, who signed himself Bill Arp: "Didn't the rebellyun klose rite up behind him, like shettin a pair of waful irons?" Pollard of the *Examiner* agreed. "His campaign comes to nought if he cannot reach Grant; nothing left of it but the brilliant zig-zag of a raid, vanishing as heat lightning in the skies."

Clergymen throughout the South, of varied denominations, prepared to undertake a new crusade designed to reunite their congregations, along with any number of strayed sheep, in resistance to the unholy fate it now was clear the enemy had in mind to impose in the wake of their defeat. Army units began sending home letters signed in mass, expressing confidence in victory if only those behind the lines would emulate the soldiers at the front. In response, a hundred Mobile citizens established the League of Loyal Confederates, dedicated to the promotion of such support, ánd vowed to expand the society to cover every section of the nation, whether occupied or still free of blue contamination. Congress too was caught up in the fervor of the occasion. Indignant over Lincoln's reported terms at Hampton Roads, both houses voted overwhelmingly for a set of resolutions asserting that "no alternative is left to the people of the Confederate States, but a continuance of the war or submission to terms of peace alike ruinous and dishonorable." The choice was plain, and Congress made it with no opposing vote in the Senate and only one in the House. Fighting would continue, the joint resolution declared, until "the independence of the Confederate States shall have been established."

Davis thus gained more than he had planned for when, at the urging of Old Man Blair, he first decided to send the trio of submissionists to confer with Lincoln on the prospect of "securing peace to the two countries." Not only had they returned discredited, as he had expected and assured in their instructions, but the nature of their failure — made evident by Hunter when he repeated at rallies the harsh terms laid out for them aboard the *River Queen* — united the clashing factions within the Confederacy more effectively than any single event had done since far-off Chancellorsville. Elation had been the causative reaction then. Now it was indignation, quite as heady an emotion and even more cohesive in effect, since not to feel it was to confess a lack of honor sensible to insult. And yet there was a measure of elation, too, this cold first week in February, based on the simultaneous elevation of Lee as general-in-chief, the replacement of Northrop with Isaac St John as commissary general, and the appointment of Breckinridge — even more popular as the hero of New Market than he had been as the South's favorite candidate in the presidential election that brought on the current struggle for independence — to the post vacated by Seddon, who was associated with all the military disasters that had occurred since he took office, two long years ago. Men noted these administrative changes and found in them a cause for hope that the war, which Lincoln had just made clear would have to be fought to the finish, had taken a sharp turn for the better, at least in the way it would be run.

How deep the emotion went was another matter. It might be what Pollard, reverting to type, would call "a spasmodic revival, or short fever of the popular mind"; in which case not even the indignation, let alone the tentative elation, would outlast the march begun that week by Sherman, north through the Carolinas from Savannah. "The South's condition is pitiable," Seward had told his wife after talking with Blair on the eve of the Hampton Roads conference, "but it is not yet fully realized there." That too might be true; in which case, deep or shallow, the unifying reaction came too late. Davis had silenced his most vociferous critics, driving them headlong from the public view; but he knew well enough, from hard experience, that they were only waiting in the wings. One bad turn of fortune, left or right, would bring them back, stage center and full-voiced.

※ 4 ※

Lee received formal notice of his appointment to command of all the armies on February 6, midway through a heavy three-day attack on his right flank at Hatcher's Run, word of which had reached him the day before, a Sunday, while he was at church in Petersburg. Contrary to his usual custom, though he waited out the service, he went with the first group to the chancel for Communion before he left to ride down the Boydton Plank Road, where guns were growling and infantry was engaged on the far side of the frozen stream. Some green recruits, exposed to their first large-scale action, were in a state of panic along one critical part of the line, and when the good gray general rode out to rally them — a heroic figure, accustomed to exciting worshipful fervor in veterans who then would set up a shout of "Lee to the rear! Lee to the rear!" — one badly rattled soldier flung both hands above his head in terror and exclaimed: "Great God, old man, get out of the way! You don't know nothing!"

Grant had made no serious effort to attack or flank the Petersburg defenses since his late-October drive to cut the Southside Railroad was turned back at Burgess Mill, where the Boydton Plank Road straddled Hatcher's Run. Mindful however of Lincoln's admonition on the eve of Hampton Roads — "Let nothing which is transpiring change, hinder, or delay your military movements or plans" — he considered it time, despite the bitterness of the weather, to give the thing another try, less ambitious both in size and scope, but profitable enough if it worked out. This time he would not attempt to seize the railroad; he would be content to reach and hold the Boydton pike, which ran northeast from Stony Creek and Dinwiddie Courthouse, believing that this was the route Lee's supply wagons took from the new Petersburg & Weldon railhead at Hicksford, just beyond the Meherrin River. Accordingly, on February 4 — the Saturday the three rebel envoys returned to their own lines from City Point — Warren and Humphreys were instructed to move out next morning, each with two of his three divisions, preceded by Gregg's troopers, who were to strike and patrol the objective from Dinwiddie to Burgess Mill, capturing whatever enemy trains were on it, until the infantry arrived to establish permanent occupation. So ordered: Gregg set out before dawn Sunday, and Warren followed from his position on the Union left, two miles west of Globe Tavern. Humphreys brought up the rear, his marchers breathing steam in the frosty air while their boots crunched ice in puddles along the way.

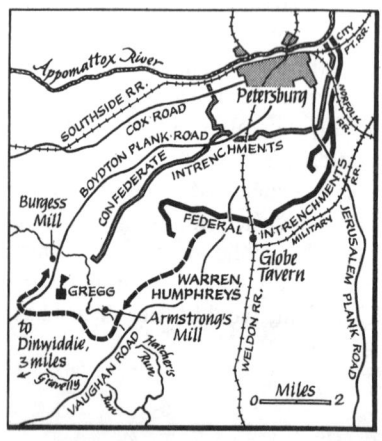

Hard as the weather was on men in the open, mounted or afoot, it had much to do with their success, first in reaching the Boydton Road unchallenged and then in holding their own through most of the three-day action which presently went into the books as the Battle of Hatcher's Run. Thinly clad and poorly fed, shivering in their trenches north of the stream, the Confederates apparently had not believed that any general, even Grant, would purposely expose his troops to the cutting wind, whistling over a bleak landscape frozen iron hard, for a prize of so little worth. As it turned out, Lee was scarcely using the Dinwiddie artery as a supply route at all, considering it too vulnerable to just such a strike as now was being made. Early on the scene, the blue troopers captured only a few wagons out on a foraging expedition, and when the infantry came up — Warren on the left, confronting Burgess Mill, and Humphreys opposite Armstrong's Mill, two miles below — there was little for them to do but dig in under long-range fire from guns in the rebel works beyond the run. Late that afternoon the graybacks tried a sortie against Humphreys, who rather easily turned it back. Reinforced that night by two divisions sent by Meade from the lines on the far side of Petersburg — one from Wright, the other from Parke — he was joined before daylight by Warren and Gregg, who gave up holding and patrolling the unused Boydton Plank Road in favor of a concentration of all available forces. Next morning (February 6; Lee was notified of his confirmation as general-in-chief, and Davis would speak that night in Metropolitan Hall) scouts reported the defenders hugging their works, but a probe by Warren that afternoon provoked a counterattack that drove him back in some disorder until he stiffened alongside Humphreys. Together they broke up the butternut effort, which turned out to have involved all three of Gordon's divisions, as well as one of Hill's. Despite this evidence of compacted danger and a total of 1474 casualties — most of them Warren's; Humphreys lost 155, all told — the Federals remained on the south bank of the creek well into the following day, then recrossed to take up a new position extending Grant's left to the Vaughan Road crossing of Hatcher's Run, three miles downstream from Burgess Mill and about the same distance southwest of where his flank had rested prior to this latest attempt to turn his adversary's right.

Militarily, the results of this latest flanking try were negligible except on two counts. One was that it required a corresponding three-mile extension of Lee's own line, now stretched to a length of more than 37 miles, exclusive of recurrent jogs and doublings, while the army that held it was reduced by casualties and desertion to a strength of 46,398, the number listed as "present for duty" although many among them were too weak for anything more rigorous than answering roll call from their widespread posts along the fire step. The other negative outcome was the loss of John Pegram, the only professional among Gordon's three division commanders. Shot through the heart, he fell leading the counterattack on the second day of battle, two weeks past his thirty-third birthday, and was buried two days later from St Paul's Church in Richmond, just three weeks after he was married there. Such a loss came hard. But hardest of all, perhaps, was the feeling of what the three-day fight portended, coming as it did at a time when the food reserve was quite exhausted. Throughout the action, the troops received no issue of meat, only a scant handful of meal per man. Lee protested to the War Department about this and the absence of his cavalry, dispersed for lack of forage. "Taking these facts in connection with the paucity of our numbers," he informed his superiors in the capital at his back, "you must not be surprised if calamity befalls us."

At the same time, he spoke to those below him not of calamity but of fortitude and courage. On February 11, four days after the fighting subsided along Hatcher's Run, he issued with the concurrence of the President a final offer of pardon for all deserters who would return to the colors within twenty days. Included in this general order, the first since he took over as general-in-chief, was an address to all the nation's soldiers, present and absent. The choice, he said, had been narrowed "between war and abject submission," and "to such a proposal brave men with arms in their hands can have but one answer. They cannot barter manhood for peace, nor the right of self-government for life or property.... Taking new resolution from the fate which our enemies intend for us," Lee's appeal concluded, "let every man devote all his energies to the common defense. Our resources, wisely and vigorously employed, are ample, and with a brave army, sustained by a determined and united people, success with God's assistance cannot be doubtful. The advantages of the enemy will have but little value if we do not permit them to impair our resolution. Let us then oppose constancy to adversity, fortitude to suffering, and courage to danger, with the firm assurance that He who gave freedom to our fathers will bless the efforts of their children to preserve it."

Sherman by then was eleven days out of Savannah, and though all was confusion in his path and ruin in his rear, his purpose was becoming clearer with every northward mile he covered toward a link-up with Schofield, moving inland from Fort Fisher against Wilmington and Bragg. So too was Grant's purpose, which Lee believed was to act on his own before the intended conjunction. Petersburg now had been under seige for eight relentless months — five times the length of Vicksburg's previous forty-eight-day record — but the chances were that the blue commander wanted to avoid having it said that he could never have taken the place without the help of the forces coming up through the Carolinas. "I think Genl Grant will move against us soon," Lee wrote his wife some ten days later, "within a week if nothing prevents, and no man can tell what may be the result."

★ ★ ★

"I want to see the long deferred chastisement begin. If we don't purify South Carolina it will be because we *can't get a light,*" an Illinois major wrote home while awaiting orders to cross the Savannah River. Six weeks later, when he got his next chance to post a letter, he could look back on a job well done and satisfaction achieved. "The army burned everything it came near in the State of South Carolina," he informed his wife, "not under orders, but in spite of orders. The men 'had it in' for the state, and they took it out in their own way. Our track through the state is a desert waste."

In some commands — Judson Kilpatrick's, for one — there were at least informal orders for such destruction. "In after years," the cavalry leader told his staff at a dinner he gave on the eve of setting out, "when travelers passing through South Carolina shall see chimney stacks without houses, and the country desolate, and shall ask, 'Who did this?' some Yankee will answer, 'Kilpatrick's Cavalry.'" Moreover, he did what he could to fulfill this prophecy en route. Descending on Barnwell four days later, just beyond the Salkehatchie, his troopers left little behind them but ashes and the suggestion that the town be renamed Burnwell.

"It seems to be decreed that South Carolina, having sown the wind, shall reap the whirlwind," a veteran infantryman asserted, and was echoed by a comrade: "South Carolina has commenced to pay an installment, long overdue, on her debt to justice and humanity. With the help of God, we will have principal and interest before we leave her borders. There is a terrible gladness in the realization of so many hopes and wishes."

Sherman, having cast himself in the role of avenging angel, saw his long-striding western veterans as crusaders, outriders for the Union, charged with imparting to the heathen Carolinians a wisdom that began with fear, and they in turn were proud to view their service in that light; "Do Boys," they called themselves, happy to be at the bidding of a commander who did not intend to restrain his army unduly, "lest its vigor and energy should be impaired." Anticipating a two-way profit from such license — high spirits within the column, panic in its path — he was hard put to say which of these benefits he valued most. "It is impossible to conceive of a march involving more labor and exposure," he would say, "yet I cannot recall an instance of bad temper." Throughout what was known from the outset as the Smoky March, a free-swinging jocularity obtained, as if to demonstrate that the damage, however severe, was being inflicted in high good humor, not out of meanness or any such low motivation. "There goes your damned old gospel shop!" the soldiers crowed, by way of a warmup for the march, as they pulled down the steeple and walls of a church in Hardeeville. "Vandalism, though not encouraged, was seldom punished," according to an artillery captain who also served as an undercover reporter for the New York *Herald.* He noted that, while "in Georgia few houses were burned, here few escaped," with the result that "the middle of the finest day looked black and gloomy" because of the dense smoke rising on all sides. Here again the cavalry did its share, Kilpatrick being under instructions to signal his whereabouts out on the flank by setting fire to things along the way. "Make a smoke like Indians do on the plains," Sherman had told him.

By way of further protection against the pangs of conscience, in case any tried to creep in, the marchers developed a biding dislike for the natives, especially those who had anything to lose. "In Georgia we had to respect the high-toned feelings of the planters," the *Herald*'s artillerist explained, "for they yielded with a dignity that won our admiration. In Carolina, the inhabitants, with a fawning, cringing subserviency, hung around our camps, craving a bite to eat." Enlarging on this, a Massachusetts colonel declared that he felt no sympathy for these victims of the army's wrath or high jinks. "I might pity individual cases brought before me," he wrote home, "but I believe that this terrible example is needed in this country as a warning to those men in all time to come who may cherish rebellious thoughts; I believe it is necessary in order to show the strength of this Government and thoroughly to subdue these people."

For the most part, though, no matter how amusing all this was for the soldiers trudging northward, or painful for the victims in their path, such depredations had little more to do with the success or failure of the operation, at least at this stage, than did the marksmanship or battle skill of the invaders, who went unchallenged except by skittish bands of butternut horsemen on the flanks. What mattered now was endurance, the ability of the marchers to cover a dozen miles of icy calf-deep bog a day, and the dexterity of the road-laying pioneers, charged with getting the 3000-odd wagons and ambulances through, as well as the 68 guns. On the right, where Howard had taken a steam-propelled head start up Port Royal Sound, then overland to Pocotaligo, this was not so much of a problem; he had only the Salkehatchie to cross before he reached the railroad linking Charleston and Augusta, Sherman's initial tactical objective; whereas Slocum, on the left, had first the Savannah River and then the Coosawhatchie Swamp to get across before he even approached the Salkehatchie. Howard made it in seven days. The wonder was that Slocum took only two days longer, considering the obstacles he encountered — especially the Coosawhatchie, which was three rain-swollen miles across and belt-buckle-deep, or sometimes worse, for nearly a mile on either side of the main channel. "Uncle Billy seems to have struck this river end-ways," one floundering veteran complained, submerged to his armpits in liquid muck and crackling skim-ice.

In addition to a 300-foot bridge that spanned the deeper-bottomed channel, the pioneers had to corduroy both approaches, in and out of the morass, and pin down the split-sapling mats, laid crosswise two and three feet underwater, to keep them from floating away. All this was managed handily, using materials on the scene; the six divisions crossed with a minimum of delay, if not of discomfort. By February 9 Slocum had all his men and vehicles over the Salkehatchie and in camp along the railroad west of Blackville, alongside Howard, who had reached and begun wrecking it two days ago, east to Bamberg, within fifteen miles of Branchville. For two more days they stayed there, converting thirty miles of track into twisted scrap iron, and then both wings were off again, slogging northward for the Congaree and the capital on its opposite bank, some fifty miles away. In addition to the "terrible gladness" the marchers felt because of the destruction they had wrought, official and unofficial, along and on both sides of their line of march, they also felt considerable hindsight amazement at the speed they had made through the midwinter swamps.

Nor were they by any means the only ones to feel this. Up in western North Carolina, where he was awaiting the outcome of efforts by friends in Richmond to achieve his reinstatement to the command from which he had been removed just over half a year before, Joe Johnston was even more amazed than were the soldiers who had accomplished this near miracle of stamina and logistics. He had been told by experts that the South Carolina hinterland was impenetrable at this season of the year, all the roads being under water, and he had believed it. "But when I learned that Sherman's army was marching through the Salk swamps, making its own corduroy roads at the rate of a dozen miles a day and more," he said later, "I made up my mind that there had been no such army in existence since the days of Julius Caesar."

Sherman rather agreed with this assessment. He had ridden with Howard on the less-obstructed right, northwest from Pocotaligo across the Salkehatchie, and when Slocum came up on the left along the railroad, having also encountered little formal opposition, the red-haired general's enthusiasm flared. For one thing, it was evident that his strategy of striking at a central objective while feinting simultaneously at others beyond his flanks was still effective, and for another it was equally clear that his policy of giving his troops a freer hand, not only to forage but also to visit their frisky wrath on the property of aboriginal secessionists along both routes of march, was bearing fruit; soldiers and civilians alike, the Confederates seemed unstrung by indecision and alarm. So far, the only resistance had come from cavalry snapping ineffectively at his wingtips, and already he could see that Magrath's appeal for South Carolinians to ambuscade the bluecoats in their midst was even less productive than Joe Brown's had been, two months ago in Georgia — with the result that, in his attitude toward the enemy ahead, Sherman become more confident and high-handed than ever. "I had a species of contempt for these scattered and inconsiderable forces," he afterwards declared, and the record sustained his claim. Midway of the two-day pause for railroad twisting, for example, when he received a flag-of-truce note from Wheeler, offering to quit burning cotton in the path of the invaders if they in turn would "discontinue burning houses," he kept his answer brief and to the point. He was unwilling to waste time now in an argument over the propriety of gratuitous destruction, nor did he intend to fall into the fibrous trap that had snared Banks last spring up the Red River. In short, he declined to enter into any discussion of the matter, except to tell the rebel cavalryman: "I hope you will burn all cotton and save us the trouble. All you don't burn I will."

Next day — February 9 — he was off again, across the Edisto, hard on the go for the Congaree and Columbia, just beyond. The two wings marched in near conjunction now, and once more it was as if the friction match had replaced the rifle as the basic infantry weapon. Barns exploded in flame as soon as the foragers emptied them of stock and corn; deserted houses loosed heavy plumes of smoke on the horizon; even the split-rail fences crackled along roadsides, and Kilpatrick was complaining of how "the infernal bummers," outstripping his troopers in the race for booty, "managed to plunder every hamlet and town before the cavalry came up." Aware that their next prize was the state capital, the very cradle of secession, the veterans chanted as they swung along the roads converging northward on their goal:

> "Hail Columbia, happy land!
> If I don't burn you, I'll be damned."

Riding among them, his spirits as high as their own — "sandy-haired, sharp-featured," an associate described him; "his nose prominent, his lips thin, his gray eyes flashing fire as fast as lightning on a summer's day; his whole face mobile as an actor's, and revealing every shade of thought or emotion that flitters across his active mind" — Sherman would have been in even higher feather if he had known that Schofield's troops, long ice-bound up the Potomac, began unloading that same day at Fort Fisher, preparatory to moving against Wilmington and points inland, as agreed upon beforehand. Not only would this provide the northward marchers with supplies and reinforcements when the time came; it would create still more confusion for Beauregard, who was confused enough already by his instructions from Richmond to intercept the invaders with a force that was even more "scattered and inconsiderable" than his adversary knew.

The Creole had returned from Mississippi the week before, called back to conduct the defense of the Carolinas, where his name retained a measure of the magic it once evoked, first as the Hero of Sumter and then as the deliverer who turned back Du Pont's iron fleet. On February 2, the day after his arrival in Augusta, he assembled a council of war for discussion of how to go about intercepting Sherman's double-pronged advance, which had begun in earnest just the day before. Hardee was there, summoned by rail from Charleston, as were G. W. Smith, in command of the Georgia militia, and D. H. Hill, who had volunteered, as at Petersburg nine months before, for service under Beauregard in a time of national trial. Taking count, the council came up with a figure of 33,450 men available for the task. But this was a considerable overestimate, since it included some 7500 veterans from the Army of Tennessee, only 3000 of whom were yet on hand, as well as Hoke's 6000, pinned down at Wilmington by the fall of Fort Fisher, and Smith's 1500 Georgians, forbidden by law to move outside their home state. The actual number available was just over 20,000, barely more than a third as many as Sherman had moving against them from Sister's Ferry and Pocotaligo. Moreover, they were grievously divided. Hardee had 12,500 in and around Charleston — 8000 in two divisions under Major Generals Lafayette McLaws and Ambrose Wright, 3000 South Carolina militia under Brigadier General William Taliaferro, and M. C. Butler's 1500 troopers, recently detached from the Army of Northern Virginia — while Harvey Hill had 9500 near Augusta, including Stevenson's 3000, just off the cars from Tupelo, and Wheeler's 6500 cavalry, already in motion to challenge the invaders in case they tried to cross the "impassable" Salkehatchie. Beauregard's decision, made in the absence of any information as to which blue wing was making the main effort, was to defend both cities, 120 miles apart, until such time as evidence of a feint allowed the troops in that direction to be shifted elsewhere. He himself would set up headquarters at Columbia, he said. If worse came to worse, both Hardee and Hill could fall back and join him there, evacuating Charleston and Augusta rather than suffer the loss of their commands to overwhelming numbers, and thus combine for an attack on one or another of the two blue columns toiling northward.

Poor as the plan was in the first place, mainly because of its necessary surrender of the initiative to the enemy, it was rendered even poorer — in fact inoperative — by the speed with which Sherman moved through the supposedly impenetrable swamps. By the time Beauregard set up headquarters in the capital on February 10, the invaders, having reached and wrecked the railroad between Charleston and Augusta, were over the Edisto and hard on the march for the Congaree, no longer by two routes but in a single unassailable column; Sherman, like a diving hawk, had closed his wings for a rapid descent on Columbia before either Hill or Hardee, outflanked on the left and right, had time to react as planned for the combined attack on some lesser segment of the Union host. Despondent, Beauregard wired Hill to leave Augusta and join him at once with Stevenson's men at Chester, fifty miles north of the South Carolina capital. Similar orders to Hardee struck a snag, however. Though he promptly detached Butler's remounted troopers to assist Wheeler in delaying the blue advance, Richmond had urged him not to abandon Charleston until it was absolutely necessary, and he wanted his chief to make that judgment in person, on the scene. Unable to end the Georgian's indecision by telegraph, Beauregard went to Charleston on February 14, convinced him there was no longer any choice in the matter, prepared written instructions for the evacuation, and returned that night to Columbia: only to learn next day that Hardee had suffered another change of heart, prompted by still another Richmond dispatch urging him to postpone the evacuation until it was certain that Beauregard could not stop the Federals on his own. Exasperated, the Creole wired peremptory orders for Hardee to get the endangered garrison aboard the cars for Chester while there still was time. Sherman by then was maneuvering for a crossing of the Congaree, upstream and down, and Columbia itself was being evacuated in hope of sparing the capital the destruction that would attend any attempt to defend it against the 60,000 bluecoats on its doorstep.

That was February 15. Beauregard stayed through the following day and set out north by rail for Chester after nightfall, leaving Wade Hampton, whose splendid peacetime mansion rivaled the new brick State House as the showplace of the capital, to conduct the final stage of the withdrawal before the Federals arrived. Placed in command of all the cavalry, the post he had filled in Virginia until Lee detached him for his present task, the South Carolina grandee was promoted to lieutenant general over Wheeler, who, though nearly two decades his junior in age — Hampton would be forty-seven next month; Wheeler was twenty-eight — had half a year's seniority on him as a major general. Like most evacuations under pressure, this one was attended with considerable disorder and a confusion enlarged by particular circumstances. Columbia, a neat, well-laid-out little city with a charm befitting its uplands heritage as a center for culture and commerce, had grown in the course of the past two years from a population of about 8000 to better than 20,000, largely as a result of the influx of people from threatened areas on the seacoast and, more recently and in even larger numbers, from regions along or near the Georgia border thought to lie in the path of Sherman's burners. Convinced that the capital was strategically unimportant, especially in comparison with directly menaced Charleston and Augusta, prominent landowners and businessmen sought refuge here for their families, as well as for their valuables and house slaves. Before the war, there had been three banks in Columbia; now there were fourteen, including all of bombarded Charleston's, shifted beyond reach of the heaviest naval guns. Moreover, this notion of inland security persisted well beyond the time that Sherman left Savannah. Just last week, on February 9, the editor of the local *South Carolinian* had assured his readers that there was "no real tangible cause" for supposing that the Yankees had Columbia in mind.

Then suddenly they knew better; Sherman was two days off, then one, then none, guns booming from the Congaree bottoms, just across the way; there was neither time nor means for removing their sequestered goods beyond his reach. Offers as large as $500 hired no wagons, and men and women competed testily for seats or standing room on every northbound train. Earlier, the authorities had ordered all cotton transported from intown warehouses for burning in open fields beyond the city limits, and the bales were trundled into the streets for rapid loading when the time came. They sat there still, spilling their fluffy, highly combustible fiber through rents in the jute bagging. Columbia thus was a tinderbox, ready to burst into flame at the touch of a match or a random spark, by the time the rear-guard handful of gray troopers pulled out Friday morning, February 17, and Mayor T. J. Goodwyn set out with three aldermen in a carriage flying a white flag, charged by Hampton with surrendering the capital to the bluecoats already entering its outskirts.

Sherman rode in about midday, close on the heels of Howard's lead brigade. Part of Logan's XV Corps, whose mere proximity he had said would obviate the need for sowing any hated place with salt, its members were given the customary privilege, as the first troops in, of policing the captured town and enjoying all it had to offer in the way of food and fun. A blustery wind had risen and was blowing the spilled cotton about the streets in wisps and skeins. Asked later why, under these explosive circumstances, he had not kept his veterans in formation and under control while they were in occupation of the surrendered capital, the red-haired Ohioan replied indignantly: "I would not have done such a harshness to save the whole town. They were men, and I was not going to treat them like slaves."

Liquor shops were among the first establishments to be looted when the troops broke ranks and scattered. But this was more from habit than from need, since friendly house slaves stood in front of many residences, offering the soldiers drinks from bottles they had brought up from abandoned cellars. "Lord bless you, Massa. Try some dis," a genial white-haired butler said, extending a gourd dipper he kept filled with fine old brandy from a bucket in his other hand. Breakfastless and exuberant, a good part of the command was roaring drunk in short order. Slocum, whose left wing crossed upstream and went into camp beyond the city, saw in this the main cause for what would follow after sundown. "A drunken soldier with a musket in one hand and a match in the other is not a pleasant visitor to have about the house on a dark, windy night," he afterwards remarked, "particularly when for a series of years you have urged him to come so that you might have an opportunity of performing a surgical operation on him." Sherman apparently thought so, too. "Look out," he told Howard, observing the effect of all this proffered whiskey, "or you'll have hell to pay. You'd better go and see about it in person."

Howard did go and see about it. Alarmed, he stopped the informal distribution of spirits and, after nightfall, ordered the drunken brigade relieved by another from the same division, which had marched through the city earlier to camp on the far side. But it was altogether too late by then. The men of the first having scattered beyond recall, the practical outcome was that a second XV Corps brigade was added to the milling throng of celebrants and looters. By then, moreover, the frightened citizens had learned what the soldiers meant when, passing through the windy streets that afternoon, they told them: "You'll catch hell tonight." Sherman could have interpreted for them, though as it happened he only found out about the prophecy after it had been fulfilled. Weary, he took an early supper and lay down to rest in a bedroom of the house his staff had commandeered for headquarters. "Soon after dark," he would remember, "I became conscious that a bright light was shining on the walls."

Columbia was burning, and burning fiercely, in more than a dozen places simultaneously. Hampton's mansion was one of the first to go, along with Treasury Secretary Trenholm's, and lest it be thought that these had been singled out because of their owners' wealth or politics, the Gervais Street red-light district was put to the torch at the same time, as well as Cotton Town, a section of poorer homes to the northwest, and stores and houses along the river front. One object of special wrath was the Baptist church where the South Carolina secession convention had first assembled, but the burners were foiled by a Negro they asked for directions. As it happened, he was the sexton of the church they sought and he pointed out a rival Methodist establishment just up the block, which soon was gushing flames from all its windows. So presently was the nearby Ursuline convent, whose Mother Superior was known to be the sister of Bishop Patrick N. Lynch, an outspoken secessionist who had celebrated the breakup of the Union, back in '61, with thanksgiving rites in his Charleston cathedral. Hardest hit of all was the business district. Terrified pigeons flapped and wheeled in the drifting smoke, unable to find a place to light, and the hysterical screams of women combined strangely with the lowing of cattle trapped in their stalls. "All around us were falling thickly showers of burning flakes," a seventeen-year-old girl wrote in her diary next day. "Everywhere the palpitating blaze walled the streets as far as the eye could reach, filling the air with its terrible roar. On every side [was] the crackling and devouring fire, while every instant came the crashing of timbers and the thunder of falling buildings. A quivering molten ocean seemed to fill the air and sky."

Mindful perhaps of a statement he had made to Mayor Goodwyn, who served as his guide on an afternoon tour of inspection: "Go home and rest assured that your city will be as safe in my hands as if you had controlled it," Sherman himself turned out to fight the flames, along with his staff, a number of unit commanders, and as many of their troops as could be rounded up and persuaded to serve as firemen. Of the rest, unwilling to end their fun or too drunk to follow orders, 370 were placed in arrest, two were shot and killed, and thirty wounded. That still left enough at large to defeat the efforts being made to confine the conflagration. Some among them hurried from block to block, carrying wads of turpentine-soaked cotton for setting fire to houses so far spared, while others used their rifles to bayonet hoses and cripple pumpers brought into play by the civilian fire department. Before the night was over, another whole division was summoned into the city to help subdue the arsonists and the flames, but even that did not suffice until about 4 o'clock in the morning, when the wind relented enough to let the flames die down and save the capital from annihilation. As it was, when the sun rose two hours later, blood red through the murk of heavy smoke, two thirds of Columbia lay in ashes. Fire had raged through 84 of its 124 blocks, with such effect that the girl diarist could see nothing from her position near the center "but heaps of rubbish, tall dreary chimneys, and shattered brick walls." Burned-out families gathered in the parks and on the common, huddled among such possessions as they had managed to save. Some of the women were weeping uncontrollably. Others were dry-eyed, either from shock or from a sharpened hatred of the Yankees. An Illinois surgeon moved among them for a time, then withdrew sadly. "I talked with some," he wrote in his diary that night, "but it made me feel too bad to be endured."

Sherman had a different reaction. "Though I never ordered it, and never wished it," he was to say of the burning, "I have never shed any tears over it, because I believe that it hastened what we all fought for — the end of the war." As for blame, he fixed that on Hampton for starting the fire and on God for enlarging it. He charged the rebel general with "ripping open bales of cotton, piling it in the streets, burning it, and then going away"; at which point "God Almighty started wind sufficient to carry that cotton wherever He would." Originally, while the fire was in progress, he had seen whiskey as the overriding cause of the catastrophe, available in quantity because the departed graybacks had foolishly made "an evacuated city a depot of liquor for an army to occupy." Under its influence, he admitted, his soldiers "may have assisted in spreading the fire after it once began, and may have indulged in unconcealed joy to see the ruin of the capital of South Carolina," but he did not dwell long on this aspect of the case, saying instead: "I disclaim on the part of my army any agency in this fire, but, on the contrary, claim that we saved what of Columbia remains unconsumed. And without hesitation I charge General Wade Hampton with having burned his own city of Columbia, not with malicious intent, or as the manifestation of a silly 'Roman stoicism,' but from folly and want of sense in filling it with lint, cotton, and tinder." So he declared in his formal report of the campaign, although he conceded in his memoirs, ten years later, that there had been method in his arraignment of his adversary for the burning. "I distinctly charged it to General Wade Hampton," he wrote then, "and confess I did so pointedly, to shake the faith of his people in him, for he was in my opinion a braggart, and professed to be the special champion of South Carolina."

For two more days the army remained in and around Columbia, probing the rubble for overlooked spoils and expanding the destruction by burning down the Confederate arsenal and a Treasury printing office, legitimate targets which somehow had survived the conflagration. The Preston mansion, where Hood had visited his fiancée on his way to Richmond two weeks back, escaped entirely: first, because John Logan occupied it during the three-day stay, and finally because Sherman gave permission for the homeless wards of the Ursuline convent to take up residence there on February 20, the day his troops moved out. Logan was supervising the placement of barrels of pitch in the cellar, intending to set them ablaze on his departure, when the white-clad pupils were herded in by the Mother Superior, armed with Sherman's order. Black Jack loosed a string of oaths at this sparing of a rebel general's ornate property, but had no choice except to let the house go unburned when he took up the march.

It was northward, as before. The feint now was at Chester, fifty miles away, and at Charlotte, about the same distance farther on, across the North Carolina line. Beyond Winnsboro, however — which the outriding bummers set afire next day, though not soon enough to keep the main body from coming up in time to save most of it from the flames — both infantry wings turned hard right for a crossing of the Wateree River, a dozen miles to the east, and a fast march on Cheraw, en route to Fayetteville and Goldsboro, where Sherman had arranged for Schofield to meet him with supplies brought inland from Wilmington and New Bern.

Alas, it was just at this critical stage, with by far the worst stretch of the march supposedly behind him, that the pace slowed to a crawl. Coming down to the Wateree on February 23, Howard's wing made it over the river in a driving rain, but only half of Slocum's crossed before the bridge collapsed under pressure from logs and driftwood swept downstream by the rush of rising water; Davis's XIV Corps was left stranded on the western bank, and the other three, having made it over, soon had cause to wish they hadn't. The mud, though thinner, was slick as grease on the high red ground beyond the river, and grew slicker and deeper throughout the record three-day rainfall, until at last — "slipping, stumbling, swearing, singing, and yelling" — the head of the column reached Hanging Rock Post Office on February 26, having covered barely twenty miles in the past four days; while the XIV Corps, still on the far side of the Wateree, had made no miles at all. Furious, Sherman called a halt and ordered Slocum to ride back and expedite a crossing. If necessary, he was to have Davis burn his wagons, spike his guns, shoot the mules, and ferry or swim his troops across; he was in fact to do anything, within reason or beyond, that would avoid prolonging the delay now that a solid half of the long trek to Goldsboro was behind the main body, slathered with mud and resting close to exhaustion at Hanging Rock, within twenty air-line miles of the North Carolina line.

No such drastic steps were needed. That afternoon the sun came out, beaming down on "bedraggled mules, toiling soldiers, and seas of mud," and by the next the river had fallen enough for Davis to improvise a bridge; his laggard corps got over that night with its guns and train, followed by the cavalry, which had kept up the feint against Chester after the infantry swung east. Sherman meanwhile improved the interim by sending a reinforced brigade to nearby Camden, with instructions to destroy all "government property, stores, and cotton." Reinspired despite their bone-deep weariness, the detached troops accomplished this and more, burning a large flour mill and both depots of the South Carolina Railroad, along with the Masonic Hall, and looting almost every private residence in town, then returned to Hanging Rock in time to take their place in column when the reunited army resumed its march on Cheraw, just under fifty miles away. They had recovered their high spirits, and so too, by now, had their commander. He had learned from newspapers gathered roundabout that Charleston, evacuated by Hardee on the night Columbia burned, had been occupied next morning by units from Foster's garrison at Savannah: a splendid example of what Sherman had meant when he told him to be ready to "pick up the apples." Symbolically, at any rate — for it was here, not quite two months under four long years ago, that the war began — this was the biggest apple of them all. Four days later, moreover, while the inland marchers were turning east to cross the Wateree, Schofield had captured Wilmington, freeing his and Terry's men for the appointed meeting in the interior next month.

One other piece of news there was, but Sherman was not sure, just yet, whether he was glad or sorry to receive it. Joe Johnston, he learned, had replaced Beauregard as commander of the "scattered and inconsiderable forces" assembling in his front.

Often, down the years, it would be said that Lee's first exercise of authority, following his confirmation as general-in-chief, had been to recall Johnston to active duty; whereas, in fact, one of his first acts at his new post was the denial of a petition, signed by the Vice President and seventeen prominent Senators, urging him to do just that by restoring his fellow Virginian to command of the Army of Tennessee. "The three corps of that army have been ordered to South Carolina and are now under the command of Genl Beauregard," he replied on February 13, one week after his elevation. "I entertain a high opinion of Genl

Johnston's capacity, but think a continual change of commanders is very injurious to any troops and tends greatly to their disorganization. At this time, as far as I understand the condition of affairs, an engagement with the enemy may be expected any day, and a change now would be particularly hazardous. Genl Beauregard is well known to the citizens of South Carolina, as well as to the troops of the Army of Tennessee, and I would recommend that it be certainly ascertained that a change was necessary before it was made." Besides, he told Stephens and the others, "I do not consider that my appointment ... confers the right which you assume belongs to it, nor is it proper that it should. I can only employ such troops and officers as may be placed at my disposal by the War Department."

Old Joe it seemed would have to bide his time in the Carolina piedmont, awaiting the outcome of further efforts by his supporters. But developments over the course of the next week provoked a reassessment of the situation. For one thing, Beauregard's health was rumored to be "feeble and precarious," which might account for his apparent shakiness under pressure. Shifting his headquarters, formerly at Augusta, from Columbia to Chester, then to Charlotte, the Creole seemed confused and indecisive in the face of Sherman's "semi-amphibious" march through the boggy lowlands. "General Beauregard makes no mention of what he proposes or what he can do, or where his troops are," Lee complained to Davis. "He does not appear from his dispatches to be able to do much." Columbia by then had been abandoned, along with outflanked Charleston, and Wilmington was under heavy pressure from Schofield; at which point, on February 21, Davis received and passed on to Lee a wire just in from Beauregard, once more proposing a "grand strategy" designed to bring the Yankees to their knees. In the Louisianian's opinion, Sherman (who would not turn east, away from Chester, until the following day) was advancing upon Charlotte and Salisbury, North Carolina, on his way to a conjunction with Grant in rear of Richmond, and Old Bory saw in this — as he so often had done before, under drastic circumstances — the opportunity of a lifetime. "I earnestly urge a concentration of at least 35,000 infantry and artillery at [Salisbury], if possible, to give him battle there, and crush him, then to concentrate all forces against Grant, and then to march on Washington and dictate a peace. Hardee and myself can collect about 15,000 exclusive of Cheatham and Stewart, not likely to reach in time. If Lee and Bragg can furnish 20,000 more, the fate of the Confederacy would be secure."

Unknowingly, Beauregard had proposed his last air-castle strategy of the war. "The idea is good, but the means are lacking," Lee told Davis two days later. He had by then made up his mind that the Creole had to go, and by way of providing a successor he had already sounded out Breckinridge on the matter. "[Sherman] seems to have everything his own way," he informed the War Secretary on February 19, the day after Charleston fell, adding that he could get little useful information from the general charged with contesting the blue advance through the Carolinas. "I do not know where his troops are, or on what lines they are moving. His dispatches only give movements of the enemy. He has a difficult task to perform under present circumstances, and one of his best officers, Genl Hardee, is incapacitated by sickness. I have also heard that his own health is indifferent, though he has never so stated. Should his strength give way, there is no one on duty in the department that could replace him, nor have I anyone to send there. Genl J. E. Johnston is the only officer whom I know who has the confidence of the army and people, and if he was ordered to report to me I would place him there on duty. It is necessary to bring out all our strength...."

Puzzled by Lee's indirectness, the Kentuckian asked just what it was he wanted, and when. Lee replied that he had intended "to apply for Genl J. E. Johnston, that I might assign him to duty, should circumstances permit." Understanding now that by "circumstances" Lee meant the President's objections, Breckinridge passed the request along, and Davis — despite his recent expression of "a conviction so settled that it would be impossible for me again to feel confidence in [Johnston] as the commander of an army in the field" — agreed, however reluctantly, to the recall and appointment, though he was careful to point out that he did so only "in the hope that General Johnston's soldierly qualities may be made serviceable to his country when acting under General Lee's orders, and that in his new position those defects which I found manifested by him when serving as an independent commander will be remedied by the control of the general-in-chief."

That was how it came about that Johnston received on February 23, the day after they were issued, simultaneous orders from the War Department and from Lee, recalling him to active duty and assigning him to command of the troops now under Beauregard, including the Army of Tennessee. He was then at Lincolnton, North Carolina — "I am in the regular line of strategic retreat," Mrs Chesnut, who preceded him there in her flight from threatened Mulberry, had remarked sarcastically when she learned that he was expected any day — thirty miles northwest of Charlotte, where Beauregard had established headquarters after falling back from Chester. Instructed to "concentrate all available forces and drive back Sherman," Johnston replied much as he had done on his arrival in Mississippi just under two years ago, preceding the fall of Vicksburg: "It is too late.... The remnant of the Army of Tennessee is much divided. So are the other troops.... Is any discretion allowed me? I have no staff."

Before taking over he went by rail to Charlotte to confer with his predecessor, now designated his second in command. Beauregard assured him of his support, having just wired Lee that he would "at all times be happy to serve with or under so gallant and patriotic a soldier." Privately, though, the Louisianian was bitterly disappointed at having once more been relegated to a subordinate position, as at Manassas, Shiloh, and Petersburg. "My greatest desire has always been to command a good army in the field," he had recently declared. "Will I ever be gratified?" Now in the Carolinas — as in Mississippi nearly three years before, following his canny withdrawal from Halleck's intended trap at Corinth — another chance had come and gone, and he knew this was the last; Fate and Davis had undone him, now as then.

Johnston was by no means correspondingly elated. Though he was grateful for Beauregard's loyalty, he believed the post afforded little opportunity for success or even survival. He had, as he informed one of his Richmond supporters, "not exactly no hope, but only a faint hope," and even this was presently seen to have been an overstatement of the case. He said later that he took over in Charlotte, February 25, "with a full consciousness... that we could have no other object, in continuing the war, than to obtain fair terms of peace; for the Southern cause must have appeared hopeless then, to all intelligent and dispassionate Southern men."

Sherman by now was astride Lynch's Creek, midway between the Wateree and the Pee Dee, closing fast on Cheraw, his final intermediary objective before he entered North Carolina. Moreover, the invaders by then had still another powerful column in contention; Wilmington's fall, on the day of Johnston's restoration by the War Department, freed Schofield to join Sherman for a northward march across the Roanoke, the last strong defensive line south of the Appomattox. Lee pointed out that the only way to avoid the consequences of such a penetration would be for him to combine with Johnston for a strike at Sherman before that final barrier was crossed, even though this would require him not only to give up his present lines covering Petersburg and the national capital, but also to manage the evacuation so stealthily that Grant would not know he was gone until it was too late to overtake and crush him on the march. How long the odds were against his achieving such a deliverance Lee did not say, yet he did what he could to warn his superiors of the sacrifice involved in the attempt. On the day after Foster occupied Charleston — February 18: the fourth anniversary of Davis's provisional inauguration in Montgomery — he notified Breckinridge: "I fear it may be necessary to abandon all our cities, and preparation should be made for this contingency." Similarly, on the day after Wilmington fell — February 22: the third anniversary of Davis's permanent inauguration in Richmond — he made it clear to Davis himself that any attempt to "unite with [Johnston] in a blow against Sherman" would "necessitate the abandonment of our position on James River, for which contingency every preparation should be made." One other alternative there was, and he mentioned it one week later in a different connection.

This was the acceptance of Lincoln's terms, as set forth aboard the *River Queen* four weeks ago in Hampton Roads. "Whether this will be acceptable to our people yet awhile," he told Davis, "I cannot say."

"Yet awhile" was as close as Lee had come, so far, to foreseeing surrender as the outcome of the present situation. As for himself, this detracted not a whit from the resolution he had expressed in a letter to his wife the week before: "Sherman and Schofield are both advancing and seem to have everything their own way. But trusting in a merciful God, who does not always give the battle to the strong, I pray we may not be overwhelmed. I shall however endeavor to do my duty and fight to the last."

CHAPTER

7

Victory, and Defeat

★ ✗ ☆

"EVERYTHING LOOKS LIKE DISSOLUTION in the South. A few more days of success with Sherman will put us where we can crow loud," Grant wrote his congressional guardian angel Elihu Washburne on the day after Schofield captured Wilmington, hard in the wake of Foster's occupation of Charleston and Sherman's burning of Columbia. By coincidence, this February 23 was also the day Lee warned Davis of the need for abandoning Richmond when the time came for him to combine with Johnston in a last-ditch effort to stop Sherman and Schofield before they crossed the Roanoke River, sixty miles in what had been his rear until he was cooped up in Petersburg. Far from being one of the things Grant looked forward to crowing about, however, such a move by his adversary, even though it would mean possession of the capital he had had under siege for eight long months, was now the Union commander's greatest fear. Looking back on still another of those "most anxious periods," he afterwards explained: "I was afraid, every morning, that I would awake from my sleep to hear that Lee had gone, and that nothing was left but a picket line. He had his railroad by the way of Danville south, and I was afraid that he was running off his men and all stores and ordnance except such as it would be necessary to carry with him for his immediate defense. I knew he could move much more lightly and more rapidly than I, and that, if he got the start, he would leave me behind so that we would have the same army to fight again farther south." In other words, he feared that Lee might do to him what he had done to Lee after Cold Harbor; that is, slip away some moonless night while the bluecoats, snug in their trenches across the way, engaged in lackadaisical speculation on "a good run of Johnnies." The result would be recovery by the old fox of his freedom to maneuver, a resumption of the kind of warfare at which he and his lean gray veterans had shown themselves to be past masters, back in May and early June; in which case, Grant summed it up, still shuddering at the prospect, "the war might be prolonged another year."

Three factors prevented or delayed effective Federal interference with either the preparation or execution of such a breakout plan. One was the weather, which had turned the roads into troughs of mud and the fields into quagmires, unfit for pursuit or maneuver if Lee, who had the use of the Danville and Southside lines for the removal of all he chose to put aboard them, was to be overtaken and overwhelmed before he achieved a link-up with Johnston in the Carolinas. Another was the strength of the Richmond-Petersburg defenses, which, combined with his skill in tactical anticipation, had withstood all efforts to penetrate or outflank them. The third was the prevailing cavalry imbalance, occasioned by Sheridan's protracted absence with two of his three divisions in the Shenandoah Valley, which made it highly inadvisable to attempt a strike at the tenuous rail supply lines deep in Lee's rear, vital though they were, not only to the subsistence of his army, but also to its breakout when the time came. There was little or nothing Grant could do about the first two of these three discouraging factors, except wait out a change in the weather and the continuous sapping effect of rebel desertions, neither of which was likely to prove decisive before Lee found a chance to slip away. However, the third factor was quite another matter, and Grant had already begun to do something about it three days ago, on February 20, in a letter assigning Sheridan the task of slamming shut Lee's escape route, west or southwest, through Lynchburg or Danville.

He had decided, as a result of his fear of the growing risk of a getaway by Lee, on an alteration in the bandy-legged cavalryman's role in the close-out plan devised to bring the Confederacy to its knees. Instead of awaiting a fair-weather summons, Sheridan was to leave the Valley "as soon as it is possible to travel," and instead of rejoining Meade by the shortest route, down the Virginia Central, he was to move with his two mounted divisions against Lynchburg, where the Southside Railroad and the Orange & Alexandria came together to continue west as the Virginia & Tennessee. A thorough wrecking of that important junction, together with an adjacent stretch of the James River Canal, would cut Lee off from supplies coming in from Southwest Virginia and would also end any hope he had for a flight beyond that point. "I think you will have no difficulty about reaching Lynchburg with a cavalry force alone," Grant wrote. "From there you could destroy the railroads and canal in every direction, so as to be of no further use to the rebellion." Then came the real surprise. "From Lynchburg, if information you might get there would justify it, you could strike south, heading the streams in Virginia to get to the westward of Danville, and push on and join Sherman."

Explaining this change — not only of route, in order to deny Lee both the Southside and the Richmond & Danville lines for use as all-weather avenues for escape, but also of destination — Grant tied what he called "this additional raid" in with those about to be launched by Canby and Wilson through Alabama and by Stoneman into North Carolina. Seen in that light, with these three on the rampage and Sherman "eating out the vitals of South Carolina," the proposed operation was "all that will be wanted to leave nothing for the rebellion to stand upon." There followed a final touch of the spur, applied as insurance against discouragement or delay. "I would advise you to overcome great obstacles to accomplish this. Charleston was evacuated on Tuesday last."

Sheridan seldom needed much urging on either count, and he did so less than ever now, having engaged in no large-scale fighting in the four months since his celebrated mid-October "ride" from Winchester to Cedar Creek, where he turned apparent defeat into a smashing victory and drove the shattered remnant of Early's army headlong out of the Valley. This was not to say that he had been idle all this time; far from it; but his activity was rather in the nature of common labor, directed more against enemy resources than against enemy soldiers, of which by now there were none on the scene; or almost none, if guerillas (or "rangers," as they preferred to call themselves) were taken into account. Such times as his troops were engaged in the devastation Grant had ordered, burning mills and barns, rounding up or butchering livestock, and removing or destroying all food and forage, they were in danger of being bushwhacked, and wagon trains also had to be heavily escorted, going and coming, to keep them from being captured. Not only did this interfere with the speedy conversion of the once-lush region into a wasteland, it was also hard on morale, requiring the blue troopers to turn out in freezing weather, at night and on days better spent in bed or round the campfire. Sometimes, indeed, the damage was far worse. For example, at 3 o'clock in the morning of the day Grant's letter arrived — February 21 — a small party of guerillas stole into Cumberland, Maryland, on the Potomac and the Baltimore & Ohio, fifty-odd miles above Harpers Ferry, and into the hotel room of George Crook himself, recently promoted to major general and put in charge of the Department of West Virginia as a reward for his performance as Sheridan's star corps commander at Winchester and Fisher's Hill. Undetected, they grabbed Crook and his ranking subordinate, Brigadier General B. F. Kelley, and got them onto waiting horses for a fast ride south, once more through the unsuspecting pickets, all the way to Libby Prison. Both generals were presently released by the terms of a special exchange worked out between Richmond and Washington, but the incident rankled badly as an example of what such brigands could accomplish without fear of personal reprisal.

That had not always been the case. At the outset, with the approval of Grant, Sheridan adopted a policy of reprisal that was personal in-

Victory, and Defeat [805]

deed, especially against members of Colonel John S. Mosby's Partisan Rangers, two battalions with just under a hundred men in each, who claimed as their own a twenty-mile-square district containing most of Loudon and Fauquier counties; "Mosby's Confederacy," they dubbed it, cradled between the Bull Run Mountains and the Blue Ridge, through whose passes they raided westward across the Shenandoah River. Farmers by day, they rode mostly by night, and their commander, a former Virginia lawyer, thirty-three years old and sandy-haired, weighing less than 130 pounds in his thigh-high boots, red-lined cape, and ostrich plume, was utterly fearless, quite uncatchable, and altogether skillful in the conduct of operations which Lee himself, though he had small use for partisans in general, had praised as "highly creditable." In the past six months, in addition to keeping his superiors accurately informed of enemy activities in the Valley, he had killed, wounded, or captured more than a thousand Federals of all ranks, at a cost of barely twenty casualties of his own, and had taken nearly twice that many beeves and horses, along with a considerable haul of rations and equipment. Most of this came from Sheridan, who arrived on the scene in August. Appealing to Grant for permission to deal harshly with such guerillas as he was able to lay hands on, by way of deterring the rest, he was told: "When any of Mosby's men are caught, hang them without trial."

Promptly Sheridan passed the word to his subordinates, and in late September, having captured six of the rangers in a sudden descent on Front Royal, Custer shot four and hanged the other two, leaving their bodies dangling with a crudely lettered placard around the neck of one. "This will be the fate of Mosby and all his men," it read.

Mosby bided his time, even though another ranger was similarly captured, hanged, and placarded the following month in Rappahannock County. All this time, however, he was taking captives of his own, some 700 within a six-week span, and forwarding them to Richmond: unless, that is, they were from Custer's division, in which case they were set apart and kept under guard in an abandoned schoolhouse near Rectortown, just across the Blue Ridge from Front Royal. By early November he had 27 of Custer's men in custody, and he lined them up to draw folded slips of paper from a hat, informing them beforehand of his purpose. Twenty of the slips were blank; the rest, numbered 1 to 7, signified that those who drew them would be executed in retaliation for the postcapture death of his seven rangers. Harrowing as the lottery was for the participants, the game took an even crueler turn when it developed that one of the hard-luck seven was a beardless drummer, barely into his teens; Mosby had the delivered twenty draw again to determine who would take the boy's place. This done, a detail escorted the seven losers out into the night, under orders to hang them in proximity to Custer's headquarters at Winchester. One scampered off in the rainy darkness as they approached the scene of execution near Berryville, where three of the remaining six were hanged and the other three were lined up to be shot. One of these also managed to get away in the confusion, but Mosby later said that he was glad the two troopers escaped to "relate in Sheridan's camps the experience they had with Mosby's men." Meantime, under a flag of truce, a ranger scout — his safe conduct ensured by the remaining hostages — was on his way to deliver in person a note to Sheridan, informing him of what had been done, and why. "Hereafter," it concluded, "any prisoners falling into my hands will be treated with the kindness due to their condition, unless some new act of barbarity shall compel me reluctantly to adopt a line of policy repugnant to humanity. Very respectfully, your obedient servant, John S. Mosby."

Deterred himself, Sheridan called off the hanging match and agreed to deal henceforward with Mosby's men as he did with other prisoners of war. It came hard for him just now, though, for the rangers lately had wrecked and robbed a B. & O. express, dividing among themselves a $73,000 Federal payroll, and followed up this "Greenback Raid," as they called it, by capturing Brigadier General Alfred Duffié, out for a buggy ride near Bunker Hill, within ten miles of army headquarters. Besides, the Valley commander had more or less carried out by then his instructions to "peel this land"; little remained to protect or patrol except the trains bringing in rations for his troops, whose number had dwindled steadily as the infantry — first Wright's whole corps, then most of Crook's, and finally part of Emory's — was detached, all but a couple of rest-surfeited divisions, for transfer to more active theaters. Grant's letter, outlining plans for an all-out cavalry strike at Lynchburg and a subsequent link-up with Sherman, was greeted by Sheridan as a reprieve from boredom, a deliverance from uncongenial idleness in what had become a backwash of the war. He did not much like the notion of a detour into Carolina, preferring to be in on the smashing of Lee from the outset, but he was pleased to note that Grant had left him room for discretion in the matter, just as he had done about the date for setting out, saying merely that Sheridan could take off southward "as soon as it is possible to travel."

Unleashed, he wasted no time in getting started, even though, as he later reported, "the weather was very bad.... The spring thaw, with heavy rains, had already come on, [and] the valley and surrounding mountains were covered with snow which was fast disappearing, putting all the streams nearly past fording." A more cautious man would have waited; but not this one. Soon after sunrise, February 27 — one week from the date on Grant's letter — he had 10,000 veteran troopers pounding south up the turnpike out of Winchester, leaving Mosby and boredom and other such problems to Hancock, who returned to active duty to replace him in command of all he left behind in the lower Valley. Thirty miles the two divisions made that day, and thirty the next, to make camp at the end of the third day out — March 1 — within seven miles of Staunton, where Early had established headquarters after his rout at Cedar Creek. Next morning Sheridan rode into town to find Old Jube had departed eastward the day before, apparently headed for Charlottesville by way of Rockfish Gap. The question was whether to take out after him, in hope of completing his destruction, or press on south without delay to Lynchburg, leaving Early's remnant stranded in his wake; perhaps to bedevil Hancock. Sheridan chose the former course, and scored next day, as a result, a near Cannae that abolished what little remained of Stonewall Jackson's fabled Army of the Valley.

Twelve miles east out the Virginia Central almost to Waynesboro, a hamlet perched on the slope leading up to the snowy pass through the Blue Ridge in its rear, he came upon the thrice-whipped rebels posted in what he termed "a well chosen position" on the near side of a branch of the South Fork of the Shenandoah. They numbered about 1200 of all arms, all but a handful of Rosser's troopers being still en route from their rest camp forty miles west of Staunton. Early had stopped here in hope of delaying the bluecoats long enough to get his eleven guns across the mountain in double-teamed relays; otherwise, lacking horses enough to haul them up the slippery grade, he would have had to abandon five of them. "I did not intend making my final stand on this ground," he afterwards explained, "yet I was satisfied that if my men would fight, which I had no reason to doubt, I could hold the enemy in check until night, and then cross the river to take position in Rockfish Gap; for I had done more difficult things than that during the war."

He had indeed done more difficult things, but not with the disjointed skeleton of a command that had been trounced, three times running, by the general now closing fast upon his rear. As it turned out, holding his ground was not only difficult; it was impossible, mainly because Sheridan would not be denied even an outside chance at the total smash-up he had been seeking from the start. One division, under Brigadier General Thomas Devin — successor to Wesley Merritt, who had replaced Torbert as chief of cavalry — was delayed by orders to clean out a depot of supplies on the far side of Staunton, and though this left only Custer's division for the work at hand, Sheridan judged it would be enough, not only because he still enjoyed a better than four-to-one numerical advantage, but also because of Custer's nature, which he knew to be as aggressive as his own. He knew right. Told to move against the position, the yellow-haired Michigander — lately brevetted a major general on the eve of his twenty-fifth birthday — sent one brigade to strike the rebel left, which was somewhat advanced, and led the other two in a saber-swinging charge on the hastily thrown-up breastworks dead ahead. He had his favorite mount shot from under him in the assault, but that did not disrupt the breakthrough in either direction or slow down the lunge for the one bridge over the river in the Confederate rear. The result, according to the cartographer Jed Hotchkiss, posted by Early as a lookout, was "one of the most terrible panics and stampedes I have ever seen." Early himself agreed, though he caught no more than a tail-end glimpse of the rout. "I went to the top of a hill to reconnoiter," he later wrote, "and had the mortification of seeing the greater part of my command being carried off as prisoners, and a force of the enemy moving rapidly toward Rockfish Gap."

What was worse, "the greater part" was a considerable understatement. Merritt claimed "over 1000 prisoners" — a figure enlarged by Sheridan to 1600 and by Custer to 1800 in their reports, although the latter came to half again more than Early had on hand — along with 11 guns, close to 200 wagons, and 17 flags. Best of all, according to Sheridan, was the seizure of Rockfish Gap, "as the crossing of the Blue Ridge, covered with snow as it was, at any other point would have been difficult." The other division coming up next morning, March 3, he sent his captives and spoils back to Winchester under escort — all but the rebel battle flags, which he kept to flaunt in the faces of future opponents, if any — then moved on to make camp that night at Charlottesville, twenty miles away. For two days he rested his men and horses there, what time he did not have them ripping up track on the Virginia Central, before he set out southwest down the Orange & Alexandria on March 6, wrecking it too in his wake, bound for Lynchburg in accordance with the instructions in Grant's letter, written two weeks ago that day.

Old Jubilee had a harder road to travel. Escaping over the mountains with a few members of his staff — all that managed a getaway when Wharton's two brigades collapsed — he turned up at Lee's headquarters two weeks later. He had left with a corps, nine months ago; now he returned with nothing. Lee comforted him as best he could, but instead of restoring him to the post occupied by Gordon, ordered him back to the Valley. Although there was little to command there, Rosser's 1200 troopers having been summoned to Petersburg in partial replacement for the division still with Hampton in the Carolinas, Lee's hope was that he would be able to collect and attract such fugitives and under- or over-aged volunteers as remained in that burned-out region. Early departed on this mission, but before the month ended Lee rescinded the order, explaining to Breckinridge that he did so, despite his fellow Virginian's "great intelligence, good judgment, and undoubted bravery," because it was clear that his defeats in the lower Valley, capped by the recent final debacle at Waynesboro, had cost him the confidence of those he would be attempting to reassemble or recruit. To Early himself, at the same time, went a letter expressing Lee's "confidence in your ability, zeal, and devotion to the cause" and thanking him "for the fidelity and energy with which you have always supported my efforts, and for the courage and devotion you have ever manifested in the service."

Victory, and Defeat

This letter remained Old Jube's most treasured possession down the years, and did much to relieve the bitterness of the next few weeks — no doubt for him the hardest of the war — while he waited at home in Franklin County for orders to return to duty; orders that never came.

★ ★ ★

On March 3, about the time Sheridan's troopers were approaching Charlottesville, still jubilant over yesterday's lopsided victory at Waynesboro, Lincoln was up at the Capitol signing last-minute bills passed by Congress in preparation for adjournment tomorrow on Inauguration Day. He was interrupted by Stanton, who had just received a wire from Grant requesting instructions on how to reply to a formal query from Lee "as to the possibility of arriving at a satisfactory adjustment of the present unhappy difficulties, by means of a military convention."

There was more behind this than many people knew; Grant gave some of the details in his wire. Longstreet and Ord, it seemed, had met between the lines ten days ago, ostensibly to arrange a prisoner exchange, and Ord had advanced the notion that, the politicians having failed to agree on terms for peace at Hampton Roads, it might be well for the contestants themselves — the men, that is, who had been doing the actual bleeding all along — to "come together as former comrades and friends and talk a little." Grant and Lee could meet for an exchange of views, as could others, not excluding a number of their wives; Mrs Grant and Mrs Longstreet, for example, intimates before the war, could visit back and forth across the lines, along with their husbands, so that "while General Lee and General Grant were arranging for better feeling between the armies, they could be aided by intercourse between the ladies and officers until terms honorable to both sides could be found." Thus Ord spoke to his old army friend James Longstreet, who went to Lee with the proposal. Lee in turn conferred with Davis and Breckinridge. Both agreed the thing was worth a try: particularly the Kentuckian, who, as Old Peter later remarked, "expressed especial approval of the part assigned for the ladies." So Lee returned to Petersburg and sent his letter across the lines to Grant, suggesting "a military convention" as a means of ending the bloodshed, and Grant wired the War Department for instructions, saying: "I have not returned any reply, but promised to do so at noon tomorrow."

Noon tomorrow would be the hour at which Lincoln was scheduled to take the inaugural oath to "preserve, protect, and defend the Constitution of the United States" against what he conceived to be its domestic foes, and he did not intend to break — or, what might be worse, stand by while a clubby group of West Point professionals, North and South, broke for him — either that or another public oath he had taken just under nine months ago in Philadelphia: "We accepted this war for an object, a worthy object, and the war will end when that object is attained. Under God, I hope it never will until that time." The thing to do, as he saw it, was to nip this infringement in the bud. Accordingly, he wrote out in his own hand, for Stanton's signature, a carefully worded reply to Grant's request for instructions. "The President directs me to say to you that he wishes you to have no conference with General Lee unless it be for the capitulation of Gen. Lee's army, or on some minor and purely military matter. He instructs me to say that you are not to decide, discuss, or confer upon any political question. Such questions the President holds in his own hands; and will submit them to no military conferences or conventions. Meantime you are to press to the utmost your military advantages."

That ended that; Grant informed Lee next day that he had "no authority to accede to your proposition.... Such authority is vested in the President of the United States alone." Lincoln meantime had wound up his bill-signing chores and returned to the White House for the last night of his first term in office, having received on February 12 — his fifty-sixth birthday — formal notice from the Electoral College of his victory over McClellan, back in November, by a vote of 212 to 21.

Inauguration Day broke cold and rainy. High on the dome of the Capitol, unfinished on this occasion four years ago, Thomas Crawford's posthumous bronze Freedom, a sword in one hand, a victory wreath in the other, peered out through the mist on a scene of much confusion, caused in part by deepening mud that hampered the movement of the throng of visitors jammed into town for the show, and in part by Mrs Lincoln, who, growing impatient at a long wait under the White House portico, ordered her carriage to proceed up Pennsylvania Avenue at a gallop, disrupting the schedule worked out by the marshals. Her husband had already gone ahead to a room in the Senate wing, and was occupied with signing another sheaf of bills rammed through to beat the deadline now at hand. The rain let up before midmorning, though the sun did not break through the scud of clouds, and around 11 o'clock a small, sharp-pointed, blue-white diamond of a star — later identified as the planet Venus — appeared at the zenith, directly over the Capitol dome, bright in the murky daylight sky.

First the Senate would witness the swearing in of Andrew Johnson; for which purpose, shortly before noon, all the members of both houses and their distinguished guests fairly packed the Senate chamber. Diplomats in gold lace and feathers rivaled the crinolined finery of the ladies in the gallery. Joe Hooker, hale and rosy in dress blues, represented the army, Farragut the navy; "The dear old Admiral," women cooed as the latter entered, wearing all of his sixty-three years on his balding head. Governors of most loyal states were there, together with the nine Supreme Court justices, clad, as one observer noted, in "long black silk nightgowns (so to speak) though it's all according to law." These last — five of them of Lincoln's making, including the new Chief

Victory, and Defeat

Justice — were seated in the front row, to the right of the chair, while the Cabinet occupied the front row on the left. Lincoln sat between the two groups, looker trimmer than usual because of a shorter clip to his beard and hair.

As the clock struck 12, Vice President Hamlin entered, arm in arm with the man who would replace him. They had no sooner taken their seats than Hamlin rose and opened the ceremony by expressing his "heartfelt and undissembled thanks" to his colleagues for their kindness over the past four years. He paused, then asked: "Is the Vice President elect now ready to take and subscribe the oath of office?" Johnson got up. "I am," he said firmly, and launched without further preamble into an unscheduled oration. "Senators, I am here today as the chosen Vice President of the United States, and as such, by constitutional provision, I am made the presiding officer of this body." He wore his habitual scowl, as if to refute some expected challenge to his claim. "I therefore present myself here, in obedience to the high behests of the American people, to discharge a constitutional duty, and not presumptuously to thrust myself in a position so exalted." He spoke impromptu, without notes, and his words boomed loud against a hush more puzzled than shocked; just yet. "May I at this moment — it may not be irrelevant to the occasion — advert to the workings of our institutions under the Constitution which our fathers framed and George Washington approved, as exhibited by the position in which I stand before the American Senate, in the sight of the American people? Deem me not vain or arrogant; yet I should be less than man if under the circumstances I were not proud of being an American citizen, for today one who claims no high descent, one who comes from the ranks of the people, stands, by the choice of a free constituency, in the second place in this Government."

By now a buzz had begun in the chamber, spreading from point to point as his listeners gradually perceived that his near incoherence was not the result of faulty hearing or a lapse of comprehension on their part. "All this is in wretched bad taste," Speed whispered to Welles on his right. Welles agreed, saying to Stanton on his other side: "Johnson is either drunk or crazy." Stanton wagged his head. "There is evidently *some*thing wrong," he admitted. Then Welles had another thought. "I hope it is sickness," he said.

It was, in part. Six weeks ago, emerging shaky from a bout with typhoid and the strain of the campaign, the Tennessean had sought permission to stay in Nashville for the taking of the oath, but when Lincoln urged him to come to Washington he did so, though he still was far from well. "I am not fit to be here, and ought not to have left my home," he said that morning after he reached Hamlin's office in the Capitol. Someone brought him a tumbler of whiskey, which he drank to settle his nerves and get his strength up, then followed it with another just before he entered the overheated Senate chamber, saying: "I need all the strength for the occasion I can have." The result was the present diatribe, which continued despite tugs on his coattail from Hamlin, seated behind him, and unseen signals from his friends in front. He had stumped his way through a long campaign and he was stumping still. "Humble as I am, plebeian as I may be deemed," he went on, red-faced and unsteady, "permit me in the presence of this brilliant assemblage to enunciate the truth that courts and cabinets, the President and his advisers, derive their power and their greatness from the people." He wore on, croaking hoarsely toward the end, and when at last the oath had been administered he turned to the crowd with the Bible in both hands and kissed it fervently, saying as he did so: "I kiss this Book in the face of my nation of the United States."

Reactions varied. A reporter noted that, while Seward remained "bland and serene as a summer's day" and Charles Sumner "wore a saturnine and sarcastic smile," few others among those present managed to abide the harangue with such aplomb or enjoyment. Lincoln, for example, kept his head down throughout the blusterous display, apparently engaged in profound study of his shoe tips. Later he would discount the fears and rumors going round about the man who might replace him at any tragic moment. "I have known Andy for many years," he would say. "He made a bad slip the other day, but you need not be scared. Andy aint a drunkard." Just now, though, he had had enough embarrassment on so solemn an occasion. As he rose to join the procession filing out onto the inaugural platform set up along the east face of the building, he said pointedly to a marshal: "Do not let Johnson speak outside."

Emerging, he saw beneath the overcast of clouds what a journalist described as "a sea of heads in the great plaza in front of the Capitol, as far as the eye could reach, and breaking in waves along its outer edges." When he came out to take his seat a roar of applause went up from the crowd, which subsided only to rise again when the sergeant-at-arms, performing in dumb show, "arose and bowed, with his shining black hat in hand ... and Abraham Lincoln, rising tall and gaunt among the groups about him, stepped forward." Just as he did so, the sun broke through and flooded the platform with its golden light. "Every heart beat quicker at the unexpected omen," the reporter declared. Certainly Lincoln's own did. "Did you notice that sunburst?" he later asked. "It made my heart jump." He moved to the lectern, unfolding a single large sheet of paper on which his speech was printed in two broad columns. "Fellow countrymen," he said.

There was, as he maintained, "less occasion for an extended address" than had been the case four years ago, when his concern had been to avoid the war that began soon afterward. Nor would he much concern himself just now with purely military matters or venture a prediction as to the outcome, though his hope was high in that regard. "Both parties deprecated war; but one of them would make war rather than let the nation survive, and the other would accept war rather than let it perish. And the war came.... Neither party expected for the war the magnitude or the duration which it has already attained. Neither anticipated that the cause of the conflict might cease with, or even before, the conflict itself should cease. Each looked for an easier triumph, and a result less fundamental and astounding. Both read the same Bible and pray to the same God, and each invokes His aid against the other. It may seem strange that any men should dare to ask a just God's assistance in wringing their bread from the sweat of other men's faces; but let us judge not, that we be not judged. The prayers of both could not be answered; that of neither has been answered fully. The Almighty has His own purposes. 'Woe unto the world because of offenses! for it must needs be that offenses come; but woe to that man by whom the offense cometh!'"

"Bless the Lord!" some down front cried up: Negroes mostly, who took their tone from his, and responded as they would have done in church. Lincoln kept on reading from the printed text in a voice one hearer described as "ringing and somewhat shrill."

"If we shall suppose that American slavery is one of those offenses which, in the providence of God, must needs come, but which, having continued through His appointed time, He now wills to remove, and that He gives to both North and South this terrible war, as the woe due to those by whom the offense came, shall we discern therein any departure from those divine attributes which the believers in a living God always ascribe to Him? Fondly do we hope — fervently do we pray — that this mighty scourge of war may speedily pass away. Yet, if God wills that it continue until all the wealth piled by the bondman's two hundred and fifty years of unrequited toil shall be sunk, and until every drop of blood drawn with the lash shall be paid by another drawn with the sword, as was said three thousand years ago, so still it must be said: 'The judgments of the Lord are true and righteous altogether.'"

"Bless the Lord!" came up again through the thunder of applause, but Lincoln passed at once to the peroration. He was beyond the war now, into the peace which he himself would never see.

"With malice toward none; with charity for all; with firmness in the right, as God gives us to see the right, let us strive on to finish the work we are in; to bind up the nation's wounds; to care for him who shall have borne the battle, and for his widow, and his orphan — to do all which may achieve and cherish a just and a lasting peace, among ourselves and with all nations."

Thus ended, as if on a long-held organ note, the shortest inaugural any President had delivered since George Washington was sworn in the second time. When the applause subsided, Chase signaled the clerk of the Supreme Court to come forward with the Bible held open-faced before him; Lincoln rested one hand on it while repeating the oath of office. "So help me God," he said, then bent and kissed the Book. Cheers went up as he rose once more to his full height and guns began thudding their shotless, flat-toned salutes in celebration. He turned to the crowd and bowed in several directions before he reëntered the Capitol and emerged again from a basement entrance, where a two-horse barouche waited to take him and Tad back to the White House in time for him to rest up for the reception scheduled there that evening. Between 8 and 11 o'clock, newsmen reckoned, he shook hands with no less than six thousand people, though these were by no means all who tried to get close enough to touch him. Walt Whitman, caught in the press of callers, was one of those who had to be content with watching from a distance. "I saw Mr Lincoln," the poet wrote in his notebook that night, "dressed all in black, with white kid gloves and a clawhammer coat, receiving, as in duty bound, shaking hands, looking very disconsolate ... as if he would give anything to be somewhere else."

He was concerned about the reception of his speech that afternoon. "What did you think of it?" he asked friends as they passed down the line. He had heard and seen the cheers and tears of people near the platform, but tonight he was like a neglected author in wistful search of a discerning critic. Later, writing to Thurlow Weed, he said that he expected the address "to wear as well — perhaps better than — anything I have produced; but I believe it is not immediately popular. Men are not flattered by being shown that there has been a difference of purpose between the Almighty and them." Actually, the difficulty lay elsewhere. Some among his hearers and readers found his style as turgid, his syntax as knotty to unravel, as that of the new Vice President in the tirade staged indoors. "While the sentiments are noble," a disgruntled Pennsylvanian would complain this week in a private letter, "[Lincoln's inaugural] is one of the most awkwardly expressed documents I ever read — if it be correctly printed. When he knew it would be read by millions all over the world, why under the heavens did he not make it a little more creditable to American scholarship? Jackson was not too proud to get Van Buren to slick up his state papers. Why could not Mr Seward have prepared the Inaugural so as to save it from the ridicule of a sophomore in a British university?"

In point of fact, the British reaction was quite different from the one this Keystone critic apprehended. "It was a noble speech," the Duke of Argyll wrote his friend Sumner, "just and true, and solemn. I think it has produced a great effect in England." The London *Spectator* thought so, too, saying: "No statesman ever uttered words stamped at once with the seal of so deep a wisdom and so true a simplicity." Even the *Times*, pro-Confederate as it mostly was, had praise for the address. Nor was approval lacking on this side of the Atlantic, even among those with valid claims to membership in the New World aristocracy. "What think you of the inaugural?" C. F. Adams Junior wrote his ambassador father. "That rail-splitting lawyer is one of the wonders of the day. Once at Gettysburg and now again on a greater occasion he has shown a capacity for rising to the demands of the hour which we should not expect from orators or men of the schools. This inaugural strikes me in its grand simplicity and directness as being for all time the keynote of this war; in it a people seemed to speak in the sublimely simple utterance of ruder times. What will Europe think of this utterance of the rude ruler, of whom they have nourished so lofty a contempt? Not a prince or minister in all Europe could have risen to such an equality with the occasion."

Others besides Adams drew the Gettysburg comparison, being similarly affected, and presently there was still another likeness in what followed. Lincoln fell ill, much as he had done after the earlier address, except then it had been varioloid, a mild form of smallpox, and this was a different kind of ailment — noninfectious, nonspecific, yet if anything rather more debilitating. In fact, that was at the root of his present indisposition. He was exhausted. "Nothing touches the tired spot," he had begun to say within a year of taking office, and lately he had been referring again to "the tired spot, which can't be got at," somewhere deep inside him, trunk and limbs and brain. "I'm a tired man," he told one caller. "Sometimes I think I'm the tiredest man on earth."

If so, he had cause. In the past five weeks — hard on the heels of a bitter campaign for reëlection, which only added to the cumulative strain of leadership through four bloody years of fratricidal conflict — he had cajoled and logrolled Congress into passing the Thirteenth Amendment, dealt with the Confederate commissioners aboard the *River Queen* in Hampton Roads, and kept a watchful eye on Grant while raising the troops and money required to fuel the war machine. All this, plus the drafting and delivery of the second inaugural, was in addition to his usual daily tasks as Chief Executive, not the least of which consisted of enduring the diurnal claims of office-seekers and their sponsors, often men of political heft and high position. Two cabinet changes followed within a week, both the result of his acceding to Fessenden's plea that the time had come for him to leave the Treasury and return to his seat in the Senate. Lincoln replaced him on March 7 with Hugh McCulloch, a Maine-born Hoosier banker, only to have Interior Secretary John P. Usher resign on grounds that he too was from Indiana. Iowa Senator James Harlan was named to take his place, a felicitous choice, since he was a close family friend and the President's son Robert was courting the senator's daughter with the intention of marrying her as soon as he completed his military service.

This too was a problem for Lincoln — or, more specifically, for his wife; which came to the same thing. Just out of college, the young man wanted to enter the army despite strenuous objections by his mother, who grew sick with fear of what might happen to him there. As a result, Lincoln had worked out a compromise, back in January, that might satisfy them both, depending on Grant's response to a proposal made him at the time: "Please read and answer this letter as though I was not President, but only a friend. My son, now in his twenty-second year, having graduated from Harvard, wishes to see something of the war before it ends. I do not wish to put him in the ranks, nor yet to give him a commission to which those who have already served long are better entitled, and better qualified to hold. Could he, without embarrassment to you or detriment to the service, go into your military family with some nominal rank, I, and not the public, furnishing his necessary means? If no, say so without the least hesitation, because I am as anxious, and as deeply interested that you shall not be encumbered, as you can be yourself." Grant replied that he would be glad to have the young man on his staff as an assistant adjutant, his rank to be that of captain and his pay to come from the government, not his father. In mid-February the appointment came through. Soon after attending the inaugural ceremonies in the hard-galloping carriage with his mother and his prospective father-in-law, Robert set out down the coast for City Point. Lincoln was glad to have the difficult matter settled, but it came hard for him that he had had to settle it this way, knowing as he did that he had drafted into the shot-torn ranks of the nation's armies hundreds of thousands of other sons whose mothers loved and feared for them as much as Mary Lincoln did for hers.

As a result of all these pressures and concerns, or rather of his delayed reaction to them, what should have been for him a time of relieved tension — Congress, having adjourned, was not scheduled to reconvene until December, so that he had hope of ending the war in much the same way he had begun it; that is, without a host of frock-coated politicians breathing down his neck — turned out instead to be the one in which he looked and felt his worst. It was as if, like a spent swimmer who collapses only after he has reached the shore, he had had no chance till now, having been occupied with the struggle to keep afloat in a sea of administrative and domestic frets, to realize how close he was to absolute exhaustion. "His face was haggard with care and seamed with thought and trouble," Horace Greeley noted after a mid-March interview. "It looked care-ploughed, tempest-tossed and weather-beaten." One reporter diagnosed the ailment as "a severe attack of influenza," but another remarked more perceptively that the President was "suffering from the exhausting attentions of office hunters." In any case, on March 14 — ten days after the inauguration — Lincoln was obliged to hold the scheduled Tuesday cabinet meeting in his bedroom, prone beneath the covers but with his head and shoulders propped on pillows stacked against the headboard of his bed.

That day's rest did some good, and even more came from a new rule setting 3 o'clock as the close of office hours, so far at least as scheduled callers went. By the end of the week he felt well enough to go with his wife and guests to a performance of Mozart's *Magic Flute* at Grover's Theatre, enjoying it so much indeed that when Mrs Lincoln suggested leaving before the final curtain reunited the fire-tested lovers, he protested: "Oh, no. I want to see it out. It's best, when you undertake a job, to finish it." Much of his fascination was with one of the sopranos, whose feet were not only large but flat. "The beetles wouldn't have much of a chance there," he whispered, nodding toward the stage.

Here was at least one sign that he was better, though it was true he often joked in just this way to offset the melancholia that dogged him all his life. He still felt weary — "flabby," as he called it — and no amount of rest, by night or day, got through to the tired spot down somewhere deep inside him. He considered a trip, perhaps a visit to the army in Virginia, "immediately after the next rain." Then on March 20 a wire from Grant seemed to indicate that the general either had read his mind or else had spies in the White House. "Can you not visit City Point for a day or two? I would like very much to see you, and I think the rest would do you good."

Lincoln at once made plans to go. He would leave in the next day or two, aboard the fast, well-armed dispatch steamer *Bat*. "Will notify you of exact time, once it shall be fixed upon," he replied to Grant. But when he told his wife, she announced that she too would be going; it had been two weeks since Robert left for City Point, and she would see him there. So the expanded party shifted to the more commodious *River Queen*, retaining the *Bat* for escort. Tad would go, along with Mrs Lincoln's maid, a civilian bodyguard, and a military aide. Lincoln had heard from Grant on Monday, and on Thursday he was off down the Potomac, sailing from the Sixth Street wharf in the early afternoon.

✗ 2 ✗

That same Thursday — March 23 — Sherman reached Goldsboro, the goal of his 425-mile slog up the Carolinas, to find Schofield waiting for him with reinforcements enough to lift his over-all strength to just under 90,000 of all arms. Both had run into their first hard fighting of the double-pronged campaign, and both had come through it more or less intact, despite losses they would rather have avoided until they combined to inflict the utter destruction of whatever gray fragments presumed to stand in the path of their northward conjunction with Grant at the gates of Richmond.

What was more, for all the wretched weather and sporadic opposition, the two blue columns — themselves divided and out of touch, each with the other, until they arrived at their common objective — had made good time. Two weeks after Columbia went up in smoke, Sherman got both wings of his army up to the Pee Dee River and called a halt at Cheraw, March 3–5, to give his bedraggled troops a chance to dry their clothes and scrape away the mud they had floundered through while crossing the rain-bulged Wateree and soft-banked Lynch's Creek. Then he was off again, out of the Palmetto State at last. Reactions differed, up and down the long line of marchers; some looked back with cackling glee on the destruction, while others felt a softening effect. "South Carolina may have been the cause of the whole thing," a Michigan lieutenant wrote in a running letter home, "but she has had an awful punishment."

She had indeed, and now ahead lay the Old North State; a quite different prospect, Sherman believed, one that entailed a much higher degree of Union sentiment, which he intended to woo and play upon en route. "Deal as moderately and fairly by North Carolinians as possible," he told subordinates, "and fan the flame of discord already subsisting between them and their proud cousins of South Carolina. There never was much love lost between them. Touch upon the chivalry of running away, always leaving their families for us to feed and protect, and then on purpose accusing us of all sorts of rudeness."

Accordingly, guards were posted at the gates or on the steps of roadside houses, barring entrance to the marchers filing past, and the women, emboldened by this protection, came out on their porches to watch the invaders go by, shoulders hunched against the rain, feet made heavy with balled-up mud, and spirits considerably dampened. The women looked at the men, and the men looked back. "We glanced ruefully at them out of the shadow of our lowering, drenched hat rims," one soldier was to say, recalling freer times a week ago, when their red-haired commander had scorned to practice such restraint. Denied access to residences, they exercised their arsonist proclivities on the forests of pine through which they passed between the Pee Dee and Cape Fear rivers — and found the result even more spectacular than those produced when they set fire to barns and gins, back in Georgia and South Carolina. Notched for the drawing of sap, the trees burned like enormous torches, often hundreds at a time, when a match was put to them. Overhead, "the smoke could hardly escape through the green canopy, and hung like a pall," an Ohio colonel noted. "It looked like a fire in a cathedral." A New York private, highly conscious of being part of what he saw, found himself awed by the tableau, "all to be heard and seen only by glimpses under the smoke and muffled by the Niagara-like roar of the flames as they licked up turpentine and pitch. Now came rolling back from the depths of the pine forest the chorus of thousands singing 'John Brown's body lies a-moldering.' " He considered it "at once a prophecy and a fulfillment."

This final leg of the march, just over a fourth of the whole, would be covered in two sixty-mile jumps, with a rest halt in between: Cheraw to Fayetteville, a major Confederate supply base, and Fayetteville to Goldsboro, where Sherman had arranged to meet Schofield, barring serious complications. Driving rains and deepening mud, together with the washout of all bridges over the Wateree, had thrown him a bit off schedule by now, but he hoped to get back on it by making better time through the piny highlands. And so he did, despite the unrelenting downpour. "It was the damndest marching I ever saw," he said of an Illinois regiment's covering fifteen soggy miles in five hours. Delighted, he detached three enlisted volunteers — two of them disguised as rebel officers, the third as a civilian — to pick their way through enemy country, ninety-odd miles east to Wilmington, with a note for whoever Schofield had left in charge there: "If possible, send a boat up Cape Fear River.... We are well and have done finely. The rains make our roads difficult, and may delay us about Fayetteville, in which case I would like to have some bread, sugar, and coffee. We have abundance of all else. I expect to reach Goldsboro by the 20th instant." He kept going, crossing the Lumber River by the light of flaming pine knots, and made it into Fayetteville before midday, March 11, five days out of Cheraw; Hardee, he learned, had left the night before, and Hampton had come close to being captured by the first blue troopers riding in that morning. After running the national flag up over the market place and establishing headquarters in the handsome former U.S. arsenal — now U.S. again — his first concern was to find out whether anything had been heard from downriver in response to the note, written three days ago, which the three-man detail had been charged with getting through to Wilmington.

Nothing had. But at noon next day the Sabbath quiet was shattered by the scream of a steamboat whistle; Alfred Terry, in command at Wilmington, had sent the army tug *Davidson* upriver in response to Sherman's note, all three copies of which had reached him the day before. Armored with cotton bales to shield her crew from snipers, the boat's main cargo was not sugar, coffee, or hardtack, but news of the outside world, as set forth in dispatches and a bundle of the latest papers, North and South. "The effect was electric," Sherman was to say, "and no one can realize the feeling unless, like us, he has been for months cut off from all communication with friends and compelled to listen to the croakings and prognostications of open enemies." He ordered the tug to return downriver at sunset, passing the word that she would take with her all the letters anyone cared to write, and gave instructions for a larger vessel to be sent back up as soon as possible, this time with the hardtack, coffee, and sugar he had requested in the first place, plus all the shoes, stockings, and drawers that could be spared. Which done, he put his men back to work destroying rebel installations, including the Fayetteville arsenal itself, and spent much of the night and the following day studying the dispatches and perusing newspapers crammed with speculations as to his whereabouts and fate.

The best of the news was that Schofield, his strength increased above 30,000 by the addition of two new divisions, one made up of convalescents sent from Washington, the other of troops from coastal garrisons such as Beaufort, was hard on the go for Goldsboro and seemed likely to get there well within the time allotted. Leaving Terry to hold Wilmington with his X Corps, in case improbable rebel combinations obliged Sherman to veer in that direction at the last minute, he had sent Jacob Cox by sea to New Bern with his beefed-up XXIII Corps, under instructions to move west along the Atlantic & N.C. Railroad — which was not only shorter and more repairable than the Wilmington & Weldon, but was also provided with locomotives and cars, as the other was not — thus establishing a rapid-transit link between Goldsboro and the coast, not at the mouth of the Cape Fear River, as originally intended, but instead at the mouth of the Neuse in Pamlico Sound, which afforded the navy far better all-weather harbor facilities for unloading the mountain of supplies Sherman's 60,000 footsore, tattered veterans would need at the end of their long swing through the Carolinas. Cox had set out from New Bern on March 1, repairing the railroad as he went, and Schofield had left Wilmington to join him, wanting to be on hand in case he ran into serious opposition from Hoke, whose division, flung out of Wilmington two weeks before, was reported to have fallen back on Kinston, where the Atlantic & N.C. crossed the Neuse, about midway between Goldsboro and New Bern.

Sherman was pleased with this news of Schofield's progress across the way, promising as it did an early combination for the follow-up march into Virginia. He had grown more cautious since learning that Johnston, his wily Georgia adversary, was back in command of the forces in his front. So far, here inland, nothing had come of the shift, however, and Terry's report assured him that all was well in the other direction, too. "Jos. Johnston may try to interpose between me here and Schofield about New Bern," he had written Grant in a letter the *Davidson* carried downriver at sunset, March 12, "but I think he will not try that." His notion was that the Virginian would "concentrate his scattered armies at Raleigh": in which case, he told his friend the general-in-chief, "I will go straight at him as soon as I get our men reclothed and our wagons reloaded." Meantime, before he moved on, there was the arsenal to be disposed of, a handsome cluster of cream-colored brick structures whose well-kept grounds served Fayetteville as a municipal park. "The arsenal is in fine order, and has been much enlarged," he informed Stanton in a letter that went along with Grant's. "I cannot leave a detachment to hold it, therefore shall burn it, blow it up with gunpowder, and then with rams knock down its walls. I take it for granted the United States will never again trust North Carolina with an arsenal to appropriate at her leisure."

In point of fact, he had been right to suspect that Johnston was up to something, and wrong to think that all he was up to was a concentration at Raleigh. Terry's latest information about Schofield's other column, toiling westward out the Atlantic & N.C., was three days old; within which span, as a result of Johnston's caginess, Cox had had to fight a battle on disadvantageous ground. Schofield had reached New Bern by sea from Wilmington on March 7, and when he went forward next morning, beyond the spike-hammer din of rail repair crews, he found the head of the infantry column under fire from graybacks who had lain in wait along the high ground just this side of Southwest Creek, the western limit of Dover Swamp, a thirty-mile-wide marsh through which the railroad threaded its way to within three miles of Kinston and the Neuse. A sudden, unexpected attack had struck and scattered two blue regiments in advance, capturing three fourths of the men, and the attackers seemed determined to expand this opening setback into a full-scale defeat. What was more, they might be able to do just that, by the sheer weight of their numbers. Prisoners taken were found to be not only from Hoke's division, already suspected of lurking up ahead, but also from Stewart's and S. D. Lee's corps of the Army of Tennessee, a good five hundred miles from home.

It was Johnston, urged by R. E. Lee to strike before the Federals united in his front, who had made this possible by reinforcing the troops opposing Cox. Moreover, he had other such moves in mind, and was even now in the process of effecting them: not so much with the intention of actually defeating his red-haired antagonist — each of whose two wings, like Schofield's two-corps army over toward the coast, was nearly half again larger than his total force — but rather in the hope of delaying the blue combination until Lee could give Grant the slip and join him, here in Carolina, for an offensive combination of their own. Although by ordinary he was far from being the cut-and-slash sort of general who seized upon long chances as a means of redressing odds that were even longer, desperation had made him bold. Indeed, there was no better indication of the extent of Confederate desperation, at this stage, than Joseph E. Johnston's overnight conversion into the kind of commander he became, at least for a time, hard on the heels of having told Lee, while en route to take over from Beauregard at Charlotte: "It is too late," and following this with a letter in which, having studied the strength reports on hand, he said flatly: "In my opinion these troops form an army too weak to cope with Sherman."

He had at the time fewer than 20,000 men, considerably scattered. Hardee's 10,000 at Cheraw, the rail terminus he fell back on after evacuating Charleston, were joined by Hampton's 4000 cavalry, three fourths of them under Wheeler and the rest under Butler, while another 4000 infantry, on hand or still on the way from the Army of Tennessee, brought the total to 18,000 of all arms. Presently, on March 4, this figure was enlarged by Lee's extension of Johnston's authority to include Hoke's 5500, withdrawn by Bragg to Goldsboro after the fall of Wilmington. By then, however, Hardee had been obliged to evacuate Cheraw, under pressure from Howard and Slocum, and had fallen back on Fayetteville, reduced to about 8000 by desertions and the detachment of his South Carolina militia, who were forbidden by law to follow him out of the state. Sherman continued his march, obviously toward Fayetteville now, but Johnston was hard put to determine whether his adversary would be headed next for Goldsboro or for Raleigh. Splitting the difference, he decided to concentrate at Smithfield, on the railroad midway between the two, for a strike at one or another of Sherman's wings before they came together at whichever city was their goal. There was hope in this, but only by contrast with the surrounding gloom of the piecemeal and seemingly endless retreat. Desertions were heavy and getting heavier, particularly by Carolinians, South and North, whose homes lay in the path or wake of the blue despoilers tramping northward. Ambrose Wright, commanding one of Hardee's two divisions, took the occasion to return to his native Georgia, where he had been elected *in absentia* to the senate; Taliaferro took over his undersized division, adding the Sumter garrison to its roll — a disgruntled body in which tempers ran short among men unaccustomed to marching or going hungry. A sergeant, for example, on being reproved for advising comrades to desert, drew his pistol and attempted to use it on the lieutenant who had reproached him. Arrested, he was tried before a drumhead court and sentenced to be shot. He died without the consolation of religion. "Preacher, I never listened to you at Fort Sumter," he said bitterly to the chaplain who came to pray with him on the night before his execution, "and I won't listen to you now."

These were brave men; Wright had been one of the Army of Northern Virginia's hardest-hitting brigadiers, all the way from the Seven Days to the Siege of Petersburg, and the sergeant had stood up to everything the U.S. Navy had to throw at him in the rubble and brick dust of Sumter. What they mainly suffered from was despair, a discouragement verging into disgust as they were shuttled about, invariably rearward, to avoid being crushed by the compact masses of bluecoats in their front. Johnston knew well enough that the best correction for flagging morale lay in delivery of the blow he planned to throw as soon as he completed the concentration now in progress around Smithfield, although this was a necessarily slow procedure, scattered as his 21,500 soldiers were in their attempt to confront the 90,000 invaders moving against them from the south and east, unchecked so far, and scarcely even delayed. Then Bragg suggested an interim maneuver that might not only lift morale but also disrupt the Federal convergence. Schofield had divided his army, holding one corps at Wilmington while the other went to New Bern; Bragg's notion was for Johnston to reinforce him at Goldsboro for an attack, just east of Kinston, on the corps slogging westward along the Atlantic and N.C. Railroad; after which he would hurry back east by rail in time for a share in the strike at one of Sherman's wings before they closed on Raleigh or Goldsboro, whichever they headed for after reaching Fayetteville. "A few hours would suffice to unite the forces at Smithfield with mine and assure a victory," he telegraphed headquarters on March 6. Johnston thought it over, and then next day — uncharacteristically; for the shift involved a division of force in the presence of a greatly superior foe — decided to give the thing a try. All he had on hand just now were some 3000 men from the Army of Tennessee, forwarded by Beauregard, who had remained in Charlotte to expedite such movements; but he alerted them for the shift, and notified Bragg that they were at his disposal. "Send trains when fight is impending," he wired, "and send back troops as soon as it is over."

That was how it came about that Bragg was able to surprise and crumple the head of Cox's column next morning, March 8, just before it reached the western rim of Dover Swamp. Encouraged by this initial rout, which netted him close to a thousand prisoners, he pressed his assault on the main body. Schofield had arrived by then, however, and had ordered light intrenchments thrown up during the lull that followed the opening attack: with the result that Bragg rebounded to search elsewhere along Southwest Creek for a breakthrough point. He never found it, though he tried for the rest of that day and the next, when Cox brought up the remainder of his 15,000-man corps, including the railroad workers, to stand fast against the graybacks, whom he estimated at better than twice their actual number of 8500. On the third day, March 10, Bragg withdrew across the Neuse, burning the wagon and railway bridges in his rear, and got his troops aboard the cars for a fast ride west to Smithfield, as he had said he would do, in time for a share in the sequential attack on Sherman. The Battle of Kinston — or Wise's Forks, as the Federals sometimes called it — was a long way short of the triumph he had predicted, but the respective casualty lists went far toward sustaining his claim that he had scored a tactical success. He lost 134 men in all, while Cox lost 1257, most of them captured at the outset. What was more, the engagement had served its larger purpose as a check to Schofield's progress toward Goldsboro. It was March 14 before he got the bridges rebuilt across the Neuse, and still another week, after summoning Terry up from Wilmington, before he reached his appointed goal. Even so, he reached it well before Sherman, whom Johnston had struck not once but twice in the course of Schofield's final week of marching west along the railroad toward their common objective.

Old Joe was of course disappointed that Bragg had not been able to do Schofield all the damage promised in his plea for reinforcements, but he was grateful for the resultant easing of pressure from the east while he continued his efforts to pull his scattered units together for the projected strike at Sherman, about to move out of Fayetteville by now. Still uncertain whether this main blue force was headed for Raleigh or Goldsboro, he held Bragg and the Tennessee contingent near Smithfield, midway between them, and divided his cavalry to patrol the roads in both directions, Butler's troopers on the left and Wheeler's on the right, the latter covering Hardee's northward withdrawal from Fayetteville under instructions to slow down, if he could, the march of the Federals in his rear. For all his grave numerical disadvantage, Johnston at least had no shortage of brass in the corps-sized army he planned to unite and throw at one or another of Sherman's wings; Bragg was a full general, Hardee, Stewart, and Hampton lieutenant generals, and in addition he had fourteen major generals and innumerable brigadiers, not

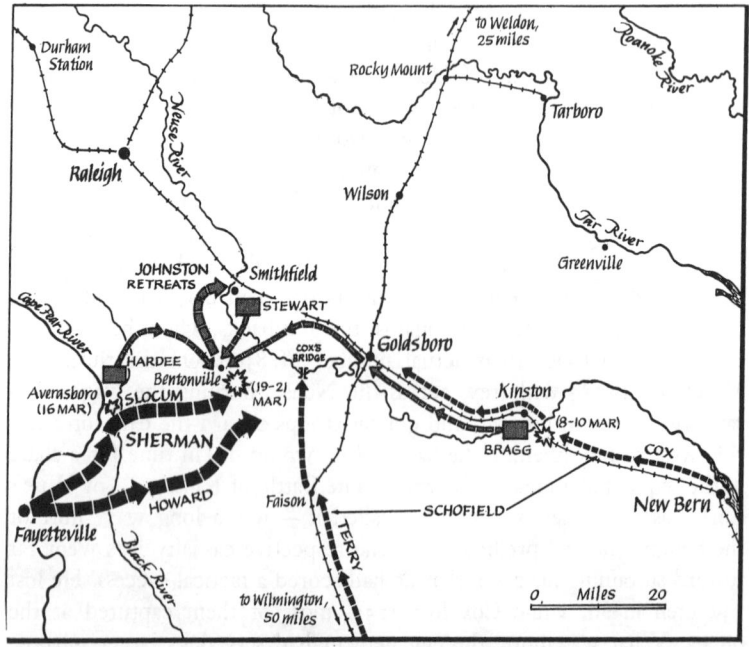

to mention another full general, Beauregard, expediting the movement of troops through Charlotte, and still a fourth lieutenant general, S. D. Lee, present but not yet recovered enough from his post-Nashville wound to take the field. For all their various prickly characteristics — including, in several paired cases, a stronger dislike for each other than for anything in blue — they made a distinguished roster, one that augured well for the conduct of the impending battle. Johnston took much comfort from that, and also from something else he learned about this time. Texas Senator Louis Wigfall, one of his most ardent supporters in the capital, wrote that both the President and Mrs Davis appeared to be in deep distress over the current situation. The Virginian replied on March 14: "I have a most unchristian satisfaction in what you say of the state of mind of the leading occupants of the Presidential Mansion. For me, it is very sufficient revenge."

Sherman began his march out of Fayetteville that same day, and by the next — having completed his demolition of the arsenal by alternately blowing it up and battering it down — had both wings over the Cape Fear River, trudging north for a feint at Raleigh before he turned east to keep his March 20 appointment with Schofield at Goldsboro, five days off. Terry had not been able to send shoes or clothing on the *Davidson*'s return upriver, but he had sent coffee and sugar, to the delight of the tattered, half-barefoot veterans, and he had relieved the column of "twenty to thirty thousand useless mouths," started downriver by Sherman under escort, white and black, to be herded into refugee camps at Wilmington; "They are a dead weight to me and consume our supplies," the red-haired commander explained. He was in higher spirits than ever, having learned that Sheridan would likely be joining him in a week or two. Far from resenting the prospect of sharing laurels with the man who next to himself was the chief hero of the day, he looked forward to his fellow Ohioan's arrival as "a disturbing element in the grand and beautiful game of war.... If he reaches me, I'll make all North Carolina howl," he told Terry, adding the further inducement: "I will make him a deed of gift of every horse in the state, to be settled for at the day of judgment."

For all his lightness of heart as he set out on the final leg of his march, he was thoroughly aware of possible last-minute dangers in his path. Indeed, he was overaware of them, not only because of his great respect for Johnston, who had shown in the past a capacity for reading his mind as accurately as if he were reading his mail, but also because he more than doubled his adversary's true numerical strength with an estimate of 45,000 of all arms; a not unreasonable error after all, since the Virginian had been in command for better than two weeks, presumably with every Confederate resource at his disposal for fending off this ultimate strike through the Carolinas. Properly cautious now that he was within a few days of his goal, Sherman ordered four divisions in each wing to travel light, ready for action, while the others — two in Slocum's case, three in Howard's — accompanied the train and guns to help them along through the mud, thereby assuring speed in case of breakdowns and alertness in case of attack. "I can whip Joe Johnston if he don't catch one of my corps in flank," he had written Terry from Fayetteville, "and I will see that my army marches hence to Goldsboro in compact form."

So he said. But compactness was no easy thing to achieve on roads that varied greatly in condition, especially under the pelting of rain, which now began to come down harder than ever. Besides, in the opening stage of this final leg of the march, while Howard's wing traveled a fairly direct route (a little north of east) toward Cox's Bridge, a dozen miles above Goldsboro on the Neuse, Slocum's followed a more circuitous route (a little east of north) up the Fayetteville-Raleigh road along the left bank of the Cape Fear River — a move designed to mislead Johnston into assembling all his troops for the defense of the state capital, in the belief that it was the Federal objective. If successful, this would remove the graybacks from contention; for Slocum meantime would have swung due east at Averasboro, twenty miles upriver from Fayetteville, to get back in touch with Howard near Bentonville, twelve miles short of Cox's Bridge, where both would cross for an on-schedule meeting with Schofield at Goldsboro and a brief pause for rest and refitment before turning to deal with Johnston, once and for all, preparatory to setting out for Virginia to join Grant. In any case, that was Sherman's plan, and he rode with Slocum to see that all went well.

All did, despite frequent clashes between Kilpatrick's horsemen, screening the outer flank, and Wheeler's. On the first night out, March 15, Slocum made camp about eight miles south of Averasboro, where he would swing east tomorrow to reunite the two blue columns before they reached the Neuse, ninth of the nine major rivers between Savannah and their goal. Or so Sherman thought until Slocum took up the march next morning, shortly after sunrise, only to run into heavy infantry fire from dead ahead.

It was Hardee. Instructed by Johnston to keep between Sherman and Raleigh for the double purpose of slowing the bluecoats down and determining their objective (if it was the capital, as seemed likely, he would be joined by Bragg and the Tennesseans for a strike before the Federals got there. If not, if instead they were marching somewhat roundabout on Goldsboro, he would move toward Smithfield, where Bragg and the Tennesseans were posted, for a combined attack somewhere short of the Neuse) he had decided the night before to make a stand, as he later explained, "to ascertain whether I was followed by Sherman's whole army, or part of it, and what was its destination." Half a dozen miles south of Averasboro, where the Cape Fear and

Black rivers were only four miles apart, he came upon suitable ground for such a delaying action. Adopting the tactics used by Daniel Morgan eighty-four years ago at Cowpens, just under two hundred miles away in northwest South Carolina, he placed Taliaferro's less experienced troops in a double line out front, astride the Fayetteville-Raleigh road and facing south between the rivers, with orders to fall back on McLaws' veterans, dug in along another double line 600 yards to the north, as soon as the attackers pressed up close enough to overrun them. These six infantry brigades — Taliaferro's two were mostly converted artillerists from the Sumter garrison — together with Wheeler's two mounted brigades, gave Hardee an overall strength of about 11,000. How many the Federals had, except that they had a lot, the Georgian did not know. He expected to find out soon, however, since that was one of his three main reasons for stopping to fight them in the first place, the other two being to slow them down and find out for certain whether their march was a feint or a true drive on the North Carolina capital, thirty-odd miles in his rear.

They had about twice his number, as it turned out, immediately available under Kilpatrick and in the four divisions Sherman had ordered to travel light for ready use, plus half again as many more who could be called up from the train if they were needed; which they were not. Slocum advanced two divisions in support of the skirmishing troopers, and when at last around 10 o'clock, their progress badly hampered by muddy ravines and a driving rain, they encountered Taliaferro's makeshift force in position astride the road, they halted, pinned down by spattering fire, and sent back word that they had struck Hardee's main line of resistance, intrenched across the swampy neck of land between the rivers. Anxious to waste no more time, Sherman had Slocum commit a third division for an immediate assault. That burned still more daylight, however. It was 3 o'clock before the concerted push could be made, and though it was altogether successful in flinging the graybacks rearward with the loss of three guns and more than two hundred prisoners, the attackers pursued them less than a quarter of a mile before they were pinned down again by fire from a stronger line of works, some 600 yards in rear of the first. "It would have been worse than folly to have attempted a farther advance," one division commander would report, and Sherman and Slocum agreed. Long-range fire continued past sundown into dusk, then stopped. Hardee, who had suffered about 500 casualties, pulled back after nightfall, leaving Wheeler's horsemen to cover his rear, and issued next day a congratulatory order commending his troops, green and seasoned alike, for "giving the enemy the first check he has received since leaving Atlanta."

There was truth in that, and it was also true that Sherman wanted no more of it just now. Unlike Johnston, he was not seeking to fight his enemy piecemeal; he wanted him whole, for total destruction when the time came — after his and Schofield's forces were combined beyond the Neuse. Averasboro had gained him nothing more than control of the field next morning, and had cost him 682 casualties, 149 of them dead or missing, which left 533 wounded to fill the left-wing ambulances and hinder still further the train's hard-grinding progress through the mire. It had also cost him a day of critical time, both for Slocum and for Howard, who had to be told to slow his pace across the way, lest the space between them grow so great that mutual support would no longer be possible in a crisis. There seemed little likelihood of this last, however; Wheeler's troopers faded back up the Raleigh pike which Hardee's men had traveled the night before, apparently in delayed obedience to Johnston's orders for a concentration in front of the threatened capital. Satisfied that his feint had worked, Sherman turned the head of Slocum's column east for Bentonville and Cox's Bridge, as originally planned, when he came in sight of Averasboro at midday, March 17. The rain was pouring down harder than ever, and one officer later testified that St Patrick's Day and the two or three that followed were "among the most wearisome of the campaign. Incessant rain, deep mud, roads always wretched but now nearly impassable, seemed to cap the climax of tedious, laborious marching.... In spite of every exertion," he added, "the columns were a good deal drawn out, and long intervals separated the divisions."

In short, aside from the irreducible disparity in numbers, blue and gray, Johnston could scarcely have asked for a situation more favorable to his purpose than the one reported to him before daybreak, March 18. As a result — for the first time since Seven Pines, nearly three years ago, with his back to Richmond's eastern gates — he went over to the offensive. Informed by Hardee, who had fallen back not on Raleigh but to a point where the road forked east to Smithfield, and by Hampton, who was in touch with Butler and Wheeler, that both of Sherman's wings were across Black River, bound for Goldsboro in separate columns, a day's march apart and badly strung out on sodden, secondary roads, Old Joe called for a concentration at Bentonville that night and an all-out strike just south of there next morning, first at one and then the other of Slocum's corps toiling eastward through the mud. By the time Bragg and the Tennesseans left Smithfield, shortly after sunrise, he had matured his plan so far that he could direct Hardee, a day in advance, to take position "immediately on their right" when he arrived. Hampton, already with Butler on the chosen field, two miles beyond the town, would skirmish with Slocum's leading elements in an attempt to fix him in position for the execution Johnston had designed.

Sherman, having remained with the left wing so long as he supposed it was in graver danger than the other, set out crosscountry next morning — Sunday, March 19 — to join Howard for the crossing of the Neuse and the meeting with Schofield the following day, as scheduled. Soon after he started he heard what he called "some cannonading over about Slocum's head of column," but he kept going, on the assumption that it amounted to nothing more than another try by Hampton to divert and slow him down. Nine air-line miles to the south and east, after a wearing day spent doubling the right-wing column — as badly strung out, tail to head, as was Slocum's across the way — he came upon Howard at Falling Creek, where the roads from Fayetteville and Averasboro came together, four miles from Cox's Bridge; Howard had made camp there, less than twenty miles from Goldsboro, to give his two corps a chance to close up before crossing the river next day. All seemed well in this direction, and any worries Sherman might have had about the cannonade that erupted in his rear when he set out that morning, just short of Bentonville, had been allayed by a staff officer Slocum sent to overtake him with word that the clash was with butternut cavalry, which he was "driving nicely." Still, the rumble and thump of guns had continued from the northwest all day and even past sundown, when a courier reached Falling Creek with another left-wing message, altogether different from the first. Headed 1.30 p.m. and written under fire, it read: "I am convinced the enemy are in strong force to my front. Prisoners report Johnston, Hardee, Hoke and others present. They say their troops are just coming up. I shall strengthen my position and feel of their lines, but I hope you will come up on their left rear in strong force. Yours, truly, H. W. Slocum, Major General."

After reading the message in Howard's tent, where he had removed his boots and uniform to get some rest, Sherman rushed out to stand ankle-deep in the ashes of a campfire, hands clasped behind him — a lanky figure dressed informally, to say the least, in a red flannel undershirt and a pair of drawers. He seemed bemused, but not for long. Presently he was barking orders, and there was much of what one startled witness called "hurrying to and fro and mounting in hot haste." Once a courier was on the way with a note advising Slocum to fight a purely defensive action until the rest of the army joined him, Sherman told Logan, whose corps was in the lead today, to march for Bentonville on the road from Cox's Bridge, and sent word for Blair to follow by the same route; which hopefully would put them in the rebel rear, provided Slocum could hold his position until they got there. Whether this last was possible, however, in the light of subsequent dispatches from the field, was highly doubtful. "I deem it of the greatest importance that the Right Wing come up during the night," Slocum urged in a message written an hour after dark.

That could scarcely be; Bentonville was a good ten miles by road from Falling Creek. Moreover, by way of indicating the fury of the conflict up to now, he requested "all the ammunition and empty ambulances and wagons that can be spared," and added that he had positive information that "the corps and commands of Hardee, Stewart, Lee, Cheatham, Hill, and Hoke are here."

Which Lee? Which Hill? Sherman might have wondered as he stood amid the ashes, convinced as he had been till now that Old Joe would not risk fighting with the Neuse at his back. Still, as a roster — a Confederate order of battle — the list was not only accurate but complete: although it had not been the latter until past midday, when Hardee at last came up. Otherwise Slocum might not have survived the ambush Johnston had devised for his piecemeal destruction.

Bragg and the Tennesseans had reached Bentonville the night before, as ordered, and were deployed for combat by midmorning, two miles south of town. Hoke's 5500 were posted athwart the road on which Slocum was advancing, slowed by Hampton's skirmishing troopers, while the 4000 western veterans were disposed behind a dense screen of scrub oaks, north of the road and parallel to it, facing south. Johnston's plan was for Hoke to bring the bluecoats to a jumbled halt with a sudden blast of fire from dead ahead, at which point they would be struck in flank by the Tennesseans and Hardee, charging unexpectedly out of the brush. The trouble was that Old Reliable's 7500 — more than a third of the gray total, mounted and afoot — were not yet there to extend and give weight to the strike force stretching westward along the north side of the road. Misled by Johnston, who had himself been misled by a faulty map, Hardee had found yesterday's march twice its reckoned length; with the result that he had had to go into camp, long after dark, some six miles short of Bentonville. He notified his chief of this, but said that he hoped to make up for it by setting out again at 3 a.m. Even so, he did not reach the town until around 9 o'clock, and then found the single road leading south through the blackjack thickets badly clogged by rearward elements of the units already in position. It was well past noon before he approached the field, and by that time the trap had been sprung by pressure on Hampton, whose vedettes were driven back through the line of works Hoke's men had thrown across the road to block the Federal advance.

The trap snapped, but lacking Hardee it lacked power in the jaw that was intended to bite deeply into the flank of the startled Union column. Brigadier General William Carlin's division of Davis's corps had the lead today, and when the woods exploded in his front — a crash of rifles, with the roar of guns mixed in — he recoiled, then rallied and came on again, having called for help from Brigadier General James D. Morgan, whose other XIV Corps division was close behind. While Carlin pressed forward, as if to storm Hoke's light intrenchments, Morgan came up in time to help resist the rebel effort against the flank. They made a good team: Carlin, a thirty-five-year-old Illinois West

Pointer, and Morgan, twenty years his senior, an Illinoisian too, but born and raised in Massachusetts, a workhorse type who had risen by hard fighting. Holding in front, the Federals fell back south of the road and took up a new position facing north, where the graybacks were regrouping in the thickets for a follow-up assault. These were the three corps, so called, of the Army of Tennessee, though all three combined amounted to little more, numerically, than a single full division in the old days, and not one of the three was led today by its regular commander; Harvey Hill had replaced S. D. Lee, still out with his wound, while Bate had charge of his own and the remnant of Cleburne's division, Cheatham not having arrived with the third, and Loring had taken over from Stewart, whose rank gave him command of the whole. They lacked the strength for an overwhelming strike at the bluecoats intrenching rapidly in the woods, and not even Hardee's arrival from Bentonville at this critical juncture was of much help, as it turned out. From the left, dug in athwart the road, Bragg sent word that Hoke was on the verge of being overrun; whereupon Johnston — "most injudiciously," he later said — responded by ordering Hardee to send McLaws to his assistance. That left only Taliaferro's division to reinforce the effort on the right, and it was not enough.

It was especially not enough in light of the fact that Williams by now had his two available XX Corps divisions hurrying forward to close the gap between him and Davis, and the other two divisions, one from each corps, were presently summoned to move up from escort duty with the train. Methodical as always, Hardee extended Stewart's line with Taliaferro's Carolinians, hoping to overlap the enemy left, and then at last, soon after 3 o'clock, resumed the attack on the Federals intrenched by then in the woods to the south of the road. He suffered heavy losses in coming to grips with Morgan's men, and though he was successful in driving a good part of them from their hastily improvised works, taking three guns in the process — "We however showed to the Rebs as well as to our side some of the best running ever did," a Wolverine lieutenant would write home — it was only for a few hundred yards before they stiffened, and he had to call a halt again to realign his strike force in the tangled underbrush. While he did so, Williams' lead division came up and the Union right held firm against a belated attempt by Bragg to add to the confusion. Both commanders then had about 15,000 infantry on the field, and now that surprise was no longer a factor there was scant hope of an advantage for either side in any fighting that might ensue: barring, of course, the arrival of substantial reinforcements. In regard to this last, Slocum already had the other half of his two-corps wing moving up, and what was more he had hopes that Sherman, in response to repeated crosscountry pleas, would land Howard's wing in the Confederate rear tonight, or early tomorrow morning at the latest. But for Johnston there was no such hope and no such reassurance. He could expect no additional troops even in his own rear, let alone the enemy's; he could only try to make better use of those he had — including the solid fourth of his infantry under McLaws, whose division, after groping blind around unmapped ponds and impenetrable thickets, finally reached the left to find that it was not only unneeded for the defense of Hoke's position, but was also too late for a share in the follow-up demonstration against Carlin. As a result of Hardee's miscalculated approach march and McLaws' futile detachment, Seven Pines now had a rival for the distinction of being at once the best-planned and worst-conducted battle of the war.

Still Hardee pressed on, as thorough as he was methodical. Cheered by the western veterans he had last commanded back in Georgia, he was also saddened by the thinness of their ranks. For example, the 1st, 13th, and 19th Tennessee, each of which had contained an average of 1250 effectives at the outset of the war, now had 65, 50, and 64 respectively present for duty; nor were these by any means the worst-off units in this gaunted aggregation, the ghost of the one-time Army of Tennessee, fighting southward now and farther from home than it had been even at Perryville, the northernmost of its lost victories. "It was a painful sight," one of Hoke's men wrote after watching these transplanted remnants of a departed host surge forward in their first charge since Franklin, "to see how close their battle flags were together, regiments being scarcely larger than companies and a division not much larger than a regiment should be." Blown as they were, their third attack — launched shortly after 5 o'clock, within an hour of sunset — was less successful than their second, two hours before; Morgan's men, stoutly dug in and reinforced by Williams' lead division, yielded nothing. The graybacks rebounded, then came on again, and the wierd halloo of the rebel yell rang out in the dusky Carolina woods, given with a fervor that seemed to signify a knowledge by the tattered Deep South veterans that this would be their last. "The assaults were repeated over and over again until a late hour," Slocum reported, "each assault finding us better prepared for resistance."

Convinced by now, if not sooner, that all had been done that could be done once his plan for exploiting the initial shock had gone awry, Johnston instructed Hardee to pull Stewart's and Taliaferro's men back in the darkness to their original position north of the road, confronting with Bragg the reunited half of Sherman's army under Slocum, while Wheeler's troopers, just arrived from their decoy work in front of Raleigh, proceeded east toward Cox's Bridge to delay the advance of the other half under Howard, who was no doubt hard on the way from that direction in response to the eight-hour boom and growl of guns near Bentonville today. (In point of fact, Old Joe would have had to do this, or something like it, in any case — preferably an outright skedaddle — since, even if he had succeeded in abolishing Slocum's wing entirely,

Victory, and Defeat

despite its three-to-two preponderance in numbers, Sherman could then have brought Schofield across the Neuse to combine with Howard for a counterattack with the odds extended to three-to-one or worse.) Hardee managed the withdrawal before dawn, and when Wheeler sent word that he was in contact with Howard's advance, some half-dozen miles in rear of Hoke's division, Johnston had Bragg pull Hoke back, too, and place him in a newly intrenched position from which he would confront the blue right wing when it came up. Formerly concave, the gray line was now convex, a spraddled V, one arm opposing Slocum, the other Howard, whose first corps arrived by noon, followed shortly by the second. Before the day was over — March 20: the vernal equinox — Sherman thus had close to 60,000 soldiers on or near the field, while Johnston, bled down by his losses in yesterday's failed assault, had fewer than 20,000.

Here then for the red-haired Ohioan was a rare chance, not only to score the Cannae every general prayed for, but also to refute the charge leveled by scorners that he lacked the moral courage to commit his whole army in a single all-out effort. It was true he had never done so, yet it was also true he had never before had such an opportunity as this. Discouraged by their failure to snap shut the trap Old Joe had laid for Slocum, frazzled by hard fighting well into the previous night, confronted left and right today by three times their number, the Confederates clung to the spraddled V whose apex was three miles from the lone bridge over Mill Creek in their rear, and though their purpose was to afford the medical details time to evacuate the wounded, they knew well enough that in remaining within this snare of their own making they were also giving Sherman time to accomplish their destruction — provided, of course, he was willing to attempt it; which he was not. "I would rather avoid a general battle," he cautioned Slocum when the New Yorker concluded his report, "but if [Johnston] insists, we must accommodate him."

He stayed his hand, not so much from lack of moral courage as from mistrust of his own impulsive nature, which he only gave free rein in times of relaxation, while writing letters, say, or dealing with civilians, and almost never when men's lives were at stake. There was that deterrent, plus the fact that he knew little of Johnston's position, except that it was skillfully intrenched, or of his strength, except that it seemed great indeed, to judge by the number of units yielding prisoners from the Army of Tennessee; Sherman, unaware that most of its regiments had dwindled to company size, could assume that the whole army was in his front, as formidable in North Carolina as it had been in Georgia. Besides, his Bentonville casualties, though unreported yet, were clearly heavy; in fact, they would come to 1646 in all, and of these 1168 were wounded. Combined with the 533 from Averasboro, that gave him 1700 sufferers to find room for in his train. Any more such — and who knew how many more there would be if he pressed the issue here? — would overflow the ambulances and crowd the aid stations far beyond the capacity of his surgeons to give them even minimal attention. At Goldsboro, on the other hand, he would be in touch by rail with mountains of supplies, medical and otherwise, unloaded from ships at New Bern and Wilmington, and that was where he wanted to go, as soon as possible, for a combination with Schofield in the open country beyond the Neuse, where he could deal with Johnston at his leisure, fully rested and with half again more men than he had now. Ten days ago, he had promised Schofield to meet him there today, and though Averasboro and Bentonville had thrown him a couple of days off schedule, he hoped to arrive without further delay. If Johnston would only pull back, he himself would be free to go his way, and he was somewhat puzzled by his opponent's apparent reluctance to cooperate by retiring — as he plainly ought to do. "I cannot see why he remains," Sherman complained, but added: "[I] still think he will avail himself of night to get back to Smithfield."

In this he was mistaken, or at any rate premature. Night fell, ending the first day of spring, and the following dawn, March 21, showed Old Joe still in occupation of the works across the way. His reason for staying — concern for his wounded — was similar to Sherman's for wanting to leave, except that in Johnston's case the problem was evacuation, with heavier losses and even slimmer means of transportation. He suffered 2606 casualties in the battle, almost a thousand more than his adversary, and of these 1694 were wounded, who, for lack of enough wagons, had to be taken rearward across Mill Creek Bridge in relays; all of which took time, and time was why he stayed, gambling that the greatly superior enemy force would not overrun him while the work was in progress.

As it turned out, that was nearly what happened: not by Sherman's orders, but rather by a flaunting of them by one of Blair's division commanders, Major General Joseph Mower. Vermont-born, a Massachusetts carpenter in his youth, Mower had served as a private in the Mexican War, and staying on in the army had been commissioned a second lieutenant by the time of Sumter. Since then, he had risen steadily, always as an officer of the line; "the boldest young soldier we have," Sherman had said of him the year before, when he was a thirty-six-year-old brigadier, and here today, posted on the far right, he demonstrated that such praise was deserved. Slipping the leash, he committed his division in a headlong charge that broke through on the rebel left, then drove hard for the single bridge in Johnston's rear. Struck front and flank by a sudden counterattack, he paused and called on Blair and Howard for reinforcements, certain that if he got them nothing could prevent him from closing the only Confederate escape hatch. What he got instead was a peremptory order from Sherman to return to his original position.

Hardee had stopped him with reinforcements brought over from the right, including the 8th Texas Cavalry, which sixteen-year-old Willie Hardee, the general's only son, had joined that morning after finally overcoming his father's objections that he was too young for army duty. "Swear him into service in your company, as nothing else will suffice," Old Reliable told the captain who reported to headquarters with him. Then he kissed the boy and sent him on his way for what turned out to be a share in the critical job of checking Mower's penetration. Elated by the retirement of the bluecoats — which he did not know had been ordered by Sherman — Hardee grinned and said to Hampton, as they rode back from directing the counteraction: "General, that was nip and tuck, and for a while I thought Tuck had it." Laughing, they continued across the field, only to encounter a pair of litter bearers bringing Willie from the front, badly wounded in his first charge. It was also his last; he would die three days later, with his father at his side, and be buried in a Hillsborough churchyard after the military funeral he would have wanted. For the present, Hardee could only dismount and spend a moment with him before rejoining Hampton for deployment of their troops in case the Yankees tried for another breakthrough, somewhere else along the line.

There was no such attempt, and Johnston, having completed the evacuation of his wounded, pulled back that night across Mill Creek and took the road for Smithfield the next morning, unpursued. He had failed to carry out his plan for wrecking Slocum, but he had at least achieved the lesser purpose of delaying Sherman's march to the back door of Richmond, thereby gaining time for Lee to give Grant the slip and combine with him for another, more substantial lunge at the blue host slogging north. As for himself, now that all six Union corps were about to consolidate at Goldsboro, close to 90,000 strong — "I wonder if Minerva has stamped on the earth for our foes?" Beauregard marveled, contemplating their numbers in intelligence reports — Johnston was convinced that he could accomplish nothing further on his own, and he said as much in a wire to Lee when he crossed the Neuse the following day, March 23.

"Sherman's course cannot be hindered by the small force I have. I can do no more than annoy him," he told the general-in-chief. His only hope, slight as it was, lay in the proposed combination of the two gray armies for a sudden strike, here in the Old North State, and he continued to urge the prompt adoption of such a course. "I respectfully suggest that it is no longer a question whether you leave present position; you have only to decide where to meet Sherman. I will be near him."

In point of fact he was near him now; Sherman by then was in

Goldsboro, barely twenty miles from Smithfield, a morning's boatride down the Neuse. Schofield had been there for two days, awaiting the arrival of his other corps under Terry, which Sherman had diverted from its direct route up the Wilmington & Weldon, with instructions to prepare a pontoon crossing for Slocum and Howard at the site of Cox's Bridge, burned by the rebels while the fighting raged a dozen miles to the west. As a result, there was no delay when the lead wing reached the river on March 22; Sherman rode into Goldsboro next morning, only three days off the time appointed. Fifty days out of Savannah, ten of which he had had his troops devote to halts for rest or intensive destruction, he had covered well over four hundred miles of rough terrain in wretched weather, crossing rivers and plunging full-tilt through "impenetrable" swamps, and now, after three battles of mounting intensity — Kinston, Averasboro, Bentonville — he combined his four corps with Schofield's two for a total of 88,948 effectives, half again more than he had had when he set out on what he called "one of the longest and most important marches ever made by an organized army in a civilized country." Best of all, from the tactical point of view, Goldsboro was within eighty miles of Weldon, and Weldon was more than halfway to Richmond, already under pressure from 128,046 Federal besiegers. Combined, as they soon could be, the two forces would give Grant 217,000 veterans for use in closing out R. E. Lee, whose own force had been ground down by combat and depleted by desertion to less than one fourth that number of all arms. Impatient for the outcome, which seemed to him foregone, Sherman said later, "I directed my special attention to replenishing the army for the next and last stage of the campaign."

First off, by way of preparation for the prospective meeting with the paper-collar Easterners, the outriding "bummers" were unhorsed and told to rejoin their units for reconversion into soldiers of the line. That came hard for them, accustomed as they had become to hard-handed, light-fingered living and the special pleasure of frightening civilians on their own, independent of the usual military restrictions. What might have been worse, their red-haired commander took it into his head to stage an impromptu review as they came striding into town, mud-spattered and ragged as they were. Oddly enough, the notion appealed to them about as much as it did to him; they saw that he was eager to show them off, and they were glad to please him. "They don't march very well, but they will fight," he told Schofield, who had ridden out to meet him. Half were shoeless, and their trousers were in tatters; "a sorry sight," one brigadier admitted, while a staff colonel noted that "nearly every soldier had some token of the march on his bayonet, from a pig to a potato." Uncle Billy was altogether delighted by their appearance, even their rags, which lent a rollicking touch to the column, and was amused by their unavailing efforts, as they swung past him, to close files that had not been closed in months. When Frank Blair remarked, "Look at those poor fellows with bare legs," Sherman scoffed at such misplaced sympathy.

"Splendid legs! Splendid legs!" he sputtered between puffs on his cigar. "I'd give both of mine for any one of them."

He had never cared for parades and such, and even in this case, for all his pride in the weathered marchers and his amusement at the show they made, he seemed to a reporter "to be wishing it was over. While the troops are going by he must be carrying on a conversation or smoking or fidgeting in some way or other." Self-distracted as he was, the approach of the colors nearly caught him unaware; "he looks up just in time to snatch off his hat. And the way he puts that hat on again! With a jerk and drag and jam, as if it were the most objectionable hat in the world and he was specially entitled to entertain an implacable grudge against it." So great was his impatience, indeed, that he cancelled the rest of the review as soon as the second regiment passed. However, there was more to this than the reporter knew. Sherman had just found out that neither railroad was in working order to the coast, and in his anger he fired off a wire to Schofield's chief quartermaster — now his own — demanding to know the whereabouts of "the vast store of supplies I hoped to meet here.... If you can expedite the movement of stores from the sea to the army, do so, and don't stand on expenses. There should always be three details of workers, of eight hours each, making twenty-four hours per day of work on every job, whether building a bridge, unloading vessels, loading cars, or what not. Draw everything you need from Savannah, Port Royal, Charleston, &c. for this emergency.... I must be off again in twenty days, with wagons full, men reclad, &c."

As a result of this round-the-clock prodding, the road to New Bern was in operation within two days, and Sherman himself was one of its first eastbound passengers, March 25. He was off on a trip: first to, then up, the coast. "If I get the troops all well placed, and the supplies working," he had written Grant when he entered Goldsboro, "I might run up to see you for a day or two before diving again into the bowels of the country." A year ago this week, he and the new general-in-chief had huddled over their maps in a Cincinnati hotel room, planning the vast campaign that was about to enter its final stage. He had not seen him since, and it occurred to him, now that his soldiers were at last in camp, idly awaiting delivery of their new clothes and other luxuries, that this would be a good time for him and his chief to get back in touch, to put their heads together again over plans for the close-out maneuver. Privately, in a jesting mood, he remarked to friends that he was going to see Grant in order to "stir him up," fearing that so long a time behind breastworks might have "fossilized" him. Actually, though, he saw the prospective conference as a means of saving time and lives by hastening the showdown operation and avoiding misunderstandings once it began. By way of preamble, he suggested in a follow-up letter, March 24, his notion of what could be done. "I think I see pretty clearly how, in one more move, we can checkmate Lee, forcing him to unite Johnston with him in the defense of Richmond, or, by leaving Richmond, to abandon the cause. I feel certain if he leaves Richmond, Virginia leaves the Confederacy."

Next day he was off. Leaving Schofield in command at Goldsboro, he took the cars for New Bern, where he spent the night before getting aboard the steamer *Russia* Sunday morning, March 26, for the trip to City Point. "I'm going up to see Grant for five minutes and have it all chalked out for me," he said, "and then come back and pitch in."

★ ★ ★

"How d'you do, Sherman."

"How are you, Grant."

Smiles broadened into laughter for them both as they shook hands on the wharf at City Point late Monday afternoon, then proceeded at once to headquarters for the reunion that ended their year-long separation. En route, the red-head launched into a description of his two marches, first across Georgia to the sea, then up through the Carolinas to within 150 miles of where they presently were sitting, Grant smoking quietly and Sherman talking, talking. He spoke for the better part of an hour, scarcely pausing — "Columbia; pretty much all burned, and burned *good*," a staffer heard him say — until his companion, jogged by a sudden recollection, interrupted to remark that the President too was there on a visit. Arriving late Friday he had spent the past three nights tied up to the City Point dock, aboard the *River Queen*. "I know he will be anxious to see you. Suppose we go and pay him a visit before supper?"

Lincoln was indeed on hand, and what was more, in leaving Washington four days ago for the double purpose of escaping the press of executive duties and seeing something of the war first-hand, he had arrived in time to have his first night's sleep disrupted before dawn, March 25, by what seemed to him a tremendous uproar over toward Petersburg, as if all the guns in this part of Virginia were being fired at once, barely half a dozen miles from his stateroom on the presidential yacht. They boomed and they kept booming; he thought surely a full-scale battle must be raging; that is until his son Robert, still proud of his untarnished captain's bars, came aboard for breakfast and informed him that there had been "a little rumpus up the line this morning, ending about where it began." There must have been more to it than that, however, because when Lincoln expressed a desire to visit the scene of the fight — or "rumpus," as Robert had it, affecting the jargon of the veterans whose life he had shared these past two weeks — Grant

Victory, and Defeat

sent word that he couldn't permit the Commander in Chief to expose himself to the danger of being shot.

Presently, though, the general relented. Lincoln not only could view the scene of this morning's disturbance; he would also — along with Tad and Mrs Lincoln, as well as a number of visiting army wives — attend a review by a V Corps division, previously scheduled for noon, but postponed now till 3 o'clock, to be staged in rear of a sector adjoining the one where the predawn uproar had erupted.... Here, for those who could spot it in passing, was another of those unobtrusive but highly significant milestones on the long road to and through the war. This prompt rescheduling of the review, combined with young Robert's offhand reference to "a little rumpus up the line," was indicative of the extent to which the strength of the pent-up rebels had declined in the past few months. For what had awakened Lincoln before daylight was the last of the Army of Northern Virginia's all-out offensive strikes, so awesome in effect these past three years, but now more pitiful than savage. Despite casualties totaling close to 7000 on both sides — more, in fact, than had been suffered in all three battles down in North Carolina during the past two weeks — the only tangible result, once the smoke cleared, was a three-hour postponement of a formal review by part of a corps that had stood idle, within easy supporting distance, while another contained and repelled, unassisted, the heaviest assault the Confederates could manage at this late stage of the drawn-out siege of Petersburg and their national capital. Here indeed was a milestone worth remarking by those on the lookout, blue or gray, aboard the juggernaut fast approaching the end of its four-year grind across the landscape of the South.

No one knew better than Lee himself the odds against survival, by his army or his country — the two were all but synonymous by now, in most men's eyes — of the showdown that drew nearer as the lengthening days wore past. Early's defeat at Waynesboro not only had abolished his last conceivable infantry reserve, it had also cleared the way for a rapid descent on his westward supply lines by Sheridan's win-prone troopers; "against whom," Lee told a colleague, "I can oppose scarcely a vedette." At the same time he learned of this reverse, March 4, he received from Grant a reply to his proposal that ranking officers of their two armies meet to discuss a possible armistice. Declining, Grant informed him that all such matters were up to Lincoln, whose reinauguration day this was and who had said flatly, a month ago in Hampton Roads, that negotiations must follow, not precede, surrender. Lee perceived that his only remaining course, if he was to stave off disaster, was to set out southward for a combination with Johnston before Sherman overwhelmed or moved around him to combine with Grant and serve Petersburg's defenders in much the same fashion. Such a march, he had warned Davis nine days back, would "necessitate the abandonment of our position on James River, for which contingency every preparation should be made." Now he went in person to the capital, that same day, to notify the President that the time for such a shift — and such an abandonment — was closer at hand than he had presumed before Early's defeat and Grant's concomitant refusal to enter into negotiations that might have led to peace without more bloodshed.

In confirmation of what Lee called "his unconquerable will power," Davis did not flinch at the news that Richmond might have to be given up sooner than had been supposed till now. In fact, he countered by asking whether it wouldn't "be better to anticipate the necessity by withdrawing at once." Lee replied that his horses were too weak to haul his guns and wagons through the still-deep mud; he would set out when the roads had dried and hardened. What he had in mind for the interim, he went on, was a strike at Grant that might disrupt whatever plans he was making, either for a mass assault on the Confederate defenses or another westward extension of his line. The Mississippian approved that too, hoping, as he said later, that such a blow would "delay the impending disaster for the more convenient season for retreat." Nothing in his manner indicated that he viewed the loss of Richmond as anything worse than yet another shock to be absorbed in the course of resistance to forces that would deny him and his people the right to govern themselves as they saw fit, and Lee returned to Petersburg impressed and sustained by his chief's "remarkable faith in the possibility of still winning our independence."

That he termed such faith "remarkable" was a measure of his discouragement at this stage, as well as of his military realism in assessing the likely outcome of the problems he and his hungry soldiers faced. Yet in planning the strike just mentioned to Davis he demonstrated anew that none of his old aggressive fire was lacking. "His name might be Audacity. He will take more desperate chances, and take them quicker, than any other general in the country, North or South," a subordinate had said of him when he first assumed command of the army now clinging precariously to its 37 miles of works from White Oak Swamp to Hatcher's Run, and that this was as true now as the Seven Days had proved it to be then, nearly three years back, was shown by his reaction to a report from John Gordon, whom he instructed to study the works confronting his part of the line — due east of Petersburg and closer to the enemy defenses than either Hill's, winding off to the west, or Longstreet's, north of the James — with a view to recommending the point most likely to crumple under attack.

The Georgian chose Fort Stedman, a somewhat run-down Federal installation, midway between the Appomattox and the Crater, only 150 yards from the nose of a bulge in his own line known as Colquitt's Salient. His plan was to use all three of his divisions in a predawn assault, preceded by fifty axmen, whose job it would be to chop a path through

Victory, and Defeat [841]

the sharp-pointed abatis in front of the objective, and three groups of a hundred men each, who would make their way into the Union rear to seize three open-ended forts Gordon had spotted there, turning their captured guns on the works to the right and left of Stedman, so that the main body could widen the breach in both directions. One beauty in the choice of this location was that it lay in close proximity to the City Point Railroad, a vital supply route leading rearward to Grant's headquarters and main base; Grant would have little choice, if the operation went as planned, except to withdraw troops from his far left to meet the danger, thus shortening his line in just the direction Lee would be moving when the time came for him to set out on his march to join Joe Johnston.

Lee not only approved, he expanded the operation. Leaving the tactical details to Gordon, much as he had done in the old days with Jackson, he reinforced him with four brigades from Hill and two from Anderson — which lifted the total to about half of his southside infantry — as well as with Rooney Lee's cavalry division, summoned up from Stony Creek to be used in spreading havoc in the Union rear once the breakthrough had succeeded.

Although he thus would be stripping the Petersburg front practically bare of men except at the point of concentration, he was more than willing to accept the risk for the sake of the possible gain. For one thing, having told his wife some weeks ago that he intended to "fight to the last," he was going about it in his familiar style: all out. For another, in the nearly three weeks since his talk with Davis in Richmond, the over-all situation had worsened considerably. Sheridan, after disposing of Early, was reported to be moving toward a junction with Grant that would give the besiegers the rapid-fire mobility they had been needing for a raid-in-force around the Confederate right, which would not only menace the tenuous gray supply lines but would also block the intended escape route for the link-up down in Carolina. Moreover, things had gone from bad to worse in that direction too. On March 11 Johnston warned that if Sherman and Schofield combined, "their march into Virginia cannot be prevented by me." Twelve days and three lost battles later, on March 23, he sent word that the two blue armies had met at Goldsboro. "I can do no more than annoy him," he said of Sherman, whose 90,000 troops were closer to Grant at Globe Tavern, say — a ten-day march at worst — than Johnston, with scarcely one fifth that number around Smithfield, was to Lee at Petersburg.

Time had all but run out. Lee called Gordon in that night and told him to assemble his force next day for the strike at Fort Stedman before dawn, March 25. Gordon requested that Pickett's division be detached from Longstreet to strengthen the effort, and Lee agreed, though he doubted that it would arrive in time from beyond the Appomattox. "Still we will try," he said, adding by way of encouragement to the young corps commander, who at thirty-three was twenty-five years his junior: "I pray that a merciful God may grant us success and deliver us from our enemies."

Gordon cached his reinforced corps in Colquitt's Salient the following day, as ordered, and after nightfall had the obstructions quietly removed to clear the way for the attack. Exclusive of Pickett, who was not up, and the division of cavalry en route from Stony Creek, he had 12,000 infantry poised for the 4 o'clock jump-off, an hour before dawn and two hours before sunrise. Lee arrived on Traveller after moonset and took position on a hill just in rear of the trenches; he would share in the waiting, though he would of course be able to see nothing until daylight filtered through to reveal Fort Stedman, out ahead on Hare's Hill; by which time it should be in Gordon's possession, along with a considerable stretch of line in both directions. On schedule, the signal — a single rifle shot, loud against the bated silence — rang out, and the skirmishers overwhelmed the drowsy enemy pickets, followed by the fifty axmen and the 300-man assault force, all wearing strips of white cloth across their breasts and backs for ready identification in the darkness.

There was no alarm until the first wave started up the rising ground directly under the four guns in the fort. Then suddenly there was. All four guns began to roar, and the force of their muzzle blasts and the wind from passing shells tore at the hats of the attackers. "We went the balance of the way with hats and guns in hand," one would recall. At the moat, the axmen came forward to hack at the chevaux-de-frise, and the charging graybacks went up and over the parapet so quickly that the defenders, some 300 members of a New York heavy artillery outfit, had no time to brace themselves for hand-to-hand resistance. Stedman fell in that first rush, along with its guns, which were seized intact and turned on the adjacent works. Battery 10, on the immediate left, was promptly taken, as was Battery 11 on the right. Gordon was elated. A lean-faced man with a ramrod bearing, long dark hair, and glowing eyes — "as fierce and nearly cruel blue eyes as I ever looked into," a reporter was to note — he was much admired by his men, one of whom said of him: "He's most the prettiest thing you ever did see on a field of fight. It would put heart in a whipped chicken just to look at him." Happy and proud, he sent back word of his success and his intention to enlarge it, left and right and straight ahead.

Dawn had glimmered through by then, and the three 100-man assault teams pressed on beyond the captured works, toward the rim of sky tinted rose by the approaching sun. Trained artillerists were among them, assigned to serve the guns in the three backup forts, once they were taken, and thus bring them to bear on the rear of front-line redoubts north and south of fallen Stedman and its two companion batteries. This unexpected shelling from the rear, combined with pressure from the front and flanks, would assure enlargement of the gap

Victory, and Defeat [843]

through which the waves of graybacks could push eastward, perhaps within reach of City Point itself, where the wide-ranging cavalry would take over the task of rounding up high-rank prisoners — conceivably including U. S. Grant himself, whose headquarters was known to be in the yard of the Eppes mansion — while setting fire to the main enemy supply base and disrupting the very nerve center of the encircling Union host. Gordon saw that the pressure from the rear had better come soon, though, for the bluecoats in Batteries 9 and 12 were standing firm, resisting all efforts to widen the breach. Then at sunup he got the worst possible news from runners sent back by officers in charge of the assault teams. They could not locate the three open-ended forts on the rearward ridge: for the simple reason, discovered later, that they did not exist, being nothing more than the ruins of old Confederate works along the Dimmock line, abandoned back in June by Beauregard. Meantime the counterbattery fire was getting heavier and more accurate from adjoining redoubts and Fort Haskell, within easy range to the south, as well as from massed batteries of field artillery, brought forward to help contain the penetration. Fort Stedman and its two flank installations were subjected to converging fire from every Yankee gun along this portion of the line; a fire so intense that the air seemed filled with shells whose burning fuzes, one observer said, made them resemble "a flock of blackbirds with blazing tails beating about in a gale." Pinned down, the stalled attackers huddled under what shelter they could find, waiting for the metallic storm to lift.

Instead of lifting it grew heavier as the red ball of the sun bounced clear of the landline. Gordon saw plainly that without help from the nonexistent forts he not only could not deepen or widen the dent he had made, he would not even be able to hold what he had won by the predawn rush. Accordingly, he notified Lee of his predicament, and word came back, shortly before 8 o'clock, for him to call off the attack and withdraw. The Georgian was altogether willing to return to his own lines, but the same could not be said for hundreds of his soldiers, who preferred surrender to running the gauntlet of fire that boxed them in. As a result, Confederate losses for this stage of the operation came to about 3500 men, half of them captives, as compared to a Federal total of 1044. Nor was that all. Convinced that Lee must have stripped the rest of his southside line to provide troops for the strike at Stedman, Grant ordered a follow-up assault to be launched against the rebel right, where Hill's intrenched picket line was overrun near Hatcher's Run, inflicting heavy casualties and taking close to a thousand additional prisoners, not to mention securing a close-up hug on Hill's main line of resistance. By the time a truce was called that afternoon for collecting the dead and wounded on both sides, the casualty lists had grown to 4800 for Lee and 2080 for Grant. The bungled affair of the Crater — which today's effort so much resembled, both in purpose and in outcome — had been redressed, although with considerably heavier losses all around.

Another difference was that the southern commander could ill afford what his opponent had shrugged off, eight months ago and less than a mile down the line, with no more than a brief loss of temper. Riding rearward, Lee met Rooney coming forward in advance of his division. With him was his younger brother Robert, now a captain on his staff. Both greeted their father, who gave them the news that there would be no cavalry phase of the operation. The assault had failed, and badly, at great cost. "Since then," Robert declared long afterwards, "I have often recalled the sadness of his face, its careworn expression."

Lee's depression was well founded. On no single day since the Bloody Angle was overrun at Spotsylvania had he lost so many prisoners, and these combined with the killed and wounded had cost him a solid tenth of his command, as compared to Grant's loss of less than a sixtieth. "The greatest calamity that can befall us is the destruction of our armies," he had warned Davis eleven days ago, while Gordon was planning the Stedman operation. "If they can be maintained, we may recover from our reverses, but if lost we have no resource." Today marked a sizeable step toward the destruction of the first army of them all. Moreover, it had gained him nothing, while costing him Hill's outer defenses, now occupied by Grant, who could be expected to launch a swamping assault from this new close-up position — a sort of Stedman in reverse — in just the direction Lee would be obliged to move when he tried for a breakout west and south: no longer for the purpose of combining with Johnston for a lunge at Sherman before the red-head crossed the Roanoke, but simply as the only remaining long-shot chance of postponing the disaster he foresaw. Notifying Breckinridge of the failed attack, he made no complaint of Gordon's miscalculations; he merely remarked that the troops had "behaved most handsomely." But next day, in following this with a report to the President, he confessed himself at a loss as to his next move, except that he knew he had to get away, and soon. "I fear now it will be impossible to prevent a junction between Grant and Sherman," he frankly admitted, "nor do I deem it prudent that this army should maintain its position until the latter shall approach too near."

He was warning again that Richmond would have to be given up any day now, but what would follow that abandonment he did not say; perhaps because he did not know. All he seemed to have in mind was a combination with Johnston for the confrontation that was bound to ensue. "I have thought it proper to make the above statement to Your Excellency of the condition of affairs," he concluded, "knowing that you will do whatever may be in your power to give relief."

But the power was Grant's, and Grant knew it. When Lincoln

came to headquarters, shortly after the Confederates began their withdrawal from Fort Stedman — those of them, that is, who did not choose surrender over running the gauntlet of fire — the general observed that the assault had been less a threat to the integrity of the Union position than it was an indication of Lee's desperation in regard to the integrity of his own. Accordingly, he rescheduled the V Corps review, which would be staged in rear of a sector just south of the one where Gordon's attack had exploded before dawn, and decided as well that the President would be safe enough in taking a look at the ground where the struggle had raged between 4 and 8 o'clock that morning.

So it was that Lincoln, going forward on the railroad to the margin of that field, saw on a considerably larger scale what he had seen at Fort Stevens eight months earlier, just outside Washington. Mangled corpses were being carted rearward for burial in the army cemetery near City Point — which incidentally, like everything else in that vicinity, had been much expanded since his brief visit in June of the year before — and men were being jounced on stretchers, writhing in pain as they were lugged back for surgeons to probe their wounds or remove their shattered arms and legs. There was pride and exhilaration in statements that Parke, cut off from communication with Meade and Grant while the fighting was in progress, had used only his three IX Corps divisions to contain and repulse the rebels without outside help. But for Lincoln, interested though he always was in military matters, the pleasure he would ordinarily have taken in such reports was greatly diminished by the sight of what they had cost. He looked "worn and haggard," an officer who accompanied him declared; "He remarked that he had seen enough of the horrors of war, that he hoped this was the beginning of the end, and that there would be no more bloodshed."

Still another shock was in store for him before the day was over, this one involving his wife. For some time now, particularly since the death of her middle and favorite son, eleven-year-old Willie, Mary Lincoln had been displaying symptoms of the mental disturbance that would result, a decade later, in a medical judgment of her case as one of insanity. Her distress, though great, was scarcely greater than her family misfortunes — exclusive of the greatest, still to come. Four of her five Kentucky brothers had gone with the South, and three of them died at Shiloh, Baton Rouge, and Vicksburg. Similarly, three of her four sisters were married to Confederates, one of whom fell at Chickamauga. Such losses not only brought her grief, they also brought on a good deal of backhand whispering about "treason in the White House." All this, together with Lincoln's lack of time to soothe her hurts and calm her fears, combined to produce a state in which she was quick to imagine slights to her lofty station and threats to all she valued most, including her two surviving sons and her husband.

It was the latter who was in danger today, or so she conceived from something she heard as she rode with Mrs Grant and Lieutenant Colonel Adam Badeau, Grant's military secretary, in an ambulance on the way to the review that had been rescheduled for 3 o'clock. Badeau happened to remark that active operations could not be far off, since all army wives had recently been ordered to the rear: all, that is, but the wife of Warren's ranking division commander, Mrs Charles Griffin, who had been given special permission by the President to attend today's review. The First Lady flared up at this. "What do you mean by that, sir? Do you mean to say that she saw the President alone? Do you know that I never allow the President to see any woman alone?" Speechless with amazement at finding her "absolutely jealous of poor, ugly Abraham Lincoln," the colonel tried to assume a pleasant expression in order to show he meant no malice; but the effect was otherwise. "That's a very equivocal smile, sir," Mrs Lincoln exclaimed. "Let me out of this carriage at once! I will ask the President if he saw that woman alone."

Badeau and Mrs Grant managed to persuade her not to alight in the mud, but it was Meade who saved the day. Coming up to pay his respects on their arrival, he was taken aside by Mrs Lincoln for a hurried exchange from which she returned to fix the flustered staffer with a significant look. "General Meade is a gentleman, sir," she told him. "He says it was not the President who gave Mrs Griffin the permit, but the Secretary of War." Badeau afterwards remarked that Meade, the son of a diplomat, "had evidently inherited some of his father's skill."

Unfortunately, the Pennsylvanian was not on hand for a similar outburst the following day, when the troops reviewed were Ord's, beyond the James. Arriving late, again in an ambulance with the staff colonel and Mrs Grant, Mrs Lincoln found the review already in progress, and there on horseback beside her husband, who was mounted too — he wore his usual frock coat and top hat, though his shirt front was rumpled and his strapless trouser legs had worked up to display "some inches of white socks" — was Mrs Ord. She was neither as young nor as handsome as Mrs Griffin, but that was no mitigation in Mary Lincoln's eyes. "What does the woman mean by riding by the side of the President? And ahead of me! Does she suppose that *he* wants *her* by the side of *him*?" She was fairly launched, and when Mrs Grant ventured a few words of reassurance she turned on her as well, saying: "I suppose you think you'll get to the White House yourself, don't you?" Julia Grant's disclaimer, to the effect that her present position was higher than any she had hoped for, drew the reply: "Oh, you had better take it if you can get it. 'Tis very nice."

Mrs Ord, seeing the vehicle pull up, excused herself to the dignitaries around her. "There come Mrs Lincoln and Mrs Grant; I think I had better join them," she said, unaware of the tirade in progress across the way, and set out at a canter. It was not until she drew rein beside the ambulance that she perceived that she might have done better to ride in the opposite direction. "Our reception was not cordial," an aide who accompanied her later testified discreetly. Badeau, a former newsman, gave a fuller account of Mrs Ord's ordeal. "Mrs Lincoln positively insulted her, called her vile names in the presence of a crowd of officers, and asked what she meant by following up the President. The poor woman burst into tears and inquired what she had done, but Mrs Lincoln refused to be appeased, and stormed till she was tired. Mrs Grant tried to stand by her friend, and everybody was shocked and horrified. But all things come to an end, and after a while we returned to City Point."

Things were no better there, however: certainly not for Lincoln, who was host that night at a dinner given aboard the *Queen* for the Grants and Grant's staff. Mrs Lincoln, with the general seated on her right, spent a good part of the evening running down Ord, who she said was unfit for his post, "not to mention his wife." Making no headway here, she shifted her scorn toward her husband, up at the far end of the table, and reproached him for his attentions to Mrs Griffin and Mrs Ord. Lincoln "bore it," Badeau noted, "with an expression of pain and sadness that cut one to the heart, but with supreme calmness and dignity. He called her Mother, with old-time plainness; he pleaded with eyes and tones, and endeavored to explain or palliate the offenses." Nothing worked, either at table or in the saloon afterwards; "she turned on him like a tigress," until at last "he walked away, hiding that noble, ugly face that we might not catch the full expression of its misery." Yet that did not work either; she kept at him. After the guests had retired, she summoned the skipper of the *Bat*, Lieutenant Commander John S. Barnes, who had been present at today's review, and demanded that he corroborate her charge that the President had been overattentive to Mrs Ord. Barnes declined the role of "umpire," as he put it, and earned thereby her enmity forever. He left, and when he reported aboard next morning to inquire after the First Lady, Lincoln replied that "she was not at all well, and expressed the fear that the excitement of the surroundings was too great for her, or for any woman."

By then it was Monday, March 27. Sherman's courtesy call that evening, within an hour of his arrival from down the coast, was all the more welcome as a diversion: for Lincoln at any rate, if not for the red-haired Ohioan, who had accepted Grant's suggestion — "Suppose we pay him a visit before supper?" — with something less than delight at the prospect. "All right," he said. He had small use for politicians, including this one, whom he had met only once, four years ago this week, at the time when the Sumter crisis was heading up. Introduced at the White House by his senator brother as a first-hand witness of recent activities in the South, he testified that the people there were preparing for all-out conflict. "Oh, well," he heard the lanky Kentuckian say, "I guess we'll manage to keep house." Disgusted, he declined to resume his military career, and though he relented when the issue swung to war, he retained down the years that first impression of a lightweight President.

Now aboard the *Queen*, however — perhaps in part because he could later write, "He remembered me perfectly" — he found himself in the presence of a different man entirely, one who was "full of curiosity about the many incidents of our great march" and was flatteringly concerned "lest some accident might happen to the army in North Carolina in my absence." Sherman's interest, quickened no doubt by Lincoln's own, deepened into sympathy as the exchange continued through what he called "a good, long, social visit." He saw lights and shadows unsuspected till now in a figure that had been vague at best, off at the far end of the telegraph wire running back to Washington. "When at rest or listening," he would say of his host, now three weeks into a second term, "his arms and legs seemed to hang almost lifeless, and his face was careworn and haggard; but, the moment he began to talk, his face lighted up, his tall form, as it were, unfolded, and he was the very impersonation of good-humor and fellowship."

Taking their leave, the two generals returned to Grant's quarters, where Mrs Grant, laying out tea things, asked if they had seen the First Lady. They had not; nor had they thought to tender their respects. "Well, you are a pretty pair!" she scolded.

After some badinage about the risk of having Julia within earshot ("Know all men by these presents," he observed, might just as well read "Know one woman," if what you wanted was to spread the word) Grant brought his companion up to date on the progress of other forces involved in his plan for closing out the rebellion. Mainly it had been a vexing business, especially in regard to the strikes by Canby, Stoneman, and Wilson, from which so much had been expected, both on their own and by way of diversion, if they had been launched in conjunction with Sherman's march through the Carolinas; which they had not. Canby was the worst offender, delaying his movement against Mobile while he gathered materials and built up a construction corps for laying seventy miles of railroad supply line. Moreover, he had put Gordon Granger in charge of one wing of his army, despite Grant's known dislike of the New Yorker, and had wanted to give Baldy Smith the other, until Grant vetoed the notion and flatly told him to get moving with what he had. Finally he did. Two columns of two divisions each, one under Granger, the other under A. J. Smith, together with a division of cavalry and a siege train, were put in motion around the east side of Mobile Bay, while a third column, also of two divisions, set out from Pensacola under Frederick Steele, resurrected from Arkansas, where he had spent the past ten months recuperating from his share in the Red River expedition. This brought a total of 45,000 men converging on an estimated 10,000 defenders in the works that rimmed Mobile; surely enough to assure reduction in short order. But it was March 17 by the time Canby got started, more than a month behind schedule, and March 26 — just yesterday — by the time Spanish Fort, an outwork up at the head of the bay, nine miles east of the city, was taken under fire. How long it might be at this rate before the Mobile garrison surrendered or skedaddled, Grant did not try to guess, but he saw clearly enough that it would not be in time to free any portion of Canby's army for the projected march on Selma in coöperation with the mounted column Thomas had been ordered to send against that vital munitions center, the loss of which would go far toward ending Confederate resistance in the western theater.

There was however another rub, no less vexing because it had been more or less expected with Old Slow Trot in command. Late as Canby was in setting out, Thomas was even later: not only in getting Wilson headed south for Selma, but also in launching Stoneman eastward into the Carolinas, where he had been told to operate against the railroad between Charlotte and Columbia and thus disrupt the rebel effort to assemble troops in the path of Sherman's army slogging north. As it turned out, Sherman had fought at Averasboro and was midway through the Bentonville eruption, within a day's march of his Goldsboro objective, by the time Stoneman left Knoxville on March 20, and it took him and his 4000 horsemen a week, riding through Morristown, Bull's Gap, and Jonesboro, before he crossed the Smokies to approach the western North Carolina border. By then — today, March 27; Sherman would reach City Point at sundown — there was little raiders could do in that direction; so Grant wired Thomas to have Stoneman turn north into Southwest Virginia instead, and there "repeat the raid of last fall, destroying the [Virginia & Tennessee] railroad as far toward Lynchburg as he can." That way, at least he might be able to cripple Lee's supply line and be on hand in case the old fox tried a getaway westward. Perhaps it would even work out better, Grant reasoned, now that Sherman had managed to come through on his own. But it was vexing, in much the same way Sigel's and Butler's ineptitudes had been vexing at the outset of the previous campaign, back in May of the year before.

Wilson posed a somewhat different problem, in part because Grant had a fondness for him dating back to their Vicksburg days, when the young West Pointer had been a lieutenant colonel on his staff, and also because real danger was involved. Danger was always an element in military ventures, but in Wilson's case the danger was Bedford Forrest, who could be depended on to try his hand at interfering with this as he had done with other Deep South raids, all too often disastrously — as Abel Streight, Sooy Smith, and Samuel Sturgis could testify, along with Stephen Hurlbut, A. J. Smith, Cadwallader Washburn, and several others who had encountered him at various removes, including Grant and Sherman. However, his recent promotion to lieutenant general was no measure of the number of soldiers he now had at his disposal; Wilson, with 12,500 troopers armed to a man with Spencer carbines, three batteries of horse artillery, and a supply train of 250 wagons (a command he described, on setting out, as being "in magnificent condition, splendidly mounted, perfectly clad and equipped") would outnumber his adversary two-to-one in any likely confrontation. Even without the distraction Canby would fail to supply, and even though the long delay had given Forrest and Richard Taylor an extra month to prepare for its reception, Grant believed the blue column would be able to ride right over anything they were able to throw in its path.

Still, this delay was as vexing as the others — and even longer, as it turned out. It was March 18 before Wilson, who had been having remount troubles, was able to start crossing the Tennessee, swollen by the worst floods the region had ever known. The steamboat landing at Eastport, his crossing point into Mississippi's northeast corner, was so far under water that he needed three whole days to get his horsemen over the river and reassembled on the southern bank. Finally, on March 22, he set out across the hilly barrens of Northwest Alabama, hard on the go for Selma, two hundred miles to the southeast. Five days later — March 27; Sherman was steaming up the James for a handshake with Grant, a visit with Lincoln, and later that night the present informal briefing by the general-in-chief — Wilson began to cross the upper forks of the Black Warrior River near Jasper, almost halfway to his goal. So far, he had encountered nothing he could not brush aside with a casual motion of one hand; but up ahead, somewhere between there and Selma, Forrest no doubt was gathering his gray riders for whatever deviltry he had in mind to visit on the invading column's front or flank or rear. Grant, conferring with Sherman that evening in his quarters, could only hope it was nothing his twenty-seven-year-old former staff engineer couldn't handle on his own.

By way of contrast with Canby, Stoneman, and Wilson — whose efforts, as Grant declared in his vexation, might turn out to be "eminently successful, but without any good results" because they were launched too near the end they had been designed to hasten — Phil Sheridan had demonstrated, here in the eastern theater, the virtue of promptness when striking deep into enemy territory. Leaving Winchester a month ago today, within a week of receiving orders to set out "as soon as it is possible to travel," he had caught Early unprepared at Waynesboro, his back to the Blue Ridge, and after wrecking him there moved on through Rockfish Gap to Charlottesville, where he tore up track on two vital rail supply lines, first the Virginia Central and then the Orange & Alexandria, the latter while proceeding south in accordance with his instructions to cross the James for a link-up with Sherman beyond the Carolina line. As he approached Lynchburg, however — the main objective of his raid, as defined by Grant, because it was there that the Orange & Alexandria and Lee's all-important Southside Railroad came together to continue west as the Virginia & Tennessee — he received reports from scouts that the place had been reinforced too heavily for him to move against it. What was more, the rebels had burned all the nearby bridges over the James, which was swollen to a depth past fording and a width beyond the span of his eight pontoons. Accordingly, he drew rein, thought the matter over briefly, and turned east, intending to move down the north bank of the river to the vicinity of Richmond, where he would rejoin Grant. This was not a difficult decision, since it led to what he had wanted in the first place. Regardless of orders, which required him either to cross the James or turn back to the Valley, he wanted to be where the action was. And in his eyes, the action — the real action: so much of it as remained, at any rate — was not with Sherman in North Carolina, opposing Johnston, but here in Virginia with Grant, opposing Lee. "Feeling that the war was approaching its end," he afterwards explained in fox-hunt terms, "I desired my cavalry to be in at the death."

At Columbia on March 10, fifty-odd miles upstream from the rebel capital, he gave his troopers a day's rest from their exertions, which included the smashing of locks on the James River Canal, and got off a crosscountry message to Grant, "notifying him of our success, position, and condition, and requesting supplies to be sent to White House." That was his goal now, McClellan's old supply base on the Pamunkey River, well within the Union lines on the far side of Richmond. To reach it, he turned away from the James next day at Goochland and rode north across the South Anna to Beaver Dam Station, which he had visited back in May on the raid that killed Jeb Stuart. From there he turned east and south again, down the Virginia Central to Hanover Courthouse, then crossed the North Anna to proceed down the opposite bank of the Pamunkey to White House, arriving on March 20 after three full weeks on the go. Though his loss in horses had been "considerable — almost entirely from hoof-rot," he noted — his loss in men "did not exceed 100," including some "left by the wayside, unable to bear the fatigues of the march." The rest, he said, "appeared buoyed up by the thought that we had completed our work in the Valley of the Shenandoah, and that we were on our way to help our brothers-in-arms in front of Petersburg in the final struggle."

Assurance that he and they would have a share in the close-out operation against Lee was contained in a dispatch the general-in-chief had waiting for him at White House, along with the supplies he had requested. Dated yesterday, the message instructed him to cull out his broken-down horses and men, give the others such rest and refitment as they needed to put them back in shape, and prepare to cross the James for a strike around Lee's right flank at Petersburg, in conjunction with some 40,000 infantry who would be shifted in that direction. "Start for this place as soon as you conveniently can," Grant told him. His assignment would be to wreck the Southside and Danville railroads, "and then either return to this army or go on to Sherman, as you may deem most practicable." Which of the two he chose, Grant said, "I care but little about, the principal thing being the destruction of the only two roads left to the enemy at Richmond."

Sheridan was delighted, knowing already which course he would "deem most practicable" when the time came. Next day, March 21, a follow-up message arrived. "I do not wish to hurry you," it began, and then proceeded to do just that, explaining: "There is now such a possibility, if not probability, of Lee and Johnston attempting to unite that I feel extremely desirous not only of cutting the lines of communication between them, but of having a large and properly commanded cavalry force ready to act with in case such an attempt is made." Elsewhere, Grant added, things were moving at last. "Stoneman started yesterday from Knoxville"; "Wilson started at the same time from Eastport"; "Canby is in motion, and I have reason to believe that Sherman and Schofield have formed a junction at Goldsboro." As for Sheridan, "I think that by Saturday next you had better start, even if you have to stop here to finish shoeing up."

Saturday next would be March 25. On Friday, still busy getting his horses and troopers reshod and equipped, the bandy-legged cavalryman received from Grant a letter — copies of which also went to Meade and Ord, as heads of armies: proof, in itself, of his rise in the military hierarchy since his departure for the Valley, back in August — giving details of the maneuver designed to accomplish Lee's undoing. "On the 29th instant the armies operating against Richmond will be moved by our left, for the double purpose of turning the enemy out of his present position around Petersburg and to insure the success of the cavalry under General Sheridan, which will start at the same time, in its efforts to reach and destroy the South Side and Danville railroads." That was the opening sentence; specific instructions followed. Ord was to cross the James with four of his seven divisions, including one of cavalry, and take over the works now occupied by Humphreys and Warren on the Federal left, thus freeing their two corps to move west beyond Hatcher's Run, where Sheridan's three mounted divisions — 13,500 strong — would plunge north, around Lee's right, to get astride the vital rail supply routes in his rear. Meantime, Ord's other three divisions under Weitzel, north of the James and across Bermuda Hundred, together with the two corps under Parke and Wright and Ord's four divisions south of the river, were to keep a sharp lookout and attack at once if they saw signs that Lee was drawing troops from the works in their front to meet the threat to his flank and rear.

In short, what Grant had devised was another leftward sidle, the maneuver he had employed all the way from the Rapidan to the James, with invariable success in obliging his adversary to give ground. Since then, in the nine months spent on this side of the James, the maneuver had been a good deal less successful, achieving little more in fact than a slow extension of the rebel earthworks, along with his own, more or less in ratio to his lengthening casualty lists. Much of that time, however, Sheridan had been on detached service up the country; whereas, this time, Little Phil and his hard-hitting troopers would not only be on hand — "the left-hand man of Grant the left-handed," someone dubbed him — but would also lead the strike intended to dispossess Lee, first of his tenuous rail supply lines and then of Petersburg itself, whose abandonment would mean the loss of his capital as well.

Presently it developed that Grant intended to dispossess him of even more than that, right here and now. Sheridan began crossing his horsemen on March 26, riding ahead for a talk with his chief at City Point. Pleased though he was at having been told he could do as he chose, "return to this army or go on to Sherman" once he and his troops had completed their share in the upcoming sidle, he still worried that Grant might change his mind and send him south against his will. And, indeed, further written instructions he found waiting for him at headquarters reinforced this fear by stressing the possibility of having him "cut loose from the Army of the Potomac" and continue his ride "by way of the Danville Railroad" into North Carolina. Watching him scowl as he read that part of the order, Grant took him aside, out of earshot of the staff, and quietly told him: "General, this portion of your instructions I have put in merely as a blind." He explained that if the sidle failed, as others had done in the course of the past nine months, he would be able to head off criticism by pointing to these orders as proof that it had been designed as nothing more than a sidelong slap at Lee by Sheridan, en route to a junction with Sherman. Actually, Grant assured him, he had no intention of sending him away. He wanted him with him, in the forefront of the strike about to be launched and the chase that would ensue. Little Phil began to see the light; a light that grew swiftly into a sunburst when he heard what his chief said next. "I mean to end the business here," Grant told him. The cavalryman's raid-weathered face brightened at the words; Lee was to be dispossessed, not only of Petersburg and Richmond, but also of his army — here and now. Sheridan grinned. "I am glad to hear it," he said. He slapped his thigh. "And we can do it!" he exclaimed.

Elated by this private assurance from the general-in-chief (and flattered by Lincoln, who told him later that morning, in the course of a boatride down the James: "General Sheridan, when this peculiar war began I thought a cavalryman should be at least six feet four inches high, but I have changed my mind. Five feet four will do in a pinch") he was alarmed the following afternoon by news that Sherman was expected at City Point that evening. His concern proceeded from awareness that his fellow Ohioan was not only badly in need of mounted reinforcements, still having only Kilpatrick's frazzled division on hand at Goldsboro, but was also an accomplished talker, possessed of considerable "zeal and powers of emphasis," which might well enable him to persuade his friend Grant to revise his plan for keeping Sheridan and all three of his divisions in Virginia. Disturbed by the threat, he got the last of his troopers over the James by nightfall — one month, to the day, since they left Winchester — then boarded a train and set out for headquarters. Breakdowns delayed his arrival till nearly midnight, just as Grant and Sherman were ending the conference that followed their meeting with Lincoln aboard the *River Queen*. So far as he could tell, the interloper had not changed their chief's mind about the use of cavalry in the pending operation against Lee, if indeed the subject had come up. Still the danger remained, and Sheridan continued to fret about it, even after all three of them had turned in for the night. His alarm increased next morning, March 28, when the red-head came to his room and woke him up, talking earnestly of "how he would come up through the Carolinas and hinting that I could join him." Sheridan responded so angrily, however, that Sherman dropped the subject and retired.

There was by now little time for argument, even if Sherman had thought it would do any good. He and Grant were scheduled to see Lincoln again this morning, and the President's concern for the safety of his army in his absence had led him to promise that he would start back for Goldsboro as soon as this second meeting aboard the *Queen* was over; in which connection David Porter, who was there to give advice on naval matters, had volunteered to substitute the converted blockade-runner *Bat* for the sluggish *Russia*, thus assuring the western general a faster voyage down the coast. This time, coming aboard the presidential yacht, Grant remembered to tender his and Sherman's respects to the First Lady, but when her husband went to her stateroom she sent word that she hoped they would excuse her; she was unwell. Whereupon the four men — Grant and Sherman, Porter and Lincoln — took their seats in the saloon, and the high-level conference began.

It was not, properly speaking, a council of war; "Grant never held one in his life," a staffer was to note; but it did begin with a discussion of the military situation here and in North Carolina. In regard to the former, Grant explained that Sheridan's horsemen had crossed the James in preparation for a strike at Lee's rail supply lines, which, if successful, would leave the old fox no choice except to surrender or (as he had done on a lesser scale three days ago at Fort Stedman, no doubt to his regret) come out and fight: unless, that is, he managed to slip away beforehand, in which case Meade and Ord would be close on his heels in pursuit. As for the danger to Sherman, in the event that Lee made it south to combine with Johnston, the red-head assured Lincoln that

Victory, and Defeat

his army at Goldsboro was strong enough to hold its own against both rebel forces, "provided Grant could come up within a day or so." As for a matching attempt by Johnston to give him the slip, either on foot or by rail, he saw little chance of that; "I have him where he cannot move without breaking up his army, which, once disbanded, can never be got together."

Tactically, the Commander in Chief was satisfied that victory was at last within reach. But it seemed to him, from what had just been pointed out, that all this squeezing and maneuvering was leading to a high-loss confrontation, an Armageddon that would serve no purpose on either side except to set the seal on a foregone conclusion. "Must more blood be shed?" he asked. "Cannot this last bloody battle be avoided?" Both generals thought not. In any case, that was up to the enemy; Lee being Lee, there was likely to be "one more desperate and bloody battle." Lincoln groaned. "My God, my God," he said. "Can't you spare more effusions of blood? We have had so much of it."

In the pause that followed — for they had no answer, except to repeat that the choice was not with them — Sherman observed again, as he had done the night before, the effect four years of war had had on the leader charged with its conduct all that time. "When in lively conversation, his face brightened wonderfully, but if the conversation flagged his face assumed a sad and sorrowful expression." Presuming somewhat on his feeling of sympathy, and wanting to be prepared for what was coming, he then "inquired of the President if he was all ready for the end of the war" and, more specifically, "What was to be done with the rebel armies when defeated?" That was the question, as he recalled it a decade later, when he also set down Lincoln's answer. "He said he was all ready; all he wanted of us was to defeat the opposing armies, and to get the men composing the Confederate armies back to their homes, at work on their farms and in their shops." Warming to the subject, Lincoln went on to expand it. He was also ready, he declared, "for the civil reorganization of affairs in the South as soon as the war was over." In this connection, the general would remember, "he distinctly authorized me to assure Governor Vance and the people of North Carolina that, as soon as the rebel armies laid down their arms, and resumed their civil pursuits, they would at once be guaranteed all their rights as citizens of a common country," and he added that in order to avoid anarchy in the region, "the state governments then in existence, with their civil functionaries, would be recognized by him as the government *de facto* till Congress could provide others."

Sherman, "more than ever impressed by his kindly nature, his deep and earnest sympathy with the afflictions of the whole people, resulting from the war and the march of hostile armies through the South," perceived (or gathered) from these remarks, uttered offhand and in private, that Lincoln's "earnest desire seemed to be to end the war speedily, without more bloodshed or devastation, and to restore all the men of both sections to their homes." *All,* he said; but did he mean it? Did that apply to the fire-eaters who had engineered secession; to the stalwarts, in and out of uniform, who sustained the rebellion after the fire-eaters fell by the wayside? Coming down to the most extreme example, Sherman wanted to know: Did the hope for such restoration apply to Jefferson Davis?

Now it was Lincoln's turn to pause, though not for long. As Chief Executive, the possible reviewing authority for any future legal action taken in the matter, he was "hardly at liberty to speak his mind fully," he declared, yet he was willing to reply, as he had done so often down the years, with a story. "A man once had taken the total-abstinence pledge. When visiting a friend he was invited to take a drink, but declined, on the score of his pledge; when his friend suggested lemonade, which was accepted. In preparing the lemonade, the friend pointed to the brandy bottle, and said the lemonade would be more palatable if he were to pour in a little brandy; when his guest said, if he could do so 'unbeknown' to him, he would not object." Thus Sherman retold the story, no doubt tightening it up a bit in the transcription, from which he inferred that the northern President hoped his southern counterpart would "escape, 'unbeknown' to him" — clear out, leave the country — "only it would not do for him to say so openly."

By then it was close to leaving time; Barnes had steam up on the *Bat,* waiting for Sherman to come aboard, and Lincoln was no less anxious for him to get started down the coast, where he could look to the security of his army and prepare for the movement scheduled to begin on April 10, first on Raleigh to dispose of Johnston, then north across the Virginia line to Burkeville, chosen as his objective because it was there that the Southside and Danville railroads crossed, fifty miles west of Petersburg; which meant that, once he reached that point, he would not only have cut Lee's two remaining all-weather supply lines — if, indeed, they survived till then — but would also be in position to intercept him if he retreated in that direction. Before he left, however, he and Grant and the President took a walk along the river bank, glad of a chance to stretch their legs after confinement in cramped quarters on the *Queen* for the past three hours. A reporter saw and described them as they strolled. "Lincoln, tall, round-shouldered, loose-jointed, large-featured, deep-eyed, with a smile upon his face, is dressed in black and wears a fashionable silk hat. Grant is at Lincoln's right, shorter, stouter, more compact; wears a military hat with a stiff, broad brim, has his hands in his pantaloon pockets, and is puffing away at a cigar. Sherman, tall, with a high, commanding forehead, is almost as loosely built as Lincoln; has sandy whiskers, closely cropped, and sharp, twinkling eyes, long arms and legs, shabby coat, slouched hat, his pantaloons tucked into his boots." As usual, the red-head did most of the talking —

"gesticulating now to Lincoln, now to Grant," the newsman noted, "his eyes wandering everywhere" — but at one point the President broke in to ask: "Sherman, do you know why I took a shine to Grant and you?"

"I don't know, Mr Lincoln," he replied. "You have been extremely kind to me, far more than my deserts."

"Well, you never found fault with me," Lincoln said.

This was not true. Sherman had found a good deal of fault with the President over the past four years, beginning with the day he heard him say, almost blithely, "Oh, well, I guess we'll manage to keep house." But it was true from this day forward. For one thing, Lincoln had in fact managed to "keep house," though sometimes only by the hardest, and for another, now that Sherman knew him he admired him, perhaps beyond all the men he had ever known. Again at the wharf, he boarded the *Bat* and set out down the James. Afterwards, looking back, he said of Lincoln, who had walked him to the gangplank: "I never saw him again. Of all the men I ever met, he seemed to possess more of the elements of greatness, combined with goodness, than any other."

※ 3 ※

Grant began his close-out sidle in earnest the following day. Ord's four divisions, after crossing the James in the wake of Sheridan's troopers, had replaced the six under Humphreys and Warren at the far end of the line the night before, freeing them to move in support of the cavalry strike around Lee's right, and Grant was leapfrogging his headquarters twenty miles southwest down the Vaughan Road, beyond the western limit of his intrenchments at Hatcher's Run, so he could watch the progress of events and make, first hand, such last-minute adjustments as might be needed in that direction. After breakfast, around 8.30, while he and his staff waited beside the tracks at City Point for their horses and gear to be loaded onto boxcars, Lincoln joined them and stood talking with the general for a time. Finally, after handshakes with the President all round — including one for Robert, about to take the field in his first campaign — Grant and his military family got aboard the cars. As the engine began to strain they raised their hats in salute to Lincoln, who lifted his in turn to them, and the train chuffed off, south then west, behind the long slow curve of trenches the army had dug in the course of the past nine months of stalemate here in front of Petersburg, a type of warfare the present shift had been designed to end.

In Richmond, that same March 29, Brigadier General Josiah Gorgas received at his office in the Ordnance Department, which he headed, a hastily written note signed Jefferson Davis. "Will you do me the favor to have some cartridges prepared for a small Colt pistol, of which

I send the moulds?" Gorgas, a Pennsylvania-born West Pointer who had married south — and who, starting with next to nothing in the way of machinery, skilled labor, raw materials, or the means of producing them, in the past four years had turned out seventy million rounds of small-arms ammunition, along with so much else, including weapons, that no Confederate army, whatever it suffered from being deprived of food and clothing, ever lost a battle for lack of ordnance equipment or supplies — filled the requisition overnight. The cartridges were not for Davis himself, but for his wife. He gave her the pistol and showed her how to load, aim, and fire it, saying: "You can at least, if reduced to the last extremity, force your assailants to kill you."

Four days ago, at the time of Lee's latest warning that Richmond was to be given up, he had told her she must prepare to leave without him. "My headquarters for the future may be in the field, and your presence would embarrass and grieve me instead of giving comfort." Though she begged to stay and help relieve the tension, he was firm in refusal. "You can do this in but one way: by going yourself and taking the children to a place of safety. If I live, you can come to me when the struggle is ended," he said: adding, however, that he did not "expect to survive the destruction of constitutional liberty." Regretfully she began her preparations for departure, hampered by his insistence that she not ask friends to look after the family silver, lest they be "exposed to inconvenience or outrage" when the Yankees took the city. So she sent the silver, together with some of the furniture, to an auctioneer for sale under the hammer. Then she "made the mistake," as she later said, of telling her husband that she intended to take along several barrels of flour she had bought — at the going price of $1500 a barrel — to help withstand the expected siege. He forbad this, saying flatly: "You can't take anything in the shape of food from here. The people need it." Saddened, she turned to packing what little was left, mainly clothes for herself and the four children, who ranged in age from ten years to nine months.

Others had done what Varina Davis was doing now, though with less conscientious interference by their husbands with regard to such household items as flour and silver. Since early February, foreseeing that the end of winter meant the end of Richmond, men of substance had been sending their wives and children to outlying estates, north and west of the threatened capital, or to North Carolina towns and cities so far spared a visit from Sherman. All through March the railway stations were crowded with well-off "refugees" boarding trains to avoid the holocaust at hand. Having no choice, those with nowhere to go (and no money either to pay the fare or live on when they got there) remained, as did the heads of families whose government duties or business interests required their presence; with the result that by the time the First Lady started packing, alerted for a sudden removal to

Charlotte, where Davis had rented a house for her and the children, Richmond's population was predominantly black and poor and male. A sizeable group among these last had been composed of the 105 congressmen and 26 senators, most of them eager for adjournment so they too could get aboard the cars rattling westward, away from the seven-hilled capital and the blue flood lapping the earthworks east and south — muddy dikes buttressed only by the scarecrow infantry under Lee, who was rumored to have given the government notice that they would not be there long.

In any case, these 131 elected representatives of the people felt that they had done all they could by March 18, when they adjourned and scattered for their homes, those who still had them. And, indeed, they had done much this term: including the unthinkable. After long and sometimes acrimonious debate, the House on February 20 and the Senate on March 8 authorized the enlistment of Negroes for service in the armies of the Confederacy. On March 13 a joint bill to that effect was forwarded for approval by the Chief Executive, who promptly signed it despite objections that it fell considerably short of what he — and Pat Cleburne, fifteen months ago — had wanted. For one thing, the recruits must all be volunteers, and at second hand at that; only "such able-bodied slaves as might be patriotically rendered by their masters" were to be accepted, although the President was authorized to call on the states to fill their respective quotas, limited in each case to no more than one fourth of its male slaves between the ages of eighteen and forty-five. Moreover, while it was stipulated that Negro soldiers were to receive the same pay, rations, and clothing as other troops, no mention was made of emancipation as a reward for military service, and it was even stressed in a final rider that nothing in the act was "to be construed to authorize a change in the relation which the said slaves shall bear toward their owners, except by the consent of their owners and of the states in which they may reside." Mainly, though, Davis regretted the extended debate that had kept the bill so long from his desk. "Much benefit is anticipated from this measure," he remarked, "though far less than would have resulted from its adoption at an earlier date, so as to afford time for organization and instruction during the winter months."

Grim as the warnings leading up to passage of the act had been, the fulminations that followed were even grimmer. "If we are right in passing this measure," Robert Hunter told his fellow senators, "we were wrong in denying the old government the right to interfere with the institution of slavery and to emancipate slaves." Howell Cobb agreed, writing from Georgia: "Use all the Negroes you can get, for the purposes for which you need them" — cooking, digging, chopping, and such — "but don't arm them. The day you make soldiers of them is the beginning of the end of the revolution. If slaves will make good soldiers our whole theory of slavery is wrong." Even Robert Kean, head of the Bureau of War, who knew better than most the urgent need for men in the ranks of the nation's armies, saw nothing but evil proceeding from a measure which, he noted in his diary, "was passed by a panic in the Congress and the Virginia Legislature, under all the pressure the President indirectly, and General Lee directly, could bring to bear. My own judgment of the whole thing is that it is a colossal blunder, a dislocation of the foundations of society from which no practical results will be reaped by us." Robert Toombs, after his brief return to the service during Sherman's march through Georgia, was strongest of all in condemnation of this attempt to convert the Negro into a soldier; a Confederate soldier, anyhow. "In my opinion," he wrote from his plantation in Wilkes County, where he had put down a full crop of cotton last year in response to a Davis proclamation calling on planters to shift to food crops, "the worst calamity that could befall us would be to gain our independence by the valor of our slaves. ... The day that the army of Virginia allows a negro regiment to enter their lines as soldiers they will be degraded, ruined, and disgraced."

Toombs need not have fretted about the prospect of disgrace to his former comrades, either in Virginia or elsewhere. For though the army, by and large, had favored adoption of the measure (144 out of 200 men in an Alabama regiment, for example, signed a petition addressed to Congress in its favor, and the proportion was about the same in a Mississippi outfit) the legislation failed in application: not so much because of the shortness of "time for organization and instruction," of which Davis had complained, as because of a lack of support by the owners of prospective black recruits — and possibly by the slaves themselves, though of the latter there was little chance to judge. Some few came or were sent forward to Richmond before the end of March; new gray uniforms were somehow found for them, and there was even a drill ceremony in Capitol Square, performed to the shrill of fifes and throb of drums; but that was all. Small boys jeered and threw rocks at the paraders, not one of whom reached the firing line while there was still a firing line to reach.

Nor was it only on this side of the Atlantic that the proposal to invoke the assistance of the Negro in the struggle which so intimately concerned him failed to achieve its purpose. Judah Benjamin, ever willing to play any last card in his hand, had written to Mason and Slidell in late December, instructing them to sound out the British prime minister and the French emperor, respectively, as to what effect a Confederate program for emancipation — "not suddenly and all at once, but so far as to insure abolition in a fair and reasonable time" — might have on their views with regard to recognition of the Confederacy and possible intervention in the war. Napoleon rather blandly replied that slavery had never been an issue so far as France was concerned, and Lord Palmerston said much the same of England in an interview on March 14 with Mason, who wrote Benjamin that he was "satisfied that the most ample concessions on our part in the matter referred to would have produced no change in the course determined by the British government." Twelve days later, in conversation with the Earl of Donoughmore, a Tory leader friendly to the South, the Virginian's view was confirmed by a franker response to the same question. If the proposal had been made in midsummer of 1863, while Lee was on the march in Pennsylvania, the earl did not doubt that recognition would have followed promptly. But that was then. What about now? Mason asked, and afterwards informed the Secretary: "He replied that the time had gone by."

It would have been at best a deathbed conversion, and as such would have lacked the validity of conviction and free will. Meantime, opponents of the earlier and more limited proposal — to induct blacks into the army, even without the promise of freedom as a reward for any suffering short of death — were no doubt pleased that, in practical application, the Lost Cause was spared this ultimate "stain" on its record. In any case the Confederacy's chief opponent, Abraham Lincoln, professed not to care one way or another about the success or failure of the experiment. "There is one thing about the Negro's fighting for the rebels which we can know as well as they can," he remarked, "and that is that they cannot at the same time fight in their armies and stay home and make bread for them. And this being known and remembered, we can have but little concern whether they become soldiers or not." Something else he saw as well, and when news of the action by the Richmond lawmakers reached Washington he expressed it in an address to an Indiana regiment passing through the capital on March 17, six days before he set out down the coast for City Point. "I am rather in favor of the measure," he told the Hoosiers, "and would at any time, if I could, have loaned them a vote to carry it. We have to reach the bottom of the insurgent resources, and that they employ or seriously think of employing the slaves as soldiers gives us glimpses of the bottom. Therefore I am glad of what we learn on this subject."

Davis by now had caught more than "glimpses" of the scraped bottom. Yet for all his West Point training and his regular army background, both of which contributed to the military realism that had characterized his outlook as Commander in Chief — and paradoxically, because of his unblinking recognition of the odds, had made him a believer in long chances and a supporter of those generals who would take them — it was also in his nature, as the leader of his people, to deny, even to himself, the political consequences of whatever of this kind he saw, even with his own eyes. "I'd rather die than be whipped," Jeb Stuart had said at Yellow Tavern, ten months back. So would Davis, but he took this a step further in his conviction that no man was ever whipped until he admitted it; which he himself would never do. Earlier this month, writing to thank a Virginia congressman for support "in an hour when so many believed brave have faltered and so many esteemed true have fallen away," he declared his faith in survival as an act of national will. "In spite of the timidity and faithlessness of many who should give tone to the popular feeling and hope to the popular heart, I am satisfied that it is in the power of the good man and true patriots of the country to reanimate the wearied spirit of our people. The incredible sacrifices made by them in the cause will be surpassed by what they are still willing to endure in preference to abject submission, if they are not deserted by their leaders. Relying upon the sublime fortitude and devotion of my countrymen, I expect the hour of deliverance."

His resolution was to be tested to the full before the month was out. Gordon's failure at Fort Stedman prompted Lee to state unequivocally next day that he would have to give up Richmond before Sherman and Grant effected a junction he could do nothing to prevent, and two days later, March 28, in response to a query from Breckinridge as to how much notice the capital authorities could expect — "I have given the necessary orders in regard to commencing the removal of stores, &c.," the Secretary wrote, "but, if possible, would like to know whether we may probably count on a period of ten or twelve days" — Lee replied: "I know of no reason to prevent your counting upon the time suggested." So he said. But next morning he learned that Grant had begun another crablike sidle around his thin-stretched right. Both infantry and cavalry were involved, and the movement was across Monk's Neck Bridge, over Rowanty Creek just below the confluence of Hatcher's and Gravelly runs; their initial objective seemed to be Dinwiddie Courthouse, a scant half-dozen miles beyond, which would give them a clear shot north at Five Forks, a critical intersection out the White Oak Road, about the same distance west of Burgess Mill, the right-flank anchor of Lee's line. Five Forks, defended now by no more than a handful of gray vedettes, was within three miles of the Southside Railroad, whose loss would interfere grievously — perhaps disastrously — with the army's projected withdrawal, not only from its lines below the James but also from those above, since the Richmond & Danville would also be exposed beyond the Appomattox.

Informed of this, Davis requisitioned from Gorgas ammunition for the pistol he gave his wife next day, along with instructions on how to use it. By that time Lee had troops in motion westward to meet the threat, which further reports had identified as substantial; Sheridan was at Dinwiddie with his cavalry, and two blue corps had also crossed the Rowanty, apparently to lend heft to the roundhouse left Lee believed was about to be thrown at Five Forks. Unable to stretch his line that far, lest it snap, the gray commander detached Pickett from Longstreet,

Victory, and Defeat

reinforcing his division to a strength of 6400, and posted him there, four miles beyond the farthest reach of the intrenchments on that side of Hatcher's Run. Fitzhugh and Rooney Lee's divisions, as well as Rosser's, lately arrived from the Valley — a total of 5400 troopers; all but a handful of all the army had — were called in from roundabout and sent to bolster Pickett. Nor was that all Lee did. Aggressive as always, he visited the outpost position the following morning, March 30, and ordered an advance toward Dinwiddie the following day, hoping thus to seize the initiative and throw the flankers into confusion, despite odds he knew were long. This done, he rode back to Petersburg. "Don't think he was in good humor," a young lieutenant entered in his diary.

Heavy rain had been falling with scarcely a let-up since the night before, and it continued through the final day of March, hampering last-minute preparations for the departure that evening of Mrs Davis, made urgent by the threat to the Danville line. Guns boomed daylong east of Richmond, mixed with peals of thunder; Grant no doubt was feeling the works in that direction, as well as elsewhere along the nearly forty random miles of their extent, for evidence that Lee had weakened them to confront the movement around his right. Soon after dark an overloaded carriage set out from the White House for the railroad station, bearing Mrs Davis and her sister Margaret Howell, the four children and their nurse, a young midshipman assigned as escort, and Burton Harrison, the President's secretary, who was to help them get settled in Charlotte, then rejoin his chief — wherever he might be by then. They arrived well before leaving time, 8 o'clock, and boarded a passenger coach which, though dilapidated and "long a stranger to paint," was the best the Confederacy could provide for its First Lady at this late stage of its existence. She looked with dismay at the lumpy seats, with threadbare plush the color of dried blood, and made the children as comfortable as she could; Billy, three, and the baby Pie were stretched out asleep by the time their father arrived to see them off. He sat talking earnestly with his wife, ten-year-old Maggie clinging to him all the while and eight-year-old Jeff trying hard to keep from crying. When the whistle blew, an hour and a half past schedule, he rose, kissed the children, embraced Varina, and turned to go, still with an appearance of great calm, though he came close to giving way to his emotion when Maggie persisted in clinging to him, sobbing, and Little Jeff begged tearfully to remain with him in Richmond. "He thought he was looking his last upon us," Mrs Davis later wrote.

There was a further wait on the station platform; he walked up and down it, talking with Harrison until 10 o'clock, when the train gave a sudden lurch that left the secretary barely time to leap aboard. Davis stood and watched the tail light fade and vanish, then rode back to the big empty-seeming house at Clay and 12th streets, there to await word from Lee that he too must leave the city.

All the evidence was that it would not be long, and next morning — All Fools Day — a message from the general-in-chief served notice that the time was shorter than he or anyone else had known. Pickett's advance the day before, supported by Fitz Lee's troopers, had driven the startled Federals back on Dinwiddie by sunset, but there they rallied, pumping lead from their rapid-fire carbines, and Pickett felt obliged to pull back in the rainy predawn darkness, leaving the situation much as it had been when he set out from Five Forks yesterday morning. Sheridan still held Dinwiddie, cutting the Stony Creek supply line, and had followed up Pickett's withdrawal so closely as to deny him use of the critical White Oak Road leading east to Hatcher's Run. Supported as it was by at least two corps of infantry, Lee told Davis, this movement of Grant's "seriously threatens our position and diminishes our ability to maintain our present lines in front of Richmond and Petersburg.... I fear he can cut both the South Side and the Danville railroads, being far superior to us in cavalry. This in my opinion obliges us to prepare for the necessity of evacuating our position on James River at once, and also to consider the best means of accomplishing it, and our future course."

★ ★ ★

"Grant has the bear by the hind leg while Sherman takes off the hide," Lincoln had told a White House caller some weeks back, explaining the situation as it then obtained. But now the holder-skinner roles were to be reversed, and Sheridan — much to his delight — was the catalytic agent injected by Grant to bring the change about. At Dinwiddie on the 29th, just as the rain began to patter on the roof of the tavern where he had set up for the night, he received a dispatch that sent his spirits fairly soaring. "I feel now like ending the matter, if it is possible to do so, before going back," his chief informed him. "In the morning, push around the enemy, if you can, and get onto his right rear. The movements of the enemy's cavalry may, of course, modify your action, [but] we will all act together as one army until it is seen what can be done."

"Onto," Grant said, not *into* Lee's rear: meaning that the strike at the two railroads had become incidental to his main purpose, which was to crush the rebel army where it stood. "My hope was that Sheridan would be able to carry Five Forks, get on the enemy's right flank and rear, and force them to weaken their center to protect their right so that an assault in the center might be successfully made." That was how he put it later; Warren and Humphreys would support the cavalry effort west of Hatcher's Run, and Wright was to lunge at Petersburg on signal, supported on the left and right by Ord and Parke, while Weitzel maintained pressure on Richmond's defenses beyond the James, partly to hold Longstreet in position, but also to be ready to move in when

Victory, and Defeat [865]

the breakthrough came, beyond the Appomattox. Glad to find his superior following through on what he had told him in private, three days back — "I mean to end the business here" — Sheridan briefed his subordinates on their share in the operation. All during the conference, however, rain drummed hard and harder on the tavern roof;

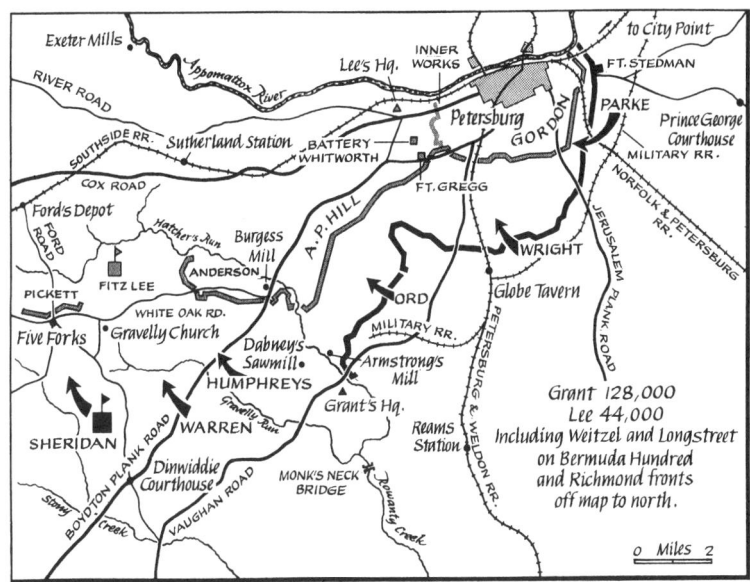

daylight showed a world in flood, with no sign of a let-up; roads were practically bottomless, preventing the movement of supplies, and the rain continued to fall in sheets, converting meadows into ponds. To make things worse, a bogged observer noted, "the soil was a mixture of clay and sand, partaking in some places of the nature of quicksand." Grant could testify to this, his headquarters beside the Vaughan Road being one such place. Formerly a cornfield, it now resembled a slough, with effects at once comic and grim on men and mounts, coming and going or even trying to stand still. "Sometimes a horse or mule would be standing apparently on firm ground," he later wrote, "when all at once one foot would sink, and as he commenced scrambling to catch himself, all his feet would sink and he would have to be drawn by hand out of the quicksands so common in that part of Virginia."

Veterans wagged their heads, remembering Burnside's Mud March, and some declared the situation was no worse than might have been expected, what with all the glib predictions that Bobby Lee was about to be outfoxed. They had heard that kind of talk before, with results that varied only in the extent of their discomfort when the smoke cleared. "Four years of war, while it made the men brave and valorous," a Pennsylvania private would point out, "had entirely cured them of imagining that each campaign would be the last." Still they were not dispirited; soggy crackers and soaked blankets often went with soldiering, especially on occasions like the present; "When are the gunboats coming up?" they called to one another as they slogged along the spongy roads or stood about in fields too wet for sitting.

Sheridan, on the other hand, fumed and fretted. He had scouting parties working northward out of Dinwiddie in accordance with his orders, but he feared the arrival of a dispatch changing those orders because of the weather. Sure enough, just such a message came from Grant around midmorning. "The heavy rain of today will make it impossible for you to do much until it dries up a little, or we get roads around our rear repaired." His suggestion was that Sheridan "leave what cavalry you deem necessary to protect the left" and return with the rest to a station on the military railroad, where he could draw rations and grain for his troopers and their mounts. Or, better yet: "Could not your cavalry go back by the way of Stony Creek Depot and destroy or capture the store of supplies there?"

Go back! Sheridan frowned as he read the words, then set out instead for Grant's command post, seven miles northeast, to argue for all he was worth against postponement of the forward movement. Hoping to save time — "a stumpy, quadrangular little man," a subsequent acquaintance was to say, "with a forehead of no promise and hair so short that it looks like a coat of black paint" — he rode a long-legged Kentucky pacer, much admired for its mile-eating gait. But the going was slow on the mud-slick roads, pelted by unrelenting rain, and slower still around midday when he turned off the Vaughan Road, a mile beyond Gravelly Run, and urged his mount across the drowned headquarters cornfield. "Instead of striking a pacing gait now," a staffer noted, "[the horse] was at every step driving its legs knee-deep into the quicksand with the regularity of a pile driver." Grant was in conference just then, but Little Phil, "water dripping from every angle of his face and clothes," launched forthwith into his protest to such listeners as were handy. Give him his head, he said, and Lee would be whipped in short order. How about forage? someone asked; to his disdain. "Forage?" he snorted. "I'll get all the forage I want. I'll haul it out if I have to set every man in the command to corduroying roads, and corduroy every mile of them from the railroad to Dinwiddie. I tell you I'm ready to strike out tomorrow and go to smashing things!"

Such enthusiasm was contagious. Twenty minutes alone with the general-in-chief, once he was free, resulted in agreement that the cavalry would "press the movement against the enemy with all vigor." Ord, Wright, and Parke were to remain on the alert for the signal to assault the rebel works in their front, and Sheridan would not only have the diversionary support of Humphreys and Warren, he would also be given direct command of the latter's corps at any time he requested it, thereby assuring full coöperation despite any difference of opinion that might arise. "Let me know, as early in the morning as you can, your judgment of the matter," Grant told him in parting, "and I will make the necessary orders." Elated, the bandy-legged Ohioan remounted and set out to rejoin his troopers around Dinwiddie, waving goodbye to the admiring group of staffers who came out into the still-driving rain to see him off, most of them as happy as he was over his success in getting their chief to cancel the postponement.

Still, a day had been lost to mud and indecision. And so, as it developed, was another — the last in March — not so much because of the weather, though rain continued to pelt the roads and sodden fields, as because of a double-pronged attack by Lee, who went over to the offensive in an attempt to disconcert the combinations moving against him west of Hatcher's Run. True to his word, Sheridan put Custer's whole division to work that morning, corduroying the Dinwiddie supply routes, while Devin probed northwest up the road to Five Forks, reinforced by a brigade from the third division, formerly Gregg's but now under George Crook; Gregg had resigned in February, exhausted or disheartened by a winter spent on the Petersburg front, and Crook was exchanged, one month after his capture up in Maryland, in time to take Gregg's place on the eve of the present maneuver, covering Dinwiddie today with his two remaining brigades while the other moved out with Devin for a share in what turned out to be a retreat in the face of heavy odds.

Approaching Five Forks around noon Devin encountered Pickett, who had been instructed by Lee to move out with his nearly 12,000 infantry and cavalry in order to beat the advancing Federals to the punch; which he did, emptying more than 400 U.S. saddles in the process. Outnumbered almost three to one, Devin had all he could do to make it back to Dinwiddie by sunset, still under heavy pressure. Crook's and Custer's troopers, called up and thrown dismounted into line alongside Devin's, managed to stop the graybacks in plain view of Sheridan's headquarters. Night came down, and with it came word of a similar repulse suffered by Warren across the way. Advancing in the direction of Lee's right, which he had been told to "feel," the New Yorker's corps was badly strung out on the muddy byroads, various units marking time while others ran heavy-footed to catch up; Brigadier General Romeyn Ayres' division, struck a sudden blow by a butternut host that came screaming out of the dripping woods ahead, took off rearward in such haste that Crawford's, next in line and with no chance to brace for the shock, was also overrun. The attack was delivered by veterans from Bushrod Johnson's division — all that remained of Anderson's improvised corps — reinforced by others brought over from A. P. Hill beyond the run, and was directed by Lee himself, who had no way of knowing that this would be his and the Army of Northern Virginia's last. In any case, the drive did not falter until it reached Griffin's division, posted in reserve, and even then was only contained with help from Humphreys, whose corps was advancing in better order on the right. After sundown, the attackers — some 5000 in all, of whom about 800 had fallen or been captured — withdrew to their works apparently satisfied with the infliction of just over 1400 casualties on Warren and just under 400 on Humphreys, both of whom testified that the call had been a close one, indicative of the need for caution while groping for contact with the rebel flank.

Sheridan did not agree. Nettled, but no more daunted by Devin's repulse than he was by Warren's, he was convinced that what had been learned from these two encounters far outweighed the loss of 2700 men on the Union left, today and yesterday. After all there still were some 50,000 blue-clad veterans west of Hatcher's Run, mounted and afoot, and he believed in using them all-out, with emphasis on getting the job done, rather than on caution. Lee had scarcely that many troops in his whole command, from White Oak Swamp to Five Forks, and if Little Phil had his way tonight the old fox would have a good many less before the sun went down tomorrow. What he had in mind was Pickett's detachment. Its movement against him today, while tactically successful, had increased its isolation and thereby exposed it to destruction, if only the right kind of pressure could be brought to bear. Even before sundown, with the issue still apparently in doubt, he said as much to a staff colonel sent over by Grant, who expressed alarm at finding Devin's troopers thrown back on the outskirts of Dinwiddie, skirmishing hotly within carbine range of the headquarters tavern. "This force is in more danger than I am," Sheridan told him. "If I am cut off from the Army of the Potomac, it is cut off from Lee's army, and not a man in it should ever be allowed to get back to Lee. We at last have drawn the enemy's infantry out of its fortifications, and this is our chance to attack it."

One doubt he had, which he also expressed. He would need a corps of infantry to help inflict Pickett's destruction, and today's encounter across the way had increased his mistrust of Warren as a fit partner, or even subordinate, in such an undertaking. Consequently, recalling how well he and Wright had worked together in the Valley, he urged the staffer to pass on to Grant his fervent request that the VI Corps be sent to him instead. Departing after nightfall, the colonel promised to support the plea, despite doubts that the change would be made this late, and presently these doubts were confirmed. Near midnight, word came from Grant — whose headquarters had been shifted that afternoon to Dabney's Sawmill, a mile northwest of the boggy Vaughan Road cornfield — that Wright could not be sent: first, because he was too far away to make the march tonight, and second because he would be needed where he was, to score the breakthrough scheduled to follow upon the smashing of Lee's right. In any case, Warren had been detached from Meade and ordered to proceed down the Boydton Plank Road to Dinwiddie, where he would report for such duty as Sheridan had in mind for him. He and his three divisions should arrive by midnight, Grant wrote, followed next morning by Brigadier General Ranald Mackenzie's troopers, one of the four divisions brought over from beyond the James two days ago. This would raise Sheridan's total to around 30,000 effectives, half cavalry, half infantry; quite enough, presumably, for the resumption of his stalled offensive. "You will assume command of the whole force sent to operate with you," the message ended, "and use it to the best of your ability to destroy the force which your command has fought so gallantly today."

More or less reconciled, Little Phil turned in for a few hours' sleep, only to have his wrath flare up again when he rose at dawn to find none of Warren's troops on hand. The rain had stopped at last, but even so their march had been a snarl of mud and confusion, including a four-hour jumbled wait for the washed-out bridge over Gravelly Run to be rebuilt. It was broad open daylight by the time the head of the 16,000-man column reached Dinwiddie, and crowding noon before Warren himself came up with his third division, eleven hours behind the schedule sent by Grant, but apparently satisfied that he and his men had done their best under difficult conditions. Sheridan took a less tolerant view. "Where's Warren?" he growled at a brigadier who arrived with the first of the mud-slathered infantry. Back toward the rear, attending to some tangle, the other replied. "That's where I expected to find him," the cavalryman snapped.

His impatience mounted with the fast-climbing sun, right up to midday, when he rode over to give the New Yorker instructions for his share in the attack. Pickett had withdrawn to Five Forks this morning and reoccupied breastworks along the White Oak Road, on both sides of the Ford Road crossing; Sheridan's plan was for his troopers, advancing northwest up the road from Dinwiddie — which bisected the southeast quadrant of the intersection and gave it the name Five Forks — to apply and maintain pressure in front, thus pinning the defenders in position while the infantry attacked their eastern flank in a turning movement whose main effort would be against the angle where their line bent north to confront a possible blue approach out the White Oak Road from Hatcher's Run, where Lee's intrenchments ended. By hitting this knuckle with one division and rounding the brief northward extension with the other two, Warren could throw two thirds of his corps — a force equal to everything Pickett had, mounted and dismounted — into their rear, and perhaps bag the lot when they gave way under double pressure, front and flank, in full flight for their lives. The important thing just now, the cavalryman stressed, was to get going before the rebs escaped or used still more of the time allowed them to improve their position. Warren nodded agreement, but it did not seem to Sheridan that much of his western enthusiasm had been communicated to the paper-collar Easterner, who left to rejoin his tired and sleepy men, muttering something about "Bobby Lee getting people into difficulties."

Actually, for all his chafing, Sheridan was to find that the delay had worked to his advantage by lulling the defenders into believing there would be no serious confrontation at Five Forks today: so much so, indeed, that when the attack did come — as it finally did, around 4 o'clock — neither the infantry nor the cavalry commander was even present to oppose him.

Reporting this morning on his two-day movement to Dinwiddie and back, Pickett was somewhat miffed by the tone of Lee's reply. "Hold Five Forks at all hazards," he was told. "Protect road to Ford's Depot and prevent Union forces from striking the Southside Railroad. Regret exceedingly your forced withdrawal, and your inability to hold the advantage you had gained." Not only did this seem tinged with unaccustomed panic, it also seemed to the long-haired hero of Gettysburg inappreciative of his efforts yesterday, which he was convinced had shocked the Federals into deferring whatever maneuver they had intended before he struck and drove them back. At any rate, on his return he put his five brigades of infantry in line along the White Oak Road, astride the Ford Road intersection, and covered their flanks and rear with cavalry, Rooney Lee's division on the right, Fitz Lee's on the left, and Tom Rosser's on guard with the train beyond Hatcher's Run, two miles to the north. All seemed well; he had no doubt that he could maintain his position against Sheridan's horsemen, even if they ventured to attack, and there had been no word of a farther advance by the blue infantry whose reported presence west of Gravelly Run had provoked his withdrawal this morning. Consequently, when an invitation came from Rosser to join in an alfresco meal of shad caught in the Nottoway River on his way from Stony Creek, Pickett gladly accepted, as did Fitzhugh Lee, who turned his division over to Colonel T. T. Munford around 1 o'clock, then set out for the rear with his ringleted superior for a share in their fellow Virginian's feast. Neither told any subordinate where he was going or why, perhaps to keep from dividing the succulent fish too many ways; with the result that when the attack exploded — damped from their hearing, as it was, by a heavy stand of pines along Hatcher's Run — no one knew where to find them. Pickett only made it back to his division after half its members had been shot or captured, a sad last act for a man who gave his name to the most famous charge in a war whose end was hastened by his three-hour absence at a shad bake.

Nor was he the only Gettysburg hero whose reputation suffered from his participation — or, strictly speaking, nonparticipation — in the fight that raged at Five Forks during the final daylight hours of April 1. Sheridan's wrath had continued to mount as the sun declined past midday and the V Corps plodded wearily up the road past Gravelly Run Church to execute its share of the fix-and-shatter maneuver already begun by the dismounted troopers banging away with their rapid-fire weapons in front of the enemy right and center. "This battle must be fought and won before the sun goes down," he grumbled on being told that it would be 4 o'clock by the time the three infantry divisions were deployed. "All the conditions may be changed in the morning; we have but a few hours of daylight left us. My cavalry are rapidly exhausting their ammunition, and if the attack is delayed much longer they may have none left." Warren, however, "seemed gloomy and despondent," Little Phil said later, and "gave me the impression that he wished the sun to go down before dispositions for the attack could be completed." If so, the New Yorker was in graver danger than he knew. Another staff colonel had arrived from Grant with a message for Sheridan, authorizing Warren's removal "if in your judgment the V Corps would do better under one of its division commanders." Sheridan saw this not only as an authorization but also as a suggestion, knowing that his chief was as displeased as he was by Warren's performance these past two days, despite his aura as the savior of Little Round Top, twenty-one months ago in Pennsylvania. All the same, he stayed his hand, controlling his temper by the hardest, and finally, not long after 4 o'clock, all three divisions started forward on a thousand-yard front, Ayres on the left, Crawford on the right, and Griffin in support, intending to strike and turn the rebel left, preliminary to the combined assault that would sweep the graybacks from the field and net them as they fled northward.

Alas, it was just at this critical moment that the bill for the worst of the day's inadvertencies came due. Informed by Sheridan that the road past Gravelly Run Church entered the White Oak Road at the point where the enemy works bent north, Warren had aligned his left division on it as a guide for the attack. Emerging from the woods, however, Ayres saw that the rebel angle — his objective — was in fact about half a mile west of the junction he was approaching. Accordingly, he swung left as he crossed the White Oak Road, then lunged westward: only to find that he was charging on his own. Crawford, on the right, kept going north, followed by Griffin close in his rear, while Mackenzie, who had arrived that morning to support the turning movement, led his troopers eastward, as instructed, to block the path of any reinforcements Lee might send across the three-mile gap between him and Pickett. Alarmed at the widening breach in the ranks of his supposed attackers, Warren spurred after the two divisions trudging north. He overtook Griffin and ordered him to turn west, where Ayres was taking concentrated punishment from guns that bucked and fumed along that end of the gray line. Then he rode on after Crawford, who continued to drift into the northward vacuum, unaware of the battle raging ever farther in his rear.

Sheridan reacted fast. Over on the left and center, Custer and Devin surged forward on schedule, their clip-fed weapons raising a clatter that sounded to one observer "as if a couple of army corps had opened fire," while Crook stood by for the mounted pursuit that was to follow. Just now, however, their chief gave his attention to the infantry in trouble on the right. "Where's my battle flag?" he cried. Snatching the swallow-tailed guidon from its bearer, he spurred Rienzi into the confusion Ayres had encountered on his lonely approach to the fuming rebel flank. "Come on, men!" he shouted, brandishing his twin-starred banner along their cowered ranks, a prominent if diminutive target, high on his huge black horse amid twittering bullets. "Go at 'em with a will. Move on at a clean jump or you'll not catch one of them! They're all getting ready to run now, and if you don't get on to them in five minutes they'll every one get away from you." Converted by such assertiveness, the wavering troops responded by resuming their advance. It was as if he addressed them individually: as, indeed, he sometimes did. Just then a nearby skirmisher was struck in the throat, blood gushing from the severed jugular. "I'm killed," he moaned as his legs gave way. But Sheridan would not have it. "You're not hurt a bit," he told the fallen soldier. "Pick up your gun, man, and move right on to the front." Dazed but convinced, the skirmisher rose, clutching his rifle, and managed to take a dozen forward steps before he toppled over, dead beyond all doubt.

For all the certainty in his voice and manner while hoicking the laggards into line, Little Phil's assurance that the rebs were "ready to run" was based not on what he could discern beyond the flame-stabbed bank of smoke that boiled up from their breastworks (he could in fact see very little, even at close range) but rather on his conviction of what would happen once the blue machine got rolling in accordance with his orders. With close to three times as many troops, and well over half of them deployed as flankers, he had no doubt about the outcome — if only they could be brought to bear as he intended. Then suddenly they were. No sooner had Ayres resumed his stalled advance than the lead elements of Griffin's division, redirected west just now by Warren, began to come up on his right, overlapping the northward extension of the enemy works. "By God, that's what I want to see: general officers at the front!" Sheridan greeted a commander who rode at the head of his brigade. He put these late arrivers in line alongside Ayres, adding others as they came up in rapidly growing numbers, then ordered the attack pressed home, all out.

Still brandishing his red and white guidon, he was in the thick of the charge that shattered the rebel left, where more than a thousand prisoners were trapped within the confines of the angle. He leaped Rienzi over the works and landed amid a group of startled graybacks. Hands shot skyward in surrender all around him. "Whar do you want us-all to go to?" one asked, and he replied, suddenly conversational if not quite genial, grinning down at them: "Go right over there. Go right along now. Drop your guns; you'll never need them any more. You'll all be safe over there. Are there any more of you? We want every one of you fellows."

There were in fact a great many more such fellows to be gathered up. Devin — known as "Sheridan's hard hitter" — broke through in front, just west of the shattered angle, and Mackenzie, finding no reinforcements on the way from Lee, returned to assist in the round-up; Griffin was into the rebel rear, and so by now was Crawford, overtaken at last by Warren and hustled westward to arrive in time for a share in the butternut gleaning. All told, at a cost of 634 casualties, the V Corps took 3422 prisoners; while the dead, plus fugitives who slipped through the infantry dragnet only to be snagged by the wider-ranging Federal troopers, raised the Confederate total above 5000; more, even, than had been lost at Fort Stedman, a week ago today. Sheridan, though exhilarated, was far from satisfied. When a jubilant brigadier reported the capture of five rebel guns, he roared back at him: "I don't care a damn for their guns — or you either, sir! What I want is the Southside Railway." He said as much to the troops themselves as they crowded round him, cheering and waving their caps. "I want you men to understand we have a record to make before that sun goes down that will make hell tremble." He stood in his stirrups, pointing north toward the railroad three miles off. "I want you there!" he cried. Encountering Griffin beyond Five Forks, shortly after sunset at 6.20, he told him: "Get together all the men you can, and drive on while you can see your hand before you."

Griffin — crusty Griffin, whom Grant had advised Meade to place in arrest for insubordination on his second day over the Rapidan — now headed the V Corps. Warren, deep in the rebel rear with Crawford, corralling prisoners as they came streaming north across the fields and up Ford Road, had sent a staff colonel to inform headquarters of his whereabouts and his success in carrying out the flanking operation, only to have Sheridan scoff at the report. "By God, sir," he interrupted hotly, "tell General Warren he wasn't in that fight." Astonished, the colonel replied that he would dislike to deliver any such message verbally. Might he take it down in writing? "Take it down, sir!" Sheridan barked. "Tell him by God he was not at the front." Nor was that all. At their sundown meeting he formally notified Griffin that he was to take over in place of Warren, to whom a hastily scrawled field order soon was on its way: "Major General Warren, commanding the Fifth Army Corps, is relieved from duty, and will at once report for orders to Lieutenant General Grant, commanding Armies of the United States. By command of Major General Sheridan."

All the same, though he now felt he had an infantry chief he could depend on, he called off the pursuit he had been urging. In part this was because of the encumbrance of so many grayback prisoners that he used their discarded rifles to corduroy the worst stretches of road; but mainly it was because, on second thought — detached as he was from the rest of the army — he concentrated instead on bracing his victory-scattered troops for the counterattack Lee's opponents had long since learned to expect in such a crisis. Nightfall cooled his blood, and with it his temper, even to the point where he came close to a downright apology for some of the rough talk he had unloaded on subordinates today. "You know how it is," he told a group of V Corps officers gathered around a Five Forks campfire. "We had to carry this place, and I was fretted all day until it was done." None of this applied to their former chief, however, and he had said as much to Warren himself when the New Yorker rode up to headquarters in the gathering dusk and asked him to reconsider the order issued for his removal in the heat of battle. "Reconsider, hell," Sheridan snorted; "I don't reconsider my decisions. Obey the order."

Sedgwick, Burnside, Hancock, Warren: now all four of the men commanding infantry corps at the time of the Rapidan crossing had departed, the last under conditions not unlike those attending the removal of his predecessor Fitz-John Porter, with whom he had shared an admiration for George McClellan, rejected like them by the powers that were. Reporting as ordered to headquarters at Dabney's Mill about 10 o'clock that night, he found a celebration of Sheridan's victory in progress. Grant, he said later, "spoke very kindly of my past services and efforts," though the best he could do for him now, apparently, was put him in charge of the inactive City Point area, where he sat in the backwash while the guns boomed westward.... Warren began at once to press for a court of inquiry to right the hot-tempered wrong he believed had been done him today. He finally got it, fourteen years later, and after nearly three more years of hearings and deliberation he also received a measure of vindication by the court, which not only cleared him of Sheridan's charges that he had been negligent at Five Forks, but also criticized the manner of his relief. However, that came three months after Warren himself was in his grave. Buried, as he directed in his will, in civilian clothes and without military ceremony, he would in time stand fully accoutered in bronze on the crest of Little Round Top, where he had saved Meade and, some would say, the Union.

Back at Dabney's, before Warren's appearance put something of a damper on the scene, the victory celebration had been set off by Horace Porter's arrival from Five Forks about an hour after dark; he had sent couriers, but overtook the last and most joyously burdened of these in his haste to share the good news with his friends and fellow members of the staff. They were sitting around a blazing campfire — Grant among them, wrapped in a long blue overcoat and smoking his usual cigar — when the young colonel rode into the firelight, shouting from horseback of Sheridan's success. "For some minutes," he would recall, "there was a bewildering state of excitement, grasping of hands, tossing up of hats, and slapping of each other on the back. It meant the beginning of the end, the reaching of the 'last ditch.' It pointed to peace and home."

Only the general-in-chief remained seated, puffing stolidly at his cigar while Porter burbled of six guns captured along with thirteen rebel flags. "How many prisoners have been taken?" Grant asked. More than 5000, he was told. He rose, went into his tent, and began to write telegraphic dispatches by the flickering light of a candle. When these were done he gave them to an orderly for transmission, then came back out to resume his seat beside the fire. "I have ordered an immediate assault along the lines," he said.

Hearing before sunset of the reverse at Five Forks (though not of its extent, which would leave Pickett gunless by nightfall and unable to muster 2000 infantry in his shattered ranks next morning) Lee ordered Anderson to have Bushrod Johnson march his three remaining brigades at once to Sutherland Station, three miles north on the Southside Railroad, to combine with Pickett and Fitz Lee for the defense of that vital supply line and the even more vital Richmond & Danville, farther west. In partial compensation for this stripping of his right, and though the shift reduced by about 400 the number of defenders in A. P. Hill's two divisions east of Burgess Mill — already so thin-spread, one of them declared, that the pickets were "as far apart as telegraph poles" — he brought two of Heth's regiments across Hatcher's Run to patrol the empty works along the south bank of that stream. Still robbing Peter to pay Paul, when he returned to his headquarters near the Appomattox, two miles west of Petersburg, he wired Longstreet to bring Field's division south by rail tonight from beyond the James. That would leave only Kershaw's reduced division and Ewell's reservists to cover Richmond: a grave risk, but no graver than the one Lee ran in gambling that Grant would not launch an all-out southside attack before Old Peter arrived to help prevent the breaking of Hill's line. Situated as he was, his right flank turned and a deep river at his back, if he had known that Pickett's losses today, combined with those a week ago at Stedman, had cost him a solid fourth of his army, he probably would have evacuated Petersburg that night. Instead, he held on where he was, shifting and sidling his few troops to meet a crisis whose true dimensions were unknown to him, in hope of deferring his departure until such time — quite possibly tomorrow night — as would allow him to alert his subordinate commanders, not to mention the Richmond authorities, at least a few hours in advance.

In any case, having done what he could within his means to meet the problem caused by the loss of Five Forks, he turned in early, so weary that he only removed his boots and outer garments before lying down to sleep. It was as well; for he had no sooner rested his head on the pillow, shortly after 9 o'clock, than guns began to growl all up and down the long curve of Union works, possibly signifying that he would have to turn out in a hurry to meet what Grant had in mind to do when the bombardment lifted. Whatever it was, he hoped it would not come before Field arrived to chink the undermanned stretches of his line. At 1.45 (April 2 now, a Sunday, though dawn was three hours off) a sudden ripple of picket fire intensified the duller rumble of artillery. Awake or asleep, Lee may or may not have heard it, intermittent at first and then a rising clatter. Certainly A. P. Hill did, for he appeared at the Turnbull house, Lee's command post, about an hour before dawn. Disturbed by the weakness of his six-mile front along the Boydton Plank Road leading down to Burgess Mill — especially those portions of it whose outworks had been overrun by the Federals in reaction to Gordon's storming of Fort Stedman, eight days back — Little Powell had returned from sick leave yesterday, though he still was far from well. Unable to sleep tonight, what with the roar of cannons and the stutter of small-arms fire, he had ridden from his own headquarters, back on the outskirts of Petersburg, a mile and a half out Cox Road to the Turnbull house to inquire whether anyone there knew what the Yankees were up to in the rackety, flame-stabbed darkness out beyond his front.

Lee was awake, though still in bed, when Hill arrived, hazel eyes glittering feverishly above his auburn beard, high-set cheekbones hectic with the illness that had kept him from duty so much of the past year. Nearly two decades apart in age — one fifty-eight and looking it, prone beneath the bedclothes, the other eight months short of forty, slim and immaculately uniformed as always — the two generals began a discussion of what could be done if, as seemed likely from the step-up in the firing with the swift approach of dawn, a blue assault preceded Field's arrival from beyond the James. Then Longstreet entered, burly and imperturbable despite the persistent lameness of his sword arm from the bullet that had cut him down at the height of his Wilderness flank attack, just one month less than a year ago this week. His arrival, as commander of the reinforcements ordered southward in all haste, was encouraging until he explained that he and his staff had ridden ahead on horseback to save space on the crowded cars for Field's 4600 infantry. They were still on the way, so far as he knew, though he could not say how long it would be before the first of them reached Petersburg, let alone the front. Daylight was glimmering through by now, and Lee was indicating on a map the route he wanted these troops to take as soon as they detrained, when a staff colonel rushed into the room exclaiming that panicked teamsters were dashing their wagons "rather wildly" up the Cox Road past the Turnbull gate, apparently in flight from a Federal breakthrough somewhere down near Hatcher's Run. A wounded officer, hobbling back on crutches, had even told of being driven from his quarters more than a mile behind the center of Hill's line.

Alarmed — as well he might be, since this first word of a penetration also indicated the likelihood of a rout — Lee drew a wrapper around him and went to the front door. Sure enough, though swirls of ground fog obscured the color of their uniforms in the growing light, long lines of men resembling skirmishers were moving toward him from the southwest, the nearest of them not over half a mile away. Uncertain whether they were retreating Confederates or advancing Federals, he sent an aide to take a closer look. Just then, however, they halted as if in doubt, and as they did the quickening daylight showed their clothes were blue. Lee turned to Longstreet and told him to go at once to the Petersburg station and hurry Field's men westward, relay by relay, as fast as they unloaded from the cars. Then he turned to speak to Hill; but Hill was already running toward his horse, intent on reaching and rallying the troops in rear of his broken line. He mounted and rode south, accompanied by Sergeant G. W. Tucker, his favorite courier. Disturbed by something desperate in his fellow Virginian's manner — or perhaps because he had heard that during the recently interrupted sick leave, spent with kinsmen in a Richmond rife with rumors of impending evacuation, Little Powell had said he had no wish to survive the fall of the capital — Lee sent a staffer to caution Hill not to expose himself unduly.

Out front, across the open fields to the southwest, the line of bluecoats remained halted in a swale. Apparently made cautious by the activity in the Turnbull yard, they seemed to be waiting for reinforcements to come up before they continued their advance. Lee studied them briefly, then went into the house to finish dressing. When he reappeared, he wore his best gray uniform and had buckled on his sword. This last was so unusual that it occurred to at least one member of his staff that the general had decided to be in "full harness" in case he was obliged to surrender before the rising sun went down. In any event, he mounted Traveller and rode out for a closer examination of whatever calamity was at hand.

Piecemeal, in the absence of reports from subordinates who were too busy just then to do anything but fight to hang on where they were or hurry rearward to avoid capture, he managed to gather at least a notion of what had happened as a result of the massive three-corps blue assault launched at daybreak, 60,000 strong, against nearly the whole twelve miles of works, defended by less than one fourth that number, from the Appomattox down to Burgess Mill. On the left, east and directly south of Petersburg, Gordon's front-line troops were driven back on their inner fortifications by the force of Parke's attack. There they rallied, supported by Pendleton's reserve artillery, which Lee had massed in their rear the day before, and not only resisted all further efforts to dislodge them, but were counterattacking even now to recover the outworks they had lost. Southwest along the thinly manned stretch of Hill's line, whose forward positions had been overrun the week before, events took a different turn. Attacking from close up, one of Wright's three divisions broke through a single line of works defended by two of Wilcox's brigades. Swept from their trenches, these veterans fell back north through the soggy woods, firing as they went. Beyond the Boydton Plank Road — within two miles of the Turnbull house, where Lee was conferring with A. P. Hill and Longstreet — their pursuers fanned out to the left, southwest down the plank road toward Hatcher's Run, in rear of that part of the gray line under assault by Ord. Heth's division and the other half of Wilcox's, pressed in front and threatened from the rear, gave way in turn, withdrawing northwest up the left bank of the run, and Ord's and Wright's men followed for a time, then veered northeast into the angle between the Boydton Plank Road and Cox Road. These were the bluecoats Lee discerned through wisps of fog when he came to the Turnbull front door in his wrapper, and this was the breakthrough — the two breakthroughs, really — that had more or less abolished Hill's half dozen miles of line between Gordon's right and Hatcher's Run.

Fortunately for him, at this stage the attackers were about as disorganized by their sudden gains as his own troops were by their retreat. Straggling was heavy among the pursuers, and various units were intermingled, shaken loose from their regular order of battle and strung out in long lines like skirmishers. Their pause for realignment and the ensuing wait for reinforcements, at a time when absolutely nothing stood between them and his headquarters, gave Lee the chance to dress and mount Traveller for a first-hand study of the situation. Westward there was scattered firing, and a heavier clatter rolled in from the east, where the sun by now was rising over Petersburg, obscured by smoke from Pendleton's guns supporting Gordon in his fight to hold back Parke. Southward, however, there was an ominous silence along the lines where Ord and Wright had undone Heth and Wilcox. Riding toward the Turnbull gate for a look across the fields in that direction, Lee saw a group of horsemen turn in from the road: members of Hill's staff, he observed as they drew nearer, and then noted with a pang of apprehension that the man astride the corps commander's handsome dapple-gray was Sergeant Tucker. This could only mean that Hill was dead or wounded.

He was dead; Tucker, who had been with him when he fell, told how it happened. Proceeding south from the Turnbull house before sunrise, just short of the Boydton Plank Road they found Union soldiers cavorting among the huts the men of Mahone's division had occupied, as the army's one reserve, until they were detached and shifted north of the Appomattox to take over Pickett's position on Bermuda Hundred. This in itself showed the depth of the breakthrough, but Hill, skirting the celebration being staged a mile behind his lines, was determined to continue the search for his missing troops, even though all that could be seen in any direction were random groups of blue-clad stragglers from the attack that had swept this way and then moved on. Beyond the plank road he turned right, explaining that he hoped to reach Heth on the far side of the break that seemed to have made a clean sweep of Wilcox and all four of his brigades. The two rode west about a mile along a screening fringe of woods, through which from time to time they sighted still more clots of Federals on the prowl, but no Confederates at all. "Sergeant," Hill said at last, for the sense of danger grew as they proceeded, "should anything happen to me, you must go back to General Lee and report it." Tucker responded by taking the lead, and removed his navy Colt from its holster to be prepared for whatever loomed. Presently he drew rein, having spotted a squad-sized cluster of bluecoats in the woods directly ahead, the two closest of whom scuttled for shelter behind a large tree and extended their rifle barrels around its trunk, one above the other. "We must take them," Hill said, coming forward. But Tucker would not have it. "Stay there: I'll take them," he said, and shouted to the hidden pair, some twenty yards away: "If you fire you'll be swept to hell! Our men are here. Surrender." Beside him now, Hill too had drawn his pistol and held it at the ready. "Surrender!" he cried, his gauntleted left hand extended palm-out toward the two blue soldiers crouched behind their tree. "I can't see it," Tucker heard one of them say, and then: "Let's shoot them." One rifle had been lowered. Now it rose and both went off. A bullet whistled past the courier's head: but not past Little Powell's. Unhorsed, he lay sprawled and motionless on the ground, arms spread. Later, when his body was recovered, friends discovered that the bullet had passed through the gauntlet, cutting off his thumb, before it entered his heart and dropped him, dead perhaps before he struck the earth. Tucker dodged and grabbed the bridle of the riderless gray horse, spurring his own mount back the way they had come. Beyond range of the two soldiers — Corporal John W. Mauk and Private Daniel Wolford, stragglers from a Pennsylvania regiment in one of Wright's divisions — he changed to the faster horse and made good time, first to Hill's headquarters, then to Lee's, where he told and retold what had happened to his chief, back there amid the wreckage of what had been his rear until this morning.

Lee's eyes brimmed with tears. "He is at rest now, and we who are left are the ones to suffer," he said on learning thus of his loss of fiery, high-strung Little Powell, the hard-hitting embodiment of his army's offensive spirit and the one troop commander Stonewall Jackson had called on in his last delirium, back in the days when that spirit burned its brightest. "Go at once, Colonel, and get Mrs Hill and her children across the Appomattox," he told the Third Corps chief of staff, adding: "Break the news to her as gently as possible."

As it turned out, there was no gentle way to break such news. Hesitating at the front door of the cottage she and Hill and their two small daughters had shared on an estate near Petersburg, the staffer could hear the unsuspecting widow singing as she went about her housework. He entered without knocking, hoping to spare her so abrupt a summons. But when Mrs Hill — John Morgan's younger sister Kitty, auburn-haired like the husband she did not yet know had fallen, though she had learned to live with apprehension of such loss throughout the nearly four years of her marriage — heard his slow footsteps in the hall, then turned and saw him, the singing stopped. "The general is dead," she said in a strained voice, numbed by shock. "You would not be here unless he was dead."

Back at the Turnbull house by then, Lee had begun planning to do for his southside units what he had told the colonel to do for Hill's widow and children; that is, get them over the Appomattox before the victory-flustered Union host completed its mission of cutting them off from a crossing. Tucker's account of all that he and his chief had seen, en route to their encounter with the two blue stragglers in rear of the crumpled right, was enough to convince him that the time had come — if, indeed, it was not already past — for him to order the evacuation not only of Petersburg but also of Richmond. Beyond Burgess Mill, Humphreys by now had added a fourth corps to the general assault, and Sheridan was reported driving north and east with his and Griffin's men, lifting the total to six full corps, any one of which had more troops on its roster than Lee had in all on this side of Hatcher's Run, including those in flight. Moreover, this would continue to be the case until Field arrived: if, in fact, he did arrive in time to stop or hinder Wright and Ord, whose buildup southwest of headquarters had continued to the point where they seemed ready to resume their stalled advance, unopposed by anything more than Lee and his staff and a single battery of guns just unlimbered in the Turnbull yard.

Around 10 o'clock, firing over the heads of infantry massing for attack, Federal gunners ended the providential four-hour lull by opening on the battery and the house itself. Before disconnecting the telegraph for departure, Lee dictated a series of dispatches to the Secretary of

Victory, and Defeat [881]

War, the President, and Ewell, who had taken over from Longstreet north of the James. "I see no prospect of doing more than holding our position here till night. I am not certain that I can do that. If I can I shall withdraw tonight north of the Appomattox, and if possible it will be better to withdraw the whole line tonight from James River." This was the message to Breckinridge, ending summarily: "I advise that all preparation be made for leaving Richmond tonight." The one to Davis added that he was sending "an officer to Your Excellency to explain the routes by which the troops will be moved," as well as "a guide and any assistance that you may require." Ewell in turn was cautioned to "make all preparations quietly and rapidly to abandon your position.... Have your field transportation ready and your troops prepared for battle or marching orders, as circumstances may require."

But the time was short. When Lee came out again into the yard, where the gray cannoneers were getting badly knocked about in the process of limbering their pieces for withdrawal, a shell tore over his head and into the house, starting fires that soon would leave only four tall chimneys standing where his headquarters had been. "This is a bad business," he remarked as he mounted for the ride to find shelter in the inner fortifications, which Field's troops were to man when they arrived. Still, he waited for the guns to complete their displacement before he set out eastward, trailed by his staff. He rode at a walk, not looking back until a shell exploded close behind him, disemboweling a horse. Others followed rapidly, now that the enemy gunners had the range, and an officer riding beside him watched as Lee reacted to what he evidently considered a highly personal affront. "He turned his head over his right shoulder, his cheeks became flushed, and a sudden flash of the eye showed with what reluctance he retired before the fire directed upon him." Rearward he saw blue infantry moving out ahead of the bucking guns, their rifle barrels gleaming in the sunlight. Suppressing his defiance, if not his anger, he gave Traveller the spur and rode on nearly a mile to the thinly-held works about the same distance west of Petersburg. "Well, Colonel," he said to one of his staff as he drew rein, "it has happened as I told them it would at Richmond. The line has been stretched until it has broken."

These inner fortifications, where he and his staff took refuge from the shells that pursued them on their ride, were the so-far unused western portion of the old Dimmock Line, other parts of whose original half-oval had been put to such good use in June. Beauregard then had been grievously outnumbered, but Lee's predicament now was even worse. East and south, on the far side of town, Gordon had all he could do to hold off Parke, and Field's veterans had not yet appeared. The few garrison troops available to man this empty stretch of works extending from Gordon's hard-pressed right, northward a mile and a half to the Appomattox, were scarcely enough to delay, let alone prevent, a breakthrough by Ord and Wright, whose renewed advance, if undeterred, would end the war in the streets of Petersburg before the midday sun went down. Lee's hope, pending Field's arrival, was in two small earthworks under construction out the Boydton Plank Road, half a mile in front of the main line; Fort Gregg and Battery Whitworth, they were called. Less than a quarter-mile apart and mutually supporting, they were occupied by four slim regiments from Nathaniel Harris's Mississippi brigade — some 400 men in all, left on line when the rest of Mahone's division was shifted north — together with about a hundred North Carolinians, fugitives cut off from Wilcox by the collapse of his left center. Harris put just under half his troops into Gregg, along with two of his five guns, and took the rest with him to Whitworth, 300 yards north of the plank road. A Natchez-born former Vicksburg lawyer, thirty years old, he passed Lee's orders to Gregg's defenders when he left. "Men," he told them, shouting above the uproar of the opening cannonade, "the salvation of the army is in your keep. Don't surrender this fort. If you can hold out for two hours, Longstreet will be up." Behind him, as he turned to go, he heard someone call out after him: "Tell them we'll not give up."

It was noon by now, and presently they showed that they meant what their spokesman said, and more. Given the reduction assignment, Ord passed it along to John Gibbon and the two 6000-man divisions he had brought southside from his XXIV Corps, one against each of the outworks, intending to overrun them in short order. The attack on Whitworth was delayed by a wait for some huts set afire by the rebels to burn out in its front, but the one on Gregg was launched promptly at 1 o'clock, as soon as the bombardment lifted. A brigade in each, the advance was in three columns, which converged as they drew near the objective. Hit by massed volleys, they fell back in some disorder to reform, and then came on again; only to have the same thing happen. "In these charges," a defender would recall, "there was no shooting but by us, and we did cruel and savage work with them." Between attempts, observers back on the Confederate main line, where Field's leading elements were at last beginning to file into the trenches, heard faint cheering from the fort, as well as from Battery Whitworth, still not under immediate pressure. Lee watched from a high vantage point: as did Longstreet, who thought he recognized his old friend Gibbon when he studied the close-packed attackers through his glasses. "[I] raised my hat," he later wrote, "but he was busy and did not see me."

Gibbon was indeed busy, having learned by now that the only way he was going to reduce the two-gun earthwork was by swamping it. Fortunately he had the men, and the men themselves were willing. He brought down a brigade from the division standing idle in front of Whitworth, thus increasing the assault force to 8000, and sent them forward, no longer in successive waves but in a single flood. Inside the

Victory, and Defeat [883]

place, wounded graybacks loaded rifles taken from the dead and dying, and passed them up to rapid-firing marksmen perched atop the walls. Still the attackers came on, taking their losses to sweep past the flanks and into the rear of the uncompleted installation. Near the end, a butternut captain noted, "The battle flags of the enemy made almost a solid line of bunting around the fort. The noise was fearful, frightful, indescribable. The curses and groaning of frenzied men could be heard over the din of our musketry. Savage men, ravenous beasts — we felt there was no hope for us unless we could keep them at bay. We were prepared for the worst, and expected no quarter." Tumbling over the parapets, sometimes onto the lifted bayonets of the defenders, the Federals gained the interior, and there the struggle continued, hand to hand. One gun was out by then, but the other, trained on the still-advancing bluecoats on the far side of the ditch, was double shotted with canister, its lanyard held taut by a single cannoneer. "Don't fire that gun! Drop the lanyard or we'll shoot!" the attackers yelled, their rifles leveled at him. "Shoot and be damned!" he shouted back, leaning on the lanyard. Canister plowed the ranks out front, and the cannoneer, riddled with bullets, sprawled dead across the trail of the smoking gun.

For another twenty minutes the fight continued at close quarters with clubbed muskets, rammer staffs, and any weapons that were handy, including brickbats from a toppled chimney. By the time it ended, Gibbon's loss of 122 killed and 592 wounded more than tripled the rebel garrison of 214 men, of whom 55 were dead, 129 wounded — 86 percent — and only 30 surrendered uninjured. Northward, their flank exposed by Gregg's collapse and the huts at last burned out in front, Whitworth's defenders scuttled rearward, losing about 60 captives in the final rush by Gibbon's other division's other two brigades. By then it was just after 3 o'clock. Harris's Mississippians and the Tarheel fugitives had given Lee the two hours he asked of them, plus still another for good measure.

Something else they gave as well: an example for Field's veterans, now on line, to follow when and if the Federals tried to continue their advance: which they did not. "The enemy, not finding us inclined to give way for him," Field afterwards reported, "contented himself with forming line in front of us, but out of range. We stood thus in plain view of each other till night, when the army began its retreat."

While the contest for Gregg was in progress Lee and his staff worked on plans for the removal that night of the divided army, northward over the Appomattox and southward over the James, and its subsequent concentration at Amelia Courthouse on the Richmond & Danville, forty miles west-northwest and west-southwest, respectively, of Petersburg and the capital. From there, reunited for the first time since Cold Harbor, ten months back, the command was to follow the line of the railroad, via Burkeville, for a combination with Joe Johnston somewhere beyond Danville, which was just over a hundred miles from Amelia. What Grant would do with his greatly superior force, by way of interfering with this proposed march of a hundred and fifty miles or more, depended in part on how much of a head start Lee managed to gain between nightfall and daylight — at the latest — when the Union lookouts woke to find him gone. Accordingly: "The movement of all troops will commence at 8 o'clock," the evacuation order read, "the artillery moving out quietly first, infantry following, except the pickets, who will be withdrawn at 3 a.m." Copies went to Longstreet and Gordon, close at hand, to Ewell in Richmond and Mahone on the Bermuda Hundred line, and to Anderson, who was instructed to collect the shattered remnants of Pickett's, Johnson's, Heth's, and Wilcox's divisions beyond Hatcher's Run, cut off from Petersburg by the enemy now astride the Southside Railroad east of Sutherland Station.

Except for his anger at the Federals for their shelling of the Turnbull house that morning, the southern commander kept his temper all through this long and trying day; save once. This once was when he received a wire from Davis in the capital, protesting that "to move tonight will involve the loss of many valuables, both for the want of time to pack and of transportation. Arrangements are progressing," the President added, however, "and unless you otherwise advise, the start will be made." Lee bristled at the implied rebuke — perhaps forgetting that five days ago he had promised Breckinridge a ten- or twelve-day warning — and ripped the telegram to pieces. "I am sure I gave him sufficient notice," he said testily, and dictated a reply that left no doubt whatever about his intentions: "I think it is absolutely necessary that we should abandon our position tonight. I have given all necessary orders on the subject to the troops, and the operation, though difficult, I hope will be performed successfully."

It was, and on schedule. Less than an hour after dark, Pendleton, close in rear of the Second Corps, began withdrawing the reserve artillery through the cobbled streets of Petersburg and then across the Appomattox bridges, followed by other batteries from all parts of the line. Field's First Corps division led the infantry displacement under Longstreet, who had also been put in charge of those Third Corps units cut off east of this morning's breakthrough. Assigned the rear-guard duty, Gordon pulled his three divisions back in good order, with little need for stealth and none at all for silence, since any noise his departing soldiers made was drowned by the nightlong roar of Union guns, firing all-out in apparent preparation for another dawn assault; an assault which, if made at all, would be made upon a vacuum. Beyond the river, approaching a road junction whose left fork Longstreet had taken to ease the crowding when his own corps took the right, Gordon came upon Lee, dismounted and holding Traveller's rein in one gauntleted hand. All the troops left in Petersburg at sundown — fewer than 15,000 of all arms — would pass this way, and the gray-bearded commander had chosen this as his post for supervising the final stage of the evacuation. About the same number of graybacks were in motion elsewhere, miles away in the chilly early-April darkness. Kershaw was with Ewell up in Richmond, withdrawing too by then, along with reservists from the capital fortifications, guncrews from the heavy batteries on James River, and even a battalion of sailors, homeless landsmen now that they had burned their ships to keep them out of enemy hands. Mahone was on the march from Bermuda Hundred, just to the north, and Anderson presumably was working his way west along the opposite bank of the Appomattox with the remnants of Johnson's and Pickett's divisions, as well as parts of Hill's two, driven in that direction by the collapse of his line at daybreak, and Fitz Lee's troopers. South of the river, from point to scattered point along the otherwise empty eight-mile curve of intrenchments, the pickets kept their shell-jarred vigil. Soon now they too would be summoned rearward and engineer details would carry out their work of demolition, first on the abandoned powder magazines and then on the bridges, which were to be fired when the last man crossed, leaving Petersburg to the bluecoats who, at a cost of well over 40,000 casualties, had been doing all they could to take it for the past two hundred and ninety-three days.

Lee did not wait for that. About an hour before midnight, having observed that both gray columns were well closed up as they slogged past him there in the fork of the two roads, he mounted and set out westward for Amelia Courthouse, just under forty miles away.

By that time, up in the capital, Davis and his cabinet were departing from the railway station where, two nights ago, he had seen his wife and children off for Charlotte, three hundred miles to the southwest. His own destination was Danville, half as far away, just short of the North Carolina line. That was to be the new seat of government at least until Lee and his army got there, en route to a combination with Johnston; at which time another shift would no doubt be required, though how far and in what direction — still within or else beyond the borders of the Old Dominion, every vestige of whose "sacred soil" would in the latter case be given over to the invader — no one could say at this stage of a crisis that had become acute some twelve hours earlier, when a War Department messenger brought to the presidential pew in St Paul's Church, midway through the morning service, Lee's telegram advising that "all preparation be made for leaving Richmond tonight."

Nearby worshipers saw "a sort of gray pallor creep over his face" as he read the dispatch, then watched him rise and stride back down the aisle "with stern set lips and his usual quick military tread." Some few rose to follow, knowing the summons must be urgent for him to leave before taking Communion this first-Sunday; but for the most part, he said later, "the congregation of St Paul's was too refined to make a scene at anticipated danger." He went directly to the War Office to confer with Breckinridge and other cabinet members available at short notice on the Sabbath. One such was Judah Benjamin, who strolled over from his quarters on North Main, apparently unperturbed, "his pleasant smile, his mild Havana, and the very twirl of his slender gold-headed cane contributing to give casual observers an expression of casual confidence."

Davis's manner was almost as calm, though by no means as debonair, as he told the assembled ministers of the breaking of Lee's line and the impending evacuation, then directed them to have their most valuable records packed for delivery to the Richmond & Danville Depot, where they would meet that evening for departure as a group. Special instructions for the Treasury Department covered the boxing of Confederate funds on hand — some $528,000 in double-eagle gold pieces, Mexican silver coins, gold and silver bricks and ingots — for shipment aboard a special train, with a guard of sixty midshipmen from their academy training vessel *Patrick Henry*. These last would of course be furnished by Mallory, who was also told to pass the word for Raphael Semmes to see to the destruction of this and all other ships of the James River Squadron, iron and wood; after which their crews would proceed to Danville for service under Lee.

Later that afternoon, his desk cleared and his office put in order for tomorrow's faceless blue-clad occupant — Grant himself, for all he knew, or whoever else would command the occupation force — Davis set out through Capitol Square for the last of his familiar homeward walks to the White House, where he still had to pack for the journey south. More people were abroad today than usual, but they were strangely quiet, shocked by rumors that they and their city were about to be abandoned to the foe. Asked if it was true, he replied that it was, adding however that he hoped to return under better auspices. Some wept at the news, while others replaced false hope with resolution. "If the success of the cause requires you to give up Richmond, we are content," one matron came out of her house to tell him as he walked by, and he afterwards declared that "the affection and confidence of this noble people in the hour of disaster were more distressing to me than complaint and unjust censure would have been."

At the mansion there was much to do, including the disposition of certain effects he could not take with him yet did not want to have fall into enemy hands: the family cow, for instance, lent by a neighbor and now returned: a favorite easy chair, which he had carted to Mrs R. E. Lee's home on Franklin Street with a message expressing hope that it would comfort her arthritis: an oil painting, "Heroes of the Valley," and a marble bust of Davis himself, both turned over to a friend who offered to put them where "they will never be found by a Yankee." While a servant packed his valise he gave final instructions to the housekeeper, emphasizing that everything must be in decent order, swept and dusted, when the Federals arrived to take possession tomorrow morning. This done, he dressed carefully — trousers and waistcoat of Confederate gray, a dark Prince Albert frock coat, polished Wellingtons, a full-brimmed planter's hat — brushed his hair and tuft of beard, and waited in his pale-rugged private office — long the terror of muddy-booted officers reporting from the field — for word that the special train was ready for boarding. Shortly after 8 o'clock it came. He went out the front door and down the steps, mounted his saddle horse Kentucky, and set out for the railway station beside the James on the far side of town.

The ride was just over half a mile through crowded streets, and his impressions now were very different from those he had received four hours ago, in the course of his walk home from Capitol Square. Numbed decorum had given way to panic, a hysteria that grew more evident as he drew near the river and the depot. Government warehouses stocked with rations for the anticipated siege were there, and word had spread that the food was to be distributed to the public, on a first-come first-served basis, before the buildings were destroyed along with whatever remained in them by the time the army left. Some among those gathered were marauders out for spoils in the business district, their number swollen by convicts who, deserted by their guards, had broken out of jail and were rifling shops for clothing to replace their prison garb; "a crowd of leaping, shouting demons," one observer called these last, "in parti-colored clothes and with heads half-shaven. . . . Many a heart which had kept its courage to this point quailed at the sight." All in all, another witness would declare, this was "the saddest of many of the sad sights of war — a city undergoing pillage at the hands of its own mob, while the standards of an empire were being taken from its capitol and the tramp of a victorious enemy could be heard at its gates." Davis rode on, forcing his way through the throng, and finally reached the station. There the cabinet awaited his arrival; all but Breckinridge, who would remain behind to supervise the final stages of the evacuation, then follow Lee to observe and report on the military situation before rejoining his colleagues at Danville, or wherever they might be by then.

All got aboard the waiting coach, but there was another long delay while the treasure train, preceding them with its cargo of precious metals and its sixty nattily-uniformed midshipmen, cleared the southbound track and the bridge across the James. Glum but resigned, the ministers took their seats on the dusty plush. Trenholm, down with neuralgia and attended by his wife, the only woman in the party, had brought along a demijohn of peach brandy, presumably for medicinal purposes though it helped to ease the tension all around: especially for Benjamin, who smiled in his curly beard as he spoke from his fund of historical examples of other national causes that had survived reverses even more dismal than the one at hand. Mallory however remained somber, aware that the flotilla he had improvised for the capital's defense — three small ironclads and half a dozen wooden vessels — would be abolished, by his own orders, before dawn. By contrast, Attorney General George Davis was limited to theoretical regrets, his department having existed only on paper from the outset: and paper, unlike ships, could be replaced. Finally, at 11 o'clock — as Lee headed Traveller west from the roadfork on the near side of the Appomattox, twenty miles to the south — the train creaked out of the station. While the gaslit flare of Richmond faded rearward beyond the river, the fleeing President could reflect on the contrast between his departure tonight and his arrival, four bright springs ago, when the city had been festooned with flowers to bid him welcome. Whatever he was thinking, though, he kept his thoughts to himself. So did John Reagan, the selfmade Texan who had kept the mail in motion, if not on time, throughout the shrinking Confederacy all those years. He chewed morosely at his habitual quid, a colleague would recall, "whittling a stick down to the little end of nothing without ever reaching a satisfactory point."

Behind them as the train crept southward, worn wheels clacking on worn track, Richmond trembled for the last time from the tramp of gray-clad soldiers through her streets; Ewell was leaving, and only a cavalry rear guard, a small brigade of South Carolina troopers, stood between the city and some 20,000 bluecoats confronting the unmanned fortifications north of the James. On their way through town, demolition squads set fire to tobacco warehouses near the river, while others stood by to put the torch to buildings stocked with munitions of all kinds. City officials protested, but to no avail; the army had its orders, and no ranking member of the government was available to appeal to, all having left by midnight except John A. Campbell, who was not available either; he had last been seen at sundown, talking rapidly to himself as he walked along 9th Street with two books under his arm. A south wind sprang up, spreading flames from the burning tobacco, and soon the great waterside flour mills were on fire. Around 2 o'clock, a huge explosion jolted the city with the blowing of a downstream magazine, followed presently by another, closer at hand, that shattered plate glass windows all over Shockoe Hill. This last was a sustained eruption, volcano-like in its violence, for its source was the national arsenal, reported to contain 750,000 loaded projectiles, which continued to go off for hours. "The earth seemed fairly to writhe as if in agony," a diarist recorded; "the house rocked like a ship at sea, while stupendous thunders roared around." When the three ironclads went, near Rocketts Landing shortly afterward, Semmes pronounced the spectacle "grand beyond description," especially the one produced by his flagship, C.S.S. *Virginia Number 2*. "The explosion of her magazine threw all the shells, with their fuses lighted, into the air. The fuses were of different lengths, and as the shells exploded by twos and threes, and by the dozen, the pyrotechnic effect was very fine." By then both railway bridges were long lines of fire, reflected in the water that ran beneath them. Only Mayo's Bridge remained, kept open for the rear guard, though barrels of tar were stacked at intervals along it, surrounded by pine knots for quick combustion when the time came. At last it did. Shortly after dawn, having seen the last of his troopers across, the South Carolina brigadier rode out onto the span and touched his hat to the engineer in charge. "All over. Goodbye. Blow her to hell," he said, and trotted on.

From where he stood, looking back across the river at the holocaust in progress along Richmond's waterfront, a butternut horseman afterwards observed, "The old war-scarred city seemed to prefer annihilation to conquest." What was more, she appeared well on the way toward achieving it. Both the Haxall and Gallego mills, reportedly the largest in the world, were burning fiercely, gushing smoke and darting tongues of flame from their hundreds of windows, while beyond them, after spreading laterally the better part of a mile from 8th to 18th streets, the fire licked northward from Canal to Cary, then on to Main, dispossessing residents and driving looters from the shops. Within this "vista of desolation," known henceforward as "the burnt district," practically everything was consumed, including two of the capital's three newspaper offices and plants. Only the *Richmond Whig* survived to continue the long-term verbal offensive against the departed government. "If there lingered in the hearts of our people one spark of affection for the Davis dynasty," its editor would presently declare, "this ruthless, useless, wanton handing over to the flames [of] their fair city, their homes and altars, has extinguished it forever." But that was written later, under the once-dread Union occupation. Just now, with the Confederate army gone and the fire department unequal to even a fraction of the task at hand, the only hope of stopping or containing the spread of destruction lay with the besiegers out on the city's rim, who perhaps would restore order when they arrived: if, indeed, they arrived in time for there to be anything left to save.

They barely did, thanks to the lack of opposition and an urgent plea by the mayor himself that they not delay taking over. From near the crest of Chimborazo, easternmost of Richmond's seven hills, a hospital matron watched the first of the enemy infantry approach. "A single bluejacket rose over the hill, standing transfixed with astonishment at what he saw. Another and another sprang up, as if out of the earth, but still all remained quiet. About 7 o'clock there fell upon the ear the steady clatter of horses' hoofs, and winding around Rocketts came a small and compact body of Federal cavalry in splendid condition, riding closely and steadily along." At that distance she did not perceive that the enemy troopers were black, but she did see, moving out the road at the base of the hill to meet them, a rickety carriage flying a white flag. In it was eighty-year-old Mayor Joseph Mayo. Dressed meticulously, as another witness remarked, "in his white cravat and irrepressible ruffles, his spotless waistcoat and his blue, brass-buttoned coat," he had set out from Capitol Square with two companions to urge the invaders to hasten their march, which he hoped would end with their bringing the mob and the fire under control, and he took with him, by way of authentication, a small leather-bound box containing the seal of the city he intended to surrender.

About that time — already some eight hours behind schedule, with other delays to follow — the presidential special crossed the Roanoke River and rolled creakily into Clover Station, two thirds of the way to Danville. A young lieutenant posted there had watched the treasure train go through at daybreak, loaded with bullion and cadets, and now came the one with the Chief Executive and his ministers aboard, all obviously feeling the strain of a jerky, sleepless night. "Mr Davis sat at a car window. The crowd at the station cheered. He smiled and acknowledged their compliment, but his expression showed physical and mental exhaustion." Finally the engine chuffed on down the track and over Difficult Creek, drawing its brief string of coaches and boxcars. Others followed at various intervals. Increasingly as they went by, jammed to overflowing with the archives and employees of the Treasury Department, Post Office, and Bureau of War, the conviction grew in the young officer that all, or nearly all, was lost; "I saw a government on wheels." Moreover, as he watched the passage of car after car, burdened with "the marvelous and incongruous débris of the wreck of the Confederate capital," it seemed to him that each grew more bizarre in its contents than the one before — as if whoever was loading them was getting closer and closer to the bottom of some monstrous grab bag. "There were very few women on these trains, but among the last in the long procession were trains bearing indiscriminate cargoes of men and things. In one car was a cage with an African parrot, and a box of tame squirrels, and a hunchback! Everybody, not excepting the parrot, was wrought up to a pitch of intense excitement." Then at last, near midday, the final train passed through. "Richmond's burning. Gone; all gone!" a man called from the rear platform, and it occurred to the lieutenant that Clover Station, within forty miles of the Carolina line, "was now the northern outpost of the Confederacy."

This was to discount or overlook Lee, whose army was even then making its way west from Richmond and Petersburg to converge on Amelia Courthouse, sixty miles back up the track. Davis, when he reached Danville in the midafternoon, did not make that mistake. Weary though he was — the normal four-hour run had taken just four times that long, and sleep had been impossible, what with the cinders and vibration, not to mention the crowds at all the many stops along the way — he had no sooner established headquarters in a proffered residence on Main Street than he set out on an inspection tour of the nearly four-year-old intrenchments rimming the town. Finding them "as faulty in location as in construction," he said later, "I promptly proceeded to correct the one and improve the other." So far, despite anxious inquiries, he had heard nothing of or from the general-in-chief, yet he was determined to do all he could to prepare for his arrival, not only by strengthening the fortifications Lee's men were expected to occupy around Danville, but also by collecting food and supplies with which to feed and refit them when they got there. "The design, as previously arranged with General Lee," he afterwards explained, "was that, if he should be compelled to evacuate Petersburg, he would proceed to Danville, make a new defensive line of the Dan and Roanoke rivers, unite his army with the troops in North Carolina, and make a combined attack upon Sherman. If successful," Davis went on, "it was expected that reviving hope would bring reinforcements to the army, and Grant being then far removed from his base of supplies, and in the midst of a hostile population, it was thought we might return, drive him from the soil of Virginia, and restore to the people a government deriving its authority from their consent."

Although this was unquestionably a great deal to hope or even wish for, it was by no means out of proportion to his needs; that is, if he and the nation he represented were to survive the present crisis. He went to bed that night, still with no word from Lee or any segment of his army, and woke Tuesday morning, April 4, to find that none had come in, either by wire or by courier, while he slept. Around midday Raphael Semmes arrived with 400 crewmen from the scuttled James flotilla; Davis made him a brigadier, reorganized his sailors into an artillery brigade, and put him in charge of the Danville fortifications, with orders to defend and improve them pending Lee's arrival from Amelia, one hundred miles to the northeast. This done, he retired to his office to compose a proclamation addressed "To the People of the Confederate States of America," calling on them to rally for the last-ditch struggle now so obviously at hand.

"It would be unwise, even if it were possible, to conceal the great moral as well as material injury to our cause that must result from the occupation of Richmond by the enemy." He admitted as much from the outset, but promptly added: "It is equally unwise and unworthy of us, as patriots engaged in a most sacred cause, to allow our energies to falter, our spirits to grow faint, or our efforts to become relaxed under reverses, however calamitous. . . . It is for us, my countrymen, to show by our bearing under reverses how wretched has been the self-deception of those who have believed us less able to endure misfortune with fortitude than to encounter danger with courage." Squaring his shoulders for the test to come, he urged his compatriots to do likewise. "We have now entered upon a new phase of the struggle, the memory of which is to endure for all ages and to shed an increasing luster upon our country. Relieved from the necessity of guarding cities and particular points, important but not vital to our defense; with an army free to move from point to point and strike in detail the garrisons and detachments of the enemy; operating in the interior of our own country, where supplies are more accessible and where the foe will be far removed from his own base and cut off from all succor in case of reverse, nothing is now needed to render our triumph certain but the exhibition of our own unquenchable resolve. Let us but will it, and we are free — and who, in the light of the past, dare doubt your purpose in the future?" He asked that, then continued. "Animated by that confidence in your spirit and fortitude which never yet has failed me, I announce to you, fellow countrymen, that it is my purpose to maintain your cause with my whole heart and soul; that I will never consent to abandon to the enemy one foot of the soil of any one of the States of the Confederacy.... If by stress of numbers we should ever be compelled to a temporary withdrawal from [Virginia's] limits, or those of any other border State, again and again will we return, until the baffled and exhausted enemy shall abandon in despair his endless and impossible task of making slaves of a people resolved to be free. Let us not then despond, my countrymen, but, relying on the never-failing mercies and protecting care of our God, let us meet the foe with fresh defiance, with unconquered and unconquerable hearts."

Davis himself said later that the appeal had been "over-sanguine" in its expression of what he called his "hopes and wishes" for deliverance; but to most who read it, South as well as North, the term was all too mild. To speak of the present calamitous situation as "a new phase of the struggle," which ultimately would result in the withdrawal of Grant's "baffled and exhausted" armies, seemed now — far more than two months ago, when Aleck Stephens applied the words to Davis's speech in Metropolitan Hall — "little short of demention," if indeed it was short at all. However, this was to ignore the alternative which to Davis was unthinkable. He was no readier to submit, or even consider submission, than he had been when fortune's scowl was a broad smile. Now as in the days when he played Hezekiah to Lincoln's Sennacherib, he went about his duties as he saw them, his lips no less firmly set, his backbone no less rigid.

Mainly, once the proclamation had been composed and issued, those duties consisted of overseeing the pick-and-shovel work Brigadier Admiral Semmes's landlocked sailors were doing on the fortifications Lee and his men were to occupy when they arrived from Amelia. In the two days since his and their abandonment of Petersburg and Richmond, there had been no news of them whatever. Davis could only wait, as he had done so often before, for some word of their progress or fate, which was also his.

Lincoln spent the better part of that Tuesday in the capital Davis had left two nights ago, and slept that night aboard a warship just off Rocketts Landing, where he had stepped ashore within thirty hours of the arrival of the first blue-clad troops to enter the city in four years. The two-mile walk that followed, from the landing to the abandoned presidential mansion — Weitzel had set up headquarters there, as chief of occupation, less than twelve hours after Davis's departure — was a fitting climax to three days of mounting excitement that began soon after sundown, April 1, when he learned of Sheridan's coup at Five Forks. "He has carried everything before him," Grant wired, exulting over the taking of "several batteries" and "several thousand" prisoners. Other trophies included a bundle of captured flags, which he sent to City Point that evening by a special messenger. Lincoln was delighted. "Here is something material," he said as he unfurled the shot-torn rebel colors; "something I can see, feel, and understand. This means victory. This *is* victory."

Mrs Lincoln had left for Washington that morning, frightened by a dream of her husband's that the White House was on fire, and Lincoln, perhaps feeling lonesome, had decided to sleep on board Porter's flagship *Malvern*, a converted blockade runner. As a result, having declined the admiral's offer of his own commodious quarters, he spent an uncomfortable night in a six- by four-foot cubicle whose built-in bunk was four inches shorter than he was. Asked next morning how he had slept, he replied somewhat ruefully: "You can't put a long blade into a short scabbard. I was too long for that berth." In the course of the day — Sunday, April 2 — Porter had the ship's carpenter take down the miniature stateroom and rebuild it, together with the bed and mattress, twice as wide and half a foot longer. Lincoln however knew nothing of this; he was up at the telegraph office, reading and passing along to Stanton in Washington a series of high-spirited messages from the general-in-chief. Lee's line had been shattered in several places; Grant was closing in on what remained; "All looks remarkably well," the general wired at 2 o'clock, and followed this with a 4.30 dispatch — Fort Gregg and Battery Whitworth had just been overrun — announcing that "captures since the army started out will not amount to less than 12,000 men and probably 50 pieces of artillery." He had no doubt he would take Petersburg next morning, and he urged the President to "come out and pay us a visit." Lincoln replied: "Allow me to tender to you, and all with you, the nation's grateful thanks for this additional and magnificent success. At your kind suggestion, I think I will visit you tomorrow."

Back aboard the *Malvern* after dark, he and Porter watched from her deck the flash of guns against the sky to the southwest, where Grant had ordered a dawn assault if Lee was still in Petersburg by then. "Can't the navy do something now to make history?" Lincoln asked, unsated by the daylong flow of good news from the front. The admiral pointed out that the fleet had quite enough to do in standing by to counter a downriver sally by the Richmond flotilla, but he did send instructions for all the ships above Dutch Gap to open on the rebel forts along both banks of the James. Presently the northwest sky was aglow with flashes too, and Lincoln, his impatience relieved to some degree, turned in for another presumably fitful sleep in the cramped quarters he did not yet know had been enlarged. Next morning, rising early and well rested, he announced that a miracle had happened in the night. "I shrunk six inches in length, and about a foot sideways," he told Porter, straight-faced.

Their laughter was interrupted by a dispatch Lincoln passed along to Stanton at 8 o'clock: "Grant reports Petersburg evacuated, and he is confident Richmond also is. He is pushing forward to cut off, if possible, the retreating army. I start to join him in a few minutes." Accompanied by Tad and a civilian White House guard, he also took Porter with him on the train ride to the outskirts of Petersburg, where Robert was waiting with an escort and horses for them to ride the rest of the way. Tightly shuttered, the town seemed deserted except for a few Negroes on the roam amid the wreckage; Robert explained that Meade had been told to leave only a single division in occupation while he pressed on after Lee with all the rest. Proceeding up Market Street, the riders came to a house where Grant was waiting on the porch. A staffer watched as the President "dismounted and came in through the gate with long and rapid strides, his face beaming." Grant rose and met him on the steps. When they had shaken hands and exchanged congratulations, Lincoln said with a smile: "Do you know, General, I have had a sort of a sneaking idea for some days that you intended to do something like this." Grant replied that, rather than wait for Sherman and his Westerners to come up from Goldsboro, he had thought it better to let the Armies of the Potomac and the James wind up, unassisted, their long-term struggle against Lee's Army of Northern Virginia. That way, he believed a good deal of sectional jealousy and discord, East and West, would be avoided. Lincoln nodded. He could see that now, he said, but his anxiety had been so great that he had not cared what help was given, or by whom, so long as the job got done.

They talked for more than an hour, not only of the pursuit in progress but also of the peace to come, and it seemed to the staffer, listening while the President spoke, that "thoughts of mercy and magnanimity were uppermost in his mind." Before long the yard was crowded with former slaves, drawn by reports that Lincoln was there in the flesh: proof, if proof was needed, of their sudden deliverance from bondage. Round-eyed, they looked at him, and he at them, intently, neither saying a word to the other. Grant was eager to be off, yet he lingered in hope of hearing that Richmond had been taken before he set out to join the long blue columns toiling westward on this side of the Appomattox, intent on intercepting Lee when he turned south, as Grant felt sure he would try to do, for a link-up with Johnston in North Carolina. Finally he could wait no longer. He and Lincoln shook hands and parted; Lincoln stood on the porch and watched him ride off down the street.

Near Sutherland Station, eight miles out the Southside Railroad, a courier overtook the general and handed him a message. He read it with no change of expression, then said quietly: "Weitzel entered Richmond this morning at half past eight." Word spread rapidly down the line of marchers, accompanied by cheers. "Stack muskets and go home!" some cried, although there was no slackening of the pace. At Sutherland, Grant stopped long enough to wire Sherman the news, adding that he was hard on the go for Burkeville, the railroad crossing where he would block the route to Danville. If Lee got there first, he told Sherman, "you will have to take care of him with the force you have for a while," but if Lee lost the race and was thus obliged to keep moving west toward Lynchburg, "there will be no special use in you going any farther into the interior." In other words, the Army of the Potomac would need no assistance in disposing of its four-year adversary, and two closing sentences reflected the pride Grant felt in what had been achieved these past two days. "This army has now won a most decisive victory and followed the enemy. This is all it ever wanted to make it as good an army as ever fought a battle."

Back at City Point by sundown, Lincoln found a telegram Stanton had sent that morning in response to the one informing him that the President intended to visit Grant in Petersburg. "Allow me respectfully to ask you to consider whether you ought to expose the nation to the consequences of any disaster to yourself in the pursuit of a treacherous and dangerous enemy like the rebel army. If it was a question concerning yourself only I should not presume to say a word. Commanding Generals are in the line of their duty running such risks. But is the political head of a nation in the same condition?" Amused by the Secretary's alarm, and no doubt even more amused by the thought of his reaction to what he now had in mind to do, Lincoln replied: "Yours received. Thanks for your caution, but I have already been to Petersburg, staid with Gen. Grant an hour & a half, and returned here. It is certain now that Richmond is in our hands, and I think I will go there tomorrow. I will take care of myself."

He did "go there tomorrow," Tuesday, April 4, but the added promise to "take care" went unkept — indeed, could scarcely *be* kept: partly because of the inherently dangerous nature of the expedition, which was risky in the extreme, and partly because of unforeseen developments, which included the subtraction of all but a handful of the men assigned to guard him on the trip upriver and into the fallen capital itself. Still he went, and apparently would not have it otherwise. Once he learned at breakfast that the fire and the mob had been brought under control by the force in occupation since about that time the day before, he was determined to be off. "Thank God I have lived to see this," he told Porter. "It seems to me that I have been dreaming a horrid dream for four years, and now the nightmare is gone. I want to see Richmond."

So they set out, Lincoln and Tad and the White House guard on board the flagship with Porter, escorted by the *Bat*, which brought along a complement of marines detailed to accompany the President ashore. Approaching Dutch Gap by noon, they cleared the farthest upstream Union installation within another hour and entered a more dangerous stretch of river. Swept by now of floating and underwater mines, which lay along the banks like stranded fish, the channel was littered with charred timbers, the bloated, stiff-legged carcasses of horses, and other wreckage that made for cautious navigation. Past Chaffin's Bluff, under the spiked guns of Fort Darling, the admiral found the unremoved Confederate obstructions afforded too narrow passage for either the *Malvern* or the *Bat*, both sidewheelers. Accordingly, unwilling to wait on the tedious clearance operations, he unloaded a twelve-oared barge, commandeered a naval tug to tow him and his guests the rest of the way to Richmond, and put thirty of the marines aboard her to serve as guards when they arrived. Near the city, however, the tug ran hard aground, and Porter decided to proceed under oars, leaving the stuck vessel and the marines behind. Amused by this diminution of the flotilla, Lincoln told a story about "a fellow [who] once came to ask for an appointment as a minister abroad. Finding he could not get that, he came down to some more modest position. Finally he asked to be made a tide-waiter. When he saw he could not get that, he asked for an old pair of trousers. It is well to be humble."

Porter was more amused by the joke than he was by a situation whose difficulty grew obvious when he put in at Rocketts, on the outskirts of the city, to find not a single Federal soldier anywhere in sight. Apparently the occupation did not extend this far from the hilltop Capitol, visible through rifts in the smoke from the burned-out district between the river and Capitol Square, an air-line mile and a half to the northwest. Perturbed — as well he might be, with who knew how many diehard rebels and wild-eyed fanatics on the prowl in the toppled citadel of secession, wanting nothing on earth so much as they did a shot or a swing at the hated Yankee leader in his charge — the admiral landed ten of the twelve oarsmen, leaving two to secure the barge, and armed them with carbines to serve as presidential escorts, six in front and four behind, during the uphill walk toward the heart of town, where he hoped to find more adequate protection. They comprised a strange group in that setting, ten sailors in short jackets and baggy trousers, clutching their stubby, unfamiliar weapons; tall Abraham Lincoln in his familiar long black tailcoat, made even taller by contrast with the stocky Porter, whose flat-topped seaman's cap was more than a foot lower than the crown of the high silk hat beside him; the civilian guard holding Tad by the hand, and Tad himself, twelve years old today and looking somewhat possessively around him, as if his father had just given him Richmond for a birthday present. Before they could start they were set upon by a dozen jubilant Negroes, including one old white-haired man who rushed toward Lincoln shouting, "Bless the Lord, the great Messiah! I knowed him as soon as I seed him. He's been in my heart four long years, and he come at last to free his children from their bondage. Glory, hallelujah!" With that, he threw himself at the President's feet, as did the rest, much to Lincoln's embarrassment. "Don't kneel to me," he said. "That is not right. You must kneel to God only, and thank Him for the liberty you will enjoy hereafter." They responded with a hymn, "All Ye People, Clap Your Hands," and Lincoln and the others waited through the singing before they set out on their climb toward Capitol Square.

Behind them, as they trudged, the dozen celebrants were joined by many dozens more, and up ahead, as news of the Emancipator's coming spread, still larger clusters of people began to gather, practically all of them Negroes. The White House guard, whose name was William Crook, grew more apprehensive by the minute. "Wherever it was possible for a human being to gain a foothold there was some man or woman or boy straining his eyes after the President," he would recall. "Every window was crowned with heads. Men were hanging from tree-boxes and telegraph poles. But it was a silent crowd. There was something oppressive in those thousands of watchers, without a sound either of welcome or of hatred. I think we would have welcomed a yell of defiance. I stole a sideways look at Mr Lincoln. His face was set. It had the calm in it that comes over the face of a brave man when he is ready for whatever may come." Within half an hour they passed Libby Prison, empty now, still with its old ship chandler's sign attached. "We'll pull it down!" someone offered, but Lincoln shook his head. "No; leave it as a monument," he said. Skirting the burned district just ahead, the group began climbing Capitol Hill, and it occurred to Crook that he and his companions "were more like prisoners than anything else." Presently they saw their first evidence of welcome from anyone not black. A young white woman stood on the gallery spanning the street in front of the Exchange Hotel, an American flag draped over her shoulders. But she was the exception. A few blocks farther on, "one lady in a large and elegant building looked a while, then turned away her head as if from a disgusting sight." For the most part, such houses were shuttered, curtains drawn across the windows; but there were watchers in them as well, peering out unseen. "I had a good look at Mr Lincoln," one young matron wrote a friend next day. "He seemed tired and old — and I must say, with due respect to the President of the United States, I thought him the ugliest man I had ever seen."

By now they had encountered their first Union soldier, a cavalryman idly sitting his horse and gawking like all the others in the crowd. "Is that Old Abe?" he asked Porter, who sent him to summon a mounted escort. Soon it came, and for the first time since the landing at Rocketts the group had adequate protection.

Lincoln continued to plod along with the shambling, flat-footed stride of a plowman, past the Governor's Mansion, then three more blocks out 12th Street to Weitzel's headquarters, the former Confederate White House. Sweaty and tired from his two-mile walk, he entered the study Davis had vacated two nights ago. Perhaps it was for this he had been willing to risk the danger — the likelihood, some would have said — of assassination in the just-fallen rebel capital: this moment of feeling, for the first time since his first inauguration, four years and one month ago today, that he now was President of the whole United States. One witness described him as "pale and haggard, utterly worn out," while another saw "a serious, dreamy expression" on his face. In any case, exhausted or bemused, he crossed the cream-colored rug and sank wearily into the chair behind his fugitive rival's desk. "I wonder if I could get a glass of water?" he inquired.

After a light midafternoon lunch, John A. Campbell, the only prominent member of the Confederate government remaining in Richmond, turned up to propose returning Virginia to the Union by means of an appeal to her elected officials, who knew as well as he did, he declared, that the war was lost and over. Lincoln had not been impressed by the Alabama jurist at Hampton Roads two months ago, but now that he came less as an envoy than as a supplicant, having reported his "submission to the military authorities," his acceptability was considerably improved. "I speak for Virginia what would be more appropriate for a Virginian," he said, and quoted: "When lenity and cruelty play for a kingdom, the gentler gamester is the soonest winner." Lincoln liked the sound of that, along with the notion of Old Dominion soldiers — including, presumably, R. E. Lee — being removed, by authority of their own state government, from those rebel forces still arrayed against him. He told the former Assistant Secretary of War that he would be staying overnight in Richmond and would confer with him next morning on the matter. Just now, though, he was joining Weitzel for a carriage tour of the fallen capital.

He sat up front with one of the three division commanders Ord had left behind; Tad and Porter sat in back with Brigadier General George F. Shepley, Weitzel's chief of staff and the newly appointed military governor of Richmond, a post for which he had been schooled by service as Ben Butler's right-hand man in Louisiana. Weitzel himself — another Butler trainee, from New Orleans to Fort Fisher — rode alongside the carriage with a cavalcade of some two dozen officers, line and staff, who comprised a guard of honor for the sightseeing expedition. Their first stop was Capitol Square, where they pulled up east of Thomas Crawford's equestrian statue of the first President, posed gazing west, with one bronze arm extended majestically southward. "Washington is looking at me and pointing at Jeff Davis," Lincoln said. Refugees huddled about the Square, guarding the few household possessions they had managed to save from yesterday's fire, and the Capitol had been looted by vandals and souvenir hunters, military and civilian. From there the carriage rolled through the burned district, whose streets were choked with toppled masonry and littered with broken glass, on down Cary Street to Libby Prison, which Lincoln had passed earlier on his way uptown. It held captive rebels now, and in fact had had no Federal inmates since last May, when they were transferred to a new prison down in Georgia; but the thought of what it once had been caused one horseman to remark that Jefferson Davis should be hanged. Lincoln turned and looked at him. "Judge not, that ye be not judged," he said quietly. Soon afterwards Weitzel took the opportunity to ask if the President had any suggestions as to treatment of the conquered people in his charge. Lincoln replied that, while he did not want to issue orders on the subject, "If I were in your place I'd let 'em up easy; let 'em up easy."

Suddenly there was the boom of guns a mile downriver, which to everyone's relief turned out to be the *Malvern*; she had made it through the rebel obstructions to drop anchor at last off Rocketts, and was firing a salute in celebration. Porter was especially relieved. He still considered the President's welfare his responsibility, and he was in a state of dread from the risk to which he had let him expose himself today. Refusing to take no for an answer, he insisted that Lincoln sleep that night aboard the flagship, where he could be isolated from all harm. Weary from the strain of a long, exciting day, his charge turned in shortly after an early dinner, and presumably got another good night's sleep in the refurbished stateroom, this time with a guard posted outside his door.

One hundred miles to the north, few citizens of his own capital got any such rest, either that night or the one before. Washington was a blaze of celebration, and had been so ever since midmorning yesterday, when a War Department telegrapher received from Fort Monroe, for the first time in four years, the alerting message: "Turn down for Richmond," meaning that he was to relieve the tension on the armature spring of his instrument so that it would respond to a weak signal. He did, and the dit-dahs came through, distant but distinct. "We took Richmond at 8.15 this morning." Church bells pealed; fire engines clattered and clanged through the streets. Locomotives in the yards and steamboats on the river added the scream of their whistles to the uproar. Schools dismissed; clerks spilled out of government buildings; extras hit the stands. "Glory!!! Hail Columbia!!! Hallelujah!!! Richmond Ours!!!" the *Star* exulted. Army batteries fired an 800-gun salute that went on forever, three hundred for Petersburg, five hundred more for the fall of the rebel capital, while the Navy added another hundred from its biggest Dahlgrens, rattling windows all over town. "From one end of Pennsylvania Avenue to the other," a reporter noted, "the air seemed to burn with the bright hues of the flag.... Almost by magic the streets were crowded with hosts of people, talking, laughing, hurrahing and shouting in the fullness of their joy. Men embraced one another, 'treated' one another, made up old quarrels, renewed old friendships, marched arm-in-arm singing and chatting in that happy sort of abandon which characterizes our people when under the influence of a great and universal happiness. The atmosphere was full of the intoxication of joy." Stanton gave a solemn, Seward a light-hearted speech, both wildly cheered by the celebrants outside their respective offices: especially when the former read a dispatch from Weitzel saying Richmond was on fire. What should he reply? "Burn it, burn it! Let her burn!" the cry came up. "A more liquorish crowd was never seen in Washington than on that night," the newsman declared, and told of seeing "one big, sedate Vermonter, chief of an executive bureau, standing on the corner of F and 14th streets, with owlish gravity giving fifty-cent 'shin plasters' to every colored person who came past him, brokenly saying with each gift, 'Babylon has fallen.'"

That was Monday. The formal celebration — or "grand illumination," as it was called — was set for the following evening. All day Tuesday, while Lincoln walked and rode through the cluttered streets of Richmond, workmen swarmed over Washington's public buildings, preparing them for the show that would start at dusk. When it came it was altogether worth the waiting. "This is the Lord's doing; it is marvellous in our eyes" was blazoned in huge letters on a gaslighted transparency over the western pediment of the Capitol, which glittered from its basement to its dome. City Hall, the Treasury, the Post Office, the Marine Barracks, the National Conservatory, the prisons along First Street, even the Insane Asylum, lonely on its hill, burned like beacons in the night.

All Washington turned out to cheer and marvel at the candle-light displays, but the largest crowd collected in front of the Patent Office, where flaring gas jets spelled out U N I O N across the top of its granite pillars. A speaker's stand had been erected at their foot; for this was the Republican mass rally, opened by Judge David Cartter of the district supreme court, who got things off to a rousing start by referring in racetrack terms to Jefferson Davis as "the flying rascal out of Richmond," by way of a warm-up for the principal speaker, Andrew Johnson. He had been lying rather low since the inauguration, yet he showed this evening that he had lost none of his talent for invective on short notice. He too mentioned Davis early on, and when his listeners shouted, "Hang him! Hang him!" the Vice President was quick to agree: "Yes, I say hang him twenty times." Nor was the rebel leader the only one deserving of such treatment. Others like him were "infamous in character, diabolical in motive," and Johnson had a similar prescription for them all, including confiscation of their property. "When you ask me what *I* would do, my reply is — I would arrest them, I would try them, I would convict them, and I would hang them.... Treason must be made odious," he declared; "traitors must be punished and impoverished."

Other remarks, public and private — all in heady contrast to Lincoln's "Let 'em up easy," spoken today in the other capital after the interview in which Campbell described "the gentler gamester" as "the soonest winner" — followed as the celebration went on into and through the night. Long after the candles had guttered out and the flares had been extinguished, serenaders continued to make the rounds and corks kept popping in homes and hotel bars all over town.

Headaches were the order of the day in Washington by 10 o'clock Wednesday morning, April 5; at which time, as agreed on yesterday, the President received the Alabama jurist aboard the *Malvern*, riding at anchor off Rocketts Landing. Campbell brought a Richmond lawyer with him, Gustavus Myers, a member of the Virginia legislature, and their suggestion was that this body, now adjourned and scattered about the state, be reassembled for a vote withdrawing the Old Dominion from the Confederacy and formally returning her to her old allegiance. Weitzel, who was present, later summarized their proposal. "Mr Campbell and the other gentleman assured Mr Lincoln that if he would allow the Virginia Legislature to meet, it would at once repeal the ordinance of secession, and that then General Robert E. Lee and every other Virginian would submit; that this would amount to virtual destruction of the Army of Northern Virginia, and eventually to the surrender of all the other rebel armies, and would assure perfect peace in the shortest possible time."

Lincoln liked the notion, in part because it provided a way to get local government back in operation, but mainly because it offered at least a chance of avoiding that "last bloody battle" Grant and Sherman had told him would have to be fought before the South surrendered. Accordingly, he gave Campbell a document repeating his three Hampton

Roads conditions—"restoration of the national authority throughout all the states"; "no receding by the Executive on the slavery question"; "no cessation of hostilities short of an end to the war and the disbanding of all forces hostile to the government" — in return for which, confiscations of property would be "remitted to the people of any state which shall now promptly and in good faith withdraw its troops and other support from further resistance." In addition, though he declined to offer a general amnesty, he promised to use his pardoning power to "save any repentant sinner from hanging." Finally he agreed to reach an early decision in regard to permitting the Virginia legislators to reassemble.

This last he did next day, informing Weitzel that "the gentlemen who have acted as the legislature of Virginia, in support of the rebellion, may now desire to assemble at Richmond and take measures to withdraw the Virginia troops and other support from resistance to the general government. If they attempt it, give them permission and protection, until, if at all, they attempt some action hostile to the United States, in which case you will notify them and give them reasonable time to leave.... Allow Judge Campbell to see this, but do not make it public." Sending word to Grant of his decision, he added: "I do not think it very probable that anything will come of this, but I have thought it best to notify you, so that if you should see signs you may understand them," then closed with the familiar tactical warning: "Nothing I have done, or probably shall do, is to delay, hinder, or interfere with you in your work."

He was back at City Point by then, having steamed downriver at Porter's insistence as soon as the meeting with Campbell ended. Today — Thursday — made two full weeks he had been gone from Washington, and in response to a wire from Seward the day before, offering to come down for a conference on several matters "important and urgent in conducting the government but not at all critical or serious," he had informed the Secretary: "I think there is no probability of my remaining here more than two days longer. If this is too long come down." For one thing, he was awaiting the arrival next day of Mrs Lincoln. Having found her husband's dream of a White House fire a false alarm, she was returning with a number of distinguished visitors, all eager for a look at fallen Richmond. This might prolong his stay; or so he thought until bedtime Wednesday, when he received news that threatened to cut his vacation even shorter than he had supposed. Seward, he learned, had been thrown from his carriage that afternoon and had been so seriously injured, it was feared, that Lincoln might have to return to Washington at once. A follow-up wire from Stanton next morning, however, informed him that while the New Yorker's injuries were painful they were almost certainly not fatal; Lincoln could stay away as long as he chose. So he went down to the wharf at noon, this April 6, to meet his wife and the party of sightseers she had brought along on the boatride down the coast.

Irked to find that her husband had already been to the rebel capital and would not be going there again, Mrs Lincoln decided to make the trip herself on the *River Queen,* which would afford overnight accommodations for her guests, Senator and Mrs Harlan, Attorney General Speed and his wife, Charles Sumner and a young French nobleman friend, the Marquis de Chambrun. They left that afternoon and reached Richmond in time for a cavalry-escorted tour of the city before returning to sleep aboard the *Queen,* anchored in the James. Sumner was especially gratified by all he had seen, including the looted Capitol, where he asked in particular to examine the ivory gavel of the Congress. When it was brought he put it in his pocket — as a souvenir, or perhaps as further recompense for the caning he had suffered at the hands of Preston Brooks, nine years ago this spring — and brought it back with him to City Point next morning. Once more Lincoln was waiting on the dock, this time with an offer to take them by rail to Petersburg for a look at what ten months of siege and shelling had accomplished.

He was in excellent spirits, Harlan noted. "His whole appearance, pose, and bearing had marvelously changed. He was, in fact, transfigured. That indescribable sadness which had previously seemed to be an adamantine element of his very being had been suddenly changed for an equally indescribable expression of serene joy, as if conscious that the great purpose of his life had been attained." Partly this was the salutary effect of being removed for two full weeks from Washington and the day-in day-out frets that hemmed his White House office there, but a more immediate cause was a series of dispatches from Grant, all of them so encouraging to Lincoln that, in telling the general of his decision to let the Virginia legislature assemble, he remarked that Grant seemed to be achieving on his own, by "pretty effectually withdrawing the Virginia troops from opposition to the government," what he had hoped the legislators would effect by legal action. Not only had the blue pursuers won the race for Burkeville, thereby preventing Lee from turning south to combine with Johnston; they had also netted some 1500 grayback captives in the process. "The country is full of stragglers," Grant reported, "the line of retreat marked with artillery, burned or charred wagons, caissons, ambulances, &c." Gratifying as this was, he capped the climax with a wire sent late the night before, telling of a victory scored that afternoon by Humphreys, Wright, and Sheridan, some eight miles beyond Burkeville. Five rebel generals had been taken, including Richard Ewell and Custis Lee, along with "several thousand prisoners, fourteen pieces of artillery with caissons, and a large number of wagons." Such were the spoils listed by Sheridan in a message Grant passed along to Lincoln. "If the thing is pressed," the cavalryman urged his chief in closing, "I think Lee will surrender." Lincoln's enthusiasm soared, and he replied at 11 o'clock this Friday morning, about the time his wife and her guests returned from their overnight cruise to Richmond: "Sheridan says, 'If the thing is pressed I think that Lee will surrender.' Let the *thing* be pressed."

Two distractions, one slight and rather easily dismissed, the other a good deal more poignant in effect, broke into this three-day span of high good feeling. The first was a note from Andrew Johnson, who had come down on an army packet, now anchored nearby, and wanted to pay the President a visit before proceeding upriver for a tour of the fallen capital. Lincoln frowned, having read in the Washington papers of the Tennessean's call for all-out vengeance in his speech at the Republican mass rally Tuesday night. "I guess he can get along without me," he said distastefully, and did not reply to the note. That had been yesterday afternoon, and the second distraction followed that evening. He was taking the air after supper on the top deck of the *Malvern*, once more in a happy frame of mind, when he looked down from the rail and saw a group of rebel prisoners being loaded for shipment north aboard a transport moored alongside. The guard Crook, with him as usual, watched them too. "They were in a pitiable condition, ragged and thin; they looked half starved. When they were on board they took out of their knapsacks the last rations that had been issued to them before capture. There was nothing but bread, which looked as if it had been mixed with tar. When they cut it we could see how hard it was and heavy. It was more like cheese than bread." He watched, and as he did so he heard Lincoln groan beside him: "Poor fellows. It's a hard lot. Poor fellows." Crook turned and looked at his companion. "His face was pitying and sorrowful. All the happiness had gone."

Next morning's dispatch from the general-in-chief revived his genial spirits. "Let the *thing* be pressed," he replied, echoing Sheridan, and looked forward to the brightest news of all, which would be that Lee had at last been run to earth. Once that happened, he believed, commanders of other gray armies were likely to see the folly of further resistance on their part — if, indeed, they managed to survive that long. Developments elsewhere finally seemed to be moving at a pace that matched the stepped-up progress of events here in Virginia: particularly in South and Central Alabama. Canby had a close-up grip on Mobile's outer defenses, Spanish Fort and Fort Blakely, whose fall would mean the fall of the city in their rear, and he was preparing to assault, with results that were practically foregone, considering his better than four-to-one numerical advantage. Similarly — and incredibly, in the light of what had happened to those who tried it in the past — James Wilson, after crossing the Black Warrior, then the Cahaba, had driven Bedford Forrest headlong in the course of a two-day running skirmish, fifty miles in length, to descend on Selma, April 2, the day Richmond itself was abandoned. By now the all-important manufactories there were a mass of smoking rubble, and Wilson had his troopers hard on the go for Montgomery, where the Confederacy began. Neither Canby nor Wilson had started in time to be of much help to each other, as originally intended; nor had Stoneman crossed the Smokies in time to strike in Johnston's rear for Sherman's benefit. But now, in accordance with Grant's revised instructions, he turned his raiders north for Lynchburg, where Lee was apparently headed too.

No wonder, then, that Harlan found Lincoln "transfigured" as he stood on the dock at City Point to welcome his wife and her guests back from Richmond, or that he took increased encouragement from what he saw on the trip to Petersburg that afternoon. "Animosity in the town is abating," he told Chambrun; "the inhabitants now accept accomplished facts, the final downfall of the Confederacy and the abolition of slavery. There still remains much for us to do, but every day brings new reason for confidence in the future."

Aboard the *River Queen* that night — April 7; Good Friday was a week away — Elihu Washburne, en route to the front for another visit with Grant, whose rise he had done so much to promote through the first three years of a war that now had stretched to nearly four, called on Lincoln and found him "in perfect health and exuberant spirits," voluble in recounting for his guests the events of the past week, including his walk through the streets of Richmond. "He never flagged during the whole evening," the Illinois congressman would recall. Chambrun, however — a liberal despite his privileged heritage and the conservative domination of his homeland under the Second Empire — observed in his host contrasting traits often remarked by others in the past: Crook for one, just the night before, and Sherman at the conference held on this same vessel, ten days back. "He willingly laughed either at what was being said to him, or at what he said himself," the Frenchman later wrote. "But all of a sudden he would retire within himself; then he would close his eyes, and all his features would bespeak a kind of sadness as indescribable as it was deep. After a while, as though it were by an effort of his will, he would shake off this mysterious weight under which he seemed bowed; his generous and open disposition would again reappear. In one evening I happened to count over twenty of these alternations and contrasts."

Part of this intermittent sadness no doubt came from realization that he was approaching the end of the only real vacation he had taken in the past four years. All day Saturday preparations went forward for departure of the *Queen* that night, including a thorough check on the records of her crew, ordered by Porter in reaction to the belated fright he felt at the risk he had run in taking the President to and through the rebel capital, all but unescorted. That evening a military band came on board for a farewell concert. After several numbers, Lincoln requested the "Marseillaise," which he liked so well that he had it repeated. "You must, however, come over to America to hear it," he said wryly to the young marquis, knowing the Emperor had banned the piece in France. Then he called for "Dixie," much to the surprise of his guests and the musicians, as well as to listeners in the outer darkness on the docks and blufftop. "That tune is now Federal property," he told Chambrun. An hour before midnight, the *Queen* cast off and began to steam down the winding moonlit river, escorted by the *Bat*. Reaching Hampton Roads before dawn, she stopped long enough to board a pilot at Fort Monroe and was off again by sunrise, up Chesapeake Bay toward the mouth of the Potomac.

It was April 9; Palm Sunday. Eastward the sky was a glory of red, but the rising sun was presently dimmed by clouds rolling in from the sea with a promise of rain. The President and his guests rose early, and after breakfast went on deck to watch the gliding tableau of the coreline. Soon after they entered the Potomac, paddle wheels churning against the current, they passed Stratford Hall, the birthplace of Robert Lee — presumably still in flight for his life, a hundred-odd miles to the southwest — and within the hour, on that same bank, saw the birth-sites too of Washington and James Monroe. Almost in view of the capital, as they steamed past Mount Vernon just at sundown, someone remarked that Springfield would someday be equally honored. Lincoln, who had been musing at the rail, came out of himself on hearing his home town mentioned. "Springfield!" he exclaimed. He smiled and said he would be happy to return there, "four years hence," and live in peace and tranquillity. Mainly though, according to Chambrun, "the conversation dwelt upon literary subjects." Lincoln read to the assembled group from what Sumner called "a beautiful quarto Shakespeare," mainly from *Macbeth*, perhaps his favorite, with emphasis on the scenes that followed the king's assassination.

> "Duncan is in his grave;
> After life's fitful fever he sleeps well;
> Treason has done his worst: nor steel, nor poison,
> Malice domestic, foreign levy, nothing
> Can touch him further."

He paused, then read the lines again, something in them responding to something in himself. After the reading he was again withdrawn, although presently when his wife spoke of Jefferson Davis—saying, as the staff officer had said five days ago in Richmond, "He must be hanged"—he replied, as he had then: "Judge not, that ye be not judged." Contradiction was risky in that direction, inviting "malice domestic" as it did, but he ventured to repeat it when they came within sight of the roofs of Washington and he heard her tell Chambrun, "That city is filled with our enemies." Lincoln made a gesture of impatience. "Ene-

Victory, and Defeat

mies," he said, as if with the taste of something bitter on his tongue. "We must never speak of that."

Rain was coming down hard in the twilight by the time the steamer reached the wharf at the foot of Sixth Street. The President's carriage was waiting to take him to the White House, but he let Tad and Mrs Lincoln off there and went on alone to Seward's house, nearby on Franklin Square, where the Secretary lay recovering from the injuries he had suffered. They were extensive, the right shoulder badly dislocated, the jaw broken on both sides; the pain had been so great that he had been in delirium for three of the four days since his fall. Indeed, he was scarcely recognizable when his friend entered the upstairs bedroom to find him stretched along the far edge of the bed, his arm projected over the side to avoid pressure on the bruised socket, his face swathed in bandages, swollen and discolored, his jaw clamped in an iron frame for healing. "You are back from Richmond?" he said in a hoarse whisper, barely able to speak because of the damage and the pain. "Yes, and I think we are near the end at last," Lincoln told him. First he sat gingerly on the bed, then sprawled across it, resting on an elbow, his face close to Seward's while he described much that had happened down near City Point in the course of the past two weeks. He stayed half an hour, by which time the New Yorker had fallen into a feverish sleep. Then he came out, gesturing for silence in the hall, and tiptoed down the stairs to the front door, where his carriage was waiting to take him back to the White House.

Later that evening, undressing for sleep, he felt the familiar weariness all men feel on their first night home from a vacation. Then there came a knock, and he opened the bedroom door to find a War Department messenger in the hall with a telegram that made Lincoln forget that weariness had anything to do with living. It was from Grant and had been sent from a place called Appomattox Courthouse.

April 9, 1865 — 4.30 p.m.

Hon. E. M. Stanton,
Secretary of War:
 General Lee surrendered the Army of Northern Virginia this afternoon upon terms proposed by myself. The accompanying additional correspondence will show the conditions fully.
U. S. GRANT,
Lieutenant General.

✗ 4 ✗

What had begun as a retreat the previous Sunday night, when Lee abandoned Petersburg and Richmond with the intention of marching southwest beyond the Roanoke, developed all too soon into a race against Grant and starvation, which in turn became a harassed flight that narrowed the dwindling army's fate to slow or sudden death. For six days this continued, ever westward. Then on the seventh — April 9, Palm Sunday — Lee made his choice. The agony ended, as his opponent said in the bedtime telegram to Lincoln, "upon terms proposed by myself."

Few at the start, in the column he accompanied, apparently thought it would turn out so: least of all Lee himself, who told a companion when they took up the march on Monday morning: "I have got my army safely out of its breastworks, and in order to follow me, the enemy must abandon his lines and can derive no further benefit from his railroads or James River." Others felt a similar elation at their successful withdrawal across the Appomattox, unpursued, and the exchange of their cramped trenches for the spread-out landscape, where sunlight glittered on greening fields and new-fledged trees along the roadside. Whatever the odds, this was Chancellorsville weather, with its reminders of their old skill at maneuver. "A sense of relief seemed to pervade the ranks at their release from the lines where they had watched and worked for more than nine weary months," a staff brigadier would recall. "Once more in the open field, they were invigorated with hope, and felt better able to cope with their powerful adversary."

But that applied only to the central column, the 13,000 infantry under Longstreet and Gordon, Pendleton's 3000 cannoneers, and Mahone's 4000-man division on its way from Bermuda Hundred via Chesterfield Courthouse. Most of these 20,000 effectives had stood fast the day before, had conducted the nighttime withdrawal in good order, and had sustained their group identity in the process. It was different for the 6000 coming down from beyond the James with Ewell. Less than a third were veterans under Kershaw, while the rest — combined extemporaneously under Custis Lee, who had lately been promoted to major general though he had never led troops in action outside the capital defenses — were reservists, naval personnel, and heavy artillerymen, so unaccustomed to marching that the road in their rear was already littered with stragglers, footsore and blown from a single night on the go. Nor was their outlook improved by the view they had had, back over their shoulders the night before, of Richmond in flames on the far side of the river. Even so, they were in considerably better shape than the 3500 men with Anderson beyond the Appomattox, rattled fragments of the four divisions of Pickett, Johnson, Heth, and Wilcox, working their way west in the wake of Fitz Lee's 3500 jaded troopers on worse-than-jaded horses. Badly trounced at Five Forks, two days back, and scattered by yesterday's breakthrough on the right — which had now become the left — they had been whipped, and knew it. "There was an attempt to organize the various commands," a South

Carolina captain later said of this smallest and worst-off of the three infantry columns; "to no avail. The Confederacy was considered as 'gone up,' and every man felt it his duty, as well as his privilege, to save himself. I do not mean to say there was any insubordination whatever, but the whole left of the army was so crushed by the defeats of the past few days that it straggled along without strength and almost without thought. So we moved on in disorder, keeping no regular column, no regular pace. When a soldier became weary he fell out, ate his scanty rations — if, indeed, he had any to eat — rested, rose, and resumed the march when his inclination dictated. There were not many words spoken. An indescribable sadness weighed upon us. The men were very gentle toward each other, very liberal in bestowing the little of food that remained to them."

All that day, well into darkness, Anderson's fugitive survivors kept up their march northwest along the south bank of the Appomattox. Around midnight, when a halt was called at last, the weary captain watched as his men "fell about and slept heavily, or else wandered like persons in a dream. I remember, it all seemed to me like a troubled vision. I was consumed by fever, and when I attempted to walk I staggered about like a drunken man." A night's sleep helped, and Tuesday morning when they encountered Longstreet's veterans, crossing the river with Lee himself at the head of the central column, they were comforted to find that the rest of the army was by no means as badly off as they were. Small bodies of blue cavalry, attempting to probe their flank and interrupt the march, were driven off and kept at a respectful distance. "We revived rapidly from our forlorn and desolate feeling," the captain would recall.

Hunger was still a problem, to put it mildly, but there was also comfort for that; at any rate the comfort of anticipation. Amelia Courthouse lay just ahead on the Richmond & Danville, five miles west of the river, and Lee had arranged for meat and bread to be sent there from the 350,000 rations amassed in the capital in the course of the past two months. Or so he thought until he arrived, shortly before noon, to find a generous shipment of ordnance equipment — 96 loaded caissons, 200 crates of ammunition for his guns, and 164 boxes of artillery harness — waiting aboard a string of cars pulled onto a siding; but no food. His requisition had not been received, the commissary general afterwards explained, until "all railroad transportation had been taken up."

If Lee's face, as a cavalry staffer noted, took on "an anxious and haggard expression" at the news, it was no wonder. At the close of a march of nearly forty miles in about as many hours, with nothing to eat but what they happened to have with them at the outset or could scrounge along the way, he had 33,000 soldiers — the number to which his army, including reservists, had been reduced in the past ten days by its losses at Fort Stedman and Five Forks and during the Sunday breakthrough, each of which had cost him just under or over 5000 men — converging on a lonely trackside village where not a single ration could be drawn. His only recourse was to call a halt while commissary details scoured the countryside for such food as they could find. This they soon began to do, armed with an appeal "To the Citizens of Amelia County," signed *R. E. Lee* and calling on them "to supply as far as each one is able the wants of the brave soldiers who have battled for your liberty for four years."

In point of fact, there would have been a delay in any case, since nothing had yet been heard from Ewell, and the rest of the army could not push on down the railroad until this laggard column was on hand. Meantime, Lee got off a telegram to Danville, directing the immediate rail shipment of rations from the stores St John had waiting for him there, though whether the requisition would get through was doubtful, the wires having been cut near Jetersville, a hamlet six miles down the track and twelve miles short of Burkeville. After supper, a message came from Ewell announcing that he had been delayed by flooded bridges; he expected to cross the Appomattox tonight and would arrive next morning. Lee could do nothing but wait for him and the commissary wagons, hopefully loaded with whatever food had been volunteered or impressed. Even so, he was aware that he had lost a good part of the head start he had gained when he slipped away from Grant two nights ago, and knowledge of this, together with the anguish he felt for the hungry troops still hobbling in, was reflected in his bearing. "His face was still calm, as it always was," an artillery sergeant major later wrote, "but his carriage was no longer erect, as his soldiers had been used to see it. The troubles of these last days had already plowed great furrows in his forehead. His eyes were red as if with weeping, his cheeks sunken and haggard, his face colorless. No one who looked upon him, as he stood there in full view of the disastrous end, can ever forget the intense agony written upon his features."

Such distress was general that evening. While the wagon details were out scouring the picked-over region for something the men or animals could eat, the half-starved troops, bedded down in fields around the rural county seat or still limping toward a concentration that should have been completed before nightfall, evidenced a discouragement more profound than any they had known in the darkest days of the siege that now had ended. "Their strength was slowly drained from them," an officer declared, "and despondency, like a black and poisonous mist, began to invade the hearts before so tough and buoyant." Some were taken with a restlessness, a sort of wanderlust that outweighed their exhaustion: with the result that there were further subtractions from the army's ranks. "Many of them wandered off in search of food, with no thought of deserting at all. Many others followed the example of their government, and fled."

A hard shock followed next morning, April 5, when the foraging details came rattling back, their wagons all but empty. So thoroughly had Northrop's and St John's agents done their work these past ten months, impressing stock and grain to feed the trench-bound men at Petersburg, few of the farmers roundabout had anything left to give, even in response to a personal appeal from Robert Lee. Still, he had no choice except to keep moving. To stay where he was meant starvation, and every hour's delay was another hour's reduction of his head-start gain: if, indeed, there was any of it left. All the troops were up by now, and he had done what he could to ease the strain, including a culling of nearly one third of the 200 guns and 1000 wagons — which, fully spread out, covered more than twenty miles of road — to provide replacements for those draft animals exhaustion had subtracted from the teams needed to keep the other two thirds rolling; the culls were to be forwarded, if possible, by rail. A cold rain deepened the army's gloom when the fall-in sounded for still a third day of marching on empty stomachs. Longstreet took the lead, Gordon the rear-guard duty; Anderson and Ewell slogged between, while Fitz Lee's troopers ranged well to the front on their gaunt, weak-kneed horses, left and right of the railroad leading down to Danville, a hundred miles to the southwest.

Five of those miles from Amelia by early afternoon, the outriders came upon bluecoats intrenched in a well-chosen position just short of Jetersville, a dozen miles from Burkeville, where the Southside and the Danville railroads crossed. This was no surprise; enemy cavalry had been active in that direction yesterday. Longstreet shook out skirmishers, preparing to brush these vedettes from his path, but shortly before 2 o'clock, when Lee arrived, reports came back that the force in front amounted to a good deal more than cavalry. One corps of Union infantry was already on hand, in support of Sheridan's horsemen, and another was rapidly approaching. Lee's heart sank at the news. His adversary had won the race for the critical Burkeville crossing; he was blocked, and so were the rations he had ordered sent from Danville in hope of intercepting them en route. Regretfully he lowered his glasses from a study of the position, which he knew was too strong for an attack by his frazzled army, heavily outnumbered as it was by the three blue corps, with others doubtless hard on the way to join them. Rejecting the notion, if it crossed his mind, of going out in an Old Guard blaze of glory, he turned his thoughts to another plan of action — another route — still with the intention, or anyhow the hope, of combining with Joe Johnston somewhere to the south.

He would veer west, across the upper quadrant of the spraddled X described by the two railroads, to the vicinity of Farmville on the upper Appomattox, where rations could be sent to meet him, via the Southside line, from stores collected at Lynchburg by St John. Then, having fed his hungry men and horses, he would move south again, across the western quadrant of the X, bypassing the Burkeville intersection — Grant's reported point of concentration — to resume his march down the Danville line for a combination with Johnston, beyond the Roanoke, before turning on his pursuers. Admittedly this was a long-odds venture, difficult at best. Farmville was five miles farther away than Burkeville, and he knew little of the roads he would have to travel, except that they were poor. Moreover, he was by no means sure that his half-starved troops and animals could manage a cross-country slog of perhaps twenty roundabout miles without food, especially since they would have to begin it with still another night march if he was to avoid being overtaken and overwhelmed, practically at the start. Here again, however, he had no choice but to attempt it or face the narrowed alternatives of surrender or annihilation. Accordingly, instructions for the westward trek went out; "the most cruel marching order the commanders had ever given the men in four years of fighting," a later observer was to say. As always, all that time, "Lee's miserables" responded as best they could when the move began near sundown. "It is now a race for life or death," one wrote in his diary at the outset.

It was indeed. "Night was day. Day was night," a groggy cannoneer was to recall. "There was no stated time to sleep, eat, or rest, and the events of morning became strangely intermingled with the events of evening. Breakfast, dinner, and supper were merged into 'something to eat,' whenever and wherever it could be found." Four miles out, a bridge collapsed into Flat Creek, stalling the guns and wagons for hours before it could be repaired, and though the infantry got over by fording, the discomfort of wet feet was added to those of hunger and exhaustion. Confusion and sleeplessness made the marchers edgy, quick to panic: as when a runaway stallion broke loose from a fence where he was tethered and came pounding down the road, the rail still tied to his rein. Abrupt and point-blank exchanges of fire by several units, in response to what they assumed was a night attack by Yankee cavalry, resulted in an undetermined number of casualties. Straggling was heavy, and many who kept going simply dropped their rifles as they hobbled along, too weak to carry them any farther, or else planted them by the roadside, bayonet down, each a small monument to determination and defeat.

Dawn showed the effects of this harrowing night, not only in the thinness of the army's ranks, but also in the faces of the survivors, the sullen lines of strain around their mouths, the red etchings of fatigue along their lower eyelids. Many staggered drunkenly, and some found, when they tried to talk, that their speech was incoherent. They had reached what later came to be called "poor old Dixie's bottom dollar," and for the most part they were satisfied that even that was spent. One of Longstreet's Deep South veterans put it strongest, dropping back toward the tail of the column as he struggled to keep up, tattered and barefoot, yet still with some vestige of the raucous sense of humor that had brought him this far along the four-year road he had traveled. "My shoes are gone; my clothes are almost gone. I'm weary, I'm sick, I'm hungry. My family has been killed or scattered, and may now be wandering helpless and unprotected." He shook his head. "I would die; yes, I would die willingly," he said, "because I love my country. But if this war is ever over, I'll be damned if I ever love another country!"

This was Grant's doing, the outcome of his steadiness and simplicity of purpose, designed to accomplish in short order the destruction of his opponent now that he had flushed him out of his burrow, into the open field, and had him on the run. He became again, in brief, the Grant of Vicksburg. "There was no pause, no hesitancy, no doubt what to do," a staff colonel afterwards declared. "He commanded Lee's army as much as he did ours; caused and knew beforehand every movement that Lee made, up to the actual surrender.... There was no let up; fighting and marching, and negotiating, all at once."

Mindful perhaps of Sherman's dictum, "A stern chase is a long one," the northern commander had decided at the outset that he stood to gain more from heading his adversary off than he did from pursuing him across the Appomattox. That way, once he was in his front, he could bag him entire, rather than engage in the doubtful and drawn-out process of attempting his piecemeal destruction by means of a series of attacks upon his rear, not to mention avoiding ambuscades at practically every step along the way. Moreover, a comparison of the two probable routes, Union and Confederate, showed clearly enough the advantage the former offered. Lee doubtless intended to assemble his army somewhere along the upper stretch of the Danville Railroad, with a march to follow down it, through Burkeville, for a combination with Johnston beyond the Carolina line. From all three of his starting points, Richmond, Bermuda Hundred, and Petersburg, the distance to Burkeville was just under sixty miles, and two of his three columns would have to make two time-consuming river crossings, one at the start and one near the end of the move toward concentration; whereas Grant's route, due west along the Southside Railroad, from Sutherland Station to Burkeville — blue chord of the gray arc — not only spanned no river, but was also twenty miles shorter; which in itself was enough to abrogate the head start Lee had gained by taking off at first-dark Sunday. Accordingly, before his meeting with Lincoln in Petersburg next morning, Grant issued orders for winning the race as he conceived it. Sheridan of course would lead, fanning out to the right to keep tabs on the graybacks still on the near side of the Appomattox, and

Griffin would press along in the wake of the troopers as fast as his men could manage afoot, under instructions to support them in any action that developed, whether defensive or offensive. Humphreys and Wright would follow Griffin, while Ord and Parke stuck to the railroad, the latter repairing track as he went, thereby providing an all-weather supply line that led directly into the moving army's rear.

Speed was the main requirement, and the blue-clad veterans gave it willingly. "We never endured such marching before," a footsore private later wrote. As a result, they won the Monday-Tuesday race with time to spare. By Wednesday morning, April 5, when Lee began his delayed movement down the railroad from Amelia, Griffin was in position athwart his path, in close support of Sheridan's dug-in troopers; Humphreys was coming up fast in his rear, and Wright was expected before sundown. Confronted thus by twice his dwindled number, Lee called a halt that afternoon, just short of Jetersville, and Meade — who had traveled by ambulance for the past two days, a victim of wrought-up nerves and indigestion — decided that the army's best course would be to get some food and rest, including a good night's sleep, then pitch into the rebel host next morning. Sheridan fumed at this imposed restraint; rest was the last thing on earth he wanted at that stage, either for his own soldiers or anyone else's, blue or gray. "I wish you were here," he protested in a message to Grant, who was with Ord, some twelve miles off at Nottoway Courthouse. "I feel confident of capturing the Army of Northern Virginia if we exert ourselves. I see no escape for Lee."

In response to the summons, Grant undertook a cross-country ride over unfamiliar ground, with no more escort than a quartet of staff officers and a squad of cavalry, but arrived too late to overrule Meade, if in fact that was what he had had in mind when he set out. In any case, next morning's dawn proved Little Phil's concern well founded; Lee was gone. He had swung westward on a night march, scouts reported, apparently headed for Farmville, eighteen miles away on the upper Appomattox and the Southside Railroad, down which he could draw supplies from Lynchburg, then continue his getaway toward the fastness of the Blue Ridge, or turn back south in a renewal of his effort to combine with Johnston. Such disappointment as Grant felt at this loss of contact, this postponement of the showdown that was to have been his reward for winning the race to Burkeville, was more than offset by another consideration, stated later: "We now had no other objective than the Confederate armies, and I was anxious to close the thing up at once." In other words, the race was now a chase — "a matter of legs," as the saying went — and he had confidence in the outcome, not only because he had had a chance to compare the legs of the two armies, these past three days on the march from Petersburg, but also because he understood the temper of his soldiers and the motive that impelled them. "They began to see the end of what they had been fighting four years for. Nothing seemed to fatigue them. They were ready to move without rations and travel without rest until the end. Straggling had entirely ceased, and every man was now a rival for the front."

Pursuit began without delay, and even before contact was reëstablished — first by Sheridan, whose horsemen lapped the rebel flank, probing for a gap, and then by Humphreys, whose lead division overtook the tail of the slow-grinding butternut column within a couple of hours of setting out — all the indications were that the course would not be long. Abandoned rifles and blanket rolls, cluttering the roadsides west of Amelia, testified to the weariness of the marchers who had carried them this far, while the roads themselves were clogged from point to point by broken-down or mud-stalled wagons, as well as by the creatures who had hauled them. "Dropped in the very middle of the road from utter exhaustion," one pursuer would recall, "old horses, literally skin and bones, [were] so weak as scarcely to be able to lift their heads when some soldier would touch them with his foot to see if they really had life." But the best, or worst, evidence in this regard was the condition of the stragglers encountered in increasing numbers as the chase wore on. Collapsed in ditches or staggering through the woods and sodden fields, near delirium from hunger and fatigue, they not only offered little resistance to being gathered up; they seemed to welcome capture as a comfort. For them at least the war was over, won or lost, and winning or losing made less difference than they had thought before they reached the end of their endurance. Not that all of them, even now, had abandoned the last vestige of that cackling sense of the ridiculous they had flaunted from the start, four years ago. A squad of well-clad, well-fed bluecoats, for example, descended on a tattered, barefoot North Carolina private who had wandered off, lone and famished, in search of food. "Surrender, surrender! We've got you!" they cried as they closed in with leveled weapons. "Yes, you've got me," the Tarheel scarecrow replied, dropping his rifle to raise his hands, "and a hell of a git you got."

Any army in this condition, more or less from top to bottom, was likely to stumble into some error that would cost it dearly, and that was what happened this April 6, known thereafter as the Black Thursday of the Confederacy. Longstreet, still in the lead, was under orders to march hard for Rice, a Southside station three miles short of the Appomattox, lest Ord's corps, reported to be on its way up the track from Burkeville, get there first and cut the hungry graybacks off from the rations St John had waiting for them at Farmville. Behind the First Corps train came Anderson, then Ewell, followed by the guns and wagons of the other three corps — so called, though none was larger than a division had been in the old days — including Gordon's, which had been fighting a rear-guard action against Humphreys since 8.30 that morning, west of the Flat Creek crossing where the march had been delayed. By then Old Peter had reached Rice at the head of his lead division, not only in advance of Ord but also in time to send Rosser's horsemen in pursuit of a flying column of 600 Federals who had just passed through on their way north to burn the bridges the army would need if it was to cross the river. This too was successful. Overtaken and surrounded, outnumbered two to one, the raiders — two regiments of infantry, sent forward by Ord with a squadron of cavalry — were killed or captured, to a man, before they reached their objective. The bridges were saved, along with the rations still awaiting the arrival of the half-starved troops approaching from the south and, presumably, the east.

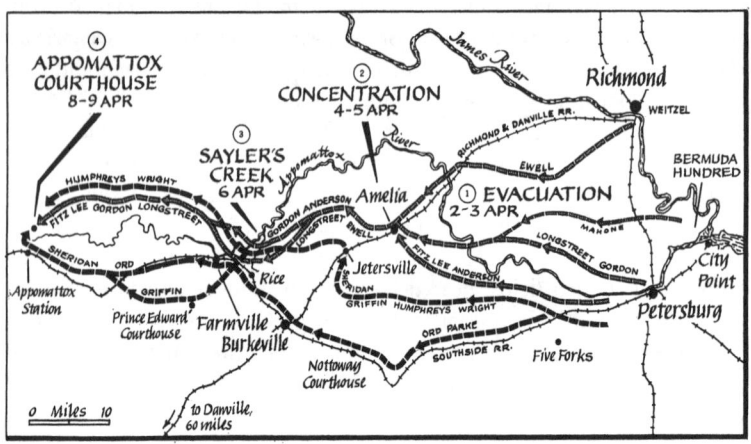

Lee's relief at this turn of events, which encouraged hope for a successful getaway, was soon replaced by tension from a new development, one that left him in the dark as to what might have happened to the other half of his army. Anderson, obliged to halt from time to time to fight off mounted attacks on his flank, had lost touch with Longstreet's rear; so that by noon, with three of the four First Corps divisions deployed near Rice to contest Ord's advance from the southeast, the gray commander could only guess at what might have occurred or be occurring rearward, beyond the gap Sheridan's troopers had created by delaying Anderson. There was mean ground in that direction, as Lee knew from just having crossed it: particularly between the forks of Sayler's Creek, which combined to flow into the Appomattox half a dozen miles below Farmville, athwart the westward march of all four corps. Riding north, then east in an attempt to find out for himself, he approached the point where the boggy little stream ran into the river, and saw beyond it a skirmish in progress between Gordon's rear-guard elements and heavy columns of blue infantry in pursuit. Not only was this dire in itself; it also deepened the mystery of the disappearance of Anderson and Ewell, supposedly on the march between Gordon and

Longstreet. Lee turned south and rode in search of them, only to encounter a staffer who informed him that enemy horsemen had struck the unprotected train between the two branches of Sayler's Creek, setting fire to wagons and creating panic among the teamsters. Eastward, guns were booming in earnest now, and Lee still knew nothing as to the fate or whereabouts of his two missing corps. "Where is Anderson? Where is Ewell?" he said testily. "It is strange I can't hear from them."

It was worse than strange: far worse, he soon found out. Proceeding eastward with Mahone, whose division he summoned from its position in rear of Longstreet's other three near Rice, he topped a ridge overlooking the valley of Sayler's Creek, and there he saw, spread out below him and scrambling up the slope, the answer to his questions about Anderson and Ewell. Union batteries were firing rapidly from a companion ridge across the way, pounding the shattered remnant of both gray corps as the fugitives streamed out of the bottoms where they had met defeat; "a retiring herd," Mahone would later call them, made up of "hurrying teamsters with their teams and dangling traces, infantry without guns, many without hats — a harmless mob." Instinctively, Lee straightened himself in the saddle at the sight. "My God!" he cried, staring downhill at the worst Confederate rout he had seen in the thirty-four months since Davis placed him in command amid the confusion of Seven Pines. "Has the army been dissolved?"

That portion of it had at any rate, largely because of errors of omission by the two corps commanders and the redoubled aggressiveness of the blue pursuers, mounted and afoot, once they became aware of the resultant isolation of the graybacks slogging westward into the toils of Sayler's Creek. Just as Anderson, in failing to notify Longstreet of his need to stop and fight off cavalry attacks upon his flank, had created the gap into which enemy troopers had plunged, so presently had Ewell lost touch with Gordon through a similar oversight. Informed that the rear guard was heavily engaged, he too halted to let part of the intervening train move on, then diverted the rest onto a secondary road that led directly to High Bridge, where the railroad crossed the Appomattox, three miles north of Rice, before looping back to recross it at Farmville, four miles to the west. In resuming his march to overtake Anderson, however, he neglected to tell Gordon of the change: with the result that Gordon, still involved with the bluecoats close in his rear, took the same route as the wagons he had been trailing all along, unaware that he was alone, that his corps had become one of three unequal segments into which Lee's army had been divided by this double failure on the part of the two generals in charge of the central segment. This was now the most gravely endangered of the three, though neither of the two commanders knew it. Ewell, in fact, did not even know that he had rear-guard duties until he came under fire from guns of the VI Corps, which was coming up fast and massing for an assault in conjunction with Sheridan's horsemen, still on Anderson's flank and cavorting among the burning wagons up ahead.

Sheridan had spotted the opportunity almost as soon as it developed. While Humphreys kept on after Gordon, pressing him back toward the crossing of the creek above the junction of its branches — this was the contest Lee had observed when he rode north from Rice in search of the missing half of his command — Little Phil sent word to Wright, whose corps was next in line, that together they could wipe out that portion of the rebel army stalled by his harassment of its flank and his probe of the resultant gap in front. Just then, about 2 o'clock, Anderson struck at Custer, who had made the penetration, and when Custer recoiled Sheridan threw in Devin to contain the drive. Then, hearing Wright's guns open against Ewell, a mile to the northeast, he committed Crook's division against Anderson's center, locked in position by Custer and Devin, front and rear. "Never mind your flanks," he shouted to his troopers as they dismounted for the assault. "Go through them! They're demoralized as hell."

He was right. Resistance by the jangled, road-worn survivors of the Petersburg breakthrough, four hungry days ago, was as brief and ineffectual as their commander later admitted when he reported that they "seemed wholly broken down and disheartened. After a feeble effort ... they gave way in confusion." Only Wise's brigade of Virginians retired from the field as a military unit of any size. In all the rest it was more or less every man for himself, including those of highest rank; Anderson escaped on horseback, along with Pickett and Bushrod Johnson, but a solid half of the 3000 troops who had managed to stay with him this far on the retreat were killed or captured as they fled through the tangled brush and clumps of pine. Sheridan, leaving this roundup work to Custer, plunged on north with the other two divisions, intent on dealing with Ewell in much the same fashion. At Five Forks he had delivered the unhinging blow to Lee's army; now he was out to make Sayler's Creek the coup de grâce. And in fact that was what it came to, at least for that part of the bedraggled rebel host within his reach.

One-legged Ewell, strapped to the saddle to keep from falling off his horse, had his two undersized divisions facing east along the west side of the creek in an attempt to keep Wright from crossing before Anderson unblocked the road to Rice. Down to 3000 effectives as a result of the straggling by Custis Lee's reservists, he relied mainly on Kershaw's veterans in position on his right. Despite heavy shelling from the ridge across the way and mounting pressure from the three blue divisions in his front, he managed to hold his own until Kershaw's outer flank and rear were suddenly assailed by Sheridan's rapid-firing troopers, who had just overrun Anderson and came storming northward through the brush. "There's Phil! There's Phil!" the VI Corps infantrymen yelled as they splashed across the creek to join the attack being made by their old Valley comrades.

"On no battlefield of the war have I felt a juster pride in the conduct of my command," Joe Kershaw was to say, and Custis Lee was equally proud of what remained of his scratch division, though both saw clearly now that further resistance was useless. So did Ewell, who afterwards reported that "shells and even bullets were crossing each other from front and rear over my troops, and my right was completely enveloped. I surrendered myself and staff to a cavalry officer who came in by the same road General Anderson had gone out on." Some 200 of Kershaw's Georgians and Mississippians managed to escape in the confusion, but they were about all that got away. The rest were taken, along with their commanders at all levels. These 2800, combined with those lost earlier by Anderson, brought the total to 4300 graybacks snared in the fork of Sayler's Creek that afternoon. No wonder, then, that a Federal colonel visiting Sheridan's headquarters that evening found Richard Ewell "sitting on the ground hugging his knees, with his face bent down between his arms." Old Bald Head now bore little resemblance to the self he had been when he was Stonewall Jackson's mainstay, two years ago in the Shenandoah Valley. "Our cause is lost. Lee should surrender before more lives are wasted," he was reported to have told his captors. Watching him, the colonel remarked that "if anything could add force to his words, the utter despondency of his air would do it."

Sheridan provided a study in contrast. Elated, he got off a sundown message to Grant reporting the capture of one lieutenant general, two major generals, and three brigadiers, together with thousands of lesser prisoners, fourteen pieces of artillery, and an uncounted number of wagons. "I am still pressing on with both cavalry and infantry," he informed his chief, and added the flourish that would catch Lincoln's eye next morning: "If the thing is pressed I think Lee will surrender."

That might be, but Lee by then was in a better frame of mind than Sheridan supposed. Mahone, who was beside him on the western ridge when he exclaimed, in shock at what he saw in the valley down below, "My God! Has the army been dissolved?" replied stoutly, in reference to his division coming up behind: "No, General. Here are troops ready to do their duty." Lee at once recovered his composure, and turned his thoughts to preventing the enlargement of the disaster by the bluecoats in pursuit of the remnant of Anderson's corps streaming toward him up the hillside. "Yes, General," he said; "there are some true men left. Will you please keep those people back?"

Leaving Mahone to prepare a line of defense against "those people," he rode forward to meet and comfort his own. From somewhere, perhaps from the hand of a passing color bearer, or else from the ground where another had dropped it in flight, he secured a Confederate battle flag; with the result that Anderson's panicked fugitives, toiling uphill, saw him waiting astride Traveller near the crest, a gray general on a gray horse, over whose head the red folds of the star-crossed bunting caught the rays of the sun declining beyond the ridge. Some kept going, overcome by fear, while others stopped to cheer and cluster round him, though with more than a touch of delirium in their voices. "It's General Lee!" they cried. "Where's the man who won't follow Uncle Robert?" As at Gettysburg when they came limping back across the mile-wide valley from the carnage on Cemetery Hill, they found solace in his words and manner. Mahone's troops would cover their withdrawal, he said; they must go to the rear and form again. They did as he asked, most of them at any rate, and presently Mahone came forward to relieve him of the flag and escort him within the lines his veterans had drawn in case the Federals launched a follow-up assault.

No such attack ensued. Despite Sheridan's message assuring Grant that he was "pressing on," Custer had all he could handle in rounding up captives in the brush, as did Crook and Devin, a mile to the north; Wright went into bivouac, and Humphreys' clash with Gordon was still in progress near the Appomattox. Mahone remained in position till after dark, as Lee directed, then marched for High Bridge, four miles northeast, under instructions to cross and set it and an adjacent wagon span afire as soon as Gordon passed over with what remained of the three-corps train. Lee meantime had rejoined Longstreet at Rice for a night march to Farmville, where he too would cross the river and burn the bridges in his rear. A dispatch from Gordon, received soon after sundown, informed his chief that he was "fighting heavily" with Humphreys. "My loss is considerable," he reported, "and I am still closely pressed." By the time he was able to break contact, after nightfall, he had left some 1700 men behind as prisoners, together with a good part of the train. This brought the total to 6000 Confederates made captive today, with perhaps another 2000 killed, wounded, or otherwise knocked loose from their commands. Ewell's corps had been abolished, all but a couple of hundred survivors who made it through the lines that night. ("What regiment is that?" someone asked an officer at the head of the arriving column. "Kershaw's *division*," he replied.) Anderson's corps had been reduced by half, its units shattered except for one brigade, and Gordon's three divisions were cut to skeleton proportions, as Lee would see for himself when they came up next morning. "That half of our army is destroyed," he said of the troops engaged along Sayler's Creek this black Thursday.

Still, even though it was done at a cost of 8000 casualties — not half, but in any case a solid third of all that remained with the colors —

he had accomplished what he set out to do when he left Amelia the day before. Old Peter's corps was intact, having had little trouble holding off Ord's advance up the Southside Railroad. Moreover, rations in plenty were waiting ahead at Farmville, and once there, with the bridges burned behind him, he could put the swollen Appomattox between him and his pursuers, feed and rest his weary men, and perhaps, by moving westward on the north side of the river, get enough of a new head start to try again for a turn south to combine with Johnston in North Carolina. Or, failing that, he might press on to gain the fastness of the Blue Ridge Mountains, where he once had said he could hold out "for years."

The night was cold, with flurries of snow reported in nearby Burkeville next morning. Lee went ahead of Longstreet's men, who trudged on a poor cross-country road, and got a few hours' rest in a house at Farmville. When he rose at dawn, April 7, the First Corps troops were filing through the town, their step quickened by the promise of rations awaiting issue in boxcars parked on the northside tracks. Anxious for some first-hand word of the Sayler's Creek survivors, who were crossing downriver, with instructions to follow the railroad to the vicinity of Farmville, he again doubled Old Peter's column and proceeded eastward, beyond the Appomattox, until he encountered the first of his missing veterans in the person of Henry Wise, who had shared with him the rigors of his first campaign, out in western Virginia in the fall of '61. Arriving on foot at the head of his brigade — the only one to survive, as a unit more or less intact, Anderson's debacle of the day before — the former governor presented an outlandish picture of a soldier. He had lost not only his horse and baggage in yesterday's fight, but also much else in the hurried withdrawal, including his headgear and overcoat, which he had replaced with a jaunty Tyrolean hat, acquired en route, and a coarse gray blanket held together in front by a wire pin. His face, moreover, was streaked with red from having washed it in a puddle. This gave him, as he later said, the appearance of an aged Comanche brave. Lee thought so, too, and recovered a measure of his accustomed good humor at the sight. "I perceive that you, at any rate, have not given up the contest," he told his fellow Virginian, "as you are in your warpaint this morning." Wise drew himself up, shoulders back; he and Lee were of an age, just under two years short of sixty. "Ready for dress parade," he responded proudly to a question about the condition of his command.

Other good news he had as well. Mahone was over the river, too, in position to cover the downstream bridges; Gordon had crossed with all that remained of the train, preceded by a number of Anderson's stragglers, and Mahone was waiting for still others to get over before he gave the engineers word to fire both spans; that is, unless the Yankees came in sight beforehand, which they had not done by the time Wise left at sunup. Encouraged, Lee rode back to where his staff had set up headquarters opposite Farmville. Here he was visited presently by the Secretary of War, who had come on horseback by a different route from Richmond and was off again for Danville as soon as he had conferred with the general-in-chief. In a wire sent to the President next day, while moving roundabout to join him, Breckinridge reported that Lee had been "forced across the Appomattox" to find "temporary relief" from the heavy columns of Federals in pursuit, but that he would "still try to move around [them] toward North Carolina," once he resumed his westward march up the left bank of the river shielding his flank. So he had said at any rate. A military man himself, however, the Kentuckian added his own appraisal of Lee's chances as he saw them: "The straggling has been great, and the situation is not favorable."

In point of fact the situation was considerably less favorable than he had known when the brief conference ended. He had no sooner left, around midmorning, than a courier reached headquarters with news of a development that threatened to undo all Lee's plans for his next move, if indeed there was to be one. Bluecoats were over the Appomattox in strength at High Bridge, four miles east, and were closing even now upon the famished graybacks filing into the fields across from Farmville to draw their first issue of rations in five days. Mahone, it seemed, had pulled out behind Wise and Gordon without giving the engineers orders to fire the two bridges, and the resultant delay, while an officer spurred after him and returned, brought a heavy enemy column in sight before a match was struck. High Bridge itself, an open-deck affair on sixty-foot trusses of brick and pine, burned furiously at once, dropping four of its dozen spans into the water; but the low wagon bridge alongside, built of hardwood, caught fire so slowly that the whooping Federals arrived in time to stamp out the flames. By 9 o'clock Humphreys had his lead division over the river and a second arriving to reinforce the bridgehead to a strength too great for Mahone to retake it, though he countermarched and tried. As for Lee, when he got word of what had happened he lost his temper entirely. "He spoke of the blunder," a staffer observed, "with a warmth and impatience which served to show how great a repression he ordinarily exercised over his feelings."

His rage at this sudden removal of the advantage of having the swollen river between him and his pursuers — not to mention the loss of the anticipated rest halt, which was to have given his road-worn soldiers time to cook and eat their rations and perhaps even get some badly needed sleep before setting out once more to regain the head start that would enable them to turn south for Danville, across the front of the blue column, or anyhow win the race for Lynchburg, where St John had still more rations waiting just over forty miles away — was subdued by the need for devising corrective defensive measures, lest his approximately 20,000 survivors, effective and noneffective, suffer destruction at the hands of more than 80,000 Federals converging upon them from the east and south, on both sides of the Appomattox. Because of a deep bend in the river above Farmville, the Lynchburg pike ran north for about three miles before it turned west near Cumberland Church, where a road from High Bridge joined it. Lee's orders were for Mahone, falling back under pressure from Humphreys, to take up a position there and hold the enemy off until Gordon and Longstreet cleared the junction. At the same time, he summoned Brigadier General E. P. Alexander, the First Corps chief of artillery, and gave him the double task of sending a battalion of guns to support Mahone and of destroying the two bridges at Farmville, as soon as Old Peter's men and wagons finished crossing, to prevent the bluecoats in their rear from joining Humphreys in his attempt to end the campaign, and with it the Army of Northern Virginia, here and now.

Alexander, a Georgia-born West Pointer, not quite thirty and a veteran of nearly all the army's major battles, got the guns off promptly to Cumberland Church, where they presently were in action against the Federals arriving from High Bridge, and prepared the railroad and wagon spans for burning as soon as the last of the gray infantry on the march from Rice were safely over. There was time for that, but not for the horsemen covering their rear; Alexander was taking no chances on a repetition of what had happened earlier, four miles downstream. Closely pursued by Crook, whose division had been sent over by Sheridan after a good night's rest, Fitz Lee was obliged to turn and fight on the outskirts of Farmville in order to give the tail of Longstreet's column a chance to clear the bridges. By the time he was able to break off the action and retire under fire through the streets of the town, both spans were ablaze from end to end; Fitz had to veer west in a race for an upstream ford, which he hoped would not prove too deep for his bone-tired horses to cross before Crook overtook them and used his guns to bloody the waters at that point. His uncle, watching from the opposite bank, took alarm at the thought of his cavalry being cut off, as well as at the sight of the hard-driving VI Corps, which arrived just then from Sayler's Creek and appeared on the hills overlooking the river from the south. Displaying the first real agitation he had shown on the retreat, Lee rode to where Longstreet's earliest arrivers had begun to frizzle bacon and boil cornmeal over newly kindled fires. In response to his urgent orders, and despite Old Peter's remonstrance that Fitz and his troopers could look out for themselves, the issue of rations was discontinued, amid groans from men still waiting to receive them, and those that had been partly cooked were dumped from skillets and kettles which then were flung over the tailgates of wagons whose drivers were in a panic to be off. In a state of torment from the smell of food they had not gotten to eat, the First Corps veterans fell in for the march beyond Cumberland Church, where Mahone was making his stand.

When they got there they found the road still open to the west, but they were unable to take it because Mahone, hard pressed by Humphreys' flankers, had to be reinforced if he was to continue holding out against bluecoats whose attacks grew harder to withstand as more and more of them arrived from downriver, eager to make the most of the opportunity their rapid, dry-shod crossing had afforded them, first to bring the fleeing rebs to bay — which they had done already — and then to overrun them, while the rest of the blue army effected a crossing in their rear to cut them off and help complete their destruction. Neither of these two last things happened, however. Supported by Gordon and Longstreet when they came up, Mahone not only held firm, he also counterattacked with a fury that went far toward making up for this morning's lapse at High Bridge, which had brought on the present crisis. Longstreet, informed that the enemy was menacing the left, detached a brigade from Field's division "with orders to get around the threatening force and break it up. Mahone so directed them through a woodland," he later wrote, "that they succeeded in over-reaching the threatened march and took in some 300 prisoners, the last of our troubles for the day."

The sun by then was going down. When it had set, and the fighting sputtered into a silence broken only by the mewls and groans of the wounded trapped between the lines, Old Peter rode through the twilight to a cottage where Lee had set up headquarters near Cumberland Church. He found him in a much better frame of mind than when he last saw him that morning, agitated by the news of Humphreys' easy coup, which voided his plans for a rest halt and a shielded march upriver, as well as by the threat of having his cavalry overwhelmed by the superior force of blue troopers in a race for the perhaps unusable ford northwest of the bridges on fire at Farmville. As it happened, though their best pace was no more than a shaky gallop, Fitz Lee's horsemen not only effected their escape across the Appomattox; they also managed to turn the tables on their pursuers once they reached the other side. Crossing by the ford, hard on the heels of the gray riders, Crook's lead brigade soon came in sight of Longstreet's train, grinding northward on a poor road near the river, and sought to repeat its successful foray at Sayler's Creek the day before. Fitz saw his chance and prepared to take it. Posting his own division to block the attack by receiving it head on, he sent Rosser against the Union flank, which crumpled when he struck it. Surprised and routed, the former aggressors scurried hard for the ford they had crossed when the pursuit was in the opposite direction, roles reversed.

Lee's spirits rose as he watched his nephew's rousing counterstroke, and lifted again when he learned of Mahone's success in keeping Humphreys' flankers off his line of retreat near Cumberland Church. There still was fight in his diminished army, fight in the style that had won it fame, and while he could not react as he once would have done by going over to the offensive against a divided foe, he was much encouraged by what had been achieved in the course of a day that opened with threats of disaster, left and right, and closed with his forces reunited after inflicting heavier casualties than they suffered. Although it was clear that another night march would have to be undertaken — the third in a row, and the fourth since leaving Petersburg and Richmond — by sundown his trains were rolling westward on the Lynchburg turnpike, unmolested, and his still-hungry soldiers were preparing to follow after moonrise. "Keep your command together and in good spirits, General," he had told his son Rooney that afternoon. "Don't let them think of surrender. I will get you out of this."

Surrender. Though the word was spoken in buoyant reaction to his nephew's savage counterslash at Crook, Lee's use of it showed that he knew his weary, half-starved troops were thinking of that contingency: as indeed he himself was, if only to counsel rejection. Grant, by contrast, was thinking of it quite purposely by then — in reverse, of course — as a proposal to end the drawn-out agony of his adversary's retreat, which he perceived was doomed in any case, and as a duty he presently said he felt "to shift from myself the responsibility of any further effusion of blood."

He had arrived from Burkeville around midday, shortly after Wright's infantry topped the hills overlooking Farmville from the south, and established headquarters in the local hotel, a rambling brick structure on the main street, two blocks short of where the still-burning wreckage of the town's two bridges released twin plumes of smoke above the swollen Appomattox, now a barrier to pursuit of the Confederates, who apparently were free at last to take some badly needed rest on the far side. Couriers soon were coming and going, however, back and forth across the broad hotel veranda, and all the news was good. Yesterday's forays along Sayler's Creek, which had netted some 6000 butternut prisoners, had cost the attackers fewer than 1200 casualties, only 166 of them killed. Best of all, though, was the news that Humphreys was over the river, four miles below, and moving westward to deny the rebels the rest they thought they had won when they fired the bridges in their rear. He was, as Grant said later, "in a very hazardous position," but the sound of his guns, roaring nearer and nearer from the northeast, gave evidence that his boldness was paying off. Besides, he would not stay unsupported long; Grant told Wright to throw a footbridge over the Appomattox, tied to the charred pilings of the railroad span, and use it to reinforce Humphreys as soon as possible with his whole corps. Including Crook's troopers, who would cross by an upstream ford, close to 40,000 Federals would then be on the north bank of the river. That was twice the strength to which Lee by now had dwindled or been cut: surely enough for Wright and Humphreys to perform the task of simultaneously driving and delaying him when he continued (as he would be obliged to do, if he could get away to try) his efforts to move westward to Lynchburg, where rations were known to be waiting in abundance.

For all its heft, this northside push involved no more than half Grant's army, and only half his plan for Lee's undoing. The other half — exclusive of Parke's corps, which had been given the laborious noncombat chore of shifting one track of the Southside Railroad an inch and a half inward, all the way from Petersburg to Burkeville, to accommodate the narrower-gauged Union cars and locomotives and thus provide a high-speed supply line running close in the moving army's rear from the high-piled docks at City Point — would move south of the Appomattox, and also westward, unimpeded, to outmarch and cut the old fox off before he reached his goal. Sheridan, in fact, after sending Crook to support the convergence on Farmville, had already set out in that direction from Sayler's Creek this morning with his other two divisions, riding hard for Prince Edward Courthouse, a dozen miles west of Rice, on the chance that Lee might succeed in giving his pursuers the slip and pass through there, en route to Danville and a combination with Johnston. Nothing came of that, but presently a wire reached headquarters from the bandy-legged cavalry commander, who had covered better than twenty miles of winding road by early afternoon. He was moving instead to Appomattox Station, twenty-five miles out the Southside line from Farmville, to intercept eight supply trains loaded with rations Lee had ordered shipped from Lynchburg to feed his troops when they rounded the nearby headwaters of the Appomattox River. Grant was quick to act on this; indeed, had begun to act on it before he received the information, by sending Griffin after Sheridan with instructions to do all he could to keep up with the fast-riding horsemen then on their way to Prince Edward. Now he added Ord's corps to this southside interception force, with the difference that Ord was to move by a more direct route, due west out the railroad. This too would be a 40,000-man effort, and Grant himself would go along to see that everything went as planned, leaving to Meade the supervision of the march beyond the river, until such time as the two halves, slogging westward along its opposite banks, came together near its source, like upper and nether millstones, to grind between them whatever remained by then of Lee's bedraggled army.

That should occur by tomorrow evening, or Sunday morning at the latest. Meantime he had little to do but wait for Wright to complete his footbridge, just up the street from the hotel, and Ord to get started out the railroad; Griffin was already west of Rice, slogging after Sheridan, and Humphreys' guns were still booming aggressively, two or three miles beyond the river. Despite his mud-spattered clothes, which he had not been able to change since getting separated from his baggage on the twilight ride to Jetersville two nights back, Grant was in a pleasant frame of mind. "Let the *thing* be pressed," Lincoln had wired him this morning, and he was proceeding to do just that, being similarly convinced that the iron was hot for striking. He saw the end in sight at last. What was more, he believed that Lee must see it, too, outnumbered two-to-one as he was by each half of the well-fed and superbly equipped army that soon would be driving him westward up the opposite bank of the dwindling Appomattox. According to Wright, who had talked with him yesterday after his capture, even so stout a fighter as Dick Ewell had confessed that the Confederate cause was lost "and it was the duty of the authorities to make the best terms they could while they still had a right to claim concessions." To continue the conflict under present conditions, he added, "would be but very little better than murder."

Grant rather thought so, too, and presently said as much. Shortly before 5 o'clock, Ord and Gibbon came by headquarters for a final check with him before setting out westward, and as the conference drew to a close he suddenly fell silent, musing, then looked up, and in what Gibbon called "his quiet way," remarked: "I have a great mind to summon Lee to surrender." He seemed to have surprised himself almost as much as he surprised his listeners, but there was no doubt that he meant what he said, for he called at once for ink and paper and began to write accordingly.

> Headquarters Armies of the United States,
> April 7, 1865 — 5 p.m.
>
> General R. E. Lee,
> Commanding C. S. Army.
>
> General: The results of the last week must convince you of the hopelessness of further resistance on the part of the Army of Northern Virginia in this struggle. I feel that it is so, and regard it as my duty to shift from myself the responsibility of any further effusion of blood by asking of you the surrender of that portion of the C. S. Army known as the Army of Northern Virginia.
>
> Very respectfully, your obedient servant,
> U. S. GRANT, Lieutenant General,
> Commanding Armies of the United States.

Brigadier General Seth Williams, Grant's inspector general, charged with delivery of the message under a flag of truce, set out at once for High Bridge to cross the river there and make his way through Humphreys' lines to Lee's. He would have saved time, and spared himself and his orderly and their mounts two thirds of the roundabout nine-mile ride, if he had waited for the VI Corps engineers to complete their footbridge over the Appomattox. They did so by sundown, and Wright's lead division began crossing shortly afterwards, marching three abreast up the street in front of headquarters, where Grant came out and took a seat on the veranda to watch the troops swing past "with a step that seemed as elastic," a staffer observed, "as on the first day of their toilsome tramp." On that day he had called them "as good an army as ever fought a battle," and now they returned the compliment in kind. Passing thus in review, they spotted their rather stumpy, dark-bearded commander on the hotel porch, his cigar a ruby point of light in the deepening shadows, and cheered him lustily to show that whatever reservations they had felt in the past were as gone as his own. He left his chair and came to the railing, still quietly smoking his cigar, and they cheered louder at this reduction of the distance between them. When night fell, bonfires were kindled for illumination along both sides of the street. The effect was one of a torchlight parade as the men broke ranks to snatch brands from the fires, then fell back in to flourish them overhead, roaring the John Brown song while they slogged on toward the river and Lee's army on the other side.

Grant did not wait for the last of Wright's cheering veterans to march past the hotel. After finishing his smoke he turned in early, retiring to a room in which the manager falsely assured him Lee had slept the night before.

Three miles to the north, where Mahone still held his position near Cumberland Church, Captain H. H. Perry, adjutant of the brigade sent by Longstreet to reinforce the left, went forward around 9 o'clock to investigate a report that a flag of truce had been advanced by the enemy in front. He proceeded with caution, for there had been a similar incident about an hour earlier, which ended when the butternut pickets, suspecting a Yankee trick, opened fire at the first hail from the twilit woods across the way. Now here were the truce-seekers back again, if that was what they had been in the first place. The young Georgia captain picked his way carefully to a point some fifty yards in front of the lines, where he stopped amid a scattering of blue-clad dead and wounded, hit in the last assault, and called for the flag: if that was what it was. It was: for now there appeared before him, resplendent in the light of the rising moon, what he later described as "a very handsomely dressed Federal officer" who introduced himself as Brigadier General Seth Williams of Grant's staff. Highly conscious of the contrast they presented, no less in looks than in rank — "The truth is, I had not eaten two ounces in two days, and I had my coattail then full of corn, waiting to parch it as soon as the opportunity might present itself" — Perry said later, "I drew myself up as proudly as I could, and put on the appearance as well as possible of being perfectly satisfied with my personal exterior."

Williams measured up to the occasion. Formerly the "efficient and favorite" prewar adjutant at West Point, including a time while R. E. Lee was superintendent, he had served McClellan, Burnside, Hooker, and Meade in the same capacity, with emphasis on his ability to celebrate the amenities. Now, as Grant's I.G. and special envoy — despite the loss, an hour ago, of his orderly in the fire that greeted his first attempt to open communications — he demonstrated that same ability in the moon-lit clearing between the lines of Humphreys and Mahone. Once the formal introductions were concluded, he produced a handsome silver flask and remarked, as Perry afterwards recalled, "that he hoped I would not think it an unsoldierly courtesy if he offered me some very fine brandy." The Georgian, who had nothing to offer in return but the unparched corn in the tail of his coat, found himself in a dilemma. "I wanted that drink awfully," he said later. "Worn down, hungry and dispirited as I was, it would have been a gracious godsend if some old Confederate and I could have emptied that flask between us in that dreadful hour of misfortune. But I raised myself about an inch higher, if possible, bowed and refused politely, trying to produce the ridiculous appearance of having feasted on champagne and pound cake not ten minutes before." Williams — "a true gentleman," his then companion would declare — returned the flask unopened to his pocket, and for this Perry was most grateful down the years. "If he had taken a drink, and my Confederate olfactories had obtained a whiff of the odor of it, it is possible that I should have caved." Spared this disgrace, he received from Williams the letter from Grant to Lee, together with a request for its prompt delivery; after which the ragged captain and the well-groomed brigadier "bowed profoundly to each other and turned away," each toward his own lines.

A courier soon reached Lee's headquarters in the cottage near Cumberland Church. Longstreet, still with his chief though the time by now was close to 10 o'clock, watched as he studied the message. There was no emotion in his face, and he passed it to his lieutenant without comment. Old Peter read the surrender request, then handed it back. "Not yet," he said.

Lee made no reply to that, but he did to Grant's letter; first, to refuse acceptance of the responsibility therein assigned him for such blood as might still be shed, and second, to explore the possibility — however remote — that his adversary might be willing to reopen the Ord-Longstreet peace discussions he had broken off so abruptly the month before, disclaiming any "authority" in such matters. As soon as Old Peter went out into the night, rejoining his troops for the march that had begun to get under way at moonrise, Lee wrote his answer on a single sheet of paper and gave it to the courier to be sent across the lines.

7th Apl '65

Genl
    I have recd your note of this date. Though not entertaining the opinion you express of the hopelessness of further resistance on the

part of the Army of N. Va. I reciprocate your desire to avoid useless effusion of blood, & therefore before considering your proposition, ask the terms you will offer on condition of its surrender.

> Very respy your obt Svt
> R. E. LEE, Genl

Lt Genl U. S. Grant,
Commd Armies of the U States.

Old Peter cleared his camps well before midnight, but presently, in accordance with instructions to assume the more rigorous task of guarding the rear, halted to let Gordon take the lead on the westward march up the left bank of the Appomattox. The army thus had a head and a tail, but no middle now that the other two corps had been "dissolved" in battle and by Lee; Wise's still sizeable brigade — practically all that remained of Johnson's division — was assigned to Gordon, in partial compensation for his losses at Sayler's Creek, while skeletal fragments of the other three divisions, under Pickett, Heth, and Wilcox, were attached to Longstreet, thereby rejoining comrades they had not seen since the Petersburg breakthrough sundered them, six days back. That left Richard Anderson and Bushrod Johnson troopless, and George Pickett not much better off with only sixty armed survivors; Lee solved the problem by formally relieving all three of duty, with authorization to return to their homes before reporting to the War Department. Anderson and Johnson left that afternoon, but Pickett's orders apparently went astray. In any case he was still around, that day and the next, still nursing grievances over rejection of a report in which he had sought to fix the blame on others for his Gettysburg repulse. Lee may or may not have known about the Five Forks shad bake, a week ago today, but subsequently, when he saw his fellow Virginian ride by headquarters, ringlets jouncing, air of command intact, he reacted with dark surprise. "I thought that man was no longer with the army," he remarked.

Otherwise, aside from continuing hunger and fatigue, there was much that was pleasant about this sixth day's march, especially by contrast with the five that had gone before. Not only had the weather improved, the plodding graybacks noted when the sun came up this Saturday morning, but so had the terrain, barely touched by war till now. It was a day, one pursuing Federal wrote, "of uneventful marching; hardly a human being was encountered along the way. The country was enchanting, the peach orchards were blossoming in the southern spring, the fields had been peacefully plowed for the coming crops, the buds were beginning to swell, and a touch of verdure was perceptible on the trees and along the hillsides. The atmosphere was balmy and odorous; the hamlets were unburnt, the farms all tilled." Best of all, no roar of guns disturbed what a South Carolinian called "the soft airs, at once warm and invigorating, which blew to us along the high ridges we traversed." Fitz Lee, whose horsemen trailed the column at a distance of two miles, reported the enemy infantry no closer to him than he was to his own, while the blue cavalry seemed equally disinclined to press the issue. Still, there was a driving urgency about the march, an apprehension unrelieved by the lack of direct pressure, and the need for it was evident from even a brief study of the map. On the left, the dwindling Appomattox soon would cease to be a barrier to whatever Union forces were in motion on the other side. A dozen miles beyond that critical point, westward across a watershed traversed by the Southside Railroad, the James River flowed northeast to reënter the tactical picture as a new barrier — one that was likely to be controlled by whichever army rounded the headwaters of the Appomattox first. If it was Lee's, he could feed his men from the supply trains he had ordered sent to Appomattox Station, then press on next day to take shelter behind the James. If on the other hand the Federals got there in time to seize his provisions and in strength enough to block his path across the twelve-mile watershed, the campaign would be over. Alexander, the First Corps artillerist, saw this clearly. Examining on the map the "jug-shaped peninsula between the James and the Appomattox," he noted that "there was but one outlet, the neck of the jug at Appomattox Station." Both armies were headed there now, north and south of the river that had its source nearby — and "Grant had the shortest road."

What was likely to come of this was plain enough to a number of high-ranking officers who had conferred informally about it the previous evening while waiting to set out on what they judged might well be their last march. Concluding that surrender would soon be unavoidable, they requested William Pendleton, the senior of the group, to communicate their view to Lee and thus, as Alexander put it, "allow the odium of making the first proposition to be placed upon them," rather than on him. Neither Longstreet nor Gordon took part in the discussion, and when Pendleton told them of it next morning, seeking their endorsement, both declined. Old Peter, in fact — saying nothing of the message from Grant, which he had read the night before — was quick to point out that the Articles of War provided the death penalty for officers who urged capitulation on their commanders. As for himself, he said angrily, "If General Lee doesn't know when to surrender until *I* tell him, he will never know."

Pendleton, who had been at West Point with Lee before leaving the army to enter the ministry, bided his time until midday, when he found his fellow graybeard resting in the shade of a large pine beside the road. Like Longstreet, after hearing him out, Lee said nothing of Grant's message — or of his own reply, in which, by requesting terms, he had already begun the negotiations Pendleton was recommending

— but rather expressed surprise at the proposal. "I trust it has not come to that," he said sternly, even coldly. "We certainly have too many brave men to think of laying down our arms."

Snubbed and embarrassed, convinced, in Alexander's words, that Lee "preferred himself to take the whole responsibility of surrender, as he had always taken that of his battles," Pendleton rejoined the troops slogging past on the road beside the river, which narrowed with every westward mile through the long spring afternoon. The going was harder now that this morning's hunger and exertion had been added to those of the past five days. Tailing the march, Longstreet observed that "many weary soldiers were picked up, and many came to the column from the woodlands, some with, some without, arms — all asking for food." There were also those who were too far gone for rescue, sitting as Ewell had sat two days ago, his arms on his knees, his head down between them. Others were even worse undone, "lying prone on the ground along the roadside, too much exhausted to march farther, and only waiting for the enemy to come and pick them up as prisoners, while at short intervals there were wagons broken down, their teams of horses and mules lying in the mud, from which they had struggled to extricate themselves until complete exhaustion forced them to wait for death to glaze their wildly staring eyes." A Virginia trooper saw them thus, but added: "Through all this, a part of the army still trudged on, with their faith still strong, only waiting for General Lee to say whether they were to face about and fight."

Fortunately, no such turnabout action was required before nightfall ended the march with the head of the column approaching Appomattox Courthouse, some three miles short of Appomattox Station. Part of the train was already parked in the fields around the county seat, and the reserve batteries, which had also gone ahead, were in position over toward the railroad. Lee was just dismounting to make camp beside the pike, about midway between Gordon and Longstreet, when a courier overtook him at last with a sealed message that had come through the lines earlier in the day. By the light of a candle held by an aide, he saw that it was Grant's reply to last night's request for his terms of surrender. "Peace being my great desire," the Union commander wrote, "there is but one condition I would insist upon — namely, that the men and officers surrendered shall be disqualified for taking up arms against the Government of the United States until properly exchanged." Not only was this a far cry from the "unconditional" demand that had won him his nom-de-guerre three years ago at Donelson, but Grant considerately added: "I will meet you, or will designate officers to meet any officers you may name for the same purpose, at any point agreeable to you, for the purpose of arranging definitely the terms upon which the surrender of the Army of Northern Virginia will be received."

Nothing of Lee's reaction showed in his face. "How would you answer that?" he asked the aide, who read it and replied: "I would answer no such letter." Lee mused again, briefly. "Ah, but it must be answered," he said, and there by the roadside, still by the flickering light of the candle, he proceeded to do so. Parole was infinitely preferable to imprisonment, but he had to weigh his chances of getting away westward, beyond the James, against the advantage of negotiating while surrender remained a matter of choice. Moreover, he still clung to the notion of resuming more general peace discussions that might lead to something less than total capitulation. "In mine of yesterday," he now told Grant, "I did not intend to propose the surrender of the Army of N. Va., but to ask the terms of your proposition. To be frank, I do not think the emergency has arisen to call for surrender of this Army, but as the restoration of peace should be the sole object of all, I desired to know whether your proposals would lead to that end. I cannot therefore meet you with a view to surrender the Army of N. Va.; but as far as your proposal may affect the C. S. forces under my command, and tend to the restoration of peace, I shall be pleased to meet you at 10 a.m. tomorrow on the old stage road to Richmond, between the picket lines of the two armies."

Soon after the courier set out rearward with this reply, a roar of guns erupted from over near the railroad, three miles off. It swelled and held, then subsided, and after a time — around 9 o'clock — Pendleton arrived from that direction to explain that he had ridden forward, a couple of miles beyond the courthouse village just ahead, to check on the reserve artillery, which had left Farmville with the train the day before. Sixty pieces were in park, awaiting resumption of the march tomorrow; all seemed well, he said, until a sudden attack by Union cavalry exploded out of the twilight woods, full in the faces of the lounging cannoneers. Two batteries were ordered to hold off the blue troopers while the rest pulled back, and there ensued what a participant called "one of the closest artillery fights in the time it lasted that occurred during the war. The guns were fought literally up to the muzzles. It was dark by this time, and at every discharge the cannon were ablaze from touchhole to mouth. There must have been six or eight pieces at work, and the small arms of some three or four hundred men packed in among the guns in a very confined space. It seemed like the very jaws of the infernal regions." Pendleton by then had left to help withdraw such pieces as might be saved, but narrowly avoided capture himself by enemy horsemen who came swarming up the wagon-crowded road. He feared perhaps half the guns had been lost, he told Lee, including those in the two batteries left behind, which soon fell silent in the darkness, three miles to the southwest.

As it turned out, two dozen of them were taken, there and on the road. But that was by no means the worst of the news, or the worst of its implications. Just beyond the overrun gun park was Appomattox

Station, where the supply trains had been ordered to await the arrival of the army. Most likely they had been captured too. If so, that meant still another rationless march tomorrow: if, indeed, a march could be made at all. No one could even guess at the number of Federals involved in the night attack across the way, and though they appeared to be cavalry, to a man — so far at least as anyone had been able to tell in the darkness and confusion — there was no way of knowing what other forces were at hand, including division after division of blue infantry near the end of their unhindered daylong westward tramp up the opposite bank of the river. One thing was certain in any case. If they were there in any considerable strength, corking the James-Appomattox jug, the way across the twelve-mile watershed was blocked and the campaign was over, all but the formal surrender on whatever terms Grant might require at the 10 o'clock meeting Lee had just requested.

Not even now, with the probable end in sight, did Lee show the mounting tension he had been under since the collapse of his flank at Five Forks, a week ago today. He did react swiftly to Pendleton's report, however, by summoning his two infantry corps commanders, as well as his nephew Fitz, who was told to alert his troopers for a shift from the tail of the column to its head. Before long, all three joined him at his camp, pitched near a large white oak on the last low ridge overlooking the north branch of the Appomattox, and the council of war began. Longstreet sat on a log, smoking his pipe; Gordon and Fitz shared a blanket spread on the ground for a seat. The new-risen moon, only two nights short of the full, lighted the scene while Lee, who stood by a fire that had been kindled against the chill, explained the tactical situation, so far as he knew it, and read them Grant's two letters, together with his replies. Then he did something he had not done, at least in this collective way, since the eve of the Seven Days, shortly after he took over as their leader. He asked for their advice. "We knew by our own aching hearts that his was breaking," Gordon was to say. "Yet he commanded himself, and stood calmly facing and discussing the long-dreaded inevitable."

So did they, and the decision accordingly reached was that the army would try for a breakout, a getaway westward beyond the glow of enemy campfires rimming the horizon on all sides except the barren north. While Fitz brought his horsemen forward to lead the attack out the Lynchburg pike, Gordon would prepare to move in support of the mounted effort. If successful in unblocking the road, they would then wheel left to hold it open for the passage of the train, which would be reduced to two battalions of artillery and the ammunition wagons, and Longstreet would follow, guarding the rear in case the pursuing Federals tried to interfere from that direction. It was a long-odds gamble at best; moreover, Gordon pointed out, "The utmost that could be hoped for was that we might reach the mountains of Virginia and Tennessee with

Victory, and Defeat

a remnant of the army, and ultimately join General Johnston." Still it was no more, or less, than could be expected of men determined to keep fighting so long as a spark of hope remained. If the bluecoats could not be budged, if more than cavalry had arrived to bar the way, there would be time enough then, as Fitz Lee put it, "to accede to the only alternative left us."

While his lieutenants rode off to issue instructions for their share in the predawn movement, Lee prepared to take his last sleep under the stars. Before he turned in, however, a member of Gordon's staff returned to ask where the head of the column was to make camp next night on its westward march. The question was put as if there could be no doubt that the breakthrough would succeed, and Lee's reply, though grim and not without a touch of irony, was in much the same vein. "Tell General Gordon I should be glad for him to halt just beyond the Tennessee line," he said, much to the staffer's chagrin; for the Tennessee line was nearly two hundred miles away.

Grant too was bedded down by then, some fifteen miles to the east in an upstairs room of a deserted house beside the pike; but not to sleep. He had a splitting headache — on this of all days, which had opened with a spirit-lifting message from Lee requesting terms in response to last night's suggestion that he surrender. After stating them in a note that was soon on its way through the lines, Grant changed his mind about riding with the southside column, and crossed the river instead to be where Lee's reply could reach him with the least delay. "Hello, old fellow!" he greeted Meade, to the shock of both their staffs, when he overtook the grizzled Pennsylvanian, still confined to his ambulance by dyspepsia and the added discomfort of chills and fever. All through the bright warm morning the march continued without incident; Grant's spirits continued to mount. At the midday halt, aware that Lincoln was on his way up the coast, he got off an exuberant telegram to Stanton, briefing him on the tactical situation and concluding: "I feel very confident of receiving the surrender of Lee and what remains of his army tomorrow." His terms in this morning's note, he felt, were too generous for his opponent to decline them in his present condition, which was evident from the dolorous state of the stragglers Humphreys and Wright were gleaning while they pressed on westward in the littered wake of the butternut throng. All the same, as the day wore on and there still was no response to his predawn offer, sent forward some eight hours before, he began to wonder at the delay and at the ability of the half-starved graybacks to keep beyond reach of their pursuers. Then out of nowhere, just as the rim of the declining sun glittered below the brim of his hat, the blinding headache struck.

It struck and it kept striking, even after he stopped for the night in a large frame house beside the pike, a dozen miles from Farmville.

The pain was by no means lessened by the banging some aide was giving a piano in the parlor directly below Grant's upstairs bedroom, nor by assurances from another staffer that his migraine attacks were usually followed by good news. Indeed, the arrival of just such a dispatch from Sheridan around 10 o'clock failed to bring relief, although the news was about as good as even he could have hoped for. The cavalryman reported that he had reached Appomattox Station at dusk, ahead of the leading elements of Lee's army. Not only had he captured four and chased off the rest of the supply trains waiting there for the hungry rebels to arrive from Cumberland Church; he had also followed through with a night attack by Custer toward Appomattox Courthouse, which had netted him some two dozen guns, a considerable haul of prisoners and wagons, and — best of all — a dug-in position athwart the Lynchburg road, blocking Lee's escape in the only direction that mattered. Moreover, by way of assuring that the road stayed blocked, he had urged Ord and Griffin to press on westward with their six divisions in a forced-march effort to join him before daylight. "If [they] can get up tonight we will perhaps finish the job in the morning," he told Grant, adding suggestively: "I do not think Lee means to surrender until compelled to do so."

Presently Grant had cause to agree with this closing assessment, and what was more he received it from Lee himself in a message that arrived soon after Sheridan's. Denying that he had intended to propose surrender in his previous response, or that an emergency had arisen which called for him to adopt so drastic a course, the southern commander said only that he would be willing to meet between the lines for a general discussion that might "tend to a restoration of peace." Grant studied the note, more saddened than angered by what he discerned, and shook his head. "It looks as if Lee meant to fight," he said.

He was disappointed. But that was mild compared to the reaction of his chief of staff, with whom he was sharing the bed in the upstairs room. "He did not propose to surrender!" Rawlins scoffed, indignant. "Diplomatic, but not true. He did propose, in his heart, to surrender. . . . He now wants to entrap us into making a treaty of peace. You said nothing about that. You asked him to surrender. He replied by asking what terms you would give. You answered by stating the terms. Now he wants to arrange for peace — something beyond and above the surrender of his army; something to embrace the whole Confederacy, if possible. No, sir. No, sir. Why, it is a positive insult — an attempt, in an underhanded way, to change the whole terms of the correspondence." Grant demurred. "It amounts to the same thing, Rawlins. He is only trying to be let down easy. I could meet him as requested, in the morning, and settle the whole business in an hour." But Rawlins would not have it so. Listeners downstairs heard him shout that Lee had purposely shifted his ground "to gain time and better terms." He saw the Virginian as a sharper, a wriggler trying to squirm from under the retribution about to descend on his guilty head. "He don't think 'the emergency has arisen'! That's cool, but another falsehood. That emergency has been staring him in the face for forty-eight hours. If he hasn't seen it yet, we will soon bring it to his comprehension! He has to surrender. He shall surrender. By the eternal, it shall be surrender or nothing else."

Grant continued to defend his year-long adversary, protesting that in his present "trying position," the old warrior was "compelled to defer somewhat to the wishes of his government.... But it all means precisely the same thing. If I meet Lee he will surrender before I leave." At this, Rawlins was quick to remind his chief of last month's wire from Stanton, forbidding him to treat with the enemy on such matters. "You have no right to meet Lee, or anyone else, to arrange terms of peace. That is the prerogative of the President, or the Senate. Your business is to capture or destroy Lee's army." Obliged to admit the force of this, Grant yielded; "Rawlins carried his point," one downstairs listener was to say, "as he always did, when resolutely set." Grant yielded; but he insisted that he still must do Lee the courtesy of answering his letter, if only to decline the suggested meeting. "I will reply in the morning," he said.

That ended the discussion, but not the throb in his head. Before daybreak, a staff colonel found him pacing about the yard of the house, both hands pressed to his aching temples. At the colonel's suggestion, he tried soaking his feet in hot water fortified with mustard, then placed mustard plasters on his wrists and the back of his neck; to no avail. When dawn began to glimmer through he went over to Meade's headquarters, just up the road, and had a cup of coffee. Feeling somewhat better, though not much, he composed a sort of open-ended refusal of Lee's request for a meeting between the lines this Sunday morning. "Your note of yesterday is received," he wrote. "I have no authority to treat on the subject of peace; the meeting proposed for 10 a.m. today could lead to no good. I will state, however, General, that I am equally anxious for peace with yourself, and the whole North entertains the same feeling. The terms upon which peace can be had are well understood. By the South laying down their arms they will hasten that most desirable event, save thousands of human lives, and hundreds of millions of property not yet destroyed. Seriously hoping that all our difficulties may be settled without the loss of another life, I subscribe myself, &c. *U. S. Grant*, Lieutenant General.

After a sunrise breakfast he went forward to find Humphreys and Wright again on the march. Meade was still in his ambulance, but Grant declined the offer of one for himself, despite the headache that made jogging along on horseback a constant torture, apparently having decided to put up with the pain, much as he was putting up with the rumpled and muddy uniform he had been wearing ever since his baggage went astray near Burkeville. Up ahead, though contact had not yet been established with the rebel rear, guns were thumping faintly in the distance. What this meant, or what might come of it, he did not know. He decided, however, that the best way to find out would be to approach the conflict not from this direction, with the column in pursuit, but from the front with Sheridan, who was in position over beyond Appomattox Courthouse. Accordingly, he told Meade goodbye and doubled back, accompanied by his staff, for a crossing of the river and a fast ride west on the far side. So he intended; but there were delays. "We had to make a wide detour to avoid running into Confederate pickets, flankers, and bummers," a reporter who went with him would recall. "It proved to be a long rough ride, much of the way without any well-defined road, often through fields and across farms, over hills, ravines, and 'turned out' plantations, across muddy brooks and bogs of quicksand." Once they even got lost in a pathless stretch of woods, narrowly avoiding capture by a band of rebel stragglers on the roam there. All this time, the rumble of guns up ahead had been swelling and sinking, swelling and sinking, until finally it hushed; a matter for wonder, indeed, though it might well flare up again, as it had before. The sun was nearing the overhead when the riders stopped at last to rest their horses in a roadside clearing whose timber had been cut and heaped for burning. While they dismounted to light cigars from the fuming logs, the reporter later wrote, "someone chanced to look back the way we had come, and saw a horseman coming at full speed, waving his hat above his head and shouting at every jump of his steed."

Soon recognized as one of Meade's lieutenants — a young man well acquainted with army protocol, and observant of it even under the excitement of his current mission — the rider drew rein in front of the chief of staff, saluted stiffly, and presented him with a sealed envelope. Rawlins tore one end open slowly, withdrew the message, and read it deliberately to himself. Nothing in his manner revealed his feelings as he passed the single sheet to Grant, who read it with no more expression on his face, the reporter noted, "than in a last year's bird's nest." Handing it back, he said quietly: "You had better read it aloud, General." Rawlins did so, in a deep voice that by now was a little shaky with emotion.

April 9th, 1865

General: I received your note of this morning on the picket line, whither I had come to meet you and ascertain definitely what terms were embraced in your proposal of yesterday with reference to the surrender of this army. I now request an interview, in accordance with the offer contained in your letter of yesterday, for that purpose.

Very respectfully, Your obt servt
R. E. LEE.

Victory, and Defeat [939]

The celebration that followed was unexpectedly subdued. "No one looked his comrade in the face," the reporter would declare years later. One staffer hopped on a stump, waved his hat, and called for three cheers; but the hurrahs were few and feeble. Most throats were too constricted for speech, let alone cheers. "All felt that the war was over. Every heart was thinking of friends — family — home."

Grant was the first to recover his voice: perhaps in happy reaction to finding his headache cured, as he afterwards testified, "the instant I saw the contents of the note." This time Lee had said nothing about a broad-scale discussion that might "tend to the restoration of peace." He spoke rather of "the surrender of this army," and sought, as he said, an interview "for that purpose." Negotiations were back on the track, and the track was Grant's.

"How will that do, Rawlins?" he asked, smiling as he recalled his friend's tirade in their upstairs bedroom, late the night before.

"I think *that* will do," the other said.

Lee had foreseen the outcome from the start, and showed it when he joined his staff around the campfire that morning, a couple of hours before daylight, dressed in a splendid new gray uniform. His linen was snowy, his boots highly polished, and over a deep red silken sash, gathered about his waist, he had buckled on a sword with an ornate hilt and scabbard. When Pendleton expressed surprise at finding him turned out in such unaccustomed finery, he replied: "I have probably to be General Grant's prisoner, and thought I must make my best appearance."

No considerable insight was required for this assessment of what was likely to come of today's effort. Including 2000 cannoneers available to serve the remaining 61 guns, he had by now some 12,500 effectives in his ranks — fewer, in all, than Sheridan had in bivouac just to the west and south, their horses tethered athwart his one escape route, and only about one third of the skeleton force that began its withdrawal from Richmond, Bermuda Hundred, and Petersburg, a week ago tonight. Nearly as many more were present or scattered roundabout in various stages of collapse from hunger and exhaustion, but that was the number still fit for fight and still with weapons in their hands. Closing on Fitz, whose 2400 troopers were assembled in the yards and lanes of the little courthouse hamlet up ahead, Gordon was down to no more than 2000 infantry, while Longstreet, in motion behind the train of creaking wagons, had barely 6000 to cover the rear. Lee could hear them shuffling past in the darkness, along the road and in the woods surrounding the low glow of his headquarters fire, where the staff was breakfasting on gruel heated in a single metal cup and passed from hand to hand, more or less in the order of rank. He did not share in this, but when the meal was over, such as it was, and daylight began to glimmer through, he mounted Traveller and rode forward to watch his nephew and Gordon try for the breakout that at best would mean that the long retreat would continue beyond the dawn of this Palm Sunday.

Eastward the rim of sky was tinged with red by the time Fitz sent his horsemen forward on the right of Gordon, whose three-division corps — not much larger now than a single good-sized brigade had been when Grant first crossed the Rapidan, just one month less than a year ago this week — attacked due west out the Lynchburg pike, where the Federals had thrown up a gun-studded line of fieldworks in the night. The volume of fire was heavy, but because of a dense ground fog, which the growing light seemed to thicken, Lee could see little from his position on a hill overlooking the town and the fields beyond. If he could have observed the action, screened from his view by the mist that filled the valley, his heart would have lifted, as it had done so often at the start of one of his pulse-quickening offensives. Infantry and cavalry alike, the gray veterans reached and overran the enemy works in a single rush, taking two brass Napoleons and screaming with their old savage delight as the bluecoats scattered rearward to avoid the onslaught. Gordon, exultant, wheeled his cheering men hard left to hold the road open for the passage of the train. All the enemy dead and wounded had on spurs, and he took this for assurance that the breakthrough would be sustained. But then, as he watched the outdone troopers scuttle left and right, across the fields on both sides of the road, it was as if a theater curtain parted to show what he least wanted to see in all the world. There in rear of the gap, rank on rank and growing thicker by the minute, stood long lines of Union infantry, braced and ready, facing the risen sun, their blue flags snapping in the breeze that by now was beginning to waft the fog away.

It was Ord and it was Griffin, with close to 15,000 men apiece. They had arrived at dawn, after an all-night march undertaken in response to the summons from Sheridan, and each had two of his three divisions in position by sunup — in time to hear the high-throated caterwaul of the rebels bearing down on the dismounted cavalry up front. "The sweetest music I ever heard," Stonewall Jackson had called what the Federals themselves variously referred to as "that hellish yell," scarcely human either in pitch or duration, apparently with no hint of brain behind it, and "nothing like a hurrah, but rather a regular wildcat screech." A Wisconsin soldier put it best, perhaps, without even trying for a description. "There is nothing like it this side of the infernal region," he declared, "and the peculiar corkscrew sensation that it sends down your backbone under these circumstances can never be told. You have to *feel* it, and if you say you did not feel it, and heard the yell, then you have never *been* there." They heard it now, through the mist ahead, and for them too, as the cavalry scuttled rearward and sideways, the effect was one of a curtain parting on dread. There stood the butternut infantry, full in front, their regiments so diminished by attrition that their flags took the breeze not in intersticed rows, as in the old days, but in clusters of red, as if poppies or roses had suddenly burst into crowded bloom amid the smoke of their rapid-firing batteries. "We grew tired and prostrated," a blue veteran said of the hard six-day pursuit, "but we wanted to be there when the rebels found the last ditch of which they had talked so much." Now here it was, directly before them, and they were not so sure. Persuaded last night to press on westward out the railroad for the sake of getting a hot breakfast at Appomattox Station, they instead found graybacks in their front, scarecrow thin and scarecrow ragged, but still about as dangerous, pound for pound, as so many half-starved wolves or panthers. It might be the end, as some were saying, yet nobody wanted to be the last man to fall. "We were angry at ourselves," one candidate for that distinction later wrote, "to think that for the sake of drawing rations we had been foolish enough to keep up and, by doing so, get in such a scrape." It was not so much the booming guns they minded, he explained; "We dreaded the moment when the infantry should open on us."

Such dread was altogether mutual. Fitz Lee recoiled, and while the other two blue divisions came up to extend the triple Union line to a width of about three miles — 10,000 men to the mile, afoot — Sheridan remounted and alerted his troopers for an all-out strike at the rebel left as soon as the infantry started forward. "Now smash 'em, I tell you; smash 'em!" he was urging his subordinates, and Gordon knew only too well that, given the opportunity at hand, this was what Little Phil would be saying. Exposed to attack on both flanks and his center, the Georgian perceived that he had to pull back if he was to avoid being cut off and annihilated. He kept his sharpshooters active and stepped up the fire of his batteries, hoping at best to effect a piecemeal withdrawal that would discourage a swamping rush by the Federals in his front. Just then — about 8 o'clock — a staff colonel arrived from the fogbound army command post to inquire how things were going. Gordon gave him a straight answer. "Tell General Lee I have fought my corps to a frazzle and I fear I can do nothing unless I am heavily supported by Longstreet."

Blind on his hilltop, Lee received the message without flinching, though he saw clearly enough what it meant. If so stalwart a fighter as Gordon could "do nothing" without the help of Longstreet, who had just been warned that Humphreys and Wright had resumed their advance and soon would pose as grave a threat to his rear as Ord and Griffin now presented in his front, he had lost all choice in the matter. What was more he admitted as much, however regretfully, in the presence of his staff. "Then there is nothing left me to do but go and see General Grant," he said, "and I would rather die a thousand deaths."

It was by now about 8.30. With more than an hour to wait before setting out for the meeting he had suggested in last night's letter across the lines, Lee returned to his headquarters beside the pike and sent for Longstreet. Leaving Field in charge of the rear guard, which had halted behind the stalled train and was digging in to confront the two blue corps reported to be advancing from the east, Longstreet brought Mahone and Alexander along, apparently in the belief that their advice would be helpful at the council of war he thought had been called to determine the army's next move. As it turned out, however, he had not been summoned for that purpose, but rather to give his opinion on the question of surrender. Countering with a question of his own, he asked whether the sacrifice of the Army of Northern Virginia would in any way help the cause elsewhere. Lee said he thought not. "Then your situation speaks for itself," Old Peter told him. Mahone felt the same. A slight, thin man in a long brown linen duster — so thin, indeed, that his wife, once informed that he had received a flesh wound, replied in alarm: "Now I know it is serious, for William has no flesh whatever" — he was shivering, and he wanted it understood that this was from the chill of the morning, not from fear. All the same, he too could recommend nothing but surrender under the present circumstances. Alexander disagreed. Ten years younger than Mahone, who was crowding forty, he proposed that the troops take to the woods, individually and in small groups, under orders to report to the governors of their respective states. That way, he believed, two thirds of the army would avoid capture by the Yankees; "We would be like rabbits or partridges in the bushes, and they could not scatter to follow us." Lee heard the young brigadier out, then replied in measured tones to his plan. "We must consider its effect on the country as a whole," he told him. "Already it is demoralized by the four years of war. If I took your advice, the men would be without rations and under no control of officers. They would be compelled to rob and steal in order to live. They would become mere bands of marauders, and the enemy's cavalry would pursue them and overrun many sections they may never have occasion to visit. We would bring on a state of affairs it would take the country years to recover from. And as for myself, you young fellows might go bushwhacking, but the only dignified course for me would be to go to General Grant and surrender myself and take the consequences of my acts." Alexander was silenced, then and down the years. "I had not a single word to say in reply," he wrote long afterwards. "He had answered my suggestion from a plane so far above it that I was ashamed of having made it."

Nothing much had been accomplished by all this, but at least Lee had managed to get through the better part of a hard hour: which had probably been his purpose in sending for Longstreet in the first place. Now the time was at hand, and he prepared to set out for the 10 o'clock meeting, rearward between the lines, with his young adjutant, Walter Taylor, and Lieutenant Colonel Charles Marshall, his military secretary; Sergeant George Tucker — Hill's courier, who had attached himself to Lee after the fall of his chief, a week ago this morning — would go along as bearer of the flag of truce. They rode eastward, the four of them, through the cheering ranks of First Corps troops waiting beside the road, and on beyond a stout log barricade under construction for reception of the enemy, due to arrive at any moment. Reaching the picket line, they paused for Tucker to break out the white flag — a soiled handkerchief, tied by one corner to a stick — then continued, half a mile or so, until they saw blue skirmishers approaching. They drew rein, and Marshall rode out front with Tucker, expecting to encounter Grant and his staff. Instead, a single Federal officer appeared, also a lieutenant colonel and also accompanied by an orderly with a flag of truce. He introduced himself as a member of Humphreys' staff, but said that he knew nothing about any meeting, here or elsewhere. All he knew was that he had been given a letter to deliver through the lines, together with instructions to wait for an answer, if one was made. Marshall took the envelope, which was addressed to Lee, and trotted back to hand it to him.

Lee broke it open and read the note Grant had written at Meade's headquarters before sunup, declining the proposed conference on grounds that he had "no authority to treat on the subject of peace," and declaring that hostilities could only be ended "by the South laying down their arms." It was, then, to be "unconditional" surrender; Grant had reverted to type, and Lee had no choice except to repeat his request for a meeting, this time in accordance with whatever preconditions were required. Accordingly, he dictated the message Rawlins would read aloud two hours later, on the far side of the Appomattox. Marshall took it back to the waiting colonel, told him of its contents, and asked that fighting be suspended on this front until it could be delivered and replied to. The Federal turned and rode back through the line of halted skirmishers. While waiting, Lee sent a note to Gordon, through Longstreet, authorizing him to request a similar truce of the enemy moving against him from the opposite direction.

A cease-fire, even a brief one, was likely to prove a good deal easier to ask for than to receive from either direction: especially westward, where Sheridan might have a voice in the matter. And so it was. "Damn them," the cavalryman said angrily on learning that a white flag had come out from Gordon, whose troops by then had fallen back through the town in their rear, "I wish they had held out an hour longer and I would have whipped hell out of them." Suspecting a trick, he wanted no let-up until he bagged the lot. "I've got 'em; I've got 'em like that!" he cried, and he brandished a clenched fist. But Ord outranked and overruled him, and the guns fell silent along the rebel front. Meade, however, reacted much as Sheridan did. Four miles to the east, coming up in the rear of the stalled gray army, he was for pressing the advantage he had worked so hard to gain, flat on his back though he was with chills and fever. "Hey! What?" he exclaimed, emerging from his ambulance when Humphreys' truce-flag colonel delivered Lee's request. "I have no authority to grant such a suspension. General Lee has already refused the terms of General Grant. Advance your skirmishers, Humphreys, and bring up your troops. We will pitch into them at once." He sent the colonel back to inform Lee that Grant had left that part of the field some hours ago; the letter could not reach him in time to stop the attack.

Marshall's reply was that if Meade would read Lee's note to Grant he would surely agree that a truce was in order, but even as the staffer rode back to deliver this suggestion the blue skirmishers resumed their advance. Lee held his ground, determined to do all he could to prevent unnecessary bloodshed, and when another white-flag officer emerged to warn him to withdraw, he responded — over Meade's head, so to speak — with a second message to Grant: "I ask a suspension of hostilities pending the adjustment of the terms of the surrender." Still the skirmishers came on, along and on both sides of the road where Lee and his three companions sat their horses. Only when the bluecoats were within one hundred yards, and he was peremptorily informed that their advance could not be halted, did he turn Traveller's head and ride back up the road, past his own pickets and beyond the now finished barricade. Longstreet was there, bracing his troops for the attack that seemed about to open. Instead — it was close to 11 o'clock by then — the Federal colonel reappeared with a note from Meade, agreeing to an informal one-hour truce and suggesting that Lee might be able to get in touch with Grant more quickly through some other part of the line. Lee accordingly rode on toward the front, which Gordon had established on the near side of the north fork of the Appomattox, and dismounted in a roadside apple orchard to compose his third message of the day to Grant, repeating his request for "an interview, at such time and place as you may designate, to discuss the terms of the surrender of this army."

He was weary from the strain of the long morning. After the messenger set out — this time through Gordon's lines, in accordance with Meade's suggestion — he lay down on a blanket-covered pile of fence rails in the shade of one of the trees. Longstreet presently joined him, and when Lee expressed concern that Grant was stiffening his terms, replied that he did not think so. Well acquainted with the northern commander for years before the war, he believed he would demand nothing that Lee would not demand if the roles were reversed. Lee still had doubts, however, and continued to express them until shortly after noon, when they saw riding toward them, from the direction of Gordon's lines, a well-mounted Federal officer under escort. Presuming that he had been sent by Grant to summon Lee to the meeting requested in one of his earlier notes, Old Peter told his chief: "Unless he offers us honorable terms, come back and let us fight it out." Lee sat up, squaring his shoulders, and Longstreet observed that "the thought of another round seemed to brace him."

Dismounting, the blue-clad emissary saluted and introduced himself as Lieutenant Colonel Orville Babcock of Grant's staff, then presented a note the Union commander had scribbled in his order book half an hour ago, five miles southeast of Appomattox Courthouse, in reply to Lee's first message that morning — the one that Rawlins had finally said would "do." Not mentioning terms or conditions, Grant merely wrote that he would "push forward to the front for the purpose of meeting you. Notice sent to me on this road where you wish the interview to take place will meet me."

Lee only delayed his departure to attend to two comparatively minor matters. One was to have Grant's aide send a dispatch to Meade, directing him to extend the truce until further orders, and the other was to grant a plea from his young adjutant, Walter Taylor, to be spared the heartbreak of attending the surrender. Then he set out, riding alongside Babcock and preceded by Marshall and Tucker, who led the way through Gordon's thin and silent line of battle, down the slope to the creek-sized north branch of the Appomattox. Here he paused to let Traveller drink, then continued his ride toward the courthouse village less than half a mile beyond the stream. Remembering at last that his adversary had left it to him to appoint a meeting place, he sent Marshall ahead, along with the flag-bearing sergeant, to select a proper house for the occasion.

By then it was close to 1 o'clock. Within half an hour Grant arrived from the southeast to find Sheridan waiting for him on the outskirts of town, still eager, as he said later, "to end the business by going in and forcing an absolute surrender by capture." Though this was the first time they had met since the start of the pursuit, a week ago tomorrow, the greetings exchanged were casual.

"How are you, Sheridan?"

"First rate, thank you. How are you?"

"Is Lee up there?"

"Yes, he is in that brick house."

"Very well. Let's go up."

The house Sheridan pointed out belonged to a man named Wilmer McLean, who had agreed to let it be used when Marshall rode in ahead of Lee in search of a place for the meeting with Grant. By the oddest of chances, McLean had owned a farm near Manassas Junction, stretching along the banks of Bull Run, at the time of the first of the two battles fought there. In fact, a shell had come crashing through one of his windows during the opening skirmish, and after that grim experience he had resolved to find a new home for his family, preferably back in the rural southside hill country, "where the sound of battle would never reach them." He found what he wanted at Appomattox Courthouse — a remote hamlet, better than two miles from the railroad and clearly of no military value to either side — only to discover, soon after midday on this fateful Palm Sunday, that the war he had fled was about to end on his doorstep; indeed in his very parlor, where Lee and Marshall waited a long half hour until Babcock, watching beside a window for his chief's arrival, saw him and his staff turn in at the gate, then crossed the room and opened the door into the hall.

Grant entered and went at once to Lee, who rose to meet him. They shook hands, one of middle height, slightly stooped, his hair and beard "nut-brown without a trace of gray," a little awkward and more than a little embarrassed, as he himself later said, mud-spattered trouser legs stuffed into muddy boots, tunic rumpled and dusty, wearing no side arms, not even spurs, and the other tall and patrician-looking, immaculately groomed and clad, with his red sash and ornate sword, fire-gilt buttons and polished brass, silver hair and beard, demonstrating withal, as one observer noted, "that happy blend of dignity and courtesy so difficult to describe." Fifteen years apart in age — the younger commander's forty-third birthday was just over two weeks off — they presented a contrast in more than appearance. Surprised at his own reaction to the encounter, Grant did not know what to make of Lee's at all. "As he was a man of much dignity, with an impassable face," he afterwards declared, "it was impossible to say whether he felt inwardly glad that the end had finally come, or felt sad over the result and was too manly to show it. Whatever his feelings they were entirely concealed from my observation; but my own feelings, which had been quite jubilant on the receipt of his letter, were sad and depressed. I felt like anything rather than rejoicing at the downfall of a foe who had fought so long and valiantly, and had suffered so much for a cause, though that cause was, I believe, one of the worst for which a people ever fought."

Lee resumed his seat, while Marshall remained standing beside him, leaning against the mantel over the unlighted fireplace. Grant took a chair near the middle of the room. Meantime his staff officers were filing in, as one would note, "very much as people enter a sick chamber where they expect to find the patient dangerously ill." Some found seats, but most stood ranged along one wall, looking intently at the old gray fox — the patient — cornered at last and seated across the room from them in his fine clothes. Grant tried to relieve the tension. "I met you once before, General Lee," he said, recalling a time in Mexico when the Virginian had visited his brigade. "I have always remembered your appearance and I think I should have recognized you anywhere." Lee nodded. "Yes, I know I met you on that occasion," he replied, "and I have often thought of it and tried to recollect how you looked. But I have never been able to recall a single feature." If this was a snub Grant did not realize it, or else he let it pass. He went on with his Mexican recollections, warming as he spoke, until Lee, feeling the strain of every dragging moment, broke in at the first pause to say: "I suppose, General Grant, that the object of our present meeting is fully understood. I asked to see you to ascertain upon what terms you would receive the surrender of my army." Grant's response was made with no change of expression, either on his face or in his voice. "The terms I propose are those stated substantially in my letter of yesterday — that is, the officers and men surrendered to be paroled and disqualified from taking up arms again until properly exchanged, and all arms, ammunition, and supplies to be delivered up as captured property." Inwardly, Lee breathed a sigh of vast relief: Longstreet had been right about Grant, and his own worst fears had been groundless. Now, though, it was his turn to mask his emotion, and he did so. "Those are about the conditions I expected would be proposed," he said quietly.

Grant spoke then of a possible "general suspension of hostilities," which he hoped would follow shortly throughout the land, but Lee, anxious to end the present surrender ordeal, once more cut him short, albeit courteously. "I would suggest that you commit to writing the terms you have proposed, so that they may be formally acted upon," he said, and the other replied: "Very well, I will write them out." He called for his order book, bound sheets of yellow flimsy with alternate carbons, and opened it flat on the small round marble-topped table before him. "When I put my pen to the paper," he later declared, "I did not know the first word I should make use of in writing the terms. I only knew what was in my mind, and I wished to express it clearly so that there could be no mistaking it." He succeeded in doing just that. Rapidly and in fewer than two hundred words, he stipulated that officers would "give their individual paroles not to take up arms against the Government of the United States until properly exchanged," that unit commanders would "sign a like parole for the men of their commands," and that "the arms, artillery and private property [were] to be parked and stacked and turned over to the officer appointed by me to receive them." He paused, looking briefly at Lee's dress sword, then added the two last sentences. "This will not embrace the side arms of the officers, nor their private horses or baggage. This done, each officer and man will be allowed to return to their homes, not to be disturbed by the United States authority so long as they observe their paroles and the laws in force where they may reside."

Lee made something of a ritual of examining the document now passed to him. No doubt in an effort to master his nerves, he placed the book on the table before him — small and marble-topped like Grant's, but square — took out his steel-rimmed spectacles, polished them very carefully with a handkerchief, crossed his legs, set the glasses deliberately astride his nose, and at last began to read. Nothing in his expression changed until he reached the closing sentences. Having read them he looked up at Grant and remarked in a warmer tone than he had used before: "This will have a very happy effect on my army." When his adversary said that he would have a fair copy made for signing, "unless you have some suggestions in regard to the form in which I have stated the terms," Lee hesitated before replying. "There is one thing I would like to mention. The cavalrymen and artillerists own their own horses in our army. Its organization in this respect differs from that of the United States. I would like to understand whether these men will be permitted to retain their horses." Grant overlooked what he later called "this implication that we were two countries," but said flatly: "You will find that the terms as written do not allow this." Lee perused again the two sheets of yellow flimsy. He was asking a favor, and he did not enjoy the role of supplicant. "No," he admitted regretfully, "I see the terms do not allow it. That is clear." Then Grant relented. Perhaps recalling his own years of hardscrabble farming near St Louis before the war — or Lincoln's remark at City Point, less than two weeks ago, that all he wanted, once the time came, was "to get the men composing the Confederate armies back to their homes, at work on their farms or in their shops" — he relieved Lee of the humiliation of having to plead for a modification of terms already generous. "Well, the subject is quite new to me," he mused, feeling his way as he spoke. "Of course I did not know that any private soldiers owned their animals, but I think this will be the last battle of the war — I sincerely hope so — and that the surrender of this army will be followed soon by all the others, and I take it that most of the men in the ranks are small farmers, and as the country has been so raided by the two armies it is doubtful whether they will be able to put in a crop to carry themselves and their families through the next winter without the aid of the horses they are now riding, I will arrange it this way; I will not change the terms as now written, but I will instruct the officers I shall appoint to receive the paroles to let all the men who claim to own a horse or mule take the animals home with them to work their little farms." Lee's relief and appreciation were expressed in his response. "This will have the best possible effect upon the men," he said. "It will be very gratifying, and will do much toward conciliating our people."

Grant passed the document to his adjutant for copying, and while this was in progress Lee had Marshall draft a letter of acceptance. In the wait that followed, the northern commander introduced his staff, together with Ord and Sheridan. Shaking hands with those who offered theirs, the Virginian bowed formally to the others, but spoke only to Seth Williams, his former West Point associate, and even then, for all his studied courtesy, could not manage a smile in response to a pleasantry of the old days. The introductions over, he informed Grant that he had a number of Federal prisoners he would like to return to their own lines as soon as it could be arranged, "for I have no provisions for them. I have, indeed, nothing for my own men. They have been living for the last few days principally on parched corn, and are badly in need of both rations and forage." Grant said he wanted his troops back as soon as possible, and would be glad to furnish whatever food the surrendered army needed. "Of about how many men does your present force consist?" Lee scarcely knew; casualties and straggling had been heavy, he admitted. "Suppose I send over 25,000 rations. Do you think that will be a sufficient supply?" "Plenty, plenty; an abundance," Lee replied.

Marshall having completed his draft of the brief acceptance, Lee made a few corrections — "Don't say, 'I have the honor to acknowledge receipt of your letter.' He is here. Just say, 'I accept the terms' " — and while he waited for the finished copy, Grant, whose appearance Marshall would charitably describe as "rather dusty and a little soiled" — in contrast to a quip by one of his own staffers, who remarked that he "looked like a fly on a shoulder of beef" — came over again and apologized for his rumpled clothes and lack of side arms. His baggage had gone astray, he said, "and I thought you would rather receive me as I was than be detained." Lee replied that he was much obliged; "I am very glad you did it that way." He signed the completed fair copy of his letter of acceptance, which Marshall then sealed and handed to Grant's adjutant, receiving in turn the signed and sealed terms of surrender. Lee broke the envelope open and read them through for the third time, but Grant did not bother with reading the letter to him just yet, later explaining that Lee's spoken acceptance of the terms was surety enough for him, without the formality of words set down on paper.

It was close to 4 o'clock by now, and all that protocol required had been performed. After nearly three hours in the McLean parlor — half of one spent waiting and the rest in what could scarcely be called negotiation, since his adversary had freely given all he asked and more than he had hoped for: including immunity, down the years, from prosecution on any charge whatever in connection with the war — Lee was free to go. He rose, shook hands with Grant again, bowed to the others, and passed from the room, followed by Marshall. Out on the porch, several blue-clad officers came to attention and saluted as he emerged. He put on his hat to return their salute, then crossed to the head of the steps leading down to the yard. There he drew on his gauntlets, distractedly striking the fist of one hand three times into the palm of the other as he looked out across the valley to where the men of his army were waiting to learn that they had been surrendered. "Orderly! Orderly!" he called hoarsely, not seeing Tucker close by with Traveller, whose bit had been slipped to let him graze. "Here, General, here," Tucker replied, and Lee came down the steps to stand by the horse's head while he was being bridled. A cavalry major, watching from the porch, noted that "as the orderly was buckling the throat latch, the general reached up and drew the forelock out from under the brow band, parted and smoothed it, and then gently patted the gray charger's forehead in an absent-minded way, as one who loves horses, but whose thoughts are far away, might all unwittingly do." Mounted, Lee waited for Marshall and Tucker, then started at a walk across the yard. Grant had come out of the house and down the steps by then, also on his way to the gate where his own horse was tethered. Stopping, he removed his hat in salute, as did the staff men with him. Lee raised his own hat briefly in return, and passed out through the gate and up the road. Presently, northward beyond the dwindled, tree-lined Appomattox, listeners on the porch heard cheers, and then a poignant silence.

Indoors behind them, as they watched him go and heard the choked-off yells subside beyond the tree line, scavengers were at work. "Relic-hunters charged down upon the manor house," a staff colonel would recall, "and began to bargain for the numerous pieces of furniture." Ord paid forty dollars for Lee's table, and Sheridan gave half as much for Grant's — though 'bargain' and 'paid' were scarcely words that applied to either transaction; Wilmer McLean, not wanting to sell his household possessions, threw the money on the floor or had it flung there when he declined to accept it. No matter; the rest of the furniture was quickly snapped up, beginning with the chairs the two commanders had sat in. Sheridan's brother Michael, a captain on his staff, made off with a stone inkstand, and an enterprising brigadier secured two brass candlesticks for ten dollars. Once these and other prize items were gone, mainly to persons whose rank had placed them early on the scene, what remained was up for grabs, and something close to pandemonium set in. "Cane-bottomed chairs were ruthlessly cut to pieces," a reporter was to write, "the cane splits broken into pieces a few inches long and parceled out among those who swarmed around. Haircloth upholstery, cut from chairs and sofas, was also cut into strips and patches and carried away." McLean was left surveying a Tacitean wilderness his enemies called peace. They made off with their spoils, exulting as they went, and a few years later — with still more rank, and again with the advantage of working close to the man in charge — some of them would try their hand at doing much the same thing to the country at large, with considerable success.

Grant knew nothing of this, of course, just as he would know little or nothing of their later endeavors along that line. He rode on toward his headquarters tent, which had been found at last, along with his baggage, and pitched nearby. He had not gone far before someone asked if he did not consider the news of Lee's surrender worth passing on to the War Department. Reining his horse in, he dismounted and sat on a large stone by the roadside to compose the telegram Lincoln would receive that night. By the time he remounted to ride on, salutes were beginning to roar from Union batteries roundabout, and he sent word to have them stopped, not only because he feared the warlike racket might cause trouble between the victors and the vanquished, both of them still with weapons in their hands, but also because he considered it unfitting. "The war is over," he told his staff. "The rebels are our countrymen again."

Lee by then was back in the apple orchard he had left four hours ago. The yells that greeted him as he reëntered Gordon's lines had come in part by force of custom; the troops, for all their cumulative numbness from hunger, weariness, and stress, cheered him as they had always done when he moved among them. Moreover, despite the grinding week-long retreat and its heavy losses, more from straggling than in combat — despite last night's red western glow of enemy campfires and this morning's breakout failure; despite the coming and going of couriers, blue and gray, and his own outward passage through their line of battle, accoutered for something more solemn even than church on this Palm Sunday — many of them were still not ready to believe the end had come. One look at his face as he drew near, however, confirmed what they had been unwilling to accept. They broke ranks and crowded round him. "General, are we surrendered? Are we surrendered?" they began asking.

Hemmed in, Lee removed his hat and spoke from horseback to a blurred expanse of upturned faces. "Men, we have fought the war together, and I have done the best I could for you. You will all be paroled and go to your homes until exchanged." Tears filled his eyes as he tried to say more; he could only manage an inaudible "Goodbye." Their first stunned reaction was disbelief. "General, we'll fight 'em yet," they told him. "Say the word and we'll go in and fight 'em yet." Then it came home to them, and though most responded with silence, one man threw his rifle down and cried in a loud voice: "Blow, Gabriel, blow! My God, let him blow, I am ready to die!"

Grief brought a sort of mass relaxation that let Traveller proceed, and as he moved through the press of soldiers, bearing the gray commander on his back, they reached out to touch both horse and rider, withers and knees, flanks and thighs, in expression of their affection. "I love you just as well as ever, General Lee!" a ragged veteran shouted, arms held wide above the crowd. At the orchard he drew rein, dismounted, and walked through the trees to one well back from the road, and there began pacing back and forth beneath its just-fledged branches, too restless to sit down on this morning's pile of fence rails. "He seemed to be in one of his savage moods," a headquarters engineer declared, "and when these moods were on him it was safer to keep out of his way." His own people knew to let him alone, but Federal officers kept arriving, "mostly in groups of four or five and some of high rank. It was evident that they came from curiosity, or to see General Lee as friends in the old army." He had small use for any of them just now though, whether they were past acquaintances or strangers. Coming up to be presented, they removed their hats out of deference and politeness, but he did not respond in kind, and sometimes did not even touch his hatbrim in return to their salutes. When he saw one of his staff approach with another group of such visitors, "he would halt in his pacing, stand at attention, and glare at them with a look which few men but he could assume." Finally, near sundown, when the promised rations began arriving from the Union lines, he remounted and rode back to a less exposed position, under the white oak tree on the ridge where he had slept the night before.

This second ride was through the ranks of the First Corps, and Longstreet saw him coming. "The road was packed by standing troops as he approached," Old Peter was to write, "the men with hats off, heads and hearts bowed down. As he passed they raised their heads and looked at him with swimming eyes. Those who could find voice said goodbye; those who could not speak, and were near, passed their hands gently over the sides of Traveller." From point to point there were bursts of cheers, which the dark-maned gray acknowledged by arching his neck and tossing his head, but Longstreet observed that Lee had only "sufficient control to fix his eyes on a line between the ears of Traveller and look neither to the right nor left." He too had his hat off, and tears ran down his cheeks into his beard. Back on the white oak ridge he stood for a time in front of his tent — "Let me get in. Let me bid him farewell," the men were crying as they thronged forward — then went inside, too choked for speech. Later he came out and sat by the fire with his staff. He told Marshall to prepare an order, a farewell to the army, but he had little heart for talk and turned in early, weary from the strain of perhaps the longest and no doubt the hardest day he had ever known.

A cold rain fell next morning. He kept mainly to his tent until shortly after 9 o'clock, when word came that Grant, on the way to see him, had been stopped by pickets who had been put out yesterday to prevent the troops of the two armies from engaging in possible squabbles. Embarrassed, Lee set out at a gallop and found his distinguished visitor waiting imperturbably on a little knoll beside the road, just south of the north branch of the Appomattox. He lifted his hat in greeting, as did the other; then they shook hands, sitting their horses in the rain while their aides retired beyond earshot, and began to talk. Grant had come to ask Lee to use his influence — "an influence that was supreme," he later said — to help bring the war to an early end by advising his subordinates, in command of the other armies of the South, to lay down their arms under the terms he himself had received the day before. Lee replied, in effect, that he agreed that further resistance was useless, but that he felt obliged as a soldier to leave all such matters to his Commander in Chief; in any case, he could do nothing without conferring with him beforehand. Grant did not persist — "I knew there was no use to urge him to do anything against his ideas of what was right" — but he deeply regretted the refusal, he declared long afterward, because "I saw that the Confederacy had gone a long way beyond the reach of President Davis, and that there was nothing that could be done except what Lee could do to benefit the Southern people. I was anxious to get them home and have our armies go to their homes and fields."

He was also anxious to get himself to Burkeville, where, thanks to the hard-working IX Corps, he could take the cars for City Point and get aboard a fast packet for Washington. By now the war was costing four million dollars a day, and he wanted to get back to the capital and start cutting down on expenses. So the two parted, Grant to set out for Burkeville and Lee to return to his own lines. Within them, the latter encountered Meade, who had recovered from his indisposition and ridden over to see him. Lee at first did not recognize his old friend. Then he did, but with something of a shock. "What are you doing with all that gray in your beard?" he asked, and his Gettysburg opponent replied genially: "You have to answer for most of it." As they rode together toward headquarters, the soldiers camped along the road began to cheer, and Meade, not wanting to misrepresent himself, told his color bearer, who had the flag rolled up: "Unfurl that flag." The bearer did, and drew a sharp retort. "Damn your old rag!" a butternut veteran called from beside the road. "We are cheering General Lee."

Back in his tent Lee talked for a time with Meade, then turned to the writing of his report on the campaign that now was over. "It is with pain that I announce to Your Excellency the surrender of the Army of Northern Virginia," the document began. Walter Taylor did most of the work on this, as he had on all the others, but Lee also conferred with Charles Marshall, whom he had instructed to draw up an order bidding the troops farewell. Marshall, a former Baltimore lawyer and grandnephew of the illustrious Chief Justice, had delayed preparing the address — because all the coming and going around headquarters had left him no time, he said, but also because of a certain reluctance, a feeling of inadequacy for the task. "What can I say to those people?" he asked a friend this morning, still avoiding getting down to putting pen to paper. Lee settled this by ordering the colonel to get into his ambulance, parked nearby with a guard on duty to fend off intruders, and stay there until he finished the composition. Marshall, his writer's block effectively broken, soon emerged with a penciled draft. Lee looked it over and made a few changes, including the deletion of a paragraph he thought might "tend to keep alive the feeling existing between the North and South"; after which the Marylander returned to the ambulance, wrote out the final version of the order, and turned it over to a clerk for making inked copies which Lee then signed for distribution to the corps commanders and ranking members of his staff.

Having signed his parole he might have left then, as Grant had done by noon on this rainy Monday; yet he did not. The formal surrender ceremony was set for Wednesday — the required turning over of all "arms, artillery and public property," in accordance with the terms accepted — and he stayed on, not to take an active role as a participant, but simply to be on hand, if not in view, when his men faced the sad ritual of laying down their shot-torn flags and weapons. He continued to keep to his tent, however, through most of the waiting time, while all around him, despite the pickets both sides had posted to discourage fraternization, blue-clad visitors of all ranks drifted through the camps for a look at their one-time enemies. For the most part they were received without animosity; "Success had made them good-natured," one grayback uncharitably observed. A Federal colonel noted that the Confederates "behaved with more courtesy than cordiality," and it was true. "Affiliation was out of the question; we were content with civility," one explained. Union troops, on the other hand, were friendly and outgoing; "in fact almost oppressively so," a butternut declared. "We've been fighting one another for four years. Give me a Confederate five-dollar bill to remember you by," a bluecoat said, and his hearers found nothing offensive in his manner. Sometimes, though, a discordant note would be struck and would bring on a fiery answer — as when a Federal major, seeking a souvenir to take home, asked a Confederate staff captain for the white towel he had carried as a flag of truce on Sunday. "I'll see you in hell first!" the angered staffer replied. "It is humiliating enough to have had to carry it and exhibit it; I'm not going to let you preserve it as a monument of our defeat." Similarly, when a visiting sergeant tried to open a friendly discussion by remarking: "Well, Johnny, I guess you fellows will go home now to stay," he found that he had touched a nerve. The rebel was in no mood to be gloated over. "You *guess*, do you?" he said hotly. "Maybe we are. But don't be giving us any of your impudence. If you do, we'll come back and lick you again."

Much of Tuesday, with rain still murmurous on the canvas overhead, Lee spent working on his last report. He finished and signed it next morning, April 12, while his veterans, in Longstreet's words, "marched to the field in front of Appomattox Courthouse, and by divisions and parts of divisions deployed into line, stacked their arms, folded their colors, and walked empty-handed to find their distant, blighted homes." The weather having faired, they made as brave a show as their rags and sadness would permit; "worn, bright-eyed men," a

Federal brigadier would call them. They seemed to him "purged of the mortal, as if knowing pain or joy no more," and he asked himself as he watched them pass before him "in proud humiliation... thin, worn, and famished, but erect, and with eyes looking level into ours... Was not such manhood to be welcomed back into a Union so tested and assured?" They had been whipped about as thoroughly as any American force had ever been or ever would be, short of annihilation, but it was part of their particular pride that they would never admit it, even to themselves. "Goodbye, General; God bless you," a ragged private told his brigadier commander over a parting handshake at the close of the surrender ceremony. "We'll go home, make three more crops, and try them again."

They left in groups, dispersing by routes as varied as their destinations, and one of the smallest groups was Lee's. He rode with Taylor and Marshall northeast into Buckingham County, bound for Richmond, and stopped for the night, some twenty miles out, in a strip of woods beside the road. To his surprise he found Longstreet there before him, likewise headed for a reunion with his family. Once more they shared a campsite, then next morning diverged to meet no more. The burly Georgian was assailed by mixed emotions, partly as a result of having encountered his friend Grant on Monday, shortly before the blue commander's departure for Burkeville. "Pete, let's have another game of brag to recall the old days," Grant had said, and though there was no time for cards he gave him a cigar, which Longstreet said "was gratefully received." Moved by the reunion, he later wondered: "Why do men fight who were born to be brothers?" and remarked, not without bitterness, that the next time he fought he would be sure it was necessary.

But that was by no means a reaction characteristic of the veterans now trudging the roads in all directions from the scene of their surrender. They were content with "the satisfaction that proceeds from the consciousness of duty faithfully performed." The words were part of Lee's final behest they took with them from the farewell issued two days ago, near Appomattox Courthouse.

Headquarters Army of N. Va.
April 10, 1865

General Orders
No. 9

After four years of arduous service marked by unsurpassed courage and fortitude, the Army of Northern Virginia has been compelled to yield to overwhelming numbers and resources.

I need not tell the brave survivors of so many hard fought battles, who have remained steadfast to the last, that I have consented to this result from no distrust of them. But feeling that valor and devotion could accomplish nothing that could compensate for the loss that must have attended the continuance of the contest, I determined to avoid the useless sacrifice of those whose past services have endeared them to their countrymen.

By the terms of the agreement, officers and men can return to their homes and remain until exchanged. You will take with you the satisfaction that proceeds from the consciousness of duty faithfully performed, and I earnestly pray that a merciful God will extend to you His blessing and protection.

With an unceasing admiration of your constancy and devotion to your Country, and a grateful remembrance of your kind and generous consideration for myself, I bid you all an affectionate farewell.

R. E. Lee
General.

In addition to the copies made by Marshall's clerk for normal distribution, others were transcribed and taken to the general for his signature, and these remained for those who had them the possession they cherished most. One such was Henry Perry, the young infantry captain who had refused a drink from Seth Williams' silver flask three nights before, near Cumberland Church. Later he told how he got it and how he felt, then and down the years, about the man who signed it. "I sat down and copied it on a piece of Confederate paper," he recalled, "using a drumhead for a desk, the best I could do. I carried this copy to General Lee, and asked him to sign it for me. He signed it and I have it now. It is the best authority, along with my parole, that I can produce why after that day I no longer raised a soldier's hand for the South. There were tears in his eyes when he signed it for me, and when I turned to walk away there were tears in my own eyes. He was in all respects the greatest man who ever lived, and as a humble officer of the South, I thank heaven I had the honor of following him."

CHAPTER
* 8 *

Lucifer in Starlight

★ ✘ ☆

GUNS BOOMED THE NEWS OF APPOMATTOX as dawn broke over Washington next morning, April 10, one week after a similar uproar hailed the fall of Richmond. If the reaction now was less hysterical, if many loyal citizens were content to remain abed, counting the five hundred separate thuds of the salute — as compared to nine hundred the Monday before — that was not only because of the earlier drain on their emotions, it was also because of rain drumming hard on their bedroom windows and mud slathered more than shoetop-deep outside. Still, a carousing journalist observed, the streets were soon "alive with people singing and cheering, carrying flags and saluting everybody, hungering and thirsting for speeches." They especially wanted a speech from Lincoln, whose presence in town, after his return from down the coast last evening, was in contrast to his absence during the previous celebration. At the Treasury Department, for example, when the clerks were told they had been given another holiday, the same reporter noted that they "assembled in the great corridor of their building and sang 'Old Hundredth' with thrilling, even tear-compelling effect," then trooped across the grounds to the White House, where, still in excellent voice, they serenaded the President with the national anthem.

He was at breakfast and did not appear, but a night's sleep had done nothing to diminish the excitement he felt on reading Grant's wire at bedtime. "Let Master Tad have a Navy sword," he directed in a note to Welles, and added in another to the Secretary of War (omitting the question mark as superfluous on this day of celebration): "Tad wants some flags. Can he be accommodated." Stanton evidently complied in short order, for when a procession arrived from the Navy Yard a couple of hours later, dragging six boat howitzers which were fired as they rolled up Pennsylvania Avenue, the boy stood at a second-story window and flaunted a captured rebel flag, to the wild applause of a crowd that quickly swelled to about three thousand. Presently Lincoln himself appeared at the window, and the yells redoubled. "Speech! Speech!" men cried from the lawn below. But he put them off. He would speak tonight, or more likely tomorrow, "and I shall have nothing to say if you dribble it all out of me before." As the laughter subsided he took up a notion that had struck him. "I see you have a band of music with you," he said, and when a voice called up: "We have two or three!" he proposed closing the interview by having the musicians play "a particular tune which I will name.... I have always thought 'Dixie' one of the best tunes I ever heard. Our adversaries over the way attempted to appropriate it, but I insisted yesterday that we fairly captured it. I presented the question to the Attorney General and he gave it as his legal opinion that it is now our lawful prize. I now request the band to favor me with its performance."

The band did, to roars of approval from the crowd, then followed the irreverent rebel anthem with a lively rendition of "Yankee Doodle," after which Lincoln called for "three good hearty cheers for General Grant and all under his command." These given, he requested "three more cheers for our gallant navy," and when they were over he retired, as did the rollicking crowd. Near sundown, a third crew of celebrants turned up, to be similarly put off on grounds that he had to be careful what he said at times like this. "Everything I say, you know, goes into print. If I make a mistake it doesn't merely affect me nor you, but the country. I therefore ought at least to try not to make mistakes. If, then, a general demonstration be made tomorrow evening, and it is agreeable, I will endeavor to say something and not make a mistake without at least trying carefully to avoid it."

Next night he was back, as promised, and they were there to hear him in their thousands, packed shoulder to shoulder on the White House lawn and looking up at the same window. Off in the drizzly distance, Arlington House — R. E. Lee's former home, long since commandeered by the government he had defied — glittered on its hillside beyond the Potomac, illuminated tonight along with all the other public buildings, while nearer at hand, gilded with light from torches and flares, the Capitol dome seemed to float like a captive balloon in a gauzy mist that verged on rain. To one observer yesterday, seeing him for the first time, Lincoln "appeared somewhat younger and more off-hand and vigorous than I should have expected. His gestures and countenance had something of the harmless satisfaction of a young politician at a ratification meeting after his first election to the Legislature. He was happy, and glad to see others happy." Tonight, though, he was different. Appearing after Tad had once more warmed the crowd by flourishing the Confederate banner, he seemed grave and thoughtful, and he had with him, by way of assuring that he would "not make a mistake without at least trying carefully to avoid it," a rolled-up manuscript he had spent most of the day preparing. What he had in mind to deliver tonight was not so much a speech as it was a closely written document, a state paper dealing less with the past, or even the present, than with the future; less with victory than with the problems victory brought. The crowd below did not know this yet, however, and Noah Brooks — a young newsman who was slated to replace one of his private secretaries — saw "something terrible in the enthusiasm with which the beloved Chief Magistrate was received. Cheers upon cheers, wave after wave of applause rolled up, the President patiently standing quiet until it was over."

"Fellow Citizens," he said at last. Holding a candle in his left hand to light the papers in his right, he waited for new cheers to subside, and then continued. "We are met this evening not in sorrow but in gladness of heart. The evacuation of Petersburg and Richmond, and the surrender of the principal insurgent army, give hope of a righteous and speedy peace whose joyous expression cannot be restrained." Cheered again, he sought relief from the difficulty of managing both the candle and his manuscript by signaling to Brooks, who stood behind one of the window drapes beside him, with what the journalist called "a comical motion of his left foot and elbow, which I construed to mean that I should hold his candle for him." With both hands free to grip the sheaf of papers, and Brooks extending the light from behind the curtain, he went on with his speech, dropping each read page as he began the next. Unseen by the crowd, Tad scrambled about on the balcony floor to catch the sheets as his father let them flutter down. "Another, another," he kept saying impatiently all through the reading, heard plainly because of a hush that soon descended on the celebrants on the lawn below.

Referred to afterwards by Brooks as "a silent, intent, and perhaps surprised multitude," they were in fact both silent and surprised, but they were more confused than they were intent. Until Lincoln began speaking they had not supposed tonight was any occasion for mentioning sadness, even to deny it, and as he continued along other lines, equally unexpected at a victory celebration, their confusion and discomfort grew. After this brief introduction, scarcely fitting in itself, he spoke not of triumphs, but rather of the problems that loomed with peace; in particular one problem. "By these recent successes," he read from the second of the sheets that fell fluttering to his feet, "the re-inauguration of the national authority — reconstruction — which has had a large share of thought from the first, is pressed much more closely upon our attention. It is fraught with great difficulty. Unlike the case of a war between independent nations, there is no authorized organ for us to treat with — no one man has authority to give up the rebellion for any other man. We simply must begin with, and mold from, disorganized and discordant elements. Nor is it a small additional embarrassment that we, the loyal people, differ among ourselves as to the mode, manner, and means of reconstruction."

This then was his subject — "the mode, manner, and means of reconstruction" — and he stayed with it through Tad's retrieval of the last dropped sheet, addressing himself less to his listeners, it seemed, than to the knotty problem itself, and in language that was correspondingly knotty. For example, in dealing with the claim that secession, while plainly illegal, had in fact removed from the Union certain states which now would have to comply with some hard-line requirements before they could be granted readmission, he pronounced it "a merely pernicious abstraction," likely to "have no effect other than the mischievous one of dividing our friends" left and right of the stormy center. "We all agree that the seceded states, so called, are out of their proper practical relation with the Union, and that the sole object of the government, civil and military, in regard to those states, is to again get them into that proper practical relation. I believe it is not only possible, but in fact easier, to do this without deciding or even considering whether these states have even been out of the Union, than with it. Finding themselves safely at home, it would be utterly immaterial whether they had ever been abroad. Let us all join in doing the acts necessary to restoring the proper practical relations between these states and the Union, and each forever after innocently indulge his own opinion whether, in doing the acts, he brought the states from without into the Union, or only gave them proper assistance, they never having been out of it."

In regard to the new state government in Louisiana, which had the support of only ten percent of the electorate, he acknowledged the validity of criticism that it was scantly based and did not give the franchise to the Negro. All the same, though he himself wished its constituency "contained fifty, thirty, or even twenty thousand [voters] instead of only twelve thousand, as it does," and though he preferred to have the ballot extended to include the blacks — at least "the very intelligent" and "those who serve our cause as soldiers" — he did not believe these shortcomings invalidated the present arrangement, which in any case was better than no arrangement at all. "Concede that the new government of Louisiana is only to what it should be as the egg is to the fowl, we shall sooner have the fowl by hatching the egg than by smashing it." For one thing, the state legislature had already voted to ratify the 13th Amendment, and the sooner its authority was recognized by Congress, the sooner all men would be free throughout the land. He had thought long and hard about the problem, as well as about various proposals for its solution, "and yet so great peculiarities pertain to each state, and such important and sudden changes occur in the same state, and withal, so new and unprecedented is the whole case, that no exclusive and inflexible plan can safely be prescribed as to details and collaterals.... In the present 'situation,' as the phrase goes, it may be my duty to make some new announcement to the people of the South. I am considering, and shall not fail to act when satisfied that action will be proper."

That was the end, and he let it hang there, downbeat, enigmatic, inconclusive, as perfunctory and uncertain, even in its peroration, as the applause that followed when his listeners finally understood that the speech — if that was what it had been — was over. Tad gathered up the last sheet of manuscript, and as Lincoln stepped back into the room he said to Brooks, still holding the candle out from behind the window drape: "That was a pretty fair speech, I think, but you threw some light on it." Down on the lawn, the misty drizzle had turned to rain while he spoke, and the crowd began to disperse, their spirits nearly as dampened as their clothes. Some drifted off to bars in search of revival. Others walked over to Franklin Square to serenade Stanton, who might do better by them.

Not that there were no repercussions. There were, and they came fast — mostly from disaffected radicals who contended that secession had been a form of suicide from which no state could be resurrected except on conditions imposed by them at the end of the struggle now drawing rapidly to a close. Differing from Lincoln in this, or at any rate on what those terms should be, they believed they saw clearly enough what he was up to. Congress would not meet again until December, and he had it in mind to unite the people behind him, between now and then, and thus confront his congressional opponents with an overwhelming majority of voters whom he would attract to his lenient views by a series of public appeals, such as the one tonight from the high White House window or last month's inaugural, adorned with oratorical phrases as empty as they were vague. "Malice toward none" had no meaning for them, as here applied, and "charity for all" had even less; for where was the profit in winning a war if then you lost the peace? They asked that with a special urgency now that they had begun to suspect the Administration of planning to neglect the Negro, who was in fact what this war had been about from start to finish. Lincoln's reference tonight to a possible limited extension of the franchise to include those who were "very intelligent" only served to increase their apprehension that the cause of the blacks was about to be abandoned, possibly in exchange for the support of certain reactionary elements in the reunited country — not excluding former Confederates — in putting together a new and powerful coalition of moderates, unbeatable at the polls for decades to come. One among those perturbed was Chase, who had written this day to his former chief of his fears in regard to that neglect. The most acceptable solution, he said, was "the reorganization of state governments under constitutions securing suffrage to all citizens.... This way is recommended by its simplicity, facility, and, above all, justice," the Chief Justice wrote. "It will be hereafter counted equally a crime and a folly if the colored loyalists of the rebel states shall be left to the control of restored rebels, not likely in that case to be either wise or just, until taught both wisdom and justice by new calamities."

Lincoln found the letter on his desk when he came into the office next morning, and Chase followed it up with another, that same Wednesday, midway of Holy Week, suggesting an interview "to have the whole subject talked over." Others had the same notion; Charles Sumner, for example. He had not heard the speech last night, but his secretary reported that it was "not in keeping with what was in men's minds. The people had gathered, from an instructive impulse, to rejoice over a great and final victory, and they listened with respect, but with no expressions of enthusiasm, except that the quaint simile of 'the egg' drew applause. The more serious among them felt that the President's utterances on the subject were untimely, and that his insistence at such an hour on his favorite plan was not the harbinger of peace among the loyal supporters of the government." The Massachusetts senator felt this, too, and regretted it, his secretary noted; "for he saw at hand another painful controversy with a President whom he respected, on a question where he felt it his duty to stand firm." Already his mail was filled with urgings that he do just that. "Magnanimity is a great word with the disloyal who think to tickle the President's ear with it," a prominent New Yorker wrote. "Magnanimity is one thing. Weakness is another. I know you are near the throne, and you must guard its honor." A Boston constituent knew where to fix the blame: on Lincoln, whose reconstruction policy was "wicked and blasphemous" in its betrayal of the cause of freedom by his failure to take the obvious next step after emancipation. "No power but God ever has or could have forced him up to the work he has been instrumental of, and now we see the dregs of his backwardness."

Mainly these were old-line abolitionists, men with a great capacity for wrath. Ben Wade, for one, expressed the hope that such neglect would goad the southern blacks to insurrection. "If they could contrive to slay one half of their oppressors," he asserted, "the other half would hold them in the highest regard, and no doubt treat them with justice." But even this was mild compared to the reaction that followed disclosure that Lincoln had authorized John A. Campbell to reassemble the Virginia legislature, composed in part of the very men who had withdrawn the Old Dominion from the Union in the first place. As it happened, the Joint Committee on the Conduct of the War was down at Richmond now, aboard the steamer *Baltimore*, and one of its members went ashore this morning to get the daily papers. He came back, much excited, with a copy of the Richmond *Whig*, which carried an Address to the People of Virginia by some of the legislators then about to assemble. Moreover, Weitzel had indorsed it, and Wade went into a frenzy at this evidence of official sanction for the outrage. Fuming, he declared — "in substance, if not in exact words," a companion afterwards testified — "that there had been much talk of the assassination of Lincoln; that if he authorized the approval of that paper ... by God, the sooner he was assassinated the better!" Others felt as strongly about this development, which seemed to them to undo all they had worked for all these years. Zachariah Chandler, according to the same report, "was also exceedingly harsh in his remarks," and none of the other members took offense at the denunciations.

In Washington, the Secretary of War was apparently the first to get the news. He went at once to Lincoln, then to Sumner, who wrote Chase: "I find Stanton much excited. He had a full and candid talk with the President last eve, and insisted that the proposed meeting at Richmond should be forbidden. He thinks we are in a crisis more trying than any before, with the chance of losing the fruits of our victory. He asks if it was not Grant who surrendered to Lee, instead of Lee to Grant. He is sure that Richmond is beginning to govern Washington."

But Lincoln by then had revoked his authorization for the Virginians to assemble. At a cabinet meeting the day before, he had found Stanton and Speed vehement in their opposition, and none of the rest in favor of creating a situation in which, as Welles pointed out, "the so-called legislature would be likely to propose terms which might seem reasonable, but which we could not accept." To these were added the protests of various other advisers, by no means all of them die-hard radicals. Lincoln considered the matter overnight — aside, that is, from the time he spent delivering his speech from the balconied window — and though, as he said, he rather fancied the notion of having the secessionists "come together and undo their own work," at 9 o'clock Wednesday morning he telegraphed Weitzel a question and a suggestion: "Is there any sign of the rebel legislature coming together on the basis of my letter to you? If there is any sign, inform me of what it is; if there is no such sign you may as [well] withdraw the offer."

Although it was true he had no wish just now for a knockdown drag-out fight with either wing of his party, his decision to revoke what he called his 'offer' was in fact less political than it was practical in nature. The conditions under which it had been extended no longer obtained; the gains sought in exchange had since been won. His purpose in approving Campbell's proposal, just under a week ago, had been to encourage Virginia's legislators, in return for certain "remissions" on his part, to withdraw her troops from the rebel armies and the state itself from the Confederacy. Grant had accomplished the first of these objectives on Palm Sunday — the formal surrender ceremony was getting under way at Appomattox Courthouse even as Lincoln's telegram went over the wire to Weitzel — and the second scarcely mattered, since there was no longer any sizeable body of armed graybacks within the borders of the Old Dominion. So much for that. As for the problem of keeping or breaking his promise to Campbell, that was merely personal; which was only another way of saying it didn't count. "Bad promises are better broken than kept," he had said in his speech the night before, with reference to assurances he had given those who set up the provisional Louisiana government. "I shall treat this as a bad promise, and break it, whenever I shall be convinced that keeping it is adverse to the public interest." And so it was in this case; he simply labeled the promise 'bad' — meaning profitless — and broke it.

When he heard from Weitzel that afternoon that "passports have gone out for the legislators, and it is common talk that they will come together," Lincoln wired back a definite order that their permission to assemble be revoked. He prefaced this, however, with some lawyerly explication of the events leading up to his decision, which he said was based on statements made by Campbell in a letter informing certain of the prospective legislators what their task would be in Richmond. He had talked the matter over with the President on two occasions, the Alabama jurist declared, and both conversations "had relation to the establishment of a government for Virginia, the requirement of oaths of allegiance from the citizens, and the terms of settlement with the United States." Lincoln flatly denied this in his sundown wire to Weitzel. "[Judge Campbell] assumes, as appears to me, that I have called the insurgent legislature of Virginia together, as the rightful legislature of the state, to settle all differences with the United States. I have done no such thing. I spoke of them not as a legislature, but as 'the gentlemen who have *acted* as the Legislature of Virginia in support of the rebellion.' I did this on purpose to exclude the assumption that I was recognizing them as a rightful body. I dealt with them as men having power *de facto* to do a specific thing; to wit, 'to withdraw the Virginia troops and other support from resistance to the general government.' . . . I meant this and no more. Inasmuch however as Judge Campbell misconstrues this, and is still pressing for an armistice, contrary to the explicit statement of the paper I gave him, and particularly as Gen. Grant has since captured the Virginia troops, so that giving a consideration for their withdrawal is no longer applicable, let my letter to you and the paper to Judge Campbell both be withdrawn, or countermanded, and he be notified of it. Do not allow them to assemble; but if any have come, allow them safe-return to their homes."

Word of this revocation spread rapidly over Washington and out across the land, to the high delight of those who lately had seethed with indignation: particularly the hard-war hard-peace Jacobins, who saw in the action near certain proof that, in a crunch, the President would always come over to their side of the question — provided, of course, the pressure was kept on him: which it would be. James Speed, who had no sooner been confirmed as Attorney General than he went over to the radicals all-out, presently wrote to Chase that Lincoln "never seemed so near our views" as he did now, with Holy Week drawing rapidly toward a close.

Davis by then was in Greensboro, North Carolina, just under fifty miles south of the Virginia line. Once more "a government on wheels," he and his cabinet had left Danville late Monday night in a driving rainstorm that only added to the depression and confusion brought on by the arrival of simultaneous reports, no less alarming for being unofficial and somewhat vague, that Lee had surrendered to Grant the day before, near Appomattox Courthouse, and that a heavy column of enemy cavalry was approaching from the west. Nothing more was heard for a time about the extent of Lee's removal from the war — that is, whether all or only part of his army had been surrendered — but the other report was soon confirmed by word that a detachment from the column of blue troopers, some 4000 strong under Stoneman, had burned the Dan River bridge a few hours after the fugitive President's train rattled across it and on into Carolina. Informed of his narrow escape from capture, Davis managed a smile of relief. "A miss is as good as a mile," he remarked, and his smile broadened.

Such pleasure as he took from this was soon dispelled by the coolness of his reception when the train crept into Greensboro next morning. Though news of his coming had been wired ahead, no welcoming group of citizens turned out to greet him or even acknowledge his presence, which made their town the Confederacy's third capital in ten days. For the most part, like many in this Piedmont region of the Old North State, they had never been enthusiastic about the war or its goals, and their pro-Union feeling had been considerably strengthened by reports, just in, that Stoneman's raiders were headed in their direction and that Sherman had begun his advance from Goldsboro the day before, first on Raleigh, with Johnston known to be falling back, and then on them. Fearing reprisal for any courtesy offered Davis and his party, they extended none — except to the wealthy and ailing Trenholm; he and Mrs Trenholm were taken in by a banker who, it was said, hoped to persuade the Secretary to exchange some gold from the treasure train for his Confederate bonds. Davis himself would have had no place to lay his head if an aide, John T. Wood — former skipper of the *Tallahassee* and the President's first wife's nephew — had not had his family refugeeing in half of a modest Greensboro house. Despite protests from the landlord, who feared that his property would go up in flames as soon as Stoneman or Sherman appeared, Wood's wife had prepared a small upstairs bedroom for the Chief Executive. While Trenholm was being made comfortable in the banker's mansion across town, the rest of the cabinet adapted themselves as best they could to living in the dilapidated coaches, which had been shunted onto a siding near the depot.

Beauregard and his staff were similarly lodged in three boxcars parked nearby. He had arrived the previous night, en route to Danville in response to a summons from the Commander in Chief, and now he crossed the tracks to report aboard the presidential coach. Davis greeted him cordially, eager for news of the situation around Raleigh. Dismayed, the Creole told of Johnston's hurried evacuation of Smithfield, under pressure from Sherman, and of his present withdrawal toward the state capital, which he did not plan to defend against a force three times his size. In short, Beauregard said, the situation was hopeless. Davis disagreed. Lee's surrender had not been confirmed; some portion of his army might have escaped and could soon be combined with Johnston's, as originally intended. The struggle would continue, whatever the odds, even if it had to be done on the far side of the Mississippi. Beauregard was amazed, but by no means converted from his gloom, when Davis got off a wire instructing Johnston to come at once to Greensboro for a strategy conference. "The important question first to be solved is what point of concentration should be made," the President declared. He had no intention of giving up the war, and he wanted the Virginian to be thinking of his next move before they met, though he was frank to admit that "your more intimate knowledge of the data for the solution of the problem deters me from making a specific suggestion on that point."

Johnston arrived next morning — Wednesday, April 12 — and took up quarters in one of Beauregard's boxcars. Yesterday in Raleigh, Zeb Vance had warned him that Davis, "a man of imperfectly constituted genius, . . . could absolutely *blind himself* to those things which his prejudices or hopes did not desire to see." Johnston readily agreed, having observed this quality often in the past. But he had never seen it demonstrated more forcefully than he did today, when he and his fellow general entered the presidential coach for the council of war to which he had been summoned from his duties in the field. "We had supposed that we were to be questioned concerning the military resources of our department in connection with the question of continuing or terminating the war," he later wrote. Instead, "the President's object seemed to be to give, not obtain information." Quite as amazed as his companion had been the day before, he listened while Davis spoke of raising a large army by rounding up deserters and conscripting men who previously had escaped the draft. Both generals protested that those who had avoided service in less critical times were unlikely to come forward now, and when Johnston took the occasion to advise that he be authorized to open a correspondence with Sherman regarding a truce that might lead to a successful conclusion of the conflict, this too was rejected out of hand. Any such effort was sure to fail, he was informed, and "its failure would have a demoralizing effect on both the troops and the people, neither of [whom]" — as Davis later summed up his reply — "had shown any disposition to surrender, or had any reason to suppose that their government contemplated abandoning its trust."

There was a pause. All three men sat tight-lipped, brooding on the impasse they had reached. Davis at last broke the silence by remarking that Breckinridge was expected to arrive at any moment from Virginia with definite information about the extent of Lee's disaster, and he suggested that they adjourn until the Secretary got there. The two generals were glad to retire from a situation they found awkward in the extreme — something like being closeted with a dreamy madman — although the encounter was not without its satisfactions for them both, convinced as they were, not only that they were right and he was wrong about the military outlook, but also that he would presently be obliged to admit it; if not to them, then in any case to Grant and Sherman.

In point of fact, they were righter than they would have any way of knowing until reports came in from close at hand and far afield. On this fourth anniversary of the day Beauregard opened fire on Sumter, Lee's men — not part: all — were formally laying down their arms at Appomattox Courthouse, just over a hundred miles away, and James Wilson, after visiting destruction upon Selma, even now was riding unopposed into Montgomery, the Confederacy's first capital, in bloodless celebration of the date the shooting war began. Nor was that all by any means. Canby marched this morning into Mobile, which Maury had abandoned in the night to avoid encirclement and capture; while here in North Carolina itself, some eighty miles to the east, Sherman was closing on Raleigh, whose occupation tomorrow would make it the ninth of the eleven seceded state capitals to feel the tread of the invader; all, that is, but Austin and Tallahassee, whose survival was less the result of their ability to resist than it was of Federal oversight or disinterest. Even nearer at hand — but unaware that Jefferson Davis was a prize within their reach — Stoneman's raiders had bypassed Greensboro to strike today at Salisbury, fifty of the ninety miles down the railroad to Charlotte, rounding up 1300 prisoners and putting the torch to supplies collected in expectation that Lee would move that way from Burkeville. Also taken were 10,000 stands of small arms and 14 pieces of artillery, the latter commanded by Lieutenant Colonel John C. Pemberton, who had surrendered Vicksburg, three months under two years ago, as a lieutenant general. Enlarging his destruction to include the railway bridges for miles in both directions before he swung west from Salisbury to return to Tennessee, Stoneman, though still uninformed of its proximity, ensured that when the fugitive rebel government resumed its flight — Meade and Ord hovered northward;

Sherman was advancing from the east — Davis and his ministers would no longer have the railroad as a means of transportation, swift and tireless and more or less free of the exigencies of weather, but would have to depend on horses for keeping ahead of the fast-riding bluecoats who soon would be hard on their trail.

Arriving that evening after his roundabout ride from Richmond by way of Farmville, Breckinridge knew even less of most of this than Johnston and Beauregard did. He did know, however, that Lee's surrender included the whole of his army, and this in itself was enough to convince the two generals that any further attempt to continue the conflict "would be the greatest of crimes." Johnston said as much to the Secretary when he called on him that night, adding that he wanted the opportunity to tell Davis the same thing, if Davis would only listen. Breckinridge assured him he would have his chance at the council of war, which he had been informed would be resumed next morning in the house John Wood had provided across town.

When the two generals entered the small upstairs room at 10 o'clock Thursday morning the atmosphere was grim. "Most solemnly funereal," Reagan later called it; for he and his fellow cabinet members, Benjamin, Mallory, and George Davis — Trenholm, still ailing, was absent — had just concluded a session during which Breckinridge presented his report, and "it was apparent that they had to consider the loss of the cause." Only the President and the imperturbable Benjamin seemed unconvinced that the end was at hand. Davis in fact not only did not believe that Lee's surrender meant the death of Confederate hopes for survival; he began at once, after welcoming Johnston and Beauregard, a further exposition of his views that resistance could and must continue until the northern people and their leaders grew weary enough to negotiate a peace that acknowledged southern independence. "Our late disasters are terrible," he admitted, "but I do not think we should regard them as fatal. I think we can whip the enemy yet, if our people will turn out." After a pause, which brought no response, he turned to the senior of the two field commanders. "We should like to hear your views, General Johnston."

The Virginian had been told he would have his chance, and now he took it. In a tone described by Mallory as "almost spiteful" he spoke directly to the man he had long considered his bitterest enemy, North or South. "My views are, sir, that our people are tired of the war, feel themselves whipped, and will not fight." Overrun by greatly superior Union forces, the Confederacy was "without money, or credit, or arms, or ammunition, or means of procuring them," he said flatly, driving home the words like nails in the lid of a coffin. "My men are daily deserting in large numbers. Since Lee's defeat they regard the war as at an end." There was, he declared in conclusion, no choice but surrender. "We may perhaps obtain terms which we ought to accept."

Davis heard him out with no change of expression, eyes fixed on a small piece of paper which he kept folding, unfolding, and folding. After the silence that followed Johnston's declaration of defeat, he asked in a low even tone: "What do you say, General Beauregard?" The Creole too had his moment of satisfaction. "I concur in all General Johnston has said," he replied quietly. Another silence followed. Then Davis, still holding his eyes down on the paper he kept folding and refolding, addressed Johnston in the same inflectionless voice as before: "You speak of obtaining terms...." The general said he would like to get in touch with Sherman to arrange a truce during which they could work out the details required for surrender. All those present except Benjamin agreed that this was the thing to do, and Davis accepted their judgment, but not without a reservation he considered overriding. "Well, sir, you can adopt this course," he told Johnston, "though I am not sanguine as to ultimate results." At the general's insistence, he dictated a letter to Sherman for Johnston's signature. "The results of the recent campaign in Virginia have changed the relative military condition of the belligerents," it read. "I am, therefore, induced to address you in this form the inquiry whether, to stop the further effusion of blood and devastation of property, you are willing to make a temporary suspension of active operations ... the object being to permit the civil authorities to enter into the needful arrangements to terminate the existing war."

Tomorrow was Good Friday; Davis spent it preparing to continue his flight southward. Others might treat for peace, not he. Nor would he leave the country. He had, he said when urged to escape to Mexico or the West Indies by getting aboard a ship off the Florida coast, "no idea whatever of leaving Confederate soil as long as there are men in uniform to fight for the cause." Fortunately, the treasure train had been sent ahead to Charlotte before Stoneman wrecked the railroad above and below Salisbury, but Davis and his party would have to take their chances on the muddy roads and byways. Nothing in his manner showed that he had any doubt of getting through, however, any more than he doubted the survival of the nation he headed. Only in private, and only then in a note he wrote his wife that same Good Friday, did he show that he had anything less than total confidence in the outcome of a struggle that had continued unabated for four years and was moving even now into a fifth.

"Dear Winnie," he wrote to her in Charlotte, employing her pet name before signing with his own, "I will come to you if I can. Everything is dark. You should prepare for the worst by dividing your baggage so as to move in wagons.... I have lingered on the road to little purpose. My love to the children and Maggie. God bless, guide and preserve you, ever prays Your most affectionate Banny."

★ ★ ★

There was a ceremony that same holy day in Charleston Harbor, held in accordance with War Department instructions which Stanton himself had issued back in March. "*Ordered.* That at the hour of noon on the 14th day of April, 1865, Brevet Major General Anderson will raise and plant upon the ruins of Fort Sumter the same United States flag which floated over the battlements of that fort during the rebel assault, and which was lowered and saluted by him and the small force of his command when the works were evacuated on the 14th day of April, 1861."

At first there was only minor interest in the occasion, even when it was given out that Henry Ward Beecher, the popular Brooklyn minister, would be the principal speaker. Presently, however, the fall of Richmond, followed within the week by Lee's surrender, placed the affair in a new light, one in which it could be seen as commemorating not only the start but also the finish of the war, in the same place on the same date, with precisely four years intervening between the hauling down and running up of the same flag. People began to plan to attend from all directions, especially from Boston and Philadelphia, where abolitionist sentiment ran strong, as well as from the sea islands along the Georgia and Carolina coasts, where uplift programs had been in progress ever since their occupation. Prominent men were among them, and women too, who for decades had been active in the movement. "Only listen to that — in Charleston's streets!" William Lloyd Garrison marveled, tears of joy brimming his eyes as a regimental band played "John Brown's Body" amid the ruins created by the long bombardment, which another visitor noted "had left its marks everywhere, even on gravestones in the cemeteries." So many came that the navy was hard put, this mild Good Friday morning, to provide vessels enough to ferry them from the Battery wharves out to the fort. More than four thousand were on hand, including a number of blacks from nearby plantations, though it was observed that there were scarcely a dozen local whites in the throng pressed close about the platform where the dignitaries awaited the stroke of noon.

Except for the bunting draped about the rostrum, the polished brass of army and navy officers, and the colorful silks on some of the women, the scene was bleak enough. Sumter, a Union soldier declared at the time it was retaken, "was simply an irregular curved pile of pulverized masonry, which had with enormous labor been industriously shoveled back into place as fast as we knocked it out of shape, and was held up on the inside by gabions and timber work. So many tons of projectiles had been fired into it that the shot and shell seemed to be mixed through the mass as thick as plums in a pudding." Somewhere in the pudding mass of the central parade, where the crowd gathered, was the grave of Private Daniel Hough, who had died in a flare-back while firing the fifty-gun salute of departure, four years ago today, and thus had been the first to fall in a war that by now had cost well over 600,000 lives. What was more, the man generally credited with firing from nearby Cummings Point the first shot of that war — white-haired Edmund Ruffin, past seventy and still hating, as he said in a farewell note this week, "the perfidious, malignant and vile Yankee race" — was dead too now from a bullet he put through his head when he heard the news from Appomattox.

Few if any were thinking of either Hough or Ruffin, however, as noon approached and Robert Anderson arrived with Quincy Gillmore, the department commander. Two months short of sixty, Anderson looked much older; sickness had worn him down and deprived him, except for a brief period of command in his native Kentucky, of any part in the struggle that followed the bloodless two-day bombardment in Charleston Harbor, which had turned out to be the high point in his life. He carried himself with military erectness, but he appeared somewhat confused: perhaps because, as a journalist would report, he "could see nothing by which to recognize the Fort Sumter he had left four years ago."

Still, this was another high point, if not so high as the one before, and as such had its effect both on him and on those who watched from in front of the canopied platform, where a tall new flagstaff had been erected. After a short prayer by the chaplain who had accompanied the eighty-odd-man force into the fort on the night after Christmas, 1860 — six days after South Carolina left the Union — and a responsive reading of parts from several Psalms, selected for being appropriate to the occasion — "When the Lord turned again the captivity of Zion, we were like them that dream" — a sergeant who was also a veteran of the bombardment stepped forward, drew from a leather pouch the scorched and shot-ripped flag Anderson had kept for use as a winding sheet when the time came, and began to attach it to the rope that would run it up the pole.

"We all held our breath for a second," a young woman from Philadelphia was to write many years later, "and then we gave a queer cry, between a cheer and a yell; nobody started it and nobody led it; I never heard anything like it before or since, but I can hear it now." Then, as she watched, "General Anderson stood up, bareheaded, took the halyards in his hands, and began to speak. At first I could not hear him, for his voice came thickly, but in a moment he said clearly, 'I thank God that I have lived to see this day,' and after a few more words he began to hoist the flag. It went up slowly and hung limp against the staff, a weather-beaten, frayed, and shell-torn old flag, not fit for much more work, but when it had crept clear of the shelter of the walls a sudden breath of wind caught it, and it shook its folds and flew straight out above us, while every soldier and sailor instinctively saluted."

What happened next was confused in her memory by the emotion of the moment. "I think we stood up; somebody started 'The Star-Spangled Banner,' and we sang the first verse, which is all that most people know. But it did not make much difference, for a great gun was fired close to us from the fort itself, followed, in obedience to the President's order, 'by a national salute from every fort and battery that fired upon Fort Sumter.' The measured, solemn booming came from Fort Moultrie, from the batteries on Sullivan and Folly Islands, and from Fort Wagner.... When the forts were done it was the turn of the fleet, and all our warships, from the largest — which would look tiny today — down to the smallest monitor, fired and fired in regular order until the air was thick and black with smoke and one's ears ached with the overlapping vibrations."

All this was prelude, so to speak, to the main event, the address to be delivered by the reverend Mr Beecher, the fifty-two-year-old younger brother of the author of *Uncle Tom's Cabin*, whom Lincoln was said to have greeted once as "the little lady who started this great war." Beecher's specialty was flamboyance: as when, some years before, he staged in his church a mock auction of a shapely mulatto who stood draped in white beside the pulpit, her loosened hair streaming down her back. "How much am I bid? How much am I bid for this piece of human flesh?" he intoned, and men and women in their enthusiasm removed their jewelry and unhooked their watches for deposit in the collection baskets which then were passed. There was no such heady reaction here today, however, perhaps because, as another Philadelphia visitor noted, the Brooklyn pastor "spoke very much by note, and quite without fire. [He] *read* his entire oration." His performance was also cramped by the wind, which rose briskly, once the flag was aloft, and presented him with some of the problems Lincoln had had at the White House window, two nights back, in trying to manage a candle at the same time he delivered a quite different kind of speech. Beecher's problem, while the stiff breeze off the ocean whipped his hair and threatened to scatter his manuscript broadcast, was his hat. His solution was to clap it firmly on his head and jam it down tight against his ears, thus freeing both hands to grip the wind-fluttered leaves of his text.

Even so, a measure of the old fiery rhetoric came through the awkwardness of his disadvantaged performance. For though he predicted that the common people North and South would soon unite to rule the country, he entertained no notion of forgiveness for those "guiltiest and most remorseless traitors," the secessionist aristocrats. They were the villains; "polished, cultured, exceedingly capable and wholly unprincipled," they were the ones who had "shed this ocean of blood," and he foresaw eternal agony for them on the Day of Judgment, when they would be confronted by their victims. "Caught up in black clouds full of voices of vengeance and lurid with punishment,

[they] shall be whirled aloft and plunged downward forever and forever in endless retribution." He paused for a brief rest and a drink of water, then passed on to the subject of reconstruction, which he believed posed no problems not easily solved. *"One nation, under one government, without slavery,* has been ordained, and shall stand.... On this base, reconstruction is easy, and needs neither architect nor engineer." In closing, though he had been one of Lincoln's harshest critics throughout the war — "Not a spark of genius has he; not an element for leadership. Not one particle of heroic enthusiasm" — Beecher wound up his address by offering the President "our solemn congratulations that God has sustained his life and health under the unparalleled burdens and sufferings of four bloody years, and permitted him to behold this auspicious confirmation of that national unity for which he has waited with so much patience and fortitude, and for which he has labored with such disinterested wisdom."

Robert Anderson, having performed what he called "perhaps the last act of my life, of duty to my country," had a somewhat let-down feeling as the ceremony ended and he and the rest got aboard boats to return to Charleston. At the outset he had urged Stanton to keep the program brief and quiet, but it had turned out to be neither. What was more, he faced still another speaking ordeal that night at a formal dinner Gillmore was giving for him and other guests of honor, including the old-line abolitionist Garrison, who had been hanged and burned in effigy on a nearby street corner, thirty-odd years before, in reaction to the Nat Turner uprising in Virginia. Garrison spoke, as did Beecher again — impromptu this time, and to better effect — and John Nicolay, who had been sent from Washington to deliver the Chief Executive's regrets that he himself was unable to attend. Others held forth at considerable length, interrupted from time to time by the crump and crackle of a fireworks display being staged in the harbor by Dahlgren's fleet, with Battery wharves and rooftops nearly as crowded as they had been for a grimmer show of pyrotechnics, four years ago this week. In the banquet hall of the Charleston Hotel the evening wore on as speaker after speaker, not sharing Anderson's aversion to exposure, had his say. At last, the various orators having subsided, the Kentuckian's turn came round.

He rose, glass in hand, and haltingly, with no mention of Union victory or Confederate defeat, of which so much had already been said by the others, proposed a toast to "the man who, when elected President of the United States, was compelled to reach the seat of government without an escort, but a man who now could travel all over our country with millions of hands and hearts to sustain him. I give you the good, the great, the honest man, Abraham Lincoln."

★ ★ ★

The man to whom the celebrants raised their glasses down in Charleston this Good Friday evening was seated in a box at Ford's Theater, attentive to the forced chatter of a third-rate farce which by then was into its second act. Apparently he was enjoying himself, as he generally did at the theater, even though he had come with some reluctance, if not distaste, and more from a sense of obligation than by choice. "It has been advertised that we will be there," he had said that afternoon, "and I cannot disappoint the people. Otherwise I would not go. I do not want to go."

In part this was because of a last-minute withdrawal by Grant, who earlier had accepted an invitation for him and his wife to come along, and whose presence, as the hero of Appomattox, would have lent the presidential box a glitter that outdid anything under limelight on the stage. Besides, Lincoln had looked forward to the general's company as a diversion from the strain of the daily grind, which the advent of peace had not made any less daily or less grinding. Today, for example, he was in his office by 7 o'clock as usual, attending to administrative matters in advance of the flood of supplicants who would descend on him later. After issuing a call for a cabinet meeting at 11, he went back upstairs for breakfast with Mrs Lincoln and their two sons. Robert, just up from Virginia, brought with him a photograph of R. E. Lee which he presented to his father at the table, apparently as a joke. Lincoln did not take it so. He polished his glasses on a napkin, studied the portrait, then said quietly: "It's a good face. I am glad the war is over."

This last was repeated in varied phrasings through the day. Returning to his office he conferred first with Speaker Colfax, who was slated for a cabinet post — probably Stanton's, who more than anything wanted a seat on the Supreme Court as soon as one became vacant — and then with Senator John Creswell, who had done much to keep Maryland in the Union during the secession furor. "Creswell, old fellow," Lincoln hailed him, "everything is bright this morning. The war is over. It has been a tough time, but we have lived it out. Or some of us have." His face darkened, then lightened again. "But it is over. We are going to have good times now, and a united country." He approved a number of appointments, granted a military discharge, sent a messenger over to Ford's on 10th Street to reserve the State Box for the evening performance — not forgetting to inform the management that Grant would be a member of his party, which would help to increase the normally scant Good Friday audience — and wrote on a card for two Virginians requesting passes south: "No pass is necessary now to authorize anyone to go and return from Petersburg and Richmond. People go and return just as they did before the war." Presently, as the hour approached for the cabinet meeting he had called, he walked over to the War Department, hoping for news from Sherman of Johnston's surrender. There was nothing, but he was not discouraged. He said later at the meeting that he was convinced some such news was on the way, and soon would be clicking off the wire, because of a dream he had had the night before.

Grant was there by special invitation, having arrived from City Point just yesterday. Welcomed and applauded as he entered the cabinet room, he told of his pursuit of Lee and the closing scene at Appomattox, but added that no word had come from Carolina, where a similar campaign was being mounted against Joe Johnston, hopefully with similar results. The President said he was sure they would hear from Sherman soon, for he had had this dream the night before. What sort of dream? Welles asked. "It relates to your element, the water," Lincoln replied, and told how he had been aboard "some singular, indescribable vessel" which seemed to be "floating, floating away on some vast and indistinct expanse, toward an unknown shore." The dream was not so strange in itself, he declared, as in the fact that it was recurrent; that "each of its previous occurrences has been followed by some important event or disaster." He had had it before Sumter and Bull Run, he said, as well as before such victories as Antietam, Stones River, Gettysburg, Vicksburg, and Wilmington. Grant — who seldom passed up a chance to take a swipe at Rosecrans — remarked that Stones River was no victory; he knew of no great results it brought. In any case, Lincoln told him, he had had this dream on the eve of that battle, and it had come to him again last night. He took it as a sign that they would "have great news very soon," and "I think it must be from Sherman. My thoughts are in that direction."

After a brief discussion of dreams and their nature, the talk returned to Appomattox. Grant's terms there had assured that no member of the surrendered army, from Lee on down, would ever be prosecuted by the government for treason or any other crime, so long as he observed the conditions of his parole and the laws in force where he resided. Lincoln's ready approval of this assurance gave Postmaster General William Dennison the impression that he would like to have it extended to the civilian leaders — a number of whom by now were fugitives, in flight for their lives amid the ruins of the rebellion — if only some way could be found to avoid having them hauled into court. "I suppose, Mr President," he half-inquired, half-suggested, "that you would not be sorry to have them escape out of the country?" Lincoln thought it over. "Well, I should not be sorry to have them out of the country," he replied, "but I should be for following them up pretty close to make sure of their going." Having said as much he said still more to others around the table. "I think it is providential that this great rebellion is crushed just as Congress has adjourned and there are none of the disturbing elements of that body to hinder and embarrass us. If we are wise and discreet we shall reanimate the states and get their governments in successful operation, with order prevailing and the Union reëstablished before Congress comes together in December." Returning to the question of what should be done with the rebel leaders, he became more animated both in speech and gesture. "I hope there will be no persecution, no bloody work after the war is over. No one need expect me to take any part in hanging or killing these men, even the worst of them. Frighten them out of the country; open the gates; let down the bars." He put both hands out, fluttering the fingers as if to frighten sheep out of a lot. "Shoo; scare them off," he said; "enough lives have been sacrificed."

It was for this, the consideration of reconstruction matters and incidentals preliminary to them, that the cabinet had been assembled in the first place, midway between its regular Tuesday gatherings. In the absence of Seward — still on his bed of pain, he was represented at the meeting by his son Frederick — Stanton had come armed with a plan, drawn up at the President's request, for bringing the states that had been "abroad" back into what Lincoln, in his speech three nights ago, had called "their proper practical relation with the Union." The War Secretary's notion was that military occupation should precede readmission, and in this connection he proposed that Virginia and North Carolina be combined in a single district to simplify the army's task. Welles took exception, on grounds that this last would destroy the individuality of both states and thus be "in conflict with the principles of self-government which I deem essential." So did Lincoln. After some earnest discussion, back and forth across the green-topped table, he suggested that Stanton revise his plan in this regard and provide copies for the other cabinet members to study between now and their next meeting, four days off. Congress would no doubt have its say when it returned in December, but as for himself he had already reached certain bedrock conclusions. "We can't undertake to run state governments in all these southern states. Their own people must do that — though I reckon that at first some of them may do it badly."

By now it was close to 2 o'clock, and the meeting, nearly three hours long, adjourned. Grant however remained behind to talk with Lincoln: not about army matters, it turned out, but to beg off going to the theater that night. His wife, he said, was anxious to catch the late-afternoon train for Philadelphia, en route to a visit with their young sons in Burlington, New Jersey. Lincoln started to press him, but then refrained, perhaps realizing from the general's embarrassed manner that the real reason was Julia Grant, who was determined not to expose herself to another of Mary Lincoln's tirades, this time in full view of the audience at Ford's. Disappointed, Lincoln accepted the excuse — reinforced just then by a note from Mrs Grant, reminding her husband not to be late for their 6 o'clock departure — and went upstairs for lunch, faced with the unpleasant job of informing his wife that the social catch of the season would not be going with them to the theater that evening. If he also told her, as he would tell others between now and curtain time, that he too no longer wanted to go, it made no difference; Grant or no Grant, she was set on attending what the papers were calling the "last appearance of Miss Laura Keene in her celebrated comedy of *Our American Cousin.*"

He was back in his office by 3 o'clock, in time for an appointment with the Vice President, the first since the scandalous scene at his swearing in. They talked for twenty minutes or so, and though neither left any record of what was said, witnesses noted that Lincoln called him "Andy," shaking him vigorously by the hand, and that Johnson seemed greatly relieved to find himself greeted cordially after nearly six weeks of pointed neglect. This done, Lincoln attended to some paper work, including an appeal on behalf of a soldier convicted for desertion. So far in the war he had approved 267 death sentences for military offenses, but not this one. "Well, I think the boy can do us more good above ground than under ground," he drawled as he fixed his signature to a pardon. Before setting out on a 4.30 carriage ride with his wife — "Just ourselves," he had said at lunch when she asked if he wanted anyone else along — he walked over to the War Department, in hope that some word had come at last from Sherman. Again there was nothing, which served to weaken his conviction that the news of "some important event or disaster" would shake the capital before the day was over. Time was running out, and he was disappointed. It was then, on the way back from the telegraph office, that he told his bodyguard Crook that he did not want to go to the theater that night, and would not go, except for notices in the papers that he would be there. Crook was about to go off shift, and when they reached the White House door Lincoln paused for a moment and turned to face him. He seemed gloomy, depressed. "Goodbye, Crook," he said, to the guard's surprise. Always before, it had been "Good night, Crook," when they parted. Now suddenly it was goodbye; "Goodbye, Crook."

Still, by the time the carriage rolled out of the driveway a few minutes later, on through streets that glittered with bright gold April sunshine, he had recovered his spirits to such an extent that he informed his wife: "I never felt better in my life." What was more — even though, just one month ago today, he had been confined to his bed with what his doctor described as "exhaustion, complete exhaustion" — he looked as happy as he said he felt. The recent City Point excursion, his first extended vacation of the war, had done him so much good that various cabinet members, after observing him at the midday meeting — in contrast to the one a month ago, when they gathered about his sickbed — remarked on the "expression of visible relief and content upon his face." One said that he "never appeared to better advantage," while another declared that "the weary look which his face had so long worn ... had disappeared. It was cheerful and happy." They were glad to see him so. But Mary Lincoln, whose moods were quite as variable as his own, had a different reaction when he told her he had never felt better in his life. "Don't you remember feeling just so before our little boy died?" she asked. He patted her hand to comfort her, and spoke of a trip to Europe as soon as his term was up. After that they would return to Springfield, where he would resume the practice of law and perhaps buy a farm along the Sangamon. "We must both be more cheerful in the future," he told her. "Between the war and the loss of our darling Willie, we have both been very miserable."

The good mood held. Seeing two old friends just leaving as the open barouche turned into the White House driveway an hour later, he stood up and called for them to wait. They were Richard Oglesby, the new governor of Illinois, and his adjutant general Isham Haynie, a combat brigadier who had left the army to work for him and Lincoln in the recent campaign. Lincoln led the way inside, where he read to them from the latest collection of "Letters" by Petroleum V. Nasby, a humorist he admired so much that he once said he would gladly swap his present office for the genius to compose such things. "Linkin rides into Richmond!" he read from the final letter. "A Illinois rale-splitter, a buffoon, a ape, a goriller, a smutty joker, sets hisself down in President Davis's cheer and rites dispatchis! . . . This ends the chapter. The Confederasy hez at last consentratid its last consentrate. It's ded. It's gathered up its feet, sed its last words, and deceest. . . . Farewell, vane world." The reading went on so long — four letters, with time out for laughter and thigh-slapping all around — that supper was delayed, as well as his departure for the theater. Even so, with the carriage waiting, he took time to see Colfax, who called again to ask if a special session of Congress was likely to interrupt a Rocky Mountain tour he was planning. The President said there would be no special session, and they went on talking until Mrs Lincoln appeared in the office doorway. She wore a low-necked evening dress and was pulling on her gloves, by way of warning her husband that 8 o'clock had struck.

He excused himself and they started out, only to be interrupted by two more men, a Massachusetts congressman and a former congressman from Illinois, both of whom had political favors to collect. One wanted a hearing for a client who had a sizeable cotton claim against the government; Lincoln gave him a card that put him first on tomorrow's list of callers. What the other wanted no one knew, for he whispered it into the presidential ear. Lincoln had entered and then backed out of the closed carriage, cocking his head to hear the request. "Excuse me now," he said as he climbed in again beside his wife. "I am going to the theater. Come and see me in the morning."

Stopping en route at the home of New York Senator Ira Harris to pick up their substitute guests, the senator's daughter Clara and her fiancé, Major Henry Rathbone, the carriage rolled and clopped through intersections whose streetlamps glimmered dimly through the mist. It was close to 8.30, twenty minutes past curtain time, when the coachman drew rein in front of Ford's, on 10th Street between E and F, and the two couples alighted to enter the theater. Inside, about midway of Act I, the performance stopped as the President and his party came down the side aisle, and the orchestra struck up "Hail to the Chief" as they entered the flag-draped box to the right front. A near-capacity crowd of about 1700 applauded politely, masking its disappointment at Grant's absence. Clara Harris and Rathbone took seats near the railing; the First Lady sat a little behind them, to their left, and Lincoln slumped into a roomy, upholstered rocker toward the rear. This last represented concern for his comfort and was also the management's way of expressing thanks for his having been here at least four times before, once to see Maggie Mitchell in *Fanchon the Cricket*, once to see John Wilkes Booth in *The Marble Heart* — "Rather tame than otherwise," John Hay had complained — and twice to see James Hackett play Falstaff in *Henry IV* and *The Merry Wives of Windsor*. Tonight's play resumed, and Lincoln, as was his habit, at once grew absorbed in the action down below: though not so absorbed that he failed to notice that the major was holding his fiancée's hand, for he reached out and took hold of his wife's. Pleased by the attention he had shown her on their carriage ride that afternoon, and now by this further expression of affection, Mary Lincoln reverted to her old role of Kentucky belle. "What will Miss Harris think of my hanging onto you so?" she whispered, leaning toward him. Lincoln's eyes, fixed on the stage, reflected the glow of the footlights. "Why, she will think nothing about it," he said, and he kept his grip on her hand.

Act I ended; Act II began. Down in Charleston the banqueters raised their glasses in response to Anderson's toast, and here at Ford's, in an equally festive mood, the audience enjoyed *Our American Cousin* with only occasional sidelong glances at the State Box to see whether Grant had arrived. He might have done so without their knowledge, for though they could see the young couple at the railing and Mrs Lincoln half in shadow behind them, the President was screened from view by the box curtains and draped flags. Act II ended; Act III began. Lincoln, having at last released his wife's hand and settled back in the horsehair rocker, seemed to be enjoying what was happening down below. In the second scene, which opened shortly after 10 o'clock, a three-way running dialogue revealed to Mrs Mountchessington that Asa Trenchard, for whom she had set her daughter's cap, was no millionaire after all.

— No heir to the fortune, Mr Trenchard?
— Oh, no.
— What! No fortune!
— Nary a red. . . .

Consternation. Indignation.

— Augusta, to your room.

— Yes, ma. The nasty beast!

— I am aware, Mr Trenchard, that you are not used to the manners of good society, and that alone will excuse the impertinence of which you have been guilty.

Exit Mrs Mountchessington, trailing daughter. Trenchard alone.

— Don't know the manners of good society, eh? Wal, I guess I know enough to turn you inside out, you sockdologizing old mantrap!

Then it came, a half-muffled explosion, somewhere between a boom and a thump, loud but by no means so loud as it sounded in the theater, then a boil and bulge of bluish smoke in the presidential box, an exhalation as of brimstone from the curtained mouth, and a man coming out through the bank and swirl of it, white-faced and dark-haired in a black sack suit and riding boots, eyes aglitter, brandishing a knife. He mounted the ledge, presented his back to the rows of people seated below, and let himself down by the handrail for the ten-foot drop to the stage. Falling he turned, and as he did so caught the spur of his right boot in the folds of a flag draped over the lower front of the high box. It ripped but offered enough resistance to bring all the weight of his fall on his left leg, which buckled and pitched him forward onto his hands. He rose, thrust the knife overhead in a broad theatrical gesture, and addressed the outward darkness of the pit. "Sic semper tyrannis," he said in a voice so low and projected with so little clarity that few recognized the state motto of Virginia or could later agree that he had spoken in Latin. "Revenge for the South!" or "The South is avenged!" some thought they heard him cry, while others said that he simply muttered "Freedom." In any case he then turned again, hobbled left across the stage past the lone actor standing astonished in its center, and vanished into the wings.

Barely half a minute had passed since the jolt of the explosion, and now a piercing scream came through the writhing tendrils of smoke — a full-voiced wail from Mary Lincoln. "Stop that man!" Rathbone shouted, nursing an arm slashed by the intruder, and Clara Harris, wringing her hands, called down from the railing in a tone made falsely calm by shock: "Water. Water." The audience began to emerge from its trance. "What is it? What happened?" "For God's sake, what is it?" "What has happened?" The answer came in a bellow of rage from the curtained orifice above the spur-torn flag: "He has shot the President!" Below, men leaped from their seats in a first reaction of disbelief and denial, not only of this but also of what they had seen with their own eyes. "No. For God's sake, no! It can't be true." But then, by way of reinforcement for the claim, the cry went up: "Surgeon! A surgeon! Is there a surgeon in the house?"

The young doctor who came forward — and at last gained admission to the box, after Rathbone removed a wooden bar the intruder had used to keep the hallway door from being opened while he went about his work — thought at first that he had been summoned to attend a dead man. Lincoln sat sprawled in the rocker as if asleep, knees relaxed, eyes closed, head dropped forward so that his chin was on his chest. He seemed to have no vital signs until a closer examination detected a weak pulse and shallow breathing. Assuming that he had been knifed, as Rathbone had been, the doctor had him taken from the chair and laid on the floor in a search for a stab wound. However, when he put his hands behind the patient's head to lift it, he found the back hair wet with blood from a half-inch hole where a bullet had entered, three inches to the right of the left ear. "The course of the ball was obliquely forward," a subsequent report would state, "toward the right eye, crossing the brain in an oblique manner and lodging a few inches behind that eye. In the track of the wound were found fragments of bone driven forward by the ball, which was embedded in the anterior lobe of the left hemisphere of the brain." The doctor — Charles A. Leale, assistant surgeon, U.S. Volunteers, twenty-three years old and highly familiar with gunshot wounds — did not know all this; yet he knew enough from what he had seen and felt, here in the crowded box for the past five minutes, as well as in casualty wards for the past year, to arrive at a prognosis. Everything was over for Abraham Lincoln but the end. "His wound is mortal," Leale pronounced. "It is impossible for him to recover."

Two other surgeons were in the box by then, both senior to Leale in rank and years, but he remained in charge and made the decision not to risk a removal to the White House, six cobblestone blocks away. "If it is attempted the President will die before we reach there," he replied to the suggestion. Instead, with the help of four soldier volunteers, the three doctors took up their patient and carried him feet first down the stairs and aisle, out onto 10th Street — packed nearly solid with the curious and grieving, so that an infantry captain had to draw his sword to clear a path for the seven bearers and their awkward burden, bawling excitedly: "Out of the way, you sons of bitches!" — up the front steps, down a narrow hall, and into a small back ground-floor bedroom in one of a row of modest houses across the way. Let by the night by its owner, a Swedish tailor, the room was mean and dingy, barely fifteen by nine feet in length and width, with a threadbare rug, once Turkey red, and oatmeal-colored paper on the walls. The bed itself was too short for the long form placed diagonally on the cornshuck mattress; Lincoln's booted feet protruded well beyond the footboard, his head propped on extra pillows so that his bearded chin was on his chest, as it had been when Leale first saw him in the horsehair rocker, back at

Ford's. By then the time was close to 11 o'clock, some forty-five minutes after the leaden ball first broke into his skull, and now began a painful, drawn-out vigil, a death watch that would continue for another eight hours and beyond.

Three more doctors soon arrived, Surgeon General Joseph Barnes, his chief assistant, and the family physician, who did what he could for Mary Lincoln in her distress. Barnes took charge, but Leale continued his ministrations, including the removal of the patient's clothing in a closer search for another wound and the application of mustard plasters in an attempt to improve his respiration and heartbeat. One did as little good as the other; for there was no additional wound and Lincoln's condition remained about the same, with stertorous breathing, pulse a feeble 44, hands and feet corpse-cold to the wrists and ankles, and both eyes insensitive to light, the left pupil much contracted, the right dilated widely. Gideon Welles came in at this point and wrote next day in his diary of "the giant sufferer" as he saw him from his post beside the bed. "He had been stripped of his clothes. His large arms, which were occasionally exposed, were of a size which one would scarce have expected from his spare appearance. His slow, full respiration lifted the bedclothes with each breath that he took. His features were calm and striking. I had never seen them appear to better advantage than for the first hour, perhaps, that I was there." Presently, though, their calm appearance changed. The left side of the face began to twitch, distorting the mouth into a jeer. When this desisted, the upper right side of the face began to darken, streaked with purple as from a blow, and the eye with the ball of lead behind it began to bulge from its socket. Mary Lincoln screamed at the sight and had to be led from the room, while a journalist noted that Charles Sumner, "seated on the right of the President's couch, near the head, holding the right hand of the President in his own," was about equally unstrung. "He was sobbing like a woman, with his head bowed down almost on the pillow of the bed on which the President was lying."

By midnight, close to fifty callers were in the house, all of sufficient prominence to gain entrance past the guards and most of them wedged shoulder to shoulder in the death chamber, at one time or another, for a look at the final agony of the man laid diagonally on the bed in one corner. Andrew Johnson was there — briefly, however, because his presence was painful to Mrs Lincoln, who whimpered at the sight of her husband's imminent successor — as were a number of Sumner's colleagues from the House and Senate, Robert Lincoln and John Hay, Oglesby and Haynie again, a pair of clergymen — one fervent, the other unctuous — and Laura Keene, who claimed a star's prerogative, first in the box at the theater, where she had held the President's bleeding head in her lap, and now in the narrow brick house across the street, where she helped Clara Harris comfort the distraught widow-to-be in the tailor's front parlor, what time she was not with her in the crowded bedroom toward the rear. All members of the cabinet were on hand but the Secretary of State, and most of the talk that was not of Lincoln was of him. He too had been attacked and grievously wounded, along with four members of his household, by a lone assassin who struck at about the same time as the one at Ford's: unless, indeed, it was the same man in rapid motion from one place to the other, less than half a mile away. Seward had been slashed about the face and throat, and he was thought to be dying, too, except that the iron frame that bound his jaw had served to protect him to some extent from the knife. "I'm mad, I'm mad," the attacker had said as he ran out into the night to vanish as cleanly as the other — or he — had done when he — or the other — leaped from the box, crossed the stage, entered the wings, and exited into the alley behind Ford's, where he — whoever, whichever he was — mounted his waiting horse and rode off in the darkness.

In this, as in other accounts concerning other rumored victims — Grant, for one, and Andrew Johnson for another, until word came that the general was safe in Philadelphia and the Vice President himself showed up unhurt — there was much confusion. Edwin Stanton undertook on his own the task of sifting and setting the contradictions straight, in effect taking over as head of the headless government. "[He] instantly assumed charge of everything near and remote, civil and military," a subordinate observed, "and began issuing orders in that autocratic manner so superbly necessary to the occasion." Among other precautions, he stopped traffic on the Potomac and the railroads, warned the Washington Fire Brigade to be ready for mass arson, summoned Grant back to take charge of the capital defenses, and alerted guards along the Canadian border, as well as in all major eastern ports, to be on the lookout for suspicious persons attempting to leave the country. In short, "he continued throughout the night acting as president, secretary of war, secretary of state, commander in chief, comforter, and dictator," all from a small sitting room adjacent to the front parlor of the tailor's house on 10th Street, which he turned into an interrogation chamber for grilling witnesses to find out just what had happened in the theater across the street.

From the outset, numbers of people who knew him well, including members of his profession, had identified John Wilkes Booth as Lincoln's attacker, and by now the twenty-six-year-old matinee idol's one-shot pocket derringer had been found on the floor of the box where he had dropped it as he leaped for the railing to escape by way of the stage and the back alley. Identification was certain. Even so, and though a War Department description eventually went out by wire across the land — "height 5 feet 8 inches, weight 160 pounds, compact build; hair jet black, inclined to curl, medium length, parted behind; eyes black, heavy dark eyebrows; wears a large seal ring on little finger; when talking inclines head forward, looks down" — Stanton was intent on larger game. Apparently convinced that the President could not have been shot by anyone so insignificant as an actor acting on his own, he was out to expose a full-scale Confederate plot, a conspiracy hatched in Richmond "and set on foot by rebels under pretense of avenging the rebel cause."

So he believed at any rate, and though he gave most of his attention to exploring this assumption — proceeding with such misdirected and disjointed vigor that he later aroused revisionist suspicions that he must have wanted the assassin to escape: as, for instance, by his neglect in closing all city bridges except the one Booth used to cross into Maryland — he still had time for periodic visits to the small back room, filled with the turmoil of Lincoln's labored breathing, and to attend to such incidental administrative matters as the preparation of a message giving Johnson formal notice that the President had died. His purpose in this, with the hour of death left blank to be filled in later, was to avoid delay when the time came, but when he read the rough draft aloud for a stenographer to take down a fair copy he produced a premature effect he had not foreseen. Hearing a strangled cry behind him, he turned and found Mary Lincoln standing in the parlor doorway, hands clasped before her in entreaty, a stricken expression on her face. "Is he dead? Oh, is he dead?" she moaned. Stanton tried to explain that what she had heard was merely in preparation for a foreseen contingency, but she could not understand him through her sobbing and her grief. So he gave it up and had her led back into the parlor, out of his way; which was just as well, an associate declared, for "he was full of business, and knew, moreover, that in a few hours at most she must be a widow."

It was by then about 1.30; Good Friday was off the calendar at last, and Mary Lincoln was into what everyone in the house, doctors and laymen alike, could see would be the first day of her widowhood. At intervals, supported on either side by Clara Harris and Laura Keene, she would return to the crowded bedroom and sit or stand looking down at her husband until grief overcame her again and the two women would half-guide half-carry her back to the front parlor, where she would remain until enough strength returned for her to repeat the process. She made these trips about once an hour, and each was more grueling than the last, not only because of her own cumulative exhaustion, but also because of the deteriorating condition of the sufferer on the bed, which came as a greater shock to her each time she saw him. Earlier, there had been a certain calm and dignity about him, as if he were in fact aboard "some singular, indescribable vessel... floating, floating away on some vast and indistinct expanse, toward an unknown shore." Now this was gone, replaced by the effects of agony. The dream ship had become a rack, and the stertorous uproar of his breathing, interspersed with drawn-out groans, filled the house as it might have filled a torture chamber. "Doctor, save him!" she implored first one and then another of the attending physicians, and once she said in a calmer tone: "Bring Tad. He will speak to Tad, he loves him so." But all agreed that would not do, either for the boy or for his father, who was beyond all knowledgeable contact with anything on earth, even Tad, and indeed had been so ever since Booth's derringer crashed through the laughter in the theater at 10.15 last night. All the while, his condition worsened, especially his breathing, which not only became increasingly spasmodic, but would stop entirely from time to time, the narrow chest expanded between the big rail-splitter arms, and then resume with a sudden gusty roar through the fluttering lips. On one such occasion, with Mrs Lincoln leaning forward from a chair beside the bed, her cheek on her husband's cheek, her ear near his still, cyanotic mouth, the furious bray of his exhalation — louder than anything she had heard since the explosion in the box, five hours ago — startled and frightened her so badly that she shrieked and fell to the floor in a faint. Stanton, interrupted in his work by the piercing scream, came running down the hall from his improvised Acting President's office up front. When he saw what it was he lost patience entirely. "Take that woman out," he ordered sternly, thrusting both arms over his head in exasperation, "and do not let her in again."

He was obeyed in this as in all his other orders, and she remained in the front parlor until near the very end. Meantime dawn came through, paling the yellow flare of gas jets. A cold rain fell on the people still keeping their vigil on the street outside, while inside, in the dingy room made dingier by daylight, Lincoln entered the final stage of what one doctor called "the saddest and most pathetic deathbed scene I ever witnessed." Interruptions of his breathing were more frequent now, and longer, and whenever this happened some of the men about the bed would take out their watches to note the time of death, then return them to their pockets when the raucous sound resumed. Robert Lincoln — "only a boy for all his shoulder straps," the guard Crook had said — "bore himself well," according to one who watched him, "but on two occasions gave way to overpowering grief and sobbed aloud, turning his head and leaning on the shoulder of Senator Sumner." At 7 o'clock, with the end at hand, he went to bring his mother into the room for a last visit. She tottered in, looked at her husband in confusion, saying nothing, and was led back out again. Stanton was there full-time now, and strangely enough had brought his hat along, standing motionless with his chin on his left hand, his right hand holding the hat and supporting his left elbow, tears running down his face into his beard.

By this time Lincoln's breathing was fast and shallow, cheeks pulled inward behind the closed blue lips. His chest heaved up in a last deep breath, then subsided and did not rise again. It was 7.22; the nine-hour agony was over, and his face took on what John Hay described as "a look of unspeakable peace." Surgeon General Barnes leaned forward, listened carefully for a time to the silent chest, then straightened up, removed two silver half-dollars from his pocket, and placed them carefully on the closed eyes. Observing this ritual, Stanton then performed one of his own. He stretched his right arm out deliberately before him, clapped his hat for a long moment on his head, and then as deliberately removed it, as if in salute. "Now he belongs to the ages," he said, or anyhow later saw to it that he was quoted as having said. "Let us pray," one of the parsons intoned, and sank to his knees on the thin red carpet beside the bed.

Soon thereafter Mary Lincoln was brought back into the room. "Oh, why did you not tell me he was dying?" she exclaimed when she saw her husband lying there with coins on his eyes. Then it came home to her, and her grief was too great to be contained. "Oh my God," she wailed as she was led out, weeping bitterly, "I have given my husband to die!" Presently she was taken from the house, and the other mourner witnesses picked their way through the wet streets to their homes and hotels near and far.

Bells were tolling all over Washington by the time Lincoln's body, wrapped in a flag and placed in a closed hearse, was on its way back to the White House, escorted (as he had not been when he left, twelve hours before) by an honor guard of soldiers and preceded by a group of officers walking bareheaded in the rain. He would lie in state, first in the East Room, then afterwards in the Capitol rotunda, preparatory to the long train ride back to Springfield, where he would at last be laid to rest. "Nothing touches the tired spot," he had said often in the course of the past four years. Now Booth's derringer had reached it.

At 10 o'clock that Saturday morning, less than three hours after Lincoln died in the tailor's house two blocks away, Andrew Johnson took the oath of office in the parlor of his suite at the Kirkwood House, just down Pennsylvania Avenue from the mansion that was soon to be his home. After kissing the Bible held out to him by Chase, he turned and made a short speech, a sort of extemporaneous inaugural, to the dozen senators and cabinet members present, all with faces that showed the strain of their all-night vigil. "Gentlemen," he said, "I have been almost overwhelmed by the announcement of the sad event which has so recently occurred." Other than this he made no reference to his predecessor, and as for any policy he would adopt, "that must be left for development as the Administration progresses.... The only assurance I can now give of the future is reference to the past. Toil, and an honest advocacy of the great principles of free government, have been my lot. The duties have been mine; the consequences are God's."

If this sounded at once conventional and high-handed, if some among the new President's hearers resented his singular omission of any reference to the old one — "Johnson seemed willing to share the glory of his achievements with his Creator," a New Hampshire senator observed, "but utterly forgot that Mr Lincoln had any share of credit in the suppression of the rebellion" — there were those beyond reach of his voice just then who were altogether delighted with the change, as they saw it, from a soft- to a hard-peace Chief of State. Back from Richmond that same day, most of the members of the Joint Committee on the Conduct of the War spent the afternoon at a caucus held to consider "the necessity of a new cabinet and a line of policy less conciliatory than that of Mr Lincoln." They had been upset by a number of things, including his recent speech from the White House window, and Julian of Indiana complained that "aside from his known tenderness to the rebels, Lincoln's last public avowal, only three days before his death, of adherence to the plan of reconstruction he had announced in December 1863, was highly repugnant." All in all, "while everybody was shocked at his murder," Julian declared, "the feeling was nearly universal that the accession of Johnson to the Presidency would prove a godsend to the country."

Sure enough, when they requested through their chairman a meeting with the new President — himself a member of the committee until he left the Senate, three years ago, to take up his duties as military governor of Tennessee — he promptly agreed to see them the following day, not at the White House, which was in a turmoil of preparation for the funeral, but next door at the Treasury Department. It was Easter Sunday, and Ben Wade, as chairman, got things off to a rousing start. "Johnson, we have faith in you," he said. "By the gods, there will be no trouble *now* in running the government."

Lincoln's life had ended, so to speak, in a tailor shop; Johnson's could be said to have begun in one, plying needle and thread while his wife taught him to read. Since then, he had come far — indeed, all the way to the top — with much of his success attributable to his skill as a stump speaker whose specialty was invective. Nor did he disappoint his Jacobin callers now in that regard. One year older and half a foot shorter than his predecessor, he thanked Wade for the warmth of his greeting and launched at once into a statement of his position on the burning issue of the day, repeating, with some expansion and adjustment of the words, what he had said on the steps of the Patent Office, twelve days back. "I hold that robbery is a crime; rape is a crime; murder is a crime; *treason* is a crime — and crime must be punished. Treason must be made infamous, and traitors must be impoverished." The impression here was as strong as the one produced at the Republican rally, two days after the fall of Richmond, and it was also encouraging to learn that the text under his lips when he kissed the Bible held out to him by Chase the day before, open to the lurid and vengeful Book of Ezekiel, carried a similar burden of blame and retribution: *And I will give them one heart, and I will put a new spirit within you; and I will take the stony heart out of their flesh, and will give them an heart of flesh: That they may walk in my statutes, and keep mine ordinances, and do them: and they shall be my people, and I will be their God. But as for them whose heart walketh after the heart of their detestable things and their abominations, I will recompense their way upon their own heads, saith the Lord God.* Although he made them no commitment as to changes in the cabinet he had inherited — not even regarding dismissal of the twice-injured Seward, whom they detested — they did not expect that; not just yet. It was enough, for the present, that he was with them. They knew him of old; he was *of* them, a long-time colleague, and they counted on him to come down stronger on their enemies all the time. They knew, as their chairman had said at the outset, there would be no trouble in running the government now.

Anyhow they thought they knew, and when Johnson presently issued a proclamation offering rewards that ranged from $100,000 to $10,000 for the capture of Jefferson Davis and certain of his "agents," on charges of having conspired to incite the murder of Abraham Lincoln, their cup nearly ran over. Zachariah Chandler, for one, was pleased with the prospect brought about by the assassination, and he said as much in a letter he wrote his wife in Michigan, one week after the Easter meeting. "Had Mr Lincoln's policy been carried out, we should have had Jeff Davis, Toombs, etc. back in the Senate at the next session of Congress, but now their chances to stretch hemp are better.... So mote it be."

※ 2 ※

Escorted by a small band of Tennessee cavalry, Davis and his official family left Greensboro on the morning Lincoln died, April 15, all on horseback except the ailing Trenholm, accompanied in his ambulance by Adjutant General Samuel Cooper, crowding seventy years of age, and Judah Benjamin, for whom a saddle was an instrument of torture. While they toiled southwest over clay roads made slippery by recent heavy rains, Joe Johnston waited in his Hillsboro headquarters, forty miles northwest of Union-occupied Raleigh, for a reply to his request, sent through the lines the day before — Good Friday; Lincoln had been right, after all, about good news in the offing — for "a temporary suspension of active operations ... to permit the civil authorities to enter into the needful arrangements to terminate the existing war." Reluctant to have the overture made, even though he himself, under pressure from his advisers, had written the message the Virginian signed, Davis had said he was not "sanguine" as to the outcome. But the response, received by Johnston on Easter Sunday, showed Sherman to be a good deal more receptive to the notion than the departed President had expected. "I am fully empowered," the Ohioan replied, "to arrange with you any terms for the suspension of further hostilities between the armies commanded by you and those commanded by myself, and will be willing to confer with you to that end." He proposed surrender on the same terms Grant had given Lee, a week ago today, and spoke in closing of his "desire to save the people of North Carolina the damage they would sustain by the march of this army through the central or western parts of the state."

In point of fact, Sherman was even more pleased than he sounded: not only because, as he later said, "the whole army dreaded the long march to Charlotte" and beyond, "back again over the thousand miles we had just accomplished," but also because of his own fear that Johnston, overtaken, might "allow his army to disperse into guerrilla bands" and thereby cause the war to be "prolonged indefinitely." Surrender of course would obviate both of these unwanted eventualities, and Sherman, with Grant's example before him — "Glory to God and our country," he had exclaimed in a field order passing the news of Appomattox along to his troops, "and all honor to our comrades in arms, toward whom we are marching! A little more labor, a little more toil on our part, the great race is won, and our Government stands regenerated after four long years of war" — fairly leaped at the invitation thus extended. Accordingly, after assuring Washington that he would "be careful not to complicate any points of civil policy" in the terms he planned to offer, he arranged with Johnston to meet at noon on Monday, April 17, midway between the picket lines of the two armies.

That would be somewhere between the Confederate rear at Hillsboro and his own advance at Durham Station, twenty-odd miles up the track from Raleigh. Monday morning, as he was boarding the train that would take him and his staff to the midday meeting, a telegrapher came hurrying down the depot stairs with word that a coded message from the War Department, sent by steamer down the coast, was just coming over the wire from Morehead City. Sherman waited nearly half an hour for it to be completed and decoded, then took it from the operator, who came running back much excited. It was from Stanton and it had been nearly two days in transit. "President Lincoln was murdered about 10 o'clock last night in his private box at Ford's Theatre in this city, by an assassin who shot him through the head by a pistol ball." Seward too had been gravely hurt, and Andrew Johnson was about to take over even as Stanton wrote the final words of the message: "I have no time to add more than to say that I find evidence that an assassin is also on your track, and I beseech you to be more heedful than Mr Lincoln was of such knowledge."

Sherman thrust the sheet of flimsy into his pocket and said nothing of it to anyone but the telegrapher, whom he swore to secrecy. Aboard the train as it chuffed along he sat tight-lipped all the way to Durham, where he and his staff changed to horses for the flag-of-truce ride toward Hillsboro to meet Johnston. They encountered him and his party about five miles out, also under a flag of truce, and here, midway between their lines of battle, the two generals met for the first time in person: although, as Sherman put it afterwards, looking back on the hundred-mile minuet they had danced together in North Georgia from early May through mid-July, "We knew enough of each other to be well acquainted at once." Riding side by side — forty-five-year-old "Uncle Billy," tall and angular, and his spruce, spare companion, thirteen years his senior, "dressed in a neat gray uniform," a blue staffer noted, "which harmonized gracefully with a full beard and mustache of silvery whiteness, partly concealing a genial and generous mouth" — they led the small blue-gray column to a roadside house owned by a farmer named James Bennett, whose permission they asked for its use, and then went in, leaving their two staffs in the yard. Once they were alone Sherman took the sheet of flimsy from his pocket and handed it over without comment. As Johnston read it, "perspiration came out in large drops on his forehead," his companion observed, and when he had finished he denounced the assassination as "the greatest possible calamity to the South," adding that he hoped Sherman did not connect the Confederate government with the crime. "I told him," the red-head would recall, "I could not believe that he or General Lee, or the officers of the Confederate army, could possibly be privy to acts of assassination; but I would not say as much for Jeff Davis . . . and men of that stripe."

Johnston made no reply to this, and the two proceeded at once to the subject arranged beforehand. Both agreed that any resumption of the fighting would be "the highest possible crime," the Virginian — outnumbered four to one by enemy troops in the immediate vicinity, and ten to one or worse by others who could be brought to bear within a week — even going so far as to define the crime as "murder." All the same, they soon reached an apparent impasse. For while Sherman rejected any proposal designed to lead to negotiations between the civil authorities, Davis had consented to the meeting only if it was to be conducted on that basis; which, incidentally, was why he had not been "sanguine as to ultimate results." Johnston, however, stepped over the barrier by proposing that he and Sherman "make one job of it," then and there, by settling "the fate of all armies to the Rio Grande." Taken aback, the Ohioan questioned whether his companion's authority was that broad. Johnston replied that it was, or anyhow could be made so by the Secretary of War, whose orders would be obeyed by Taylor, Forrest, Maury, and all the others with forces still under arms, including Kirby Smith beyond the Mississippi. In fact, he said, he could send a wire requesting Breckinridge to join them overnight. Sherman demurred; he could not deal with a member of the rebel cabinet, no matter how desirable the outcome. However, when Johnston pointed out that the

Kentuckian was also a major general, and could be received on that basis, Sherman agreed. They would meet tomorrow, same time, same place, soldier to soldier, and work out the details, all of which would of course be dependent on approval by his Washington superiors, civil as well as military.

They parted "in extreme cordiality," Johnston later declared, he to wait near Greensboro for Breckinridge to arrive from Salisbury, which Davis and his party had reached by then, and Sherman to face the problem of how to go about informing his troops of Lincoln's death. So far, the occupation of the North Carolina capital had been orderly and forbearing; "Discipline was now so good that the men didn't know themselves," an Illinois infantryman observed. But their commander, nursing his bombshell of news on the trainride back to Raleigh, was aware that "one single word by me would have laid the city in ashes and turned its whole population homeless upon the country, if not worse." Accordingly, he ordered all units back to their camps before releasing a bulletin in which he was careful to exonerate the Confederate army from complicity in the assassination. It seemed to work. At least there was no violent reaction within the guarded bivouacs. However: "The army is crazy for vengeance," a private wrote home, remarking that "if we make another campaign it will be an awful one." Some even went so far as to hope that Johnston would not surrender; in which case they planned to turn loose with both hands. "God pity this country if he retreats or fights us," the soldier closed his letter.

From what he had heard today in the roadside farmhouse Sherman believed there was little chance of that; Johnston, he knew, was eager to surrender, and he intended to give him every chance. He would do so in part because of his soldier's pride in being generous to a disadvantaged foe who asked for mercy. "The South is broken and ruined and appeals to our pity," he would tell Rawlins before the month was out. "To ride the people down with persecutions and military exactions would be like slashing away at the crew of a sinking ship." There was that, and there was also his reaction to the Good Friday assassination, which was quite the opposite of the angered private's hope that Old Joe would not surrender. Lincoln's death brought Lincoln himself into sharper focus in Sherman's memory: particularly as he had come to know him at City Point, three weeks ago. Remembering his concern for avoiding "this last bloody battle," his eagerness "to get the men composing the Confederate armies back to their homes, at work on their farms and in their shops," he was resolved, as he set out for the second meeting Tuesday morning, "to manifest real respect for his memory by following after his death that policy which, if living, I felt certain he would have approved." Grant had removed from the contest the most feared and admired of the rebel armies; now Sherman would remove all the rest by taking Johnston up on his soldier-to-soldier proposal that they "make one job of it," here and now in the Bennett farmhouse, and settle "the fate of all armies to the Rio Grande."

He arrived first and went in alone, his saddlebags over one arm. They contained writing materials, together with something else he mentioned when Johnston entered the room with Breckinridge. "Gentlemen, it occurred to me that perhaps you were not overstocked with liquor, and I procured some medical stores on my way over. Will you join me before we begin work?" Johnston afterwards described his companion's expression — till now "rather dull and heavy" — as "beatific" when he heard these words. For some days the Kentuckian had been deprived of his customary ration of bourbon and had had to make do with tobacco, which he was chewing vigorously with a steady sidewise thrust of his jaw beneath the outsized mustache of a Sicilian brigand. When the bottle appeared, along with a glass, he tossed his quid into the fireplace, rinsed his mouth with water, and "poured out a tremendous drink, which he swallowed with great satisfaction. With an air of content he stroked his mustache and took a fresh chew of tobacco," while Sherman returned the bottle to his saddlebags. Thus refreshed, the three generals then got down to business, and Johnston observed that the former Vice President "never shone more brilliantly than he did in the discussions which followed. He seemed to have at his tongue's end every rule and maxim of international and constitutional law." Indeed, he cited and discoursed with such effect that Sherman — "confronted by the authority, but not convinced by the eloquence" — pushed his chair back from the table and registered a complaint. "See here, gentlemen," he protested. "Who is doing this surrendering anyhow? If this thing goes on, you'll have me sending a letter of apology to Jeff Davis."

Certain of his superiors would presently accuse him of having done just about that in the "Memorandum, or Basis of Agreement" arrived at in the course of the discussion. He wrote it himself, after rejecting a draft of terms prepared that morning in Greensboro by John Reagan — who had also come up from Salisbury but was not admitted to the conference because of his nonmilitary status — as "too general and verbose." Having said as much, he settled down to composing one of his own, more soldierly and direct, based on Reagan's and the agreements reached with Johnston yesterday and the silver-tongued Kentuckian today. As he worked he grew increasingly absorbed, until at one point, pausing to arrange his thoughts, he stopped writing, rose from the table, walked over to his saddlebags, and fumbled absentmindedly for the bottle. Seeing this, Breckinridge removed his quid in anticipation of another treat. But that, alas, was not to be. Still preoccupied, the Ohioan poured himself a couple of fingers of whiskey, recorked the bottle and returned it to the bag, then stood gazing abstractedly out of a window, sipping the drink while he got his thoughts in order; which done, he set the empty glass down, still without so much as a sidelong glance at his companions, and returned to his writing. In a state of near shock, his face taking on what Johnston called "an injured, sorrowful look," the Kentuckian solaced himself as best he could with a new chew of tobacco. Finally Sherman completed his draft of the terms and passed it across the table, saying: "That's the best I can do."

It was enough, perhaps indeed even more than enough from the rebel point of view. In seven numbered paragraphs, the memorandum provided that the present truce would remain in effect pending approval by superior authorities on both sides; that the troops in all Confederate armies still in existence would be "disbanded and conducted to their several state capitals, there to deposit their arms and public property in the state arsenals"; that federal courts would be reëstablished throughout the land; that the U.S. President would recognize existing state governments as soon as their officials took the required oath of loyalty, and would guarantee to all citizens "their political rights and franchises, as well as their rights of person and property, as defined by the Constitution," pledging in addition that neither he nor his subordinates would "disturb any of the people by reason of the late war, so long as they live in peace and quiet, abstain from acts of armed hostility, and obey the laws in force at the place of their residence." Such, in brief, were the terms set forth, and though Sherman knew that they went far beyond those given Lee, and knew too that he had violated his promise "not to complicate any points of civil policy," he felt more than justified by the assurance, received in return, that all the surviving gray armies — not one of which had been brought to bay, let alone hemmed in, as Lee's had been at Appomattox — would disband en masse, rather than fragment themselves into guerilla bands which might disrupt and bedevil the nation for years to come. In any case, nothing he had promised would be given until, and unless, it was approved by his superiors. Moreover, even if all he had written was rejected — which, on second thought, seemed possible, and on third thought seemed likely — he still would be the gainer by the provisional arrangements he had made. "In the few days it would take to send the papers to Washington, and receive an answer," he rather slyly pointed out, "I could finish the railroad up to Raleigh, and be the better prepared for a long chase."

Once he and Johnston had signed the copies then drawn up, Sherman shouldered his saddlebags and walked out into the gathering dusk, convinced that he had found a simple, forthright, soldierly solution to the multifarious problems of reconstruction by declaring, in effect, that there would be no reconstruction; at any rate none that would involve the politicians. They might not be willing to go along with the instrument which achieved this — the "Memorandum, or Basis of Agreement" — but he believed he knew a solution to that, too. "If you will get the President to simply indorse the copy and commission me to carry out the terms," he told Grant in a letter sent north by courier with the document next morning, "I will follow them to the conclusion."

Johnston too seemed in good spirits as he walked out of the Bennett house and across the yard with his fellow Confederate, who, on the other hand, had reverted to the "full and heavy" condition that preceded the one drink he had been offered before their host recorked the bottle and stuffed it back into his saddlebag. Hoping to divert him, and perhaps dispel the gloom, the Virginian asked his companion what he thought of Sherman. Breckinridge glowered. "He is a bright man, a man of great force," he replied. "But, General Johnston" — his voice rose; his face took on a look of intensity — "General Sherman is a hog. Yes, sir, a hog. Did you see him take that drink by himself?" Johnston suggested that the Ohioan had merely been absent-minded, but Breckinridge had been offended past endurance. He could overlook charges of pillage and arson; not this, which he found quite beyond the pale. "No Kentucky gentleman would ever have taken away that bottle," he said hotly. "He knew we needed it, and needed it badly."

There was a five-day wait, both armies remaining in position as agreed, and then on April 24 the staff courier sent to Washington returned, accompanied — much to Sherman's surprise — by Grant, who had come down the coast to say in person that the proposed "agreement" wouldn't do; wouldn't do at all, in fact, from several points of view.

He himself had seen as much in a single hurried reading when the document first reached him, late in the afternoon three days ago, and got in touch at once with Stanton to have the President call a meeting of the cabinet that night. This was done, and when he read them what Sherman had written, the reaction of the assembled dignitaries was even more vehement than he had expected. Lincoln's body, on display for the past three days in the East Room of the White House and the Capitol rotunda, had been put aboard a crepe-draped train that morning for the burial journey back to Illinois; now, hard in the wake of that emotional drain — that sense of loss which swept over them as they watched the train fade down the track, the smell of cinders fading too — came this documentary evidence that one of the nation's top generals wanted to end the war by reproducing the conditions that began it. Not only was there no mention of the Negro in any of the seven numbered paragraphs Grant read, but the provision for home-bound rebel soldiers to deposit their arms in state arsenals sounded suspiciously like a plan for keeping them ready-stacked for re-rebellion once the men who had carried them for the past four years grew rested enough to try their hand again at tearing the fabric of the Union. Hard to take, too, was the suggested exculpation of all Confederates from all blame, which contrasted strongly with the new President's post-inaugural statement lumping treason with rape and murder as a crime that "must be punished." Johnson was particularly angered by this attempt to override his bedrock pronouncement on the issue of guilt. Angriest of all, however, was the Secretary of War, who saw Sherman's so-called "memorandum" as a bid for the "Copperhead nomination for President" three years hence — if, indeed, he was willing to wait that long and was not planning a military coup when he marched north. Speed, "prompted by Stanton, who seemed frantic," according to Welles, "expressed fears that Sherman, at the head of his victorious legions, had designs upon the government" right now.

Grant defended his friend as best he could; defended his motives, that is, even though he agreed that what they had led to "could not possibly be approved." Nor was he displeased with instructions from his superiors to go in person down to Raleigh and inform his out-of-line subordinate that, his plan having been rejected, he was to "notify General Johnston immediately of the termination of the truce, and resume hostilities against his army at the earliest moment." Their notion was that he should be there in case the red-head attempted defiance of the order, whereas his own purpose was to be on hand to blunt the sting of the rebuke; which was also why he kept the trip a secret, thereby avoiding speculation and gossip about his mission, as well as embarrassment for the man he was going to see. He left at midnight, steaming away from the 6th Street wharf, and two mornings later, after a trainride from the coast, was with Sherman at his headquarters in the North Carolina capital.

Actually, when told of the disapproval of his plan for bringing peace "from the Potomac to the Rio Grande," the Ohioan was not as shocked as Grant expected him to be. Just yesterday he had received a bundle of newspapers reflecting anger throughout the North at the shock of Lincoln's murder, and he sent them along to Johnston with the comment: "I fear much the asassination of the President will give such a bias to the popular mind, which, in connection with the desires of the politicians, may thwart our purpose of recognizing 'existing local governments.'" This last, in fact, was what Grant chose to stress as the principal reason for disapproval of the terms proposed. Making no mention of Johnson's or Stanton's fulminations, he produced a copy of the War Department telegram he had received in early March while still in front of Petersburg. "You are not to decide, discuss, or confer upon any political question," he had been told. "Such questions the President holds in his own hands; and will submit them to no military conference or conventions." Sherman read the dispatch through, then remarked that he wished someone had thought to send him a copy at the time. "It would have saved a world of trouble," he said dryly, and promptly notified Johnston that Washington had called off their agreement. "I am instructed to limit my operations to your immediate command and not to attempt civil negotiations," he wrote, serving notice that hostilities would resume within forty-eight hours unless the Virginian surrendered before that time, "on the same terms as were given General Lee at Appomattox on April 9, instant, purely and simply."

This was plainly an ultimatum; events had taken the course predicted by Davis even as he approved the now repudiated "Basis of Agreement." Dismayed, Johnston wired Breckinridge for instructions, but when these turned out to be a suggestion that he fall back toward Georgia with his cavalry, light guns, and such infantry as could be mounted on spare horses, he replied that the plan was "impracticable," and instead got in touch with Sherman to arrange a third meeting and work out the details for surrender in accordance with the scaled-down terms. Two days later — April 26; Grant, still concerned with avoiding any show of interference, did not attend — they met again in the Bennett farmhouse and the matter was soon disposed of, including an issue of ten days' rations for 25,000 paroled graybacks, offered by Sherman "to facilitate what you and I and all good men desire, the return to their homes of the officers and men composing your army." Johnston replied that "the enlarged patriotism manifested in these papers reconciles me to what I previously regarded as the misfortune of my life — that of having had you to encounter in the field." On this high note of mutual esteem they parted to meet no more, though Johnston would die some twenty-six years later from the effects of a severe cold he contracted in New York while standing bareheaded in raw February weather alongside the other pallbearers at Sherman's funeral. "General, please put on your hat," a friend urged the eighty-four-year-old Virginian; "you might get sick." Johnston refused. "If I were in his place," he said, "and he were standing here in mine, he would not put on his hat."

But that would be a full generation later. Just now all the talk was of surrender, at any rate in the Federal camps; for though a Confederate staffer had remarked on "the eagerness of the men to get to their homes" through these past ten days of on-and-off negotiations, another observed that on the day when the actual news came down, "they scarcely had anything to say." Such dejection was offset by the elation of the bluecoats in their bivouacs around Raleigh. One wrote home of how the birds woke him that morning with their singing — four years and two weeks, to the day, since the first shot was fired in Charleston harbor. "I never heard them sing so sweetly, and never saw them flit about so merrily," he declared, adding that "the green groves in which we were camped had a peculiar beauty and freshness, and as the sun rose above the steeples, it seemed as if we could float right up with it."

Presently there was other news, to which reactions also varied. On that same April 26, about midway between Washington and Richmond, Lincoln's assassin, run to earth at last, was shot and killed by a platoon of New York cavalry. After a week spent hiding in the woods and swamps of southeast Maryland, suffering all the while from pain in the leg he had broken in his leap from the box at Ford's, Booth and an associate succeeded in crossing the Potomac near Port Tobacco on April 22, then two days later made it over the Rappahannock, some twenty miles below Fredericksburg, only to be overtaken the following night on a farm three miles from the river. Surrounded by their pursuers they took refuge in a tobacco shed, and though his companion surrendered when ordered out (and was carried back to the capital next day to stand trial along with seven other alleged conspirators, including one who had made the knife attack on Seward and another who had been slated to dispose of the Vice President but had lacked the nerve to try) Booth himself refused to emerge, even after the tinder-dry structure was set afire. The troopers could see him in there, a crippled figure with a crutch and a carbine, silhouetted against the flames. Then one fired and he fell, dropped by a bullet that passed through his neck, "perforating both sides of the collar." He was still breathing when they dragged him out of the burning shed and onto the porch of a nearby house, but he was paralyzed below the point where his spinal cord had been struck. Two weeks short of his twenty-seventh birthday, he was so much the worse for wear — and the loss of his mustache, which he had shaved off the week before — that he scarcely resembled the darkly handsome matinee idol he had been before his ordeal of the past eleven days. "I thought I did for the best," he managed to say. Just at sunup he asked to have his hands lifted so he could see them, and when this was done he stared at them in despair. "Useless, useless," he muttered. Then he died.

So tight a grip had been kept on official news of the assassination — particularly southward, where Stanton believed the plot had been hatched and where such information might be of use to the conspirators in their flight from justice — most citizens did not know of the murder, except as one more piece of gossip among many that were false, until the murderer himself had been dispatched. Down in rural Georgia, for example, a full week after Lincoln's death and four days before Booth's, a young woman wrote in her diary: "None of our people believe any of the rumors, thinking them as mythical as the surrender of General Lee's army." Presently though, when the truth came out, there were those who reacted with a bitterness nurtured by four long years of a war that now was lost. Another Georgian, an Augusta housewife, writing to her mother-in-law on the last day of April, saw the northern leader's violent fall as a "righteous retribution," a minor comfort in a time of shock. "One sweet drop among so much that is painful is that he at least cannot raise his howl of diabolical triumph over us," she declared. Some in Johnston's army, waiting around Greensboro for the details of their surrender to be worked out, reacted initially in much the same fashion; that is, until Beauregard heard them whooping outside his tent. An aide later testified that this was the only time he saw Old Bory lose his temper all the way. "Shut those men up," he said angrily. "If they won't shut up, have them arrested. Those are my orders."

For the most part, however, even those celebrations that went unchecked lasted only about as long as it took the celebrants to turn their thoughts to Andrew Johnson, who was now in a position to exact the vengeance he had been swearing all along. Jefferson Davis perceived this from the outset. In Charlotte on April 19, when he learned from Breckinridge of his war-long adversary's sudden removal from the scene, he saw in the Tennessean's elevation a portent of much woe. "Certainly I have no special regard for Mr Lincoln," he remarked, "but there are a great many men of whose end I would rather hear than his. I fear it will be disastrous to our people, and I regret it deeply."

That was his first reaction, and he held to it down the years. Though, like Beauregard, he was quick to silence those in his escort who cheered the news, he never engaged in pious homilies over the corpse of his chief foe, but rather stressed his preference for him over the "renegade" who replaced him. "For an enemy so relentless in the war for our subjugation, we could not be expected to mourn," he wrote afterwards; "yet, in view of its political consequences, [Lincoln's assassination] could not be regarded otherwise than as a great misfortune to the South. He had power over the Northern people, and was without personal malignity toward the people of the South; [whereas] his successor was without power in the North, and [was] the embodiment of malignity toward the Southern people, perhaps the more so because he had betrayed and deserted them in the hour of their need."

★ ★ ★

As long ago as late September, before Hood set out on the northward march that turned his fine-honed army into a skeow — "s-k-e-o-w, bubble, bubble, s-k-e-o-w, bust" — Richard Taylor had told Davis that "the best we could hope for was to protract the struggle until spring." Now spring had come, and all he had left for the defense of his Department of Alabama, Mississippi, and East Louisiana were some 10,000 troops under Forrest and Maury, recently flung out of Selma and Mobile, plus something under half that number in garrisons scattered about the three-state region west of the Chattahoochee. Clearly enough, the time was at hand "for statesmen, not soldiers, to deal with the future." Accordingly, when he learned of the week-old "Basis of Agreement" worked out by Sherman, Johnston, and Breckinridge near Durham Station on April 18, he got in touch at once with Canby to arrange a similar armistice here in the western theater, pending approval by the civil authorities of terms that would, in Sherman's words, "produce peace from the Potomac to the Rio Grande." Canby — who knew no more than Taylor did of Washington's quick rejection of those terms — was altogether willing, and a meeting was scheduled for the last day in April, twelve miles up the railroad from Mobile.

Magee's Farm, the place was called. Canby, waiting at the appointed hour beside the tracks, had a full brigade drawn up as a guard of honor, along with a band and a brassy array of staffers, all turned out in their best. The effect, when Taylor at last pulled in, was anticlimactic to say the least. Arriving from Meridian on a handcar — practically the only piece of rolling stock left unwrecked by Wilson's raiders — he had been "pumped" down the line by two Negroes and was accompanied by a single aide whose uniform was as weathered as his own. Nothing daunted, for all his awareness that "the appearance of the two parties contrasted the fortunes of our respective causes," he then retired with the Federal commander to a room prepared in a nearby house, where they promptly agreed to observe a truce while awaiting ratification by their two governments of the terms given Johnston twelve days ago by Sherman, copies of which had been forwarded to them both. This done, they came out into the yard to share an al fresco luncheon that included a number of bottles of champagne, the drawing of whose corks provided what the Louisianian said were "the first agreeable explosive sounds I had heard for years." Presently, when the musicians struck up "Hail, Columbia," Canby ordered a quick switch to "Dixie," but Taylor, not to be outdone, suggested that the original tune continue, the time having come when they could "hail Columbia" together, as in the old days.

Back in Meridian next day he heard from Canby that the Sherman-Johnston agreement had been disavowed; that fighting would resume within forty-eight hours unless he surrendered — as Johnston had done, five days ago — on the terms accorded Lee at Appomattox, three weeks back. Taylor had neither the means nor the inclination to continue the struggle on his own; his task as he saw it, now that the Confederacy had crumbled, was "to administer on the ruins as residuary legatee," and he said as much in his reply, May 2, accepting Canby's scaled-down offer. Two days later they met again, this time at Citronelle, also on the Mobile & Ohio, twenty miles north of Magee's Farm, where, as Taylor later put it, "I delivered the epilogue of the great drama in which I had played a humble part." In Alabama, Mississippi, and East Louisiana, as had already been done in Virginia, North and South Carolina, and Georgia, all butternut survivors were to lay down their arms in exchange for assurance by the victors that they were not to be "disturbed" by the U.S. government "so long as they continue to observe the conditions of their parole and the laws in force where they reside." Although Sherman's proposal for restoring peace "from the Potomac to the Rio Grande" had been rejected, more or less out of hand, the arrangement that replaced it — commander to individual army commander, blue and gray, after the pattern set by Grant and Lee — achieved as much, in any case, for all of that region east of the Mississippi.

Or did it? Would it? Some, indeed many, believed it would not: including Sherman. "I now apprehend that the rebel armies will disperse," he had written Grant the week before, "and instead of dealing with six or seven states, we will have to deal with numberless bands of desperadoes, headed by such men as Mosby, Forrest, Red Jackson, and others who know not and care not for danger and its consequences."

One at least of these, despite the Ohioan's assertion that "nothing is left for them but death or highway robbery," had already proved him wrong. On April 21, soon after learning of Lee's capitulation, John Mosby formally disbanded his Rangers and presently — remarking, as if in specific response to Sherman: "We are soldiers, not highwaymen" — made official application for parole in order to hang up his shingle and resume the life he had led before the war. So much then for baleful predictions as to the postsurrender activities of Virginia's leading partisan, who soon was practicing law in the region where he and his men had given the blue authorities so much trouble for the past two years. As for Forrest and his red-haired subordinate, W. H. Jackson, there was considerable doubt, even in their own minds, as to what course they would follow. Between Taylor's final meeting with Canby, May 4 at Citronelle, and the issuance of paroles four days later, a staff colonel would recall, "all was gloom, broken only by wild rumors." This was especially the case in Forrest's camps around Gainesville, Alabama, fifty miles northeast of Meridian. There was much talk of "going to Mexico" as an alternative to surrender, and the general himself was said to be turning the notion over in his mind.

He was in fact in a highly disgruntled state, one arm in a sling from his fourth combat wound, suffered during a horseback fight with a young Indiana captain at Ebenezer Church, just north of Selma on the day before Wilson overran him there. The Federal hacked away at the general's upraised arm until Forrest managed to draw his revolver and kill him. "If that boy had known enough to give me the point of his saber instead of the edge," he later said, "I should not have been here to tell about it." Instead the Hoosier captain became his thirtieth hand-to-hand victim within a four-year span of war that also saw twenty-nine horses shot from under him, thereby validating his claim that he was "a horse ahead at the close." What rankled worse, despite the mitigating odds, was the drubbing Wilson had given him in what turned out to be his last campaign. Unaccustomed to defeat, this only soldier on either side who rose from private to lieutenant general had no more fondness for surrender now than he had had when he rode out of Donelson, nearly forty months ago. Mexico seemed preferable — at any rate up to the day before the one on which he and his troopers were scheduled to lay down their arms. That evening he and his adjutant set out on a quiet, thoughtful ride. Neither spoke until they drew rein just short of a fork in the road. "Which way, General?" his companion asked, and Forrest replied glumly: "Either. If one road led to hell and the other to Mexico, I would be indifferent which to take." They sat their horses in the moonlight for a time, the adjutant doing most of the talking, which had to do with the duty they owed their native land, whether in victory or defeat: particularly Forrest, who could lead into the ways of peace the young men who had followed him in war. "That settles it," the general said, and turned back toward camp.

As usual, once he made up his mind to a course of action, he followed it all-out: as did his men, who dropped all talk of Mexico when they learned that he had done so before them. Whatever doubt they had of this was dispelled by the farewell he addressed to them at Gainesville on May 9, soon after they furled their star-crossed flags and gave their parole to fight no more against the Union he and they rejoined that day.

SOLDIERS:

By an agreement made between Lieutenant General Taylor, commanding the Department of Alabama, Mississippi, and East Louisiana, and Major General Canby, commanding U.S. forces, the troops of this department have been surrendered. I do not think it proper or necessary at this time to refer to the causes which have reduced us to this extremity, nor is it now a matter of material consequence as to how such results were brought about. That we are beaten is a self-evident fact, and any further resistance on our part would be justly regarded as the height of folly and rashness. . . . Reason dictates and humanity demands that no more blood be shed. Fully realizing and feeling that such is the case, it is your duty and mine to lay down our arms, submit to the "powers that be," and aid in restoring peace and establishing law and order throughout the land. The terms upon which you were surrendered are favorable, and should be satisfactory and acceptable to all. They manifest a spirit of magnanimity and liberality on the part of the Federal authorities which should be met on our part by a faithful compliance with all the stipulations and conditions therein expressed. . . .

Civil war, such as you have just passed through, naturally engenders feelings of animosity, hatred, and revenge. It is our duty to divest ourselves of all such feelings, and, so far as it is in our power to do so, to cultivate feelings toward those with whom we have so long contested and heretofore so widely but honestly differed. Neighborhood feuds, personal animosities, and private differences should be blotted out, and when you return home a manly, straightforward course of conduct will secure the respect even of your enemies. Whatever your responsibilities may be to government, to society, or to individuals, meet them like men. The attempt made to establish a separate and independent confederation has failed, but the consciousness of having done your duty faithfully and to the end will in some measure repay for the hardships you have undergone. . . . I have never on the field of battle sent you where I was unwilling to go myself, nor would I now advise you to a course which I felt myself unwilling to pursue. You have been good soldiers, you can be good citizens. Obey the laws, preserve your honor, and the government to which you have surrendered can afford to be and will be magnanimous.

N. B. FORREST,
Lieutenant General.

★ ★ ★

On April 26, the day of Booth's death and Johnston's renegotiated surrender, Davis met for the last time with his full cabinet and decided to end his week-long stay in Charlotte by pressing on at once to the southwest. He had not been surprised at Washington's rejection of the Sherman-Johnston "Basis of Agreement," which he himself had approved two days before, since his opinion of the new northern leader and "his venomous Secretary of War," as he said afterwards, did not permit him to expect "that they would be less vindictive after a surrender of the army had been proposed than when it was regarded as a formidable body defiantly holding its position in the field." What did surprise and anger him, some time later, was the news that Johnston, ignoring the suggestion that he fall back with the mobile elements of his army to draw Sherman after him, had laid down his arms without so much as a warning note to superiors he knew were in flight for their lives. Davis's indignation was heightened all the more when he learned that the Virginian, in his last general order, had blamed "recent events in Virginia for breaking every hope of success by war." Lee had fought until he was virtually surrounded and a breakout attempt had failed; whereas Johnston not only had not tried for the getaway suggested and expected, but had also, by a stroke of the pen, ended all formal resistance in three of the states through which his fugitive superiors would be traveling in their attempt to reach Dick Taylor or Kirby Smith, on this or the far side of the Mississippi River.

Hope for escape by that route had been encouraged by a series of dispatches from Wade Hampton, who did not consider himself or his troopers bound by the surrender negotiations then in progress. "The military situation is very gloomy, I admit," he wrote Davis on the day after the Sherman-Johnston-Breckinridge meeting near Durham Station, "but it is by no means desperate, and endurance and determination will produce a change." His notion was that the struggle should continue wherever there was ground to stand on, in or out of the country, whatever the odds. "Give me a good force of cavalry and I will take them safely across the Mississippi, and if you desire to go in that direction it will give me great pleasure to escort you.... I can bring to your support many strong arms and brave hearts — men who will fight to Texas, and who, if forced from that state, will seek refuge in Mexico rather than in the Union." Hoping to confer with the President in Salisbury, he reached Greensboro three days later, April 22, and found that the government had been transferred to Charlotte. "My only object in seeing you," he declared in a follow-up message, "was to assure you that many of my officers and men agree with me in thinking that nothing can be as disastrous to us as a peace founded on the restoration of the Union. A return to the Union will bring all the horrors of war, coupled with all the degradation that can be inflicted on a conquered people.... If I can serve you or my country by any further fighting you have only to tell me so. My plan is to collect all the men who will stick to their colors, and to get to Texas. I can carry with me quite a number, *and I can get there.*"

Heartened by this stalwart reassurance from the South Carolina grandee, whose views — delusions, some would say — were in accordance with his own, Davis took time out next day for the first real letter he had had a chance to write his wife since he left Richmond, three weeks back. In it were mingled the hopes expressed by Hampton and the private doubts that surfaced when he shifted his attention from his duty to his country, as the symbol of its survival, to his concern for the welfare of his four children and their mother. Threatened by Stoneman's descent on Salisbury, they had left Charlotte ten days ago, six days before he got there, and were now in Abbeville, South Carolina, down near the Georgia line. He spoke first of the difficulty of his position in deciding whether to urge his people to continue their resistance to what he saw as subjugation. "The issue is one which it is very painful for me to meet," he told Varina. "On one hand is the long night of oppression which will follow the return of our people to the 'Union'; on the other, the suffering of the women and children, and carnage among the few brave patriots who would still oppose the invader, and who, unless the people would rise en masse to sustain them, would struggle but to die in vain. I think my judgment is undisturbed by any pride of opinion, [for] I have prayed to our Heavenly Father to give me wisdom and fortitude equal to the demands of the position in which Providence has placed me. I have sacrificed so much for the cause of the Confederacy that I can measure my ability to make any further sacrifice required, and am assured there is but one to which I am not equal — my wife and my children.... For myself," he added, "it may be that a devoted band of cavalry will cling to me and that I can force my way across the Mississippi, and if nothing can be done there which it will be proper to do, then I can go to Mexico, and have the world from which to choose a location." That such a choice would come hard for him was shown by the emotion that swept over him when, having faced the prospect of spending the rest of his life in exile, he closed his letter. "Dear Wife, this is not the fate to which I invited [you] when the future was rose-colored to us both; but I know you will bear it even better than myself, and that, of us two, I alone will ever look back reproachfully on my past career.... Farewell, my dear. There may be better things in store for us than are now in view, but my love is all I have to offer, and that has the value of a thing long possessed, and sure not to be lost."

Three days later, in reaction to the news that Sherman's terms had been rejected, Davis and his advisers — fugitives in a profounder sense now that the new enemy President had branded them as criminals not eligible for parole — concluded that the time had come to press on southward, out of the Old North State. This was the last full cabinet meeting, for it was no sooner over than George Davis submitted his resignation on grounds that his motherless children required his attention at Wilmington. Concerned as he was about his own homeless family up ahead, Jefferson Davis had sympathy for the North Carolinian's view as to where his duty lay, and the Confederacy — which had never had any courts anyhow, Supreme or otherwise — no longer had an Attorney General by the time its government pulled out of Charlotte that same afternoon. At Fort Mill two mornings later, just over the South Carolina line, Trenholm also resigned, too ill to continue the journey even by ambulance. Davis thanked the wealthy Charlestonian for his "lofty patriotism and personal sacrifice," then shifted John Reagan to the Treasury Department, leaving the postal service headless and the cabinet score at two down, four to go.

"I *cannot* feel like a beaten man," he had remarked before setting out, and now on the march his spirits rose. In part this was because of his return to the field, to the open-air soldier life he always fancied. Four more cavalry brigades — so called, though none was as large as an old-style regiment, and all five combined totaled only about 3000 men — had turned up at Charlotte, fugitive and unattached, in time to swell the departing column to respectable if not formidable proportions. Breckinridge took command of the whole, and Davis had for company three military aides, all colonels, John Wood, Preston Johnston — son of his dead hero, Albert Sidney Johnston — and Francis Lubbock, former governor of Texas. Like Judah Benjamin, who had an apparently inexhaustible supply of wit and prime Havanas, these were congenial traveling companions. Moreover, progress through this section of South Carolina, which had been spared the eastward Sherman torch, was like a return to happier times, the crowds turning out to cheer their President and wish him well. This was the homeland of John C. Calhoun, and invitations poured in for one-night stays at mansions along the way. Davis responded accordingly. "He talked very pleasantly of other days," Mallory would recall, "and forgot for a time the engrossing anxieties of the situation." He spoke of Scott and Byron, of hunting dogs and horses, in a manner his fellow travelers found "singularly equable and cheerful" throughout the six-day ride to Abbeville, which they reached on May 2.

Mrs Davis and the children were not there, having moved on into Georgia three days ago. "Washington will be the first point I shall 'unload' at," she informed her husband in a note brought by a courier who met him on the road. That was less than fifty miles off, the closest they had been to one another in more than a month, and though she planned to "wait a little until we hear something of you," she urged him not to risk capture by going out of his way to join her, saying: "Let me beseech you not to calculate upon seeing me unless I happen to cross your shortest path toward your bourne, be that what it may." Stragglers and parolees from Lee's and Johnston's armies had passed through in large numbers, she also cautioned, and "not one has talked fight. A stand cannot be made in this country; do not be induced to try it. As to the Trans-Mississippi, I doubt if at first things will be straight, but the spirit is there and the daily accretions will be great when the deluded on this side are crushed out between the upper and nether millstone."

Speed then was the watchword, lest he be gathered up by blue pursuers or victimized by butternut marauders, hungry alike for the millions in treasury bullion he was rumored to have brought with him out of Richmond. At 4 o'clock that afternoon he summoned Breckinridge and the brigade commanders to a large downstairs parlor in the house where his family had stayed while they were here. Through a large window opening westward the five could see a rose garden in full bloom, and one among them later remarked that he had "never seen Mr Davis look better or show to better advantage. He seemed in excellent spirits and humor, and the union of dignity, graceful affability, and decision, which made his manner usually so striking, was very marked in his reception of us." After welcoming and putting them at ease, as was his custom at such meetings — even when the participants were familiars, as these were not; at least not yet — he passed at once to his reason for having called them into council. "It is time that we adopt some definite plan upon which the further prosecution of our struggle shall be conducted. I have summoned you for consultation. I feel that I ought to do nothing now without the advice of my military chiefs." He smiled as he said this last: "rather archly," according to one hearer, who observed that while "such a term addressed to a handful of brigadiers, commanding altogether barely 3000 men, by one who so recently had been the master of legions, was a pleasantry; yet he said it in a way that made it a compliment." What followed, however, showed clearly enough how serious he was. "Even if the troops now with me be all that I can for the present rely on," he declared, "3000 brave men are enough for a nucleus around which the whole people will rally when the panic which now afflicts them has passed away."

A tense silence ensued; none of the five wanted to be the first to say what each of them knew the other four were thinking. Finally one spoke, and the rest chimed in. What the country was undergoing wasn't panic, they informed their chief, but exhaustion. Any attempt to prolong the war, now that the means of supporting it were gone, "would be a cruel injustice to the people of the South," while for the soldiers the consequences would be even worse; "for if they persisted in a conflict so hopeless they would be treated as brigands and would forfeit all chance of returning to their homes." Breaking a second silence, Davis asked why then, if all hope was exhausted, they still were in the field. To assist in his escape, they replied, adding that they "would ask our men to follow us until his safety was assured, and would risk them in battle for that purpose, but would not fire another shot in an effort to continue hostilities." Now a third silence descended, in which the gray leader sat looking as if he had been slapped across the face by a trusted friend. Recovering, he said he would hear no suggestion that had only to do with his own survival, and made one final plea wherein, as one listener said, "he appealed eloquently to every sentiment and reminiscence that might be supposed to move a Southern soldier." When he finished, the five merely looked at him in sorrow. "Then all is indeed lost," he muttered, and rose to leave the room, deathly pale and unsteady on his feet. He tottered, and as he did so Breckinridge stepped forward, hale and ruddy, and offered his arm, which Davis, aged suddenly far beyond his nearly fifty-seven years, was glad to take.

Now it was flight, pure and simple — flight for flight's sake, so to speak — with no further thought of a rally until and unless he reached the Transmississippi. That was still his goal, and all agreed that the lighter he traveled the better his chances were of getting there. One encumbrance was the treasury hoard, which had got this far by rail, outracing Stoneman, but could go no farther. Of this, $39,000 had been left in Greensboro for Johnston to distribute among his soldiers (which he did; all ranks drew $1.15 apiece to see them home) and now the balance was dispersed, including $108,000 in silver coins paid out to troopers of the five brigades, the cadet guards, and other members of the presidential party; officers and men alike drew $26.25 each. Transferred to wagons, $230,000 in securities was sent on to a bank in Washington, just beyond the Georgia line, for deposit pending its return to Richmond and the banks that owned it, while $86,000 in gold was concealed in the false bottom of a carriage and started on its way to Charleston, there to be shipped in secrecy to England and drawn on when the government reached Texas. That left $30,000 in silver bullion, packed in trunks and stored in a local warehouse, and $35,000 in gold specie, kept on hand to cover expenses on the journey south and west. Relieved at last of their burden and "detached," the cadets promptly scattered for their homes.

Before leaving-time, which was midnight that same May 2, others expressed their desire to be gone, and one of these was Stephen Mallory. Pleading "the dependent condition of a helpless family," he submitted his resignation as head of the all-but-nonexistent C. S. Navy. He would leave soon after they crossed the Savannah River into Georgia, he said, and join his refugee wife and children in La Grange. That would bring the cabinet tally to three down, three to go. Or rather, four down, two to go; for by then still another member had departed. Plump and chafed, Judah Benjamin took off informally the following night, after a private conversation with his chief. His goal was the Florida coast, then Bimini, and he set out disguised variously as a farmer and a Frenchman, with a ramshackle cart, a spavined horse, and a mismatched suit of homespun clothes. Davis wished him well, but again declined an offer from Mallory, when the Floridian parted from him in Washington on May 4, of a boat then waiting up the Indian River to take him to Cuba or the Bahamas. He said, as he had said before — unaware that, even as he spoke, Dick Taylor was meeting with Canby at Citronelle to surrender the last gray army east of the Mississippi — that he could not leave Confederate soil while a single Confederate regiment clung to its colors.

Here again, as at Abbeville two days ago, he found that his family, fearful of being waylaid by marauders, had moved on south. "I dread the Yankees getting news of you so much," his wife had written in a note she left behind. "You are the country's only hope, and the very best intentioned do not calculate upon a stand this side of the river. Why not cut loose from your escort? Go swiftly and alone, with the exception of two or three.... May God keep you, my old and only love," the note ended.

He had it in mind to do just that, or anyhow something close, and accordingly instructed Breckinridge to peel off next day with the five brigades of cavalry, leaving him only an escort company of Kentucky horsemen; which, on second thought — for they were, as he said, "not strong enough to fight, and too large to pass without observation" — he ordered reduced to ten volunteers. He would have with him after that, in addition to a handful of servants and teamsters, only these men, his three military aides, and John Reagan. The Texan had been with him from the start and was determined to stick with him to the finish, which he hoped would not come before they reached his home beyond the Mississippi and the Sabine. Davis was touched by this fidelity, as he also was by a message received when he took up the march next morning. Robert Toombs lived in Washington, and though none of the party had called on him, or he on them, he sent word that all he had was at the fugitive President's disposal. "Mr Davis and I have had a quarrel, but we have none now," he said. "If he desires, I will call all my men around here to see him safely across the Chattahoochee at the risk of my life." Davis, told of this, replied: "That is like Bob Toombs. He always was a whole-souled man. If it were necessary, I should not hesitate to accept his offer."

No such thoughts of another Georgia antagonist prompted a side trip when he passed within half a dozen miles of Liberty Hall, the Vice President's estate near Crawfordville; nor did he consider getting in touch with Joe Brown at Milledgeville, twenty-five miles to the west, when he reached Sandersville, May 6. Pressing on — as if aware that James Wilson had issued that day in Macon, less than fifty miles away, a War Department circular announcing: "One hundred thousand dollars Reward in Gold will be paid to any person or persons who will apprehend and deliver JEFFERSON DAVIS to any of the military authorities of the United States. Several millions of specie reported to be with him will become the property of the captors" — the now fast-moving column of twenty men and three vehicles made camp that evening on the east side of the Oconee, near Ball's Ferry. Their intention was to continue southwest tomorrow for a crossing of the Chattahoochee "below the point where the enemy had garrisons," but something Preston Johnston learned when he walked down to the ferry before supper caused a sudden revision of those plans. Mrs Davis and the children, escorted by Burton Harrison, had crossed here that morning, headed south, and there was a report that a group of disbanded soldiers planned to attack and rob their camp that night. Hearing this, Davis remounted his horse. "I do not feel that you are bound to go with me," he told his companions, "but I must protect my family."

What followed turned out to be an exhausting all-night ride beyond the Oconee. Though the escort horses finally broke down, Davis and his better-mounted aides kept on through the moonlit bottoms until shortly before dawn, near Dublin, close to twenty miles downstream, they came upon a darkened camp beside the road. "Who's there?" someone called out in an alarmed, determined voice which Davis was greatly relieved to recognize as Harrison's. He and his wife and children were together again for the first time since he put them aboard the train in Richmond, five weeks back.

Having rested their mounts, the escort horsemen arrived in time for breakfast, and the two groups — with Davis so bone-tired that he agreed for the first time to ride in an ambulance — pushed on south together to bivouac that night some twenty miles east of Hawkinsville, where 3000 of Wilson's raiders were reported to be in camp. Alarmed, Mrs Davis persuaded her husband to proceed without her the following day, May 8. Once across the Ocmulgee at Poor Robin Bluff, however, he heard new rumors of marauders up ahead, and stopped on the outskirts of Abbeville to wait for her and the children, intending to see them through another day's march before turning off to the southwest. They arrived that night, and next morning the two groups, again

Lucifer in Starlight

combined, continued to move south. Lee had surrendered a month ago today; tomorrow would make a solid month that Davis had been on the go from Danville, a distance of just over four hundred miles, all but the first and last forty of which he had spent on horseback; he was understandably weary. Yet the arrangement, when they made camp at 5 o'clock that afternoon in a stand of pines beside a creek just north of Irwinville, was that he would take some rest in his wife's tent, then press on with his escort after dark, presumably to see her no more until she rejoined him in Texas.

Outside in the twilight, seated with their backs against the boles of trees around the campfire, his aides waited for word to mount up and resume the journey. They too were weary, and lately they had been doubtful — especially during the two days spent off-course because of Davis's concern for the safety of his wife and children — whether they would make it out of Georgia. But now, within seventy miles of the Florida border, they felt much better about their chances, having come to believe that Breckinridge, when he peeled off near Washington with the five brigades, had decoyed the Federals onto his track and off theirs. In any case, the President's horse was saddled and waiting, a brace of pistols holstered on its withers, and they were waiting, too, ready to move on. They sat up late, then finally, receiving no call, dozed off: unaware that, even as they slept and dawn began to glimmer through the pines, two regiments of Union cavalry — 4th Michigan and 1st Wisconsin, tipped off at Hawkinsville that the rebel leader and his party had left Abbeville that morning, headed for Irwinville, forty-odd miles away — were closing in from opposite sides of the camp, one having circled it in the darkness to come up from the south, while the other bore down from the northwest. The result, as the two mounted units converged, was the last armed clash east of the Mississippi. Moreover, by way of a further distinction, all the combatants wore blue, including the two killed and four wounded in the rapid-fire exchange. "A sharp fight ensued, both parties exhibiting the greatest determination," James Wilson presently would report, not without a touch of pride in his men's aggressiveness, even when they were matched against each other. "Fifteen minutes elapsed before the mistake was discovered."

All was confusion in the night-drowsed bivouac. Wakened like the others by the sudden uproar on the fringes of the camp — he had lain down, fully dressed, in expectation of leaving before midnight, but had slept through from exhaustion — Davis presumed the attackers were butternut marauders. "I will go out and see if I can't stop the firing," he told his wife. "Surely I will have some authority with Confederates." When he lifted the tent flap, however, he saw high-booted figures, their uniforms dark in the pearly glow before sunrise, dodging through the woods across the creek and along the road on this side. "Federal cavalry are upon us!" he exclaimed. Terrified, Varina urged him to flee while there was time. He hesitated, then took up a lightweight sleeveless raincoat — which he supposed was his own but was his wife's, cut from the same material — and started out, drawing it on along with a shawl she threw over his head and shoulders. Before he had gone twenty paces a Union trooper rode up, carbine at the ready, and ordered him to halt. Davis paused, dropping the coat and shawl, and then came on again, directly toward the trooper in his path. "I expected, if he fired, he would miss me," he later explained, "and my intention was in that event to put my hand under his foot, tumble him off on the other side, spring into his saddle, and attempt to escape." It was a trick he had learned from the Indians, back in his early army days, and it might have worked except for his wife, who, seeing the soldier draw a deliberate bead on the slim gray form advancing point-blank on him, rushed forward with a cry and threw her arms around her husband's neck. With that, all chance for a getaway was gone; Davis now could not risk his life without also risking hers, and presently other blue-clad troopers came riding up, all with their carbines leveled at him and Varina, who still clung to him. "God's will be done," he said in a low voice as he turned away and walked slowly past the tent to take a seat on a fallen tree beside the campfire.

Elsewhere about the camp the struggle continued on various levels of resistance. Four days ago, a wagon had gone south from Sandersville with most of the $35,000 in gold coin; the remaining $10,000, kept for travel expenses between there and the Gulf, was distributed among the aides and Reagan, who carried it in their saddlebags; as the bluecoats now discovered. Reagan, with his own and the President's portion of the burden — some $3500 in all — turned it over with no more than a verbal protest, but his fellow Texan Lubbock hung onto his in a tussle with two of the soldiers, despite their threats to shoot him if he did not turn loose. "Shoot and be damned!" he told them. "You'll not rob me while I'm alive and looking on." They did, though, and Preston Johnston lost his share as well, along with the pistols his father had carried when he fell at Shiloh. Only John Wood was successful in his resistance, and that was by strategy rather than by force. Knowing that he would be charged with piracy for his work off the New England coast last August, the former skipper of the *Tallahassee* took one of his captors aside, slipped him two $20 gold pieces, and walked off unnoticed through the pines — eventually to make it all the way to Cuba with Breckinridge, whom he encountered down in Florida two weeks later, determined like himself to leave the country rather than stay and face charges brought against him by the victors in their courts.

But that was later. For the present, all Wood's friends knew was that he was missing, and only one of his foes knew even that much. Besides, both groups were distracted by the loud bang of a carbine, followed at once by a shriek of pain. Convinced that the reported millions in coin and bullion must be cached somewhere about the camp, one unfortunate trooper had used his loaded weapon in an attempt to pry open a locked trunk, and the piece had discharged, blowing off one of his hands. Others took over and got the lid up, only to find that all the trunk contained was a hoop skirt belonging to Mrs Davis. Despite their disappointment, the garment turned out to have its uses, being added to the cloak and shawl as evidence that the rebel chieftain had tried to escape in women's clothes. Three days later, Wilson would inform the War Department that Davis, surprised by the dawn attack, "hastily put on one of Mrs Davis' dresses and started for the woods, closely pursued by our men, who at first thought him a woman, but seeing his boots while running suspected his sex at once. The race was a short one, and the rebel President soon was brought to bay. He brandished a bowie knife of elegant pattern, and showed signs of battle, but yielded promptly to the persuasion of Colt revolvers without compelling our men to fire." This was far too good to let pass unexploited, providing as it did a counterpart to the story of Lincoln's passage through Baltimore four years ago, similarly clad in a Scotch-plaid garment borrowed from his wife, on the way to his first inauguration. "If Jefferson Davis was captured in his wife's clothes," Halleck recommended after reading Wilson's dispatch, "I respectfully suggest that he be sent North in the same habiliments."

That too would come later, along with the many jubilant cartoons and a tableau staged by Barnum to display the Confederate leader in flight through brush and briers, cavorting in hooped calico and brandishing a dagger. Just now his worst indignity came from having to look on powerless while the treasure-hungry bluecoats rifled his and Varina's personal luggage, tossing the contents about and only pausing to snatch from the fire and gulp down the children's half-cooked breakfast. "You are an expert set of thieves," he told one of them, who replied: "Think so?" and kept on rifling. Presently the Michigan colonel approached and stood looking down at the Mississippian, seated on his log beside the campfire. "Well, old Jeff, we've got you at last," he declared with a grin. Davis lost his temper at this and shouted: "The worst of it all is that I should be captured by a band of thieves and scoundrels!" Stiffening, the colonel drew himself up. "You're a prisoner and can afford to talk that way," he said.

Davis knew well enough that he was a prisoner. What was more, in case it slipped his memory during the three-day trip to Wilson's headquarters at Macon, the soldiers took pains to keep him well reminded of the fact. "Get a move on, Jeff," they taunted him from time to time. He rode in an ambulance with his wife and a pair of guards, while her sister Margaret followed in another with the children, all four of whom were upset by her weeping. The other captives were permitted to ride their own horses, which were "lent" them pending arrival. There was a carnival aspect to the procession, at least among the troopers riding point. "Hey, Johnny Reb," they greeted paroled Confederates by the roadside, "we've got your President!" That was good for a laugh each time save one, when an angered butternut replied: "Yes, and the devil's got yours." A supposed greater shock was reserved for Davis along the way, when he was shown the proclamation Andrew Johnson had issued charging him with complicity in Lincoln's assassination. He took it calmly, however, remarking that there was one man who knew the document to be false — "the one who signed it, for he at least knew that I preferred Lincoln to himself."

After a night spent in Macon, May 13, he and his wife, together with Margaret Howell and the children, Reagan, Lubbock, and Preston Johnston, were placed in a prison train for an all-day roundabout journey to Augusta, where they were driven across town to the river landing and put on a tug waiting to take them down the Savannah to the coast. Already aboard, to his surprise, were two distinguished Confederates, now prisoners like himself. One was Joe Wheeler, who had been captured five days ago at Conyer Station, just east of Atlanta, frustrated in his no-surrender attempt to reach the Transmississippi with three members of his staff and eleven privates. The other was Alexander Stephens, picked up last week at Liberty Hall after Davis passed nearby. Pale and shaken, the child-sized former Vice President looked forlorn in the greatcoat and several mufflers he wore despite the balmy late-spring weather. Davis gave him a remote but courteous bow, which was returned in kind. At Port Royal, on the morning of May 16, the enlarged party transferred to an ocean-going steamer, the side-wheeler *William P. Clyde*. Presumably, under escort by the multigunned warship *Tuscarora*, she would take them up the coast, into Chesapeake Bay, then up the Potomac to the northern capital.

So they thought. But three days later, after a stormy delay while rounding Hatteras, the *Clyde* dropped anchor off the eastern tip of the York-James peninsula, and there she lay for three more days, under the guns of Fort Monroe, "the Gibraltar of the Chesapeake," whose thirty-foot granite walls, close to a hundred feet thick at their base, had sheltered its Union garrison throughout the four years of the war. Next day, May 20, Stephens and Reagan were transferred to the *Tuscarora* for delivery to Fort Warren in Boston harbor. The day after that, Wheeler, Lubbock, and Johnston were sent on their way to Fort Delaware, downriver from Philadelphia. Then on May 22 came Davis's turn, though he had nothing like as far to go. His destination was there at hand, and the delay had been for the purpose of giving the fort's masons time to convert a subterranean gunroom into a prison cell: strong evidence that, for him as for the others gone before, the charges and the trial to follow would be military, not civil.

"In leaving his wife and children," a witness informed Stanton,

"Davis exhibited no great emotion, though he was violently affected." This last was clearly true, in spite of the prisoner's efforts to conceal what he was feeling. "Try not to cry. They will gloat over your grief," he told Varina as he prepared to board the tug that would take him ashore. She managed to do as he asked, but then, having watched him pass from sight across the water, rushed to her cabin and gave way to weeping. It was as if she had read what tomorrow's New York *Herald* would tell its readers: "At about 3 o'clock yesterday, 'all that is mortal' of Jeff'n Davis, late so-called 'President of the alleged Confederate States,' was duly, but quietly and effectively, committed to that living tomb prepared within the impregnable walls of Fortress Monroe.... No more will Jeff'n Davis be known among the masses of men. He is buried alive."

X 3 X

On May 10, unaware that the Confederate leader had been captured before sunup down in Georgia, Andrew Johnson issued a proclamation declaring that "armed resistance to the authority of this Government in the said insurrectionary States may be regarded as virtually at an end." This was subsequently taken by some, including the nine Supreme Court justices, to mark the close of the war, and it was followed twelve days later — the day Davis entered the granite bowels of Fort Monroe — by another presidential edict announcing that all the reunited nation's seaports would be open to commerce, with the exception of Galveston and three others along the Texas coast, and that civilian trade in all parts of the country east of the Mississippi would be resumed without restrictions.

That was May 22, and this second pronouncement, like the first, not only reflected the widespread public hope for a swift return to the ways of peace, but also served to clear the Washington stage for still another victory celebration, a two-day Grand Review planned for tomorrow and the next day, larger in scale, and above all in panoply, than the other two combined. Meade's and Sherman's armies had come north from Appomattox and Raleigh, and by then were bivouacked around the capital; which gave rise to a number of problems. In addition to the long-standing rivalry between paper-collar Easterners and roughneck Westerners, the latter now had a new burden of resentment to unload. Soon after the Administration's rejection of the original Durham Station terms, the papers had been full of Stanton's denunciation of the red-haired general who composed them, including charges that he was politically ambitious, with an eye on the Copperhead vote, and quite possibly had been seduced by Confederate gold, slipped to him out of the millions the fugitive rebel leader carried southward when Sherman obligingly called a halt to let him pass across his front. Angered by the slander of their chief, western officers no sooner reached the capital than they began leaping on saloon bars to call for "three groans for the Secretary of War," and the men in the ranks provoked fistfights with the Potomac veterans, whom they saw as allied with Stanton if only because of proximity. Eventually Grant solved the problem, in part at least, by having the two armies camp on opposite sides of the river; yet the bitterness continued.

The showdown would come tomorrow and the following day, not in a direct confrontation — though by now large numbers of men in the ranks of both might have welcomed such a test — but rather in a tandem display, whereby the public would judge their respective merits in accordance with their looks, their martial demeanor as they swung up Pennsylvania Avenue toward a covered stand erected in front of the White House for the President and his guests, including Grant and other dignitaries, civil as well as military. By prearrangement, the Army of the Potomac would parade on May 23 and the Westerners would take their turn next day. Sherman had qualms about the outcome: as well he might, for close-order marching was reported to be the chief skill of the bandbox Easterners, who moreover would be performing on home turf to long-term admirers, whereas his own gangling plowboys, though they had slogged a thousand roundabout miles through Georgia and the Carolinas, then north across Virginia, had done scarcely any drilling since they set out south from Chattanooga, a year ago this month. Then too there was the matter of clothes and equipment, another comparative disadvantage for members of the Armies of the Tennessee and the Cumberland. Their uniforms had weathered to "a cross between Regulation blue and Southern gray," a New England soldier observed, and the men inside were no less outlandish in his eyes. "Their hair and beards were uncut and uncombed; huge slouched hats, black and gray, adorned their heads; their boots were covered with the mud they had brought up from Georgia; their guns were of all designs, from the Springfield rifle to a cavalry carbine." That was how they looked to him on their arrival, three days before the start of the Grand Review. Sherman, with only that brief span for preparation, could only order such intensified drill instruction as there was time for, between hours of refurbishing dingy leather and dull brass, and hope meanwhile for the best; or in any case something better than the worst, which would be to have his veterans sneered or laughed at by people along the route of march or, least bearable of all, by those in the reviewing stand itself.

Washington — midtown Washington anyhow; the outlying sections were practically deserted — had never been so crowded as it was on the day when the first of more than 200,000 blue-clad victors, up from Virginia and the Carolinas, stepped out for the start of their last parade. In brilliant sunshine, under a cloudless sky, bleachers lining the avenue from the Capitol, where the march began, overflowed with citizens dressed this Tuesday in their Sunday best to watch the saviors of the Union swing past in cadence, twelve abreast. All the national flags were at full staff for the first time since April 15, and the crepe had been removed from public buildings as a sign that nearly six weeks of mourning for Lincoln were to be rounded off with two days of rejoicing for the victory he had done so much to win but had not lived to see completed. Meade led the column of march today, and after saluting Johnson and Grant, who stood together against a frock-coated backdrop of dignitaries massed in the stand before the White House, dismounted and joined them to watch his troops pass in review. Zouaves decked in gaudy clothes, Irish units with sprigs of greenery in their caps, engineers with ponderous equipment, artillerists riding caissons trailed by big-mouthed guns, all lent their particular touches to a show dominated in the main by close-packed throngs of infantry, polished bayonets glittering fiery in the sunlight, and seven unbroken miles of cavalry, steel-shod hoofs clopping for a solid hour past any given point. Spectators marveled at the youth of many commanders: especially Custer, whose "sunrise of golden hair" rippled to his shoulders as if in celebration of his latest promotion, one week after Appomattox. Barely four years out of West Point, not yet twenty-six and already a major general of volunteers, he came close to stealing the show when his horse, spooked by a wreath tossed from the curb, bolted just short of the White House. "Runaway!" the crowd shrieked, frightened and delighted. A reporter, watching the general's hat fly off and "his locks, unskeined, stream a foot behind him," was put in mind — more prophetically than he knew — of "the charge of a Sioux chieftain." The crowd cheered as Custer brought the animal under control, though by then he had passed the grandstand and, as Sherman said, "was not reviewed at all."

Wedged among the politicians, diplomats, and other honored guests, the red-haired Ohioan studied today's parade with all the intentness of an athletic coach scouting a rival team. His eye was peeled for shortcomings, and he found them. Observing for example that the Potomac soldiers "turned their heads around like country gawks to look at the big people on the stand," he would caution his ranking subordinates tonight not to let their men do that tomorrow. "I will give [them] plenty of time to go to the capital and see everything afterwards," he promised, "but let them keep their eyes fifteen feet to the front and march by in the old customary way." Still, for all his encouragement, he decided he would do well to register a disclaimer in advance, and accordingly, as today's review wore toward a close, he found occasion to remark to Meade: "I am afraid my poor tatterdemalion corps will make a poor appearance tomorrow when contrasted with yours." The Pennsylvanian, pleased with his army's performance today, was sympathetic in response. People would make allowances, he assured him.

Hopeful, but still deeply worried about what kind of showing his Westerners would manage now that their turn had come, Sherman rose early next morning to observe his six corps as they filed out of their Virginia camps — a march likened by one journalist to "the uncoiling of a tremendous python" — first across the Potomac, then on to the assembly area back of Capitol Hill. There they formed, not without a good deal of confusion, and there at 9 o'clock a cannon boomed the starting signal. He was out front on a handsome bay, hat in hand, sunlight glinting coppery in his close-cropped hair, and though the tramp of Logan's XV Corps marchers sounded solid and steady behind him during breaks in the cheers from the bleachers on both sides, he lacked the nerve to glance rearward until he topped the rise beside the Treasury Building, where a sharp right would bring into view the stand in front of the White House. Then at last he turned in the saddle and looked back. What he saw down the long vista, a full mile and a half to the Capitol shining on its hilltop, brought immeasurable relief. "The sight was simply magnificent. The column was compact, and the glittering muskets looked like a solid mass of steel, moving with the regularity of a pendulum." So he later wrote, adding: "I believe it was the happiest and most satisfactory moment of my life." Now, though, he was content to grin as he released his bated breath. "They have swung into it," he said.

They had indeed swung into it, and the crowd responded in kind. A reporter noted "something almost fierce in the fever of enthusiasm" roused by the sight of these lean, sunburnt marchers, all "bone and muscle and skin under their tattered battle flags." Risking fiasco, their commander had decided to go with their natural bent, rather than try for the kind of spit-and-polish show their rivals had staged the day before, and the gamble paid off from the moment the first of them set out, swinging along the avenue with a proud, rolling swagger, their stride a good two inches longer than the mincing twenty-two inches required by regulations, and springier as well. "They march like the lords of the world!" spectators exclaimed, finding them "hardier, knottier, weirder" than yesterday's prim, familiar paraders. Moreover, they provided additional marvels, reminders of their recent excursion across Georgia, some grim, others hilarious in effect. Hushes came at intervals when ambulances rolled past in the wake of each division, blood-stained stretchers strapped to their sides, and there was also laughter — rollicksome, however: not the kind Sherman had feared — when the crowd found each corps trailed by a contingent of camp followers, Negro men and women and children riding or leading mules alongside wagons filled with tents and kettles, live turkeys and smoked hams. Pet pigs trotted on leashes and gamecocks crowed from the breeches of cannon, responding to cheers. "The acclamation given Sherman was without precedent," the same reporter wrote. "The whole assemblage raised and waved and shouted as if he had been the personal friend of each and every one of them."

He had approached the White House stand by then, delivered his salute, dismounted, and walked over to take his guest-of-honor place among the reviewers, intent on securing a satisfaction only slightly less rewarding than the one he had experienced when he turned in the saddle, a few minutes ago, and thrilled at the compact, rhythmic beauty of the column stretching all the way back to the marble Capitol. The men who composed it had already protested, in their hard-handed way, the recent slanders directed at their chief — and so, now that the time had come, would Sherman himself, in person. He had Edwin Stanton in mind, up there in the stand, and he was resolved, as he said later, not only "to resent what I considered an insult," but also to do so "as publicly as it was made." Accordingly, after shaking hands with the President he moved on to Stanton, who was standing with his hand out, next in line. "Sherman's face was scarlet and his red hair seemed to stand on end," one among the startled watchers noted, as he drew himself up, glared at the Secretary for a couple of baleful seconds, then stepped deliberately past him to shake hands with the other cabinet members before returning to take his post on the left of Johnson. For more than six hours his long-striding troops surged by, applauded enthusiastically by everyone who saw them. "On the whole, the grand review was a splendid success," he afterwards declared, "and was a fitting conclusion to the campaign and the war."

It was also, in its way, a valedictory. "In a few weeks," another journalist was to write, "this army of two or three hundred thousand men melted back into the heart of the people from whence it came, and the great spectacle of the Grand Army of the Republic ... disappeared from sight." In point of fact, a considerable portion of that army had already disappeared — or "melted back," as the reporter put it — in the course of the four years leading up to this and other last parades at various assembly points throughout the beaten South. A total of just over 110,000 northern soldiers had died on the field of battle or from wounds received there; which meant that, for every two men who marched up Pennsylvania Avenue on both days of the Grand Review, the ghost of a third marched with them. There were indeed skeletons at that feast, at any rate for those along the route who remembered this army of the fallen, equal in number to the survivors who swung past the grandstand, twelve abreast, for six long hours on either day.

One among the last to have joined this ghostly throng — later, even, than Abraham Lincoln, and like him the victim of a northern bullet — was a young V Corps lieutenant, George H. Wood, a line officer in a regiment from Maine. On the march north from Appomattox, two weeks back, his unit made camp one night just outside Fredericksburg, surrounded by memories of corpses lying frozen where they had been dropped in trying to reach the rebel-held sunken road at the base of Marye's Heights, and next morning, while the lieutenant and his platoon were getting ready to depart, a teamster accidentally fired a round from a carbine he was handling. It passed through several tents, then struck Wood. He had seen too much of death these past three years, as a veteran of all the major battles of the Army of the Potomac within that span, to find anything exceptional in his own, which the surgeons now informed him was at hand. His regret was not so much that he was dying, but rather that he had spent the past three years as he had done. A devout young man, he doubted that what he had been engaged in was the work of the Lord, and in this connection, hoping fervently for mercy in the hereafter, he expressed a further wish to the minister who was with him when the end drew near. "Chaplain," he said, "do you suppose we shall be able to forget anything in heaven? I would like to forget those three years."

Another veteran, of considerably higher rank, also missed the Grand Review: not as the result of any mishap — no piece of flying metal ever so much as grazed him, though it had been his practice, throughout an even longer war career, to go where there was least room between bullets — but rather because of last-minute orders that took him elsewhere. This was Sheridan. Arriving in Washington on May 16, one week before he and his seven miles of horsemen were scheduled to clop up Pennsylvania Avenue, he was informed next day by Grant that he was to proceed without delay to the Transmississippi and take charge of operations designed to restore West Louisiana and Texas to the Union. Although he would command a force of better than 50,000 seasoned effectives — Canby's army from Mobile, already alerted for the move, plus one corps each from Ord and Thomas at City Point and Nashville — Little Phil did not covet an assignment that would deny him a role in next week's big parade and separate him, permanently perhaps, from his hard-riding troopers. Moreover, while the Transmississippi would be the scene of what little fighting there was left, it did not seem to him to offer much in the way of a chance for distinction, especially by contrast with all he had achieved in the past year. As he had done on the eve of the Appomattox campaign, when the plan had been to send him down to Sherman, he protested for all he was worth at being shifted from stage center, out of the limelight.

Now as then, Grant explained that there was more to these new orders than met the eye, "a motive not explained by the instructions themselves." In addition to the task of closing down Kirby-Smithdom, there was also the problem of ending defiance of the Monroe Doctrine by the French in Mexico, where their puppet Emperor had been on the throne for a full year, usurping the power of the elected leader, President Benito Juárez. Maximilian had been pro-Confederate from the outset, Juárez pro-Union, and the time had come to persuade or compel the French "to quit the territory of our sister republic." The State Department — meaning Seward, who by now was on the mend from the slashing he had received on assassination night, just over a month ago — was "much opposed to the use of our troops along the border in any active way that would involve us in a war with European powers." Grant however went on to say that he did not think it would come to that; the French would remain in Mexico no longer than it took them to find that he had sent his most aggressive troop commander to patrol the border with 50,000 of the hardest-handed soldiers the world had known since Napoleon's illustrious uncle retired to Saint Helena. Flattered, Sheridan was more amenable to the shift, which he now perceived might involve him in still another war, despite his superior's confidence that his presence would serve rather to prevent one. Though he complained that he could not see why his departure could not be delayed a couple of days, so he could ride up the avenue at the head of his column of troopers, he later declared that, "under the circumstances, my disappointment at not being permitted to participate in the review had to be submitted to, and I left Washington without an opportunity of seeing again in a body the grand Army of the Potomac."

Whatever might come of the projected border venture, he soon discovered that he had been right to suspect that little or no additional glory awaited him for subduing what remained of the Confederacy beyond the Mississippi. Leaving the capital on May 21, two days short of the start of the Grand Review, he learned before he reached New Orleans, where he planned to confer with Canby on the upcoming campaign, that Kirby Smith had already agreed to surrender on the terms accepted earlier by Taylor, Johnston, and Lee.

Smith in fact had had little choice in the matter. Credited with 36,000 troops on paper, he commanded practically none in the flesh, and even these few, as he complained, were "deaf alike to the dictates of duty, reason, and honor." Price's ill-starred Missouri raid, from August through November, had used up their hope along with their dash. Such things as they did now were done on their own, usually under enemy compulsion: for example, a two-day engagement at Palmito Ranch, May 12–13, on the east bank of the Rio Grande near Brownsville, down at the very tip of Texas. Andrew Johnson's May 10 declaration that armed resistance was "virtually at an end" had thus been premature, but only by three days; for this was the last sizeable clash of arms in the whole war. Two Union regiments of white and colored infantry, plus one of cavalry, marched upriver from Brazos Santiago to attack the rebel camp. At first they were successful. Then they were driven back. Next day they tried again, and again succeeded, only to be repulsed when the defenders once more rallied and drove them from the ranch with a loss of 115 killed, wounded, and missing. It was Wilson's Creek all over again, reproduced in miniature and stretched out over a period of two days. When it was done, the Federals withdrew downriver to the coast. They had gained nothing except the distinction of having made the last attack of the four-year conflict, as well as the last retreat.

Ironically, this last fight, like the first, was a Confederate victory; yet the news was scarcely noticed in the excitement over the outcome of a conference held at the opposite end of the state while the second day of battle was in progress. Responding to a call from the department commander, the exiled governors of Louisiana, Arkansas, and Missouri met that day in Marshall, forty miles west of Shreveport, to assess the current situation, political as well as military, so far as it affected the four Transmississippi states, including Texas, whose ailing chief executive sent a spokesman in his place. Lee's surrender had been known for about three weeks now, together with the southward flight of the government from Richmond. Kirby Smith informed the assembled heads of states that he considered himself duty bound to hold out "at least until President Davis reaches this department, or I receive some definite orders from him." The governors, for all their admiration of his soldierly commitment, did not agree. Speaking for their people, whose despair they understood and shared, they considered it "useless for the Trans-Mississippi Department to undertake to do what the Cis-Mississippi Department had failed to do," and accordingly recommended an early surrender — if liberal, or anyhow decent, terms could be secured. In line with this, they appointed one of their number, Governor Henry W. Allen of Louisiana, to go to Washington and confer with the Federal authorities to that end.

But there was nothing like time enough for that. Returning to Shreveport with the threats of bitter-enders ringing in his ears — Jo Shelby, for one, wanted to turn him out if he so much as thought of capitulation — Smith rejected on May 15 terms proposed by an emissary from John Pope in Missouri, who presented him with a choice between outright surrender and "all the horrors of violent subjugation." Pope, as usual, overplayed his hand. Speaking for himself as well as his country, Smith replied that he could not "purchase a certain degree of immunity from devastation at the expense of the honor of its army." So he said. Yet he had no sooner done so than news of a series of disasters began arriving from beyond the Mississippi: first, that Johnston and Sherman had come to terms, and then that Taylor and Canby had followed suit. He now commanded, such as it was, the Confederacy's only unsurrendered department, and in reaction he ordered his headquarters moved from Shreveport to Houston, where he would be less vulnerable to attack in the campaign he knew was about to be launched against him. Before he could make the shift, however, word came that Davis himself had been captured in South Georgia. That did it. Convinced at last that he no longer had anything left to hope for, let alone fight for, Smith decided to reopen negotiations: not with Pope, up in Missouri, but with Canby, who was en route from Mobile to New Orleans. Rather than go himself he sent his chief of staff, Lieutenant General Simon Buckner, with full authority to accept whatever terms were offered. That was fitting. At Donelson, three years and three months ago, the Kentuckian had surrendered the first Conferedate army to lay down its arms. Now he was charged with surrendering the last.

His mission was soon accomplished. Steaming under a flag of truce, first down the Red and then the Mississippi, he reached New Orleans on May 25, the same day Canby got there. They conferred, and next morning, having accepted the terms afforded Lee and Johnston and Taylor, Buckner signed the surrender agreement with Peter Osterhaus, Canby's own chief of staff. One week later, on June 2, Kirby Smith came down to Galveston, boarded the Federal steamer *Fort Jackson* out in the harbor, and fixed his signature to the document brought from New Orleans for that purpose. Before he left Houston he had already issued his farewell to such troops as were still with him, if only on paper. "Your present duty is plain," he told them. "Return to your families. Resume the occupations of peace. Yield obedience to the laws. Labor to restore order. Strive both by counsel and example to give security to life and property. And may God, in his mercy, direct you aright and heal the wounds of our distracted country."

Thus the final place of refuge within the vanished Confederate borders passed from being, no longer a goal for die-hards such as Wheeler, who had been trying to get there when he was taken near Atlanta, three weeks back. Similarly, four days ago at Natchez, unaware that Buckner had come to terms with Canby a couple of hundred winding miles downstream, John B. Hood and two aides were picked up by Federal patrollers before they could get across the river. He had stopped off in South Carolina long enough for Sally Preston to break her engagement to him, and then, aggrieved, had ridden on, intent on reaching his adoptive Texas. Paroled on May 31, the day after his capture, he continued his journey, no longer as a general in search of recruits for the army he had promised Jefferson Davis he would raise there, but rather as one more one-legged civilian who had to find some way to make a living.

Thousands of others in the region had that problem, too, and only a handful solved it without changing the life style they had known for the past four years. These exceptions came mainly from the ranks of the guerillas, some of whom enlisted in the Union army, thereby avoiding government prosecution, while others simply moved on west and resumed on the frontier such wartime activities as bank and stagecoach robbery, with cattle rustling thrown in for a sideline. One among them was W. C. Quantrill, except that he went east, not west, bent on bringing off a coup that would outdo in notoriety even his sacking of Lawrence, Kansas, late in the summer of '63. Back in Missouri after Price retreated, Quantrill assembled some two dozen followers, including Frank James and Jim Younger — but not George Todd or Bill Anderson, who had been killed within a month of the Centralia massacre — and set out for a crossing of the Mississippi on New Year's Day, just north of Memphis, at the head of a column of blue-clad horsemen he identified as a platoon from the nonexistent 4th Missouri Cavalry, U.S. His plan, announced at the outset, was to proceed by way of Kentucky and Maryland to Washington, and there revive Confederate hopes by killing Abraham Lincoln. He took up so much time en route, however, that he never got there. In the Bluegrass by mid-April he learned that J. Wilkes Booth had beat him to the act. Still in Kentucky three weeks later, he was wounded in a barnyard skirmish on May 10, thirty miles southeast of Louisville. Like Booth he was struck in the spine and paralyzed, though he lived for nearly a month in that condition. Recognizing one of the physicians at his bedside, he asked if he had not treated him previously, in another part of the state. "I am the man. I have moved here," the doctor replied. "So have I," Quantrill said, enigmatic to the end, which came on June 6.

By that time Kirby Smith had returned from Galveston; the last outlying remnants of organized resistance were submitting or departing. On June 23 at Doaksville, near Fort Towson in the Indian Territory, Brigadier General Stand Watie, a Cherokee chief who had held out with a third of his people when the other two thirds renewed their allegiance to the Union, surrendered and disbanded his battalion of Cherokees, Creeks, Seminoles, and Osages, all proscribed as tribal outlaws for refusing to repudiate the treaty made with Richmond in the early days of the war. Close to sixty, a veteran of Wilson's Creek, Elkhorn Tavern, Prairie Grove, and a hundred lesser fights — not to mention the long march out the "trail of tears" from Georgia, nearly thirty years ago — Watie, his gray-shot hair spread fanwise on his shoulders, was the last Confederate general to lay down his arms.

One who did not surrender was Jo Shelby, who had sworn he never would. When news of the Buckner-Smith capitulation reached him he assembled his division on the prairie near Corsicana, Texas, for a speech. "Boys, the war is over and you can go home. I for one will not go home. Across the Rio Grande lies Mexico. Who will follow me there?" Some two hundred of his veterans said they would, and next morning, after parting with comrades who chose to stay behind, set out southward. Proceeding through Waco, Austin, and San Antonio, they picked up recruits along the way, together with a number of dignitaries in and out of uniform: John Magruder and Sterling Price, for instance, as well as Henry Allen of Louisiana and Texas Governor Pendleton Murrah, who rose from his sickbed to join the horsemen riding through his capital, five hundred strong by then. Finally, beyond San Antonio, Kirby Smith himself caught up with the column. He was bound for Mexico, like all the rest, but not as a soldier, having discovered for the first time since he left West Point, twenty years ago this month, "the feeling of lightness and joy experienced by me when I felt myself to be plain Kirby Smith, relieved from all cares and responsible only for my own acts."

Clearing Eagle Pass by the last week in June, Shelby paused to weight his tattered battle flag with stones and sink it in the Rio Grande before crossing into Mexico. At Monterrey the column lost most of its distinguished civilian hangers-on, who scattered variously for Cuba, Brazil, and other regions where ex-Confederates were reported to be welcome. But Shelby and his body of troopers, grown by now to the size of a small brigade, kept on for Mexico City, having decided — such was their proclivity for lost causes — to throw in with Maximilian, rather than Juárez. The Emperor, whose subjects already were showing how much they resented his foreign support, knew better than to enlist the help of *gringo* mercenaries. Still, he was friendly enough to offer them a plot of land near Vera Cruz for colonization. Most declined and went their several ways, being far from ready to settle down to the farming life they had left four years ago, but Shelby and a few others accepted and even sent for their families to join them; which they did, though not for long. The settlement — dubbed Carlota, in honor of the Empress — scarcely outlasted Maximilian, who fell in front of a firing squad two Junes later, after the troops supporting Juárez rushed into the vacuum left by the departing French. Grant had been right about Napoleon's reaction, once Sheridan reached the Texas border and bristled along it, much as he had done in the old days up and down the Shenandoah Valley.

Afloat, whether on salt water or fresh, the wind-down of the rebellion seemed likely to prove a good deal more erratic and explosive than on land, depending as it would on the attitude and nature of the individual skipper operating on his own, as so many did in the Confederate navy, up lonely rivers or far out to sea. "Don't give up the ship" — a proud tradition sometimes taken to irrational extremes: as in duels to the death, with eight-inch guns at ranges of eight feet — might apply no less at the finish than at the start. A case in point was Lieutenant Charles W. Read, whose handling of the steam ram *William H. Webb* in a late-April dash for freedom down the Red and the Mississippi provided a possible forecast of instances to come.

A twenty-four-year-old Mississippian, Read had finished at Annapolis in 1860, one year ahead of his Union counterpart William Cushing, and like him had had a colorful war career. He fought with distinction against Farragut below New Orleans, then again at Vicksburg as a gunnery officer on the *Arkansas*, and next aboard the *Florida* in her great days, when Maffitt gave him a captured brig, along with a crew of twenty and one boat howitzer, and set him up as an independent raider. In twenty-one days, cruising the Atlantic coast from Norfolk to New England, he took twenty-one prizes before he himself was taken, off Portland, Maine, in June of 1863, and confined at Fort Warren. Exchanged in October of the following year, he was assigned to duty with the James River squadron below Richmond until March of 1865, when Mallory chose him to command the *Webb*, languishing in far-off Louisiana for the past two years. Reported to be "the fastest thing afloat," she had seen no substantial action since her sinking of the monster ironclad *Indianola*, back in the early spring of '63, and it was Mallory's belief that she could be put to highly effective use against Yankee merchantmen and blockaders, if Read could only get her out into the open waters of the Gulf of Mexico.

Arriving by the end of the month he found the 206-foot sidewheel steamer tied up eighty miles below Shreveport, "without a single gun on board, little or no crew, no fuel, and no small arms save a few cutlasses." Undaunted, he took her up to department headquarters and secured from the army a 30-pounder Parrott rifle, which he mounted on her bow, and two 12-pounder smoothbores, one for each broadside, as well as fifty-one soldier volunteers and sixteen officers. Back at Alexandria, while training his new green crew, he put carpenters to work constructing a rough bulwark around the *Webb*'s forecastle and loaded close to two hundred bales of cotton for use as a shield for her machinery until he reached Cuba and could exchange them for a longer-burning fuel than the pine knots he now had stacked about her decks. By that time, news had come of Lee's surrender and the government's flight south. He knew he would have to hurry, and on April 22, as he prepared to cast off down the Red, he learned of Lincoln's assassination, which might or might not add to the confusion he hoped to encounter during his run past Baton Rouge and New Orleans and the warships on patrol above and below them both. "As I will have to stake everything upon speed and time," he wrote Mallory that day, "I will not attack any vessel in the passage unless I perceive a possibility of her arresting my progress. In this event I am prepared with five torpedoes ... one of which I hold shipped on its pole on the bows."

He left that evening and reached the mouth of the river about 8.30 the following night, the first Sunday after Easter. Displaying the lights of a Federal transport and running slow to reduce the engine noise, he hoped to sneak past the blue flotilla on patrol there, which included two ironclads and a monitor. For a time it seemed the *Webb* was going to steam by undetected, but then a rocket swooshed up from the deck of one of the blockaders, giving the signal: "Strange vessel in sight, positively an enemy." Read shouted, "Let her go!" and the engineer opened the throttle all the way. As the ram shot forward, whistles screamed and drums rolled beat-to-quarters along the line of warships dead ahead. "Keep for the biggest opening between them," Read told the pilot. Out in the moonless night, the monitor *Manhattan* swung her big guns in their turret and hurled two 11-inch shells at the rebel churning past. Both missed, and the *Webb* was soon out of range, driving hard as she began her intended 300-mile run down the Mississippi to the Gulf. Unpursued by anything that had even an outside chance of overtaking him, Read tied up to the east bank and sent a detail ashore to cut the telegraph wires, then set out again, gliding past Baton Rouge in the darkness, unseen or unrecognized, and on to Donaldsonville by daylight, still carrying the signals of a Union transport. Here too the ram passed unchallenged, though some who saw her booming along with the midstream current later testified that she was making a good 25 knots as she went by. That may well have been; for by 1 o'clock that afternoon, April 24, the church spires of low-lying New Orleans came in view.

Read hoisted the U.S. flag at half mast, brought his boiler pressure up to maximum, and began his run past the Crescent City. No warning message had got through, thanks to the cutting of the wires the night before; lookouts here, like those at Donaldsonville that morning, took the *Webb* to be a friendly transport, mourning with her lowered colors the death of Abraham Lincoln. They did, that is, until about midway through the run, when a bluejacket who had fought against her, a couple of years ago upriver, recognized her and gave the alarm, setting off a din of bells and drums and whistles, soon punctuated by the roar of guns. Most of the shots went wild, but three struck the ram before she cleared the fleet, one through her chimney, one into a bale of cotton, and one just above the waterline at her bow, damaging the torpedo mechanism so badly that the explosive had to be jettisoned. Stopping to accomplish this, Read took down the half-staffed Union emblem, ran up to the peak his true Confederate colors, and continued downriver at full speed, bound for the open waters of the Gulf.

Behind him New Orleans was abuzz with rumors that Jeff Davis and John Wilkes Booth were aboard the ram, headed for South America with millions in gold bullion. Read knew nothing of this, of course, but he did know that the two fastest gunboats in the enemy flotilla, *Hollyhock* and *Florida*, were churning downstream after him. Confident that he could outrun them, the young Mississippian was alarmed only so far as their pursuit might interfere with his plan for not reaching Forts Jackson and St Philip, sixty winding miles away, before night came down to help screen him from the plunging crossfire of guns on both sides of the river. He considered stopping to dispose of them, despite their superior armament, but up ahead just then, twenty-five miles below the city, he saw something that commanded all his attention. It was the veteran screw sloop *Richmond*, mounting twenty-one guns, anchored for engine repairs and now being cleared for action. He studied her briefly, regretting the loss of his spar torpedo, then told the pilot: "Make straight for the *Richmond*'s bow, and ram." "I can't reach her bow because of a shoal," the pilot replied, "but I can come in under her broadside." Read shook his head at that suggestion. "I've been under the *Richmond*'s broadside before, and don't wish to try it again," he said. He assembled all hands on the foredeck and informed them of what he knew he had to do. "It's no use. The *Richmond* will drown us all — and if she doesn't, the forts below will, as they have a range of three miles each way up and down the river, and they know by this time that we are coming." He turned to the helmsman. "Head for shore," he told him.

Fifty yards from bank the *Webb* struck bottom, and while most of the crew began climbing down ropes thrown over the bow, others went about dousing the deck and cabins with turpentine before they too abandoned ship. Read started fires with a lighted match, then went over the side, the last to leave the flaming ram. He and his men lay in waiting in the brush till they heard her magazine explode, after which they broke into groups and scattered. By daybreak, half of them had been rounded up, including Read, who suffered the indignity of being placed on public display in New Orleans; but not for long. Presently he and the rest were paroled and allowed to return to their homes. At a cost of one man wounded, and of course the *Webb* herself, he had given the victors notice of what they might expect in the way of naval daring between now and the time the final curtain fell.

Whatever might come of such fears as this aroused, a river mishap of far bloodier proportions occurred six hundred miles upstream in the early morning hours of April 27, the day Read was put on display in New Orleans. En route for Cairo with an outsized cargo of surplus army mules and discharged soldiers who had crowded aboard at Vicksburg and Helena after their release from Deep South prison camps, the sidewheel steamer *Sultana*, one of the largest on the Mississippi, blew her boilers near Paddy's Hen and Chickens, north of Memphis two hours before dawn. Although her authorized capacity was less than 400 passengers, she had about six times that number packed about her decks and in her hold — mostly Ohio, Illinois, and Indiana veterans, men who had fought perhaps the hardest war of all, sweating out its finish in stockades beyond reach of the various columns of invasion. So sudden was the blast and the fire that followed, those who managed to make it over the side had to dive through flames into muddy water running swift and cold as any millstream. A body count put the official death toll at 1238, but there was really no way of telling how many troops had been aboard or were consumed by shrimp and gars before all those hundreds of other blue-clad corpses bobbed up downstream in the course of the next month. Estimates ran as high as 1800 dead and presumed dead, with 1585 as the figure most generally agreed on. That was more than the number killed on both sides at First Bull Run and Wilson's Creek combined, and even by the lowest count the loss of the *Sultana* went into the books as the greatest marine disaster of all time. Just under one month later, as if to emphasize the shock that came with sudden peace, on May 25 — the day after the Grand Review up Pennsylvania Avenue ended, and the day before Simon Buckner surrendered to Canby in New Orleans for his chief — a warehouse on the Mobile waterfront, stocked with some twenty tons of surrendered ammunition, blew up and "shook the foundations" of the city. An estimated 300 people were killed outright, and the property loss was reckoned at $5,000,000.

By way of consolation for these subtractions — unexpected and all the more tragic because they were self-inflicted, so to speak — fears regarding those other losses, anticipated because of the example set by Read in his abortive downstream dash, turned out to be quite groundless. Joe Johnston's capitulation, followed within two weeks by Richard Taylor's — the former on the day before the *Sultana* blew her boilers above Memphis — brought about the surrender of the few surviving rebel warships east of the Mississippi, bloodlessly and practically without fanfare. On May 10, four that had taken refuge up the Tombigbee almost a month ago, after the evacuation of Mobile, struck their colors in accordance with a commitment by the flotilla captain to hand over to the Federals "all public property yet afloat under his command." On May 27, down in West Florida, the gunboat *Spray* was the last to go. Stationed up the St Marks River to cover the water approaches to Tallahassee, her skipper agreed to surrender when he learned that the troops defending the capital in his rear had laid down their arms the week before. Then came Kirby Smith's formal capitulation at Galveston, and next day, June 3, the *Webb*'s one-time consorts up the Red hauled down their flags. One among them was the ironclad *Missouri*, completed at Shreveport in late March and taken down to Alexandria, not in time to fight, but at any rate in time to be handed over with the rest. "A most formidable vessel," one Union officer pronounced her, though after a closer look he added an assessment that might have served as an epitaph for all the improvised warships knocked together by backwoods carpenters and blacksmiths, here and elsewhere throughout the South: "She is badly built of green lumber, caulked with cotton, leaks badly, and is very slow."

By that time, too, the gravest of all the Union navy's current fears had been allayed. These concerned still another ironclad, a seagoing armored ram described by those who had seen her as the most powerful thing afloat. Built not by amateur shipwrights in the rebel hinterland, but rather by French craftsmen at Bordeaux, she was commissioned the C.S.S. *Stonewall* — "an appellation not inconsistent with her character," the purchasing agent proudly declared — and in mid-January set out down the European coast on the first leg of a voyage across the Atlantic, under instructions to lift the blockade at Wilmington and elsewhere by sinking the blockaders: an assignment considered by no means beyond her capability, since in addition to her defensive attributes, which reportedly made her unsinkable, she featured such dread offensive devices as a protruding underwater beak, heavy enough to drive through the flank and bottom of any rival, wood or metal, and a 300-pounder Armstrong rifle mounted on her bow. Damaged by rough weather, she put into Ferrol, Spain, for repairs. By the time these were made, two multigunned U.S. frigates were on station outside the harbor, apparently waiting to take her on when she emerged. When she did so, however, on March 24, both refrained and stood aside to let her go, one blue skipper afterwards explaining that "the odds in her favor were too great and too certain, in my humble judgment, to admit of the slightest hope of being able to inflict upon her even the most trifling injury."

As it turned out, that one negative triumph, achieved by a bluff for whose success the Federal commander was court-martialed, was the *Stonewall*'s only contribution to the struggle whose tide of victory her purchasers had hoped she would reverse. After filling with coal at Lisbon, down the coast, she set out across the ocean on March 28, still unchallenged. Obliged to make another refueling stop in the Canaries, she did not reach Nassau until May 6. Not only had she made poor time; her bunkers were nearly empty again, and her skipper, Captain T. J. Page, a Virginian in his middle fifties, was shaking his head at her lumbering performance and the sharpness of French salesmen. "You must not expect too much of me," he wrote his superiors; "I fear the power and effect of this vessel have been much exaggerated." On May 11 he dropped anchor at Havana. News had not yet arrived of the capture of Jefferson Davis the day before, but he soon learned that both Lee and Johnston had surrendered their armies. While he pondered what to do, word came that Taylor had followed suit, ending all possibility of resistance east of the Mississippi. By now, moreover, Union warships of all types were assembling outside the harbor from all directions, including the monitors *Canonicus* and *Monadnock*, veterans of Fort Fisher and the first of their type to leave home waters. "*Canonicus* would have crushed her, and the *Monadnock* could have taken her beyond a doubt," the admiral in command of the blue flotilla later said of the holed-up *Stonewall*. No one would ever know for sure, however. On May 19, having reached his decision, Page turned over to the Captain

General of Cuba, for a decision by Spain as to her eventual disposition, the only ironclad ever to fly the Confederate flag on the high seas.

That flag still flew on the high seas, but only at one ever-moving point, the peak of the cruiser *Shenandoah*. "An erratic ship, without country or destination," Gideon Welles quite accurately described her, urging his otherwise unemployed frigate captains to locate and run down this last Confederate raider, which lately had been reported raising havoc in the South Pacific. By now, though, she was elsewhere; Welles was warm, yet far from hot, in the game of hide-and-seek the rebel privateer was playing with his men-of-war. James Waddell had sailed her north from Melbourne in mid-February, intent on "visiting," as his instructions put it, "the enemy's distant whaling grounds." He had no luck in that regard until April 1, when he approached Ascension Island in the eastern Carolines and found a quartet of the blubber-laden vessels anchored in Lea Harbor like so many sitting ducks. After putting the crews ashore he set all four afire and continued northward, past Japan, into the northwest reaches of the Sea of Okhotsk, where he took one more prize during the final week in May. So far, the pickings had been rather slim, but now he had accurate, up-to-date whaling charts, as well as a number of volunteers from the captured ships, to show him where to go: south, then north, around the Kamchatka Peninsula, into the Bering Sea. There the forty-year-old North Carolinian found what he had been seeking all along.

Off Cape Navarin on June 22 he came upon two whalers, one of which — a fast bark out of New Bedford, aptly named the *Jerah Swift* — tried to make a run for it. *Shenandoah* gave chase, dodging ice floes as she went, and after a hard three-hour pursuit, drew close enough to put a round from a 32-pounder Whitworth rifle across her bow; whereupon her captain "saw the folly of exposing the crew to a destructive fire and yielded to his misfortunes with a manly and becoming dignity." So Waddell later wrote, unaware at the time — as, indeed, he would remain for weeks to come — that he had just fired the last shot of the American Civil War. He burned the two ships, then started after more. Next day he took a trading vessel, only two months out of San Francisco, and found aboard her a newspaper dated April 17, containing the latest dispatches from the eastern theater. Lee had surrendered: Richmond had fallen: the Government had fled. Shaken though he was by this spate of disasters, he also read that Johnston had won a victory over Sherman in North Carolina, back in March, and that the President, resettled with his cabinet in Danville, had issued a proclamation announcing "a new phase of the struggle," which he urged all Confederates to wage with "fresh defiance" and "unconquered and unconquerable hearts." Waddell took his cue from that, and was rewarded three days later when he steamed into a cluster of six whalers lying becalmed off St Lawrence Island. Five he burned; the sixth he ransomed to take on board the crews of all the rest. Two days later, on June 28, he made his largest haul near the narrows of Bering Strait, where he fell in with a rendezvous of eleven whalers. He put all the crews aboard two of these, bonded as before, and set the other nine ablaze in a single leaping conflagration, rivaling with its glow of burning oak and sperm oil, reflected for miles on the ice that glittered roundabout, the brilliance of the Aurora Borealis. In nine months of sailing close to 40,000 miles, the *Shenandoah* now had taken an even two dozen whalers, along with 1053 prisoners and another 14 merchant vessels, destroying all but six of the 38, whose total value Waddell placed at $1,361,983. Wanting still more, he steamed next day into the Arctic Ocean.

But there were no more. He discovered, after searching, that he had abolished the whaling trade, so far at least as his one-time fellow countrymen were concerned. Narrowly escaping getting ice-bound, he turned back and passed once more between the outpost capes of Asia and North America. Propeller triced up to save coal, he crowded on all sail and set out for the coast of Baja California, intending to make prizes of the clippers plying between Panama and San Francisco. By July 4 he was clear of the chain of the Aleutians and back into the icefree waters of the North Pacific. For a month he held his southward course, sailing well out of sight of land, and then on August 2 encountered the English bark *Barracouta*, less than two weeks out of Frisco. Newspapers on her told of Kirby Smith's capitulation, two months ago today; Jefferson Davis was in prison, and the Confederacy was no longer among the nations of earth. Despite earlier indications, the news came hard for those on board the *Shenandoah*. "We were bereft of ground for hope or aspiration," her executive officer wrote in his journal that night, "bereft of a cause for which to struggle and suffer." Waddell now was faced with the problem of what to do with his ship and his people: a decision, he said, "which involved not only our personal honor, but the honor of the flag entrusted to us which had walked the waters fearlessly and in triumph." Though he ordered the battery struck below and the crew disarmed, he was determined to avoid capture if possible. Accordingly, after rejecting the notion of surrendering at some port close at hand, where treatment might be neither fair nor unprejudiced, he decided to make a nonstop run, by way of Cape Horn, for England.

The distance was 17,000 miles, very little of it in sight of land, and required three full months of sailing, never speaking another vessel from start to finish lest the *Shenandoah*'s whereabouts became known to Federal skippers who by now were scouring the seas under orders to take or sink her. Rounding the Horn in mid-September, she was driven off course by a northeast gale and did not cross the equator until October 11. Then she took the trades, with smooth going all the way to the western coast of England. "I believe the Divine will directed and protected that ship in all her adventures," her captain was to say. On November 5 she reached St George's Channel and dropped anchor to wait for a pilot, then steamed next morning up the Mersey to Liverpool, the Stars and Bars flying proudly at her peak. She had covered better than 58,000 miles, circumnavigated the globe, visited all its oceans except the Antarctic, and taken in the course of her brief career more prizes than any other Confederate raider except the *Alabama*. Anchored beside a British ship-of-the-line, she lowered her abolished country's last official flag and was turned over to the port authorities for adjudication. Two days later, Waddell and his crew were unconditionally released to go ashore for the first time since they left Melbourne, almost nine months ago. Looking back with pride and satisfaction on all the *Shenandoah* had accomplished in her thirteen months at sea, he later wrote: "I claim for her officers and men a triumph over their enemies and over every obstacle.... For myself," he added, "I claim having done my duty."

By that time, no more than a handful of Confederates remained in Federal custody, locked up awaiting trial or other disposition of their cases. On May 27, the day after Canby's provisional acceptance of the surrender of the last armed grayback in the Transmississippi, Andrew Johnson had ordered the discharge, with but few exceptions, of all persons imprisoned by military authorities. Two days later a presidential Proclamation of Amnesty offered pardon to all who had participated, directly or indirectly, in "the existing rebellion," with full restitution of property rights — except of course slaves — on the taking of an oath by such people that they would "henceforth" support and defend the Constitution and abide by the laws of the reunited land. In this latter instance, however, so many exceptions were cited that the document was about as much a source of alarm as it was of solace. Among those excluded were all who held civil or diplomatic offices in the secessionist regime and the governors of its member states; former U.S. congressmen, senators, and judges; West Pointers, Annapolis men, and members of the armed forces who had resigned or deserted to join the South; those engaged in the destruction of commerce or mistreatment of prisoners, officers above the rank of army colonel or navy lieutenant, and finally all "voluntary" participants with taxable property worth more than $20,000. The list ran on, and though it was stated that even those ineligibles could apply directly to the President for pardon, with assurance that "such clemency will be liberally extended as may be consistent with the facts of the case and the peace and dignity of the United States," few took much consolation in that provision, knowing as they did the views of Johnson with regard to treason and its consequences, which he had proclaimed so often in the course of the past four years. Kirby Smith, for example, no sooner read the offer than he rode off after Jo Shelby, bound for Mexico, as he informed his wife, in order "to place the Rio Grande between myself and harm."

Some measure of his concern, and that of others in flight from northern justice, was aroused by the savagery with which the eight accused of complicity with Booth in his assassination plot were being prosecuted at the time. Shackled at their trial, as no prisoner had been in an English-speaking court for more than a hundred and fifty years, they were kept hooded in their cells, with thick cotton pads over eyes and ears, lest they see or hear each other or their guards, and two small slits in the canvas for the admission of food and air. The military trial, presided over by nine high-ranking army officers in Washington's Arsenal Penitentiary, began on May 10 and ended June 30, when verdicts were returned. Johnson approved them on July 5, and two days later they were carried out. All eight had been found guilty. Four were soon on their way to the Dry Tortugas, three with life sentences, including a Virginia doctor who had set Booth's broken leg, and one, a stagehand at Ford's, with a six-year term for having allegedly helped the actor leave the theater. The other four got death: Lewis Paine, an ex-Confederate soldier who had made the knife attack on Seward, George Atzerodt, an immigrant carriage-maker who had lacked the nerve to attempt his assignment of killing the Vice President, David Herald, a slow-witted Maryland youth who had served as a guide for the fugitive in his flight, and Mary E. Surratt, the widowed proprietor of a boarding house where Booth was said to have met with some of the others in planning the work only he carried out in full. All were in their twenties except Mrs Surratt, who was forty-five and whose principal offense appeared to be that her twenty-year-old son had escaped abroad before he could be arrested for involvement in the crime. Some objections arose to the execution of a woman, but not enough to prevent her being one of the four who were hanged and buried in the yard of the penitentiary where Booth had been buried in secret, under the dirt floor of a cell, ten weeks before.

Despite this evidence of how ruthless the government — mainly Stanton, who had engineered the trial — could be in pursuit and removal of those it was determined to lay hands on, Johnson proved quite as liberal in granting clemency as he had said he would be in his amnesty proclamation. By mid-October, not only had all the arrested secessionist governors been released on their application for pardon, but so too had such once high-placed rebels as John Reagan and George Trenholm, John A. Campbell, and even Alexander Stephens. In November there was one sharp reminder of the claws inside the velvet Federal glove, when Captain Henry Wirz, the Swiss-born commandant of Andersonville, was convicted on trumped-up testimony of deliberate cruelty to the prisoners in his care. He was tried in violation of his parole, as well as of other legal rights, but Stanton had more or less assured a guilty verdict by appointing Lew Wallace president of the court; Wallace had consistently voted against the accused in the trial of the Lincoln conspirators, and Wirz was duly hanged on November 10, four days after the *Shenandoah* lowered the last Confederate flag. Meantime, Johnson continued granting amnesty to ex-rebels. By April 2 of the following year, when he declared the insurrection officially "at an end," Stephen Mallory had been relieved of long-pending charges of having promoted the willful destruction of commerce. Two weeks later Raphael Semmes was similarly released, along with Clement C. Clay, another Alabamian, who had been detained all this time on suspicion of having "incited, concerted, and procured" Lincoln's assassination from his post as a special commissioner in Canada. Now only Jefferson Davis remained behind bars in his cell at Fort Monroe.

Clay's release on April 17 resulted in a good deal of speculation about his former chief, who was being held on the same charge. Nothing came of that, for the present, but just over two weeks later, on May 3 — one week less than a year after his capture down in Georgia — Varina Davis was permitted to see her husband for the first time since they parted aboard the vessel that brought them up the coast to Hampton Roads. She was conducted past three lines of sentries, each requiring a password, then through a guardroom, until at last she approached and saw him beyond the bars of his quarters, moving toward her. His "shrunken form and glassy eyes" nearly caused her to collapse from shock, she later said. "His cheek bones stood out like those of a skeleton. Merely crossing the room made his breath come in short gasps, and his voice was scarcely audible."

He had had a harder time than she or anyone else not in the fort with him for the past year could know. What was more, it had begun in deadly earnest before the end of his first full day of incarceration. Near sundown, he looked up from reading his small-print Bible, the only possession allowed him except the clothes he wore, and saw that a guard captain had entered the casemate, accompanied by two men who seemed to be blacksmiths. One of them held a length of chain with a shackle at each end, and suddenly he knew why they were there, though he still could not quite believe it. "My God," he said. "You don't intend to iron me?" When the captain replied that those were indeed his orders, the prisoner rose and protested for all he was worth. "But the war is over; the South is conquered. For the honor of America, you cannot commit this degradation!" Told again that the orders were peremptory, Davis met this as he had met other challenges in the past, whatever the odds. "I shall never submit to such an indignity," he exclaimed. "It is too monstrous. I demand that you let me see the commanding general."

Here a certain irony obtained, unknown as yet to the captive in his cell. For it was the fort commander, Brigadier General Nelson A. Miles, who, in prompt response to a War Department directive authorizing him "to place manacles and fetters upon the hands and feet of Jefferson Davis...whenever he may think it advisable in order to render [his] imprisonment more secure," had made the decision to shackle him forthwith, not for the reason stated, but rather because he was eager to give his superiors what they wanted. Miles was cruel, in this as in other instances to follow, not so much by nature as by design. Not yet twenty-six, a one-time Massachusetts farm boy who had left the farm to clerk in a Boston crockery shop, he had achieved a brilliant record in the war, suffering four wounds in the course of his rise from lieutenant to brigadier, with the prospect of still another promotion if he did well at his current post, to which he had been assigned in part because of his lack of such West Point and Old Army ties as were likely to make him stand in awe of the prisoner in his charge. That he felt no such awe he quickly demonstrated, beginning with Davis's first full day in his care, and his reward would follow. By October he would be a major general. In a couple of years he would marry a niece of Sherman's, and before the century was out he would succeed Grant, Sherman, and Sheridan as general-in-chief; William McKinley, himself a former sergeant, would make him a lieutenant general, and he would live until 1925, when he died at a Washington circus performance and was buried at Arlington in a mausoleum he had built some years before. His was an American success story—Horatio Alger in army braid and stars—and part of the story was the time he spent as Jefferson Davis's jailer, giving his superiors what he saw they wanted, including the fetters now about to be applied.

Davis subsided after registering his protest, and the guard captain supposed him resigned to being ironed. "Smith, do your work," he said. But when the man came forward, kneeling to attach the shackles, the prisoner unexpectedly grabbed and flung him across the room. Recovering, the smith charged back, hammer lifted, and would have struck his assailant if the captain had not stopped him. One of the two armed sentries present cocked and leveled his rifle, but the captain stopped him too, instructing the four men "to take Mr Davis with as little force as possible." The struggle was brief, though it took more force than they had thought would be required; Davis, the captain later reported, "showed unnatural strength." While his helper and the sentries pinned the frail gray captive to the cot, the blacksmith riveted one clasp in place and secured its mate around the other ankle with a large brass lock, "the same as is in use on freight cars." The struggle ceased with the snap of the lock; Davis lay motionless, flat on his back, as the smith and his helper retired, their job done. Looking over his shoulder as he left, the captain saw the prisoner sit up, turn sideways on the cot, and with a heavy effort drop both feet to the stone floor. The clank of the chain was followed by unrestrained weeping, and the departing captain thought it "anything but a pleasant sight to see a man like Jefferson Davis shedding tears."

Mercifully, this particular humiliation was brief. Within five days, vigorous private and public objections — first by the post surgeon, who protested that the captive was being denied even such limited exercise as he could get from pacing up and down his cell, and then by a number of northern civilians who, though willing to keep on hating the former Confederate leader, disapproved of tormenting him in this fashion — caused the removal of the shackles. Other hardships continued in force, however, including the constant presence of two sentries under orders to keep tramping back and forth at all hours, a lamp that burned day and night, even while he slept or tried to, and the invariable dampness resulting from the fact that the floor of his cell was below the level of the water in the adjacent moat. Davis's health declined and declined, from neuralgia, failing eyesight, insomnia, and a general loss of vitality. Passing his fifty-seventh birthday in early June, he had to wait until late July, more than two months after his arrival, to be permitted an hour's daily exercise on the ramparts, and still another month went by before he was allowed to read the first letter from his wife. In October he was moved from the casemate to a second-story room in the fort's northwest bastion, but it was mid-December, after nearly seven months of seeing no one but the surgeon and his guards — including Miles, who sneered at him and called him Jeff — before he received his first visitor, his wartime pastor, who came down from Richmond to give him Communion and found him changed in appearance by long confinement, but not in spirit. "His spirit could not be subdued," the minister later wrote, "and no indignity, angry as it made him at the time, could humiliate him."

By that time, prominent Northerners — especially those in the legal profession — had seen the weakness of the government's case against Davis and the handful of Confederates yet being held. One who saw it was the Chief Justice who would rule on their appeal in the event that one was needed, which he doubted. "If you bring these leaders to trial it will condemn the North," Chase had warned his former cabinet colleagues in July, "for by the Constitution secession is not rebellion." As for the rebel chieftain, the authorities would have done better not to apprehend him. "Lincoln wanted Jefferson Davis to escape, and he was right. His capture was a mistake. His trial will be a greater one. We cannot convict him of treason. Secession is settled. Let it stay settled." Charles O'Conor, the distinguished New York attorney who had volunteered his services in Davis's behalf, was convinced that he would eventually be freed. "No trial for treason on any like offense will be held in the civil courts," he predicted, and as for his client's chances of being railroaded by the army, as Wirz and Mrs Surratt had been, "the managers at Washington are not agreed as to the safety of employing military commissions to color a like outrage upon any eminent person." Horace Greeley had come over, early on, and was saying in the *Tribune* that Davis should either be tried or turned loose without delay. Even so stalwart an Abolitionist as the philanthropist Gerrit Smith, a backer of John Brown, was persuaded that an injustice was in progress and was willing to sign a petition to that effect, as were others who wanted liberty for all men, black and white, by due process of law.

Clement Clay's release in mid-April, 1866, showed clearly enough the government's abandonment of the charge that he and Davis had been instigators of the assassination, but it also permitted total concentration on what was left of the case against the one prisoner still held. Stanton and Judge Advocate General Joseph Holt were determined, as Schuyler Colfax put it, to see the Mississippian "hanging between heaven and earth as not fit for either." Despite the Chief Justice's opinion, given in private nine months ago, that no such accusation could be sustained, they fell back on a vague charge of "treason," and persisted in it even after the distinguished jurist Francis Lieber, handed all the War Department evidence to study for recommendations on procedure, told them flatly: "Davis will not be found guilty and we shall stand there completely beaten." All the same, in early May an indictment was handed down by the U.S. Circuit Court, District of Virginia. "Jefferson Davis, yeoman," it began, "not having fear of God before his eyes, nor weighing the duty of his said allegiance, but being moved and seduced by the institution of the devil, and wickedly devising against the peace and tranquillity of the United States to subvert and to stir, move, and incite insurrection, rebellion, and war — " There was more, much more, but this alone was enough to rally support all over the South for its fallen leader. "That such a creature should be allowed to dispense justice is a perfect farce," Mrs R. E. Lee remarked of the judge presiding. "I think his meanness and wickedness have affected his brain."

By then Varina Davis was with her husband and had even begun to get accustomed to the change in his looks and condition, which had shocked her at first sight. Given quarters in the fort, and allowed to visit with him once a day, she could tell him of the growth of affection in the hearts of many who had turned blameful while the war was on the down slope. Recently she had written from New Orleans: "It is impossible to tell you the love which has been expressed here for you — the tenderness of feeling for you. People sit and cry until I am almost choked with the effort to be quiet. But it is a great consolation to know that a nation is mourning your suffering with me, and to be told hourly how far above reproach you are — how fair your fame. I am overwhelmed by the love which everything of your name attracts." Now that feeling had been extended and enlarged by the harsh indictment and the passing of the anniversary of his capture. To many of his former fellow countrymen it seemed that he alone was undergoing punishment for them all, and presently still another measure was added to the debt they felt they owed him. In late May, Mrs Davis secured an appointment with the President in Washington to plead for her husband's release. To her surprise, Johnson informed her that he was on her side. "But we must wait," he said. "Our hope is to mollify the public to Mr Davis." Meantime, he suggested, the prisoner's best course would be to make application for a pardon. Varina replied that she felt certain he would never do so, and she was right. When she returned to Fort Monroe and told Davis of Johnson's advice, he declined it on grounds that to ask for pardon would be to confess a guilt he did not feel. In this he resembled Robert Toombs, who, having gone abroad to avoid arrest, was counseled by northern friends to apply for pardon. "Pardon for what?" he said with an unreconstructed glare. "I have not pardoned you-all yet." So it was with Davis, and when word got round of his refusal, the growing affection for him grew still more. So long as he declined to ask forgiveness, it was as if they too had never humbled their pride. It was even as if they had never been defeated — except in fact, which mattered less and less as time wore on.

    Reassured by such reports from the home front, so to speak, as well as by his attorneys, with whom he now was permitted to confer, Davis suffered a legal setback on June 5, two days after his fifty-eighth birthday, when his plea for an early trial was declined by the Richmond court on grounds that he had never been in its custody, despite the indictment recently handed down, but rather was being held as a State Prisoner "under order of the President, signed by the Secretary of War." A follow-up motion for his release on bail was also disallowed, but it was more or less clear by then that Stanton and Holt were fighting a holding action, with scarcely a hope of securing a conviction. They scheduled a trial for early October, overriding O'Conor's protest at the delay.

    All Davis could do was wait. He found this easier, however, now that he had his wife to comfort him, unrestricted access to his mail, and a steady stream of visitors, including ex-President Franklin Pierce, Richard Taylor, and Wade Hampton. August brought two encouraging developments. One was the petition signed by Gerrit Smith and other prominent Northerners, addressed to Johnson in his behalf, and the other was a presidential order removing Nelson Miles as fort commander, after fifteen months of personal abuse. Miles's replacement soon gave the State Prisoner freedom of the post and better quarters, which he and Varina shared. A second Christmas came and went, the trial having been postponed; New Year's 1867 was far different from the one before.

The plan now was to force his release by a writ of habeas corpus, and among those willing to put up $25,000 each for bail were Horace Greeley and Cornelius Vanderbilt.

Spring came on, greening the York-James peninsula from the Chickahominy bottoms to its tip at Old Point Comfort, where "the world's most famous prisoner" was lodged. On the first Monday in May, the trial having been postponed again, an aide left for Richmond to secure the signature of the District Court clerk, as required by law, to the writ O'Conor and his associates had prepared. He returned to Fort Monroe on Friday, May 10 — the second anniversary of the then President's capture in South Georgia — to deliver the authenticated document to the fort commander, who was directed "to present the body of Jefferson Davis" in court three days later. Packed and ready, the State Prisoner and his wife set out upriver the following day. Still under guard, but hopefully not for long now, he saw from the rail that clusters of people had gathered at plantation landings along the James to salute him as he passed, and when the boat approached the capital that Saturday afternoon the wharves and streets along the rebuilt waterfront were so jammed that it seemed all Richmond had assembled to pay him its respects. Men removed their hats as he came ashore, and women fluttered handkerchiefs from balconies and windows along the route his carriage followed toward the heart of town. At the Spotswood, he and Varina were given the same rooms he had occupied when he arrived from Montgomery, six years back, and some declared that a greater number of people turned out to greet him now than had done so when he first arrived to take up his duties in the new capital. "I have never seen this city in such a state of pleased excitement," a visitor wrote home, "except upon the news of a Confederate victory. Men and women in tears was a common sight, and the ladies say they are very much afraid they will have to love the Yankees a little."

On Sunday the Davises kept to their rooms except for a secret trip to Hollywood Cemetery to lay flowers on the grave where their son Joe had lain since his fall from the White House balcony in that other fateful spring, three years ago. After church, old friends came by the hotel, some bringing daughters and nieces who had emerged from girlhood during the past two years, and it was noted that while Davis kissed them all on arrival, "he kissed the prettiest again on their departure." Still, the tension was unmistakable. Tomorrow he would appear before Judge John C. Underwood, who had composed the scabrous charge under which he had been indicted the previous May, and it was feared that he would no sooner have escaped the clutches of the military than Underwood would have him jailed on some new civil pretext of his own.

Next morning, leaving his wife to wait and pray at the hotel, he rode down Main Street — heavily thronged, especially for a Monday, with townspeople and others who had come in hope of witnessing his deliverance — to the old Customs House, where the hearing would be held, and went inside to join his lawyers — six of them, three northern and three southern — seated at a table within the bar. After the first shock of recognition, those watching in the close-packed chamber were pleased to see that the change he had undergone was mainly on the surface. "He wears a full beard and mustache," a reporter had observed in the *Enquirer* the day before, "but his countenance, although haggard and careworn, still preserves the proud expression and the mingled look of sweetness and dignity for which it was ever remarkable. His hair is considerably silvered, but his eye still beams with all the fire that characterized it in the old time." Now one among the spectators, watching him enter the courtroom "with his proud step and lofty look," was convinced that "a stranger would have sworn that he was the judge and Underwood the culprit."

What followed was not only brief and to the point; it also proved yesterday's fears to be groundless. Presented with "the body of Jefferson Davis," as he had required in response to the writ, Underwood declared that the prisoner had passed from the control of martial law to the custody of the local U.S. marshal. O'Conor then requested a trial without delay, and when the district attorney replied that the case could not be heard at the present term, the judge received and granted a motion for bail, which he fixed at $100,000. Horace Greeley was there, along with other one-time enemies who had agreed to give their bond for that amount, and while they came forward to sign the necessary papers, one among the applauding spectators crossed to a window and shouted down to the crowd below on Main Street: "The President is bailed!" A roar came up in response to the news, and those inside the courtroom could hear the cry being passed from street to street, all over Richmond and its seven hills: "The President is bailed!"

They still called him that, and always would: thanks in part to Stanton and his subordinates, whose harshness had recovered for him an affection and devotion as profound as any he had received when the title was his in fact. Presently, when he came out of the Customs House and got into his carriage, the roar of approval grew shrill with the weird halloo of the rebel yell, loosed by veterans who had been waiting two years now to give it. This continued vociferously all the way to the Spotswood, where a crowd of about 5000 had gathered. Then a strange thing happened. When the coachman pulled up in front of the entrance a grave hush came down, as if everyone in the throng had suddenly felt too deeply moved for cheers. "Hats off, Virginians!" a voice rang out. All uncovered and stood in silence as Davis stepped from the carriage, free at last, and entered the hotel where his wife was waiting.

※ 4 ※

All things end, and by ending not only find continuance in the whole, but also assure continuance by contributing their droplets, clear or murky, to the stream of history. Anaximander said it best, some 2500 years ago: "It is necessary that things should pass away into that from which they are born. For things must pay one another the penalty and compensation for their injustice according to the ordinance of time." So it was with the Confederacy, and so one day will it be for the other nations of earth, if not for earth itself. Appomattox was one of several endings; Durham Station, Citronelle, Galveston were others; as were Johnson's mid-May proclamation and the ratification of the 13th Amendment, which seven months later freed the slaves not freed in the course of a four-year struggle that reunited the nation Lincoln's election had split asunder. But at what cost — if not in suffering, which was immeasurable, then at any rate in blood — had the war been won and lost?

In round numbers, two million blue-clad soldiers and sailors were diminished by 640,000 casualties — more than a fourth — while the 750,000 in gray, all told, lost 450,000 — well over half. Of the former, 110,000 had been killed in battle, as compared to 94,000 of the latter. Death from diseases (dysentery, typhus, malaria, pneumonia, smallpox, measles, tuberculosis) or mishaps out of combat (murder, suicide, drowning, sunstroke, execution, adjunctive to a host of unstated causes) raised these totals to 365,000 and 256,000 respectively, and the addition of the wounded — 275,000 Federals, 194,000 Confederates — yielded the figures quoted above. Minimal computations (deceptive in their specificity, for they too were little more than educated guesses, especially with regard to the southern forces) showed a North-South total of 623,026 dead and 471,427 wounded. The butcher's bill thus came to no less than 1,094,453 for both sides, in and out of more than 10,000 military actions, including 76 full-scale battles, 310 engagements, 6337 skirmishes, and numerous sieges, raids, expeditions, and the like. For the most part, having fewer troops on any given field, the rebels lost fewer in the fighting, but in at least one category the ratio was reversed and extended. Out of 583 Union generals, 47 were killed in action; whereas, of the 425 Confederate generals, 77 fell — roughly one out of twelve, as compared to one out of five. Moreover, much the same awesome ratios obtained when applied to the number slain or maimed out of the total number available for conscription on each side. Approximately one out of ten able-bodied Northerners was dead or incapacitated, while for the South it was one out of four, including her noncombatant Negroes. Some notion of the drain this represented, as well as of the poverty the surrendered men came home to, was shown by the fact that during the first year of peace the state of Mississippi allotted a solid fifth of its revenues for the purchase of artificial arms and legs for its returning veterans.

Few wars — western wars, that is; for in China the Tai-ping Rebellion, which began in 1850 and ended only a year before our own, cost an estimated twenty million lives — had been so proportionately expensive, either in money or in blood. And yet, for all the hard-earned cynicism that prompted them to echo Bill Arp, saying: "I've killed as many of them as they have of me. I'm going home," veterans on both sides knew that, even as they headed for their farms and shops and the girls they left behind, something momentous was passing from them, something that could never be recaptured. "I have no idea that many of them will ever see as happy times as they have had in the army," Rutherford Hayes wrote his wife from West Virginia as he watched his discharged troops depart. They would no doubt have hooted at this, eager for home as they were just then, although some among them already had experienced intimations of nostalgia. "None of us were fond of war," an Indiana infantryman would recall, looking back on the farewell review Thomas staged in Nashville, "but there had grown up between the boys an attachment for each other they never had nor ever will have for any other body of men." For others, there were doubts and fears about the future; a future now at hand. "I do feel so idle and lost to all business," an Iowa cavalryman told his diary on the eve of the Grand Review, "that I wonder what will become of me. Can I ever be contented again? *Can I work?* Ah! how doubtful — it's raining tonight."

Among the shocks awaiting homebound northern soldiers, especially those who had been gone the longest, was the fact that while wages had been rising 43 percent in the course of the war, the cost of living had gone up 117 percent. "Democracies are prone to war, and war consumes them," Seward had said, fifteen years before, and doubtless that was part of what he meant. In any case, demobilization proceeded apace. Within six months of Kirby Smith's surrender, the Union army had declined from just over a million men to 183,000. By the end of the following year it was down to 54,000, and would continue to decline for thirty years. For Southerners there was of course no waiting to be mustered out; a man's parole was his discharge, and he started home as soon as he received it. What awaited him there, particularly if home was a place Sherman or Wilson had given their passing attention, had little or nothing to do with wages. All too often there were no wages, and the cost of living was measured less in dollars than in sweat. Some notion of the waiting desolation was given by a former Georgia slave, who recalled his own departure: "The master had three boys to go to war, but there wasn't one come home. All the children he had was killed. Master, he lost all his money, and the house soon begun dropping away to nothing. Us niggers one by one left the old place, and the last time I seed the home plantation I was standing on a hill. I looked back on it for the last time through a patch of scrub pine, and it looked so lonely. There wasn't but one person in sight, the master. He was a-setting in a wicker chair in the yard looking out over a small field of cotton and corn. There was four crosses in the graveyard on the side lawn where he was setting. The fourth one was his wife."

Whatever else the veterans brought or failed to bring home with them, and whether they returned to snugness or dilapidation, with or without back pay, bonuses, and pensions, they had acquired a sense of nationhood, of nationality. From the outset Lincoln had had the problem of uniting what remained of his divided country if he was to recover by conquest the segment that had departed, and though he succeeded well enough in this to achieve his immediate purpose, true fulfillment came after his death, after the victory that brought the soldiers home. They knew now they had a nation, for they had seen it; they had been there, they had touched it, climbed its mountains, crossed its rivers, hiked its roads; their comrades lay buried in its soil, along with many thousands of their own arms and legs. Nor did this apply only to those whose return was northward, above the Mason-Dixon line. Below it, too, men who never before had been fifty miles from their places of birth now knew, from having slept and fought in its fields and woods and cane brakes, gawked at its cities, such as they were, and trudged homeward through its desolation, that they too had had a country. Not secession but the war itself, and above all the memories recurrent through the peace that followed — such as it was — created a Solid South, more firmly united in defeat than it had been during the brief span when it claimed independence. Voided, the claim was abandoned, but the pride remained: pride in the segment reabsorbed, as well as in the whole, which now for the first time was truly indivisible. This new unity was best defined, perhaps, by the change in number of a simple verb. In formal as in common speech, abroad as well as on this side of its oceans, once the nation emerged from the crucible of that war, "the United States *are*" became "the United States *is*."

It would continue so, but toward what goal? Walt Whitman, for one, believed he saw what was to come of this forged unity. "I chant the new empire, grander than before. I chant commerce opening!" he exulted. John Sherman was more specific, telling his soldier brother: "The truth is, the close of the war with our resources unimpaired gives an elevation, a scope to the ideas of leading capitalists, far higher than anything ever undertaken before. They talk of millions as confidently as formerly of thousands." Soon the nation was into a raucous era whose inheritors were Daniel Drew, Jay Gould, Jim Fisk, and others of that stripe, operating in "a riot of individual materialism, under which," as Theodore Roosevelt was to say, "complete freedom for the individual ...

turned out in practice to mean perfect freedom for the strong to wrong the weak." The big fish ate the little fish, and once the little fish got scarce or learned to hide among the rocks, the big fish ate each other. *Laissez faire* meant *laissez nous faire,* and free enterprise reached its symbolic apogee with the attempt by a gang of thieves, one night late in 1876, to steal and ransom for $200,000 the body of Abraham Lincoln. They made it into his Springfield tomb and had begun removing the casket from its sarcophagus when they were caught.

Freedom then was variously interpreted, and these differences of stance and opinion — especially as they applied to the Negro in the procedure for getting the seceded states back into what Lincoln had called "their proper practical relation with the Union" — lay at the knotty heart of Reconstruction, the four-year war's lurid twelve-year epilogue. It was in fact a sequel, a drama in three acts, of which the first was much the shortest and the mildest. Johnson, in the remaining six months of the 1865 congressional recess, put into operation his predecessor's lenient plan for allowing the defeated rebels to form their own state governments and return to their old allegiance, on condition that they pledge obedience to the national laws and promise to deal fairly with their former slaves. Summer and fall wore by; Johnson declared the process of reconstruction all but complete. Then in December Congress reassembled for Act Two, the longest and quite the rowdiest of the three. Indignant over what had been done in their absence — particularly southward, where ex-Confederates were demonstrating their notion that the black man's preparation for freedom, after two hundred years of bondage, should include an indefinite interlude of peonage — the Republican majority repudiated the new state governments and declined to seat their elected senators and representatives. Vengeance-minded, the hard-war men were out for blood. "As for Jeff Davis," George Julian told the House, "I would indict him, I would convict him and hang him in the name of God. As for Robert E. Lee, unmolested in Virginia, hang him too. And stop there? Not at all. I would hang liberally while I had my hand in."

They were above all out to get Johnson, who had jumped as it were from their pocket, where he himself had assured them he was lodged, and betrayed them while their backs were turned. The battle, promptly joined, raged through the year that followed, beginning with the passage, over the President's veto, of the first civil rights bill. That was on the anniversary of Appomattox, and two months later came the 14th Amendment, which, together with other legislation barreled through, assured full citizenship to former slaves and disqualified former Confederate leaders from holding office or casting ballots in local or national elections. Victory at the polls in November having increased the close-knit, radical-dominated Republican majority to better than two thirds in both houses, Congress then was ready to move in for the kill. Impeached by the House in February 1868 for "high crimes and misdemeanors," chief among which was his "usurpation of power," Johnson avoided conviction in May by one vote in the upper chamber. Disappointed at not having replaced him with one of their own — Ben Wade, president pro tempore of the Senate — the Jacobins concentrated on winning the fall election, and got something even better for their pains. They got U. S. Grant; which was another way of saying they got their way through most of the next eight years. Grant, with his profound mistrust of intellectuals and reformers — "narrow headed men," he called them, with eyes so close-set they could "look out of the same gimlet hole without winking" — provided the perfect foil by which the Vindictives could secure what they were after. He admired their forthrightness, as he did that of certain high-powered businessmen, who also profited from his trust; with the result that the country would wait more than fifty years for an administration as crooked in money matters, and a solid hundred for one as morally corrupt.

In the end it was the sum of these excesses that brought down the second-act curtain and moved the drama into Act Three. Shock and indignation paled to boredom as news of the scandals grew, and this, combined with the effects of the financial panic of 1873, alienated enough voters to give the Democratic candidate, Samuel J. Tilden of New York, a substantial majority of the ballots cast in the presidential election three years later. Tilden did not get into the White House, though. An engineered deal, whereby the Republicans agreed to withdraw the last Union troops from occupation of the South in exchange for the electoral votes of Louisiana and Florida, put Rutherford Hayes — three times governor of Ohio by then — into office by an electoral count of 185 to 184. All this time the play had been winding down anyhow, as state after state reëstablished "home rule": Tennessee in 1869, Virginia and North Carolina in 1870, Georgia in 1871, Arkansas, Alabama, and Texas in 1874, and Mississippi in 1875. Now with the departure in 1877 of the occupation forces, Louisiana, Florida, and South Carolina also threw off the Federal yoke, and the final curtain fell. Reconstruction, so called, was over.

Home rule, as both sides knew, meant white supremacy. The Negro, then, was bartered: or his gains were, which came to the same thing. "Bottom rail on top!" he had cried in 1870 when Hiram Revels of Mississippi, the first black man to become a member of the U.S. Senate, took Jefferson Davis's former seat. After Revels came Blanche K. Bruce, also of Mississippi. He was the second Negro senator, and the last for ninety years. In 1883 the Supreme Court would invalidate the Civil Rights Act of 1875, and would follow through, before the turn of the century, by approving racial segregation on condition that "separate" accommodations also be "equal," which they seldom were. Bottom rail was back on bottom. The 14th and 15th Amendments remained as legacies of Reconstruction, along with greatly expanded free school facilities for both races, but until the government and the courts were ready again to take the Constitution at its word, the Negro — locked in a caste system of "race etiquette" as rigid as any he had known in formal bondage — could repeat, with equal validity, what an Alabama slave had said in 1864 when asked what he thought of the Great Emancipator whose proclamation went into effect that year. "I don't know nothing bout Abraham Lincoln," he replied, "cep they say he sot us free. And I don't know nothing bout that neither."

It so happened that the year that marked the end of Reconstruction, 1877, was also the watershed year in which the United States, well on its way toward becoming a — and, ultimately, the — major industrial power, began regularly exporting more than it imported. Simultaneously, the invention of what seemed at first to be little more than toys, together with their eventual mass production, was about to change the way of life, first of its own people, then the world's. Just the year before, Alexander Bell had sent the first telephone message; this year Thomas Edison had a phonograph playing, and within another two years George B. Selden would apply for a patent for a "gasoline carriage." Change was at hand, and there were those who observed its coming with mingled approval and apprehension. "I tell you these are great times," young Henry Adams had written his brother from London during the war. "Man has mounted science, and is now run away with. I firmly believe that before many centuries more, science will be the master of man. The engines he will have invented will be beyond his strength to control. Some day science may have the existence of mankind in its power, and the human race commit suicide by blowing up the world. Not only shall we be able to cruise in space, but I see no reason why some future generation shouldn't walk off like a beetle with the world on its back, or give it another rotary motion so that every zone should receive in turn its due portion of heat and light."

North and South, the veterans were part of this, but mainly as observers rather than participants, and least of all as profiteers. Few or no tycoons had served in the northern armies, and southern talents seemed not to lie in that direction, except for a prominent few who lent their names for use on letterheads. Well into what passed for middle age by then, they had something of the studied indifference of men who had spent their lives in another world. Visiting regions where they had fought, ten, then twenty, then thirty years ago, they found the distances not as great as they remembered, but the hills a good deal steeper. Certain tags of poetry had a tendency to hang in their minds, whether from a dirge by Whitman:

> *Beautiful that war and all its deeds of carnage*
> *must in time be utterly lost,*
> *That the hands of the sisters Death and Night*

> *incessantly softly wash again,*
> *and ever again, this soil'd world —*

or, more likely, a snatch from a rollicking cavalry tune, sung in time with hoofbeats pounding the moon-drenched highways of their youth:

> *He who has good buttermilk aplenty,*
> *And gives the soldiers none,*
> *Shan't have any of our buttermilk*
> *When his buttermilk is gone.*

Time played its tricks, distorting and subtracting. The rebel yell, for instance — "shrill, exultant, savage," a one-time blue infantryman recalled, "so different from the deep, manly, generous shout of the Union soldiers" — would presently be lost to all who had never heard it on the field of battle. Asked at the close of a U.D.C. banquet to reproduce it, a Tennessee veteran explained that the yell was "impossible unless made at a dead run in full charge against the enemy." Not only could it not be given in cold blood while standing still; it was "worse than folly to try to imitate it with a stomach full of food and a mouth full of false teeth." So it perished from the sound waves. Wildcat screech, foxhunt yip, banshee squall, whatever it had been, it survived only in the fading memories and sometimes vivid dreams of old men sunning themselves on public benches, grouped together in resentment of the boredom they encountered when they spoke of the war to those who had not shared it with them.

Once a year at least — aside, that is, from regimental banquets and mass reunions, attended more and more sparsely by middle-aged, then old, then incredibly ancient men who dwindled finally to a handful of octogenarian drummer boys, still whiskered for the most part in a clean-shaven world that had long since passed them by — these survivors got together to honor their dead. Observed throughout the North on May 30, Memorial Day hopscotched the calendar in the South, where individual states made their choice between April 26, May 10, and June 3. In any case, whenever it came, this day belonged to the veterans and their fallen comrades, and they made the most of it, beginning with their choice of a speaker, always with the hope that he would rival the "few appropriate remarks" Lincoln had uttered at Gettysburg on a similar occasion. None ever did, but one at least came close at Keene, New Hampshire, in 1884, twenty years after that day on the outskirts of Washington when he yelled at the since-martyred leader, high on the parapet of Fort Stevens: "Get down, you damn fool!" Young Captain Holmes, thrice gravely wounded in three years of service, was forty-three by now, not halfway into a distinguished life that would continue through more than a third of the approaching century. He would deliver, in the course of his ninety-four years, many speeches highly admired for their pith and felicity of expression, yet he never spoke more to the point, or more to the satisfaction of his hearers, than he did on this Memorial Day in his native New England.

He began by expressing his respect, not only for the veterans gathered to hear him, but also for the men they had fought, and he told why he felt it. "You could not stand up day after day, in those indecisive contests where overwhelming victory was impossible because neither side would run as they ought when beaten, without getting at last something of the same brotherhood for the enemy that the north pole of a magnet has for the south, each working in an opposite sense to the other, but unable to get along without the other." Such scorn as he felt he reserved for those who had stood aside when the call came for commitment. "I think that, as life is action and passion, it is required of a man that he should share the passion and action of his time at peril of being judged not to have lived." Memorial Day was for him and his listeners "the most sacred of the year," and he believed it would continue to be observed with pride and reverence. "But even if I am wrong, even if those who are to come after us are to forget all that we hold dear, and the future is to teach and kindle its children in ways as yet unrevealed, it is enough for us that to us this day is dear and sacred.... For one hour, twice a year at least — at the regimental dinner, where the ghosts sit at table more numerous than the living, and on this day when we decorate their graves — the dead come back and live with us. I see them now, more than I can number, as once I saw them on this earth." He saw them, and he saw what they stood for, even now in the midst of what Mark Twain had dubbed the Gilded Age. "The generation that carried on the war has been set aside by its experience. Through our great good fortune, in our youth our hearts were touched with fire. It was given to us to learn at the outset that life is a profound and passionate thing. While we are permitted to scorn nothing but indifference, and do not pretend to undervalue the worldly rewards of ambition, we have seen with our own eyes, beyond and above the gold fields, the snowy heights of honor, and it is for us to bear the report to those who come after us."

No wonder, then, if they looked back on that four-year holocaust — which in a sense was begun by one madman, John Brown, and ended by another, J. Wilkes Booth — with something of the feeling shared by men who have gone through, and survived, some cataclysmic phenomenon; a hurricane or an earthquake, say, or a horrendous railway accident. Memory smoothed the crumpled scroll, abolished fear, leached pain and grief, and removed the sting from death. "Well," a former hospital steward testified, recalling the moribund patients in his ward, "they would see that the doctor gave them up, and they would ask me about it. I would tell them the truth. I told one man that, and he asked how long? I said not over twenty minutes. He did not show any fear — they never do. He put his hand up, so, and closed his eyes with his own fingers, then stretched himself out and crossed his arms over his breast. 'Now, fix me,' he said. I pinned the toes of his stockings together; that was the way we laid corpses out; and he died in a few minutes. His face looked as pleasant as if he was asleep, and smiling. Many's the time the boys have fixed themselves that way before they died." In time, even death itself might be abolished. Sergeant Berry Benson, a South Carolina veteran from McGowan's brigade, Wilcox's division, A. P. Hill's corps, Army of Northern Virginia — he had enlisted three months before Sumter, aged eighteen, and served through Appomattox — saw it so when he got around to composing the Reminiscences he hoped would "go down amongst my descendants for a long time." Reliving the war in words, he began to wish he could relive it in fact, and he came to believe that he and his fellow soldiers, gray and blue, might one day be able to do just that: if not here on earth, then afterwards in Valhalla. "Who knows," he asked as his narrative drew toward its close, "but it may be given to us, after this life, to meet again in the old quarters, to play chess and draughts, to get up soon to answer the morning roll call, to fall in at the tap of the drum for drill and dress parade, and again to hastily don our war gear while the monotonous patter of the long roll summons to battle? Who knows but again the old flags, ragged and torn, snapping in the wind, may face each other and flutter, pursuing and pursued, while the cries of victory fill a summer day? And after the battle, then the slain and wounded will arise, and all will meet together under the two flags, all sound and well, and there will be talking and laughter and cheers, and all will say: Did it not seem real? Was it not as in the old days?"

★ ★ ★

By then they had nearly all come round, both sides having entered into a two-way concession whereby the victors acknowledged that the Confederates had fought bravely for a cause they believed was just and the losers agreed it was probably best for all concerned that the Union had been preserved. The first step lay in admission of defeat, and one of the first to take it publicly was Joe Johnston. Aboard a Chesapeake Bay steamer, not long after his surrender, the general heard a fellow passenger insisting that the South had been "conquered but not subdued." Asked in what command he had served, the bellicose young man — one of those stalwarts later classified as "invisible in war and invincible in peace" — replied that, unfortunately, circumstances had made it impossible for him to be in the army. "Well, sir, I was," Johnston told him. "You may not be subdued, but I am."

Similarly, R. E. Lee encouraged all who sought his advice to take the loyalty oath required by the President's amnesty proclamation as a prerequisite to recovery of their rights as citizens, and even did so himself, barely two months after Appomattox, though nothing came of it then or later; he would go to his grave disfranchised. However, news that he had "asked for pardon" spread rapidly through the South, producing consternation, which was followed for the most part, even among those who had been die-hards up till then, by prompt acceptance and emulation. "You have disgraced the family, sir!" Ex-Governor Henry Wise sputtered when he learned that one of his sons had taken the oath. "But, Father," the former captain said, "General Lee advised me to do it." Taken aback, Wise paused only a moment before he replied: "That alters the case. Whatever General Lee advises is right."

Neither of these attitudes or reactions — Johnston's admission that he had been "subdued," Lee's willingness to pledge loyalty to a government he had sought to overthrow — was acceptable to Jefferson Davis in his own right. He did not object intrinsically to their view, so long as they applied it to themselves, but as the symbolic leader of a nation, even one that had been abolished by force of arms, he had other factors to consider. For him, the very notion of subdual was something to be rejected out of hand, if acceptance, as he conceived it, meant abandoning the principles of constitutional government. The war had been lost beyond denial, but not the cause. Nothing would ever bend him from that. He clung to the views he had held in 1861, and indeed ever since he entered public life some twenty years before. As for anything resembling an apology — which he believed was what he would be offering if he took the oath required — he would say repeatedly, first and last: "I have no claim to pardon, not having in any wise repented." No wonder, then, that Andrew Johnson referred to him as Lucifer incarnate, "the head devil of them all."

To his own people he was something else, in part because of all he had suffered, first in the granite bowels of Fort Monroe — where Miles, acting on Stanton's orders, martyred him about as effectively as Booth had martyred Lincoln — and then through much of the decade following his release on bail, a time referred to by his wife as one spent "floating uprooted." From Richmond, his trial having been put off until November, he went to Canada, where the two older of his four children were in school, then came back by way of Cuba for his health's sake, his trial having been postponed again till March of 1868, then still again until the following February. Impeachment was heading up by now in Washington, and the danger loomed of Johnson's being replaced by bluff Ben Wade, who was not above Star Chamber proceedings. On the advice of his attorneys, Davis and his family planned to sail for Europe, and did so in July, though Wade by then had been kept from becoming President by one senatorial vote. In England the former State Prisoner was entertained by high-born sympathizers and had the pleasure of dining with his old companion Judah Benjamin, fast on the rise as a distinguished member of the bar. A visit to France at the end of the year also gave him the satisfaction of declining an audience with

Napoleon and Eugénie, who, he said, had "played us false" at a time when the need for friends was sore.

He had by now had more than enough of "floating," and his pride would not allow him to accept indefinitely from admirers the financial help he was obliged to live on while his trial was pending. Then suddenly it no longer was. Early in 1869, with the indictment quashed at last, he was free to come home and accept employment as president of the Carolina Life Insurance Company, headquartered in Memphis. He returned without his family, got settled in the business, and went back to England in late summer, 1870, for his wife and children. Docking at Baltimore in mid-October he learned that Robert Lee had died that week. "Virginia has need of all her sons," the general had replied when asked by veterans what he thought of their going elsewhere to escape the strictures of poverty and Reconstruction, and he himself had set them an example by serving, at a salary of $1500 a year, as president of Washington College, a small, all but bankrupt institution out in the Shenandoah Valley. He aged greatly in the five years left him after Appomattox, suffering from the heart ailment which his doctors now could see had been what plagued him through much of the war, when the symptoms were diagnosed as rheumatism. Stricken in late September, he lingered till October 12. Back in battle toward the end, like Stonewall before him, he called in his delirium on A. P. Hill: "Tell Hill he must come up." Then he quieted, as Jackson too had done before he crossed the river. "Strike the tent," he said, and then he died.

"Of the man, how shall I speak? His moral qualities rose to the height of genuis," Davis declared at a memorial service held in Richmond in early November. It was his first public address since the end of the war, and though he was encouraged by the fervor of his reception in the one-time national capital, the passing of the great Confederate captain was the signal for the onset of a series of reversals for his former chief, the heaviest of which came two years later with the death of one of his two surviving sons. Eleven-year-old Billy, conceived in Montgomery during the secession furore and born after the removal of the government to Virginia, fell victim to diphtheria in Memphis. Settled in a house of his own for the first time in six years, and released at last, as he thought, from the life his wife described as "floating uprooted," Davis suffered this sudden deprivation only to have it followed by still another during the financial panic of '73, precipitated by the failure of Jay Cooke & Company in New York, which had marketed the huge war loans of the Federal government. Carolina Life went under, too, a chip among the flotsam, taking with it his last $15,000 and the only job he had ever had. Afloat again, he sought other ventures, some involving trips to Europe in search of backers, but nothing came of them. Though he kept his home in Memphis, even managing the expense of a wedding for his daughter Maggie in 1875, the result was that he again found himself floating rootless, his life no longer a career, but rather an existence.

When at last he found the answer, a way out of this dilemma, it was neither in Memphis nor in business. Ever since his release from prison he had had it in mind to write a personal history of the war, and even as early as his stay in Canada he had begun to look through such papers as were then available for his purpose, including duplicates of messages sent commanders in the field. One of the first he examined, however — a telegram he had addressed to Lee from Danville on the day of Appomattox, unaware that the surrender was in progress — put an end to this preliminary effort. "You will realize the reluctance I feel to leave the soil of Virginia," he had wired, "and appreciate my anxiety to win success north of the Roanoke." Mrs Davis, who was there to help him sort the documents, saw a stricken look come on his face at the memories the words called up. He pushed the papers away. "Let us put them by for a while. I cannot speak of my dead so soon," he told her. That had been nearly ten years ago, and he had not returned to them since, despite the urging of such friends as Preston Johnston, who admonished him: "I do not believe any man ever lived who could dare to tell in the light more fully what was done in the dark, than you can. It seems to be a friendly duty to warn you not to forget your design." Davis did not forget, but he was fully occupied by the insurance business: until it vanished, that is, along with what little he had left in the way of funds. Failure freed him to return to his old design; failure and necessity, and something else as well. Recently, old comrades who had shared the glory and pain of battles won and lost — ex-Confederates for the most part, though the victors also had their differences in public — had begun to turn on each other, quarreling over what they considered a proper distribution of praise and blame, especially the latter. One of the hottest of these arguments had to do with Gettysburg; Fitzhugh Lee and Jubal Early crossed swords with Longstreet, who had compounded their enmity by going over to the Republicans and his old friend Grant. Davis stayed well out of it, reserving his ire for a long-time adversary, Joseph E. Johnston, who had brought out in 1874 his *Narrative of Military Operations Directed During the Late War Between the States*, much of it devoted to unburdening himself of grievances against his former superior. "The advance sheets exhibit his usual malignity and suppression of the truth when it would affect his side of the case unfavorably," Davis informed his wife by way of warming up for the counteroffensive he now had it in mind to launch. He would write his own account, quartering much of the same ground, of course, and accordingly signed a contract with Appleton's of New York, who agreed to cover such expenses as he required for secretarial assistance.

Bustling Memphis, hot in summer, cold in winter — the scene of his loss, moreover, of the third of his four sons — seemed unconducive to the peace he believed he needed for such work. Who could write anything there, let alone a full-fledged two- or three-volume history of the war? He had found the atmosphere he wanted on a trip to the Mississippi Coast the previous November, when he wrote his wife that "the moaning of the winds among the pines and the rolling waves of the Gulf on the beach gave me a sense of rest and peace which made me wish to lay me down and be at home." Midway between New Orleans and Mobile was "Beauvoir," an estate belonging to Sarah E. Dorsey, a wealthy, recently widowed childhood friend of Varina's; "a fine place," Davis called it, with a "large and beautiful house" set among spreading live oaks "and many orange trees yet full of fruit." Receiving him now as a visitor, Mrs Dorsey offered him the use of a cottage on the grounds, "a refuge without encumbrances" in which to write his book. He quickly accepted, on condition of paying board, and by February 1877 he and a body servant had moved in. Quarters were found nearby for Major W. T. Walthall, his research assistant, and work began at once, with the added help of Sarah Dorsey herself. She had written four novels under the nom de plume "Filia," and was delighted to serve as an amanuensis, having long admired her house guest as "the noblest man she had ever met on earth."

Varina, who had never enjoyed the notion of sharing Jefferson Davis with anyone — least of all another woman, childhood friend or not — was considerably less pleased with this outcome of his quest for domestic tranquillity. She had been in Germany most of the past eight months, getting twelve-year-old Winnie settled in a girls' school in Carlsruhe, and despite urgings from her husband and Mrs Dorsey that she join them on the Coast, she remained in Europe for another eight, determined not to be a party to any such *ménage à trois* arrangement. Finally in October she returned, not to Beauvoir but to Memphis, where twenty-year-old Jeff Junior, after an unsatisfactory year at V.M.I., had accepted a place in a bank with his sister Maggie's husband. Davis himself came up at once, hoping to take her back with him, but she refused. She was pleased, however, to see him looking well, absorbed in his work and eager to get back to it. A new urgency was on him, caused in part by the recent passing of some of the principal characters in the story he was attempting to retell. Braxton Bragg, for example, had dropped dead on the street in Galveston last year, and Raphael Semmes had been buried only the month before in Mobile. Another great raider, Bedford Forrest, was dying in Memphis even now, wasted by diabetes to a scant one hundred pounds. "I am completely broke up," he confessed to friends. "I am broke in fortune, broke in health, broke in spirit." Davis sat by his bedside the day before he died, then served as a pallbearer at his funeral on the last day of October. In the carriage, en route to Elmwood Cemetery, a companion remarked on Forrest's greatness as a soldier. "I agree with you," the former President said. "The trouble was that the generals commanding in the Southwest never appreciated him until it was too late. Their judgment was that he was a bold and enterprising raider and rider. I was misled by them, and never knew how to measure him until I read the reports of his campaign across the Tennessee River in 1864. This induced a study of his earlier reports, and after that I was prepared to adopt what you are pleased to name as the judgment of history." Someone mentioned Brice's Crossroads, and Davis replied as before: "That campaign was not understood in Richmond. The impression made upon those in authority was that Forrest had made another successful raid.... I saw it all after it was too late."

He returned alone to Beauvoir, Sarah Dorsey, and his work. Varina was willing to help by mail, amplifying his recollections with her own, but not in person. "Nothing on earth would pain me like living in that kind of community," she had written from Europe, and she still felt that way about it. At any rate she did for another eight months before she relented, in part because of the heat of a Memphis summer, but mainly because her husband by then had offered to give up his present living arrangement if she would join him elsewhere. Apparently it was this she had been waiting for all along, for he no sooner made the offer than she consented to join him where he was. She arrived in July, 1878, and at once took over the job of amanuensis. Indignant at the unrelenting vindictiveness of Washington in excluding Davis from the benefits of a pension bill for veterans of the Mexican War, they settled down to work amid reports of a yellow fever epidemic moving upriver from New Orleans. Memphis and other cities and towns were still under quarantine in October when a wire reached Beauvoir to inform them that Jeff Junior had come down with the disease. Then five days later another arrived to tell them he had rallied and then died. Davis had lost the fourth of his four sons; Samuel, Joseph, William, and now Jeff. "I presume not God to scorn," he wrote a kinsman, "but the many and humble prayers offered before my boy was taken from me are hushed in the despair of my bereavement."

Work was the answer, as much for Varina as for her husband, and they got on with it, sometimes into the small hours of the night. In February the domestic strain was relieved by Mrs Dorsey, who sold Beauvoir to Davis for $5500, to be paid in three installments, then went to New Orleans to consult a physician for what turned out to be cancer. By July she was dead. Childless, she left Beauvoir to Davis, absolving him from making the other two payments. Nor was that all. "I hereby give and bequeath all my property, wherever located and situated, wholly and entirely, without hindrance or qualification," her will read, "to my most honored and esteemed friend, Jefferson Davis, ex-President of the Confederate States, for his sole use and benefit, in fee simple forever.... I do not intend," she had said in closing, "to share in the ingratitude of my country towards the man who is in my eyes the highest and noblest in existence." He was now the master of Beauvoir, along with much else, including three plantations in Louisiana, and Varina was its mistress.

The work went on. Reconstruction was over, but Davis still fought the war, landing verbal blows where armed strokes had failed. Soon the first of what were to be two large volumes was ready for the printer. *Rise and Fall of the Confederate Government,* he would call it: not *Our Cause,* as he had originally intended. He moved into and steadily through the second volume. On an afternoon in April, 1881, he took a long nap, then at 8 o'clock that evening resumed dictation. Speaking slowly and distinctly, so that Varina would not miss a word, he tugged firmly on the drawstrings of his logic for a final explication of his thesis that the North, not the South, had been the revolutionary party in the struggle, malevolent in its effort to subvert, subjugate, and destroy, respectively, the states, the people, and the Union as it had been till then. "When the cause was lost, what cause was it?" he asked, and answered: "Not that of the South only, but the cause of constitutional government, of the supremacy of law, of the natural rights of man." It was by then well past midnight, and only the rhythmic plash of waves on the beach came through the stillness of the dark hours before dawn. He kept on, launched now onto the last of nearly 1500 pages, restating his conviction "that the war was, on the part of the United States Government, one of aggression and usurpation, and, on the part of the South, was for the defense of an inherent, unalienable right." He paused, then continued.

> In asserting the right of secession, it has not been my wish to incite to its exercise: I recognize the fact that the war showed it to be impracticable, but this did not prove it to be wrong. And now that it may not be again attempted, and that the Union may promote the general welfare, it is needful that the truth, the whole truth, should be known, so that crimination and recrimination may forever cease, and then, on the basis of fraternity and faithful regard for the rights of the States, there may be written on the arch of the Union, *Esto perpetua.*

He leaned back, sighed, and closed his eyes against the glare of lamplight. It was 4 o'clock in the morning and he was within two months of being seventy-three years old. Her pen poised above the paper, Varina looked up, ready for the next sentence. "I think I am done," he said with a tired smile.

He was done, and the book — already in type, except these final pages — came out in June. In the South it was hailed and praised. No home that could afford them was without the two thick volumes, often bound in calf, on a parlor table. The trouble was, so few could afford them, and in the North the book was largely ignored, save in a few grudging magazine reviews. Financially, it was a failure; Appleton's lost money, and Davis himself made little, despite a drawn-out lawsuit with the publisher which ensued. In August he and Varina sailed for Europe to get Winnie, and returned in late November. "The Daughter of the Confederacy," born in the Richmond White House while the guns of Kennesaw were booming, was tall and fair, with clear gray eyes and a quiet manner; she spoke, to her father's surprise, with traces of a German accent which she would never lose. Settled again at Beauvoir he looked forward to a peaceful life through whatever years were left him. Then in mid-December came news that Joe Johnston had wondered aloud to a reporter what had become of all the treasury gold Davis had taken along on his flight through Georgia. It came, he heard, to $2,500,000; yet "Mr Davis has never given any satisfactory account of it." In the hue and cry that followed, the general was obliged to run for cover, and letters poured into Beauvoir from all parts of the country, expressing outrage at the slander and admiration for its victim. Davis had won his last skirmish with Johnston, who perhaps was confirmed in his distaste for the offensive.

Still, no amount of adulation North or South could temper the former President's resolution not to ask for pardon; not even pleas from his home-state Legislature that he do so in order to be returned to his old seat in the U. S. Senate. He did however agree to come to Jackson in March, 1884, for a ceremony staged to honor him as "the embodied history of the South." Standing in the high-ceilinged Capitol chamber where he had stood just over two decades ago, near the midpoint of the war, and told the assembled dignitaries, "Our people have only to be true to themselves to behold the Confederate flag among the recognized nations of the earth," he spoke now much as he had then: "It has been said that I should apply to the United States for a pardon. But repentance must precede the right of pardon, and I have not repented. Remembering, as I must, all which has been suffered, all which has been lost — disappointed hopes and crushed aspirations — yet I deliberately say, if it were all to do over again, I would again do just as I did in 1861." His hearers caught their breath at this, then applauded with all their might the fallen leader who represented, almost alone, the undefeat of which they boasted from stumps across the land, now and for years to come. Unforgiving, he was unforgiven, and he preferred it so, for their sake and his own.

Late in the spring of the following year a Boston paper called on Davis for an expression of his views on U. S. Grant, who was dying at Mount McGregor, New York, of cancer of the throat. Bankrupt by a brokerage partner who turned out to be a swindler, the general had lost even his sword as security for an unpaid loan, and was now engaged in a race with death to complete his *Memoirs,* hoping the proceeds would provide for his family after he was gone. He won, but only by the hardest. Reduced by pain to communicating with his doctor on slips of paper — "A verb is anything that signifies to be; to do; to suffer," one read. "I signify all three" — he managed to finish the book within a week of his death in July, and royalties approaching half a million dollars went to Julia and his sons. Davis had declined to comment on the career of this man whose name, in the course of his two White House terms, had come to stand for plunder and repression. "General Grant is dying," he replied to the request from Boston. "Instead of seeking to disturb the quiet of his closing hours, I would, if it were in my power, contribute to the peace of his mind and the comfort of his body." Similarly, he had withheld comment on the passing of other former enemies, beginning with George Thomas, whose weight rose above three hundred pounds within five years of the end of the war, when he died on duty of a stroke in the same year as his fellow Virginian, R. E. Lee. Henry Halleck and George Meade, who also stayed in the army, followed him two years later. George McClellan, after serving three years as governor of New Jersey, died three months after Grant, and was followed in turn by Winfield Hancock, who had run against Garfield in the presidential election six years back, just over three months later.

By then it was 1886, the silver anniversary of Sumter. Memorial services and reunions were being planned throughout the South, and Davis was pressed to attend most of them as guest of honor. He declined, pleading frailty, until someone thought to point out that Winnie might never know how dear he was to the hearts of his people unless he gave them the chance to show their love in public. That persuaded him. "I'll go; I'll go," he said, and accepted invitations from Montgomery, Atlanta, and Savannah. In late April he sat on the portico of the Alabama capitol, where he had been inaugurated twenty-five years before, and heard a eulogy pronounced by John B. Gordon, former U. S. senator and now a candidate for governor of Georgia, who also presented Winnie to the crowd, to wild applause. Next day Davis spoke briefly at the laying of the cornerstone for a monument to the Confederate dead — repeating once more his contention that the seceded states had launched no revolution; "Sovereigns never rebel," he said — then set out for Atlanta, where 50,000 veterans were assembling for a May Day reunion. He was on the platform, receiving the cheers of all that host, when he looked out beyond its distant fringes and saw a man approaching on horseback, portly and white-haired, with cottony muttonchop whiskers, decked out in Confederate gray with the looped braid of a lieutenant general on his sleeves. It was Longstreet. Uninvited because of his postwar views — "The striking feature, the one the people should keep in view," he had said at the outset of Reconstruction, "is that we are a conquered people. Recognizing this fact, fairly and squarely, there is but one course left for wise men to pursue, and that is to accept the terms that now are offered by the conquerers" — Old Peter had risen that morning at his home in nearby Gainesville, put on his full uniform, come down by train, and ridden out to show the throng that he was of them, whether they wanted him there or not. Dismounting, he walked up the steps of the platform where Davis was seated, and everyone wondered what Davis would do. They soon found out, for he rose and hurried to meet Lee's old warhorse. "When the two came together," a witness declared, "Mr Davis threw his arms around General Longstreet's neck and the two leaders embraced with great emotion. The meaning of the reconciliation was clear and instantly had a profound effect upon the thousands of veterans who saw it. With a great shout they showed their joy."

One occasion of the Atlanta visit was the unveiling of a statue to the late Senator Benjamin Hill, always a loyal friend in times of crisis. "We shall conquer all enemies yet," he had assured his chief within two weeks of Appomattox, but admitted nine years later, looking back: "All physical advantages are insufficient to account for our failure. The truth is, we failed because too many of our people were not determined to win." Davis knew the basic validity of this view, yet he preferred to stress the staunchness of his people and the long odds they had faced. Northern journalists had begun to note the "inflammatory" effect of his appearances, and he tried next week in Savannah to offset this by remarking at a banquet given by the governor in his honor: "There are some who take it for granted that when I allude to State sovereignty I want to bring on another war. I am too old to fight again, and God knows I do not want you to have the necessity of fighting again." He paused to let the reporters take this down, but while he waited he saw the faces of those around him, many of them veterans like himself; with the result that he undid what had gone before. "However, if the necessity *should* arise," he said, "I know you will meet it, as you always have discharged every duty you felt called upon to perform."

Although he returned to Beauvoir near exhaustion, he recovered in time, the following year, to challenge the prohibition movement as still another "monstrous" attempt to limit individual freedom. His words were quoted by the liquor interests and he was denounced by a Methodist bishop for advocating "the barroom and the destruction of virtue." But the fact was he had mellowed, partly under the influence of strong nationalist feelings never far below the surface of his resistance. When he went back to Georgia in October, to meet "perhaps for the last time" with veterans at a reunion staged in Macon — where he had first been taken after his capture near Irwinville, more than twenty-two years ago — he spoke to them of the North and South as indivisibly united. "We are now at peace," he said, "and I trust will ever remain so.... In referring therefore to the days of the past and the glorious cause you have served ... I seek but to revive a memory which should be dear to you and to your children, a memory which teaches the highest lessons of manhood, of truth and adherence to duty — duty to your State, duty to your principles, duty to your buried parents, and duty to your coming children." That was the burden of what he had to say through the time now left him, including his last speech of all, delivered the following spring at Mississippi City, only a six-mile buggy ride from Beauvoir.

Within three months of being eighty years old, he had not thought he would speak again in public; but he did, this once, for a particular reason. The occasion was a convention of young Southerners, and that was why — their youth. He did not mention the war at all, not even as "a memory which should be dear," though he did refer at the outset to the nation he had led. "Friends and fellow citizens," he began, and stopped. "Ah, pardon me," he said. "The laws of the United States no longer permit me to designate you as fellow citizens. I feel no regret that I stand before you a man without a country, for my ambition lies buried in the grave of the Confederacy." Then he went on to tell them what he had come to say. "The faces I see before me are those of young men; had I not known this I would not have appeared before you. Men in whose hands the destinies of our Southland lie, for love of her I break my silence to speak to you a few words of respectful admonition. The past is dead; let it bury its dead, its hopes and its aspirations. Before you lies the future, a future full of golden promise, a future of expanding national glory, before which all the world shall stand amazed. Let me beseech you to lay aside all rancor, all bitter sectional feeling, and to take your places in the ranks of those who will bring about a consummation devoutly to be wished — a reunited country."

Those were his last public words, and they seemed withal to have brought him a new peace, one that fulfilled a hope he had recently expressed to an old friend: "My downs have been so many, and the feeling of injustice so great, that I wish to hold on and see whether the better days may not come." A reporter who came to Beauvoir for his eightieth birthday, June 3, not only found him "immaculately dressed, straight and erect, with traces of his military service still showing in his carriage, and with the flush of health on his pale, refined face," but also observed that he retained "a keen interest in current topics, political, social, religious." He kept busy. In the course of the next year he wrote three magazine articles, a *Short History of the Confederate States*, and even got started on an autobiography, though he soon put this aside. In early November, 1889, he set out for New Orleans to catch a steamer upriver for his annual inspection trip to Brierfield, which he had lost and then recovered by a lawsuit. Usually his wife went along but this time she remained behind with guests. Exposed to a sleety rain, he came down with a cold and was so ill by the time the boat reached Brierfield Landing, late at night, that he continued on to Vicksburg. Going ashore next morning, he rode down to the plantation, only to spend the next four days in bed, sick with bronchitis and a recurrence of the malaria that had killed his bride and nearly killed him, more than fifty years before, at the same place.

Alarmed, for Davis by then was near delirium, the plantation manager got him back to Vicksburg and onto a steamer headed south. Downriver that night the boat was hailed by another coming up with Varina on board. Warned by telegraph of her husband's condition, she had set out to join him, and now she did so, transferring in midstream to claim her place at his bedside. New Orleans doctors pronounced him too ill to be taken to Beauvoir, so he was carried on a stretcher to a private home in the Garden District. He seemed to improve in the course of the next week. "It may seem strange to you," he told an attending physician, "that a man of my years should desire to live; but I do. There are still some things that I have to do in this world." He wanted above all to get back to the autobiography he had set aside. "I have not told what I wish to say of my college-mates Sidney Johnston and Polk. I have much more to say of them. I shall tell a great deal of West Point — and I seem to remember more every day." Presently, though, it was clear that he would do none of these things, including the desired return to Beauvoir. Another week passed; December came in. On December 5, within six months of being eighty-two years old, he woke to find Varina sitting beside him, and he let her know he knew the time was near. "I want to tell you I am not afraid to die," he said, although he seemed no worse than he had been the day before.

That afternoon he slept soundly, but woke at dusk with a violent chill. Frightened, Varina poured out a teaspoon of medicine, only to have him decline it with a meager smile and a faint shake of his head. When she insisted he refused again. "Pray excuse me. I cannot take it," he murmured. These were the last words of a man who had taken most of the knocks a hard world had to offer. He lapsed into a peaceful sleep that continued into the night. Once when his breathing grew labored the doctors turned him gently onto his right side, and he responded childlike by raising his arm to pillow his cheek on his hand, the other resting lightly on his heart. Midnight came and went, and less than an hour later he too obeyed Anaximander's dictum, breathing his last so imperceptibly that Varina and the others at his bedside could scarcely tell the moment of his going.

He died on Friday and was buried on Wednesday, time being needed to allow for the arrival of friends and relatives from distant points. Meanwhile, dressed in a civilian suit of Confederate gray, his body lay in state at City Hall, viewed in the course of the next four days by an estimated hundred thousand mourners. Then the day of the funeral came, December 11, and all the church bells of New Orleans tolled. Eight southern governors served as pallbearers, the Washington Artillery as guard of honor; interment would be at Metairie Cemetery in the tomb of the Army of Northern Virginia, which was crowned with a statue of Stonewall Jackson atop a fifty-foot marble shaft. "The end of a long and lofty life has come. The strange and sudden dignity of death has been added to the fine and resolute dignity of living," the Episcopal bishop of Louisiana declared on the steps of City Hall as the casket was brought out to begin the three-hour march to Metairie. After the service at the tomb, when Taps had sounded, he spoke again. "In the name of God, amen. We here consign the body of Jefferson Davis, a servant of his state and country and a soldier in their armies; sometime member of Congress, Senator from Mississippi, and Secretary of War of the United States; the first and only President of the Confederate States of America; born in Kentucky on the third day of June, 1808, died in Louisiana on the sixth day of December, 1889, and buried here by the reverent hands of his people."

Much else was said in the way of praise across the land that day, and still more would be said four years later, when his body would be removed to its permanent resting place in Hollywood Cemetery, Richmond, to join his son Joe and others who had died nearby in Virginia during the war. Lincoln by now had been a full generation in his Springfield tomb, and all he had said or written would be cherished as an imperishable legacy to the nation, including the words he had spoken in response to a White House serenade on the occasion of his reëlection: "What has occurred in this case must ever recur in similar cases. Human nature will not change. In any future great national trial, compared with the men of this, we shall have as weak and as strong, as silly and as wise, as bad and as good. Let us therefore study the incidents of this, as philosophy to learn wisdom from, and none of them as wrongs to be revenged." Davis could never match that music, or perhaps even catch its tone. His was a different style, though it too had its beauty and its uses: as in his response to a recent Beauvoir visitor, a reporter who hoped to leave with something that would help explain to readers the underlying motivation of those crucial years of bloodshed and division. Davis pondered briefly, then replied.

"Tell them — " He paused as if to sort the words. "Tell the world that I only loved America," he said.

List of Maps
Bibliographical Note

LIST OF MAPS

PAGE
- 2. Grant's Plan, Spring '64.
- 63. Red River Campaign; Camden Expedition.
- 124. Six Against Richmond.
- 154. Wilderness, 5May: Contact.
- 162. Wilderness, Second Attack.
- 180. Wilderness; Flankers.
- 195. A Race for Spotsylvania.
- 217. The Bloody Angle, 12May.
- 227. Sheridan's Richmond Raid.
- 245. Sigel; Crook, Averell.
- 252. Bottling Butler, 6–17May.
- 266. March to the North Anna.
- 272. Lee's Inverted V, 24May.
- 277. March to the Totopotomoy.
- 289. Cold Harbor, 3Jun.
- 314. Grant Shifts to James.
- 324. Dalton to Resaca.
- 336. Resaca to Cassville.
- 346. Kingston to Pine Top, via Dallas.
- 366. Brice's Crossroads, 10Jun.
- 396. Kennesaw Mountain, 27Jun.
- 407. Chattahoochee Crossings.
- 429. Southside Convergence.
- 437. Petersburg Assault.
- 448. Early Heads North.
- 474. Peachtree Creek, 20July.
- 476. Atlanta, 22July.
- 489. Ezra Church, 28July.
- 496. Mobile Bay, 5Aug.
- 521. Atlanta Envelopment.
- 546. Petersburg, August.
- 554. Winchester, 19Sep.
- 566. Cedar Creek, 19Oct.
- 578. Price Raids Missouri.
- 600. Forrest in Tennessee.
- 618. Hood and Sherman Part.
- 628. Petersburg: Fall '64.
- 642. The March to the Sea.
- 655. Hood Sets Out North.
- 657. Schofield Flanked.
- 668. Franklin, 30Nov.
- 689. Nashville, 15Dec.
- 699. Nashville: Second Day.
- 734. The Close-Out Plan.
- 752. Sherman Heads North.
- 784. Hatcher's Run, 5–7Feb.
- 824. Kinston, Averasboro, Bentonville, 8–21Mar.
- 865. Dinwiddie, Five Forks.
- 916. To Appomattox, 2–9Apr.

ENDPAPERS.
Front: Theater of War.
Back: Atlanta Campaign.
Virginia, Grant vs Lee.

Maps drawn by Rafael Palacios, from originals by the author. All are oriented north.

BIBLIOGRAPHICAL NOTE

So there now. Twenty years have come and gone and I can say with Chaucer, "Farwel my book and my devocion." All through the second of these two decades — the drawn-out time it took to write this third and final volume — my debt to those who went before me, dead and living, continued to mount even as the Centennial spate diminished to a trickle and then ran dry. Previous obligations were enlarged, and new ones acquired, on both sides of the line defining the limits of the original material: especially on the near side, where the evidence was assembled and presented in general studies, biographies, and secondary accounts of individual campaigns. Chief among these last, to take them in the order of their use, were the following: *Red River Campaign* by Ludwell H. Johnson, *Lee's Last Campaign* by Clifford Dowdey, *Autumn of Glory* by Thomas L. Connelly, *Jubal's Raid* by Frank E. Vandiver, *The Decisive Battle of Nashville* by Stanley F. Horn, *Sherman's March Through the Carolinas* by John G. Barrett, and two recitals of the Appomattox chase, *An End to Valor* by Philip Van Doren Stern and *Nine April Days* by Burke Davis. Similarly, my long-term obligation to works on naval matters was extended by Virgil Carrington Jones's *Civil War at Sea: The Final Effort* and Edward Boykin's *Ghost Ship of the Confederacy*.

No one who has read or even scanned these books can fail to see my debt to them, as well as to the biographies cited earlier, two of which had concluding volumes that came out just as the need for them was sorest: Hudson Strode's *Jefferson Davis: Tragic Hero* and Bruce Catton's *Grant Takes Command*. Having had them, I cannot see how I could have managed without them, and the same applies to J. G. Randall's *Lincoln the President*, completed after his death by Richard N. Current in *Last Full Measure*, and Jim Bishop's *Day Lincoln Was Shot*. Clifford Dowdey's *Lee* brought his subject into sharper focus, and T. Harry

Williams filled a sizeable gap with his *Hayes of the Twenty-third,* as E. B. Long did many others with *The Civil War Day by Day: An Almanac.* Nash K. Burger's and John K. Bettersworth's *South of Appomattox* helped get me down to the wire, and Kenneth M. Stampp, who was with me at the start in *And the War Came,* was also with me at the finish in *The Era of Reconstruction,* another old friend among the many I know only through their work.

To all these I am grateful, as I was and am to those mentioned in the end notes to the first two volumes of this iliad, most of whom continued their contribution through the third. Originally I intended to list my obligations in a complete bibliography here at the close of the whole, but even this chore has been spared me — along with a considerable added bulkiness for you — by Ralph G. Newman and E. B. Long, whose 1964 pamphlet, *A Basic Civil War Library,* first published in the *Journal of the Illinois State Historical Society,* enumerates by category the 350-odd books I owe most to, old and new and in and out of print. Other such compilations are readily available, including a much fuller one in Long's own *Almanac,* yet this one is to me the best in its inclusion of the works I mainly relied on, at any rate up to its date of issue. While I hope I have acknowledged my heaviest contemporary debts in this trio of notes, there are two I would like to stress in particular. One is to Bruce Catton, whose *Centennial History of the Civil War* was finished in time for its third volume, *Never Call Retreat,* to be available, together with his earlier *Stillness at Appomattox,* as a source and guide all through the writing of my own third volume. I was, as Stonewall Jackson said in another connection on his deathbed, "the infinite gainer" from having him thus meet his deadline even as I was failing to reach mine. My other chief debt is to the late Allan Nevins, whose close-packed *Organized War to Victory,* the last in his four-volume *War for the Union,* was similarly available during the past two years. Both gave me a wealth of useable material, but at least as valuable was their example of dedication and perseverance, double-barreled proof that such an undertaking could be carried to a finish. In that sense my debt to them is personal, though not as much so, nor as large, as the ones I owe my editor, Robert Loomis, and my wife, Gwyn Rainer Foote, both of whom bore with me all the way.

Perhaps in closing I might add that, although nowhere along the line have I had a "thesis" to argue or maintain — partly no doubt because I never saw one yet that could not be "proved," at least to the satisfaction of the writer who advanced it — I did have one thing I wanted to do, and that was to restore a balance I found lacking in nearly all the histories composed within a hundred years of Sumter. In all too many of these works, long and short, foreign and domestic, the notion prevailed that the War was fought in Virginia, while elsewhere — in an admittedly large but also rather empty region known vaguely as "the West" — a sort of running skirmish wobbled back and forth, presumably as a way for its participants, faceless men with unfamiliar names, to pass the time while waiting for the issue to be settled in the East. I do not claim that the opposite is true, but I do claim that it is perhaps a little closer to the truth; that Vicksburg, for example, was as "decisive" as Gettysburg, if not more so, and that Donelson, with its introduction of Grant and Forrest onto the national scene, may have had more to do with the outcome than either of the others had, for all their greater panoply, numbers, and documentation. In any case, it was my hope to provide what I considered a more fitting balance, East and West, in the course of attempting my aforesaid purpose of re-creating that war and making it live again in the world around us.

So, anyhow, "Farwel my book and my devocion," my rock and my companion through two decades. At the outset of this Gibbon span, plunk in what I hope will be the middle of my writing life, I was two years younger than Grant at Belmont, while at the end I was four months older than Lincoln at his assassination. By way of possible extenuation, in response to complaints that it took me five times longer to write the war than the participants took to fight it, I would point out that there were a good many more of them than there was of me. However that may be, the conflict is behind me now, as it is for you and it was a hundred-odd years ago for them.

—S.F.

Index

A

Abbeville, 1003–4, 1007, 1008
Abingdon, 245, 246, 721
Abolitionists, 91, 377, 534, 728, 962, 970, 973, 1036
Acworth, 352, 353, 355, 609, 611
Adairsville, 337, 338, 339
Adams, Charles F., 100, 815
Adams, Charles F., Jr., 186, 815
Adams, Henry, 1045
Adams, John, 670
Alabama (cruiser), 442, 508, 587, 590, 765, 1031
   sinking of, 380–90, 587
Alabama River, 493, 759
Albemarle (ironclad), 113–17, 257–58, 407, 745
   sinking of, 591–95
Albemarle Sound, 113, 115, 593
Alden, James, 498, 501
Alexander, Edward P., 923, 931, 932, 942
Alexandria, 26, 28–30, 31, 33, 38–40, 52, 54, 78–80, 85, 87, 88, 320, 1024
   Federal withdrawal to, 56–61, 62, 64, 73, 76
Allatoona, 320, 347, 409, 609, 611, 613
Allatoona Pass, 343–45, 346, 352, 353, 409, 611–12
Allen, Henry W., 1020, 1023
Amelia Courthouse, 883–84, 885, 890, 891, 892, 909, 911, 921
American Revolution, 101, 764
Anaximander, 1040, 1059
Anderson, George T., 176–78
Anderson, Richard H., 165, 236, 316, 540, 544–46, 553, 867
   and Cold Harbor, 284, 286, 293
   Fort Harrison assault, 561

and North Anna, 265, 266, 268, 272–73, 274
and Petersburg, 435, 438, 439, 631, 841, 884, 885
   withdrawal, 908, 909, 911, 915–921, 930
   relieved of duty, 930
   Sayler's Creek rout, 917, 918–19, 921
   Spotsylvania battle, 192–93, 194, 195, 196–97, 200, 201, 215, 220, 222
   Totopotomoy confrontation, 278, 279, 280
   in the Wilderness, 165, 176
Anderson, Robert, 970, 971–72, 973, 979
Anderson, William "Bloody Bill," 578–79, 1022
Andersonville (prisoner-of-war camp), 416–17, 486, 488, 1032–33
   transfer of prisoners from, 604
Annapolis, 18, 122, 136
Antietam, *see* Sharpsburg
Antietam Creek, 448
Appleton's (publishing company), 1051, 1054–55
Appomattox Courthouse, 907, 932, 938, 945–56, 963–64, 965, 967, 975, 1013, 1018, 1040
Appomattox River, 251, 252, 255, 257, 301, 305–6, 314, 428, 430, 433, 434, 437, 439, 533, 540, 543, 548, 627, 633, 773, 800, 840, 862, 865, 878–80, 881
   and Lee's withdrawal, 908, 909, 913, 914, 916, 921–27, 931, 934, 945, 952
Appomattox Station, 926, 931, 932, 933–34, 936
Aransas Pass, 26
Arapahoe Indians, 726
Arcadian people, 31
Arctic Ocean, 591, 1030
Argyll, George, Duke of, 814

[1070] INDEX

Arkadelphia, 27, 62–63, 64, 65, 66, 68, 76
Arkansas (vessel), 113, 493, 591, 1024
Arkansas River, 71, 575, 576, 584, 585
Arlington House, 958
Arnold, Benedict, 58
Arnold, Richard, 58, 59
Arnold, Dr. Richard D., 736
Arp, Bill, *see* Smith, Charles H.
Ascension Island, 1029
Ashby's Gap, 564–65
Atchafalaya River, 30, 53, 84–86, 87–88, 90, 124
Athens, Tennessee, 598, 621, 677
Atlanta, 14, 55, 92, 118, 320, 326, 337, 344, 391, 404, 406, 409, 410–24, 598, 622, 623, 735, 1012
    burning of, 640–41, 654
    defense reserve force, 17
    evacuation of civilians, 601–3
    fall of, 519–30
    occupation of, 530
        Davis's prediction on, 608, 610
        Sherman's supply line, Forrest's harassment and, 596–601
    refugees, 410–11, 491
    sabbath prayers, 414
Atlanta, battle for, 472–92, 552–53, 559, 575, 596, 640, 657, 685, 730, 754, 760, 780
    artillery bombardments, 480, 492, 521, 522
    casualties, 483, 487, 490–91, 528, 529
    city rail connections, 480, 486–87, 488, 520–21, 523–24, 526, 527
    Confederate raid (in the Union rear), 519–20, 522
    end of, 530
    at Ezra Church, 489–91, 521
    Federal envelopment, 519–30
    at (and around) Jonesboro, 520–21, 524, 525, 526, 527–28, 529, 530
    loss of Macon road, 523–24, 525, 526, 529
    at Peachtree Creek, 472–75
        Confederate withdrawal, 476–77
    Union supply lines, 485–86, 491, 519, 520, 522
    Utoy Creek repulse, 491
Atlanta & West Point Railroad, 486, 521–22, 523, 604
Atlantic Monthly, 469
Atlantic & N.C. Railroad, 820, 821, 823
Atlee Station, 276, 278, 280, 283, 284, 304, 307
Atzerodt, George A., 1032
Augur, Christopher C., 458
Augusta, 604, 607, 643, 646, 648, 751, 753, 792, 1012
Australia, 591, 1029, 1031
Averasboro, 826–28, 829, 834, 849
    casualties, 828, 833

Averell, William W., 302, 304, 358
    Fisher's Hill pursuit, 557
    triple-pronged offensive, 243–46
Avoyelles Prairie, 30, 31, 85
Ayres, Romeyn B., 867, 871–72

B

Babcock, Orville E., 945, 946
Badeau, Adam, 846, 847
Bahia harbor, 587–89
Bailey, Joseph, 78–79, 83–84, 88
Baja California, 1030
Bald Hill (Leggett's Hill), 475, 477, 479–80, 481, 482, 483, 640, 654
Baldwyn, 366, 367
Ball's Bluff, 461
Baltimore, 480, 624
    Early's northward march and, 446–61
Baltimore (steamer), 962
Baltimore Convention, 377, 378
Baltimore & Ohio Railroad, 448, 449, 453, 545, 804, 806
Banks, Nathaniel P., 15–16, 17, 22, 24, 126, 252, 510, 568, 739
    march up the Teche, 28
    New Orleans meeting, 29
    Pleasant Hill conference, 41
    Red River campaign, 124, 250, 267, 320, 340, 374, 492, 496, 575, 790
        Camden Expedition, 61–77
    seizure of contraband goods, 28
    Transmississippi operations, 25–77, 104
Banks, Mrs. Nathaniel P., 39
Barlow, Francis C., 291
    in the Wilderness, 161, 163, 168, 173, 174, 175
Barnes, John S., 847, 856
Barnes, Joseph K., 982, 986
Barnum, P. T., 1011
Barnum's Museum (New York City), 725
Barracouta (bark), 1030
Bat (steamer), 817, 847, 854, 857, 896, 906
Bate, William B., 350, 351, 355, 660
    Atlanta battle, 477, 479, 481
    and Bentonville, 831
    Franklin battle, 666, 670, 677, 678
    and Murfreesboro, 677–78
    Nashville battle, 692, 694, 695, 698, 700, 701, 702, 703–4
Bates, Edward, 727–28
Baton Rouge, 647, 1024, 1025
Battery Wagner, 741
Battery Whitworth, 882–83, 893
"Battle Hymn of the Republic," 3, 641
Bazaine, Marshal Achille, 87
Beatty, Samuel, 692

Index [1071]

Beaufort, 716, 718, 720, 741, 753, 820
Beauregard, P. G. T., 121, 139, 152, 265, 273, 305, 315, 316, 317, 606–9, 616, 620, 645, 712, 835, 843
    Augusta Council, 790–91
    bottling of Butler, 251–65, 278, 280, 281, 628
    Charlotte headquarters, 799, 821–22, 823, 825
    Chester headquarters, 792, 799
    Columbia headquarters, 791, 792
    Gadsden meeting with Hood (October 21), 616–18
    Grant's Jamesward strategy and, 305, 315, 316, 317
    in Greensboro, 966, 968, 969
    and Hood's march north, 655, 680, 709–10
    inspection of Charleston defenses, 606
    Lee on, 798
    and Petersburg, 427–46, 533–34, 536
    number of troops, 433
    reaction to Lincoln's death, 998
    as second in command, 799–800, 821–22
    and Sherman's march to the Carolinas, 757, 758, 759, 764, 768, 769, 792, 799
    triple-pronged offensive and, 242
    at Tupelo, 758, 759
Beauregard, René, 355
Beauvoir plantation, 1052–55, 1057, 1058
Beaver Dam, 225, 226, 227, 233, 234, 266, 279, 301
Beaver Dam Creek, 279, 281
Beaver Dam Station, 225, 228, 851
Bee, Barnard E., 58
Bee, Hamilton P., 43, 44, 54, 58–59
Beecher, Henry Ward, 970, 972–73
Bell, Alexander Graham, 1045
Bell, Tyree H., 365, 366, 367, 369, 370, 372
Belle Plain, 214, 269
Belmont, 82
Benjamin, Judah P., 99, 416, 467, 773, 776, 860, 861, 886, 888, 968–69, 988, 1004, 1007, 1049
Bennett, James, 996
Bennett, James Gordon, 559
Bennett farmhouse, 992, 996
Benson, Berry G., 1048
Bentonville, 826, 828–35, 849
    casualties, 833, 834
    Mill Creek Bridge withdrawal, 833, 834, 835
Bering Sea, 591, 1029
Bering Strait, 1030
Bermuda Hundred, 151–52, 251–65, 278, 279–80, 281, 313, 314, 533, 740, 852, 908, 913
    casualties, 253, 254, 262, 263, 264

    naval operations, 251–54, 257–58
    use of torpedoes, 254
    prisoners-of-war, 262
    See also Butler, Benjamin F.
Bermuda Landing, 634–35
Bermuda Neck, 253, 257, 258, 261, 265, 270, 301, 305–6, 315, 438, 628, 631
Bethesda Church, 279, 280, 281, 282, 283, 287, 288
Big Bethel, 113
Big Blue River, 580, 581, 582
Big Shanty, 353, 357, 380, 393, 609, 611
Birney, David B., 240, 445
    Fort Gilmer strike, 560–61
    and Petersburg, 437, 439–41, 442, 444, 445
    in the Wilderness, 161–62, 163
Black Kettle, Chief, 726–27
Black Warrior River, 850, 904
Blair, Francis P., 456, 460
    Richmond peace mission, 770–73, 776, 783
Blair, Francis P., Jr., 353, 392, 456, 603, 837
    Atlanta battle, 479–81, 483–85, 490, 527
    and Bentonville, 829, 834–35
    Carolinas march, 754
    electioneering stumping, 562, 603, 642
    and Ezra Church, 490
    march to the sea, 642, 648
Blair, Montgomery, 353, 456, 460, 728
    resignation of, 559–60
Blair's Landing, 50, 53, 56, 68
Bliss, P. P., 612
Bloody Angle, 210–24, 547, 669, 844
    abortive breakthrough, 207–10, 226
    casualties, 223
    disengagement of forces, 223
    nightmare fighting at, 221–22
    at the U perimeter (the "Mule Shoe"), 215–23, 232, 235, 660
Blue Ridge Mountains, 23, 24, 128, 142, 152, 247, 270, 304, 309, 311, 442, 461, 558, 564, 722, 914, 921
Blunt, James G., 580, 581, 584, 585
Bocock, Thomas S., 766
Bolivar Heights, 448, 553
"Bonnie Blue Flag, The," 645
Booneville, 365, 366, 369, 579
Booth, John Wilkes, 979, 983–84, 985, 986, 1022, 1025, 1047, 1049
    assassination of Lincoln, 980
    burial of, 1032
    death of, 996–97, 1002
Bordeaux, France, 1028
Boston *Evening Transcript*, 469
Boston Navy Yard, 389
Boteler's Ford, 448
Bouton, Edward, 371, 372, 510
Bowling Green, 357

Boydton Plank Road, 561, 573, 628, 784, 785, 869, 876, 878, 879, 882
Bradford, Augustus W., 461
Brady, Mathew, 8–9
Bragg, Braxton, 16, 98, 101, 113, 117–18, 119, 120, 122, 170, 187, 280, 294, 511, 549, 605, 606, 613, 616, 632, 640, 674, 678, 702, 706, 707, 709–10, 741, 798
 at Bentonville, 830, 831, 832
 and Bermuda Hundred, 257, 260, 264
 in the Carolinas, 821–24, 830–32
 death of, 1052
 departure for Atlanta, 416
 Fort Fisher garrison, 743, 744, 746
 Grant's Jamesward strategy and, 305–6, 317
 Johnston's withdrawal strategy and, 326, 328, 341, 345, 357, 358, 414, 416–18, 422
 meeting with Johnston, 417–18
 military advisory role, 113, 116
 and Petersburg, 433, 434
 and Sheridan's raid on Richmond, 228, 229, 230, 232, 235
 at Wilmington, 756, 758, 764, 786
Branchville, 789
Brandy Station, 8, 9–12, 23, 277, 581
Brazil, 574, 587–89, 590, 1023
Breckinridge, John C., 121, 152, 567, 721
 and Cold Harbor, 286, 287, 291, 293
 and Early's northward march, 446–47, 450, 452, 456, 460
 escape of, 1007, 1009, 1010
 and Grant's Jamesward strategy, 304, 306, 309, 311, 312
 at Lynchburg, 445, 446, 447
 Monocacy battle, 452
 and North Anna, 265, 266, 273, 276
 as Secretary of War, 766, 783, 798–99, 800, 808, 809, 844, 862, 881, 884, 886, 887, 922, 967, 968, 990–92, 996, 998, 1004, 1005, 1006, 1009
 surrender discussions with Sherman, 992, 994, 1002
 triple-pronged offensive and, 242, 247, 248, 249, 250–51
Brentwood, 673, 676, 680–81, 698, 699, 705–6
Brice's Crossroads, 362–73, 374, 415, 510, 597, 1053
 "bulge" tactics, 368, 373
 casualties, 372
 movement to, 362–66
Brierfield plantation, 1058–59
Broadway Landing, 428, 433
Brock Road, 156–58, 161–63, 168, 171, 173, 174, 178, 184, 189–91, 193, 197–99, 223
Brock's Bridge, 151, 152
Brook Turnpike, 229, 232
Brooklyn (ship), 498–502
Brooklyn Navy Yard, 493, 509, 562–63, 724

Brooks, Noah, 959, 961
Brooks, Preston, 903
Brough, John, 463
Brown, John, 641, 1036, 1046
Brown, John C., 660, 666
 Franklin battle, 666, 668–69, 670–72, 674
Brown, Joseph E., 92–93, 94, 95, 96, 328, 411, 412, 419, 604, 605, 642, 644, 645, 646, 647, 652, 735, 781, 789, 1008
Browning, Orville H., 470
Brownsville, 765, 1019
 occupation of, 26
Bruce, Blanche K., 1044
Brush Mountain, 353, 355, 391
Buchanan, Franklin, 493–95, 498, 502–4, 507
Buchanan, James, 456, 644, 728, 749
 election of 1856, 377
Buckland, Ralph P., 516, 517
Buckland Races, 24
Buckner, Simon B., 1021, 1022, 1027
Buell, Don Carlos, 124, 736–37
Buford, Abraham, 106, 108, 365, 369, 370, 372–73
 Hermitage assignment, 678
 in Middle Tennessee, 597, 599, 600, 677
 in North Mississippi, 514
 wounded, 708
Bull Run, *see* Manassas
Bull's Gap, 595, 849
Burbridge, Stephen G., 358–62, 471
Burgess Mill, 628, 631, 784, 785, 862, 875, 876, 878, 880
Burkeville, 444, 450, 548, 856, 883, 895, 903, 904, 910–12, 921, 925, 926, 938, 953, 955, 967
Burnside, Ambrose E., 17–18, 123, 261, 270, 271, 281, 285, 295, 313, 315, 865, 928
 Crater fiasco, 531–38
 Grant's Plan (Spring '64) and, 16, 17–78, 20, 24, 122, 123, 133, 136–37
 march to Totopotomoy, 276
 and Petersburg, 432, 435, 436–37, 531–38, 541
 Rapidan crossing, 874
 removal of, 634
 Spotsylvania battle, 202, 204, 205, 206, 207, 209, 210, 211, 212, 217, 219
 triple-pronged offensive and, 236, 239, 241
 in the Wilderness, 147, 148, 149, 153, 158, 164
 race to Spotsylvania, 189
 second day (May 6th), 167, 171, 172, 173, 180, 181
Burnt Hickory, 346, 347, 391
Butler, Benjamin F., 19, 147, 204, 242, 320, 467, 531, 541, 542, 545, 948, 889
 and Bermuda Hundred, 251–65, 270,

Index [1073]

278, 279–80, 300–1, 303, 305, 306, 471, 508, 628
  assignment, 252
  conference with Grant, 428
  disembarkation, 151–52
  naval operations, 251–54, 257–58
  double-pronged offensive (Forts Harrison and Gilmer), 560–61
  at Fair Oaks, 573
  Fort Fisher (Wilmington) expedition, 684, 685, 715–21, 737, 739, 740–42, 747, 750
    casualties, 715
    failure of, 721
  Grant's Plan (Spring '64) and, 20, 22, 116, 127, 133, 136
  hearing before the Joint Committee, 740–41, 747
  and Petersburg, 427, 428, 429, 431, 433, 434, 435, 437, 439, 441, 639, 714
    June assault casualties, 633
  relieved of command, 739–40
  and Sheridan's raid on Richmond, 225, 226, 232, 233, 234
Butler, M. Calbraith, 762, 791
  in the Carolinas, 822, 824, 828
Butterfield, Daniel, 342, 348
Buzzard Roost, 324, 325, 337, 344
Byron, Lord, 1005

C

Cabell, William L., 583, 584
Cadwallader, Sylvanus, 186–87
Cahaba River, 904
Cairo, 14, 576, 1026
Calhoun, James M., 530, 602, 603
Calhoun, John C., 530, 1004
Calhoun, Georgia, 337, 338, 519, 522, 615
Camden, Arkansas, 27
Camden, S.C., Federal destruction of, 797
Camden Expedition, 52, 53, 61–77, 104, 575
  casualties, 69–70, 72, 74, 75, 76
  departure from Little Rock, 62–65, 66
  at Jenkins Ferry, 74–75, 76, 78, 104
  preliminary skirmishes, 65–69
  troop strength, 64–65, 66, 68, 74
Cameron, Simon, 549
Campbell, John A., 767, 770, 888, 898, 901–2
  authorized to reassemble Virginia Legislature, 962, 963, 964
  Blair's peace feeler and, 772–73
  pardoned, 1032
  shipboard conference in Hampton Roads, 773–78, 780
Campbelltown, 486, 487, 608, 611

Canada, 466, 467, 470, 509, 551, 586, 587, 767, 983, 1049, 1051
  Confederate operations from, 586–87, 725, 1033
Canary Islands, 1028
Canby, Edward R. S., 415, 496, 508, 511, 514, 738, 758, 759, 1020
  Alabama raid, 804, 848–49, 850, 904, 905, 967, 1018, 1019
  Far West campaign, 89
  New Orleans meeting, 1019, 1021, 1027, 1031
  Red River campaign, 89–90
  and Taylor's surrender negotiations, 998–99, 1000, 1007
Cane Hill, 585
Cane River, 54, 57, 58, 517
Canonicus (monitor), 742, 1028
Cantey, James, 327
Cape Fear River, 121, 509, 717, 741, 752–53, 818, 819, 820, 825, 826
Cape of Good Hope, 591
Carlin, William P., 830–31, 832
Carlota (settlement), 1023
Carolinas march (Savannah to Goldsboro), 736, 750–54, 756, 757, 786, 787–801, 825–38, 848, 851, 858, 1029
  beginning of, 753–54, 759
  burnings and vandalism, 787–88, 790, 802, 818, 838
  casualties, 833–34
  at Columbia, 792–96, 802, 818, 838
  crossing of the Neuse, 828–29, 836
  in Fayetteville, 819–21, 824, 825, 826
  link-up with Schofield, 817–18, 819, 820, 821, 824, 829, 833, 834, 836–38, 841, 852
  astride Lynch's Creek, 800, 818
  in North Carolina, 818–38
  number of miles, 752
  offer from Wheeler, 789–90
  parade in Goldsboro, 836–37
  plan for, 736, 751–52, 826
  proposal to Johnston for restoring peace, 988–96, 998
  through the Salk swamps, 788–89
Carondolet (gunboat), 83
Carr, Eugene A., 72–73
Carter, John C., 670
Carter, Theodore H. (Tod), 674
Carter's Creek Pike, 666, 670
Cartter, David K., 901
Cassville, 339, 340, 341, 342, 343, 347, 418, 473–74, 519
Casualties:
  from disease, 1040
  total number of (North and South), 1040
  See also Naval operations; names of battles

[1074]   INDEX

Catharpin Road, 148, 151, 152, 158, 165, 166, 174, 192, 199
Cedar Creek, 250, 302, 564, 565, 566–72, 574, 631, 804
    casualties, 571–72
    See also Fisher's Hill
Cedar Mountain, 20, 24
Cedar Point, 495, 506
Centerville, 122
Central Georgia Railroad, 646, 647
    demolition of, 648
Centralia, 578
Chaffin's Bluff, 254, 261, 304, 435, 438, 545, 560, 561, 628, 896
Chalmers, James R., 106–7, 108, 597, 601, 670
    Memphis patrol, 597
    Nashville battle, 679–80, 690, 698, 700, 705, 707
    in North Mississippi, 513, 514, 515, 518
Chambersburg, 451
    burning of, 539
Chambrun, Marquis de, 903, 905–6
Chancellorsville, 113, 134, 135, 142, 146, 147, 150, 174, 179, 188, 189, 190, 347, 475, 477, 485, 555, 566, 639, 783, 908
Chandler, Zachariah, 464–65, 559, 963, 988
Chantilly, 20
Charles I, King, 776
Charles City Courthouse, 313
Charleston, 17, 121, 256, 258, 427, 507, 586, 614, 624, 635, 645, 646, 736, 751, 753, 764, 799, 1006
    evacuated, 797, 804, 822
    expulsion of British consul, 99
    Fort Sumter ceremonies (April, 1865), 969–73, 979
    goods run into (1864), 741
    occupation of, 800
Charleston Convention of 1860, 19
Charleston & Savannah Railroad, 652–53
Charlotte, Empress, 376, 1023
Charlotte, North Carolina, 796, 798, 859, 863, 885, 967, 969, 989, 998
    Confederate government headquarters, 1002–4
Charlottesville, 270, 302, 306, 309, 311, 445, 450, 565, 807, 808, 850
Chase, Salmon P., 38, 462–63, 471, 558, 559, 562, 814, 963, 965, 987–88
    on reorganization of state governments, 961–62
    on secession, 1035
    Supreme Court appointment, 728
    swearing in of Johnson, 986
Chattahoochee River, 320, 321, 343, 344, 347, 353, 392, 394, 395, 399, 412, 413, 417, 418, 419, 473, 485–87, 521–23, 524, 604, 607–9, 611, 614, 998, 1007
    Federal crossing of, 402–10, 411, 415, 419

Chattanooga, 4, 13, 27, 112, 117, 135, 187, 319–21, 322, 323, 331, 337, 344, 347, 391, 395, 485, 491, 492, 519, 598, 599, 615, 621, 622, 636, 681, 1014
Chattanooga Railroad, *see* Nashville & Chattanooga Railroad
Chattooga River, 615
Cheatham, Benjamin F., 605, 606, 759, 798
    Atlanta battle, 473–76, 477, 482, 483, 490
    at Bentonville, 830, 831
    Franklin battle, 663, 667–70, 671, 673, 674
    and Hood's march north, 656, 657, 659, 660–61
    at Kennesaw Mountain, 396–97, 398, 399
    Nashville battle, 676–77, 678, 679, 690, 692, 694, 698–703, 706, 707
    and Peachtree Creek, 473–76
Cheraw, 751, 796, 800, 818, 819, 822
Cherbourg harbor, 508, 587, 765
Cherokee Indians, 1022
Chesapeake Bay, 127, 450, 457, 906, 1012
Chesnut, James, Jr., 755
Chesnut, Mary Boykin, 755, 760, 799
Chester, 791–92, 796, 798, 799
Chesterfield Bridge, 266, 268, 269, 270, 274
Chesterfield Courthouse, 908
Cheyenne Indians, 726
Chicago, Convention, 378–79, 470, 549, 551–52, 713
Chicago Times, 186
Chicago Tribune, 574
Chickahominy, 233, 260, 264, 275, 277, 279, 280, 281, 285, 286, 287, 292, 300, 303, 313, 315, 316, 430, 439, 628, 631
Chickamauga, 13–14, 16, 122, 171, 244, 257, 258, 330, 349, 350, 370, 399, 408, 458, 549, 606, 640, 660
Chickasaw (ship), 497, 499, 505
Chilesburg, 225, 307
Chillicothe (steamer), 83
China, 1041
Chivington, John M., 725–27
Choctaw Indians, 68, 69, 585
Churchill, Thomas J., 36–37, 42–44, 45, 47–49, 53, 54, 73, 75, 76
Cincinnati, 13, 21, 24, 108, 133, 616, 837
Cincinnati Convention, 470
Cincinnati Gazette, 471
Citronelle, 999, 1040
City Belle (transport), 79–80
City Point, 19, 127, 151–52, 251–53, 255, 256, 261, 263, 313, 436, 442, 443, 450, 458, 548, 554, 560, 614, 623, 637, 650, 710–11, 715, 739, 784, 853–54, 893, 895, 903, 926, 953, 975, 1018
City Point Railroad, 429, 433, 841
Civil Rights Act of 1875, 1044
Clark, John S., 41

Index

Clark's Mountain, 135, 142–44, 145, 146, 149, 197–98
Clay, Clement C., 1033, 1036
Clayton, Henry DeL., 699–700, 703
Cleburne, Patrick R., 349, 350, 351, 423, 690, 706, 831
  Atlanta battle, 475, 476, 477, 479, 481, 526, 528
  death of, 671, 700, 710
  Franklin battle, 663, 666, 668–70, 671, 700
  and Hood's march north, 659, 660, 661
  on recruitment of Negroes, 754, 859
Cleveland, Ohio, 323
Cleveland Convention, 377
Clinch River, 519
Close-Out Plan, the, 735–54, 836, 848
  Confederate authorities and, 754–83
  double-pronged, see Schofield; drive to Wilmington; Sherman; march to the Carolinas
  and Hatcher's Run battle, 783–86
  naval operations, 739
  Negro troops, 741
  outline of, 736–38
Clover Station, 890
Cloyd's Mountain, 243–44, 245
Coal torpedoes, 635
Cobb, Howell, 643–44, 645, 781
  on enlistment of Negroes, 859–60
Cobb plantation, 646
  burning of, 643–44
Cockrell, Francis M., 670, 672
Coggins Point, 560
Cold Harbor, 280, 281–99, 300, 301, 304, 306, 307, 311, 312, 314, 315, 316, 427–29, 432, 436, 440, 461, 462, 531, 539, 540, 802, 883
  beginning of the battle 290–92
  casualties, 286, 291–92, 293, 294, 295–96, 297, 352, 380, 672
  Grant on (quoted) 294
  movement to, 281–85
  postponement of attack, 288–90
  total military strength at, 288
  truce, 296–97
Coldwater River, 516
Colfax, Schuyler, 471, 748, 974, 978, 1036
Collierville, 364, 373
Collins, Napoleon, 587–90
Colorado Territory, 725–27
Colquitt, Alfred H., 260, 262
Columbia, South Carolina, 609–10, 736, 751, 753, 760, 790, 792–96, 798, 851
  burning of, 794–95, 802
  evacuation of, 792–93
Columbia, Tennessee, 598, 599–600, 654–56, 657, 658, 659, 663, 676, 681, 708
Columbia Pike, 664, 665, 666, 670–71, 707
Columbus, Georgia, 738, 759, 781
Columbus, Mississippi, 106, 108

Comanche Indians, 726
Committee on Foreign Affairs (Confederate States of America), 767
Commodore Jones (double-ender), 253–54
Comstock, Cyrus B., 303, 313
Conestoga (vessel), 33
Confederate Point (Federal Point) peninsula, 716, 717, 741
Congaree River, 752–53, 789, 790, 791, 792
Congressional Globe, 748
Connasauga River, 332
Connecticut, election of 1864, 625
Conscription, 359, 410, 469–70, 639, 640, 730, 966
  bounty substitutes, 128, 129
  Confederate, 99, 112, 124–26, 172
  quotas, 756
  removal of $300 exemption clause, 463, 470
  riots against (in the North), 89, 548
  Union draft substitutes, 129
Contraband goods, seizure of, 28
Conyer Station, 1012
Cooke, James W., 114–15, 116
Cooper, Samuel, 419, 769, 988
Coosa River, 320, 607, 613, 616, 621
Coosawhatchie Swamp, 788
Copper, scarcity of (in the South), 630
Copperheads, 102, 296, 377, 466, 551, 562, 995, 1013
Corinth, 25, 108, 364, 365, 366, 427, 601, 616, 709, 800
Corps d'Afrique, 38, 40
Corse, John M., 611–12
Cotton,
  as contraband of war, 38–39
  prices (in Boston, 1864), 28
Courtland, 618
Coushatta Chute, 56
Covington, 487, 488
Covington (gunboat), 80
Cowpens, 827
Cowslip (tender), 497
Cox, Jacob D., 349, 820
  Franklin battle, 664, 665, 669
Cox Road, 876, 877, 878
Cox's Bridge, 826, 828, 829, 832, 836
Crapsey, Edward, 298, 299, 303
Crater fiasco, the, 530–38, 539, 541, 544, 545, 628, 717, 773, 840, 843
  casualties, 536, 537
  results of, 537–38
Craven, Tunis A., 499–500
Crawford, Samuel W., 867, 871, 873
  in the Wilderness, 159–60
Crawford, Thomas, 810, 899
Crawfordville, 93, 781, 1008
Creek Indians, 1022
Creswell, John, 974
Cricket (gunboat), 59, 60
Crockett's Cove, 246, 358

[1075]

[1076] INDEX

Crook, George, 18–19, 302, 304, 309, 763, 806
  and Cedar Creek, 564, 566, 568, 570
  and Fisher's Hill, 556–57, 804
  Five Forks battle, 867, 872
  guerrilla abduction of, 804, 867
  near Kernstown, 539
  and Petersburg, 542
  promoted to major general, 804
  pursuit of Lee's army, 918, 920, 923, 925–26
  triple-pronged offensive, 243–45, 246
  and Winchester, 555, 804
Crook, William H., 897, 904, 905, 977, 985
Cuba, 389, 1007, 1010, 1023, 1024, 1029, 1049
Culpeper, 23, 24, 108, 127, 132, 133, 138, 143, 540
Culpeper Mine Ford, 146
Cumberland (ship), 589
Cumberland Church, 923, 924, 928, 929, 936, 956
Cumberland River, 636, 676, 678, 680, 682, 685, 758
Cummings Point, 971
Curtis, Samuel R., 723, 747
  pursuit of Price, 579–85
  transferred to Department of the Northwest, 747
Cushing, Alonzo H., 592
Cushing, William B., 592–95, 745, 1024
Custer, George A., 564, 570, 571, 572, 722, 807, 808, 918
  Appomattox Courthouse attack, 936
  brevetted major general, 807
  and Cold Harbor, 282
  December strike (1864), 722–23
  at Dinwiddie supply routes, 867, 872
  Grand Review parade, 1015
  and Sheridan's raid on Richmond, 225, 230, 231
  Winchester headquarters, 805–6
Cutler, Lysander, 267
Cynthiana, 360, 362, 373, 380, 471

D

Dahlgren, John A., 750, 751, 753
Dallas, 346, 354, 380, 391, 612
Dallas Road, 396, 397, 398
Dalton, 13, 16, 17, 92, 117, 119, 137, 318–30, 333, 416, 418, 423, 486, 519, 613
  Confederate withdrawal from, 330, 331
Dalton to Resaca march, 318–30, 363
  casualties, 324
  railroad supply lines, 319, 329
  Tunnel Hill attack, 323–24, 334, 338

Dan River, 891, 965
Dana, Charles A., 572, 573
Danville, 717, 802, 803, 884, 885, 887, 890, 895, 910, 911, 922, 926
  Confederate government headquarters at, 890–93, 965, 1009, 1029, 1051
Danville Railroad, 629, 863
Dardanelle, 576, 585
Dauphin Island, 495, 496, 497, 506
Davidson (tug), 819, 820, 825
Davis, David, 378
Davis, George, 888, 968, 1004
Davis, Henry Winter, 464, 465, 471, 558–59
Davis, Jefferson, 19, 34, 92–103, 112–13, 115–17, 120, 121–26, 139–42, 151–52, 247, 260, 264, 278, 280, 287–88, 293–94, 306, 466, 467, 469, 508, 509, 596, 623–24, 632, 647, 654, 711, 756, 757, 761–73, 798, 800, 802, 809, 825, 857–64, 953, 1021, 1044, 1049–60
  accused of near treason, 772
  attempts to curtail power of, 768–69, 770
  at Beauvoir plantation, 1052–55, 1057, 1058
  Blair's peace feeler to, 770–73
  cabinet reorganization, 766
  in Canada, 1049, 1051
  captured, 1010–13, 1021, 1028, 1033, 1038
  Confederacy's efforts (1864) and, 96–103
    core of the Confederacy, 102–3
    impossibility of peace negotiations, 96–97
    military offensive, 97–98
    securing foreign recognition, 98–101
    self-perception of, 96
  criticism of (in the South), 92–96, 118–19
  Danville government, 890–93, 965, 1009, 1029, 1051
  death of, 1059–60
  departure from Richmond, 885–93, 1002–13
    dispersal of the treasury, 1006, 1010
    in Georgia, 1007–12
    last full cabinet meeting, 1004
    in North Carolina, 965–69, 988, 991, 1002–4, 1009, 1029
    rewards for capture of, 988, 1008
    in South Carolina, 1003–6
  in England, 1049, 1050
  escape in women's clothes story, 1011
  exchange of letters with Vance, 95, 96, 97, 101
  in France, 1049–50

Index [1077]

imprisonment, 1012–13, 1030, 1033–39, 1049
  in custody of Richmond authorities, 1038–39
  Federal tormenting during, 1035 and shackled, 1033–35
  trial postponements, 1037–38, 1049
  weakness of government case against, 1035–36, 1037
  insurance company career, 1050
  Johnson (Andrew) on, 901, 1049
  legal action against, 856
  Lincoln's assassination and, 988, 990, 998, 1012, 1036
  Lincoln's public reference to, 729
  Metropolitan Hall speech, 779–80, 781, 785, 892
  opposition to prohibition movement, 1057
  outlook as Commander in Chief (1865), 861–62
  Petersburg siege and, 434, 539–40, 881, 884
  proclamation to shift food crops, 860
  refusal to seek pardon, 1055
  released on bail, 1039, 1051
  on secession, 1054
  Sherman's campaign and, 326, 344, 345, 357, 642, 644, 649
    reaction to Johnston's withdrawal strategy, 411–19, 420, 421
  Silver Anniversary reunion (1886), 1056–57
  on slavery, 468
  spirit-lifting task (September '64), 604–11, 613, 614, 617, 623
    Augusta meeting with Beauregard, 608–9
    in Columbia, 609
    in Macon, 607–8
    in Montgomery, 608
    Palmetto meeting with Hood, 604–7
  State of the Nation address, 102
Davis, Jefferson, Jr., 140, 610, 863, 1052, 1053
Davis, Jefferson C., 335, 338, 398, 527–28
  at Bentonville, 830, 831
  Carolinas march, 754, 796–97
Davis, Joseph Evan, 140–41, 1038, 1053, 1060
Davis, Margaret "Maggie," 610, 863, 969, 1050, 1052
Davis, Samuel, 1053
Davis, Varina Anne "Winnie," 610, 863, 1052, 1055, 1056
Davis, Varina Howell, 140, 141, 388, 610, 768–69, 771, 825, 969, 1003–4, 1005, 1007–10, 1011, 1033, 1036–39, 1051–53, 1058, 1059

appointment with Johnson (Andrew), 1037
departure from Richmond, 858–59, 862, 863
in Germany, 1052, 1053
Davis, William H. "Billy," 610, 863, 1050, 1053
Decatur, 112, 409, 410, 477, 481–83, 486–88, 520, 598, 607, 618, 621, 677
Declaration of Independence, 93
Deep Bottom, 253, 317
Deerhound (yacht), 387, 388
Delaware, election of 1864, 625
Demopolis, 17, 92, 759
Dennison, William, 975
Desertions, army, 130, 640, 785, 786, 822, 966, 977
Detroit, 625
Devin, Thomas C., 807, 918
  Five Forks, battle, 867, 868, 872, 873
Dilger, Hubert, 355–56, 357
Dimmock, Charles H., 430
Dimmock Line, 430, 433, 436, 843, 881
Dinwiddie Courthouse, 784, 862–63, 864, 866, 867
  See also Five Forks
Disease casualties, total number (North and South), 1040
Dispatch Station, 313
District of Columbia, *see* Washington, D.C.
"Dixie," 906, 958, 999
Dodge, Grenville M., 724, 747
  Atlanta battle, 479–84, 490, 525, 527
Dog River, 493
Donaldson, James L., 686
Donaldsonville, 90, 1025
Donelson, 4, 16, 25, 212, 416, 633, 690, 932
Donoughmore, Earl of, 861
Dorsey, Sarah E., 1052, 1053–54
Douglas, Kyd, 460
Douty, Jacob, 535
Dover Swamp, 821, 823
Draft, the, *see* Conscription
Draft Act, 463
Drayton, Percival, 498, 500, 503, 504, 507
Drew, Daniel, 1042
Drewry's Bluff, 254, 256, 259, 260, 261, 263, 306, 315, 316, 434
Du Pont, Samuel F., 790
Dublin, 244, 246, 646, 1008
Duck River, 599, 654, 655, 657–59, 660, 674, 681, 692, 707–9
Duffié, Alfred N. A., 806
Dug Gap, 321, 323, 324, 325, 329
Dunlavy, James, 583–84
Durham, 989–90
Durham, Station, 989, 998, 1013, 1040
Dutch Gap, 894, 896
Dwight, William, 50, 89

[1078]   INDEX

E

Eads, James B., 83
Eagle Pass, 1023
Early, Jubal A., 280, 311–12, 316, 317, 610, 722, 771, 1051
  accused of incompetence, 572
  and Cold Harbor, 283, 284, 286, 287
  defeat at Winchester, 553–55, 605, 804
  end of army career, 808–9
  northward march, 446–61, 465, 469, 531, 539, 540
    assessment of town merchants, 449, 539
    casualties, 452
    commandeered supplies, 461
    Lee's instructions to, 446
    at Monocacy, 448–50, 451, 452, 453, 457, 461
    Potomac crossing, 448
    results of, 461
    Valley Turnpike hike, 446–49
    withdrawal, 459–61, 539
  and Petersburg, 435, 439, 442, 445
  rout at Cedar Creek, 566–72, 631, 804, 807
  in Shenandoah Valley, 539–40, 544, 545, 553–55, 556–72, 631, 632, 638, 762–63, 804, 807
    at Fisher's Hill, 555–58, 559
    harassment of B & O, 545
    at Lynchburg, 445
  Spotsylvania battle, 192, 193, 198, 215, 217, 218, 219
  Staunton headquarters, 807
  Totopotomoy confrontation, 277, 278, 279, 280
  Waynesboro rout, 807–9, 839, 840, 841, 850
  in the Wilderness, 155, 173, 181
East Point, 486, 521, 523, 524
East Tennessee & Georgia Railroad, 323, 408, 410, 421, 423, 473, 475, 486, 643
Eastport, 850
Eastport (ironclad), 33, 59–60, 73, 83
Ebenezer Church, 1000
Ebenezer Creek, 649–50
Eckert, Thomas T., 774, 775
Ector, Matthew D., 679, 690, 692, 693, 695, 698, 701, 705
Edgefield, 680, 682
Edison, Thomas A., 1045
Edisto River, 752–53, 790, 791
Election of 1856, 377
Election of 1864, 624–26
  campaign funding, 562–63
  results of, 625–26, 810
Eliza (cook), 308

Elizabeth City, 114
Elk River, 598–99
Elkhorn Tavern, 1022
Elliott, George Washington, 694–95
Elliott, Gilbert, 114
Ely's Ford, 135, 143, 144, 146, 147, 187, 190, 191
Emancipation Proclamation, 729–30, 777, 1045
  slavery and, 750
Emma (transport), 79
Emory, William H., 542, 806
  and Cedar Creek, 566, 568, 570
  and Fisher's Hill, 556
  Red River campaign, 50, 58, 84–85
  and Winchester, 554, 555
England, 98, 99–101, 508, 590, 861, 1006
  Confederate ambassador in, 99
  reaction to Lincoln's Inaugural Address, 814–15
English Channel, 380, 383, 387, 388, 390, 442
Etowah River, 320, 335, 337–39, 340, 343, 344, 345, 347, 352, 363, 519, 522, 609, 622
Eugénie, Empress, 99, 1050
Evans, Clement A., 638, 639
Everett, Edward, 747–48
Ewell, Richard S., 142, 145, 226, 232, 311, 447
  captured, 903, 919, 927
  Federal triple-pronged offensive and, 235, 237, 239, 240, 241
  and North Anna, 265, 266, 273
  Richmond reservist command, 631–32, 639, 761, 762, 875, 881, 884, 885, 888
  Sayler's Creek rout, 917, 918–19
  sick leave, 277
  Spotsylvania battle, 191, 194, 197, 198, 202, 208, 215, 216, 217, 219, 222
  in the Wilderness, 151, 154, 163, 164, 165–66, 167
    designated objective, 150–51, 153, 154
    positions, 156
    second day (May 6th), 167, 171, 173, 176–77, 181, 182–83
    turnpike engagement (May 5), 154–56, 157
Ewing, Thomas, 577
Ezra Church, 489–91, 521
  casualties, 490

F

Fagan, James F., 576, 580, 881–83
  Camden Expedition, 66, 67–68, 71–72, 74, 75
Fair Oaks, 573
Fairburn, 521–22, 523

Index [1079]

Farmville, 911–12, 914, 916, 917, 920, 921, 923, 925, 926, 933, 935, 968
Farragut, David G., 17, 385–86, 595, 613, 810, 1024
  created vice admiral, 724
  in Mobile Bay, 492–508, 521, 530, 552, 724
Farrar's Island, 252
Fayetteville, Arkansas, 585
Fayetteville, North Carolina, 151, 796, 822, 824, 825, 826, 829
  demolition of the arsenal, 819–21, 825
  occupation of, 819–21
Fayetteville, Tennessee, 599, 601
Federal Point (Confederate Point) peninsula, 716, 717, 741
Ferrero, Edward, 533, 534–35, 537, 538
  removal of, 634
Ferrol, Spain, 1028
Fessenden, William Pitt, 463, 728
Field, Charles W., 166, 196
  and Cold Harbor, 285, 286
  and Petersburg, 435, 437, 875, 876–77, 880, 881, 882, 883
    withdrawal, 924, 941
  in the Wilderness, 166, 170, 173, 176–77, 178, 179, 180
Field, David Dudley, 470
Fifteenth Amendment, 1044–45
Finegan, Joseph, 104, 124, 291
Fisher's Hill, 544, 555–58, 563, 564, 568, 571
  casualties, 558
  See also Cedar Creek
Fisk, Jim, 1042
Five Forks, 862, 864–75, 876, 908, 910, 918, 930, 934
  casualties, 868, 873
Flat Creek, 173, 912, 916
Flint River, 523, 524, 525
Florence, 374, 597–98, 600, 621, 622, 654, 676, 677, 708
Florida, 14, 19, 104, 116, 181, 288, 604, 1010, 1044
Florida (cruiser), 587–90, 591, 1024, 1025
Folly Island, 972
Foote, Henry Stuart, 767
Force, Manning F., 482
Ford's Theatre, 974, 976, 978–81, 983, 989, 997, 1032
Forrest, Jesse, 516–17
Forrest, Nathan Bedford, 58, 319, 328–29, 339, 340, 358, 412, 414–15, 737, 759, 850, 990, 1000–1
  at Brice's Crossroads, 366–74, 415
  death of, 1052–53
  farewell address to the army, 1001–2
  foraging expeditions, 104–13, 124, 328–29
    casualties, 107, 111
    cavalry strength, 105–6
  complaints about, 106
  Fort Pillow operations, 108–12, 329, 364
  letter to Davis, 112–13
  and Hood's march north, 654, 656, 657, 658, 661
    Duck River crossing, 656
    at Franklin, 666, 667, 669, 673
    at Hurt's Corner, 657
    Lynnville surprise attack, 708
    at Murfreesboro, 677–78, 679, 681, 707
    at Nashville, 677, 681
    rear-guard assignment, 707–8, 757
    return to Alabama line, 708–9
    Thompson's Station clash, 659, 661
  Johnsonville raid, 617–21, 654
  Memphis raid, 510, 516–17, 518, 549, 596
  in North Alabama, 365, 374
  in North Mississippi, 362–74, 509–19, 596
  promoted to major general, 104
  promoted to lieutenant general, 849
  Tennessee raid (September–October), 596–601, 603, 608, 614
    casualties, 600
    main objective, 598–99, 601
    prisoners-of-war, 598, 600
    unconditional surrender policy, 598
    wrecking operations, 598, 600
Forrest, William, 516–17
Fort Baxter, 579
Fort Blakely, 904
Fort Darling, 896
Fort Davidson, 576, 577, 579
Fort De Russy, 30, 31, 34, 459
Fort Fisher, 262, 509, 634, 685, 717, 773, 786, 899, 1028
  Butler-Porter expedition to, 715–21
  fall of, 740–47, 754, 763, 791
Fort Gaines, 495, 496, 497, 506, 507
Fort Gilmer, 560–61
Fort Granger, 665, 669
Fort Gregg, 882–83, 893
Fort Harrison, 560–61, 610
Fort Henry, fall of (1862), 60
Fort Hindman (tinclad), 60, 81, 82
Fort Jackson, 495, 1025
Fort Jackson (steamer), 1021
Fort Lafayette, 725
Fort Leavenworth, 581, 584
Fort McAllister, 653, 679, 711, 715
  fall of, 615–52, 679, 711, 715, 730
Fort Mahone (Fort Damnation), 628, 773
Fort Monroe, 19, 127, 128, 137, 253, 450, 451, 713, 899, 1012
  imprisonment of Davis at, 1033–38
Fort Morgan, 495, 496, 498, 502, 503, 506

[1080] INDEX

Fort Moultrie, 972
Fort Pickering, 515, 517, 518
Fort Pillow, 108–12, 139, 329, 362
 casualties, 111
 congressional investigation of, 111–12
 Negro soldiers at, 108, 111, 112, 364, 538
Fort Powell, 494–95, 506
Fort Rosecrans, 677–78
Fort St. Philip, 495, 1025
Fort Sedgwick (Fort Hell), 628
Fort Smith, 27, 65, 66, 67, 576, 585
Fort Stedman, 854, 862, 875, 876
 assault at, 840–44, 845, 873, 910
Fort Stevens, 453–54, 458, 459, 460, 469, 845, 1046
Fort Sumter, 128, 139, 160, 207, 362, 427, 550, 748, 975
 raising of U.S. flag at, 969–73, 979
Fort Warren, 1012, 1024
Foster, John G., 652–53, 711, 712, 737, 750
 occupation of Charleston, 800, 802
Fourteenth Amendment, 1043, 1044–45
France, 98, 860, 1018–19, 1028
 Confederate ambassador in, 99
 occupation of Mexico, 376–77
Franklin, William B., 541
 Red River campaign, 40, 41, 43, 45–52, 79, 84–85, 89
Franklin, battle for, 656, 662–74, 675, 676, 677, 679, 681, 691, 697, 699, 758, 760, 832
 casualties, 670–71, 672, 673–74
 number of troops at, 664
 Schofield's withdrawal from, 672–74
Franklin, Tennessee, 656, 657, 658, 705, 707
Franklin Turnpike, 663, 676, 688, 696, 698, 699, 700, 701, 702, 703, 705, 706
Frederick, Maryland, 448, 449, 451, 452, 465
Fredericksburg, 24, 143, 148, 153, 171, 174, 176–77, 188, 191, 196, 198, 204, 206, 214, 224, 247, 267, 272, 537, 997, 1018
Fredericktown, 576, 577
Frémont, John C., 22, 24, 624
 presidential candidacy of, 377, 559
French, Samuel G., 396–97, 398, 399, 423, 606, 611–12
 Franklin battle, 666, 669, 670, 679
 Nashville battle, 690, 692
Front Royal, 248, 555–56, 557, 565, 567, 571, 805
Fugitive Slave Law, repealed, 463

G

Gadsden, 607, 615, 616, 621
Gaines, Dr. William, 287
Gaines (gunboat), 494, 502

Gaines Mill, 233, 287, 292, 294, 314, 316, 666
Gainesville, 1000, 1001
Gallego Mill, burning of, 889
Galveston, 26, 53, 1013, 1021, 1022, 1027, 1040
Garfield, James A., 1056
Garrard, Kenner, 335, 338, 352, 396, 401, 402, 404–5, 409
 Atlanta battle, 486–87, 488, 520
 in Marietta, 402
Garrison, William Lloyd, 970, 973
Gasconade River, 578
Gauley Bridge, 243, 244, 246
Gaylesville, 615, 621
Geary, John W., 347–48, 735
Georgetown, Ky., burning of, 360
Georgia campaign, 318–424, 472–530, 640–723
 battle for Atlanta, 475–92, 552–53, 559, 575, 596, 640, 657, 685, 730, 754, 760, 780
 Chattahoochee crossings, 402–10, 411, 415, 419
 Confederate raiders, 358–74
  in Kentucky, 358–62
  in North Mississippi, 362–74
 consternation in Atlanta, 410–24
 Dalton to Resaca march, 318–30, 363
 Hood's march to the north, 654–710
 Kingston to Pine Top via Dallas march, 345–57
 probe at the flank tactics, 322, 327, 331, 336, 341, 346, 393, 394, 395–96, 412
 Resaca to Cassville march, 331–45
 Sherman's march to the sea, 622–23, 640–54, 655, 674, 679, 681, 684, 723–24, 730, 747, 754
 total casualties, 400–1
 See also names of cities
Germanna Ford, 135, 143, 144, 146, 147, 158, 161, 164, 185, 187
Germanna Plank Road, 147, 154, 158, 159, 164, 182, 184–85
Germany, 1052, 1053
Getty, George W., 161
Gettysburg, 9, 10, 11, 21, 98, 99, 101, 153, 164, 174, 181, 207, 256, 290, 299, 330, 347, 356, 403, 432, 447, 533, 569, 581, 782, 920, 975, 1051
Gettysburg Address, 748, 1046
Gibbon, John, 547, 882–83, 927
 casualties suffered by, 144
 and Petersburg, 444
 in the Wilderness, 161, 162, 177
Gilgal Church, 353, 355, 392
Gillis House (Kansas City), 581
Gillmore, Quincy A., 19, 560, 652, 971, 973
 and Bermuda Hundred, 253, 255–56, 261, 262
Gilmore, James R., 467–68, 469

Index

Gist, States Rights, 670
Glendale, 316
Globe Tavern, 545–46, 547, 548, 561, 841
Godwin, Parke, 471
Gold, price of (1864), 341, 462
Gold Hoax of 1864, 375–76, 379
Goldsboro, 258, 737, 751, 752, 796, 797, 817–19, 820, 822–24, 826, 828, 829, 834, 835, 841, 854, 855, 894
Goode, R. R., 359
Goodwyn, T. J., 793, 794
Gordon, George W., 670
Gordon, James B., 227, 228, 229, 230, 232, 233
Gordon, John B., 808, 1056
  and Cedar Creek, 566–70, 571
  and Early's northward march, 446–47, 450, 452, 453, 459
  Fort Stedman assault, 840–44, 845, 862, 876
  Hatcher's Run battle, 785
  Monocacy battle, 452
  named acting corps commander, 638, 639
  and Petersburg, 637, 840, 878, 881–82, 884–85
    withdrawal, 908, 911, 915–17, 920–24, 930, 931, 932, 934–35, 939–41, 943, 944, 945, 951
  Spotsylvania battle, 191, 192, 193, 217–19, 220
  in the Wilderness, 155, 160, 312
    second day (May 6th), 173, 181, 182, 185
  and Winchester, 555
Gordonsville, 122, 123, 133, 145, 150, 151, 173, 307, 308–9, 722
Gorgas, Josiah, 857–58, 862
Gould, Jay, 1042
Govan, Daniel C., 528
Gracie, Archibald, 259
  and Bermuda Hundred, 258
  death of, 640
  and Petersburg, 433, 436, 437, 438
Grahamville Station, 652, 653
Granbury, Hiram B., 350, 528, 671, 690
Grand Design plan (Spring '64), 3–145
  authorities in Richmond and, 92–126
  criticism of Davis, 92–96, 118–19
  efforts to "conquer a peace," 96–103
  question of survival, 103–26
  final preparations, 126–45
    in the North, 126–39
    in the South, 139–45
  over-all command strategy, 3–24
  Transmississippi operation, 25–92
    Camden Expedition, 61–77
    prolonging of, 77–92
    Red River campaign, 25–77

Grand Ecore, 32, 33, 38, 39, 40, 43, 46, 48, 50–51, 52, 53, 54, 55, 68, 69, 70, 84, 87
  Federal withdrawal from, 56–61, 62
Grand Junction, 514
Grand Review parade, 1013–18, 1027, 1041
Granger, Gordon, 496–97, 506, 507, 677, 848
Granny White Pike, 688, 695, 698, 700–1, 705
Grant, Fred D., 5, 7
Grant, Julia Dent, 13, 24, 554, 809, 846–47, 848, 976–77, 1056
Grant, Ulysses S., 3–9, 21, 376, 390, 408, 420, 519, 530, 579, 610, 613–14, 615, 617, 628, 631, 837, 957, 967, 993–94, 1018–19, 1023, 1034, 1051
  Baltimore Convention votes (1864), 378
  battle at Nashville and, 681, 682, 683, 684, 685, 686, 690, 696, 701, 710–11
  Close-Out Plan, 735–54, 836, 848
  Confederate authorities and, 754–83
  fall of Fort Fisher, 740–47
  Hatcher's Run battle, 783–86
  leftward sidle operation, 852–53, 862
  and Sherman's march northward, 736, 750–54, 756, 757, 786, 787–801, 825–38, 848, 851, 858, 1029
  total combat force, 739
  Transmississippi region, 739, 747
  death of, 1055–56
  election of 1868, 1044
  Grand Design plan (Spring '64), 3–145
    army reorganization, 126–32
    authorities in Richmond and, 92–126
    command arrangement, 24, 127, 128
    final preparations, 126–45
    principles of action, 14–15
    Transmississippi region, 25–92
  Grand Review parade, 1014, 1015
  Mexican War, 9, 13
  Nashville meeting (1864), 16, 29, 31
  number of combat soldiers serving under, 13
  pendulum strikes, 560–62, 628, 631
  promoted to general-in-chief, 3–9, 24
    acceptance speech, 7–8
  River Queen conference, 847–48, 854–57
  Robert Lincoln's appointment and, 816
  tone-deafness, 9
  Vicksburg campaign, 4, 11, 29, 64, 136, 184, 187, 295, 313, 322, 363, 403, 427, 428, 541, 737, 913

Grant, Ulysses S. (*Cont.*)
　Virginia campaign, 3–317, 427–72, 530–74, 802–956
　　to Appomattox, 907–56
　　and Butler at Bermuda Hundred, 251–65
　　Close-Out Plan, 735–54
　　at Cold Harbor, 281–99, 380, 429, 672
　　and Confederate drive toward Washington, 446–61
　　Grand Design for (Spring '64), 3–145
　　at North Anna, 265–76, 375
　　Petersburg siege, 427–46, 530–49, 627–40
　　race for Spotsylvania, 189–91, 191–224
　　and Sheridan's raid on Richmond, 224–35
　　and Sheridan's Shenandoah Valley operations, 553–58, 563–73, 574, 763, 803–4, 1023
　　and Sheridan's two-pronged strike (December), 722–23
　　and Sherman's march through Georgia, 318, 319, 320, 322–23, 332, 362, 364, 374, 375, 376, 378, 380, 390, 394, 408, 420, 613–14, 623, 641, 649, 650, 713, 714, 715, 721, 730
　　strategy shift to James River, 299–317
　　Totopotomoy confrontation, 276–81
　　triple-pronged operations, 235–51
　　victory, 802–956
　　in the Wilderness, 146–91, 332, 375
Grant's Pass, 495
Grapevine Bridge, 288
Gravelly Run, 628, 862, 866, 869, 870
Gravelly Run Church, 871
Greeley, Horace, 465–66, 467, 469, 471, 558, 816, 1036, 1038, 1039
Green, Thomas, 36, 37, 42, 43, 44, 48, 49, 53–54, 56, 68
"Greenback Raid," 806
Greenbrier River, 244, 246, 302
Greeneville, 117, 595–96
Greensboro, 312, 717, 991, 992, 997, 1003, 1006
　flight of Confederate government to, 965–69, 988
Gregg, David M., 225, 233, 282, 283, 285
　Boydton Plank Road mission, 561
　at Hatcher's Run, 784–85
　railroad destruction by, 308–9
　Reams Station strike, 547
　resignation of, 867
　Spotsylvania battle, 199

　Weldon Railroad assignment, 637
Gregg, John, 169–70, 640
Greyhound (steamer), 634–35
Grierson, Benjamin H., 363–64, 367–69
　in North Mississippi, 510, 511, 514
　at Tupelo, 511
Griffin, Charles, 201, 926, 936, 940, 941
　and Dinwiddie, Five Forks, 868, 871, 873
　and Petersburg, 880
　race for Burkeville, 914
　in the Wilderness, 159–60, 161
Griffin, Mrs. Charles, 846, 847
Grimes, Bryan, 638–39
Griswoldville, 646, 651, 652
Ground Squirrel Bridge, 226, 228, 229
Grover's Theatre (Washington, D.C.), 817
Guiney Station, 269
Guntersville, 616, 618
Guntown, *see* Brice's Crossroads

H

Habeas corpus, writ of, 471, 768, 1038
Hackett, James H., 979
Hagerstown, 449
Hahn, Michael, 29
Halifax, Nova Scotia, 509, 590
Halleck, Henry W., 7, 15, 16, 25, 26, 28, 29, 34, 39, 62, 64, 69, 89, 116, 126, 132, 135–37, 147, 149, 276, 290, 299, 300, 301, 303, 470, 491, 492, 565, 576, 602, 633, 736, 751, 753, 800, 1011
　created chief of staff, 24
　death of, 1056
　and Early's northward march, 450, 455
　Grant's letter to (May 11), 211–12
　Nashville battle communication with Thomas, 682, 683, 684, 685, 686, 696, 710
　and Petersburg, 430, 445, 540, 542, 543, 548
　Sherman's campaign and, 332, 345, 347, 357, 391, 399, 404, 405, 410, 530, 649, 713, 714–15, 736, 753, 800
Hamilton's Crossing, 148, 152
Hamlin, Hannibal, 378, 811, 812
Hampton, Wade, 194, 239–40, 304, 305, 306–8, 309, 312, 316, 444, 561, 573, 762, 794, 795–96, 1037
　along Hatcher's Run, 631
　at Bentonville, 828, 829, 830, 835
　in the Carolinas, 808, 819, 822, 824
　Mississippi plan, 1002–3
　evacuation of Columbia, 792–93
　at Haw's Shop, 277–78
　named chief of cavalry, 309

Index

and Petersburg, 533, 631, 637
promoted to lieutenant general, 792
Hampton Roads, 589, 591, 595, 635, 906, 1033
Hampton Roads Conference, 773-83, 784, 801, 839, 898, 901-2
Southern reaction to, 778-83
"Hampton's Cattle Raid," 560
Hancock, Winfield S., 313, 314, 315, 560, 573, 633-34
and Cold Harbor, 285, 288, 291, 292, 295
death of, 1056
at Deep Bottom Run, 545
march to Totopotomoy, 276, 281
and North Anna, 265, 268, 269, 270, 271, 274
and Petersburg, 427, 428, 431-32, 436-37, 440, 444, 533-35, 541, 545-47, 548
Rapidan crossing, 874
return to active duty, 806, 807
Spotsylvania battle, 202, 205, 206, 207, 209, 210-11, 212-13, 217, 219, 220, 221, 222, 232
triple-pronged offensive and, 236, 238-43, 250
Weldon Railroad assignment, 637
in the Wilderness, 147, 151, 161-63, 164, 165
designated objective, 148, 158
race to Spotsylvania, 189, 190-91
second day (May 6th), 167-68, 170, 171, 172, 173, 174-75, 177, 180, 182, 184
Hanging Rock Post Office, 796
Hanover Courthouse, 851
Hanover Junction, 153, 191-92, 228, 241, 242, 251, 256, 265, 266, 272, 273, 275, 276, 277, 283
Hardee, William J., 606, 609, 611, 798, 799
Atlanta battle, 473-79, 483-84, 490, 523-30, 605-6
Augusta Council meeting, 790-91
in the Carolinas, 819, 822
at Averasboro, 826-27, 828
at Bentonville, 828-32, 833
Fayetteville withdrawal, 824
Charleston headquarters, 606, 756, 758, 759, 762, 764, 791-92
evacuation of the city, 797
on Cleburne's death (quoted), 671
Macon headquarters, 645-46
and Peachtree Creek, 473-75
at Rocky Face Ridge, 321, 327
Sherman's campaign and, 411, 417, 421, 423, 645-46, 652-53
evacuation of Savannah, 711-12, 730
Kennesaw Mountain, 391-93, 397, 398, 399
Kingston and Pine Top and Dallas, 347, 349, 350, 353, 355, 356
Resaca and Cassville, 332-34, 338-41
Hardee, William J., Jr., 835
Hardeeville, 787
Harding Turnpike, 679, 688, 690, 691
Harlan, James, 815-16, 903, 905
Harpers Ferry, 446, 447, 451, 455, 461, 539, 542, 544, 553, 555, 560, 804
Harper's Weekly, 562
Harpeth River, 656, 660, 662, 664-66, 669, 672-73, 675, 681, 696, 697, 698, 705, 707
Harris, Clara H., 978-79, 980, 982-83, 984
Harris, Ira, 978
Harris, Nathaniel H., 220, 882-83
Harrisburg, Mississippi, 511, 513
burning of, 512
Harrison, Burton N., 100, 140, 863, 1008
Harrisonburg, 558, 722
Hartford (flagship), 493-94, 496, 498-504, 507, 724
Harvard University, 816
Hatch, Edward, 655
Hatcher's Run, 573, 628, 638, 763, 783-86, 840, 843, 852, 857, 862-64, 867-69, 875, 877-80
casualties, 785
Hatchie River, 371
Hatteras (gunboat), 381, 382, 384
Hatteras Inlet, 593
Hawkinsville, 1008, 1009
Haw's Shop, 276, 277-78, 280, 281
Hawthorne, Nathaniel, 375, 376
Haxall Mill, burning of, 889
Haxall's Landing, 233, 236
Hay, John, 466, 979, 982, 986
Hayes, Rutherford B., 244, 1041, 1044
Haynie, Isham N., 978
Hays, Alexander, 163
Hazen, William B., 651-52
Helena, 403
Helm, Ben Hardin, 350
Henderson's Hill, 31, 34
Henry, Patrick, 94, 103
Henry IV (Shakespeare), 979
Herald, David E., 1032
Hermitage (estate), 678
Hernando, 516-17
Heth, Henry, 156, 267-68
and Petersburg siege, 875, 878, 879, 884
withdrawal, 908, 930
Spotsylvania battle, 193, 214, 215
in the Wilderness, 156, 157, 162, 163, 165, 166
second day (May 6th), 167, 168, 170, 176-77
Hichakala Creek, 515-16
Hicksford, 638, 784
High Bridge, 920, 922, 923, 924, 927

[1084] INDEX

Hill, Ambrose Powell, 142, 143, 145, 235, 283, 316, 317, 573, 867, 1048, 1050
  along Hatcher's Run, 631, 785
  and Cold Harbor, 284, 286, 287, 291, 293
  death of, 879–80, 943
  and North Anna, 265, 266, 267, 270, 271–72, 273
  Peebles Farm, 561
  and Petersburg, 435, 438, 440, 441, 444, 445, 631, 638, 840, 841, 843, 844, 875–80, 885
  Spotsylvania battle, 193, 194, 198, 214
  Totopotomoy confrontation, 278, 279, 280
  Weldon Railroad attack and, 546–48
  in the Wilderness, 151, 153, 161, 164, 166
    designated objective, 150–51, 153, 154
    plank road engagement (May 5th), 154, 156–57
    second day (May 6th), 167, 168, 169, 171, 173, 175, 176–77, 178, 181, 182
Hill, Benjamin H., 411–15, 416, 418–19, 781, 1057
Hill, Catherine Morgan, 880
Hill, Daniel Harvey, 262, 263
  Augusta Council with Beauregard, 791
  at Bentonville, 830, 831
  and Bermuda Hundred, 257, 258
Hillsboro, 488, 988–89
Hillsboro Pike, 679, 688, 691, 693, 694, 695, 696, 698
Hilton Head, 652, 712
Hincks, Edward W., 428–29, 431, 432, 433, 444
Hindman, Thomas C., 348, 393
Hobson, Edward H., 358–61
Hobson's Bay, 591
Hoke, Robert F., 113, 115–16, 124, 153, 306
  and Bermuda Hundred, 256, 257, 258, 259, 260, 262, 278, 280
  in the Carolinas, 821, 822, 829, 830–32, 833
  and Cold Harbor, 281, 282, 284, 285, 286, 291, 293
  and Petersburg, 433, 434, 631, 639
  Wilmington defense, 639, 717, 720, 743, 744, 762, 791, 820
Hollow Tree Gap, 705, 706, 707
Holly Springs, 514
Hollyhock (gunboat), 1025
Hollywood Cemetery (Richmond), 140–41, 235, 1038, 1060
Holmes, Oliver Wendell, 469
Holmes, Oliver Wendell, Jr., 458–59, 1046–47
Holmes, Theophilus H., 36
Holston River, 519

Holt, Joseph, 1036, 1037
Honey Hill, 653, 711
Hood, John Bell, 169, 287, 576, 597, 601, 632, 697
  baptism of, 329–30, 339
  captured and paroled, 1021
  Dalton conference, 329
  defense of Atlanta, 475–92, 509, 514, 549, 575, 760
    assault plan, 524–25, 526
    evacuation plan, 527
    loss of the city, 519–30
    at Peachtree Creek, 472–75
    transfer of command to, 420–23
    Wheeler's raid and, 519–20, 522
  and Forrest's raiders in North Mississippi, 509–19
  Gadsden meeting with Beauregard, 616–18
  and Kennesaw Mountain, 391–93, 394, 399, 401
  Kingston and Pine Top and Dallas, 347, 349, 351, 353, 355
  at LaFayette (October 17th), 613, 616
  march to the north strategy, 654–710, 724, 730, 998
    Duck River crossing, 655–56
    flanking movements, 656, 657, 660, 662
    at Franklin, 662–74
    at Nashville, 674–710
    retreat from Nashville, 705–10, 738, 757–58
    Spring Hill fiasco, 658–62
  meeting with Davis, 604–7
  Palmetto headquarters, 604–7
  plan for recruiting volunteers, 760, 765
  rearward strikes (after fall of Atlanta), 602–4, 609, 610, 611–13, 615–16, 636
  reduced in rank, 765
  relieved of command, 758
  at Resaca (October, 12th), 613, 615
  Resaca and Cassville, 332–34, 339–43
  return to Richmond, 760–71
  and Rocky Face Ridge, 321, 327
  "spread-eagle" plan, 616–17
  strategy shift (October '64), 616–22
Hooker, Joseph, 10, 17, 18, 24, 122, 123, 134, 135, 139, 143, 144, 146, 149–50, 305, 403, 476, 477, 521, 538, 566, 810, 928
  failure of offensive against Lee, 17, 18
  and the "Hell Hole," 347–49
  at Kennesaw Mountain, 392, 393, 396
  Kingston to Pine Top, via Dallas march, 347, 351, 356
  in Northern Department, 485
  Resaca to Cassville march, 336, 342
  Richmond campaign, 17, 18, 123, 275, 295
  in the Wilderness, 171–72, 183, 186, 188

Index [1085]

Hot Springs, 64, 67
Hotchkiss, Jedediah, 566, 808
Hough, Daniel, 970-71
Houston, 27, 1020-21
Howard, Joseph, 376
Howard, Oliver O., 337-53, 355, 403, 603, 611, 622, 658, 672
   Atlanta battle, 485, 486, 488-92, 521-28, 530
   Carolinas march, 751, 753, 788-89, 793-94, 826, 828
      at Bentonville, 831, 832, 833, 834-35
      at Cheraw, 822
      crossing of the Neuse, 828-29, 836
      Falling Creek camp, 829
   at Kennesaw Mountain, 394, 398
   on Sherman's march to the sea, 640, 642, 643, 645-46, 648
Howe, Julia Ward, 3
Howell, Beckett K., 388
Howell, Margaret, 863, 1011, 1012
Howlett Line, 433, 434, 437, 438, 439, 628
Huey's Mill, 656
Huff, John A., 231
Hullihen, Walter Q., 231
Humphreys, Andrew A., 857
   Five Forks battle, 864, 866-67, 868
   at Hatcher's Run, 784-85
   and Petersburg, 634, 637, 880
   pursuit of Lee's army, 918, 920, 922-27, 929, 935, 937-38, 941, 943, 944
   race for Burkeville, 903, 914, 915
Hunter, David, 448, 450, 456, 460, 461, 539, 540, 542, 558, 563
   Grant's Jamesward strategy and, 304-5, 306, 309-11, 312
   coup at Piedmont, 301-2
   destruction at Lexington, 309-10, 311
   at Lynchburg, 439, 445, 446, 447
   and Petersburg, 427, 439, 442, 445, 446
Hunter, Robert M. T., 766, 767, 770
   Blair's peace feeler and, 772-73
   on enlistment of Negroes, 859
   Hampton Roads Conference, 773-78, 779, 780
Huntsville, Alabama, 599, 600
Hurlbut, Stephen A., 362, 516, 849

I

Illinois, election of 1864, 625
Imboden, John D., 247, 248, 249
   B & O wrecking operations, 448
Independence, 580, 582
Indian Territory, 28, 65, 66, 68, 73, 575, 576, 585, 747, 1022

Indiana, October elections (1864), 562
Indianola (ironclad), 1024
Indians, 67, 68, 69, 70, 563, 725-27, 1022
   Minnesota uprising, 725
   Sand Creek Massacre, 725-27
   Sheridan's policy on, 727
Iron Mountain Railroad, 578
Ironton, 576, 577
Irwinville, 1009, 1057

J

Jackson, Andrew, 378, 456, 678, 728, 770, 814
Jackson, Henry R., 619, 669, 677, 703, 704
Jackson, Thomas J. "Stonewall," 18, 34, 35, 42, 58, 139, 149, 179, 181, 182, 192, 205, 217, 228, 235, 250, 257, 271, 310, 357, 363, 446, 453, 460, 476, 477, 489, 539, 555, 565, 568, 639, 656, 807, 841, 880, 919, 940, 1050, 1059
Jackson, William H. "Red," 353, 519, 520, 522-23, 525
Jackson, Mississippi, 647, 1055
Jackson, Tennessee, 106, 107
James, Frank, 579, 1022
James, Jesse, 579
James River, 14, 19, 121, 127, 151-52, 226, 230, 232, 233, 251, 257, 266, 270, 276, 278, 280, 427-28, 431, 432, 435, 543, 560, 561, 610, 627, 633, 638, 722, 840, 851, 852-53, 876, 881, 883, 885, 887, 888, 894, 903, 908, 931, 933
   Grant's shift to, 299-317
James River Canal, 311, 312, 803, 851
James River Squadron, 765, 1024
   destruction of, 886, 888-89
Japan, 1029
Jaquess, James F., 467-68, 469
Jay Cooke & Company, 1050
Jefferson City, 54, 576, 578, 579, 580
Jenkins, Albert G., 244, 247
Jenkins, Micah, 178, 180
Jenkins Ferry, 74-75, 76, 78, 104
Jericho Mills, 267, 268, 269, 270, 274, 279
Jerusalem Plank Road, 436, 439, 442, 444, 445, 533, 545-46, 628, 773
Jetersville, 910, 911, 914, 907
"John Brown's Body," 770, 819, 928, 970
Johnson, Andrew, 378-79, 596, 682, 683, 982, 983, 984, 986-87, 988, 994-95, 998, 1012, 1013, 1019, 1037, 1040
   amnesty proclamation, 1031-32, 1033, 1048-49
   Grand Review parade, 1015, 1017
   impeached, 1044, 1049
   on Jefferson Davis (quoted), 901, 1049
   as military governor of Tennessee, 987

Johnson, Andrew (*Cont.*)
  oath of office, 986
  Reconstruction policy, 1043
  Republican vengeance speech, 901, 904
  as Vice-President, 810, 811-12, 977
Johnson, Bradley T., 449, 457, 459, 460-61
Johnson, Bushrod R., 762, 867
  and Bermuda Hundred, 257, 278
  and Petersburg, 433, 434, 436, 631, 875, 884, 885
    withdrawal, 908, 918, 930
    relieved of duty, 930
Johnson, Edward, 154-55, 660, 661, 663, 667
  captured, 660, 702, 703
  Nashville battle, 692, 694, 695, 698, 700, 702, 703
  Spotsylvania battle, 215, 216, 217, 218, 219, 660
  in the Wilderness, 154-55
Johnson, William A., 366, 368-69, 597
Johnson's Island (prison), 182, 777
Johnsonville, 601, 617, 619-20, 654, 681
Johnston, Albert Sidney, 139, 284, 357, 677, 1004, 1059
Johnston, James D., 494, 503, 505
Johnston, Joseph E., 13, 16, 17, 18, 91-92, 94, 97-98, 108, 112, 117-18, 119, 124, 126, 133, 605, 607, 613, 661, 767, 768, 769, 789, 1051
  admission of defeat, 1048, 1049
  Army of Tennessee command, 117
  baptism of, 339-40
  in the Carolinas, 802, 803, 820-38, 839, 851, 856, 905, 965, 974, 975, 1006, 1029
  army desertions, 822
  Davis (Jefferson) and, 825, 839
  Greensboro strategy conference, 966-69
  and Kinston, Averasboro, and Bentonville, 820-38
  Lee's attempt to combine with, 839, 840, 841, 844, 852, 854-55, 884, 885, 891, 895, 903, 911, 912, 913, 914, 921, 926, 935, 966
  Smithfield evacuation, 966
  surrender negotiations with Sherman, 988-96, 998
  on Confederate treasury gold, 1055
  death of, 996
  recalled to active duty, 797-800
  Sherman's campaign and, 318-424, 472, 473-74, 476, 486, 491, 519, 990
    Dalton and Resaca, 318-30
    Federal crossing of the Chattahoochee, 402-10
    Forrest's North Mississippi raids, 362-74
    Kennesaw Mountain, 391-401
    Kingston and Pine Top and Dallas, 345-57, 391
  letter to Army of Tennessee, 340-41
  meeting with Bragg, 417-18
  reaction of Richmond authorities to, 411-19, 420, 421
  relieved of command, 419-22, 467, 472
  Resaca and Cassville, 331-45
  surrender of, 1019, 1020, 1021, 1027, 1028
Johnston, Louisa McL., 339
Johnston, Robert D., 181
Johnston, W. Preston, 1004, 1008, 1010, 1012, 1051
Joint Committee on the Conduct of the War, 10, 111-12, 740-41, 747, 962, 987
Jones, John M., 155
Jones, William E., 302, 304
Jonesboro, 486, 487, 520-21, 524-30, 607, 643, 645, 849
Journal of Commerce, 376
Juárez, Benito, 1019, 1023
Julian, George W., 464, 987, 1043
Juliet (gunboat), 60

K

Kamchatka Peninsula, 1029
Kanawah River, 243, 455
Kansas, 574, 576, 579, 580, 582, 585, 586, 726, 747
Kansas City, 579, 580, 581
Kautz, August V., 560
  and Bermuda Hundred, 254-55, 257, 258, 261
  and Petersburg, 429, 442, 444, 445
Kean, Robert, 860
Kearsarge (sloop), 380-90, 442, 587
  armaments aboard, 381-82
  gunnery effectiveness, 385
  refitted, 389-90
Keatchie, 37, 42, 44, 49
Keene, Laura, 977, 982-83, 984
Keitt, Lawrence M., 284-85
Kell, John McI., 384-88
Kelley, Benjamin F., 804
Kennesaw Mountain, 344, 353, 391-402, 407, 410, 411, 412, 610, 665, 1055
  beginning of attack, 397-98
  casualties, 393, 398, 399-400
  Confederate abandonment of, 401-402
  Culp's Farm assault, 392-93
  at the Dead Angle, 398-99
  flank attacks, 395-96
Kentucky:
  draft riots, 548
  election of 1864, 625
  judgeship election (1864), 471

Index

Morgan's raid (June '64), 358-62, 373, 374, 380
Kernstown, 569
Kershaw, Joseph B., 540, 544, 545, 553, 564, 762
   and Cedar Creek, 567, 568, 571
   and Cold Harbor, 284, 285, 286
   and Petersburg, 875
      withdrawal, 908, 918, 919, 920
   in Richmond, 885
   Spotsylvania battle, 192, 196, 197
   in the Wilderness, 170, 173, 176-77, 178
Kilpatrick, Hugh Judson, 105, 232, 331-32, 335, 337, 622
   Atlanta battle, 520-21, 526
   Carolinas march, 751, 754, 787-88, 789, 826, 827, 854
   on Sherman's march to the sea, 640, 645, 647, 648
Kimball, Nathan, 664, 694-95
Kingston, 117, 320, 326, 335, 337-38, 339, 341, 363, 613, 616, 622, 721
Kingston to Pine Top, via Dallas march, 345-57
   casualties, 348, 350, 351-52
   at New Hope Church (the "Hell Hole"), 347-49, 352, 354
   Pine Top salient, 355-57
Kinston, 820, 821-25
   casualties, 823
   Lee's urging for, 821
   purpose of, 823-24
Kiowa Indians, 726
Kirke, Edmund, *see* Gilmore, J. R.
Knipe, Joseph F., 738
Knoxville, 16, 117, 261, 322, 323, 595, 597, 721-22, 737, 849
Kolb's Farm, 392-93

L

La Grange, 510, 513, 781, 1007
Lackawanna (sloop), 498, 499, 502, 504-5
Lacy farmhouse, 159, 160, 161, 163, 164
Lacy Springs, 248
LaFayette, 613, 615, 616
Lairds of Liverpool, 100, 388
Lake Erie (prison camp), 777
Lamb, William, 717, 719, 720, 741, 743, 744, 745, 746
Lancaster, John, 388
Lash, Jacob A., 703, 704
Law, Evander McI., 274, 287, 293
   in the Wilderness, 170, 171, 172
Lawrence, Kansas, sacking of, 1022
Lawrence Hill, 688, 691, 696
Lawrenceburg, 654, 655
Laynesport, 586, 723

[1087]

Lay's Ferry, 335-37
League of Loyal Confederates, 782
Leale, Charles A., 981-82
Ledlie, James H., 534-36, 537, 538
   removal of, 634
Lee, Albert L., 41-44, 50, 55, 58, 89
Lee, Fitzhugh, 304, 307, 308, 309, 540, 544, 545, 1051
   and Cold Harbor, 280, 281, 282-83
   at Dinwiddie, Five Forks, 863, 864, 870
   and Fisher's Hill, 556, 557
   at Haw's Shop, 277-78
   and Petersburg, 875, 885
      withdrawal, 908, 911, 923, 924, 931, 934, 935, 939, 940, 941
   and Sheridan's raid on Richmond, 227, 228-29, 230, 231, 232, 233, 235
   Spotsylvania battle, 194-96, 197, 199
   at Winchester, 554-55
Lee, George Washington Custis, 761-62, 908, 918, 919
   captured, 919
   promoted to major general, 908
Lee, Mary Custis, 886, 1036
Lee, Robert E., 11-12, 94, 99, 489, 506, 576, 606, 610, 617, 644, 655, 661-62, 705, 707, 711, 736, 737, 741, 958, 974, 1043, 1057
   appointment as general-in-chief, 768, 769-70, 783, 785
   recall of Johnston, 797-800
   army withdrawal, 802-956
      and abandonment of Richmond, 857-64, 885-93
      to Amelia Courthouse, 890, 891, 892, 909, 911, 913
      to Appomattox, 907-56
   and Dinwiddie, Five Forks battles, 862-75
   fall of Petersburg, 875-85, 893
   Farmville route, 911-12, 914, 921, 922
   food shortages, 909-10, 911
   Fort Stedman assault and, 840-44, 845
   last battle attack, 867-68
   meeting with Breckinridge, 922
   and plan to combine with Johnston, 839-40, 841, 844, 852, 854-55, 884, 885, 891, 895, 903, 911, 912, 913, 914, 921, 926, 935, 966
   race for Burkeville crossing, 903, 911, 913-14, 915
   Sayler's Creek rout, 917-21
   confidence in Army of Northern Virginia, 123, 242, 764
   death of, 1050, 1056
   farewell to the army (General Orders No. 9), 955-56
   Federal offensive launched against, 17-18, 21, 24

Lee, Robert E. (*Cont.*)
   Grant's campaign and:
      Beauregard's bottling of Butler, 251–65
      Cold Harbor, 281–99, 429, 802
      Confederate authorities, 754–83
      Early's northward march, 446–61
      Federal triple-pronged offensive, 235–51
      Grant's shift to the James, 299–317
      Grant's third pendulum strike (September), 560–62
      Hatcher's Run, 783–86
      North Anna, 265–76
      Petersburg (Fall '64), 627–40
      Petersburg (June '64), 427–46
      Petersburg (July-August) and, 530–49
      race for Spotsylvania, 191–224, 332
      Sheridan's operations, 224–35, 553–58, 563–73, 574
      Totopotomoy confrontation, 276–81
      in the Wilderness, 146–91, 323, 424
   Grant's Plan (Spring '64) and, 11–12, 13, 17–18, 19, 98, 101, 105, 108, 116–23, 127, 133–35, 136, 137–139, 140, 142
      Clark's Mountain prediction, 142–44, 145, 197–98
      prospects for invading the enemy, 98
   loyalty oath to U.S., 1048–49
   on need to abandon Richmond, 844, 858, 862, 864
   offer of pardon for deserters, 786
   as president of Washington College, 1050
   surrender of, 938, 939–56, 965, 966, 968, 970, 975, 989, 996, 1000, 1019, 1021, 1024, 1028, 1029
   on using Negro soldiers, 755
Lee, Robert E., Jr., 449, 844
Lee, Samuel P., 709
Lee, Stephen D., 112, 338, 340, 365, 415, 575, 821, 830, 831
   Atlanta battle, 509, 523–24, 525, 526, 530
   at Ezra Church, 489–90
   Franklin battle, 662, 663, 672
   and Hood's march north, 654, 656, 657, 659, 660, 674, 759
   march from Columbia, 662, 663
   Nashville battle, 676–77, 680, 692, 695, 698, 700, 702, 703, 708
   in North Mississippi, 511–12, 514
   promoted to lieutenant general, 489
Lee, W. H. F. "Rooney," 194, 213–14, 227, 841, 844, 863, 870
Lee & Gordon's Mill, 323
Leesburg, 361, 461, 539

Leggett, Mortimer D., 480, 481
Leggett's Hill (Bald Hill), 475, 477, 479–80, 481, 482, 483, 640, 654
Letcher, John, 310, 311, 460
Lewis, Joseph H., 350
Lewisburg, 244, 599
Lewisburg Pike, 657, 666
Lexington, Kentucky, 358, 359–60
   looting of, 360
Lexington, Missouri, 579, 580, 581
Lexington, Virginia, 244, 247, 309, 446, 449
   burning of, 309–10, 311
Lexington (timberclad), 82
Libby Prison, 804, 897, 899
Liberty Hall (estate), 93, 94, 781, 1008
Lickskillet Road, 489–90
Lieber, Francis, 1036
Lincoln, Abraham, 148, 247, 312, 457–58, 508, 519, 558–60, 574, 595, 596, 636, 736, 739–40, 749, 857, 861, 893–94, 895–96, 903, 927, 950, 973–88, 1017, 1042, 1060, 1067
   assassination of, 980–88, 989, 991, 995, 1024, 1033, 1049
      conspirator's trial, 1032
      public mourning, 1015, 1025
      reaction in the South, 997–98
   Blair's peace feeler and, 770–73
   burial journey to Illinois, 986, 994
   criticism of, 973
   death sentences for military offenses, 977
   draft calls, 124, 129, 300, 376
   and Early's drive to Washington, 446, 449, 454–59
      conference with Grant, 541
      evacuation plan, 455
      tour of fortifications, 457–58, 459
   Emancipation Proclamation, 729–30, 750, 777, 1045
   Georgia campaign and, 353, 362, 377–80, 390, 423, 642, 650–51, 713, 723–24
      Nashville battle, 684, 701
      renomination (1864), 377–80
   Gettysburg Address, 748, 1046
   Gold Hoax forgery and, 375–76, 379
   Grant's Grand Design and, 12, 15, 18, 21, 22, 97, 101, 103, 104, 112, 134, 135, 136, 137, 138–39
      appointment of Grant as general-in-chief, 3–9, 124
      cotton trade permits, 38–39
      first strategy conference, 8
      Red River campaign, 34, 38, 48, 85, 89
      White House reception, 5–7
   Hampton Roads and, 773–78, 780, 782, 784, 801, 839, 847–48, 854–57
   illness, 815, 816–17
   inaugural ceremonies (March '65), 809–17

Index

on legal action against Davis, 856
message to Congress (1864), 727-31, 748, 776
as national leader, 462-72
nomination of (1864), 377-80
Petersburg siege and, 428, 442-43, 445, 838-39, 845
   visit to Negro troops, 443
in Philadelphia, 442-43, 809-10
Proclamation of Thanksgiving and Prayer, 552
reaction to *Alabama* sinking, 390
Reconstruction policy, 957-65, 976
reelection of, 623, 624-26, 632, 727
removal of Butler from command, 739-40
request for son's army appointment, 816
review of Minnesota Sioux trial, 725
on slavery, 813
suspension of habeas corpus, 471
Ten Percent plan, 27
trade permits signed by, 38-39
on treatment of the conquered, 899, 906-7, 948, 975-76
use of patronage, 559
visit to City Point, 817, 857
visit to occupied Richmond, 893, 896-901
war strains on, 375
Lincoln, Mary Todd, 6, 12, 810, 816, 817, 839, 845-47, 893, 902-3, 906, 907, 974, 976-77, 978
   at Ford's Theatre, 978-80
   mental illness of, 845-47
   reaction to husband's assassination, 982, 984-85, 986
   visit to City Point, 817
Lincoln, Robert T., 816, 838, 857, 894, 974, 982, 985
Lincoln, Thomas T. "Tad," 814, 839, 896, 897, 899, 907, 957, 958, 959, 960, 961, 985
Lincoln, Willie, 845
Lisbon, Portugal, 1028
Little Big Horn, 723
Little Blue River, 580
Little Hattie (blockade runner), 717-18
Little Missouri River, 37, 51, 53, 62, 65, 67, 68
Little North Mountain, 556
Little Osage River, 584
Little River, 273
Little Rock, 27, 28, 31, 62-65, 66, 67, 71-73, 74, 76, 77, 576, 585, 647
Little Sante Fe, 583
Llewellyn, David, 386
Locke, David R. (Petroleum V. Nasby), 978
Locust Grove, 151

Logan, John A., 397, 603, 684-85, 723-24, 736
   Atlanta battle, 479, 482-85, 489, 490, 524-26, 527
   Carolinas march, 754, 796, 829
   in Columbia, 796
   electioneering stumping, 562, 642
   at Ezra Church, 490
   Grand Review parade, 1016
Logan Courthouse, 243
Loggy Bayou, 51, 52, 56
Lomax, Lunsford L., 228, 230, 556, 564, 571
London *Spectator*, 814-15
London *Times*, 388, 461
Longstreet, James, 117, 118, 119, 121, 122, 123, 136, 142, 143, 145, 235, 256, 271, 283-84, 311, 328, 349, 475, 565, 569, 570, 596, 691, 722, 762, 809, 862, 1051, 1056-57
   admiration for Lee, 170
   and Petersburg, 631, 840, 841, 875-77, 878, 881, 882, 884
      withdrawal, 908, 909, 911, 913, 915-17, 920, 921, 923, 924, 928-32, 939, 941-45, 952, 954, 955
   postwar views, 1056
   in the Wilderness, 153, 156, 157, 161, 164, 165, 166, 169, 192, 876
      battle tactics, 175
      designated objective, 150-51, 152-53, 154, 165
      second day (May 6th), 168, 170, 171, 173, 174, 175-76, 177, 178, 179
      wounded, 179-80, 182
Longstreet, Mrs. James, 809
Lookout Mountain, 101
Loring, W. W., 831
   Franklin battle, 666, 669-70
   and Kennesaw Mountain, 391, 393, 394, 397, 399
   Nashville battle, 692, 694, 695
Lost Mountain, 353, 355, 391, 611, 612
Louisa, 229, 309, 450
Louisiana:
   abolition convention, 91
   April Fool election, 91
   readmitted to the Union, 27
   Reconstruction, 960-61, 964, 1004
Louisiana (iron gunboat), 716-19
Louisville, 112, 319, 362, 685, 1022
Louisville (gunboat), 83
Louisville *Courier*, 682
Lovejoy Station, 487, 488, 520, 529, 530, 602, 604, 691
Lovell, Mansfield, 411
Lubbock, Francis R., 1004, 1010, 1012
Lumber River, 752-53, 819
Lumsden, Charles L., 692
Luray Valley, 555-56, 557
Lyman, Theodore, 237-38

Lynch, Bishop Patrick, 794
Lynchburg, 270, 302, 304, 306, 309, 311, 312, 447, 450, 461, 610, 722, 737, 807, 808, 849, 850, 895, 905, 912, 914, 922, 923, 926, 934
Lynch's Creek, 800, 818
Lynnville, 708
Lyon, Hylan B., 365, 366, 367, 368–69
Lyons, Lord Richard, 100

M

McArthur, John, 694, 695, 702
Macbeth (Shakespeare), 906
McCausland, John, 448–50, 453, 459
  assessment of Hagerstown merchants, 449, 539
  burning of Chambersburg, 539
McClellan, George B., 15, 17–18, 22, 36, 119, 123, 142–43, 172, 284, 290, 303, 305, 363, 448, 573, 636, 672, 684, 851, 874, 928
  death of, 1056
  departure from the war, 492
  European tour, 625
  of failure of offensive against Lee, 17–18
  presidential candidacy, 470, 551–52, 558, 562, 563, 624, 728, 749
    defeat, 625–26, 810
  in retirement, 538
  Richmond campaign, 123, 250, 275, 279, 295, 297, 311, 380, 430, 633, 770
McClellan, Henry, 166
McClernand, John A., 85, 736–37
McCook, Alexander, 458
McCook, Edward M., 486–88, 519
McCulloch, Ben, 579–80
McCulloch, Hugh, 815
McDonough Road, 476, 530, 640
McDowell, Irvin, 24, 123, 295
McGowan, Samuel, 168–69, 1048
Mackall, W. W., 341, 342, 343
Mackenzie, Ranald S., 869, 871, 873
McKinley, William, 1034
McLaws, Lafayette, 791, 827, 831, 832
McLean, Wilmer, 945, 950
McMillen, William L., 363, 364, 367–69, 370
Macon, 408, 422, 480, 487, 488, 603, 607–8, 643, 645, 646, 648, 652, 738, 757, 759, 781, 1008, 1011–12, 1057
Macon & Western Railroad, 486, 487, 488, 520, 521, 524, 530, 604, 642, 645
McPherson, James B., 16, 20, 684–85
  Atlanta battle, 473–78, 479–81, 484, 486, 491
  Chattahoochee crossing, 402–5, 409, 410
  Dalton to Resaca march, 321–23, 325, 326–27, 329
  death of, 481–82, 483, 484, 640
  and Kennesaw Mountain, 392, 394, 397, 401
  Kingston to Pine Top, via Dallas march, 346, 349, 350, 351, 353, 354, 357
  and Peachtree Creek, 473–75
  at Resaca, 331–33, 401
  Resaca to Cassville march, 335–40, 342
Maffitt, John N., 587, 1024
Magee's Farm, 999
Magic Flute (Mozart), 817
Magnolia (boat), 24
Magrath, Andrew G., 762, 765, 789
Magruder, John B., 36, 1023
Mahone, William, 176–78, 193, 218, 220, 537, 538
  Bermuda Hundred Line, 884, 885
  and Petersburg, 879, 882
    withdrawal, 908, 917, 919, 920, 922–24, 928, 929, 941
Major, James, 43, 44
Mallory, Stephen, 590–91, 605, 886, 888, 968, 1004–5, 1024
  pardoned, 1033
  resignation of, 1007
Malvern (flagship), 744, 893, 894, 896, 899, 901, 904
Malvern Hill, 233, 254, 279, 314, 316, 434
Manassas (railroad junction), 9, 328
Manassas Gap Railroad, 248
Manassas, First (Bull Run), 13–14, 52, 172, 176, 475, 530, 555, 741, 945, 975, 1027
Manassas, Second (Bull Run), 11, 24, 166, 176, 239, 247, 477, 530, 945
Maney, George E., 477, 478–79
Manhattan (ship), 497, 500, 1025
Manigault, Arthur M., 672
Mankato, hanging of Indians at, 725
Mansfield, 37, 39, 41, 42, 43–44, 51, 53, 56, 85, 86, 91, 104
Mansura, 86, 87, 90, 104
Marais des Cygnes River, 583
"Marching Through Georgia," 713
Marietta, 320, 344, 345, 346, 353, 355, 391, 392, 393, 396, 401, 409, 412, 414, 418, 519, 604, 611
  occupation of, 402, 411
Marks Mill, 72, 73, 76
Marmaduke, James S., 576, 577, 580–83
  Camden Expedition, 66, 67–68, 69, 72, 73, 74, 75, 78
  captured, 583–84
Marmiton River, 584
"Marseillaise," 905–6
Marshall, Charles, 942–43, 944, 945, 946, 948, 949, 950, 953–54, 955, 956
Marshall, John, 728, 953

Index

Marshall, Texas, 27, 1020
Martinsburg, 447, 448, 556
Marye's Heights, 1018
Maryland, election of 1864, 625
Mason, James M., 99, 589, 860-61
Massachusetts, election of 1864, 624
Massanutton Mountain, 248, 555-56, 557, 558, 563, 565, 566
Matagorda Bay, 26
Matamoros, Mexico, 765
Mattaponi River, 225, 238, 241, 266, 269, 276, 304
Mauk, John W., 879
Maury, Dabney, 509, 511, 575, 967, 990, 998
Maxey, Samuel B., 66, 67-68, 69, 72, 73
Maximilian, Emperor, 376-77, 771, 1019
  death of, 1023
Maxwell, John, 543-44
Mayo, Joseph, 890
Meade, George G., 9, 270, 300, 301, 303, 306, 469, 491, 572, 685, 737, 751, 773, 778, 785, 803, 845, 846, 852, 854, 869, 874, 894, 914, 926, 929, 935, 937, 943-44, 953, 967
  and Cold Harbor, 283, 285-86, 289, 293, 297-99, 352
  death of, 1056
  at Gettysburg, 9, 11
  Grand Review parade, 1013, 1015-16
  Grant's Plan (Spring '64) and, 9-11, 12, 16, 17, 18, 19, 20, 22, 24, 122, 123, 127, 128, 129, 133, 134, 135, 143, 144
  preliminary objective, 137-38
  and Petersburg, 428, 431, 432, 434-42, 445, 446, 450, 457, 539, 541, 542, 545, 548, 553, 634, 637, 639, 714
    Crater fiasco, 531-38
    June assault casualties, 633
  right-left strikes by, 560, 563
  and Sheridan's raid on Richmond, 224, 232
  Sherman's campaign and, 318, 320, 323, 340, 352, 408, 424
  Spotsylvania battle, 199, 201-2, 203, 204, 205-6, 207, 210, 219
  stalemate against Lee, 18, 123, 295
  triple-pronged offensive and, 237, 243
  in the Wilderness, 147, 148, 153, 157-58, 323, 424
    crossing of the Rapidan, 152
    Lacy meadow headquarters, 159, 160, 161, 163, 164, 175, 185, 186, 188
    race to Spotsylvania, 189-90
Meadow Bluff, 244, 246
Meadow Bridge, 233, 234, 281
Mechanicsville, 279, 280, 281, 287
Meherrin River, 637, 638, 784
Melbourne, Australia, 1029
Melville, Herman, 574
Memminger, Christopher G., 766

Memoirs (Grant), 1055-56
Memorial Day reunions, 1046-48
Memphis, 104, 105, 106, 107, 108, 111, 363-65, 367, 373, 510, 513, 515, 516, 518-19, 599, 1022, 1026, 1027, 1050-52
  Forrest's raid on, 510, 516-17, 518, 549, 596
Memphis & Charleston Railroad, 598
Mercer, Hugh W., 479
Meridian, 17, 30, 319, 509, 575, 596, 759, 999, 1000
Merrimac (ironclad), 493, 508, 589, 591
Merritt, Wesley, 199, 225, 230, 233, 282, 564, 807, 808
  and Cedar Creek, 570, 571, 572
Merry Wives of Windsor, The (Shakespeare), 979
Metacomet (vessel), 500, 501, 502
Metz, Battle of, 87
Mexican War, 9, 53, 64, 160, 347, 381, 478, 775, 834, 1053
Mexico, 15, 26, 389, 771, 1000, 1003, 1019, 1022-23, 1032
Mexico City, 376-77, 1023
Miami (steamer), 114-15
Middletown, 568, 570, 571
Miles, Nelson A., 1034, 1035, 1037, 1049
Milford Station, 238, 241
Mill Creek, 569
Mill Creek Gap, 320, 321, 325
Milledgeville, 93, 94, 615, 643, 645-47, 648, 753, 759, 781, 1008
Millen, 615, 645, 647, 648, 649
Mine Run, 133, 134, 135, 142, 143, 151
Minnesota, Sioux uprising in, 725
Missionary Ridge, 16, 101, 103, 119, 136, 328, 349, 395, 399, 422, 691, 702, 706, 710, 754
Mississippi Central Railroad, 514
Mississippi River, 14, 15, 16, 29, 33, 105, 320, 493, 583, 759, 765, 1002, 1003, 1021
  last armed clash east of, 1009
Mississippi Sound, 494, 495, 497
Mississippi & Tennessee Railroad, 515
Missouri (ironclad), 1027
Missouri River, 576, 583, 586
Mitchell, Margaret, 979
Mobile, 17, 102, 126, 326, 345, 374, 408, 415, 480, 486, 511, 514, 575, 603, 604, 624, 716, 738, 755, 758, 759, 764, 765, 904, 998, 1018, 1021, 1052
  abandonment of, 967
  expulsion of British consul from, 99
  Red River campaign and, 25, 26, 32, 46, 55, 60-61, 90, 92
  warehouse explosion, 1027
Mobile Bay, 492-508, 509, 848
  casualties, 500, 502, 506
  prisoners-of-war, 507

Mobile & Ohio Railroad, 364, 365, 366, 511, 999
Monadnock (monitor), 1028
Monett's Ferry, 54, 57, 58
Monitor (ironclad), 493, 508, 591
Monk's Neck Bridge, 862
Monocacy Junction, 451, 542
Monocacy River, 448-50, 451, 452, 453, 457, 461, 558
Monongahela (sloop), 498, 502, 504
Monroe, James, 906
Monroe Doctrine, 376-77, 771, 1018-19
Montgomery, 326, 408, 486, 607, 608, 758, 759, 905, 967, 1038, 1050, 1056
Montgomery Hill, 688, 691, 693, 695, 698
Moreauville, 86, 87
Morgan, Daniel, 827
Morgan, Edwin D., 462
Morgan, James D., 830, 831, 832
Morgan, John H., 105, 113, 245-46, 247, 319, 412, 414-15, 471, 880
 death of, 595-96, 721
 East Tennessee raid, 595-96
 Kentucky raid, 358-62, 373, 374, 380, 593
Morgan, Mattie Ready, 596
Morgan (gunboat), 494, 502
Morris, Charles M., 587-88, 589
Morton, John W., 365, 366, 367, 369-70
 at Johnsonville, 619-20
 in Middle Tennessee, 598, 599, 601
 in North Mississippi, 514, 515
Morton, Oliver P., 549
Mosby, John S., 805-6, 1000
Mott, Gershom, 161-62, 177
 Spotsylvania battle, 209, 210, 212, 213
Moulton, Alfred, 42, 44, 49
Mound City (gunboat), 83
Mount Jackson, 248, 250
Mount Pleasant, 654, 655, 663
Mount Sterling, 361, 362
 Confederate looting of, 358-59
Mount Vernon, 906
Mower, Joseph A., 834, 835
Mozart, Wolfgang Amadeus, 817
Munford, Thomas T., 870
Murdoch, James E., 574
Murfreesboro, *see* Stones River
Murrah, Pendleton, 1023
Muscle Shoals, 708, 709
Myers, Gustavus A., 901

N

Nancy's Creek, 409-10
Napoleon I, 29, 157, 608, 610, 675, 679, 780, 1019

Napoleon III, 15, 25, 99, 860, 1019, 1023, 1050
 occupation of Mexico, 376-77
Nasby, Petroleum V., *see* Locke, D. R.
Nashville, 7, 13, 21, 31, 64, 92, 102, 108, 112, 117, 357, 365, 395, 522, 598, 600, 607, 614, 616, 617, 619, 621, 636, 647, 654-60, 662, 666, 672, 673, 750, 1018, 1041
Nashville, battle for, 674-710, 737, 738
 casualties, 678, 695, 700, 705, 706, 708
 city fortifications, 676
 first day, 688-95
 Murfreesboro strike, 677-78, 679, 681
 prisoners-of-war, 704-5, 709
 second day, 698-705
 withdrawal of Confederate army, 705-10, 757
Nashville & Chattanooga Railroad, 519, 599, 601, 677
Nashville Military Institute, 704
Nashville & Northwestern Railroad, 601
Nassau, 717, 1028
Nassau bacon, 629
Nat Turner uprising, 973
Natchez, 735
Natchitoches, 32, 34, 35, 38, 39, 40, 54, 56-57, 68, 85, 91, 92, 575
 burning of, 57
National Union party, 378
Naval operations, 14, 17, 30, 100, 109, 110, 309, 315, 317, 587-95, 614, 709
 at Bermuda Hundred, 251-54, 257-58
 blockade runners, 493, 507, 591, 614, 717, 737, 741, 754
 off Brazil, 587-90
 Butler-Porter expedition (to Wilmington), 715-21
  casualties, 715
  failure of, 721
 off Carolina coast, 113-17, 591-95
 off Cherbourg harbor, 380-90, 442, 587
 defense of Washington, 457
 on the high seas, 590-91, 1028-31
 James River Squadron, 765, 886, 888-89, 1024
 last shot of the Civil War, 1029
 late-April through November (1865), 1023-31
 in Mobile Bay, 492-508
 off New England coast, 508-9, 1010, 1024
 North Atlantic Blockading Squadron, 589
 Red River campaign, 26, 28, 30, 32-33, 38-39, 51, 52-56, 59-60, 61, 68, 73, 85, 88, 104
  casualties, 88-89
  cotton seizure policy, 38-39
  divergence from land forces, 39-40

Index [1093]

salvation of the flotilla, 77-84, 85
in the South Pacific, 1029
Sultana disaster, 1026-27
Tennessee River (north of Johnsonville), 619
use of torpedoes, 254, 634-35
White River gunboat probe, 574-75
See also names of ships
Nebraska, 747
Negroes, 38, 57, 60, 305-6, 314, 371, 510, 523, 534, 615, 645, 690, 700, 741, 813, 894, 897, 960, 961, 1043
    camp followers, 1016-17
    citizenship, 1043
    Confederate enlistment of, 859-61
    Davis on, 97
    first to practice before Supreme Court, 749
    first U.S. senator, 1044
    at Fort Pillow, 108, 111, 112, 538
    oath of vengeance, 364
    Reconstruction era, 1044, 1045
    as refugees (Sherman's march to the sea), 649-50
    segregation, 1044, 1045
    Sherman on, 533
    total number of soldiers (North and South), 756
    See also Slavery
Nelson, William "Bull," 527
Nelson, Lord Horatio, 608
Nelson, Samuel, 767
Neosho (monitor), 81, 82
Neuse River, 752-53, 820, 821, 823, 824, 826, 834, 836
Nevada, admitted to the Union, 625
New Bern, 116, 256, 257, 258, 508, 737, 751, 796, 820, 834
New Castle, 281, 282
New Hope Church, 347-50, 352, 354, 380, 400, 412, 418, 612
New Jersey, election of 1864, 624, 625
New Market, 247, 248, 250, 264, 302, 304, 447, 556, 557, 572
New Mexico campaign of 1862, 53, 89, 725
New Orleans, 14, 17, 102, 260, 411, 415, 450, 493, 503, 511, 716, 738, 899, 1024, 1036, 1052
    occupation of, 19
    Red River campaign and, 29, 32, 34, 38, 39, 47, 48, 52, 55, 91
    yellow fever epidemic (1878), 1053
New River, 243, 244, 245, 246
New York City:
    Confederate terrorist activities in, 725
    draft riots, 89, 548
    election of 1864, 625
New York *Evening Post*, 471
New York *Herald*, 186, 787, 788, 1013
New York Stock Market, 341, 462

New York Times, The, 378, 549, 718
New York *Tribune*, 32, 465, 469, 558, 1036
New York World, 376, 379, 461
Newton, John, 398
Newtonia, 584-85
Ni River, 204, 206, 225, 239, 240, 265
Nickajack Creek, 402, 403
Nicolay, John G., 7, 8, 378, 728, 729, 730, 973
Nitre and Mining Corps, 761
Noonday Creek, 355
Norfolk, 589, 716, 720, 1024
Norfolk & Petersburg Railroad, 432, 436
North Anna River, 150, 151, 152, 158, 225, 227, 241, 265-76, 277, 283, 285, 288, 290, 307, 309, 316, 375
    casualties, 267-68, 276
    Chesterfield Bridgehead assault, 268, 269-70
    departure from Spotsylvania to, 265-71
    Lee's inverted V strategy, 272-73, 274, 275
North Atlantic Blockading Squadron, 589
Northrop, Lucius B., 761, 783, 911
Nottoway Courthouse, 914
Nottoway River, 254, 258, 870
Nova Scotia, 509, 590
Noyes Creek, 392

O

Ocmulgee River, 487, 488, 1008
Oconee River, 643, 646, 647, 1008
O'Conor, Charles, 1035-36, 1037, 1038, 1039
Ogeechee River, 648, 649, 651, 652, 711, 713, 730
Oglesby, Richard J., 978, 982
Ohio, October elections (1864), 562
Ohio River, 105, 112, 360, 374
Okolona, 67, 104, 105, 112, 365, 510, 511, 513
Olley's Creek, 393
Olustee, 104, 105, 181, 291
Oneida (sloop), 495, 501, 502-3
Oostanaula River, 320, 321, 323, 325, 326, 329, 330, 332, 333-35, 336, 363, 613
Opdycke, Emerson, 665, 667, 669, 670, 673
Opequon Creek (Third Winchester), 553-55
Orange & Alexandria Railroad, 23, 122, 133, 302, 722, 803, 808, 850, 851
Orange Plank Road, 148, 150, 151, 192
Orange Turnpike, 147, 148, 150, 151
Ord, Edward O. C., 740, 809, 846, 847, 852, 854, 1018
    Five Forks battle, 864, 866

INDEX

Ord, Edward O. C. (*Cont.*)
  Fort Gilmer strike, 560–61
  named commander of Army of the James, 740
  and Petersburg, 541, 878, 882
  pursuit of Lee's army, 916, 921, 926, 927, 936, 940, 941, 943, 948, 967
  race for Burkeville, 914
Ord, Mrs. Edward O. C., 846–47
Osage (monitor), 81, 82
Osage Indians, 1022
Osage River, 578, 583
Ossabaw Sound, 651, 652, 654
Ossipee (sloop), 495, 498, 502
Osterhaus, Peter J., 642, 646, 647, 1021
Ouachita River, 62, 64, 65, 66, 71, 73, 76
Ould, Robert, 467
Our American Cousin, 977, 979–80
Overton Hill, 698, 699–700, 701, 703, 704, 705
Ox Ford, 266, 267, 268, 270, 271, 272, 273
Oxford, 514, 515
  burning of, 518
Ozark (monitor), 83

P

Pacific Railroad, 578, 579
Paducah, 107, 108, 329
Page, Richard L., 506–7
Page, Thomas J., 1028–29
Paine, Lewis, 1032
Palmer, John M., 350, 398, 403, 527
Palmerston, Lord Henry J. T., 861
Palmetto, 604–6, 616
Palmito Ranch, 1019–20
Pamlico Sound, 116, 258, 820
Pamunkey River, 234, 276, 277, 278, 279, 281, 304, 307, 309, 851
Panic of 1873, 1044, 1050
Panola, 515, 517, 518
Parke, John G., 543, 845, 926
  Boydton Plank Road mission, 561
  Five Forks battle, 864, 866
  Hatcher's Run battle, 785
  and Petersburg, 541, 878, 881
  race for Burkeville, 914
Parker's Store, 148, 151, 154, 156, 158, 162, 165, 168, 192, 199
Parsons, Mosby M., 75–76
Partisan Rangers, 805–6
Pass Cavallo, 85
Patapsco (ship), 751
Patrick Henry (training vessel), 886
Pea Ridge, 247, 579, 581, 585, 747
Peace Democrats, 551

Peace feelers, 465–69
  Blair's attempt at, 770–73
  Confederacy's efforts, Davis and, 96–97
  Stephens' proposal for, 768
  See also Hampton Roads Conference
Peachtree Creek, 406, 407, 408, 419, 422, 423, 472–75, 489
  casualties, 475, 496
  Confederate withdrawal from, 476–77
Peck, John J., 116
Pee Dee River, 752–53, 800, 818
Peebles Farm, 561, 610
Pegram, John, 156, 218
  and Cedar Creek, 567, 571
  death of, 785–86
  and Petersburg, 637, 639
  Wilderness battle, 156, 187, 567
Pemberton, John C., 12, 101, 967
Pendleton, George H., 552, 562, 748
Pendleton, William N., 192, 193–94
  and Petersburg, 878, 884, 908, 931–32, 933, 934, 939
Pennsylvania:
  draft riots, 548
  election of 1864, 625
  October elections (1864), 562
Pensacola, 493, 497, 648, 848
Perry, H. Henry, 928, 929, 956
Perryville, 98, 832
Petersburg, 19, 121, 127, 252, 255, 256, 258–60, 263, 300, 301, 305–6, 314, 315, 462, 606, 737, 751, 800, 822, 838–39, 786, 840, 913, 926
  evacuated, 894, 959
  Fort Stedman assault, 840–44, 845, 862
  Richmond rail connections, 152, 252–53, 441–42, 722
  siege of 1864 (June), 427–46, 491, 716–17, 743
    casualties, 441, 443, 444–45, 633
    Dimmock Line, 430, 433, 436
    Howlett Line, 433, 434, 437, 438, 439
    Lincoln's visit to, 443, 445
    Negro troops at, 428–29, 431, 443
    and rail connection to Richmond, 441–42
    relieving pressure on (Early's northward march), 446–61
    southside convergence, 427–30
  siege of 1864 (July–August), 530–49
    casualties, 538–39
    Crater fiasco, 531–38, 539, 541, 544, 545, 628, 717, 773, 840, 843
  siege of 1864–65 (Fall to April), 627–40, 653
    Bermuda Hundred line, 884, 885
    casualties, 630, 883, 886, 893

Index [1095]

Confederate army shortages, 629–30
confidence of Lee, 630–32
control for Fort Gregg, 882–83, 893
morale, 756
railroad wrecking, 637–38
See also Richmond, abandonment of
Petersburg & Weldon Railroad, 254, 441–42, 444, 531, 545–46, 548, 561, 637, 763, 784
Phelps, S. Ledyard, 59
Philadelphia, 624
Philadelphia *Inquirer*, 298–99, 303
Ph 'lips, P. J., 646
Pickett, George E., 173, 174, 175, 266, 547
   and Bermuda Hundred, 256–58, 259, 265, 879
   and Cold Harbor, 283, 285, 286
   convalescence of, 153
   Dinwiddie, Five Forks battle, 862–63, 864, 867, 868–71
   Foft Stedman assault, 841–42
   and Petersburg, 435, 437, 875, 884, 885
   withdrawal, 908, 918, 930
   relieved of duty, 930
Pickett's Charge, 592, 669
Pickett's Mill, 349, 354, 380, 400
Piedmont, 301–2, 304, 312, 445, 453
Pierce, Franklin, 1037
Pilot Knob, 576, 579
Pine Bluff, 65, 66, 71, 72, 74
Pine Mountain, 353, 355
Pine Top, 355–57, 390, 391
Pittsburg (gunboat), 83
Pleasant Hill, 39, 41, 46–50, 62, 68, 70, 75, 104
   casualties, 50
Pleasants, Henry, 531–33, 535, 536
Pleasonton, Alfred, 579–85, 723
Plymouth, 113–14, 115, 116, 139, 258, 497, 508, 591–95
Po River, 193, 196, 199, 205, 206, 207, 209, 212, 218, 225, 235, 236, 265
Poague, William, 169, 171, 172
Pocahontas, Arkansas, 576
Pocket veto, use of, 465
Pocotaligo, 653, 753, 754, 791
Pocotaligo River, 788
Point Lookout, 457, 459
   Confederate prisoners at, 449
Point of Rocks, 255, 453
Poison Spring, 69–70, 71, 72, 104
Pole Green Church, 288
Polecat Creek, 266
Polignac, Camille Armand Jules Marie, Prince de, 44, 48–49, 50, 53, 57
Polk, Leonidas, 17, 92, 112, 117, 133, 365, 415, 418, 663, 1059

in Alabama, 320, 321, 322, 326
arrival in Georgia, 327–30
baptism of Hood, 329–30
baptism of Johnston, 339–40
Dalton conference, 329
death of, 356–57, 390, 391
and Kingston, Pine Top and Dallas, 347, 349, 353, 355–57, 390
and Resaca and Cassville, 332–34, 338–43
Pollard, Edward A., 95–96, 779, 781, 783
Pontotoc, 366, 510–11
Pool, David, 579
Poor Robin Bluff, 1008
Pope, John, 11, 123, 188, 205, 239, 295, 310, 311, 363, 538
   defeats of, 20–21
   failure of offensive against Lee, 17–18
   Grant's Plan (Spring '64) and, 11, 17–18, 20, 24, 122, 123, 143
   in Minnesota, 563, 725
   in Missouri, 1020, 1021
Port Hudson, 38, 52, 78, 82, 90, 458, 495, 503, 690
   surrender of, 25, 26
Port Royal, 269, 741, 1012
Port Royal Sound, 753, 788
Port Walthall, 252, 253, 254, 305
Port Walthall Junction, 253, 255, 257, 260, 262, 435
Porter, David D., 492, 589–90, 595, 634–35
   Fort Fisher (Wilmington) expedition, 715–21, 737, 740, 741–47, 751
   Red River campaign, 28, 30, 32–33, 40, 48, 51, 53, 55–56, 59, 61, 68, 73, 77–84, 104
   cotton seizures, 38–39
   salvation of the flotilla, 77–84, 85
   River Queen conference, 854–57
Porter, Fitz-John, 287, 666, 874
Porter, Horace, 290, 303, 313, 633, 874–75, 893, 894, 896–99, 902
Posey, Carnot, 220
Potomac River, 9, 214, 224, 303, 305, 443, 445, 462, 544, 545, 572, 750, 804, 906, 958, 997, 1012
Potter, Robert B., 531, 534
Pound Gap, 358, 359
Powder Springs, 611
Powhite Creek, 281, 282, 287
Prairie d'Ane, 68, 104
Prairie Grove, 1022
Prentice, George D., 682
Prentiss, Benjamin, 736–37
Preston, John S., 760
Preston, Sally Buchanan, 760, 1021
Preston, Willie, 760
Prestonburg, 359

INDEX

Price, Sterling, 36, 51, 91, 723, 747, 1023
   and Camden Expedition, 65–68, 69, 70, 71, 73, 75, 104
   Missouri raids, 574–86, 739, 1019, 1022
      casualties, 577, 585
      purpose of, 576
      results of, 586
Prince Edward Courthouse, 926
Prince George Courthouse, 431, 432, 434
Princeton, 74, 75, 576
Prisoners-of-war, exchanging, 131
Proclamation of Amnesty and Reconstruction, 464, 468, 1031–32
Pulaski, 598, 599, 600, 654–56, 663, 677, 707, 708, 709

Q

Quantrill, William C., 579, 1022
Quarles, William, 670
Quintard, Charles, 657

R

Radical Reconstruction, 464–65, 1043–44
Radicals, 10, 378, 470, 963
   Cleveland Convention, 377
   party plank, 378
Raleigh, 95, 717, 737, 751, 820–22, 823, 824–26, 832, 856, 965–67, 989, 993, 995, 1013
   occupation of, 967, 988
Ramseur, S. Dodson, 567, 637, 640
   death of, 571
   and Early's northward march, 447, 450, 452
   Winchester battle, 554–55
Ransom, Robert, 433, 436
   and Bermuda Hundred, 256, 259, 260, 262
   "buttermilk rangers" command, 447
Rapidan River, 9, 12, 18, 19, 23, 24, 105, 116, 120, 121, 123, 130, 134, 135, 137, 142, 143–44, 145, 146–50, 151, 165, 185, 190, 191, 240, 285, 297, 300, 323, 439, 444, 722, 852
Rapidan Station, 133
Rappahannock, 23, 120, 124, 130, 131, 133, 134, 143, 150, 190, 214, 269, 272, 293, 997
Rappahannock Station, 147
Rathbone, Henry R., 978–79, 980, 981
Rawlins, John A., 7, 12, 185–86, 294, 299, 541, 936–37, 938, 939, 945, 991
Raymond, Henry J., 278, 549–50
Read, Charles W., 1023–26, 1027

Read, Thomas Buchanan, 574
Reagan, John H., 293, 888, 968, 992, 1004, 1007, 1010
   captured, 1010, 1012
   pardoned, 1032
Reams Station, 444, 547
Rebel yell, the, 1046
Reconstruction, 97, 961, 976, 1043–44, 1045, 1050, 1056
   end of, 1044, 1045, 1054
   Johnson's policy, 1043
   Lincoln's policy, 957–65, 1043
   Radical, 464–65, 1043–44
Rectortown, 805
Red Clay, 323, 324
Red Oak, 521–22, 523
Red River, 15, 17, 575, 586, 1021
Red River campaign, 25–77, 98, 126, 264, 320, 340, 374, 376, 450, 790, 848
   beginning of, 25–61
   Camden Expedition, 61–77, 104
   casualties, 30, 45, 46, 48, 50, 58, 69–70, 72, 74, 75, 76, 80, 88–89, 91
   cotton speculators, 27–28, 32, 38–39, 47, 62, 72
   Federal withdrawal to Alexandria, 56–61, 62, 64, 73, 76
   "gorilla" operations, 34, 35, 40, 42, 51, 52, 56, 57, 62, 84, 92
   naval operations, 26, 28, 30, 32–33, 38–39, 51, 52–56, 59–60, 61, 68, 73, 85, 88, 104
      salvation of the flotilla, 77–84, 85
   at Pleasant Hill, 39, 41, 46–50, 62, 68, 70, 75, 104
   results of, 90–92
   at Sabine Crossroads, 42–46, 48, 49, 51, 52, 68, 70, 85
Reese, Harry, 535
Reid, Whitelaw, 471
Republican National Executive Committee, 549
Resaca, 320, 331, 332–34, 338, 401, 418, 519, 613, 616, 665
Resaca to Cassville march, 331–45
   casualties, 337
Revels, Hiram R., 1044
Revolution of 1848, 248
Reynolds, Joseph J., 691
Rhind, Alexander C., 718
Rice, 915–16, 917, 918, 926
Richard's Shop, 151, 152, 166
Richland Creek, 599, 691, 693, 708
Richmond, 55, 92–103, 147, 204, 206, 293, 300, 414, 466–68, 519, 623–24, 764, 838, 955, 1006, 1038
   abandonment of, 857–64, 885–93, 894, 957, 959
   Lee on, 844, 858, 862, 864
   communication between Transmissis-

Index [1097]

sippi and, 104
foreign consuls in, 99
mob pillaging of, 887, 889, 890
occupation of, 893-907
prisoners-of-war in, 105
rail connections with Petersburg, 152, 252-53, 441-42, 722
Sheridan's raid on (May '64), 224-35, 259, 260, 270, 309
See also Virginia campaign
Richmond (sloop), 498, 502, 1026
Richmond & Danville Railroad, 261, 312, 444, 548, 804, 852, 856, 862, 864, 875, 883, 886, 909, 911, 912, 913
Richmond *Dispatch*, 736
Richmond *Enquirer*, 778, 779, 782, 1039
Richmond *Examiner*, 95, 472, 552-53, 736, 768
Richmond, Fredericksburg & Potomac Railroad, 191, 229, 238, 266, 267, 275
Richmond *Whig*, 472, 889, 962
Ricketts, James B., 164, 181, 450-52, 454
Riddell's Shop, 313, 315, 316, 435
Rienzi, 364, 365, 367, 369, 570, 574, 872, 873
Ringgold, 321, 323, 325
Ringgold Gap, 349, 706
Rio Grande, 26, 990, 992, 995, 1019-20, 1022, 1023
Ripley, 363, 364, 365-66, 372, 510
Rise and Fall of the Confederate Government (Davis), 1054-55
River Queen (steamer), 775, 778, 779, 783, 801, 815, 817, 838, 847-48, 854-57, 903, 905-6
Rives, William C., 766-67
Roanoke Island, 116
Roanoke River, 113, 257, 800, 802, 844, 890, 891, 908, 912
Robinson, John C., 199-201, 209
Rock, John S., 749
Rocketts Landing, 888, 889, 893, 896, 899, 901
Rockfish Gap, 309, 312, 722, 807, 808, 850
Rockville, 453, 455, 459, 460, 461
Rocky Face Ridge, 320-21, 323, 324, 325, 327, 328, 330, 331, 344
Rodes, Robert E., 567, 640
death of, 555, 556, 639
and Early's northward march, 447, 450, 454, 459
Spotsylvania battle, 217, 219, 220
in the Wilderness, 154-55
Rolla, 577, 579
Rome, 320, 326, 328, 329, 335, 338, 352, 611, 613, 622
Roosevelt, Theodore, 1042
Rosecrans, William S., 349, 576, 613, 636, 658-59, 672, 684, 736-37, 795
Grant's Plan (Spring '64) and, 16, 124

as Missouri Department commander, 576, 577-78, 579, 581, 584, 599, 724
Rosser, Thomas L., 194, 196, 197, 638, 722, 762, 807, 808, 924
Beverly raid, 763
and Cedar Creek, 567, 571
Dinwiddie, Five Forks battle, 863, 870
and Fisher's Hill, 564
Rough & Ready Station, 521, 523, 524, 525, 526, 527, 602
Rosseau, Lovell H., 486, 599
at Murfreesboro, 677-78
Roswell, 404-6, 409
Rottenwood Creek, 402
Rowanty Creek, 862
Rucker, Edmund W., 365, 366, 367, 368-69, 705
Ruffin, Edmund, 971
Ruger, Thomas H., 664, 669
Russell, David A., 208
Russell, Lord John, 100-1
Russia, 98
Russia (steamer), 838, 854
Rutherford Creek, 657, 658, 659, 660, 664, 707, 708

S

Sabine Crossroads, 42-46, 48, 49, 51, 52, 68, 70, 85, 320
casualties, 45, 46, 48
Sabine River, 26, 36, 1007
St Albans raid (Vermont), 586-87, 590, 725
Saint Helena, island of, 1019
St James Church (Richmond), 235
St. John, Isaac M., 761, 783, 910, 911, 912, 915, 922
St. John Church (Richmond), 233
Saint Johns River, 104
St. Lawrence Island, 1029-30
St. Louis, 62, 77, 91, 575-76, 584
St. Louis *Republican*, 31, 90
St. Marks River, 1027
Saint Paul's Church (Richmond), 101, 786, 885-86
Salem, Mississippi, 364, 372
Salem, Virginia, 244, 245
Saline River, 62, 65, 66, 71-73, 74, 75-76, 92, 124
Salisbury, 798, 967, 969
Confederate government headquarters at 991, 1003
Salkehatchie River, 752-53, 787, 788, 789, 791
Sallacoa, 337
Salomon, Frederich S., 69, 72-73
Saltville, 243, 245, 246, 358, 721

[1098] INDEX

San Antonio, 27, 1022, 1023
Sand Creek Massacre, 725-27
Sand Island, 497
Sandersville, 647, 1008, 1010
Sandtown, 522, 523
Sandusky Bay, 182
Sandy Hook, 508, 509
Sangamon County, 625
Sangamon River, 978
Santa Cruz de Tenerife (coaling station), 587
Santee Sioux Indians, 725
Sarah Boyce (schooner), 508
Savannah, 102, 408, 486, 613-14, 615, 623, 624, 645, 646, 648, 684, 730, 752, 753, 764, 826, 836
    evacuation of, 711-12, 730
    expulsion of British consul from, 99
    occupation of, 711-15, 722, 735-36, 757
    railroad link with Charleston, 652-53
Savannah River, 648, 713, 752-53, 754, 787, 788, 1007
Sayler's Creek, 916, 917-20, 921, 923, 924, 925, 926, 930
Schofield, John M., 17, 414, 423, 621
    Atlanta battle, 473, 474, 476, 479, 480, 482-86, 488, 489, 491, 520-22, 525-30
    Chattahoochee crossing, 402, 404, 405, 406, 408-9, 410
    Dalton to Resaca march, 321-25
    drive to Wilmington, 737-38, 750, 751, 773, 786, 790, 796, 797, 798, 800, 801, 802
    and the "Hell Hole," 348-49
    Hood's march north and, 654-55, 657-59, 661, 675
        escape from the trap, 655-62, 672-73
        Franklin battle, 663-65, 669, 672-73, 677
        Nashville battle, 681, 683, 684, 686, 687, 691, 693-99, 701-2, 705, 709
        race to the Duck River, 655-56
        Thompson's Station clash, 659, 661
    at Kennesaw Mountain, 392-94, 396, 399, 401
    Kingston to Pine Top, via Dallas march, 346-52, 353, 357
    in Knoxville, 603
    and Peachtree Creek, 473, 474
    Resaca to Cassville March, 331-39, 341
    link-up with Sherman (at Goldsboro), 817-18, 819, 820, 821, 824, 829, 833, 834, 836-38, 841, 852
Scott, Sir Walter, 1005
Scott, Dred, 728, 749
Scott, Thomas M., 670
Scott, Winfield, 15
Sea of Japan, 591
Sea King, see *Shenandoah*

Sea of Okhotsk, 1029
Sears, Claudius W., 692, 694, 695
Second Empire (France), 905
Sedalia, 580
Seddon, James A., 118, 119, 167, 294, 358, 548, 632, 680, 754, 757, 758, 761, 766, 783
Sedgwick, John, 147, 312, 874
    death of, 203, 207, 235
    Spotsylvania battle, 197, 198, 201, 202, 203, 206, 207
    in the Wilderness, 147, 148, 159-60, 161, 164
        race to Spotsylvania, 189, 190-91
        second day (May 6th), 167, 173, 175, 181, 182, 184-85
Seldon, George B., 1045
Selma, 104, 105, 326, 494, 603, 607, 645, 738, 759, 849, 850, 967, 998, 1000
Selma (gunboat), 494, 502, 506
Seminole Indians, 1022
Seminole War, 478
Semmes, Raphael, 380-90, 588, 765, 886, 888-89
    created a brigadier, 891
    in Danville, 891, 892-93
    death of, 1052
    pardoned, 1033
    promoted to rear admiral, 389, 765
Seven Days, 233, 279, 293, 301, 311, 316, 672, 705, 822, 840, 934
Seven Pines, 284, 828, 832, 917
Seward, Frederick W., 976
Seward, William H., 6, 100, 457-58, 590, 728, 767, 771, 774-78, 783, 812, 814, 900, 902, 907, 983, 988, 989, 997, 1019, 1032
Seymour, Horatio, 551-52
Seymour, Truman, 181, 182
Shady Grove, 194, 199, 205
Shady Grove Church, 148, 152, 158, 192, 197, 284
Shakespeare, William, 906
Shaler, Alexander, 182
Sharpsburg, 22, 98, 244, 448, 975
Shawneen (gunboat), 254
Shelby, J. O., 66, 71, 72
    in Mexico, 1022-23, 1032
    Missouri raids, 576, 577, 580-85
Shelbyville, 707
Shenandoah (cruiser), 1033
    commissioned, 590
    on the High Seas, 590-91
    nonstop run to England, 1030-31
    whaling raids by, 1029-31
Shenandoah River, 248, 556, 805
Shenandoah Valley, 18-19, 24, 34, 121, 126, 152, 181, 204, 225, 242, 243, 246, 247, 250, 260, 270, 275, 301, 302, 305, 309, 316, 427, 445, 453, 539, 629, 632, 737
    Sheridan in, 553-58, 563-73, 574, 763, 803-4, 1023

Index [1099]

Shepley, George F., 899
Sheridan, Michael V., 950
Sheridan, Philip H., 135-36, 236, 238, 423, 450, 451, 455, 533, 542-58, 563-74, 575, 579, 737, 1018, 1034
  City Point meeting with Grant, 853
  and Cold Harbor, 281, 282, 283, 284, 285, 287
  and Dinwiddie, Five Forks, 862, 864-65, 866, 868-75, 893
  Grant's Close-Out Plan and, 737, 803-9, 850-54
  Grant's Jamesward strategy and, 302, 303, 304, 305, 306-8, 312, 316
  Haw's Shop battle, 276, 277-78
  Indian policy, 727
  march to Totopotomoy, 276, 277-78
  Mosby's guerrilla tactics and, 805-6
  and Petersburg, 427, 436, 442, 446, 533, 542-53, 880
  promoted, 555
  pursuit of Lee's army, 916, 918-19, 920, 923, 936, 938-41, 943, 945, 948
  race for Burkeville, 903-4, 911, 913-15
  Richmond raid, 224-35, 259, 260, 270, 309
  Shenandoah Valley operations, 553-58, 563-73, 574, 763, 803-4, 1023
    and Cedar Creek, 566-72, 804
    at Fisher's Hill, 555-58, 559
    at Winchester, 553-55, 556, 804
  Spotsylvania battle, 198-99, 201, 202, 204, 214
  Transmississippi operations, 1018, 1023
  two-pronged strike (December '64), 722-23
  Waynesboro victory, 807-8, 809, 839, 841, 850
"Sheridan's Ride" (Read), 569, 574
Sherman, John, 21, 650
Sherman, William T., 16-17, 456, 469, 471, 573, 576, 633, 635, 894, 895, 901, 913, 1034, 1041, 1042
  advance from Goldsboro, 965
  City Point meeting with Lincoln, 991
  death of, 996
  Georgia campaign and, 318-424, 558, 599, 601, 697, 743, 838, 860, 940
    battle for Atlanta, 475-92, 513, 519-30, 549, 552, 730
    Confederate raiders, 358-62, 362-74
    crossing the Chattahoochee, 402-10
    Dalton to Resaca, 318-30, 363
    Forrest's Middle Tennessee raids, 596-601
    Hood (October-November), 611-23
    at Kennesaw Mountain, 391-402, 442
    Kingston to Pine Top via Dallas, 345-57
    march to the sea, 640-54
    occupation of Atlanta, 601-11
    Peachtree crossing, 472-75
    renomination of Lincoln, 377-80
    Resaca to Cassville, 331-45
    and Smith (A. J.) in North Mississippi, 509-19
  Grand Review parade, 1014, 1015-17
  Grant's Plan (Spring '64) and, 10, 11, 12, 13, 14, 15, 16, 17, 20, 21, 126, 128, 133, 137
    Cincinnati meeting, 13, 21, 133, 837
    destruction of Meridian, 104-5
    Nashville meeting, 13, 16, 29, 31
    Transmississippi region, 28, 29, 30, 31-32, 46, 47, 53, 55, 79, 84, 88, 91, 92, 104-5
  march to the Carolinas (from Savannah to Goldsboro), 736, 750-54, 756, 757, 786, 787-801, 825-38, 848, 851, 858, 1029
    beginning of, 753-54, 759
    burnings and vandalism, 787-88, 790, 802, 818, 838
    casualties, 833-34
    at Columbia, 792-96, 802, 818, 838
    crossing of the Neuse, 828-29, 836
    in Fayetteville, 819-21, 824, 825, 826
    link-up with Schofield, 817-18, 819, 820, 821, 824, 829, 833, 834, 836-38, 841, 852
    astride Lynch's Creek, 800, 818
    in North Carolina, 818-38
    offer from Wheeler, 789-90
    parade in Goldsboro, 836-37
    plan for, 736, 751-52, 826
    proposal to Johnston for restoring peace, 988-96, 998
    railroad crews, 753
    through the Salk swamps, 788-89
  march to the sea, 622-23, 640-54, 655, 674, 679, 681, 684, 723-24, 730, 747, 754
    casualties, 646-47, 652, 653, 713
    fall of Fort McAllister, 651-52, 679, 711, 715, 730
    foraging operations, 641, 642, 643-44, 645, 647
    Grant and, 613-14, 623, 635-36, 641, 649, 650, 713, 714, 715, 721, 730
    Honey Hill attack, 653
    Milledgeville layover, 647
    Millen layover, 648
    Negro refugees and, 649-50

Sherman, William T. (*Cont.*)
proposal for, 613-14
ripping up railroad tracks, 643, 647, 648
Savannah goal, 648-54, 679
Savannah occupation, 711-15, 722, 735-36, 750, 764, 782
supply rations, 641-42, 653-54
total damage inflicted (in U.S. dollars), 645
use of prisoners-of-war, 647-48
on Negro troops, 533
physical appearance, 319-20
River Queen conference, 847-48, 854-57
shipboard meeting with Grant, 838
on war (quoted), 602
Vicksburg to Meridian march, 319, 321
Sherman, Mrs. William T., 400, 713
Shiloh, 16, 39, 44, 82, 103, 136, 139, 184, 328, 356, 362, 416, 451, 475, 633, 665, 672, 737, 800
Shreveport, 15, 16, 104, 1020, 1024, 1027
industrial complex at, 27
Red River campaign and, 26, 27, 28, 31, 32, 34, 35, 36, 37, 38, 39, 42, 43, 45, 46-47, 48, 50, 51, 53, 55, 61, 62, 64, 66, 67, 70, 71, 77, 90
Shy, William M., 698, 702
Shy's Hill, 698, 699, 700, 701, 702, 704, 705
Sigel, Franz, 152, 204, 264, 270, 301, 320, 450, 455, 456, 461, 849
Grant's Plan (Spring '64) and, 18-19, 20, 22, 23, 24, 126, 127, 133, 136
at Martinsburg, 447-48
relieved of command, 250
triple-pronged offensive, 242, 243-50
Signal (gunboat), 80
Silver Spring, 453, 456, 459
Simsport, 30, 31, 84, 86, 87, 89
Sioux Indians, 726
Sister's Ferry, 753, 754, 791
Slavery, 378, 464, 465, 551, 644, 649, 730, 748, 754-55
abolished (in U.S.), 748-50
Confederate program for emancipation, 860-61
Davis on, 97, 468
Emancipation Proclamation and, 750
Lincoln on, 813
recruitment controversy, 754-55
See also Negroes
Slidell, John, 99, 589, 860-61
Slocum, Henry W., 485, 622
Atlanta battle, 485, 521, 524, 528-30, 552, 615
Carolinas march, 751, 753, 788-89, 793, 796-97, 826
at Averasboro, 826-27, 828
at Bentonville, 828-33, 835
at Cheraw, 822
crossing of the Neuse, 836
at Milledgeville, 647
occupation of Atlanta, 611, 612
and Sherman's march to the sea, 640, 642, 643, 646, 647, 649
Smith, Andrew J., 415, 848, 849
in Missouri, 576-77, 578, 581, 599, 621
at Nashville, 681, 686, 687, 690, 691, 693-97, 699, 700, 701-2, 705
North Mississippi operation, 509-19
Red River campaign, 30, 32, 34, 39-40, 46, 47, 48, 49, 50, 52, 55, 56-57, 84, 86, 88, 89, 92, 374, 510, 738
Smith, Charles H. (Bill Arp), 782, 1041
Smith, Edmund Kirby, 575, 576, 680, 765, 990, 1002
farewell to troops, 1021
in Mexico, 1032
Red River campaign, 28, 34, 35, 36, 37, 38, 40, 42, 45, 51, 53, 54, 56, 61, 80, 87, 90-91, 92, 98, 104, 124
Camden Expedition, 62, 66, 70, 71, 72, 73-74, 75, 76
Mansfield meeting, 37
Shreveport meeting, 53-54
surrender of, 1019-22, 1027, 1030, 1031, 1041
Smith, Gerrit, 1036, 1037
Smith, Giles A., 483
Smith, Gustavus W., 645-46
in Augusta, 756, 790-91
Georgia militia command, 790-91
at Honey Hill, 653
in Savannah, 652
Smith, James A., 700, 701
Smith, Martin L., 175-76, 178
Smith, Morgan L., 397
Smith, Thomas B., 703, 704
Smith, Thomas Kilby, 30-31, 34-35, 48, 50
Smith, W. Sooy, 510, 849
Smith, William "Extra Billy," 754-55, 779
Smith, William F. "Baldy," 270-71, 300, 301, 313, 315, 533, 560, 634, 848
and Bermuda Hundred, 253, 255, 261, 262, 279-80
and Cold Harbor, 281, 282, 285, 286, 289-90, 291, 292, 297
and Petersburg, 427-34, 437, 441
relieved of command, 541, 634
Smithfield, 822, 823, 826, 828, 834, 835, 836, 841, 966
Smyrna, 393, 401, 402, 413
Smyrna Station, 392, 399
Smyth, Thomas D., 483
Snake Creek Gap, 321, 322, 325, 327, 329, 331, 332, 613
Snapfinger Creek, 487
Soap Creek, 405, 409
Sorrel, G. Moxley, 176-78, 179, 180

Index

South Anna River, 226, 228, 276, 307, 851
South Carolina, Sherman's march through, 787–97
South Carolina Railroad, 797
South Carolinian (newspaper), 792
South Mountain, 450, 452, 465
Southfield (steamer), 114–15, 593
Southside Railroad, 302, 311, 312, 441–42, 444, 561, 573, 629, 784, 803, 851, 852, 862, 870, 875, 883, 895, 911, 912–14, 921, 926, 931
Spain, 1028, 1029
Spangler's Mill, 571
Spanish Fort, 849, 904
Speed, James, 727, 811, 903, 995
   Reconstruction policy, 963, 964–65
Speed, Mrs. James, 903
Spotswood Hotel (Richmond), 467, 1039
Spotsylvania, 189–224, 250, 251, 265, 268, 274, 284, 285, 288, 310, 316, 375, 547, 669, 844
   at Bloody Angle, 210–24, 547, 669, 844
   abortive breakthrough, 207–10, 226
   disengagement of forces, 223
   total casualties, 223
   at the U perimeter (the "Mule Shoe"), 215–23, 232, 235, 660
   casualties, 200, 208, 209, 210, 214, 221–22, 223
   departure to North Anna, 265–71
   movement to, 189–210
Spray (gunboat), 1027
Spring Hill, 68, 656, 657, 658–62, 663, 664, 665, 676, 677, 707, 757
Springfield, Illinois, 625, 906, 978
   attempted theft of Lincoln's body, 1043
Springfield, Missouri, 579
Springfield Landing, 39, 48
Squirrel Level Road, 561
Stafford, Leroy A., 156
Stanley, David S., 621, 654–55, 658–59, 690
   Atlanta battle, 485, 527, 528
   wounded, 691
   Franklin battle, 664, 673
Stanton, Edwin M., 6, 8, 112, 256, 376, 457, 542, 555, 563, 635, 636, 684, 696, 728, 730, 739, 751, 767, 774, 809, 810, 811, 821, 893, 900, 902, 907, 937, 957, 961, 963, 970, 973, 974, 983, 984, 985, 986, 989, 994, 995, 997, 1012–13, 1014, 1017, 1032, 1036, 1037, 1039, 1049
Staunton, 19, 243, 244, 246, 247, 248, 250, 270, 302, 304, 306, 309, 445, 446, 453, 558, 563, 571, 722, 807
Steedman, James B., 622
   Nashville battle, 681, 683, 686–92, 699, 700, 703, 705

Steele, Frederick, 15, 16, 64, 126
   advance on Little Rock, 27, 28
   Camden Expedition, 53, 61–77, 575
   crossing of Little Missouri, 37, 51, 53
   Mobile operation, 848
   Red River campaign, 25, 27, 31, 32, 35, 36–37, 51, 78, 91, 104, 124, 126
Stephens, Alexander H., 93–94, 95, 605, 755, 770, 798, 892, 1008
   antipathy toward Davis, 94, 95, 96, 767–68
   Blair's peace feeler and, 772–73
   captured, 1012
   Hampton Roads Conference, 773–78, 780
   pardoned, 1032
   peace negotiations proposal, 768
   in retirement, 781
Stephens, John A., 777–78
Stephens, Linton, 94
Steuart, George H., 215, 216, 217
Stevens, Thaddeus, 464, 465
Stevenson, Carter L., 348, 393, 699–700, 703, 707, 759, 760, 791
Stevenson, Thomas G., 207
Stevenson, Alabama, 618
Stewart, Alexander P., 348, 351, 418, 421, 490, 606, 759, 798
   Acworth strike, 611
   Atlanta battle, 473–77, 489, 490, 524–26, 530
   in the Carolinas, 821, 824, 830, 831, 832
   Franklin battle, 663, 667, 669, 670
   and Hood's march north, 654, 655–60, 674
   Nashville battle, 676–77, 679, 691–95, 698, 700, 701, 702, 703, 709
   at Peachtree Creek, 473–75
Stone, Charles P., 47–48, 55, 89
Stone, John M., 176–77, 178
Stone Mountain, 409, 410, 486, 643
Stoneman, George, 352, 404, 405, 409, 737
   Atlanta battle, 486, 487, 488, 519
   captured, 488, 721
   descent on Saltville, 721–22, 723
   North Carolina raid, 804, 848, 849, 850, 852, 905, 965, 967, 1006
   Northeast Tennessee command, 721–22
   at Salisbury, 1003
Stones River (Murfreesboro), 117, 621, 677–78, 679, 681, 707, 975
Stonewall (ironclad), 1028
Stonewall Brigade, 217
Stony Creek, 254, 258, 546, 547, 637, 638, 784, 841, 842, 864, 870
Stony Mountain, 133, 134, 149
Stowe, Harriet Beecher, 972
Strahl, Otho F., 670–71, 673
Strasburg, 250, 544, 555, 556, 564, 567, 571
Strawberry Plains, 519, 597

Streight, Abel D., 58, 849
Stuart, Flora C., 228, 234, 235
Stuart, J. E. B., 564, 581, 763, 861
  death of, 223-24, 231-32, 234-35, 286, 287, 306, 851
  and Sheridan's raid on Richmond, 224-35
  Spotsylvania battle, 191, 194, 196, 197, 198, 201, 202, 206, 214, 223-24
  in the Wilderness, 148, 152, 153, 154, 156, 166, 174
Stubbs Farm, 366, 367, 371, 372
Sturgis, Samuel D., 415, 849
  at Brice's Crossroads, 362-73, 510
Sugar Creek, 477, 479
Sugar Valley, 326, 329
Sultana (sidewheel steamer), 1026-27
Sumner, Charles, 464, 471, 749, 812, 814, 903
  reaction to Lincoln's assassination, 982
  Reconstruction policy, 962, 963
Sumter (raider), 382, 389
Sunshine Church, 488
Surratt, Mary E., 1032, 1036
Sutherland Station, 875, 884, 895, 913
Swainsboro, 647
Sweeny, Thomas W., 335, 336
Swift Creek, 255, 256, 258, 263
Swinton, William, 441

T

Ta River, 225
Tahlequah, 585
Tai-ping Rebellion, 1041
Taliaferro, William B., 791
  at Bentonville, 831, 832
  in the Carolinas, 822, 827, 831, 832
Talladega, 326
Tallahassee, 967, 1027
Tallahassee (raider), 508-9, 549, 590, 965, 1010
Tallahatchie River, 510, 513, 514, 515, 517
Taney, Roger B., 728
Tapp farmhouse, 156, 157, 168, 176, 191, 193
Taylor, Richard, 575, 755, 757, 758-59, 764, 769, 850, 990, 998-99, 1002, 1037
  Forrest's Tennessee expedition and, 596-97, 599, 601
  Macon headquarters, 645
  Meridian headquarters, 596-97, 599, 601, 606
  Red River campaign, 34-39, 42-59, 62, 66, 77, 79, 80, 85, 86-88, 90-91, 92, 104
    Mansfield meeting, 37
    Shreveport meeting, 53-54

Selma headquarters, 608, 617, 619
  surrender of, 998-1001, 1007, 1019, 1020, 1021, 1027, 1028
Taylor, Walter, 942-43, 945, 953, 955
Taylor, Zachary, 34, 508
Tazewell, 245, 246
Tecumseh (ship), 497, 499-500, 501, 503, 506
Telegraph Road, 224, 225, 227, 228, 265, 267
Tenallytown, 453
Tennessee:
  divided loyalties in, 595-96
  end of Reconstruction in, 1044
  Forrest expedition (September-October), 596-601
  Morgan raid (Sept. 4th), 595-96
  Wheeler raids, 597, 601
Tennessee (ironclad), 493-94, 497-99, 502-6, 508, 591
Tennessee & Alabama Railroad, 598, 599-600, 601
Tennessee River, 59, 105, 117, 124, 321, 365, 374, 519, 520, 522, 597, 599, 600, 610, 616, 621, 674, 677, 707, 708-9, 711, 850, 1053
Terre Noir Creek, 66
Terre Rouge Creek, 68
Terry, Alfred H., 740, 741-43, 744, 746, 751, 797, 819, 820, 821, 824, 825, 826, 836
Texas, 15-16, 25-26, 28, 35, 36, 104, 575, 586, 765, 1003, 1006, 1009, 1019-20, 1044
Thayer, John M., 65, 66, 67, 68-69, 72-73
Third Winchester, 567
Thirteenth Amendment, 777, 815
  adoption of, 748-49
  ratification of, 960, 1040
Thomas, George H., 16, 20, 135, 573, 642, 723, 737, 738, 759, 1018
  Atlanta battle, 473-76, 484-85, 486, 488, 489, 521-30
    at Red Oak and Fairburn, 521-22
  death of, 1056
  Georgia campaign, 423, 473-76, 484-85, 486, 488, 489, 521-30
    Chattahoochee crossing, 402, 403-4, 409-10
    Dalton to Resaca march, 321-25, 327
    the "Hell Hole," 348-49
    Kennesaw Mountain, 392, 396, 398-99, 400
    Kingston to Pine Top, via Dallas march, 346-51, 353, 354, 357
    Marietta occupation, 402
    at Resaca, 331-32
    Resaca to Cassville march, 331, 332, 335-37, 339, 340-42
  at Peachtree Creek, 473-76
  in Tennessee, 599, 603, 611, 614-18, 621, 622, 636-37, 653, 730, 737, 756, 849

Index [1103]

farewell review, 1041
Hood's march north and, 654, 655, 658, 664, 673, 674, 677, 724
Nashville battle, 675-88, 693, 696, 697, 698, 701-5, 709, 710, 711
Thomasville, 652
Thompson Station, 659, 661
Tilden, Samuel J., 1044
Times (of London), 815
Tishomingo Creek, *see* Brice's Crossroads
Todd, George, 579, 1022
Todd's Tavern, 148, 152, 158, 161, 165, 174, 189, 190, 191-92, 195, 198, 199
Tom's Brook, 564, 565
Toombs, Robert A., 781, 860, 1007-8, 1037
Torbert, Alfred T. A., 199, 225, 308, 309, 564
  and Cedar Creek, 571
  and Cold Harbor, 282, 285
  December strike (1864), 722-23
  in Luray Valley, 556, 557
  replaced, 807
Toronto, Ontario, 725
Torpedoes, use of, 635, 647-48, 719-20
Totopotomoy Creek, 276-81, 282, 283, 284, 286, 287, 292, 316, 442
  Atlee conference, 278
  Federal march to, 276-77
Tower Island, 495
Town Creek, 512
Toxie Creek, 75
Transmississippi region, 15-16, 25-92, 98, 126, 139, 574-86, 680, 998
  communication between Richmond and, 104
  Grant's Close-Out Plan and, 739
  Grant's Plan (Spring '64) and, 25-92
    Camden Expedition, 61-77
    prolonging of operations, 77-92
    Red River campaign, 27-77
  last attack of the war, 1020
  last Confederate general to surrender, 1022
  Missouri raids, 574-86
  surrender of, 998-1002
  White River gunboat probe, 574-75
Traveller (horse), 122, 144, 153, 169-70, 191, 217, 218, 220, 265, 287, 435, 842, 877, 878, 881, 884-85, 888, 920, 940, 945, 949-50, 951, 952
Treasury, Confederate, 886, 965, 969, 1005, 1013-14, 1055
  dispersal of, 1006, 1010, 1011
Trenholm, George A., 766, 887-88, 965-66, 968, 988
  pardoned, 1032
  resignation of, 1004
Trenholm, Mrs. George A., 965
Trent (steamer), 377, 589
Trent's Reach, 428

Trevilian Station, 307-9, 311, 444
Tucker, George W., 877, 879, 880, 943, 945, 949-50
Tullahoma, 601
Tumbling Run, 556
Tunnel Hill, 323-24, 325, 474, 490, 613
Tupelo, 365, 366, 367, 510, 512, 597, 709, 751-58, 759, 760, 791
Turkey Bend, 254
Turkey Hill, 287, 288, 291
Turnbull house, 876, 878, 879, 880, 884
Turner, Nat, 973
Tuscarora (warship), 1012
Tuscumbia, 374, 519, 618-19, 620, 654, 676, 757, 758
Twain, Mark, 1047
Tyler, Robert, 240
Tyler, Texas, 27

U

Uncle Tom's Cabin (Stowe), 972
Unconditional surrender, policy of, 14, 101, 212, 598, 612, 778, 779, 943
Underwood, John C., 1038-39
Undine (gunboat), 619, 620
Union City, surrender of, 106-7
United States Constitution, 14, 94, 552, 562, 729, 730, 811, 993, 1031, 1035, 1044-45
  Fifteenth Amendment, 1044-45
  Thirteenth Amendment, 748-49, 777, 815, 960, 1040
United States Supreme Court, 470, 728, 749
  first Negro admitted to practice before, 749
  separate but equal doctrine, 1044
University of Alabama, 694
Upton, Emory, 226, 295, 299
  Spotsylvania battle, 207-10, 211, 215, 220, 221
Usher, John P., 815
Utah, 747
Utoy Creek, 491, 521, 527

V

Vallandigham, Clement L., 551, 558
Valley Turnpike, 446-49, 722
Van Buren, Martin, 378, 814
Vance, Zebulon B., 94-95, 96, 97, 101, 781-82, 855, 966
Vanderbilt, Cornelius, 1038
Varnell Station, 324, 325
Vaughan Road, 561, 785, 857, 865, 866, 868

[1104] INDEX

Venus (transport), 619, 620
Vera Cruz, Mexico, 376, 377, 1023
Verdiersville, 149, 151, 152, 153, 154, 165
Vermont, 471, 558, 574
Vicksburg, 4, 11, 16, 21, 24, 25, 28, 29, 30, 33, 64, 88, 92, 99, 101, 102, 103, 104, 105, 119, 136, 139, 175, 184, 187, 295, 313, 319, 322, 363, 374, 403, 480, 485, 492, 503, 541, 552, 633, 735, 782, 975, 1024
Villanow, 322
Vining Station, 403-4, 408
Virginia (vessel), 113
Virginia campaign (1864-65), 3-317, 427-72, 530-74, 802-956
　at Bermuda Hundred, 251-65
　Close-Out Plan, 735-54
　　Butler-Porter expedition, 715-21
　　Confederate authorities and, 754-83
　　fall of Fort Fisher, 740-47
　　Hatcher's Run battle, 783-86
　　and Sherman's march northward, 736, 750-54, 756, 757, 786, 787-801, 825-38, 848, 851, 858, 1029
　at Cold Harbor, 281-99
　Grant's Grand Design (Spring '64) and, 3-145
　　authorities in Richmond, 92-126
　　final preparations, 126-45
　　over-all command strategy, 3-24
　Jamesward strategy, 299-317
　at North Anna, 265-76
　pendulum strikes against Richmond-Petersburg (September), 560-62
　Petersburg siege:
　　Crater fiasco, 530-38
　　and Early's drive toward Washington, 446-61
　　Fall, 627-40
　　July-August, 530-49
　　June, 427-46
　and politicking in Washington, 549-53, 558-60, 562-63
　race for Spotsylvania, 189-91, 191-224
　raid on Richmond, 224-35
　Shenandoah Valley operations, 553-58, 563-73, 574
　Totopotomoy confrontation, 276-81
　triple-pronged offensive, 235-43, 243-51
　victory and defeat, 802-956
　　abandonment of Richmond, 857-64, 885-93
　　to Appomattox, 907-56
　　at Dinwiddie, Five Forks, 862-75
　　fall of Petersburg, 875-85, 893
　　surrender of Army of Northern Virginia, 938, 939-56
　in the Wilderness, 146-91

　See also names of generals; naval operations
Virginia Central Railroad, 19, 126, 133-34, 191, 225, 228, 243, 260, 266, 270, 275, 276, 278, 301, 304, 306, 307, 309, 311, 312, 427, 539, 540, 553, 563, 722, 802, 807, 808, 850
Virginia Military Institute, 247, 248, 447, 694, 1052
　burning of, 310
Virginia Number 2 (flagship), 889
Virginia & Tennessee Railroad, 19, 243, 244, 302, 721, 803, 849, 851

W

Wachusett (ship), 587, 588-90
Waddell, James I., 590, 591, 1029-31
Wade, Benjamin F., 464, 465, 471, 558-59, 728, 987, 1044, 1049
　Reconstruction policy, 962, 963
Wade-Davis Bill, 463-64
Wade-Davis Manifesto, 465-66, 549, 558-59
Wadsworth, James S., 159-60, 163, 164, 171, 172-74, 175, 267
Wagner, George D., 658, 659-60
　Franklin battle, 665, 667, 671, 673, 676, 694
Walker, John G., 42, 44, 48, 49, 53, 54, 73, 75, 76, 92
Walker, Tandy, 68, 69
Walker, W. H. T., 333-34
　Atlanta battle and, 477, 478, 479, 481
　death of, 479, 484
Wallace, Lew, 450-51, 452, 455, 1033
Walnut Grove Church, 287
Walthall, Edward C., 666, 669-70, 757
　Nashville battle, 692, 693, 694, 695, 700, 707, 708, 709
Walthall, William T., 1052
Walthall Junction, 301, 437
Warfield Station, 708
Warner (transport), 80
Warren, Gouverneur K., 313, 315, 537, 573, 846, 857
　Boydton Plank Road mission, 561
　and Cold Harbor, 281, 285, 295
　Five Forks battle, 864, 866-74
　and Hatcher's Run, 784-85
　march to Totopotomoy, 276
　and North Anna, 269-70, 271, 274
　and Petersburg, 432, 435, 436, 533
　　Globe Tavern attack, 545-46, 547
　Rapidan crossing, 874
　relieved from duty, 873-74
　Spotsylvania battle, 196, 197, 198, 199-200, 202, 205-6, 207, 210, 211, 212, 220, 222

Index

[1105]

triple-pronged offensive and, 236, 239–40, 241
Weldon Railroad assignment, 545–46, 547, 637
in the Wilderness, 147, 151, 158, 159–60, 161
race to Spotsylvania, 189, 190–91
second day (May 6th), 167, 173
Warrenton, 722
Washburn, Cadwallader C., 362, 363, 510, 513, 515–17, 518, 759, 849
Washburne, Elihu B., 211–12, 362, 518, 549, 802, 905
Washington, George, 811, 814, 906
Washington, Arkansas, 27, 64, 67, 69
Washington, D.C., 3–9, 20, 24, 108, 135–36, 147, 188, 275, 445, 565 650
Early's northward march and, 446–61
naval defense, 457
plan to evacuate Lincoln, 455
Grand Review parade, 1013–18
Washington, Georgia, 1007–8, 1009
Washington College, 310, 449, 1050
Wateree River, 752–53, 796, 797, 800, 818, 819
Watie, Stand, 1022
Wauhatchie, 347
Waynesboro, 563, 654, 807–9, 839, 840, 841, 850
Webber's Falls, 585
Weed, Thurlow, 549, 814
Weitzel, Godfrey, 719–20, 742, 852
Richmond occupation headquarters, 895, 898–99, 900, 901, 902, 963–64
Weldon, 113, 121, 152, 256, 258, 836
Welles, Gideon, 6, 78, 389, 464, 562, 563, 590, 595, 720–21, 724, 728, 747, 811, 957, 963, 976, 982, 995, 1029
West Point, Georgia, 486, 487
West Point, Mississippi, 759
West Virginia, 18, 244, 245, 302, 445, 763, 776, 1041
Western & Atlantic Railroad, 319, 323, 326, 333–34, 335, 337, 338, 339, 343, 345, 352, 353, 355, 391, 393, 395, 401, 486, 519, 522, 609, 611, 614, 615–16, 622
Westport, 580, 581, 582, 583, 586
Wharton, Gabriel C., 567, 568, 571, 638, 762, 808
Wheeler, Joseph, 331–32, 339, 347, 645, 648, 787–88, 789–90, 791
Atlanta battle, 473–78, 482, 483, 487–89, 519–22
in the Union rear, 519–20, 522
captured, 1012, 1021
in the Carolinas, 822, 824, 826, 827, 828, 832, 833
cavalry skirmish with Kilpatrick, 331–32
defense of Dalton, 321, 324
and Kennesaw Mountain, 392–93
at Peachtree Creek, 473–75
Tennessee raids, 597, 601, 603, 604, 614
Whipple, William D., 683
White House Landing, 279, 281, 309, 313, 427
White Oak Road, 862, 864, 869, 870, 871
White Oak Swamp, 303, 314, 316, 434, 628, 638, 840, 868
White River, 574–75
White's Ford, 461
Whiting, W. H. C., 741, 743–45, 746
and Bermuda Hundred, 259, 261, 262–63
death of, 746
Whitman, Walt, 395, 814, 1042, 1045–46
Wickham, Williams C., 228, 230
Wigfall, Louis T., 825
Wilcox, Cadmus M., 267, 1048
and Petersburg, 878, 879, 882, 884
withdrawal, 908, 930
Spotsylvania battle, 193, 217, 219
in the Wilderness, 156, 157, 163, 165, 166, 168
Wilcox Landing, 315, 427, 428, 439
Wilderness, the, 24, 122, 134, 135, 137, 143, 144, 146–91, 284, 285, 290, 298, 311, 316, 323, 332, 375, 441, 476, 547, 567, 569, 631
casualties, 156, 163, 173, 182, 188, 323
contact (May 5th), 154–64, 165, 166, 167
flankers, 176–82, 184–85, 186
Grant and:
assignment of objectives, 148, 150, 158
crossing the Rapidan, 146–50, 211, 240
"hit now, worry later" policy, 157–59
troop strength, 149
victory formula, 164
Lee and:
assignment of objectives, 150–53, 165
change of objectives, 165
combat strength, 153
departure of Longstreet, 179–80, 182
reconnaissance operations, 171, 175, 178
surrender of the initiative, 184
pattern of fighting, 156
prisoners-of-war, 163, 182
second day of attack (May 6th), 167–87
Wilderness Run, 159
Wilderness Tavern, 147, 149, 151, 154, 158
Wilkes, Charles, 589, 590
Willard's Hotel, 3–5, 7, 135–36, 137, 685
Willcox, Orlando B., 534

William P. Clyde (side-wheeler), 1012
William H. Webb (steam ram), 1023–26, 1027
Williams, Alpheus S., 348, 485, 642, 754, 831, 832
Williams, Seth, 927, 928–29, 948, 956
Wilmington, 492–93, 507, 509, 614, 624, 634, 648, 684, 685, 751, 764, 819, 834, 975, 1028
  fall of, 800, 802, 822
  Federal expedition to, 715–21, 737, 740, 741–47, 751
  goods run into (1864), 741
  refugee camps, 825
Wilmington & Weldon Railroad, 820, 836
Wilson, James H., 186, 225, 233, 294, 656, 657, 658, 738, 1009, 1041
  Alabama raid, 804, 848, 849–50, 852, 904–5, 967, 999
  dispatch on Davis' capture, 1011
  Franklin battle, 664, 669
  Grant's Jamesward strategy and, 313–14, 315
  at Hollow Tree Gap, 707
  Macon headquarters, 1011–12
  Nashville battle, 681, 686–87, 690, 691, 693–94, 697–702, 709
  and Petersburg, 432, 435–36, 442, 444–45, 446
  promoted to Major General, 622
  Spotsylvania battle, 198, 199
  War Department circular of, 1008
Wilson's Creek, 68, 579–80, 581, 1020, 1022, 1027
Winchester, 137, 181, 243, 246, 247, 248, 447, 539, 544, 553–55, 556, 563, 564, 567, 569, 722, 804, 806, 808, 850
  casualties, 554, 555
Windmill Point, 427, 428, 431, 434, 436, 439
Winnebago (ship), 497
Winslow, John A., 380–90, 587, 588
Winstead Hill, 663–65, 666, 667, 670, 673, 707
Wirz, Henry, 1032–33, 1036
Wise, Henry A., 433, 434, 918, 921–22, 930, 1049
Witherspoon, William W., 670
Wofford, William T., 176–78
Wolford, Daniel, 879

Wood, George H., 1017–18
Wood, John T., 508–9, 965, 968, 1004, 1010
Wood, Thomas J., 349–50, 664, 707
  Nashville battle, 681, 686, 690–95, 699, 700, 701, 703, 705
Woodstock, 563, 564, 565
Wright, Ambrose R., 791, 822
Wright, Horatio G., 236, 239, 241, 313, 314, 315, 563, 564, 565, 566, 806, 852
  and Cedar Creek, 568, 569, 571
  and Cold Harbor, 281, 285, 286, 289, 291, 292, 295
  and Early's northward march, 450, 454, 457, 459–60, 531
  at Fisher's Hill, 556, 557
  Five Forks battle, 864, 866, 868–69
  march to Totopotomoy, 276
  and North Anna, 270, 271, 274
  and Petersburg, 432, 436, 437, 442, 444, 445, 592, 637–38, 785, 878, 879, 880, 882
  pursuit of Lee's army, 918, 920, 925–28, 935, 937–38, 941
  race for Burkeville, 903, 914
  Spotsylvania battle, 207, 209, 211, 212, 219–20, 221, 222
  in the Wilderness, 159–60, 181
Wright, Rebecca, 553
Wright, W. W., 345
Wytheville, 243, 245, 246, 358, 721

Y

"Yankee Doodle," 958
Yazoo River, 186
Yellow Bayou, 86–88, 90, 104, 340
"Yellow Rose of Texas," 710
Yellow Tavern, 229, 230, 232, 861
York-James peninsula, 36, 105, 119, 127, 251, 328, 1012, 1038
York River, 270, 276, 280, 313
York River Railroad, 313
Yorktown, 251
Young, Bennett H., 586–87
Younger, Jim, 1022

COMPREHENSIVE TABLE OF CONTENTS

Volume One

I.

CHAPTER 1. PROLOGUE—THE OPPONENTS
1. Secession: Davis and Lincoln
2. Sumter; Early Maneuvers
3. Statistics North and South

CHAPTER 2. FIRST BLOOD; NEW CONCEPTIONS
1. Manassas—Southern Triumph
2. Anderson, Frémont, McClellan
3. Scott's Anaconda; the Navy
4. Diplomacy; the Buildup

CHAPTER 3. THE THING GETS UNDER WAY
1. The West: Grant, Fort Henry
2. Donelson—The Loss of Kentucky
3. Gloom; Manassas Evacuation
4. McC Moves to the Peninsula

II.

CHAPTER 4. WAR MEANS FIGHTING...
1. Pea Ridge; Glorieta; Island Ten
2. Halleck-Grant, Jston-Bgard: Shiloh
3. Farragut, Lovell: New Orleans
4. Halleck, Beauregard: Corinth

CHAPTER 5. FIGHTING MEANS KILLING
1. Davis Frets; Lincoln-McClellan
2. Valley Campaign; Seven Pines
3. Lee, McC: The Concentration
4. The Seven Days; Hezekiah

III.

CHAPTER 6. THE SUN SHINES SOUTH
1. Lincoln Reappraisal; Emancipation?
2. Grant, Farragut, Buell
3. Bragg, K. Smith, Breckinridge
4. Lee vs. Pope: Second Manassas

CHAPTER 7. TWO ADVANCES; TWO RETREATS
1. Invasion West: Richmond, Munfordville
2. Lee, McClellan: Sharpsburg
3. The Emancipation Proclamation
4. Corinth-Perryville: Bragg Retreats

CHAPTER 8. LAST, BEST HOPE OF EARTH
1. Lincoln's Late-Fall Disappointments
2. Davis: Lookback and Outlook
3. Lincoln: December Message

Volume Two

I.

CHAPTER 1. THE LONGEST JOURNEY
1. Davis, Westward and Return
2. Goldsboro; Fredericksburg
3. Prairie Grove; Galveston
4. Holly Springs; Walnut Hills
5. Murfreesboro: Bragg Retreats

CHAPTER 2. UNHAPPY NEW YEAR
1. Lincoln; Mud March; Hooker
2. Arkansas Post; Transmiss; Grant
3. Erlanger; Richmond Bread Riot
4. Rosecrans; Johnston; Streit
5. Vicksburg—Seven Failures

CHAPTER 3. DEATH OF A SOLDIER
1. Naval Repulse at Charleston
2. Lee, Hooker; Mosby; Kelly's Ford
3. Suffolk: Longstreet Southside
4. Hooker, Stoneman: The Crossing
5. Chancellorsville; Jackson Dies

II.

CHAPTER 4. THE BELEAGUERED CITY
1. Grant's Plan; the Run; Grierson
2. Eastward, Port Gibson to Jackson
3. Westward, Jackson to Vicksburg
4. Port Hudson; Banks vs. Gardner
5. Vicksburg Siege, Through June

CHAPTER 5. STARS IN THEIR COURSES
1. Lee, Davis; Invasion; Stuart
2. Gettysburg Opens; Meade Arrives
3. Gettysburg, July 2: Longstreet
4. Gettysburg, Third Day: Pickett
5. Cavalry; Lee Plans Withdrawal

CHAPTER 6. UNVEXED TO THE SEA
1. Lee's Retreat; Falling Waters
2. Milliken's Bend; Helena Repulse
3. Vicksburg Falls; Jackson Reburnt
4. Lincoln Exults; N.Y. Draft Riot
5. Davis Declines Lee's Resignation

III.

CHAPTER 7. RIOT AND RESURGENCE
1. Rosecrans; Tullahoma Campaign
2. Morgan Raid; Chattanooga Taken
3. Charleston Seige; Transmississippi
4. Chickamauga—First Day
5. Bragg's Victory Unexploited

CHAPTER 8. THE CENTER GIVES
1. Sabine Pass; Shelby; Grant Hurt
2. Bristoe Station; Buckland Races
3. Grant Opens the Cracker Line
4. Davis, Bragg; Gettysburg Address
5. Missionary Ridge; Bragg Relieved

CHAPTER 9. SPRING CAME ON FOREVER
1. Mine Run; Meade Withdraws
2. Olustee; Kilpatrick Raid
3. Sherman, Meridian; Forrest
4. Lincoln-Davis, a Final Contrast
5. Grant Summoned to Washington

Volume Three

I.

CHAPTER 1. ANOTHER GRAND DESIGN
1. Grant in Washington—His Plan
2. Red River, Camden: Reevaluation
3. Paducah, Fort Pillow; Plymouth
4. Grant Poised; Joe Davis; Lee

CHAPTER 2. THE FORTY DAYS
1. Grant Crosses; the Wilderness
2. Spotsylvania—"All Summer"
3. New Market; Bermuda Hundred
4. North Anna; Cold Harbor; Early

CHAPTER 3. RED CLAY MINUET
1. Dalton to Pine Mountain
2. Brice's; Lincoln; "Alabama"
3. Kennesaw to Chattahoochee
4. Hood Replaces Johnston

II.

CHAPTER 4. WAR IS CRUELTY...
1. Petersburg; Early I; Peace?
2. Hood vs. Sherman; Mobile Bay; Memphis Raid; Atlanta Falls
3. Crater; McClellan; Early II
4. Price Raid; "Florida"; Cushing; Forrest Raids Mid-Tenn.
5. Hood-Davis; Lincoln Reelected.

CHAPTER 5. YOU CANNOT REFINE IT
1. Petersburg Trenches; Weldon RR
2. March to Sea; Hood, Spring Hill
3. Franklin; Hood Invests Nashville
4. Thomas Attacks; Hood Retreats
5. Savannah Falls; Lincoln Exultant

III.

CHAPTER 6. A TIGHTENING NOOSE
1. Grant; Ft. Fisher; 13th Amendment
2. Confed Shifts; Lee Genl-in-Chief?
3. Blair Received; Hampton Roads
4. Hatcher's Run; Columbia Burned

CHAPTER 7. VICTORY, AND DEFEAT
1. Sheridan, Early; Second Inaugural
2. Goldsboro; Sheridan; City Point
3. Five Forks—Richmond Evacuated
4. Lee, Grant Race for Appomattox

CHAPTER 8. LUCIFER IN STARLIGHT
1. Davis-Johnston; Sumter; Booth
2. Durham; Citronelle; Davis Taken
3. K. Smith; Naval; Fort Monroe
4. Postlude: Reconstruction, Davis

ABOUT THE AUTHOR

SHELBY FOOTE was born in Greenville, Mississippi, and attended school there until he entered the University of North Carolina. During World War II he served in the European theater as a captain of field artillery. He has written five novels: *Tournament, Follow Me Down, Love in a Dry Season, Shiloh* and *Jordan County*. He has been awarded three Guggenheim fellowships. He died in 2005.

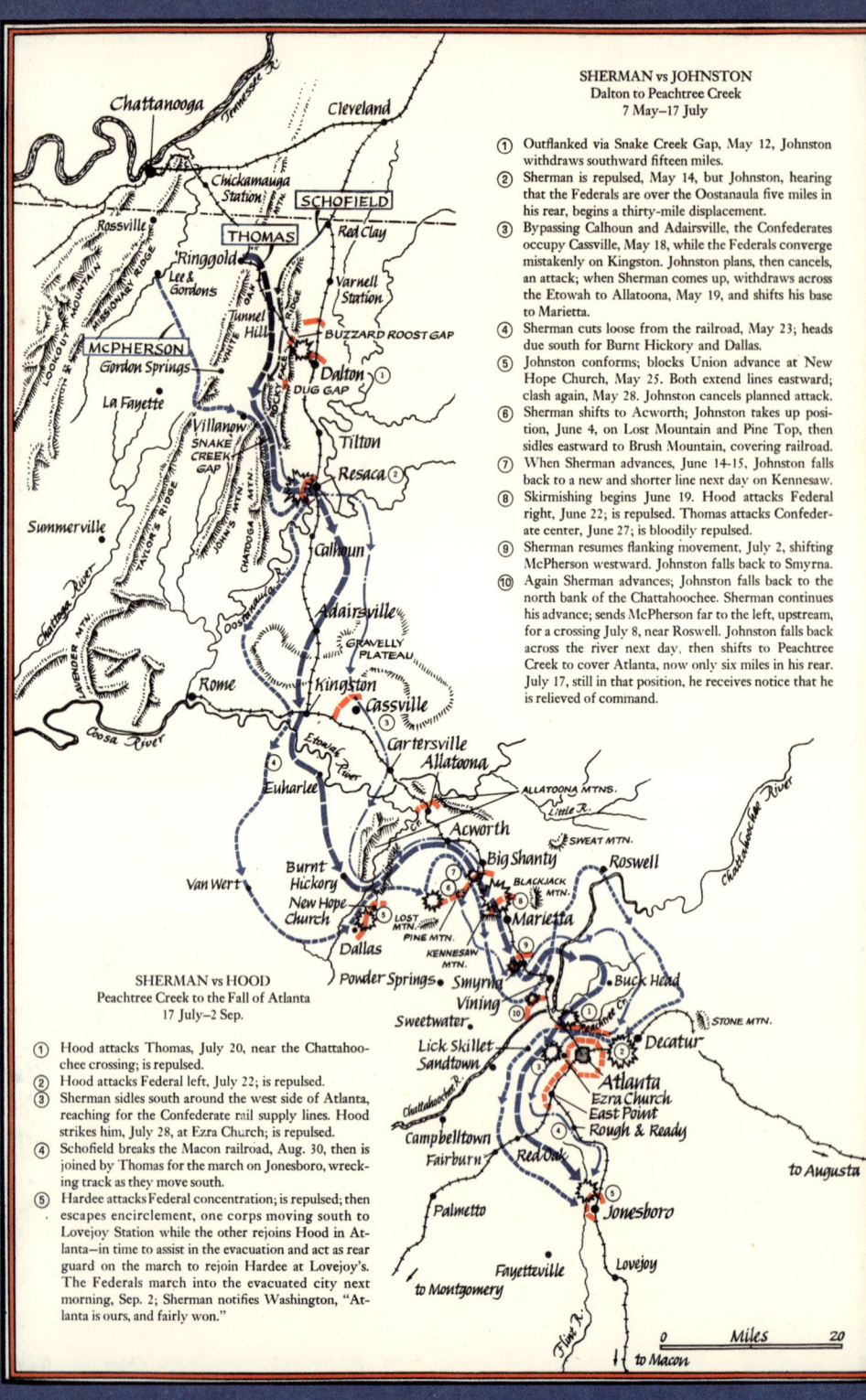

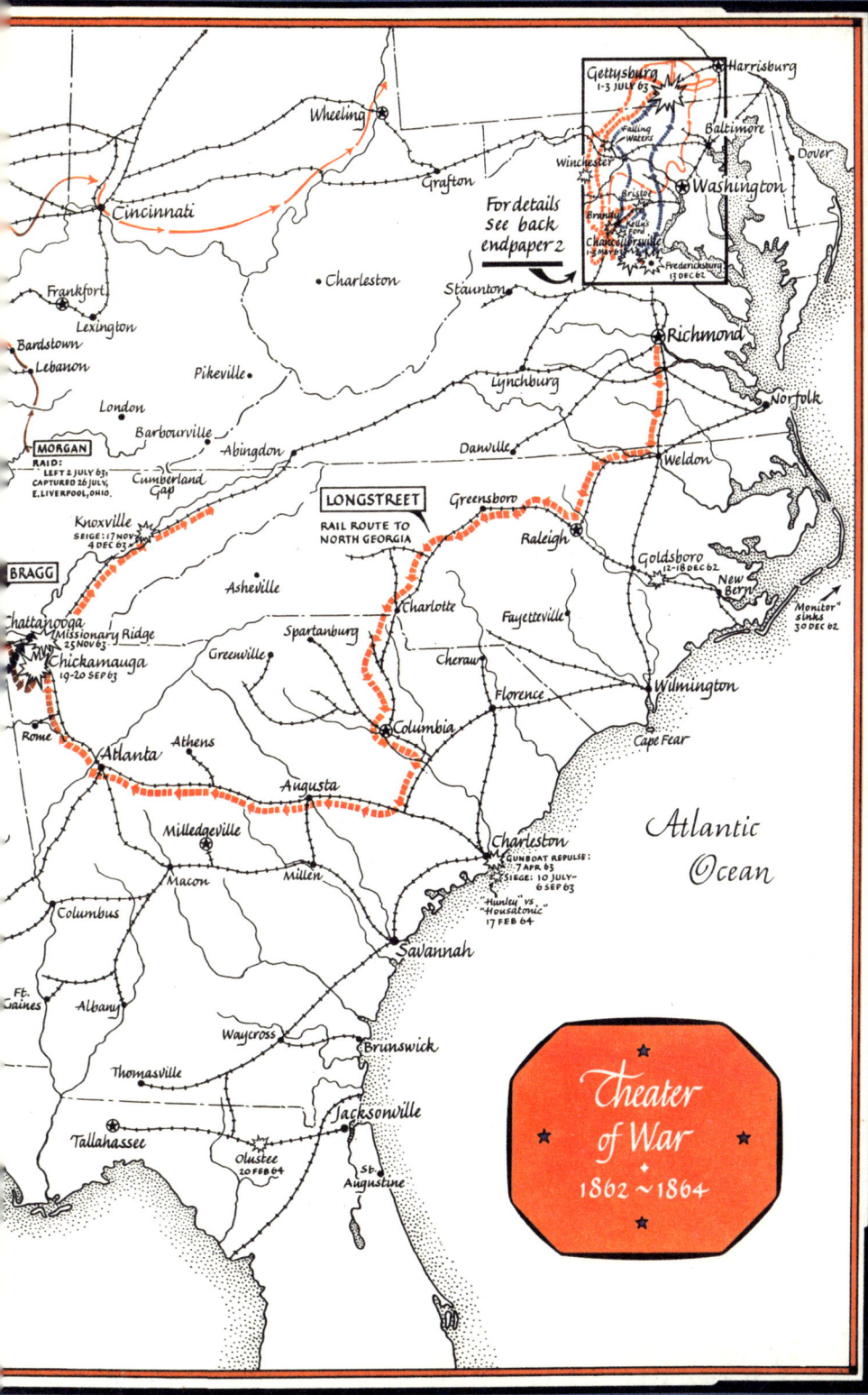

The Civil War
A Narrative

ALL THESE WERE HONOURED IN THEIR GENERATIONS

AND WERE THE GLORY OF THEIR TIMES

THERE BE OF THEM

THAT HAVE LEFT A NAME BEHIND THEM

THAT THEIR PRAISES MIGHT BE REPORTED

AND SOME THERE BE WHICH HAVE NO MEMORIAL

WHO ARE PERISHED AS THOUGH THEY HAD NEVER BEEN

AND ARE BECOME AS THOUGH THEY HAD NEVER BEEN BORN

AND THEIR CHILDREN AFTER THEM

BUT THESE WERE MERCIFUL MEN

WHOSE RIGHTEOUSNESS HATH NOT BEEN FORGOTTEN

WITH THEIR SEED SHALL CONTINUALLY REMAIN

A GOOD INHERITANCE

AND THEIR CHILDREN ARE WITHIN THE COVENANT

THEIR SEED STANDETH FAST

AND THEIR CHILDREN FOR THEIR SAKES

THEIR SEED SHALL REMAIN FOR EVER

AND THEIR GLORY SHALL NOT BE BLOTTED OUT

THEIR BODIES ARE BURIED IN PEACE

BUT THEIR NAME LIVETH FOR EVERMORE

Ecclesiasticus xliv

THE
Civil War

---- ★ ★ ----

FREDERICKSBURG
to MERIDIAN

---- ★ ★ ----

By SHELBY FOOTE

RANDOM HOUSE · NEW YORK

2011 Modern Library Edition

Copyright © 1963 and copyright renewed 1991 by Shelby Foote

All rights reserved.

Published in the United States by Modern Library, an imprint of
The Random House Publishing Group, a division of
Random House, Inc., New York.

MODERN LIBRARY and the TORCHBEARER Design are
registered trademarks of Random House, Inc.

This work was originally published in hardcover in 1963 by
Random House, an imprint of The Random House Publishing Group,
a division of Random House, Inc.

ISBN 978-0-679-64370-8

Printed in China on acid-free paper

www.modernlibrary.com

2 4 6 8 9 7 5 3 1

Case and box photographs: Library of Congress

CONTENTS

★ ✗ ☆

I

1. The Longest Journey   3
2. Unhappy New Year   107
3. Death of a Soldier   221

II

4. The Beleaguered City   323
5. Stars in their Courses   428
6. Unvexed to the Sea   582

III

7. Riot and Resurgence   663
8. The Center Gives   769
9. Spring Came on Forever   870

List of Maps, Bibliographical Note, and Index   967

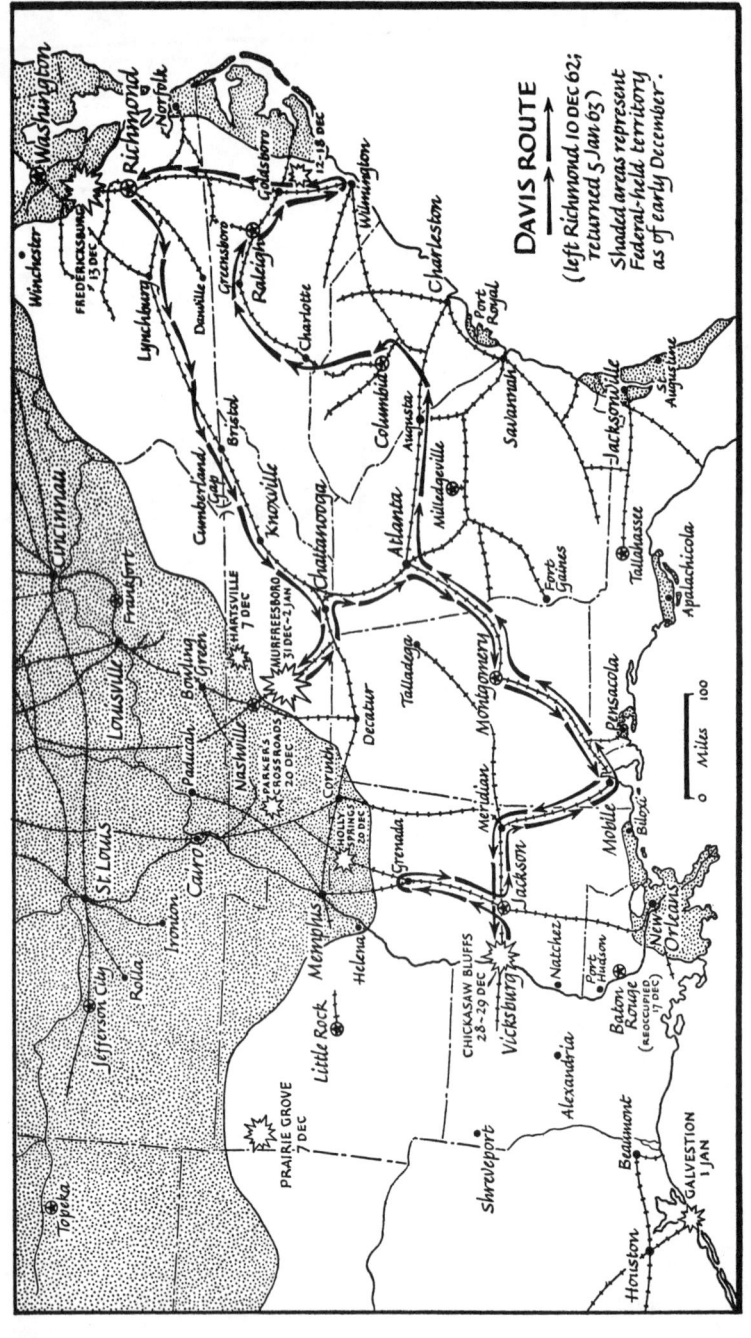

CHAPTER 1

The Longest Journey

★ ✗ ☆

"AFTER AN ABSENCE OF NEARLY TWO YEARS," Jefferson Davis told the legislators assembled under the golden dome of his home-state capitol on the day after Christmas, 1862 — twenty months and two weeks, to the day, since the guns of Charleston opened fire on Sumter to inaugurate the civil war no one could know was not yet halfway over — "I again find myself among those who, from the days of my childhood, have ever been the trusted objects of my affection, those for whose good I have ever striven and whose interests I have sometimes hoped I may have contributed to subserve.... I left you to assume the duties which have devolved upon me as the representative of the new Confederacy. The responsibilities of this position have occupied all my time, and have left me no opportunity for mingling with my friends in Mississippi or for sharing in the dangers which have menaced them. But, wherever duty may have called me, my heart has been with you, and the success of the cause in which we are all engaged has been first in my thoughts and prayers."

In February of the year before, he had left for Montgomery, Alabama, to assume his role as President of the newly established provisional government, believing, as he said now, "that the service to which I was called could be but temporary." A West Pointer and an authentic hero of the Mexican War, he had considered his primary talent — or, as he termed it, his "capacity" — to be military. He had thought to return to the duty he found congenial, that of a line officer in the service of his state, "to lead Mississippians in the field, and to be with them where danger was to be braved and glory won.... But it was decided differently. I was called to another sphere of action. How, in that sphere, I have discharged the duties and obligations imposed on me, it does not become me to constitute myself the judge. It is for others to decide that question. But, speaking to you with that frankness and that confidence with which I have always spoken to you, and which partakes of the nature of thinking aloud, I can say with my hand upon my heart that whatever I have done has been done with the sincere purpose of promoting the noble cause in which we are engaged. The period which has elapsed since I left you is short; for the time which may appear long in the life of a man is short in the history of a nation. And in that short period remarkable changes have been wrought in all the circumstances by which we are surrounded."

Remarkable changes had indeed been wrought, and of these the most immediately striking to those present, seated row on row beneath him or standing close-packed along the outer aisles, was in the aspect of the man who stood before them, tall and slender, careworn and oracular, in a mote-shot nimbus of hazy noonday sunlight pouring down from the high windows of the hall. When they had seen him last on this same rostrum, just short of twenty-three months ago this week, he had not appeared to be within a decade of his fifty-two years of age. Now, though, he was fifty-four, and he looked it. The "troubles and thorns innumerable" which he foretold on his arrival in Montgomery to take the oath of office, back in the first glad springtime of the nation, had not only come to pass; they had also left their marks — as if the thorns, being more than figurative, had scored his brow and made of him what he had never seemed before, a man of sorrows. The gray eyes, one lustrous, the other sightless, its stone gray pupil covered by a film, were deeply sunken above the jut of the high cheekbones, and the thin upper lip, indicative of an iron will and rigid self-control, was held so tightly against the teeth, even in repose, that you saw their shape behind it. The accustomed geniality was there, the inveterate grace and charm of manner, along with the rich music of the voice, but the symptoms of strain and overwork were all too obvious. These proceeded, it was said, not only from having had to await (as he was awaiting even now) the outcome of battles in which he could have no active part, whatever his inclination, but also, it was added, from a congenital inability to relegate authority, including the minor paperwork which took up such a disproportionate share of his existence.

Other changes there were, too, less physical and therefore less immediately obvious, but on closer inspection no less profound. In this case, moreover, the contrast between now and then was emphasized by mutuality, involving others besides Davis. It was two-sided; reciprocal, so to speak. Arriving in Jackson to accept his appointment as commander of Mississippi troops after his farewell to the Senate in January of what had presently turned out to be the first year of the conflict some men had still believed could be avoided, he had been met at the station by Governor J. J. Pettus, whom he advised to push the procurement of arms. "We shall need all and many more than we can get," he said, expressing the conviction that blood would soon be shed. "General, you overrate the risk," the governor protested, and Davis replied: "I only wish I did." So thoroughly had this prediction been fulfilled in the past twenty months — Kentucky and Missouri irretrievably gone, along with most of Tennessee and the northwest quarter of Virginia, New Orleans fallen, Nashville and Memphis occupied, and North Mississippi itself aswarm with bluecoats — that now it was Governor Pettus who was calling for reassurance, and calling for it urgently, from the man to whom he previously had offered it so blandly.

"You have often visited the army of Virginia," he wired Richmond in early December. "At this critical juncture could you not visit the army of the West? Something must be done to inspire confidence."

By way of reinforcement for this plea there came a letter from Senator James Phelan, whose home lay in the path of the invaders. "The present alarming crisis in this state, so far from arousing the people, seems to have sunk them in listless despondency," he wrote. "The spirit of enlistment is thrice dead. Enthusiasm has expired to a cold pile of damp ashes. Defeats, retreats, sufferings, dangers, magnified by spiritless helplessness and an unchangeable conviction that our army is in the hands of ignorant and feeble commanders, are rapidly producing a sense of settled despair.... I imagine but one event that could awaken from its waning spark the enthusiastic hopes and energy of Mississippians. Plant your own foot upon our soil, unfurl your banner at the head of the army, tell your own people that you have come to share with them the perils of this dark hour.... If ever your presence was needed as a last refuge from an 'Iliad of woes,' this is the hour. It is not a point to be argued. [Only] you can save us or help us save ourselves from the dread evils now so imminently pending."

Flattering as this was, in part — especially the exhortation to "unfurl your banner," which touched the former hero of Buena Vista where his inclination was strongest and his vanity was most susceptible — the senator's depiction of regional gloom and fears, tossed thus into the balance, added weight to the governor's urgent plea that the Commander in Chief undertake the suggested journey to his homeland and thereby refute in the flesh the growing complaint that the authorities in Richmond were concerned only for the welfare of the soldiers and civilians in Virginia, where if anywhere the war was being won, rather than for those in the western theater, where if anywhere the war was being lost. Not that the danger nearest the national capital was slight. Major General Ambrose Burnside, a month in command of the Army of the Potomac as successor to Major General George McClellan, who had been relieved for a lack of aggressiveness, was menacing the line of the Rappahannock with a mobile force of 150,000 men, backed by another 50,000 in the Washington defenses. To oppose this host General Robert E. Lee had something under 80,000 in the Army of Northern Virginia moving toward a concentration near Fredericksburg, where the threat of a crossing seemed gravest, midway of the direct north-south hundred-mile line connecting the two capitals. That the battle, now obviously at hand, would be fought even closer to the Confederate seat of government appeared likely, for Davis wrote Lee on December 8: "You will know best when it will be proper to make a masked movement to the rear, should circumstances require you to move nearer to Richmond."

Something else he said in this same letter. Hard as it was for him to leave the capital at a time when every day might bring the battle that would perhaps decide his country's fate, he had made up his mind to heed the call that reached him from the West. "I propose to go out there immediately," he told Lee, "with the hope that something may be done to bring out men not heretofore in service, and to arouse all classes to united and desperate resistance." After expressing the hope that "God may bless us, as in other cases seemingly as desperate, with success over our impious foe," he added, by way of apology for not having reviewed the Virginian's army since it marched northward on the eve of Second Manassas: "I have been very anxious to visit you, but feeble health and constant labor have caused me to delay until necessity hurries me in the opposite direction." He sent the letter by special courier that same December 8; then, two days later, he himself was off.

He left incognito, aboard a special car and accompanied by a single military aide, lest his going stir up rumors that the capital was about to be abandoned in the face of the threat to the line of the Rappahannock. His planned itinerary was necessarily roundabout: not only because the only direct east-west route was closed to him by the Federal grip on the final hundred miles of the Memphis & Charleston Railroad, but also because he had decided to combine the attempt to restore morale among the distraught civilians of the region, as suggested by Governor Pettus and Senator Phelan, with a personal inspection of the two main armies charged with the defense of the theater bounded east and west by the Blue Ridge Mountains and the Mississippi River. The Army of Tennessee, the larger of the two, northwest of Chattanooga and covering that city by pretending to threaten Nashville, was under General Braxton Bragg; the other, the Army of Mississippi under Lieutenant General John C. Pemberton, covered Vicksburg. Both were menaced by superior forces, or combinations of forces, under Major Generals William S. Rosecrans and Ulysses S. Grant, and Davis had lately appointed General Joseph E. Johnston to co-ordinate the efforts of both armies in order to meet the double menace by operating on interior lines, much as Lee had done for the past six months in Virginia, on a smaller scale but with such success as had won for Confederate arms the admiration of the world.

Johnston's was the more difficult task, albeit one on which the survival of the nation was equally dependent. Whether it could be performed — specifically, whether it could be performed by Johnston — remained to be seen. So far, though, the signs had appeared to the general himself to be anything but promising. Pemberton was falling back under pressure from Grant in North Mississippi, and Bragg's preparations for the defense of Middle Tennessee, though they had not yet been tested by Federal pressure, did not meet with the new commander's approval when he inspected them this week. In fact, he found in them full justification for a judgment he had delivered the week before, when he first established headquarters in Chattanooga. "Nobody ever assumed a command under more unfavorable circumstances," he wrote to a friend back East. "If Rosecrans had disposed our troops himself, their disposition could not have been more unfavorable to us."

Davis did not share the Virginian's gloom; or if he did he did not show it as he left Richmond, December 10, and rode westward through Lynchburg and Wytheville and across the state line to Knoxville, where, beginning his attempt to bolster civilian morale by a show of confidence, he made a speech in which he characterized "the Toryism of East Tennessee" as "greatly exaggerated." Joined by Lieutenant General Edmund Kirby Smith, the department commander whose march north in August and September had cleared the region of bluecoats and delivered Cumberland Gap, but whose strength had been reduced by considerably more than half in the past month as a result of orders to reinforce Bragg in the adjoining department, the President reached Chattanooga by nightfall and went at once to pay a call on Johnston.

He found him somewhat indisposed, waiting in his quarters. Short of stature, gray and balding, a year older than Davis despite the fact that he had been a year behind him at West Point, the general had a high-colored, wedge-shaped face, fluffed white side whiskers, a grizzled mustache and goatee, eyes that crinkled attractively at their outer corners when he smiled, and a jaunty, gamecock manner. Mrs Johnston, in attendance on her husband, was able to serve their visitor a genuine cup of coffee: the "real Rio," she reported proudly to a friend next day, describing the event. She claimed nonetheless the saddest heart in Chattanooga. Whatever Davis might have accomplished elsewhere on this arduous first day of the journey he had undertaken "to arouse all classes to united and desperate resistance," he obviously had had little success in her direction. "How ill and weary I feel in this desolate land," she added in the letter to her friend in the Old Dominion, which she so much regretted having left, "& how dreary it all looks, & how little prospect there is of my poor husband doing ought than lose his army. Truly a forlorn hope it is."

The general himself was far from well, suffering from a flareup of the wound that had cost him his Virginia command, six months ago at Seven Pines, and from a weariness brought on by his just-completed inspection of the Army of Tennessee. So Davis, postponing their strategy conference until such time as he would be able to see for himself the condition of that army, left next day for Bragg's headquarters at Murfreesboro, ninety miles away and only thirty miles from Nashville.

It was a two-day visit, and unlike Johnston he was heartened by what he saw. Serenaded at his hotel by a large and enthusiastic crowd, he announced that he entertained no fears for the safety of Richmond, that Tennessee would be held to the last extremity, and that if the people would but arouse themselves to sustain the conflict, eventual if not immediate foreign intervention would assure a southern victory and peace on southern terms. His listeners, delighted by a recent exploit beyond the northern lines by Colonel John H. Morgan, did not seem to doubt for a moment the validity of his contentions or predictions. Whatever dejection he might encounter in other portions of the threatened region, he found here an optimism to match his own. The thirty-seven-year-old Morgan, with four small regiments of cavalry and two of infantry — just over 2000 men in all, most of them Kentuckians like himself — had crossed the icy Cumberland by starlight, in order to strike at dawn on Sunday, December 7, a Union force of equal strength in camp at Hartsville, forty miles upstream from Nashville. Another enemy force, three times his strength, was camped nine miles away at Castalian Springs, within easy hearing distance of his guns, but had no chance to interfere. After less than an hour of fighting, in which he inflicted more than 300 casualties at a cost of 125, Morgan accepted the surrender of Colonel Absalom B. Moore of Illinois. By noon he was back across the Cumberland with 1762 prisoners and a wagon train heavily loaded with captured equipment and supplies, riding hard for Murfreesboro and the cheers that awaited him there. "A brilliant feat," Joe Johnston called it, and recommended that Morgan "be appointed brigadier general immediately. He is indispensable."

Davis gladly conferred the promotion in person when he arrived, receiving from Morgan's own hands in return one of the three sets of enemy infantry colors the cavalryman had brought home. A formal review of one corps of the Army of Tennessee next day, followed that evening by a conference with Bragg and his lieutenants, was equally satisfying, fulfilling as it did the other half of the President's double-barreled purpose. "Found the troops there in good condition and fine spirits," he wired the Secretary of War on December 14, after his return to Chattanooga the night before. "Enemy is kept close in to Nashville, and indicates only defensive purposes."

This last had led to a strategic decision, made on the spot and before consultation with Johnston. As Davis saw it, comparing Pemberton's plight with Bragg's, the Mississippi commander was not only more gravely threatened by a combination of army and naval forces, above and below the Vicksburg bluff; he was also far more heavily outnumbered, and with less room for maneuver. Practically speaking, despite the assurance lately given the serenaders, the loss of Middle Tennessee would mean no more than the loss of supplies to be gathered in the region; whereas the loss of Vicksburg would mean the loss of the Mississippi River throughout its length, which in turn would mean the loss of Texas, West Louisiana, Arkansas, and the last tenuous hope for the recovery of Missouri. Consequently, in an attempt to even the odds — east and west, that is; North and South the odds could never be evened, here or elsewhere — Davis decided to reinforce Pemberton with a division from Bragg. When the latter protested that this would encourage Rosecrans to attack him, he was informed that he would have to take his chances, depending on maneuver for deliverance. "Fight if you can," Davis told him, and if necessary "fall back beyond the Tennessee."

Bragg took the decision with such grace as he could muster; but not Johnston. When Davis returned to Chattanooga with instructions for the transfer to be ordered, the Virginian protested for all he was worth against a policy which seemed to him no better than robbing Peter to pay Paul. Both western armies, he declared, were already too weak for effective operations; to weaken either was to invite disaster, particularly in Tennessee, which he referred to as "the shield of the South." But in this matter the President was inflexible. Apparently reasoning that if the general would not do the job for which he had been sent here — a balancing and a taking of calculated risks in order to make the most of the advantage of operating on interior lines — then he would do it for him, Davis insisted that the transfer order be issued immediately. This Johnston did, though with a heavy heart and still protesting, convinced that he would be proved right in the end.

Whatever Davis's reaction was on learning thus that one of his two ranking commanders was opposed to availing himself of the one solid advantage strategically accruing to the South, he had other worries to fret him now: worries that threatened not a long-range but an immediate collapse, not of a part but of the whole. On his return from Murfreesboro he heard from the War Department that the national capital was menaced from two directions simultaneously. A force of undetermined strength was moving inland from coastal North Carolina against Goldsboro and the vital Weldon Railroad, and Burnside was across the Rappahannock. "You can imagine my anxiety," Davis wrote his wife, chafed by distance and the impossibility of being in two places at once. "If the necessity demands, I will return to Richmond, though already there are indications of a strong desire for me to visit the further West, expressed in terms which render me unwilling to disappoint the expectation." Presently, however, his anxiety was relieved. The Carolina invasion, though strongly mounted, had been halted at the Neuse, well short of the vital supply line, and Lee had inflicted another staggering defeat on the main northern army, flinging it back across the Rappahannock. Davis was elated at the news, but Johnston's reaction was curiously mixed. "What luck some people have," he said. "Nobody will ever come to attack me in such a place."

After a day of rest and conferences, political as well as military, Davis left Chattanooga late on the afternoon of December 16, accompanied by Johnston, who would be making his first inspection of the western portion of his command. However, with the Memphis & Charleston in Federal hands along the Tennessee-Mississippi line, their route at first led south to Atlanta, where they spent the night and Davis responded to another serenade. Continuing south to Montgomery next morning, he spoke at midday from the portico of the Alabama capitol, where he had delivered his first inaugural a week after being notified of his unexpected election to head the newly established Confederate States of America. That was nearly two years ago. Whatever thoughts he had as to the contrast between now and then, as evidenced by the demeanor of the crowd that gathered to hear him, he kept to himself as he and Johnston rode on that night to Mobile, where he spoke formally for the second time that day. Next morning, December 19, they reached Jackson, but having agreed to return for a joint appearance before the Mississippi legislature on the day after Christmas, they only stayed for lunch and left immediately afterwards for Vicksburg.

This too was a two-day visit, and mainly they spent it inspecting the town's land and water defenses, which had been extended northward a dozen miles along a range of hills and ridges overlooking the Yazoo and its swampy bayous — Chickasaw Bluffs, the range was called, or sometimes Walnut Hills — and southward about half that far to Warrenton, a hamlet near the lower end of the tall red bluff dominating the eastern shank of the hairpin bend described at this point by a whim of the Mississippi. To an untrained eye the installations might look stout indeed, bristling with guns at intervals for nearly twenty miles, but Johnston was not pleased by what he saw. To his professional eye, they not only left much to be desired in the way of execution; their very conception, it seemed to him, was badly flawed. Nor was he any slower to say so now than he had been eight months ago at Yorktown, in a similar situation down the York-James peninsula from Richmond. "Instead of a fort requiring a small garrison," which would leave the bulk of available troops free to maneuver, he protested, the overzealous engineers had made the place into "an immense intrenched camp, requiring an army to hold it." Besides, scattered as they were along the high ground north and south "to prevent the bombardment of the town, instead of to close the navigation of the river to the enemy," the batteries would not be able to concentrate their fire against naval attack. In these and other matters Johnston expressed his discontent. Davis, a professional too, could see the justice in much of this, and though he did not order the line contracted, he moved to strengthen it by wiring the

War Department of the "immediate and urgent necessity for heavy guns and long-range fieldpieces at Vicksburg."

Two bits of news, one welcome, one disturbing, reached them here in the course of their brief visit. The first was that a Federal ironclad, the *Cairo*, had been sunk up the Yazoo the week before, the result of an experiment with torpedoes by Commander Isaac N. Brown, builder and skipper of the *Arkansas*, which single-handedly had raised the midsummer naval siege by an all-out attack on the two enemy fleets before she steamed downriver to her destruction in early August. The other news was that Major General Nathaniel P. Banks, whose troops were escorted upriver from New Orleans by the deep-draft fleet under Rear Admiral David G. Farragut, had reoccupied Baton Rouge, abandoned three months before by his predecessor, Major General Benjamin F. Butler. Whatever comfort the bluff's defenders found in the mishap encountered by the Yankees in their probe of the Yazoo was more than offset by the news that they were approaching in strength from the opposite direction. Johnston, for one, was convinced that, in addition to the 9000-man division already on the way from Bragg, another 20,000 troops would be required if Vicksburg and Port Hudson, another strong point on another bluff three hundred miles downriver, were to be held against the combined forces of Grant and Banks. What was more, he thought he knew just where to get them: from the adjoining Transmississippi Department, commanded by Lieutenant General Theophilus H. Holmes.

"Our great object is to hold the Mississippi," Johnston told Davis. In this connection, he firmly believed "that our true system of warfare would be to concentrate the forces of the two departments" — his and Holmes's — "on this side of the Mississippi, beat the enemy here, then reconquer the country beyond it, which [the Federals] might have gained in the meantime."

Davis had already shown his appreciation of this "true system" by recommending, a month before he left Richmond and two weeks before Johnston himself had been assigned to the western command, that Holmes send reinforcements eastward to assist in the accomplishment of the "great objective." Since then, unfortunately, and by coincidence on the December 7 of Morgan's victory at Hartsville, the Arkansas army under Major General Thomas C. Hindman, the one mobile force of any size in the department beyond the river, had fought and lost the Battle of Prairie Grove, up in the northwest corner of the state. This altered considerably Holmes's ability to comply with the request. However, instead of pointing out this and other drawbacks to Johnston's argument — 1) that to lose the Transmississippi temporarily might be to lose it permanently, as a result of losing the confidence of the people of the region; 2) that the Confederacy, already suffering from the strictures of the Federal blockade, could not afford even a brief stoppage of the flow of supplies from Texas and the valleys of the Arkansas and the Red; and 3) that the transfer east of men in gray would result in a proportional transfer of men in blue, which would lengthen rather than shorten the odds on both sides of the river unless the blow was delivered with unaccustomed lightning speed — Davis was willing to repeat the recommendation in stronger terms. Accordingly, on this same December 21, he wrote to Holmes in Little Rock, apprising him of the growing danger and urging full co-operation with Johnston's plan as set forth in that general's correspondence, which was included. It was a long letter, and in it the President said in part: "From the best information at command, a large force is now ready to descend the Mississippi and co-operate with the army advancing from Memphis to make an attack upon Vicksburg. Large forces are also reported to have been sent to the lower Mississippi for the purpose of ascending the river to attempt the reduction of Port Hudson.... It seems to me then unquestionably best that you should reinforce Genl Johnston." After reminding Holmes that "we cannot hope at all points to meet the enemy with a force equal to his own, and must find our security in the concentration and rapid movement of troops," Davis closed with a compliment and an admonition: "I have thus presented to you my views, and trusting alike in your patriotism and discretion, leave you to make the application of them when circumstances will permit. Whatever may be done should be done with all possible dispatch."

Johnston's enthusiasm on reading the opening paragraphs of the letter, which was shown to him before it was given to a courier bound for Little Rock, was considerably dampened by the close. Judging perhaps by his own reaction the week before, when he protested against the detachment of a division from Bragg for this same purpose, he did not share the President's trust in the "patriotism and discretion" Holmes was expected to bring to bear, and he noted regretfully that, despite the final suggestion as to the need for haste, "circumstances" had been left to govern the application of what Davis called his "views."

Two days later, moreover, the general's gloom was deepened when they returned to Jackson and proceeded north a hundred miles by rail to Grenada, where Pemberton had ended his southward retreat in the face of Grant's advance and had his badly outnumbered field force hard at work in an attempt to fortify the banks of the Yalobusha River while his cavalry, under Major General Earl Van Dorn, probed for Grant's rear in an attempt to make him call a halt, or anyhow slow him down, by giving him trouble along his lengthening supply line. Here as at Vicksburg, Johnston found the intrenchments "very extensive, but slight — the usual defect of Confederate engineering." Nor was he pleased to discover, as he said later, that "General Pemberton and I advocated opposite modes of warfare." He would have continued the retreat to a better position farther south, hoping for a stronger concentration; but as usual Davis discounted the advantage of withdrawal and sided with the commander who was opposed to delaying a showdown.

Christmas Day they returned to Jackson, which gave the President time for an overnight preparation of the speech he would deliver tomorrow before his home-state legislature. This was not so large a task as might be thought, despite the fact that he would speak for the better part of an hour. In general, what he would say here was what he had been saying for more than two weeks now, en route from Virginia, through Tennessee, Georgia, and Alabama, and elsewhere already in Mississippi. His overnight task was mainly one of consolidating his various impromptu responses to serenades and calls for "remarks" from station platforms along the way, albeit with added emphasis on his home ties and the government's concern for the welfare of the people in what he called "the further West."

That was why he began by addressing his listeners as "those who, from the days of my childhood, have ever been the trusted objects of my affection," and adding: "Whatever fortunes I may have achieved in life have been gained as a representative of Mississippi, and before all I have labored for the advancement of her glory and honor. I now, for the first time in my career, find myself the representative of a wider circle of interest, but a circle of which the interests of Mississippi are still embraced.... For, although in the discharge of my duties as President of the Confederate States I had determined to make no distinction between the various parts of the country — to know no separate state — yet my heart has always beat more warmly for Mississippi, and I have looked on Mississippi soldiers with a pride and emotion such as no others inspired."

Flanked on the rostrum by Governor Pettus and Senator Phelan, he waited for the polite applause to subside, then launched at once into an excoriation of the northern government: not only its leaders but also its followers, in and out of the armies of invasion.

"I was among those who, from the beginning, predicted war... not because our right to secede and form a government of our own was not indisputable and clearly defined in the spirit of that declaration which rests the right to govern on the consent of the governed, but because I saw that the wickedness of the North would precipitate a war upon us. Those who supposed that the exercise of this right of separation could not produce war have had cause to be convinced that they had credited their recent associates of the North with a moderation, a sagacity, a morality they did not possess. You have been involved in a war waged for the gratification of the lust of power and aggrandizement, for your conquest and your subjugation, with a malignant ferocity and with a disregard and a contempt of the usages of civilization entirely unequaled in history. Such, I have ever warned you, were the characteristics of the northern people.... After what has happened during the last two years, my only wonder is that we consented to live for so long a time in association with such miscreants and have loved so much a government rotten to the core. Were it ever to be proposed again to enter into a Union with such a people, I could no more consent to do it than to trust myself in a den of thieves.... There is indeed a difference between the two peoples. Let no man hug the delusion that there can be renewed association between them. Our enemies are a traditionless and homeless race. From the time of Cromwell to the present moment they have been disturbers of the peace of the world. Gathered together by Cromwell from the bogs and fens of the north of Ireland and England, they commenced by disturbing the peace of their own country; they disturbed Holland, to which they fled; and they disturbed England on their return. They persecuted Catholics in England, and they hung Quakers and witches in America."

He spoke next of the conscription act, defending it against its critics; reviewed the recent successes of Confederate arms, sometimes against odds that had amounted to four to one; recommended local provision for the families of soldiers in the field; urged upon the legislators "the necessity of harmony" between the national government and the governments of the states; then returned to a bitter expression of his views as to the contrast between the two embattled peoples.

"The issue before us is one of no ordinary character. We are not engaged in a conflict for conquest, or for aggrandizement, or for the settlement of a point of international law. The question for you to decide is, Will you be slaves or will you be independent? Will you transmit to your children the freedom and equality which your fathers transmitted to you, or will you bow down in adoration before an idol baser than ever was worshiped by Eastern idolators? Nothing more is necessary than the mere statement of this issue. Whatever may be the personal sacrifices involved, I am confident that you will not shrink from them whenever the question comes before you. Those men who now assail us, who have been associated with us in a common Union, who have inherited a government which they claim to be the best the world ever saw — these men, when left to themselves, have shown that they are incapable of preserving their own personal liberty. They have destroyed the freedom of the press; they have seized upon and imprisoned members of state legislatures and of municipal councils, who were suspected of sympathy with the South; men have been carried off into captivity in distant states without indictment, without a knowledge of the accusations brought against them, in utter defiance of all rights guaranteed by the institutions under which they live. These people, when separated from the South and left entirely to themselves, have in six months demonstrated their utter incapacity for self-government. And yet these are the people who claim to be your masters. These are the people who have determined to divide out the South among their Federal troops. Mississippi they have devoted to the direst vengeance of all. 'But vengeance is the Lord's,' and beneath His banner you will meet and hurl back these worse than vandal hordes."

Having attempted thus to breathe heat into what Senator Phelan had called "a cold pile of damp ashes," Davis spoke of final success as certain. "Our people have only to be true to themselves to behold the Confederate flag among the recognized nations of the earth. The question is only one of time. It may be remote, but it may be nearer than many people suppose. It is not possible that a war of the dimensions that this one has assumed, of proportions so gigantic, can be very long protracted. The combatants must soon be exhausted. But it is impossible, with a cause like ours, that we can be the first to cry, 'Hold, enough.' " He spoke of valor and determination, of his pride in the southern fighting man, and assured his listeners that the Confederacy could accomplish its own salvation. This last led him into a statement unlike any he had made before:

"In the course of this war our eyes have often been turned abroad. We have expected sometimes recognition, and sometimes intervention, at the hands of foreign nations; and we had a right to expect it. Never before in the history of the world have a people so long a time maintained their ground, and shown themselves capable of maintaining their national existence, without securing the recognition of commercial nations. I know not why this has been so, but this I say: 'Put not your trust in princes,' and rest not your hopes on foreign nations. This war is ours; we must fight it out ourselves. And I feel some pride in knowing that, so far, we have done it without the good will of anybody."

When the applause that echoed this had died away he defined what he believed to be the "two prominent objects in the program of the enemy. One is to get possession of the Mississippi River, and to open it to navigation, in order to appease the clamors of the [Northwest] and to utilize the capture of New Orleans, which has thus far rendered them no service. The other is to seize upon the capital of the Confederacy, and hold this but as proof that the Confederacy has no existence." The fourth full-scale attempt to accomplish the latter object had just been frustrated by Lee at Fredericksburg, he informed the legislature, "and I believe that, under God and by the valor of our troops, the capital of the Confederacy will stand safe behind its wall of living breasts." As for the likelihood that the Unionists might accomplish the first-mentioned object, Davis admitted that this had caused him grave concern, and was in fact the reason for his present visit.

"This was the land of my affections," he declared. "Here were situated the little of worldly goods I possessed." He had, he repeated, "every confidence in the skill and energy of the officers in command. But when I received dispatches and heard rumors of alarm and trepidation and despondency among the people of Mississippi; when I heard, even, that people were fleeing to Texas in order to save themselves from the enemy; when I saw it stated by the enemy that they had handled other states with gloves, but Mississippi was to be handled without gloves — every impulse of my heart dragged me hither, in spite of duties which might have claimed my attention elsewhere. When I heard of the sufferings of my own people, of the danger of their subjugation by a ruthless foe, I felt that if Mississippi were destined for such a fate, I would wish to sleep in her soil." However, now that he had seen for himself the condition of the army and the people of his homeland, "I shall go away from you with a lighter heart ... anxious, but hopeful."

In closing he spoke as a man who had kept a vigil through darkness into dawn, so that now he stood in sunlight. "I can, then, say with confidence that our condition is in every respect greatly improved over what it was last year. Our armies have been augmented; our troops have been instructed and disciplined. The articles necessary for the support of our troops and our people, and from which the enemy's blockade has cut us off, are being produced by the Confederacy.... Our people have learned to economize and are satisfied to wear homespun. I never see a woman dressed in homespun that I do not feel like taking off my hat to her, and although our women never lose their good looks, I cannot help thinking that they are improved by this garb. I never meet a man dressed in homespun but I feel like saluting him. I cannot avoid remarking with how much pleasure I have noticed the superior morality of our troops and the contrast which in this respect they present to the invader. On their valor and the assistance of God I confidently rely."

The applause that followed had begun to fade, when suddenly it swelled again, provoked and augmented by loud calls for "Johnston! Johnston!" At last the general rose and came forward, modestly acknowledging the cheers, which were redoubled. When they subsided he spoke with characteristic brevity and the self-effacement becoming to a soldier. "Fellow citizens," he said. "My only regret is that I have done so little to merit such a greeting. I promise you, however, that hereafter I shall be watchful, energetic, and indefatigable in your defense." That was all; but it was enough. According to one reporter, the applause that burst forth as he turned to resume his seat was "tremendous, uproarious, and prolonged." Apparently the general was more popular than the Chief Executive, even in the latter's own home state.

Despite this evidence of enthusiastic support from the civilians of the region, now that he had completed his military inspection Johnston was more dissatisfied than ever with the task which had been thrust into his hands. His command, he told Davis as soon as they were alone, was "a nominal one merely, and useless.... The great distance between the Armies of Mississippi and Tennessee, and the fact that they had different objects and adversaries, made it impossible to combine their action." The only use he saw for his talents, he continued in a subsequent account of the interview, was as a substitute commander of one of the armies, "which, as each had its own general, was not intended or desirable." In short, he told the President, he asked to be excused from serving in a capacity "so little to my taste."

Davis replied that distance was precisely the factor which had caused Johnston to be sent here. However far apart the two armies were, both were certainly too far from Richmond for effective control to be exercised from there; someone with higher authority than the two commanders should be at hand to co-ordinate their efforts and "transfer troops from one army to another in an emergency." Unpersuaded, still perturbed, the general continued to protest that, each being already "too weak for its object," neither army "could be drawn upon to strengthen the other," and with so much distance between the two, even "temporary transfers" were "impracticable." In point of fact, he could see nothing but ultimate disaster resulting from so unorthodox an arrangement. Once more Davis disagreed. Johnston was not only here; he was *needed* here. He must do the best he could. Or as the general put it, his "objections were disregarded."

On this discordant note the two men parted, Johnston to establish a new headquarters in the Mississippi capital and Davis to visit his eldest brother Joseph at his new plantation near Bolton, on the railroad west of Jackson. Their previous holdings on Davis Bend, just below Vicksburg — Joseph's, called The Hurricane, and his own, called Brierfield — had been overrun and sacked by Butler's men during their abortive upriver thrust, made in conjunction with Farragut's fleet the previous summer: which, incidentally, was why Davis had used the past tense in reference to "the little of worldly goods I possessed," and which, in part, was also why he referred to the Federals as "worse than vandal hordes."

In the course of his two-day visit with his septuagenarian brother, good news reached him on December 27 which seemed to indicate that Johnston's unwelcome burden already had been made a good deal lighter than he had protested it to be. Grant's army in North Mississippi was in full retreat; Van Dorn had broken loose in its immediate rear and burned its forward supply base at Holly Springs, capturing the garrison in the process, while Brigadier General Nathan Bedford Forrest, even farther in the northern commander's rear, was wrecking vital supply lines and creating general havoc all over West Tennessee. The following day, however, on the heels of these glad tidings, came word that Vicksburg itself was under assault by Major General William Tecumseh Sherman, who had come downriver from Memphis with the other half of Grant's command, escorted by Rear Admiral David Porter's ironclad fleet, and was storming the Chickasaw Bluffs. With the main body off opposing Grant, this was the worst of all possible news, short of the actual capture of the place; but on the 29th the President's anxiety was relieved and his spirits lifted by word that Sherman's repulse had been accomplished as effectively and as decisively, against even longer odds, as Burnside's had been at Fredericksburg two weeks before. What was more, the means by which it had been done went far toward sustaining Davis's military judgment, since the victory had been won in a large part by two brigades from the division he had recently detached, under protest, from the Army of Tennessee.

Vicksburg, then, had been delivered from the two-pronged pressure being applied from the north. If Bragg could do even partly as well in keeping Rosecrans out of Chattanooga, and if the garrison at Port Hudson could stop Banks and Farragut in their ascent of the Mississippi, the multiple threats to the western theater would have been smashed all round, or anyhow blunted for a season, despite the dire predictions made only that week by its over-all commander. One thing at any rate was certain. The President's long train ride back to Richmond would be made in a far more genial atmosphere, militarily speaking, than he had encountered at successive stops in the course of the outward journey.

He left Jackson on the last day of the year, and after speaking again that evening from a balcony of the Battle House in Mobile, received while retracing in reverse his route through Alabama and Georgia a double — indeed, a triple — further measure of good tidings. "God has granted us a happy New Year," Bragg wired from Murfreesboro. Rosecrans had ventured out of his intrenchments to attack the Army of Tennessee, which had then turned the tables with a dawn assault, jackknifing the Union right against the Union left. Not only was Chattanooga secure, but from the sound of the victorious commander's dispatch, Nashville itself might soon be recovered. "The enemy has yielded his strong position and is falling back," Bragg exulted. "We occupy whole field and shall follow him."

The pleasure Davis felt at this — augmented as it was by information that John Morgan had outdone himself in Kentucky on a Christmas raid, wrecking culverts, burning trestles, and capturing more than two thousand men, while Forrest and Van Dorn were returning safely from their separate and equally spectacular raids, the former after escaping a convergence designed for his destruction at Parker's Crossroads, deep inside the enemy lines — was raised another notch by word that a Federal reconnaissance force, sent upriver by Banks from Baton Rouge, had turned tail at the unexpected sight of the guns emplaced on Port Hudson's bluff and steamed back down without offering a challenge. And when this in turn was followed by still a third major item in the budget of good news, the presidential cup ran over. Major General John B. Magruder, recently arrived to take command of all the Confederates in Texas, had improvised a two-boat fleet of "cotton-clads" and had retaken Galveston in a New Year's predawn surprise attack, destroying one Yankee deep-water gunboat and forcing another to strike its colors. With the surrender of the army garrison in occupation of the island town, Texas was decontaminated. The only bluecoats still on her soil were Magruder's prisoners.

Leaving Mobile, Davis again visited Montgomery and Atlanta, but passing through the latter place he proceeded, not north to Chattanooga, but eastward to Augusta, where he spent the night of January 2. Next morning he entered South Carolina for the first time since the removal of the government to Richmond, back in May, and after a halt for a speech in Columbia, the capital, went on that night across the state line to Charlotte. At noon the following day he spoke in Raleigh, the North Carolina capital, then detoured south to Wilmington, the principal east coast port for blockade-runners, where he received the first really disturbing military news that had reached him since he left Virginia, nearly a month before. Instead of "following" the defeated Rosecrans, as he had said he would do, Bragg had waited a day before resuming the offensive, and then had been repulsed; whereupon, having been informed that the enemy had been reinforced — and bearing in mind, moreover, the Commander in Chief's recent advice: "Fight if you can, and fall back [if you must]" — he fell back thirty miles to a better defensive position on Duck River, just in front of Tullahoma and still protecting Chattanooga, another fifty-odd miles in his rear. As at Perryville, three months ago, he had won a battle and then retreated. Not that Murfreesboro was not still considered a victory; it was, at least in southern eyes. Only some of the luster had been lost. Davis, however, placing emphasis on the odds and the fact that Chattanooga was secure, counted it scarcely less a triumph than before. In response to a Wilmington serenade, tendered just after he received word that Bragg had fallen back, he spoke for a full hour from his hotel balcony. Employing what one hearer called "purity of diction" and a "fervid eloquence" to match the enthusiasm of the torchlight serenaders, he characterized recent events as a vindication of the valor of southern arms, and even went so far as to repeat the words he had spoken to a similar crowd from a Richmond balcony on the jubilant morrow of First Manassas: "Never be humble to the haughty. Never be haughty to the humble."

That was a Sunday. Next day, January 5, he covered the final leg of his long journey, returning to Richmond before dark. He was weary and he looked it, and with cause, for in twenty-five days he had traveled better than twenty-five hundred miles and had made no less than twenty-five public addresses, including some that had lasted more than an hour. However, his elation overmatched his weariness, and this too was with cause. He knew that he had done much to restore civilian morale by appearing before the disaffected people, and militarily the gains had been even greater. Though mostly they had been fought against odds that should have been oppressive, if not completely paralyzing, of the several major actions which had occurred during his absence from the capital or on the eve of his departure — Prairie Grove and Hartsville, Fredericksburg and Goldsboro, Holly Springs and Chickasaw Bluffs, Galveston and Murfreesboro — all were resounding victories except the first and possibly the last. Taken in conjunction with the spectacular Christmas forays of Morgan and Forrest, the torpedoing of the *Cairo* up the Yazoo River, and Grant's enforced retreat in North Mississippi, these latest additions to the record not only sustained the reputation Confederate arms had gained on many a field during the year just passed into history; they also augured well for a future which only lately had seemed dark. Defensively speaking, indeed, the record could scarcely have been improved. Of the three objectives the Federals had set for themselves, announcing them plainly to all the world by moving simultaneously against them as the year drew to a close, Vicksburg had been disenthralled and Chattanooga remained as secure as Richmond.

Davis himself had done as much as any man, and a good deal more than most, to bring about the result that not a single armed enemy soldier now stood within fifty air-line miles of any one of these three vital cities. It was therefore a grateful, if weary, President who was met by his wife and their four children on the steps of the White House, late that Monday afternoon of the first week of the third calendar year of this second American war for independence.

✗ 2 ✗

Of all these various battles and engagements, fought in all these various places, Fredericksburg, the nearest to the national capital, was the largest — in numbers engaged, if not in bloodshed — as well as the grandest as a spectacle, in which respect it equaled, if indeed it did not outdo, any other major conflict of the war. Staged as it was, with a curtain of fog that lifted, under the influence of a genial sun, upon a sort of natural amphitheater referred to by one of the 200,000 participants, a native of the site, as "a champaign tract inclosed by hills," it quite fulfilled the volunteers' early-abandoned notion of combat as a picture-book affair. What was more, the setting had been historical long before the armies met there to add a bloody chapter to a past that had been peaceful up to now. John Paul Jones had lived as a boy in the old colonial town that gave its name and sacrificed the contents of its houses to the battle. Hugh Mercer's apothecary shop and James Monroe's law office were two among the many points of interest normally apt to be pointed out to strangers by the four thousand inhabitants, most of whom had lately been evacuated, however, by order of the commander of the army whose looters would presently take the place apart and whose corpses would find shallow graves on its unwarlike lawns and in its gardens. Here the widowed Mary Washington had lived, and it was here or near here that her son was reported to have thrown a Spanish silver dollar across the Rappahannock. During the battle itself, from one of the dominant hills where he established his forward command post, R. E. Lee would peer through rifts in the swirling gunsmoke in an attempt to spot in the yard of Chatham, a mansion on the heights beyond the river, the old tree beneath whose branches he had courted Mary Custis, granddaughter of the woman who later married the dollar-flinging George and thus became the nation's first first lady.

Yet it was Burnside, not Lee, who had chosen the setting for the impending carnage. Appointed to succeed his friend McClellan because of that general's apparent lack of aggressiveness after the Battle of Antietam, he had shifted the Army of the Potomac eastward to this point where the Rappahannock, attaining its head of navigation, swerved suddenly south to lave the doorsteps of the town on its right bank. Washington lay fifty miles behind him; Richmond, his goal, lay fifty miles ahead. Mindful of the President's admonition that his plan for eluding Lee in order to descend on the southern capital would succeed "if you move very rapidly, otherwise not," he had indeed moved rapidly; but, as it turned out, he had moved to no avail. Though he had successfully given Lee the slip, the pontoons he had requisitioned in advance from Harpers Ferry, altogether necessary if he was to cross the river, did not reach the Fredericksburg area until his army had been massed in jump-off positions for more than a week; by which time, to his confoundment, Lee had the opposite ridges bristling with guns that were trained on the prospective bridge sites. Burnside was so profoundly distressed by this turn of events that he spent two more weeks looking down on the town from the left-bank heights, with something of the intentness and singularity of purpose which he had displayed, back in September at Antietam, looking down at the little triple-arched bridge that ever afterwards bore his name as indelibly as if the intensity of his gaze had etched it deep into the stone. Meanwhile, by way of increasing his chagrin as Lee's butternut veterans clustered thick and thicker on the hills across the way, it was becoming increasingly apparent, not only to the northern commander but also to his men, that what had begun as a sprint for Richmond had landed him and them in coffin corner.

He had troubles enough, in all conscience, but at least they were not of the kind that proceeded from any shortage of troops. Here opposite Fredericksburg, ready to execute his orders as soon as he could decide what those orders were going to be, Burnside had 121,402 effectives in his six corps of three divisions each. Organized into three Grand Divisions of two corps each, these eighteen divisions were supported by 312 pieces of artillery. Nor was that all. Marching on Dumfries, twenty miles to the north, were two more corps with an effective strength of 27,724 soldiers and 97 guns. In addition to this field force of nearly 150,000 men, supported by more than 400 guns, another 52,000 in the Washington defenses and along the upper Potomac were also included in his nominal command; so that his total "present for duty" during this second week of December — at any rate the first part of it, before the butchering began — was something over 200,000 of all arms. He did not know the exact strength of the rebels waiting for him beyond the town and at other undetermined positions downriver, but he estimated their strength at just over 80,000 men.

In this — unlike McClellan, who habitually doubled and sometimes even tripled an enemy force by estimation — he was not far off. Lee had nine divisions organized into two corps of about 35,000 each, which, together with some 8000 cavalry and artillery, gave him a total of 78,511 effectives, supported by 275 guns. He had, then, not quite two thirds as many troops in the immediate vicinity as his opponent had. By ordinary, as he had lately told the Secretary of War, he thought it preferable, considering the disparity of force, "to attempt to baffle [the enemy's] designs by maneuvering rather than to resist his advance by main force." However, he found his present position so advantageous — naturally strong, though not so formidable in appearance as to rule out the possibility of an attempted assault — that he was determined to hold his ground, despite the odds, in the belief that the present situation contained the seeds of another full-scale Federal disaster.

Except for two detached brigades of cavalry, his whole army was at hand. So far, though, he had effected the concentration of only one corps, leaving the other spread out downstream to guard the crossings all the way to Port Royal, twenty miles below. The first corps, five divisions under Lieutenant General James Longstreet — "Old Peter," his men called him, adopting his West Point nickname; Lee had lately dubbed him "my old warhorse" — was in position on the slopes and crest of a seven-mile-long range of hills overlooking the mile-wide "champaign tract" that gave down upon the town and the river, its flanks protected right and left by Massaponax Creek and the southward bend of the Rappahannock. Forbidding in appearance, the position was even more formidable in fact; for the range of hills — in effect, a broken ridge — was mostly wooded, affording concealment for the infantry, and the batteries had been sited with such care that when Longstreet suggested the need for another gun at a critical point, the artillery commander replied: "General, we cover that ground now so well that we comb it as with a fine-tooth comb. A chicken could not live on that field when we open on it."

The other corps commander, Lieutenant General Thomas Jonathan Jackson — "Old Jack" to his men, redoubtable "Stonewall" to the world at large — had three of his four divisions posted at eight-mile in-

The Longest Journey   [23]

tervals downstream, one on the south bank of Massaponax Creek, one at Skinker's Neck, and one near Port Royal, while the fourth was held at Guiney Station, on the Richmond, Fredericksburg & Potomac Railroad, eight miles in rear of Longstreet's right at Hamilton's Crossing. Despite the possibility that Burnside might swamp Longstreet with a sudden assault, outnumbering him no less that three-to-one, Lee accepted the risk of keeping the second corps widely scattered in order to be able to challenge the Union advance at the very outset, whenever and wherever it began. Jackson, on the other hand, would have preferred to fight on the line of the North Anna, a less formidable stream thirty miles nearer Richmond, rather than here on the Rappahannock, which he believed would be an effective barrier to pursuit of the beaten Yankees when they retreated, as he was sure they would do, under cover of their superior artillery posted on the dominant left-bank heights. "We will whip the enemy, but gain no fruits of victory," he predicted.

In point of fact, whatever validity Jackson might have as a prophet, Lee not only accepted the risk of a sudden, all-out attack on Longstreet; he actually preferred it. Though he expected the crossing to be attempted at some point downriver, in which case he intended to challenge it at the water's edge, it was his fervent hope that Burnside could be persuaded — or, best of all, would persuade himself — to make one here. In that case, Lee did not intend to contest the crossing itself with any considerable force. The serious challenge would come later, when the enemy came at him across that open, gently undulating plain. He had confidence that Old Peter, securely intrenched along the ridge, his guns already laid and carefully ranged on check points, could absorb the shock until the two closest of Stonewall's divisions could be summoned.

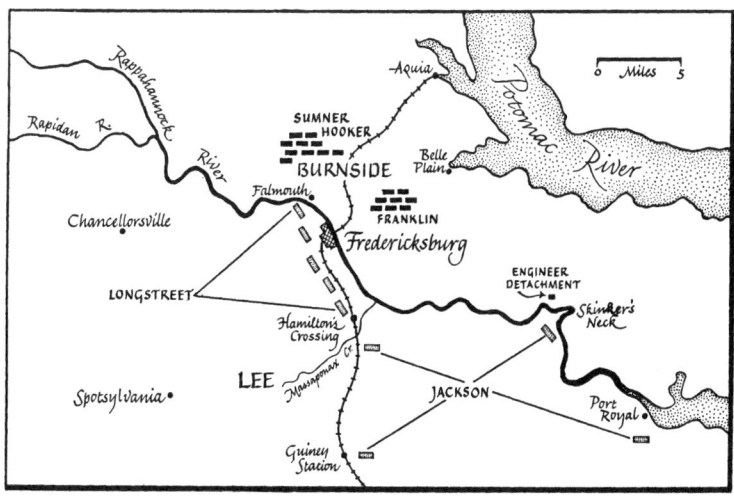

Their arrival would give the Confederate infantry the unaccustomed numerical wealth of six men to every yard of their seven-mile line: which Lee believed would be enough, not only to repulse the Federals, but also to enable the graybacks to launch a savage counterstroke, in the style of Second Manassas, that would drive the bluecoats in a panicky mass and pen them for slaughter against the unfordable river, too thickly clustered for escape across their pontoon bridges and too closely intermingled with his own charging troops for the Union artillery to attempt a bombardment from the opposite heights. It was unlikely that Burnside would thus expose his army to the Cannae so many Southerners believed was overdue. It was, indeed, almost too much to hope for. But Lee did hope for it. He hoped for it intensely.

Burnside, too, was weighing these possibilities, and it seemed to him also that the situation was heavy with the potentials of disaster: much more so, in fact, than it had been before he shifted his army eastward in November from the scene of Pope's late-August rout. Though so far he had escaped direct connection with a military fiasco, he had not been unacquainted with sudden blows of adversity in the years before the war. Once as a newly commissioned lieutenant on his way to the Mexican War he had lost his stake to a gambler on a Mississippi steamboat, and again in the mid-50's he had failed to get a government contract for the manufacture of a breech-loading rifle he had invented and put his cash in after leaving the army to devote full time to its promotion, which left him so broke that he had to sell his sword and uniforms for money to live on until his friend McClellan gave him a job with the land office of a railroad, where he prospered. Between these two financial upsets, he had received his worst personal shock when a Kentucky girl, whom he had wooed and finally persuaded to accompany him to the altar, responded to the minister's final ceremonial question with an abrupt, emphatic "No!" Hard as they had been to take, these three among several lesser setbacks had really hurt no one but himself, nor had they seriously affected the thirty-eight-year-old general's basically sunny disposition. But now that he had the lives of two hundred thousand men dependent on his abilities, not to mention the possible outcome of a war in which his country claimed to be fighting for survival, he did not face the likelihood of failure with such equanimity as he had shown in those previous trying situations. Formerly a hearty man, whose distinctive ruff of dark brown whiskers described a flamboyant double parabola below a generous, wide-nostriled nose, a pair of alert, dark-socketed eyes, and a pale expanse of skin that extended all the way back to the crown of his head, he had become increasingly morose and fretful here on the high left bank of the Rappahannock. "I deem it my duty," he had advised his superiors during the interim which followed the nonarrival of the pontoons at the climax of his rapid cross-country march, "to say that I cannot make the promise of probable success with the faith that I did when I supposed that all the parts of the plan would be carried out."

This was putting it rather mildly. Yet, notwithstanding his qualms, he had evolved a design which he believed would work by virtue of its daring. His balloons were up, despite the blustery weather, and the observers reported heavy concentrations of rebels far downstream. He had intended to throw his bridges across the river at Skinker's Neck, ten miles beyond Lee's immediate right, then march directly on the railroad in the southern army's rear, thus forcing its retreat to protect its supply line. However, the balloon reports convinced him that Lee had divined his purpose, and this — plus the difficulty of concealing his preparations in that quarter, which led him to suspect that he would be doing nothing more than side-stepping into another stalemate — caused him to shift the intended attack back to the vicinity of Fredericksburg itself, where he could use the town to mask the crossing. It was a bold decision, made in the belief that, of all possible moves, this was the one his opponent would be least likely to suspect until it was already in execution: which, as he saw it from the Confederate point of view, would be too late. The troops below were Jackson's, the renowned "foot cavalry" of the Army of Northern Virginia, but a good part of them were as much as twenty miles away. By the time they arrived, if all went as Burnside intended, there would be no other half of their army for them to support; he would have crushed it, and they would find that what they had been hastening toward was slaughter or surrender.

Accordingly, early on December 9, a warning order went out for Grand Division commanders to report to army headquarters at noon, by which time they were to have alerted their troops, supplied each man with sixty rounds of ammunition, and begun the issue of three days' cooked rations. They would have the rest of today to get ready, he told them, and all of tomorrow. Then, in the predawn darkness of Thursday, December 11, the engineers would throw the six bridges by which the infantry and cavalry would cross for the attack, followed at once by such artillery as had been assigned to furnish close-up support. The crossing would be made in two general areas, one directly behind the town and the other just below it, with three bridges at each affording passage for the left and right Grand Divisions, commanded respectively by Major Generals William B. Franklin and Edwin V. Sumner. The center Grand Division, under Major General Joseph Hooker, would lend weight to the assault by detaching two of its divisions to Franklin and the other four to Sumner, giving them each a total of approximately 60,000 men, including cavalry and support artillery. Burnside's intention — not unlike McClellan's at Antietam, except that the flanks were reversed — was for Franklin's column to attack and carry the lower end of the ridge on which the Confederates were intrenched, then wheel and sweep northward along it while the enemy was being held in place by attacks delivered simultaneously by Sumner on the right. It was simple enough, as all such designs for destruction were meant to be. In fact, Burnside apparently considered it so readily comprehensible as to require little or no incidental explanation when the three generals reported to him at noon.

One additional subterfuge he would employ, but that was all. The engineers at Skinker's Neck, assisted by a regiment of Maine axmen, would be kept at work felling trees and laying a corduroy approach down to the riverbank at that point, as if for the passage of infantry with artillery support. The sound of chopping, along with the glow of fires at night, would help to delude the rebels in their expectation of a crossing there. However, even this was but a strengthening of the original subterfuge, the shifting of the main effort back upstream, on which the ruff-whiskered general based his belief, or at any rate his hope, that he would find Lee unprepared and paralyze him with his daring.

That was a good deal more than any of the northern commander's predecessors had been able to do, but Burnside's gloom had been dispelled; his confidence had risen now to zenith. As he phrased it in a dispatch telegraphed to Washington near midnight, outlining his attack plan and divulging his expectations, "I think now that the enemy will be more surprised by a crossing immediately in our front than in any other part of the river. The commanders of Grand Divisions coincide with me in this opinion, and I have accordingly ordered the movement. ... We hope to succeed."

Lee was indeed surprised, though not unpleasantly. Already a firm believer in the efficacy of prayer, he might have seen in this development a further confirmation of his faith. Nor was the surprise as complete as Burnside had intended. On Wednesday night, December 10, a woman crept down to the east bank of the Rappahannock and called across to the gray pickets that the Yankees had drawn a large issue of cooked rations — always a sign that action was at hand. Then at 4.45 next morning, two hours before dawn, two guns boom-boomed the prearranged signal that the enemy was attempting a crossing here in front of Fredericksburg. At once the Confederate bivouacs were astir with men turning out of their blankets to take the posts already assigned them along the ridge overlooking the plain that sloped eastward to the old colonial town, still invisible in the frosty darkness.

In it there was one brigade of Mississippi infantry, bled down to 1600 veterans under Brigadier General William Barksdale, a former congressman with long white hair and what one of his soldiers called "a thirst for battle glory." He had had his share of this in every major engagement since Manassas, but today was his best chance to slake that thirst; for Lee, being unwilling to subject the town to shelling, had left to these few Deep South troops the task of contesting the crossing — not with any intention of preventing it, even if that had been possible in the face of all those guns on the dominant heights, but merely to make it as costly to the Federals as he could. Barksdale received the assignment gladly, posting most of his men in stout brick houses whose rear walls, looking out upon the river, they loopholed so as to draw their beads with a minimum of distraction in the form of return fire from the men they would be dropping when the time came. Shortly after midnight, hearing sounds of preparation across the way — the muffled tread of soldiers on the march, the occasional whinny of a horse or bray of a mule, the clank of trace-chains, and at last the ponderous rumble of what he took to be pontoons being brought down from the heights — he knew the time was very much at hand. After sending word of this to his superiors, he saw to it that the few remaining civilians, mostly women and children, with a sprinkling of old men, either hastened away to the safety of the hills or else took refuge in their cellars.

He was in no hurry to open fire, preferring not to waste ammunition in the darkness. Long before daylight, however, his men could hear the Federal engineers at work: low-voiced commands, the clatter of lumber, and at intervals the loud crack of half-inch skim ice as another pontoon was launched. This last drew closer with every repetition as the bridge was extended, unit by six-foot unit, across the intervening four hundred feet of water. At last, judging by the sound that the pontoniers had reached midstream, the waiting riflemen opened fire. They aimed necessarily by ear, but the result was satisfactory. After the first yelp of pain there was the miniature thunder of boots on planks, diminishing as the runners cleared the bridge; then silence, broken presently by the boom-boom of the two guns passing the word along the ridge that the Yanks were coming.

Soon they returned to the bridge-end, working as quietly as possible since every sound, including even the squeak of a bolt, was echoed by the crack of rifles from the western bank. It was perilous work, but it was nothing compared to the trouble brought by a misty dawn and a rising sun that began to burn the fog away, exposing the workers to aimed shots from marksmen whose skill was practically superfluous at a range of two hundred feet. A pattern was quickly established. The pontoniers would rush out onto the bridge, take up their tools, and work feverishly until the fire grew too hot; whereupon they would drop their tools and run the gauntlet back to bank. Then, as they got up their nerve again, their officers would lead or chevy them back onto the bridge, where the performance would be repeated. This went on for hours, to the high delight of the Mississippians, who jeered and hooted as they shot and waited, then shot and waited to shoot some more.

By 10 o'clock the northern commander's patience had run out.

The movement was already hours off schedule; Longstreet's signal guns had announced Lee's alertness, and Jackson's lean marchers might well be on the way by now. Rifle fire having proved ineffective against the snipers behind the brick walls of the houses along the riverbank, Burnside ordered his chief of artillery, Brigadier General Henry Hunt, to open fire with the 147 heavy-caliber guns posted on Stafford Heights, frowning down on the old town a hundred feet below. The response was immediate and uproarious, and it lasted for more than an hour, Hunt having instructed his gun crews to maintain a rate of fire of one shot every two minutes. Seventy-odd solid shot and shells a minute were thrown until 5000 had been fired. During all that time, a correspondent wrote, "the earth shook beneath the terrific explosions of the shells, which went howling over the river, crashing into houses, battering down walls, splintering doors, ripping up floors."

As a spectacle of modern war it was a great success, and it was also quite successful against the town. It wrecked houses, setting several afire; it tore up cobblestones; it shook the very hills the armies stood on. But it did not seem to dampen the spirits or influence the marksmanship of the Mississippians, who rose from the rubble and dropped more of the pontoniers, driving them again from the work they had returned to during the lull that followed the bombardment. When Barksdale sent a message asking whether he should have his men put out the fires, Longstreet replied: "You have enough to do to watch the Yankees." Back at Lee's observation post, the sight of what the Union guns had done to the Old Dominion town so riled the southern commander that he broke out wrathfully against the cannoneers and the officers who had given them orders to open fire. "Those people delight to destroy the weak and those who can make no defense," he said hotly. "It just suits them!" However, when he sent to inquire after the welfare of Barksdale's men and to see if there was anything they wanted, that general sent back word that he had everything he needed. But he added, "Tell General Lee that if he wants a bridge of dead Yankees, I can furnish him with one."

It was well past noon by now. Hunt, admitting that his guns could never dislodge the rebels, suggested that infantry use the pontoons as assault boats in order to get across the river and pry the snipers out of the rubble with bayonets. A Michigan regiment drew the duty, supported by two others from Massachusetts, and did it smartly, establishing a bridgehead in short order. During the street fighting, which used up what was left of daylight, the bridges were laid and other regiments came to their support. Barksdale's thirst was still unslaked, however. When he received permission to withdraw, he declined and kept on fighting, house to house, until past sundown. Not till dusk had fallen was he willing to call it a day, and even then he had trouble persuading some of his men to agree. This was particularly difficult in the case of the rear-guard company, whose commander somehow discovered in the course of the engagement that the Federal advance was being led by a Massachusetts company whose commander had been his classmate at Harvard. The Mississippi lieutenant called a halt and faced his men about, determined to whip his blue-clad friend then and there, until his colonel had him placed in arrest in order to continue the withdrawal. It was 7 o'clock by the time the last of Barksdale's veterans crossed the plain to join their admiring comrades on the ridge, leaving Fredericksburg to the bluecoats they had been fighting for fifteen hours.

Not until well after dark did Lee order Jackson to bring his two nearest divisions to Longstreet's support, and not even then did he summon the other two from Port Royal and Skinker's Neck, where the Maine axmen on the opposite bank had kindled campfires around which they were resting from their daylong chopping. Pleased though he was with the day's work — his eyes had lighted up at each report that a new attempt to extend the bridge had been defeated — Lee simply could not believe that his hopes had been so completely fulfilled that the enemy was concentrating everything for an attack against the ridge where his guns had been laid for weeks now and his infantry was disposed at ease in overlapping lines of battle.

Across the way, on Stafford Heights, Burnside too was pleased. Despite delays that had been maddening, he had his six bridges down at last (the three lower ones, below the town, had been down since noon, but he had hesitated to use them so long as the Fredericksburg force of unknown strength was in position on their flank) and his army was assembled for the crossing. Besides, he had received balloon reports at sundown informing him that the other half of the rebel army was still in its former positions down the river, with no signs of preparation for a move in this direction. The delay, it seemed, had cost him nothing more than some nervous twinges and a few expendable combat engineers; Lee might be caught napping yet. So confidently did the ruff-whiskered general feel next morning, when observers reported Jackson's troops still in position at Skinker's Neck and Port Royal, twenty miles away, that he decided he could afford to spend another day assembling his army on the west bank of the Rappahannock for the assault across the empty plain and against the rebel ridge.

Fog shrouded the entire valley while the long blue lines of men came steeply down to the riverbank and broke step as they crossed the swaying bridges. On the heights above, the Union guns fired blindly over their heads, in case the Confederates attempted to challenge the crossing. They did not. At noon, however, the fog lifted; Lee, with a close-up view of the bluecoats massed in their thousands beyond the plain, saw at once that this was no feint, but a major effort. He sent for Jackson's other two divisions, instructing them to begin their long marches immediately in order to arrive in time for the battle, which he now saw would be fought tomorrow. Beyond that he could do no more.

Though he was outnumbered worse than three-to-two, and knew it, he was in good spirits as he rode on a sundown inspection of his lines. Returning to headquarters, he seemed pleased that the Federals on the flat were about to charge him. "I shall try to do them all the damage in our power when they move forward," he said.

Down in the town, meanwhile, the Union soldiers had been having themselves a field day. Cavalrymen ripped the strings from grand pianos to make feed troughs for their horses, while others cavorted amid the rubble in women's lace-trimmed underwear and crinoline gowns snatched from closets and bureau drawers. Scarcely a house escaped pillage. Family portraits were slashed with bayonets; pier glass mirrors were shattered with musket butts; barrels of flour and molasses were dumped together on deep-piled rugs. It was all a lot of fun, especially for the more fortunate ones who found bottles of rare old madeira in the cellars. Gradually, though, the excitement paled and the looters began to speculate as to why the rebs had made no attempt to challenge the crossing today, not even with their artillery. Some guessed it was because they had no ammunition to spare, others that they were afraid of retaliation by "our siege guns." One man had a psychological theory: "General Lee thinks he will have a big thing on us about the bombardment of this town. He proposes to rouse the indignation of the civilized world, as they call it. You'll see he won't throw a shell into it. He is playing for the sympathies of Europe." Still another, a veteran private, had a different idea. "Shit," he said. "They *want* us to get in. Getting out won't be quite so smart and easy. You'll see."

★ ★ ★

They would see; but not just yet. Day broke on a fog so thick that the sun, which rose at 7.17 beyond the Union left, could not pierce it, but rather gave an eerie, luminous quality to the mist that swathed the ridge where Lee's reunited army awaited the challenge foretold by sounds of preparation on the invisible plain below; "an indistinct murmur," one listener called it, "like the distant hum of myriads of bees."

Longstreet held the Confederate left. Four of his five divisions were on line, commanded north to south by Major Generals Richard Anderson, Lafayette McLaws, George Pickett, and John Bell Hood; the fifth and smallest, a demi-division under Brigadier General Robert Ransom, was in reserve. Jackson, on the right, had posted Major General A. P. Hill's large division along his entire front, backed by a second line of two close-packed divisions under Brigadier Generals William Taliaferro and Jubal Early, which in turn was supported by Major General D. H. Hill's division, just arrived from Port Royal after an all-night march. Major General J. E. B. Stuart's cavalry guarded the flank, extending it southward from Hamilton's Crossing to Massaponax Creek. Since this end of the ridge was considerably lower than the other, and

The Longest Journey

consequently much less easy to defend, Lee had assigned five miles of the line to Longstreet and only two to Jackson, who thus had no less than ten men to every yard of front and could distribute them in depth. It was no wonder, then, that he replied this morning to a staff officer's expression of qualms about the enemy strength and the lowness of the ridge in this direction: "Major, my men have sometimes failed to take a position, but to defend one, never! I am glad the Yankees are coming."

Lee and Longstreet stood on an eminence known thereafter as Lee's Hill because that general had set up his forward command post here, about midway of Longstreet's line, with an excellent view — or at any rate what would be an excellent view, once the curtain of fog had lifted — of the lines in both directions, including most of Jackson's line to the south, as well as of Fredericksburg and the snow-pocked plain where the blue host was massing under cover of their guns on Stafford Heights, preparing even now to give the lower ridge across the way a long-range pounding. Today as yesterday, however, the southern commander was in good spirits. Tall and comely — nothing less, indeed,

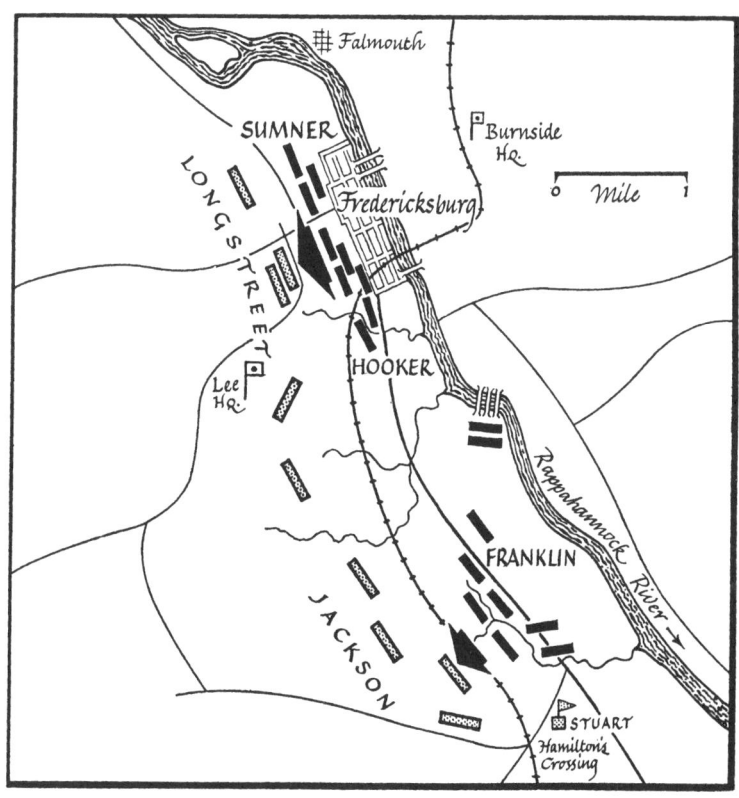

than "the handsomest man in Christendom," according to one who saw him there this morning — neatly dressed, as always, with only the three unwreathed stars on the collar of his thigh-length gray sack coat to show his rank, he gave no sign of nervousness or apprehension. Above the short-clipped iron-gray beard and beneath the medium brim of a sand-colored planter's hat, his quick brown eyes had a youthfulness which, together with the litheness of his figure and the deftness of his movements, disguised the fact that he would be fifty-six years old next month.

His companion seemed to share his confidence, if not his handsomeness of person, though he too was prepossessing of appearance. A burly, shaggy man, six feet tall, of Dutch extraction and just past forty-one, Longstreet gave above all an impression of solidity and dependability. His men's great fondness for him was based in part on their knowledge of his concern for their well-being, in and out of combat. Yesterday, for example, when some engineers protested to him that the gun crews were ruining their emplacements by digging them too deep, Old Peter would not agree to order them to stop. "If we only save the finger of a man, that's good enough," he told the engineers, and the cannoneers kept digging. Often phlegmatic, this morning he was in an expansive mood: especially after he and Lee were joined by the third-ranking member of the army triumvirate, who came riding up from the south. It was Jackson, but a Jackson quite unlike the Stonewall they had known of old. Gone were the mangy cadet cap and the homespun uniform worn threadbare since its purchase on the eve of the Valley Campaign, through the miasmic nightmare of the Seven Days, the suppression of the "miscreant Pope" at Cedar Mountain and Second Manassas, the invasion of Maryland and the hard fight at Sharpsburg. Instead he wore a new cap bound with gold braid, and more braid — "chicken guts," Confederate soldiers irreverently styled the stuff — looped on the cuffs and sleeves of a brand-new uniform, a recent gift from Jeb Stuart. Even his outsized boots were brightly polished. For all his finery, he looked as always older than his thirty-eight years. His pale blue eyes were stern, his thin-lipped mouth clamped forbiddingly behind the scraggly dark-brown beard; but this had not protected him from the jibes of his men, who greeted him with their accustomed rough affection as he rode among them. "Come here, boys!" they yelled. "Stonewall has drawed his bounty and bought hisself some new clothes." Others shook their heads in mock dismay at seeing him tricked out like some newly commissioned quartermaster lieutenant. "Old Jack will be afraid for his clothes," they said, doleful amid the catcalls, "and will not get down to work."

He had ridden all this way, exposing himself to all that raillery, for a purpose which he was quick to divulge. Turning aside Longstreet's banter, he muttered that the finery was "some doing of my friend Stuart,

I believe," and passed at once to the matter that had brought him here. He wanted permission to attack. If his men surged down the ridge and onto the plain before the fog had lifted, he explained, they would be hidden from the guns on Stafford Heights and could fling the startled bluecoats into the river. Lee shook his head. He preferred to have the superior enemy force worn down by repeated charges and repulses, in the style of Second Manassas, before he passed to the offensive. Stonewall had his answer. As he turned to leave, Longstreet began to bait him again. "General, do not all those multitudes of Federals frighten you?" Old Peter's humor was heavy-handed, but Jackson had no humor at all. "We shall see very soon whether I shall not frighten *them*," he said as he put one foot in the stirrup. But Longstreet kept at him. "Jackson, what are you going to do with all those people over there?" Stonewall mounted. "Sir, we will give them the bayonet," he said, and he turned his horse and rode away.

By 10 o'clock the fog had begun to thin. It drained downward, burned away by the sun, layer by upper layer, so that the valley seemed to empty after the manner of a tub when the plug is pulled. Gradually the town revealed itself: first the steeples of two churches and the courthouse, then the chimneys and rooftops, and finally the houses and gardens, set upon the checkerboard of streets. Dark lines of troops flowed steadily toward two clusters, one within the town, masked by the nearer buildings, the other two miles down the Richmond Stage Road, which ran parallel to the river and roughly bisected the mile-wide plain. Already the more adventurous Federal batteries had opened, arching their shells through sunlit rifts in the thinning mist, but the Confederates made no reply until 10.30 when Lee passed the word: "Test the ranges on the left." Longstreet's guns began to roar from Marye's Heights, the tall north end of the long ridge, directly opposite the center of the town, where the first of the two clusters of blue-clad men was thickening. All the fog was gone by now, replaced by brilliant sunlight. The drifting smoke made shifting patterns on the plain. High over Stafford Heights, where the long-range guns were adding their deeper voices to the chorus of the Union, two of Burnside's big yellow observation balloons bobbed and floated, the men in their swaying baskets looking down on war reduced to miniature.

First blood was drawn in a brief dramatic action staged in front of the Confederate right. Here the fog had rolled away so rapidly that the scene was exposed as if by the sudden lift of a curtain, showing a three-division Federal corps advancing westward in long lines so neatly dressed that watchers on the ridge could count the brigades and regiments — ten of the former, forty-six of the latter, plus eleven batteries of artillery — each with its attendant colors rippling in the sunlight. From Lee's Hill, the southern commander was surprised to see two horse-drawn guns, toy-sized in the distance, go twinkling out to the old stage road and go into position in the open, within easy range of the left flank of the 18,000 Federals, which was thrown into some disorder and came to a milling halt as the two guns began to slam their shots endwise into the blue ranks, toppling men like tenpins.

They had been brought into action by Stuart's chief of artillery, twenty-four-year-old Major John Pelham of Alabama, who in his haste to join the southern army had left West Point on the eve of graduation in '61. He had often done daring things, similar to this today, but never before with so large an audience to applaud him. As the men of both armies watched from the surrounding heights, he fired so rapidly that one general involved in the blue confusion estimated his strength at a full battery. Four Union batteries gave him their undivided attention, turning their two dozen guns against his two. One, a rifled Blakely, was soon disabled and had to be sent to the rear, but Pelham kept the other barking furiously, a 12-pounder brass Napoleon, and shifted his position each time the enemy gunners got his range. The handsome young major was in his glory, wearing bound about his cap, at the request of a British army observer, a necktie woven of red and blue, the colors of the Grenadier Guards. When Stuart sent word for him to retire, Pelham declined, though he had lost so many cannoneers by then that he himself was helping to serve the gun. "Tell the general I can hold my ground," he said. Three times the order came, but he obeyed only when his caissons were nearly empty. Back at Hamilton's Crossing, he returned the smoke-grimed necktie-souvenir to the English visitor, blushing with pleasure and embarrassment at the cheers. Lee on his hill took his glasses down, smiling as he exclaimed: "It is glorious to see such courage in one so young!"

While the Federals remained halted on the plain, recovering the alignment Pelham had disturbed, their artillery began to pound the lower ridge in earnest, probing the woods in an attempt to knock out Jackson's hidden batteries before the battle passed to the infantry. The Confederate gunners made no reply, being under orders not to disclose their positions until the enemy came within easy range. At last he did, and the graybacks got their revenge for the punishment they had had to accept in silence. When the advance came within 800 yards, all of Stonewall's guns cut loose at once. The blue flood stopped, flailed ragged along its forward edge, and then reversed its flow.

The Union guns resumed the argument, having spotted their targets by the smoke that boiled up through the trees, but the infantry battle now shifted northward to where the bluecoats had been massing under cover of the town. At 11.30 they emerged and began to surge across the plain toward Marye's Heights, less than half a mile away. A thirty-foot spillway, six feet deep, lay athwart their path, however, and the rebel gunners caught them close-packed as they funneled onto three bridges whose planks had been removed but whose stringers had been left in place, apparently to lure them across in single file. "Hi! Hi! Hi!" the Federals yelled as they pounded over, taking their losses in order to gain the cover of a slight roll or "dip" of ground that hid them from the guns on the heights beyond.

"It appeared to us there was no end of them," a waiting cannoneer observed. But Longstreet was not worried; he had a surprise in store for them. Along the base of Marye's Heights ran a road, flanked by stone walls four feet high, which Brigadier General T.R.R. Cobb had had his Georgians deepen, throwing the spoil over the townward wall, to add to its effectiveness as a breastwork and to hide it from the enemy. This was the advance position of the whole army, and as such it might be outflanked or enfiladed. However, when Cobb was given permission to fall back up the hill in case that happened, he replied grimly in the spirit of Barksdale and Pelham: "Well, if they wait for me to fall back, they will wait a long time."

Presently he got the chance to begin to prove his staunchness; for the Federals leaped to their feet in the swale and made a sudden rush, as if they intended to scale the heights whose base was only 400 yards away. High up the slope the guns crashed, darting tongues of flame, and the Georgians along the sunken road pulled trigger. It was as if the charging bluecoats had struck a trip wire. When the smoke of that single rifle volley rolled away, all that were left in front of the wall were writhing on the ground or scampering back to safety in the swale. After a wait, they rose and came forward again, deploying as they advanced. This time the reaction was less immediate, since they knew what to expect; but it was no different in the end. The guns on the slope and the rifles down along the wall broke into a clattering frenzy of smoke and flame, and more men were left writhing as others fell back off the blasted plain and into the swale. Again they rose. Again, incredibly, they charged. They came forward, one of them afterwards recalled, "as though they were breasting a storm of rain and sleet, their faces and bodies being only half turned to the storm, with their shoulders shrugged." Another observed that "everybody, from the smallest drummer boy on up, seemed to be shouting to the full extent of his capacity." Like the first and second, except that more men fell because it lasted longer, this third charge broke in blood and pain before a single man got within fifty yards of the wall. The survivors flowed back over the roll of earth and into the "dip," where reinforcements were nerving themselves for still a fourth attempt.

"They are massing very heavily and will break your line, I am afraid," Lee told Longstreet. But Old Peter did not believe it. He was ready for the whole Yankee nation, provided it would come at him from the direction this portion of it had done three times already, and he said so: "General, if you put every man now on the other side of the Potomac in that field to approach me over that same line, and give me plenty of ammunition, I will kill them all before they reach my line. Look to your right; you are in some danger there," he said. "But not on my line."

It was true; Lee's line was in considerable danger southward. While Sumner's men were charging the sunken road, repeatedly and headlong, taking their losses, Franklin was taking stock of the situation as Pelham's brass Napoleon and Jackson's masked batteries had left it when they disrupted his first and second advances. Both had been tentative, at best, but now he believed he knew what he had to deal with. However, as in Pleasant Valley preceding the battle on Antietam Creek, he was inclined to be circumspect: an inclination which had not been lessened here on the Rappahannock by Burnside's instructions that, once he was over the river "with a view to taking the heights," he was to be "governed by circumstances as to the extent of your movements." Further instructions had arrived this morning, warning him to keep his attack column "well supported and its line of retreat open." Accordingly, before going forward for the third time, he took care to protect the flank in Stuart's direction. The attack was delivered by the same corps, commanded by Major General John F. Reynolds, whose three divisions were under Major General George G. Meade and Brigadier Generals Abner Doubleday and John Gibbon. Doubleday was ordered to wheel left, guarding the bruised flank (sure enough, Pelham came out promptly and began to pound him) while the other two went forward in an attempt to storm the ridge. Gibbon, on the right, got as far as the railroad embankment, where he ran into murderous pointblank fire, was himself wounded, and had to be brought out on a stretcher. He was followed shortly by his men, who were not long in discovering that the Johnnies had drawn them into a trap.

That left Meade, whose division was the smallest of the three. Out of 60,000 soldiers available for the intended assault on the Confederate right, Franklin managed to get only these 4500 Pennsylvanians into slugging contact with the enemy, but they did what they could to make up in spirit for what they lacked in weight. Charging first to the railroad, then beyond it, they struck a boggy stretch of ground, about 500 yards in width, which A. P. Hill had left unmanned in the belief that it was impenetrable. It was not. Meade's troops slogged through it, burst upon and scattered a second-line brigade of startled rebels, and were still driving hard toward the accomplishment of Franklin's assignment — that is, to get astride the lower ridge and then sweep northward along it, dislodging men and guns as he went — when they themselves were struck in front and on both flanks by a horde of screaming graybacks.

These were Early's men, from over on the right. Told that Hill's line had been pierced, they came on the run, hooting as they passed the fugitives: "Here comes old Jubal! Let old Jubal straighten out that

The Longest Journey

fence!" Then they struck. The Pennsylvanians were driven back through the boggy gap and out again across the open fields, where the pursuers stabbed vengefully at their rear and Confederate guns to the left and right tore viciously at their flanks. Unsupported, heavily outnumbered, thrown off balance by surprise, they paid dearly for their daring; more than a third of the men who had gone in did not come out again. There was no safety for the survivors until they regained the cover of their artillery, which promptly drove the pursuers back with severe losses and shifted without delay to the rebel batteries, blanketing them so accurately with shellbursts that the fire drew an indirect compliment from Pelham himself, who happened to be visiting this part of the line at the time. "Well, you men stand killing better than any I ever saw," he remarked as he watched the cannoneers being knocked about.

At any rate, the break had been repaired, the line restored. Lee on his hill had seen it all, the penetration and repulse on Jackson's front, coincident with the bloody disintegration of the third attack on Longstreet. The ground in front of both was carpeted blue with the torn bodies of men who had challenged unsuccessfully the integrity of his line. Beyond the river, Stafford Heights were ablaze with guns whose commanding elevation and heavier metal enabled them to rake the western ridge almost at will. Even now, one of them put a large-caliber shell into the earth at the southern commander's feet, but it did not explode. A British observer saw "antique courage" in Lee's manner as he turned to Longstreet, lowering his glasses after a long look at the blasted plain where still more Federals were massing to continue their assault over the mangled remains of comrades who had tried before and failed. "It is well that war is so terrible," the gray-bearded general said. "We should grow too fond of it."

If the assault was to be resumed after the comparative lull that settled over the field about 3.30, following the double failure at opposite ends of the line, it would have to be launched against that portion of the ridge where Longstreet's men were ranked four-deep in the sunken road, their rifles cocked and primed for firing at whatever came at them across the fields beyond their breast-high wall of stone and dirt. To the south, Franklin had shot his bolt with Meade's quick probe of the hole in Jackson's front: in reaction to which he was not unlike a man who has managed to salvage a good part of one hand after groping about in the dark and finding a bear trap. There might be other holes, for all he knew, but after that one costly venture the commander of the left Grand Division seemed less concerned about finding than he was about avoiding them. Whoever might deliver another attack, it was not going to be Franklin. That left Sumner and Hooker. Burnside sent them instructions to continue the assault with their right and center

Grand Divisions, in hopes that the Confederates along the ridge could be breached or budged or somehow thrown into confusion as a prelude to their downfall.

Sumner, a crusty veteran of forty-four years' service, nearly forty of which had been spent accomplishing the slow climb from second lieutenant to colonel, was altogether willing, despite his heavy losses up to now. So was Hooker, whose nickname was "Fighting Joe." Shortly before 4 o'clock, the men crouched in the swale caught sight of what they thought was their best chance to storm the ridge. A whole battalion of rebel artillery began a displacement from the slopes of Marye's Heights. Quickly the word passed down the Union line; men braced themselves for the order to charge. It came and they surged forward, followed this time by several batteries, which ventured out to within 300 yards of the fuming wall, adding the weight of their metal to the attack but losing cannoneers so fast that the guns could only be served slowly. As it turned out, this was worse than ever. The artillery displacement they had spotted was not the beginning of a retreat, as they had supposed, but a yielding of the position to a fresh battalion, which arrived with full caissons in time to aid in contesting this fourth assault. Down in the sunken road, Tom Cobb had been hit by a sharpshooter firing from the upper story of a house on the edge of town; he had bled to death by now; but his men were still there, reinforced by several regiments of North Carolinians from Ransom's reserve division. Shoulder to shoulder along the wall, they loosed their volleys, then stepped back to reload while the rank behind stepped up to fire. So it went, through all four ranks, until the first had reloaded and taken its place along the wall, which flamed continuously under a mounting bank of smoke as if the defenders were armed with automatic weapons. This attack, like the three preceding it, broke in blood. The Federals fell back, leaving the stretch of open ground between the swale and a hundred yards of the wall thick-strewn with corpses and writhing men whose cries could be heard above the diminishing clatter of musketry.

While the carnage was being continued here ("Oh, great God!" a division commander groaned in anguish from his lookout post in the cupola of the courthouse. "See how our men, our poor fellows, are falling!") Jackson was burning to take the offensive against the inactive bluecoats at the other end of the line: so much so, indeed, that according to one observer "his countenance glowed, as from the glare of a great conflagration." If all those thousands of Federals on the plain could not be persuaded to approach the ridge, he ached to go down after them. "I want to move forward," he said impatiently; "to attack them — drive them into the river yonder," and as he spoke he threw out his arm, by way of lending emphasis to his words. The risk was great, he knew, for a repulse would expose his men to annihilation by the guns on the opposite heights. But at last, out of urgency, he devised a plan by which he hoped to nullify his prediction that the Confederates would "gain no fruits" from their victory. If the counterstroke were preceded by a bombardment, he believed, the enemy might be so stunned that the sudden charge across the plain might be made without undue sacrifice of life, and if it were launched just at sundown he could withdraw under cover of darkness in case it failed.

So conceived, it was so ordered. However, the almanac put sunset at 4.34; there was little time for preparation. Word was passed to the four divisions assigned to the attack, and as they got ready for the jump-off Stonewall's batteries went forward, out into the open, to begin their work of stunning or confusing the enemy. Instead, it was they who were stunned and confused, and in short order. Beyond the river, Stafford Heights seemed to buck and jump in flame and thunder as the guns on the crest redoubled their fire at the sight of these easy targets down below. Jackson quickly recalled his badly pounded artillerymen and canceled the attack, which he now saw would be shattered as soon as the infantry emerged from the woods. At that, the demonstration was not without its effect: especially on Franklin, who had already notified Burnside that "any movement to my front is impossible at present. . . . The truth is, my left is in danger of being turned. What hope is there of getting reinforcements across the river?" Of his eight divisions, only three had been employed offensively, and one whole corps of 24,000 men, the largest in the army, saw no action at all; yet he was asking after reinforcements. At the height of Jackson's abortive demonstration, orders came from Burnside for Franklin to take the offensive, but he declined. He was in grave danger here, he repeated. Besides, there was no time; the sun was down behind the western ridge.

Sunset did not slow the tempo of the fighting to the north, where a fifth major assault on Marye's Heights had been repulsed in much the same manner as all the others, though the officers in charge had attempted a somewhat different approach. Their instructions were for the men to veer northward when they left the swale and thus confront the sunken road from the right, which perhaps would enable them to lay down an enfilade as they gained the flank and bore down at an angle. But it did not work out that way. As the men went forward, attempting to bear off to the right, they encountered a marsh that forced them back to the left and a repetition of the direct approach to the stone wall, which seemed thus to draw them like a magnet. From behind it, all this while, the rebels — many of whom were shoeless, without overcoats or blankets to protect them from the penetrating mid-December chill — taunted the warmly clad Federals coming toward them in a tangle-footed huddle after their encounter with the bog: "Come on, blue belly! Bring them boots and blankets! Bring 'em hyar!" And they did bring them, up to within fifty yards of the flame-stitched wall at any rate. There the forward edge of the charge was frayed and broken, the survivors crawling or running to regain the protection of the swale, which by now they were convinced they never should have left.

Sumner had done his best, or worst but the carnage was by no means over. Hooker's men had crossed the river, under orders to continue the assault, and the commander of one of his divisions, Brigadier General Andrew Humphreys, believed he knew a way to get his troops up to and over the wall, so they could come to grips with the jeering scarecrows in the sunken road. While they were deploying in the dusk he rode among them, telling them not to fire while they were charging. It was obvious by now, he said, that firing did the rebels little damage behind their ready-made breastwork; it only served to slow the attack and expose the attackers to more of the rapid-fire volleys from beyond the wall. The object was to get there fast — much as a man might hurry across an open space in a shower of rain, intending to be as dry as possible when he reached the other side — then rely on the bayonet to do the work that would remain to be done when they got there.

They went forward in the twilight, stumbling over the human wreckage left by five previous charges. Prone men, wounded and unwounded, called out to them not to try it; some even caught at their legs as they passed, attempting to hold them back; but they ignored them and went on, beckoned by voices that mocked them from ahead, calling them blue-bellies and urging them to bring their boots and blankets within reach. Humphreys sat his horse amid the bullets, a slim veteran of aristocratic mien. He had left West Point in '31, two years behind R. E. Lee, and his record in the peacetime army had been a good one; yet his advancement since then, it was said, had been delayed because of suspicions aroused by his prewar friendship with Jefferson Davis. Now he was out to prove those suspicions false. As he watched he saw the stone wall become "a sheet of flame that enveloped the head and flanks of the column." Its formations unraveled by sudden attrition, the charge was brought to a stumbling halt about forty yards from the wall. For a moment the Federals hung there, beginning to return the galling fire; but it was useless, and they knew it. Despite the shouts and pleas of their officers — including Humphreys, who remained mounted yet incredibly went unhit — the men turned and stumbled back through the gathering darkness. Or anyhow the survivors did, having added a thousand casualties to the wreckage that cluttered the open slope, ghastly under the pinkish yellow flicker of muzzle-flashes still rippling back and forth along the crest of the stone wall.

"The fighting is about over," a Union signal officer reported at 6 o'clock from the heights across the way; "only an occasional gun is heard."

It was over, as he said, but not as the result of instructions from Burnside. Hooker was the one who finally called a halt to the carnage.

"Finding that I had lost as many men as my orders required me to lose," he later declared in his official report, "I suspended the attack."

Burnside himself took a much less gloomy view of the state of affairs when he crossed the river late that night for an inspection of the front. Unquestionably a great deal of blood had been shed — far more, in fact, than he would know until he received the final casualty returns — but he had little doubt that a continuation of today's work would break Lee's line tomorrow. At any rate he was determined to try it, and he sent out orders to that effect, alerting his front-line commanders. Recrossing the Rappahannock at 4 o'clock in the morning, he got off a wire to Washington: "I have just returned from the field. Our troops are all over the river. We hold the first ridge outside the town, and 3 miles below. We hope to carry the crest today."

Once more Lee had divined his opponent's purpose. "I expect the battle to be renewed at daylight," he wired Richmond, three hours after the final assault had failed, and this opinion was reinforced within another three hours by the capture, shortly before midnight, of a courier bearing orders to Burnside's front-line commanders for tomorrow's continuation of the attack. But Sunday's dawn, December 14, brought only the soup-thick fog of yesterday, without the familiar hum of preparation from down on the curtained plain. Indeed, even after the rising sun had burned away the mist, the only change apparent to the eye was in the lines along the western ridge. Expecting a turning movement, Lee had instructed his men to improve their fortifications in order to free all but a comparative handful for action on the flanks. So well had they plied their tools, these soldiers who six months ago had sneered at digging as cowardly work "unfit for a white man" and in derision had dubbed their new commander "the King of Spades," that Lee remarked with pleasure at the sight: "My army is as much stronger for these new intrenchments as if I had received reinforcements of 20,000 men."

No longer in need of prodding, or even suggestion, they kept digging. As the sun rose higher, so did the parapets. But the observers on Lee's Hill discerned no corresponding activity among the Federals on the plain, portions of whose forward edge were carpeted solid blue with the thick-fallen dead and wounded. The only sign of preparation was that the near ends of the east-west streets of Fredericksburg had been barricaded, as if in expectation of receiving, not delivering, an attack. The morning wore on. Noon came and went: then afternoon: and still no sign that the bluecoats were about to launch the assault that had been ordered in the dispatch captured the night before. As the shadows lengthened, Lee turned at last to Longstreet, who had been acquainted with the northern commander in the peacetime army. "General," he said, "I am losing faith in your friend General Burnside."

He was by no means alone in this, although the principal loss of faith in Old Peter's friend had occurred within the luckless commander's own ranks. Refreshed by a short sleep, and still convinced that he would break Lee's line by continuing yesterday's headlong tactics, Burnside had risen early that morning, only to be confronted by Sumner, who had been five years in the army before his present chief was born. He was known to be no quitter; in fact, so pronounced was his fondness for personal combat, Burnside had ordered the old man to remain at his left-bank headquarters yesterday, lest he get himself killed leading charges. Today, though, he was quite unlike himself in this respect.

"General," he said, obviously unstrung by all he had seen the day before, if only from a distance, "I hope you will desist from this attack. I do not know of any general officer who approves of it, and I think it will prove disastrous to the army."

Burnside was taken aback, having expected to encounter a different spirit. However, as he later wrote, "Advice of that kind from General Sumner, who had always been in favor of an advance whenever it was possible, caused me to hesitate." To his further dismay, he found his other Grand Division commanders of the same opinion. Franklin did not surprise him greatly in this regard — ironically, that general had served him on the left at Fredericksburg in much the same fashion as he himself had served McClellan on the left at Antietam — but when Hooker, the redoubtable Fighting Joe, was even more emphatic than Sumner in advising no renewal of the attack, he knew the thing was off. His first reaction was one of frantic despair. He had a wild impulse to place himself at the head of his old corps and lead an all-out, all-or-nothing charge against the sunken road, intending to break Lee's line or else be broken by it. Dissuaded from this, he retired to his tent, bitter with the knowledge that all yesterday's blood had been shed to no advantage: except to the rebels, who would be facing that many fewer men next time the two armies came to grips. A corps commander, Major General W. F. Smith, followed him into the tent and found him pacing back and forth, distracted. "Oh, those men! Oh, those men!" he was saying. What men? Smith asked, and Burnside replied: "Those men over there," pointing across the river, where portions of the plain were carpeted blue: "I am thinking of them all the time!"

Sunset closed a day that had witnessed nothing more than a bit of long-range firing on one side and a great deal of digging on the other. Such spectacle as there was, and it was much, came after nightfall. A mysterious refulgence, shot with fanwise shafts of varicolored light, predominantly reds and blues — first a glimmer, then a spreading glow, as if all the countryside between Fredericksburg and Washington were afire — filled a wide arc of the horizon beyond the Federal right. It was the aurora borealis, seldom visible this far south and never before seen by most of the Confederates, who watched it with amazement. The Northerners might make of it what they chose by way of a portent (after all, these were the *Northern* Lights) but to one Southerner it seemed "that the heavens were hanging out banners and streamers and setting off fireworks in honor of our great victory."

As if to rival this gaudy nighttime aerial display, morning brought a terrestrial phenomenon, equally amazing in its way. The ground in front of the sunken road, formerly carpeted solid blue, had taken on a mottled hue, with patches of startling white. Binoculars disclosed the cause. Many of the Federal dead had been stripped stark naked by shivering Confederates, who had crept out in the darkness to scavenge the warm clothes from the bodies of men who needed them no longer.

That afternoon, as a result of a request by Burnside for a truce during which he could bury his dead and relieve such of his wounded as had survived two days and nights of exposure without medicine for their hurts or water for their fever-parched throats, the men of both armies had a nearer view of the carnage. No one assigned to one of the burial details ever forgot the horror of what he saw; for here, close-up and life-size, was an effective antidote to the long-range, miniature pageantry of Saturday's battle as it had been viewed from the opposing heights. Up close, you heard the groans and smelled the blood. You saw the dead. According to one who moved among them, they were "swollen to twice their natural size, black as Negroes in most cases." They sprawled "in every conceivable position, some on their backs with gaping jaws, some with eyes as large as walnuts, protruding with glassy stare, some doubled up like a contortionist." Here, he wrote — approaching incoherency as the memory grew stronger — lay "one without a head, there one without legs, yonder a head and legs without a trunk; everywhere horrible expressions, fear, rage, agony, madness, torture; lying in pools of blood, lying with heads half buried in mud, with fragments of shell sticking in oozing brain, with bullet holes all over the puffed limbs."

Not even amid such scenes as this, however, did the irrepressible rebel soldier's wry sense of humor — or anyhow what passed for such; mainly it was a biting sense of the ridiculous — desert him. One, about to remove a shoe from what he thought was a Federal corpse, was surprised to see the "corpse" lift its head and look at him reproachfully. "Beg pardon, sir," the would-be scavenger said, carefully lowering the leg; "I thought you had gone above." Another butternut scarecrow, reprimanded by a Union officer for violating the terms of the truce by picking up a fine Belgian rifle that had been dropped between the lines, looked his critic up and down, pausing for a long stare at the polished boots the officer was wearing. "Never mind," he said dryly. "I'll shoot you tomorrow and git them boots."

So he said. But as the thing turned out, neither he nor anyone else was going to be doing any shooting on that field tomorrow: not unless the Confederates started shooting at each other. Night brought a storm of sleet and driving rain, with a hard wind blowing eastward off the ridge and toward the river. When the fog of December 16 rolled away, the plain was empty. A hurried and red-faced investigation disclosed the fact that not a single live, unwounded Federal remained on the west bank of the Rappahannock. Covered by darkness, the sound of their movements drowned by the howling wind, the bluecoats had made a successful withdrawal in the night, taking up their pontoons after such a good job of salvaging equipment that one signal officer proudly reported that he had not left a yard of wire behind.

Burnside was distressed that a campaign which had opened so auspiciously should have so ignominious a close. What was more, reports of the battle were appearing by now in the northern papers, and the correspondents, ignoring the general's plea that they not treat "the affair at Fredericksburg" as a disaster, pulled out all the descriptive stops and figuratively threw up their hands in horror at the bungling and the bloodshed. An account in the New York *Times* so infuriated Burnside that he summoned the reporter to his tent and threatened to run him through with his sword. By ordinary a mild-natured man, he was souring under the goads of criticism, such as those made by two of his own colonels: one that he and his men had been committed piecemeal — "handed in on toasting forks," he phrased it — and the other that the defeat had been "owing to the heavy fire in front and an excess of enthusiasm in the rear." Nor was his temper soothed when he read such comments as the following, from an Ohio journal: "It can hardly be in human nature for men to show more valor, or generals to manifest less judgment, than were perceptible on our side that day."

In truth, the casualties were staggering: especially by contrast. The Federals had lost 12,653 men, the Confederates well under half as many: 5309. The latter figure was subsequently adjusted to 4201, just under one third of the former, when it was found that more than a thousand of those reported missing or wounded had taken advantage of the chance at a Christmas holiday immediately after the battle.

Longstreet was not unhappy with the results, despite the bloodless withdrawal. Suffering fewer than 2000 casualties, he had inflicted about 9000, and he was looking forward to a repetition of the tactics which had made this exploit possible. But Jackson, whose losses were not much less than his opponent's on the right, was far from satisfied, even though 11,000 stands of arms had been gleaned from the field after the departure of the Yankees. "I did not think a little red earth would have frightened them," he said. "I am sorry they are gone. I am sorry that I fortified." Lee agreed, saying of Burnside and the punishment that general had absorbed: "Had I divined that was to have been his only effort, he would have had more of it."

That evening he wrote his wife, "They went as they came — in the night. They suffered heavily as far as the battle went, but it did not go far enough to satisfy me." His anger had been aroused by the evidence of rabid vandalism he saw when he rode into Fredericksburg that afternoon. So had Jackson's. "What can we do?" a staff officer asked helplessly when he saw how thoroughly the Federals had taken the town apart. "Do?" Stonewall replied promptly. "Why, shoot them."

The stern-lipped Jackson's ire would never cool (later he expanded this remark; "We must do more than defeat their armies," he said. "We must destroy them") but Lee's was influenced considerably by the advent of the season of the Nativity. On Christmas Day he wrote his wife: "My heart is filled with gratitude to Almighty God for His unspeakable mercies with which He has blessed us in this day, for those He has granted us from the beginning of life, and particularly for those He has vouchsafed us during the past year. What should have become of us without His crowning help and protection? Oh, if our people would only realize it and cease from vain self-boasting and adulation, how strong would be my belief in final success and happiness to our country! But what a cruel thing is war; to separate and destroy families and friends, and mar the purest joys and happiness God has granted us in this world; to fill our hearts with hatred instead of love for our neighbors, and to devastate the fair face of this beautiful world. I pray that, on this day when only peace and good-will are preached to mankind, better thoughts may fill the hearts of our enemies and turn them to peace." But he added a sort of postscript in a letter to his youngest daughter, remarking that he was "happy in the knowledge that General Burnside and his army will not eat their promised Christmas dinner in Richmond today."

� 3 ✝

Near the far end of the thousand-mile-long firing line that swerved and crooked its way between North and South — westward across northern Virginia, East and Middle Tennessee, North Mississippi, central Arkansas, and thence on out to Texas — Theophilus Holmes, with less rank and not one half as many soldiers in a department better than twenty times as large, had troubles which, in multiplicity at any rate, made Lee's seem downright single. From his Transmississippi headquarters in Little Rock the lately appointed North Carolinian looked apprehensively north and west and south; he was threatened from all those quarters; while from the east he was being jogged by repeated pleas and suggestions from Johnston and the President, not to mention such comparatively minor figures as Pemberton and the Secretary of War, that he send his hard-pressed and outnumbered troops to the aid of his fellow department commander on the opposite bank of the big river that ran between them. A grim-featured man, deaf as a post, at fifty-seven Holmes was the oldest of the Confederate field commanders. Moreover, his rigidity of face, indicative of arteriosclerosis, was matched by a rigidity of mind which augured ill in a situation that called for nothing so much as it called for flexibility.

By way of compensation for this drawback, he had under him three major generals whose outstanding characteristic, individually and collectively, was the very flexibility he lacked. John Magruder, Richard Taylor, and Thomas Hindman, respectively in charge of Texas, West Louisiana, and Arkansas, were remarkable men, battle tested and of proved resourcefulness. In this regard the last was not the least accomplished of the three. A prewar Helena lawyer, thirty-four years old, Hindman had preceded his present chief to his home state, and within six months of his arrival in late May, stepping into the vacuum left by Van Dorn's April crossing of the Mississippi with all the men and weapons that could be salvaged from the defeat at Elkhorn Tavern, had created and equipped, by strict enforcement of the new conscription act and the establishment of factories and foundries where none had been before, an army of 20,000 recruits, armed and uniformed more or less in accordance with regulations and supported by 46 guns. This in itself was about as close to a miracle of improvised logistics as any general ever came in the whole war, but Hindman expected to accomplish a great deal more before he was through. Dapper, jaunty, dandified, addicted to patent leather boots and rose-colored kidskin gloves, frilled shirt fronts and a rattan cane, perhaps by way of compensation for his Napoleonic five feet two of height, he was accustomed to getting what he wanted, whether it was a fine brick house, a seat in Congress, or a wife whose father had sought to keep her from him by locking her away in a convent: all of which he had won, despite the odds, by extending his credit, demolishing opponents from the stump, and scaling the convent wall. What he had in mind just now, though, was not only the scourging of all bluecoats from the soil of Arkansas — including Helena, where the Federal commander of the force in occupation had taken over the fine brick house for his headquarters — but also the recovery of Missouri.

Arriving in mid-August to find the diminutive Arkansan already far along with his plans, Holmes had been infected by his enthusiasm and had approved his preparations for a counterinvasion. It was gotten under way at once. By October Hindman's advance, a combined command of cavalry and Indians, was across the Missouri border, but suffered a repulse at the hands of a superior Union force under Brigadier

General John M. Schofield, in command of three divisions styled the Army of the Frontier. The Indians scattered like chaff before a fan, and the cavalry fell back to the security of the Boston Mountains, skirmishing as they went. Hindman, coming forward to Fort Smith with the main body, was not discouraged by this turn of events. Indeed, as he saw it, the Federals were being lured to their destruction in the wilds of northwest Arkansas. Accordingly, he crossed the Arkansas river and concentrated his infantry at Van Buren. All he wanted, he told Holmes, was a chance to hit the Yankees with something approaching equal strength, after which he would "move into Missouri, take Springfield, and winter on the Osage at least."

Presently he got that chance, and at odds considerably better than he had dared even to hope for. Schofield, believing in mid-November that hostilities had ended for the winter, left the largest of his three divisions near Fayetteville under Brigadier General James G. Blunt, with the assignment of blocking the path of another Confederate incursion, and withdrew to Springfield with the other two, which he placed under Brigadier General Francis J. Herron while he himself took off on sick leave. Hindman, with a mobile force of 11,500 men and 22 guns, was preparing to take advantage of this chance to strike at Blunt, who had 7000 men and 20 guns, when word came from Holmes (who by now had received instructions from the Secretary of War, urging the necessity for reinforcing Vicksburg) for him to return posthaste to Little Rock with all his men, in preparation for an eastward march across the Mississippi. Hindman protested for all he was worth. To fall back would cost him heavily in desertions, he knew, since many of his conscripts were natives of the region through which they would be retreating. Besides, he told Holmes, "to withdraw without fighting at all would . . . so embolden the enemy as to insure his following me up." Without waiting for a reply he put his army in motion on December 3, intending to precede the retrograde movement with an advance and a victory that would leave the Federals in no condition to pursue. Slogging next day through the brushy Boston Mountains, the highest and most rugged section of the Ozark chain, he printed and distributed an address to his soldiers, designed to steel their arms for the strike at Blunt. "Remember that the enemy you engage has no feeling of mercy or kindness toward you," he told them. "His ranks are made up of Pin Indians, free negroes, Southern tories, Kansas jayhawkers, and hired Dutch cut-throats. These bloody ruffians have invaded your country; stolen and destroyed your property; murdered your neighbors; outraged your women; driven your children from their homes, and defiled the graves of your kindred. If each man of you will do what I have here urged upon you, we will utterly destroy them."

Blunt now had his troops in bivouac about twenty miles southwest of Fayetteville, near the hamlet of Cane Hill, from which he had driven the grayback cavalry that week. When he got word that Hindman was across the Arkansas with an estimated 25,000 men he reacted according to his nature, rejecting the notion of retreat. A Maine-born Kansan who had practiced medicine en route in Ohio, he was a militant abolitionist and a graduate of the border wars. Round-faced, stocky, pugnacious in manner, he was thirty-six years old and no part of his training had prepared him for running from rebels, whatever their numbers. Determined to hold his ground, he wired for reinforcements and began to organize his position for defense.

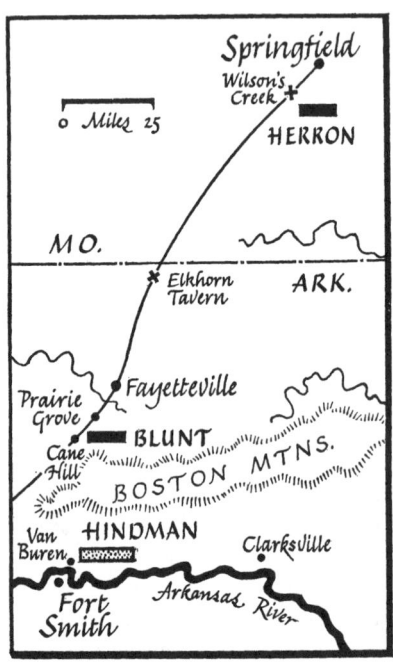

The trouble with this was that the only reinforcements available were the two small divisions under Herron, a scant 6000 men with 22 guns, and they were back near Springfield, well over a hundred miles away, whereas Hindman's camp at Van Buren was little more than a third that distance from Cane Hill, so that the chances were strong that the rebels would arrive before the reinforcements did. However, this was leaving two factors out of account. The first was that Hindman's route of march lay through the mountains; his men would be climbing and descending about as much as they would be advancing along the rugged trails. The other factor was Frank Herron. An adopted Iowan, already in command of two divisions at the age of twenty-five, he intended to accomplish a great deal more in the way of fulfilling his military ambitions before returning to civilian life as head of the Dubuque bank established for him by his wealthy Pennsylvania parents. Just now, more than anything, he wanted a chance to command those two divisions in actual battle, and he got it much sooner than he had expected. At 8 o'clock on the morning of December 3 — by which hour, unknown to him or Blunt, Hindman had put his army on the road for its trek across the Boston Mountains — Herron received the summons from Cane Hill, one hundred and thirty miles from his present camp on the somber fields where the Battle of Wilson's Creek had been fought and lost by Nathaniel Lyon, almost a year and a half ago. Drums and bugles sounded assembly and the men fell in to receive instructions for the march. It would be made without tents or baggage, they were told, except for knapsacks which would be hauled in wagons. By noon they were headed south, and before they stopped at dawn next morning, slogging at route step down the pike, they had made twenty miles. After a short rest they were off again. Across the state line on December 5, munching hardtack and raw bacon as they walked, they skirted the granite slopes of Pea Ridge and saw the nine-months-old scars on the Elkhorn Tavern, where Van Dorn had come to grief. At midnight the following day, having covered better than one hundred blistering miles of road, the head of the column entered Fayetteville, where the weary marchers slept in the streets, sprawled around fires they kindled and fed by ripping pickets from front-yard fences. Another twenty miles tomorrow and they would be at Cane Hill with Blunt, ready for whatever came at them from beyond the mountains whose foothills they could presently see by the glimmer of dawn on Sunday, December 7.

The first sign they had that they were not going to make it — at least not on schedule — came later that morning, twelve miles down the pike, when they encountered long-range cannonfire as they were approaching Illinois Creek. Soon they saw that the Confederates had drawn a line of battle around the hilltop village of Prairie Grove, a couple of miles beyond the creek, blocking the path of the road-worn bluecoats eight miles short of their goal. Herron shook out a regiment of skirmishers and advanced them to the protection of the creekbank, where to his horror he discovered that his men were so weary that once they were off their feet they promptly dropped to sleep with rebel shells and bullets whistling and twittering over their heads. Undaunted, he built up his firing line and put his batteries in position, partly by way of returning the hostile fire, but mostly by way of letting Blunt know from the racket that he had arrived, or almost arrived, and needed help. The trouble was, with all those graybacks swarming in his front, he was not even sure that Blunt and his men were still in existence. For all he knew, Hindman might have gobbled them up while he himself was on the march from Wilson's Creek.

Hindman had not gobbled up Blunt; he had gone around him. Approaching Cane Hill late the afternoon before, after a march across the shoulder of the mountains in weather so cold that water froze in the men's canteens and icicles tinkled on the beards of the horses, he had put his troops in position for a dawn attack, only to learn that Herron was on the way, already approaching Fayetteville with a force which, once it was joined to Blunt's, would give the Federals the advantage of numbers, both in men and guns. In command of a brigade at Shiloh, where he had been wounded and commended for gallantry, Hindman decided to profit from the example of that battle by preventing what had caused its loss, the arrival of Buell after Grant had been pushed to the edge of desperation. That is, he would strike at the reinforcements first, then turn on the main body. Accordingly, he built up the campfires along his outpost line, left a skeleton brigade of cavalry to keep up the bluff next morning, and set off after moonset on a circuitous march with 10,000 men to intercept and defeat the blue column hurrying southward out of Fayetteville. That was how it came about that Herron encountered long-range cannonfire at the crossing of Illinois Creek and the bristling line of battle at Prairie Grove, eight miles short of a junction with Blunt at Cane Hill.

Blunt had spent the morning in constant expectation of being swamped by the rebels maneuvering boldly to his front, apparently in overwhelming numbers. Near noon, however, hearing the sudden boom of guns from across the hills to his left rear, he realized that he had been outflanked; whereupon he fell back hastily to Rhea's Mills, six miles north, in order to protect his trains. Finding them secure he turned southeast in the direction of the booms and at 4 o'clock reached Prairie Grove, where he came upon the battle still in full swing after nearly five hours of doubtful contest. Two rounds from his lead battery announced his arrival — announced it all too emphatically, in fact, for both shots landed among Herron's skirmishers, causing them to think that they were being flanked by their foes instead of being supported by their friends. Herron had been holding his own despite the weariness of his foot-sore men. Two charges against the ridge had failed, breaking in blood against the rim of the rebel horseshoe line, but Hindman had had no better luck in attempting a counterattack with his green conscripts, who fell apart whenever he ordered them forward. The fighting continued, left and right, muzzle flashes stabbing the early darkness. Despite their superiority of numbers, especially in guns — 42 to 22, now that the Union forces were united — Blunt's fresh troops could make no more of a penetration of the rebel line than Herron's weary ones had been able to achieve. Gradually the firing died to a sputter. Then it stopped. The battle was over.

Losses in killed, wounded, and missing totaled 1317 for the Confederates and 1251 for the Federals. Of the latter only 333 were from Blunt's command, indicating how much heavier a proportion of the conflict Herron's men had borne, despite the fact that both laid claim to a lion's share in having brought the victory about. Hindman's only claim in that respect was the not inconsiderable one that he had managed to hold his ground throughout the fighting. Whether he had also accomplished his main objective — to shock the enemy into immobility, escaping pursuit while he fell back southward in compliance with the previous orders from Holmes — would soon be known; for he retreated that night under cover of darkness, wrapping the iron tires of his gun and caisson wheels with blankets to muffle the sound of his withdrawal. The ruse worked, and so did another he tried next morning. Not only did Blunt not hear him go, but at dawn he also granted a request for a truce, which Hindman sent forward under a white flag, to allow for tending the wounded and burying the dead. Discovering presently that the Confederate main body had departed in the night, Blunt canceled the truce, on grounds that the rebels were gleaning abandoned arms from the field, and prepared to follow. By that time, however, Schofield was on the scene. Up from his sickbed and furious that his army had been committed to battle in his absence, he censured both commanders: Blunt for not withdrawing to meet the reinforcements hurrying toward him, and Herron for attacking with troops so badly blown that some of them were found dead on the field, not from wounds but from exhaustion and exposure after their long march from Wilson's Creek. If Schofield's purpose in this was to prevent his subordinates' advancement by discrediting their valor, that purpose failed. By way of showing its appreciation for a victory won by northern arms as the year drew to a close — a victory which presently shone the brighter by contrast with the several full-scale disasters that developed elsewhere along the thousand-mile-long firing line before the month was out — the government promptly awarded major general's stars not only to Blunt but also to Herron, who then succeeded Lew Wallace as the youngest man to hold that rank in the U.S. Army. Moreover, as soon as these promotions came through, both men would outrank their present commander.

Hindman's discomfort was considerably increased in late December, when Schofield finally unleashed his cavalry for a forced march against the Confederates who, down to about 4000 men as a result of straggling and desertions, had taken sanctuary behind the Arkansas River. Three days after Christmas the blue riders struck Van Buren, destroying five steamboats at the wharf and all of the supplies of corn and bacon Hindman had gathered over the months in order to keep his army from starvation. Once more he was thrown into dispirited retreat, losing still more soldiers as he went. The Federals withdrew to Fayetteville, and thence on back to comfortable winter quarters in Missouri, but now there was no question of Hindman's returning to Little Rock with the prospect of marching his army to the relief of Vicksburg. Practically speaking he had no army. So much of it as did not lie in shallow graves at Prairie Grove was scattered over northern Arkansas, hiding from conscription agents in Ozark coves and valleys.

Thus it was that the battle lost in northwest Arkansas had repercussions far beyond the theater it was fought in. Holmes had opposed the eastward transfer from the start, protesting that the march led through a region barren of supplies and would require no less than thirty days. "Solemnly, under the circumstances," he had informed the Adjutant General earlier that month, "I regard the movement ordered as equivalent to abandoning Arkansas." All the same, against his better judgment, he had been preparing to go along with the plan. But now, with Hindman's army practically out of existence and only the local reserves to protect Little Rock itself against an advance from occupied Helena, he had what he considered the best of specific reasons for declining to comply with the government's wishes. On December 29, the day after Schofield's cavalry hit Van Buren, he wrote Johnston in reply to the correspondence the President had forwarded from Vicksburg during his inspection of that place the week before: "My information from Helena is to the effect that a heavy force of the enemy has passed down the Mississippi on transports.... Thus it seems very certain that any force I can now send from here would not be able to reach Vicksburg, and if at all not before such a reinforcement would be useless, while such a diversion would enable the enemy to penetrate those portions of the Arkansas Valley where the existence of supplies of subsistence and forage would afford them leisure to overrun the entire state and gradually reduce the people to ... dependence."

★ ★ ★

It was bad enough that the Yankees were steaming down the Mississippi, but they were also steaming up it — simultaneously. Banks had reoccupied Baton Rouge in mid-December and now was giving every sign that he intended to continue the northward penetration, shortening the stretch of river necessarily rebel-held if Holmes was to keep open the supply lines vital to the feeding and reinforcement, if not indeed to the survival, of all the armies of the South. Since the loss of the armed ram *Arkansas*, three months back, the Confederacy had had no vestige of a navy with which to oppose this two-pronged challenge designed for her riving and destruction; the threat would have to be stopped, if at all, not on the river itself, but from its banks. On the east bank the responsibility was Pemberton's, and to help him meet it he had two stout high-ground bastions one hundred air-line miles apart, commanding bends of the river at Vicksburg and Port Hudson. On the west bank it was Richard Taylor's, who had nothing: not only no lofty fortresses bristling with heavy-caliber guns emplaced to blow the Union ironclads out of the water, but also no army. In fact, on his arrival from Virginia in late August, he had found that his total force consisted of two troops of home-guard cavalry, a scattering of guerillas hidden from friends and foes in the moss-hung swamps and bayous, and a battalion of mounted infantry just arrived from Texas — in all, fewer than 2000 effectives for the defense of the whole Department of Louisiana. Nonetheless, Holmes had confidence that this second of his three major generals would be ingenious and tireless in his efforts to reduce the nearly immeasurable odds, and this confidence was not misplaced.

Commander of a division used as shock troops by Stonewall Jackson throughout the Shenandoah Valley campaign, Taylor had been one of the stars of that amazing chapter in military history, and had found in that experience ample compensation for his lack of formal training in the art of war. Gripped on the eve of the Seven Days by a strange paralysis of the legs, which seemed to portend the close of a promising career and a denial of any further share in winning his country's independence, this son of Zachary Taylor had recovered in time to receive his present assignment, together with a promotion, from his brother-in-law Jefferson Davis. Happy over what in fact would be a home-coming, for he had commanded Louisianians in the Valley and had spent his antebellum years on a Louisiana plantation, he came West with an enthusiasm that was only slightly dampened by the discovery of conditions in his new department, as of August 20, when he established headquarters in Alexandria. Undismayed by the shortage of soldiers, which kept him from any immediate accomplishment of big things — such as the retaking of New Orleans, which was very much a part of his plans for the future — he decided to be content at first with small ones. Within two weeks of his arrival he mounted a surprise attack that captured a four-gun battery and two companies of infantry at Bayou des Allemands, a Federal post near his plantation home, fifty miles downriver from Donaldsonville and less than half that far above New Orleans. If he could not retake the Crescent City just yet, he could at least draw near it — and profitably, too.

Slight though it was, this first success gained locally by Confederate arms in the four months since the fall of the South's first city was heartening indeed to the people of the district. Not even the recapture of the post in late October, when the resurgent Louisianians were driven away by a Federal amphibious force that included four regiments of infantry and a quartet of light-draft gunboats, detracted from the brilliance of that first strike. What was more, Taylor was planning others of still larger scope. Denied access to the Lafourche, that fertile region lying between the Mississippi and the Atchafalaya, he moved into the Teche country, which lay between the Atchafalaya basin and the Gulf of Mexico, and here, despite the fact that his government, as he said, "had no soldiers, no arms or munitions, and no money within the limits of the district," he set about the task of raising, equipping, and training the army with which he hoped, in time, not only to capture but also to hold the series of fortified posts that blocked the path between him and his goal, New Orleans. Meanwhile, intent on preventing further enemy penetrations, he had to disperse what forces he had in order to meet threats from all directions. With few trained subordinates and almost no telegraph or railway lines, the problem of central control was well-nigh insoluble. However, now that December had come on and the year drew toward a close, Taylor went far toward solving it. By using relays of fast-stepping mules and an ambulance in which he could sleep while traveling, the thirty-six-year-old general managed to employ what might have been his immobile hours for visits to the various scattered points in his large department. "Like the Irishman's bird," he subsequently wrote, "I almost succeeded in being in two places at the same time."

In this respect, as well as in several others, he was easily distinguishable from his opposite number, the newly arrived commander of all the Union forces in the region. Ten years Taylor's senior, of humbler birth but with much larger accomplishments in public life, having been a three-term governor of Massachusetts and speaker of the national House of Representatives, Nathaniel Banks was nothing like the Irishman's bird and had nothing like his opponent's nighttime mobility — though the fact was, he had perhaps an even greater need for it if he was to carry out the multiple assignment given him by his superiors when he set out from Hampton Roads on his voyage down and around the coast to relieve his fellow Bay State politician, Benjamin Butler, as military ruler of New Orleans and commander of the Department of the Gulf. Vicksburg and Mobile were his primary objectives, he was told, and after the fall of the former place had opened the Mississippi to Union traffic throughout its length he was to move up the Red in order to gain control of northern Louisiana and, eventually, Texas. It was a large order, particularly for a general who not only had not a single battlefield victory to his credit, but rather had been whipped twice already in open contest — once at Winchester, in the Shenendoah Valley, and again at Cedar Mountain, both times by Stonewall Jackson, whose lean marchers had captured so many of his supplies that they had dubbed him "Commissary" Banks — but he apparently had no doubt that it could be filled and that he was the man to fill it. He docked at New Orleans, December 14, and took over formally next day from Butler, who issued an address to his army — "I greet you, my brave comrades, and say farewell!" it began, and ended: "Farewell, my comrades! Again, Farewell!" — and promptly departed for Washington to take the government to task for having made what seemed to him an improvident substitution.

Banks wasted no time on speeches. On the day he took command he issued orders for one of the divisions he had brought along to proceed at once upriver, without unloading from its transports, and to reoccupy Baton Rouge, which Butler had abandoned after repulsing an all-out attack on the place in early August. Two days later, when the Louisiana capital fell without even a show of resistance, Banks was greatly pleased at having made so prompt and effective a beginning toward fulfilling his government's outsized expectations. Including the reinforcements still arriving after their long voyage from New York and Fort Monroe, he had 36,508 effectives in his department, exclusive of navy personnel, and he felt that these were ample for the accomplishment of his task. What was more, he reported that he had found in Farragut, who was to be his partner in continuing the bold upriver thrust, a sailor who was "earnest for work." After a conference with the Tennessee-born admiral he added that he was delighted with his enthusiasm and frankness, and that he looked forward to "a most satisfactory result from our mutual labors." Banks was feeling chipper, and he said so. "All the indications of our campaign are auspicious," he notified Washington on December 18, the day after the fall of Baton Rouge, "and I hope to make good the most sanguine expectations in regard to my expedition."

There were, however, two previously unsuspected matters for concern, one military, one civil, and both grave. The first was the presence, thirty-five miles above Baton Rouge, which in turn was a hundred miles above New Orleans, of the fortifications at Port Hudson. Neither his Washington superiors nor Banks himself, until he arrived, had known of the existence of any such obstacle south of Vicksburg, another 250 winding miles upstream; yet intelligence reports informed him now that the Confederates had no less than 12,000 troops in the place, strongly intrenched on the landward side and with 21 heavy guns emplaced on the high bluff, waiting to sink or blow sky high whatever came their way across the chocolate-colored surface of the river. This in itself, placing as it did a new complexion on the problem of ascent, was enough to give Banks pause. But the other concern, the civil one, was even more disturbing in its way, since it showed that the command of the department was going to be a far more complex occupation than he had supposed, early that month, when he set out from Virginia. Less than two weeks after his arrival, for example, he received a note from one C. A. Smith, commission agent for certain northern interests, and Andrew Butler, whose brother Ben had set him up in business when he took over as military ruler of New Orleans. "Dear Sir," it read. "If you will allow our commercial program to be [carried] out as projected previous to your arrival in this department, giving the same support and facilities as your predecessor, I am authorized on [receiving] your assent to place at your disposal $100,000."

In the course of his rise from bobbin boy to the top of the heap in Massachusetts politics Banks no doubt had encountered other offers of this nature, but hardly one that was made so blatantly or with such apparent confidence in his basic corruptibility. "It was no temptation," he told his wife. "I thank God every night that I have no desire for dishonest gains." All the same, he felt obliged to report to Washington "that as much, or more, attention has been given to civil than to military matters," including the training of his army, and that, in consequence, the troops were "not in condition for immediate service." Though he declared on Christmas Eve, "We hope to move up the river at the close of the week," he was still in New Orleans after New Year's, complaining that he was cramped by a shortage of siege artillery. "The enemy's works at Port Hudson have been in progress many months and are formidable," he explained. "Our light field guns would make no impression on them." In fact, having learned by now of the reverses lately suffered by the column supposed to be working its way southward out of Memphis while he moved northward from New Orleans, he was beginning to "feel some anxiety as to the defenses of this city.... The enemy is concentrating all available forces on the river, and in the event of disasters North will not fail to turn their attention to this quarter."

So it was that, now in January — while Taylor kept busy raising and training an army in the bayous, lulled to sleep each night in his ambulance by the clopping of hoofs as he traveled the moon-drenched roads of the Teche and dreamed of retaking the South's first city — Banks stayed where he was, bedeviled by itchy-handed speculators, made apprehensive by rebel successes upriver, and fretted by shortages while he continued his preparations for the upstream movement which he had assured his superiors in December would be launched without delay.

Another part of his assignment, albeit one that was no more than incidental, he had also placed in the way of execution, though so far on a scale that was small indeed. Its conception was provoked by the shortage of cotton for the textile mills of New England, 3,252,000 of whose 4,745,750 spindles had fallen idle by the middle of the year, with the result that production was down to less than one fourth of normal before its close. New Orleans having failed to yield more than a comparative handful of bales, the hungry manufacturers had cast their eyes on Texas. What they had in mind was conquest and colonization; they saw their chance to make of it what one observer called "another and a fairer Kansas," where Yankee know-how and industry, replacing the slovenly farming methods now employed, would produce more cotton in a single year than had previously been grown in all the history of the vast Lone Star expanse. That way, the idle spindles would be fed, the mill hands would return to work, and the owners would get rich. First, however, the army would have to clear the path for immigration, and in this connection Banks had in his entourage a Texas Unionist, Andrew Jackson Hamilton, upon whom the War Department, at the behest of the New England manufacturers, had conferred the rank of brigadier general, together with appointment as military governor of Texas. He would take office, preparing the way for the textile-sponsored "colonists," when and if Banks won control of some portion of the state for him to govern.

So far, all there was for him in this regard was Galveston harbor, seized two months ago by the navy and now being patrolled by gunboats of the West Coast Blockading Squadron, part of Farragut's command. Texas was far down on the list of Banks's assigned objectives; though his department had been enlarged to include that state, its occupation was scheduled to follow the opening of the Mississippi and the conquest of the Red River Valley in northwest Louisiana; but at Hamilton's urging he agreed to send a Massachusetts regiment to take and hold the island town at once, thus giving the newly appointed governor at least the shadow of a dry-land claim to his high title. Accordingly, an advance party of three companies left New Orleans on December 22, before they had had time for more than a hurried look at the sights of the city, and landed at Galveston on Christmas Eve. There, under the muzzles of the gunboats anchored in the harbor, they set to work barricading the wharf as a precaution against attack from the landward side while awaiting the arrival of the rest of the infantry by sea, together with attached units of cavalry and field artillery.

They had need for greater caution than they suspected, for this action brought them into immediate contact with the first in rank of Holmes's three major generals, John Magruder. Known to be unpredictable and tricky, he was also first in reputation; "Prince John" he had been called in the old army, partly because of his aristocratic manner and his fondness for staging amateur theatricals, partly too because of his flared mustache, luxuriant sideburns, gaudy clothes, and imperial six-feet-two of height. As flamboyant in the Transmississippi as he had been in his native Virginia — where, previous to becoming somewhat unstrung in the jangle of the Seven Days, he had put on such a show of strength with a handful of men that McClellan had been awed into immobility before Yorktown — his ache for distinction and love of flourish were no less pronounced in the Lone Star state. The difference here, eight months later, was that Magruder was thinking offensively. For some time now, in fact ever since his assignment to command the District of Texas, Arizona, and New Mexico on October 10, five days after the Union flotilla steamed in and put Galveston under its guns, he had had it in mind not only to liberate the island town, less than fifty miles southeast of his Houston headquarters, but also to sink or capture the warships riding insolently at anchor in the harbor. So far as Prince John was concerned, the addition of those three companies of Massachusetts infantry, now barricading the wharf against attack, only fattened the prize within his grasp and added to the glory about to be won.

Nor was his plan for making a naval assault deterred by his lack of anything resembling a navy. If he had none then he would build one, or at any rate improvise one, and he did so in short order. Workmen off the Houston docks piled bales of cotton around the paddle boxes and decks of the *Bayou City*, a two-story side-wheel Mississippi steamboat, and the stern-wheeler *Neptune*, a smaller vessel. The former was armed with a rifled 32-pounder, located forward of her stacks, and the latter's bow was faced with railroad iron to stiffen her punch as a ram.

Their crews were army volunteers, including some 300 riflemen stationed about the decks as sharpshooters. These two "cotton-clads" would stage the naval assault, descending Buffalo Bayou to come booming down on the five Union gunboats, *Westfield, Harriet Lane, Owasco, Clifton,* and *Sachem,* which had a combined displacement of over 3000 tons and mounted a total of 28 guns, mostly heavy. For the land attack there were in all about 500 men; Texans under Colonel Tom Green, who had led them at Valverde, they were survivors of Brigadier General Henry Sibley's nightmare expedition up the Rio Grande, back in the spring. Magruder divided them into three assault columns, taking the center one himself. By New Year's Eve his preparations were complete. He gave the signal and the attack got under way, bringing in the new year with a bang.

Crossing from the mainland by the unguarded bridge, he struck the barricade shortly after midnight — only to find that his scaling ladders were too short. All he could do was work his men up close and keep exchanging shots with the defenders, who had turned out at the first alarm and were laying down a heavy fire. Everything depended now on the untried two-boat navy. The first the Federals knew of its existence was when lookouts on the *Westfield,* Commander W. B. Renshaw's flagship, spotted two ungainly-looking steamboats, apparently overloaded with cotton bales, driving hard toward the anchored flotilla. Attempting to take evasive action, the *Westfield* went aground on Pelican Island Bar, removed from the fight as effectively as if she had been sunk. Aboard the *Bayou City,* bearing down on the *Harriet Lane,* the gun captain of the 32-pounder shouted: "Well, here goes for a New Year's present!" and pulled the lanyard. The first shot missed, as did the second, and on the third the gun exploded at the breech, killing him and four of its crew; whereupon the *Neptune* came up, churning the water in her wake, and struck the *Lane* such a tremendous thump that she broke her own nose and had to run up on the flats to keep from sinking. Afloat as ashore, the battle seemed lost by mishap or miscalculation.

By now, however, the *Bayou City* had pulled up alongside the *Lane,* her upper-deck riflemen firing down on the rattled bluejackets while a boarding party swarmed over the bulwarks and began slashing at the survivors in the style of John Paul Jones. In the course of this melee the Union skipper was killed and his lieutenant ran up the white flag of surrender; observing which, the other three nearby captains did the same. Across the way, still hard aground, Renshaw saw that the *Westfield* was next on the rebel target list. Determined not to have her fall into enemy hands, he ordered the crew to abandon ship while he lowered into an open magazine a barrel of turpentine equipped with a slow fuze which he set and started before he turned to go. That was his last act on earth or water, for the fuze was defective or wrongly set.

Before he made it out of range, a flame-shot column of black smoke roared skyward and the *Westfield* blew apart, her wreckage enveloped in fire and steam.

Watching this abrupt disintegration of the naval support for the defenders of the wharf, the Texans in front of the barricade took heart and the Federals behind it were dejected; so much so, indeed, that the three Massachusetts companies, warned by a step-up in the firing that an assault was about to be launched, surrendered in a body. But the commanders of the gunboats *Clifton, Owasco,* and *Sachem,* claiming that this forcing of the issue ashore was in violation of the naval "truce" — for so they had considered it, they later affirmed by way of rebuttal to the outrage expressed by the rebels — hauled down their white flags and made a sudden run for open water. The Confederates, unable to pursue out into the Gulf, could do nothing but howl in protest at foul play. They had lost 143 killed and wounded. Including captives the Federals had lost about 600 soldiers and sailors: plus, of course, two gunboats and the town. At a single stroke, boldly conceived and boldly delivered, Magruder had cleared Texas of armed bluecoats. Nor did he intend to grant them another foothold. Moving his headquarters triumphantly to Galveston, he notified his government next day: "We are preparing to give them a warm reception should they return."

The navy might (and in fact did, the following week, withdrawing the 2000-ton screw steamer *Brooklyn* and six gunboats from the blockade squadron off Mobile and bringing them to Galveston, where they were careful however to maintain station well outside the harbor and thus beyond reach of another eruption of Magruder's cotton-clads) but Banks had no intention of returning, not even with a token force. He counted himself lucky that the whole Bay State regiment, together with its artillery and cavalry supports, had not landed in time to be gobbled up, and he brought the still-loaded transports back to New Orleans, turning a deaf ear to Would-Be-Governor Hamilton's disgruntled protestations. That gentleman and his party — a sizable group, characterized by one critic as "friends, patrons, and creditors," who had meant to be front runners in the intended Lone Star colonization — returned instead to Washington, complaining bitterly that they had been "deliberately and purposely humbugged."

Though Holmes of course was quick to congratulate Magruder, whose amphibious coup made the one bright spot in the entire Transmississippi as the new year came in, Hamilton's dejection and disgust were not matched by any corresponding elation on the part of the overall commander of the Confederate Far West. Though he had managed, on the face of it, to achieve a sort of balance within the limits of his department — defeat in northwestern Arkansas, stalemate in West Louisiana, victory in coastal Texas — he knew that it was precarious in nature, tenuous at best and, in consideration of the odds, most likely temporary.

Nor was the maintenance of that shaky balance only dependent on what occurred within the borders of the monster region. Cut off, Holmes and all those under him would be left as it were to wither on the vine; so that what happened beyond or along those borders was equally important, and this was true in particular as to what happened along the eastern border, the Mississippi itself, down which he had reported the "heavy force" of Union ironclads and transports steaming the week before past Helena. It was headed, according to his conjecture, for Vicksburg, the linchpin whose loss might well result in the collapse of the whole Confederate wagon.

✗ 4 ✗

Haste made waste and Grant knew it, but in this case the haste was unavoidable — unavoidable, that is, unless he was willing to take the risk of having another general win the prize he was after — because he was fighting two wars simultaneously: one against the Confederacy, or at any rate so much of its army as stood between him and the river town that was his goal, and the other against a man who, like himself, wore blue. That was where the need for haste came in, for the rival general's name was John McClernand. A former Springfield lawyer and Illinois congressman, McClernand was known to have political aspirations designed to carry him not one inch below the top position occupied at present by his friend, another former Springfield lawyer and Illinois congressman, Abraham Lincoln. Moreover, having decided that the road to the White House led through Vicksburg, he had taken pains to see that he traveled it well equipped, and this he had done by engaging the preliminary support, the active military backing, not only of his friend the President, but also of the Secretary of War, the crusty and often difficult Edwin M. Stanton. With the odds thus lengthened against him, Grant — when he belatedly found out what his rival had been up to — could see that this private war against McClernand might well turn out to be as tough, in several ways, as the public one he had been fighting for eighteen months against the rebels.

In the first place, he had not even known that he had this private war on his hands until it was so well under way that his rival had already won the opening skirmish. McClernand had gone to Washington on leave in late September, complaining privately that he was "tired of furnishing brains" for Grant's army. Arriving in the capital he appealed to Lincoln to "let one volunteer officer try his abilities." His plan was to return to his old political stamping ground and there, by reaching also into Indiana and Iowa, raise an army with which he would descend the Mississippi, capture Vicksburg, "and open navigation to New Orleans." Lincoln liked the sound of that and took him to see Stanton, who liked it too. McClernand left Washington in late October, armed with a confidential order signed by Stanton and indorsed by Lincoln, giving official sanction to his plan. By early November Grant was hearing rumors from upriver in Illinois: rumors which were presently reinforced by a dispatch from General-in-Chief Henry W. Halleck, whom the three former lawyers had not taken into their confidence. Memphis, which was in Grant's department, was to "be made the depot of a joint military and naval expedition on Vicksburg." Alarmed at hearing the rumors confirmed, Grant wired back: "Am I to understand that I lie still here while an expedition is fitted out from Memphis, or do you want me to push south as far as possible?" Halleck was something of a lawyer, too, though he now found himself at cross-purposes with the men who had not let him in on the secret. "You have command of all troops sent to your department," he replied, " and have permission to fight the enemy where you please."

Grant considered himself unleashed. Organizing his mobile force of about 40,000 effectives into right and left wings, respectively under Major General W. T. Sherman and Brigadier General C. S. Hamilton, with the center under Major General J. B. McPherson, he began to move at once, southward along the Mississippi Central Railroad from Grand Junction. Ordinarily he would have preferred to wait for reinforcements, but not now. "I feared that delay might bring McClernand," he later explained. Vicksburg was 250 miles away, and as he saw it the town belonged to the man who got there first. By mid-November he was in Holly Springs, where he set up a depot of supplies and munitions, then continued on across the Tallahatchie, leapfrogging his headquarters to Oxford while the lead division was fording the Yocknapatalfa, eight miles north of Water Valley, which was occupied during the first week of December. The movement had been rapid and well coordinated; so far, it had encountered only token resistance from the rebels, who were fading back before the advance of the bluecoats. Presently Grant discovered why. Pemberton — whose strength he considerably overestimated as equal to his own — was avoiding serious contact while seeking a tactical advantage, and at last he found it. He called a halt near Grenada, another twenty-five miles beyond Water Valley, and put his gray-clad troops to work improving with intrenchments a position of great natural strength along the Yalobusha. Approaching Coffeeville on December 5, midway between Water Valley and Grenada, the Federal cavalry was struck a blow that signified the end of easy progress. Still 150-odd miles from Vicksburg, Grant could see that the going was apt to be a good deal rougher and slower from here on.

Something else he could see as well, something that disturbed him even more. While he was being delayed in the piny highlands of north-central Mississippi, facing the rebels intrenched along the high-banked Yalobusha, McClernand might come down to Memphis, where advance contingents of his expedition were awaiting him already, and ride the broad smooth highway of the Mississippi River down to Vicksburg unopposed: in which case Grant would not only have lost his private war, he would even have helped his opponent win it by holding Pemberton and the greater part of the Vicksburg garrison in position, 150 miles away, while McClernand captured the weakly defended town with little more exertion than had been required in the course of the long boat ride south from Cairo. That was what rankled worst, the thought that he would have helped to pluck the laurels that would grace his rival's brow. But as he thought distastefully of this, it began to occur to him that he saw here the possibility of a campaign of his own along these lines. "You have command of all troops sent to your department," Halleck had told him, and presumably this included the recruits awaiting McClernand's arrival at Memphis. So Grant, still at his Oxford headquarters on December 8, sent a note to Sherman, whose command was at College Hill, ten miles away: "I wish you would come over this evening and stay tonight, or come in the morning. I would like to talk with you."

Sherman did not wait for morning. Impatient as always, he rode straight over, a tall red-haired man with a fidgety manner, concave temples, glittering hazel eyes, and a scraggly, close-cropped beard. "I never saw him but I thought of Lazarus," one observer was to write. A chain smoker who, according to another witness, got through each cigar "as if it was a duty to be finished in the shortest possible time," he was forty-two, two years older than the comparatively stolid Grant and once his military senior, too, until Donelson brought the younger brigadier fame and a promotion, both of which had been delayed for Sherman until Shiloh, where he fought under — some said, saved — his former junior. He felt no resentment at that. In fact, he saw Grant as "the coming man in this war." But he had never had better reason for this belief than now at Oxford, when he was closeted with him and heard his plan for the sudden capture of Vicksburg with the help of a kidnaped army.

As usual in military matters, geography played a primary part in determining what was to be done, and how. Various geographic factors made Vicksburg an extremely difficult nut to crack. First there was the bluff itself, the 200-foot red-clay escarpment dominating the hairpin bend of the river at its base, unscalable for infantry and affording the guns emplaced on its crest a deadly plunging fire — as Farragut, for one, could testify — against whatever naval forces moved against or past it. As for land forces, since they could not scale the bluff itself, even if they had been able to approach it from the front, their only alternative was to come upon it from the rear; that is, either to march overland down the Mississippi Central to Grenada, as Grant was now attempting to do, and thence along the high ground lying between the Yazoo and the Big Black Rivers, or else debark from their transports somewhere

The Longest Journey [63]

short of the town and make a wide swing east, in order to approach it from that direction. However, the latter was nearly impossible, too, because of another geographic factor, the so-called Yazoo-Mississippi alluvial delta. This incredibly fertile, magnolia-leaf-shaped region, 200 miles in length and 50 miles in average width, bounded east and west by the two rivers that gave it its compound name, and north and south by the hills that rose below and above Memphis and Vicksburg, was nearly roadless throughout its flat and swampy expanse, was subject to floods in all but the driest seasons, and — except for the presence of a scattering of pioneers who risked its malarial and intestinal disorders for the sake of the richness of its forty-foot topsoil, which in time, after the felling of its big trees and the draining of its bayous, would make it the best cotton farmland in the world — was the exclusive domain of moccasins,

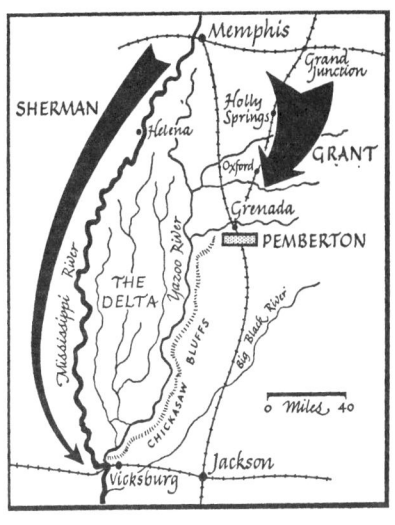

bears, alligators, and panthers. It was, in short, impenetrable to all but the smallest of military parties, engaged in the briefest of forays. An army attempting to march across or through it would come out at the other end considerably reduced in numbers and fit for nothing more strenuous than a six-month rest, with quinine as the principal item on its diet. Anyhow, Grant did not intend to try it that way. He had his eye fixed on the mouth of the Yazoo, twelve miles above Vicksburg, and it seemed to him that an amphibious force could ascend that river for a landing on the southeast bank, which would afford the troops a straight shot at the town on the bluff. True, there were hills here, too — the Walnut Hills, they were called, the beginning of the long ridge known as the Chickasaw Bluffs, which lay along the left bank of the Yazoo, overlooking the flat morass of the delta — but they were by no means as forbidding as the heights overlooking the Mississippi, a dozen miles below. It was Grant's belief that determined men, supported by the guns of the fleet, could swarm over these comparatively low-lying hills, brushing aside whatever portion of the weakened garrison tried to stop them, and be inside the town before nightfall of the day they came ashore.

That was why he had sent for Sherman, who seemed to him the right man for the job. Sherman happily agreed to undertake it, and Grant gave him his written orders that same evening. He was to return at once to Memphis with one of his three divisions, which he would combine with McClernand's volunteers, already waiting there. This would give him 21,000 troops, and to these would be added another 12,000 to be picked up at Helena on the way downriver, bringing his total strength to four divisions of 33,000 men, supported by Porter's fleet. Grant explained that he himself would continue to bristle aggressively along the line of the Yalobusha "so as to keep up the impression of a continuous move," and if Pemberton fell back prematurely he would "follow him even to the gates of Vicksburg," in which event he and Sherman would meet on the Yazoo and combine for the final dash into the town. Delighted with the prospect, Sherman was off next day for Memphis, altogether mindful of the need for haste if he was to forestall both McClernand and Pemberton. "Time now is the great object," he wired Porter. "We must not give time for new combinations."

He did not make it precisely clear whether these feared "combinations" were being designed in Richmond or in Washington — whether, that is, they threatened the successful prosecution of Grant's public or his private war. By mid-December, however, Grant's worries in regard to the latter were mostly over. Sherman was in Memphis, poised for the jump-off, and McClernand's men had become organic parts of the army the redhead was about to take downriver. There was still one danger. McClernand outranked him; which meant that if he arrived before Sherman left, he would assume command by virtue of seniority. But Grant considered this unlikely. Sherman was thoroughly aware of the risk and would be sure to avoid the consequences. Besides, with Halleck's telegram in his files as license for the kidnap operation, Grant felt secure from possible thunder from on high. "I doubted McClernand's fitness," he later wrote, "and I had good reason to believe that in forestalling him I was by no means giving offense to those whose authority to command was above both him and me."

The arrival of a telegram from Washington on the 18th, instructing him to divide his command (now and henceforward to be called the Army of the Tennessee) into four corps, with McClernand in charge of one of those assigned to operations down the Mississippi — which meant of course that, once he joined it, he would be in charge of the whole column by virtue of his rank, unless Grant himself came over and took command along the river route — did not disturb the plans Grant had described in a letter home, three days ago, as "all complete for weeks to come," adding: "I hope to have them all work out just as planned." Sherman was ready to leave, he knew, and in fact would be gone tomorrow, before McClernand could possibly arrive from Illinois. Blandly he wired his new subordinate word of the Washington order, which dispelled McClernand's illusion that his command was to be an independent one. Instructing him to come on down to Memphis, Grant even managed to keep a straight face while remarking: "I hope you will find all the preliminary preparations completed on your arrival and the expedition ready to move."

★ ★ ★

McClernand found no such thing, of course. All he found when at last he reached Memphis on December 29 were the empty docks his men had departed from, ten days ago under Sherman, and Grant's telegram, delayed eleven days in transmission. Nor did Grant's own plans, "all complete for weeks to come," work out as he had intended and predicted. In both cases — entirely in the former and largely in the latter — the cause could be summed up in three two-syllable nouns: Nathan Bedford Forrest.

"He was the only Confederate cavalryman of whom Grant stood in much dread," a friend of the Union general's once remarked. Then he told why. "Who's commanding?" Grant would ask on hearing that gray raiders were on the prowl. If it was some other rebel chieftain he would shrug off the threat with a light remark; "but if Forrest was in command he at once became apprehensive, because the latter was amenable to no known rules of procedure, was a law unto himself for all military acts, and was constantly doing the unexpected at all times and places."

Grant's apprehensions were well founded as he looked back over his shoulder in the direction of his main supply base at Columbus, Kentucky; or, more specifically, since the far-off river town was adequately garrisoned against raiders, as he traced on the map the nearly two hundred highly vulnerable, not to say frangible, miles of railroad which were his sole all-weather connection with the munitions and food his army in North Mississippi required if it was to continue to shoot and eat. Without that base and those railroads, once he had used up the reserve supplies already brought forward and stored at Holly Springs, his choice would lie between retreat on the one hand and starvation or surrender on the other. Just now, moreover, the reason his apprehensions were so well founded was that Forrest was looking — and not only looking, but moving — in that direction, too: as Grant learned from a dispatch received December 15 from Jackson, Tennessee, a vital junction about midway of his vulnerable supply line. "Forrest is crossing [the] Tennessee at Clifton," the local commander wired. Four days later, Jackson itself was under attack by a mounted force which the Federal defenders estimated at 10,000 men, with Forrest himself definitely in charge.

Pemberton had begun it by appealing to Bragg in late November for a diversion in West Tennessee, which he thought might ease the pressure on his front, and Bragg had responded by sending Forrest instructions to "throw his command rapidly over the Tennessee River and precipitate it upon the enemy's lines, break up railroads, burn bridges, destroy depots, capture hospitals and guards, and harass him generally." Receiving these orders December 10 at Columbia, forty miles south of Nashville, Forrest was off next day with four regiments of cavalry and a four-gun battery, 2100 men in all, mostly recruits newly brigaded under his command and mainly armed with shotguns and flintlock muskets. Four days later and sixty miles away, he began to cross the Tennessee at Clifton on two flatboats which he had built for the emergency and which he afterwards sank in a nearby creek in case he needed them coming back. Deep in enemy country, with the bluecoats warned of his crossing while it was still in progress, he encountered on the 18th, near Lexington, two regiments of infantry, a battalion of cavalry, and a section of artillery, all under Colonel Robert G. Ingersoll, who had been sent out to intercept him. The meeting engagement was brief and decisive. Falling back on the town, Ingersoll took up what he thought was a good defensive position and was firing rapidly with his two guns at the rebels to his front, when suddenly he "found that the enemy were pouring in on all directions." The fight ended quite as abruptly as it had begun. "If he really believed that there is no hell," one grayback later said of the postwar orator-agnostic, "we convinced him that there was something mightily like it." Captured along with his two guns and 150 of his men, while the rest made off "on the full run" for Jackson, twenty-five miles to the west, Ingersoll greeted his captors with aplomb: "Is this the army of your Southern Confederacy for which I have so diligently sought? Then I am your guest until the wheels of the great Cartel are put in motion."

Following hard on the heels of the fugitives, who he knew would stumble into Jackson with exaggerated stories of his strength, Forrest advanced to within four miles of the place and began to dispose his "army" as if for assault, maneuvering boldly along the ridge-lines and beating kettledrums at widely scattered points to keep up the illusion, or, as he called it, "the skeer." It worked quite well. Convinced that he was heavily outnumbered, though in fact he had about four times as many troops inside the town as the Confederates had outside it, Brigadier General Jeremiah Sullivan prepared to make a desperate house-to-house defense. All next day the rebel host continued to gather, waxing bolder hour by hour. When dawn of the 20th showed the graybacks gone, Sullivan took heart and set out after them, pushing eastward — into emptiness, as it turned out, for Forrest had swung north. Today in fact, having thrown the Federal main body off his trail, he began in earnest to carry out his primary assignment, the destruction of the sixty miles of the Mobile & Ohio connecting Jackson and Union City, up near the Kentucky line. The common complaint of army commanders, that cavalry could seldom be persuaded to get down off their horses for the hard work that was necessary if the damage to enemy installations was to be more than temporary, was never leveled against Forrest's men.

Besides forcing the surrender of the several blue garrisons in towns along the line, they tore up track, burned crossties and trestles, and wrecked culverts so effectively that this stretch of the M&O was out of commission for the balance of the war. In Union City on Christmas Eve, resting his troopers after their four-day rampage with axes and sledges, Forrest reported by courier to Bragg that, at a cost so far of 22 men, he had killed or captured more than 1300 of the enemy, "including 4 colonels, 4 majors, 10 captains, and 23 lieutenants." That he considered this no more than a respectable beginning was shown by his closing remark: "My men have all behaved well in action, and as soon as rested a little you will hear from me in another quarter."

His problem now, after paroling his captives and sending them north to Columbus to spread bizarre reports of his strength — reports that were based on bogus dispatches, which he had been careful to let them overhear while their papers were being made out at his headquarters — was, first, what further damage to inflict and, second, how to get back over the river intact before the various Federal columns, still chasing phantoms all over West Tennessee, converged on him with overwhelming numbers. The first was solved on Christmas Day, when he marched southeast out of Union City and spent the next two days administering to the Nashville & Northwestern the treatment already given the M&O. Reaching McKenzie on the 28th in an icy, pelting rain, he headed south across the swampy bottoms of the swollen Obion River, and now began his solution of the second part of his problem. Instead of trying to make a run for the Tennessee, with the chance of being caught half-over and hamstrung, he decided to brazen out the game by thrusting in among the Federals attempting a convergence, and by vigorous blows, struck right or left at whatever came within his reach, stun them into inaction or retreat, while he continued his movement toward the security of Middle Tennessee.

The fact was, he had little to fear from the direction of Columbus. Brigadier General Thomas A. Davies, commander of the 5000 bluecoats gathered there, had been so alarmed by demonstrations within ten miles of the town on Christmas Eve, as well as by the parolees coming in next day with reports of 40,000 infantry on the march from Bragg, that he had spiked the guns at New Madrid and Island Ten, throwing the powder into the Mississippi to keep it out of rebel hands, and now was concentrating everything in order to protect the $13,000,000 worth of supplies and equipment being loaded onto steamboats at the Columbus wharf for a getaway in case Forrest broke his lines. Conditions were scarcely better, from the Union point of view, 250 miles downriver at Memphis, where the citizens had become so elated over rumors that their former alderman was coming home, along with thousands of his troopers, that Major General S. A. Hurlbut, perturbed by their reaction and the fact that his garrison was down to a handful since the departure of

Sherman, telegraphed Washington: "I hold city by terror of heavy guns bearing upon it and the belief that an attack would cause its destruction." Grant, however, was of a different breed. He was thinking not of his safety, but of the possible destruction of Forrest and his men. "I have directed such a concentration of troops that I think not many of them will get back to the east bank of the Tennessee," he informed a subordinate. Nor was this opinion ill-founded. One superior blue force was coming south from Fort Henry, another north from Corinth, and both were now much closer to the Clifton crossing than Forrest was. So, for that matter, were Jere Sullivan and his three brigades, two of which were back by now from their goose chase east of Jackson and headed north. Undiscouraged by his lack of luck so far, he believed he knew just where the raiders were, and he intended to bag them. "I have Forrest in a tight place," he wired Grant on December 29. "My troops are moving on him from three directions, and I hope with success."

Forrest was indeed in a tight place, and that place was about to get tighter. Emerging from the flooded Obion bottoms, which he had crossed by an abandoned causeway, he paused on December 30 to let Sullivan's unsuspecting lead brigade go by him, then resumed his march past Huntingdon and toward Clarksburg, nearing which place on the morning of the last day of the year he encountered the other brigade, forewarned and drawn up to meet him at Parker's Crossroads. By way of precaution he had sent four companies to guard the road from Huntingdon and warn him in case the lead brigade turned back, and now, secure in the belief that his rear was well protected against surprise, he settled down to a casualty-saving artillery duel with the blue force to his front. It lasted from about 9 o'clock until an hour past noon, by which time he had captured three of the enemy guns and 18 wagonloads of ammunition and had driven the skirmishers back on their supports. He had in fact ceased firing, in response to several white flags displayed along the Union line, and was sending in his usual demand for "unconditional surrender to prevent the further effusion of blood," when an attack exploded directly in his rear. For the first last only time in his career, Forrest was completely surprised in battle. His reaction was immediate. Quickly resuming the fight to his front, he simultaneously charged rearward, stalling the surprise attackers with blows to the head and flanks, and withdrew sideways before his opponents recovered from the shock. It was smartly done — later giving rise to the legend that his response to a staff officer's flustered question, "What shall we do? What shall we do?" was: "Charge both ways!" — but not without sacrifice. The captured guns were abandoned, along with three of his own, for lack of horses to draw them, as well as the 18 wagonloads of ammunition. Three hundred men who had been fighting afoot were taken, too, while trying to catch their mounts, which had bolted at the sudden burst of gunfire from the rear. Sullivan, coming up from behind Jackson with his third brigade next day, was elated. "Forrest's army completely broken up," he wired Grant. "They are scattered over the country without ammunition. We need a good cavalry regiment to go through the country and pick them up."

So he said. But while he and his three brigades were waiting for that "good regiment," Forrest and his troopers were riding hard for the Tennessee and eluding the columns approaching cautiously from Corinth and Fort Henry. All in high spirits on New Year's Day — except possibly the captain who by now had been verbally blistered for taking yesterday's rear-guard companies up the wrong road and thus permitting the Federals to march past him unobserved — they reached Clifton about midday, raised the sunken flatboats, and were across the icy river before dawn. The basis for their high spirits was a sense of accomplishment. They had gone out as green recruits, miserably armed, and had returned within less than three weeks as veterans, equipped with the best accouterments and weapons the U.S. government could provide. In the course of a brief midwinter campaign, which opened and closed with a pontoonless crossing of one of the nation's great rivers, and in the course of which they more than made up in recruits for what they lost in battle or on the march, they had killed or paroled as many men as they had in their whole command and had kept at least ten times their number of bluecoats frantically busy for a fortnight. Besides the estimated $3,000,000 they had cost the Federals in wrecked installations and equipment, they had taken or destroyed 10 guns and captured 10,000 rifles and a million badly needed cartridges. Above all, they had accomplished their primary assignment by cutting Grant's lifeline, from Jackson north to the Kentucky border. They saw all this as Forrest's doing, and it was their pride, now and for all the rest of their lives — whether those lives were to end next week in combat or were to stretch on down the years to the ones they spent sunning their old bones on the galleries of crossroads stores throughout the Deep and Central South — that they had belonged to what in time would be known as his Old Brigade.

Pemberton was highly pleased, not only with the results of this cavalry action outside the limits of his department, but also with another which had been carried out within those limits and which he himself had designed as a sort of companion piece or counterpart to the raid-in-progress beyond the Tennessee line. Both had a profound effect on the situation he had been facing ever since he called a halt and began intrenching along the Yalobusha, preparatory to coming to grips with Grant's superior army: so profound an effect, indeed, that it presently became obvious that if he and Grant were to come to grips, it would be neither here nor now. Like that of the first, the success of this second horseback exploit — which in point of fact was simultaneous rather than sequential, beginning later and ending sooner — could also be summed up in three nouns, though in this case the summary was even briefer, since all three were single-syllabled: Earl Van Dorn.

"Buck" Van Dorn, as he had been called at West Point and by his fellow officers in the old army, had leaped at the chance for distinction, not only because it was part of his nature to delight in desperate ventures, but also because he was badly in need just now of personal re-

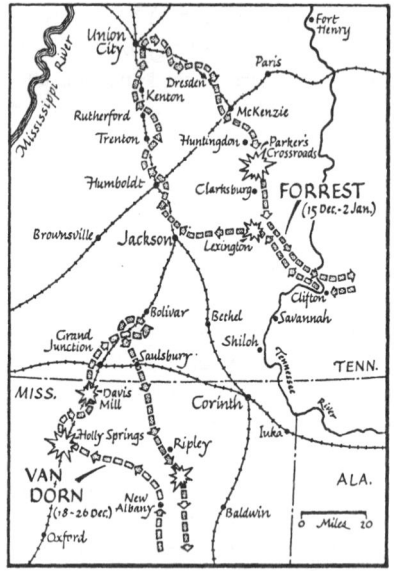

demption. After a brilliant pre-Manassas career in Texas, he had been called to Virginia, then reassigned to Arkansas, where his attempt at a double envelopment had been foiled disastrously at Elkhorn Tavern. Crossing the Mississippi after Shiloh, he had suffered an even bloodier repulse at Corinth in October, which gave him so evil a reputation in his home state that a court had been called to hear evidence of his bungling. Although he was cleared by the court, the government soon afterwards promoted Pemberton over the head upon which the public was still heaping condemnations. The accusation that he was "the source of all our woes," Senator Phelan wrote President Davis, was "so fastened in the public belief that an acquittal by a court-martial of angels would not relieve him of the charge." Van Dorn was depressed, but he was not without hope. A court-martial of angels was one thing; a brilliant military exploit, characterized by boldness and attended by great risk, was quite another. So when Pemberton summoned him to army headquarters and gave him his assignment — an all-out raid on Grant's communications and supply lines, including the great depot lately established at Holly Springs — the diminutive Mississippian saw in it the opportunity to retrieve his reputation and bask once more in the warmth of his countrymen's affection. Always one to grasp the nettle danger, he embraced the offered chance without delay.

He left Grenada on December 18 with 3500 cavalry, heading east at first to skirt Grant's flank, then north as if for a return to Corinth. Next day, however, he turned west beyond New Albany and came thundering into Holly Springs at dawn, December 20. The Federal commander there, Colonel R. C. Murphy, had been placed in a similar uncomfortable position in September at Iuka, which he had abandoned without a fight or even destruction of the stores to keep them from falling into enemy hands. Grant had forgiven him then because of his youth and inexperience, and now he was given another chance to prove his mettle. He did no better. In fact, despite advance warning that a heavy column of graybacks was moving in his direction, he did far worse. This time, he lost not only the stores in his charge but also the soldiers, 1500 of whom were captured and paroled on the spot by the jubilant rebels, caracoling their horses at the sight of the mountains of food and equipment piled here for Grant's army. "My fate is most mortifying," he reported that night amid the embers which were all that remained of the million-dollar depot of supplies. "I have done all in my power — in truth, my force was inadequate."

Grant reacted "with pain and mortification" at the news of his loss and ordered Murphy dismissed from the service, as of "the date of his cowardly and disgraceful conduct." With Forrest loose on the railroad north of Jackson that same day, and his own wife spared embarrassment at Holly Springs only because she had left to join him in Oxford the day before, Grant began to design combinations of forces in North Mississippi, not unlike those already sent out after Forrest in West Tennessee, to accomplish Van Dorn's destruction before he could return to safety behind the Yalobusha. "I want those fellows caught, if possible," he said.

The trouble with this was that by the time the various columns could be put in motion Van Dorn was no longer in North Mississippi. Instead of racing for home, and perhaps into the arms of superior forces already gathering in his rear, he pushed on northward into Tennessee. Before he left his native state, however, the commander of a small outpost at Davis Mill, twenty miles north of Holly Springs and just south of the Tennessee line, gave him — and, incidentally, Murphy — a lesson in how well an "inadequate" force could hold its own against "overwhelming" numbers. His name was Colonel W. H. Morgan and he had less than 300 men for the defense of a point made critical by the presence of a trestle by which the Mississippi Central crossed Wolf River. Hearing that the raiders were coming his way, he converted an old sawmill into a blockhouse, reinforcing its walls with cotton bales and crossties, and a nearby Indian mound into a moated earthwork, both of which covered the railroad approach with converging fire. About noon of the 21st, the Confederates came up and launched a quick assault, which was repulsed. After a two-hour long-range skirmish, finding the fire too hot for a storming party to reach and ignite the trestle, let alone cross the river, the attackers sent forward, under a flag of truce, a note asking whether the defenders were ready to surrender. Morgan replied with what he later termed "a respectful but decided negative," and the Confederates withdrew, leaving 22 dead and 30 wounded on the field, along with another 20 prisoners who had ventured up too close to be able to pull back without exposing themselves to slaughter. Morgan's loss was 3 men slightly wounded.

Except for the further damage it did to his former opinion that one Southerner was worth ten Yankee hirelings in a scrap, Van Dorn was not greatly disturbed by this tactical upset. In the course of his approach to the fight, and even while it was in progress, he had done the railroad enough damage to be able to afford to let the trestle go. Bypassing Morgan's improvised blockhouse, he crossed upstream and pushed on northward between Grand Junction and LaGrange, where he tore up sections of the Memphis & Charleston for good measure. Near Bolivar on the 23rd, he circled Middleburg, still ripping up track and wrecking culverts, and headed back south on Christmas Eve, riding through Van Buren and Saulsbury to re-enter Mississippi. South of Ripley on Christmas Day, he had a brush with one of the converging Union colums, but pressed on without delay, through Pontotoc and thence on back to Grenada, which he reached by midafternoon of December 28. He had carried out his mission in fine style, destroying Grant's reserve supplies of food, forage, and munitions. What was more, at least from a particular point of view, he had refurbished his tarnished reputation. Households which formerly had mentioned his name only with frowns of disapproval or downright scowls of condemnation now drank his health with shouts of joy and praised him to the skies.

Pemberton, then, was delighted at the manner in which Van Dorn had achieved redemption; but not Grant, who paid the bill which thus was added to all that Forrest was costing him simultaneously. With Columbus in a panic, Memphis cowed by heavy guns, his communications disrupted, and his supply line almost a continuous wreck from Holly Springs north to the Kentucky border, he was stymied and he knew it. Van Dorn having destroyed his supplies on hand and Forrest having made it impossible for him to bring up more, he could neither move forward nor stand still. There was no way he could go but back, and this he proceeded to do, meanwhile solving the problem of immediate subsistence by sending out "all the wagons we had, under proper escort, to collect and bring in all supplies of forage and food from a region of fifteen miles east and west of the road from our front back to Grand Junction." At the news of this, the broad smiles caused by Van Dorn's coup faded from the faces of the people around Oxford. Their former mocking question, "What will you do now?" was changed to: "What are *we* to do?" Grant replied that he had done his best to feed his soldiers from their own northern resources, but now that these had been cut off "it could not be expected that men, with arms in their hands, would starve in the midst of plenty." In short, as he said later, "I advised them to emigrate east, or west, fifteen miles and assist in eating up what we left."

To his amazement — for he had thought the pickings would be slim and had lately advised his government that an army could not "subsist itself on the country except in forage"; "Disaster would result in the end," he had predicted — the wagons returned heavy-laden with hams, corn on the cob, field peas and beans, sweet and Irish potatoes, and fowls of every description, accompanied by herds of beef on the hoof. "It showed that we could have subsisted off the country for two months instead of two weeks without going beyond the limits designated," he subsequently wrote, adding: "This taught me a lesson."

The knowledge thus gained might prove to be of great use in the future, but for the present one thing still bothered him beyond all others. This was the thought that, putting it baldly, he was leaving his friend Sherman in the lurch. He had promised to hold Pemberton in position, 150 miles from Vicksburg, while Sherman was storming its thinly held defenses; yet Pemberton was already hurrying troops in that direction, as Grant knew, and might well arrive in time to smother the attackers in the Yazoo bottoms. However, there was little Grant could do about it now, except depend on Sherman to work out his own salvation. Out of touch as he was, because of his ruptured communications, Grant did not even know whether Sherman had left Memphis yet — or, if so, whether he was still in command of the river expedition; McClernand, in event of delay, might have arrived in time to take over. All Grant could do was send a courier to Memphis with a message addressed to "Commanding Officer Expedition down Mississippi," advising him, whoever he was, "that farther advance by this route is perfectly impracticable" and that he and his men were falling back, while Pemberton did likewise. Whether this would arrive in time to forestall disaster, he did not know.

★ ★ ★

Sherman was already downriver, and so far his only thought of disaster had been the intention to inflict it. "You may calculate on our being at Vicksburg by Christmas," he wrote Grant's adjutant on December 19, the day he left Memphis. "River has risen some feet, and all is now good navigation. Gunboats are at mouth of Yazoo now, and there will be no difficulty in effecting a landing up Yazoo within twelve miles of Vicksburg." Two days later at Helena, where he picked up his fourth division, he received from upriver his first intimation that Grant might be having trouble in the form of rebel cavalry, which was reported to have captured Holly Springs. If this was so, then Sherman's first letter most likely had not got through to Oxford; nor would a second. Nevertheless, he refused to be disconcerted, and wrote again. "I hardly know what faith to put in such a report," he said, "but suppose whatever may be the case you will attend to it."

All was indeed "good navigation" for the fifty-odd army transports and the 32,500 soldiers close-packed on their decks, steaming rapidly toward their destiny below, as well as for the naval escort of three ironclads, two wooden gunboats, and two rams. But for the rest of Porter's fleet — three ironclads and two "tinclads," so called because their armor was no more than musket-proof — the going had been less easy. Sent downriver two weeks before, they had succeeded in clearing the Yazoo from its mouth upstream to Haines Bluff, where a stout Confederate battery defined the limit of penetration, 23 winding miles from the point of entrance. This had not been accomplished without cost, however, for the defenses were in charge of Isaac Brown, and Brown was known to be hungry for vengeance because of the recent loss above Baton Rouge of the steam ram *Arkansas*, which he had built up this same river the summer before and with which he had charged and sundered the two flotillas then besieging Vicksburg. He had no warship now, but he had notions about torpedoes, five-gallon whiskey demijohns packed with powder, fuzed with artillery friction tubes, and each suspended a few feet below a float on the muddy surface. On December 12 the five-boat Union reconnaissance squadron appeared up the Yazoo, shelling the banks and fishing up Brown's torpedoes as it advanced. Approaching Haines Bluff, the ironclad *Cairo* made contact with one of the glass demijohns at five minutes before noon, and at 12.03 she was out of sight, all but the tips of her stacks, in thirty feet of water.

Celerity and good discipline made it possible for the crew to abandon ship within the allowed eight minutes. No lives were lost, but the *Cairo*'s skipper, Lieutenant Commander T. O. Selfridge, Jr., a young man with a lofty forehead and luxuriant sideburns, was greatly disturbed by the loss of his boat and the possible end of his career as well, depending on the admiral's reaction to the news. Steaming back down the Yazoo aboard one of the tinclads, he found Porter himself at the mouth of the river, just arrived from Memphis, and stiffly requested a court of inquiry. "Court!" the admiral snorted. "I have no time to order courts. I can't blame an officer who puts his ship close to the enemy. Is there any other vessel you would like to have?" Without waiting for an answer he turned abruptly to the flag captain standing beside him on the bridge. "Breese, make out Selfridge's orders to the *Conestoga*."

Porter was like that, when he chose to be. Just short of fifty and rather hard-faced, with a hearty manner and a full dark beard, he had been given his present assignment, together with the rank of acting rear admiral, over the heads of eighty seniors. For the present, though, despite this cause for self-congratulation, the heartiness and bluster were cover for worry. Most of his old sailors had broken down, with the result that his heavy boats were half-manned, while ten light-draft vessels were laid up for lack of crews, and he was complaining to Washington that a draft of new men, lately arrived from New York, were "all boys and very ordinary landsmen." Characteristically, however, in a letter written this week to Sherman, after protesting of these and other matters, including a shortage of provisions, fuel, medicines, and clothing — not to mention the loss of the *Cairo* — he closed by observing: "I expected that the government would send men from the East, but not a man will they send or notice my complaints, so we will have to go on with what we have."

Reaching Milliken's Bend, on the west bank of the Mississippi ten miles above the mouth of the Yazoo, Sherman landed a brigade on Christmas Day and sent it out to wreck a section of the railroad connecting Vicksburg and Monroe, Louisiana. Next morning, while the brigade was returning, its mission accomplished, the rest of the armada proceeded downstream, entered the Yazoo, and steamed up its intricate channel. A light gunboat and an ironclad led the way, followed by twenty transports, each with two companies of riflemen charged with returning the fire of snipers. Then came another ironclad and twenty more transports, similarly protected. So it went, to the tail of the 64-boat column, until a landing was made at Johnson's Farm, on the Vicksburg shore of the Yazoo ten miles above its mouth. Alertness had paid off, or else it had been unnecessary. "Some few guerilla parties infested the banks," Sherman explained, "but did not dare to molest so strong a force as I commanded." It occurred to some of his soldiers, though, that the rebels were going to let geography do their fighting for them. Wide-eyed as the Illinois and Indiana farmboys were in this strange land, that seemed altogether possible. First there had been the big river itself — or himself; the Old Man, natives called the stream, taking their cue from the Indians, who had named it the Father of Waters — the tawny, mile-wide Mississippi, so thick with silt that recruits could almost believe the steamboat hands who solemnly assured them that if you drank its water for as much as a week "you will have a sandbar in you a mile long." Then had come the smaller stream, with its currentless bayous and mazy sloughs, whose very name was the Indian word for death. And now there was this, the land itself, spongelike under their feet as they came ashore, desolate as the back side of the moon and brooded over by cypresses and water oaks with long gray beards of Spanish moss. North was only a direction indicated by a compass — if a man had one, that is, for otherwise there was no north or south or east or west; there was only the brooding desolation. If this was the country the rebs wanted to take out of the Union, the blue-coated farmboys were ready to say good riddance.

The molestation Sherman had said the Confederates did not dare to attempt began the following day, December 27, against the navy. Commander William Gwin, a veteran of all the river fights since Fort Henry, took his ironclad *Benton* upstream to shell out some graybacks lurking in the woods on the left flank, but got caught in a narrow stretch of the river and was pounded by a battery on the bluffs. Three of the more than thirty hits came through the *Benton*'s ports, cutting her crew up badly, and Gwin, who refused to take cover in the shot-proof pilothouse — "A captain's place is on the quarterdeck," he protested when urged to step inside — was mortally wounded by an 8-inch solid that took off most of his right arm and breast, exposing the ribs and lung in a sudden flash of white and scarlet. Meanwhile the army was having its share of opposition, too, as it floundered about in the Yazoo bottoms and tried to get itself aligned for the assault on the Walnut Hills. The four division commanders, Brigadier Generals A. J. Smith, M. L. Smith, G. W. Morgan, and Frederick Steele, were in the thick of things next morning, dodging bullets like all the rest, when suddenly their number was reduced to three by a sniper who hit the second Smith in the hip joint and retired him from the campaign.

These two high-placed casualties only added to a confusion that was rife enough already. Johnson's Farm, which was little more than a patch of cleared ground in the midst of swampy woods, was separated from the hills ahead by a broad, shallow bayou, a former bed of the Yazoo, and hemmed in on the flanks by two others, Old River Bayou on the right and Chickasaw Bayou on the left. All three looked much alike to an unpracticed eye, so that there was much consequent loss of direction, misidentification of objectives, and countermarching of columns. A bridge ordered constructed over the shallow bayou to the front was built by mistake over one of the others, too late to be relaid. Whole companies got separated from their regiments and spent hours ricocheting from one alien outfit to another. As a result of all this, and more, it was Monday morning, December 29, before the objectives could be assigned and pointed out on the ground instead of on the inadequate maps. Sherman's plan for overrunning the hilltop defenses was for all four divisions to make "a show of attack along the whole front," but to concentrate his main effort at two points, half a mile apart, which seemed to him to afford his soldiers the best chance for a penetration. One of these was in front of Morgan's division, and when Sherman pointed it out to him and told him what he wanted, Morgan nodded positively. "General, in ten minutes after you give the signal I'll be on those hills," he said.

His timing was a good deal off. Except for one brigade, which "took cover behind the [opposite] bank, and could not be moved forward," as Sherman later reported in disgust, Morgan not only did not reach "those hills," he did not even get across the bayou, in ten or any other number of minutes after the signal for attack was given by the batteries all along the Federal line. Presently, however, it was demonstrated that, all in all, this was perhaps the best thing to have done in the situation in which their red-headed commander had placed them. A brigade of Steele's division, led by Brigadier General Frank Blair, Jr., a former Missouri congressman and brother of the Postmaster General, got across in good order and excellent spirits, only to encounter a savage artillery crossfire that sent it staggering back, leaving 500 killed, wounded, and captured at the point where it had been struck. One regiment kept going but was stopped by the steepness of the bluff and a battery firing directly down the throats of the attackers. With their hands they began to scoop out burrows in the face of the nearly perpendicular hillside, seeking overhead cover from enemy riflemen who held their muskets out over the parapet and fired them vertically into the huddled, frantically digging mass below. Indeed, so critical was their position, as Sherman later said, "that we could not recall the men till after dark, and then one at a time." He added, in summation of the day's activities: "Our loss had been pretty heavy, and we had accomplished nothing, and had inflicted little loss on our enemy."

"Pretty heavy" was putting it mildly, as he would discover when he found time for counting noses, but the rest of this estimation was accurate enough. Federal losses reached the commemorative figure 1776, of whom 208 were killed, 1005 were wounded, and 563 were captured or otherwise missing. The Confederates lost 207 in all: 63 killed, 134 wounded, and 10 missing.

Unwilling to let it go at that — "We will lose 5000 men before we take Vicksburg," he had said, "and may as well lose them here as anywhere else" — Sherman decided to reload Steele's division aboard transports and move it upstream for a diversionary strike in the vicinity of Haines Bluff, which might induce the defenders to weaken their present line. Porter was no less willing than before. Moreover, by way of disposing of Brown's remaining torpedoes, he conceived the idea of using one of the rams to clear the path. "I propose to sent her ahead and explode them," he explained. "If we lose her, it does not matter much." Colonel Charles R. Ellet, youthful successor to his dead father as commander of the former army vessels, did not take to this notion of a sacrificial ram. With Porter's consent, he added a 45-foot boom extending beyond the prow and equipped it with pulleys and cords and hooks for fishing up the floats and demijohns. Ram and transports set out by the dark of the moon on the last night of the year, while Sherman alerted his other three divisions for a second all-out assault on the Walnut Hills as soon as they heard the boom of guns upstream. What came instead, at 4 a.m. on New Year's Day, was a note from Steele, explaining that the boats were fog-bound and could not proceed. So Sherman called a halt and took stock. He had been waiting all this time for some word from Grant, either on the line of the Yalobusha or here on the Yazoo, but there had been nothing since the rumor of the fall of Holly Springs. From Vicksburg itself, ten air-line miles away, its steeples visible from several points along his boggy front, he had been hearing for the past three days the sound of trains arriving and departing. It might be a ruse, as at Corinth back in May. On the other hand, it might signify what it sounded like: the arrival from Grenada or Mobile or Chattanooga, or possibly all three, of reinforcements for the rebel garrison. Also, rain had begun to fall by now in earnest, and looking up he saw watermarks on the trunks of trees "ten feet above our heads." In short, as he later reported, seeing "no good reason for remaining in so unenviable a position any longer," he "became convinced that the part of wisdom was to withdraw."

Withdraw he did, re-embarking his soldiers the following day and proceeding downriver without delay. There was more room on the decks of the transports now, and Sherman was low in spirits: not because he was dissatisfied with his direction of the attempt — "There was no bungling on my part," he wrote, "for I never worked harder or with more intensity of purpose in my life" — but because he knew that the journalists, whom he had snubbed at every opportunity since their spreading of last year's rumors that he was insane, would have a field day writing their descriptions of his repulse and retreat. Presently he was hailed by Porter, who signaled him to come aboard the flagship. Sherman did so, rain-drenched and disconsolate.

"I've lost 1700 men," he said, "and those infernal reporters will publish all over the country their ridiculous stories about Sherman being whipped."

"Pshaw," the admiral replied. "That's nothing; simply an episode of the war. You'll lose 17,000 before the war is over and think nothing of it. We'll have Vicksburg yet, before we die. Steward! Bring some punch."

When he got the red-head settled down he gave him the unwelcome news that McClernand was at hand, anchored just inside the mouth of the Yazoo and waiting to see him. Sherman, who could keep as straight a face as his friend Grant when so inclined, afterwards remarked of his rival's sudden but long-expected appearance on the scene: "It was rumored he had come down to supersede me."

McClernand, too, had news for him when they met later that day. Grant was not coming down through Mississippi; he had in fact been in retreat for more than a week, leaving Pemberton free to concentrate for the defense of Vicksburg. Sherman suggested that this meant that any further attempt against the town with their present force was hopeless. Indeed, in the light of this disclosure, he began to consider himself most fortunate in failure, even though it had cost him a total of 1848 casualties for the whole campaign. "Had we succeeded," he reasoned, "we might have found ourselves in a worse trap, when General Pemberton was at full liberty to turn his whole force against us."

Dark-bearded McClernand agreed that the grapes were sour, at least for now. Next day, January 3, he and Sherman withdrew their troops from the Yazoo and rendezvoused again at Milliken's Bend, where McClernand took command.

"Well, we have been to Vicksburg and it was too much for us and we have backed out," Sherman wrote his wife from the camp on the west bank of the Mississippi. Reporting by dispatch to Grant, however, he went a bit more into detail as to causes. "I attribute our failure to the strength of the enemy's position, both natural and artificial, and not to his superior fighting," he declared; "but as we must all in the future have ample opportunities to test this quality, it is foolish to discuss it."

Pemberton would have agreed that it was foolish to discuss it, not for the reason his adversary gave, but because he considered the question already settled. The proof of the answer, so far as he was concerned, had been demonstrated in the course of the past two weeks, during which time he had stood off and repulsed two separate Union armies, each superior in numbers to his own. What was more, he had gained new confidence in his top commanders: in Van Dorn, whose lightning raid, staged in conjunction with Forrest's in West Tennessee, had abolished the northward menace: in the on-the-spot Vicksburg defenders, Major General Martin L. Smith and Brigadier General Stephen D. Lee, who with fewer than 15,000 soldiers, most of whom had arrived at the last minute from Grenada, had driven better than twice as many bluecoats out of their side yard, inflicting in the process about nine times as many casualties as they suffered: and in himself, who had engineered the whole and had been present for both repulses. Not that he did not expect to have to fight a return engagement. He did. But he considered that this would be no more than an occasion for redemonstrating what had been proved already.

"Vicksburg is daily growing stronger," he wired Richmond soon after New Year's. "We intend to hold it."

✗ 5 ✗

Rosecrans too was aware that haste made waste, but unlike Grant he was having no part of it. In reply to Halleck's frequent urgings that he move against Bragg and Chattanooga without delay — it was for this, after all, that he had been appointed to succeed his fellow Ohioan, Don Carlos Buell, whose characteristic attitude had seemed to his superiors to be one of hesitation — he made it clear that he intended to take his time. He would move when he got ready, not before, and thus, as he put it, avoid having to "stop and tinker" along the way. His policy, he explained in a series of answers to the telegraphic nudges, was "to lull [the rebels] into security," then "press them up solidly" and "endeavor to make an end of them." When Halleck at last lost patience altogether, informing the general in early December that he had twice been asked to designate a successor for him — "If you remain one more week in

Nashville," he warned, "I cannot prevent your removal" — Rosecrans set his heels in hard and bristled back at the general-in-chief: "I need no other stimulus to make me do my duty than the knowledge of what it is. To threats of removal or the like I must be permitted to say that I am insensible."

"Old Rosy" the men called him, not only because of his colorful name, but also because of his large red nose, which one observer classified as "intensified Roman." He was a tall, hale man, a heavy drinker but withal an ardent Catholic; he carried a crucifix on his watch chain and a rosary in his pocket, and he so delighted in small-hours religious discussions that he sometimes kept his staff up half the night debating such fine points as the distinction between profanity, which he freely employed, and blasphemy, which he eschewed. One such discussion achieved marathon proportions, going on for ten nights running, and though this was hard on the staff men, who missed their sleep, Rosecrans considered the problem solved beforehand by the fact that, like himself, they were all blond; "sandy fellows," he remarked upon occasion, were "quick and sharp," and, being more industrious by nature than brunets, required less rest — although he, for his own part, often slept till noon on the day following one of the all-night sessions devoted to eschatology or the question of how many angels could stand tiptoe on a pinpoint. Like Bardolph, whom he so much resembled in physiognomy, he could swing rapidly from gloom to equanimity or from abusiveness to affability. The bristly reply to Halleck was characteristic, for he would often flare up on short notice; but he was likely to calm down just as fast. All of a sudden, on the heels of an outburst of temper, he would be all smiles and congeniality, stroking and cajoling the very man he had been reviling a moment past, and if this was sometimes confusing to those around him, it was also a rather welcome relief from the dour and noncommittal Buell. Rosecrans was forty-three, two years younger than his present opponent Bragg, who had graduated five years ahead of him at West Point, where each had stood fifth in his class. Sometimes he seemed older than his years, sometimes not, depending on his mood, but in general he was liked and even admired, especially by the volunteers, who found him approachable and amusing. For instance, he would stroll through the camps after lights-out, and if he saw a lamp still burning in one of the tents he would whack on the canvas with the flat of his sword. The response, if not blasphemous, would at any rate be profane and abusive. Prompt to apologize when they saw the red-nosed face of their general appear through the tent flap, the soldiers would explain that they had thought he was some rowdy prowling around in the dark. He took it well, including the muffled laughter that followed the extinguishing of the lamp on his departure, and the result was a steady growth of affection between him and the men of the army which Halleck was protesting he was slow to commit to battle.

That army's present over-all strength was 81,729 effectives, divided like Grant's into Left Wing, Center, and Right Wing, commanded respectively by Major Generals T. L. Crittenden, George Thomas, and Alexander McCook, all veterans of the bloody October fight at Perryville, Kentucky, under Buell. By mid-December — Halleck having more or less apologized for the previous nudgings by explaining that they had not been intended as "threats of removal or the like," but merely as expressions of the President's "great anxiety" over the fact that, Middle Tennessee being the Confederacy's only late-summer gain which had not been erased, pro-Southern members of the British parliament, scheduled to convene in January, might find in this apparent stalemate persuasive arguments for the intervention France was already urging — Rosecrans became more optimistic, despite the drouth which kept the Cumberland River too shallow for it to serve as a dependable supply line. "Things will be ripe soon," he assured his nervous superiors on the 15th, and followed this dispatch with another, put on the wire within an hour: "Rebel troops say they will fight us.... Cumberland still very low; rain threatens; will be ready in a few days."

The few days stretched on to Christmas, and still he had not moved. By then, however, he had received encouraging reports from scouts and spies beyond the rebel lines. In the first place, Morgan and Forrest were on the prowl, and though normally this would have been considered alarming information, in this case it was not so, for the former was now so far in his rear as not to be able to interfere with any immediate action south or east of Nashville, while the latter was clean outside his department. Whatever harm they might do in Kentucky and West Tennessee (which, as it turned out, was considerable) Rosecrans could wish them Godspeed, so long as they kept their backs in his direction. Moreover, he had learned of the visit to Murfreesboro by Jefferson Davis and the subsequent detachment of one of Bragg's six divisions to Pemberton. Now if ever was the time to strike, and the Union commander was ready. Orders went out Christmas Day for the advance to begin next morning in three columns: Crittenden on the left, marching down the Murfreesboro turnpike through La Vergne and paralleling the Nashville & Chattanooga Railroad; McCook in the middle, cross-country through Nolensville; Thomas on the right, due south through Brentwood, then eastward across McCook's rear to take his rightful position in the center. Each of the three "wings" was well below its normal three-divisional strength because of guard detachments. Thomas, for example, had left a whole division on garrison duty at Nashville, in case Morgan or Forrest turned back or some other pack of raiders struck in that direction while the main body was attending to Bragg, and Crittenden and McCook were almost equally reduced by piecemeal detachments on similar duty elsewhere along the lines of supply and communication. The result was that Rosecrans had barely

44,000 troops in his three columns — Crittenden 14,500, Thomas 13,500, McCook 16,000 — or only a little more than half of his total effective strength. But he was not ruffled by this reduction of the numerical odds in his favor; he knew that he was still a good deal stronger than his opponent. What was more, his deliberate preparations had paid off. Not only would he be free of the necessity to "stop and tinker" for lack of engineering equipment; he had within reach "the essentials of ammunition and twenty days' rations." Thus he had notified Washington on Christmas Eve, while planning the movement of his eight attack divisions, and he added in regard to the enemy, thirty miles southeastward down the pike: "If they meet us, we shall fight tomorrow; if they wait for us, next day."

It was neither "tomorrow" nor the "next day" — which was in fact the day he actually got started. Nor was it the day after that, or the day after that, or even the day after that. Still, Rosecrans was not unduly perturbed. Delay had already gained him much, including the loss by the Confederates of one infantry division and two brigades of cavalry; further delay might gain him more. Such was not the case, as it turned out, but what fretted him most just now was the slashing efficiency of the cavalry retained by Bragg, which cost the advancing Federals portions of their wagon train, as well as isolated detachments of their own horsemen assigned to protect the flanks and rear of the main body, slogging forward in three columns. As these drew near Murfreesboro on the 29th and 30th, consolidating at last to form a continuous line of battle along the west bank of the south fork of Stones River, two miles short of the town, they began to encounter infantry resistance, spasmodic at first and then determined, which seemed to promise fulfillment of the vow Rosecrans had passed along to Halleck two weeks before: "Rebel troops say they will fight us." However, he had followed this with a vow of his own, which he also believed was moving toward fulfillment: "If we beat them, I shall try to drive them to the wall."

Bragg had 37,713 effectives, well under half as many as his opponent, but he had them all at hand, with the result that the attackers were only about fifteen percent stronger than the defenders. Not that he considered himself committed to the tactical defensive. If the opportunity arose he intended to hit Rosecrans first, and hard. By way of preparation, however, he wanted him within reach, and therefore he gave his outpost commanders instructions to offer the advancing blue columns no more than a token resistance. "General Bragg sent us word not to fight them too much, but to let them come on," one gray cavalryman afterwards recalled.

In the course of the four-day Federal approach march — which was impeded, but not "too much," by the nearly 4000 troopers under

The Longest Journey [83]

Brigadier General Joseph Wheeler — Bragg assembled his 34,000 infantry at Murfreesboro, the center of the wide arc along which his five divisions had been disposed so as to cover the roads out of Nashville. Lieutenant General Leonidas Polk's two-division corps was there already, and Lieutenant General William J. Hardee's came in on December 28 from Triune, fifteen miles west. With the arrival next day of Major General John McCown's division from Readyville, a dozen miles east, the concentration was complete, and the army formed for combat astride Stones River, which was fordable at practically all points because of the drouth. Hardee was on the right, northwest of the town and with a bend of the river to his front; Polk was on the left, due west of the town and with another bend of the river to his rear; McCown was in reserve behind the center, which

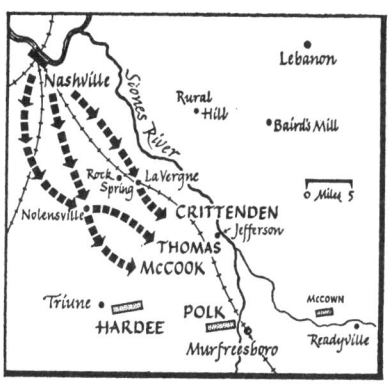

was pierced by the Nashville turnpike and the Nashville & Chattanooga Railroad, pointing arrow-straight in the direction from which Rosecrans was expected. Except for Wheeler's horsemen, who, now that the consolidation of the infantry had been effected with time to spare, were turned loose with a vengeance on the flanks and rear of the still approaching Federals, the Confederates settled down to wait for the opening of the battle everyone knew was about to be fought.

Many of them — particularly the officers, whose opportunities were larger in this respect — were still suffering from the aftereffects of a Christmas which they had celebrated with the fervor of men who knew only too well that the chances were strong that it would be their last. "I felt feeble," a Georgia lieutenant wrote in his diary the morning after, "but, being anxious to be with my men, reported for duty." Things had been that way for weeks now. Murfreesboro, a former state capital named for a colonel in the Revolution, was a lively place whose citizens, decidedly pro-rebel no matter which army happened to be in occupation, afforded their gray-clad defenders entertainments and amusements of all kinds, including horse races, balls, whist parties, and midnight gatherings in their parlors. President Davis's visit, two weeks before, had been the occasion for much rejoicing and pride, but all agreed that the social high point of the season had been the marriage on December 14, the day after the President's departure, of John Morgan and a local belle. Spirited in her defense of all things southern, when she heard some northern officers disparaging the raider during the Union occupation the previous summer, she told them off so roundly that one of the bluecoats asked her name. "It's Mattie Ready now," she said. "But by the grace of God one day I hope to call myself the wife of John Morgan." Hearing the story, the widower cavalryman came to call on her as soon as the town was again in southern hands, and in due time — for the young lady was apparently as skilled in her brand of tactics as the colonel was in his — they became engaged. Because of the size of the guest list, which included Bragg and his ranking commanders, Morgan's fellow officers and kinsmen from Kentucky, and a host of civilians invited from round about by the bride's family, the wedding was held in the courtroom of the Murfreesboro courthouse, Leonidas Polk officiating and wearing over the uniform of a Confederate lieutenant general the vestments of an Episcopal bishop. Thus it was that Mattie Ready, by the grace of God, became Mrs John Hunt Morgan.

Within a week, apparently not content with his exploit at Hartsville earlier that month, the bridegroom was off on what would be known as his Christmas Raid, a twofold celebration of his marriage and the brigadier's commission recently handed him by the President himself. His goal, assigned by Bragg, was Rosecrans' supply line, specifically the Louisville & Nashville Railroad north of Bowling Green, with particular attention to be paid to the great trestles at Muldraugh's Hill. He left Alexandria, thirty miles northeast of Murfreesboro, on December 21 with 2500 horsemen, crossed the Cumberland the following day, and re-entered his home state the day after that. Passing through Glasgow on the 24th, he forded the Green on Christmas Day, skirmishing as he went and taking prisoners by the hundreds, and struck suddenly north of Munfordville to lay siege to the Federal garrison at Elizabethtown, which surrendered on the 27th, opening the way to Muldraugh's Hill, where the garrison also surrendered. After burning the trestles, enormous structures five hundred feet long and eighty feet tall, he continued east through Bardstown to Springfield, then turned south, skirting heavily garrisoned Lebanon and fighting off pursuers for a getaway through Campbellsville, Columbia, and Burkesville, to reach Smithville, Tennessee, on January 5, fifteen miles southeast of his starting point at Alexandria. In two weeks, having covered better than 400 miles, he had fought four engagements and numerous skirmishes. At a total cost of 2 men killed and 24 wounded, plus about 300 stragglers — victims not of enemy guns but of the weather, which was bitter, and of confiscated bourbon — he had destroyed the vital railroad trestles and four important bridges, along with an estimated $2,000,000 in Union stores, and had torn up more than twenty miles of L&N track, while capturing and paroling 1887 enemy soldiers.

Joe Wheeler, West Point '59, was not to be outdone by Morgan or Forrest, who were his subordinates as a result of Bragg's appointment of the twenty-six-year-old Georgian as commander of all the cavalry in the Army of Tennessee. Unleashed on the night of December 29, after screening the concentration of the gray infantry in his rear and delaying the advance of the blue columns to his front, he rode north on the Lebanon pike with 2000 troopers, then swung west to Jefferson, where he attacked a brigade of infantry on the march and gobbled up a 20-wagon segment of Crittenden's supply train. At La Vergne by noon, halfway to Nashville and well in the Union rear, he captured and burned McCook's whole train of 300 wagons, packed with stores valued by Wheeler at "many hundred thousands of dollars," and paroled 700 prisoners, including the teamsters and their escort. "The turnpike, as far as the eye could reach, was filled with burning wagons," a Federal officer reported when he rode through the town next morning and surveyed the ruin the graybacks left behind. "The country was overspread with disarmed men [and] broken-down horses and mules. The streets were covered with empty valises and trunks, knapsacks, broken guns, and all the indescribable débris of a captured and rifled army train." Wheeler and his horsemen were over the southwest horizon by then, having taken two more trains, one at Rock Spring and another at Nolensville. Beyond there, more prisoners were paroled while the weary raiders snatched a few hours' sleep before swinging back into their saddles and heading east for Murfreesboro to rejoin the infantry drawn up along Stones River. Completing his two-day circuit of Rosecrans — in the course of which he had captured more than a thousand men, destroyed all or parts of four wagon trains, brought off enough rifles and carbines to arm a brigade, remounted all of his troopers who needed fresh horses, and left a train of devastation along both flanks and around the rear of the entire Union army — Wheeler made contact with Bragg's left at 2 a.m. on the last day of the year, in time for a share in the battle which was now about to open.

A certain amount of reshuffling had occurred during his absence. Rosecrans, coming forward with his main body on the 30th while Wheeler was clawing at his flanks and rear, put his three corps in line, left to right, Crittenden and Thomas and McCook, the first opposite Hardee, the second opposite Polk, and the third — the largest of the three — opposite nothing more than a thin line of skirmishers extending the rebel left. Because of skillful screening by the gray cavalry during the approach march, the Federal commander was not aware of the opportunity he had created for a lunge straight into Murfreesboro around the Confederate flank; but Bragg was, and he moved at once to correct his dispositions, shifting McCown's reserve division from its post behind the center to a position on Polk's left, extending his line of battle southward to meet the threat. Rosecrans meanwhile was planning and issuing orders for an attack. His intention was to execute a right wheel, sending Crittenden forward on the north, with instructions to pivot on the left of Thomas, who would also move forward in sequence to assist in the capture of the town, cutting the rebels off from their supplies and setting them up for annihilation. McCook was thus to serve as anchor man. "If the enemy attacks you," Rosecrans told him, "fall back slowly, refusing your right, contesting the ground inch by inch. If the enemy does not attack you, you will attack him, not vigorously but warmly." As an added piece of deception, McCook was ordered about 6 p.m. to build a line of fires beyond his right, simulating a prolongation of his line so as to draw Bragg's attention away from the main effort at the far end of the field.

The southern commander was indeed deceived, and quite as thoroughly as Rosecrans had intended, but his reaction was something different from what the northern commander had hoped for. Or, rather, it was what he had hoped for, only more so. When Bragg observed the fires and heard sounds of movement on the Federal right, not only did he take the bait, but he proceeded, so to speak, to run away with it. Devising an offensive of his own to meet what he conceived to be a new threat to his left, he instructed Hardee, whose two divisions were under Major Generals John C. Breckinridge and Patrick R. Cleburne, to leave the former posted where it was, guarding the river crossings on the right, and move the latter southward to a position in support of McCown, who had been shifted earlier that day. Hardee himself was to come along, moreover, and take command of these two divisions on the left for a slashing assault on the Federals seemingly massed in that direction. Bragg's plans called for a right wheel by both corps on the west bank of Stones River, with the pivot on Polk's right division near the Nashville pike, the brigades attacking in rapid sequence from left to right, obliquing northward as they advanced, in order to throw the bluecoats back against the stretch of river whose crossings were covered by Breckinridge's guns and infantry.

Just before tattoo, while this additional shift was being completed under cover of darkness and orders were going out for the assault next morning, the military bands of both armies began to play their respective favorite tunes. Carrying sweet and clear on the windless wintry air, the music of any one band was about as audible on one side of the line as on the other, and the concert thus became something of a contest, a musical bombardment. "Dixie" answered the taunting "Yankee Doodle"; "Hail Columbia" followed "The Bonnie Blue Flag." Finally, though, one group of musicians began to play the familiar "Home Sweet Home," and one by one the others took it up, until at last all the bands of both armies were playing the song. Soldiers on both sides of the battle line began to sing the words, swelling the chorus east and west, North and South. As it died away on the final line — "There's no-o place like home" — the words caught in the throats of men, who, bluecoat and butternut alike, would be killing each other tomorrow in what already gave promise of being one of the bloodiest battles in that fratricidal war.

* * *

As at First Manassas, a year and a half ago, both commanders had identical plans of battle: in this case, an advance on the left to strike the enemy right. Here as there, if they had moved simultaneously, the two armies might have grappled and swung round and round, like a pair of dancers clutching each other and twirling to the accompaniment of cannon. So it might have been, but it was not. For one thing, the lines were closer together on the south than on the north, and there was no natural obstacle such as the river to delay the Confederate attack in its initial stages. For another, with his usual attention to preparatory matters, Rosecrans had told his generals to advance as soon as possible after breakfast; whereas Bragg, with less concern for the creature comforts, had called for a dawn assault, and that was what he got.

McCown went forward in the steely twilight before sunrise, Cleburne following 400 yards behind. Between them they had 10,000 men and McCook had 16,000, but the latter were still preparing breakfast when the rebel skirmishers, preceding a long gray double line of infantry extending left and right, shoulder to shoulder as far as the eye could reach, broke through the cedar thickets and bore down on them, yelling. Coming as it did, with all the advantage of surprise, the charge was well-nigh irresistible. A Tennessee private later recalled that his brigade, in the front rank of the attackers, "swooped down on those Yankees like a whirl-a-gust of woodpeckers in a hail storm." The fact was, in this opening phase, everything went so smoothly for the aggressors that even their mistakes seemed to work to their advantage. When McCown, who had had little combat experience, having been left behind in command of Knoxville during the invasion of Kentucky, drifted wide because he neglected to oblique to the right as instructed, Pat Cleburne, whose soldierly qualities had grown steadily since Shiloh despite the wounds he had taken at Richmond and Perryville, moved neatly forward into the gap without even the need to pause for alignment. Advancing on this extended front the two divisions swept everything before them, their captures including several front-line batteries taken before the cannoneers could leap to their posts and get a round off. Such knots of bluecoats as managed to form for individual resistance in clumps of cedar or behind outcroppings of rock, finding themselves suddenly outflanked on the left or right, cried as they had cried under Buell twelve weeks before: "We are sold! Sold again!" and broke for the rear, discarding their weapons as they ran.

McCook's three divisions, on line from right to left under Brigadier Generals R. W. Johnson, Jefferson Davis, and Philip Sheridan, caught the full force of the initial assault. Johnson and Davis were under personal clouds, the former because he had been captured by Morgan early that month and exchanged on the eve of battle, the latter because of his assassination of Major General William Nelson in a Lousiville hotel lobby back in September; but they had little chance to earn redemption here. Johnson's division, on the far right of the army, practically disintegrated on contact, losing within the opening half-hour more than half its members by sudden death, injury, or capture. Davis, next in line, fared scarcely better, though most of his men at least had time to put up a show of resistance before falling back, dribbling skulkers as they went. That left Sheridan. As pugnacious here as he had been at Perryville, where he first attracted general attention, the bandy-legged, bullet-headed Ohioan was determined to yield no ground except under direct pressure, and only then when that pressure buckled his knees. "Square-shouldered, muscular, wiry to the last degree, and as nearly insensible to hardship and fatigue as is consistent with humanity" — thus a staff man saw him here, on the eve of his thirty-second birthday — he rode his lines, calling on his men to stand firm while the storm of battle drew nearer, then broke in fury against his front.

Polk's corps, with its two divisions under Major Generals J. M. Withers and Benjamin Cheatham, had taken up the assault by now, and it was Withers who struck Sheridan first — and suffered the first Confederate repulse. The Federals were in a position described by one of its defenders as "a confused mass of rock, lying in slabs, and boulders interspersed with holes, fissures, and caverns which would have made progress over it extremely difficult even if there had been no timber." But there was timber, a thick tangle of cedars whose trunks "ran straight up into the air so near together that the sunlight was obscured." Fighting here, with all that was happening on the right or left hidden from them "except as we could gather it from the portentous avalanches of sound which assailed us from every direction," Sheridan's men repulsed three separate charges by Withers. Then Cheatham came up. A veteran of Mexico and all the army's battles since Belmont, where he had saved the day, Cheatham was forty-two, a native Tennessean, and had earned the distinction of being the most profane man in the Army of Tennessee, despite the disadvantage in this respect of having as his corps commander the distinguished and watchful Bishop of Louisiana. "Give 'em hell, boys!" he shouted as he led his division forward. Polk, who was riding beside him, approved of the intention if not of the unchurchly language. "Give them what General Cheatham says, boys!" he cried. "Give them what General Cheatham says!"

That was what they gave them, though they received in return a goodly measure of the same. Sheridan, down to his last three rounds and having lost the first of his three brigade commanders, his West Point classmate Brigadier General Joshua Sill — he would lose the other two before the day was over — fell back under knee-buckling

The Longest Journey

pressure from Cheatham in front and Cleburne on the flank, abandoning eight guns in the thicket for lack of horses to draw them off. He then replenished his ammunition and took a position back near the Nashville turnpike, facing south and east alongside Brigadier General J. S. Negley's division, one of the two belonging to Thomas, who had been forced to give ground during the struggle. It was now about 10 o'clock; Bragg's initial objectives had been attained, along with the capture of 28 guns and no less than 3000 soldiers. The enemy right had been driven three miles and the center had also given way, until now the Union line of battle resembled a half-closed jackknife, most of it being at right angles to its original position. Bragg was about to open the second phase, intending to break the knife at the critical juncture of blade and handle; after which would come the third phase, the mop-up.

Rosecrans meanwhile had used to good advantage the interlude afforded him by Sheridan's resistance, though it was not until the battle had been raging for more than an hour that he realized he was face to face with probable disaster. For some time, indeed, having joined Crittenden on the left so as to supervise the opening attack, he assumed that what was occurring on the right — the uproar being considerably diminished by distance and acoustical peculiarities — was in accordance with his instructions to McCook, whereby Bragg had been deceived

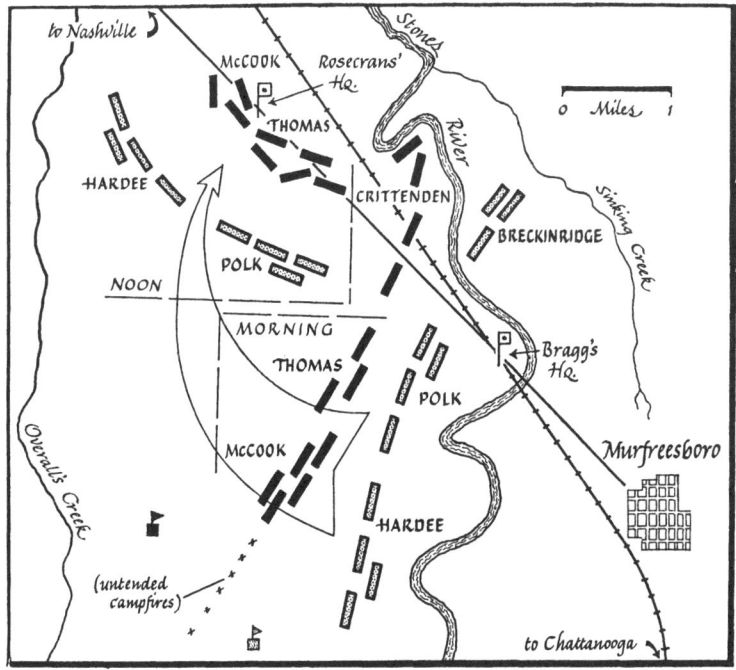

into stripping the flank about to be assaulted, in order to bolster the flank beyond which the untended campfires had been kindled the night before. One of Crittenden's divisions was already crossing Stones River, and he was preparing to follow with the other two. Not even the arrival of a courier from McCook, informing Rosecrans that he was being assailed and needed reinforcements, changed the Federal commander's belief in this regard.

"Tell General McCook to contest every inch of ground," he told the courier, repeating his previous instructions. "If he holds them we will swing into Murfreesboro with our left and cut them off." To his staff he added, with apparent satisfaction: "It's working right."

Discovering presently, however, that it was "working" not for him but for Bragg, who was using his own battle plan against him and had got the jump in the process — with the result that McCook, far from being able to conduct an inch-by-inch defense, had lost control of two of his three divisions before he was able to conduct a defense that was even mile-by-mile — Rosecrans reacted fast. To one observer he seemed "profoundly moved," but that was putting it rather mildly. Even his florid nose "had paled and lost its ruddy luster," the officer added, the glow apparently having been transferred to his eyes, which "blazed with sullen fire." Canceling the advance on the left, he told Crittenden to send the two uncrossed divisions of Brigadier Generals John Palmer and Thomas Wood to reinforce the frazzled right. Brigadier General Horatio Van Cleve's division was to be recalled from the opposite bank of the river and sent without delay after the others, except for one brigade which would be left to guard against a crossing, in case the rebels tried to follow up the withdrawal in this quarter. Crittenden passed the word at once, and: "Goodbye, General," Wood replied as he set out in the direction of the uproar, which now was swelling louder as it drew nearer. "We'll all meet at the hatter's, as one coon said to another when the dogs were after them."

Rosecrans had no time for jokes. His exclusive concern just now was the salvation of his army, and it seemed to him that there was only one way for this to be accomplished. "This battle must be won," he said. He intended to see personally to all the dispositions, especially on the crumbling right, but first he needed a feeling of security on the left — if for no other purpose than to be able to forget it. Accordingly, accompanied by his chief of staff, he rode to the riverbank position of the one brigade Van Cleve had left behind to prevent a rebel crossing, and inquired who commanded.

"I do, sir," a colonel said, stepping forward. He was Samuel W. Price, a Union-loyal Kentuckian.

"Will you hold this ford?" Rosecrans asked him.

"I will try, sir," Price replied.

Unsatisfied, Rosecrans repeated: "Will you hold this ford?"

"I will die right here," the colonel answered stoutly.

Still unsatisfied, for he was less interested in the Kentuckian's willingness to lay down his life than he was in his ability to prevent a rebel crossing, the general pressed the question a third time: "Will you hold this ford?"

"Yes, sir," Price said.

"That will do," Rosecrans snapped, and having at last got the answer he wanted, turned his horse and galloped off.

As he drew near the tumult of battle, which by now was approaching the turnpike on the right, he received another shock in the form of a cannonball which, narrowly missing him, tore off the head of his chief of staff, riding beside him, and so bespattered Rosecrans that whoever saw him afterwards that morning assumed at first sight that he was badly wounded. "Oh, no," he would say, in response to expressions of concern. "That is the blood of poor Garesché." However, this did nothing to restrict or slow his movements; he would not even pause to change his coat. "At no one time, and I rode with him during most of the day," a signal officer afterwards reported, "do I remember of his having been one half-hour at the same place." To Crittenden, whose troops he was using as a reserve in order to shore up the line along the turnpike, he "seemed ubiquitous," and to another observer he appeared "as firm as iron and fixed as fate" as he moved about the field, rallying panicked men and hoicking them into line. "This battle must be won," he kept repeating.

Arriving in time to meet Sheridan, who had just been driven back, he directed him to refill his cartridge boxes from the ammunition train and to fall in alongside Negley and Major General Lovell Rousseau, commanding Thomas's other division. As a result of such stopgap improvisations, adopted amid the confusion of retreat, there was much intermingling of units and a resultant loss of control by division and corps commanders. Some of Crittenden's brigades were on the right with McCook, who had set up a straggler line along which he was doing what he could to rally the remnants of Johnson and Davis, and some of McCook's brigades were on the left with Crittenden, who was nervously making his dispositions on unfamiliar ground. Between them, with his two divisions consolidated and supported by Van Cleve, George Thomas was calm as always, whatever the panic all around him. Where his left joined Crittenden's right there was a salient, marking the point where the half-closed knife blade joined the handle, and within this angle, just east of the pike and on both sides of the railroad, there was a slight elevation inclosed by a circular four-acre clump of cedars, not unlike the one Sheridan had successfully defended against three separate all-out rebel assaults that morning. Known locally as the Round Forest, this tree-choked patch of rocky earth was presently dubbed "Hell's Half-Acre" by the soldiers; for it was here that Bragg seemed most determined to score a breakthrough, despite the heavy concentration of artillery of all calibers which Rosecrans had massed on the high ground directly in its rear.

He struck first, and hard, with a brigade of Mississippians from Withers. They surged forward across fields of unpicked cotton, yelling as they had yelled at Shiloh, where they had been the farthest to advance, and were staggered by rapid-fire volleys from fifty guns ranked hub to hub on the high ground just beyond the clump of dark-green trees. At that point-blank range, one cannoneer remarked, the Federal batteries "could not fire amiss." Deafened by the uproar, the Confederates plucked cotton from the fallen bolls and stuffed it in their ears. Still they came on — to be met, halfway across, by sheets of musketry from the blue infantry close-packed under cover of the cedars; whereupon, some regiments having lost as many as half a dozen color-bearers, the Mississippians wavered and fell back, leaving a third of their number dead or wounded in the furrows or lying crosswise to the blasted rows. Next to try it, about noon, was a Tennessee brigade from Cheatham, which lately had helped throw Sheridan out of a similar position. They charged through the rattling dry brown stalks, yelling with all the frenzy of those who had come this way before, but with no better luck. They too were repulsed, and with even crueler losses. More than half of the men of the 16th Tennessee were casualties, while the 8th Tennessee lost 306 out of the 424 who had started across the fields in an attempt to drive the bluecoats out of the Round Forest.

Bragg was by no means resigned, as yet, to the fact that this could not be done. Though he had no reserves at hand — McCown and Cleburne were still winded from their long advance, around and over the original Federal right, and Withers and Cheatham had just been fought to a frazzle by the newly established left — the five-brigade division of Breckinridge, the largest in the army, was still posted beyond the river, having contributed nothing to the victory up to this point except the shells its batteries had been throwing from an east-bank hill which the former Vice President had been instructed to hold at all costs, as "the key to the position." So far, he had had no trouble doing this, despite an early-morning cavalry warning that a large body of enemy troops had crossed the river well upstream and was headed in his direction. This was of course Van Cleve's division, whose advance had been spotted promptly, but whose subsequent withdrawal had gone unnoticed or at any rate unreported; so that when Bragg's order came, about 1 o'clock, for him to leave one brigade to guard the right while he marched to the support of Polk and Hardee with the other four, Breckinridge was alarmed and sent back word that it was he who needed reinforcements; the enemy, in heavy force, was moving upon him even now, intending to challenge his hold on "the key to the position." Bragg's reply was a peremptory repetition of the order, which left the Kentuckian no choice except to obey. He sent two brigades at 2 o'clock, and followed with the other two himself, about an hour later.

That way, they came up piecemeal, and piecemeal they were fed into the hopper. The Federals, allowed an hour or more in which to improve their dispositions in the Round Forest and replenish the ammunition for the guns posted just behind it, caught the third wave of attackers much as they had caught the first and second, naked in the open fields, with devastating effect. Here again there was no lack of valor. One defender said of the charge that it was "without doubt the most daring, courageous, and best-executed attack which the Confederates made on our line between pike and river." But it broke in blood, as the others had done, and the survivors fell back across the fields, leaving their dead and wounded behind with the dead and wounded Tennesseans and Mississippians. Again there was a lull, until about 4 o'clock, when the last two brigades arrived from Breckinridge and the fourth gray wave rolled out across the fields of cotton.

"The battle had hushed," a Union brigadier reported, "and the dreadful splendor of this advance can only be conceived, as all descriptions must fall vastly short." While the attackers moved forward, "steadily, and, as it seemed, to certain victory," he added, "I sent back all my remaining staff successively to ask for support, and braced up my own lines as perfectly as possible." The bracing served its purpose; for though the defenders suffered heavily, too — it was here that Sheridan lost the third of his three brigade commanders — the charge was repulsed quite as decisively as the others. The sun went down at 4.30 and the racket died away. After eleven hours of uproar, a mutual hush fell over the glades and copses, and the brief winter twilight faded into the darkness before moonrise.

Bragg's losses had been heavy — about 9000 — but he had reason to believe that the enemy's, which included several thousand prisoners, had been much heavier. Moreover, in thus reversing the usual casualty ratio between attacker and defender, he had not only foiled the attempt to throw him out of his position covering Murfreesboro and Chattanooga; he had overrun the original Union position at every point where he had applied pressure, driving major portions of the blue line as far as three miles backward and taking guns and colors in abundance as he went. By all the logic of war, despite their stubborn stand that afternoon in the Round Forest, the Federals were whipped, and now they would have to accept the consequences. As Bragg saw it, they had little choice in this respect. They could stay and suffer further reverses, amounting in the end to annihilation; or they could retreat, hoping to find sanctuary in the Nashville intrenchments. Perhaps because it was the one he himself would have chosen, he believed the latter course to be the one Rosecrans was most likely to adopt. At any rate, this opinion seemed presently to have been confirmed by the arrival of outpost reports informing him that long lines of wagons had been heard rumbling through the darkness behind the Union lines and along the Nashville pike. Elated by this apparent chance to catch the northern army strung out on the roads and ripe for slaughter, Bragg prepared to follow in the morning. Proudly reviewing today's accomplishments while anticipating tomorrow's, he got off a wire to Richmond before he went to bed: "The enemy has yielded his strong position and is falling back. We occupy whole field and shall follow him.... God has granted us a happy New Year."

He was mistaken, at least in part. The rumble of wagons, northwestward along the turnpike, had not signified an attempt on the part of the Federal commander to save his trains before the commencement of a general retreat, but rather was the sound made by a long cavalcade of wounded — part of today's total of about 12,000 Union casualties — being taken back to the Tennessee capital for treatment in the military hospitals established there as another example of foresight and careful preparation. Not that Rosecrans had given no thought to a withdrawal. He had indeed. In fact, in an attempt to make up his mind as to the wisdom of retreating, he was holding a council of war to debate the matter and share the responsibility of the decision, even as Bragg was composing his victory message. It was a stormy night, rain beating hard on the roof of the cabin which Rosecrans had selected the day before as his headquarters beside the Nashville pike, never suspecting that the battle line would be drawn today practically on its doorstep. All three of his corps commanders were present, along with a number of their subordinates, and all presented a rather bedraggled aspect, "battered as to hats, tousled as to hair, torn as to clothes, and depressed as to spirits." An adjutant in attendance described them thus, and added: "If there was a cheerful-expressioned face present I did not see it."

After a long silence, broken only by the drumming of rain on shingles, Rosecrans began the questioning, addressing the several generals in turn, clockwise as they sat about the room. "General McCook, have you any suggestions for tomorrow?" Smooth-shaven and round-faced, the thirty-one-year-old McCook was somewhat more subdued tonight than he had been on the night after Perryville — where, as here, his had been the corps that was surprised and routed — but he showed by his reply that at least a part of his rollicking nature still remained. "No," he said. "Only I would like for Bragg to pay me for my two horses lost today." Others were gloomier and more forthright, advising retreat as the army's best way out its predicament. Characteristically, George Thomas had fallen asleep in his chair before the discussion got well under way. When the word "retreat" came through to him, he opened his eyes. "This army doesn't retreat," he muttered, and fell back into the sleep he had emerged from. The discussion thus interrupted was resumed, but it led to no clear-cut decision before the council broke up and the commanders returned to their units. Except for incidental tactical adjustments, specifically authorized from above, they would hold their present positions through tomorrow, unless they received alternate instructions before dawn.

Still undecided, Rosecrans rode out for a midnight inspection of his lines, in the course of which he looked out across the fields and saw an alarming sight. On the far side of Overall's Creek, which crossed the turnpike at right angles and covered his right flank and rear, firebrands were moving in the night. The explanation was actually simple: Federal cavalrymen, suffering from the cold, had disobeyed orders against kindling fires and were carrying brands from point to point along the outpost line: but Rosecrans, never suspecting that his orders would be flaunted in this fashion, assumed that they were rebels. "They have got entirely in our rear," he said, "and are forming line of battle by torchlight!" With retreat no longer even a possibility, let alone an alternative — or so at any rate he thought — he returned at once to army headquarters and, adopting the dramatic phraseology of the Kentucky colonel which he had rejected that morning beside the upper Stones River ford, sent word for his subordinates to "prepare to fight or die."

Except for the surgeons and the men they worked on, blue and gray, whose screams broke through the singing of the bone saws, both sides were bedded down by now amid the wreckage and the corpses, preparing to sleep out as best they could the last night of the year. Simultaneously, from a balcony of the Mobile Battle House, Jefferson Davis lifted the hearts of his listeners with a review of recent Confederate successes, unaware that even as he spoke the list was about to be lengthened by John Magruder, whose two-boat navy of cotton-clads was steaming down Buffalo Bayou to recapture Galveston. Lee's Army of Northern Virginia still occupied the field of its two-weeks-old long-odds victory on the southwest bank of the Rappahannock, and the Federal invaders from coastal North Carolina were back beneath the shelter of their siege guns, licking the wounds they had suffered in their repulse along the Neuse. In North Mississippi, where Van Dorn was resting his troopers after their exploits in Holly Springs and beyond the Tennessee line, Grant was in retreat on Memphis, while Sherman, three hundred winding miles downriver, was counting his casualties under Chickasaw Bluff and preparing to give it one more try before falling back down the Yazoo to meet the general whose army he had kidnaped and depleted to no avail. Forrest and Morgan, the former moving east from Parker's Crossroads, the latter riding south through Campbellsville, both having eluded their pursuers, were returning in triumph from disruptive raids on their respective home regions in West Tennessee and Kentucky. In all these scattered theaters, where so recently the Confederacy had seemed at best to be approaching near-certain disaster, fortune had smiled on southern arms; yet nowhere did her smile seem broader than here, southeast of Nashville and northwest of vital Chattanooga, where Bragg with such alacrity had snatched up the gage flung down by Rosecrans and struck him smartly with it, first on the flank, a smashing blow, and then between the eyes. Now both rested from their injuries and exertions. Wrapped in their blankets, those who had them, the soldiers of both armies huddled close to fires they had kindled against orders. The waxing moon set early and the wind veered and blew coldly from the north; the screams of the wounded died away with the singing of the bone saws. Unlike the night before, on the eve of carnage, there were no serenades tonight, no mingled choruses of "Home Sweet Home," for even the bandsmen had fought in this savage battle, and expected to have to fight again tomorrow, bringing in the new year as they had ushered out the old.

★ ★ ★

So they thought; but they were wrong, at least so far as the schedule was concerned. Though there were tentative skirmishes, fitful exchanges of artillery fire, and some readjustment of the tactical dispositions on both sides, New Year's Day saw nothing like the carnival of death that had been staged on New Year's Eve. In point of fact, the two armies were rather like two great jungle cats who, having fought to mutual exhaustion, were content — aside, that is, from the more or less secret hope on the part of each that the other would slink away — to eye one another balefully, limiting their actions to licking their wounds and emitting only occasional growls and rumbles, while storing up strength to resume the mortal contest.

Considerably surprised, in the light of last night's cavalry reports of a withdrawal, to find the enemy not only still there, but still there in line of battle, Bragg sent Polk forward about midmorning to discover what effect a prod would have. He soon found out. Though the troops moved unopposed into the Round Forest, which Rosecrans had ordered evacuated so as to straighten out his line, and which in turn gave validity to the bishop's subsequent claim that "the opening of the new year found us masters of the field," Polk encountered resistance just beyond it too stiff to permit his men to emerge from the woods on the far side. All he had gained for his pains were more blue corpses, along with the unwelcome task of digging their graves in order to rid his nostrils of their stench. Likewise, on the Union left, Rosecrans advanced Van Cleve's division — now under Colonel Samuel Beatty; Van Cleve had caught a bullet in the leg — beyond Stones River, retracing the route it had taken the previous morning by moving today into the vacuum created by the withdrawal of Breckinridge the afternoon before, and occupied a hill overlooking the ford. These were the only major read-

The Longest Journey [97]

adjustments, North or South, though the Federals were reinforced by a brigade arrived from Nashville, accompanied as one officer said by "an army of stragglers" picked up along the pike. For the most part, the soldiers on both sides roved the field, looking for fallen comrades among the wounded and the slain. The search for food was even more intensive, and for once, as a result of Wheeler's depredations in the course of his prebattle ride around the Union forces, the Yankees were worse off in this respect than the rebels. One brigade commander later recorded that he made his supper off a piece of raw pork and a few crackers he found in his pocket. No food had ever tasted sweeter, he declared. Even so high-ranking an officer as Crittenden was not exempt from want, but as he went to bed, complaining of hunger pangs, he was delighted to hear his orderly say he could get him "a first-rate beefsteak." The Kentuckian accepted the offer gladly, and presently, when the promised meal was brought, consumed it with gusto — only to learn next morning that the "beefsteak" had been cut from a horse that had been killed in the battle. "I didn't know this at the time I ate it," he afterwards explained, somewhat ruefully.

Day ended; night came down. Although Rosecrans had no apparent notion of resuming the offensive, or indeed any definite plan at all beyond holding onto the ground he had fallen back to, he was pleased to have had this day-long opportunity to consolidate his forces and recover in some measure from the shock to his army and his nervous system. Bragg on the other hand seemed to have no more of a plan than his opponent. Convinced that he had won a victory, he apparently did not know what to do with it beyond setting various details to work collecting the arms and matériel scattered about the field and paroling the thousands of captives he had taken the day before. What he mainly wanted, still, was for the enemy to admit defeat by retreating, and thus substantiate his claim; then he would follow, as he had promised in his wire to Richmond, hoping to catch the blue mass in motion on the pike and tear its flanks and rear, which now were inaccessible to him beyond the guns parked hub to hub behind the long lines of close-spaced bayonets weaving in and out of the cedar brakes and among the gray outcroppings of rock that scarred the landscape. The prospect was altogether grim. After nightfall, however, he was again encouraged by cavalry reports that well-guarded Federal trains were in motion on the roads leading back to Nashville. If this meant what Bragg hoped it did, that the Unionists were finally admitting they were whipped and were preparing to retire, bag and baggage, he would be up and after them tomorrow.

Tomorrow's dawn showed the prospect unimproved. Whatever might be moving along the rearward roads, the bayonets defining the Union front glinted quite as close-spaced as ever and the guns frowned every bit as grim. In fact, as Bragg conducted a personal inspection of his lines that morning, combining with it a long-range binocular reconnaissance of the enemy position, he began to perceive that, despite his bloodless occupation of the Round Forest, which increased his claim to the honors of the field, it was his own army which was in the graver danger as a result of yesterday's tactical readjustments. The advance of Van Cleve's division, which put it in possession of the hill just east of the river, gave him particular concern. Artillery emplaced on that height could fire across the stream and enfilade Polk's flank if he attempted to advance. With this in mind, Bragg decided the enemy guns must be dislodged. Accordingly he sent for Breckinridge, whose troops had returned to their east-bank position north of Murfreesboro, along a ridge about a mile short of the hill overlooking the ford. When the former Vice President reached army headquarters, under a large sycamore that stood alongside the Nashville pike just west of the wrecked bridge that had spanned Stones River, Bragg told him what he wanted. He was going to resume the offensive by sending Polk forward, he explained. First, though, he wanted Van Cleve's men flung off the dominant height. This was admittedly a tough assignment, he continued, but to protect the attackers from the added strain of having to repulse a counterattack, he was directing that the movement be made less than an hour before sundown, which would give the Federals no time to reorganize or bring up reinforcements before dark. Then next morning Polk could jump off, not only with his flank secure, but also with the enemy mouse-trapped out of position to his front.

Breckinridge, who was not yet forty-two despite his distinguished prewar career in national politics — a hearty-looking man with a prominent forehead, somewhat bulging eyes, a plump but firm jaw, and the swooping dark mustache of a Sicilian brigand, he was a leading contender among the many candidates for the title of the handsomest general in the southern army — protested at once and for all he was worth. The hill was well-nigh impregnable, he said, and Van Cleve's division had now been reinforced by two brigades from Palmer; besides which, he added, guns from the main Union line across the river would tear his flank as he advanced, thus exposing his men to the very horror he would be sparing Polk's if he was successful, which was doubtful. Warming to the subject, he took up a stick and began to draw in the soft dirt a map that emphasized the difficulty of the terrain. Bragg stopped him in mid-sketch. The Kentuckian had delayed the battle two days ago with similar protests which had turned out to be ill-founded, and the army commander was having no more of that. "Sir," Bragg said curtly, "my information is different. I have given the order to attack the enemy in your front and expect it to be obeyed."

That was that, and Breckinridge returned to his troops, most of whom were Bluegrass natives like himself, exiles from their homeland since midwinter nearly a year ago; "my poor orphans," he sometimes called them, jokingly but not without an undertone of sadness and homesickness. Rejoining them he sought out his friend Brigadier General William Preston — now commanding one of his brigades, but formerly chief of staff to his brother-in-law Albert Sidney Johnston, who had died in his arms at Shiloh — to whom he now addressed himself concerning the assignment he had just been given. "General Preston," he said, speaking formally and with a tone that strangely combined dejection and determination, "this attack is made against my judgment and by the special orders of General Bragg. Of course we all must try to do our duty and fight the best we can. But if it should result in disaster and I be among the slain, I want you to do justice to my memory and tell the people that I believed this attack to be very unwise and tried to prevent it." And having thus unburdened his mind he ordered his five brigades to form for the assault.

Across the way, Crittenden was inspecting his dispositions along the west bank of Stones River, accompanied by his chief of artillery Captain John Mendenhall, when he looked over the ford near the base of the occupied hill beyond and saw the graybacks forming in heavy columns along the ridge to the south, obviously preparing for a blow at Beatty, who commanded not only Van Cleve's division but also the two brigades of reinforcements which had joined him that morning. It was now about 3.30; the sun was within an hour of the landline. According to Mendenhall, "The general asked me if I could not do something to relieve Colonel Beatty with my guns." The Indiana-born West Pointer could indeed, and he moved to do so promptly. Assembling within the next half hour a total of 58 pieces of various calibers, he stationed 37 of these on the crest of a west-bank hill, cradled by a bend of the stream and overlooking the opposite bank, and placed the other 21 along its eastern base for flat-trajectory fire that would catch the rebel columns end-on as they charged across the rolling slopes beyond the river. Then he waited; but not for long.

The five Confederate brigades, with a total effective strength of 4500 men, started down off their sheltering ridge at 4 o'clock, moving steadily across the valley which lay between them and the hill from whose crest Beatty's cannoneers and riflemen soon took them under fire. As at Baton Rouge five months ago, where they had fought in isolation while the rest of Bragg's army was preparing to set out for their native Bluegrass, the Kentuckians did not falter as they swung down the long slope of the intervening valley, crossed its floor, and began to climb the other side. Halfway up the face of the hill, taking heavier losses now at closer range, they fired their first volleys and then, beginning to yell, broke into a run for the crest. The bluecoats did not wait for them, but whirled and fled from the threat of contact, and the attackers came on after them, yelling now with shrill screams of triumph as they topped the rise and pursued the defenders down the rearward slope.

However, they could not close the gap created by the quick retreat, and this gave Mendenhall the chance he had been waiting for all this time, to shoot at his foes without injuring his friends. At the signal "Fire!" his 58 double-shotted guns began to roar in chorus, flinging more than a hundred rounds a minute against the flank of the butternut mass across the way. "Thinned, reeling, broken under that terrible hail" — thus one reporter described the instantaneous effect — the graybacks milled in confusion, scarcely knowing at first what had struck them. When they saw what it was, they attempted to change front to the left and move against the fuming hill beyond the ford; but to no avail. "The very forest seemed to fall before our fire," one Federal observer wrote — without exaggeration, for men in the gray ranks were actually crushed under fallen limbs that were torn from the trees by exploding shells when they tried to find shelter in a patch of woods — "and not a Confederate reached the river." Shattered, they changed front again to the left, of one accord, and ran for the ridge that had marked their line of departure. A Union colonel, watching this sudden turn of events, was the amused witness of a double, simultaneous retreat. "It was difficult to say which was running away the more rapidly," he later reported, "the division of Van Cleve to the rear, or the enemy in the opposite direction."

Breckinridge watched his men come stumbling back through the dusk that followed sunset of the brief winter day. They had been gone just seventy minutes in all, and of their number 1700 had fallen: which meant that better than one man out of every three who descended the slope did not return unhurt. As their commander, who had protested the slaughter in advance and done what he could to prevent it, watched them close ranks to fill the gaps as they formed their line behind their own ten guns on the ridge, his eyes filled with tears. "My poor orphans! My poor orphans!" he exclaimed.

The lament for the fallen need not have been limited to the Confederate right, nor indeed to either side of the line of battle; for the overall Federal losses had been even heavier. According to final reports and computations, in two days of conflict — the day-long struggle of the 31st and the sunset repulse on the 2d — only a dozen less than 25,000 casualties had been suffered by the two armies. (Which, incidentally, indicated something of the fury of western fighting. With fewer than half as many troops involved, the butcher bill at Murfreesboro, Tennessee, was more than one-third greater than the one presented at Fredericksburg, Virginia, three weeks back.) The South lost 1294 killed, 7945 wounded, and 2500 captured or missing, a total of 11,739. The North lost 1730 killed, 7802 wounded, and 3717 captured or missing, a total of 13,249. The over-all total thus was 24,988: which was to say, and more could scarcely *be* said, that the battle had been bloodier than Shiloh or Sharpsburg.

At any rate, though neither commander yet recognized the fact, the carnage was over. Polk, who had learned of the sunset assault only just before it was launched, when Bragg came to his headquarters for a better view of the action across the river, had protested almost as vehemently as Breckinridge had done, but with no more success; Bragg's mind was quite made up. And now that the attack had met with predicted disaster, the blue defenders returned to the abandoned hill in greater strength than ever, reinforced by another whole division. Tactically, all was as it had been before the assault was launched, only more so; Polk would be less able to advance tomorrow than he had been today. Whether the enemy was under a similar disadvantage he did not know, but his two division commanders were not only doubtful that such was the case, they were also doubtful that their troops were in any fit condition to block the way: as was shown by a letter they wrote, shortly after midnight, and sent through channels to Bragg. "We deem it our duty to say to you frankly," Cheatham and Withers declared, "that, in our judgment, this army should be promptly put in retreat. . . . We do fear great disaster from the condition of things now existing, and think it should be averted if possible." Polk added his endorsement to the unusual document: "I greatly fear the consequences of another engagement at this place in the ensuing day. We could now, perhaps, get off with some safety and some credit, if the affair is well managed," and forwarded it to Bragg. Waked at 2 a.m., the grim-faced commander sat up in bed and read the letter halfway through, then stopped and told the aide who had disturbed his sleep: "Say to the general we shall maintain our position at every hazard."

When he rose at daylight, however, he began to discover how great that hazard was. Rain was falling steadily and the river was rising fast, threatening to isolate the two wings of his army. Moreover, unlike the previous ones, this morning's cavalry reports gave no hint of signs in the night that the enemy was considering withdrawal, but rather informed him that another fresh brigade of reinforcements had just arrived on the Union right, accompanying a train of supplies from the Tennessee capital. By now, too, his staff had found time to study the papers captured when McCook's headquarters were overrun, which indicated an effective strength of nearly 70,000 bluecoats to his front. This gave Bragg pause, and having paused he wavered. At 10 o'clock that morning he sent for Polk and Hardee, who found him in a different frame of mind from the one he had shown eight hours ago, when he was roused out of sleep to read the letter advising retreat. With the enemy heavily reinforced, as he believed and later wrote in his report, "Common prudence and the safety of my army, upon which even the safety of our cause depended, left no doubt on my mind as to the necessity of my withdrawal from so unequal a contest." The retrograde movement got under way that night, January 3, and was conducted with such skill that not even a rear-guard action was fought with the unsuspecting Federals, who seemed no more anxious to pursue than Bragg had been to stay. He himself went to Winchester, fifty miles southeast, planning to establish a new line along Elk River. Polk was instructed to fall back on Shelbyville, Hardee on Tullahoma, respectively twenty-three and thirty-five miles from Murfreesboro, but when the former reached his goal and reported that the bluecoats had not ventured beyond Stones River, Bragg ordered Hardee to stop at Wartrace, on line with Polk. Returning at once to establish headquarters at Tullahoma, on the railroad about midway between Nashville and Chattanooga, he began to organize a new defensive position along the Duck, whose rich valley offered much in the way of subsistence and adequate camp sites, including level fields for the daily hours of close-order drill in which he placed great store as a disciplinarian.

His pride in his army and its conduct during the battle — which was in a way a coda to the Kentucky excursion, launched soon after he took command at Tupelo, Mississippi, back in June — was expressed in his report, where he listed with satisfaction the capture of 6273 prisoners and enemy colors in abundance, along with 31 cannon and 6000 small arms, as well as "a large amount of other valuable property, all of which was secured and appropriated to proper uses." Moreover, he declared by way of final proof of moral superiority over his antagonist, "the army retired to its present position behind Duck River without giving or receiving a shot." Within the ranks of that army, however, though the men agreed that they had won a victory, there were fewer signs of elation. The retreat was made in wretched weather, and as they plodded southward through the mud, alternately drenched with rain and pelted with sleet, bent beneath the weight of their sodden packs, it seemed to them that the Perryville technique — fight; win; fall back — had been repeated. "What does he fight battles for?" they grumbled, beginning to discern a discouraging pattern to their efforts under Bragg. Similarly at home, as one civilian diarist recorded, "It was small surcease to the sob of the widow and the moan of the orphan that 'the retreat to Tullahoma was conducted in good order.'"

Rosecrans, on the other hand — who had not made a single offensive move since the explosive attack on his right wing at dawn of the 31st, who had allowed a foe he claimed was beaten to withdraw from his immediate front without so much as a threat of molestation, and who was so cautious in pursuit that his eventual movement to the east bank of Stones River, from which he had withdrawn on the night of January 3 lest the rising waters expose his troops to destruction in detail, amounted to practically no pursuit at all — was praised not only by those below and above him in the army, but also by the public at large, including the Ohio legislature, which tendered him before the month was out a resolution of thanks "for the glorious victory resulting in the capture of Murfreesboro and the defeat of the rebel forces at that place." Cheered by his soldiers as he rode among them, he received equally gratifying responses to the dispatches by which he announced his victory to the authorities in Washington. "God bless you, and all of you," the President replied, and the Secretary of War (who had said of Rosecrans' appointment at the outset, "Well, you have made your choice of idiots. Now you can await the news of a terrible disaster") was quite expansive, wiring: "The country is filled with admiration of the gallantry and heroic achievement of yourself and the officers and troops under your command.... There is nothing you can ask within my power to grant to yourself or your noble command that will not be cheerfully given." Even Halleck, who had prodded and nudged him for weeks beyond endurance, eventually joined the chorus of praise, though not before he had waited a few days for verification in Confederate newspapers smuggled across the border. "Rebel accounts fully confirm your telegrams from the battlefield," he wired, and added: "You and your brave army have won the gratitude of your country and the admiration of the world.... All honor to the Army of the Cumberland — thanks to the living and tears for the lamented dead."

Bragg, he knew, was playing a cagey game at Tullahoma ("We shall fight him again at every hazard if he advances, and harass him daily if he does not," the terrible-tempered general was telling his superiors even now) but Rosecrans was firm in his intentions and had already reverted to the use of vigorous phrases he had been employing two weeks back, on the eve of battle. "We shall press them as rapidly as our means of traveling and subsistence will permit," he notified Stanton on January 5. Next day, though he was still at Murfreesboro, he boldly repeated words he had used at Nashville in mid-December: "I now wish to press them to the wall."

★ ★ ★

When Davis returned to Richmond that same January 5, to be met on the portico of the White House by his wife and their four children — three sons and a daughter, stair-stepped at two-year intervals so that their ages ranged from just past one to almost eight — Mrs Davis, observing that her husband was near exhaustion, insisted that he retire at once to rest from the exertions of his journey. Presently, however, they heard the thump and blare of drums and horns and the cheers of a crowd that had gathered in front of the house to welcome him back with a serenade. Weary though he was, and despite his desire to be alone with his family — "Every sound is the voice of my child and every child renews the memory of a loved one's appearance," he had written home from Tennessee, "but none can equal their charms, nor can any compare with my own long-worshipped Winnie" — he felt that he could not ignore the shouts of the crowd or fail to acknowledge the courtesy being tendered.

The cheers were redoubled as the big front door swung ajar once more and the President came out onto the steps. Captain J. B. Smith's Silver Band played "Listen to the Mocking Bird" and several other airs which the crowd enjoyed while waiting for the speech they had come to hear. Davis did not disappoint them. Carried forward perhaps by a sort of verbal secondary inertia, he spoke as he had been speaking now for more than three weeks, to similar crowds and with similar words, in the course of his nearly three-thousand-mile trip to "the further West" and back.

"I am happy to be welcomed on my return to the capital of the Confederacy — the last hope, as I believe, for the perpetuation of that system of government which our forefathers founded — the asylum of the oppressed, and the home of true representative liberty." His voice, as he thus began, showed the strain to which it had been exposed, but as usual it gathered strength as he continued, reverting to the deeds of olden days in the Old Dominion, where the earlier Revolution had been proclaimed and, finally, won. Now once more, he told these latter-day Virginians, "anticipating the overthrow of that government which you had inherited, you assumed to yourselves the right, as your fathers had done before you, to declare yourself independent, and nobly have you advocated the assertion which you have made. Here, upon your soil, some of the fiercest battles of the Revolution were fought, and upon your soil it closed by the surrender of Cornwallis. Here again are men of every state; here they have congregated, linked in the defense of a most sacred cause. They have battled, they have bled upon your soil, and it is now consecrated by blood which cries for vengeance against the insensate foe of religion as well as of humanity, of the altar as well as of the hearthstone." Thus he repeated the bitterness he had voiced in his home state, ten days ago. Nor, with first-hand accounts of the sack of Fredericksburg now added to the list of northern depredations — not the least of them being the recently issued Emancipation Proclamation, which, as he saw it, incited the slaves to the murder of their masters — had that reaction been tempered by second thought. Rather, the bitterness had increased: as he now showed. "It is true," he told his listeners, "you have a cause which binds you together more firmly than your fathers were. They fought to be free from the usurpations of the British crown, but they fought against a manly foe. You fight against the offscourings of the earth."

Applauded, he passed on to a brief review of recent Confederate successes in the field, which he predicted would bring discord to northern councils, and then returned to his condemnation, not only of the conduct of the Federal armies of invasion, but also of the men who had sent them South. "Every crime which could characterize the course of demons has marked the course of the invader ... from the burning of defenseless towns to the stealing of silver forks and spoons." In this last he had particular reference to Ben Butler, known as "Beast" Butler and "Spoons" Butler as a result of his alleged brutality and deftness in the exercise of his authority in command of the occupation of New Orleans, and Davis made the charge explicit, asserting that the Massachusetts general had "exerted himself to earn the excoriations of the civilized world, and now returns [to Washington] with his dishonors thick upon him to receive the plaudits of the only people on earth who do not blush to think he wears the human form.... They have come to disturb your social organization on the plea that it is a military necessity. For what are they waging war? They say to preserve the Union. Can they preserve the Union by destroying the social existence of a portion of the South? Do they hope to reconstruct the Union by striking at everything which is dear to man? — by showing themselves so utterly disgraced that if the question was proposed to you whether you would combine with hyenas or Yankees, I trust every Virginian would say: 'Give me the hyenas.'"

"Good! Good!" his listeners cried, and there was laughter. They wanted more along these lines.

But Davis spoke calmly now, as if to refute the charge made by his critics that he was cold in his attitude toward the people, unconcerned for their welfare, and anxious to avoid commingling with them — as if, indeed, he had brought back East from his journey West an increased awareness of the warmth and strength proceeding from contact with those who looked to him for leadership not only as their President but also as a man. "My friends, constant labor in the duties of office, borne down by care, and with an anxiety which has left me scarcely a moment for repose, I have had but little opportunity for social intercourse among you. I thank you for this greeting, and hope the time may come soon when you and I alike, relieved of the anxieties of the hour, may have more of social intercourse than has heretofore existed." Flushed with confidence as a result of the victories won by the nation's armies in the course of his trip, he added: "If the war continues we shall only grow stronger and stronger as each year rolls on. Compare our condition today with that which existed one year ago. See the increasing power of the enemy, but mark that our own has been proportionately greater, until we see in the future nothing to disturb the prospect of the independence for which we are struggling. One year ago, many were depressed and some were despondent. Now deep resolve is seen in every eye; an unconquerable spirit nerves every arm. And gentle woman, too;

who can estimate the value of her services in this struggle? ... With such noble women at home, and such heroic soldiers in the field, we are invincible."

He waited for the applause to die away, and then concluded his remarks, once more on a personal note. "I thank you, my friends, for the kind salutation tonight; it is an indication that at some future time we shall be better acquainted. I trust we shall all live to enjoy some of the fruits of the struggle in which we are engaged. My prayers are for your individual and collective welfare. May God prosper our cause, and may we live to give to our children untarnished the rich inheritance which our fathers gave us. Good night!"

CHAPTER

⚔ 2 ⚔

Unhappy New Year

★ ✵ ☆

NEW YEAR'S 1863 WAS FOR ABRAHAM LINCOLN perhaps the single busiest day of his whole presidential life, and it came moreover at dead center of what was perhaps his period of deepest gloom and perplexity of spirit. Not only was there political division within his party, and even within his own official family, but with the possible exception of Rosecrans, whose battle was in mid-career and appeared worse than doubtful, all his hand-picked commanders had failed him utterly, through enemy action or their own inaction, in his hopes for a multifaceted early-winter triumph in which he himself had assigned them the parts they were to play in putting a quick end to rebellion. One by one, sometimes two by two, they had failed him. Burnside and his fellow generals on the Rappahannock, having blundered into defeat at Fredericksburg, were engaged in a frenzy of backbiting such as not even the highly contentious Army of the Potomac had ever known before. Grant, according to the New York *Times*, remained "stuck in the mud of northern Mississippi, his army of no use to him or anybody else." Banks, caught in a toil of imported New Orleans cotton speculators, was stymied by a previously unsuspected fort on the Mississippi, two hundred and fifty miles downstream from his assigned objective. And McClernand, from whom the Commander in Chief had perhaps expected most, was apparently the worst off of all. He not only had done nothing with his army; the last Lincoln had heard from him, he could not even find it.

Nor had these and other failures of omission and commission gone unnoticed by the country at large, the voters and investors on whose will and trust the prosecution of the war depended. The Democrats, still on the outside looking in, but with substantial gains in the fall elections to sharpen their appetite for more, had seen to that: especially Ohio Representative Clement L. Vallandigham, who was savagely pointing out, from the vantage point of his seat in Congress, the administration's errors. "Money you have expended without limit," he told Republicans in the House, "and blood poured out like water. Defeat, debt, taxation, and sepulchers — these are your only trophies." Others, less violent but no less earnest, including his disaffected former allies, were accusing the President in a similar vein; so that now, perhaps, with his own critics crying out against him, he could feel more sympathy for James K. Polk than he had felt when he spoke against him in Congress, fifteen years ago this month, in the midst of another war. "I more than suspect already," the youthful Lincoln had declared from a seat in the rear of the House, "that he is deeply conscious of being in the wrong; that he feels the blood of this war, like the blood of Abel, is crying to heaven against him; that originally having some strong motive ... to involve the two countries in a war, and trusting to escape scrutiny by fixing the public gaze upon the exceeding brightness of military glory ... he plunged into it and has swept on and on, till, disappointed in his calculation ... he now finds himself he knows not where.... His mind, tasked beyond its power, is running hither and thither, like some tortured creature on a burning surface, finding no position on which it can settle down and be at ease.... He is a bewildered, confounded, and miserably perplexed man. God grant he may be able to show there is not something about his conscience more painful than all his mental perplexity!"

The words rebounded from the target, boomeranged down the years, and came back in other forms to strike the sender. Orestes Brownson, the prominent Boston author and former transcendentalist, wrote of Lincoln: "His soul seems made of leather, and incapable of any grand or noble emotion. Compared with the mass of men, he is a line of flat prose in a beautiful and spirited lyric. He lowers, he never elevates you. You leave his presence with your enthusiasm dampened, your better feelings crushed, and your hopes cast to the winds. You ask not, can this man carry the nation through its terrible struggles? but can the nation carry this man through them, and not perish in the attempt?" Brownson was of no uncertain mind where Lincoln was concerned. "He is thickheaded; he is ignorant; he is tricky, somewhat astute, in a small way, and obstinate as a mule.... He is wrong-headed, the attorney not the lawyer, the petty politician not the statesman, and, in my belief, ill-deserving of the soubriquet of Honest. I am out of all patience with him," he added, rather anticlimactically, and inquired: "Is there no way of inducing him to resign, and allow Mr Hamlin to take his place?" Senator William Pitt Fessenden, a Maine Republican high in the party's councils, replied in somewhat the same vein when told that he should be a member of the cabinet in order to be at Lincoln's elbow and give the nation the full benefit of his advice. "No friend of mine should ever wish to see me there," he answered. "You cannot change the President's character or conduct. He remained long enough in Springfield, surrounded by toadies and office-seekers, to persuade himself that he was specially chosen by the Almighty for this crisis, and well chosen. This conceit has never yet been beaten out of him, and until it is, no human wisdom can be of much avail. I see nothing for it but to let the ship of state drift along, hoping that the current of public opinion may bring it safely into port." Similarly, a Boston philanthropist, railroad magnate J. M. Forbes, convinced that Lincoln was badly off the track, was asking: "Can nothing be done to reach the President's ear and heart? I hear he is susceptible to religious impressions; shall we send our eloquent divines to talk to him, or shall we send on a deputation of mothers and wives, or can we, the conservators of liberty, who have elected him, combine with Congress in beseeching him to save the country?"

In point of fact, one such group of "eloquent divines" as Forbes suggested did come to call on Lincoln at this time, protesting with considerable heat the lack of progress in the war; but he gave them little satisfaction beyond a brief, short-tempered lecture comparing the administration's predicament to that of a tightrope walker in mid-act. "Gentlemen," he told them, "suppose all the property you were worth was in gold, and you had put it in the hands of Blondin to carry across the Niagara River. Would you shake the cable or keep shouting out to him, 'Blondin, stand up a little straighter!' 'Blondin, stoop a little more!' 'Go a little faster'; 'Lean a little more to the north'; 'Lean a little more to the south'? No. You would hold your breath as well as your tongue, and keep your hands off until he was safe over. The government is carrying an immense weight. Untold treasures are in their hands. They are doing the very best they can. Don't badger them. Keep silence, and we'll get you safe across." The visit, he said afterwards, made him "a little shy of preachers" for a time. "But the latchstring is out," he added, "and they have the right to come here and preach to me if they will go about it with some gentleness and moderation."

Gentleness and moderation were easier to prescribe than they were to practice. An infinitely patient man, he was beginning to lose patience: with the result that some who formerly had complained that he lacked firmness were now protesting that he had assumed the prerogatives of a dictator, spurning their counsels and high-handedly overruling their objections. It was true in some respects. His accustomed tact sometimes failed him under pressure nowadays, and he gave short answers, though rarely without the saving grace of humor, the velvet glove that softened the clutch of the iron hand. This was evident, for example, in a clash with Secretary of the Treasury Salmon P. Chase about this time. An economist came to Lincoln with a plan for issuing greenbacks. Lincoln heard him out, liked the notion, but told him: "You must go to Chase. He is running that end of the machine." The man left, then presently returned, saying that the Secretary had dismissed him with the objection that the proposal was unconstitutional. Lincoln grimaced. "Go back to

Chase," he said, "and tell him not to bother himself about the Constitution. Say that I have that sacred instrument here at the White House, and am guarding it with great care."

Such brusque, not to say cavalier, treatment of his highly respected Treasury chief was prologue to an even rougher handling of that dignitary in mid-December, when he tripped him neatly from behind as he tried a sprint up several rungs of the political ladder. This was a time of crisis and division, in the cabinet as in the nation at large. One member, Secretary of the Interior Caleb Blood Smith, who had received his appointment as the result of a convention bargain, was leaving to accept a judgeship Lincoln had offered him in his native Indiana; his post would go to John Palmer Usher, another Hoosier, at present the Assistant Secretary. The other six members were split on the question of whether to admit West Virginia as a state under an act just passed by Congress, divorcing Virginia's northwest counties from the Old Dominion and validating the rump government set up in Charleston during the Sumter furor. Three cabinet officers — Chase, Stanton, and Secretary of State William H. Seward — wanted Lincoln to sign the bill, converting slave soil into free soil by the stroke of a pen, and incidentally adding good Republican votes on whatever questions Congress might decide needed settling in the future; while three others — Secretary of the Navy Gideon Welles, Attorney General Edward Bates, and Postmaster General Montgomery Blair — recommended that he veto it, on grounds that the act was in a sense a ratification of secession. Though he could not reconcile their views, Lincoln quickly solved the problem to his own approximate satisfaction. "The division of a state is dreaded as a precedent," he reasoned. "But a measure made expedient by a war is no precedent for times of peace. It is said that the admission of West Virginia is secession, and tolerated only because it is *our* secession. Well, if we call it by that name, there is still difference enough between secession against the Constitution and secession in favor of the Constitution." On the last day of the year, though he did so with a wry face, he signed the bill. West Virginia would become in June a full-fledged state of the Union, the thirty-fifth, not discounting the eleven who had no representation in Congress pending the settlement of their claim to have abolished their old ties.

Seward and Chase had voted together on the issue, but that was rare. In general they were diametrically opposed, as they had been in the old days when they were rivals for the office which, by a fluke, had gone to Lincoln. Chase, who was jealous of Seward's position as the President's chief adviser, wanted not only the seat closest to the one at the head of the table, but also, as time would show, the principal seat itself. In this connection, noting the way the wind blew, he had aligned himself with the radicals in Congress, the so-called Jacobins who had come to see Seward as the stumbling block in the way of adoption of their notions as to how the war should be fought and the country run, just as Chase had come to see him as a hurdle that would have to be removed or overleaped if he was to fulfill his own ambitions. By way of undoing their common adversary, he fanned the flames of the radicals' hatred by reporting Seward's every private opposition to their aims (the New Yorker, for example, had delayed the promulgation of the Preliminary Emancipation Proclamation by advising Lincoln to wait for a more propitious season before releasing it to the world; than which, indeed, there could be no crime greater in radical eyes) as well as by giving them a blow-by-blow account of every cabinet crisis, omitting nothing that served to thicken the atmosphere of discord and indecision. So it was that at last, on December 17 — four days after the Fredericksburg fiasco, which seemed to them to prove emphatically that the prosecution of the war was in quite the wrong hands — all but one of the thirty-two Republican senators met in secret caucus on Capitol Hill and passed unanimously the following resolution, by way of advice to the leader of their party: *"Resolved, that . . . the public confidence in the present administration would be increased by a change in and partial reconstruction of the cabinet."* It was Seward they were after, Seward alone, and lest there be any doubt on that score a committee of nine was appointed to present the resolution to Lincoln and explain to him just what it was they meant.

The one abstaining senator was New York's Preston King, who went at once to Seward and warned his former senatorial colleague that the Jacobins, "thirsty for a victim" in the wake of recent misfortunes, had selected his neck for the ax. Seward reacted fast when he learned thus of the resolution about to be presented. "They may do as they please about me," he said, "but they shall not put the President in a false position on my account." Accordingly he took a sheet of paper, and having scrawled a few words across it —"Sir, I hereby resign from the office of Secretary of State, and beg that my resignation be accepted immediately" — sent it forthwith to the White House. Lincoln was shocked. "What does this mean?" he asked as he put on his hat and set out for Seward's house, which was just across the street. Seward explained what had happened, along with what was about to happen, and added that he personally would be glad to get from under the burden of official duties and political harassment. "Ah yes, Governor," Lincoln said, shaking his head. "That will do very well for you, but I am like the starling in Sterne's story. 'I can't get out.'" He pocketed the resignation and went sadly back across the White House lawn.

At any rate, next morning when the committee spokesman called, he knew what to expect. He set the time for the presentation at 7 o'clock that evening; he would receive the full committee then. This was a crisis, not only for Lincoln but also for the nation, and he knew it. "If I had yielded to that storm and dismissed Seward," he said later, "the thing would have all slumped over one way, and we should have been left with a scant handful of supporters." Knowing what had to be done was a quite different thing, however, from knowing how to do it. Ben Wade of Ohio, George W. Julian of Indiana, Zachariah Chandler of Michigan: these and others like them were men of power and savage purpose, accomplished haters who would be merciless in revenging even an imagined slight, let alone an outright rebuff. Whatever Lincoln did had better be done without incurring their personal enmity. Besides, he not only had to avoid their anger; he also needed their support. What he required just now was someone to draw their wrath, someone to serve him much as a billygoat serves the farmer who places him in a barnlot to draw fleas. By evening, not without a certain sense of political and even poetical justice, he had chosen the someone. All that remained was to make him serve, and that could be done quite simply by branding him, in the eyes of all, for what he was.

The nine committeemen were prompt; Lincoln received them in his office. By way of a beginning, seventy-one-year-old Jacob Collamer of Vermont, who had been elected spokesman, read the resolution and followed it with a paper which summed up the conclusions reached in caucus the day before. The war should be prosecuted vigorously; cabinet members should be "cordial, resolute, unwavering" in their devotion to the principles of the Republican majority; the cabinet itself, once it had been stripped and rebuilt so as to contain only such stalwarts, should have a larger voice in the running of the government. Wade rose next, a vigorous man with "burning" eyes and bulldog flews, protesting hotly that the President had "placed the direction of our military affairs in the hands of bitter and malignant Democrats." He spoke at length, going somewhat afield from the central issue, and was followed by Fessenden, who agreed that the war was "not sufficiently in the hands of its friends," then brought the discussion back on target by charging specifically "that the Secretary of State [is] not in accord with the majority of the cabinet and [has] exerted an injurious influence upon the conduct of the war." Others had their say along these lines, also at considerable length, but Lincoln kept his temper and said little. After three hours of listening, however, he suggested that the meeting adjourn until the following night. The senators agreed. Alone at last, he saw clearly, as he presently remarked, that if he let these men have their way "the whole government must cave in; it could not stand, could not hold water; the bottom would be out."

He knew what to do and, by now, how to do it; but he was saddened. "What do those men want?" he asked his friend Senator Orville Browning of Illinois next day. "I hardly know, Mr President," Browning replied, "but they are exceedingly violent...." Lincoln knew well enough what they wanted, though, and he said so: "They wish to get rid of me — and I am sometimes half disposed to gratify them." Browning protested, but Lincoln shook his head. "We are now on the brink of destruction," he said. "It appears to me the Almighty is against us, and I can hardly see a ray of hope." Again Browning protested. Though he was not a member of the committee, he had attended the caucus and had voted for the resolution: which, he explained defensively, "was the gentlest thing that could be done. We had to do that, or worse." The trouble he said was Seward. While he personally had a high regard for the Secretary, others were saying that the New Yorker had the President under his thumb. "Why should men believe a lie," Lincoln broke in, "an absurd lie, that could not impose on a child, and cling to it and repeat it in defiance of all evidences to the contrary?" His sadness deepened. "The committee is to be up to see me at 7 o'clock. Since I heard last night of the proceedings of the caucus I have been more distressed than by any event of my life."

If this was so, it did not show in his manner when he welcomed the committeemen that evening for a second round of grievance presentations. Before the discussion got under way, however, he announced to the assembled senators that he had thought it fitting to have the cabinet officers — minus Seward, of course, since even aside from the fact that his resignation was pending, that would have been too indelicate — present to answer the charge that there was discord among them and that the President seldom followed or even asked for their advice. Whereupon the door opened and the six gentlemen in question filed into the room. Lincoln had invited them at the cabinet meeting that morning, after telling them of the matter afoot and of Seward's submission of his resignation. Mostly they had welcomed the chance to confront their accusers, although two of their number — Chase in particular — had protested that they "knew of no good that could come of an interview." In the end, however, the two — the other was Bates — had been obliged to go along with the majority. Now here they were, face to face with critics whose accusations were based, at least in part, on information supplied in private by Chase in order to curry favor with them. Already he was squirming, as if the fleas had jumped at the sight of his large, handsome person: but the worst was still to come.

If Chase and some of the senators were embarrassed by the confrontation, Lincoln certainly was not. He began the proceedings by reading aloud yesterday's bill of particulars, admitting as he went along that he had not consulted the cabinet on all affairs of state or war, and that he had not always followed their advice, even when he had sought it; but in the main, he said, he had valued and used their abilities, individually and collectively. As for discord, he did not think it reasonable to expect seven such independent-minded men to agree on every issue that came before them; but here again, he said, he thought they worked together mainly as a unit, and certainly he himself had no complaint. He paused, then turned to the six cabinet members present, beginning to poll them one by one. Did they or did they not agree with his statement of the case? They did; or so they said, one by one; until he came to Chase. Chase, as it turned out, also agreed, though not without considerable hemming and hawing by way of preamble. He would never have come to the meeting, he said, if he had known he was "to be arraigned." He seemed angry. He seemed to feel that he was being "put upon"—as indeed he was. In the end, with Wade and the others watching balefully, he admitted that matters of prime importance had usually come before the cabinet, though perhaps "not so fully as might be desired," and that there had been "no want of unity in the cabinet, but a general acquiescence in public measures." Thus he wound up, and the Jacobins watched him cold-eyed, contrasting what he said now, in the presence of Lincoln and his colleagues, with what he had said in private. The President did not prolong his suffering. Having more or less settled these two points of contention, he shifted the talk to the question of Seward, defending his chief minister against yesterday's charges, and then began to poll the committeemen on their views. At that point Fessenden recoiled. "I do not think it proper," he said, "to discuss the merits or demerits of a member of the cabinet in the presence of his associates." Chase was quick to agree. "I think the members of the cabinet should withdraw," he said. In solemn procession they did so, some amused, some disgruntled, and one, at least, discredited in the eyes of men whose favor he had sought.

Like Simon Cameron a year ago, the Treasury chief had learned the hard way what it meant to tangle with Lincoln. Cameron was in Russia now, a victim of political decapitation, and Chase was determined to avoid such punishment. He would forestall the headsman by submitting, however regretfully, his resignation. This was exactly what Lincoln wanted: as was shown next morning, December 20, when he came into his office and found Chase, Welles, and Stanton grouped around the fire. Chase began to complain of yesterday's damage to his dignity. It had affected him most painfully, he said, for it seemed to indicate a lack of confidence. In fact—he hesitated—he had written out his resignation at home the night before.... Lincoln's reaction to this was not at all what the Secretary had expected. His expression was one of downright joy.

"Where is it?" he said eagerly.

"I brought it with me," Chase replied, taking a letter from his inside coat pocket.

"Let me have it," Lincoln said, and he put out a long arm.

Chase drew back, but not in time. Lincoln already had hold of the paper, and the Secretary suffered the added shock of having it snatched from his grasp. Reading it quickly through, Lincoln laughed; "a triumphal laugh," Welles called it in his diary. "This cuts the Gordian knot," he exclaimed. "I can dispose of this subject now without difficulty. I see my way clear." Stanton, who had been guilty of some of the same backstairs maneuvers—though he did not know whether the President suspected him, or what he might do if he did—remarked stiffly that he was prepared to tender his resignation, too. But Lincoln already had what he had been working toward. "You may go to your department," he said gaily. "I don't want yours. This"— he held up Chase's letter —"is all I want; this relieves me; the case is clear; the trouble is ended. I will detain neither of you longer."

His satisfaction was obvious, amounting to delight. What he had had in mind all along, and had achieved through skillful handling, was a balance: Chase's resignation against Seward's, which the Jacobins were still urging him to accept. Now, however, with Chase's inseparably included —"If one goes, the other must," he presently notified the senators; "they must hunt in couples"— they would be much less insistent; for, whatever their disgust with the Treasury chief's performance the day before, they still believed that he could be useful to them within the administration's private councils. Lincoln himself described the situation with a metaphor out of his boyhood in Kentucky, where he had seen farmers riding to market with a brace of pumpkins lodged snugly in a bag, one at each end in order to make a balanced load across the horse's withers. "Now I can ride," he said. "I have got a pumpkin in each end of my bag." Accordingly, he sent polite, identical notes to the two ministers, declining to accept their resignations and requesting them to continue as members of his official family. Seward, who had watched the maneuvers with amusement from a seat behind the scene, agreed at once; but Chase held off, still suffering from the fleabites, which were no less painful for being figurative. "I will sleep on it," he said. However, after a day of meditation and prayer — for it was a Sunday and he was intensely religious, spending a good part of each Sabbath on his knees — he agreed to remain at his post, as Lincoln had confidently expected.

Here was a case of double salvation, in more ways than one. Within the confines of his office in the White House, Lincoln had planned and fought a three-day battle as important to the welfare of the nation, and the progress of the war through united effort, as many that raged in the open field with booming guns and casualties by the thousands. In addition to retaining the services of Seward and Chase, both excellent men at their respective posts, he had managed to turn aside the wrath of the Jacobins without increasing their bitterness toward himself or incurring their open hatred, which might well have been fatal. Nor was that all. Paradoxically, because of the way he had gone about it, in avoiding the disruption of his cabinet he had achieved within it a closer harmony than had obtained before. This was partly because of the increased respect his actions earned him, but it was also because of the effect the incident had on the two ministers most intimately concerned. For all his loyalty to Lincoln through the storm, Seward had not previously abandoned the notion that he was the man directly in line for his job. Now, though, with all but one of the senators in his own party having expressed a desire to see him removed from any connection with the executive branch of the government, the presidential itch was cured. From that hour, his devotion to his duties was single-minded and his loyalty acquired an added zeal. So much could hardly be said for Chase, exactly, but he too had been sobered, and his ambition taken down a notch, by the cold-eyed looks the radical leaders had given him while he squirmed. It was no wonder, then, that Lincoln indulged in self-congratulation when he reviewed the three-day maneuver. "I do not see how I could have done better," he remarked.

Few would disagree with this assessment, even among the frock-coated politicians he had bested, whether senators or members of his cabinet. In point of fact, whatever shocks they had suffered along the way, there should have been little surprise at the outcome; for the matter had been essentially political, and politics (or statesmanship, if you will, which he once defined as the art of getting the best from men who all too often were intent on giving nothing better than their worst) was a science he had mastered some time back. The military art was something else. Whether Lincoln would ever do as well as Commander in Chief of the nation's armies as he had done as its Chief Executive was more than doubtful — particularly in the light of current testimony as to the condition of the largest of those armies, still on the near bank of the Rappahannock attempting to recover from the shock of its mid-December blood bath.

"Exhaustion steals over the country. Confidence and hope are dying," the Quartermaster General wrote privately this week to its commander. "The slumber of the army since [the attack at Fredericksburg] is eating into the vitals of the nation. As day after day has gone, my heart has sunk and I see greater peril to our nationality in the present condition of affairs than I have seen at any time during the struggle." Complaints were heard from below as well as above, and though these were not addressed to Burnside personally, accusing fingers were leveled in his direction and even higher. "Our poppycorn generals kill men as Herod killed the innocents," a Massachusetts private declared, and a Wisconsin major called this winter "the Valley Forge of the war." A bitterness was spreading through the ranks. "Alas my poor country!" a New York corporal wrote home. "It has strong limbs to march and meet the foe, stout arms to strike heavy blows, brave hearts to dare. But the brains, the brains — have we no brains to use the arms and limbs and eager hearts with cunning? Perhaps Old Abe has some funny story to tell, appropriate to the occasion.... Mother, do not wonder that my loyalty is growing weak," he added. "I am sick and tired of disaster and the fools that bring disaster upon us."

There was a snatch of doggerel, sung to the tune of the old sea chanty "Johnny, Fill up the Bowl," making the rounds:

> *Abram Lincoln, what yer 'bout?*
> *Hurrah! Hurrah!*
> *Stop this war. It's all played out.*
> *Hurrah! Hurrah!*
> *Abram Lincoln, what yer 'bout?*
> *Stop this war. It's all played out.*
> *We'll all drink stone blind:*
> *Johnny, fill up the bowl!*

Veterans in the Army of the Potomac took up the refrain, "all played out," and made it their own. Once they had pretended cynicism as a cover for their greenness and their fears, but now they felt they had earned it and they found the phrase descriptive of their outlook through this season of discontent. "The phrensy of our soldiers rushing to glory or death has, as our boys amusingly affirm, *been played out*," a regimental chaplain wrote. "Our battle-worn veterans go into danger when ordered, remain as a stern duty so long as directed, and leave as soon as honor and duty allow." Case-hardened by their recent experience over the river, particularly in the repeated fruitless assaults on the stone wall at the base of Marye's Heights, they had no use for heroic postures or pretensions nowadays. When they saw magazine illustrations showing mounted officers with drawn sabers leading smartly aligned columns of troops unflinchingly through shellbursts, they snickered and jeered and whooped their motto: "All played out!"

Lincoln already knew something of this, but he learned a good deal more on December 29 when two disgruntled brigadiers hurried from Falmouth to Washington on short-term passes, intending to warn their congressmen of what they believed was imminent disaster. Burnside was planning to recross the Rappahannock any day now, having issued three days' cooked rations the day after Christmas, along with orders for the troops to be held in readiness to move on twelve hours' notice. What alarmed the two brigadiers — John Newton and John Cochrane, the latter a former Republican congressman himself — was that the army, which they were convinced was in a condition of near-mutiny, would come apart at the seams if it was called upon to repeat this soon the tragic performance it had staged two weeks ago in the same arena, and therefore they had come to warn the influential Bay State senator Henry Wilson, chairman of the Senate Military Committee, in hopes that he could get the movement stopped. In the intensity of their concern, as they discovered when they reached the capital, they had failed to take into account the fact that Congress was in recess over the holidays; Wilson had gone home. Undeterred, they went to see the Secretary of State, a former political associate of Cochrane's. When Seward heard their burden of woes he took them straight to the President, to whom — though they were somewhat daunted now, never having intended to climb this high up the chain of command — they repeated, along with hasty assurances that the basis for their admittedly irregular visit was patriotism, not hope for advancement, their conviction that if the Army of the Potomac was committed to battle in its present discouraged state it would be utterly destroyed. Not only would it be unable to hold the line of the Rappahannock; it would not even be able to hold the line of the river from which it took its name. Lincoln, who had known nothing of the pending movement, and scarcely more of the extent of the demoralization Cochrane and Newton claimed was rampant, was infected with their fears and got off a wire to Burnside without delay: "I have good reason for saying that you must not make a general movement without first letting me know of it."

Burnside, though his infantry had already been alerted for a downstream crossing while his cavalry was in motion for a feint upstream —"a risky expedition but a buster," one trooper called the plan — promptly complied with the President's telegram by canceling the movement, but he was angered and saddened by the obvious lack of confidence on the part of his superiors. The army, too — whatever its gladness over the postponement of another blood bath — was aggrieved as it filed back into its camps, feeling mistrusted and mistrustful. "Such checks destroy the enthusiasm of any army," the same trooper dolefully protested.

Yet it was at this point, near the apparent nadir of its self-confidence and pride, with disaffection evident in all of its components, from the commander down to the youngest drummer boy, that the one truly imperishable quality of this army first began to be discerned, like a gleam that only shone in darkness. If men could survive the unprofitable slaughter of Fredericksburg — the patent bungling, the horror piled on pointless horror, and the disgust that came with the conclusion that their comrades had died less by way of proving their love for their country than by way of proving the ineptness of their leaders — it might well be that they could survive almost anything. There were those who saw this. There were those who, unlike Newton and Cochrane, did not mistake the vociferous reaction for near-mutiny, who knew that griping was not only the time-honored prerogative of the American soldier, from Valley Forge on down, but was also, in its way, a proof of his basic toughness and resilience. "The more I saw of the Army of the Potomac," one correspondent wrote from the camps around Falmouth, "the more I wondered at its invincible spirit, which no disaster seemed able to destroy." A *Harper's Weekly* editor perhaps overstated the case —"All played out!" the soldiers who read it doubtless jeered — but was also thinking along these lines in an issue that came out about this time: "Like our forefathers the English, who always began their wars by getting soundly thrashed by their enemies, and only commenced to achieve success when it was thought they were exhausted, we are warming to the work with each mishap."

Lincoln thought so, too, what time he managed to shake off the deep melancholy that was so much a part of his complex nature. He probed and, probing, he considered what emerged. As of the first day of the year which was opening so inauspiciously, the Union had 918,211 soldiers under arms, whereas the Confederacy had 446,622, or a good deal less than half as many. At several critical points along the thousand-mile line of division the odds were even longer — out in Middle Tennessee, for instance, or down along the Rappahannock — and the troubled Commander in Chief found solace in brooding on the figures, even those that reached him from the field of Fredericksburg. "We lost fifty percent more men than did the enemy," a member of the White House staff remarked after hearing his chief discuss the outcome of the fighting there, "and yet there is sense in the awful arithmetic propounded by Mr Lincoln. He says that if the same battle were to be fought over again, every day, through a week of days, with the same relative results, the army under Lee would be wiped out to the last man, [while] the Army of the Potomac would still be a mighty host. The war would be over, the Confederacy gone." There was error here. Northern losses in the battle had exceeded southern losses, not by fifty, but by considerably better than one hundred percent. And yet there was validity in Lincoln's premise as to the end result, and especially was there validity in the conclusion the staff man heard him draw: "No general yet found can face the arithmetic, but the end of the war will be at hand when he shall be discovered."

Scott and McDowell, Pope and McClellan, and now Burnside: none of these was the killer he was seeking. Already he saw that this search was perhaps after all the major problem. All else — while, like Blondin, Lincoln threaded his way, burdened by untold treasures — was, in a sense, a biding of time until the unknown killer could be found. Somewhere he existed, and somewhere he would find him, this unidentified general who could face the grim arithmetic being scrawled in blood across these critical, tragic pages of the nation's history.

★ ★ ★

These and other matters were much on the President's mind when he woke on January 1. After an early-morning conference with Burnside, who had come up from Falmouth to ask in person just what the Commander in Chief's "good reason" had been for not allowing him to handle his own army as he saw fit, Lincoln spent the usual half hour with his barber, then got into his best clothes and went downstairs for the accustomed New Year's White House reception. For three hours, beginning at 11 o'clock, it was "How do you do?" "Thank you." "Glad to see you." "How do you do?" as the invited guests — high government officials, members of the diplomatic corps, and other important dignitaries, foreign and domestic — having threaded their way through the crowd of uninvited onlookers collected on the lawn, alighted from their carriages, came into the parlor, and filed past Lincoln for handshakes and refreshments. At 1 o'clock the long ordeal was over; he went back upstairs to his office for the day's — or, some would say, the century's — most important business, the signing of the Emancipation Proclamation.

Throughout the ninety-nine days since September 23, when the preliminary announcement of intention had been made, there had been much speculation as to whether he would issue or withdraw the final proclamation. Some were for it, some against. His friend Browning, for example, reflecting the view of constituents in the President's home state, thought it "fraught with evil, and evil only." The senator believed that the "useless and mischievous" document would serve "to unite and exasperate" the South, and to "divide and distract us in the North." Lincoln himself, if only by his neglect of the subject while the hundred days ticked off, had seemed to see the point of this objection. In his December message to Congress he had barely mentioned the projected edict, but had reverted instead to his original plan for compensated emancipation, a quite different thing indeed. Alarmed by this apparent failure of nerve, Abolitionists looked to their hero Senator Charles Sumner of Massachusetts, who went to Lincoln three days after Christmas for a straight talk on the matter. He found him hard at work on the final draft of the proclamation, writing it out in longhand. "I know very well that the name connected with this document will never be forgotten," Lincoln said, by way of explanation for his pains, and Sumner returned to his own desk to reassure a qualmish friend in Boston: "The President says he would not stop the Proclamation if he could, and he could not if he would.... Hallelujah!"

So it was. Seward brought the official copy over from the State Department, where a skilled penman had engrossed it from Lincoln's final draft, just completed the night before. All it lacked was the President's signature. He dipped his pen, then paused with it suspended over the expanse of whiteness spread out on his desk, and looked around with a serious expression. "I never in my life felt more certain that I was doing right," he said, "than I do in signing this paper. But I have been receiving calls and shaking hands since 9 o'clock this morning, till my arm is stiff and numb. Now this signature is one that will be closely examined, and if they find my hand trembled they will say, 'He had some compunctions.' But anyway it is going to be done." Slowly and carefully he signed, not the usual *A. Lincoln,* but his name in full: *Abraham Lincoln.* The witnesses crowded nearer for a look at the result, then laughed in relief of nervous tension; for the signature, though "slightly tremulous," as Lincoln himself remarked, was bold and clear. Seward signed next, the quick, slanting scrawl of the busy administrator, and the great seal was affixed, after which it went to its place in the State Department files (where it later was destroyed by fire) and in the hearts of men, where it would remain forever, though some of them had doubted lately that it would even be issued.

★ ★ ★

It was one thing to claim that by the stroke of a pen the fetters had been struck from the limbs of five million slaves and that their combined worth of more than a billion dollars was thereby automatically subtracted from enemy assets. It was quite another, however, to translate the announcement into fact, especially considering its peculiar limitations. All of Delaware, Maryland, Kentucky, Tennessee, and Missouri were exempt by specific definition within the body of the edict, along with those portions of Virginia and Louisiana already under Federal control. Lincoln himself explained that the proclamation had "no constitutional or legal justification, except as a military measure. The exemptions were made because the military necessity did not apply to the exempted localities." He freed no slave within his reach, and whether those beyond his reach would ever be affected by his pronouncement was dependent on the outcome of the war, which in turn depended on the southward progress of his armies. Just now that progress, East and West — once more with the possible exception of Middle Tennessee, where the issue remained in doubt — was negligible at best and nonexistent for the most part. Nor did the signs in either direction give promise of early improvement. Here in the East, in fact, if this morning's conference with Burnside was any indication of what to expect, the outlook was downright bleak.

The ruff-whiskered general had arrived in a state of acute distress, obviously fretted by more than the discomforts of his all-night ride from Falmouth, and Lincoln was distressed in turn to see him so. He liked Burnside — almost everyone did, personally — for his courage, for his impressive military bearing, and for what one subordinate called his "single-hearted honesty and unselfishness." All these qualities he had, and Lincoln, with a feeling of relief after weeks of trying to budge the balky McClellan, had chosen him in expectation of aggressiveness. The Indiana-born Rhode Islander had certainly given him that at Fredericksburg, in overplus indeed, but with a resolution so little tempered by discretion that critics now were remarking that he waged war in much the same way some folks played the fiddle, "by main strength and awkwardness." He himself was the first to admit his shortcomings. He had done so from the start, and recently in testimony given under oath before a congressional committee he had taken on his shoulders the whole blame for the late repulse. This was in a way disarming; it had the welcome but unfamiliar sound of natural modesty, so becoming in a truly capable man. However, there were those who saw it merely as further proof of his unfitness for the job he had accepted under protest. Burnside, they said, had not only admitted his incompetency; he had sworn to it.

When he opened the New Year's conference by asking what lay behind the telegram advising him not to move against the enemy without notifying Washington beforehand, Lincoln told him of the interview with the two brigadiers, in which they had stated that the army lacked confidence in its commander and was in no fit shape to be committed. Bristling at this evidence of perfidy from below, Burnside demanded to know their names, but Lincoln declined to divulge them for fear of the reprisal which he now saw would be visited upon their heads. This further increased the general's depression. It might well be true, he said, that his army had no faith in him; certainly not a single one of his senior commanders had approved of the movement he had canceled at Lincoln's suggestion. In fact, he added, plunging deeper into gloom, "It is my belief that I ought to retire to private life." When Lincoln demurred, Burnside's spirits rose a bit: enough, at least, to allow a sudden shift to the offensive. However low his own stock might have fallen, he said earnestly, he wanted the President to know that in his opinion neither Stanton's nor Halleck's was any higher. A man was apt to be a poor judge of his own usefulness and the loyalty of his subordinates, but of one thing he was sure. Neither the Secretary of War nor the general-in-chief had the confidence of the army — or of the country either for that matter, he quickly added, though he admitted that Lincoln was probably better informed on this latter point than he was. At any rate it was his belief that they too should be removed.... Lincoln expressed no opinion as to whether he could spare Stanton or Halleck, but he assured the unhappy Burnside that he valued his services highly. He urged him to return at once to his command and do the best he could, as he was sure he had done invariably in the past. Burnside replied that his plan was still to cross the Rappahannock, somewhere above or below Fredericksburg, and attack the rebels on their own ground. Lincoln said that was what he wanted, too, but prudence sometimes had to be applied, especially when risky ventures were involved. Whereupon, having secured this approval, however qualified, the general took his leave, apparently in a somewhat better frame of mind.

Still the fact remained that he was returning to his army with the intention of requiring it to pursue a course of action which, by his own admission, did not have the approval of the ranking subordinates who would be charged with its execution. The situation was, to say the least, loaded with possibilities of disaster. Here, Lincoln saw, was where the general-in-chief would fit into the picture; here was where Halleck could begin to perform the principal duty for which he had been summoned to the capital almost six months ago. He could go down to Falmouth for a first-hand look at the lay of the land and a talk with the disaffected corps commanders, then come back and submit his recommendations as to whether Burnside should be given his head or halted and replaced. Accordingly, before going upstairs to dress for the New Year's reception, Lincoln took out a sheet of paper and wrote the owl-eyed general a letter explaining what it was he wanted him to do. "If in such a difficulty as this you do not help," he wrote, "you fail me precisely in the point for which I sought your assistance." The tone was somewhat tart, doubtless because Lincoln was irked at having to ask for what should have been forthcoming as a matter of course, and he added: "Your military skill is useless to me, if you will not do this."

The letter was forwarded through Stanton, who gave it to Halleck that same morning at the reception. "Old Brains," as he was called, was taken aback. Twice already in this war he had ventured into the field — one occasion was the inchworm advance on Corinth, back in May, when all he got for his pains was an empty town, plus the guffaws that went with being hoodwinked; the other was his trip to see McClellan down on the York-James peninsula, shortly after his arrival East in late July, when he ordered the withdrawal that had permitted Lee to concentrate against Pope with such disastrous results on the plains of Manassas — and he was having no more of such exposure to the jangle of alarums and excursions. He prized the sweatless quiet of his office, where he could scratch his elbows in seclusion and ponder the imponderables of war. Lincoln's letter was a wrench, not so much because of what it said — which was, after all, little more than a definition of Halleck's duties — but because of the way it said it. The fact that his chief had thought it necessary to put the thing on record, in black and white, instead of making the suggestion verbally, which would have left no blot, seemed to him to indicate a lack of confidence. His reaction was immediate and decisive. As soon as the reception was over he went to his office, wrote out his resignation, and sent it at once to the Secretary of War.

Lincoln heard of this development from Stanton late that afternoon, following the signing of the Emancipation Proclamation. Saddened though he was by the general's reaction, which deprived him, as he said, of the professional advice he badly needed at this juncture, he still did not want to lose the services of Old Brains, such as they were. To mollify the offended man he recalled the letter that same day and put it away in his files with the indorsement: "Withdrawn, because considered harsh by General Halleck." He was pleased when the general then agreed to remain at his post, even though he amounted, as Lincoln subsequently remarked, to "little more ... than a first-rate clerk." The fact was, in spite of his objection to what he called "Halleck's habitual attitude of demur," he valued his opinions highly, especially those on theoretical or procedural matters. "He is a military man, has had a military education. I brought him here to give me military advice." So Lincoln defended him, and added: "However you may doubt or disagree [with] Halleck, he is very apt to be right in the end." Then too, since he knew something of the unfortunate general's sufferings from hemorrhoids, which made him gruff as a sore-tailed bear and caused him to be avoided by all who could possibly stay beyond his reach, Lincoln's sympathy was aroused. Once when he was asked why he did not get rid of so unpleasant a creature, he replied: "Well, the fact is the man has no friends. [He] should be taken care of."

All in all, it had been a wearing day, and as Lincoln went to bed that night (having attended to several other less important matters, such as the complaint made to him by "an old lady of genteel appearance" that, despite previous assurances to the contrary, her boarding house near the corner of Tenth and E Streets was about to be commandeered by the War Department; "I know nothing about it myself," he wrote Stanton, "but promised to bring it to your notice") he might well have slept the sleep of nervous exhaustion: unless, that is, he was kept awake by an aching right hand, which had been squeezed and pumped by more than a thousand people in the course of this busy New Year's, or by the knowledge that from now on — or at any rate until he found the man who, as he said, could "face the arithmetic"— he would have to continue to act as his own general-in-chief, as in fact he had been doing all along, leaving the West Pointer who occupied the post at present to act as little more than a clerk, albeit a first-rate one.

In the days that followed hard on this, the one touch of relief in a prevailing military gloom was the news that Bragg had retreated from Stones River and that Rosecrans had taken Murfreesboro. Lincoln would have preferred a bolder pursuit, but he was grateful all the same for what he got. "I can never forget, while I remember anything," he told Rosecrans some months later, looking back, "that at about the end of last year, and beginning of this, you gave us a hard-earned victory which, had there been a defeat instead, the nation could scarcely have lived over." The law of diminishing utility obtained here in reverse; by contrast, this one glimmer swelled to bonfire proportions. All else was blackness — even afloat, where up to now the salt-water navy (so long at least as it had kept to its proper medium and stayed out of the muddy Mississippi) had suffered not a single major check in all the more than twenty months since the opening shots were fired at Sumter. Now suddenly all the news was bad and the checks frequent: not only at Galveston, where Magruder's cotton-clads had wrecked and panicked the Union warships, driving them from the bay, but also at other points along and off the rebel shore, before and after that disaster.

The first of these several naval wounds was self-inflicted, so to speak, or at any rate was not the result of enemy action. This did not make it any less painful or sad, however, for though the loss amounted to only one ship, that one was the most famous in the navy. Under tow off stormy Hatteras, with waves breaking over her deck and starting the oakum from her turret seam, the little ironclad *Monitor* — David to the *Merrimac*'s Goliath in Hampton Roads almost ten months ago — foundered and went to the bottom in the first hour of the last day of the year, taking four of her officers and a dozen of her crew down with her. This was hard news for the North, and close on its heels came word of what happened in Galveston harbor the following day. By way of reaction, the squadron commander at Pensacola ordered the 24-gun screw steamer *Brooklyn* and six gunboats to haul off from the blockade of Mobile and proceed at once to Texas to retrieve the situation. They arrived on January 8, but found there was little they could do except resume the blockade outside the harbor and engage in long-range shelling of the island town, now fast in rebel hands. They kept this up for three days, with little or no profit, until on January 11 they were handed another jolt.

About an hour before sundown the *Brooklyn*'s lookout spotted a bark-rigged vessel, apparently a merchantman, approaching from the south. When she saw the blockaders she halted as if surprised, and the Union flag officer, finding her manner suspicious, ordered the 10-gun sidewheel steamer *Hatteras* to heave her to for investigation of her papers. As the gunboat approached, she drew off and the chase began. It was a strange business. She ran awkwardly, despite the trimness of her lines, and though she managed to maintain her distance, on through twilight into a moonless darkness relieved only by the stars, the blockader had no difficulty in keeping her within sight. At last she hove to, as if exhausted, her sails furled. The *Hatteras* closed to within a hundred yards, stopped dead, and put a boat out. Before the boarding party reached her, however, a loud clear voice identified the vessel: "This is the Confederate States steamer *Alabama;* FIRE!" and a broadside lurched her sideways in the water, striking the *Hatteras* hard amidships so that she too recoiled, as if in horror. Ten guns to eight, the Federal outweighed her adversary by one hundred tons, but the advantage of surprise was decisive. Though she promptly returned the fire, the fight was brief. Within thirteen minutes, her walking beam shot away and her magazine flooded, she hoisted the signal for surrender.

"Have you struck?"

"I have."

"Cease fire! Cease fire!"

Within another six minutes she was on the bottom, thirty-fifth on the list of vessels taken, sunk, or ransomed by Captain Raphael Semmes, who would add another thirty-six to the list before the year was out.

He had read in captured Boston newspapers that the 30,000-man expedition under Banks was scheduled to rendezvous off Galveston on January 10 for the conquest of Texas, and he had shown up the following day, intending to get among the transports under cover of darkness, just outside the bar, and sink them left and right. When he saw the gunboats shelling the town, however, he knew it had been retaken, and he seized the opportunity to realize his life's ambition to stage a hand-to-hand fight with an enemy warship, provided he could lure one into pursuit and single combat: which he had done, fluttering just beyond her reach like a wounded bird until, having her altogether to himself, he turned and pounced. He was proud of the outcome of this "first yardarm engagement between steamers at sea," but just now his problem was to get away before his victim's friends, warned of the hoax by the flash and roar of guns, came up to avenge her. Pausing long enough to pick up the 118 survivors — about as many as he had in his whole crew, whose only casualty was a carpenter's mate with a cheek wound — he doused his lights and made off through the night. The *Brooklyn* and the other gunboats, arriving shortly thereafter, saw no sign of the *Hatteras* until dawn showed bits of her wreckage tossed about by the waves. By that time the *Alabama* was a hundred miles away, running hard for Jamaica, where Semmes and his crew — that "precious set of rascals," as he called them, being known in turn as "Old Beeswax" because of the needle-sharp tips to his long black mustache — would parole their captives and celebrate their exploit. Chagrined, the Union skippers turned back to resume their fruitless shelling of the island, bitterly conscious of the fact that instead of redeeming the late Galveston disaster, as they had intended, they had enlarged it.

 Word of this no sooner reached Washington than it was followed, four days later, by news that was potentially even worse. At Mobile, where the departure of the *Brooklyn* and her consorts had weakened the cordon drawn across the entrance to the bay, the other famous Confederate raider *Florida* had been bottled up since early September, when she slipped in through the blockade with her crew and captain, Commander John N. Maffitt, down with yellow fever. By now they were very much up and about, however: as they proved on the night of January 15, when they steered the rebel cruiser squarely between two of the largest and fastest ships in the blockade squadron and made unscathed for the open sea, leaving her frantic pursuers far behind. Within ten days she had captured and sunk three U.S. merchantmen, the first of more then twenty she would take before midsummer, in happy rivalry with her younger sister the *Alabama*. Secretary Welles had been so furious over her penetration of the cordon, four months back, that he had summarily dismissed the squadron commander from the navy, despite the fact that he was a nephew of Commodore Edward Preble of *Constitution* fame; but this repetition of the exploit, outward bound, was seen by some as a reflection on the Secretary himself and a substantiation of the protest a prominent New Yorker had made to Lincoln, on the occasion of the Connecticut journalist's appointment, that if he would "select an attractive figurehead, to be adorned with an elaborate wig and luxuriant whiskers, and transfer it from the prow of a ship to the entrance of the Navy Department, it would in my opinion be quite as serviceable ... and less expensive."

Nor was this by any means the last bad news to reach the Department from down on the Gulf before the month was out. On January 21, at the end of the week that had opened with the *Florida*'s escape, John Magruder staged in Texas — apparently, like Browning's thrush, lest it be thought that the first had been no more than a fine careless rapture — a re-enactment of the previous descent on the Union flotilla in Galveston harbor. This time the scene was Sabine Pass, eighty miles to the east, and once more two cotton-clad steamboats were employed, with like results. The *Morning Light*, a sloop of war, and the schooner *Velocity*, finding themselves unable to maneuver in all the confusion, struck their flags and surrendered 11 guns and more than a hundred seamen to the jubilant Confederates who had come booming down the pass with a rattle of small arms and a caterwaul of high-pitched rebel yells. Next day the blockade was re-established by gunboats sent over from the flotilla cruising off Galveston, but there was little satisfaction in the fact, considering the increase of tension in the wardrooms and on lookout stations. However, a lull now followed, almost as if the crowing rebels were giving the bluejackets time to digest the three bitter pills administered in the course of the past three weeks.

For Lincoln there was no such lull, nor did there seem likely to be one so long as the present commander of the Army of the Potomac remained at his post. He had chosen Burnside primarily as a man of action, and however far the ruff-whiskered general had fallen short of other expectations, from the day of his appointment he had never done less than his fervent best to measure up to this one. The Fredericksburg fight, pressed despite a snarl-up of preparatory matters which had turned it into something quite different from what had been intended at the outset, was an instance of that determination to be up and doing, and Lincoln was in constant trepidation that a similar sequence of snarl-ups — the canceled year-end maneuver, for example — presaged a similar disaster. The signs were unmistakably there.

Four days after the New Year's conference Burnside informed the President that he still intended to attempt another Rappahannock crossing, and had in fact alerted his engineers, although his generals practically unanimously remained opposed to the movement. Inclosed with the note was his resignation; Lincoln could either sustain him or let him return to civilian life. Another letter went to Halleck this same day. "I do not ask you to assume any responsibility in reference to the mode or place of crossing," Burnside wrote, "but it seems to me that, in making so hazardous a movement, I should receive some general directions from you as to the advisability of crossing at some point, as you are necessarily well informed of the effect at this time upon other parts of the army of a success or a repulse." However, this attempt to wring a definite personal commitment from the general-in-chief was no more productive than Lincoln's had been. Halleck — described by a correspondent as resembling "an oleaginous Methodist parson in regimentals," with a "large, tabular, Teutonic" face — replied on January 7, administering an elementary textbook strategy lecture. He had always been in favor of an advance, he said, but he cautioned Burnside to "effect a crossing in a position where we can meet the enemy on favorable or even equal terms.... If the enemy should concentrate his forces at the place you have selected for a crossing, make it a feint and try another place. Again, the circumstances at the time may be such as to render an attempt to cross the entire army not advisable. In that case theory suggests that, while the enemy concentrates at that point, advantages can be gained by crossing smaller forces at other points, to cut off his lines, destroy his communication, and capture his rear guards, outposts, &c. The great object is ... to injure him all you can with the least injury to yourself.... As you yourself admit, it devolves upon you to decide upon the time, place, and character of the crossing which you may attempt. I can only advise that an attempt be made, and as early as possible. Very respectfully, your obedient servant, H. W. Halleck, General-in-Chief."

Burnside had asked for "general directions." What he got was very general advice. Tacked onto it, however, was a presidential indorsement in which, after urging him to "be cautious, and do not understand that the Government or the country is driving you," Lincoln added: "I do not yet see how I could profit by changing the command of the Army of the Potomac, and if I did, I should not do it by accepting the resignation of your commission." The "yet" might well have given Burnside pause, but at any rate he had a sort of left-handed reply to his ultimatum demanding that the President either fire or sustain him. He prepared therefore to go ahead with his plan for an upstream crossing, beyond Lee's left, and a southward march to some rearward point athwart the Confederate lines of supply and communication. This time he intended to guard against failure by feeling his way carefully beforehand. After originally selecting United States Ford as the bridgehead, a dozen miles above Fredericksburg, he rejected it when a cavalry reconnaissance showed the position well covered by Confederate guns, and selected instead Banks Ford, which was not only less heavily protected but was also less than half as far away. By January 19 his preparations were complete. Next morning his soldiers assembled under full packs for the march, stood there while a general order was read to them, and set out with its spirited phrases ringing in their ears: "The commanding general announces to the Army of the Potomac that they are about to meet the enemy once more.... The auspicious moment seems to have arrived to strike a great and mortal blow to the rebellion, and to gain that decisive victory which is due to the country."

It took several hours for so many men to clear their camps, but once this had been done the march went well — indeed, auspiciously — until midafternoon, when a slow drizzle began. For a time it seemed no more than a passing shower, but the sun went down behind a steely curtain of true rain, which was pattering steadily by nightfall. All night it fell; by morning it was drumming without letup. Looking out from their sodden bivouacs, in which they could find not even enough dry twigs for boiling coffee, the soldiers could hardly recognize yesterday's Virginia. "The whole country was an ocean of mud," one wrote. "The roads were rivers of deep mire, and the heavy rain had made the ground a vast mortar bed." Presently, as the troops fell in coffeeless to resume the march in a downpour that showed no sign of slacking, broad-tired wagons loaded with big pontoons (despite all Burnside's precautions against snarl-ups, the pontoniers had been late in getting the word) churned the roads to near-impassability. Their six-mule teams were doubled and even tripled, but to small avail. Then long ropes were attached to the cumbersome things, affording hand-holds for as many as 150 men at a time, but this still did no real good according to a correspondent who watched them strain and fail: "They would flounder through the mire for a few feet — the gang of Lilliputians with their huge-ribbed Gulliver — and then give up breathlessly." Guns were even more perverse. Whole regiments pulled them along with the help of prolonges, leaving deep troughs in the roadbed to mark their progress, but if they stopped for a breather, without first putting brush or logs under the axle, the gun would begin to sink and, what was worse, would keep on sinking until only its muzzle showed, and the men would have to dig it out with shovels. "One might fancy that some new geologic cataclysm had overtaken the world," a reporter declared, surveying the desolation, "and that he saw around him the elemental wrecks left by another Deluge." When Burnside himself, trailing a gaudy kite-tail of staff officers, came riding through this waste of mired confusion, one irreverent teamster whose mules and wagon were stalled like all the rest called out to him across the sea of mud: "General, the auspicious moment has arrived!"

He was undaunted, even in the face of this. Though the rain was still coming down steadily, without a suggestion of a pause, and though most of his soldiers were thinking, as one recalled, that "it was no longer a question of how to go forward, but how to get back," Burnside no more had it in mind to quit now than he had had six weeks ago, when he had kept throwing some of these same men against the fuming base of Marye's Heights. Today was finished but there was still tomorrow, and he gave orders that the march would be resumed at dawn. However, in an attempt to raise the dejected spirits of the troops, he directed that a ration of whiskey be issued to all ranks. Somehow the barrels were brought up in the night and the distribution made next morning. The result, in several cases — for the officers poured liberally and the stuff went into empty stomachs — was spectacular. For example, rival regiments from Pennsylvania and Massachusetts promptly decided the time had come for them to settle a long-term feud, and when a Maine outfit stepped in to try and stop the scuffle, the result was the biggest three-sided fist fight in the history of the world. Meanwhile, from grandstand seats on the crests of hills across the way, the rebels were enjoying all of this enormously. Pickets jeered from the south bank of the Rappahannock, and one butternut cluster went so far as to hold up a crudely lettered placard: THIS WAY TO RICHMOND, underlined with an arrow pointing in the opposite direction. Finally, about noon, even Burnside saw the hopelessness of the situation. He gave orders and the long, bedraggled files of men faced painfully about. The Mud March — so called in the official records — was over.

It was over, that is for most of them, except for the getting back to camp and the consequences. For some, though, it was over then and there; they kept slogging northward, right on out of the war. Desertion reached an all-time high. Sick lists had never been so long. Morale hit an all-time low. "I never knew so much discontent in the army before," an enlisted diarist wrote. "A great many say that they 'don't care whether school keeps or not,' for they think there is a destructive fate hovering over our army." This reaction was by no means limited to the ranks, and what was more the men in higher positions were specific in their placement of the blame. "I came to the conclusion that Burnside was fast losing his mind," Franklin was presently saying, and Hooker was even more emphatic in the expression of his views. Without limiting his criticism to the luckless army commander, whom he considered merely inept, he told a newsman that the President was an imbecile, not only for keeping Burnside on but also in his own right, and that the administration itself was "all played out." What the country needed, Fighting Joe declared, and the sooner the better, too, was a dictator. ... Much of this reached army headquarters in one form or another, and Burnside's thin-stretched patience finally snapped under the double burden of abuse and ridicule. Early next evening, January 23, while his troops were still straggling forlornly back to their camps, he wired Lincoln: "I have prepared some very important orders, and I want to see you before issuing them. Can I see you alone if I am at the White House after midnight?"

In mud and fog and darkness he left headquarters about 9 o'clock in an ambulance, lost the road, found it, then lost it again, bumping into dead mules, stalled caissons, and other derelicts of the late lamented march. Finally, near midnight, he arrived at the Falmouth railhead, two miles from his starting point, only to learn that the special locomotive he had ordered held had given him up and chuffed away on other business. He took a lantern and set out down the track to meet it coming back, flagged and boarded it, and at last got onto a steamer at Aquia Landing. It was midmorning before he was with Lincoln at the White House, but the orders he brought for his perusal were no less startling for having been delayed. What Burnside was suggesting — in fact *ordering*, "subject to the approval of the President" — was the immediate dismissal of four officers from the service and the relief of six from further duty with the Army of the Potomac. The first group was headed by Joe Hooker, who was referred to as "a man unfit to hold an important commission during a crisis like the present, when so much patience, charity, confidence, consideration, and patriotism are due from every soldier in the field." Next came Brigadier General W.T.H. Brooks, a division commander accused of "using language tending to demoralize his command." The other two, lumped together in one paragraph, were Newton and Cochrane, whose names Burnside had learned simply by checking the morning reports to see what general officers had been on pass at the time of their late-December conference with Lincoln. These four were to be cashiered. The six who were to be relieved were two major generals — Franklin and W. F. Smith, Newton's and Cochrane's corps commander — three brigadiers (including, by some strange oversight, Cochrane, who supposedly had just been cashiered) and one lieutenant colonel, a lowly assistant adjutant who was apparently to be struck by an incidental pellet from the blast that was to bring down all those other, larger birds.

Burnside left the order with the startled President, telling him plainly to make a choice between approving it or accepting its author's resignation from command of an army that included such a set of villains. The order was dated the 23d, a Friday. Lincoln took what was left of Saturday to think the matter over. Then on Sunday, January 25, the ruff-whiskered general got his answer in the form of a general order of Lincoln's own, directing: 1) that Burnside be relieved of command, upon his own request; 2) that Sumner be relieved, also upon his own request; 3) that Franklin be relieved, period; and 4) "that Maj. Gen. J. Hooker be assigned to the command of the Army of the Potomac."

This last was a hard thing for the departing commander to accept. He had planned to blow up Hooker, but instead he had blown himself up, and Hooker into his place. It was hard, too, for Sumner and for Franklin; the fact that both were the new commander's seniors necessitated their transfer after long association with the eastern army. Lincoln did not so much regret having to sidetrack Franklin, whose lack of aggressiveness at South Mountain and Fredericksburg was notorious, but he was sorry to have to offend the superannuated Sumner, who had saved the day at Fair Oaks and fought well on every field until his soul was sickened by the slaughter at Antietam. Nor had he hurt without regret the normally good-natured Burnside, whose forthright honesty in admission of faults and acceptance of blame was so different from what was ordinarily encountered. However, what there had been of hesitation was mainly based on what Lincoln knew of Fighting Joe himself, who was next in line for the assignment. He had heard from others beside Burnside of Hooker's infidelity to his chief, and also of his excoriation of the Washington authorities. In fact, when the *Times* reporter who had talked recently with Hooker came to Lincoln on this Sunday and told him of what the general had said about the administration's shortcomings and the need for a dictator, Lincoln showed no trace of surprise. "That is all true; Hooker does talk badly," he admitted. But he decided, all the same, that Hooker was what the army and the country needed in the present crisis — a fighter who, unlike Burnside, had self-confidence and a reputation for canniness. "Now there is Joe Hooker," Lincoln had remarked a short time back. "He can fight. I think that is pretty well established."

And so it was. Without consulting Halleck or Stanton or anyone else, and despite the admitted risk to the national cause and the incidental injury to Burnside and Sumner, he made his choice and acted on it. However, before the new commander had been two days at his post, Lincoln sent for him and handed him a letter which was calculated to let him know how much he knew about him, as well as to advise him of what was now expected:

> General:
> I have placed you at the head of the Army of the Potomac. Of course I have done this upon what appear to me to be sufficient reasons, and yet I think it best for you to know that there are some things in regard to which I am not quite satisfied with you. I believe you to be a brave and a skillful soldier, which of course I like. I also believe you do not mix politics with your profession, in which you are right. You have confidence in yourself, which is a valuable if not an indispensable quality. You are ambitious, which, within reasonable bounds, does good rather than harm; but I think that during General Burnside's command of the army you have taken counsel of your ambition and thwarted him as much as you could, in which you did a great wrong to the country and to a most meritorious and honorable brother officer. I have heard, in such way as to believe it, of your recently saying that both the army and the government needed a dictator. Of course it was not for this, but in spite of it, that I have given you the command. Only those generals who gain successes can set up dictators. What I now ask of you is military success, and I will risk the dictatorship. The government will support you to the utmost of its ability, which is neither more nor less than it has done and will do for all commanders. I much fear that the spirit which you have aided to infuse into the army, of criticising their commander and withhold-

ing confidence from him, will now turn upon you. I shall assist you as far as I can to put it down. Neither you nor Napoleon, if he were alive again, could get any good out of an army while such a spirit prevails in it.

And now, beware of rashness. Beware of rashness, but with energy and sleepless vigilance go forward and give us victories.

Yours very truly
A. LINCOLN

✵ 2 ✵

McClernand, conferring with Sherman at Milliken's Bend on the day after his arrival from upriver — it was January 3; the two were aboard the former Illinois politician's headquarters boat, the *Tigress*, tied up to bank twenty-odd miles above Vicksburg — did not blame the redhaired Ohioan for the repulse suffered earlier that week at Chickasaw Bluffs; Sherman, he said in a letter to Stanton that same day, had "probably done all in the present case anyone could have done." The fault was Grant's, and Grant's alone. Grant had designed the operation and then, taking off half-cocked in his eagerness for glory that was rightfully another's, had failed to co-operate as promised, leaving Sherman to hold the bag and do the bleeding. So McClernand said, considerably embittered by the knowledge that a good part of the nearly two thousand casualties lost up the Yazoo were recruits he had been sending down from Cairo for the past two months, only to have them snatched from under him while his back was turned. "I believe I am superseded. Please advise me," he had wired Lincoln as soon as he got word of what was afoot. But permission to go downriver had not come in time for him to circumvent the circumvention; the fighting was over before he got there. He took what consolation he could from having been spared a share in a fiasco. At least he was with his men again — what was left of them, at any rate — and ready to take over. "Soon as I shall have verified the condition of the army," he told Stanton, "I will assume command of it."

He did so the following day. Christening his new command "The Army of the Mississippi" in nominal expression of his intentions, or at any rate his hopes, he divided it into two corps of two divisions each, the first under George Morgan and the second under Sherman — which, incidentally, was something of a bitter pill for the latter to swallow, since he believed a large share of the blame for the recent failure up the Yazoo rested with Morgan, who had promised that in ten minutes he would "be on those hills," but who apparently had forgot to wind his watch. However that might be, McClernand now had what he had been wanting all along: the chance to prove his ingenuity and demonstrate his mettle in independent style. His eyes brightened with anticipation of triumph as he spoke of "opening the navigation of the Mississippi," of "cutting my way to the sea," and so forth. For all the expansiveness of his mood, however, the terms in which he expressed it were more general than specific; or, as Sherman later said, "the *modus operandi* was not so clear."

In this connection — being anxious, moreover, to balance his recent defeat with a success — the Ohioan had a suggestion. During the Chickasaw Bluffs expedition the packet *Blue Wing*, coming south out of Memphis with a cargo of mail and ammunition, had been captured by a Confederate gunboat that swooped down on her near the mouth of the Arkansas and carried her forty miles up that river to Arkansas Post, an outpost established by the French away back in 1685, where the rebels had constructed an inclosed work they called Fort Hindman, garrisoned by about 5000 men. So long as this threat to the main Federal supply line existed, Sherman said, operations against Vicksburg would be subject to such harassment, and it was his belief that, by way of preamble to McClernand's larger plans — whatever they were, precisely — he ought to go up the Arkansas and abolish the threat by "thrashing out Fort Hindman."

McClernand was not so sure. He had suffered no defeat that needed canceling, and what was more he had larger things in mind than the capture of an obscure and isolated post. However, he agreed to go with Sherman for a discussion of the project with Porter, whose co-operation would be required. They steamed downriver and found the admiral aboard his headquarters boat, the *Black Hawk*, anchored in the mouth of the Yazoo. It was late, near midnight; Porter received them in his nightshirt. He too was not so sure at first. He was short of coal, he said, and the ironclads, which would be needed to reduce the fort, could not burn wood. Presently, though, as Sherman continued to press his suit, asking at least for the loan of a couple of gunboats, which he offered to tow up the river and thus save coal, Porter — perhaps reflecting that he had on his record that same blot which a victory would erase — not only agreed to give the landsmen naval support; "Suppose I go along myself?" he added. Suddenly, on second thought, McClernand was convinced: so much so, indeed, that instead of merely sending Sherman to do the job with half the troops, as Sherman had expected, he decided it was worth the undivided attention of the whole army and its commander, whose record, if blotless, was also blank. With no minus to cancel, this plus would stand alone, auspicious, and make a good beginning as he stepped off on the road that led to glory and the White House.

He took three days to get ready, then (but not until then) sent a message by way of Memphis to notify Grant that he was off — one of his purposes being, as he said, "the counteraction of the moral effect of the failure of the attack near Vicksburg and the reinspiration of the forces repulsed by making them the champions of new, important, and successful enterprises." He left Milliken's Bend that same day, January 8, his 30,000 soldiers still aboard their fifty transports, accompanied by 13 rams and gunboats, three of which were ironclads and packed his Sunday punch. By way of deception the flotilla steamed past the mouth of the Arkansas, then into the White, from which a cutoff led back into the bypassed river. Late the following afternoon the troops began debarking three miles below Fort Hindman, a square bastioned work set on high ground at the head of a horseshoe bend, whose dozen guns included three 9-inch Columbiads, one to each riverward casemate, and a hard-hitting 8-inch rifle. A good portion of the defending butternut infantry, supported by six light pieces of field artillery, occupied a line of rifle-pits a mile and a half below the fort, but these were quickly driven out when the gunboats forged ahead and took them under fire from the flank. Late the following afternoon, when the debarkation had been completed and the four divisions were maneuvering for positions from which to launch an assault, the ironclads took the lead. The *Louisville*, the *De Kalb*, and the *Cincinnati* advanced in line abreast to within four hundred yards of the fort, pressing the attack bows on, one to each casemate, while the thinner-skinned vessels followed close behind to throw in shrapnel and light rifled shell. It was hot work for a time as the defenders stood to their guns, firing with precision; the *Cincinnati*, for example, took eight hits from 9-inch shells on her pilot house alone, though Porter reported proudly that they "glanced off like peas against glass"; the only naval casualties were suffered from unlucky shots that came in through the ports. When the admiral broke off the fight because of darkness, the fort was silent, apparently overwhelmed. But when Sherman, reconnoitering by moonlight, drew close to the enemy outposts he could hear the Confederates at work with spades and axes, drawing a new line under cover of their heavy guns and preparing to continue to resist despite the long numerical odds. Crouched behind a stump in the predawn darkness of January 11 he heard a rebel bugler sound what he later called "as pretty a reveille as I ever listened to."

    Shortly before noon he sent word that he was ready. His corps was on the right, Morgan's on the left; both faced the newly drawn enemy line which extended across the rear of the fort, from the river to an impassable swamp one mile west. McClernand, having established a command post in the woods and sent a lookout up a tree to observe and report the progress of events, passed the word to Porter, who ordered the ironclads forward at 1.30 to renew yesterday's attack. Sherman heard the clear ring of the naval guns, the fire increasing in volume and rapidity as the range was closed. Then he and Morgan went forward, the troops advancing by rushes across the open fields, "once or twice falling to the ground," as Sherman said, "for a sort of rest or pause." As they approached the fort they saw above its parapet the pennants of the ironclads, which had smothered the heavy guns by now and were giving the place a close-up pounding. Simultaneously, white flags began to break out all along the rebel line. "Cease firing! Cease firing!" Sherman cried, and rode forward to receive the fort's surrender.

But that was not to be: not just yet, at any rate, and not to Sherman. Colonel John Dunnington, the fort's commander, a former U.S. naval officer, insisted on surrendering to Porter, and Brigadier General Thomas J. Churchill, commander of the field force, did not want to surrender at all. As Sherman approached, Churchill was arguing with his subordinates, wanting to know by whose authority the white flags had been shown. (He had received an order from Little Rock the night before, while there was still a chance to get away, "to hold out till help arrives or until all dead" — which Holmes later explained with the comment: "It never occurred to me when the order was issued that such an overpowering command would be devoted to an end so trivial.") One brigade commander, Colonel James Deshler of Alabama, a fiery West Pointer in his late twenties — "small but very handsome," Sherman called him — did not want to stop fighting even now, with the Yankees already inside his works. When Sherman, wishing as he said "to soften the blow of defeat," remarked in a friendly way that he knew a family of Deshlers in his home state and wondered if they were relations, the Alabamian hotly disclaimed kinship with anyone north of the Ohio River; whereupon the red-headed general changed his tone and, as he later wrote, "gave him a piece of my mind that he did not relish." However, all this was rather beside the point. The fighting was over and the butternut troops stacked arms. The Federals had suffered 31 navy and 1032 army casualties, for a total of 140 killed and 923 wounded. The Confederates, on the other hand, had had only 109 men hit; but that left 4791 to be taken captive, including a regiment that marched in from Pine Bluff during the surrender negotiations.

McClernand, who had got back aboard the *Tigress* and come forward, was tremendously set up. "Glorious! Glorious!" he kept exclaiming. "My star is ever in the ascendant." He could scarcely contain himself. "I had a man up a tree," he said. "I'll make a splendid report!"

Grant by now was in Memphis. He had arrived the day before, riding in ahead of the main body, which was still on the way under McPherson, near the end of its long retrograde movement from Coffeeville, northward through the scorched wreckage of Holly Springs, then westward by way of Grand Junction and LaGrange. Having heard no word from Sherman, he knew nothing of his friend's defeat downriver — optimistic as always, he was even inclined to credit rumors that the Vicksburg defenses had crumbled under assault from the Yazoo —

until the evening of his arrival, when he received McClernand's letter from Milliken's Bend informing him of the need for "reinspiration of the forces repulsed."

This was something of a backhand slap, at least by implication — McClernand seemed to be saying that he would set right what Grant had bungled — but what disturbed him most was the Illinois general's expressed intention to withdraw upriver for what he called "new, important, and successful enterprises." For one thing, if Banks was on the way up from New Orleans in accordance with the instructions for a combined assault on Vicksburg, it would leave him unsupported when he got there. For another, any division of effort was wrong as long as the true objective remained unaccomplished, and Grant said so in no uncertain terms next morning when he replied to McClernand's letter: "I do not approve of your move on the Post of Arkansas while the other is in abeyance. It will lead to the loss of men without a result. . . . It might answer for some of the purposes you suggest, but certainly not as a military movement looking to the accomplishment of the one great result, the capture of Vicksburg. Unless you are acting under authority not derived from me, keep your command where it can soonest be assembled for the renewal of the attack on Vicksburg. . . . From the best information I have, Milliken's Bend is the proper place for you to be, and unless there is some great reason of which I am not advised you will immediately proceed to that point and await the arrival of reinforcements and General Banks' expedition, keeping me fully advised of your movements."

He expressed his opinion more briefly in a telegram sent to Halleck that afternoon: "General McClernand has fallen back to White River, and gone on a wild-goose chase to the Post of Arkansas. I am ready to reinforce, but must await further information before knowing what to do." The general-in-chief replied promptly the following morning, January 12: "You are hereby authorized to relieve General McClernand from command of the expedition against Vicksburg, giving it to the next in rank or taking it yourself."

Grant now had what he wanted. Formerly he had moved with caution in the prosecution of his private war, by no means sure that in wrecking McClernand he would not be calling down the thunder on his own head; but not now. Halleck almost certainly would have discussed so important a matter with Lincoln before adding this ultimate weapon to Grant's arsenal and assuring him that there would be no restrictions from above as to its use. In short, Grant could proceed without fear of retaliation except from the victim himself, whom he outranked. However, two pieces of information that came to hand within the next twenty-four hours forestalled delivery of the blow. First, he learned that Port Hudson was a more formidable obstacle than he had formerly supposed, which meant that it was unlikely that Banks's upriver thrust would reach Vicksburg at any early date. And, second, he received next day from McClernand himself the "splendid report" announcing the fall of Arkansas Post and the capture of "a large number of prisoners, variously estimated at from 7000 to 10,000, together with all [their] stores, animals, and munitions of war." Not only was the urgency for a hookup with Banks removed, but to proceed against McClernand now would be to attack a public hero in his first full flush of victory; besides which, Grant had also learned that the inception of what he had called the "wild-goose chase" had been upon the advice of his friend Sherman, and this put a different complexion on his judgment as to the military soundness of the expedition. All that remained was to play the old army game — which Grant well knew how to do, having had it played against him with such success, nine years ago in California, that he had been nudged completely out of the service. When the time came for pouncing he would pounce, but not before. Meanwhile he would wait, watching and building up his case as he did so.

This did not mean that he intended to sit idly by while McClernand continued to gather present glory; not by a long shot. Four days later, January 17 — McClernand having returned as ordered to the Mississippi, awaiting further instructions at Napoleon, just below the mouth of the Arkansas — Grant got aboard a steamboat headed south from the Memphis wharf. Before leaving he wired McPherson, who had called a halt at LaGrange to rest his troops near the end of their long retreat from Coffeeville: "It is my present intention to command the expedition down the river in person."

★ ★ ★

Banks was going to be a lot longer in reaching Vicksburg than Grant knew, and more was going to detain him than the guns that bristled atop the bluff at Port Hudson. After a sobering look at this bastion he decided that his proper course of action, before attempting a reduction of that place or a sprint past its frowning batteries, would be a move up the opposite bank of the big river, clearing out the various nests of rebels who otherwise would interfere with his progress by harassing his flank as he moved upstream. Brigadier General Godfrey Weitzel, a twenty-eight-year-old West Pointer who already had been stationed in that direction by Ben Butler, was reinforced by troops from the New Orleans and Baton Rouge garrisons and told to make the region west of those two cities secure from molestation. He built a stout defensive work at Donaldsonville, commanding the head of Bayou La Fourche, and threw up intrenchments at Brashear City, blocking the approach from Berwick Bay. Then, crossing the bay with his mobile force on January 13, he entered and began to ascend the Teche, accompanied by three gunboats. This brought him into sudden contact next morning with Richard Taylor, who fought briefly and fell back, sinking the armed steamer *Cotton* athwart the bayou as he did so, corking it against farther penetration. Weitzel, who had lost 33 killed and wounded, including one of the navy skippers picked off by a sniper, reported proudly as he withdrew: "The Confederate States gunboat *Cotton* is one of the things that were.... My men behaved magnificently. I am recrossing the bay."

As a successful operation — the first of what he intended would be many — this was unquestionably gratifying to Banks, who made the most of it in reporting the action to Washington as a follow-up to the bloodless reoccupation of the Louisiana capital. Yet even as he tendered his thanks to Weitzel for "the skillful manner in which he has performed the task confided to him," he could also see much that was foreboding in this small-scale expedition up the Teche. For one thing, the rebels were very much there, though in what numbers he did not know, and for another they would fight, but only as it suited them, choosing the time and place that gave them the best advantage, fading back into the rank undergrowth quite as mysteriously as they had appeared, and then moving forward again as the bluecoats withdrew from what Taylor himself, who knew all its crooks and byways, called "a region of lakes, bayous, jungle, and bog." How long it might take to clear such an army of phantoms from the district, or whether indeed it could ever be done, Banks could not tell. By mid-January, however, he had decided that it would have to be done. His expectations, described in mid-December as "most sanguine," were tempered now by prudence and better acquaintance with the peculiar factors involved. He perceived that they would have to be refashioned to conform to a different schedule before he attempted the reduction of Port Hudson and the eventual link-up with Grant in front of Vicksburg, all those devious hundreds of miles up the tawny Mississippi.

In Northwest Arkansas and South Missouri things were not going much better for John Schofield, who had risen from a sickbed to resume command of his army on the morrow of Prairie Grove. They could in fact be said to be going a good deal worse, so far at least as personal vexation was concerned. He had won a battle (or anyhow Blunt and Herron had, with the result that they were about to be promoted over his head) and had followed it up with a lunge at Van Buren, resulting in the destruction of Hindman's stores, before withdrawing to Fayetteville; but he had no sooner regained the presumed security of this pro-Union district, where he expected to enjoy in comparative relaxation his belated but welcome promotion to major general, than he was distracted by a series of explosions in his rear. First, Hindman unleashed his cavalry under Brigadier General John S. Marmaduke, a Missouri-born West Pointer, for an all-out raid on the main Federal supply base at Springfield, a hundred miles north of the point where Schofield was in the process of drawing his lines facing south. On New Year's Eve Marmaduke left Lewisburg, on the north bank of the Arkansas River midway across the state, and reached his objective one week later at the head of 2300 horsemen, many of them picked up along the way and added to the original brigade of veterans under Colonel J. O. Shelby, who had led them on every field since Wilson's Creek. Attacking on January 8 the raiders burned the Springfield depot of supplies and withdrew eastward 45 miles to strike at Hartville on the 11th, with similar results after savage fighting, then turned south through a gale of sleet and snow, gobbling up enemy detachments as they went, and recrossed the White River at Batesville on January 25.

Casualties in the two main fights had been about 250 on each side, in addition to which Marmaduke not only had captured and paroled more than 300 of the enemy in the course of the raid, for the most part turning them loose in bitter weather without their outer garments — "In winter," one observer remarked, "the overcoat-bearing Federal was esteemed especially for his pelt" — but also had destroyed vital reserve supplies and refitted his troopers with arms and equipment greatly superior to the ones they had carried northward. All this came out of Schofield's pocket, so to speak, but that was by no means the most painful aftereffect of the operation. Major General Samuel Curtis, promoted to command of the department as a result of his Pea Ridge victory back in March, took alarm and ordered the Army of the Frontier withdrawn from Fayetteville to protect the penetrated region across the state line in its rear, abolishing at a stroke the hard-won gains of Prairie Grove. Schofield protested, to no avail; Missouri soon had greater need than ever for on-the-spot protection, Marmaduke's excursion having served to bring the guerillas out of hiding and onto the highways, along which new recruits hastened to join the bands reassembling under such leaders as George Todd, David Pool, William C. Anderson, called "Bloody Bill," and William C. Quantrill. Enrolling was a simple process. All a recruit had to do was answer "Yes" to the question: "Will you follow orders, be true to your fellows, and kill all those who serve and support the Union?"

In the wake of this sudden activity, in effect not unlike the upsetting of a beehive, came violent dissension in the ranks of the Union leaders. Curtis, a former Iowa Republican congressman and abolitionist, represented the radical faction, while Schofield, with the support of Governor Hamilton R. Gamble, became the champion of conservative views. Militarily, as well, the two generals were divergent in opinion. Curtis wanted to hold all available troops within the borders of the state in order to use them in putting down troublemakers of all sorts, armed or unarmed; Schofield on the other hand believed in taking the offensive against the Confederates to his front in Arkansas. At length, as the situation grew more tense between the two, Lincoln was appealed to as arbitrator. He backed the department commander, ordering Schofield east of the Mississippi and leaving the hero of Pea Ridge in full control. However, the storm of protest which followed this decision gave promise of greater trouble than ever, and caused him to seek a different solution. Transferring Curtis out to Kansas, where his political views would be more in accord with those of the majority of the people, Lincoln appointed as the new commander of the Department of Missouri old Edwin V. Sumner, lately relieved of duty with the Army of the Potomac. But this did not work either; Sumner died en route. . . . It was March 21. Breaking his journey at Syracuse, New York, the old soldier lay in a coma, as if in belated reaction to the horror of Antietam, where he had begun to lose the grip that had been strong enough to save the day at Fair Oaks. "The Second Corps never lost a flag or a cannon!" he suddenly cried out. When his aide came over he opened his eyes. "That is true; never lost one," he said weakly. At sixty-six he was nearing the end of forty-four years of army service, and except for his long sharp nose he resembled a death's-head. The aide raised him to a more comfortable position on the bed and poured him a glass of wine, prescribed by the doctor to keep up his strength. Sumner took a sip, saying across the rim of the glass by way of a toast: "God save my country, the United States of America," then dropped the glass and died. . . . Lincoln, receiving the news of Sumner's death, decided that Schofield was probably the best man to take charge in Missouri after all. In reassigning him to duty there, however, he thought it proper to give him some advice on how to proceed among people who were engaged in what he called "a pestilent factional quarrel among themselves." It was, he said in the accents of Polonius, "a difficult role, and so much greater will be the honor if you perform it well. If both factions, or neither, shall abuse you, you will probably be about right. Beware of being assailed by one and praised by the other."

The trouble with this, as advice, was that it was the counsel of perfection, since the only way a man could avoid factions, being championed on the one hand and excoriated on the other, was to stay out of Missouri in the first place. Schofield, a rather plump New York West Pointer who wore a long thin growth of curly whiskers in partial compensation for the fact that he was already balding at the age of thirty-two, was quite aware of this, of course, but promised to do his best in that regard. At the same time, however — it was late spring by then, well up in May — he had to forgo his plans for an offensive into Arkansas, not only because of guerilla troubles within his department (they continued to grow worse as time went by, until at last they exceeded in horror the wildest nightmares Curtis or anyone else, except possibly Bill Anderson and Quantrill — not to mention old John Brown — had ever had) but also because he lacked the troops, Missouri having become in effect a recruiting ground for the support of operations far down the big river that laved its eastern flank. Schofield could only give what he had promised, his best, and if this was not a great deal, under the nearly impossible circumstances it was enough.

He could take consolation, however, in the fact that the Confederates to the south were quite as bedeviled as he himself was, though in a different way: with the result that throughout this unhappy season, when so much of military importance was moving inexorably toward a climax on the east flank of the theater, they were no more able to assume the offensive than Schofield was. Not only were they suffering from an even more acute shortage of troops, but a sequence of rapid-fire shifts in command, beginning at the very top, quite paralyzed whatever movements they might otherwise have undertaken.

Not that the shifts were avoidable. It had in fact already become apparent that Holmes had been given a good deal more than he could handle. In mid-January, a week after his return to Richmond from his western journey, Davis sent for Kirby Smith, whom he admired, and assigned him to command the newly created Department of West Louisiana and Texas, intending in this way to relieve Holmes of the task of co-ordinating the efforts of Taylor and Magruder. "Am I thus to be sent into exile?" Smith asked wistfully. Not yet thirty-nine, he ranked second among the nation's seven lieutenant generals, and Lee himself had lately said that he would be pleased to have him as a corps commander, alongside Longstreet and Jackson. Davis explained that the assignment, far from amounting to exile, was as important as any in the whole Confederacy, since his main duty "would be directed to aiding in the defense of the Lower Mississippi and keeping that great artery of the West effectually closed to Northern occupation or trade." Acquiescing, Smith set out in early February, only to learn en route that his command had been enlarged to include the entire Transmississippi. In the light of this he arranged with Pemberton for the transfer of Major General Sterling Price, who was much admired in the Far West and had formerly been governor of Missouri, the scene of his early victories at Wilson's Creek and Lexington. It was hoped that Price would repeat them presently, although a sadly large proportion of the men with whom he had won them were buried now in shallow graves around Corinth and Iuka, and the survivors, few as they were in number, were too badly needed around Vicksburg to be allowed to recross the river. How he would replace them Smith did not know, for the region had been stripped of troops, first by Van Dorn, who had brought them east after his defeat at Elkhorn Tavern, and then by Hindman, who, by stringent enforcement of the conscription laws, had raised the army which he had taken across the Boston Mountains and then returned with no more than a comparative handful. Smith soon found his worst fears confirmed. "The male population remaining are old men, or have furnished substitutes," he reported, "are lukewarm, or are wrapped up in speculation and money-making."

Crossing at Port Hudson, he ascended Red River in a steamboat Richard Taylor had waiting for him by prearrangement, and on March 7 at Alexandria, Louisiana, he assumed command of all troops west of the Mississippi. What he encountered first-off gave his Regular Army nature quite a shock. "There was no general system, no common head," he later reported; "each district was acting independently." It was necessary, he said, to "begin *de novo* in any attempt at a general systematizing and development of the department resources." Accordingly he set out at once on a preliminary tour of inspection, which only served to increase his first dismay. Conferring with Holmes at Little Rock — the North Carolinian now had charge of the subdepartment including Arkansas, Missouri, and Indian Territory — he found him anxiously awaiting the arrival of Price to command the army remnant left by Hindman, who had resigned in a huff at having been superseded by Holmes on the occasion of that officer's step-down from command of the whole theater. Price arrived before the end of the month, yet there was little he could do until he got his men in condition to fight, which obviously would not be soon. Smith meantime established his headquarters at Shreveport. He considered it "a miserable place with a miserable population," but it had the virtue of central location, at the head of navigation of Red River and on the direct route between Texas and Richmond. Here he set to work, laying the groundwork for organization of the enormous region which in time would be known as Kirby-Smithdom. He worked long hours and did not spare himself or his subordinates; but spring had come, and so had Banks and Grant, before his command — which included, in all, about 30,000 soldiers between the Mississippi and the Rio Grande, fewer even than Bragg had in the Duck River Valley or Pemberton had at Vicksburg and Port Hudson — was in any condition to offer them anything more than a token resistance.

★ ★ ★

After an all-night boat ride down the Mississippi, from Memphis past the mouth of the Arkansas, Grant reached Napoleon on January 18 to find McClernand, Porter, and Sherman awaiting his arrival with mixed emotions — mixed, that is, so far as McClernand's were concerned; Porter and Sherman were united, if by nothing more than a mutual and intense dislike of the congressman-turned-commander. To them, Grant came as something of a savior, since he outranked the object of their scorn. To McClernand, on the other hand, he seemed nothing of the sort; McClernand plainly suspected another attempt to steal his thunder, if not his army. He had enlarged his Arkansas Post exploit by sending a pair of gunboats up White River to drive the rebels from St Charles and wreck their installations at De Valls Bluff, terminus of the railroad running east from Little Rock toward Memphis. It was smartly done, accomplishing at the latter place the destruction of the depot and some rolling stock, as well as the capture of two 8-inch guns which the flustered garrison was trying to load aboard the cars for a getaway west. Still at Fort Hindman while this was in progress, McClernand received Grant's curt and critical letter ordering him back to the Mississippi at once, and he bucked it along to Lincoln with a covering letter of his own.

"I believe my success here is gall and wormwood to the clique of West Pointers who have been persecuting me for months," he wrote, imploring his friend and fellow-townsman not to "let me be clandestinely destroyed, or, what is worse, dishonored, without a hearing." He asked, "How can General Grant at a distance of 400 miles intelligently command the army with me?" and answered his own question without a pause: "He cannot do it. It should be made an independent command, as both you and the Secretary of War, as I believe, originally intended."

Grant was about to get in some licks of his own in this regard, if not through out-of-channels access to Lincoln — whom he had not only never met, but had never even seen, despite the fact that both had gone to war from Illinois — then at any rate through Halleck, which was the next-best thing. For the present he merely conferred with the three officers, collectively and singly, and ordered the return of the whole expedition to Milliken's Bend for a renewal of the drive on Vicksburg by the direct route. By now, however, as a result of his talk with these men who had been there, he was beginning to see that the only successful approach, after all, might have to be roundabout. "What may be necessary to reduce the place I do not yet know," he wired the general-in-chief, "but since the late rains [I] think our troops must get below the city to be used effectually."

He spent the night ashore at Napoleon, whose partial destruction by incendiaries the day before caused Sherman to declare that he was "free to admit we all deserve to be killed unless we can produce a state of discipline when such disgraceful acts cannot be committed unpunished." One solution, he decided, would be "to assess the damages upon the whole army, officers included," but no such drastic remedy was adopted. The following morning Grant saw the transports and their escort vessels steam away south, in accordance with his orders, and returned that evening to Memphis. Next day, January 20, he sent Halleck a long dispatch explaining the tactical situation as he saw it and announcing that, by way of a start, he intended to try his hand at redigging the canal across the base of the hairpin bend in front of Vicksburg, abandoned the previous summer by Butler's men when the two Union fleets were sundered and repulsed by the rebel warship *Arkansas*, now fortunately at the bottom of the river. Grant suggested that, in view of the importance of the campaign he was about to undertake, it would be wise to combine the four western departments, now under Banks, Curtis, Rosecrans, and himself, under a single over-all commander in order to assure co-operation. "As I am the senior department commander in the West," he wrote — apparently unaware that Banks was nine months his senior and in point of fact had been a major general before Grant himself was even a brigadier — "I will state that I have no desire whatever for such combined command, but would prefer the command I now have to any other than can be given." From which disclaimer he passed at once to the subject of John McClernand: "I regard it as my duty to state that I found there was not sufficient confidence felt in General McClernand as a commander, either by the Army or Navy, to insure him success. Of course, all would co-operate to the best of their ability, but still with a distrust. This is a matter I made no inquiries about, but it was thrust upon me." (As a later observer pointed out, there was "a touch of artfulness" in this; Grant "elevated Sherman and Porter to speak for entire branches of the service, then sought audiences with them so that the issue might be forced upon him!") However, he continued, "as it is my intention to command in person, unless otherwise directed, there is no special necessity of mentioning this matter; but I want you to know that others besides myself agree in the necessity of the course I had already determined upon pursuing."

His belief that Old Brains was on his side was strengthened the following day by a quick reply to his suggestion that "both banks of the Mississippi should be under one command, at least during the present operations." "The President has directed that so much of Arkansas as you may desire to control be temporarily attached to your department," Halleck wired. "This will give you control of both banks of the river." Pleased to learn of Lincoln's support, even at second hand, Grant kept busy with administrative and logistical matters preparatory to his departure from Memphis at the earliest possible date. McPherson was marching in from LaGrange with two divisions to accompany him downriver; these 14,979, added to the 32,015 already there, would give him an "aggregate present" of 46,994 in the vicinity of Vicksburg, with more to follow, not only from his own Department of the Tennessee, which included a grand total of 93,816 of all arms, but also from the Department of Missouri, now under Curtis and later under Schofield. On January 25 he received further evidence of Lincoln's interest in the campaign for control of the Lower Mississippi, whose whimsical habit of carving itself new channels the Chief Executive knew from having made two flatboat voyages down it to New Orleans as a youth. "Direct your attention particularly to the canal proposed across the point," Halleck urged. "The President attaches much importance to this."

Grant himself was about ready to embark by now, wiring the general-in-chief this same day: "I leave for the fleet . . . tomorrow." Last-minute details held him up an extra day, but on the 27th he was off. "The work of reducing Vicksburg will take time and men," he had told Halleck the week before, "but can be accomplished."

Sherman was already hard at work on the project which had drawn Lincoln's particular attention, and with his present arduous endeavor — in effect a gigantic wrestling match with Mother Nature herself, or at any rate with her son the Father of Waters — added to his previous bloody experience up the Yazoo, he could testify as to the validity of Grant's long-range observation that the conquest of Vicksburg would "take time and men." In fact, he was inclined to think it might require so much of both commodities as to prove impossible. Both were expendable in the ordinary sense, but after all there were limits. He was discouraged, he wrote his senator brother John this week, by the lack of substantial progress by Union arms, East and West, and by the unexpected resilience of the Confederates, civilian as well as military: "Two years have passed and the rebel flag still haunts our nation's capital. Our armies enter the best rebel territory and the wave closes in behind. The utmost we can claim is that our enemy respects our power to do them physical harm more than they did at first; but as to loving us any more, it were idle even to claim it. . . . I still see no end," he added, "or even the beginning of the end."

Perhaps the senseless burning of Napoleon the week before was on his mind or conscience, but the truth was he had enough on his hands to distress him here and now. The rain continued to come down hard — even harder, perhaps, than it was falling along the Rappahannock, where Burnside's Mud March was coming to its sticky close and the soldiers were composing a parody of a bedtime prayer:

> *Now I lay me down to sleep*
> *In mud that's many fathoms deep.*
> *If I'm not here when you awake*
> *Just hunt me up with an oyster rake*

— with the result that Sherman's men, in addition to having to widen and deepen the old canal, which was little more than a narrow ditch across the base of the low-lying tongue of land, had to work day and night at throwing up a levee along its right flank in order not to be washed away by water from the flooded bayous in their rear. Besides, even if the river could be persuaded to scour out a new channel along this line and thus "leave Vicksburg out in the cold," as Sherman said, it would be no great gain so far as he could see. The Confederates would merely shift their guns southward along the bluff to command the river at and below the outlet, leaving the shovel-weary Federals no better off than before. So he told his brother. And Porter, watching his red-haired friend slosh around in the mud and lose his temper a dozen times a day — "half sailor, half soldier, with a touch of the snapping turtle," he called him — once more found it necessary to bolster Sherman's spirits with hot rum and rollicking words. "If this rain lasts much longer we will not need a canal," he ended a note to the unhappy general on January 27. "I think the whole point will disappear, troops and all, in which case the gunboats will have the field to themselves."

Next day, however, Grant arrived, and Porter, reporting the fact to Welles, could say: "I hope for a better state of things."

※ 3 ※

The word *shoddy* was comparatively new, having originated during the present century in Yorkshire, where it was used in reference to almost worthless quarry stone or nearly unburnable coal. Crossing the ocean to America it took on other meanings, at first being used specifically to designate an inferior woolen yarn made from fibers taken from worn-out fabrics and reprocessed, then later as the name for the resultant cloth itself. "Poor sleezy stuff," one of Horace Greeley's *Tribune* reporters called it, "woven open enough for sieves, and then filled with shearmen's dust," while *Harper's Weekly* used even harsher words in referring to it as "a villainous compound, the refuse and sweepings of the shop, pounded, rolled, glued, and smoothed to the external form and gloss of cloth, but no more like the genuine article than the shadow is to the substance." Thoroughly indignant, the magazine went on to tell how "soldiers, on the first day's march or in the earliest storm, found their clothes, overcoats, and blankets scattering to the wind in rags or dissolving into their primitive elements of dust under the pelting rain."

It followed that the merchants and manufacturers who supplied the government with such cloth became suddenly and fantastically rich in the course of their scramble for contracts alongside others of their kind, the purveyors of tainted beef and weevily grain, the sellers of cardboard haversacks and leaky tents. No one was really discomforted by all this — so far, at least, as they could see — except the soldiers, the Union volunteers whose sufferings under bungling leaders in battles such as Fredericksburg and Chickasaw Bluffs were of a nature that made their flop-soled shoes and tattered garments seem relatively unimportant, and the Confederate jackals who stripped the blue-clad corpses after the inevitable retreat. If the generals were unashamed, were hailed in fact as heroes after such fiascos, why should anyone else have pangs of conscience? The contractors asked that, meanwhile raking in profits that were as long as they were quick. The only drawback was the money itself, which was in some ways no more real than the sleazy cloth or the imitation leather, being itself the shadow of what had formerly been substance. With prosperity in full swing and gold rising steadily, paper money declined from day to day, sometimes taking sickening drops as it passed from hand to hand. All it seemed good for was spending, and they spent it. Spending, they rose swiftly in the social scale, creating in the process a society which drew upon itself the word that formerly had been used to describe the goods they bartered — "shoddy" — and upon their heads the scorn of those who had made their money earlier and resented the fact that it was being debased. One such was Amos Lawrence, a millionaire Boston merchant. "Cheap money makes speculation, rising prices, and rapid fortunes," Lawrence declared, "but it will not make patriots." He wanted hard times back again. Closed factories would turn men's minds away from gain; then and only then could the war be won. So he believed. "We must have Sunday all over the land," he said, "instead of feasting and gambling."

For the present, though, all that was Sunday about the leaders of the trend which he deplored was their clothes. They wore on weekdays now the suits they once had reserved for wear to church, and as they prospered they bought others, fine broadcloth with nothing shoddy about them except possibly what they inclosed. So garbed, and still with money to burn before it declined still further, the feasters and gamblers acquired new habits and pretensions, with the result that the disparaging word was attached by the New York *World* not only to the new society, but also to the age in which it flourished:

> The lavish profusion in which the old southern cotton aristocracy used to indulge is completely eclipsed by the dash, parade, and magnificence of the new northern shoddy aristocracy of this period. Ideas of cheapness and economy are thrown to the winds. The individual who makes the most money — no matter how — and spends the most money — no matter for what — is considered the greatest man. To be extravagant is to be fashionable. These facts sufficiently account for the immense and brilliant audiences at the opera and the theatres, and until the final crash comes such audiences undoubtedly will continue. The world has seen its iron age, its silver age, its golden age, and its brazen age. This is the age of shoddy.
> The new brown-stone palaces on Fifth Avenue, the new equipages at the Park, the new diamonds which dazzle unaccustomed eyes, the new silks and satins which rustle overloudly, as if to demand attention, the new people who live in the palaces, and ride in the carriages, and wear the diamonds and silks — all are shoddy.... They set or follow the shoddy fashions, and fondly imagine themselves à la mode de Paris, when they are only à la mode de shoddy. They are shoddy brokers on Wall Street, or shoddy manufacturers of shoddy goods, or shoddy contractors for shoddy articles for a shoddy government. Six days in the week they are shoddy business men. On the seventh day they are shoddy Christians.

Nor were journalists and previously wealthy men the only ones to express a growing indignation. Wages had not risen in step with the rising cost of food and rent and other necessities of life, and this had brought on a growth of the trade-union movement, with mass meetings held in cities throughout the North to protest the unequal distribution of advantages and hardships. (Karl Marx was even now at work on *Das Kapital* in London's British Museum, having issued with Friedrich Engels *The Communist Manifesto* fifteen years ago, and Lincoln himself had said in his first December message to Congress: "Labor is prior to, and independent of, capital. Capital is only the fruit of labor, and could never have existed if labor had not first existed. Labor is the superior of capital, and deserves much the higher consideration.") One such meeting, held about this time at Cooper Union, filled the building to capacity while hundreds of people waited outside for word to be passed of what was being said within by delegates on the rostrum; whatever it was was being received with cheers and loud applause, along with a sprinkling of hisses and vehement boos. A representative of the hatters, one McDonough Bucklin, believed that the war was being used by the rich as an excuse for increased exploitation of the poor. As Bucklin put it, "The machinery is forging fetters to bind you in perpetual bondage. It gives you a distracted country with men crying out loud and strong for the Union. Union with them means no more nor less than that they want the war prolonged that they may get the whole of the capital of the country into their breeches pocket and let it out at a percentage that will rivet the chain about your neck." It was the old story: "Every day the rich are getting richer, the poor poorer." Apparently at this point Bucklin got carried away, for a *World* reporter noted that "the speaker made some concluding remarks strongly tainted with communism, which did not meet with general approval."

And yet, for all the offense to the sensibilities of the Boston millionaire, who had made his pile in a different time, as well as to those of the New York journalist, whose indignation was one of the tools he used in earning a living, and the labor delegate, who after all was mainly concerned with the fact that he and his hatters were not getting what he considered a large fair slice of the general pie, much of the undoubted ugliness of the era — the Age of Shoddy, if you will — was little more than the manifest awkwardness of national adolescence, a reaction to growing pains. Unquestionably the growth was there, and unquestionably, too — despite the prevalent gaucherie, the scarcity of grace and graciousness, the apparent concern with money and money alone, getting and spending — much of the growth was solid and even permanent. The signs were at hand for everyone to read. "Old King Cotton's dead and buried; brave young Corn is king," was the refrain of a popular song written to celebrate the bumper grain crops being gathered every fall, of which the ample surpluses were shipped to Europe, where a coincidental succession of drouths — as if the guns booming and growling beyond the Atlantic had drawn the rain clouds, magnet-like, and then discharged them empty — resulted in poor harvests which otherwise would have signaled the return of Old World famine. More than five million quarters of wheat and flour were exported to England in 1862, whereas the total in 1859 had been less than a hundred thousand. In the course of the conflict the annual pork pack nearly doubled in the northern states, and the wool clip more than tripled. Meanwhile, industry not only kept pace with agriculture, it outran it. In Philadelphia alone, 180 new factories were established between 1862 and 1864 to accommodate labor-saving devices which had been invented on the eve of war but which now came into their own in response to the accelerated demands of the boom economy of wartime: the Howe sewing machine, for example, which revolutionized the garment industry, and the Gordon McKay machine for stitching bootsoles to uppers, producing one hundred pairs of shoes in the time previously required to finish a single pair by hand. All those humming wheels and clamorous drive-shafts needed oil; and got it, too, despite the fact that no such amounts as were now required had even existed before, so far at least as men had suspected a short while back; for within that same brief three-year span the production of petroleum, discovered in Pennsylvania less than two years before Sumter, increased from 84,000 to 128,000,000 gallons. The North was fighting the South with one hand and getting rich with the other behind its back, though which was left and which was right was hard to say. In any case, with such profits and progress involved, who could oppose the trend except a comparative handful of men and women, maimed or widowed or otherwise made squeamish, if not downright unpatriotic, by hard luck or oversubscription to Christian ethics?

A change was coming upon the land, and upon the land's inhabitants; nor was the change merely a dollars-and-cents affair, as likely to pass as to last. Legislation which had long hung fire because of peacetime caution and restraints imposed by jealous Southerners, now departed, came out of the congressional machine about as fast as proponents could feed bills into the hopper. Kansas had become a state and Colorado, Dakota, and Nevada were organized as Territories before the war was one year old, with the result that no part of the national area remained beyond the scope of the national law. Wherever a man went now the law went with him, at least in theory, and this also had its effect. Helping to make room on the eastern seaboard for the nearly 800,000 immigrants who arrived in the course of the conflict — especially from Ireland and Germany, where recruiting agents were hard at work, helping certain northern states to fill their quotas — no less than 300,000 people crossed the prairies, headed west for Pike's Peak or California, Oregon or the new Territories, some in search of gold as in the days of '49 and others to farm the cornlands made available under the Homestead Act of 1862, whereby a settler could stake off a claim to a quarter-section of public land and, upon payment of a nominal fee, call those 160 acres his own; 15,000 such homesteads were settled thus in the course of the war, mostly in Minnesota, amounting in all to some 2,500,-000 acres. In this way the development of the Far West continued, despite the distraction southward, while back East the cities grew in wealth and population, despite the double drain in both directions. Nor were the cultural pursuits neglected, and these included more than attendance of the opera as a chance to show off the silks and satins whose rustling had disturbed the *World* reporter. Not only did university enrollments not decline much below what could be accounted for by the departure of southern students, but while the older schools were expanding their facilities with the aid of numerous wartime bequests, fifteen new institutions of higher learning were founded, including Cornell and Swarthmore, Vassar and the Massachusetts Institute of Technology. Campus life was not greatly different as a whole, once the undergraduates and professors grew accustomed to the fact that armies were locked in battle from time to time at various distances off beyond the southern horizon. Interrupted in 1861, for example, the Harvard-Yale boat races were resumed three years later in the midst of the bloodiest season of the war, and not a member of either crew volunteered for service in the army or the navy.

The draft, passed in early January as if in solution of the problem of Fredericksburg losses, hardly affected anyone not willing to be affected or else so miserably poor in these high times as not to be able to scrape up the $300 exemption fee as often as his name or number came up at the periodic drawings, in which case it might be said that he was about as well off in the army as out of it, except for the added discomfort of being drilled and possibly shot at. Large numbers of men from the upper classes, whether recently arrived at that level or established there of old, went to the expense of hiring substitutes (usually immigrants who were brought over by companies newly formed to supply the demand, trafficking thus in flesh to an extent unknown since the stoppage of the slave trade, and who were glad of the chance to earn a nest egg, which included the money they got from the men whose substitutes they were, plus the bounty paid by that particular state to volunteers — minus, of course, the fee that went to the company agent who had got them this opportunity in the first place) not only because it meant that the substitute-hirer was done with the problem of the draft for the duration, but also because it was considered more patriotic. All the same, the parody *We Are Coming, Father Abraham, Three Hundred Dollars More* was greeted with laughter wherever it was heard; for there was no stigma attached to the man who stayed out of combat, however he went about it short of actual dodging or desertion.

"In the vast new army of 300,000 which Mr Lincoln has ordered to be raised," one editor wrote, marveling at this gap disclosed in the new prosperity, "there will not be *one* man able to pay $300. Not one! Think of that!"

Washington itself was riding the crest of the wave thrown up by the boom, its ante-bellum population of 60,000 having nearly quadrupled under pressure from the throng of men and women rushing in to fill the partial vacuum created by the departure of the Southerners who formerly had set the social tone. Here the growing pains were the worst of all, according to Lincoln's young secretary John Hay, who wrote: "This miserable sprawling village imagines itself a city because it is wicked, as a boy thinks he is a man when he smokes and swears." In this instance Hay was offended because he and the President, riding back from the Soldiers Home after an interesting talk on philology — for which, he said, Lincoln had "a little indulged inclination" — encountered "a party of drunken gamblers and harlots returning in the twilight from [*erased*]." The fact was, the carousers might have been returning from almost any quarter of the city; for the provost marshal, while unable to give even a rough estimate of the number of houses of prostitution doing business here beside the Potomac, reported 163 gambling establishments in full swing, including one in which a congressman had lately achieved fame by breaking the bank in a single night and leaving with $100,000 bulging his pockets. It was a clutch-and-grab society now, with a clutch-and-grab way of doing business, whether its own or the government's, though it still affected a free and easy manner out of office hours. Nathaniel Hawthorne, in town for a look-round, found that the nation's pulse could be taken better at Willard's Hotel, especially in the bar, than at either the Capitol or the White House. "Everybody may be seen there," he declared. "You exchange nods with governors of sovereign states; you elbow illustrious men, and tread on the toes of generals; you hear statesmen and orators speaking in their familiar tones. You are mixed up with office-seekers, wire pullers, inventors, artists, poets, editors, army correspondents, attachés of foreign journals, long-winded talkers, clerks, diplomats, mail contractors, railway directors, until your own identity is lost among them. You adopt the universal habit of the place, and call for a mint julep, a whiskey skin, a gin cocktail, a brandy smash, or a glass of pure Old Rye; at any hour all these drinks are in request."

Not that there were no evidences of war aside from the uniforms, which were everywhere, and the personal experience of wounds or bereavement. There were indeed. War was the central fact around which life in Washington revolved, and what was more there were constant reminders that war was closely involved with death in its more unattractive forms. Although men with wrecked faces and empty sleeves or trouser-legs no longer drew the attention they once had drawn, other signs were not so easily ignored. Under huge transparencies boasting their skill at embalming, undertakers would buttonhole you on the street and urgently guarantee that, after receiving payment in advance, they would bring you back from the place where you caught the bullet "as lifelike as if you were asleep," the price being scaled in accordance with your preference for rosewood, pine, or something in between. One section of the city ticked like an oversized clock as the coffinmakers plied their hammers, stocking their shops against the day of battle, the news of which would empty their storerooms overnight and step up the tempo of their hammers in response to the law of supply and demand, as if time itself were hurrying to keep pace with the rush of events. In the small hours of the night, when this cacophonous ticking was stilled, men might toss sleepless on their beds, with dread like a presence in the room and sweat breaking out on the palms and foreheads even of those who knew the horror only by hearsay; but the outward show, by daylight or lamplight, was garish. Pennsylvania Avenue was crowded diurnally, to and beyond its margins of alternate dust and mud, and the plumes and sashes of the blue-clad officers, setting off the occasional gaudy splash of a Zouave, gave it the look of a carnival midway. This impression was heightened by the hawkers of roasted chestnuts and rock candy, and the women also did their part, contributing to the over-all effect the variegated dresses and tall hats that had come into fashion lately, the latter burdened about their incongruously narrow brims "with over-hanging balconies of flowers."

A future historian described them so, finding also in the course of her researches that the ladies "were wearing much red that season." Magenta and Solferino were two of the shades; "warm, bright, amusing names," she called them, derived from far-off battlefields "where alien men had died for some vague cause." Search as she might, however, she could find no shade of red identified with Chickasaw Bluffs, and it was her opinion that the flightiest trollop on the Avenue would have shrunk from wearing a scarlet dress that took its name from Fredericksburg.

★ ★ ★

Across the Atlantic, unfortunately for Confederate hopes of official acceptance into the family of nations, the Schleswig-Holstein problem, unrest in Poland, and the rivalry of Austria and Prussia gave the ministries of Europe a great deal more to think about than the intricacies of what was called "the American question." Aware that any disturbance of the precarious balance of power might be the signal for a general conflagration, they recalled Voltaire's comment that a torch lighted in 1756 in the forests of the new world had promptly wrapped the old world in flames. Russia, by coincidence having emancipated her serfs in the same year the western conflict began, was pro-Union from the start, while France remained in general sympathetic to the South; but neither could act without England, and England could not or would not intervene, being herself divided on the matter. The result, aside from occasional fumbling and inopportune attempts at mediation — mostly on the part of Napoleon III, who had needs and ambitions private and particular to himself — was that Europe, in effect, maintained a hands-off policy with regard to the blood now being shed beyond the ocean.

The double repulse, at Sharpsburg and Perryville, of the one Confederate attempt (so far) to conquer a peace by invasion of the North did not mean to Lord Palmerston and his ministers that the South would necessarily lose the war; far from it. But it did convince these gentlemen that the time was by no means ripe for intervention, as they had recently supposed, and was the basis for their mid-November rejection of a proposal by Napoleon that England, France, and Russia join in urging a North-South armistice, accompanied by a six-month lifting of the blockade. The result, if they had agreed — as they had been warned in no uncertain terms by Seward in private conversations with British representatives overseas — would have been an immediate diplomatic rupture, if not an outright declaration of war: in which connection the London *Times* remarked that "it would be cheaper to keep all Lancashire in turtle and venison than to plunge into a desperate war with the Northern States of America, even with all Europe at our back." No one knew better than Palmerston the calamity that might ensue, for he had been Minister at War from 1812 to 1815, during which period Yankee privateers had sunk about 2500 English ships, almost the entire marine. At that rate, with all those international tigers crouched for a leap in case the head tiger suffered some crippling injury, England not only could not afford to risk the loss of a sideline war; she could not even afford to win one.

Besides, desirable though it was that the flow of American cotton to British spindles be resumed — of 534,000 operatives, less than a quarter were working full time and more than half were out of work entirely; including their dependents, and those of other workers who lost their jobs in ancillary industries, approximately two million people were without means of self-support as a result of the cotton famine — the over-all economic picture was far from gloomy. In addition to the obvious example of the munitions manufacturers, who were profiting handsomely from the quarrel across the way, the linen and woolen industries had gained an appreciable part of what the cotton industry had lost, and the British merchant marine, whose principal rival for world trade was being chased from the high seas by rebel cruisers, was prospering as never before, augmented by more than seven hundred American vessels which transferred to the Union Jack in an attempt to avoid capture or destruction. And though there were those who favored intervention on the side of the South as a means of disposing permanently of a growing competitor, if by no other way then by assisting him to cut himself in two — the poet Matthew Arnold took this line of reason even further, speaking of the need "to prevent the English people from becoming, with the growth of democracy, *Americanized*" — the majority, even among the hard-pressed cotton operatives, did not. The Emancipation Proclamation saw to that, and Lincoln, having won what he first had feared was a gamble, was quick to press the advantage he had gained. When the workingmen of Manchester, the city hardest hit by the cotton famine, sent him an address approved at a meeting held on New Year's Eve, announcing their support of the North in its efforts to "strike off the fetters of the slave," Lincoln replied promptly in mid-January, pulling out all the stops in his conclusion: "I know and deeply deplore the sufferings which the workingmen at Manchester and in all Europe are called upon to endure in this crisis. . . . Under these circumstances, I cannot but regard your decisive utterance upon the question as an instance of sublime Christian heroism which has not been surpassed in any age or in any country. It is, indeed, an energetic and reinspiring assurance of the inherent power of truth and of the ultimate and universal triumph of justice, humanity, and freedom. I do not doubt that the sentiments you have expressed will be sustained by your great nation, and, on the other hand, I have no hesitation in assuring you that they will excite admiration, esteem, and the most reciprocal feelings of friendship among the American people. I hail this interchange of sentiment, therefore, as an augury that whatever else may happen, whatever misfortune may befall your country or my own, the peace and friendship which now exist between the two nations will be, as it shall be my desire to make them, perpetual."

Palmerston could have made little headway against the current of this rhetoric, even if he had so desired. In point of fact he did not try. Having resisted up to now the efforts of Confederate envoys to rush him off his feet — which they had done their best to do, knowing that it was their best chance to secure European intervention: aside, that is, from such happy accidents as the *Trent* affair, which unfortunately after a great deal of furor had come to nothing — he would have little trouble in keeping his balance from now on. Napoleon, across the Channel, was another matter. Practically without popular objection to restrain him, he continued to work in favor of those interests which, as he saw them, coincided with his own. Through the prominent Paris banking firm, Erlanger et Cie — whose president's son had lately married Matilda Slidell, daughter of the Confederate commissioner — a multi-million-dollar loan to the struggling young nation across the Atlantic was arranged, not in answer to any plea for financial assistance (it had not occurred to the Southerners, including John Slidell, despite the recent matrimonial connection, that asking would result in anything more than a Gallic shrug of regret) but purely as a gesture of good will. So the firm's representatives said as they broached the subject to Secretary of State Judah P. Benjamin in Richmond, having crossed the ocean for that purpose. However, being bankers — and what is more, French bankers — they added that they saw no harm in combining the good-will gesture with the chance to turn a profit, not only for the prospective buyers of the bonds that would be issued, but also for Erlanger et Cie. Then came the explanation, which showed that the transaction, though ostensibly a loan, was in fact little more than a scheme for large-scale speculation in cotton. Each 8% bond, which the firm would obtain at 70 for sale at approximately 100, was to be made exchangeable at face value, not later than six months after the end of the war, for New Orleans middling cotton at 12¢ a pound. There was the catch; for cotton was worth twice that much already, and was still rising. Benjamin, who was quite as sharp as the visiting bankers or their chief — Erlanger was a Jew and so was he; Erlanger was a Frenchman and so was he, after a manner of speaking, being Creole by adoption — saw through the scheme at once, as indeed anyone but a blind man would have done; but he also saw its propaganda value, which amounted at least to financial recognition of the Confederacy as a member of the family of nations. After certain adjustments on which he insisted, though not without exposing himself to charges of ingratitude for having looked a gift horse in the mouth — the original offer of $25,000,000 was scaled down to $15,000,000 and the interest rate to 7%, while the price at which the firm was to secure the bonds was raised to 77 — the deal was closed.

That was in late January, and at first all went well. Issued in early March at 90 — which gave Erlanger a spread of 13 points, plus a 5% commission on all sales — the bonds were enthusiastically oversubscribed and quickly arose to 95½. But that was the peak. Before the month was out they began to fall, and they kept falling, partly because of the influence of U.S. foreign agents who, basing their charge on the fact that Jefferson Davis himself had been a prewar advocate of the repudiation of Mississippi state bonds, predicted vociferously that the Southerners, if by some outside chance they won the war, would celebrate their victory by repudiating their debts. This had its effect. As the price declined, the alarmed Parisian bankers brought pressure on James M. Mason, the Confederate commissioner in London, to bull the market by using the receipts of the first installment for the purchase of his government's own bonds. Reluctantly, with the agreement of Slidell, he consented and, before he was through, put $6,000,000 into the attempt. But even this caused no more than a hesitation. When the artificial respiration stopped, the decline resumed, eventually pausing of its own accord at a depth of 36 before the bonds went off the board entirely. By that time, however, Erlanger et Cie was well in the clear, with a profit of about $2,500,000: which was more than the Confederacy obtained in all from a bond issue for which it had pledged six times that amount in capital and 7% in interest. The real losers, though, were the individual purchasers, mostly British admirers of the Confederacy, who left to their descendants the worthless scroll-worked souvenirs of a curious chapter in international finance.

As a fund-raising device the experiment was nearly a total failure — for the Confederates, that is, if not for the French bankers — but it did provide an additional incentive for Napoleon, who had taken considerable interest in the transaction, to hope for a southern victory. On February 3, after the bond issue had been authorized but before it had begun, the Emperor had his minister at Washington, Henri Mercier by name, present an offer of mediation, suggesting that representatives of the North and South meet on neutral soil for a discussion of terms of peace. The reaction to this was immediate and negative, at least on the part of the North. Seward replied that the Federal government had not the slightest notion of abandoning its efforts to save the Union, and certainly not by any such relinquishment of authority as the French proposal seemed to imply. This was seconded emphatically by Congress on March 3, when both houses issued a joint resolution denouncing mediation as "foreign interference" and reaffirming their "unalterable purpose" to suppress a rebellion which had for its object the tearing of the fabric of the finest government the world had ever known. In short, all that came of this latest effort by Napoleon to befriend the South was a further reduction of his possible influence. And Palmerston, watching the outcome from across the Channel, was more than ever convinced that no good could proceed from any such machinations. Dependent as his people were on U.S. grain to keep them from starvation, with Canada liable to seizure as a hostage to fortune and the British merchant marine exposed to being crippled if not destroyed, it seemed to him little short of madness to step into an argument which was after all a family affair. "Those who in quarrels interpose, Are apt to get a bloody nose," he intoned, falling back on doggerel to express his fears.

A. Dudley Mann, third in the trio of Confederate commissioners in Europe, had opened the year by complaining to his government that "the conduct of [England and France] toward us has been extremely shabby" and deploring their lack of spirit in the face of "the arrogant pretensions of the insolent Washington concern." Now in mid-March, as the third spring of the war began its green advance across the embattled South, all those thousands of miles away, Slidell in Paris was becoming increasingly impatient with Napoleon, whose avowed good will and favors never seemed to lead to anything valid or substantial, and Mason in London was lamenting bitterly that he had "no intercourse, unofficial or otherwise, with any member of the [British] Government." It was his private opinion, expressed frequently to Benjamin these days, that instead of continuing to put up with snubs and rebuffs, he would do better to come home.

★ ★ ★

If he had come home to Virginia now — as he did not; not yet — he would have done well to brace himself for the shock of finding it considerably altered from what it had been when he left it, a year and a half ago, to begin his aborted voyage on the *Trent*. That was perhaps the greatest paradox of all: that the Confederacy, in launching a revolution against change, should experience under pressure of the war which then ensued an even greater transformation, at any rate of the manner in which its citizens pursued their daily rounds, than did the nation it accused of trying to foist upon it an unwanted metamorphosis, not only of its cherished institutions, but also of its very way of life.

That way of life was going fast, and some there were, particularly among those who could remember a time when a society was judged in accordance with its sense of leisure, who affirmed that it was gone already. Nowhere was the change more obvious than in Richmond. Though the city was no longer even semi-beleaguered, as it had been in the time of McClellan, the outer fortifications had been lengthened and strengthened to such an extent that wags were saying, "They ought to be called fiftyfications now." Within that earthwork girdle, where home-guard clerks from government offices walked their appointed posts in their off hours, an ante-bellum population of less than 40,000 had mushroomed to an estimated 140,000, exclusive of the Union captives and Confederate wounded who jammed the old tobacco warehouses converted to prisons and hospitals. Yet the discomfort to which the older residents objected was not so much the result of the quantity of these late arrivers as it was of their quality, so to speak, or lack of it. "Virginians regarded the newcomers much as Romans would regard the First Families of the Visigoths," a diarist wrote. In truth, they had provocation far beyond the normal offense to their normal snobbery. Tenderloin districts such as Locust Alley, where painted women helped furloughed men forget the rigors of the field, and Johnny Worsham's gambling hell, directly across from the State House itself, had given the Old Dominion capital a reputation for being "the most corrupt and licentious city south of the Potomac." A Charlestonian administered the unkindest cut, however, by writing home that he had come to Richmond and found an entirely new city erected "after the model of Sodom and New York." According to another observer, an Englishman with a sharper ear for slang and a greater capacity for shock, the formerly decorous streets were crowded now with types quaintly designated as pug-uglies, dead rabbits, shoulder-hitters, "and a hundred other classes of villains for whom the hangman has sighed for many a long year."

Richmond saw and duly shuddered; but there was grimmer cause for shuddering than the wrench given its sense of propriety by the whores and gamblers who had taken up residence within its gates. As new-mounded graves spread over hillsides where none had been before, the population of the dead kept pace with the fast-growing population of the living. Though the Confederates in general lost fewer men in battle than their opponents, the fact that they had fewer to lose gave the casualty lists a greater impact, and it was remarked that "funerals were so many, even the funerals of friends, that none could be more than sparsely attended." Even more pitiful were the dying; Richmonders had come to know what one of them called "the peculiar chant of pain" that went up from a line of springless wagons hauling wounded over a rutted road or a cobbled street. You saw the maimed wherever you looked. For the city's hospitals — including the one on Chimborazo Heights, which had 150 buildings and was said to be the largest in the world — were so congested during periods immediately following battles that men who had lost an arm three days before had to be turned out, white-faced and trembling from shock and loss of blood, to make room for others in more urgent need of medical attention. It was up to the people to take them into their houses for warmth and food, and this they did, though only by the hardest, for both were dear and getting further beyond their means with every day that passed.

A gold dollar now was worth four in Confederate money, and even a despised $1 Yankee greenback brought $2.50 in a swap. Of coined money there was none, and in fact there had never been any, except for four half-dollars struck in the New Orleans mint before the fall of that city caused the government to abandon its plans for coinage. Congress's first solution to the small-change problem had been to make U.S. silver coins legal tender up to $10, along with English sovereigns, French napoleons, and Spanish and Mexican doubloons, but presently a flood of paper money was released upon the country, bills of smaller denominations being known as "shinplasters" because a soldier once had used a fistful to cover a tibia wound. Sometimes, as depreciation continued, that seemed about all they were good for. A War Department official, comparing current with prewar household expenses — flour, then $7, now $28 a barrel; bacon, then 20¢, now $1.25 a pound; firewood, then $3 or $4, now $15 a cord — found, as many others were finding, that he could not make ends meet; "My salary of $3000 will go about as far as $700 would in 1860." Wool and salt, drugs and medicines, nails and needles were scarcely to be had at any price, though the last were often salvaged from sewing kits found in the pockets of dead Federals. Dress muslin was $6 to $8 a yard, calico $1.75, coal $14 a cartload, and dinner in a first-class hotel ran as high as $25 a plate. In addition to genuine shortages, others were artificial, the result of transportation problems. Items that were plenteous in one part of the country might be as rare as hen's teeth in another. Peaches selling for 25¢ a dozen in Charleston, for instance, cost ten, fifteen, even twenty cents apiece in Richmond nowadays. For men perhaps the worst shock was the rising price of whiskey. As low as 25¢ a gallon in 1861, inferior stuff known variously as bust-head, red-eye, and tangle-foot now sold for as high as $35 a gallon. For women, on the other hand, the main source of incidental distress was clothes, the lack of new ones and the unsuitability of old ones through wear-and-tear and changing styles, although the latter were of necessity kept to a minimum. "Do you realize the fact that we shall soon be without a stitch of clothes?" a young woman wrote to a friend in early January. "There is not a bonnet for sale in Richmond. Some of the girls smuggle them, which I for one consider in the worst possible taste." Apparently ashamed to have let her mind turn in this direction at this time, she hastened to apologize for her flightiness, only to fall into fresh despair. "It seems rather volatile to discuss such things while our dear country is in such peril. Heaven knows I would costume myself in coffee-bags if that would help, but having no coffee, where would I get the bags?"

One provident source of amusement and delivery from care was the theater, which was popular as never before, though it did not escape the censure of the more respectable. "The thing took well, and money flowed into the treasury," a manager afterwards recalled, "but often had I cause to upbraid myself for having fallen so low in my own estimation, for I had always considered myself a gentleman, and I found that in taking control of this theatre and its vagabond company I had forfeited my claim to a respectable stand in the ranks of Society." A prominent Baptist preacher's complaint from his pulpit that "twenty *gentlemen* for the chorus and the ballet" might be more useful to their country in the army, where they could do more than "mimic fighting on the stage," met with the approval of his congregation; but the S.R.O. signs continued to go up nightly beside the ticket windows. When the Richmond Theatre burned soon after New Year's, an entirely new building was promptly raised on the old foundations. Opening night was greeted with an "Inaugural Poem" by Henry Timrod, concluding:

> *Bid Liberty rejoice! Aye, though its day*
> *Be far or near, these clouds shall yet be red*
> *With the large promise of the coming ray.*
> *Meanwhile, with that calm courage which can smile*
> *Amid the terrors of the wildest fray*
> *Let us among the charms of Art awhile*
>   *Fleet the deep gloom away;*
> *Nor yet forget that on each hand and head*
> *Rest the dear rights for which we fight and pray.*

If the production itself — Shakespeare's *As You Like It;* "but not as *we* like it," one critic unkindly remarked — left much to be desired in the way of professional excellence, Richmonders were glad to have found release "among the charms," and even the disgruntled reviewer was pleased to note "that the audience evinced a disposition at once to stop all rowdyism." For example, when the callboy came out from behind the curtain to fasten down the carpet, certain ill-bred persons began to yell, "Soup! Soup!" but were promptly shushed by those around them.

An even better show, according to some, was presented at the Capitol whenever Congress was in session, though unfortunately — or fortunately, depending on the point of view — these theatricals were in general unavailable to the public, being conducted behind closed doors. It was not so much what occurred in the regular course of business that was lively or amusing (for, as was usual with such bodies, there was a good deal more discussion of what to do than there was of doing. One member interrupted a long debate as to a proper time for adjournment by remarking, "If the House would adjourn and not meet any more, it would benefit the country." Others outside the legislative assembly agreed, including a Deep South editor who, learning that Congress had spent the past year trying without success to agree on a device for the national seal, suggested "A terrapin *passant*," with the motto "Never in haste"); it was what happened beside the point, so to speak, that provided the excitement. In early February the Alabama fire-eater William L. Yancey, opposing the creation of a Confederate Supreme Court — which, incidentally, never came into being because of States Rights obstructionists — so infuriated Benjamin H. Hill of Georgia, a moderate, that he threw a cutglass inkstand at the speaker and cut his cheek to the bone. As Yancey, spattered with blood and ink, started for him across the intervening desks, Hill followed up with a second shot, this time a heavy tumbler, which missed, and the sergeant-at-arms had to place both men in restraint and remove them from the chamber. Less fortunate was the chief clerk, shot to death on Capitol Square two months later by the journal clerk, who was angry at having been accused of slipshod work by his superior. The killer was sentenced to eighteen years in the penitentiary, but nothing at all was done to a woman who appeared one day on the floor of the House and proceeded to cowhide a Missouri congressman. She too was a government clerk, but it developed that her wrath had been aroused by information that Congress, in connection with enforcement of the Conscription Act, was about to require all clerks to divulge their ages. Deciding that the woman was demented, the House voted its confidence in the unlucky Missourian, who apparently had been selected at random. No such vote was ever given Jefferson Davis's old Mississippi stump opponent Henry S. Foote, who worked hard to deserve the reputation of being the stormiest man in Congress. He fought with his fists, in and out of the chamber, and was always ready to fall back on dueling pistols, with which he had had considerable experience. An altercation with an expatriate Irishman and a Tennessee colleague, who struck Foote over the head with an umbrella and then dodged nimbly to keep from being shot, caused all three to be brought into the Mayor's Court and placed under a peace bond. Another three-sided argument occurred in the course of a congressional hearing in which a Commissary Department witness was so badgered by Foote that the two came to blows. Foote tore off his adversary's shirt bosom, and when Commissary General Lucius B. Northrop came to the witness's assistance Foote knocked him into a corner. According to some who despised Colonel Northrop, asserting that he was attempting to convert the southern armies to vegetarianism, this was Foote's one real contribution to the Confederate war effort. But he was by no means through providing excitement. In the course of a speech by E. S. Dargan of Alabama, Foote broke in to call him a "damned rascal," which so infuriated the elderly congressman that he went for the Mississippian with a knife. Foote avoided the lunge, and then — Dargan by now had been disarmed and lay pinned to the floor by colleagues — stepped back within range and, striking an attitude not unworthy of Edwin Booth, whose work he much admired, hissed at the prostrate Alabamian: "I defy the steel of the assassin!"

All this was part and parcel of the revolution-in-progress, and if much of it was scandalous and distasteful, most Confederates could take that too in stride, along with spiraling prices and increasing scarcities. A native inclination toward light-heartedness served them well in times of strain. What the newcomers to Richmond lacked in tone they more than made up for in gaiety. Practically nothing was exempt from being laughed at nowadays, not even the sacred escutcheon of Virginia, whose motto *Sic semper tyrannis*, engraved below the figure of Liberty treading down Britannia, was freely rendered as "Take your foot off my neck!" Officers and men on leave and furlough from the Rappahannock line opened Volume I, "Fantine," of Victor Hugo's *Les Misérables*, which had come out in France the year before, and professed surprise at finding that it was not about themselves, "Lee's Miserables, Faintin'." One whose spirits never seemed to falter was Judah Benjamin, who remarked in this connection that it was "wrong and useless to disturb oneself and thus weaken one's energy to bear what was foreordained." This hedonistic fatalist went his way, invariably smiling, whether in attendance at government councils or at Johnny Worsham's green baize tables across the way. He once assured Varina Davis that with a glass of McHenry sherry, of which she had a small supply, and beaten biscuits made of flour from Crenshaw Mills, spread with a paste made of English walnuts from a tree on the White House grounds, "a man's patriotism became rampant." She found him amusing, an ornament to her receptions, and an excellent antidote to the FFV's who currently were condemning her as "disloyal to the South" because of a rumor that she had employed a white nurse for her baby.

The easy laughter was infectious, though some could hear it for what it was, part of an outward pose assumed at times to hide or hold back tears. What was happening behind the mask — not only Benjamin's, but the public's at large — no one could say for certain. Presently, however, there were signs that the mask was beginning to crack, or at any rate slip, and thus disclose what it had been designed to cover. When the President proclaimed March 5 another "day of fasting and prayer," this too was not exempt from unregenerate laughter; "Fasting in the midst of famine!" some remarked sardonically. Then, just short of one month later, on Holy Thursday — Easter came on April 5, a week before the second anniversary of Sumter — a demonstration staged on the streets of the capital itself gave the authorities cause to question whether all was as well concerning public morale here in the East as they had supposed, especially among those citizens who could not enjoy the relaxations afforded by such places as Johnny Worsham's, where a lavish buffet was maintained for the refreshment of patrons at all hours. The Holy Thursday demonstration, at least at the start, was concerned with more basic matters: being known, then and thereafter, as the Bread Riot.

Apparently it began at the Oregon Hill Baptist church, where Mary Jackson, a huckster with "straight, strong features and a vixenish eye," harangued a group of women who had gathered to protest the rising cost of food. Adjourning to Capitol Square they came under the leadership of a butcher's Amazonian assistant, Minerva Meredith by name. Six feet tall and further distinguished by a long white feather that stood up from her hat and quivered angrily as she tossed her head, she proposed that they move on the shops to demand goods at government prices and to take them by force if this was refused. As she spoke she took from under her apron, by way of emphasis, a Navy revolver and a Bowie knife. Brandishing these she set out for the business section at the head of a mob which quickly swelled to about three hundred persons, including the children some of the women had in tow. "Bread! Bread!" they shouted as they marched. Governor John Letcher, who had watched from his office as the demonstration got under way, had the mayor read the Riot Act to them, but they hooted and surged on past him, smashing plate-glass windows in their anger and haste to get at the goods in the shops on Main and Cary. It was obvious that they were after more than food, for they emerged with armloads of shoes and clothes, utensils and even jewelry, which some began to pile in to handcarts they had thought to bring along. Governor Letcher sent for a company of militia and threatened to fire on the looters when it arrived, but the women sneered at him, as they had done at the mayor, and went on with their vandalism. Just then, however, those on the outer fringes of the mob saw a tall thin man dressed in gray homespun climb onto a loaded dray and begin to address them sternly. They could not hear what he was saying, but they saw him do a strange thing. He took money from his pockets and tossed it in their direction. Whereupon they fell silent and his voice came through: "You say you are hungry and have no money. Here is all I have. It is not much, but take it." His pockets empty of all but his watch, he took that out too, but instead of throwing it at them, as he had done the money, he stood with it open in his hand, glancing sidelong at the militia company which had just arrived. "We do not desire to injure anyone," he said in a voice that rang clear above the murmur of the crowd, "but this lawlessness must stop. I will give you five minutes to disperse. Otherwise you will be fired on."

Recognizing the President — and knowing, moreover, that he was not given to issuing idle threats — the mob began to disperse, first slowly, then rapidly as the deadline approached. By the time the five minutes were up, there was no one left for the soldiers to fire at. Davis put his watch back in his pocket, climbed down off the dray, and returned to his office. Outwardly calm, inwardly he was so concerned that he did something he had never done before. He made a special appeal to the Richmond press, requesting that it "avoid all reference directly or indirectly to the affair," and ordered the telegraph company to "permit nothing relative to the unfortunate disturbance . . . to be sent over the telegraph lines in any direction for any purpose." He feared the reaction abroad, as well as in other parts of the South, if it became known that the streets of the Confederate capital had been the scene of a riot that had as its cause, if only by pretense, a shortage of food. Two days later, however, the *Enquirer* broke the story by way of refuting defeatist rumors that were beginning to be spread. Identifying the rioters as "a handful of prostitutes, professional thieves, Irish and Yankee hags, gallows birds from all lands but our own," the paper denounced them for having broken into "half a dozen shoe stores, hat stores and tobacco houses and robbed them of everything but bread, which was just the thing they wanted least."

This one attempt at suggesting censorship was as useless as it was ineffective: Richmond was by no means the only place where such disturbances occurred in the course of Holy Week. Simultaneously in Atlanta a group of about fifteen well-dressed women entered a store on Whitehall Street and asked the price of bacon. $1.10 a pound, they were told: whereupon their man-tall leader, a shoemaker's wife "on whose countenance rested care and determination," produced a revolver with which she covered the grocer while her companions snatched what they wanted from the shelves, paying their own price or nothing. From there they proceeded to other shops along the street, repeating the performance until their market baskets were full, and then went home. A similar raid was staged at about the same time in Mobile, as well as in other towns and cities throughout the South. Presently countrywomen took their cue from their urban sisters. North Carolina experienced practically an epidemic of demonstrations by irate housewives. Near Lafayette, Alabama, a dozen such — armed, according to one correspondent, with "guns, pistols, knives, and tongues" — attacked a rural mill and seized a supply of flour, while a dozen more came down out of the hills around Abingdon, Virginia, and cowered merchants into handing over cotton yarn and cloth; wagon trains were stopped at gunpoint and robbed of corn near Thomasville and Marietta, Georgia. All these were but a few among the many, and there were those who saw in this ubiquitous manifestation of discontent the first crack in the newly constructed edifice of government. If the Confederacy could not be defeated from without, then it might be abolished from within; for the protests were not so much against shortages, which were by no means chronic at this stage, as they were against the inefficiency which resulted in spiraling prices. These observers saw the demonstrations, in fact — despite the recent successes of southern arms, both East and West — as symptoms of war weariness, the one national ailment which could lead to nothing but defeat. The new government could survive, and indeed had survived already, an assortment of calamities; but that did not and could not include the loss of the will to fight, either by the soldiers in its armies or by the people on its home front.

No one saw the danger more clearly than the man whose principal task — aside, that is, from his duties as Commander in Chief, which now as always he placed first — was to do all he could to avert it. Recently he had undertaken a 2500-mile year-end journey to investigate and shore up crumbling morale, with such apparent success that on his return he could report to Congress, convening in Richmond for its third session on January 12, that the state of the nation, in its civil as well as in its military aspect, "affords ample cause for congratulation and demands the most fervent expression of our thankfulness to the Almighty Father, who has blessed our cause. We are justified in asserting, with a pride surely not unbecoming, that these Confederate States have added another to the lessons taught by history for the instruction of man; that they have afforded another example of the impossibility of subjugating a people determined to be free, and have demonstrated that no superiority of numbers or available resources can overcome the resistance offered by such valor in combat, such constancy under suffering, and such cheerful endurance of privation as have been conspicuously displayed by this people in the defense of their rights and liberties." Moreover, he added, flushed by the confidence his words had generated: "By resolute perseverance in the path we have hitherto pursued, by vigorous efforts in the development of all our resources for defense, and by the continued exhibition of the same unfaltering courage in our soldiers and able conduct in their leaders as have distinguished the past, we have every reason to expect that this will be the closing year of the war."

Since then, despite continued successful resistance by the armies in the field, symptoms of unrest among civilians had culminated in the rash of so-called Bread Riots, the largest of which had occurred in the capital itself and had been broken up only by the personal intervention of the Chief Executive. Two days later — on April 10, just short of three months since his confident prediction of an early end to the conflict — Davis issued, in response to a congressional resolution passed the week before, a proclamation "To the People of the Confederate States." Observing that "a strong impression prevails throughout the country that the war . . . may terminate during the present year," Congress urged the people not to be taken in by such false hopes, but rather to "look to prolonged war as the only condition proffered by the enemy short of subjugation." The presidential proclamation, issued broadcast across the land, afforded the people the unusual opportunity of seeing their President eat his words, not only by revoking his previous prediction, but by substituting another which clearly implied that what lay ahead was a longer and harder war than ever.

Though "fully concurring in the views thus expressed by Congress," he began with the same boldness of assertion as before. "We have reached the close of the second year of the war, and may point with just pride to the history of our young Confederacy. Alone, unaided, we have met and overthrown the most formidable combination of naval and military armaments that the lust of conquest ever gathered together for the subjugation of a free people. . . . The contrast between our past and present condition is well calculated to inspire full confidence in the triumph of our arms. At no previous period of the war have our forces been so numerous, so well organized, and so thoroughly disciplined, armed, and equipped as at present." Then he passed to darker matters. "We must not forget, however, that the war is not yet ended, and that we are still confronted by powerful armies and threatened by numerous fleets. . . . Your country, therefore, appeals to you to lay aside all thoughts of gain, and to devote yourselves to securing your liberties, without which those gains would be valueless. . . . Let fields be devoted exclusively to the production of corn, oats, beans, peas, potatoes, and other food for man and beast; let corn be sown broadcast for fodder in immediate proximity to railroads, rivers, and canals, and let all your efforts be directed to the prompt supply of these articles in the districts where our armies are operating. . . . Entertaining no fear that you will either misconstrue the motives of this address or fail to respond to the call of patriotism, I have placed the facts fully and frankly before you. Let us all unite in the performance of our duty, each in his own sphere, and with concerted, persistent, and well-directed effort . . . we shall maintain the sovereignty and independence of these Confederate

States, and transmit to our posterity the heritage bequeathed to us by our fathers."

As usual, the people responded well for the most part to a clear statement of necessity. But there were those who reacted otherwise. The Georgia fire-eater Robert Toombs, for example, who had left the cabinet to join the army on the day of First Manassas and then had left the army to re-enter politics after his one big day at Sharpsburg, petulantly announced that he was increasing his plantation's cotton acreage. Nor were opposition editors inclined to neglect the opportunity to launch the verbal barbs they had been sharpening through months of increasing dissatisfaction. "Mr Davis is troubled by blindness," the Mobile *Tribune* told its subscribers, "is very dyspeptic and splenetic, and as prejudiced and stubborn as a man can well be, and not be well."

Thus did the Confederacy enter upon its third year of war.

4

Disenchantment was mainly limited to civilians, but it was by no means limited to the sphere of civilian activities. Illogically or not — that is, despite the lopsided triumphs at Fredericksburg and Chickasaw Bluffs, the flood-reversing coups at Holly Springs and Galveston, the brilliant cavalry forays into Kentucky and West Tennessee, and the absence of anything resembling a clear-cut defeat east of the Mississippi — there was a growing impression that victory, on field after field, brought little more than temporary joy, which soon gave way to sobering realizations. The public's reaction was not unlike that of a boxer who delivers his best punch, square on the button, then sees his opponent merely blink and shake his head and bore back in. People began to suspect that if the North could survive Fredericksburg and the Mud March, Chickasaw Bluffs and the loss of the *Cairo* to a demijohn of powder, it might well be able to survive almost anything the South seemed able to inflict. A whole season of victories apparently had done nothing to bring peace and independence so much as one day closer. Howell Cobb of Georgia could say, not altogether in jest, "Only two things stand in the way of an amicable settlement of the whole difficulty: the Landing of the Pilgrims and Original Sin," while the Richmond *Examiner* could simultaneously call attention to the chilling fact that, aside from Sumter, "[Lincoln's] pledge once deemed foolish by the South, that he would 'hold, occupy, and possess' all the forts belonging to the United States Government, has been redeemed almost to the letter."

Fredericksburg had been hailed at the outset as the turning point of the war. Presently, however, as Lee and his army failed to find a way to follow it up, the triumph paled to something of a disappointment. In time, paradoxically, the more perceptive began to see that it had indeed been a turning point, though in a sense quite different from the one originally implied; for no battle East or West, whether a victory or a defeat, showed more plainly the essential toughness of the blue-clad fighting man than this in which, judging by a comparison of the casualties inflicted and received, he suffered the worst of his several large-scale drubbings. But this was an insight that came gradually and only to those who were not only able but also willing to perceive it. Murfreesboro was more immediately disappointing in respect to Confederate expectations, and no such insight was required. Here the contrast between claims and accomplishments was as stark as it was sudden. First it was seen to be a much less brilliant victory than the southern commander had announced before his guns had hushed their growling. Then it was seen to be scarcely a victory at all. It was seen, in fact, to have several of the aspects of a typical defeat: not the least of which was the undeniable validity of the Federal claim to control of the field when the smoke had cleared. "So far the news has come in what may be called the classical style of the Southwest," the *Examiner* observed caustically near the end of the first week in January, having belatedly learned of Bragg's withdrawal. "When the Southern army fights a battle, we first hear that it has gained one of the most stupendous victories on record; that regiments from Mississippi, Texas, Louisiana, Arkansas, &c. have exhibited an irresistible and superhuman valor unknown in history this side of Sparta and Rome. As for their generals, they usually get all their clothes shot off, and replace them with a suit of glory. The enemy, of course, is simply annihilated. Next day more dispatches come, still very good, but not quite as good as the first. The telegrams of the third day are invariably such as make a mist, a muddle, and a fog of the whole affair."

No mist, muddle, or fog could hide Bragg from the ire aroused when the public learned the premature and insubstantial basis for his wire announcing that God had granted him and them a Happy New Year. What saved him from the immediate consequences of their anger was his adversary Rosecrans, who, despite his recent promise to "press [the rebels] to the wall," not only refused to follow up the victory he claimed, but resisted with all his strength — as he had done through the months preceding the march out of Nashville, pleading the need to lay in "a couple of millions of rations"— the efforts by his superiors to prod him into motion. Crittenden, who had commanded the unassailed left wing throughout the first day's fight and then repulsed his fellow-Kentuckian Breckinridge on the second, stated the case as it appeared to many in the Union ranks: "The battle was fought for the possession of Middle Tennessee. We went down to drive the Confederates out of Murfreesboro, and we drove them out. They went off a few miles and camped again. And we, although we were the victors, virtually went into hospital for six months before we could march after them again." He added, by way of developing a theory: "As in most of our battles, very meager fruits resulted to either side from such partial victories as were for the most part won. Yet it was a triumph. It showed that in the long run the big purse and the big battalions — both on our side — must win; and it proved that there were no better soldiers than ours."

Rosecrans disagreed with much of this critique, particularly the remark that the army had gone "into hospital," but he not only subscribed to Crittenden's opinion about the big purse and the big battalions, he also took it a step further by insisting that the last ounce be wrung from the advantage. What good were riches, he seemed to be asking, unless they were at hand? When he swung the purse he wanted it to be heavy. "I believe the most fatal errors of this war have begun in an impatient desire of success, that would not take time to get ready," he protested in mid-February, by way of reply to Halleck's continuous urging. So the general-in-chief changed his tack. "There is a vacant major generalcy in the Regular Army," he wired on March 1, "and I am authorized to say that it will be given to the general in the field who first wins an important and decisive victory." The implication was that Rosecrans had better get to Chattanooga before Grant got to Vicksburg; but Old Rosy did not react at all in the way that had been intended. "As an officer and a citizen, I feel degraded to see such auctioneering of honor," he replied. "Have we a general who would fight for his own personal benefit, when he would not for honor and the country? He would come by his commission basely in that case, and deserve to be despised by men of honor." Halleck in turn resented this show of righteous indignation, and said so, which only served to increase their differences. Rosecrans was convinced by now that all of Washington was against him: especially Stanton, who had promised, in the first flush of excitement over the news of a hard-fought triumph, to withhold "nothing ... within my power to grant," but who lately had bridled at filling the balky commander's many requisitions and requests, including one that his latest promotion be predated so as to give him rank over Grant and all the other western generals. Finally he protested to the President himself, who gave him little satisfaction beyond assurances of admiration. "I know not a single enemy of yours here," Lincoln wrote, and added: "Truth to speak, I do not appreciate this matter of rank on paper as you officers do. The world will not forget that you fought the battle of Stones River, and it will never care a fig whether you rank Gen. Grant on paper, or he so ranks you."

By then it was mid-March. The bloody contest, ten weeks back, had done much to increase Old Rosy's appreciation of the dangers involved in challenging the rebs on their own ground. The rest of March went by, and all of April. Still he would not budge. May followed. Still he would not move until he was good and ready, down to the final nail in the final horseshoe. As June came on, approaching the end of the six-month term which Crittenden said the army spent "in hospital," Rosecrans made a virtue of his immobility, claiming that by refraining from driving Bragg southward he was preventing him from co-operating with Pemberton against Grant. Besides, he added, he had held a council of war at which it had been decided to "observe a great military maxim, not to risk two great and decisive battles at the same time." He thought it best to wait till Vicksburg fell or Grant abandoned the effort to take it, whereupon he himself would advance against Bragg and Chattanooga. Halleck by now was fairly frantic. A master of maxims, he fired one back at Rosecrans: "Councils of war never fight." But this had no more effect than the earlier proddings had done; Old Rosy stayed exactly where he was. If Bragg would only leave him alone, he would gladly return the favor, at any rate until he was good and ready to advance. Just when that would be he would not say.

He might have taken some measure of consolation, amid the proddings, from the fact that his opponent's troubles quite overmatched his own. The difference was that Rosecrans' woes came mainly from above, whereas Bragg's came mainly from below. As a result, the latter were not only more widely spread, they were also frequently sharper barbed. His harsh discipline in camp, unbalanced by conspicuous victories in the field, and his reputation as a commander who invariably retreated after battle, whether his troops won or lost, had resulted in bitter censure from all sides, civil as well as military, in and out of the newspapers. Riding one day near his Tullahoma headquarters, soon after his withdrawal behind Duck River, he encountered a man wearing butternut garb and requested information about the roads. When this had been given, the general thanked him and, unable to tell from his clothes whether the man was a soldier or a civilian — the kindest thing that could be said about dress in the Army of Tennessee was that it was informal — asked if he belonged to Bragg's army. "Bragg's army?" the countryman replied, scowling at the grim-faced man on horseback. "Bragg's got no army. He shot half of them himself, up in Kentucky, and the other half got killed at Murfreesboro."

Bragg laughed and rode on, curbing for once his terrible temper. But the experience rankled under pressure of newspaper criticisms leveled at him while his troops were getting settled along their new defensive line: particularly the charge, widely printed and reprinted, that he had pulled out of Murfreesboro against the advice of his lieutenants. This was patently untrue, as he could prove by the note from Cheatham and Withers, urging immediate retreat, which he had rejected, at least at first, despite Polk's indorsement of their plea. Accordingly, he decided to make an issue of it, addressing on January 11 a letter to his chief subordinates. "It becomes necessary for me to save my fair name," he wrote, and "stop the deluge of abuse which [threatens to] destroy my usefulness and demoralize this army." He asked them to acquit him of the fabrication that he had gone against their wishes in ordering a retreat, which in point of fact "was resisted by me for some time after [it was] advised by my corps and division commanders.... Unanimous as you were in council in verbally advising a retrograde movement," he added, "I cannot doubt that you will cheerfully attest the same in writing." So far, he was on safe ground. Unwilling to let it go at that, however, he closed with something of a flourish: "I desire that you will consult your subordinate commanders and be candid with me.... I shall retire without a regret if I find I have lost the good opinion of my generals, upon whom I have ever relied as upon a foundation of rock."

This last was what opened the floodgates. Though none could fail to exonerate him from the specific charge that he had originated the notion of retreat, his closing statement that he would retire if he found that he had lost their good opinion presented the generals with a once-in-a-lifetime opportunity, which they did not neglect. Hardee, after pointing out that neither he nor his division commanders had proposed a withdrawal, though they had made no objection once the decision had been announced, replied that he had consulted his subordinates, as requested, and found them "unanimous in the opinion that a change in the command of this army is necessary. In this opinion I concur." He had "the highest regard for the purity of your motives, your energy, and your personal character," he told Bragg, but he was "convinced, as you must feel, that the peril of the country is superior to all personal considerations." His lieutenants replied in a similar vein. "I have consulted with my brigade commanders," Cleburne wrote, "and they unite with me in personal regard for yourself... but at the same time they see, with regret, and it has also met my observation, that you do not possess the confidence of the army in other respects in that degree necessary to secure success." Breckinridge was as forthright, and what was more — the officers and men of his division having found Bragg's report of the recent battle so disparaging to themselves and their dead comrades that they had urged their chief to challenge him to a duel — took perhaps the greatest satisfaction of all in seizing the present chance to sit in judgment. "Acting with the candor which you invoke," the former Vice President replied, "[my brigade commanders] request me to say that, in their opinion, the conduct of the military operations in front of Murfreesboro made it necessary for our army to retire." Lest the irony of this be lost, he passed at once to a summation. "They also request me to say that while they entertain the highest respect for your patriotism, it is their opinion that you do not possess the confidence of the army to an extent which will enable you to be useful as its commander. In this opinion I feel bound to state that I concur."

Polk was away on leave at the time, visiting his refugee family in North Carolina, and in his absence Cheatham and Withers merely replied with an acknowledgment that they had made the original suggestion to withdraw. When the bishop returned at the end of the month he found the army a-buzz with talk of this latest development. Since there was some difference of opinion as to whether Bragg had really intended to call down all this thunder on his head, Polk wrote to ask whether his chief had meant for him to answer both questions — 1) as to who was responsible for bringing up the subject of retreat, and 2) as to whether the army commander had lost the confidence of his subordinates — or only the first. Bragg by now had had quite enough "candid" responses to the second question, and stated that he had only wanted to get an opinion on the inception of the retreat; "The paragraph relating to my supercedure was only an expression of the feeling with which I should receive your replies." In that case, Polk responded, he believed the original battlefield note would suffice as a documentary answer. He was content to let the matter drop. But learning presently that Hardee and his officers felt that he had dodged the issue, thereby leaving them in the position of insubordinate malcontents, he decided to write directly to his friend the President, attaching the rather voluminous correspondence he had had with Bragg. "I feel it my duty to say to you," he told Davis, "that had I and my division commanders been asked to answer, our replies would have coincided with those of the officers of the other corps.... My opinion is he had better be transferred." The best place for him, Polk believed, was Richmond, where "his capacity for organization and discipline, which has not been equaled among us, could be used by you at headquarters with infinite advantage to the whole army. I think, too," he added, "that the best thing to be done in supplying his place would be to give his command to General Joseph E. Johnston. He will cure all discontent and inspire the army with new life and confidence. He is here on the spot, and I am sure will be content to take it."

Davis was quite aware that Johnston was at Tullahoma, having ordered him there two weeks ago, when Bragg's circular, together with the replies of Hardee and his lieutenants, first landed on the presidential desk. "Why General Bragg should have selected that tribunal, and have invited its judgment upon him, is to me unexplained; it manifests, however, a condition of things which seems to me to require your presence." So Davis wrote Johnston, who was engaged at the time in an inspection of the Mobile defenses, instructing him to proceed at once to Bragg's headquarters and determine "whether he had so far lost the confidence of the army as to impair his usefulness in his present position.... You will, I trust, be able, by conversation with General Bragg and others of his command, to decide what the best interests of the service require, and to give me the advice which I need at this juncture. As that army is part of your command," the President added, knowing the Virginian's meticulosity in such matters, "no order will be necessary to give you authority there, as, whether present or absent, you have a right to direct its operations and do whatever else belongs to the general commanding."

However, Johnston's squeamishness went further than Davis reckoned. He found much that was improper in the conduct of an inquiry which might result in the displacement of the officer under investigation by the one who was doing the investigating. Besides, he had a high regard for the grim-faced North Carolinian's abilities. "Bragg has done wonders, I think," he wrote privately. "No body of troops has done more in proportion to numbers in the same time." Accordingly on February 3, ten days after his arrival, although "incessant rain has permitted me to see but a fourth of the troops as yet," he reported them "in high spirits, and as ready as ever for fight." He found his confidence in Bragg not only unshaken but "confirmed by his recent operations, which, in my opinion, evince great vigor and skill." In short: "It would be very unfortunate to remove him at this juncture, when he has just earned, if not won, the gratitude of the country." He would report more fully, Johnston said, when he had completed his inspection. Meanwhile, "I respectfully suggest that, should it appear to you necessary to remove General Bragg, no one in this army or engaged in this investigation ought to be his successor." Nine days later, his final report buttressed his first impression. He had found the men "well clothed, healthy, and in good spirits," which gave "positive evidence of General Bragg's capacity to command.... To me it seems that the operations of this army in Middle Tennessee have been conducted admirably. I can find no record of more effective fighting in modern battles than that of this army in December, evincing great skill in the commander and courage in the troops." He had heard, he said in closing, that Polk and Hardee had advised their present chief's removal and his own appointment to the command; but "I am sure that you will agree with me that the part I have borne in this investigation would render it inconsistent with my personal honor to occupy that position.... General Bragg should not be removed."

With that, he left for Chattanooga. Davis replied that he was "truly gratified at the language of commendation which you employ in relation to General Bragg," but he considered it "scarcely possible," in the light of Polk's and Hardee's formal disapproval, "for [Bragg] to possess the requisite confidence of the troops." He still thought Johnston should take over, and he could not see that this involved any breach of military etiquette. Johnston was already in command, by rank and title, whenever he was on the scene; "The removal of General Bragg would only affect you so far as it deprived you of his services." However, Davis assured him, "You shall not be urged by me to any course which would wound your sensibility of views of professional propriety." In early March, Johnston having made no reply to this, the Secretary of War added his pleas to those of the Commander in Chief. It was his opinion that Bragg should be "recalled altogether," but if Johnston's conscience would not permit this, then he suggested that he keep him at hand, "as an organizer and disciplinarian," in the post of assistant commander. "Let me urge you, my dear general," Seddon wrote, "to think well, in view of all the great interests to our beloved South ... and, if possible, make the sacrifice of your honorable delicacy to the importance of the occasion and the greatness of our cause." When Johnston still did not reply — he was back in Mobile by now, though Davis and Seddon supposed he was still in Chattanooga — the matter was taken out of his hands by a wire from Richmond, which reached him on March 12: "Order General Bragg to report to the War Department here for conference. Assume yourself direct charge of the army in Middle Tennessee."

Perhaps Davis and Seddon had decided that what Johnston had been wanting all along, and even hinting at, was for them to *order* him to the post in spite of his objections; that way, the conditions of honor would be met, since he would have done all he could to avoid the outcome. If so, they were wrong. Johnston really did not want the command. The fact was, he did not want the larger one he had already — his duties, he said disparagingly, were those of an "inspector general"— despite the President's and the Secretary's insistence that it was the most important post in the Confederacy. If that was the case, Lee should have it as a reward for his recent accomplishments; then "with great propriety," Johnston wrote in confidence to a friend, he himself could return to his native Virginia and resume command of the army he had lost at Seven Pines, "where the Yankee bullets found me." Now it looked as if that hope was going up in smoke. He was ordered to Middle Tennessee, with no alternative to compliance except submission of his resignation.

So it seemed. When he returned to Tullahoma on March 19, however, he found a way — still on grounds of sparing offense to what Seddon had called his "honorable delicacy"— at least to delay what he had sought all this time to avoid. Bragg's wife was down with typhoid, despaired of by the doctors, and her husband had given over his official duties in order to be at her bedside round the clock. It was therefore no more than normal courtesy, under the circumstances, for Johnston to carry out that portion of the orders which required him to take command of the army; but as for increasing the distracted general's present woes by instructing him to report at once to Richmond, that was manifestly impossible, Johnston wired the authorities, "on account of Mrs Bragg's critical condition." Besides, he added, the country was "becoming practicable" now that the rains had slacked and the roads were drying; "Should the enemy advance, General Bragg will be indispensable here." Apparently he intended to take the Secretary's earlier suggestion that he keep the unpopular general at hand as his assistant. But presently even this went by the board. By the time Mrs Bragg had recovered sufficiently from her illness to permit her husband's return to active duty, Johnston himself was bedridden, suffering from a debility brought on by a flare-up of his wounds. "General Bragg is therefore necessary here," he notified Richmond on April 10. "If conference with him is still desirable, might not a confidential officer visit him, for the purpose, in Tullahoma?"

* * *

That was that; Bragg remained at his post by default, so to speak. Meanwhile — principally by courtesy of Rosecrans, who, though the methods employed to avoid compliance were quite different in each case, would no more be budged by his superiors than Johnston would be influenced by his — the Army of Tennessee enjoyed, throughout the opening half of the year, the longest period of inaction afforded any considerable body of Confederates in the whole course of the war. Polk's corps was on the left at Shelbyville, Hardee's on the right at Wartrace, with cavalry extending the long defensive line westward to Columbia and eastward to McMinnville, seventy air-line miles apart. Breastworks protected by abatis were thrown up along the critical center, and behind them, once the countryside emerged from the quagmires created by the late winter and early spring rains — which had afforded one self-styled etymologist the opportunity to remark that the name of the little railroad town where Bragg had his headquarters was derived from the conjunction of two Greek words: *tulla*, meaning "mud," and *homa*, meaning "more mud" — the infantry enjoyed the foison of the lush Duck River Valley and indulged in such diversions as attending church services and revival meetings (Bragg set an example here by allowing himself to be baptized in an impressive ceremony) or chuck-a-luck games and cockfights, depending on individual inclinations. The army's effective strength had risen by now to almost 50,000 of all arms, including better than 15,000 cavalry, who passed the time in a quite different manner by probing at Rosecrans' flanks and rear and harassing his front.

Joe Wheeler got things off to a rousing start on January 13 with a strike at Harpeth Shoals, midway between Nashville and Clarksville, where he captured or sank four loaded packets and one lightly armored gunboat, taking them under fire from the bank, and thus effectively suspended the flow of goods up the Cumberland River, the main Federal supply line. But this accomplishment was more than offset, another fifty miles downstream, by the repulse he suffered on February 3 when he launched an ill-conceived and poorly co-ordinated assault on an outnumbered but stout blue garrison at Dover, two weeks short of the anniversary of the fall of adjacent Fort Donelson to Grant. Bedford Forrest, who had not only lost some of his best men but had also had two fine horses shot from under him in the course of attacks which he had advised against making in the first place, was so incensed by Wheeler's handling of the affair that he bluntly told the young commander that he would resign from the army before he would fight again under his direction. The discouraged graybacks limped back to Columbia, the western tip of Bragg's long crescent. Meanwhile, far out the opposite horn, Morgan was doing no better, if indeed as well. With two of his regiments de-

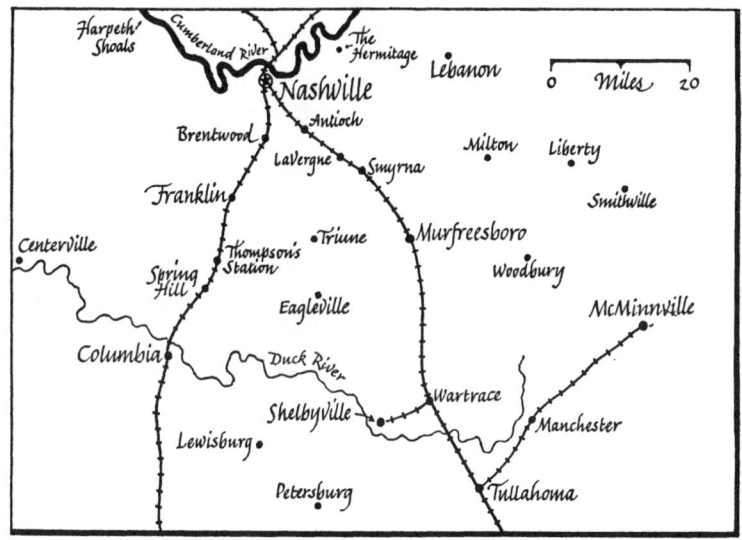

tached to stir up excitement in Kentucky, he too suffered a bloody repulse at the hands of an inferior force on March 20 at Milton, fifteen miles northeast of Murfreesboro, and still another, two weeks later, at nearby Liberty, which resulted in his being driven in some confusion back on his base at McMinnville. Perhaps the best that could be said for all these various affairs, at any rate from the Confederate point of view, was that they all occurred within the Union lines and therefore served, victories and defeats alike, to keep Rosecrans off balance by increasing his native caution and apprehensiveness. "Their numerous cavalry goads and worries me," he had informed Washington at the outset, "but I will try to be equal to them."

This was going to be more difficult than he knew. Even as he wrote, Earl Van Dorn, the South's ranking major general — ordered north by Johnston over Pemberton's frantic protest at thus being practically stripped of cavalry despite the skill he recently had shown in handling that arm — was on the way from Mississippi with two divisions of horsemen, all thirsty for more of the glory they lately had tasted when they threw a whole Yankee army into retreat from Holly Springs. In this respect, their leader was the thirstiest man among them. After the Transmississippi disasters and the Corinth fiasco, which had resulted, amid wholesale condemnation, in his being superseded as commander of his home state forces, his bad luck had suddenly turned good, and he was eager to take further advantage of the switch. Presently, soon after his arrival on February 22 at Columbia, where he assumed responsibility for protecting the left horn of Bragg's crescent while Wheeler protected the right, Rosecrans gave the diminutive Mississippian just the chance he had been seeking ever since his return to his first love, cavalry. The Federal plan was for a convergence of two infantry columns, one out of Murfreesboro under Phil Sheridan, the other out of Franklin, directly south of Nashville, under Colonel John Coburn; they would unite at Spring Hill, a dozen miles north of Columbia, then move together against that place, foraging as they went. Coburn set out on March 4, with just under 3000 of all arms. Van Dorn was waiting for him next morning at Thompson's Station, just above the intended point of convergence, with twice as many men — including Forrest, who had been transferred in consideration of his vow to serve no more under Wheeler. The result was a sudden and stunning victory, cinched by Forrest, who came in on the flank and rear while Van Dorn maintained pressure against the front, and a bag of 1221 prisoners, including Coburn, whose artillery and cavalry, along with one of his infantry regiments assigned to guard the forage train, had fled at the first detection of the odds. His thirst unslaked, Van Dorn sent his captives south and turned east to tackle Sheridan, intending thus to sweep the board of all available opponents, but found that the other column had taken warning from the boom of guns and pulled back out of danger.

Rosecrans too had taken alarm, and though his present-for-duty strength now stood at 80,124, as compared to Bragg's 49,068, he began to suspect that he was outnumbered. "I am not, as you know, an alarmist," he wired Halleck on the day after Coburn's defeat, "but I do not think it will do to risk as we did before." He reinforced the threatened quarter, causing the rebel horsemen to pull back. But when the blue tide once more receded, Van Dorn returned again, cutting and slashing, left and right, and playing all the while on Rosecrans' fears. On March 24, having leapfrogged his headquarters to Spring Hill, he sent Forrest against Brentwood (ten miles north of Federal-held Franklin) where a garrison of about 800 Wisconsin and Michigan infantry protected army stores and a stockaded railroad bridge across the Little Harpeth River. Forrest appeared before the place next morning, demanding an unconditional surrender. "Come and take us," Colonel Edward Bloodgood replied stoutly, until he saw the graybacks preparing to do just that: whereupon he changed his mind and hauled down his flag. Setting fire to the stockade and packing the stores for removal along with his captives, Forrest sent one regiment up the Nashville pike to spread the scare in that direction — which it did, penetrating the southern environs of the city and riding within plain sight of the capitol tower — while the main body, after pausing to fight a confused rear-guard action provoked by a blue column that moved up from Franklin, made its getaway eastward before turning south to safety. In a general order issued on the last day of the month, Bragg expressed the "pride and gratification" he felt as a result of the "two brilliant and successful affairs recently achieved by the forces of the cavalry of Major General Van Dorn."

Unwilling to rest on his laurels now that fortune's smile was broadening still further, Van Dorn moved on April 10 against Franklin itself. A forced reconnaissance, he called it afterwards, though the defenders insisted that it had been an all-out attempt to take the place by storm. In support of the former contention was the fact that casualties were fewer than a hundred on each side; anyhow, he disengaged and withdrew when he found that the Union commander, Major General Gordon Granger, had been reinforced to a strength of about 8000. Back at Spring Hill, he continued to design projects for the discomfiture of the enemy, assisting Bragg to hold onto the fruitful region despite the odds which favored a Federal advance. On through April he labored, and into May, though apparently not so exclusively as to require him to abandon other pursuits; for at 10 o'clock on the morning of May 7, Dr George B. Peters, a local citizen, walked into headquarters, where Van Dorn was hard at work at his desk, and shot him in the back of the head with a pistol. He died about 2 o'clock that afternoon, by which time the assassin was safe within the Union lines, having ridden off in the buggy he had left parked outside while he stepped indoors to carry out his project. The accepted explanation was that the doctor had chosen this emphatic means to protest the general's attention to his young wife, though there were some who claimed that he had done the shooting for political reasons. At any rate, that was the end of the saga of Buck Van Dorn. Fortune's smile had turned out fickle after all, and they buried him in Columbia next day.

Wheeler had got back in stride by then with a double blow at Rosecrans' rail supply lines on April 10, the day Van Dorn tested the Franklin defenses and found them strong. The first was scored northeast of Nashville, beyond Andrew Jackson's Hermitage, by secretly posting guns along the near bank of a bend that took the Cumberland River within 500-yard range of the Louisville & Nashville tracks. After a wait of two hours, Wheeler reported, "a very large locomotive came in view, drawing eighteen cars loaded with horses and other stock." Though the target was moving his marksmanship was excellent, according to a Federal brigadier. "The first shot knocked off the dome of the locomotive, the next went through the boiler, one shot broke out a spoke in one of the driving-wheels." When the engine stalled in a cloud of steam, the gunners continued to pump shells into the cars, scattering bluecoats, horses, and cattle in all directions. Meanwhile, on the Nashville & Chattanooga side of the Tennessee capital, another group of Wheeler's men rode into Antioch, where they ambushed and derailed a train by spreading the tracks and took from the wreckage about seventy Union captives — including twenty officers, three of whom were members of Rosecrans' staff — along with some forty Confederates en route to Ohio prison camps, $30,000 in greenbacks, and a large mail containing much useful information. Loaded with booty, the raiders got away eastward to join their friends, who by now had ridden back past the Hermitage after their shooting-gallery fun on the Cumberland. Wheeler's total cost for both accomplishments was one man wounded.

He was cheered all round and greeted with smiles on his return, for both actions had a somewhat comic tinge. But the loudest cheers and the broadest smiles were reserved for Bedford Forrest, who began to win his *nom de guerre* "the Wizard of the Saddle" with an exploit which took him, through the closing days of April and the opening days of May, into parts of three states and across the northern width of Alabama. He was drawn in that direction by a Federal project which got under way, by coincidence on that same April 10, with the embarkation at Nashville of an expedition designed to sever Bragg's main supply line, the Western & Atlantic Railroad, between Atlanta and Chattanooga. This had been attempted once before, a year ago this week, but had resulted in the Great Locomotive Chase and the capture of the twenty-two spies who tried it. The new plan, while perhaps equally daring, was of a quite different nature. Taking a page from the book the rebel cavalry fought by — particularly John Morgan and Forrest himself — Colonel Abel D. Streight, New-York-born commander of a regiment of Hoosier infantry, proposed to Rosecrans that a large body of men, say 2000, be mounted for a quick but powerful thrust, into and out of the South's vitals. Rosecrans, who so often had been on the receiving end of this kind of thing, was delighted at the prospect of turning the tables, and his delight increased when Streight removed his final objection by agreeing to mount the men on mules instead of horses, of which there was a shortage; mules, he said, were not only more sure-footed, they were also more intelligent. (Which was true, so far as it went, though that was by no means all of the story. Mules had other, less admirable qualities: as he would presently discover.) At any rate, Rosecrans gave his approval to the project, designated Streight as commander, and assigned him three more regiments of Ohio, Indiana, and Illinois infantry, together with two companies of North Alabama Unionists — a breed of men who were known to their late compatriots as "homemade Yankees," but who were expected to prove invaluable as guides through a region unfamiliar to everyone else in the flying column — and a requisition for some nine hundred quartermaster mules. This would mount only about half of the troops, but Rosecrans explained that the rest could secure animals by commandeering them from rebel sympathizers while on the way to their starting point in the northeast corner of Mississippi.

So Streight got his men and mules aboard the transports and steamed next morning down the Cumberland to unload at Palmyra, on the left bank just around the bend from Clarksville, for a stock-gathering march to Fort Henry, where they again met the transports for the long ride south up the Tennessee to Eastport, Mississippi. That was the true starting point, tactically speaking, but Streight — a broad-chested man of soldierly appearance, just past forty, with a tall forehead, light-colored eyes, a fleshy, powerful-looking nose, and a dark, well-trimmed beard framing a wide, determined mouth exposed below a clean-shaven upper lip — had already encountered complications well outside the original margin he had allowed for error. For one thing, after waiting to pick up rations and forage on the Ohio, the navy did not turn up at Fort Henry on time, with the result that he did not reach Eastport until April 19, three days behind schedule. For another, a delayed check disclosed that a large proportion of the quartermaster mules were sadly afflicted with distemper, while many others were unbroken colts, not over two years old. This last exposed a further drawback; for he found that his converted infantrymen, as one of them remarked, "were at first very easily dismounted, frequently in a most undignified and unceremonious manner." Practice might improve the men's equestrian skill, but the mules were going to remain a problem. About five hundred had been commandeered on the course of the overland march, which more than made up for the hundred-odd who died of sickness and exhaustion while en route; but this gain was canceled on the evening of his arrival at Eastport. Returning to headquarters about midnight from a conference with Brigadier General Grenville M. Dodge, who had brought a 7500-man column over from Corinth to serve as a screen for the raiders' departure, he learned that some four hundred of the creatures — naturally the most intelligent of the lot — had escaped from their crudely built corrals and now were scattered about the countryside, disrupting the stillness of the night and mocking his woes with brays that had the sound of fiendish laughter. Two more days were spent here in rounding them up; half of them, that is, for the rest were never recovered. However, Dodge made up the difference with animals out of his pack train, and Streight at last got started in earnest, moving eastward across Bear Creek on the morning of April 22.

Five days behind schedule, but still protected from inquisitive eyes by the screen Dodge's troops had drawn along the south bank of the Tennessee River, he reached Tuscumbia late on the 24th and called a final two-day rest halt before resuming the march at 11 p.m. of the 26th, his force reduced to 1500 by a rigid inspection in which the surgeons culled such men as they judged unfit for the rigorous work ahead. All next day, and the next, as the column moved south to Russellville, then eastward to Mount Hope, rain and mud held its progress to a crawl and 300 of the fledgling troopers were reconverted to infantry because their mounts were too weak to carry anything heavier than a saddle. On the 29th, however, the sun broke through, giving "strong hopes of better times," as Streight declared in his last rearward message, and he began to pick up speed, along with replacements for his ailing mules. Thirty-five miles he made that day, clearing Moulton to make camp that night at the western foot of Day's Gap, a narrow defile piercing a lofty ridge that signaled the advent of the Appalachians. At this point, with the tactically dangerous flatlands left behind, he was about halfway to his first objective: Rome, Georgia, where the Confederacy had a cannon foundry and machine shops for the Western & Atlantic, whose main line was barely a half-day's ride beyond. Starting early next morning, the last day of April, Streight rode at the head of the column toiling upward through the gap. "The sun shone out bright and beautiful as spring day's sun ever beamed," his adjutant later recalled, "and from the smouldering campfires of the previous night the mild blue smoke ascended in graceful curves and mingled with the gray mist slumbering on the mountain tops above." There was in fact much that was dreamlike and idyllic about the scene —"well calculated to inspire and refresh the minds of our weary soldiers," the admiring lieutenant phrased it — until suddenly, without previous intimation of a transition, as Streight and the forward elements of the column neared the crest, the dream shifted kaleidoscopically into nightmare. From downhill, in the direction of last night's camp, the deep-voiced booms of guns, mixed in with the tearing rattle of musketry, abruptly informed him that he was under attack.

It was Forrest. A week ago today — the day after Streight left Eastport — he had received at Spring Hill, Tennessee, orders from Bragg to proceed south to the Florence-Tuscumbia region and assist the inadequate local defense units to oppose the force moving eastward under Dodge. He left next morning, April 24, and thirty-six hours later had his 1577-man brigade at Brown's Ferry, Alabama, ninety miles away. Leaving one of his three regiments to guard the north bank of the Tennessee in case Dodge decided to strike in that direction, he ferried the others across on the 26th and moved west through Courtland to Town Creek, which he reached in time to challenge a Federal crossing. The long-range skirmish continued until dusk of the following day, when Forrest received word from a scout that a mounted column estimated at 2000 men had left Mount Hope that morning, headed east. This was the first he had heard of Streight's existence, but he decided at once that this was the major threat, not the larger force immediately to his front. Accordingly, leaving Dodge to the local defenders and the regiment already posted beyond the river, he took off southward at dawn of the 29th for Moulton, which Streight had cleared six hours before. At midnight, having covered fifty miles of road with just over a thousand horsemen and eight guns, he went into bivouac, four miles short of Streight's camp at Day's Gap, in order to give his saddle-weary troopers some rest for tomorrow, and soon after sunrise was banging away at the Federal rear.

In the course of the three-day running fight which followed, the pursued had certain definite advantages. The first was a superiority of numbers, although Streight's enjoyment of this was considerably diminished by the fact that he did not know he had it. All the same, the numerical odds were with him, three to two, whether he knew it or not, and what was more they grew as he moved eastward past well-stocked farms untouched by war till now. When his mules gave out, as they frequently did, he could remount his men by seizing others; whereas for Forrest, coming along in the raiders' clean-swept wake, a broken-down horse meant a lost rider. Another tactical advantage accruing to the blue commander was that whenever he chose to make a stand he could not only select the terrain best suited for defensive fighting, he could also lay small-scale ambushes by which a rear-guard handful could shock the pursuers with surprise fire, forcing them to halt and deploy, then hurry ahead to rejoin the main body before the attack was delivered. Streight was altogether aware of this advantage, and used it first within three miles of the point where he heard the opening boom of guns. Selecting a position along a wooded ridge, with a boggy creek protecting his left and a steep ravine his right, he sent back word for the rear-guard Alabama Unionists, still skirmishing in Day's Gap, to retreat on the run through the newly drawn line and thus draw the graybacks into ambush. It worked to perfection. As the pursuers rode fast to overtake the homemade Yankees, the waiting bluecoats rose from the underbrush and shattered the head of the column with massed volleys. When reinforcements came up to repeat the attempt, this time advancing a section of artillery to counterbalance the two 12-pounder mountain howitzers firing rapidly from the ridge, the defenders followed up a second repulse with a counterattack and captured both of the guns, then drew off, leaving the rebels rocked back on their heels.

Forrest was thrown into a towering rage by the loss of his guns and the fact that the raiders had won first honors and drawn first blood — including that of his brother, Captain William Forrest, who had led his company of scouts in the charge and had been unhorsed by a bullet that broke his thigh — but by the time he got his troopers back into line for a third attack, the bluecoats had pulled out. He pushed on, closing again on their rear at Crooked Creek, where Streight again formed line of battle, six miles beyond the first. Here, from about an hour before dark until 10 o'clock that night, the two forces engaged in a fire fight. Determined to give the raiders no rest, Forrest kept forcing the issue by moonlight, and his orders, though brief, were conclusive: "Shoot at everything blue and keep up the scare." Finally, with one flank about to crumple, Streight "resumed the march," leaving the two captured guns behind him, spiked. At midnight, then again two hours later, he laid ambushes, but Forrest kept crowding him and did not call a halt till daylight, when he paused long enough to water and feed the horses and give the weaker ones an opportunity to catch up. Streight meanwhile pushed on to the outskirts of Blountsville, which he reached about midmorning of May Day, having covered forty-three miles over mountain roads since the skirmishing began soon after sunrise yesterday. However, before his men could finish feeding their weary mounts, Forrest once more was driving in the pickets, and the two commands went through the town in a whirl of dust and gunsmoke, shooting at one another over the ears of their horses or the cruppers of their mules.

So it went, all that day and the next, eastward another fifty miles, then northeastward along the near bank of the Coosa River, with Streight making stands behind the east fork of the Black Warrior River and Big Will's Creek, laying ambushes in the heavily wooded valley off the southern end of Lookout Mountain, and burning the only bridge across Black Creek, just short of Gadsden. Forrest kept the pressure on, however. He got over the last-named obstacle by using a ford that was shown him, under fire from the opposite bank, by a sixteen-year-old farm girl, Emma Sanson — in appreciation of whose courage he took time and pains to leave an autograph note of thanks:

> *Hed Quaters in Sadle*
> *May 2 1863*
> *My highest regardes to miss Ema Sanson for hir Gallant conduct while my posse was skirmishing with the Federals across Black Creek near Gadesden Allabama.*
> *N. B. Forrest*
> *Brig Genl Comding N. Ala —*

and pressed on after the blue raiders, engaging them in another running fight through Gadsden and beyond, where they soon were forced to make another stand. He had the advantage of singleness of purpose, plus the chance to give his men a breather when he chose, pursuing as it were in shifts, some resting while others kept up the chase; whereas Streight not only had to keep fending off the myriad and apparently inexhaustible graybacks hot on his trail — a profitless business at best — but also had to keep pushing on toward the accomplishment of his mission in North Georgia. After nearly three days of riding and fighting, and two nights without rest, his men were falling asleep on muleback and even in line of battle whenever he called a halt to lay another ambush or defend another opportune position, and now that his pursuers had avoided delay at Black Creek, thanks to Emma Sanson, he faced another sleepless night. "It now became evident to me," he later reported, "that our only hope was in crossing the river at Rome and destroying the bridge, which would delay Forrest a day or two and give us time to collect horses and mules and allow the command a little time to sleep, without which it was impossible to proceed."

Accordingly, when he reached Turkeytown, eight miles beyond Gadsden, he selected two hundred of the best-mounted men and sent them ahead to seize the bridge across the Oostanaula River at Rome and hold it until the main body came up. At sunset, four miles farther along, he formed again for battle "as it was impossible to continue the march through the night without feeding and resting." In the course of the preliminary skirmish, however, he discovered that much of the men's

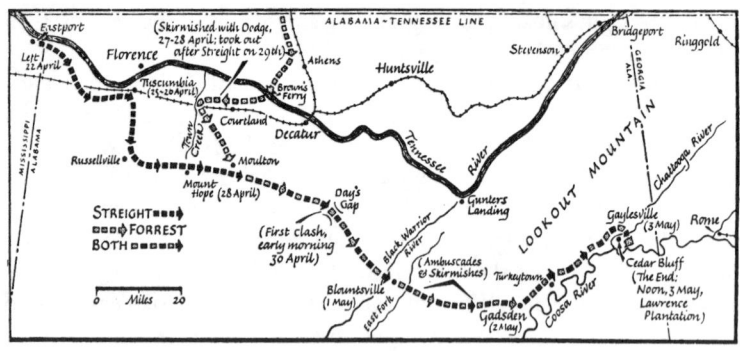

ammunition had been ruined by dampness and abrasion. Instead of risking another general engagement under these circumstances, he decided to disengage — "unobserved, if possible" — and lay another ambush in a thicket half a mile ahead. When Forrest detected the ruse and began to move out on the flank, Streight had to pull back and make a run for it in the dusk, beginning another horrendous night march with men who by now had the look of somnambulists and mules that were "jaded, tender-footed, and worn out." But the worst development, so far, was encountered when they reached the Cedar Bluff ferry across the Chattooga River, just above its confluence with the Coosa. The 200-man detail had passed this way a short while back, headed for Rome, but had neglected to post a guard: with the result that some citizens had spirited the ferryboat away, leaving Streight with the sort of problem he had been leaving Forrest all along.

Yet he was nothing if not persevering. Turning left, he plodded wearily through the darkness along the west bank of the Chattooga, intent on reaching a bridge near Gaylesville, half a dozen miles upstream. Whereupon — while Forrest was giving his troopers a few hours' sleep: all but one squadron, which he instructed to stay on the trail of the raiders and "devil them all night" — Streight and his muleback soldiers entered the worst of their several Deep South nightmares. The way led through extensive "choppings" where the timber had been cut and burned to furnish charcoal for nearby Round Mountain Furnace, which in turn supplied the Rome foundry with pig iron. Though the raiders succeeded in wrecking part of the smelting plant — the one substantial blow they struck in the course of their long ride across Alabama — they paid a high price in the extra miles they covered in order to bring it within reach. Lost in a maze of wagon trails, segments of the blue column were scattered about the choppings until daylight showed them the way back to the river and then to the bridge, which they crossed and burned in their wake. Wobbly with fatigue, animals and men alike, they staggered along the opposite bank, again to the vicinity of Cedar Bluff, then turned eastward five more miles to the Lawrence plantation, which they reached about 9 a.m. The Georgia line was only five miles ahead, with Rome barely another fifteen miles beyond, but Streight had no choice except to drop from exhaustion or halt for rest and food. He had no sooner begun the distribution of rations, however, than the graybacks once more were driving in his pickets.

Forrest had swum the Chattooga at sunup, using long ropes to drag two of his guns across, submerged on the sandy bottom. Down to six hundred men by now, he was outnumbered worse than two to one and knew it, even if Streight did not. All along he had had to avoid the obvious maneuver of circling the flank of the blue column in order to block its path; for in that case, goaded by desperation, the Federals might have run right over him, swamping his line with the sheer weight of numbers. Even now, in fact, though his troopers were considerably refreshed by the sleep they had enjoyed while the bluecoats were stumbling around in the choppings south of Gaylesville, he preferred not to risk a pitched battle if he could accomplish his purpose otherwise. So he did as he had done before, in similar circumstances: sent forward, under a flag of truce, an officer with a note demanding immediate surrender "to stop the further and useless effusion of blood."

Streight, who had had to wake his men to put them into line of battle — where they promptly fell asleep again, with bullets whistling overhead — replied that he was by no means ready to give up, but that, sharing Forrest's humane views as to unnecessary bloodshed, he was willing to parley. He insisted further, when the guns fell silent and the two commanders met between the lines, that he would not even consider laying down his arms unless his opponent would prove that he had an overwhelming superiority of numbers. Forrest declined to show his hand in any such manner; but all the while, acting under previous instructions, the officer in charge of the section of artillery kept bringing his two guns over a distant rise in the road, then back under cover and over the rise again, producing for the benefit of Streight, who had been placed so as to watch all this over Forrest's shoulder, the appearance of a stream of guns arriving at intervals to bolster the rebel line. "Name of God!" Streight cried at last. "How many guns have you got? There's fifteen I've counted already." Forrest looked around casually. "I reckon that's all that has kept up," he said. So Streight went back to his own lines for a conference with his regimental commanders, most of whom, as he later reported, "had already expressed the opinion that, unless we could reach Rome and cross the river before the enemy came up with us again, we should be compelled to surrender." At this juncture, a messenger arrived from the 200-man detail sent ahead the night before and reported that the bridge across the Oostanaula was strongly held by rebel troops in Rome. That did it; Streight returned and announced his willingness to surrender. Forrest replied, "Stack your arms right along there, Colonel, and march your men away down that hollow."

The total bag, including the 200-man detail picked up on the way into Rome that same Sunday afternoon as it returned from its fruitless mission, was 1466 bluecoats, and though they had been feared as would-be conquerors — a fear which had thrown the Rome citizenry into such a panic of feverish activity that the Federal scouts, observing from across the Oostanaula, had mistaken the milling for preparedness — they were welcomed and fed generously as captives. Forrest's own entrance was the occasion for the presentation of a horseshoe wreath of flowers, hailing him as the town's deliverer, and a fine saddle horse, which helped to make up for the two that had been shot from under him in the course of the long chase. Then began a famous celebration, attended by what one matron called "just a regular wholesale cooking of hams and shoulders and all sorts of provisions" to relieve the hunger pangs of the gray heroes. Nor were the prisoners excluded from this bounty; "We were quite willing to feed the Yankees when they had no guns," she added. But the Roman holiday was cut short on the night of May 5 by the arrival of word that another column of blue raiders had left Tuscumbia that afternoon, headed southeast for Jasper and possibly Montgomery. Forrest and his men were back in the saddle next morning. Riding once more through Gadsden the following day, they learned that the rumor was groundless, Dodge having returned to Corinth; so they swung north, recovering the third regiment en route, to resume their accustomed work in Tennessee. On May 10, however — another Sunday — Forrest was handed orders from Bragg, instructing him to have his brigade continue its present march but for him to report in person to army headquarters, where he would receive, along with a recommendation for promotion to major general, appointment to the command Van Dorn had vacated three days ago, when he came under the Spring Hill doctor's pistol.

✘ 5 ✘

Along toward sunset of January 28, completing a 400-mile overnight trip from Memphis down the swollen, tawny, mile-wide Mississippi, a stern-wheel packet warped in for a west-bank landing at Young's Point, just opposite the base of the long hairpin bend in front of Vicksburg and within half a dozen air-line miles of the guns emplaced along the lip of the tall clay bluff the city stood on. First off the steamboat, once the deck hands had swung out the stageplank, was a slight man, rather stooped, five feet eight inches in height and weighing less than a hundred and forty pounds, who walked with a peculiar gait, shoulders hunched "a little forward of the perpendicular," as one observer remarked, so that each step seemed to arrest him momentarily in the act of pitching on his face. He had on a plain blue suit and what the same reporter called "an indifferently good 'Kossuth' hat, with the top battered in close to his head." Forty years old, he looked considerably older, partly because of the crow's-feet crinkling the outer corners of his eyes — the result of intense concentration, according to some, while others identified them as whiskey lines, plainly confirming rumors of overindulgence and refuting the protestations of friends that he never touched the stuff — but mainly because of the full, barely grizzled, light brown beard, close-cropped to emphasize the jut of a square jaw and expose a mouth described as being "of the letterbox shape," clamped firmly shut below a nose that surprised by contrast, being delicately chiseled, and blue-gray eyes that gave the face a somewhat out-of-balance look because one was set a trifle lower than the other. Wearing neither sword nor sash, and indeed no trappings of rank at all, except for the twin-starred straps of a major general tacked to the weathered shoulders of his coat, he was reading a newspaper as he came down the plank to the Louisiana shore, and he chewed the unlighted stump of a cigar, which not only seemed habitual but also appeared to be a more congruous facial appendage than the surprisingly aquiline nose.

"There's General Grant," an Illinois soldier told a comrade as they stood watching this unceremonious arrival.

"I guess not," the other replied, shaking his head. "That fellow don't look like he has the ability to command a regiment, much less an army."

It was not so much that Grant was unexpected; he had a habit of turning up unannounced at almost any time and place within the limits of his large department. The trouble was that he bore such faint resemblance to his photographs, which had been distributed widely ever since Donelson and which, according to an acquaintance, made him look like a "burly beef-contractor." In person he resembled at best a badly printed copy of one of those photos, with the burliness left out. Conversely, the lines of worry — if his friends were right and that was what they were — were more pronounced, as was perhaps only natural when he had more to fret about than the discomfort of holding still for a camera. Just now, for instance, there was John McClernand, who persisted in considering the river force a separate command and continued to issue general orders under the heading, "Headquarters, Army of the Mississippi." Before Grant had been downriver two days he received a letter from McClernand, noting "that orders are being issued directly from your headquarters directly to army corps commanders, and not through me." This could only result in "dangerous confusion," McClernand protested, "as I am invested, by order of the Secretary of War, indorsed by the President, and by order of the President communicated to you by the General-in-Chief, with the command of all the forces operating on the Mississippi River.... If different views are entertained by you, then the question should be immediately referred to Washington, and one or the other, or both of us, relieved. One thing is certain; two generals cannot command this army, issuing independent and direct orders to subordinate officers, and the public service be promoted."

Grant agreed at least with the final sentence — which he later paraphrased and sharpened into a maxim: "Two commanders on the same field are always one too many" — but he found the letter as a whole "more in the nature of a reprimand than a protest." The fact was, it approached outright insubordination, although not quite close enough to afford occasion for the pounce Grant was crouched for. "I overlooked it, as I believed, for the good of the service," he subsequently wrote. By way of reply, instead of direct reproof, he issued orders announcing that he was assuming personal command of the river expedition and instructing all corps commanders, including McClernand, to report henceforth directly to him; McClernand's corps, he added by way of a stinger, would garrison Helena and other west-bank points well upriver. Outraged at being the apparent victim of a squeeze play, the former congressman responded by asking whether, "having projected the Mississippi River expedition, and having been by a series of orders assigned to the command of it," he was thus to be "entirely withdrawn from it." Grant replied to the effect that he would do as he saw fit, since "as yet I have seen no order to prevent my taking command in the field." McClernand acquiesced, as he said, "for the purpose of avoiding a conflict of authority in the presence of the enemy," but requested that the entire matter be referred to their superiors in Washington, "not only in respect for the President and Secretary, under whose authority I claim the right to command the expedition, but in justice to myself as its author and actual promoter." Grant accordingly forwarded the correspondence to Halleck, saying that he had assumed command only because he lacked confidence in McClernand. "I respectfully submit the whole matter to the General-in-Chief and the President," he ended his indorsement. "Whatever the decision made by them, I will cheerfully submit to and give a hearty support."

In bucking all this up to the top echelon Grant was on even safer ground than he supposed. Just last week McClernand had received, in reply to a private letter to Lincoln charging Halleck "with wilful contempt of superior authority" because of his so-far "interference" in the matter, "and with incompetency for the extraordinary and vital functions with which he is charged," a note in which the President told him plainly: "I have too many *family* controversies (so to speak) already on my hands to voluntarily, or so long as I can avoid it, take up another. You are now doing well — well for the country, and well for yourself — much better than you could possibly be if engaged in open war with

General Halleck. Allow me to beg that for your sake, for my sake, and for the country's sake, you give your whole attention to the better work." So it was: McClernand already had his answer before he filed his latest appeal. Lincoln would not interfere. The army was Grant's, and would remain Grant's, to do with as he saw fit in accomplishing what Lincoln called "the better work."

His problem was how best to go about it. Now that he had inspected at first hand the obstacles to success in this swampy region, much of which was at present under water and would continue to be so for months to come, he could see that the wisest procedure, from a strategic point of view, "would have been to go back to Memphis, establish that as a base of supplies, fortify it so that the storehouses could be held by a small garrison, and move from there along the line of the [Mississippi & Tennessee] railroad, repairing as we advanced to the Yalobusha," from which point he would have what he now so gravely lacked: a straight, high-ground shot at the city on the rebel bluff. So he wrote, years later, having gained the advantage of hindsight. For the present, however, he saw certain drawbacks to the retrograde movement, which in his judgment far outweighed the strictly tactical advantages. For one thing, the November elections had gone against the party that stood for all-out prosecution of the war, and this had turned out to be a warning of future trouble, with the croakers finding encouragement in the reverse. There was the question of morale, not only in the army itself, but also on the home front, where even a temporary withdrawal would be considered an admission that Vicksburg was too tough a nut to crack. At this critical juncture, both temporal and political, with voluntary enlistment practically at a standstill throughout much of the North and the new conscription laws already meeting sporadic opposition, such a discouragement might well prove fatal to the cause. "It was my judgment at the time," Grant subsequently wrote, "that to make a backward movement as long as that from Vicksburg to Memphis, would be interpreted, by many of those yet full of hope for the preservation of the Union, as a defeat, and that the draft would be resisted, desertions ensue, and the power to capture and punish deserters lost. There was nothing left to be done but to *go forward to a decisive victory*. This was in my mind from the moment I took command in person at Young's Point."

In his own mind at least that much was settled. He would stay. But this decision only brought him face to face with the basic problem, as he put it, of how "to secure a footing upon dry ground on the east side of the river, from which the troops could operate against Vicksburg ... without an apparent retreat." Aside from a frontal assault, either against the bluff itself or against the heights flanking it on the north — which Sherman, even if he had done nothing more last month, had proved would not only be costly in the extreme but would also be fruitless, and which Grant said "was never contemplated; certainly not by me" — the choice lay between whether to cross upstream or down, above or below the rebel bastion. One seemed about as impossible as the other. Above, the swampy, fifty-mile-wide delta lay in his path, practically roadless and altogether malarial. Even if he were able to slog his foot soldiers across it, which was doubtful, it was worse than doubtful whether he would be able to establish and maintain a vital supply line by that route. On the other hand, to attempt a crossing below the city seemed even more suicidal, since this would involve a run past frowning batteries, not only at Vicksburg itself, but also at Warrenton and Grand Gulf, respectively seven and thirty-five miles downriver. Armored gunboats — as Farragut had demonstrated twice the year before, first up, then down, with his heavily gunned salt-water fleet — might run this fiery gauntlet, taking their losses as they went, but brittle-skinned transports and supply boats would be quite another matter, considering the likelihood of their being reduced to kindling in short order, with much attendant loss of life and goods.... In short, the choice seemed to lie between two impossibilities, flanking a third which had been rejected before it was even considered.

Two clear advantages Grant had, however, by way of helping to offset the gloom, and both afforded him comfort under the strain. One was the unflinching support of his superiors; the other was an ample supply of troops, either downstream with him or else on call above. "The eyes and hopes of the whole country are now directed to your army," Halleck presently would tell him. "In my opinion, the opening of the Mississippi River will be to us of more advantage than the capture of forty Richmonds. We shall omit nothing which we can do to assist you." Already, before Grant left Memphis, Old Brains had urged him: "Take everything you can dispense with in Tennessee and [North] Mississippi. We must not fail in this if within human power to accomplish it." His total effective strength within his department, as of late January, was approximately 103,000 officers and men, and of these, as a result of abandoning railroads and other important rear-area installations, Grant had been able to earmark just over half for the downriver expedition: 32,000 in the two corps under McClernand and Sherman, already at hand, and 15,000 in McPherson's corps, filing aboard transports southbound from Memphis even now. In addition to these 47,000 — the official total, "present for duty, equipped," was 46,994 — another 15,000 were standing by under Hurlbut, who commanded the fourth corps, ready to follow McPherson as soon as they got the word. Just now, though, there not only was no need for them; there actually was no room. Because of the high water and the incessant rain overflowing the bayous, there was no place to camp on the low-lying west bank except upon the levee, with the result that the army was strung out along it for more than fifty miles, north and south, under conditions that were anything but healthy.

As morale declined, the sick-lists lengthened; desertions were up; funerals were frequent. "Go any day down the levee," one recruit wrote home, "and you could see a squad or two of soldiers burying a companion, until the levee was nearly full of graves and the hospitals still full of sick. And those that were not down sick were not well by a considerable." Pneumonia was the chief killer, with smallpox a close second. Some regiments soon had more men down than up. The food was bad. Paymasters did not venture south of Helena, which increased the disaffection, and the rumor mills were grinding as never before. When the mails were held up, as they frequently were, it was reported from camp to camp, like a spark moving along a fifty-mile train of powder, that the war was over but that the news was being kept from the troops "for fear we could not be held in subjection if we knew the state of affairs." They took out at least a share of their resentment on such rebel property as came within their reach. "Farms disappear, houses are burned and plundered, and every living animal killed and eaten," Sherman informed his senator brother. "General officers make feeble efforts to stay the disorder, but it is idle." Then when the mail came through at last they could read in anti-administration newspapers of the instability and incompetence of the West Pointers responsible for their welfare, including Sherman — "He hates reporters, foams at the mouth when he sees them, snaps at them; sure symptoms of a deep-seated mania" — and the army commander himself: "The confidence of the army is greatly shaken in General Grant, who hitherto undoubtedly depended more upon good fortune than upon military ability for success."

The wet season would continue for months, during which all these problems would be with him. As Grant said in retrospect, "There seemed to be no possibility of a land movement before the end of March or later." Yet "it would not do to lie idle all this time. The effect would be demoralizing to the troops and injurious to their health. Friends in the North would have grown more and more insolent in their gibes and denunciations of the cause and those engaged in it." So he launched (or rather, continued) what he called "a series of experiments," designed not only "to consume time," but also to serve the triple purpose of diverting "the attention of the enemy, of my troops, and of the public generally." Two failures were already behind him in his campaign against Vicksburg: the advance down the Mississippi Central and the assault on the Chickasaw Bluffs, both of which had ended in retreat. Now there followed five more failures, bringing the total to seven. Looking back on them later he was to say — quite untruthfully, as the record would show — that he had "never felt great confidence that any of the experiments resorted to would prove successful," though he had always been "prepared to take advantage of them in case they did."

The third of these seven "experiments" — the attempt, by means of a canal across the base of the tongue of land in front of Vicksburg, to divert the channel of the river and thus permit the column of warships, transports, and supply boats to bypass the batteries on the bluff — had been in progress ever since the return of the army from Arkansas Post, but Sherman, who had assigned a thousand men a day to the digging job, was not sanguine of results. "The river is about full and threatens to drown us out," he was complaining as he sloshed about in a waste of gumbo, with the rain coming down harder every week. "The ground is wet, almost water, and it is impossible for wagons to haul stores from the river to camp, or even horses to wallow through." Conversely, as if to preserve a balance of optimism, Grant's expectations rose with the passage of time. In early March he wired Halleck: "The canal is near completion.... I will have Vicksburg this month, or fail in the attempt." But this was the signal for disaster. "If the river rises 8 feet more, we would have to take to the trees," Sherman had said, and presently it did. The dam at the upper end of the cut gave way, and the water, instead of scouring out a channel — as had been expected, or anyhow intended — spread all over the lower end of the peninsula, forcing the evacuation of the troops from their flooded camps, with the resultant sacrifice of many horses and much equipment. "This little affair of ours here on Vicksburg Point is labor lost," Sherman reported in disgust, announcing the unceremonious end of the third experiment.

But Grant already had a fourth in progress. Fifty-odd miles above Vicksburg, just west of the river and south of the Arkansas line, lay Lake Providence, once a bend of the Mississippi but long since abandoned by the Old Man in the course of one of his cataclysmic whims. Though the lake now was land-locked, separated moreover from the river by a levee, Bayou Baxter drained it sluggishly westward into Bayou Macon, which in turn flowed into the Tensas River, just over a hundred winding miles to the south. Still farther down, the Tensas joined the Ouachita to form the Black, and the Black ran into the Red, which entered the Mississippi a brief stretch above Port Hudson. Despite its roundabout meandering, a distance of some 470 miles, this route seemed to Grant to offer a chance, once the levee had been breached to afford access to Lake Providence and the intricate system of hinterland bayous and rivers, for a naval column to avoid not only the Vicksburg batteries but also those below at Warrenton and Grand Gulf. Accordingly, two days after his arrival at Young's Point, he sent an engineer detail to look into the possibilities indicated on the map, and the following week, in early February, he went up to see for himself. It seemed to him that "a little digging" — "less than one-quarter," he said, of what Sherman had done already on the old canal — "will connect the Mississippi and Lake, and in all probability will wash a channel in a short time." If so, the way would be open for a bloodless descent, at the end of which he would join Banks for a combined attack on Port Hudson, and once that final bastion had been reduced the Confederacy would

have been cut in two and the Great Lakes region would have recovered its sorely missed trade connection with the Gulf. Impressed by this vista, Grant sent at once for McPherson to come down with a full division and get the project started without delay. "This bids fair to be the most practicable route for turning Vicksburg," he told him in the body of the summons.

He could scarcely have assigned the task to an officer better prepared to undertake it. McPherson, who was thirty-three and a fellow Ohioan, had been top man in the West Point class of '53 and had returned to the academy as an engineering instructor; he also had worked on river and harbor projects in the peacetime army, and had served at the time of Shiloh, when he was a lieutenant colonel, as chief engineer on Grant's staff. His advancement since then had been rapid, though not without some grousing, on the part of line officers he had passed on his way up the ladder, that a man who had never led troops in a major action should be given command of a corps. Sherman, on the other hand, considered him the army's "best hope for a great soldier," not excepting Grant and himself; "if he lives," he added. A bright-eyed, pleasant-faced young man, alternately bland and impulsive, McPherson came quickly down from Memphis with one of his two divisions and set to work at once. Without waiting for the levee to be cut, he horsed a small towboat overland, launched it on the lake, and got aboard for a reconnaissance — with the result that his high hopes took a sudden drop. The Bayou Baxter outlet led through an extensive cypress brake, and what could be found of its channel, which was but little at the present flood stage, was badly choked with stumps and snags that threatened to knock or rip the bottom out of whatever came their way. He put his men to work with underwater saws, but it was clear that at best the job would be a long one, if not impossible. Besides, Grant now saw that, even if a passage could be opened in time to be of use, he would never be able to get together enough light-draft boats to carry his army down to the Red River anyhow. McPherson and his staff meanwhile enjoyed something of a holiday, taking a regimental band aboard the little steamer for moonlight excursions, to and from the landing at one of the lakeside plantation houses which turned out to have a well-stocked cellar. Soldiers too found relaxation in this quiet backwater of the war, mainly in fishing, what time they were not taking turns on the underwater saws. By early March it was more or less obvious that nothing substantial was going to come of this fourth attempt to take or bypass Vicksburg, but Grant declared, later and rather laconically: "I let the work go on, believing employment was better than idleness for the men."

All seven of these experiments, four of which by now had gone by the board, anticipated some degree of co-operation from the navy. For the most part, indeed, they were classically amphibious, depending as much on naval as on army strength and skill. But if Porter, whatever his other shortcomings — one acquaintance called him "by all odds the greatest humbug of the war" — was not the kind of man to withhold needed help, neither was he the kind to be satisfied with a supporting role if he saw even an outside chance at stardom. And he believed he saw one now: had seen it, in fact, from the outset, and had already made his solo entrance on the stage. One of the two main reasons for attempting the reduction of Vicksburg and Port Hudson — in addition, that is, to opening a pathway to New Orleans and the Gulf — was to choke off rebel traffic along and across the nearly three hundred miles of river that flowed between them, particularly that segment of it tangent to the mouth of Red River, the main artery of trade connecting the goods-rich Transmississippi's far-west region with the principal Confederate supply depots in Georgia and Virginia. To accomplish this, the admiral perceived, it would not be absolutely necessary to capture either of the two bastions anchoring opposite ends of the long stretch of river. All that was needed, really, was to control what lay between them, and this could be done by sending warships down to knock out whatever vestiges of the rebel fleet remained and to establish a sort of internal blockade by patrolling all possible crossings. In early February, accordingly, while Sherman's men were still digging their way across soggy Vicksburg Point and Grant was steaming upriver for a preliminary look at cypress-choked Lake Providence, Porter gave orders which put his plan in the way of execution.

First off, this would require a run past the batteries on the bluff, and he gave the assignment to the steam ram *Queen of the West*, which had done it twice before, back in July, in an unsuccessful attempt to come to grips with the *Arkansas*. She was one of the navy's best-known vessels, having led the ram attack at the Battle of Memphis, where she had been commanded by her designer and builder, Colonel Charles Ellet, Jr., who had died of the only wound inflicted on a Northerner in that one-sided triumph. His son, nineteen-year-old Colonel Charles R. Ellet — who, as a medical cadet, had gone ashore in a rowboat, accompanied by three seamen, to complete the Memphis victory by raising the Stars and Stripes over the post office — had succeeded his uncle, Brigadier General A. W. Ellet, who had succeeded the first Ellet as commander of the ram fleet, as skipper of the *Queen*. Patched up from the two poundings she had taken from Vicksburg's high-perched guns, and fitted out now with guns of her own for the first time — previously she had depended solely on her punch — she made her run at daybreak, February 4, taking an even dozen hits, including two in the hull but none below the water line, and pulled up at a battery Sherman had established on the west bank, just around the bend, for the protection of his diggers. Above the town, two nights later, Porter set adrift a barge loaded with 20,000 bushels of coal, which made it downstream on schedule and without mishap, apparently not having been spotted by the lookouts on the bluff. "This gives the ram nearly coal enough to last a month," the admiral proudly informed Secretary Welles, "in which time she can commit great havoc, if no accident happens to her."

Though at first it seemed an unnecessary flourish — he knew the rebels had nothing afloat to match the *Queen* — that final reservation was prophetic. Setting out on the night of February 10, accompanied by an ex-Confederate steamboat, the *DeSoto*, which had been captured by the army below Vicksburg, Ellet began his career as a commerce raider in fine style, slipping past the Warrenton batteries undetected and going to work at once on enemy shipping by destroying skiffs and flatboats on both banks. He burned or commandeered hundreds of bales of cotton, taking some aboard for "armoring" the wheelhouse, destroyed supply trains heavily loaded with grain and salt pork being sent to collection points, and in reprisal for a sniper bullet, which struck one of his sailors in the leg, burned no less than three plantation houses, together with their outbuildings, apparently undismayed even when one planter's daughter sang "The Bonny Blue Flag" full in his face as the flames crackled. His greatest single prize, however, was the corn-laden packet *Era No. 5*, which he captured after passing Natchez and entering the Red River. But at that point, or just beyond it — seventy-five miles from the mouth of the river and with Alexandria in a turmoil less than half that far ahead — he and the *Queen* ran out of luck. On Valentine's Day, approaching Gordon's Landing, where a battery of guns had been reported, the ram stuck fast on a mud flat and was taken suddenly under fire by enemy gunners who yelled with delight at thus being offered a stationary target at a range of four hundred yards. In short order the boat's engine controls were smashed, her escape-pipe shot away, her boiler fractured. As she disappeared in hissing clouds of steam — one survivor later claimed to have avoided scalding his lungs because "I had sufficient presence of mind to cram the tail of my coat into my mouth" — officers and men began to tumble bales of cotton over the rail, then leap after them into the river, clinging to them in hope of reaching the *DeSoto* or the *Era*, a mile below. By now it was every man for himself, including the wounded, and the youthful skipper was not among the last to abandon the *Queen* in favor of a downstream ride astride a bale of cotton.

Picked up by the *DeSoto*, Ellet and the others were alarmed to discover that in the excitement she had unshipped both rudders and become unmanageable; so they set her afire and abandoned her, too, in favor of the more recently captured *Era*. Their career as raiders had lasted just four days. From now on, their only concern was escape, which seemed unlikely because of reports that the Confederates had at Alexandria a high-speed steamboat, the *William H. Webb*, which would surely be after them as soon as the news arrived upriver. She mounted only one gun, they had heard, and would never have dared to tackle the *Queen*, but now the tables were more or less turned; the pursuers became the pursued. "With a sigh for the poor fellows left behind, and a hope that our enemies would be merciful," a survivor wrote, "the prow of the *Era* was turned toward the Mississippi." They made it by daylight, after a race through stormy darkness unrelieved except for blinding flashes of lightning, and started north up the big river, heaving overboard all possible incidentals, including rations, in an attempt to coax more speed from their unarmed boat. Next morning, February 16, just below Natchez, with the *Webb* reportedly closing fast on their stern, they were startled to see an enormous, twin-stacked vessel bearing down on them from dead ahead. Their dismay at the prospect of being ground between two millstones was relieved, however, when the lookout identified her as the *Indianola*. The latest addition to the ironclad fleet and the pride of the Federal inland-waters navy, she mounted two great 11-inch smoothbores forward and a pair of 9-inch rifles amidships, casemated between her towering sidewheel-boxes, while for power she boasted four engines, driving twin screws in addition to her paddles, and she had brought two large barges of coal along, one lashed to starboard and one to port, to insure a long-term stay on the previously rebel-held 250-mile stretch of river above Port Hudson. Porter had sent her down past the Vicksburg batteries three nights ago, intending for her to support the *Queen* and thus, as he said, "make matters doubly sure."

Learning from Ellet that the *Queen* had been lost, Lieutenant Commander George Brown, captain of the *Indianola*, decided at once to proceed downriver, accompanied by the *Era*. Presently they sighted the *Webb*, in hot pursuit, and once more the tables were turned; for the *Webb* took one quick look at the iron-clad monster and promptly made use of her superior speed to withdraw before coming within range of those 11-inch guns, two short-falling shots from which only served to hurry her along, as one observer said, "for all the world like a frightened racehorse." Brown gave chase as far as the mouth of Red River, up which the rebel vessel disappeared, but there he called a halt, Porter having warned him not to venture up that stream without an experienced pilot, which he lacked. While Brown continued on patrol, guarding against a re-emergence of the *Webb*, Ellet took off northward in the *Era* with the unpleasant duty of informing Porter that he had lost the *Queen*. Two days later, still on patrol at the mouth of the Red, Brown received astounding news. The Confederates had resurrected the *Queen of the West*, patching up her punctured hull and repairing her fractured steam drum. Even now, in company with the skittish *Webb* and two cottonclad boats whose upper decks were crowded with sharpshooters, she was preparing to come out after the *Indianola*. Brown thought it over and decided to retire.

He would have done better to leave without taking time to think it over; the fuze was burning shorter than he knew. However, he was in for a fight in any event because of the two coal barges, which he knew would decrease his upstream speed considerably, but which he was determined to hold onto, despite the fact that the *Indianola*'s bunkers were chock-full. Partly this decision was the result of his ingrained peacetime frugality, but mostly it was because he wanted to have plenty of fuel on hand in case Porter complied with his request, forwarded by Ellet, that another gunboat be sent downriver as a replacement for the *Queen*. Brown left the mouth of the Red on Saturday, February 21, and stopped for the night at a plantation landing up the Mississippi to take on a load of cotton bales, which he stacked around the ironclad's low main deck to make her less vulnerable to boarders. Next morning he was off again in earnest, all four engines straining to offset the drag of the two barges lashed alongside. He did not know how much of a head start he had, but he feared it was not enough. In point of fact, it was even less than he supposed; for the four-boat Confederate flotilla, including the resurrected *Queen*, set out after him at about the same hour that Sunday morning, ninety miles astern of the landing where the *Indianola* had commandeered the cotton. The race was on.

It was not really much of a race. Major Joseph L. Brent, commanding the quartet of rebel warships, each of which was in the charge of an army captain, could have overtaken Brown at almost anytime Tuesday afternoon, the 24th, but he preferred to wait for darkness, which would not only make the aiming of the ironclad's big guns more difficult but would also give the Grand Gulf batteries a chance at her as she went by. Held to a crawl though she was by the awkward burden of her barges, the *Indianola* got past that danger without mishap; but Brown could see the smoke from his pursuers' chimneys drawing closer with every mile as the sun declined, and he knew that he was in for a fight before it rose again. He also knew by now that no reinforcing consort was going to join him from the fleet above Vicksburg, in spite of which he held doggedly to his barges, counting on them to give him fender protection from ram attacks. As darkness fell, moonless but dusky with starlight, he cleared for action and kept half of his crew at battle stations: "watch and watch," it was called. At 9.30 he passed New Carthage, which put him within thirteen miles of the nearest westbank Union battery, but by that time the rebel boats were in plain sight. Abreast of Palmyra Island, heading into Davis Bend — so called because it flowed past the Confederate President's Brierfield Plantation — Brown swung his iron prow around to face his pursuers at last, thus bringing his heavy guns to bear and protecting his more vulnerable stern.

As the *Queen* and the *Webb* came at him simultaneously, the former in the lead, he fired an 11-inch shell point-blank at each. Both missed, and the *Queen* was on him, lunging in from port with such force that the barge on that side was sliced almost in two. Emerging unscathed from this, except for the loss of the barge, which was cut adrift to sink, the *Indianola* met the *Webb* bows on, with a crash that knocked most of both crews off their feet and left the Confederate with a gash in her bow extending from water line to keelson, while the Federal was comparatively unhurt. Nevertheless the *Webb* backed off and struck again, crushing the remaining barge so completely as to leave it hanging by the lashings. Meanwhile the *Queen*, having run upstream a ways to gain momentum, turned and came charging down, striking her adversary just abaft the starboard wheelhouse, which was wrecked along with the rudder on that side, and starting a number of leaks along the shaft. Likewise the *Webb*, having gained momentum in the same fashion, brought her broken nose down hard and fair on the crippled ironclad's lightly armored stern, starting the timbers and causing the water to pour in rapidly. All this time the *Indianola* had kept throwing shells into the smoky darkness, left and right, but had scored only a single hit on the *Queen*, which did no considerable damage to the boat herself though it killed two and wounded four of her crew. Brown, having done his worst with this one shot, was now in a hopeless condition, scarcely able to steer and with both of his starboard engines flooded. After waiting a while in midstream until the water had risen nearly to the grate-bars of the ironclad's furnaces, planning thus to avoid her capture by making sure that she would sink, he ran her hard into the more friendly west bank and hauled down his colors just as the two cottonclads came alongside, crowded with yelling rebels prepared for boarding. Quickly they leaped down and attached two ropes by which the steamers could haul the *Indianola* across the river to the Confederate-held east bank, barely making it in time for her to sink in ten feet of water. As soon as they got their prisoners ashore they went to work on the captured dreadnought, intending to raise her, as they had raised the *Queen of the West* the week before, for service under the Stars and Bars.

Though he had heard the heavy nighttime firing just downriver, Porter did not know for certain what had happened until two days later, when a seaman who had escaped from the *Indianola* during her brief contact with the western bank came aboard his flagship *Black Hawk* and gave him an eyewitness account of the tragedy. Coming as it did on the heels of news of the loss of the *Queen* — which in turn had been preceded, two months back, by the destruction of the *Cairo* — the blow was hard, especially since it included the information that the *Queen* had been taken over by the enemy and had played a leading part in the defeat of her intended consort, which was now about to be used in the same manner as soon as the rebels succeeded in getting her afloat. What made it doubly hard, for Porter at any rate, was the contrast between his present gloom and his recent optimism. "If you open the Father of Waters," Assistant Navy Secretary G. A. Fox had wired the acting rear admiral in response to reports of his progress just two weeks ago, "you will at once be made an admiral; besides we will try for a ribboned star.... Do your work up clean," Fox had added, "and the public will never be in doubt who did it. The flaming army correspondence misleads nobody. Keep cool, be very modest under great success, as a contrast to the soldiers." At any rate, such strain as there had been on Porter's modesty was removed by the awareness that all he had really accomplished so far — aside from the capture of Arkansas Post, which had had to be shared with the army — was the loss of three of his best warships, two of which were now in enemy hands. What filled his mind just now was the thought of what this newest-model ironclad, the former pride of the Union fleet, could accomplish once she went into action on the Confederate side. Supported as she would be by the captured ram, she might well prove invincible in an upstream fight. In fact, any attempt to challenge her en masse would probably add other powerful units to the rebel flotilla of defected boats, since any disabled vessel would be swept helplessly downstream in such an engagement. Far from opening the Father of Waters, and gaining thereby a ribboned star and the permanent rank of admiral, Porter could see that he would be more likely to lose what had been won by his predecessors. Besides, even if he had wanted to launch such an all-out attack, he had no gunboats in the vicinity of Vicksburg now; they had been sent far upriver to co-operate in another of Grant's ill-fated amphibious experiments.

Porter was inventive in more ways than one, however, and his resourcefulness now stood him in good stead. If he had no available ironclad, then he would build one — or anyhow the semblance of one. Ordering every man off the noncombatant vessels to turn to, he took an old flat-bottomed barge, extended its length to three hundred feet by use of rafts hidden behind false bulwarks, and covered it over with flimsy decking to support a frame-and-canvas pilothouse and two huge but empty paddle-wheel boxes. A casemate was mounted forward, with a number of large-caliber logs protruding from its ports, and two tall smokestacks were erected by piling barrels one upon another. As a final realistic touch, after two abandoned skiffs were swung from unworkable davits, the completed dummy warship was given an all-over coat of tar. Within twenty-four hours, at a reported cost of $8.63, the navy had what appeared, at least from a distance, to be a sister ship of the *Indianola*. Belching smoke from pots of burning tar and oakum installed in her barrel stacks, she was set adrift the following night to make her run past the Vicksburg batteries. They gave her everything they had, but to no avail; her black armor seemingly impervious to damage, she glided unscathed past the roaring guns, not even deigning to reply. At daybreak she grounded near the lower end of Sherman's canal, and the diggers pushed her off again with a cheer. As she resumed her course downriver, the *Queen of the West*, coming up past Warrenton on a scout, spotted the dark behemoth in the distance, bearing down with her guns run out and her deck apparently cleared for action. The ram spun on her heel and sped back to spread the alarm: whereupon — since neither the *Queen* nor the broken-nosed *Webb* was in any condition for another fight just yet — all four of the Confederate vessels made off southward to avoid a clash with this second ironclad. Aboard the *Indianola*, still immobile and now deserted by her new friends, the lieutenant in charge of salvage operations was for holding onto her and fighting it out, despite repeated orders for him to complete her destruction before she could be recaptured. At a range of about two miles, the dreadnought halted as if to look the situation over before closing in for the bloody work she was bent on. Still the lieutenant held his ground until nightfall, when he decided to comply with the instructions of his superiors. After heaving the 9-inch rifles into the river, he laid the 11-inch smoothbores muzzle to muzzle and fired them with slow matches. When the smoke from this had cleared, he came back and set fire to what was left, burning the wreckage to the water line and ending the brief but stormy career of the ironclad *Indianola*.

Next morning, seeing the black monster still in her former position, some two miles upriver — one observer later described her as "terrible though inert" — a party of Confederates went out in a rowboat to investigate. Drawing closer they recognized her for the hoax she was, and saw that she had come to rest on a mudbank. Nailed to her starboard wheelhouse was a crudely lettered sign. "Deluded people, cave in," it read.

"Then, too," Grant added, continuing the comment on his reasons for keeping McPherson's men sawing away at the underwater stumps and snags clogging the Bayou Baxter exit from Lake Providence even after he knew that, in itself, the work was unlikely to produce anything substantial, "it served as a cover for other efforts which gave a better prospect of success." What he had in mind — in addition, that is, to Sherman's canal, which was not to be abandoned until March — was a fifth experimental project, whose starting point was four hundred tortuous miles upriver from its intended finish atop the Vicksburg bluff. In olden days, just south of Helena and on the opposite bank, a bayou had afforded egress from the Mississippi; Yazoo Pass, it was called, because it connected eastward with the Coldwater River, which flowed south into the Tallahatchie, which in turn combined with the Yalobusha, farther down, to form the Yazoo. Steamboats once had plied this route for trade with the planters of the delta hinterland. In fact, they still steamed up and down this intricate chain of rivers, but only by entering from below, through the mouth of the Yazoo River; for the state of Mississippi had sealed off the northern entrance, five years before the war, by constructing across the mouth of Yazoo Pass a levee which served to keep the low-lying cotton fields from going under water with every rise of the big river. Now it was Grant's notion that perhaps all he needed to do, in order to utilize this old peacetime trade route for his wartime purpose, was cut the levee and send in gunboats to provide cover for transports, which then could be unloaded on high ground — well down the left bank of the Yazoo but short of Haines Bluff, whose fortifications blocked an ascent of that river from below — and thus, by forcing the outnumbered defenders to come out into the open for a fight which could only result in their defeat, take Vicksburg from the rear. Accordingly, at the same time he ordered McPherson down from Memphis to Lake Providence, he sent his chief topographical engineer, Lieutenant Colonel James H. Wilson, to inspect and report on the possibility of launching such an attack by way of Yazoo Pass.

Wilson, described by a contemporary as "a slight person of a light complexion and with rather a pinched face," was enthusiastic from the start. An Illinois regular, only two years out of West Point and approaching his twenty-sixth birthday, he recently had been transferred from the East, where he had served as an aide to McClellan at Antietam, and he had approached his western assignment with doubts, particularly in regard to Grant, whose "simple and unmilitary bearing," as the young man phrased it, made a drab impression by contrast with the recent splendor of Little Mac, whose official family had included an Astor and two genuine French princes of the blood. But in this case familiarity bred affection; Wilson soon was remarking that his new commander was "a most agreeable companion both on the march and in camp." What drew him more than anything, however, was the trust Grant showed in sending him to take charge of the opening phase of this fifth and latest project for the reduction of the Gibraltar of the West. After a bit of preliminary surveying and shovel work, he wasted no time. On the evening of February 3 — while Ellet prepared to take the *Queen* past the Vicksburg bluff at daybreak and Grant himself was about to head upriver for a first-hand look at Lake Providence — Wilson mined and blew the levee sealing the mouth of Yazoo Pass. The result was altogether spectacular, he reported, "water pouring through like nothing else I ever saw except Niagara." After waiting four days for the surface level to equalize, east and west of the cut, he boarded a gunboat, steamed "with great ease" into Moon Lake, a mile beyond, and "ran down it about five miles to where the Pass leaves it." Hard work was going to be involved, he wrote Grant's adjutant, but he was confident of a large return on such an investment. Grant was infected at once with the colonel's enthusiasm. Wilson already had with him a 4500-man division from Helena; now a second division was ordered to join him from there. Presently, when he reported that he had got through to the Coldwater, McPherson was told to be prepared to follow with his whole corps. "The Yazoo Pass expedition is going to prove a perfect success," Grant informed Elihu B. Washburne, his home-state Representative and congressional guardian angel.

Hard work had been foreseen, and that was what it took. Emerging from Moon Lake, Wilson found the remaining twelve-mile segment of the pass sufficiently deep but so narrow in some places that the gunboat could not squeeze between giant oaks and cypresses growing on opposite banks. These had to be felled with axes, a patience-testing business but by no means the most discouraging he encountered. Warned of his coming, the Confederates had brought in working parties of slaves from surrounding plantations and had chopped down other trees, some of them more than four feet through the bole, so that they lay athwart the bayou, ponderous and apparently immovable. Undaunted, Wilson borrowed navy hawsers long enough to afford simultaneous handholds for whole regiments of soldiers, whom he put to work snaking the impediments out of the way. They did it with such ease, he later remarked, that he never afterwards wondered how the Egyptians had lifted the great stones in place when they built the Pyramids; enough men on a rope could move anything, he decided. Still, he had no such span of time at his disposal as the Pharaohs had had, and this was at best a time-consuming process. February was almost gone before he reached the eastern end of the pass. South of there, however, he expected to find clear sailing. The Coldwater being "a considerable stream," he reported, vessels of almost any length and draft could be sent from the Mississippi into the Tallahatchie in just four days. And so it proved when a ten-boat flotilla, including two ironclads, two steam rams, and six tinclads — the 22 light transports were to come along behind — tried it during the first week in March. In fact, it was not until the warships were more than a hundred miles down the winding Tallahatchie, near its junction with the Yalobusha, that Wilson realized he was in for a great deal more trouble, and of a kind he had not encountered up to now.

The trouble now was the rebels themselves, not just the various obstructions they had left in his path before fading back into the swamps and woods. Five miles above Greenwood, a hamlet at the confluence of the rivers, they had improvised on a boggy island inclosed by a loop of the Tallahatchie a fort whose parapets, built of cotton bales and reinforced with sandbags, were designed not only to deflect heavy projectiles but also to keep out the river itself, which had gone well past the flood stage when the Yankees blew the levee far upstream. Fort Pemberton, the place was called, and it had as its commander a man out of the dim Confederate past: Brigadier General Lloyd Tilghman, who had fought against Grant and the ironclads under similar circumstances at Fort Henry, thirteen months ago. Exchanged and reinstated, he was determined to wipe out that defeat, though the odds were as long and the tactical situation not much different. His immediate superior, Major General W. W. Loring, was also a carry-over from the past, and as commander of the delta subdepartment he intended to give the Federals even more trouble than he had given Lee and Jackson in Virginia the year before, which was considerable. A third relic on the scene was the former U.S. ocean steamer *Star of the West,* whose name had been in the scareheads three full months before the war, when the Charleston batteries fired on her for attempting the relief of Sumter. Continuing on to Texas, she had been captured in mid-April by Van Dorn at Indianola and was in the rebel service as a receiving-ship at New Orleans a year later, when Farragut provoked her flight up the Mississippi and into the Yazoo to avoid recapture. Here above Greenwood she ended her days afloat, but not her career, for she was sunk in the Tallahatchie alongside Fort Pemberton, blocking the channel and thus becoming an integral part of the outer defenses of Vicksburg. Three regiments, one from Texas and two from Mississippi, were all the high command could spare for manning the breastworks and the guns, which included one 6.4-inch rifle and half a dozen smaller pieces. This was scarcely a formidable armament with which to oppose 11-inch Dahlgrens housed in armored casemates, but on March 11 — while northward a long column of approaching warships and transports sent up a winding trail of smoke, stretching out of sight beyond the heavy screen of woods — the graybacks were a determined crew as they sighted their guns up the straight stretch of river giving down upon the fort.

Lieutenant Commander Watson Smith, who had charge of the ten-boat Union flotilla, was by now in a state of acute distress; he had never experienced anything like this in all his years afloat. Coming through Yazoo Pass into the Coldwater and down the Tallahatchie, all of which were so narrow in places that the gunboats had to be warped around the sharper bends with ropes, one tinclad had shattered her wheel and was out of action, while another had lost both smokestacks. All the rest had taken similar punishment in passing over rafts of driftwood or under projecting limbs that came sweeping and crashing along their upper works. The most serious of these mishaps was suffered when the *Chillicothe,* one of the two ironclads, struck a snag and started a plank in her bottom, which had to be held in place by beams shored in from the deck above. Smith's distress was greatly increased this morning, however, when this same unlucky vessel, at the head of the column, rounded the next-to-final bend leading down to the Yazoo and was struck hard twice on the turrets by high-velocity shells from dead ahead. She pulled back to survey the damage and fortify with cotton bales, then came on again that afternoon, accompanied by the other ironclad, the *De Kalb.* She got off four rounds at 800 yards and was about to fire a fifth — the loaders had already set the 11-inch shell in the gun's muzzle and were stripping the patch from the fuze — when a rebel shell came screaming through the port; both projectiles exploded on contact, killing 2 and wounding 11 of the gun crew. The two ironclads withdrew under urgent orders from Smith, whose distress had increased to the point where, according to Porter's subsequent report, he was showing "symptoms of aberration of mind."

Twice more, on the 13th and the 16th — without, however, attempting to close the range — the ironclads tried for a reduction of the fort at the end of that tree-lined stretch of river, as straight and uncluttered as a bowling alley: with similar results. Unable to maneuver in the narrow stream, the two boats took a terrible pounding, but could do little more than bounce their big projectiles off the resilient enemy parapet. The infantry, waiting rearward in the transports, gave no help at all; for the flooded banks made debarkation impossible, and any attempt at a small-boat attack — even if such boats had been available, which they were not — would have been suicidal. By the time the third day's bombardment was over, both ironclads were badly crippled; the *De Kalb* had lost ten of her gun-deck beams and her steerage was shot to pieces, while the luckless *Chillicothe* had more of her crew felled by armor bolts driven inward, under the impact of shells from the hard-hitting enemy rifle, to fly like bullets through the casemate. On March 17, in an apparent moment of lucidity, Smith ordered the flotilla to withdraw. Everyone agreed that this was the wisest course: everyone but Wilson, who complained hotly to Grant that the issue had not been pressed. "To let one 6½-inch rifle stop our navy. Bah!" he protested, and put the blame on "Acting Rear Admiral, Commodore, Captain, Lieutenant-Commander Smith" and the other naval officers. "I've talked with them all and tried to give them backbone," he said, "but they are not confident."

Returning up the Coldwater two days later — while Loring and Tilghman were celebrating the repulse in victory dispatches sent downriver to Vicksburg — the disconsolate Federals met the second Helena division on its way to reinforce them under Brigadier General Isaac Quinby, who outranked all the brass at hand and was unwilling to retreat without so much as a look at what stood in the way of an advance. So the expedition turned around and came back down again. Stopping short of the bend leading into the bowling alley, the men aboard the transports and gunboats slapped at mosquitoes and practiced their marksmanship on alligators, while Quinby conducted a boggy twelve-day reconnaissance which finally persuaded him that Smith had been right in the first place. Besides, even Wilson was convinced by now that the game was not worth the candle, for the rebels had brought up another steamboat which they were "either ready to sink or use as a boarding-craft and ram," and it seemed to the young colonel that they were "making great calculations 'to bag us' entire." He agreed that the time had come for a final departure. This began on April 5 and brought the Yazoo Pass experiment to a close. Being, as he said, "solicitous for my reputation at headquarters," Wilson ended a letter to Grant's adjutant with a request for the latest staff gossip, and thought to add: "Remember me kindly to the general."

His fears, though natural enough in an ambitious young career officer who had failed in his first independent assignment, were groundless. For unlike Porter, who no sooner learned the details of the Tallahatchie nightmare than he relieved Watson Smith of duty with the fleet and sent him North — where presently, by way of proving that his affliction had been physical as well as mental, he died in a delirium of fever and chagrin — Grant did not hold the collapse of this fifth experiment against his subordinate, but rather, when Wilson returned at last to Young's Point after an absence of more than two months, welcomed him back without reproach into the fold. By then the army commander had a better appreciation of the problems that stood in the way of an amphibious penetration of the delta, having been involved simultaneously in a not unsimilar nightmare of his own. In point of fact, however, no matter how little he chose to bring it to bear, Porter had even greater occasion for such charity, since he had been more intimately involved, not only as the author but also as the on-the-scene director of this latest fiasco, the sole result of which had been the addition of a sixth to the sequence of failures designed for the reduction of Vicksburg.

Left with time more or less on his hands after the downriver loss of two of his best warships, and being anxious moreover to offset the damage to his reputation with an exploit involving something less flimsy than a dummy ironclad, the admiral pored over his charts and made various exploratory trips up and down the network of creeks and bayous flowing into the Yazoo River below Haines Bluff, whose guns he had learned to respect back in December. Five miles upstream from its junction with the Mississippi, the Yazoo received the sluggish waters of Steele Bayou, and forty miles up Steele Bayou, Black Bayou connected eastward with Deer Creek, which in turn, at about the same upstream distance and by means of another bayou called Rolling Fork, connected eastward with the Sunflower River. That was where the payoff came within easy reach; for the Sunflower flowed into the Yazoo, fifty miles below, offering the chance for an uncontested high-ground landing well above the Haines Bluff fortifications, which then could be assaulted from the rear or bypassed on the way to the back door of Vicksburg. Though the route was crooked and the distance great — especially by contrast; no less than two hundred roundabout miles would have to be traversed by the column of gunboats and transports in order to put the troops ashore no more than twenty air-line miles above their starting point — Porter was so firmly convinced he had found the solution to the knotty Vicksburg problem that he called at Young's Point and persuaded Grant to come aboard the *Black Hawk* for a demonstration. Steaming up the Yazoo, the admiral watched the tree-fringed north bank for a while, then suddenly to his companion's amazement signaled the helm for a hard turn to port, into brush that was apparently impenetrable. So far, high water had been the curse of the campaign, but now it proved an asset. As the boat swung through the leafy barrier, which parted to admit it, the leadsman sang out a sounding of fifteen feet — better than twice the depth the ironclads required. Formerly startled, Grant was now convinced, especially when Porter informed him that they were steaming above an old road once used for hauling cotton to the river. Practically all the lower delta was submerged, in part because of the seasonal rise of the rivers, but mostly because of the cut Wilson had made in the levee, four hundred miles upstream at Yazoo Pass; a tremendous volume of water had come down the various tributaries and had spread itself over the land. It was Porter's contention, based on limited reconnaissance, that as a result all those creeks and bayous would be navigable from end to end by vessels of almost any size, including the gunboats and transports selected to thread the labyrinth giving down upon the back-door approach to Vicksburg. Infected once more with contagious enthusiasm, Grant returned without delay to Young's Point, where he issued orders that same night for the army's share in what was known thereafter as the Steele Bayou expedition.

Sherman drew the assignment, along with one of his two divisions of men who just that week had been flooded out of their pick-and-shovel work on the doomed canal, and went up the Mississippi to a point where a long bend swung eastward to within a mile of Steele Bayou. On the afternoon of March 16, after slogging across this boggy neck of land, he made contact with the naval units, which had come up by way of the Yazoo that morning. As soon as he got his troops aboard the waiting transports the column resumed its progress northward, five ironclads in the lead, followed by four all-purpose tugs and a pair of mortar boats which Porter, not knowing what he might encounter in the labyrinth ahead, had had "built for the occasion." With his mind's eye fixed on permanent rank and the ribboned star Fox had promised to try for, the admiral was taking no chances he could avoid. All went well — as he had expected because of his preliminary reconnaissance — until the gunboats approached Black Bayou, where the unreconnoitered portion of the route began. This narrow, four-mile, time-forgotten stretch of stagnant water was not only extremely crooked, it was also filled with trees. Porter used his heavy boats to butt them down, bulldozer style, and hoisted them aside with snatch blocks. This was heavy labor, necessarily slow, and as it progressed the column changed considerably in appearance. Overhead branches swept the upper decks of the warships, leaving a mess of wreckage in the place of boats and woodwork. Occasionally, too, as Porter said, "a rude tree would throw Briarean arms" around the stacks of the slowly passing vessels, "and knock their bonnets sideways." After about a mile of this, Sherman's men were put to work with ropes and axes, clearing a broader passage for the transports, while the sturdier ironclads forged ahead, thumping and bumping their way into Deer Creek, where they resumed a northward course next morning.

But this was worse in several ways, one of them being that the creek was even narrower than the bayou. If the trees were fewer, they were also closer together, and vermin of all kinds had taken refuge in them from the flood; so that when one of the gunboats struck a tree the quivering limbs let fall a plague of rats, mice, cockroaches, snakes, and lizards. Men were stationed about the decks with brooms to rid the vessels of such unwelcome boarders, but sometimes the sweepers had larger game to contend with, including coons and wildcats. These last, however, "were prejudiced against us, and refused to be comforted on board," the admiral subsequently wrote, "though I am sorry to say we found more Union feeling among the bugs." To add to the nightmare, Deer Creek was the crookedest stream he had ever encountered: "One minute an ironclad would apparently be leading ahead, and the next minute would as apparently be steering the other way." Along one brief stretch, less than half a mile in length, the five warships were steaming in five quite different directions. Moreover, this was a region of plantations, which meant that there were man-made obstacles such as bridges, and though these gave the heavy boats no real trouble — they could plow through them as if they were built of matchsticks — other impediments were more disturbing. For example, hearing of the approach of the Yankees, the planters had had their baled cotton stacked along both creekbanks and set afire in order to keep it out of the hands of the invaders: with the result that, from time to time, the gunboats had to run a fiery gauntlet. The thick white smoke sent the crews into spasms of coughing, while the heat singed their hair, scorched their faces, and blistered the paint from the vessels' iron flanks.

So far, despite the crowds of field hands who lined the banks to marvel at the appearance of ironclads where not even flat-bottomed packets had ventured before, Porter had not seen a single white man. He found this odd, and indeed somewhat foreboding. Presently, however, spotting one sitting in front of a cabin and smoking a pipe as if nothing unusual were going on around him, the admiral had the flagship stopped just short of another bridge and summoned the man to come down to the landing; which he did — a burly, rough-faced individual, in shirt sleeves and bareheaded; "half bulldog, half bloodhound," Porter called him. When the admiral began to question him he identified himself as the plantation overseer. "I suppose you are Union, of course?" Porter said. "You all are so when it suits you." "No, by God, I'm not, and never will be," the man replied. "As to the others, I know nothing about them. Find out for yourself. I'm for Jeff Davis first, last, and all the time. Do you want any more of me?" he added; "for I am not a loquacious man at any time." "No, I want nothing more with you," Porter said. "But I am going to steam into that bridge of yours across the stream and knock it down. Is it strongly built?" "You may knock it down and be damned," the overseer told him. "It don't belong to me." Catching something in his accent, Porter remarked: "You're a Yankee by birth, are you not?" "Yes, damn it, I am," the man admitted. "But that's no reason I should like the institution. I cut it long ago." And with this he turned on his heel and walked away. Porter had the skipper ring "Go ahead fast," and the ironclad smashed through the bridge about as easily as if it had not been there. When he looked back, however, to see what impression this had made on the overseer, he saw him seated once more in front of the cabin, smoking his pipe, not having bothered even to turn his head and watch. Deciding that the fellow "was but one remove from a brute," Porter was disturbed by the thought that "there were hundreds more like him" lurking somewhere in the brush. At any rate, he fervently hoped that Sherman's men — particularly one regiment, which had the reputation of being able to "catch, scrape, and skin a hog without a soldier leaving the ranks" — would "pay the apostate Yankee a visit, if only to teach him good manners."

Under the circumstances, even aside from the necessary halts, half a mile an hour was the best speed the ironclads could make on this St Patrick's Day. Nightfall overtook them a scant eight miles from the morning's starting point. Twelve miles they made next day, but the increased speed increased the damage to the boats, including the loss of all the skylights to falling debris, and when they stopped engines for the night, Porter heard from up ahead the least welcome of all sounds: the steady chuck of axes, informing him that the rebels were warned of his coming. He wished fervently for Sherman, whose men were still at work in Black Bayou, widening a pathway for their transports, and consoled himself with the thought that the red-haired general would be along eventually; "there was only one road, so he couldn't have taken the wrong one." For the present, however, he did what he could with what he had, sending the mortar boats forward in the darkness; and when their firing stopped, so had the axes. Next morning, March 19, he pushed on. Despite the delay involved in hoisting the felled trees aside, he made such good progress that by nightfall he was within half a mile of the entrance to Rolling Fork. At daybreak he steamed north again, but the flagship had gone barely two hundred yards when, just ahead and extending all the way across the creek, the admiral saw "a large green patch . . . like the green scum on ponds." He shouted down from the bridge to one of the admiring field hands on the bank: "What is that?" "It's nuffin but willers, sah," the Negro replied, explaining that in the off season the plantation workers often went out in skiffs and canoes to cut the willow wands for weaving baskets. "You kin go through dat lak a eel."

That this last was an overstatement — based on a failure to realize that, unlike skiffs and canoes, the gunboats moved *through* rather than *over* the water, and what was more had paddle wheels and overlapping plates of armor — Porter discovered within a couple of minutes of giving the order to go ahead. Starting with a full head of steam, the ironclad made about thirty yards before coming to a dead stop, gripped tightly by the willow withes, not unlike Gulliver when he woke to find himself in Lilliputian bonds. The admiral called for hard astern; but that was no good either; the vessel would not budge. Here was a ticklish situation. The high creekbanks rendered the warships practically helpless, for their guns would not clear them even at extreme elevation. Not knowing what he would do if the Confederates made a determined boarding attack, Porter fortified a nearby Indian mound with four smoothbore howitzers and put the flagship's crew over the side with knives and hooks and orders to cut her loose, twig by twig. It was slow work; "I wished ironclads were in Jericho," he later declared. Just then his wish seemed about to be fulfilled. The shrill shrieks of two rifle shots, which he recognized as high-velocity Whitworths, were followed at once by a pair of bursts, abrupt as blue-sky thunder and directly over the mound. Suddenly, in the wake of these two ranging shots — within six hundred yards of Rolling Fork and less than ten miles from clear sailing down the broad and unobstructed Sunflower River — two six-gun rebel batteries were firing on the outranged smoothbores from opposite directions, and the naval commander was shocked to see his cannoneers come tumbling down the rearward slope of the mound, seeking cover from the rain of shells. Continuing to hack at the clinging willows, he got his mortars into counterbattery action and, with the help of half a dollar, persuaded a "truthful contraband" (so Porter termed him later, but just then he called him Sambo; which drew the reply, "My name aint Sambo, sah. My name's Tub") to attempt to get a message through to Sherman and his soldiers, wherever downstream they might be by now. "Dear Sherman," the note began: "Hurry up, for Heaven's sake."

Tub reached Sherman on Black Bayou late that night, having taken various short cuts, and Sherman started northward before daylight, accompanied by all the troops on hand. Retracing the messenger's route through darkness, they carried lighted candles in their hands as they slogged waist-deep through swamps and canebrakes. "The smaller drummer boys had to carry their drums on their heads," the general afterwards recalled, "and most of the men slung their cartridge boxes around their necks." All the following day they pushed on, frequently losing their way, and into darkness again. At dawn Sunday, March 22, they heard from surprisingly close at hand the boom of Porter's mortars, punctuated by the sharper crack of the Whitworths. Presently they encountered rebels who had got below the ironclads and were felling trees to block their escape downstream. Sherman chased them from their work and pushed on. Soon he came within sight of the beleaguered flotilla, but found it woefully changed in appearance. After finally managing to extricate the willow-bound flagship with winches, Porter had unshipped the rudders of all five gunboats and was steaming backward down the narrow creek, fighting as he went. He had not only heard the sound of axes in his rear; what was worse, he had suddenly realized that the Confederates might dam the creek upstream with cotton bales and leave him stranded in the mud. The arriving bluecoats ran the snipers off — they were not actually so numerous as they seemed; just industrious — and came up to find the admiral on the deck of the flagship, directing the retreat from behind a shield improvised from a section of smokestack. "I doubt if he was ever more glad to meet a friend than he was to see me," Sherman later declared. For the present, though, he asked if Porter wanted him to go ahead and "clean those fellows out" so the navy could resume its former course. "Thank you, no," the admiral said. He had had enough, and so had Sherman, who complained hotly that this was "the most infernal expedition I was ever on." As Porter subsequently put it, "The game was up, and we bumped on homeward."

All the way downstream, from Deer Creek through Black Bayou, the sailors took a ribbing from the soldiers who stood along the banks to watch them go by, in reverse and rudderless. "Halloo, Jack," they would call. "How do you like playing mud turtle?" "Where's all your masts and sails, Jack?" "By the Widow Perkins, if Johnny Reb hasn't taken their rudders away and set them adrift!" But an old forecastleman gave as good as he got. "Dry up!" he shouted back at them. "We wa'n't half as much used up as you was at Chickasaw Bayou." So it went until the gunboats regained Steele Bayou and finally the mouth of the Yazoo, where they dropped anchor — those that still had them — and were laid up for repairs. Within another week they were supplied with new chimneys and skylights and woodwork; they glistened with fresh coats of paint, and according to Porter, "no one would have supposed we had ever been away from a dock-yard." By then, too, the officers had begun to discuss their share in this sixth of Grant's Vicksburg failures with something resembling nostalgia. There was an edge of pride in their voices as they spoke of the exploit, and some even talked of being willing to go again. But they did so, the admiral added, much "as people who have gone in search of the North Pole, and have fared dreadfully, wish to try it once more."

. . .

Despite the high hopes generated during the preliminary reconnaissance up Steele Bayou, Grant was no more discouraged by this penultimate failure, reported in no uncertain terms by a disgusted Sherman, than he had been by the preceding five. Now as before, he already had a successive experiment in progress, which served to distract the public's attention and occupy his mind and men. Besides, for once, he had good news to send along to Washington with the bad — the announcement of the first real success achieved by Federal arms on the river since his arrival in late January — although his pleasure in reporting it was considerably diminished by the fact that it had been accomplished not in his own department but in Banks's, not by the army but by the navy, and not by Porter but by Farragut.

Banks himself had been having troubles that rivaled Grant's, if not in number — being limited by a lack of corresponding ingenuity and equipment in his attempts to come to grips with the problem — then at any rate in thorniness. Port Hudson was quite as invulnerable to a frontal assault as Vicksburg, so that here too the solution was restricted to two methods: either to attack the hundred-foot bluff from the rear or else to go around it. He worked hard for a time at the latter, seeking a route up the Atchafalaya, into the Red, and thence into the Mississippi, fifty miles above the Confederate bastion. At first this appeared to be ready-made for his use, but it turned out to be impractical on three counts. 1) He had only one gunboat designed for work on the rivers; 2) a large portion of the Atchafalaya basin was under water as a result of breaks in the neglected levees; and 3) he became convinced that to leave the rebel garrison alive and kicking in his rear would be to risk, if not invite, the recapture of New Orleans. This last was so unthinkable that it no sooner occurred to him than he abandoned all notion of such an attempt. As for attacking Port Hudson from the rear, he perceived that this would be about as risky as attacking it from the front. Knowing nothing of Grant's success or failure upriver, except the significant fact that something must have happened to delay him, Banks did not know but what the Confederates would be free to concentrate against him from all directions, including the north, as soon as he got his troops ashore; which would mean, at best, that he would lose his siege train in a retreat from superior numbers, and at worst that he would lose his army. Thus both methods of approaching a solution to the problem seemed to him likely to end in disaster; he did not know what to do, at least until he could get in touch with Grant upstream. Consequently, he did nothing.

This reverse approach, with its stress on what the enemy might do to him, rather than on what he intended to do to the enemy, had not been Grant's way of coming to grips with the similar problem, some three hundred miles upstream; nor was it Farragut's. The old sea dog —

approaching sixty-two, he was Tennessee-born and twice married, both times to Virginians, which had caused some doubt as to his loyalty in the early months of the war — had surmounted what had seemed to be longer odds below New Orleans the year before, and he was altogether willing to try it again, "army or no army." In early March, when he received word that the rebels, by way of reinforcing their claim to control of the whole Red River system, along with so much of the Mississippi as ran between Vicksburg and Port Hudson, had captured the steam ram *Queen of the West*, he took the action as a challenge to personal combat; especially when they emphasized it by sinking and seizing the ironclad *Indianola*, which for all he knew was about to join the *Queen* in defying the flag she once had flown. He promptly assembled his seven wooden ships off Profit's Island, seven miles below Port Hudson, intending to take them past the fortified heights for a showdown with the renegade boats upriver. He had with him the three heavy sloops-of-war *Hartford, Richmond,* and *Monongahela,* the old sidewheeler *Mississippi,* and three gunboats. All were ocean-going vessels, unarmored but mounting a total of 95 guns, mostly heavy — the flagship *Hartford* alone carried two dozen 9-inch Dahlgrens — with which to oppose the 21 pieces manned by the Confederates ashore. This advantage in the weight of metal would be offset considerably, however, by the plunging fire of the guns on the hundred-foot bluff and by the five-knot current, which would hold the ships to a crawl as they rounded the sharp bend at its foot. In an attempt to increase the speed and power of his slower and larger ships, Farragut gave instructions for the three gunboats to be lashed to the unengaged port sides of the three sloops; the *Mississippi,* whose paddle boxes would not allow this, would have to take her chances unassisted. It was the admiral's hope that the flotilla would steam past undetected in the moonless darkness, but a greenhorn chaplain, watching the gun crews place within easy reach "little square, shallow, wooden boxes filled with sawdust, like the spittoons one used to see in country barrooms," was shocked to learn that the contents were to be scattered about the deck as "an absorbent" to keep the men from slipping in their own blood, when and if the guns began to roar and hits were scored. At 9.30 p.m. March 14, the prearranged signal — two red lights described by the same impressionable chaplain as "two distinct red spots like burning coals" — appeared just under the stern of the flagship in the lead, and the run began.

At first it went as had been planned and hoped for. Undetected, unsuspected, the *Hartford* led the way up the long straight stretch of river leading due north into the bend that would swing the column west-southwest; she even cleared the first battery south of town, her engines throbbing in the darkness, her pilot hugging the east bank to avoid the mudflat shallows of the point across the way. Then suddenly the night was bright with rockets and the glare of pitch-pine bonfires ignited by west-bank sentinels, who thus not only alerted the gun crews on the bluff, but also did them the service of illuminating their targets on the river down below. The fight began as it were in mid-crescendo. Still holding so close to the east bank that the men on her deck could hear the shouts of the enemy cannoneers, the flagship opened a rolling fire which was taken up in turn by the ships astern. The night was misty and windless; smoke settled thick on the water, leaving the helmsmen groping blindly and the gunners with nothing to aim at but the overhead muzzle flashes. In this respect the *Hartford* had the advantage, steaming ahead of her own smoke, but even she had her troubles, being caught by the swift current and swept against the enemy bank as she turned into the bend. Helped by her gunboat tug, she backed off and swung clear, chugging upstream at barely three knots, much damaged about her top and spars, but with only three men hit. Attempting to follow, the *Richmond* was struck by a plunging shot that crashed into her engine room and caromed about, cracking both port and starboard safety valves and dropping her boiler pressure below ten pounds. Too weak to make headway, even with the assistance of the gunboat lashed to her flank, she went with the current and out of the fight, leaking steam from all her ports, followed presently by the *Monongahela*, which suffered the same fate when her escort's rudder was wedged by an unlucky shot, one of her own engines was disabled by an overheated crankpin, and her captain was incapacitated by a shell that cut the bridge from under him and pitched him headlong onto the deck below. Between them, the two sloops and their escorts lost 45 killed and wounded before they veered out of range downriver. But the veteran frigate *Mississippi* — Commodore Matthew Perry's flagship, ten years ago, when he steamed into Tokyo Bay and opened Japan to the Western world — took the worst beating of the lot, not only from the Confederates on the bluff, but also from the gunners on the *Richmond*, who, not having gotten the word that the sloop had turned in the opposite direction, fired at the flashes of the side-wheeler's guns as they swept past her. Blind in the smoke, pounded alike by friend and foe, the pilot went into the bend and put the ship hard to larboard all too soon: with the result that she ran full tilt onto the mudflats across the way from the fuming bluff. Silhouetted against the glare of bonfires and taking hit after hit from the rebel guns, she tried for half an hour to pull loose by reversing her engines, but to no avail. Her captain ordered her set afire as soon as the crew — 64 of whom were casualties by now — could be taken off in boats, and it was only through the efforts of her executive, Lieutenant George Dewey, that many of her wounded were not roasted, including a badly frightened ship's boy he found hiding under a pile of corpses. Burning furiously, the *Mississippi* lightened before dawn and drifted off the flats of her own accord, threatening to set the other repulsed vessels afire as she passed unmanned among them and piled up at last on the head of Profit's Island, where she exploded with what an observer called "the grandest display of fireworks I ever witnessed, and the costliest."

It had been quite a costly operation all around. Thirty-five of the flotilla's 112 casualties were dead men — only two less than had been killed in the venture below New Orleans by a force almost three times as large — and of the seven ships that had attempted to run Port Hudson, one was destroyed and four had been driven back disabled. As a box score, this gave the Confederates ample claim to the honors of the engagement; but the fact remained that, whatever the cost, Farragut had done what he set out to do. He had put warships north of the bluff on the Mississippi, and he was ready to use them to dispute the rebel claim to control of the 250 miles of river below Vicksburg. Dropping down at dawn to just beyond range of Port Hudson's upper batteries, he fired the prearranged three-gun signal to let the rest of the flotilla know that he was still afloat, then set out upriver and anchored next morning off the mouth of the Red, up which he learned that the renegade *Queen* and the fast-steaming *Webb* had taken refuge after their flight from Porter's dummy ironclad. Both were too heavily damaged, as a result of their ram attacks on the *Indianola*, to be able to fight again without extensive repairs. So he heard; but he was taking no chances. Lowering the *Hartford*'s yards to the deck, he lashed them there and carried a heavy anchor chain from yard tip to yard tip, all the way round, to fend off attackers. Still unsatisfied, he improvised water-line armor by lashing cypress logs to the sides of the vessel and slung hawsers from the rigging, thirty feet above the deck, with heavy netting carried all the way down to the rail to frustrate would-be boarders. Then, accompanied by her six-gun escort *Albatross*, the *Hartford* — whose own builders would scarcely have recognized her, dressed out in this manner — set out northward, heading for Vicksburg in order to open communications with the upper fleet.

Passing Grand Gulf on March 19 the two ships came under fire that cost them 2 more killed and 6 more wounded, almost three times the number they had lost five nights ago; otherwise they encountered no opposition between Port Hudson and the point where they dropped anchor next morning, just beyond range of the lower Vicksburg batteries. Porter was up Steele Bayou, but conferring that afternoon with Grant and A. W. Ellet, the ram fleet commander, Farragut asked that he be reinforced by units from the upper flotilla. Ellet volunteered to send two of his boats, the *Switzerland* and the *Lancaster*, respectively under C. R. Ellet, the former captain of the *Queen*, and his uncle Lieutenant Colonel J. A. Ellet. They made their run at first light, March 25. The *Lancaster* was struck repeatedly in her machinery and hull, but she made it downstream, where a week's patchwork labor would put her back in shape to fight again. Not so the *Switzerland;* she received a shell in her boilers and others which did such damage to her hull that she went to pieces and sank, affording her nineteen-year-old skipper another ride on a bale of cotton. Unperturbed, Grant reported her loss as a blessing in disguise, since it served to reveal her basic unfitness for combat: "It is almost certain that had she made one *ram* into another vessel she would have closed up like a spy-glass, encompassing all on board."

In point of fact, whatever the cost and entirely aside from his accustomed optimism, he and all who favored the Union cause had much to be joyful about. As a result of this latest naval development, which would establish a blockade of the mouth of the Red and deny the rebels the use of their last extensive stretch of the Mississippi, Farragut had cut the Confederacy in two. The halves were still unconquered, and seemed likely to remain so for no one knew how long, but they were permanently severed one from the other. When the *Hartford* and the *Albatross* passed Port Hudson and were joined ten days later below Vicksburg by the steam ram *Lancaster*, the cattle and cereals of the Transmississippi, together with the goods of war that could be smuggled in through Mexico from Europe, became as inaccessible to the eastern South as if they were awaiting shipment on the moon.

This was not to say, conversely, that the Mississippi was open throughout its length to Federal commerce or even to Federal gunboats; that would not be the case, of course, until Vicksburg and Port Hudson had been taken or abolished. Continuing his efforts to accomplish this end, or anyhow his half of it, Grant was already engaged in the seventh of his experiments — which presently turned out to be the seventh of his failures. Work on the canal across the base of Vicksburg Point having been abandoned, he sent an engineering party out to find a better site for such a project close at hand. Receiving a report that a little digging south of Duckport, just above Young's Point, would give the light-draft vessels access to Roundaway Bayou, which entered the main river at New Carthage, well below the Vicksburg and Warrenton batteries, Grant gave McClernand's men a turn on the picks and shovels. For once, however, he had no great hope that much would come of the enterprise, even if it went as planned — only the lightest-draft supply boats would be able to get through; besides, there would still be the Grand Gulf batteries to contend with — and for once he was right. Even this limited success depended on a rise of the river; whereupon the river, perverse as always, began to fall, leaving Grant with a seventh failure on his hands.

"This campaign is being badly managed," Cadwallader Washburn, a brigadier in McPherson's corps, informed his congressman brother Elihu in Washington. "I am sure of it. I fear a calamity before Vicksburg. All Grant's schemes have failed. He knows that he has got to do something or off goes his head. My impression is that he intends to attack in front." (Washburn's fears were better founded than he knew. Grant had just written a long letter to Banks, reviewing his lack of progress up to now, and in it he had stated flatly: "There is nothing left for me but to collect my strength and attack Haines Bluff. This will necessarily be attended with much loss, but I think it can be done." On April Fools' Day, however, accompanying Porter up the Yazoo for a reconnaissance of the position, he decided that such an attack "would be attended with immense sacrifice of life, if not defeat," and abandoned the notion, adding: "This, then, closes out the last hope of turning the enemy by the right.") Nor were others, farther removed from the scene of action, more reticent in giving their opinion of the disaster in store for the Army of the Tennessee. For example Marat Halstead, editor of the *Cincinnati Commercial*, addressed his friend the Secretary of the Treasury on the matter: "You do once in a while, don't you, say a word to the President, or Stanton, or Halleck, about the conduct of the war? Well, now, for God's sake say that Genl Grant, entrusted with our greatest army, is a jackass in the original package. He is a poor drunken imbecile. He is a poor stick sober, and he is most of the time more than half drunk, and much of the time idiotically drunk.... Grant will fail miserably, hopelessly, eternally. You may look for and calculate his failures, in every position in which he may be placed, as a perfect certainty. Don't say I am grumbling. Alas! I know too well I am but feebly outlining the truth." Alarmed, Chase passed the letter on to Lincoln with the reminder that the *Commercial* was an influential paper, and the indorsement: "Reports concerning General Grant similar to the statements made by Mr Halstead are too common to be safely or even prudently disregarded." Lincoln read it with a sigh. "I think Grant has hardly a friend left, except myself," he told his secretary, and when a delegation came to protest Grant's alleged insobriety he put these civilians off with the remark, "If I knew what brand of whiskey he drinks I would send a barrel or so to some other generals." About this time a Nebraska brigadier, in Washington on leave from Vicksburg, called on the President and the two men got to talking. "What I want, and what the people want, is generals who will fight battles and win victories," Lincoln said. "Grant has done this, and I propose to stand by him."

The evidence was conflicting. Some said the general never touched a drop; others declared that he was seldom sober; while still others had him pegged as a spree drinker. "He tries to let liquor alone but he cannot resist the temptation always," a Wisconsin brigadier wrote home. "When he came to Memphis he left his wife at LaGrange, and for several days after getting here was beastly drunk, utterly incapable of doing anything. Quinby and I took him in charge, watching him day and night and keeping liquor away from him." According to this witness, the bender was only brought to an end when "we telegraphed to his wife and brought her on to take care of him." On the other hand, Mary Livermore — later famous as a suffragette — led a Sanitary Commission delegation down to Young's Point to investigate the rumors, and it was her opinion that the general's "clear eye, clean skin, firm flesh, and steady nerves ... gave the lie to the universal calumnies then current concerning his intemperate habits." Still unsatisfied, Stanton sent the former Brook Farm colonist and Greeley journalist Charles Dana down the Mississippi, ostensibly as an inspector of the pay service, but actually as a spy for the War Department. He arrived in early April, became in effect a member of the general's military family, and soon was filing reports that glowed with praise not only of Grant but also of Sherman and McPherson, declaring that in their "unpretending simplicity" the three Ohioans were "as alike as three peas." McClernand did not fare so well in these dispatches; for if Dana acquired a fondness for the army commander's friends, he also developed a dislike for his enemies. Later he summed up his findings by describing Grant as "the most modest, the most disinterested, and the most honest man I ever knew, with a temper that nothing could disturb and a judgment that was judicial in its comprehensiveness and wisdom. Not a great man except morally; not an original or brilliant man, but sincere, thoughtful, deep, and gifted with courage that never faltered."

Aside from the rhetoric here included, practically all of the general's soldiers would have agreed with this assessment of his character and abilities, even though it was delivered in the wake of seven failures. "Everything that Grant directs is right," one declared. "His soldiers believe in him. In our private talks among ourselves I never heard a single soldier speak in doubt of Grant." According to a New York reporter, this was not only because of "his energy and disposition to do something," it was also because he had "the remarkable tact of never spoiling any mysterious and vague notions which [might] be entertained in the minds of the privates as to the qualities of the commander-in-chief. He confines himself to saying and doing as little as possible before his men." Another described him as "a man who could be silent in several languages," and it was remarked that, on the march, he was more inclined to talk of "Illinois horses, hogs, cattle, and farming, than of the business actually at hand." In general he went about his job, as one observer had stated at the outset, "with so little friction and noise that it required a second look to be sure he was doing anything at all." One of his staff officers got the impression that he was "half a dozen men condensed into one," while a journalist, finding him puzzling in the extreme because he seemed to amount to a good deal more than the sum of all his parts, came up with the word "unpronounceable" as the one that described him best. Grant, he wrote, "has none of the soldier's bearing about him, but is a man whom one would take for a country merchant or a village lawyer. He had no distinctive feature; there are a thousand like him in personal appearance in the ranks.... A plain, unpretending face, with a comely, brownish-red beard and a square forehead, of short stature and thick-set. He is we would say a good liver, and altogether an unpronounceable man; he is so like hundreds of others as to be only described in general terms." The soldiers appreciated the lack of "superfluous flummery" as he moved among them, "turning and chewing restlessly the end of his unlighted cigar." They almost never cheered him, and they did not often salute him formally; rather, they watched him, as one said, "with a certain sort of familiar reverence." Present discouragements were mutual; so, someday, would be the glory. Somehow he was more partner than boss; they were in this thing together. "Good morning, General," "Pleasant day, General," were the usual salutations, more fitting than cheers or hat-tossing exhibitions; "A pleasant salute to, and a good-natured nod from him in return, seems more appropriate." All these things were said of him, and this: "Here was no McClellan, begging the boys to allow him to light his cigar on theirs, or inquiring to what regiment that exceedingly fine-marching company belonged.... There was no nonsense, no sentiment; only a plain business man of the republic, there for the one single purpose of getting that command over the river in the shortest time possible."

Yet the fact remained that he and they were into their third month of camping almost within the shadow of the Vicksburg bluff, and all they had accomplished so far was the addition of five to their previous two failures; they were still not "over the river." However, as the flood waters receded, defining the banks of the bayous and even the network of greasy-looking roads hub deep in mud, there were rumors that Grant was evolving an entirely new approach to the old problem. "As one after another of his schemes fail," Congressman Washburne heard from his brigadier brother — who had dropped the final euphonious "e" from his surname, presumably as superfluous baggage for a soldier — "I hear that he says he has a plan of his own which is yet to be tried [but] in which he has great confidence." Just what this was Grant would not say, either to subordinates or superiors, but his staff observed that he spent long hours in the former ladies' cabin of his headquarters boat the *Magnolia*, blueing the air with cigar smoke as he pored over maps and tentative orders, not so much inaccessible ("I aint got no business with you, General," they heard one caller tell him; "I just wanted to have a little talk with you, because folks will ask me if I did") as removed, withdrawn behind a barrier of intense preoccupation. After several days of this, McPherson came into the cabin one evening, glass in hand, and stood facing Grant across the work-littered desk. "General, this won't do," he said. "You are injuring yourself. Join us in a few toasts, and throw this burden off your mind." Mrs Livermore, for one, would have been horrified, but what followed would have quickly reassured her. Grant looked up, smiled, and replied that whiskey was not the answer; if McPherson really wanted to help him, he said, he could give him a dozen cigars and leave him alone. McPherson did so, and Grant returned to brooding over his papers, still seeking a way to come to grips with the Confederates in their hilltop citadel.

Death of a Soldier

★ ✗ ☆

PIERRE GUSTAVE TOUTANT BEAUREGARD WAS as flamboyant by nature as by name, and over the course of the past two years this quality, coupled all too often with a readiness to lay down the sword and take up the pen in defense of his reputation with the public, had got him into considerable trouble with his superiors, who sometimes found it difficult to abide his Creole touchiness off the field of battle for the sake of his undoubted abilities on it. Called "Old Bory" by his men, though he was not yet forty-five, the Hero of Sumter had twice been relieved of important commands, first in the East, where he had routed McDowell's invasion attempt at Manassas, then in the West, where he had saved his badly outnumbered army by giving Halleck the slip at Corinth, and now he was back on the scene of his first glory in Charleston harbor. Here, as elsewhere, he saw his position as the hub of the wheel of war. Defying Union sea power, Mobile on the Gulf and Wilmington, Savannah, and Charleston on the Atlantic remained in Confederate hands, and of these four it was clear at least to Beauregard that the one the Federals coveted most was the last, variously referred to in their journals as "the hotbed of treachery," "the cradle of secession," and "the nursery of disunion." Industrious as always, the general was determined that this proud South Carolina city should not suffer the fate of his native New Orleans, no matter what force the Yankees brought against it. Conducting frequent tours of inspection and keeping up as usual a voluminous correspondence — a steady stream of requisitions for more guns and men, more warships and munitions, nearly all of which were returned to him regretfully unfilled — he only relaxed from his duties when he slept, and even then he kept a pencil and a note pad under his pillow, ready to jot down any notion that came to him in the night. "Carolinians and Georgians!" he exhorted by proclamation. "The hour is at hand to prove your devotion to your country's cause. Let all able-bodied men, from the seaboard to the mountains, rush to arms. Be not exacting in the choice of weapons; pikes and scythes will do for exterminating your enemies, spades and shovels for protecting your friends. To arms, fellow citizens! Come share with us our dangers, our brilliant success, or our glorious death."

Two approaches to Charleston were available to the Federals. They could make an amphibious landing on one of the islands or up one of the inlets to the south, then swing northeastward up the mainland to move upon the city from the rear; or they could enter through the harbor itself, braving the massed batteries for the sake of a quick decision, however bloody. Twice already they had tried the former method, but both times — first at Secessionville, three months before Beauregard's return from the West in mid-September, and again at Pocotaligo, one month after he reassumed command — they had been stopped and flung back on their naval support before they could gather momentum. This time he thought it probable that they would attempt the front-door approach, using their new flotilla of vaunted ironclads to spearhead the attack. If so, they were going to find they had taken on a good deal more than they expected; for the harbor defenses had been greatly improved during the nearly two years that had elapsed since the war first opened here. Fort Moultrie, Castle Pinckney, and Fort Sumter, respectively on Sullivan's Island, off the mouth of the Cooper River, and opposite the entrance to the bay, had not only been strengthened, each in its own right, but now they were supported by other fortifications constructed at intervals along the beaches and connected by a continuous line of signal stations, making it possible for a central headquarters, itself transferrable, to direct and consolidate their fire. First Beauregard, then Pemberton, and now Beauregard again — both accomplished engineers and artillerists, advised moreover by staffs of specialists as expert as themselves — had applied all their skill and knowledge to make the place as nearly impregnable as military science and Confederate resources would allow. A total of seventy-seven guns of various calibers now frowned from their various embrasures, in addition to which the harbor channels were thickly sown with torpedoes and other obstructions, such as floating webs of hemp designed to entangle rudders and snarl propellers. Not content with this, the sad-eyed little Creole had not hesitated to dip into his limited supply of powder in order to improve the marksmanship of his cannoneers with frequent target practice. Like his idol Napoleon he believed in a lucky star, but he was leaving as little as possible to chance; for which reason he had set marker buoys at known ranges in the bay, with the corresponding elevations chalked on the breeches of the guns. As a last-ditch measure of desperation, to be employed if all else failed, he encouraged the organization of a unit known as the Tigers, made up of volunteers whose assignment was to hurl explosives down the smokestacks of such enemy ships as managed to break through the ring of fire and approach the fortress walls or the city docks. The ironclads might indeed be invincible; some said so, some said not; but one thing was fairly certain. The argument was likely to be settled on the day their owners tested them in Charleston harbor.

This was not to say that Beauregard had abandoned all notion of assuming the offensive, however limited his means. He had at his disposal two homemade rams, the *Palmetto State* and the *Chicora*, built with funds supplied by the South Carolina legislature and the Ladies' Gunboat Fair. The former mounted an 80-pounder rifle aft and an 8-inch shell gun on each broadside, while the latter had two 9-inch smoothbores and four rifled 32-pounders. Both were balky and slow, with cranky, inadequate engines and armor improvised from boiler plate and railroad iron, but as January drew to a close the general was determined to put them to the test by challenging the blockade squadron off the Charleston bar. Orders were handed Flag Officer Duncan Ingraham on the 30th, instructing him to make the attempt at dawn of the following day. Beauregard meanwhile had in mind a more limited offensive of his own, to be launched against the 9-gun screw steamer *Isaac Smith*, which had been coming up the Stono River almost nightly to shell the Confederate camps on James and John's islands. That night he lay in wait for her with batteries of field artillery, allowed her to pass unchallenged, then took her under fire as she came back down. The opening volley tore off her stack, stopped her engines, riddled her lifeboats, and killed eight of her crew. Her captain quickly surrendered himself and his ship and the 94 survivors, including 17 wounded. Repaired and rechristened, the *Smith* became the *Stono* and served under that name as part of Charleston's miniature defense squadron, the rest of which was already on its way across the bay, under cover of darkness, in accordance with Ingraham's orders to try his hand at lifting the Union blockade.

Palmetto State and *Chicora*, followed by three steam tenders brought along to tow them back into the harbor in case their engines failed, were over the bar and among the wooden-walled blockaders by first light. Mounting a total of one hundred guns, the Federal squadron included the 1200-ton sloop-of-war *Housatonic*, two gunboats, and seven converted merchantmen. A lookout aboard one of these last, the 9-gun steamer *Mercedita*, was the first to spot the misty outline of an approaching vessel. "She has black smoke!" he shouted. "Watch, man the guns! Spring the rattle! Call all hands to quarters!" This brought the captain out on deck, clad only in a pea jacket. When he too spotted the stranger, nearer now, he cupped his hands about his mouth and called out: "Steamer, ahoy! You will be into us! What steamer is that?" It was the *Palmetto State*, but for a time she did not deign to answer. Then: "Halloo!" her skipper finally replied, and with that the ram put her snout into the quarter of the *Mercedita* and fired her guns. Flames went up from the crippled steamer. "Surrender," the rebel captain yelled up, "or I'll sink you!" The only answer was a cloud of oily smoke shot through with steam. "Do you surrender?" he repeated. This brought the reply, "I can make no resistance; my boiler is destroyed!" "Then do you surrender?" "Yes!" So the *Palmetto State* backed off, withdrawing her snout, and turned to go to the help of the *Chicora*, which meanwhile had been serving the 10-gun sidewheel steamer *Keystone State* in much the same fashion. Riddled and aflame, the Federal hauled down her flag to signify surrender, then ran it up again and limped out to sea as the two rams moved off in the opposite direction. At the far end of the line, the *Housatonic* and the gunboats held their station, thinking the racket had been provoked by a blockade runner venturing out. By full daylight the two improvised ironclads were back in Charleston harbor, their crews accepting the cheers of a crowd collected on the docks.

Beauregard was elated by the double coup. Quick to claim that the blockade had been lifted, at least for a time, he took the French and Spanish consuls out to witness the truth of his words that "the outer harbor remained in the full possession of the two Confederate rams. Not a Federal sail was visible, even with spyglasses." Next day the blockaders were back again, presumably too vigilant now to permit him to risk another such attempt, but he did not admit that this detracted in the slightest from the brilliance of the exploit. He bided his time, still improving his defenses for the all-out attack which he believed was about to be launched. "Already six monitors ... are in the waters of my department, concentrating about Port Royal, and transports with troops are still arriving from the North," he reported in mid-March. "I believe the drama will not much longer be delayed; the curtain will soon rise." Three more weeks went past before his prediction was fulfilled. Then on Monday, April 6, the day after Easter — it was also the first anniversary of Shiloh and within a week of the second anniversary of the opening of the war in this same harbor — not six but nine brand-new Union ironclads, some single- and some double-turreted, crossed the Charleston bar and dropped anchor in the channel, bringing their great 15-inch guns to bear on the forts and batteries Beauregard had prepared for their reception. The curtain had indeed risen.

Rear Admiral Samuel Du Pont had the flag. It was he who, back in early November of 1861, had conceived and executed the elliptical attack on Port Royal, thereby giving the North its first substantial victory of the war, and it was hoped by his superiors — his desk-bound superiors in Washington, that is, for he had no superiors afloat — that he would repeat the triumph here in Charleston harbor. Son of a wealthy New York importer and nephew of an even wealthier Delaware powder maker, the admiral was approaching sixty, a hale, well-set-up aristocrat with a dignified but genial manner and a growth of luxuriant whiskers describing a bushy U about his chops and under his cleanshaven mouth and chin, all of which combined to give at least one journalist the impression that he was "one of the stateliest, handsomest, and most polished gentlemen I have ever seen." Gideon Welles admired him, too; up to a point. "He is a skillful and accomplished officer," the Secretary confided in his diary. "Has a fine address, [but] is a courtier with perhaps too much finesse and management." This edge of mistrust was returned by the man who was its object. It seemed to Du Pont, whose enthusiasm had been tempered by close association, that the Navy Department was suffering from an affliction which might have been diagnosed as "ironclads on the brain."

This had not always been the case, particularly in the days when John Ericsson was trying to persuade the brass to give him authority for construction of the *Monitor*. Grudgingly, despite grave objections, they had finally let him go ahead with a contract which stipulated that he would not be reimbursed in case of failure. But after Hampton Roads and the draw engagement that put an end to the overnight depredations of the *Merrimac*, the Department not only reversed itself, but went all-out in the opposite direction. Ericsson received an order for half a dozen sister ships of the one already delivered, and other builders were engaged for the construction of twenty-one more, of various shapes and sizes. Assistant Secretary Fox was especially enthusiastic, informing Du Pont that after he had used the new-fangled warships to reduce Charleston he was to move on to Savannah, then send them down to the Gulf to give Mobile the same treatment. Ironclads were trumps, according to Fox. He told Ericsson he had not "a shadow of a doubt as to our success, and this confidence arises from a study of your marvelous vessels." The Swede was less positive. "The most I dare hope is that the contest will end without loss of that prestige which your ironclads have conferred upon the nation abroad," he replied, adding the reminder: "A single shot may sink a ship, while a hundred rounds cannot silence a fort." Unwilling to have his confidence undermined or his ebullience lessened, Fox assured a congressional committee that the monitors (such was the generic name, adopted in honor of the first of what was intended to be a long line of invincible vessels) could steam into southern harbors, flatten the defenses, and emerge unscathed. His only note of caution was injected into a dispatch addressed to Du Pont. "I beg of you," he pleaded, "not to let the Army spoil it." He wanted the show to be all Navy, with the landsmen merely standing by to be ferried in to pick up the pieces when the smoke cleared. In late March, having gained nothing from nudging Porter with the promise of a ribboned star and permanent promotion, he informed Du Pont that it was up to him to make up for the reverses lately suffered in the West: "Farragut has had a setback at Port Hudson and lost the noble old *Mississippi*. It finally devolves upon you by great good fortune to avert the series of disasters that have fallen upon our Navy. That you will do it most gloriously I have no misgivings whatever."

In point of fact, Du Pont by this time had misgivings enough for them both. What was more, these doubts were shared by a majority of his ironclad skippers — and with cause. Near the mouth of the Ogeechee River, just beyond the Georgia line, the Confederates had constructed as part of the Savannah defenses a 9-gun earthwork called Fort McAllister, which Du Pont decided to use as a sort of test range to determine how well the monitors would do, offensively and defensively, under fire. He gave the reduction assignment to the *Montauk*, which meant that he was giving the best he had; for her captain was Commander John L. Worden, who had skippered the *Monitor* in her fight with the *Merrimac*. Worden made his first attack on January 27 and, after expending all his ammunition in a four-hour bombardment, withdrew undamaged despite repeated hits scored by the guns of the fort, which was not silenced. Returning February 1 he tried again, with like results. Neither the ship nor the fort had done much damage to the other, aside from the concussive strain on the eardrums of the *Montauk*'s crew from the forty-six hits taken on her iron decks and turret. A third attack, February 27, was more fruitful, although not in the way intended. Finding the rebel cruiser *Nashville* aground beyond Fort McAllister, Worden took her under long-range fire with his 11- and 15-inch guns, set her ablaze, and had the satisfaction of watching her destruction when her magazine exploded. Struck only five times by the guns of the fort, the ironclad pulled back without replying, well satisfied with her morning's work, only to run upon a torpedo which blew such a hole in her bottom that she had to be beached in the mud at the mouth of the river. While she was undergoing repairs that soon restored her to full efficiency, three more monitors came down from Port Royal on March 3 and tried their hand with an eight-hour bombardment of the fort: with similar results. Neither silenced or seriously damaged the other, and the ironclads withdrew to try no more.

Fruitless though the experiment had been in positive results — aside, that is, from the fortunate interception of the *Nashville* — a lesson had been learned, on the negative side, as to the capabilities of the monitors. "Whatever degree of impenetrability they might have," Du Pont reported, "there was no corresponding degree of destructiveness as against forts." He felt much as one sailor had felt on a test run. "Give me an oyster-scow!" the man had cried. "Anything — only let it be of wood, and something that will float over instead of under the water." Most of the captains were of a similar mind, and when they looked beyond the present to the impending future, their doubts increased. If these vaunted engines of destruction could not humble a modest 9-gun sand fort, what could they hope to accomplish against multi-gunned bastions like Sumter and Moultrie? They asked the question and shook their heads. "I do not feel as sure as I could wish," one skipper admitted, while another was more positive in expressing his reservations. "I begin to rue the day I got into the iron clad business," he wrote home. Still, orders were orders, and as April came in Du Pont completed his final preparations for the attack. In addition to his flagship the *New Ironsides*, a high-bulwarked 3500-ton frigate whose ponderous armor and twenty heavy guns mounted in broadside made her the most powerful battleship in the world, he had eight low-riding monitors, mounting one or two guns each in revolving turrets: which meant that, in all, he would be opposing 77 guns ashore with 33 afloat. These odds were rather evened by the fact that the naval guns, in addition to being mounted on moving targets, which made them far more difficult to hit, were heavier in caliber and threw about an equal weight of metal. Other odds were irreducible, however, one being that in order to reach the city from the sea his ships would have to steam for seven winding miles in a shoal-lined channel, much of which had been fiendishly obstructed and practically all of which was exposed to the plunging fire of forts whose gun crews had been anticipating for months this golden opportunity to disprove the claim that monitors were indestructible. On April 2, despite increasing doubts and reservations, Du Pont left Port Royal and reached Edisto Island, twenty-odd miles below the entrance to Charleston harbor, before nightfall. There the ships were cleared for action, the exposed armor of their decks and turrets covered over with slippery untanned hides and their bulwarks slopped with grease to lessen the "bite" of enemy projectiles. (That at least was the hoped-for effect, when the vessels should come under fire. The more immediate result, however, was that they stank fearfully under the influence of the Carolina sun.) On the 5th — Easter Sunday — they cleared North Edisto and crossed the Charleston bar next morning. Du Pont had intended to attack at once, but finding the weather hazy, which as he said "prevent[ed] our seeing the ranges," he decided to drop anchors and wait for tomorrow, in hopes that it would afford him better visibility. (It would also afford the same for the gunners in the forts; but Du Pont was not thinking along these lines, or else he would have made a night attack.) Finally, against his better judgment — and after much prodding from above, including jeers that he had "the slows" and taunts that identified him as a sea-going McClellan, overcautious and too mindful of comparative statistics — he was going in.

Tomorrow — April 7 — brought the weather he thought he wanted, and soon after noon the iron column started forward, the nine ships moving in single file, slowly and with a certain ponderous majesty not lost on the beholders in the forts. Originally the admiral had intended to lead the way in the flagship, but on second thought he decided to take the center position from which "signals could be better made to both ends of the line," so that the resultant order of battle was *Weehawken, Passaic, Montauk, Patapsco; New Ironsides; Catskill, Nantucket, Nahant, Keokuk.* There was an exasperating delay of about an hour when the lead monitor's heavy anchor chain became entangled with the bootjack raft designed to protect her bow from torpedoes; then the column resumed its forward motion, passing Morris Island in an ominous silence as the rebel cannoneers on Cummings Point held their fire. As the ships approached the inner works, however, the Confederate and Palmetto flags were hoisted over Sumter and Moultrie, while bands on the parapets struck up patriotic airs and the guns began to roar in salute. Captain John Rodgers of the *Weehawken,* spotting the rope obstructions dead ahead, commanded the helmsman to swing hard to starboard in order to avoid becoming entangled in the web and immobilized under the muzzles of guns whose projectiles were already hammering the monitor like an anvil. This was well short of the point at which Du Pont had intended to open fire, however, and the result was that the whole line was thrown into confusion by the abrupt necessity, confronting each ship in rapid sequence, of avoiding a collision with the ship ahead. Moreover, as the *Weehawken* turned she encountered a torpedo which exploded directly under her. "It lifted the vessel a little," Rodgers later reported, "but I am unable to perceive that it has done us any damage."

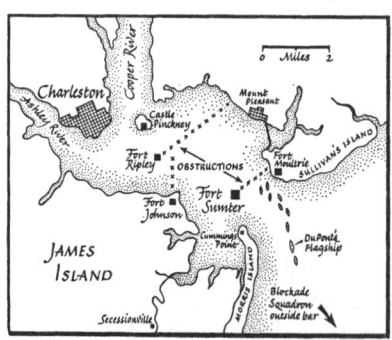

Aboard the flagship, with her deeper draft, the confusion was at its worst. When she lost headway she had to drop her anchor to keep from going aground, and as she hung there, trying to get her nose into the tide, she received two disconcerting butts from two of the monitors astern as they swept past in response to her signal to move up and join the action. Hoisting anchor at last, the *Ironsides* chugged forward a short distance, only to have to drop it again in order to avoid piling up on a shoal. This brought her, unbeknownst, directly over a huge submerged torpedo which the Confederates had fashioned by packing an old boiler with explosives and connecting it to an observation post ashore, to be used to detonate the charge at the proper time. Now the proper time was very much at hand; the rebel electrician later said that if he himself had been allowed to spot the Yankee flagship he could not have placed her more precisely where he wanted her. However, his elation quickly faded, turning first to dismay and then to disgust, when the detonating mechanism failed time after time to send a spark to the underwater engine of destruction. Meanwhile, happily unaware that he and his ship were in mortal danger of being hoisted skyward in sudden flame and smoke, Du Pont signaled the monitors to "disregard motions of commander in chief" and continue to press the attack without his help. The *Ironsides*, as one of her surgeons complained, was as completely out of the fight as if she had been moored to a dock in the Philadelphia Navy Yard, but this did not prevent her taking long-range punishment from the rebel guns. Presenting if not the closest, then at any rate the largest and least mobile target in the harbor, she was struck no less than ninety-five times in the course of the engagement. Despite the din, according to one of her officers, "the sense of security the iron walls gave to those within was wonderful, a feeling akin to that which one experiences in a heavy storm when the wind and hail beat harmlessly against the windows of a well-protected house."

No such feeling was experienced by the crews of the monitors, the officer added; "for in their turrets the nuts that secured the laminated plates flew wildly, to the injury and discomfiture of the men at the guns." Up closer, they were harder hit. "The shots literally rained around them," a correspondent wrote, "splashing the water up thirty feet in the air, and striking and booming from their decks and turrets." The flagship was a mile from Sumter, the nearest monitors about half that far, but the captain of the twin-turreted *Nahant* quickly found what it would cost to close the range. "Mr Clarke, you haven't hit anything yet," he protested to the ensign in charge of the 15-inch gun, which was throwing its 420-pound shells at seven-minute intervals. When the young man replied, "We aint near enough, Captain," the skipper went into a rage. "Not near enough? God damn it," he cried, "I'll put you near enough! Starboard your helm, Quartermaster!" As the ship came about, a rebel projectile slammed against the sight-slit, killing the helmsman and mangling the pilot. "Retire! Retire!" the captain shouted. Others caught it as hard or harder, with similar results: smokestacks perforated, turrets jammed, decks ripped up, guns knocked out of action. The only effect on the enemy a journalist could see, examining the brick northeast face of Sumter through his glasses, was that of "increasing pock marks and discolorations on the walls, as if there had been a sudden breaking out of cutaneous disease." But there was no corresponding slackening of fire from within the fort, whose cannoneers were jubilant over the many hits they scored. Frenzied at being kept from a share in the fun of pummeling the ironclads, Confederates locked in the Moultrie guardhouse screamed above the roar of the bombardment: "For God's sake, let us come out and go to the guns!"

After peering through the drifting smoke for about two hours, Du Pont was told that it was nearly 5 o'clock. "Make signal to the ships to drop out of fire," he said quietly. "It is too late to fight this battle tonight. We will renew it early in the morning." Below decks, when the gun captains received word of this decision, they sent up an urgent request that they be allowed to fire at least one broadside before retiring. It was granted, and as the *Ironsides* turned to steam down the channel an eight-gun salvo was hurled at Moultrie, the only shots she fired in the course of the engagement. This brought the total to an even 150 rounds expended by the flotilla, and of these 55 were scored as hits. The Confederates, on the other hand, had fired 2209, of which no less than 441 had found their mark, despite the fact that the targets had not only been comparatively small, and moving, but had also been mostly submerged. That this was remarkably effective shooting Du Pont himself began to appreciate when the retiring monitors came within hailing distance of the flagship and he got a close-up look at their condition. The first to approach was the *Keokuk*, limping badly. Last in and first out, she had ventured nearest to Sumter's 44 guns, and she had the scars of 90 point-blank hits to prove it. She was "riddled like a colander," one witness remarked, "the most severely mauled ship one ever saw." That night, in fact, she keeled over and sank at her anchorage off Morris Island. Others also had been roughly handled; *Weehawken* had taken 53 hits, *Nantucket* 51, *Patapsco* 47, *Nahant* 36, *Passaic* 35, *Catskill* 20, and *Montauk* 14. In general, the damage suffered was in inverse ratio to the individual distance between them and the rebel guns, and none had been closer than 600 yards.

The admiral's intention to "renew [the battle] early in the morning" was modified by the sight of his crippled monitors. Five of the eight were too badly damaged to be able to engage if ordered, and of these five, one would sink before the scheduled time for action. Equally conclusive were the reports and recommendations of the several captains when they came aboard the flagship that evening. "With your present means," John Rodgers advised, "I could not, if I were asked, recommend a renewal of the attack." The redoubtable Worden was no less emphatic. "After testing the weight of the enemy's fire, and observing the obstructions," he reported, "I am led to believe that Charleston cannot be taken by the naval force now present, and that had the attack been continued [today] it could not have failed to result in disaster." This gave Du Pont pause, and pausing he reflected on the risks. Here was no New Orleans, where the problem had been to run the fleet through a brief, furious gauntlet of fire in order to gain a safe haven above the forts and place a defenseless city under the muzzles of its guns; this was Charleston, whose harbor, in the words of a staff officer, "was a *cul-de-sac*, a circle of fire not to be passed." The deeper you penetrated the circle, the more you were exposed to destruction from its rim. Moreover, as the admiral saw the outcome, even if he pressed the attack "in the end we shall retire, leaving some of our ironclads in the hands of the enemy, to be refitted and turned against our blockade with deplorable effect." This last was unthinkable — though he thought about it in his cabin all night long. By daybreak he had made up his mind. "I have decided not to renew the attack," he told his chief of staff. "We have met with a sad repulse; I shall not turn it into a great disaster."

Next afternoon he recrossed the bar. "I attempted to take the bull by the horns, but he was too much for us," he admitted to the army commander whose troops had been standing by to pick up the pieces. By the end of the week the flotilla again was riding at anchor inside Port Royal, swarmed over by armorers hammering the vessels back into shape. The admiral knew the reaction in Washington would be severe, coming as it did on the heels of such great expectations, but he also knew that he had the support of his monitor captains, who stood, as one of them said, "like a wall of iron" around his reputation, agreeing with his chief of staff's opinion that "Admiral Du Pont never showed greater courage or patriotism than when he saved his ships and men, and sacrificed himself to the clamor and disappointment evoked by his defeat." In point of fact, however, part of the expressed disappointment, if not the outright clamor, occurred within the fleet itself. A chief engineer was clapped in arrest for complaining in his ship's mess that the attack had not been pressed to the victory point, and at least one junior officer remarked wryly that "the grim sort of soul like Farragut was lacking." Welles and Fox, though hot enough at the outcome and in no doubt at all as to where the blame lay, were considerably hampered in their criticisms by the political necessity for delay in bringing the matter out into the open with the publication of the adverse battle reports. After all, it was they — especially Fox — who had announced that the monitors were irresistible, and contracts already had been signed for the delivery of eighteen more of the expensive naval monsters. Two weeks after the repulse, Welles was attempting to shrug it off by telling his diary: "I am by no means confident that we are acting wisely in expending so much strength and effort on Charleston, a place of no strategic importance."

The grapes had soured for him; but not for Beauregard. The Louisiana general's only regrets were that the boiler-torpedo had not gone off beneath the *Ironsides* and that the Yankees had slunk away without attempting a renewal of the assault, which he felt certain would have been even more decisively repulsed. In a congratulatory address to his troops, his enthusiasm knew no bounds. He spoke of "the stranded, riddled wreck" of the *Keokuk*, whose big guns now were part of the harbor defenses, and of the ignominious flight of "her baffled coadjutors," whose defeat had reinspired world-wide confidence in the ultimate and glorious triumph of the Confederate cause. In his official report to Richmond, though — for he had recently confided to a friend that, from now on, he was adopting a more restrained style in his dispatches, in order to counteract a rumor that he was prone to exaggerate his accomplishments — the little Creole, with his bloodhound eyes, his swarthy face, and his hair brushed forward in lovelocks at the temples, contented himself for the most part with factual observations. "It may be accepted, as shown," he wrote, "that these vaunted monitor batteries, though formidable engines of war, after all are not invulnerable or invincible, and may be destroyed or defeated by heavy ordnance, properly placed and skillfully handled." However, in the glow and warmth of congratulations being pressed upon him, including one that he had made Sumter "a household word, like Salamis and Thermopylae," he could not resist the temptation to add a closing flourish to the report: "My expectations were fully realized, and the country, as well as the State of South Carolina, may well be proud of the men who first met and vanquished the iron-mailed, terribly armed armada, so confidently prepared and sent forth by the enemy to certain and easy victory."

※ 2 ※

Though he grew snappish at the first report that the fleet had been repulsed — "Hold your position inside the bar near Charleston," he instructed Du Pont in a message sent posthaste down the coast; "or, if you shall have left it, return to it, and hold it till further orders" — Lincoln was in a better frame of mind for the reception of bad news than he had been for months. The reason for this was that he had just returned from a five-day Easter vacation combined with a highly satisfactory inspection of the Army of the Potomac, whose tents were pitched along the Rappahannock in the vicinity of Falmouth. The visit was a heartening experience, not only because it showed him that the condition of the troops was excellent, but also because it abolished his main previous doubt as to the fitness of the man he had appointed as their commander. After saying, "Now there is Joe Hooker. He can fight. I think that is pretty well established," Lincoln had added: "But whether he can 'keep tavern' for a large army is not so sure." If the trip down the bay had done nothing else, it had reassured the President on that score. Fighting Joe had taken hold with a vengeance, and the results were plain to see on the faces and in the attitude of the men. Fredericksburg and the Mud March, though the letters of the former were embroidered on the rippling blue of their regimental colors, were no longer even a part of their vocabulary.

Hooker could indeed keep tavern. Within a week of his assumption of command he jolted the commissary department by ordering the issue of rations expanded to include fresh vegetables and soft bread; he supervised a thorough cleanup of the unsanitary camps, shrinking the overlong sick lists in the process, and he instituted a liberal system of furloughs which, combined with a tightening of security regulations, did much to reduce desertion. "Ah! the furloughs and vegetables he gave!" one infantryman still marveled years later, "How he did understand the road to the soldier's heart!" In the midst of all this welcome reform, army paymasters came down from Washington with bulging satchels and surprised the troops with six months' back pay. It was no wonder another veteran recalled that "cheerfulness, good order, and military discipline at once took the place of grumbling, depression, and want of confidence." Idleness, that breeder of discontent, was abolished by a revival of the old-time grand reviews, with regiment after regiment swinging past the reviewing stand so that when the men executed the command "eyes right" they saw their chieftain's clean-shaven face light up with pleasure at seeing their appearance improved by their diurnal spit-and-polish preparations. Unit pride, being thus encouraged, increased even more when Hooker, expanding the use of the so-called Kearny patch — a device improvised by the late Phil Kearny, about this time last year, to identify the men of his division in the course of their march up the York-James peninsula — ordered the adoption of corps insignia of various shapes, cut from red, white, or blue cloth, thus indicating the first, second, or third division, and stitched to the crown of the caps of the troops, so that he and they could tell at a glance what corps and division a man was gracing or disgracing, on duty or off. Moreover, after the gruff and dish-faced Pope and the flustered and fantastically whiskered Burnside, Hooker himself, by the force of his personality and the handsomeness of his presence, infused some of the old McClellan magnetism into the reviving army's ranks. "Apollo-like," a Wisconsin major called the forty-eight-year-old Massachusetts-born commander, and a visiting editor wrote of him as "a man of unusually handsome face and elegant proportions, with a complexion as delicate and silken as a woman's." Another remarked, along this same line, that the general looked "as rosy as the most healthy woman alive."

Some claimed that this glow, this rosiness, had its origin in the bottle (the men themselves apparently took pride in the assertion;

*"Joe Hooker is our leader —
He takes his whiskey strong!"*

they sang as they set off on practice marches) while other dissenters from the prevalent chorus of praise, although admitting that the general was "handsome and picturesque in the extreme," directed attention to what one of them called his "fatally weak chin." Still others believed they detected inner flaws, below the rosy surface. "He could play the best game of poker I ever saw," a former West Coast intimate recollected, "until it came to the point when he should go a thousand better, and then he would flunk." But the harshest judgment of all came from a cavalry officer, Charles F. Adams, Jr. According to this son of the ambassador to England, the new commander was "a noisy, low-toned intriguer" under whose influence army headquarters became "a place to which no self-respecting man liked to go, and no decent woman could go. It was a combination of barroom and brothel." Young Adams' own "tone" was exceptionally high, which made him something less than tolerant of the weakness of others — particularly the weaknesses of the flesh, from which he himself apparently was exempt — but in support of at least a part of the accusation was the fact that, from this time on, the general's surname entered the language as one of the many lower-case slang words for prostitute. As for the rest, however, a friend who was with him almost daily insisted that Hooker had gone on the wagon the day he took command. Headquarters might have some of the aspects of a barroom, as Adams said, but according to this observer the general himself did not imbibe.

The fact was, it did indeed appear that he as well as the army had experienced a basic change of character. Much of his former bluster was gone; he had even acquired a dislike for his *nom-de-guerre,* though perhaps this was largely because the story was beginning to get around that he had come by it as the result of an error made in a New York composing room during the Peninsula Campaign, when a last-minute dispatch arrived from the front with additional news involving his division. "Fighting — Joe Hooker," the follow-up was tagged, indicating that it was to be added to what had gone before, but the typesetter dropped the dash and it was printed as a separate story, under the resultant heading. The nickname stuck despite the general's objections. "Don't call me Fighting Joe," he said. "[It] makes the public think that I am a hot-headed, furious young fellow, accustomed to making furious and needless dashes at the enemy." Nor was this the only change in Hooker. All his military life, at West Point, in Mexico, and in the peacetime army — from which he had resigned in 1853, after sixteen years of service, in order to take up California farming and civil engineering, only to fail at both so utterly that when news came that the war had begun his friends had to pass the hat to get up money for his fare back East — he had been quick to resent the authority and criticize the conduct of his superiors. Just recently, he had sneered at the President and the Cabinet as a flock of bunglers and had asserted that what the country needed was a dictator, making it more or less clear that the man he had in mind for the job was himself. Now, though, all that had gone by the board. He had not even resented Lincoln's "beware of rashness. Beware of rashness" letter, calling him to account for his derogations while appointing him to command the army. Soon afterwards, in the privacy of his tent, Hooker read the letter to a journalist, only taking exception to the charge that he had "thwarted" Burnside. "The President is mistaken. I never thwarted Burnside in any way, shape, or manner," he broke off reading to say — though even now he could not resist adding: "Burnside was pre-eminently a man of deportment. He fought the battle of Fredericksburg on his deportment; he was defeated on his deportment; and he took his deportment with him out of the Army of the Potomac, thank God." He returned to the letter, and when he had finished reading it he folded it and put it back into his breast pocket, as if to emphasize the claim that he had taken it to heart. "That is just such a letter as a father might write to his son," he mused aloud, and the reporter thought he saw tears beginning to mist the general's pale blue-gray eyes. "It is a beautiful letter," Hooker went on, "and although I think he was harder on me than I deserved, I will say that I love the man who wrote it." Again he paused. Then he said, "After I have got to Richmond I shall give that letter to you to have published."

This last, variously phrased as "When I get to Richmond" or "After we have taken Richmond," cropped up more frequently in his talk as the spirit and strength of his army grew, and it was one of the few things that struck Lincoln unfavorably when he arrived for his Easter visit. "If you get to Richmond, General —" he remarked at their first conference, only to have Hooker break in with "Excuse me, Mr President, but there is no 'if' in this case. I am going straight to Richmond if I live." Lincoln let it pass, though afterwards he said privately to a friend: "That is the most depressing thing about Hooker. It seems to me that he is over-confident." Presently, however, as the inspection tour progressed, he began to see for himself that the general's ready assurance was solidly based on facts and figures. Even after the detachment of Burnside's old corps — which took with it, down the coast to Newport News, whatever resentment its members might be feeling as a result of the supersession of their former chief — Hooker still had seven others, plus a newly consolidated corps of cavalry, including in all no less than twenty divisions of infantry and three of horsemen, here on the Rappahannock, with a present-for-duty total of 133,450 effectives, supported by seventy batteries of artillery with a total of 412 guns. Across the way, the Confederates had less than half as many men and a good deal less than half as many guns, and Hooker not only knew the approximate odds, he was also preparing to take advantage of them. On the eve of Lincoln's arrival he had put his corps commanders on the alert by ordering all surplus baggage sent to the rear, and he had warned the War Department to have siege equipment ready for shipment to him in front of the rebel capital. In addition to 10,000 shovels, 5000 picks, 5000 axes, and 30,000 sandbags, he wanted authentic maps of the Richmond defenses, to be used in laying out saps and parallels, and he requested that a flotilla of supply boats be kept standing by at all times, ready to deliver 1,500,000 rations up the Pamunkey River as soon as the army got that far. He did not say "if," he said "as soon as," and when this was repeated at Falmouth on Easter Sunday Lincoln shook his head in some perplexity. He admired determination and self-reliance, especially in a military man, but he also knew there was such a thing as whistling in the dark. He had known men — John Pope, for one — who assumed those qualities to hide their doubts, not only from their associates but also from themselves. In fact, the louder a man insisted that there was no room for doubt in his make-up, the more likely he was to belong to the whistler category, and Lincoln feared that Hooker's brashness might be assumed for some such purpose. "It is about the worst thing I have seen since I have been down here," he remarked.

Most of what he saw he found encouraging, however. He agreed with Hooker's estimation of the army as "the finest on the planet," and he particularly enjoyed the temporary relief the visit afforded him from the day-to-day pressure of White House paperwork and the importunities of favor-seekers. Not that he was entirely delivered from the latter. Now that the career officers had him where they could get at him, out of channels and yet with no great strain on their ingrained sense of propriety, they did not neglect the opportunity. Even so stiff a professional as Meade, whose testiness had caused his troops to refer to him as "a God-damned old goggle-eyed snapping turtle," could not resist the chance to curry favor, difficult though he found it to unbend. "In view of the vacant brigadiership in the regular army," he wrote his wife, "I have ventured to tell the President one or two stories, and I think I have made decided progress in his affections." But this was all comparatively mild and even enjoyable — even the stories — in contrast to what the Chief Executive had left behind, and presently would be returning to, in Washington. What was more, his wife and younger son, who accompanied him on the outing, appeared to enjoy it every bit as much as he did. Mary Lincoln responded happily to the all-too-rare opportunity of being with her husband, in and out of office hours, and playing the role of First Lady in a style she considered fitting. Riding one day through a camp of Negro refugees, who crowded about the presidential carriage and lifted their children overhead for a look at the Great Emancipator, she asked her husband how many of "those piccaninnies" he supposed were named Abraham Lincoln. "Let's see," he calculated. "This is April, 1863. I should say that of all those babies under two years of age perhaps two thirds have been named for me." Mrs Lincoln, who enjoyed the notion — it was fairly customary in her native Bluegrass for slaves to name their offspring for the master — smiled. But ten-year-old Tad had an entirely different notion of what was fun. He wanted to see some real, live rebels. And Lincoln obliged him. Proceeding one blustery morning to Stafford Heights, they looked across the Rappahannock and down into the ruined streets of Fredericksburg, where the army had staged its two-day carnival before crossing the "champaign tract" to be brought up short in front of the sunken road at the foot of Marye's Heights, and to Tad's delight they saw floating from the eaves of one of the town's few unwrecked houses the Stars and Bars. Nearby, moreover, alongside a tall scorched chimney like a monument erected to commemorate a home, stood two sentinels: genuine, armed graybacks, though one of them —

perversely, as if to lessen Tad's pleasure — wore a light-blue U. S. Army overcoat. Their voices faint with distance, they began yelling across the river at the Yankee spectators, something about Fort Sumter and the ironclads being "licked," which brought an officer out of one of the Fredericksburg bomb-proofs to investigate the shouting. He took out his binoculars, beginning to sweep the opposite heights, and when he spotted the presidential group he paused, adjusted the focus, and peered intently. Whether or not he recognized the tall form, made still taller by the familiar stovepipe hat, they never knew; but at any rate he seemed to. He lowered the glasses and struck an attitude of dignity, then removed his wide-brimmed hat, made a low, formal bow, and retired.

For the Confederates across the way — less than 60,000 in all, including the punctilious officer and the two sentinels, one of whom had been lucky enough to scavenge a Yankee overcoat to put between him and the chill of Virginia's early spring — there had been no corresponding improvement, but rather a decline, in the quantity as well as the quality of the supplies provided by their government. The basic daily ration at this time consisted of a quarter-pound of bacon, often rancid, and eighteen ounces of cornmeal, including a high proportion of pulverized cob, supplemented about every third day by the issue of ten pounds of rice to each one hundred men, along with an occasional few peas and a scant handful of dried fruit when it was available, which was seldom. "This may give existence to the troops while idle," Lee complained to the War Department, "but [it] will certainly cause them to break down when called upon for exertion." Scurvy had begun to appear, and though he attempted to combat this by sending out details to gather sassafras buds, wild onions, and such antiscorbutics — together with other, more substantial windfalls, unofficial and in fact illegal; "Ah, General," he chided Hood, "when you Texans come about, the chickens have to roost mighty high" — Lee felt, as he said, "painfully anxious lest the spirit and efficiency of the men should become impaired, and they be rendered unable to sustain their former reputation or perform the service necessary for our safety."

Yet their morale was as high as ever, if not higher: not only because they managed to forget, or at least ignore, their hunger pangs by staging regimental theatricals and minstrel shows, attending the mammoth prayer meetings which were a part of the great religious revival that swept like wildfire through the army at this time, and organizing brigade-size snowball battles which served much the same purpose on this side of the river as Hooker's grand reviews were serving on the other; but also because they could look back on a practically uninterrupted series of victories which they had grounds for believing would be continued, whatever the odds. In the ten months Lee had been in command of the Army of Northern Virginia, including the past three spent in winter quarters, they had fought no less than thirteen battles, large and small, and in all but one of these — South Mountain, where they had been outnumbered ten to one — they had maintained the integrity of their position from start to finish, and in all but one other — Sharpsburg, where the odds were never better than one to three and mostly worse — they had dominated the field when the smoke cleared. Although they had generally assumed the more costly tactical role of the attacker, they had inflicted more than 70,000 casualties, at a cost of less than 50,000 of their own, and had captured about 75,000 small arms while losing fewer than one tenth as many. In guns, the advantage was greatest of all in this respect; losing 8, they had taken 155. ("I declare," a North Carolina private said as his Federal captors were taking him rearward through their lines. "You-uns has got about as many of them 'U.S.' guns as we have.") The over-all result was confidence, in Lee and in themselves, and a pride that burned fiercely despite privation and grim want. One Confederate, writing home, expressed amazement at the contrast between the army's bedraggled appearance in camp and its efficiency in combat. He marveled at the spirit of his companions, "so ragged, slovenly, sleeveless, without a superfluous ounce of flesh upon their bones, with wild matted hair, in mendicants' rags — and to think when the battle-flag goes to the front how they can and do fight!" Nor was praise of Lee's scarecrow heroes limited to those who stood in his army's ranks. An exchanged Union officer, returning to his own lines this spring after a term spent beyond them as a captive, put his first-hand observations on the record in a letter home. "Their artillery horses are poor, starved frames of beasts, tied to their carriages and caissons with odds and ends of rope and strips of raw hide; their supply and ammunition trains look like a congregation of all the crippled California emigrant trains that ever escaped off the desert out of the clutches of the rampaging Comanche Indians. The men are ill-dressed, ill-equipped, and ill-provided, a set of ragamuffins that a man is ashamed to be seen among, even when he is a prisoner and can't help it. And yet they have beaten us fairly, beaten us all to pieces, beaten us so easily that we are objects of contempt even to their commonest private soldiers, with no shirts to hang out the holes of their pantaloons, and cartridge-boxes tied around their waists with strands of rope."

 Lee himself could silence grousing with a jest. "You ought not to mind that," he reassured a young officer who complained about the toughness of some biscuits; "they will stick by you the longer." He referred in much the same tone of levity to the threats made by his new opponent, who had no sooner taken charge of the blue army than he began showing signs of living up to his nickname, Fighting Joe. "General Hooker is obliged to do something," the gray commander wrote home in early February. "I do not know what it will be. He is playing the Chinese game, trying what frightening will do. He runs out his guns, starts wagons and troops up and down the river, and creates an excitement generally. Our men look on in wonder, give a cheer, and all again subsides *in statu quo ante bellum.*" When nothing came of all this show of force before the month was out, Lee expressed a wry impatience. "I owe Mr F. J. Hooker no thanks for keeping me here," he told his wife. "He ought to have made up his mind long ago what to do." At the same time, though, he was warning subordinates that the bluecoats would "make every effort to crush us between now and June, and it will require all our strength to resist them." His confidence, while as firm as that of the men he led, did not cause him to ignore the present odds or the fact that if they continued to lengthen they would stretch beyond endurance. Within a month of the destructive but fruitless repulse of the Federal host that ventured across the river in mid-December, he made his warning explicit in a dispatch to the Secretary of War. "More than once have most promising opportunities been lost for want of men to take advantage of them, and victory itself has been made to put on the appearance of defeat because our diminished and exhausted troops have been unable to renew a successful struggle against fresh numbers of the enemy. The lives of our soldiers are too precious to be sacrificed in the attainment of successes that inflict no loss upon the enemy beyond the actual loss in battle." And he added, with a new note of bitterness which had come with the sack of Fredericksburg and the issuance of the Emancipation Proclamation: "In view of the vast increase of the forces of the enemy, of the savage and brutal policy he has proclaimed, which leaves us no alternative but success or degradation worse than death, if we would save the honor of our families from pollution [and] our social system from destruction, let every effort be made, every means be employed, to fill and maintain the ranks of our armies, until God in his mercy shall bless us with the establishment of our independence."

Instead of an increase, what followed hard on the heels of this appeal was a drastic reduction of his fighting strength, beginning January 14 with the detachment of D. H. Hill to contest the further invasion of the crusty Tarheel general's home state, presaged by the Federals' mid-December advance on Goldsboro. Lee himself went to Richmond two days later to confer with Davis on this and other problems, but had to hurry back to the Rappahannock on the 18th — the eve of his fifty-sixth birthday — when the high-level council of war was disrupted by news that Burnside's army was astir in its camps around Falmouth. As it turned out, all that came of this was the Mud March and Joe Hooker's elevation; Lee detached Robert Ransom's demi-division, which had played a leading role in Longstreet's defense of the sunken road the month before, and sent it south to North Carolina, as he had agreed to do at the interrupted strategy conference. Shortly afterwards, however, word came that Burnside's old corps had boarded transports at Aquia Landing and steamed down Chesapeake Bay to Hampton Roads. It seemed likely that these men were being returned to the scene of their year-old triumph below Norfolk, with instructions to extend their conquest eastward to the Weldon Railroad, Lee's vital supply connection with the factories and grainfields of Georgia and the Carolinas, or to Petersburg, whose fall would give them access to the back door of the capital itself. This two-pronged menace could not be ignored, whatever risk might be involved in attempting to contest it by a further weakening of the Rappahannock line. On February 15 the dismemberment of Longstreet's corps was resumed. Pickett's division was hastened south to Richmond; Hood's followed two days later, accompanied by Old Peter himself, who was charged with the defense of the region beyond the James. These two divisions combined with the troops already there would give him 44,000 men in all, whereas the Federals had 55,000 on hand, exclusive of the corps that presumably was about to join them from Hampton Roads. It was at best a chancy business for the Confederates, north and south of their threatened capital; for even if these blue reinforcements arrived, as was expected momentarily, the command on the south side of the James would be no worse outnumbered than the one on the south side of the Rappahannock, now that more than a fourth of the latter's strength had been subtracted in favor of the former. All Lee could do in this extremity was urge Longstreet to be ready to hurry northward, if possible — that is, if he could find a way to disengage without inviting the destruction of his command or the capture of Richmond — as soon as he got word that Hooker had left off playing the Chinese game and was on the move in earnest. "As our numbers will not admit of our meeting [the enemy] on equality everywhere," the gray commander wrote his detached lieutenant in mid-March, "we must endeavor, by judicious dispositions, to be enabled to make our troops available in any quarter where they may be needed [and] after the emergency passes in one place to transfer them to any other point that may be threatened."

With fewer First Corps troops on hand than had departed, he was down to 58,800 effectives and 170 guns, to be used in opposing a good deal better than twice as many of both. He was almost precisely aware of his opponent's numerical preponderance, not only because of information he received from spies beyond the northern lines, but also because he read the northern papers, one of which was quite specific on the point. Quoting Hooker's medical director, this journal showed 10,777 men on the current sick list, and then went on to state that the sick-well ratio was 67.64 per 1000. By computation Lee arrived at a figure close to 160,000. (Awesome though this total was, it was even a bit low. In late March the Federal commander, lumping teamsters, cooks, and other extra-duty personnel with all the rest, reported an "aggregate present" of 163,005.) Against such odds, and with the knowledge that Hooker would choose the time and place of attack, Lee's only hope for salvation was superior generalship — his own and that of his chief subordinates — coupled with the valor of his soldiers and the increased efficiency of his army. To help achieve this last, he reorganized the artillery into battalions of four four-gun batteries each, four of which battalions were attached to each of the two corps, with two more in general reserve. His hope was that this arrangement, besides strengthening the close-up support of the infantry on the defensive, would provide the "long arm" with a flexibility that would permit a more rapid massing of fire from several quarters of the field at once, either for counterbattery work or for softening an enemy position as a prelude to attack. Whether such measures would produce the desired effect remained to be seen in combat, but another innovation required no testing, its effectiveness being apparent even to a casual eye. This was a legacy left by Longstreet on his departure beyond the James: left, indeed, not only to the Army of Northern Virginia, but also to military science, since in time it would be recognized as perhaps the Confederacy's main contribution to the art of war, which was never the same thereafter.

In mid-January, while Lee was away on his brief trip to Richmond, Old Peter had been left in command on the Rappahannock by virtue of his seniority. His corps, still intact at the time, occupied the northern half of the position, from Hamilton's Crossing to Banks Ford, five miles above Fredericksburg, while Jackson's occupied the rest, from Massaponax Creek down to Port Royal, twenty miles below the town. Lee had no sooner left than Longstreet invited Stonewall to inspect the First Corps defenses, and what the grim Virginian saw when he arrived

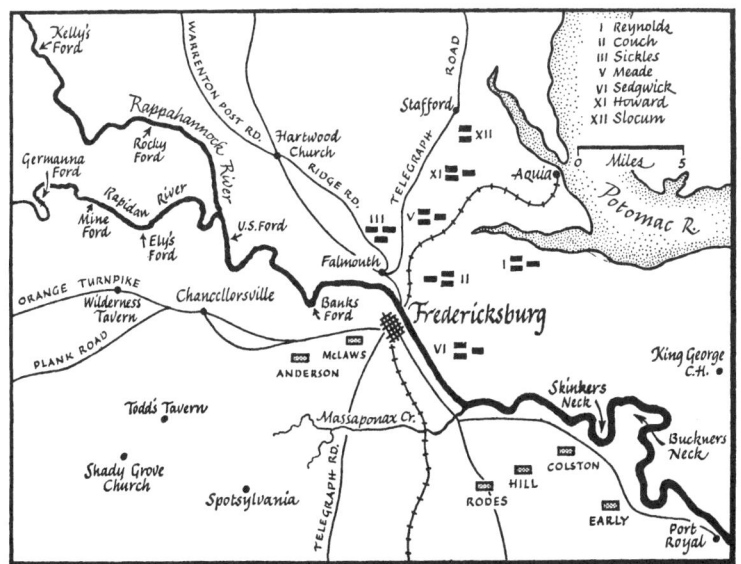

was in the nature of a revelation. Located so as to dominate the roads and open ground, the fieldworks had been designed for use by a skeleton force which could hold them against a surprise attack until supports came up from the reserve. There was nothing new about that; Lee had conceived and used intrenchments for the same purpose on the Peninsula, nearly a year ago. The innovation here involved was the traversed trench. Formerly such works had been little more than long, open ditches, with the spoil thrown forward to serve as a parapet, which gave excellent protection from low-trajectory fire from dead ahead but were vulnerable to flank attack and the lateral effect of bursting shells. To offset these two disadvantages — particularly the latter, intensified by the long-range rifled cannon of the Federals, firing from positions well beyond the reach of most Confederate batteries — Longstreet's engineers had broken the long ditches into quite short, squad-sized rifle trenches, staggered in depth, disposed for mutual support, and connected by traverses which could be utilized against flank attacks and afforded solid protection from all but direct artillery hits. Jackson took a careful look, then returned to his own lines, where the dirt began at once to fly anew. From such crude beginnings, fathered by the necessity for defending a fixed position against a greatly superior foe, grew the highly intricate field fortifications of the future. Presently the whole Rappahannock line, from Banks Ford to Port Royal, was thus protected throughout its undulant, winding, 25-mile length, and when Old Peter left next month with more than half of his men, so well had he and they designed and dug, Lee did not find it necessary to reinforce the two-division remnant by shifting troops from Jackson. "The world has never seen such a fortified position," a young Second Corps artillerist declared some weeks later. "The famous lines at Torres Vedras could not compare with them. ... They follow the contour of the ground and hug the bases of the hills as they wind to and from the river, thus giving natural flanking arrangements, and from the tops of the hills frown the redoubts for sunken batteries and barbette batteries *ad libitum*, far exceeding the number of our guns; while occasionally, where the trenches take straight across the fields, a redoubt stands out defiantly in the open plain to receive our howitzers." Hooker might, as Lee said, "make every effort to crush [the defenders] between now and June," but he was going to find it a much harder job, from here on out, if he tried anything like the approach his predecessor had adopted in December.

On the face of it, that seemed unlikely; Hooker did not resemble Burnside in manner any more than he did in looks. Clearly, if he continued to develop along the lines he had followed so far, Lee was going to have a far thornier problem on his hands, even aside from the lengthened numerical odds, than any he had overcome in frustrating the two all-out offensives that had succeeded his repulse of McClellan, within sight and sound of Richmond, nine months back. The new chieftain's reorganization of his mounted force was a case in point; "Hooker *made* the Federal cavalry," an admiring trooper later declared. Formerly parceled out, regiment by regiment, to infantry commanders whose handling of them had been at best inept, whether in or out of combat, the three divisions — 11,500 strong, with about 13,000 horses — were grouped into a single corps under Brigadier General George Stoneman, a forty-year-old West Pointer, all of whose previous service had been with the mounted arm, before and during the present war, except for a brief term as an infantry corps commander, in which capacity he had won a brevet for gallantry at Fredericksburg. His current rank was one grade below that of the other seven heads of corps; Hooker was withholding promotion until Stoneman proved that he could weld his inherited conglomeration of horsemen into an effective striking force. That was his basic task, and he seemed well on the way toward pushing it to fulfillment, helped considerably by the fact that, after nearly two years in the saddle, the early blue-jacket volunteers — formerly sneered at by their fox-hunt-trained opponents as "white-faced clerks and counter jumpers" who scarcely knew the on side from the off — were becoming seasoned troopers, no longer mounted on crowbait nags fobbed off on the government by unprincipled contractors, but on strong-limbed, sound-winded, well-fed animals who, like their riders, had learned the evolutions of the line and had mastered the art of survival in all weathers.

This improvement came moreover at a time of crisis for the gray cavalry on the opposite bank of the Rappahannock. Not only was there a critical shortage of horses in the Army of Northern Virginia; there was also the likelihood that those on hand, survivors for the most part of a year of hard campaigning, would die for lack of forage. This second danger increased the threat implicit in the first. So clean had the region been swept of fodder that such few remounts as could be found outside the immediate theater of war could not be brought northward. For example, four hundred artillery horses procured that winter in Georgia had to be kept in North Carolina because they could not be foraged with the army, all but a dozen of whose batteries had already been withdrawn from the lines in order to save the animals from starvation. A man could subsist, at least barely, on a couple of pounds of food a day, whereas a horse required about ten times that amount, and this was a great deal more than the rickety single-track railroad from Richmond could bring forward, even if that much grain had been available there. The result was that the cavalry's activity was severely limited. Brigadier General Wade Hampton's brigade, for instance — the first of Stuart's three, which contained in all about 5000 men — had staged three highly successful small-scale raids, deep in the Federal rear at Dumfries and Occoquan, immediately before and after the Battle of Fredericksburg, returning with some 300 captives and their mounts, mostly unwary vedettes picked up in the course of the gray column's advance by starlight, together with a sizeable train of mule-drawn wagons loaded with captured stores, including 300 pairs of badly needed boots — a real windfall. But the end result of these three coups was that Hampton's underfed horses were so utterly broken down by their exertions that the whole brigade had to be sent south to recover, thus weakening Lee still further at a time when he expected Hooker to make up his mind to come booming over the river any day.

Stuart chafed under the restriction thus imposed. His one exploit this winter was an 1800-trooper raid on Fairfax Courthouse, fifteen miles from the Federal capital, beginning the day after Christmas and ending New Year's Day; but all it earned him — in contrast to the enormously successful forays by Forrest and Morgan, launched simultaneously in the West — was 200 mounted prisoners, 20 wagons, and the contents of a dozen sutler stalls; which scarcely made up for the wear and tear of the long ride. Though as usual he made the most of the adventure in his report, it was followed by two months spent in winter quarters, where he was obliged to give less attention to the fast-developing enemy cavalry than to the problem of finding forage for his hungry horses. In such surroundings, though he sought diversion for himself and his men in regimental balls and serenades, the plumed hat, red-lined cape, and golden spurs lost a measure of their glitter, at least in certain eyes. "Stuart carries around with him a banjo player and a special correspondent," one high-ranking fellow officer remarked. "This claptrap is noticed and lauded as a peculiarity of genius, when in fact it is nothing else but the act of a buffoon to attract attention." Down to two brigades after Hampton's departure — one under W. H. F. Lee, called "Rooney," and the other under Fitzhugh Lee, respectively the commanding general's son and nephew — Jeb was obliged to take his pleasure at second hand, from the occasional exploits of subordinates and even ex-subordinates. Among the latter was Captain John S. Mosby, a former cavalry scout who had been given permission in January to recruit a body of partisans for operations in the Loudoun Valley, part of a region to be known in time as "Mosby's Confederacy," so successful were he and his Rangers in bedeviling and defeating the bluecoats sent there to capture or destroy him. Twenty-eight years old and weighing barely 125 pounds, the slim, gray-eyed Virginian first attracted wide attention by his capture, at Fairfax on a night in early March, of Brigadier General E. H. Stoughton, a Vermont-born West Pointer, together with two other officers, 30 men, and 58 horses. Mosby, who at present had fewer men than that in his whole command, entered the general's headquarters, stole upstairs in the darkness, and found the general himself asleep in bed. Turning down the covers, he lifted the tail of the sleeper's nightshirt and gave him a spank on the behind.

"General," he said, "did you ever hear of Mosby?"

"Yes," Stoughton replied, flustered and half awake; "have you caught him?"

"He has caught you," Mosby said, by way of self-introduction, and got his captive up and dressed and took him back through the lines, along with virtually all of his headquarters guard, for delivery to Fitzhugh Lee the following morning at Culpeper.

Fitz Lee, a year younger than the clean-shaven Mosby, though he disguised the fact behind an enormous shovel beard that outdid even Longstreet's in length and thickness, could appreciate a joke as well as the next man, and in this case he could appreciate it perhaps a good deal better, since he and the captive Vermonter had been schoolmates at the Point. Besides, he was in an excellent frame of mind just now, having returned the week before from a similar though less spectacular exploit involving still another fellow cadet of his and Stoughton's: New York–born Brigadier General W. W. Averell, who commanded the second of Stoneman's three divisions. Young Lee was sent by his uncle to investigate a rumor that Hooker was about to repeat McClellan's strategy by transferring his army to the Peninsula. Crossing the Rappahannock well upstream at Kelly's Ford on February 24, Lee's 400-man detachment pushed on to the Warrenton Post Road, then down it, penetrating the blue cavalry screen to the vicinity of Hartwood Church, eight miles short of Falmouth. Here the graybacks encountered their first serious opposition in the form of the 3d Pennsylvania Cavalry, Averell's old regiment before his promotion to divisional command. Lee promptly charged and routed the Keystone troopers, capturing 150 of them at a cost to himself of 14 killed and wounded. Then, having secured the information he had come for — Hooker, whose headquarters were a scant half-dozen miles away by now, obviously was planning no such move as had been rumored — Lee successfully withdrew without further incident, leaving behind him a note for his former schoolmate, whose entire division had been turned out, along with two others of infantry, in a vain attempt to intercept the raiders and avenge the defeat of one of its best regiments. The note was brief and characteristic. "I wish you would put up your sword, leave my state, and go home," Fitz told his old friend, adding in reference to the speed with which the bluecoats had retreated when attacked: "You ride a good horse, I ride a better. Yours can beat mine running." The close was in the nature of a challenge. "If you won't go home, return my visit and bring me a sack of coffee."

Averell returned the visit within three weeks, and he took care to bring along a sack of coffee in his saddlebags. What was more, he repaid the call in force, splashing through the shallows of Kelly's Ford on the morning of March 17 with 3000 troopers. Lee had fewer than 1000 at the time, but his pickets put up such a scrap at the crossing that Averell, though he was pleased to have captured about two dozen of them in the skirmish, persuaded himself that it would be wise to leave a third of his force there to protect his rear, thereby of his own accord reducing the odds to only a little better than two to one. Also, being aware of his old schoolmate's impulsive nature, he halted about midmorning, less than a mile beyond the river, dismounted his men, and took up a strong defensive position behind a stone wall crossing a pasture on the farm of a family named Brooks. Sure enough, at noon Lee came riding hard from Culpeper and attacked without delay, his lead regiment charging dragoon-style, four abreast. The result, as the defenders poured a hot fire from behind their ready-made breastworks, was a quick and bloody repulse. Averell cautiously followed it up, but was struck again, one mile north, with like results. While the blue riders held their ground, the Confederates crossed Carter's Run and reassembled; whereupon the two commands settled down to long-range firing across the creek, relieving the monotony from time to time with limited charges and countercharges which did nothing to alter the tactical stalemate. This continued until about 5.30, when Averell, having learned from captured rebels that Stuart and his crack artillerist Pelham were on the field, decided that the time had come for him to recross the Rappahannock. "My horses were very much exhausted. We had been successful so far. I deemed it proper to withdraw." So he stated later in his report. However, before terminating the requested "visit" he took care to observe the amenities by leaving the sack of coffee Lee had asked for, together with a note: "Dear Fitz. Here's your coffee. Here's your visit. How do you like it? Averell."

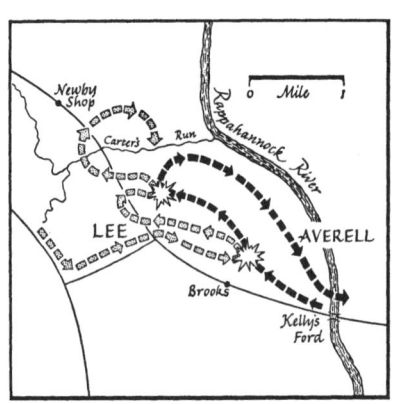

The truth was, Fitz did not much like it. Though he could, and did, claim victory on grounds that he had remained in control of the field after the enemy withdrew, this was not very satisfactory when he considered that the Federals could make the same claim with regard to every similar Confederate penetration, including his own recent raid on Hartwood Church and Stuart's dazzling "rides" the year before. Then too, there was the matter of casualties. Suffering 133, Lee had inflicted only 78, or not much over half as many. If this was a victory, it was certainly a strange one. But there was more that was alarming about this St Patrick's Day action: much more, at least from the southern point of view. For the first time on a fair field of fight — the two-to-one odds were not unusual; moreover, they had been the source of considerable underdog glory in the past — Confederate cavalry had fallen back repeatedly under pressure from Federal cavalry. Nothing could have demonstrated better the vast improvement of this arm of the Union war machine, especially when it was admitted that only Averell's lack of the true aggressive instinct, which twice had left the rebel horsemen unmolested while they reformed their broken ranks, had kept the blue troopers from converting both repulses into routs. Unquestionably, this proof that the Federal cavalry had come of age, so to speak, meant future trouble for the men who previously had ridden around and through and over their awkward opponents almost at will.... Nor was that all either. This light-hearted exchange of calling cards, accompanied in one case by the gift of a pound of coffee, had its more immediate somber consequences, too. After all, a man who died on this small field was every bit as dead as a man who died in the thunderous pageantry of Fredericksburg, and his survivors were apt to be quite as inconsolable in their sorrow. They might possibly be even more inconsolable, since their grief did not take into account the battle or skirmish itself, but rather the identity of the man who fell. What made Kelly's Ford particular in this respect was that it produced one casualty for whom the whole South mourned.

One of Averell's reasons for withdrawing had been the report that Stuart was on the field. It was true, so far as it went; Jeb was there, but he had brought no reinforcements with him, as Averell supposed; he had come to Culpeper on court-martial business, and thus happened to be on hand when the news arrived that bluecoats were over the river. Similarly, the day before, John Pelham had left cavalry headquarters to see a girl in Orange, so that he too turned up in time to join Fitz Lee on the ride toward Kelly's Ford; "tall, slender, beautifully proportioned," a friend called the twenty-three-year-old Alabamian, and "as grand a flirt as ever lived." With his own guns back near Fredericksburg — including the brass Napoleon with which he had held up the advance of a whole Federal division for the better part of an hour — he was here supposedly as a spectator, but anyone who knew him also knew that he would never be content with anything less than a ringside seat, and would scarcely be satisfied even with that, once the action had been joined. And so it was. When the first charge was launched against the stone wall, the young major smiled, drew the sword which he happened to be wearing because he had gone courting the night before, and waved it gaily as he rode hard to overtake the van. "Forward! Forward!" he cried. Just then, abrupt as a clap of blue-sky thunder, a shell burst with a flash and a roar directly overhead. Pelham fell. He lay on his back, full length and motionless, his blue eyes open and the smile still on his handsome face, which was unmarked. Turning him over, however, his companions found a small, deep gash at the base of his skull, just above the hair line, where a fragment of the shell had struck and entered. When Stuart, who had ridden to another quarter of the field, heard that his young chief of artillery was dead he bowed his head on his horse's neck and wept. "Our loss is irreparable," he said.

Others thought so, too: three girls in nearby towns, for instance, who put on mourning. Word spread quickly throughout the South, and men and women in far-off places, who had known him only by reputation, received with a sense of personal bereavement the news that "the gallant Pelham" had fallen. Robert Lee, who had attached the adjective to the young gunner's name in his report on their last great battle, made an unusual suggestion to the President. "I mourn the loss of Major Pelham," he wrote. "I had hoped that a long career of usefulness and honor was still before him. He has been stricken down in the midst of both, and before he could receive the promotion he had richly won. I hope there will be no impropriety in presenting his name to the Senate, that his comrades may see that his services have been appreciated, and may be incited to emulate them." Davis promptly forwarded the letter, with the result that Pelham was promoted even as he lay in state in the Virginia capitol. For once, the Senate had acted quickly, and the dead artillerist, who just under two years ago had left West Point on the eve of graduation in order to go with his native state, went home to Alabama as Lieutenant Colonel Pelham.

At this time of grief, coupled with uncertainty as to the enemy's intentions, Lee fell ill for the first time in the war. A throat infection had settled in his chest, giving him pains that interfered with his sleep and made him testy during his waking hours. By the end of March his condition was such that his medical director insisted that he leave his tent and take up quarters in a house at Yerby's, on the railroad five miles south of Fredericksburg. He did so, much against his wishes, and complained in a home letter that the doctors were "tapping me all over like an old steam boiler before condemning it." After the manner of most men unfamiliar with sickness, he was irritable and inclined to be impatient with those around him at such times (which in turn provoked his staff into giving him the irreverent nickname "the Tycoon") but he never really lost the iron self-control that was the basis of the character he presented to the world. Once, for example, when he was short with his adjutant over some administrative detail, that officer drew himself up with dignity and silently defied his chief; whereupon Lee at once got hold of himself and said calmly, "Major Taylor, when I lose my temper don't let it make you angry." Nor did his illness detract in any way from the qualities which, at the time of his appointment to command, had led an acquaintance to declare: "His name might be Audacity. He will take more desperate chances, and take them quicker, than any other general in this country, North and South." Confirmation of these words had come in the smoke and flame of the Seven Days, in the fifty-mile march around Pope with half of an outnumbered army, and in the bloody defense of the Sharpsburg ridge with his back to a deep river. Yet nothing gave them more emphasis than his reaction now to the early-April news that Burnside's old corps, after lingering all this time at Newport News, was proceeding west to join its old commander, who had been assigned to head the Department of the Ohio. This signified trouble for Johnston and Bragg in Tennessee, since it probably meant that these troops would reinforce Rosecrans. At Charleston, moreover, Beauregard even now was under what might well be an irresistible attack by an ironclad fleet, with thousands of bluecoats waiting aboard transports for the signal to steam into the blasted harbor and occupy the city. Lee's reaction to this combination of pressures, sick though he was, and faced with odds which he knew were worse than two to one here on the Rappahannock, was to suggest that, if this bolstering of the Union effort down the coast and in the West indicated a lessening of the Union effort in the East, the Army of Northern Virginia should swing over to the offensive. "Should Hooker's army assume the defensive," he wrote the Secretary of War on April 9, "the readiest method of relieving the pressure on General Johnston and General Beauregard would be for this army to cross into Maryland." The wretched condition of the roads, plus the cramping shortage of provisions and transportation, made such a move impossible at present, he added; "But this is what I would recommend, if practicable."

Such audacity, though ingrained and very much a part of the nature of the man, was also based on the combat-tested valor of the soldiers he commanded. He knew there was nothing he could ask of them that they would not try to give him, and he believed that with such a spirit they could not fail; or if they failed, it would not be their fault. "There never were such men in an army before," he said this spring. "They will go anywhere and do anything if properly led." And if his admiration for them was practically boundless, so too was his concern. "His theory, expressed upon many occasions," a staff officer later wrote, "was that the private soldiers — men who fought without the stimulus of rank, emolument, or individual renown — were the most meritorious class of the army, and that they deserved and should receive the utmost respect and consideration." Not one of them ever appealed to him without being given a sympathetic hearing, sometimes in the very heat of battle, and he turned down a plan for the formation of a battalion of honor because he did not believe there would be room in its ranks for all who deserved a place there. Quite literally, nothing was too good for them in the way of reward, according to Lee, and this applied without reservation. To him, they all were heroes. One day he saw a man in uniform standing near the open flap of his tent. "Come in, Captain, and take a seat," he said. When the man replied, "I'm no captain, General; I'm nothing but a private," Lee told him: "Come in, sir. Come in and take a seat. You ought to be a captain."

. . .

Lincoln apparently felt much the same way about the enlisted men in blue. One correspondent observed that at the final Grand Review, staged on the last full day of his Falmouth visit, "the President merely touched his hat in return salute to the officers, but uncovered to the men in the ranks." Seated upon a short, thick-set horse with a docked tail, the tall civilian in the stovepipe hat and rusty tailcoat presented quite a contrast to the army commander, who wore a dress uniform and rode his usual milk-white charger. A Maine soldier noticed Hooker's "evident satisfaction" as the long blue files swung past in neat array, and spoke of "the conscious power shown on his handsome but rather too rosy face," whereas another from Wisconsin remarked that "Mr Lincoln sat his cob perfectly straight, and dressed as he was in dark clothes, it appeared as if he was an exclamation point astride of the small letter m." He seemed oddly preoccupied with matters far removed from the present martial business of watching the troops pass in review. This was shown to be the case when he turned without preamble to Major General Darius N. Couch, the senior corps commander, and asked: "What do you suppose will become of all these men when the war is over?" Couch was somewhat taken aback; his mind had not been working along those lines; but he said later, "It struck me as very pleasant that somebody had an idea that the war would sometime end."

Four days of intimate acquaintance with the Army of the Potomac had indicated to Lincoln, despite the blusterous symptoms of overconfidence on the part of the man beside him on the big white horse — despite, too, the rumored repulse of the ironclads at Charleston, the loss of the Union foothold on Texas, the upsurge of guerillas in Missouri, the apparent stalemate in Middle Tennessee, and Grant's long sequence of failures in front of Vicksburg — that the end of the war might indeed be within reach, once Hooker decided the time had come for a jump-off. Morale had never been higher, the Chief Excutive found by talking with the troops in their renovated camps and hospitals. Moreover, the reorganizational shake-up seemed to have brought the best men to the top. Sumner and Franklin were gone for good, along with the clumsy Grand Division arrangement which had accomplished little more than the addition of another link to the overlong chain of command, and of the seven major generals now at the head of the seven infantry corps, less than half — Couch, Reynolds, and Henry W. Slocum had served in the same capacity during the recent Fredericksburg fiasco, while the remaining four were graduates of the hard-knocks school of experience and therefore could be presumed to have achieved their current eminence on merit. Daniel E. Sickles, the only nonregular of the lot, had taken over from Stoneman after that officer's transfer to the cavalry; Meade had succeeded Dan Butterfield, who had moved up to the post of army chief of staff; John Sedgwick had inherited the command of W. F. Smith, now in charge of Burnside's old corps on its way

Death of a Soldier

out to Ohio; Oliver O. Howard, who had lost an arm last year on the Peninsula, had replaced Sigel when that general, already miffed because Hooker had been promoted over his head, resigned in protest because his corps, being next to the smallest of the seven, was incommensurate with his rank. Lincoln had known most of these men before, but in the course of the past four days he had come to know them better, with the result that he felt confident, more confident at any rate than he had felt before, as to the probable outcome of a clash between the armies now facing each other across the Rappahannock. In fact his principal admonition, in a memorandum which he prepared in the course of his visit — perhaps on this same April 9 of the final Grand Review, while Lee was recommending to his government that the Army of Northern Virginia swing over to the offensive in order to break up the menacing Federal combinations — was that "our prime object is the enemy's army in front of us, and is not . . . Richmond at all, unless it be incidental to the main object." Having observed from Stafford Heights the strength of the rebel fortifications, he did not think it would be wise to "take the disadvantage of attacking [Lee] in his intrenchments; but we should continually harass and menace him, so that he shall have no leisure or safety in sending away detachments. If he weakens himself, then pitch into him."

One further admonition he had, and he delivered himself of it the following morning as he sat with Hooker and Couch before departing for Aquia Landing, where the steamer was waiting to take him and his party back to Washington. "I want to impress upon you two gentlemen," he said, "in your next fight, put in all your men." He pronounced the last five words with emphasis, perhaps recalling that in the December fight a good half of the army had stood idle on the left while the conflict wore toward its bloody twilight finish on the right, and then he was off to join his wife and son for the boat ride up the Potomac. Although the trip unquestionably had done him good, providing him with a rare chance to relax, it was after all no more than an interlude in the round of administrative cares, a brief recess from the importunities of men who sought to avail themselves of the power of his office. When a friend remarked that he was looking rested and in better health as a result of his visit to the army, Lincoln replied that it had been "a great relief to get away from Washington and the politicians. But nothing touches the tired spot," he added.

※ 3 ※

Longstreet, on his own at last — at least in a manner of speaking — was finding no such opportunities for glory beyond the James as his fellow corps commander Jackson had found the year before, on detached service out in the Shenandoah Valley. There Stonewall had not only added a brisk chapter to military history and several exemplary paragraphs to future tactics manuals, but had also earned for himself, according to admirers, the one thing his senior rival, according to detractors, wanted more than anything on or off the earth: a seat among the immortals in Valhalla. However, this southside venture, being a different kind of thing, seemed quite unlikely to be productive of any such reward. Designed less for the gathering of laurels than for the gathering of the hams and bacon which for generations had made and would continue to make the Smithfield region famous, it was aimed at satisfying the hunger of the stomach, rather than the hunger of the soul. What was more, throughout his ten weeks of "independent" command, Old Peter was obliged to serve three masters — Davis, Seddon, and Lee — who saddled him with three separate, simultaneous, and sometimes incompatible assignments: 1) the protection of the national capital, threatened by combinations of forces superior to his own, 2) the gathering of supplies in an area that had been under Federal domination for nearly a year, and 3) the disposition of his troops so as to be able to hurry them back to the Rappahannock on short notice. To these, there presently was added a fourth, the investment of Suffolk, which had more men within its fortifications than he could bring against them. The wonder, under such conditions as obtained, was not that he failed in part, but that he succeeded to any degree at all in fulfilling these divergent expectations.

In Richmond itself there had been no talk of failure at the outset, only a feeling of vast relief as the battle-hardened divisions of Hood and Pickett arrived to block the approach of blue forces reported to be gathering ominously, east and southeast of the city, beyond the rim of intrenchments mainly occupied by part-time defenders recruited in the emergency from the host of clerks and other government workers who had escaped conscription up to now. One of these, an industrious diarist, influenced perhaps by a far-fetched sense of rivalry — or perhaps by the fact that in the past six months, since Lee's army had set out northward after Pope, he had forgot what a combat soldier looked like — thought the First Corps veterans "pale and haggard" when he saw them on February 18, slogging through snow deposited calf-deep in the streets by a heavy storm the night before. Four days later, however, Seddon wrote Lee that their "appearance, spirit, and cheerfulness afforded great satisfaction," not only to the authorities but also to the fretful populace. "General Longstreet is here," the Secretary added, "and under his able guidance of such troops no one doubts as to the entire security of the capital." On February 25 he appointed the burly Georgian commander of the Department of Virginia and North Carolina, which was created by combining the three departments of Richmond, Southern Virginia, and North Carolina, respectively under Major Generals Arnold Elzey, Samuel G. French, and D. H. Hill, together with the independent Cape Fear

River District under Brigadier General W. H. C. Whiting, who was charged with protecting Wilmington from attack by land or water. Longstreet's total number of men present for duty, including those in the two divisions he brought with him, plus Ransom's demi-division forwarded earlier, was 44,193 of all arms, mostly scattered about the two states in ill-equipped and poorly administered garrisons of defense. Already outnumbered by the Federals on hand — whose current strength of 50,995 effectives he considerably overestimated — he was alarmed by reports, received on the day he assumed command, that transports were arriving daily in Hampton Roads, crowded to the gunwales with reinforcements for the intended all-out drive on Richmond. So far, they had unloaded an estimated "40,000 or 50,000" troops at Newport News, he wired Lee, and there were rumors that Joe Hooker himself had been seen at Fort Monroe, presaging the early arrival of the balance of the Army of the Potomac.

In such alarming circumstances, and schooled as he had been in strategy under Lee, Old Peter reasoned that the time had come for him to attack, if only by way of creating a diversion. As he put it, "We are much more likely to succeed by operating ourselves than by lying still to await the enemy's time for thorough preparations before he moves upon us." However, it was in the attempted application of this commendable principle that his troubles really began; for it was then that he came face to face with the fact that the exercise of independent command, especially in the armies of the Confederacy, involved a good deal more than a knowledge of tactics and logistics. Like him, his three ranking subordinates were West Pointers in their early or middle forties, and like him, too, they had their share of temperamental peculiarities — as he discovered when he issued instructions for a joint attack on New Bern. Held by the Federals for nearly a year now, the town had been the base for their mid-December advance against the Wilmington & Weldon Railroad, sixty miles away at Goldsboro, and it was Longstreet's belief that an attack on both banks of the Neuse River, farther down, would pinch off the blue garrison and expose it to capture or destruction. His plan was for Hill to move against the place with his whole command, reinforced by one of Whiting's two brigades, which would give him about 14,000 men in all. Hill was altogether willing, having recently excoriated the Yankee invaders by calling upon his infantry to "cut down to 6 feet by 2 the dimensions of the farms which these plunderers propose to appropriate." But Whiting was not, even though the brigade asked for was Ransom's, detached from the First Corps and forwarded to him only the month before. In response to Longstreet's call for "half your force and as many more as can be spared from the Wilmington garrison," along with one of his three long-range Whitworth guns, Whiting — a brilliant thirty-nine-year-old Mississippian who, three years after Old Peter had finished near the bottom of the

West Point class of '42, had not only graduated at the top of his class, but had done so with the highest marks any cadet had ever made — promptly wrote: "I perceive you are not acquainted with this vicinity. ... So far from considering myself able to spare troops from here, I have applied for and earnestly urged that another brigade be sent here immediately. The works here are by no means completed and I need the services of every man I can raise."

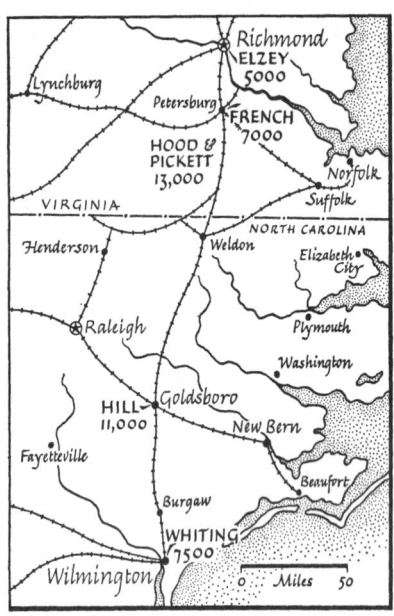

The result was that Hill moved against New Bern without the help of Whiting's men or the loan of the precious long-range gun, and though he converted what was to have been an attack into a demonstration — it was March 14, the anniversary of the fall of the town to the Federals as a follow-up of their capture of Roanoke Island — even that was repulsed decisively when the defenders towed gunboats up the river from Pamlico Sound and opened a scorching fire against the Confederates on both banks, inflicting 30-odd casualties at a cost of only 6. Back in Goldsboro two days later, Hill was furious. "The spirit manifested by Whiting has spoiled everything," he protested in his report. As he saw it, the proper correction for this was for the government to keep its word that he would be given command of all the troops in the state, including those at Wilmington, in which case he would be able to bend the fractious Whiting to his will. "I have received nothing but contemptuous treatment from Richmond from the very beginning of the war," he complained hotly, "but I hope they will not carry matters so far as to perpetuate a swindle." Longstreet, receiving his caustic friend's report, sought to protect him from the wrath of their superiors. "I presume that this was not intended as an official communication," he replied, "and have not forwarded it. I hope that you will send up another account of your trip." Hill neither insisted that the document stand nor offered to withdraw it, but he declined to submit a new or expurgated account of what Old Peter referred to as his "trip."

For all his obstreperous ways of protesting the injustice he saw everywhere around him, Hill was only one among the many when it came to presenting his chief with problems. Arnold Elzey, in charge of the Richmond defenses north of the James, had only recently returned to duty after a long and painful convalescence from the face wound he had suffered at Gaines Mill. A Marylander, he originally had had the last name Jones, but had dropped it in favor of his mother's more distinctive maiden name. Erratic and moody, perhaps because of his disfigurement and the internal damage to his mouth which made his words scarcely intelligible, he was said to be drinking heavily — a particular yet not uncommon type among the casualties of war, injured as much in pride as in body. At any rate, neither he nor his command could be counted on for anything more than the desperate last-ditch resistance that was his and their assignment. Moreover, Longstreet had no high opinion of the abilities of Sam French, who was charged with the defense of Petersburg, that vital nexus of rail supply lines connecting Virginia and the deeper South. A New-Jersey-born adoptive Mississippian and a veteran of the Mexican War, French had attained high rank without distinction in the field of the present conflict, and Old Peter had the usual combat officer's prejudice in this and other such cases he encountered when he crossed the James. Because of Lee's policy of quietly getting rid of men he found unsatisfactory, not by cashiering them but by transferring them to far or adjoining theaters where he considered their shortcomings would cost their country less, Longstreet might have thought he was back with the old Army of the Potomac, as it had been called before the advent of Lee and its transfiguration into the Army of Northern Virginia, so familiar were the faces of many of the officers he found serving under him when he took over his new department. All too many of those faces reflected failure, and all too many others identified men who were inexperienced in combat.

Not that there appeared to be any considerable need for such experience just now. Foraging operations were in full swing, with commissary details scouring the countryside and sending back long trains of wagons heavily loaded with hams and bacon, side meat, salted fish, and flour and cornmeal, all of which were plenteous in the region. Increasingly, as the Federals failed to press their rumored drive on Richmond, the removal of such badly needed stores was becoming the prime concern of the department commander and his troops.

On March 17 their work was interrupted by a dispatch from Lee. Bluecoats were over the Rappahannock at Kelly's Ford; Longstreet was to hurry north with Hood and Pickett to help drive them back. Before he could obey, however, the order was countermanded. The threat had been no more than a cavalry raid; the enemy troopers had retired. Old Peter returned to his foraging duties with new zeal. Now that the nearer counties had been picked clean, he wanted to move eastward into those beyond the Blackwater and Chowan Rivers, out of reach for the past year because of the Union occupation. He figured that if the Yankees could be driven back within their works and held there for a reasonable length of time, his commissary agents — unhampered by the enemy and aided by the citizens of those regions, who had remained intensely loyal to the Confederacy through long months when they might have thought themselves forsaken — would be able to effect a quick removal of the stores. However, this was at best a risky business for him to undertake. He would not only have to keep his two most effective divisions ready to disengage on short notice, in order to be able to speed them north on call from Lee; he would also have to detail a considerable portion of his force for commissary duties behind the lines if he was to accomplish the main purpose underlying his reason for advancing in the first place. In short, with these two disadvantages added to the fact that he was outnumbered before he even began, he would be reversing the required two-to-one numerical ratio between the two parties engaged in siege operations. But he decided to give the thing a try in any event, for the sake of all those thousands of slabs of bacon and barrels of herring awaiting removal from areas previously inaccessible to the soldiers who were fighting here and elsewhere for their eventual deliverance from the blue forces now in occupation.

He made his plans accordingly. Hood and Pickett would join French for a movement against Suffolk, which would serve the double purpose of bringing the fertile Blackwater-Chowan watersheds within the grasp of his commissary agents and of blocking the path of a Federal drive on Petersburg from the lower reaches of the James. Nor was that all. Hill — reinforced at last by Ransom's brigade, pried loose from Whiting over that general's violent protest that he was being stripped of two thirds of his infantry on the eve of an all-out assault on Wilmington by the ironclad fleet Du Pont was assembling at Port Royal — would move simultaneously against Washington, North Carolina, the Tar River gateway to a region which was lush with agricultural produce and gave access to the fisheries of upper Pamlico Sound. This lower movement under Hill, while equally rich in foraging possibilities, was more in the nature of a diversion, favoring the main effort against Suffolk, which would be under Longstreet's personal direction. It was Old Peter's hope that the Unionists, being threatened in two places at once, would not only be prevented from strengthening either at the expense of the other, but would also be thrown off balance by the expectation of additional strikes, all down the long perimeter of their coastal holdings. Though he made it clear at the outset, to his superiors as well as to his subordinates, that both advances were intended to be no more than demonstrations, staged primarily to drive the bluecoats within their works so that his foraging details would be free to scour the area unmolested, he did not overlook the possibility of taking advantage of any opening the enemy might afford. Food for Lee's soldiers was his main concern, but he intended to draw blood, too — despite the numerical odds — whenever and wherever the tactical risk appeared slight enough to justify grasping the nettle. "The principal object of the expedition was to draw out supplies for our army," he reminded the War Department after the movement against Suffolk was under way. "I shall confine myself to this unless I find a fair opportunity for something more."

Hill took off first, however, advancing so rapidly from Goldsboro that on March 30 he had Washington invested before the Federal department commander, Major General John G. Foster, had a chance to reinforce its 1200-man garrison. With ten times that many troops on hand, the Confederates would have little trouble keeping the defenders penned up, but Hill did not believe their capture would be worth the casualties he would suffer in an assault. Consequently, while his foragers were busily rounding up hogs and cattle, he continued to hover about the place, making threatening gestures from time to time in the face of highly accurate fire from gunboats anchored off the town. His chief worry was that Foster — one of Burnside's three aggressive brigadiers in last year's smashing attack on Roanoke Island — would order an advance against his rear by the Union force at New Bern, only thirty miles away. As the siege progressed through the first week in April he vibrated with alternate emotions of jubilation and despair, much to the confusion of Longstreet, who scarcely knew what to make of his lieutenant's fluctuant dispatches. "Up to the 2d instant," he replied from Petersburg on April 7, apparently in something of a daze, "you gave me no reason to hope that you could accomplish anything.... Then came your letter of the 2d, which was full of encouragement and hope.... After your letter of the 2d came one of the 4th, which I believe was more desponding than your previous letters.... Your letter of the 5th revives much hope again." Old Peter was understandably confused, but in point of fact Hill was doing much better than he knew or would admit. Not only were large quantities of supplies moving swiftly back to Goldsboro for forwarding to Richmond and the Rappahannock line, but Foster was reacting exactly as the Confederates had hoped he would do to their pretense of great strength and earnestness. Drawing in his horns in expectation of being struck next at almost any point in his department, he left Hill's commissary agents a clear field for exploitation. "I am confident," he warned Halleck on Easter Sunday, "that heavy operations will be necessary in this state, and that the most desperate efforts are and will continue to be made to drive us from the towns now occupied."

At any rate Longstreet's main concern was centered presently on matters closer at hand than Hill's pendulum swings from gloom to elation down on the banks of the Tar. On April 9 — the day Lee recommended an advance into Maryland as the best Confederate strategy for contesting the over-all Union menace, East and West, and also the day Hooker staged the last of the Grand Reviews in honor of Lincoln's Falmouth visit — First Corps troops moved out of their camps near Petersburg and took up the march southeastward in the direction of the lower Blackwater crossings less than twenty miles from Suffolk, which the Federals had been fortifying ever since they occupied it formally in September. Two divisions were quartered there now, under Major General John J. Peck and Brigadier General George W. Getty, with a combined total of 21,108 effectives. Hood, Pickett, and French had 20,192 between them; but Peck, estimating the rebel strength at "40,000 to 60,000 men," reacted much as Foster had done, ten days ago, to Hill's advance on Washington. Calling in all his detachments from the surrounding countryside, he skirmished briefly along the Blackwater to gain time for a concentration, then fell back on Suffolk, where he buttoned himself up tightly. While his troops were at work improving the intrenchments, he notified his superiors at Fort Monroe and Washington that he was prepared to fight to the last man, despite the enemy's "great preponderance of artillery as well as other branches." Longstreet moved up deliberately. On April 11 he invested the town, taking the bluecoats under fire from the opposite bank of the Nansemond River while extending his right southward all the way to Dismal Swamp. Behind this long, concave front, which he held with a minimum number of men in order to provide details for his all-important foraging operations, commissary officers were soon busy purchasing everything in sight that a man could eat or wear. Long trains of wagons, piled high with goods and forage, soon were grinding westward amid a din of cracking whips, ungreased axles, and teamster curses. After unloading at newly established dumps along the Petersburg & Norfolk Railroad, they returned eastward, rattling empty across the muddy landscape, for new loads. Day and night, to Longstreet's considerable satisfaction — as well as to that of the hungry men on the Rappahannock, whose rations improved correspondingly — the shuttle work continued. Supplies appeared inexhaustible in this region scarcely touched by war till now.

Meanwhile, by way of keeping up the bluff, the troops on line were demonstrating noisily, as if in preparation for an assault on the blue intrenchments across the way. Although the duty was mostly dull, there were occasional incidents that provided all the excitement a man could want, and more. For instance, there was the affair at Fort Huger, an old Confederate redoubt constructed originally as part of the Suffolk defenses but abandoned by the Federals when they took over. As it turned out, they showed wisdom by this action. On April 16, French moved five guns and three companies of infantry into the fort on the far left of his line, intending to deny enemy gunboats the use of the adjoining Nansemond River. Three nights later, however, six companies of Connecticut infantry crossed the river, a quarter of a mile upstream, and swooped down in a surprise attack that captured the works, along with all five of the guns and 130 officers and men. Joined before dawn by the other four companies of their regiment, they held the place all the following day and returned to their own lines after dark, taking along the captured men and guns. Longstreet had scarcely had time to absorb the news of this setback when he heard from Hill that the Washington siege had been abandoned on the same day Fort Huger was occupied by French. Two weeks had sufficed for the removal of most of the stores from the region; so that when, at the end of that span, the Federals succeeded in running in two ships to replenish the supplies of the garrison, Hill decided the time had come for him to withdraw. Back at Goldsboro before the week was out, he praised his troops for their "vigilance on duty and good behavior everywhere." His scorn he reserved for homeguarders, especially those of lofty rank, whose avoidance of combat duty he blamed for his lack of the strength required to drive the detested Yankees not only "into their rat holes at New Bern and Washington," but into Pamlico Sound as well. "And such noble regiments they have," he sneered at these stay-at-home Tarheel warriors. "Three field officers, four staff officers, ten captains, thirty lieutenants, and one private with a misery in his bowels.... When our independence is won, the most trifling soldier in the ranks will be more respected, as he is now more respectable, than an army of these skulking exempts."

Longstreet accepted vexation far more philosophically. Even the overrunning of Fort Huger, though it showed, as he said, "a general lack of vigilance and prompt attention to duties," did not arouse his ire. "Many of the officers were of limited experience," he concluded his report of the affair, "and I have no doubt acted as they thought best. I do not know that any of them deserve censure. This lesson, it is hoped, will be of service to us all." Others reacted differently as the Suffolk siege wore on. Hood, for example, had small use for this buttoned-up style of warfare. "Here we are in front of the enemy again," he wrote Lee toward the end of April. "The Yankees have a very strong position, and of course they increase the strength of their position daily. I presume we shall leave here so soon as we gather all the bacon in the country." Boyishly the Kentucky-born Texan added: "When we leave here it is my desire to return to you. If any troops come to the Rappahannock please don't forget me." Thirty-one and a bachelor, Hood was bored. But that could scarcely be said of his fellow division commander Pickett. This thirty-eight-year-old widower, a handsome if rather doll-faced man with long chestnut curls which he anointed regularly with perfume, was in the full flush of a sunset love affair with a southside girl not half his age. LaSalle Corbell was her name; he styled her "the charming Sally" — his dead wife had been called Sally, too — and wrote her ardent letters signed "Your Soldier" despite the fact that he saw her almost nightly, riding up to her home at Chuckatuck by twilight and back to his lines before the first red glow of dawn. When Longstreet at last began to frown on this inattentiveness to duty, not to mention the abuse of horseflesh, Pickett tried to persuade the corps adjutant, Major G. Moxley Sorrel, to give him permission to take off without Old Peter's knowledge.

Sorrel, who did not approve of what he called "such carpet-knight doings in the field," declined to accept the responsibility for what might happen in Pickett's absence, and referred him back to Longstreet. "But he is tired of it and will refuse," the ringleted Virginian protested. "And I must go; I must see her. I swear, Sorrel, I'll be back before anything can happen in the morning." Sorrel still said no; but recalling the scene years later he added that "Pickett went all the same. Nothing could hold him back from that pursuit."

Increasingly, as spring wore on and the end of the campaign drew near — he himself had set a May 3 closing date by notifying Richmond on April 19 that two more weeks would suffice for draining the region of its stores — Longstreet grew dissatisfied: not so much with what he had done, which was after all considerable, as with the thought of what he had not done. While it was true that he had carried out, practically to the letter, his difficult triple assignment — that is, he had kept the Yankees out of Petersburg, he had secured enormous quantities of previously inaccessible supplies, and he had kept his First Corps troops on the alert for a swift return to Lee — it was also painfully true that he had accomplished nothing that would compare in tactical brilliance with even the smallest battlefield victory scored by Jackson out in the Valley a year ago. As a result, the taking of Suffolk, along with its thousands of bluecoats and tons of matériel, began to appeal to him more and more as a fitting end to these two months of detached service. Moreover, as the notion grew more attractive in his mind's eye, it also began to appear more feasible to his military judgment, despite the fact that the Federals inside the place were stronger now, by some 9000 reinforcements brought in from Hampton Roads, than they had been at the outset. There were several ways of assessing this last, however, and one was that the grandeur of the triumph would be in direct ratio to the plumpness of the prize. Accordingly, Old Peter wrote to Lee, telling him what he had in mind and asking if he could not be sent the rest of his corps in order to assure the success of his assault on the blue intrenchments. Foreseeing objections — as well he might — he suggested that Lee, if need be, could fall back to the line of the Annas, though it was his own conviction that one corps would be able to stand fast on the Rappahannock in the event of an attack. Lee replied on April 27 that Hooker was far too strong, and just now far too active, for him to consider a further weakening of his army. In fact, he countered by asking his lieutenant if he could spare him any of the troops in North Carolina. But he certainly did not veto the proposal for ending the southside siege with an assault. "As regards your aggressive movement upon Suffolk," he wrote, "you must act according to your good judgment. If a damaging blow could be struck there or elsewhere of course it would be advantageous." He added some doubts as to whether the game would be worth the candle in this case, but Longstreet could see in the letter a relaxation of the urgency for keeping his First Corps divisions practically uncommitted in order to have them ready to hurry north on short notice. Consequently, while his foraging crews kept busy, hauling out the last of the precious wagonloads of hogs and corn and herring, he turned his thoughts to tactical details of the assault that would cap the climax by adding the one element — glory — so far lacking in a campaign already productive of much else.

Three days later, however — April 30 — his plans were shattered by a wire from Adjutant General Cooper in Richmond, quoting a dispatch just received from Lee. Hooker was over the Rappahannock in great strength, above as well as below Fredericksburg, Lee had announced, "and it looks as if he was in earnest." Cooper's instructions to Longstreet were brief and to the point: "Move without delay your command to this place to effect a junction with General Lee."

Longstreet inquired by telegraph whether this meant that he was to abandon his wagons, still scattered about on foraging operations, and risk a quick withdrawal of his men, which would bring out the Federals hot on his heels. By no means, Cooper replied on May Day. What had been intended was for him "to secure all possible dispatch without incurring loss of trains or unnecessary hazard of troops." Having thus avoided going off half-cocked, Old Peter turned to the always difficult task of designing a disengagement. After the wagons had been called in and sent rearward, orders were issued on May 2 for all the troops to withdraw from the intrenchments the following evening and retire westward under cover of darkness, burning bridges and felling trees in their wake to discourage pursuit. This came off on schedule, and after some sharp skirmishing by rear-guard elements, the whole command was across the Blackwater by sundown of the 4th. Leaving French to defend that line, Hood and Pickett moved to Petersburg next day. Dawn of the 6th found them on the march for the James, leg-weary but eager, and Longstreet himself was in Richmond before noon, making preparations to speed both divisions northward by rail for a share in the great battle reportedly still raging along the near bank of the Rappahannock. All this ended the following day, however, when he received a wire from Lee: "The emergency that made your presence so desirable has passed for the present, so far as I can see, and I desire that you will not distress your troops by a forced movement to join me, or sacrifice for that purpose any public interest that your sudden departure might make it necessary to abandon."

※ 4 ※

"Go forward, and give us victories," Lincoln had written, and that was what Hooker had in mind when he crossed the Rappahannock. Nor was that all. "I not only expected victory," he would recall when the smoke had cleared, "I expected to get the whole [rebel] army." That this had indeed been his intention was confirmed by his chief of staff, who also declared in retrospect that the real purpose of the campaign had been "to destroy the army of General Lee where it then was." Earlier, on the eve of committing what he called "the finest body of soldiers the sun ever shone on," Fighting Joe had expressed his resolution in terms that were even more expansive. "My plans are perfect," he announced, "and when I start to carry them out, may God have mercy on Bobby Lee; for I shall have none."

Just what those plans were he was not saying, even to those whose task it would be to translate them into action. In point of fact, however, they were influenced considerably by the man who had preceded him in command. In addition to having demonstrated the folly of launching headlong attacks against prepared intrenchments — intrenchments which, incidentally, had been enormously strengthened and extended since December — Burnside had explored, at least on paper, several other approaches to the problem of how to prise the rebels loose from their works and come to grips with them in the open, where the advantage of numbers would be likely to decide the issue in favor of the Union. Now he had departed, taking "his deportment with him out of the Army of the Potomac, thank God," but Hooker could remember how the lush-whiskered general had stressed the need for secrecy and then proceeded to talk with all and sundry about his plans, with the result that his opponent's only surprise had been at his foolhardiness. So the new commander, who, by ordinary, was anything but a closemouthed man, profited in reverse from his predecessor's example. He kept his plans to himself.

Not that he did not have any; he did, indeed, and he did not care who knew it, so long as the particulars remained hidden. These too had been inherited, however, for the most part. Originally, like Burnside on the eve of his bloody mid-December commitment, Hooker had planned to cross the Rappahannock well below Fredericksburg; but this had two serious disadvantages. It would uncover the direct route to Washington, which he knew would distress Lincoln, and it would have to be announced to the Confederates in advance by the laying of pontoons. Upstream, on the other hand, the river narrowed and was comparatively shallow. There were fords in that direction — Banks Ford, five miles above the town, and United States Ford, seven miles farther west — behind which he could mass and conceal his troops in order to send them splashing across in a rush that would smother the south-bank gray outpost detachments, thus forcing Lee to face about and meet his assailants without the advantage of those formidable intrenchments. This had been Burnside's intention in the campaign that ground to a soggy halt in January, but Hooker, by waiting for the advent of fair weather, had greatly reduced the likelihood of the movement's coming to any such premature and ignominious end. Besides, there would be tactical embellishments, designed to increase the Federal chances for an all-out victory. Principal among these was a plan for taking advantage of the recently demonstrated improvement of the blue cavalry. With Stoneman outnumbering Stuart better than three to one — just over 11,500 sabers opposed to just under 3500 — it was Hooker's belief that if his troopers crossed the river in strength they would be able to have things pretty much their own way in the Confederate rear. Damage to Lee's communications and supply lines, coupled with strikes at such vital points as Gordonsville and Hanover Junction, might throw him into sudden retreat; in which case the Federal infantry, coming down on the run from the upstream crossings, would catch him in flight, strung out on the roads leading southward, and destroy him. No one so far in this war had been able to throw Lee into such a panic, it was true, but the reason for this might be that no one had dared to touch him where he was tender. At any rate Hooker thought it worth a try, and he had his adjutant general draw up careful instructions for Stoneman. His entire corps, less one brigade but accompanied by all 22 of its guns, was to cross Rappahannock Bridge, thirty miles above Fredericksburg, not later than 7 a.m. on April 13, "for the purpose of turning the enemy's position on his left, throwing the cavalry between him and Richmond, isolating him from his supplies, checking his retreat, and inflicting on him every possible injury which will tend to his discomfiture and defeat." Lest there be any doubt that the cavalry chief was to be vigorous in his treatment of the fleeing Lee, the adjutant then broke into what might one day have become the model for a pregame Rockne pep talk: "If you cannot cut off from his column large slices, the general desires that you will not fail to take small ones. Let your watchword be fight, fight, fight, bearing in mind that time is as valuable to the general as rebel carcasses."

Stoneman and his 10,000 chosen troopers, along with their 22 guns and a train of 275 wagons containing enough additional food and forage to sustain them for nine days beyond the lines, were poised for a crossing at the specified hour. One brigade had already forded the river a few miles above Rappahannock Bridge, with instructions to come sweeping down and clear out the rebel horsemen watching from across the way. But as the three divisions stood to their mounts, awaiting the order that would send them about their task of cutting slices large and small from Lee's retreating column, rain began to patter and then to drum, ominously reminiscent of the downpour that had queered the Mud March. Now as then, roads became quagmires and the river began to swell, flooding the fords and tugging at the shaky pilings of the bridge. Stoneman decided to wait it out. Recalling the brigade that had crossed, he wired headquarters that his rolling stock was stalled. Hooker replied that he was to shuck his guns and wagons and proceed without them. Stoneman said he would, and set dawn of the 15th as his new jump-off time. Then the wire went dead. Hooker, having promised to keep the President posted on the progress of the movement, struck an optimistic note in a dispatch sent to Washington on that date: "I am rejoiced that Stoneman had two good days to go up the river, and was able to cross it before it had become too much swollen. If he can reach his position [deep in the enemy rear] the storm and mud will not damage our prospects." Lincoln was not so sure. It was his belief, he replied within the hour, that "General S. is not moving rapidly enough to make the expedition come to anything. He has now been out three days, two of which were unusually fair weather, and all three without hindrance from the enemy, and yet he is not 25 miles from where he started. To reach his point he still has 60 to go, another river (the Rapidan) to cross, and will be hindered by the enemy. By arithmetic, how many days will it take him to do it? ... I greatly fear it is another failure already."

His fears were confirmed the following day when a courier reached Falmouth with a letter from upstream. "I cannot say what has been the state of affairs away from this vicinity," Stoneman wrote, "but here, at the hour of my last dispatch, the condition of things may be judged of when I tell you that almost every rivulet was swimming, and the roads next to impassable for horses or pack-mules.... The railroad bridge has been partly carried away by the freshet. The river is out of its banks, and was still on the rise a few hours ago.... My dispatch [setting a new date for the crossing] was based upon the expectation that we were to be favored with a continuation of fair weather. It certainly was not predicated upon the expectation of being overtaken by one of the most violent rainstorms I have ever been caught in." There was much else by way of explanation and excuse, including the news that three men and several horses had been drowned that morning while attempting to cross what had been a nearly dry stream bed the day before. But the gist of the long letter came about midway: "The elements seem to have conspired to prevent the accomplishment of a brilliant cavalry operation."

Hooker was disappointed. He told Stoneman to stay where he was, keep up his reserve supply of rations, and be ready to take off southward "as soon as the roads and rivers will permit." However, the rain showed no sign of a real letup. For nearly two weeks it kept falling, with only a few fair days mixed in to mock the army's immobility, and all this time Hooker was champing at the bit, anxious to put his troops in motion for the kill. As the days went by, his bitterness increased. He began to doubt that Stoneman and the cavalry were up to carrying out the mission he had assigned them; he began, in fact, to see room for improvement in the plans he had called perfect. Since he had the Confederates outnumbered better than two to one — as he knew by reports from the excellent intelligence service he had established as part of his staff — he had a rare chance to attack them, front and back, with separate columns each of which would be superior to the gray mass clamped between them. Instead of 10,000 cavalry, he would put 60,000 infantry and artillery in Lee's immediate rear, blocking his retreat while the other 60,000 pounded his front and the troopers far in his rear slashed at his lines of supply and communication. Isolated and surrounded, prised out of his intrenchments and grievously outnumbered, Lee would be pulverized; Hooker would "get the whole army." It was a pleasant thing to contemplate, not only because of its classic tactical simplicity, but also because it would involve what might be called poetic justice, a turning of the tables on the old fox who so often had divided his own army, but without the advantage of numbers, in hopes of destroying the very soldiers who now were about to destroy him.

What was more, as Hooker pored over his maps to plan the logistical details of the proposed envelopment, he found that the terrain seemed made to order for just such a maneuver. Banks Ford was stoutly defended from across the way, the rebels having honeycombed the dominant south-bank heights with trenches that formed the left-flank anchor of their line, and U. S. Ford was guarded nearly as heavily by an intrenched outpost detachment; besides which, the recent rains had swollen them both well past wading depth, so that his previous design to seize them in a sudden, splashing rush was now impractical. On the other hand Kelly's Ford, fifteen miles above the junction of the Rappannock and the Rapidan, which occurred just over a mile above U. S. Ford, was lightly held, unfortified, and comparatively shallow. Although crossing there would call for a long approach march and would involve another river crossing when the column reached the Rapidan, the advantages greatly outweighed the drawbacks. For one thing, Kelly's Ford was far enough out beyond the enemy flank to give hope that, with luck, the march and perhaps both crossings could be accomplished before the rebs knew what was afoot, and for another it would afford a covered approach, along excellent roads traversing a wooded region known locally as the Wilderness, to within striking distance of the Confederate rear. Moreover, as the column moved eastward along the south bank of the Rappahannock it would uncover both U.S. and Banks Fords, which would not only shorten considerably its lines of supply and communication, thereby making it possible for the two halves of the blue army to reinforce each other quickly if an emergency arose in either direction, but would also give the flankers, in the case of the Banks Ford defenses, control of high ground that dominated much of the present rebel line of fortifications; Lee would be obliged to come out into the open, whether he wanted to or not. All this sounded fine to Hooker. Admittedly he was about to engage in the risky business of dividing his army in the presence of the enemy, but Lee had proved on more than one occasion that the profits more than justified the risk, even though he had done so with the numerical odds against him; whereas with Hooker it would be the other way around. It was this last that gave him substantial reason to hope for the Cannae which so far, and for all his vaunted skill in battle, had eluded Lee.

Translating theory into action, Fighting Joe sent orders on April 26 for the corps of Slocum, Howard, and Meade to march for Kelly's Ford at sunrise the following morning. They were to be in position there not later than 4 p.m. of the 28th, at which time they were to head south for the Rapidan, cross that river at Ely's and Germanna Fords, and take the roads leading southeast to the Orange Turnpike, then proceed due east along it to a position covering a crossroads hamlet called Chancellorsville, eight miles west of Lee's line and less than half that far from the ragged eastern rim of the Wilderness. Couch — minus Gibbon's division, which could not be moved just yet because its Falmouth camp was in plain view of the enemy on Marye's Heights — was to march at dawn of the 29th to a position in the rear of Banks Ford and stand ready to throw pontoons for a crossing as soon as Slocum's advance flanked the rebels out of the trenches across the way. Meanwhile, with 60,000 Federal soldiers marching against the Confederate rear, the corps of Sedgwick, Reynolds, and Sickles, aggregating another 60,000, would move down to the riverbank south of Fredericksburg, near the point of Franklin's crossing in December, where they would establish a west-bank bridgehead on the 29th for the purpose of demonstrating against Lee's front, thus distracting his attention from what would be going on behind him and keeping him in doubt as to where the heaviest blow would fall. Stoneman would add to the confusion by striking first at the Virginia Central Railroad, then eastward along it to the Richmond, Fredericksburg & Potomac, where he was to harass and slow down the gray army if it attempted to escape the jaws of the blue vise by falling back on its threatened capital. Still mindful of the need for secrecy, Hooker enjoined the generals with the upstream column to regard the "destination of their commands as strictly confidential." Apparently his left hand was to be kept from knowing what his right hand was about, but he lifted the veil a little by telling Sedgwick, who was in charge of the downstream column, to carry the enemy works "at all hazards" in case Lee detached "a considerable part of his force against the troops operating ... west of Fredericksburg." Whether the main attack would be delivered against the enemy's front or his rear — that is, by Sedgwick's 60,000 or by Slocum's — remained to be seen. At

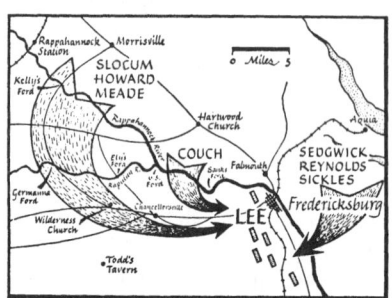

the critical moment, probably on the 30th but certainly by May Day, Hooker would ride to Chancellorsville, make his estimate of the situation, and then, like an ambidextrous boxer, swing with either hand for the knockout.

The upstream march began on schedule Monday, April 27, despite a slow drizzle that threatened to undo the good which three days of fair weather had done the roads. Slogging toward Hartwood Church and Morrisville, where they would turn off south for Kelly's Ford, the veterans chanted as they trudged:

> *"The Union boys are moving on the left and on the right,*
> *The bugle call is sounding, our shelters we must strike;*
> *Joe Hooker is our leader, he takes his whiskey strong,*
> *So our knapsacks we will sling, and go marching along."*

Sweating under fifty to sixty pounds of weight, which included eight days' rations, a pair of blankets, a thick wool overcoat, and forty rounds of ammunition each, they interpreted the word "sling" as they saw fit, shedding knapsacks by the roadside to be gleaned by civilian scavengers — "ready finders," the army called them — who moved in their wake and profited from their prodigality. Hooker's administrative sensibilities were offended by the waste, but he was consoled by the fact that the march was otherwise orderly and rapid in spite of the showers, which fortunately left off before midday without softening the roads. In response to a wire that afternoon from a fretful Lincoln — "How does it look now?" — he managed to be at once reticent and reassuring: "I am not sufficiently advanced to give an opinion. We are busy. Will tell you all soon as I can, and have it satisfactory." Riding next day up to Morrisville, through rain that had come on again to slow the march and throw it several hours behind schedule, he was pleased all the same to note that the column had turned south for the Rappahannock, and he sent an aide ahead with a message urging Slocum to make up for lost time: "The general desires that not a moment be lost until our troops are established at or near Chancellorsville. From that moment all will be ours."

He sounded buoyant, and presently he had cause for feeling even more so. By dusk the head of the flanking column was approaching Kelly's Ford, and Hooker received word from his chief of staff at Falmouth that Couch had his two divisions in position behind Banks Ford, as ordered, and was improving the waiting time by extending the telegraph to U.S. Ford, in case that proved to be a better point for crossing. Sedgwick had been delayed by the rain, Butterfield added, but he had his three corps on the march and would begin throwing five pontoon bridges across the river below Fredericksburg on schedule in the morning. Moreover, though the weather had been too gusty to permit spyglass observation from the bobbing gondolas of Professor T. S. C. Lowe's two balloons, the ruse of leaving Gibbon's division in its exposed camp seemed to have worked as intended; Lowe reported that, from what he could see, the Confederate trenches "appeared to be occupied as usual," indicating that Lee almost certainly had no intimation that the various Federal columns were on the move for positions from which to accomplish his destruction. All this was about as encouraging as could be, but Hooker, being painfully familiar with the tricks of the old fox across the way, was leaving as little as possible to chance. He wired Lowe to send a balloon up anyhow, despite the wind and darkness, "to see where the enemy's campfires are," not forgetting to add: "Someone acquainted with the position and location of the ground and of the enemy's forces should go up."

By the time the Professor — the title was complimentary; his official designation was "Chief of Aeronauts, Army of the Potomac," and his basic uniform was a voluminous linen duster — got a balloon up into the windy night for a look at the rebel campfires, Howard's corps was over the Rappahannock, crossing dry-shod on a pontoon bridge just completed by the engineers, and had taken up a position on the south bank to guard against a surprise attack while the other two corps were crossing. Slocum came over at dawn, followed by Meade, who struck out southeastward for Ely's Ford; then Howard fell in behind Slocum, who had already headed south for Germanna Ford. Behind all three came Stoneman, a full day late and complaining bitterly that the alert order had not allowed him time to call in his 10,000 horsemen from their camps around Warrenton. He set out for Raccoon Ford, ten miles west of Germanna, for a descent on the Virginia Central in the vicinity of Louisa Courthouse, leaving Hooker a single 1000-man brigade of three slim regiments to accompany the infantry on the march and another 500 troopers to guard the deserted north-bank camps and installations. The foot soldiers pushed ahead, stepping fast but warily now; for it was here in the V of the rivers that Pope, for all his bluster, had nearly come to grief in August. Neither column encountered any real difficulty, however, in the course of its daylong hike to the Rapidan. Nor did Slocum's run into much trouble after it got there. His advance guard, splashing its way through the chest-deep water, surprised a drowsy 100-man rebel detachment at Germanna, capturing a number of graybacks before they knew what was upon them. Finding timbers collected here on the south bank for the construction of a bridge, the jubilant bluecoats set to work and put them to use in short order, with the result that the rest of their corps, and all of Howard's, made a second river crossing without having to wet their socks.

Meade's troops had no such luck. Though he too encountered no opposition in the V, his march to Ely's was longer than Slocum's to Germanna, and he found no bridge materials awaiting him at its end.

Coming down to the ford at sunset the advance guard plunged across the cold, swift-running Rapidan, chased off the startled pickets on the opposite bank, and set to work building fires to light the way for the rest of the corps approaching the crossing in the dusk. Regiment by regiment the three road-worn divisions entered the foam-flecked, scrotum-tightening water and emerged to toil up the steep south bank, which became increasingly slippery as the slope was churned to gumbo by the passage of nearly 16,000 soldiers, all dripping wet from the armpits down. Once across, they gathered about the fires for warmth, some in good spirits, some in bad, each arriving cluster somewhat muddier than the one before, but all about equally wet and cold. By midnight the last man was over. Low in the east, the late-risen moon, burgeoning toward the full, had the bruised-orange color of old gold, and while all around them the whippoorwills sang plaintively in the moon-drenched woods, the men lay rolled in their blankets, feet to the fire, catching snatches of sleep while awaiting the word to fall back into column. Meade had them on the go again by sunup of the last day of April, still marching southeast, but now through an eerie and seemingly God-forsaken region; the Wilderness, it was called, and they could see why. Mostly a tangle of second-growth scrub oak and pine, choked with vines and brambles that would tear the clothes from a man's back within minutes of the time he left the road, it was interrupted briefly at scattered points by occasional small clearings whose abandoned cabins and sag-roofed barns gave proof, if such was needed, that no amount of hard work could scratch a living from this jungle. To make matters worse, rebel cavalry slashed at the column from time to time, emerging suddenly from ambush, then back again, apparently for the purpose of taking prisoners who would identify their units. Meade did not like the look of things any better than the men did. He rode with the van and set a rapid pace, wanting to get them out of here, and for once they were altogether willing. Chancellorsville was less than half a dozen miles from the ford, and though it was still a good three miles short of open country where he could deploy his troops and bring his guns to bear, he remembered that Hooker had said that once the flankers were "established" in that vicinity, "all will be ours."

Arriving about an hour before noon, still without having encountered anything more than token resistance from the enemy cavalry and none at all from the famed, hard-marching rebel infantry, he found that for all its grand-sounding name the crossroads hamlet — if it could be called even that — consisted of nothing more than a large, multi-chimneyed brick-and-timber mansion, with tall slim pillars across its front supporting a double-decked veranda, and three or four outbuildings scattered about the quadrants of the turnpike intersection. There was, however, a hundred-acre clearing, which seemed expansive indeed after what he had just emerged from and would re-enter when he moved on, and there were also four ladies, of various ages and in bright spring dresses, who likewise were a relief of sorts despite their show of pique at having to receive unwelcome guests. At any rate, Meade's spirits rose as he waited for Slocum and Howard, whose troops had the longer march today. Much that he previously had not understood, mainly because of Hooker's refusal to give out details of his plan — "It's all right" had been his usual and evasive reply to questions from commanders of all ranks — suddenly became much clearer to Meade, now that he was within a half-day's march of Lee's rear without its having cost him anything more than the handful of men gobbled up by the graybacks in the course of his plunge through the heart of the Wilderness. Now that he believed he saw the whole design, his dourness gave way to something approaching exaltation. By 2 o'clock, when Slocum arrived at the head of his two-corps column, Meade was fairly beside himself. "This is splendid, Slocum," he cried, displaying an exuberance that seemed all the more abandoned because it was so unlike him; "hurrah for Old Joe! We are on Lee's flank and he doesn't know it."

What he wanted now, he added with no slackening of enthusiasm, was to push on eastward without further delay, at least another couple of miles before nightfall, "and we'll get out of this Wilderness." Slocum felt much the same way about it. But while they talked a courier arrived with a dispatch signed by Butterfield, relaying an order from Hooker: "The general directs that no advance be made from Chancellorsville until the columns are concentrated. He expects to be at Chancellorsville tonight."

Somewhat crestfallen, and nearly as puzzled now as he had been before he saw what he had believed was the light, Meade went about the business of getting his troops into bivouac. Slocum and Howard were doing the same when presently, at about 4.30 and true to his word, Fighting Joe himself came riding up on his big white horse, cheered lustily by the men along the roadside, and explained the logic behind the restraining order. The easterly advance along the turnpike had already flanked the rebels out of their U.S. Ford defenses, permitting Couch to sidle upstream for a crossing there instead of at Banks Ford, where the defenders were still in occupation; he was on the march for Chancellorsville even now, and Gibbon had been alerted to join him from Falmouth with his third division. This would put four whole corps in the Confederate rear, as had been intended from the start, but the northern commander had it in mind to do even more by way of cinching the victory already within reach. Sedgwick's bridgehead having been established across the river below Fredericksburg with a minimal resistance from the rebels on the heights — who thus were clamped securely between two superior Union forces which now could reinforce each other, rapidly and at will, by way of U.S. Ford — Hooker had decided to summon Sickles from the left to add the weight of his corps to the blow about to be delivered against the more vulnerable enemy rear. His arrival tonight or tomorrow morning would bring the striking force up to a strength of 77,865 effectives within the five corps. With three regiments of cavalry added, along with several batteries detached from the artillery reserve, engineer troops, and headquarters personnel, the total would reach about 80,000 of all arms, who then could be flung in mass against Lee's rear to accomplish his destruction with a single May Day blow.

Meade was considerably reassured; he saw in fact, or believed he saw, a brighter light than ever. A rare attention to detail — pontoons in place on time, road space properly allotted to columns on the march, surprise achieved through ruse and secrecy — had made possible, at practically no cost at all, one of the finest maneuvers in military history. Now this same attentiveness, with regard to the massing of troops for the ultimate thrust, would also make possible one of the grandest victories. Sure enough, Couch arrived before nightfall and went into bivouac a mile north of the crossroads; Sickles sent word that he was on the way. Once more careful planning had paid off. A New York *Herald* correspondent who had accompanied the flankers shared the pervading optimism. "It is rumored that the enemy are falling back toward Richmond," he wrote, "but a fight tomorrow seems more than probable. We expect it, and we also expect to be victorious." Hooker expected it, too, because he knew the rumor to be untrue. Sedgwick, from his low-lying, close-up position south of Fredericksburg, and Professor Lowe, from the gondola of one of his big yellow balloons riding high over Stafford Heights, had both assured him that the Confederates still occupied the ridge beyond the town. Reynolds, in fact, had reported to headquarters this afternoon that he believed some of the troops in his front had just arrived from Richmond: which brought the reply, "General Hooker hopes they are from Richmond, as the greater will be our success."

His spirits were high, and so were those of his men, who cheered him to the echo, especially when a congratulatory order was read to them that evening in their camps around Chancellorsville: "It is with heartfelt satisfaction that the commanding general announces to the army that the operations of the last three days have determined that our enemy must either ingloriously fly, or come out from behind his defenses and give us battle on our own ground, where certain destruction awaits him."

★ ★ ★

Battle on his "own ground" — setting aside for the moment the question of whether any part of the Old Dominion could ever properly be so termed in relation to the man Lee called Mr F. J. Hooker — was exactly what Stonewall Jackson had been aching to give him for the past three months. "We must make this campaign an exceedingly active one," the Virginian declared as spring approached. "Only thus can a weaker country cope with a stronger. It must make up in activity what it lacks in strength." Fredericksburg, for all its one-sided tactical brilliance, had been a strategic disappointment to him, and he hoped to compensate for this in the great battle he knew would be fought as soon as the Federals decided the time had come for them to attempt another Rappahannock crossing. "My trust is in God," he said quietly, seated one day in his tent and musing on the future. But then, anticipating the hour when the blue host would venture within his reach, his patience broke its bounds and he rose bristling from his chair, eyes aglow. "I wish they would come!" he cried.

These past three months had been perhaps the happiest of his military life. In fact, despite his eagerness to interrupt any or all of them with bloodshed, February, March, and April, following as they did his thirty-ninth birthday in late January, had been idyllic, at least by Jacksonian standards. Aside from administrative concerns, such as the usual spate of court-martials and the preparation of battle reports, grievously neglected up to now because he had been too busy fighting to find time for writing — the total was fourteen full-scale battles in the previous eight months, with the reduction and capture of Harpers Ferry added for good measure — his principal occupation was prayer and meditation, relieved from time to time by evenings of unaccustomed social pleasure. His quarters, an office cottage on the grounds of a Moss Neck estate, were comfortable to the point of lavishness, which prompted Jeb Stuart to express mock horror at the erstwhile Presbyterian deacon's evident fall from spirituality, and Lee himself, in the course of a particularly fine meal featuring oysters, turkey, and a waiter decked out in a fresh white apron, taunted the high-ranking guests and their host with the remark that they were merely playing at being soldiers; they should come and dine with him, he said, if they wanted to see how a real soldier lived. Stonewall took the raillery and the chiding in good part, at once flustered and delighted. But the best of the idyl came at its close. The last nine days, beginning April 20, were spent with the wife he had not seen in just over a year and the five-month-old daughter he had never seen at all.

He had moved by then, back into his tent near Hamilton's Crossing, which did much to reduce the Calvinistic twinges. "It is rather a relief," he said, "to get where there will be less comfort in a room." But for the occasion of the long-anticipated visit he accepted the hospitality of the Yerby house, in which Lee had stayed for a time under doctor's orders, and was given a large room, with no less than three beds, where he could be alone with his wife and get to know the baby. Outside duty hours, the couple took walks in the woods and along the heights overlooking the Fredericksburg plain whose December scars were beginning to be grassed over. It was the happiest of times for them both. The days went by in a rush, however, for there in full view across the way were the enemy guns and the yellow observation balloons, reminders that the idyl was likely to have a sudden end. And so it was. Dawn, Wednesday, April 29; booted feet on the stairs and a knock at the bedroom door; "That looks as if Hooker were crossing," Jackson said. He drew on some clothes and went out, was gone ten minutes, and then returned to finish dressing. The visit was over, he told Anna as he buckled on his sword. He would come back if he could, but if he could not he would send an aide to see her to the train. After a last embrace, and a last long look at the baby, he was gone. Presently the staff chaplain arrived to tell her the general would not be coming back. While she was packing she began hearing the rattle of musketry from down by the river. It grew louder behind her, all the way to Guiney Station, where she boarded an almost empty train for Richmond.

Lee expressed even less surprise when an aide sent by Jackson came into his tent before sunup to give him the news. Still abed, Lee said teasingly: "Captain, what do you young men mean by waking a man out of his sleep?" Hooker had thrown his pontoons near the site of the lower December crossing, the aide replied; he was over the river in force. "Well, I thought I heard firing," Lee said, "and I was beginning to think it was time some of you young fellows were coming to tell me what it was all about. You want me to send a message to your good general, Captain? Tell him that I am sure he knows what to do. I will meet him at the front very soon."

Shortly afterwards, peering through rifts in the early morning fog, he saw for himself that the Federals had one bridge down and others under construction, all near the point now known as Franklin's Crossing, just over a mile below the town. They did not attempt an advance across the plain, but seemed content to stay within their bridgehead, at least for the present, covered by the long-range guns on Stafford Heights. Resisting the temptation to attack while the build-up was in progress, Lee decided to make his defense along the ridge, as he had done in December. Accordingly, he told Jackson to bring up the rest of his corps from below, and ordered the reserve artillery to leave its rearward camps and move forward into line. In notifying Richmond of these developments, although he knew it was unlikely that the two detached divisions would arrive in time for a share in the battle now shaping up, he requested that Longstreet be alerted for a return from Suffolk as soon as possible. Before noon, the situation was complicated by a dispatch from Stuart, informing Lee that a blue force of about 14,000 infantry and six guns had crossed at Kelly's Ford and appeared to be headed for Gordonsville. This was corrected a few hours later, however, when the cavalry commander sent word that the enemy column had turned in the direction of Ely's and Germanna Fords; so far, Jeb added, he had taken prisoners from three different Union corps, though he did not say whether he thought all three were present in full strength. In reaction, Lee sent instructions for Stuart to move eastward at once and thus avoid being cut off from headquarters. This would leave the Federal cavalry free to operate practically unmolested against his lines of supply; yet, bad as that was, it was by no means as bad as having to fight blind when he and the greatly superior Federal main body came within grappling distance of each other, here on Marye's Heights or elsewhere. Just after sundown a third courier arrived to report the bluecoats across both Rapidan fords. Though Lee still had no reliable information as to the strength of this flanking column, it was clear by now that some part of Hooker's army — a considerable part, for all he knew — was in the Confederate rear and moving closer, hour by hour. Whatever its strength, the threat it offered was too grave to be ignored. Nor did he ignore it. Two brigades of Richard Anderson's division were already at U.S. Ford; Lee instructed him to draw them in and move the others rearward to meet them in the vicinity of Chancellorsville, where the roads leading south and east from Ely's and Germanna Fords came together, "taking the strongest line you can and holding it to the best advantage." To McLaws, who commanded Longstreet's other remaining division, went orders alerting him for a possible westward march, in case it turned out that Anderson was not strong enough to stop the blue columns last reported to be moving in his direction. Anderson pulled out of the line at 9 o'clock, and after a three-hour march through driving rain informed headquarters that his division was concentrated near Chancellorsville by midnight. Knowing that his rear was protected at least to this extent, Lee turned in to rest for tomorrow.

Morning of the 30th disclosed a total of five bridges spanning the river below Fredericksburg. Though the bluecoats had enlarged their west-bank foothold, they showed no disposition to advance. In fact, they were intrenching their perimeter — as if in expectation, not of delivering, but of receiving an attack. Jackson, for one, was eager to give it to them, whereas Lee preferred to draw them farther away from their heavy guns on Stafford Heights. Both men thus reacted as they had done to the similar situation in December; but this time Lee offered to defer to his lieutenant's judgment. "If you think you can effect anything," he said, "I will give orders for the attack." While Stonewall went about conducting a more thorough examination of the bridgehead, preparatory to moving against it, Lee received another cavalry report that the Federals were advancing eastward from Germanna Ford, along the Orange Turnpike, while a substantial train of wagons and artillery was across Ely's Ford with a heavy infantry escort, following in the wake of the column that had crossed at that point the night before. A little later — it was now past noon — Anderson sent word that he had taken up a good defensive position east of Chancellorsville, along the near fringe of the Wilderness, and was preparing to resist the blue advance. So far, all he had seen of the enemy were cavalry outriders, he added, but he thought he was going to need support when the infantry came up. Lee replied at 2.30 that Anderson was to dig in where he was, providing hasty fortifications not only for his own division but also for McLaws', which was on call to join him in case it was needed. "Set all your spades to work as vigorously as possible," Lee urged, and sent him some engineers to assist in drawing his line, as well as a battalion of artillery from the reserve. Then he turned back to see how Jackson was doing.

The fact was, Jackson was not doing so well, at least by his own interpretation. A careful reconnaissance had shown the enemy bridgehead to be stronger than he had supposed; he regretfully admitted that an assault would be unwise. Lee took out his binoculars for a better look at the bluecoats massed on the plain below and on the heights beyond the river. He took his time, evaluating reports while he peered. There was by now much disagreement among his officers as to whether Hooker was planning to deliver his heaviest blow from upstream or down. Presently, however, Lee returned the glasses to their case and snapped it shut with a decisive gesture. "The main attack will come from above," he said.

Having made this estimate of the situation he proceeded to act on it with an urgency required by the fact that a farther advance by the Federals approaching his rear would put them between him and Richmond, in which case he would have no choice except to retreat. He might have to do so anyhow, under the menace of Hooker's skillful combinations, but he was determined, now as always, to yield no ground he saw any chance of holding. His decision, then — announced in orders which he retired to his tent to write and issue soon after nightfall — was to turn on the rearward Union column with a preponderance of his badly outnumbered army, leaving a skeleton force to defend his present position against a possible frontal assault by the blue mass on the plain. Early's division of Jackson's corps drew the latter assignment, reinforced by a brigade from McLaws, whose other three brigades were to proceed at once to join Anderson in the intrenchments he was digging four miles east of Chancellorsville. Jackson was to follow McLaws with his remaining three divisions "at daylight tomorrow morning ... and make arrangements to repulse the enemy." This would give Lee a total of 45,000 troops, plus Stuart when he came up, to block the path of the enemy columns moving eastward through the Wilderness, and barely 10,000, including the artillery reserve, to hold the Fredericksburg ridge, which by tomorrow would have become his rear. The risks were great, but perhaps no greater than the odds that led him to accept them. At any rate, if it came to a simultaneous fight in both directions, he would have the advantage of interior lines, even though he would have gained it by inviting annihilation.

McLaws pulled back at midnight, leaving Barksdale's Mississippians behind for a possible repetition of their mid-December exploit. Early spread his lone division all up and down the five-mile stretch of intrenchments from Marye's Heights to Hamilton's Crossing, mindful of Lee's admonition that he was to keep up a bristling pretense of strength and aggressive intentions. Jackson, told to move at daylight, was on the march by 3 a.m. Riding ahead of his troops he arrived soon after sunrise at Tabernacle Church, the left-flank anchor of Anderson's newly established line, which McLaws was busy extending northward to the vicinity of Duerson's Mill, covering Banks Ford. His instructions were to "make arrangements to repulse the enemy," and to Stonewall this meant, quite simply, to attack him. If he had no orders to proceed beyond this point, neither did he have any to remain here. Besides, there was no enemy in sight except an occasional scampering blue horseman in brief silhouette against the verdant background of the Wilderness. Before he could repulse the enemy he would have to find him, and the obvious way to find him would be to go where he was — reportedly, four miles dead ahead at Chancellorsville. So he told Anderson and McLaws to leave off digging and get their men in motion. He would go forward with them. If they ran into trouble up ahead, and it was clear by now that trouble was what they definitely were going to find in that direction, his three divisions would soon be up to lend support.

It was about 11 o'clock of a fine May Day morning by the time they got their troops into march formation and set out, preceded by clouds of skirmishers. The advance was by two main roads, the turnpike on the right and the plank road on the left; McLaws took the former, Anderson the latter, accompanied by Jackson himself. Almost as soon as they entered the green hug of the Wilderness, McLaws made contact with the enemy advancing on the turnpike. At 11.20 the first gun of the meeting engagement boomed. Then others began to roar in that direction. Jackson's instructions were for both divisions to keep pushing west until they ran into something solid. Presently he received a dispatch from Stuart, who was near at hand. "I will close in on the flank," Jeb wrote, "and will help all I can when the ball opens.... May God grant us victory." Stonewall replied, "I trust that God will grant us a great victory." But he added, by way of showing what he had in mind to reinforce his trust: "Keep closed on Chancellorsville."

★ ★ ★

Hooker too had started forward at 11 o'clock, so that the meeting engagement occurred about midway between Chancellorsville and Tabernacle Church. Sickles having come up that morning, the northern commander was set to throw a five-corps Sunday punch. This was no time for wild blows, however, and he made his preparations with the same concern for detail as before. Slocum would advance along the plank road on the right, supported by Howard; Meade would take the left, along the turnpike, supported by Couch; Sickles would remain in general reserve, on call to add the extra weight that might be needed in either direction. Nor was Fighting Joe committing the amateur's gaffe of forgetting he had another hand to box with. Orders had gone the previous evening to Sedgwick: "It is not known, of course, what effect the advance will have upon the enemy, and the general commanding directs that you observe [Lee's] movements with the utmost vigilance, and, should he expose a weak point, attack him in full force and destroy him." This was made even more specific by instructions sent to Sedgwick as the advance got under way. No matter whether the rebels weakened their Fredericksburg line or not, he was "to threaten an attack in full force at 1 o'clock and to continue in that attitude until further orders. Let the demonstration be as severe as can be," Hooker added, "but not an attack," unless of course the enemy afforded a real opening, in which case the earlier instructions would obtain and Sedgwick would go for a left-hand knockout.

Slocum and Meade stepped off smartly, much encouraged by a circular prescribing the order of march and closing: "After the movement commences, headquarters will be at Tabernacle Church." It sounded as if Hooker meant business this time. Also it made considerable tactical sense, for the turnpike and the plank road, after branching off from one another at Chancellorsville, converged near that objective. Out of the woods at last, the two lead corps would be concentrated for the final lunge, supported by Howard, Couch, and Sickles, who would follow close behind. For more than half the distance, however, these two main Wilderness arteries diverged: with the result that as the two columns moved eastward, hemmed in by the dense jungle of stunted trees and brambly underbrush, they lost contact with each other. As an additional complication, Meade had one division on the pike and two on the River Road, which curved northward to outflank the rebel intrenchments at Banks Ford; so that here, too, contact was quickly lost. Two miles from its crossroads starting point, out of touch with Slocum on the right and the rest of its own corps on the left, the division on the turnpike came under fire from enemy skirmishers as it plodded up a long slope whose crest would bring the eastern rim of the Wilderness in view. It so happened that this division, commanded by Major General George Sykes, could lay substantial claims to being the sturdiest in the Army of the Potomac, two of its three brigades being composed exclusively of U.S. regulars, while the third was made up of battle-hardened New York volunteers who had stood fast on Henry Hill and thereby saved the fleeing remnant of Pope's army from utter destruction at Bull Run. As steady now as then, they went smoothly into attack formation and drove the rebel skirmishers back to the crest of the low ridge. There, however, they came upon the Confederate main body, long gray lines of infantry supported by clusters of guns that broke into a roar at the sight of bluecoats. Calling a halt, Sykes sent back word that he was badly in need of help. Then, as the gray mass started forward, overlapping both of his open flanks, he began a rearward movement down the pike, dribbling casualties as he went. What would be known as the Battle of Chancellorsville had opened.

Couch was already coming up with Major General Winfield S. Hancock's division, which he threw into the line at once to stabilize the situation preparatory to resuming the advance. Before this last could be accomplished, however, a courier arrived with orders from Hooker: "Withdraw both divisions to Chancellorsville." Couch was amazed. Here he was, as he later said, with "open country in front and the commanding position," yet his chief was telling him to retire. Sykes and Hancock were equally puzzled. They too wanted to push ahead in accordance with the original instructions. With their approval, Couch sent an aide to inform Hooker that the situation was under control and the troops were about ready to continue their drive along the pike. Off to the right, a mounting bank of smoke and the rumble of guns told them that Slocum was likewise engaged and seemed to be holding his own, while Meade's other two divisions apparently had encountered no resistance at all on the left. But within half an hour the aide returned with a peremptory repetition of the order: Pull back to Chancellorsville without delay. Couch considered outright disobedience. Brigadier General G. K. Warren, chief engineer of the army, urged him to adopt just such a course while he himself rode back to explain its advantages to Hooker. He spurred rearward; but as soon as he left, Couch's West-Point-inculcated instinct for obedience took over. Complying with the order to retire, he withdrew the two divisions, first Sykes, then Hancock. The disengagement had been completed, except for two rear-guard regiments still in line, when a third message arrived from Hooker: "Hold on until 5 o'clock." Evidently Warren had stated his case persuasively, but Couch by now was disgusted. "Tell General Hooker he is too late," he replied testily. "The enemy are already on my right and rear. I am in full retreat."

In point of fact, his right was more seriously threatened than he knew. Slocum, followed as closely by Anderson as Couch himself was being followed by McLaws, had already fallen back down the plank road in accordance with similar instructions from headquarters. Meade too was backtracking by now, but unpursued, having encountered nothing substantial in the way of resistance on the left. As a result he was even more astounded than Couch had been at receiving the order to withdraw. Within sight of Duerson's Mill, he had been within easy reach of Banks Ford, control of which would shorten greatly the lines of supply and communication between the army's divided wings. To be told to fall back under such circumstances, with clear going to his front and his lines extending along the crest of the eastward rise, was more exasperating than anything he had encountered up to now. Once again Hooker had built up his hopes only to dash them with a peremptory order which not only called for a halt, as before, but also insisted on a retirement. Meade was furious. "If he thinks he can't hold the top of a hill, how does he expect to hold the bottom of it?" the Pennsylvanian stormed as he complied with the instructions to fall back.

That was about 2 o'clock. All three corps commanders were hard put to understand what had come over Fighting Joe in the scant three hours since they had set out from the crossroads they now were under orders to return to. At the outset, with the announcement that his headquarters would be leapfrogged four miles forward while the movement was in progress, he had seemed confident of delivering a knockout blow. Then suddenly, at the first sputter of musketry on the turnpike, he had abandoned all his aggressive intentions and ordered everything back for a defense of Chancellorsville, deep in the Wilderness. Why? They did not know, but already they were beginning to formulate theories which they and others down the years would enlarge on. For one thing, that excellent intelligence section back at Falmouth was hard at work, forwarding information disturbing enough to jangle the nerves of the steadiest man alive. According to one rebel deserter, brought in for interrogation the night before, Longstreet's whole corps had left Suffolk, presumably by rail, and had "gone to Culpeper," which would place it directly in rear of the Union flanking column and scarcely a day's march away. The prisoner added "that Lee said it was the only time he should fight equal numbers," which if true was alarming in the extreme, considering all the old fox had been able to accomplish with inferior numbers in the past. Another deserter — "from New York state originally; an intelligent man," Butterfield commented — avowed that Hood's division was already with Lee; he knew this, he said, because he had "asked the troops as they passed along." One of the two informers must be lying, at least so far as Longstreet's location was concerned. Indeed, both might be lying; it was not unusual for the Confederates to send out bogus "deserters" to confuse an opponent with misleading information. But the fact was, Lee was not reacting to his present predicament at all as he ought to be doing if he was heavily outnumbered. He was reacting, in fact, as if the numerical advantage was with him even more than either deserter claimed. And just what that reaction was Hooker had learned shortly after Meade and Slocum left him. Until that time, Professor Lowe's balloons had been fogbound high over Stafford Heights, but all of a sudden the weather faired, permitting the aeronaut to tap out a steady flow of information regarding the panorama now spread out before his eyes. He could see various rebel columns in motion, he wired Hooker at 11 o'clock, but the largest of these was "moving on the road toward Chancellorsville." This tallied with the intelligence summation forwarded shortly thereafter by Butterfield. Completing his tabulation of the Confederate order of battle, the chief of staff declared: "Anderson, McLaws, A. P. Hill, and Hood would, therefore, be in your front."

It also explained — all too clearly — the sudden clatter of musketry and the boom of guns, first down the turnpike, then down the plank road, not long after the two columns set out eastward through the forest. In part, as well, it accounted for Hooker's reaction, which in effect was a surrendering of the initiative to Jackson, who plunged deeper into the Wilderness in pursuit. But there was a good deal more to it than this: a good deal more that was no less valid for being less specific. Perhaps Hooker at last had recalled Lincoln's admonition, "Beware of rashness." Perhaps at this critical juncture he missed the artificial stimulus of whiskey, which formerly had been part of his daily ration but which he had abjured on taking command. Perhaps he mistrusted his already considerable accomplishment in putting more than 70,000 soldiers in Lee's immediate rear, with practically no losses because he had met practically no resistance. It had been altogether too easy; Lee must have wanted him where he was, or at any rate where he had been headed before he called a halt and ordered a pull-back. Or perhaps it was even simpler than that. Perhaps he was badly frightened (not physically frightened: Hooker was never that: but morally frightened) after the manner of the bullfighter Gallo, who, according to Hemingway, "was the inventor of refusing to kill the bull if the bull looked at him in a certain way." This Gallo had a long career, featuring many farewell performances, and at the first of these, having fought the animal bravely and well, when the time came for killing he faced the stands and made three eloquent speeches of dedication to three distinguished aficionados; after which he turned, sword in hand, and approached the bull, which was standing there, head down, looking at him. Gallo returned to the barrera. "You take him, Paco," he told a fellow matador; "I don't like the way he looks at me." So it was with Hooker, perhaps, when he heard that Lee had turned in his direction and was, so to speak, looking at him. Lowe had signaled at noon that the rebels were "considerably diminished" on the heights behind Fredericksburg. Consequently, at 2 o'clock, Fighting Joe wired Butterfield: "From character of information have suspended attack. The enemy may attack me — I will try it. Tell Sedgwick to keep a sharp lookout, and attack if can succeed." In effect, now that Lee had turned his attention westward, Hooker was telling Sedgwick: "You take him, Paco. I don't like the way he looks at me."

None of this perturbation showed in his manner, however, when the returning generals confronted him at the Chancellor house, which he had taken over as his headquarters. "It's all right, Couch; I've got Lee just where I want him," he said expansively. "He must fight me on my own ground." Couch had a cold eye for this blusterous performance. "The retrograde movement had prepared me for something of the kind," he wrote years later, "but to hear from his own lips that the advantages gained by the successive marches of his lieutenants were to culminate in fighting a defensive battle in that nest of thickets was too much.... I retired from his presence with the belief that my commanding general was a whipped man."

Whether or not this was the case remained to be seen. For the present, the order was for the army to intrench itself along lines prescribed with the usual attention to detail. On the map they resembled a double-handled dipper. Couch and Slocum, with two divisions each in the vicinity of Chancellorsville — Gibbon had stayed at Falmouth after all — formed the cup, bulging south of the crossroads to include some comparatively high ground known as Fairview. The cup was just over a mile wide at the rim, tapering slightly toward the base, and just under a mile deep. Sickles' three divisions were in reserve, poised for a leap into the cup or a quick march out either of the handles, which were between two and three miles long and extended generally northeast and due west. Meade's three divisions connected the eastern lip of the cup with the Rappahannock, his left resting on a bend of the river south of U. S. Ford, which thus was covered. Howard's three divisions, the dipper's western handle, extended out the turnpike past Wilderness Church, where the plank road came in from the southwest, and thus presumably could block the approach of an enemy moving up from that direction. The troops worked into the night with picks and shovels, intrenching the six-mile line from flank to flank. At 2 a.m. Couch, Slocum, and Howard reported themselves satisfied that their respective sectors could be held against assault. Advantageously disposed along Mineral Spring Run, a small boggy creek that covered his front and rendered his position doubly secure, Meade had reported the same thing earlier. Hooker, with his accustomed thoroughness, seemed to have allowed for all eventualities before he retired to a bedroom in the crossroads mansion to sleep and store up strength for whatever tomorrow was going to bring.

He hoped it would bring an all-out Confederate attack; or so at least he had been saying, all afternoon and evening. "The rebel army is now the legitimate property of the Army of the Potomac," he announced to the officers gathered about him in the May Day sunshine on the Chancellor veranda. The fact that nearly all of his cavalry had ridden well beyond his reach, while nearly all of Lee's was in what Hooker called "my immediate presence," did not seem to him a cause for alarm, but rather an advantage, "which I trust will enable Stoneman to do a land-office business in the interior. I think the enemy in his desperation will be compelled to attack me on my own ground.... I am all right." Thus he wired the Washington authorities, thinking that such information, besides relieving the President's concern, might "have an important bearing on movements elsewhere." If the other Union armies would only keep step with this one, the war would soon be over and done with — won. As the daylight hours wore on and his intrenchments were extended, still with no full-scale rebel assault, his show of confidence reached its zenith. He feared nothing and he wanted it known; not even the artillery of heaven. "The enemy is in my power," he exulted, "and God Almighty cannot deprive me of them." In the late afternoon he issued another circular for the encouragement of subordinates: "The major general commanding trusts that a suspension in the attack today will embolden the enemy to attack him."

✘ 5 ✘

Lee and Jackson met at sundown, on the plank road just over a mile southeast of Chancellorsville, for the purpose of deciding how best to go about giving Hooker what he claimed he wanted. They began their conference on the road itself, at the junction where a trail came in from Catharine Furnace, a rural ironworks on Lewis Creek a mile and a half to the west, but they withdrew presently into a nearby clump of pines when a Federal sharpshooter began ranging in on them from a perch in a tree just up the road, beyond the line along which Anderson's and Slocum's pickets were keeping up a rackety contention. Seated side by side on a log, the two men continued their discussion in the May Day twilight, the gray-bearded elder impeccably dressed as always, his neat gray tunic devoid of trappings except for the three unwreathed stars on each side of the turned-down collar, and the younger wearing the rather gaudy uniform which had provoked such hoots and catcalls on the day of Fredericksburg. Reconnoitering on the right this afternoon, Lee had found the terrain unpromising, hemmed in as it was by a bend of the Rappahannock, and the few heavily wooded approaches well guarded by troops already dug in along the far side of a marsh. To attempt to come to grips with them in that quarter, he said, would be to invite destruction. How about the center and the left? Jackson had not been far to the west, but he had made a long-range examination of the enemy lines in front of Chancellorsville itself and had found the bluecoats disposed three-deep, hard at work with picks and shovels, and supported by many batteries of artillery. However, he was inclined to believe that the question of how to get at Hooker, here in the Wilderness tomorrow, was largely academic. The ease with which he had repulsed the advancing Union columns today made him suspect that their recoil was prelude to a withdrawal. "By tomorrow morning there will not be any of them on this side of the river," he declared.

Lee shook his head. So far he had deferred to Stonewall's judgment, but not in this. Though he too was puzzled by his opponent's sudden, turtle-like reaction to moderate pressure, he was convinced that Hooker was planning to make his main effort right here. Anyhow, even if that were not the case, they must prepare to deal with him tomorrow on even the outside chance that he would still be in his present intrenched position. Without quite giving over his belief that dawn would show the forest empty to their front, Jackson could not disagree with the logic of Lee's contention; besides which, he found the prospect so attractive as to overrule his inclination to think that it would not be offered. For him, as for his commander, to "deal with" Hooker meant to attack him. But how? And where? One possibility was that the Federal center might not appear as stout to a close-up view as it had seemed from a distance. The two generals accordingly dispatched an engineer officer from each of their staffs to go take a look at the intrenchments there and report on what they saw.

While this night reconnaissance was in progress, and while Lee and Jackson continued to speculate on ways of bringing the blue army's current excursion to a violent close, Jeb Stuart came jingling up from Catharine Furnace in fulfillment of his promise to "help all I can when the ball opens." Glad as he was to see his friend Stonewall decked out in the handsome uniform he had given him, he deferred comment in favor of some interesting information which had just come to hand. According to Fitzhugh Lee, who had ridden west to scout it, Hooker's right flank was "in the air" on the Orange Turnpike, wide open to attack from that direction. Though this was news of a kind to set both him and his chief lieutenant on tremble, the southern commander suppressed his excitement to ask whether roads were available for a covered approach to that critical point by troops in large numbers. Stuart replied that he did not know but he would do what he could to find out, and with that he swung back onto his horse and rode off westward, his red-lined cape and cinnamon whiskers glistening in the light of the new-risen moon.

From this time on, Lee and Jackson gave little attention to anything but the possibility of launching the suggested flank attack. When the two engineers returned to announce that the Union center was too strongly intrenched to be assaulted, Lee received the anticlimactic report with a nod and kept peering at a map spread on his knees; he peered so intently, indeed, that he seemed to be trying to make it give him information which it did not contain. "How can we get at those people?" he asked, half to himself and half to Jackson, who replied in an equally distracted manner, as he too searched the map for roads that were not on it: "You know best. Show me what to do, and we will do it." Finally, Lee traced a fingertip westward along the map from their present location, as if to sketch in an ideal route past the front of the enemy position, then northward to intersect the turnpike, where the latter veered abruptly east to address the Union flank end-on. In naval parlance, he was crossing Hooker's T. That would be the movement, he said; Jackson would lead it and Stuart would cover his march. Smiling, Jackson stood erect and saluted. "My troops will move at 4 o'clock," he said. In his eagerness, he not only seemed unable to remain seated, he also seemed to have forgotten his prediction that Hooker would clear out before sunup. Lee checked him with a reminder. If there was any doubt about this next morning, he said, Jackson could open from an exposed position with a couple of guns, then judge by the response as to whether the blue army was still behind its Wilderness fortifications.

There was much to be done between now and sunrise: especially by Jackson, to whom Lee had left the choice of a route, the composition of the force to be employed, and the decision as to when and in what manner the flank attack would be delivered. But what both men needed for the present, at the close of a strenuous day and on the eve of what promised to be an even more strenuous morrow, was a few hours' sleep: again especially Jackson, who had demonstrated on several occasions — the Seven Days, for one — that without at least a minimum of profound rest he would be reduced to a state of somnambulism. They lay down where they were, in separate quarters of the grove, spreading their saddle blankets on the pine needles for a bed and using their saddles for a pillow. Both were soon asleep, but Lee was wakened presently by an officer he had sent to look into conditions on the turnpike to the north. "Ah, Captain, you have returned, have you?" he said, and he sat up slowly. "Come here and tell me what you have learned on the right." It was the same young man from Jackson's staff who had wakened him two mornings ago to tell him Hooker was crossing; J. P. Smith was his name, a divinity student before the war. He hesitated, in awe of the general whose massive features and gray beard looked so imposing in the moonlight, but as he leaned forward the seated man put an arm about his shoulder and drew him down by his side while he finished his report. Lee thanked him and then, still retaining his grip, began to chide him by saying that he regretted that Smith and the other "young men about General Jackson" had not done a better job today of locating and silencing an enemy battery that had held up the advance. Young men nowadays, he declared in the accents of Nestor, were a far remove from the young men of his youth. The captain, seeing, as he later said, that the general "was jesting and disposed to rally me," broke away from the hold Lee tried to retain on his shoulder. As he moved off through the moonlit pines he could hear the Virginian laughing heartily there in the Wilderness where many men now sleeping would be laid in their graves tomorrow and the next day and the next, blue and gray alike, as a result of instructions he had given just before he himself lay down, in apparently excellent spirits, to rest for what he knew was coming with the dawn.

When Lee woke he saw the gaunt figure of Jackson bending over a small fire a courier had built. Rising, he joined him and the two sat on a couple of hardtack boxes the Federals had left behind the day before. It was already past 4 o'clock, the hour set for the column to move out, but Jackson explained that he was awaiting the return of his staff chaplain, who once had had a church hereabouts and was familiar with the region. For this reason he had sent him, together with a skilled cartographer, to explore the roads leading west from Catharine Furnace and then north to the plank road, up which he expected to make his strike. The two sat talking, warming their hands at the meager fire, until the glimmer of dawn showed the staff officers returning from their scout. Major Jedediah Hotchkiss, the cartographer, approached the generals and spread his map on another hardtack box which he placed between them. It was obvious from his manner, before he said a word, that he had found the route he had been seeking, and as he spoke he traced it on the map: first due west to the furnace, then due south, away from the enemy, along a trail that gradually turned back west to enter the Brock Road, which ran northward to the plank road and the turnpike. However, he explained that the column must not turn north at this point, since that would bring it within sight of a Federal signal station at Fairview, but south again for a short distance to another road leading north and paralleling the Brock Road, which it rejoined a couple of miles above in some heavy woods just short of its junction with the plank road. That way, practically the entire route — some ten miles in length from their present position and firm enough throughout to support wagons and artillery — would be screened from the eyes of enemy lookouts. Completing his exposition, Hotchkiss looked from one to another of the generals, both of whom kept their eyes fixed on the map for what seemed to him an inordinately long time. Finally Lee spoke, raising his head to look at his lieutenant: "General Jackson, what do you propose to do?" Jackson put out his hand and retraced, with a semicircular motion of his wrist, the route just drawn. "Go around here," he said. Lee kept looking at him. "What do you propose to make this movement with?" he asked, and Jackson promptly replied: "With my whole corps."

Now there was a pause while Lee absorbed the shock the words had given him. "What will you leave me?" he asked. The question was rhetorical; he already knew the answer. But Jackson answered it anyhow, as readily as before. "The divisions of Anderson and McLaws." This meant that he would have better than 30,000 soldiers off to the rear and on the flank, necessarily out of contact with the enemy and the rest of his own army for most of the day, while Lee would be left with scarcely half as many troops planted squarely across the path of a greatly superior blue host which might resume its forward movement at any minute. However, having weighed the odds — which had to include the by no means improbable chance that Hooker might learn what was afoot and react accordingly — the southern commander made and announced his decision. "Well, go on," he said.

While they talked the sun had reddened the east, and now it broke clear, fiery above the treetops back toward Fredericksburg, where Early was facing odds almost as long as Lee's would be when the flanking column left. Jackson informed his chief that the march would be led by D. H. Hill's old division, now under Brigadier General Robert Rodes; next would come his own old division, commanded by its senior brigadier, Raleigh Colston; A. P. Hill's division would bring up the rear. He would take all his artillery with him, dispersed along the column, and depend on Stuart to cover his advance. Lee took notes on this, then retired to write the necessary orders while his lieutenant went about making preparations to move out. As Jackson rode past one brigade camp the lounging veterans rose to cheer him, but seeing what one of them later called "battle in his haste and stern looks," they merely gazed at him and wondered what exertion he was about to require of them. The preliminary dispositions were a time-consuming business, involving the extraction of some units already committed, but at last they were completed. Shortly before 8 o'clock, the lead regiment — Georgians who had fought under him in every battle since McDowell, the prologue to the Valley Campaign, which had opened exactly a year ago today with his descent through Brown's Gap to put his troops aboard the cars for Staunton — turned off the plank road and set out westward for Catharine Furnace and Hooker's right. Though he was four hours behind the starting time he had set the night before, Stonewall did not appear to be disturbed by the delay. He was alert but not impatient, one observer remarked, and spoke tersely "as though all were distinctly formed in his mind and beyond all question." Under the lowered bill of his cap, the battle light was already shining fiercely in his pale blue eyes.

Lee came up and joined him at the turn-off where the sniper had tried to draw a bead on them at sunset. Both mounted — Lee on Traveller, a tall dapple gray, and Jackson on stocky, ox-eyed Little Sorrel — they spoke briefly against a background of skirmish fire which had begun to sputter along the two-mile front now occupied exclusively by Anderson and McLaws, with just over 15,000 troops between them. Nothing in Lee's manner showed the strain involved in gambling that his opponent, whether or not he became aware in the meantime of what was happening in his front and on his flank, would not exploit his five-to-one numerical advantage by launching an all-out attack — frontal or otherwise; either would be about equally destructive — before the widely divided Confederate wings were reunited. Moreover, Lee was proceeding not only on the assumption that Jackson could gain and strike the Union flank before the bluecoats recovered from their current puzzling lethargy, here in the Wilderness or back in front of Marye's Heights; he was also proceeding on the belief, or at any rate the hope, that Hooker would be completely unstrung by the explosion on his right. Nothing less would serve. For if Hooker could absorb and then recover from the shock, he might still take the offensive against the outnumbered and divided graybacks to the west and south, or signal eastward for an assault upon the thinly held Fredericksburg ridge in Lee's immediate rear. This was, in short, the longest gamble of a career which had been crowded with risks throughout the eleven months since Lee first took command at Seven Pines. Now, their brief conversation ended, the two men parted, the elder to stay, the other to go. As they did so, the dark-bearded younger general raised his arm and pointed west, in the direction he was headed. Lee nodded, and Stonewall rode off into the forest, out of sight.

Fighting Joe had been up for hours, conducting a flank-to-flank inspection of his lines. "How strong! How strong!" he marveled as he examined the hastily improvised but elaborate fortifications: particularly those out on the right, where so many of the regiments were composed of foreign-born troops who performed such labor with Germanic thoroughness and a meticulous attention to detail rivaling Hooker's own. Wherever he went this morning, tall in the saddle and rosy-looking, flushed with confidence and trailing a kite-tail of staff officers behind his big white high-stepping horse, the soldiers cheered him lustily, delighted to see their commander sharing with them the rigors of the field. His mood was as expansive as before; more so, in fact; and with cause. For he had received, the night before, a report from a trusted operative just in from Richmond, who not only had documentary evidence that Lee was receiving barely 59,000 daily rations, but also reported that the southern commander could hope for no reinforcements except from Longstreet, both of whose divisions — despite the contrary fabrications passed on by yesterday's rebel deserters — were still in front of Suffolk. This last was confirmed by Peck himself, who wired that he had taken prisoners from Hood and Pickett that same day. In reaction, Hooker's last move before retiring had been to direct that Reynolds' corps be detached from Sedgwick and sent to join him here at Chancellorsville. When it arrived — as it should do before long, the summons having been issued at 1.55 this morning — he would have better than 90,000 men on hand to repulse the attack Lee seemed to be preparing to deliver against the bulging center of the Union line. If the old fox really believed what he was rumored to have said the day before, that this "was the only time he should fight equal numbers," he was in for a large surprise. What Fighting Joe was planning was Fredericksburg in reverse, with Lee in the role of Burnside, and himself in the role of Lee: except that this time, when the attackers were exhausted and bled white as a result of their attempts to storm his fortifications, he would be in a position to swing over to the offensive that had been impossible for the Confederates, back in December, because of their numerical inferiority and the guns on Stafford Heights. Hereabouts there were no heights for Lee to mass his guns on, only the blinding and restricting thickets, and Hooker had men aplenty for the delivery of an all-out counterattack and the administration of the

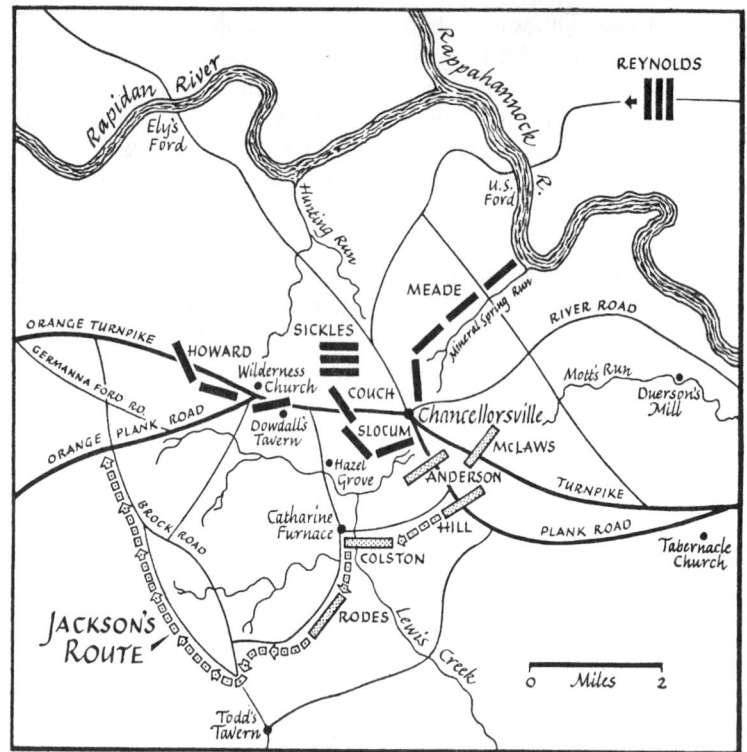

windup *coup de grâce* which would end the final spasmodic twitch of the dying rebel army.

He was in excellent spirits when he got back to headquarters at 9 o'clock to find a courier waiting for him from Brigadier General David Birney, commander of a division Sickles had sent out to some unoccupied high ground southwest of Fairview — Hazel Grove, it was called on the map — for a look at what the graybacks might be up to. According to the information brought back by the courier, they were up to a great deal. Hazel Grove afforded a clear but limited view of Catharine Furnace, less than one mile south, and the advancing bluecoats had spotted a rebel column moving due south of there along a stretch of road that disappeared into the woods. Apparently endless, the column included infantry, artillery, wagons, and ambulances; Birney thought it must signify an important development in the enemy's plans. Hooker agreed. In fact, after referring to his map, which showed that the road in question veered west beyond the screen of trees, he believed he knew just what that development was. The Confederates were in retreat, probably on Gordonsville, where Stoneman must have struck by now, severing one of their two main supply lines. However, on the off-chance that Lee was attempting at this late date to come up with something out of his bag of tricks, Hooker decided it would be wise to warn Howard of what was going on, and he sent him a message advising him to be vigilant in protecting the western flank: "We have good reason to suppose that the enemy is moving to our right. Please advance your pickets for purposes of observation as far as may be safe to obtain timely information of their approach." He might have followed to see for himself that his instructions were carried out, but presently a dispatch arrived from Howard, sent before his own had been received, stating that he too had sighted the rebel column "moving westward on a road parallel with this," and adding, of his own accord: "I am taking measures to resist an attack from the west." It was clear that Howard required no supervision to assure that he did his duty; he had performed it before he was even told what it was, thereby leaving Hooker free to concentrate on the question of pursuit.

In this connection he thought again of Sedgwick, who had been kept by a faulty telegraph connection from getting yesterday's instructions until the hour was too late for an attack. First Sickles and now Reynolds had been detached from the downstream force, but Sedgwick's was the largest corps in the army. With Gibbon's division still available at Falmouth, he had close to 30,000 effectives, plus the support of the long-range guns on Stafford Heights, and though Professor Lowe had reported earlier that a hard wind was bumping him around so much he could not use his telescope, the headquarters intelligence section informed Hooker that only Early's division remained on the Fredericksburg ridge. Accordingly, he directed Butterfield to pass the word along to Sedgwick and authorize him to attack if there was "a reasonable expectation of success." Meanwhile Hooker kept his staff busy preparing orders designed to put the whole army on Lee's trail if he still appeared to be in retreat next morning. A circular issued at 2.30 instructed corps commanders to load up with forage, provisions, and ammunition so as "to be ready to start at an early hour tomorrow." By the time this was distributed, reports had begun to come in from Sickles, who had been given permission at noon to advance with two divisions to investigate the movement Birney had spotted from Hazel Grove. He sent back word that he had pierced the rebel column near Catharine Furnace, capturing men and wagons, but that practically all of it had moved westward beyond his reach by now. Hooker took fire at this, his confidence soaring: Lee was unquestionably in full retreat, intending to follow the heavily escorted train with the Confederate main body. At 4.30 the jubilant Federal commander wired Butterfield to order Sedgwick to throw his entire force across the river, "capture Fredericksburg and everything in it, and vigorously pursue the enemy." Previous instructions had been discretionary, and so were these; but Hooker made it clear that a fine opportunity lay before him. "We know that the enemy is fleeing, trying to save his trains," he added. "Two of Sickles' divisions are among them."

As might have been expected with the rebel column filing through the woods to the army's front, there was a good deal of excitement along the outpost lines. Couriers and even unit commanders began to turn up at the Chancellor house with frantic, sometimes near-hysterical warnings of an impending flank attack. Staff officers had all they could do to keep some of them — especially one persistent artilleryman with the lowly rank of captain, who claimed to have ridden out and seen the graybacks massing — from bothering Hooker himself with their perturbations. When these men finally could be made to understand that the high command was already aware of the alleged danger and had taken steps to meet it in case it developed, they returned to their units, most of them feeling rather sheepish at having presumed to believe they knew more than their superiors. Others, however, remained unconvinced: particularly those through whose ranks the rebel prisoners had been taken rearward after their capture near Catharine Furnace. They were Georgians, hale-looking men in neat butternut clothes, and for the most part they seemed cheerful enough, considering their plight. They had come over, they replied to taunts, to help "eat up them eight-day rations." But some were surly and in no mood to be chided. Told by a bluecoat, "We'll have every mother's son of you before we go away," one snapped back: "You'll catch hell before night." Another was more specific as to how calamity was to be visited upon them, and by whom. "You think you've done a big thing just now," he said, "but wait till Jackson gets around on your flank." This seemed to its hearers well worth passing on to headquarters, but when they went there to report it they were told to return to their outfits; Lee was in retreat, no matter what the butternut captives said, and Hooker was making plans even now for an orderly pursuit.

Far out on the right flank, as the shadows lengthened toward 5 o'clock and beyond, Howard's men were taking it easy. They had seen no action so far in the campaign, but that was much as usual; they had seen little real action anywhere in the war, save for a great deal of marching and countermarching, and were in fact a sort of stepchild corps, collectively referred to by the rest of the army as "a bunch of Dutchmen." Indeed, nothing demonstrated more conclusively Hooker's lack of concern for his western flank than the fact that he had posted these men here. Mostly New Yorkers and Pennsylvanians, large numbers of them were immigrants, lately arrived and scarcely able to speak English; "Hessians," their enemies called them, with a contempt dating back to the days of the Revolution. Schurz, Steinwehr, and Schimmelfennig were three of their generals, while their colonels had names such as Von

Gilsa, Krzyzanowski, Einsiedel, Dachrodt, and Schluemback. Howard himself was by no means popular with them, despite his sacrifice of an arm to the cause and a record of steady progress up the ladder of command. After his maiming, a year ago at Fair Oaks, he had returned to lead a brigade at Antietam and a division at Fredericksburg, both with such distinction that now — to the considerable displeasure of men whose proudest boast had been "I fights mit Sigel" and who rather illogically put the blame for their hero's departure on his successor — he had a corps. He had had it, in fact, exactly a month today; but in his anxiety to make good he not only had borne down hard on discipline, he also had tried to influence the out-of-hours activities of his troops by distributing religious tracts among them. The latter action was resented even more than the former, for many of the men were freethinkers, lately emerged from countries where the church had played a considerable part in attempting their oppression, and they drew the line somewhere short of being preached at, prayed over, or uplifted. The result of all this, and more, was that army life was not a happy one for them or their commander, whose ill-concealed disappointment at their reaction to his attempt to play the role of Christian Soldier only served to increase their mistrust and dislike of him, empty sleeve and all.

Today was one of the better days, however, with a minimum of work, no drill whatsoever, and a maximum of rest. Extended for more than a mile along the turnpike west of Dowdall's Tavern, an oversized cabin just east of the junction where the plank road came in from the southwest, they lounged behind the elaborate southward-facing breastworks Hooker himself had admired. Like his chief, Howard was convinced that he was onto the rebel strategy, which seemed to him to be designed to cover a retreat with a pretense of strength and boldness. He too rejected various cries of wolf, including those from an outpost major who sent back a stream of frantic messages from beyond the flank, all patterned after the first at 2.45: "A large body of the enemy is massing in my front. For God's sake make disposition to receive him!" At the outer end of the intrenched line, two guns were posted hub-to-hub on the pike itself, facing west, and two regiments of infantry — not over 900 men in all — were disposed at right angles to the road, strung out northward from the point where the guns were posted. These two regiments and guns were all the flank protection Howard had provided after notifying Hooker that he was "taking measures to resist an attack from the west," but he considered them ample, since nothing could approach him from that direction except along the turnpike, covered by the two guns, or through a tangle of second-growth timber and briery underbrush which he had pronounced impenetrable. Moreover, there was a half-mile stretch of unoccupied ground between his left and Slocum's right, marking the former position of his one reserve brigade, which had been detached in the midafternoon and still had not returned from its mission of guarding Sickles' flank in the course of his advance from Hazel Grove. This gap was critical. Though it went unnoticed, or at any rate unfilled, it meant that if anything struck Howard a hard enough blow from the west, he would be in much the same predicament as a man attempting to sit on a chair he did not know had been removed.

That, or something like that, was what happened. Not long after 5 o'clock, with some regiments already eating supper and others lounging about while waiting for it, their rifles neatly stacked, the troops at the far end of the line were alarmed and then amused to see large numbers of deer break out of the thickets to the west and come bounding toward them, accompanied by droves of rabbits darting this way and that in the underbrush, as if pursued by invisible beaters. The men cheered and hallooed, waving their caps at the startled forest creatures, until presently something else they heard and saw froze the laughter in their throats. Long lines of men in gray and butternut, their clothes ripped to tatters by the briers and branches, were running toward them through the "impenetrable" thickets. They were screaming as they came on, jaws agape, and their bayonets caught angry glints from the low-angled sun pouring its beams through the reddened treetops and over their shoulders.

★ ★ ★

For all its explosive force, its practically complete surprise, and its rapid gathering of momentum, Stonewall's flank attack was launched with only about two hours of daylight left for the accomplishment of the destruction he intended. One of the two main reasons for this tardiness was that the start itself had been late, and the other was that the finish was delayed by an extension of the march. Between these two untoward extremes, however, all went smoothly, despite attempted enemy interruptions. The roads, described by one of the marchers as "just wet enough to be easy to the feet and free from dust," were narrow but firm, so that the column was elongated but its progress was not impeded. Like his men, who were enthused by a sense of adventure before they had even had time to guess what the adventure was going to be, Jackson was in excellent spirits, and though he did not push them to the limit of their endurance as he had done so often in the past, being concerned for once to conserve their energy for the work that lay ahead, he took care to deal with emergencies in a manner that would not hold up the main body. For instance, when the head of the column came under fire from a section of guns just north of Catharine Furnace, he detached the lead regiment of Georgians, with instructions for them to block a possible infantry probe at that point, and had the remaining units double-time across the clearing, being willing to suffer whatever incidental losses this involved rather than to burn more daylight by taking a roundabout route. Similarly A. P. Hill, whose division did not clear the starting point until well after 11 o'clock, dropped off his two rear brigades to assist the hard-pressed Georgians — forty of them had been captured and most of the rest were about to be captured — in fending off an infantry attack launched by the Federals just as he was approaching the furnace about noon, and forged ahead with his other four brigades. Far in the lead and quite unmindful of his rear, which he left to look out for itself after making the original provision, Jackson kept the main body on the go. "Press forward. Press forward," he urged his subordinate commanders. Including 1500 attached cavalry and 2000 artillerymen in support of his 70 regiments of infantry, Stonewall had better than 31,000 effectives in the column, and his only regret was that he did not have more. "I hear it said that General Hooker has more men than he can handle," he remarked in the course of the march. "I should like to have half as many more as I have today, and I should hurl him into the river!"

His eyes glowed at the thought, and presently they had occasion to blaze even more fiercely, not only at a thought, but also at what was actually spread before them. About 2 o'clock, as he approached the Orange Plank Road — the intended objective, up which he expected to turn the column northeastward for an attack that would strike the Orange Turnpike just west of Dowdall's Tavern, where Hooker's flank presumably was anchored — he was met by Fitz Lee, who approached from the opposite direction, drew rein alongside Little Sorrel, and announced with a barely suppressed excitement that explained his lack of ceremony: "General, if you will ride with me, halting your column here out of sight, I will show you the enemy's right." The two officers, accompanied by a single courier so as not to increase the risk of detection, rode past the plank road intersection, then turned off eastward through the trees to a little hill which they climbed on horseback. From the summit, parting the curtain of leaves, Stonewall saw what had provoked the excitement Lee would still be feeling, years later, when he came to write about it: "What a sight presented itself before me! Below, and but a few hundred yards distant, ran the Federal line of battle... with abatis in front and long lines of stacked arms in the rear. Two cannon were visible in the part of the line seen. The soldiers were in groups in the rear, laughing, smoking, probably engaged, here and there, in games of cards and other amusements indulged in while feeling safe and comfortable, awaiting orders. In rear of them were other parties driving up and butchering beeves." As he observed the peaceful scene, Jackson's mind was on a different kind of butchery. According to Lee, "his eyes burned with a brilliant glow, lighting his sad face. His expression was one of intense interest; his face was colored slightly with the paint of the approaching battle, and radiant in the success of his flank movement."

The salient fact was that Hooker's flank was as completely "in the air" as had been reported the night before, but that an attack up the plank road, such as had been intended, would strike it at an angle, about midway, rather than end-on; which would not do. Correction of this, however, called for a two-mile extension of the march in order to get beyond the farthest western reach of the Union intrenchments and approach them on the perpendicular. That meant a further delay of at least an hour, to which of course would be added the time required to form the three divisions for assault. With the sun already well past the overhead — by now, in fact, the hands of his watch were crowding 2.30 — there might not be enough daylight left for the execution of his plans. But Jackson did not hesitate beyond the few minutes it took him to make a careful examination of what was spread before his eyes. Seeing his lips moving as he looked at the enemy soldiers down below, Lee assumed that he was praying. If this was so, there was no evidence of it in his voice as he turned to the courier and snapped out an order for him to take back to the head of the column, halted on the Brock Road to await instructions: "Tell General Rodes to move across the plank road, halt when he gets to the old turnpike, and I will join him there." The courier took off. Jackson turned for a final look at the lounging bluecoats, disposed as they were for slaughter, then "rode rapidly [back] down the hill, his arms flapping to the motion of his horse, over whose head it seemed, good rider as he was, he would certainly go." Lee saw him thus; then he too turned and followed, somewhat chagrined that he had not received the thanks he had expected in return for making a discovery which not only would save many Confederate lives but also had made possible what gave promise of being the most brilliant tactical stroke of Stonewall's career.

Jackson had already forgotten him, along with practically everything else preceding the moment when his mind became fixed on what he was going to do. Retracing his horse's steps back down the Brock Road he passed Rodes, who had his men slogging northward for the turnpike, and returned to the plank road intersection, where he met and detached Colston's lead brigade — his own old First Manassas outfit, the Stonewall Brigade — to advance a short distance up the plank road and take position at a junction where the road from Germanna Ford came in from the northwest. With his rear and right flank thus screened and protected, he took a moment to scrawl a note briefly explaining the situation to Lee, who he knew must be fretting at the delay. "I hope as soon as practicable to attack," he wrote, and added: "I trust that an ever kind Providence will bless us with great success." The note was headed, "Near 3 p.m."; time was going fast. He hurried northward to the turnpike, overtook Rodes, and gave him the instructions he had promised. Rodes accordingly moved eastward on the pike for about a mile — unopposed and apparently unobserved, although this brought him within 1000 yards of the western knuckle of Howard's intrenchments — then formed his division along a low, north-south ridge. Four brigades were in line, two to the right and two to the left, extending about a mile in each direction from the turnpike, which would be the guide for the assault. The fifth brigade took position behind the extreme right, and Colston's remaining three brigades prolonged this second line northward, 200 yards in rear of the first. Jackson's orders were that the charge would be headlong. Under no circumstances was there to be even a pause in the advance. If a first-line brigade ran into trouble, it was to call for help from the brigade in its immediate rear, without taking time to notify either division commander. The main thing, he emphasized as he spoke to his subordinates in turn, was to keep rolling, to keep up the pressure and the scare.

Maneuvering the stretched-out column off the road and into a compact mass, like a fist clenched for striking, was a time-consuming business, however, especially when it had to be done in woods so dense that visibility scarcely extended beyond the limits of a single regiment. Also there was the problem of fatigue. Though by ordinary standards the march had been neither long nor hard — an average dozen miles in an average eight hours — none of the troops had had anything to eat since breakfast, and many of them had not had even that. Hunger made them trembly. Moreover, there had been a tormenting shortage of water all along the way, and the men were spitting cotton as they filed into position to await the signal that would send them plunging eastward through the thickets to their front. They knew now, for certain, what they had only assumed before: Hooker's flank lay dead ahead and they were about to strike it. But the waiting was long. It was 4.30 by the time Colston had formed in rear of Rodes, and Hill was not yet off the road. Another half hour sufficed to get Little Powell's two leading brigades into position in rear of Colston's left, while the center two were coming forward on the turnpike; but the last two were miles back down the road, delayed by their rear-guard action at Catharine Furnace. Jackson waited as long as he could, watch in hand. Rodes stood beside him, waiting too; he was a V.M.I. graduate, just past his thirty-fourth birthday, and like his chief a former professor of mathematics. Tall and slender, a Virginia-born Alabamian with a tawny mustache that drooped below the corners of his mouth, he had fought well in almost every major battle since First Manassas, taking time off only for wounds, but he would be leading a division in combat for the first time today. At 5.15 — an hour and a half before sundown — Jackson looked up from his watch. His proposed third line was not half formed, but he and the sun could wait no longer.

"Are you ready, General Rodes?"
"Yes sir."
"You can go forward then."

He spoke calmly, almost matter-of-factly; yet what followed within the next quarter hour approximated pandemonium. Crashing through the half-mile screen of brush and stunted trees, whose thorns and brittle, low-hanging limbs quickly stripped the trail-blazing skirmishers near-naked, the long lines of Confederates broke suddenly into the clear, where the sight of the enemy brought their rifles to their shoulders and the quavering din of the rebel yell from their throats; "that hellish yell," one bluecoat called it, though Jackson himself had once referred to the caterwaul as "the sweetest music I ever heard." He was getting his fill of such music now. All across the nearly two-mile width of his front, the woods and fields resounded with it as the screaming attackers bore down on the startled Federals, who had just risen to whoop at the frightened deer and driven rabbits. Now it was their turn to be frightened — and driven, too. For the Union regiments facing west gave way in a rush before the onslaught, and as they fled the two guns they had abandoned were turned against them, hastening their departure and increasing the confusion among the troops facing south behind the now useless breastworks they had constructed with such care. These last, looking over their shoulders and seeing the fugitives running close-packed on the turnpike immediately in their rear, took their cue from them and began to pull out, too, in rapid succession from right to left down the long line of intrenchments, swelling the throng rushing eastward along the road. Within twenty minutes of the opening shots, Howard's flank division had gone out of military existence, converted that quickly from organization to mob. The adjoining division was sudden to follow the example set. Not even the sight of the corps commander himself, on horseback near Wilderness Church, breasting the surge of retreaters up the turnpike and clamping a stand of abandoned colors under the stump of his amputated arm while attempting to control his skittish horse with the other, served to end or even slow the rout. Bareheaded and with tears in his eyes, Howard was pleading with them to halt and form, halt and form, but they paid him no mind, evidently convinced that his distress, whether for the fate of his country or his career or both, took no precedence over their own distress for their very lives. Some in their haste drew knives from their pockets and cut their knapsack straps as they ran, unburdening themselves for greater speed without taking the time to fumble at buckles, lest they be overtaken by the horde of tatterdemalion demons stretching north and south as far as the eye could follow and screaming with delight at the prospect of carnage.

Jackson was among the pursuers, riding from point to point just in rear of the crest of the wave, exultant. "Push right ahead," he told his brigadiers and colonels, and as he spoke he made a vigorous thrusting gesture, such as a man would make in toppling a wall. When a jubilant young officer cried, "They are running too fast for us. We can't keep up with them!" he replied sternly: "They never run too fast for me, sir. Press them, press them!" It was 6.30 by now; the sun was down behind the rearward treetops. Dowdall's Tavern lay dead ahead, and from the east the answering thunder of guns and clatter of musketry told Stonewall that Lee had heard or learned of the attack and was applying pressure to keep the tottering Union giant off balance, even though he could scarcely hope to break through the endless curve of fortifications south and east of Chancellorsville. Here to the west, on the other hand, whenever a clump of bluecoats more stalwart than their fellows tried to make a stand, they found themselves quickly outflanked on the left and right by the overlapping lines of the attackers, and they had to give way in a scramble to avoid being surrounded. Every time Jackson heard the wild yell of victory that followed such collapses he would lift his head and smile grimly, as if in thanks to the God of battle. Conversely, whenever he came upon the bodies of his own men, lying where panicky shots had dropped them, he would frown, draw rein briefly, and raise one hand as if blessing the slain for their valor. A staff officer later remarked, "I have never seen him so well pleased with the progress and results of a fight."

On through sundown his pleasure was justified by continuing success, and presently it was increased. By 7 o'clock, with darkness settling fast in the clearings and the woods already black, his triumph over Howard was complete as the Federals gave way around Dowdall's Tavern and began their flight across the reserveless gap that yawned between them and the rest of the blue army. On the right, just south of the turnpike, there was a meeting engagement with a column of Union cavalry, which resulted in its repulse, and enemy guns were booming on Fairview Heights, firing blind to discourage pursuit, but Jackson did not believe there was anything substantial between him and the loom of forest screening Chancellorsville itself, just over a mile ahead. The only deterrent beyond his control was the darkness, and soon there was not even that. As if in response to a signal from the southern Joshua, the full moon came up, huge and red through the drifting smoke, then brightened to gold as it rose to light the way for pursuit. Many times in the past Stonewall had ached to launch a night attack; now he not only had the chance, he believed it was downright necessary if he was to prevent the enemy from recovering from the shock and attempting to turn the tables on the still-divided Confederates. Two immediate objectives he had in mind. One was to strike deep in Hooker's rear, cutting him off from U.S. Ford so as to prevent his escape across the Rappahannock, and the other was to reunite with Lee for a combined assault on the bluecoats who thus would be hemmed in for slaughter. It was more or less obvious by now that Rodes and Colston had done their worst, at least for the present; they would need a breathing spell in which to regain control of their troops, hopelessly mingled in a single wave that was already ebbing because of exhaustion; but Hill's four brigades were still intact, available as a reserve, and Jackson was determined to use them for a moonlight advance along the pike and up the roads leading northeastward to the single river crossing in Hooker's rear. Soon he found Little Powell and gave him his instructions. There was no studied calmness about him now, such as there had been three hours ago when he told Rodes he could go forward. His excitement was evident to everyone he met, and his sense of urgency was communicated with every word he spoke, including those in the orders he gave Hill: "Press them! Cut them off from the United States Ford, Hill. Press them!"

Hooker by then was doing all he could to avert disaster, but for the better part of an hour after the first wave of attackers struck and crumpled the tip of his western wing — three miles from the Chancellor gallery where he sat chatting amiably with members of his staff — he had been under the tactical disadvantage of not even knowing that he had been surprised. Because of acoustic peculiarities of the terrain and the cushioning effect of brush and trees, the roar of battle reached him but faintly and indirectly. He and his aides supposed that the racket, such as it was, came from down around Catharine Furnace, a couple of miles to the south, and were exchanging conjectures as to the havoc Sickles must be making among Lee's trains in that direction. Just before sundown, however, one of the officers strolled out to the road and casually gazed westward. "My God — here they come!" the others heard him shout. Then they saw for themselves what he meant. A stumbling herd of wild-eyed men, the frantic and apparently unstoppable backwash of Howard's unstrung corps, was rushing eastward, filling the pike from shoulder to shoulder. Fighting Joe reacted fast. At hand was Sickles' third division — his own in the days before his elevation to corps and army command — left in reserve when the other two moved south; Hooker ordered it to wheel right and stem the rout. "Receive them on your bayonets! Receive them on your bayonets!" he cried, not making it clear whether he meant the demoralized Dutchmen or the rebels somewhere in their rear, as he rode westward through the failing light and into the teeth of the storm.

At Hazel Grove, sealed off from the uproar which by now was just over a mile away, a regiment of Pennsylvania cavalry received at about this same time, between sunset and moonrise, orders to join Howard near Wilderness Church. With no suggestion of urgency in the message and no hint that a clash had occurred, let alone a retreat, the troopers mounted and set out northwestward on a trail too narrow for anything more than a column of twos. They rode at a walk, talking casually among themselves, their weapons sheathed, until they approached the turnpike: at which point the major in command barely had time to cry, "Draw sabers! Charge!" before they ran spang into a whole Confederate division moving eastward through darkness that all of a sudden was stitched with muzzle flashes and filled with yells and twittering bullets. One side was about as startled as the other. The riders managed to hack their way out of the melee, though by the time they reassembled in the moonlight back near Chancellorsville a good many saddles had been emptied and a number of troopers had been captured, along with their unmanageable horses.

For blue and gray alike, whether mounted or afoot, the meeting engagement had some of the qualities of a nightmare too awful to be remembered except in unavoidable snatches. But for other Union soldiers, east of there, such an experience would have been counted almost mild in comparison with the one they blundered into a few hours later, in which blue was pitted not only against gray, but also against blue. Down around Catharine Furnace, deep in enemy territory, Dan Sickles knew nothing of what had been happening until well past sundown, when he heard the roar of batteries massed on the heights at Hazel Grove and Fairview, far in his rear. Informed at last of the enemy flank attack, which placed his two divisions precariously between the superior halves of the rebel army and thus exposed him to the danger of being pinched off and surrounded, he pulled hurriedly back to Hazel Grove — unhindered, so far, but by no means out of the trap whose jaws seemed likely to snap shut at any moment. By now it was past 9 o'clock, and except for occasional bellows by the 22 guns posted here and the 34 at Fairview, the firing had died to a mutter. Placing one division on the left and the other on the right of a trail leading northward through the forest, Sickles prepared to continue his march to the comparative safety of the turnpike. He had scarcely set out, however, before the two columns lost the trail and drifted apart, one veering east and the other west, with the result that they ran into horrendous trouble in both directions. The division on the left angled into a line of Confederates, alert behind hastily improvised intrenchments, while the one on the right stumbled into a similar line along which one of Slocum's divisions was deployed. Both broke into flames on contact, and a three-sided fight was in progress as suddenly as if someone had thrown a switch. Caught in what a participant called "one vast square of fire," Sickles' troops milled aimlessly, throwing bullets indiscriminately east and west. Shouts of "Don't fire! We're friends!" brought heavier volleys from both sides of the gauntlet, and consternation reached a climax when rival batteries started pumping shell and canister into the frantic mass hemmed thus between the lines. Somehow, though, despite the darkness and confusion, Sickles finally managed to effect a withdrawal southward, in the direction he had come from. By midnight he had what was left of his two divisions back at Hazel Grove, where the men bedded down to wait for daylight, barely four hours off, and restore their jangled nerves as best they could.

Elsewhere along his contracted line — albeit the contraction had been accomplished more by Jackson's efforts than his own — Hooker saw to it that the rest of his army did likewise. He did not know what tomorrow was going to bring, but he intended to be ready for it. And in point of fact he had cause for confidence. Reynolds was over the river by now; his three divisions were available as a reserve. Even Howard's three, or anyhow a good part of them, had managed to reassemble in the vicinity of U.S. Ford, where they were brought to a halt after ricocheting northward off Lee's intrenchments east of Chancellorsville. Meade's three had been unaffected by the turmoil across the way. Couch and Slocum, under cover of the 56-gun barrage from Hazel Grove and Fairview, had adapted their four divisions to the altered situation, along with the one Sickles had left behind. Moreover, another brigade of cavalry was at hand, Averell having been called in from near Rapidan Station, where Stoneman had dropped him off, ostensibly to check Stuart's pursuit but actually, since there was no pursuit, to play little or no part in the southward raid. His total loss, after three days in enemy country, was 1 man killed and 4 wounded; Hooker was furious and relieved him on the spot. "If the enemy did not come to him, he should have gone to the enemy," Fighting Joe protested with unconscious irony. Apparently he could not see that this applied in his own case. He still depended on Sedgwick for the delivery of any blow that was to be struck, repeating in greater detail at 9 p.m. the instructions sent him earlier in the day. This time they were peremptory; Sedgwick was to "cross the Rappahannock at Fredericksburg on the receipt of this order." Leaving Gibbon to hold the town, he was to march at once on Chancellorsville and "attack and destroy any force he may fall in with on the road." This would bring him promptly into contact with Lee's rear, "and between us we will use him up.... Be sure not to fail." The pattern was unchanged. Now as before, Gallo-Hooker was leaving the confrontation of the bull to Paco-Sedgwick, while he himself stood fast behind the barrera to cheer him on.

Lulled by what one insomniac called "the weird, plaintive notes of the whippoorwills," who would not let even a battle the size of this one cancel their serenade to the full, high-sailing moon, the army slept. From point to point the Wilderness was burning — "like a picture of hell," a cavalryman said of the scene as he viewed it from a hilltop — but the screams of the wounded caught earlier by the flames had died away, together with the growl and rumble of the guns. It was midnight and the Army of the Potomac took its rest.

Though the Army of Northern Virginia was doing the same, west and south of the now one-handled Union dipper, it did so in an atmosphere of tragedy out of all ratio to the success it had scored today. Not only had Stonewall's plan for continuing the eastward drive by moonlight been abandoned, but Stonewall himself had been taken rearward, first on a stretcher and then in an ambulance, to a hospital tent near Wilderness Tavern, where even now, as midnight came and went, surgeons were laying out the probes and knives and saws they would use in their fight to save his life. Intimations of national tragedy, intensified by a sense of acute personal loss, pervaded the forest bivouacs as the rumor spread that Jackson had been wounded.

After telling Hill to bring his men forward in order to resume the stalled pursuit, he had proceeded east along the turnpike in search of a route that would intercept the expected blue retreat to U.S. Ford. As he and several members of his staff rode past the fringe of Confederate pickets, taking a secondary road that branched off through the woods on the left, they began hearing the sound of axes from up ahead, where the Federals were trimming and notching logs for a new line of breastworks. "General, don't you think this is the wrong place for you?" an officer asked. Jackson did not agree. "The danger is all over," he said. "The enemy is routed. Go back and tell A. P. Hill to press right on." Presently, though, with the ring of axes much nearer at hand, he drew rein and listened carefully. Then he turned and rode back the way he had come, apparently satisfied that the bluecoats, for all their frenzy of preparation, would be unable to resist what he intended to throw at them as soon as Hill got his troops into position. Soon he came upon Little Powell himself, riding forward with his staff to examine the ground over which he expected to advance, and the two parties returned together. To the pickets crouched in the brush ahead — North Carolinians whose apprehensiveness had been aroused by the meeting engagement, a short while ago, with the saber-swinging Pennsylvanians over on the turnpike — the mounted generals and their staffs, amounting in all to nearly a score of horsemen, must have had the sound of a troop of Union cavalry on the prowl or the advance element of a wave of attackers. At any rate that was the premise on which they acted in opening fire. "Cease firing! Cease firing!" Hill shouted, echoed by one of Jackson's officers: "Cease firing! You are firing into your own men!" Fortunately, no one had been hit by the sudden spatter of bullets, but the Tarheel commander believed he saw through a Yankee trick. "Who gave that order?" he cried. "It's a lie! Pour it into them, boys!" The boys did just that. Not only the pickets but the whole front-line battalion opened fire at twenty paces and with such devastating effect that the bodies of no less than fourteen horses were counted later in the immediate area.

Little Sorrel was not among them, having returned by then to the allegiance from which Stonewall had removed him, nearly two years ago, with his capture at Harpers Ferry. Frightened by the abrupt first clatter of fire from the pickets crouched in the brush ahead, he whirled and made a rearward dash through the woods. Jackson managed to turn him, though he could not slow him down, and was coming back west, his right arm raised to protect his face from low-hanging branches, when the second volley crashed. Once more Little Sorrel whirled and scampered toward the enemy lines, completely out of control now because his rider had been struck by three of the bullets, two in the left arm, which hung useless at his side, and one through the palm of the upraised hand, which he lowered and used as before, despite the pain, to turn the fear-crazed animal back toward his own lines. There one of the surviving officers, dismounted by the volley, caught hold of the horse's bridle and brought him to a stop, while another came up and braced the general in the saddle. He seemed dazed. "Wild fire, that, sir; wild fire," he exclaimed as he sat staring into the darkness lately stitched with muzzle flashes. All around them they could hear the groans and screams of injured men and horses. "How do you feel, General?" one of the officers asked, with the simplicity of great alarm, and Jackson replied: "You had better take me down. My arm is broken." They did so, finding him already so weak from shock and bleeding that he could not lift his feet from the stirrups. Freed at last of the restraining weight, Little Sorrel turned and ran for the third time toward the Union lines, and this time he made it. Meanwhile the two staffers laid the general under a tree. While one went off in search of a surgeon and the other was doing what he could to staunch the flow of blood from an artery severed in the left arm, just below the shoulder, Jackson began muttering to himself, as if in disbelief of what had happened. "My own men," he said.

That was about 9.30; the next two hours were a restless extension of the nightmare as Federal batteries at Fairview began firing, the gunners having spotted the moonlit confusion just over half a mile away. Presently the second of Jackson's two attendant staff officers returned through the storm of bursting shells with a regimental surgeon, who administered first aid and ordered the general taken rearward on a stretcher. This had to be done under artillery fire so intense that the bearers were forced to stop and lie flat from time to time, as much for Jackson's protection as their own. On several such occasions they almost dropped him, and once they did, hard on the injured arm, which made him groan with pain for the first time. At last they found an ambulance and got him back to the aid station near Wilderness Tavern, where his medical director, Dr Hunter McGuire, took one look at "the fixed, rigid face and the thin lips, so tightly compressed that the impression of the teeth could be seen through them," and ordered the patient prepared for surgery. "What an infinite blessing... blessing... blessing," Stonewall murmured as the chloroform blurred his pain. Then McGuire removed the shattered left arm, all but a two-inch stump. Coming out of the anesthetic, half an hour later — it was now about 3 o'clock in the morning — Jackson said that during the operation he had experienced "the most delightful music," which he now supposed had been the singing of the bone-saw. At that point, however, he was interrupted by a staff officer just arrived from the front. Tragedy had succeeded tragedy.

Hill had been incapacitated, struck in both legs by shell fragments, and had called on Jeb Stuart to take command instead of Rodes, the senior infantry brigadier, who until today had never led anything larger than a brigade. Stuart had come at a gallop from Ely's Ford, altogether willing. Knowing little of the situation and almost nothing of Stonewall's plans, however, he had sent to him for instructions or advice. Jackson stirred, contracting his brow at the effort. For a moment the light of battle returned to his eyes. Then it faded; his face relaxed. Even the exertion of thought was too much for him in his weakened condition. "I don't know — I can't tell," he stammered. "Say to General Stuart he must do what he thinks best."

Stuart would do that anyhow, of course, and so would Lee, who was informed at about this same time of the progress of the flank attack and the climactic wounding of his chief lieutenant. "Ah, Captain," he said; he shook his head; "Any victory is dearly bought which deprives us of the services of General Jackson, even for a short time." When the officer started to give him further details of the accident Lee stopped him. "Ah, don't talk about it. Thank God it is no worse." He was quick to agree, however, when the young man expressed the opinion that it had been Stonewall's intention to continue the attack. "Those people must be pressed today," Lee said decisively, and he put this into more formal language at once in a note to Stuart: "It is necessary that the glorious victory thus far achieved be prosecuted with the utmost vigor, and the enemy given no time to rally.... Endeavor, therefore, to dispossess them of Chancellorsville, which will permit the union of the army."

★ ★ ★

Hooker did not wait for Stuart or anyone else to dispossess him of Chancellorsville. He dispossessed himself. After establishing in the predawn darkness a secondary line of defense — a formidable V-shaped affair, with Reynolds deployed along Hunting Run, Meade at the southern apex, where the roads from Ely's and U.S. Fords came together in rear of army headquarters, and the fragments of Howard reassembled in Meade's old position along Mineral Spring Run, so that the flanks were anchored, right and left, on the Rapidan and the Rappahannock — he rode forward at first light, past the works still held by Couch and Slocum around Fairview, to confer in person with Sickles. Despite last night's horrendous experience of being mauled by foes and friends, Sickles had got his nerve back and was all for holding his ground; but Hooker would not hear of it, and ordered him to withdraw at once. It was this well-intentioned readjustment, designed to tidy up his lines and consolidate his defenses south of the vital crossroads, which resulted in his dispossession. Hazel Grove turned out to be the key to the whole advance position, since rebel artillery posted there could enfilade the intrenchments around Fairview, which in turn were all that covered Chancellorsville itself. The result was that everything south of the improvised V came suddenly unglued, and Hooker was left, scarcely twelve hours after his apparent delivery from the first, with a possible second disaster on his hands.

Stuart's advance, south of the turnpike and into the rising sun, coincided with Sickles' withdrawal, the final stages of which became a rout as the graybacks swarmed into Hazel Grove and overran the tail of the blue column. Immediately behind the first wave of attackers came the guns, 30 of them slamming away from the just-won heights at the Federals massed around Fairview, while another 30 assailed the western flank from a position near Howard's former headquarters, back out the pike, and 24 more were roaring from down the plank road to the southeast. Lee's midwinter reorganization of the Confederate long arm, for increased flexibility in close-up support, was paying short-term dividends this morning. Caught in the converging fire of these 84 guns, along with others west and south, the troops of Couch and Slocum were infected by the panic Sickles' men brought out of the smoke at Hazel Grove. North of the pike, sheltered by the breastworks Jackson had heard them constructing the night before, the bluecoats held fast against repeated assaults by the rebel infantry, but they were galled by the crossfire from batteries whose shots were plowing the fields around the crossroads in their rear and smashing their lines of supply and communication. Not even the Chancellor mansion, converted by now into a hospital as well as a headquarters by surgeons who took doors off their hinges and propped them on chairs for use as operating tables, was safe from the bombardment — as Hooker himself discovered presently, in a most emphatic manner. Shortly after 9 o'clock he was standing on the southwest veranda, leaning against one of the squat wooden pillars, when a solid projectile struck and split it lengthwise. He fell heavily to the floor, stunned by the shock. His aides gathered round and took him out into the yard, where they laid him on a blanket and poured a jolt of brandy down his throat. Revived by this first drink in weeks, Fighting Joe got up, rather wobbly still, and walked off a short distance, calling for his horse. It was well that he did, for just after he rose a second cannonball landed directly on the blanket, as if to emphasize the notion suggested by the first that the war had become an intensely personal matter between the Union commander and the rebel gunners who were probing for his life. He mounted awkwardly, suffering from a numbness on the side of his body that had been in contact with the shattered pillar, and rode for the rear, accompanied by his staff.

Despite the fact that he would succeed to command of the army in the event that its present chief was incapacitated, Couch knew nothing of Hooker's precipitate change of base until about 10 o'clock, when he received a summons to join him behind Meade's lines, where the apex of the secondary V came down to within a mile of the Chancellor house. Though he had his hands quite full just then — it was during the past half hour that the lines around Fairview had begun to come unglued in earnest — Couch told Hancock to take charge, and set out rearward in the wake of his chief, whom he found stretched out on a cot in a tent beside the road to U.S. Ford. "Couch, I turn the command of the army over to you," the injured general said, raising himself on one elbow as he spoke. However, his next words showed that he did not really mean what he had said. Whether or not he had control of himself at this point was open to question, but there was no doubt that he intended to retain control of the army. "You will withdraw it and place it in the position designated on this map," he added, indicating a field sketch with the V drawn on it to show where the new front lines would run. Couch perhaps was relieved to hear that he would not be given full control, along with full responsibility — "If he is killed, what shall I do with this disjointed army?" he had asked himself as soon as he heard that Hooker had been hurt — but others were hoping fervently that he would take charge; for he was known to be a fighter. "By God, we'll have some fighting now," a colonel said stoutly as Couch emerged from the tent. Meade looked inquiringly at his friend, hoping to receive at last the order for which he had been waiting all morning: Go in. Instead, Couch shook his head by way of reply and relayed Hooker's instructions for a withdrawal.

In any event, such instructions were superfluous by now except as they applied to Hancock, whose division was the only one still maintaining, however shakily, its forward position in a state that even approached cohesiveness. The choice, if the army's present disjointed condition allowed for any choice at all, lay not in whether or not to withdraw, as Hooker expressly directed, but in whether or not to counterattack and thus attempt to recover what had been lost by the retreat already in progress; which manifestly would be difficult, if not downright impossible, since the Confederates had just seized the heights at Fairview and with them domination of the open fields across which the troops of Sickles, Couch, and Slocum were streaming to find sanctuary within the line of breastworks to the north. Hancock's rear-guard division was having to back-pedal fast to keep from being cut off or overrun by a horde of butternut pursuers who were screaming as triumphantly now, and with what appeared to be equally good cause, as they had done when they bore down on Howard's startled Dutchmen yesterday. While Stuart pressed eastward, making his largest gains on the south side of the turnpike, Lee had been pushing north and west up the plank road and reaching out simultaneously to the left, past Catharine Furnace, for the anticipated hookup. It was his belief that the best and quickest way to accomplish the reunion of the two wings of his army would be to uncover Chancellorsville, after which it was his intention to launch a full-scale joint assault that would throw Hooker back against the Rappahannock and destroy him.

For a time it looked as if that might indeed be possible in the ten full hours of daylight still remaining. Never before, perhaps, had the Army of Northern Virginia fought with such frenzy and exaltation, such apparent confidence in its invincibility under Lee. Accompanied by the roar of artillery from the dominant heights, McLaws and Anderson moved steadily westward up the turnpike and the plank road, while Rodes, Colston, and Henry Heth — the senior brigadier in Hill's division — plunged eastward along both sides of the turnpike, cheered on by Stuart, who rode among them, jaunty in his red-lined cape, hoicking them up to the firing line and singing at the top of his voice some new words set to a familiar tune: "Old Joe Hooker, won't you come out the Wilderness?" All advanced rapidly toward the common objective, east and west, as the bluecoats faded back from contact. Shortly before 10.30 the two wings came together with a mighty shout in the hundred-acre clearing around the Chancellor mansion, which had been set afire by the bombardment. Lee rode forward from Hazel Grove, past Fairview, on whose crown two dozen guns had been massed to tear at the rear of the retreating enemy columns, and then into the yard of the burning house, formerly headquarters of the Union army, where the jubilant Confederates, recognizing the gray-bearded author of their victory, tendered him the wildest demonstration of their lives. "The fierce soldiers with their faces blackened with the smoke of battle, the wounded crawling with feeble limbs from the fury of the devouring flames, all seemed possessed with a common impulse," a staff man later wrote. "One long, unbroken cheer, in which the feeble cry of those who lay helpless on the earth blended with the strong voices of those who still fought, rose high above the roar of battle and hailed the presence of the victorious chief. He sat in the full realization of all that soldiers dream of — triumph.... As I looked upon him in the complete fruition of the success which his genius, courage, and confidence in his army had won," the officer added, "I thought that it must have been from such a scene that men in ancient times rose to the dignity of gods."

In the midst of this rousing accolade a courier arrived with a dispatch from Jackson, formally reporting that the extent of his wounds had compelled him to relinquish command of his corps. Lee had not known till now of the amputation, and the news shook him profoundly. His elation abruptly replaced by sadness, he dictated in reply an expression of regret. "Could I have directed events," he told his wounded lieutenant, "I would have chosen for the good of the country to be disabled in your stead," and added: "I congratulate you upon the victory, which is due to your skill and energy." This done, he returned to the business at hand. He had, as he said, won a victory; but if it was to amount to much more than the killing, as before, of large numbers of an enemy whose reserves were practically limitless, the present advantage would have to be pressed to the point at which Hooker, caught in the coils of the Rappahannock and with the scare still on him, would have to choose between slaughter and surrender. Before this could be accomplished, however, or even begin to be accomplished by a resumption of the advance, the attackers themselves would have to be reorganized and realigned for the final sweep of the fields and thickets stretching northward to the river. Lee gave instructions for this to be done as quickly as possible, and while waiting got off a dispatch to Davis in Richmond. "We have again to thank Almighty God for a great victory," he announced.

His hope was that he would be sending another announcement of an even greater victory by nightfall. But just as he was about to order the attack, a courier on a lathered horse rode in from the east with news of a disaster. At dawn that morning, with a rush across the pontoon bridge they had thrown under cover of darkness, the Federals had occupied Fredericksburg. Sedgwick then had feinted at the thinly held defenses on the ridge beyond the town, first on the far left and then the right, by way of distracting attention from his main effort against the center. This too had been repulsed, not once but twice, before the weight of numbers told and the bluecoats swarmed up and over Marye's Heights. In accordance with previous instructions designed for such a crisis, Early had withdrawn southward to protect the army's trains at Guiney Station; but Sedgwick had not pursued in that direction. Instead, he had moved — was moving now — due west along the plank road, which lay open in Lee's rear. This was the worst of all possible threats, and the southern commander had no choice except to meet it at this worst of all possible times. Postponing the assault on Hooker, he detached McLaws to head eastward and delay Sedgwick, if possible, while Anderson extended his present right out the River Road to prevent a junction of the two Union forces in case Sedgwick managed to sidestep McLaws or brush him out of the way. By now it was close to 3 o'clock. Holding Rodes and Heth in their jump-off positions, Lee ordered Colston to move up the Ely's Ford Road in order to establish and maintain contact with Hooker, who might be emboldened by this new turn of events. "Don't engage seriously," Lee told Colston, "but keep the enemy in check and prevent him from advancing. Move at once."

Now as before, he was improvising, dividing his badly outnumbered army in order to deal with a two-pronged menace. While McLaws swung east to throw his 7000 soldiers in the teeth of Sedgwick's 20,000 or more, Lee would endeavor to hold Hooker's 80,000 in position with his own 37,000. When and if he managed to stabilize the situation — as Jackson had done, two days ago, with the advance beyond Tabernacle Church — he would decide which of the two enemy wings to leap at, north or east. Meanwhile, as usual, he was prepared to take advantage of any blunder his opponents might commit, and he was determined to recover the initiative. Above all, he kept his head and refused to take counsel of his fears. When an excited officer, alarmed by the threat to the army's rear, arrived with a lurid eyewitness account of the loss of Marye's Heights, Lee cut him short. "We will attend to Mr Sedgwick later," he said calmly.

What with the relentless depletion of his forces, siphoned off westward at the rate of a corps a day for the past two days, and the spate of discretionary orders, generally so delayed in transmission that the conditions under which they had been issued no longer obtained by the time they came to hand, John Sedgwick — "Uncle John" to his troops, a fifty-year-old bachelor New Englander with thirty years of army service, including West Point, the Mexican War, the Kansas border troubles, and frontier Indian uprisings, in all of which he had shown a good deal more of plodding dependability than of flash — had difficulty in maintaining the unruffled disposition for which he was beloved. Even the peremptory dispatch received last night, after the uproar subsided in the thickets across the way, had left him somewhat puzzled. Hooker told him to "cross the Rappahannock at Fredericksburg on receipt of this order," which was clear enough, so far as the words themselves went; but what did it mean? Surely the army commander knew he was already across the Rappahannock, and in fact had been across it for the past three days.... Deciding that it meant what it ought to mean, he told Gibbon, whose division was still at Falmouth, to cross the river at dawn and seize the west-bank town, preparatory to joining in the attack Sedgwick was planning to launch against the fortified ridge with his other three divisions. He had not taken part in the December battle, having been laid up with three wounds received at Antietam, but he knew well enough what Burnside had encountered on this ground. For a time, indeed, it appeared that Sedgwick was going to do no better, despite his usual methodical preparations. After feinting on the left and right, he sent ten regiments in mass against the sunken road at the foot of the heights where so many men had come to grief, five months ago, when two of Longstreet's divisions held this section of the line. Now, however, so well had the feints misled the defenders, all that were there were two slim regiments and sixteen guns. Even so, the first two assaults were bloodily repulsed. As the bluecoats dropped back into the swale for a breather, preparatory to giving the thing another try, the colonel of a Wisconsin regiment made a short speech to the men who would lead the third assault. "When the signal *forward* is given you will advance at double-quick," he told them. "You will not fire a gun and you will not stop until you get the order to halt." He paused briefly, then added: "You will never get that order."

The Badgers gulped, absorbing the shock of this, then cheered and went in fast, the other nine regiments following close on their heels. Beyond the stone wall to their front, Barksdale's two Mississippi regiments turned loose with everything they had, attempting to shatter the head of the column of assault, while four batteries of the Washington Artillery, a crack New Orleans outfit, broke into a frenzied roar on the ridge beyond. The attackers took their losses and kept going, over the wall and among the defenders with the bayonet, then across the sunken road and up the slope of Marye's Heights with scarcely a pause, staring directly into the muzzles of the flaming guns on the crest. These too were taken in a rush as the cannoneers got off a final volley and broke for the rear. Within half an hour, and at a cost of no more than 1500 casualties, Sedgwick had his flags aflutter on ground that Burnside had spent 6300 men for no more than a fairly close-up look at, back in December. The bluecoats went into a victory dance, hurrahing and thumping each other on the back in celebration of their triumph; whereas the Confederates, several hundred of whom had been captured, were correspondingly dejected or wrathful, depending on the individual reaction to defeat. One cannoneer, who had managed to get away at the last moment, just as the Union wave broke over his battery, was altogether furious. "Guns be damned!" he replied hotly when a reserve artillerist twitted him by asking where his guns were. "I reckon now the people of the Southern Confederacy are satisfied that Barksdale's Brigade and the Washington Artillery can't whip the whole damned Yankee army!"

Having broken Jubal Early's line and thrown him into retreat, Sedgwick would have enjoyed pursuing his West Point classmate down the Telegraph Road, but another classmate, Hooker himself, had forbidden this by insisting that he push westward without delay, so that between them, as Fighting Joe put it, they could "use up" Lee. Moreover, at 10 o'clock — less than an hour after being stunned by the split pillar, and at about the same time, as it turned out, that his forward defenses began to come unglued — Hooker had his adjutant send Sedgwick a dispatch reminding him of his primary mission: "You will hurry up your column. The enemy's right flank now rests near the plank road at Chancellorsville, all exposed. You will attack at once." This reached Sedgwick at about 11.30, amid the victory celebration on Marye's Heights, and he did what he could to comply. Leaving Gibbon to hold Fredericksburg in his rear, he began to prepare his other three divisions for the advance on Lee. It was a time-consuming business, however, to break up the celebration and get the troops into formation for the march. The lead division did not get started until 2 o'clock, and it was brought to a sudden halt within the hour, just over a mile from Marye's Heights, by the sight of Confederate skirmishers in position along a ridge athwart the road. Despite Hooker's assurance that Lee's flank was "all exposed," the graybacks seemed quite vigilant, and what was more they appeared to be present in considerable strength, with guns barking aggressively in support. Sedgwick was obliged to halt and deploy in the face of the resistance, at the cost of burning more daylight.

Slowly the rebels faded back, bristling as they went, leapfrogging their guns from ridge to ridge and flailing the pursuers all the time. Near Salem Church, a mile ahead and a mile short of the junction of the plank road and the turnpike, they stiffened. It was 4 o'clock by now; the day was going fast, and Sedgwick was still a good half-dozen miles from Chancellorsville. Without waiting for the others to come up, he sent the troops of his lead division forward on the run. At first they made headway, driving the graybacks before them, but then they encountered a heavy line of battle. Repulsed, they came streaming back across the fields. The second division was up by now, however, with the third not far behind, and between them they managed to check the pursuit, though by the time Sedgwick got them rallied and into attack formation the day was too far gone for fighting. Aware by now that he had run into something considerably stronger than a mere rear guard, he set up a perimetrical defense and passed the word for his 22,000 soldiers to bed down.

Today had been a hard day. Tomorrow gave promise of being even harder. He had set out to put the squeeze on Lee, but it had begun to seem to him that he was the one in danger now. All around him, south and east as well as west, he could hear enemy columns moving in the darkness. "Sedgwick scarcely slept that night," an observant soldier later recalled. "From time to time he dictated a dispatch to General Hooker. He would walk for a few paces apart and listen; then returning he would lie down again in the damp grass, with his saddle for a pillow, and try to sleep. The night was inexpressibly gloomy."

The night was inexpressibly gloomy, and he was in graver danger than he knew. All that had stood in his way at the outset, when he began his march from Marye's Heights, had been a single brigade of Alabamians, stationed for the past three days on outpost duty at Banks Ford, from which point their commander, Brigadier General Cadmus Wilcox, had shifted them, on his own initiative, when he learned that Early's defenses had been pierced. Determined to do what he could to protect Lee's unguarded rear, he had taken up a position athwart the plank road, spreading his men in the semblance of a stout line of skirmishers, and thus had managed to bluff Sedgwick into caution, delaying his advance until McLaws had had time to post his division near Salem Church and rock the charging bluecoats on their heels. As a result, when darkness ended the fighting here to the east of Chancellorsville, Lee had what he had been hoping for: a more or less stable situation and the opportunity, as he had said, to "attend to Mr Sedgwick." Early, he learned, had retreated only a couple of miles down the Telegraph Road, then had halted on finding that he was unpursued. Lee wrote him, just after sunset, that McLaws was confronting the Federals east of Salem Church; "If...you could come upon their left flank, and communicate with General McLaws, I think you would demolish them." A similar message went to McLaws, instructing him to co-operate with Early. "It is necessary to beat the enemy," Lee told him, "and I hope you will do it."

A dawn reconnaissance — Monday now: May 4 — showed Hooker's intrenchments well laid out and greatly strengthened overnight, the flanks securely anchored below and above the U.S. Ford escape hatch, and the whole supported by batteries massed in depth. While this discouraged attack, it also seemed to indicate that the Federals had gone entirely on the defensive in the region north of Chancellorsville. At any rate Lee proceeded on that assumption. Canceling a projected feeling-out of the enemy lines along Mineral Spring Run, he shifted half of Heth's division from the far left, beyond Colston and Rodes, to take up Anderson's position on the right, and ordered Anderson east to join with McLaws and Early in removing the threat to his rear. His plan, if daring, was simple enough. Stuart and the 25,000 survivors of Jackson's flanking column were given the task of keeping Hooker's 80,000 penned in their breastworks, while the remaining 22,000 Confederates disposed of Sedgwick, who had about the same number to the east. This last was now the main effort, and Lee decided to supervise it in person. Riding over to Salem Church at noon, he conferred with McLaws, who was awaiting Anderson's arrival before completing his dispositions for attack, and then proceeded east, skirting the southward bulge of Sedgwick's perimeter, to see Early. He found him on Marye's Heights, which he had reoccupied soon after sunrise, posting the remnant of Barksdale's brigade in the sunken road to resist another possible advance by Gibbon, who had retired into Fredericksburg. The plan of attack, as McLaws and Early had worked it out, was for Anderson to take up a position between them, confronting Sedgwick from the south, while they moved against him, simultaneously, from the east and west. The result, if all went well, would be his destruction. Lee gave his approval, though he saw that this would involve a good deal of maneuvering over difficult terrain, and rode back toward the center.

It was past 2 o'clock by now, and Anderson was not yet in position. Time was running out for Lee today, as it had done the day before for Sedgwick. Already he was finding what it cost him to be deprived even temporarily of the services of Jackson, of whom he would say before the week was over: "He has lost his left arm, but I have lost my right." More hours were spent examining the approaches and correcting the alignment of the columns so as to avoid collisions. While Anderson continued to balk, McLaws was strangely apathetic and Early floundered in the ravines across the way; it was 6 o'clock before all the troops were in position and the signal guns were fired. The fighting was savage

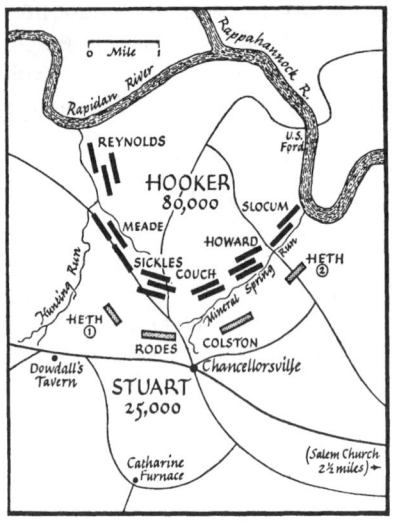

at scattered points, especially on Early's front, but McLaws got lost in a maze of thickets and scarcely made contact, either with the enemy or with Anderson, whose men added to the confusion by firing into each other as they advanced. Fog thickened the dusk and the disjointed movement lurched to a halt within an hour. Sedgwick had been shaken, though hardly demolished. Anxious to exploit his gains, such as they were, before the Federals reintrenched or got away across the river, Lee for the first time in his career ordered a night attack. While the artillery shelled Banks Ford in the darkness, attempting to seal off the exit, the infantry groped about in the fog, dog-tired, and made no progress. At first light, the skirmishers recovered their sense of direction, pushed forward, and found that the works to their front were empty; Sedgwick had escaped. Though his casualties had been heavy — worse than 4600 in all, including the men lost earlier — he had got his three divisions to safety across a bridge the engineers had thrown a mile below Banks Ford, well beyond range of the all-night interdictory fire.

Word came presently from Barksdale that Gibbon too had recrossed the river at Fredericksburg and cut his pontoons loose from the west bank. This meant that for the first time in three days no live, uncaptured bluecoats remained on the Confederate side of the Rappahannock except the ones intrenched above Chancellorsville; Lee had abolished the threat to his rear. Though he was far from satisfied, having failed in another of a lengthening sequence of attempts to destroy a considerable segment of the Union army, he had at least restored — and even improved — the situation that had existed yesterday, when he was preparing to give Hooker his undivided attention. Once more intent on destruction, he allowed the men of McLaws and Anderson no rest, but ordered them to take up the march back to Chancellorsville, intending for them to resume the offensive they had abandoned for Sedgwick's sake the day before. Stuart reported that the Federals, though still present in great strength behind their V, had made no attempt to move against him, either yesterday or so far this morning; yet Lee did what he could to hasten the march westward, not so much out of fear that Hooker would lash out at Stuart, whom he outnumbered better than three to one, as out of fear that he would do as Sedgwick had done and make his escape

Death of a Soldier

across the river before the Confederates had time to reconcentrate and crush him.

In point of fact, Lee's fears on the latter count were more valid than he had any way of knowing, not having attended a council of war held the night before at his opponent's headquarters. At midnight, while Sedgwick was beginning his withdrawal across the Rappahannock, Hooker had called his other corps commanders together to vote on whether they should do the same. Couch, Reynolds, Meade, Howard, and Sickles reported promptly, but Slocum, who had the farthest to come, did not arrive until after the meeting had broken up. Hooker put the question to them — remarking, as Couch would recall, "that his instructions compelled him to cover Washington, not to jeopardize the army, etc." — then retired to let them talk it over among themselves. Reynolds was much fatigued from loss of sleep; he lay down in one corner of the tent to get some rest, telling Meade to vote his proxy for attack. Meade did so, adding his own vote to that effect. Howard too was for taking the offensive; for unlike Meade and Reynolds, whose two corps had scarcely fired a shot, he had a reputation to retrieve. Couch on the other hand voted to withdraw, but made it clear that he favored such a course only because Hooker was still in charge. Sickles, whose corps had suffered almost as many casualties as any two of the other five combined, was in favor of pulling back at once, Hooker or no Hooker. Fighting Joe returned, was given the three-to-two opinion, and adjourned the council with the announcement that he intended to withdraw the army beyond the river as soon as possible. As the generals left the tent, Reynolds broke out angrily, quite loud enough for Hooker to overhear him: "What was the use of calling us together at this time of night when he intended to retreat anyhow?"

Their instructions were to cut whatever roads were necessary, leading from their present positions back to U.S. Ford, while the army engineers were selecting a strong inner line, anchored a mile above and a mile below the two pontoon bridges, for Meade's corps to occupy in covering the withdrawal. All were hard at work on their various assignments before dawn on the 5th, at which time Hooker crossed in person, accompanied by his staff. Then at noon, with the pull-back to the inner line completed, rain began to fall.

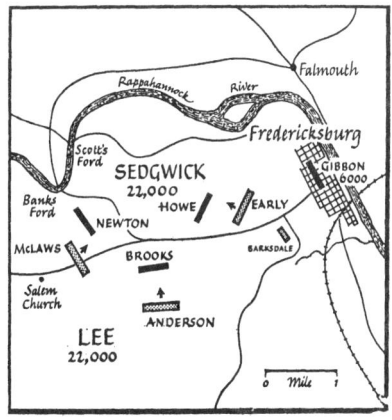

It fell in earnest, developing quickly into what one diarist called "a tremendous cold storm." By midnight the river had risen six feet, endangering the bridges and interrupting the retreat before more than a handful of regiments had reached the opposite bank. Cut off from Hooker, Couch believed he saw his chance. "We will stay where we are and fight it out," he announced. But peremptory orders arrived at 2 a.m. for the movement to be continued. One of the bridges was cannibalized to piece out the other, and the crossing was resumed. By midmorning Wednesday, May 6, it was completed. Except for the dead and missing, who would not be coming back, the army's week-long excursion south of the river had come full circle.

Lee was up by then, after being delayed by the storm the day before, but when his skirmishers pushed forward through the dripping woods they found the enemy gone. He lost his temper at the news and scolded the brigadier who brought it. "That is the way you young men always do," he fumed. "You allow those people to get away. I tell you what to do, but you won't do it!" He gestured impatiently. "Go after them, and damage them all you can!" But no further damage was possible; the bluecoats were well beyond his reach. At a cost of less than 13,000 casualties he had inflicted more than 17,000 and had won what future critics would call the most brilliant victory of his career, but he was by no means satisfied. He had aimed at total capture or annihilation of the foe, and the extent to which he had fallen short of this was, to his mind, the extent to which he had failed. Leaving a few regiments to tend the wounded, bury the dead, and glean the spoils abandoned by the Unionists on the field, he marched the rest of his army back through the rain-drenched Wilderness to Fredericksburg and the comparative comfort of the camps it had left a week ago, when word first came that the enemy was across the Rappahannock.

Back at Falmouth that evening, while his army straggled eastward in his wake, Hooker learned that Stoneman's raid, from which so much had been expected, had been almost a total failure. Intending, as he later reported, to "magnify our small force into overwhelming numbers," the cavalryman had broken up his column into fragments, none of which, as it turned out, had been strong enough to do more than temporary damage to the installations in Lee's rear. According to one disgusted trooper, "Our only accomplishments were the burning of a few canal boats on the upper James River, some bridges, hen roosts, and tobacco houses." Stoneman returned the way he had come, recrossing at Raccoon Ford on the morning of May 7, while other portions of his scattered column turned up as far away as Yorktown. His total losses, in addition to about 1000 horses broken down and abandoned, were 82 men killed and wounded and 307 missing. These figures seemed to Hooker to prove that Stoneman had not been seriously engaged, and it was not long before he removed him from command. However, his own casualties, while quite as heavy as anyone on his own side of the line could have desired — the ultimate total was 17,287, as compared to Lee's 12,821 — were equally condemning, though in a different way, since a breakdown of them indicated the disjointed manner in which he had fought and refrained from fighting the battle. Meade and Reynolds, for example, had lost fewer than 1000 men between them, while Sedgwick and Sickles had lost more than four times that number each. Obviously Lincoln's parting admonition, "Put in all your men," had been ignored. Hooker was quick to place the blame for his defeat on Stoneman, Averell, Howard, and Sedgwick, sometimes singly and at other times collectively. It was only in private, and some weeks later, that he was able to see, or at any rate confess, where the real trouble had lain. "I was not hurt by a shell, and I was not drunk," he told a fellow officer. "For once I lost confidence in Joe Hooker, and that is all there is to it."

In time that would become the registered consensus, but for the present many of his compatriots were hard put to understand how such a disaster had come about. Horace Greeley staggered into the *Tribune* managing editor's office Thursday morning, his face a ghastly color and his lips trembling. "My God, it is horrible," he exclaimed. "Horrible. And to think of it — 130,000 magnificent soldiers so cut to pieces by less than 60,000 half-starved ragamuffins!" An Episcopal clergyman, also in New York, could not reconcile the various reports and rumors he recorded in his diary that night. "It would seem that Hooker has beaten Lee, and that Lee has beaten Hooker; that we have taken Fredericksburg, and that the rebels have taken it also; that we have 4500 prisoners, and the rebels 5400; that Hooker has cut off Lee's retreat, and Lee has cut off Sedgwick's retreat, and Sedgwick has cut off everybody's retreat generally, but has retreated himself although his retreat was cut off.... In short, all is utter confusion. Everything seems to be everywhere, and everybody all over, and there is no getting at any truth." Official Washington was similarly confused and dismayed. When Sumner of Massachusetts heard that Hooker had been whipped, he flung up his hands and struck an attitude of despair. "Lost — lost," he groaned. "All is lost!" But the hardest-hit man of them all was Lincoln, whose hopes had had the longest way to fall. Six months ago, on the heels of Emancipation, he had foreseen clear sailing for the ship of state provided the helmsman kept a steady hand on the tiller. "We are like whalers who have been on a long chase," he told a friend. "We have at last got the harpoon into the monster, but we must now look how we steer, or with one flop of his tail he will send us all into eternity." Then had come Fredericksburg, and he had said: "If there is a worse place than Hell, I am in it." Now there was this, a still harder flop of the monster's tail, and Hooker and the Army of the Potomac had gone sprawling. Even before the news arrived, a White House caller had found the President "anxious and harassed beyond any power of description." Yet this was nothing compared to his reaction later in the day, when he reappeared with a telegram in his hand. "News from the army," he said in a trembling voice. The visitor read that Hooker was in retreat, and looking up saw that Lincoln's face, "usually sallow, was ashen in hue. The paper on the wall behind him was of the tint known as 'French gray,' and even in that moment of sorrow ... I vaguely took in the thought that the complexion of the anguished President's visage was like that of the wall." He walked up and down the room, hands clasped behind his back. "My God, my God," he exclaimed as he paced back and forth. "What will the country say? What will the country say?"

Within the ranks of the army itself, slogging down the muddy roads toward Falmouth, the reaction was not unlike the New York clergyman's. "No one seems to understand this move," a Pennsylvania private wrote, "but I have no doubt it is all right." He belonged to Meade's corps, which had seen very little fighting, and he could not quite comprehend that what he had been involved in was a defeat. All he knew for certain was that the march back to camp was a hard one. "Most of the way the mud was over shoe, in some places knee deep, and the rain made our loads terrible to tired shoulders." Others knew well enough that they had taken part in a fiasco. "Go boil your shirt!" was their reply to jokes attempted by roadside stragglers. Turning the matter over in their minds, they could see that Hooker had been trounced, but they could not see that this applied to themselves, who had fought as well as ever — except, of course, the unregenerate Dutchmen — whenever and wherever they got the chance. Mostly, though, they preferred to ignore the question of praise or blame. "And thus ends the second attempt on the capture of Fredericksburg," a Maine soldier recorded when he got back to Falmouth. "I have nothing to say about it in any way. I have no opinions to express about the Gen'ls or the men nor do I wish to. I leave it in the hands of God. I don't want to think of it at all."

★ ★ ★

Unquestionably, this latest addition to the lengthening roster of Confederate victories was a great one. Indeed, considering the odds that had been faced and overcome, it was perhaps in terms of glory the greatest of them all; *Chancellorsville* would be stitched with pride across the crowded banners of the Army of Northern Virginia. But its ultimate worth, as compared to its cost, depended in large measure on the outcome of Stonewall Jackson's present indisposition. As Lee had said on Sunday morning, when he first learned that his lieutenant had been wounded, "Any victory is dearly bought which deprives us of the services of General Jackson, even for a short time."

So far — that is, up to the time when Hooker threw in the sponge and the northern army fell back across the Rappahannock — Dr McGuire's prognosis had been most encouraging and the general himself had been in excellent spirits, despite the loss of his arm. "I am wounded but not depressed," he said when he woke from the sleep that followed the amputation. "I believe it was according to God's will, and I can wait until He makes his object known to me." Presently, when Lee's midday note was brought, congratulating him on the victory, "which is due to your skill and energy," Jackson permitted himself the one criticism he had ever made of his commander. "General Lee is very kind," he said, "but he should give the praise to God." Next day, May 4, with Sedgwick threatening the army's rear, he was removed to safety in an ambulance. The route was south to Todd's Tavern, then southeast, through Spotsylvania Court House, to Guiney Station, where he had met his wife and child, two weeks ago today, to begin the idyl that had ended with the news that Hooker was on the march. All along the way, country people lined the roadside to watch the ambulance go by. They brought with them, and held out for the attendants to accept, such few gifts as their larders afforded in these hard times, cool buttermilk, hot biscuits, and fried chicken. Jackson was pleased by this evidence of their concern, and for much of the 25-mile journey he chatted with an aide, even responding to a question as to what he thought of Hooker's plan for the battle whose guns rumbled fainter as the ambulance rolled south. "It was in the main a good conception, sir; an excellent plan. But he should not have sent away his cavalry. That was his great blunder. It was that which enabled me to turn him, without his being aware of it, and to take him by the rear." Of his own share in frustrating that plan, he added that he believed his flank attack had been "the most successful movement of my life. But I have received more credit for it than I deserve. Most men will think that I had planned it all from the first; but it was not so. I simply took advantage of circumstances as they were presented to me in the providence of God. I feel that His hand led me."

By nightfall he was resting comfortably in a cottage on the Chandler estate near Guiney Station. He slept soundly, apparently free from pain, and woke next morning much refreshed. His wounds seemed to give him little trouble; primary intention and granulation were under way. All that day and the next, Tuesday and Wednesday, he rested easy, talking mainly of religious matters, as had always been his custom in times of relaxation. The doctor foresaw a rapid recovery and an early return to duty. Then — late Wednesday night and early Thursday morning, May 7 — a sudden change occurred. McGuire woke at dawn to find his patient restless and in severe discomfort. Examination showed that the general faced a new and formidable enemy: pneumonia. He was cupped, then given mercury, with antimony and opium, and morphine to ease his pain. From that time on, as the drugs took effect and the pneumonia followed its inexorable course, he drifted in and out of sleep and fuddled consciousness. His wife arrived at midday, having been delayed by Stoneman's raiders, to find him greatly changed from the husband she had left eight days ago. Despite advance warning, she was shocked at the sight of his wounds, especially the mutilated arm. Moreover, his cheeks were flushed, his breathing oppressed, and his senses numbed. At first he scarcely knew her, but presently, in a more lucid moment, he saw her anxiety and told her: "You must not wear a long face. I love cheerfulness and brightness in a sickroom." He lapsed into stupor, then woke again to find her still beside him. "My darling, you are very much loved," he murmured. "You are one of the most precious little wives in the world." Toward evening, he seemed to improve. Once at least, in the course of the night, he appeared to be altogether himself again. "Will you take this, General?" the doctor asked, bending over the bed with a dose of medicine. Stonewall looked at him sternly. "Do your duty," he said. Then, seeing the doctor hesitate, he repeated the words quite firmly: "Do your duty." Still later, those in the room were startled to hear him call out to his adjutant, Alexander Pendleton, who was in Fredericksburg with Lee: "Major Pendleton, send in and see if there is higher ground back of Chancellorsville! I must find out if there is high ground between Chancellorsville and the river.... Push up the columns; hasten the columns! Pendleton, you take charge of that.... Where is Pendleton? Tell him to push up the columns." In his delirium he was back on the field of battle, doing the one thing he did best in all the world.

All that day and the next, which was Saturday, he grew steadily worse; McGuire sent word to Fredericksburg and Richmond that recovery was doubtful. Lee could not believe a righteous cause would suffer such a blow. "Surely General Jackson will recover," he said. "God will not take him from us now that we need him so much." The editor of the Richmond *Whig* agreed. "We need have no fears for Jackson," he wrote. "He is no accidental manifestation of the powers of faith and courage. He came not by chance in this day and to this generation. He was born for a purpose, and not until that purpose is fulfilled will his great soul take flight." Jackson himself inclined to this belief that he would be spared for a specific purpose. "I am not afraid to die," he said in a lucid moment Friday. "I am willing to abide by the will of my Heavenly Father. But I do not believe I shall die at this time. I am persuaded the Almighty has yet a work for me to perform." On Saturday, when he was asked to name a hymn he would like to hear sung, he requested "Shew Pity, Lord," Isaac Watts's paraphrase of the Fifty-first Psalm:

> "*Shew pity, Lord; O Lord, forgive;*
> *Let a repenting rebel live —*"

This seemed to comfort him for a time, but night brought a return of suffering. He tossed sleepless, mumbling battle orders. Though these

Death of a Soldier

were mostly unintelligible, it was observed that he called most often on A. P. Hill, his hardest-hitting troop commander, and Wells Hawks, his commissary officer, as if even in delirium he strove to preserve a balance between tactics and logistics.

Sunday, May 10, dawned fair and clear; McGuire informed Anna Jackson that her husband could not last the day. She knelt at the bedside of the unconscious general, telling him over and over that he would "very soon be in heaven." Presently he stirred and opened his eyes. She asked him, "Do you feel willing to acquiesce in God's allotment if He will you to go today?" He watched her. "I prefer it," he said, and she pressed the point: "Well, before this day closes you will be with the blessed Savior in his glory." There was a pause. "I will be the infinite gainer to be translated," Jackson said as he dozed off again. He woke at noon, and once more she broached the subject, telling him that he would be gone before sundown. This time he seemed to understand her better. "Oh no; you are frightened, my child. Death is not so near. I may yet get well." She broke into tears, sobbing that the doctor had said there was no hope. Jackson summoned McGuire. "Doctor, Anna informs me that you have told her I am to die today. Is it so?" When McGuire replied that it was so, the general seemed to ponder. Then he said, "Very good, very good. It is all right." After a time he added, "It is the Lord's day; my wish is fulfilled. I have always desired to die on Sunday."

At 1.30 the doctor told him he had no more than a couple of hours to live. "Very good; it's all right," Jackson replied as before, but more weakly, for his breathing was high in his throat by now. When McGuire offered him brandy to keep up his strength, he shook his head. "It will only delay my departure, and do no good," he protested. "I want to preserve my mind, if possible, to the last." Presently, though, he was back in delirium, alternately praying and giving commands, all of which had to do with the offensive. Shortly after 3 o'clock, a few minutes before he died, he called out: "Order A. P. Hill to prepare for action! Pass the infantry to the front.... Tell Major Hawks —" He left the sentence unfinished, seeming thus to have put the war behind him; for he smiled as he spoke his last words, in a tone of calm relief. "Let us cross over the river," he said, "and rest under the shade of the trees."

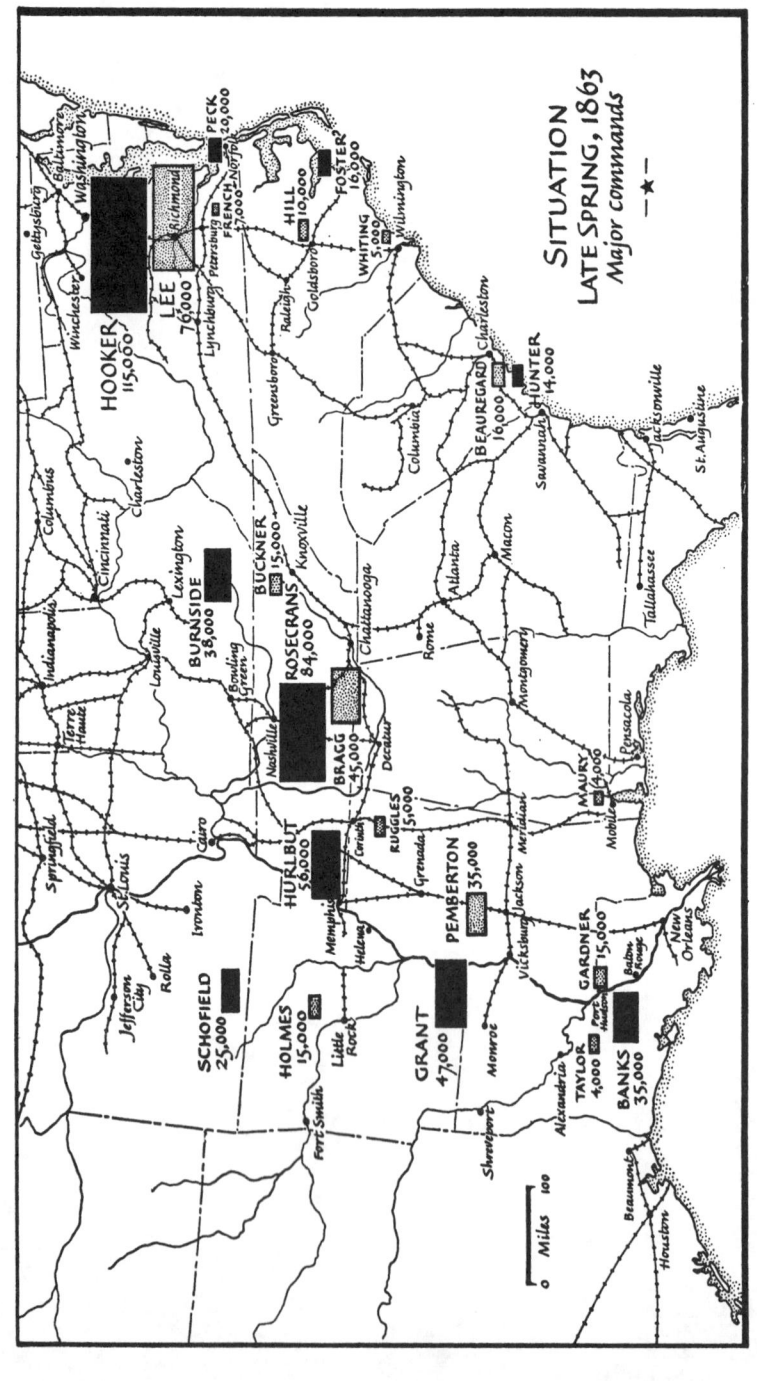

CHAPTER
4

The Beleaguered City

★ ✗ ☆

WHILE HOOKER WAS CROSSING THE RAPPA-
hannock, unaware as yet that he would come to grief within a week, Grant, having caught what he believed was a gleam of victory through the haze of cigar smoke in the former ladies' cabin of the *Magnolia*, was putting the final improvisatorial touches to a plan of campaign that would open, two days later, with a crossing of the greatest river of them all. He too might come to grief, as two of his three chief lieutenants feared and even predicted, but he was willing to risk it for the sake of the prize, which had grown in value with every sore frustration. As spring advanced and the roads emerged from the drowned lands adjacent to the Mississippi — although so far they were little more than trails of slime through the surrounding ooze, not quite firm enough for wagons nor quite wet enough for boats — the Illinois general, with seven failures behind him in the course of the three months he had spent attempting to take or bypass Vicksburg, reverted in early April to what he had told Halleck in mid-January, before he left Memphis to assume command in person of the expedition four hundred miles downriver: "[I] think our troops must get below the city to be used effectively."

His plan, in essence, was to march his army down the Louisiana bank to a position well south of the fortified bluff, then cross the river and establish a bridgehead from which to assail the Confederate bastion from the rear. The Duckport canal, designed to give his transports access to Walnut and Roundaway bayous, and thus allow them to avoid exposure to the plunging fire of the batteries at Vicksburg and Warrenton, had failed; only one small steamer had got through before the water level fell too low for navigation; but exploration of the route had shown that, by bridging those slews that could not be avoided by following the crests of levees flanking the horseshoe curves of the several bayous, it might be practicable to march dry-shod all the way from Milliken's Bend to New Carthage, a west-bank hamlet about midway between Warrenton and Grand Gulf, third of the rebel east-bank strongholds. In late March, by way of preparation, Grant had assigned McClernand the task of putting this route into shape for a march by his own corps as well as the two others, which would follow. This, if it worked, would get the army well south of its objective. Getting the troops across the river was quite another matter, however, depending as it did on the co-operation of the navy, which, as Grant said, "was absolutely essential to the success (even to the contemplation) of such an enterprise." For the navy to get below, in position to ferry the men across and cover the east-bank landing, it would have to run the batteries, and this had been shown in the past to be an expensive proposition even for armored vessels, let alone the brittle-skinned transports which would be required for the ferrying operation. Moreover, Porter was no more under Grant's command than Grant was under Porter's. The most Grant could do was "request" that the run be made. But that was enough, as it turned out.

The admiral — who had returned only the week before from the near-disastrous Steele Bayou expedition, considerably the worse for wear and with his boats still being hammered back into shape — expressed an instant willingness to give the thing a try, though not without first warning of what the consequences would be, not only in the event of initial failure but also in the event of initial success, so far at least as the navy was concerned. He could make a downstream run, he said, and in fact had proved it twice already with the ill-fated *Queen of the West* and the equally ill-fated *Indianola*, but his underpowered vessels could never attempt a slow-motion return trip, against the four-knot current, until Vicksburg had been reduced. "You must recollect that when these gunboats once go below we give up all hopes of ever getting them up again," he replied, wanting it understood from the start that this would be an all-or-nothing venture. Moreover: "If I do send vessels below, it will be the best vessels I have, and there will be nothing left to attack Haines Bluff, in case it should be deemed necessary to try it." Grant replied on April 2 that McClernand's men were already at work on the circuitous thirty-mile road down to New Carthage; he had no intention of turning back, even if that had been possible; and in any case Haines Bluff had cost the army blood enough by now. "I would,

Admiral, therefore renew my request to prepare for running the blockade at as early a day as possible."

Two days later he wrote Halleck: "My expectation is for a portion of the naval fleet to run the batteries of Vicksburg, whilst the army moves through by this new route [to New Carthage]. Once there, I will move either to Warrenton or Grand Gulf; most probably the latter. From either of these points there are good roads to Vicksburg, and from Grand Gulf there is a good road to Jackson and the Black River Bridge without crossing the Black River." Much could be said for making the landing at either place. Warrenton, for example, was some fifteen air-line miles closer to his objective. But he knew well enough that a straight line was not always the surest connection between two military points. A Grand Gulf landing, in addition to giving him access to Vicksburg's main artery of supply, would also afford him a chance to supplement his own. By holding the newly established bridgehead with part of his army and sending the balance downstream to assist in the reduction of Port Hudson by Banks, who presumably was working his way upstream at the same time, he then would have an unbroken, all-weather connection with New Orleans and would no longer be exclusively and precariously dependent on what could be brought down from Memphis, first by steamboat, then by wagon over the new road skirting the westbank complex of bayous across from the fortified bluff, and then again by steamboat in order to get the supplies over the river and into the east-bank bridgehead. Grant pondered the alternatives, and by April 11, a week after the dispatch giving Halleck a brief statement of the problem, he had made his choice: "Grand Gulf is the point at which I expect to strike, and send an army corps to Port Hudson to co-operate with General Banks."

He did not know how Old Brains, whose timidity had been demonstrated in situations far less risky than this one, would react to a plan of campaign that involved 1) exposing the irreplaceable Union fleet to instantaneous destruction by batteries that had been sited on commanding and impregnable heights with just that end in mind, 2) crossing a mile-wide river in order to throw his troops into the immediate rear of a rebel force of unknown strength which, holding as it did the interior lines, presumably could be reinforced more quickly than his own, and 3) remaining dependent all the while, or at least until the problematical capture of Port Hudson, on a supply line that was not only tenuous to the point of inadequacy, but was also subject to being cut by enemy intervention or obliterated by some accident of nature, by no means unusual at this season, such as a week of unrelenting rain, a sudden rise of the river, and a resultant overflow that would re-drown the west-bank lowlands and the improvised road that wound its way around and across the curving bayous and treacherous morasses into which a wagon or a gun could disappear completely, leaving no more trace than a man or a mule whose bones had been picked clean by gars and crawfish. Whether Halleck would approve the taking of all these risks, Grant did not know; but he was left in no such doubt as to the reaction closer at hand. So far, of his three corps commanders, only his archrival McClernand had indicated anything resembling enthusiasm for the plan. Hard at work constructing makeshift bridges from materials found along the designated route to New Carthage, which he reached before mid-April, the former Illinois politician was in high spirits and predicted great results, for both the country and himself, because his corps had been assigned to lead the way. By contrast, though perhaps for the same reason — that is, because the nonprofessional McClernand had the lead — Sherman and McPherson, along with Dana and practically every member of Grant's own staff, considered the proposed operation not only overrisky and unwise, but also downright unmilitary. Sherman in fact was so alarmed at the prospect that he sat down and wrote Grant a long letter, insisting that the proper course would be for the army to return at once to Memphis and resume from there the overland advance along the Mississippi Central, abandoned in December. When his friend and chief replied that he had no intention of canceling his plans, Sherman had no choice except to go along with them, although he still did not approve. "I confess I don't like this roundabout project," he told one of his division commanders, "but we must support Grant in whatever he undertakes." He was loyal and he would remain so, but he also remained glum, writing home even as he ordered his men out of their camps at Milliken's Bend to join the movement: "I feel in its success less confidence than in any similar undertaking of the war."

Porter too had doubts as to the over-all wisdom of Grant's plan, as well as fears in regard to the specific risk the plan required the navy to assume, but he took no counsel of them aside from the more or less normal precautions the prospect of such exposure always prompted, as in the case of a farmer sending eggs to market in a springless wagon over a bumpy road. Unlike Sherman, he wrote no Cassandran letters and made no protest after his initial warning that once the fleet had gone below it could not come back up again until the batteries had been silenced in its rear. Instead, he kept busy preparing his crews and vessels for the passage of bluffs that bristled with 40-odd pieces of artillery, light and heavy, manned by cannoneers whose skill had improved with every chance to show it. By April 16 he was ready. Seven armored gunboats, mounting a total of 79 guns, were assigned to make the run, accompanied by three army transports, loaded with commissary stores instead of troops, and a steam ram captured the year before at Memphis when the Confederate flotilla was abolished in a brief half-morning's fight. At 9.30, two hours after dusk gave way to a starry but moonless night, the column cleared the mouth of the Yazoo, Porter leading aboard the flagship *Benton*.

The "run," so called, was in fact more creep than sprint, however, at least in its early stages; stealth was the watchword up and down the line of eleven boats steaming southward in single file on the dark chocolate surface of what one observer called "the great calm river, more like a long winding lake than a stream." Furnaces had been banked in advance, so as to show a minimum of smoke. All ports were covered and all deck lights doused, except for hooded lanterns visible only from dead astern for guidance. It was hoped that such precautions would hide the column from prying eyes. To reduce the likelihood of noise, which also might give the movement away, low speed was prescribed and exhaust pipes were diverted from the stacks to the paddle boxes, where the hiss of steam would be muffled. Pets and poultry were put ashore, moreover, lest a sudden mewing or cackling alert the rebel sentries. The admiral was leaving as little as possible to chance; but in the event of discovery he was prepared to shift at once from stealth to boldness. Coal-laden barges were lashed to the starboard flanks of the warships, leaving their port-side weapons free to take up any challenge from the high-sited batteries on the Mississippi shore, and water-soaked bales of hay were stacked around the otherwise unprotected boilers and pilothouses of the transports. Instructed to maintain a fifty-yard interval, each helmsman was also told to steer a little to one side of the boat he followed, so as not to have to slow engines or change course to avoid a collision in case of a breakdown up ahead. Thus, though he wanted no trouble he could avoid, Porter was prepared to give as well as receive it in the event that his carefully woven veil of secrecy was ripped away. Passing Young's Point at about 10.30, the dark and silent column swung north as it approached the mouth of Sherman's abandoned canal, then rounded the final turn at 11 sharp, altering course again from north to south, and headed down the straightaway eastern shank of the hairpin bend that led past Vicksburg's dark and silent bluff. Ten minutes later all hell broke loose.

Grant was there to see the show, and he had his two families with him, one military and the other personal, the former consisting of his staff, the latter of his wife and their two sons, who had come downriver from Illinois to afford him a sort of furlough-in-reverse. Both were gathered tonight on the upper deck of the *Magnolia*, which was anchored three miles below Young's Point, just beyond range of the heaviest enemy guns, so that they watched as if from a box in a darkened theater, awaiting the raising of the curtain. The general and Mrs Grant occupied deck chairs near the starboard rail — front row center, as it were — with twelve-year-old Fred beside them; Ulysses Junior, who was ten, sat nearby in young Colonel Wilson's lap. Behind and on both sides of them stood twenty-odd men in uniform, staff officers and two high-ranking observers. One was Dana, who had been sent by Stanton to watch Grant, and the other was no less a personage than Adjutant General Lorenzo Thomas, who had arrived five days ago, five days after Dana, to watch them both. Or so it was said at any rate, so deep was the supposed mistrust the War Department felt. Just now though, whatever truth there was to the rumored assignment, there was a good deal more to watch than the unimpressive-looking department commander. First there was the passage of the hooded and muffled warships, disappearing northward in the direction of the bend that swung them south toward the rebel batteries; then a long wait in the blackness; then, eastward — across the narrow tongue of land called Vicksburg Point, beyond which the dark loom of bluff reared up to blot out the low-hanging stars — a sudden burgeoning incandescence, exposed as if by a rapid lifting of the awaited curtain. The show was on. It began, so to speak, in mid-crescendo as the guns came alive on the bluff and were replied to by those down on the brightly lighted river, growling full-throated, jarring the earth and water for miles around, and adding their muzzle flashes to the vivid illumination of the scene. "Magnificent, but terrible," Grant later called the sight. For the present, however, aside from ordering the younger boy to bed when he heard him whimper and saw him press his face against Wilson's chest in terror at the holocaust of flame and thunder, he said nothing. He merely smoked and watched the fireworks, holding all the while to his wife's hand. After ninety minutes of uproar, during which Dana tallied 525 shots fired by the Confederates, the bluff was once more dark and silent except for the reflection of fires still burning fitfully on the lower level where the boats had been. How much damage had been done and suffered, no one aboard the *Magnolia* could tell, although presently it was clear that some at least of the vessels had got past, for the Warrenton batteries came alive downstream, reproducing in miniature the earlier performance. Finally these too fell silent; which told the watchers exactly nothing, save that the final curtain had come down. Near and far, the fires burned out and the former blackness returned to the bluff and the river.

Unable to wait for word from below — news, perhaps, that the indispensable fleet had gone out of existence — Grant went ashore, got on his horse, and rode south under the paling stars, galloping along the crude and pot-holed road McClernand's corps had spent the past three weeks constructing. This was quite unlike the old Grant, who had never seemed in a hurry about anything at all. Something had come over him, here lately. "None who had known him the previous years could recognize him as being the same man," one officer observed. He had never seen the general ride at even a fast trot, let alone a gallop; but now, he said, "[Grant's] energies seemed to burst forth with new life," with the result that he rode at top speed practically all the time and "seemed wrought up to the last pitch of determination and energy." Shiloh and the long hot unproductive summer of 1862, the ill-wind fiasco near Iuka and the fruitless victory at Corinth, the period of indecision in

Memphis and the recent seven failures above Vicksburg, all were behind him now; he was launched at last on an all-or-nothing effort, a go-for-broke campaign, of which the passage of the batteries by the fleet was the first stage. If this failed, all failed; he would never get his troops across the mile-wide Mississippi. It was no wonder he rode fast.

Near New Carthage about midday he drew rein and breathed a sigh of relief at the sight of the fleet riding at anchor, apparently intact. Closer inspection showed that the boats had been knocked about considerably, however. All were damaged to various degrees, some in their hulls and others in their machinery. One was missing altogether: a transport, as it turned out, set afire by repeated hits and sunk to the accompaniment of cheers from the rebel batteries. But all the rest were seaworthy, or soon would be, after the completion of repairs already under way by bluejackets swarming over their ripped-up decks and pounded bulwarks. Porter and his captains were in excellent spirits, though they were frank to admit that last night's experience had been little short of horrendous. For one thing, all their precautions involving stealth and secrecy had availed them nothing. As they proceeded, dark and silent, down the straightaway eastern shank of the hairpin bend, Confederate sentries posted in skiffs on the river spotted them quickly; whereupon some rowed eastward to give the alarm to the Vicksburg cannoneers, while others, risking capture, crossed to the opposite bank, where they set fire to prepared stacks of pitch-soaked wood, as well as to the abandoned De Soto railroad station midway up the point. Quick-leaping flames floodlighted the approaching Yankee gunboats and the alerted rebel gunners promptly took these well-defined targets under fire. Another difficulty was that the prescribed low speed left the vessels to the mercy of the eddying current, which caught them alternately on the bow and quarter, swinging them broadside to the stream and in some cases even spinning them halfway around, so that they were obliged to come full circle under the plunging fire, as if responding to cruel encores that held them on the brightly lighted stage for further pelting by an irate audience. Clear at last, they played a brief epilogue at Warrenton, then swept on south to anchor above New Carthage in the predawn darkness. Assessing damages, Porter was grateful to discover that, despite a total of 68 hits received, the transport *Henry Clay* was the flotilla's only loss. Not a man had been killed, even aboard the missing boat, and only 13 — in this case a decidedly lucky number — had been wounded. Give him a couple of days in which to complete repairs, he said, and he would be quite ready to co-operate with the army.

Grant returned to Milliken's Bend, much pleased with the outcome, and prepared for another run within the week, this time by transports alone, in order to provide more ferries for the crossing. "If I do not underestimate the enemy," he wrote Halleck on April 21, "my force is abundant, with a foothold once obtained, to do the work." Next night six river steamers, loaded with rations, forage, and medical supplies, attempted the second run under instructions "to drop noiselessly down with the current... and not show steam until the enemy's batteries began firing, when the boats were to use all their legs." This was an all-army show, the steamers being army-owned and manned by army volunteers, since the civilian crews had balked at exposing their persons to what they had watched six nights ago from a safe distance. Now as then, Grant was there to see the show; an Illinois private later told how he "saw standing on the upper deck of his headquarters boat a man of iron, his wife by his side. He seemed to me the most immovable figure I ever saw." Then came the fireworks across the way, the sudden illumination and the uproar of the guns on the fuming bluff. Grant took it calmly, the soldier recalled; "No word escaped his lips, no muscle of his earnest face moved." Presently the batteries fell silent and word arrived from below that, now as before, only a single vessel had failed to survive the run — the steamer *Tigress*, McClernand's former headquarters boat, which Grant had ridden to Shiloh a year ago. Loaded with medicines and surgical equipment, she was hulled a dozen times or more and broke in two and sank, her skeleton crew floating downstream to safety on bits of wreckage. Once more not a man had been killed and the wounded were only a handful. Half the steamers had their engines permanently smashed, but that was no real drawback, since they would hold as many troops as ever and could be pushed or towed across the river as barges. As Grant saw it, this second run had been quite as successful as the first, and he was twice as pleased.

Belittling the loss of the *Tigress* and her cargo, which he said amounted to nothing more than "little extras for the men," he set off southward again on horseback to join Porter for a naval reconnaissance of Grand Gulf, designated as the point where the army would obtain a foothold once the navy had blasted its batteries out of existence. Porter was experiencing misgivings, and Grant, looking the place over from just beyond range of its guns on the 24th, saw that he had indeed given the navy a tough nut to crack. Its batteries were sited high, as at Donelson and Vicksburg, and what was more they seemed altogether ready for whatever came their way. "I foresee great difficulties in our present position," he informed Sherman on his return from the exploratory boat ride, "but it will not do to let these retard any movements." In this connection it seemed to him there might be a chance for an assault to succeed at last up the Yazoo, despite the previous fiasco. "It may possibly happen," he wrote Sherman, "that the enemy may so weaken his forces about Vicksburg and Haines Bluff as to make the latter vulnerable, particularly with a fall of water to give you an extended landing." However: "I leave the management of affairs at your end of the line to you," he added by way of making it clear that he was not definitely ordering an assault.

Monday, April 27, was Grant's forty-first birthday. It also marked the completion of his first-stage preparations for getting his troops across the river in order to come to grips with the rebels on dry ground, which was what he had been after from the start. By now all four divisions of McClernand's corps, having extended their march southward around Bayou Vidal and Lake Saint Joseph, were at Hard Times, Louisiana, the designated point of embarkation for the landing at Grand Gulf, five miles downstream. One of McPherson's divisions was also there and the other two were closing fast, while Sherman's three remained at Young's Point, on call to follow but held in place for the present so as to confuse the lookouts on the Vicksburg bluff. Seven warships and seven transports were available below, and though Porter was still troubled by misgivings — he thought his gunboats could suppress the Grand Gulf batteries, all right, but he warned that they might get so knocked about in the process that they would not be able to provide adequate cover for the crossing that would follow — Grant himself, as usual, expressed no doubt as to the outcome. He foresaw "great difficulties," but he did not admit that they were any occasion for delay. All he asked of the navy was that the rebel guns be silenced, after which there would be no need for cover. Before the anniversary was over, he sent McClernand word to go ahead: "Commence immediately the embarkation of your corps, or so much of it as there is transportation for."

The showdown was unquestionably at hand; but Grant was disclosing nothing he could avoid disclosing until the final moment. He had, in fact, devised three separate feints or demonstrations, two of them designed to mislead the enemy as to his chosen point of attack, well downstream, and a third whereby he hoped not only to distract his opponent by diverting his attention from front to rear, but also to add to his confusion, throughout this critical period, by disrupting the lines of supply and communication leading back into the interior of the state whose welfare and defense were the southern commander's assigned concern.

Sherman was organically involved in two of these, one of which had already been accomplished during the first ten days of April. Lest Pemberton call in the troops disposed to guard against a penetration of the Delta, and thereby strengthen the Vicksburg garrison in time for the showdown fight now imminent, Fred Steele's division was sent a hundred miles up the Mississippi to Greenville, where the men went ashore and thrashed about for a week in the interior, giving the impression that they were merely the advance contingent for another major drive on the Gibraltar of the West. Having done so — to the extreme alarm of the local planters, who bemoaned the attendant loss of cotton, cattle, and Negroes, and the home-guard commanders, who called loudly for reinforcements — they got back aboard their transports and rejoined Sherman at Young's Point for a share in the second and more important feint, this time against Haines Bluff. Grant had suggested it in his letter of the 24th, after a look at the Grand Gulf defenses, but now on his birthday he returned to the matter in more persuasive terms. "The effect of a heavy demonstration in that direction would be good so far as the enemy are concerned," he wrote Sherman from Hard Times, where McClernand's men were preparing to embark, "but I am loth to order it, because it would be hard to make our own troops understand that only a demonstration was intended and our people at home would characterize it as a repulse. I therefore leave it to you whether to make such a demonstration."

In referring thus to the probable adverse reaction by "our people at home," who of course would get their information from the papers, many of which were hostile — particularly toward Sherman, who returned the hostility in full measure — Grant may or may not have intended to use psychology on his journalist-hating friend. But at any rate it worked. "Does General Grant think I care what the newspapers say?" Sherman exclaimed as soon as he read the letter. And despite his growing antipathy for the strategy his superior had evolved ("I tremble for the result," he wrote his wife that week; "I look upon the whole thing as one of the most hazardous and desperate moves of this or any other war") he replied at once with a pledge of full co-operation. "We will make as strong a demonstration as possible," he declared. "The troops will all understand the purpose and not be hurt by the repulse. The people of the country must find out the truth as best they can; it is none of their business. You are engaged in a hazardous enterprise, and for good reason wish to divert attention; that is sufficient for me, and it shall be done." Warming as he wrote, the red-haired general bristled with contempt for public opinion. "The men have sense, and will trust us. As to the reports in newspapers, we must scorn them, else they will ruin us and our country. They are as much enemies to good government as the secesh, and between the two I like the secesh best, because they are a brave, open enemy and not a set of sneaking, croaking scoundrels."

Accordingly, he spent the next two days in preparation, and on the final day of April — previously designated by Lincoln, at the request of Congress, "as a day of national humiliation, fasting, and prayer" because, in the words of the proclamation, the people had "forgotten God" and become "too proud to pray" — set off up the Yazoo with ten regiments from Frank Blair's division, escorted by the flotilla remnant Porter had left behind, three gunboats, four tinclads, and three mortars, under Lieutenant Commander K. R. Breese. Intent on making the greatest possible show of strength, Sherman spread his troops over the transport decks with orders for "every man [to] look as numerous as possible." Short of Haines Bluff and near the scene of their December repulse, the bluecoats went ashore; marching and countermarching, banners flying and bands playing for all they were worth in the boggy woodland, they demonstrated in sight of the fortified line of hills, while the gunboats closed to within point-blank range of the bluff itself. For three hours the naval attack was pressed, as if in preparation for an infantry assault. However, the defenders clearly had their backs up; nor was there anything wrong with their marksmanship. The overaged *Tyler*, a veteran of all the fights since Henry, retired early with a shot below the water line, and the other two hauled off at 2 p.m. roughly handled, one having taken a total of forty-six hits. Sherman might have let it go at that, but he was determined to play out the game to full advantage. May Day morning he wrote Grant: "At 3 p.m. we will open another cannonade to prolong the diversion, and keep it up till after dark, when we shall drop down to Chickasaw and go on back to camp." The other two divisions, waiting at Young's Point under Steele and Brigadier General James M. Tuttle, were alerted for the long march to Hard Times, while Blair was told to keep up the pretense of attack until darkness afforded cover for withdrawal, at which time he would "let out for home," meaning Milliken's Bend, where he was to shield the rear of the two divisions moving southward to join Grant. Meanwhile, Sherman told him, "I will hammer away this p.m. because Major Rowley, [a staff observer] now here, says that our diversion has had perfect success, great activity being seen in Vicksburg, and troops pushing up this way. By prolonging the effort, we give Grant more chance." The infantry continued to mass as if for attack, and the gunboats moved again within range of Haines Bluff, keeping up the action until 8 o'clock that evening. Then Blair's men got back aboard their transports and withdrew, returning to the west bank of the Mississippi, followed by the somewhat battered but undaunted ten-boat flotilla, which dropped anchor off the mouth of the Yazoo. Steele and Tuttle took up the march for Hard Times at first light next morning, accompanied by Sherman himself, who sent a courier ahead with a full account of the two-day affair. Casualties had been negligible, he reported, afloat and ashore. Whether matters had gone as well for Grant, far downriver at Grand Gulf, he did not know; but he was satisfied that the feint from above had held a considerable portion of the Vicksburg garrison in position north of the city, away from the simultaneous main effort to the south. "We will be there as soon as possible," he assured his friend and superior.

Such were the first two of the three diversions intended to confuse and distract the Confederate defenders in the course of this highly critical span of time during which Grant was preparing to launch, and indeed was launching, his main effort a good forty miles downriver from the bluff that was his goal. Though both appeared to have exceeded strategic expectations, the third, while altogether different in scope and composition, was even more successful, and in fact was referred to afterwards by Sherman, who had no direct connection with the venture, as nothing less than "the most brilliant expedition of the war." Grant was as usual more restrained in judgment, qualifying his praise by calling the exploit "one of the most brilliant," but he added that it would "be handed down in history as an example to be imitated."

In point of fact, it was itself an imitation. For two years now, in the West as in the East, the Federal cavalry had suffered from a well-founded inferiority complex; Stuart and Morgan and Forrest had quite literally ridden rings around the awkward blue squadrons and the armies in their charge. Now, perhaps, the time had come for them to emulate the example set by the exuberant gray riders. Hooker thought so, in Virginia, and so did Grant in Mississippi. Back in February he had suggested to Hurlbut, commanding in Memphis, that a cavalry force, "with about 500 picked men, might succeed in making [its] way south and cut the railroad east of Jackson, Miss. The undertaking would be a hazardous one," he added, "but would pay well if carried out. I do not direct that this shall be done, but leave it for a volunteer enterprise." A month later, in mid-March, his instructions were more specific. The conception had been enlarged, tripling the strength of the force to be employed, and the volunteer provision had been removed. Hurlbut was to have all "the available cavalry put in as good condition as possible in the next few weeks for heavy service.... The date when the expedition should start will depend upon movements here. You will be informed of the exact time for them to start." In early April the date was set and a leader chosen: Colonel Benjamin H. Grierson, of Grant's home state of Illinois. Hurlbut saw to it that the raiders got away on schedule, April 17, riding south out of La Grange, forty miles east of Memphis, into the dawn that saw Porter's battered gunboats drop anchor near New Carthage after their fiery run past the Vicksburg bluff. "God speed him," Hurlbut said of Grierson, who led the 1700-man column in the direction of the Mississippi line, "for he has started gallantly on a long and perilous ride. I shall anxiously await intelligence of the result."

The wait would necessarily be a long one. Before the raid was over, the blue riders would have covered more than six hundred miles of road and swamp, through hostile territory. At the outset, however, none of the troopers in the three regiments, two from Illinois and one from Iowa, nor of the cannoneers in the attached six-gun battery of 2-pounders, suspected that the warning order, "Oats in the nosebag and five days rations in haversacks, the rations to last ten days," was prelude to so deep a penetration. "We are going on a big scout to Columbus, Mississippi, and play smash with the railroads," one predicted. Only Grierson himself, riding at the head of the column, knew that the true objective was Pemberton's main supply line, the Southern Railroad east of Jackson, connecting Vicksburg with Meridian and thence with Mobile and the arsenals in Georgia and the East. Pennsylvania-born and just short of thirty-seven years of age, with a spade beard and an acquired mistrust of horses dating back to a kick received from a pony in childhood, which smashed one of his cheekbones, split his forehead, and left him scarred for life — he had protested his assignment to the cavalry in the first place, though to no avail; Halleck, who made the appointment, insisted that he looked "active and wiry enough to make a good cavalryman" — Grierson eighteen months ago had been a music teacher and bandmaster at Jacksonville, Illinois, but all that was left to remind him or anyone else of that now was a jew's-harp he carried inside his blouse, along with a pocket compass and a small-scale map of the region he and his men would be traversing in the course of their strike at the railroad some two hundred air-line miles away. Riding where no bluecoat had ever been before, he could expect to be surrounded en route by small bodies of home guardsmen, who would outnumber him badly if they were consolidated, as well as by sizable detachments of regulars, horse and foot, which Pemberton would certainly send to oppose him, front and rear, once his presence and intention became known. Even if he succeeded in his mission — that is, reached and wrecked an appreciable stretch of the railroad between Jackson and Meridian, temporarily severing the one connection by which reinforcements could reach Vicksburg swiftly from outside Mississippi — he would then be deep in the heart of a land where every man's hand would be raised against him. One suggestion, included in his orders, was that he return to Tennessee by swinging east, then north through Alabama; another was that he plunge on south and west for a hookup with Grant in the vicinity of Grand Gulf, anticipating a successful crossing by McClernand and McPherson at that point, or else take sanctuary within Banks's outpost lines at Baton Rouge, which would give him about as far to go from the railroad south as he would have come already in order to reach it. In any case, whatever escape plan he adopted as a result of the unfolding course of events, the tactical requisites were vigilance, speed, boldness, and deception. Without any one of these four, he and his troopers, in the cavalry slang of the time, would be "gone up."

Across the Mississippi line by sunup, they made thirty miles the first day — a good average march for cavalry, though Grant himself covered nearly as great a distance before noon, galloping south from Milliken's Bend to check on the condition of Porter's gunboats at New Carthage — and called a halt that night just short of Ripley, which they passed through next morning, brushing aside the few startled gray militia they encountered, to camp beyond New Albany at sundown. On the third day, April 19, they continued due south through Pontotoc. Eighty miles from base, with rebel detachments no doubt alerted in his front and rear, Grierson began his fourth day with an inspection, culled out 175 victims of dysentery, chills and fever, and saddle galls — "the Quinine Brigade," the rejected troopers promptly dubbed themselves — and sent them back, under a staff major, with one of the 2-pounders and instructions to "pass through Pontotoc in the night, marching by fours, obliterating our tracks, and producing the impression that we have all returned." He himself continued south with the main body, to Houston and beyond. Deciding to throw a still larger tub to the Confederate whale, he detached Colonel Edward Hatch's regiment of Iowans next morning, along with another of the guns, and gave its commander orders to strike eastward for the Mobile & Ohio, inflicting what damage he could to that vital supply line before heading north in the wake of the Quinine Brigade, thus spreading the scare and increasing the impression that all the raiders were returning. Hatch, a transplanted New Englander hungry for fame and advancement — tomorrow would be his thirty-second birthday — now began a five-day adventure on his own. Though he did not succeed in breaking the well-guarded railroad to the east, he fought two severe skirmishes — one at the outset, a delaying action which allowed Grierson to get away southward, the other near the finish, which allowed his own getaway northward — burned several cotton-stocked warehouses in Okolona, and succeeded handsomely in his primary mission of drawing most of the North Mississippi home guardsmen pell-mell after him and away from Grierson. At a cost of ten men lost en route, he reported that he had inflicted ten times as many casualties on the enemy and "accumulated 600 head of horses and mules, with about 200 able-bodied negroes to lead them." Returning to La Grange on Sunday morning, April 26, he brought Hurlbut the first substantial news of the raiders' progress since their departure, nine days back.

    The unavailable news was a good deal better; Grierson by then had not only reached his objective, he was already forty hours beyond it, having formulated and put into execution his tactics for escape. Relieved of the threat to his rear on the 21st by Hatch's decoy action south of Houston, he and his 1000 troopers — all Illinoisans now, including the fifty cannoneers with the four remaining guns — rode on past Starkville, where he detached one company for a strike at Macon, twenty-odd miles southeast on the M&O, then took up the march at dawn and cleared Louisville by sundown. Beyond Philadelphia on the 23d he called a halt at nightfall, and made an early start next morning in order to reach the Southern Railroad before noon. Preceded by scouts who seized the telegraph office and thus kept the alarm from being spread — "Butternut Guerillas," these outriders called themselves, for they wore Confederate uniforms, risking hanging for the advantage gained — the raiders burst into Newton Station, a trackside hamlet twenty-five miles west of Meridian and about twice as far east of Jackson, where they at once got down to the work for which they had ridden all this way. Two locomotives were captured and wrecked, along with three dozen freight cars loaded with ordnance and commissary supplies, including artillery ammunition on consignment for Vicksburg, which afforded a rackety fire-

The Beleaguered City

works display when set aflame. Meantime other details were ripping up miles of track and crossties, burning trestles and bridges, tearing down telegraph wires all the way to the Chunky River, and setting fire to a government building stocked with 500 small arms and a quantity of new gray uniforms. By 2 o'clock the destruction was complete; Grierson had his bugler sound the rally to assemble the smoke-grimed raiders, some of whom were showing the effects of rebel whiskey they had "rescued" from the flames, then took his accustomed post at the head of the column and led them away from the charred and smoldering evidence of their efficiency as wreckers. Now as before, the march was south. They did not bivouac till near midnight, having covered a good fifty miles of road despite the arduous delay at Newton Station. Next day, April 25, was the easiest of the raid, however, since the blue raiders spent most of it on a plantation in the piny highlands just short of the Leaf River valley, resting their mounts, gorging themselves on smokehouse ham, and presumably nursing their hangovers. Sunday followed, and while

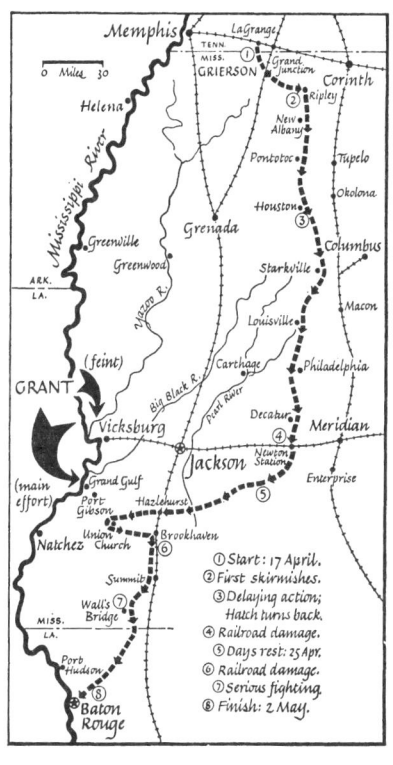

Hatch was riding into La Grange at the end of his five-day excursion through North Mississippi, the raiders turned west. In time, according to Grierson's calculations, this would bring them either to Grand Gulf, in case Grant had effected a crossing as planned, or to Natchez, which had been under intermittent Federal occupation for nearly a year.

Either place would afford refuge for his saddle-weary troopers if all went as he hoped and planned, but he knew well enough that the most dangerous part of the long ride lay before him. By now, doubtless, every grayback in the state would have learned of the presence of his two regiments at Newton Station two days ago, with the result that a considerable number of them must be hot on his trail or lying in wait for him in all directions. However, this had its compensations as well as its drawbacks. Scarcely less important than the temporary severing of Vicksburg's main supply line was the disruption of its defenses, preventing the hasty concentration of its outlying forces against Grant in the early stages of his river crossing. In point of fact, Grierson was more successful in this regard than he had any way of knowing. Orders flew thick and fast from Pemberton's headquarters in the Mississippi capital, directing all units within possible reach to concentrate on the capture of the ubiquitous blue column. An infantry brigade, en route from Alabama to reinforce Vicksburg, was halted at Meridian to protect that vital intersection of the Southern Railroad and the Mobile & Ohio, while another moved east from Jackson in the direction of the break at Newton Station. Forces at Panola and Canton, under James Chalmers and Lloyd Tilghman, were shifted to Okolona and Carthage to block the northern escape route. All of these troops, amounting to no less than a full division, not counting the various home-guard units caught up in the swirl, were thus effectively taken out of the play and removed from possible use at this critical time against either Grant or Grierson, who were off in the opposite corner of the map. Not that Pemberton was neglecting matters in that direction, at least so far as Grierson was concerned. Detachments of fast-riding cavalry were ordered eastward from Port Hudson and Port Gibson — the latter a scant half dozen miles from Grant's intended point of landing at Grand Gulf — in case the marauders tried for a getaway to the south or the southwest. In short, Pemberton's reaction to the widespread confusion in his rear and along his lines of supply and communication, while altogether commendable from a limited point of view, amounted to full co-operation with the raiders in the accomplishment of their secondary mission, which was to divert his attention, as well as his reserves, away from the point at which Grant was preparing to hurl two thirds of the blue army.

Grierson wasted no time. Monday, April 27 — Grant's birthday; Sherman prepared for his feint up the Yazoo, and McClernand was told to get his troops aboard the transports at Hard Times — the blue riders pushed westward across Pearl River, aided considerably by the capture of a ferryboat by scouts who masqueraded as Confederates. While the crossing was in progress the company detached five days ago near Starkville rejoined the main body, reporting that in addition to throwing a scare into the defenders of Macon, as instructed, it had also made a feint at Enterprise, twelve miles below Meridian, thus adding to the difficulties of the rebel high command's attempt to pinpoint the location of the invaders. Safely across the Pearl, the reunited 1000-man column pressed on west to Hazlehurst, where a string of boxcars was set afire on a siding of the New Orleans, Jackson & Great Northern Railroad. Flames spreading to a nearby block of buildings, the erstwhile incendiaries turned firemen and worked side by side with the citizens in preventing the loss of the whole town. At dusk, in a driving rain which had helped to contain the fire, the colonel ordered his troopers to remount. The march was west; Grand Gulf was only forty miles away and he hoped to make it there tomorrow, in case Grant had crossed the Mississippi. However, morning brought no indication that any part of the Army of the Tennessee was on this side of the river, so Grierson veered a bit to the south for Natchez, his alternate sanctuary, which was only twenty miles farther away than Grand Gulf. But that too was not to be. Beyond Union Church that afternoon, the raiders were enjoying a rest halt when they were charged by what one of them called "a crowd of graylooking horsemen galloping and shooting in a cloud of dust and smoke." The result at first was panic and the beginning of a rout, but presently they stiffened and repulsed the attackers, who turned out to be nothing more than a couple of understrength companies on the prowl. The colonel prepared to push on next day to Natchez, but was warned that night by one of the Butternut Guerillas, who had ridden ahead and struck up a conversation with a rebel outpost group, that seven companies of cavalry from Grand Gulf were planning to ambush him when he moved westward in the morning. So Grierson once more changed his plans, abandoning Natchez as his destination. Determined now to press on down to Baton Rouge, though this added another hundred miles to the distance his weary men would have to ride, he turned back east at dawn of April 29, avoiding the ambush laid so carefully in what was now his rear.

By early afternoon they were in Brookhaven, twenty-five miles east, astride the railroad they had crossed two days ago, twenty miles to the north, when the march was west. "There was much running and yelling" on the part of the startled citizens, Grierson later reported, "but it soon quieted into almost a welcome." Here, as at Hazlehurst on Monday, sparks from the burning railroad station and another string of boxcars set a section of the town ablaze, and the troopers once more turned firemen to help the natives keep the flames from spreading. Meantime, however, a wrecking crew kept busy tearing up track and burning crossties, thus abolishing the possibility of a locomotive pursuit by troops from Jackson. Back in the saddle, the raiders moved south along the railroad and made camp that night, eight miles below Brookhaven and just over a hundred miles from Baton Rouge. At Summit before sundown of the last day of April, the colonel spared the depot lest his men have to turn firefighters again to save the town, but there was another unfortunate — or fortunate, depending on the point of view — encounter with rebel spirits when the troopers uncovered a cache of rum in fifty-gallon barrels. Grierson broke up the binge, got the revelers mounted at last, drunk or sober, and pressed on south another half dozen miles before stopping for the night. Dawn of May Day completed two full weeks the men had spent in the saddle, with only a half day's rest aside from the minimal halts for sleep and food. Once more the march was west. "A straight line for Baton Rouge, and let speed be our safety," Grierson told his officers as the column was put in motion.

Speed there was — the raiders covered no less than seventy-five miles of road in the following twenty-eight hours — but there was fighting, too, the first and only serious opposition the main body encountered in the course of the long raid. Even so, it was not much. At Wall's Bridge, which spanned the Tickfaw River just north of the Louisiana line, three companies of Confederates from Port Hudson laid a noonday ambush that cost the leading Union company eight casualties. Grierson promptly brought his artillery to the front, shelled the opposite bank, and ordered a charge that not only cleared the bridge but threw the rebels into headlong flight. Riding south all night, with no time out for rest or food, the blue column reached and crossed the Amite River, the last unfordable stream this side of Baton Rouge, before the aroused graybacks could bar the way. Six miles short of the Louisiana capital next morning, his troopers reeling in their saddles from lack of sleep, Grierson called a halt at last. The men tumbled from their mounts and slept where they fell, along the roadside, but the colonel himself, as befitted a former music teacher with an ingrained mistrust of horses, was refreshing himself by playing the piano in the parlor of a nearby plantation house when a picket burst in with news that they were about to be overwhelmed and captured. A rebel force was approaching from the west, he said, with skirmishers out! Grierson, knowing better, rode out to meet the reported enemy, who turned out to be members of the garrison at Baton Rouge, sent to investigate an improbable-sounding rumor "that a brigade of cavalry from General Grant's army had cut their way through the heart of the rebel country, and were then only five miles outside the city." Somewhat restored by their naps, the men remounted and rode into the capital that afternoon. Cheered by spectators, civilians as well as soldiers, the two-mile-long procession of road-worn men and animals, so weathered and dust-caked that they could scarcely be distinguished from the prisoners and Negroes they had gathered along the way, wound slowly around the public square, then south out of town to a grove of magnolias two miles south, where they dismounted, unsaddled, and fell so soundly asleep that they could not be aroused to accept hot coffee.

They had cause for weariness, having covered more than six hundred miles in less than sixteen days, and for thankfulness as well: thankfulness that Pemberton had lost Van Dorn to Bragg three months before, along with nearly all his cavalry, and that it was Abel Streight and not themselves who had been made the prime concern of Bedford Forrest. Streight had left Fort Henry on the day they left La Grange, and was surrendering in East Alabama while Grierson's men, having caught up on their sleep at last, were enjoying their first midday meal in the magnolia grove just south of the Louisiana capital. Different circumstances might well have led to different results, including perhaps a reversal of their current roles as prisoners on the one hand and heroes on the other, but the fact remained that the Illinois troopers had dealt with conditions as they found them. And having done so, they had cause for pride. At a total cost of barely two dozen casualties — "3 killed, 7 wounded, 5 left on the route sick ... and 9 men missing, supposed to have straggled" — they had "killed and wounded about one hundred of the enemy, captured and paroled over 500 prisoners, many of them officers, destroyed between fifty and sixty miles of railroad and telegraph, captured and destroyed over 3000 stand of arms, and other army stores and government property to an immense amount." So Grierson later reported, adding as if by afterthought, despite his continued mistrust of all equine creatures: "We also captured 1000 horses and mules."

Within three days the colonel was on a steamboat for New Orleans, where he was feted and presented with a horse by the admiring citizenry. "My dear Alice," he wrote his wife that night, "I like Byron have had to wake up one morning and find myself famous. Since I have been here it has been one continuous ovation." In early June, with his picture on the covers of both *Harper's Weekly* and *Leslie's Illustrated*, he was promoted to brigadier general. But perhaps the finest tribute of all came from a man by no means given to using superlatives, on or off the record. Assessing the value of the raid in its relation to the over-all campaign for the taking of Vicksburg, of which it was very much a part, Grant said flatly: "It was Grierson who first set the example of what might be done in the interior of the enemy's country without any base from which to draw supplies."

For the present, however, Grant at Hard Times had no more knowledge of Grierson's progress, across the way, than Grierson had had of Grant's while riding west from Hazlehurst. All the cavalryman learned for certain as he pressed on toward the river was that the army had not crossed as planned, which meant that something must have gone awry. Something had indeed. When the raiders turned back east from Union Church at dawn of April 29, avoiding the ambush laid in what had been their front, they missed hearing the guns of the attackers and defenders at Grand Gulf, less than thirty air-line miles away. It was just as well, for otherwise they might have been lured into what would have been a trap. Except for the rather negative advantage of proving that this was no place to attempt an east-bank landing, the attack was an utter failure, and an expensive one at that.

Porter's doubts had been increasing all week, ever since his April 22 reconnaissance of the stronghold on the bluff across the way. Though he had kept up a show of confidence in his talks with Grant, privately he was airing his misgivings in dispatches to his Washington superiors, not only by way of preparing them for bad news, but also by way of divesting himself in advance of any responsibility for the failure he saw looming. "I am quite depressed with this adventure," he wrote Fox, "which as you know never met with my approval." This last was something less than strictly true, though when he signaled the flotilla captains to move against Grand Gulf at 8 o'clock next morning, April 29, his forebodings soon turned out to have been well founded. The navy's task was to silence the rebel batteries, then cover the crossing by the transports bringing the army over to take the place by storm; but when four of the seven ironclads closed to within pistol shot of the 75-foot bluff — so at least it seemed to Grant, who watched the contest from aboard a tug — they were severely mauled. The flagship *Benton* took 70 hits, the *Tuscumbia* 81; the *Lafayette* took 45, the *Pittsburg* 35. The other three boats, *Carondelet, Mound City,* and *Louisville,* all veterans of the river war from its beginning, did their fighting at long range, lobbing shells into the blufftop works, and consequently suffered little damage. Even so, when Porter hoisted the pennant for the flotilla to drop back out of action at 12.30 — all but the *Tuscumbia,* which had been struck in her machinery and swept powerless downstream until she fetched up short against the Louisiana bank — a total of 75 casualties, including 18 dead, had been subtracted from its crews. By contrast, although time would disclose that they had lost 3 killed and 15 wounded, the defenders seemed unhurt behind their earthwork fortifications. Grand Gulf was as much a failure for the Union navy as Fort Donelson had been, just over a year ago. Porter frankly admitted as much. A crossing might be managed elsewhere, he told Grant, but not here, under the muzzles of those guns across the way.

Grant had not expected a repulse, but he was prepared for what he considered the outside chance of one. Now that a repulse had been encountered, an alternate plan was put into execution without delay. McClernand's men would debark at Hard Times, march south across the point of land to De Shroon's, a plantation landing some four miles downstream, and be ready before dawn to get back aboard the transports, which were to steal past Grand Gulf under cover of darkness, hugging the western bank while the gunboats re-engaged the batteries. All this went as planned, afloat and ashore. The navy lost only one man in its renewal of the duel with the blufftop cannoneers, and the army made its night march unobserved, to find the transports waiting unscathed in the predawn darkness at De Shroon's. "By the time it was light," Grant later wrote, "the enemy saw our whole fleet, ironclads, gunboats, river steamers, and barges, quietly moving down the river three miles below them, black, or rather blue, with National troops."

Accomplishing this he showed the flexibility that would characterize his planning throughout the various stages of the campaign which now was under way in earnest. Other characteristics he also showed. An officer was to remember seeing the general sitting his horse beside the road at a point where a narrow bridge had been thrown across a bog. "Push right along, men," he told the marchers, speaking in almost a conversational tone. "Close up fast and hurry over." The soldiers recognized him and were obviously pleased to see their commander sharing their exertions, but the officer noted that their only reply was to do as he directed. They did not cheer him; they just "hurried over." It was as if, in the course of the long winter of repeated failures, they had caught his quality of quiet confidence. Charles Dana, for one, had begun to think so. He had come down here three weeks ago to report on Grant's alleged bad habits. So far, though, he not only had detected none of these; he had never even heard him curse or seen him lose his temper. Dana was puzzled. "His equanimity was becoming a curious spectacle to me," the former journalist later recalled. Tonight, for example, riding beside the general along the dark road from Hard Times to De Shroon's, he saw Grant's horse stumble. "Now he will swear," he thought, half expecting to see the rider go tumbling over the animal's head; "For an instant his moral status was on trial." But Grant lost neither his balance nor his temper. "Pulling up his horse, he rode on, and, to my utter amazement, without a word or sign of impatience."

Nor did the night march across the point of land, from Hard Times to De Shroon's, put an end to the need for sudden improvisation. Having bypassed Grand Gulf — which he could not allow to remain alive for long, so close in his rear — Grant still was faced with the problem of where to effect a landing on the Mississippi bank, in order to return for a strike at the fortified bluff from its vulnerable landward flank. A look at the map suggested Rodney, another twelve miles downstream. But that would not only give the troops a considerable distance to march, and the defenders time to improve their position and call in reinforcements, it would also place the bluecoats on the far side of Bayou Pierre, which would have to be crossed when they turned back north. Yet to make a landing short of the point where the bayou flowed westward into the river, five miles below, might be to founder the army in some unmapped and unsuspected swamp. What was needed was a guide, a sympathetic native of the region, and Grant sent a detachment of soldiers across the river in a skiff, with instructions to bring back what he wanted. They returned before midnight with an east-bank slave who filled the bill. At first he had been unwilling to come, and in fact had had to be taken by force, but now that he found himself in the lamp-lighted headquarters tent, facing the Union commander across an unrolled chart, he turned co-operative. "Look here," Grant said. "Tell me where this road leads to — starting where you see my finger here on the map and running down that way." The Negro studied the problem, then shook his head. "That road fetches up at Bayou Pierre," he said. "But you can't go that way, 'cause it's plum full of backwater." The thing to do, he replied to further questions, was to go ashore at Bruinsburg, six miles below De Shroon's. This would still be south of Bayou Pierre, but at least it was only half as far as Rodney. Moreover, there was a good road leading from there to Grand Gulf by way of Port Gibson, which lay ten miles inland, well back from the trackless swamps and canebrakes of the river bottoms. At Bruinsburg, the captive slave explained, "you can leave the boats and the men can walk on high ground all the way. The best houses and plantations in all the country are there, sir, all along that road."

So Bruinsburg it was. By midmorning of this last day of April — while Sherman was launching his demonstration against Haines Bluff, fifty air-line miles to the north, and Grierson was pressing southward along the railroad below Brookhaven, the same distance to the east — all four of McClernand's divisions and one of McPherson's, some 23,000 men in all, had completed their debarkation and were slogging inland toward Port Gibson. "When this was effected," Grant declared years later, "I felt a degree of relief scarcely ever equaled since." Then he told why. "I was now in the enemy's country, with a vast river and the stronghold of Vicksburg between me and my base of supplies. But I was on dry ground on the same side of the river with the enemy. All the campaigns, labors, hardships, and exposures from the month of December previous to this time that had been made and endured were for the accomplishment of this one object."

※ 2 ※

For all his northern birth and starchy manner, which some continued to find personally distasteful, Pemberton by now had either sustained or won the confidence not only of his military superiors but also of the people of Mississippi, who came within his charge. His four-month sequence of successes in the face of threats from all points of the compass far outweighed their original prejudice against him. On May Day, for example — unaware that Sherman was knocking at Vicksburg's upper gate or that Grant, with half his army over the river, already was marching inland from below — an editor in the capital, where the department commander had his headquarters, was taking a sanguine view of the situation. "It would be idle to say that our state and country was not in a position of great peril," he declared. "Yet, strange as it may seem to our readers, we have never felt more secure since the fall of Donelson. The enemy will never reach Jackson; we are satisfied of that.... General Pemberton, assisted by vigilant and accomplished officers, is watching the movements of the enemy, and at the proper time will pounce upon him. Let us give the authorities all the assistance we can, and trust their superior and more experienced judgment as to the management of the armies. We know we have a force sufficient, if properly handled, not only to defeat but to rout and annihilate Grant if he ventures far from his river base." As for doubts as to the proper handling of this sufficient force: "Let any man who questions the ability of General Pemberton only think for a moment of the condition the department was in when he was first sent here. No general has evinced a more sleepless vigilance in the discharge of his duty, or accomplished more solid and gratifying results." Nor was this merely the opinion of one uninformed civilian. With reservations, Joe Johnston shared his view. Despite the gloom into which his inspection of the Vicksburg defenses had thrown him, back in December, the Virginian since had warmed to the Pennsylvanian as a result of his apparent skill in fending off the combinations designed for his destruction. In mid-March, reviewing the situation from three hundred miles away in Tennessee, he congratulated him handsomely. "Your activity and vigor in the defense of Mississippi must have secured for you the confidence of the people of Mississippi," he wrote, and added: "I have no apprehension for Port Hudson from Banks. The only fear is that the canal may enable Grant to unite their forces. I believe your arrangements at Vicksburg make it perfectly safe, unless that union should be effected."

Applause was one thing, assistance quite another: as Pemberton soon found out. Despite the denial of help from the vast department across the river, and despite the January transfer of three quarters of his cavalry to Middle Tennessee, he was so encouraged by the flooding of Grant's canal in March that he mistook the subsequent withdrawal of the diggers to Milliken's Bend for an abandonment by the Federals of their entire campaign. On April 11 he notified Johnston that the canal was no longer a danger, that Grant appeared to be pulling back to Memphis, and that he was therefore sending, as requested, a brigade to reinforce Bragg at Tullahoma. Five days later, however, with the blue army still in evidence on the opposite bank and Porter's gunboats preparing for their run past the batteries that night, he recalled the detached brigade, which by then was in northern Mississippi. "[Grant's] movement up the river was a ruse," he wired Johnston. "Certainly no more troops should leave this department." In fact, he said, it was he who stood in gravest need of help. Nothing came of that. Then on April 20, with Porter's ironclads riding at anchor near New Carthage, McClernand moving farther down the Louisiana bank, and Grierson on the rampage east of Grenada — "part and parcel of the formidable invasion preparing before my eyes" — Pemberton stepped up his plea for reinforcements: especially for the return of his 6000 troopers under Van Dorn, the loss of whom had left him three-fourths blind. "Heavy raids are making from Tennessee deep into this state," he warned. "Cavalry is indispensable to meet these expeditions. The little I have is ... totally inadequate. Could you not make a demonstration with a cavalry force on their rear?" He protested that he had "literally no cavalry from Grand Gulf to Yazoo City, while the enemy is threatening to [cross] the river between Vicksburg and Grand Gulf, having now twelve vessels below the former place." Johnston, obliged as he presently was to send Forrest to Alabama after Streight, not only would not agree to make a demonstration against West Tennessee; he also declined to lessen the strength of Bragg's mounted arm, which included Wheeler and Morgan as well as Forrest and Van Dorn, despite the fact that Van Dorn was nominally on loan from Pemberton. It turned out, moreover, that the Pennsylvanian's previous successes worked against him now. Matters had seemed as dark several times before, in the course of the past four months, and he had managed to survive without assistance; apparently Johnston believed he would do as well again. At any rate he was still of his former opinion: "Van Dorn's cavalry is absolutely necessary to enable General Bragg to hold the best part of the country from which he draws supplies."

In effect this amounted to signing Van Dorn's death warrant, since it kept him within range of the Tennessee doctor's wife and her husband's pistol. Pemberton was inclined to think that in the end it might amount to much the same thing for Vicksburg, which Jefferson Davis referred to as "the nailhead that held the South's two halves together." For suddenly now the news grew more alarming. Two nights later, April 22, five unarmored steamboats ran the batteries, obviously to provide the means for a crossing, somewhere below, by the bluecoats slogging down the western bank. Throughout the week that followed, Pemberton sent what little cavalry he had in pursuit of Grierson, whose raiders were disrupting the interior of the state and playing havoc with his lines of supply and communication. Then on April 29 word came from Brigadier General John S. Bowen, commanding at Grand Gulf, that the place was under heavy attack by gunboats attempting to soften him up for an assault by infantry waiting in transports across the river at Hard Times. Scarcely had the news arrived next morning that the ironclads had retired, severely battered, than Pemberton was notified that Haines Bluff was under similar pressure to the north. By the time he learned that this too had been beaten off, a follow-up message from Bowen informed him that the Union fleet had slipped past Grand Gulf in the darkness, transports and all, and was unloading soldiers in large numbers at Bruinsburg, ten miles below. Then came word that the Federals had resumed their pounding of Haines Bluff. Deciding that the downriver threat was the graver of the two, Pemberton resolved to reinforce Bowen, whom he instructed to contest the blue advance on Port Gibson.

On May Day, with the issue still in doubt below — so he thought, though it could scarcely be in doubt for long; the enemy strength was reported at 20,000 men, while Bowen had considerably less than half that many — he appealed once more to Johnston for assistance, bolstering his plea with a wire directly to the President. Davis replied that, in addition to urging Johnston to send help from Tennessee, he was doing all he could to forward troops from southern Alabama. Secretary Seddon, alerted to the danger, informed Pemberton that "heavy reinforcements" would start at once by rail from Beauregard in Charleston. Both messages were gratifying, communicating assurance of assistance from above. But all the harassed Vicksburg commander got from Johnston was advice. "If Grant's army lands on this side of the river," the Virginian replied from Tullahoma, "the safety of Mississippi depends on beating it. For that object you should unite your whole force."

A Georgia-born West Pointer, Bowen had left the old army after a single hitch as a lieutenant and had prospered as a St Louis architect before he was thirty, at which age he offered his sword to the newly formed Confederacy. Promoted to brigadier within ten months, he now was thirty-two and eager for further advancement, having spent more than a year in grade because of a long convalescence from a wound taken at Shiloh, where he led his brigade of Missourians with distinction. On the afternoon of April 30, marching his 5500 soldiers out of Grand Gulf and across Bayou Pierre to meet Grant's 23,000 moving inland from Bruinsburg after their downriver creep past his blufftop guns in the darkness, he carried proudly in his pocket a dispatch received last night from Pemberton, congratulating him on the repulse of Porter's ironclads: "In the name of the army, I desire to thank you and your troops for your gallant conduct today. Keep up the good work.... Yesterday I warmly recommended you for a major-generalcy. I shall renew it." Bowen had it very much in mind to keep up the good work. Despite the looming four-to-one odds and the changed nature of his task now that he and the blue invaders were on the same bank of the river, he welcomed this opportunity to deal with them ashore today as he had dealt with them afloat the day before. Four miles west of Port Gibson before nightfall, he put his men in a good defensive position astride a wooded ridge just short of a fork in the road leading east from Bruinsburg. Presently the Federals came up and his pickets took them under fire in the moonlight. Artillery deepened the tone of the argument, North and South, but soon after midnight, as if by mutual consent, both sides quieted down to wait for daylight.

McClernand opened the May Day fight soon after sunrise, advancing all four of his divisions under Brigadier Generals Peter Osterhaus, A. J. Smith, Alvin Hovey, and Eugene Carr. The road fork just ahead placed him in something of a quandary, lacking as he did an adequate map, but this was soon resolved by a local Negro who informed him that the two roads came together again on the near side of Port Gibson, his objective. He sent Osterhaus to the left as a diversion in favor of the other three commanders, who were charged with launching the main effort on the right. Grant came up at midmorning to find the battle in full swing and McClernand in some confusion, his heavily engaged columns being out of touch with each other because the two roads that wound along parallel ridges — "This part of Mississippi stands on edge" was how Grant put it — were divided by a timber-choked ravine that made lateral communication impossible. The result was that McClernand's right hand quite literally did not know what his left was doing, though the fact was neither was doing well at all. In his perplexity he called for help from McPherson, who supplied it by sending one brigade of Major General John A. Logan's division to the left and another to the right. "Push right along. Close up fast," the men heard Grant say as they went past the dust-covered general sitting a dust-covered horse beside the road fork. They did as he said, and arrived on the left in time to stall a rebel counterattack that had already thrown Osterhaus off balance, while on the right they added the weight needed for a resumption of the advance. Outflanked and heavily outnumbered on the road to the south, Bowen at last had to pull back to the outskirts of Port Gibson, where he rallied his men along a hastily improvised line and held off the blue attackers until nightfall ended the fighting.

Casualties were about equal on both sides; 832 Confederates and 875 Federals had fallen or were missing. Bowen had done well and he knew it, considering the disparity of numbers, but he also knew that to fight here tomorrow, against lengthened odds and without the advantage of this morning's densely wooded terrain, would be to invite disaster. At sundown he notified Pemberton that he would "have to retire under cover of night to the other side of Bayou Pierre and await reinforcements." Pemberton, who had arrived in Vicksburg from Jackson by now, had already sent word that he was "hurrying reinforcements; also ammunition. Endeavor to hold your own until they arrive, though it may be some time, as the distance is great." At 7.30, having received Bowen's sundown message, he rather wistfully inquired: "Is it not probable that the enemy will himself retire tonight? It is very important, as you know, to retain your present position, if possible.... You must. however, of course, be guided by your own judgment. You and your men have done nobly." But Bowen by then had followed up his first dispatch with a second: "I am pulling back across Bayou Pierre. I will endeavor to hold that position until reinforcements arrive." He withdrew skillfully by moonlight, unpursued and unobserved, destroying the three bridges over the bayou and its south fork, northwest and northeast of Port Gibson, and took up a strong position on the opposite bank, covering the wrecked crossing of the railroad to Grand Gulf, which he believed would be Grant's next objective.

But Grant did not come that way, at least not yet. Finding Port Gibson empty at dawn, he pressed on through and gave James Wilson a brigade-sized detail with which to construct a bridge across the south fork of Bayou Pierre, just beyond the town. Wilson was experienced in such work, having built no less than seven such spans in the course of the march from Milliken's Bend, and besides he had plenty of materials at hand, in the form of nearby houses which he tore down and cannibalized. By midafternoon the job was finished, "a continuous raft 166 feet long, 12 feet wide, with three rows of large mill-beams lying across the current, and the intervals between them closely filled with buoyant timber; the whole firmly tied together by a cross-floor or deck of 2-inch stuff." So Wilson later described it, not without pride, adding that he had also provided side rails, corduroy approaches over quicksand, and abutments "formed by building a slight crib-work, and filling in with rails covered by sand." Grant was impressed, but he did not linger to admire the young staff colonel's handiwork. The second of McPherson's three divisions having arrived that morning, he was given the lead today, with orders to march eight miles northeast to Grindstone Ford, which he reached soon after dark. He was prevented from crossing at once because the fine suspension bridge had been destroyed at that point, but Wilson was again at hand and had it repaired by daylight of May 3, when McPherson pressed on over. Near Willow Springs, two miles beyond the stream, he encountered and dislodged a small hostile force which retreated toward Hankinson's Ferry, six miles north, where the main road to Vicksburg crossed the Big Black River. Instructing McPherson to keep up the march northward in pursuit, Grant detached a single brigade to accompany him westward in the direction of Grand Gulf.

McClernand, coming along behind McPherson, whom he was ordered to follow north, was alarmed to learn what Grant had done, striking off on his own like that, and sent a courier galloping after him with a warning: "Had you not better be careful lest you may personally fall in with the enemy on your way to Grand Gulf?" But Grant was not only anxious to reach that place as soon as possible, and thus reestablish contact with the navy and with Sherman, who was on the march down the Louisiana bank; he also believed that Bowen, chastened by yesterday's encounter, would fall back beyond the Big Black as soon as he discovered that his position on Bayou Pierre had been turned upstream. And in this the northern commander was quite right. Reinforcements had reached Bowen from Jackson and Vicksburg by now, but they only increased his force to about 9000, whereas he reckoned the present enemy strength at 30,000, augmented as it was by a full division put ashore at Bruinsburg the night before. When he learned, moreover, that this host had bridged both forks of Bayou Pierre to the east of Port Gibson and was headed for the crossings of the Big Black, deep in his rear, he lost no time in reaching the decision Grant expected. At midnight, finding that his staff advisers "concurred in my belief that I was compelled to abandon the post at Grand Gulf," he "then ordered the evacuation, the time for each command to move being so fixed as to avoid any delay or confusion." The retrograde movement went smoothly despite the need for haste. Bringing off all their baggage — which Pemberton, when informed of their predicament, had authorized them to abandon lest it slow their march, but which Bowen declared he was "determined to and did save" — the weary veterans and the newly arrived reinforcements set off northward, leaving the blufftop intrenchments, which they had defended so ably against the ironclad assault four days ago, yawning empty behind them in the early morning sunlight.

Soon after they disappeared over the northern horizon Porter arrived with four gunboats, intending to launch a new attack. He approached with caution, remembering his previous woes and fearing a rebel trick, but when he found the Grand Gulf works abandoned he did not let that diminish his claim for credit for their reduction. "We had a hard fight for these forts," he wrote Secretary Welles, "and it is with great pleasure that I report that the Navy holds the door to Vicksburg." He announced that his fire had torn the place to pieces, leaving it so covered with earth and debris that no one could tell at a glance what had been there before the bombardment. "Had the enemy succeeded in finishing these fortifications no fleet could have taken them," he declared, quite as if he had subdued the batteries in the nick of time, and added: "I hear nothing of our army as yet; was expecting to hear their guns as we advanced on the forts."

He heard from "our army" presently with the arrival of its commander, who had got word of the evacuation while en route from Grindstone Ford and had ridden ahead of the infantry with an escort of twenty troopers. Grant was glad to see the admiral, but most of all — after seven days on a borrowed horse, with "no change of underclothing, no meal except such as I could pick up sometimes at other headquarters, and no tent to cover me" — he was glad to avail himself of the admiral's facilities. After a hot bath, a change of underwear borrowed from one of the naval officers, and a square meal aboard the flagship, he got off a full report to Halleck on the events of the past four days. "Our victory has been most complete, and the enemy thoroughly demoralized," he wrote. Bowen's defense of Port Gibson had been "a very bold one and well carried out. My force, however, was too heavy for his, and composed of well-disciplined and hardy men who know no defeat and are not willing to learn what it is." After this unaccustomed flourish he got down to the matter at hand. "This army is in the finest health and spirits," he declared. "Since leaving Milliken's Bend they have marched as much by night as by day, through mud and rain, without tents or much other baggage, and on irregular rations, without a complaint and with less straggling than I have ever before witnessed.... I shall not bring my troops into this place, but immediately follow the enemy, and, if all promises as favorable hereafter as it does now, not stop until Vicksburg is in our possession."

He was on his own, however, in a way he had neither intended nor foreseen. His plan had been to use Grand Gulf as a base, accumulating a reserve of supplies and marking time with Sherman and McPherson, so to speak, while McClernand took his corps downriver to co-operate with Banks in the reduction of Port Hudson, after which the two would join him for a combined assault on Vicksburg. But he found waiting for him today at Grand Gulf a three-week-old letter from Banks, dated April 10 and headed Brashear City — 75 miles west of New Orleans and equally far south of Port Hudson — informing him of a change in procedure made necessary, according to the Massachusetts general, by unexpected developments in western Louisiana which would threaten his flank and rear, including New Orleans itself, if he moved due north from the Crescent City as originally planned. Instead, he intended to abolish this danger with an advance up the Teche and the Atchafalaya, clearing out the rebels around Opelousas before returning east to Baton Rouge for the operation against Port Hudson with 15,000 men. He hoped to open this new phase of the campaign next day, he wrote, and if all went as planned he would return to the Mississippi within a month — that is, by May 10 — at which time he would be ready to co-operate with Grant in their double venture.... Reading the letter, Grant experienced a considerable shock. He had expected Banks to have twice as many troops already in position for a quick slash at Port Hudson, to be followed by an equally rapid boat ride north to assist in giving Vicksburg the same treatment. Now all that went glimmering. Some 30,000 men poorer than he had counted on being, he was on his own: which on second thought had its advantages, since the Massachusetts general outranked him and by virtue of his seniority would get the credit, from the public as well as the government, for the reduction of both Confederate strongholds and the resultant clearing of the Mississippi all the way to the Gulf. Grant absorbed the shock and quickly made up his mind that he was better off without him. Banks having left him on his own, he would do the same for Banks. "To wait for his co-operation would have detained me at least a month," he subsequently wrote in explanation of his decision. "The reinforcements would not have reached 10,000 men after deducting casualties and necessary river guards at all high points close to the river for over 300 miles. The enemy would have strengthened his position and been reinforced by more men than Banks could have brought. I therefore determined to move independently of Banks, cut loose from my base, destroy the rebel force in rear of Vicksburg, and invest or capture the city."

So much he intended, though he had not yet decided exactly how he would go about it. One thing he knew, however, was that the change of plans called for an immediate speed-up of the accumulation of supplies, preliminary to launching his all-out drive on the rebel citadel two dozen air-line miles to the north. A look at the Central Mississippi interior, with its lush fields, its many grazing cattle, and its well-stocked plantation houses — "of a character equal to some of the finest villas on the Hudson," a provincial New York journalist called these last — had convinced him that the problem was less acute than he had formerly supposed. "This country will supply all the forage required for anything like an active campaign, and the necessary fresh beef," he informed Halleck. "Other supplies will have to be drawn from Milliken's Bend. This is a long and precarious route, but I have every confidence in succeeding in doing it." Accordingly, he ordered this supply line shortened, as soon as the river had fallen a bit, by the construction of a new road from Young's Point to a west-bank landing just below Warrenton. "Everything depends upon the promptitude with which our supplies are forwarded," he warned. He had already directed that two towboats make a third run past the Vicksburg guns with heavy-laden barges. "Do this with all expedition," he told the quartermaster at Milliken's Bend, "in 48 hours from receipt of orders if possible. Time is of immense importance." Hurlbut was ordered to forward substantial reinforcements from Memphis without delay, as well as to lay in a sixty-day surplus of rations, to be kept on hand for shipment downriver at short notice. To Sherman, hurrying south across the way, went instructions to collect 120 wagons en route, load them with 100,000 pounds of bacon, then pile on all the coffee, sugar, salt, and crackers they would hold. "It is unnecessary for me to remind you of the overwhelming importance of celerity in your movements," Grant told him, outlining the situation as he saw it now on this side of the river: "The enemy is badly beaten, greatly demoralized, and exhausted of ammunition. The road to Vicksburg is open. All we want now are men, ammunition, and hard bread. We can subsist our horses on the country, and obtain considerable supplies for our troops."

With all this paper work behind him, he left Grand Gulf at midnight and rode eastward under a full moon to rejoin McPherson, who had reached Hankinson's Ferry that afternoon and had already dispatched cavalry details to probe the opposite bank of the Big Black River. From his new headquarters Grant kept stressing the need for haste. "Every day's delay is worth 2000 men to the enemy," he warned a supply officer, and kept goading him with questions that called for specific answers: "How many teams have been loaded with rations and sent forward? I want to know as near as possible how we stand in every particular for supplies. How many wagons have you ferried over the river? How many are still to bring over? What teams have gone back for rations?" His impatience was such that he had no time for head-shaking or regrets. Learning on May 5 that one of the two towboats and all the barges had been lost the night before in attempting the moonlight run he had ordered, he dismissed the loss with the remark: "We will risk no more rations to run the Vicksburg batteries," and turned his attention elsewhere. This touch of bad luck was more than offset the following day by news that Sherman had reached Hard Times, freeing McPherson's third division from guard duty along the supply route, and was already in the process of crossing the river to Grand Gulf. The red-haired general was in excellent spirits, having learned that four newspaper reporters had been aboard the towboat that was lost. "They were so deeply laden with weighty matter that they must have sunk," he remarked happily, and added: "In our affliction we can console ourselves with the pious reflection that there are plenty more of the same sort."

One thing Grant did find time for, though, amid all his exertions at Hankinson's Ferry. On the 7th he issued a general order congratulating his soldiers for their May Day victory near Port Gibson, which he said extended "the long list of those previously won by your valor and endurance." He was proud of what they had accomplished so far in the campaign, he assured them, and proudest of all that they had endured their necessary privations without complaint. Then he closed on a note of exhortation. "A few days' continuance of the same zeal and constancy will secure to this army the crowning victory over the rebellion. More difficulties and privations are before us. Let us endure them manfully. Other battles are to be fought. Let us fight them bravely. A grateful country will rejoice at our success, and history will record it with immortal honor."

Pemberton at this stage was by no means "badly beaten." Neither was he "greatly demoralized," any more than Vicksburg's defenders were "exhausted of ammunition." Nor was the road to the city "open," despite Grant's suppositions in his May 3 note urging Sherman to hurry down to get in on the kill. It was true, on the other hand, that the southern commander had been acutely distressed by the news that the blue invaders were landing in force on the east bank of the river below Grand Gulf, for he saw only too clearly the dangers this involved. "Enemy movement threatens Jackson, and, if successful, cuts off Vicksburg and Port Hudson from the east," he wired Davis on May Day, before he knew the outcome of the battle for Port Gibson, and he followed this up next morning, when he learned that Bowen had withdrawn across Bayou Pierre, with advice to Governor Pettus that the state archives be removed from the capital for safekeeping; Grant most likely would be coming this way soon. Another appeal to Johnston for "large reinforcements" to meet the "completely changed character of defense," now that the Federals were established in strength on this side of the river, brought a repetition of yesterday's advice: "If Grant crosses, unite all your troops to beat him. Success will give back what was abandoned to win it."

If this proposed abandonment included Vicksburg, and presumably it did, Pemberton was not in agreement. He already had ordered all movable ordnance and ammunition sent to that place from all parts of the state, in preparation for a last-ditch fight if necessary, and he arrived in person the following day, about the same time Grant rode into Grand Gulf with a twenty-trooper escort. For all his original alarm, Pemberton felt considerably better now. Davis and Seddon had promised reinforcements from Alabama and South Carolina — 5000 were coming from Charleston by rail at once, the Secretary wired, with another 4000 to follow — and Sherman had withdrawn from in front of Haines Bluff, reducing by half the problem of the city's peripheral defense. Johnston moreover had agreed at last, now that Streight had been disposed of, to send some cavalry under Forrest to guard against future raids across the Tennessee line. Much encouraged, Pemberton telegraphed Davis: "With reinforcements and cavalry promised in North Mississippi, think we will be all right."

His new confidence was based on a reappraisal of the situation confronting him now that Bowen, with his approval, had fallen back across the Big Black River, which curved across his entire right front and center. Not only did this withdrawal make a larger number of troops available for the protection of a much smaller area; it also afforded him the interior lines, so that a direct attack from beyond the arc could be met with maximum strength by defenders fighting from prepared positions. Presumably Grant would avoid that, but Pemberton saw an even greater advantage proceeding from the concentration behind the curved shield of the Big Black. It greatly facilitated what he later called "my great object," which was "to prevent Grant from establishing a base on the Mississippi River, above Vicksburg." Until the invaders accomplished this they would be dependent for supplies on what could be run directly past the gun-bristled bluff, a risky business at best, or freighted down the opposite bank, along a single jerry-built road that was subject to all the ravages of nature. As Pemberton saw it, his opponent's logical course would be to extend his march up the left bank of the Big Black, avoiding the bloodshed that would be involved in attempting a crossing until he was well upstream, in position for an advance on Haines Bluff from the rear and the establishment there of a new base of supplies, assisted and protected by Porter's upper flotilla, which would have returned up the Yazoo to meet him. But the southern commander did not intend to stand idly by, particularly while the latter stages of the movement were in progress. "The farther north [Grant] advanced, toward my left, from his then base below, the weaker he became; the more exposed became his rear and flanks; the more difficult it became to subsist his army and obtain reinforcements." At the moment of greatest Union extension and exposure, the defenders — reinforced by then, their commander hoped, from all quarters of the Confederacy — would strike with all their strength at the enemy's flanks and rear, administering a sudden and stunning defeat to a foe for whom, given the time and place, defeat would mean disaster, perhaps annihilation. Such was the plan. And though there were obvious drawbacks — the region beyond the Big

Black, for example, would be exposed to unhindered depredations; critics would doubtless object, moreover, that Grant might adopt a different method of accomplishing his goal — Pemberton considered the possible consummation of his design well worth the risk. Having weighed the odds and assessed his opponent's probable intentions from his actions in the past, he was content to let the outcome test the validity of his insight into the mind of his adversary. "I am a northern man; I know my people," he was to say. Besides, he believed that the Federals, obliged to hold onto one base to the south while reaching out for another to the north, had little choice except to act as he predicted. It was true that in the interim they "might destroy Jackson and ravage the country," he admitted, "but that was a comparatively small matter. To take Vicksburg, to control the valley of the Mississippi, to sever the Confederacy, to ruin our cause, a base upon the eastern bank immediately above was absolutely necessary."

Whatever else was desirable in the conflict now about to be resumed, he knew he would need all the soldiers he could get for the close-up defense of the line on the Big Black. In this connection, at the same time he informed Richmond of the pending evacuation of Grand Gulf he requested permission to bring the so-far unthreatened garrison of Port Hudson north for a share in the coming struggle. "I think Port Hudson and Grand Gulf should be evacuated," he wired Davis on May 2, "and the whole force concentrated for defense of Vicksburg and Jackson." Accordingly, in conformity with Johnston's advice to "unite all your troops," he ordered Major General Franklin Gardner, commanding the lower fortress, to strip the garrison to an absolute minimum and move with all the rest of the men to Jackson; those remaining behind would follow as soon as Richmond confirmed his request for total evacuation. On May 7, however, Davis replied that he approved of the withdrawal from Grand Gulf, but that "to hold both Vicksburg and Port Hudson is necessary to a connection with the Trans-Mississippi." So Pemberton countermanded the order to Gardner. He was to return at once to Port Hudson "and hold it to the last. President says both places must be held."

Such discouragement as this occasioned had been offset in advance, at least in part, by the defeat three nights ago of Grant's third attempt to run supplies downriver past the Vicksburg batteries. The sunken towboat and the flaming barges — not to mention the four Yankee journalists, who had not drowned, as Sherman had so fervently hoped, but had been fished out of the muddy water as prisoners of war — were evidence of improvement in the marksmanship of the gunners on the bluff, although it had to be conceded that the brilliant moonlight gave them an advantage they had lacked before. Another encouragement came soon afterwards from Johnston, who replied on May 8 to a report in which Pemberton explained his preparations for defense: "Disposition of troops, as far as understood, judicious; can be readily concentrated against Grant's army." If this was guarded, it was also approving, which was something altogether new from that direction. Then next day came the best news of all: Johnston himself would be coming soon to Vicksburg to inspirit the men and lend the weight of his genius to the defense of the Gibraltar of the West. Acting under instructions from Davis, Seddon ordered the general to proceed from Tullahoma "at once to Mississippi and take chief command of the forces, giving to those in the field, as far as practicable, the encouragement and benefit of your personal direction." Johnston was suffering at the time from a flare-up of his Seven Pines wound, but he replied without apparent hesitation: "I shall go immediately, although unfit for service." He left Tennessee next morning, May 10, having complied with the Secretary's further instructions to have "3000 good troops" follow him from Bragg's army as reinforcements for Pemberton.

Pemberton took new hope at the prospect of first-hand assistance from on high; now he could say, with a good deal more assurance than he had felt when he used the words the week before, "Think we will be all right." But there were flaws in the logic of his approach to the central problem, or at any rate errors in the conclusion to which that logic had led him. His assessment of Grant's intention was partly right, but it was also partly wrong: right, that is, in the conviction that what his opponent wanted and needed was a supply base above Vicksburg, but wrong as to how he would go about getting what he wanted. By now Grant had nine of his ten divisions across the Mississippi and had reached the final stage of his week-long build-up for an advance, though not in the direction Pemberton had supposed and planned for.

McPherson had been shifted eight miles east to Rocky Springs, leaving Hankinson's Ferry to be occupied by Sherman, two of whose three divisions were with him, while McClernand was in position along the road between those two points. In connection with the problem of supply, Grant had been collecting all the transportation he could lay hands on, horses, mules, oxen, and whatever rolled on wheels, ever since the Bruinsburg crossing. The result was a weird conglomeration of vehicles, ranging from the finest plantation carriages to ramshackle farm wagons, with surreys and buckboards thrown in for good measure, all piled to the dashboards and tailgates with supplies — mainly crates of ammunition and hardtack, the two great necessities for an army on the move — constantly shuttling back and forth between the Grand Gulf steamboat landing and Rocky Springs, where Grant had established headquarters near McPherson. Sherman, being farthest in the rear, had a close-up view of vehicular confusion that seemed to him to be building up to the greatest traffic snarl in history, despite the fact that there was still not transportation enough to supply more than a fraction of the army's needs. It was his conclusion that Grant's headlong impatience to be up and off was plunging him toward a logistic disaster. By May 9 he could put up with it no longer. "Stop all troops till your army is partially supplied with wagons, and then act as quickly as possible," he advised his chief, "for this road will be jammed as sure as life if you attempt to supply 50,000 men by one single road." The prompt reply from Rocky Springs gave the redhead the shock of his military life. Previously he had known scarcely more of Grant's future plans than Pemberton knew from beyond the Big Black River, but suddenly the veil of secrecy was lifted enough to give him considerably more than a glimmer of what he had never suspected until now. "I do not calculate upon the possibility of supplying the army with full rations from Grand Gulf," Grant told him. "I know it will be impossible without constructing additional roads. What I do expect, however, is to get up what rations of hard bread, coffee, and salt we can, and make the country furnish the balance."

This clearly implied, if it did not actually state, that he intended to launch an invasion, much as Cortez and Scott had done in Mexico, without a base from which to draw supplies. And so he did. Back in December, returning through North Mississippi to Memphis after the destruction of his forward depot at Holly Springs, he had discovered that his troops could live quite easily off the country by the simple expedient of taking what they wanted from the farmers in their path. "This taught me a lesson," he later remarked, and now the lesson was about to be applied. Moreover, the success of Grierson, whose troopers had lacked for nothing in the course of a 600-mile ride that had "knocked the heart out of the state" — so Grant himself declared in passing along to Washington the news of the raid — was a nearer and more recent example of what might be accomplished along those lines. For his own part, in the course of his march from Bruinsburg through Port Gibson to Rocky Springs, he had observed that "beef, mutton, poultry, and forage were found in abundance," along with "quite a quantity of bacon and molasses." What was more, every rural commissary "had a run of stone, propelled by mule power, to grind corn for the owners and their slaves. All these [could be] kept running ... day and night ... at all plantations covered by the troops." He felt sure there would be enough food and forage of one sort or another for all his men and animals, leaving room in the makeshift train for ammunition and such hard-to-get items as salt and coffee, provided there were no long halts during which the local supplies would be exhausted. All that was required was that he keep his army moving, and that was precisely what he intended to do, from start to finish, for tactical as well as logistic reasons. His 45,000 effectives were roughly twice as many as Pemberton had behind the curved shield of the Big Black River; he was convinced that he could whip him in short order with a frontal attack. "If Blair were up now," he told Sherman, who was still awaiting the arrival of the division that had feinted at Haines Bluff, "I believe we could be in Vicksburg in seven days." But that would leave some 10,000 rebels alive in his rear at Jackson, which was connected by rail not only to Vicksburg but also to the rest of the Confederacy, so that reinforcements could be hurried there from Bragg and the East until they outnumbered him as severely as he had outnumbered Pemberton, thus turning the tables on him. His solution was to strike both north and east, severing the rail connection between Jackson and Vicksburg near the Big Black crossing, while simultaneously closing in on the capital. He would capture the inferior force at that place, if possible, but at any rate he would knock it out of commission as a transportation hub or a rallying point; after which he would be free to turn on Vicksburg unmolested, approaching it from the east and north, and thus either take the citadel by storm or else establish a base on the Yazoo from which to draw supplies while starving the cut-off defenders into surrender.

Sherman had much of this explained to him when he rode over to Rocky Springs that afternoon, in considerable perturbation, for what he called "a full conversation" with the army commander. But his doubts persisted, much as they had done after he had agreed to stage the Haines Bluff demonstration. "He is satisfied that he will succeed in his plan," he said of Grant in a letter urging Blair to hasten his crossing from Hard Times, "and, of course, we must do our full share." Though he would "of course" co-operate fully in carrying out his chief's design, he wanted it understood from the start — and placed indelibly on the record — that he was doing so with something less than enthusiasm and against his better judgment. Grant by now was accustomed to his lieutenant's mercurial ups and downs, and he did not let them discourage him or influence his thinking. The following day, May 10 — the Sunday Joe Johnston left Tullahoma for Jackson — he heard again from Banks, who informed him, in a letter written four days ago at Opelousas, that he was making steady progress up the Teche, clearing out the rebels on his flank, and expected to turn east presently for Port Hudson. "By the 25th, probably, and by the 1st certainly, we will be there," he promised. Convinced more than ever that he had done right not to wait for Banks, Grant replied that he was going ahead on his own. Previously he had told him nothing of his plans, not even that he would not be meeting him; but now he did, on the off-chance that Banks might be of assistance. "Many days cannot elapse before the battle will begin which is to decide the fate of Vicksburg," he wrote, "but it is impossible to predict how long it may last. I would urgently request, therefore, that you join me or send all the force you can spare to co-operate in the great struggle for opening the Mississippi River." Similarly, at this near-final moment, he got off a dispatch to the general-in-chief, announcing that he was leaving Banks to fend for himself against Port Hudson while the Army

The Beleaguered City [359]

of the Tennessee cut loose from its base at Grand Gulf and plunged inland in order to come upon Vicksburg from the rear. "I knew well that Halleck's caution would lead him to disapprove of this course," he subsequently explained; "but it was the only one that gave any chance of success." Besides, such messages were necessarily slow in transmission, having to be taken overland from Hard Times to Milliken's Bend, then north by steamboat all the way to Cairo before they could be put on the wire, and Grant saw a certain advantage in this arrangement. "The time it would take to communicate with Washington and get a reply would be so great that I could not be interfered with until it was demonstrated whether my plan was practicable."

This done, he turned to putting the final touches to the plan he had evolved. McClernand would move up the left bank of the Big Black, guarding the crossings as he went, and strike beyond Fourteen Mile Creek at Edwards Station, on the railroad sixteen miles east of Vicksburg. McPherson would move simultaneously against Jackson, and Sherman would be on call to assist either column, depending on which ran into the stiffest resistance. On the 11th, Grant advanced all three to their jump-off positions: McClernand on the left, as near Fourteen Mile Creek as possible "without bringing on a general engagement," Sherman in the center, beyond Cayuga, and McPherson on the right, near Utica. "Move your command tonight to the next crossroads if there is water," Grant told McPherson, "and tomorrow with all activity into Raymond.... We must fight the enemy before our rations fail, and we are equally bound to make our rations last as long as possible."

Before dawn the following morning, May 12, they were off. The second phase of the campaign designed for the capture of Vicksburg was under way.

Advancing through a rugged and parched region, McClernand's troops found that the only way they could quench their thirst, aggravated by the heat of the day and the dust of the country roads, was to drive the opposing cavalry beyond Fourteen Mile Creek, which was held by a rebel force covering Edwards Station, some four miles to the north. By midafternoon they had done just that. "Our men enjoyed both the skirmish and the water," the commander of the lead division reported. Sherman, coming up on the right, accomplished this same purpose by throwing "a few quick rounds of cannister" at the gray vedettes, who promptly scampered out of range. Pioneers rebuilt a bridge the Confederates had burned as they fell back, and several regiments crossed the creek at dusk, establishing a bridgehead while the two corps went into bivouac on the south bank, prepared to advance on Edwards in the morning.

But that was not to be. McPherson, when within two miles of Raymond at 11 o'clock that morning, had encountered an enemy force of undetermined strength, "judiciously posted, with two batteries of artillery so placed as to sweep the road and a bridge over which it was necessary to pass." This was in fact a single brigade of about 4000 men, recently arrived from Port Hudson under Brigadier General John Gregg, who had come out from Jackson the day before, under orders from Pemberton to cover the southwest approaches to the capital. Informed that the Federals were moving on Edwards, over near the Big Black River, he assumed that the blue column marching toward him from Utica was only "a brigade on a marauding excursion," and he was determined not only to resist but also, if possible, to slaughter the marauders. The result was a sharp and — considering the odds — surprisingly hot contest, in which seven butternut regiments took on a whole Union corps. McPherson threw Logan's division against the wooded enemy position, only to have it bloodily repulsed. While the other two were coming forward, Logan rallied in time to frustrate a determined counterattack and follow it up with one of his own. By now, however, having learned what it was he had challenged — and having suffered 514 casualties, as compared to McPherson's 442 — Gregg had managed to disengage and was withdrawing through Raymond. Five miles to the east, one third of the distance to Jackson, he met Brigadier General W. H. T. Walker, who had marched out to join him with a thousand men just arrived from South Carolina. Gregg halted and faced about, ready to try his hand again; but there was no further action that day. Entering Raymond at 5 o'clock, McPherson decided to stop for the night. "The rough and impracticable nature of the country, filled with ravines and dense undergrowth, prevented anything like an effective use of artillery or a very rapid pursuit," he explained in a sundown dispatch to the army commander.

Grant was seven miles away, at the Dillon plantation on Fourteen Mile Creek with Sherman, and when he learned the outcome of the battle whose guns he had heard booming, five miles off at first, then fading eastward into silence, he revised his over-all plan completely. Edwards could wait. If Jackson was where the enemy was — and the determined resistance at Raymond seemed to indicate as much — he would go after him in strength; he would risk no halfway job in snuffing out a segment of the rebel army concentrated near a rail hub that gave it access to reinforcements from all quarters of the South. Accordingly, at 9.15 he sent orders assigning all three of his corps commanders new objectives for tomorrow and prescribing that each would begin his march "at daylight in the morning." McPherson would move against Clinton, on the railroad nine miles north, then eastward that same distance along the right-of-way to Jackson. Sherman would turn due east from his present bivouac at Dillon, swinging through Raymond so as to come upon the objective from the south. McClernand, after detaching one division to serve as a rear guard in the event that the Confederates at Vicksburg attempted to interfere by crossing the Big Black, would come along behind Sherman and McPherson, prepared to move in support of either or both as they closed in on the Mississippi capital. Such were Grant's instructions, and presently he had cause to believe that he had improvised aright. Two days ago McPherson had passed along a rumor that "some of the citizens in the vicinity of Utica say Beauregard is at or near Jackson." If the Charleston hero was there it was practically certain he had not come alone. And now there arrived a second dispatch from McPherson, headed 11 p.m. and relaying another rumor that heavy Confederate reinforcements were moving against him out of Jackson, intending to fight again at Raymond soon after sunup. He did not know how much fact there was in this, he added, but he would "try to be prepared for them." Grant had confidence in McPherson, especially when he was forewarned as he was now, and did not bother to reply. Besides, whether it was true or false that the rebels were marching in force to meet him west of their capital, he already had made provisions to counter such a threat by ordering all but one of his ten divisions, some 40,000 men in all, to move toward a convergence on that very objective "at daylight in the morning."

All three columns moved on schedule. By early afternoon McPherson was in Clinton, nine miles from Jackson, and Sherman was six miles beyond Raymond, about the same distance from the Mississippi capital. A lack of determined resistance seemed to indicate that last night's rumor of heavy reinforcements was in error, and this, plus reports from scouts that Pemberton had advanced in force to the vicinity of Edwards, caused Grant to modify his strategy again. McPherson was instructed to spend the rest of the day wrecking the railroad west of Clinton, then resume his eastward march at first light tomorrow, May 14, tearing up more track as he went. Sherman, half a dozen miles to the south, would regulate his progress so that both corps would approach the Jackson defenses simultaneously. McClernand, instead of following along to furnish unneeded support, would turn north at Raymond and march on Bolton Depot, eight miles west of Clinton, occupying a strong position in case Pemberton attempted a farther advance along the railroad toward his threatened capital. There was of course the possibility that the Confederate commander might lunge southward, across Fourteen Mile Creek, with the intention of attacking the Federal army's rear and severing its connection with Grand Gulf: in which case he would be removing himself from the campaign entirely, at least for the period of time required for him to discover that he had plunged into a vacuum. For Grant not only had no supply line; he had no rear, either, in the sense that Pemberton might suppose. Such rear as Grant had he had brought with him, embodied in McClernand, who now had orders to take up a position at Bolton, astride the railroad about midway between Vicksburg and Jackson, facing west. Moreover, once the capital had fallen and the blue army turned its attention back to its prime objective, the blufftop citadel forty-five miles away, what was now its rear would automatically become its front; McClernand, already in position for an advance, once more would take the lead, with Sherman and McPherson in support. For all the improvisatorial nature of his tactics, Grant, like any good chess player, was keeping a move or two ahead of the game.

By midmorning of May 14, slogging eastward under a torrential rain that quickly turned the dusty roads into troughs of mud, Sherman was within three miles of Jackson. At 10 o'clock, while peering through the steely curtain of the downpour to examine the crude fortifications to his front, he heard the welcome boom of guns off to the north; McPherson was on schedule and in place. While Sherman reconnoitered toward Pearl River for an opening on the flank, McPherson deployed for a time-saving frontal attack, to be launched astride the railroad. He waited an hour in the rain, lest the cartridge boxes of his troops be filled with water, like buckets under a tap, when they lifted the flaps to remove their paper-wrapped ammunition, and then at 11 o'clock, the rain having slacked to a drizzle at last, ordered his lead division forward across fields of shin-deep mud. The rebel pickets faded back to the shelter of their intrenchments, laying down a heavy fire that stopped the bluecoats in their tracks and flung them on their faces in the mud. By now it was noon. McPherson impatiently reformed his staggered line, having lost an even 300 men, and sent the survivors forward again. This time they found the rebel infantry gone. Only a handful of cannoneers had remained behind to serve the seven guns left on line and be captured by McPherson's jubilant soldiers. Sherman had the same experience, two miles to the south, except that he found ten guns in the abandoned works he had outflanked. Not only were his spoils thus greater than McPherson's; his casualties were fewer, numbering only 32. The Confederates, under Gregg and Walker, who had fallen back from east of Raymond the night before, had lost just over 200 men before pulling out of their trenches to make a hairbreadth getaway to the north. The Battle of Jackson was over, such as it was, and Grant had taken the Mississippi capital at a bargain price of 48 killed, 273 wounded, and 11 missing.

He was there to enjoy in person the first fruits of today's sudden and inexpensive victory. Sherman, riding in from the south — and noting with disapproval some "acts of pillage" already being committed by early arrived bluecoats under the influence "of some bad rum found concealed in the stores of the town" — was summoned by a courier to the Bowman House, Jackson's best hotel, where he found Grant and McPherson celebrating the capture of Jeff Davis's own home-state capital, the third the South had lost in the past two years. From the lobby they had a view, through a front window, of the State House where the rebel President had predicted, less than six months ago, that his fellow Mississippians would "meet and hurl back these worse than vandal hordes." Quick as the two generals had been to reach the heart of town, riding in ahead of the main body, they were slower than the army commander's young son Fred. His mother and brother had gone back North after the second running of the Vicksburg batteries, but Fred had stayed on to enjoy the fun that followed, wearing his father's dress sword and sash — which the general himself had little use for, and almost never wore — as badges of rank. Grant, an indulgent parent, later explained that the boy "caused no trouble either to me or his mother, who was at home. He looked out for himself and was in every battle of the campaign. His age, then not quite thirteen, enabled him to take in all he saw, and then to retain a recollection of it that would not be possible in more mature years." Fred's recollection of the capture of Jackson was saddened, however, by his failure to get a souvenir he badly wanted. He and a friendly journalist had seen from the outskirts of town a large Confederate flag waving from its staff atop the golden dome of the capitol. Mounted, they hurried ahead of the leading infantry column, tethered their horses in front of the big stone building, and raced upstairs — only to meet, on his way down, "a ragged, muddy, begrimed cavalryman" descending with the rebel banner tucked beneath his arm. For Fred, a good measure of the glory of Jackson's capture had departed, then and there.

Grant could sympathize with the boy's disappointment, but he had just been handed something considerably more valuable to him than the lost flag or even the seventeen guns that had been taken in the engagement that served as prelude to the occupation of the capital. Charles Dana arrived in mid-celebration with a dispatch just delivered by a courier from Grand Gulf. Signed by the Secretary of War and dated

May 5, it had been sent in response to a letter in which Dana had given him a summation of Grant's plan "to lose no time in pushing his army toward the Big Black and Jackson, threatening both and striking at either, as is most convenient.... He will disregard his base and depend on the country for meat and even for bread." Now Stanton replied:

> General Grant has full and absolute authority to enforce his own commands, to remove any person who, by ignorance, inaction, or any cause, interferes with or delays his operations. He has the full confidence of the Government, is expected to enforce his authority, and will be firmly and heartily supported; but he will be responsible for any failure to exert his powers. You may communicate this to him.

There was more here than met the eye. Stanton of course had authority over Halleck, so that if — or rather, as Grant believed from past experience, *when* — the time came for the general-in-chief to protest that Grant had disobeyed orders by abandoning Banks and striking out on his own, he would find — if indeed he had not found already — that Stanton, and presumably Lincoln as well, had approved in advance the course Grant had adopted. Nor was that all. Dana, having long since taken a position alongside the army commander in his private war against McClernand, had been keeping the Secretary copiously posted on the former congressman's military shortcomings, large and small, and feeling him out as to what the administration's reaction would be when Grant decided the time had come for him to swing the ax. Now the answer was at hand. Grant not only had "full and absolute authority" to sit in judgment; he would in fact be held "responsible for any failure to exert his powers" in all matters pertaining to what he considered his army's welfare and the progress of what Stanton called his "operations," whether against the rebels or McClernand.

It was no wonder then — protected as he now was from the wrath of his immediate superior, as well as from the machinations of his ranking subordinate — that he was in good spirits during the hotel-lobby victory celebration. All around him, meanwhile, the town was in a turmoil. "Many citizens [had] fled at our approach," one Federal witness later recalled, "abandoning houses, stores, and all their personal property, without so much as locking their doors. The Negroes, poor whites, and it must be admitted some stragglers and bummers from the ranks of the Union army, carried off thousands of dollars worth of property from houses, homes, shops and stores, until some excuse was given for the charge of 'northern vandalism,' which was afterwards made by the South. The streets were filled with people, white and black, who were carrying away all the stolen goods they could stagger under, without the slightest attempt at concealment and without let or hindrance from citizens or soldiers.... In addition ... the convicts of the penitentiary, who had been released by their own authorities, set all the buildings connected with that prison on fire, and their lurid flames added to the holocaust elsewhere prevailing." He observed that "many calls were made upon [Grant] by citizens asking for guards to protect their private property, some of which perhaps were granted, but by far the greater number [of these petitioners] were left to the tender mercies of their Confederate friends."

After all, Grant had not brought his army here to protect the private property of men in revolution against the government that army represented; nor, for that matter, had it ever been his custom to deny his soldiers a chance at relaxation they had earned, even though that relaxation sometimes took a rather violent form. His purpose, rather, was to destroy all public property such as might be of possible comfort to the Confederacy. This applied especially to the railroads, the wrecking of which would abolish the Mississippi capital as a transportation hub, at least through the critical period just ahead. But that other facilities were not neglected was observed by a witness who testified that "foundries, machine shops, warehouses, factories, arsenals, and public stores were fired as fast as flames could be kindled." Sherman was the man for this work, Grant decided, and he gave him instructions "to remain in Jackson until he destroyed that place as a railroad center and manufacturing city of military supplies."

Meanwhile there was the campaign to get on with; Pemberton was hovering to the west, already on the near side of the Big Black, and beyond him there was Vicksburg, the true object of all this roundabout marching and such bloodshed as had so far been involved. McPherson was told to get his corps in hand and be prepared to set out for Bolton Depot at first light tomorrow to support McClernand, whose corps was no longer the army's rear guard, but rather its advance. Having attended to this, Grant joined Sherman for a little relaxation of his own; namely, a tour of inspection to determine which of the local business establishments would be spared or burned. In the course of the tour they came upon a cloth factory which, as Grant said later, "had not ceased work on account of the battle nor for the entrance of Yankee troops." Outside the building "an immense amount of cotton" was stacked in bales; inside, the looms were going full tilt, tended by girl operatives, weaving bolts of tent cloth plainly stamped C.S.A. No one seemed to notice the two generals, who watched for some time in amused admiration of such oblivious industry. "Finally," Grant said afterwards, "I told Sherman I thought they had done work enough. The operatives were told they could leave and take with them what cloth they could carry. In a few minutes cotton and factory were in a blaze."

This done, Grant returned to the Bowman House for his first

night's sleep on a mattress in two weeks. Joe Johnston, he was told, had occupied the same room the night before.

✗ 3 ✗

Johnston — not Beauregard, as rumor had had it earlier — had arrived at dusk the day before, at the end of a grueling three-day train ride from Tennessee by way of Atlanta, Montgomery, Mobile, and Meridian, only to find the Mississippi capital seething with reports of heavy Union columns advancing from the west. As night closed in, a hard rain began to fall, shrouding the city and deepening the Virginian's gloom still further: as was shown in a wire he got off to Seddon after dark. "I arrived this evening finding the enemy's force between this place and General Pemberton, cutting off communication. I am too late." To Pemberton, still on the far side of the Big Black, he sent a message advising quick action on that general's part. To insure delivery, three copies were forwarded by as many couriers. "I have lately arrived, and learn that Major General Sherman is between us, with four divisions, at Clinton," Johnston wrote. "It is important to re-establish communications, that you may be reinforced. If practicable, come up in his rear at once. To beat such a detachment would be of immense value. The troops here could cooperate. All the strength you can quickly assemble should be brought. Time is all important."

He had at Jackson, he presently discovered, only two brigades of about 6000 men with which to oppose the 25,000 Federals who were knocking at the western gates next morning. After a sharp, brief skirmish and the sacrifice of seventeen guns to cover a withdrawal, he retreated seven miles up the Canton road to Tugaloo, where he halted at nightfall, unpursued, and sent another message to Pemberton, from whom he had heard nothing since his arrival, informing him that the capital had been evacuated. He was expecting another "12,000 or 13,000" troops from the East, he said, and "as soon as [these] reinforcements are all up, they must be united to the rest of the army. I am anxious to see a force assembled that may be able to inflict a heavy blow upon the enemy.... If prisoners tell the truth, the force at Jackson must be half of Grant's army. It would decide the campaign to beat it, which can only be done by concentrating, especially when the remainder of the eastern troops arrive." He himself could do little or nothing until these men reached him, reducing the odds to something within reason, but he did not think that Pemberton should neglect any opportunity Grant afforded meanwhile, particularly in regard to his lines of supply and communication. "Can he supply himself from the Mississippi?" Johnston asked. "Can you not cut him off from it, and above all, should he be compelled to fall back for want of supplies, beat him?"

This last was in accord with Pemberton's own decision, already arrived at before the second message was received. The first, delivered by one of the three couriers that morning at Bovina Station, nine miles east of Vicksburg, had taken him greatly by surprise. He had expected Johnston to come to his assistance in defense of the line along or just in front of the Big Black; yet here that general was, requesting him "if practicable" to come to *his* assistance by marching against the enemy's rear at Clinton, some twenty miles away. Pemberton replied that he would "move at once with the whole available force," explaining however that this included only 17,500 troops at best, since the remaining 9000 under his command were required to man the Warrenton-Vicksburg-Haines Bluff defenses, as well as the principal crossings of the Big Black, which otherwise would remain open in his rear, exposing the Gibraltar of the West to sudden capture by whatever roving segment of the rampant blue host happened to lunge in that direction. "In directing this move," he felt obliged to add, by way of protest, "I do not think you fully comprehend the position Vicksburg will be left in; but I comply at once with your request."

So he said. However, when he rode forward to Edwards, where his mobile force of three divisions under Loring, Stevenson, and Bowen was posted four miles east of the Big Black, he learned that a Union column, reportedly five divisions strong — it was in fact McClernand's corps, with Blair attached as guard for the wagon train — was at Raymond, in position for a northward advance on Bolton. If Pemberton marched on Clinton, as Johnston suggested, ignoring this threat to his right flank as he moved eastward along the railroad, he would not only be leaving Vicksburg and the remaining two divisions under Major Generals M. L. Smith and John H. Forney in grave danger of being gobbled up while his back was turned; he would also be exposing his eastbound force to destruction at the hands of the other half of the Northern army. Perplexed by this dilemma, and mindful of some advice received two days ago from Richmond that he "add conciliation to the discharge of duty" — "Patience in listening to suggestions ... is sometimes rewarded," Davis had added — he decided the time had come for him to call a council of war, something he had never done before in all his thirty years of military service. Assembling the general officers of the three divisions at Edwards Station shortly after noon, he laid Johnston's message before them and outlined the tactical problems it posed. Basically, what he had to deal with was a contradiction of orders from above. As he understood the President's wishes, he was not to risk losing Vicksburg by getting too far from it, whereas Johnston was suggesting a junction of their forces near Jackson, forty miles away, in order to engage what he called a "detachment" of four — in fact, five — divisions, without reference to or apparent knowledge of the five-division column now at Raymond, both of which outnumbered the Confederates at Edwards. Pemberton, on the other hand, did not strictly agree with either of his two superiors, preferring to await attack in a prepared position near or behind the Big Black River, with a chance of following up a repulse with a counterattack designed to cut off and annihilate the foe. These three views could not be reconciled, but neither did he consider that any one of them could be ignored; so that, like the nation at large, this Northerner who sided with the South was torn and divided against himself. That was his particular nightmare in this nightmare interlude of his country's history. According to an officer on his staff, the Pennsylvanian's trouble now and in the future was that he made "the capital mistake of trying to harmonize instructions from his superiors diametrically opposed to each other, and at the same time to bring them into accord with his own judgment, which was averse to the plans of both."

Nor was the council of much assistance to him in finding a way around the impasse. Though a majority of the participants favored complying with Johnston's suggestion that the two forces be united, they were obliged to admit that it could not be accomplished by a direct march on Clinton, which was plainly an invitation to disaster. Meanwhile Pemberton's own views, as he told Johnston later, "were strongly expressed as unfavorable to any advance which would remove me from my base, which was and is Vicksburg." Apparently he limited himself to this negative contention. But finally Loring — known as "Old Blizzards" since his and Tilghman's spirited repulse of the Yankee gunboats above Greenwood — suggested an alternate movement, southeast nine miles to Dillon, which he believed would sever Grant's connection with Grand Gulf and thus force him either to withdraw, for lack of supplies, or else to turn and fight at a disadvantage in a position of Pemberton's choice. Stevenson agreed, along with others, and Pemberton, though he disliked the notion of moving even that much farther from Vicksburg, "did not, however, see fit to put my own judgment and opinions so far in opposition as to prevent a movement altogether." He approved the suggestion, apparently for lack of having anything better to offer, and adjourned the council after giving the generals instructions to be ready to march at dawn. At 5.40, on the heels of the adjournment, he got off a message informing Johnston of his intentions. "I shall move as early tomorrow morning as practicable with a column of 17,000 men," he wrote, explaining the exact location of Dillon so that Johnston would have no trouble finding it on a map which was enclosed. "The object is to cut the enemy's communications and to force him to attack me, as I do not consider my force sufficient to justify an attack on the enemy in position or to attempt to cut my way to Jackson."

Johnston received this at 8.30 next morning, May 15, by which time he had withdrawn another three miles up the Canton road, still farther from the intended point of concentration at Clinton. Though

The Beleaguered City

the message showed that Pemberton had anticipated the Virginian's still unreceived suggestion that he attempt to "cut [Grant] off from [the Mississippi]," Johnston no longer favored such a movement. "Our being compelled to leave Jackson makes your plan impracticable," he replied, and repeated — despite Pemberton's objection to being drawn still farther from his base — his preference for an eastward march by the mobile force from Vicksburg: "The only mode by which we can unite is by your moving directly to Clinton, informing me, that [I] may move to that point with about 6000 troops. I have no means of estimating the enemy's force at Jackson. The principal officers here differ very widely, and I fear he will fortify if time is left him. Let me hear from you immediately."

Evidently Johnston believed that Grant was going to hole up in the Mississippi capital and thus allow him time to effect a junction between the Vicksburg troops and his own, including the "12,000 or 13,000" reinforcements expected any day now from the East. If so, he was presently disabused. A reply from Pemberton, written early the following morning but not delivered until after dark, informed him that the advance on Dillon — badly delayed anyhow by the need for building a bridge across a swollen creek — had been abandoned, in accordance with his wishes, and the direction of march reversed. It was Pemberton's intention, as explained in the message, to move north of the railroad, swing wide through Brownsville to avoid the mass of Federals reported to be near Bolton, and converge on Clinton as instructed. "The order of countermarch has been issued," he wrote, and followed a description of his proposed route with the words: "I am thus particular, so that you may be able to make a junction with this army."

The Vicksburg commander at last had abandoned his objections to what Johnston had called "the only mode by which we can unite." He was, or soon would be, moving east toward his appointed destination. But there was an ominous postscript to the message, written in evident haste and perhaps alarm: "Heavy skirmishing is now going on to my front."

What that portended Johnston did not know; but Grant did. Before he retired to the hotel room his adversary had occupied the night before the fall of Jackson, he received from McPherson one of the three copies of Johnston's message urging Pemberton to "come up in [Sherman's] rear at once." This windfall was the result of a ruse worked some months ago by Hurlbut, who banished from Memphis, with considerable fanfare, a citizen found guilty of "uttering disloyal and threatening sentiments," though he was in secret, as Hurlbut knew, a thoroughly loyal Union man. The expulsion, along with his continued expression of secessionist views after his removal to the Mississippi capital, won him the sympathy and admiration of the people there: so much so, indeed, that he was one of the three couriers entrusted with copies of Johnston's urgent message. He delivered it, however, not to Pemberton but to McPherson, who passed it promptly along to Grant. "Time is all important," the Virginian had written. Grant agreed. By first light next morning, May 15, McPherson was marching west from the capital, leaving Sherman to accomplish its destruction while he himself moved toward a junction with McClernand, who had been instructed simultaneously by Grant: "Turn all your forces toward Bolton station, and make all dispatch in getting there. Move troops by the most direct road from wherever they may be on the receipt of this order."

McPherson's three divisions had seventeen miles to go, and McClernand's four — five, including Blair — were variously scattered, from Raymond back to Fourteen Mile Creek. Each corps got one division to Bolton by late afternoon — Hovey and Logan, in that order — while the others camped along the roads at sundown. Carr and Osterhaus were three miles south, with A. J. Smith between them and Raymond, where Blair was. Brigadier Generals John McArthur and Marcellus Crocker, commanding McPherson's other two divisions, were bivouacked beside the railroad leading back to Clinton. Riding out from Jackson to that point before nightfall, Grant ordered McClernand to move on Edwards in the morning, supported by McPherson, but warned him "to watch for the enemy and not bring on an engagement unless he felt very certain of success." The fog of war, gathering again to obscure the Confederate purpose, had provoked this note of caution; but it was dispersed once more at 5 o'clock next morning, when two Union-sympathizing employes of the Vicksburg-Jackson Railroad were brought to Grant at Clinton. They had passed through Pemberton's army in the night, they said, and could report that it was moving east of Edwards with a strength of about 25,000 men. Though this was in fact some 7500 high, it was still some 10,000 fewer than Grant had on hand. But he was taking no unavoidable chances. Deciding to ignore Johnston, who by now was a day's march north of Jackson at Calhoun Station, he ordered Sherman to "put one division with an ammunition train on the road at once, with directions to its commander to march with all possible speed until he comes upon our rear." The remaining division was to hurry its demolition work and follow along as soon as might be. The orders to McClernand and McPherson were unaltered; all that was changed by this second dispersal of the war fog was the weight of the blow about to be delivered. Now that he knew Pemberton's strength and had him spotted, Grant intended to hit him with everything he had.

At about the time the railroad men were telling all they knew, McClernand started forward in high spirits. "My corps, again, led the advance," he was to say proudly in a letter giving his friend Lincoln an account of the campaign. Such was indeed the case. Three roads led west from the vicinity of Bolton to a junction east of Edwards, and McClernand used all three: Hovey on the one to the north, Osterhaus and Carr on the one in the middle, and Smith on the one to the south. Blair followed Smith, and McPherson's three divisions followed Hovey. Rebel cavalry was soon encountered, gray phantoms who fired and scampered out of range while the blue skirmishers flailed the woods with bullets. Then at 7.30, five miles short of Edwards, Smith came upon a screen of butternut pickets and dislodged them, exposing a four-gun battery, which he silenced. He wanted to plunge on, despite the signs that the high ground ahead was occupied in strength, but McClernand told him to hold what he had till Blair came up to keep his exposed left flank from being turned. Immediately on the heels of this, a rattle of gunfire from the north signified that Osterhaus and Hovey had also come upon johnnies to their front. McClernand inspected the rebel position as best he could from a distance and, finding it formidable, decided to hang on where he was until the situation could be developed. Having obeyed Grant's instructions "to watch for the enemy," he was also mindful of the injunction "not [to] bring on an engagement unless he felt very certain of success." At this point, with his various columns a mile or two apart and facing a wooded ridge a-swarm with graybacks, he was not feeling very certain about anything at all. What he mainly felt was lonely.

Countermarching in obedience to the message received early that morning from Johnston, Pemberton had been warned by his outriders of the Union host advancing westward along the three roads from Bolton and Raymond. When this danger was emphasized by the "heavy skirmishing" mentioned in the postscript to his reply that he was moving north and east toward a junction at Clinton, he knew he had a fight on his hands, wanted or not, and to avoid the risk of being caught in motion, strung out on the road to Brownsville, he hastily put his troops in position for receiving the attack he knew was coming. Whether his choice of ground was "by accident or design," as Grant ungenerously remarked, there could be no doubt that Pemberton chose well. Just south of the railroad and within a broad northward loop of rain-swollen Baker's Creek, a seventy-foot eminence known as Champion Hill — so called because it was on a plantation belonging to a family of that name — caused the due-west road from Bolton to veer south around its flank, joining the middle road in order to cross a timbered ridge that extended southward for three miles, past the lower of the three roads along which the enemy was advancing. Pemberton placed Stevenson's division on the hill itself, overlooking the direct approach from Bolton, and Bowen's and Loring's divisions along the ridge, blocking the other two approaches. Here, in an opportune position of great natural strength, he faced as best he could the consequences of his reluctant and belated compliance with his superior's repeated suggestion that he abandon the security of his prepared lines, along and just in front of the Big Black, for an attack on the Federal "detachment" supposed to be at Clinton. Now, however, as the thing turned out, it was Pemberton who was about to be attacked, a dozen miles short of his assigned objective. And here, precisely midway between Vicksburg and Jackson, both of which were twenty-two miles away, was fought what at least one prominent western-minded historian was to call "the most decisive battle of the Civil War."

Grant did not much like the look of things when he came riding out from Bolton and reached the front, where the road veered south beyond the Champion house, to find Hovey exchanging long-range shots with the enemy on the tall hill just ahead. It seemed to him, as he said later, that the rebels "commanded all the ground in range." However, unlike McClernand on the two roads to the south, he was not content to hold his own while waiting for the situation to develop more or less of its own accord. Logan's division having arrived, he sent it to the right, to prolong the line and feel for an opening in that direction. This was about 10 o'clock; he preferred to wait for Crocker to come up and lend the weight of McPherson's second division to the attack. But Hovey by now was hotly engaged, taking punishment from the batteries on the height and protesting that he must either go forward or fall back. Grant unleashed him. A former Indiana lawyer, of whom it was said that he had taken to the army "just as if he expected to spend his life in it," Hovey drove straight up the steep acclivity to his front, flinging back successive Confederate lines, until he reached and seized the eleven guns that had been pounding him from near the crest. His men were whooping with delight, proud but winded, when they were struck in turn by a powerful counterattack launched from a fringe of woods along the crest. "We ran, and ran manfully," one among them declared, explaining how he and his fellows had been swept back from the captured guns and down the slope they had climbed. Reinforced by Crocker's lead brigade, which had just arrived under Colonel George Boomer, they managed to hang on at the foot of the hill; but only by the hardest. One officer called the fighting there "unequal, terrible, and most sanguinary." For half an hour, he said, the troops "on each side took their turn in driving and being driven."

It was obvious that Hovey, who had left about one third of his division lying dead or wounded on the hillside, could not hold out much longer unassisted. Then one of the survivors looked over his shoulder and saw the army commander speaking to the colonel in charge of Crocker's second brigade, which was coming forward along the road behind them. "I was close enough to see his features," the man was to recall. "Earnest they were, but sign of inward movement there was none." This was the Grant of Belmont, Donelson, and Shiloh, reacting to adversity here as he had reacted there. If the face was "cool and calculating," the soldier observed, it was also "careful and half-cynical." He could not catch the spoken words across the distance, but they were as characteristic as the calm, enigmatic mask or the habitual cigar stump that was wedged between its teeth. "Hovey's division and Boomer's brigade are good troops," Grant was saying. "If the enemy has driven them he is not in good plight himself. If we can go in again here and make a little showing, I think he will give way."

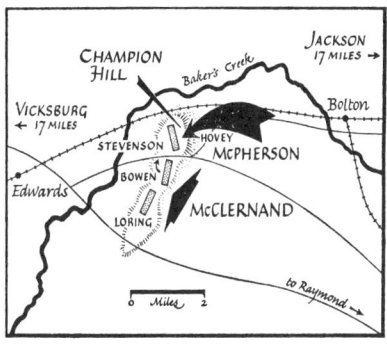

But it developed that a good deal more than this one additional brigade would have to join the melee at the base of Champion Hill if Grant was to make what he called "a little showing." With McPherson's third division still too far away to be of help in time, he had to call on Logan, who had been sent to probe the rebel left. And this, as Grant admitted later, was the salvation of Pemberton today. Logan had ridden around the north end of the hill, where the terrain was more open and gently rolling. He was sitting on horseback, surveying the scene, when a private who had wandered on his own came up to him and remarked laconically, gesturing off to the right: "General, I've been over the rise yonder, and it's my idea that if you'll put a regiment or two over there you'll get on their flank and lick 'em easy." Logan took a look for himself and saw that the man was right; Pemberton's left was "in the air" and the way to his rear was practically unobstructed, including the single bridge over Baker's Creek by which he could fall back. Just then, however, the order to return and support the hard-pressed Hovey was received; Logan had to defer pressing the advantage the amateur tactician had discovered. Learning of this when it was too late to take full advantage of the maneuver, Grant remarked with hindsight: "Had McClernand come up with reasonable promptness, or had I known the ground as I did afterwards, I cannot see how Pemberton could have escaped with any organized force."

The reference to McClernand was something more, this time, than merely another point scored in the private war Grant waged on paper against the former congressman from his home state. Pemberton, observing the lack of enemy aggressiveness to the south, had reinforced his staggered left by shifting troops northward from his center, which was disposed along the ridge. Bowen brought them to Stevenson's assistance on the run, arriving just in time to launch the savage counterattack that drove Hovey's exultant soldiers back down the hill. Like Grant, however, Pemberton was finding that he would need more than this to keep up the pressure or even hold what he had won; so he sent for Loring. That general — referred to as "a scared turkey" by a member of Stonewall Jackson's staff during the Romney controversy, two Christmases ago, which had almost resulted in Jackson's retirement from the army and which had been settled only with Loring's transfer to the West — was already in a state of agitation because Bowen's departure had left him alone on the ridge, with four blue divisions in plain sight. When the summons came for him to follow Bowen he declined. It would be suicidal, he protested. All this time, the pressure against Stevenson was mounting, and when Logan added the weight of his division it became unsupportable. Old Blizzards moved at last, in response to repeated calls from Pemberton; but too late. He was scarcely in motion northward, about 4 o'clock, when the whole Confederate left flank gave way. Stevenson's men fell back in a panic, and though Pemberton managed to rally them with a personal appeal, the damage was done. The eleven retaken guns were lost again, this time for good, and Bowen's division — having, as one officer remarked, "sustained its reputation by making one of its grand old charges, in which it bored a hole through the Federal army" — now found itself unsupported and nearly surrounded; whereupon it "turned around and bored its way back again," following Stevenson's pell-mell flight down to Baker's Creek, where it formed a rear-guard line in an attempt to hold off the bluecoats until Loring too had made his escape across the stream. Darkness fell and there was still no sign of Loring. Bowen waited another two hours, still maintaining his position, then gave it up and crossed in good order, burning the bridge when his last man was safe on the west bank.

Casualties here, after three hours of skirmishing and four of actual battle, had been much the heaviest of the campaign. Grant had lost 2441 men, Pemberton 3624, including prisoners cut off in the retreat — plus 11 guns and, as it turned out, all of Loring's division. Finding his path along the ridge blocked by victorious Federals, he swung west, then back south, and after a brief skirmish in which Lloyd Tilghman was killed by a cannonball while covering the withdrawal, made a rapid getaway around McClernand's open flank. By the following evening he was in Crystal Springs, twenty-five miles south of Jackson, and two days later he was with Johnston at Canton, an equal distance north of the capital. Except for the loss of Tilghman, whose courage and ability had been proved at Fort Henry and Fort Pemberton, Loring's disappearance was more a source of mystery than regret for the army of which he had lately been a part, since he had contributed little to the battle except to assist in the show of strength that immobilized McClernand. Grant felt much the same way about McClernand, whose 15,000-man command — including Blair but not Hovey, who fought beyond McClernand's control and suffered almost half the army's casualties — had lost a total of 17 dead and 141 wounded in the course of what a brigade commander with McPherson called "one of the most obstinate and murderous conflicts of the war." Despite the fact that not a single man had been killed in three of the four divisions to the south, elation over the victory scored by the three divisions to the north was tinged with sorrow at its cost. "I cannot think of this bloody hill without sadness and pride," Hovey was to say, and an Illinois soldier, roaming the field when the fighting was over, was struck by the thought that no moral solution had been arrived at as a result of all the bloodshed. "There they lay," he said of the dead and wounded all around him, "the blue and the gray intermingled; the same rich, young American blood flowing out in little rivulets of crimson; each thinking he was in the right."

Grant was more interested just now in military solutions, and he believed he had reached one. "We were now assured of our position between Johnston and Pemberton," he subsequently declared, "without a possibility of a junction of their forces." Others in his army believed they saw an even more profitable outcome of the struggle on Champion Hill. "Vicksburg must fall now," a participant wrote home that night; "I think a week may find us in possession. It may take longer," he added on second thought, "but the end will be the same."

While Pemberton's depleted army fell back through the darkness to a position covering the Big Black crossing, eight miles to the west, Grant let his soldiers sleep till dawn, by which time Wilson's engineers had the bridge over Baker's Creek rebuilt, then took up the pursuit. McClernand once more had the lead, though Blair was detached to rejoin Sherman, who by now was close at hand with his other two divisions. "We have made good progress today in the work of destruction," he had written Grant the day before, as he prepared to leave the Mississippi capital. "Jackson will no longer be a point of danger. The land is devastated for thirty miles around." Next morning — Sunday, May 17 — while Grant was crossing Baker's Creek to come to grips with Pemberton again, Sherman passed through Bolton and encountered other signs of devastation. Seeing some soldiers drawing water from a well in front of "a small hewn-log house" beside the road, he turned his horse in at the gate to get a drink. The place had been rifled, its furnishings wrecked and strewn about the yard, and though such acts of vandalism were fairly common at this stage of the campaign — brought on, so to speak, by an excess of skylark energy and delight that things were going so well for the army of invasion — this one appeared to have been committed with an extra measure of glee and satisfaction. When Sherman had one of the men hand him a book he saw lying on the ground beside the well, he found out why. It was a copy of the United States Constitution, with the name Jefferson Davis written on the title page. This was the property the Confederate President's brother had secured for him the year before, when Brierfield was occupied by Butler, and though in the course of his December visit Davis had expressed the hope that he would be spared further depredations, it had not turned out that way. For him, as for his septuagenarian brother, the blue pursuit had been unrelenting. "Joe Davis's plantation was not far off," Sherman later recalled. "One of my staff officers went there, with a few soldiers, and took a pair of carriage horses, without my knowledge at the time. He found Joe Davis at home, an old man, attended by a young and affectionate niece; but they were overwhelmed with grief to see their country overrun and swarming with Federal troops."

Grant meanwhile was pushing west. About 7 o'clock he came upon Pemberton's new position — and found it even stronger, in some respects, than the one the rebels had occupied "by accident or design" the day before. This time, however, it was clearly by design. Not only had the position been prepared overnight for just such an emergency as the Confederates now faced; it was here, in fact, that Pemberton had wanted to do his fighting in the first place. The railroad bridge, which had been floored to provide for passage of his artillery and wagons, was at the apex of a horseshoe bend of the Big Black, whose high west bank afforded the guns emplaced along it an excellent field of fire out over the low-lying eastern bank and the mile-long line of rifle pits already dug across the open end of the horseshoe. Parapeted with bales of cotton brought from surrounding plantations, the line was a strong one, even without the concentric support of the guns emplaced to its rear, its front being protected by a shallow bayou that abutted north on the river and south on an impenetrable cypress brake. Whatever came at the men in these pits would have to come straight up the narrow railroad embankment, a suicidal prospect in the face of all that massed artillery, or across the rain-swollen bayou, beyond which open fields stretched for nearly half a mile, allowing the attackers little or no cover except for a single copse of woods about three hundred yards in front of the far left, where guns were also grouped in expectation. Still unaware that Loring had skedaddled, Pemberton held this intrenched bridgehead in hopes that Old Blizzards would show up in time for a share in the impending fight at the gates of Vicksburg, which was less than a dozen miles back down the road.

What showed up instead was the Yankees. One look at the position his opponent had selected — Pemberton, after all, was a trained engineer, with a reputation for skill in the old army — told Grant that he stood an excellent chance of suffering the bloodiest of repulses if he attempted a frontal attack. Fortunately, though, he had instructed Sherman to swing north of Edwards for a crossing at Bridgeport, five miles upstream; so that all Grant had to do here, for the present, was keep up a show of strength to hold Pemberton in place while Sherman got his three divisions over the river above and came down on his flank. But McClernand had other ideas. Troubled perhaps by his poor showing yesterday — though he would not hesitate presently to claim a lion's share of the credit for the Champion Hill success, on grounds that Hovey's division was from his corps — he moved vigorously today, sending Carr and Osterhaus, the Pea Ridge companions, respectively north and south of the railroad to confront the rebels crouched behind their cotton parapets. An assault was a desperate thing to venture against the dug-in Confederates and all those high-sited batteries in their rear, he knew, but he was quite as determined as Grant to "make a little showing," if not a big one. So was Brigadier General Michael Lawler, commanding Carr's second brigade, which had worked its way into the copse on the far right. A big man, over 250 pounds in weight and so large of girth that he had to wear his sword belt looped over one shoulder, Lawler was Irish, forty-nine years old, and lately an Illinois farmer. His favorite Tipperary maxim, "If you see a head, hit it," was much in his mind as he peered across the chocolate-colored bayou at the rebel intrenchments three hundred yards away. Many heads were visible there, inviting him to hit them, and at last he could bear it no longer. Stripped to his shirt sleeves because of the midday heat, he stood up, swinging his sword, and ordered his four regiments forward on the double. The bayou was shoulder-deep in places, but the Iowa and Wisconsin soldiers floundered straight across it in what a reporter called "the most perilous and ludicrous charge I witnessed during the war," and came mud-plastered up to the enemy line with a whoop, having suffered 199 casualties in the three minutes that had elapsed since they left the copse. The loss was small compared to the gain, however, for the rebels broke rearward, avoiding contact, only to find that the bridge had been set afire in their rear to keep the close-following bluecoats from surging across in their wake. Lawler's reward was 1200 prisoners — more men, he said, than he himself had brought into action — out of a final total of 1751 Confederates killed and captured, along with 18 guns, when the other brigades took fire from his example and rushed forward, breaking the gray line all down its length. Grant's losses were 276 killed and wounded, plus 3 missing, presumably left at the bottom of the bayou now in his rear.

Across the way, Pemberton had watched the disintegration of his skillfully drawn line and the quick subtraction of a brigade from his dwindling army. Neither was truly catastrophic; he still held the high west bank of the river, and the bridge the Federals might have used for a crossing was burning fiercely in the noonday sunlight; but he was depressed by the failure of his men to hold a position of such strength. If they would not stand fast here, where would they stand fast? Years later, a member of his staff was to say: "The affair of Big Black bridge was one which an ex-Confederate participant naturally dislikes to record." It was unpleasant to remember, and it had been even more unpleasant to observe. Presently, moreover, word came from upstream that Sherman had forced a crossing at Bridgeport, capturing the dozen pickets on duty at that point. There was nothing for it now but to continue the retreat or be outflanked. Pemberton gave the necessary orders and the westward march got under way, as it had done after yesterday's bloodier action, except that this time there would be no halt until Vicksburg itself was reached. Then what? He did not know how well his troops would fight with their backs to the wall, but this most recent action was not an encouraging example of their mettle. Some thirty hours ago he had had 17,500 effectives in his mobile force, and now he was down to a good deal less than half that many. In fact it was nearer a third, 5375 having been killed, wounded, or captured, while as many more had wandered off with Loring. As he rode westward, accompanied by his chief engineer, young Major Samuel Lockett, Pemberton's distress increased and his confidence touched bottom. "Just thirty years ago," he said at last, breaking a long and painful silence, "I began my military career by receiving my appointment to a cadetship at the U.S. Military Academy, and today — that same date — that career is ended in disaster and disgrace." Lockett tried to reassure the general by reminding him that two fresh divisions stood in the Vicksburg intrenchments, which had been designed to withstand repeated assaults by almost any number of men. Besides, he said, Joe Johnston would be reinforced at Canton in the event of a siege, and would come to the beleaguered city's relief with all the skill for which he was famous, North and South. "To all of which," the major recalled afterwards, "General Pemberton replied that my youth and hopes were the parents of my judgment; he himself did not believe our troops would stand the first shock of an attack."

A dispatch had already gone to Johnston that morning, announcing the results of yesterday's battle and warning that Haines Bluff would have to be abandoned if the Big Black position was outflanked or overrun. Accordingly, as the retreat got under way, orders were sent for the garrison on the Yazoo to fall back, all but two companies, who were to forward all stores possible and destroy the rest, "making a show of force until the approach of the enemy by land should compel them to retire." Provisions were much on Pemberton's mind, despite his dejection, and he issued instructions that, from Bovina on, "all cattle, sheep, and hogs belonging to private parties, and likely to fall into the hands of the enemy, should be driven within our lines." Similarly, corn was pulled from the fields along the way, "and all disposable wagons applied to this end." If it was to be a siege, food was likely to be as vital a factor as ammunition, and he did all he could in that respect. The march continued, accompanied by the lowing of cows, the bleating of sheep, and the squealing of pigs, steadily westward. For all the Confederates knew, Sherman might have moved fast around their flank and beaten them to the goal. Then up ahead, as Pemberton was to remember it years later, "the outlines of the hill city rose slowly through the heated dust — Vicksburg and security. Passing raddled fields turning colorless from the powdered earth that rose beneath their tramp, the gray soldiers slacked off the turnpikes along the high ground until they came inside the city's breastworks. As word carried down the crooked line of march that the race to Vicksburg had been won, the footsore remnants in the rear flooded down the pike."

Sunset made a red glory over the Louisiana bayous; "The sky faded to a cool green and it was dark." Pemberton and his aides worked through the night, seeing to the comfort of the troops who had fought today and yesterday, bivouacked now in rear of the intrenchments, and inspecting the front-line defenses manned by the two divisions which had remained in the city all this time. Dawn gave light by which to check the overlapping fields of fire commanded by the 102 guns, light and heavy, emplaced along the semicircular landward fortifications. Midmorning brought reports from scouts that the two companies left at Haines Bluff were on their way to Vicksburg, having complied with the order to hold out as long as possible. Heavy columns of Federals were close behind them, while other blue forces were hard on the march from Bovina. Before they arrived — as they presently did, to begin the investment — a messenger came riding in with a reply to yesterday's dispatch to Johnston, who had moved southwest from Canton to a position northeast of Brownsville. Pemberton's spirits had risen considerably since his confession of despair as he fell back from the Big Black the day before, but what his superior had to say was scarcely of a nature to raise them further. For one thing, the Virginian said nothing whatsoever about relief, either now or in the future. As he saw it, the choice had been narrowed to evacuation or surrender.

May 17, 1863.

LIEUTENANT GENERAL PEMBERTON:

Your dispatch of today ... was received. If Haines Bluff is untenable, Vicksburg is of no value and cannot be held. If, therefore, you are invested at Vicksburg, you must ultimately surrender. Under such circumstances, instead of losing both troops and place, we must, if possible, save the troops. If it is not too late, evacuate Vicksburg and its dependencies, and march them to the northeast.

Most respectfully, your obedient servant,
J. E. JOHNSTON, General.

Even if Pemberton had wanted to follow this advice — which he did not, considering it in violation of orders from the Commander in Chief that the place be held at all costs — compliance was altogether beyond his means. Before he had time for more than brief speculation as to what effect these words might have on his chances of survival, Union guns were shelling his outer works. The siege had begun, and Grant was jockeying for positions from which to launch an all-out assault, intending to bring the three-week-old campaign, which had opened on his birthday, to the shortest possible end.

Yesterday's rout on the Big Black had seemed to indicate what the result of one hard smash at the rebel lines would be, and Grant's spirits had risen more or less in ratio to the droop of his opponent's. If roads could be found, he said as he watched the enemy abandon the high western bank, he intended to advance in three columns of one corps each, "and have Vicksburg or Haines Bluff tomorrow night." While Wilson and his engineers were collecting materials for replacing the burned railroad bridge, he rode up to Bridgeport and found Sherman hard at work laying India-rubber pontoons for a crossing in force. Soon after dark the first of his three divisions started over, their way lighted by pitch pine bonfires on both banks. Grant and his red-haired lieutenant sat on a log and watched the troops move westward over the Big Black, faces pale in the firelight and gun barrels catching glints from the flames as "the bridge swayed to and fro under the passing feet." Sherman was to remember it so. A water-colorist of some skill back in the days when there had been time for such diversions, he thought the present scene "made a fine war picture."

By daybreak all three divisions were across. Riding south to see whether McClernand and McPherson had done as well, Grant left instructions for Sherman to march northwest in order to interpose between Vicksburg and the forts on the Yazoo. By 10 o'clock this had been done. A detachment sent northward found Haines Bluff unoccupied, its big guns spiked, and made contact with the Union gunboats on the river below, signaling them to steam in close and tie up under the frowning bluff that had defied them for so long. Grant now had the supply base he wanted, north of the city. Presently he came riding up, to find his friend Sherman gazing down from the Walnut Hills at the Chickasaw Bayou region below, from which he had launched his bloody and fruitless assault against these heights five months ago. Up to now, the Ohioan had had his reservations about this eighth attempt to take or bypass Vicksburg, saying flatly, "I tremble for the result. I look upon the whole thing as one of the most hazardous and desperate moves of this or any other war." But now his doubts were gone, replaced by enthusiasm: as was shown when he turned to Grant, standing quietly by, and abruptly broke the silence.

"Until this moment I never thought your expedition a success," he said; "I never could see the end clearly until now. But this is a campaign. This is a success if we never take the town."

Grant shared his friend's enthusiasm, if not his verbal exuberance, with regard to a situation brought about by a combination of careful strategy, flawlessly improvised tactics, sudden marches, and hard blows delivered with such triphammer rapidity that the enemy had never been given a chance to recover the balance he lost when the blue army, feinting coincidentally at Haines Bluff, swarmed ashore at Bruinsburg, forty-five air-line miles away. At no time in the past three weeks, moreover, had the outlook been so bright as it was now. All three corps had crossed the Big Black, the final natural barrier between them and their goal, and were converging swiftly upon the hilltop citadel by three main roads so appropriate to their purpose that they might have been surveyed with this in mind. Sherman advanced from the northeast on the Benton road, McPherson from due east, along the railroad and the Jackson turnpike, and McClernand from the southeast on the Baldwin's Ferry road. By nightfall, after a few brief skirmishes along the ill-organized line of rebel outposts — invariably abandoned at the first suggestion of real pressure — the lead elements of all three columns were in lateral contact with each other and in jump-off positions for tomorrow's assault. Next morning, May 19, while they completed their dispositions, the men were in high spirits. They were in fact, like Sherman, "a little giddy with pride" at the realization of all they had accomplished up to now. In the twenty days since they crossed the Mississippi, they had marched 180 miles to fight and win five battles — Port Gibson, Raymond, Jackson, Champion Hill, Big Black River — occupy a Deep South capital, inflict over 7000 casualties at a cost of less than 4500 of their own, and seize no less than fifty pieces of

field artillery, not to mention two dozen larger pieces they found spiked in fortifications they outflanked. In all this time, they had not lost a gun or a stand of colors, and they had never failed to take an assigned objective, usually much more quickly than their commanders expected them to do. And now, just ahead, lay the last and largest of their objectives: Vicksburg itself, the ultimate prize for which the capture of all those others had served as prelude. Their belief that they would carry the place by storm, here and now, was matched by Grant, who issued his final orders before noon. "Corps commanders will push forward carefully, and gain as close position as possible to the enemy's works, until 2 p.m.; at [which] hour they will fire three volleys of artillery from all the pieces in position. This will be the signal for a general charge of all the army corps along the whole line." A closing sentence, intended to forestall the lapse of discipline that would attend a too-informal victory celebration, expressed the measure of his confidence that the assault would be successful, bringing the campaign to a triumphant close today: "When the works are carried, guards will be placed by all division commanders to prevent their men from straggling from their companies."

At the appointed hour, the guns boomed and the blue clots of troops rushed forward, shoulder to shoulder, cheering as they vied for the honor of being first to scale the ridge: whereupon, as if in response to the same signal, a long low cloud of smoke, torn along its bottom edge by the pinkish yellow stabs of muzzle flashes, boiled up with a great clatter from the rebel works ahead. The racket was so tremendous that no man could hear his own shouts or the sudden yelps of the wounded alongside him. What was immediately apparent, however, amid a confusion of sound so uproarious that it was as if the whole mad scene were being played in pantomime, was that the assault had failed almost as soon as it got started. Sherman, watching from a point of vantage near the north end of the line, put it simplest in a letter he wrote home that night: "The heads of the columns have been swept away as chaff thrown from the hand on a windy day." Others, closer up, had a more gritty sense of what had happened. Emerging into the open, an Illinois captain saw "the very sticks and chips, scattered over the ground, jumping under the hot shower of rebel bullets." Startled, he and his company plunged forward, tumbled into a cane-choked ravine at the base of the enemy ridge, and hugged the earth for cover and concealment. All up and down the line it was much the same for those who had not scattered rearward at the first burst of fire; once within point-blank musket range, there was little the attackers could do but try to stay out of sight until darkness gave them a chance to pull back without inviting a bullet between the shoulder blades. As they lay prone the fire continued, cutting the stalks of cane, one by one, so that "they lopped gently upon us," as if to assist in keeping them hidden. Through the remaining hours of daylight they stayed there, with bullets twittering just above the napes of their necks. Then they returned through the gathering dusk to the jump-off positions they had left five hours ago. Reaching safety after a hard run, the captain and other survivors of his company "stopped and took one long breath, bigger than a pound of wool."

Pemberton was perhaps as surprised as the bluecoats were at their abrupt repulse. In reporting to the President — the message would have to be smuggled out, of course, before it could be put on the wire for Richmond — that his army was "occupying the trenches around Vicksburg," he added proudly: "Our men have considerably recovered their morale." Meanwhile he strengthened his defenses and improved the disposition of his 20,000 effectives. M. L. Smith's division had the left, Forney's the center, and Stevenson's the right, while Bowen's was held in immediate reserve, under orders to be prepared to rush at a moment's notice to whatever point needed bolstering. There was a crippling shortage of intrenching tools, only about five hundred being on hand. "They were entirely inadequate," an engineer officer later declared, but "the men soon improvised wooden shovels [and used] their bayonets as picks." They had indeed "considerably recovered," now that they had stopped running, and they were hungry for revenge for the humiliations they had been handed, particularly day before yesterday on the Big Black River. If the Yankees would keep coming at them the way they had come this afternoon, the Confederates hoped they would keep it up forever.

In point of fact, that was pretty much what Grant had in mind. He had suffered 942 casualties and inflicted less than 200, thus coming close to reversing the Big Black ratio, but he still thought the ridge could be carried by assault. Conferring next morning with his corps commanders he found them agreed that this first effort had failed, in Sherman's words, "by reason of the natural strength of the position, and because we were forced by the nature of the ground to limit our attacks to the strongest part of the enemy line, viz., where the three principal roads entered the city." Nothing could be done about the first of these two drawbacks, but the second could be corrected by careful reconnaissance. Better artillery preparations would also be of help, it was decided, in softening up the rebel works; moreover, the navy could add the weight of its metal from the opposite side of the ridge, Porter having returned from a two-week expedition up the Red River to Alexandria, where he had met Banks coming north from Opelousas on May 6. Grant told McClernand, Sherman, and McPherson to spend today and tomorrow preparing "for a renewed assault on the 22d, simultaneously, at 10 a.m." Riding his line while the work was being pushed, he found the men undaunted by their repulse the day before, though they were prompt to let him know they were weary of the meat-and-vegetables diet on which they had been subsisting for the past three weeks. Turkey and sweet potatoes were fine as a special treat, it seemed, but such rich food had begun to pall as a regular thing. A private looked up from shoveling, recognized Grant riding by, and said in a pointed but conversational tone: "Hardtack." Others took up the call, on down the line, raising their voices with every repetition of the word, until finally they were shouting with all their might. "Hardtack! Hardtack!" they yelled as the army commander went past. "Hardtack! Hardtack!" Finally he reined in his horse and informed all those within earshot that the engineers were building a road from the Yazoo steamboat landing, "over which to supply them with everything they needed." At this, as he said later, "the cry was instantly changed to cheers." That night there was hardtack for everyone, along with beans, and coffee to wash it down. The soldiers woke next morning strengthened for the work that was now at hand.

For the first time in history, a major assault was launched by commanders whose eyes were fixed on the hands of watches synchronized the night before. This was necessary in the present case because the usual signal guns would not have been heard above the din of the preliminary bombardment, which included the naval weapons on both flanks, upstream and down, and six mortar boats already engaged for the past two days in what one defender contemptuously called "the grand but nearly harmless sport of pitching big shells into Vicksburg." All night the 13-inch mortars kept heaving their 200-pound projectiles into the checkerboard pattern of the city's streets and houses, terrifying citizens huddled under their beds and dining-room tables. ("Vertical fire is never very destructive of life," the same witness remarked. "Yet the howling and bursting shells had a very demoralizing effect on those not accustomed to them.") Then at dawn the 200 guns on the landward side chimed in, raising geysers of dirt on the ridge where the Confederates were intrenched and waiting. At 9.30, in compliance with Grant's request, Porter closed the range with four gunboats from below and took the lower water batteries under fire. He was supposed to keep this up until 10.30, half an hour past the scheduled time for the infantry assault to open, but since he could see no indication that the army had been successful in its storming attempt, he kept up the fire for an extra hour before dropping back downriver and out of range. One ironclad, the *Tuscumbia*, was severely battered and forced to retire before the others. Otherwise, though he reported that this was altogether the hottest fire his boats had yet endured, Porter suffered little damage in the bows-on fight, aside from a few men wounded. He could not see, however, that he had accomplished much in the way of punishing the defenders. Nor was there any evidence that the army had done any better.

As a matter of fact, the army had done a good deal worse, though not for lack of trying. At the appointed hour the men of all three corps rushed forward, the advance waves equipped with twenty-foot scaling ladders to be used against steep-walled strongpoints, of which there were many along the ridge ahead. "The rebel line, concealed by the parapet, showed no sign of unusual activity," Sherman observed from his point of vantage to the north, "but as our troops came in fair view, the enemy rose behind their parapet and poured a furious fire upon our lines.... For about two hours we had a severe and bloody battle, but at every point we were repulsed." It was much the same with McPherson and McClernand, to the south, who also lost heavily as a result of these whites-of-their-eyes tactics employed by the Confederates. At several points, left and right and center, individual groups managed to effect shallow penetrations, despite what an Illinois colonel called "the most murderous fire I ever saw," but were quickly expelled or captured by superior forces the enemy promptly brought to bear from his mobile reserve. Those bluecoats who crouched in the ravines and ditches at the base of the ridge, taking shelter there as they had done three days ago, were dislodged by the explosion in their midst of 12-inch shells which the defenders rolled downhill after lighting the fuzes. On McClernand's front a heavier lodgment was effected at one point, and the general, taking fire at the sight of his troops flaunting their banners on the rebel works, sent word to Grant that he had "part possession of two forts, and the stars and stripes are floating over them." If the other two corps "would make a diversion in my favor," he thought he could enlarge his gains and perhaps score an absolute breakthrough. At any rate, he earnestly declared, "a vigorous push ought to be made all along the line."

Grant was with Sherman when the message reached him. "I don't believe a word of it," he said. Sherman protested that the note was official and must be credited. Though he had just called off his own attack, admitting failure, he offered to renew it at once in the light of this appeal from McClernand. Grant thought the matter over, then told the redhead he "might try it again" at 3 o'clock, if no contrary orders reached him before that time. Riding south, he detached one of McPherson's divisions to support McClernand and authorized a resumption of the attack on the center as well. Promptly at 3, Sherman launched his promised second assault, but found it "a repetition of the first, equally unsuccessful and bloody." McPherson had the same unpleasant experience. McClernand, still afire with hope, threw the borrowed division into the fray — though not in time to maintain, much less widen or deepen, the penetration of which he had been so proud. A whooping counterattack by Colonel T. N. Waul's Texas Legion killed or captured all but a handful of Federals at that point. By sundown the firing had died to a sputter, and at nightfall the survivors crept back across the corpse-pocked fields to the safety of the lines they had left with such high hopes that morning. Some measure of their determination and valor was shown by a comparison of their losses today with those of three days ago. The previous assault had ended with two stands of colors left on the forward slope of the enemy ridge; this time there were five. Moreover, the casualties exceeded this five-two ratio. Less than a thousand men had fallen the time before, including 165 killed or missing, whereas this time the figures went above three thousand — 3199, to be exact — with 649 in the killed-or-missing category. In other words, Grant had lost in the past three days almost as many soldiers as he had lost in the past three weeks of nearly continuous battle and maneuver which had brought him within sight of the ramparts of Vicksburg only to be repulsed.

He was furious. "This last attack only served to increase our casualties without giving any benefit whatever," he wrote some twenty years later, still chagrined. Quick as ever to shift the blame for any setback or evidence of shortcoming — at Belmont it had been overexcited "higher officers"; at Donelson it had been McClernand; at Shiloh it had been Prentiss and Lew Wallace, although the former most likely had saved him from defeat; at Iuka it had been Rosecrans and the wind — he notified Halleck, two days after the second Vicksburg repulse: "The whole loss for the day will probably reach 1500 killed and wounded. General McClernand's dispatches misled me as to the real state of facts, and caused much of this loss. He is entirely unfit for the position of corps commander, both on the march and on the battlefield. Looking after his corps gives me more labor and infinitely more uneasi-ness than all the remainder of my department." And yet, on the day of battle itself, he included that general's misleading claims in his own dispatch informing Halleck of the outcome. "Vicksburg is now completely invested," he declared. "I have possession of Haines Bluff and the Yazoo; consequently have supplies. Today an attempt was made to carry the city by assault, but was not entirely successful. We hold possession, however, of two of the enemy's forts, and have skirmishers close under all of them. Our loss was not severe." As he wrote, his optimism grew; for that was the reverse of the coin. He would no more admit discouragement than he would entertain self-blame. "The nature of the ground about Vicksburg is such that it can only be taken by a siege," he judged, but added: "It is entirely safe to us in time, I would say one week if the enemy do not send a large army upon my rear."

He did not regret having made the assaults; he only regretted that they had failed. Besides, he subsequently explained, his high-spirited troops had approached the gates of Vicksburg with a three-week cluster of victories to their credit; they would never have settled down willingly to the tedium of siege operations unless they had first been given the chance to prove that the place could not be taken by storm. Now that this had been demonstrated, though at the rather excessive price of 4141 casualties, they took to spadework with a will, constructing their own complex system of intrenchments roughly parallel to those of the rebels, which in a few places were not much more than fifty yards away. As they delved in the sandy yellow clay of the hillsides or drew their beads on such heads as appeared above the enemy parapets, they were encouraged by news of tangential victories, particularly on the part of the navy, which was on a rampage now that the outlying Confederate defenses had been abandoned. An expedition made up of the *DeKalb* and three tinclads, all under Lieutenant Commander John Walker, had been sent up the Yazoo on May 20, the day after the first assault, and returned on the 23d, the day after the second, to report that the rebels had set their Yazoo City navy yard afire at the approach of the Union vessels, the flames consuming three warships under construction on the stocks, for an estimated loss of $3,000,000. This meant that there would be no successor to the *Arkansas*, which was welcome news indeed. But Porter was unsatisfied; he sent the expedition back upriver the next morning. This time Walker steamed to within a dozen miles of Fort

Pemberton, destroying steamboats and sawmills as he went, then came back downstream to push 180 miles up the winding Sunflower River, where he caught and burned still more fugitive rebel steamboats. Returning this second time, he could report that these streams were no longer arteries of supply for the Confederates below the confluence of the Tallahatchie and the Yalobusha, nearly one hundred air-line miles from the beleaguered Vicksburg bluff.

Pemberton took the news of this without undue distress. After all, the Yazoo and the Sunflower were no longer of much interest to him; the Father of Waters was now his sole concern, and only about a dozen miles of that. "I have decided to hold Vicksburg as long as possible," he had replied to Johnston's last-minute dispatch urging evacuation, "with the firm hope that the Government may yet be able to assist me in keeping this obstruction to the enemy's free navigation of the Mississippi River. I still conceive it to be the most important point in the Confederacy." His outlook improved with the repulse of the first Federal assault, and on the eve of the second he was asking: "Am I to expect reinforcements? From what direction, and how soon? ... The men credit and are encouraged by a report that you are near with a large force. They are fighting in good spirits, and the reorganization is complete." After the second repulse, however, the defenders were faced with an unpleasant problem. For three days — six, in the case of those who had fallen in the first assault — Grant's dead and injured lay in the fields and ditches at the base of the Confederate ridge, exposed to the fierce heat of the early Mississippi summer. The stench of the dead, whose bodies were swollen grotesquely, and the cries of the wounded, who suffered the added torment of thirst, were intolerable to the men who had shot them down; yet Grant would not ask for a truce for burial or treatment of these unfortunates, evidently thinking that such a request would be an admission of weakness on his part. Finally Pemberton could bear it no longer. On the morning of May 25 he sent a message through the lines to the Union commander: "Two days having elapsed since your dead and wounded have been lying in our front, and as yet no disposition on your part of a desire to remove them being exhibited, in the name of humanity I have the honor to propose a cessation of hostilities for two hours and a half, that you may be enabled to remove your dead and dying men." To Pemberton's relief, Grant at last "acceded" to this proposal. At 6 p.m. all firing was suspended while the Federals came forward to bury the dead where they lay and bring comfort to such few men as had survived the three-day torture. This done, they returned through the darkness to their lines and the firing was resumed with as much fury as before.

In nothing was Grant more "unpronounceable" than in this. He would berate, and in at least one case attack with his fists, any man he saw abusing a dumb animal; he had, it was said to his credit, no stomach for suffering; he disliked above all to ride over a field where there had been recent heavy fighting; he would not eat a piece of meat until it had been cooked to a char, past any sign of blood or even pinkness. Yet this he could do to his own men, this abomination perhaps beyond all others of the war, without expressed regret or apparent concern. However, this too was the reverse of a coin, the other side of which was his singleness of purpose, his quality of intense preoccupation with what he called "the business," meaning combat. He took his losses as they came — they had, in fact, about been made up already with the arrival that week of a division of reinforcements from Memphis, and would be more than made up with the arrival, early the following week, of a second such division, while four more were being alerted even now for the trip downriver from Tennessee, Missouri, and Kentucky to bring his mid-June total to 71,000 effectives — for the sake of getting on with the job to which he had set his hand. Long ago in Mexico, during a lull in the war, he had written home to the girl he was to marry: "If we have to fight, I would like to do it all at once and then make friends." He felt that way about it still, and now that he was calling the turn, he wanted no interludes or delays; he wanted it finished, and he believed the finish was in sight. "The enemy are now undoubtedly in our grasp," he told Halleck the day before the burial truce. "The fall of Vicksburg and the capture of most of the garrison can only be a question of time."

This was not to say there would be no more setbacks and frustrations. There would indeed, war being the chancy thing it was, and Grant knew it: which perhaps was why he had dropped his prediction, made two days before, that the fall of the city would be accomplished within "I would say one week." And in fact there was one such mishap three days later, two days after the burial truce, this time involving the navy. In the course of drawing his lines for the siege, Sherman had begun to suspect, from the amount of artillery fire he drew, that the Confederates were shifting guns from their upper water batteries to cover the landward approaches, particularly on their far left. Requested by Grant to test the facts of the case, Porter on May 27 sent the *Cincinnati* to draw the fire of the guns "if still there," covering her movements with four other ironclads at long range. She started downriver at 7 o'clock in the morning, commanded by Lieutenant G. M. Bache, and by 10 the matter had been settled beyond doubt. Not only were the guns still there, but they sank the *Cincinnati*. Rounding to in order to open fire, she took a pair of solids in her shell room and a third in her magazine. As she tried to make an upstream escape, a heavy shot drove through her pilot house and her starboard tiller was carried away, along with all three flagstaffs. Hulled repeatedly by plunging fire, she began filling rapidly. Bache, with five of his guns disabled in short order, tried to get beyond range and tie the vessel up to the east bank before she sank, but could not make it. She went down in three fathoms of water, still within range of the enemy guns, and what remained of her crew had to swim for their lives. The total loss, aside from the *Cincinnati* herself, was 5 killed, 14 wounded, and 15 missing, presumed drowned.

Convinced that Bache and his crew had done their best under disadvantageous circumstances, Porter accepted the loss of the ironclad — the third since his arrival in early December — as one of the accidents of war, and did not relax on that account his pressure against the rebels beleaguered on their bluff. He already had the approval of Grant for his conduct of naval affairs. Replying to a message in which the admiral informed him that Banks, although he had wound up his West Louisiana campaign at last, would "not [be] coming here with his men. He is going to occupy the attention of Port Hudson, and has landed at Bayou Sara, using your transports for the purpose," Grant told Porter: "I am satisfied that you are doing all that can be done in aid of the reduction of Vicksburg. There is no doubt of the fall of the place ultimately, but how long it will be is a matter of doubt. I intend to lose no more men, but to force the enemy from one position to another without exposing my troops."

※ 4 ※

Banks had done a good deal more by now than merely "occupy the attention of Port Hudson." Crossing the Mississippi on the day after Grant's second repulse at Vicksburg, he completed his investment of the Louisiana stronghold on May 26, and next morning — simultaneous with the sinking of the *Cincinnati*, 240 winding miles upriver — launched his own all-out assault, designed to bring to a sudden and victorious end a campaign even more circuitous than Grant's. That general had covered some 180 miles by land and water before returning to his approximate starting point and placing his objective under siege, whereas Banks had marched or ridden about three times that far, as the thing turned out, to accomplish the same result. However, not only was the distance greater; the numerical odds had been tougher, at least at the start. Back in mid-March, when Farragut ran two ships past the fuming hundred-foot bluff, Banks had maneuvered on the landward side, only to discover that the defenders had more men inside the works than he had on the outside. This gave him pause, as well it might, and while he pondered the problem he learned that Grant, whom he had expected to join him in reducing Port Hudson as a prelude to their combined movement against Vicksburg, was stymied north of the latter place, involved in a series of canal and bayou experiments which seemed likely to delay him for some time. Thinking it over, Banks decided to accomplish his assignment on his own. If he could not take Port Hudson, he would do as Grant was trying to do upriver. He would go around it.

It was not only that he was disinclined to wait and share the glory, politically ambitious though he was. He also believed he could not, and with cause. Nearly half of the 35,000 troops in his department were nine-month volunteers whose enlistments would be expiring between May and August; they would have to be used before summer or not at all. However, there was about as much need for caution as there was for haste, since more than half of this total, long- and short-term men alike, were required to garrison Baton Rouge, New Orleans, and various other points along the Mississippi and the Gulf. As a result of these necessary smaller detachments, his five divisions were reduced to about 5000 men each. Three of the five were with him near Port Hudson, under Major General C. C. Augur and Brigadier Generals William Emory and Cuvier Grover, while the fourth was at New Orleans under Brigadier General Thomas W. Sherman. Leaving Augur to hold Baton Rouge, Banks set out downriver with the other two on March 25 to join Godfrey Weitzel, commanding his fifth division at Brashear City, near Grand Lake and the junction of the Atchafalaya River and Bayou Teche. Back in January, Weitzel had ascended the former stream for a few miles, intending to establish an alternate route, well removed from the guns of Port Hudson, from the mouth of Red River to the Gulf. In this he had failed, not so much because of interference from Richard Taylor's scratch command of swamp-bound rebels, which he had thrown into precipitate retreat, but mainly because he had found the Atchafalaya choked with brush at that season of the year. Banks believed that this time he would succeed, and he hoped to abolish Taylor as a continuing threat. He intended in fact to capture him, bag and baggage, having worked out his plans with that in mind.

Taylor had about 4000 troops between the Teche and the Atchafalaya, his flanks protected right and left by two captured Union warships, the gunboat *Diana* and the armed ram *Queen of the West*, the former having been ambushed and seized that week near Pattersonville, when she imprudently ventured up the bayou, and the latter having been brought down from the Red River the week before to prevent her destruction or recapture by Farragut after his run past Port Hudson. Banks had four Gulf Squadron gunboats with which he planned to neutralize these two turncoat vessels, and he intended to bag Taylor's entire land force by sending one division from his 15,000-man command across Grand Lake to land in the rear of the rebels while he engaged them in front with his other two divisions. Hemmed in and outnumbered nearly four to one, Taylor would have to choose between surrender and annihilation. On April 11, in accordance with his design, Banks moved Emory and Weitzel from Brashear across the Atchafalaya to Berwick, and while they were advancing up the left bank of the Teche next day, skirmishing as they went, Grover put his troops aboard transports, escorted by the quartet of gunboats, and set out across the lake for a landing on the western shore within a mile of Irish Bend, an eastward loop of the Teche, control of which would place him squarely athwart the only Confederate line of retreat. Despite some irritating delays, the maneuver seemed to be going as planned; the skirmishing continued in front and Grover got his division ashore six miles in the enemy rear; Banks anticipated a Cannae. But Taylor got wind of what was up and reacted fast. Leaving a handful of men to put up a show of resistance to the two blue divisions in his front, he swung rearward with the rest to attack Grover and if possible drive him into the lake. On the 13th heavy fighting ensued. The shoestring force managed to delude and delay Emory and Weitzel while the main body fell on Grover. Though the latter was not driven into the lake, he was held in check while Taylor withdrew up the Teche in the darkness, foiling the plans so carefully laid for his destruction. In three days of intermittent action the Federals had lost 577 killed and wounded, the Confederates somewhat less, although there was considerable disagreement between the two commanders, then and later, as to the number of prisoners taken on each side, Taylor afterwards protesting that Banks had claimed the capture of more men than had actually opposed him.

Whatever the truth of his claims in this regard, and despite his failure to bring off the Cannae he intended, there could be no doubt that Banks, after a season of rather spectacular defeats in Virginia at the hands of Stonewall Jackson, had won his first clear-cut victory in the field. And next day, when he received word that the *Diana* and the *Queen* had been destroyed — the former burned by the rebels, who could not take her with them up the narrow Teche, and the latter sunk by the four Union gunboats, who blew her almost literally out of the water as soon as she entered Grand Lake and came within their range — his elation knew no bounds. Moreover, two of the gunboats steamed forthwith up the Atchafalaya and found it open to navigation all the way to the mouth of the Red, fifty miles above Port Hudson. This meant that Banks had the bypass he had been seeking, though of course it would be of small practical use until Vicksburg had likewise been bypassed or reduced. Since there was no news that Grant had succeeded in any of his experimental projects in that direction, the Massachusetts general decided to explore some vistas he saw opening before him as a result of Taylor's defeat and withdrawal. Within two weeks New Orleans would have been returned to Federal control a solid year, and yet this principal seaport of the South had even less commerce with the outside world today than she had enjoyed in the days of the blockade runners, mainly because the rebel land forces had her cut off from those regions that normally supplied her with goods for shipment. One of the richest of these lay before him now: the Teche. Return of the Teche country to Union control, along with its vast supplies of cotton, salt, lumber, and foodstuffs, would restore New Orleans to her rightful place among the world's great ports and would demonstrate effectively, as one observer pointed out, "that the conquests of the national armies instead of destroying trade were calculated to instill new life into it." There was one drawback. Such a movement up the long riverlike bayou stretching north almost to Alexandria, even though unopposed, might throw him off his previously announced schedule, which called for a meeting with Grant at Baton Rouge on May 10 for a combined attack, first on Port Hudson and then on Vicksburg. But Banks decided the probable gains were worth the risk. Besides, May 10 was nearly a month away, and he hoped to have completed his conquest of the region before then. If not, then Grant could wait, just as he had kept Banks waiting all this time.

Eager for more victories now that he had caught the flavor, the former Bay State governor put his three divisions on the march up the right bank of the Teche without delay. Two days later — April 16: Porter's bluejackets were steeling themselves for their run past the Vicksburg batteries that night, and Grierson's troopers would ride out of La Grange the following morning — he entered New Iberia and pushed on next day to the Vermilion River, which branched southward from the Teche near Vermilionville. Finding Taylor's rear guard drawn up on the opposite bank to contest a crossing, the bluecoats forced it with a brief skirmish, rebuilt the wrecked bridge, and on April 20 marched into Opelousas, evacuated two days earlier by the Louisiana government

which had moved there a year ago when Farragut steamed upriver from New Orleans and trained his guns on Baton Rouge. Taylor did not challenge the occupation of this alternate capital, but continued to fall back toward Alexandria, having received from Kirby Smith at Shreveport, his Transmississippi headquarters, a message expressing "gratification at the conduct of the troops under your command" and congratulating Taylor for the skill he had shown "in extricating them from a position of great peril." Banks called a halt in order to rest his men for a few days and consolidate his gains, which were considerable. Conquest of the Teche had brought within his grasp large quantities of lumber, 5000 bales of cotton, many hogsheads of sugar, an inexhaustible supply of salt, and an estimated 20,000 head of cattle, mules, and horses. He later calculated the value of these spoils to have been perhaps as high as $5,000,000 and pointed out that even this liberal figure should be doubled, since the goods it represented had not only come into Federal hands but had also been kept from the Confederates beyond the Mississippi, for whom they had been in a large part intended. Nor was that all. There were human spoils as well. Back in New Orleans the year before, Ben Butler had begun to enlist freedmen and fugitive slaves in what he called his Corps d'Afrique; now Banks continued this recruitment in the Teche. Two such regiments were organized at Opelousas, with about 500 men in each. Styled the 1st and 3d Louisiana Native Guards, the former was composed of "free Negroes of means and intelligence," with colored line officers and a white lieutenant colonel in command, while the latter was made up largely of ex-slaves whose officers were all white. There was considerable speculation, in the army of which they were now a part, as to how they would behave in combat — when and if they were exposed to it, which many of their fellow soldiers thought inadvisable — but Banks was willing to abide the issue until it had been settled incontrovertibly under fire.

Taylor by now had reached the Red at Gordon's Landing, where the *Queen of the West* had been blasted and captured back in February, thirty miles below Alexandria. Renamed Fort De Russy, the triple-casemated battery had held the low bluff against all comers, and on May 4 its staunchness was proved again when it was attacked by the two gunboats that had come up the Atchafalaya from Grand Lake after sinking the *Queen*. Leading the way, however, was the *Albatross*, which had got past Port Hudson with Farragut in mid-March. She closed the range to five hundred yards and kept up a forty-minute bombardment, supported by the other two ships at longer range, before dropping back with eleven holes punched in her hull and most of her spars and rigging shot away. Fifty miles downriver next morning, having given up hope of reducing the fort on their own, the three ships met Porter — who, after completing the ferrying of Grant's two lead divisions across the Mississippi, had taken possession of Grand Gulf three days ago — coming up the Red with three of his ironclads, a steam ram, and a tug. This seemed quite enough for the task of reduction, but when he reached Fort De Russy late that afternoon, prepared to throw all he had at the place, he found it abandoned, its casemates yawning empty. Threatened from the rear by Banks, who had ended his Opelousas rest halt and resumed his northward march beyond the headwaters of the Teche, the garrison had retreated to avoid capture. Porter continued on to Alexandria next day, May 6, to find that Taylor had also fallen back from there. A couple of hours later, Banks marched in at the head of his three-division column. He was in fine spirits, still wearing his three-week-old aura of victory, and Porter was impressed — particularly by the outward contrast between this new general and the one he had been working alongside for the past four months around Vicksburg. "A handsome, soldierly-looking man," the admiral called the former Speaker of the House, "though rather theatrical in his style of dress." The impression was one of nattiness and sartorial elegance; Banks in fact was something of a military dude. "He wore yellow gauntlets high upon his wrists, looking as clean as if they had just come from the glove-maker; his hat was picturesque, his long boots and spurs were faultless, and his air was that of one used to command. In short, I never saw a more faultless-looking soldier."

Banks was about as proud as he was dapper, and with cause. His Negro recruits more than made up — in numbers at any rate, though it was true their combat value was untested — for the casualties he had suffered in the course of his profitable campaign up the Teche, and his present position at Alexandria gave him access to the entire Red River Valley, a region quite as rich as the one he had just traversed, and far more extensive. With elements already on the march for Natchitoches, fifty air-line miles upriver, and Taylor still fading back from contact, he saw more vistas opening out before him. He also realized, however, that they were unattainable just yet. "The decisive battle of the West must soon be fought near Vicksburg," Kirby Smith was telling a subordinate even now. "The fate of the Trans-Mississippi Department depends on it, and Banks, by operating here, is thrown out of the campaign on the Mississippi." The Massachusetts general agreed, although unwillingly, that he must first turn back east to resume his collaboration with Grant for the reduction of Vicksburg and Port Hudson. Then perhaps, with the Mississippi unshackled throughout its length, he would return up the Red to explore those new vistas stretching all the way to Texas. Grant meanwhile, having won the Battle of Port Gibson, crossed Bayou Pierre, and put his three divisions into jump-off positions for the advance on Jackson, was calling urgently for Banks to join him at once in front of Vicksburg; "But I must say, without qualifications," the latter replied on May 12, "that the means at my disposal do not leave me a shadow of a chance to accomplish it." Though he was "dying with a kind of vanishing hope to see [our] two armies acting together against the strong places of the enemy," he had "neither water nor land transportation to make the movement by the river or by land. The utmost I can accomplish," he told Grant, "is to cross for the purpose of operating with you against Port Hudson."

Once more having reached a decision he wasted no time. Two days later, ending a week's occupation in the course of which he sent no less than 2000 spoils-laden wagons groaning south, he began his withdrawal from Alexandria. The march prescribed was via Simmesport for a crossing at Bayou Sara, a dozen miles above Port Hudson, but Banks himself did not accompany the three divisions on their overland trek; he went instead by boat, first down the Red, then down the Atchafalaya to Brashear City, where he caught a train for New Orleans. With him rode the fifty-two-year-old Emory, whose health had failed in the field and who had been succeeded by Brigadier General Halbert Paine, fifteen years his junior and the only non-West Pointer in Banks's army with so much rank — aside from Banks himself, of course — though he could claim the distinction of having shared a law office with Lincoln's friend Carl Schurz before the war. In New Orleans, Banks gave Emory the task of defending the city with a stripped-down garrison left behind by Thomas Sherman, who was instructed to put most of his men aboard transports bound for Baton Rouge to join Augur for an advance on Port Hudson. As Banks planned it, the two divisions marching north from Baton Rouge would converge on the objective at the same time as the three marching south from Bayou Sara. For all the omnivorous reading he had done since his days as a bobbin boy in his home-state spinning mills, he may or may not have known that in thus intending to unite two widely divided columns on the field of battle he was attempting what Napoleon had called the most difficult maneuver in the book. If so, nonprofessional though he was, he showed no qualms beyond those normally involved in getting some 20,000 troops from one place — or in this case two places — to another. What was more, he brought it off. Advancing simultaneously north and south, the two bodies converged on schedule, May 25. Next day they completed their investment, and the following morning they launched an all-out assault on the 7000 rebels penned up inside Port Hudson.

Like Pemberton, who was nine years his senior, Franklin Gardner was a northern-born professional who married South — his father-in-law was ex-Governor Alexander Mouton, who presided over the legislative body that voted Louisiana out of the Union — then went with his wife's people when the national crisis forced a choice. New York born and Iowa raised, the son of a regular army colonel who had been Adjutant General during the War of 1812, he had graduated from West Point in the class of '43, four places above Ulysses Grant and one below Christopher Augur, whose division was part of the blue cordon now drawn around the bastion Gardner was defending. A brigadier at Shiloh and with Bragg in Kentucky, he had been promoted to major general in December, shortly before his fortieth birthday, and sent to command the stronghold Breckinridge had established at Port Hudson after being repulsed at Baton Rouge in August. By early April his strength had risen beyond 15,000 men, but it had since been whittled down to less than half that as a result of levies by the department commander, reacting to upriver pressure from Grant while Banks was off in the Teche. On May 4, in response to what turned out to be Pemberton's final call, Gardner set out for Jackson with all but a single brigade, only to receive on May 9 at Osyka, just north of the Mississippi line, a dispatch instructing him to return at once to Port Hudson and hold it "to the last," this being Pemberton's interpretation of the President's warning that "both Vicksburg and Port Hudson [are] necessary to a connection with Trans-Mississippi." Gardner did as he was told, and got back there barely ahead of Banks. His strength report of May 19 — the date of Grant's first assault on the Vicksburg intrenchments, 120 air-line miles upriver — showed an "aggregate present" of 5715 in his three brigades, plus about one thousand artillerists in the permanent garrison. That was also the date on a message Joe Johnston addressed to Gardner from north of the Mississippi capital, which had fallen on the day after his arrival the week before: "Evacuate Port Hudson forthwith, and move with your troops toward Jackson to join other troops which I am uniting. Bring all the fieldpieces that you have, with their ammunition and the means of transportation. Heavy guns and their ammunition had better be destroyed, as well as the other property you may be unable to remove." By the time the courier got there, however, he found a ring of Federal steel drawn tightly around the blufftop fortress. He could only report back to Johnston that Port Hudson, like Vicksburg 240 roundabout miles upriver, was besieged.

The Union navy had reappeared ahead of the Union army. On May 4, meeting Porter at the mouth of the Red, Farragut gave over his blockade duties from that point north and steamed back down the Mississippi to Port Hudson. For three days, May 8-10, he bombarded the bluff from above and below, doing all he could to soften it up for Banks, who was still at Alexandria. Upstream were the *Hartford* and the *Albatross*, patched up since her recent misfortune at Fort De Russy, while the downstream batteries were engaged by the screw sloops *Monongahela* and *Richmond*, the gunboat *Genesee*, and the orphaned ironclad *Essex*, which had been downriver ever since her run past Vicksburg the summer before. Coming overland down the western bank, Farragut conferred with Banks on his arrival from New Orleans, May 22. The rebels had given him shell for shell, he said, and shown no sign of weakening under fire, but he assured the general that the navy would continue to do its share until the place had been reduced. Banks thanked him and proceeded to invest the bluff on its landward side, north and east and south, depending on the fleet to see that the beleaguered garrison made no westward escape across the river and received no reinforcements or supplies from that direction. Assisted meanwhile by Grierson's well-rested troopers, who had ridden up from Baton Rouge with the column from the south, he drew his lines closer about the rebel fortifications. On May 26, with ninety guns in position opposing Gardner's thirty-one, he issued orders for a full-scale assault designed to take the place by storm next morning. Weitzel, Grover, and Paine were north of the Clinton railroad, which entered the works about midway, Augur and Sherman to the south. The artillery preparation would begin at daybreak, he explained, augmented by high-angle fire from the navy, and the five division commanders would "dispose their troops so as to annoy the enemy as much as possible during the cannonade by advancing skirmishers to kill the enemy's cannoneers and to cover the advance of the assaulting column." This was somewhat hasty and Banks knew it, but he had reasons for not wanting to delay the attempt for the sake of more extensive preparations. First, like Grant eight days ago at Vicksburg, he believed the rebels were demoralized and unlikely to stand up under a determined blow if it were delivered before they had time to recover their balance. Second, and more important still, he was anxious to wind up the campaign and return to New Orleans; Emory was already complaining that he was in danger of being swamped by an attack from Mobile, where the Confederates had some 5000 men — twice as many as he himself had for the defense of the South's first city — or from Brashear, to which Taylor was free to return now that Banks had left the Teche. This was indeed a two-pronged danger; in fact, despite the cited lack of transportation, it had been the real basis for the Massachusetts general's refusal to join Grant in front of Vicksburg. However, for all his haste, the special orders he distributed on the 26th for the guidance of his subordinates in next day's operation were meticulous and full. Attempting to forestall confusion by assigning particular duties, he included no less than eleven numbered paragraphs in the order, all of them fairly long except the last, which contained a scant half-dozen words: "Port Hudson must be taken tomorrow."

At first it appeared that the order would be carried out, final paragraph and all; but around midmorning, when the thunder of the preliminary bombardment subsided and Weitzel went forward according to plan, driving the rebel skirmishers handsomely before him, he found that this unmasked their artillery, which opened point-blank on his troops with murderous effect. The bluecoats promptly hit the dirt and hugged it while their own batteries came up just behind them and unlimbered, returning the deluge of grape and canister at a range of two hundred and fifty yards. Crouched under all that hurtling iron and lead from front and rear, the men were badly confused and lost what little sense of direction they had retained during their advance through a maze of obstructions, both natural and man-made. "The whole fight took place in a dense forest of magnolias, mostly amid a thick undergrowth, and among ravines choked with felled and fallen timber, so that it was difficult not only to move but even to see," a participant was to recall, adding that what he had been involved in was not so much a battle or a charge as it was "a gigantic bush-whack." Paine and Grover, moving out in support of Weitzel, ran into the same maelstrom of resistance, with the same result. So did Augur, somewhat later, when his turn came to strike the Confederate center just south of the railroad. But all was strangely quiet all this while on the far left. At noon Banks rode over to look into the cause of this inaction, and found to his amazement that Tom Sherman had "failed utterly and criminally to bring his men into the field." The fifty-two-year-old Rhode Islander was at lunch, surrounded by "staff officers all with their horses unsaddled." As usual, despite the multiparagraphed directive, someone — in this case about 3500 someones, from the division commander down to the youngest drummer — had not got the word. Nettled by the dressing-down Banks gave him along with peremptory orders to "carry the works at all hazards," Sherman got his two brigades aligned at last and took them forward shortly after 2 o'clock. He rode at their head, old army style; but not for long. A conspicuous target, he soon tumbled off his horse, and the surgeons had to remove what was left of the leg he had been shot in.

Command of the division passed to Brigadier General William Dwight, who had resigned as a West Point cadet ten years ago to go into manufacturing in his native Massachusetts at the age of twenty-one, but had returned to military life on the outbreak of the war. However, for all the youth and vigor which had enabled him to survive three wounds and a period of captivity after being left for dead on the field of Williamsburg a year ago next month, Dwight could do no more than Sherman had done already. His pinned-down men knew only too well that to attempt to rise, with all those guns and rifles trained on them from behind the red clay parapets ahead, would mean at best a trip back to the surgery where the doctors by now were sawing off their former commander's leg. To attempt a farther advance, either here or on the east, was clearly hopeless; yet Banks was unwilling to call it a day until he had made at least one more effort. Weitzel's division, which had opened the action that morning around to the north, had gained more ground than any of the other four, causing one observer to remark that if he had "continued to press his attack a few minutes longer he would probably have broken through the Confederate defense and taken their whole line in reverse." Now that the defenders were alert and had the attackers zeroed in, that extra pressure would be a good deal harder to exert, but Banks at any rate thought it worth a try. Orders were sent to the far right for a resumption of the assault, and were passed along to the colonel commanding the two regiments lately recruited in the Teche, the 1st and 3d Louisiana Native Guards. Held in reserve till now, they were about to receive their baptism of fire: a baptism which, as it turned out, amounted to total immersion. A Union staff officer who watched them form for the attack described what happened. "They had hardly done so," he said, "when the extreme left of the Confederate line opened on them, in an exposed position, with artillery and musketry and forced them to abandon the attempt with great loss." However, that was only part of the story. Of the 1080 men in ranks, 271 were hit, or one out of every four. They had accomplished little except to prove, with a series of disjointed rushes and repulses over broken ground and through a tangle of obstructions, that the rebel position could not be carried in this fashion. And yet they had settled one other matter effectively: the question of whether Negroes would stand up under fire and take their losses as well as white men. "It gives me pleasure to report that they answered every expectation," Banks wrote Halleck. "In many respects their conduct was heroic. No troops could be more determined or more daring."

Yet this was but a fraction of the day-long butcher's bill, which was especially high by contrast; 1995 Federals had fallen, and only 235 Confederates. In reaction, Banks told Farragut next day that Port Hudson was "the strongest position there is in the United States." Though he frankly admitted, "No man on either side can show himself without being shot," he was no less determined than he had been before the assault was launched. "We shall hold on today," he said, "and make careful examinations with reference to future operations." That morning — unlike Grant after his second repulse, five days earlier at Vicksburg — he had requested "a suspension of hostilities until 2 o'clock this afternoon, in order that the dead and wounded may be brought off the field." Gardner consented, not only to this but also to a five-hour extension of the truce when it was found that the grisly harvest required a longer time for gleaning. Meanwhile Banks was writing to Grant, bringing him up to date on events and outlining the problem as he saw it now. "The garrison of the enemy is 5000 or 6000 men," he wrote. "The works are what would ordinarily be styled 'impregnable.' They are surrounded by ravines, woods, valleys, and bayous of the most intricate and labyrinthic character, that make the works themselves almost inaccessible. It requires time even to understand the geography of the position. [The rebels] fight with determination, and our men, after a march of some 500 or 600 miles, have done all that could be expected or required of any similar force." A postscript added an urgent request: "If it be possible, I beg you to send me at least one brigade of 4000 or 5000 men. This will be of vital importance to us. We may have to abandon these operations without it." No such reinforcements would be coming either now or later from Grant, who had his hands quite full upriver; but Banks had no real intention of abandoning the siege. "We mean to harass the enemy night and day, and to give him no rest," he declared in a message to Farragut that same day, and he followed this up with another next morning: "Everything looks well for us. The rebels attempted a sortie upon our right last evening upon the cessation of the armistice, but were smartly and quickly repulsed." Two days later, May 31, when the admiral informed him that three Confederate deserters had stated that "unless reinforcements arrive they cannot hold out three days longer," Banks replied: "Thanks for your note and the cheering report of the deserters. We are closing in upon the enemy, and will have him in a day or two."

So he said. But presently a dispatch arrived from Halleck, dated June 3, which threatened to cut the ground from under the besieging army's feet. Like Grant, and perhaps for the same reasons, Banks had kept the general-in-chief in the dark as to his intentions until it was too late for interference, and Old Brains expressed incredulity at the second-hand reports of what had happened. "The newspapers state that your forces are moving on Port Hudson instead of co-operating with General Grant, leaving the latter to fight both Johnston and Pemberton. As this is so contrary to all your instructions, and so opposed to military principles, I can hardly believe it true." That it was true, however, was shown by a bundle of letters he received that same day from Banks, announcing his intention to move southeast from Alexandria. "These fully account for your movement on Port Hudson, which before seemed so unaccountable," Halleck wrote next morning. But he still did not approve, and he said so in a message advising Banks to get his army back on what the general-in-chief considered the right track. "I hope that you have ere this given up your attempt on Port Hudson and sent all your spare forces to Grant. . . . If I have been over-urgent in this matter, it has arisen from my extreme anxiety lest the enemy should concentrate all his strength on one of your armies before you could unite, whereas if you act together you certainly will be able to defeat him." Banks bristled at being thus lectured to. It irked him, moreover, that the authorities did not seem to take into account the fact that he was the senior general on the river. If any reproach for nonco-operation was called for, it seemed to him that it should have been aimed at Grant. "Since I have been in the army," he replied in mid-June, when the second message reached him, "I have done all in my power to comply with my orders. It is so in the position I now occupy. I came here not only for the purpose of co-operating with General Grant, but by his own suggestion and appointment." In time Halleck came round. "The reasons given by you for moving against Port Hudson are satisfactory," he conceded in late June. "It was presumed that you had good and sufficient reasons for the course pursued, although at this distance it seemed contrary to principles and likely to prove unfortunate." If this was not altogether gracious, Banks did not mind too much. He considered that he had already disposed of Halleck's bookish June 4 argument with a logical rebuttal, written by coincidence on the same day: "If I defend New Orleans and its adjacent territory, the enemy will go against Grant. If I go with a force sufficient to aid him, [bypassing Port Hudson,] my rear will be seriously threatened. My force is not large enough to do both. Under these circumstances, my only course seems to be to carry this post as soon as possible, and then to join General Grant. . . . I have now my heavy artillery in position, and am confident of success in the course of a week."

Here again he underestimated the rebel garrison's powers of resistance; Port Hudson was not going to fall within a month, much less a week. Gardner had drawn his semicircular lines with care, anchoring both extremities to the lip of the hundred-foot bluff overlooking the river, and had posted his troops for maximum effect, whatever the odds.

The Beleaguered City

North of the railroad there were two main forts, one square, the other pentagonal, with a small redoubt between them, all three surrounded and tied together by a network of trenches, occupied by two brigades under Colonels I. G. W. Steedman and W. R. Miles. Brigadier General William Beall, a Kentucky-born West Pointer, had his brigade, which was as big as the other two combined, disposed to the south along a double line of bastions, the largest of which surmounted the crest of a ridge and was called the Citadel because it dominated all the ground in that direction. These various major works, together with their redans, parapets, ditches, and gun emplacements, were mutually supporting, so that an advance on one invited fire from those adjoining it. Banks had discovered this first, to his regret, while launching the May 27 assault. Since then, he had limited his activities mainly to long-range bombardments and the digging of lines of contravallation, designed to prevent a breakout and to protect his troops from sorties. After two weeks of this, in the course of which a considerable number of his men were dropped by snipers, he grew impatient and ordered a probing night action which he characterized as an endeavor "to get within attacking distance of the works in order to avoid the terrible losses incurred in moving over the ground in front." Informed that the sudden lunge was to be preceded by a twenty-hour bombardment, Farragut, whose ships by now were getting low on ammunition, protested mildly that he did not think the constant shelling did much good. "After people have been harassed to a certain extent, they become indifferent to danger, I think," he said. But he added: "We will do all in our power to aid you." That power was not enough, as it turned out. At 3 o'clock in the morning, June 11, the blue infantry crept quietly forward under cover of darkness — and found the defenders very much on the alert. Though some men got through the abatis and up to the hostile lines, once the alarm was sounded they were quickly driven back, while those who chose not to run the gauntlet to regain their jump-off positions were taken captive. Except for lengthening the Federal casualty lists and increasing Confederate vigilance in the future, the action had no effect on anything whatsoever, so far as Banks and his shovel-weary, sniper-harassed men could discern: least of all on the siege, which continued as before.

His spirits were revived, however, by a message received two days later from Dwight, who reported that he had interrogated a quartet of Confederate deserters and had learned from them that the garrison, reduced by sickness to 3200 infantry and 800 artillerymen, was down to "about five days' beef." There were "plenty of peas, plenty of corn," but "no more meal." Starvation was staring the rebels in the face. In fact, a Mississippi regiment was said to be in such low spirits that it "drove about 50 head of cattle out of the works about a week ago," intending thereby to hasten the inevitable end. In short, Dwight wrote, "The troops generally wish to surrender, and despair of relief." Next morning, June 13, Banks decided to test the validity of this report. His plan, as he explained it to Farragut, whose co-operation was requested, was to "open a vigorous bombardment at exactly a quarter past eleven this morning, and continue it for exactly one hour.... The bombardment will be immediately followed by a summons to surrender. If that is not listened to, I shall probably attack tomorrow." The guns roared on schedule, then stopped at the appointed time, and Banks sent forward under a white flag his demand for instant capitulation. "Respect for the usages of war, and a desire to avoid unnecessary sacrifice of life, impose on me the necessity of formally demanding the surrender of the garrison of Port Hudson." That was the opening sentence of the page-long "summons," and it was balanced by another very like it at the close: "I desire to avoid unnecessary slaughter, and I therefore demand the immediate surrender of the garrison, subject to such conditions only as are imposed by the usages of civilized warfare. I have the honor to be, sir, very respectfully, your most obedient servant, *N. P. Banks,* Major General, Commanding." The Confederate reply was prompt and a good deal briefer. "Your note of this date has just been handed to me, and in reply I have to state that my duty requires me to defend this position, and therefore I decline to surrender. I have the honor to be, sir, very respectfully, your most obedient servant, *Frank. Gardner,* Major General, Commanding C. S. Forces."

Banks had said that if his demands were not "listened to" he probably would launch a second full-scale assault next morning, all along the line. At daybreak, following a vigorous one-hour cannonade which apparently served little purpose except to warn the Confederates he was coming, he did just that. When the smoke cleared it was found that he had suffered the worst drubbing of the war, so far at least as a comparison of the casualties was concerned. On the far left, Dwight was misdirected by his guides, with the result that he was blasted into retreat before he even knew he was exposed. In the center, Augur and Paine attacked with vigor and were bloodily repulsed when they struck what turned out to be the strongest point of the enemy line, the priest-cap near the Jackson road; Paine himself fell, badly wounded, and was carried off the field. On the right, Grover and Weitzel were stopped in midcareer when it was demonstrated that no man could clear the fire-swept ridge along their front and live. "In examining the position afterward," a Union officer declared, "I found [one] grass-covered knoll shaved bald, every blade cut down to the roots as by a hoe." By noon it was apparent that the assault had failed in every sector. All that had been accomplished was a reduction of the range for the deadly snipers across the way, and the price exacted was far beyond the worth of a few yards of shell-torn earth. There was hollow mockery, too, in the respective losses, North and South. The Federals had 1792 killed, wounded, and missing subtracted from their ranks, while the Confederates had lost an over-all total of 47.

Four weeks of siege, highlighted by two full-scale assaults and one abortive night attack, had cost Banks more than 4000 casualties along his seven concave miles of front. His men, suspecting that they had inflicted scarcely more than one tenth as many casualties on the enemy, were so discouraged that the best he could say of them, in a note to Farragut that evening, was that they were "in tolerable good spirits." Presently, though, even this was more than he could claim. "The heat, especially in the trenches, became almost insupportable, the stenches quite so," a staff major later recalled. "The brooks dried up, the creek lost itself in the pestilential swamp, the springs gave out, and the river fell, exposing to the tropical sun a wide margin of festering ooze. The illness and mortality were enormous." Counting noses four days after the second decisive repulse, Banks reported that he was down to 14,000 effectives, including the nine-month volunteers whose enlistments were expiring. This too was a source of discontent, which reached the stage of outright mutiny in at least one Bay State regiment, and the reaction was corrosive. Men whose time was nearly up did not "feel like desperate service," Banks told Halleck, while those who had signed on for the duration did not "like to lead where the rest will not follow." Old Brains had a prescription for that, however. "When a column of attack is formed of doubtful troops," he answered, "the proper mode of curing their defection is to place artillery in their rear, loaded with grape and canister, in the hands of reliable men, with orders to fire at the first moment of disaffection. A knowledge of such orders will probably prevent any wavering, and, if not, one such punishment will prevent any repetition of it in your army."

This was perhaps reassuring, though in an unpleasant sort of way, since it showed the general-in-chief to be considerably more savage where blue rebels were concerned than he had ever been when his opponents wore butternut or gray. However, Banks had even larger problems than mutiny on his hands by then. Emory was crying havoc in New Orleans, which he protested was in grave danger of being retaken by the rebels any day now. "The railroad track at Terre Bonne is torn up. Communication with Brashear cut off," he notified Banks on June 20, adding: "I have but 400 men in the city, and I consider the city and the public property very unsafe. The secessionists here profess to have certain information that their forces are to make an attempt on the city." Five days later — by which date Port Hudson had been under siege a month — he declared that the rebels bearing down on him were "known and ascertained to be at least 9000, and may be more.... The city is quiet on the surface, but the undercurrent is in a ferment." "Something must be done for this city, and that quickly," he insisted four days later.

His anxiety continued to mount in ratio to his estimate of the number of graybacks moving against him, until finally he said flatly: "It is a choice between Port Hudson and New Orleans.... My information is as nearly positive as human testimony can make it that the enemy are 13,000 strong, and they are fortifying the whole country as they march from Brashear to this place, and are steadily advancing. I respectfully suggest that, unless Port Hudson is already taken, you can only save this city by sending me reinforcements immediately and at any cost." What was more, he said, the danger was not only from outside New Orleans. "There are at least 10,000 fighting men in this city (citizens) and I do not doubt, from what I see, that these men will, at the first appearance of the enemy within view of the city, be against us to a man. I have the honor to be &c. *W. H. Emory*, Brigadier General, Commanding."

But Banks had no intention of loosening his grip on the upriver fortress, which he believed — despite the nonfulfillment of all his earlier predictions — could not hold out much longer. Emory would have to take his chances. If it came to the worst and New Orleans fell, Farragut would steam down and retake it with the fleet that would be freed for action on the day Port Hudson ran up the white flag. Meanwhile the signs were good. On June 29, no less than thirty deserters stole out of the rebel intrenchments and into the Union lines, and though by now Banks knew better than to judge the temper of the garrison by that of such defectors, he was pleased to learn from those who arrived in the afternoon that their dinner had been meatless. In the future, they had been told, the only meat they would get would be that of mules. Judging by the adverse reaction of his own troops to a far more palatable diet, Banks did not think the johnnies would be likely to sustain their morale for long on that. However, one of the butternut scarecrows brought with him a copy of yesterday's *Port Hudson Herald*, which featured a general order issued the day before by Gardner, "assuring the garrison that General Johnston will soon relieve Vicksburg, and then send reinforcements here." The southern commander declared as well, Banks pointed out in passing the news along to Halleck, "his purpose to defend the place to the last extremity."

Confident none the less "of a speedy and favorable result" — so at least he assured the general-in-chief — Banks kept his long-range batteries at work around the clock, determined to give the Confederates no rest. The fire at night was necessarily blind, but that by day was skillfully directed by an observer perched on a lofty yardarm of the *Richmond*, tied up across the river from the bluff. He communicated by wigwag with a battery ashore, which also had a signalman, and the two kept up a running colloquy, not only to improve the marksmanship, but also to relieve the tedium of the siege.

"Your fifth gun has hit the breastwork of the big rifle four times. Its fire is splendid. Can dismount it soon."

"You say our fifth gun?"

"Yes, from the left." But the next salvo brought a shift of attention. "Your sixth gun just made a glorious shot. . . . Let the sixth gun fire 10 feet more to the left."

"How now about the fifth and sixth guns?"

"The sixth gun is the bully boy."

"Can you give it any directions to make it more bully?"

"Last shot was little to the right."

Just then, however, the cannoneers were forced to call a halt. "Fearfully hot here," the battery signalman explained. "Several men sunstruck. Bullets whiz like fun. Have ceased firing for a while, the guns are so hot. Will profit by your directions afterward." Presently they resumed firing, though with much less satisfactory results, according to the observer high in the rigging of the *Richmond*.

"Howitzer shell goes 6 feet over the guns every shot; last was too low, little too high again." Exasperated, he added: "Can't they, or won't they, depress that gun?"

"Won't, I guess. . . . Was that shot any better, and that?"

"Both and forever too high."

"We will vamose now. Come again tomorrow."

"Nine a.m. will do, will it not?"

"Yes; cease signaling."

✘ 5 ✘

The forces threatening New Orleans were no such host as Emory envisioned, but they were under the determined and resourceful Richard Taylor, who earlier, though much against his will, had struck at Grant's supposedly vital supply line opposite Vicksburg. "To break this would render a most important service," Pemberton had told Kirby Smith in early May, in one of his several urgent appeals for help across the way. Returning to Alexandria as soon as Banks pulled out, Taylor prepared to move at once back down the Teche, threaten New Orleans, and thereby "raise such a storm as to bring General Banks from Port Hudson, the garrison of which could then unite with General Joseph Johnston in the rear of General Grant." On May 20, however, before he could translate his plan into action, he received instructions from Smith directing him to march in the opposite direction. "Grant's army is now supplied from Milliken's Bend by Richmond, down the Roundaway and Bayou Vidal to New Carthage," the department commander explained, and if Taylor could interrupt the flow of supplies along this route, the

Federal drive on Vicksburg would be "checked, if not frustrated." He sympathized with Taylor's desire "to recover what you have lost in Lower Louisiana and to push on toward New Orleans," Smith added, "but the stake contended for near Vicksburg is the Valley of the Mississippi and the Trans-Mississippi Department; the defeat of General Grant is the *terminus ad quem* of all operations in the West this summer; to its attainment all minor advantages should be sacrificed." Taylor agreed as to the object, but not as to the method, much preferring his own. However, as he said later, "remonstrances were of no avail." He turned his back on New Orleans, at least for the present, and set out up the Tensas, where he was joined by a division of about 4000 men under Major General John G. Walker, a Missourian lately returned from Virginia, where he had commanded a division in Lee's army and was one of the many who could fairly be said to have saved the day at Sharpsburg.

Debarking June 5 on the east bank of the Tensas, some twenty-five miles west of Grant's former Young's Point headquarters, Taylor sent his unarmed transports back downstream to avoid losing them in his absence. Next day he surprised and captured a small party of Federals at Richmond, midway between the Tensas and the Mississippi, only to learn that Grant had established a new base up the Yazoo, well beyond the reach of any west-bank forces, and was no longer dependent on the one at Milliken's Bend. "Our movement resulted, and could result, in nothing," Taylor later admitted. All the same, he carried out his instructions by attacking, at dawn of the 7th, both Young's Point and Milliken's Bend, sending a full brigade against each. Like Banks, Grant had been recruiting Negroes, but since he intended to use them as laborers rather than as soldiers, he had given them little if any military training apart from the rudiments of drill. Surprised in their camps by the dawn attacks, they panicked and fled eastward over the levee to the protection of Porter's upstream flotilla. The gunboats promptly took up the quarrel, blasting away at the exultant rebels, and Taylor, observing that the panic was now on the side of the pursuers, ordered Walker to retire on Monroe, terminus of the railroad west of Vicksburg, while he himself went back down the Tensas and up the Red to Alexandria. Once there, he returned his attention to Banks and New Orleans, glad to have done with what he called "these absurd movements" against a supposedly vital supply line which in fact had been abandoned for nearly a month before he struck it.

Though the losses had been unequal — 652 Federals had fallen or were missing, as compared to 185 Confederates — Grant was not disposed to be critical of the outcome. Agreeing with Porter that the rebels had got "nothing but hard knocks," he was more laconic than reproachful in his mid-June report of the affair: "In this battle most of the troops engaged were Africans, who had little experience in the use of firearms. Their conduct is said, however, to have been most gallant, and I doubt

The Beleaguered City [407]

not but with good officers they will make good troops." Anyhow, this was beyond the circle of his immediate attention, which was fixed on the close-up siege of Vicksburg itself. Six divisions had been added by now to his original ten, giving him a total of 71,000 effectives disposed along two lines, back to back, one snuggled up to the semicircular defenses and the other facing rearward in case Joe Johnston got up enough strength and nerve to risk an attack from the east. Three divisions arrived in late May and early June from Memphis, the first of which, commanded by Brigadier General Jacob Lauman, was used to extend the investment southward, while the other two, under Brigadier Generals Nathan Kimball and William Sooy Smith, made up a fourth corps under Washburn, now a major general, and were sent to join Osterhaus, who had been left behind to guard the Big Black crossings while the two assaults were being launched. Frank Herron, who at twenty-five had won his two stars at Prairie Grove to become the Union's youngest major general, arrived from Missouri with his division on June 11 and extended the line still farther southward to the river, completing Grant's nine-division bear hug on Pemberton's beleaguered garrison. The final two were sent by Burnside from his Department of the Ohio. Commanded by Brigadier Generals Thomas Welsh and Robert Potter, they constituted a fifth corps under Major General John G. Parke and raised the strength of the rearward-facing force to seven divisions. "Our situation is for the first time in the entire western campaign what it should be," Grant had written Banks in the course of the build-up. And now that it was complete, so was his confidence as to the outcome of the siege, which he expressed not only in official correspondence but also in informal talks with his officers and men. "Gen. Grant came along the line last night," an Illinois private wrote home. "He had on his old clothes and was alone. He sat on the ground and talked with the boys with less reserve than many a little puppy of a lieutenant. He told us that he had got as good a thing as he wanted here."

One item he would have liked more of was trained engineers. Only two such officers were serving in that capacity now in his whole army. However, as one of them afterwards declared, this problem was solved by the "native good sense and ingenuity" of the troops, Middle Western farm boys for the most part, who showed as much aptitude for such complicated work as they had shown for throwing bridges over creeks and bayous during the march that brought them here. According to the same officer, "Whether a battery was to be constructed by men who had never built one before, [or] a sap-roller made by those who had never heard the name ... it was done, and after a few trials well done." Before long, a later observer remarked, "those who had cut wood only for stoves would be speaking fluently of gabions and fascines; men who had patiently smoothed earth so that radishes might grow better would be talking affectionately of terrepleins for guns." In all of this they were inspired by the same bustling energy and quick adaptability on the part of the generals who led them; for one thing that characterized Grant's army was the youth of its commanders. McClernand, who was fifty-one, was the only general officer past fifty. Of the twenty-one corps and division commanders assigned to the Army of the Tennessee in the course of the campaign, the average age was under forty. And that promotion had been based on merit was indicated by the fact that the average age of the nine major generals was as low as that of the dozen brigadiers; indeed, excepting McClernand, it was better than one year lower. Moreover, nine of these twenty-one men were older than Grant himself, and this too was part of the reason for his confidence in himself and in the army which had come of age, so to speak, under his care and tutelage. He considered it more than a match for anything the Confederates could bring against him — even under Joe Johnston, whose abilities he respected highly. One day a staff officer expressed the fear that Johnston was planning to fight his way into Vicksburg in order to help Pemberton stage a breakout; but Grant did not agree. "No," he said. "We are the only fellows who want to get in there. The rebels who are in now want to get out, and those who are out want to stay out. If Johnston tries to cut his way in we will let him do it, and then see that he don't get out. You say he has 30,000 men with him? That will give us 30,000 more prisoners than we now have."

This was not to say that the two repulsed assaults had taught him nothing. They had indeed, if only by way of confirming a first impression that the rebel works were formidable. One officer, riding west on the Jackson road, had found himself confronted by "a long line of high, rugged, irregular bluffs, clearly cut against the sky, crowned with cannon which peered ominously from embrasures to the right and left as far as the eye could see." Beyond an almost impenetrable tangle of timber felled on the forward slopes, "lines of heavy rifle pits, surmounted with head-logs, ran along the bluffs, connecting fort with fort, and filled with veteran infantry." The approaches, he said, "were frightful enough to appall the stoutest heart." Sherman agreed, especially after the two assaults which had cost the army more than four thousand casualties. "I have since seen the position at Sevastopol," he wrote years later, "and without hesitation I declare that at Vicksburg to have been the more difficult of the two." Skillfully constructed, well sited, and prepared for a year against the day of investment, the fortifications extended for seven miles along commanding ridges and were anchored at both extremities to the lip of the sheer 200-foot bluff, north and south of the beleaguered city. Forts, redoubts, salients, redans, lunets, and bastions had been erected or dug at irregular intervals along the line, protected by overlapping fields of fire and connected by a complex of trenches, which in turn were mutually supporting. There simply was no easy way to get at the defenders. Moreover, Grant's three-to-one numerical advantage was considerably offset, not only by the necessity for protecting his rear from possible attacks by the army Johnston was assembling to the east, but also by the fact that, because of the vagaries of the up-ended terrain, his line of contravallation had to be more than twice the length of the line he was attempting to confront. "There is only one way to account for the hills of Vicksburg," a Confederate soldier had said a year ago, while helping to survey the present works. "After the Lord of Creation had made all the big mountains and ranges of hills, He had left on His hands a large lot of scraps. These were all dumped at Vicksburg in a waste heap." One of Grant's two professional engineers was altogether in agreement, pronouncing the Confederate position "rather an intrenched camp than a fortified

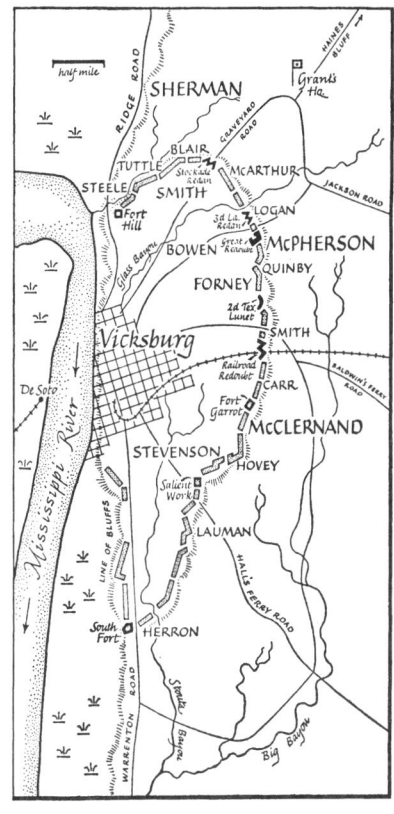

place, owing much of its strength to the difficult ground, obstructed by fallen trees to its front, which rendered rapidity of movement and *ensemble* in an assault impossible."

Yet even this ruggedness had its compensations. Although the hillsides, as one who climbed them said, "were often so steep that their ascent was difficult to a footman unless he aided himself with his hands," the many ravines provided excellent cover for the besiegers, and Grant had specified in his investment order: "Every advantage will be taken of the natural inequalities of the ground to gain positions from which to start mines, trenches, or advance batteries." With the memory of slaughter fresh in their minds as a result of their two repulses, the men dug with a will. Knowing little or nothing at the outset of the five formal stages of a siege — the investment, the artillery attack, the construction of parallels and approaches, the breaching by artillery or mines, and the final assault — they told one another that Grant, having failed to go over the rebel works, had decided to go under them instead. Fortunately the enemy used his artillery sparingly, apparently conserving ammunition for use in repelling major assaults, but snipers were quick to shoot at targets of opportunity: in which connection a Federal major was to recall that "a favorite amusement of the soldiers was to place a cap on the end of a ramrod and raise it just above the head-logs, betting on the number of bullets which would pass through it within a given time." Few things on earth appealed to them more, as humor, than the notion of some butternut marksman flaunting his skill when the target was something less than flesh and blood. Mostly, though, they dug and took what rest they could, sweating in their wool uniforms and cursing the heat even more than they did the snipers. Soon they were old hands at siege warfare. "The excitement . . . has worn away," a lieutenant wrote home from the trenches in early June, "and we have settled down to our work as quietly and as regularly as if we were hoeing corn or drawing bills in chancery."

Life in the trenches across the way — though the occupants did not call them that; they called them "ditches" — was at once more sedentary and more active. With their own 102 guns mostly silent and Grant's opposing 220 roaring practically all the time, they did nearly as much digging as the bluecoats, the difference being that they did it mainly in the same place, time after time, repairing damages inflicted by the steady rain of shells. Nor were they any less inventive. "Thunder barrels," for example — powder-filled hogsheads, fuzed at the bung — were found to be quite effective when rolled downhill into the enemy parallels and approaches. Similarly, such large naval projectiles as failed to detonate, either in the air or on contact with the ground, could be dug up, re-fuzed, and used in the same fashion to discourage the blue diggers on the slopes. However, despite such violent distractions, after a couple of weeks of spadework the two lines were within clod-tossing distance of each other at several points, and this resulted in an edgy sort of existence for the soldiers of both sides, as if they were spending their days and nights at the wrong end of a shooting gallery or in a testing chamber for explosives. "Fighting by hand grenades was all that was possible at such close quarters," a Confederate was to recall. "As the Federals had the hand grenades and we had none, we obtained our supply by using such of theirs as failed to explode, or by catching them as they came over the parapet and hurling them back."

Resistance under these circumstances implied a high state of morale, and such was indeed the case. Grant's heavy losses in his two assaults — inflicted at so little cost to the defenders that, until they looked out through the lifting smoke and saw the opposite hillsides strewn with the rag-doll shapes of the Union dead, they could scarcely believe a major effort had been made — convinced them that the Yankees could never take the place by storm. What was more, they had faith in "Old Joe" Johnston, believing that he would raise the siege as soon as he got his troops assembled off beyond the blue horizon, whereupon the two gray forces would combine and turn the tables on the besiegers. Until then, as they saw it, all that was needed was firmness against the odds, and they stood firm. Thanks to Pemberton's foresight, which included pulling corn along the roadside and driving livestock ahead of the army during its march from the Big Black, food so far was more plentiful inside the Confederate lines than it was beyond them. The people there were the first to feel the pinch of hunger; for the Federals, coming along behind the retreating graybacks, had consumed what little remained while waiting for roads to be opened to their new base on the Yazoo. "The soldiers ate up everything the folks had for ten miles around," a Union private wrote home. "They are now of necessity compelled to come here and ask for something to live upon, and they have discovered that they have the best success when the youngest and best-looking one in the family comes to plead their case, and they have some very handsome women here." This humbling of their pride did not displease him; it seemed to him no more than they deserved. "They were well educated and rich before their niggers ran away," he added, but adversity had brought them down in the world. "If I was to meet them in Illinois I should think they were born and brought up there."

Whether this last was meant as a compliment, and if so to whom, he did not say. But at least these people beyond the city's bristling limits were not being shot at; which was a great deal more than could be said of those within the gun-studded belt that girdled the bluff Vicksburg had been founded on, forty-odd years ago, by provision of the last will and testament of the pioneer farmer and Methodist parson Newitt Vick. In a sense, however, the bluff was returning to an earlier destiny. All that had been here when Vick arrived were the weed-choked ruins of a Spanish fort, around which the settlement had grown in less than two generations into a bustling town of some 4500 souls, mostly devoted to trade with planters in the lower Yazoo delta but also plagued by flatboat men on the way downriver from Memphis, who found it a convenient place for letting off what they called "a load of steam" that would not wait for New Orleans. As it turned out, though, the ham-fisted boatmen with knives in their boots and the gamblers with aces and derringers up their sleeves were mild indeed compared to what was visited upon them by the blue-clad host sent against them by what had lately been their government. Now the bluff was a fort again, on a scale beyond the most flamboyant dreams of the long-departed Spaniards, and the residents spent much of their time, as one of them said, watching the incoming shells "rising steadily and shiningly in great parabolic curves, descending with ever-increasing swiftness, and falling with deafening shrieks and explosions." The "ponderous fragments" flew everywhere, he added, thickening the atmosphere of terror until "even the dogs seemed to share the general fear. On hearing the descent of a shell, they would dart aside [and] then, as it exploded, sit down and howl in a pitiful manner." Children, on the other hand, observed the uproar with wide-eyed evident pleasure, accepting it as a natural phenomenon, like rain or lightning, unable to comprehend — as the dogs, for example, so obviously did — that men could do such things to one another and to them. "How is it possible you live here?" a woman who had arrived to visit her soldier husband just before the siege lines tightened asked a citizen, and was told: "After one is accustomed to the change, we do not mind it. But becoming accustomed: that is the trial." Some took it better than others, in or out of uniform. There was for instance a Frenchman, "a gallant officer who had distinguished himself in several severe engagements," who was "almost unmanned" whenever one of the huge mortar projectiles fell anywhere near him. Chided by friends for this reaction, he would reply: "I no like ze bomb: I cannot fight him back!" Neither could anyone else "fight him back," least of all the civilians, many of whom took refuge in caves dug into the hillsides. Some of these were quite commodious, with several rooms, and the occupants brought in chairs and beds and even carpets to add to the comfort, sleeping soundly or taking dinner unperturbed while the world outside seemed turned to flame and thunder. "Prairie Dog Village," the blue cannoneers renamed the city on the bluff, while from the decks of ironclads and mortar rafts on the great brown river, above and below, and from the semicircular curve of eighty-nine sand-bagged battery emplacements on the landward side, they continued to pump their steel-packaged explosives into the checkerboard pattern of its streets and houses.

Like the men in the trenches, civilians of both sexes and all ages were convinced that their tormentors could never take Vicksburg by storm, and whatever their fright they had no intention of knuckling under to what they called the bombs. For them, too, Johnston was the one bright hope of deliverance. Old Joe would be coming soon, they assured each other; all that was needed was to hold on till he completed his arrangements; then, with all the resources of the Confederacy at his command, he would come swooping over the eastern horizon and down on the Yankee rear. But presently, as time wore on and Johnston did not come, they were made aware of a new enemy. Hunger. By mid-June, though the garrison had been put first on half and then on quarter rations of meat, the livestock driven into the works ahead of the army back in May had been consumed, and Pemberton had his foragers impress all the cattle in the city. This struck nearer home than even the Union shells had done, for it was no easy thing for a family with milk-thirsty children to watch its one cow being led away to slaughter by a squad of ragged strangers. Moreover, the army's supply of bread was running low by now, and the commissary was directed to issue instead equal portions of rice and flour, four ounces of each per man per day, supplementing a quarter-pound of meat that was generally stringy or rancid or both. When these grains ran low, as they soon did, the experiment was tried of baking bread from dough composed of equal parts of corn and dried peas, ground up together until they achieved a gritty consistency not unlike cannon powder. "It made a nauseous composition," one who survived the diet was to recall with a shudder, "as the corn meal cooked in half the time the peas meal did, so the stuff was half raw.... It had the properties of india-rubber, and was worse than leather to digest." Soon afterwards came the crowning indignity. With the last cow and hog gone lowing and squealing under the sledge and cleaver, still another experiment was tried: the substitution of mule meat for beef and bacon. Though it was issued, out of respect for religious and folk prejudices, "only to those who desired it," Pemberton was gratified to report that both officers and men considered it "not only nutritious, but very palatable, and in every way preferable to poor beef." So he said; but soldiers and civilians alike found something humiliating, not to say degrading, about the practice. "The rebels don't starve with success," a Federal infantryman observed jokingly from beyond the lines about this time. "I think that if I had nothing to eat I'd starve better than they do." Vicksburg's residents and defenders might well have agreed, especially when mule meat was concerned. Even if a man refused to eat such stuff himself, he found it disturbing to live among companions who did not. It was enough to diminish even their faith in Joe Johnston, who seemed in point of fact a long time coming.

Though at the outset the Virginian had sounded vigorous and purposeful in his assurance of assistance, Pemberton himself by now had begun to doubt the outcome of the race between starvation and delivery. "I am trying to gather a force which may attempt to relieve you. Hold out," Johnston wrote on May 19, and six days later he made this more specific: "Bragg is sending a division. When it comes, I will move to you. Which do you think is the best route? How and where is the enemy encamped? What is your force?" Receiving this last on May 29 — the delay was not extreme, considering that couriers to and from the city had to creep by darkness through the Federal lines, risking capture every foot of the way — the Vicksburg commander replied as best he could to his superior's questions as to Grant's dispositions and strength. "My men are in good spirits, awaiting your arrival," he added. "You may depend on my holding the place as long as possible." After waiting nine days and receiving no answer, he asked: "When may I expect you to move, and in what direction?" Three more days he waited, and still there was no reply. "I am waiting most anxiously to know your intentions," he repeated. "I have heard nothing from you since [your dispatch of] May 25. I shall endeavor to hold out as long as we have anything to eat." Three days more went by, and then on June 13 — two weeks and a day since any word had reached him from the world outside — he received a message dated May 29. "I am too weak to save Vicksburg," Johnston told him. "Can do no more than attempt to save you and your garrison. It will be impossible to extricate you unless you co-operate and we make mutually supporting movements. Communicate your plans and suggestions, if possible." This was not only considerably less than had been expected in the way of help; it also seemed to indicate that Johnston did not realize how tightly the Union cordon was drawn about Vicksburg's bluff. In effect, the meager trickle of dispatches left Pemberton in a position not unlike that of a man who calls on a friend to make a strangler turn loose of his throat, only to have the friend inquire as to the strangler's strength, the position of his thumbs, the condition of the sufferer's windpipe, and just what kind of help he had in mind. So instead of "plans and suggestions," Vicksburg's defender tried to communicate some measure of the desperation he and his soldiers were feeling. "The enemy has placed several heavy guns in position against our works," he replied on June 15, "and is approaching them very nearly by sap. His fire is almost continuous. Our men have no relief; are becoming much fatigued, but are still in pretty good spirits. I think your movement should be made as soon as possible. The enemy is receiving reinforcements. We are living on greatly reduced rations, but I think sufficient for twenty days yet."

Having thus placed the limit of Vicksburg's endurance only one day beyond the Fourth of July — now strictly a Yankee holiday — Pemberton followed this up, lest Johnston fail to sense the desperation implied, with a more outspoken message four days later: "I hope you will advance with the least possible delay. My men have been thirty-four days and nights in the trenches, without relief, and the enemy within conversation distance. We are living on very reduced rations, and, as you know, are entirely isolated." He closed by asking bluntly, "What aid am I to expect from you?" This time the answer, if vague, was prompt. On June 23 a courier arrived with a dispatch written only the day before. "Scouts report the enemy fortifying toward us and the roads blocked," Johnston declared. "If I can do nothing to relieve you, rather than surrender the garrison, endeavor to cross the river at the last moment if you and General Taylor communicate." To Pemberton this seemed little short of madness. Taylor had made his gesture against Young's Point and Milliken's Bend more than two weeks ago; by now he was all the way down the Teche, intent on menacing New Orleans. But that was by no means the worst of Johnston's oversights, which was to ignore the presence of the Union navy. The bluejacket gun crews would have liked nothing better than a chance to try their marksmanship on a makeshift flotilla of skiffs, canoes, and rowboats manned by the half-starved tatterdemalions they had been probing for at long range all these weeks. Besides, even if the boats required had been available, which they were not, there was the question of whether the men in the trenches were in any condition for such a strenuous effort. They looked well enough to a casual eye, for all their rags and hollow-eyed gauntness, but it was observed that they tired easily under the mildest exertion and could serve only brief shifts when shovel work was called for. The meager diet was beginning to tell. A Texas colonel reported that many of his men had "swollen ankles and symptoms of incipient scurvy." By late June, nearly half the garrison was on the sick list or in hospital. If Pemberton could not see what this meant, a letter he received at this time — June 28: exactly one week short of the date he had set, two weeks ago, as the limit of Vicksburg's endurance — presumed to define it for him in unmistakable terms. Signed "Many Soldiers," the letter called attention to the fact that the ration now had been reduced to "one biscuit and a small bit of bacon per day," and continued:

> The emergency of the case demands prompt and decided action on your part. If you can't feed us, you had better surrender us, horrible as the idea is, than suffer this noble army to disgrace themselves by desertion. I tell you plainly, men are not going to lie here and perish, if they do love their country dearly. Self-preservation is the first law of nature, and hunger will compel a man to do almost anything.... This army is now ripe for mutiny, unless it can be fed. Just think of one small biscuit and one or two mouthfuls of bacon per day. General, please direct your inquiries in the proper channel, and see if I have not stated the stubborn facts, which had better be heeded before we are disgraced.

★ ★ ★

"Grant is now deservedly the hero," Sherman wrote home in early June, adding characteristically — for his dislike of reporters was not tempered by any evidence of affection on their part, either for himself or for Grant, with whom, as he presently said, "I am a second self" — that his friend was being "belabored with praise by those who a month ago accused him of all the sins in the calendar, and who next will turn against him if so blows the popular breeze. Vox populi, vox humbug."

In point of fact, however, once the encompassing lines had been drawn, the journalists could find little else to write about that had not been covered during the first week of the siege. And it was much the same for the soldiers, whose only diversion was firing some fifty to one hundred rounds of ammunition a day, as required by orders. Across the way — though the Confederates lacked even this distraction, being under instructions to burn no powder needlessly — the main problem, or at any rate the most constant one, was hunger; whereas for the Federals it was boredom. "The history of a single day was the history of all the others," an officer was to recall. Different men had different ways of trying to hasten the slow drag of time. Sherman, for instance, took horseback rides and paid off-duty visits to points of interest roundabout, at least one of which resulted in a scene he found discomforting, even painful. Learning that the mother of one of his former Louisiana Academy cadets was refugeeing in the neighborhood — she had come all the way from Plaquemine Parish to escape the attentions of Butler and Banks, only to run spang into Grant and Sherman — he rode over to tender his respects and found her sitting on her gallery with about a dozen women visitors. He introduced himself, inquired politely after her son, and was told that the young man was besieged in Vicksburg, a lieutenant of artillery. When the general went on to ask for news of her husband, whom he had known in the days before the war, the woman suddenly burst into tears and cried out in anguish: "You killed him at Bull Run, where he was fighting for his country!" Sherman hastily denied that he had "killed anybody at Bull Run," which was literally true, but by now all the other women had joined the chorus of abuse and lamentation. This, he said long afterwards, "made it most uncomfortable for me, and I rode away."

Other men had other spare-time diversions. Grant's, it was said, was whiskey. Some denied this vehemently, protesting that he was a teetotaler, while some asserted that this only appeared to be the case because of his low tolerance for the stuff; a single glass unsteadied him, and a second gave him the glassy-eyed look of a man with a heavy load on. He himself seemed to recognize the problem from the outset, if only by the appointment and retention of John A. Rawlins as his assistant adjutant general. A frail but vigorous young man, with a "marble pallor" to his face and "large, lustrous eyes of a deep black," Rawlins at first had wanted to be a preacher, but had become instead a lawyer in Galena, where Grant first knew him. His wife had died of tuberculosis soon after the start of the war, and he himself would die of the same disease before he was forty, but the death that seemed to have affected him most had been that of his father, an improvident charcoal burner who had died at last of the alcoholism that had kept him and his large family in poverty all his life. Rawlins, a staff captain at thirty and now a lieutenant colonel at thirty-two, was rabid on the subject of drink. He was in fact blunt in most things, including his relationship with Grant. "He bossed everything at Grant's headquarters," Charles Dana later wrote, adding: "I have heard him curse at Grant when, according to his judgment, the general was doing something that he thought he had better not do." Observing this, many wondered why Grant put up with it. Others believed they knew. "If you hit Rawlins on the head, you'll knock out Grant's brains," they said. But they were wrong. Rawlins was not Grant's brain; he was his conscience, and a rough one, too, especially where whiskey was concerned. "I say to you frankly, and I pledge you my word for it," he had written eighteen months ago to Elihu Washburne, the general's congressional guardian angel, "that should General Grant at any time become an intemperate man or an habitual drunkard, I will notify you immediately, will ask to be removed from duty on his staff (kind as he has been to me) or resign my commission. For while there are times when I would gladly throw the mantle of charity over the faults of my friends, at this time and from a man of his position I would rather tear the mantle off and expose the deformity." Grant had cause to believe that Rawlins meant it. And yet, despite the danger to his career and despite what a fellow staffer called Rawlins' "insubordination twenty times a day," he kept him on, both for his own good and the army's.

Since writing to Washburne, however, the adjutant had either changed his mind about disturbing the mantle or else he had been singularly forgetful. Despite periodic incidents thereafter, in which Grant was involved with whiskey, Rawlins limited his remarks to the general himself, apparently in the belief that he could handle him. And so he could, except for lapses. Anyhow, there was never any problem so long as Mrs Grant was around; "If she is with him all will be well and I can be spared," he later confided to a friend. The trouble seemed in part sexual, as in California nine years ago, and it was intensified by periods of boredom, such as now. Three weeks of slam-bang fighting and rapid maneuver had given way to the tedium of a siege, and Mrs Grant had been six weeks off the scene. On June 5 Rawlins found a box of wine in front of the general's tent and had it removed, ignoring Grant's protest that he was saving it to toast the fall of Vicksburg. He learned, moreover, that the general had recently accepted a glass of wine from a convivial doctor. These were danger signs, and there were others that evening. Rawlins sat down after midnight and wrote Grant a letter. "The great solicitude I feel for the safety of this army leads me to mention, what I had hoped never again to do, the subject of your drinking. ... Tonight when you should, because of the condition of your health if nothing else, have been in bed, I find you where the wine bottle has just been emptied, in company with those who drink and urge you to do likewise, and the lack of your usual promptness and decision, and clearness in expressing yourself in writing conduces to confirm my suspicion." Rawlins himself had become rather incoherent by now, whether from anger or from sorrow; but the ending was clear enough. Unless Grant would pledge himself "[not] to touch a single drop of any kind of liquor, no matter by whom asked or under what circumstances," Rawlins wanted to be relieved at once from duty in the department. Grant, however, left early next morning — apparently before the letter reached him — on a tour of inspection up the Yazoo River to Satartia, near which he had posted a division in case Johnston came that way. The two-day trip, beyond the sight and influence of Rawlins, became a two-day bender.

Dana went with him, and on the way upriver from Haines Bluff they met the steamboat *Diligent* coming down. Grant hailed the vessel, whose captain was a friend of his, transferred to her, and had her turned back upstream for Satartia. Aboard was Sylvanus Cadwallader, a Chicago *Times* correspondent on the prowl for news. It was he who had ridden into Jackson with Fred Grant in mid-May, when they lost the race for the souvenir flag atop the capitol, and it was he who was to leave the only detailed eyewitness account of Grant on a wartime bender — specifically the two-day one which already was under way up the Yazoo. In some ways, for Cadwallader at least, it was more like a two-day nightmare. "I was not long in perceiving that Grant had been drinking," he wrote long afterwards, "and that he was still keeping it up. He made several trips to the bar room of the boat in a short time, and became stupid in speech and staggering in gait." The reporter of course had heard rumors of Grant's predilection, but this was the first time he had seen him show it to the extent of intoxication. Alarmed by the general's "condition, which was fast becoming worse," he tried to get the captain and a lieutenant aide to intervene. Neither would; so Cadwallader undertook to do it himself. He got Grant into his stateroom, locked the door, "and commenced throwing bottles of whiskey which stood on the table, through the windows, over the guards, into the river." Grant protested, to no avail; the reporter "firmly, but good-naturedly declined to obey," and finally got him quieted. "As it was a very hot day and the stateroom almost suffocating, I insisted on his taking off his coat, vest and boots, and lying down on one of the berths. After much resistance I succeeded, and soon fanned him to sleep."

But that was only the beginning. Shortly before dark, when the *Diligent* neared Satartia, she met two gunboats steaming down, and a naval officer came aboard to warn that it was not safe for the unarmed vessel to proceed. Dana — who later reported tactfully in his *Recollections* that "Grant was ill and went to bed soon after we started" — knocked on the stateroom door to ask whether the boat should turn back. Grant, he said, was "too sick to decide," and told him: "I will leave it to you." Now that he was awake, however, though still not "recovered from his stupor," Cadwallader said, the general took it into his head "to dress and go ashore," despite the naval officer's warning. Once more the reporter prevailed, and got him back to bed. While he slept, the *Diligent* returned downstream in the darkness to Haines Bluff. Next morning, according to Dana, Grant was "fresh as a rose, clean shirt and all, quite himself," when he came out to breakfast. "Well, Mr Dana," he observed, "I suppose we are at Satartia."

Cadwallader relaxed his guard, despite the 25-mile geographical error, presuming that "all necessity for extra vigilance on my part had passed," and was profoundly shocked to discover, an hour later, "that Grant had procured another supply of whiskey from on shore and was quite as much intoxicated as the day before." Again the reporter managed to separate the general from his bottle, only to have him insist on proceeding at once to Chickasaw Bayou. This would have brought them

The Beleaguered City

there "about the middle of the afternoon, when the landing would have been alive with officers, men, and trains from all parts of the army." Conferring with the captain as to the best means by which to avoid exposing Grant to "utter disgrace and ruin," Cadwallader managed to delay the departure so that they did not arrive until about sundown, when there was much less activity at the landing. As luck would have it, however, they tied up alongside a sutler boat whose owner "kept open house to all officers and dispensed free liquors and cigars generously." Alarmed at the possibilities of disaster, the reporter slipped hastily over the rail, warned the sutler of what was afoot, and "received his promise that the general should not have a drop of anything intoxicating on his boat." Back aboard the *Diligent*, Cadwallader helped the escort to unload the horses for the five-mile ride to army headquarters northeast of Vicksburg; but when this was done he looked around and could find no sign of Grant. Fearing the worst, he hurried aboard the sutler boat "and soon heard a general hum of conversation and laughter proceeding from a room opening out of the ladies' cabin." There he saw his worst fears realized. The sutler was seated at "a table covered with bottled whiskey and baskets of champagne," and Grant was beside him, "in the act of swallowing a glass of whiskey." Cadwallader once more intervened, insisting that "the escort was waiting, and it would be long after dark before we could reach headquarters." Grant came along, though he plainly resented the interruption. His horse was a borrowed one called Kangaroo "from his habit of rearing on his hind feet and making a plunging start whenever mounted." That was his reaction now; for "Grant gave him the spur the moment he was in the saddle, and the horse darted away at full speed before anyone was ready to follow." The road was crooked, winding among the many slews and bayous, but the general more or less straightened it out, "heading only for the bridges, and literally tore through and over everything in his way. The air was full of dust, ashes, and embers from campfires, and shouts and curses from those he rode down in his race." Cadwallader, whose horse was no match for Kangaroo, thought he had lost his charge for good. But he kept on anyhow, hoping against hope, and "after crossing the last bayou bridge three-fourths of a mile from the landing," caught up with him riding sedately at a walk. Finding that Grant had become "unsteady in the saddle" as a result of the drink or drinks he had had from the sutler, and fearing "discovery of his rank and situation," the reporter seized Kangaroo's rein and led him off into a roadside thicket, where he helped the general to dismount and persuaded him to lie down on the grass and get some sleep. While Grant slept Cadwallader managed to hail a trooper from the escort, whom he instructed to go directly to headquarters "and report at once to Rawlins — and no one else — and say to him that I want an ambulance with a careful driver."

Waking before the ambulance got there, Grant wanted to resume his ride at once, but the reporter "took him by the arm, walked him back and forth, and kept up a lively rather one-sided conversation, till the ambulance arrived." Then there was the problem of getting the general into the curtained vehicle, which he refused to permit until, as Cadwallader said, "we compromised the question by my agreeing to ride in the ambulance also, and having our horses led by the orderly." They reached headquarters about midnight to find the dark-eyed Rawlins and Colonel John Riggin, another staff officer, "waiting for us in the driveway." The reporter got out first, "followed promptly by Grant," who now gave him perhaps the greatest shock of the past two days. "He shrugged his shoulders, pulled down his vest, 'shook himself together,' as one just rising from a nap, and seeing Rawlins and Riggin, bid them good night in a natural tone and manner, and started to his tent as steadily as he ever walked in his life." Cadwallader turned to Rawlins, who was pale with rage — "The whole appearance of the man indicated a fierceness that would have torn me into a thousand pieces had he considered me to blame" — and said he was afraid, from what they had just seen, that the adjutant would think it was he, not Grant, who had been drinking. "No, no," Rawlins said through clenched teeth. "I know him, I know him. I want you to tell me the exact facts, and all of them, without any concealment. I have a right to know them, and I will know them."

He heard them all, from start to finish, but he never reported the incident to Washburne, any more than Dana did to the War Department, not only out of loyalty and friendship, but also perhaps on reflecting that if anything brought about Grant's removal, or even his suspension during an inquiry, command of the army would pass automatically to McClernand, whom they both despised. As for Cadwallader, despite assurances from Rawlins — "He will not send you out of the department while I remain in it," the adjutant told him — he spent an anxious night, "somewhat in doubt as to the view of the matter Gen. Grant would take next day," and "purposely kept out of his way for twenty-four hours to spare him the mortification I supposed he might feel." As it turned out, he need not have worried. "The second day afterward I passed in and out of his presence as though nothing unusual had occurred. To my surprise he never made the most distant allusion to [the matter] then, or ever afterward." From that time on, he said, it was "as if I had been regularly gazetted a member of his staff." Passes from Grant enabled the reporter to go anywhere he wanted; he could requisition transportation and draw subsistence from quartermaster and commissary authorities; his tent was always pitched near Grant's, and his dispatches often were sent in the official mail pouch; in short, he "constantly received flattering personal and professional favors and attentions shown to no one else in my position." All this was in return for his respecting a confidence which he kept for more than thirty years. In 1896, a seventy-year-old sheep raiser out in California, he wrote his memoirs, including an account of Grant's two-day trip up the Yazoo and back. For nearly sixty years they remained in manuscript, and when at last they were published, ninety years after the war was over, they were attacked and the writer vilified by some of the general's long-range admirers, who claimed that what Cadwallader called "this Yazoo-Vicksburg adventure" never happened.

At any rate, no harm had resulted from the army commander's two-day absence from headquarters, drunk or sober. The repulse of Taylor at Milliken's Bend and Young's Point by the gunboats, on the second day, increased Grant's confidence rather than his fretfulness, which in fact seemed to be cured. "All is going on here now just right," he wrote to a friend on June 15, and added: "My position is so strong that I feel myself abundantly able to leave it and go out twenty or thirty miles with force enough to whip two such garrisons." He had small use for Pemberton, characterizing him as "a northern man [who] got into bad company." Nor did he fear Joe Johnston. Though he respected his ability, he said he did not believe the Virginian could save Vicksburg without "a larger army than the Confederates now have at any one place." Next day, moreover, the watchful eye of former congressman Frank Blair enabled Grant to dispose of his third opponent, John McClernand, and thus wind up the private war he had been waging all this time. Scanning the columns of the Memphis *Evening Bulletin*, Blair spotted a congratulatory order McClernand had issued to his corps, claiming the lion's share of the credit for the victory he foresaw. Blair sent the clipping to Sherman, who forwarded it to Grant next day, calling it "a catalogue of nonsense" and "an effusion of vain-glory and hypocrisy ... addressed not to an army, but to a constituency in Illinois." He also cited a War Department order, issued the year before, "which actually forbids the publication of all official letters and reports, and requires the name of the writer to be laid before the President of the United States for dismissal."

Grant had waited half a year for this, passing over various lesser offenses in hopes that one would come along which would justify charges that could not fail to stick. But now that he had it he still moved with deftness and precision, completing the adjustment of the noose. That same day, June 17, he forwarded the clipping to McClernand with a note: "Inclosed I send you what purports to be your congratulatory address to the Thirteenth Army Corps. I would respectfully ask if it is a true copy. If it is not a correct copy, furnish me one by bearer, as required both by regulations and existing orders of the Department." Next day McClernand acknowledged the validity of the clipping. "I am prepared to maintain its statements," he declared. "I regret that my adjutant did not send you a copy as he ought, and I thought he had." With the noose now snug, Grant sprang the trap: "Major General John A. McClernand is hereby relieved from command of the Thirteenth Army Corps. He will proceed to any point he may select in the state of Illinois and report by letter to Headquarters of the Army for orders." Grant signed the order after working hours, supposing that it would be delivered the following morning, but when James Wilson came in at midnight and heard what was afoot — there was bad blood between him and McClernand; the two had nearly come to blows a couple of weeks ago — he urged Rawlins to let him deliver the order in person, without delay, lest something come up — a rebel sortie at dawn, for example, which might enable McClernand to distinguish himself as he had done at Shiloh — to cause its suspension or cancellation. Rawlins agreed, and Wilson put on his dress uniform, summoned the provost marshal and a squad of soldiers, and set out through the darkness for McClernand's headquarters. Arriving about 2 o'clock in the morning, he demanded that the general be roused. Presently he was admitted to McClernand's tent, where he found the former congressman seated at a table on which two candles burned. Apparently he knew what to expect, for he too was in full uniform and his sword lay before him on the table. Wilson handed him the order, remarking that he had been instructed to see that it was read and understood. McClernand took it, adjusted his glasses, and perused it. "Well, sir, I am relieved," he said. Then, looking up at Wilson, whose expression did not mask his satisfaction, he added: "By God, sir, we are both relieved!"

He did not intend to take this lying down, but he soon found that Grant had played the old army game with such skill that his opponent was left without a leg to stand on. "I have been relieved for an omission of my adjutant. Hear me," McClernand wired Lincoln from Cairo on his way to Springfield, their common home. From there he protested likewise to Halleck, suggesting the possible disclosure of matters that were dark indeed: "How far General Grant is indebted to the forbearance of officers under his command for his retention in the public service, I will not undertake to state unless he should challenge it. None know better than himself how much he is indebted to that forbearance." That might be, but it was no help to the general up in Illinois; Grant challenged nothing, except to state that he had "tolerat[ed] General McClernand long after I thought the good of the service demanded his removal." In time, there came to Springfield a letter signed "Your friend as ever, A. Lincoln," in which the unhappy warrior was told: "I doubt whether your present position is more painful to you than to myself. Grateful for the patriotic stand so early taken by you in this life-and-death struggle of the nation, I have done whatever has appeared practicable to advance you and the public interest together." However: "For me to force you back upon Gen. Grant would be forcing him to resign. I cannot give you a new command, because we have no forces except such as already have commanders." In short, the President had nothing to offer his fellow-townsman in the way of balm, save his conviction that a general was best judged by those "who have been with him in the field.... Relying on these," Lincoln said in closing, "he who has the right needs not to fear."

This was perhaps the unkindest cut of all, since McClernand knew only too well what was likely to happen to his reputation if judgment was left to Sherman and McPherson and their various subordinate commanders, including the army's two remaining ex-congressmen Blair and Logan. Among all these, and on Grant's staff, there was general rejoicing at his departure. Major General Edward O. C. Ord, who had fought under Grant at Iuka, had just arrived to take charge of a sixth corps intended to consist of the divisions under Herron and Lauman; instead, he replaced McClernand. Three days later, on June 22, Sherman was given command of the rearward line, which was strengthened by shifting more troops from in front of Vicksburg. "We want to whip Johnston at least 15 miles off, if possible," Grant explained. Steele succeeded Sherman, temporarily, and the siege went on as before. No less than nine approaches were being run, all with appropriate parallels close up to the enemy trenches, so that the final assault could be launched with the lowest possible loss in lives. Mines were sunk under rebel strongpoints, and on June 25 two of these were exploded on McPherson's front, the largest just north of the Jackson road. It blew off the top of a hill there, leaving a big, dusty crater which the attackers occupied for a day and then abandoned, finding themselves under heavy plunging fire from both flanks and the rear. The mine accomplished little, but contributed greatly to the legend of the siege by somehow lofting a Negro cook, Abraham by name, all the way from the Confederate hilltop and into the Federal lines. He landed more or less unhurt, though terribly frightened. An Iowa outfit claimed him, put him in a tent, and got rich charging five cents a look. Asked how high he had been blown, Abraham always gave the same answer, coached perhaps by some would-be Iowa Barnum. "Donno, massa," he would say, "but tink bout tree mile."

Mostly, though, the weeks passed in boredom and increasing heat, under whose influence the Confederates appeared to succumb to a strange apathy during the final days of June. A Federal engineer remarked that their defense "was far from being vigorous." It seemed to him that the rebel strategy was "to wait for another assault, losing in the meantime as few men as possible," and he complained that this had a bad effect on his own men, since "without the stimulus of danger ... troops of the line will not work efficiently, especially at night, after the novelty has worn off." Another trouble was that they foresaw the end of the siege, and no man coveted the distinction of being the last to die. Not that all was invariably quiet. Occasionally there were flare-ups, particularly where the trenches approached conjunction, and the snipers continued to take their toll. Though the losses were small, the suffering was great. "It looked hard," a Wisconsin soldier wrote, "to see six or eight poor fellows piled into an ambulance about the size of Jones's meat wagon and hustled over the rough roads as fast as the mules could trot and to see the blood running out of the carts in streams almost." Taunts were flung as handily as grenades, back and forth across the lines, the graybacks asking, "When are you folks going to come on into town?" and the bluecoats replying that they were in no hurry: "We are holding you fellows prisoner while you feed yourselves." There was much fraternization between pickets, who arranged informal truces for the exchange of coffee and tobacco, and the same Federal engineer reported that the enemy's "indifference to our approach became at some points almost ludicrous." Once, for example, when the blue sappers found that as a result of miscalculation a pair of approach trenches would converge just inside the rebel picket line, the two sides called a cease-fire and held a consultation at which it was decided that the Confederates would pull back a short distance in order to avoid an unnecessary fire fight. At one stage of the discussion a Federal suggested that the approaches could be redesigned to keep from disturbing the butternut sentries, but the latter seemed to think that it would be a shame if all that digging went to waste. Besides, one said, "it don't make any difference. You Yanks will soon have the place anyhow."

Grant thought so, too. By now, in fact — though he kept his soldiers burrowing, intending to launch his final assault from close-up positions in early July — he was giving less attention to Pemberton than he was to Johnston, off in the opposite direction, where Sherman described him as "vibrating between Jackson and Canton" in apparent indecision. Blair had reported earlier, on returning from a scout, that "every man I picked up was going to Canton to join him. The negroes told me their masters had joined him there, and those who were too old to go, or who could escape on any other pretext, told me the same story." This had a rather ominous sound, as if hosts were gathering to the east, but Grant was not disturbed. He had access, through the treacherous courier, to many of the messages that passed between his two opponents. He knew what they were thinking, what the men under them were thinking, and what the beleaguered citizens were thinking. He spoke of their expectations in a dispatch he sent Sherman on June 25, the day the slave Abraham came hurtling into the hands of the Iowans: "Strong faith is expressed by some in Johnston's coming to their relief. [They] cannot believe they have been so wicked as for Providence to allow the loss of their stronghold of Vicksburg. Their principal faith seems to be in Providence and Joe Johnston."

By then — the fortieth day of siege — it had been exactly a month since the man in whom Vicksburg's garrison placed its "principal faith" assured Pemberton: "Bragg is sending a division. When it joins I will come to you." The division reached him soon afterwards, under Breckinridge, and was combined with the three already at hand under

Loring, French, and Walker; Johnston's present-for-duty strength now totaled 31,226 men, two thirds of whom had joined him since his arrival in mid-May. But he found them quite deficient in equipment, especially wagons, and deferred action until such needs could be supplied. In the interim he got into a dispute with the Richmond authorities, protesting that he had only 23,000 troops, while Seddon insisted that the correct figure was 34,000. Finally the Secretary told him: "You must rely on what you have," and urged him to move at once to Pemberton's relief. But Johnston would not be prodded into action. "The odds against me are much greater than those you express," he wired on June 15, and added flatly: "I consider saving Vicksburg hopeless." Shocked by his fellow Virginian's statement that he considered his assignment an impossible one, Seddon took this to mean that Johnston did not comprehend the gravity of the situation or the consequences of the fall of the Gibraltar of the West, which in Seddon's eyes meant the probable fall of the Confederacy itself. It seemed to him, moreover, that the general — in line with his behavior a year ago, down the York-James peninsula — was moving toward a decision not to fight at all, and to the Secretary this was altogether unthinkable. "Your telegram grieves and alarms me," he replied next day. "Vicksburg must not be lost without a desperate struggle. The interest and honor of the Confederacy forbid it. I rely on you still to avert the loss. If better resources do not offer, you must hazard attack. It may be made in concert with the garrison, if practicable, but otherwise without; by day or night, as you think best." Still Johnston would not budge. "I think you do not appreciate the difficulties in the course you direct," he wired back, "nor the probabilities or consequences of failure. Grant's position, naturally very strong, is intrenched and protected by powerful artillery, and the roads obstructed.... The defeat of this little army would at once open Mississippi and Alabama to Grant. I will do all I can, without hope of doing more than aid to extricate the garrison." Fairly frantic and near despair over this prediction that the Father of Waters was about to pass out of Confederate hands, severing all practical connection with the Transmississippi and its supplies of men and food and horses, Seddon urged the general "to follow the most desperate course the occasion may demand. Rely upon it," he told him, "the eyes and hopes of the whole Confederacy are upon you, with the full confidence that you will act, and with the sentiment that it were better to fail nobly daring than, through prudence even, to be inactive.... I rely on you for all possible to save Vicksburg."

But no matter what ringing tones the Secretary employed, Johnston would not be provoked into what he considered rashness. "There has been no voluntary inaction," he protested; he simply had "not had the means of moving." By then it was June 22. Two days later he received a message from Pemberton, suggesting that he get in touch with Grant and make "propositions to pass this army out, with all its arms and equipages," in return for abandoning Vicksburg to him. Johnston declined, not only because he did not believe the proposal would be accepted, but also because "negotiations with Grant for the relief of the garrison, should they become necessary, must be made by you," he replied on June 27. "It would be a confession of weakness on my part, which I ought not to make, to propose them. When it becomes necessary to make terms, they may be considered as made under my authority." In other words, any time Pemberton wanted to throw in the sponge, it would be all right with Johnston. However, he prefaced this by saying that the Pennsylvanian's "determined spirit" encouraged him "to hope that something may yet be done to save Vicksburg," and two days later, June 29, "field transportation and other supplies having been obtained," he put his four divisions on the march for the Big Black, preceded by a screen of cavalry.

He had never been one to tilt at windmills, nor was he now. The march — or "expedition," as he preferred to call it — "was not undertaken in the wild spirit that dictated the dispatches from the War Department," he later explained, and added scornfully: "I did not indulge in the sentiment that it was better for me to waste the lives and blood of brave soldiers 'than, through prudence even,' to spare them." He never moved until he was ready, and then his movements were nearly always rearward. The one exception up to now had been Seven Pines, which turned out to be the exception that proved the rule, for it had cost him five months on the sidelines, command of the South's first army, and two wounds that were still unhealed a year later. Moreover, it had resulted in his present assignment, which was by no means to his liking, though his resultant brusqueness was reserved for those above him on the ladder of command, never for those below. To subordinates he was invariably genial and considerate, and they repaid him with loyalty, affection, and admiration. "His mind was clear as a bell," a staff officer had written from Jackson to a friend, two weeks ago, while the build-up for the present movement was still in progress. "I never saw a brain act with a quicker or more sustained movement, or one which exhibited a finer sweep or more striking power.... I cannot conceive surroundings more intensely depressing. Yet amidst them all, he preserved the elastic step and glowing brow of the genuine hero."

Desperation never rattled him; indeed, it had rather the opposite effect of increasing his native caution. And such was the case now as he approached the Big Black, beyond which Grant had intrenched a rearward-facing line. On the evening of July 1, Johnston called a halt between Brownsville and the river, and spent the next two days reconnoitering. Convinced by this "that attack north of the railroad was impracticable," he "determined, therefore, to make the examinations necessary for the attempt south of the railroad." On July 3, near Birdsong's Ferry, he wrote Pemberton that he intended "to create a diversion, and thus enable you to cut your way out if the time has arrived for you to do this. Of that time I cannot judge; you must, as it depends upon your condition. I hope to attack the enemy in your front [on] the 7th.... Our firing will show you where we are engaged. If Vicksburg cannot be saved, the garrison must."

Next morning, however, before he took up the march southward he noticed a strange thing. Today was the Fourth — Independence Day — but the Yankees over toward Vicksburg did not seem to be celebrating it in the usual fashion. On this of all days, the forty-eighth of the siege, the guns were silent for the first time since May 18, when the bluecoats filed into positions from which to launch their first and second assaults before settling down to the digging and bombarding that had gone on ever since; at least till now. Johnston and his men listened attentively, cocking their heads toward the beleaguered city. But there was no rumble of guns at all. Everything was quiet in that direction.

CHAPTER 5

Stars in Their Courses

★ ✗ ☆

WHATEVER LACK OF NERVE OR INGENUITY had been demonstrated in Mississippi throughout the long hot hungry weeks that Vicksburg had shuddered under assault and languished under siege, there had been no shortage elsewhere in the Confederate States of either of these qualities on which the beleaguered city's hopes were hung. Indeed, a sort of inverse ratio seemed to obtain between proximity and daring, as if distance not only lent enchantment but also encouraged boldness, so far at least as the western theater was concerned. A case in point was Beauregard, 650 air-line miles away on the eastern seaboard. Charleston's two-time savior was nothing if not inventive: especially when he had time on his hands, as he did now. In mid-May, with the laurels still green on his brow for the repulse of Du Pont's ironclad fleet the month before, he unfolded in a letter to Joe Johnston — with whom he had shared the triumph of Manassas, back in the first glad summer of the war, and to whom, under pressure from Richmond, he had just dispatched 8000 of his men — a plan so sweeping in its concept that the delivery of the Gibraltar of the West, whose plight had started him thinking along these lines, was finally no more than an incidental facet of a design for sudden and absolute victory over all the combinations whereby the North intended to subjugate the South. According to his "general views of the coming summer campaign," propounded in the letter to his friend, Johnston would be reinforced by troops from all the other Confederate commanders, who would stand on the defensive, east and west, while Johnston joined Bragg for an all-out offensive against the Union center, wrecking Rosecrans and driving the frazzled remnant of his army beyond the Ohio. Johnston would follow, picking up 10,000 recruits in Middle Tennessee and another 20,000 in Kentucky, and if this threat to the Federal heartland had not already prompted a withdrawal by the bluecoats from in front of Vicksburg, he could march west to the Mississippi, above Memphis, "and thus cut off Grant's communications with the north." When the besiegers moved upriver, as they would be obliged to do for want of supplies, Johnston would draw them into battle on a field of his choice, "and the result could not be doubtful for an instant." With Grant thus disposed of, the victorious southern Army of the Center, some 150,000 strong by then, could split in two, one half crossing the big river to assist Kirby Smith and Price in the liberation of Louisiana and Missouri, while the other half joined Lee in Virginia to complete "the terrible lesson the enemy has just had at Chancellorsville." Meanwhile, by way of lagniappe, a fleet of special torpedo boats would be constructed in England, from designs already on hand at Charleston, to steam westward across the Atlantic and "resecure" the Mississippi, upwards from its mouth. The war would be over: won.

Thus Beauregard. But after waiting five weeks and receiving no sign that his suggestions had been received, much less adopted, he felt, as he told another friend, "like Samson shorn of his locks." Time was slipping away, he complained in a postscript to his retained copy of the letter, despite the fact that "the whole of this brilliant campaign, which is only indicated here, could have been terminated by the end of June." On July 1 he heard at last from Johnston, though only on an administrative matter and without reference to his proposals of mid-May. Assuming that the original must have gone astray, he sent him at once a copy of the letter, together with the postscript stressing the need for haste in the adoption of the plan which he called brilliant. "I fear, though, it is now too late to undertake it," he admitted, and added rather lamely: "I hope everything will yet turn out well, although I do not exactly see how."

Nothing came of the Creole general's dream of reversing the blue flood, first in the center and then on the left and right; but others with easier access to the authorities in Richmond had been making similar, if less flamboyant, proposals all the while. Longstreet for example, on his way to rejoin Lee in early May, hard on the heels of Chancellorsville and the aborted Siege of Suffolk, outlined for the Secretary of War a plan not unlike Beauregard's, except that it had the virtue of comparative simplicity. It was Old Peter's conviction "that the only way to equalize the contest was by skillful use of our interior lines," and in this connection he proposed that Johnson give over any attempt to go directly to Pemberton's assistance and instead reinforce Bragg at Tullahoma, while Longstreet, with his two divisions now en route from Suffolk, moved by rail to that same point for that same purpose; Rosecrans would be swamped by overwhelming numbers, and the victors then could march for the Ohio. Grant's being the only force that could be used to meet this threat, his army would be withdrawn upriver and Vicksburg thereby would be relieved.... Seddon listened attentively. Though he liked the notion of using Hood and Pickett to break the enemy's grip on the Mississippi south of Memphis, he preferred the more direct and still simpler method of sending them to Jackson for a movement against Grant where he then was. However, this presupposed the approval of Lee: which was not forthcoming. Lee replied that he would of course obey any order sent him, but he considered the suggestion less than wise. "The adoption of your proposition is hazardous," he wired Seddon, "and it becomes a question between Virginia and the Mississippi." The date was May 10; Stonewall Jackson died that afternoon. But Lee suppressed his grief in order to expand his objections to the Secretary's proposal in a letter that same Sunday. He not only thought the attempt to rescue Pemberton by sending troops from Virginia unduly risky; he also considered it unnecessary. "I presume [the reinforcements] would not reach him until the last of this month," he wrote. "If anything is done in that quarter, it will be over by that time, as the climate in June will force the enemy to retire."

Seddon doubted that climate alone would be enough to cause the Federals to abandon, even for a season, their bid for source-to-mouth control of the Mississippi. Whatever Lee might think of Grant, the Secretary considered him "such an obstinate fellow that he could only be induced to quit Vicksburg by terribly hard knocks." In fact, that had been his objection to Longstreet's claim that a strike at Rosecrans would abolish the threat downriver; Grant might simply ignore the provocation and refuse to loosen his grip. Davis agreed. Moreover, he shared Seddon's reservations about Johnston, who had just been ordered to Jackson, as a deliverer of hard knocks. Between them, under pressure of the knowledge that something had to be done, and done quickly, now that the bluecoats were on the march in Pemberton's rear, the President and the Secretary decided that the time had come for a high-level conference to determine just what that something was to be. On May 14, the day Johnston abandoned the Mississippi capital to Union occupation, they summoned Lee to Richmond for a full discussion of the problem.

He arrived next day, which was one of sorrow and strain for the whole Confederacy; Stonewall Jackson was being buried, out in the Shenandoah Valley, and Joe Johnston was retreating to Canton while Grant turned west for a leap at Vicksburg from the rear. Davis and Seddon hoped that, face to face with Lee, they might persuade him to continue the risk of facing Hooker with a depleted army, so that Longstreet could join Johnston for a strike at Grant. However, they found him still convinced that such an attempt, undertaken for the possible salvation of Mississippi for a season, would mean the loss of Virginia forever; and that for him was quite unthinkable. "Save in defense of my native State, I never again desire to draw my sword," he had said two years ago, on the day he resigned from the U.S. Army. Apparently he still felt that way about it: with one refinement. His proposal now —

for he agreed that something drastic had to be done to reverse the blue flood of conquest in the center and on the far left of the thousand-mile Confederate line of battle — was that he launch a second invasion of the North. The first, back in September, had come to grief in Maryland because of a combination of mishaps, not the least of which had been McClellan's luck in finding the lost order issued by Lee when he snapped at the bait left dangling at Harpers Ferry. This time, though, he would profit by that experience. He would march without delay into Pennsylvania, deep in Washington's rear, where a victory might well prove decisive, not only in his year-long contest with the Army of the Potomac, in which he had never lost a major battle, but also in the war. It might or might not cause the withdrawal of Grant from in front of Vicksburg, but at least it would remove the invaders from the soil of Virginia during the vital harvest season, while at best it would accomplish the fall of the northern capital and thus encourage the foreign intervention which Davis long had seen as the key to victory over the superior forces of the Union.... The President and Seddon were impressed. Having heard Lee out, Davis asked him to return the following morning for a presentation of his views to the entire cabinet.

That too was a critical day for the young republic. Before it was over, Grant had thrown Pemberton into retreat from Champion Hill, continuing his lunge for the back door of Vicksburg, and Banks had ended his week-long occupation of Alexandria in order to move against Port Hudson. Lee spent most of it closeted with Davis and the cabinet at the White House, presenting his solution to the national crisis. He spoke not in his former capacity as military adviser to the President, and certainly not as general-in-chief — no such office existed in the Confederacy; Halleck's only counterpart was Davis, or at least a fraction of him — but rather as commander of the Department of Northern Virginia. Having rejected the notion of reinforcing Vicksburg — "The distance and the uncertainty of the employment of the troops are unfavorable," he told Seddon — Lee based his present advice on what was good or bad for his department and the soldiers in his charge. "I considered the problem in every possible phase," he subsequently explained, "and to my mind, it resolved itself into a choice of one of two things: either to retire to Richmond and stand a siege, which must ultimately have ended in surrender, or to invade Pennsylvania." Placed in that light, the alternatives were much the same as if the cabinet members were being asked to choose between certain defeat and possible victory. In fact, "possible" became *probable* with Robert E. Lee in charge of an invasion launched as the aftermath of Fredericksburg and Chancellorsville, triumphs scored against the same adversary and against longer odds than he would be likely to encounter when he crossed the Potomac with the reunited Army of Northern Virginia. Seddon and Benjamin, Secretary of the Treasury Christopher G. Memminger,

Attorney General Thomas H. Watts, and Secretary of the Navy Stephen R. Mallory all agreed with the gray-bearded general "whose fame," as one of them said, "now filled the world." They were not only persuaded by his logic; they were awed by his presence, his aura of invincibility. And this included Davis, who had seldom experienced that reaction to any man.

It did not include Postmaster General John H. Reagan. He was by no means persuaded by Lee, and such awe as he felt for any living man was reserved for Jefferson Davis, whom he considered self-made and practical-minded like himself. Born in poverty forty-five years ago in Tennessee, Reagan had been a schoolteacher and a Mississippi plantation overseer before he was eighteen, when he moved to Texas with all he owned tied up in a kerchief. Passing the bar, he had gone into Lone Star politics and in time won election to Congress, where service on the postal committee prepared him for his present assignment. In this he already had scored a singular triumph, unequaled by any American postmaster in the past seventy-five years or indeed in the next one hundred. Under Reagan's watchful eye, the Confederate postal department did not suffer an annual deficit, but yielded a clear profit. He accomplished this mainly by forcefulness and vigor, and now he employed these qualities in an attempt to persuade Davis and his fellow cabinet members that no victory anywhere, even in Washington itself, could offset the disaster that would result from the loss of the Mississippi. The only man present whose home lay beyond that river, he said plainly that he thought Lee was so absorbed in his masterful defense of Virginia that he did not realize the importance of the Transmississippi, which would be cut off from the rest of the country with the fall of Vicksburg. It had been claimed that Lee's advance might result in Grant's withdrawal to meet the challenge, but Reagan did not believe this for an instant. Grant was committed, he declared. The only way to stop him from accomplishing his object was to destroy him, and the only way to destroy him was to move against him with all possible reinforcements, including Longstreet's two divisions from Lee's army. As for the talk of co-operation expected from those with antiwar sentiments in the North — this too had been advanced as an argument for invasion; the peace movement had been growing beyond the Potomac — Reagan agreed with Beauregard as to "the probability that the threatened danger to Washington would arouse again the whole Yankee nation to renewed efforts for the protection of their capital." In short, he saw everything wrong with Lee's plan and everything right about the plan it had superseded. Grant was the main threat to the survival of the Confederacy, and it was Grant at whom the main blow must be aimed and struck.

Davis and the others heard both men out, and when the two had had their say a vote was taken. In theory, the cabinet could reject Lee's proposal as readily as that of any other department commander, Bragg or

Pemberton or Beauregard, for example, each of whom was zealous to protect the interests of the region for which he was responsible. But that was only in theory. This was Lee, the first soldier of the Confederacy — the first soldier of the world, some would assert — and this was, after all, a military decision. The vote was five to one, in the general's favor. Davis concurring, it was agreed that the invasion would begin at the earliest possible date.

Pleased with the outcome and the confidence expressed, Lee went that evening to pay his respects to a Richmond matron who had done much to comfort the wounded of his army. As he took his leave, it seemed to a young lady of the house — much as it had seemed earlier to five of the six cabinet members — that he was clothed in glory. "It was broad moonlight," she was to write years later, "and I recall the superb figure of our hero standing in the little porch without, saying a last few words, as he swung his military cape around his shoulders. It did not need my fervid imagination to think him the most noble looking mortal I had ever seen. We felt, as he left us and walked off up the quiet leafy street in the moonlight, that we had been honored by more than royalty."

Again Reagan had a different reaction. Unable to sleep because of his conviction that a fatal mistake had been made that day at the White House, he rose before dawn — it was Sunday now, May 17; Pemberton would be routed at high noon on the Big Black, and Johnston was advising the immediate evacuation of Vicksburg — to send a message urging Davis to call the cabinet back into session for a reconsideration of yesterday's decision. Davis did so, having much the same concern for Mississippi as Lee had for Virginia — his brother and sisters were there, along with many lifelong friends who had sent their sons to help defend the Old Dominion and now looked to him for deliverance from the gathering blue host — but the result of today's vote, taken after another long discussion, was the same as yesterday's: five to one, against Reagan. Lee returned to the Rappahannock the following day, which was the first of many in the far-off Siege of Vicksburg.

The problems awaiting him at Fredericksburg were multitudinous and complex. Chancellorsville, barely two weeks in the past and already being referred to as "Lee's masterpiece," had subtracted nearly 13,000 of the best men from his army. Of these, in time, about half would be returning; but the other half would not. And of these last, as all agreed, the most sorely missed was Jackson. "Any victory would be dear at such a price," Lee declared. He found it hard to speak of him, so deep was his emotion at the loss. "I know not how to replace him," he said — and, indeed, he did not try. Instead he reorganized the army, abandoning the previous grouping of the infantry into two corps, of four divisions each, for a new arrangement of three corps, each with three divisions. The new ninth division thus required was created by detaching two brigades from A. P. Hill's so-called Light Division, the largest in the army, and combining them with two brought up from Richmond and North Carolina; Henry Heth, Hill's senior brigadier, was given command, along with a promotion to major general. Similarly, one division was taken from each of the two existing corps — Anderson's from the First and what was left of Hill's from the Second — in order to fill out the new Third. The problem of appointing corps commanders was solved with equal facility. Longstreet of course would remain at the head of the First Corps, whose composition was unchanged except for the loss of Anderson; McLaws, Pickett, and Hood were in command of their three divisions, as before. The Second Corps went to Richard S. Ewell, Jackson's former chief subordinate, who opportunely returned to the army at this time, having recovered from the loss of a leg nine months ago at Groveton. A. P. Hill got the new Third Corps, which was scarcely a surprise; Lee had praised him weeks ago to Davis as the best of his division commanders, and moreover a good half of the troops involved had been under him all along. Promotion to lieutenant general went to both Ewell and Hill. Jubal Early kept the division he had led since Ewell's departure, and W. Dorsey Pender succeeded Hill, under whom he had served from the outset. He was promoted to major general, as was Robert Rodes, who was confirmed as commander of the division that had spearheaded the flank attack on Hooker. Major General Edward Johnson, returning to duty after a year-long absence spent healing the bad leg wound he had suffered at McDowell, the curtain raiser for Jackson's Valley Campaign, completed the roster of corps and division commanders by taking over the Second Corps division which had been temporarily under Colston. The artillery was reshuffled, too, and the general reserve abolished, so that each corps now had five battalions; William Pendleton, the former Episcopal rector, retained his assignment as chief of the army's artillery, though the title was merely nominal now that the reserve battalions had been distributed, and he remained a brigadier. Stuart, on the other hand, gained three new brigades of Virginia cavalry, brought in from various parts of the state in order to add their weight to the three he already had for the offensive. As a result of all these acquisitions, supplemented by volunteers and conscripts forwarded from all parts of the nation as replacements for the fallen, the army was almost up to the strength it had enjoyed before the subtractions of Fredericksburg and Chancellorsville. Approximately 75,000 effectives — in round figures, 5000 artillery, 10,000 cavalry, and 60,000 infantry — stood in its ranks. The infantry order of battle was as follows:

I. Longstreet	II. Ewell	III. A. P. Hill
McLaws	Early	Anderson
Pickett	Johnson	Heth
Hood	Rodes	Pender

The arrangement seemed pat and apt enough, but there were those who had objections no less sharp for being silent. Longstreet for instance, perhaps chagrined that Lee had not consulted him beforehand, resented Hill's promotion over the head of McLaws, whom he considered better qualified for the job. Aside from that, Old Peter was of the opinion that the post should have gone to Harvey Hill, on duty now in his home state of North Carolina. "His record was as good as that of Stonewall Jackson," the Georgian later wrote, "but, not being a Virginian, he was not so well advertised." There was, he thought, "too much Virginia" on the roster — and there were, in fact, apparent grounds for the complaint. Of the fifteen most responsible assignments in the army, ten were held by natives of the Old Dominion, including Lee himself, Ewell and Hill, Stuart, Early and Johnson, Pickett, Rodes and Heth, and Pendleton. Georgia had two, Longstreet and McLaws; Texas had Hood, South Carolina Anderson, and North Carolina, which furnished more than a quarter of Lee's troops, had only the newly promoted Pender; while Mississippi and Alabama, which furnished three brigades apiece, had no representative on the list at all.

Lee too saw possible drawbacks and shortcomings to the arrangement, though not with regard to the states his leading generals came from. His concern was rather with the extent of the reorganization, which placed two of his three corps and five of his nine divisions under men who previously had served either briefly or not at all in their present capacities. Moreover, though his brigadiers were the acknowledged backbone of his army, six of the thirty-seven brigades were under new commanders, and another half dozen were under colonels whom he considered unready for promotion. This troubled him, though not as much as something else. Always in his mind was the missing Jackson, whose death had been the occasion for the shake-up now in progress and of whom he said, "I never troubled myself to give him detailed instructions. The most general suggestions were all that he needed." Lee's proposed solution was characteristically simple. "We must all do more than formerly," he told one general. And this applied as much to himself as it did to anyone; especially as far as "detailed instructions" were concerned. The sustaining factor was the army itself, the foot soldiers, troopers, and cannoneers who had never failed him in the year since the last day of May, 1862, when Davis gave him the command amid the half-fought confusion of Seven Pines. He was convinced, he declared within ten days of the anniversary of his appointment, "that our army would be invincible if it could be properly organized and officered." Of the troops themselves, the rank and file who carried the South's cause on their bayonets, he had no doubts at all. "There never were such men in an army before," he said. "They will go anywhere and do anything if properly led."

Another known quantity, or at any rate an assumed one, was

James Longstreet. "My old warhorse," Lee had called him after Sharpsburg, a battle which Old Peter had advised against fighting — "General," he had said to Lee on entering Maryland, "I wish we could stand still and let the damned Yankees come to us" — but which at least was fought in the style he preferred, with the Confederates taking up a strong defensive position against which the superior blue forces were shattered, like waves against a rock. Fredericksburg, where his corps had suffered fewer than 2000 casualties while inflicting about 9000, had confirmed his predilection in that respect, and he considered Chancellorsville the kind of flashy spectacle the South could ill afford. Facing what Lincoln called "the arithmetic," he perceived that four more such battles, in which the Confederates were outnumbered two to one and inflicted casualties at a rate of three for four, would reduce Lee's army to a handful, while Hooker would be left with the number Lee had had at the outset. Disappointed by the rejection of his proposal that he take Hood and Pickett west for an assault on Rosecrans, the burly Georgian listened with disapproval as Lee announced his intention to launch an offensive in the East. He protested, much as Reagan had done, but with no more success; Lee's mind was made up. So Longstreet contented himself with developing his theory — or, as he thought, advancing the stipulation — that the proposed invasion be conducted in accordance with his preference for receiving rather than delivering attack when the two armies came to grips, wherever that might be. As he put it later, quite as if he and Lee had been joint commanders of the army, "I then accepted his proposition to make a campaign into Pennsylvania, provided it should be offensive in strategy but defensive in tactics, forcing the Federal army to give us battle when we were in strong position and ready to receive them."

Lee heard him out with the courtesy which he was accustomed to extend to all subordinates, but which in this case was mistaken for a commitment. He intended no such thing, of course, and when he was told years later that Longstreet had said he so understood him, he refused to believe that his former lieutenant had made the statement. But Old Peter had said it, and he had indeed received that impression at the time; whereby trouble was stored up for all involved.

In any case, once Lee had completed the groundwork for his plans, he wasted no time in putting them into execution. Four days after his May 30 announcement of the army's reorganization, and just one month after Chancellorsville, he started McLaws on a march up the south bank of the Rappahannock to Culpeper, near which Hood and Pickett had been halted on their return from Suffolk. Rodes followed on June 4, and Early and Johnson the next day, leaving Hill's three divisions at Fredericksburg to face alone the Union host across the river. Hooker's balloons were up and apparently spotted the movement, for the bluecoats promptly effected a crossing below the town. It was rumored that Lee had expressed a willingness to "swap queens," Richmond for Washington, in case Hooker plunged south while his back was turned. However, the validity of the rumor was not tested; Hill reported the bridgehead was nothing he could not handle, and Lee took him at his word. Riding westward in the wake of Longstreet and Ewell, he joined them at Culpeper on June 7.

Stuart had been there more than two weeks already, getting his cavalry in shape for new exertions, and two days before Lee's arrival he had staged at nearby Brandy Station a grand review of five of his brigades, including by way of finale a mock charge on the guns of the horse artillery, which lent a touch of realism to the pageant by firing blank rounds as the long lines of grayjackets bore down on them with drawn sabers and wild yells. Stirred or frightened by this gaudy climax, several ladies fainted, or pretended to faint, in the grandstand which Jeb had had set up for them along one side of the field. To his further delight, the army commander agreed to let him restage the show for his benefit on the day after his arrival, though he insisted that the finale be omitted as a waste of powder and horseflesh. Despite this curtailment, the performance was a source of pride to the plumed chief of cavalry, who, as Lee wrote home, "was in all his glory." It was something more, as well; for another result of this second review was that he still had most of his 10,000 troopers concentrated near Brandy on June 9 for what turned out to be the greatest cavalry battle of the war.

Thirty-nine-year-old Alfred Pleasonton, recently promoted to major general as successor to Stoneman, had eight brigades of cavalry, roughly 12,000 men, grouped in three divisions under Brigadier Generals John Buford, David Gregg, and Judson Kilpatrick. All were West Pointers, like himself, and all were of the new hell-for-leather style of horsemen who had learned to care more for results than they did for spit and polish. Buford, the oldest, was thirty-seven; Gregg was thirty; Kilpatrick was twenty-seven. Supported by two brigades of infantry, Pleasonton moved upriver from Falmouth on June 8, with six of his brigades, which gave him a mounted force equal in strength to Stuart's, and crossed at dawn next morning at Beverly and Kelly's fords, above and below Rappahannock Station. Instructed to determine what Lee was up to, there in the V of the rivers where Pope had nearly come to grief the year before, he got over under cover of the heavy morning fog and surprised the rebel pickets, who were driven back toward Brandy, five miles away, with the blue riders hard on their heels. And so it was that Stuart, who had pitched his headquarters tent on Fleetwood Hill overlooking the field where the two reviews were held, got his first sight of the Yankees at about the same time he received the first message warning him that they were over the river at Beverly Ford. Two of his present five brigades, under Rooney Lee and Brigadier General William E. Jones, were already in that direction, contesting the advance. Fitz Lee's brigade was seven miles north, beyond the Hazel River, and the other two, under Wade Hampton and Brigadier General Beverly Robertson, were in the vicinity of Kelly's Ford, where Pelham had fallen twelve weeks ago today. Stuart sent couriers to alert the brigades to the north and south, then rode forward to join the fight Lee and Jones were making, about midway between Beverly Ford and Fleetwood Hill. However, he had no sooner gotten the situation fairly well in hand on that quarter of the field than he learned that another enemy column of equal strength had eluded the pickets at Kelly's Ford and was riding now into Brandy Station, two miles in his rear. The result, as he regrouped his forces arriving from north and south to meet the double threat, was hard fighting in the classic style, headlong charges met by headlong countercharges, with sabers, pistols, and carbines employed hand to hand to empty a lot of saddles. He lost Fleetwood Hill, retook it, lost it again, and again retook it. Near sundown, spotting rebel infantry on the march from Brandy — his own infantry had been engaged only lightly — Pleasonton fell back the way he had come, effecting an orderly withdrawal. He had lost 936 men, including 486 taken prisoner, as compared to the Confederate total of 523, but he was well satisfied with his troopers and their day's work on the rebel side of the Rappahannock.

Stuart expressed an equal if not greater satisfaction. After all, he retained possession of the field, along with three captured guns, and had inflicted a good deal more damage than he had suffered: except perhaps in terms of pride. For there could be no denying that he had been surprised, on his own ground, or that the Yankees had fought as hard — and, for that matter, as well — as his own famed gray horsemen, at least one of whom was saying, even now, that the bluecoats had been successful because he and his fellows had been "worried out," all the preceding week, by the grand reviews Jeb staged out of fondness for "military foppery and display." One thing was clear to Stuart at any rate. Such exploits as he hoped to perform in the future, enhancing his already considerable reputation, were going to be more difficult to bring off than those he had accomplished in the days when the blue troopers were comparatively inept. Doubtless his solution was the same as the army commander's. "We must all do more than formerly," Lee had said, and for Jeb this meant more, even, than the two rides around McClellan.

Approaching the field of battle that afternoon, Lee experienced the double shock of learning that his normally vigilant chief of cavalry had suffered a surprise and of seeing his son Rooney being carried to the rear with an ugly leg wound. However, he did not let either development change his plans for the march northward; which were as follows. While Longstreet remained at Culpeper, in position to reinforce Hill in case Hooker tried to swamp him, Ewell would move into and down the

Shenandoah Valley, preceded by Stuart's sixth brigade of cavalry, en route from Southwest Virginia under Brigadier General Albert Jenkins. When Ewell reached the Potomac, he was to cross into Maryland and strike out for Pennsylvania without delay. Longstreet then would advance northward, east of the Blue Ridge, thus preventing Union penetration of the passes, while Hill marched west from Fredericksburg and followed Ewell down the Valley and over the Potomac, to be followed in turn by Longstreet, who would leave Stuart to guard the Blue Ridge passes until the combined advance of 60,000 butternut infantry into Pennsylvania caused the Washington authorities to call the Army of the Potomac northward across the river from which it took its name.

Lee's plan was a bold one, but it had worked well against Lincoln and McClellan in September and it seemed likely to work as well against Lincoln and Hooker nine months later. The most questionable factor was Ewell, whose corps would not only set the pace for the rest of the army, but would also be the first to encounter whatever trouble lay in store for the Confederates in the North. In effect, this meant that he was being required to march and fight with the same fervor and skill as his former chief and predecessor, and whether he could ever become another Jackson was extremely doubtful, especially since he was not even the same Ewell, either to the ear or eye, who had fought under and alongside the dead Wizard of the Valley. In partial compensation for the loss of his leg — though this seemed in fact to bother him very little, either on horseback or afoot — he had made two acquisitions. One was religion, which tempered his language, and the other was a wife, which tempered his whole outlook. Formerly profane, he now was mild in manner. Formerly of modest means, he now was wealthy, having won the hand of a rich widow who in her youth had rejected his suit in order to marry a man with the undistinguished name of Brown. Now that she and her extensive property were in his charge, Old Bald Head could scarcely believe his luck, and sometimes he forgot himself so far as to introduce her as "My wife, Mrs Brown." Whether this new, gentled Ewell would measure up to such high expectations was the subject of much discussion around the campfires of all three corps, particularly his own; but it soon appeared that all the worry had been for nothing. Out in the Valley, the scene of former military magic, his firm grasp of strategy and tactics, coupled with a decisiveness of judgment, a good eye, and an eagerness to gather all the fruits of sudden victory, made it seem to former doubters that another Stonewall had indeed been found to lead the Second Corps and inspire the army.

He moved northward on the day after Stuart's fight at Brandy Station, entered the Valley by way of Chester Gap, and on June 13, having divided his corps at Front Royal the day before, marched on Winchester with Early and Johnson while Rodes and the cavalry struck at Berryville. Major General Robert Milroy had 5100 bluecoats at the former place, and Ewell was out to get them, along with an 1800-man detachment at the latter, ten miles east. As it turned out, the Berryville force made its getaway due to blunders by Jenkins, who was unfamiliar with the kind of work expected of horsemen in Lee's army, but the success of the operation against Winchester more than made up for the disappointment. Warned to fall back, Milroy chose to stand his ground, much as Banks had done in a similar predicament the year before. That hesitation had led to Banks's undoing, and so now did it lead to Milroy's. Charged by Early on the 14th from the west, he retreated northeastward in the darkness, only to be intercepted at dawn by Johnson some four miles up the Harpers Ferry road at Stevenson's Depot, where he was routed. The Union general managed to escape with a couple of hundred of his troopers, but his unmounted men had no such luck in outrunning their pursuers, who gathered them up in droves. Johnson himself — called "Old Clubby" by his soldiers because he preferred to direct their combat maneuvers with a heavy walking stick instead of a sword — asserted happily that he had taken thirty prisoners "with his opera glass" before he ended his private chase by falling off his horse and into Opequon Creek. Milroy was presently removed from command by Lincoln, but that was a rather superfluous gesture, since practically all of his command had already been removed from him by Ewell. The total bag, in addition to the infliction of 443 casualties on the immediate field of battle, was 700 sick and 3358 able-bodied prisoners, 23 fine guns, and some 300 well-stocked wagons: all at a cost of 269 Confederate casualties, less than fifty of whom were killed. Ewell's triumph over Milroy was even greater than Jackson's had been over Banks on that same field: a fact that was not lost on the men of the Second Corps, whose final doubts as to the worth of their new commander were forgotten. Moreover, like Stonewall, Old Bald Head did not sit down to enjoy in leisure the spoils and glory he had won. Pushing Jenkins forward to the Potomac before sundown, he had Rodes follow on June 16 for a crossing at Williamsport, Maryland, where a halt was called to allow the other two divisions to catch up for a combined advance into Pennsylvania.

 Lee had already put the other two corps in motion. On June 15, while Ewell was gathering prisoners in the woods and fields near Winchester, Longstreet started north from Culpeper, and Hill — who reported that Hooker had abandoned his west-bank bridgehead and withdrawn his army from its camps around Falmouth the day before, apparently for a concentration at or near Manassas, where he would stand athwart Lee's path in case the unpredictable Virginian launched a direct drive on Washington from Culpeper — left Fredericksburg, under instructions to follow Ewell's line of march to the Potomac. Two days later, Lee himself moved north, establishing headquarters at Berryville on the 19th, while Stuart fought a series of thunderous cavalry engagements at Aldie, Middleburg, and Upperville, in all of which he was successful at keeping his hard-riding blue opponents from discovering what was afoot beyond the mountains that screened the Valley from the Piedmont. Pleased with Jeb's recovery of his verve, the army commander listened with sympathy to the cavalry chief's suggestion that he leave two brigades of horsemen to plug the gaps of the Blue Ridge and move with the other three into Hooker's rear, the better to annoy and delay him when he started north across the Potomac. Lee approved, in principle, but warned that once it became clear that Fighting Joe was crossing the river, Stuart "must immediately cross himself and take his place on our right flank," where he would be needed to screen the northward advance and keep the invading army informed of the movements of the defenders. Aware of his former cadet's fondness for adventure at any price, Lee sent him written instructions on June 22, repeating the warning that he must not allow himself to be delayed in joining the rest of the column when the time came. Next day, when Stuart reported the bluecoats lying quiet in their camps north of Manassas and suggested that a crossing of the Potomac to the east of them by his three mobile brigades would help to mislead Hooker as to Lee's intentions, Lee followed his first message with a second, re-emphasizing the need for close observance of the Federals, but adding: "You will, however, be able to judge whether you can pass around their army without hindrance, doing them all the damage you can, and cross the river east of the mountains. In either case, after crossing the river, you must move on and feel the right of Ewell's troops, collecting information, provisions, etc." The dispatch ended on a note of caution. "Be watchful and circumspect in all your movements," Lee told Stuart.

Meanwhile the infantry was marching rapidly. By June 24, Ewell's main body had cleared Hagerstown and his lead division was at Chambersburg, twenty miles beyond the Pennsylvania line, with orders to press on to the Susquehanna. Presumably the North was in turmoil, having been warned that the penetration would be deep. "It is said," the Richmond *Whig* had reported the week before, "that an artificial leg ordered some months ago awaits General Ewell's arrival in the city of Philadelphia." Hill and Longstreet crossed the Potomac that same day, at Shepherdstown and Williamsport, and Lee himself made camp that night on the south bank, opposite the latter place, intending to cross over in the morning. Before he did so, however, he received from the President a reply to a letter written two weeks before, in which Lee had made certain admissions in regard to the present national outlook and had suggested some maneuvers he thought might be available to the Confederacy, not only on the military but also on the diplomatic front. "Our resources in men are constantly diminishing," he had written, "and the disproportion in this respect between us and our enemies, if they continue united in their efforts to subjugate us, is steadily augmenting." This being so, he thought the proper course would be to promote divi-

sion in the northern ranks by encouraging those who favored arbitration as a substitute for bloodshed. "Should the belief that peace will bring back the Union become general," Lee continued, "the war would no longer be supported, and that, after all, is what we are interested in bringing about. When peace is proposed to us, it will be time enough to discuss its terms, and it is not the part of prudence to spurn the proposition in advance, merely because those who wish to make it believe, or affect to believe, that it will result in bringing us back to the Union." If this was sly, it was also rather ingenuous, particularly in its assumption of such a contrast between the peoples of the North and South that the latter would be willing to resume fighting if negotiations produced no better terms than a restoration of the Union, whereas the former would be willing to concede the Confederacy's independence rather than have the war begin again. Perceiving the risk involved — after all, it might turn out the other way around — Davis contented himself with remarking that encouragement of the followers of the northern peace party was a commendable notion, especially now that a second invasion was being launched at them. Lee replied next morning, as he prepared to cross the Potomac, that he was "much gratified" by the President's approval of his views. He suggested, moreover, that Bragg at Tullahoma and Buckner at Knoxville take the offensive against the Union center and thus "accomplish something in Ohio." Beauregard, too, could share in the delivery of the all-out blow about to be struck for southern independence, Lee said, by bringing to Culpeper such troops as he could scrape together on the Seaboard for a feint at Washington. This "army in effigy," as Lee called it, would have at least a psychological effect, particularly with the Hero of Manassas at its head, since it probably would cause Lincoln to make Hooker leave a portion of his army behind when he started north to challenge the invaders of Pennsylvania. Of course, it was rather late for such improvisations, but Lee suggested them anyhow. "I still hope that all things will end well for us in Vicksburg," he said in closing, unaware that this was the day Grant exploded the mine that transferred the slave Abraham's allegiance to the Union. "At any rate, every effort should be made to bring about that result." And with that, having advanced such recommendations as he thought proper in connection with the supreme endeavor he was about to make with the Army of Northern Virginia, he mounted Traveler and rode in a heavy rain across the shallow Potomac.

This was the week of the summer solstice, and the land was green with promise as Lee rode northward, this day and the next. "It's like a hole full of blubber to a Greenlander!" Ewell had exclaimed as he passed this way the week before. Hill and Longstreet agreed, finding that his heavy requisitions of food and livestock had scarcely diminished the pickings all around. Marches were so rapid over the good roads that some outfits enjoyed "breakfast in Virginia, whiskey in Maryland, and supper in Pennsylvania." Struck by the contrast to the ravaged, fought-over region in which they had spent most of the past two years, the Confederates gazed wide-eyed at the lush fields and cattle and the prosperity of the citizens who tilled and tended them. A Texas private wrote home in amazement that the barns hereabouts were "positively more tastily built than two thirds of the houses in Waco." The sour looks of the natives had no repressive effect on the soldiers, who "would ask them for their names so we could write them on a piece of paper, so we told them, and put it in water as we knew it would turn to vinegar." Spirits were high all down the long gray column. "Och, mine contree!" the lean marchers called out to the stolid men along the roadside, or: "Here's your played-out rebellion!" The Pennsylvanians in turn were impressed by the butternut invaders, so different from their own well-turned-out militiamen, who had fallen back northward at the approach of Ewell's outriders the week before. "Many were ragged, shoeless, and filthy," a civilian wrote, but all were "well armed and under perfect discipline. They seemed to move as one vast machine." Others found that the obvious admiration the rebels felt for this land of plenty did not necessarily mean that they preferred it to their homeland. The farms were too close together for their liking, and they complained of the lack of trees and shade, which made the atmosphere seem cramped and unfit for leisure. Even the magnificent-looking horses, the great Percherons and Clydesdales, turned out to be a disappointment in the end. Consuming about twice the feed, they could stand only about half the hardship required of what one artilleryman called "our compact, hard-muscled little horses. . . . It was pitiful later," he added, "to see these great brutes suffer when compelled to dash off at full gallop with a gun, after pasturing on dry broom sedge and eating a quarter of feed of weevil-eaten corn." Nor was the qualified reaction limited to those from whom it might have been expected. A housewife, questioning a Negro body servant who was attending his North Carolina master on the march, tested his loyalty by asking him if he was treated well, and she got a careful answer. "I live as I wish," he told her, "and if I did not,

I think I couldn't better myself by stopping here. This is a beautiful country, but it doesn't come up to home in my eyes."

Apparently Lee felt much the same way about it, for at Chambersburg on June 27 — he had arrived the day before and pitched his headquarters tent just east of town in a roadside grove called Shetter's Woods, where the townspeople came in normal times for picnics and such celebrations as the one planned for the Fourth of July, a week from now — he told "a true Union woman" who asked him for his autograph: "My only desire is that they will let me go home and eat my bread in peace." He said this despite the fact that his ride northward had in some ways resembled a triumphal procession, beginning with a gift of fresh raspberries just after he crossed the Potomac. Though Marylanders noted that he had aged considerably in the ten months since his previous visit, the gray commander on the iron-gray horse still impressed them as quite the handsomest man they had ever seen. "Oh, I wish he was ours!" a girl who was waving a Union flag exclaimed with sudden fervor as he passed through Hagerstown, and in Pennsylvania when a civilian whispered in awe as he rode by, "What a large neck he has," a nearby Confederate was quick with an explanation: "It takes a damn big neck to hold his head." The "perfect discipline" remarked on by civilians as the butternut columns wound past their houses and left them unmolested was the result of a decision Lee had made before leaving Virginia. "I cannot hope that Heaven will prosper our cause when we are violating its laws," he said. "I shall therefore carry on the war in Pennsylvania without offending the sanctions of a high civilization and of Christianity." Accordingly, he had instructed his commissary officers to meet all the necessities of the army by formal requisition on local authorities or by direct purchase with Confederate money. Exhorting his troops "to abstain with most scrupulous care from unnecessary or wanton injury to private property," he issued at Chambersburg today a general order commending them for their good behavior so far on the march. "It must be remembered that we make war only upon armed men," he told them, "and that we cannot take vengeance for the wrongs our people have suffered without lowering ourselves in the eyes of all whose abhorrence has been excited by the atrocities of our enemies, and offending against Him to whom vengeance belongeth, without whose favor and support our efforts must all prove in vain."

In part these words were written, and enforced, with an eye to the encouragement of the northern peace movement. Whether anything would come of that remained to be seen, but the effect on the men to whom the order was addressed was all that could have been desired. No army had ever marched better or with so little straggling. Longstreet and Hill had their two corps in bivouac at Chambersburg and Fayetteville, six miles east, and their men were in excellent spirits, well rested and far better shod and clad and fed than they had been when they were up this way the year before. Ewell by now was well along with his independent mission; Early was within half a dozen miles of York, and the other two divisions were at Carlisle, a short day's march from the Susquehanna and Harrisburg, which Ewell had been authorized to capture if it "comes within your means." This now seemed likely, and Lee was prepared to follow with the other two corps as soon as Stuart arrived to shield his flank and bring him news of what the Federals were up to on the far side of the Potomac. But there was the rub; Lee had heard nothing from Stuart in three days. This probably meant that Jeb and his picked brigades were off on the "ride" Lee had authorized on the 23d, but he seemed either to have ignored the admonition to "take his place on our right flank," which was highly improbable, or else to have run into unforeseen difficulties: which might mean almost anything, including annihilation, except that it was hard to imagine the irrepressible Stuart being caught in any box he could not get out of. Still, the strain of waiting was beginning to tell on Lee, who spent much of his time poring over a large-scale map of western Maryland and southern Pennsylvania which Stonewall Jackson had had prepared that winter, with just such a campaign as the present one in mind.

Another legacy from Jackson was a sixty-one-year-old West Pointer named Isaac Trimble, one of his favorite brigadiers, who reported for duty to Lee in Shetter's Woods today, having recovered at last from a leg wound received ten months ago. "Before this war is over," he had told Stonewall, "I intend to be a major general or a corpse." His promotion having come through in April, he had been slated for command of the division that had gone to Edward Johnson, but his injuries had been so slow to heal — in part, no doubt, because of his age — that it had been necessary to go ahead without him. There could be no question of his superseding Old Clubby, who had done so well at Winchester, yet Lee had no intention of losing the services of so hard a fighter as this veteran of all the Second Corps victories from First through Second Manassas, even though there was no specific command to give him that was commensurate with his rank. Ewell was moving against Harrisburg, Lee told Trimble; "go and join him and help him take the place." Before he left, however, Lee drew him into conversation about the terrain just beyond the mountains to the east. Trimble, who had been chief engineer of a nearby railroad before the war, replied that there was scarcely a square mile in that direction that did not contain excellent ground for battle or maneuver. Lee seemed pleased at that, and he told why. "Our army is in good spirits, not overfatigued, and can be concentrated in twenty-four hours or less." Not having heard from Stuart to the contrary — as he surely would have done if such had been the case — he assumed that the Federals were still on the far side of the Potomac, and he outlined for Trimble his plans for their destruction. "When they hear where we are, they will make forced marches to interpose their forces between us and Baltimore and Philadelphia. They will come up, probably through Frederick, broken down with hunger and hard marching, strung out on a long line and much demoralized. When they come into Pennsylvania, I shall throw an overwhelming force on their advance, crush it, follow up the success, drive one corps back on another, and by successive repulses and surprises, before they can concentrate, create a panic and virtually destroy the army."

Stirred by this vision of the Army of the Potomac being toppled like a row of dominoes, Trimble said that he did not doubt the outcome of such a confrontation, especially since the morale of the Army of Northern Virginia had never been higher than it was now. "That is, I hear, the general impression," Lee replied, and by way of a parting gesture he laid his hand on the dead Jackson's map, touching the region just east of the mountains that caught on their western flanks the rays of the setting sun. "Hereabouts we shall probably meet the enemy and fight a great battle," he said, "and if God gives us the victory, the war will be over and we shall achieve the recognition of our independence."

One of the place names under his hand as he spoke was the college town of Gettysburg, just over twenty miles away, from which no less than ten roads ran to as many disparate points of the compass, as if it were probing for trouble in all directions.

★ ★ ★

At sundown of that same June 27, as Trimble said goodbye to Lee and left for Carlisle to join Ewell, a courier left Washington aboard a special train for Hooker's headquarters, established just that afternoon at Frederick. Though he thus was risking capture by rebel cavalry, which was known to be on the loose, the documents he carried would admit of no delay. In the past ten months, the army had fought four major battles under as many different commanders — Bull Run under Pope, Antietam under McClellan, Fredericksburg under Burnside, and Chancellorsville under Hooker — all against a single adversary, Robert Lee, who could claim unquestionable victory in three out of the four: especially the first and the last, of which about the best that could be said was that the Federal army had survived them. Now it was about to fight its fifth great battle, and the import of the messages about to be delivered was that it would fight it under still a fifth commander.

Not that Hooker had not done well in the seven weeks since Chancellorsville. He had indeed: especially in the past few days, when by dint of hard and skillful marching he managed to interpose his 100,000 soldiers between Lee and Washington without that general's knowledge that the blue army had even crossed the river from which it took its name. The trouble was that, despite his efforts to shift the blame for the recent Wilderness fiasco — principally onto Stoneman and Sedgwick and Howard's rattled Dutchmen — he could not blur a line of the picture fixed in the public mind of himself as the exclusive author of that woeful chapter. In early June, for example, the Chicago *Tribune* defined its attitude in an editorial reprinted in papers as far away as Richmond: "Under the leadership of 'fighting Joe Hooker' the glorious Army of the Potomac is becoming more slow in its movements, more unwieldy, less confident of itself, more of a football to the enemy, and less an honor to the country than any army we have yet raised." There was much in this that was unfair — particularly in regard to slowness, a charge Hooker had refuted once and would refute again — but it was generally known, in and out of army circles, that his ranking corps commander, Darius Couch, had applied for and been granted transfer to another department in order to avoid further service under a man he judged incompetent. Moreover, this mistrust was shared to a considerable extent by the authorities in Washington. Stanton and Halleck had never liked Joe Hooker, and Lincoln had sent him at the outset a letter which made only too clear the doubts that had attended his appointment. These doubts had been allayed for a time by the boldness and celerity of his movements preceding the May Day confrontation in the Wilderness, when he came unglued under pressure and revived them. Now they were back, and in force: as was shown by the day-to-day correspondence between himself and Lincoln, made voluminous by his determination to avoid all possible contact with Halleck, whom he regarded with reciprocal distaste.

On June 4, when Lowe's balloonists reported some Confederates gone from their camps across the Rappahannock, Hooker interpreted this as the opening movement of an offensive elsewhere, probably upriver, and reasoned that the most effective way to stop it was to launch one of his own, here and now. Next morning, after directing the establishment of a west-bank bridgehead for this purpose, he wired Lincoln that he thought his best move would be "to pitch into [Lee's] rear," and he asked: "Will it be within the sphere of my instructions to do so?" Lincoln replied promptly, to the effect that it would not. He had, he said, "but one idea which I think worth suggesting to you, and that is, in case you find Lee coming to the north of the Rappahannock, I would by no means cross to the south of it. . . . In one word, I would not take any risk of being entangled upon the river, like an ox jumped half over a fence and liable to be torn by dogs, front and rear, without a fair chance to gore one way or kick the other." Halleck followed this up with some advice of his own. "Lee will probably move light and rapidly," he warned. "Your movable force should be prepared to do the same." Hooker did as he was told, alerting his troops for a sidling movement up the north bank, but he maintained the bridgehead, not only as a possible means of learning what the enemy was up to, but also on the off-chance that the authorities might decide to give him his head after all. On June 10, hearing from Pleasonton that rebel infantry had been spotted in force at Brandy Station the day before, he showed that he too, though he considered the Washington defenses quite strong enough to withstand attack, was willing to risk a swap of queens in the presently deadly chess game. If Lee had taken a good part of his army west to Culpeper, Hooker wired Lincoln, "will it not promote the true interest of the cause for me to march to Richmond at once? ... If left to operate from my own judgment, with my present information, I do not hesitate to say that I should adopt this course as being the most speedy and certain mode of giving the rebellion a mortal blow." Once more Lincoln was prompt in reply. Unlike Davis, who believed that the best defense of his capital was a threat to the enemy's, he was plainly horrified at this notion of removing the army from its present tactical position between Lee and Washington. Besides, he said, "If you had Richmond invested today, you would not be able to take it in twenty days; meanwhile your communications, and with them your army, would be ruined. I think Lee's army, and not Richmond, is your true objective point. If he comes toward the Upper Potomac, follow on his flank and on his inside track, shortening your lines whilst he lengthens his. Fight him, too, when opportunity offers. If he stays where he is, fret him and fret him."

Next morning Hooker began the movement north, conforming to the pattern set by Lee, but maintaining what Lincoln called the "inside track." This meant that he was required to keep between the Confederates and the capital in his rear, a limitation he found irksome. Moreover, though he knew the rebels had been reinforced for the campaign now fairly under way, his own army was far below the strength it had enjoyed when it marched on Chancellorsville. Nearly 17,000 men had fallen there, and an equal number of short-term enlistments had expired in the past six weeks. As a result of these subtractions, by no means offset by the trickle of recruits, barely 100,000 effectives left the familiar camps around Falmouth in the course of the next four days. To facilitate the march, which would be a hard one, he divided his army into two unequal wings, one led by John Reynolds, consisting of his own corps and those under Sickles and Howard, and the other by Hooker himself, consisting of those under Meade, Sedgwick, Slocum, and Hancock, who had succeeded Couch. "If the enemy should be making for Maryland, I will make the best dispositions in my power to come up with him," he assured Lincoln on June 14: only to receive from him a message sent at the same time. Foreseeing disaster in the present threat to Milroy, the Commander in Chief wanted something more from Fighting Joe than words of reassurance. "If the head of Lee's army is at Martinsburg and the tail of it on the Plank road between Fredericksburg and Chancellorsville," he wired, "the animal must be very slim somewhere. Could you not break him?" Strung out on the roads as he was by now, having abandoned the bridgehead he had held for more than a week, there was nothing Hooker could do for the present but keep marching, and that was what he did. Hancock's corps, the last to go, pulled out of Falmouth on June 15, the day that A. P. Hill left Fredericksburg and Ewell's lead division began its crossing of the Potomac. A simultaneous dispatch from Halleck, warning against "wanton and wasteful destruction of public property," snapped the string of Hooker's patience, and he got off an urgent wire to Lincoln: "You have long been aware, Mr President, that I have not enjoyed the confidence of the major general commanding the army, and I can assure you so long as this continues we may look in vain for success." This sounded as if he was saying he lacked confidence in himself, "the major general commanding the army," but it was Old Brains he meant, and Lincoln knew it. "To remove all misunderstanding," he replied, "I now place you in the strict military relation to General Halleck of a commander of one of the armies to the general-in-chief of all the armies. I have not intended differently, but as it seems to be differently understood, I shall direct him to give you orders and you to obey them."

The sting of this was somewhat relieved by a covering letter in which the Chief Executive explained that all he asked was "that you will be in such mood that we can get into our action the best cordial judgment of yourself and General Halleck, with my own poor mite added, if indeed he and you shall think it entitled to any consideration at all." However, it had begun to seem to Hooker that Lincoln's advice in regard to Lee — "fret him and fret him" — was also being applied in regard to himself, not only by the general-in-chief but also by the President, whose "poor mite" often made up in sharpness for what it lacked in weight. It seemed to Hooker that he was being goaded, and unquestionably he was. One after another his proposals had been dismissed as rash, or else they had been urged upon him only after subsequent instructions had placed his army in an attitude from which they could no longer be accomplished. Urgent appeals for reinforcements were rejected out of hand, as were others that his authority be extended to include the soldiers in the capital defenses. More and more, as the long hot days of hard and dusty marching went by, it came to seem to Fighting Joe that he commanded his army only in semblance, though it was clear enough at the same time that his was the head on which the blame would fall in event of the disaster he saw looming. Leapfrogging his headquarters northward, first to Dumfries and then to Fairfax, with no information as to what was occurring beyond his immediate horizon, he complained at last to Halleck, on June 24, that "outside of the Army of the Potomac I don't know whether I am standing on my head or feet." The next two days were spent crossing the Potomac at Edwards Ferry and effecting a concentration around Frederick. His plan was to strike westward into the Cumberland Valley, severing Lee's communications with Virginia, and for this he wanted the co-operation of the 10,000 men at Harpers Ferry, which was beyond the limits of his control, but which he thought should be evacuated before Lee turned and gobbled up the garrison as he had done in September. On the evening of June 26, believing that the authorities might have learned from that example — at least they had learned to post the troops on Maryland Heights, occupation of which had permitted the Confederates to take the place in short order the time before, along with some 12,000 men and 73 cannon — Hooker wired Halleck: "Is there any reason why Maryland Heights should not be abandoned after the public stores and property are removed?" Halleck replied next morning: "Maryland Heights have always been regarded as an important point to be held by us, and much expense and labor incurred in fortifying them. I cannot approve their abandonment, except in case of absolute necessity."

Convinced that the garrison was "of no earthly account" on its perch above the Ferry, Hooker decided to appeal through channels to Stanton and Lincoln. "All the public property could have been secured tonight," he wired back, "and the troops marched to where they could have been of some service. Now they are but a bait for the rebels, should they return. I beg that this may be presented to the Secretary of War and His Excellency the President." While waiting for an answer, he either decided the appeal should be strengthened or else he lost his head entirely. Or perhaps, having taken all he could take from above, he really wanted to get from under. At any rate, before the general-in-chief replied, Fighting Joe got off a second wire to him, hard on the heels of the first. "My original instructions require me to cover Harpers Ferry and Washington," it read. "I have now imposed upon me, in addition, an enemy in my front of more than my number. I beg to be understood, respectfully, but firmly, that I am unable to comply with this condition with the means at my disposal, and earnestly request that I may at once be relieved from the position I occupy." This was sent at 1 p.m. The long afternoon wore slowly away; the sun had set and night had fallen before he received an answer addressed to "Major General Hooker, Army of the Potomac." Whether the word *commanding* had been omitted by accident or design he could not tell. Nor was the body of the message at all conclusive on that point. "Your application to be relieved from your present command is received," Halleck told him. "As you were appointed to this command by the President, I have no power to relieve you. Your dispatch has been duly referred for Executive action."

The wire was headed 8 p.m. and that was where duplicity came in. Halleck knew that the special train had left Washington half an hour before that time, for the courier aboard it was Colonel James A. Hardie, his own assistant adjutant general, and Old Brains himself had written the documents he carried, one an order relieving Hooker of command

and the other a letter of instructions for his successor. Reaching Frederick well after midnight, Hardie did not wait for morning. Nor did he call first on Joe Hooker. Rather, he went directly to the tent of the man who would succeed him: George Meade.

This would come as something of a shock to the army, especially to Reynolds and Sedgwick, who ranked him, but no one was more surprised than Meade himself. His immediate reaction, on waking out of a sound sleep at 3 o'clock in the morning to find the staff officer standing beside his cot, was alarm. He thought he was about to be arrested. Sure enough, after a brief exchange of greetings, during which Meade wondered just what military sin he had committed, Hardie's first words were: "General, I'm afraid I've come to make trouble for you." And with that, changing the nature if not the force of the shock, he handed him Halleck's letter of instructions, which began: "You will receive with this the order of the President placing you in command of the Army of the Potomac."

Shortly before, in a letter to his wife, Meade had commented on "the ridiculous appearance we present of changing our generals after each battle," and only two days ago, amid rumors that Hooker was slated for removal, he had written her that he stood little chance of receiving the appointment, not only because he was outranked by two of his six fellow corps commanders, but also "because I have no friends, political or others, who press or advance my claims or pretensions." Yet now he had it, against all the odds, and with it a cluster of problems inherited on what was obviously the eve of battle. Partly, though — if he could believe what Halleck told him — these problems were reduced at the very outset. "You will not be hampered by any minute instructions from these headquarters," the letter read. "Your army is free to act as you may deem proper under the circumstances as they arise." His main duty would be to cover Washington and Baltimore. "Should General Lee move upon either of these places, it is expected that you will either anticipate him or arrive with him so as to give him battle." By way of stressing the fact that the new commander would have a free hand, Halleck added: "Harpers Ferry and its garrison are under your direct orders." Knowing the difficulties Hooker had encountered on this question, Meade could scarcely believe his eyes. "Am I permitted, under existing circumstances," he inquired by telegraph, later that same day, "to withdraw a portion of the garrison of Harpers Ferry, providing I leave sufficient force to hold Maryland Heights against a *coup de main?*" Promptly the reply came back: "The garrison at Harpers Ferry is under your orders. You can diminish or increase it as you think the circumstances justify."

Meanwhile the new commander had called on Hooker, who reacted to the order with as much apparent relief as Lincoln and Halleck had felt in issuing it. In fact, nothing in Fighting Joe's five-month tenure, in the course of which the army had experienced much of profit as well as pain, became him more than the manner in which he brought it to a close. Conferring with Meade on his plans and dispositions, he was cooperative and pleasant, except for one brief flare-up when Meade, looking over the situation map, remarked that the various corps seemed "rather scattered." Then Hooker quieted down, issued a farewell address urging support for his successor — "a brave and accomplished officer, who has nobly earned the confidence and esteem of this army on many a well-fought field" — and got into a spring wagon, alongside Hardie, for the ride to the railroad station. Meade shook his hand, stood for a moment watching the wagon roll away, then turned and entered the tent Hooker had just vacated. Presently he was interrupted by Reynolds, who had put on his dress uniform to come over and congratulate his fellow Pennsylvanian. This had a good effect on those who had wondered what his reaction would be: the more so because those closest to him knew that he had gone to Washington early that month, when it was rumored that Fighting Joe was about to get the ax, to tell Lincoln that he did not want the command — for which, with Couch gone, he was next in line — unless he was allowed more freedom of action than any of the army's five unfortunate chieftains had been granted up to then. Now, if not before, Reynolds had his answer, and he took it with aplomb. Sedgwick too arrived to offer congratulations and assurance of support, having managed to assuage the burning in his bosom which the announcement had provoked. News that it was Meade who would head the army, and not himself, had reached Uncle John while he was out for his morning ride. For him, as for most old soldiers, the tradition of seniority was a strong one. Putting the spurs to his horse, he led his staff on a hard gallop for some distance to relieve his agitation, then rode over to shake the hand of the man who had passed him by.

That hand was a busy one just now, getting the feel of the controls even as the vehicle was headed for a collision. Meade's own elevation called for other promotions and advancements beyond those recently conferred in the wake of Chancellorsville, which in turn had followed hard upon another extensive shake-up after bloody Fredericksburg. As a result, not one of the seven army corps was commanded now by the general who had led it into battle at Antietam, and the same was true of all but two of the nineteen infantry divisions — Humphreys' and Alpheus S. Williams' — only four of which were commanded by major generals: Doubleday, Birney, Newton, and Carl Schurz. Of the fifteen brigadiers in charge of divisions, seven had been appointed to their posts since early May: John C. Caldwell, Alexander Hays, James Barnes, Romeyn B. Ayres, Samuel W. Crawford, Horatio G. Wright, and Francis Barlow. Equally new to their positions were Hancock and George Sykes, successors to Couch and Meade as corps commanders. In fact, only Reynolds and Slocum had the same division commanders they had had at Chancellorsville: Doubleday, James S. Wadsworth, and John C. Robinson with the former, Williams and John W. Geary with the latter. Other drawbacks there were, too. In contrast to Lee, all of whose corps and division commanders were West Pointers except for one V.M.I. man, Meade had only fourteen academy graduates among the twenty-six generals who filled those vital positions in the Army of the Potomac. This meant that nearly half were nonprofessionals, and of these a number were political appointees: Dan Sickles for example, for whom Meade had small use, either military or private. He had, however, for whatever it was worth, a better geographical distribution among his generals than Lee had achieved. Eight were Pennsylvanians and seven were New Yorkers, while three were from Connecticut, two from Maine, two from Germany — Schurz and Adolf von Steinwehr, both of course in Howard's corps — and one each from Vermont, Massachusetts, Maryland, and Virginia. The revised order of battle was as follows:

I. REYNOLDS	II. HANCOCK	III. SICKLES	V. SYKES
Wadsworth	Caldwell	Birney	Barnes
Doubleday	Gibbon	Humphreys	Ayres
Robinson	Hays		Crawford

VI. SEDGWICK	XI. HOWARD	XII. SLOCUM
Wright	Barlow	Williams
Howe	Steinwehr	Geary
Newton	Schurz	

Doubtful as were the qualities of a sizable proportion of these men, one third of whom had been assigned to their current posts within the past eight weeks, none was more of a military question mark than the man who had just been given the most responsible job of all. This doubt was not so much because of any lack of experience; Meade had performed well, if not brilliantly, in combat as the commander of a brigade, a division, and a corps. If at Chancellorsville, through no fault of his own, he had been denied an appreciable share in the battle, at Fredericksburg his had been the only division to achieve even a brief penetration of the rebel line, and surely this had been considered by Lincoln — along with Reynolds' unacceptable stipulation and Sedgwick's alleged poor showing in early May, of which Hooker had complained — in making his choice as to who was to become the army's sixth commander. The question, rather, was whether Meade could inspire that army when pay-off time came round, as it was now about to do. He seemed utterly incapable of provoking the sort of personal enthusiasm McClellan and Hooker could arouse by their mere presence; Burnside and Pope, even the hapless McDowell, seemed downright gaudy alongside Meade, who gave an impression of professorial dryness and lack of juice. What he lacked in fact was glamour, not only in his actions and dispatches, but also in his appearance, which a journalist said was more that of "a learned pundit than a soldier." Two birthdays short of fifty, he looked considerably older, with a "small and compact" balding head, a grizzled beard, and outsized pouches under eyes that were "serious, almost sad," and "rather sunken" on each side of what the reporter charitably described as "the late Duke of Wellington class of nose." The over-all effect, although "decidedly patrician and distinguished," was not of the kind that brought forth cheers or a wholesale tossing of caps, particularly when it was known to be combined with a hair-trigger temper and a petulance which tested in turn the patience of his staff. "What's Meade ever done?" was a common response among the men — those outside his corps, at least — when they heard that he was their new commander. The general himself had few delusions on this score. "I know they call me a damned old snapping turtle," he remarked.

Whatever other shortcomings he might have, in addition to lacking glamour, it presently was shown that indecision was not one of them: at least not now, in these first hours. "So soon as I can post myself up, I will communicate more in detail," he had closed an early-morning telegram accepting the appointment to command. By midafternoon, having studied Hooker's plans and dispositions, along with intelligence reports on Lee — reports which, incidentally, turned out to be extremely accurate; "The enemy force does not exceed 80,000 men and 275 guns," he was told by Maryland observers who kept tally on what passed through Hagerstown, and this was within 5000 men and 3 guns of agreement with Lee's own figures, which included his scattered cavalry — Meade had decided on a course of action and had already begun to issue orders that would put it into execution. "I propose to move this army tomorrow in the direction of York," he wired Halleck at 4.45 p.m. This meant that he had rejected Hooker's plan for a westward strike at Lee's supply line. Moreover, the decision was made irrevocable by dispatches, not only recalling the units that had gone in that direction, but also ordering French to march eastward to Frederick with 7000 men while the remainder of the garrison served as train guards for the Harpers Ferry stores, which were to be removed at once to the capital defenses. Meade thus was adopting what had seemed to him at the outset the only proper course for him to take in conformity with his orders from above: "I must move toward the Susquehanna, keeping Washington and Baltimore well covered, and if the enemy is checked in his attempt to cross the Susquehanna, or if he turns toward Baltimore, to give him battle." Reynolds was retained as commander of the three corps in the lead on the swing north, and a warning order went out soon after sundown for the whole army to "be ready to march at daylight tomorrow.... Strong exertions are required."

That meant early reveille and breakfast in the dark, but the men had grown accustomed to this in the two weeks they had spent on the road since leaving the Rappahannock. All the same, and even though they had taken what Lincoln called the "inside track," the pace had been killing — Slocum's corps, as an extreme example, had covered thirty-three hot dusty miles in a single day while moving up to Fairfax — with the result that straggling had been worse than at any time since the berry-picking jaunt to First Bull Run, just three weeks short of two full years ago. For the most part, those who fell out managed to catch up at night and start out with their units in the morning, but enough had dropped out permanently, skulking in barns along the way, to bring the army's total down to 94,974 effectives of all arms. Then — on June 28, by coincidence a Sunday — had come a day of rest, occasioned by the change of commanders, and now they were off again. Although they did not know just where they were going, at any rate they were glad it was not back to the Old Dominion. "We have marched through some beautiful country," a colonel wrote home. "It is refreshing to get out of the barren desert of Virginia and into this land of thrift and plenty." One thing was practically certain, however, and this was that the road they now were taking led to battle. But that was all right, too, apparently, despite the tradition of defeat which had been lengthened under Burnside and Hooker and was a part of Meade's inheritance. "We felt some doubt about whether it was ever going to be our fortune to win a victory in Virginia," another soldier afterwards recalled, "but no one admitted the possibility of a defeat north of the Potomac."

★ ★ ★

For Lee, this same Sunday had been a day of puzzlement, mounting tension, and frustration. He not only did not know of the early-morning switch in blue commanders; he did not even know that for the past two days the whole Federal army had been on the same side of the Potomac as his own. Such ignorance might have been expected to be the opposite of disturbing — a maxim even described it as "bliss"— except that, as he knew only too well, having had occasion to prove it to several opponents, a lack of information was all too often the prelude to disaster. A recent prime example of this was Hooker, of whom Jackson had said on the ride to Guiney Station: "He should not have sent away his cavalry. That was his great blunder. It was that which enabled me to turn him, without his being aware of it, and to take him by the rear." Now Lee himself was in somewhat the same danger, and for somewhat the same reason. For the better part of a week he had heard nothing at all from Stuart, on whom he had always depended for information, or from any of his six brigades. One was at Carlisle with Ewell, approaching the Susquehanna; two were guarding the Blue Ridge passes, far to the south; while the other three, presumably, were off on another of those circumferential "rides" that had brought fame to their plumed leader. This last was not in itself the reason for Lee's anxiety. After all, he himself had authorized the adoption of such a course. What bothered him was the silence, which was as complete as if a sound-proof curtain had been dropped between him and his one best source of information. Scarcely an officer who approached him there in Shetter's Woods today escaped the question: "Can you tell me where General Stuart is?" or: "Where on earth is my cavalry?" or even: "Have you any news of the enemy's movements? What is the enemy going to do?"

No one had ever heard him ask such things before, for the simple reason that he had never needed to ask them; Stuart had generally supplied the answers in advance. And now, for lack of answers, he was obliged — as most of his opponents, to their distress in the course of the past year, had been obliged — to fall back on uninformed conjecture. This summoned up a host of alarming possibilities, including the danger that the bluecoats might be contemplating an attack on thinly defended Richmond or on his even more thinly defended supply line in the Cumberland Valley: both of which maneuvers had in fact been proposed by Hooker and disallowed by Lincoln. One would be about as unwelcome to Lee as the other in the present dispersed condition of his army, one third of which was a good forty miles from Chambersburg, where the remaining two thirds were in profitless bivouac and so completely stripped of cavalry that the foraging was being done by soldiers mounted on horses from the artillery and the wagon train. However, for all his inward anxiety, which he masked as best he could behind a show of being calm and even cheerful, Lee not only let his dispositions stand; he sent word for Ewell to continue the advance on Harrisburg, and prepared to move the rest of his army in that direction the following day, first Longstreet and then Hill, both of whom were put on the alert. "If the enemy does not find us," he explained, "we must try to find him, in the absence of the cavalry, as best we can." So he said, continuing the attempt to mask his growing concern. But still he asked all comers: "Can you tell me where General Stuart is?" and "Where on earth is my cavalry?"

Perhaps it was just as well, so far at least as his temper was concerned, that no one within range of his voice could give him the answer, which was not of a nature to relieve his qualms. In fact, it might well have upset him more than did the tantalizing silence. For even as he inquired of various callers as to the whereabouts of his cavalry on this Sunday afternoon, Stuart and the more than 5000 troopers of his three best brigades were on the northeast fringe of Washington, some seventy miles away. That was as the crow flew, moreover, and for anyone but a crow it would have been considerably farther, not only because Jeb had no more notion of Lee's whereabouts than Lee had of his, but also because a good many of those intervening miles were occupied by the Federal army, which Lee mistakenly assumed to be still south of the Potomac but which in fact was being alerted even now for a resumption of its northward march at dawn. This meant that Stuart would face tomorrow the same frustration he had faced today, and indeed for the past three days as well, in attempting to carry out his instructions to make contact with the right flank of the Confederate army of invasion; Hooker had stood in his path, and so would Meade. It had been that way from the outset, just after midnight June 24, when he first left Salem and moved east, beyond the Bull Run Mountains, to find a heavy column of blue infantry marching squarely athwart the route he had chosen for what was intended to be not only the greatest of all his "rides," but also indemnity for the ugly things some of the southern papers had been saying about him ever since the surprise they claimed he had suffered a couple of weeks ago at Brandy Station.

His plan, based on information that the bluecoats were inactive in their camps east of the mountains and were scattered over so wide an area that he would be able to push his way between two of their corps in order to get beyond them for a crossing of the Potomac in their rear, had been workable the day before, when the information was true; but it was true no longer. By coincidence, Hooker began his northward march to the Potomac shortly before Stuart emerged from Glasscock's Gap on the morning of June 25, and that was how it happened that Jeb found his progress blocked by a whole corps of Federals in motion across his front. Promptly he unlimbered the six guns he had brought along and began to shell the passing column, which extended north and south for a greater distance than the eye could follow. He thus was mindful of Lee's instructions to do the enemy "all the damage you can," but the admonition included in the same letter, that he was not to attempt his favorite maneuver unless he found he could do so "without hindrance," was ignored. Turning off to the south, he camped for the night near Buckland, intending to swing wide around the enemy rear next morning. However, dawn showed the Federals gone, and he rode east through Bristoe and Brentsville, not sighting a single bluecoat all day long, to bivouac just south of Occoquan Creek, which he crossed at Wolf Run Shoals next morning, June 27. In better than fifty hours he had covered less than forty miles of road, and he was about as far from the nearest Potomac ford as he had been when he started. Moreover, horses and men were beginning to show how hard they had been worked these past two weeks, fending off the aggressive blue troopers at such places as Middleburg and Aldie before undertaking their present exertions deep in the enemy rear. Frequent halts were necessary for rest and feeding, no matter how Stuart chafed when he remembered that his orders had been to cross the Potomac as soon as practicable after the 24th, three days ago.

Pressing northward, first through Fairfax Station, where he captured most of a 100-man detachment of New York cavalry, and then to Fairfax Court House, where he called a halt to let his hungry troopers "go through" several sutler shacks and graze their horses, he struck the

Leesburg-Alexandria turnpike and turned left along it for Dranesville, which he reached soon after sundown. Smoldering campfires were evidence that Federal infantry had recently passed this way and were still in the vicinity, guarding the better Potomac fords upstream; so he swung due north for a crossing at Rowser's Ford, which was deep and wide and booming. "No more difficult achievement was accomplished by the cavalry during the war," a staff officer later declared. The guns went completely out of sight, and the ammunition was distributed among the men, who kept it above water by carrying it over in their arms. By 3 o'clock in the morning, June 28 — as Meade awoke to find Hardie standing beside his cot — the entire command, one member said, "stood wet and dripping on the Maryland shore." Stuart let his troopers sleep till dawn, then resumed the march, mindful of his orders to "take position on General Ewell's right, place yourself in communication with him, guard his flank, keep him informed of the enemy's movements, and collect all the supplies you can for the use of the army." The trouble was he did not know Ewell's position, any more than he knew Lee's, except that Ewell would "probably move toward the Susquehanna." Jeb's decision to move in that direction, too, was easily arrived at. The whole Union army was to the west; the heavily-manned Washington defenses were to the east; all that was left — unless he gave the project up and retraced his steps southward, which apparently never crossed his mind — was north, and that was the way he went.

By midday he was in Rockville, a town on the National Road, which ran from Washington through Frederick, present headquarters of the Army of the Potomac, and thence on out to Ohio. Rockville was thus on the main Federal supply route, and scouts reported a train of 150 mule-drawn wagons on the way there from the capital, whose outskirts were less than a dozen miles away. Soon they came in sight and the raiders bore down on them, whooping in hungry anticipation of a feast. "The wagons were brand new, the mules fat and sleek, and the harness in use for the first time," one trooper later wrote. "Such a train we had never seen before and did not see again." Though almost half were captured at that first swoop, the other teamsters got their wagons turned around and took off down the road at a hard trot. For a time it looked as if they might be able to outrun the weary rebel horses, but presently a wagon overturned and caused a pile-up, blocking the road for all but about two dozen of the others, whose drivers continued their race for safety, still pursued, until the gray riders came within full view of Washington itself and abandoned the chase. Even without the ones that got away, the spoils were rich, including 400 teamsters, 900 mules, and 125 wagons loaded with hams, bacon, sugar, hardtack, bottled whiskey, and enough oats to feed the 5000 half-starved mounts of the raiders for several days. Much time was spent at Rockville, paroling the prisoners, feeding the horses, and accepting the admiring glances of some young ladies from a local seminary, who came out waving improvised Confederate flags and requesting souvenir buttons. While all this was going on, Stuart toyed with the notion of making a quick dash into the northern capital, but then rejected it regretfully — for lack of time, he subsequently explained — and resumed his northward march at sundown, hampered somewhat by the "one hundred and twenty-five best United States model wagons and splendid teams with gay caparisons" which he was determined to turn over to Lee, as a sort of super trophy of the ride, when and if he managed to find him.

A twenty-mile night march brought the raiders into Cooksville, where they captured another detachment of blue cavalry on the morning of June 29 before pushing on to Hood's Mill, a station on the B&O about midway between Baltimore and Frederick. While further disrupting the Federal lines of supply and communication by tearing up the tracks there and burning a bridge at Sykeston, three miles east, Stuart inquired of friendly Marylanders as to Ewell's whereabouts. None of them could tell him anything, but newspapers just in from the north reported Confederate infantry at York and Carlisle, moving against Wrightsville and Harrisburg; so Jeb pressed on to Westminster, fifteen miles north, on the turnpike connecting Gettysburg and Baltimore. Arriving in the late afternoon, he gobbled up another mounted blue detachment and made camp for the night. Scouts brought word that Union cavalry was in strength at Littletown, twelve miles ahead and just beyond the Pennsylvania line. Next morning — it was now the last day of June, the sixth he had spent out of touch with the rest of the army — he took the precaution of placing Fitz Lee on the left of the column, assigned Hampton to guard the captured wagons, and rode in the lead with Colonel John R. Chambliss, successor to the wounded Rooney Lee. His immediate objective, another fifteen miles to the north, was Hanover, where he would be able to choose between two good roads, one leading northwest to Carlisle and the other northeast to York, for a hook-up with one or the other of Ewell's reported columns of invasion. What he encountered first at Hanover, however, was a fight. It was an unequal affair, the enemy force amounting to no more than a single brigade, but what the blue horsemen lacked in numbers they made up for in vigor. A sudden charge struck and shattered the head of the gray column, and Stuart himself was obliged to take a fifteen-foot ditch jump to avoid being captured along with his blooded mare Virginia. "I shall never forget the glimpse I then saw of this beautiful animal away up in midair over the chasm," a staff officer later wrote, "and Stuart's fine figure sitting erect and firm in the saddle." Bringing up reserves, Jeb drove off the attackers, who in turn were reinforced by another brigade. No serious fighting ensued, however, for while the Federals seemed content to block the road to Gettysburg, a dozen miles to the west, Stuart wanted only to take the road to York, twenty miles to the northeast.

After some desultory long-range firing, the two forces drew apart, the Confederates still hampered by the train of captured wagons and some 400 prisoners, taken here and elsewhere in the past two days since leaving Rockville, where the previous 400 had been paroled.

This called for another night march, and the riders who made it remembered it ever after as a nightmare. "It is impossible for me to give you a correct idea of the fatigue and exhaustion of the men and beasts," a lieutenant afterwards said. "Even in line of battle, in momentary expectation of being made to charge, [the men] would throw themselves upon their horses' necks, and even to the ground, and fall to sleep. Couriers in attempting to give orders to officers would be compelled to give them a shake and a word, before they could make them understand." Reaching Dover soon after dawn of the hot first day of July, Stuart learned to his chagrin that there were no Confederates at York, six miles east. They had been there, two days ago, but now they were gone and no one would say where. So he turned the head of the column hard left toward Carlisle, 25 miles northwest, supposing that Ewell had ordered a concentration there. He was wrong: as he discovered when he approached the town that afternoon and found it occupied by Pennsylvania militia, who peremptorily rejected his demand for a surrender. Jeb and his road-worn troopers were in no shape for a fight, even with raw home guardsmen, one of his officers frankly admitted. "Weak and helpless as we were," he wrote home later, "our anxiety and uneasiness were painful indeed. Thoughts of saving the wagons now were gone, and we thought only of how we, ourselves, might escape." Contenting himself with a token long-range shelling of the U.S. cavalry barracks, the plumed commander was at a loss for a next move until well after nightfall, when two scouts who had left the column near York, with instructions to search westward for signs of the army, reported back to Stuart outside Carlisle. They had found Lee and the main body that day at Gettysburg, where a battle was in progress, and Lee had sent them to find and summon the long-absent Jeb, who thus was placed in the unusual position of having the army commander report to him the location of the infantry he had been ordered to get in touch with and protect.

At 1 o'clock in the morning, July 2 — one week, to the hour, since he first set out on the ride that was designed, in part, to retrieve his slipping reputation — Stuart had his troopers on the march for Gettysburg, which was thirty miles away by the nearest road. This was their fifth night march in the past eight days, and it was perhaps the hardest of them all. Southward the weary horses plodded, over Yellow Breeches Creek, through Mount Holly Pass, and across the rolling farmland of Adams County, of which Gettysburg was the county seat. The riders were so exhausted, it was noted, that one who tumbled from his mount slept sprawled across the fence that broke his fall. At dawn they still had miles to go, and even the indefatigable Jeb, though he still clung tenaciously to the train of captured wagons as the one substantial trophy of his ride, could see that a rest halt had to be called if he was to arrive with more than a remnant of his three brigades. It was late afternoon before he reached the field of the greatest battle of the war, having missed all of the first day and most of the second. Lee received him with an iciness which a staff officer found "painful beyond description."

Reddening at the sight of his chief of cavalry, the gray commander raised one arm in a menacing gesture of exasperation. "General Stuart, where have you been?" he said. "I have not heard a word from you in days, and you the eyes and ears of my army." Jeb wilted under this unfamiliar treatment and became so flustered that he played his trump card at the outset. "I have brought you 125 wagons and their teams, General," he announced: only to have Lee reply, "Yes, General, but they are an impediment to me now." Then suddenly Lee softened. Perhaps it was Stuart's obvious dismay or his somewhat bedraggled appearance after eight days in the saddle; or perhaps it was a recollection of all the service this young man had done him in the past. At any rate, a witness recalled years later, Lee's manner became one "of great tenderness" as he added: "Let me ask your help now. We will not discuss this longer. Help me fight these people."

The reason Stuart had encountered none of Ewell's men at York or Carlisle the day before — a Wednesday — was that Lee, acting on information that reached him Sunday night, had recalled them Monday morning. As it was, the tail of Early's column, marching westward on the road through East Berlin and Heidlersburg, had been less than ten miles from the head of Stuart's own at the time he took the risky ditch jump near Hanover on Tuesday. In fact, the foot soldiers had heard the guns of that brief engagement, but had not investigated because Lee, despite his repeated warning to Stuart to be on the lookout for Ewell, had neglected to warn Ewell to be on the lookout for Stuart: with the result that the cavalry's roundabout hegira was prolonged for two more days, including some thirty-odd hours beyond the opening of the battle, which in turn resulted from Lee's groping his way across the Pennsylvania landscape, deprived of his eyes and ears, as he said, and with little information as to the enemy's whereabouts or intentions. Because that ten-mile gap had been ignored — not only ignored, but unsuspected — whatever Lee encountered, good or bad, was bound to come as a surprise, and surprise was seldom a welcome thing in war. And so it was. Coincidents refused to mesh for the general who, six weeks ago in Richmond, had cast his vote for the long chance. Fortuity itself, as the deadly game unfolded move by move, appeared to conform to a pattern of hard luck; so much so, indeed, that in time men would say of Lee, as Jael had said of Sisera after she drove the tent peg into his temple, that the stars in their courses had fought against him.

Such information as he had, and it was meager, had come to him not from Robertson or Jones, whom Stuart had left to guard the Blue Ridge passes, nor from Jenkins, who was off with Ewell, but from a spy — "scout" was the euphemistic word — sent out some weeks before by Longstreet, with instructions to pick up what useful tips he could in the lobbies and barrooms of Washington. His name was Harrison, and no one knew much about him except that he was a Mississippian, bearded and of average height, with sloping shoulders, pale hazel eyes, and an abiding dislike of all Yankees. Lee, for one, apparently considered him unsavory and declined at first to see him when he was brought to Shetter's Woods that Sunday night. "I have no confidence in any scout," he said. Informed by a staff officer, however, that Harrison claimed the Federal army had crossed the Potomac — which Lee could scarcely credit, in the absence of any such report from Stuart — he changed his mind and sent for him, shortly before midnight. Travel-stained and weary, the spy told Lee that

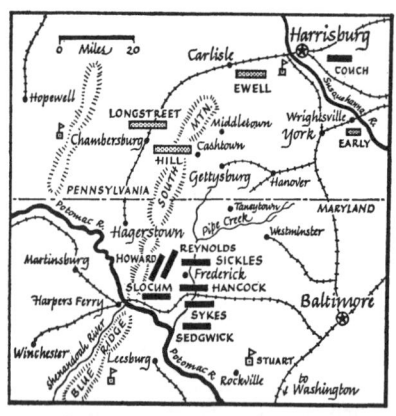

he had been in Frederick that morning, having heard in Washington that Hooker had transferred his headquarters to that place. Arriving he had found it true. At least two corps were there, he said, and others were in the vicinity, with two more pushed out toward South Mountain. After observing all this he had procured a horse and ridden hard for Chambersburg to report to Longstreet, who had sent him on to Lee. Incidentally, he remarked in closing, Hooker had been replaced that day by Meade.

Lee reacted fast — as well he might — to this news that the blue army had been for the past two days on the same side of the Potomac as his own, one of whose corps, in addition to being divided itself, was thirty-odd miles away from the other two, which were threatened in turn by a possible movement against their rear. It was not so much that he feared for his supply line; he was prepared to abandon contact with Virginia anyhow. The trouble was, if the Federals crossed South Mountain and entered the lower Cumberland Valley — as Harrison had claimed they were about to do, and as Hooker in fact had intended — they would force Lee to conform, in order to meet the threat to his rear, and thus deprive him of the initiative he had to retain if he was to conduct the sort of campaign he had in mind. In the absence of his cavalry, moreover, the dispersed segments of his army were in danger of being surprised and swamped by overwhelming numbers: Meade, in short, might do to him what he had planned to do to Hooker — defeat him in detail. What was called for, in the face of this, was a rapid concentration of all his forces, preferably east of the mountains so as to compel the enemy to abandon the threat to his rear. Orders designed to effect this went out promptly. Ewell was instructed to give up his advance on Harrisburg and return at once to Chambersburg with all three of his divisions. Hill and Longstreet, who had just been alerted for a northward march to the Susquehanna, were told to prepare instead for a move on Cashtown, eighteen miles to the east and just beyond South Mountain; the former would start today — it was morning by now, June 29 — the latter tomorrow, which would keep the single road from being clogged. On second thought, and for the same purpose of avoiding a jam, Lee sent a follow-up message to Ewell, suggesting that he remain on the far side of the mountains and march directly to Cashtown or Gettysburg, another eight miles to the east. Simultaneously, couriers hurried south to urge Robertson and Jones to leave the Blue Ridge and join the army in Pennsylvania as soon as possible. A seventh brigade of cavalry, under Brigadier General John B. Imboden, assigned to Lee for use on the invasion but so far only used to guard the western approaches to the lower Cumberland Valley, was also summoned, but since it would be at least two days before these horsemen could get to Chambersburg, Lee told Longstreet to leave one division behind to protect the trains until Imboden arrived. Meanwhile the rest of the army would converge on Cashtown, from which point it could threaten both Washington and Baltimore, thus retaining the initiative by forcing the enemy to turn back east or remain there, in order to keep between the gray invaders and those two vital cities.

All this had been arranged within eight hours of Harrison's report to Lee. But neither the spy nor anyone else could tell him anything of Stuart, who had vanished as if into quicksand. However, an officer who arrived from the south that morning reported that he had met two cavalrymen who told him they had left Stuart on June 27, all the way down in Prince William County, on the far side of Occoquan Creek. Lee was startled to hear this, having learned from Harrison that Hooker had begun to cross the Potomac two full days before that time. Though he kept up a show of confidence for the benefit of subordinates — "Ah, General, the enemy is a long time finding us," he told a division commander; "If he does not succeed soon, we must go in search of him" — Lee was obviously disturbed, and he kept asking for news of Stuart from all callers, none of whom could tell him anything. One more item concerned him, though few of his lieutenants agreed that it should do so. They were saying that Meade was about as able a general as Hooker, but considerably less bold, and they were exchanging congratulations on Lincoln's appointment of another mediocre opponent for them. Lee, who had known the Pennsylvanian as a fellow engineer in the old army, did not agree. "General Meade will commit no blunder on my front," he said, "and if I make one he will make haste to take advantage of it."

While Longstreet marked time at Chambersburg, waiting for Hill to clear the road on which his three divisions were proceeding east to Cashtown, Ewell began his southward march from Carlisle. Greatly disappointed by the cancellation of his plan to occupy the Pennsylvania capital, which he saw as a fitting climax to the campaign that had opened so auspiciously at Winchester and continued for the next two weeks as a triumphal procession through one of the most prosperous regions of the North, Old Bald Head was puzzled by the apparent indecisiveness of his chief. Jackson's orders, enigmatic though they often were, had always been precise and positive; whereas Lee had not only reversed himself by ordering a return to Chambersburg, he had also modified this further by changing the objective to Cashtown or Gettysburg and leaving it up to the corps commander to choose between the two. Unaccustomed to such leeway, which Jackson had never allowed him on any account, Ewell deferred making a final choice until next day, when he would reach Middletown, aptly named because it was equidistant from both of these alternative objectives. Sending word for Early to head west from York and taking up the southward march himself with Rodes while Johnson came along behind with the spoils-laden wagon train, he was also nettled by Lee's additional instructions that if at any point he encountered what he judged to be a large force of the enemy, he was to avoid a general engagement, if practicable, until the other two corps were at hand. This seemed to Ewell a plethora of ifs, and he fumed under the added burden of responsibility, not only for the safety of his corps, but also for the safety of the army, in a situation which, for him at least, was far from clear. Much as he missed his amputated leg, he missed even more the iron guidance of the man under whom he had been serving when he lost it.

Those same precautionary instructions had gone of course to Hill, who was known to have little caution in his make-up. His policy, throughout his year of service under Lee — beginning with the attack that opened the Seven Days offensive, which he had started rolling for the simple reason that he could no longer abide the strain of standing idle — had been to pitch into whatever loomed in his path, with little or no regard for its strength or composition. This had stood the Confederacy in good stead from time to time, especially at Cedar Mountain, where he had saved Stonewall from defeat, and at Sharpsburg, where he had done the same for Lee, whose reference to him in the official report of that battle, "And then A. P. Hill came up," had become a byword in the army. Little Powell was the embodiment of the offensive spirit, here in Pennsylvania as well as back home in Virginia, and so were the troops of his command, who took a fierce pride in the fact. Completing the march to Cashtown that first day, Heth's division went into camp while the other two were still on the road, and hearing that Early's men had overlooked a supply of shoes while passing through Gettysburg the week before, Heth sent his lead brigade forward next morning, June 30, to investigate the rumor. Its commander, Brigadier General Johnston Pettigrew, mindful of Lee's warning not to bring on a battle until the whole army was at hand, prudently withdrew when he encountered Federal troopers along a creekbank west of town, not knowing what number of blue soldiers of all arms might be lurking in rear of the cavalry outposts. He returned to Cashtown late that afternoon, having put his men into bivouac about midway between there and Gettysburg, and reported on the day's events. Heth did not think highly of such wariness. What was more, he wanted those shoes. So he took Pettigrew to Hill and had him repeat the account of what he had seen. Hill agreed with Heth. "The only force at Gettysburg is cavalry," he declared, "probably a detachment of observation." Meade's infantry forces were still down in Maryland, he added, "and have not struck their tents."

Heth was quick to take him up on that. "If there is no objection," he said, "I will take my division tomorrow and go to Gettysburg and get those shoes."

"None in the world," Hill told him.

★ ★ ★

One strenuous objector was there, however, in the person of John Buford, a tough, Kentucky-born regular with a fondness for hard fighting and the skill to back it up. And though Hill was strictly correct in saying that the only bluecoats now in Gettysburg were cavalry, Buford's two brigades were formidable in their own right, being equipped with the new seven-shot Spencer carbine, which enabled a handy trooper to get off twenty rounds a minute, as compared to his muzzle-loading adversary, who would be doing well to get off four in the same span. Moreover, in addition to having five times the firepower of any equal number of opponents, these two brigades were outriders for the infantry wing under Reynolds, whose own corps was camped tonight within six miles of the town, while those under Howard and Sickles were close behind him. Meade had set up army headquarters just south of the state line at Taneytown, about the same distance from Reynolds as Reynolds was from Gettysburg, and all but one of his seven corps — Sedgwick's, off to the east at Manchester — were within easy marching distance of the latter place. He was, in fact, about as well concentrated as Lee was on this last night of June. The Confederates had the advantage of converging on a central point — Ewell at Heidlersburg and Longstreet in rear of Cashtown were each about ten miles from Gettysburg, and Hill was closer than either — whereas the Federals would be marching toward a point that was beyond their perimeter, but Meade had the advantage of numbers and a less congested road net: plus another advantage which up to now, except for the brief September interlude that ended bloodily at Sharpsburg, had been with Lee. The northern commander and his soldiers would be fighting on their own ground, in defense of their own homes.

His march north, today and yesterday, after the day spent getting the feel of the reins, had been made with the intention, announced to Halleck at the outset, "of falling upon some portion of Lee's army in detail" with the full strength of his own. His "main point," he said, was "to find and fight the enemy," since in his opinion "the attitude of the enemy's army in Pennsylvania presents us the best opportunity we have had since the war began." But this morning, receiving information "that the enemy are advancing, probably in strong force, on Gettysburg," he had begun to doubt that that was really what he wanted after all. "Much oppressed with a sense of responsibility and the magnitude of the great interests intrusted to me," as he wrote his wife, he had begun to think that his best course would be to take up a strong defensive position, covering Washington and Baltimore, and there await attack. It was his intention, he declared in a circular issued that afternoon, "to hold this army pretty nearly in the position it now occupies until the plans of the enemy shall have been more fully developed," adding that it was "not his desire to wear the troops out by excessive fatigue and marches, and thus unfit them for the work they will be called upon to perform." He found what he considered an excellent position along the south bank of Pipe Creek, just to the rear of his present headquarters at Taneytown, and he had his engineers start laying it out on the morning of July 1, planning to rally his army there in case Lee came at him in dead earnest. "The commanding general is satisfied that the object of the movement of the army in this direction has been accomplished," he announced in another circular, "viz. the relief of Harrisburg, and the prevention of the enemy's intended invasion of Philadelphia, &c. beyond the Susquehanna. It is no longer his intention to assume the offensive until the enemy's movements or position should render such an operation certain of success." If this was reminiscent of Hooker in the Wilderness, Meade went Fighting Joe one better by making it plain that every corps commander was authorized to initiate a retirement to the Pipe Creek line, not only by his own corps but also by the others, in the event that the rebels made a lunge at him: "The time for falling back can only be developed by circumstances. Whenever such circumstances arise as would seem to indicate the necessity for falling back and assuming this general line indicated, notice of such movement will be at once communicated to these headquarters and to all adjoining corps commanders."

That was a long way from the intention expressed two days ago, "to find and fight the enemy." But the fact was, Meade had already lost control of events before he made this offer to abide by the decision of the first of his chief subordinates who took a notion that the time had come to backtrack. Even as the circular was being prepared and the engineers were laying out the proposed defensive line behind Pipe Creek, John Reynolds was committing the army to battle a dozen miles north of the headquarters Meade was getting ready to abandon. And Reynolds in turn had taken his cue from Buford, who had spread his troopers along the banks of another creek, just west of Gettysburg; Willoughby Run, it was called. "By daylight of July 1," he later reported, "I had gained positive information of the enemy's position and movements, and my arrangements were made for entertaining him until General Reynolds could reach the scene."

Buford was all business and hard action, now as always. A former Indian fighter, he drove himself as mercilessly as he did his men, with the result that he would be dead within six months, at the age of thirty-seven, of what the doctors classified as "exposure and exhaustion." Convinced now that the fate of the nation was in his hands, here on the outskirts of the little college town, the Kentuckian was prepared to act accordingly. A journalist had recently described him as being "of a good-natured disposition, but not to be trifled with," a "singular-looking party... with a tawny mustache and a little, triangular gray eye, whose expression is determined, not to say sinister." The night before, when one of his brigade commanders expressed the opinion that the rebels would not be coming in any considerable strength and that he would be able to hold them off without much trouble, Buford had not agreed at all. "No, you won't," he said. "They will attack you in the morning and they will come booming — skirmishers three-deep. You will have to fight like the devil until supports arrive."

✷ 2 ✷

That was how they came, three-deep and booming; Heth was on his way to "get those shoes." In the lead today, by normal rotation of the honor, was the Alabama brigade of Maryland-born James Archer. A Princeton graduate who had discovered an aptitude for war in Mexico and had gone on to become a U.S. Army captain and now a Confederate brigadier at the age of forty-six, Archer had fought in every major battle under Lee, from the Seven Days through Chancellorsville, where he led the charge on Hazel Grove that broke the back of the Federal defense. Hill had fallen sick in the night and was confined to his tent in Cashtown this morning, too weak to mount a horse, but with Archer out front he would have all the aggressiveness even he could desire — as was presently demonstrated. Though Pettigrew had warned him the previous evening that he was likely to run into trouble short of

Gettysburg, Archer moved his Alabamians rapidly eastward, down the Chambersburg Pike, until they topped a rise and came under fire, first from the banks of a stream in the swale below and then from the slopes of another north-south ridge beyond, on whose crest a six-gun battery was in action at a range of three quarters of a mile. That was about 8 o'clock. Archer ordered up a battery of his own, and while it took up the challenge of the guns across the way, he shook out a triple line of skirmishers, textbook style, and prepared to continue the advance. But Heth, who had come to the head of the column by now, decided to make doubly sure there would be no further delay. He called up a Mississippi brigade commanded by Brigadier General Joseph R. Davis, put it on the left of Archer, north of the pike, and sent them forward together, down into the shallow valley that was floored with the shimmering gold of ripened wheat fields. The two brigades started downhill through the standing grain, the skirmishers whooping and firing as they went. Just as the Deep South had led the way to secession — Alabama had been fourth and Mississippi second among the original seven states to leave the Union — so was it leading the way into the greatest battle of the war that had been provoked by that withdrawal.

Buford's troopers, back across Willoughby Run by now and in position on McPherson's Ridge, fired their carbines rapidly as the butternut riflemen came at them down the east side of Herr Ridge. But it was obvious to their general, who had a good view of the scene from the cupola of a Lutheran seminary on the crest of the next rearward ridge, about midway between Gettysburg and the one they were defending a mile from town, that his two brigades of dismounted men, one out of four of whom had to stay behind to hold the horses of the other three, were not going to be able to hang on long in the face of all that power. Moreover, reports had reached him from outposts he had established to the north, toward Heidlersburg, that substantial rebel forces were advancing from there as well. Unless Federal infantry came up soon, and in strength, he would have to pull out to avoid being swamped from both directions. At about 8.30, however, as he started down the ladder, perhaps to give the order to retire, he heard a calm voice asking from below: "What's the matter, John?" It was Reynolds, whom many considered not only the highest ranking but also the best general in the army. Buford shook his head. "The devil's to pay," he said, and he came on down the ladder. But when Reynolds asked if this meant that he could not hang on till the I Corps got there, most likely within an hour, the cavalryman said he reckoned he could; at any rate he would try. That was enough for Reynolds. He sent at once for Howard and Sickles, urging haste on the march to join him, then turned to an aide and gave him a verbal message for Meade at Taneytown. "Tell him the enemy are advancing in strong force, and that I fear they will get to the heights beyond the town before I can. I will fight them inch by inch, and if driven into the town I will barricade the streets and hold them back as long as possible."

He himself rode back to bring up Wadsworth's division, which was leading the march up the Emmitsburg Road, and guided it cross-country, over Seminary Ridge and up the Chambersburg Pike toward McPherson's Ridge, where by now, after two full hours of fighting, Buford's troopers were approaching both the crest of the ridge, uphill in their rear, and the limit of their endurance. Reynolds directed one of Wadsworth's two brigades to the right and the other to the left, to bolster the cavalry and oppose the rebel infantry coming at them. The race was close; he knew that unless he hurried he would lose it. Already the time was past 10 o'clock, and he could see Confederates among the trees of an apple orchard just to the left of where the pike went out of sight beyond the ridge. He turned in the saddle and called back over his shoulder to the infantry trudging behind him: "Forward, forward, men! Drive those fellows out of that! Forward! For God's sake, forward!" Those were his last words. He suddenly toppled from his horse and lay quite still, face-down on the soil of his native Pennsylvania. No one knew what had hit him — including Reynolds himself, most likely — until an aide saw the neat half-inch hole behind his right ear, where the rifle bullet had struck. When they turned him over he gasped once, then smiled; but that was all. He was dead at the age of forty-two, brought down by a rebel marksman in the orchard just ahead. "His death affected us much," a young lieutenant later wrote, "for he was one of the *soldier* generals of the army."

Beyond the ridge, Heth had decided by now that the time had come for him to press the issue with more than skirmishers. He passed the word and Davis and Archer went in with their main bodies, left and right of the turnpike, intending to overrun the rapid-firing blue troopers spread out on the slope before them. Archer's men were thrown into some disorder by a fence they had to climb just west of Willoughby Run, but at last they got over and splashed across the stream. As they started up McPherson's Ridge, however, the woods along the crest were suddenly filled with flame-stabbed smoke and the crash of heavy volleys. This was musketry, not sporadic carbine fire, and then they saw why. Not only were these new opponents infantry, but their black hats told the startled and stalled attackers that this was the Iron Brigade, made up of hard-bitten Westerners with a formidable reputation for hard fighting and a fierce pride in their official designation as the first brigade of the first division of the first corps of the first army of the Republic. Staggered by the ambush and outnumbered as they were, the butternut survivors perceived that the time had come to get out of there, and that was what they did. Splashing back across the stream, however, they piled up again at the high fence and were struck heavily on the outer flank by a Michigan regiment that had worked its way around through the woods to the south. Most got over, but about 75 Confederates were captured while awaiting their turn at the fence: including Archer, who was grabbed and mauled by a hefty private named Patrick Maloney. Exuberant over the size of his catch — as well he might be; no general in Lee's army had ever been captured before — Maloney turned Archer over to his captain, who refused to accept the sword that was offered in formal surrender. "Keep your sword, General, and go to the rear," he told him. "One sword is all I need on this line." A staff lieutenant who had taken no part in the fighting did not see it that way, however, and insisted on having the trophy even after the prisoner explained that it had been declined by the man who was entitled to it. Archer was furious, not only at this but also because of the roughing-up the big Irishman had given him; which accounted in part for his reaction when he was presented to Doubleday, who had succeeded Reynolds as corps commander. "Archer! I'm glad to see you," the New Yorker cried, striding forward with his hand out. They had been friends in the old army, but apparently that meant nothing to Archer now. "Well, I'm not glad to see you by a damn sight," he said coldly, and he kept his hand at his side.

North of the turnpike, the other half of Heth's attack had better success, at least at the start. Though Reynolds even in death had won his race on the Union left, where the Iron Brigade arrived in time to prepare for what was coming, the brigade on the right not only had a longer way to go, and consequently less time for getting set, it also found no covering woods along that stretch of McPherson's Ridge. Davis's men — five regiments scraped together from the Richmond defenses and the Carolina littoral, none of whom had worked together previously and only two of which had ever fought in Virginia — could see what lay before them, and they advanced with all the eagerness of green troops glad of a chance to demonstrate their mettle. One of the five was a North Carolina outfit whose colonel went down early in the charge, shot as he took up the fallen colors, and when another Tarheel officer bent over him to ask if he was badly hurt, he replied: "Yes, but pay no attention to me. Take the colors and keep ahead of the Mississippians." By then the whole line was going in on the double. On the crest ahead, the Federals wavered and then, as Wadsworth sought to forestall a rout by ordering a withdrawal, fell back hastily toward Seminary Ridge. Davis was elated. The President's nephew, he was aware of muttered complaints of nepotism, and he was happy to be proving his worth and his right to the stars on his collar. Yelling in anticipation of coming to grips with the fleeing bluecoats, the attackers swept over the crest of McPherson's Ridge and into the quarter-mile-wide valley beyond. There they funneled into the deep cut of an unfinished railroad bed, which seemed to offer an ideal covered approach to the Federal rear, but which in fact turned out to be a trap. Once in, they found the sides of the cut so high and steep that they could not fire out, and Doubleday, spotting the opportunity, quickly took advantage of it by sending two regiments over from south of the pike, where Archer had just been routed. "Throw down your muskets! Throw down your muskets!" the men in the cut heard voices calling from overhead, and they looked up into the muzzles of rifles slanted down at them from the rim above. Caught thus in a situation not unlike that of fish in a rainbarrel, some 250 graybacks surrendered outright, dropping their weapons where they stood, while casualties were heavy among those who chose to attempt escape by running the gauntlet westward. The reversal was complete. Davis and his survivors fell back across McPherson's Ridge, profoundly shaken by the sudden frown of fortune and considerably reduced from the strength they had enjoyed when they first came whooping over the crest, headed in the opposite direction. Here on the Confederate left, after so brave a beginning, the attackers had wound up with an even worse disaster than had been suffered on the right. Though Davis himself, unlike Archer, had avoided capture, a good half of his men had either been taken prisoner or shot, and the rest were too demoralized to be of any present use at all.

Doubleday was as elated as Davis had been, a short while back. Moreover, his hard-won feeling of security was strengthened by the arrival of the other two divisions of the corps, his own and Robinson's, and close on their heels came Howard, riding in advance of his own corps, which was coming fast and would be there within an hour. Eleven years younger than forty-four-year-old Doubleday, Howard assumed command of the field by virtue of his seniority. While the skirmishers of both armies kept up a racket down in the valley, banging away at each other from opposite banks of Willoughby Run, he reinforced Wadsworth on McPherson's Ridge and continued the long-range artillery duel with rebel batteries on Herr Ridge. It was noon by now; the XI Corps was arriving, under Schurz, and the lines were much the same as they had been four hours ago, when Buford's dismounted troopers were all that held them. Unquestionably, there were a great many butternut soldiers on the field — you could see them plainly across the valley, "formed in continuous double lines of battle," a staff man noted, adding that "as a spectacle it was striking" — but Howard believed he was ready for whatever came his way. Sickles ought to be arriving soon, and he had sent for Slocum as well; that would give him five more divisions, a total of eleven, perhaps by nightfall.... Just then, however, a shell burst in rear of the Union center, followed quickly by another and another, all with such startling accuracy that one regimental commander sent an angry complaint that the supporting guns were firing short. But those were not friendly shells, dropped in error; they were Confederate. A mile north of the Chambersburg Pike, the two eastern ridges merged at a dominant height called Oak Hill, and there an enemy battery was in action, signaling danger to the Federal right, which extended only about half that distance. Coming south across the fields around Oak Hill, directly toward the vulnerable flank, was another gray flood of rebel infantry. One-armed Howard, knowing he had to move fast to meet the threat, bent the north end of Doubleday's line back east, astride Seminary Ridge, and hurried the first two divisions of his own corps across the rolling farmland north of Gettysburg, with instructions for Schurz to form a new line there, at right angles to the first. They barely had time to arrive before the storm burst.

This new gray pressure was brought to bear by Rodes. Like Heth, he was going into battle for the first time as a major general, and just as his fellow Virginian had faced the test without his corps commander at hand to advise him, so too was Rodes on his own, not because Ewell lay sick in his tent, as had been the case with Hill, but because he preferred to ride near the tail of the column in his buggy. Old Bald Head was in a strange mood anyhow, confused by discretionary orders and aggrieved by the sudden abandonment of his advance on Harrisburg, just as he had the place within his grasp. At Middletown that morning, confronted with the necessity for choosing between his alternate objectives, he had had his mind made up for him at last by a note from Hill, informing him that the Third Corps was on its way to Gettysburg; so he had directed Rodes to take the left fork, which led there. Besides, that seemed a convenient point for a junction with Early who was marching from the west, while Johnson, off to the east with the train, could join them there by turning east when he reached Cashtown. By nightfall the corps would be reunited for the first time in a week, but until then Ewell preferred to allow all three division commanders to function independently. Rodes no doubt appreciated the confidence this implied. At any rate, hearing heavy firing up ahead at noon, he quickened the pace and reached Oak Hill about 1.30 to find a golden opportunity spread before him. On parallel ridges extending south from where he stood, Confederates and Federals were disposed in an attitude not unlike that of two animals who had just met and scrapped and then drawn back, still growling, for a better assessment of each other before coming to grips again. What attracted Rodes at first glance was the fact that the enemy flank, half a mile down the eastern ridge, was wide open to an oblique attack from the road along which his division was advancing. He would have to move fast, however, for already the near end of the Union line was beginning to curl back in response to his appearance, and reinforcements were pouring in large numbers from the streets of Gettysburg, taking up positions from which to defend it. This last was quite all right with Rodes. It was not the town he wanted, dead ahead; it was the blue force on the ridge to his right front. Accordingly, after posting one of his five brigades out to the left, with instructions to hold off the still-arriving defenders of the town in case they went over to the offensive — which they well might do; their number by now was larger than his own — he held another brigade in reserve and put the remaining three in line abreast, facing south, for a charge against the flank of the bluecoats on the ridge. All this was quickly done, with no time spared for a preliminary reconnaissance or even the advancement of a skirmish line. By 2 o'clock the alignment had been completed, and Rodes gave his three attack brigades the order to go forward.

They did go forward, but into chaos. Left on its own by the other two brigades — one stalled at the outset; the other drifted wide — the center brigade stepped in midstride into slaughter when a line of Federals, hidden till then, rose from behind a low stone wall, diagonal to the front, and killed or wounded about half of the advancing men with a series of point-blank volleys pumped directly into their flank. Such was the price they paid for the time Rodes saved by foregoing a reconnaissance. The survivors hit the ground alongside the fallen, some making futile attempts to return the decimating fire, while others began waving scraps of cloth in token of surrender. Observing this, their shaken commander, Brigadier General Alfred Iverson, sent word to Rodes that one whole regiment had raised the white flag and gone over to the enemy on first contact. Though Rodes did not credit the hysterical report, he saw only too clearly that he had the makings of a first-class disaster on his hands. Like Heth to the south, he had paid in disproportionate blood for the ready aggressiveness which in the past had been the hallmark of the army's greatest victories, but which now seemed mere rashness and the hallmark of defeat. It had been so for the captured Archer and for Davis, and now it was the same for Iverson, who was so demoralized by what he had seen, or thought he had seen, that he had to turn over to his adjutant the task of trying to extricate his shattered regiments.

It was at this critical juncture that Lee drew near. Riding through the mountains east of Chambersburg that morning, he had heard the rumble of guns in the distance and wondered what it meant. Hill, who had risen from his sickbed at the sound, pale and feeble though he was, and called for his horse in order to go forward and investigate, could tell Lee nothing more than he already knew — namely, that Heth had marched on Gettysburg, with Pender in support — nor could Anderson, whose division was just beyond Cashtown and within half a dozen miles of the ominous booming. Despite repeated warnings that a general engagement was to be avoided until the army was reunited, the noise up ahead was too loud, or anyhow too sustained, for a mere skirmish. Moreover, Lee was aware of Napoleon's remark that at certain edgy times a dogfight could bring on a battle, and it seemed to him that with his infantry groping its way across unfamiliar hostile terrain, in an attempt to perform the proper function of cavalry, this might well be one of those times. He was worried and he said so.

"I cannot think what has become of Stuart," he told Anderson. "I ought to have heard from him long before now. He may have met with disaster, but I hope not." As he spoke he gazed up the road, where the guns continued to rumble beyond the horizon. "In the absence of reports from him, I am in ignorance of what we have in front of us here. It may be the whole Federal army, or it may be only a detachment. If it is the whole Federal force, we must fight a battle here." For once, he did not seem pleased at the prospect of combat, and he spoke of a withdrawal before he knew what lay before him: "If we do not gain a victory, those defiles and gorges which we passed this morning will shelter us from disaster." And having used the word disaster twice within less than a minute, he hurried ahead, as Hill had done before him, to see for himself what grounds there might be for such forebodings.

About 2.30, after passing through Pender's division, which was formed for attack on both sides of the pike but was so far uncommitted, he ascended Herr Ridge to find the smoky panorama of a battle spread before him — a battle he had neither sought nor wanted. Heth had three brigades in line on the slope giving down upon Willoughby Run, and Lee now learned that he had attacked some three hours earlier, due east and on a mile-wide front, only to encounter Federal infantry whose presence he had not even suspected until he saw what was left of his two attack brigades streaming back from a bloody repulse. Since then, belatedly mindful of the warning not to bring on a battle, he had contented himself with restoring his shattered front while engaging the enemy guns in a long-range contest. Lee could see for himself the situation that had developed. Across the way, disposed along the two parallel ridges that intervened between the one on which he stood and Gettysburg, plainly visible two miles to the southeast, the Federals confronted Heth in unknown strength, their right flank withdrawn sharply in the direction of the town, from whose streets more bluecoats were pouring in heavy numbers, in order to meet a new Confederate threat from the north. This was Rodes, just arrived from Heidlersburg, Lee was told, and though his attack was opportune, catching the bluecoats end-on and almost unawares, he was making little headway because he had launched it in a disjointed fashion. At that point Heth came riding up, having heard that Lee was on the field. Anxious to make up for a slipshod beginning, he appealed to the commanding general to let him go back in.

"Rodes is heavily engaged," he said. "Had I not better attack?"

Lee was reluctant. "N-no," he said slowly, continuing to sweep the field with his glasses. It was not that he lacked confidence in Heth, who was not only a fellow Virginian and a distant cousin, but was also the only officer in the army, aside of course from his own sons, whom he addressed by his first name. It was because Lee still had no real notion of the enemy strength, except that it was obviously considerable, and he was by no means willing to risk the apparent likelihood of expanding a double into a triple repulse. "No," he said again, more decisively than before; "I am not prepared to bring on a general engagement today. Longstreet is not up."

But suddenly his mind was changed by what he saw before him. Rodes's right brigade, after drifting wide, came down hard on the critical angle where the Union line bent east, and his reserve brigade, committed after the wreck of Iverson, dislodged the Federals from their position behind the diagonal stone wall, while his left brigade recovered momentum and plunged into a quarter-mile gap between the two blue corps, north and west of Gettysburg. Assailed and outflanked, the eastward extension of Doubleday's line began to crumble as the men who had held it retreated stubbornly down Seminary Ridge. Simultaneously, Howard's two divisions under Schurz—his own, now led by Brigadier General Alexander Schimmelfennig, and Barlow's; the third, Von Steinwehr's, had been left in reserve on the other side of the town —were assaulted by a new gray force that came roaring down the Harrisburg Road—it was Early, arriving from York—to strike their right at the moment when Rodes was probing the gap beyond their left. As a result, this line too began to crumble, but much faster than the other.... On Herr Ridge, Lee saw much of this through his binoculars. Blind chance having reproduced in miniature the conditions of Second Manassas, with Chancellorsville thrown in for good measure, he dropped his unaccustomed cloak of caution and told Hill, who rode up just then, to send both Heth and Pender forward to sweep the field.

They did just that, but only after fierce and bloody fighting, particularly on McPherson's Ridge, south of the pike, where the Iron Brigade was posted. Unleashed at last, Heth's men went splashing across Willoughby Run and up the opposite slope, to and finally over the fuming crest. Heth himself did not make it all the way, having been unhorsed by a fragment of shell which struck him on the side of the head, knocked him unconscious, and probably would have killed him, too, except that the force of the blow was absorbed in part by a folded newspaper tucked under the sweatband of a too-large hat acquired the day before in Cashtown. Hundreds of others in both armies were not so fortunate. Told by Doubleday to maintain his position at all costs, Brigadier General Solomon Meredith, commander of the Iron Brigade, came close to following these instructions to the letter, although he himself, like Heth, was knocked out before the action was half over. The 24th Michigan, for example, had come onto the ridge with 496 officers and men; it left with 97. This loss of just over eighty percent was exceeded only by the regiment that inflicted it, Pettigrew's 26th North Carolina, whose two center companies set new records for battlefield losses that

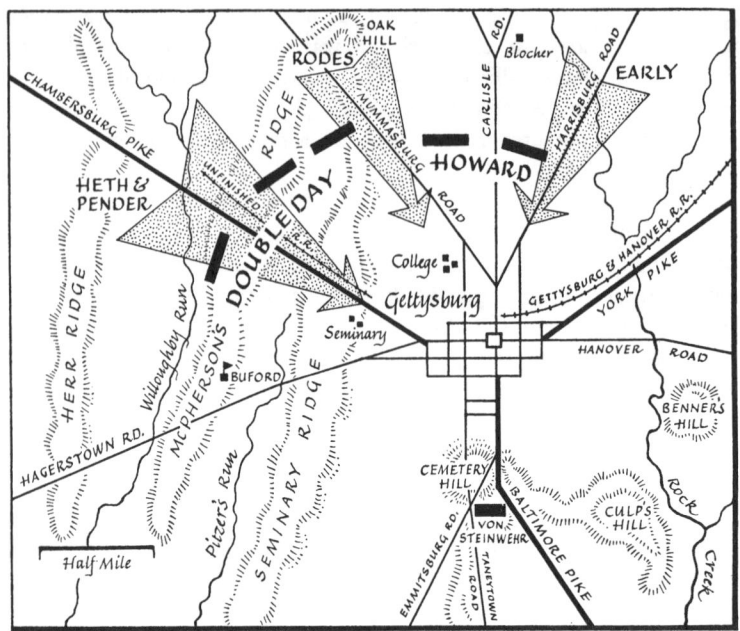

would never be broken, here or elsewhere; one took 83 soldiers into the fight and emerged with only 2 unhit, while the other went in with 91, and all were killed or wounded. Pender, sent forward by Hill as the struggle approached a climax, overlapped the south flank of the defenders and added the pressure that forced them off the ridge. The men of the Iron Brigade fell back at last — 600 of them, at any rate, for twice that many were casualties out of the original 1800 — ending the brief half hour of concentrated fury. "I have taken part in many hotly contested fights," Pettigrew's adjutant later declared, "but this I think was the deadliest of them all." Coming up in the wake of the attack he heard "dreadful howls" in the woods on the ridge, and when he went over to investigate he found that the source of the racket was the wounded of both sides. Several were foaming at the mouth, as though mad, and seemed not even to be aware that they were screaming. He attributed their reaction to the shock of having been exposed to "quick, frightful conflict following several hours of suspense."

Across the way, Ewell's two divisions were having a much easier time than Hill's. While Rodes was pressing Doubleday steadily southward down Seminary Ridge, widening the gap on the left of the line Schurz had drawn north of the town, Early struck hard at the far right of the Union front, which was exposed to just such a blow as the one that had crumpled that same flank at Chancellorsville, two months ago tomorrow. Most of the men opposing him had been through that experience, and now that they foresaw a repetition of it, they reacted in the same fashion. They broke and ran. First by ones and twos, then by squads and platoons, and finally by companies and regiments, they forgot that they had welcomed the chance to refute in action the ugly things the rest of the army had been saying about them; instead, they took off rearward in headlong flight. Barlow, a twenty-nine-year-old New York lawyer who had finished first in his class at Harvard and volunteered at the start of the war as a private in a militia company, tried desperately to rally the division he had commanded for less than six weeks, but was shot from his horse and left for dead on the field his men were quitting. It was otherwise with Schimmelfennig. A former Prussian officer, ten years older than Barlow and presumably that much wiser, he went along with the rush of his troops, all the way into Gettysburg, until he too was unhorsed by a stray bullet while clattering down a side street, and took refuge in a woodshed, where he remained in hiding for the next three days.

Yelling with pleasure at the sight of the blue flood running backwards across the fields as if the landscape had been tipped, the rebel pursuers cut down and gathered in fugitives by the hundreds, all at comparatively small cost to themselves, since but little of their fire was being returned. "General, where are your dead men?" an elated young officer called to Brigadier General John B. Gordon, whose six Georgia regiments had led the charge that threw the bluecoats into retreat before contact was established. Still intent on the pursuit, Gordon did not pause for an answer. "I haven't got any, sir!" he shouted as he rode past on his black stallion. "The Almighty has covered my men with his shield and buckler."

Lee observed from atop Herr Ridge the sudden climax of this latest addition to his year-long string of victories. Riding forward in the wake of Pender's exultant attack, which was delivered with the cohesive, smashing power of a clenched fist, he crossed McPherson's Ridge, thickly strewn with the dead and wounded of both armies, and mounted the opposite slope just as the Federals abandoned a fitful attempt to make a stand around the seminary. Ahead of him, down the remaining half mile of the Chambersburg Pike, they were retreating pell-mell into the streets of Gettysburg, already jammed with other blue troops pouring down from the north, under pressure from Ewell, as into a funnel whose spout extended south. Those who managed to struggle free of the crush, and thus emerge from the spout, were running hard down two roads that led steeply up a dominant height where guns were emplaced and the foremost of the fugitives were being brought to a halt, apparently for still another stand; Cemetery Hill, it was called because of the graveyard on its lofty plateau, half a mile from the town square. Another half mile to the east, about two miles from where Lee stood, there was a second eminence, Culp's Hill, slightly higher than the first, to which it was connected by a saddle of rocky ground, similarly precipitous and forbidding. These two hills, their summits a hundred feet above the town, which in turn was about half that far below the crest of Seminary Ridge, afforded the enemy a strong position — indeed, a natural fortress — on which to rally his whipped and panicky troops, especially if time was allowed for the steadily increasing number of defenders to improve with their spades the already formidable advantages of terrain. Lee could see for himself, now that he had what amounted to a ringside view of the action, that his victory had been achieved more as the result of tactical good fortune than because of any great preponderance of numbers, which in fact he did not have. Prisoners had been taken from two Union corps, six divisions in all, and they reported that the rest of the blue army was on the march to join them from bivouacs close at hand. Some 25,000 attackers, just under half of Lee's infantry, had faced 20,000 defenders, just over one fourth of Meade's, and the resultant casualties had done little to change the over-all ratio of the two armies, on and off the field. Nearly 8000 Confederates had fallen or been captured, as compared to 9000 Federals, about half of whom had been taken prisoner. It was clear that if the tactical advantage was not pressed, it might soon be lost altogether, first by giving the rattled bluecoats a chance to recompose themselves, there on the dominant heights just south of town, and second by allowing time for the arrival of heavy reinforcements already on the way. Moreover, both of these reasons for continuing the offensive were merely adjunctive to Lee's natural inclination, here as elsewhere, now as always, to keep a beaten opponent under pressure, and thus off balance, just as long as his own troops had wind and strength enough to put one foot in front of the other.

Ill though he was, ghostly pale and "very delicate," as one observer remarked, A. P. Hill was altogether in agreement that the new Federal position had to be carried if the victory was to be completed. But when Lee turned to him, there on Seminary Ridge, and proposed that the Third Corps make the attack, Little Powell declined. Anderson's division was still miles away; Heth's was shattered, the commander himself unconscious, and Pender's blown and disorganized by its furious charge and wild pursuit. The survivors were close to exhaustion and so was their ammunition, which would have to be replenished from the train back up the pike. Regretfully Hill replied that his men were in no condition for further exertion just now, and Lee, knowing from past experience that Hill invariably required of them all that flesh could endure, was obliged to accept his judgment. That left Ewell. Rodes had been roughly handled at the outset, it was true, but Early was comparatively fresh, had suffered only light casualties in driving the skittish Dutchmen from the field, and was already on the march through the streets of the town, rounding up herds of prisoners within half a mile of the proposed objective; besides which, it seemed fitting that the Second Corps continue its Jacksonian tradition of hard-legged mobility and terrific striking power, demonstrated recently at Winchester, a month after Stonewall was laid to rest nearby in the Shenandoah Valley, and redemonstrated here today in Pennsylvania. Having made the decision, Lee gave a staff officer oral instructions to take Ewell. As usual, not being in a position to judge for himself the condition of the troops or the difficulties the objective might present when approached from the north, he made the order discretionary; Ewell was "to carry the hill occupied by the enemy, if he found it practicable" — so Lee paraphrased the instructions afterwards in his formal report — "but to avoid a general engagement until the arrival of the other divisions of the army."

That was about 4.30; barely an hour had passed since Hill threw Pender into the follow-up attack on Seminary Ridge, sweeping it clear of defenders within less than half an hour, and a good four hours of daylight remained for Ewell's follow-up attack on Cemetery Hill, which would complete the victory by annihilating or driving the survivors from the scene before Meade could accomplish his convergence there.

Presently, as Lee continued to search the field for signs that the intended attack was under way, Longstreet arrived, riding well in advance of his troops, who had marked time short of Cashtown all morning, under instructions to yield the single eastward road to Johnson, who was hurrying to join the other divisions of the Second Corps. While Lee explained what had happened so far today, and pointed out the hill aswarm with bluecoats across the valley, Old Peter took out his binoculars and made a careful examination of the front. A broad low ridge, parallel to and roughly three quarters of a mile east of the one on which he stood, extended two miles southward from Cemetery Hill to a pair of conical heights, the nearer of which, called Little Round Top, was some fifty feet taller than the occupied hill to the north, while the farther, called simply Round Top, was more than a hundred feet taller still. On the map, and in the minds of students down the years, this complex of high ground south of Gettysburg conformed in general to the shape of a fishhook, with Round Top as the eye, Cemetery Ridge as the shank, Cemetery Hill as the bend, and Culp's Hill as the barb. Neither of the dominant heights to the south appeared to have been occupied yet by the enemy, though it was fairly clear that either would afford the Federals another rallying point in the event of another retreat. However, if this bothered Lee, he did not show it as he stood waiting for Ewell to open the attack from the north. Certainly it did not bother Longstreet, who had the look of a man whose prayers had been answered. Completing his survey of the field, he lowered his glasses, turned to his chief, and declared with evident satisfaction that conditions were ideal for pursuing the offensive-defensive campaign on which he presumed they had agreed before they left Virginia.

"If we could have chosen a point to meet our plans of operation," he said, "I do not think we could have found a better one than that upon which they are now concentrating. All we have to do is throw our army around by their left, and we shall interpose between the Federal army and Washington. We can get a strong position and wait, and if they fail to attack us we shall have everything in condition to move back tomorrow night in the direction of Washington, selecting beforehand a good position into which we can place our troops to receive battle next day. Finding our object is Washington and that army, the Federals will be sure to attack us. When they attack, we shall beat them, as we proposed to do before we left Fredericksburg, and the probabilities are that the fruits of our success will be great."

The southern commander's reaction to this proposed surrender of the initiative to Meade was immediate and decisive. "No," he said, and gestured with his fist in the direction of Cemetery Hill as he spoke. "The enemy is there, and I am going to attack him there."

"If he is there," Old Peter countered, unimpressed, "it will be because he is anxious that we should attack him: a good reason, in my judgment, for not doing so."

Lee still did not agree. He had made an auspicious beginning on his plan for toppling the Federal units piecemeal as they came up, like a row of dominoes, and he was determined to go ahead with it. "No," he said again. "They are there in position, and I am going to whip them or they are going to whip me."

For the present, Longstreet let it go at that, observing that his chief "was in no frame of mind to listen to further argument," but he resolved to return to the subject as soon as Lee had simmered down. "In defensive warfare he was perfect," he wrote years later. "When the hunt was up, his combativeness was overruling."

Just then a courier arrived with a message from Ewell, sent before the one from Lee had reached him. Rodes and Early believed they could take Cemetery Hill, he reported, if Hill would attack it simultaneously from the west. Lee replied that he was unable to furnish this support, except by long-range artillery fire, and after repeating his instructions for Ewell to take the height alone, if possible, added that he would ride over presently to see him. Once more Longstreet spoke up. Minute by minute, he had watched the number of bluecoats increasing on the hill, while those already there were making the dirt fly as they worked at improving the natural strength of the position. He was still opposed to the attack, he said, but if it was going to be made at all, it had better be made at once. Lee did not reply to this immediately. Instead, after sending the courier back to Ewell, he asked where the First Corps divisions were by now. McLaws was a couple of miles this side of Cashtown, Old Peter replied, with Hood somewhere behind him, awaiting road space on the pike. When Lee explained that he could not risk a general assault until these fresh units arrived, Longstreet again fell silent — whether in agreement or disagreement, he did not say — and soon rode off, apparently to hasten the march of the column whose head was half a dozen miles away.

It was now past 5.30 and the guns had stopped their growling on both sides. The staff officer returned to report that he had delivered the hour-old message to Ewell, but there was no other evidence that it had been received. Down below, the streets of the town were still crowded with Confederates, busy flushing Union fugitives out of cellars and back alleys, and there was no sign whatsoever that Ewell was preparing to launch the attack he had twice been told to make if he believed it would be successful. Meantime, the sun was dropping swiftly down the sky and the survivors of the two blue corps were hard at work improving their defenses. One welcome interruption there was, in the form of a pair of Stuart's troopers who brought word to Seminary Ridge of the skirmish near Hanover the day before, the fruitless grope toward York, and the subsequent decision to push on to Carlisle. Relieved to learn that Jeb had managed to avoid personal disaster, whatever trouble he might have made for others, Lee told the horsemen to ride the thirty miles north at once, with orders for the cavalry to rejoin the army as soon as possible. That could not be sooner than tomorrow, of course, but at least he could anticipate removal of the blindfold he had worn throughout the week of Stuart's absence. Near 7 o'clock, with sunset half an hour away and full darkness a good hour beyond that — which left just time enough, perhaps, for launching the attack on Cemetery Hill — Lee mounted Traveller and rode toward Gettysburg, intending not only to pay Ewell the visit he had promised, but also to discover for himself the reason for the long delay.

★ ★ ★

At Taneytown, a dozen miles from the hill where the men of the two wrecked blue corps were plying their shovels in frantic anticipation of the overdue assault, Meade had heard nothing of the eight-hour battle aside from the note in which Reynolds announced that he would "fight [the rebels] inch by inch... and hold them back as long as possible." Not even the booming of the guns came through; for though the east wind carried their rumble as far as Pittsburgh, 150 miles to the west, it was not audible ten miles to the south, apparently having been absorbed by the Round Tops and the sultry air, which served as a soundproof curtain in that direction. In the early afternoon, however, a New York *Times* correspondent came riding back from Gettysburg on a lathered horse and requested the use of the army telegraph in order to file a story on the fighting. Taken at once to headquarters, he could only report that the conflict had been fierce, that the issue had been in doubt when he left, and that one among the many who had fallen was John Reynolds. All of this was a shock for Meade. Not only had he lost the officer on whom he had depended most for guidance during these first days of command, but one fourth of his army had been committed, perhaps beyond the possibility of disengagement, a hard day's march north of his chosen position along Pipe Creek, which the engineers were still mapping and preparing for occupation. Moreover, a 2 o'clock dispatch from Howard, confirming the newsman's statement and adding that he had sent for Sickles and Slocum — which would mean the commitment, once they arrived, of just over half the army — was followed by one from Buford, addressed to Pleasonton, announcing that two enemy corps — two thirds of the rebel army, it would seem — had made a junction on the heights northwest of town and seemed determined to press the issue to a conclusion, however bloody. Outnumbered and outflanked on the left and right, the defenders had been severely crippled, Buford added, by the untimely death of Reynolds and the resultant loss of co-ordination all along the line. "In my opinion," the cavalryman closed his dispatch, "there seems to be no directing person.... P.S. We need help now."

The note was headed 3.20 p.m., by which time help had been on the way for better than an hour: substantial help, moreover, though it consisted of only one general and his staff. Hancock's corps had reached Taneytown shortly before noon, and Meade had held it there while waiting to hear from Reynolds. When he heard instead of that general's death, he told Hancock to turn his corps over to Gibbon and ride to Gettysburg as a replacement for their fellow Pennsylvanian, with full authority to assume command of all units there and recommend whether to reinforce or withdraw them. He himself would remain in Taneytown, Meade said, to control the movements of the other corps and continue work on the Pipe Creek line, which would be needed worse than ever in the event of a northward collapse. Hancock was thirty-nine, a year older than Sickles and six years older than Howard; all three had been promoted to major general on the same day, back in November, but the other two had been made brigadiers before him and therefore outranked him still. When he suggested that this might make for trouble up ahead, Meade showed him a letter from Stanton, stating that he would be sustained in such arrangements by the President and the Secretary of War. So Hancock set out. He rode part of the way in an ambulance, thus availing himself of the chance to study a map of the Gettysburg area, which he had never previously visited though he was born and raised at Norristown, less than a hundred miles away. Coming within earshot of the guns, which swelled to a sudden uproar about 3.30, he shifted to horseback and rode hard toward the sound of firing. At 4 o'clock, the hour that Lee climbed Seminary Ridge to find a Confederate triumph unfolding at his feet, Hancock appeared on Cemetery Hill, a mile southeast across the intervening valley, to view the same scene in reverse. "Wreck, disaster, disorder, almost the panic that precedes disorganization, defeat and retreat were everywhere," a subordinate who arrived with him declared.

One-armed Howard was there by the two-story arched brick

gateway to the cemetery, brandishing his sword in an attempt to stay the rout, but he was doing little better now than he had done two months ago at Chancellorsville, under similar circumstances. Von Steinwehr, an old-line Prussian and a believer in fortifications, had put his troops to digging on arrival, and the work had gone well, even though one of his two brigades had been called forward when the line began to waver north of town. The trouble was, there were so few men left to hold the hilltop, intrenched or not. Out of the 20,000 on hand for the battle, nearly half had fallen or been captured, while practically another fourth were fugitives who had had their fill of fighting: as was indicated by the fact that the provost guardsmen of a corps that came up two hours later herded ahead of them some 1200 skulkers encountered on the Baltimore Pike, which was only one of the three roads leading south. Fewer than 7000 soldiers — the equivalent of a single Confederate division — comprised the available remnant of the two wrecked Union corps, including the brigade that had remained in reserve on the hilltop all along. With all too clear a view of the jubilant mass of rebels in the town and on the ridge across the way, Howard foresaw an extension of the disaster, the second to be charged against his name in the past two months. Anxious as ever to retrieve his reputation, which had been grievously damaged in the Wilderness and practically demolished north of Gettysburg today, he was chagrined to hear from Hancock that Meade had sent him forward to take charge. "Why, Hancock, you cannot give orders here," he exclaimed. "I am in command and I rank you." When the other repeated that such were Meade's instructions all the same, he still would not agree. "I do not doubt your word, General Hancock," he said stiffly, "but you can give no orders while I am here." Possessed of a self-confidence that required no insistence on prerogatives, Hancock avoided having the exchange degenerate into a public squabble by pretending to defer to Howard's judgment in deciding whether to stand fast or fall back. "I think this is the strongest position by nature on which to fight a battle that I ever saw," he said, looking east and south along the fishhook line of heights from Culp's Hill to the Round Tops, "and if it meets with your approbation I will select this as the battlefield." When Howard replied that he agreed that the position was a strong one, Hancock concluded: "Very well, sir. I select this as the battlefield."

Howard later protested that he had selected and occupied Cemetery Hill as a rallying point long before Hancock got there. This was true; but neither could there be any doubt, when the time came for looking back, that it was the latter who organized the all-round defense of the position, regardless of who had selected it in the first place. Meade had chosen well in naming a successor to the fallen Reynolds. Fourteen months ago, in the course of his drive up the York-James peninsula, McClellan had characterized Hancock as "superb," and the word stuck; "Hancock the Superb," he was called thereafter, partly because of his handsome looks and regal bearing — "I think that if he were in citizen's clothes, and should give commands in the army to those who did not know him," one officer observed, "he would be likely to be obeyed at once"— but also because of his military record, which was known and admired by those below as well as by those above him. The army's craving for heroes, or at any rate a hero, had not been diminished by the fact that so many who supposedly qualified as such had melted away like wax dolls in the heat of combat; Hancock seemed an altogether likelier candidate. A Maine artilleryman, for example, recalling the Pennsylvanian's sudden appearance on Cemetery Hill, later asserted that his "very atmosphere was strong and invigorating," and added: "I remember (how refreshing to note!) even his linen clean and white, his collar wide and free, and his broad wrist bands showing large and rolling back from his firm, finely molded hands." Carl Schurz, who might have been expected to side with Howard, his immediate superior, found Hancock's arrival "most fortunate" at this juncture. "It gave the troops a new inspiration," he declared. "They all knew him by fame, and his stalwart figure, his proud mien, and his superb soldierly bearing seemed to verify all the things that fame had told about him. His mere presence was a reinforcement, and everybody on the field felt stronger for his being there."

His first order was for the troops to push forward to the stone walls that ran along the northern face of the hill, in order to present a show of strength and thus discourage an advance by the rebels down below. "I am of the opinion that the enemy will mass in town and make an effort to take this position," he told the captain of a battery posted astride the Baltimore Pike at the rim of the plateau, "but I want you to remain here until you are relieved by me or by my written order, and take orders from no one." It was clear to all who saw him that he meant business, and though Howard had chosen to defend only a portion of the hill, Hancock soon extended the line to cover it from flank to flank; after which he turned his attention to Culp's Hill. Half a mile to the east and slightly higher than the ground his present line was drawn on, that critical feature of the terrain had not been occupied, despite the obvious fact that Cemetery Hill itself could not be held if this companion height was lost. He told Doubleday to send a regiment over there at once. "My corps has been fighting, General, since 10 o'clock," the New Yorker protested, "and they have been all cut to pieces." Hancock replied: "I know that, sir. But this is a great emergency, and everyone must do all he can." With that he turned away, as if there could be no question of not obeying, and when he came back presently he found that Doubleday, whose regiments had been reduced to the size of companies in the earlier fighting, had sent Wadsworth's whole division to occupy the hill and the connecting saddle of high ground. It was, in fact, the shadow of a division, no larger than a small brigade, but the position was a strong one, heavily timbered and strewn with rocks that varied in size, as one defender wrote, "from a chicken coop to a pioneer's cabin." Moreover, the lead division of Slocum's corps soon arrived and was posted there, too. Feeling considerably more secure, Hancock got off a message to Meade in which he stated that he believed he could hold his ground till nightfall and that he considered his present position an excellent one for fighting a battle, "although somewhat exposed to be turned by the left."

Across the way, on Seminary Ridge, Longstreet was expressing that same opinion even now. The difference was that Old Peter was a subordinate, whereas Hancock was in actual command and therefore in a position to do something about it. Weak though the line was on those two hills to the north, he saw that it could not be held, even in strength, if those two commanding heights to the south — the Round Tops — were occupied by the enemy, whose batteries then would enfilade all the rest of the fishhook. And having noted this, he acted in accordance with his insight. Slocum's second division (but still not Slocum himself; he refused to come forward in person and take command by virtue of his rank, judging that Meade's plans for the occupation of the Pipe Creek line were being perverted by this affair near Gettysburg, which seemed to be going very badly. He would risk his men, but not his career; heads were likely to roll, and he was taking care that his would not be among them) was approaching the field soon after 5 o'clock, when its commander reported to Hancock near the cemetery gate. "Geary, where are your troops?" he was asked, and replied: "Two brigades are on the road advancing." Hancock gestured south, down Cemetery Ridge. "Do you see this knoll on the left?" He was pointing at Little Round Top. "That knoll is a commanding position. We must take possession of it, and then a line can be formed here and a battle fought.... In the absence of Slocum, I order you to place your troops on that knoll."

This was promptly done, and with the continuing forbearance of the Confederates, who obligingly refrained from launching the attack Hancock had predicted, Federal confidence gradually was restored. Here and there, along the heights and ridges, men began to say they hoped the rebels would come on, because when they did they were going to get a taste of Fredericksburg in reverse. Arriving with his lead division about 6 o'clock, Sickles was posted on the northern end of Cemetery Ridge, just in rear of Howard's and Doubleday's position on Cemetery Hill, which thus was defended in considerable depth. His other division would arrive in the night, as would Hancock's three under Gibbon, if Meade released them, to extend the line southward along the ridge leading down to the Round Tops. Once this had been done, the fishhook would be defended from eye to barb, and if Meade would also send Sykes and Sedgwick, reserves could be massed behind the high ground in the center, where they would have the advantage of interior lines in moving rapidly to the support of whatever portion of the convex front might happen to be under pressure at any time. All this depended on Meade, however, and when Slocum at last came forward at 7 o'clock (apparently he had decided to risk his reputation after all, or else he had decided that it was more risky to remain outside events in which his soldiers were involved) Hancock transferred the command to him and rode back to Taneytown to argue in person for a Gettysburg concentration of the whole army, nine of whose nineteen divisions were there already, with a tenth one on the way.

He arrived at about 9.30 to find his chief already persuaded by the message he had sent him four hours earlier. "I shall order up the troops," Meade had said, after brief deliberation, and orders had gone accordingly to Gibbon, Sykes, and Sedgwick, informing them that the Pipe Creek plan had been abandoned in favor of a rapid concentration on the heights just south of Gettysburg, where the other half of the army was awaiting their support. However, instead of going forward at once himself — there would be no time for a daylight reconnaissance anyhow — Meade decided to get some badly needed sleep. At 1 a.m. he came out of his tent, mounted his horse, and rode the twelve miles north with his staff and escort, a full moon floodlighting the landscape of his native Pennsylvania. At 3 o'clock, barely an hour before dawn, he dismounted at the cemetery gate, through which there was a rather eerie view of soldiers sprawled in sleep among the tombstones. Across the way, on the western ridge and down in the moon-drenched town below, he saw another sobering sight: the campfires of the enemy, apparently as countless as the stars. Slocum, Howard, and Sickles were there to greet him, and though he had seen but little of the position Hancock had so stoutly recommended, all assured him that it was a good one. "I am glad to hear you say so, gentlemen," Meade replied, "for it is too late to leave it."

By the time he had made a brief moonlight inspection of Culp's and Cemetery hills, dawn was breaking and Hancock's three divisions were filing into position on Cemetery Ridge, having completed their all-night march from Taneytown. Sykes had reached Hanover and turned west in the darkness; he would arrive within a couple of hours. Only Sedgwick's corps was not at hand, the largest of the seven. Uncle John had promised to make it from Manchester by 4 o'clock that afternoon, and though it seemed almost too much to hope that so large a body of men could cover better than thirty miles of road in less than twenty hours, Meade not only took him at his word; he announced that he would attack on the right, as soon as Sedgwick got there.

✻ 3 ✻

Lee's headquarters tents were pitched in a field beside the Chambersburg Pike, on the western slope of Seminary Ridge. When he rose from sleep, an hour before dawn — about the same time Meade drew rein beside the gate on Cemetery Hill — his intention, like his opponent's, was to attack on the right. He had arrived at this decision the previous evening, in the course of a twilight conference north of Gettysburg with Ewell, whom he found gripped by a strange paralysis of will, apparently brought on, or at any rate intensified, by Lee's stipulation that an assault on the bluecoats attempting a rally on the hilltop south of town, though much desired, not only could not be supported by troops outside his corps, as Ewell had requested, but also was to be attempted only if he found it "practicable," which Ewell interpreted as meaning that he must be certain of success. It occurred to him that in war few things were certain, least of all success; with the result that he refrained from taking any risk whatever. First he waited for Johnson, whose division did not come onto the field until past sundown, and finally he called the whole thing off, finding by then that the heights beyond the town bristled with guns and determined-looking infantry, deployed in overlapping lines, well dug in along much of the front, and heavily reinforced.

Though it was not Lee's way to challenge an assessment made by a general on ground which he himself had not examined, when he arrived for the conference he indicated his regret by expressing the hope that Ewell's decision would not apply to next day's operations. "Can't you, with your corps, attack on this front tomorrow?" he asked. Ewell said nothing; nor did Rodes, whose accustomed fieriness had been subdued by his narrow escape from disaster in his first action as a major general, and Johnson was not present. That left Early, who did not hesitate to answer for his chief that an offensive here on the left, after the Federals had spent the night preparing for such a move, would be unwise. However, he added, indicating the Round Tops looming dimly in the distance and the dusk, an attack on the right, with the mass of bluecoats concentrated northward to meet the expected threat from Ewell, offered the Confederates a splendid opportunity to seize the high ground to the south and assail the Union flank and rear from there. Ewell and Rodes nodded agreement, but when Lee replied: "Then perhaps I had better draw you around towards our right, as the line will be very long and thin if you remain here, and the enemy may come down and break through," Early again was quick to disagree. In his view, that would spoil the whole arrangement by allowing the foe to turn and give his full attention to the blow aimed at his rear. As for the integrity of the present line, Lee need have no qualms; whatever its shortcomings as a base from which to launch an offensive, the position was an excellent one for defense. Besides, Early went on to say, much captured material and many of the wounded could not be moved on such brief notice, not to mention the effect on morale if the troops were required to give up ground they had won so brilliantly today.

Lee heard him out, then pondered, head bent forward. The main thing he disliked about the proposal was that it would require a change in his preferred style of fighting, typified by Manassas, where he had used the nimble Second Corps to set his opponent up for the delivery of a knockout punch by the First Corps, whose specialty was power. Early was suggesting what amounted to a change of stance, which was neither an easy nor a wise thing for a boxer to attempt, even in training, let alone after a match was under way, as it was now. Head still bowed in thought, Lee mused aloud: "Well, if I attack from the right, Longstreet will have to make the attack." He raised his head. "Longstreet is a very good fighter when he gets in position and gets everything ready, but he is so slow." The extent of his perplexity was shown by this criticism of one subordinate in the presence of another, a thing he would never have done if he had not been upset at finding the commander of the Second Corps, famed for its slashing tactics under Jackson, content to fall back on the defensive with a victory half won. However, when Early, still speaking for his chief, who seemed to have lost his vocal powers along with those employed to arrive at a decision, assured him that the three divisions would be prompt to join the action as soon as the attack was launched across the way, Lee tentatively accepted the plan and rode back through the darkness to Seminary Ridge.

Once he was beyond the range of Early's persuasive tongue, however, his doubts returned. He reasoned that the blow, wherever it was to be delivered — and he had not yet decided on that point — should be struck with all the strength he could muster. If Ewell would not attempt it on the left, he would bring him around to the right, thus shortening the line while adding power to the punch. Accordingly, he sent him instructions to shift his three divisions west and south at once if he was still of the opinion that he could launch no drive from where they were. This not only restored Ewell's powers of speech; it brought him in person to army headquarters. Dismounting with some difficulty because of his wooden leg, he reported that Johnson had examined the Federal position on Culp's Hill and believed he could take it by assault. This changed the outlook completely; for if Culp's Hill could be taken, so could the main enemy position on Cemetery Hill, which it outflanked. Happy to return to his accustomed style, which was to use his left to set his opponent up for the knockout punch he planned to throw with his right, Lee canceled Ewell's instructions for a shift and directed instead that he remain where he was, with orders to seize the high ground to his front as soon as possible. By now it was close to midnight; Ewell rode back to his own headquarters north of Gettysburg. Lee pondered the matter further. Since Longstreet, who would deliver the major blow, was not yet up, whereas Ewell was already in position, he decided to time the latter's movements by the former's, and sent a courier after Ewell with instructions for him not to advance against Culp's Hill until he heard Longstreet open with his guns across the way. This done, Lee turned in at last to get some sleep, telling his staff as he did so: "Gentlemen, we will attack the enemy as early in the morning as practicable."

Rising at 3 a.m. he ate breakfast in the dark and went forward at first light to the crest of the ridge, preceded by a staff engineer whom he sent southward, in the direction of the Round Tops, to reconnoiter the ground where the main effort would be made. To his relief, as he focused his glasses on the enemy position, though he saw by the pearly light of dawn that the Federals still held Cemetery Hill in strength, the lower end of the ridge to the south appeared to be as bare of troops as it had been at sunset. Longstreet soon arrived to report that McLaws and Hood were coming forward on the pike, having camped within easy reach of the field the night before — all but one of Hood's brigades, which was on the way from New Guilford, more than twenty miles to the west. Pickett too was on the march, having been relieved by Imboden the day before at Chambersburg, but could scarcely arrive before evening. Glad at any rate to learn that Hood and McLaws were nearby, Lee then was startled to hear Old Peter return to yesterday's proposal that the Confederates maneuver around the Union left and thus invite attack instead of attempting one themselves against so formidable a position as the enemy now held. While Longstreet spoke, the force of his words was increased by the emergence on Cemetery Ridge of brigade after brigade of blue-clad soldiers, extending the line southward in the direction of the Round Tops. However, Lee rejected his burly lieutenant's argument out of hand, much as he had done the previous afternoon, although by sunup it was apparent that his plan for a bloodless occupation of the enemy ridge would have to be revised. Longstreet lapsed into a troubled silence, and at that point A. P. Hill came up, still pale and weak from illness. Except to report that his whole corps was at hand, Anderson having arrived in the night, he had little to say. Heth was with him, his head wrapped in a bandage, too badly shaken by yesterday's injury to resume command of his division, which was to remain in reserve today under Pettigrew, the senior brigadier. Hood rode up soon afterwards, ahead of his men. As he watched the bluecoats cluster thicker on the ridge across the mile-wide valley, Lee told him what he had told his corps commander earlier. "The enemy is here," he said, "and if we do not whip him, he will whip us." Hood interpreted this to mean that Lee intended to take the offensive as soon as possible, but Longstreet took him aside and explained in private: "The general is a little nervous this morning. He wishes me to attack. I do not wish to do so without Pickett. I never like to go into battle with one boot off."

Hood could see that both men were under a strain; but whatever its cause, it was mild compared to what followed presently. As the sun climbed swiftly clear of the horizon, Lee worked out a plan whereby he would extend his right down Seminary Ridge to a point beyond the enemy left, then attack northeast up the Emmitsburg Road, which ran diagonally across the intervening valley, to strike and crumple the Union flank on Cemetery Ridge. Though he said nothing of this to Longstreet, who had expressed his disapproval in advance, he explained it in some detail to McLaws when he rode up shortly after 8 o'clock. "I wish you to place your division across this road," Lee told him, pointing it out on the map and on the ground. "I wish you to get there if possible without being seen by the enemy. Can you do it?" McLaws said he thought he could, but added that he would prefer to take a close-up look at the terrain in order to make certain. Lee replied that a staff engineer had been ordered to do just that, "and I expect he is about ready." He meant that the officer was probably about ready to report, but McLaws understood him to mean that he was about ready to set out. "I will go with him," he said. Before Lee could explain, Longstreet broke in, having overheard the conversation as he paced up and down. "No, sir," he said emphatically, "I do not wish you to leave your division." As he spoke he leaned forward and traced a line on the map, perpendicular to the one Lee had indicated earlier. "I wish your division placed so," he said. Quietly but in measured tones Lee replied: "No, General, I wish it placed just opposite." When the embarrassed McLaws repeated that he would like to go forward for a look at the ground his division was going to occupy, Longstreet once more refused to permit it and Lee declined to intervene further. So McLaws retired in some bewilderment to rejoin his troops and await the outcome of this unfamiliar clash of wills.

Presently the staff engineer, Captain S. R. Johnston, returned from his early-morning reconnaissance on the right, and his report was everything Lee could have hoped for. According to him, the Federals had left the southern portion of Cemetery Ridge unoccupied, along with both of the Round Tops. When Lee asked pointedly, "Did you get there?" — for the information was too vital to be accepted as mere hearsay — Johnston replied that his report was based entirely on what he had seen with his own eyes, after climbing one of the spurs of Little Round Top. Lee's pulse quickened. This confirmed the practicality of his plan, which was for Longstreet to launch an oblique attack up the Emmitsburg Road, get astride the lower end of Cemetery Ridge, and then sweep northward along it, rolling up the Union flank in order to get at the rear of the force on Cemetery Hill, kept under pressure all this time by Ewell, who was to attack on the left, fixing the bluecoats in position and setting them up for the kill, as soon as he heard the guns open fire to the south. Moreover, while Lee was considering this welcome intelligence, Longstreet received a report that his reserve artillery, eight batteries which were to lend the weight of their metal to the assault, had just arrived. It was now about 9 o'clock. Except for Pickett's division and Brigadier General Evander Law's brigade, on the march respectively from Chambersburg and New Guilford, the whole First

Corps was at hand. Still, Lee did not issue a final order for the attack, wanting first to confer with Ewell and thus make certain that the Second Corps understood its share in the revised plan for the destruction of "those people" across the way.

Leaving Hill and Longstreet on Seminary Ridge, he rode to Ewell's headquarters north of Gettysburg, only to find that the general was off on a tour of inspection. Trimble was there, however, serving in the capacity of a high-ranking aide and advisor, and while they waited for Ewell to return he conducted Lee to the cupola of a nearby almshouse, which afforded a good view of the crests of Culp's and Cemetery hills, above and beyond the rooftops of the town below. Observing that the defenses on the two heights had been greatly strengthened in the course of the sixteen hours that had elapsed since Ewell first declined to attack the rallying Federals there, Lee said regretfully: "The enemy have the advantage of us in a short and inside line, and we are too much extended. We did not or could not pursue our advantage of yesterday, and now the enemy are in a good position." When Ewell at last returned, Lee repeated what he had told Trimble, stressing the words, "We did not or could not pursue our advantage," as if to impress Ewell with his desire that the Second Corps would neglect no such opportunity today. Though it was plain that the Union stronghold had been rendered almost impregnable to attack from this direction, he explained his overall plan in detail, making it clear that all three divisions here on the left were to menace both heights as soon as Longstreet's guns began to roar, and he added that the demonstration was to be converted into a full-scale assault if events disclosed a fair chance of success. This done, he rode back toward Seminary Ridge, along whose eastern slope two of Hill's divisions were already posted, well south of the Chambersburg Pike. Anderson's, which had not arrived in time for a share in yesterday's fight, was farthest south, under orders to join Longstreet's attack as it came abreast, rolling northward, and Pender's was to do the same in turn, simultaneously extending its left to make contact with the Second Corps southwest of Gettysburg. Heth's division, which was in about as shaken a state as its shell-shocked commander, would remain in reserve on the far side of Willoughby Run, not to be called for except in the event of the threat of a disaster.

It was just past 11 o'clock when Lee returned to Seminary Ridge, suffering en route from what an officer who rode with him called "more impatience than I ever saw him exhibit upon any other occasion," and gave Longstreet orders to move out. Observing his chief's disappointment at finding the two First Corps divisions still occupying the stand-by positions in which he had left them two hours earlier, Longstreet did not presume to suggest that he wait for Pickett — as he had told Hood he preferred to do, even though this would have postponed the attack until sundown at the soonest — but he did request a half-hour delay to allow for the arrival of Law, whose brigade was reported close at hand by now. Lee agreed, although regretfully, and when Law came up shortly before noon, completing a 24-mile speed march from New Guilford in less than nine hours, the two divisions lurched into motion, headed south under cover of Herr Ridge, which screened them from observation by enemy lookouts on the Round Tops. Apparently Meade had begun to rectify his neglect of those bastions, for signal flags were flapping busily from the summit of the nearer of the two. Lee was not disturbed by this, however. Now that the march was under way, his calm and confidence were restored. "Ah, well, that was to be expected," he said when scouts reported that the enemy left was being extended southward along Cemetery Ridge. "But General Meade might as well have saved himself the trouble, for we'll have it in our possession before night."

Longstreet's veterans agreed. The march was far from an easy one, the day being hot and water scarce, but they were accustomed to such hardships, which were to be endured as prelude to the delivery of the assault that would determine the outcome of the battle. Moreover, they considered it standard procedure that theirs was the corps selected for that purpose. "There was a kind of intuition, an apparent settled fact," one of its members later declared, "that after all the other troops had made their long marches, tugged at the flanks of the enemy, threatened his rear, and all the display of strategy and generalship had been exhausted in the dislodgment of the foe, and all these failed, then when the hard, stubborn, decisive blow was to be struck, the troops of the First Corps were called on to strike it." As it turned out, however, the march was a good deal harder and longer than they or anyone else, including Lee and Longstreet, had expected when they began it. The crow-flight distance of three miles, from their starting point near Lee's headquarters to their jump-off position astride the Emmitsburg Road just opposite the Round Tops, would be doubled by the necessity for taking a roundabout covered route in order to stay hidden from Meade, who would be able to hurry reinforcements to any portion of his line within minutes of being warned that it was threatened. Nor was that all. This estimated distance of six miles had to be redoubled in turn, at least for some of the marchers, when it was discovered that the movement eastward would be disclosed to the enemy if the butternut column passed over the crest of Herr Ridge here to the south where the woods were thin. Plainly upset by this sign of the guide's incompetence — but no more so than the guide himself, Captain Johnston of Lee's staff, who had neither sought nor wanted the assignment, who had not reconnoitered west of Seminary Ridge at all, and who later protested that he "had no idea that I had the confidence of the great General Lee to such an extent that he would entrust me with the conduct of an army corps moving within two miles of the enemy line" — Longstreet halted the column and reversed its direction of march, back northward to a point near the Chambersburg Pike again, where the ridge could be crossed under cover of heavy woods. Some time was saved by giving the lead to Hood, who had followed McLaws till then, but nearly two full hours had been wasted in marching and countermarching, only to return to the approximate starting point. Longstreet's anger soon gave way to sadness. A soldier who watched him ride past, "his eyes cast to the ground, as if in deep study, his mind disturbed," recorded afterwards that Old Peter today had "more the look of gloom" than he had ever seen him wear before.

Southward the march continued, under cover of McPherson's Ridge, then around its lower end, eastward across Pitzer's Run and through the woods to Seminary Ridge, which here approached the Emmitsburg Road at the point desired. The head of the column — Law's brigade, which by now had spent twelve blistering hours on the march — got there shortly after 3 o'clock. This was not bad time for the distance hiked, but the better part of another hour would be required to mass the two divisions for attack. Worst of all, as Hood's men filed in on the far right, confronting the rocky loom of Little Round Top, they saw bluecoats clustered thickly in a peach orchard half a mile to the north, just under a mile in advance of the main Federal line on Cemetery Ridge and directly across the road from the position McLaws had been assigned. This came as a considerable surprise. They were not supposed to be there at all, or at any rate their presence was not something that had been covered by Lee's instructions.

★ ★ ★

Neither was their presence in the orchard covered by any instructions from their own commander. In fact, at the time Hood's men first spotted them, Meade did not even know they were there, but supposed instead that they were still back on the ridge, in the position he had assigned to them that morning. Since 9 o'clock — six hours ago, and within six hours of his arrival — his dispositions for defense had been virtually complete. Slocum's two divisions, reunited by shifting Geary north from Little Round Top, occupied the southeast extremity of Culp's Hill, while Wadsworth's I Corps division was posted on the summit and along the saddle leading west to Cemetery Hill. There Howard's three divisions held the broad plateau, supported by the other two divisions of the First Corps, now under Virginia-born John Newton, whom Meade had ordered forward from Sedgwick's corps because he mistrusted Doubleday. Thus eight of the sixteen available divisions were concentrated to defend the barb and bend of the fishhook, with Sykes's three in general reserve, available too if needed. South of there, along the nearly two miles of shank, the five divisions under Hancock and Sickles extended the line down Cemetery Ridge to the vicinity of Little Round

Top, though the height itself remained unoccupied after Geary's early-morning departure. Buford's cavalry guarded the left flank, Gregg's the right, and Kilpatrick's the rear, coming west from Hanover.

Meade had established headquarters in a small house beside the Taneytown Road, half a mile south of Cemetery Hill and thus near the center of his curved, three-mile line. Here, once the posting of his men and guns had been completed, he busied himself with attempts to divine his opponent's intentions. With Ewell's three divisions in more or less plain view to the north, he expected the rebel attack to come from that direction and he had massed his troops accordingly. However, as the sun climbed swiftly up the sky, the apparent inactivity of the other two enemy corps disturbed him, knowing as he did that Lee was seldom one to bide his time. It seemed to him that the Virginian must have something up his sleeve — something as violent and bloody, no doubt, as Chancellorsville, where Hooker had been unhorsed — and the more he considered this possibility, the less he liked the present look of things. At 9.30, thinking perhaps the proper move would be to beat his old friend to the punch, he asked Slocum to report from Culp's Hill on "the practicability of attacking the enemy in that quarter." When Slocum replied an hour later that the terrain on the right, though excellent for defense, was not favorable for attack, Meade abandoned the notion of taking the offensive when Sedgwick arrived. In point of fact, he already had his chief of staff at work in the low-ceilinged garret of his headquarters cottage, preparing an order for retirement. Not that he meant to use it unless he had to, he explained later; but with so large a portion of Lee's army on the prowl, or at any rate out of sight, he thought it best to be prepared for almost anything, including a sudden necessity for retreat. At 3 o'clock, still with no substantial information as to his adversary's intentions, he wrote Halleck that he had his army in "a strong position for defensive." He was hoping to attack, he said, but: "If I find it hazardous to do so, or am satisfied the enemy is endeavoring to move by my rear and interpose between me and Washington, I shall fall back to my supplies at Westminster.... I feel fully the responsibility resting upon me," he added, "and will endeavor to act with caution."

At least one of his corps commanders — Sickles, whose two divisions were on the extreme left of the line — had serious reservations about the defensive strength of the position, at least so far as his own portion of it was concerned. Cemetery Ridge lost height as it extended southward, until finally, just short of Little Round Top, it dwindled to comparatively low and even somewhat marshy ground. Three quarters of a mile due west, moreover, the Emmitsburg Road crossed a broad knoll which seemed to Sickles, though its crest was in fact no more than twelve feet higher than the lowest point of the ridge, to dominate the sector Meade had assigned him. The only cover out there was afforded by the scant foliage of a peach orchard in the southeast corner of a junction formed by a dirt road leading back across the ridge; artillery from either side could bludgeon, more or less at will, that otherwise bald hump of earth and everything on it. But to Sickles, gazing uphill at it from his post on the low-lying far left of the army, the situation resembled the one that had obtained when his enforced abandonment of Hazel Grove caused the Union line to come unhinged at Chancellorsville, and he reasoned that the same thing would happen here at Gettysburg unless something more than skirmishers were advanced to deny the Confederates access to that dominant ground directly to his front. As the morning wore on and Meade did not arrive to inspect the dispositions on the left, Sickles sent word that he was grievously exposed. Meade, concerned exclusively with the threat to his right and having little respect anyhow for the former Tammany politician's military judgment, dismissed he warning with the remark: "Oh, generals are apt to look for the attack to be made where they are." To Sickles this sounded more than ever like Hooker, and at midmorning he went in person to headquarters to ask if he was or was not authorized to post his troops as he thought best. "Certainly," Meade replied, "within the limits of the general instructions I have given you. Any ground within those limits you choose to occupy I leave to you." So Sickles rode back, accompanied by Henry Hunt, whom Meade sent along to look into the complaint, and though the artillerist rather agreed that it was valid, he also pointed out the danger of establishing a salient — for that was what it would amount to — so far in advance of the main line, so open to interdictory fire, and so extensive that the available troops would have to be spread thin in order to occupy it. In short, he declined to authorize the proposed adjustment, though he promised to discuss it further with the army commander and send back a final decision. As the sun went past the overhead and no word came from headquarters, Sickles continued to fume and fret. Learning finally that Buford's cavalry had been relieved from its duty of patrolling the left flank, which he believed exposed him to assault from that direction, he could bear it no longer. If Meade was blind to obvious portents of disaster, Sickles certainly was not. He decided to move out on his own.

At 3 o'clock, while Meade was writing Halleck that his position was a strong one "for defensive," the veterans of Hancock's corps, playing cards and boiling coffee along the northern half of Cemetery Ridge, taking it easy as the long hot day wore on and no attack developed, were surprised to hear drums rolling and throbbing, off to the left, and when they looked in that direction they saw Sickles' two divisions of better than 10,000 men advancing westward across the open fields in formal battle order, bugles blaring and flags aflutter, lines carefully dressed behind a swarm of skirmishers all across the front. "How splendidly they march!" one of the watchers cried, and another remarked in round-eyed admiration: "It looks like a dress parade, a review." The movement was so deliberate, so methodical in execution, that John Gibbon, sitting his horse alongside Hancock, who had dismounted, wondered if the II Corps had somehow failed to receive an order for a general advance. Hancock knew better. Leaning on his sword and resting one knee on the ground, he tempered his surprise with amusement at the sight of Old Dan Sickles leading his soldiers to the war. "Wait a moment," he said, and he smiled grimly as he spoke, "you'll see them tumbling back."

Some among Sickles' own officers were inclined to agree with this prediction: especially after they had reached and examined their new position, half a mile and more in front of the rest of the army. In ordering the maneuver, one brigadier observed, the corps commander had shown "more ardor to advance and meet the fight than a nice appreciation of the means to sustain it." Old soldiers reviewing the situation down the years expressed the same thought in simpler terms when they said that Sickles "stuck out like a sore thumb." Not only was there little cover or means of concealment, out here on the broad low hump of earth; there was also a half-mile gap between the extreme right of the salient and the left of Hancock's corps, back on the ridge. Moreover, Hunt's theoretical objection that Sickles did not have enough troops for the operation he proposed was sustained by the fact that his new line — extending from near the Cordori house, well up the Emmitsburg Road, to the peach orchard, where it bent sharply back to form an angle, and then across the southwest corner of a large wheat field, to end rather inconclusively in front of a mean-looking jumble of boulders known appropriately as the Devil's Den, just west of Little Round Top — was about twice the length of the mile-long stretch of ridge which now lay vacant in its rear. As a result, the position had little depth, practically no reserves or physical feature to fall back on, and was unsupported on both ends. To some, it seemed an outright invitation to disaster: an impression that was strengthened considerably, within half an hour of the march out, by a full-scale bombardment from rebel guns across the way, in the woods along the eastern slope of Seminary Ridge.

Riding down at last in response to the sudden uproar, Meade was appalled to see what Sickles had improvised here on the left. "General, I am afraid you are too far out," he said, understating the case in an attempt to keep control of his hair-trigger temper. Still in disagreement, Sickles insisted that he could maintain his position if he were given adequate support: a stipulation he had not made before. "However, I will withdraw if you wish, sir," he added. Meade shook his head as the guns continued to growl and rumble in the woods beyond the Emmitsburg Road. "I think it is too late," he said. "The enemy will not allow you." He was calculating his chances as he spoke. The situation had been greatly improved by the arrival of Sedgwick, whose three divisions now were filling up the Baltimore Pike, across Rock Creek, and onto the field, ending on schedule their long march from Manchester. They could replace Sykes in general reserve and thus free those three well-rested divisions to move in support of Sickles. "If you need more artillery, call on the reserve!" Meade shouted above the thunder of the bombardment. "The V Corps and a division of Hancock's will support you —"

But that was as far as he got. His horse reared in terror at the roar of a nearby gun and suddenly bolted, the bit in his teeth. For a moment all Meade's attention was on the fear-crazed animal, which seemed as likely to carry him into the enemy lines as to remain within his own, but presently he got him under control again and galloped off to order up supports for Sickles in the salient.

It was clear by now that they would be needed soon; for behind him, as he rode, he could hear above the uproar of the guns the unnerving quaver of the rebel yell, which signified all too clearly that Lee was launching another of those savage attacks that had won fame for him and his scarecrow infantry.

★ ★ ★

Although Lee's ready acceptance of the role of attacker seemed to indicate otherwise, the odds were decidedly with Meade. Sedgwick's arrival completed the concentration of the Army of the Potomac, which remained some 80,000 strong after deductions for stragglers and yesterday's casualties. Lee on the other hand, with Pickett's division and six of the seven cavalry brigades still absent, had fewer than 50,000 effectives on the field after similar deductions. Moreover, the tactical deployment of the two forces extended these eight-to-five odds considerably. Meade's 51 brigades of infantry and seven of cavalry were available for the occupation of three miles of line, which gave him an average of 27,000 men per mile, or better than fifteen to the yard — roughly twice as heavy a concentration as the Confederates had enjoyed at Fredericksburg — whereas Lee's 34 brigades of infantry and one of cavalry were distributed along a five-mile semicircle for an average of 10,000 men to the mile, or fewer than six per yard. As for artillery, Meade had 354 guns and Lee 272, or 118 to the mile, as compared to 54.

Nor were numbers the whole story. If the attacker enjoyed the advantage of being able to mass his troops for a sudden strike from a point of his choice along the extended arc, this was largely offset by the defender's advantage of being able to rush his ample reserves along the chord of that arc, first to bolster the threatened point and then to counterattack; so that the problem for Lee was not only to achieve a penetration, but also to maintain it afterwards in order to exploit it, which might prove an even greater difficulty. What was more, as he had warned Ewell the evening before, any thinning of the circumferential line to provide a striking force elsewhere would expose the weakened sector to being swamped and broken by the kind of powerful assault Meade could launch, more or less at will, from his interior lines. In short, if Sickles had exposed his two divisions to possible destruction by his occupation of the salient, the same might be said of Lee, in the light of all this, with regard to his whole army and the manner in which he had disposed it.

Longstreet had discerned a good deal of this at first glance; at any rate he had recognized the potentials of disaster, even though he had no access to figures comparing the tactical strengths of the two armies. The two positions were there to look at, Meade's and Lee's, and the only thing he liked about the latter was that it could be abandoned without much trouble. When Lee declined his suggestion that the Confederates move around the Federal left and take up a similar position of their own, thus reversing the present assignment of roles, Old Peter was dismayed. Failure by Hill and Ewell to complete the victory by driving the blue fugitives from the heights they had fallen back on, which was his second choice as a proper course of action, only increased his despondency. "It would have been better had we not fought at all than to have left undone what we did," he had said the night before, in response to a staff officer's exuberance over the day's success. Renewing his plea for a withdrawal this morning, the burly Georgian had been rebuffed again: whereupon he turned sulky. Though he had of course obeyed all orders given him, he had not anticipated them in the best tradition of the Army of Northern Virginia, with the result that he was partly to blame for the delays encountered in the course of the unreconnoitered flank march. As it approached its close, however, his spirits rose — as they always did in proximity to the enemy. Above all, by a sort of extension if not reversal of his native stubbornness, he was determined to carry out Lee's orders to the letter.

Just how determined Longstreet was in this respect was demonstrated to McLaws and Hood shortly after they halted their divisions in wooded jump-off positions due west of the Peach Orchard and the Devil's Den. McLaws rode forward, then dismounted and walked to the edge of the woods, about a quarter of a mile from the Emmitsburg Road, for a look at the ground over which his troops would be advancing. There in plain sight he saw two blue divisions, one posted north along the road and the other southeast in the direction of the Round Tops. "The view presented astonished me," he later recalled, "as the enemy was massed in my front, and extended to my right and left as far as I could see." Whatever validity they might have had when they were conceived, two miles away and something over five hours ago, Lee's plans for an attack up the Emmitsburg Road, in order to get astride the lower end of Cemetery Ridge, were obviously no longer practicable. Not only was the Union left not overlapped, as had been presupposed, but McLaws would be exposing his flank to end-on fire if he attacked in accordance with instructions. He notified Longstreet of this turn of events, only to be told that the orders were not subject to alteration. "There is no one in your front but a regiment of infantry and a battery of artillery," the staff man who brought this message informed him. McLaws replied that he knew better, having seen with his own eyes what was out there. But this had no effect. Three times he protested, and three times he was told to attack as ordered. And the same was true of Hood. Never in his military life had the sad-eyed blond young giant requested a modification of an order to attack, but he took one look at the situation and reacted much as McLaws was doing, half a mile to the north. Before protesting, however, he sent out scouts to search for an alternative to what appeared to him to be a suicidal venture. They promptly found one. All the country south of the Round Tops was unoccupied, they reported; Meade's far left was wide open to just such an attack as Lee had contemplated. So Hood sent word to Longstreet that it was "unwise to attack up the Emmitsburg Road, as ordered," and requested instead that he be allowed "to turn Round Top and attack the enemy in flank and rear."

Longstreet's reply — based, as he said later, on Lee's repeated earlier refusal to permit any maneuver around the enemy left — was brief and to the point: "General Lee's orders are to attack up the Emmitsburg Road." Supposing there must have been some misunderstanding, Hood repeated his request, and again his chief replied with that one sentence: "General Lee's orders are to attack up the Emmitsburg Road." By now Hood had been in position for nearly an hour, confronting the fissured tangle of the Devil's Den and the rocky frown of Little Round Top, and the longer he looked at what his men were being required to face, the more he became convinced that they were doomed. "In fact," he declared afterwards, "it seemed to me that the enemy occupied a position so strong — I may say impregnable — that, independently of their flank fire, they could easily repel our attack by merely throwing or rolling stones down the mountain side as we approached." Once more he urged Longstreet to grant him freedom to maneuver, only to have Old Peter deny him for still a third time: "General Lee's orders are to attack up the Emmitsburg Road." All that was lacking to complete the symbolism was a cockcrow. What came instead was a staff officer with peremptory instructions for him to go forward without delay, and while Hood was making last-minute adjustments in the alignment of his brigades, the corps commander himself rode up. It was 4 o'clock. With his troops already in motion, Hood made a fourth and final appeal for permission to maneuver around Round Top for a strike at the open flank and rear of the blue army. Longstreet still would not agree, though he did at least change the wording of his one-sentence reply. "We must obey the orders of General Lee," he said.

Lee's instructions called for the attack to be launched in echelon, from right to left, not only by divisions — first Hood, then McLaws, and finally Anderson, with Pender alerted to strike in turn if additional pressure was needed — but also by the brigades within those divi-

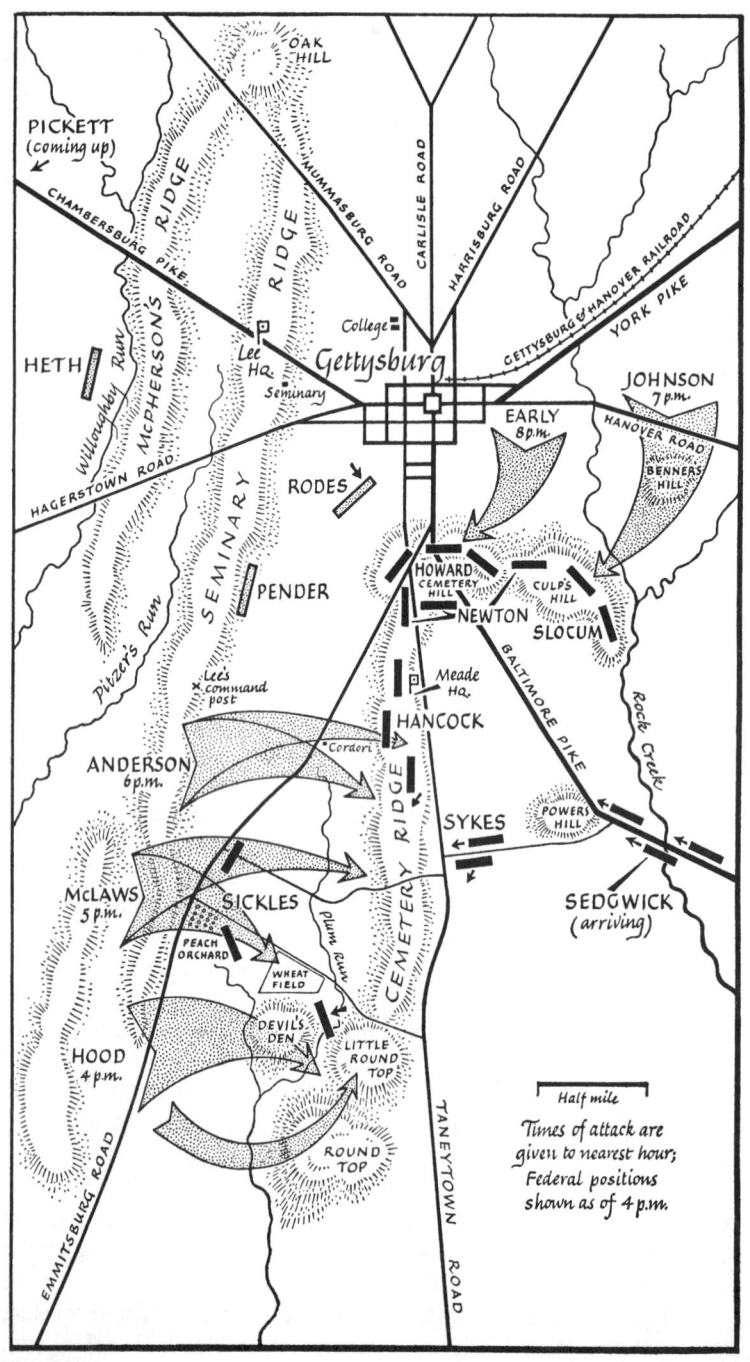

sions, so that the attack would gather strength as it rolled northward. This meant that Law, on Hood's and therefore the army's right, would be the first to step off. And so he did, promptly at 4 o'clock: but not as ordered. If Longstreet would not disregard or modify Lee's instructions, nor Hood Longstreet's, Law — a month short of his twenty-seventh birthday and next to the youngest of Lee's generals — had no intention of exposing first the flank and then the rear of his troops to the destructive fire of the Yankees in the Devil's Den, as would necessarily be the case if he advanced with his left aligned on the Emmitsburg Road. His unwillingness was not the result of any lack of courage, a quality he had demonstrated on field after field, beginning with Gaines Mill, where his brigade had charged alongside Hood's to break Fitz-John Porter's apparently unbreakable triple line and give the Army of Northern Virginia its first victory. He would make whatever sacrifice was called for, but he saw that to advance as ordered would be to spill the blood of his five Alabama regiments to little purpose and with no chance of return. Consequently, in flat disobedience of orders, he charged due east, in a frontal not an oblique attack on the Devil's Den and Little Round Top itself, which he saw as the key to control of the field.

Brigadier General J. B. Robertson's Texas brigade conformed, being next in line, and the result, as Lee's far right and Meade's far left came to grips in that vine-laced maze of boulders and ravines, "was more like Indian fighting," one participant would recall, "than anything I experienced during the war." By the time Hood's other two brigades, both from Georgia and under Georgians, Brigadier Generals Henry L. Benning and G. T. Anderson, joined the melee in the Devil's Den, they found the conflict quite as confused as it was fierce. Hood was down, unhorsed by a shell fragment much as Heth had been the day before, except that he was struck in the arm and carried out of the battle on a stretcher. Such control as remained was on the company level, or even lower. "Every fellow was his own general," a Texan later wrote. "Private soldiers gave commands as loud as the officers; nobody paying any attention to either."

While this highly individualistic struggle was building toward a climax half a mile west of Little Round Top, Law gave twenty-seven-year-old Colonel William Oates instructions to veer southward with two regiments and flush a troublesome detachment of Union sharpshooters out of some woods at the foot of the steep northwest slope of Round Top. It was done in short order, though not without galling casualties; after which the five hundred survivors continued their uphill charge, scrambling hand over hand around and across huge boulders and through heavy underbrush, to call a halt at last on the lofty summit, panting for breath and wishing fervently that they had not sent their canteens off to be filled just before they received the order to advance. Unlike the lower conical hill immediately to the north, which had been cleared of timber in the fall and thus afforded an excellent all-round view of the countryside, this tallest of all the heights in Adams County — sometimes called Sugarloaf by the natives — was heavily wooded from base to crown, a condition detracting considerably from its tactical usefulness. Through the trees due north, however, just over a hundred feet below and less than half a beeline mile away, Oates could see the barren, craggy dome of Little Round Top, deserted except for a handful of enemy signalmen busily wagging their long-handled flags, while off to the left, on lower ground, smoke boiled furiously out of the rocks where the fight for the Devil's Den was raging at the tip of the left arm of the spraddled V drawn by Sickles, its apex in the Peach Orchard and its right arm extended for the better part of a mile up the Emmitsburg Road, south and west of the main Federal position along the upper end of Cemetery Ridge and on the dominant heights to the north and east, bend and barb of the fishhook Meade had chosen to defend. All this lay before and below the young Alabama colonel, who continued to look it over while his troops were catching their breath on the crest of Round Top. Victory seemed as clear to him, in his mind's eye, as the town of Gettysburg itself, which he could see through the drifting smoke, and the green fields rolling northward out of sight. He believed that with his present force he could hold this hilltop stronghold against the whole Yankee army, if necessary, so steep were the approaches on all sides, and if a battery of rifled guns could somehow be manhandled up here, piece by piece and part by part if need be, not a cranny of Meade's fishhook line would be tenable any longer than it would take a detail of axmen to clear a narrow field of fire. So he believed. But just then a courier arrived from Law with instructions for him to push on and capture Little Round Top. Oates protested briefly, to no avail, then got his parched and weary men to their feet — feet that had covered no less than thirty miles of road and mountainside since 3 o'clock that morning at New Guilford — and started them down the northern face of Round Top, intent on carrying out the order.

It did not seem to him that this would be too difficult, particularly after he crossed the wooded valley between the Round Tops and was joined by a third regiment of Alabamians and two of Texans who had fought their way eastward through the lower fringes of the Devil's Den. Earlier, looking down from the taller of the two peaks, he had seen that the lower was not only undefended but also unoccupied, except by a handful of signalmen, and the confidence he derived from this was strengthened as the uphill march began and then continued without an indication that a single enemy rifleman stood or crouched among the rocks ahead. Two thirds of the way up, however, as the butternut skirmishers approached a ledge that formed a natural bastion around the southwest face of the hill, a heavy volley of musketry exploded in their faces. Oates knew at once, from the volume of fire — he afterwards described it as the most destructive he had ever encountered — that it had been delivered by nothing less than a brigade, and probably a veteran one at that. This meant that he had a fight on his hands, against troops in a position that afforded the same advantages he had contemplated enjoying in defense of the hilltop he had just abandoned under protest that he could hold it against all comers with two regiments of about 500 badly winded men and no artillery at all. It was obvious here on Little Round Top, though, that a good many more men than that were shooting at him from the rocky ledge ahead, and what was more they had artillery, two guns spraying canister from the crest above and beyond them. As soon as he could establish a firing line of his own, the three Alabama regiments on the right and the two Texas regiments on the left, Oates gave the order for an all-out uphill charge to drive the Federals back on their guns and off the mountaintop.

That the blue defenders had taken position on Little Round Top, even as Oates was on his way down from the companion height to seize it, was due to the vigilance and perception of one man, a staff brigadier who, strictly speaking, had no direct command over troops at all. Gouverneur K. Warren, the army's thirty-three-year-old chief engineer, a frail-looking New Yorker, thin-faced and clean-shaven except for a drooped mustache and a tuft of beard just below his lower lip, had ridden over to inspect the hill's defenses at about the same time Meade's brief talk with Sickles was being interrupted by his horse's antic reaction to the rebel cannonade. Disturbed to find the high ground all but unoccupied, despite its obvious tactical value, Warren told the signalmen to keep up their wigwag activity, simply as a pretense of alertness, whether they had any real messages to transmit or not — which was why Oates had found them so busy when he looked down at them from across the valley — and quickly notified Meade of the grave danger to his left. Meade passed the word to Sykes, whose corps by now was in motion to reinforce Sickles, and Sykes passed it along to Barnes. Barnes, who at sixty-two was the oldest division commander in the army, was not with his troops at the time, but Colonel Strong Vincent, who at twenty-six was the army's youngest brigade commander, responded by marching at once to occupy the hill. Arriving less than a quarter of an hour before the Texans and Alabamians, he advanced his brigade — four regiments from as many different states, Pennsylvania, New York, Maine, and Michigan — to the far side of the crest, well downhill in order to leave room for reinforcements, and took up a stout position in which to wait for what was not long in coming. Warren meanwhile had ordered up two guns of First Lieutenant Charles Hazlett's battery, helping to manhandle them up the rocky incline and onto the summit. This done, he went in search of infantry supports, which he could see were about to be needed badly, and found Brigadier General Stephen

H. Weed's brigade of Ayres's division marching west on the road leading out to the Peach Orchard. When the commander of the rear regiment, Colonel Patrick O'Rorke — by coincidence it was the 140th New York, which Warren himself had commanded before he moved up to staff — protested that he and his men were under orders to join Sickles, Warren did not waste time riding to the head of the column to find Weed. "Never mind that, Paddy," he said. "Bring them up on the double-quick, and don't stop for aligning. I'll take the responsibility." O'Rorke did as Warren directed, and Weed soon followed with his other three regiments, double-timing them as best he could up the steep, boulder-clogged incline and over the crest, to find the struggle raging furiously below him on the equally steep and rocky southwest face of the fuming hill.

Vincent by then had fallen, shot through the heart as he ranged up and down the firing line. "Don't yield an inch!" was his last command, and though his men tried their hardest to do as he said, one officer was to recall that, under the influence of no less than five charges and countercharges, "the edge of the fight swayed back and forward like a wave." The conflict was particularly desperate on the far left, where the 20th Maine, made up of lumberjacks and fishermen under Colonel Joshua Chamberlain, a former minister and Bowdoin professor, opposed the 15th Alabama, Oates's own regiment, composed for the most part of farmers. Equally far from home — Presque Isle and Talladega were each 650 crowflight miles from Little Round Top, which lay practically on the line connecting them — the men of these two outfits fought as if the outcome of the battle, and with it the war, depended on their valor: as indeed perhaps it did, since whoever had possession of this craggy height on the Union left would dominate the whole fishhook position. "The blood stood in puddles in some places on the rocks," Oates said later. Losses were especially heavy among Federals of rank. O'Rorke, who was barely twenty-three and an officer of much promise, having been top man in the West Point class of '61, was killed along with more than two dozen of his men in the first blast of musketry that greeted his arrival. Weed, coming up behind him with the rest of the brigade, was shot in the head by a sniper down in the Devil's Den, and as Hazlett, who was standing beside him directing the fire of his two guns, bent forward to catch any last words the twenty-nine-year-old brigadier might utter, he too was dropped, probably by the same long-range marksman, and fell dead across Weed's body.

Casualties on the Confederate side were as heavy, if not heavier, and increased steadily as blue reinforcements continued to come up, unmatched by any on the downhill side. With all but one of the field officers killed or wounded in the Texas regiments, and no replacements anywhere in sight, Major J. C. Rogers, who had succeeded to leadership of the 5th Texas by elimination, might have thought he had been forgotten by the high command, except that presently a courier from division came up the hillside, dodging from boulder to boulder among the twittering bullets and screaming ricochets. He brought no expected word of reinforcements, but he did have a message from the wounded Hood's successor. "General Law presents his compliments," he told Rogers, "and says to hold the place at all hazards." This was altogether too much for the hard-pressed major. "Compliments, hell!" he roared above the clatter of battle. "Who wants compliments in such a damned place as this? Go back and ask General Law if he expects me to hold the world in check with the 5th Texas regiment!"

Oates could see that the struggle could have but one end if it continued at this rate, five regiments fighting uphill against eight who were supported by artillery in defense of a position he had judged to be nearly impregnable in the first place. So long as there was a hope of reinforcements he would fight — "Return to your companies; we will sell out as dearly as possible," he told his captains — but presently, after the courier arrived with nothing more substantial than Law's compliments, he ordered a withdrawal. Just as the word was passed, the Maine men launched a bayonet attack. "When the signal was given we ran like a herd of wild cattle," Oates later admitted.

Near the base of the hill they rallied, being joined by the rest of Law's and Robertson's brigades, together with those of Anderson and Benning, who had succeeded by now in driving the Federals out of the Devil's Den, capturing three guns in the process. Not that the fighting had abated; Sykes had brought up two of his divisions in support of Sickles, with the result that the odds were as long down here as they had been above. There on the lower western slopes of Little Round Top the survivors began collecting rocks of all shapes and sizes, constructing a barricade to fight behind, and all the while the soldiers of both armies kept up a hot fire, banging away at whatever showed itself or perhaps at nothing at all. "Both sides were whipped," a Texas private explained afterwards, "and all were mad about it."

McLaws was also engaged by now, in part at least, and though this finally helped to relieve the pressure on the men who were fighting for their lives at the base of the rocky hill, the wait had been a long one, Longstreet having held him back in hopes that when he went forward at last he would find the enemy line greatly weakened by the shift of troops to meet Hood's attack on Little Round Top, which after all was not the assigned objective. Such withholding tactics had made possible the one-punch knockout Old Peter had scored at Second Manassas, a year ago next month, and he planned to repeat that coup today. If this was hard on Hood, whose men were thus required to absorb the single-minded attention of the entire Federal left wing for more than an hour, it was not easy on McLaws and his four brigade commanders, who were burning to advance: particularly Barksdale, whose thirst for glory was as sharp in Pennsylvania as it had been on his great day at Fredericksburg, where Lee to his delight had let him challenge the whole Yankee army. From the eastern fringe of the woods in which his troops awaited the signal to move out, the Mississippian could see bluecoats milling about in the Peach Orchard, as if they had it in mind to advance against him, and a battery posted temptingly at the apex of the salient, less than six hundred yards away. "General, let me go; General, let me charge," he kept begging McLaws, who declined, being under orders to wait for corps to inform him when the time was ripe. Soon Longstreet came riding northward through the woods and drew rein to talk with McLaws. Born within a week of each other, forty-two years ago, the two Georgians had been classmates at West Point. Equally burly of form and shaggy of hair and beard, they even resembled one another, not only in looks but also in their deliberative manner. Barksdale approached them and renewed his plea. "I wish you would let me go in, General," he appealed to the corps commander; "I will take that battery in five minutes." Longstreet looked out at the guns in the orchard, then back at the tall, white-maned Mississippian, who was trembling with excitement. Old Peter liked Barksdale, who was half a year his junior but looked older because of the prematurely gray hair worn shoulder-length, and greatly admired his spirit; but he would not be hurried. "Wait a little," he said in a calm, deep voice. "We are all going in presently."

It was near 5.30 before he gave the signal that opened the secondary attack. McLaws went in as Hood had done, his brigades committed in echelon from the right, which meant that Barksdale had some more waiting to do, being stationed on the left. South Carolinians under Brigadier General J. B. Kershaw — one of the five generals the town of Camden was to contribute to the Confederacy before the war was over — went forward with a shout, headed straight for the big wheat field north of the Devil's Den, about midway between Little Round Top and the Peach Orchard. Longstreet walked out with them as far as the Emmitsburg Road, where he stopped and waved them on with his hat, adding his own deep-throated version of the rebel yell to the tumult. They struck the center of Birney's division, which was posted behind a low stone wall along the near edge of the shimmering field of wheat, with Barnes's two remaining brigades in close support. As the fighting mounted swiftly toward a climax, Brigadier General Paul J. Semmes — younger brother of the *Alabama*'s captain — brought his Georgians out to join the stand-up fight, and behind them came the third brigade, still more Georgians, under Brigadier General W. T. Wofford, who had led them since the death of Tom Cobb in the sunken road at Fredericksburg. The Union line began to crumble under this added pressure, men dropping all along it and others scrambling rearward to get a head start in the race for safety.

Just then Semmes fell mortally wounded, which resulted in some confusion among his troops; but the loss was overbalanced at this critical point by one on the other side. Sickles was riding his line, erect on horseback, ignoring the whistle of bullets and the scream of shells, until one of the latter came along that could not be ignored because it struck his right leg, just above the knee, and left it hanging in shreds. He fell heavily to the ground, but kept cool enough to save his life by ordering a tourniquet improvised from a saddle strap. As he lay there, pale from the sudden loss of blood, his thigh bone protruding stark white against the red of mangled flesh, a staff officer rode up and asked solicitously, if superfluously: "General, are you hurt?" Normally, Sickles would have laughed at the simplicity of the question, but not now. "Tell General Birney he must take command," he replied. Lifted onto a stretcher, he heard through the waves of pain and shock that a rumor was being spread that he was dead; so he called the bearers to a halt while one of them lit a cigar for him, then rode the rest of the way to the aid station with it clenched at a jaunty angle between his teeth, puffing industriously at it by way of disproving the rumor that he had stopped breathing. Thus did Old Dan Sickles leave the war, to proceed in time to other fields of endeavor, including a well-publicized liaison with the deposed nymphomaniac Queen of Spain.

There was to be a great deal of discussion, beginning tonight and continuing down the years, as to whether his occupation of the salient, half a mile and more in front of the main Union line, had been a colossal blunder or a tactically sound maneuver. Whatever else it was or wasn't — and entirely aside from the fact that it helped to discourage Longstreet's men from attacking as Lee had ordered, straight up the Emmitsburg Road, which probably would have meant utter destruction for them if Sickles had stayed back on the ridge to tear their flank as they went by — the movement resulted at any rate in the wrecking of his corps, whose two divisions, formerly under Phil Kearny and Joe Hooker and therefore among the most famous in the army, were to suffer well over four thousand casualties in the two hours before sunset. The worst of the damage occurred when the line gave way at the western rim of the wheat field. "It is too hot; my men cannot stand it!" Barnes cried, and he ordered a retreat. Birney's were quick to follow, despite his efforts to stop them. But as the elated Confederates started forward, in close and hot pursuit, they were met by a fresh division under Caldwell, whom Hancock had alerted to stand by for trouble after predicting — quite accurately, as it turned out — that Sickles' troops would "come tumbling back" from the salient. Caldwell struck with all his strength, holding nothing in reserve. And now, though he lost three of his four brigade commanders, two of them killed on contact, it was the rebels who fell back through the trampled grain, the steam gone out of their drive. From Little Round Top to the northern edge of the wheat field, the fighting degenerated into a bloody squabble as regiment fought regiment, alternately driving and being driven. "What a hell is there down in that valley!" a Federal lieutenant exclaimed after viewing the carnage from up on Cemetery Ridge. Birney's men were out of it by then, such as remained uncaptured and alive, and now the turn had come of those with Humphreys in the orchard and strung out along the road northeast of there.

Longstreet's "presently" had begun to seem interminable to Barksdale and his soldiers, held under cover and straining at the leash all the time the other three brigades were taking on most of Birney's and Barnes's divisions and finally all of Caldwell's, which came in fresh to stop them short of the ridge. Though opinion was divided as to the distinguishing characteristics of these troops from the Deep South — a Virginia artilleryman, for example, having learned to feel secure whenever his battery had the support of the Mississippians, was to say that theirs was the brigade "I knew and loved best of all in Lee's army"; whereas a Chambersburg civilian, observing the various rebel outfits that passed through his town, decided quite to the contrary that "those from Mississippi and Texas were more vicious and defiant" than the rest — the men themselves not only would have considered both of these remarks complimentary, but also would have been hard put to say which compliment they preferred. Certainly their viciousness and defiance were apparent to the Federals in the orchard, just over a quarter-mile away, as they came running eastward out of the woods, unleashed at last and eager to come to grips. Barksdale was out in front of the whole line, his face "radiant with joy," as one observer remarked, to be leading what a Confederate lieutenant and a Union colonel referred to afterwards, respectively, as "the most magnificent charge I witnessed during the war" and "the grandest charge that was ever made by mortal man." His earlier assurance that he could "take that battery in five minutes" had sounded overconfident at the time, mainly because the stout rail fences on both sides of the Emmitsburg Road seemed likely to slow his advance while they were being torn down or climbed over. As it turned out, however, the fences were no deterrent at all. They simply vanished under the impact of the charging Mississippians, who reached the Peach Orchard even sooner than their general had predicted, whooping with delight as they swarmed over the battery and such of its defenders as had resisted the impulse to get out of the path of that savage assault. Four of the guns and close to a thousand prisoners were taken in one swoop, but that was only a part of what Barksdale was after. Still out front, hatless so that his long white hair streamed behind him as he ran, he shouted: "Forward, men! Forward!" pointing with his sword at the blue line half a mile ahead on Cemetery Ridge.

He did not make it that far, nor did any of his men. A Federal brigadier, watching the conspicuous figure draw nearer across the stony floor of the valley, assigned a whole company of riflemen the task of bringing him down; which they did. As for his men, the vigilant Hunt had prepared a reception for them by massing forty guns along the crest and down the slope of the ridge. Meade had seen to it that these batteries had infantry support by shifting troops southward from his overcrowded right, but the guns themselves, blasting the attackers wholesale as they came within easy range, turned out to be enough. Still they came on, overrunning the first line of artillery on the slope, where the cannoneers fought them with pistols and rammer staffs and whatever came to hand, and all the while the guns on the crest flung canister point-blank at them, mangling blue and gray alike. Finally, unsupported on the left or right, Barksdale's men fell back westward to a line along Plum Run, midway between the road and the ridge, leaving half their number dead or wounded on the field, including their commander. Scouts from a Vermont regiment were to bring him into their lines that night, shot through both legs and the breast, and he would die by morning, his thirst for glory slaked at last.

Hood and McLaws had done their worst, and the 15,000 men in their eight brigades, having taken on six full enemy divisions, together with major portions of three others — a total of 22 Federal brigades, disposed with all the advantages of the defensive and containing better than twice as many troops as came against them — were fought to a standstill along an irregular line stretching northward from the Round Tops to the Peach Orchard, anywhere from half a mile to a mile beyond the Emmitsburg Road, which had marked the line of departure. Proud of what his soldiers had accomplished against the odds, though he knew it was less than Lee had hoped for, Longstreet was to say: "I do not hesitate to pronounce this the best three hours' fighting ever done by any troops on any battlefield." The cost had been great — more than a third of the men in the two divisions had been hit; Hood would be out of combat for some time, a grievous loss, and Semmes and Barksdale forever — but so had been the gain: not so much in actual ground, though that had been considerable, as in its effect of setting the bluecoats up for the kill. Meade had been stripping his center, along with his right, to reinforce his left. And now the offensive passed to Hill, or more specifically to Richard Anderson, whose division was on the right, adjoining McLaws, and who now took up his portion of the echelon attack from a position directly opposite the weakened Union center.

In this as in the other two divisional attacks the brigades were to be committed in sequence from the right, and it opened with all the precision of a maneuver on the drill field. Nor was there any such delay as there had been in the case of McLaws, held in check by Longstreet while Hood's men were storming the Devil's Den and fighting for their lives on Little Round Top. At 6.20, when Barksdale's survivors began their withdrawal from the shell-swept western slope of Cemetery Ridge, Anderson sent Wilcox and his Alabamians driving hard for a section of the ridge just north of where the Mississippians had struck and been repulsed. Next in line, Colonel David Lang's small brigade of three Florida regiments followed promptly, supported in turn by Brigadier General Ambrose R. Wright's Georgians, who came forward on the left. But that was where the breakdown of the echelon plan began. Brigadier General Carnot Posey, having already committed three of his four Mississippi regiments as skirmishers, had not understood that he was to charge with the fourth, and his doubts became even graver when he discovered that his left would not be covered by Brigadier General William Mahone, who could not be persuaded that his Virginia brigade, posted all day in reserve, was intended to have a share in the attack. Wilcox by now had sent his adjutant back to ask for reinforcements, and Anderson had sent him on to Mahone with full approval of the request. But Mahone refused to budge. "I have my orders from General Anderson himself to stay here," he kept insisting, despite the staff man's protest that it was the division commander who had sent him. As a result, Posey advanced his single regiment only as far as the Emmitsburg Road, where he came under heavy artillery fire, and Wright, after pausing briefly to give the two laggard brigades a chance to catch up and cover his left, went on alone when he saw that the Mississippians would come no farther and that the Virginians had no intention of advancing at all.

The fault was primarily Anderson's. Missing the firm if sometimes heavy hand of Longstreet, under whom he had always fought before — except of course at Chancellorsville, where Lee himself had taken him in charge — he was unaccustomed to Hill's comparatively light touch, which allowed him to be less attentive to preparatory details. Furthermore, Hill had understood that his right division was more or less detached to Longstreet, whereas Longstreet had interpreted Lee's instructions merely to mean that Hill would be in support and therefore still in command of his own troops. Consequently, neither exercised any control over Anderson, who followed suit by leaving the conduct of the attack to his subordinates, with the result that it broke down in midcareer.

At this point, however, with Wilcox, Lang, and Wright driving hard for Cemetery Ridge, the question of blame seemed highly inappropriate. A more likely question seemed to concern a proper distribution of praise among the three attacking brigades for having pierced the Union center. Hancock certainly saw it in that light, and with good cause. Meade having placed him in command of the III Corps as well as his own when Sickles fell, he had sent one of his three divisions to reinforce the left an hour ago, and since then he had been using elements of the two remaining divisions to bolster the line along Plum Run, where McLaws was keeping up the pressure. As a result, he had found neither the time nor the means to fill the gap on his left, where Caldwell had been posted until his departure, and the even larger gap that had yawned beyond it ever since Sickles moved out to occupy the salient. To his horror, Hancock now saw that Wilcox was headed directly for this soft spot, driving the remnant of Humphreys' division pell-mell before him as he advanced, with Lang on his left and Wright on the left of Lang. Gambling that no simultaneous attack would be launched against his right, just below Cemetery Hill, Hancock ordered Gibbon and Hays to double-time southward along the ridge and use what was left of their commands to plug the gap the rebels were about to strike.

He hurried in that direction, ahead of his troops, and arrived in time to witness the final rout of Humphreys, whose men were in full flight by now, with Wilcox close on their heels and driving hard for the scantly defended ridge beyond. As he himself climbed back up the slope on horseback, under heavy fire from the attackers, Hancock wondered how he was going to stop or even delay them long enough for a substantial line of defense to be formed on the high ground. Gibbon and Hays "had been ordered up and were coming on the run," he later explained, "but I saw that in some way five minutes must be gained or we were lost." Just then the lead regiment of Gibbon's first brigade came over the crest in a column of fours, and Hancock saw a chance to gain those five minutes, though at a cruel price.

"What regiment is this?" he asked the officer at the head of the column moving toward him down the slope.

"First Minnesota," Colonel William Colvill replied.

Hancock nodded. "Colonel, do you see those colors?" As he spoke he pointed at the Alabama flag in the front rank of the charging rebels. Colvill said he did. "Then take them," Hancock told him.

Quickly, although scarcely a man among them could have failed to see what was being asked of him, the Minnesotans deployed on the slope — eight companies of them, at any rate; three others had been detached as skirmishers, leaving 262 men present for duty — and charging headlong down it, bayonets fixed, struck the center of the long gray line. Already in some disorder as a result of their run of nearly a mile over stony ground and against such resistance as Humphreys had managed to offer, the Confederates recoiled briefly, then came on again, yelling fiercely as they concentrated their fire on this one undersized blue regiment. The result was devastating. Colvill and all but three of his officers were killed or wounded, together with 215 of his men. A captain brought the 47 survivors back up the ridge, less than one fifth as many as had charged down it. They had not taken the Alabama flag, but they had held onto their own. And they had given Hancock his five minutes, plus five more for good measure.

Those ten minutes were enough. By the time Wilcox reached the foot of the ridge, with Lang bringing up his three regiments on the left, Gibbon's division had taken position on the crest and was pouring heavy volleys of musketry into the ranks of both brigades from dead ahead. Staggered by this, and torn on his unprotected right by fire from the massed batteries that had repulsed Barksdale half an hour before, Wilcox looked back across the valley and saw that his appeal for reinforcements had not been answered. Regretfully he ordered a retreat. So did Lang at the same time. And as the Alabamians and Floridians began their withdrawal from the base of the ridge, Wright's Georgians struck with irresistible force, some four hundred yards to the north. "On they came like the fury of a whirlwind," a Pennsylvania captain later recalled. The impetus of their drive carried them swiftly up the slope and into the breaking ranks of the defenders, then through the line of guns, whose cannoneers scattered, and onto the crest. They did not stay there long — Gibbon and Hays had them greatly outnumbered, as well as outflanked on the right and left, and Meade had already ordered another three divisions to converge on the threatened point from Cemetery Hill, three quarters of a mile to the north, and Culp's Hill, about the same distance across the eastern valley — but while they were there Wright believed that he had victory within his reach. On the reverse slope, bluecoats were streaming rearward across the Taneytown Road, and half a mile beyond it the Baltimore Pike was crowded with fugitives. Yet these were only the backwash of the battle. Nearer at hand, on the left and right, he saw heavy blue columns bearing down on him, and he saw too — like Wilcox and Lang before him, though they had achieved no such penetration of the main Union line — that to stay where he was, unsupported, meant capture or annihilation. He ordered a withdrawal, which was achieved only by charging a body of Federals who had gained his rear by now, and then fell back across the Emmitsburg Road, taking punishment all the way from the two dozen guns he had captured and then abandoned. Like Wilcox and Lang, Wright had lost nearly half his men in that one charge, and he found this a steep price to pay for one quick look at the Union rear, even though he believed ever after that the end of the war had been within his reach if only he had been supported while he was astride the crest of Cemetery Ridge, midway of the Yankee line and within plain sight of the cottage Meade was using as headquarters for his army.

The hard fact that no supports were at hand when the Georgians crested the ridge and stood poised there, silhouetted against the eastern sky for one brief fall of time as they pierced the enemy center, did not mean that none had been available. Though Posey and Mahone had hung back, declining for whatever reasons to go forward — the former calling a halt halfway across the valley and the latter refusing to budge from the shade of the trees on Seminary Ridge, directly behind Lee's command post — there still was Pender, whose division was to the Third Corps what Hood's and Johnson's were to the First and Second, the hardest-hitting and fiercest of the three. And yet Pender was not there after all: not Pender in person. Like Heth and Hood, at about the same time yesterday and earlier today, he had been unhorsed by a casual fragment of shell while riding his line to inspect and steady his men for their possible share in the attack then rolling northward. The wound in his leg, though ugly enough, was not thought to be very serious, or at any rate not fatal. But it was. Two weeks later the leg was taken off, infection having set in during the long ambulance ride back to Virginia, and he did not survive the amputation. "Tell my wife I do not fear to die," the twenty-nine-year-old North Carolinian said in the course of his suffering, which was intense. "I can confidently resign my soul to God, trusting in the atonement of our Lord Jesus Christ. My only regret is to leave her and our children." If this had the tone of Stonewall Jackson, under whom Pender had developed into one of the best of all Lee's generals despite his youth, his last words sounded even more like his dead chief: "I have always tried to do my duty in every sphere of life in which Providence has placed me." Few doubted afterwards that he would have done that duty here today at Gettysburg by leading his four brigades across the valley to assault the ridge just north of where Wright had struck it. There was in fact little to stop him once he got there. Not only had Hancock shifted his two divisions south to counter Anderson's attack; Meade had also moved Newton's two in that direction from their position supporting Howard on Cemetery Hill. But that was beside the point, as it turned out. The decision whether to join the charge had been discretionary anyhow, according to Lee's orders, and when Pender was hit and carried off the field, his temporary successor Brigadier General James Lane, having watched Anderson's two adjoining brigades falter, decided that it was no longer advisable for his troops to advance, since they would not be supported on the right. Moreover, A. P. Hill was not there at the time, having ridden northward to confer with Rodes, and did not urge Lane on.

With that, the three-hour-long assault on Cemetery Ridge broke down completely. Hood, McLaws, and Anderson — some 22,000 men in all, including the cannoneers — had tried their hands in sequence against a total of no less than 40,000 blue defenders. Better than 7000 of the attackers had fallen in the attempt, and all they had to show for this loss of one third of the force engaged was the Devil's Den, plus the Peach Orchard, which had been proved to be practically indefensible in the first place, and a few acres of stony ground on the floor of the valley between the ridges. "The whole affair was disjointed," a member of Lee's staff admitted later. "There was an utter absence of accord in the movements of the several commands."

The truth was, the army had slipped back to the disorganization of the Seven Days, except that here at Gettysburg there was no hardcore tactical plan to carry it through the bungling. There was in fact scarcely any plan at all, Lee's instructions for an attack up the Emmitsburg Road having been rejected out of necessity at the start. This, together with the refusal of the Federals to panic under pressure, as they had done so often before when the graybacks came screaming at them, had stood in the way of victory. And yet, in light of the fact that each of the three attacking divisions in turn had come close to carrying the day, there was more to it than that. Specifically, there was Warren and there was Hancock, both of whom had served their commander in a way that none of Lee's chief lieutenants had served him. Warren had acted on his own to save Little Round Top and the battle, and Hancock had done the same to prevent a breakthrough, first at the lower end and then at the center of Cemetery Ridge; but no one above the rank of colonel — Oates, the exception, lacked the authority to make it count — had acted with any corresponding initiative on the other side. There was, as always, no lack of Confederate bravery, and the army's combat skill had been demonstrated amply by the fact that, despite its role as the attacker, it had inflicted even more casualties than it had suffered, yet these qualities could not make up for the crippling lack of direction from above and the equally disadvantageous lack of initiative just below the top.

Longstreet sensed a good part of this, of course — perhaps even his own share of the blame, at least to a degree — but once more his reaction was a strange one. Though he was saddened by the wounding of Hood and the death or capture of Barksdale, which he believed were the main reasons he had failed to break Meade's line, he was by no means as gloomy as he had been in the course of the roundabout march into position. "We have not been so successful as we wished," he told an inquirer, and that was all he said. He seemed glad, for once, that his share of the fighting was over. If Hill had broken down, it was not his fault; he had small use for Little Powell anyhow. And now the battle passed to Ewell.

Stung by Lee's complaint that he had failed to "pursue our advantage of yesterday," Ewell was eager to make a redemptive showing today, despite the difficulties of terrain on this northern quarter of the field. After Lee had departed he had kept busy, all through what was left of the morning and most of the afternoon, inspecting his three divisions, which were disposed along a convex arc on three sides of Gettysburg, Rodes to the west, Early just south, and Johnson to the east, confronting the two dominant heights at the bend and barb of the Union fishhook. His instructions required him to guard the Confederate left, keeping as many bluecoats occupied there as possible, and to stage a vigorous demonstration, by way of insuring that effect, when Longstreet's guns began to roar at the far end of the line. Moreover — and this was the prospect he found most attractive, in connection with his desire to make a showing — if Ewell decided that he could strike with a fair chance of success, he was to convert the demonstration into a real attack, driving the enemy from Cemetery and Culp's hills, which commanded the Taneytown Road and the Baltimore Pike, both vital to the Federals if they were thrown into retreat from these two northern heights and the ridge leading southward to the Round Tops. The wait was a long one, anxious as Ewell was, and some time after 4 o'clock, when the distant booming at last informed him that Longstreet's artillery preparation had begun, he decided to respond in the same fashion. Six batteries, held under cover till then by Major Joseph Latimer, Johnson's twenty-year-old chief of artillery, were sent to the crest of Benner's Hill, a solitary eminence one mile east of town, with orders to pummel Culp's Hill, half a mile southwest across the valley of Rock Creek. Ewell felt that this would not only serve as a "vigorous demonstration," fixing the blue defenders in position as required, but would also afford him an opportunity to study their reaction and thus determine the advisability of launching an all-out uphill infantry assault.

The answer was both sudden and emphatic, as might have been expected if a proper reconnaissance had been made. Benner's Hill was not only fifty feet lower than the height across the way; it was also bald, which meant that the two dozen guns found neither cover nor concealment when they went into action there, whereas the Federal cannoneers had spent the past twenty hours digging lunettes and piling up embankments to add to the security of their densely wooded battery positions. Lashing their teams up the reverse slope of the isolated hill, the Confederates opened fire from its crest soon after 5 o'clock, and within a few minutes of the prompt and wrathful response by the heavier guns directly across the valley, as well as by those a mile away on Cemetery Hill, it was obvious that there could be no doubt as to the outcome of the duel, but only as to how long it could be sustained against the odds. Starkly exposed on the naked summit, the gray gunners stood to their work under a deluge of hot metal and amid sudden pillars of smoke and flame reared by exploding caissons. After about an hour of this, Latimer, who was known as the "Boy Major" and was said to be developing fast into another Pelham, felt compelled to send word that his position was untenable, a thing he had never done before in the two years since he had interrupted his sophomore year at VMI to join the army. Johnson at once authorized him to withdraw all but four of the guns, which were to remain there in support of the attack Ewell had just ordered all three of his divisions to make, despite this graphic evidence of the fury they were likely to encounter as they approached the hilltop objectives he assigned them. Latimer's withdrawal was necessarily slow, his crews having been reduced to skeletons by the counterbattery fire, and he himself was mortally wounded before it was completed, a high price to pay for confirming what should have been apparent before the one-sided contest even began.

On the face of it, the infantry attempt seemed equally doomed. Actually this was not the case, however, for the paradoxical reason that Ewell had failed in his primary mission of holding the blue forces in position on his front. By 6 o'clock, when the attack order was issued, Meade had taken thorough alarm at the series of threats to his left and center, and by 7 o'clock, when the advance began against his right, he had shifted two of Newton's three divisions southward, together with all but a single brigade from the two divisions in Slocum's corps. All that remained by then on Cemetery Hill, which Early and Rodes were to assault in sequence from the north and the northwest, were the three battered divisions under Howard, while Culp's Hill was even more scantly held by Wadsworth's division of the I Corps, down to half its normal strength after yesterday's drubbing on Seminary Ridge, and the one brigade Slocum had left behind. That was where the paradox came in. If Ewell had succeeded in holding the departed bluecoats in position, as Lee had instructed him to do, the attack would have been as suicidal as any ever attempted by either army in the whole course of the war; but as it was, with the defenses manned only by Howard's jumpy Dutchmen, Wadsworth's thin line of survivors from the rout of the day before, and the single brigade from Geary's division, the chances of a Confederate breakthrough here on the north were considerably better than fair, despite the obvious difficulties of the terrain. For one thing, thanks to Meade's alarm at the unrelenting fury of the three-hour-long assault on the Round Tops and Cemetery Ridge, Ewell's troops outnumbered the defenders to their front, an advantage no other attacking force had enjoyed on any portion of the field today.

Johnson's division, which had arrived too late for a share in the battle yesterday, had remained in the same position for nearly twenty-four hours, a mile east of Gettysburg and north of the Hanover Road, its four brigades posted from right to left under Colonel J. M. Williams and Brigadier Generals John M. Jones, George H. Steuart, and James A. Walker. The men of the first were Louisianians, and the rest were nearly all Virginians, like Old Clubby himself, who took them forward at 7 o'clock, brandishing the post-thick hickory stick from which his nickname was derived. That left half an hour till sunset, but they had more than a mile to go and armpit-deep Rock Creek to cross before they came within musket range of their Culp's Hill objective. As a result, the sun was well down behind it by the time they came surging up the northeast slope, yelling fiercely as they approached the crest. They did not make it all the way; Wadsworth's troops, including the remnant of the Iron Brigade, were well dug in and quite as determined as they had been when they shattered Heth's attack the day before. Jones was wounded early in the fight, and his and Williams's men, unsupported because Walker and his famed Stonewall Brigade remained in reserve on the far side of the creek, had all they could do to keep from being driven off the hillside. Around to the left, Steuart had better luck, the trenches down the southern nose of the hill having yawned vacant ever since Slocum's departure, half an hour before the rebel advance got under way. The gray attackers swarmed into and along them, whooping as they swung northward in the twilight, apparently unopposed, only to strike a new line of fortifications, drawn at right angles to the old and occupied by the brigade Slocum had left behind. The struggle here was as bitter as on the right, and the defenders — five regiments of upstate New Yorkers under Brigadier General George S. Greene — fought with a determination every bit as grim as Wadsworth's.

Rhode-Island-born, with a seagoing son who had served as executive officer on the *Monitor*, Greene was sixty-two, a few months older than the ineffectual Barnes and therefore the oldest Federal on the field. "Old Man Greene," his soldiers called him, or sometimes merely "Pop," for though he had finished second in his class at West Point forty years ago, he affected an easy style of dress that made him look more like a farmer than a regular army man. What he was, in fact, was a civil engineer; he had left the service early to build railroads and design municipal sewage and water systems for Washington, Detroit, and several other cities, including New York, whose Central Park reservoir was his handiwork, along with the enlarged High Bridge across the Harlem River. Such experience, as he applied it now to laying out intrenchments, stood him and his 1300 men in good stead this evening on Culp's Hill. Rather than attempt to hold the empty trenches on his right with his one brigade, which would have stretched it beyond the breaking point, he had dug a traverse, midway of the line and facing south behind a five-foot-thick embankment of earth and logs. Here his troops fought savagely, holding their own against Steuart's frantic lunges, and were reinforced at last by two regiments Wadsworth was able to spare when the pressure eased on the north end of the hill. When the commander of the first of these reported to him on the firing line, the battle racket was so terrific that Greene had to give up trying to shout above the uproar, and instead wrote his name on a card which he handed to the colonel by way of identification. For two hours, from twilight well into darkness, the firing hardly slacked. Then gradually it did, dying away to a sputter of individual shots, as if by mutual agreement that the blind slaughter had grown pointless: as indeed it had. Johnson was forced to content himself with what was after all a substantial lodgment on the far Union right, and Greene was more or less satisfied that he had been able to keep it from being enlarged, though it was clear to the fighters on both sides that the lull would not last past daylight.

Although it started later and ended sooner, Early's attack on Cemetery Hill, launched when he heard Johnson open fire on the far left, not only accomplished a deeper penetration, but also came even closer than Wright's had done, two hours ago, to achieving a complete breakthrough and the consequent disruption of Meade's whole fishhook system of defense. His four brigades were from four different states, Virginia, Louisiana, North Carolina, and Georgia; Gordon commanded the last of these, and the other three were respectively under Brigadier Generals William Smith and Harry T. Hays and Colonel Isaac Avery. Smith had no share in the assault, having been posted two miles out the York Pike to fend off a rumored threat to the rear. Nor did Gordon, as the thing turned out; Early held him in reserve. But the North Carolinians and Louisianians did all they could, in fury and hard-handed determination, to make up for these subtractions. Hays advanced on the right and Avery on the left, headed straight for the steep northeast face of the hundred-foot hill, and neither brigade would be stopped. Avery fell at the outset, mortally wounded, but his men kept going, over and past three successive lines of bluecoats disposed behind stone walls, defying the frantic overhead fire of infantry and artillery massed on the summit. Hays, a Tennessee-born and Mississippi-raised New Orleans lawyer whose brigade had first won fame under Dick Taylor in the Shenandoah Valley, refused to be outdone, though he too had to contend with three successive blue lines, the first along the far side of a ravine at the foot of the hill, the second behind a stone wall halfway up, and the third in well-dug rifle pits just short of the crest, protected by an abatis of felled trees. Losses were surprisingly light, partly because the downhill-firing Federals tended to overshoot the climbing graybacks, but mostly, as Hays said later, because of "the darkness of the evening, now verging into night, and the deep obscurity afforded by the smoke." Another reason was that the defenders here were Howard's men, who had yesterday's disaster fresh in mind. Hays called no names, merely reporting that his troops, having taken the third Yankee line at small cost to themselves, "found many of the enemy who had not fled hiding in the pits for protection." While these were being rousted out and told to make their own way to the rear as prisoners, the two rebel brigades surged over the lip of the plateau, in hot pursuit of the fugitive survivors. One-armed Howard was there, again the unhappy witness of a scene that by now was becoming familiar. "Almost before I could tell where the assault was made," he afterwards declared, "our men and the Confederates came tumbling back together."

Once more, having failed to stem the rout, he was left with a choice of joining it or exposing himself to capture, along with the guns his cannoneers had abandoned when the attackers reached point-blank range. "At that time," Hays noted proudly, "every piece of artillery which had been firing upon us was silent." The Louisianians and Tarheels swarmed among them, in full possession of the Union stronghold at the bend of the three-mile fishhook. Like Wright before him, a mile to the south, though darkness permitted him no such view of the enemy rear, Hays experienced a feeling of elation as he looked about the plateau for the reinforcements he had been told to expect. For a moment he thought he saw them; heavy masses of infantry were coming up from the southwest in the gloom. He could not be sure they were not Federals, in which case he would take them under fire, but he had been "cautioned to expect friends" from that direction, either Longstreet or Hill, or Rodes from his own corps. Even when they fired at him, dropping a number of his men, he did not shoot back, not wanting to compound the error if they were Confederates. They fired again and kept coming on through the darkness; still he held his fire, perhaps remembering the fall of Jackson in the Wilderness, two months ago tonight. A third volley crashed, much nearer now, and he saw by the fitful glare of the muzzle flashes that the uniforms were blue. A close look even showed the trefoil insignia of the II Corps on the flat-top forage caps of the still advancing Federals, whose "Clubs Are Trumps" motto Hays and his men knew only too well from hard experience. They were, in fact, Colonel S. S. Carroll's brigade of Hancock's third division, and Hancock himself had sent them. He had been talking just now with Gibbon in the twilight, gazing westward from the point on Cemetery Ridge where Wright's breach had been sealed, when the racket of Early's attack erupted on the north slope of Cemetery Hill. "We ought to send some help over there," he told Gibbon, who was acting as corps commander while his chief undertook the larger duties Meade had assigned him. As the uproar drew nearer, signifying the progress of the attackers, Hancock added with rapid decision: "Send a brigade. Send Carroll."

Carroll it was. And Hays, already staggered by the three unanswered volleys — the third had been especially destructive, delivered as it was at such close range — gave the order at last for his men to return the fire. This they did, glad to be released from hard restraint, and kept it up as fast as they could ram cartridges and draw triggers, bringing the blue mass to a stumbling halt. Beyond it, however, Hays could see other such masses forming in the flame-stabbed darkness; Howard's fugitives were rallying to support the troops who had opened ranks to let them through and then gone on to stop the rebels in their tracks. Looking back over his shoulder for some sign that Gordon was advancing, and wishing fervently that at any moment he would see Rodes and his five brigades come charging across the plateau from the west, Hays held his own for a time against the odds, but then, abandoning all hope of support, gave the necessary commands for a withdrawal. Unpursued past the line of abandoned guns, the two brigades fell back in good order, firing as they went, and called a halt at the bottom of the hill, angry that neither Gordon nor Rodes had mounted the slope to help them exploit the greatest opportunity of the day.

This lack of support — which, if supplied, might well have made up for all the miscalculations and fumbled chances of the past two days — resulted from a series of interrelated hesitations and downright failures of nerve on the part of several men. Early had withheld Gordon because he saw at the last moment that Rodes was not advancing on his right, and Rodes had called off his attack for the same reason, with regard to Lane. In a sense, it all went back to the fall of Pender and the curious defection of Mahone; or perhaps it went even further back than that, to the near escape from disaster Rodes had experienced yesterday. Restrained at first by a fear of being involved in another fiasco if he charged unsupported up Cemetery Hill, he now was prodded by a desire to retrieve what his restraint had cost him. When he heard the clatter of gunfire on the overhead plateau, which signified unmistakably that the blue defenses had been breached, he repented his inaction and decided to go forward anyhow, with or without support. But by the time he got his troops in position to advance — most of them had been waiting all day in Gettysburg itself, which meant that they had to be disentangled from the complex of streets and houses before they could form for attack — the hilltop clatter had subsided; Hays had brought his two brigades back down the northeast slope. Rodes took a careful, close-up look at the objective, which bristled with guns, and decided — no doubt wisely, at this late hour — that "it would be a useless sacrifice of life to go on." However, instead of bringing his five brigades back to their various starting points, he put them in line along the hollow of an old roadbed southwest of town, a position, he later reported, "from which I could readily attack without confusion." He did not explain why he had not done this sooner, in order to be able to move promptly in support of Hays, but he added: "Everything was gotten ready to attack at daybreak."

So he said. But for now the fighting was over, all but the final stages of Johnson's blind assault on Old Man Greene's well-engineered intrenchments, a mile across the way. Presently this too sputtered into silence, and moonlight glistened eerily on the corpse-strewn valleys and hillsides, its refulgence no longer broken by the fitful and ubiquitous pinkish-yellow stabs of muzzle flashes. Here and there, the wounded troubled the stillness with their cries for water and assistance, but for the most part the veterans of both armies were inured to this by now; they slept to rest their minds and bodies for tomorrow.

Thus ended the second day of what was already the bloodiest battle of the war to date, with no one knew how much more blood still to be shed on this same field.

★ ★ ★

Their lines drawn helter-skelter in the darkness, the soldiers could sleep; but not the two commanders and their staffs, who had the task of assessing what had been done today, or left undone, in order to plan for tomorrow. In this, the two reacted so literally in accordance with their native predilections — Lee's for daring, Meade's for caution —

that afterwards, when their separate decisions were examined down the tunnel of the years — which provides a diminished clarity not unlike that afforded by a reversed telescope — both would be condemned for having been extreme in these two different respects.

Lee had spent the battle hours at his command post on Seminary Ridge, midway of that portion of the line occupied by Hill's two divisions, and though this gave him a clear view of most of the fighting in the valley below and on the ridge across the way, he had made no attempt to control or even influence the action once the opening attack had been launched on the far right. An observer who was with him recorded that he sent only one message and received only one all afternoon, despite what another witness described as "an expression of painful anxiety" on his face as the assault rolled north toward its breakdown — just at the point where he stood, between Anderson and Pender, with Mahone's brigade taking it easy in the woods directly behind the command post — then shifted across to Culp's Hill and moved back toward him through the gathering dusk, only to stall again when it got to Rodes. Both breakdowns were particularly untimely, since in each case they had occurred at the moment when the echeloned build-up of pressure resulted at last in a penetration of the enemy defenses, hard by the point that had been scheduled to be struck next. If there was bitter mockery in these two near-successes, which had had to be abandoned for lack of support, there was also much encouragement in the over-all results of the five-hour contest. All that had been lacking, Lee perceived and later reported, was "proper concert of action." Substantial lodgments had been effected and maintained by Hood and Johnson, on the far right and far left; Meade was clamped as in a vise. Moreover, high ground along the Emmitsburg Road had been taken by McLaws in the vicinity of the Peach Orchard, which afforded good positions for the massing of artillery to support an attack on the enemy center or left center. It was just at that point, shortly before sundown and directly opposite the command post, that Lee had focused his binoculars to watch Wright's Georgians storm Cemetery Ridge, driving off the defending infantry and cannoneers, and then stand poised on the crest for a long moment, as if balanced on a knife blade, before they had to fall back for want of support. What had almost been achieved today could be achieved tomorrow, Lee believed, with "proper concert of action" and artillery support.

Basically, what he intended was a continuation of the tactics employed today. Longstreet and Ewell would strike simultaneously on the right and left, driving for the Taneytown Road and the Baltimore Pike, just in rear of their primary objectives, while Hill stood by to assist either or both in exploiting whatever opportunities proceeded from the exertion of this double pressure on an enemy Lee presumed was badly shaken by the headlong routs and heavy losses of the past two days. Not that there was no room for doubt or occasion for hesitation. There was indeed. If the fighting today had shown nothing else, it certainly had shown that this was a difficult undertaking. However, the situation was not without its compensations and attractions from the Confederate point of view. In at least one sense, the very strength of the close-knit Federal position worked to the disadvantage of the men who occupied it, and this was that any collapse at all was likely to be total and disastrous. Lee could never forget the breakthrough Hood and Law had scored a year ago at Gaines Mill, where they had launched a frontal assault on Turkey Hill under conditions not unlike those the army faced at Gettysburg. What he hoped for, in short, was a repetition of that exploit tomorrow: by Pickett.

That general had marched his three Virginia brigades to within three miles of the field by 6 o'clock, an hour and a half before sunset; but when he notified Lee of his arrival and asked if he was to press on and join the battle he could hear raging toward its climax just ahead, Lee had sent him instructions to go into bivouac where he was, apparently wanting the men to be fully rested for the work he already had in mind for them tomorrow. These 5000 soldiers would come a good deal short of making up for the nearly 9000 who had fallen here today, not to mention the nearly 8000 who had fallen or been captured the day before, but there were others to be taken into account in comparing the force of the blow he planned to strike with the one he had struck already, which had failed. In addition to Pickett, whose newly arrived division would supply the extra power Lee believed would insure an initial breakthrough, two of Hill's divisions and one of Ewell's had taken little or no part in the fighting today, and the same could be said of two of Anderson's brigades, two of Early's, and one of Johnson's. Longstreet alone had put in all the men he had on hand. In point of fact, only 16 of the army's 37 infantry brigades had been seriously engaged today, which left 21 presumably well rested for tomorrow. Moreover, Stuart's three veteran brigades of cavalry would also be available — two had arrived by sundown and the third was expected before sunrise — to harry the retreat of whatever remnant of the blue army survived the collapse that would attend the rapid exploitation of Pickett's breakthrough.... Such then were the factors that contributed to Lee's decision to renew the attack next morning. All this seemed not only possible but persuasive to a man who had determined to stake everything on one blow and whose confidence in his troops — "They will go anywhere and do anything, if properly led" — had been strengthened by the sight of what they had accomplished, rather than weakened by the thought of what they had failed to accomplish because of a lack of "concert" on the part of their commanders. Just as yesterday's successes had led to a continuation of the offensive today, so did today's successes — such as they were — lead to a continuation of the offensive tomorrow. And both were a part of what would be meant, in the years ahead, when it came to be said of Lee that the stars had fought against him in Pennsylvania.

By midnight, when he retired to his tent to get some sleep, his plans had been developed in considerable detail. A message had gone to Ewell, instructing him to open the action on the left at daybreak, and another to Hill, directing him to detach two brigades from Rodes to reinforce Johnson on Culp's Hill for that purpose, while Pendleton had been told to advance the artillery, under cover of darkness, into positions from which to support the attack on the left and right and center. No orders reached Longstreet, however; nor was Pickett alerted for the night march he would have to make if he was to have any share in the daybreak assault. Perhaps this was an oversight, or perhaps Lee had decided by then to attack at a later hour and thus give his troops more rest, though if so he neglected to inform Ewell of the change. In any event, none of the three corps commanders visited headquarters that evening to discuss their assignments for tomorrow; Lee neither summoned them nor rode out to see them, and though he sent instructions to Ewell and Hill, he did not get in touch with Longstreet at all, apparently being satisfied that the man he called his old warhorse would know what was expected of him without being told.

Across the way, on Cemetery Ridge, the northern leader was taking no such chances. An hour before Lee retired for the night, Meade assembled his corps commanders for a council of war in the headquarters cottage beside the Taneytown Road. He sent for them not only because he wanted to make sure they understood their duties for tomorrow, but also because he wanted to confer with them as to what those duties should be. Moreover, he wanted their help in solving a dilemma in which he had placed himself earlier that evening, the unguarded victim of his own enthusiasm. Elated by Warren's success in holding Little Round Top, as well as by Hancock's subsequent ejection of the rebels who pierced his center near sundown, he had gotten off an exultant message to Halleck. "The enemy attacked me about 4 p.m. this day," he wrote, "and, after one of the severest contests of the war, was repulsed at all points." This last was untrue and he knew it, though he might contend that, strictly speaking, neither the Devil's Den nor the Peach Orchard was an integral part of his fishhook system of defense. In any case, he closed the dispatch with a flat assurance: "I shall remain in my present position tomorrow, but am not prepared to say, until better advised of the condition of the army, whether my operations will be of an offensive or defensive character."

The courier had scarcely left with the message — it was headed 8 p.m. — when Johnson's attack exploded on the right. His troops swarmed into and along the trenches Slocum had vacated half an hour before, and while their advance was being challenged by Wadsworth and

Greene, Early struck hard at Cemetery Hill, driving Howard's panicky Dutchmen from the intrenchments on the summit. Thanks to Hancock, the nearer of these two dangers was repulsed, at least for the time, but the graybacks maintained the lodgment they had effected at the far end of the line. To Meade, this meant that his position — already penetrated twice today, however briefly, first left, then right of center — was gravely menaced at both extremities: from the Devil's Den, hard against Little Round Top, and on Culp's Hill itself. The inherent possibilities were unnerving. Though he ordered Slocum to return to the far right with all his troops and prepare to oust the rebels at first light, Meade now began to regret the flat assurance he had given Halleck that he would not budge from where he was. He foresaw disaster, and not without cause. Five days in command, he already had suffered about as many casualties as the bungling Hooker had lost in five whole months, and it appeared fairly certain that he was going to suffer a good many more tomorrow. In fact, considering what Lee must have learned today from his exploratory probes of the Union fishhook, it was by no means improbable that he had plans for breaking it entirely. And if that happened, the chances were strong that the Army of the Potomac would be abolished right here in its new commander's own home state. The more he thought about it, the more it seemed to Meade that the best way to avoid that catastrophe would be to pull out before morning and retire to the Pipe Creek line, which had seemed to him much superior in the first place. By now, moreover, his chief of staff had completed the formal orders for withdrawal; they could be issued without delay. As for his untimely assurance to Washington — "I shall remain in my present position tomorrow" — it occurred to him that a negative vote on the matter by his corps commanders would release him from his promise. Accordingly, he sent word for them to come to headquarters at once for a council of war.

All seven came, and more. Pleasanton was off on cavalry business — he later testified that he had been ordered to prepare for covering the withdrawal — but since Hancock and Slocum had brought Gibbon and Williams along, nine generals were present in addition to Meade and two staff advisers, Butterfield and Warren. A dozen men made quite a crowd in the little parlor, which measured barely ten feet by twelve and whose furnishings included a deal table in the center, with a cedar water bucket, a tin cup, and a pair of lighted candles on it, a somewhat rickety bed in one corner, and five or six chairs. These last were soon filled, as was the bed, which served as a couch, leaving three or four of the late arrivers, or their juniors, with nothing to sit on but the floor. A witness remarked afterwards that, for all their rank, those in attendance were "as modest and unpretentious as their surroundings" and "as calm, as mild-mannered, and as free from flurry or excitement as a board of commissioners met to discuss a street improvement." By

11 o'clock all were there. Meade opened the council by announcing that he intended to follow whatever line of action was favored by a majority of those present. Then he submitted three questions for a formal vote: "1. Under existing circumstances, is it advisable for this army to remain in its present position, or to retire to another nearer its base of supplies? 2. It being determined to remain in present position, shall the army attack or wait the attack of the enemy? 3. If we wait attack, how long?" As was the custom in such matters, the junior officer voted first, the senior last. From Gibbon through Slocum, with Butterfield keeping tally, all nine agreed that the army should neither retreat nor attack. Only on the third question was there any difference of opinion, and this varied from Slocum's "Stay and fight it out" to Hancock's "Can't wait long," which perhaps was some measure of how much fighting each had done already. At any rate, Meade had his answer. His lieutenants having declined to take him off the hook, the assurance he had given Halleck remained in effect. "Well, gentlemen," he said when all the votes were in, "the question is settled. We will remain here."

By now it was midnight. On the far side of the valley, Lee had retired, and on this side the Union council of war was breaking up. As the generals were departing to rejoin their commands, along and behind the three-mile curve of line, Meade stopped Gibbon, whose troops were posted on the nearby crest of Cemetery Ridge, due west of the headquarters cottage. "If Lee attacks tomorrow, it will be in your front," he told him. Gibbon asked why he thought so. "Because he has made attacks on both our flanks and failed," Meade said, "and if he concludes to try it again it will be on our center." Nearly a quarter-century later Gibbon recalled his reaction to this warning that it was his portion of the fishhook line that Lee would strike at: "I expressed the hope that he would, and told General Meade, with confidence, that if he did we would defeat him."

※ 4 ※

July 3; Lee rose by starlight, as he had done the previous morning, with equally fervent hopes of bringing this bloodiest of all his battles to a victorious conclusion before sunset. Two months ago today, Chancellorsville had thundered to its climax, fulfilling just such hopes against longer odds, and one month ago today, hard on the heels of a top-to-bottom reorganization occasioned by the death of Stonewall Jackson, the Army of Northern Virginia had begun its movement from the Rappahannock, northward to where an even greater triumph had seemed to be within its reach throughout the past forty-odd hours of savage fighting. Today would settle the outcome, he believed, not only of the battle — that went without saying; flesh and blood, bone and sinew and nerve could only stand so much — but also, perhaps, of the war; which, after all, was why he had come up here to Pennsylvania in the first place. He woke to a stillness so profound that one of Gibbon's officers, rolled in his blankets near a small clump of trees on Cemetery Ridge, two thirds of the way up the shank of the Union fishhook, heard the courthouse clock a mile away in Gettysburg strike three. Lee emerged from his tent soon afterwards, fully dressed for the fight, and shared a frugal breakfast with his staff. Three miles northwest, Pickett's men were stirring, too, in a grove of oaks where they had made camp beside the Chambersburg Pike at sundown. Well rested though still a little stiff from yesterday's long march, which had ended not in battle, as they had expected, but in bivouac, they were the shock troops Lee would employ today in an ultimate attempt to achieve the breakthrough he had been trying for all along. It was for this reason, this purpose, that he had withheld them from the carnage they might otherwise have arrived in time to share the day before.

With sunrise only an hour away, however, it was obvious that he had abandoned his plan for a dawn attack. A good two hours would be required for Pickett to move his three brigades from their present bivouac area and mass them in a jump-off position well down Seminary Ridge. For them to have any share in an attack at dawn, they had to have been in motion at least an hour ago, and Lee not only had not sent Pickett or his corps commander any word of his intentions; he did not even do so now. Perhaps, on second thought, he had reasoned that more deliberate preparations were required for so desperate an effort, including another daylight look at the objective, which the enemy might have reinforced or otherwise rendered impregnable overnight. Besides, the assault would necessarily be a one-shot endeavor; late was as good as early, and maybe better, since it not only would permit a more careful study of all the problems, but also would lessen the time allowed the Federals for mounting and launching a counterattack in event of a Confederate repulse. Or perhaps it was even simpler than that. Perhaps Lee merely wanted time for one more talk with the man he called his warhorse, whose three divisions he had decided to use in the assault. At any rate, it was Longstreet he set out to find as soon as he mounted Traveller in the predawn darkness and rode eastward up the reverse slope of Seminary Ridge, delaying only long enough to send a courier to Ewell with word that the proposed attack, though still designed as a simultaneous effort on the right and the far left, would be delayed until 10 o'clock or later.

From the crest of the ridge, as he gazed southeast to where the first pale streaks of dawn had just begun to glimmer, he was greeted by a sudden eruption of noise that seemed to have its source in the masked valley beyond Cemetery Hill. It was gunfire, unmistakably, a cannonade mounting quickly to a sustained crescendo; but whose? In the absence of reports, Lee could not tell, but he knew at once that one of two regrettable things had happened. Either his message had failed to reach Ewell in time, in which case his plan for the synchronization of the two attacks had gone awry, or else Meade had gotten the jump on him in that direction, leaving Ewell no choice whatsoever in the matter of when to fight.

In point of fact, it was something of both. The courier had not yet reached Second Corps headquarters (indeed, he had not had time to) and Meade *had* seized the initiative. Slocum, returning to the Federal right with both of his divisions before midnight, had massed them along the Baltimore Pike for the purpose of driving the Confederates from the lower end of Culp's Hill, where they had effected a lodgment soon after his sundown departure. At 3.45, accordingly, he opened with four batteries he had posted along the northern slope of Powers Hill, blasting away at the rebels crouched in the trenches his own men had dug the day before. For fifteen minutes he kept up the fire, taking care that the guns did not overshoot and drop their shells on Greene's troops just beyond, then paused briefly to survey the damage as best he could in the dim light. Apparently unsatisfied, he resumed the cannonade, joined now by a battery firing southeast from Cemetery Hill, and continued it for the better part of an hour, after which he intended to launch an infantry assault.

This time, though, it was the Confederates who got the jump on their opponents in this struggle for possession of the barb of the Union fishhook. Unable to bring artillery over Rock Creek and the rough ground he had crossed to gain the position he now held, Johnson had his men lie low among the rocks and in the trenches while the shells burst all around them. Then, as soon as the hour-long bombardment ended, he sent them surging forward, determined to gain control of the Baltimore Pike in accordance with last night's orders from Lee and Ewell. In this he was unsuccessful, though he gave it everything he had, including the added strength of the two brigades from Rodes, under Brigadier General Junius Daniel and Colonel Edward O'Neal. Slocum's troops refused to yield, and now that the graybacks were out of their holes the guns resumed their firing on the left and on the right, their targets clearly defined for them against the risen sun. Presently word arrived from Ewell that Lee had ordered a postponement of the attack here on the left so that it might be co-ordinated with Longstreet's on the right, which had been delayed; but Old Clubby, fighting less by now in hope of gain than for survival — to attempt even to disengage would be to invite destruction — no longer had any say-so in the matter. Unrelentingly severe, the contest degenerated into a series of brief advances and sudden repulses, first by one side, then the other. For better than five hours this continued, Slocum being reinforced by a brigade from Sedgwick's corps and Johnson adding Smith's brigade of

Early's division to his ranks, but neither could gain a decided advantage over the other, except in the weight of metal thrown. The unopposed Federal guns made the real difference, and they were what told in the end. By 10.30 the Confederates had been driven off Culp's Hill, approximately back to the line at its eastern base along Rock Creek, from which they had launched their attack the day before. Slocum, having recovered his lost trenches, was content to hold them, and Johnson was obliged to forgo any attempt to retake them. All he could do today he had done already, for the casualties in his seven brigades had been heavy and the survivors were fought to a frazzle. Whatever Longstreet was going to accomplish, around on the far side of the fishhook, would have to be accomplished on his own.

Lee had already taken this into account, however, and he had not seen in it any cause for cancellation of his plans. Ewell's share in them had been secondary anyhow, a diversionary effort designed to mislead his opponent into withholding reinforcements from that portion of the Federal line assigned to Longstreet for a breakthrough, with consequent disruption of the whole. If Meade had taken the offensive against Ewell, Lee's purpose might be served even better in that regard, since this would require the northern commander to employ more troops at the far end of his position than if he had remained on the defensive there. A more serious question was whether he could be prevented from turning the tables on the Confederates by scoring a breakthrough of his own, but Lee was no more inclined to worry about the possibility of such a mishap here at Gettysburg than Jackson had been at Fredericksburg, when he remarked of the soldiers now under fire on Culp's Hill, "My men have sometimes failed to take a position, but to defend one, never!" Lee might have said the same thing now, and he also might have added on Ewell's behalf, as Jackson had done on his own, "I am glad the Yankees are coming." At any rate, after pausing on the crest of Seminary Ridge to listen to the cannonade a mile across the way, he turned Traveller's head southward, noting with pleasure by the spreading light of dawn that Meade did not seem to have strengthened his center overnight, and continued his ride in search of Longstreet.

He found him shortly after sunrise, three miles down the line, in a field just west of Round Top. The burly Georgian had emerged at last from the gloom into which his heavy losses, following hard upon the rejection of his counsel, had plunged him the previous evening. Moreover, his first words showed the reason for this recovery of his spirits. "General," he greeted Lee, "I have had my scouts out all night, and I find that you still have an excellent opportunity to move around to the right of Meade's army and maneuver him into attacking us." Apparently he believed that yesterday's experience must have proved to the southern commander the folly of attempting to storm a position of great natural strength, occupied by a numerically superior foe who had demonstrated forcefully his ability to maintain it against the most violent attempts at dislodgment. But Lee was as quick to set Old Peter straight today as he had been the day before, and he did so with nearly the same words. "The enemy is there," he said, pointing northeast as he spoke, "and I am going to strike him." Longstreet's spirits took a sudden drop. He knew from Lee's tone and manner that his mind was quite made up, that no argument could persuade him not to continue the struggle on this same field. Accordingly, after giving instructions canceling the intended shift around the south end of the Federal line, Old Peter turned again to his chief to receive his orders for the continuation of the battle he did not want to fight, at least not here.

These orders only served to deepen his gloom still further. What Lee proposed was that Longstreet strike north of the Round Tops with his whole corps, now that Pickett was at hand, in an attempt to break the Union line on Cemetery Ridge. Essentially, this was what Old Peter had tried and failed to do the day before, after protesting to no avail, and he did not believe that his chances for success had been improved by the repulse already suffered, especially in view of the fact that all three of the attacking divisions had been fresh and up to full strength when they were committed yesterday, whereas two of the three Lee intended to employ today were near exhaustion and had lost no less than a third of their men by way of demonstrating that the attempt had been unwise in the first place. In opposing the selection of troops for the assault, Longstreet pointed out that to withdraw his two committed divisions from the vicinity of the Devil's Den and the Wheat Field would be to expose the right flank of the attacking column to assault by the bluecoats now being held in check in that direction. Lee thought this over briefly, then agreed. McLaws and Law would hold their ground; Pickett would be supported instead by two of Hill's divisions, and the point of attack would be shifted northward, from the left center to the right center of the enemy ridge, though this would afford the attackers less cover and a greater distance to march before they came to grips with the defenders on the far side of the nearly mile-wide valley.

Longstreet did some rapid calculations. Pickett had just under 5000 men, his division being the smallest in the army, and the chances were that Hill's would be no larger, if as large, after his losses of the past two days. That gave a rough total of 15,000 or less, and Longstreet did not believe this would be enough to do the job Lee had in mind. Perhaps he had reproached himself the night before for not having made a firmer protest yesterday against what he had believed to be an unwise assignment. If so, he made sure now, at the risk of being considered insubordinate, that he would have no occasion for self-reproach on that account tonight. "General," he told Lee in a last face-to-face endeavor to dissuade him from extending what he believed was an invitation to disaster, "I have been a soldier all my life. I have been with soldiers engaged in fights by couples, by squads, companies, regiments, divisions, and armies, and should know as well as anyone what soldiers can do. It is my opinion that no 15,000 men ever arrayed for battle can take that position."

Lee's reply to this was an order for Pickett to be summoned. He was to post his three brigades behind Seminary Ridge, just south of the army command post near the center of the line, and there await the signal to attack. Two of Anderson's brigades, those of Lang and Wilcox, already posted in the woods adjoining Pickett's assembly area, would be on call for his support if needed. On his left, north of the command post and also under cover of the ridge, Heth's four brigades — under Pettigrew, for Heth was still too jangled to resume command — would be massed for the same purpose, supported in turn by two brigades from Pender, who was also incapacitated. Longstreet was to be in over-all command of the attack, despite his impassioned protest that it was bound to fail, and would give the signal that would launch it, though only three of the eleven brigades involved were from his corps. The plan itself, as Lee explained it to his lieutenant while they rode northward for an inspection of the terrain and the units selected to cross it, had at least the virtue of simplicity. The objective was clearly defined against the skyline: a little clump of umbrella-shaped trees, four fifths of a mile away on Cemetery Ridge, just opposite the Confederate command post. Pickett and Pettigrew, each with two brigades in support, would align on each other as they emerged from cover and advanced, guiding on the distinctive landmark directly across the shallow valley from the point where their interior flanks would come together. By way of softening up the objective, the assault would be preceded by a brief but furious bombardment from more than 140 guns of various calibers: 80 from the First Corps, disposed along a mile-long arc extending from the Peach Orchard to the command post back on Seminary Ridge, and 63 from the Third Corps, strung out north of the command post, along the east slope of the ridge. This would be the greatest concentration of artillery ever assembled for a single purpose on the continent, and Lee appeared to have no doubt that it would pave the way for the infantry by pulverizing or driving off the batteries posted in support of the Union center.

Longstreet displayed considerably less confidence than did his chief as they rode north along the line McLaws had fallen back to in the darkness, after charging eastward across the wheat field and part way up the western slope of Cemetery Ridge. "Never was I so depressed as upon that day," Old Peter declared years later. Presently they came to Wofford, who proudly reported to Lee that his brigade had nearly reached the crest of the ridge the day before, just north of Little Round Top, in pursuit of the troops Dan Sickles had exposed. But when the army commander inquired if he could not go there again, the Georgian's jubilation left him.

"No, General, I think not," he said.

"Why not?" Lee asked, and Wofford replied:

"Because, General, the enemy have had all night to intrench and reinforce. I had been pursuing a broken enemy, and the situation now is very different."

Longstreet looked at Lee to see what effect this might have on him, but apparently it had none at all. The two men continued their ride northward, all the way to the sunken lane where Rodes's three remaining brigades were posted on the outskirts of Gettysburg, and then back south again. Twice they rode the full length of the critical front, and all this time Lee refused to be distracted by the clatter of Ewell's desperate back-and-forth struggle across the way, smoke from which kept boiling out of the hidden valley in rear of Lee's prime objective on Cemetery Ridge. He was leaving as little as possible to chance, including the posting of individual batteries for the preliminary bombardment.

Only once, in the three hours required for this careful examination of the ground over which the attack would pass, did he admit the possibility that it might not be successful, and this was when A. P. Hill, who joined him and Longstreet in the course of the reconnaissance, suggested that instead of using only eight of his thirteen brigades, as instructed, he be allowed to send his whole corps forward. Lee would not agree. "What remains of your corps will be my only reserve," he said, "and it will be needed if General Longstreet's attack should fail."

By now it was 9 o'clock; Pickett's three brigades of fifteen veteran regiments — 4600 men in all, and every one a Virginian, from the division commander down — were filing into position behind Seminary Ridge, there to await the signal which Longstreet, who would give it, believed would summon them to slaughter. Pickett himself took no such view of the matter. He saw it, rather, as his first real chance for distinction in this war, and he welcomed it accordingly, his hunger in that regard being as great as that of any man on the field, on either side. This was not only because he had missed the first two days of battle, marking time at Chambersburg, then eating road dust on the long march toward the rumble of guns beyond the horizon, but also because it had begun to appear to him, less than two years short of forty and therefore approaching what must have seemed the down slope of life, that he was in danger of missing the whole war. That came hard; for he had already had one taste of glory, sixteen years ago in Mexico, and he had found it sweet.

After a worse than undistinguished record at West Point — the class of 1846 had had fifty-nine members, including George McClellan and T. J. Jackson, and Pickett had ranked fifty-ninth — he went to war, within a year of graduation, and was the first American to scale the ramparts at Chapultepec, an exploit noted in official reports as well as in all the papers. Twelve years later he made news again, this time by defying a British squadron off San Juan Island in Puget Sound; "We'll make a Bunker Hill of it," he told his scant command; for which he was commended by his government and applauded by the press. Then came secession, and Pickett resigned his commission and headed home from Oregon. Arriving too late for First Manassas, he was wounded in the shoulder at Gaines Mill, just too early for a part in the charge that carried the day. That was a year ago this week, and he had seen no large-scale fighting since, not having returned to duty till after Second Manassas and Sharpsburg. At Fredericksburg his division had been posted in reserve, with scarcely a glimpse of the action and no share at all in the glory; after which, by way of capping the anticlimax, as it were, the Suffolk excursion had caused him to miss Chancellorsville entirely. But now there was Gettysburg, albeit the contest was two thirds over before he reached the field, and when he was offered this opportunity to deliver what Lee had designed as the climactic blow of the greatest battle of them all, he perceived at last what fate had kept in store for him through all these tantalizing months of blank denial. He grasped it eagerly, not only for his own sake, but also for the sake of the girl he called "the charming Sally," his letters to whom were always signed "Your Soldier."

So eager was he, indeed, that an English observer who saw him for the first time here today, just after Pickett learned of his assignment, described him as a "desperate-looking character." But the fact was he might have given that impression almost anywhere, on or off the field of battle, if only because of his clothes and his coiffure. Jaunty on a sleek black horse, he wore a small blue cap, buff gauntlets, and matching blue cuffs on the sleeves of his well-tailored uniform. Mounted or afoot, he carried an elegant riding crop. His boots were brightly polished and his gold spurs glinted sunlight, rivaling the sparkle of the double row of fire-gilt buttons on his breast. Of middle height, slender, graceful of carriage — "dapper and alert," a more familiar witness termed him, while another spoke of his "marvelous pulchritude" — he sported a curly chin-beard and a mustache that drooped beyond the corners of his mouth and then turned upward at the ends. To add to the swashbuckling effect, his dark-brown hair hung shoulder-length in ringlets which he anointed with perfume. There were those who alleged that he owed his rapid advancement to his friendship with the corps commander, which dated back to the peacetime army, rather than to any native ability, which in fact he had had little chance to prove. "Taking Longstreet's orders in emergencies," the corps adjutant would recall, "I could always see how he looked after Pickett, and made us give him things very fully; indeed, sometimes stay with him to make sure he did not go astray."

His three brigadiers were all his seniors in years, and one had been his senior in rank as well, until Pickett's October promotion to major general. James L. Kemper, the youngest, was just past his fortieth birthday. A former Piedmont lawyer and politician, twice elected speaker of the House of Delegates, he was the only nonprofessional soldier of the lot, and though he retained a fondness for high-flown oratory — "Judging by manner and conversation alone," an associate observed, "he would have been classed as a Bombastes Furioso" — his combat record was a good one, as was that of his troops, whose three previous commanders now commanded the three corps of the army. Kemper had been with the brigade from the outset, first at the head of a regiment, and had fought in all its battles, from First Manassas on. He and his men shared another proud distinction, dating back to what Southerners liked to refer to as the "earlier" Revolution; one of the five regiments was a descendant of George Washington's first command, and Kemper's grandfather had served as a colonel on the future President's staff. By contrast, though he too was of a distinguished Old Dominion family — one that had given the Confederacy the first of its seventy-seven general officers who would die of wounds received in action — Richard B. Garnett was a comparative newcomer to the division and had never led his present brigade in a large-scale battle. Forty-five years old, strikingly handsome, a West Pointer and a regular army man, he had advanced rapidly in the early months of the war and had succeeded Jackson as commander of the Stonewall Brigade. Then at Kernstown, where he ordered a withdrawal to avoid annihilation, had come tragedy; Jackson removed him from his post and put him in arrest for retreating without permission. Garnett promptly demanded a court-martial, convinced that it would clear him of the charge, but the case dragged on for months, interrupted by battle after battle — all of which he missed — until Lee took a hand in the matter, immediately after Sharpsburg, and transferred him to Longstreet's corps to take command of Pickett's brigade when that general, whom he had previously outranked, was promoted to command of the division. Neither Fredericksburg nor Suffolk brought Garnett the opportunity by which he hoped to clear his record of the Kernstown stain, and now in Pennsylvania he was not only limping painfully from an injury lately suffered when he was kicked in the knee by a horse; he was also sick with chills and fever. Medically speaking, he should have been in bed, not in the field, but he was determined to refute — with blood, if need be — the accusations Jackson had leveled against his reputation. The third and oldest of the three brigadiers, forty-six-year-old Lewis Armistead, was also something of a romantic figure, though less by circumstance than by inclination. A widower, twice brevetted for gallantry in Mexico, he was a great admirer of the ladies and enjoyed posing as a swain. This had earned him the nickname "Lo," an abbreviation of Lothario, which was scarcely in keeping with his close-cropped, grizzled beard or receding hairline. He had, however, a sentimental turn of mind and fond memories of life in the old army. For example, he and Hancock, who was waiting for him now across the way though neither knew it, had been friends. "Hancock, goodbye," he had said in parting, two years ago on the West Coast as he prepared to cross the continent with Albert Sidney Johnston; "you can never know what this has cost me." As he spoke he put both hands on his friend's shoulders, and tears stood in his eyes. Now he and Dick Garnett stood together on the crest of Seminary Ridge, looking out across the gently rolling valley toward the little clump of umbrella-shaped trees which had been pointed out to them as their objective, a mile away on Cemetery Ridge. Both men were experienced soldiers, and both knew at a glance the ordeal they and their brigades would be exposed to when the signal came for them to advance. Finally Garnett broke the silence. "This is a desperate thing to attempt," he said. Armistead agreed. "It is," he replied. "But the issue is with the Almighty, and we must leave it in His hands."

Completing what was described as "a shady, quiet march" of about five miles, southeast along the turnpike, then due south through the woods along the far bank of a stream called Pitzer's Run, Pickett's men were unaware of what awaited them beyond the screening ridge; or as one among the marchers later put it, "No gloomy forebodings hovered over our ranks." Not since Sharpsburg, nearly ten months ago, had the troops in these fifteen regiments been involved in heavy fighting, and this encouraged them to believe — quite erroneously, but after the custom of young men everywhere — that they were going to live forever. Near the confluence of Pitzer's and Willoughby Runs, they were halted and permitted to break formation for a rest in the shade of the trees. The sun had burned the early morning clouds away, and though the lack of breeze gave promise of a sultry afternoon, the impression here in this unscarred valley behind Seminary Ridge was of an ideal summer day, no different from any other except in its perfection. "Never was sky or earth more serene, more harmonious, more aglow with light and life," one among the loungers afterwards wrote. Presently they were called back into ranks, told to leave their extra gear in the care of a single guard from each regiment, and marched eastward over the crest of the ridge, then down its opposite slope and into a wooded swale a couple of hundred yards beyond, where they were halted. Here too they were shielded from hostile observers by the low bulge of earth extending northward from the Peach Orchard, along which they could see the corps artillery disposed in a slow curve from the right, the cannoneers silhouetted against the skyline directly in their front. Two brigades of infantry were up there, too, under Wilcox, but Pickett's orders were for his own troops to take it easy here in the swale, doing nothing that might attract the enemy's attention. Soon after they were in position, Lee arrived and began to ride along the lines of reclining men. Mindful of their instructions not to give away their presence, they refrained from cheering; but as the general drew abreast of each company, riding slowly, gravely past, the men rose and took off their hats in silent salute. Lee returned it in the same manner, the sunlight in his gray hair making a glory about his head.

If he seemed graver than usual this morning, he had cause. He had just come from making a similar inspection of the troops disposed northward along the densely wooded eastern slope of Seminary Ridge, where they too were waiting under cover for the signal to move out, and he had noticed that a good number of them wore bandages about their heads and limbs. "Many of these poor boys should go to the rear; they are not able for duty," he remarked. Drawing rein before one hard-hit unit, he looked more closely and realized, apparently for the first time, how few of its officers had survived the earlier fighting. "I miss in this brigade the faces of many dear friends," he said quietly. Riding away, he looked back once and muttered to himself, as if to fend off such tactical doubts as were provoked by personal sorrow: "The attack must succeed."

His choice of the half-dozen brigades that made up the left wing of the assault force — Heth's four, plus two from Pender — was doubly logical, in that all the troops so chosen were handy to the jump-off position and had not been engaged the day before, which not only lessened the chance of disclosing his intention to the enemy by their preliminary movements, but also was presumed to mean that they were fresh, or at any rate well rested, for the long advance across the valley and the subsequent task of driving the bluecoats off the ridge on the far side. What had not been taken into account, however — at least not until Lee saw for himself the thinned ranks and the bandaged wounds of the survivors — was the additional and highly pertinent fact that five of the six had suffered cruelly in the first day's fighting. Both division commanders were out of action, and only two of the six brigades were still under the leaders who had brought them onto the field. The one exception on both counts was Lane's brigade, which had not been heavily engaged and still had its original commander; but this was offset by the misfortune of the other brigade from Pender's division, which had lost its leader, Brigadier General Alfred Scales, together with all but two of its officers above the rank of captain and more than half of those of that rank or below. This was the unit Lee had paused in front of this morning to remark that he missed "the faces of many dear friends," and it was led now by Colonel William Lowrance, who never before had commanded anything larger than a regiment. Moreover, because Lee did not consider Lane experienced enough to succeed the wounded Pender, he had summoned old Isaac Trimble over from Ewell and put him in charge of the two brigades, though he too had never served in such a capacity before, despite his recent promotion to major general, and had

had no previous acquaintance, on or off the field of battle, with the troops he was about to lead across the valley in support of the four brigades under Pettigrew.

These last made up the first wave of the attack, here on the left, and they too had been more severely mauled in the earlier fighting than the army commander or his staff took into account. "They were terribly mistaken about Heth's division in the planning," Lee's chief aide declared afterwards. "It had not recovered, having suffered more than was reported on the first day." In point of fact, whether the planners knew it or not, the division had lost no less than forty percent of its officers and men. Ordinarily, this would have ruled out its employment as a fighting force, particularly on the offensive, until it had been reorganized and brought back up to strength; but in this case it had been selected to play a major role in the delivery of an attack designed as the climax of the army's bloodiest battle. Whether the choice proceeded from ignorance, indifference, or desperation (there was evidence of all three; Longstreet, while admitting his own profound depression, later said flatly that Lee had been "excited and off his balance") some measure of the condition of the division should have been perceived from the fact that only one of the original four commanders remained at the head of his brigade, and this was the inexperienced Davis, whose troops had lost so heavily when he led them into an ambush on the opening day. The captured Archer had been replaced by Colonel B. D. Fry, Colonel John M. Brockenbrough by Colonel Joseph Mayo, and Pettigrew by Colonel J. K. Marshall. All three were thus as new to command of their brigades as Pettigrew was to command of the division, which in turn had not been organized till after Chancellorsville and had gone into its first fight as a unit less than fifty hours ago. It had in all, after the cooks, the extra-duty men, and the lightly wounded were given rifles and brought forward into its ranks, about the same number of troops as Pickett had; that is, about 4600. Trimble had 1750 in the second line. If Wilcox and Lang added their 1400 to the assault, this Pickett-Pettigrew-Trimble total of just under 11,000 would be increased to roughly 12,500 effectives, a figure well below the 15,000 which the man in over-all command of the attack had already said would not be enough to afford him even the possibility of success.

In addition to Armistead and Garnett, who agreed that the maneuver was "a desperate thing to attempt," a good many other high-ranking officers had had a look at the ground in front by now, and their impressions were much the same. To a staff major, on a midmorning visit to the command post near the center, the long approach to the Union position across the shallow valley — more than half a mile out to the Emmitsburg Road, past a blue skirmish line "almost as heavy as a single line of battle," then another quarter-mile up the gradual slope of Cemetery Ridge, where the main enemy line was supported from the crest above by guns that could take the attackers under fire throughout most of their advance — resembled "a passage to the valley of death." Impressions mainly agreed, but reactions varied. For example, an artillerist observed that Pickett was "entirely sanguine of success in the charge, and was only congratulating himself on the opportunity," whereas Pettigrew seemed more determined than elated. Tomorrow would be his thirty-fifth birthday, and though his intellectual accomplishments were perhaps the highest of any man on the field — a scholar in Greek and Hebrew, fluent as well in most of the modern languages of Europe, he had made the best grades ever recorded at the University of North Carolina, where he had also excelled in fencing, boxing, and the single stick, then had traveled on the continent and written a book on what he had seen before returning to settle down to a brilliant legal career, only to have it interrupted by the war and the experience of being left for dead on the field of Seven Pines — he now was devoting his abilities to the fulfillment of his military duties. Slender and lithe of figure, with a neatly barbered beard, a spike mustache, and a dark complexion denoting his Gallic ancestry, Pettigrew was quite as eager as Pickett for distinction, but his eagerness was tempered by a sounder appreciation of the difficulties, since he had fought on this same field two days ago, against this newest version of the Army of the Potomac. Perhaps he recalled today what he had written after a visit to Solferino: "The invention of the Minié ball and the rifled cannon would, it was thought, abolish cavalry and reduce infantry charges within a small compass." On the other hand, if he was remembering his comments on that battle, fought four years ago in Italy, he might have drawn encouragement from the fact that in it the French had crushed the Austrian center, much as Lee intended to crush the Union center here today, with a frontal assault delivered hard on the heels of an intense bombardment.

The men themselves, though few of them had the chance to examine the terrain over which they would be advancing, knew only too well what lay before them; Lee and Longstreet had directed that they be told, and they had been, in considerable detail. "No disguises were used," one wrote afterwards, "nor was there any underrating of the difficult work at hand." They were told of the opportunities, as well as of the dangers, and it was stressed that the breaking of the Federal line might mean the end of the war. However, there were conflicting reports of their reaction. One declared that the men of Garnett's brigade "were in splendid spirits and confident of sweeping everything before them," while another recalled that when Mayo's troops, who were also Virginians, were informed of their share in the coming attack, "from being unusually merry and hilarious they on a sudden had become as still and thoughtful as Quakers at a love feast." Some managed to steal a look at the ground ahead, and like their officers they were sobered by what they saw. One such, a Tennessee sergeant from Fry's brigade, walked forward to the edge of the woods, looked across the wide open valley at the bluecoats standing toylike in the distance on their ridge, and was so startled by the realization of what was about to be required of him that he spoke aloud, asking himself the question: "June Kimble, are you going to do your duty?" The answer, too, was audible. "I'll do it, so help me God," he told himself. He felt better then. The dread passed from him, he said later. When he returned to his company, friends asked him how it looked out there, and Kimble replied: "Boys, if we have to go it will be hot for us, and we will have to do our best."

All this time, the waiting soldiers had been hearing the clatter of Ewell's fight beyond the ridge. By 10.30 it had diminished to a sputter and withdrawn eastward, indicating only too plainly how he had fared; Lee knew unmistakably, before any such admission reached him from the left, that what he had designed as a two-pronged effort had been reduced, by Ewell's failure, to a single thrust which the enemy would be able to oppose with a similar concentration of attention and reserves. However, he did not cancel or revise his plans in midcareer. That was not his way. Like Winfield Scott, on whose staff he had served in Mexico, he believed it "would do more harm than good," once the selected units were in position, for him to attempt to interfere. "It would be a bad thing if I could not rely on my brigade and division commanders," he told a Prussian observer three days later. "I plan and work with all my might to bring the troops to the right place at the right time. With that, I have done my duty." The same rule applied to a brisk skirmish that broke out, at 11 o'clock, around a house and barn on the floor of the valley, half a mile east-northeast of the command post and about midway between the lines. Confederate sharpshooters posted in the loft of the barn had been dropping Federal officers on the opposing ridge all morning, and finally two blue regiments moved out and drove the snipers back; whereupon Hill's guns opened thunderously with a half-hour bombardment. This in turn made the house and barn untenable for the new occupants, who set them afire and withdrew to their own lines, having solved the problem they had been sent to deal with. Lee watched from the command post and made no protest, either at the expenditure of ammunition, which was considerable, or at the resultant disclosure of the battery positions, which up to now the crews had been so careful to conceal. "I strive to make my plans as good as human skill allows," he told the Prussian inquirer, in further explanation of the hands-off policy he practiced here today, "but on the day of battle I lay the fate of my army in the hands of God."

By now it was noon, and a great stillness came down over the field and over the two armies on their ridges. Between them, the burning house and barn loosed a long plume of smoke that stood upright in the hot and windless air. From time to time some itchy-fingered picket would fire a shot, distinct as a single handclap, but for the most part the silence was profound. For the 11,000 Confederates maintaining their mile-wide formation along the wooded slope and in the swale, the heat was oppressive. They sweated and waited, knowing that they were about to be launched on a desperate undertaking from which many of them would not be coming back, and since it had to be, they were of one accord in wanting to get it over with as soon as possible. "It is said, that to the condemned, in going to execution, the moments fly," a member of Pickett's staff wrote some years later, recalling the strain of the long wait. "To the good soldier, about to go into action, I am sure the moments linger. Let us not dare say, that with him, either individually or collectively, it is that 'mythical love of fighting,' poetical but fabulous; but rather, that it is nervous anxiety to solve the great issue as speedily as possible, without stopping to count the cost. The Macbeth principle — *'Twere well it were done quickly* — holds quite as good in heroic action as in crime."

Colonel E. P. Alexander, a twenty-eight-year-old Georgian and West Pointer, had been up all night and hard at work all morning, supervising the movement into position of the 80 guns of the First Corps. By noon the job had been completed; the batteries were disposed along their mile-long arc, southward from the command post to the Peach Orchard and beyond, and the colonel, having taken time to breakfast on a crust of cornbread and a cup of sweet-potato coffee, was awaiting notification to fire the prearranged two-gun signal that would open the 140-gun bombardment. Young as he was, he had been given vital assignments from the outset of the war and had fought in all the army's major battles, first as Beauregard's signal officer, then as Johnston's chief of ordnance, and later as commander of an artillery battalion under Longstreet. Serving in these various capacities, he had contributed largely to the curtain-raising victory at Manassas, as well as to the subsequent effectiveness of Confederate firepower, and since his transfer from staff to line he had been winning a reputation as perhaps the best artillerist in Lee's army, despite the flashier performances of men like Latimer and Pelham. His had been the guns that defended Marye's Heights at Fredericksburg and accompanied Jackson on the flank march at Chancellorsville. However, his most challenging assignment came today from Longstreet, who instructed him to prepare and conduct the First Corps' share of the bombardment preceding the infantry attack. When the objective was shifted northward along Cemetery Ridge, after the early morning conference between Lee and Longstreet, Alexander rearranged his dispositions "as inoffensively as possible," seeking to hide his intentions from enemy lookouts on the heights, and took care to keep his crews from "getting into bunches." He listened with disapproval as Hill's 60-odd guns began their premature cannonade, northward along Seminary Ridge, and would not allow his own to join the action, lest they give away the positions he had taken such pains to conceal. As the uproar subsided and was followed by the silence that came over the field at noon, he received an even greater shock from his own corps commander, who informed him that he would be required to make the decision, not only as to when the infantry attack was to begin, but also as to whether it was to be launched at all. "If the artillery fire does not have the effect to drive off the enemy or greatly demoralize him, so as to make our effort pretty certain," Longstreet wrote in a message delivered by an aide, "I would prefer that you should not advise Pickett to make the charge. I shall rely a great deal upon your judgment to determine the matter and shall expect you to let General Pickett know when the moment offers."

Alexander experienced a violent reaction to this sudden descent of command responsibility. "Until that moment, though I fully recognized the strength of the enemy's position," he recalled years later, "I had not doubted that we would carry it, in my confidence that Lee was ordering it. But here was a proposition that *I* should decide the question. Overwhelming reasons against the assault at once seemed to stare me in the face." He replied at some length, declining the heavy burden Old Peter appeared to be attempting to unload. "General," he protested, "I will only be able to judge of the effect of our fire on the enemy by his return fire, for his infantry is but little exposed to view and the smoke will obscure the whole field. If, as I infer from your note, there is any alternative to this attack, it should be carefully considered before opening our fire, for it will take all the artillery ammunition we have left to test this one thoroughly, and if the result is unfavorable, we will have none left for another effort. And even if this is entirely successful it can only be so at a very bloody cost." Longstreet's answer was not long in coming. Having failed to persuade the colonel to join him in resubmitting his protest that the charge was bound to fail — which was what he had been suggesting between the lines of his rather turgid note — he merely rephrased the essential portion of what he had said before. "Colonel," he wrote, "The intention is to advance the infantry if the artillery has the desired effect of driving the enemy's off, or having other effect such as to warrant us in making the attack. When that moment arrives advise General P., and of course advance such artillery as you can use in aiding the attack."

This left one small loophole — "*if* the artillery has the desired effect" — and Alexander saw it. No cannonade had ever driven Union batteries from a prepared position, and he certainly had no confidence that this one would accomplish that result. But before he replied this second time he decided to confer with two men of higher authority than his own. The first was his fellow Georgian A. R. Wright, who had stormed the enemy ridge the day before, achieving at least a temporary penetration, and could therefore testify as to the difficulty involved.

"What do you think of it?" Alexander asked him. "Is it as hard to get there as it looks?" Wright spoke frankly. "The trouble is not in going there," he said. "I was there with my brigade yesterday. There is a place where you can get breath and re-form. The trouble is to stay there after you get there, for the whole Yankee army is there in a bunch." Alexander took this to mean that the attack would succeed if it was heavily supported, and he assumed that Lee had seen to that. Thus reassured, he went to see how Pickett was reacting to the assignment. He not only found him calm and confident, but also gathered that the ringleted Virginian "thought himself in luck to have the chance." So the colonel returned to his post, just north of the Peach Orchard, and got off a reply to Old Peter's second message. "When our fire is at its best," he wrote briefly, even curtly, "I will advise General Pickett to advance."

Word came soon afterwards from Longstreet: "Let the batteries open. Order great care and precision in firing."

By prearrangement, the two-gun signal was given by a battery near the center. According to a Gettysburg civilian, a professor of mathematics and an inveterate taker of notes, the first shot broke the stillness at exactly 1.07, following which there was an unpropitious pause, occasioned by a misfire. Nettled, the battery officer signaled the third of his four pieces and the second shot rang out. "As suddenly as an organ strikes up in church," Alexander would recall, "the grand roar followed from all the guns."

★ ★ ★

The firing was by salvos, for deliberate precision, and as the two-mile curve of metal came alive in response to the long-awaited signal, the individual pieces bucking and fuming in rapid sequence from right to left, a Federal cannoneer across the valley was "reminded of the 'powder snakes' we boys used to touch off on the Fourth of July." To a man, the lounging bluecoats, whose only concern up to then had been their hunger and the heat, both of which were oppressive, knew what the uproar meant as soon as it began. "Down! Down!" they shouted, diving for whatever cover they could find on the rocky forward slope of Cemetery Ridge. By now the rebel fire was general, though still by salvos within the four-gun units, and to Hunt, who was up on Little Round Top at the time, the sight was "indescribably grand. All their batteries were soon covered with smoke, through which the flames were incessant, whilst the air seemed filled with shells, whose sharp explosions, with the hurtling of their fragments, formed a running accompaniment to the deep roar of the guns." That was how it looked and sounded to a coldly professional eye and ear, sited well above the conflict, so to speak. But to Gibbon, down on the ridge where the shots were landing, the bombardment was "the most infernal pandemonium it has ever been my fortune to look upon." One of his soldiers, caught like him in the sudden deluge of fire and whining splinters, put it simpler. "The air was all murderous iron," he declared years later, apparently still somewhat surprised at finding that he had survived it.

In point of fact, despite the gaudiness of what might be called the fireworks aspect of the thing, casualties were few among the infantry. For the most part they had stone walls to crouch behind; moreover, they were disposed well down the slope, and this, as it turned out, afforded them the best protection of all. At first the fire was highly accurate, but as it continued, both the ridge and the batteries at opposite ends of the trajectory were blanketed in smoke, so that the rebel gunners were firing blind, just as Alexander had foretold. As the trails dug in, the tubes gained elevation and the shellbursts crept uphill, until finally almost all of the projectiles were either landing on the crest, where most of the close-support artillery was posted, or grazing it to explode in the rearward valley. "Quartermaster hunters," the crouching front-line soldiers called these last, deriving much satisfaction from the thought that what was meant for them was making havoc among the normally easy-living men of the rear echelon.

Havoc was by no means too strong a word, especially in reference to what was occurring around and in army headquarters. The small white cottage Meade had commandeered, immediately in rear of that portion of the ridge on which the rebels had been told to mass their hottest fire, became untenable in short order. Its steps were carried away by a direct hit at the outset, along with the supports of the porch, which then collapsed. Inside the house, a solid shot crashed through a door and barely missed the commanding general himself, while another plowed through the roof and garret, filling the lower rooms with flying splinters. Meade and his staff retired to the yard, where sixteen of their horses lay horribly mangled, still tethered to a fence; then moved into a nearby barn, where Butterfield was nicked by a shell fragment; and finally transferred in a body all the way to Powers Hill, where Slocum had set up the night before. Here at last they found a measure of the safety they had been seeking, but they were about as effectively removed from what was happening back on Cemetery Ridge, or was about to happen, as if they had taken refuge on one of the mountains of the moon.

Meanwhile, other rear-area elements had been catching it nearly as hard. Down and across both the Taneytown Road and the Baltimore Pike, fugitives of all kinds — clerks and orderlies, ambulance drivers and mess personnel, supernumeraries and just plain skulkers — were streaming east and south to escape the holocaust, adding greatly to the panic in their haste and disregard for order. Nor were such noncombatants the only ones involved in the confusion and the bloodshed. Returning to its post on the left, the VI Corps brigade that had been lent to Slocum that morning to assist in the retaking of Culp's Hill — he had not had to use it, after all — was caught on the road and lost 23 killed and wounded before it cleared the zone of fire. More important still, tactically speaking, the parked guns of the reserve artillery and the wagons of the ammunition train, drawn up in assumed safety on the lee side of the ridge, came under heavy bombardment, losing men and horses and caissons in the fury of the shellbursts, and had to be shifted half a mile southward, away from the point where they would be needed later. All in all, though it was more or less clear already that the gray artillerists were going to fail in their attempt to drive the blue defenders from the ridge, they had accomplished much with their faulty gunnery, including the disruption of army headquarters, the wounding of the chief of staff, and the displacement of the artillery reserve, not to mention a good deal of incidental slaughter among the rearward fugitives who had not intended to take any part in the fighting anyhow. Unwittingly, and in fact through carelessness and error, the Confederates had invented the box barrage of World War One, still fifty-odd years in the future, whereby a chosen sector of the enemy line was isolated for attack.

Awaiting that attack, crouched beneath what seemed a low, impenetrable dome of screaming metal overarching the forward slope of their isolated thousand yards of ridge, were three depleted divisions under Hancock, six brigades containing some 5700 infantry effectives, or roughly half the number about to be sent against them. This disparity of forces, occupying or aimed at the intended point of contact, was largely the fault of Meade, whose over-all numerical superiority was offset by the fact that his anticipations did not include the threat which this small segment of his army was about to be exposed to. Despite his midnight prediction to Gibbon that today's main rebel effort would be made against "your front," he not only had sent him no reinforcements; he had not even taken the precaution of seeing that any were made immediately available by posting them in proximity to that portion of the line. Daylight had brought a change of mind, a change of fears. He no longer considered that the point of danger, partly because his artillery enjoyed an unobstructed field of fire from there, but mostly because he recollected that his opponent was not partial to attacks against the center. As the morning wore on and Ewell failed to make headway on the right, Meade began to be convinced that Lee was planning to assault his left, and he kept his largely unused reserve, the big VI Corps, massed in the direction of the Round Tops. At 12.20, when Slocum sent word that he had "gained a decided advantage on my front, and hope to be able to spare one or two brigades to help you on some other part of the line," the northern commander was gratified by the evidence of staunchness, but he took no advantage of the offer. Then presently, under the distractive fury of the Confederate bombardment, which drove him in rapid, headlong sequence from house to yard, from yard to barn, and then from barn to hilltop, he apparently forgot it. Whatever defense of that critical thousand yards of ridge was going to be made would have to be made by the men who occupied it.

They amounted in all to 26 regiments, including two advanced as skirmishers, and their line ran half a mile due south from Ziegler's Grove, where Cemetery Hill fell off and Cemetery Ridge began. Gibbon held the center with three brigades, flanked on the left and right by Doubleday and Hays, respectively with one and two brigades; Gibbon had just over and Hays just under 2000 infantry apiece, while Doubleday had about 1700. For most of the long waiting time preceding the full-scale Confederate bombardment, these 5700 defenders had been hearing the Slocum-Johnson struggle for Culp's Hill, barely a mile away. At first it made them edgy, occurring as it did almost directly in their rear, but as it gradually receded and diminished they gained confidence. Finally it sputtered to a stop and was succeeded by a lull, which in turn was interrupted by the brief but lively skirmish for possession of the house and barn down on the floor of the western valley. The half-hour rebel cannonade that followed accomplished nothing, one way or the other, except perhaps as a bellow of protest at the outcome of the fight. By contrast, hard on the heels of this, the midday silence was profound. "At noon it became as still as the Sabbath day," a blue observer later wrote. He and his fellows scarcely knew what to make of this abrupt cessation, in which even the querulous skirmishers held their fire. "It was a queer sight to see men look at each other without speaking," another would recall; "the change was so great men seemed to go on tiptoe not knowing how to act." This lasted a full hour, during which they tried to improvise shelter from the rays of the sun and sought relief from the pangs of hunger. There was precious little of either shade or food, there on the naked ridge, but shortly after 1 o'clock, when the curtain of silence was suddenly ripped to tatters by the roar of what seemed to be all the guns in the world, they forgot the discomforts of heat and hunger, acute as these had been, and concentrated instead on a scramble for cover behind the low stone walls. However, as the pattern of shellbursts moved up the slope and stayed there — except for an occasional round, that is, that tumbled and fell short — they found that, once they grew accustomed to the whoosh and flutter of metal just overhead, the bombardment was not nearly so bad as it seemed. "All we had to do was flatten out a little thinner," one of the earth-hugging soldiers afterwards explained, "and our empty stomachs did not prevent that."

Despite the feeling of security that came from lying low, it seemed to another crouching there "that nothing four feet from the ground could live." Presently, however, he and his companions all along that blasted thousand yards of front were given unmistakable proof that such was not the case, at least so far as one man was concerned. As the bombardment thundered toward crescendo, they were startled to see Hancock, mounted on a fine black horse and trailed by most of his staff, riding the full length of his line amid the hiss and thud of plunging shells and solids. He rode slowly, a mounted orderly beside him displaying the swallow-tailed corps guidon. Resisting the impulse to weave or bob when he felt the breath of near misses on his face, the general only stopped once in the course of his excursion, and that was when his horse, with less concern for show than for survival, became unmanageable and forced him to take over the more tractable mount of an aide, who perhaps was not unhappy at the exchange since it permitted him to retire from the procession. Hancock resumed his ride at the same deliberate pace, combining a ramrod stiffness of backbone with that otherwise easy grace of manner expected of top-ranking officers under fire — a highly improbable mixture of contempt and disregard, for and of the rebel attempt to snuff out the one life he had — whereby the men under him, as one of them rather floridly explained, "found courage to endure the pelting of the pitiless gale." Intent on giving an exemplary performance, he would no more be deterred by friendly counsel than he would swerve to avoid the enemy shells that whooshed around him. When a brigadier ventured a protest: "General, the corps commander ought not to risk his life that way," Hancock replied curtly: "There are times when a corp commander's life does not count," and continued his ride along the line of admiring soldiers, who cheered him lustily from behind their low stone walls, but were careful, all the same, to remain in prone or kneeling positions while they did so.

Another high-ranking Federal was riding better than three times that length of line at the same time, but he did so less by way of staging a general show, as Hancock was doing to bolster the spirits of the men along his portion of the front, than by way of assuring conformity with Army Regulations. "In the attack," these regulations stated, "the artillery is employed to silence the batteries that protect the [enemy] position. In the defense, it is better to direct its fire on the advancing troops." It was the second of these two statements that here applied, and no one knew this better than Henry Hunt, who had been an artillery instructor at West Point and had spent the past two years in practical application, on the field of battle, of the theories he had expounded in the classroom. On Cemetery Hill, on Little Round Top, and along the ridge that ran between them, he had twenty batteries in position, just over one hundred guns that could be brought to bear on the shallow western valley and the ridge at its far rim. Just now there were no "advancing troops" for the long line of Union metal "to direct its fire on," but Hunt was convinced there soon would be, and his first concern — after observing, from his lofty perch at the south end of the line, the "indescribably grand" beginning of the Confederate bombardment — was that his cannoneers not burn up too much of their long-range ammunition in counterbattery fire, lest they run short before the rebel infantry made its appearance. Accordingly, after instructing Lieutenant B. F. Rittenhouse to keep up a deliberate fire with his six-gun battery on Little Round Top, Hunt rode down onto the lower end of Cemetery Ridge and ordered Lieutenant Colonel Freeman McGilvery, commanding seven batteries of 37 guns from the artillery reserve, to refrain from taking up the enemy challenge until the proper time. The same instructions went to Captain John G. Hazard, commanding the six II Corps batteries whose 29 guns were posted north of there, above and below the little umbrella-shaped clump of trees. On Cemetery Hill, completing the two-mile ride from Little Round Top, Hunt repeated what he had told Rittenhouse at the outset; Major T. W. Osborn was to keep up a deliberate counterbattery fire with the 29 guns of his six XI Corps batteries. By this arrangement, one third of the 101 guns were to do what they could to disconcert the rebel gunners by maintaining a crossfire from the high-sited extremities of the Federal position, while the remaining two thirds kept silent along the comparatively low-lying ridge that ran between them. However, it did not work out that way entirely. Completing his slow ride along his thousand-yard portion of the front, Hancock observed that his cannoneers were idle (if idle was quite the word for men who were hugging the earth amid a deluge of shells) and promptly countermanded Hunt's instructions. He did so, he explained afterwards, because he believed that his infantry needed the deep-voiced encouragement of the guns posted in close support on the crest of the ridge directly in their rear. Whatever comfort the blue foot soldiers derived from the roar and rumble in response to the fire of the rebel guns down in the valley, Hunt watched with disapproval as the half-dozen II Corps batteries came alive, but there was nothing he could do about it, since the corps commander had every right to do as he thought best with his own guns, no matter what any and all staff specialists might advise.

All this time the Confederates kept firing, exploding caissons, dismounting guns, and maiming so many cannoneers — particularly in those batteries adjacent to the little clump of trees — that replacements had to be furnished from nearby infantry outfits, supposedly on a volunteer basis, but actually by a hard-handed form of conscription. "Volunteers are wanted to man the battery," a Massachusetts captain told his company. "Every man is to go of his own free will and accord. Come out here, John Dougherty, McGivern, and you Corrigan, and work those guns." For a solid hour the bombardment did not slacken, and when another half hour was added to this, still with no abatement, McGilvery ordered his seven batteries to open fire at last, convinced that by now the rebels must be getting low on ammunition and would have to launch their infantry attack, if they were going to launch it at all, before his own supply ran low. That was about 2.30; all the surviving

Union guns were in action, bucking and roaring along the whole two miles of line. From down in the valley, Alexander peered through the billowing smoke and it seemed to him that both enemy heights and the connecting ridge were "blazing like a volcano." On Cemetery Hill, where he availed himself of the excellent observation post established by the XI Corps chief of artillery, Hunt watched with gratification this tangible proof that, for all its prolonged fury, the rebel cannonade had failed to drive his gun crews from their pieces or the guns themselves from their assigned positions. It occurred to him, however, that in the light of this evidence, as plain from below as from above, the Confederates might not attempt their infantry assault at all, and he considered this regrettable. Standing beside him, Osborn suddenly asked: "Does Meade consider an attack of the enemy desirable?" When Hunt replied that the army commander had expressed a fervent hope that the rebels would try just that, "and he had no fear of the result," the major added: "If this is so, why not let them out while we are all in good condition? I would cease fire at once, and the enemy could reach but one conclusion, that of our being driven from the hill."

Hunt thought this over briefly, then agreed. Moreover, while the batteries on the hill fell silent one by one, he rode down onto Cemetery Ridge to increase the effectiveness of the ruse by passing the word along to the remaining two thirds of his guns. At closer range, however, he found the II Corps batteries so badly mauled by the rebel cannonade and so low on ammunition that he decided they might as well use up what few long-range rounds were still on hand. For example, Lieutenant Alonzo Cushing's battery, posted just north of the clump of trees, had only three of its six guns still in working order and only two of these in action, casualties having reduced the number of cannoneers to barely enough for two slim crews; Cushing himself, a twenty-two-year-old West Pointer from Wisconsin, had twice been hit by fragments of exploding shells, one of which had struck him in the crotch and groin. Despite the pain, he refused to leave the field or relinquish his command, and Hunt let him stay, together with his handful of survivors. A Rhode Island battery just south of the clump was in even worse shape, its ammunition practically exhausted, all of its officers dead or wounded, and barely enough men left to serve the three remaining guns; Hunt took a quick look at the wreckage and gave the survivors permission to withdraw, which they did in a rather helter-skelter fashion, being leaderless, but took their three guns with them. Riding on south, Hunt passed the cease-firing order along to McGilvery, down near the far end of the ridge, and finally to Rittenhouse, whose six guns had been firing all the while from Little Round Top. When the weary and badly cut-up batteries of the II Corps had gotten off their few remaining rounds, thus adding to the effectiveness of the pretense by giving the impression that the guns were being knocked out group by group, spasmodically, the whole Union line fell silent under the continuing rain of rebel projectiles.

That was about 2.45, and it soon became apparent that the ruse had worked, at least in part. Within another five or ten minutes, the Confederates also stopped firing, and what Osborn later referred to as "a singularly depressing silence" settled over the field. Whether the ruse had worked entirely would not be known until the enemy infantry started forward across the valley, but the Federal cannoneers were taking no chances that it had failed. The cooling tubes were swabbed to remove the gritty residue of powder and thus prepare them for the rapid-fire work that lay ahead, while in those batteries that had used up all their long-range ammunition, the pieces were carefully loaded with canister. Forty-four-year-old Alex Hays, a Pennsylvanian like his corps and army commanders, was certain that the rebs would soon be coming through the screening smoke. "Now, boys, look out; you will see some fun!" he called to the men of his two brigades, posted north of the clump of trees. In confirmation of his prediction, shortly after 3 o'clock, Warren wigwagged a message from the Little Round Top signal station, which afforded a clear view beyond the hump of earth that Sickles had claimed and lost the day before: "They are moving out to attack." Presently, all along the bend and shank of the Union fishhook, the waiting troops could see for themselves, through or below the rifting, lifting smoke, that what Warren had signaled was true. "Here they come!" men exclaimed as they caught sight of the long gray lines moving toward them across the shallow basin inclosed by the two ridges.

Reactions to this confrontation varied. "Thank God! Here comes the infantry!" one exuberant bluecoat cried. Though it was obvious at a glance that the attackers, moving steadily forward under their red and blue flags, outnumbered the defenders by no less than two to one, he and others like him looked forward to the slaughter, anticipating a Fredericksburg in reverse. A New Yorker, on the other hand, remembering the sight two days later, wrote in a home letter: "Beautiful, gloriously beautiful, did that vast array appear in the lovely little valley." Then he and his fellows — first the cannoneers, who took up their work with a will, and then the foot soldiers, no less eager — settled down to the task of transforming those well-dressed long gray lines into something far from beautiful.

There they came. And for them, advancing eastward over the gently undulating floor of the shallow valley, the relief of tension was as great as it was for the men awaiting their arrival on the ridge just under a mile across the way. In fact, if a comparison of losses was any measure of the strain, it was probably greater. The Federal infantry had suffered a good deal less from the bombardment than the Federal artillery had done, but for the Confederates, whose infantry was posted behind instead of in front of their fuming line of metal, it was the other way around. Both sides were overshooting, with the unequal result that the eastbound "overs" spared the bluecoats on the forward slope of their ridge, whereas a high proportion of their long shots landed squarely in the ranks of the gray soldiers drawn up to await the order to advance. Fewer than 200 of the former were hit, while the latter suffered approximately twice that number of casualties in the course of the nearly two-hour-long exchange. "Such a tornado of projectiles it has seldom been the fortune or misfortune of anyone to see," one of Pickett's veterans declared. It seemed to go on forever, he recalled, under a high hard hot blue sky that soon became "lurid with flame and murky with smoke," until presently the sun was in a red eclipse, "shadowing the earth as with a funeral pall," though this gave little relief from the heat, which was even more oppressive here in the swale than it was for the blue soldiers on the high ground in the distance. "Many a poor fellow thought his time had come," another grayback wrote. "Great big, stout-hearted men prayed — loudly, too." Stretcherbearers were kept on the run, answering the sudden, high-pitched yells of the wounded up and down the sweaty, mile-long formation. One of Kemper's men, attempting later to describe what he had been through, finally gave it up and contented himself with a four-word description of his ordeal by fire: "It was simply awful." Even so, not all the accustomed butternut risibility was suppressed. Near one badly pounded company, when a rabbit suddenly broke from a clump of bushes and went bounding for the rear: "Run, old hare," a man called after him. "If I was a old hare, I'd run too."

Officers of rank, commanders of the nine brigades and three divisions, kept moving among the waiting troops, seeking to encourage them by example, much as Hancock was doing at the same time across the way. However, the response was somewhat different on this side of the valley. When Longstreet rode along the front of Pickett's division and a round shot plowed the ground immediately under his horse's nose, the general kept the startled animal under control, "as quiet as an old farmer riding over his plantation on a Sunday morning, and looked neither to the right or left." Thus an admiring captain described the scene; but the men themselves, apparently resentful of the implication that they needed steadying, had a different reaction. "You'll get your old fool head knocked off!" one of them called out to him, while others shouted angrily: "We'll fight without you leading us!" Similarly, in Armistead's brigade, where the troops had been instructed to remain prone throughout the bombardment, there was resentment that their commander felt it necessary to move erect among them with encouraging remarks and a showy disregard for the projectiles whooshing past him. One soldier rose in protest, and when Armistead ordered him to lie back down, pointed out that he was only following his general's example. Armistead, however — like Hancock on the ridge across the valley — had a ready answer. "Yes, but never mind me," he said. "We want men with guns in their hands."

Out front, on the low bulge of earth crowned by the peach orchard Barksdale's men had seized the day before, Alexander had been watching all this time for evidence that the cannonade was accomplishing its mission, which was to wreck the enemy batteries or drive them from the ridge that was the infantry's objective. So far, although an hour had elapsed since his guns first opened, the young colonel had seen little that encouraged him to believe that he was going to succeed in his assignment. Volcano-like, the enemy ridge and its two flanking heights not only continued to return the fire directed at them, but presently that return fire grew more furious than ever, despite an occasional burst of flame and the sudden resultant erection of a pillar of smoke whose base marked the former location of a caisson. Earlier, Wright and Pickett had persuaded him that all Lee intended would be accomplished in short order. After more than an hour of steady firing, however, Alexander's doubts returned in strength. Moreover, the pressure of command responsibility grew heavier by the minute, until at last, as he wrote later, "It seemed madness to order a column in the middle of a hot July day to undertake an advance of three fourths of a mile over open ground against the center of that line." What was worse, another half hour reduced the ammunition supply to the point where the attack would have to be launched without delay if it was to have artillery support. Shortly after 2.30, with the counterbattery fire approaching crescendo, Alexander dispatched a courier with a note informing Pickett of the situation. "If you are to come at all, you must come at once," he told him, "or we will not be able to support you as we ought. But the enemy's fire has not slackened materially and there are still 18 guns firing from the cemetery." This last had reference to the little clump of trees, which the colonel had been told was a cemetery, and though he was mistaken in this, his estimate as to the number of guns still active in that vicinity was accurate enough. And presently, as he kept peering through the smoke to catch the slightest encouraging reaction by the blue gunners in the distance, he observed with gratification that the Federals had ceased firing on the hill to the left, and soon afterwards he spotted a rearward displacement by some guns near the critical center. It was the battered Rhode Islanders, whom Hunt had given permission to withdraw their three surviving pieces, but in his elation — for the enemy fire continued to slacken all along the ridge and on both adjoining heights — Alexander persuaded himself that the withdrawal had been considerably more substantial than it was in fact. In other words, the blue ruse had worked far better than its authors would have any way of knowing until they saw the long gray lines of infantry advancing. He got off a second note to Pickett, hard on the heels of the first: "For God's sake come quick. The 18 guns have gone. Come quick or my ammunition will not let me support you properly."

Pickett by then had already acted on the first of the two dispatches. Glad to receive anything that might end the strain of waiting, he mounted his horse and rode at once to Longstreet, whom he found sitting on a snake rail fence out front, observing the bombardment. Dismounting, he handed him the note. Old Peter read it deliberately, but said nothing. "General, shall I advance?" Pickett asked eagerly. Longstreet, who later explained: "My feelings had so overcome me that I could not speak, for fear of betraying my want of confidence," responded with a silent nod. That was enough for the jaunty long-haired Virginian. "I am going to move forward, sir," he said. Then he saluted, remounted, and rode back to join his men.

Front and center of his division, he delivered from horseback what one of his officers called "a brief, animated address" which only those soldiers nearest him could hear but which ended on a ringing note: "Up, men, and to your posts! Don't forget today that you are from old Virginia!" There was, however, no disconcerting haste as the troops were placed in attack formation. For the most part, they simply rose to their feet and began to dress their regimental lines while their colonels passed among them repeating the instructions received from above: "Advance slowly, with arms at will. No cheering, no firing, no breaking from common to quick step. Dress on the center." In at least one outfit, a survivor would recall, one of the captains led in the singing of a hymn and a white-haired chaplain offered prayer. Nor was the step-off itself unduly precipitate. Pettigrew gave the signal on the left to the new leader of his old brigade: "Now, Colonel, for the honor of the good Old North State, forward!" The advance was somewhat ragged at first, as if the Virginians, Mississippians, Alabamians, and Tennesseans of his division supposed that the spoken order only applied to the Carolinians, but the laggard brigades soon restored the alignment by double-timing to catch up. Meanwhile, in the wooded swale to the south, others had taken up the cry. Armistead, whose brigade comprised the supporting line on the right, as Trimble's two did on the left, did not neglect the opportunity afforded for another display of determination. "Sergeant, are you going to plant those colors on the enemy works today?" he asked a nearby colorbearer, and when the sergeant gave the staunch expected answer, "I will try, sir, and if mortal man can do it, it shall be done," the general removed his wide-brimmed black felt hat, placed it on the point of his sword, and raised it high for all to see, shouting in a voice that carried from flank to flank of his brigade: "Attention, 2d Battalion, the battalion of direction! Forward, guide centerrr, *march!*" and led the way. Beyond the left, within the lower limits of the town of Gettysburg, onlookers from Rodes's division, seeing Pettigrew's troops emerge from the woods and begin their downhill march into the valley, called out to the Federal surgeons who had remained behind to tend the captured wounded of their army: "There go the men who will go through your damned Yankee line for you!"

Longstreet had preceded them out to the line of guns and was conferring with Alexander. Pleased though he had been at seeing the enemy artillery first slack then cease its fire, he was anything but pleased when he saw his own guns follow suit immediately after he gave Pickett the nod that would send him forth to what he himself had predicted would be slaughter. But his greatest surprise was at Alexander's explanation that he had suspended firing in order to save ammunition, being doubtful whether enough remained on hand for proper support of the infantry on its way across the valley. Old Peter was plainly horrified, despite the colonel's earlier statement that the supply was limited. "Go and stop Pickett right where he is, and replenish your ammunition!" he exclaimed. Now it was Alexander's turn to be surprised. "We can't do that, sir," he protested. "The train has but little. It would take an hour to distribute it, and meanwhile the enemy would improve the time." Longstreet made no reply to this. For a long moment he stood there saying nothing. Then he spoke, slowly and with deep emotion. "I do not want to make this charge," he said; "I do not see how it can succeed. I would not make it now but that General Lee has ordered it and expects it."

With that he stopped, gripped by indecision and regret, though in point of fact he had been given no authority to halt the attack even if he had so chosen. The young artillerist volunteered nothing further. Just then, however, the issue was settled for once and all by the appearance of Garnett's and Kemper's brigades from the swale behind the guns. Garnett was mounted, having been granted special permission to ride because of his injured knee and feverish condition, and Alexander went back to meet him; they had been friends out on the plains in the old army. Apparently the Virginian was experiencing a chill just now, for he wore an old blue overcoat buttoned close to his throat despite the July heat. Alexander walked beside the horse until they reached the slope leading down to the Emmitsburg Road and the Union ridge beyond. There he stopped and watched his friend ride on. "Goodbye," he called across the widening gap, and he added, as if by afterthought: "Good luck."

★ ★ ★

By now — some twenty or thirty minutes after the Union guns stopped firing, and consequently about half that long since Alexander followed suit — much of the smoke had been diffused or had drifted off, so that for the attackers, many of whom had stepped at a stride from the dense shade of their wooded assembly areas into the brilliant sunlight that dappled the floor of the valley, the result was not only dazzling to their eyes but also added to their feeling of elation and release. "Before us lay bright fields and fair landscape," one among them would recall.

It was not until the effect of this began to wear off, coincidental with the contraction of their pupils, that they saw at last the enormity of what was being required of them, and by then, although the vista afforded absolute confirmation of their direst apprehensions, the pattern of exhilaration had been set. Under the double influence of secondary inertia and terrific deliberation, the long gray lines came on, three brigades to the south under Pickett and six to the north under Pettigrew and Trimble, with a quarter-mile gap between the interior flanks of the two formations, the former composed of fifteen and the latter of twenty-seven regiments, all with their colors flying at more or less regular intervals along the rows of nearly 11,000 striding men. Harvey Hill was to say of the individual Confederate, as he had observed him in offensive action: "Of shoulder-to-shoulder courage, spirit of drill and discipline, he knew nothing and cared less. Hence, on the battlefield, he was more of a free-lance than a machine. Whoever saw a Confederate line advancing that was not crooked as a ram's horn? Each ragged rebel yelling on his own hook and aligning on himself." But Hill, though he was to see about as much combat as any general on either side before the war was over, was not at Gettysburg. If he had been, he would have had to cite it as the exception. Forbidden to step up the cadence or fire their rifles or even give the high-pitched yell that served at once to steady their own nerves and jangle their opponents', the marchers concentrated instead on maintaining their alignment, as if this in itself might serve to awe the waiting bluecoats and frighten them into retreat. And in point of fact, according to one among the watchers on the ridge across the way — a colonel commanding a brigade adjacent to the little clump of trees — it did at least produce the lesser of these two reactions. For him, the advancing graybacks had "the appearance of being fearfully irresistible," while a foreign observer, whose point of vantage was on the near side of the valley, used the same adjective to communicate the impression the attackers made on him: "They seemed impelled by some irresistible force." Out front with the rebel skirmishers, a captain had a closer view of the troops as they strode down the slope toward where he crouched, and he remembered ever afterwards the "glittering forest of bayonets," the two half-mile-wide formations bearing down "in superb alignment," the "murmur and jingle" of trouser-legs and equipment, and the "rustle of thousands of feet amid the stubble," which stirred up dust and chaff beneath and before them "like the dash of spray at the prow of a vessel."

They came on at a steady rate of about one hundred yards a minute, and before they had been three minutes in the open — barely clear of the line of friendly guns, whose cannoneers raised their hats in salute and wished them luck as they passed through — the Union batteries, as if in quick recovery from the shock of seeing them appear thus, massed for slaughter, began to roar. The gray lines dribbled rag-doll shapes, each of which left a gap where it had been while still in motion. Flags plunged with sudden flutters in the windless air, only to be taken up at once as the fallen colorbearers were replaced. This happened especially often in the regiments on the flanks, which came under galling long-range fire delivered in enfilade from the two heights, Cemetery Hill on the left and Little Round Top on the right. Pettigrew's troops had farther to go, since they had begun their march from Seminary Ridge itself, but this had been foreseen and allowed for; Pickett had been charged with closing the quarter-mile interval between the two formations, which would lengthen the distance his three brigades would have to cover in the course of their advance. Accordingly, once they were clear of the line of guns, in plain view of the little clump of trees just over half a mile ahead, he gave his troops the order, "Left oblique!" They obeyed it neatly, executing in midstride a half-face to the north, which, at every full step of their own, brought them half a step closer to the flank of the undeviating marchers on their left. All this time, both groups were taking losses, a more or less steady leakage of killed and wounded, who lay motionless where they fell or turned and hobbled painfully up the slope they had descended. Coming presently to a slight dip, about midway of the valley — a swale not deep enough to hide them from the enemy gunners, but conveniently parallel to the ridge that was their objective — Pickett's men received their second order, which was to halt, close up the gaps their casualties had left, and dress the line. They did so, once more with the deliberate precision of the drill field, but with the difference that such gaps continued to appear at an even more alarming rate as the Union gunners, delighted with this sudden transformation of a moving into a stationary target, stepped up their rate of fire. The result was the first evidence of confusion in the Confederate ranks. A soldier would look toward the comrade on his right, feeling meanwhile with his extended hand for the shoulder of the comrade on his left, and there would be a constant sidling motion in the latter direction, as men continued to fall all down the line, leaving additional gaps that had to be closed. This might have gone on indefinitely, or at any rate until there were no survivors left to dress or dress on, but at last the order came for them to continue the advance, still on the oblique.

This they did, to the considerable relief of most of the bluecoats on the ridge ahead, whose reaction to the maneuver was one of outrage, as if they had been exposed to a blatant indecency, such as the thumbing of a nose, though for others the feeling of revulsion was tempered by awe and incredulity. "My God, they're dressing the line!" some among the waiting infantry exclaimed, more by way of protest than applause. In the course of the ten- or fifteen-minute lull allowed by the enemy guns before the attackers first appeared on the far side of the valley, the defenders had improved the time by repairing what little damage had been done to their improvised earthworks by the rebel cannonade. Now there was nothing left to do but wait, and in some ways that was the hardest thing of all. In fact, some among them found it downright impossible. Despite the renewed Confederate bombardment, they stood up behind their low stone walls or their meager scooped-up mounds of dirt and began to shoot at the graybacks half a mile away, only to have their officers tell them gruffly to hold their fire until the Johnnies came within decent range. Hays, who was jumpy enough himself, being of an excitable nature, found a way to pass the time for the men of his two brigades; he put them through a few stiff minutes of drill in the manual of arms, despite the overhead hiss and flutter of going and coming projectiles. Meanwhile the Union cannoneers kept busy, at any rate those who had husbanded their long-range ammunition for the opportunity now at hand, including the men in a six-gun battery that came up with full limbers just as the lull was ending and replaced the departed Rhode Islanders in the position directly south of the clump of trees. Rittenhouse and Osborn had the best of it in this respect, slamming their shells in at angles that caught the advancing lines almost end-on, but others were by no means idle. "We had a splendid chance at them," one of McGilvery's captains later testified, "and we made the most of it." Watching the effects of this — the gnawed flanks and the plunging flags, the constantly recurring gaps all up and down the long gray front — the bluecoats cheered, and from time to time a man would holler "Fredericksburg!" elated by the thought that he was seeing, or was about to see, a repetition of that fiasco, though with certain welcome differences. On that field, for example, only the last four hundred yards of the attack had been made in full view of the defenders behind their wall of stone and dirt, yet not a single one of the attackers had come within twenty yards of the objective. Here the critical distance was more than three times as great, and the waiting soldiers took much consolation in the fact that the respective roles of the two armies, as attackers and defenders, had been reversed. "Come on, Blue Belly!" the rebs had yelled, but now it was the other way around; now it was the Federals who were yelling, "Come on, Johnny! Keep on coming!" even though the Confederates were bringing no blankets or overcoats along and their worn-out shoes would not be worth stripping from their corpses.

On Pickett's right, Kemper's brigade was taking cruel punishment from the half-dozen guns on Little Round Top, whose gunners tracked their victims with the cool precision of marksmen in a monstrous shooting gallery, except that in this case the targets were displayed in depth, which greatly increased the likelihood of hits. Moreover, the slightest excess in elevation landed their shots in Garnett's ranks "with fearful effect," as one of his officers would report, "sometimes as many as ten men being killed [or] wounded by the bursting of a single shell." But worse by far was the predicament of the troops on Pettigrew's left. Here Mayo's brigade — Virginians too, but fewer by half in number; their heavy losses at Chancellorsville had never been made up, and they had been under a series of temporary commanders for nearly a year, with the result that their morale had been known to be shaky even before the bloody action two days ago had taken its further toll — caught the end-on fire, not of six but of 29 high-sited guns, with correspondingly greater suffering and disruption. As they tottered forward under the merciless pounding from the batteries on Cemetery Hill, these unfortunates had all they could do to maintain their alignment and keep their four flags flying. Whereupon, about two hundred yards short of the Emmitsburg Road, having passed the still-hot ashes of the house and barn set afire by the forenoon bombardment, they were struck on the flank by a regiment of Ohioans from the Union skirmish line, whose colonel massed and launched them in an assault as unexpected as it was bold. The reaction of the Virginians — it was they who "on a sudden had become as still and thoughtful as Quakers at a love feast" when they first learned that the attack was to be made and that they were to have a share in it — was immediate and decisive. Despite their four-to-one numerical advantage and their well-earned heritage of valor, they took off rearward at a run, flags and all, to the considerable dismay of the onlookers who had told the Federal surgeons, "There go the men who will go through your damned Yankee line for you," and did not stop until they regained the cover of Seminary Ridge. By quick subtraction, four of Pettigrew's regiments, nearly one fourth of the total in his division, thus were removed from his calculations as effectively as if they had stepped into bottomless quicksand. Osborn's gunners, observing the flight of the brigade which up to now had been their sole concern, cheered lustily and swung their muzzles without delay along a short arc to the left. Their first shell burst in the midst of Davis's brigade, killing five men in one of his Mississippi regiments.

Nothing quite like this abrupt defection had ever happened before, at least not in Lee's army, though the sight had been fairly common in the ranks of its opponents over the past two years, beginning at First Manassas and continuing through Second Winchester. Most Confederate witnesses reacted first with unbelief and then with consternation; but not Longstreet, who had steeled himself at the outset by expecting the very worst. Still seated on the snake rail fence at the far end of the field, he moved at once to counteract what he had seen through the shellbursts to the north, sending word for Anderson to commit his three remaining brigades — Wright's and Posey's and Mahone's; Lang and Wilcox had already been instructed to furnish such help for Pickett if it was needed — in support of the line thus weakened. No one could know whether the sudden collapse of this one brigade was indicative of what the others would do when the pressure intensified, but there was always the danger, even in quite sound units, that when a flank started to crumble, as this one had done, the reaction would continue all down the line. And in fact it did continue in one regiment under Davis, some of whose green troops took off rearward in the wake of the Virginians, but the other three held steady, taking in turn the end-on pounding from the batteries on the height as they kept up their steady progress across the valley. By now the interior flanks of Pettigrew and Pickett had come together on the near side of the fence-lined Emmitsburg Road, beyond which the blue skirmishers fired a volley or two before hurrying back to their own line, some four hundred yards up the slope behind them. The resultant crowding of Fry's and Garnett's brigades, which occurred before the latter received the order that brought its marchers off the oblique, presented a close-packed target the Union gunners did not neglect from point-blank range on the ridge ahead. "Don't crowd, boys!" a rebel captain shouted, his voice as lackadaisical amid the bursting shells as that of a dancing master. There was in fact a certain amount of formal politeness as the two brigades came together, Tennesseans on the one hand and Virginians on the other, under circumstances designed to favor havoc. Southern courtesy had never been more severely tried, yet such protest as was heard was mild in tone. It was here that the classic Confederate line was spoken: "Move on, cousins. You are drawing the fire our way."

Armistead was hard on Garnett's heels by now, and Kemper's men had drifted left, not only in an attempt to keep in touch with the latter's contracting line, but also in obedience to a natural inclination to flinch from the increasingly effective fire directed at their exposed flank from Little Round Top as well as from the south end of the Federal ridge, where McGilvery's seven batteries were massed. From close in rear of his advancing troops, Pickett saw his and Pettigrew's lead brigades, crowded into a blunted wedge perhaps five hundred yards in width, surge across the road and its two fences, taking severe losses from the opening blasts of canister loosed by guns that had been silent until now, and begin their climb up the slope toward the low stone wall behind which the blue infantry was crouched. He saw that his men were going to make it, a good part of them anyhow; but he saw, too — so heavy had their casualties been on the way across the valley, and so heavy were they going to be in storming the wall itself, which extended the length of the front and beyond — that unless the survivors were stoutly reinforced, and soon, they would not be able to hold what they were about to gain. Accordingly, he sent a courier to inform Longstreet of this close-up estimate of the situation. The courier, a staff captain, galloped fast to find Old Peter, but even so he took time to draw rein in an attempt to rally some stragglers he found trotting toward the rear. "What are you running for?" he demanded, glaring down at them.

One of the men looked up at him as if to say the question was a foolish waste of breath, though what he actually said was: "Why, good gracious, Captain, aint you running yourself?" Too flustered to attempt an answer, the courier gave his horse the spur and continued on his mission, feeling rather baffled by the encounter.

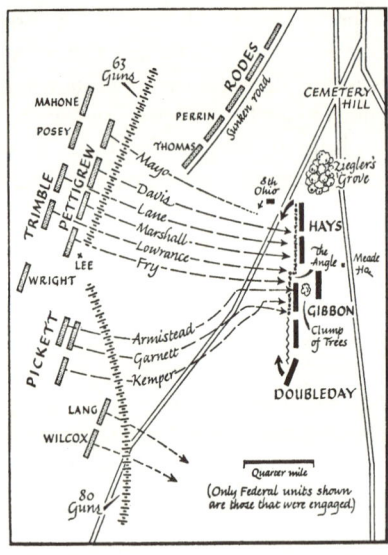

He found Old Peter still perched atop the snake rail fence, observing through his binoculars the action on the ridge. The general listened attentively to Pickett's message, but before he could reply a distinguished British visitor rode up: Lieutenant Colonel Arthur Fremantle, of Her Majesty's Coldstream Guards. Despite his high rank in a famous regiment, this was his first experience of battle. "General Longstreet," he said, breathless with excitement, "General Lee sent me here, and said you would place me in a position to see this magnificent charge." Then, observing for himself the struggle in progress on the ridge across the way, he exclaimed: "I wouldn't have missed this for anything!" Old Peter laughed, an incongruous sound against that backdrop of death and destruction. "The devil you wouldn't!" he said; "I would like to have missed it very much. We've attacked and been repulsed. Look there." All the colonel could see, amid swirls of smoke on the slope at which the general was pointing, half a mile in the distance, was that men were fighting desperately; but Longstreet spoke as if the issue was no longer in doubt. "The charge is over," he said flatly. And then, having attended in his fashion to the amenities due a guest, he turned to the courier and added: "Captain Bright, ride to General Pickett and tell him what you have heard me say to Colonel Fremantle." The courier started off, but the general called after him: "Captain Bright!" Drawing rein, Bright looked back and saw Old Peter pointing northward. "Tell General Pickett that Wilcox's brigade is in that orchard, and he can order him to his assistance."

The courier galloped off at last, and the burly Georgian returned to watching the final stages of the action, pausing only to countermand his recent order for Anderson's three reserve brigades to be committed. Wilcox and Lang could go forward, in accordance with Lee's original arrangements — Longstreet's final instructions, shouted after the courier when he first started back to Pickett, were more in the nature of a reminder than a command — but if what was happening on the ridge was only the prelude to a repulse, as he believed, then Anderson's three and Pender's two uncommitted brigades would be needed to meet the counterattack Meade would be likely to launch in the wake of the Confederates as they fell back down the slope and recrossed the valley. Fremantle marveled at his companion's self-possession under strain, remarking afterwards that "difficulties seem[ed] to make no other impression on him than to make him a little more savage." In point of fact, though Old Peter kept his binoculars trained on the flame-stabbed turmoil halfway up the enemy ridge, he watched the fighting not so much in suspense as to the outcome — for that had been settled already, at least to his own disgruntled satisfaction — as to study the manner in which it came about. Convinced that the attack had failed, even before the first signs of retreat were evident, he was mainly interested in seeing how many of his soldiers would survive it.

But they themselves had no such detached view of the holocaust in which they were involved. Massed as they were on a narrow front, flailed by canister from both flanks and dead ahead, the men of the five lead brigades were mingled inextricably; few of them had any knowledge of anything except in their immediate vicinity, and very little of that. "Everything was a wild kaleidoscopic whirl," a colonel would recall. Fry, for one, thought victory was certain. "Go on; it will not last five minutes longer!" he shouted as he fell, shot through the thigh while urging his brigade to hurry up the slope. Nearby a lieutenant waved his sword and exulted as if he saw the end of the war at hand. "Home, boys, home!" he cried. "Remember, home is over beyond those hills!" Sheets of flame leaped out at the charging graybacks as the blue infantry opened fire along the wall, but they held their own fire until Garnett passed the word, which was taken up by officers all up and down the front: "Make ready. Take good aim. Fire low. *Fire!*" Uphill sheets of flame flashed in response and blue-capped heads dropped from sight beyond the wall. "Fire! Fire!" they could hear the Federal officers shouting through the smoke and muzzle-flashes. Still wrapped in his old army overcoat, Garnett rocked back in the saddle and fell heavily to the ground, dead, the Kernstown stain removed at last. Kemper meanwhile had turned and called to Armistead, who was close in his rear: "Armistead, hurry up! I am going to charge those heights and carry them, and I want you to support me!" His friend called back, "I'll do it!" and added proudly: "Look at my line. It never looked better on dress parade." But Kemper by then was in no condition to observe it; he had fallen, shot in the groin as he ordered the final assault. Pickett thus was down to a single brigade commander, and Pettigrew was in the same condition on the left, where only Davis remained, Marshall having been killed at about the same time Fry went down. Unhorsed by a shell on his way across the valley, Pettigrew had crossed the Emmitsburg

Road on foot and then had been wounded painfully in the hand as he began to climb the ridge. He remained in command, though his troops were mingled beyond the possibility of over-all control, even if he could have managed to make himself heard above the tremendous clatter of firing and the high screams of the wounded. Nevertheless, like Pickett's leaderless two on the right, his three brigades continued their uphill surge, eager to come to grips with their tormentors beyond the wall, and for the first time on this field today the rebel yell rang out.

On the Union right, near Ziegler's Grove, Hancock watched with admiration as Hays, whose northern flank considerably overlapped the enemy left, swung his end regiment forward, gatelike, to make contact with the Ohioans who had halted after routing Mayo and had taken up a position facing southwest with their left on the Emmitsburg Road. As a result of this pivoting maneuver, which was accompanied by two brass Napoleons firing double-shotted canister, some 450 men who otherwise would have had no share in the fighting after the rebels actually struck the blue defenses, well down the line and beyond their angle of sight, were placed where they could and did pump heavy volleys into the mangled flank of the attackers, adding greatly to the confusion and the carnage. Hancock shouted approval of this happy improvisation and took off southward at a gallop, intending to see whether the same could not be done at the opposite end of the position, which likewise extended well beyond the huddled mass of graybacks driving hard against his center. He rode fast, but even so he had cause to fear he would be too late. The stone wall along which his five brigades were deployed ran due south for a couple of hundred yards from Ziegler's Grove, then turned sharply west for eighty yards, thus avoiding the clump of umbrella-shaped trees, before it made as sharp a turn again to resume its former direction. The jog in the wall — described thereafter as The Angle — had caused Gibbon's men to be posted eighty yards in advance of Hays's, which meant that they would be struck first: as indeed they were. Galloping southward along the ridge, Hancock was hailed by Colonel Arthur Devereux, who commanded one of two regiments Gibbon had placed in reserve, well up the slope behind his center. "See, General!" Devereux cried, pointing. "They have broken through; the colors are coming over the stone wall. Let me go in there!" Reining his horse in so abruptly that he brought the animal back on its haunches, Hancock looked and saw that the report was all too true. Less than two hundred yards away, due west and northwest of the clump of trees, which partly obscured his view, he saw a host of butternut soldiers, led by a gray-haired officer who brandished a sword with a black hat balanced on its point, boiling over the wall in hot pursuit of a blue regiment that had bolted. Some two hundred undefended feet of the south leg of the angle had been overrun. "Go in there pretty God-damned quick!" the general shouted, and spurred on southward to order Doubleday to repeat the flanking maneuver that was working so well at the far end of the line. That way, the breakthrough might at least be limited in width, and if Devereux got there in time it might even be contained.

Arriving, Hancock found that Doubleday, or anyhow the commander of the one I Corps brigade attached for defense of the Union center, had anticipated the order; Brigadier General G. J. Stannard, a former Vermont dry-goods merchant and militia officer, had already begun the pivot maneuver and was wheeling two of his three regiments into an advance position from which to tear the flank of the attackers pressing forward to exploit their narrow penetration of the south leg of the angle, directly in front of the clump of trees and less than two hundred yards north of the point where Stannard's gatelike swing was hinged. Vermonters all, the 900 men of these two outsized regiments were nine-month volunteers; "nine monthlings hatched from $200 bounty eggs," scornful veterans had dubbed them on their recent arrival from the soft life of the Washington defenses. They had seen their first action yesterday and their army time was almost up, but they were determined to give a good account of themselves before returning home. Now the opportunity was at hand. Company by company, they opened fire as they wheeled into line, blasting the rebel flank, and as they delivered their murderous volleys they continued to move northward, closing the range until their officers were able to add the fire of their revolvers to the weight of metal thrown into the writhing mass of graybacks. "Glory to God! Glory to God!" Doubleday shouted, swinging his hat in approval as he watched from up the slope. "See the Vermonters go it!"

Hancock too was delighted, but while he was congratulating Stannard on the success with which his green troops had executed the difficult maneuver, a bullet passed through the pommel of his saddle and buried itself in the tender flesh of his inner thigh, along with several jagged bits of wood and a bent nail. Two officers caught him as he slumped, and when they had lowered him to the ground Stannard improvised a tourniquet — a knotted handkerchief wound tight with a pistol barrel — to stanch the flow of blood from the ugly wound. Hancock himself extracted the saddle nail unaided, though he mistook its source. "They must be hard up for ammunition when they throw such shot as that," he said wryly. Stretcherbearers came on the run, but he refused to be carried off the field just yet. He insisted on staying to watch the action, which now was mounting swiftly toward a climax.

The gray-haired Confederate officer he had glimpsed through the screen of trees as he rode southward in rear of the center was his old friend Armistead, whom he had seen last in California and did not recognize now because of the distance and the smoke. Working his way forward to assume command of the frantic press of troops after Garnett and Kemper had fallen, Armistead found himself at the stone wall, midway of the 200-foot stretch from which a regiment of Pennsylvanians had bolted to avoid contact with the charging rebels. There the gray advance had stopped, or anyhow paused, while those in front knelt behind its welcome cover and poured a heavy fire into the secondary blue line up the slope. He saw, however, that it would not do to lose momentum or allow the Federals time to bring up reinforcements. "Come on, boys! Give them the cold steel!" he cried, and holding his saber high, still with the black hat balanced on its tip for a guidon, he stepped over the wall, yelling as he did so: "Follow me!" Young Cushing's two guns were just ahead, unserved and silent because Cushing himself was dead by now, shot through the mouth as he called for a faster rate of fire, and Gibbon had been taken rearward, a bullet in his shoulder. Then Armistead fell too, killed as he reached with his free hand for the muzzle of one of the guns, and the clot of perhaps 300 men who had followed him over the wall was struck from the right front by the two regiments Devereux had brought down "pretty God-damned quick" from the uphill slope beyond the clump of trees. The fight was hand to hand along the fringes, while others among the defenders stood back, left and front and right, and fired into the close-packed, heaving mass of rebel troops and colors. "Every man fought on his own hook," a bluecoat would recall, with little regard for rank or assignment, high or low. Even Hunt was there, on horseback, emptying his revolver into the crush. "See 'em! See 'em!" he cried as he pulled trigger. Then his horse went down, hoofs flailing, with the general underneath. Men on both sides were hollering as they milled about and fired, some cursing, others praying, and this, combined with the screams of the wounded and the moans of the dying, produced an effect which one who heard it called "strange and terrible, a sound that came from thousands of human throats, yet was not a commingling of shouts and yells but rather like a vast mournful roar."

Neither on the left nor on the right of the shallow penetration of the center, assailed as they were from north and south by the double envelopment Hays and Stannard had improvised, could the Confederates make real headway. Pettigrew's troops, advancing up their additional eighty yards of slope, which one of them noted incongruously was "covered with clover as soft as a Turkish carpet," were in fact outnumbered by the defenders of the two hundred yards of wall above the angle. Fry's brigade and part of Marshall's having gone in with the Virginians to the south, all that remained were Davis's brigade and Marshall's remnant, and though they kept coming on, torn by rifle fire and canister from the flank and dead ahead, they had not the slightest chance of scoring a breakthrough and they knew it. The most they could hope to accomplish was to keep the enemy units in their front from being shifted to meet the threat below the angle, and this they did, though at a cruel cost. A Mississippi regiment — including the University Greys, a company made up exclusively of students from the state university, which suffered a precisely tabulated loss of 100% of its members killed or wounded in the charge — managed to plant its colors within arm's length of the Union line before it was blasted out of existence, and a sergeant from a North Carolina outfit, accompanied by one man bearing the regimental colors, got all the way up to the wall itself, but only because the admiring defenders held their fire as they drew near. "Come over to this side of the Lord!" a bluecoat shouted: whereupon the two surrendered and crossed over with their flag. Some others availed themselves of the same mercy at various points along the line, but these were all. Except as captives, or as corpses tumbling headlong under pressure from the rear, not an attacker got over the wall north of the angle.

Blood dripping from his wounded hand, Pettigrew sent word for Trimble to bring his two supporting brigades forward and add their weight to the attack. Trimble did so, ordering Lowrance to the right, against the angle, and Lane to reinforce the battered left. Mounted, he watched with pride as they swung past him. "Charley, I believe those fine fellows are going into the enemy's line," he told an aide. But he was wrong. Moreover, as he watched them waver and recoil under the impact of the heavy fire the Federals brought to bear, he was hit a bone-splintering blow in the leg he had nearly lost at Manassas, just over ten months back, from a wound that had kept him all those fretful months out of combat. He passed the command to Lane, whom he had succeeded only four hours ago, but stayed to watch the outcome of the action. Discouraged by what he saw, the sixty-one-year-old Marylander, whose reputation for hard-handed aggressiveness was unsurpassed by any man in either army, went rapidly into shock from pain and loss of blood, and declined to permit his aide to attempt to rally the troops for a renewal of the assault, which he now perceived could not succeed. "No," he said slowly, sadly, in response to the aide's request. "The best thing the men can do is get out of this. Let them go."

They did go, here and on the right and in the center — at any rate, those who had not surrendered and were still in any condition, either physical or mental, to undertake the long walk back across the shell-torn valley. This was harder for those within the angle, not only because they had to run the longest gauntlet between the two converging wings under Hays and Stannard, but also because they were the last to realize that the assault had failed. For them, the let-down was abrupt and sickening. "I looked to the right and left," a Virginia lieutenant would recall, "and felt we were disgraced. . . . We had, for the first time, failed to do our duty." It was only after he started back and saw for himself that the friends he missed were casualties, not skulkers, that he began to comprehend the nature of the failure, and "felt that after all we were not disgraced." He made it back across, as did June Kimble, the

Tennessee sergeant who had resolved to do his duty and had done it, but who now admitted frankly: "For about a hundred yards I broke the lightning speed record." Once more, however, his conscience intervened. With a horror of being shot in the back, he turned to face the bluecoats firing downhill at him and walked backwards until he was out of musket range, then turned again and plodded uphill amid shellbursts that plowed the farther reaches of what a Federal observer called "a square mile of Tophet." Fortunately, the final stages of the withdrawal were favored somewhat by the advance of Wilcox and Lang, who came forward in response to calls from Pickett. Although Wilcox later reported that by the time he emerged from cover "not a man of the division that I was ordered to support could I see," his limited advance had at least the effect of causing Stannard, who was wounded too by now, to order his Vermonters back into line to meet this new menace to their flank, thus easing the pressure on those Confederates who were last to leave the angle and the more stubbornly defended portions of wall above and below it.

Even so, barely more than half of the 11,000 men in the nine-brigade assault force — including Mayo's defectors, whose losses had been comparatively light, and those disabled stalwarts who managed to hobble or crawl the westward distance across the valley — returned to the ridge they had left with such high hopes an hour ago. The rest, some 5000 in all, were either killed or captured. Further allowance for the wounded among the survivors, as well as for those who were killed or injured during the preliminary bombardment and in the belated advance of Lang and Wilcox, raised the total to about 7500 casualties, which amounted to sixty percent of the 12,500 Confederates engaged from first to last. In the five leading brigades under Pickett and Pettigrew the ratio of losses was considerably higher, no less indeed than seventy percent; so that it was no wonder that the former, writing five days later to his fiancée, spoke of "my spirit-crushed, wearied, cut-up people," especially if he had reference to his subordinate commanders. Not only had he lost all three of his brigadiers, but of his thirteen colonels eight were killed and all the rest were wounded. In fact, of his thirty-five officers above the rank of captain only one came back unhit, a one-armed major, and Pettigrew's losses were almost as grievous in that regard. In Fry's brigade two field officers escaped, in Marshall's only one, and in Davis's all were killed or wounded. Moreover, the Union infantry force, with half as many troops as came against them, suffered no more than 1500 casualties, barely one fifth of the number they inflicted while maintaining the integrity of their position. "We gained nothing but glory," a Virginia captain wrote home before the week was out; "and lost our bravest men."

The gloom that settled over the western ridge was more than

matched, at least in intensity, by the elation of the victors on the one across the way. On Cemetery Hill, watching as the rebel lines began to come unhinged, a captain shouted: "By God, boys, we've got 'em now. They've broke all to hell!" And down on the blood-splotched ridge below, when it became apparent that such was indeed the case, a wild celebration got under way before the gunfire stopped. Hays, who had had two horses shot from under him and had lost all but six of his twenty orderlies, was so exuberant that he grabbed and kissed young David Shields, a lieutenant on his staff. "Boys, give me a flag!" he cried. "Get a flag, Corts, get a flag, Dave, and come on!" There was no shortage of such trophies; for of the 38 regimental flags that had been brought within musket range of the wall, here on the right and on the left, no less than 30 had been captured. Hays and the two staff officers he had invited to join him in a horseback victory dance rode up and down the division line, each trailing a stand of rebel colors in the dust behind his mount, cheered by those of their grinning soldiers who were not still busy taking pot shots at the butternut figures retreating in disorder across the valley. Recalling his excitement, Shields wrote later: "My horse seemed to be off the ground traveling through the air." His impression was that if he could survive what he had just been through, he could survive almost anything, in or out of the catalogue of war. He was going to live forever. "I felt though a shot as large as a barrel should hit me in the back, it would be with no more effect than shooting through a fog bank."

Meanwhile the nearly 4000 rebel prisoners, wounded and unwounded, were being rounded up and sent to the rear. "Smart, healthy-looking men," one Federal called them, adding: "They move very quick, walk like horses." It was strange to see them thus, close up and de-fanged, without their guns and yells. They had a simple dignity about them which their ragged clothes served more to emphasize than lessen. Nor were all of them in rags. "Many of their officers were well dressed, fine, proud gentlemen," another observer wrote soon afterwards, "such men as it would be a pleasure to meet, when the war is over. I had no desire to exult over them, and pity and sympathy were the general feelings of us all upon the occasion." This last was not entirely true. At least one Union officer was alarmed by the thought that the prisoners — who, after all, numbered only a few hundred less than the surviving defenders of the ridge — might take it into their heads to renew the fight with the discarded weapons thickly strewn about the ground at their feet. There was, as it turned out, no danger of this; but the commander of a reserve battery, galloping forward in response to belated orders to reinforce the badly pounded guns along the center, received a different kind of shock. As he came up the reverse slope of the ridge he saw a mass of gray-clad men come over the crest ahead, and his first thought was that the position had been overrun. He signaled a halt and was about to give the order to fall back, when he saw that the Confederates bore no arms and were under guard.

Meade had much the same original reaction. Arriving at last from Powers Hill, he too mistook the drove of prisoners for evidence of a breakthrough. Then, as he realized his mistake and rode on past them toward the crest, he encountered a lieutenant from Gibbon's staff. "How is it going here?" he asked eagerly, and received the reply: "I believe, General, the enemy's attack is repulsed." Meade could scarcely credit the information, welcome though it was. "What!" he exclaimed. "Is the assault already repulsed?" By that time he had reached the crest, however, and the lieutenant's assurance, "It is, sir," was confirmed by what he saw with his own eyes: more captives being herded into clusters along the left and right and center, his own troops cavorting with abandoned rebel flags, and the fugitives withdrawing amid shellbursts on the far side of the valley, all unmistakable evidence of a victory achieved. "Thank God," he said fervently. The lieutenant observed that Meade's right hand jerked involuntarily upward, as if to snatch off his slouch hat and wave it in exultation, but then his concern for dignity prevailed. Instead he merely waved his hand, albeit rather self-consciously, and cried, just once: "Hurrah!" This done, he gave the staffer instructions for the posting of reinforcements expected shortly, "as the enemy might be mad enough to attack again." Adding: "If the enemy does attack, charge him in the flank and sweep him from the field," he rode on down the ridge, where he was greeted with cheers of recognition and tossed caps. A band had come up by now from somewhere, and when it broke into the strains of "Hail to the Chief" a correspondent remarked, not altogether jokingly: "Ah, General Meade, you're in very great danger of being President of the United States."

Despite the evidence spread before him that the Confederates were in a state of acute distress, and therefore probably vulnerable to attack, the northern commander's words had made it clear that he had no intention of going over to the offensive. No one on the other side of the valley had heard those words, however. If they had, their surprise and relief would have been at least as great as his had been on learning that their attempt to pierce his center had been foiled. This was especially true of Longstreet. A counter-puncher himself, he expected Meade to attack without delay, and he moved at once to meet the threat as best he could, sending word for Wright, whom he had halted when he saw the charge must fail, to collect and rally the fugitives streaming back toward the center, while he himself attended to that same function on the right. Now that the painful thing he had opposed was over, he recovered his bluff and hearty manner. He rode among the returning troops and spoke reassuringly to them, meantime sending word for Mc-

Laws and Law to pull back to the line they had taken off from yesterday and thus place their divisions in position to assist in the defense of the weakened center. When one commander protested that his men could not be rallied, Old Peter mocked at his despair. "Very well; never mind then, General," he told him. "Just let them remain where they are. The enemy's going to advance, and will spare you the trouble." Fremantle thought the Georgian's conduct "admirable," and when he paused at one point to ask if the colonel had anything to drink, the Britisher not only gave him a swig of rum from a silver flask but also insisted that he keep the rest, together with its container, as a token of his esteem. Longstreet thanked him, put the flask in his pocket for future reference, and continued to move among the fugitives with words of cheer and encouragement, preparing to meet the counterattack which he believed Meade would be delivering at any moment now.

But most of the survivors came streaming back the shortest way, straight across the valley toward the command post midway of its western rim, like hurt children in instinctive search of solace from a parent: meaning Lee. There the southern commander had remained throughout their advance and their brief, furious struggle on the distant ridge, until he saw them falter and begin their slow recoil; whereupon he rode forward to meet them coming back, to rally them with words of reassurance, and to share with them the ordeal of the counterattack he believed would soon be launched. Nor did he disappoint them in their expectations of solace and sustainment. "All this will come right in the end," he told them. "We'll talk it over afterwards. But in the meantime all good men must rally. We want all good and true men just now." He made it clear to all he met that he considered the failure of the charge not their fault, but his, for having asked of them more than men could give. To Fremantle, who had ridden over from the right, he said: "This has been a sad day for us, Colonel. A sad day. But we can't always expect to win victories." After advising the visitor to find a safer point for observation, he continued to move among his soldiers in an attempt to brace them for the storm he thought was coming. "Very few failed to answer his appeal," Fremantle noted, "and I saw many badly wounded men take off their hats and cheer him."

One among the fugitives most in need of encouragement was Pickett, who came riding back with an expression of dejection and bewilderment on his face. Leading his division into battle for the first time, he had seen two thirds of it destroyed. Not only had his great hour come to nothing; tactically speaking, it added up to considerably less than nothing. Lee met him with instructions designed to bring him back to the problem now at hand. "General Pickett, place your division in rear of this hill," he told him, "and be ready to repel the advance of the enemy should they follow up their advantage." At least one bystander observed that in his extremity Lee employed the words "the enemy" rather than his usual "those people." But Pickett was in no state to observe anything outside his personal loss and mortification.

"General Lee, I have no division now," he said tearfully; "Armistead is down, Garnett is down, and Kemper is mortally wounded —"

"Come, General Pickett," Lee broke in. "This has been my fight, and upon my shoulders rests the blame. The men and officers of your command have written the name of Virginia as high today as it has ever been written before.... Your men have done all that men can do," he added after a pause for emphasis. "The fault is entirely my own."

He repeated this as he rode from point to point about the field: "It's all my fault," "The blame is mine," and "You must help me." To Wilcox, who was about as unstrung as Pickett in reporting that he was not sure his troops would stand if the Federals attacked, Lee was particularly solicitous and tender. "Never mind, General," he told him, taking his hand as he spoke. "All this has been my fault. It is I who have lost this fight, and you must help me out of it the best way you can." Fremantle, who had not followed his advice to find a place of safety, thought it "impossible to look at him or listen to him without feeling the strongest admiration," and when he rode forward to the line of guns, the Britisher found the cannoneers ready to challenge any blue attack on the disrupted center. They had much the same reaction as his own to Lee's appeal. "We've not lost confidence in the old man," they assured him, speaking defiantly, almost angrily, as if someone had suggested otherwise. "This day's work will do him no harm. Uncle Robert will get us into Washington yet. You bet he will."

By no means all responded in that fashion, however — especially among the troops who had been all the way to the enemy ridge and back, as the artillerists had not — and even concerning those who did there was considerable doubt as to whether they would stand their ground, this soon after their delivery from chaos, if they were exposed to more than the possibility of further danger. In point of fact, there was strong evidence that they would not. When some officers managed to form a line along the forward slope of Seminary Ridge, still in plain view of the Union batteries, the rallied fugitives broke badly under the long-range fire their concentration drew. "Then commenced a rout, that increased to a stampede," an indignant witness later wrote. Fleeing rearward over the crest, the mass of several hundred fear-crazed men was funneled into a ravine along the western slope, and there, without regard for orders or appeals from their officers, who were swept along in the crush, they "pushed, poured, and rushed in a continuous stream, throwing away guns, blankets, and haversacks," until at last a straggler line, composed of the more stalwart few among them, was thrown across their path and "dammed [them] up."

Lee did not reproach them even then, knowing as he did that time alone could heal the wounds their morale had suffered in the hour just past. What was more, his ready acceptance of total blame for the failure of the assault was not merely a temporary burden he assumed for the sake of encouraging his troops to resist the counterattack he believed Meade was about to launch at them; he continued to say the same things in the future, after the immediate need for them was past and the quite different but altogether human need for self-justification might have been expected to set in. "It's all my fault. I thought my men were invincible," he told Longstreet the next day, perhaps by way of making specific admission that he had been wrong in overruling his chief lieutenant's objection that the charge was bound to fail. And in his official report to the President, forwarded on the last day of the month, he repeated for the record his assertion that such fault as might be found could not properly be applied to the men who had bled and died to sustain his pride in them. "The conduct of the troops was all that I could desire or expect," he wrote, "and they deserved success so far as it can be deserved by heroic valor and fortitude. More may have been required of them than they were able to perform, but my admiration of their noble qualities and confidence in their ability to cope successfully with the enemy has suffered no abatement from the issue of this protracted and sanguinary conflict."

※ 5 ※

Protracted the conflict had certainly been, and sanguinary too, three days of fighting having produced a combined total of about 50,000 casualties North and South. Nor was it quite over yet. Although Lee could not and Meade would not renew the infantry action, two indecisive and as it were extraneous cavalry engagements — one three miles east of Gettysburg, deep in the Federal right rear, and the other just west of Round Top, on the Confederate right flank — were, respectively, still to be ended and begun. The former, which reached a climax at about the time Pickett and Pettigrew surged up Cemetery Ridge, was the result of Jeb Stuart's attempt to carry out his instructions for placing his troopers in a position from which to harry the expected, or at any rate hoped-for, blue retreat; whereas the latter, fought about an hour after the gray attackers fell back across the valley, was the result of Judson Kilpatrick's attempt, in the absence of instructions, to strike while the tactical iron was hot and thus not only throw the rebels into retreat but also provoke a panic that would prevent them from achieving a getaway. Neither Stuart nor Kilpatrick, quite different in makeup and ability, but altogether similar in their thirst for action and applause, succeeded in accomplishing what he set out to do. In fact, as the two things turned out, both generals would have done better to remain within their respective lines, together with all their men: especially Kilpatrick.

At midday Stuart rode eastward out the York Pike with the brigades of Chambliss and Jenkins, the latter now under Colonel M. J. Ferguson since its regular commander had been wounded the day before; Hampton and Fitz Lee followed at a distance, bringing the total to just over 6000 sabers. One night's rest could scarcely have restored either the men or their mounts after a week on the go, but Jeb was eager for a fight. On Evelington Heights a year ago this morning, by way of providing the just-concluded drama of the Seven Days with an upbeat epilogue, he had opened fire with a single howitzer on McClellan's blue host encamped at Harrison's Landing, and though he had been criticized for flushing the game in this fashion, he would have liked nothing better today than another such opportunity, especially after the chilling reception his chief had given him yesterday when he rejoined the army that had been groping blindfold in his absence. For more than two miles, however, he did not sight a single enemy soldier. The Pennsylvania countryside looked altogether peaceful, its rolling farmlands untouched by war, despite the thunder of the great cannonade behind him, south of Gettysburg, which began soon after 1 o'clock and continued to rumble without diminution as he turned south about 2.30 along Cress Ridge, which extended down to the Hanover Road and the Baltimore Pike beyond. Presently he spotted horsemen a mile to the east on the Low Dutch Road, a lane that paralleled the ridge, and promptly decided to defeat or drive them off, thus clearing his path to the Union rear. Accordingly, after posting Chambliss behind a screen of woods, he dismounted Ferguson's men and sent them forward to take position around a large barn on the farm of a family named Rummel. They would serve as bait to draw the Federals, whose strength was so far undisclosed, after which Stuart planned to attack with Chambliss, then sweep the field with Hampton and Lee, whom he warned by courier to remain under cover of the ridge as they came up, thereby adding the shock of surprise to the weight of their horseback assault on the unsuspecting bluecoats whose attention would be fixed on the dismounted and presumably vulnerable band of graybacks in the Rummel barnyard.

It did not work out quite that way, for several reasons. For one, the blue riders were in much greater numbers than he knew. Two brigades of David Gregg's division, reinforced by one brigade from Kilpatrick's, were at hand, 5000 strong, armed with repeating carbines, and apparently as eager for a clash as Stuart was. This by itself would have been all right — the Confederates still had the numerical advantage — but it presently developed that Ferguson's men, through a misinterpretation of instructions, had drawn only ten rounds of ammunition each, with the result that they ran out of bullets almost as soon as the fight got started. Stuart had to send in Chambliss prematurely, in order to keep the bait from being gobbled before he was set to spring the trap. Even this was not too bad, or anyhow it need not have been, if Hampton and Lee had come up as planned; but they did not. Disclosing their presence while still too far away to achieve surprise, they gave the Federals time to fall back from the melee around the barn and form their ranks to receive the charge. In fact, a good many of the bluecoats did a great deal more than that. They moved to meet it. The brigade attached from Kilpatrick included four Michigan regiments commanded by a recently promoted brigadier named George A. Custer, bottom man in the West Point class of '61, which had lost its top man yesterday on Little Round Top. Custer, whose love of combat was only exceeded by his ache for glory, saw the rebel column approaching and moved fast. "Come on, you Wolverines!" he shouted, four lengths in front of the lead regiment, his long yellow ringlets streaming in the wind. A Federal witness described what followed. "As the two columns approached each other, the pace of each increased, when suddenly a crash, like the falling of timber, betokened the crisis. So sudden and violent was the collision that many of the horses were turned end over end and crushed their riders beneath them. The clashing of sabers, the firing of pistols, the demands for surrender and cries of the combatants now filled the air."

Gregg dealt ably with the situation that developed, sending in other units to strike the flanks of the gray column which Custer had brought to a standstill by meeting it head-on, and while the saber-to-saber conflict was in progress, cannoneers on both sides threw in shell and canister whenever they could do so without too great risk of hitting their own men. Hampton went down with a deep gash in his head, but was brought off the field in time to prevent his capture. Stuart, perhaps reasoning that it was not after all his mission to stage a cavalry fight at this stage of the battle — which he had no way of knowing was now at its climax, back on Cemetery Ridge, with Armistead crying "Follow me!" as he stepped over the low stone wall along Meade's center — withdrew his troopers to the ridge from which they had charged, and Gregg, who had cause to be well satisfied, was content to let them go. The artillery exchange continued till past sundown, at which time the Confederates retired northward and went unmolested into bivouac alongside the York Pike, near the point where they had left it six hours back. Gregg reported 254 casualties, most of them Custer's, whose Michiganders would suffer, before the war was over, a larger number of killed and wounded than any other cavalry brigade in the Union army. Stuart listed 181, but since this was exclusive of Ferguson's brigade and the artillery, the losses probably were about equal on both sides. Jeb made the most of the affair in his report, praising the conduct of some of his regiments by saying that "the enemy's masses vanished before them like grain before the scythe." Yet the fact remained that, for once, he had failed to drive an outnumbered foe from a fair field of fight. "Defeated at every point, the enemy withdrew," Gregg declared, and while Stuart objected strenuously to the claim — he had withdrawn when he got good and ready, he maintained — there could be no denying that he had failed in his purpose of reaching the Union rear, even though it later developed that there was no retreat for him to harry and therefore no real work for him to do if he had been there.

Four miles southwest of the Rummel farm, the other cavalry action was over too by now. Beginning some two hours later, it ended some two hours earlier, and if, despite this brevity, its potential fruits were greater — the intention had been to throw Lee's right into confusion, hard on the heels of the Pickett-Pettigrew repulse, and thus set him up for a crumpling assault to be launched by the blue infantry from the western slopes of the Round Tops — so too was the failure, which amounted to nothing more or less than a fiasco. Kilpatrick's remaining brigade, commanded by twenty-six-year-old Brigadier General Elon J. Farnsworth, was in position on the rebel flank, opposed by a skirmish line of Texans from Law's division, which extended from the base of Round Top west to the Emmitsburg Road. A year older than Farnsworth, and four years older than Custer, who had been a West Point classmate, Kilpatrick rode back and forth among his troopers, expressing what one of them called "great impatience and eagerness for orders." There was nothing unusual in this, for that was his accustomed manner, all the way back to his boyhood in New Jersey. "A wiry, restless, undersized man with black eyes [and] a lantern jaw," as a fellow officer described him, he had stringy blond side whiskers, bandy legs that gave him a rolling gait, and a burning ambition which he attempted to assuage and advance with constant aggressiveness and bluster. The result was not uncomical, at least to some observers; Sherman, for one, was to call him "a hell of a damned fool," and a member of Meade's staff remarked that "it was hard to look at Kilpatrick without laughing." But this last was not always the case for those who served under him — "Kill Cavalry," they had dubbed him, somewhat ruefully — and it was especially not the case today, so far as Farnsworth was concerned; for Kilpatrick kept insisting that he make horseback probes at the rebel skirmish line, despite the boulder-strewn terrain, which was highly unsuitable for cavalry operations, and the renowned marksmanship of the Texans, who had emptied a good many saddles by now and were backed up, moreover, by Law's old brigade of Alabamians, whose skill was scarcely less in that respect. However, the worst was still to come for Farnsworth and his men.

It came shortly before 5 o'clock, when an orderly arrived on a lathered horse from Cemetery Ridge, shouting as he drew near: "We turned the charge! Nine acres of prisoners!" That was enough for Kilpatrick. Though he had no instructions to go over to the offensive, he assumed that Meade was on the lookout for a chance to strike at the rebel line, especially if some part of it could be thrown into confusion beforehand, and he quickly determined to provide such an opportunity for the forces gazing down from the slopes of Round Top. Turning to Farnsworth, he told him to commit a West Virginia regiment at once, with orders to hack a gap in the butternut skirmish line, then go for the Confederate main body, deployed along the base of the height beyond Plum Run, opposing the blue infantry above. The West Virginians tried it and were repulsed, losing heavily when the Texans rose from behind a rail fence and slammed massed volleys at them. They tried it again — and again, by way of demonstration that the terrain was unsuited to horseback maneuver, were driven back. But Kilpatrick was not satisfied. Having often maintained that cavalry could "fight anywhere except at sea," he was out to prove it here today. He told Farnsworth to send in a second regiment, this time one of Vermonters who had suffered cruelly in the earlier skirmishing. Farnsworth had shown his mettle in some forty engagements since the first days of the war, and only four days ago he had been promoted from captain to brigadier in recognition of his bravery under fire. There could scarcely be any question of his courage, but after what they had both just seen he could not believe he had heard his chief aright. "General, do you mean it?" he asked. "Shall I throw my handful of men over rough ground, through timber, against a brigade of infantry? The 1st Vermont has already been fought half to pieces. These are too good men to kill." But Kilpatrick not only meant it; he wanted it done without question or delay. "Do you refuse to obey my orders?" he snapped. "If you are afraid to lead this charge, I will lead it." Farnsworth rose in his stirrups, flushed with anger. "Take that back!" he cried, and an observer thought the tall young man "looked magnificent in his passion." Kilpatrick bristled back at him for a moment, but then repented and apologized. "I didn't mean it. Forget it," he said. Farnsworth's anger subsided as quickly as it had risen. "General, if you order the charge, I will lead it," he replied; "but you must take the responsibility." Kilpatrick nodded. "I take the responsibility," he said.

  The Texans were even readier now than they had been before. Posted within earshot, they had overheard the hot exchange between the two young brigadiers: with the result that they not only had time to brace themselves for what was coming, but also time to pass the word along to Law that his rear would be threatened if the troopers managed to punch a hole in the widespread skirmish line. The Vermonters were prepared to do just that, though one of them later wrote: "Each man felt, as he tightened his saber belt, that he was summoned to a ride to death." Farnsworth having massed them in depth, they broke through on a narrow front about midway of the line, taking losses along both flanks as they made their penetration, then swung hard east to strike the rear of the rebel infantry on the far side of Plum Run, which was bone dry at this season. They crossed, still at a gallop, but it would have been far better for them if they had not. As they approached what they thought was the Confederate rear, their drawn sabers flashing sunlight, it was as if the head of the column struck a trip wire. Oates, forewarned, had faced his Alabamians about, ignoring the enemy infantry uphill, and presented a solid front to the blue riders. The survivors turned sharply north again, in an attempt to avoid a second volley; but that too was a mistake, since it carried them directly along the line of marksmen who did not neglect the rare opportunity for point-blank firing at cavalry in profile. For some, indeed, it was like a return to happier days. A company commander, seeing a horse collapse in midstride with a bullet through the brain, heard a private alongside him shout: "Captain, I shot that black!" Asked why he had not aimed for the rider instead of the horse, the Alabamian grinned. "Oh, we'll get him anyhow," he said. "But I'm a hunter, and for two years I haven't looked at a deer's eye. I couldn't stand it."

By that time Law had reinforced the skirmishers with another regiment; so that when the blue survivors turned back west and south, they found the entry gap resealed. What had been intended as a havoc-spreading charge now degenerated into a sort of circus, Roman style, with the penned-in horsemen riding frantically in large circles, ricocheting from cluster to cluster of whooping rebels as they tried to find a way out of the fire-laced coliseum. Farnsworth had his mount shot from under him, took another from a trooper who was glad to go afoot, and in final desperation — perhaps with Kilpatrick's taunt still ringing in his ears — made a suicidal one-man charge, saber raised, against a solid mass of Confederates who brought him down with five mortal wounds. Some 65 of his men had fallen with him by the time the remnant found an exit and regained the safety of the Union lines. No earthly good had been accomplished, except by way of providing a show for the spectators, blue and gray, who had watched as in an amphitheater. Still, Kilpatrick did not regret having ordered the attempt; he only regretted that the infantry onlookers, high on the slopes of Round Top, had failed to seize the advantage offered them by the Vermonters on the plain below; in which case, he reported, "a total rout would have ensued." As for Farnsworth: "For the honor of his young brigade and the glory of his corps, he gave his life.... We can say of him, in the language of another, 'Good soldier, faithful friend, great heart, hail and farewell.' " Thus Kilpatrick, who had sent him to his death with words of doubt as to his courage.

The infantry had not come down to join the mix-up in the valley for the sufficient reason that it had received no instructions to do so, although there were those who urged this course on Meade in no uncertain terms. One such was Pleasonton, who was quite as cocky as his lieutenants. "I will give you half an hour to show yourself a great general," he told his chief, soon after the latter's arrival on Cemetery Ridge. "Order the army to advance, while I take the cavalry and get in Lee's rear, and we will finish the campaign in a week." But Meade was having no part of such advice. Six days in command, he had spent the last three locked in mortal combat, all of it defensive on his side, and he had no intention of shifting to the offensive on short notice, even if that had been possible, simply because another in the sequence of all-out rebel assaults on his fishhook line had been repulsed. Besides, he was by no means convinced that this was the last of them. "How do you know Lee will not attack me again?" he replied. "We have done well enough." Pleasonton continued to press the point, maintaining that the Confederates, low on supplies by now and far from base, would be obliged to surrender if nailed down; to which Meade's only response was an invitation for the cavalryman to accompany him on the triumphal ride along the ridge to Little Round Top. It seemed to Pleasonton that the cheers of the troops "plainly showed they expected the advance," but the army commander did not swerve from the opinion he had just expressed: "We have done well enough."

Hancock made a similar appeal, with similar results. Lifted into an ambulance after the charge had been repulsed, he ordered the vehicle halted as soon as it reached the Taneytown Road, where shells from long-range Whitworths north of Gettysburg were still landing, and began to dictate a message to be delivered at once to Meade. After explaining that he had been "severely but I trust not seriously wounded," he made it clear that he had not left his troops "so long as a rebel was to be seen upright." Interrupted by the attending surgeon, who protested against the delay, especially under enfilading fire from the rebels, the wounded general replied testily: "We've enfiladed *them*, God damn 'em," and went on with his dictation. He urged his chief to hurl Sedgwick and Sykes at Seminary Ridge without delay — if, indeed, this had not been done already. "If the VI and V corps have pressed up, the enemy will be destroyed," he predicted, and he added, by way of reinforcing his claim that Lee was in no condition to withstand a determined attack: "The enemy must be short of ammunition, as I was shot with a tenpenny nail." However, all he heard from Meade was a verbal message that avoided the central issue altogether. "Say to General Hancock," his fellow Pennsylvanian replied, "that I regret exceedingly that he is wounded, and that I thank him for the country and for myself for the service he has rendered today."

By this time McLaws had begun the withdrawal Longstreet ordered, and when the Federal skirmishers followed the graybacks out to the Emmitsburg Road, reclaiming the salient lost the day before, they were met by heavy volleys from guns and rifles; which tended to confirm the wisdom of Meade's decision, as he afterwards explained, not to advance on Seminary Ridge "in consequence of the bad example [Lee] had set for me, in ruining himself attacking a strong position." Nor was the northern commander alone in this belief. Henry Hunt, who had been pulled from under his toppled horse at the climax of the rebel assault and suffered only minor aches and pains from the injuries received, sided absolutely with his chief. "A prompt counter-charge after combat between two small bodies of men is one thing," the artillerist later wrote; "the change from the defensive to the offensive of an army, after an engagement at a single point, is quite another. To have made such a change to the offensive, on the assumption that Lee had made no provision against a reverse, would have been rash in the extreme." Warren thought so, too. It was generally felt, he subsequently declared, "that we had saved the country for the time and that we had done enough; that we might jeopardize all that we had done by trying to do too much." Such were the opinions of the two surviving members of the quartet of generals — the dead Reynolds and the wounded Hancock were the other pair — who were commonly given credit, then and later, for having done most to prevent another defeat from being added to the Union record: a defeat, moreover, which, given the time and place, some would maintain the Union could not have survived.

In point of fact, the greatest deterrent was the mute but staggering testimony of the casualty lists. Including Reynolds, Sickles, and Hancock, the three most aggressive of its corps commanders, a solid fourth of the Federal army had been killed or wounded or captured, and well over half again as many skulkers and stragglers had simply wandered off or been knocked loose from their units. A head count next morning would show 51,414 present of all ranks. Of the more than 38,000 men who thus were absent, the actual casualties numbered 23,049 — precisely tabulated a few days later at 3155 killed, 14,529 wounded, 5365 captured — which left some 15,000 not accounted for, just now at least, and encouraged the belief that the losses had been even greater than they were in fact. Moreover, they were quite unevenly distributed. Of Meade's seven infantry corps, the four led into action by Reynolds, Hancock, Sickles, and Howard had suffered almost ninety percent of the casualties, and if this had its brighter aspect — Sedgwick's corps, the largest in the army, had scarcely been engaged at all, and might therefore be considered available for delivery of the counterstroke urged by Pleasonton and Hancock — it also cast a corresponding gloom over those who had done the bleeding. All in all, when they became available, these figures did much to support the judgment of the responsible commander that, notwithstanding the tactical desirability of launching an immediate mass assault, which was as clear to him as it was to any man on the field, the troops were in no condition to sustain it.

On the other hand there was testimony from Lee's own ranks that the Confederates were in no condition to resist an assault if one had been made against them. "Our ammunition was so low," Alexander confessed, "and our diminished forces at the moment so widely dispersed along the unwisely extended line, that an advance by a single fresh corps, [Sedgwick's] for instance, could have cut us in two." Few on that same side of the line agreed with this, however. After all, it was not Lee's army that had been shattered in the desperate charge that afternoon, but only eight of his thirty-seven brigades, five of which — Anderson's other three and Pender's two: the same number that had stood fast for Meade across the way — were on hand to defend his center. Moreover, all his cavalry was up by now, including Imboden's 2000 troopers who had arrived at midday, and not one piece of artillery had been lost. Far from being depressed by the repulse, many along the rebel line had been angered by what they had seen and were eager for revenge; they asked for nothing better than a chance to serve the blucoats in the same manner, if they could be persuaded to attack. "We'll fight them, sir, till hell freezes over," one grayback told an observer, "and then, sir, we will fight them on the ice." Indeed, adversity seemed to knit them closer together as a family, which was what they had become in the past year under Lee, and brought out the high qualities that would stand them in good stead during the downhill months ahead. Longstreet, for example, riding out after dark to inspect his skirmish line, found a battery still in position near the Peach Orchard, though he had ordered all his artillery withdrawn to the cover of the western ridge some time before. "Whose are these guns?" he demanded; whereupon a tall man with a pipe in his mouth stepped out of the shadows. "I am the captain," he said quietly, and when the general asked why he had stayed out there in front of the infantry, the artilleryman replied: "I am out here to have a little skirmishing on my own account, if the Yanks come out of their holes." Amused by the prospect of a skirmish with 12-pounder howitzers, and heartened by such evidence of staunchness in a time of strain, Old Peter threw back his head and let his laugh ring out once more across that somber field.

Incongruous as his laughter had seemed that afternoon, just before the 11,000-man assault wave broke and began to ebb, it sounded even stranger now in the darkness, under cover of which the extent of the army's losses could begin to be assessed. From the top down, they were unremittingly grievous. Of the 52 Confederate generals who had crossed the Potomac in the past three weeks, no less than 17 — barely under one third — had become casualties in the past three days. Five were killed outright or mortally wounded: Semmes and Barksdale, Pender, Armistead and Garnett. Two were captured: Archer, who had been taken on the first day, and Trimble, who had not been able to make it back across the valley today with a shattered leg: and this figure would be increased to three when the army began its withdrawal, since Kemper was too badly injured to be moved. Nine more were wounded:

some lightly, such as Heth and Pettigrew, others gravely, such as Hood, whose arm might have to be taken off, and Hampton, who had received not one but two head cuts and also had some shrapnel in his body. When the list was lengthened by 18 colonels killed or captured, many of them officers of high promise, slated for early promotion, it was obvious that the Army of Northern Virginia had suffered a loss in leadership from which it might never recover. A British observer was of this opinion. He lauded the offensive prowess of Lee's soldiers, who had marched out as proudly as if on parade in their eagerness to come to grips with their opponents on the ridge across the way; "But they will never do it again," he predicted. And he told why. He had been with the army since Fredericksburg, ticking off the illustrious dead from Stonewall Jackson down, and now on the heels of Gettysburg he asked a rhetorical question of his Confederate friends: "Don't you see your system feeds upon itself? You cannot fill the places of these men. Your troops do wonders, but every time at a cost you cannot afford."

That might well be. Certainly there was no comfort in a comparison of the representation on the list of those of less exalted rank. Here, too, no less than a third had fallen — and possibly more, for the count was incomplete. Lee recorded his losses as 2592 killed, 12,709 wounded, and 5150 captured or missing, a total of 20,451: which was surely low, for a variety of reasons. For one, a few units that had fought made no report, and for another he had directed in mid-May that troops so lightly wounded that they could remain with their regiments were not to be listed as casualties, although such men were included in the Federal tabulations. Moreover, his figure for the number captured or missing could not be reconciled with the prisoner-of-war records in the Adjutant General's office at Washington, which bore the names of 12,227 Confederates captured July 1-5. The true total of Lee's losses in Pennsylvania could hardly have been less than 25,000 and quite possibly was far heavier; 28,063 was the figure computed by one meticulous student of such grisly matters, in which case the butcher's bill for Gettysburg, blue and gray together, exceeded 50,000 men. This was more than Shiloh and Sharpsburg combined, with Ball's Bluff and Belmont thrown in for good measure. And while there was considerably less disparity of bloodshed among the several corps of the attackers — Hill had suffered most and Ewell least, but both were within a thousand of Longstreet, who had lost perhaps 8500 — this was by no means true of smaller units within the corps. Gordon's exultation, "The Almighty has covered my men with his shield and buckler," could scarcely have been echoed by any commander of the eight brigades that went up Cemetery Ridge, and even within these there was a diversity of misfortune. Most regiments came back across the valley with at least a skeleton cadre to which future recruits or conscripts could be attached; but not all. The 14th Tennessee, for example, had left Clarksville in 1861 with 960 men on its muster roll, and in the past two years, most of which time their homeland had been under Union occupation, they had fought on all the major battlefields of Virginia. When Archer took them across Willoughby Run on the opening day of Gettysburg they counted 365 bayonets; by sunset they were down to barely 60. These five dozen survivors, led by a captain on the third day, went forward with Fry against Cemetery Ridge, and there — where the low stone wall jogged west, then south, to form what was known thereafter as the angle — all but three of the remaining 60 fell. This was only one among the forty-odd regiments in the charge; there were others that suffered about as cruelly; but to those wives and sweethearts, parents and sisters and younger brothers who had remained at its point of origin, fifty miles down the Cumberland from Nashville, the news came hard. "Thus the band that once was the pride of Clarksville has fallen," a citizen lamented, and he went on to explain something of what he and those around him felt. "A gloom rests over the city; the hopes and affections of the people were wrapped in the regiment.... Ah! what a terrible responsibility rests upon those who inaugurated this unholy war."

No one felt the responsibility harder than Lee, though, far from inaugurating, he had opposed the war at the outset, when some who now were loudest in their lamentations had called for secession or coercion, whatever the consequences, and had allowed themselves to be persuaded that all the blood that would be shed could be mopped up with a congressman's pocket handkerchief; whereas it now turned out that, at the modest rate of a gallon for every dead man and a pint for each of the wounded, perhaps not all the handkerchiefs in the nation, or both nations, would suffice to soak up the blood that had been spilled at Gettysburg alone. Such macabre calculations might be of particular interest down the years — a fit subject, perhaps, for a master's thesis when centennial time came round — but Lee's tonight were of a different nature. From the moment he saw the shattered brigades of Pickett and Pettigrew begin their stumble back across the valley, it was obvious that what was left of his army, low on food and with only enough ammunition on hand for one more day of large-scale action, would have to retreat. After riding forward to help rally the fugitives and thus present as bold a front as possible to discourage a counterattack, he went to his tent and there, by candlelight, resumed his study of the maps over which he had pored throughout the hectic week preceding the blindfold commitment to battle. If his problems now were no less difficult, they were at least much simpler, having been reduced to the logistics of withdrawing his survivors, together with his wounded, his supply train, and his prisoners, from the immediate front of a victorious opponent deep in hostile territory. He chose his routes, decided on the order of march, and then, despite the lateness of the hour and his bone-deep weariness after three days of failure and frustration, went in person to make certain that his plans were understood by the responsible commanders. By dawn, Ewell and Longstreet were to have their troops disposed along Seminary Ridge, north and south of Hill's present position in the center. All day tomorrow, whether Meade attacked or not, they were to hold their ground and thus afford a head start for the wounded, as well as for the supply train and the captives; after which they were to take up the march themselves, under cover of darkness, with Hill in the lead, followed by Longstreet, and Ewell bringing up the rear. Pickett's remnant — a scant 800 of his badly shaken men would be on hand at daylight — was assigned to guard the 5000-odd Federal prisoners on the return, and Imboden's troopers would escort the miles-long column of ambulances and forage wagons loaded with such of the wounded as the surgeons judged could survive the long ride home. By this arrangement, the last infantry division to reach the field, as well as the last cavalry brigade, would be the first to depart. Before leaving his tent, Lee sent word for Imboden to report to headquarters and wait for his return, intending to give him detailed instructions for the conduct of the march. Then he went out into the night.

Unlike the vague and discretionary orders he had issued throughout the week leading up to battle and even during the past three days of fighting, in the course of which his messages had been verbal and for the most part tentative, his instructions now were written and precise, allowing no discretion whatsoever to anyone at all. In Hill's case, moreover, since his was the corps that would mark the route and set the pace, Lee took the added precaution of conferring with him in person, tracing for him the line of march on the map and making certain there was no possibility of a misunderstanding. This might have waited for morning; the infantry movement would not begin until the following evening at the earliest; but evidently Lee felt that he should not, or could not, sleep until the matter had been disposed of to his satisfaction. Delegation of authority, under orders that not only permitted but encouraged a wide degree of latitude in their execution by subordinates, had been the basis for his greatest triumphs, particularly during the ten months he had had Jackson to rely on; Second Manassas and Chancellorsville were instances in point. But at Gettysburg, with Stonewall just seven weeks in his grave, the system had failed him, and his actions tonight were an acknowledgment of the fact. Though he would return to the system in time, out of necessity as well as from choice, on this last night of his greatest and worst-fought battle he abandoned it entirely. He relied on no one but himself.

It was late, well after midnight, by the time he left Hill and rode back through the quiet moonlit camps along Seminary Ridge to his headquarters beside the Chambersburg Pike. Imboden was waiting for him there, as instructed, though no one else was stirring; his staff had gone to sleep so tired that not even a sentry had been posted. Lee drew rein and sat motionless for a time, apparently too weary to dismount, but as the cavalryman stepped forward, intending to assist him, he swung down and leaned for another long moment against Traveller, head bowed and one arm thrown across the saddle for more rest. Imboden watched him, awed by the tableau — "The moon shone full upon his massive features and revealed an expression of sadness that I had never before seen upon his face" — then, hoping, as he said later, "to change the silent current of his thoughts," ventured to speak of his obvious fatigue: "General, this has been a hard day on you." Lee raised his head, and his fellow Virginian saw grief as well as weariness in his eyes. "Yes, this has been a sad, sad day to us," he replied, emphasizing the word he had used that afternoon in speaking to Fremantle. Again he fell silent, but presently he "straightened up to his full height" and spoke "with more animation and excitement" than Imboden had ever seen him display: "I never saw troops behave more magnificently than Pickett's division of Virginians did today in that grand charge upon the enemy. And if they had been supported as they were to have been — but, for some reason not yet fully explained to me, were not — we would have held the position and the day would have been ours." This last was a strange thing for him to say, for he himself had denied Hill permission to throw his whole corps into the assault. However, there was no mistaking the extent of his regret. "Too bad; too bad," he groaned; "Oh, too bad!"

Suppressing his emotion, he invited Imboden into his tent for a study of the map and the long road home, which he was about to take. "We must now return to Virginia," he said.

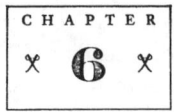

Unvexed to the Sea

★ ✕ ☆

ALL NEXT MORNING, HAVING COMPLETED THE perilous nighttime disengagement of both wings in order to form a continuous line of defense along Seminary Ridge, from Oak Hill on the north to the confronting loom of Round Top on the south, the Confederates awaited the answer to the question that was uppermost in their minds: Would the Federals attack? Apparently they would not. "What o'clock is it?" Longstreet finally asked an artillerist standing beside him. "11.55," the officer replied, and ventured a prediction: "General, this is the 'Glorious Fourth.' We should have a salute from the other side at noon." Noon came and went but not a gun was fired. Old Peter believed he knew why. "Their artillery was too much crippled yesterday to think of salutes," he said with satisfaction. "Meade is not in good spirits this morning."

Presently there was evidence that he was wrong. Across the way, in the vicinity of the Peach Orchard, a Union brigade was seen deploying for battle. Nothing came of this, however; for just at that time — about 1 o'clock — rain began to fall, first a drizzle, then a steady downpour; the bluecoats jammed their fixed bayonets into the ground to keep the water from running down their rifle barrels, then squatted uncomfortably beside them, shoulders hunched against the rain. Obviously they had abandoned all notion of attack, if indeed they had had any such real intention in the first place. On their separate ridges, an average mile apart, the men of both armies peered at one another through the transparent curtain of rain as it sluiced the bloodstains from the grass and rocks where they had fought so savagely the past three days, but would not fight today.

Lee appeared calm and confident as he watched the departure of the long column of wounded at the height of the afternoon rainstorm and continued his preparations for the withdrawal of the infantry and artillery that night. Beneath the surface, however, he was testy: as was shown by his response to a well-meant pleasantry from one of Ewell's young staff officers who came to headquarters with a report from his chief. "General," he said encouragingly, "I hope the other two corps are in as good condition for work as ours is this morning." Lee looked at him hard and said coldly, "What reason have you, young man, to suppose they are not?" Even before it became evident that the Federals were not going to attack he proposed, by means of a flag of truce, a man-for-man exchange of prisoners, thus risking a disclosure of his intentions in hope of lightening his burden on the march. Nothing came of this; Meade prudently declined, on grounds that he had no authority in such matters, and Lee continued his preparations for the withdrawal, prisoners and all. Imboden and the wounded were to return by way of Cashtown and Chambersburg, Greencastle and Hagerstown, for a Potomac crossing near Williamsport, a distance of forty-odd miles, while the infantry would follow a route some dozen miles shorter, southwest through Fairfield to Hagerstown for a crossing at the same point, its left flank protected by units of Stuart's cavalry on the road to Emmitsburg. Though he felt confident that his opponent would be restricted in maneuver by the continuing obligation to cover Baltimore and Washington, Lee recognized the impending retrograde movement as probably the most hazardous of his career. His troops did not seem greatly dispirited by the failure of the campaign, but their weariness was apparent to even a casual eye and a good third of those who had headed north with such high hopes a month ago would not be returning. Including the walking wounded who remained with their commands, he had fewer than 50,000 effectives of all arms. Moreover, Meade by now must have received heavy reinforcements from the surrounding northern states, as well as from his nearby capital: whereas Lee could expect no such transfusions of strength until he crossed the Potomac, if at all.

Leaving his campfires burning on the ridge, Hill began the withdrawal soon after nightfall. Longstreet followed, still in a driving rain that served to muffle the sound of the army's departure from its opponent across the valley. There were delays, however, and it was 2 o'clock in the morning before Ewell began his march. By now the roads were troughs of mud, which made for heavy going: so heavy, indeed, that it was 4 o'clock in the afternoon by the time the lead elements of the Second Corps plodded into Fairfield, only nine miles from the now deserted ridge just west of Gettysburg. Part of the delay was caused by free-swinging Union troopers, who got among the trains and captured a number of wagons, together with their guards and drivers. Old Bald Head was so outraged by this development that he was for facing about and fighting, then and there. But Lee would not agree. "No, no, General Ewell," he said; "we must let those people alone for the present. We will try them again some other time." Hill and Longstreet, well beyond Fairfield before sundown, had no such difficulties. The latter, in fact, was in high good spirits when he called a halt that evening, conveniently near a roadside tavern where his staff had arranged for dinner to be served. Apparently the troops outside were getting theirs, too, for in the course of the meal there was a sound of scuffling in the adjoining chamber, followed by the appearance of a hard-faced farmwife who pushed her way into the dining room, exclaiming as she advanced: "Which is the General? Where is the great officer? Good heavens, they are killing our fat hogs! Our milk cows now are going!" On the march northward, such a complaint would have brought sudden and heavy reprisal on the offenders, but not now. "Yes, Madam," Old Peter told her, shaking his head in disapproval, "it's very sad; very sad. And this sort of thing has been going on in Virginia for more than two years. Very sad."

He took over the lead from Hill next day, July 6, and though the rain continued to fall and the mud to deepen, the men stepped out smartly once they were clear of Monterey Pass and beyond South Mountain. "Let him who will say it to the contrary," a Texan wrote home, "we made Manassas time from Pennsylvania." At 5 p.m. Longstreet entered Hagerstown, and Lee, who rode with him as usual, was relieved to learn that the train of wounded had passed through earlier that day and should have reached the Potomac by now, half a dozen miles away. Imboden had made good speed with his 17-mile-long column, though at the cost of much suffering by the wounded, whose piteous cries to be left by the road to die were ignored by the drivers in obedience to orders that there were to be no halts for any reason whatever, by day or night. Many of the injured men had been without food for thirty-six hours, he later wrote, and "their torn and bloody clothing, matted and hardened, was rasping the tender, inflamed, and still oozing wounds. Very few of the wagons had even a layer of straw in them, and all were without springs.... From nearly every wagon as the teams trotted on, urged by whip and shout, came such cries and shrieks as these: 'Oh, God! Why can't I die?' 'My God, will no one have mercy and kill me?' 'Stop! Oh, for God's sake, stop just for one minute; take me out and let me die on the roadside!' 'I am dying, I am dying!' ... During this one night," the cavalryman added, "I realized more of the horrors of war than I had in all the two preceding years." Bypassing Chambersburg in the darkness, the lead escort regiment rode through Greencastle at dawn, and when the troopers were a mile beyond the town, which had offered no resistance at all in the course of the march north the week before, some thirty or forty citizens rushed out of their houses and "attacked the train with axes, cutting the spokes out of ten or a dozen wheels and dropping the wagons in the streets." Imboden sent a detachment of troopers back, and this put an end to the trouble there. Beyond Hagerstown, however, the Union cavalry appeared in strength from Frederick and began to harass the column. At Williamsport, finding the pontoon bridge destroyed by raiders from downstream on the opposite bank, Imboden called a halt and deployed his men and vehicles in the style employed by wagon trains when attacked by Indians on the plains. Arming his drivers with spare rifles and placing his 23 guns at regular intervals along the half-circle of wagons, he faced northeast, the river at his back, and managed to hold off the attackers until Fitz Lee arrived and drove them away.

The army commander got there the following morning, still riding with Longstreet at the head of the infantry column, and though he was pleased to learn that Imboden and his nephew Fitz had staved off the immediate threat by the blue horsemen, who had greatly outnumbered the defenders until now, he could see for himself that his predicament, here on the north bank of the river he had marched so hard to reach, was worse by far than the one in which he had found himself three days ago at Gettysburg, after the failure of his final attempt to break the Union fishhook. Not only was the pontoon bridge destroyed, but the recent torrential rains had swollen the Potomac well past fording. Low on food, as well as ammunition for its guns, the army was cut off from Virginia, together with its prisoners and its wounded. Lee's first thought was for these last; he directed that all the ferryboats in the region were to be collected and used in transporting the injured men to the south bank; the wagons, like the infantry and the artillery, would have to wait until the river subsided or the bridge could be rebuilt. Meanwhile, if Meade attacked, the Confederates, with small chance to maneuver and none at all to retreat, would have to give him battle under conditions whereby victory would yield but little profit and defeat would mean annihilation.

Accordingly, the engineers began their task of laying out a system of defense that extended some three miles in each direction, upstream and down from Williamsport, where in normal times a man could wade across. Both of its extremities well covered, the six-mile curve of line was anchored north on Conococheague Creek and south on the Potomac below Falling Waters, the site of the wrecked bridge. As at Gettysburg, Hill took the center and Ewell and Longstreet the left and right — they had by now about 35,000 effectives between them, including the cannoneers whose limber chests were nearly empty — while Stuart's troopers reinforced the flanks and patrolled the front. By next day, July 8, the dispositions were complete, though the men continued to improve them with their shovels, and Lee received the welcome news that ammunition for his guns was on the way from Winchester; it would arrive tomorrow and could be brought across by the ferries already hard at work transporting the wounded to the Virginia bank. Foam-flecked and swollen, the river was still on the boom, however, farther than ever past fording and with no decrease predicted. So far, Meade's infantry had not appeared, but Lee did not believe it would be long in coming — and in strength much greater than his own. He kept up a show of calmness, despite a precarious shortage of food and the personal strain of having been informed that his son Rooney, taken to Hanover County to recover from his Brandy Station wound, had been captured by raiders and hauled off to Fort Monroe, where he was being held as a hostage to insure the safety of some Federal prisoners charged with various crimes against the people of the Old Dominion. Despite the fret of such distractions, Lee wrote that night to the President, proposing once more that Beauregard's "army in effigy" march at once for the Rappahannock and thus create a diversion in his favor through this anxious time of waiting for the Potomac to subside.

"I hope Your Excellency will understand that I am not in the least discouraged," he added, somewhat apologetic over this second appeal for help from outside his department, "or that my faith in the protection of an all-merciful Providence, or in the fortitude of this army, is at all shaken. But, though conscious that the enemy has been much shattered in the recent battle, I am aware that he can be easily reinforced, while no addition can be made to our numbers. The measure, therefore, that I have recommended is altogether one of a prudential nature."

Learning from scouts the following evening that the Federal main body was on the march from Frederick, he was convinced that his army would soon have to fight for its survival, which in turn meant the survival of the Confederacy itself. In this extremity he occupied himself with the inspection and improvement of his defenses, the distribution of the newly arrived ammunition for his batteries, and the nerving of his troops for the shock he believed was coming. Though the river continued to rise in his rear and food and forage were getting scarcer by the hour — the men were now on half rations and the horses were getting nothing to eat but grass and standing grain — he kept up a show of confidence and good cheer. Only those who knew him best detected his extreme concern: Alexander, for example, who later testified that he had never seen his chief so deeply anxious as he appeared on July 10, one week after the guns of Gettysburg stopped roaring. This did not show, however, in a dispatch the general sent Davis that night from his still bridgeless six-mile bridgehead on the north bank of the still unfordable Potomac. "With the blessing of Heaven," he told the President, "I trust that the courage and fortitude of the army will be found sufficient to relieve us from the embarrassment caused by the unlooked-for natural difficulties of our situation, if not to secure more valuable and substantial results. Very respectfully, your obedient servant, R. E. LEE."

In all this time, Sunday through Saturday, no two opposing infantrymen had looked at one another along the barrels of their rifles, and the source of this week-long lethargy on the part of those who should have been pursuers lay in the make-up of the man who led them. His caution, which had given the blue army its first undeniable large-scale victory to balance against the five major defeats it had suffered under as many different leaders in the past two years, was more enlarged than reduced by the discovery, on the morning of July 5, that the Confederates were no longer in position on the ridge across the way; so that while the first half of Lee's prediction — "General Meade will commit no blunder on my front" — had been fulfilled, the second half — "If I make one, he will make haste to take advantage of it" — had not. Not that there was no occasion for this increase of caution. The defenders had suffered heavily in the three-day conflict, particularly in the loss of men of rank. Schimmelfennig, who emerged from his woodshed hiding place when Gettysburg was reoccupied on the 4th, was meager compensation for the sixteen brigade and division commanders killed or wounded in the battle, let alone for the three corps commanders who had fallen. Besides, avoidance of risk having gained him so much so far, Meade had no intention of abandoning that policy simply because the winds of chance appeared to have shifted in his favor for the moment.

Whether they had in fact shifted, or had merely been made to seem to, was by no means certain. Lee was foxy, as Meade well knew from old acquaintance. He was known to be most dangerous when he appeared least so: particularly in retreat, as McClellan had discovered while pursuing him under similar circumstances, back in September, after presuming to have taken his measure at South Mountain. Moreover, he was not above tampering with the weather vane, and there was evidence that such was the case at present. Francis Barlow, who had been wounded and captured on the opening day of battle while commanding one of Howard's overrun divisions north of town, was left behind in Gettysburg when the rebels withdrew to their ridge on the night of July 3. He got word to headquarters next morning that Lee's plan, as he had overheard it from his sick-bed, was to feign retreat, then waylay his pursuers. Meade took the warning much to heart and contented himself that afternoon, at the height of the sudden rainstorm, with issuing a congratulatory order to the troops "for the glorious result of the recent operations." That those operations had not ended was evident to all, for the graybacks were still on Seminary Ridge, less than a mile across the rain-swept valley. "Our task is not yet accomplished," the order acknowledged, "and the commanding general looks to the army for greater efforts to drive from our soil every vestige of the presence of the invader."

It was read to all regiments that evening. In one, when the reading was over, the colonel waved his hat and called for three cheers for Meade. But the men were strangely silent. This was not because they had no use for their new chief, one of them afterwards observed; it was simply because they did not feel like cheering, either for him or for anyone else, rain or no rain. Many of them had been engaged all day in burying the dead and bringing in the wounded of both armies, and this was scarcely the kind of work that put them in the frame of mind for tossing caps and shouting hurrahs. Mostly though, as the man explained, the veterans, "with their lights and experiences, could not see the wisdom or the occasion for any such manifestation of enthusiasm." They had done a great deal of cheering over the past two years, for Hooker and Burnside and Pope and McDowell, as well as for Little Mac, and in the course of time they had matured; or as this witness put it, their "business sense increased with age." Someday, perhaps, there would be a reason for tossing their caps completely away and cheering themselves hoarse, but this did not seem to them to be quite it. So they remained silent, watching the colonel swing his hat for a while, then glumly put it back on his head and dismiss them.

That evening the corps commanders voted five to two to hold their present ground until it was certain that Lee was retreating. Next morning — Sunday: Meade had been just one week in command — they found that he was indeed gone, but there was doubt as to whether he was retreating or maneuvering for a better position from which to renew the contest. Sedgwick moved out in the afternoon, only to bog down in the mud, and fog was so heavy the following morning that he could determine nothing except that the Confederates had reached Monterey Pass, southwest of Fairfield. "As soon as possible," Meade wired Halleck, "I will cross South Mountain and proceed in search of the enemy." On second thought, however, and always bearing in mind his instructions to "maneuver and fight in such a manner as to cover the capital and Baltimore," he decided that his best course would be to avoid a direct pursuit, which might necessitate a costly storming of the pass, and instead march south into Maryland, then westward in an attempt to come up with Lee before he effected a crossing near Williamsburg, where French's raiders had wrecked the pontoon bridge the day before. In Frederick by noon of July 7, fifty-odd hours after finding that his opponent had stolen away from his front under cover of darkness, the northern commander indulged himself in the luxury of a hot bath in a hotel and put on fresh clothes for the first time in ten days. This afforded him considerable relief, but it also provided a chance for him to discover how profoundly tired he was. "From the time I took command till today," he wrote his wife, "I . . . have not had a regular night's rest, and many nights not a wink of sleep, and for several days did not even wash my face and hands, no regular food, and all the time in a state of mental anxiety. Indeed, I think I have lived as much in this time as in the last thirty years."

The men, of course, were in far worse shape from their exertions. Four of the seven corps had been shot almost to pieces, and some of the survivors had trouble recognizing their outfits, so unequal had been the losses in the various commands, including more than 300 field and company grade officers lost by the quick subtractive action of shells and bullets and clubbed muskets. III Corps veterans, who were among the hardest hit in this respect, sardonically referred to themselves as "the III Corps as we understand it." Their uniforms were in tatters and their long marches through dust and mud, to and from the three-day uproar, had quite literally worn the shoes off their feet. Meade's regular army soul was pained to see them, though the pain was salved considerably by a wire received that afternoon from Halleck: "It gives me pleasure to inform you that you have been appointed a brigadier general in the Regular Army, to rank from July 3, the date of your brilliant victory." This welcome message was followed however by two more from Old Brains that were not so welcome, suggesting as they did a lack of confidence in his aggressive qualities. "Push forward and fight Lee before he can cross the Potomac," one directed, while the other was more specific: "You have given the enemy a stunning blow at Gettysburg. Follow it up, and give him another before he can reach the Potomac.... There is strong evidence that he is short of artillery ammunition, and if vigorously pressed he must suffer." Meade wanted it understood that the suffering was unlikely to be as one-sided as his superior implied. He too was having his troubles and he wanted them known to those above him, who presumed to hand down judgments from a distance. "My army is assembling slowly," he replied, still in Frederick on July 8. "The rains of yesterday and last night have made all roads but pikes almost impassable. Artillery and wagons are stalled; it will take time to collect them together. A large portion of the men are barefooted.... I expect to find the enemy in a strong position, well covered with artillery, and I do not desire to imitate his example at Gettysburg and assault a position where the chances were so greatly against success. I wish in advance to moderate the expectations of those who, in ignorance of the difficulties to be encountered, may expect too much. All that I can do under the circumstances I pledge this army to do."

Apparently Halleck did not like the sound of this, for he replied within the hour: "There is reliable information that the enemy is crossing at Williamsport. The opportunity to attack his divided forces should not be lost. The President is urgent and anxious that your army should move against him by forced marches." Meade had not heard a word from Lincoln, either of thanks for his recent victory or of encouragement in his present exertions, and now there was this indirect expression of a lack of confidence. Forced marches! The Pennsylvanian bristled. "My army is and has been making forced marches, short of rations and barefooted," he wired back, pointing out in passing that the information as to a rebel crossing differed from his own, and added: "I take occasion to repeat that I will use my utmost efforts to push forward this army." Old Brains protested that he had been misconceived. "Do not understand me as expressing any dissatisfaction," he replied; "on the contrary, your army has done most nobly. I only wish to give you opinions formed from information received here." But having entered this disclaimer he returned to his former tone, ignoring Meade's denial that any appreciable part of the rebel force had crossed the Potomac, either at Williamsport or elsewhere. "If Lee's army is so divided by the river," he persisted, "the importance of attacking the part on this side is incalculable. Such an opportunity may never occur again.... You will have forces sufficient to render your victory certain. My only fear now is that the enemy may escape."

At Middletown on July 9, having replaced Butterfield with Humphreys as chief of staff and thus got rid of the last reminder of Hooker's luckless tenure, Meade was pleased that no rain had fallen since early the day before. Though the Potomac remained some five feet above its normal level and therefore well past fording, the roads were drying fast and permitted better marching. Moreover, Halleck was keeping his word as to reinforcements. The army had 85,000 men present for duty and 10,000 more on the way, which meant that its Gettysburg losses had been made good, although a number of short-term militia and grass-green conscripts were included. "This army is moving in three columns," Meade informed Halleck before midday, "the right column having in it three corps.... I think the decisive battle of the war will be fought in a few days. In view of the momentous consequences, I desire to adopt such measures as in my judgment will tend to insure success, even though these may be deemed tardy." Delighted to hear that Meade was in motion again, however tardy, the general-in-chief was careful to say nothing that might cause him to stop and resume the telegraphic argument. "Do not be influenced by any dispatch from here against your own judgment," he told him. "Regard them as suggestions only. Our information here is not always correct." In point of fact, now that contact seemed imminent, it was Old Brains who was urging caution. More troops were on the way, he wired next day, and he advised waiting for them. "I think it will be best for you to postpone a general battle till you can concentrate all your forces and get up your reserves and reinforcements.... Beware of partial combats. Bring up and hurl upon the enemy all your forces, good and bad."

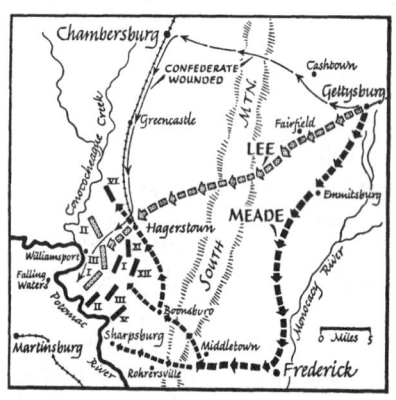

Meade agreed. He spent the next two days, which continued fair, examining the curved shield of Lee's defenses and jockeying for a position from which to "hurl" his army upon them. By early afternoon of

July 12 — Sunday again: he now had been two full weeks in command — he was ready, though the skies again were threatening rain. Selected divisions from the II, V, and VI Corps confronted a rebel-held wheat field, pickets out, awaiting the signal to go forward, when a Pennsylvania chaplain rode up to the command post and protested the violation of the Sabbath. Couldn't the battle be fought as well tomorrow? he demanded. For once Meade kept his temper, challenged thus by a home-state man of the cloth, and explained somewhat elaborately that he was like a carpenter with a contract to construct a box, four sides and the bottom of which had been completed; now the lid was ready to be put on. The chaplain was unimpressed. "As God's agent and disciple I solemnly protest," he declared fervently. "I will show you that the Almighty will not permit you to desecrate his sacred day.... Look at the heavens; see the threatening storm approaching!" Whereupon there were sudden peals of thunder and zigzags of lightning, as in a passage from the Old Testament, and rain began to pour down on the wheat field and the troops who were about to move against it. Meade canceled the probing action, returned to his quarters, and got off a wire to Halleck. "It is my intention to attack them tomorrow," he wrote; but then — perhaps with the chaplain's demonstration in mind — he added, "unless something intervenes to prevent it."

So he said. But a council of war he called that evening showed that his chief subordinates were opposed to launching any attack without a further examination of Lee's position. Only Wadsworth, commanding the I Corps in the absence of Newton, who was sick, agreed with Meade wholeheartedly in favoring an assault, although Howard, anxious as always to retrieve a damaged reputation, expressed a willingness to go along with the plan. Despite reports that the Potomac was falling rapidly after four days of fair weather, Meade deferred to the judgment of five of his seven corps commanders, postponed the scheduled advance, and spent the next day conducting a further study of the rebel dispositions. Informing Halleck of the outcome of the council of war, he told him: "I shall continue these reconnaissances with the expectation of finding some weak point upon which, if I succeed, I shall hazard an attack." Old Brains was prompt to reply that he disapproved of such flinching now that the two armies were once more face to face. "You are strong enough to attack and defeat the enemy before he can effect a crossing," he wired. "Act upon your own judgment and make your generals execute your orders. Call no council of war. It is proverbial that councils of war never fight. Reinforcements are pushed on as rapidly as possible. Do not let the enemy escape."

It was plain that the advice as to councils of war amounted to an attempt to lock the stable after the pony had been stolen. And so too did the rest of it, as the thing turned out. When Meade at last went forward next morning, July 14, he found the rebel trenches empty and all but a rear-guard handful of graybacks already on the far bank of the Potomac. Aside from a number of stragglers picked up in the rush, together with two mud-stalled guns — the only ones Lee lost in the whole campaign — attacks on the remnant merely served to hasten the final stages of the crossing, after which the delivered Confederates cut their rebuilt pontoon bridge loose from the Maryland shore and looked mockingly back across the swirling waters, which were once more on the rise as a result of the two-day rainstorm the chaplain had invoked.

Meade was not greatly disappointed, or at any rate he did not seem so in a dispatch informing Halleck of Lee's escape before it had even been completed. The closing sentence was downright bland: "Your instructions as to further movements, in case the enemy are entirely across the river, are desired."

For Lee, threatened in front by twice his number and menaced within the perimeter by starvation, the past three days had been touch and go, all the time with the receding but still swollen Potomac mocking his efforts to escape. In the end it was Jackson's old quartermaster, Major John Harman, who managed the army's extraction and landed it safe on the soil of Virginia, having improvised pontoons by tearing down abandoned houses for their timbers and floating the finished products down to Falling Waters, where they were linked and floored; "a good bridge," Lee called the result, and though a more critical staff officer termed it a "crazy affair," it served its purpose. Its planks overlaid with lopped branches to deaden the sound of wheels and boots, it not only permitted the secret withdrawal of the guns and wagons in the darkness; it also made possible the dry-shod crossing of the two corps under Longstreet and Hill, while Ewell managed to use the ford at Williamsport, his tallest men standing in midstream, armpit deep, to pass the shorter waders along. By dawn the Second Corps was over, but the First and Third were still waiting for the trains to clear the bridge. At last they did, and Longstreet crossed without interference, followed by Hill's lead division: at which point guns began to roar.

"There!" Lee exclaimed, turning his head sharply in the direction of the sound. "I was expecting it — the beginning of the attack."

He soon learned, however, that Heth, who had recovered from his head injury and returned to the command of his division, had faced his men about and was holding off the attackers while Hill's center division completed the crossing; whereupon Heth turned and followed, fighting as he went. It was smartly done. Despite an official boast by Kilpatrick that he captured a 1500-man Confederate brigade, only about 300 stragglers failed to make it over the river before the bridge was cut loose from the northern bank, and the loss of the two stalled guns, while regrettable, was more than made up for by the seven that had been taken in Pennsylvania and brought back. Another loss was more grievous.

On Heth's return to duty, Johnston Pettigrew had resumed command of what was left of his brigade, which served this morning as rear guard. He had his men in line, awaiting his turn at the bridge, when suddenly they were charged by a group of about forty Union cavalrymen who were thought at first to be Confederates brandishing a captured flag, so foolhardy was their attack. Pettigrew, one of whose arms was still weak from his Seven Pines wound, while the other was in a sling because of the hand that had been hit at Gettysburg, was tossed from his startled horse. He picked himself up and calmly directed the firing at the blue troopers, who were dashing about and banging away with their carbines. Eventually all of them were killed — which made it difficult to substantiate or disprove the claim that they were drunk — but meantime one took a position on the flank and fired so effectively that the general himself drew his revolver and went after him in person. Determined to get so close he could not miss, Pettigrew was shot in the stomach before he came within easy pistol range. He made it over the bridge, refusing to be left behind as a prisoner, and lived for three days of intense suffering before he died at Bunker Hill, Virginia, the tenth general permanently lost to the army in the course of the invasion. The whole South mourned him, especially his native North Carolina, and Lee referred to him in his report as "an officer of great merit and promise."

Saddened by this last-minute sacrifice of a gallant fighter, but grateful for its delivery from immediate peril, the army continued its march that day and the next to Bunker Hill, twenty miles from the Potomac, and there it went into camp, as Lee reported, for rest and recruitment. "The men are in good health and spirits," he informed Richmond, "but want shoes and clothing badly.... As soon as these necessary articles are obtained we shall be prepared to resume operations." That he was still feeling aggressive, despite the setback he had suffered, was shown by his reaction on July 16 to information that the enemy was preparing to cross the river at Harpers Ferry. "Should he follow us in this direction," Lee wrote Davis, "I shall lead him up the Valley and endeavor to attack him as far from his base as possible."

Meade's exchanges with his government, following his laconic report of a rebel getaway, were of a different nature. Halleck was plainly miffed. "I need hardly say to you," he wired, "that the escape of Lee's army without another battle has created great dissatisfaction in the mind of the President, and it will require an active and energetic pursuit on your part to remove the impression that it has not been sufficiently active before." This was altogether more than Meade could take, particularly from Lincoln, who still had sent him no word of appreciation or encouragement, by way of reward for the first great victory in the East, but only second-hand expressions of doubt and disappointment. The Pennsylvanian stood on his dignity and made the strongest protest within his means. "Having performed my duty conscientiously and to the best of my ability," he declared, "the censure of the President conveyed in your dispatch... is, in my judgment, so undeserved that I feel compelled most respectfully to ask to be immediately relieved from the command of this army." There Halleck had it, and Lincoln too. They could either refrain from such goadings or let the victorious general depart. Moreover, Meade strengthened his case with a follow-up wire, sent half an hour later, in which he passed along Kilpatrick's exuberant if erroneous report of capturing a whole rebel brigade on the near bank of the Potomac. Old Brains promptly backtracked, as he always seemed to do when confronted with vigorous opposition from anyone, blue or gray, except Joe Hooker. "My telegram, stating the disappointment of the President at the escape of Lee's army, was not intended as a censure," he replied, "but as a stimulus to an active pursuit. It is not deemed a sufficient cause for your application to be relieved."

In the end Meade withdrew his resignation, or at any rate did not insist that it be accepted, and on July 17, 18, and 19 — the last date was a Sunday: he now had been three weeks in command — he crossed the Potomac at Harpers Ferry and Berlin, half a dozen miles downstream, complying with his instructions to conduct "an active and energetic pursuit," although he was convinced that such a course was overrisky. "The proper policy for the government would have been to be contented with driving Lee out of Maryland," he wrote his wife, "and not to have advanced till this army was largely reinforced and reorganized and put on such a footing that its advance was sure to be successful." In point of fact, however, he had already been "largely reinforced." His aggregate present on July 20 was 105,623 men, including some 13,500 troopers, while Lee on that same date, exclusive of about 9000 cavalry, had a total of 50,178, or barely more than half as many infantry and cannoneers as were moving against him. Confronted with the danger of being cut off from Richmond, he abandoned his plan for drawing the enemy up the valley and instead moved eastward through Chester Gap. On July 21 — the second anniversary of First Manassas, whose twice-fought-over field lay only some thirty miles beyond the crest of the Blue Ridge — Federal lookouts reported dust clouds rising; the rebels were on the march. Lee reached Culpeper two days later, and Meade, conforming, shifted to Warrenton, from which point he sent a cavalry and infantry column across the Rappahannock on the last night of the month. Gray horsemen opposed the advance, but Lee, aware of the odds against him and unwilling to take the further risk of remaining within the V of the two rivers, decided to fall back beyond the Rapidan. This was accomplished by August 4, ending the sixty days of marching and fighting which comprised the Gettysburg campaign. Both armies were back at their approximate starting points, and Meade did not pursue.

He had at last received from Washington the accolade that had been withheld so long, though the gesture still was not from Lincoln. "Take it altogether," Halleck wrote, "your short campaign has proved your superior generalship, and you merit, as you will receive, the confidence of the government and the gratitude of your country." But Meade had already disclaimed such praise from other sources. "The papers are making a great deal too much fuss about me," he wrote home. "I claim no extraordinary merit for this last battle, and would prefer waiting a little while to see what my career is to be before making any pretensions.... I never claimed a victory," he explained, "though I stated that Lee was defeated in his efforts to destroy my army." Thin-skinned and testy as he was, he found it hard to abide the pricks he received from his superiors. He doubted, indeed, whether he was "sufficiently phlegmatic" for the leadership of an army which he now perceived was commanded from Washington, and he confided to his wife that he would esteem it the best of favors if Lincoln would replace him with someone else. Who that someone might be he did not say, but he could scarcely have recommended any of his present subordinates, whose lack of energy he deplored. Most of all, he missed his fellow Pennsylvanians, the dead Reynolds and the convalescing Hancock. "Their places are not to be supplied," he said.

With nine of his best generals gone for good, and eight more out with wounds of various depth and gravity, Lee had even greater cause for sadness. Just now, though, his energies were mainly confined to refitting his army, preparing it for a continuation of the struggle he had sought to end with one hard blow, and incidentally in putting down a spirit of contention among his hot-tempered subordinates as to where the blame for the recent defeat should go. Few were as frank as Ewell, who presently told a friend that "it took a dozen blunders to lose Gettysburg and [I] committed a good many of them," or as selfless as Longstreet, who wrote to a kinsman shortly after the battle: "As General Lee is our commander, he should have the support and influence we can give him. If the blame, if there is any, can be shifted from him to me, I shall help him and our cause by taking it. I desire, therefore, that all the responsibility that can be put upon me shall go there, and shall remain there." Later he would vigorously decline the very chance he said he hoped for, but that was in the after years, where there was no longer any question of sustaining either the army commander or the cause. Others not only declined it now but were quick to point out just where they thought the blame should rest: Pickett, for instance, whose report was highly critical of the other units involved in the charge tradition would give his name to. Lee returned the document to him with the suggestion that it be destroyed, together with all copies. "You and your men have covered yourselves with glory," he told him, "but we have the enemy to fight and must carefully, at this critical moment, guard against dissensions which the reflections in your report would create.... I hope all will yet be well."

His own critique of the battle, from the Confederate point of view, was given five years later to a man who was contemplating a school history. Referring the writer to the official accounts, Lee avoided personalities entirely. "Its loss was occasioned by a combination of circumstances," he declared. "It was commenced in the absence of correct intelligence. It was continued in the effort to overcome the difficulties by which we were surrounded, and [a success] would have been gained could one determined and united blow have been delivered by our whole line. As it was, victory trembled in the balance for three days, and the battle resulted in the infliction of as great an amount of injury as was received and in frustrating the Federal campaign for the season." Reticent by nature in such matters, he was content to let it go at that, except for once when he was out riding with a friend. Then he did speak of personalities, or anyhow one personality. "If I had had Stonewall Jackson with me," he said, looking out over the peaceful fields, "so far as man can see, I should have won the battle of Gettysburg."

That was still in the future, however. For the present he reserved his praise for the men who had been there. "The army did all it could," he told one of his numerous cousins in late July. "I fear I required of it impossibilities. But it responded to the call nobly and cheerfully, and though it did not win a victory it conquered a success. We must now prepare for harder blows and harder work."

※ 2 ※

Having failed in his effort to "conquer a peace" by defeating the principal Union army north of its capital, Lee had failed as well in his secondary purpose, which had been to frighten the Washington authorities into withdrawing Grant and Banks from their strangle-hold positions around Vicksburg and Port Hudson, thereby delivering from danger not only those two critical locations but also the great river that ran between them, the loss of which would cut the South in two. But Lee's was not the only attempt to forestall that disaster. In addition to Joe Johnston, whose primary assignment it was, Kirby Smith too had plans for the relief of Pemberton and Gardner, on whose survival depended his hope of remaining an integral part of the Confederacy. Though these included nothing so ambitious as an intention to end the war with a single long-odds stab at the enemy's vitals, they were at least still in the course of execution when Pickett's and Pettigrew's men came stumbling back from Cemetery Ridge, leaving the bodies of their comrades to indicate the high-water mark of Lee's campaign, which now was on the ebb. Nor were these Transmississippi plans without the element of boldness. Encouraged by Magruder's success in clearing Texas of all trace of the invader, Smith hoped his other two major generals, Holmes in Arkansas and Taylor in West Louisiana, might accomplish as much in their departments. If so, he might attain the aforementioned secondary purpose of causing the Federal high command to detach troops from Grant and Banks, in an attempt to recover what had been lost across the river from their respective positions, and thus lighten the pressure on Vicksburg and Port Hudson. At any rate Smith thought it worth a try, and in mid-June, being frantically urged by Richmond to adopt some such course of action — Davis and Seddon by then had begun losing confidence that anything was going to come of their increasingly strident appeals to Johnston along those lines — he instructed Taylor and Holmes to make the effort.

Taylor, who had just returned disgruntled to Alexandria after his strike at Milliken's Bend — a tactical success, at least until Porter's gunboats hove onto the scene, but a strategic failure, since the objective turned out to be little more than a training camp for the Negro recruits Grant had enlisted off the plantations roundabout — was pleased to be ordered back onto what he considered the right track, which led down to New Orleans. His plan, as he had outlined it before the fruitless excursion opposite Vicksburg, was to descend the Teche and the Atchafalaya, recapture Berwick Bay and overrun the Bayou Lafourche region, which lay between Grand Lake and the Mississippi, deep in Banks's rear, interrupting that general's communications with New Orleans and threatening the city itself; whereupon Banks would be obliged to raise his siege of Port Hudson in order to save New Orleans, whose 200,000 citizens he knew to be hostile to his occupation, and Gardner then could march out to join Johnston for an attack on Grant's rear and the quick delivery of beleaguered Vicksburg. Such at least were Taylor's calculations — or more properly speaking, his hopes; for his resources were admittedly slim for so ambitious a project. He had at Alexandria three small cavalry regiments just arrived from Texas under Colonel J. P. Major, a twenty-seven-year-old Missouri-born West Pointer whose peacetime army career had included service in Albert Sidney Johnston's 2d Cavalry, which already had provided the South with eight and the North with two of their leading generals. Awaiting instructions on the upper Teche, to which they had returned in the wake of Banks's withdrawal in mid-May, were five more such mounted regiments under Thomas Green, the Valverde hero who had been promoted to brigadier for his share in the New Year's triumph at Galveston, along with three regiments of Louisiana infantry under Brigadier General Alfred Mouton, thirty-four years old and a West Pointer, a Shiloh veteran and native of nearby Vermilionville, son of the former governor and brother-in-law to Frank Gardner, whose rescue was the object of the campaign.

The combined strength of the three commands was about 4000 effectives, barely one tenth of the force available to Banks, but Taylor intended to make up in boldness for what he lacked in numbers.

The advance was made in two widely divided columns. While Mouton and Green swung down the west bank of the Teche, marching unopposed through Opelousas and New Iberia, Taylor rode with Major across the Atchafalaya, then down Bayou Fordoche to within earshot of the guns of Port Hudson. At that point he left him, on June 18, with orders to move rapidly to the rear of Brashear City, the objective upon which the two forces were to converge for a simultaneous attack five days later. The distance was one hundred miles, entirely through occupied territory, but Major made it on schedule. Skirmishing briefly that afternoon with the bluecoats on guard at Plaquemine, a west-bank landing below Baton Rouge, he bypassed fortified Donaldsonville after nightfall and set off next morning down Bayou Lafourche, which left the Mississippi just above the town. Some thirty miles below on the 20th, he rode into Thibodaux, whose garrison had fled at the news of his approach, and next day he struck the railroad at Terrebonne, thirty miles east of Brashear, then turned due west to complete his share of the convergence Taylor had designed. Moving crosscountry with relays of quick-stepping mules hitched to his ambulance, that general had joined Mouton and Green on their unopposed march through Franklin to Fort Bisland. By nightfall of June 22 they were at Berwick and were poised for an amphibious attack, having brought with them a weird collection of "small boats, skiffs, flats, even sugar-coolers," which they had gathered for this purpose during their descent of the Teche. Batteries were laid under cover of darkness for a surprise bombardment in support of the scheduled dawn assault on the Brashear fortifications, just eastward across the narrow bay. Taylor's old commander in the Shenandoah Valley doubtless would have been proud to see how well his pupil, whose preparatory work had been done not at West Point but at Yale, had learned the value of well-laid plans when the object was the capture or destruction of an enemy force in occupation of a fixed position.

Old Jack's pride would have swelled even more next morning, when the Louisianian gathered the fruits of his boldness and careful planning. While some 300 dismounted Texans manned the 53 boats of his improvised flotilla — it was fortunate that there was no wind, Taylor said later, for the slightest disturbance would have swamped them — Green's cannoneers stood to their pieces. At first light they opened fire, and as they did so the sea-going troopers swarmed ashore, encouraged by the echoing boom of Major's guns from the east. Flustered by the sudden bombardment, which seemed to erupt out of nowhere, and by the unexpected assault from both directions, front and rear, the blue defenders milled about briefly, then surrendered. The take was great, for here at the western terminus of the railroad Banks had cached the ordnance and quartermaster supplies he intended to use in his planned return up the Teche and the Red. In addition to 1700 prisoners, a dozen heavy-caliber guns and 5000 new-style Burnside repeaters and Enfield rifles were captured, together with two locomotives and their cars, which were unable to get away eastward because Major had wrecked the bridge at Lafourche Crossing, and commissary and medical stores in such abundance that they brought to more than $2,000,000 the estimated profit from Taylor's well-engineered strike. The general's pleasure was as great as that of his men, who wasted no time before sitting down to gorge themselves on the spoils. Their main concern was food, but his was the acquisition of the implements with which to continue his resistance to the invasion of his homeland. "For the first time since I reached western Louisiana," he exulted afterwards, "I had supplies."

All in all, it was the largest haul any body of Confederates had made since Stonewall followed up his raid on Manassas Junction with the capture of Harpers Ferry, back in September. Like his mentor, however, Taylor did not allow his exultation to delay his plans for the further discomfiture of his adversary. Next morning, leaving one regiment to sort the booty and remove it to Alexandria for safekeeping, he pressed on north and east, once more in two columns. While Green and Major marched for Donaldsonville, near which they were to establish batteries for the purpose of disrupting traffic on the Mississippi and thus sever the main line of supply and communications available to the besiegers of Port Hudson, Mouton's infantry went by rail to Thibodaux, from which point he sent pickets down the line to Bayou des Allemands, within twenty-five miles of New Orleans. It was during the early morning hours of June 28 that Taylor encountered his first setback, though not in person. Approaching Donaldsonville the night before, Green had meant to bypass it, as Major had done on his way south, but the existence of an earthwork at the junction of the Lafourche and the Mississippi proved irresistible, perhaps in part because the Yankees had given it a hated name: Fort Butler. He disposed 800 dismounted troopers for attack and sent them forward two hours before dawn. The result was a bloody repulse, administered by the 225 defenders and three gunboats that arrived in time to support them. Green, who had suffered 261 casualties and inflicted only 24, pulled back, chagrined, and went about his proper business of establishing his three batteries on the west bank of the river, some ten miles below the town. He opened fire on July 7 and for three days not only kept the Mississippi closed to transports and unarmored supply boats, but also sent out mounted patrols as far downstream as Kenner, barely a dozen miles from the heart of New Orleans, which was already in a turmoil of expectancy as a result of Mouton's continued presence at Thibodaux and nearby Bayou des Allemands.

Secessionists were joyously predicting the imminent entry of the graybacks who were knocking at the gates, and William Emory, with fewer than 1000 men to oppose a rebel host he reckoned at 13,000, was altogether in agreement that the place was the Confederacy's for the taking. What was more, as we have seen already, he had said as much to Banks. "It is a choice between Port Hudson and New Orleans," he informed him on July 4, adding: "You can only save this city by sending me reinforcements immediately and at any cost." Dick Taylor thus had accomplished the preliminary objective of his campaign; that is, he had brought the pressure he intended upon Banks, who now would be obliged to withdraw from Port Hudson, permitting Gardner to join Johnston for the delivery of Pemberton by means of an attack on Grant's intrenchments from the rear. So much Taylor had planned or anyhow hoped for. But Banks, as we have also seen, refused to cooperate in the completion of the grand design. If New Orleans fell, he told Halleck, he would retake it once the business at hand was completed and his army was free to be used for that purpose; but meantime he would hang on at Port Hudson till it surrendered, no matter what disasters threatened his rear. Observing this perverse reaction, Taylor was obliged to admit that once again, as at Milliken's Bend a month ago, though his tactics had been successful his strategy had failed. He had gained much in his brief campaign — particularly at Brashear City, whose spoils would greatly strengthen his future ability to resist the blue invaders — but he had not accomplished the recapture of New Orleans, which he saw as a cul-de-sac to be avoided, or the raising of the siege at Port Hudson.

Theophilus Holmes, though neither as energetic nor as inventive as Zachary Taylor's son and Stonewall Jackson's pupil, was also under compunction to do something toward relieving their hemmed-in friends across the way. Since the turn of the year, when Marmaduke made his successful raid into Missouri, burning the Springfield supply base and bringing a hornetlike swarm of guerillas out of the brush and canebrakes, all the elderly North Carolinian had attempted in this regard was a repeat performance by that same general in late April, this time with twice as many men and instructions to put the torch to the well-stocked military depots along the west bank of the Mississippi north of Cairo, particularly Cape Girardeau, from which Grant was drawing much of his subsistence for the campaign far downriver. Little came of this, however. Marmaduke and his 5000 troopers — the largest body of horsemen ever assembled in the Transmississippi — struck and routed an inferior blue force at Fayetteville on April 18, then crossed the line into his native state and rode eastward across it in two columns, one through Fredericktown and the other through Bloomfield, driving Yankee outpost garrisons before him as he advanced. Secessionists, many of whom had kinsmen riding with him, greeted their favorite with cheers. His father had been governor before the war and he himself would be governor after it, a bachelor just past thirty now, tall and slender, quick-tempered and aristocratic in manner, with a full beard, delicate hands and feet, and fine hair brushed smooth on top and worn long in back so that it flared in a splendid ruff behind his head. His eyes were kindly and intelligent, though they had a disconcerting squint that came from his being at once near-sighted and unwilling to disfigure himself with glasses. He had studied both at Harvard and Yale before his graduation from West Point six years ago, but neither this formal preparation nor his success on the similar mission back in January stood him in much stead on April 25, when he completed his investment of Cape Girardeau with a demand for an immediate surrender; to which Brigadier General John McNeil, a fifty-year-old former Boston hatter and St Louis insurance agent, who had increased the strength of the garrison to 1700 by bringing in his brigade the day before, replied with an immediate refusal. Marmaduke attacked and found the resistance stiff, all the approaches being covered by well-served artillery. Not only was he repulsed, but scouts reported steamers unloading reinforcements from St Louis at the Cape Girardeau dock. So he withdrew next morning, after launching one more attack designed to discourage pursuit. It failed in its purpose, however, and the retreat southward across the St Francis bottomlands of the Missouri boot heel required all his skill to avoid being intercepted by the now superior forces of the enemy. By May Day he was back in Arkansas, having suffered 161 casualties, and though he claimed that Federal losses "must have been five times as great as mine in killed and wounded" — McNeil and the others who had opposed him admitted a scant 120, combined — all he had to show for his pains, aside from some 150 recruits picked up in the course of the 400-mile-long ride, was "a great improvement in the number and quality of horses" in his command.

Grant was over the river by then, hard on the march for Jackson, but Holmes attempted nothing more in the way of interference until he received in mid-June an excerpt from a letter the Secretary of War had written Johnston in late May, after Pemberton was besieged, suggesting that he urge the Transmississippi commanders to "make diversions for you, or, in case of the fall of Vicksburg, secure a great future advantage to the Confederacy by the attack on, and seizure of, Helena, while all the available forces of the enemy are being pushed to Grant's aid." Seddon added that, though he was cut off from those commanders and therefore had no means of ordering the adoption of his suggestion, its tactical soundness was "so apparent that it is hoped it will be voluntarily embraced and executed." He was right, so far at least as concerned its being "embraced," for Holmes had already conferred with Sterling Price on the same notion, and Price, who had taken command in early June of two brigades of infantry, not only declared that his men were "fully rested and in excellent spirits," but also expressed confidence that if Holmes would bring up two more brigades, together they could "crush the foe" at Helena. He had, moreover, an up-to-the-minute report from "an intelligent lady" just arrived from the west-bank Arkansas town, in which she described the enemy garrison as "exceedingly alarmed," much reduced by downriver calls for reinforcements, "and apprehensive that you will attack them daily." Seddon's suggestion reached Holmes at Little Rock on June 14, together with a covering letter from Kirby Smith, who left its adoption or rejection up to him. Holmes was eager, for once, being greatly encouraged by Price's coincidental approval of the project. "I believe we can take Helena. Please let me attack it," he replied next day, and Smith consented promptly. "Most certainly do it," he told him. That was on June 16. Two days later Holmes issued orders for a concentration of his forces, preparatory to launching the attack.

He had available for the effort just under 5000 infantry in Price's two brigades and a third under Brigadier General James Fagan, a thirty-five-year-old Kentucky-born Arkansan who was a veteran of the Mexican War as well as of Shiloh and Prairie Grove, and just over 2500 cavalry in the two brigades remaining with Marmaduke — two others had been detached since his repulse at Cape Girardeau — and a third under Brigadier General Lucius Walker, who was thirty-three, a nephew of Tennessee's James K. Polk and a West Point graduate, though he had abandoned army life to enter the mercantile business in Memphis until Sumter put him back in uniform. Holmes's instructions called for a cavalry screen to be thrown around Helena as soon as possible, in order to conceal from its blue defenders the infantry concentration scheduled for June 26 across the St Francis River at Cotton Plant and Clarendon, within fifty miles of the objective. Walker and Marmaduke moved out promptly, followed by Price and Fagan. Anxious to get back onto the victory trail that had led to Wilson's Creek and Lexington, up in his home state, before he was sidetracked into defeat at Pea Ridge and more recently at Iuka and Corinth, Price had announced to his troops that they would "not only drive the enemy from our borders, but pursue him into his own accursed land." The men, who idolized him and affectionately called him Pap, cheered at the news that these words were about to be translated into action, and Fagan likewise reported that his brigade was "ready and in high condition and spirit" as the march got under way. Those spirits were soon dampened, however, by torrents of rain that turned the roads to quagmires and flooded the unbridged streams past fording. As a result, it was June 30 before the infantry reached the areas designated. Holmes remained calm, despite the strain of a four-day wait, and engaged in no useless criminations. "My dear general," he wrote Price while the former Missouri governor was still on the march through calf-deep mud, "I deeply regret your misfortune." Revising his schedule accordingly, he moved out from Clarendon and Cotton Plant on July 1, arrived within five miles of Helena on the evening of July 3, and issued detailed instructions for an attack at dawn next morning. Much depended on concert of action, for the Union position featured mutually supporting earthworks and intrenchments, but Holmes counted also on his assumed superiority in numbers. His strength was 7646 effectives, and he reckoned that of the enemy at "4000 or 5000" at the most.

It was in fact much closer to the lower than to the higher figure; 4129 bluecoats were awaiting him in the Helena defenses. But what he did not know was that they had been warned of his coming and had made special preparations to receive him, including arrangements for the support of the gunboat *Tyler*, whose 8-inch guns had helped to save the day at Shiloh under similar circumstances. The post commander, Benjamin M. Prentiss, had done even stouter service on that bloody field by holding the Hornets Nest until he and his division were overrun and captured. Exchanged in October, the Virginia-born Illinois lawyer had won promotion to major general and assignment to command of the District of East Arkansas — meaning Helena, since this was the only Union-occupied point in the region below Memphis. For the past four days, disturbed by the rebel cavalry thrashing about in the brush outside his works, Prentiss had had the garrison up and under arms by 2.30 each morning, and just yesterday he had issued an order forbidding a Fourth of July celebration his officers had planned for tomorrow. However, the most effective preparation of all had begun in late December, when Fred Steele went downriver with Sherman and three fourths of his corps, leaving the remnant exposed to a sudden thrust such as Holmes was launching now. At that time, six months ago, the total defense consisted of a single bastioned earthwork, called Fort Curtis for the then commander of the department, whose guns could sweep the gently rising ground of the hills that cradled the low-lying town beside the river, but since then Prentiss had constructed breastworks and dug rifle pits along the brow of the ridge, an average half mile beyond the fort, overlooking the timber-choked terrain of its more precipitous eastern slopes, and on the three dominant heights, Rightor Hill on the right, Graveyard Hill in the center, and Hindman Hill on the left, he had installed batteries which he designated, north to south, as A, B, C, D. Stoutly emplaced and mutually supporting, so that if one fell those adjoining could turn their fire on it, those four batteries and their protective intrenchments, which linked them into an iron chain of defense, covered the six roads that passed over the semicircular ridge and converged on Fort Curtis like so many spokes on the hub of half a wheel, and the cannoneers who manned them could feel secure — especially after a look back over their shoulders at the *Tyler* riding at anchor beyond the town — in the knowledge that Prentiss and his engineers had made the most of what nature had placed at their disposal,

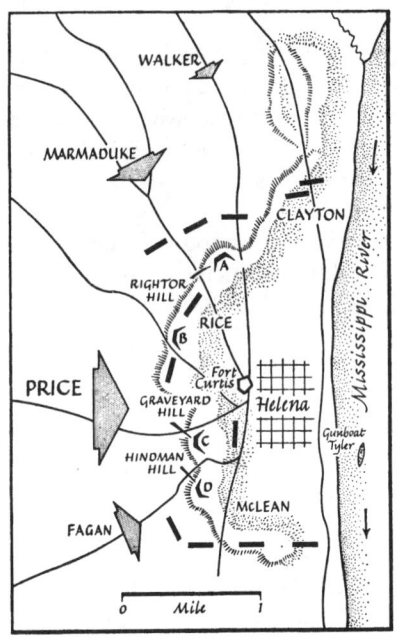

Brigadier General Frederick Salomon commanded the division Steele had left behind. One of four immigrant brothers who served the Union through this crisis — three of them as colonels and brigadiers and the fourth as wartime governor of Wisconsin, to which they had fled from their native Prussia to avoid the consequences of having fought on the losing side in the Revolution of 1848 — he had three small brigades, each led by a colonel: two of infantry, under William McLean and Samuel Rice, and one of cavalry under Powell Clayton. Like Salomon, these three officers were all in their middle or early thirties, nonprofessionals who had risen strictly on merit if not in action, and their troops were Westerners to a man, mostly farm boys out of Missouri, Iowa, and Wisconsin. Except for a single regiment of Hoosiers who had served with Pope in the taking of New Madrid and Island Ten, some fifteen months ago, the total field experience of the garrison had been the recent Yazoo Pass fiasco, in which they had been matched primarily against gnats and mosquitoes while the navy tried in vain to reduce Fort Pemberton. Still irked by the memory of that unhappy experience, and in accordance with Prentiss's standing instructions, they turned out of their bunks and took their posts at 2.30, an hour before dawn and a good two hours before sunrise of this Independence Day. Clayton's troopers were on the far right, guarding the river road north of town; McLean's and Rice's cannoneers and riflemen were disposed along the hilltop chain of batteries and intrenchments. Half an hour after they were in position, Holmes's attack opened against the left center. At first it was rather tentative, driving the Federal outpost pickets back up the rugged western slopes of Hindman and Graveyard hills, but presently it exploded in full fury as the butternut pursuers came yelling after them, massed shoulder to shoulder in a solid drive for possession of the two high-sited batteries Prentiss had labeled C and D.

Their repulse was not as sudden as their eruption, but it was equally emphatic. In part this was because they had found the last five miles of road, which they covered after dark, in even worse shape than the hundred-odd they had traversed so painfully during the past week:

with the result that they had been unable to bring their guns along and therefore had to attack without artillery support, of which the Federals had plenty. Fagan's brigade struck first, storming Hindman Hill — so called because it was here that the former Confederate commander had built the fine brick house Curtis had taken for his headquarters soon after occupying the town the year before. Three successive lines of half-bastions were rapidly penetrated and seized, but not the hilltop battery itself, which met the attackers with volleys of grape that shattered their formation, sent them scrambling for cover, and pinned them down so effectively that they could not even retreat. Price's two brigades did better, at least at first. Battery C was taken in a rush, the graybacks swarming over Graveyard Hill and whooping among the captured guns. The weaponless rebel artillerymen came up, prepared to turn the pieces on their late owners, only to find that the retreating cannoneers had carried off all the friction primers, which left the guns about as useless to their captors as so much scrap iron. Moreover, they came under enfilade fire from the two adjoining batteries and took a pounding as well from Fort Curtis, dead ahead at the foot of the gradual eastern slope. Nor was that all. Receiving word that Hindman Hill was under assault, Prentiss had signaled Lieutenant Commander J. M. Prichett of the *Tyler:* "Open fire in that direction." Now Prichett did, and with a vengeance, the fuzes of his 8-inch shells cut at ten and fifteen seconds. So demoralized were the attackers by the sudden deluge of heavy-caliber projectiles that, according to one blue officer, two groups of about 250 men each responded "by hoisting a white flag, their own sharpshooters upon the ridge in their rear firing from cover upon and cursing them as they marched out prisoners of war."

Holmes did what he could to expand the lodgment, sending one of Price's brigades to co-operate with Fagan in the stalled drive on Battery D. But to no avail; McLean and Rice held steady, backed up stoutly by Fort Curtis and the *Tyler,* whose bow and stern guns were firing north and south, respectively, while her ponderous broadside armament tore gaps in the rebel center. The early morning coolness soon gave way to parching heat; men risked their lives for sips of water from the canteens of the dead. Around to the north, Marmaduke had even less success against the defenders of Rightor Hill, and though he later complained vociferously that Walker had not supported him on his vulnerable left flank, the fact was he had already found Batteries A and B too hot to handle. He and Walker together lost a total of 66 men, only a dozen of whom were killed. As usual, it was the infantry that suffered, and in this case most of the sufferers wore gray. Including prisoners, the three brigades under Price and Fagan lost better than 1500 men between them. Holmes was not only distressed by the disproportionate losses, which demonstrated the unwisdom of his unsupported assault on a fortified opponent; he also saw that the attack would have been a mistake even if it had been successful, since the force in occupation would have been at the mercy of the *Tyler* and other units of the Federal fleet, which would make the low-lying river town untenable in short order. By 10.30, after six hours of fighting, all this was unmistakably clear; Holmes called for a withdrawal. By noon it had been accomplished, except for some minor rear-guard skirmishing, although better than one out of every five men who had attacked was a casualty. His losses totaled 1590, nearly half of them captives pinned down by the murderous fire and unable to retreat.

Prentiss lost 239: less than six percent of his force, as compared to better than twenty percent of the attackers. However, even with the odds reduced by this considerable extent, he still had too few men to risk pursuit. Reinforcements arrived next day from Memphis, together with another welcome gunboat, but he was content to break up a rebel cavalry demonstration which he correctly judged to be nothing more than a feint designed to cover a general retirement. By dawn of July 6 the only live Confederates around Helena were captives, many of them too gravely wounded to be moved. In praising his troops for their stand against nearly twice their number, Prentiss did not neglect his obligation to the *Tyler*, whose skipper in time received as well a letter of commendation from the Secretary of the Navy. "Accept the Department's congratulations for yourself and the officers and men under your command," the Secretary wrote, "for your glorious achievement, which adds another to the list of brilliant successes of our Navy and Army on the anniversary of our nation's independence."

※ 3 ※

It was indeed a Glorious Fourth, from the northern point of view; Gideon Welles did not exaggerate in speaking wholesale of a "list of brilliant successes" scored by the Union, afloat and ashore, on this eighty-seventh anniversary of the nation's birth. For the South, however, the day was one not of glory, but rather of disappointment, of bitter irony, of gloom made deeper by contrast with the hopes of yesterday, when Lee was massing for his all-or-nothing attack on Cemetery Ridge and Johnston was preparing at last to cross the Big Black River, when Taylor was threatening to retake New Orleans and Holmes was moving into position for his assault on Helena. All four had failed, which was reason enough for disappointment; the irony lay in the fact that not one of the four, Lee or Johnston, Taylor or Holmes, was aware that on this Independence Eve, so far at least as his aspirations for the relief of Vicksburg or Port Hudson were concerned, he was too late. At 10 o'clock that morning, July 3, white flags had broken out along a portion of Pemberton's works and two high-ranking officers, one a colonel, the other a major general, had come riding out of their lines and into those of the besiegers, who obligingly held their fire. The senior bore a letter from his commander, addressed to Grant. "General," it began: "I have the honor to propose to you an armistice for several hours, with a view to arranging terms for the capitulation of Vicksburg."

Pemberton's decision to ask for terms had been reached the day before, when he received from his four division commanders, Stevenson, Forney, Smith, and Bowen, replies to a confidential note requesting their opinions as to the ability of their soldiers "to make the marches and undergo the fatigues necessary to accomplish a successful evacuation." After forty-six days and forty-five nights in the trenches, most of the time on half- and quarter-rations, not one of the four believed his troops were in any shape for the exertion required to break the ring of steel that bound them and then to outmarch or outfight the well-fed host of bluecoats who outnumbered them better than four to one in effectives. Forney, for example, though he expressed himself as "satisfied they will cheerfully continue to bear the fatigue and privation of the siege," answered that it was "the unanimous opinion of the brigade and regimental commanders that the physical condition and health of our men are not sufficiently good to enable them to accomplish successfully the evacuation." There Pemberton had it, and the other three agreed. "With the knowledge I then possessed that no adequate relief was to be expected," the Pennsylvania Confederate later wrote, "I felt that I ought not longer to place in jeopardy the brave men whose lives had been intrusted to my care." He would ask for terms. The apparent futility of submitting such a request to a man whose popular fame was based on his having replied to a similar query with the words, "No terms except an unconditional and immediate surrender can be accepted," was offset — at least to some extent, as Pemberton saw it — by two factors. One was that the Confederates had broken the Federal wigwag code, which permitted them to eavesdrop on Grant's and Porter's ship-to-shore and shore-to-ship exchanges, and from these they had learned that the navy wanted to avoid the troublesome, time-consuming task of transporting thousands of grayback captives far northward up the river. This encouraged the southern commander to hope that his opponent, despite his Unconditional Surrender reputation, might be willing to parole instead of imprison the Vicksburg garrison if that was made a condition of avoiding at least one more costly assault on intrenchments that had proved themselves so stout two times before. The other mitigating factor, at any rate to Pemberton's way of thinking, was that the calendar showed the proposed surrender would occur on Independence Day. Some among the defenders considered a capitulation on that date unthinkable, since it would give the Yankees all the more reason for crowing, but while Pemberton was aware of this, and even agreed that it would involve a measure of humiliation, he also counted it an advantage. "I am a northern man," he told the objectors on his staff. "I know my people. I know their peculiar weaknesses and their national vanity; I know we can get better terms from them on the Fourth of July than on any other day of the year. We must sacrifice our pride to these considerations."

One other possible advantage he had, though admittedly it had not been of much use to Buckner at Donelson the year before. John Bowen had known and befriended Grant during his fellow West Pointer's hard-scrabble farming days in Missouri, and it was hoped that this might have some effect when the two got down to negotiations. Although Bowen was sick, his health undermined by dysentery contracted during the siege — he would in fact be dead within ten days, three months short of his thirty-third birthday — he accepted the assignment, and that was how it came about that he was the major general who rode into the Union lines this morning, accompanied by a colonel from Pemberton's staff. However, it soon developed that the past seventeen months had done little to mellow Grant in his attitude toward old friends who had chosen to do their fighting under the Stars and Bars. He not only declined to see or talk with Bowen, but his reply to the southern commander's note, which was delivered to him by one of his own officers, also showed that he was, if anything, even harsher in tone than he had been in the days when Buckner charged him with being "ungenerous and unchivalrous." Pemberton had written: "I make this proposition to save the further effusion of blood, which must otherwise be shed to a frightful extent." Now Grant replied: "The useless effusion of blood you propose stopping by this course can be ended at any time you may choose, by an unconditional surrender of the city and garrison.... I do not favor the proposition of appointing commissioners to arrange terms of capitulation, because I have no terms other than those indicated above."

There were those words again: Unconditional Surrender. But their force was diminished here at Vicksburg, as they had not been at Donelson, by an accompanying verbal message in which Grant said that he would be willing to meet and talk with Pemberton between the lines that afternoon. Worn by strain and illness, Bowen delivered the note and repeated the off-the-record message, both of which were discussed at an impromptu council of war, and presently — by then it was close to 3 o'clock, the hour Grant had set for the meeting — he and the colonel retraced in part the route they had followed that morning, accompanied now by Pemberton, who spoke half to himself and half to his two companions as he rode past the white flags on the ramparts. "I feel a confidence that I shall stand justified to my government, if not to the southern people," they heard him say, as if he saw already the scapegoat role in which he as an outlander would be cast by strangers and former friends for whose sake he had alienated his own people, including two brothers who fought on the other side. First, however, there came a ruder shock. Despite the flat refusal expressed in writing, he had interpreted Grant's spoken words, relayed to him through Bowen, as an invitation to parley about terms. But he soon was disabused of this impression. The three Confederates came upon a group of about a dozen Union officers awaiting them on a hillside only a couple of hundred yards beyond the outer walls of the beleaguered city. Ord, McPherson, Logan, and A. J. Smith were there, together with several members of Grant's staff and Grant himself, whom Pemberton had no trouble recognizing, not only because his picture had been distributed widely throughout the past year and a half, but also because he had known him in Mexico, where they had served as staff lieutenants in the same division. Once the introductions were over, there was an awkward pause as each waited for the other to open the conversation and thereby place himself in somewhat the attitude of a suppliant. When Pemberton broke the silence at last by remarking that he understood Grant had "expressed a wish to have a personal interview with me," Grant replied that he had done no such thing; he had merely agreed to such a suggestion made at second hand by Bowen.

Finding that this had indeed been the case, though he had not known it before, Pemberton took a different approach. "In your letter this morning," he observed, "you state that you have no other terms than an unconditional surrender." Grant's answer was as prompt as before. "I have no other," he said. Whereupon the Pennsylvanian — "rather snappishly," Grant would recall — replied: "Then, sir, it is unnecessary that you and I should hold any further conversation. We will go to fighting again at once." He turned, as if to withdraw, but fired a parting salvo as he did so. "I can assure you, sir, you will bury many more of your men before you will enter Vicksburg." Grant said nothing to this, nor did he change his position or expression. The contest was like poker, and he played it straight-faced while his opponent continued to sputter, remarking, as he later paraphrased his words, that if Grant "supposed that I was suffering for provisions he was mistaken, that I had enough to last me for an indefinite period, and that Port Hudson was even better supplied than Vicksburg." Grant did not believe there was much truth in this, but he saw clearly enough from Pemberton's manner that his unconditional-surrender formula was not going to obtain without a good deal more time or bloodshed. So he unbent, at least to the extent of suggesting that he and Pemberton step aside while their subordinates talked things over. The Confederate was altogether willing — after all, it was what he had proposed at the outset, only to be rebuffed — and the two retired to the shelter of a stunted oak nearby. In full view of the soldiers on both sides along this portion of the front, while Bowen and the colonel talked with the other four Union generals, the blue and gray commanders stood together in the meager shade of the oak tree, which, as Grant wrote afterwards, "was made historical by the event. It was but a short time before the last vestige of its body, root and limb had disappeared, the fragments taken as trophies. Since then the same tree has furnished as many cords of wood, in the shape of trophies, as 'The True Cross.'"

But that was later, after the souvenir hunters had the run of the field. For the present, the oak remained as intact as almost seven weeks of bullets and shells from both sides had allowed, and Grant and Pemberton continued their pokerlike contest of wills beneath its twisted branches. If the Confederate played a different style of game, that did not necessarily mean that he was any less skillful. In point of fact — at any rate in the limited sense of getting what he came for — he won; for in the end it was the quiet man who gave way and the sputterer who stood firm. In the adjoining group, Bowen proposed that the garrison "be permitted to march out with the honors of war, carrying with them their arms, colors, and field batteries," which was promptly denied, as he no doubt had expected; whereupon Pemberton, after pointing out that his suggestion for the designation of commissioners had been rejected, observed that it was now Grant's turn to make a counteroffer as to terms. Grant agreed; Pemberton would hear from him by 10 o'clock that evening, he said; and with that the meeting broke up, though it was made clear that neither opponent was to consider himself "pledged." Both returned to their own lines and assembled councils of war to discuss what had developed. Pemberton found that all his division commanders and all but two of his brigade commanders favored capitulation, provided it could be done on a basis of parole without imprisonment. Grant found his officers of a mind to offer what was acceptable, although he himself did not concur; "My own feelings are against this," he declared. But presently, being shielded in part from the possible wrath of his Washington superiors by the overwhelming vote of his advisers, he "reluctantly gave way," and put his terms on paper for delivery to Pemberton at the designated hour. Vicksburg was to be surrendered, together with all public stores, and its garrison paroled; a single Union division would move in and take possession of the place next morning. "As soon as rolls can be made out, and paroles signed by officers and men," he stipulated, "you will be allowed to march out of our lines, the officers taking with them their side-arms and clothing, and the field, staff, and cavalry officers one horse each. The rank and file will be allowed all their clothing, but no other property." Remembering Pemberton's claim that he had plenty of provisions on hand, Grant added a touch that combined generosity and sarcasm: "If these conditions are accepted, any amount of rations you may deem necessary can be taken from the stores you now have, and also the necessary cooking utensils for them. . . . I am, general, very respectfully, your obedient servant, U. S. GRANT, Major General."

Now that he had committed his terms to paper, he found them

much more satisfactory than he had done before. "I was very glad to give the garrison of Vicksburg the terms I did," he afterwards wrote. To have shipped the graybacks north to Illinois and Ohio, he explained, "would have used all the transportation we had for a month." Moreover, "the men had behaved so well that I did not want to humiliate them. I believed that consideration for their feelings would make them less dangerous foes during the continuance of hostilities, and better citizens after the war was over." So he said, years later, making a virtue of necessity and leaving out of account the fact that he had begun with a demand for unconditional surrender. For the present, indeed, he was so admiring of the arrangement, from the Union point of view, that he did what he could to make certain Pemberton could not reject it — as both had reserved the right to do — without risking a mutiny by the beleaguered garrison. He had Rawlins send the following note to his corps commanders: "Permit some discreet men on picket tonight to communicate to the enemy's pickets the fact that General Grant has offered, in case Pemberton surrenders, to parole all the officers and men and to permit them to go home from here."

He could have spared himself the precaution and his courier the ride. "By this time," a Confederate declared, "the atmosphere was electric with expectancy, and the wildest rumors raced through camp and city. Everyone had the air of knowing something vital." What was more, a good deal of back-and-forth visiting had begun on both sides of the line. "Several brothers met," a Federal remarked, "and any quantity of cousins. It was a strange scene." Whatever the blue pickets might say, on whatever valid authority, was only going to add to the seethe of speculation within and without the hilltop fortress which was now about to fall, just under fourteen months after its mayor replied to the first demand for surrender, back in May of the year before: "Mississippians don't know, and refuse to learn, how to surrender to an enemy. If Commodore Farragut and Brigadier General Butler can teach them, let them come and try." The upshot was that Grant had come and tried, being so invited, and now Pemberton had been taught, although it galled him. Assembling his generals for a reading of the 10 o'clock offer, he remarked — much as his opponent had done, an hour or two ago, across the way — that his "inclination was to reject these terms." However, he did not really mean it, any more than Grant had meant it, and after he had taken the all but unanimous vote for capitulation, he said gravely: "Gentlemen, I have done what I could," then turned to dictate his reply. "In the main, your terms are accepted," he told Grant, "but in justice both to the honor and spirit of my troops, manifested in the defense of Vicksburg, I have to submit the following amendments, which, if acceded to by you, will perfect the agreement between us...." The added conditions, of which there were two, were modest enough in appearance. He proposed to march his soldiers out of the works, stack arms, and then move off before the Federals took possession, thus avoiding a confrontation of the two armies. That was the first. The second was that officers be allowed "to retain their ... personal property, and [that] the rights and property of citizens ... be respected." But Grant declined to allow him either, and for good cause. As for the first, he replied, it would be necessary for the troops to remain under proper guard until due process of parole had been formally completed, and as for the second, while he was willing to give all citizens assurance that they would be spared "undue annoyance or loss," he would make no specific guarantees regarding "personal property," which he privately suspected was intended to include a large number of slaves, freed six months ago by Lincoln's Proclamation. "I cannot consent to leave myself under any restraint by stipulations," he said flatly. Denial of the proposed amendments was contained in a dispatch sent before sunrise, July 4. Pemberton had until 9 a.m. to accept the original terms set forth in last night's message; otherwise, Grant added, "I shall regard them as having been rejected, and shall act accordingly."

Now it was Pemberton's turn to bend in the face of stiffness, and this he did the more willingly since the morning report — such had been the ravages of malnutrition and unrelieved exposure — showed fewer than half his troops available for duty as effectives. "General," he answered curtly about sunrise: "I have the honor to acknowledge the receipt of your communication of this day, and in reply to say that the terms proposed are accepted." The rest was up to Grant, and it went smoothly. At 10 o'clock, in response to the white flags that now fluttered along the full length of the Confederate line, John Logan marched his division into the works. Soon afterwards the Stars and Stripes were flying over the Vicksburg courthouse for the first time in two and a half years. If the victors were somewhat disappointed professionally that seven weeks of intensive shelling by 220 army cannon, backed up by about as many heavier pieces aboard the gunboats and the mortar rafts, had done surprisingly little substantial damage to the town, it was at least observed that the superficial damage was extensive. Not a single pane of glass remained unbroken in any of the houses, a journalist noted. It was also observed that, despite the southern commander's claim that he had ample provisions, the gauntness of the disarmed graybacks showed only too clearly, not only that such was not the case, but also that it apparently had not been so for some time. One Federal quartermaster, bringing in a train of supplies for the troops in occupation, was so affected by the hungry looks on the faces of the men of a rebel brigade that he called a halt and began distributing hardtack, coffee, and sugar all around. Rewarded by "the heartfelt thanks" of the butternut scarecrows, he said afterwards that when his own men complained that night about the slimness of their rations, "I swore by all the saints in the calendar that the wagons had broken down and the Johnny Rebs had stolen all the grub." Not only was there little "crowing," which some Confederates had feared would be encouraged and enlarged by a Fourth of July surrender, but according to Grant "the men of the two armies fraternized as if they had been fighting for the same cause." Though that was perhaps an overstatement of the case, there was in fact a great deal of mingling by victors and vanquished alike — "swapping yarns over the incidents of the long siege," as one gray participant put it — and even some good-natured ribbing back and forth. "See here, Mister; you man on the little white horse!" a bluecoat called out to Major Lockett, whose engineering duties had kept him on the move during lulls in the fighting. "Danged if you aint the hardest feller to hit I ever saw. I've shot at you more'n a hundred times." Lockett took it in good part, and afterwards praised his late adversaries for their generosity toward the defeated garrison. "General Grant says there was no cheering by the Federal troops," he wrote. "My recollection is that on our right a hearty cheer was given by one Federal division 'for the gallant defenders of Vicksburg!'"

Pemberton did not share in the fraternization, not only because of his present sadness, his sense of failure, and his intimation of what the reaction of his adoptive countrymen would be when they got the news of what had happened here today, but also because of his nature, which was invariably distant and often forbidding. For him, congeniality had been limited mainly to the family circle he had broken and been barred from when he threw in with the South. Even toward his own officers he had always been stiffly formal, and now toward Grant, who came through the lines that morning on his way to confer with Porter at the wharf, he was downright icy; indeed, rude. Perhaps it was the northern commander's show of magnanimity, when he knew that such concessions as had been granted — parole of the garrison, for example, instead of a long boat ride to prison camps in Ohio and Illinois — had been the result of hard bargaining and a refusal to yield to his original demand for unconditional surrender. In any event, one of his staff found Pemberton's manner "unhandsome and disagreeable in the extreme." No one offered Grant a seat when he called on Pemberton in a house on the Jackson road, this officer protested, and when he remarked that he would like a drink of water, he was told that he could go where it was and help himself. He did not seem perturbed by this lack of graciousness, however; he went his way, taking no apparent umbrage, content with the spoils of this Independence Day, which were by far the greatest of the war, at any rate in men and materiel. Confederate casualties during the siege had been 2872 killed, wounded, and missing, while those of the Federals totaled 4910; but now the final tally of captives was being made. It included 2166 officers, 27,230 enlisted men, and 115 civilian employees, all paroled except one officer and 708 men, who preferred to go north as prisoners rather than risk being exchanged and required to fight again. In ordnance, too, the harvest was a rich one, yielding 172 cannon, surprisingly large amounts of ammunition of all kinds, and nearly 60,000 muskets and rifles, many of such superior quality that some Union regiments exchanged their own weapons for the ones they found stacked when they marched in.

One additional prize there was, richer by far than all the rest combined and to which they had served as no more than prologue. The Mississippi would return to its old allegiance as soon as one remaining obstruction had been removed, and that allegiance would be secure as soon as one continuing threat had been abolished. The obstruction — Port Hudson — was not really Grant's concern except for the dispatching of reinforcements, which he could now quite easily afford, to help Banks get on with the job. He kept his attention fixed on Joe Johnston — the threat — who continued to hover, off to the east, beyond the Big Black River. Conferring with Porter, Grant requested his co-operation in flushing out the rebels up the Yazoo, re-established there by Johnston while the Federals were concentrating on the reduction of Vicksburg. As usual, the admiral was altogether willing; he assigned an ironclad and two tinclads the task of escorting 5000 infantry upstream to retake Yazoo City, which the Confederates had refortified since their flight from the approaching gunboats back in May. But the northern army commander's main concern was Johnston himself and the force he was assembling west of Jackson. Yesterday, while surrender negotiations were under way, Grant had notified Sherman, whose troops were already faced in that direction, that he was to strike eastward as soon as Vicksburg fell. "I want Johnston broken up as effectually as possible, and roads destroyed," he wired. This message was followed shortly by another, in which he was more specific as to just what breakage was expected. "When we go in," he told his red-haired lieutenant, "I want you to drive Johnston from the Mississippi Central Railroad, destroy bridges as far as Grenada with your cavalry, and do the enemy all the harm possible. You can make your own arrangements and have all the troops of my command, except one corps — McPherson's, say. I must have some troops to send to Banks, to use against Port Hudson."

As it turned out, there was no need for more troops at Port Hudson. All that was required was valid evidence that its companion bluff 240 miles upriver was in Union hands, and this arrived before the reinforcements: specifically, during the early hours of July 7. That evening Gardner received from one of his three brigade commanders — Miles, whose position on the far right afforded him a view of the river, as well as of the extreme left of the Federal intrenchments — a report of strange doings by the enemy, ashore and afloat: "This morning all his land batteries fired a salute, and followed it immediately [by another] with shotted guns, accompanied by vociferous yelling. Later in the day the fleet fired a salute also. What is meant we do not know. Some of them hallooed over, saying that Vicksburg had fallen on the 4th instant. My own impression is that some fictitious good news has been given to his troops in order to raise their spirits; perhaps with a view of stimulating them to a charge in the morning. We will be prepared for them should they do so."

The colonel's men shared his skepticism as well as his resolution, even when confronted with documentary evidence in the form of a "flimsy" tossed into their lines, bearing the signature of the Federal adjutant-general and announcing Pemberton's surrender three days ago. "That's another damned Yankee lie!" a butternut defender shouted back. But Gardner himself was not so sure. He had fought well, inflicting 4363 casualties at a cost of only 623 of his own, and though by now the trenches were less than twenty feet apart in places and the enemy was obviously about to launch another massive assault, which was likely to succeed at such close range, he was prepared to fight still longer if need be. On the other hand, it was no part of his duty to sacrifice the garrison for no purpose — and obviously Port Hudson's purpose, or anyhow its hope of survival, was tied to that of Vicksburg. If the Mississippi bastion had fallen, so must the Louisiana one, exposed as it would be to the possible combination of both Union armies. So Gardner adopted the logical if somewhat irregular course of inquiring of his opponent, by means of a flag of truce next morning, as to whether the report of Vicksburg's fall was true. And when Banks supplied confirming evidence, in the form of a dispatch Grant had sent on the surrender date, Gardner decided that the time for his own capitulation was at hand. Final details were not worked out until the following day, July 9, when the besiegers marched in and took possession, but a train of wagons had already entered Port Hudson the previous afternoon, loaded with U.S. Army rations for the half-starved garrison. Banks combined firmness and generosity. Though his terms had been unconditional, he paroled his 5935 enlisted captives and sent only their 405 officers to New Orleans to await exchange or shipment north. Moreover, having acquired some 7500 excellent rifles and 51 light and heavy guns, he closed the formal surrender ceremony with "a worthy act, well merited." Thus his adjutant characterized the gesture in describing it years later. "By General Banks's order, General Gardner's sword was returned to him in the presence of his men, in recognition of the heroic defense."

If there was haste in the northern commander's method, including parole of all his enlisted prisoners, there was also method in his haste. Albeit they were the sweeter, being his first, Banks was no more inclined than Grant to sit down and enjoy the fruits of his victory; for just as the latter took out after Joe Johnston as soon as Vicksburg fell, so did the former concern himself with Dick Taylor as soon as Port Hudson followed suit. Faced as he was with the departure of the nine-month volunteers who made up a considerable portion of his army, Banks had to choose between using the remainder as guards for the captured garrison or as a mobile force for driving out the reported 13,000 Confederates who had moved into his rear and were threatening New Orleans from Bayou Lafourche and Berwick Bay. Quite aside from the pleasure he derived from being generous to a defeated foe, that was why he paroled nearly 6000 of his 6340 prisoners: to get them off his hands and thus be free to deal with Taylor. Having decided, he wasted no time. While the surrender ceremony was in progress he put Weitzel's and Grover's divisions aboard transports and sent them at once to Donaldsonville, where they would begin their descent of the Lafourche, disposing of infiltrated rebels as they went. The debarkation was completed on July 11; next afternoon the two blue divisions began their advance down opposite banks of the bayou. Early the following morning, however — July 13 at Koch's Plantation, six miles from Donaldsonville — Weitzel's two west-bank brigades, and indirectly Banks himself, were given a cruel demonstration of the fact that haste sometimes made waste, even in pursuit.

Tom Green, with his own and Major's brigade of mounted Texans, had been having a fine time disrupting traffic on the Mississippi with the guns he had established on its right bank, ten miles below the town. Though they could do no real damage to the *Essex*, which came down to challenge them, they did succeed in driving the ironclad off and puncturing the steam-drums of several less heavily armored vessels. A battery commander referred to the 12-foot levee as "the best of earthworks," and Green was prepared to stay there indefinitely, finding balm in his present success for the sting of the recent setback at Fort Butler. After three days of such fun, however, he learned of the arrival of ten transports at Donaldsonville and the debarkation of two blue divisions with better than five times his number of men. Determined not to leave without a fight, whatever the odds, he pulled back from the river, crossed the Lafourche, and lay in wait for what was coming. What was coming was Weitzel, supported by Grover across the way. Green struck hard, soon after sunrise of July 13, caught the bluecoats off guard, and threw them into such hasty retreat that they abandoned three of their guns to their pursuers. They lost 50 killed, 223 wounded, and 186 captured or missing, while Green lost 9 killed and 24 wounded. He withdrew westward, unmolested, and rejoined Taylor at Vermilionville, that general having retired with all his spoils from Brashear City when he learned of Gardner's surrender and the intended return downriver of the besieging army. By no means strong enough for a full-scale battle with the greatly superior forces of the Federals near their base, he was content to wait for them to attempt a second ascent of the Teche. They would find him better equipped for resistance than he had been before his recent brief but profitable drive to the outskirts of New Orleans.

Banks accepted the Koch's Plantation check with his usual easy grace, even setting aside a court-martial's findings that one of Weitzel's brigade commanders had been guilty of drunkenness on duty and misconduct in the presence of the enemy. The former Speaker was looking for no scapegoat; he would take whatever blame there was, along with the praise, as designer and director of the campaign from start to finish. And of praise there was much. It was Banks, after all, who had removed the final obstruction to Union control of the Mississippi, following Grant's extraction of "the nail that held the South's two halves together." On July 16, one week after the fall of Port Hudson, the unarmed packet *Imperial* tied up at New Orleans and began unloading cargo she had brought unescorted from St Louis. For the first time in thirty months, the Father of Waters was open to commerce from Minnesota to the Gulf.

Meanwhile Porter and Sherman had gone about their assignments, though for both there had been irksome delays followed by mishaps for which irksome was all too mild a word; Porter's, in fact, had occurred on the same day as Weitzel's, and while it had been considerably less bloody it was also a good deal more expensive. Originally intended as reinforcements for Banks, since they had spent less than a month in the Vicksburg trenches, 5000 men of Herron's division were shifted to lighter-draft transports on July 11, when news of the fall of Port Hudson arrived, and set out up the Yazoo next morning, escorted by two 6-gun tinclads and the 14-gun ironclad *Baron de Kalb*, formerly the *St Louis* but rechristened when it developed that the navy already had a warship by that name. One of the original seven built by James Eads in the fall of '61 and a veteran of all the major engagements on the Tennessee, the Cumberland, and the Mississippi north of Vicksburg, she had carried the flag eight weeks ago on a similar expedition to Yazoo City and beyond, which had resulted in much damage to the enemy at no cost to the fleet. This last was not to be the case this time, however. Isaac Brown, who had sunk the *De Kalb*'s sister ship *Cairo* with a demijohn of powder up this same winding river in December, was back again with forty survivors of the crew from his lost ram *Arkansas*, and he had plans for a repeat performance. His navy artillerists managed to drive the ironclad back around the bend when she appeared below the town at noon of July 13, but a Tarheel regiment assigned to the place by Johnston withdrew on learning that Herron had landed three of his own with instructions to bag the defenders. Obliged to pull back for lack of support, Brown and his sailors left something behind them in addition to their guns: as Porter and Herron presently discovered. The two were on the bridge of the flagship, steaming slowly upstream toward the undefended town, when — just after sunset, abreast of the yards where, about this time a year ago, the *Arkansas* had acquired her rusty armor — one of Brown's improvised torpedoes exploded directly under her bow.

As she began to settle, another went off under her stern, which hastened her destruction. Within fifteen minutes, though all aboard managed to escape with nothing worse than bruises, she was on the muddy bottom, providing a multichambered home for gars and catfish. Herron, having survived this violent introduction to one of the dangers involved in combined operations, went ashore to complete his share of the mission, afterwards reporting the destruction of the Yazoo City fortifications and five of the nine rebel steamboats found lurking in the vicinity, together with the capture of some 300 prisoners, six guns, and about 250 small-arms, as well as 2000 bales of cotton and 800 horses and mules which he commandeered from the planters roundabout. He was enthusiastic; no less than 50,000 more bales were awaiting discovery and seizure in the region, he declared. Porter, on the other hand, summed up the operation somewhat ruefully. "But for the blowing up of the *Baron de Kalb*, it would have been a good move," he informed his superiors, and he added, by way of extenuating this loss of his fourth ironclad since December: "While a rebel flag floats anywhere the gunboats must follow up. The officers and men risk their lives fearlessly on these occasions, and I hope the Department will not take too seriously the accidents which happen to the vessels when it is impossible to avoid them."

Sherman made no such apology, though his particular mishap had occurred the day before and had been preceded by a week of hot and profitless activity. Grant's instructions for him to "do the enemy all the harm possible," accompanied as they were by the prospect of having close to 50,000 troops with which to carry them out, had put the red-haired Ohioan in what he liked to call "high feather," and when they were followed next day — July 4 — by the news that Vicksburg had fallen, his excitement reached fever pitch. "I can hardly restrain myself," he replied. Nor did he: adding, "This is a day of jubilee, a day of rejoicing to the faithful.... Already are my orders out to give one big huzza and sling the knapsack for new fields." Those new fields lay on the far side of the Big Black, however, which was now past fording because of a sudden four-foot rise resulting from heavy rains upstate. Sherman spent two days throwing bridges at Birdsong's Ferry and Messinger's Ford and due east of Bovina, thus providing a crossing for each of his three corps, and on July 6 the "Army of Observation," so called from the days of the siege, passed over the river in pursuit of Johnston, who had retired toward Jackson the day before, on learning of Pemberton's surrender. As the rebels withdrew eastward along roads that were ankle-deep in dust — no matter how many inches of rain had fallen upstate, not a drop had fallen here in weeks — they made things difficult for their pursuers by leading animals into such few ponds as had not dried in the heat, then killing them and leaving their carcasses to pollute the water. It was Johnston's intention not only to delay his opponent by such devices, but also to goad him into attempting a reckless, thirst-crazed assault on the

Jackson intrenchments, which the Confederates had repaired and improved since Grant's departure and in which they had taken refuge by the time the superior Federal force completed its crossing of the Big Black, twenty-five miles away.

The crafty Virginian's attempt to discourage and torment his pursuers with thirst was unsuccessful, however, for several reasons. For one, the siege-toughened bluecoats simply dragged the festering carcasses from the ponds, gave the water a few minutes to settle, then brushed the scum aside and drank their fill, apparently with no ill effects at all. For another, the rain soon moved down from the north, sudden thunderous showers under which the marchers unrolled their rubber ponchos and held them so that the water trickled into their mouths as they slogged along. Lifted so recently by the greatest victory of the war, their spirits were irrepressible, whether the problem was too little moisture or too much. "The dirt road would soon be worked into a loblolly of sticky yellow mud," one veteran was to recall. "Thereupon we would take off our shoes and socks, tie them to the barrel of our muskets, poise the piece on the hammer on either shoulder, stock uppermost, and roll up our breeches. Splashing, the men would swing along, singing 'John Brown's Body,' or whatever else came handy." They gloried in their toughness and took pride in the fact that they never cheered their generals, not even "Uncle Billy" Sherman. A surgeon wrote home that they were "the noisiest crowd of profane-swearing, dram-drinking, card-playing, song-singing, reckless, impudent daredevils in the world." They would have accepted all this as a compliment, second only to one Joe Johnston had paid them in warning his Richmond superiors not to underrate Grant's Westerners, who in his opinion were "worth double the number of northeastern troops." They thought so, too, and were ready to prove it on July 10 when their three columns converged on the rebel intrenchments outside Jackson and took up positions before them, Ord's four divisions to the south, Steele's three in the center, and Parke's two on the north.

Within the semicircular works — which, as usual, he considered "miserably located" — Johnston had four divisions of infantry confronting the Union nine, plus a small division of cavalry which he used to patrol the flanks along Pearl River, above and below the town. He made several brief sorties in an attempt to provoke the bluecoats into attacking, but Sherman, though he enjoyed a better than two-to-one numerical advantage, had had too much experience with earthworks these past eight weeks to be tempted into rashness. Instead, he spent two days completing his investment, meantime sending raiders north and south to break the Mississippi Central and thus cut Jackson off from any possible rail connection with the outside world, the bridge in its rear not having been rebuilt since its destruction back in May. Then on July 12, despite his admonitions as to caution, the mishap came. On Ord's front, Lauman was advancing his division through an area obscured by trees and brush, when the lead brigade of 880 veterans suddenly found itself exposed to a withering crossfire from guns and rifles, losing 465 men and three stands of colors, as well as most of the cannoneers and horses of a section of artillery, before the remnant could recover from the shock and backpedal. "I am cut all to pieces," Lauman lamented; Ord relieved him of command. Sherman approved the brigadier's removal, but refused to be disconcerted by the affair, which had at least confirmed his assumption that Joe Johnston was a dangerous man when cornered: so much so, in fact, that the Ohioan began to wish the Virginian gone. "I think we are doing well out here," he informed Grant two days later, "but won't brag till Johnston clears out and stops shooting his big rifle guns at us. If he moves across Pearl River and makes good speed, I will let him go."

That was just what Johnston had in mind, now that Sherman had the capital invested on three sides. "It would be madness to attack him," he wired Richmond that same day. "In the beginning it might have been done, but I thought then that want of water would compel him to attack us." By next morning, July 16, he was convinced that his only hope for survival lay in retreat. "The enemy being strongly reinforced, and able when he pleases to cut us off," he notified Davis, "I shall abandon this place, which it is impossible for us to hold." Accordingly, after nightfall, he proceeded to carry out the most skillful of his withdrawals so far in the war. Previously — at Manassas and Yorktown, as well as here at Jackson two months ago yesterday, on the day after his arrival from Tennessee — it had been his practice to leave guns and heavy equipment in position lest their removal, which was likely to be noisy, warn the enemy of his intention; but not now. Silently the guns were withdrawn by hand from their forward emplacements while the sick and wounded were being sent eastward across the river, followed by brigade after brigade of soldiers who had been kept busy with picks and shovels till after midnight, drowning out the sounds of the evacuation. Breckinridge's Orphans, who had accomplished Lauman's discomfiture four days ago, went last. The lines of the aborted siege, which had cost the Federals 1122 casualties and the Confederates 604, yawned empty in the darkness and remained so until daylight brought a blue advance and the discovery that Johnston had escaped across the Pearl, much as Lee had done across the Potomac three nights earlier with somewhat less success.

He took with him everything movable but he could not take the railroad or the town. Undefended, Jackson was reoccupied — and reburned. That task was assigned to Sherman's old corps, primarily to Blair's division, which was fast becoming proficient in such work, while Ord moved south with instructions to break up the Mississippi Central "absolutely and effectually" for a distance of ten miles, and Parke did the same in the opposite direction. Steele's men did a thorough job on the capital, sparing little except the State House and the Governor's Mansion. Pettus had departed, but the victorious generals held a banquet in his mansion on the second night of the occupation, and when one brigadier was missing next morning he was found asleep beneath the table, so freely had the wine flowed. "You can return slowly to Black River," Grant replied to news that the town had fallen, but Sherman stayed on for a week, supervising the extensive demolition his chief had prescribed at the outset. Added to what had been done in May, this new damage converted the Mississippi capital into what he referred to as "one mass of charred ruins." (Blair's exuberant veterans had a briefer, more colorful description of the place; "Chimneyville," they called it.) Though he found the stripping of the countryside by his foragers for fifteen miles around "terrible to contemplate," Sherman thought it proper to add that such was "the scourge of war, to which ambitious men have appealed rather than [to] the judgment of the learned and pure tribunals which our forefathers have provided for supposed wrongs and injuries." Characteristically, however, before his departure he distributed supplies to civilian hospitals and turned over to a responsible committee enough hard bread, flour, and bacon to sustain five hundred people for thirty days, his only condition being that none of this food was to be converted "to the use of the troops of the so-called Confederate states." Despite the damage to their pride, the committeemen were glad to accept the offer, whatever the condition. "The inhabitants are subjugated. They cry aloud for mercy," Sherman informed his commander back at Vicksburg.

How lasting the damage would be, either to their pride or to their property, was open to some question. Up to now, particularly in regions where the occupation had been less than constant, the rebels had shown remarkable powers of recovery from blows about as heavy. On the march eastward from the Big Black, for example, one of the Federal columns had crossed a portion of the field that took its name from Champion Hill, which the shock of battle had left all torn and trampled, scorched and scored by shells and strewn with wreckage. That was how the marchers remembered the scene from their passage this way a little less than two months back; but now, to their considerable surprise, they found that much of the field had been plowed and planted and corn stood four feet tall in neat, lush rows, not only as if the battle had never been fought, but also as if, except for the reappearance of the soldiers, there had never been a war at all, either here or anywhere else. It was in a way discouraging. This time, though, as Johnston faded back before them without fighting, they were less distracted and could give their full attention to the destruction which had been more or less incidental on the western march. They blazed a trail of devastation; gins, barns, farmhouses, almost everything burnable went up in flames and smoke; rearward the horizon was one long smudge. Looting took on new dimensions, sometimes of absurdity. One officer, watching a cavalryman stagger along with a grandfather's clock in his arms, asked what on earth he planned to do with it, and the trooper explained that he was going to take it apart "and get a pair of the little wheels out of it for spur rowels." There was time, too, for bitterness. A colonel viewing a porticoed mansion set back from the road in a grove of trees, neatly fenced and with a well-kept lawn and outbuildings, including slave quarters, burst out hotly: "People who have been as conspicuous as these in bringing this thing about *ought* to have things burned! I would like to see those chimneys standing there without any house." That his troops had taken his words to heart was evident on the return from Jackson, when the regiment passed that way again. His wish had been fulfilled. All that remained of the plantation house was its blackened chimneys. "Sherman monuments," they were called; or, perhaps more aptly, "Sherman tombstones."

Some among the Confederates in and out of uniform, but most particularly Richmond friends of Davis and Seddon, put the blame for much of this on Johnston, whose policy it had ever been to sacrifice mere territory, the land and all it nourished, rather than risk avoidable bleeding by any soldier in his charge. Always, everywhere in this war except at Seven Pines — which battle, poorly fought as it was, had done more to sustain than refute his theory: especially from the personal point of view, since it had cost him two wounds and command of the South's first army — he had backed up after a minimum of fighting, leaving the civilians of the evacuated region to absorb the shocks he evaded. So some said, angered by his apparent lack of concern for the fate of Vicksburg, which he had been sent to save. Others not only disagreed; they even pointed to the recent campaign as an example of his superior generalship. Unlike Pemberton, who had lost his army by accepting risks Johnston had advised him to avoid, the Virginian had saved his men to fight another day, and in the process had inflicted nearly twice as many casualties as he suffered. Mainly such defenders were members of his army, who not only had good cause to feel thankful for his caution, but also had come under the sway of his attractive personality. A genial companion, as invariably considerate of subordinates as he was critical of superiors, he won the affection of associates by his charm. There were, however, a few who were immune, and one among them was Pemberton, though this was only recently the case. At the outbreak of the war they had been friends; Johnston in fact had chosen the Pennsylvanian as his adjutant before the northern-born officer's transfer to South Carolina. But that was far in the past, in the days before the siege one friend had waited in vain for the other to raise.

Soon afterwards, in mid-July and in accordance with Grant's instructions for the paroled lieutenant general to report to his immediate superior, Pemberton found the Virginian "sitting on a cleared knoll on a moonlight night surrounded by members of his staff." Thus a witness described the scene, adding that when Johnston recognized the "tall, handsome, dignified figure" coming toward him up the slope, he sprang from his seat and advanced to meet him, hand outstretched.

"Well, Jack old boy," he cried. "I'm certainly glad to see you!"

Pemberton halted, stood at attention, and saluted.

"General Johnston, according to the terms of parole prescribed by General Grant, I was directed to report to you."

The two men stood for a moment in silence as Johnston lowered his unclasped hand. Then Pemberton saluted once more, punctiliously formal, and turned away.

They never met again.

✗ 4 ✗

News that Meade had stopped Lee at Gettysburg sent Lincoln's expectations soaring; he foresaw the end of the war, here and now, if only the victory could be pressed to its logical conclusion with "the literal or substantial destruction" of the rebel host before it recrossed the Potomac. Then came the letdown, first in the form of the northern commander's Fourth of July congratulatory order to his troops, calling for still "greater efforts to drive from our soil every vestige of the presence of the invader." Lincoln's spirits took a sudden drop. "My God, is that all?" he exclaimed, and presently he added: "This is a dreadful reminiscence of McClellan.... Will our generals never get that idea out of their heads? The whole country is our soil." His fears were enlarged the following day by word that Lee had stolen away in the night, and no dispatch from Meade, that day or the next, gave any assurance of a vigorous pursuit. Lincoln fretted as much *after* as he had done before or during the three-day battle, so high were his hopes and so great was his apprehension that they would be unfulfilled. At a cabinet meeting on July 7 his expression was one of "sadness and despondency," according to Welles, "that Meade still lingered at Gettysburg, when he should have been at Hagerstown or near the Potomac, in an effort to cut off the retreating army of Lee." That afternoon he was conferring with Chase and a few others in his office, pointing out Grant's progress to date on a map of Mississippi, when Welles came running into the room with a broad smile on his face and a telegram from Porter in his hand. The admiral had sent a fast boat up to Cairo, the Memphis wirehead having broken down, and beat the army in getting the news to Washington: "I have the honor to inform you that Vicksburg has surrendered to the U.S. forces on this 4th day of July."

Lincoln rose at once. "I myself will telegraph this news to General Meade," he said, then took his hat as if to go, but paused and turned to Welles, throwing one arm across the shoulders of the bearer of good tidings. "What can we do for the Secretary of the Navy for this glorious intelligence? He is always giving us good news. I cannot in words tell you my joy over this result. It is great, Mr Welles; it is great!" The Secretary beamed as he walked to the telegraph office with his chief, who could not contain his pleasure at the outcome of Grant's campaign. "This will relieve Banks. It will inspire me," he said as he strode along. He thought it might also inspire Meade, and he had Halleck pass the word to him that Vicksburg had surrendered; "Now if General Meade can complete his work so gloriously prosecuted thus far ... the rebellion will be over."

A wire also went to Grant: "It gives me great pleasure to inform you that you have been appointed a major general in the Regular Army, to rank from July 4, the date of your capture of Vicksburg." Moreover, on Grant's recommendation, Sherman and McPherson soon were made permanent brigadiers, the reward that had gone to Meade at Frederick that same day. The following day, however, when Grant's own announcement of Pemberton's capitulation came limping in behind Porter's — which had said nothing about terms — there was cause to think that his victory was by no means as complete as had been supposed before details of the surrender were disclosed. Surprise and doubt were the reaction to the news that practically all of the nearly 30,000-man garrison had been paroled. Halleck, for instance, protested by return wire that such terms might "be construed into an absolute release, and that the men will immediately be placed in the ranks of the enemy." Grant had already noted that the arrangement left his and Porter's "troops and transports ready for immediate service" against Johnston and Gardner, which otherwise would not have been the case, and when he explained that the parolees had been turned over to an authorized Confederate commissioner for the exchange of prisoners, which made the contract strictly legal, Old Brains was mollified. So was Lincoln, who was a lawyer himself and knew the dangers that lurked in informalities, though what appealed to him most was Grant's further contention that the surrendered troops were "tired of the war and would get home just as soon as they could." There, he believed, they would be likely to create more problems for the Confederacy than if they had been lodged in northern prison camps, a headache for the Union, which would be obliged to feed and guard them while awaiting their exchange.

Others not only disagreed, but some among them formed a delegation to call on Lincoln with a protest against Grant's dereliction and a demand for his dismissal from command. What rebel could be trusted? they asked, and predicted that within the month Pemberton's men would violate their parole and be back in the field, once again doing their worst to tear the fabric of the Union. Referring to his callers as "crossroads wiseacres," though they must have included some influential dignitaries, Lincoln afterwards described to a friend his handling of the situation. "I thought the best way to get rid of them was to tell the story of Sykes's dog. Have you ever heard about Sykes's yellow dog? Well, I must tell you about him. Sykes had a yellow dog he set great store by —" And he went on to explain that this affection was not shared by a group of boys who disliked the beast intensely and spent much of their time "meditating how they could get the best of him." At last they hit upon the notion of wrapping an explosive cartridge in a piece of meat, attaching a long fuze to it, and whistling for the dog. When he came out and bolted the meat, cartridge and all, they touched off the fuze, with spectacular results. Sykes came running out of the house to investigate the explosion. "What's up? Anything busted?" he cried. And then he saw the dog, or what was left of him. He picked up the biggest piece he could find, "a portion of the back with part of the tail still hanging to it," and said mournfully: "Well, I guess he'll never be much account again — as a dog." Lincoln paused, then made his point. "I guess Pemberton's forces will never be much account again as an army." He smiled, recalling the reaction of his callers. "The delegation began looking around for their hats before I had got quite to the end of the story," he told his friend, "and I was never bothered any more after that about superseding the commander of the Army of the Tennessee."

Now as always he shielded Grant from the critics who were so quick to come crying of butchery, whiskey, or incompetence. "I can't spare this man. He fights," he had said after Shiloh, and more than a month before the surrender of Vicksburg he had called the campaign leading up to the siege "one of the most brilliant in the world." In a sense, this latest and greatest achievement was a vindication not only of Grant but also of the Commander in Chief who had sustained him. Perhaps Lincoln saw it so. At any rate, though previously he had corresponded with him only through Halleck, even in the conferring of praise and promotions, this curious hands-off formality, which had no counterpart in his relations with any of the rest of his army commanders, past or present, ended on July 13, when he wrote him the following letter:

> My dear General
> I do not remember that you and I ever met personally. I write this now as a grateful acknowledgment for the almost inestimable service you have done the country. I wish to say a word further. When you first reached the vicinity of Vicksburg, I thought you should do what you finally did — march the troops across the neck, run the batteries with the transports, and thus go below; and I never had any faith, except a general hope that you knew better than I, that the Yazoo Pass expedition and the like could succeed. When you got below and took Port Gibson, Grand Gulf, and vicinity, I thought you should go down the river and join General Banks; and when you turned north-

ward, east of the Big Black, I feared it was a mistake. I now wish to make the personal acknowledgment that you were right and I was wrong.

> Yours very truly
> A. LINCOLN

Though in time, when news of the fall of Port Hudson arrived, a congratulatory dispatch also went to Banks, expressing Lincoln's "thanks for your very successful and very valuable military operations this year" — "The final stroke in opening the Mississippi never should, and I think never will, be forgotten," he wrote — no such letter went to Meade, nor did Lincoln mention him by name in responding to a White House serenade on the evening of July 7, tendered in celebration of the double victory. "These are trying occasions," he said, adding a somber note to the tone of jubilation, "not only in success, but also for want of success." He withheld personal praise of Meade because he was waiting for a larger occasion that did not come, though he kept hoping against hope. Finally, his hopes dwindling, he turned cynical. On July 12, when the general wired that he would attack the flood-stalled Confederates next day "unless something intervenes to prevent it," Lincoln ventured a prediction: "They will be ready to fight a magnificent battle when there is no enemy there to fight." Nevertheless, the news two days later that Lee had made a getaway came as an awful shock to him. "We had them in our grasp," he groaned. "We had only to stretch forth our hands and they were ours. And nothing I could say or do could make the army move." He told his son Robert, home from Harvard: "If I had gone up there, I could have whipped them myself." So great was his distress, he adjourned a cabinet meeting on grounds that he was in no frame of mind for fit deliberation. Nor was he. In his extremity — having passed in rapid succession from cynicism, through puzzlement and exasperation, to the edge of paranoia — he questioned not only the nerve and competence of Meade and his subordinates, but also their motives. "And that, my God, is the last of this Army of the Potomac!" he cried as he walked out with the Secretary of the Navy. "There is bad faith somewhere. Meade has been pressed and urged, but only one of his generals was for an immediate attack, was ready to pounce on Lee; the rest held back. What does it mean, Mr. Welles? Great God, what does it mean?"

Halleck did not exaggerate in wiring Meade of Lincoln's "great dissatisfaction" on that day; Welles recorded in his diary that "on only one or two occasions have I ever seen the President so troubled, so dejected and discouraged." Meade's request to be relieved of command, submitted promptly in response to Halleck's wire, shocked Lincoln into recovering his balance. For this was more than a military matter; it was a downright political threat, with sobering implications. The Administration simply could not afford to be placed in the position of having forced the resignation of the man who, in three hard days of fighting, had just turned back the supreme Confederate effort to conquer a peace: an effort, moreover, launched hard on the heels of Union defeats at Fredericksburg and Chancellorsville, which had been fought under leaders now recognized as hand-picked incompetents, both of whom had been kept in command for more than a month after their fiascos. No matter what opinion the citizenry might have as to whether or not the rebels had been "invaders," politically it would not do to make a martyr of the hero who had driven them from what he called "our soil." After instructing Old Brains to decline the general's request to be relieved, Lincoln sat down and wrote Meade a letter designed to assuage the burning in his breast. So great was his own distress, however, that the words came out somewhat differently from what he had intended. In the end it was Lincoln's burning that was assuaged, at least in part. For example, yesterday's letter to Grant had begun: "My dear General," whereas today's bore no salutation at all, merely the heading: "Major General Meade." He opened by saying, "I am very — *very* — grateful to you for the magnificent success you gave the cause of the country at Gettysburg, and I am sorry now to [have been] the author of the slightest pain to you. But I was in such deep distress myself that I could not restrain some expression of it." Whereupon he proceeded to extend that expression of dissatisfaction in a review of the events of the past ten days. Meade had "fought and beat the enemy," with losses equally severe on both sides; then Lee's retreat had been halted by the swollen Potomac, and though Meade had been substantially reinforced and Lee had not, "yet you stood and let the flood run down, bridges be built, and the enemy move away at his leisure, without attacking him." The words were cutting, but those that followed were sharper still. "Again, my dear general, I do not believe you appreciate the magnitude of the misfortune involved in Lee's escape. He was within your easy grasp, and to have closed upon him would, in connection with our other late successes, have ended the war. As it is, the war will be prolonged indefinitely.... It would be unreasonable to expect, and I do not expect you can now effect much. Your golden opportunity is gone, and I am distressed immeasurably because of it."

He ended with a further attempt at reassurance: "I beg you will not consider this a prosecution or persecution of yourself. As you had learned that I was dissatisfied, I have thought it best to kindly tell you why." But on reading the letter over he could see that it was perhaps not so "kindly" after all; that, in fact, rather than serve the purpose of soothing the general's injured feelings, it was more likely to provoke him into resubmitting his request to be relieved of his command. So Lincoln put the sheets in an envelope labeled "To General Meade, never sent or signed," filed it away in his desk, and having thus relieved his spleen contented himself with issuing next day a "Proclamation of Thanksgiving," expressing his gratitude, not to Grant or Meade or Banks or Prentiss, but to Almighty God for "victories on land and on the sea so signal and so effective as to furnish reasonable grounds for augmented confidence that the Union of these States will be maintained, their Constitution preserved, and their peace and prosperity permanently restored." He further besought the public to "render the homage due to the Divine Majesty, for the wonderful things He has done in the nation's behalf, and invoke the influence of His Holy Spirit to subdue the anger which has produced and so long sustained a needless and cruel rebellion, to change the hearts of the insurgents, to guide the counsels of the Government with wisdom adequate to so great a national emergency, and to visit with tender care and consolation throughout the length and breadth of our land all those who, through vicissitudes of marches, voyages, battles, and sieges, have been brought to suffer in mind, body, or estate, and finally to lead the whole nation, through the paths of repentance and submission to the Divine Will, back to the perfect enjoyment of Union and fraternal peace. In witness whereof," the Proclamation ended, "I have hereunto set my hand and caused the seal of the United States to be affixed."

Though it was in large part a reaction to the knowledge that the suffering and bloodshed of the past two years would continue indefinitely past the point at which he believed they could have been stopped, Lincoln's extreme concern over the fact that one of his two great victories had been blunted was also based on fear that if he did not win the war in the field, and soon, he might lose it on the home front. There appeared to be excellent grounds for such apprehension. Ever since the fall elections, which had gone heavily against him in certain vital regions of the country, the loyal and disloyal opposition had been growing, not only in size but also in boldness, until now, in what might have been his hour of triumph, he was faced with the necessity for dealing with riots and other domestic troubles, the worst of which reached a climax in the nation's largest city on the day he issued his Proclamation of Thanksgiving. Though he could assign a measure of the blame to Meade, whose timidity had cost him the chance, as Lincoln saw it, of ending the war with a single stroke, he knew well enough that the discontent had been cumulative, the product of an almost unbroken seven-month sequence of military reverses, a good many of which he had engineered himself, and that the failure might be defined more reasonably as one of leadership at the top. Indeed, many did so define it, both in speeches and in print. During the past two years, while healing the split in his cabinet and winning the respect of those who were closest to him, he had grown in the estimation of the great mass of people who judged him solely from a distance, by his formal actions and utterances and by the gathering aura of his honesty and goodness. There were, however, senators and congressmen, together with other federal and state officials of varying importance, who saw him only occasionally and were offended by what they saw.

"The lack of respect for the President in all parties is unconcealed," Richard Dana, a U.S. district attorney from Massachusetts, had written home from the national capital at the beginning of a visit in late February. Author of *Two Years Before the Mast*, a founder of the Free Soil party and now a solid Republican, Dana spent two weeks looking and listening, then delivered himself of a still harsher judgment based on what he had seen and heard: "As to the politics of Washington, the most striking thing is the absence of personal loyalty to the President. It does not exist. He has no admirers, no enthusiastic supporters, none to bet on his head. If a Republican convention were to be held tomorrow, he would not get the vote of a State. He does not act, or talk, or feel like the ruler of a great empire in a great crisis. This is felt by all, and has got down through all the layers of society. It has a disastrous effect on all departments and classes of officials, as well as on the public. He seems to me to be fonder of details than of principles, of tithing the mint, anise, and cummin of patronage, and personal questions, than of the weightier matters of empire. He likes rather to talk and tell stories with all sorts of persons who come to him for all sorts of purposes than to give his mind to the noble and manly duties of his great post. It is not difficult to detect that this is the feeling of his cabinet. He has a kind of shrewdness and common sense, mother wit, and slipshod, low-leveled honesty, that made him a good Western jury lawyer. But he is an unutterable calamity to us where he is. Only the army can save us."

If there was some perception here, there was also much distortion, and in any event the judgment was merely personal. More serious were the signs of organized obstruction. "Party spirit has resumed its sway over the people," Seward had lamented in the wake of the fall elections, and Sumner had written a friend soon after the turn of the year: "The President tells me that he now fears 'the fire in the rear' — meaning the Democracy, especially at the Northwest — more than our military chances." When the Bay State senator spoke of "the Democracy" he meant the Democrats, particularly that wing of the party which opposed the more fervent innovations of his own: Emancipation, for example, and the draft. At any rate Lincoln's anxiety seemed well founded. "I am advised," Governor Oliver P. Morton of Indiana had wired the Secretary of War, "that it is contemplated when the Legislature meets in this State to pass a joint resolution acknowledging the Southern Confederacy and urging the States of the Northwest to dissolve all constitutional relations with the New England States. The same thing is on foot in Illinois." The same thing, or something resembling it, was indeed on foot in the President's home state, where the legislature had likewise gone Democratic in the fall. However, though the Illinois house passed resolutions praying for an armistice and recommending a convention of all the states North and South to agree upon some adjustment of their differences, the senate defeated by a few votes the proposal to discuss the matter; Governor Richard Yates was not obliged to exercise the veto. On the other hand, Morton did not allow matters to progress even that far in Indiana. He had spies in the opposition ranks, and when he saw what he believed was coming he dissolved the legislature by the simple expedient of advising the Republican minority to withdraw, which left the body without a quorum. The trouble with this was that it also left the Hoosier governor without funds for running the state for the next two years. But he solved the dilemma by strenuous and unconstitutional efforts. After obtaining loans from private sources and the counties, amounting to $135,000 in all, he appealed to Lincoln for the necessary balance. Lincoln referred him to Stanton, who advanced him $250,000 from a special War Department fund. Morton had what he needed to keep Indiana loyal and going, though it bothered him some that the law had been severely bent if not broken in the process. "If the cause fails, you and I will be covered with prosecutions, imprisoned, driven from the country," he told Stanton, who replied: "If the cause fails I do not wish to live."

Stanton believed in rigorous methods, especially when it came to dealing with whatever seemed to him to smack or hint of treason, and he had been given considerable sway in that regard. Perceiving at the outset that the septuagenarian Bates was unequal to the task, Lincoln had put Seward in charge of maintaining internal security, which included the power to arrest all persons suspected of disloyalty in those regions where habeas corpus had been suspended despite the protest of the courts, including the Supreme Court itself. The genial New Yorker did an effective job, particularly in Maryland and Kentucky during their periods of attempted neutrality; judges and legislators, among others who seemed to the government or the government's friends to favor the government's enemies, were haled from their benches and chambers, sometimes from their beds, and clapped into prisons, more often than not without being told of the charges or who had preferred them. When protests reached Lincoln he turned them aside with a medical analogy, pointing out that a limb must sometimes he amputated to save a life but that a life must never be given to save a limb; he felt, he said, "that measures, however unconstitutional, might become lawful by becoming indispensable to the preservation of the Constitution, through the preservation of the nation." After Seward came Stanton, who assumed the security duties soon after he entered the cabinet in early '62. In addition to the fierce delight he took in crushing all advocates of disunion, he enjoyed the exercise of power for its own sake. "If I tap that little bell," he told a visitor, obviously relishing the notion, "I can send you to a place where you will never hear the dogs bark." Apparently the little bell rang often; a postwar search of the records disclosed the names of

13,535 citizens arrested and confined in various military prisons during Stanton's tenure of office under Lincoln, while another survey (not concerned with names, and therefore much less valid) put the total at 38,000 for the whole period of the war. How many, if indeed any, of these unfortunates had been fairly accused — and, if so, what their various offenses had been — could never be known, either then or later, since not one of all those thousands was ever brought into a civil court for a hearing, although a few were sentenced by military tribunals.

One of these last was Ohio's Vallandigham, who had continued to fulminate against the abuses of the minority by the majority, including the gerrymandering of his district by the addition of a Republican county, which had resulted in his defeat in the fall election. "I learned my judgment from Chatham: 'My lords, you cannot conquer America.' And you have not conquered the South. You never will.... The war for the Union is, in your hands, a most bloody and costly failure," he told his fellow congressmen during the following lame duck session. His main targets were the Emancipation Proclamation and the Conscription Act. With the former, he declared, "war for the Union was abandoned, war for the Negro openly begun, and with stronger battalions than before. With what success? Let the dead at Fredericksburg and Vicksburg answer.... Will men enlist now at any price? Ah, sir, it is easier to die at home. I beg pardon, but I trust I am not 'discouraging enlistments.' If I am, then first arrest Lincoln, Stanton, and Halleck and some of your other generals, and I will retract; yes, I will recant. But can you draft again? Ask New England, New York; ask Massachusetts; [but] ask not Ohio, the Northwest. She thought you were in earnest, and gave you all, all — more than you demanded. Sir, in blood she has atoned for her credulity, and now there is mourning in every house and distress and sadness in every heart. Shall she give you any more? Ought this war to continue? I answer, no; not a day, not an hour. What then? Shall we separate? Again I answer, no no, no! What then? ... Stop fighting, Make an armistice."

So he counseled, and though a Republican member wrote in his diary that this was "a full exhibition of treason" and downright "submission to the rebels," Vallandigham and others like him considered themselves dedicated rather to opposing men like Thaddeus Stevens, whose avowed intent it was to "drive the present rebels as exiles from this country" and to "treat those states now outside of the Union as conquered provinces and settle them with new men." Democrats knew only too well who these "new men" would be: Republicans. To ask them to support this redefined conflict was asking them to complete the stripping of their minority of its former greatest strength, the coalition with conservatives of the South, and thus assure continuing domination by the radical majority down the years. Faced with this threat of political extinction, and having seen their friends arrested by thousands in defiance of their rights, diehard anti-Republicans banded together in secret organizations, especially in Ohio, Indiana, and Illinois, where a prewar society known as "Knights of the Golden Circle," so called because it had been founded to promote the advancement of national interests around the sun-drenched rim of the Caribbean, was revived and enlarged; "Order of American Knights," its new members called it, and later changed the name again to "Sons of Liberty." Their purpose was to promote the success of the Democratic party — first in the North, while the war was on, and then in the South when it was over, which they hoped would be soon — and to preserve, as they said, "the Constitution as it is, the Union as it was." By way of identification to one another, in addition to such intricate handclasps and unpronounceable passwords as were common in secret fraternities, they wore on their lapels the head of Liberty cut from an old-style penny; "Copperheads," their enemies called them, in scornful reference to the poisonous reptile by that name.

Vallandigham was their champion, and when Congress adjourned in March he came home and addressed them from the stump, along the same lines he had followed in addressing his former colleagues. A tall man in his early forties, handsome and gifted as a speaker, with clear gray eyes, a mobile mouth, and a dark fringe of beard along his lower jaw and chin, he found his words greeted with more enthusiasm here than they had received in Washington, where one or another of his opponents had threatened from time to time to cut his throat. On May Day, with Hooker stalled in the Wilderness and Grant on the march across the Mississippi, the Ohioan addressed a crowd of thousands assembled in his home state for a mass Democratic meeting at Mount Vernon. He made a rousing speech, asserting that the war could be concluded by negotiation but that the Republicans were prolonging the bloodshed for political purposes. The Union had gone by the board as a cause, he added; what was being fought for now, he said, was liberation of the blacks at the cost of enslaving the whites. This brought him more than the cheers of the crowd, which included a large number of men wearing copper Liberty heads in their buttonholes. It also resulted, four days later — or rather three nights later, for the hour was 2.30 a.m. May 5 — in his arrest by a full company of soldiers at his home in Dayton, by order of Major General Ambrose Burnside, commander of the Department of the Ohio.

Still smarting from the whips and scorns that followed Fredericksburg and the Mud March, the ruff-whiskered general had established headquarters in Cincinnati in late March and, outraged by Copperhead activities in the region, issued on April 13 a general order prescribing the death penalty for certain overt acts designed to aid or comfort the Confederacy. Moreover, he added, "the habit of declaring sympathy for the enemy will not be allowed.... It must be distinctly understood that treason, expressed or implied, will not be tolerated in this department."

Then on May Day had come Vallandigham's speech at Mount Vernon, reported to Burnside by two staff captains he had sent there in civilian clothes to take notes. Clearly this was a violation of the general order, and on May 4, without consulting his superiors or subordinates or even an attorney, he instructed an aide-de-camp to proceed at once to Dayton and arrest the offender. The aide boarded a special train, taking a company of soldiers along, and by 2.30 next morning was banging on Vallandigham's door. Refused admittance, the soldiers broke it down, seized the former congressman in his bedroom, and carried him forthwith to prison in Cincinnati. Brought before a military commission eight days later — though he declined to plead, on grounds that the tribunal had no jurisdiction over a civilian — he was given a two-day trial, at the close of which he was found guilty of violating the general order and was sentenced to close confinement for the duration of the war. Burnside approved the findings and the sentence that same day, May 16, and designated Fort Warren in Boston Harbor as the place of incarceration.

From the outset, though he promptly assured the general of his "firm support," Lincoln had doubted the wisdom of the arrest. Now his doubts were abundantly confirmed. Vallandigham had declined to plead his case before the tribunal, but he did not hesitate to plead it before the public in statements issued from his cell in Cincinnati. Denouncing Burnside as the agent of a despot, he asserted: "I am here in a military bastille for no other offense than my political opinions." Newspapers of various shades of opinion were quick to champion his basic right to freedom of speech, war or no war. As a result, he progressed overnight from regional to national prominence, his cause having been taken up by friends and sympathizers who sponsored rallies for him all across the land. Vallandigham in jail was a far more effective critic of the Administration than he had been at large; Lincoln was inclined to turn him loose, despite his previous assurance of "firm support" for Burnside and his subsequent reply to a set of resolutions adopted at a protest meeting in Albany, New York: "Must I shoot a simple-minded soldier boy who deserts, while I must not touch a hair of a wily agitator who induces him to desert? ... I think that in such a case to silence the agitator and save the boy is not only constitutional but withal a great mercy." However, this was leaving out of account the fact that the soldier and the agitator came under different codes of law, and the last thing Lincoln wanted just now was for the legality of Burnside's general order to be tested in the civil courts. He cast about, and as usual he came up with a solution. Burnside had warned that offenders might be sent "beyond our lines and into the lines of their friends." Early the previous year, moreover, Jefferson Davis had done just that to Parson Brownlow, arrested under suspicion of treasonous activities in East Tennessee. Wherever the notion came from, Lincoln found in it the solution to his problem of what to do with Vallandigham, and on May 26 commuted his sentence to banishment, thereby creating the prototype for "The Man Without a Country." Soon afterwards, south of Murfreesboro, the Ohioan was delivered by a detachment of Federal cavalry, under a flag of truce, to a Confederate outpost north of Tullahoma. Informed that he could not remain in the South if he considered himself a loyal citizen of the Union, he made his way to Wilmington, where he boarded a blockade-runner bound for the West Indies. On July 5, two months after his arrest, he turned up in Nova Scotia. Ten days later — having been nominated unanimously for governor by the state Democratic convention, which had been held at Columbus in mid-June — he opened his campaign for election to that high office with an address to the people of Ohio, delivered from the Canadian side of the border at Niagara Falls. Under the British flag, he said, he enjoyed the rights denied him by "usurpers" at home, and he added that he intended to "return with my opinions and convictions... not only unchanged, but confirmed and strengthened."

In time he did return, wearing false hair on his face and a large pillow strapped beneath his waistcoat. Presently he threw off these Falstaffian trappings and campaigned openly, despite the warning that the original sentence would be imposed if he broke the terms of his commutation. Lincoln did not molest him this time, however, nor would he allow the military to do so, having learned from the experience in May. Moreover, he had acted by then to prevent further unnecessary roiling of the citizenry by Burnside. In early June, encouraged by his apparent success in suppressing freedom of speech in his department, the general moved against the press in a similar heavy-handed manner. At 3 o'clock in the morning, June 3, cavalry vedettes rode up to the offices of the Chicago *Times*, which he had charged with "repeated expression of disloyalty and incendiary statements." Reinforced an hour later by two companies of infantry from Camp Douglas, they stopped the presses, destroyed the papers already printed, and announced that the *Times* was out of business. The reaction was immediate and uproarious. A noon meeting of prominent Chicagoans, presided over by the mayor, voted unanimously to request the President to revoke the suppression, and in Court House Square that evening a crowd of "20,000 loyal citizens," including many Republicans, gathered to hear speeches against such arbitrary seizures of power by the military and to cheer the news that in Springfield that afternoon the legislature had denounced the general for his action. Confronted with such outbursts of indignation, which seemed likely to spread rapidly beyond his home-state borders, much as the Vallandigham affair had spread beyond the borders of Ohio, Lincoln rescinded Burnside's order the following morning. What was more, he followed this up by having Stanton direct his over-zealous subordinate to arrest no more civilians and suppress no more newspapers without first securing the approval of the War Department.

In all conscience, he had troubles enough on his hands without the help or hindrance of the fantastically whiskered general in Cincinnati, whose brief foray against the Illinois paper was by no means an isolated example of all-out censorship. From start to finish, despite Lincoln's instructions for department commanders to exercise "great caution, calmness, and forbearance" in the matter, no less than 300 newspapers large and small, including such influential publications as the New York *World,* the Louisville *Courier,* the New Orleans *Crescent,* the Baltimore *Gazette,* and the Philadelphia *Evening Journal* — Democratic all — were suppressed or suspended for a variety of offenses, ranging from the usual "extension of aid or comfort to the enemy" to the release of a bogus proclamation which had the President calling for "400,000 more." In thus increasing the public's apprehension of an extension of the draft, he was treading on dangerous ground — dangerous to the government, that is — for nothing so inflamed resentment as did the Conscription Act which Congress had passed in early March and which had begun to be placed in operation by early summer. This resentment was directed less against the draft itself, which was plainly necessary, than it was against the way the act was written and administered. Actually, though it provoked a good deal of volunteering by men who sought to avoid the stigma of being drafted and the discomfort of not being able to choose their branch of service, it was far from effective in accomplishing its avowed purpose, as postwar records would show; 86,724 individuals escaped by paying the $300 commutation fee, while of the 168,649 actually drafted, 117,986 were hired substitutes, leaving a total of 50,663 men personally conscripted, and of these only 46,347 went into the ranks. Though barely enough to make up the losses of two Gettysburgs, draftees and substitutes combined amounted to less than ten percent of the force the Union had under arms in the course of the war; in fact, they fell far short of compensating for the 201,397 deserters, many of whom had been drafted in the first place. However, the popular furor against conscription was provoked not by its end results, which of course were unknown at the time, but rather by the vexations involved in its enforcement, which brought the naked power of military government into play on the home front and went very much against the national grain. While provost marshals conducted house-to-house searches, often without the formality of warrants, boards of officers sentenced drafted boys as deserters for failing to report for induction, and troops were used without restraint to break up formal protest meetings as well as rowdy demonstrations. In retaliation, conscription officials were roughed up on occasion, a few being shot from ambush as they went about their duties, and others had their property destroyed by angry mobs, all in the good old American way dating back to the Revolution. So-called "insurrections," staged at scattered points throughout the North, invariably met with harshness at the hands of soldiers who did not always bother to discriminate between foreign and domestic "rebels," especially when brought back from the front to deal with this new home-grown variety. In mid-June, for example, an uprising in Holmes County, Ohio, was quelled so rigorously by the troops called in for that purpose that their colonel felt obliged to account for their enthusiasm when he made his report of the affair. "The irregularities committed by some of the men," he wrote, "were owing more to their having campaigned in the South than to any intention on their part of violating my express orders to respect private property."

This rash of draft disturbances, which broke out during the long hot summer leading up to and continuing beyond the two great early-July victories, was by no means limited to the Old Northwest or the Ohio Valley, where secret societies were most active in opposition to the Administration and its measures. Boston and Newark had their clamorous mobs, as did Albany and Troy, New York, and Columbia and Bucks counties, Pennsylvania. There were uprisings in Kentucky and New Hampshire, and the governor of Wisconsin had to call out the state militia to deal with demonstrations in Milwaukee and Ozaukee County, where immigrants from Belgium, Holland, and Germany, especially vigorous in resisting what they had left Europe to escape, attacked the draft headquarters with guns and clubs and stones. By far the greatest of all the riots, however, was the one that exploded in New York City, hard on the heels of Vicksburg and Gettysburg, while Lincoln was writing his sent and unsent letters to Grant and Meade. Partly the trouble was political; protests had been made by party orators that Democratic districts were being required to furnish more than their fair share of conscripts and that ballot boxes were being stuffed with imported Republican soldier votes. Partly, too, it was racial; charges were also made that Negro suffrage was a device for overthrowing the white majority, including Tammany Hall, and that Negroes were being shipped in from the South to throw the Tammany-loyal workers, mostly Irish, out of work. Whatever began it, the three-day riot soon degenerated into violence for its own sake. On Monday, July 13, a mob wrecked the draft office where the drawing of names had begun two days before, then moved on to the Second Avenue armory, which was seized and looted, along with jewelry stores and liquor shops. By nightfall, with the police force overpowered, much of the upper East Side had been overrun. Segments of the mob were reported to be "chasing isolated Negroes as hounds would chase a fox," and the chase generally ended beneath a lamppost, which served conveniently as a gibbet. All next day this kind of thing continued, and nearly all of the next. A colored orphanage was set afire and the rioters cheered the leaping flames, seeing the Negroes not only as rivals for their jobs but also as the prime cause of the war. According to one witness of their fury, "three objects — the badge of a defender of the law, the uniform of the Union army, the skin of a helpless and outraged race — acted upon these madmen as water acts upon a rabid dog." By morning of the third day, however, representatives of all three of these hated categories were rare. The mob had undisputed control of the city.

In Washington, Lincoln and Stanton reacted to news of the violence by detaching troops from Meade to deal with the situation. They arrived on Wednesday evening and got to work at once. "We saw the grim batteries and weatherstained and dusty soldiers tramping into our leading streets as if into a town just taken by siege," another witness recorded in his diary. According to him, the action was brief and bloody. "There was some terrific fighting between the regulars and the insurgents; streets were swept again and again by grape, houses were stormed at the point of the bayonet, rioters were picked off by sharpshooters as they fired on the troops from housetops; men were hurled, dying or dead, into the streets by the thoroughly enraged soldiery; until at last, sullen and cowed and thoroughly whipped and beaten, the miserable wretches gave way at every point and confessed the power of the law." Estimates of the casualties ranged from less than 300 to more than 1000, though some Democrats later protested that the figures had been enlarged by Republican propagandists and that there was "no evidence that any more than 74 possible victims of the violence of the three days died anywhere but in the columns of partisan newspapers." Whether the dead were few or many, one thing was clear: Lincoln was determined to enforce the draft. "The government will be able to stand the test," Stanton had replied by wire to Mayor George Opdyke's request for troops at the height of the trouble, "even if there should be a riot and mob in every ward of every city."

Conscription resumed on schedule, August 19, and though there was grumbling, there was no further violence in the nation's largest city; the Secretary had seen to the fulfillment of his prediction by sending in more troops, with orders to crack down hard if there was any semblance of resistance. Lincoln stood squarely behind him, having denied Governor Horatio Seymour's plea for a suspension of the draft. "Time is too important," he told the Democratic leader, and while he agreed to look into the claim that the state's quota was unfair, he made it clear that there would be no delay for that or any other purpose. "We are contending with an enemy who, as I understand, drives every able-bodied man he can reach into his ranks, very much as a butcher drives bullocks into a slaughter pen. No time is wasted, no argument is used. This produces an army ... with a rapidity not to be matched on our side if we first waste time to re-experiment with the volunteer system." His intention, he said in closing, was to be "just and constitutional, and yet practical, in performing the important duty with which I am charged, of maintaining the unity and free principles of our common country." And so it was. Under Lincoln there was Stanton, and under Stanton there was Provost Marshal General James B. Fry, who headed a newly created bureau of the War Department. Under Fry, in charge of enrollment districts corresponding roughly to congressional districts all across the land, were the provost marshals, who were responsible not only for the functioning of the conscription process but also for the maintenance of internal security within their individual districts. Each could call on his neighboring marshals for help in case of trouble, as well as on Fry in Washington, and Fry in turn could call on Stanton, who was prepared to lend the help of the army if it was needed and the Commander in Chief approved. Lincoln's long arm now reached into every home in the North, as well as into every home in the South that lay in the wake of his advancing armies, east and west.

Now that he had had time to absorb the shock Lee's getaway had given him, he felt better about the outcome of the battle in Pennsylvania and the capacity of the general who had won it. Though he was still regretful — "We had gone through all the labor of tilling and planting an enormous crop," he complained, "and when it was ripe we did not harvest it" — he was also grateful. That was the word he used: saying, "I am very grateful to Meade for the service he did at Gettysburg," and asking: "Why should we censure a man who has done so much for his country because he did not do a little more?" All the same, he could scarcely help contrasting the eastern victory with the western one, which had left him not even "a little more" to wish for. Nor could he avoid comparing the two commanders. More and more, he was coming to see Grant as the answer to his military problem: not only because of his obvious talent, demonstrated in the capture of two rebel armies intact, but also because of his attitude toward his work. For example, when Lorenzo Thomas was sent to Mississippi to direct the recruiting of Negro troops, Grant had been instructed to assist him, and though he said quite frankly, "I never was an abolitionist, not even what could be called anti-slavery," he had replied forthrightly: "You may rely upon it I will give him all the aid in my power. I would do this whether the arming the negro seemed to me a wise policy or not, because it is an order that I am bound to obey and I do not feel that in my position I have a right to question any policy of the government."

Lincoln liked the tone of that. In contrast to the petulance he had encountered in his dealings with five of the six commanders of the eastern army (McDowell, the exception, had also turned sour in the end, after two months of service under Pope) Grant had the sound of a man he could enjoy working closely with, and apparently he had the notion of bringing him East, although Halleck and Charles Dana, who had returned to Washington shortly after the fall of Vicksburg, were certain that the general would prefer to continue his service in the West. Presently there was first-hand evidence that such was indeed the case; for

Dana wrote to Grant in late July, telling him what was afoot, and got a reply in early August. "General Halleck and yourself were both very right in supposing that it would cause me more sadness than satisfaction to be ordered to the command of the Army of the Potomac. Here I know the officers and men and what each general is capable of as a separate commander. There I would have all to learn. Here I know the geography of the country and its resources. There it would be a new study. Besides, more or less dissatisfaction would necessarily be produced by importing a general to command an army already well supplied with those who have grown up, and been promoted, with it. ... While I would disobey no order, I should beg very hard to be excused before accepting that command." This too was forthright; the President, if he saw the letter, was left in no doubt as to Grant's own preference in the matter. At any rate Lincoln decided to stick with Meade for the time being, much as he had done with Burnside and Hooker after telling a friend that "he was not disposed to throw away a gun because it missed fire once; that he would pick the lock and try it again." Grant would keep, Grant would be there in case he was needed; Grant was his ace in the hole.

Meanwhile there was the war to get on with, on the political front as well as on the firing line. In mid-June out in Illinois, at the height of the Vallandigham controversy and two weeks after Burnside's suppression of the Chicago *Times,* a monster protest rally had been staged in Lincoln's own home town; Copperhead orators had whipped the assembly into frenzies of applause, and the meeting had closed with the adoption of peace resolutions. Now, with the fall elections drawing near, Republicans were calling for loyal Democrats to join them, under the banner of a "National Union" party, in campaigning for support of the Administration's war aims. They planned a record-breaking turnout at Springfield in early September, to offset whatever effect the previous gathering might have had on voters of the region, and the arrangements committee invited Lincoln to come out and speak. He considered going — after all, except for military conferences, he had not left Washington once in the thirty months he had been there — but found the press of business far too great. Instead, he decided in late August to write a letter to the chairman of the committee, James Conkling, to be read to the assembly and passed on to the rest of the country by the newspapers, giving his views on the conflict at its present stage. He began by expressing his gratitude to those "whom no partizan malice, or partizan hope, can make false to the nation's life," then passed at once, since peace seemed uppermost in men's minds nowadays, to a discussion of "three conceivable ways" in which it could be brought about. First, by suppressing the rebellion; "This I am trying to do. Are you for it? If you are, so far we are agreed." Second, by giving up the Union; "I am against this. Are you for it? If you are, you should say so plainly." Third, by negotiating some sort of armistice based on compromise with the Confederates; but "I do not believe any compromise, embracing the maintenance of the Union, is now possible. All I learn leads to a directly opposite belief."

After disposing thus, to his apparent satisfaction, of the possibility of achieving peace except by force of arms, he moved on to another matter which his opponents had lately been harping on as a source of dissatisfaction: Emancipation. "You say you will not fight to free negroes. Some of them seem willing to fight for you; but no matter. Fight you, then, exclusively to save the Union. I issued the Proclamation on purpose to aid you in saving the Union. Whenever you shall have conquered all resistance to the Union, if I shall urge you to continue fighting, it will be an apt time then for you to declare you will not fight to free negroes. I thought that in your struggle for the Union, to whatever extent the negroes should cease helping the enemy, to that extent it weakened the enemy in his resistance to you. Do you think differently? I thought that whatever negroes can be got to do, as soldiers, leaves just so much less for white soldiers to do in saving the Union. Does it appear otherwise to you? But negroes, like other people, act upon motives. Why should they do anything for us if we will do nothing for them? If they stake their lives for us, they must be prompted by the strongest motive — even the promise of freedom. And the promise, being made, must be kept."

And having progressed so far in what an associate called a "stump speech" delivered by proxy, Lincoln passed to the peroration. Here he broke into a sort of verbal buck-and-wing:

> The signs look better. The Father of Waters again goes unvexed to the sea. Thanks to the great Northwest for it. Nor yet wholly to them. Three hundred miles up, they met New England, Empire, Keystone, and Jersey, hewing their way right and left. The Sunny South, too, in more colors than one, also lent a hand. On the spot, their part of the history was jotted down in black and white. The job was a great national one, and let none be banned who bore an honorable part in it. And while those who have cleared the great river may well be proud, even that is not all. It is hard to say that anything has been more bravely and well done than at Antietam, Murfreesboro, Gettysburg, and on many fields of lesser note. Nor must Uncle Sam's web-feet be forgotten. At all the watery margins they have been present. Not only on the deep sea, the broad bay, and the rapid river, but also up the narrow muddy bayou, and wherever the ground was a little damp, they have been and made their tracks. Thanks to all. For the great republic, for the principle it lives by and keeps alive, for man's vast future — thanks to all.

> Peace does not appear so distant as it did. I hope it will come soon, and come to stay, and so come as to be worth the keeping in all future time. It will then have been proved that among free men there

can be no successful appeal from the ballot to the bullet, and that they who take such appeal are sure to lose their case and pay the cost. And then there will be some black men who can remember that, with silent tongue and clenched teeth and steady eye and well-poised bayonet, they have helped mankind on to this great consummation, while I fear there will be some white ones unable to forget that, with malignant heart and deceitful speech, they have strove to hinder it.

Still, let us not be over-sanguine of a speedy final triumph. Let us be quite sober. Let us diligently apply the means, never doubting that a just God, in his own good time, will give us the rightful result.

※ 5 ※

In their first reports of Gettysburg, southern newspapers hailed the battle as a climactic triumph. "A brilliant and crushing victory has been achieved," the Charleston *Mercury* exulted on July 8, and two days later the Richmond *Examiner* informed its readers that the Army of Northern Virginia, with upwards of 30,000 prisoners in tow, was on the march for Baltimore. Presently, when it was learned that the graybacks had withdrawn instead to the Potomac, these and other southern journals assured the public that there was "nothing bad in this news beyond a disappointment"; Lee, whose "retrograde movement" had been "dictated by strategy and prudence," was "perfectly master of the situation." Though the victory "had not been decisive" because of "the semblance of a retreat," the outcome of the Pennsylvania conflict remained "favorable to the South." Not until the last week of the month did the *Examiner* refer to the "repulse at Gettysburg." By that time, however, the *Mercury*'s editor had also come full circle and like his Richmond colleague had recovered, through hindsight, his accustomed position as an acid critic of the Administration's conduct of the war. "It is impossible for an invasion to have been more foolish and disastrous," he pronounced.

For the most part, Lee's weary soldiers were content to leave such public judgments to the home-front critics, but privately there were some who agreed with the angry Carolinian. They had been mishandled and they knew it. "The campaign is a failure," a Virginia captain wrote home on his return to native soil, "and the worst failure the South has ever made. Gettysburg sets off Fredericksburg. Lee seems to have become as weak as Burnside. And no blow since the fall of New Orleans had been so telling against us." News of the loss of Vicksburg, which the strike across the Potomac had been designed in part to prevent, served to deepen the gloom, especially for those whose lofty posts afforded them a long-range view of the probable consequences. Longstreet, for example, wrote years later, looking back: "This surrender, taken in connection with the Gettysburg defeat, was, of course, very discouraging to our superior officers, though I do not know that it was felt as keenly by the rank and file. For myself, I felt that our last hope was gone, and that it was now only a question of time with us." Officials in Richmond also were staggered by the double blow, and of these perhaps the hardest hit was Seddon, who had put his faith in Johnston. Nowadays, according to a War Department clerk, the Secretary resembled "a galvanized corpse which has been buried two months. The circles around his eyes are absolutely black." Others about the office were as grim, particularly after reading the preliminary reports of the commanders in the field. "Gettysburg has shaken my faith in Lee as a general," R. G. H. Kean, chief of the Bureau of War, recorded in his diary on July 26. "To fight an enemy superior in numbers at such terrible disadvantage of position in the heart of his own territory, when the freedom of movement gave him the advantage of selecting his own time and place for accepting battle, seems to have been a great military blunder. [Moreover] the battle was worse in execution than in plan.... God help this unhappy country!" Two days later another high-placed diarist, Chief of Ordnance Josiah Gorgas, who had worked brilliantly and hard to provide the enormous amounts of matériel lost or expended, west and east, confessed an even darker view of the situation. "It seems incredible that human power could effect such a change in so brief a space," he lamented. "Yesterday we rode on the pinnacle of success; today absolute ruin seems to be our portion. The Confederacy totters to its destruction."

The one exception was Davis, who neither contributed to nor shared in the prevailing atmosphere of gloom that settled over the capital as a result of the triphammer blows struck by the Federals east and west. It was not that he failed to appreciate the gravity of the situation, the extent and intensity of the danger in both directions. He did. "We are now in the darkest hour of our political existence," he admitted in mid-July. Rather, it was as if defeat, even disaster, whatever else it brought, also brought release from dread and a curious inverse lift of the spirit after a time of strain which had begun with Grant's crossing of the Mississippi River and the death of Stonewall Jackson. Visitors to the White House in mid-May found him "thin and frail and gaunt with grief," and the tension increased tremendously when Vicksburg was besieged and Lee started north on June 3, the President's fifty-fifth birthday. Mrs Davis said afterwards that throughout this time her husband was "a prey to the acutest anxiety": so much so, indeed, that he found it nearly intolerable to have to wait deskbound in Richmond while his and the nation's fate was perhaps being decided in Pennsylvania and far-off Mississippi. He yearned for the field, a return to his first profession, and like Lincoln — who would declare somewhat later, under a similar press of anxiety: "If I had gone up there I could have whipped them myself" — he considered personal intervention. At any rate he expressed such a hope aloud, if only to his wife. "If I could take one wing and Lee the other," she heard him say one hot June night, "I think we could between us wrest a victory from those people." But that was not to be, either for him or his opponent, though presently there was disquieting news from Bragg and Buckner that Rosecrans and Burnside were on the march in Middle and East Tennessee, and hard on the heels of this came the first vague reports of Lee's retreat and Pemberton's surrender. Moreover, on July 10, when Vicksburg's fall was officially confirmed and Lee reported his army marooned on the hostile northern bank of the Potomac, bad news arrived from still another quarter. Beauregard wired that the enemy had effected a sudden lodgment on Morris Island; Fort Wagner had not been taken, the Creole declared, but the build-up and the pressure were unrelenting. Three days later, however, with Bragg in full retreat and the possible loss of Charleston increasing the strain on the President's frayed nerves, word came from Lee that his army was over the swollen river at last and back on the soil of Virginia, unpursued. Davis seized upon this one gleam of brightness in the gloom, and the clerk who had noted the black circles around Seddon's eyes recorded in his diary: "The President is quite amiable now. The newspaper editors can find easy access and he welcomes them with a smile."

There was more to this than a grasping at straws, though of course there was that as well; nor was his smile altogether forced, though of course it was in part. Davis saw in every loss of mere territory a corresponding gain, if only in the sense that what had been lost no longer required defending. Just as the early fall of Nashville and New Orleans had permitted a tighter concentration of the Confederacy's limited military resources and had given its field commanders more freedom of action by reducing the number of fixed positions they were obliged to defend, so might the loss of the Mississippi make the defense of what remained at once more compact and more fluid. What remained after all was the heartland. Contracted though its borders were, from the Richmond apex south through the Carolinas to Savannah on the Atlantic and southwest through East Tennessee and Alabama to Mobile on the Gulf, the nation's productive center remained untouched. There the mills continued to grind out powder, forge guns, weave cloth; there were grown the crops and cattle that would feed the armies; there on the two seaboards were the ports into which the blockade-runners steamed. In the final analysis, as Davis saw it, everything else was extra — even his home state, which now was reduced to serving as a buffer. Besides, merely because the far western portion of the country had been severed from the rest, it did not follow that the severed portion would die or even, necessarily, stop fighting. In point of fact, some of the advantages he saw accruing to the East as a result of the amputation might also obtain in the Transmississippi, if only the leaders there were as determined as he himself was. Accordingly, after making himself accessible to the Richmond editors so that they might spread these newest views among the defenders of the heartland, he took as his first task next day, July 14, the writing of a series of letters designed to encourage resolution among the leaders and people whose duties and homes lay beyond the great river just fallen to the Union.

Of these several letters the first went to Kirby Smith, commander of that vast region which in time would be known as Kirby-Smithdom. "You now have not merely a military, but also a political problem involved in your command," Davis told him, and went on to suggest that necessity be made a virtue and a source of strength. Cut off as it was, except by sea, the Transmississippi "must needs be to a great extent self-sustaining," he wrote, urging the development of new plants in the interior to manufacture gun carriages and wagons, tan leather for shoes and harness, and weave cloth for uniforms and blankets, as well as the establishment of a rolling mill for the production of ironclad vessels, "which will enable you in some contingencies to assume the offensive" on the Arkansas and the Red. In any case, he added, "the endurance of our people is to be sorely tested, and nothing will serve more to encourage and sustain them than a zealous application of their industry to the task of producing within themselves whatever is necessary for their comfortable existence. And in proportion as the country exhibits a power to sustain itself, so will the men able to bear arms be inspired with a determination to repel invasion.... May God guide and preserve you," the long letter ended, "and grant to us a future in which we may congratulate each other on the achievement of the independence and peace of our country." This was followed by almost as long a letter to Theophilus Holmes, the only one of Smith's three chief subordinates who had suffered a defeat. Far from indulging in criminations for the botched assault on Helena, the details of which were not yet known in Richmond, Davis chose rather "to renew to you the assurance of my full confidence and most friendly regards.... The clouds are truly dark over us," he admitted, but "the storm may yet be averted if the increase of danger shall arouse the people to such a vigorous action as our situation clearly indicates." Nor were the military leaders the only ones to whom the President wrote in this "darkest hour." He also addressed himself, in a similar vein of encouragement, to Governors Harris Flanagin of Arkansas, Francis R. Lubbock of Texas, and Thomas C. Reynolds of Missouri. And having received from Senator R. W. Johnston a gloomy report of dissatisfaction in Arkansas, including some talk of seceding from the sundered Confederacy, he replied on this same July 14: "Though it was well for me to know the worst, it pained me to observe how far your confidence was shaken and your criticism severe on men who I think deserve to be trusted. In proportion as our difficulties increase, so must we all cling together, judge charitably of each other, and strive to bear and forbear, however great may be the sacrifice and bitter the trial. ... The sacrifices of our people have been very heavy both of blood and of treasure; many like myself have been robbed of all which the toil of many years had gathered; but the prize for which we strive — freedom, and independence — is worth whatever it may cost. With union and energy, the rallying of every man able to bear arms to the defense of his country, we shall succeed, and if we leave our children poor we shall leave them a better heritage than wealth."

In urging these Westerners to "judge charitably of each other, and strive to bear and forbear," he was preaching what he practiced in the East in regard to Lee and Pemberton. Both had come under a storm of criticism: especially the latter, who not only had suffered a sounder defeat, but also had no earlier triumphs to offset it. So bitter was the feeling against him in the region through which he marched his Vicksburg parolees on their way to Demopolis, Alabama — a scarecrow force, severely reduced by desertions which increased with every mile it covered — that the President was obliged in mid-July to detach Hardee from Bragg, despite the touch-and-go situation in Tennessee, and send him to Demopolis to gather up the stragglers and assume the task of remolding them into a fighting unit. This left Pemberton without a command, though he had been exchanged and was available for duty. In early August, Davis wrote him a sympathetic letter: "To some men it is given to be commended for what they are expected to do, and to be sheltered, when they fail, by a transfer of the blame which may attach. To others it is decreed that their success shall be denied or treated as a necessary result, and their failures imputed to incapacity or crime. ... General Lee and yourself have seemed to me to be examples of the second class, and my confidence has not been diminished because 'letter writers' have not sent forth your praise on the wings of the press. I am no stranger to the misrepresentation of which malignity is capable, nor to the generation of such feeling by the conscientious discharge of duty." However, it was no easy thing to find employment for a discredited lieutenant general. Bragg at first expressed a willingness to take him, but presently, having conferred with his officers, reported somewhat cryptically that it "would not be advisable." Pemberton returned to Richmond, and after waiting eight months for an assignment, appealed to the Commander in Chief to release him for service "in any capacity in which you think I may be useful." Davis replied that his confidence in him was unimpaired — "I thought and still think that you did right to risk an army for the purpose of keeping command of even a section of the Mississippi River. Had you succeeded none would have blamed; had you not made the attempt, few if any would have defended your course" — but ended, two months later, by accepting the Pennsylvanian's resignation as a lieutenant general, at which rank he was unemployable, and by presenting him with a commission as a lieutenant colonel of artillery, the rank he had held in that same branch when he first crossed over and threw in with the South. In this capacity Pemberton served out the war, often in the thick of battle, thereby demonstrating a greater devotion to the cause he had adopted than did many who had inherited it as a birthright.

To Lee, too, went sustaining letters expressive of the President's confidence after the late reverse in Pennsylvania. "I have felt more than ever before the want of your advice during the recent period of disaster," Davis wrote in late July, closing "with prayers for your health, safety and happiness," and in early August, after assuring the general that he could "rely upon our earnest exertions to meet your wants," he offered the opinion that the Virginian might do well to withdraw his army closer to Richmond and thus encourage the enemy to attack him in a position that could be reinforced more readily; but he made it clear that now as always he was leaving the final decision to the commander in the field, who might prefer to defend the line of the Rappahannock, as he had done so successfully twice before. In closing, Davis spoke again of how sorely Lee had been missed throughout the fourteen months since he had left his post as presidential adviser: "I will not disturb your mind by reciting my troubles about distant operations. You were required in the field and I deprived myself of the support you gave me here. I need your counsel, but must strive to meet the requirements of the hour without distracting your attention at a time when it should be concentrated on the field before you.... As ever, truly your friend, Jeffn Davis."

No such letter went to Joe Johnston, though the correspondence between the Chief Executive and this other top-ranking Virginian was a good deal more voluminous. When a friend remarked, one day amid these troubles, that Vicksburg had fallen "apparently from want of provisions," Davis replied scathingly: "Yes, from want of provisions inside, and a general outside who wouldn't fight." First his anger and then his scorn had been aroused by efforts on the part of Johnston and his friends to free the general of all responsibility for the loss not only of Vicksburg and Port Hudson, but even of Jackson, their claim being based on a renewal of the complaint that he had not been allowed enough authority to permit decisive action. Davis replied on July 15 with a fifteen-page letter in which he reviewed the entire case, order by order, dispatch by dispatch, showing that Johnston had been given unlimited authority to act as he thought best, and he concluded in summation: "In no manner, by no act, by no language, either of myself or of the Secretary of War, has your authority ... been withdrawn, restricted, or modified." Johnston's response was a request that he be relieved of all responsibility for the disaster that seemed to be shaping up for Bragg, and Davis was prompt to comply. On July 22 the Department of Tennessee was removed from the Virginian's control. However, the apparent effect of this was to afford the general and his staff more time for self-justification.

There now began to appear, in various anti-Administration journals throughout the South, excerpts from a 5000-word "letter" written by Dr D. W. Yandell, Johnston's medical director, ostensibly to a fellow physician in Alabama. Secret dispatches and official orders were quoted, certain evidence that the writer had had access to the general's private files, and Johnston was praised extravagantly at the expense of Pemberton and the Commander in Chief, who were charged with indecision and lack of foresight. On August 1 Davis sent a copy of this "article-letter," which was being passed around in Richmond, directly to Johnston with a covering note that combined irony and contempt: "It is needless to say that you are not considered capable of giving countenance to such efforts at laudation of yourself and detraction of others, and the paper is sent to you with the confidence that you will take the proper action in the premises." The effect, of course, was to widen the rift between the two leaders, whose rupture was soon complete. An acquaintance observed that from this time forward Johnston's "hatred of Jeff Davis became a religion with him." Davis, on the other hand, was content to restrict himself to slighting references such as those he had made while the latest of the Virginian's "retrograde adjustments" was still in progress. "General Johnston is retreating on the east side of Pearl River," he informed Lee on the second anniversary of Manassas, "and I can only learn from him of such vague purposes as were unfolded when he held his army before Richmond." A week later the veil lifted a bit, but only to descend again. "General Johnston, after evacuating Jackson, retreated to the east, to the pine woods of Mississippi," Davis wrote Lee on July 28, "and if he has any other plan than that of watching the enemy, it has not been communicated."

Meanwhile Johnston, having advised the War Department of his intention "to hold as much of the country as I can and to retire farther only when compelled to do so," was enjoying a brief vacation in Mobile with his wife, who told a friend in early August that she had found her husband looking well and in "tolerable spirits, as cheerful as if Jeff was throwing rose leaves at him, instead of nettles and thorns."

"Misfortune often develops secret foes," Davis had said in a letter written earlier that week to Lee, "and oftener still makes men complain. It is comfortable to hold someone responsible for one's discomfort." Lee could testify to the truth of this, having seen it demonstrated first on his return from western Virginia, back in the rainy fall of '61, and now again on his return from Pennsylvania, when some of the same irate critics took him to task for blunders in the field. But the President had something else to say, of which Lee, concerned almost exclusively with army matters throughout the past year, was perhaps much less aware. Convinced that "this war can only be successfully prosecuted while we have the cordial support of the people," Davis had been pained to observe what he set down next: "In various quarters there are mutterings of discontent, and threats of alienation are said to exist, with preparation for organized opposition.... If a victim would secure the success of our cause," he added in closing, "I would freely offer myself."

This last was scarcely necessary, however, since a good many influential men had already singled him out for that distinction. In Charleston, for instance, the Robert Barnwell Rhetts, Senior and Junior, stepped up their attacks against him in the columns of their *Mercury*, and the father was in Columbia even now, suggesting as a member of the South Carolina convention, still in session, that Davis be impeached. There was considerable disagreement as to whether his sins were mainly ones of omission or commission, but his critics agreed that, whichever they were, he had them to a ruinous extent. Old Edmund Ruffin, Virginia's secession leader who had gone down to Sumter to fire the first shot of the war, referred contemptuously nowadays to "our tender conscienced and imbecile President," while James L. Alcorn, a fellow Mississippian of doubtful loyalty to the Confederacy, pulled out all the stops in calling him a "miserable, stupid, one-eyed, dyspeptic, arrogant tyrant." Two of his more vehement opponents, W. L. Yancey and seventy-year-old Sam Houston, were removed from the political scene by death before the end of July — the former as a result of a kidney ailment, though some editors hostile to Davis claimed the Alabamian died of a broken heart and acute regret at having presented "the man and the hour" to the inaugural crowd thirty months ago in Montgomery — but plenty of others remained: Robert Toombs, for example, whose wounded pride continued to fester down in Georgia. "Toombs is ready for another revolution," a diarist observed, "and curses freely everything Confederate from the President down to a horse boy." North Carolina's Governor Zebulon Vance, who had fought against secession as a Unionist and then against the Yankees as an officer of the line, was equally ready to take on the Richmond government as a champion of States Rights. "I can see but little good, but a vast tide of inflowing evil from these inordinate stretches of military powers which are fast disgracing us equally with our northern enemies," he told his constituents, and he was so zealous in his concern for their comfort and welfare that he was said to have in his warehouses, on the chance they might be needed some day, more uniforms than were on the backs of the ragged soldiers in Lee's army, to which he himself had belonged until he resigned and came home to campaign for the election he had won last fall.

How a nation which at the outset had been practically without industrial facilities for warfare, which had lost more than half its harbors and had the remaining few blockaded, which was penetrated from the landward side by large and well-organized columns of invasion, and which was outnumbered worse than five to one in available manpower for its armies, could hope to survive unless its people were united in diehard resistance Vance did not say. His concern at that particular time had been the suspension of habeas corpus during a crisis, and apparently his concern stopped there, whatever concomitant problems loomed alongside it or lurked in the background. Other leaders had other concerns as exclusive. Georgia's Joe E. Brown — "Joseph the Governor of all the Georgias," a home-state editor dubbed him; another said that he suffered from delusions in which he was "alternately the State of Georgia and the President of the Confederate States" — saw conscription as the great evil to be feared and fought. "The people of Georgia will refuse to yield their sovereignty to usurpation," he had notified Davis in October, and since then he had done much to prove he meant it, beginning with an executive order forbidding the taking or shipment of firearms from the state. Under his guidance the legislature elected Herschel V. Johnson, Stephen Douglas's 1860 running mate, to the Confederate senate on a program of opposition to the central government. Its members cheered wildly an address Johnson delivered before his departure, protesting the concentration of power in Richmond, and were joined in their applause by a fellow Georgian in whose hands a good part of that power had supposedly been placed: Vice President Alexander Stephens. There was nothing unusual in his presence at Milledgeville on this occasion, for he had early become disenchanted with the republic he had helped to establish and now he spent more time at home in nearby Crawfordville than he did at his duties in the national capital. Nor was there anything unusual, by now, in his indorsement of a speech against the Administration of which he was nominally a part. Like his friend Toombs, he was "ready for another revolution" whose cause would be the same as the First and Second, staged respectively in 1776 and 1861: both of which, as Stephens saw it, had since been betrayed. What he feared most, whether it was dressed in red or blue or gray, was what he later termed "the Demon of Centralism, Absolutism, Despotism!" That was the true enemy, and with it there could be no compromise whatever. "Away with the idea of getting independence first, and looking after liberty afterward," he declared. "Our liberties, once lost, may be lost forever."

Such opinions, voiced by such leaders — "impossiblists," they would be called one day — made waverers of many among their listeners who had been steadfast up to then, and defeatists of those who were wavering already. Moreover, their influence ranged well beyond the halls and stumps from which they spoke, for their words were broadcast far and wide by newspapers whose editors shared their views. The Rhetts and Edward Pollard of the *Examiner*, who referred to Davis as "a literary dyspeptic [with] more ink than blood in his veins, an intriguer busy with private enmities," were only three among the many, including the editors and owners of the Lynchburg *Virginian*, the Atlanta *Southern Confederacy,* the Macon *Telegraph* and *Intelligencer,* the Columbus *Sun,* and the Savannah *Republican.* Georgians were thus predominant, but the most blatant in his approach to downright treason was William Holden of the Raleigh *Standard.* Unsuppressed (for the Confederate government never censored so much as a line in a single paper throughout the war) Holden continued to rail against the Administration and all it stood for, uninterrupted except for one day in September when a brigade from Lee's army, passing through the North Carolina capital, indignantly wrecked the office of the *Standard.* Holden resumed publication without delay; but meanwhile, the soldiers having departed, a crowd of his admirers marched in retaliation on the plant of the rival *State Journal,* a Davis-loyal paper just up the street, and destroyed its type, presses, and machinery. Despite a presidential warning that those who sowed "the seeds of discontent and distrust" were preparing a "harvest of slaughter and defeat," hostile editors not only continued their attacks on the government, but also carried in their news columns the identification of military units in their areas, plans of yet unfought battles and campaigns, the arrival and departure times of blockade-runners, descriptions and locations of vital factories and munition works, all in such detail, a diarist remarked, that the North had no need for spies; "Our newspapers tell every word there is to be told, by friend or foe." Helpful though all this was to the enemy, the worst effect on the nation's chances for survival lay in the undermining of the public's confidence in eventual victory. Profoundly shaken by the double defeat of Gettysburg and Vicksburg, the people looked to their leaders for reassurance. From some they got it, while from others all they got was "I told you so" — as indeed they had, with a stridency that increased with every setback. All too often, as a result, enthusiasm was replaced by apathy. "They got us into it; let them get us out," men were saying nowadays, and by "them" they meant the authorities in Richmond.

In point of fact, if the public's faith in its government's paper money was a fair reflection of its attitude in general, the decline of confidence had begun much earlier. For the first two years of the war — that is, through April of the present year — the dollar had fallen gradually, if steadily, to a ratio of about four to one in gold. This was not too bad; the Federal greenback had fallen to about three to one in the same period. However, in the next four months, while Union money not only held steady but even rose a bit, Confederate notes declined nearly twice as much in value as they had done in the course of the past two years. In May, despite the splendid victory at Chancellorsville, the dollar fell from 4.15 to 5.50, the worst monthly drop to date. In June, moreover, with Lee on the march in Pennsylvania to offset Grant's progress in Mississippi, it took an even greater drop, from 5.50 to 7. In July, with Vicksburg lost and Lee in retreat, it tumbled to 9, and by the end of August, with the full impact of the two defeats being felt by all the people, one gold dollar was worth an even dozen paper dollars. To some extent, though the figures themselves could not be argued with, their effect could be discounted; men — some men; particularly money men — were known to be more touchy about their pocketbooks than they were about their lives, withholding the former while risking the latter for a cause. Davis, for one, could maintain that the shrinking of the dollar, even though the damage was to a large extent self-inflicted, was only one more among the hardships to be endured if independence was to be achieved. "Our people have proven their gallantry and patriotic zeal," he had written Lee; "their fortitude is now to be tested. May God endow them with all the virtue which is needed to save a suffering country and maintain a just cause."

Beyond the northern lines, as we have seen, there were many who agreed with Davis that his cause was just; who at any rate were willing to have the Confederates depart in peace. Similarly, or conversely, there were many behind the southern lines who disagreed with him; who were also for peace, but only on Union terms. Some had lost heart as a result of the recent reverses, while others had had no heart for the war in the first place. The latter formed a hard core of resistance around which the former gathered in numbers that increased with every Federal success. It was these men Davis had in mind when, after referring to "mutterings of discontent," he spoke of downright "threats of alienation" and "preparation for organized opposition." Such preparations had begun more than a year ago, but only on a small scale, as when some fifty men in western North Carolina raised a white flag and marched slowly around it praying for peace. Since then, the movement had grown considerably, until now the South too had its secret disloyal societies: Heroes of America, they called themselves, or Sons of America, or sometimes merely "Red Strings," from the identifying symbol they wore pinned to their lapels. While neither as numerous nor as active as their counterparts in the North, they too had their passwords, their signs and grips and their sworn objectives, which were to discourage enlistment, oppose conscription, encourage desertion, and agitate for an early return to the Union. Mostly the members were natives of a mountainous peninsula more than a hundred miles in width and six hundred miles in length, extending from the Pennsylvania border, southwest through western Virginia and eastern Tennessee, down into northern Georgia and Alabama. Owning few or no slaves, and indeed not much of anything else in the way of worldly goods, a good portion of these people wanted no part of what they called "a rich man's war and a poor man's fight." War or fight, its goals were those of the Piedmont and Tidewater regions, not their own, and they contributed substantially to the total of 103,400 Confederate desertions computed to have occurred in the course of the war. So far, they had amounted more to a potential than to an actual danger; Streight's raid across North Alabama, for example, had been planned with their support in mind, but they had not been of much use to him with Forrest close in his rear. However, the coming months would show that Davis had been quite right to give them his attention in late July, when they made their first significant gains outside the fastness of the Appalachian chain.

Reverses in the field, increasingly forthright opposition to the central government by regional States Rights leaders, the formation and expansion of societies dedicated to sabotage of the entire Confederate effort, all combined to increase the discouragement natural to the hour. If not convictions of defeat, then anyhow widespread doubts of ultimate victory took root for the first time. In the present "gloom of almost despondency," a Richmond editor wrote in mid-August, "many fainthearted regard all as lost." This was Pollard, who tended to exaggerate along these lines for reasons of his own; but even so staunch a supporter of the Administration as Congressman Dargan of Alabama — who had proved his mettle, if not his effectiveness, by making an unsuccessful bowie knife attack on his opprobrious colleague Henry Foote — fell into a midsummer state of desperation. "We are without doubt gone up; no help can be had," he wrote Seddon from Mobile in late July. "The failure of the Government to reinforce Vicksburg, but allowing the strength and flower of the Army to go north when there could be but one fate attending them, has so broken down the hopes of our people that even the little strength yet remaining can only be exerted in despair." He pinned his own hopes, such as they were, on foreign intervention, and since he believed that what stood in the way of this was slavery, he favored some form of Confederate emancipation. "So would the country," he declared, if the people were given the choice between abolition and defeat — especially in light of the fact that defeat would mean abolition anyhow. At any rate, he told his friend the Secretary of War, "If anything can be done on any terms in Europe, delay not the effort. If nothing can, God only knows what is left for us."

Dargan would perhaps have done better to write to the Secretary whose proper business was diplomacy. But it was as well he did not; Benjamin's department was having the least success of all this summer, both at home and abroad. In June, for example, Davis had had a letter from the Vice President down in Georgia, suggesting that he be sent on a mission to Washington, ostensibly to alleviate the sufferings of prisoners and humanize the conduct of the war, but actually, once negotiation on these matters was under way, to treat for peace on a basis of "the recognition of the sovereignty of the States and the right of each in its sovereign capacity to determine its own destiny." Just what he meant by this was not clear, and anyhow his disapproval of the government was too well known to permit his use as a spokesman, particularly at a conference on peace with the government's enemies. But Davis too was distressed by the growth of what he considered barbarism in the conflict, and he wired for Stephens to come to Richmond at once. Though he had no intention of allowing the Georgian any large authority — "Your mission is one of humanity, and has no political aspects," he informed him — he thought it might be advantageous to have an emissary on northern soil, whatever his basic persuasion, when Lee delivered the knockout blow he planned as a climax to the invasion about to be launched. Armed with two identical letters, one from Commander in Chief Davis to Commander in Chief Lincoln, the other from President Davis to President Lincoln — his instructions were to deliver whichever was acceptable — Stephens set off down the James, July 3, on the flag-of-truce steamer *Torpedo*. His hopes were high, despite the imposed restrictions, for he and Lincoln had been fellow congressmen and friends before the war. Off Newport News next morning, however, he submitted to the Union commander a request that he be allowed to proceed to Washington, only to be kept sweltering for two days aboard the motionless *Torpedo* while waiting for an answer. At last it came, in the form of a wire from Stanton on July 6: "The request is inadmissible. The customary agents and channels are adequate for all needful military communications and conference between the United States forces and the insurgents." Back at Richmond next day, the frail and sickly Georgian, who was barely under average height but weighed less than one hundred pounds with his boots on, learned that Gettysburg had been fought and lost — which explained, as a later observer remarked, why "Lincoln could afford to be rude" — and that evening the first reports of the fall of Vicksburg arrived. Discomfited and disgruntled, Stephens remained in Richmond for a couple of months, then returned to Crawfordville before Congress reconvened. A guidebook to the capital, listing the office and home addresses of government officials, contained the note: "The Vice President resides in Georgia."

Events abroad had taken a turn no more propitious than those on the near side of the Atlantic, although this too came hard on the heels of revived expectations. Despite the North's flat rejection of Mercier's offer to mediate a truce in February, friends of the Confederacy had been encouraged since then by what seemed to them an increasing conviction in Europe that the South could never be conquered. Chancellorsville had served to confirm this impression, even in the minds of men unwilling to admit it, and the London *Times* on May 2, unaware that the Wilderness battle was in mid-career, had noted that the Union was "irreparably divided." Looking back on the earlier Revolution, the editor said of the former Colonies: "We have all come to the conclusion that they had a right to be independent, and it was best they should be. Nor can we escape from the inference that the Federals will one day come to the same conclusion with regard to the Southern States." James Mason drew much solace from such remarks. Observing the hard times the cotton shortage had brought to the British spinning industry, he found himself emerging from the gloom into which more than a year of diplomatic unsuccess had plunged him. "Events are maturing which must lead to some change in the attitude of England," he informed Benjamin. Across the way in Paris, John Slidell was even more hopeful. "I feel very sanguine," he wrote, "that not many months, perhaps not many weeks, will elapse without some decided action on Napoleon's part." Grant's slam-bang May campaign in Mississippi offset considerably the brilliance of Lee's triumph over Hooker, but when it was followed by the determined resistance of Vicksburg under siege, with Johnston supposedly closing on Grant's rear, the Confederate flame of independence burned its brightest. Moreover, it was at this point that Lee set out on his second invasion of the North. The first, launched just under ten months ago, had come closer to securing foreign intervention than anyone outside the British cabinet knew; now if ever, with the second invasion in progress, was the time for an all-out bid for intervention. To ease the way, Benjamin assured a distinguished English visitor — Arthur Fremantle, who passed through Richmond in mid-June on his way to join Lee in Pennsylvania — that the South's demands were modest. To draw up a treaty of peace acceptable to the Confederacy, he said, it would only be necessary to write the word "self-government" on a blank sheet of paper. "Let the Yankees accord that," he told the colonel, "and they might fill up the paper in any manner they choose.... All we are struggling for is to be let alone."

There were those in the British Parliament who not only saw the opportunity as clearly as did anyone in the Confederate State Department, but also were willing to act. Two such were William S. Lindsay and John A. Roebuck, opposition stalwarts who, perceiving their chance for action after months of forced delay, crossed the Channel for an interview with Napoleon on June 20. Informed of his views that the time was ripe for joint intervention in the war across the sea, they hastened back to present them in a motion Roebuck brought before the house on June 30, requesting the Queen to enter into negotiations with foreign powers for the purpose of welcoming the Confederacy into the family of nations. They hoped thereby to place the government in a dilemma between recognition and resignation; however, they had neglected in their enthusiasm to make sure of their forces. When the ministry replied that no such proposal had been received from France, Napoleon failed to confirm their account of the interview, and thus exposed their veracity to question. John Bright and W. E. Forster, long-time Liberal proponents of the Union, both made powerful speeches against the motion, laced with sarcastic remarks on Roebuck's efforts to represent the Emperor on the floor of Parliament. What was more, as the debate wore on it developed that other pro-Confederate members did not approve of such overzealous methods, and Benjamin Disraeli, the Conservative leader, declined to commit the party to what amounted in the popular mind to a defense of slavery. Finally, on July 13, after waiting two weeks in vain for word of a victory won by Lee on northern soil, Roebuck — a diminutive individualist of somewhat ridiculous aspect; "Don Roebucco," *Punch* had dubbed him, "the smallest man 'in the House' " — admitted defeat by moving the discharge of his motion. Three days later the first reports of Gettysburg reached London, followed within the week by news of the fall of Vicksburg; after which there was no hope of a revival of the motion, either by Roebuck or anyone else. In fact, the ill-managed debate had done a good deal more to lower than to raise the Confederacy's chances of securing foreign recognition, particularly in England, where some of the ineptness and downright absurdity of its champions was connected, as a general impression, with the cause they had sought to further.

Benjamin perceived in this another instance of the attitude he had complained of earlier: "When successful fortune smiles on our arms, the British cabinet is averse to recognition because 'it would be unfair to the South by the action of Great Britain to exasperate the North to renewed efforts.' When reverses occur ... 'it would be unfair to the North in a moment of success to deprive it of a reasonable opportunity of accomplishing a reunion of the States.' " Davis agreed with this bleak assessment of the situation. " 'Put not your trust in princes,' " he had told his people before New Year's, "and rest not your hopes on foreign nations. This war is ours; we must fight it out ourselves." All the same, he had kept Mason in London all this time, suffering under snubs, on the off-chance that something would occur, either on this or that side of the water, to provoke a rupture between the Unionists and the British, who in that case would be glad to find an ally in the South. But this latest development, with its tarnishing absurdities, was altogether too much for him to bear. The game was no longer worth the candle, and he had Benjamin notify Mason of his decision. On August 4 the Secretary wrote as follows to the Virginian in England: "Perusal of the recent debates in the British Parliament satisfies the President that the government of Her Majesty has determined to decline the overtures made through you for establishing, by treaty, friendly relations between the two governments, and entertains no intention of receiving you as the accredited minister of this government near the British court. Under these circumstances, your continued residence in London is neither conducive to the interests nor consistent with the dignity of this government, and the President therefore requests that you consider your mission at an end, and that you withdraw, with your secretary, from London."

A private letter accompanied the dispatch, authorizing the envoy to delay his departure "in the event of any marked or decisive change in the policy of the British cabinet." But Mason too had had all he could bear in the way of snubs by now. Before the end of the following month he gave up his fashionable West End residence, removed the diplomatic archives, and took his leave of England, sped on his way by a hectoring editorial in the *Times* on the South's folly in demanding recognition before it had earned it. Despite the high hopes raised at the start of his mission by the *Trent* Affair, all he had to show for twenty months of pains was a note in which the foreign minister, Lord John Russell, after explaining that his reasons for declining the Virginian's overtures were "still in force, and it is not necessary to repeat them," expressed "regret that circumstances have prevented my cultivating your personal acquaintance, which, in a different state of affairs, I should have done with much pleasure and satisfaction." Joining Slidell in Paris, only a day away from London by train and packet, Mason kept himself and his staff in readiness for a return to England on short notice. Moreover, he believed he knew what form, if any, this notice was likely to take. Translating his diplomatic problems into British political terms, he pinned his remaining hopes on a Tory overthrow of Palmerston's coalition government, whose continuance in power he felt depended on the survival of the elderly Premier, and his correspondence with friends he had left behind, across the Channel, was peppered from this time forward with anxious inquiries as to the octogenarian's health. But Lord Palmerston — who, in point of fact, had been friendlier to the South than Mason knew — had a good two years of life left in him, and those two, as it turned out, were six months more than quite enough.

  The shock felt by Davis at this all but final evidence that the Confederacy would have to "fight it out," as he had said, without the hope of foreign intervention — for it was generally understood that France could not act without England, and Russia had been pro-Union from the start — was lessened somewhat, or at any rate displaced, by an even greater shock which he received on reading a letter the South's first soldier had written him four days after Benjamin wrote Mason. From Orange Courthouse, his new headquarters south of the Rapidan, Lee sent the President on August 8 what seemed at first to be some random musings on the outcome of the Gettysburg campaign. His tone was one of acceptance and resolution, of confidence in what he called "the virtue of the whole people.... Nothing is wanting," he declared, "but that their fortitude should equal their bravery to insure the success of our cause. We must expect reverses, even defeats. They are sent to teach us wisdom and prudence, to call forth greater energies, and to prevent our falling into greater disasters. Our people have only to be true and united, to bear manfully the misfortunes incident to war, and all will come right in the end." Davis agreed. In fact he had spent the past month saying much the same thing, not only to the public at large, but also, more specifically, to the heads of the nation's armies, including Lee. Nor did he disagree with what came next, having heard it before from his dead friend and hero Albert Sidney Johnston, who had been the subject of far more violent attacks by the press in another time of crisis. "I know how prone we are to censure," Lee continued, "and how ready [we are] to blame others for the non-fulfillment of our expectations. This is unbecoming in a generous people, and I grieve to see its expression. The general remedy for want of success in a military commander is his removal. This is natural, and in many instances proper. For no matter what may be the ability of the officer, if he loses the confidence of his troops disaster must sooner or later ensue." For all his basic agreement with the principle here expressed, Davis was by no means prepared for the application Lee made in the sentence that followed: "I have been prompted by these reflections more than once since my return from Pennsylvania to propose to Your Excellency the propriety of selecting another commander for this army."

There was where the shock came in. Davis read on with mounting apprehension as Lee explained what had brought him to make this request. Moreover, the care with which he had chosen his words indicated plainly that the letter had not been written as a mere gesture, but rather with publication in mind, as the closing document of a career that had ended in failure and sadness, but not in bitterness or despair:

> I have seen and heard of expression of discontent in the public journals at the result of the expedition. I do not know how far this feeling extends in the army. My brother officers have been too kind to report it, and so far the troops have been too generous to exhibit it. It is fair, however, to suppose that it does exist, and success is so necessary to us that nothing should be risked to secure it. I therefore, in all sincerity, request Your Excellency to take measures to supply my place. I do this with the more earnestness because no one is more aware than myself of my inability for the duties of my position. I cannot even accomplish what I myself desire. How can I fulfill the expectations of others? In addition I sensibly feel the growing failure of my bodily strength. I have not yet recovered from the attack I experienced the past spring. I am becoming more and more incapable of exertion, and am thus prevented from making the personal examinations and giving the personal supervision to the operations in the field which I feel to be necessary. I am so dull that in making use of the eyes of others I am frequently misled. Everything, therefore, points to the advantages to be derived from a new commander, and I the more anxiously urge the matter upon Your Excellency from my belief that a younger and abler man than myself can readily be obtained....
>
> I have no complaints to make of anyone but myself. I have received nothing but kindness from those above me, and the most considerate attention from my comrades and companions at arms. To Your Excellency I am specially indebted for uniform kindness and consideration. You have done everything in your power to aid me in

the work committed to my charge, without omitting anything to promote the general welfare. I pray that your efforts may at length be crowned with success, and that you may long live to enjoy the thanks of a grateful people.

With sentiments of great esteem,

I am very respectfully and truly yours,
R. E. LEE, General

Davis was dismayed. He had by now become reconciled to the permanent loss of some 15,000 of the South's best fighting men at Gettysburg, but if that defeat was also going to cost him Lee, who had held the North's main army at bay for more than a year and had provoked the removal of four of its commanders in the process, the loss might well be insupportable. Moreover, recent adversity East and West had drawn the two men even closer to one another, in their service to an imperiled cause, than they had been fifteen months ago in Richmond during a similar time of strain. Whether the nation could survive without Lee at the head of its first-line army Davis did not know, but he doubted that he himself could. "I need your counsel," he had written him earlier that week. Besides, for Davis, loyalty rendered was invariably returned, and Lee was not only personally loyal, he was also modest, magnanimous, and unselfish. Contrasting these qualities with those lately encountered in that other Virginian, that other Johnston — Joe — Davis could tell his ranking field commander: "Were you capable of stooping to it, you could easily surround yourself with those who would fill the press with your laudations, and seek to exalt you for what you had not done rather than detract from the achievements which will make you and your army the subject of history and object of the world's admiration for generations to come." Such words might serve to ease the sting of the lashings the journalists had been handing out. As for the general's failing health, this too could be set aside as no valid reason for resigning, Davis believed, even without the example of his own debilitation, which included loss of sight in one eye and searing pain that sometimes made the other almost useless. "I am truly sorry to know that you still feel the effects of the illness you suffered last spring, and can readily understand the embarrassment you experience in using the eyes of others, having been so much accustomed to make your own reconnaissances. Practice will however do much to relieve that embarrassment, and the minute knowledge of the country which you have acquired will render you less dependent for topographical information."

These things he could and did say, along with much else, in an attempt to dissuade Lee from resigning and thus spare the nation the calamitous loss of his service in the field. Fully conscious of the importance of choosing the proper tone and phrasing, he spent two days studying the general's letter and composing his own thoughts by way of rebuttal. Then on August 11, incorporating the sentences quoted above, he wrote his answer:

> General R. E. Lee,
> Commanding Army of Northern Virginia:
> Yours of the 8th instant has been received. I am glad to find that you concur so entirely with me as to the want of our country in this trying hour, and am happy to add that after the first depression consequent upon our disasters in the West, indications have appeared that our people will exhibit that fortitude which we agree in believing is alone needful to secure ultimate success.
> It well became Sidney Johnston, when overwhelmed by a senseless clamor, to admit the rule that success is the test of merit, and yet there has been nothing which I have found to require a greater effort of patience than to bear the criticisms of the ignorant, who pronounce everything a failure which does not equal their expectations or desires, and can see no good result which is not in the line of their own imaginings. I admit the propriety of your conclusions, that an officer who loses the confidence of his troops should have his position changed, whatever may be his ability; but when I read the sentence I was not at all prepared for the application you were about to make. Expressions of discontent in the public journals furnish but little evidence of the sentiment of an army....
> But suppose, my dear friend, that I were to admit, with all their implications, the points which you present, where am I to find that new commander who is to possess the greater ability which you believe to be required? I do not doubt the readiness with which you would give way to one who could accomplish all that you have wished, and you will do me the justice to believe that if Providence should kindly offer such a person for our use, I would not hesitate to avail of his services.
> My sight is not sufficiently penetrating to discover such hidden merit, if it exists, and I have but used to you the language of sober earnestness when I have impressed upon you the propriety of avoiding all unnecessary exposure to danger, because I felt our country could not bear to lose you. To ask me to substitute you by someone in my judgment more fit to command, or who would possess more of the confidence of the army or of the reflecting men in the country, is to demand of me an impossibility.
> It only remains for me to hope that you will take all possible care of yourself, that your health and strength may be entirely restored, and that the Lord will preserve you for the important duties devolved upon you in the struggle of our suffering country for the independence which we have engaged in war to maintain.
> As ever, very respectfully and truly yours,
> JEFFERSON DAVIS

After this, there was no more talk of Lee resigning. As long as the Army of Northern Virginia existed he would remain at its head.

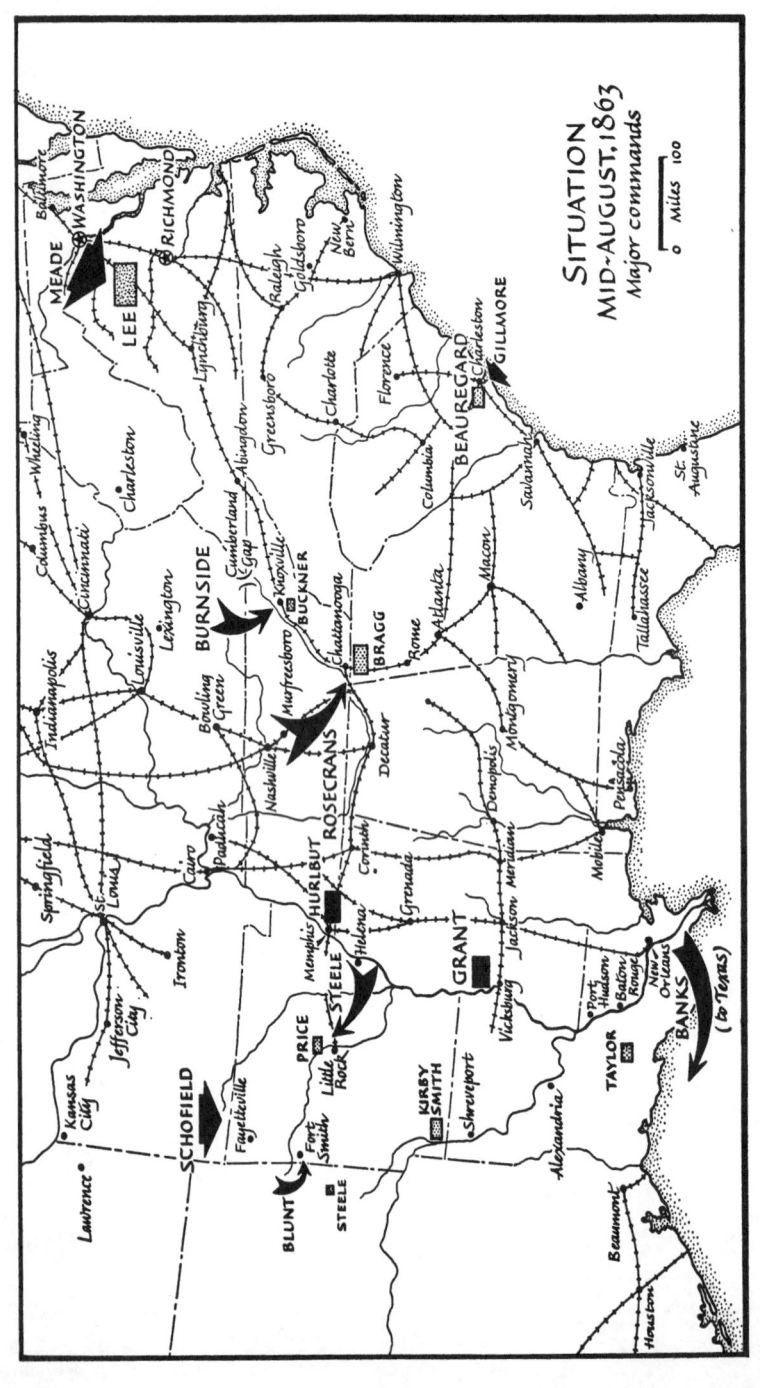

CHAPTER

7

Riot and Resurgence

★ ✘ ☆

AS JUNE WORE ON, ROSECRANS AND HIS ARMY of the Cumberland approached the end of their six-month convalescence from the rigors of Stones River. The narrowness of his escape from total disaster on that field having convinced him more than ever of the wisdom of meticulous preparation — which, as he saw it, had made the hairbreadth difference between victory and defeat — he would no more respond to prodding now than he had done in the months leading up to that horrendous New Year's confrontation just short of Murfreesboro. Directly or indirectly, but mostly directly, Lincoln and Stanton and Halleck all three had tried their hand at getting him to move: to no avail. He would not budge, though he would sometimes agree blandly, as if for the sake of prolonging the argument, that an advance was highly desirable.

Immediately after Chancellorsville, for instance, when Stanton reported — quite erroneously — that Hooker had inflicted as many casualties as he suffered, Rosecrans replied: "Thanks for your dispatch. It relieves our great suspense. What we want is to deal with their armies. Piece for piece is good when we have the odds. We shall soon be ready here to try that." So he said. But May went by, and still he would not budge. "I would not push you to any rashness," Lincoln wrote, "but I am very anxious that you do your utmost, short of rashness, to keep Bragg from getting off to help Johnston against Grant." The Ohioan's answer was both prompt and brief: "Dispatch received. I will attend to it." But he did not. June came in, and still he would not budge. "If you can do nothing yourself," Halleck wired, "a portion of your troops must be sent to Grant's relief." Old Rosy was unperturbed by this threat of amputation. "The time appears now nearly ripe," he responded, "and we have begun a movement, which, with God's blessing, will give us some good results." He omitted, however, a definition of "nearly." June wore on; he would not budge. By June 16 Lincoln's patience was exhausted, and he had the general-in-chief put a point-blank question to the Middle Tennessee commander: "Is it your intention to make an immediate movement forward? A definite answer, yes or no, is required." Halleck asked for a yes or a no, but Rosecrans gave him both. "In reply to your inquiry," he wired back, "if immediate means tonight or tomorrow, no. If it means as soon as all things are ready, say five days, yes."

At any rate this fixed the jump-off day; Washington settled back to wait for word, June 21, that the Army of the Cumberland was in motion. What came instead, by way of anticlimax on that date, was another wire, so little different in substance from the many received before that the whole sheaf might have been shuffled and refiled, indiscriminate of sequence, with little or no disturbance of its continuity, since in point of fact it had none. Bulky though it was — Old Brains had already complained to Rosecrans of the strain his frequent telegrams had placed on the military budget — the file was not so much a series of pertinent dispatches as it was a loose collection of secondhand maxims designed to strengthen his brief for refusing to expose his troops to bloodshed. "We ought to fight here," he wired, "if we have a strong prospect of winning a decisive battle over the opposing force, and upon this ground I shall act. I shall be careful" he added, "not to risk our last reserve without strong grounds to expect success." It was exasperating, to say the least; for it was becoming increasingly apparent, on evidence supplied by himself, that what Old Rosy was doing was fighting a verbal holding action, not so much against the rebels in his front as against his own superiors in his rear. Lincoln's patience almost snapped again. Three days later, however — on June 24, in a telegram headed barely two hours after midnight — the longed-for word came through: "The army begins to move at 3 o'clock this morning. W. S. Rosecrans, Major General."

The "strong grounds" on which he based his expectation of success were twofold, logistical and tactical, and he had neglected no detail in either category. Logistically he had adopted what might be called a philosophy of abundance. His requisitions, submitted practically without remission, reflected a conviction that there simply could not be too much of anything. As long ago as mid-April, for example, one of his brigadiers had been awed by the sight, at the Murfreesboro depot, of 40,000 cases of hard bread stacked in a single pile, while there were also gathered roundabout, in orderly profusion, such quantities of flour, salt pork, vinegar, and molasses as the brigadier had never seen before; he marveled at the wealth and prodigality of the government he was defending. Nor was food by any means the commander's sole or even main concern. Operating as he would be in a region that called for long supply trains and numerous cavalry to guard them and protect the flanks and front of the infantry line-of-march, he had put in for and received since December 1 no fewer than 18,450 horses and 14,067 mules. Exclusive of culls, this gave him — or should have given him, according to the quartermaster general, when combined with the number shown on hand — a total of 43,023 animals, or about one for every two men in his army. Rosecrans did not consider this one beast too many, especially since he had evacuated some 9000 of them as unserviceable and was complaining even then that over a fourth of those remaining were worn out. So it went; he kept demanding more of everything. The same applied to men. He had, as of mid-June, a total of 87,800 effectives, a considerable preponderance when compared to his estimated total for Bragg of 41,680 of all arms. However, this left out of account the necessary garrisons for Nashville, Donelson, Clarksville, and other such vital places in his rear — including Murfreesboro itself, when move-out time came round — which reduced, or would reduce, his total to 65,137 strictly available for the offensive. That was still a preponderance, but it was scarcely a man too many, as he saw it, to assure him what he called "a strong prospect of winning a decisive battle over the opposing force." Moreover, to this would be added, as he had complained soon after the bloodletting at Stones River, multiple difficulties of terrain. "The country is full of natural passes and fortifications," he informed the impatient Washington authorities, "and demands superior forces to advance with any success."

Lacking what he considered strength enough to assure a victory as the result of any direct confrontation, he had decided to depend instead on guile, and with this approach to the problem he began to perceive that the tricky terrain of which he had complained in January could be employed to his advantage. Bragg had his infantry disposed along the near side of Duck River, two divisions at Shelbyville under Polk and two at Wartrace under Hardee, about twenty miles from Murfreesboro and roughly half that far from Tullahoma, his headquarters and supply base on the Nashville & Chattanooga Railroad leading down across Elk River and the Tennessee, respectively twenty-five and sixty miles in rear of the present line of intrenchments north of the Duck. Just to the front of this line, and occupied by rebel outpost detachments, an almost mountainous ridge, broadening eastward into a high plateau, stood in the path of a direct advance by the superior blue force. Formerly Rosecrans had seen this as a barrier, further complicating the tactical problem Bragg had set for him, but presently he began to conceive of it

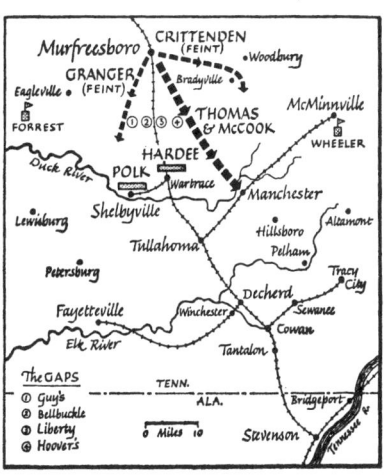

as a convenient screen, behind which he could mass his army for a surprise maneuver designed to turn the graybacks out of the works they had spent the past five months improving. Four main passes, each accommodating a road, pierced the ridge and gave access to the lush valley just beyond. In the center were Bellbuckle Gap, through which the railroad ran, and Liberty Gap, a mile to the east, with a wagon road also leading down to Wartrace. The remaining two gaps, Guy's and Hoover's, were respectively six miles west and east of the railroad, the former accommodating the Shelbyville pike and the latter the macadamized road from Murfreesboro to Manchester, which was sixteen miles east of Wartrace and twelve miles northeast of Tullahoma. It was in this tangled pattern of gaps and roads, so forbidding at first inspection, that Rosecrans found the answer to the problem Bragg had posed him.

He had no intention of advancing due south, through Bellbuckle or Liberty Gap, for a frontal assault on the Confederate intrenchments, which presumably was just what Bragg was hoping he would do. Nor was it any part of his design to launch an isolated attack on either of the rebel corps alone, since their positions were mutually supporting. His plan was, rather, to outflank them, thereby obliging the graybacks to come out into the open for a fight against the odds — or, better yet, to throw them into headlong retreat by threatening their rear, either at Tullahoma, where their supplies were stored, or somewhere else along the sixty brittle miles of railroad leading down past the Alabama line. This could be done, he figured, by forcing one of the outer gaps, Guy's or Hoover's, and swinging wide around the western or eastern flank of the rebel infantry. The western flank was favored by the terrain, which was far more rugged to the east; but it also had the disadvantage of being the more obvious, and therefore expected, approach. Then too, Polk's was the stronger of the two enemy corps, Hardee's having been weakened by detachments sent to Johnston in Mississippi. Rosecrans weighed the alternatives, one against the other, and chose the eastern flank. He would send his main body, the two corps of Thomas and McCook, southeastward through Hoover's Gap, then down the macadamized road to Manchester, from which place he could lunge at Tullahoma, in case the rebels remained in position north of the Duck, or continue his march southeastward for a strike at some point farther down. By way of initial deception, however, he would feint to the west, sending Granger's corps through or around Guy's Gap and down the pike toward Shelbyville, thus encouraging his opponent to believe that it was there the blow would land. Simultaneously — and here was where the deepest guile and subtlety came in — he would feint to the east with Crittenden's corps, through Bradyville toward McMinnville: with the difference that this supplementary feint was intended to be recognized as such, thereby convincing Bragg (who, he knew, took great pride in his ability to "see through" all such tactical deceptions) that the main effort was certainly in the opposite direction.... Looking back over the plan, now that he had matured and refined it during months of poring over maps and assembling supplies, meantime resisting impatient and unscientific proddings from above, Old Rosy was delighted with his handiwork. And indeed he had good cause to be pleased by the look of the thing on paper. If he reached the unfordable Tennessee before the rebels did, he would be between them and Chattanooga, his true goal, the capture of which he knew was one of Lincoln's fondest hopes; he could turn on the outnumbered and probably demoralized Bragg, who would be confined by necessity to the north bank of the river, and destroy him at his leisure. Or at its worst, if the Confederates somehow avoided being cut off from a crossing, he still would have driven them, brilliantly and bloodlessly, out of Middle Tennessee.

Secrecy being an all-important element of guile, he played his cards close to his vest. He said nothing of the particulars of his plan to either his subordinates or his superiors when, on June 16, he confided to the latter — prematurely, as it turned out — that he would advance in "say five days." Not even on June 24, in the telegram sent at 2.10 in the morning to announce that the army would be on the march within fifty minutes, did he say in what direction or strength the movement would be made. He was taking no chance on a Washington leak, even at that late hour, though of course his corps and division commanders had been informed of their share in the grand design and told to have their units deployed on schedule. Gordon Granger, with the one division remaining in his reserve corps after heavy detachments for garrison duty at Nashville and other points, began his march down the pike toward Shelbyville, preceded by a full division of cavalry, with instructions to kindle campfires on a broad front every night in order to encourage Polk, and therefore Bragg, to believe that this was the Federal main effort. Crittenden, one of whose three divisions remained on guard at Murfreesboro, began to execute the transparent feint eastward in the direction of McMinnville with the other two, preceded by a brigade of cavalry. George Thomas, whose four-division corps was much the largest in the army, took up the march for Hoover's Gap and Manchester, followed by Alex McCook, who had been told to make a disconcerting attack on Liberty Gap with one of his three divisions, thereby fixing Hardee in position at Wartrace, just beyond the gap, while Thomas circled his flank to threaten his rear. As usual, with Old Rosy in charge, no detail had been neglected. The foot soldiers were massed in their respective assembly areas, all ten divisions of them under carefully briefed commanders, and staff officers checked busily to see that all was as it should be, not only among the combat elements, but also in the rear echelon, including the various supply trains loaded with rations for twelve days. Nothing that could be calculated had been overlooked. Half the beef had been salted, for example, and loaded in wagons for ready distribution, while the other half was on the hoof: self-propelled, so to speak, for speed and ease of transportation.

Whereupon, just as the troops stepped out in the predawn darkness, beginning to weave the network of marches designed to accomplish Bragg's discomfiture, something uncalculated — indeed, incalculable — occurred. What Rosecrans later described as "one of the most extraordinary rains ever known in Tennessee at that period of the year" began to fall; "no Presbyterian rain, either," an Illinois soldier called it, "but a genuine Baptist downpour."

That was only the beginning. Crittenden afterwards maintained that, from this day forward, it "rained incessantly for fifteen days," and reports by lesser commanders bore witness to the difficulties involved. "Rain poured in torrents the entire night"; "Train not up in consequence of difficult traveling"; "Wet weather all day"; "Troops and animals much jaded." There was small comfort in knowing that the rain also fell on the rebels, but the men derived a kind of bitter satisfaction from the knowledge that they could learn to put up with almost anything. "It rained so much and so hard," one declared, "that we ceased to regard it as a matter of any consequence and simply stood up and took it, without attempting to seek shelter or screen ourselves in the least. Why should we, when we were already wet to the skin?" Besides, they had been heartened at the outset, before the fields and secondary roads were churned shin-deep in mud, by reports of a solid achievement that opened the way for the column under Thomas, who had been given the leading role in the present act of the drama Rosecrans was directing. More specifically, the accomplishment had been scored by Colonel John T. Wilder's brigade of Major General J. J. Reynolds' division.

It had been Wilder, a former Indiana industrialist, who surrendered Munfordville to Bragg, together with more than 4000 soldiers and 10 guns, as an incident of the Confederate advance into the Bluegrass region of Kentucky the previous September. The memory of that still rankled, and Wilder and his command, two regiments of fellow Hoosiers and two from Illinois, exchanged soon after their captors released them on parole — though not in time to fight at Perryville — were determined to make the rebels pay for that indignity. Just now they were in an excellent position to do so, for they were the lead element of the column that would deliver the main effort intended to throw Bragg into confusion. Moreover, they were superbly equipped for the work at hand, both in mobility and firepower, partly as a result of efforts by Rosecrans and partly as a result of efforts of their own. Short of cavalry, the army commander had mounted two of his infantry brigades, and one of these was Wilder's, who had also seen to it that his troops were armed with seven-shot Spencer carbines, the first unit in the West to be so accoutered. He had done this by signing a personal note upon which security bankers in his home town of Greensburg had a .vanced funds for purchase of the Spencers, the men having agreed to periodic deductions from their pay in order to reimburse their commander, pending their own reimbursement by the army once the red tape had been cleared away. So armed and mounted, 2000 strong, they left their camps above Murfreesboro at exactly 3 a.m. and by midmorning were herding enemy pickets into the northern mouth of Hoover's Gap, the prompt seizure of which was prerequisite to the success of the whole campaign. Wilder did not hesitate in fear of a trap or ambush, but plunged straight ahead through the three-mile-long pass with all the strength and speed he could muster, his mounted infantry driving the graybacks before them with the considerable help of their rapid-fire weapons. The works at the southern end of the gap were taken in a rush, together with the silk-embroidered colors of the 1st Kentucky Infantry, an elite Confederate outfit. Unlimbering their six guns, the Hoosiers and Prairie Staters broke up a savage counterattack and held the pass alone until the other two brigades of the division came plodding up to reinforce them, swinging their caps and cheering despite the rain. As a result of Wilder's daring and resolution, and at a relatively minor cost of 14 killed and 47 wounded, the way now lay open for an advance by Thomas around Hardee's flank and into his rear.

Bragg personally was not in good shape, either physically or mentally, for resisting the strain his opponent was about to apply as a test of his staunchness and perception. He had weathered the criticisms leveled at him by his chief subordinates, the steady depletion of his army by detachments ordered to Pemberton and Johnston, and the near-fatal illness of his wife, only to undergo a siege of boils which, by his own admission, had culminated in "a general breakdown" of his health by early summer. None of these troubles, particularly the last, had had the effect of sweetening his temper, lengthening his patience, or enabling him to abide the shortcomings of his associates, most of whom he considered unfit for their present duties. Unfortunately, too, these various woes and discomforts had served to increase, if anything, his accustomed savagery of looks and reflexes. "This officer in appearance is the least prepossessing of the Confederate generals," the ubiquitous Colonel Fremantle had recorded in his diary when he visited Bragg that spring, en route from Texas to Richmond. "He is very thin; he stoops; and has a sickly, cadaverous, haggard appearance; rather plain features, bushy black eyebrows which unite in a tuft on the top of his nose, and a stubby, iron-gray beard; but his eyes are bright and piercing. He has the reputation of being a rigid disciplinarian, and of shooting freely for insubordination. I understand he is rather unpopular on this account, and also by reason of his occasional acerbity of manner."

Not that the Tennessee commander lacked grounds for pride in what he and his men had accomplished during their sojourn in the lush

Duck River Valley. After all — though admittedly it was with the determined co-operation of an adversary who resisted all urgings to advance — he had held his ground and managed to feed and refit his badly outnumbered army in the process. "Our transportation is in fine condition," Polk was writing home, "horses and mules all fat, and battery horses and batteries in fine condition. The troops have plenty of clothes and are well shod. We have plenty of food also, and so far as the fields before us are any indication, there never was such a wheat harvest." Moreover, despite the permanent loss of some 6000 men at Murfreesboro and the detachment since of at least that many more, including Breckinridge's whole division, Bragg's mid-June strength of 46,250 effectives (for once in this war, at any rate, a Union commander had underestimated the force arrayed against him) was appreciably greater than it had been before New Year's. Primarily he had accomplished this by rigid enforcement of the conscription laws in the region threatened by a Federal advance, for he knew only too well that this might be his last chance to get at this particular reservoir of manpower, Davis having given him permission beforehand to fall back across the Tennessee as soon as he judged the pressure against his front to be insupportable. Rosecrans, however, for all his underestimation of Bragg's strength, had exerted almost no pressure at all in the past five months; so that Bragg had had ample opportunity to drill and condition his soldiers for the work that lay ahead. This was the sort of thing he did best, and the results had been gratifying. Even Fremantle, a product of the most rigid sort of training, admitted that the citizen soldiers "drilled tolerably well, and an advance in line was remarkably good." That was high praise indeed from an officer of the Coldstream Guards, though he could not repress a shudder on observing that some of the men had removed their jackets because of the heat and marched past the reviewing stand in shirt sleeves. When he expressed a desire to see them "form squares," he was told by his host that they had not been taught this maneuver, since "the country does not admit of cavalry charges, even if the Yankee cavalry had the stomach to attempt it." Similarly, he noted that the absence of the bayonet as a standard piece of equipment was a matter of small concern to the troops, "as they assert that they have never met any Yankee who would wait for that weapon." This last, of course, was far from true — as any stormer of the Hornets Nest or the Round Forest could have testified — but it was a measure of the men's high spirits that they made the claim to the credulous Englishman, who closed the account of his visit by remarking that "the discipline in this army is the strictest in the Confederacy."

In round numbers, 32,000 infantry and artillery were with Polk and Hardee on the Shelbyville-Wartrace line, while 14,000 cavalry were with Wheeler and Forrest, strung out for thirty miles east and west, respectively, with headquarters at McMinnville and Columbia.

These 46,000 effectives, comprising the Army of Tennessee, did not include some 15,000 under Buckner, who was charged with the defense of Knoxville against Burnside. That general, what time he was not fulminating against the Copperheads in his rear, was known to be preparing for an advance by the Army of the Ohio, though he had been crippled even more sorely than Bragg by detachments sent to Mississippi. To help discourage the threat in that direction, and also to continue the harassment of his Middle Tennessee opponent's lines of supply, Bragg had recently agreed to a proposal by John Morgan that he stage another of his famous "rides" into Kentucky with his 2500 Bluegrass troopers. Nettled by the defeats suffered in late March and early April at Milton and Liberty — he had in fact accomplished nothing significant since his spectacular Christmas Raid, hard on the heels of his marriage to Mattie Ready — Morgan had sought permission to extend his field of operations beyond the Ohio River, for the double purpose of carrying the scourge of war into the heartland of the North and restoring the glitter to his somewhat tarnished reputation; but Bragg (unlike Lee, who assented, though with misgivings, to a somewhat similar proposal by Jeb Stuart that same week in Virginia, preliminary to his crossing of the Potomac) had withheld approval of this extension of the raid, not wanting the Kentuckian and his men to be too far away in case Rosecrans lurched into motion in their absence. As it turned out, however, when he received word from his outposts on June 24 that the Federals were indeed in motion, not only on the left and right but also against his center, Morgan was already beyond reach, and Bragg did not discover until some weeks later, along with news of the disastrous consequences, that the freewheeling cavalryman had simply disobeyed the restrictive portion of the orders he had received.

Just now, though, Bragg had troubles enough on his hands, without looking afield for others. Correctly identifying the movements on Bradyville and Guy's Gap as feints, he left Crittenden and Granger to the attention of Forrest and Wheeler, and concentrated instead on opposing with his infantry the more immediate danger to his front. On the 25th he counterattacked at Liberty Gap, which had fallen to McCook the previous evening. Hardee failed to drive the bluecoats from the pass but he did succeed in holding them there, and Bragg, encouraged by this, sent orders for Polk to advance next day through Guy's Gap, then swing east for a descent on the rear of the troops opposing Hardee. Polk, as usual, protested, and Bragg as usual insisted. He reversed himself that night, however, on learning that the column under Thomas was approaching Manchester, still preceded by Wilder's rapid-firing horseback infantry and followed by Crittenden, who had abandoned his feint toward McMinnville and turned south at Bradyville. There was nothing for it now, as Bragg assessed the situation, but to call off the proposed attack on Liberty Gap and fall back on Tullahoma to protect his base and his present flank and rear. This he did with all possible speed, though the going was heavy; Polk left Shelbyville early on the 27th and did not reach Tullahoma, eighteen muddy miles away, until late next afternoon, soon after Hardee completed his march down the railroad in the rain. At any rate Bragg's army now was concentrated, protected by works prepared in advance, and he was determined to give the Yankees battle there.

Once more Rosecrans was unco-operative. Having reached Manchester the day before, June 27, he spent a day replenishing supplies brought forward on the hard-surfaced pike, and then resumed his march, not toward Tullahoma, as Bragg expected, but southeastward as before, toward Hillsboro and Pelham, still threatening the railroad on which his adversary depended for subsistence. At a council of war held on the night of the 28th, when Polk expressed some uneasiness that the Federals would continue their previously successful tactics by circling the right flank, Bragg taunted him by asking: "Then you propose that we shall retreat?" The bishop did indeed. "I do," he said firmly, "and that is my counsel." Hardee was less positive; he thought perhaps protection of the rear could be left to the cavalry while the infantry fought in its present intrenched position, outflanked or not; Rosecrans might gain the Confederate rear only to find the Confederates in his own. Bragg adjourned the council without making any definite decision. He would await developments, he said.

Developments were not long in coming. Granger and McCook had occupied Shelbyville and Wartrace that same day, moving in behind the departed graybacks, and though Rosecrans had no intention of attacking Tullahoma from the north, the presence of these two divisions at the crossings of the Duck was a menace Bragg could not ignore. Meanwhile Thomas, with McCook's other two divisions in support and Crittenden close behind, continued his march from Manchester to Hillsboro, a dozen miles due east of Bragg's right flank, and sent Wilder's hard-riding foot soldiers — already dubbed "The Lightning Brigade" as a result of their rapid seizure of Hoover's Gap on the opening day of the campaign — ahead to Pelham for an independent crossing of Elk River and a strike at the railroad near Decherd or Cowan, twenty miles in rear of the rebel works at Tullahoma. High trestles over gorges along this mountainous stretch of the line presented inviting targets, since the destruction of even one of them would be about as effective, so far as the flow of supplies was concerned, as the destruction of them all. Wilder's men rode fast and hard, anticipating further revenge for the Munfordville indignity. Reaching Decherd on June 28, they attacked a small detachment of rebel guards and drove them from a stockade: only to discover that a railroad might be vulnerable in some ways, yet still be highly defensible in others. No less than six gray regiments of infantry, responding to a telegraphic summons from the guards, arrived suddenly aboard cars from up the line. The blue raiders had barely time to get away on their horses, avoiding capture by the superior force and contenting themselves with the wrecking of an alternate trestle near Winchester, on the branch line to Fayetteville. Next morning, after a fireless bivouac in the brush, they tried the main line again, this time below Cowan, but with similar results; the ultramobile Confederate infantry once more drove them off before they could inflict any serious damage. Wilder fell back toward Pelham, pausing near Sewanee to wreck another trestle on the branch line to Tracy City, then continued his withdrawal, hastened by the interception of information that Forrest was on his trail. Aided by a driving rain, which obliterated his tracks, he eluded his pursuers and rode back into Manchester at noon of the 30th. Though he had failed to carry out his primary assignment, which had been to interrupt traffic on the Nashville & Chattanooga by destroying one of its main-line trestles, he had at any rate demolished one on each of the two branch lines, east and west, and he reported proudly that he had done so without the loss of a single man on the three-day expedition deep in the enemy rear. Thankful for what he had done, rather than critical for what he had not done, both Thomas and Rosecrans praised him highly for his resourcefulness and daring.

So did Bragg, though indirectly, not so much in words as by reaction. Wilder's strike, deep in his rear, plus the presence of Thomas on his flank with eight divisions, convinced him at last that retreat was the wisest policy at this juncture. The two-day wait having gained him time for removal of his stores and heavy equipment, he issued orders on the last night of June for a withdrawal. At Decherd next day he asked his corps commanders for advice: "The question to be decided instantly [is] shall we fight on the Elk or take post at the foot of the mountain at Cowan?" Polk favored Cowan, but Hardee was more explicit. "Let us fight at the mountain," he advised. Bragg did neither. The retreat being under way, he preferred to continue it rather than risk a long-odds battle with the unfordable Tennessee immediately behind him. While the infantry plodded southward under the unrelenting rain, Forrest guarded the rear. On July 3, with Polk and Hardee safely across Sewanee Mountain and out of the unsprung trap Old Rosy had devised, Federal cavalry in heavy numbers forced the pass near Cowan, and as the rear-guard Confederate troopers fell back rapidly through the streets of the town a patriotic lady came out of her house and began reviling them for leaving her and her neighbors to the mercy of the Yankees. "You great big cowardly rascal!" she cried, singling out Forrest himself for attack, not because she recognized him (it presently was made clear that she did not) but simply because he happened to be handy; "why don't you turn and fight like a man instead of running like a cur? I wish old Forrest was here. He'd make you fight!" Old Forrest, as she called him, did not pause for either an introduction or an explanation, though later he joined in the laughter at his expense, declaring that he would rather have faced an enemy battery than that one irate female.

Bragg could find nothing whatever to laugh about in his present situation. He had saved his army, but at the cost of abandoning Middle Tennessee. Moreover, with every horseback mile a torture to his boils, he was nearer than ever to the physical breakdown of which he had spoken earlier, and when a solicitous chaplain remarked from the roadside that he seemed "thoroughly outdone," he replied: "Yes, I am utterly broken down." Nor did he deny that he had been outdone tactically as well. "This is a great disaster," he confided dolefully, leaning from his saddle to whisper the words into the chaplain's ear.

Beyond Cowan he transferred to a railway car for less discomfort and more speed. After pausing at Bridgeport to send a dispatch notifying the Adjutant General of his retreat, he reached Chattanooga early on July 4, at about the same time his telegram reached Richmond, where it served as a forecast of even darker ones that followed at staggered intervals with the staggering information of what had occurred on that same day at Gettysburg, Helena, and Vicksburg. Meantime his army continued its withdrawal. Descending the slopes of the Cumberland Plateau, it entered the lovely Sequatchie Valley, then turned south along the right bank of the Tennessee for a crossing downstream at Bridgeport, just beyond the Alabama line. Here Forrest gave over his rearguard duties to a brigade from Cheatham's division, which was charged with maintaining a temporary bridgehead to discourage pursuit, and crossed the river in the wake of the rest of the army on the night of July 6, just three days short of the anniversary of his crossing northward as the spearhead of the advance into Kentucky. After a year of marching nearly a thousand miles and fighting two great battles, both of which he claimed as victories though both were preludes to retreat, Bragg was back where he started.

Rosecrans was willing to leave him there for the present. At a cost of 570 casualties, including less than a hundred dead and barely a dozen missing, the Federals had captured no fewer than 1634 prisoners — many of them Middle Tennessee conscripts who came into the northern lines of their own accord, wanting no more of the war now that their homeland was no longer being fought for — and had inflicted, despite their role as attackers, about as many wounds as they had suffered. They were proud of themselves and proud of the chief who had planned and supervised the campaign that ended, so far as the foot soldiers were concerned, with Bragg's retreat across the Elk on July 2. On that day, having moved into the abandoned rebel works at Tullahoma, they settled down for the first true rest they had enjoyed since setting off in their predawn marches from Murfreesboro, nine days back. Rain and mud, short rations, and all too little sleep had been their portion all this time; "It would be hard to find a worse set of used-up boys," an Indiana infantryman confessed. But they were well enough rested, a few days later, to cheer heartily at the news of Vicksburg's fall. Tremendously set up by their own recent success in a campaign which even the enemy newspapers were already calling "masterful" and "brilliant," they figured that Chattanooga was next on the list, and they were ready to take it whenever Old Rosy gave the word.

✗ 2 ✗

In Washington, too, there was delight that the campaign had gone so well, although the fact that so much had been accomplished with so little bloodshed seemed rather to validate the opinion, urged for months, that the issue could have been forced much sooner to the same conclusion with a corresponding gain in time. The first discordant note, struck amid the general rejoicing, was sounded by Stanton on July 7 in a telegram informing Rosecrans that Vicksburg had fallen and that the Gettysburg attackers were in full retreat. "Lee's army overthrown; Grant victorious," the Secretary wired. "You and your noble army now have the chance to give the finishing blow to the rebellion. Will you neglect the chance?" Nettled that the goading thus was resumed almost before his weary men had time to catch their breath and scrape the mud from their boots and clothes — not to mention that the taunt preceded any official congratulations for an achievement which even the enemy had begun to refer to as masterful — Rosecrans managed, as was usual in such verbal fencing matches with his superiors, to give as good as, if not better than, he got. "You do not appear to observe the fact that this noble army has driven the rebels from Middle Tennessee," he replied on that same day. "I beg in behalf of this army that the War Department may not overlook so great an event because it is not written in letters of blood." Four days later, in hope of avoiding further prods and nudges of this kind, he listed for Halleck some of the difficulties he faced. These included the necessary replacement of a 350-foot railroad bridge across Duck River, as well as a long trestle south of there, the relaying of several miles of track, both on the main line down to Tullahoma and on the branch line out to Manchester and McMinnville, and the construction of new corduroy roads in order to get his wagon trains across the seas of mud. Then too, he noted, there was the problem of Burnside and his delayed advance on Knoxville, which would not only protect the flank of the Army of the Cumberland when move-out time came round, but would also complicate matters for the enemy on the opposite bank of the Tennessee. In short, Rosecrans wanted it understood by the general-in-chief and those with whom he was in daily contact, meaning Stanton and Lincoln, that "the operations now before us involve a great deal of care, labor, watchfulness, and combined effort, to insure the successful advance through the mountains on Chattanooga."

The result was that Halleck stepped up the prodding. "You must not wait for Johnston to join Bragg," he wired on July 24, "but must move forward immediately.... There is great dissatisfaction felt here at the slowness of your advance. Unless you can move more rapidly, your whole campaign will prove a failure." A confidential letter written that same day put the issue even more bluntly: "The patience of the authorities here has been completely exhausted, and if I had not repeatedly promised to urge you forward, and begged for delay, you would have been removed from your command." This was a familiar threat, and Rosecrans met it much as he had done before. "I say to you frankly," he replied on August 1, "that whenever the Government can replace me by a commander in whom they have more confidence, they ought to do so, and take the responsibility of the result." He followed this with an expanded list of the difficulties in his path, but once more with results quite different from the ones he had hoped to bring about. "Your forces must move forward without further delay," Halleck snapped back at him three days later. "You will daily report the movement of each corps till you cross the Tennessee River." Rosecrans could scarcely believe his eyes. But when he inquired, by return wire, "if your order is intended to take away my discretion as to the time and manner of moving my troops," Old Brains replied that this was precisely his intention: "The orders for the advance of your army, and that its movements be reported daily, are peremptory." On August 6, a Thursday, the Middle Tennessee commander started a dispatch with what seemed a definite commitment — "My arrangements for beginning a continuous movement will be completed and the execution begun by Monday next" — only to proceed at once to enlarge on the difficulties and to request either that the order be modified or else that he be relieved of his command. He may or may not have been bluffing; in any case it did not work. Halleck was relentless. "I have communicated to you the wishes of the Government in plain and unequivocal terms," he replied next day. "The object has been stated, and you have been directed to lose no time in reaching it. The means you are to employ, and the roads you are to follow, are left to your own discretion. If you wish to promptly carry out the wishes of the Government, you will not stop to discuss mere details."

Old Rosy had one string left to his bow: an out-of-channels appeal made early that month to Lincoln, in hopes that he would intervene on the side of the field commander. "General Halleck's dispatches imply that you not only feel solicitude for the advance of this army but dissatisfaction at its supposed inactivity," he had written, thus extending to the Commander in Chief an invitation to step into the argument with a denial that this was so. On August 10 — the "Monday next" which Rosecrans had set as the date on which he would march, though he did not — Lincoln replied at length. "I have not abated in my kind feeling for and confidence in you," the letter began encouragingly, but then went into a review of the anxiety the writer had felt because of the Middle Tennessee general's immobility while Bragg was sending troops to Johnston for the relief of Vicksburg. As strategy, Lincoln added, this "impressed me very strangely, and I think I so stated to the Secretary of War and General Halleck." In the present case, moreover, he had doubts about the wisdom of accumulating such vast amounts of food and equipment as a prelude to the move on Chattanooga. "Does preparation advance at all? Do you not consume supplies as fast as you get them forward? ... Do not misunderstand," he said in closing. "I am not casting blame upon you. I rather think, by great exertion, you can get to East Tennessee. But a very important question is, Can you stay there? I make no order in the case — that I leave to General Halleck and yourself." In other words, he would not intervene. Old Rosy's bow was quite unstrung, even though the President ended his letter with further expression of his personal good will. "And now, be assured that I think of you in all kindness and confidence, and that I am not watching you with an evil eye. Yours very truly, A. Lincoln."

Having lost this ultimate appeal for a delay, Rosecrans finally began his march on August 16. This time, the recuperative halt had lasted not six months, as at Murfreesboro, but six weeks. It was time enough, however, for his purpose. Now as then, once he got moving he moved fast, with much attention to detail and much dependence on deception.

Burnside had begun his march on Knoxville the day before, after similar difficulties with the Washington authorities were brought to a head by a similar direct order for him to get moving, ready or not. In point of fact, despite the impatience of those above him, he had had excellent reasons for delay. First, when he was about to move in early June he was stripped of his veteran IX Corps, which went to Vicksburg under Parke. While waiting for its return he began assembling another, composed of inexperienced garrison troops brought forward from such places as Cincinnati, and sent a mixed brigade of 1500 cavalry and mounted infantry under Colonel William P. Sanders to look into conditions beyond the mountainous bulge of the horizon. Sanders, a thirty-year-old Kentucky-born West Pointer, set out on June 14, and in the course of the next nine days he not only disrupted rebel communications throughout East Tennessee, but also destroyed a number of bridges along the vital Tennessee & Virginia Railroad, including a 1600-foot span across the Holston River. He returned on June 23, elated by his success, which he reported was due in large part to the friendliness of natives whose loyalty to the Union had not been shaken by more than two years of waiting in vain for deliverance from Confederate oppression. Much encouraged, Burnside might have set out then and there with his green corps — thus matching Old Rosy's advance on Tullahoma, which got under way next morning — except that it was at this point that John Hunt Morgan exploded in his rear, necessitating the employment of all his cavalry in a chase through the Copperhead-infested region north of the Ohio, which the raiders crossed near Brandenburg on the night of July 8 after a wild ride northward through Kentucky, capturing blue detachments as they went and provoking alternate reactions of fear and elation in the breasts of the loyal and disloyal in their path.

On July 2, about midway between Nashville and Barbourville, Morgan crossed the upper Cumberland with eleven regiments, 2460 men in all, and a section of rifled guns. Four of his five brothers rode with him, Calvin, Richard, Charlton, and Thomas, and his brother-in-law Colonel Basil Duke commanded the larger of his two brigades; so that the raid was in a sense a family affair. Indeed, in an even more limited sense, it was a private affair. His disobedience of Bragg's orders regarding a crossing of the Ohio, which he had intended from the start, was based on the conviction that no mere "ride," even if the itinerary included Louisville, Frankfort, and Lexington, would accomplish his objective of stopping Rosecrans or Burnside, who would simply let the Bluegrass region look out for itself while they marched south, respectively, through Middle and East Tennessee. On the other hand, a strike into Indiana and Ohio could not so easily be ignored, either by them or by their superiors, for political as well as military reasons. As for the danger, though admittedly it was great, Morgan thought it might not prove so extreme as it appeared. Boldness was sometimes its own best protection, as he had demonstrated often in the past, and this was the epitome of boldness. Once across the Ohio he intended to ride east, through or around Cincinnati, always keeping within reach of the river, which was reported to be seasonally low, for a recrossing into Kentucky whenever the pressure on the north bank grew too great. Or at the worst, if this maneuver proved impractical, he would continue east and north for a juncture with Lee in Pennsylvania and a return by easy stages to his proper theater of the war. This would be an affair not only for the history books and tactics manuals of the future, but also for the extension and enlargement of the legends and songs already being told and sung in celebration of earlier, lesser horseback exploits by Morgan and his "terrible" men: an inheritance, in short, to be handed down to Confederate patriots yet unborn, including the child his young wife was about to bear him down in Tennessee. And so it was; so it became; though not precisely in the form intended.

At least the beginning was propitious, the entry into Kentucky despite the presence of some 10,000 soldiers Burnside had posted along the Cumberland with instructions to prevent just that. The raiders penetrated the screen without encountering anything more substantial than a small detachment of cavalry beyond Burkesville, which they easily brushed aside. Late the following night, however, while taking a rest halt at Columbia, they heard bluecoats on the north bank of the Green preparing earthworks from which to challenge any attempt to cross the bridge. They were five companies of Michigan infantry, and next morning, not wanting to leave them active in his rear, Morgan sent in a demand for their surrender. "On any other day I might," the Federal colonel replied, smiling, "but on the Fourth of July I must have a little brush first." By way of testing his earnestness and the strength of his position, the raiders gave him what he sought: to their regret, for they were repulsed with a loss of 80 killed and wounded, out of less than 600 engaged, having inflicted fewer than 30 enemy casualties, most of whose hurts were superficial. Morgan crossed the river elsewhere, convinced by now that he should have done so in the first place, and pressed on through Campbellsville to camp that night near Lebanon, where he had his second fight next day. Here the challengers were a regiment of Union-loyal Kentuckians, whose colonel replied in the Wolverine vein to a note demanding instant capitulation. "I never surrender without a struggle," he said grimly. This time the attack was made by both Confederate brigades for a quick settlement of the issue, however bloody. After some savage house-to-house fighting, the Federals fell back to the railroad station, where they finally yielded under assault. More than 400 prisoners were taken, along with valuable medical supplies, again at a cost of about 80 casualties for the attackers. But for Morgan personally the price was steeper than any comparison of cold figures could possibly indicate. Tom, the youngest of the brothers with him, was killed in the final volley fired before the white flag went up. The four surviving brothers buried him in the garden of a sympathetic Lebanon preacher, then resumed their ride northward, though with much of the glory and all of the gladness already gone from the raid for them.

In Bardstown on July 6, hoping to throw his pursuers off his trail, Morgan feinted simultaneously north and east by sending fast-riding columns toward Louisville and Harrodsburg, but swung the main body westward through Garnettsville to Brandenburg, where an advance detachment seized two small steamers for crossing the wide Ohio. This was accomplished between noon and midnight, July 8, despite some interference from a prowling Union gunboat that hung around, exchanging shots with the two rebel guns, till it ran out of ammunition. Their crossing completed, the raiders burned the steamers against the Indiana bank and pushed on six miles northward before halting for what little was left of the night. As they approached the town of Corydon next morning they found a sizable body of Hoosier militia drawn up to contest their entrance. Not wanting to take time to go around them, Morgan decided to go through them; which he did, scattering the home guardsmen in the process — they suffered a total of 360 casualties, of whom 345 were listed as missing — but at a cost to himself of 8 men killed and 33 wounded. Nor was that the worst of it. Taking the midday meal at a Corydon hotel, he learned from the innkeeper's daughter that Lee had been whipped six days ago at Gettysburg and was on his way back to Virginia. This meant that Morgan's alternate escape plan, involving a hookup with the invaders in Pennsylvania, was no longer practical, if indeed it had ever been. Apparently undaunted, he pressed on northward, that day and the next, through Palmyra to Salem, just over forty air-line miles from the Ohio and less than twice that far from Indianapolis. The Indiana capital was in a turmoil, its celebration of the great double victory at Gettysburg and Vicksburg brought to an abrupt and woeful end by news that Morgan was over the river with 10,000 horsemen and on his way even now to capture and sack the city. Church and fire bells rang the alarm, and a crowd turned out in front of the Bates House to hear Governor Morton read the latest dispatches. More than 60,000 citizens responded throughout the state to his appeal for militia volunteers, as many as possible of those who were immediately available being posted along the southern outskirts of the capital, toward Martinsville and Franklin, with orders to stop the gray raiders at all costs.

But they were not coming that way after all. Morgan had veered east from Salem on July 10, through Vienna to Lexington, where he allowed himself, if not his companions, the luxury of a night's rest in a hotel — and narrowly avoided, as it turned out, the ignominy of being captured in bed by a detachment of blue troopers who rode up to the building while he slept, then fell back hastily when his orderly gave the alarm, never suspecting the prize that lay within their grasp. Doubling the column to regain the lead, the Kentucky brigadier took up a zigzag course next day, through Paris and Vernon, for a small-hours halt at Dupont. Back in the saddle by dawn of the 12th, he rode that night into Sunman, fifteen miles short of the Indiana-Ohio line, which he crossed next day into Harrison, barely twenty miles from downtown Cincinnati. With Vicksburg lost, Lee defeated, and Bragg in full retreat, his purpose was no longer to cut railroads, wreck supply dumps, or even disrupt communications — except, of course, to the extent that such depredations would serve to confuse his pursuers — but simply to stretch out the expedition and thus prolong the inactivity of Burnside, who could not advance on Knoxville, in conjunction with Rosecrans' advance on Chattanooga, until his cavalry rejoined him. Morgan's proper course, in line with this reduced objective, was to move rapidly, appear suddenly at unexpected points, and then slip away before the superior forces combined against him could involve him in time-consuming fights that would only serve to exhaust his men and horses. Yet there was the rub. In the past ten days he had covered nearly 400 miles, including the crossing of three major rivers, at a cost of some 500 casualties and stragglers. Men and horses were beginning to break down at an alarming rate, just as he was about to call on them for even more strenuous exertions. However, he had no choice in the matter. What had begun as a raid, a foray as of a fox upon a henhouse, had turned into a foxhunt — and, hunting or hunted, Morgan was still the fox. He pressed on, southeastward now, in the direction of Cincinnati and the Ohio, which he was obliged to keep close on his right for a crossing in case he was cornered.

Down to fewer than 2000 men, he rode fast that night through the northeast suburbs of Cincinnati, not wanting to risk their dispersion in the labyrinth of its streets or to expose them to the temptations of its downtown bars and shops, overburdened as some of them were already with plunder they had gathered along the way. He did not call a halt for sleep until the column reached Williamsburg late that afternoon, some two dozen miles beyond the city, having covered no less than ninety miles in the past day and a half. Next morning, July 15, Morgan was feeling confident and expansive as his troopers took up the march. "All our troubles are now over," he told his staff, anticipating a three-day ride by easier stages to the fords upstream from Buffington, which he had had reconnoitered by scouts before he left Tennessee and which had been reported as an excellent point for a crossing back into Kentucky. While he traversed the southern tier of Ohio counties, through or around Locust Grove, Jasper, and Jackson, newspaper editors in his rear recovered sufficiently from their fright to begin crowing. "John Morgan's raid is dying away eastward," the Chicago *Tribune* exulted, "and his force is melting away as it proceeds. Their only care is escape and their chances for that are very slight." This was on July 16, and two days later the editor felt spry enough to manage a verbal sally. "John Morgan is still in Ohio," he wrote, "or rather is in Ohio without being allowed to be still."

It was true; Morgan was still in Ohio, delayed by militiamen quite as determined as the Hoosiers he had encountered on his first day on northern soil. Bypassing Pomeroy that morning, 150 miles east of Cincinnati, he had had to call a halt at Chester, just beyond, to wait for stragglers: with the result that the head of the column did not approach the river above Buffington until well after dark. Here he received his worst shock to date. Swollen by two weeks of rain, the Ohio was on an unseasonal boom, and the fords — if they could be called that, deep as they were — were guarded by 300 enemy infantry who had been brought upstream on transports, together with two guns which they had emplaced on the north bank, covering the approaches to the shallowest of the fords. Moreover, if transports could make it this far upriver, so could gunboats; which was something the general had not counted on. Deciding to wait for daylight before attacking, he gave his men some badly needed sleep, then sent two regiments forward at dawn, only to discover that the bluecoats had abandoned their position in the darkness, tumbling their guns into the river unobserved and leaving the crossing unguarded for most of the night. However, there was no time for crimination or even regret for this lack of vigilance on the part of the scouts; for just then two things happened, both calamitous. A gunboat rounded the lower bend, denying the raiders access to the ford, and heavy firing broke out at the rear of the long gray line of weary men on weary horses. Two heavy columns of Federal cavalry, 5000 strong and well rested, had come up from Pomeroy after an overnight boat ride from downstream and had launched an immediate all-out attack on the raiders, who were wedged in a mile-long valley beside the swollen river, awaiting their turns at a ford they could not use. Morgan reacted with his usual quick intelligence, leading the head of the column out of the unblocked northern end of the narrow valley while the rear guard did what it could to fight off the attackers. But resistance quickly crumpled and the withdrawal became a rout. He was fortunate, under the circumstances, to lose no more than half of his command, including 120 killed or wounded and some 700 captured — Duke and two more of the Morgan brothers, Richard and Charlton, were among the latter — together with both of his guns and such of his wagons as had managed to keep up. One of these belonged to an old Tennessee farmer who had intended to trade for a load of salt at Burkesville, then return to his home on Calf-killer Creek, near Sparta. Unable to turn back for lack of an escort, he had stayed with the column, and now he found himself in far-off Ohio, beside an alien river, with Yankee troopers charging full-tilt at him and shooting as they came. Exhausted though he was, and badly frightened, he delivered extemporaneously one of the great, wistful speeches of the war. "Captain," he said to an officer standing beside him amid the twittering bullets, "I would give my farm in White County, Tennessee, and all the salt in Kentucky, if I had it, to stand once more safe and sound on the banks of Calf-killer Creek."

So would the thousand survivors who got away from Buffington with Morgan have liked to be back on their farms in Tennessee and Kentucky; but that was not to be, at least not soon, except for some 300 who made it across the river that afternoon at Blennerhassett's Island, a few miles below Parkersburg, West Virginia. The ford was deep, the current swift, and a number of riders and their mounts were swept away and drowned. Moreover, the crossing had scarcely begun when the gunboat reappeared from below, guns booming, and slammed the escape hatch shut. In midstream aboard a powerful horse, Morgan himself could have made it across, yet he chose instead to return to the north bank and stay with the remaining 700 to the bitter end of what, from this point on, was not so much a raid as it was a frantic attempt to avoid capture by the greatly superior forces converging from all points of the compass upon the dwindling column of graybacks. Northward they rode, through Eagleport and across the Muskingum River, twisting and turning for six more days, still following the right bank of the Ohio in search of another escape hatch. But there was none; or at any rate there was none that was not blocked. On July 26, down to fewer than 400 now because of the increasing breakdown of their horses, the survivors were brought to bay at Salineville, on Beaver Creek, near New Lisbon, and there — just off the tip of West Virginia's tiny panhandle, less than a hundred miles from Lake Erie and only half that far from Pittsburgh — Morgan and the 364 troopers still with him laid down their arms. In the thirty days since leaving Sparta on June 27, they had ridden more than 700 miles, averaging twenty hours a day in the saddle from the time they crossed the Ohio, and though they met with disaster in the end, they had at least accomplished their primary objective of preventing an early march southward by Burnside, in conjunction with Rosecrans' advance on Tullahoma, which would have made Bragg's retreat across the Tennessee a far more difficult maneuver than the unharassed withdrawal it actually was.

Morgan and his chief lieutenants, captured at Salineville and elsewhere, were brought in triumph back to Cincinnati, where Burnside pronounced them ineligible for parole. Nor was that the worst of it. Acting on misinformation that Abel Streight had been so treated after his capture in Alabama three months earlier, the authorities ordered that the Ohio raiders were to be confined in the State Penitentiary at Columbus for the duration of the war. And there they were lodged before the month was out. "My sleep was very much disturbed," a Kentuckian recorded in his diary, "by the terrible impression made upon my mind by our confinement in such a place." It was, he said, "enough to shock the sensibilities of any refined gentleman." Now that Burnside had his hands on Morgan he was taking no chance whatever of his escaping. All visitors were denied access to the prisoners, even the general's mother, presumably on the suspicion that she might smuggle in a bustle full of hacksaws. Hardest of all for them to bear, however, was the indignity of being dressed in convict clothes and shorn of their hair and beards. This last was the ultimate in inhumanity, according to one of the four reunited Morgan brothers, who had the full horror of war brought home to him by the loss of his mustache and imperial. Presently Governor Tod himself tendered what one of the captives called "a most untimely apology for an outrageous and disgraceful act." The shearing had been an administrative error, the governor explained, but Morgan's brother Charlton expressed a harsher opinion of the action. "The entire world will stamp it as disgraceful to this nation and the present age," he fervently protested.

Pleased with the capture and prompt disposition of the raiders — and encouraged as well, although it scarcely bore out his previous contention that they had been waiting for just such a treacherous chance, by the failure of the Copperheads to come to the aid of these outlaws deep in his rear — Burnside ordered his cavalry to rejoin the three divisions of infantry marking time all this while on the line of the Cumberland, gave them a couple of weeks to rest and get their horses back in shape, and then came forward himself in mid-August to direct in person the maneuver he had devised, under pressure from Washington, for delivering East Tennessee from the grip of the rebels under Buckner. Like Rosecrans, who was to advance simultaneously on his right, he counted heavily on deception to offset the disadvantages of terrain, and in this connection, by way of increasing his opponent's confusion and alarm, he had resolved to make his approach march in four columns. Two were of cavalry, one to advance on the left through Big Creek Gap and the other on the right through Winter's Gap, while the third, made up of two divisions of infantry, marched between them on Kingston, which lay at the confluence of the Clinch and Tennessee rivers, forty miles below Knoxville, the objective of all three columns. The fourth, composed of the remaining infantry division, would move directly on Cumberland Gap, which the Federals had taken in June of 1862 and then been obliged to abandon when Bragg and Kirby Smith outflanked it on their way to Kentucky, a year ago this month, and which was occupied now by a garrison of about 2500 graybacks, well entrenched, heavily armed, and amply supplied with provisions for a siege. Burnside had some 24,000 effectives in all, a comfortable preponderance; but the way was long, the roads steep, and the adversary tricky. Consequently, he planned carefully and gave his full attention to details, substituting pack mules for wagons in his trains, for instance, and mounting the lead regiments of both infantry columns so that they would set a fast pace for the troops who slogged along behind them. Learning at the last minute that his long-lost IX Corps veterans were finally on the way to rejoin him, though sadly decreased by casualties and sickness in the Mississippi lowlands — the two divisions, in fact, were down to about 6000 men between them — he decided not to wait. They could join him later, after they had rested, got the fever out of their bones, and been brought back up to strength. Besides, having planned without them and waited all this time in vain for their return, he preferred to move without them. And once he got moving he moved fast, with a march that matched the mid-November performance of the Army of the Potomac when he shifted it from the upper to the lower Rappahannock by way of preparation for the mid-December nightmare at Fredericksburg, which had haunted him, waking or sleeping, ever since.

This time it was otherwise. Though the two marches were alike in the sense that he encountered no opposition en route, this one differed profoundly in that he encountered none at the end, either. Reaching Kingston on September 1, unchallenged, he entered Knoxville with the infantry main body two days later, to find that the mounted column that had proceeded by way of Winter's Gap had arrived the day before.

Buckner had pulled out, bag and baggage, abandoning everything east of Loudon and west of Morristown, except Cumberland Gap, which the one-division column was attacking from the north. Delighted by his first large-scale victory since Roanoke Island, nineteen months ago, Burnside made a triumphal entrance at the head of the two-division column, September 3, and was hailed by the joyous citizens as their deliverer from oppression; "a rather large man, physically," an observer noted, "about six feet tall, with a large face and a small head, and heavy side-whiskers." These last added considerably to the over-all impression of the general as "an energetic, decided man, frank, manly, and well educated." He was, in brief, what was called a show officer. "Not that he *made* any show," the witness added; "he was naturally that."

Discontent with anything less than the whole loaf, he left two thirds of his infantry and cavalry to maintain his grip on Knoxville and that vital stretch of the only railroad directly connecting the rebel East and West, and set out three days later with the rest for Cumberland Gap, where the garrison still held out. He covered sixty miles of mountainous road in two days and four hours, completing the investment from the south as well as the north, and on the day of his arrival, September 9, forced the unconditional surrender of the 2500 defenders, together with all their equipment and supplies, including fourteen guns. Hearing next day from Rosecrans that Bragg was in full retreat upon Rome, Georgia, Burnside assumed that everything was under control in that direction; he turned his attention eastward instead, intending to complete his occupation of East Tennessee, to and beyond the North Carolina line, and to seize, by way of lagniappe, the important Confederate saltworks near Abingdon, Virginia. After a long season of blight and personal disappointment, he had rediscovered the heady delight of victory, and he was hard after more of the same.

With as little bloodshed — which, in effect, meant none at all — Rosecrans had marched on as rigid a schedule, over terrain no less forbidding, to accomplish as much against more seasoned defenders of an even tougher objective. For him too, once he got started, speed and dexterity were the keynotes. His army completed its crossing of the Tennessee on September 4, the day after Burnside rode into Knoxville, and five days later — September 9, the day Cumberland Gap came back into Union hands — he occupied Chattanooga, long recognized as the gateway to the heartland of the South, whose seizure Lincoln had said a year ago was "fully as important as the taking and holding of Richmond." Not only were many Confederates inclined to agree with this assessment, but they also considered the fall of one to be quite as unlikely as the fall of the other. On the face of it, in fact, the western bastion seemed to them the stronger of the two. Though it lacked the protective genius of Lee, it had its geographical compensations, such as the Tennessee

River to serve as a moat and the surrounding mountains and ridges to serve as ramparts in its defense, both of them the gift of God himself. "I tell you," a high-ranking Deep South officer later told a Federal correspondent, "when your Dutch general Rosencranz commenced his forward movement for the capture of Chattanooga, we laughed him to scorn. We believed that the black brow of Lookout Mountain would frown him out of existence, that he would dash himself to pieces against the many and vast natural barriers that rise all around Chattanooga, and that then the northern people and the government at Washington would perceive how hopeless were their efforts when they came to attack the real South."

In determining a solution to the problem during his six-week halt at Tullahoma and McMinnville, on the northwest side of the Cumberland Plateau, Rosecrans had reached deeper than ever into the bag of tricks that was always part of his military luggage. Bragg had Polk's corps disposed for a close-up defense of the city and Hardee's off to the east, protecting the railroad to Cleveland and beyond, while Wheeler's cavalry guarded the river crossings below and Forrest's those above. The obvious Federal strategy called for a movement toward the left, the better to make contact with Burnside. But this would not only take the army across the Sequatchie River and over Walden's Ridge, away from its railroad supply line back to Nashville; it also had the disadvantage of being expected, with Bragg already half deployed to meet it. The alternative was a move to the right for a crossing downstream, in the vicinity of the new forward supply base at Stevenson, and this was the one Old Rosy chose. It too would have its drawbacks, once he was over the river, since it would give him a longer way to go and three steep ridges to cross before he got to Chattanooga; but the reward would be correspondingly great. That way, with skill and luck, he might trap Bragg's whole army in its city fortress beside the river to the north, much as Grant had trapped Pemberton's at Vicksburg. Or if Bragg grew alert to the danger in his rear and fell back southward, down the line of the Western & Atlantic Railroad to Dalton or Rome, Rosecrans might catch him badly strung out and destroy him. However, if either of these aims was to be accomplished, it was necessary meanwhile to keep his opponent's attention fixed northward or northeastward, for the double purpose of making an undelayed crossing well downstream and a rapid march eastward, across the ridges in Northwest Georgia, to gain the rebel commander's rear before he became aware of what was looming. And here again was where guile and deception came in.

Keeping his main body well back from the river to screen his true intention, he demonstrated upstream with three brigades. Every night they lighted bonfires in rear of all possible crossings, from opposite Chattanooga itself clear up to Washington, a distance of forty miles, and while special details sawed the ends from planks and threw the scraps into creeks flowing into the Tennessee, others pounded round the clock on empty barrels in imitation of shipyard workers, thereby encouraging rebel scouts across the way to report that boats were being constructed for an amphibious assault somewhere along that stretch of the river. On August 21, by way of adding punch to the show, a battery went into action on Stringer's Ridge, directly across from the city, throwing shells into its streets and scoring hits on two steamboats at its wharf, one of which was sunk and the other disabled. Bragg's reaction was to withdraw the brigade from the north-bank bridgehead he had been holding all this time near Bridgeport, fifty miles downstream, and before the week was out a crossing by the mass of the blue army was underway in that vicinity: by Thomas at Bridgeport itself, where pontoons were thrown in replacement of the burned railroad bridge: by McCook, twelve miles below at Caperton's Ferry: and by Crittenden, ten miles above at Shellmound, which was twenty air-line miles due west of Chattanooga and twice that far by river. None of the three met any substantial resistance, so well had the upstream deception served its purpose. Except for Granger's one-division reserve corps, on guard at the Stevenson depot of supplies, and the three detached brigades, which kept making threatening gestures to fix Bragg's attention northward, Rosecrans had his whole army across the Tennessee by September 4, including all his artillery and trains loaded with ammunition enough for two great battles and rations for better than three full weeks, in case he remained that long out of touch with his base on the north bank. The main thing, as he saw it, was to keep moving and move fast. And that he did.

It took some doing, for the terrain was rugged; but Old Rosy had planned for that as well, directing the formation of company-sized details equipped with long ropes for hauling guns and wagons up difficult grades when the mules faltered. Perpendicular to his line of march, the three lofty ridges — actually long, narrow mountains, with deep valleys intervening — were Raccoon Mountain, Lookout Mountain, and Missionary Ridge. Lookout, which extended all the way to the bend of the river just below Chattanooga, was penetrated by only two gaps: Stevens Gap, 18 miles southwest of the city, and Winston Gap, 24 miles farther down. Rosecrans planned to use them both for a fast march eastward, sending Crittenden directly along the railroad, around the sheer north face of the mountain and into the city, which Bragg would probably evacuate when he learned that the other two corps were moving through the passes in his rear — McCook by way of Winston Gap, then around the lower end of Missionary Ridge, toward Alpine and Summerville, and Thomas by way of Stevens Gap, which also pierced Missionary Ridge within a dozen miles of LaFayette — for a blow at his vital and vulnerable rail supply line from Atlanta. Here again there were drawbacks, theoretical ones at any rate. The two outer columns, Crittenden's and McCook's, would be more than forty miles apart, and neither would be within a day's march of Thomas in the center; Bragg might concentrate and strike at any one of the isolated three. But this too had been foreseen and guarded against by sending all but one brigade of the cavalry with McCook — who seemed most susceptible in that regard, being on the remoter flank — while the remaining brigade preceded Crittenden, ready to give warning in case such a threat developed. The main thing was speed, and this assured just that. Rosecrans rode with the trooperless middle column, not only to keep in closer touch with all three of his chief lieutenants, but also to act as a goad to Thomas, who had many admirable qualities but was known to be somewhat lethargic on occasion.

Proud in the knowledge that they were the first Federals to penetrate this region since the beginning of the war, the men reacted with enthusiasm to the march, particularly when they saw spread out before them such vistas as the one unrolled from atop Raccoon Mountain. "Far beyond mortal vision extended one vast panorama of mountains, forests, and rivers," an Illinois veteran later wrote. "The broad Tennessee below us seemed like a ribbon of silver; beyond rose the Cumberlands, which we had crossed. The valley on both sides was alive with the moving armies of the Union, while almost the entire transportation of the army filled the roads and fields along the Tennessee. No one could survey the grand scene on that bright autumn day unmoved, unimpressed with its grandeur and the meaning conveyed by the presence of that mighty host." Presently word came from Crittenden that Bragg had apparently had a similar reaction to the presence of all those bluecoats in his rear; for when the Kentuckian drew near Chattanooga on September 8 he learned that the Confederates were in mid-evacuation, and next morning, as the tail of the gray column disappeared through Rossville Gap and behind the screen of Missionary Ridge, the city fell without the firing of a shot. Rosecrans passed the word to the troops of the central column, who did their best to rock Lookout with their cheers as they slogged through Stevens Gap.

Simultaneously, scores of butternut deserters began to filter into the Union lines with reports of Bragg's demoralization. He was in full flight for Rome or perhaps Atlanta, they declared, quite unmanned by this latest turning movement and in no condition to resist an attack if one could be thrown at him before he got there. Convinced that he had acted wisely in accepting the risk of dispersion for the sake of speed, Old Rosy urged his cheering soldiers forward, intent on giving the panic-stricken rebels what the deserters said would amount to a coup de grâce.

★ ★ ★

Rosecrans was partly right about Bragg, but only up to a point a good way short of the whole truth. The Confederate commander had been outsmarted, and he had fallen back in haste, even in some disorder, to escape the closing jaws of the Federal trap; but that was as far as it went. He was not retreating now, nor was he avoiding a fight. Rather, he was in search of one, although on different terms, having by now devised a trap of his own. As for the butternut scarecrows who had come stumbling into the northern lines, peering nervously over their shoulders and babbling of demoralization in the fleeing press of comrades left behind, Old Rosy would have done well to bear in mind some words one of his young staffers wrote years later: "The Confederate deserter was an institution which has received too little consideration.... He was ubiquitous, willing, and altogether inscrutable. Whether he told the truth or a lie, he was always equally sure to deceive. He was sometimes a real deserter and sometimes a mock deserter. In either case he was sure to be loaded." In the present instance, a considerable number of them were indeed "loaded," being scouts sent forth by Bragg himself, who had chosen them for their ability to be convincing in misrepresentation of the true state of affairs in the army that lay in wait for the exuberant bluecoats, just beyond the last of the screening ridges.

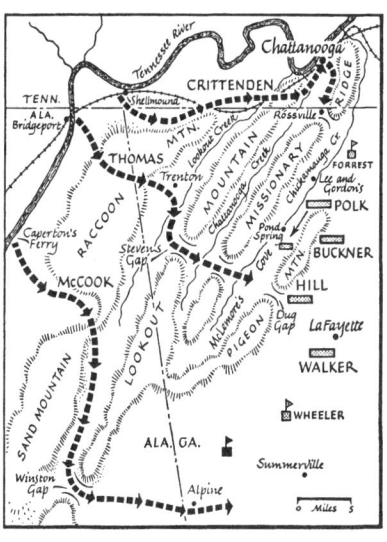

Bragg's present aggressiveness had come only after six weeks of uncertainty and confusion following his retreat across the Tennessee. Hearing from Adjutant General Cooper on August 1 that the government was anxious to reinforce him with most of Johnston's army, on condition that he recross the river for an attack on Rosecrans, he replied next day that he was willing, provided "a fight can be had on equal terms." But three days later he withdrew the offer. "After fully examining all resources," he wired, "I deem them insufficient to justify a movement across the mountains." He meant the Cumberland Plateau, which he had just traversed and which by then was serving Rosecrans as a screen to hide his preparations for pursuit. He did not like having it there at all; he wished it could be abolished. "It is said to be easy to defend a mountainous country," he complained to one of his corps commanders, "but mountains hide your foe from you, while they are full of gaps through which he can pounce upon you at any time. A mountain is like the wall of a house full of rat holes. The rat lies hidden at his hole, ready to pop out when no one is watching. Who can tell what lies hidden behind that wall?" Respectfully, while in this frame of mind, he informed Richmond that he declined to plunge his army into "a country rugged and sterile, with a few mountain roads only by which to reach a river difficult of passage. Thus situated," he explained, "the enemy need only avoid battle for a short time to starve us out." But he added, by way of final encouragement: "Whenever he shall present himself on this side of the mountains the problem will be changed."

On the strength of this last, though disappointed that Bragg was unwilling to take the offensive, the authorities decided to reinforce him anyhow. In point of fact, even aside from the evidence that Joe Johnston seemed determined to do nothing with the troops standing idle in Mississippi all this time, they had no choice; repulses or surrenders at Gettysburg and Vicksburg, Helena and Port Hudson, plus the loss of Middle Tennessee and Morgan's raiders, all within a single month, had caused them to question whether the South could survive another large-scale defeat this soon, particularly one that would swing ajar the gateway to its heartland. Informed of Richmond's decision, Bragg set about reorganizing his army so as to incorporate without delay the new brigades and divisions about to join or rejoin him from various directions. Indeed, reorganization had already begun on a limited scale. Hardee having been detached in mid-July to take over the mutinous remnant of Pemberton's band of parolees awaiting exchange at Demopolis, the irascible and highly competent D. H. Hill, promoted to lieutenant general subject to congressional approval, had come from North Carolina to replace him. Likewise the dapper and experienced, if disgruntled, Tom Hindman arrived in mid-August from the Transmississippi, and a place was made for him by transferring the less distinguished Withers to an administrative post in his native Alabama. Soon afterwards Buckner was ordered to evacuate Knoxville, and having moved southwest to Loudon, where he burned the railroad bridge across the Tennessee, he continued his march to the Hiwassee, less than forty miles from Chattanooga. There he stopped, for the time being, under orders to contest an advance by Burnside, if one developed, and stand ready to join Bragg on short notice if one did not. By that time Breckinridge had arrived with the first of two divisions being sent from Mississippi. He rejoined his old corps, formerly Hardee's, and Major General A. P. Stewart's division was detached from Hill to be combined with Buckner's and thus form a new third corps under the Kentuckian, who was summoned from the Hiwassee, Burnside having turned his attention elsewhere. When W. H. T. Walker joined Bragg with the second of the two divisions from Johnston, another division was organized by detaching and combining brigades from divisions already present, thus providing a fourth corps under his command. Practically overnight — that is, within a ten-day period extending from late August into early September — the Army of Tennessee had grown from two to four corps, each with two divisions, and a total strength of about 55,000 effectives, including cavalry.

Having in these eight infantry divisions 26 brigades with which to oppose 33 brigades in the eleven Federal divisions — considerably better odds, after all, than the ones he had prevailed against at Murfreesboro — Bragg developed, in the course of the reorganization of his expanded army, strong hopes of being able to defeat his adversary in pitched battle. He was not so sure, however, that this was what it would come to here, any more than it had at Tullahoma, where he had been outmaneuvered and given no real chance to defend a position he had been determined not to yield without a fight. In fact, there were signs that it would not. All this time Rosecrans had been demonstrating as if for a crossing well above Chattanooga, a repetition of the strategy that had won him Middle Tennessee, and Bragg had been reacting fretfully. Harvey Hill, for one, was quite unfavorably impressed. The junior lieutenant in Bragg's battery a dozen years ago in Texas — George Thomas, now commanding a blue corps across the way, and John Reynolds, recently killed at Gettysburg, were the other two lieutenants — Hill had looked forward to the reunion at Chattanooga, but was received with none of the warmth he had expected from his chief. "He was silent and reserved and seemed gloomy and despondent," Hill said later of his fellow North Carolinian. "He had grown prematurely old since I saw him last, and showed much nervousness." Moreover, as the newcomer learned from those who had been with the army all along, this was not entirely due to worry about his opponent on the far side of the river. "His relations with his next in command (General Polk) and with some others of his subordinates were known to be not pleasant. His many retreats, too, had alienated the rank and file from him, or at least had taken away that enthusiasm which soldiers feel for the successful general, and which makes them obey his orders without question." Fresh from the East, where he had been impressed by Lee's great daring, always based on sound knowledge of the enemy's dispositions, Hill was shocked by Bragg's apparent ignorance of the enemy's whereabouts and movements, which resulted in his maintaining a supine attitude while waiting for Rosecrans to show his hand. It was Hill to whom he described the Cumberlands as "the wall of a house full of rat holes," and Hill afterwards recorded that he "was most painfully impressed with the feeling that it was to be a haphazard campaign on our part."

However that might be, and it was as yet no more than an impression, it presently developed that Bragg had been quite right to suspect that Old Rosy was groping elbow-deep in his bag of tricks. No sooner was the Confederate reorganization completed than Bragg learned that the Federals were not only over the river, well downstream, but were also far in his rear, crossing Lookout and the other north-south Georgia ridges for a strike at the rail supply line whose loss would mean starvation for the defenders of Chattanooga. Determined not to be trapped as Pemberton had been at Vicksburg, he promptly evacuated the city and fell back southward through Rossville Gap to a position from which to block the continued advance of the three blue columns when they came around and over Missionary Ridge. His left was at LaFayette, two dozen miles from Chattanooga, and his right at Lee & Gordon's Mill, twelve miles north, where the road from Rossville crossed Chickamauga Creek. Walker held the former, Polk the latter, and Hill and Buckner were posted in between, confronting the westward loom of Pigeon Mountain, a crescent-shaped spur of Lookout Mountain which inclosed the lower end of Missionary Ridge and its eastern valley, a cul-de-sac known locally as McLemore's Cove. Bragg saw in this the trap he had been seeking, the trap he had encouraged Rosecrans to enter by sending out loaded deserters to dispel the Ohioan's native caution and hasten his march with the promise of an easy triumph over a demoralized opponent. Wheeler and Forrest, who had been called in and now were operating respectively on the immediate left and right, toward Alpine and Rossville, were instructed to impede the advance of McCook and Crittenden from Winston Gap and Chattanooga. This would leave the balance of the army, some 40,000 infantry and artillery, free to concentrate against Thomas, who had a total of 23,000 effectives, and destroy him there in the fastness of McLemore's Cove; after which the victors would turn on either or both of the remaining enemy columns, still well beyond supporting distance of each other, and administer the same annihilation treatment. Bragg so ordered on the evening of September 9, shortly after receiving from his scouts, civilian as well as military, reports that Thomas's lead division had entered the cove that afternoon and made a sundown camp on upper Chickamauga Creek.

His plan combined the virtues of simplicity and power, and his orders were issued with the coolness of a gambler holding four aces against a splurger whose overconfidence had been nurtured by an inordinate run of luck. While Cleburne's division of Hill's corps attacked due west through Dug Gap, corking the Pigeon Mountain outlet and fixing the bluecoats in position, Hindman's division of Polk's corps would move southwest from Lee & Gordon's Mill, up Chickamauga Creek, sealing the mouth of the cul-de-sac and striking the enemy flank and rear. Basically, the operation was intended to be like that of a meatgrinder, and if Thomas reinforced his lead division in the cove, so much the better; Breckinridge would be in support of Cleburne, Cheatham of Hindman, and the Federal reinforcements would only give them that much more meat to grind. Hindman set out an hour after midnight, September 10, and halted at dawn, four miles short of contact, waiting to hear from Cleburne. He had a long, tense wait. Finally a message came from Hill, protesting that he had not received his orders till after daylight, that Cleburne himself was sick in bed, with four of his best regiments absent on other duties, and that the proposed attack was risky in the first place, since Thomas had probably sent his lead division forward "as a bait to draw us off from below." In short, Cleburne would not be coming; not this morning at any rate. Later in the day, while still maintaining his indecisive position short of contact, Hindman received a message from Bragg, urging him to finish up his work in the cove as quickly as possible, because Crittenden's corps was on the march from Chattanooga by way of Rossville Gap, directly in his rear. This added fright to confusion, and after remaining all night in a position which he judged perilous in the extreme, the veteran of Prairie Grove decided next morning to withdraw the way he had come. By now, though, Bragg had sent Buckner to his support, with orders to force the issue promptly, and Cleburne was through Dug Gap; so Hindman returned southward. But when the two gray forces came together that afternoon in McLemore's Cove there was nothing blue between them. Thomas at last had spotted the danger, despite his lack of cavalry, and withdrawn to the far side of Missionary Ridge.

Bragg was furious, blaming the lost opportunity on Hindman's indecisiveness and Hill's "querulous, insubordinate spirit," while they in turn put the blame on him, claiming that their orders had been permissive rather than peremptory. However, he resolved to try again, in a different direction and with different commanders. Thomas had withdrawn to safety, but Crittenden had not. Polk having retired toward LaFayette at his approach, the Kentuckian had sent one of his three divisions to occupy Lee & Gordon's Mill while the other two moved against Ringgold, a station on the railroad between Chattanooga and Dalton, in accordance with his orders to break the rebel supply line. Learning of this next morning from Forrest, who was patrolling that flank of the army, Bragg directed Polk to return to his former position with his own reunited corps and Walker's, and attack the isolated Federals there at dawn, September 13. "This division crushed and the others are yours," he told him. The bishop protested that Crittenden, taking alarm, had recalled the two divisions from their march on Ringgold and now had his whole corps posted for defense behind the Chickamauga at that point. This was quite true, as it turned out, but Bragg replied that it was no matter; Polk had four divisions to the enemy's three, and he would send Buckner's two to assist him in case they were needed, which seemed unlikely; the attack was to be launched on schedule, as directed. But when he reached the field at 9 o'clock next morning he found Polk on the defensive, still unwilling to advance lest he be swamped. Madder than ever, the terrible-tempered Confederate commander finally got Polk and Walker and Buckner into assault formation by noon and sent them forward — only to discover that Crittenden, after the manner of Thomas two days ago in McLemore's Cove, had escaped the trap by withdrawing undetected beyond Missionary Ridge. In a rage of frustration and regret for the two rare chances he had lost in the past three days, Bragg pulled his whole army once more back to LaFayette, the best position from which to counter a thrust at his vital supply line by any one or all three of the blue columns across the way.

But there was small likelihood of any such thrust by then. The scales having fallen at last from his eyes, Rosecrans was doing all he could to get the three isolated segments of his army back together before they were abolished, one by one, by a rebel army which he now knew was not only not retreating in disorder, but also had been heavily reinforced. And now there followed a three-day interlude during which neither commander knew much of what the other was doing, although the graybacks at least had the physical advantage of standing still while their opponents tramped the dusty hills and valleys that lay between them and concentration. Presently the blue movements took on a new urgency, a new franticness, with the circulation of reports that Bragg was about to be even more substantially reinforced by troops already on the way by rail from Lee in Virginia; three divisions of them, rumor had it, under Longstreet. Old Rosy and his staff began to curse Burnside, who had turned east by now from Knoxville and Cumberland Gap instead of in their direction for the intended hookup: with the result, as they believed, that now it was they who were in grievous danger of being cut off from their base, exposed to the threat of starvation, and swamped by superior numbers, including a whole corps of hard-bitten killers from the far-off eastern theater.

Meanwhile at LaFayette, where the Confederates were recovering from their recent fruitless exertions in McLemore's Cove and near Lee & Gordon's Mill, Harvey Hill marveled at the apparent casualness with which these Westerners, blue and gray alike, accepted the proximity of their adversaries just on the opposite side of the intervening ridge. It was quite unlike what he had known before, back in Virginia under Lee. "When two armies confront each other in the East, they get to work very soon," he remarked to one of his veteran brigadiers. "But here you look at one another for days and weeks at a time." The brigadier, a cockfight enthusiast, laughed. "Oh, we out here have to crow and peck straws awhile before we use our spurs," he said.

All the same, as Hill, observed long afterwards in recording the exchange, "the crowing and pecking straws were now about over." A dozen to twenty miles north of there, above Lee & Gordon's Mill, the woods-choked field of Chickamauga awaited the confrontation that would result, within the week, in what would not only be the greatest battle of the West, but would also be, for the numbers engaged, the bloodiest of the war.

✗ 3 ✗

Reports that Longstreet was en route were true, but once more only up to a point, the difference being that this time the exaggeration was in the opposite direction, serving rather to deepen the blue commander's fears than to heighten his expectations. Old Peter was coming with two, not three divisions; Pickett's was still in no shape for another headlong commitment, and though it too had been detached from Lee, it was left behind to assist in the close-up defense of Richmond when the other two, under McLaws and Law — or Hood, as it turned out — passed through the capital on the first stage of their long ride to Northwest Georgia. The decision to send them to join Bragg had been arrived at during a White House conference in late August and early September, a conference not unlike the one that had preceded the march into Pennsylvania, except that this time the gray-bearded commander of the Army of Northern Virginia carried much less weight in council than he had done before his defeat at Gettysburg, which had been the direct result of the weight he exerted then in overriding the objections of Reagan. Besides, since that and the other early-July reverses in Mississippi, Arkansas, Louisiana, and Middle Tennessee, additional threats to the national existence had developed, including not only the menace to East Tennessee — which was lost while the conference was in progress — but also on the Atlantic seaboard, particularly at Charleston, and in the far-off Transmississippi. These too had served to strengthen the conviction that the country simply could not afford another defeat in the vital central theater, and therefore the decision had been to reinforce Bragg at the expense of all the others, including Lee, who would be left to face the victorious Meade with a greatly reduced force, and Beauregard, who was calling urgently for assistance in resisting an all-out Union amphibious effort to rock and wreck the cradle of secession.

Du Pont's repulse, back in April, had resulted in some sour-grapes talk on the part of Gideon Welles to the effect that Charleston, "a place of no strategic importance," had not been worth taking in the first place; but the failure rankled badly over the span of the next two months, with the result that he decided to try again with a more determined commander. Rear Admiral Andrew H. Foote, apparently recovered from the wound he had suffered while clearing the lower Tennessee and the Cumberland, as well as the Mississippi down to Memphis, was the logical choice for the job and was appointed despite his reluctance to supersede his old friend Samuel Du Pont. He died in New York in late June, however, while on the way to his new post, and the position went instead to Rear Admiral John A. Dahlgren, head of the Bureau of Ordnance, inventor of the bottle-shaped gun that had done so much to give the Union its victories afloat, and an intimate friend of Lincoln's during his command of the Washington Navy Yard in the first two years of the war. Described by a correspondent as "a light complexioned man of perhaps forty years of age," though he was in fact in his mid-fifties, Dahlgren was "slight and of medium height, [with] pale and delicate features. His countenance is exceedingly thoughtful and modest... while his eye is inevitably keen, and his thin nostrils expand as he talks, with a look of great enthusiasm." Welles believed this last proceeded from less admirable qualities than those the reporter discerned. "He is intensely ambitious," the Secretary noted in his diary, "and, I fear, too selfish. He has the heroism which proceeds from pride, and would lead him to danger and death; but whether he has the innate, unselfish courage of the genuine sailor and soldier, remains to be seen." Despite these doubts on the part of his superior, based in part on personal observation and in part on the fact that he had never been in action, Dahlgren was given command of the South Atlantic Blockading Squadron, which he took over as Du Pont's successor in early July, together with special instructions covering the employment of his patched-up ironclads to effect the reduction of the South Carolina city, defiant behind the guns and obstructions around and in its harbor.

This time there was no plea from the Department that the army not be allowed to "spoil" the show by having a vital part in it. Rather, the admiral was to work in conjunction with Brigadier General Quincy Gillmore, who had arrived three weeks earlier to assume command of the 15,000 infantrymen, artillerists, and engineers assigned to take the lead in the opening phase of the combined attack. Fort Sumter was seen as the key to control of Charleston harbor, and Gillmore, a thirty-eight-year-old Ohio-born West Pointer — top man in the otherwise undistinguished class of 1849 — had been called in, as a fortifications expert and a master of siege operations, to give an opinion on whether the army could reduce it. He replied that this could best be done by mounting heavy guns on the north end of Morris Island, held at present by the Confederates, and using them to knock the famed pentagonal fort to pieces; after which, as Gillmore saw it, the ironclads would be able to steam in and administer the same treatment to the city itself, on the far side of the harbor, until such time as the white flag went up. His plan approved, he got to work as soon as he arrived in mid-June, and by the time Dahlgren took over from Du Pont he was ready to launch his opening attack from Folly Island, where he had secretly massed a 3000-man assault force, against the adjoining southern end of Morris Island, preparatory to a drive up its narrow four-mile length to Cummings Point, which was less than 1500 yards from Sumter. On July 10, encouraged by a promotion to major general, he sprang a dawn attack which caught the rebels so thoroughly off guard that by noon he had the lower three fourths of the island in his grip. All that remained was Battery Wagner, dead ahead, and Battery Gregg, 1300 yards farther along on Cummings Point. His loss so far had amounted to scarcely more than a hundred men, only fifteen of whom were dead. Wasting no time, he ordered another all-out assault next morning. This too was launched with verve and determination, but with considerably less satisfactory results. The first wave made it up to Wagner's parapet, only to be shattered by heavy volleys of grape and musketry, while the support formations were scattered by high-angle fire from Gregg. Within an hour the attackers lost 49 killed, 167 captured or missing, and 123 wounded, and so far as the repulsed survivors could see, these 339 casualties had been expended without any effect whatever on either the earthwork or its defenders, who kept up a deadly sniping at everything blue that showed above the level of the sandy ground out front.

Undaunted, Gillmore spent a week bringing up another 3500 soldiers and emplacing 41 guns for counterbattery work; then at noon of July 18 he opened fire, which was also the signal for Dahlgren's monitors to close the range and pound both rebel works from the seaward flank. This continued for more than seven hours, and presently Battery Wagner ceased to reply, its cannoneers driven from their guns. Then at 7.30 — the attack hour had been set for twilight so that the defenders would not be able to take careful aim — the Union guns fell silent too, ashore and afloat, and the 6000 Federals started forward on a necessarily narrow front of less than 200 yards. In the lead was a Massachusetts regiment, all-Negro except for its officers, who were mostly Boston bluebloods, including its young colonel, Robert Gould Shaw, whose mother had wept for joy at the sight of her boy leading black men forth to war; "What have I done, that God has been so good to me!" she cried at the grand farewell review staged in Boston in late May. In less than seven weeks, however, it developed that God had not been so good to her after all, unless what she wanted in place of her son was a fine bronze statue on the Common. The 1000-man rebel garrison came out of the bombproof to which it had retired at the height of the cannonade and met the attackers as it had done the week before, with even more spectacular results. Here in the East, on Morris Island just outside Charleston harbor, as formerly in the West, at Milliken's Bend and Port Hudson, Negro troops proved that they could stop bullets and shell fragments as well as white men; but that was about all. When flesh and blood could stand no more, the survivors fell back from the ditch and parapet, black and white alike, and returned to the trenches they had left an hour ago. Casualties had been heavy; 1515 of the attackers had fallen, as compared to 174 of the defenders, and next morning when the latter peered out of their sight slits they saw live and dead men strewn in piles and windrows, their bodies horribly mangled by close-up artillery fire, while detached arms and legs and heads were splattered all about. A brief truce sufficed for removal of the wounded and disposal of the slain, including the twenty-six-year-old Shaw, who had taken a bullet through the heart and was buried in a common grave with his Negro soldiers, nearly half of whom had been lost in the repulse.

Somewhat daunted, but still determined, Gillmore decided to settle down to regular siege operations and take Sumter under fire from where he was, the range being only about 3000 yards. From close up, he would batter Wagner and Gregg into submission, meanwhile bringing eighteen heavy guns to bear in a round-the-clock attempt to breach the fort less than a mile across the water from the inaccessible north end of the island. By mid-August three parallels had been drawn and advanced, preparatory to launching a sudden, swamping rush upon the stubborn earthwork dead ahead, and Sumter was being bombarded at a rate of nearly 5000 shells a week, its brick walls cracking and crumbling under the impact of 300-pound projectiles, the heaviest ever employed by rifled field artillery up to then. Another innovation was the use of calcium lights, which threw the ramparts of Battery Wagner into stark relief and helped to prevent the rebels from making nighttime sorties against the gunners and diggers in their immediate front. Still a third innovation was the establishment in the marshes between Morris and James islands, off to the left and about 8000 yards from downtown Charleston, of an 8-inch Parrott rifle — promptly dubbed the "Swamp Angel" by the engineers who sweated and floundered in the salty mud to place the big gun on its platform — for the purpose of heaving its 200-pound shells, specially filled for the occasion with liquid and solidified Greek Fire, into the city's streets and houses. On August 21 the monster weapon was reported ready, and Gillmore sent a note across the lines demanding the immediate evacuation of Morris Island and Fort Sumter; otherwise, he warned, he would open fire "from batteries already established within easy and effective range of the heart of the city." No answer having been received by midnight, he sent word for the gun to go into action. At 1.30 a.m. the first shell was on the way. The sound of alarm bells and whistles, which reached them faintly across the nearly five miles of marsh and water, told the crew that the percussion-fuzed shell had found its mark, and they followed this with fifteen others, equally accurate, before dawn. At that time Gillmore received a message signed G. T. Beauregard, protesting his barbarity and rejecting his ultimatum that Wagner and Gregg and Sumter be abandoned. "It would appear, sir, that despairing of reducing these works, you now resort to the novel measure of turning your guns against the old men, the women and children, and the hospitals of a sleeping city," the Creole hotly accused his adversary, and he predicted that this "mode of warfare, which I confidently declare to be atrocious and unworthy of any soldier ... will give you 'a bad eminence' in history, even in the history of this war." Gillmore replied that the city had had forty days' notice, this being the length of time he had been battering at its gates, and despite the added protests of the Spanish and British consuls he ordered the bombardment resumed on August 23. Twenty more incendiary shells were fired, six of which exploded prematurely in the tube with spectacular pyrotechnical effects, and though no member of the crew was hurt by these sudden gushes of flame from the vent and muzzle, the gun itself was probably weakened. At any rate, on the twentieth shot the breech of the piece blew out of its jacket, just behind the vent, and the Swamp Angel ended her brief career of thirty-six rounds, thirty of which had landed squarely on target in the birthplace of secession, whatever "bad eminence" she might have gained for Gillmore in the process.

He made no attempt to replace the ruined cannon, believing as he did that he soon would have possession of Cummings Point, where the ground was firmer and the range to Charleston shorter. By August 26 his sappers were within 200 yards of Battery Wagner, and within another week the distance was half that. All this time, the bombardment of Fort Sumter had continued, with gratifying results. Most of its southern wall was down, and both the western and eastern walls were badly cracked. Practically every casemate had been breached. On the first night in September, when six of the monitors gave the crumbling fort a five-hour pounding, not a shot was fired from the rubble in reply. Gillmore stepped up the action against Wagner. On September 5 he began a relentless 42-hour cannonade during which no less than 3000 shells were rained upon the earthwork, preparatory to the final assault. But when the guns stopped firing in the predawn darkness of September 7, so that the infantry could rush forward and end the 58-day siege — in the course of which the Federals had suffered a total of 2318 casualties and inflicted 641 — it was discovered that the Confederates had evacuated both Wagner and Gregg the night before, despite the constant deluge of metal, and withdrawn in rowboats to James Island. Once more, Beauregard's uncanny sense of timing had not failed him. Advancing to emplace his heaviest guns on Cummings Point, from which he could resume his shelling of the city, Gillmore passed the word to Dahlgren that the army's share of the operation had been accomplished. Morris Island had been occupied entirely and Fort Sumter had been neutralized; now the navy's turn had come to take the lead. Proud Charleston would be brought to its knees if the ironclads would only steam across the harbor and bring it under the muzzles of their guns.

But could they? Dahlgren was far from certain: so little so, in fact, that he was unwilling to make the attempt until Sumter had not only been "neutralized," as the army claimed, but taken. Moreover, he wanted the honor of doing the taking, and he believed he saw how this could be done without exposing his valuable monitors to sudden destruction by a torpedo or by point-blank fire from a gun kept hidden amid the rubble for that purpose. Constant shelling had tumbled the bricks of the south wall down to the water's edge, affording an incline which, though steep and rugged, could be scaled without the delay the use of ladders would involve. If a surprise landing could be accomplished, a storming party would be into the place before its defenders even had time to sound the alarm. So at least the naval commander believed, or reasoned, when he called on September 7 — the same day Morris Island fell to the army — for 500 naval volunteers to make a small-boat landing by the dark of the moon the following night. By way of preamble he sent in a demand for the fort's surrender and received, at second hand, Beauregard's reply: "Tell Admiral Dahlgren to come and take it." That was just what he was preparing to do, and when the officer he had placed in charge of the venture expressed some doubts that it would succeed, Dahlgren scoffed at his fears. "You have only to go and take possession," he assured him. "You will find nothing but a corporal's guard." Accordingly, the volunteers were loaded into some thirty assault boats and towed within half a mile of Sumter before moonrise the next night. No lights were shown and the oars were muffled, but the rebel lookouts spotted them anyhow and gave the alarm, including the firing of rockets, which was the signal for batteries on James and Sullivan's islands to open fire on the waters near the fort. Caught under the resultant two-way barrage, the marines and sailors hurried ashore and were received by the 300-man garrison lying in wait for them with rifles, fire-balls, hand grenades, and brickbats, which combined to make conditions even worse on the beach than on the water. Five of the boats were captured, along with more than a hundred men and thirteen officers. The rest got away as best they could through the ring of fire, bringing their wounded with them. "Nobody hurt on our side," Beauregard reported.

Dahlgren took the check as proof that he had been wise not to risk his iron flotilla in any such challenge to the alert and tricky rebels, but he could not escape the depression that proceeded from the knowledge that he had done no better, so far, than the man he had replaced. The enervating heat, plus long confinement in the poorly ventilated monitors, had impaired his health; moreover, he was often seasick, which caused him to lose caste with his sailors and perhaps with himself as well. Worst of all, though, was the gnawing sense of failure. Victory was the cure, he knew, but he would not risk the alternative, defeat, which in this case would be utterly disastrous, not only to his ships and men, but also to his career. Nothing helped, or even seemed to. "I am better today," he confided in his journal, "but the worst of this place is that one only stops getting weaker. One does not get stronger." Torn between desire and fear, ambition and indecision, he reacted physically to the mental strain. "My debility increases, so that today it is an exertion to sit in a chair. I do not see well. How strange — no pain, but so feeble. It seems like gliding away to death. How easy it seems! Why not, to one whose race is run?" It was scarcely to be expected, with the admiral in this frame of mind, that the navy would press matters beyond the point that had been reached when Morris Island fell. Nor did it. Dahlgren perceived that Sumter had become little more than an infantry outpost, its heaviest guns having been removed in secret to Sullivan's Island during the two-month siege of Battery Wagner; Fort Moultrie was now the real obstacle to a penetration of the harbor, and the only way to close with it was by steaming through the torpedo-infested channel, which was something he was by no means willing to attempt. Meanwhile — illogically, but for lack of anything better in the way of employment for his vessels and their crews — he maintained an intermittent bombardment of Sumter. Formerly a brick masonry fort, it was now a powerful earthwork; the shells it absorbed only served to make it more impervious by stirring up and adding to the rubble any attackers would have to climb and cross, dodging fire-balls and grenades, in order to come to grips with the defenders. He had tried that once, however, and he had no intention of trying it again.

Gillmore at least had the satisfaction of knowing that he had carried out his primary assignment by securing possession of Morris Island, but even if he had had another intermediary objective in mind — which he did not — he would have had no way to get there, shipless as he was, with bottomless marshes on one flank, open sea on the other, and the mine-strewn harbor dead ahead. Like Dahlgren, he contented himself with lobbing projectiles into Sumter, barely 1400 yards away, or into Moultrie, twice that distance across the harbor mouth. By way of diversion he sometimes threw a long-range salvo or two at Charleston, which was about half a mile closer to Cummings Point than it was to the platform that had kept the ill-fated Swamp Angel out of the mud. None of these seemed to accomplish much, however. Sumter merely continued to squat there, defiant and misshapen — "a noble mass of ruins," Beauregard called it, "over which still float our colors" — responding to hits by sending up puffs of brickdust, but otherwise appearing as indifferent as an elephant to flea bites. Moultrie did not even do that much, so far as the Federal spotters could see from a range of 2800 yards, and presently they left off shooting at it. As for Charleston itself, while banks moved their resources from the lower to the upper part of town and hospitals were evacuated in the impact zone, the chief complaint of those citizens who had recovered from their early panic and returned to their homes, keeping tubs of water handy in all the rooms for fighting fires, was that the scream of the Yankee shells disturbed their sleep. They were proud of themselves, proud of their defenders out on the firing line, and proudest of all of Beauregard, their original hero, to whom Congress afterwards tendered a joint resolution of thanks for "a defense which, for the skill, heroism, and tenacity displayed during an attack scarcely paralleled in warfare ... is justly entitled to be pronounced glorious by impartial history and an admiring country."

* * *

But that was later. The Richmond conference ended on September 7, a day that seemed more the occasion for alarm than for high-flown congratulations, least of all to Beauregard, since it was then that Morris Island fell and the Charleston commander stepped up his plea for reinforcements, predicting graver disasters unless the odds he faced were shortened. All the statesmen and generals knew, as they studied the situation from their council room in the White House, was that events appeared to be mounting rapidly toward an unwelcome climax — not only down the Atlantic seaboard, but also along the opposite end of the thousand-mile frontier. In that far-western quarter the odds were even longer and the enemy had mounted a two-pronged offensive designed to restore the northern two thirds of Arkansas, including its capital, to the domain of the Union. The Confederacy having been sundered by the loss of Vicksburg and Port Hudson, the Federals seemed to be losing no time in getting to work on the disconnected halves, particularly the one that lay beyond what Lincoln called the "unvexed" Mississippi.

One prong was being driven eastward from Indian Territory, with Fort Smith as its immediate goal, and the other was being driven westward from Helena, whose garrison, flushed by its success in breaking up the Independence Day assault, had been strengthened by the return of Frederick Steele's division, which had gone downriver eight months ago with Sherman and now came back with the names of the many engagements of the Vicksburg campaign proudly stitched to its battle flags. Much to the disgruntlement of Prentiss, who submitted his resignation as a result, command of the inland expedition went to Steele, together with instructions to "break up Price and occupy Little Rock," a hundred crow-flight miles away in the heart of the state. To do this he had two divisions of infantry, totaling only about 6000 effectives — "The sick list is frightful," he reported — plus one division of cavalry, as large as the two of infantry put together, detached from Schofield. This mounted force, led by Brigadier General John W. Davidson, a forty-year-old Virginia-born West Pointer, left Bloomfield, Missouri, and proceeded south down Crowley's Ridge to Clarendon, Arkansas, which it reached on August 8, to be joined nine days later by Steele, who marched his foot soldiers from Helena and took command of the combined 12,000. Shifting his base to De Valls Bluff, a dozen miles northwest, he spent another two weeks making final preparations and then on September 1, in accordance with his instructions, set out for the capital, just under fifty miles due west. By that date the opposite prong — a scratch collection of seven regiments, three composed of Union-loyal Indian volunteers and one of Negroes, all under James Blunt, the former Ohio doctor who had been promoted to major general as a reward for Prairie Grove — had attained its initial objective with a bloodless occupation of Fort Smith, 125 miles from Little Rock and just short of

Riot and Resurgence   [703]

the western border. Back in mid-July, Blunt had prepared the way for this maneuver with an attack on the Confederates to his front at Honey Springs, fifty miles west of his goal, driving them south in disorder and destroying the stores they had collected for subsistence in that barren region of Indian Territory. Commanded by Brigadier General William Steele, a forty-year-old New Yorker and West Pointer who had married South, the rebel force of nine regiments, six of them Indian, was actually larger than Blunt's; but when the action was joined the graybacks found to their dismay that their powder, imported from Europe by way of Texas, had turned to paste in their cartridge boxes. They ran and kept on running. Satisfied merely to have them out of the way for the time being, Blunt did not pursue. He returned instead to the Arkansas River to rest and refit his victorious 3000 multicolored troops, then turned east in late August to occupy Fort Smith on September 1, the day the other Steele started west from De Valls Bluff.

About this time, while events were heading up for the recovery of most of Arkansas, word came of a "raid" some 300 miles to the north, across the Missouri-Kansas line, that provoked more excitement and indignation throughout the country than any that had been staged in the course of the nearly four years since John Brown struck at Harpers Ferry. The difference was that this one, launched against the region where Brown had got his start, was not only a good deal bloodier, and therefore more atrocious, but was also as complete a success as the other had been a failure. Heavy detachments of troops from Schofield to Grant and Steele, well downriver, had emboldened

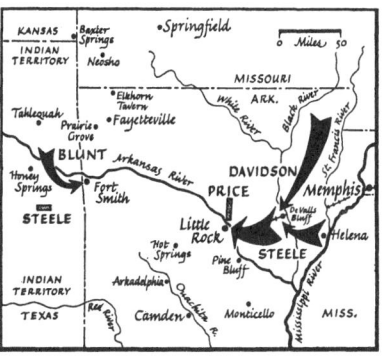

the guerillas lurking in the Missouri brush: particularly Charles Quantrill, who had secured a captain's commission from Richmond and was eager to justify his bars, as well as to pay off old scores from the prewar border troubles, by leading his irregulars on a more daring expedition than any they had attempted up to now. He favored a strike at Lawrence, an old-time abolitionist settlement forty miles beyond the Kansas line. At first his men would not agree, believing that the prize, though fat, would not be worth the risk; but two developments which occurred in rapid succession in mid-August changed their minds, adding a thirst for revenge to their already strong desire for loot. For the past three months the Federal commander of the District of the Border, Brigadier General Thomas Ewing, had been arresting women charged with giving encouragement and assistance to guerillas, many of whom were their sons and brothers and husbands. This had enraged the men in the brush, who, whatever their excesses in other directions, had invariably maintained a hands-off attitude toward the mothers and sisters and wives of their Jayhawk adversaries. The prisoners were confined in certain buildings in Kansas City, and on August 14 one of these, a dilapidated three-story brick affair with a liquor shop on the ground floor, collapsed — as Ewing had been warned it might do — killing four of the women outright and seriously injuring several others. When news of this reached Quantrill's men they promptly reconsidered their chief's proposal for a raid on Lawrence. "We can get more revenge and more money there than anywhere else in the state of Kansas," he told them. Then four days later Ewing announced in a general order that not only would more such arrests be made, but that "the wives and children of known guerillas, and also women who are heads of families and are willfully engaged in aiding guerillas, will be notified ... to remove out of this district and out of the State of Missouri forthwith." The order was dated August 18; "We could stand no more," a guerilla who had lost a sister in the Kansas City tragedy wrote later. Next day Quantrill set out from Blackwater Creek in Johnson County, headed west for Lawrence with a column of just under 300 bloody-minded men.

The distance was over seventy miles and they made it in two days, riding strapped to their saddles the second night so that they could sleep without falling off their horses. While still in Missouri they encountered a party of 104 mounted Confederate recruits proceeding south under Colonel John D. Holt, who decided to take them along on the raid as a training exercise. These, plus a number of other volunteers picked up in the course of the ride to the border, brought the column to a strength of about 450 men by the time it drew rein at daybreak of August 21 on the outskirts of Lawrence. Three weeks past his twenty-sixth birthday, wearing a gaudy, low-cut guerilla shirt, gray trousers stuffed into cavalry boots, a gold-corded black slouch hat, and four revolvers in his belt, Quantrill assigned each unit its special mission, then led the howling charge that swept from the southeast into the streets of the sleeping town. Long since warned to expect no quarter, the raiders intended to give none. With the exception of a single adult male civilian — the hated Jayhawk chieftain Senator James H. Lane, who was to be taken back to Missouri alive, if possible, for a semi-public hanging — Quantrill's orders called for the killing of "every man big enough to carry a gun." First to fall, in accordance with these instructions, was the Reverend S. S. Snyder, sometimes lieutenant of the 2d Kansas Colored Infantry, shot dead under the cow he was milking in his yard. Next were seventeen recruits encountered in the otherwise deserted camp of the 14th Cavalry, several of them pistoled before they emerged from their blankets. Thus began a three-hour orgy of killing, interspersed with drinks in commandeered saloons and exhibitions of fancy riding. Men were chased and shot down as they ran; others were dragged from their homes and murdered in front of their wives and children; still others were smothered or roasted alive when the houses in which they hid were set afire. Holt and other less bloodthirsty members of the band managed to protect a few of the fugitives, but not many; Quantrill, who had lived for a time in Lawrence before the war, had prepared a vengeance list beforehand, and all who were on it and in town this morning were disposed of, except for the man whose name was at its head. Wily Jim Lane took flight in his nightshirt, warned by the first thunder of hooves as the guerillas swept in across the prairie, and hid out undetected in a cornfield until they rode away, leaving 80 new widows and 250 fatherless children weeping in the ruins of the town. Nearly 200 buildings had been wrecked or burned, including all three newspaper offices and most of the business district, for a property loss amounting to about two million dollars. In all, though not one woman was physically harmed, no less than 150 Kansans were killed, fewer than twenty of whom were soldiers and several of whom were scarcely more than boys. Not one of them sold his life dearly, however, for the only casualty the raiders suffered was a former Baptist preacher who got drunk, passed out, and was killed and scalped by an Indian when he was discovered, shortly after his friends had ridden away. His body was dragged through the streets behind a horse by a free Negro until it was stripped naked, and the grieving citizens pelted it with stones by way of revenge.

Loaded with booty, the rest of the guerillas had pulled out southward about 9 o'clock that morning, shortly after lookouts on Mount Oread reported a heavy column of troopers approaching from the north and west, beyond the Kansas River. Setting ambushes to delay his pursuers, who converged from all points of the compass as the news from Lawrence spread across the plains, and swerving aside in the twilight to avoid a blue garrison lying in wait for him at Paola, Quantrill made it back across the Missouri line next morning with nearly all of his command. At this point the order was "Every man for himself," and the raiders faded into the brush by a hundred different trails to resume their various disguises as farmers, parolees, and Union-loyal residents of the scattered towns and hamlets. All who were detected subsequently were executed on the spot, as those had been who were caught up with when their horses went lame or collapsed from exhaustion during the chase across the prairie. "No prisoners have been taken, and none will be," Ewing informed Schofield, and four days after what became known as the Lawrence Massacre he issued, at Jim Lane's insistence, his famous General Order Number 11, directing the forcible removal of all persons, male or female, child or adult, loyal or disloyal, who lived more than a mile from a Federal post in the four Missouri counties south of the Missouri River and adjacent to the border. The time limit was fifteen days from the date of issue, August 25. By mid-September the order had been so effectively enforced that Cass County, which had had a population of 10,000 before the war, was occupied by fewer than 600 civilians; Bates County, directly south, had even less. Moreover, the vengeance-minded 15th Kansas Cavalry, delighted at having been given the assignment of seeing that Ewing's order was obeyed, went through the region so enthusiastically with torch and sword, leaving nothing but chimneys to show where houses and cabins once had stood, that it was known for years thereafter as the Burnt District. Not that Quantrill was deterred. He collected his scattered guerillas, continued his depredations, including attacks on wagon trains and steamboats on the Missouri, and finally withdrew south in early October to winter in Texas with a force of 400 hard-bitten men, most of whom had been with him on the raid that nearly wiped Lawrence from the map.

By then the issue had been settled in central Arkansas, and though Steele had failed to "break up Price," he had succeeded admirably in carrying out the rest of his assignment. In temporary command of the district after Holmes fell sick in late July, Price concentrated his 8000 effectives at Little Rock, squarely between the menacing blue prongs of Blunt and Steele, the former in occupation of Fort Smith, just under 150 miles to the west, and the latter advancing from De Valls Bluff, one third that distance to the east. Bracing to meet the nearer and heavier threat — Blunt had only about 4000 men, while Steele had three times as many — the bulky but agile Missourian intrenched a line three miles in length on the north bank of the Arkansas, protected by swamps in front and anchored to the river below the capital in his rear, access to which was provided by three pontoon bridges. Though he took the precaution of sending his accumulated stores to Arkadelphia, sixty miles southwest, he reported that his troops were "in excellent condition, full of enthusiasm, and eager to meet the enemy." So was he, despite the known disparity in numbers, if the bluecoats would only attack him where he was. But Steele, as it turned out, had a different notion. Maneuvering as if for a frontal assault, he sent Davidson's 6000 troopers on a fast ride south to strike the river well downstream from the Confederate position.

This was begun on September 6, and Price on that same day lost one of his two cavalry brigadiers, not by enemy action, but rather as the result of a quarrel between them. For the past two months Marmaduke had been openly critical of Lucius Walker's failure to support him in the attack at Helena; now as they skirmished with the advancing Federals and the Tennessean gave ground under pressure, the hot-tempered Missourian accused him of outright cowardice. Walker replied, as expected, with a challenge which was promptly accepted, the terms being "pistols at ten paces to fire and advance," and the former Memphis businessman fell mortally wounded at the second fire. The conditions of honor having been satisfied in accordance with the code — which, presumably, was one of those things the South was fighting to preserve as part of its "way of life" — presently, after a period of intense suffering by the loser, the Confederacy had one general less than it had had when the two men took position, ten paces apart, and began to walk toward one another, firing as they advanced.

Within four days of this exchange the South also had one state capital the less. Assisted no doubt by the resultant confusion across the way, Davidson got his horsemen over the river at dawn of September 10, moved them rapidly up the scantly defended right bank toward Little Rock, and after forcing a crossing of Bayou Fourche, five miles below the town, received its formal surrender by the civil authorities shortly after sundown. Price had reacted fast: as indeed he had had need to do, if he was to save his army. Outflanked by the cavalry while Steele kept up the pressure against his front, he withdrew from his north-bank intrenchments, set his pontoons afire to prevent the blue infantry from following in his wake, and put his troops on the march for Arkadelphia, to which point he had prudently removed his stores the week before. There on the south bank of the Ouachita he took up a new position extending fifty miles downstream to Camden, with detachments posted as far east as Monticello, about midway between the latter place and the Federal gunboats prowling unchallenged up and down the Mississippi. Steele did not pursue.

Casualties had been light on both sides in both operations — 137 for Steele, 64 for Price; 75 for Blunt, 181 for Steele — but they were no adequate indication of what had been won and lost in the double-pronged campaign. "If they take Fort Smith, the Indian country is gone," Holmes had remarked in February, and now in September his prediction had been unhappily fulfilled. Similarly, the loss of Little Rock — fourth on the list of fallen capitals, immediately following Jackson, which had been preceded the year before by Baton Rouge and Nashville — extended the Union occupation to include three fourths of Arkansas, a gain for which the victors presumably would have been willing to pay ten or even one hundred times the actual cost.

This too was included in the Richmond assessment of the over-all situation. Although, like Chattanooga and Cumberland Gap, Little Rock had not fallen by the time the White House conference ended on September 7 — it fell three and the others two days later — its loss, like theirs, could be anticipated as a factor to be placed in the enemy balance pan alongside Fort Smith, Knoxville, and Morris Island, all of which passed into Federal possession while the council was considering what could best be attempted to offset the reverses lately suffered at Tullahoma, Gettysburg, Vicksburg, Helena, and Port Hudson. Within that same horrendous span, late June through early September, only two events occurred which might have been considered as adding weight to the South's high-riding opposite pan, one the New York draft riot and the other the Quantrill raid on Lawrence. However, both of these were not only comparatively slight, they were also of doubtful character as assets: especially the latter, which, if claimed, would expose the Confederacy to charges of land piracy, or worse, before the bar of world opinion. In strategic terms, moreover, the outlook was no less clear for being bleak. Rosecrans was over the Tennessee River, and unless Bragg could stop him — as, apparently, he could not — the Army of the Cumberland would be free to march southeast through Georgia to the coast, which would mean that the eastern half of the nation, already severed from the western half by the loss of the Mississippi, would itself be cut in two. In that event, nothing would remain to be governed from Richmond but the Carolinas and so much of Virginia as lay south of the Rappahannock, a political and geographical fragment whose survival was already threatened from the north by the Army of the Potomac, from the west by the troops now in occupation of Knoxville and East Tennessee, and from the east by the amphibious force holding Charleston under siege, all three of which had lately been victorious, to various degrees, under Meade, Burnside, and Gillmore.

Despite the fact that it now had some 20,000 fewer effectives than it had had three months ago when its commander urged a similar course of action under similar circumstances, Davis had warmed at first to Lee's proposal, submitted at the outset of the strategy conference, that the Army of Northern Virginia once more take the offensive against Meade. On the last day of August Lee sent word to Longstreet, who had been left in charge on the Rapidan, to "prepare the army for offensive operations." Old Peter replied that he would of course obey his chief's instructions and had already passed them on to Ewell and A. P. Hill, but "I do not see that we can reasonably hope to accomplish much" by continuing to fight a war of stalemate and attrition. "I am inclined to the opinion that the best opportunity for great results is in Tennessee," he asserted. "If we could hold the defensive here with two corps and send the other to operate in Tennessee with [Bragg's] army, I think that we could accomplish more than by an advance from here." This was written on September 2, the day Burnside's cavalry rode into Knoxville, and two days later Rosecrans completed his crossing of the Tennessee River, posing the intolerable threat of a march through Georgia to the sea. Davis and Seddon — to whom Longstreet had written earlier, by invitation, renewing his pre-Gettysburg claim "that the only hope of reviving the waning cause was through the advantage of interior lines" — reacted with a sudden shift from approval of Lee's proposal to approval of his lieutenant's, except that they preferred that the Virginian himself go west to deliver in person the blow designed to bring Old Rosy to his knees. Lee demurred, asserting that the general already on the scene and familiar with the terrain could do a better job. Davis reluctantly acquiesced, and the final plan to reinforce Bragg from

Virginia, though not to supersede him, was approved. On September 6 Lee sent word for his quartermaster to arrange for transportation by rail to Northwest Georgia for two of Longstreet's divisions. Next morning the Richmond council adjourned, and he returned to Orange. By the following day, September 8, the designated troops were on the move.

Longstreet rode over to headquarters to bid his gray-bearded commander farewell. They talked for a while in the latter's tent and then emerged. Lee said nothing more until the burly Georgian had one foot in the stirrup, prepared to mount. "Now, General, you must beat those people out in the West," he told him. Old Peter took his foot from the stirrup and turned to face his chief. "If I live," he said. "But I would not give a single man of my command for a fruitless victory." This was a rather impolitic thing to say to a commander whose greatest victories had been "fruitless" in the sense that Longstreet meant, but Lee either missed or ignored the implication. He merely repeated that arrangements had been made and orders issued to assure that any success would be exploited. Then he watched the man he called "my old warhorse" mount and ride away, leaving him barely more than 45,000 troops with which to block or parry an advance by an army that lately had whipped him with nearly equal numbers and now had almost twice the strength of his own.

"Never before were so many troops moved over such worn-out railways," a First Corps staff officer later wrote, though not quite accurately, since he left out of account (as most veterans of the eastern theater, together with most eastern-born or -trained historians, were prone to do in matters pertaining to the western theater) Bragg's transfer of his whole army from Tupelo to Chattanooga by way of Mobile the previous year. "Never before were such crazy cars — passenger, baggage, mail, coal, box, platform, all and every sort wobbling on the jumping strap-iron — used for hauling good soldiers," the staffer went on. "But we got there nevertheless." Here too a degree of inaccuracy crept in; for out of a total of 12,000 men in the two divisions, only about 7500 reached the field in time for a share in the fighting that had begun before the first of them arrived. Primarily this was because the fall of Knoxville, just the week before, denied them use of the East Tennessee & Virginia Railroad, which up till then had afforded a direct 550-mile route from Gordonsville to Dalton. As a result, a roundabout route had to be taken — first by way of southern Virginia, then down through both of the Carolinas, and finally across the width of Georgia, with no possibility of using through trains because of the varying gauges of track on the dozen different lines — for a total distance of nearly 1000 miles from Orange Courthouse to Catoosa Station, which was within earshot of the battle they heard raging as they approached the end of their long journey through the heartland.

For the troops themselves — Deep Southerners to a man, except the Texans and Arkansans, now that Pickett's Virginians had been detached — the trip had all the elements of a lark, despite the cramped accommodations, the thrown-together meals, and the knowledge that possible death and suffering awaited them at its end. Many of the Carolinians and Georgians — South Carolinians, that is; for there were no North Carolinians in Longstreet's corps — passed through home towns they had not visited in two years, and though guards were posted at all the stops to assure that no unauthorized furloughs were taken, it was good to see that the old places were still there, complete with pretty girls who passed out delicacies and blushed at the whoops of admirers. For Hood's men there was an added bonus in the form of their commander, who rejoined them when they passed through Richmond, where he was recuperating from his Gettysburg wound. Though his arm was still useless in a sling, he was unable to resist the impulse to come along when he saw, as he said later, that "my old troops, with whom I had served so long, were thus to be sent forth to another army — quasi, I may say, among strangers." They cheered at the news that he was aboard and was going to Georgia with them. At Weldon, North Carolina, alternate routes — one via Raleigh, Charlotte, and Columbia, the other via Goldsboro, Wilmington, and Florence — relieved the strain on the overworked roads until they combined again at Kingsville, South Carolina, where a matron diarist watched the overloaded trains chuff past in what seemed a never-ending procession. "God bless the gallant fellows," she wrote; "not one man intoxicated, not one rude word did I hear. It was a strange sight. What seemed miles of platform cars, and soldiers rolled in their blankets lying in rows with their heads all covered, fast asleep. In their gray blankets packed in regular order, they looked like swathed mummies.... A feeling of awful depression laid hold of me. All those fine fellows going to kill or be killed, but why? A word took to beating about my head like an old song, 'The Unreturning Brave.' When a knot of boyish, laughing young creatures passed, a queer thrill of sympathy shook me. Ah, I know how your homefolks feel. Poor children!"

From Branchville, immediately south of there, the route extended due west, via Augusta, to Atlanta, where it turned northwest and ran the final 125 miles northwest to the unloading point, four miles short of Ringgold and 965 circuitous miles from Orange. McLaws and Hood had four brigades each. Two of the former's and one of the latter's would not reach the field until the action had ended — neither would McLaws himself, who was charged with hurrying the last infantry elements northward from Atlanta; nor would a single piece of the corps artillery with which Alexander, still back in the Carolinas, was bringing up the rear — but the five brigades that did arrive in time were to play a significant part in the battle that was in progress when they got there. Hood arrived on September 18, had his horse unloaded from a boxcar, then mounted, still with his arm in its sling, and rode toward the sound of firing, some half a dozen miles away along the banks of a sluggish, meandering, tree-lined creek whose name he now heard for the first time: Chickamauga, an Indian word that meant "stagnant water" or, more popularly, "River of Death." Before nightfall he and his three brigades had a share, by Bragg's direction, in forcing a crossing of the stream at a place called Reed's Bridge, near which they were joined next day by the two brigades from McLaws' division.

Longstreet reached Catoosa Station the following afternoon, September 19, but found no guide waiting to take him to Bragg or give him news of the battle he could hear raging beyond the western screen of woods. When the horses came up on a later train, he had three of them saddled and set out with two members of his staff to find the headquarters of the Army of Tennessee. He was helped in this, so far as the general direction was concerned, by the rearward drift of the wounded, although none of these unfortunates seemed to know exactly where he could find their commander. Night fell and the three officers continued their ride by moonlight until they were halted by a challenge out of the darkness just ahead: "Who comes there?" "Friends," they replied, promptly but with circumspection, and in the course of the parley that followed they asked the sentry to identify his unit. When he did so by giving the numbers of his brigade and division — Confederate outfits were invariably known by the names of their commanders — they knew they had blundered into the Union lines. "Let us ride down a little way to find a better crossing," Old Peter said, disguising his southern accent, and the still-mounted trio withdrew, unfired on, to continue their search for Bragg. It was barely an hour before midnight when they found him — or, rather, found his camp; for he was asleep in his ambulance by then.

He turned out for a brief conference, in the course of which he outlined, rather sketchily, what had happened up to now in his contest with Rosecrans, now approaching a climax here at Chickamauga, and passed on the orders already issued to the five corps commanders for a dawn attack next morning. Longstreet, though he had never seen the field by daylight, was informed that he would have charge of the left wing, which contained six of the army's eleven divisions, including his own two fragmentary ones that had arrived today and yesterday from Virginia. For whatever it might be worth, Bragg also gave him what he later described as "a map showing prominent topographical features of the ground from the Chickamauga River to Mission Ridge, and beyond to the Lookout Mountain range." Otherwise he was on his own, so far as information was concerned.

✕ 4 ✕

Before the close of the Sunday that presently was dawning — September 20; the sun both rose and set at approximately straight-up 6 o'clock, for this was the week of the autumnal equinox — Old Peter was to discover that he was on his own in other ways as well. He was up and about at first light, correcting the faulty alignment of his wing and alerting his troops for their share in the attack Bragg had ordered to be opened "at day-dawn" on the far right, where Polk was in command, and then to be taken up in sequence by the divisions posted southward along the four-mile line of battle. Sunlight dappled the topmost leaves of the trees, then moved down the branches, but there was no sound of the firing Longstreet had been told to expect from the right as the signal for his own commitment on the left. An hour he waited, then another and another, and still there was no crash of guns from the north or word from headquarters of a postponement or cancellation of the attack. Like Lee at Gettysburg, where the shoe had been on the other foot, the burly Georgian scarcely knew what to make of this, except as an indication that such things were not ordered well in the western army. However, he was not of an excitable or even impatient nature, being rather inclined, as a matter of course, to take things as they came. Besides, whatever its cause, the present delay gave him time to examine and improve his dispositions, to familiarize himself at least to some extent with the heavily wooded terrain, and to learn a good deal more than Bragg had taken the trouble to tell him of what had happened, so far, on this confusing field where the two armies had come together for the fourth of their bloody confrontations, a year and a half after Shiloh, a year after Perryville, and nine months after Murfreesboro, all three of which it gave promise of exceeding, both in fury and in bloodshed, despite the apparent — and indeed, in the light of this indication of suffering to come, quite natural — reluctance of the two forces to resume what had got started here the day before.

Bragg now had on hand all the troops he was going to have for the battle. Each of his five corps had two divisions, except Longstreet's, now under Hood, which had three or anyhow parts of three: Hood's own under Law, McLaws' under Kershaw, and one created the previous week, when two more brigades arrived from Mississippi and were combined with Brigadier General Bushrod Johnson's brigade, detached from Stewart's division of Buckner's corps, to form a new provisional division under his command. Longstreet massed this three-division corps, the bulk of which had come with him from Virginia and comprised his Sunday punch, at the right center of his portion of the line, alongside Hindman's division, which had been detached from Polk the day before. On the left and right, respectively on the outer and interior flanks, were Buckner's two divisions under Preston and Stewart. Exclusive of Wheeler's cavalry, patrolling southward beyond an eastward bend of the creek on which his left was anchored, Old Peter had some 25,000 effectives. Polk had roughly the same number in his wing, exclusive of Forrest's cavalry on his right. Hill's two divisions, under Breckinridge and Cleburne, were on the outer flank, and next to them, massed in depth along the center, were the two divisions of Walker's corps, commanded by Brigadier Generals St John Liddell and States Rights Gist. Cheatham's division was posted on the interior flank, adjoining Longstreet. All eleven of these divisions, six in the left and five in the right wing, had three brigades each, with the exception of Cheatham's, which had five, and Liddell's and Kershaw's, which had two apiece; Polk had 16, Longstreet 17 brigades. Bragg's total of 33 infantry brigades was thus the same as the number Rosecrans had in his eleven divisions, but the average blue division was somewhat larger than the average gray division, with the result that the Federals had some 56,000 infantry and artillery, as compared to the Confederate 50,000. However, this disparity was offset by the fact that Rosecrans had only just over 9000 troopers, while Bragg had nearly 15,000, so that the total for each of the opposing forces was approximately 65,000 of all arms. A further disparity in guns, 170 Federal and 200 Confederate, made little tactical difference on terrain so densely wooded that visibility seldom extended for more than fifty yards in any direction; Chickamauga was by no means an artillery contest. On the other hand, Rosecrans had the decided advantage of commanding an army he had trained and fought as a unit for nearly a year now, whereas a good third of Bragg's had joined him during the past few weeks, including five brigades that had arrived in the past two days and a wing commander who had never seen the field by daylight until dawn of the second day of battle.

Already the effect of this had seemed likely to prove fatal. To judge from the poor showing the Confederates had made in failing to spring the trap on Thomas, nine days ago in McLemore's Cove, and then again on Crittenden, two days later at Lee & Gordon's Mill — both as a result of breakdowns along the unfamiliar chain of command — the evident inability of Bragg's subordinates to work in harmony, either with him or with each other in the execution of carefully laid plans, certainly did not promise well for the outcome of future confrontations, which were unlikely to afford them any such lopsided numerical and tactical advantages as they had twice neglected. Bragg was so put out by this turn of events that he fell back on LaFayette and sulked for three whole days: during which time Rosecrans, thoroughly alarmed though unmolested, got his three divergent columns approximately back together and brought his reserve corps forward from Stevenson to Rossville. Crittenden remained at the foot of Missionary Ridge, near Lee & Gordon's Mill, and Thomas shifted to Pond Spring, midway between Crittenden and his own former post at Stevens Gap, while McCook

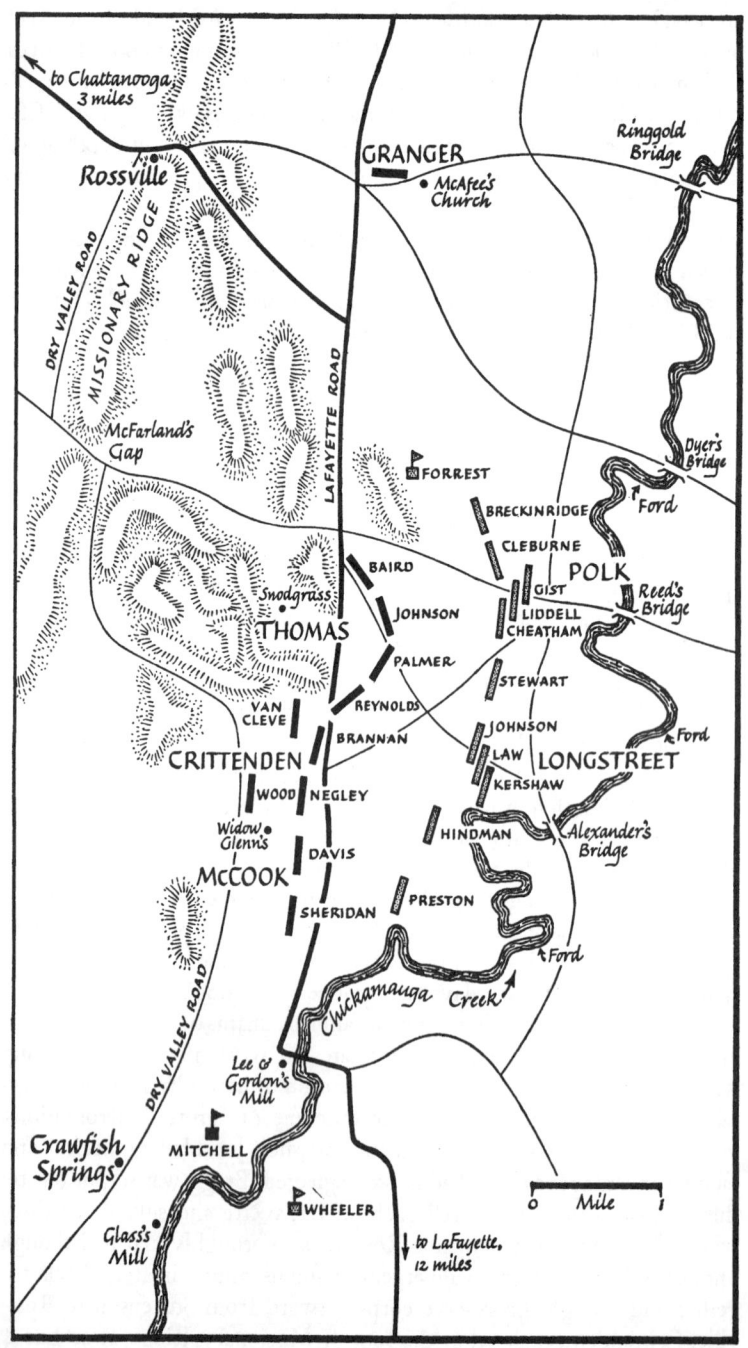

made a long march northward, in rear of Lookout Mountain, to take up the position Thomas had just vacated. By sundown, September 17, all this had been accomplished; Granger, Crittenden, Thomas, and McCook had their corps respectively in bivouac near Rossville Gap, Lee & Gordon's Mill, Pond Spring, and Stevens Gap, each within about six miles of the next one up or down the line that more or less followed the course of Chickamauga Creek, just east of Missionary Ridge. Rosecrans could draw his first easy breath since his discovery, four days back, that the rebels, far from fleeing in fear and disorder, as they had encouraged him to believe, had been intent on destroying his divided army.

He would have breathed less easily, however, if he had known what his opponent was planning, and had in fact begun to do that day, by way of accomplishing his further discomfiture. Encouraged by word that Longstreet was close at hand with reinforcements from Virginia, Bragg had emerged Achilles-like from his sulk and put his troops in motion, once more with Old Rosy's destruction as his goal. Marching north from LaFayette that morning, he massed his army before nightfall on the east side of Chickamauga Creek, his left at Glass's Mill, a mile above (that is, south of) Lee & Gordon's, and his right near Reed's Bridge, five miles downstream. Polk advised a rapid march on Rossville Gap, the seizure of which would cut the Federals off from their new base at Chattanooga and thus oblige them to attack the Confederates in a position selected in advance; but Bragg had something more ambitious in mind, involving the cul-de-sac in which Thomas had nearly come to grief a week ago tomorrow. According to orders written late that night and issued before daylight, Polk would demonstrate on the left, fixing Crittenden in position, while Buckner and Walker — supported by Hood, who was scheduled to arrive in the course of the day — crossed by fords and bridges, well below, with instructions to "sweep up the Chickamauga, toward Lee & Gordon's Mill." As they approached that point, Polk was to force a crossing and assist in driving the outflanked bluecoats southward into McLemore's Cove for another try at the meat-grinder operation. Wheeler's horsemen would plug the gaps in Pigeon Mountain, preventing a breakout, and Forrest's would guard the outer flank of the two corps — three, if Hood arrived in time — charged with executing the gatelike swing that was designed to throw Crittenden into retreat by bringing them down hard on his flank and rear. Meanwhile, opposite Glass's Mill, Hill would hold the pivot and stand ready to strike at any reinforcements from Thomas, moving north from Pond Spring toward the mouth of the cove, and pack them back into the grinder. The attack was to open in the far right at Reed's Bridge, and the jump-off hour was set for sunrise. Remembering what had happened near here a week ago, when a similar maneuver was attempted on a smaller scale, Bragg closed his field order with an admonition: "The above movements will be executed with the utmost promptness, vigor, and persistence."

Perhaps, after all that had gone wrong before, this was more an expression of hope than an expectation. At any rate he was sorely disappointed. Already nervous about his left — "It is of utmost importance that you close down this way to cover our left flank," he had wired Burnside yesterday, adding (though in vain, as it turned out) "I want all the help we can get promptly" — Rosecrans had taken alarm at sundown reports from scouts that there were rebels on the march in large numbers in the woods across the creek, and he had begun, accordingly, to sidle his army northward in the darkness. Moving Crittenden beyond Lee & Gordon's to cover the Chattanooga-LaFayette road, he advanced Thomas to Crawfish Springs, a hamlet just in rear of Glass's Mill, and McCook to the position Thomas had vacated at Pond Spring. By sunrise, as a result of these three shifts, his four corps — Granger had stayed put at Rossville Gap — were not only more tightly concentrated, the intervals between them having been reduced by half or better, but his left was also about two miles north of where it had been at sunset, when the southern commander made his calculations for an attack which thus was based on faulty or outdated information as to the blue dispositions. Then too, despite the closing admonition, there was the habitual lack of promptness in the movement of the various gray columns, plus what Bragg later referred to, rather charitably, as "the difficulties arising from the bad and narrow country roads," not to mention the stinging opposition of Federal mounted units with their rapid-fire weapons. In any event, though crossings were effected late in the day — by Hood, who arrived with his three brigades about 4 o'clock, and Walker — Buckner, Polk, and Hill were still on the east side of the creek at nightfall, with six of the ten divisions now on the field. Buckner crossed in the darkness, as did one of Polk's divisions; so that by daylight, September 19, Bragg had all of his infantry on the west bank except Hindman's division and the two with Hill. He had scarcely accomplished a fraction of all he intended today, but at any rate he was at last in a position to launch the turning movement he had designed two nights ago.

Or so he thought, still basing his calculations on a belief that the Union left was at Lee & Gordon's Mill. Actually, however, he was even wronger now than he had been the day before. Still concerned about his flank and his lines of supply and communication leading back to Chattanooga, Rosecrans had continued his sidling movement along the road toward Rossville Gap. Again leaving his position to be filled by McCook, Thomas marched across the rear of Crittenden in the darkness and extended the left another two miles north. By dawn, although Negley had not yet vacated Crawfish Springs and Reynolds was still en route, the Union-loyal Virginian's other two divisions, under Brigadier Generals Absalom Baird and J. M. Brannan, were in position at the intersection of the LaFayette Road and the road leading east to Reed's Bridge and west to McFarland's Gap, two miles south of Rossville. Consequently — though Bragg not only failed to suspect it, but in fact continued to base his attack plan on a belief that the reverse was true — the Federal left extended beyond the Confederate right. As Harvey Hill said later, with all the wisdom of hindsight, "While our troops had been moving up the Chickamauga, the Yankees had been moving down, and thus outflanked us."

The first real indication that this was so came in the emphatic form of an attack that struck and nearly crumpled the northern extremity of the Confederate line before it could begin the movement Bragg had ordered. Informed at sunup by an outpost colonel that the rebels had only a single brigade across the creek at Reed's Bridge, directly to his front, Thomas decided, on the basis of this misinformation, to attack and abolish it then and there. Brannan's division, advancing eastward, soon encountered Forrest's cavalry, out on a prowl. Dismounting his troopers, Forrest skirmished briskly to delay the bluecoats while Walker was sending Gist to his assistance. Surprised and thrown into sudden retreat when the gray infantry struck, Brannan managed to rally on Baird, sent forward by Thomas to bolster the line; but not for long. Walker threw Liddell into the conflict alongside Gist, and the two of them, with Forrest still tearing at the blue flank, drove the Federals back on their line of departure, one mile east of the LaFayette Road. Finding himself with a good deal more of a fight on his hands than he had expected, Thomas by now had called for reinforcements, and Rosecrans, still concerned about his left, responded promptly by sending Palmer of Crittenden's corps and Johnson of McCook's. The latter got there first and went in hard, stemming the near rout that had developed. Once more the line of battle swayed indecisively until the weight of numbers told. Then the graybacks began to give ground, until they in turn were reinforced by two brigades from Cheatham and the balance was restored.

That was the pattern, here and elsewhere along the four-mile line today. Always the weight of numbers decided the issue at every point in what was patently a battle not of generals but of soldiers. ("All this talk about generalship displayed on either side is sheer nonsense," Wilder declared long afterwards, looking back on the Chickamauga nightmare. "There was no generalship in it. It was a soldier's fight purely, wherein the only question involved was the question of endurance. The two armies came together like two wild beasts, and each fought as long as it could stand up in a knock-down and drag-out encounter. If there had been any high order of generalship displayed, the disasters to both armies might have been less.") What mainly distinguished the conflict from the outset was its fury. An Alabamian described the racket as "one solid, unbroken wave of awe-inspiring sound ... as if all the fires of earth and hell had been turned loose in one mighty effort to destroy each other." Fighting deep in the woods, with visibility strictly limited to his immediate vicinity, each man seemed to take the struggle as a highly personal matter between him and the blue or butternut figures he saw dodging into and out of sight, around and behind the clumps of brush and trunks of trees. "By the holy St Patrick, Colonel," a Tennessee private replied when told to pick up the flag that had fluttered down when the color-bearer fell, "there's so much good shooting around here I haven't a minute's time to waste fooling with that thing." All such interruptions, or attempts at interruption, were resented, sometimes even by men of rank. Bedford Forrest, for example, flew into a towering rage at an infantry brigadier for distracting him with messages expressing concern for his flanks. When the first of these was brought to him by an aide — "General Forrest, General Ector directed me to say to you that he is uneasy about his right flank" — the cavalryman, who wore a linen duster over his uniform today with his sword and pistol buckled outside, replied laconically: "Tell General Ector that he need not bother about his right flank. I'll take care of it." Presently, though, the staffer was back with word that his chief was uneasy again, this time about his left. Forrest, who was busy directing the fire of a battery of horse artillery, gave a roar of exasperation. "Tell General Ector that by God I am here," he shouted above the din of the guns, "and will take care of his left flank as well as his right!"

He did as he promised, but only by the hardest. All morning, here on the Confederate right, the struggle was touch and go, until the beginning was unrememberable and no end seemed possible. All there was was now, a raging fury. When an owl flew up, startled out of a tree by the battle racket, some crows attacked it in flight between the lines. "Moses, what a country!" a soldier exclaimed as he watched. "The very birds are fighting."

By now it was past midday. Rosecrans came up from Crawfish Spring about 1 o'clock, riding toward the sound of guns, and established headquarters in a small log house belonging to Mrs Eliza Glenn, the widow of a Confederate soldier. Located on a commanding elevation a bit under two miles north of Lee & Gordon's Mill and half a mile west of the road along with his army was deployed, this afforded him an excellent site, just south of the center of his line, from which to give close attention to his right, while the ablest of his corps commanders took charge of the left, which extended to the intersection not quite three miles to the north. Neatly dressed in black trousers, a white vest, and a plain blue coat, Old Rosy was in fine spirits, and with cause; Thomas had gotten the jump on the rebels this morning and seemed to be holding them handily with the reinforcements sent in prompt response to his request. Not even the capture, in the course of an early afternoon skirmish in the woods about a mile due east of headquarters, of some prisoners from Hood's division — conclusive evidence that part at least of Longstreet's corps, with an estimated strength of 17,000 effectives, was already on the scene — served to diminish the confidence displayed in the northern commander's bearing. A reporter, observing the general's flushed cheeks and sparkling eyes, considered him "very handsome," Roman nose and all, as he went over the growing collection of dispatches from subordinates, brought by couriers from all quarters of the field, and studied a rather sketchy map unrolled on the Widow Glenn's parlor table. He was in such good spirits, in fact, that he took the occasion to indulge in one of his favorite pastimes, the interrogation of a prisoner.

The man selected was a Texas captain, taken just now in the skirmish on the far side of the LaFayette Road. Rosecrans invited him to step outside, and the two sat together, apart from the officers of the staff, on a log in the side yard. Whittling as he spoke, the Ohioan conversed pleasantly for a time, then casually inquired about the Confederate dispositions.

"General, it has cost me a great deal of trouble to find your lines," the captain answered. "If you take the same amount of trouble you will find ours."

Smiling, Rosecrans went on whittling and asking questions, but to small avail. The prisoner, though he readily admitted that he was from Bragg's army, could not recall what corps or division he belonged to.

"Captain," Rosecrans said at last, "you don't seem to know much, for a man whose appearance seems to indicate so much intelligence."

Now it was the Texan's turn to smile.

"Well, General," he replied, "if you are not satisfied with my information, I will volunteer some. We are going to whip you most tremendously in this fight."

Soon after the rebel captain had been taken to the rear — alternately reticent and voluble, but about as irksome one way as the other — there was evidence that his parting remark might well turn out to be an accurate prediction. Moreover, the evidence was not only promptly presented; it was also repeated twice in the course of the next four hours, in the form of three extremely savage attacks launched against as many parts of the Federal line by Stewart, Hood, and Cleburne, three of the hardest-hitting commanders in Bragg's army.

So far, except for some minor skirmishing between the lines, there had been no action on the Union right with anything like the violence of the fighting that had continued all this time on the left, where Thomas was engaged with four of the eight blue divisions now on hand. Bragg had sent for Stewart's division of Buckner's corps, intending to throw it into the seesaw battle raging on the Confederate right; but Stewart — a forty-two-year-old Tennessean called "Old Straight" by his men, partly because of his ramrod posture, but mostly because he had taught mathematics at West Point, where he had acquired the nickname, and afterwards at Cumberland University — as he marched downstream through the woods, took a sudden turn to the west at about 2.30, either by design or error, and lunged instead at the enemy center, a mile south of where Bragg had intended to commit him. He struck Van Cleve's division of Crittenden's corps, which had seen no combat so far in the campaign and was unbraced for the shock. Having recently come into line after making their second night march in the past two days, Van Cleve and his men were not only considerably worn but were also as thoroughly confused as the Illinois soldier who later remarked wryly that "the reassembling of his three corps by Rosecrans was a tactical proceeding that even the privates could not make heads or tails of." At any rate, the three brigades broke badly under the impact of a host of screaming rebels, hurled at them from the dense woods in their front. Crittenden himself and Van Cleve, who at fifty-four was the oldest Federal brigadier — a New-Jersey-born Minnesotan and a member of the West Point class of 1831, he had been twenty-five years out of uniform when the war came — did what they could to stay the rout, though with little or no success. Stewart's troops made it up to and across the LaFayette Road to where the Glenn house, its yard crowded with staff orderlies and couriers and their mounts, was in plain view across the rolling landscape. But so, by now, was something else; two somethings else, in fact. Thomas's two remaining divisions under Reynolds and Negley, hard on their way north to join him, were halted in their tracks, still in column and nearly a mile apart, then faced right and thrown without delay into the breach, which Thomas had already begun to narrow by sending Brannan's troops — recovered by now, in part at least, from the mauling they had taken on the left — against its northern lip. As these three blue divisions converged upon his isolated gray one, Stewart fell sullenly back from contact, firing as he went. Half a mile east of the road he called a halt, and there, under cover of the woods he had emerged from, laid down a mass of fire that discouraged pursuit.

Hood was in position on the left of Stewart, due west of Alexander's Bridge. At the height of the uproar to his right front, though he was without orders, he put his two divisions in line abreast, Johnson on the left of Law, and started them forward at about 4 o'clock, by which time the racket up ahead had begun to subside. Tramping westward through the woods and brush, the Texas brigade, on the far right, went past one of Stewart's Tennessee regiments, which had just returned, blown and bloody, from its brief penetration of the Union line. "Rise up, Tennesseans," one of the advancing soldiers called, "and see the Texans go in!" Too weary to reply, let alone stand, Stewart's fought-out infantry lay there panting and watching as Hood's men swept past them, first the skirmishers, then the solid ranks of the main body, the pride of the Army of Northern Virginia, Lee's hard hitters who had shattered many a Yankee line, from Gaines Mill to the Devil's Den. Holding their attack formation as best they could in the heavy woods, these stalwarts broke into the clear near the LaFayette Road, a mile south of where Stewart had crossed it an hour ago, and went with a shout for a blue division drawn up to receive them on the west side of the road, apparently without supports on either flank.

It was Davis, of McCook. His three brigades were struck by the rebel six with predictable results; for though the bluecoats stood for a time, firing nervously but rapidly into the long line of attackers, the limit of their endurance was soon reached. Both overlapped flanks gave way at once, as if on signal, and the center promptly buckled under the strain. Once more, however, as the unstrung Federals fled westward and the Confederates pursued them to within plain view of the Widow Glenn's, yelling for all they were worth, a pair of blue divisions — the last two of the ten that would reach the field today — arrived most opportunely from the south, with all the patness of the cavalry in light fiction. Wood's division of Crittenden's corps was in the lead, coming down from Lee & Gordon's Mill, and now it was the rebels who were outflanked; Johnson had to call a halt to meet the menace to his left, as did Law, beyond him on the right. Davis rallied and led his fugitives back into the fight at about the same time Sheridan's division arrived from Crawfish Springs to tip the balance in favor of the Union. Halted, Johnson had to yield to this new pressure, and Law was obliged to conform: especially when Wilder's Lightning Brigade, still detached from Reynolds and held by Rosecrans in reserve for such emergencies, added the weight of its multishot carbines to the fray. The two butternut divisions fell back to the east side of the road, which then became and remained the dividing line between the Confederate left and the Federal right. Sheridan, in accordance with his instinct for aggression, tried to press matters with a charge, but was repulsed, and Hood settled into a new line about a mile in advance of his old one. On the right, as the men of the Texas brigade retired through the woods, badly cut up by Wilder's rapid-fire weapons in the final stage of their withdrawal, they came back to where they had called on Stewart's blown and bloody Tennesseans to "rise up ... and see the Texans go in." The regiment was still there, fairly well rested from its exertions, and one of its members did not neglect the opportunity thus afforded. "Rise up, Tennesseans," he called, "and see the Texans come out!"

By now it was sunset and the third in this sequence of savage attacks was about to be launched at the far end of the line. Summoned for one more go at the Federal left, where the fighting had slacked as if by common consent though the issue was still in doubt, Cleburne left his position opposite Lee & Gordon's at about the time Stewart's drive on the enemy center was being repulsed and Hood's was getting started against the right. Fording the Chickamauga well above Alexander's Bridge, the use of which would have delayed their march, his men found the spring-fed water icy cold and armpit deep. Wet and chilled, they continued northward through the woods for another four miles to reach their jump-off position just after sundown. Across the way, Thomas now had five divisions, Reynolds having come on to join him while Negley stayed behind to plug the gap created when Van Cleve was driven rearward. "Old Pap," as the solidly built Virginian's soldiers liked to call him, had seen to it that Baird and Johnson, who were posted at the extremity of his line, were braced for the assault he was convinced would be renewed before the day was over, while Palmer, Reynolds, and Brannan, who continued his line southward in that order, were warned to be ready to lend a hand. When the sun went down behind Missionary Ridge and no new attack had developed, they began to tell each other he was wrong; until Cleburne exploded out of the darkling woods, directly in front of Baird and Johnson, and proved him emphatically right. The three gray brigades were in line abreast, covering more than a mile from flank to flank, with Cheatham in close support. Though little could be seen in the gathering darkness, the immediate impression was one of absolute chaos as Cleburne's 5000 screaming men bore down on roughly twice that many defenders in the two blue divisions in their path. They charged with a clatter of musketry so tremendous that they seemed to be trying to make up for the disparity in numbers by the rapidity of their fire. That was in fact the case; Cleburne placed great stock in fast, well-aimed fire, and had drilled his troops relentlessly in rifle tactics, in and out of normal work hours, with just the present effect in mind. An Indiana captain later recorded that the advancing graybacks were "loading and firing in a manner that I believe was never surpassed on any battlefield during the rebellion," and Cleburne himself declared soon afterwards that "for half an hour [the firing] was the heaviest I ever heard."

This time there was no last-minute outside help; unlike Crittenden and McCook, Thomas had to fight with what he had when he was hit. After all, however, what he had was half the army, and though he lost a pair of guns, three stands of colors, some 400 captured men, and nearly a mile of ground on his outer flank, it was enough to stave off disaster. When full darkness put an end to what another Hoosier called "a display of fireworks that one does not like to see more than once in a lifetime," the blue line was severely contracted but unbroken. Baird and Brannan were forced back to the LaFayette Road on the left and right, but the three divisions between them maintained an eastward bulge of about 600 yards at its deepest. Cleburne's men, bedding down wherever they happened to be when the order reached them to stop firing, could hear the Federals hard at work beyond the curtain of night, felling trees to be used in the construction of breastworks along the contracted bulge of their new line. Shivering in their still-wet clothes, for the night was unseasonably cold for September, the listening Confederates knew only too well that they would have to try to overrun those breastworks in the morning.

Back at his campfire near Alexander's Bridge, Bragg was telling his corps commanders — all but Longstreet, who would get his instructions when he arrived near midnight, and Hill, who afterwards explained that he had not been able to locate the command post in the darkness — that the army's objective remained the same as yesterday: "to turn the enemy's left, and by direct attack force him into McLemore's Cove." Kershaw arrived after dark with his two brigades, completing a fast march from the Ringgold railhead, and was sent at once to Hood. By way of final preparation, Breckinridge was ordered to take position on Cleburne's right, extending the gray line northward in an attempt to outflank Thomas, while Hindman made a shorter march to get between Hood and Preston on the left. These three divisions, so far uncommitted, would complete the order of battle for tomorrow's attack, which Polk was scheduled to open at dawn on the far right and which would then be taken up in sequence, corps by corps, all down the line.

Hill would later refer caustically to the disjointed sequence of attacks, in which he himself had taken no part except to detach one of his divisions, as "the sparring of the amateur boxer, not the crushing blows of the trained pugilist," and Bragg in turn would describe the action, so far, as nothing more than "severe skirmishing" engaged in by his various corps and division commanders, for the most part on their own, "while endeavoring to get into line of battle." But no one knew better than Rosecrans, across the way in the Widow Glenn's lamp-lighted parlor, how near a thing it had been for him at times. In addition to the day-long pounding his left had managed to absorb — including the blood-curdling twilight assault by what sounded like tens of thousands of fiends equipped with the latest style rapid-fire weapons — two rebel penetrations, one of his center and one of his right, had surged to within plain view of army headquarters, and of these the second had come so close that he and members of his staff had had to shout at one another in order to be heard above the din.

Some measure of his mounting concern could be seen in a series of telegrams sent to the War Department in the course of the day by Charles Dana, who had arrived from Vicksburg the week before to continue his services as a behind-the-scenes observer for Stanton. "Rosecrans has everything ready to grind up Bragg's flank," he reported from Crawfish Springs that morning, and at 1 p.m. he followed this up — or, rather, he failed to follow it up — with a somewhat less encouraging or at any rate less emphatic message, sent as he left for the scene of the fighting three miles north: "Everything is going well, but the full proportions of the conflict are not yet developed." By 2.30 the telegraph line had been extended to the Glenn house, and Dana kept the operator busy. "Fight continues to rage," he wired. "Decisive victory seems assured." At 3.20 he passed along a report from Thomas "that he is driving rebels, and will force them into Chickamauga tonight." Though the center was being assailed by then, and the right was about to be, Dana was not fazed. "Everything is prosperous. Sheridan is coming up," he announced at 4 o'clock. A near commitment at 4.30 as to the outcome — "I do not yet dare to say our victory is complete, but it seems certain" — was modified in the dispatch that followed at 5.20: "Now appears to be undecided contest, but later reports will enable us to understand more clearly."

So it went; so it had gone all day. Despite his show of heartiness, what he mainly communicated was his confusion in attempting to follow a battle which, as he said, was "fought altogether in a thick forest, invisible to outsiders." In that sense, even the army commander was an outsider. Except for a rearward trickle of reports, most of them about as disconcerted as Dana's to Stanton, no one at headquarters could do much more than guess at what was happening in the smoky woods beyond the LaFayette Road. Rosecrans tried for a time, with the help of Mrs Glenn, to follow the progress of the fight by ear. She would make a guess, when a gun was heard, that it was "nigh out about Reed's Bridge" or "about a mile fornenst John Kelly's house," and he would try to match this information with the place names on the map. But it was a far from satisfactory procedure, for a variety of reasons. The map was a poor one in the first place, and after a while the roar was practically continuous all along the front. A reporter thought he had never witnessed "anything so ridiculous as this scene" between Old Rosy and the widow. Presently, when Stewart's men broke through the Federal center, she had to be removed to a place of greater safety, but Rosecrans, "fairly quivering with excitement," continued to pace back and forth, rubbing his palms rapidly together as the sound of firing swelled and quickened. "Ah! there goes Brannan!" he exclaimed with obvious satisfaction. He might have been right; besides, the noise was about all he had to go on; but it did not seem to the reporter that the general understood the situation any better than the departed countrywoman had done. Still, he kept pacing and exclaiming, perhaps in an attempt to ease the tension on his nerves and keep his spirits up. "Ah — there goes Brannan!" he would say; or, "That's Negley going in!"

Out on the line, when darkness finally put an end to the long day's fighting, the troops had a hard time of it. "How we suffered that night no one knows," a veteran was to recall. "Water could not be found; the rebels had possession of the Chickamauga, and we had to do without. Few of us had blankets and the night was very cold. All looked with anxiety for the coming of the dawn; for although we had given the enemy a rough handling, he had certainly used us very hard."

Under such conditions, despite much loss of sleep both nights before, work on the construction of breastworks was welcome as a means of keeping warm, as well as a diversion from thoughts of tomorrow. For Rosecrans, however, there could be no release from the latter; it was his job. He could take pride in the fact that his line, though obliged to yield an average mile of ground throughout its length today, was not only intact but was also considerably shorter than it had been when this morning's contest opened. Then too, word had come that Halleck at last was doing all he could to speed reinforcements to North Georgia; urgent appeals had gone from Washington to Burnside and Grant, at Knoxville and in Mississippi, directing them to send troops to Chattanooga in all haste, and similar messages had been dispatched to Hurlbut at Memphis, Schofield in Missouri, and John Pope in far-off Minnesota. It was a comfort to Rosecrans to know that in time there would be these supports to fall back on. Meanwhile, though, he had to fight with what he had on hand, and he was by no means sure that this would be enough, since prisoners had been taken from no less than a dozen regiments known to have arrived just yesterday from Virginia. How many others had come or were arriving tonight he did not know, for the captives were nearly as close-mouthed under interrogation as the Texas captain had been this afternoon, but intelligence officers had little trouble identifying these "Virginians" by their standard gray uniforms, which were in natty contrast to the "go-as-you-please" garments worn in the western armies. Occasionally, too, a scrap of information could be extracted by goading the prisoners into anger. "How does Longstreet like the western Yankees?" one was asked in a mocking tone, and he replied with a growl: "You'll get enough of Longstreet before tomorrow night."

This might be nothing more than wishful rebel thinking. On the other hand it might be an informed and accurate prediction. At any rate, whichever it was, Rosecrans decided — as he had done under similar circumstances on New Year's Eve almost nine months ago — that he would do well to call a council of war for the triple purpose of briefing his principal subordinates on the over-all situation, of obtaining their recommendations as to a proper course of action, and of enabling him, at some later date, to shift at least a share of the blame in event of a defeat. Besides, he had a natural fondness for conference discussions, especially late-at-night ones, whether the subject was strategy or religion. The council accordingly convened at headquarters at 11 o'clock that evening. Most of those present, including the three corps commanders, had attended the conference held at the close of the first day's fighting in the last great battle; the difference was in the staff. "Poor Garesché," as Rosecrans had referred to the previous chief of staff after his head was blown off by a cannonball, had been replaced in January by Brigadier General James A. Garfield, a thirty-two-year-old former Ohio schoolteacher, lawyer, lay preacher, and politician, whose warm handclasp seemed to one observer to convey the message, "Vote early. Vote right," and whose death, at the hands of an assassin who voted both early and right and then failed to get the appointment to which he believed this entitled him, would occur exactly eighteen years from today, partly as a direct result of what was going to happen here tomorrow. Big-headed, with pale eyes and a persuasive manner — like Hooker, he was a protégé of Secretary Chase's, and up to now his most notable service in the war had been as a member of the court-martial that convicted Fitz-John Porter — Garfield opened the council by displaying for the assembled generals a map with the positions of all the Union divisions indicated, along with those of the Confederates so far as they were known; after which Rosecrans called for individual opinions as to what was to be done. McCook and Crittenden — the Ohioan, according to an obviously unfriendly fellow officer, had "a weak nose that would do no credit to a baby" and a grin that gave rise to "suspicion that he is either still very green or deficient in the upper story," while the Kentuckian was characterized more briefly as "a good drinker," one of those men, fairly common in the higher echelons of all armies, who "know how to blow their own horns exceedingly well" — had little to contribute in the way of advice, each perhaps being somewhat chagrined by the loss of one of his three divisions, detached that morning to reinforce the left, and somewhat subdued by the near-destruction of one of his remaining two in the course of the afternoon. Not so Thomas, who differed as much from them in outlook, or anyhow in the emphatic expression of his outlook, as he did in appearance. Ponderous and phlegmatic, he was described by another observer as "not scrimped anywhere, and square everywhere — square face, square shoulders, square step; blue eyes with depths in them, withdrawn beneath a pent-house of a brow, features with legible writing on them, and the whole giving the idea of massive solidity, of the right kind of man to 'tie to.'" Though he slept through much of the conference — not only because it was his custom (he had done the same at Stones River) but also because he had spent the last two nights on the march and most of today under heavy attack — he repeated the same words whenever he was called on for a tactical opinion: "I would strengthen the left." But when Rosecrans replied, as he did each time, "Where are we going to take it from?" there was no answer; Thomas would be back asleep by then, propped upright in his chair.

At the council held nine months ago in the rain-lashed cabin beside the Nashville pike, the discussion had centered mainly on whether the army should retreat; but here tonight, in the small log house on the field of Chickamauga, the word was used only in connection with the rebels. The decision, committed to paper for distribution as soon as it was reached, was that the Federals would hold their ground. Unless

Bragg withdrew under cover of darkness — there was some conjecture that he might, though it was based more on hope than on tangible evidence, of which there was not a shred that indicated a change in his clear intention to destroy them — they would offer him battle tomorrow, on the same terms as today. At this late hour, in point of fact, that seemed not only the bravest but also the safest thing to do, considering the risk a retreating army would run of being caught, trains and all, strung out on the roads leading back through Rossville and McFarland's gaps to Chattanooga, which was a good ten miles from the Widow Glenn's. There would be minor readjustments, though not of Granger's three-brigade reserve force, which was instructed to remain where it was, covering Rossville Gap and holding that escape hatch open in case of a collapse. To lessen the chances of this last, which would be most likely to occur as a result of a rebel breakthrough, Rosecrans directed that his ten-division line of battle along the LaFayette Road was to be strengthened by further contraction. Thomas would hold his five divisions in their present intrenched position on the left, and McCook would move his two northward to connect with Negley's division, on Thomas's right, while Crittenden withdrew his two for close-up support of the center or a rapid shift in whichever direction they were needed, north or south. When all this had been discussed and agreed on, Garfield put it in writing and read it back, and when this in turn had been approved it was passed to the headquarters clerks for copying. By now it was midnight. While the generals were waiting for the clerks to finish their task, Rosecrans provided coffee for a social interlude, the principal feature of which was a soulful rendition by "the genial, full-stomached McCook," as one reporter called him, of a plaintive ballad entitled "The Hebrew Maiden."

Possibly Thomas slept through this as well; possibly not. In any event, it was 2 o'clock in the morning before he returned to his position on the left, where he found a report awaiting him from Baird, who warned that his division, posted on the flank, could not be extended all the way to the Reed's Bridge road, as ordered, and still be strong enough to hold if it was struck again by anything like the twilight blow that had sent it reeling for more than a mile until darkness ended the fighting. Thomas made a quick inspection by moonlight and arrived at the same conclusion, then sent a message back to headquarters, explaining the trouble and requesting that Negley, who had been halted and thrown in to shore up the crumbling center while on his way to the left that afternoon, be ordered to resume his northward march and rejoin his proper corps, the critical outer flank of which was in danger of being crushed for lack of support or turned for lack of troops to extend it. Rosecrans promptly agreed by return messenger, as he had done to all such specific requests from his senior corps commander; Negley would march at dawn. Reassured, Thomas at last bedded down under a large oak, one of whose protruding roots afforded a pillow for his head, and there resumed the sleep that had been interrupted, if not by McCook's singing, then at any rate by the breakup of the council of war, some time after midnight.

He woke to Sunday's dawn, already impatient for Negley's arrival. The sun came up blood red through the morning haze and the smoke of yesterday's battle, which still hung about the field. "It is ominous," the chief of staff was saying, back at the Widow Glenn's, as he pointed dramatically at the rising sun. "This will indeed be a day of blood." Thomas needed no sign to tell him that, but he was growing increasingly anxious about his unsupported flank, which the army commander had assured him would be reinforced without delay. The sun rose higher. Presently it was a full hour above the land-line, and still Negley had not arrived. Rosecrans himself came riding northward about this time, however, and though his face was drawn and puffy from strain and lack of sleep, he spoke encouragingly as he drew rein from point to point along the line. "Fight today as well as you did yesterday," he told his troops, "and we shall whip them!" This had a somewhat mixed effect. "I did not like the way he looked," a soldier later recalled, "but of course felt cheered, and did not allow myself to think of any such thing as defeat."

✗ 5 ✗

Bragg and his staff were up and mounted before daylight, waiting for the roar of guns that would signal Polk's compliance with his orders, received in person the night before, "to assail the enemy on our extreme right at day-dawn of the 20th." Perhaps by now, after the repeated frustrations of the past two weeks, the Confederate commander might have been expected to accept delay, if not downright disobedience, as more or less standard procedure on the part of his ranking subordinates — particularly Polk and Hill, the wing and corps commanders directly in charge of the troops who would open the attack — but such was not the case. Even if he had learned to expect it, he had by no means learned to take it calmly. Three months later, when he submitted his official account of the battle, his anger was still apparent. "With increasing anxiety and disappointment," he wrote then, "I waited until after sunrise without hearing a gun, and at length dispatched a staff officer to Lieutenant General Polk to ascertain the cause of the delay and urge him to a prompt and speedy movement."

By the time the aide located Polk, delivered the message, and returned, the sun was more than an hour high and Bragg's impatience had been mounting with it. Not a gun had yet been fired, and across the way the Yankees were hard at work improving by daylight the breastworks they had constructed in the darkness. The thought of this was enough to sour a far sweeter disposition than Bragg would ever be able to lay claim to. Moreover, what the staff officer had to report on his return brought his chief's wrath to what might be called full flower. He had found the bishop, he declared, "at a farm house three miles from the line of his troops, about one hour after sunrise, sitting on the gallery reading a newspaper and waiting, as he said, for his breakfast." Hearing this, Bragg did something rare for him. He cursed — "a terrible exclamation," the aide termed the outburst — then rode to Polk's headquarters, intending no doubt to rebuke the wing commander in person, but found that he had just left for the front, remarking as he did so: "Do tell General Bragg that my heart is overflowing with anxiety for the attack. Overflowing with anxiety, sir."

It was close to 8 o'clock by then, better than two hours past the hour scheduled for an advance on the far right, and Bragg learned from one of the bishop's aides, who had remained behind, something of what had caused the mix-up and delay. Hill had not only failed to find army headquarters last night; he had also failed to locate Polk, who in turn had been unable to find him. As a result, unlike Cheatham and Walker, who had reported to headquarters the evening before, Hill had neither received his orders to attack nor been led to suspect that Bragg or anyone else had any such plans in mind for the two divisions on the northern flank. Learning of this for the first time from the courier who returned that morning from an unsuccessful all-night search for Hill, Polk sent orders directly to Breckinridge and Cleburne, bypassing the fugitive corps commander, for them to "move and attack the enemy as soon as you are in position." Hill was with them when the message was delivered, and when they protested that their men were not only not "in position," but had not had time to eat their morning rations, he backed them up with a note in which he blandly informed the wing commander that it would be "an hour or so" before the two divisions would be ready to go forward. It was this reply, received at about 7.30, that had caused the bishop — whose overflowing heart by now outweighed his empty stomach — to interrupt his breakfast on the farmhouse gallery, or perhaps not even wait any longer for it to be served, and set out instead for the front and a conference with Hill.

Bragg got there first, however, apparently by taking a shorter route. Trailed by his staff, he rode up to where Hill had established headquarters between Breckinridge and Cleburne, whose troops had still not been placed in attack formation and were just now being fed. When Bragg inquired testily why he had not attacked at daylight in accordance with last night's order, Hill replied coolly and with obvious satisfaction, as he afterwards recalled, "that I was hearing then for the first time that such an order had been issued and had not known whether we were to be the assailants or the assailed." Bragg's anger and impatience had no discernible effect on him whatever. He would not be hurried. Miffed at having been cast in a role subordinate to that of the other two lieutenant generals, who had been made wing commanders while all he had under him was the corps he had brought onto the field, he was unmistakably determined, in the words of a later observer, "to assert to the limit what authority he retained." Soon Polk arrived, but neither he nor Bragg, scarcely on speaking terms by now with one another, was able to get their fellow North Carolinian to hurry things along; Hill's claim was that he could scarcely be held responsible for not obeying instructions that had not reached him. He took his time, and what was more he saw to it that his two division commanders took theirs as well. The troops were aligned punctiliously under cover of the woods, and all was reported ready, down to the final round in the final cartridge box, before Hill gave the nod that sent Breckinridge forward at 9.30, followed within fifteen minutes by Cleburne on his left, a full four hours past the time Bragg had set for the attack to open on the far right of the army.

Across the way, Rosecrans too had been having his troubles during the long delay, and though he began the day in a frame of mind that seemed cheerful enough for a man who had had but little sleep to ease the built-up tension on his nerves, he completely lost his temper before he returned to headquarters from his early morning ride along his still-contracting line of battle. Greeted by Thomas when he reached the left, he found him in high spirits over his successful resistance to yesterday's frantic rebel attempts to drive him from the field. "Whenever I touched their flanks they broke, General; they broke!" he exclaimed. In point of fact, as the long silence continued on through sunrise and beyond, it had become increasingly apparent that they had learned their lesson; they seemed to want no more of it today. Still, it was strange to see the phlegmatic Virginian display such exuberance, even though it lasted only until he spotted a newsman riding with the staff; whereupon he flushed and withdrew at once into the habitual reserve which he used as a shield between himself and such people. He spoke instead of possible danger to his left. Scouts had reported that the Confederates, out beyond the screening woods and thickets, were continuing to shift in that direction. "You must move up, too, as fast as they do," Rosecrans told him. Thomas agreed, but he also pointed out that this required more troops. There was the rub; Negley had not arrived. Rosecrans assured him that Negley was on the way by now, for he himself had seen to it in the course of his ride north along the line. Thomas was relieved to hear this, though he repeated that he would not consider his flank secure until reinforcements got there to extend and shore it up.

But when the Union commander rode back south, retracing his steps but not stopping now for speeches, he found to his chagrin that the reinforcements he had just assured Thomas were already on their way had not budged from their position in the center, where he had left them an hour ago with orders to march north. However, Negley had an excellent reason for his apparent insubordination. McCook still had not closed the gap created by Crittenden's withdrawal in compliance with last night's instructions, so that if Negley had pulled out in turn, as ordered, he would have left a mile-wide hole in the Federal center; which plainly, at a time when an all-out rebel assault was expected at any minute almost anywhere along the front, would not do. Nettled — as well he might be, for the sun was two hours high by now — Rosecrans hurried rearward and told Crittenden to return Wood's division to the line in place of Negley's, which then could be released to join Thomas, two miles away on the unshored northern flank. Next he rode south in search of McCook, whose slowness was at the root of the present trouble. Finding him, he stressed the need for haste and an early end to the grumbling confusion into which his two divisions had been thrown by a renewal of their sidling movement toward the left. All this time, though only by the hardest, Old Rosy had managed to keep a grip on his temper. But when he returned to the center and found Negley still in position, with Wood nowhere in sight, he lost it entirely. Pausing only long enough to order Negley to send one of his three brigades to Thomas at once, even though no replacements had arrived, he galloped rearward and presently came upon Wood, who was conferring with his staff about the unexpected and still pending movement back into line. "What is the meaning of this, sir?" Rosecrans barked at him. "You have disobeyed my specific orders. By your damnable negligence you are endangering the safety of the entire army, and by God I will not tolerate it! Move your division at once, as I have instructed, or the consequences will not be pleasant for yourself." Wood, a forty-year-old Kentuckian, flushed at being upbraided thus in the presence of his staff, but as a West Pointer, a regular army man, and a veteran of all the army's fights, from Shiloh on, he knew better than to protest. Choking back his resentment, he saluted and put his three brigades in motion.

The lead brigade was just coming into line, at about 9.45, when an uproarious clatter broke out on the far left, fulfilling Thomas's prediction that his would be the flank the rebels would assault. From the sound of it, as heard by Rosecrans at the Widow Glenn's, to which he had returned after venting his spleen in the encounter with Wood, they were putting in all they had.

They were indeed putting in all they had at that end of the line: not all at once, however, as the sudden eruption seemed to indicate by contrast with the silence which it shattered, but rather in a series of divisional attacks, as Bragg had ordered. Breckinridge struck first, on the far right. Though his left brigade came up against the north end of the mile-long curve of breastworks and was involved at once in an unequal fire fight, standing in the open to swap volleys with an adversary under cover, the other two found no such obstacle in their path. Thomas had prolonged his line by shifting one of Johnson's brigades from his center, and the brigade detached in haste from Negley had just arrived to extend the left still farther, but there had not been time enough for felling trees, much less for the heavy task of snaking and staking the trunks into position to fight behind. As a result, the two gray brigades advancing southward down the LaFayette Road met and fought the two blue ones on equal terms, first with a stand-up exchange of volleys, face to face, and then, as the defenders began to waver, with a charge that drove them rearward in a rush. However, Thomas had made good use of the time afforded him by the delaying action. Two more brigades were at hand by then, one from Brannan, which he brought over from his right, and one from Van Cleve, which Rosecrans had sent double-timing to the left when the attack first exploded in that direction. Together they stalled the advance of the jubilant graybacks, and then with the help of the other two brigades, which rallied when the pressure was relieved, drove them back northward, restoring the flank that had crumbled under assault. There was, of course, the danger that they might be reinforced to try again in greater strength; in which case Thomas would be hard put to find reinforcements of his own, for Cleburne's attack had been launched by now, due south of and adjoining Breckinridge, with such persistent savagery that not a man could be spared from the close-up defense of the long line of breastworks in order to meet a new threat to the left. All Thomas could do was continue what he had been doing ever since he reached the field; that is, call on Rosecrans for more troops from the right and center, which had been stripped to less than four divisions, as compared to the more than six already concentrated here.

Events would show that this was rather beside the point, however, for though the old one would continue with much of its original fury all morning, there was not going to be any new end-on threat to the Union left. Bragg had called for a definite series of attacks, beginning on his far right and continuing in sequence down the full length of his line, and neither Polk nor Hill (if, indeed, they were even aware of the Chancellorsville-like opportunity — which apparently they were not) was in any frame of mind to make suggestions, let alone appeals, to a commander who was already in a towering rage because his instructions had not been followed to the letter. Instead, they continued to hammer unrelentingly at the long southward curve of enemy breastworks, encouraged from time to time by reports such as one sent back by Brigadier General Lucius Polk, the bishop's thirty-year-old nephew, whose brigade of Cleburne's division smashed through the Federal outpost works, just in front of the center of the bulge, and drove the blue pickets back on their main line of resistance. Elated, he turned in mid-career to an officer on his staff. "Go back and tell the old general," he said, meaning his uncle, "that we have passed two lines of breastworks; that we have got them on the jump, and I am sure of carrying the main line." By the time this reached the wing commander, who was conferring with Cheatham, the brigade had been repulsed. But that was no part of the report, and Polk was as elated by the message as his nephew had been when he gave it to the aide. "General," he told Cheatham, "move your division and attack at once." The Tennessean, who had massed his five brigades in anticipation of the order, was prompt to comply. "Forward, boys, and give them hell!" he shouted, much as he had done nine months ago at Murfreesboro, and the bishop approved now, as he had then, of the spirit if not of the words his friend had chosen to express it. "Do as General Cheatham says, boys!" he called after the troops as they moved out.

But Cheatham had no greater success than Hill had had before him. His men went up to within easy range of the breastworks, which seemed to burst into flame at their approach, then recoiled, all in one quick involuntary movement like that of a hand testing the heat of a still-hot piece of metal. Walker's two divisions, held in reserve till then, had much the same reaction when they were committed at about 10.45, shortly after Cheatham had been repulsed. By now the entire right wing was engaged, including Forrest's dismounted horsemen, who went in with Breckinridge. "What infantry is that?" Hill asked in the course of a tour of inspection on the right. He had never seen troops like these in the East. "Forrest's cavalry," he was told. Presently, when Forrest himself came riding back to meet him, the North Carolinian removed his hat in salutation. "General Forrest," he said, "I wish to congratulate you and those brave men moving across that field like veteran infantry upon their magnificent behavior. In Virginia I made myself extremely unpopular with the cavalry because I said that so far I had not seen a dead man with spurs on. No one could speak disparagingly of such troops as yours." Whether the Tennessean blushed at this high praise could not be told, for in battle his face always took on the color of heated bronze. "Thank you, General," he replied, then wheeled his horse and with a wave of his hand galloped back into the thick of the fight that had excited Hill's admiration.

At no one point along the Confederate right had the issue been pressed to its extremity by the mass commitment of reserves to achieve a breakthrough. Rather, the pressure had been equally heavy on all points at once, as if what Bragg intended to accomplish was not so much a penetration as a cataclysm, a total collapse of the whole Union left, like that of a dam giving way to an unbearable weight of water. This was in fact what he was after, and at times it seemed to some among the defenders that he was about to get it. "The assaults were repeated with an impetuosity that threatened to overwhelm us," according to John Palmer, whose division was on loan to Thomas from Crittenden. Except on the extended flank, however, where there had been no time to throw up breastworks, casualties had been comparatively light for the Federals, who were protected by the stout log barricade they had constructed overnight and improved during the four daylight hours which Hill's delay had afforded them this morning. It was not so for the attackers; their losses had been heavy everywhere. "The rebs charged in three distinct lines," an Ohio captain wrote, "but each time they charged they were driven back with fearfully decimated ranks." Some measure of the truth of this was shown in the loss of those who led the frantic charges. Breckinridge, Cleburne, and Gist each had a brigade commander killed or mortally wounded in the course of this one hour: Brigadier Generals Ben Hardin Helm, who had married Mary Lincoln's youngest sister and recently succeeded to command of the Orphan Brigade, and James Deshler, who had been exchanged, promoted, and transferred east after his discomfiture by Sherman at Arkansas Post, and Colonel Peyton Colquitt, who had taken over Gist's brigade when that general was put in charge of the division Walker brought from Mississippi. Moreover, another of Breckinridge's brigadiers, Daniel W. Adams, an accident-prone or perhaps merely unlucky Kentucky-born Louisianan who had lost an eye at Shiloh and been severely wounded again at Murfreesboro, was shot from his horse and captured when the attack that crumpled the Union flank was repulsed by reinforcements whose arrival was unmatched by any of his own. It had gone that way, with varying degrees of success, but nowhere with complete success, all along the front of the Confederate right wing. Still, with the evidence of the casualty lists before him, Bragg could scarcely complain of any lack of determination in the fighting, no matter how disappointed he was at the outcome so far of his attempt to smash Old Rosy's left as a prologue to rolling up his entire line and packing it southward into McLemore's Cove for destruction.

By 11 o'clock all five of Polk's divisions had been committed. Now Longstreet's turn had come. Bragg passed the word for Stewart to go in, and in he went, driving hard for the enemy breastworks at the point where they curved back to the LaFayette Road immediately opposite his position on the right of the Confederate left wing.

★ ★ ★

There Reynolds was posted, with Brannan on his right, one east and the other west of the road, the latter having pulled his division back about a hundred yards in order to take advantage of the cover afforded by some heavy woods in rear of a cleared field which would have been much harder to defend. Stewart hit them both, attacking with all the fury of yesterday, when he had shattered the blue line half a mile to the south and penetrated to within sight of the Widow Glenn's before he was expelled. Today, though, there were breastworks all along the front, and he achieved nothing like his previous success. He was, in fact, flung back before he made contact, just as most of Polk's attackers had been, and had to be content, like them, with laying down a mass of fire that seemed to have little effect on the defenders beyond obliging them to keep their heads down between shots. There was, however, a good deal more to it than that, even though the result would not be evident for a while. What Stewart mainly accomplished was a further encouragement of Thomas's conviction that Bragg was throwing everything he had at the Union left, and this caused the Virginian to intensify his appeal for still more troops from the right and center, an appeal that had been communicated practically without letup, ever since the first attack exploded on his flank, by a steady procession of couriers who came to headquarters with messages warning that the left would surely be overwhelmed if it was not strengthened promptly.

Rosecrans still was quite as willing to do this as he had been earlier, when he said flatly that Thomas would be sustained in his present position "if he has to be reinforced by the entire army." In point of fact, that was what it was fast coming to by now. Shortly after 10 o'clock, with Van Cleve's remaining brigades already on their way north, McCook had been told to alert his troops for a rapid march to the left "at a moment's warning," and half an hour later the order came, directing him to send two of Sheridan's brigades at once and to follow with the third as soon as the corps front had been contracted enough for Davis to hold it alone. This would put eight divisions on the left, under Thomas, and leave only two on the right, one under Crittenden and one under McCook, but Rosecrans was preparing to send still more in that direction if they were needed. His calculations — "Where are we going to take it from?" — were interrupted at this point, however, by another of Thomas's couriers, a staff captain who, in addition to the accustomed plea for reinforcements, brought alarming news of something he had observed (or failed to observe) in the course of his ride from the left. Passing in rear of Reynolds, he had not seen Brannan's troops in the woods to the south; consequently, he reported "Brannan out of line and Reynolds' right exposed." The same opinion, derived from the same mistake, was expressed in stronger terms by another Thomas aide, who arrived on the heels of the captain and declared excitedly that there was "a chasm in the center," between the divisions of Reynolds and Wood, who had replaced Negley in the position on Brannan's right. Apparently convinced by the independent testimony of two eyewitnesses, Rosecrans did not take time to check on a report which, if true, scarcely allowed time for anything but attempting to repair an extremely dangerous error before it was discovered and exploited by the rebels. Instead, he turned to a staff major — Garfield, he later explained, "was deeply engaged in another matter" — and told him to send an order to Wood at once, correcting the situation. The major did so, heading the message 10.45 a.m.

> Brigadier General Wood, Commanding Division:
> The general commanding directs that you close up on Reynolds as fast as possible, and support him. Respectfully, &c.
> FRANK S. BOND, Major and Aide-de-Camp.

Wood received it at 10.55, barely more than an hour after the vigorous dressing-down Old Rosy had given him for slowness in obeying a previous order. This time he did not delay execution, although there was a degree of contradiction in the terms "close up on" and "support." Nor did he take time to find and confer with Crittenden, who had been bypassed as if in emphasis of the need for haste expressed in the phrase, "as fast as possible." McCook happened to be with him, though, when the message was delivered, and on receiving his assurance that Davis would sidle northward to fill the gap that would be left, the Kentuckian promptly began the shift the order seemed to require. There being no way to close on Reynolds without going around Brannan, who was in position on Reynolds' right, Wood did just that. He pulled his division straight back out of line and set out, across Brannan's rear, for the hookup with Reynolds. Riding ahead to scout the route, he encountered Thomas, told him of the order, and asked where his brigades should be posted in compliance. To his surprise, Thomas declared that Reynolds was in no need of support — he and Brannan had just repulsed Stewart without much trouble — but that Baird needed it badly, up at the far end of the line. Wood said that he was willing to go there if Thomas would take the responsibility for changing his instructions, and when the Virginian, duly thankful for a windfall that had plumped a full division of reinforcements into his empty lap, replied that he would gladly do so, Wood rode back to pass the word to his brigade commanders.

That was how it came about that in attempting to fill a gap that did not exist, Rosecrans created one; created, in fact, what Thomas's overexcited aide had referred to, half an hour ago, as "a chasm in the center." The aide had been mistaken then, but his words were now an accurate description of what lay in the path of Longstreet, who was preparing, under cover across the way, to launch an all-out assault directly upon the quarter-mile stretch of breastworks Wood's departure had left unmanned.

Old Peter had followed the progress of the fight with mounting dissatisfaction. Up to now, the piecemeal nature of the attacks had given the battle an all-too-familiar resemblance to Gettysburg, and he wanted no more of that than he could possibly avoid. At 11 o'clock, with Polk's wing unsuccessfully committed, he ventured a suggestion to the army commander, of whom he had seen nothing since the night before, "that my column of attack could probably break the enemy's line if he cared to have it go in." In referring thus to his entire wing as a "column of attack," he was recommending that the attack in echelon, which in alley-fight terms amounted to crowding and shoving and clawing and slapping, be abandoned in favor of a combined assault, which amounted in those same terms to delivering one hard punch with a clenched fist. Just then, however, Stewart moved out alone on direct orders from Bragg, who had thrown caution to the winds — and science, too — by sending word for all the division commanders to go forward on their own in a frantic, headlong, unco-ordinated effort to overrun the Federal defenses. This was altogether too much for Longstreet. Though his admiration for the naked valor of the Confederate infantry was as large as any man's, he had recently seen the South's greatest single bid for victory turned into its worst defeat by a similar act of desperation in Pennsylvania, and he was determined not to have the same thing happen here in his home state if he could help it. He rode to the front at once to restrain Hood, whom he knew to be impetuous, from committing his corps before all three of his divisions, Johnson's and Law's and Kershaw's, were massed to strike as a unit, together with Hindman's on his left.

He got there just in time; Hood already had Johnson deployed, with Law in close support, and was about to take them forward. Longstreet had him wait for Kershaw, who formed a third line behind Law, and for Hindman, who dressed in a double line on Johnson, extending the front southward for a total width of half a mile. With Stewart engaged on Hood's right and Preston held in reserve on Hindman's left, Old Peter thus had four of his six divisions, eleven of his seventeen brigades, and some 16,000 of his 25,000 soldiers massed for the delivery of his clenched-fist blow. This was roughly half again more than he had had for the "charge" on the third day at Gettysburg, and not only were the troops in better condition here in Georgia than the ones had been in Pennsylvania, where four of the nine brigades had been shot to pieces in earlier actions, but they also had less than half as far to go before making contact, as well as excellent concealment during most of their approach. Longstreet apparently had no doubt whatsoever that the attack would be successful. Earlier that morning, speaking with what Hood described as "that confidence which had so often contributed to his extraordinary success," he had assured the tawny-bearded young man "that we would *of course* whip and drive [the Yankees] from the field," and Hood said afterwards: "I could not but exclaim that I was rejoiced to hear him so express himself, as he was the first general I had met since my arrival who talked of victory." However, for all his confidence, Old Peter did not forget the dangers that lurk in military iotas. He saw to it, in person and with the help of his staff, that his preliminary instructions were followed to the letter. Then and only then, shortly before 11.15, he gave the order for the column to go forward, due west through the dense woods that had screened his preparations.

With barely a quarter mile to go before they reached it, Bushrod Johnson's lead brigades crossed the LaFayette Road within ten minutes of receiving Longstreet's nod. As they surged across the dusty road and the open field beyond — the field that Wood had recessed his line to avoid — they encountered galling fire from the left and right, where Hindman and Law were hotly engaged, but almost none from directly ahead. Welcome though this was, they thought it strange until they found out why. Entering the woods on the far side, they scrambled over the deserted breastworks and caught sight, dead ahead and still within easy reach, of the last of Wood's brigades in the act of carrying out the order to "close up on and support" Reynolds. Yelling, the Confederates struck the vulnerable blue column flank and rear, sitting-duck fashion, and, as Johnson described the brief action, "cast the shattered fragments to the right and left." Still on the run, the butternut attackers crashed on through the forest and soon emerged into another clearing, larger than the first, with Missionary Ridge looming westward beyond the tops of intervening trees. Here at last, after their half-mile run, they paused to recover their breath and alignment, and Johnson later communicated something of the elation he and those around him felt, not only at what they had accomplished so far, but also at what lay spread before them, stark against the backdrop of the green slopes of the ridge. "The scene now presented was unspeakably grand," he declared in his report. "The resolute and impetuous charge, the rush of our heavy columns sweeping out from the shadow and gloom of the forest into the open fields flooded with sunlight, the glitter of arms, the onward dash of artillery and mounted men, the retreat of the foe, the shouts of the hosts of our army, the dust, the smoke, the noise of firearms — of whistling balls and grapeshot and of bursting shell — made up a battle scene of unsurpassed grandeur."

There was little time for admiring the view, however, since it included, in addition to the items mentioned, a number of hostile guns in furious action along a low ridge half a mile away, some firing southeast, some northeast, and some due east at him. Hood rode up amid the shellbursts, managing his horse with one hand because the other still hung useless in its sling. "Go ahead," he told Johnson, who was realigning his three brigades, "and keep ahead of everything." The Ohio-born Tennessean did just that. His men had taken a six-gun Federal battery soon after they crossed the road, but this had only sharpened their appetite for more. Resuming the advance, they quickly overran a position from which nine guns were firing, then plunged ahead to seize four more whose crews did not limber them in time for a getaway, as several others managed to do along that ripple of high ground overlooking a scene of moiling confusion in the enemy rear. Here Johnson called a halt at last, having accomplished a mile-deep penetration of the Union center, the destruction or dispersal of a whole brigade of bluecoats, and the capture of nineteen pieces of artillery, all between 11.15 and noon. Bracing his troops for a possible shock, he threw out skirmishers and sent word back to Longstreet of his need for reinforcements in case the enemy launched a counterattack at his isolated division, which had lost about one fourth of its strength in the course of its long advance. Such an attack did not seem likely, though, if he could judge by what he saw from where he stood. The blue army seemed to have come apart at the seams under the impact of that one savage blow, and its fugitives were streaming in disorder up the Dry Valley Road, which curved north and west across their rear, toward Missionary Ridge and the solitary notch that indicated McFarland's Gap and possible deliverance from the terror that had suddenly come on them, less than an hour ago, after a morning of taking it easy while the battle raged at the far end of the line.

Hindman had had much to do with the creation of the blue confusion. Though he encountered a far greater number of Federals in the course of his advance on Johnson's left, and thus was limited to a shallower penetration, this gave him the chance to inflict a far greater number of casualties, and that was what he did. Johnson had struck and shattered a single brigade, but Hindman served two whole divisions in that manner within the same brief span of time, converting McCook's supposed defense of the Union right into the headlong race for safety which Johnson observed with such elation when he called a halt soon afterward on the ridge overlooking the Dry Valley Road, a mile beyond the point where he had pierced the enemy center. Much as the unmanned breastworks in his front had facilitated the Tennessean's breakthrough, so did the Arkansan have the good fortune to find both Sheridan and Davis in motion when he hit them. The former, in compliance with his orders to reinforce the left, was marching north across the latter's rear, and the latter was sidling in the same direction, under instructions to close the gap created by Wood's abrupt departure, when they were assailed by Hindman's yelling graybacks, who came swarming out of the woods before the pickets along the LaFayette Road had time to do more than get off a few wild shots by way of sounding the alarm. Davis's men scattered rearward in a panic that soon infected Sheridan's two lead brigades, whose ranks were overrun by the fugitives as a prelude to being struck by their pursuers, with the result that the two divisions were mingled in flight. "McCook's corps was wiped off the field without any attempt at real resistance," an Illinois colonel later testified, adding that he had seen artillerists cut the traces and abandon their guns in order to make a faster getaway, while others on foot, including some who might otherwise have been willing to stand their ground, were swept along by the mob, "like flecks of foam upon a river." McCook himself was one of those flecks, and Sheridan and Davis were two more; but Brigadier

General William H. Lytle was not. Commanding Sheridan's third brigade, which had been left behind as a covering force southeast of the Widow Glenn's, he ordered a countercharge in an attempt to stem the rout, but fell at the first rebel volley and died soon after his men ran off and left him, the only Union general, out of thirty of that rank on the field, to be killed or captured or even touched by metal in this bloodiest of all the western battles.

One check there was, and a bloody one at that, though not from McCook or either of his two division commanders. Detached from Reynolds, the Lightning Brigade was still posted in support of the Union right, and when Hindman routed the foot soldiers there, capturing guns and colors on the run, Wilder brought his mounted troops in hard on the rebel flank and opened fire with his repeaters. That tore it. The southernmost gray brigade lost its momentum, then collapsed in a rush as frantic as any on the other side, falling back all the way to the LaFayette Road and beyond. On the alert for some such reverse, however, Longstreet promptly threw in a brigade from Preston's reserve division, restored the line with the help of the rallied brigade, and forced the mounted bluecoats westward in the wake of their companions, who had not paused to take advantage of this respite, but had used it rather to increase their lead in the race for McFarland's Gap. Struck by an exploding shell, the Glenn house was afire by now, burning briskly under the noonday sun, with no sign of Rosecrans or his staff. Hindman called a halt, put his cannoneers to work shelling the throng of fugitives to the north and west on the Dry Valley Road, and began to reckon the fruits of his triumph, which were rich. He had taken 17 guns, ten of them abandoned, 1100 prisoners, including three full colonels, 1400 small arms, together with 165,000 rounds of ammunition, and five stands of colors, all within less than an hour and against a force considerably larger than his own.

Law and Kershaw had made similar gains, along with the infliction of a similar disruption, against much stiffer resistance by the defenders of the Union center. Watching Johnson's cheering soldiers hurdle the unmanned breastworks in their front, Law saw that they were taking cruel punishment from the bluecoats on their northern flank as they poured through the gap; so with soldierly instinct he obliqued his three brigades to the right, intending to accomplish a double purpose, first of relieving the pressure on Johnson, by drawing at least a part of the fire, and then of widening the gap by dislodging Brannan, whose own flank had been exposed by Wood's departure. Both of these objectives were attained in rapid order. Turning from the breakthrough on their right to meet this sudden menace to their front, the Federals divided their fire and wavered in the face of what seemed to them a limited choice of falling back or being ground between two rebel millstones. They chose the former course, and chose it with an individual urgency in direct ratio to each regiment's proximity to the threatened flank. Brannan's line swung gatelike, hinged on its left at the juncture with Reynolds, who held firm despite a renewal of Stewart's attack. Now it was Law's troops who were hurdling unmanned breastworks. Moreover, just as Johnson had found one of Wood's brigades defenseless in his path, so now did Law find one of Van Cleve's in that predicament as a result of having been delayed in setting off on its march to reinforce Thomas. It too was struck and shattered, quite as abruptly as the other had been: except that this time there was retribution. Hearing the uproar in its rear, which signified the destruction of its companion brigade, Wood's middle brigade was halted by its commander, Colonel Charles G. Harker, New Jersey-born, only five years out of West Point, and at twenty-five a veteran of all the western battles from Shiloh on. He faced his men about and launched a savage counterattack, not at Johnson, who had pressed on westward out of reach, but at Law, who had just knocked Brannan's gate ajar and shattered Van Cleve's sitting-duck brigade. Boldness paid off for the youthful colonel. Not only was Law stopped in his tracks by Harker's unexpected lunge, but the Texas brigade on the open flank was driven rearward in what for a time had the makings of a large-scale repulse.

Returning from his hurried conference with Johnson, midway of that general's exuberant advance, Hood arrived to find his old brigade in full retreat. This was a rare sight at any time, despite the reverse that had ended its brief penetration of the enemy line the day before, but it was particularly unwelcome in this apparent hour of victory. Blond and gigantic, though his useless arm prevented him from gesturing with his sword by way of emphasis, he rode among the fleeing Texans, exhorting them to stand their ground. They stopped in time to catch him as he toppled from the saddle, shot through the upper thigh by a rifle bullet that shattered the bone and necessitated a field amputation that would leave him barely enough of a stump to accommodate an artificial leg. As he fell he muttered incongruously, repeating in shock what he had said a few minutes ago to Johnson: "Go ahead, and keep ahead of everything." These were thought at the time to be his dying words, a fitting valedictory to battle — such wounds were all too often fatal — but that was not to be the case, and besides he had the satisfaction, as he was being taken away on a stretcher, of knowing that the line had been restored by Kershaw. Bringing up his two brigades at the critical moment of the corps commander's fall, the South Carolinian not only stemmed the incipient rout; he also resumed the advance, driving the resurgent bluecoats west and north with the help of the rallied Texans, who were eager now to get revenge for what had been done to them and their beloved Hood.

At this point, some time after noon, Longstreet rode up from the south, where he had repaired a similar reverse by sending in one of Preston's brigades to shore up Hindman's collapsed flank, and expressed great satisfaction at finding that all three elements of his clenched-fist blow — Hindman on the left, Johnson in the center, and Law and Kershaw on the right — had succeeded admirably, so far, in fulfilling his prediction that "we would of course whip and drive [the Yankees] from the field." Up to now, this only applied to about one third of the blue army, including two complete divisions and portions of three others, but Old Peter believed he had solved the problem of how best to press the issue to its desired conclusion: "As our right wing had failed of the progress anticipated, and had become fixed by the firm holding of the enemy's left, we could find no practicable field for our work except by a change of the order of battle from [a] wheel to the left, to a swing to the right." Instead of pivoting on Preston, as originally intended, he proposed to pivot on Stewart, in the opposite direction. In other words, Bragg's plan was not only to be abandoned; it was to be reversed. Pursuit of the remnant of the Union right, in flight for McFarland's Gap across the way, could be left to Wheeler, whose troopers, after exchanging shots all morning with enemy vedettes across the creek below Lee & Gordon's, had just forced a crossing at Glass's Mill and driven the Federal horsemen southward, away from the battle which was then approaching its climax three miles north. Couriers were sent at once to have him take up the chase of the fugitives on the Dry Valley Road, which passed through nearby Crawfish Springs, while the gray infantry turned sharp right to complete — with the aid of Polk's wing, which would have little to do but keep up the pressure it had been applying for better than three hours now, although without conspicuous success — the destruction of the remaining two thirds of the blue army. Law and Kershaw had faced in that direction already, drawn by the retirement of Brannan's right, but instructions had to be sent to Johnson and Hindman, as well as to Preston, who was still holding the abandoned pivot, to form their three divisions on the left of Law and Kershaw, along a new east-west line from which Longstreet intended to launch one last clenched-fist blow that would result in a knockout victory over an adversary who presumably was groggy from the effects of the punch just landed in his midriff.

However desirable it might have been, there was no question of an immediate jump-off. Preparations involving a right-angle variation in the direction of attack for an entire wing of the army, as well as changes in the posting of practically all of the elements that composed it, would of course take time, since they would require not only a great deal of shifting of units, large and small, over considerable distances — Preston, the extreme example, had nearly three miles to go before his troops would be in position — but also a prerequisite restoration of control within the five divisions themselves, most of which had been severely disorganized by the mingling of regiments and brigades in the course of their furious breakthrough and their long advance over difficult terrain.

Besides, Old Peter had never been one to begrudge time spent in preparation for the delivery of an assault, particularly in a situation such as the one that now obtained, with a good six hours of daylight still remaining and a single, well-co-ordinated effort being counted on to accomplish the objective. Orders had to be drawn up and distributed before they could be obeyed, and limber chests and cartridge boxes had to be refilled. Nor did he believe in neglecting the inner man; stomachs needed refilling, too, and that included his own. Before leaving on a tour of inspection, he directed that a lunch be spread for him to eat on his return. Dodging snipers, he reconnoitered the new defensive line the Federals had established, perpendicular to their old one along the LaFayette Road, along the irregular slopes of an eastern spur of Missionary Ridge; Snodgrass Hill was its name, according to Bushrod Johnson, whom he encountered in the course of his ride along the front. The Tennessean pointed out what he believed was "the key of the battle," a point where the bluecoats clustered thickly on the wooded slope ahead. Longstreet looked at it carefully. "It was a key, but a rough one," he said later. For the present, he instructed Buckner to establish a twelve-gun battery at the junction of the two wings, explaining that this would give him the advantage of enfilade fire down both segments of the Union line: the old one extending north, which had resisted Polk's attacks all day, and the new one extending west, which he himself was about to test for the first time. Now as before, he seemed to have little doubt as to the outcome. "They have fought their last man, and *he* is running," he said jovially, despite the evidence he had just seen to the contrary, when he returned to headquarters and sat down to his lunch of Nassau bacon and Georgia sweet potatoes. The former was an all-too-familiar item on the diet of all Confederates, East and West; "nausea bacon," it was sometimes called; but not the latter — anyhow not in the theater in which Old Peter had done all his fighting up to now. "We were not accustomed to potatoes of any kind in Virginia," he would remark more than thirty years later, still remembering the meal, "and thought we had a luxury."

There were two interruptions, both of them drastic though only the first was violent. It came in the form of a shell that burst in the woods nearby, one of whose jagged splinters ripped through a book a mounted courier was reading and struck a staff colonel, knocking him from his place at the table and to the ground, where he lay gasping as if in the throes of death. Startled, his fellow staffers leaped up to staunch the expected flow of blood, but they could not find the wound. Reacting with his usual calm, Longstreet saw that the gasping was caused by a large bite of sweet potato, which had become lodged in the colonel's windpipe when the iron fragment grazed him, and "suggested that it would be well to first relieve him of the potato and give him a chance to breathe. This done, he revived," the general recalled; "his breath came freer, and he was soon on his feet." That was the first interruption. The second came soon after the other officers rejoined their chief at the table, and if it was less violent it was also a good deal more alarming in the end. It came in the form of a message from Bragg, from whom the commander of the left wing had heard nothing since the night before, requesting his attendance at a conference a short distance in rear of the new mile-long line that was being formed in the woods to the west of the LaFayette Road. Longstreet promptly rode to meet him amid the wreckage of what had been the Union right, and after giving him a brief description of the rout that had resulted in the capture of some forty guns, together with thousands of small arms and prisoners and no less than two square miles of ground, explained his decision to wheel right instead of left, as originally instructed, in order to complete the destruction of what remained of the blue army.

Bragg did not seem to share his lieutenant's enthusiasm, and when the latter went on to suggest that the left wing be reinforced from the right, which would have little more to do than hold its ground once the attack was resumed on the south, the North Carolinian broke in testily: "There is not a man in the right wing who has any fight in him." Taken aback, Longstreet at last saw what the trouble was. Bragg was miffed because his design for herding the bluecoats into McLemore's Cove had gone astray; or as the Georgian later put it, "He was disturbed by the failure of his plan and the severe repulse of his right wing, and was little prepared to hear suggestions from subordinates for other moves or progressive work." In other words, if he could not win in just the way he wanted, he did not care about winning at all, or anyhow he wanted no personal share in such a victory. So at any rate it seemed. This fairly incredible impression was strengthened, moreover, by the manner in which Bragg brought the conference to a close. "If anything happens, communicate with me at Reed's Bridge," he said curtly, and he turned his horse and rode in that direction, which would place him well in rear of the stalled right, as far as possible from the scene of the critical attack about to be launched by Longstreet on the left.

Old Peter scarcely knew what to make of his chief's reaction. "From accounts of his former operations, I was prepared for halting work," he afterwards wrote, understating the case in an attempt to bring in a touch of humor that was altogether lacking at the time, "but this, when the battle was at its tide and in partial success, was a little surprising." However, as he returned to his new-drawn line to give the signal that would launch the assault designed to complete his half-won triumph, he soon recovered his aplomb, if not his accustomed heartiness. "There was nothing for the left wing to do but work along as best it could," he said.

Thus Bragg, in effect, removed himself from management of the battle, but only after his opponent had removed himself, in fact and person, not only from the battle but also from the field on which it was being fought. Whether out of petulance or panic, each of the two leaders reacted in accordance with his nature and his lights, for while the southern commander appeared to doubt that the contest was half won, Rosecrans had not seemed to question the evidence that it was considerably more than half lost. Not that he was a coward: Rich Mountain, Iuka, Corinth, and above all Stones River were sufficient refutation of the charge, and moreover his gloomy assessment was shared by those around him. With the exception of Lytle, whose sudden death was taken as confirmation of the majority opinion, no one with stars on his shoulders and a close-up look at the proportions of the rebel breakthrough failed to share the abrupt and general conviction that all was lost. Not only the army commander, but also his chief of staff, two of his three corps commanders, and four of his ten division commanders — in short, every man in charge of anything larger than a brigade on that quarter of the field — agreed that in the present instance, with the choice narrowed to flight or death or capture, discretion was the better part of valor. Practically of one accord, they all turned tail and ran and their troops ran with them, flecks of foam on the blue stream rushing northward up the Dry Valley Road and westward through McFarland's Gap, eager to put the bulletproof mass of Missionary Ridge between themselves and their screaming gray pursuers.

Soon after getting off the order to Wood, Rosecrans had ridden to the right, accompanied by Dana and Garfield and several other members of his staff, intending to hurry the sidling movement that would thicken the thinned center. He was sitting his horse directly in rear of Davis, whose division was in motion, when Longstreet's attack exploded dead ahead and to the immediate left front. Dana, who was badly in need of sleep, had dismounted for a nap in the grass; the first he knew of the impending breakthrough was when he was awakened by what he afterwards called "the most infernal noise I ever heard." Startled — "Never in any battle had I witnessed such a discharge of cannon and musketry" — he looked up and saw something that alarmed him even more. Old Rosy was crossing himself. "Hello!" he thought. "If the general is crossing himself, we are in a desperate situation." Sure enough, when he looked around he "saw our lines break and melt away like leaves before the wind.... The whole right of the army had apparently been routed." Rosecrans by then had reached the same conclusion, for he turned to his staff and said in a voice surprisingly calm amid the confusion of the headlong rush which Dana would compare to melting leaves: "If you care to live any longer, get away from here." His advice was so quickly taken that Dana did not even attempt a description of the dispersal or employ a single additional metaphor, mixed or otherwise. He simply remarked that "the headquarters around me disappeared."

Others "disappeared" as rapidly, even though they were out of earshot of their chief's advice. McCook's third great battle was also his third rout, and the greatest of the three. Like Davis and Sheridan, he made a brief attempt to stem the tide, then took off rearward, a leader in the race for safety, and those of his men who had not already bolted were quick to follow his example. Crittenden, too, was a part of the crush, but strictly on an individual basis. He had no troops left under him anyhow, the last of his three divisions having been detached to Thomas by midmorning, though Van Cleve himself was swept from the field with the remnant of the brigade that was wrecked by Law. Similarly, Negley became a fugitive when he led his rear brigade off on a tangent, then found his way to the left blocked by Johnson's mile-deep penetration of the center. A few among the responsible commanders, such as Wilder, maintained control of their units, but they were the exception. "Many of the officers of all ranks," according to another Indiana colonel, "showed by their wild commands and still wilder actions that they had completely lost their heads and were as badly demoralized as the private soldiers."

One among the exceptions was a young officer from McCook's staff, who managed to skirt the confusion and get through to Thomas on the left. The Virginian told him to return the way he had come and bring up Davis and Sheridan to support his dangling right. He made it back to the Dry Valley Road, and as he rode westward alongside it — for the road itself was jammed with fugitives crowding it shoulder-to-shoulder and raising a waist-high cloud of dust — he appealed to various officers in the fleeing column, but to small avail. Although the rebel pursuit had broken off by now, they either would not believe him when he said so, or else they could not see in this any reason for slowing the pace of their retreat. "See Jeff, Colonel," they told him, or "See Phil." Appeals to the men themselves were even less successful. "We'll talk to you, my son, when we get to the Ohio River!" one veteran replied, much to the amusement of his fellow trudgers. Finally, in McFarland's Gap, the young staffer overtook Davis and Sheridan, and though the former expressed a doubtful willingness to give the thing a try, the latter wanted nothing further to do with the mismanaged contest he had just put behind him. "He had lost faith," the colonel observed as he pushed on to gain the head of the column, up toward Rossville.

There where the road forked, one branch leading northwest to Chattanooga, the other east through Rossville Gap, then south to the field on whose opposite flank the scramble had begun — the distance in each case was about four miles — Rosecrans and the remnant of his staff drew rein to breathe their horses. By now the battle racket had died down, screened by the loom of Missionary Ridge, and though by dismounting and putting their ears to the ground they could hear the rattle of small arms, which signified that Thomas was still in action with at least a part of his command, the lack of any rumble from his guns seemed to indicate that the left wing had not fared much better than the right. If this was so, the thing to do was establish a straggler line on the outskirts of Chattanooga, where the two sundered portions of the army could be reunited and rallied for a last-ditch stand with the deep-running Tennessee River at its back. For his own part, Old Rosy was determined to return to the field and share with whatever troops were left the final stages of their withdrawal, leaving to his chief of staff the task of bringing the fugitives to a halt and putting them into a new defensive position before the gray wave of attackers swept over them again. However, when he turned to Garfield and began to tell him all that would have to be done — the selection of proper ground, the assignment of units to their places in line, the opening of new channels of supply and communication, and much else — the chief of staff, confused by the complexity of what he termed "the great responsibility," made a suggestion: "I can go to General Thomas and report the situation to you much better than I can give those orders." Rosecrans thought this over briefly, then reluctantly agreed. "Well," he said, "go and tell General Thomas my precautions to hold the Dry Valley Road and secure our commissary stores and artillery. [Tell him] to report the situation to me and to use his discretion as to continuing the fight on the ground we occupy at the close of the afternoon or retiring to a position in the rear near Rossville."

So while Garfield set out eastward on a ride that would take him in time to the White House — though not for long; the assassin's bullet would find him before he had been four months in office — Rosecrans took the left-hand fork that led to Chattanooga. But now the shock set in. The nearer he drew to the city the more depressed he became, as if some sort of ratio obtained between his distance from the battlefield and his realization of the enormity of his position as a commander who had deserted his army in its bloodiest hour of crisis. When he pulled rein at last, about 3.30, in front of the three-story residence where departmental headquarters had been established eleven days ago, he was so exhausted in body and broken in spirit that he had to be assisted to dismount. "The officers who helped him into the house did not soon forget the terrible look of the brave man, stunned by sudden calamity," an observer remarked, and added: "In later years I used occasionally to meet Rosecrans, and always felt that I could see the shadow of Chickamauga upon his noble face."

Dana arrived immediately behind him, having become separated from the others in what he called "the helter-skelter of the rear." That he too was much depressed by what he had seen, though his depression took a different form, was obvious from the wire he got off to Stanton at 4 o'clock, as soon as he had had time to catch his breath. "My report today is of deplorable importance," he informed the Secretary. "Chickamauga is as fatal a name in our history as Bull Run." Still badly shaken, he described the onslaught of the rebels, which was unlike anything he had seen at Vicksburg, his one previous experience of war. "They came through with resistless impulse, composed of brigades formed in divisions. Before them our soldiers turned and fled. It was wholesale panic. Vain were all attempts to rally them." He was as uncertain of what would happen next as he was of the army's losses up to now, but he ventured a guess or two in both directions. "Davis and Sheridan are said to be coming off at the head of a couple of regiments in order, and Wilder's brigade marches out unbroken. Thomas, too, is coming down the Rossville road with an organized command, but all the rest is confusion. Our wounded are all left behind, some 6000 in number. We have lost heavily in killed today. The total of our killed, wounded, and prisoners can hardly be less than 20,000, and may be much more.... Enemy not yet arrived before Chattanooga. Preparations making to resist his entrance for a time."

★ ★ ★

Some of this was useful to the Washington authorities as an estimate of the situation resulting from the sudden turn of fortune — surprisingly so, in light of the fact that it amounted to little more than guesswork by a rattled nonprofessional who had seen only a portion of the field — but much of it was about as inaccurate as might have been expected. This last applied in particular to the reference to Thomas. Not only was he not "coming down the Rossville road," as Dana claimed, but even as the telegrapher clicked away at the doleful message composed in haste and panic, the Virginian was fighting hard, resisting the combined assaults of both Confederate wings in a climactic struggle to maintain the integrity of the position he had held all morning against one. In the end — that is, before nightfall — his skill and determination in continuing this odds-on fight with what remained of the blue force after its commander had fled with a full third of the troops who had composed it at the outset, would win him the name by which he would be known thereafter: "The Rock of Chickamauga."

Indeed, there was much about him that was rocklike, not alone in the sense of being "the right kind of man to tie to," but also in appearance, especially when viewed from up close. According to a soldier observer, his "full rounded, powerful form," six feet in height and well over two hundred pounds in weight, "gradually expands upon you, as a mountain which you approach." Moreover, in addition to sheer bulk, he gave an impression of doggedness and imperturbability. "This army doesn't retreat," he had said in a similar crisis at Stones River, despite the evidence to the contrary, and it was obvious from his manner that the same thing applied here, so far at least as concerned the two thirds of the army still on the field and in his charge. Brannan's gatelike swing had ended on the rising ground in his left rear; there he posted his division, extending his right westward along the convenient eastern spur of Mis-

Riot and Resurgence [749]

sionary Ridge. Single brigades from the variously shattered and scattered commands of Wood, Van Cleve, and Negley, combined with those of Brannan, provided the equivalent of two divisions for the defense of this new line, and Thomas reinforced it further by detaching one brigade each from Johnson and Palmer, who stood at the bulging center of the north-south line confronting Polk. The east-west position was one of great natural strength, heavily wooded and uphill for attackers, but whether or not it could be held against as savage a fighter as Longstreet would depend in the final analysis on the troops who occupied it.

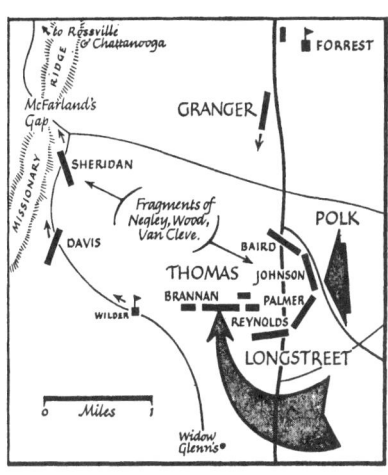

Thoroughly aware of this, as he also was of the fact that they had already backpedaled once today under pressure from the same gray veterans who were massing now for a follow-up assault, Thomas moved among them in an attempt to stiffen their resolution for what he knew was coming. "This hill must be held and I trust you to do it," he told Harker, who replied: "We will hold it or die here." Thomas rode on, and presently came to one of Harker's regimental commanders, Colonel Emerson Opdycke. "This point must be held," he told him. The Ohio colonel agreed. "We will hold this ground," he said, "or go to heaven from it." Opdycke's men nodded approval of his words, but whether they really meant it remained to be seen.

They meant it. About 2 o'clock, while Longstreet was returning from his unprofitable conference with Bragg, Kershaw assaulted the left of the new Federal position with the demidivision composed of his own South Carolina brigade and Barksdale's Mississippians, now under Brigadier General Ben G. Humphreys. "Ranks followed ranks in close order, moving briskly and bravely against us," a defender later wrote. These were the men who had taken the Wheat Field and the Peach Orchard, eighty days ago at Gettysburg, and they were determined to do as well this afternoon at Chickamauga. They did not; not yet, at any rate. Harker's troops, together with those in Brannan's left brigade and the brigade from Palmer, under Brigadier General William Hazen, fired their rifles with such steadiness and precision that the gray ranks faltered, withered, and fell back. Kershaw, who had thought one hard rap would cause the bluecoats to continue their withdrawal, was unwilling to admit that this had been disproved so quickly. After a pause for realignment he again sent his two brigades forward against the Union there. The result was the same. They surged up the slope, then fell back down it, having taken losses quite as heavy as before. Still unconvinced, he tried a third assault, and suffered a third repulse. Such uphill work was about as exhausting as it was bloody. One regimental commander reported that his men were "panting like dogs tired out in the chase." In the course of the last charge, he would recall, he had seen a fifteen-year-old soldier lagging behind and weeping, and when he told him that this was no time for hanging back out of fear, the boy explained that his trouble was not fright but exasperation. "That aint it, Colonel," he wailed between sobs. "I'm so damned tired I can't keep up with my company." Convinced at last, and perceiving that even his full-grown men were winded, Kershaw called a halt at the base of the hill to watch for some sign that the Federals were weakening their left to meet the attack that was being launched by now against their right by Johnson and Hindman, off at the far end of the line.

Thomas might well have weakened his embattled left to reinforce his threatened right, outnumbered and overlapped as it was by the two butternut divisions being massed in the woods below, except that he received unexpected help at just this critical juncture. All morning, up near McAfee's Church, which was two miles east of Rossville and about twice that distance from the hilly spur where Brannan staged his rally, Gordon Granger had fretted because his one-division Reserve Corps, charged with guarding the Rossville Gap in case it was needed as an escape hatch, was being kept from the battle he could hear raging to the south. About 11 o'clock — an hour and a half after Polk began his delayed attack and shortly before Longstreet scored the breakthrough that threw Davis and Sheridan off the field and swung Brannan out of his place in the disintegrating center of the Union line — he and his chief of staff climbed a haystack in an attempt to see something of what was going on. All they saw, far down the LaFayette Road, was a boiling cloud of dust and smoke with the fitful yellow flash of batteries mixed in at its base, but Granger soon arrived at a decision. "I am going to Thomas, orders or no orders!" he declared, snapping his glasses back in their case. The staffer was more cautious. "And if you go," he warned, "it may bring disaster to the army and you to a court martial." Granger was a career man, West Point '45, and normally an avoider of such risks; but not now. "There's nothing in our front but ragtag, bobtail cavalry," he said. "Don't you see Bragg is piling his whole army on Thomas? I am going to his assistance." And with that he climbed down off the haystack and ordered Steedman to prepare to march at once with two of his brigades, leaving the third behind to continue holding the Rossville escape hatch open in the event of a collapse by the main body, which he would soon be joining, four miles south.

Within half an hour the march was under way. Granger's remark that Bragg was "piling his whole army on Thomas" had been in error at the time he made it; Longstreet had not yet gone in. But now that the remaining half of the Confederate force had been committed, with the resultant abolition of the Federal right, the statement was in the rapid process of becoming quite literally true; so that Granger's decision, though based in part on an erroneous assumption, turned out to be militarily sound; Thomas was indeed in need of help, and it was fortunate for him that Granger began his four-mile march before the need existed, let alone before it became acute. Even so, there were delays. About noon, a mile down the LaFayette Road, the lead brigade was taken under fire by a pair of batteries in position on the flank. Steedman was obliged to go from column of march into line of battle, facing east to meet this threat from what turned out to be a sizable detachment of Forrest's men. Blue skirmishers, moving against the guns, caused the rebel troopers to give ground; yet when the skirmishers returned the graybacks followed, resuming their harassing tactics. Finally, in exasperation — for he was a short-tempered man at best — Granger sent for the third brigade to come down from McAfee's Church and hold the troublesome horsemen off while he took up his march, southwest now across the fields and through the woods in order to approach the nearly beleaguered Thomas from the rear. A mile short of the blue flank the second delay occurred; but it was brief, consisting of nothing more than a short wait for part of Negley's division to get out of the way, which it soon did, being hard on the go for Rossville and deliverance from chaos. The two columns passed each other, one headed into and the other out of the battle, and Granger rode ahead to report that his two brigades were close at hand.

He was a hard-mannered regular, originally from upper New York State, a veteran of Mexico and the Indian wars, shaggy in looks, brusque in speech, and not much liked — either by his troops, who resented a strictness that sometimes prescribed horsewhipping for minor camp offenses, or by his fellow officers, who found him uncongenial — but Thomas had seldom been as glad to see anyone as he was to see Granger, whom he greeted with a handshake and a smile that was all the broader because he had thought the column approaching his rear was hostile. That would indeed have been the final straw; for Kershaw's attack was in full career on his left by now, and Hindman and Johnson were massing their divisions for an advance on the right, which they overlapped. When they began to move forward, out of the woods and onto an intervening ridge, Granger saw the problem at a glance. "Those men must be driven back," he said. Thomas agreed. "Can you do it?" he asked. Granger nodded grimly. "Yes," he said. "My men are fresh, and they are just the fellows for that work. They are raw troops and they don't know any better than to charge up there."

Whether the basis for their conduct was ignorance, sheer heroism, or a combination of both, the men of the reserve corps were indeed "the fellows for that work." Steedman, who was forty-seven, Pennsylvania born, a former printer, Texas revolutionist, and Ohio legislator — "a great, hearty man, broad-breasted [and] broad-shouldered," whose face, according to an admirer, was "written all over with sturdy sense and stout courage" — brought them up on the double and committed them with no more delay that it took to tell a staff officer to see that his name was spelled correctly in the obituaries. Leading the charge on horseback, he saw his green troops waver at their first sight of the enemy up ahead; whereupon he grabbed the regimental colors from an Illinois bearer alongside him and waved the rippling silk to draw their attention. "Go back, boys, go back," he roared, "but the flag can't go with you!" They did not go back; they went forward, still with Steedman in the lead, but now on foot; for the rippling blue of the colors had attracted the attention of the rebels, too, with the result that his horse had been shot from under him. Badly shaken by the fall, the general got up and hobbled forward, still brandishing the flag and roaring, "Follow me!" Ahead, the graybacks gave ground before such fury and determination, then rallied and counterattacked. However, the bluecoats had the ridge by then and held it, though at the cost of losing one fifth of their number within their first twenty minutes of combat. And that was only the beginning; they would lose as many more in the next three hours. In fact, of the 3700 men in the two brigades, nearly half — 1788 — would be casualties by sundown.

Steep though the price was, the gain was great. Not only had they shored up and prolonged Brannan's overlapped western flank; they also had brought with them from McAfee's Church a hard-hitting battery of three-inch rifles, which added the weight of their metal to the blue resistance, and no less than 95,000 rounds of small-arms ammunition. This last was in particular demand, because the army's main ordnance supply train had been involved in McCook's collapse and flight, and Thomas's soldiers were burning up what they had on hand at a fearful rate; an Ohio regiment of 535 men, for example, would expend nearly 45,000 rounds of rifle ammunition before the day was over. In the face of such fiery opposition — an average expenditure of better than 80 rounds per man, including casualties — it was no wonder that Longstreet pronounced Johnson's "key of the battle," by which the Tennessean meant the hilly spur along whose slopes the east-west Union line was drawn, "a rough one."

Returning from his conference with the disgruntled Bragg, Old Peter arrived to find Kershaw checked on the right and Johnson and Hindman just going in on the left. Like them, he had thought it probable that a determined nudge would persuade the bluecoats to continue their retreat, but when the second attack was repulsed — disclosing, as he said later, that the defenders were "full of fight, even to the aggressive" — he knew he was in for trouble. Hindman, who had been struck in the neck by a fragment of shell but declined to quit the field, agreed with this revised assessment, subsequently reporting that while he "never saw Confederate soldiers fight better," he had "never known Federal troops to fight so well." However, Longstreet wasted no time on regret that Kershaw had jumped the gun, committing his two brigades before the six at the far end of the line were ready, or that Johnson, conversely, had not swept around the open flank before Granger arrived to brace it. Instead, he sent word for them to keep up the pressure on the two extremities while Preston was massing his three brigades, only one of which had seen any action so far in the battle, for an assault on the blue center. Then at last, with Law coming in on Kershaw's left and Stewart on his right, the second of Old Peter's clenched-fist blows would dispose of what had survived the devastation of the first.

Shortly before 4 o'clock, Preston — "genial, gallant, lovable William Preston," Longstreet called the forty-six-year-old Kentuckian, whom he met for the first time this afternoon — got his troops in position, two brigades advanced in echelon and one held in reserve, and sent them forward against the center of Brannan's line. By now the defenders had improvised breastworks from stones and fallen trees, anything at all that would stop a bullet, so that when the attackers emerged from the woods at the foot of the slope they were met by heavy, well-aimed fire directed confidently at them from the crest ahead. They did not stop or attempt to return this fire until they were within eighty yards of the flame-stabbed smoke that obscured the enemy position. There they halted, exposed as they were, and engaged in a deadly exchange of volleys with the sheltered bluecoats for nearly an hour. "Only new troops could accomplish such a wonderful feat," a general who opposed them declared; which perhaps was true (Hood's Texans, for example, prided themselves on knowing when to stand and when to run, and in point of fact had chosen the latter course twice already on this same field, today and yesterday) except that it left out of account the determined example of the officers who led them. The two brigades were commanded by a pair of Alabamians, Brigadier General Archibald Gracie and Colonel John H. Kelly, both of whom had had considerable experience under fire. New York born — he had distinguished kinsmen in the Union ranks — Gracie was thirty, a graduate of Heidelberg and West Point and a merchant in Mobile before secession returned him to the profession for which he had been trained, while Kelly was only twenty-three, having left West Point as a cadet to go with his native state when the war began. Both had risen fast and far, but strictly on ability, beginning respectively as an infantry captain and an artillery lieutenant; Kelly, who had soldiers under him better than twice his age, had commanded a battalion at Shiloh, a regiment at Perryville and Murfreesboro, and now a brigade at Chickamauga, which would earn him a wreath for his three stars and make him the youngest general in the army. So led, Preston's two committed brigades stood their ground and took their punishment, losing 1054 of their 2879 effectives in the process, but fixing the Federals in position while the divisions on their left and right were heartened by their example and Breckinridge finally got the twelve-gun battery posted near the junction of the two wings. Even Polk, across the way, came alive at last in response to the sustained uproar of the volleys Gracie's and Kelly's men were exchanging with their opponents, and sent word for his division commanders to match the pressure, there on the east, that Longstreet was exerting from the south.

No one knew better than Thomas, wedged as it were between anvil and sledge, that once the Confederates achieved this concert of action, east and south, the issue could not long remain in doubt. Moreover, though the two armies had begun the day with equal numbers and though each would suffer casualties of about one third its total strength before the battle ended, another third of the blue army had fled the field by early afternoon, which left Thomas with only about one third of the original Union force, as compared to Bragg's two thirds; in short, after succeeding by default to the command, the Virginian faced odds of roughly two to one, with the additional disadvantage of being pressed from two directions, in each of which the enemy strength was about equal to both Federal wings combined. He knew that under these circumstances he would have to withdraw eventually, but he hoped to prolong the struggle until he could do so under cover of darkness. As late as 4 o'clock, when Garfield arrived with his absent chief's suggestion for "retiring to a position in the rear," Thomas declined even to consider a retreat by daylight. "It will ruin the army to withdraw it now," he said. "This position must be held until night." Before another hour had passed, however, with Preston clawing at him from below and the other rebel divisions of both wings increasing the tempo of their action and inching closer to his lines, he saw that to attempt a much longer delay would be to risk a breakthrough which would be even more costly to him than a daylight disengagement, dangerous though such a maneuver was said to be in all the tactics manuals. Accordingly, about 5 o'clock, while the sun was still an hour high, he settled on a plan for withdrawal, first on the left, where the pressure was less severe, and then on the right. The divisions along the north-south line would pull out in reverse order, first Reynolds, then Palmer, then Johnson, each passing in rear of the unit on its left; Baird would be last and would serve as rear guard on the march to McFarland's Gap and Rossville, where a new line of battle would be formed to discourage pursuit beyond that point. Similarly, Brannan and Steedman, together with the brigades that had been used to reinforce them, would fall back in sequence from the east-west line, following the same route to comparative safety.

Or so at any rate Thomas hoped, knowing full well that the execution of the orders designed to bring this about would be difficult at best.

Reynolds began the movement at 5.30, and for the next two hours, from broad daylight into darkness, the battle raged with a new intensity, a new sense of urgency, as various units of both armies, obliged by the attendant confusion to operate more or less on their own, attempted on the one hand to achieve, and on the other to forestall, deliverance from slaughter. Thomas had improvised well, but in a situation so fluid that orders no longer applied by the time they were issued, let alone received, success or failure depended almost entirely on the naked valor of his infantry and the ability of his subordinate commanders to maintain control of troops who, after all, were running for their lives. In this regard, Reynolds was outstanding. Marching north on the LaFayette Road, in rear of the other three divisions, he reached the extreme left to find that Liddell had outflanked Baird and was about to strike the Union line end-on. Instead of turning west for McFarland's Gap, as ordered, the Kentucky-born Hoosier launched a savage counterattack that drove the would-be flankers back and kept open the path of retreat for the other three divisions, who were themselves under mounting pressure from Breckinridge and Cleburne. Though they lost heavily in the withdrawal, being obliged to abandon their wounded along with their dead, the four divisions managed to effect a disengagement by moving rapidly westward, outstripping their pursuers in the race for Missionary Ridge, behind which the sun had set by now. Brannan and Steedman had a harder time of it: particularly the former, who was required to hold his ground while the latter began his withdrawal in the wake of the left-wing divisions which had passed across his rear. When Steedman pulled back, Hindman's and Johnson's men boiled over the ridge in close pursuit, and Preston committed his third brigade, which plunged through the newly opened breach and then turned right to fall on Brannan's unprotected flank. Three regiments were captured in one swoop, two from Michigan and one from Ohio, and the battle abruptly disintegrated, here on the right as it had on the left, into a race. That Brannan's survivors won it was due in large part to a pair of Indiana regiments from Reynolds' division. Coming upon a broken-down ammunition wagon, abandoned by a teamster who had fled with his mules in the earlier rout, the Hoosiers filled their empty cartridge boxes and countermarched, under direct orders from Thomas himself, to serve as rear guard and cover the final stage of the retreat. This they did, checking the butternut pursuers with volleys fired blind in the gathering darkness; after which they once more faced about and took up their westward march, the last blue troops to leave the field.

In some ways, though, the hardest part of the battle still lay before them; for they marched now, down the dark valley from McFarland's Gap to Rossville, with the taste of defeat bitter in their mouths and a great weariness in their limbs. Perryville and Stones River had been bad enough, but the fact that they had remained in control of both those fields when the smoke lifted had given their generals and journalists the basis for a claim to victory. Not so here. This was absolute, unarguable defeat, and as such it was depressing beyond anything they had ever known. "Weary, worn, tired and hungry," a captain in a veteran regiment later wrote, "we sullenly dragged ourselves along, feeling a shame and disgrace that had never been experienced by the Old Sixth before." Those who fell out of the column because of wounds or exhaustion were left to their own inadequate devices by those who had the strength to keep going. Behind them, beyond the intervening ridge, they could hear the rebels celebrating their triumph with loud yells. Another officer in the retreating column, First Lieutenant Ambrose Bierce, a topographical engineer with Hazen, thought the sound "the ugliest any mortal ever heard." Presently, however, there was a stretch of road well down the valley "across which that horrible yell did not prolong itself," he added, "and through that we finally retired in profound silence and dejection, unmolested."

Back on the field of Chickamauga, their spirits lifted by the release of tension, the Confederates kept yelling, despite an almost equal physical weariness, long after their adversaries were out of earshot. As Longstreet put it, "The Army of Tennessee knew how to enjoy its first grand victory," beginning at the moment when the two wings came together, there on the reverse slopes of the hilly spur from which the Yankees had just been driven, and continuing into the night with "a tremendous swell of heroic harmony that seemed almost to lift from their roots the great trees of the forest." Harvey Hill declared years later that the cheers "were such as I had never heard before, and shall not hear again." In point of fact, along strictly practical lines, the victors had more to whoop about than anyone yet knew. Afterwards, when the field had been gleaned, Bragg would report the capture of more than 8000 prisoners, 51 guns, and 23,281 small arms, together with 2381 rounds of artillery ammunition and 135,000 rifle cartridges. The multipaged scavenger list, certified by the chief of ordnance, would include such items as 35 pounds of picket rope, 365 shoulder straps, and 3 damaged copper bugles, as well as "wagons, ambulances, and teams, medicines, hospital stores, &c., in large quantities." It was, in brief, the largest haul ever made by either side on a single field of battle. For the present, however, all the exultant graybacks knew was that they had scored a triumph of considerable proportions, and they did not delay their celebration to wait for the particulars of its scope.

Nor did others who were not there to see for themselves. After the recent and apparently interminable sequence of knee-buckling reverses, soldiers and civilians throughout the nation were elated by the news from North Georgia, which seemed to them to bear out earlier predictions that the northern armies would find what true resistance meant when they approached the southern heartland. "The effects of this great victory will be electrical," a Richmond clerk recorded in his diary. "The whole South will be filled again with patriotic fervor, and in the North there will be a corresponding depression.... Surely the Government of the United States must now see the impossibility of subjugating the Southern people, spread over such a vast expanse of territory, and the European governments ought now to interpose and put an end to this cruel waste of blood and treasure."

★ ★ ★

In war, as in love — indeed, as in all such areas of so-called human endeavor — expectation tended to outrun execution, particularly when the latter was given a head start in the race, and nowhere did this apply more lamentably, at any rate from the Richmond point of view, than in the wake of Chickamauga, probably the greatest and certainly the bloodiest of all the battles won by the South in its fight for the independence it believed to be its birthright. Harvey Hill said later that he had "never seen the Federal dead lie so thickly on the ground, save in front of the sunken wall at Fredericksburg." In point of fact, though Hill may not have seen them on his quarter of the field, the Confederate dead lay even thicker; but in any case, now that the Yankees were on the run, he and the other two lieutenant generals, commanding the two wings, were altogether in favor of a rapid and slashing pursuit of the beaten foe. Though Longstreet called a halt in the dusk that followed his second breakthrough, it was for the same purpose as the halt that had followed his first at midday; namely, to consolidate his forces for the delivery of another heavy blow. "As it was almost dark," he afterwards reported, "I ordered my line to remain as it was, ammunition boxes to be filled, stragglers to be collected, and everything [placed] in readiness for the pursuit in the morning." Polk, perhaps aware that he had done less to win the victory up to now, prepared to do more by sending out scouts to look into the possibility of continuing the slaughter of the vanished enemy. Later, when the scouts returned to report that the bluecoats had not slacked their headlong retreat, the bishop rode to headquarters and informed Bragg — whom he roused from bed, much as Old Peter had done at about the same hour the night before — "that the enemy was routed and flying precipitately from the field, and that then was the opportunity to finish the work by the capture or destruction of [Rosecrans'] army, by prompt pursuit, before he had time to reorganize or throw up defenses at Chattanooga." So an aide who rode with him testified: adding, however, that "Bragg could not be induced to look at it in that light, and refused to believe that we had won a victory."

It was true that the commanding general had received no formal notification of the outcome of the battle, but only because this had seemed to his subordinates a highly superfluous gesture. ("It did not occur to me on the night of the 20th to send Bragg word of our complete success," Longstreet explained years later. "I thought that the loud huzzas that spread over the field just at dark were a sufficient assurance and notice to anyone within five miles of us.") On the other hand, if what he wanted was an eyewitness who could testify to the behavior of the Federals after they reached the far side of Missionary Ridge — beyond which, conceivably, they might rally and lie in wait for him to commit some act of rashness — that too was available, soon after first light next morning, in the form of a Confederate private who had been captured the previous day, then escaped amid the confusion of the blue retreat, and made his way back to his outfit before dawn. When he told his captain of what he had seen across the way — for instance, that the Unionists were abandoning their wounded as they slogged northward, intent on nothing but their flight from fury — he was taken at once to repeat his story, first to his regimental and brigade commanders, then to Bragg himself. The stern-faced general heard him out, but was doubtful, if not of the soldier's capacity for accurate observation, then at any rate of his judgment on such a complicated matter. "Do you know what a retreat looks like?" he asked sharply, fixing the witness with a baleful glare. Irked by his commander's mistrust, the man replied with words that endeared him to his comrades, then and thereafter, when they were repeated, as they often were, around campfires and at future veteran gatherings. "I ought to, General," he said; "I've been with you during your whole campaign."

Whatever effect this may have had on the irascible general's disposition, a look at the field by daylight quickly convinced him that his army was in no condition for the pursuit his chief subordinates were urging him to undertake. The dead of both sides, stiffened by now in agonized postures, and the wounded, many of them with their hurts yet untended, seemed to outnumber the unhit survivors, and while this was true in the case of a dozen regiments under Longstreet — who afterwards computed his losses at 44 percent — it was of course an exaggeration in the main, proceeding from shock at the grisly scene. The fact was that the two armies had suffered a combined total of nearly 35,000 casualties, and most of them were Bragg's. Though the Federals had some 2500 more men killed and missing than the Confederates (6414, as compared to 3780) the latter had about 5000 more wounded (9756 in blue, 14,674 in gray) so that the butcher's bill, North and South, came to 16,170 and 18,454 respectively. The combined total of 34,624 was exceeded only by the three-day slaughter at Gettysburg and by the weeklong series of five battles known collectively as the Seven Days, in both of which considerably larger numbers of troops had been engaged. In all the other battles of the war so far — including Chancellorsville, which lasted one day longer and also involved about 50,000 more troops — the losses had been less than at Chickamauga, where they were greater by about 10,000 than at Shiloh, Second Manassas, or Murfreesboro, the three next bloodiest two-day confrontations. These statistics could not yet be broken down in any such manner, being as yet unknown, but they were suggested plainly enough by a tour of the field and a talk with unit commanders along the way. Nine Confederate generals had been killed or wounded, as compared to only one in the Federal ranks, and the loss of artillery horses, as a result of fighting at such close quarters, had been so heavy as to cripple that vital arm. "In one place down in the woods," a soldier wrote of a walk he took that morning, "I counted sixteen big artillery horses lying in one heap. A little way off was another heap of twelve more. And that was the way it was all through there." Without horses, Bragg could not haul his guns, and without guns he did not believe that his men could force Rossville Gap or assault the prepared defenses between there and Chattanooga. "How can I?" he replied to urgings that he press northward without delay. "Here is two-fifths of my army left on the field, and my artillery is without horses." He still felt that way about it, some weeks later, when he touched on the matter in his official report of the campaign. "Any immediate pursuit by our infantry and artillery would have been fruitless," he declared, "as it was not deemed practicable with our weak and exhausted force to assail the enemy, now more than double our numbers, behind his intrenchments."

One who did not feel that way about it, then or later, was Bedford Forrest. Early that morning, pressing forward on his own with 400 troopers, the Tennessean charged an outpost detachment of Federals who fired one volley and fled so rapidly that their lookouts had no time to desend from an observation platform they had constructed in the top of a tree on the crest of Missionary Ridge. Forrest's horse had been struck, a large artery severed in its neck, but the general staunched the spurt of blood by thrusting a finger into the bullet hole and thus gave chase. Pulling rein at last beneath the improvised tower atop the ridge, he withdrew his finger and dismounted before the animal collapsed, then summoned his prisoners down from their high perch, questioned them sharply, and climbed up to see for himself what he could see. That he could see a great deal — including the blue army, feverishly active in his front, and the gray army, immobile in his rear — was shown by a dispatch he dictated to a staff officer on the ground:

> We are in a mile of Rossville. Have been on the point of Missionary Ridge. Can see Chattanooga and everything around. The enemy's trains are leaving, going around the point of Lookout Mountain.
> The prisoners captured report two pontoons thrown across [the Tennesee River] for the purpose of retreating.
> I think they are evacuating as hard as they can go.

They are cutting timber down to obstruct our passage.
I think we ought to press forward as rapidly as possible.

The message was addressed to Polk, commander of the nearer wing, and ended with the words, "Please forward to Genl Bragg." Anticipating the response he believed this information would provoke, Forrest continued his policy of "keeping up the scare" by penetrating to within three miles of Chattanooga from the south, meanwhile shifting his guns northward along the ridge to engage the batteries posted in close defense of the town below. All this time, according to one of his troopers, the general was "almost beside himself at the delay." Finally he learned that the infantry would not be coming as he had advised; Bragg was holding it east of Missionary Ridge and near the railroad, shifting Polk to Chickamauga Station and army headquarters to Ringgold Bridge, while Longstreet remained in position to police the field and wait for McLaws, who arrived in the late afternoon with the rest of his division. Nettled by what seemed to him flagrant neglect of an opportunity gained at the cost of much suffering and bloodshed, Forrest rode back to protest in person, only to be told that the army could not move far from the railroad because of its critical lack of supplies. "General Bragg, we can get all the supplies our army needs in Chattanooga," he replied. But this too was rejected: Bragg's mind was quite made up. Forrest returned to his men, exasperated and outdone. "What does he fight battles for?" he fumed.

That was Monday. On Tuesday, unmolested even by Forrest, whose handful of troopers had been recalled, Rosecrans completed the concentration of his army within the Chattanooga defenses, and Bragg ordered the occupation of Missionary Ridge and Lookout Mountain, as well as the establishment of a line of posts across the valley that lay between them. By Wednesday, September 23, the date of the autumnal equinox, all of these abandoned points had been seized, and the Federal works, which rose and thickened hour by hour as shovels flashed along the intrenched perimeter, were under long-range fire from the surrounding heights. Three courses of action — or, rather, two of action and one of inaction — were open to the Confederates. 1.) They could attempt to turn the bluecoats out of their position by crossing the river above or below the town, thus gaining their rear and breaking their tenuous supply line. 2.) They could leave a small force to observe the enemy trapped in Chattanooga, and move with the greater part of the army against Burnside, who would then be obliged to evacuate Knoxville or fight against long odds. 3.) They could concentrate on the present investment, hoping to starve the defenders into surrender. Longstreet favored a combination of the first two — "The hunt was up and on the go," he afterwards explained, "when any move toward [the enemy's] rear was safe, and a speedy one encouraging of great results" — but Bragg, much to Old Peter's disgust and over his vigorous objections, chose the third.

This was by no means as impractical as Longstreet seemed to think. By extending his left to include the crest of Raccoon Mountain, Bragg denied his adversary use of the rail and wagon roads not only on the south but also on the immediate north bank of the Tennessee, which lay well within reach of his high-sited batteries, and thus obliged Rosecrans to haul supplies from Stevenson and Bridgeport by a roundabout and barren route, first across the bridgeless Sequatchie River, then up and over Walden's Ridge, and finally down to the steamboat landing opposite Chattanooga, a distance of some sixty tortuous miles which would become increasingly difficult when the fall rains set in and the mud deepened. Unwilling to leave the harassment entirely to the elements, Bragg on September 30, one week after getting his infantry and artillery into their interdictory positions, ordered Wheeler over the river on a raid. The diminutive Alabamian crossed next morning near Muscle Shoals with 4000 cavalry and eight guns, and on the following day he intercepted a train of 400 heavily loaded wagons at Anderson's Crossroads, deep in the Sequatchie Valley. After burning the wagons and sabering the mules, he moved north to McMinnville, then west to Shelbyville, both of which he captured, together with their supply depots, which he destroyed. By now, though, the rains had come in earnest and he was involved in a running fight with superior blue forces that converged upon him from all directions. Repulsed at Murfreesboro, he turned back south, losing four of his guns and more than a thousand of his men before he recrossed the Tennessee near Rogersville on October 9. Despite his considerable success in the execution of his mission — a Union observer afterwards declared that the disruptive and destructive strike was nearly fatal to the army besieged in Chattanooga — the cost had been high, and Wheeler did not suggest that he attempt another such raid, deep in the enemy rear. Nor did Bragg require one of him, apparently being content to watch and wait.

The fact was, he had troubles enough with his own supply lines, unmolested though they were, without concerning himself unduly about those across the way. No matter how hungry the bluecoats might be getting, down in the town, his own troops were convinced that they themselves were hungrier on the heights. "In all the history of the war," a Tennessee infantryman was to write, "I cannot remember of more privation and hardships than we went through at Missionary Ridge.... The soldiers were starved and almost naked, and covered all over with lice and camp itch and filth and dirt. The men looked sick, hollow-eyed, and heart-broken, living principally upon parched corn which had been picked out of the mud and dirt under the feet of officers' horses." There was, as usual, much bitterness over Bragg's apparent reluctance to gather the fruits of a victory they had won, but this time it was intensified by resentment of his attempts to shift the blame to other shoulders than his own. Within two days of the battle, with the army at last on the march, Polk had received a stiff note demanding an explanation of why his attack had been delayed on the morning of the 20th, and when his reply reached headquarters on the last day of September, Bragg pronounced it "unsatisfactory" and relieved the bishop of his command. Hindman received the same treatment for his conduct earlier that month at McLemore's Cove, despite his acknowledged contribution to the triumph that followed ten days later. Hill too came under fire from the army chieftain, who complained of his former lieutenant's "critical, captious, and dictatorial manner," as well as of his "want of prompt conformity to orders," and recommended to Richmond that he be suspended, like the others, from duty with the Army of Tennessee.

All three were incensed: particularly the two lieutenant generals, who in point of fact had taken care to register their protests beforehand, after a secret meeting on September 26 with Longstreet, who outranked them both. Intent on doing to Bragg what he was about to do to them — that is, accomplish his removal — they urged Old Peter to join them, in his semi-independent capacity, in complaining to Richmond of their commander's "palpable weakness and mismanagement manifested in the conduct of the military operations of this army." Polk wrote privately to his friend the President along these lines, though not in time to forestall the blow which he described as "part of [Bragg's] long-cherished purpose to avenge himself on me for the relief and support I have given him in the past.... The truth is, General Bragg has made a failure, notwithstanding the success of the battle, and he wants a scapegoat." Figuratively, but with dignity, the bishop gathered his robes about him for the train ride to Atlanta, where he was sent to await the disposition of his case. "I feel a lofty contempt for his puny effort to inflict injury upon a man who has dry-nursed him for the whole period of his connection with him, and has kept him from ruining the cause of the country by the sacrifice of its armies." So he complained in private, after the blow fell. But Longstreet had already made a stronger statement to the Secretary of War, adopting Prayer Book phraseology to add weight to his words. "Our chief has done but one thing that he ought to have done since I joined his army," Old Peter informed Seddon on the day of his meeting with Polk and Hill. "That was to order the attack upon the 20th. All other things that he has done he ought not to have done. I am convinced that nothing but the hand of God can save us or help us as long as we have our present commander."

Such was the unhappy state of affairs in the Army of Tennessee, the men hungry and disgruntled and the generals bitterly resentful, on the morrow of what Longstreet, in his letter to Richmond, called "the most complete victory of the war — except, perhaps, the first Manassas," he added, remembering past glory and gladder times.

Beyond the semicircular rim of earthworks, down in the town and off at the far end of the chain of command leading back to Washington, a scapegoat hunt was also under way. McCook and Crittenden had already been relieved, ostensibly for flight in time of danger, yet it had not escaped notice that the winner in the headlong race for safety was the man who consented to their removal. Stanton, for one, observed caustically that the two corps commanders had "made pretty good time away from the fight, but Rosecrans beat them both."

Moreover, the reverse had come in sudden and sharp contrast to expectations Old Rosy himself had aroused. "The army is in excellent condition and spirits," he had telegraphed soon after darkness ended the first day's fighting, "and by the blessing of Providence the defeat of the enemy will be total tomorrow." Lincoln did not like the sound of this, finding it reminiscent of Joe Hooker, and when he learned next evening that the army had been routed, he claimed to have foreseen such a turn of events. "Well, Rosecrans has been whipped, as I feared," he said. "I have feared it for several days. I believe I feel trouble in the air before it comes." Nor was the general's immediate reaction of a kind to encourage hope that he would make an early recovery from the setback. "We have met with a serious disaster," he notified Halleck soon after he reached Chattanooga; "extent not yet ascertained. Enemy overwhelmed us, drove our right, pierced our center, and scattered troops there." Despite his own gloom, which was heavy, Lincoln tried to lift the Ohioan's. "Be of good cheer," he wired him late that night. "We have unabated confidence in you and in your soldiers and officers. . . . We shall do our utmost to assist you. Send us your present posting." But the general, in his reply the following morning, gave no indication that he would attempt to stay in the town he had fallen back on. In fact, he expressed some doubt that he could do so, even if he tried: "Our loss is heavy and our troops worn down. . . . We have no certainty of holding our position here." Such irresolution was disturbing in a commander. What was more, when the President asked him next day to "relieve my anxiety as to the position and condition of your army," Rosecrans replied in effect that his faith was not so much in himself or his army as it was in Providence. "We are about 30,000 brave and determined men," he wired; "but our fate is in the hands of God, in whom I hope."

Lincoln soon emerged from his gloom. The important thing, as he saw it, was not that Rosecrans had been whipped at Chickamauga, but that he still held Chattanooga. As long as he did so, he could keep the Confederates out of Tennessee and also deny them use of one of their most important railroads. "If he can only maintain this position, without [doing anything] more," the President told Halleck, "the rebellion can only eke out a short and feeble existence, as an animal sometimes may with a thorn in its vitals." By now, after three days' rest and no pursuit, Rosecrans had recovered a measure of his resolution. "We hold this point, and cannot be dislodged except by very superior numbers," he wired on September 23, although he made it clear that this depended on "having all reinforcements you can send hurried up." Lincoln had been doing his best in this respect, instructing Halleck to order troops to Chattanooga from Vicksburg and Memphis, while he himself undertook to prod Burnside into marching fast from Knoxville. When Burnside replied that he was just then closing in on Jonesboro, which lay in the opposite direction, the President lost his temper. "Damn Jonesboro," he said testily, and returned to his efforts to get the ruff-whiskered general to swing west. This proved so difficult, however, that he decided in the end to leave him where he was, covering Knoxville; Rosecrans would have to be reinforced from elsewhere. And that same night, September 23, Lincoln met with Stanton, Halleck, Chase, and Seward, together with several lesser War Department officials, in an attempt to determine just where such reinforcements could be found.

Stanton, having heard that evening from Dana that the Army of the Cumberland, outnumbered, dejected, and under fire from the heights inclosing Chattanooga on the south and east, could not hold out for more than a couple of weeks unless it was promptly and substantially reinforced, had called the midnight conference to suggest a solution to the problem. Since Burnside apparently could not be budged, and since the troops ordered from Vicksburg and Memphis would have to make a slow overland march for lack of any means of transportation, the Secretary proposed that Rosecrans be sent a sizable portion of the Army of the Potomac, which could make the trip by rail. Lincoln and Halleck objected that this would prevent Meade from taking the offensive, but Stanton replied: "There is no reason to expect General Meade will attack Lee, although greatly superior in force, and his great numbers where they are are useless. In five days 30,000 could be put with Rosecrans." The President doubted this last, offering to bet that no such number of men could even be brought to Washington within that span of time. Still, it was clear that something had to be done, and when Seward and Chase sided with their fellow cabinet member Lincoln allowed himself to be persuaded. Unless Meade intended to launch an immediate offensive, two of his corps would be detached at once and sent to Chattanooga. These would be Howard's and Slocum's, and they would be commanded by Joe Hooker, who was conveniently at hand and unemployed. Aside from this reduction of the force proposed and this choice of a leader, which rather galled him, Stanton was given full charge of the transfer operation, with instructions to arrange it as he saw fit. He flew into action without delay. The meeting broke up at about 2 o'clock in the morning, and at 2.30 he got off a wire to Meade, directing him to have the two corps ready to load aboard northbound trains by nightfall, and another to Dana, informing him that the reinforcements would be sent. "[We] will have them in Nashville in five or six days from today," he declared, "with orders to push on immediately wherever General Rosecrans wants them."

Telegrams were also sent — in fact had been sent beforehand, so confident was the Secretary that the council would approve his plan — to officials of three of the several railroads involved, requesting them to "come to Washington as quickly as you can." By noon of the 24th they were in Stanton's office, poring over maps and working out the logistical details required for transporting four divisions, together with their guns and wagons, from the eastern to the western theater, 1200 circuitous miles across the intervening Alleghenies. Four changes of cars were necessary, two at unbridged crossings of the Ohio, near Wheeling and Louisville, and two more at Washington and Indianapolis, where there were no connecting tracks between the roads that must be used. Hooker was authorized to commandeer all the cars, locomotives, plants, and equipment that he deemed necessary, but no such action had to be taken, so complete was the co-operation of all the lines. Before sundown of the following day, just forty-four hours after Dana's warning reached the War Department, the first trainload of soldiers pulled into Washington from Culpeper, the point of origin down in Virginia. By the morning of the 27th, two days later, 12,600 men, together with 33 cars of field artillery and 21 of baggage, had passed through the capital, and at 10 o'clock that evening Stanton wired former Assistant Secretary Thomas A. Scott, who had returned to his prewar duties with the Pennsylvania Railroad and was posted at Louisville to regulate the operation west of the mountains: "The whole force, except 3300 of the XII Corps, is now moving." Within another two days Scott reported trains pulling regularly out of Louisville, and at 10.30 the following night — September 30 — the first eastern troops reached Bridgeport, precisely on the schedule announced at the outset, six days back. By October 2, nearly 20,000 men, 10 six-gun batteries with their horses and ammunition, and 100 carloads of baggage had arrived at the Tennessee railhead. "Your work is most brilliant," Stanton wired Scott. "A thousand thanks. It is a great achievement."

It was indeed a great achievement, this swiftest of all the mass movements of troops in history, and most of the credit belonged to the Secretary of War, who had worked feverishly and efficiently to accomplish what many, including the Commander in Chief, had said could not be done. Under his direction, the North had given its answer to the South's strategic advantage of occupying the interior lines; for though the Confederates had stolen a march and thereby managed, in Forrest's phrase, to "get there first with the most men," the Federals had promptly upped the ante by moving farther and faster with still more. In the final stages of the operation, Wheeler's raiders delayed some of the supply trains by tearing up sections of track, but all got through safely in the end. "You may justly claim the merit of having saved Chattanooga," Hooker wired Stanton on October 11, after posting his four divisions to prevent a rebel crossing below the town and a descent on the hungry garrison's rear. The Secretary was pleased to hear so, just as he had been pleased the week before at the evidence that he had been right in rejecting doleful objections that Lee would attack if Meade's army was weakened by any substantial detachment of troops to Rosecrans. " 'All quiet on the Potomac,' " he had informed the Chattanooga quartermaster on October 4. "Nothing to disturb autumnal slumbers.... All public interest is now concentrated on the Tennessee."

Bragg's complaint that the Federals had "more than double our numbers" was untrue in regard to the time he made it his excuse for not rapidly following up the advantage gained at Chickamauga. In fact, when McLaws arrived — with two of his own and one of Hood's brigades, plus the First Corps artillery, which soon was posted atop Lookout Mountain — the Confederates became numerically superior. But now that Hooker had crossed the Alleghenies with nearly 20,000 reinforcements, the situation was reversed. It was the besiegers who were outnumbered. This novel condition, rarely paralleled in military annals, was about to become more novel still; Sherman was on the way from Vicksburg, via Memphis, with another five divisions. Even when he reached Chattanooga, the Army of the Cumberland would not have "more than double" the number of troops in the Army of Tennessee, but it already had a considerable preponderance without him. Although there was still the menace of starvation — an Illinois private was complaining, tall-tale style, that since Chickamauga he and his comrades had eaten "but two meals a day, and one cracker for each meal" — Rosecrans at least could relax his fears that Bragg was going to drive him into the river with a sudden, downhill infantry assault. The rebels lacked the strength, and no one knew this better than their chief. A graver danger, so far as the northern commander was personally concerned, lurked at the far end of the telegraph wires linking his headquarters to those of his superiors in Washington. This applied in particular to the headquarters of the Secretary of War, whose original mistrust of his fellow Ohioan was being confirmed almost daily in the confidential reports he received from Dana, his special emissary on the scene.

Immediately after the battle, the former Brook Farmer had been glad to "testify to the conspicuous and steady gallantry of Rosecrans on the field"; he put the blame for the defeat on "that dangerous blunderhead McCook" and on Crittenden, whom he considered derelict and incompetent. Before the month was out, however, he had begun to sour on Old Rosy. "He abounds in friendliness and approbativeness," Dana wired on the 27th, "[but] is greatly lacking in firmness and steadiness of will. He is a temporizing man.... If it be decided to change the chief commander" — there had been no intimation that such a thing was being considered; Dana brought it up of his own accord — "I would take the liberty of suggesting that some Western general of high rank and great prestige, like Grant, for instance, would be preferable as his successor." Three days later he favored Thomas for the post, saying: "Should there be a change in the chief command, there is no other man whose appointment would be so welcome to this army." As for the present leader, Dana informed Stanton "that the soldiers have lost their attachment for [him] since he failed them in the battle, and that they do not now cheer him until they are ordered to do so." In the course of the next two weeks, the first two in October, the Assistant Secretary's conviction became even more pronounced in this regard. "I have never seen a public man possessing talent with less administrative power, less clearness and steadiness in difficulty, and greater practical incapacity than General Rosecrans. He has inventive fertility and knowledge, but he has no strength of will and no concentration of purpose. His mind scatters; there is no system in the use of his busy days and restless nights.... Under the present circumstances I consider this army to be very unsafe in his hands." Thus Dana, on the 12th. Six days later, after passing along a report that the soldiers were shouting "Crackers!" at staff officers who moved along them to inspect the fortifications, he added the finishing touches to his word portrait of a man in control of nothing, least of all himself: "Amid all this, the practical incapacity of the general commanding is astonishing, and it often seems difficult to believe him of sound mind. His imbecility appears to be contagious.... If the army is finally obliged to retreat, the probability is that it will fall back like a rabble, leaving its artillery, and protected only by the river behind it."

He might have spared himself and the telegrapher the labor of composing and transmitting this last in his series of depositions as to the general's unfitness for command; for by now, although he would not find it out until the following day, the purpose he intended had been achieved. Stanton had been passing his dispatches along to the Commander in Chief, who had found in them a ready confirmation of his own worst suspicions. Despite this, and because he had not yet decided on a replacement, Lincoln had continued his efforts to stiffen Old Rosy's resolution. On October 12, for instance, while Dana was observing the "scattered" condition of the Ohioan's mind, Lincoln wired: "You and Burnside now have [the enemy] by the throat, and he must break your hold or perish." Rosecrans replied that afternoon, complaining that the corn was ripe on the rebel side of the Tennessee, while "our side is barren." Nevertheless, and in spite of this evidence of divine displeasure, he closed by remarking, much as before, that "we must put our trust in God, who never fails those who truly trust." Commendable though such faith was, particularly after all the Job-like strain that had been placed on it of late, the President would have preferred to see it balanced by a measure of self-reliance. And not only did this quality appear to be totally lacking in the commander of the army now holed up in Chattanooga, but it had begun to seem to Lincoln that ever since Chickamauga, as he told his secretary, Rosecrans had been acting "confused and stunned, like a duck hit on the head."

Ridicule by the President was often the prelude to a general's dismissal, and this was no exception; Rosecrans was about to go, as Buell and McClellan had gone before him. But there was still the question of a successor to be settled before he went. Dana's recommendation of Thomas appealed to Lincoln, who had said of the Virginian shortly after the battle that earned him the sobriquet, "The Rock of Chickamauga": "It is doubtful whether his heroism and skill, exhibited last Sunday afternoon, has ever been surpassed in the world." Stanton felt much the same way about him. "It is not my fault that he was not in chief command months ago," he replied to Dana's observation that there was "no other man whose appointment would be so welcome to this army." However, there was also Grant, who had been comparatively idle since the fall of Vicksburg, fifteen weeks ago. This was plainly a waste the nation could ill afford. What was most desirable was some arrangement that would employ the full abilities of both, and it took Lincoln until mid-October to arrive at a solution that did just that.

The Center Gives

FOR GRANT, THE THREE-MONTH PERIOD THAT followed the fall of Vicksburg — more specifically, the ninety days that elapsed between Sherman's recapture of Jackson in mid-July and Lincoln's mid-October solution to the western command problem — had been a time of strain not unlike the one that followed Shiloh and the occupation of Corinth the year before, in which his counsel was rejected and he felt himself to be more or less a supernumerary in the conduct of the war. Now as then, he saw his army dismembered and dispersed, its various segments dispatched to critical theaters, while he himself was confined with the mere remnant to the quiet backwater which he had created along his particular stretch of the Mississippi. He did not consider submitting his resignation, as he had done before, but he suffered, as the result of a horseback accident midway of this season of frustration, an injury which for a term seemed likely to produce the same effect by removing him entirely from the scene, flat on his back on a stretcher. It was indeed a period of tension, of strain of the kind he had always borne least well, and it was attended, as all such times had been for him, by rumors of his drinking, which was said to be his only relief from the boredom that invariably descended when there was no fighting to be done and his wife was not around.

Not, of course, that he and the troops who remained with him had been completely idle all this time. While Herron was conducting his foray up the Yazoo, which had cost Porter the *De Kalb,* and Sherman was closing in on Jackson, the price of which was to run him just over 1100 casualties, Grant sent one of McPherson's brigades down to Natchez to look into a report that there was heavy rebel traffic there in goods moving to and from the otherwise cut-off Transmississippi. Brigadier General T. E. G. Ransom, who commanded the expedition, found the report to be altogether true. Moreover, by sending mounted pursuers east and west he made the simultaneous capture of a wagon train bound for Alexandria with half a million rounds of rifle and artillery ammunition and a drove of 5000 Texas cattle bound for Alabama, both of which had crossed the river the day before, headed in opposite directions. This was a sizable haul, achieved without the loss of a man, and one month later, at nearly as cheap a price, Grant made a considerably larger one at Grenada, the railroad junction south of the Yalobusha where the Confederates had collected most of the rolling stock of the Mississippi Central, trapped there since May by Johnson's precipitate burning of the bridge across the Pearl when he evacuated Jackson. The raid was two-pronged, one cavalry column sent south from Memphis by Hurlbut while another was sent north by Sherman. On August 17 they converged upon the junction, which so far had resisted all efforts to take it — including Grant's, back in December — and after a brief skirmish with the outnumbered garrison, which fled to avoid capture, went to work on the huge conglomeration of engines and cars "so closely packed as to make a small town of themselves." An elated trooper described them so, and afterwards the official tally listed no fewer than 57 locomotives and more than 400 freight and passenger cars wrecked and burned, together with depot buildings and machine shops containing a wealth of commissary and ordnance supplies. The total bill of destruction was set at $4,000,000, which made the raid one of the most profitable of the war. Presently, however, this figure had to be scaled down a bit. Learning that the Confederates had returned to Grenada in the wake of the departed bluecoats and were frugally carting away the precious locomotive driving wheels, removed from the rubble and ashes, Hurlbut advised in his report that, next time they went out on such a venture, the raiders use sledges to crack off the flanges of the wheels and thus render them unsalvageable.

Both Natchez and Grenada were satisfactory accomplishments, so far as they went, but after all they were only raids. Grant wanted something more: something comparable, in its influence on the outcome of the war, to the recent reduction of Vicksburg and the attendant opening of the Mississippi: something, in short, that would knock the flanges off the whole Confederate machine. Banks had suggested, soon after the fall of Port Hudson, an operation against Mobile, and so had Sherman, who proposed that the coastal city be taken as prelude to an advance up the Alabama River to Selma and beyond, threatening Bragg's rear while Rosecrans, who had maneuvered his adversary back across the Tennessee, brought pressure against his front. Grant approved and passed the word to Halleck. "It seems to me now that Mobile should be captured," he wired on July 18, "the expedition starting from some point on Lake Pontchartrain." Halleck replied that the plan had merit, but added characteristically that it would not do to hurry. "I think it will be best to clean up a little," he advised. "Johnston should be disposed of; also Price, Marmaduke, &c., so as to hold the line of the Arkansas River...

[and] assist General Banks in cleaning out Western Louisiana. When these things are accomplished there will be a large available force to operate either on Mobile or Texas." Just when this would be he did not say. Banks meanwhile had continued to recommend the same objective, though with no better success, and on the last day of the month he left New Orleans aboard a fast packet to confer with Grant at Vicksburg, which he reached the following morning. After putting their heads together both generals continued to urge Halleck to order the reduction of the Confederacy's only remaining Gulf port east of the Mississippi. "I can send the necessary force," Grant offered. Whereupon the general-in-chief suddenly cut the ground from under their feet by flatly rejecting the Mobile proposal in favor of an all-out effort against coastal Texas. "There are important reasons why our flag should be restored to some part of Texas with the least possible delay," he wired on August 6. He did not say what those reasons were, but three days later Lincoln himself got in touch with Grant on the matter. "I see by a dispatch of yours that you incline strongly toward an expedition against Mobile," he wrote. "This would appear tempting to me also, were it not that, in view of recent events in Mexico, I am greatly impressed with the importance of re-establishing the national authority in Western Texas as soon as possible."

Personally considerate though this was, it was not very enlightening; nor was Halleck's explanation, which he made in a covering letter to Banks, that the decision in favor of a Lone Star expedition had been "of a diplomatic rather than of a military character, and resulted from some European complications, or, more properly speaking, was intended to prevent such complications." In point of fact, the matter was more complex than anyone outside the State Department knew, including Old Brains himself, who was a student of international affairs. Benito Juárez, elected head of the Mexican government in the spring of 1861, coincident with the crisis over Sumter, had announced at the time of First Bull Run a two-year suspension of payments to foreign creditors for debts contracted by his predecessor; in response to which Spain, France, and England concluded a convention looking toward a forcible joint collection of their claims and sent some 10,000 troops to Mexico by way of proof that they meant business. By May of the following year, in the period between Shiloh and the Seven Days, while Stonewall Jackson was on the rampage in the Shenandoah Valley, England and Spain had obtained satisfaction from Juárez on the debt, and they withdrew their soldiers. France did not; Napoleon III, attracted by Mexico's wealth and weakness, had plans designed to rival in the New World those of his illustrious uncle in the Old. He stepped up his demands, including insistence on indemnity and payment of certain shady claims advanced by Swiss-French bankers, rapidly increased his occupation force to 35,000 men, and began a march inland from Vera Cruz and Tampico, which was resisted fitfully and ineffectually by guerillas operating much as they had done against Cortez and Winfield Scott, over the same route of conquest. In June of 1863, with Lee on the march for Pennsylvania and Vicksburg under siege, Mexico City fell to the invaders and a pro-French government was set up.

Such was the situation Lincoln faced when Banks and Grant proposed the Mobile expedition the following month. Entirely aside from the violation of the Monroe Doctrine, which he was willing to overlook until the present larger troubles on his hands were cleared away, he knew only too well the pro-Confederate sympathies Napoleon embraced for his own reasons. If foreign intervention came, as the Emperor had been urging for the past two years, Lincoln wanted to be ready to defend the line of the Rio Grande against the imperial forces now in occupation of the capital to the south. That, in brief, was why Mobile had gone by the board; he wanted Union troops in Texas, where none now were, and he did not believe that Banks and Grant were strong enough to accomplish both objectives at the same time. Banks was down to about 12,000 men, the enlistment period of no fewer than twenty-two of his nine-month regiments having expired since the fall of Port Hudson, and the borrowed segments of the army Grant commanded in the taking of Vicksburg were needed now by the generals who had lent them — Burnside in East Tennessee, for instance, Prentiss in Northeast Arkansas, and Schofield in guerilla-torn Missouri — as well as by Rosecrans, who claimed that a farther advance against Bragg was dependent, among other things, on reinforcements being sent him from the army lying idle in Mississippi. "On this matter," Halleck summed up in a wire to Banks on August 12, "we have no choice, but must carry out the views of the Government."

Grant was disappointed, having been convinced that the taking of Mobile, followed by a drive northward into the Confederate heartland to dispose of Bragg and put the squeeze on Lee, would have shortened the war by months — or even years, if that was what it came to — but he accepted the rejection of his counsel in good part, aware that the command decision was based on considerations beyond his ken. In any event there was little he could do about it now, even if the decision were reversed. The dismemberment of his army had begun, and it proceeded with such rapidity that within one month, mid-August to mid-September, his strength was reduced from better than five corps to less than two. Parke's IX Corps left first, dispatched to Burnside, who was marking time in Kentucky. Then Steele's division of Sherman's XV Corps was sent to Helena for the offensive against Price, followed by J. E. Smith's division of McPherson's XVII Corps. Washburn's XVI Corps also returned upriver, one division continuing on to strengthen Schofield in Missouri, while the other two debarked at Memphis to rejoin Hurlbut. Meantime, in order to beef up Banks for the top-priority Texas undertaking, Ord's XIII Corps, with Herron's division attached, proceeded downriver to New Orleans, the staging area for the drive that was intended to secure the line of the Rio Grande against Napoleon's new world dream of conquest and expansion. All that remained by then at Vicksburg were the two reduced corps of Sherman and McPherson. They were quite enough, however, in consideration of the fact that there was practically nothing left for them to do. And now there began for Grant, who was otherwise unemployed, what might be called a social interlude, a time of unfamiliar relaxation and apparent gladness, though it ended all too abruptly with the general confined to a bed of pain in a New Orleans hotel room.

He had a good deal to be glad about at the outset, both for his own sake and his friends'. His appointment as a regular army major general had lifted him almost to Halleck's level as one of the only two men of that rank on active duty. Nor had the government delayed approval of his suggestion that Sherman and McPherson be made regular brigadiers, the reward that had gone to Meade for Gettysburg. Thanks to him, moreover, seven of his colonels now wore stars on their shoulder straps, and so did Rawlins, who was jumped from lieutenant colonel to brigadier general at his chief's solicitation. "He comes the nearest being indispensible to me of any officer in the service," Grant had said of his fellow townsman in the letter of recommendation, and he added, though he must have been aware that this was spreading it rather thick: "I can safely say that he would make a good corps commander." In addition to official recognition, which included the unprecedented You-were-right-I-was-wrong letter from the President, he soon was given cause to know how much his latest victory had raised him in the public's estimation. On August 26 he attended in Memphis the first of many banquets that would be tendered in his honor over the course of the next twenty years. In front of his place at table in the Gayoso House there was a pyramid inscribed with the names of all his battles, beginning with Belmont, and he was presented to the two hundred guests with the toast, "Your Grant and my Grant," in which his reopening of the Mississippi to commerce was compared to the exploits of two other heroes much admired along the river that ran past Memphis, Hernando de Soto and Robert Fulton. He responded with an attractively awkward speech of two brief sentences, thanking the citizens for their kindness and promising to do all he could for their prosperity, then sat down amid loud, prolonged applause. Three days later, after stopping off at Vicksburg for a quick inspection of headquarters, he was in Natchez, where he found the wealthy planters entirely co-operative in their concern for the survival of their fine mansions on the bluff. Proceeding downriver to pay Banks a return visit, he reached New Orleans on September 2.

Banks knew how to entertain a guest; moreover he had all the resources of a high-living Creole society at his disposal. Two days later he staged a grand review at nearby Carrollton in honor of his visitor, who, mounted on a spirited charger procured for him on this occasion as a tribute to his horsemanship, watched Ord's veterans swing past with the names of their and his recent upriver victories on their banners. It was a stirring moment for them and him, a last reunion before they set off for new fields; but the day was grievously marred before it ended. Returning from the suburb to the heart of the city, Grant's borrowed mount shied at a hissing locomotive and, bolting, collided with a carriage that was coming from the opposite direction. Horse and rider went down hard. The animal rose from the cobblestones unassisted, but not Grant, who had suffered a badly dislocated hip, as well as a possible fracture of the skull, and was unconscious; in which condition he was carried on a litter to the nearby St Charles Hotel. Almost at once the story that he had been drinking began to make the rounds, gathering details as it went. Years later William Franklin, who had been transferred from the East to command a corps on the Texas expedition, testified in private that he "*saw* Grant tumble from his horse drunk." It even began to be said that the fall had occurred in the course of the review, which had been brought thereby to an unceremonious end, and that the general had been knocked out not so much by the blow on his head as by the whiskey in his stomach. Grant knew nothing of this at the time, nor indeed of anything else. In fact, the first he knew of having been hurt was when he regained consciousness, somewhat later, to find "several doctors" hovering over him. "My leg was swollen from the knee to the thigh," he afterwards wrote, "and the swelling, almost to the point of bursting, extended along the body up to the armpit. The pain was almost beyond endurance. I lay at the hotel something over a week without being able to turn myself in bed."

* * *

While Grant was laid up, confined to a world of pain whose limits were described by the four walls of his hotel room, Banks opened the campaign designed to carry out the instructions of his superiors to restore the flag of the Union "to some part of Texas with the least possible delay." As it turned out, however, he encountered something worse than delay in the execution of his plans, the first results of which were about as abruptly disastrous as his fellow general's fall on horseback, drunk or sober.

Halleck had advised an amphibious movement "up Red River to Alexandria, Natchitoches, or Shreveport, and the military occupation of northern Texas.... Nevertheless," he added, "your choice is left unrestricted." Banks replied with numerous logistical objections, not the least of which was that the Red was nearly dry at this season of the year. He favored a sudden descent on the coast, specifically at Sabine Pass, to be followed by an overland march on Galveston and other points beyond.

Accordingly, having been given his choice, he ordered Franklin to load a reinforced division onto transports and proceed to Sabine Pass, where he would rendezvous with a four-gunboat assault force. The rebel defenses were said to be weak, despite the reverse the navy had suffered here in January; once these had been subdued by the warships, Franklin was to put his troops ashore and move inland to the Texas & New Orleans Railroad, linking Houston and Beaumont and Orange, and there await the arrival of the balance of his corps, which by then would have been brought forward by the unloaded transports. It was all worked out in careful detail, and on September 7, three days after Grant's accident, Franklin arrived before the pass and was joined that evening by the gunboat flotilla under Lieutenant Frederick Crocker, U.S.N. Fort Griffin, the rebel work protecting Sabine City, mounted half a dozen light guns and was garrisoned by less than fifty men; Crocker attacked it the following afternoon, having six times the number of heavier guns in his four warships. The engagement was brief and decisive. Within half an hour one gunboat was hit in the boiler, losing all her steam, and a few minutes later a second ran aground in the shallow bay and was given the same treatment by the marksmen in the fort. Both vessels struck their colors, surrendering with their crews of about 300 men, including 50 killed or wounded and the luckless lieutenant in command, while the third retired out of range with the fourth, which had not engaged. Still aboard the transports with his soldiers, whom the navy was unable to put ashore, Franklin felt there was nothing to do but turn around and go back to New Orleans, and that was what he did, reporting a total loss of six men, who had been aboard the surrendered gunboats as observers, together with 200,000 rations thrown overboard to lighten a grounded transport and 200 mules served likewise when the steamer on which they were loaded lost her stack in a heavy sea on the way home.

So feeble had the attack been that Magruder at first could not believe it was anything more than a feint, designed to distract his attention from the main effort somewhere else along the coast. When no such blow was delivered in the course of the next few days, Prince John contented himself with what had been accomplished; a "brilliant victory," he called the fight, a "gallant achievement," and finally, in an excess of pride at what his gunners had done in the face of long odds, "the most extraordinary feat of the war." Congress eventually passed a resolution of thanks, "eminently due, and hereby cordially given," to the two officers and the 41 men of the garrison who had stood to their outranged guns and outfought the Yankee warships.

On the other hand, Banks assigned the reason for the failure to the "ignorance" of the naval officers involved; one of his chief regrets, no doubt, was that Farragut was not around to blister them a bit, having returned to New York for badly overdue repairs to his flagship *Hartford* in the Brooklyn Navy Yard. In any case, on Franklin's return the Massachusetts general decided that the line of advance up the Red to Northeast Texas, suggested previously by Old Brains, was probably the best invasion route after all, and he informed Lincoln that while the army was "preparing itself" for the execution of this larger plan, which would have to be delayed until rain had swelled the river, he would continue his efforts to move in directly from the Gulf against the Lone Star beaches — or, anyhow, some beach; for he left himself plenty of latitude as to just where he would strike next time, merely remarking that he proposed "to attempt a lodgment upon some point on the coast from the mouth of the Mississippi to the Rio Grande."

By then the year was well into October, and two other Federal commanders in the Transmississippi region, James Blunt and John Schofield, had unexpected problems on their hands in the departments of the Frontier and Missouri. William Steele and Pap Price had been driven from Fort Smith and Little Rock, the former deep into Indian Territory and the latter beyond the line of the Arkansas. Schofield could breathe easier; so he thought — until Jo Shelby came riding northward, all the way to the Missouri River, and Quantrill, while crossing the southeast corner of Kansas on his way to winter in Texas, gave Blunt an opportune demonstration that he had a talent for something more than murdering civilians in or under their beds.

From Arkadelphia, where he ended his retreat in mid-September, Price launched Shelby on a raid into his home state, hoping thus to discourage Schofield from reinforcing Fred Steele for a follow-up push from the Arkansas River to the Ouachita. Three months short of his thirty-third birthday, the Missouri cavalryman was still a colonel despite outstanding service in practically every major engagement fought in the region since Wilson's Creek; even now he was nursing an unhealed wound he had suffered in his sword arm during the Helena repulse, twelve weeks ago. Though, like Jeb Stuart, he took his nickname from his initials and wore a foot-long plume on his hat, there was a hard, practical core to his daring, a concentration more on results than on effect, which afterwards caused Alfred Pleasonton, who rode for three years against Stuart before transferring to the far western theater — although it perhaps should be noted in passing that he never came up against Forrest — to say flatly, after a year of fighting there as well, that "Shelby was the best cavalry general of the South." Part of the evidence in support of this contention was put on record during the present raid, which lasted longer and covered a greater distance than any undertaken by any body of horsemen from either army in the whole course of the war, including Morgan's famous raid into Ohio, which ended in disaster, whereas Shelby returned with a stronger force than he had had at the outset. He set out with 600 troopers on September 22, passing next day through Caddo Gap, forty miles northwest of Arkadelphia, and five days later crossed the Arkansas River a hundred miles above Little Rock, midway between Clarksville and Fort Smith. Riding north through Huntsville and Bentonville, he crossed the state line to reach Neosho on October 4 and promptly forced the surrender of 400 Union cavalry who had holed up in the stout brick courthouse, former capitol of the short-lived Confederate-allied Republic of Missouri, which the bluecoats had converted into a fort and were determined to hold, at any rate until the rebel cannon started knocking it to pieces. Along with the men, the victors took their horses, their fine Sharps rifles and navy revolvers, and their clothes, which were used as an effective disguise, so far at least as they went round, by the former gray-clad raiders. Next day the ride north continued, still with the stockily built and heavily bearded colonel in the lead.

His goal was Jefferson City; he had it in mind to raise the Stars and Bars over the statehouse, not only as a sign that Missouri was by no means "conquered," but also as a gesture to discourage the Union high command from detaching troops from here to exploit its recent gains in Arkansas or to shore up Rosecrans, who had been whipped two weeks ago at Chickamauga and now was under siege in Chattanooga; in furtherance of which intention Shelby sent out parties, left and right of his line of march, to cut telegraph wires, burn installations and depots of supply, attack outlying strong points, and in general spread confusion as to his strength and destination. On north he rode, through Sarcoxie and Bowers Mill, Greenfield and Stockton, Humansville and Warsaw, to Tipton on the Missouri Pacific, which he struck on October 10. Jefferson City was less than forty miles away, due east on the railroad, but his enemies were thoroughly aroused by now, expecting him to move in that direction. Instead, after tearing up track on both sides of Tipton, burning the depot, and setting fire to a large yard of freight cars, he pressed on north to Booneville, where he was greeted next day by the mayor and a delegation of citizens who came out to assure him of their southern loyalty and ask that he spare their property. This he did, except for the new $400,000 bridge across the nearby Lamine River, which he wrecked. "Now the broad bosom of the grand old Missouri lay unveiled before us in the red beams of the autumn sun," his adjutant later wrote, "and the men, forgetting all their privations and dangers, broke out in one long, loud, proud hurrah." The hurrah could indeed have been a loud one, for Shelby's strength had grown by now to more than a thousand troopers by the addition of recruits who had flocked to join him on the way. Moreover, the column was lengthened by three hundred captured wagons, drawn not by mules or draft horses, but by the hundreds of cavalry mounts he had taken in the series of surrenders that had marked his line of march, surrenders or flights which had netted him no fewer than forty stands of colors and ten "forts" of one kind or another. If the blue-clad graybacks cheered themselves hoarse with pride as they stood on the south bank of the wide Missouri, just under four hundred air-line miles from the nearest Confederate outpost, it was not without reason.

Their problem now was escape from the greatly superior Federal columns rapidly converging on them from the south and east and north. Shelby led them west along the south bank of the Missouri, in the direction of his prewar home at Waverly. Before they got there, however, they had their one full-scale engagement of the raid, October 13 near Arrow Rock, where the enemy columns finally brought them to bay, outnumbered five to one. Splitting his command in two, Shelby dismounted the larger half and fought a savage defensive action in which he lost about one hundred men while the smaller half made a mounted getaway by punching a hole in the line of the attackers; whereupon he remounted the remainder and did the same at another point, taking a different escape route to confuse and split his pursuers. On through Waverly he rode that night, still accompanied by his train, which he had brought out with him. At nearby Hawkins Mill, however, he was later to report, "finding my wagons troublesome, and having no ammunition left except what the men could carry, I sunk them in the Missouri River, where they were safe from all capture." This done he turned south. Bypassing Lexington, Harrisonville, and Butler to skirt the Burnt District, he reached Carthage on October 17 and turned east next day through Sarcoxie, which he had visited two weeks before, on his way north. Laying ambushes all the while to delay pursuers, he re-entered Arkansas on October 19 and was joined next day on the Little Osage River by the smaller force that had split off at Arrow Rock a week ago. From the Little Osage he moved by what he called "easy stages" to Clarksville, where he recrossed the Arkansas River on October 26 and made his way south through the Ouachita Mountains to Washington. There at last he called a halt, November 3, forty miles southwest of his starting point at Arkadelphia. In the forty-one days he had been gone he had covered a distance of 1500 miles, an average of better than thirty-six miles a day, and though he had suffered a total loss of about 150 killed and wounded, he had also picked up 800 recruits along the way, so that he returned with twice the number of men he had had when he set out. He listed his gains — 600 Federals killed or wounded, 500 captured and paroled; 6000 horses and mules taken, together with 300 wagons, 1200 small arms, and 40 stands of colors; $1,000,000 in U. S. Army supplies destroyed, plus $800,000 in public property — then laconically closed his report, which was addressed to Price's adjutant: "Hoping this may prove satisfactory, I remain, major, very respectfully, your obedient servant, Jo. O. Shelby, Colonel." Highly pleased — as well it might be; for there was also substance to his claim that the raid had kept 10,000 Missouri bluecoats from being sent to assist in raising the siege at Chattanooga — the government promoted him to brigadier the following month.

Quantrill by now was calling himself a colonel, too, and had even acquired a uniform in which he had his picture taken wearing three stars on the collar, a long-necked young man with hooded eyes, a smooth round jaw, and a smile as faint as Mona Lisa's. But the government — much to its credit, most historians were to say — declined to sanction his self-promotion, even after he scored a second victory in Kansas, one far more impressive, militarily, than the first, which he had scored six weeks before at Lawrence. While Shelby was preparing to set out from Arkadelphia, Quantrill was reassembling his guerillas on familiar Blackwater Creek, intending to take them to Texas for the winter. In early October the two columns passed each other, east and west of Carthage, Shelby and his 600 going north, Quantrill with about 400 going south, neither aware of the other's presence, some twenty miles away. On October 6, when the former passed through Warsaw, the latter drew near Fort Baxter, down in the southeast corner of Kansas at Baxter Springs, which was held by two companies of Wisconsin cavalry and one of Kansas infantry. Quantrill decided to take it. While the attack was in progress, however, he learned that a train of ten wagons was approaching from the north, attended by two more companies of Wisconsin and Kansas troops; so he pulled back half his men, and went to take that too. His luck was in. The train and troops were the baggage and escort of James Blunt, lately appointed commander of the District of the Frontier, on his way to establish headquarters at Fort Baxter. When Blunt saw the horsemen in line across the road ahead, he assumed they were an honor guard sent out from the fort to meet him. He halted to have his escort dress its ranks, then proceeded at a dignified pace to receive the salute of the waiting line of horsemen.

  He received instead a blast of fire at sixty yards, followed promptly by a screaming charge that threw his hundred-man escort first into milling confusion and then, when they recognized what they were up against — the guerillas, having been warned to expect no quarter, certainly would extend none — into headlong flight. This last availed all but a handful of them nothing; 79 of the hundred were quickly run down and killed, including Major Henry Curtis, Blunt's adjutant and the son of the former department commander. Blunt himself made his escape, though he was nearly unhorsed in taking a jump across a ravine. Thrown from his saddle and onto his horse's neck by the rebound, he clung there and rode in that unorthodox position for a mile or more, outdistancing his pursuers, who turned back to attend to the business of dispatching the prisoners and the wounded. Quantrill called off the attack on the fort — its garrison had suffered 19 casualties to bring the Federal total to 98, as compared to 6 for the guerillas — and proceeded to rifle the abandoned wagons. Included in the loot was all of Blunt's official correspondence, his dress sword, two stands of colors, and several demijohns of whiskey. Quantrill was so pleased with his exploit that he even took a drink or two, something none of his companions had seen him do before. Presently he became talkative, which was also quite unusual. "By God," he boasted as he staggered about, "Shelby couldn't whip Blunt; neither could Marmaduke; but *I* whipped him." He went on south to Texas, as he had intended when he left Johnson County the week before, and Blunt was removed not long thereafter from the command he had so recently acquired.

But Holmes and Price, reduced by sickness and desertion to a force of 7000, had not been greatly helped by either Shelby or Quantrill; Steele still threatened from Little Rock, and though he had not been reinforced, he outnumbered them two to one. On October 25, the day before Shelby recrossed the Arkansas River on his way back from Missouri, Holmes ordered a withdrawal of the troops left at Pine Bluff, thus loosening his last tenuous grasp on the south bank of that stream in order to prepare for what Kirby Smith believed was threatening, deep in his rear: Banks had begun another ascent of the Teche and the Atchafalaya, which could take him at last to the Red and into Texas. Once this happened, Smith's command, already cut off from the powder mills and ironworks of the East, would be cut off from the flow of goods coming in through Mexico. "The Fabian policy is now our true policy," he declared, and he advised that if further retreat became necessary, Holmes could move "by Monticello, along Bayou Bartholomew to Monroe, through a country abundant in supplies."

* * *

Grant by then had left for other fields. In mid-September, after ten days of confinement to the New Orleans hotel room, unable even to sit up in bed, he had himself carried aboard a steamboat bound for Vicksburg, and there, although as he said later he "remained unable to move for some time afterwards," he was reunited with his wife and their four children, who came down to join him in a pleasant, well-shaded house which his staff had commandeered for him on the bluff overlooking the river. Under these circumstances, satisfying as they were to his uxorious nature, his convalescence was so comparatively rapid that within a month he was hobbling about on crutches.

McPherson kept bachelor quarters in town, boarding with a family in which, according to Sherman, there were "several interesting young ladies." Not that his fellow Ohioan had neglected his own comfort. Like Grant, Sherman had his family with him — it too included four children — camped in a fine old grove of oaks beside the Big Black River, near the house from whose gallery, several weeks ago, the dozen weeping women had reviled him for the death of one of their husbands at Bull Run. He had been discomfited then, but that was all behind him now, together with his doubts about the war and his share in it. Grant had given his restless spirit a sense of direction and dedication; he could even abide the present idleness, feeling that he and his troops had earned a decent period of rest. "The time passed very agreeably," he would recall years later, "diversified only by little events of not much significance." That he was in favor of vigorous efforts at an early date, however, was shown in a letter he wrote Halleck on September 17 — the day after Grant's return from New Orleans — in response to one from the general-in-chief requesting his opinions as to "the question of reconstruction in Louisiana, Mississippi, and Arkansas.... Write me your views fully," Halleck urged him, "as I may wish to use them with the President."

Never one to require much encouragement for an exposition of his views, the red-haired general replied with a letter that was to fill eight close-spaced pages in his memoirs. He had done considerable thinking along these lines, based on his experiences in the region before and during the war, and if by "reconstruction" Halleck meant a revival of "any civil government in which the local people have much say," then Sherman was against it. "I know them well, and the very impulses of their nature," he declared, "and to deal with the inhabitants of that part of the South which borders on the great river, we must recognize the classes into which they have divided themselves." First, there were the planters. "They are educated, wealthy, and easily approached.... I know we can manage this class, but only by *action*," by "pure military rule." Second were "the smaller farmers, mechanics, merchants, and laborers.... The southern politicians, who understand this class, use them as the French do their masses — seemingly consult their prejudices, while they make their orders and enforce them. We should do the same." Third, there were "the Union men of the South. I must confess that I have little respect for this class.... I account them as nothing in this great game of war." Fourth and last, he narrowed his sights on "the young bloods of the South: sons of planters, lawyers-about-town, good billiard players and sportsmen, men who never did work and never will. War suits them, and the rascals are brave, fine riders, bold to rashness, and dangerous subjects in every sense. They care not a sou for niggers, land, or any thing." His solution to the problem they posed as "the most dangerous set of men that this war has turned loose upon the world" was easily stated: "These men must all be killed or employed by us before we can hope for peace." Just how they were to be employed by the government they were fighting Sherman did not say, but having sketched the various classes to be dealt with, he proceeded to give his prescription for victory over them all. "I would banish all minor questions, assert the broad doctrine that as a nation the United States has the right, and also the physical power, to penetrate to every part of our national domain, and that we will do it — that we will do it in our own time and in our own way; that it makes no difference whether it be in one year, or two, or ten, or twenty; that we will remove and destroy every obstacle, if need be, take every life, every acre of land, every particle of property, everything that to us seems proper; that we will not cease till the end is attained; that all who do not aid us are enemies, and that we will not account to them for our acts." Lest there be any misunderstanding, he summed up what he meant. "I would not coax them, or even meet them half way, but make them so sick of war that generations would pass away before they would again appeal to it.... The only government needed or deserved by the States of Louisiana, Arkansas, and Mississippi now exists in Grant's army." He closed by asking Halleck to "excuse so long a letter," but in sending it to Grant for forwarding to Washington, he appended a note in which he added: "I would make this war as severe as possible, and show no symptoms of tiring till the South begs for mercy.... The South has done her worst, and now is the time for us to pile on our blows thick and fast."

Halleck presently wired that Lincoln had read the letter and wanted to see it published, but Sherman declined, preferring "not to be drawn into any newspaper controversy" such as the one two years ago, in which he had been pronounced insane. "If I covet any public reputation," he replied, "it is as a silent actor. I dislike to see my name in print." Anyhow, by then he was on the move again; his troops had "slung the knapsack for new fields," and he himself had experienced a personal tragedy as deep as any he was ever to know in a long life.

Rosecrans had been whipped at Chickamauga while Sherman's letter was on its way north, and before it got to Washington the wires were humming with calls for reinforcements to relieve Old Rosy's cooped-up army. On September 23 Grant passed the word for Sherman to leave at once for Memphis with two divisions, picking up en route the division McPherson had recently sent to Helena, and move toward Chattanooga via Corinth on the Memphis & Charleston Railroad, which he was to repair as he went, thus providing a new supply line. Drums rolled in the camps on the Big Black; for the next four days the roads to Vicksburg were crowded with columns filing onto transports at the wharf. The steamer *Atlantic* was the last to leave, and on it rode Sherman and his family. He was showing the two girls and the two boys his old camp as the boat passed Young's Point, when he noticed that nine-year-old Willy, his first-born son and namesake — "that child on whose future I based all the ambition I ever had" — was pale and feverish. Regimental surgeons, summoned from below deck, diagnosed the trouble as typhoid and warned that it might be fatal. It was. Taken ashore at Memphis, the boy died in the Gayoso House, where Grant's banquet had been staged five weeks ago. Sherman was disconsolate, though he kept busy attending to details involved in the eastward movement while his wife and the three remaining children went on north to St Louis with the dead boy in a sealed metallic casket. "Sleeping, waking, everywhere I see poor Willy," he wrote her, and he added: "I will try to make poor Willy's memory the cure for the defects which have sullied my character — all that is captious, eccentric and wrong."

His grief seemed rather to deepen than to lift. A week after his son's death he was asking, "Why was I not killed at Vicksburg and left Willy to grow up and care for you?" By that time, though, his troops were all in motion, some by rail and some on foot, and on October 11 he started for Corinth aboard a train that carried his staff and a battalion of regulars. At Collierville, twenty miles out of Memphis, the train and depot, which had been turned into a blockhouse and surrounded by shallow trenches, were attacked by rebel cavalry under Chalmers, an old Shiloh adversary, whose strength he estimated at 3000. He himself had fewer than 600 and no guns, whereas the raiders had four. To gain time, he received and after some discussion declined a flag-of-truce demand for unconditional surrender, meanwhile disposing his few troops for defense and sending a wire for hurry-up assistance. The fight that followed lasted four hours, at the end of which time the rebels withdrew to avoid contact with a division marching eastward in response to the wire that, after the manner of light fiction, had got through just before the line was cut. Though it had not really been much of a fight, as such things went at this stage of the war — he had lost 14 killed, 42 wounded, and 54 captured, while Chalmers had lost 3 killed and 48 wounded — Sherman was tremendously set up. Five staff horses had been taken, including his favorite mare Dolly, and the graybacks had also confiscated his second-best uniform, but these seemed a small price to pay for the recovery of his accustomed spirits. He had escaped from gloom.

By October 16 he had his entire corps — increased to five divisions by the addition of two from Hurlbut — past Corinth, and three days later the head of the column reached Eastport to find a fleet of transports awaiting its arrival, loaded with provisions and guarded by two of Porter's gunboats. The establishment of this supply route on the Tennessee enabled Sherman to abandon the railroad west of there, but he still had 161 miles of track to rebuild and maintain, in accordance with Halleck's orders, from Iuka to Stevenson. This too he took in stride; for he was again in what he liked to call "high feather." He encouraged his men to live off the country, having decided that the best way to keep raiders out of Kentucky was to cut an arid swath across northern Mississippi and Alabama. The men took to the notion handily, not only because it agreed with their own, but also because their appetites had sharpened with the advent of early fall weather and days of working on the railroad. Sherman could scarcely contain his delight at their performance. "I never saw such greedy rascals after chicken and fresh meat," he exulted in a letter home. "I don't believe I will draw anything for them but salt. I don't know but it would be a good plan to march my army back and forth from Florence and Stevenson to make a belt of devastation between the enemy and our country."

"My army," he said, and truly; for by that time Lincoln's solution of the western command problem had been announced. On October 10, the day before Sherman left Memphis to make his spirit-restoring defense of the Collierville blockhouse, Grant received at Vicksburg a badly delayed order from Halleck directing him to report without delay to Cairo for instructions. The order, dated October 3, had taken a full week to reach him. He left at once, though he was still on crutches, and stopped off at Columbus, Kentucky, six days later — the guerilla-cut telegraph line had been restored to that point by then, only one day short of two weeks after the date on Halleck's order — to report that he was on his way upriver. Perhaps he wondered if he was to be disciplined for not keeping in touch and going off to New Orleans, as he had been after Donelson for not keeping in touch and going off to Nashville, though he could not see that he deserved any more blame in the present instance than he had deserved then. At any rate he was not much enlightened when he reached Cairo next morning, October 17, and was handed a wire directing him to proceed at once to the Galt House in Louisville, where he would receive further instructions from an officer of the War Department. He boarded a train that would take him there by way of Indianapolis. But that afternoon, as the train was pulling out of the station at the latter place, an attendant came hurrying out and flagged it to a halt. Behind him, bustling up the platform on short legs, came the Secretary of War, Edwin M. Stanton himself, whom Grant had never met. He swung aboard the last car, wheezing asthmatically, and worked his way forward, as the train gathered speed, to the car occupied by the general and his staff. "How are you, General Grant?" he said, grasping the hand of Dr Edward Kittoe, the staff surgeon. "I knew you at sight from your pictures."

This was quickly straightened out; Kittoe did not look much like his chief anyhow, though he wore a beard and a campaign hat and was also from Galena. After the amenities, exchanged while the train rocked on toward Louisville, Stanton presented Grant with two copies of a War Department order dated October 16, both of which had the same opening paragraph:

> By direction of the President of the United States, the Departments of the Ohio, of the Cumberland, and of the Tennessee, will constitute the Military Division of the Mississippi. Major General U. S. Grant, United States Army, is placed in command of the Military Division of the Mississippi, with his headquarters in the field.

The Center Gives

In brief, this was Lincoln's unifying solution to the western command problem. With the exception of the troops in East Louisiana under Banks, who outranked him, Grant was put in charge of all the Union forces between the Allegheny Mountains and the Mississippi River. That was all there was to one of the copies of the order, but the other had an added paragraph, relieving Rosecrans from duty with the Army of the Cumberland and appointing Thomas in his place. The choice was left to Grant, who had no fondness for Old Rosy; "I chose the latter," he remarked dryly, some years afterward. Sherman of course would succeed to command of the Army of the Tennessee, and Burnside would continue, at least for the present, as head of the Army of the Ohio.

At Louisville, which they reached that night, Grant and the Secretary spent the following day together at the Galt House discussing the military outlook, mostly from the Washington point of view. That evening — by which time, the general said later, "all matters of discussion seemed exhausted" — Grant and his wife, who had come from Vicksburg with him by boat and train, left the hotel to call on relatives, while Stanton retired to his room with an attack of asthma. It had been decided to defer issuance of the War Department order until the general and his staff had had time to attend to various preparatory details. Presently, however, a messenger arrived with the latest dispatch from Dana, announcing that Rosecrans intended to evacuate Chattanooga and predicting utter disaster as a result. Highly agitated, Stanton sent bellboys and staff officers to all parts of the city in a frantic search for Grant. None of them could find him until about 11 o'clock, when they all found him at once. As he returned to the hotel from his call on relatives, it seemed to him that "every person [I] met was a messenger from the Secretary, apparently partaking of his impatience to see me." Upstairs, he found Stanton pacing about in his dressing gown and clutching the fatal dispatch, which he insisted called for immediate action to prevent the loss of Chattanooga and the annihilation of the troops besieged there. Grant agreed, and at once sent two dispatches of his own: one informing Rosecrans that he was relieved of command, the other instructing Thomas to hold onto Chattanooga "at all hazards." Thomas replied promptly with a message that indicated how aptly he had been characterized as the Rock of Chickamauga. "We will hold the town till we starve," he told Grant.

✣ 2 ✣

" 'All quiet on the Potomac.' Nothing to disturb autumnal slumbers," Stanton had wired the Chattanooga quartermaster on October 4, proud of his management of the transfer west of two corps from the army down in Virginia, which apparently had been accomplished under Lee's very nose without his knowledge, or at any rate without provoking a reaction on his part. Three days later, however, Meade's signalmen intercepted wigwag messages indicating that the rebels were preparing for some sort of movement in their camps beyond the Rapidan, and two days after that, on October 9, word came from the cavalry outposts that Lee was on the march, heading west and north around Meade's flank, much as he had done when he maneuvered bold John Pope out of a similar position, fourteen months ago, and brought him to grief on the plains of Manassas. Presently things were anything but quiet on the Potomac, deep in the Federal rear; for Meade was headed in that direction, too, and the indications were that there was going to be a Third Bull Run.

Lee had been wanting to take the offensive ever since his return from Pennsylvania. "If General Meade does not move, I wish to attack him," he told Davis in late August. The detachment of Longstreet soon afterward had seemed to rule this out, however, since it reduced Lee's strength to less than 50,000, whereas the Federals had nearly twice that number in his immediate front. Also there was the problem of his health, a recurrence of the rheumatic malady that had racked him in early spring. Then had come the news of Chickamauga, which was like a tonic to him. "My whole heart and soul have been with you and your brave corps in your late battle," he wrote Old Peter. "It was natural to hear of Longstreet and Hill charging side by side, and pleasing to find the armies of the East and West vying with each other in valor and devotion to their country. A complete and glorious victory must ensue under such circumstances.... Finish the work before you, my dear general, and return to me. I want you badly and you cannot get back too soon." Glorious the victory had been, but he presently learned that it was a long way from complete, which meant that the detached third of his army would not be rejoining him anything like as soon as he had hoped. Then came a second tonic-like report. Two of Meade's corps had been sent west to reinforce Rosecrans, with the result that the odds against Lee were reduced from two-to-one to only a bit worse than eight-to-five. He had taken the offensive against longer odds in the past, and now he prepared to do so again, not only for the same reasons — to relieve the pressure on Richmond, to break up enemy plans in their formative stage, and to provide himself with more room for maneuver — but also by much the same method. What he had in mind, when reports of the Union reduction were confirmed in early October, was a repetition of the tactics he had employed against Pope in a similar confrontation on this same ground; that is, a march around the enemy flank, then a knockout blow delivered as the blue mass drew back to avoid encirclement.

Once he had decided he moved quickly. On October 9 the two

corps of the Army of Northern Virginia began their march up the south bank of the Rapidan, westward beyond the Union right, then north across the river. The last time Lee had done this, just over a year ago, he had also had only two corps in his army. Longstreet and Jackson had led them then; now it was Ewell and A. P. Hill, two very different men. Another difference was in Lee himself. He had ridden Traveller then; now he rode in a wagon, so crippled by rheumatism that he could not mount a horse.

Stuart's cavalry had been organized into two divisions, one under Wade Hampton and the other under Fitzhugh Lee, both of whom were promoted to major general. Hampton was still recuperating from his Gettysburg wounds; Stuart led his division himself, covering the right flank of the infantry on the march, and left Fitz Lee to guard the river crossings while the rest of the army moved upstream. After two days of swinging wide around Cedar Mountain — rich with memories for A. P. Hill, not only because he was a native of the region and had spent his boyhood in these parts, but also because it was here that he had saved Jackson from defeat in early August, a year ago — the gray column entered Culpeper from the southwest on the 11th. Meade had had his headquarters here, and three of his corps had been concentrated in the vicinity, with the other two advanced southward to the north bank of the Rapidan. Now he was gone, and his five corps were gone with him. Like Pope, he was falling back across the Rappahannock to avoid being trapped in the constricting apex of the V described by the confluence of the rivers. Beyond Culpeper, however, Stuart came upon the cavalry rear guard, drawn up at Brandy Station to fight a delaying action on the field where most of the troopers of both armies had fought so savagely four months before. In the resultant skirmish, which he called Second Brandy, Jeb had the satisfaction of driving the enemy horsemen back across the Rappahannock, only failing to bag the lot, he declared, because Fitz Lee did not arrive in time after splashing across the unguarded Rapidan fords. At any rate, he felt that the question of superior abilities, which some claimed had not been decided by the contest here in June, was definitely settled in his favor by the outcome of this second fight on the same ground. Elated though he was, he did not fail to show that he had learned from his mistakes on the recent march into Pennsylvania. Not that he admitted that he had made any; he did not, then or now or later; but he kept in close touch with the commanding general, sending a constant stream of couriers to report both his own and the enemy's position. "Thank you," Lee said to the latest in the series, who had ridden back to inform him that the blue cavalry was being driven eastward. "Tell General Stuart to continue to press them back toward the river. But tell him, too," he added, "to spare his horses — to spare his horses. It is not necessary to send so many messages." Turning to Ewell, whom he was accompanying today, he said of this staff officer and another who had reported a few minutes earlier: "I think these two young gentlemen make *eight* messengers sent me by General Stuart."

He was in excellent spirits, partly because of this evidence that his chief of cavalry had profited from experience; for whatever profited Stuart also profited Lee, who depended heavily on his former cadet for the information by which he shaped his plans. Then too, the pains in his back had let up enough to permit him to enter Culpeper on his horse instead of on the prosaic seat of a wagon, and though he preferred things simple for the most part, he also liked to see them done in style. Moreover, there had been an exchange which he had enjoyed in the course of the welcome extended by the old men and cripples and women and children who turned out to cheer the army that had delivered them from this latest spell of Federal occupation. Not, it seemed, that the occupation had been entirely unpleasant for everyone concerned. At the height of the celebration, one indignant housewife struck a discordant note by informing the general that certain young ladies of the town had accepted invitations to attend band concerts at John Sedgwick's headquarters, and there, according to reports, they had given every sign of enjoying not only the Yankee music, but also the attentions of the blue-coated staff officers who were their escorts. Lee heard the superpatriot out, then looked sternly around at several girls whose blushes proved their guilt of this near-treason. "I know General Sedgwick very well," he replied at last, replacing his look of mock severity with a smile. "It is just like him to be so kindly and considerate, and to have his band there to entertain them. So, young ladies, if the music is good, go and hear it as often as you can, and enjoy yourselves. You will find that General Sedgwick will have none but agreeable gentlemen about him."

Whatever effect these words had on the woman who lodged the complaint — and whose fate, after the general's departure, can only be guessed at — they served, by their vindication of youth, to heighten the gaiety of the occasion. Nor was Culpeper the only scene of rejoicing for deliverance. Bragg's great victory in North Georgia, Lee's northward march, the repulse of the Union flotilla at Sabine Pass, the apparent disinclination of the Federals to follow up their Vicksburg conquest, Beauregard's continuing staunchness under amphibious assault: all were hailed in the Richmond *Whig* on this same October 11, under the heading "The Prospect," as evidence that the South, whose resilience after admittedly heavy setbacks had now been demonstrated to all the world, could never be defeated by her present adversary. "As the campaigning season of the third year of the war approaches its close," the editor summed up, "the principal army of the enemy, bruised, bleeding, and alarmed, is engaged with all its might [at Chattanooga] digging into the earth for safety. The second largest force, the once Grand Army of the Potomac, is fleeing before the advancing corps of General Lee. The third, under Banks, a portion of which has just been severely chastised by a handful of men, is vaguely and feebly attempting some movement against Texas. The fourth, under Grant, has ceased to be an army of offense. The fifth, under Gillmore, with a number of ironclads to aid him, lays futile siege to Charleston. Nowhere else have they anything more than garrisons or raiding forces. At all points the Confederate forces are able to defy them."

Lee had it in mind to brighten his share of the prospect still further by intercepting Meade's withdrawal up the Orange & Alexandria Railroad. He could not divide his army, as he had done against Pope, using half of it to fix the enemy in place while the other half swung wide for a strike at the rear; he lacked both the transport and the strength, and besides, with the bluecoats already in motion, there wasn't time. But he could attempt a shorter turning movement via Warrenton, along the turnpike paralleling the railroad to the east, in hope of forcing Meade to halt and fight in a position that would afford the pursuers the chance, despite the disparity in numbers, to inflict what the dead Stonewall had called "a terrible wound." Accordingly, the Culpeper pause was a brief one; Little Powell had time for no more than a quick look at his home town as he passed through in the wake of Ewell, who in turn pushed his men hard to close the gap between them and the cavalry up ahead, beyond Brandy and the Rappahannock crossings. Stuart skirmished with the blue rear guard all the rest of that day and the next, banging away with his guns and gathering stragglers as he went. Lee, still riding with Ewell, reached Warrenton on the 13th to receive a report from Jeb that the Federals were still at Warrenton Junction, due east on the main line, burning stores. There seemed an excellent chance of cutting them off, somewhere up the line: perhaps at Bristoe Station, where Jackson had landed with such explosive effect that other time. Next morning Hill's lean marchers took the lead. Remembering the rewards of that other strike, they put their best foot forward, if for no other reason than the hope of getting it shod. Shoes, warm clothes, food, and victory: all these lay before them, fifteen miles away at Bristoe, if they could only arrive in time to forestall a Yankee getaway.

As they marched their hopes were heightened by the evidence that Meade, though clearly on the run, had no great head start in the race. "We found the campfires of the enemy still burning," one of Hill's men would recall. "Guns, knapsacks, blankets, etc. strewn along the road showed that the enemy was moving in rapid retreat, and prisoners sent in every few minutes confirmed our opinion that they were fleeing in haste." Another of the marchers, cheered at the outset because he had eaten a whole pot of boiled cabbage for breakfast — perhaps by way of distending his stomach for the feast he hoped to enjoy before nightfall — recorded the satisfaction he and his comrades felt at reliving the glad August days of 1862, when they had tramped these roads with the same goal ahead. "We all entered now fully into the spirit of the movement," he declared. "We were convinced that Meade was unwilling to face us, and we therefore anticipated a pleasant affair, if we should succeed in catching him." Little Powell, it was observed, had put on his red wool hunting shirt, as he generally did at the prospect of a fight, and that seemed highly appropriate today, on a march which the first soldier said "was almost like boys chasing a hare."

Meade had been prodded, these past three months since his recrossing of the Potomac, more by the superiors in his rear than by the rebels in his front. Lincoln was giving Halleck strategy lectures, and Old Brains was passing them along with interlinear comments which, to Meade at least, were about as exasperating as they were banal. As a result he had become more snappish than ever. Staff officers quailed nowadays at his glance. If Lee had caught him somewhat off balance in his reaction to the sudden advance across the Rapidan, it was small wonder.

Back in September, for instance, when he asked what the government wanted him to do — he could drive Lee back on Richmond, he said, but he failed to see the advantage in this, since he lacked the strength to mount a siege — Halleck referred the question to the President, who replied that Meade "should move upon Lee at once in the manner of general attack, leaving to developments whether he will make it a real attack." The general-in-chief rephrased and expanded this. "The main objects," he told Meade, "are to threaten Lee's position, to ascertain more certainly the condition of affairs in his army, and, if possible, to cut off some portion of it by a sudden raid." Then he, like Lincoln, stressed that these were suggestions, not orders. Meade replied that this last was precisely the trouble, so far as he was concerned. He saw no profit to be gained from the proposed endeavor, whereas he discerned in it the possibility of a good deal of profitless bloodshed, and he was therefore "reluctant to run the risks involved without the positive sanction of the government." Lincoln remained unwilling to accept the responsibility it seemed to him the general was trying to unload; "I am not prepared to order or even advise an advance in this case," he told Halleck. But he added that he saw in the present impasse "matter for very serious consideration in another aspect." If Lee's 60,000 could neutralize Meade's 90,000, he went on, why could not Meade, at that same two-three ratio, detach 50,000 men to be used elsewhere to advantage while he neutralized Lee's 60,000 with his remaining 40,000? "Having practically come to the mere defensive," Lincoln wrote, "it seems to be no economy at all to employ twice as many men for that object as are needed." And having come so far in the way of observation, he went further: "To avoid misunderstanding, let me say that to attempt to fight the enemy slowly back into his intrenchments at Richmond, and there to capture him, is an idea I have been trying to repudiate for quite a year. My judgment is so clear against it that I would scarcely allow the attempt to be made if the general in command should desire to make it. My last attempt upon Richmond was to get McClellan, when he was nearer there than the enemy was, to run in ahead of him. Since then I have constantly desired the Army of the Potomac to make Lee's army, and not Richmond, its objective point. If our army cannot fall upon the enemy and hurt him where he is, it is plain to me it can gain nothing by attempting to follow him over a succession of intrenched lines into a fortified city."

Meade perceived that he had fallen among lawyers, men who could do with logic and figures what they liked. Moreover the President, in his conclusion with regard to the unwisdom of driving Lee back into the Richmond defenses, had merely returned to the point Meade himself had made at the outset, except that now the latter found it somehow used against him. The technique was fairly familiar, even to a man who had never served on a jury, but it was no less exasperating for that, and Meade was determined that if he was to go the way of McDowell and McClellan, of Pope and McClellan again, of Burnside and Hooker, he would at least make the trip to the scrap heap under his own power. In the absence of orders or "sanction" from above, he would accept the consequences of his own decisions and no others, least of all those of which he disapproved; he would fall, if fall he must, by following his own conscience. Thus, by a reaction like that of a man alone in dangerous country — which Virginia certainly was — his natural caution was enlarged. In point of fact, he believed he had reasons to doubt not only the intentions of those above him, but also the present temper of the weapon they had placed in his hands three months ago and had recently diminished by two-sevenths. Of the five corps still with him, only two were led by the generals who had taken them to Gettysburg, and these were Sykes and Sedgwick, neither of whom had been seriously engaged in that grim struggle. Of the other three, the badly shot-up commands of Reynolds and Sickles were now under Newton and French, who had shown little in the way of ability during or since the return from Pennsylvania, and Warren, who had replaced the irreplaceable Hancock, was essentially a staff man, untested in the exercise of his new, larger duties. This too was part of what lay behind Meade's remarks, both to his wife in home letters and to trusted members of his staff in private conversations, that he disliked the burden of command so much he wished the government would relieve him.

So when Lee came probing around his right, October 9 and 10, though he knew that Lincoln and Halleck would not approve, he did as Pope had done: pulled out of the constricting V to get his army onto open ground that would permit maneuver. Unlike Pope, however, he did not stop behind the Rappahannock to wait for an explosion deep in his rear. Instead, he kept moving up the Orange & Alexandria Railroad — bringing his rear with him, so to speak. His aim was basically the same as

Lee's: the infliction of some "terrible wound," if Lee and Providence afforded him the opportunity. Meanwhile he took care to see that he afforded none to an adversary whose considerable fame had been earned at the expense of men who either had been negligent in that respect or else had been overeager in the other. He kept his five corps well closed up, within easy supporting distance of one another as they withdrew northeast along the railroad.

Not all who were with him approved of his cautious tactics; a volunteer aide, for example, considered them about as effective as trying "to catch a sea gull with a pinch of salt"; but Meade was watching and waiting, from Rappahannock Station through Warrenton Junction, for the chance he had in mind. Then suddenly on October 14, just up the line at Bristoe Station, he got it. The opportunity was brief, scarcely more indeed than half an hour from start to finish, but he made the most of it while it lasted. Or anyhow the untried Warren did.

Approaching Bristoe from the west at high noon, after a rapid march of fifteen miles, Hill saw northeastward, beyond Broad Run and out of reach, heavy columns of the enemy slogging toward Manassas Junction, a scant four miles away. He had not won the race. But neither had he lost it, he saw next; not entirely. What appeared to be the last corps in the Federal army was only about half over the run, crossing at a ford just north of the little town on the railroad, which came in arrow-straight from the southwest, diagonal to the Confederate line of march. The uncrossed half of the blue corps, jammed in a mass on the near bank of the stream while its various components awaited their turn at the ford, seemed to Little Powell to be his for the taking, provided he moved promptly. This he did. Ordering Heth, whose division was in the lead, to go immediately from march to attack formation, he put two of his batteries into action and sent word for Anderson, whose division was in column behind Heth's, to come forward on the double and reinforce the attack. Fire from the guns did more to hasten than to impede the crossing, however, and Hill told Heth, though he had only two of his four brigades in line by now, to attack at once lest the bluecoats get away. Heth obeyed, but as his men started forward he caught a glint of bayonets to their right front, behind the railroad embankment. When he reported this to Hill, asking whether he would not do better to halt for a reconnaissance, Hill told him to keep going: Anderson would be arriving soon to cover his flank. So the two brigades went on. It presently developed, however, that what they were going on to was by no means the quick victory their commander had intended, but rather a sudden and bloody repulse at the hands of veterans who had stood fast on Cemetery Ridge, fifteen weeks ago tomorrow, to serve Pickett in much the same fashion, except that here the defenders had the added and rare advantage of surprise.

They made the most of it. Behind the embankment, diagonal to the advancing line, was the II Corps under Warren, the former chief of engineers, who, demonstrating here at Bristoe as sharp an eye for terrain as he had shown in saving Little Round Top, had set for the unsuspecting rebels what a later observer called "as fine a trap as could have been devised by a month's engineering." His — not Sykes's, as Hill had supposed from a hurried look at the crowded ford and the heavy blue columns already beyond Broad Run — was the last of the five Federal corps, and when he saw the situation up ahead he improvised the trap that now was sprung. As the two gray brigades came abreast of the three cached divisions, the bluecoats opened fire with devastating effect. Back up the slope, Little Powell watched in dismay as his troops, reacting with soldierly but misguided instinct, wheeled right to charge the embankment wreathed in smoke from the enfilading blasts of musketry. This new attempt, by two stunned brigades against three confident divisions, could have but one outcome. The survivors who came stumbling back were pitifully few, for many of the startled graybacks chose surrender, preferring to remain with their fallen comrades rather than try to make the return journey up the bullet-torn slope they had just descended. Elated, the Federals made a quick sortie that netted them five pieces of artillery and two stands of colors, which they took with them when they drew off, unmolested, across the run. The worst loss to the Confederates, though, was men. Both brigade commanders were shot down, along with nearly 1400 killed or wounded and another 450 captured. The total thus was close to 1900 casualties, as compared to a Union total of about 300, only fifty of whom were killed. In the particular, the results were even sadder from the southern point of view. A North Carolina regiment on the exposed flank lost 290 of its 416 enlisted men, or just under seventy percent, plus all but three of its 36 officers. Here too fell Carnot Posey, who was struck in the thigh by a fragment of shell when he brought up his Mississippi brigade near the close of the action. The wound, though ugly, was not thought to be grave, but infection set in and he died one month later.

Indignation swept through the gray army when the rest of it arrived in the course of the afternoon and learned of what had happened at midday, down in the shallow valley of Broad Run. No segment of the Army of Northern Virginia had suffered such a one-sided defeat since Mechanicsville, which had also been the result of Little Powell's impetuosity. "There was no earthly excuse for it," a member of Lee's staff declared, "as all our troops were well in hand, and much stronger than the enemy." One North Carolinian, still angered years later by the sudden and useless loss of so many of his friends, said flatly: "A worse managed affair than this ... did not take place during the war." Hill's only reply to such critics was included in the report he submitted within two weeks. "I am convinced that I made the attack too hastily," he wrote, "and at the same time that a delay of half an hour, and there would have been no enemy to attack. In that event I believe I should equally have blamed myself for not attacking at once." Seddon and Davis both endorsed the report. "The disaster at Bristoe Station seems due to a gallant but over-hasty pressing on of the enemy," the former observed, while the latter added: "There was a want of vigilance." These comments stung the thin-skinned Virginian, but worse by far had been Lee's rebuke next morning when Hill conducted him over the field, where the dead still lay in attitudes of pained surprise, and explained what had occurred. Lee said little, knowing as he did that his auburn-haired lieutenant's high-strung impetuosity, demonstrated in battle after battle — but most profitably at Sharpsburg, of which he himself had written: "And then A. P. Hill came up" — had gained the army far more than it cost.

"Well, well, General," he remarked at last, "bury these poor men and let us say no more about it."

He was distracted by the possibility of much heavier bloodshed, four miles up the line, where so much blood had been shed twice already. It seemed to him that Meade, encouraged by Warren's coup the day before, would call a halt and prepare to fight a Third Manassas. That was very much what Lee himself wanted, despite the disparity in numbers, and when someone expressed regret that so historic a field should be widely known by the unromantic name "Bull Run," he replied that with the blessings of God they would "make it another Cowpens." Others had a different reason for wanting to push on at once to the famed junction. According to one of Stuart's men, "We were looking forward to Manassas with vivid recollections of the rich haul we had made there just prior to the second battle of Manassas, and everybody was saying, 'We'll get plenty when we get to Manassas.'" As it turned out, though, Meade wanted no part of a third fight on that unlucky ground. He marched rapidly beyond it, without even a rest halt for his army. There was no battle, and there was no "rich haul" either. "We were there before we knew it," the hungry trooper wrote. "Everything was changed. There was not a building anywhere. The soil, enriched by debris from former camps, had grown a rich crop of weeds that came halfway up the sides of our horses, and the only way we recognized the place was by our horses stumbling over the railroad tracks."

This dreary vista was repeated all around. "Never have I witnessed as sad a picture as Prince William County now presents," a young staff colonel noted in a letter home. "'Tis desolation made desolate indeed. As far as the eye can reach on every side, there is one vast, barren wilderness; not a fence, not an acre cultivated, not a living object visible, and but for here and there a standing chimney, on the ruins of what was once a handsome and happy home, one would imagine that man was never here and that the country was an entirely new one, without any virtue except its vast extent." Under such circumstances, with an inadequate wagon train and the railroad inoperable because the Federals had blown the larger bridges as they slogged northward, for Lee to remain where he was meant starvation for his men and horses. Nor could he attack, except at a prohibitive disadvantage; Meade had taken a position of great natural strength, which he promptly

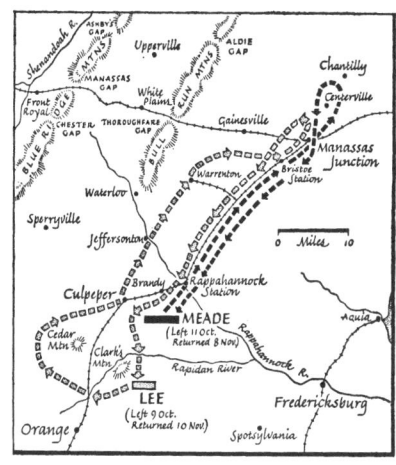

improved with intrenchments, along the Centerville-Chantilly ridge. Lee was confident he could turn him out of this, but that would be to drive him back on Washington with its 50,000-man garrison and its 589 guns (Richmond, by contrast, had just over 5000 men in its defenses and 42 guns); which plainly would not do, even if the poorly shod and thinly clad Confederates had been in any condition for pursuit, now that the weather was turning colder, along the rocky pikes of Fairfax County. Next day, October 16, a heavy rain seemed more or less to settle the question of any movement, in any direction whatever, by drenching the roads and fields, swelling the unbridged streams, and confining the southern commander to his tent with an attack of what was diagnosed as lumbago. His decision, reached before the downpour stopped that night, was to withdraw as he had come, back down the railroad, completing the destruction his opponent had begun. The march south got under way next morning, despite the mud. Stuart, assigned the task of covering the rear, did so with such zest and skill that he won another of those handy and sometimes laugh-provoking victories by which he justified his plume and his fox-hunt manner.

Meade did not pursue, except with his cavalry, and he soon had cause to regret that he had done even that much. Stuart withdrew by way of Gainesville, down the Warrenton pike, Fitz Lee by way of Bristoe, down the railroad; the arrangement was that the two would combine if either was faced with more than he could handle. Pressed by superior numbers of blue troopers — Pleasonton had three divisions, under Buford, Gregg, and Kilpatrick — Jeb fell back across Broad Run on the night of the 18th and, sending word for Fitz to reinforce him, took up a position on the south bank to contest a crossing at Buckland Mills. He was having little trouble doing this next morning, banging away with his guns at the bridge he had purposely left intact as a challenge, when a courier arrived with a suggestion from Fitz Lee, who had heard the firing and ridden ahead to assess the situation. If Stuart would fall back down the turnpike, pretending flight in order to draw the Yankees pellmell after him, the courier explained, Fitz would be able to surprise them when they came abreast of a hiding place he would select for that purpose, some distance south, behind one of the low ridges adjoining the pike; whereupon Jeb could turn and charge them, converting the blue confusion into a rout. Stuart liked the notion and proceeded at once to put it into effect. The bluecoats — Judson Kilpatrick's division, with Custer's brigade in the lead — snapped eagerly at the bait, pounding across the run in close pursuit of the fleeing graybacks, who led them on a five-mile chase to Chestnut Hill. At that point, only two miles short of Warrenton, the "chase" ended. Hearing Fitz Lee's guns bark suddenly from ambush, Jeb's horsemen whirled their mounts and charged the head of the now halted and badly rattled column in their rear. There followed another five-mile pursuit — much like the first, except that it was in the opposite direction and was not a mock chase, as the other had been, but a true flight for life — all the way back to Buckland Mills, where Stuart finally called a halt, laughing as he watched the Federals scamper across to the north bank of Broad Run. He had captured something over two hundred of them, along with several ambulances, Custer's headquarters wagon, and a good deal of dropped equipment. One regret he had, however, and this was that Kilpatrick had not kept his artillery near the front, as prescribed by the tactics manual; in which case, Jeb was convinced, "it would undoubtedly have fallen into our hands."

Lee congratulated his chief of cavalry, along with his nephew Fitz, for achieving "this handsome success" — an action known thereafter to Confederates as the "Buckland Races" — though he was also prompt to deny the permission sought by Stuart, in his elation at the outcome of the ruse, to undertake a raid behind Meade's lines while the blue troopers were trying to pull themselves together. In truth, Jeb and his men had done quite enough in the past ten days. Not only did the Buckland farce help to restore the army's morale, damaged five days ago by the Bristoe fiasco, but at a cost of 408 casualties, most of them only slightly injured, he had inflicted 1251 on the enemy cavalry, all but about three hundred of them killed or captured, and had assisted in the taking of some 600 infantry prisoners, mostly stragglers encountered during the movement north. Meade's losses totaled 2292, which was only a bit lower than Lee's for the same period, including those suffered at Bristoe. Except for that unfortunate engagement, the gray army could congratulate itself on another highly successful, if necessarily brief, campaign. With no more than 48,402 effectives, as compared to Meade's 80,789, Lee had maneuvered his adversary into a sixty-mile withdrawal, from the Rapidan to beyond Bull Run. And now, though he himself was obliged to withdraw in turn for lack of subsistence, he did what he could to insure that the inevitable Union follow-up would be a slow one. Meade had burned only the bridges on the Orange & Alexandria; now Lee burned the crossties, too, and warped the rails beyond salvation by piling them atop the burning ties. The Federals, unable to feed themselves without the use of the railroad now that the autumnal rains were turning the roads to quagmires, would advance no faster than their work gangs could lay track. Recrossing the Rappahannock, Lee called a halt and gave his men some badly needed rest while waiting for the blue army to arrive.

This took even longer than he had supposed it would do: not only because of the thorough job the blue and butternut wreckers had done on the Orange & Alexandria, but also because the Federal commander was involved again in a distractive telegraphic skirmish with the authorities in his rear. The President had been distressed by what seemed to him the supine attitude of Meade in falling back under pressure from Lee's inferior force, and this distress was increased on October 15, when the general, announcing Warren's repulse of the rebels at Bristoe Station, passed along information gleaned from prisoners "that Hill's and Ewell's corps, reinforced to a reported strength of 80,000, are advancing on me, their plan being to secure the Bull Run field in advance of me." He supposed, he said, that Lee would "turn me again, probably by the right . . . in which case I shall either fall on him or retire nearer Washington." Lincoln presumed from past performances that Meade would certainly choose the latter course, and when it did not come to that, since Lee advanced no farther than Bull Run, he took this as evidence that the Confederates were by no means as strong as the prisoners had claimed. Irked by what seemed to him a superfluity of caution, he risked a near commitment. "If Gen. Meade can now attack [Lee] on a field no worse than equal for us," he wrote Halleck next day, "and will do so with all the skill and courage which he, his officers, and men possess, the honor will be his if he succeeds, and the blame may be mine if he fails." Perhaps Meade noted the "may" in the copy Halleck sent him that same day, or perhaps he recalled that other such letters had preceded other downfalls. In any event, since neither of his superiors was willing to put the suggestion in the form of a direct order, he chose rather to continue the policy he had been following all along. Besides, he protested, this policy was no different from the one being urged on him. "It has been my intention to attack the enemy, if I can find him on a field no more than equal for us," he replied. "I have only delayed doing so from the difficulty of ascertaining his exact position, and the fear that in endeavoring to do so my communications might be jeopardized."

It seemed to Halleck that what Meade was in fear of jeopardizing was his reputation. Accordingly, with the encouragement of their Commander in Chief, he decided to crack down harder, apparently in the belief that more pressure from above might stiffen the reluctant general's backbone. Two days later, on October 18, Meade reported that Lee was again in motion, and though he did not know what the Virginian had in mind, he thought he might be headed for the Shenandoah Valley, as he had done after Chancellorsville. Halleck replied that this might be so, but he added tauntingly: "If Lee has turned his back on you to cross the mountains, he certainly has seriously exposed himself to your blows, unless his army can move two miles to your one." By evening, moreover, the general-in-chief had decided there was nothing to the report. "Lee is unquestionably bullying you," he wired. "If you cannot ascertain his movements, I certainly cannot. If you pursue and fight him, I think you will find out where he is. I know of no other way." Sooner or later, all subordinates — even the placid Grant — bridled under this kind of treatment from Old Brains, and the short-tempered Meade was by no means an exception. "If you have any orders to give me, I am prepared to receive and obey them," he shot back, "but I must insist on being spared the infliction of such truisms in the guise of opinions as you have recently honored me with, particularly as they were not asked for." By way of emphasis he added: "I take this occasion to repeat what I have before stated, that if my course, based on my own judgment, does not meet with approval, I ought to be, and I desire to be, relieved from command." This was his trump card, never played without overriding effect; for who was there in the Army of the Potomac to replace him? ("What can I do, with such generals as we have?" Lincoln had asked, some weeks ago, in response to urgings that the Pennsylvanian be relieved. "Who among them is any better than Meade?") Snail-like, Halleck pulled his horns in — as, in fact, it was his custom to do whenever they encountered resistance. "If I have repeated truisms," he wired the general next morning, "it has not been to give offense, but to give you the wishes of the government. If, in conveying these wishes, I have used words which were unpleasing, I sincerely regret it." Now it was Meade's turn to be high-handed. "Your explanation of your intentions is accepted," he replied, "and I thank you for it."

Privately, however — when he found out, as he presently did, that the Confederates were not headed for the Valley but were withdrawing as they had come, back down the railroad — he admitted that Lee had indeed bullied him, though he did not use that word. He perceived now that it had never been his adversary's real intention to come between him and Washington at all, as he had supposed, but simply to maneuver him rearward, sixty miles or more, and thus forestall a continued Union advance during the brief period of good weather that remained. Lee's had been "a deep game," Meade wrote his wife on October 21, "and I am free to admit that in the playing of it he has got the advantage of me." Accordingly, after his cavalry failed to intercept or indeed scarcely even trouble the retiring enemy, he put his repair gangs to work on the wrecked supply line and followed with his infantry. The advance was necessarily slow, being regulated to the speed with which the rails were laid and the bridges reconstructed. There was even time for a quick visit to the capital, at Halleck's urging, for a conference with the President. This was held on October 23, and Meade reported to his wife that he found Lincoln kind and considerate, though obviously disappointed that he had not got a battle out of Lee. At one point, though, the talk shifted to Gettysburg and the touchy subject of the pursuit of the rebels to the Potomac. "Do you know, General, what your attitude toward Lee for a week after the battle reminded me of?" Lincoln asked, and when Meade replied, "No, Mr President, what is it?" Lincoln said: "I'll be hanged if I could think of anything else than an old woman trying to shoo her geese across a creek."

For once, Meade kept his temper under control, but he was glad to return next day to his army, away from the Washington atmosphere. Though the advance was proceeding about as fast as could be expected with the railroad as thoroughly smashed as it was, he dispensed with none of his previous caution, wanting no part of a battle on such terms as he believed Lee (not Lincoln) would be willing to offer him. Finally, by the end of the month, he was back on the Rappahannock, whose crossings he found defended. He had been reinforced to a strength of 84,321 effectives, whereas Lee was down to 45,614 as a result of sickness brought on by exposing his thin-clad veterans to cold and rainy weather on the march. Unaware that the odds had lengthened again to almost two-to-one, Meade took a long look at the rebel defenses and, finding them formidable — Lee's soldiers had apparently been as hard at work as his own, but with shovels rather than sledges — proposed on November 2 a change of base downstream to Fredericksburg, which he said would not only put him back on the direct route to Richmond, but would also avoid the need for crossing a second river immediately after the first.

Lincoln was prompt to disapprove. He had been willing to have the army fight a Third Bull Run, but it seemed to him only a little short of madness to invite a Second Fredericksburg. So Meade looked harder than ever at what faced him here on the upper Rappahannock, where, if anywhere, he would have to do his fighting.

Despite the nearly two-to-one odds his army faced in its risky position within the constricting V of the rivers, Lee awaited Meade's advance with confidence and as much patience as his ingrained preference for the offensive would permit. "If I could only get some shoes and clothes for the men," he said, "I would save him the trouble." In electing to stand on the line of the Rappahannock — shown in the past to be highly vulnerable at Kelly's Ford, where the south bank was lower than the north — he had evolved a novel system of defense. Massing his troops in depth near the danger point, he prepared to contest a crossing there only after the blue infantry had moved beyond the effective range of its artillery on the dominant north bank, and in furtherance of this plan (patterned, so far, after the one he had used with such success at Fredericksburg, just short of eleven months ago) he maintained at Rappahannock Station, five miles upstream, a bridgehead on the far side of the river, fortified against assault by the labor-saving expedient of turning the old Federal works so that they faced north instead of south. A pontoon bridge near the site of the wrecked railroad span, safely beyond the reach of enemy batteries, made possible a quick withdrawal or reinforcement of the troops who, by their presence, were in a position to divide Meade's forces or attack him flank and rear in case he massed them for a downstream crossing. Ewell's corps guarded all these points, with Early in occupation of the tête-de-pont, Rodes in rear of Kelly's Ford, and Johnson in reserve; Hill's was upstream, beyond Rappahannock Station. For more than two weeks, October 20 to November 5, Lee waited in his Brandy headquarters for Meade's arrival. On the latter date his outpost scouts sent word that blue reconnaissance patrols were probing at various points along the river, and two days later the whole Union army was reported to be approaching in two main columns, one headed for the north-bank bridgehead, the other for Kelly's Ford.

  This report, which was just what he had expected and planned for, reached him about noon. After notifying Hill to be on the alert for orders to reinforce Ewell, he rode from Brandy to Early's headquarters near the south end of the pontoon bridge affording access to the works on the north bank. When Early explained that he was sending another of his brigades to join the one already across the river, Lee approved but he also took the precaution of ordering Hill to shift his right division over to the railroad so that it would be available as an additional reserve. Similarly, when he learned a bit later that the bluecoats had crossed in force at Kelly's Ford, he instructed Edward Johnson to move in closer support of Rodes. Old Jubal went over to the north bank late in the afternoon and returned to report that the Yankees had made so little impression there that one of his brigade commanders had assured him that, if need be, he could hold the position against the whole Federal army. Dusk came down, and presently, in the gathering darkness beyond the river, Lee and Early saw muzzle flashes winking close to the works on the north bank. A south wind carried the noise away, and anyhow the pinkish yellow flashes soon went out. Convinced that this brief twilight action had been no more than a demonstration, probably to cover the advance on Kelly's Ford — in any event, no enemy had ever made a night attack on his infantry in a fortified position — Lee rode back to Brandy under the growing light of the stars, well satisfied with

The Center Gives [801]

the results so far of the reception he had planned for Meade along the Rappahannock.

Unwelcome news awaited him at headquarters, in the form of a dispatch from Ewell. The greater part of two regiments assigned by Rodes to picket duty at Kelly's Ford had been gobbled up by the Federals, who then had laid a pontoon bridge and were sending substantial reinforcements across to the south bank. A loss of 349 veterans was not to be taken lightly, but aside from this the situation was about what Lee had expected. The thing to do now was make threatening gestures from within the bridgehead, which should serve to hold a major portion of Meade's force on the north bank, and shift two divisions of Hill's corps eastward to strengthen Rodes and Johnson for an all-out fight in rear of Kelly's Ford. That was the preconceived plan, whereby Lee intended to fall on a segment of the blue army, as he had done so often in the past, with the greater part of his own. Before this could be ordered, however, still worse news — indeed, almost incredible news — arrived from Early. Massing heavily at close range in the darkness before moonrise, the Federals had stormed and overrun the north-bank intrenchments, killing or capturing all of the troops in the two Confederate brigades except about six hundred who had swum the river or run the gauntlet over the pontoon bridge. The loss would come to 1674 men: and with them, of course, went the bridgehead itself, upon which the plan for Meade's discomfiture depended. Nor was it only the offensive that had been wrecked. Obviously the army could not remain in its present position after daylight, exposed on a shallow extended front with the Rapidan in its rear. Lee was upset but he kept his poise, thankful at any rate that Early had set the floating bridge afire to prevent a crossing by the bluecoats now in occupation of Rappahannock Station. Orders went out for Hill to retire by crossing the railroad between Culpeper and Brandy, while Ewell fell back toward Germanna Ford, contesting if necessary the advance of the blue force from Kelly's. For two days the movement continued. On November 9, when the bluecoats drew near, both corps halted and formed for battle, still within the V, but when Meade did not press the issue Lee resumed his withdrawal and crossed the Rapidan next morning. The army was back in the position it had left, marching west and north around the enemy right, a month ago yesterday.

The blue-clad veterans were elated; their 461 casualties amounted to less than a fourth of the number they had inflicted. French had moved with speed and precision on the left, seizing Kelly's Ford before the rebel pickets even had time to scamper rearward out of reach, and Uncle John Sedgwick, on the right with his own and Sykes's corps, had performed brilliantly, improvising tactics which resulted in the capture not only of the fortified tête-de-pont, supposed impregnable by its defenders, but also of the largest haul of prisoners ever secured by the army in one fell, offensive swoop. Meade's stock rose accordingly with the men in the ranks, who began to say that Bobby Lee had better look to his laurels, though there was presently some grumbling that the coup had not been followed by another, equally vigorous and even more profitable, while the rebs were on the run. Conversely, there was chagrin in the Confederate ranks. The double blow had cost a total of 2033 men: more, even, than Bristoe Station and in some ways even worse than that fiasco, which at least had not been followed by an ignominious retreat. Now it was Ewell's turn to be excoriated, as Hill had been three weeks before. "It is absolutely sickening," one of his young staff officers, a holdover from Stonewall's day, lamented. "I feel personally disgraced... as does everyone in the command. Oh, how each day is proving the inestimable value of General Jackson to us!" Early and Rodes were both intensely humiliated, and though Lee did not berate them or their corps commander, any more than he had berated Little Powell in a similar situation, neither did he attempt to reduce their burden of guilt by assigning any share of the blame to the men who had been captured and were now on their way to prison camps in the North. Quite the contrary, in fact; for he observed in his report to Richmond that "the courage and good conduct of the troops engaged have been too often tried to admit of question."

Both the elation on the one hand and the chagrin on the other were soon replaced by a sort of mutual boredom on both sides of the familiar Rapidan, where the two armies returned to their old occupation of staring at one another from the now leafless woods on its opposite banks — what time, that is, they were not engaged in the informal and illegal exchange of coffee, tobacco, and laugh-provoking insults. If there was less food on the south bank, there was perhaps more homesickness on the north, the majority of the soldiers there having come a longer way to save the Union than their adversaries had come to save the Confederacy. Presently there was rain and more rain, chill and dripping, which served to increase the discomfort, as well as the boredom, despite the snug huts put up as a sign that the armies had gone into winter quarters. A northern colonel, a staff volunteer, spoke for both sides in giving his reaction to his surroundings. "The life here is miserably lazy," he wrote home; "hardly an order to carry, and the horses all eating their heads off.... If one could only be at home, till one was *wanted*, and then be on the spot. But this is everywhere the way of war; lie still and lie still; then up and maneuver and march hard; then a big battle; and then a lot more lie still."

✗ 3 ✗

Rosecrans was relieved on the day of the Buckland Races, exactly one month after the opening day of Chickamauga, whose loss had resulted first in his retreat, then in his besiegement, and finally in his removal from command. Grant left Louisville by rail next morning, October 20, spent the night in Nashville, and went on the following day to Stevenson, Alabama, for an early evening conference with Rosecrans, who had left Chattanooga the day before, promptly on receipt of Grant's wire, because he had not wanted to encourage by his presence any demonstrations of regret at his departure from the army he would have commanded for a full year if he had lasted one week longer. It was untrue that he had intended to evacuate the beleaguered town, as Dana had told Stanton he had it in mind to do; in point of fact, he had been hard at work for the past ten days with his chief of engineers on plans for solving the acute supply problem as a prelude to resuming the offensive. Moreover, though he disliked Grant and knew quite well that Grant returned the feeling, his devotion to their common cause enabled him not only to share with the incoming general, who had just ordered his removal, his recently worked-out plans for lifting the siege, but even to do so cordially. "He came into my car," Grant subsequently wrote, "and we held a brief interview, in which he described very clearly the situation at Chattanooga, and made some excellent suggestions as to what should be done. My only wonder was that he had not carried them out."

After the conference, Old Rosy took up his journey north and Grant proceeded to Bridgeport, where he spent the night. Next morning, with his crutches strapped to the saddle like a brace of carbines — for he still could not manage afoot without them — he began the sixty-mile horseback trek up the Sequatchie Valley and over Walden's Ridge, made necessary by the long-range rebel guns on Raccoon Mountain commanding the direct approach to Chattanooga, which was less than half the roundabout distance the army trains were obliged to travel if they were to maintain a trickle of supplies for the hungry bluecoats cooped up in the town. At Jasper, ten miles out, the party stopped for a visit with Oliver Howard, who had established his corps headquarters there soon after his arrival from Virginia two weeks before. In the course of their talk Howard saw Grant looking intently at an empty whiskey bottle on a nearby table. "I never drink," the one-armed general said hastily, anxious lest his reputation for sobriety be doubted by his new commander, whatever shortcomings the latter himself might have in that regard. "Neither do I," Grant replied, straight-faced, as he rose and hobbled out on his crutches to be lifted back onto his horse. Beyond Jasper — particularly around Anderson's Crossroads, the half-way point, where Wheeler had wrought such havoc twenty days ago — he began, like Browning's Childe Roland, to get an oppressive firsthand notion of the difficulties in store for him ahead. Rain had turned low-lying stretches of the road into knee-deep bogs, and other stretches along hillsides had been made almost impassable by washouts; the crippled general had to be carried over the worst of these, which were too unsafe to cross on horseback. Ten thousand mules and horses had died by now, either by rebel bayonets or from starvation, and a great many of their carcasses were strewn along the roadway, offensive alike to eye and nose and conscience, especially for a man who loved animals as much as Grant did. Perhaps not even the field of Shiloh, with its grisly two-day harvest still upon it, offended him more than what he encountered in the course of the present two-day ride up that quiet valley and over that barren ridge, which he descended late on October 23 to regain the north bank of the Tennessee, immediately opposite the town that was his goal.

In some ways Chattanooga itself was worse; for there, in addition to more dead and dying horses, you saw the faces of the soldiers, which showed the effects not only of their hunger — "One of the regiments of our brigade," a Kansas infantryman was to testify, "caught, killed, and ate a dog that wandered into camp" — but also the dejection proceeding from their month-old defeat at Chickamauga and the apparent hopelessness of their present tactical situation, ringed as they were by the rebel victors on all the surrounding heights. Grant crossed the river just before dark, riding carefully over the pontoon bridge, and went at once to see Thomas, who had promised four days ago to "hold the town till we starve." This was something quite different, Grant now discerned, from saying that the army would be able to live there, let alone come out of the place victorious. "I appreciated the force of this dispatch ... when I witnessed the condition of affairs which prompted it," he afterwards declared. The night was cold and rainy. He could see the campfires of the Confederates, gleaming like stars against the outer darkness, above and on three sides of him, as if he stood in the pit of a darkened amphitheater, peering up and out, east and west and south.

Chattanooga was said to be an Indian word meaning "mountains looking at each other," and next morning Grant perceived the aptness of the name. He saw on the left the long reach of Missionary Ridge, a solid wall that threw its shadow over the town until the sun broke clear of its rim, and on the right the cumulous bulge of Raccoon Mountain. Dead ahead, though, was the dominant feature of this forbidding panorama. Its summit 1200 feet above the surface of the river at its base, Lookout Mountain rose, a Union correspondent had remarked, "like an everlasting thunder storm that will never pass over." Seen as Grant saw it now, wreathed in mist, the journalist continued, "it looms up ... and recedes, but when the sun shines strongly out it draws so near as to startle you." Grant was to see it that way too, in time, but for the present what impressed him most were the guns posted high on the slopes and peaks and ridges, all trained on the blue army here below. With the help of glasses he could even see the cannoneers lounging about in careless attitudes, as if to emphasize by their idleness the advantage they enjoyed. "I suppose," he said years later, "they looked upon the garrison of Chattanooga as prisoners of war, feeding or starving themselves, and thought it would be inhuman to kill any of them except in self-defense."

With two thirds of his practically useless cavalry sent away, Thomas had about 45,000 effectives in his Army of the Cumberland, and though nothing had yet been done to relieve the most pressing of their problems — the hunger that came from trying to live on quarter-rations — Dana at least had been quick to inform Stanton, on the day of Grant's arrival "wet, dirty, and well," that "the change at headquarters here [under Thomas] is already strikingly perceptible. Order prevails instead of universal chaos." For one thing, there had been a complete reorganization, a top-to-bottom shake-up, in the course of which regiments were consolidated, brigades re-formed, and divisions redistributed. Formerly there had been eleven of these last; now there were six, assigned three each to two instead of the previous four corps. Palmer had succeeded Thomas, and Granger had been placed at the head of a new corps formed by combining his own with those of the departed Crittenden and McCook. Sheridan, Wood, and Brigadier General Charles Cruft, Palmer's successor, commanded the three divisions under Palmer; Johnson, Davis, and Baird the three under Granger. The other five division commanders had been disposed of or employed in various ways; Negley was sent North, ostensibly for his health, while Steedman and Van Cleve were made post commanders of Chattanooga and Murfreesboro, and Reynolds and Brannan were respectively appointed to be chiefs of staff and artillery, directly under Thomas. Grant approved of all these arrangements, some of which had been effected by Rosecrans, but as he examined the tactical situation confronting the reorganized army — including the alarming discovery that there was not enough ammunition for one hard day of fighting — he found it altogether bleak. "It looked, indeed, as if but two courses were open," he afterwards remarked: "one to starve, the other to surrender or be captured."

Not only did the Confederates have the tactical advantage of gazing down on their opponents with something of the complacency of marksmen contemplating fish in a rain barrel; they also had a numerical advantage. Bragg had close to 70,000 veterans on those heights and in the intervening valleys. This would be considerably overmatched, of course, when and if the Federal reinforcements arrived. Hooker was already standing by, near Bridgeport, with some 16,000 effectives — exclusive, that is, of service personnel — in the four divisions he had brought from the Army of the Potomac, while Sherman was working his way east along the Memphis & Charleston Railroad with another 20,000 in the five divisions of his Army of the Tennessee, and Burnside had about 25,000 around Knoxville in the four divisions of his Army of the Ohio. This gave a total of well over 100,000 men in the four commands. Even without Burnside, who now definitely was not coming — though he was strategically useful where he was, as a bait or a menace, hovering eastward off Bragg's flank — the combination of Thomas, Hooker, and Sherman would give Grant nearly half again as many troops as stood in the ranks of his gray besiegers. First, though, he must get them into Chattanooga, and before he could do that he would have to find a way to feed them when they got there, since otherwise they would only increase the number of hungry mouths and speed the garrison's already rapid progress toward starvation. That was what it came to every time, no matter how many angles the problem was seen from: the question of how to open a new supply line, supplementing or replacing the inadequate, carcass-littered one that led back over Walden's Ridge and down the Sequatchie Valley to the railhead depots bulging with food and ammunition at Stevenson and Bridgeport.

The answer came out of a conference with Thomas and his chief engineer, W. F. Smith, who had served in the same capacity under Rosecrans. This was that same "Baldy" Smith who had led a corps at Fredericksburg but had been transferred out of the Virginia army — as a result, it was said, of his inability to get along with Hooker any better than he had with Burnside — and had commanded the Pennsylvania militia that stood off Jeb Stuart at Carlisle during the Gettysburg campaign, after which he had been given his present assignment with the army down in Tennessee. A Vermont-born West Pointer, short and portly, thirty-nine years old and described by a fellow staffer as having "a light-brown imperial and shaggy mustache, a round, military head, and the look of a German officer, altogether," Smith was still a brigadier, despite the lofty posts he had filled, because Congress refused to confirm his promotion on grounds that he had been deeply involved in the machinations against Burnside: as indeed he had, for he was by nature contentious, ever quick to spot and carp at the shortcomings of his superiors. Grant had not seen him since their Academy days, twenty years before, but he was greatly taken with him on brief reacquaintance, mainly because Smith had arrived, on his own and in conferences with Rosecrans, at what he believed was the answer to the question of how to open a new and better supply line back to Bridgeport. It was based of course on geography, but it was also based on daring. The Tennessee River, which flowed due west past Chattanooga, turned abruptly south just beyond the town, then swung back north as if by rebound from the foot of Lookout Mountain. Two miles upstream, on the western side of the point of land inclosed by this narrow bend — Moccasin Point, it was called, from its resemblance, when seen from above, to an Indian shoe — was Brown's Ferry, an excellent site for a crossing because it was beyond the reach of all but the longest-range guns on Lookout and only a mile from the pontoon bridge already in use north of the town. From Brown's Ferry the river flowed on north, then turned south again, around the long northwestern spur of Raccoon Mountain, to describe a second and longer bend, along whose base a road led westward through Cummings Gap to another Tennessee crossing known as Kelley's Ferry, and from there along the right bank of the river down to Bridgeport.

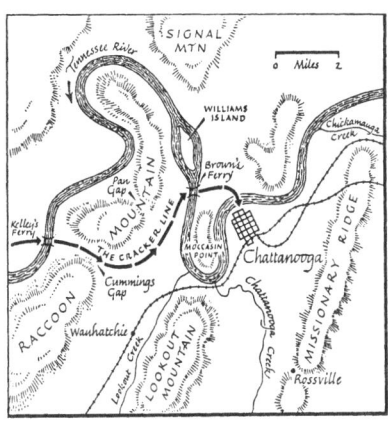

Here then was the ideal route: save for one drawback. The rebels held it. They had guns emplaced on Raccoon Mountain and pickets advanced to the river itself, squarely athwart the coveted approaches to the gap through which the road connecting the two ferries ran. But Smith had the answer to this as well, a tactical solution employing the principles of speed and stealth to achieve surprise and, with surprise, success. Crossing at Bridgeport, a force from Hooker would follow the railroad east around the south flank of the mountain, then move north under cover of darkness, still following the railroad through Wauhatchie, to close upon Brown's Ferry from the rear. Meanwhile, and also under cover of darkness, a force from Thomas would advance on the same point in two columns, one marching overland, first across the pontoon bridge at Chattanooga, then west across the narrow base of Moccasin Point, and the other floating noiselessly downriver in pontoon boats, past the sheer north face of Lookout, to spearhead the crossing at Brown's Ferry, capture the gray outpost there, and hold on while the boats were being anchored and floored over by an engineer detachment so that the column approaching by land could cross as reinforcements; whereupon the two forces, one from Hooker and one from Thomas, would combine for mop-up operations, opening Cummings Gap to clear the road leading west to Kelley's Ferry and dislodging the enemy guns on Raccoon Mountain. Once this was done, the new supply route — half the length of the old one over Walden's Ridge, and a good deal less than half as tortuous — would be securely in Federal hands; the troops in Chattanooga could go back on full rations, refill their cartridge boxes and limber chests, and prepare to deal with the graybacks still on Lookout Mountain and Missionary Ridge.

Grant liked the sound of this — particularly the notion of the silent run past Lookout, reminiscent as it was of the maneuver that opened the final phase of the Vicksburg campaign — afterwards saying of Smith: "He explained the situation of the two armies and the topography of the country so plainly that I could see it without an inspection." All the same, on the day after his arrival he rode out with Thomas and his chief engineer, back to the north bank of the Tennessee and across the base of Moccasin Point for a look at the lay of the land around Brown's Ferry. In the course of this reconnaissance Smith also showed him the work going on at a sawmill he had established for getting out the lumber needed for building the pontoons and flooring the bridge they would support after serving as transports and assault boats. Fifty of these had already been knocked together and caulked, and the workmen were also busy on an improvised steamboat, powered, as the sawmill itself was, by an engine commandeered from a nearby cotton gin. This last, Smith said, would be used for hauling supplies, once the river had been opened to traffic below the ferry. He seemed to have thought of everything. Grant was so impressed by the thoroughness and ingenuity of these preparations that as soon as he got back to Chattanooga that evening he not only issued orders for the plan to be adopted; he also directed that it was to begin within two days. Hooker was instructed to leave one division behind to guard the railroad back toward Nashville and to cross with the other three at Bridgeport on October 26, marching fast through Wauhatchie to approach Brown's Ferry from the south. Thomas was told to move the following morning, before daylight, thus allowing Hooker time to come within reach of their common objective. Grant further stipulated that Smith was to be in direct charge of the two-pronged approach from Chattanooga, later explaining that the staff engineer "had been so instrumental in preparing for the move, and so clear in his judgment about the manner of making it, that I deemed it but just to him that he should have command of the troops detailed to execute the design."

His trust was not misplaced; there was no better example, in the whole course of the war, of what the combination of careful planning, ingenuity, and great daring could accomplish under intelligent leadership. Hooker crossed on schedule at Bridgeport, leaving Slocum and one of his divisions behind to guard the Nashville & Chattanooga Railroad against saboteurs and raiders, and proceeded eastward along the Memphis & Charleston with Slocum's other division and Howard's two, a force of about 11,000 effectives. That night Smith set out across Moccasin Point with two brigades of infantry and a battalion of engineers, numbering in all about 3500 men, and at 3 o'clock the following morning, October 27, a selected group of 1500 others, who had been loaded aboard the improvised fleet of sixty pontoon-transports, cast off and started downstream from the Chattanooga wharves, two dozen men and one officer in each boat. The current was strong; there was no need for oars, except to steer with, during the nearly circuitous six-mile run. Screened by a light mist, they hugged the right bank and made the trip in just two hours, undetected by rebel lookouts despite the frantic cries of one unfortunate soldier who fell overboard and was left to drown, as he had been warned beforehand would be done if he got careless. Reaching Brown's Ferry at 5 o'clock, half an hour before dawn, the troops in the first boats swarmed ashore and captured the drowsy pickets, while oarsmen in the unloaded transports began their task of ferrying Smith's overland marchers across from the right bank, where they had waited all this time under cover of the brush and darkness.

One dispersed brigade of Confederates — for, as it turned out, this was all the force the enemy had west of Lookout Mountain — attempted to assault the beachhead in the gray dawn, but was quickly thrown into retreat by the superior blue force, which then proceeded to fortify and intrench a defensive perimeter while the engineers went hard to work on the bridge. By midmorning the pontoons had been moored and floored; reinforcements from Thomas could march across in almost any numbers Smith or Grant decided might be needed. Few would be, apparently, for those graybacks who had not been captured at the time of the landing, or knocked out during the quick repulse that followed, had withdrawn eastward across Lookout Valley, leaving Raccoon Mountain and Cummings Gap in Federal hands. Moreover, dispatches sent forward that afternoon by Hooker announced that he was approaching Wauhatchie and would arrive in person the next day. This he did, together with two of his divisions, the third having been posted as a rear guard at Wauhatchie. And now for the first time, here on the south bank of the Tennessee River, near Brown's Ferry, Union soldiers of the East and West shook hands and congratulated each other on the success of their combined operation, by which a new supply route into besieged Chattanooga was about to be opened; "The Cracker Line," they dubbed it.

Hooker had had no share in anything so obviously exciting as a six-mile run downriver through misty darkness. But the fact was, he and his troops had had perhaps the most nerve-racking time of all, if only because of the duration of the strain; and in the end they did the only real fighting involved in the operation. As he marched eastward by daylight on his first and second days away from Bridgeport, Lookout Mountain loomed nearer and taller with every mile. Rebels up there in untold numbers were watching him, alone so to speak in their own back yard, and he knew it. He counted himself fortunate when he reached Wauhatchie without being attacked, and he took the precaution of dropping John Geary's division off at that point, as a safeguard for his rear, while he continued his march north with Howard's two divisions under von Steinwehr and Carl Schurz. Presently, though, on the night of the day he made contact with Smith at Brown's Ferry — October 28 — Fighting Joe had cause to believe that what he had thought was a precautious act had in fact been an extremely rash one that might cost him no less than one third of the force he had brought across the Tennessee, and possibly much more. A sudden midnight booming of guns, loud not only at the ferry but also in the town across the way, informed him that Geary was under assault in his isolated position, three miles off. What was worse, if the attack was in sufficient force it might be launched for the purpose of overwhelming the bridgehead, in which case there would be nothing for Howard's men to do but retreat with Smith's across the river and into Chattanooga, where they would have to share the hungry garrison's meager rations and thus hasten its progress toward starvation or surrender. Determined to do what he could to avert such a fate, along with further damage to the reputation he had been given a chance to retrieve in a new theater, Hooker put Schurz on the march to reinforce the embattled Geary, the flashes of whose guns were playing fitfully on the southern horizon despite the brightness of a moon only two nights past the full, and alerted Steinwehr to stand ready to come, too, if he was needed.

The trouble, as it turned out, was by no means as serious as he had feared: not only because Geary's men gave an excellent account of themselves in defending the position at Wauhatchie, but also because the Confederates — four brigades from the absent Hood's division — became confused in their first attempt at a night attack and were unable to co-ordinate their efforts. Though the soldiers on both sides had traveled a thousand miles or more from Virginia to come to grips here in the darkness near the Tennessee-Georgia line, neither could distinguish the presence of the other except by the flashes of the shots they fired. In this sort of situation the advantage lay with the defenders, who remained in one place and at least knew where they themselves were, whereas the attackers did not even know that much for a good part of the time. Moreover, the element of surprise was by no means altogether with the latter. Geary's teamsters, for example, became frightened by the uproar and deserted their picketed mules; whereupon the mules, left to their own devices in the flame-stabbed pandemonium, broke loose from their tethers and stampeded toward the rebels, who in turn became frightened, thinking a cavalry charge had been launched at them, and stampeded too. (Just as Southerners liked to celebrate such affairs as the Buckland Races with rollicking verses, generally in parody of something at once hackneyed and heroic, so did an anonymous Ohio infantryman immortalize this "Charge of the Mule Brigade":

> *Half a mile, half a mile,*
> *Half a mile onward,*
> *Right toward the Georgia troops*
> *Broke the two hundred.*
> *"Forward, the Mule Brigade;*
> *Charge for the rebs!" they neighed.*

The Center Gives

> *Straight for the Georgia troops*
> *Broke the two hundred.*

Five stanzas later came the envoy:

> *When can their glory fade?*
> *O the wild charge they made!*
> *All the world wondered.*
> *Honor the charge they made;*
> *Honor the Mule Brigade,*
> *Long-eared two hundred.*)

In any event — aside, that is, from the disconcerting, not to say unnerving effect on the graybacks of having some two hundred fear-crazed mules come bearing down on them out of the clattering darkness — Schurz came up soon to even the odds, and the confused engagement broke off about as suddenly as it had begun. By 4 o'clock, two hours before sunrise, the Confederates had withdrawn across Lookout Creek, leaving the field to the men who had held it in the first place, and Bragg made no further attempt to interfere with the opening of the new Federal supply line. At a cost of well under five hundred casualties — 420 for Hooker, 37 for Smith — Grant had inflicted perhaps twice as many, including the prisoners taken at Brown's Ferry and picked up later on Raccoon Mountain, and had delivered the Chattanooga garrison from the grim threat of starvation, the most urgent of the several problems he had found waiting for him on his arrival, five days back. On October 30, exactly one week after he rode into town, "wet, dirty, and well," the little steamboat Smith had built tied up at Kelley's Ferry, completing a run from Bridgeport with a cargo of 40,000 rations for the troops at the opposite end of Cummings Gap. According to an officer aboard her, an orderly sent on horseback to announce the steamer's arrival returned to report "that the news went through the camps faster than his horse, and the soldiers were jubilant and cheering, 'The Cracker Line's open. Full rations, boys! Three cheers for the Cracker Line,' as if we had won another victory; and we had."

So far as Grant himself was concerned, the issue had been decided as soon as the pontoon bridge was thrown and the bridgehead secured at Brown's Ferry. His mind had moved on to other matters, even before the night action at Wauhatchie seemed for a moment to threaten the loss of what had been won. "The question of supplies may now be regarded as settled," he wired Halleck that evening, four hours before Geary came under attack. "If the rebels give us one week more time I think all danger of losing territory now held by us will have passed away, and preparations may commence for offensive operations."

✕ 4 ✕

Pleased though he was by the prospect, as he saw it from his Chattanooga headquarters now that the Cracker Line was open, Grant would have felt even more encouraged if he somehow had been able to sit in on the councils across the way, on Lookout Mountain and Missionary Ridge, and thus acquire firsthand knowledge of the bitterness that had prevailed for the past month in the camps of his adversaries. Bragg's dissatisfaction with several of his ranking lieutenants for their shortcomings during the weeks that preceded Chickamauga — willful ineptitudes, as he saw it, which had cost him the opportunity to destroy the Federal army piecemeal, in McLemore's Cove and elsewhere — was matched, if not exceeded, by their dissatisfaction with his failure, as they saw it, to gather the fruits of their great victory during the weeks that followed. Resentment bred dissension; dissension provoked criminations; recriminations led to open breaks. Polk and Hindman had departed and Harvey Hill was about to follow, relieved of duty by the army commander; while still another top subordinate — more nearly indispensable, some would say, than all the rest combined — had left under his own power. This was Forrest.

His contention that "we ought to press forward as rapidly as possible" having been ignored on the morning after the battle, the Tennessee cavalryman was sent northwest with his division, four days later, to head off or delay a supposed Union advance from Knoxville. No such threat existed, but Forrest did encounter enemy cavalry hovering in that direction and drove them helter-skelter across the Hiwassee, then through Athens and Sweetwater, slashing at their flanks and rear, to Loudon, where the survivors managed to get beyond his reach by crossing the Tennessee, eighty miles above Chattanooga and less than half that far from Knoxville. Having determined that no bluecoats were advancing from the latter place, he was on his way back across the Hiwassee, September 28, when he received a dispatch signed by an assistant adjutant on Bragg's staff. "The general commanding desires that you will without delay turn over the troops of your command previously ordered to Major General Wheeler." There was no explanation, no mention of the raid that Wheeler was about to make on the Federal supply line: just the peremptory order to "turn over the troops of your command." Forrest complied, of course, but then, having done so, dictated and sent through channels a fiery protest. "Bragg never got such a letter as that before from a brigadier," he told the staffer who took it down. A couple of days later, during an interview with the army commander, he was assured that he would get his men back as soon as they returned from over the river, and he was granted, in the interim, a ten-day leave to go to La Grange, Georgia, to see his wife for the first time since his visit to Memphis to recuperate from his Shiloh wound, a year and a half ago.

The Center Gives

While he was at La Grange, sixty miles southwest of Atlanta, he received an army order issued just after his interview with Bragg, assigning Wheeler "to the command of all the cavalry in the Army of Tennessee." Since his oath — taken in early February, after the Donelson repulse and their near duel — that he would never again serve under Wheeler was well known at headquarters, this amounted to a permanent separation of Forrest and the troopers he had raised on his own and seasoned, shortly afterward, on his December strike at Grant's supply lines in West Tennessee. Moreover, he took the order as a personal affront and he reacted in a characteristically direct manner. Interrupting his leave, he went at once to see the commanding general, accompanied by his staff surgeon as a witness.

Bragg received him in his tent on Missionary Ridge, rising and offering his hand as the Tennessean entered. Forrest declined it. "I am not here to pass civilities or compliments with you, but on other business," he said, and he launched without further preamble into a heated denunciation, which he punctuated by stabbing in Bragg's direction with a rigid index finger: "I have stood your meanness as long as I intend to. You have played the part of a damned scoundrel, and are a coward, and if you were any part of a man I would slap your jaws and force you to resent it. You may as well not issue any more orders to me, for I will not obey them ... and I say to you that if you ever again try to interfere with me or cross my path it will be at the peril of your life." And having thus attended to what he had called his "other business," he turned abruptly and stalked out of the tent. "Well, you are in for it now," his doctor companion said as they rode away. Forrest disagreed. "He'll never say a word about it; he'll be the last man to mention it. Mark my words, he'll take no action in the matter. I will ask to be relieved and transferred to a different field, and he will not oppose it."

Forrest was right in his prediction; Bragg neither took official notice of the incident nor disapproved the cavalryman's request for transfer, which was submitted within the week. He was wrong, though, in his interpretation of his superior's motives. Braxton Bragg was no coward; he was afraid of no man alive, not even Bedford Forrest. Rather, he was willing to overlook the personal affront — as the hot-tempered Tennessean, with far less provocation, had not been — for the good of their common cause. He knew and valued Forrest's abilities, up to a point, and by not pressing charges for insubordination — which would certainly have stuck — he saved his services for the country. Partly, no doubt, this was because he saw him as primarily a raider, not only a nonprofessional but an "irregular," and as such less subject to discipline for irregularities, even ones so violent as this. Others of higher rank in his army were less direct in their denunciations, but he exercised no such forbearance where they were concerned. Polk and Hindman and Hill, for instance; these he saw as regulars, and he treated them as such, writing directly to the Commander in Chief of their "want of prompt conformity to orders," as well as of their "having taken steps to procure my removal in a manner both unmilitary and un-officerlike."

He had particular reference to Hill in this, and he was right. In fact, there existed in the upper echelon of his army a cabal whose purpose was just that, to "procure [his] removal," and to do so by much the same method he himself had been employing; that is, by complaining individually and collectively to the President and the Secretary of War. Davis had received by now Polk's letter stigmatizing Bragg for "palpable weakness and mismanagement," and had also read Longstreet's note to Seddon, protesting "that nothing but the hand of God can save us or help us as long as we have our present commander." These he sought to deal with indirectly, on October 3, by explaining at some length to Bragg why he had recommended that the charges against the departed Polk not be pressed. "It was with the view of avoiding a controversy, which could not heal the injury sustained and which I feared would entail further evil," he wrote, adding that to persist would involve a full-scale investigation, "with all the crimination and recrimination there to be produced.... I fervently pray that you may judge correctly," he said in closing, "as I am well assured you will act purely for the public welfare." He hoped that this appeal to Bragg for a reduction of the pressure from above would serve to lessen the tension elsewhere along the chain of command; but he received a document, two days later, which showed that tension to be even greater than he had supposed. It came in the form of a round robin, a petition addressed to the President and signed by a number of general officers, including Hill and Buckner. While admitting "that the proceeding is unusual among military men," the petitioners contended that "the extraordinary condition of affairs in this army, the magnitude of the interests at stake, and a sense of the responsibilities under which they rest to Your Excellency and to the Republic, render this proceeding, in their judgment, a matter of solemn duty, from which, as patriots, they cannot shrink."

Their grounds for concern were stated at some length. "Two weeks ago this army, elated by a great victory which promised to be the most fruitful of the war, was in readiness to pursue the defeated enemy. That enemy, driven in confusion from the field, was fleeing in disorder and panic-stricken.... Today, after having been twelve days in line of battle in that enemy's front, within cannon range of his position, the Army of Tennessee has seen a new Sebastopol rise steadily before its view. The beaten enemy, recovering behind its formidable works from the effects of his defeat, is understood to be already receiving reinforcements, while heavy additions to his strength are rapidly approaching him. Whatever may have been accomplished heretofore, it is certain that the fruits of the victory of the Chickamauga have now escaped our grasp. The Army of Tennessee, stricken with a complete paralysis, will in a few days' time be thrown strictly on the defensive, and may deem itself fortunate if it escapes from its present position without disaster." Having thus stated the problem, the generals then went on to propose a solution that was at once tactful and explicit. "In addition to reinforcements, your petitioners would deem it a dereliction of the sacred duty they owe the country if they did not further ask that Your Excellency assign to the command of this army an officer who will inspire the army and the country with undivided confidence. Without entering into a criticism of the merits of our present commander, your petitioners regard it as a sufficient reason, without assigning others, to urge his being relieved, because, in their opinion, the condition of his health totally unfits him for the command of an army in the field."

Authorship of the document was afterwards disputed. Some said Buckner wrote it, others Hill. Bragg, for one, believed he recognized the hand of the latter in the phrasing, but Hill denied this; "Polk got it up," he said. Whoever wrote it, Davis decided that what it called for — particularly in a closing sentence: "Your petitioners cannot withhold from Your Excellency the expression of the fact that, as it now exists, they can render you no assurance of the success which Your Excellency may reasonably expect" — was another presidential journey west. "I leave in the morning for General Bragg's headquarters," he wired Lee, who was preparing to cross the Rapidan that week, "and hope to be serviceable in harmonizing some of the difficulties existing there."

He left Richmond aboard a special train, October 6, accompanied by two military aides, Colonels William P. Johnston and Custis Lee — sons of Albert Sidney Johnston and R. E. Lee — his young secretary, Burton Harrison, and the still-disconsolate John Pemberton, for whom no commensurate employment had been found in the nearly three months since his formal release from parole. Personally this saddened Davis almost as much as it did the unhappy Pennsylvanian, whom he admired for his firmness under adversity. But the truth was, there was much of sadness all around them as they traveled through the heartland of the South, in the faces of the people in their shabby towns and on their neglected farms, in the condition of the roadbeds and the cars, and even in the itinerary the presidential party was obliged to follow. The Confederacy's shrinking fortunes were reflected all too plainly in the fact that this second western journey was necessarily far more roundabout than the first had been in December, when Davis had gone directly to Chattanooga by way of Knoxville. Now the compass-boxing route led south through Charlotte and Columbia, then westward to Atlanta, and finally north, through Marietta and Dalton, to Chickamauga Station. That other time, moreover, he had extended his trip to include what he called "the further West," but this would not be possible now, the area thus referred to having fallen, like Knoxville and Chattanooga itself, under Federal occupation. Reaching Bragg's headquarters on Missionary

Ridge, October 9, he conferred in private with the general, who unburdened himself of a great many woes by placing the blame for them on his subordinates; regretfully declined the proffered services of Pemberton as a replacement for Polk, though he was still unwilling to restore the latter to duty; and, in conclusion, submitted his resignation as commander of the Army of Tennessee. This Davis refused, not wanting to disparage the abilities of the only man under whom a Confederate army had won a substantial victory since the death of Stonewall Jackson, back in May. That evening he presided over a council of war attended by Bragg and his corps commanders, Longstreet, Hill, Buckner, and Cheatham, who had taken over from Polk, pending the outcome of the bishop's current set-to with his chief. After what Davis later described as "a discussion of various programmes, mingled with retrospective remarks on the events attending and succeeding the battle of Chickamauga" — in the course of which he continued his efforts "to be serviceable in harmonizing some of the difficulties" — he inquired whether anyone had any further suggestions. Whereupon Longstreet spoke up. Bragg, he said, "could be of greater service elsewhere than at the head of the Army of Tennessee."

An embarrassing silence followed: embarrassing at any rate to Bragg, who looked neither left nor right, as well as to Davis, who after all had come here to compose differences, not to create scenes that would enlarge them. After a time, however, he asked the other generals how they felt about the matter, and all replied that they agreed with what had just been said — particularly Hill, who seemed to relish the opportunity this afforded for an airing of his views. Bragg sat immobile through the painful scene, his dark-browed face expressionless. Without giving any opinion of his own, Davis at last adjourned the council. But next day, when he sounded Longstreet on his willingness to accept the command in place of Bragg, the Georgian declined. "In my judgment," he explained later, "our last opportunity was gone when we failed to follow the success at Chickamauga, and capture or disperse the Union army, and it could not be just to the service or myself to call me to a position of such responsibility." He had, however, a suggestion: Joseph E. Johnston. Davis bridled at the name, which Longstreet said "only served to increase his displeasure, and his severe rebuke." This in turn caused Old Peter to tender his resignation, but Davis, as he said, "was not minded to accept that solution to the premise." At the close of the interview, Longstreet afterwards wrote, "the President walked as far as the gate, gave me his hand in his usual warm grasp, and dismissed me with his gracious smile; but a bitter look lurking about its margin, and the ground-swell, admonished me that the clouds were gathering about headquarters of the First Corps even faster than those that told the doom of the Southern cause."

If Davis was pained, if a bitter look did lurk in fact about the margin of his smile, it was small wonder; for he was being required to deal with a problem which came more and more to seem insoluble. Though Bragg's subordinates, or former subordinates, all agreed that he should be removed, none of those who were qualified was willing to take his place. First Longstreet, then Hardee, on being questioned, replied that they did not want the larger responsibility, while Polk and Hill, Buckner and Cheatham, either through demonstrated shortcomings in the case of the former pair or lack of experience in the latter, were plainly unqualified. Lee had been suggested, but had made it clear that he preferred to remain in Virginia, where there could be no doubt he was needed. Joe Johnston, on the other hand, had once been offered the command and once been ordered to it, and both times had refused, protesting that Bragg was the best man for the post. Besides, if past performance was any indication of what could be expected from a general, to appoint Johnston would be to abandon all hope of an aggressive campaign against the cooped-up Federals.... Davis thought the matter over for three days, and then on October 13 announced his decision in the form of a note to Bragg: "Regretting that the expectations which induced the assignment of that gallant officer to this army have not been realized, you are authorized to relieve Lieutenant General D. H. Hill from further duty with your command." It had been obvious from the outset that one of the two North Carolinians would have to go. Now Davis had made his choice. Bragg would remain as commander of the army, and Hill — an accomplished hater, with a sharp tongue he was never slow to use on all who crossed him, including now the President — would return to his home state.

In addition to concerning himself with this command decision, in which Bragg emerged the winner more by default than by virtue of his claim, Davis also inspected the defenses, reviewed the troops, and held strategy conferences for the purpose of learning what course of action the generals thought the army now should take. Basically, Bragg was in favor of doing nothing more than holding what he had; that is, of keeping the Federals penned up in the town until starvation obliged them to surrender. He felt sure that this would be the outcome, and he said so, not only now but later, in his report. "Possessed of the shortest road to the depot of the enemy, and the one by which reinforcements must reach him," he would still maintain in late December, "we held him at our mercy, and his destruction was only a question of time." When Davis expressed dissatisfaction with his apparent lack of aggressiveness, Bragg came up with an alternate plan, suggested to him earlier that week in a letter from Beauregard, who, as was often the case when he had time on his hands — Gillmore and Dahlgren were lying idle just then, licking the wounds they had suffered in the course of their recent and nearly fruitless exertions, outside and just inside Charleston harbor — had turned his mind to grand-scale operations. In Virginia and elsewhere the

Confederates should hold strictly to the defensive, he said, so that Bragg could be reinforced by 35,000 troops, mainly from Lee, in order to cross the Tennessee, flank the bluecoats out of Chattanooga, and crush them in an all-out showdown battle; after which, he went on, Bragg could assist Lee in administering the same treatment to Meade, just outside Washington. He suggested, though, that the source of the plan be kept secret, lest the President be prejudiced against it in advance by his known dislike of its originator. "What I desire is our success," Old Bory wrote. "I care not who gets the credit." So Bragg at this point, being pressed for aggressive notions, offered the program as his own, expanding it slightly by proposing that a crossing be made well upstream for a descent on the Federal rear by way of Walden's Ridge. Davis listened with interest, Bragg informed Beauregard, finding merit in the suggestion; he "admitted its worth and was inclined to adopt it, only" — here was the catch; here the Creole's spirits took a drop — "he could not reduce General Lee's army." That disposed of the scheme Bragg advanced as his own, and the true author's hopes went glimmering.

Longstreet too had an alternate plan, however, which was not greatly different except that it involved no reinforcements and called for a move in the opposite direction. He proposed a change of base to Rome, for added security, and a crossing in force at Bridgeport; a move, he said, "that would cut the enemy's rearward line, interrupt his supply train, put us between his army at Chattanooga and the reinforcements moving to join him, and force him to precipitate battle or retreat." Davis liked the sound of this much better, largely because it had the virtue of economy in attempting the same purpose. Besides, he knew only too well the danger inherent in waiting idly outside the town while Yankee ingenuity went to work on the very problems for which it was best suited. Bragg concurring, albeit with hesitation, the President hopefully ordered the adoption of Old Peter's proposal and adjourned the conference.

So far, he had not addressed the troops. In fact he had declined to do so on his arrival five days ago, when he was welcomed at Chickamauga Station by a crowd of soldiers who called for a speech as he mounted his horse for the ride to army headquarters. "Man never spoke as you did on the field of Chickamauga," Davis told them, lifting his hat in return salute, "and in your presence I dare not speak. Yours is the voice that will win the independence of your country and strike terror to the heart of a ruthless foe." Now that he had toured their camps, however, and had seen for himself how rife the discontent was, he changed his mind and did what he had said he dared not do. Referring to the men before him as "defenders of the heart of our territory," he assured them that "your movements have been the object of intensest anxiety. The hopes of our cause greatly depend upon you, and happy it is that all can securely rely upon your achieving whatever, under the blessing of Providence, human power can effect." This said, he returned to his primary task of pouring oil on troubled waters, speaking not only to the troops themselves, but also to their officers, particularly those of lofty rank. "When the war shall have ended," he declared, "the highest meed of praise will be due, and probably given, to him who has claimed least for himself in proportion to the service he has rendered, and the bitterest self-reproach which may hereafter haunt the memory of anyone will be to him who has allowed selfish aspiration to prevail over the desire for the public good.... He who sows the seeds of discontent and distrust prepares for the harvest of slaughter and defeat. To zeal you have added gallantry; to gallantry, energy; to energy, fortitude. Crown these with harmony, due subordination, and cheerful support of lawful authority, that the measure of your duty may be full." He ended with a prayer "that our Heavenly Father may cover you with the shield of his protection in the hours of battle, and endow you with the virtues which will close your trials in victory complete."

These words were spoken on October 14, the date of A. P. Hill's sudden and bloody repulse at Bristoe Station. Davis stayed on for three more days, continuing his efforts to promote "harmony, due subordination, and cheerful support of lawful authority" at all levels in the strife-torn Army of Tennessee; then on October 17 — the date Stanton overtook Grant at Indianapolis — ended his eight-day visit by reboarding the train to continue his journey south for an inspection of the Mobile defenses. As he left he was assured by Bragg that Longstreet's plan for a crossing of the Tennessee on the Federal right at Bridgeport would be undertaken as soon as the troops could be gotten ready to advance.

Two days later, after inspecting a cannon foundry and other manufacturing installations at Selma, Alabama, he addressed a large crowd from his hotel balcony, asserting that if the "non-conscripts" would volunteer for garrison duty, and thus release more regular troops for service in the field, "we can crush Rosecrans and be ready with the return of spring to drive the enemy from our borders. The defeat of Rosecrans," he added, swept along by the enthusiasm his words had aroused — and unaware, of course, that Rosecrans would be relieved that day by a wire from Grant in Louisville — "will practically end the war." From Selma he proceeded to Demopolis, where he crossed the Tombigbee River and continued west across the Mississippi line to Meridian for a visit with his septuagenarian brother at nearby Lauderdale Springs. The war had been hard on Joseph Davis. Formerly one of the state's wealthiest planters, he had had to move twice already to escape the advancing Federals, not counting refugee stops along the way, and now his wife lay dying in a dilapidated house, having conserved her ebbing strength for one last glimpse of "Brother Jeff." The weary President was distressed by what he saw here, for to him it represented what was likely to happen to all his people, kin and un-kin, if the South failed in its bid for independence. Nevertheless he managed, in the course of his stay in Meridian, to work out a solution to another thorny problem of command. On October 23 — while Grant rode south down Walden's Ridge to enter Chattanooga before nightfall — he wired instructions for Bragg and Johnston, in their now separate departments, to have Polk and Hardee swap jobs and commanders, the latter to take charge of the former's corps in the Army of Tennessee, while the bishop took over the Georgian's duties at the camp for recruitment and instruction near Demopolis. This done, Davis left next morning for Mobile. After a tour of inspection with Major General Dabney H. Maury, commander of the city's defenses, he returned to the Battle House and spoke as he had done at Selma the week before, emphasizing that "those who remain at home, not less than those in arms, have their duties to perform. Each of all can encourage the spirit which can bring success," he told his listeners, adding that "men using the opportunities given by war to make fortunes will be detested by their posterity." A local reporter, impressed by the Chief Executive's "remarkably clear enunciation," observed that, though he spoke "without the slightest apparent effort, his words penetrated far down the street and were heard distinctly by most of the vast crowd gathered on the occasion."

Davis remained in Mobile over Sunday, October 25 — cheered by news of the Buckland Races, which Stuart had staged on Monday, but disappointed by Bragg's report that rain had delayed his preparations for a crossing at Bridgeport, as well as by the returns from Ohio's second-Tuesday elections, held just under two weeks ago, which showed that Lincoln's hard-war candidates had defeated Vallandigham and his Golden Circle friends — then left the following day for Montgomery, where he had arranged to have Forrest board the train for a conference en route to Atlanta. Valuing the Tennessean's abilities, the Commander in Chief not only approved his transfer to North Mississippi, where he would have authority "to raise and organize as many troops for the Confederate service as he finds practicable," but also directed that Bragg send the cavalryman a two-battalion cadre of his veteran troopers, plus Morton's battery, and recommended to Congress his promotion to major general. Forrest left the train at Atlanta, pleased to be taking up new duties as an independent commander in a region he knew well; but for his erstwhile traveling companion there was disturbing news from the Chattanooga theater. While Bragg had been waiting for the weather to clear before he moved against the enemy right, the Federals, with no apparent concern for mud and rain, had anticipated him in that direction by crossing the river themselves. Aggressive as always, Davis saw in this a chance for offensive action. "It is reported here that the enemy are crossing at Bridgeport," he wired Bragg on the 29th. "If so it may give you the opportunity to beat the detachment moving up to reinforce Rosecrans as was contemplated.... You will be able to anticipate him, and strike with the advantage of fighting him in detail." It had become increasingly evident, though, that weather was a pretense; that Bragg was favoring his preference for the defensive, despite a presidential warning, repeated today, that "the period most favorable for actual operations is rapidly passing away, and the consideration of supplies presses upon you the necessity to recover as much as you can of the country before you." Anxious that something be done at once, in Middle or East Tennessee, to justify Longstreet's prolonged absence from Virginia — where Lee was facing grievous odds, having fallen back to the line of the Rappahannock, and might need him at any moment — Davis added: "In this connection it has occurred to me that if the operations on your left should be delayed, or not be of prime importance, that you might advantageously assign General Longstreet with his two divisions to the task of expelling Burnside and thus place him in position, according to circumstances, to hasten or delay his return to the army of General Lee."

Much might come of either of these suggestions: the destruction of the blue column that had ventured across the river, within easy reach of the Confederate left, or the expulsion of Burnside from Knoxville and East Tennessee, far upstream on the right, "to recover that country and re-establish communications with Virginia." But for the present, with whatever patience he could muster while waiting for Bragg to make up his mind and move in one direction or the other, Davis resumed his journey back to the capital by way of Savannah and Charleston, neither of which he had visited since the outbreak of the war. He was welcomed to the former place on Halloween with an exuberant torchlight procession, followed by a reception at the Masonic Hall. A young matron who stood in line for a handshake wrote her soldier brother that she and her friends "were much pleased with the affability of the President. He has a good, mild, pleasant face," she added, "and, altogether, looks like a President of our struggling country *should* look — careworn and thoughtful, and firm, and quiet."

His affability came under a strain next morning, however, when Bragg announced the failure of the attempted counterstroke on his left, three nights ago at Wauhatchie, and placed the blame on Old Peter for having used an inadequate force ineptly. "The result related is a bitter disappointment," Davis replied, "as my expectations were sanguine that the enemy, by throwing across the Tennessee his force at Bridgeport, had ensured the success of the operation suggested by General Longstreet, and confided to his execution." In any case, the way was still open for an advance around the Federal right, and he hoped it would be taken, though he was obliged as always to leave the final decision to the commander on the scene. As for himself, he faced an ordeal of his own the following day in Charleston, where Beauregard was in command and the Rhetts had been attacking him, almost without remission, for the past two years in their *Mercury*. As his train drew near the station, November 2, he heard the booming of guns being fired in his honor, and when the presidential car lurched to a stop beside the platform a welcoming committee came aboard. In the lead were Beauregard, his aide and amanuensis Colonel Thomas Jordan, and Robert Barnwell Rhett, a colonel too. As a later observer put it, Davis must have "wondered how the visit would turn out when the first three hands raised in salute to him belonged to three enemies." Perhaps it was this that threw him off his stride for the first time in the course of the autumn journey he had undertaken in the hope of harmonizing discord. At any rate, inadvertently or on purpose, here today in South Carolina he did his office, his country, and his cause the worst disservice he had done since he sent the curt, slashing note in reply to Joe Johnston's six-page letter of protest at being ranked behind Lee and the other Johnston, more than two years ago in Virginia. What made it worse in this case was that he not only passed up an easy chance to heal, he actually widened a dangerous rift, and he did so with nearly as curt a slash as he had used before, except that this time the technique involved omission.

Not that the citizens themselves were cold or unfriendly. "The streets along the line of procession were thronged with people anxious to get a look at the President," a *Courier* reporter wrote. "The men cheered and the ladies waved their handkerchiefs in token of recognition." Proud of their resistance to Du Pont's and Dahlgren's iron fleet, as well as of their standing up to Gillmore's long-range shelling — which had recently begun anew, after a respite of about a month — they were pleased that the Chief Executive had come to praise their valor and share their danger. Flags were draped across the fronts of homes and buildings, and garlands of laurel stretched from the city hall to the courthouse, supporting a large banner that bid him welcome. This was Davis's first Charleston visit since the spring of 1850, when he had accompanied the body of John C. Calhoun from Washington to its grave in St Philip's churchyard, and he recalled that sad occasion when he spoke today from the portico of the city hall. In saluting the defenders of Sumter, he had special praise for the fort's commander, Major Stephen Elliott, and predicted that if the Federals ever took the city they would find no more than a "mass of rubbish," so determined were its people in their choice of whether to "leave it a heap of ruins or a prey for Yankee spoils." ("Ruins! Ruins!" the crowd shouted.) "Let us trust to our commanding general, to those having the charge and responsibilities of our affairs," Davis said, with a sidelong glance at Beauregard, and he added a note of caution, as he had done in all his speeches this past month: "It is by united effort, by fraternal feeling, by harmonious co-operation, by casting away all personal considerations... that our success is to be achieved. He who would now seek to drag down him who is struggling, if not a traitor, is first cousin to one; for he is striking the most deadly blows that can be [struck]. He who would attempt to promote his own personal ends... is not worthy of the Confederate liberty for which we are fighting." In closing, he thanked the people and assured them of his prayers "for each and all, and above all for the sacred soil of Charleston."

At the reception held afterwards in the council chamber, people inquired of one another whether they had noticed that the President, after singling out Major Elliott for praise, not only had failed to congratulate Beauregard for his skillful defense of the city by land and water, but also had not mentioned him by name. Indeed, except for that one sidelong reference to "our commanding general," when the crowd was advised to put its trust in those in charge, Old Bory might as well not have been in Charleston at all, so far as Davis was concerned. Most of those present had noted this omission, which could scarcely have been anything but intentional, it seemed to them, on the part of a man as attentive to the amenities as the President normally was. Certainly Beauregard himself had felt the slight, and it was observed that he did not attend a dinner given that evening in Davis's honor by former governor William Aiken in his house on Wragg's Square. In point of fact, the general had already declined an invitation two days earlier. "It would afford me much pleasure to dine with you," he had told Aiken, "but candor requires me to inform you that my relations with the President being strictly official, I cannot participate in any act of politeness which might make him suppose otherwise." However, even if he had accepted earlier, he most likely would not have attended a dinner honoring a man who had just given him what amounted to a cut direct. Hard on the heels of the brief reference to him in the speech, moreover, had come the allusion to complainers as cousins to traitors, and this perhaps infuriated the Creole worst of all, touching him as it did where he was tender. Unburdening his feelings to a friend, he protested that Davis had "done more than if he had thrust a fratricidal dagger into my heart! he has *killed* my *enthusiasm* for our holy cause! ... May God forgive him," he added; "I fear I shall not have charity enough to pardon him."

Although Davis saw little or nothing of the general out of hours, according to a friendly diarist he spent a pleasant week as the former governor's house guest, "Beauregard, Rhetts, Jordan to the contrary notwithstanding.... Mr Aiken's perfect old Carolina style of living delighted him," the diarist noted, not only because of "those old greyhaired darkies and their automatic, noiseless perfection of training," but also because it afforded him the leisure, while resting from the rigors of his journey, to hear firsthand accounts of the unsuccessful but persistent siege-in-progress. Gillmore had resumed his bombardment from Cummings Point a week ago, on October 26, and while at first it had been as furious as before, it presently slacked off to an intermittent shelling. An occasional big incendiary projectile was flung at Charleston, but mostly he concentrated his attention on Sumter, chipping away at the upper casemates until it began to seem to observers that the fort, daily reduced in height as debris from the ramparts slid down the outer walls, was sinking slowly beneath the choppy surface of the harbor. The defenders were on the alert for another small-boat assault, but none was attempted; Gillmore and Dahlgren, it was said, were unwilling to risk a recurrence of the previous fiasco, though each kept insisting that the other should try his hand at reducing the ugly thing. To the Confederates, however, the squat, battered pentagon was a symbol of their long-odds resistance, and as such it took on a strange beauty. An engineer captain wrote home of the feelings aroused by the sight of its rugged outline against the night sky, lanterns gleaming in unseen hands as work crews piled sandbags on the rubble, sentinels huddled for warmth over small fires in the casemates. "That ruin is beautiful," he declared, and added: "But it is more than this, it is emblematic also.... Is it not in some respects an image of the human soul, once ruined by the fall, yet with gleams of beauty and energetic striving after strength, surrounded by dangers and watching, against its foes?"

Nor, as might have been expected with the resourceful Beauregard in charge, had the garrison's efforts been limited entirely to the defensive. Using money donated for the purpose by Charlestonians, the general had had designed and built a cigar-shaped torpedo boat, twenty feet long and five feet wide, powered by a small engine and equipped with a ten-foot spar that had at its bulbous tip a 75-pound charge of powder, primed to explode when one of its four percussion nipples came in contact with anything solid, such as the iron side of a ship. Manned by a crew of four — captain and pilot, engineer and fireman — she was christened *David* and sent forth after sunset, October 5, to try her luck on the blockading squadron just across the bar. Her chosen Goliath was the outsized *New Ironsides*, the Yankee flagship that had escaped destruction back in April when the boiler-torpedo, over which Du Pont unwittingly stopped her during his attack, failed to detonate. Undetected by enemy lookouts, the *David* made contact with her spar-tip charge six feet below the *Ironsides*' waterline, but the resultant explosion threw up a great column of water that doused the little vessel's fires when it came down and nearly swamped her. As she drifted powerless out to sea, the jolted bluejackets on the ironclad's deck opened on her with a heavy fire of musketry and grape, prompting all four of her crew to go over the side. Two of these were picked up by the Federals, the captain as he paddled about in the darkness and the fireman when he was found clinging next morning to the *Ironsides*' rudder; they were clapped in irons and later sent North by Dahlgren to be tried for employing a weapon not sanctioned by civilized nations. Nothing came of that, however; they presently were exchanged, for the captain and a seaman from a captured Union gunboat, and sent back to Charleston. The other two had been there all along. Returning to the half-swamped *David* after the firing stopped, the pilot found that the engineer had been clinging to her all this time because he could not swim. They relighted her fires with a bull's-eye lantern and, eluding searchers on all sides, steamed back into the harbor before dawn. As for the *New Ironsides*, she had not been seriously damaged, the main force of the underwater explosion having fortunately been absorbed by one of her inner bulkheads. After a trip down to Port Royal for repairs to a few leaky seams, she soon returned to duty with the squadron — though from this time on, it was observed, her crew was quick to sound the alarm and open fire whenever a drifting log or a floating patch of seaweed, or less comically an incautious friendly longboat, happened near her in the dark.

Firsthand knowledge of such events as this brief sortie by the *David*, even though it failed in its purpose, and of such reactions to destruction as those of the engineer captain to the ruins of Sumter, even though no response could be made to the diurnal pounding, served to strengthen Davis's conviction that the South could never be subdued, no matter how much of its apparently limitless wealth and strength the North expended and exerted in its attempt to bring her to her knees; Charleston, for him, was proof enough that the unconquerable spirit of his people could never be humbled, despite the odds and the malignity, as it seemed to him, with which they were brought to bear. He stayed through November 8 — his fifth Sunday away from the national capital and his wife and children — then returned the following day to the Old Dominion. Lee, he learned on arrival, was falling back across the Rapidan, having suffered a double reversal two nights ago at Kelly's Ford and Rappahannock Bridge. Davis did not doubt that the Virginian would be able to hold this new river line, whatever had happened along the old one; his confidence in Lee was complete. His concern was more for what might happen around Chattanooga, for he now was informed that Bragg, while continuing to maintain that the weather prevented a strike at the newly opened Federal supply line on his immediate left, had been quick to adopt the suggestion that Longstreet be sent against Burnside, far off on his right, thereby reducing his army by one fourth.

On the face of it, that did not seem too risky, considering the great natural strength of his position, but others as well as Davis saw the danger in that direction, not only to Bragg but also to the authority that had backed him in the recent intramural crisis. Davis had everywhere been "received with cheers" on his journey, a War Department diarist observed. "His austerity and inflexibility have been relaxed, and he has made popular speeches wherever he has gone.... The press, a portion rather, praises the President for his carefulness in making a tour of the armies and forts south of us; but as he retained Bragg in command, how soon the tune would change if Bragg should meet with a disaster!" No one understood this better than Davis, who still believed that the best defense against a Federal assault, even upon so impregnable a position as the one held by the Army of Tennessee, would be for Bragg to knock the enemy in his immediate front off balance with an offensive of his own, and this seemed all the more the proper course now that it was known that the man in command at Chattanooga was Grant, who had made the worst sort of trouble for the Confederacy almost everywhere he had been sent, so far in the war. Accordingly, two days after his return to Richmond, being still immersed in a mass of paperwork collected in his absence, Davis had Custis Lee send Bragg a reminder of this point of view. "His Excellency regrets that the weather and condition of the roads have suspended the movement [on your left]," Lee wired, "but hopes that such obstacles to your plans will not long obstruct them. He feels assured that you will not allow the enemy to get up all his reinforcements before striking him, if it can be avoided." The President, Lee added, stressing by repetition the danger in delay, "does not deem it necessary to call your attention to the importance of doing whatever is to be done before the enemy can collect his forces, as the longer the time given him for this purpose, the greater will be the disparity in numbers."

★ ★ ★

Unlike Davis, who twice in the past eleven months had visited every Confederate state east of the Mississippi except Florida and Louisiana, addressing crowds along the way and calling for national unity in them all, Lincoln in two and one half years — aside, that is, from four quick trips on army business: once to confer with Winfield Scott at West Point, twice to see McClellan, on the James and the Antietam, and once to visit with Joe Hooker on the Rappahannock line — had been no farther than a carriage ride from the White House. He had made no speeches on any of the exceptional occasions, being strictly concerned with military affairs, and for the most part even the citizens of Washington had not known he was gone until after he returned. This was not to say that he had not concerned himself with national unity or that he had made no appeals to the people in his efforts to achieve it; he had indeed, and repeatedly, in messages to Congress, in proclamations, and in public and private letters to individuals and institutions. One of the most successful of these had been his late-August letter to James Conkling, ostensibly an expression of regret that he was unable to attend a rally of "unconditional Union men" in his home town of Springfield, but actually a stump speech to be delivered by proxy at the meeting. John Murray Forbes, a prominent Boston businessman, had been so impressed with the arguments therein advanced in support of the government's views on the Negro question — "a plain letter to plain people," he called it — that he wrote directly to Lincoln in mid-September, suggesting that he also set the public mind aright on what Forbes considered the true issue of the war. "Our friends abroad see it," he declared; "John Bright and his glorious band of European republicans see that we are fighting for Democracy, or (to get rid of the technical name) for liberal institutions. ... My suggestion then is that you should seize an early opportunity, and any subsequent chance, to teach your great audience of plain people that the war is not North against South, but the *People* against the *Aristocrats*. If you can place this in the same strong light that you have the Negro question, you will settle it in men's minds as you have that."

Lincoln filed the letter in his desk and in his mind, and seven weeks later, on November 2, acting on the suggestion that he "seize an early opportunity," accepted an invitation to attend the dedication of a new cemetery at Gettysburg for the men who had fallen there in the July battle. The date, November 19, was less than three weeks off, and the reason for this lateness on the part of the committee was that he had been an afterthought, its original intention having been to emphasize the states, which were sharing the expenses of the project, not the nation. Besides, even after the thought occurred that it might be a good idea to invite the President, some doubt had been expressed "as to his ability to speak upon such a grave and solemn occasion." However, since the principal speaker, the distinguished orator Edward Everett of Massachusetts, had been chosen six weeks earlier, it was decided — as Lincoln was told in a covering letter, stressing that the ceremonies would "doubtless be very imposing and solemnly impressive" — to ask him to attend in a rather minor capacity: "It is the desire that after the oration, you, as Chief Executive of the nation, formally set apart these grounds to their sacred use by a few appropriate remarks." Duly admonished to be on his good behavior, to avoid both length and levity, Lincoln accepted the invitation, along with these implied conditions, on the day it was received.

He had not intended to crack any jokes in the first place, at least not at the ceremony itself, though in point of fact he was in higher spirits nowadays than he had been for months. For one thing, the military outlook — badly blurred by the effects of the heavy body blow Bragg landed at Chickamauga in mid-September — had improved greatly in the past ten days: specifically since October 23, when Grant rode into Chattanooga and set to work in his characteristic fashion, opening the Cracker Line and sustaining it with a victory in the night action at Wauhatchie, all within a week of his arrival, then wound up by notifying Halleck that "preparations may commence for offensive operations." If Banks had been thwarted so far in his designs on coastal Texas, that might be taken as a temporary setback, amply balanced in the far-western theater by Steele's success, on the heels of his Little Rock triumph, in driving the rebels out of Pine Bluff on October 25. Similarly, in the eastern theater, though Gillmore and Dahlgren had made but a small impression down in Charleston harbor, the news from close at hand in Virginia was considerably improved. Lee was on the backtrack from Manassas, presumably chastened by his repulse at Bristoe Station, and Meade was moving south again, rebuilding the wrecked railroad as he went. Lincoln now felt a good deal kindlier toward the Pennsylvanian than he had done in the weeks immediately following Gettysburg. If Meade had much of the exasperating caution that had characterized McClellan in the presence of the enemy, at least he was no blusterer like Pope or blunderer like Burnside, and despite his unfortunate snapping-turtle disposition he did not seem to come unglued under pressure, as McDowell and Hooker had tended to do and done. All in all, though it was evident that he was not the killer-arithmetician his Commander in Chief was seeking, the impression was that he would do till the real thing came along, and this estimate was heightened within another week, when he overtook Lee on the line of the Rappahannock, administered a double dose of what he had given him earlier at Bristoe, and drove him back across the Rapidan. "The signs look better," Lincoln had said in closing his letter to Conkling in late August. Now in November, reviewing the over-all military situation that had been disrupted by Chickamauga and readjusted since, he might have amended this to: "The signs look even better."

But it was on the political front that the news was best of all. Last year's congressional elections had been a bitter pill to swallow, but in choking it down, the Administration had learned much that could be applied in the future. For one thing, there was the matter of names. "Republican" having come to be something of an epithet in certain sections of the country, the decision was made to run this year's pro-Lincoln candidates under the banner of the National Union Party, thus to attract the votes of "loyal" Democrats. For another, with the enthusiastic co-operation of Stanton in the War Department, there were uses to which the army could be put: especially in doubtful states, where whole regiments could be furloughed home to cast their ballots, while individual squads and platoons could be assigned to maintain order at the polls and assist the local authorities in administering oaths of loyalty, past as well as present, required in several border states before a citizen could enter a voting booth. New England had gone solidly Republican in the spring. Then in August, with the help of considerable maneuvering along the lines described above, the President was pleased to note that his native Kentucky had "gone very strongly right." Tennessee followed suit, and so, presently, did all but one of the rest of the states that held elections in the fall. Only in New Jersey, where the organization was weak, did the "unconditional Unionists" lose ground. Everywhere else the outcome exceeded party expectations, particularly in Pennsylvania, Massachusetts, New York, and Maryland, in all of which the situation had been judged to be no better than touch-and-go. Ohio, where Vallandigham was opposed by John Brough in the race for governor, balloted on October 13; Lincoln said that he felt more anxious than he had done three years ago, when he himself had run. He need not have worried. With the help of 41,000 soldier votes, as compared to 2000 for Vallandigham, Brough won by a majority of 100,000. "Glory to God in the highest," Lincoln wired; "Ohio has saved the Nation." Four days later, having got this worry out of the way, he celebrated substantially by issuing another call for "300,000 more." The states were to raise whatever number of troops they could by volunteering, then complete their quotas by drafting men "to reinforce our victorious armies in the field," as the proclamation put it, "and bring our needful military operations to a prosperous end, thus closing forever the fountains of sedition and civil war."

News that the President would appear at Gettysburg reached the papers soon after his acceptance of the tardy invitation, and their reactions varied from bland to indignant, hostile editors protesting that a ceremony intended to honor fallen heroes was no proper occasion for what could only be a partisan appeal. Certain prominent Republicans, on the other hand, professed to believe it was no great matter, one way or the other, since Lincoln was by now a political cipher anyhow, a "dead card" in the party deck. "Let the dead bury the dead," Thaddeus Stevens quipped when asked for an opinion on what was about to happen just outside the little college town where he once had practiced law and still owned property. Lincoln held to his intention to attend the ceremonies, despite the quips and adverse comments in and out of print. He was, he remarked in another connection this week, not much upset by anything said about him, especially in the papers. "These comments constitute a fair specimen of what has occurred to me through life. I have endured a great deal of ridicule without much malice, and have received a great deal of kindness not quite free from ridicule. I am used to it." Meanwhile, in the scant period between the tendering of the invitation and the date for his departure, there was not much time for composing his thoughts, let alone for setting them down on paper. In addition to the usual encroachments by job- and favor-seekers, there was the wedding of Chase's sprightly daughter Kate to wealthy young Senator William Sprague of Rhode Island, the most brilliant social affair to be held in Washington in the nearly three years since the Southerners left the District; there was an urgent visit by the high-powered New York politician Thurlow Weed, who came with a plan for ending the war by means of a ninety-day armistice, a scheme that had to be heard in full and then rejected tactfully, lest Weed be offended into an enmity the cause could not afford; there was the necessity for day-to-day work on the annual year-end message to Congress, which it would not do to put off till the last minute, though the last minute was in fact about at hand already. All this there was, and more, much more: with the result that by the time the departure date came round, November 18, Lincoln had done little more than jot down a few notes on what he intended to say next day in Pennsylvania. Worst of all, in the way of distraction, Tad was sick with some feverish ailment the doctors could not identify, and Mrs Lincoln was near hysterics, remembering Willie's death, under similar circumstances, twenty months ago in this same house. But Lincoln did not let even this interfere with his plans and promise. The four-car special, carrying the President and three of his cabinet members — Seward, Blair, and Usher; the others had declined, pleading the press of business — his two secretaries, officers of the army and navy, his friend Ward Lamon, and the French and Italian ministers, left the capital around noon. Lincoln sat for a time with the others in a drawing room at the back of the rear coach, swapping stories for an hour or so, and then, as the train approached Hanover Junction, excused himself to retire to the privacy of his compartment at the other end of the car. "Gentlemen, this is all very pleasant," he said, "but the people will expect me to say something to them tomorrow, and I must give the matter some thought."

Arriving at sundown, he went to the home of Judge David Wills, on the town square, where he and Everett and Governor Curtin would spend the night. The streets and all the available beds were crowded, visitors having come pouring in for tomorrow's ceremonies, notables and nondescripts alike, many of them with no place to sleep and most of them apparently past caring. Accompanied by a band, a large group roamed about in the early dark to serenade the visiting dignitaries, including the President. He came out at last and gave them one of those brief speeches, the burden of which was that he had nothing to say. "In my position it is somewhat important that I should not say foolish things," he began. "— If you can help it!" a voice called up, and Lincoln took his cue from that: "It very often happens that the only way to help it is to say nothing at all. Believing that is my present condition this evening, I must beg you to excuse me from addressing you further." Unsatisfied, the crowd proceeded next door and called for Seward, who did better by them, though this still was evidently far from enough, since they serenaded five more speakers before calling it a night. Lincoln by then had completed the working draft of tomorrow's address and gone to bed, greatly relieved by a wire from Stanton passing along a message from Mrs Lincoln that Tad was much improved.

By morning the crowd had swelled to 15,000, most of whom were on the prowl about the town in search of breakfast or about the surrounding fields in search of relics, an oyster-colored minnie ball, a tarnished button, a fragment of shell that might or might not have killed a man. In any event, whatever disappointments there were for the hungry, the pickings were good for the souvenir hunters, for it was later calculated that 569 tons of ammunition had been expended in the course of the three-day battle. Coffins were much in evidence, too, though the work of reinterring the dead — at $1.59 a body — had been suspended for the solemn occasion now at hand. At 10 o'clock the procession began to form on the square, marshaled by Lamon and led by the President on horseback. An hour later it began to move, in what one witness referred to as "an orphanly sort of way," toward Cemetery Hill, where the ceremonies would be held. Lincoln sat erect at first, wearing a black suit, a high silk hat, and white gloves, but presently he slumped in the saddle, arms limp and head bent forward in deep thought, while behind him rode or walked the governors of six of the eighteen participating states, several generals, including Doubleday and Gibbon, and a number of congressmen, as well as the officials who had come up with him on the train. Within fifteen or twenty minutes these various dignitaries had taken their places on the crowded platform, and after a wait for Everett, who was late, the proceedings opened at noon with a prayer by the House chaplain, following which the principal speaker was introduced. "Mr President," he said with a bow, tall and white-haired, just under seventy years of age, a former governor of Massachusetts, minister to England for John Tyler, president of Harvard, successor to Daniel Webster as Secretary of State under Millard Fillmore, and in 1860 John Bell's running mate on the Constitutional Union ticket, which had carried Virginia, Kentucky, and Tennessee. "Mr Everett," Lincoln replied, and the orator launched forthwith into his address.

"Standing beneath this serene sky," with "the mighty Alleghenies dimly towering" before him, Everett raised his "poor voice to break the eloquent silence of God and Nature." He did so for two hours by the clock, having informed the committee beforehand that the occasion was "not to be dismissed with a few sentimental or patriotic commonplaces." Nor was it. He outlined the beginning of the war, reviewed the furious three-day action here, discussed and denounced the doctrine of state sovereignty, lacing his eloquence with historical and classical allusions, and came at last to a quotation from Pericles: "The whole earth is the sepulchre of illustrious men." Recognizing the advent of the peroration because he had been given advance proofs of the address, Lincoln took from his coat pocket a fair copy he had made of his own speech that morning, put on his steel-bowed spectacles, and read it through while Everett drew to a close, head back-flung, and pronounced the final sentence in a voice that had not faltered once in the whole two hours: "Down to the latest period of recorded time, in the glorious annals of our common country there will be no brighter page than that which relates the Battles of Gettysburg." Amid prolonged applause he took his seat, and after the Baltimore Glee Club had sung an ode composed for the occasion, Lamon pronounced the words: "The President of the United States." Lincoln rose, and as a photographer began setting up his tripod and camera in front of the rostrum, delivered — in what a reporter called "a sharp, unmusical treble voice," but with what John Hay considered "more grace than is his wont" — the "few appropriate remarks" which the committee had said it desired of him "after the oration."

"Fourscore and seven years ago our fathers brought forth upon this continent a new nation, conceived in liberty and dedicated to the proposition that all men are created equal. Now we are engaged in a great civil war, testing whether that nation, or any nation so conceived and so dedicated, can long endure. We are met on a great battlefield of that war. We are met to dedicate a portion of it as the final resting place of those who here gave their lives that that nation might live. It is altogether fitting and proper that we should do this. But in a larger sense we cannot dedicate, we cannot consecrate, we cannot hallow this ground. The brave men, living and dead, who struggled here, have consecrated it far above our poor power to add or detract." A polite scattering of applause was overridden at this point as Lincoln continued. "The world will little note, nor long remember, what we say here, but it can never forget what they did here. It is for us, the living, rather, to be dedicated here to the unfinished work that they have thus far so nobly carried on. It is rather for us to be here dedicated to the great task remaining before us, that from these honored dead we take increased devotion to that cause for which they here gave the last full measure of devotion; that we here highly resolve that these dead shall not have died in vain; that the nation shall, under God, have a new birth of freedom; and that government of the people, by the people, for the people, shall not perish from the earth."

He finished before the crowd, a good part of whose attention had been fixed on the photographer anyhow, realized that he was fairly launched on what he had to say. In reaction to what a later observer described as the "almost shocking brevity" of the speech, especially by contrast with the one that went before, the applause was delayed, then scattered and barely polite. Moreover, the photographer missed his picture. Before he had time to adjust his tripod and uncap the lens, Lincoln had said "of the people, by the people, for the people" and sat down, leaving the artist with a feeling that he had been robbed. Apparently many of those present felt the same, agreeing in advance with what the Chicago *Times* would say tomorrow about the President's performance here today: "The cheek of every American must tingle with shame as he reads the silly, flat and dishwatery utterances of the man who has to be pointed out to intelligent foreigners as the President of the United States." In fact, as he resumed his seat alongside his friend Lamon and heard the perfunctory spatter of applause whose brevity matched his own, the speaker himself was taken with a feeling of regret that he had not measured up to what had been expected of him. Recalling a word used on the prairie in reference to a plow that would not clean itself while shearing through wet soil, he said gloomily: "Lamon, that speech won't *scour*. It is a flat failure and the people are disappointed."

In time — for not all editors were as scathing as the one in his home state; a Massachusetts paper, for example, printed the address in full and remarked that it was "deep in feeling, compact in thought and expression, and tasteful and elegant in every word and comma" — Lincoln revised not only his opinion of what he called "my little speech," but also the text itself, improving on what a Cincinnati editor had already described as "the right thing in the right place, and a perfect thing in every respect." When Everett remarked in a letter next day, "I should be glad if I could flatter myself that I came as near the central idea of the occasion, in two hours, as you did in two minutes," he replied: "In our respective parts yesterday, you could not have been excused to make a short address, nor I a long one. I am pleased to know that, in your judgment, the little I did say was not entirely a failure." Subsequently, when the orator asked for a copy of the speech, Lincoln gladly sent him one incorporating certain workshop changes. The second "We are met" became "We have come"; "a portion of it" became "a portion of that field"; "resting place of" became "resting place for"; "the unfinished work that they have thus far so nobly carried on" became "the unfinished work which they who fought here have thus far so nobly advanced"; "the nation shall, under God," became "this nation, under God, shall." Two later drafts he also made as presentation copies, with only two additional changes, one in the first sentence, where "upon" was shortened to "on," and one in the last, where "here" was dropped from the phrase "they here gave." The final draft — only two words longer than the one he had part-read, part-improvised at the Gettysburg ceremony, though he had altered, to one degree or another, half of its ten sentences — would be memorized in the future by millions of American school children, including those of the South, despite his claim that a victory by their forebears, in their war for independence, would have meant the end of government by and for the people. That speech did indeed scour, even in dark and bloody ground.

After the ceremonies on Cemetery Hill, Lincoln returned to the Wills house for lunch, after which he held an unscheduled reception, shaking hands for about an hour, then went to a patriotic rally at the Presbyterian church, where he listened to an address by the new lieutenant governor of Ohio. Finally at 6.30 he boarded the train for Washington. Much of the time that afternoon he had seemed gloomy and listless, and now on the train he gave way to weariness and malaise, lying stretched out on one of the side seats in the drawing room, a wet towel folded across his eyes and forehead. Back in the capital by midnight, he found good news awaiting him at the White House: Tad had been up and about today, apparently as well as if he had never been sick at all. Presently it developed however that the first family still had an invalid on its hands, only this time the member who fell ill was the President himself and the doctors had no trouble identifying the ailment. It was varioloid, a mild form of smallpox. Placed in isolation by order of his physician, Lincoln for once was free of the importunities of the office-seekers who normally hemmed him in.

"There is one thing good about this," he said with a somewhat rueful smile. "I now have something I can give everybody."

✖ 5 ✖

When Grant learned on November 5 that Bragg had detached Longstreet's two divisions the day before to send them and Wheeler's cavalry against Burnside, thus reducing the strength of the besiegers of Chattanooga by one fourth, he fairly ached to attack him, then and there, despite the semicircular frown of all those guns on all those heights. Indeed, there seemed to be sore need for haste: not only because the Confederates had rail transportation as far as Loudon, two thirds of the way to Knoxville — which meant that Old Peter might be able to return within a week or ten days, including the time it would take him to defeat and capture the bluecoats there or drive them from the region they had held for two months now, thereby reopening the Tennessee & Virginia Railroad for the use of such reinforcements as the Richmond government might take the notion to send him or Bragg on an overnight ride from Lynchburg — but also because Lincoln, who was known to be touchy about East Tennessee and the protection of its Union-loyal residents, might be tempted for political reasons to disrupt the plans of the commander of the newly created Military Division of the Mississippi. Sure enough, as Grant said later, the Washington authorities no sooner heard of Longstreet's departure from his immediate front than they became "more than ever anxious for the safety of Burnside's army, and plied me with dispatches faster than ever, urging that something should be done for his relief."

He was altogether willing, but he could not see that sending part of his army to Knoxville, at this stage of the campaign, would do anything more than add to Burnside's supply problem, which was nearly as grievous as his own had been on his arrival, two weeks back. What he had in mind, instead, was to attack Bragg's right. If successful, this would break his grip on Chattanooga by dislodging him from Missionary Ridge, and even if it failed it would be likely, if it was pressed with vigor, to alarm him into recalling Longstreet. In either case, as Grant saw it, Burnside would be relieved far more effectively than by the addition of several thousand hungry mouths to his command. On November 7, however, when he suggested the attack to Thomas, whose troops would have to make it, he was told that the thing could not be done. The Cracker Line had been open barely a week, and though the men were already back on full rations, no replacements for the starved artillery horses had yet come through. The few survivors, wobbly as they were, were not enough to move the guns out of the parks, according to Thomas, much less to pull them forward in support of the advancing infantry, and without them the attack was bound to fail. Unwilling to let it go at that, Grant proposed that mules or officers' mounts be used to haul the pieces, but the Virginian explained that the former, though superb in draft, were undependable under fire, while the latter would not work in traces and lacked the heft required of gun teams anyhow. Regretfully, in the light of this, the general whose arm was infantry felt obliged to defer to the old-line artilleryman. "Nothing was left to be done," he afterwards observed, "but to answer Washington dispatches as best I could; urge Sherman forward, although he was making every effort to get forward, and encourage Burnside to hold on, assuring him that in a short time he should be relieved."

His red-haired successor in command of the Army of the Tennessee was indeed making every effort to get forward, for he had received at Iuka ten days ago an order delivered by "a dirty, black-haired individual with mixed dress and strange demeanor" — thus Sherman later described the messenger — who had left Chattanooga on the day after Grant's arrival and paddled a canoe down the Tennessee, over treacherous Muscle Shoals, to find him. The instructions were for him to leave the railroad work to one division and press on at once with the other four to Bridgeport, where he would be in position to block an attempt by Bragg to turn the Federal right, disrupt the new supply line, and flank the defenders out of Chattanooga. (Though it might have been inferred from this that Grant had been reading his opponent's mail, he did not actually know that Bragg — or, more properly speaking, Longstreet — had any such plan in mind. It just had seemed to him wise to forestall so logical a move on the part of an adversary reputed to be as bold as he was tricky.) Furthermore, as an added logistical precaution, Grant directed Sherman to abandon work on the Memphis & Charleston, west of Decatur, so that the division left behind could concentrate on repairing the Tennessee & Alabama, which ran north of there, through Columbia, to Nashville, and thus provide him with two lines connecting his railhead supply base at Stevenson with his main depot back at the capital. That way, he would not only have a spare all-weather line in case raiders broke through to the Nashville & Chattanooga; he would also be able to keep up his stocks of ammunition and food when the opportunity came for him to forward supplies to Burnside, who at present had no rail connection with the outside world.... This was a large order, for the line north of Decatur had been thoroughly wrecked by cavalry and saboteurs, but the commander of the division assigned to the task was Brigadier General Grenville M. Dodge. A capable soldier, with a wound and a promotion dating from Pea Ridge to prove it, the thirty-two-year-old New Englander was also an experienced railroad builder, civil engineer, and surveyor; "Level Eye," the Indians had dubbed him, watching him at work out on the plains before the war. Grant figured that if anyone could do the job it was Dodge, and his confidence was not misplaced. Working without a base of supplies from which to draw either rations or equipment, without skilled labor of any kind, except such as he could find in the ranks of his 8000-man division, and with nothing but axes, picks, and spades for tools, he completed the job within forty days, although it required the rebuilding of no fewer than 182 bridges and about as many culverts while re-laying 102 miles of track northward across the lowlands and uplands of North Alabama and Middle Tennessee. His troops would get none of the glory in the campaign that now was about to open in earnest, but no division in any of the three blue armies involved worked harder or deserved more credit for the outcome.

But that was still in the future. For the present, Sherman pushed on eastward, crossing the Tennessee at Eastport to reach Florence by November 1, at which point, after three weeks on the go, he was about midway between Memphis and Chattanooga. To avoid the delay that would be involved in ferrying four divisions across Elk River, wide and bridgeless this far down, he marched up its north bank for a crossing by the bridge near Decherd, then followed the railroad down to Stevenson. He reached Bridgeport in advance of his troops on the night of November 13 to find a dispatch awaiting him from Grant, urging him to hurry ahead to Chattanooga for a conference. This he did the following day, proceeding via the Cracker Line, and rode into town that evening to be greeted by the superior he had not seen since he left him on crutches at Vicksburg in September. He was pleased to see that by now the crutches had been discarded; but when they rode out together next morning on a tour of inspection, finding himself confronted by the awesome loom of Lookout Mountain on the south, while to the east, against the long, shadowy backdrop of Missionary Ridge, "rebel sentinels, in a continuous chain, were walking their posts in plain view, not a thousand yards off," Sherman was amazed. He had been told what to expect, but what he saw came as such a shock to him that he involuntarily exclaimed: "Why, General Grant, you are besieged!" Grant nodded. "It's too true," he said. And then he told him what he had in mind to do about it.

Thomas's troops, he said — according to Sherman's recollection of the briefing — "had been so demoralized by the Battle of Chickamauga that he feared they could not be got out of their trenches to assume the offensive." That was where Sherman came into the picture; "he wanted my troops to hurry up, to take the offensive *first;* after which, he had no doubt the Cumberland army would fight well." The attack was to be launched against Bragg's extreme right, Grant explained: specifically against the northern end of Missionary Ridge, which he had reconnoitered and found unfortified. After crossing at Brown's Ferry, Sherman would press on under cover of darkness and throw a pontoon bridge across the Tennessee four miles above Chattanooga, just below the mouth of Chickamauga Creek, for a surprise assault designed to strike the enemy ridge end-on and then sweep down it from the north, dislodging rebels as he went; Thomas meanwhile would fix them in position by threatening from the west, and Hooker would stand ready with his Easterners to lend a hand in whatever direction he was needed. Sherman liked the sound of this, particularly his assignment to the leading role, but said that he would prefer to take a look at the terrain by daylight. So he and Grant, accompanied by Baldy Smith, crossed over to the north bank of the river, then up it to a hill overlooking the scene of the proposed attack on the opposite bank. He studied it as carefully as distance allowed, then returned before dark, well pleased by what he had seen. There was, however, a need for haste; Longstreet had been gone for better than ten days now and might get back before Sherman's men were in position, in which case they would encounter that much more resistance. Accordingly, the Ohioan did not spend another night in Chattanooga, but returned instead to Bridgeport, again by way of the Cracker Line, to brief his four division commanders on the plan of attack and see that they got their troops on the march without delay.

He had hoped to have them in jump-off position within five days; that is, by November 20 for a dawn attack next morning; but, as he explained later, "the condition of the roads was such, and the bridge at Brown's so frail, that it was not until the 23d that we got three of my divisions behind the hills near the point indicated above Chattanooga for crossing the river."

He need not have fretted about those three lost days. They gained him much, as the thing turned out, and Grant as well. In fact, if he had been delayed one day longer, he not only would have profited still more; he would have been spared the considerable mortification he was to suffer two days later at the hands of Pat Cleburne, who in that case would not have been there. For Bragg had decided, only the day before Sherman got into his jump-off position unobserved, to double the strength of Longstreet's 11,000-man infantry column by detaching another two divisions from the lines around Chattanooga to join him for the suppression of Burnside, under siege by then at Knoxville, and one of the two was Cleburne's.

Old Peter had protested his own detachment in the first place, on the double grounds that he would not be strong enough to deal quickly with Burnside and that his departure would leave the main body, strung out along six miles of line, dangerously exposed to an assault by Grant, who already had been reinforced by Hooker and presumably would soon be joined as well by the even larger force marching eastward under Sherman. But Bragg, with what Longstreet described as a "sardonic smile," declined either to cancel or strengthen the movement against Knoxville, and "intimated that further talk was out of order." He had his reasons: largely personal ones, apparently, dating from the conference three weeks ago, at which the Georgian had volunteered the opinion that the Army of Tennessee would benefit from a change of commanders. Informing Davis, who had suggested the detachment in his letter two days earlier from Atlanta, that "the Virginia troops will move in the direction indicated as soon as practicable," Bragg had added: "This will be a great relief to me." That was on the last day of October, and four days later, despite his protest, Longstreet was detached. He took with him the divisions of McLaws and Hood — the latter now under Brigadier General Micah Jenkins, who was senior to Law and had superseded him on his arrival after Chickamauga — Alexander's artillery, and Wheeler's three brigades of cavalry. This gave him a total of about 15,000 effectives of all arms. His assignment was "to destroy or capture Burnside's army," which in turn had just over 25,000 troops in occupation of East Tennessee.

It was Longstreet's belief that his best chance for success, under the circumstances, lay in striking before his adversary had time to concentrate his forces. But that turned out to be impossible, for a variety of reasons. Not the least of these was that he lacked the means of moving his pontoons except on flatcars, which meant that he had to cross the Holston River at Loudon, where the railroad ended because the bridge was out, rather than at some point closer than thirty air-line miles from his objective. To add to his woes, not only did the trains run badly off schedule, but he found no rations on hand when he reached Sweetwater, as he had been assured they would be, and had to mark time there while they were being brought in from the country roundabout. "The delay that occurs is one that might have been prevented," he wired Bragg on November 11, "but not by myself.... As soon as I find a probability of moving without almost certain starvation, I shall move, provided the troops are up." Bragg retaliated in kind. "Transportation in abundance was on the road and subject to your orders," he shot back next day. "I regret it has not been energetically used. The means being furnished, you were expected to handle your own troops, and I cannot understand your constant applications for me to furnish them." Old Peter pushed forward on his own, crossing at Loudon on the 13th, but reviewing the situation years later he remarked: "It began to look more like a campaign against Longstreet than against Burnside."

In point of fact, although their methods differed sharply, the blue commander to his front was no less skillful an opponent than the gray one in his rear. Warned by Grant that a heavy detachment was headed in his direction, Burnside was not only on the alert for an attack; he was also mindful of his instructions to keep the enemy from returning to Chattanooga as long as possible. "Sherman's advance has reached Bridgeport," Grant wired on the day after the rebels crossed the Holston. "If you can hold Longstreet in check until he gets up, or by skirmishing and falling back can avoid serious loss to yourself and gain time, I will be able to force the enemy back from here and place a force between Longstreet and Bragg that must inevitably make the former take to the mountain passes by every available road." Accordingly, Burnside did not seriously contest the Confederate advance. Abandoning Kingston, he called his scattered forces in from all points except Cumberland Gap, thus keeping that escape hatch open in the event of a disaster, and aside from a brief delaying action at Campbell Station on the 14th, about midway between Loudon and Knoxville, did not risk a sudden termination of the contest, either by a victory or a defeat. He had some 20,000 soldiers with him; more, he knew, than were in the column advancing on him. But it was not a battle he was after. It was time.

He got it, too. Arriving before Knoxville on November 17, Longstreet found the bluecoats skillfully disposed and well dug in. "We went to work, therefore," he afterwards reported, "to make our way forward by gradual and less hazardous measures, at the same time making examinations of the enemy's entire position." For the better part of a week this continued, his caution enlarged by the knowledge that Burnside had more men inside the place than he himself had outside. Then on November 23 he received a message Bragg had written the day before, informing him that "nearly 11,000 reinforcements are now moving to your assistance." Old Peter was to go ahead and defeat Burnside now, "if practicable"; otherwise he could wait for the additional strength already on the way. Having looked the situation over carefully for the past six days, without finding a single chink in the Federal armor, Longstreet decided that the "practicable" thing to do was wait a couple more.

Bragg's decision to add weight to the blow aimed at Knoxville, seeking thereby to hasten the return of the detachment by giving it the strength to settle the issue there without additional delay, was based in part on a growing suspicion that Old Peter had been right, after all, when he warned of the danger involved in any prolonged weakening of the force in occupation of the six-mile line of intrenchments drawn around two sides of Chattanooga. Longstreet had been gone for nearly three weeks now, and all sorts of things had been happening down in the town, indicative of the fact that the blue commander had something violent in mind. Moreover, Sherman had reached Bridgeport the week before, then suddenly, after crossing at Brown's Ferry, had disappeared as mysteriously as if the earth had swallowed up all four of his divisions. Bragg inferred that the Ohioan must have marched over Walden's Ridge: in which case he was probably headed for Knoxville, with the intention not only of raising the siege but also of swamping the already outnumbered Longstreet. If this was so, the thing to do was beat him to the punch, using the speed made possible by the railroad, and settle the issue before he got there. Accordingly, having reorganized what was left of his army into two large corps of four divisions apiece — one under Hardee, who had replaced Polk, and one under Breckinridge, who had replaced Hill — Bragg decided to dispatch one division from each, Cleburne from Hardee, Buckner from Breckinridge, and send them to Knoxville at once. He no sooner reached this decision than he acted on it. Buckner being absent sick, and Preston having been called to Richmond, his troops were placed under Bushrod Johnson, who pulled them out of line on November 22 and shifted them rearward to Chickamauga Station, where they boarded the cars for a fast ride to Loudon and a march beyond the Holston. Cleburne followed next day to wait for the return of the cars that had carried Johnson up the line.

Consolidation of Walker's two small divisions had reduced the army's total from eleven to ten divisions, and of these, with Johnson and Cleburne gone, Bragg now had a scant half dozen, containing fewer than 40,000 effectives of all arms. Hardee held the left of the semicircular line, with Stevenson posted on the crest of Lookout and eastward across the valley as far as Chattanooga Creek, Walker across the rest of the valley, and Cheatham on his right, occupying the south end of the line on Missionary Ridge, the rest of which was held by Breckinridge, with Stewart adjoining Cheatham and the other two divisions — Breckinridge's own and Hindman's, respectively under William Bate and Patton Anderson, the senior brigadiers — disposed along the northern extension of the ridge, but not all the way to the end overlooking the confluence of Chickamauga Creek and the Tennessee River, where the ground was so rough that Bragg had decided a few outpost pickets would suffice to hold it. The fact was, he had need to conserve his forces, especially since the latest of his two considerable detachments. Sidling left and right to fill the gaps created by the departure of Johnson and Cleburne, the troops disposed in three lines down the western face of the ridge were a good two lateral yards apart, not even within touching distance of each other. Admittedly this was a dangerous situation, but their chief depended on the natural strength of the position to compensate for what he lacked in numbers.

However, on the afternoon of the day Cleburne pulled back to follow Johnson up to Knoxville, Bragg was given cause to believe that his judgment was about to be challenged in the stiffest kind of way. Grant advanced a large body of troops — apparently Thomas's whole army — due east from Chattanooga, as if he intended to have an all-out try at breaking the thin-spread center of the rebel line. Though the mass of bluecoats called a halt about midway across the plain and began to intrench a new line just beyond range of the batteries on Missionary Ridge, Bragg was alarmed into recalling Cleburne, whose men were loading onto the cars when the summons reached him. Early next morning, November 24, the southern commander received a still greater shock in the form of a dispatch from an outpost on the right. Four blue divisions were crossing the Tennessee River immediately below the mouth of Chickamauga Creek, apparently for an assault on the practically undefended north end of the ridge. It was Sherman, the dispatch added, and Bragg knew at last that the Ohioan had not gone off to Knoxville, as he had supposed, but rather had gone into hiding behind the hills above Chattanooga, massing for the attack now being launched.

The Center Gives

Hastily, he passed the word for Cleburne, whose troops had returned overnight from Chickamauga Station, to double-time his division northward and repulse if he could the four-division assault which, if successful, would flank the Confederates off the ridge their commander had believed to be impregnable: until now.

★ ★ ★

As was his custom when confronted with delays, long or short — including the four-month delay above Vicksburg, early this year — Grant used the three days, spent waiting for Sherman to get into position, to polish up the plan he had designed for Bragg's discomfort, improvising variations which he believed would make it at once more certain and complete. Such strain as there was, and admittedly there was much, was not so much on his own account as on Burnside's, and perhaps less on Burnside's account than on the reaction of the Washington authorities to the news that Knoxville was besieged, cut off from telegraphic communication with the outside world. "The President, the Secretary of War, and General Halleck were in an agony of suspense," Grant afterward recalled. "My own suspense was also great, but more endurable," he added, "because I was where I could do something to relieve the situation."

What he specifically had in mind to do, as he had told Burnside the week before, was to "place a force between Longstreet and Bragg" by throwing the latter into retreat and cutting the rail supply line in his rear, thus obliging Old Peter to raise his siege and "take to the mountain passes by every road" in search of food. At that time he had intended to leave the real work to Sherman and his Army of the Tennessee, with the Cumberland and Potomac troops more or less standing by to lend such help as might be needed. Thomas, for instance, was to menace but not attack the enemy center, while Hooker — reduced to a single division by the subtraction of Howard's two, which crossed at Brown's Ferry to be available as a reserve for the forces north and east of Chattanooga — stood guard at the foot of Lookout Valley, below Wauhatchie, to prevent a rebel counterstroke from there. But now, as he waited for Sherman to come up, Grant perceived that if Fighting Joe were strengthened a bit he might take the offensive on the right, against Lookout itself, and thus discourage Bragg from reinforcing his assailed right from his otherwise unmolested left. Accordingly, Thomas was ordered to send Cruft's division from Granger's corps to Hooker, and when Sherman's rear division, under Osterhaus, was kept from crossing by a breakdown of the pontoon bridge at Brown's Ferry, it too was sent to Hooker and replaced by another from Thomas, under Davis, who was detached from Palmer's corps. Thomas thus was reduced from six to four divisions, while Sherman still had four, Hooker three, and Howard two. Such a distribution seemed ideal, considering the assignments of the three commanders and the fact that the last was available as a reinforcement for the first.

These thirteen blue divisions, containing in all about 75,000 effectives, were to be employed by Grant in the following manner against the 43,000 effectives in Bragg's seven divisions. Sherman's effort on the left was still to be the main one, his orders being "to secure the heights on the northern extremity [of Missionary Ridge] to about the railroad tunnel before the enemy can concentrate against him," then drive southward down the crest, dislodging graybacks as he went. To assist in this, Thomas would menace the rebel center, fixing the defenders in position, and Howard would hold his corps "in readiness to act either with [Thomas] or with Sherman." Hooker meanwhile would deliver a secondary attack on the far right, and if successful — although this seemed unlikely, considering the difficulties of terrain on that quarter of the field — was to cross Lookout Mountain and Chattanooga Valley for a descent on Rossville, where he would turn sharp left and, matching Sherman's effort from the opposite direction, sweep northward up Missionary Ridge; at which point in the proceedings, with the rebel army clamped firmly between the two attackers north and south, Thomas's feint against the center might be converted into a true assault that would mean the end of Bragg.

One possible source of difficulty was a growing bitterness between the Federal armies, especially those of the East and West. "The

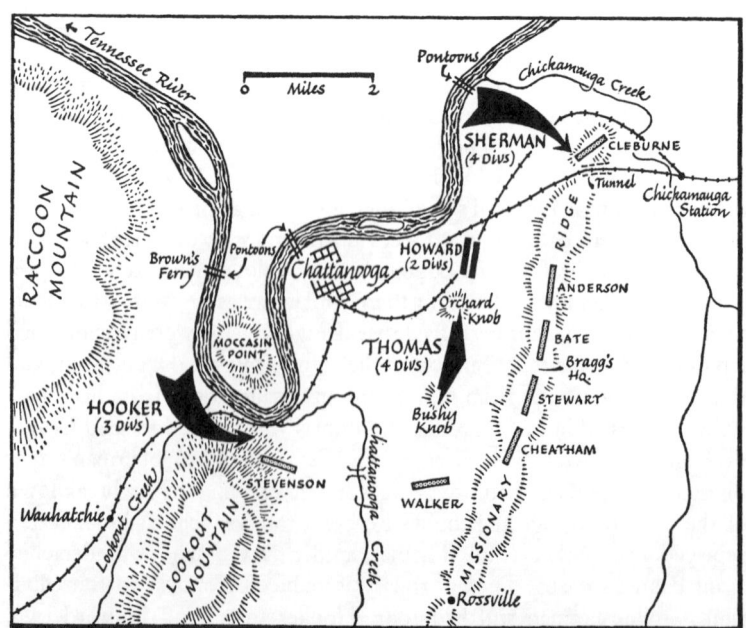

Potomac men and ours never meet without some very hard talk," one of Sherman's veterans wrote home. Westerners jeered at Easterners as paper-collar soldiers. "Bull Run!" they hooted, as if they themselves had never been whipped in battle. Resentful of the fact that the "Virginians," as they sometimes referred to these transfers from the eastern theater, had always had first call on new equipment and such luxuries as the quartermaster afforded, they would remark as they slogged past Hooker's bivouacs: "Fall back on your straw and fresh butter," and they would add, looking rearward over their shoulders: "What elegant corpses they'll make in those fine clothes!" After this would come the ultimate insult, delivered *sotto voce* from the roadside as the Easterners minced by: "All quiet on the Potomac." The latter in turn were disdainful, looking down their noses at the western soldiers, who preferred Confederate-style blanket rolls to knapsacks, walked with the long, loose-jointed stride of plowmen, and paid their officers little deference. "Except for the color of their uniforms, they looked exactly like the rebels," a New Yorker observed with unconcealed distaste. Individual confrontations were likely to produce at least a verbal skirmish. One of Blair's men, for example, wandering over for a look at Slocum's camps, was surprised to see the corps insignia — a five-pointed star — sewn or glued or stenciled onto practically everything in sight, from the flat crowns of forage caps to the tailgates of wagons. "Are you all brigadier generals?" he inquired, in real or feigned amazement. An Easterner explained that this was their corps badge, and asked: "What's yours?" The Westerner bristled. No such device had been known out here before, but he was unwilling to be outdone. "Badge, is it?" he snorted. For emphasis, he slapped the leather ammunition pouch he wore on his belt, just over his liver. "There, by Jesus! Forty rounds in the cartridge box and twenty in the pocket." In time, that would become his own XV Corps insignia — a cartridge box inscribed "Forty Rounds" — but tempers were not sweetened by such exchanges, in which neither antagonist took any care to disguise his low opinion of the other as a dude or a backwoodsman.

Nor were matters improved when the men of the three armies learned of their respective assignments in Grant's plan for lifting the siege of Chattanooga. This applied in particular to members of the Army of the Cumberland, whose role it was to stand on the defensive, merely bristling, while the other two armies "rescued" them by attacking on the left and right. Perhaps, too, they had heard by now of Grant's expressed concern that "they could not be got out of their trenches to assume the offensive." On top of all this, Thomas himself was hopping mad: not at Grant, though doubtless he masked some resentment he must have felt in that direction, but at Bragg, whose headquarters were plainly visible on the crest of the ridge across the way. A letter had arrived from the North for a Confederate officer, and Thomas, having determined that it was harmless from the security point of view, sent it through the lines with a note attached, requesting his one-time battery commander to pass it along. The letter came back promptly, with a curt indorsement on the note: "Respectfully returned to General Thomas. General Bragg declines to have any intercourse with a man who has betrayed his State." Thomas was incensed. "Damn him," he fumed; "I'll be even with him yet." Sherman, who was present, observed that the Virginian's poise, reputed to be impervious to shock, was shakable after all, at least when he was touched where he was tender. "He was not so imperturbable as the world supposes," the Ohioan testified years later, recalling Old Pap's reaction to the snub from his former superior and friend.

Hooker felt considerably better after Grant's revision of the attack plan, which changed his role from defensive to offensive, but the only change for Thomas was the loss of one third of his command, detached left and right to where the battle would be fought while he and his remaining four divisions stood by as spectators. Presently there was a further change, however, whereby they were given at least the chance for a ringside seat, a closer view of the action they were more or less barred from. On November 22 a rebel deserter reported that Bragg was about to evacuate his present lines. Though Grant mistrusted evidence so obtained, knowing how often those who imparted it were "loaded," this was altogether too serious to be ignored; Bragg might have plans for an all-out move against Burnside, availing himself of the railroad for a sudden descent on Knoxville, in which case Grant would be left holding the bag at Chattanooga. Moreover, the report gained credence when Buckner's division pulled out that afternoon, followed next morning by Cleburne's. Accordingly, Grant instructed Thomas to make a pretense of attacking Missionary Ridge by advancing his army, or what was left of it, about half the distance across the intervening plain. If he could do this, he would not only test the extent of the Confederate withdrawal, which might be greater than had been observed, and perhaps frighten Bragg into recalling the troops already detached; he would also secure a better location from which to demonstrate against the enemy center next day, November 24, when Sherman and Hooker — the former at last was moving into his jump-off position opposite the mouth of Chickamauga Creek — were scheduled to open their attacks against the flanks.

Thomas received his orders at 11 o'clock in the morning, and by 12.30 — so anxious were he and they for a share in the work — he had begun to maneuver his 25,000 veterans into positions from which to advance. In full view of their rivals from the Virginia and Mississippi theaters, as well as of the rebels out on the plain ahead and the tall ridge beyond, these soldiers of the Cumberland army made the most of this opportunity to refute the taunts that they had been permanently cowed by their defeat nine weeks ago. Granger's corps, with Wood in the lead and Sheridan in support, was the first to move out into the open. "It was an inspiring sight," a staff observer would recall. "Flags were flying; the quick, earnest steps of thousands beat equal time. The sharp commands of hundreds of company officers, the sound of drums, the ringing notes of the bugles, companies wheeling and countermarching and regiments getting into line, the bright sun lighting up ten thousand polished bayonets till they glistened and flashed like a flying shower of electric sparks, all looked like preparations for a peacetime pageant, rather than for the bloody work of death." Across the way, the Confederates thought so, too. They emerged from their trenches and stood on the parapets, calling to one another to come watch the Yankees pass in review. Palmer's corps followed Granger's; Johnson and Baird went through similar convolutions to get into line on the right. For the better part of an hour this continued. Then at about 1.30 the drums and bugles stepped up their tempo and changed their tone, beating and blaring the charge. That was the first the butternut watchers knew of the attack that was in midcareer before they got back into their trenches to resist it. Orchard Knob and Bushy Knob, fortified rebel outposts about in the center of the plain, were taken in a rush as the blue wave — flecked with shellbursts now, as if with foam — swept over them, engulfing those defenders who had not broken rearward in time for a getaway to the safety of the main line, back on Missionary Ridge. Promptly, or at any rate as soon as their officers could persuade them to leave off cheering and tossing their caps, the victors got to work with picks and shovels, turning the just-won intrenchments to face the other way, and there they settled down for the night, having taken their ringside seats for the fight which, now that the preliminaries were over and Sherman had his four divisions cached in their jump-off position on the left, was scheduled to begin soon after first light next morning.

A mile or more in advance of the line they had taken off from shortly after midday, Thomas and his Cumberlanders had drawn and shed the first blood after all, despite Grant's original intention to exclude them from any leading part in the accomplishment of their own deliverance. Their losses amounted to about 1100 killed and wounded, but they had inflicted nearly as many casualties as they suffered, including the prisoners they took. Perhaps by now, moreover, Grant had been disabused of his notion as to their reluctance to leave their trenches without the example of Sherman's men to inspire them. At any rate he seemed pleased: as well he might. Afterwards he told why. "The advantage was greatly on our side now," he wrote, "and if I could only have been assured that Burnside could hold out ten days longer" — this being the length of time he figured it would take him to finish whipping Bragg and then, if necessary, get reinforcements up to Knoxville — "I should have rested more easily. But we were doing the best we could for him and the cause."

Gathered about their campfires on the ridge, where they were disposed in three separate lines — one along its base, another about halfway up its steep western slope, and a third along its crest, four hundred feet above the plain — the Confederates admitted they had been surprised by the sudden conversion this afternoon of a two-corps "review" into an irresistible assault, but they still were not alarmed. Orchard Knob and Bushy Knob were merely outposts, no more integral to the defense of the main line of resistance than was the sheer bastion of Lookout Mountain, off on the distant left. What counted was Missionary Ridge itself. That was where the strength was, and the bluecoats, still beyond reach of all but the heaviest guns emplaced along the crest, would find a quite different reception awaiting them, when and if — although that seemed unlikely — they moved against it from their newly taken positions on the hilly plain below. "We feel we can kill all they send after us, notwithstanding our line is so thin that we are two yards apart," one of Breckinridge's Orphans wrote in his journal that night, looking down at the fires the Federals had kindled on the floor of the valley, as myriad as the stars they seemed to reflect. In this he was expressing the opinion of his army commander, who was convinced, as he said later, that Missionary Ridge could be "held by a line of skirmishers against any assaulting column."

A message wigwagged from Lookout after sundown, warning that a blue force seemed to be massing in the valley beyond for an uphill attack, gave Bragg no evident concern. Though the mountain was defended by only one brigade on its western flank and another on its summit, detached from Cheatham, he made no attempt to strengthen or adjust his dispositions there, apparently because he did not want to discourage the Federals, if they were indeed reckless enough to make the attempt, from breaking their heads against its rocky sheerness. Neither this new threat to his left, nor Thomas's advance that afternoon against his center, seemed to him sufficient cause for recalling either Johnson or Cleburne, who had pulled out yesterday and today. However, a message that reached him early next morning from the far right, warning that a sizable body of the enemy was crossing the Tennessee near the mouth of Chickamauga Creek, was quite another matter. He rode north at once to see for himself what this amounted to, and when he learned that what it amounted to was Sherman, whose troops he had thought were on their way to Knoxville, he reacted fast with a dispatch calling Cleburne back from Chickamauga Station. "We are heavily engaged," he told him, stressing the need for haste. "Move up rapidly to these headquarters."

There was in fact less need for haste than the southern commander knew. Sherman would not constitute an actual threat for some time now, though even he did not yet know that it would not be the rebels who would delay still further the opening of his carefully planned attack on the scantly defended northern end of Missionary Ridge, but geography, an unsuspected trick of the terrain. For the better part of the past week the red-haired Ohioan had been made nervously ill by the knowledge that he was falling behind the schedule Grant had set. "I feel as if I had a 30-pound shot in my stomach," he told a friend in the course of his muddy approach march. Today, though, all that was changed. Everything went smooth as clockwork. He had a thousand-man assault force over the river in boats by daylight, and behind them a pontoon bridge was thrown for a crossing by the main body before noon. Unopposed, except by a handful of butternut pickets who fled at their first sight of no less than four blue divisions coming at them, Sherman pushed forward onto the high ground he had examined nine days ago from the far side of the river. By late afternoon he had the position completely occupied: only to learn, to his acute dismay, that what he had taken was a detached hill, not actually even a part of Missionary Ridge, which lay beyond it, across a rocky valley. Red-faced, though he blamed the error on the inadequate map he had been given, he notified Grant of what had happened and instructed his troops to dig in for the night. They would continue — or, more properly speaking, begin — their assault on the enemy ridge at first light tomorrow, even though they had lost the element of surprise, which he and they had taken such precautions to achieve.

Seven miles away on the far right, southwest across the plain where the Cumberlanders occupied the ringside seats they had taken yesterday — "Thomas having done on the 23d what was expected of him on the 24th," Grant explained, "there was nothing for him to do this day except to strengthen his position" — a quite different kind of action was in progress, one in which the so-called "fog of war" prevailed in fact, not merely in the mind of the blue commander. Lookout had been wreathed in mist all morning and afternoon, except for tantalizing moments when the curtain would lift or part, only to descend or close again, affording the watchers little more than fleeting reassurance that the sheer bulk of the mountain was still there. Hooker's progress, if any, could not be determined by the eye, although, as Grant remarked from the command post shifted forward to Orchard Knob, "the sound of his artillery and musketry was heard incessantly." What was in progress, there beyond the gauzy screen, was what later would be called the "Battle Above the Clouds," despite objections by a correspondent that "there were no clouds to fight above, only heavy mist," and by Grant himself, who scoffed long afterwards: "The Battle of Lookout Mountain is one of the romances of the war. There was no such battle and no action even worthy to be called a battle on Lookout Mountain. It is all poetry."

Poetry it may have been, but if there were no clouds and no battle fought above them, there was at least some bleeding done, along with a great deal of hard work, in the course of this day-long skirmish in the mist. Hooker had about 12,000 troops, one division from each of the three armies on the field, with which to oppose the 1200-man brigade that stood between him and the crest of the mountain, where a second gray brigade was posted. Spread out along the east bank of Lookout Creek, with instructions to "fall back fighting over the rocks" if attacked, the Confederates did just that when the greatly superior Union mass forced a crossing near Wauhatchie and moved forward on a wide front, overlapping them on both flanks. Gun crews on the rearward heights were active at this stage of the attack, firing with precision into the blue ranks toiling upward, but this became increasingly difficult as the range decreased and it became necessary to raise the trails of the pieces higher and higher, until finally the tubes could not be depressed enough to keep them from overshooting; at which point the guns became only so much useless metal, so far as the defense of Lookout was concerned, and had to be removed to save them from being overrun. As they withdrew, the second gray brigade came down the rugged western slope to reinforce the first, and presently Stevenson sent a third brigade from the far side of the mountain. The three attempted to form a line among the rocks, but they soon found it was no use; the three blue divisions had caught the spirit of the chase and would not be denied. Supported by fire from batteries massed on Moccasin Point, just across the river, Geary's "paper collar" Easterners rounded the gray right flank and threatened to cut the defenders' line of retreat. There was a brief, hard fight near a farmhouse on a craggy bench about midway up the otherwise almost sheer north face of the mountain, and then once more the weight of numbers told. Again the Confederates fell back hastily, and this time Fighting Joe called a halt to consolidate his gains. Though he continued to probe upward, on through what was left of daylight into dusk — "I could see the whole thing," a rebel peering down from the crest was to say of the final stage of the contest; "It looked like lightning bugs on a dark night" — Hooker thought it best, except for a few patrols sent out to keep the enemy off balance, to rest his leg-weary men for tomorrow, which he expected to be as strenuous as today. He had suffered, or would suffer in the course of the three-day action, a total of 629 casualties, including 81 dead and 8 missing, but this seemed rather a bargain price for nearly half a mountain that practically everyone, blue or gray, had judged to be impregnable.

In point of fact he had won the whole mountain, though he would not know this until morning. Shortly after midnight, the Federal patrols having long since bedded down, Stevenson received instructions from Bragg to fall back across the eastern valley, in concert with Walker's division, and join in the defense of Missionary Ridge, where it was evident by now that the main Union effort would be centered. This he did, burning the single bridge over Chattanooga Creek as soon as his battered soldiers had crossed it in a darkness made profound by a total eclipse of the moon. Fighting Joe remained in full but isolated control of the "ever-lasting thunder storm" for which he had fought so hard today and was preparing to fight tomorrow, not knowing that it was entirely his already. Grant, of course, did not know this either, though in a wire he got off to Halleck, shortly after sundown, he sounded as if he did: "The fighting today progressed favorably. Sherman carried the end of Missionary Ridge, and his right is now at the tunnel, and his left at Chickamauga Creek. Troops from Lookout Valley carried the point of the mountain, and now hold the eastern slope and a point high up. Hooker reports two thousand prisoners taken, besides which a small number have fallen into our hands from Missionary Ridge."

Assuming from this, as well he might, that little remained to be accomplished around Chattanooga, Lincoln himself replied next morning with congratulations, gratitude, and a reminder: "Well done. Many thanks to all. Remember Burnside."

★ ★ ★

Little if any of the information Grant reported in his telegram to Halleck after sundown of November 24 had been true at the time he put it on the wire. Sherman not only had not "carried the end of Missionary Ridge," he had not even reached it; nor had Hooker, whose troops were still on the western, not the eastern slope of Lookout, "carried the point of the mountain." As for prisoners, Fighting Joe had inflicted fewer casualties than he suffered; the figure 2000 was a good deal closer to the total number of Confederates he encountered than it was to the number he had captured, which in fact was less than a tenth of the figure Grant passed on to Washington. However, before Lincoln's "Well done. Many thanks" arrived next morning, a part at least of what had been distorted was confirmed. The sun came up in a cloudless sky about 6.40; Lookout loomed with startling clarity, its curtain of mist dispelled. Watching from Orchard Knob, the Federal commander saw the rippling glitter of the Stars and Stripes break out on the 1200-foot peak, raised there by a patrol in proof that Geary's kid-glove Easterners had indeed "carried the point of the mountain" after all. Down on the plain, the Cumberland watchers broke into cheers at the sight, and Grant settled back, albeit impatiently, to wait for Hooker to complete his assignment, which was to proceed southeast across the intervening valley for a strike at Rossville and a drive northward up Missionary Ridge to meet Sherman driving south.

The wait, as it turned out, was a long one. Though the eastern slope of Lookout was less difficult than the western, and even afforded a winding road for the descent, the three divisions entered the valley below to find the bridge over fordless Chattanooga Creek destroyed and few materials at hand for constructing another; with the result that they were delayed some four hours in their advance on Rossville. Neither Grant nor the Cumberlanders, who knew that he did not intend to unleash them until the rebs intrenched to their front were firmly clamped between the two blue forces driving north and south along the ridge, took kindly to this evidence of Fighting Joe's ineptness, even though they had more or less anticipated it because of the blow-hard reputation he had brought with him from the East. This delay was mild in its effect, however, compared to the one on the far left, where no such failure had been expected of Grant's star general in command of his star army, whose reputation lately had become one of unfailing success and whose complaint had been that they could no longer get the Johnnies to fight them in the open.

Sherman went forward at dawn, as ordered, but found Cleburne in his path and was stopped cold. Rocked back — quite literally; for the defenders heaved boulders down on the heads of the attackers when their guns could no longer be brought to bear — he charged again and again, and again and again he was repulsed. "You may go up the hill if you like," he had rather casually instructed his brother-in-law Brigadier General Hugh Ewing, who commanded his lead division, adding: "Don't call for help until you actually need it." Ewing actually needed it about as soon as he got started, and Sherman not only supplied it, in the form of his three remaining divisions; he also threw in Howard's two, which were ordered to join him before midday. Yet nothing he could do would serve to move these six divisions over or around the one gray division in their path. About 3 o'clock, after eight hot hours of fighting, no appreciable gain, and more than 1500 casualties, including 261 captured when the Confederates made an unexpected sortie, Sherman admitted he had done all he could on this line. "Go signal Grant," he told a staff major. "The orders were that I should get as many as possible in front of me, and God knows there are enough. They've been reinforcing all day."

Those had not been his orders at the outset; nor were they now. "Attack again," Grant promptly replied, and Sherman did so, though with no better success. He was wrong, too, about enemy reinforcements. All he had had in his immediate front all day was Cleburne, whose five brigades had moved into position late the day before and organized it for defense by working most of the night, their task rendered more difficult by the eclipse of the moon, which for a time had made it necessary to work by sense of touch, including the spotting of the fourteen guns they employed today against the forty emplaced on the hill the Federals had occupied yesterday, off the nose of Missionary Ridge. Cleburne suffered a total of 222 casualties, less than one sixth the number he inflicted, and captured eight stands of colors, six of which were picked up from the ground where they had fallen in front of his line. Shortly before 4 o'clock Bragg sent him the first and only reinforcements of the day, the Orphan Brigade, detached from Bate to extend the

The Center Gives

right. The Kentuckians saw little action, since Sherman had desisted by then from his attempt to drive southward down the ridge, but one of them went up on his own for a look at what Cleburne's men had been doing all this time. "They had swept their front clean of Yankies," he wrote in his journal; "indeed, when I went up about sundown the side of the ridge in their front was strewn with dead yankies & looked like a lot of boys had been sliding down the hill side, for when a line of the enemy would be repulsed, they would start down hill & soon the whole line would be rolling down like a ball, it was so steep a hill side there."

While Cleburne and his troops were enjoying the respite they had earned, a message arrived from Hardee, directing him, as he afterwards reported, "to send to the center all the troops I could spare, as the enemy were pressing us in that quarter." Detaching two of his brigades, he accompanied them part of the way southward down the ridge to see that they made good time. "Before I had gone far, however," he added, still shocked by this development though his report was written some weeks later, "a dispatch from General Hardee reached me, with the appalling news that the enemy had pierced our center."

It was true; the Confederate center had been pierced. Bluecoats were clustered thick by now on Missionary Ridge, whooping and yelling in raucous celebration of a sudden, incredible victory scored less than three miles south of Sherman's all-day no-gain fight for Tunnel Hill, and hundreds of butternut prisoners were already on their way across the westward plain, taunted by their captors as they went: "You've been wanting to get there long enough. Now charge on Chattanooga!" Appalling as the news was, at least to gray-clad hearers, it became far more so when they learned of the manner in which it had come to pass. What one division had done against six, all morning and most of the afternoon on the far right, five divisions had not managed to do against four in resisting an attack that had lasted barely an hour from start to finish. Rephrasing the news only made it rankle more. Confronted by no worse than equal numbers in the vicinity of his own army headquarters, where he enjoyed positional advantages superior to those that enabled Cleburne's greatly inferior force to stand fast at the north end of the line, the vaunted southern fighting man had lost a soldiers' battle.

Joyous though the outcome was from the Union point of view, the slow hours leading up to it had been anything but pleasant for the overall Federal commander, who had stood by all this time on Orchard Knob and watched his carefully worked-out plans go by the board, or at any rate awry. After sending Howard's two divisions to Sherman, in futile hope that they would provide the added weight that would enable his old Army of the Tennessee to achieve the breakthrough on which those plans depended, Grant had Thomas detach Baird's division from his right and send it northward too. Thomas did so, but word came from the unhappy Sherman that he already had more troops than he could find room for on his present narrow front. So Baird was halted and put back into line where he then was, on Thomas's left. That was about 2 o'clock, and except for this minor rearrangement — Granger's two divisions now were flanked by Palmer's — the Army of the Cumberland had done nothing all day long; or all day yesterday either, for that matter. An hour later, two dispatches arrived from opposite directions. One was from Hooker, reporting that he had finally reached Rossville, where he had captured a quantity of supplies after driving the rebel outpost guards from the gap, and was sending Cruft's division north along the crest of Missionary Ridge, supported on the left and right by Geary and Osterhaus, who were deployed respectively on the western and eastern slopes. The other dispatch was from Sherman and was far less welcome, since what it said, in effect, was that he had shot his wad. Disgruntled, Grant clamped down tighter on his unlit cigar. With Fighting Joe at last where he wanted him, he had no intention of relaxing the pressure on either end of the enemy line. "Attack again," he signaled his red-haired lieutenant in reply, though with no different results, as we have seen.

All this time he had been getting increasingly restless, and when he saw what he took to be reinforcements moving northward along the ridge, he began to worry in earnest that Bragg — whose headquarters he could see plainly on the 400-foot crest, a mile and a half away, with couriers arriving and departing — was about to go over to the offensive against the stalled attackers off the north end of his line. Since Hooker was still a good three miles off and could scarcely be expected to get there before sunset, Grant figured that the quickest way to counteract the danger would be for Thomas to menace the rebel center. He did not like to order this, however, not only because it was an extremely hazardous undertaking, but also because the conditions he had insisted were necessary before the movement could be attempted had not been achieved; Bragg, unclamped, could give his full attention to any threat against his center. At last, although reluctantly, he inquired of the Virginian standing beside him: "Don't you think it's about time to advance against the rifle pits?" Instead of replying, Thomas continued to examine the enemy ridge through his binoculars, as if to show that he was not here to agree or disagree with opinions, but to execute orders. If Grant wanted him to move forward against that bristling triple line of intrenchments, in the face of all those guns frowning down from the crest, let him say so. Finally, at about 3.30, Grant did say so; whereupon Thomas at once passed the word to his corps commanders. Wood and Sheridan had their divisions in the center, with Baird supporting the former on the left and Johnson supporting the latter on the right. The signal for the attack would be the firing of six guns in quick succession, at which time the Cumberlanders, kept idle all day yesterday and up to

The Center Gives

now today, would advance and seize the rifle pits at the base of the ridge on the far side of the plain. At 3.40, ten minutes after Grant told Thomas to move out, the first of the six signal guns was fired under the personal direction of the ebullient and high-strung Gordon Granger, who stood on the Orchard Knob parapet, lifting and lowering his right arm in rapid sequence as he shouted: "Number One, *fire!* Number Two, *fire!* Number Three, *fire!* Number Four, *fire!* Number Five, *fire!*"

Before the sixth gun roared the leading elements were off. "Forward, guide center, march!" sixty regimental commanders shouted, and the 25,000 infantry in the four blue divisions began their plunge of nearly a mile across the wooded, hilly plain. "Number Six, *fire!*" Granger cried.

At first the only reaction on the part of the defenders was a scattering of shots from the gray pickets, who fell back hastily to gain the cover of the earthworks in their rear. Presently, though, as if recovering from the shock of unbelief that what they saw spread out below was real, the Confederate artillerists came alive. Bragg had 112 guns, and most of these were trained on the mile-wide formation of bluecoats moving toward them. "A crash like a thousand thunderclaps greeted us," one Federal was to remember, while a second observed that "the whole ridge to our front had broken out like another Ætna." The effect of this rain of projectiles, bursting over and among the close-packed ranks of the attackers, was like that of a sudden shower on a crowd of pedestrians; they quickened the pace, and those in the lead broke into a run. Well rested from their last previous advance, just over fifty hours ago, the men of the two center divisions caught something of the excitement of a race, each wanting to be first to reach the objective. Then too there was the knowledge that they were advancing in full view of their rivals on the left and right, who had been brought here from Mississippi and Virginia to extract them from the trap that had been devised to complete their defeat and destruction, but whose failure to carry out the required preliminaries had resulted in the unleashing of what had plainly been regarded, up to then, as the second team. Now the roles were more or less reversed; the second team had become the first, and those who had been intended to be saved were being called upon to do the saving. That was a pleasant thing to contemplate. Moreover there was the motive of revenge, a private matter strictly between them and the butternut soldiers just ahead. "Chickamauga! Chickamauga!" the Cumberlanders were yelling as they charged.

As they drew near the works at the base of the ridge they saw there could be no doubt they were going to take them. Already the defenders had begun to waver, flinching from the threat of contact, and presently, when the attackers closed to within pistol range, they broke. "A few rushed to the rear, and with frantic eagerness began to climb the slope," a Kansas infantryman would recall, "but nearly all, throwing down their muskets and holding up their hands in token of surrender, leaped to our side of the intrenchments and cowered behind them, for the hail of bullets raining down from the hill was as deadly to them as to us. The first line was won."

Winning it and holding it were different things, however: as the victors soon found out. Almost at once, though they were in full control of the lower works and though the ridge was so steep that few of the guns on its crest could be brought to bear on them, the position took on the aspect of a trap. Graybacks in the second line, midway up the slope, were pouring in a murderous, plunging fire, and cannoneers were rolling shells with sputtering fuzes down the hillside to explode in the lost rifle pits below. Amid all this confusion, company officers were brandishing their sabers and shouting for the new occupants to get to work with shovels, bayonets, anything that would help to reverse the parapets and throw some dirt between themselves and the marksmen overhead; but the principal reaction was a sort of aimless milling about, combined with a good deal of ducking and dodging, and a rapidly growing realization that the only practical solution was for them to get out of this untenable position as quickly as possible, either by retreating or continuing the charge. They chose the latter course, wanting more than anything to come to grips with their tormentors. By twos and threes, then by squads and platoons as the conviction took hold, blue-clad figures began to push forward, crouching low for traction on the slope.

At first their officers called after them to stop, but they paid no attention to this, and the lieutenants and captains, affected by the spirit of the men, rushed to join them, still gesturing with their swords and yelling, superfluously and illogically, out of habit: "Follow me!" Soon even the colonels and brigadiers had caught the spirit of the advance, and presently whole regiments were surging up the ridge, aligning as best they could on the colors while calling for the bearers to climb faster.

Down at the command post on Orchard Knob, this unexpected development — plainly visible, though reduced to miniature by distance — provoked the same reaction of stunned disbelief the rebel gunners had evinced when the blue mass first began its advance across the plain. Grant, for one, saw that he might have a first-class disaster on his hands if the Confederates repulsed the Cumberlanders, then followed through with a counterattack as the demoralized bluecoats tumbled down the slope and into the valley, where no reserves had been withheld to form a straggler line on which to rally. "Thomas, who ordered those men up the ridge?" he said angrily. Thomas replied in his usual quiet way: "I don't know. *I* did not." Grant turned to Granger, whom he had just reproached sharply for spending time with the guns instead of tending to his larger duties as a corps commander. "Did you order them up, Granger?" The New Yorker denied it, emphatically but enthusiastically, for he too had caught the spirit of the charge by now.

"No; they started up without orders," he said, and he added happily: "When those fellows get started all hell can't stop them." Grant turned his attention back to the action in front, remarking as he did so that somebody was going to suffer professionally if the men who had taken the bit in their teeth were repulsed.

At first that seemed altogether likely, considering the difficulties of terrain and Bragg's reputation as a counterpuncher; but not for long. Watching the upward progress of the sixty regiments as they engaged in a gallant rivalry to see which would be first to reach the crest, a staff colonel observed that "at times their movements were in shape like the flight of migratory birds, sometimes in line, sometimes in mass, mostly in V-shaped groups, with the points toward the enemy. At these points regimental flags were flying, sometimes drooping as the bearers were shot, but never reaching the ground, for other brave hands were there to seize them." That was how it looked in small from Orchard Knob. Up close, there was the gritty sense of participation, the rasp of heavy breathing, the drum and clatter of boots on rocky ground, and always the sickening thwack of bullets entering flesh and striking bone. Phil Sheridan saw and heard it so as he stood at the base of the ridge, watching his troops in their attempt to outstrip the rivals on their left in Wood's division, and accepted a drink from a silver flask held out by a staff captain. Before he drank he lifted the flask in salute to a group of gray-clad officers he saw in front of Bragg's headquarters, directly up the slope. "Here's to you!" he called. This may have failed to attract the attention of those for whom it was intended, but it certainly did not fail in the case of a pair of gunners in a nearby rebel battery. Swinging their pieces in his direction, they returned the salute with two well-placed rounds that kicked dirt over Sheridan and the captain standing beside him. "Ah, that is ungenerous!" he replied as he brushed off his uniform; "I shall take those guns for that." First, though, he took the drink, and then he started forward, necessarily on foot because his horse had been shot from under him during the advance across the plain.

There seemed an excellent chance that he would carry out his threat, for by now the second line had been overrun, midway up the slope, and his men were driving hard for the crest beyond. They had been helped considerably in advance by the Confederate dispositions, which were faulty in several respects, probably because the natural strength of the terrain had made the defenders overconfident to the point of not believing that their preparations would be tested. For example, standing orders that the troops in the lower rifle pits were to fire no more than a couple of massed volleys when the attackers came within effective range, then fall back to the intermediate position just uphill, had not been made clear to the troops involved; with the demoralizing result that while some had attempted to hold their ground, others had seemed to flee, infecting uninformed comrades with their apparent panic. Worst of all, perhaps, the officers who laid out the upper line had erred in placing it on the geographic, rather than on the "military" crest — literally along the topmost line, that is, rather than along the highest line from which the enemy could be seen and fired on — so that many of the Federal climbers found themselves protected by defilade practically all the way to the top, and once they were there they were able to take rebel strongpoints under fire from the flank, distracting the attention of the defenders from the attackers coming straight at them up the ridge. Threatened thus, the graybacks here did what those below had done already; they broke and they broke badly, despite the pleas and curses of their officers, including Bragg himself, who rode among them in a desperate, last-minute effort to persuade them to rally and drive the winded enemy troops back down the slope. "Here is your commander!" he called to them. But they either ignored him, intent as they were on getting beyond the reach of the rapid-firing bluecoats, or else they taunted him with the army catch phrase: "Here's your mule!"

When the Federals crested the ridge they saw spread out below them on the reverse slope what one of them called "the sight of our lives — men tumbling over each other in reckless confusion, hats off, some without guns, running wildly." Too blown to cheer, the victors swung their caps and gestured for the laggards to hurry forward and share the view. "My God, come see them run!" a Hoosier private shouted over his shoulder. A Kansan, writing years later, relived the excitement provoked by the tableau. This beat Bull Run, Wilson's Creek, and the opening phases of Perryville and Stones River. This beat Chickamauga. "Gray clad men rushed wildly down the hill and into the woods, tossing away knapsacks, muskets, and blankets as they ran. Batteries galloped back along the narrow, winding roads with reckless speed, and officers, frantic with rage, rushed from one panic-stricken group to another, shouting and cursing as they strove to check the headlong flight. Our men pursued the fugitives with an eagerness only equaled by their own to escape; the horses of the artillery were shot as they ran; squads of rebels were headed off and brought back as prisoners, and in ten minutes all that remained of the defiant rebel army that had so long besieged Chattanooga was captured guns, disarmed prisoners, moaning wounded, ghastly dead, and scattered, demoralized fugitives. Mission Ridge was ours."

Bragg himself had barely escaped capture, as had Breckinridge, but not their two adjutants or some 3000 other prisoners, who were taken along with 7000 abandoned small arms and 37 cannon, one third of all Bragg had. One of these last was claimed by Sheridan in person, who came running up and leaped astride one of the two guns that had fired at him a few minutes ago. Wrapping his bandy legs around the tube, he swung his hat and cheered. Harker, who commanded his third brigade, followed suit by mounting a nearby gun in a similar fashion, but scorched his seat on the hot metal and could not sit a horse for the next two weeks. In this he was less fortunate than his division commander, who either was made of sterner stuff or else had chosen a cooler piece; at any rate Sheridan stayed astride the gun and continued to cheer and swing his hat, exultant over the reversal of what had happened two months ago at Chickamauga, where he had been among those in headlong flight from fury. All round him now the men were cheering, too, having caught their breath, and Granger rode up from Orchard Knob at the height of the celebration to engage in a sort of victory dance on horseback. "I'm going to have you all court-martialed!" he shouted, laughing. "You were ordered to take the works at the foot of the hill and you've taken those on top! You have disobeyed orders, all of you, and you know that you ought to be court-martialed!"

Not that the position had been taken without cost. In fact, the cost had been about as steep as the grade up which the attack was launched: particularly to the two divisions in the center. Wood suffered 1035 casualties, as compared to a combined total of 789 for Baird and Johnson, in support on the left and right; whereas Sheridan lost 1346, a bit over twenty percent of the 6500 infantry he had had when he started forward. Moreover, there was a good deal of variation in the losses by smaller units within the larger ones, depending on the luck of the draw in their assault on different portions of the ridge. Some had cover most of the way up and therefore contributed little to the amount of blood that was shed on the slope, while others had to pass through a continuous hail of bullets and were grievously battered in the process. An Indiana regiment, for instance, started its climb with 337 effectives and lost 202 of them, or nearly sixty percent, killed and wounded in the forty-five minutes required to reach the crest. After such bleeding and exertion by the infantry, and in the absence of cavalry, which was still beyond the river because of a continuing lack of forage on the south bank, it was small wonder no true pursuit was undertaken within the brief remaining span of daylight that followed the collapse of the rebel center. Sheridan, once he had come down off his perch astride the cannon, was eager to take up the chase, but the other division commanders were not, even though they had suffered fewer casualties, and Granger declined to unleash him.

Meanwhile the Confederates made good use of the respite thus allowed them. Continuing to hold off Sherman with one hand — no difficult task, since he attempted no renewal of his attack — Cleburne prevented a widening of the breakthrough with the other, and Stewart served Hooker in much the same fashion north of Rossville. Sunset was at 4.50; Hardee rallied his and Breckinridge's fugitives on the near side of Chickamauga Creek and began a withdrawal across it under cover of darkness, one hour later. The moon rose full, drenching the fields and the lost ridge with a glistening yellow light almost bright enough to read by, if anyone had been of a mind to read. "By 9 p.m. everything was across," according to Cleburne, "except the dead and a few stragglers lingering here and there under the shadows of the trees for the purpose of being captured, faint-hearted patriots succumbing to the hardships of the war and the imagined hopelessness of the hour."

Next morning Bragg continued the withdrawal southeast into Georgia, attempting to gain the cover of Taylor's Ridge, just beyond Ringgold, and leaving a trail of charred supply dumps and broken-down wagons, as well as four more cannon, to mark the line of his retreat. He had lost, in the course of the three-day action, November 23-25, fewer than half as many killed and wounded as his adversary — 361 and 2160, as compared to 753 and 4722 in those two doleful categories — but his 4146 captured and missing, in contrast to Grant's 349, raised the Confederate total of 6667 above the Federal 5824. But that was by no means all there was to the outcome of the fighting, nor was it fitting as a yardstick by which to measure the extent of the disaster. Bragg had lost a great deal more than the scant fifteen percent of his army which these figures indicated, and a great deal more than the 41 guns his cannoneers had abandoned, even though they amounted to more than a third of all he had. Guns and men could be replaced; Chattanooga, on the other hand, was now what a northern journalist called "a gateway wrenched asunder." The road lay open into the heartland of the South, and all that stood between the bluecoats and a rapid penetration was the battered and dispirited remnant of the force they had just driven from a position its commander had deemed impregnable. And in fact he was still of that opinion, believing that all it had lacked was men determined to defend it. Unlike Lee, who at Gettysburg had said, "It's all my fault," Bragg at this stage was not inclined to shoulder even a fraction of the blame for the outcome of the contest. The burden of his official report, submitted later, was that the flaw had been in his soldiers. "No satisfactory excuse can possibly be given for the shameful conduct of the troops ... in allowing their line to be penetrated. The position was one which ought to have been held by a line of skirmishers against any assaulting column." So he said, making no reference to the faulty dispositions or the unclear orders, both of which were his responsibility.

Not many agreed with him, however, either in his own army or in the one now in control of what he had lost. An Ohio infantryman, for example, coming forward on the morning after the battle for a walk along the northern end of Missionary Ridge, encountered the body of one of the men who had fought here under Cleburne. In the course of the recent siege he himself had learned something of privation, of the effects of hunger and exposure on the human spirit in its will to persevere against the odds, and this had given him a better understanding of the problems that had been so much a part of daily living for this dead soldier and others like him, whose own commander even now was blaming him and them, along with the bolters, for the loss of a position he and they had died in an attempt to save. Bending down for a closer look at the dead Confederate, the Ohioan afterwards told of what he saw. "He was not over fifteen years of age, and very slender in size. He was clothed in a cotton suit, and was barefooted; barefooted, [in] that cold and wet ... November. I examined his haversack. For a day's ration there was a handful of black beans, a few pieces of sorghum, and a half dozen roasted acorns. That was an infinitely poor outfit for marching and fighting, but that Tennessee Confederate had made it answer his purpose."

Ultimately, if only in wry comment, at least one man on the Federal side agreed with Bragg as to the strength of the position, and that was Grant. Miffed by fortune's upset of his plans for Sherman's glorification, if not his own — on the first day, Thomas had played the leading role because Sherman was late in getting into position; on the second, Hooker had stolen the thunder from "above the clouds" while Sherman was attacking an undefended hill, just short of his true objective; on the third, Thomas once more occupied the limelight after Sherman was fought to a standstill by an opponent greatly his inferior in numbers — the over-all Union commander had sought to disassociate himself from a contest decided in outright violation not only of his wishes but also of his orders. "Damn the battle!" he was quoted as saying in that first fit of pique; "I had nothing to do with it." He recovered from this within a couple of hours, however, and got off a wire to Washington in which he had no reservations "in announcing a complete victory over Bragg." In time, he was even able to joke about it. Asked some years later whether he did not agree that his adversary had made a serious mistake in detaching Longstreet, he said he did, and when it was further suggested that Bragg must have considered his position impregnable, Grant agreed with that also, though his comment was accompanied by a smile and a shrewd look. "Well, it *was* impregnable," he said.

At any rate the Chattanooga gateway had been wrenched asunder, and what would come of this no man could say for certain, although some believed they knew, including members of the army now on the muddy and disconsolate retreat for Ringgold.

"Captain, this is the death knell of the Confederacy," a junior officer had remarked to his company commander as the withdrawal got under way from Missionary Ridge. "If we cannot cope with those fellows with the advantages we had on this line, there is not a line between here and the Atlantic Ocean where we can stop them."

"Hush, Lieutenant," the captain told him, slogging rearward through the darkness. "That is treason you are talking."

☆ ☆ ☆

Depressed by the necessity for withdrawal and retreat, following hard upon the collapse of the Confederate center, the lieutenant overlooked the effectiveness with which Cleburne, outnumbered four or five to one, had "coped" with Sherman all day on the right. Two days later at Taylor's Ridge, as if by way of a reminder, the Arkansan repeated his performance, this time with even greater success, against Hooker and odds no worse than three to one. Moreover, this repetition of his exploit was the outcome of what had been thought to be a suicide assignment. Bragg made it to Ringgold by nightfall of November 26, fifteen miles down the railroad linking Chattanooga and Atlanta, and though so far he was more or less intact, he knew the Federals were closing on him rapidly. Encumbered as he was, and they were not, by a slow-moving wagon train hub-deep in mud, they would be certain to overtake him tomorrow unless he could do something to halt or anyhow delay them long enough to give him a new head start in the race for Dalton, another fifteen miles down the track. Accordingly, as he pressed on beyond the town and through the gap in Taylor's Ridge, he sent peremptory orders for a last-ditch stand at that point by the division guarding his rear. This was Cleburne's. It seemed hard to sacrifice good soldiers for no other purpose than to gain a little time, but Bragg believed he had no choice if he was to avoid the total destruction that would be likely to ensue if he was overtaken in his present condition, strung out on the muddy roads. "Tell General Cleburne to hold this position at all hazards," he instructed the staff officer who delivered the message, "and keep back the enemy until the artillery and transportation of the army are secure."

Though he had been told to cross in the darkness and thus avoid being overtaken by the superior blue force closing on his rear, Cleburne had stopped for the night on the west side of bridgeless East Chickamauga Creek, two miles short of the town, so his men could sleep in dry clothes before resuming the march next morning. Such concern for their welfare was characteristic of him, but it was practical as well, since he was convinced that a rear-guard action, even with a deep-running stream at their backs, would cost them fewer casualties than would lengthen the sick lists after a crossing of the waist-deep ford and a chilly halt on the east bank with no sun or exercise to warm them. Bragg's orders for a stand beyond Ringgold "at all hazards" reached him shortly before midnight, and he rode ahead to reconnoiter the position by moonlight, leaving instructions for the troops to be roused and started forward three hours later. At daybreak, having crossed the creek and filed through the streets of the Georgia hamlet, they found him waiting for them at the mouth of the narrow gorge through which the railroad plunged on its way to Atlanta. After about an hour, which he spent posting them and his two guns in accordance with a plan he had worked out while they were asleep, an enemy column emerged from the nearby eastern limits of the town, the bluecoats marching four abreast, preceded by a line of skirmishers, textbook style. Cleburne had his 4100 brush-masked graybacks hold their fire until the unsuspecting skirmishers were practically upon them, then open up with everything they had, including pistols. The head of the blasted column drew back snakelike on the writhing body, which coiled itself into attack formation and then came on again, 12,000 strong. This time there was no surprise, but the repulse was as complete. Hooker — for that was who it was, and he still had the three divisions with which he had seized Lookout Mountain three days ago — paused to take stock, then probed on the right, attacking uphill, well south of the gap, in an attempt to outflank the defenders; only to find that they had shifted a portion of their force to meet him. Repulsed, he feinted again at the center and launched another uphill assault, this time on the left of the gap; but with the same result. Fighting Joe once more took stock, and decided to wait for his guns, which were toiling slowly eastward through the churned-up mud of the road from Chattanooga Valley, where they had been stalled until late yesterday for lack of a bridge strong enough to support them over Chattanooga Creek. By the time they arrived, the morning was gone and Cleburne had carried out his mission; Bragg's leading elements were in Dalton by then, safely beyond the craggy loom of Rocky Face Ridge, and the rest were not far behind, having been given the head start they needed. At a cost of 221 casualties — one less than he had suffered at Tunnel Hill — Cleburne had inflicted 442 by Hooker's admission. This was exactly double the number of his own, including more than a hundred prisoners he had taken along with three stands of colors, but Confederates were convinced the Federal losses were much larger than Fighting Joe admitted. A straggler from Walker's division, for example, watching the lop-sided contest from a grandstand seat on the ridge, pronounced it "the doggondest fight of the war." Down there below, he would recall years later, "the ground was piled with dead Yankees; they were piled in heaps. The scene looked unlike any battlefield I ever saw," he added. "From the foot to the top of the hill was covered with the slain, all lying on their faces. It had the appearance of the roof of a house shingled with dead Yankees."

Cleburne and his division, which he kept in position till well past noon and then withdrew unmolested, later received a joint resolution of thanks from Congress "for the victory obtained by them over superior forces of the enemy at Ringgold Gap, in the State of Georgia," but all that Hooker got from the engagement was a snub from his commander and an unceremonious return to inaction. When Grant came to write his report of the campaign, Ringgold Gap was referred to briefly as "a severe fight, in which we lost heavily in valuable officers and men," and he added an indorsement to Fighting Joe's own report that must have stung the glory-hungry general deeply: "Attention is called to that part of the report giving ... the number of prisoners and small arms captured, which is greater than the number really captured by the whole army." Grant was an accomplished undercutter when he chose to be, and in Hooker's case he did so choose, both now and down the years. For the present, he directed him to hold his ground, "but to go no farther south at the expense of a fight." Cast once more in a supporting role, the unhappy Easterner was told next day: "The object in remaining where you are is to protect Sherman's flank while he is moving toward Cleveland and Loudon."

Once more the volatile redhead was the star, this time in a production entitled "The Relief of Knoxville," where Longstreet was still hanging on and keeping Burnside under siege, despite Grant's prediction that he would "take to the mountain passes" once the Chattanooga Federals came between him and Bragg and stood astride the rail supply line in his rear. Sherman was altogether willing to try another turn at playing the role of savior, but he took care to have it understood that he did not want to be left stranded in the backwater region once he had wound up what he was being sent there to accomplish. He was utterly opposed to tying up masses of troops, least of all his own, for the purpose of protecting a handful of civilians, many of whom he considered of doubtful loyalty anyhow, while the main stream of the war ran on to slaughter elsewhere. "Recollect that East Tennessee is my horror," he wrote Grant on December 1 from the near bank of the Hiwassee, while preparing to set out next day for Loudon and Knoxville. "That any military man should send a force into East Tennessee puzzles me. Burnside is there and must be relieved, but when relieved I want to get out, and he should come out too."

Burnside's men were in complete agreement; in fact, they had been so all along. "If this is the kind of country we are fighting for," one of them had declared on completing the southward march across the barrens, "I am in favor of letting the rebs take their land and their niggers and go to hell, for I wouldn't give a bit an acre for all the land I have seen in the last four days." The trouble was that Lincoln very much wanted them there, for precisely the reason Sherman derided: to protect the Union-loyal citizens and relieve them of their long-borne yoke of Confederate oppression. Moreover, cooped up as they now were in Knoxville, under siege by Longstreet's two divisions plus a third that had arrived under Bushrod Johnson, the problem was not so much how to get out as it was how to survive on meager rations. They were no longer fighting for East Tennessee — which in point of fact they had abandoned, except for Knoxville itself and Cumberland Gap, the now inaccessible escape hatch fifty air-line miles due north — but for their lives.

Old Peter and his soldiers were about as unhappy outside the town — and incidentally, what with the wretched supply conditions, about as hungry — as the Federals hemmed inside it. He had probed for chinks in the blue defenses and, finding none, had waited for the reinforcements Bragg had said were on the way. Fewer than half of the promised 11,000 arrived, but at least they brought him up to a strength nearly equal to that of the force besieged. He continued to search for weak spots, though with no better success. By November 27 — the date of Cleburne's fight at Ringgold — coincident with the issuance of orders for accomplishing a breakthrough at a point he had selected, a rumor had begun to spread that Bragg had been whipped at Chattanooga. How much truth there was in this, Longstreet did not know, but in reply next day to a suggestion from McLaws that the thing to do was abandon the siege without further delay and return at once to Virginia, lest they be caught between two superior Union forces, he persisted in his belief that the best solution, if the rumor of Bragg's defeat was true, was a quick settlement of the issue here at Knoxville. His reasons were twofold: first because it would not do to leave a fellow commander in the lurch, no matter how little regard he had for him personally, and second because a victory over Burnside would dispose of at least one of the two menaces to a successful withdrawal if such a course became unavoidable. That is, if he stayed where he was, at least for a time, he might draw off a portion of the blue horde rumored to be in pursuit of Bragg, and he might also simplify his own problems, when and if the time came for him to retire eastward over the primitive mountain roads. "It is a great mistake to suppose that there is any safety for us in going to Virginia if General Bragg has been defeated," he told his fellow Georgian, "for we leave him at the mercy of his victors, and with his army destroyed our own had better be also, for we will be not only destroyed, but disgraced. There is neither safety nor honor in any other course than the one I have chosen and ordered.... The assault must be made at the time appointed, and must be made with a determination which will insure success."

The time appointed was dawn next morning, November 29, and the point selected for assault was Fort Loudon, a bastioned earthwork previously established by the Confederates at the tip of a long salient extended westward from the main line of intrenchments to include a hill 1000 yards beyond the limits of the town; Fort Sanders, the Federals had renamed it, in memory of the young cavalry brigadier who had made a successful bridge-burning raid through the region, back in June, but had been mortally wounded two weeks ago at Campbell Station, supposedly by a civilian sniper, while resisting the gray advance on Knoxville. Originally Longstreet had intended to use Alexander's artillery to soften up the objective before the infantry moved in; then later he decided to stake everything on surprise, which would be sacrificed if he employed a preliminary bombardment, and on the sheer weight of numbers massed on a narrow front. Assigning two brigades from McLaws to the assault, with a third in support from Jenkins — a total of about 3000 effectives, as compared to fewer than 500 within the fort, including the crews of its twelve guns — he posted the first wave of attackers within 150 yards of the northwest corner of the works in the cold predawn darkness of the night whose end would be the signal for the jump-off. The advance was to be conducted in columns of regiments, the theory being that such a deployment in depth would give added power to the thrust and insure that there would be no wait for reinforcements in case unexpected resistance developed in the course of the attack. It was stressed that there was to be no pause for anything whatever, front or rear, and that the main thing was to keep moving. Once the position had been overrun, the surviving remnant of the garrison, if any, was to be driven eastward through the town, so that other strongpoints along the line could be taken in reverse, thus effecting a quick reduction of the whole.

Longstreet had planned carefully, with close attention to such details as had occurred to him and the specialists on his staff. But so had Burnside: as the butternut attackers discovered when they rushed forward through the dusk of that frosty Sunday morning. The first thing they struck was wire — not barbed wire; that refinement was achieved by a later generation; but telegraph wire — looped and stretched close to the ground between stakes and stumps, which not only tripped the men at the heads of the columns and sent them sprawling and cursing, but also served as an unmistakable warning to the garrison that an assault was being launched. Nor was this innovation by any means the worst of what the Confederates encountered in the course of the next hour. Continuing through and over the wire, laced in a network knee- and ankle-high, they gained the ditch to find that it was nine feet deep — not five, as they had been informed by the staffers who had done their reconnoitering with binoculars at long range — while the parapet just beyond it, slippery with half-frozen mud and a powdering of sleet, was crowded along its crest with blue defenders, ranked shoulder to shoulder and thoroughly alert, who delivered steady blasts of musketry into the packed gray mass a dozen feet below. Without scaling ladders, which no one had thought would be needed, some men tried to get up and over the wall by standing on the shoulders of their comrades, but were either hurled back or captured. One color bearer, hoisted in this fashion, was grabbed by the neck and snatched from sight, flopping like a hooked fish being landed, and though three others managed to plant their standards on the rim of the parapet, a succession of replacements was required to keep them there. All this time, two triple-shotted guns on the flank were raking the trench with a fire that dropped the dead and injured of the two assault brigades beneath the feet of the men of the third, who came sliding down the counterscarp to add to the wedged confusion. By now, with the Federals heaving lighted shells into the ditch, where they exploded with fearful effect at such close quarters, it had become apparent, at least to the troops immediately concerned, that the only result of continuing the attack — if, indeed, it could still be called that at this stage — would be to lengthen the already considerable list of casualties. When Longstreet, coming forward with two more brigades which he intended to throw into the uproar, learned from McLaws of the woeful state of affairs up ahead, he rejected pleas by Jenkins and Johnson that they be allowed to try their hand, and ordered the recall sounded. Dazed and panicky, the survivors of the three committed brigades, or anyhow so many of them as did not prefer surrender to the further risk of catching a bullet in the back, returned through the wire they had encountered at the outset.

Generous as ever in such matters, Burnside promptly sent out a flag of truce and offered his old friend permission to remove his dead and injured from the ditch. Longstreet gratefully accepted, then requested and received an extension of the truce when this turned out to be a heavier task than he had supposed without a close-up view of the carnage. He had suffered 813 casualties — 129 killed, 458 wounded, and 226 captured — in contrast to his adversary, who lost, out of 440 effectives in Fort Sanders at the time of the attack, a total of 8 killed and 5 wounded. Thirteen was a decidedly lucky number in this instance; moreover, the high proportion of dead among the scant handful of Union casualties resulted from the fact that the defenders had exposed no more than their heads to the rattled fire of the attackers, and even then for only so long as it took them to take aim, which was scarcely necessary at that range and with a target of that size. Up to now, the Federal losses for the whole campaign had been higher than those of the besiegers, but today's losses brought the over-all totals, North and South, respectively to 693 and 1142. What was more, these figures were approximately final; for while the work of removing Old Peter's unfortunates was in progress he received a message informing him that Bragg had fallen back from Chattanooga, thirty miles down the railroad toward Atlanta, and advising him to do the same from Knoxville, either toward Georgia or Virginia, but in any case to have Wheeler report to Dalton as soon as possible with his three brigades. Having complied with the instructions for the cavalry to move out, Longstreet decided to hold his ground until he could discover whether the road to Dalton was open. He remained in front of Knoxville until he learned from a captured dispatch, two days later, that Sherman was on the way from Loudon with six divisions, which would give the Federals ten in all, as compared to the Confederate three. Accordingly, on the night of December 3 he put his trains in motion, not toward Dalton but northeast, in the direction of Virginia, and followed shortly after dark next evening with his infantry, unobserved. "Detached from General Lee, what a horrible failure is Longstreet!" an eastern diarist exclaimed, forgetful of his great day at

Chickamauga and unaware that he had been sent to East Tennessee not only against his wishes but also over his protest that the expedition was tactically unwise, both from Bragg's point of view and his own.

Sherman arrived next day, riding in ahead of the relief column, which he had stopped at Maryville, eighteen miles to the south, when he learned that the Confederates had pulled back from Knoxville. Notified that the siege had been lifted, Grant proposed that Longstreet be pursued and driven across the Blue Ridge, thus to assure his removal as a hovering threat; but the redhead wanted no part of such an assignment. "A stern chase is a long one," he protested, determined to resist all efforts to shift him farther eastward from the Mississippi Valley, which he still saw as the cockpit of the war. Now that the big river had been cleared and reclaimed from source to mouth, he preferred to deal with the rebels down in Georgia, intending to complete their destruction by driving them back on the rail transportation hub eighty air-line miles across the mountains in their rear. "My troops are in excellent heart," he declared, "ready for Atlanta or anywhere." Instructed to detach two divisions to strengthen the Knoxville garrison — in case Longstreet attempted a comeback from Rogersville, where he had ended his unpursued retreat, sixty-odd miles up the Holston — Sherman had Granger proceed north from Maryville with Sheridan and Wood, while he himself returned by easy stages to Chattanooga with his own four divisions. There he found Thomas and Hooker taking a well-earned rest from their recent exertions. Now that blustery weather had arrived, the Cumberland and ex-Potomac troops were already settling down in winter camps. Similarly, Grant had transferred his headquarters back to Nashville, and presently Sherman joined him there, enjoying such relaxations as the Tennessee capital afforded outside work hours, which the two friends spent designing further troubles for the Confederacy, to be undertaken in various directions as soon as the weather cleared.

That would not be for some time, however. Meanwhile Thomas was occupying himself with the establishment of a military cemetery on Orchard Knob. The thought had occurred to him, on the day he took it, that this would make a lovely burying ground for the Union soldiers who had fallen or were still to fall in the battles hereabout, and almost before the smoke of his involuntary assault on Missionary Ridge had cleared he had a detail at work on the project. When the chaplain who was to be in charge inquired if the dead should be buried in plots assigned to the states they represented — as was being done at Gettysburg, where Lincoln had spoken a couple of weeks ago — the Virginian lowered his head in thought, then shook it decisively and made a tumbling gesture with both hands. "No, no; mix 'em up, mix 'em up," he said; "I'm tired of states rights." Increased responsibility, accompanied by a growing and reciprocal fondness for the men in the army he now led, had brought a new geniality to the stolid Rock of Chickamauga. He had even begun to tell stories on himself: as, for example, of the soldier who had come to him recently asking for a furlough. "I aint seen my old woman, General, for four months," the man explained. If he thought this could not fail in its persuasiveness he was wrong. "And I have not seen mine for two years," Thomas replied. "If a general can submit to such privation, surely a private can." Evidently the soldier had not previously considered this connection between privates and privation. At any rate he looked doubtful. "I don't know about that, General," he said. "Me and my wife aint made that way."

No doubt the Virginian's jovial mood was also due in part to the fulfillment of his vow to be "even" with his former battery commander for the insult he had received in the course of the siege that had been lifted when his Cumberlanders took the bit in their teeth and charged, "against orders," up Missionary Ridge. What was more, his satisfaction was enlarged by the knowledge that he had obtained it despite the department commander's attempt to limit his participation in the action that had finally put revenge within his reach. In that double sense, as the outcome applied to both commanders, past and present, his gratification was doubly sweet.

As for Bragg, the reconsolidation of his army behind Rocky Face Ridge — completed on November 28 with the arrival of Cleburne, who was greeted with cheers for his rebuff of Hooker at Ringgold Gap the day before — brought with it not only a sense of relief at having been delivered from destruction, but also a certain added ruefulness, a letdown following hard upon the relaxation of tension. He knew now just how narrow his escape had been and, what was worse, how unlikely he was to be so fortunate in another contest with the foe who had just flung him out of a position he had judged impregnable. Worst of all, perhaps, was the attitude of the troops, then and since. "Here's your mule!" they had hooted in response to his attempt to rally them with "Here is your commander," and he took it as a bad sign that, far from being despondent over their disgrace, many of them were grinning at the memory of their headlong break for safety. "Flicker, flicker!" they called to one another in their camps, that being their accustomed cry when they saw a man whose legs would not behave in combat. "Yaller-hammer, Alabama! Flicker, flicker, yaller-hammer!" they would shout, adding by way of reprise: "Bully for Bragg! He's hell on retreat!" Though this might be no more than their way of shrugging off embarrassment, it did not seem to him to augur well for the outcome of the next blue-gray confrontation, wherever that might be. "We hope to maintain this position," he wired Richmond the following day, "[but] should the enemy press on promptly we may have to cross the Oostenaula," another fifteen miles to the south, beyond Resaca. "My first estimate of our disaster was not too large," he continued, "and time only can restore order and morale. All possible aid should be pushed on to Resaca." And having gone so far in the way of admission, he went one step further. "I deem it due to the cause and to myself," he added, "to ask for relief from command and an investigation into the causes of the defeat."

Perhaps this last was no more than a closing flourish, such as he had employed at the end of the letter sent out after Murfreesboro, wherein he invited his lieutenants to assess his military worth. In any event, just as they had taken him at his word then, whether he meant it or not, so did Davis now. "Your dispatches of yesterday received," the adjutant general replied on the last day of November. "Your request to be relieved has been submitted to the President, who, upon your representation, directs me to notify you that you are relieved from command, which you will transfer to Lieutenant General Hardee, the officer next in rank and now present for duty."

There he had it. Or perhaps not quite; perhaps the flourish — if that was what it was — could be recalled. At any rate, if he was thus to be brought down, he would do what he could to assure that his was not a solitary departure. In sending next day, by special messenger, "a plain, unvarnished report of the operations at Chattanooga, resulting in my shameful discomfiture," he included a letter addressed to his friend the Commander in Chief, who had sustained him invariably in the past. "The disaster admits of no palliation," he wrote, "and is justly disparaging to me as a commander. I trust, however, you may find upon full investigation that the fault is not entirely mine.... I fear we both erred in the conclusion for me to retain command here after the clamor raised against me. The warfare has been carried on successfully, and the fruits are bitter. You must make other changes here, or our success is hopeless.... I can bear to be sacrificed myself, but not to see my country and my friends ruined by the vices of a few profligate men." Specifically he charged that Breckinridge had been drunk throughout the three-day battle and "totally unfit for any duty" on the retreat, while Cheatham was "equally dangerous" in that regard. As for himself, he said in closing, "I shall ever be ready to do all in my power for our common cause, but feel that some little rest will render me more efficient than I am now. Most respectfully and truly, yours, Braxton Bragg, General, &c."

Still in Dalton the following day, December 2, he tried a different tack in a second letter — still headed "Headquarters Army of Tennessee" and still signed "General, Commanding" — in which he assessed the tactical situation and made an additional suggestion: "The enemy has concentrated all his available means in front of this army, and by sheer force of numbers has triumphed over our gallant little band. No one estimates the disaster more seriously than I do, and the whole responsibility and disgrace rest on my humble head. But we can redeem the past. Let us concentrate all our available men, unite them with this gallant little army, still full of zeal and burning to redeem its lost character and prestige, and with our greatest and best leader at its head — yourself, if practicable — march the whole upon the enemy and crush him in his power and his glory. I believe it practicable, and I trust that I may be allowed to participate in the struggle which may restore to us the character, the prestige, and the country which we have just lost."

Whatever might come of this in the future, and he knew how susceptible to flattery Davis was in that respect, there was nothing for him to do now, after waiting two whole days for them to be rescinded, but carry out the instructions he had received. Painful though the parting was, at least for him — "The associations of more than two years, which bind together a commander and his trusted troops, cannot be severed without deep emotion," he remarked in the farewell address he issued that same day — he turned his duties over to Hardee, as ordered, and took his leave. In the seventeen months he had been at its head the Army of Tennessee had fought four great battles, three of which had ended in retreat though all save the last had been claimed as victories. Similarly, in the equal span of time ahead, it would fight a great many more battles that would likewise be claimed as victories although they too — once more with a single exception, comparatively as bloody as Chickamauga — would end in retreat; but not under Bragg. His tenure had ended. "I shall proceed to La Grange, Georgia, with my personal staff," he notified Richmond, "and there await further orders."

Spring Came on Forever

★ ✗ ☆

NEWS OF THE GREAT CHATTANOOGA VICTORY, which had begun on Monday and ended on Wednesday, spread throughout the North on the following day, November 26. By coincidence, in a proclamation issued eight weeks earlier at the suggestion of a lady editor, Lincoln had called upon his fellow citizens "to set apart and observe the last Thursday of November next, as a day of thanksgiving and praise to our beneficent Father who dwelleth in the Heavens." Instituted thus "in the midst of a civil war of unequaled magnitude and severity," this first national Thanksgiving was intended not only as a reminder for people to be grateful for "the blessings of fruitful fields and healthful skies," but also as an occasion for them to "implore the interposition of the Almighty Hand to heal the wounds of the nation and to restore it, as soon as may be consistent with the Divine purposes, to the full enjoyment of peace, harmony, tranquillity, and Union." Now that word of what had happened yesterday on Missionary Ridge was added to the "singular deliverances and blessings" for which the public was urged to show its gratitude today, it seemed to many that the Almighty Hand had interposed already, answering a good part of their prayers in advance, and that the end so fervently hoped for might be considerably nearer than had been supposed when the proclamation was issued in early October, not quite two weeks after the shock of Chickamauga caused those hopes to take a sudden drop. "This is truly a day of thanksgiving," Halleck wired Grant as the news of his latest triumph went out across the land and set the church bells ringing as wildly as they had rung after Donelson and Vicksburg.

Moreover, just as Thomas had taken his revenge for Chickamauga, so had Banks obtained by now at least a degree of recompense for the drubbing he had suffered in September, when he opened his campaign against coastal Texas with Franklin's botched attack on Sabine Pass. Revising his plan by reversing it, end for end, he decided to start with a landing near the Mexican border, then work his island-hopping way back east. It was true the pickings would be much slimmer at the outset, for there was little that far down the coast that was worth taking; but the objectives were unlikely to be as stoutly defended, and he would be moving toward, rather than away from, his New Orleans base of supplies, which should serve to encourage his men to fight harder and move faster, if for no other reason than to hasten their return. Accordingly, after sending Franklin's unhappy soldiers to Berwick for a renewed ascent of the Teche — an ascent that would end abruptly on November 3 at Grand Coteau, ten miles short of Opelousas, where the column was assaulted and driven back through Vermilionville to New Iberia by Richard Taylor and Tom Green, who lost 180 and inflicted 716 casualties, including the 536 fugitives they captured — he loaded aboard transports a 3500-man division, commanded by a Maine-born major general with the resounding name of Napoleon Jackson Tecumseh Dana, who set out from New Orleans on October 26, escorted by three gunboats. This time Banks went along himself, presumably to guard against snarls and hitches. At any rate there were none. On November 2 — the day before Franklin was thrown into sudden reverse at Grand Coteau — Dana put his troops ashore at Brazos Santiago, off the mouth of the Rio Grande, and though he encountered practically no resistance, the graybacks having been withdrawn to thicken the defenses in East Texas, Banks did not let this tone down the announcement of his achievement. "The flag of the Union floated over Texas today at meridian precisely," he notified Washington. "Our enterprise has been a complete success." Four days later he occupied Brownsville, just under thirty miles inland, opposite Matamoros, and sent for the puppet governor Andrew Hamilton, who had been waiting off-stage all this time and who was established there at the southernmost tip of the state and the nation, along with his gubernatorial staff of would-be cotton factors, before the month was out. Meanwhile Banks had followed up his initial success with a series of landings on Mustang and Matagorda islands, thus gaining control of Aransas Pass and Matagorda Bay. But that was all; that was as far as he got on his way back east. Galveston and the mouth of the Brazos River were too strongly held for him to attack them with Dana's present command, reduced as it was by garrison detachments, and Halleck could not be persuaded to accede to requests for reinforcements. All Banks had gained for his pains these past three months, including the drubbing at Sabine Pass, was a couple of dusty border towns and a few bedraggled miles of Texas beach, mostly barren dunes, which he described as "inclement and uncomfortable, in consequence of the sterility of the soil and the violence of the northers."

Despite the flamboyance with which they were announced — "My most sanguine expectations are more than realized," Banks had proclaimed after occupying Brownsville; "Everything is now as favorable as could be desired" — the authorities in Washington were not inclined to include these shallow coastal lodgments, amounting in fact to little more than pinpricks along one leathery flank of the Texas elephant, among those things for which the nation should be thankful on its first Thanksgiving. Hamilton governed far too small and remote an area for his claims to be taken seriously, inside or outside the state, and it seemed to Lincoln, although he later thanked Banks politically for his "successful and valuable operations," that all the general had really done was shift some 3500 of his soldiers off to the margin of the map, where they were of about as much tactical value as if their transports had gone to the bottom of the Gulf with them aboard. Halleck expressed an even dimmer view of the proceedings. "In regard to your Sabine and Rio Grande expeditions," he protested to the Massachusetts general, "no notice of your intention to make them was received here till they were actually undertaken." Old Brains was especially irked by the setback at Grand Coteau, which he saw as the result of an unwise division of force, occasioned by the unauthorized excursion down the coast. In his opinion, the Teche, the Atchafalaya, and the Red afforded the best approach to the Lone Star State, and though he understood that these streams were at present unusable even as supply routes, being practically dry at this season of the year, he wanted the entire command standing by for the early spring rise that would convert them into arteries of invasion. For this reason, as well as for the more general one that none were available, he flatly refused to send reinforcements for an attack on Galveston by the amphibious force which by now had worked its way back east to Matagorda, explaining testily that even if such an attack were successful — and even if the place did not turn out to be a trap, as it had done before — it still would be no more than a diversion from the true path of conquest.

Besides, there were nearer and larger frets, invoking more immediate concern; Knoxville, for example. "Remember Burnside," Lincoln had wired yesterday in response to Grant's announcement that victory was within reach at Chattanooga. He could breathe easier now, for while Longstreet's siege was apparently still in progress he knew that Grant, relieved of the presence of Bragg, was free to turn his attention to East Tennessee. But there was a still nearer fret, not sixty miles southwest of Washington, and though in this case the Union force was on the offensive, the Commander in Chief had learned from long experience that the strain of waiting for news of an expected success was quite as great as waiting for news of an expected failure — particularly since experience had also taught him, all too often, that anticipated triumphs had a way of turning into the worst of all defeats; Chancellorsville, for instance. Meade at last had resumed his movement southward, having taken a two-week rest from the exertion of crossing the Rappahannock, and on this Thanksgiving morning the leading elements of his army were over the Rapidan, entering the gloomy western fringe of the Wilderness in whose depths Joe Hooker had come to grief in early May, just short of seven months ago.

His decision to cross and come to grips with Lee on that forbidding ground was based in part on a growing confidence proceeding from the fact that he had whipped him rather soundly in both of their recent face-to-face encounters, first at Bristoe Station and then at Rappahannock Bridge and Kelly's Ford. Moreover, there had come to hand on November 21 a detailed intelligence report which put the enemy strength at less than 40,000 effectives, as compared to his own 84,274 on that date. Actually, Lee's total was 48,586; Meade had just under, not just over, twice as many troops as his opponent. But in any case the preponderance was encouraging, and after four days of studying the figures and the map, he distributed on November 25 a circular directing his five corps commanders to be ready to march at 6 o'clock next morning, half an hour before sunrise. Lee's two corps were strung out along the south bank of the river, one east and the other west of Clark's Mountain, their outer flanks respectively at Mine Run and Liberty Mills, some thirty miles apart; Meade's plan called for a crossing by the downstream fords, well beyond the Confederate right, and a fast march west, along the Orange Turnpike, for a blow at the rebel east flank before Lee could bring up his other corps in support. Unlike Hooker, Meade designed no feints or diversions, preferring to concentrate everything he had for the main effort. He relied entirely on speed, which would enable him to strike before his adversary had time to get set for the punch, and on the known numerical advantage, which would be far greater than two to one if he could mass and commit his fifteen infantry divisions before the rebel six achieved a concentration. All this was explained to the responsible subordinates, whose marches began on schedule from their prescribed assembly areas near Ely's and Germanna fords, well downstream from the apparently unsuspecting graybacks in their works across the way. Aside from a heavy morning fog, which screened the movement from enemy lookouts on Clark's Mountain — more evidence, it would seem, of the interposition of the Almighty Hand in favor of the Union on this Thanksgiving Day — the weather was pleasant, a bit chilly but all the more bracing for that, and the blue troops stepped out smartly along the roads and trails leading down to the various fords that had been assigned them so that a nearly simultaneous crossing could be made by the several columns. That too had been part of the design combining speed and power.

As always, there were hitches: only this time, with speed of such vital importance, they were even more exasperating than usual. What was worse, they began to crop up almost at the outset. Meade had planned with elaborate care, issuing eight-day rations to the men, for instance, to avoid the need for a slow-rolling wagon train that would take

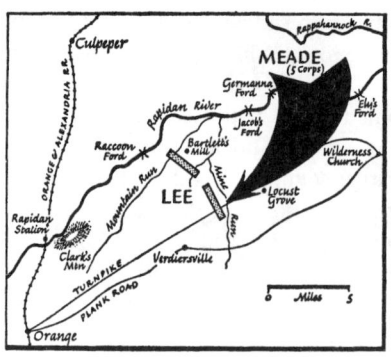

up a lot of road space and require a heavy guard; but he had neglected the human factor. In the present case, as it turned out, that factor was embodied in the person of William French, successor to Sickles as chief of the III Corps, which had been enlarged to three divisions, the same as the other four. A Maryland-born West Pointer nearing fifty, French was a tall, high-stomached man with an apoplectic look and a starchy manner, a combination that led an unadmiring staffer to remark that he resembled "one of those plethoric French colonels who are so stout, and who look so red in the face, that one would suppose someone had tied a cord tightly around their necks." So far in the war, though he had taken part in all the army's major fights except the two Bull Runs and Gettysburg, he had not distinguished himself in action. Today — and tomorrow too, for that matter, as developments would show — his performance was a good deal worse than undistinguished. Assigned to cross at Jacob's Ford, which meant that he would have the lead when the five corps turned west beyond the river, since it was the nearest of the three fords being used, he was not only late in arriving and slow in crossing, but when he found the opposite bank too steep for his battery horses to manage, he sent his artillery down to Germanna Ford and snarled the already heavy traffic there. It was dusk before he completed his crossing and called a halt close to the river, obliging those behind him to do likewise. Next morning he stepped off smartly to make up for the time lost, then promptly took the wrong fork in the road and had to countermarch. By the time he got back on the right track, the sun was past the overhead and the movement was a full day behind schedule. Red-faced and angry, for Meade was prodding him hard by now, French set out once more through the woods that screened his approach to the rebel flank, supposedly a mile away, only to run into butternut skirmishers who obliged him to call a halt and deploy his lead division. Having done so, he started forward again; but not for long. Well short of the point he had been due to reach before he encountered anything more than an outpost handful of gray pickets, the firing stepped up and he found himself involved in a full-scale engagement with what seemed to be most of the rebels in the world. Apparently Lee had made good use of the time afforded him yesterday and today by the hitches that had slowed and stalled the greatly superior mass of bluecoats closing upon him through the woods on his downstream flank.

The southern commander had indeed made use of the time so

generously allowed him. Informed by a scout on Thanksgiving Eve of the issue of eight-day rations across the way, he alerted his outposts to watch for a movement, upstream or down, and sat back to await developments. If the length of the numerical odds disturbed him, he could recall the victory he had scored against even longer odds, seven months ago, on practically this same ground. "With God's help," a young officer on his staff wrote home that night, "there shall be a Second Chancellorsville as there was a Second Manassas." Next morning, when Stuart reported the Federals crossing in force by the lower fords, Lee sent word for Hill to take up the march from beyond Clark's Mountain to join Ewell, whose corps was on the right, and shifted army headquarters the following day from Orange to Verdiersville, a dozen miles east on the plank road. He did not know yet whether Richmond or the Army of Northern Virginia was Meade's objective, but in any case he decided that his best course was to move toward him, either for an interception or for a head-on confrontation. In the absence of Ewell, who was sick, the Second Corps was under Early; Lee told him to move eastward, down the pike toward Locust Grove, and keep going until he encountered something solid. That was how it came about that French, once he recovered his sense of direction and got back on the track that afternoon, found the woods a-boil with graybacks and was obliged to engage in an unscheduled and unwanted fight, one mile short of his immediate objective. Dusk ended the brief but savage action, in which each side lost better than 500 men, and Lee had Early fall back through the darkness to a previously selected position on the far side of Mine Run, which flowed due north into the Rapidan. Hill would arrive tomorrow and extend the line southward, taking post astride the turnpike and the plank road east of Verdiersville, while Early covered the approaches to Bartlett's Mill on the far left, near the river. Anticipating with satisfaction his first purely defensive full-scale battle since Fredericksburg, just two weeks short of a full year ago, Lee instructed his men to get busy with their shovels, preparing for a repetition of that butchery.

Coming up next day through a driving rain, which made for heavy marching, the bluecoats found themselves confronted by a seven-mile line of intrenchments whose approaches had been cleared for overlapping fields of fire. They took one look at the rebel works, sited forbiddingly along a ridge on the dominant west bank of the boggy stream, and decided that for the high command to send down orders for an assault would amount to issuing death warrants for most of the troops involved. Their generals rather thought so, too, when they came forward to reconnoiter, Warren and Sedgwick on the left and right, French in the center, and Sykes and Newton in reserve. By sundown the rain had slacked and stopped, giving way to a night so cold that the water froze in the men's canteens. All next day the reconnaissance continued, and so did the spadework across the run. Meade was determined to try for a breakthrough, if one of his corps commanders would only find him a weak spot in the gray defenses. That night, when Sedgwick and Warren reported that they had found what he wanted on both flanks of the position, he issued instructions for an attack next morning. Sedgwick would open with his artillery at 7 o'clock on the right, attracting the enemy's attention in that direction, and Warren would launch an assault one hour later at the far end of the line, supported by French, who would feint at the rebel center, and by Newton, who would mass in his rear to help exploit the breakthrough. Similarly, Sykes would move up in close support of Sedgwick, whose bombardment was to be followed by an assault designed to shatter the Confederate left. With both flanks crumpled and no reserves on hand to shore them up, Lee would fall back in disarray and the blue reserves would hurry forward to complete his discomfort and destruction.

So ordered, so attempted; Uncle John opened on schedule with all his guns, while down the line the troops assigned to the assault grew tenser by the minute as the time drew near for them to go forward. Whatever the generals back at headquarters might be thinking, the men themselves, crouched in the brush and peering out across the slashings at the icy creek which they would have to cross to get within reach of the butternut infantry — dug in along the ridge to await their coming and probably smiling with anticipation as they fondled their rifles or stood by their double-shotted cannon — did not like any part of the prospect now before them. For one thing, a man even lightly hit, out there in the clearing where no stretcher bearers could get to him, would probably die in this penetrating cold. For another, they judged that their deaths would be purposeless, for they did not believe that the assault could possibly succeed. Waiting for the guns to stop their fuming, some of the soldiers passed the time by writing their names and addresses on bits of paper or chips of wood, which they fastened inside their clothes; "Killed in action, Nov. 30, 1863," a few of the gloomier or more cynical ones among them added. However, just as the artillery left off roaring and they were about to step forward into chaos, a message arrived from army headquarters: "Suspend the attack until further orders." Later they found out why. On the far left, after discovering by daylight that the rebel defenses had been greatly strengthened overnight, Warren sent word that the assault he had deemed feasible yesterday would be suicidal today. Meade rode down to see for himself, found that he agreed with this revised assessment, and canceled the attack, both left and right. Grinning, the reprieved troops discarded their improvised dogtags and thought higher than ever of Warren, who they were convinced had done the army as solid a service, in avoiding a disaster here today, as he had performed five months ago at Little Round Top or last month at Bristoe Station. What he had done, they realized, took a special kind of courage, and they were grateful not only to him but also to the commander who sustained him. Moreover, since supplies were getting low and a thaw would soften the crust of frozen mud without which no movement would be possible on the bottomless roads, Meade decided next day to withdraw the army over the same routes by which it had crossed the Rapidan, five days back, and entered this luckless woodland in the first place. So ordered, so done; the rearward movement began shortly after sunset, December 1, and continued through the night.

Glad as the departing bluecoats were to escape the wintry hug of the Wilderness, they were more fortunate than they knew. On November 30, the expected assault not having been launched against his intrenchments, Lee had been summoned to the far right by Wade Hampton, who, recovered from his Gettysburg wounds and returned to duty, had discovered an opening for a blow at the Union left, not unlike the one Hooker had received in May on his opposite flank, a few miles to the east. Looking the situation over, the southern commander liked what he saw, but decided to wait before taking advantage of it. He felt sure that Meade would attack, sooner or later, and he did not want to pass up the near certainty of another Fredericksburg, even if it meant postponing a chance for another Chancellorsville. By noon of the following day, however, with the Federals still immobile in his front, he changed his mind. "They must be attacked; they must be attacked," he muttered. Accordingly, he prepared to go over to the offensive with an all-out assault on the flank Hampton had found dangling. Sidling Early's men southward to fill the gap, Lee withdrew two of Hill's divisions from the trenches that evening and massed them south of the plank road, in the woods beyond the vulnerable enemy left, with orders to attack at dawn. Early would hold the fortified line overlooking Mine Run, while Hill drove the blue mass northward across his front and into the icy toils of the Rapidan. This time there would be no escape for Meade, as there had been for Hooker back in May, for there would be twelve solid hours of daylight for pressing the attack, not a bare two or three, as there had been when Jackson struck in the late afternoon, under circumstances otherwise much the same.

"With God's blessing," the young staffer had predicted six nights ago, "there shall be a Second Chancellorsville." But he was wrong; God's blessing was withheld. When the flankers went forward at first light they found the thickets empty, the Federals gone. Chagrined (for though he had inflicted 1653 casualties at a cost of 629 — which brought the total of his losses to 4255 since Gettysburg, as compared to Meade's 4406 — he had counted on a stunning victory, defensive or offensive), Lee ordered his cavalry after them and followed with the infantry, marching as best he could through woods the bluecoats had set afire in their wake. It was no use; Meade's head start had been substantial, and he was back across the Rapidan before he could be overtaken. In the Confederate ranks there was extreme regret at the lost opportunity, which grew in estimation, as was usual in such cases, in direct ratio to its inaccessibility. Early and Hill came under heavy criticism for having allowed the enemy to steal away unnoticed. "We miss Jackson and Longstreet terribly," the same staff officer remarked. But Lee, as always, took the blame on his own shoulders: shoulders on which he now was feeling the weight of his nearly fifty-seven years. "I am too old to command this army," he said sadly. "We should never have permitted those people to get away."

* * *

Although Davis shared the deep regret that Meade had not been punished more severely for his temporary boldness, he did not agree with Lee as to where the blame for this deliverance should rest. Conferring with the general at Orange on the eve of the brief Mine Run campaign, two weeks after his return from the roundabout western journey — it was the Commander in Chief's first visit to the Army of Northern Virginia since its departure from Richmond, nearly sixteen months before, to accomplish the suppression of Pope on the plains of Manassas — he had not failed to note the signs that Lee was aging, which indeed were unmistakable, but mainly he was impressed anew by his clear grasp of the tactical situation, his undiminished aggressiveness in the face of heavy odds, and the evident devotion of the veterans in his charge. Davis's admiration for this first of his field generals — especially by contrast with what he had observed in the course of his recent visit to the Army of Tennessee — was as strong as it had been four months ago, when he listed his reasons for refusing to accept Lee's suggestion that he be replaced as a corrective for the Gettysburg defeat. By now though, as a result of what had happened around Chattanooga the week before, he had it once again in mind to shift him to new fields. Directed to take over from Bragg, who was relieved on the day Meade began his withdrawal from the Wilderness, Hardee replied as he had done when offered the command two months ago. He appreciated "this expression of [the President's] confidence," he said, "but feeling my inability to serve the country successfully in this new sphere of duty, I respectfully decline the command if designed to be permanent." Davis then turned, as he had turned before, to Lee: with similar results. The Virginian replied that he would of course go to North Georgia, if ordered, but "I have not that confidence either in my strength or ability as would lead me of my own option to undertake the command in question."

It was Lee's opinion that Beauregard was the logical choice for the post he had vacated a year and a half ago; but Davis liked this no better than he did the notion, advanced by others, that Johnston was the best man for the job. He had small use for either candidate. Deferring action on the matter until he had had a chance to talk it over with Lee in person, he wired for him to come to Richmond as soon as possible.

Meantime the Chief Executive kept busy with affairs of state. Congress met for its fourth session on December 7, and the President's year-end message was delivered the following day.

"Gloom and unspoken despondency hang like a pall everywhere," a diarist noted on that date, adding: "Patriotism is a pretty heavy load to carry sometimes." Davis no doubt found it so on this occasion, obliged as he was to render a public account of matters better left unreviewed, since they could only thicken the gloom and add to the despondency they had provoked in the first place. In any case he made no attempt to minimize the defeats of the past fall and summer. Congress had adjourned in May; "Grave reverses befell our arms soon after your departure," he admitted at the outset. Charleston and Galveston were gleams in the prevailing murk, but they could scarcely relieve the fuliginous shadows thrown by Gettysburg and Vicksburg, along with other setbacks in that season of defeat, and the bright flame of Chickamauga had been damped by Missionary Ridge, which he confessed had been lost as the result of "misconduct by the troops." So it went, throughout the reading of the lengthy message. Gains had been slight, losses heavy. Nor did Davis hold out hope of foreign intervention, as he had done so often in the past. Diplomatically, with recognition still withheld by the great powers beyond the Atlantic, the Confederacy was about as near the end of its rope as it was financially, with $600,000,000 in paper — "more than threefold the amount required by the business of the country" — already issued by the Treasury on little better security than a vague promise, which in turn was dependent on the outcome of a war it seemed to be losing. He could only propose the forcible reduction of the volume of currency; which in itself, as a later observer remarked, amounted to "a confession of bankruptcy." The end of the contest was nowhere in sight, he told the assembled legislators, and he recommended a tightening and extension of conscription as a means of opposing the long numerical odds the Federals enjoyed. "We now know that the only reliable hope for peace is the vigor of our resistance," he declared, "while the cessation of their hostility is only to be expected from the pressure of their necessities." In closing he came back to the South's chief asset, which had won for her the sometimes grudging admiration of the world. "The patriotism of the people has proved equal to every sacrifice demanded by their country's need. We have been united as a people never were united under like circumstances before. God has blessed us with success disproportionate to our means, and under His divine favor our labors must at last be crowned with the reward due to men who have given all they possessed to the righteous defense of their inalienable rights, their homes, and their altars."

Lincoln's year-end message to the Federal Congress, which also convened on the first Monday in December, was delivered that same

Tuesday, thus affording the people of the two nations, as well as those of the world at large, another opportunity for comparing the manner and substance of what the two leaders had to say in addressing themselves to events and issues which they viewed simultaneously from opposite directions. The resultant contrast was quite as emphatic as might have been expected, given their two positions and their two natures. Not only was there the obvious difference that what were admitted on one hand as defeats were announced as victories on the other, but there was also a considerable difference in tone. While Davis, referring defiantly to "the impassable gulf which divides us," denounced the "barbarous policy" and "savage ferocity" of an adversary "hardened in crime," the northern President spoke of reconciliation and advanced suggestions for coping with certain edgy problems that would loom when bloodshed ended. He dealt only in passing with specific military triumphs, recommending the annual reports of Stanton and Halleck as "documents of great interest," and contented himself with calling attention to the vast improvement of conditions in that regard since his last State of the Union address, just one week more than a year ago today. At that time, "amid much that was cold and menacing," he reminded the legislators, "the kindest words coming from Europe were uttered in accents of pity that we were too blind to surrender a hopeless cause"; whereas now, he pointed out, "the rebel borders are pressed still further back, and by the opening of the Mississippi the country dominated by the rebellion is divided into distinct parts, with no practical communication between them." A share of the credit for this accomplishment was due to the Negro for his response to emancipation, Lincoln believed. "Of those who were slaves at the beginning of the rebellion, full one hundred thousand are now in the United States military service, about one half of which number actually bear arms in the ranks; thus giving the double advantage of taking so much labor from the insurgent cause, and supplying the places which otherwise must be filled with so many white men. So far as tested, it is difficult to say they are not as good soldiers as any."

Having said so much, and reviewed as well such divergent topics as the budget, foreign relations, immigration, the homestead law, and Indian affairs, he passed at once to the main burden of his message, contained in an appended document titled "A Proclamation of Amnesty and Reconstruction." Lately, in answer to a letter in which Zachariah Chandler, pleased by the outcome of the fall elections but alarmed by reports that the moderates were urging their views on the President during the preparation of this report on the State of the Union, had warned him to "stand firm" against such influences and pressures — "Conservatives and traitors are buried together," the Michigan senator told him; "for God's sake don't exhume their remains in your Message. They will smell worse than Lazarus did after he had been buried three days" — Lincoln had sought to calm the millionaire drygoods merchant's fears. "I am glad the elections this autumn have gone favorably," he replied, "and that I have not, by native depravity, or under evil influences, done anything bad enough to prevent the good result. I hope to 'stand fast' enough not to go backward, and yet not to go forward fast enough to wreck the country's cause." The appended document, setting forth his views on amnesty for individuals and reconstruction of the divided nation, was an example of what he meant. In essence, it provided that all Confederates — with certain specified exceptions, such as holders of public office, army generals and naval officers above the rank of lieutenant, former U.S. congressmen and judges, and anyone found guilty of mistreating prisoners of war — would receive a full executive pardon upon taking an oath of loyalty to the federal government, support of the Emancipation Proclamation, and obedience to all lawful acts in reference to slavery. Moreover, as soon as one tenth of the 1860 voters in any seceded state had taken the oath prescribed, that state would be readmitted to the Union and the enjoyment of its constitutional rights, including representation in Congress.

Reactions varied, but whether its critics thought the proclamation outrageous or sagacious, a further example of wheedling or a true gesture of magnanimity, there were the usual objections to the message as proof of Lincoln's ineptness whenever he tried to come to grips with the English language. "Its words and sentences fall in heaps, instead of flowing in a connected stream, and it is therefore difficult reading," the *Journal of Commerce* pointed out, while the Chicago *Times* was glibly scornful of the backwoods President's lack of polish. "Slipshod as have been all his literary performances," the Illinois editor complained, "this is the most slovenly of all. If they were slipshod, this is barefoot, and the feet, plainly enough, never have been shod." However, the New York *Times* found the composition "simple and yet perfectly effective," and Horace Greeley was even more admiring. He thought the proclamation "devilish good," and predicted that it would "break the back of the Rebellion," though he stopped well short of the *Tribune*'s White House correspondent's judgment that "no President's message since George Washington retired into private life has given such general satisfaction as that sent to Congress by Abraham Lincoln today."

Just how general that satisfaction might be, he did not say, but one person in emphatic disagreement was Charles Sumner, who, as he sat listening to the drone of the clerk at the joint session, favored visitors and colleagues with a demonstration of the inefficacy of caning as a corrective for infantile behavior. Watching as he "gave vent to his half-concealed anger," a journalist observed that, "during the delivery of the Message, the distinguished Senator from Massachusetts exhibited his petulance to the galleries by eccentric motions in his chair, pitching his documents and books upon the floor in ill-tempered disgust."

Sumner's disgust with this plan for reconstruction was based in part on his agreement with the New York *Herald* editor who, commenting on the proposal that ten percent of the South's voters be allowed to return the region to the Union, stated flatly that he did not believe there were "that many good men there." Besides, the Bay State senator had his own notion of the way to deal with traitors, and it was nothing at all like Lincoln's. In a recent issue of the *Atlantic Monthly* he had advocated the division of the Confederacy, as soon as it had been brought to its knees, into eleven military districts under eleven imported governors, "all receiving their authority from one source, ruling a population amounting to upward of nine millions. And this imperial domain, indefinite in extent, will also be indefinite in duration ... with all powers, executive, legislative, and even judicial, derived from one man in Washington." Although he admitted that "in undertaking to create military governors, we reverse the policy of the Republic as solemnly declared by Jefferson, and subject the civil to the military authority," he thought such treatment no worse than was deserved by cane-swinging hotheads who had brought on the war by their pretense of secession. So far as he was concerned, though he continued to deny the right of secession, he was willing to accept it as an act of political suicide. Those eleven states were indeed out of the Union, and the victors had the right to do with them as they chose, including their resettlement with good Republican voters and the determination of when and under what conditions they were to be readmitted. Most of the members of his party agreed, foreseeing a solid Republican South.

Lincoln wanted that too, of course, but he did not believe that this was the best way to go about securing it. For one thing, such an arrangement was likely to last no longer than it took the South to get back on its feet. For another, he wanted those votes now, or at any rate in time for next year's presidential and congressional elections, not at the end of some period "indefinite in duration." Therefore he considered it "vain and profitless" to speculate on whether the rebellious states had withdrawn or could withdraw from the Union, even though this was precisely the issue on which most people thought the war was being fought. "We know that they were and we trust that they shall be in the Union," he said. "It does not greatly matter whether in the meantime they shall be considered to have been in or out."

This was a rift that would widen down the years, but for the present the Jacobins kept their objections within bounds, knowing well enough that when readmission time came round, it would be Congress that would sit in judgment on the applicants. Southward, however, the reaction was both violent and sudden. Lincoln's ruthlessness — an element of his political genius that was to receive small recognition from posthumous friends who were safe beyond his reach — had long been apparent to his foes. For example, in addition to the unkept guarantees he had given slaveholders in his inaugural address, he had declared on revoking Frémont's emancipation order that such matters "must be settled according to laws made by law-makers, and not by military proclamations," and he had classified as "simply 'dictatorship'" any government "wherein a general, or a President, may make permanent rules of property by proclamation." Thus he had written in late September of the first year of the war, exactly one year before he issued his own preliminary emancipation proclamation, which differed from Frémont's only in scope, being also military, and which showed him to be a man who would hold to principles only so long as he had more to gain than lose by them. Observing this, Confederates defined him as slippery, mendacious, and above all not to be trusted.

Certainly Davis saw him in that light, increasingly so with the passing months, and never more so than in this early-December amnesty offer. "That despot," he now called Lincoln, whose "purpose in his message and proclamation was to shut out all hope that he would *ever* treat with us, on *any* terms." Acceptance would amount to unconditional surrender, Davis asserted, and by way of showing what he meant he paraphrased the offer: "If we will break up our government, dissolve the Confederacy, disband our armies, emancipate our slaves, take an oath of allegiance binding ourselves to him and to disloyalty to our states, he proposes to pardon us and not to plunder us of anything more than the property already stolen from us.... In order to render his proposals so insulting as to secure their rejection, he joins to them a promise to support with his army one tenth of the people of any state who will attempt to set up a government over the other nine tenths, thus seeking to sow discord and suspicion among the people of the several states, and to excite them to civil war in furtherance of his ends."

Thus Davis reflected a reversed mirror-image of his adversary's offer, saying: "I do not believe that the vilest wretch would accept such terms." Without exception southern editors agreed. "We who have committed no offense need no forgiveness," they protested, quoting Benjamin Franklin's reply to a British offer of amnesty. "How impudent it is," the Richmond *Sentinel* observed of Lincoln, "to come with our brothers' blood upon his accursed hands, and ask us to accept his forgiveness! But he goes further. He makes his forgiveness dependent on terms." Congress was more vigorous in its protest. Resolutions were introduced denouncing "the truly characteristic proclamation of amnesty issued by the imbecile and unprincipled usurper who now sits enthroned upon the ruins of Constitutional liberty in Washington City," while others made it abundantly clear that the people of the Confederacy, through their elected representatives, did "hereby, solemnly and irrevocably, utterly deny, defy, spurn back, and scorn the terms of amnesty offered by Abraham Lincoln in his official proclamation." All such resolutions were tabled, however, upon the protest by one member that they "would appear to dignify a paper emanating from that wretched and detestable abortion, whose contemptible emptiness and folly will only receive the ridicule of the civilized world." It was decided, accordingly, that "the true and only treatment which that miserable and contemptible despot, Lincoln, should receive at the hands of the House is silent and unmitigated contempt."

Unmitigated this contempt might be, but silent was the one thing it was not. In fact, as various members continued to plumb and scale the various depths and heights of oratory, it grew more strident all the time. Evidently they had been touched where they were sore. And indeed, in its review of Lincoln's message, the New York *World* had warned that such would be the case. Violence was a characteristic of the revolutionary impulse, the *World* declared; "You can no more control it than a flaxen hand can fetter flame"; so that if what the President was really seeking was reconciliation — or even, as Davis claimed, division within the Confederate ranks — he could scarcely have chosen a worse approach. "If Mr Lincoln were a statesman, if he were even a man of ordinary prudence and sagacity, he would see the necessity for touching the peculiar wound of the South with as light a hand as possible." What the editor had in mind was slavery, and so did the frock-coated gentlemen in Richmond, along with much else which they believed was endangered by this war of arms and propaganda. In the course of their two-month session they gave the matter a great deal of attention, and before it was over they produced a joint resolution, issued broadcast as an "Address of Congress to the People of the Confederate States." Specifically an attack on the Lincoln administration for its policies and conduct of the war, the resolution was also an exhortation for the southern people to continue their resistance to northern force and blandishments, including the recent amnesty proclamation.

> It is absurd to pretend that a government really desirous of restoring the Union would adopt such measures as the confiscation of private property, the emancipation of slaves, the division of a sovereign state without its consent, and a proclamation that one tenth of the population of a state, and that tenth under military rule, should control the will of the remaining nine tenths. The only relation possible between the two sections under such a policy is that of conqueror and conquered, superior and dependent. Rest assured, fellow citizens, that although restoration may still be used as a war cry by the northern government, it is only to delude and betray. Fanaticism has summoned to its aid cupidity and vengeance, and nothing short of your utter subjugation, the destruction of your state governments, the overthrow of your social and political fabric, your personal and public degradation and ruin, will satisfy the demands of the North.

About midway through the lengthy document, after charging that the Federals had provoked the war and were "accountable for the blood and havoc and ruin it has caused," the legislators presented a catalogue of "atrocities too incredible for narration."

> Instead of a regular war, our resistance to the unholy efforts to crush out our national existence is treated as a rebellion, and the settled international rules between belligerents are ignored. Instead of conducting the war as betwixt two military and political organizations, it is a war against the whole population. Houses are pillaged and burned. Churches are defaced. Towns are ransacked. Clothing of women and infants is stripped from their persons. Jewelry and mementoes of the dead are stolen. Mills and implements of agriculture are destroyed. Private saltworks are broken up. The introduction of medicines is forbidden. Means of subsistence are wantonly wasted to produce beggary. Prisoners are returned with contagious diseases....

The list continued, then finally broke off. "We tire of these indignities and enormities. They are too sickening for recital," the authors confessed, and passed at once to the lesson to be learned from them. "It is better to be conquered by any other nation than by the United States. It is better to be a dependency of any other power than of that.... We cannot afford to take steps backward. Retreat is more dangerous than advance. Behind us are inferiority and degradation. Before us is everything enticing to a patriot." As for how the war was to be won, the answer was quite simple: by perseverance.

> Moral like physical epidemics have their allotted periods, and must sooner or later be exhausted and disappear. When reason returns, our enemies will probably reflect that a people like ours, who have exhibited such capabilities and extemporized such resources, can never be subdued; that a vast expanse of territory with such a population cannot be governed as an obedient colony. Victory would not be conquest. The inextinguishable quarrel would be transmitted "from bleeding sire to son," and the struggle would be renewed between generations yet unborn.... There is no just reason for hopelessness or fear. Since the outbreak of the war the South has lost the nominal possession of the Mississippi River and fragments of her territory; but Federal occupation is not conquest. The fires of patriotism still burn unquenchably in the breasts of those who are subject to foreign domination. We have yet in our uninterrupted control a territory which, according to past progress, will require the enemy ten years to overrun.

In conclusion — though the words came strangely from the lips of men who, despite their nominal membership in a single national party, comprised perhaps the most fractious, factious political assembly in the western world to date — the legislators recommended "unfaltering trust," on the part of the southern people in their leaders, as the surest guide if they would tread "the path that leads to honor and peace, although it lead through tears and suffering and blood."

> Let all spirit of faction and past party differences be forgotten in the presence of our cruel foe.... We entreat from all a generous and hearty co-operation with the government in all branches of its administration, and with the agents, civil or military, in the performance of their duties. Moral aid has the "power of the incommunicable," and, by united efforts, by an all-comprehending and self-sacrificing patriotism, we can, with the blessing of God, avert the perils which environ us, and achieve for ourselves and children peace and freedom. Hitherto the Lord has interposed graciously to bring us victory, and in His hand there is present power to prevent this great multitude which come against us from casting us out of the possession which He has given us to inherit.

Such were the first bitter fruits of Lincoln's proclamation, offering amnesty to individuals and seeking to establish certain guidelines for the future reconstruction of the South.

★ ★ ★

Receiving on December 9 the President's instructions for him to come to Richmond, Lee supposed a decision had been reached to send him to North Georgia as Bragg's successor, despite his expressed reluctance to leave the Old Dominion and the army whose fame had grown with his own in the eighteen months since Davis placed him at its head. With Longstreet in East Tennessee, Ewell absent sick, and A. P. Hill as usual in poor health, the summons came at what seemed to him an unfortunate time, particularly since the latter two, even aside from their physical debility, had not fulfilled his expectations in their present subordinate positions. But orders were orders; he left at once. "My heart and thoughts will always be with this army," he said in a note to Stuart as he boarded at Orange a train that had him in the capital before nightfall.

He found to his relief, however, that no decision had been made regarding his transfer to the western theater. The President, in conference with his Cabinet on the matter of selecting a new leader for the army temporarily under Hardee, had merely wanted his ranking field commander there to share in the discussion. Lee's reluctance having been honored to the extent that it had removed him from consideration for the post, the advisers found it difficult to agree on a second choice. Not only were they divided among themselves; Davis withheld approval of every candidate proposed. Some were all for Beauregard, for instance, but the Commander in Chief had even less confidence in the Creole than he had in Joe Johnston, who was being recommended warmly in the press, on the floor of Congress, in letters from friends, and by Seddon.

While the Secretary admitted that he had been disappointed by his fellow Virginian's "absence of enterprise" in the recent Mississippi operations, he believed that "his military sagacity would not fail to recognize the exigencies of the time and position, and so direct all his thoughts and skill to an offensive campaign." Davis was doubtful. He rather agreed with Benjamin, who protested that during his six-month tenure as Secretary of War he had found in Johnston "tendencies to defensive strategy and a lack of knowledge of the environment." Others present inclined to the same view. On the evidence, Old Joe's talent seemed primarily for retreat: so much so, indeed, that if left to his own devices he might be expected to wind up gingerly defending Key West and complaining that he lacked transportation for a withdrawal to Cuba in the event that something threatened one of his flanks. Finally, however, at the close of a full week of discussion, Johnston was favored by a majority of those present, and the minority, though still unreconciled to his appointment, confessed that it had no one else to offer. According to Seddon, "the President, after doubt and with misgiving to the end, chose him ... not as with exaltation on this score, but as the best on the whole to be obtained." He wired him at Meridian that same day, December 16, two weeks after Bragg had been relieved: "You will turn over the immediate command of the Army of Mississippi to Lieutenant General Polk and proceed to Dalton and assume command of the Army of Tennessee.... A letter of instructions will be sent to you at Dalton."

Requested to inspect the capital defenses, Lee stayed on for another five days, during which time he was lionized by the public and invited by the House of Representatives to take what was infelicitously called "a seat on the floor." After the Sunday service at Saint Paul's he was given a silent ovation as he passed down the aisle, bowing left and right to friends in the congregation, and forty-year-old Mrs Chesnut, who prided herself on her sophistication, confessed in her diary that when the general "bowed low and gave me a smile of recognition, I was ashamed of being so pleased. I blushed like a schoolgirl." A four-day extension of the visit would have allowed him to spend his first Christmas with his family since two years before the war, but he would not have it so; he was thinking of his army on the Rapidan and the men there who were far from home as this gayest of holidays drew near. For their part, while they envied, they did not resent his good fortune. In point of fact, they doubted that he would take advantage of it. "It will be more in accordance with his peculiar character," a staff major wrote from Orange to his sweetheart on December 20, "if he leaves for the army just before the great anniversary; he is so very apt to suppress or deny his personal desire when it conflicts with the performance of his duty." The young officer was right. Lee returned next day, having sacrificed a Richmond Christmas with his wife in order to be with his troops and share in their frugal celebration of what had always been for Southerners a combination of all that was best in the gladdest days of the departing year.

All was quiet in the camps along the Rapidan, but the cavalry had been kept busy in his absence — and fruitlessly busy, at that — attempting to head off or break up a raid into Southwest Virginia, deep in the army's rear, by a column of hard-riding horsemen under Averell, who had been given an independent brigade after Hooker relieved him of duty amid the fury of Chancellorsville. Regaining the safety of his own lines on the day Lee returned to Orange, Averell proudly reported that in the past two weeks his troopers had "marched, climbed, slid, and swum 355 miles," avoided superior combinations of graybacks sent to scatter or capture them, and cut the Tennessee & Virginia Railroad at Salem (just west of a hamlet called Big Lick, which twenty years later would change its name to Roanoke and grow to be a city) where three depots crammed with food and equipment on consignment to the Army of Northern Virginia were set afire. At a cost of 6 men drowned, 5 wounded, and 94 missing, he had captured some 200 of the enemy, 84 of whom he brought back with him, together with about 150 horses. This time he left no sack of coffee for his friend Fitzhugh Lee, who commanded one of the columns that failed to intercept him, but he could say, as he had said before: "Here's your visit. How do you like it?" Fitz liked it no better now than he had done in March, after Kelly's Ford. Nor did Stuart, who was presented with further evidence of the decline of the advantage he had enjoyed in the days when his superior riders were mounted on superior, well-fed horses.

Meanwhile the foot soldiers took it easy, blue and gray alike. Meade's withdrawal from Lee's formidable Mine Run front — accomplished with such skill and stealth that his opponent's resultant attitude resembled that of a greenhorn lured into the Wilderness by pranksters who left him holding the bag on a "snipe hunt" — had ended all infantry operations for the year. On both sides of the river the two armies went into winter quarters, beginning what would be a five-month rest. On the north bank, for Meade despite his crankiness was liberal in such matters, generals, colonels, majors, even captains were able to bring their wives into camp on extended visits. One witness considered their presence greatly beneficial, and not only to their husbands. "Their influence softens and humanizes much that might otherwise be harsh and repulsive," he declared. "In their company, at least, officers who should be gentlemen do not get drunk." On the other hand, a high-toned Massachusetts staff man was a good deal less enthusiastic about these army ladies. "Such a set of feminine humans I have not seen often," he wrote home. "It was Lowell's factories broken loose and gone wild." However, except on the off chance that a few orderlies got lucky, all this meant little to the enlisted men, who were obliged to depend on their own resources and limit the count of their blessings to the fact that they were not to be shot at for a while. "The troops burrowed into the earth and built their little shelters," a Federal brigadier was to recall, "and the officers and men devoted themselves to unlimited festivity, balls, horse races, cockfights, greased pigs and poles, and other games such as only soldiers can devise."

For most of the people of Richmond, women and old men and children, politicians and officeholders of high and low degree, as well as for the maimed and convalescent veterans in private homes and hospitals on the city's seven hills, this holiday season was scarcely gayer than it was for their friends and kinsmen on the Rapidan with Lee. For some few others, however, owners of plantations down the country, not yet taken over by invaders, provisions had been forwarded for laying out a meal that had at least a resemblance to the feasts of olden times. Christmas dinner at Colonel and Mrs Chesnut's, for example, included oyster soup, boiled mutton, ham, boned turkey, wild duck and partridges, plum pudding, and four kinds of wine to wash it down with. "There is life in the old land yet!" the diarist exclaimed.

Among her guests that day was John Bell Hood, the social catch of the town. Taken a few miles south of the field where he lost his leg, he had spent a month in bed on a North Georgia farm and then, because it was feared he might be captured so near the enemy lines, continued his convalescence in Atlanta for another month before coming on to Richmond in late November. With his left arm still in a sling and his right trouser leg hanging empty, his eyes deep-set in a pain-gaunted face above the full blond beard of a Wagnerian hero, the thirty-two-year-old bachelor general had the ladies fluttering around him, his hostess said, "as if it would be a luxury to pull out their handkerchiefs and have a good cry." Instead, they brought him oranges and peeled and sliced them for him, prompting another guest to remark that "the money value of friendship is easily counted now," since oranges were selling in the capital markets for five Confederate dollars each. Shortly after Chickamauga, Longstreet had recommended the Kentucky-born Texan's promotion to lieutenant general "for distinguished conduct and ability in the battle of the 20th instant." Moreover, although Hood was nearly six years younger than A. P. Hill, the present youngest officer of that rank, there was little doubt that the promotion would be confirmed; for he was now an intimate of the President's and accompanied him on carriage rides and tours of inspection, in and about the city.

Another Kentuckian was being talked about on all sides this Christmas, here and elsewhere, and did much to lift the gloom resulting from the reverses lately suffered, including his own. On November 28 word flashed across the North and South that John Morgan and six of his captains, taken with him in the course of the raid that ended near Salineville four months back, had escaped the night before from the Ohio

Penitentiary by tunneling out of their cell block and scaling the outer wall. That was all that was known for the time being, except that Buckeye posses bent on his recapture were combing the region and searching the cellars and attics of all suspected Copperheads. In mid-December, two weeks later, he turned up on the near bank of the Tennessee River, below Kingston, and soon afterwards crossed the Great Smoky Mountains to Franklin, North Carolina, well beyond reach of the searchers in his rear. The particulars of his flight were as daring as the wildest of his raids. Dressed as civilians, he and his companions had boarded a fast night express at Columbus, just outside the prison walls, and reached Cincinnati before the morning bed check showed them missing from their cells. By that time they were over the Ohio, riding south on borrowed horses — there was little in the Bluegrass that John Morgan could not have for the asking — to cross the Cumberland near Burkesville. Two of the party had been lost just outside Louisville, picked up by a Federal patrol, but the others made it all the way. Morgan himself reached Danville, Virginia, in time for Christmas dinner with his wife, who was recuperating there from a miscarriage, brought on it was said by worry about her husband and resentment of Ohio's vindictive treatment of him as a felon. Now he was with her again, and soon he would be back with the army, too. He had been summoned to Richmond, where a public reception was being planned in his honor, he was informed, "thusly [to] say to the despicable foe that in their futile efforts to degrade you before the world they have only elevated you in the estimation of all Confederate citizens, and the whole civilized world."

Anticipation of his arrival, which was scheduled for January 2, gave a lift to the spirits of the people of the capital. But for many, unable to draw on such resources as were available to the Chesnuts and their guests, the holiday itself was depressing in its contrast to the ones they had enjoyed last year and the year before, when the festivities were heightened by recent victories at Fredericksburg and Ball's Bluff. No such occasions warranted celebration now. "It is a sad, cold Christmas, and threatening snow," a government clerk recorded in his diary. "The children have a Christmas tree, but it is not burdened. Candy is held at $8 per pound." Nor did he find much evidence of merriment among his fellow townsmen when he went out for a walk that afternoon. "Occasionally an *exempt,* who has speculated, may be seen drunk. But a somber heaviness is in the countenances of men as well as in the sky above." Although, like candy, a Christmas turkey was beyond his means, "[I] do not covet one. This is no time for feasting," he declared. Presently, if only out of surfeit, Mrs Chesnut was inclined to agree. "God help my country!" she exclaimed on New Year's Day, looking back somewhat ruefully on the round of holiday parties she had given or attended. "I think we are like the sailors who break into the spirits closet when they find out the ship must sink." Reviewing her correspondence for the year now past, she came upon an early draft of a letter she had written Varina Davis during a September visit to the South Carolina plantation that furnished so many delicacies for her table. It had seemed to her then, she told the first lady, that the people were divided into two main groups, one made up of enthusiasts whose "whole duty here consists of abusing Lincoln and the Yankees, praising Jeff Davis and the army of Virginia, and wondering when this horrid war will be over," while the other included "politicians and men with no stomach for fighting, who find it easier to cuss Jeff Davis and stay at home than to go to the front with a musket. They are the kind who came out almost as soon as they went into the war, dissatisfied with the way things were managed. Joe Johnston is their polar star, the redeemer!"

Polar star and redeemer he might be to the disaffected Carolinians, as well as to the western soldiers once more in his charge, but to his superiors in Richmond he was something else again. Receiving the President's telegram of December 16, the general spent a few days putting his affairs in order, including the transfer of his present command to Polk, and then on December 22 set out by rail for North Georgia. Two days after Christmas he reached Dalton, where he took over from Hardee without further delay. Awaiting him there were the instructions promised in the wire received ten days ago in Mississippi, one set from the Commander in Chief and another from the Secretary of War, both urging an early campaign against the Federals in his front. While admitting that "the army may have been, by recent events, somewhat disheartened," Seddon believed that Johnston's presence would restore its "discipline, prestige, and confidence" in preparation for the recovery of all that had been lost. "As soon as the condition of your forces will allow," the Secretary added, "it is hoped that you will be able to assume the offensive." Davis wrote in a similar vein. Information lately received encouraged "a not unfavorable view of the material of the command," he said, and "induces me to hope that you will soon be able to commence active operations against the enemy.... You will not need to have it suggested that the imperative demand for prompt and vigorous action arises not only from the importance of restoring the prestige of the army, and averting the dispiriting and injurious results that must attend a season of inactivity, but also from the necessity of reoccupying the country upon the supplies of which the proper subsistence of the armies materially depends." The general on the scene could best determine "the immediate measures to be adopted in attaining this end," the President remarked, and he urged him to "communicate fully and freely with me concerning your proposed plan of action, that all the assistance and co-operation may be most advantageously afforded that it is in the power of the government to render. Trusting that your health may be preserved, and that the arduous and responsible duties you have undertaken may be successfully accomplished, I remain very respectfully and truly yours, Jeff'n Davis."

Whereupon — in response to these conciliatory statements of confidence in the general's ability, these offers to replace past bitterness with cordiality — the old trouble rose anew, bringing with it apparent confirmation of the doubts expressed by Benjamin and others at the series of high-level conferences leading to the choice of a new commander for the Army of Tennessee. Johnston had not thought he would get the post; "The temper exhibited toward me makes it very unlikely that I shall ever again occupy an important position," he told a friend in mid-September; but when he learned of his new assignment, three months later, he was delighted. This reaction lasted no longer, however, than it took him to reach Dalton and read the letters of instruction. As always, he bridled at what he considered prodding, especially from these two, who all through June had tried to persuade him to wreck his army for no purpose, so far as he could see, except as a gesture of sympathy for the garrison penned up in Vicksburg as a result of their unwisdom. Now here they were, at it again, trying to nudge him into rashness and disaster! His reply to Seddon was edged with irony. "The duties of military administration you point out to me shall be attended to with diligence," he said. But he added flatly: "This army is now far from being in condition to 'resume the offensive.'" A similar reply went to Davis. "Your Excellency well impresses upon me the importance of recovering the territory we have lost. I feel it deeply; but difficulties appear to me in the way." These he listed in considerable detail, including a shortage of transportation and subsistence, the long numerical odds the Federals enjoyed, and the poor condition of the roads because of recent heavy rains. He might be able to resist an attack in his present position, he declared, but under the conditions now prevailing he could not even entertain the notion of delivering one. In short: "I can see no other mode of taking the offensive here than to beat the enemy when he advances, and then move forward."

There they had it — as, indeed, they had had it so often before, wherever Johnston commanded in this war. The Manassas region beyond the Rappahannock, the York-James peninsula, the Mississippi heartland, all had been given up by him on the heels of similar protests at suggestions that he "assume the offensive" or merely stand his ground. Seddon and Davis saw their worst fears realized. If past performance was any indication of what to expect, Johnston would backpedal in response to whatever pressure the enemy brought against him in North Georgia, and this time it would be the *national* heartland that would pass into Federal possession as a result. Their inclination was to remove him before that happened, but this would mean a return to the problem of finding another commander for the army, which was no more soluble now than it had been in mid-December. They had him; they would have to live with him. The result, as they continued to plead for an advance and he continued to bridle at the prodding, was increased dissatisfaction and petulance at both ends of the telegraph wires connecting Richmond and Dalton.

Whatever second thoughts his superiors might be having as to their wisdom in appointing this new commander of the Army of Tennessee, the men under him were delighted. In fact, the pleasure they had experienced on hearing of Bragg's departure was redoubled by the news that Johnston was to take his place, and according to one veteran's recollection, civilians reacted in a similar manner: "At every bivouac in the field, at every fireside in the rear, the joyous dawn of day seemed to have arisen from the night." Rations improved with the Virginian's arrival; the clothing issue was liberalized; even a system of furloughs was established. Moreover, whereas Bragg had kept to his tent between campaigns — confined there, more often than not, by dyspepsia — Johnston not only made it a point to pay frequent visits to all the camps, he also did not limit his attention to men with bars or stars on their collars. "He passed through the ranks of the common soldiers, shaking hands with every one he met," a private was to recall years later. "He restored the soldier's pride; he brought the manhood back to the private's bosom; he changed the order of roll-call, standing guard, drill, and such nonsense as that. The revolution was complete. He was loved, respected, admired; yea, almost worshipped by his troops. I do not believe there was a soldier in his army but would gladly have died for him."

This last was based in part no doubt on their knowledge that he would ask of them no dying he could spare them; that he believed, as they did, in a minimum of bloodshed, and would always sacrifice mere terrain if the price of holding it seemed to him excessive. But there was a good deal more to it than that. Veneration was deepened by affection, and the affection was returned. No matter how touchy Johnston might be in his relations with superiors, he was invariably friendly to those below him on the military ladder, considerate of their needs and never seeming to fear that this might lessen his dignity or cost him any measure of their respect. One day soon after his arrival in Dalton, for example, Cheatham brought a number of men from his division over to army headquarters in a body, accompanied by a band with which to serenade the new commander. Presently Johnston stepped hatless from his tent to thank them for the music and the visit; whereupon Cheatham performed a highly informal ceremony of introduction. "Boys," he said, affectionately patting the general's bald head two or three times as he spoke, "this is Old Joe."

✗ 2 ✗

In all seasons and all weathers, stifling heat or numbing cold, the men aboard the Federal blockaders kept their stations, stood their watches, and patrolled their designated segments of the highly irregular three thousand miles of coastline between Old Point Comfort and Matamoros. Not for them had been the thunderous runs by the frigates and gunboats under Farragut and Porter, during which the world seemed turned to flame and a man's heart pounded as if to break the confines of his ribs, or the exhilarating chases by the raiders under Semmes and Maffitt, staged hundreds of miles from the sight of land and punctuated with coaling stops in sinful foreign ports. A sailor who managed to secure a leave from one of the river fleets was sure to receive at home a hero's welcome for his share in the humbling of Vicksburg or Port Hudson, and since her sinking of the *Hatteras*, off Galveston a year ago, the *Alabama* had added an even three dozen Yankee ships and barks and schooners to her string of prizes, while the *Florida*, after her nimble sprint out of Mobile Bay, had taken just over two dozen such merchant vessels in that same span. The men on blockade duty envied blue and gray alike, not only for the stormy present but also for the future still to come. Someday perhaps, if they survived the boredom and saltpeter, there would be the question: "What did you do, Father, in the war?" Within the limitations of the truth, about the only satisfactory answer they could give — satisfactory to themselves, that is — would be: "I'd rather not talk about it."

Nor were conditions any better in that regard for the crews of ships assigned to add offensive punch to the four blockading squadrons. In contrast to 1862, when it had appeared that no salt water attack could fail, whatever the objective, the year just past had seen no fort subdued, no harbor seized, except along the scantly defended lower coast of Texas, where the year-end gains were far outweighed by the reverses suffered earlier at Galveston and Sabine Pass. If such efforts on the Gulf amounted to little, those on the Atlantic came to less. Du Pont's repulse at Charleston, and Dahlgren's protracted frustration since, had served no purpose the men could discern except to make them thankful that the brass had not seen fit to test the defenses of Wilmington or Mobile. There were dangers enough outside such places, it seemed to them, without venturing any closer: as the *Ironsides* could testify, having had her timbers shivered by the unscathed *David*. Two months later, on December 6, the monitor *Weehawken* — leader of the nine-boat iron column that had steamed into Charleston harbor back in April — met a harsher and still more ignominious fate, without an enemy in sight. Tied up to a buoy inside the bar, she had taken on an extra load of heavy ammunition which so reduced her freeboard that the ebb tide flooded an open hawse pipe and a hatch, foundering her so rapidly that she carried 31 of her crew with her on her sudden plunge to the bottom. There was small glory here for either the dead or the survivors, who were promptly transferred to other vessels to keep up the work of raising puffs of brick dust from the defiant ruin of Sumter. Morale was not helped, either, when they learned of Father Gideon's response to a request from Dahlgren — who knew something of the strain on their nerves because of the jangled state of his own — that a whiskey ration be distributed under medical supervision. Welles did not approve. He recommended that iced coffee or oatmeal mixed with water be used as a pick-me-up instead.

Boredom was the main problem, especially for the crews of the blockaders, who could not see that their day-in day-out service had much to do with fighting at all, let alone with speeding the victory which hard-war politicians and editors kept saying was just around the corner. Off Cape Fear, where the sleek gray runners steaming in from Nassau and Bermuda found cover under the unchallenged guns of Fort Fisher, a bluejacket wrote home to his mother (as the letter was paraphrased years later by a student of the era) that she could get some notion of blockade duty if she would "go to the roof on a hot summer day, talk to a half dozen degenerates, descend to the basement, drink tepid water full of iron rust, climb to the roof again, and repeat the process at intervals until she was fagged out, then go to bed with everything shut tight." Individual reactions to this monotony, which was scarcely relieved by an unbroken diet of moldy beans, stale biscuits, and sour pork, varied from fisticuffs and insubordination to homosexuality and desertion. Officers fraternized ashore with Negro women, a practice frowned on by the Navy, and mess crews specialized in the manufacture of outlaw whiskey distilled from almost any substance that would ferment in the southern heat — as in fact nearly everything would, including men. Rheumatism and scurvy kept the doctors busy, along with breakbone fever, hemorrhoids, and damage done by knuckles. These they could deal with, after their fashion, but there was no medicine for the ills of the spirit, brought on by the strain of monotony, poor food, and unhealthy living conditions, which produced much longer casualty lists than did rebel shells or torpedoes. "Give me a discharge, and let me go home," a distraught but articulate coal heaver begged his skipper after months of duty outside Charleston. "I am a poor weak, miserable, nervous, half crazy boy.... Everything jars upon my delicate nerves."

Inside the harbor, Beauregard was about as deep in the doldrums as were the blue-clad sailors beyond the bar. Disappointed that he had not been ordered west to resume command of the army Bragg had inherited from him, privately he was telling friends that his usefulness in the war had ended, and he predicted defeat for the Confederacy no later than spring or summer. He gave as the cause for both of these disasters "the persistent inability and obstinacy of our rulers." Primarily he meant Davis, of whom he said: "The curse of God must have been on our people when we chose him out of so many noble sons of the South, who would have carried us safely through this Revolution."

In addition to the frustration proceeding from his belief that presidential animosity, as evidenced by slights and snubs, had cost him the western command he so much wanted, the Creole's gloom was also due to the apparent failure of a new weapon he had predicted would accomplish, unassisted, the lifting of the Union blockade by the simple process of sinking the blockaders. There had arrived by rail from Mobile in mid-August, disassembled and loaded on two flatcars, a cigar-shaped metal vessel about thirty feet in length and less than four feet wide and five feet deep. Put back together and launched in Charleston harbor, she resembled the little *David*-class torpedo boats whose low silhouette made them hard for enemy lookouts to detect. Actually, though, she had been designed to carry this advantage a considerable step further, in that she was intended to travel under as well as on the water, and thus present no silhouette at all. She was, in short, the world's first submarine. Christened the *H. L. Hunley* for one of her builders, who had come from Alabama with her to instruct the Carolinians in her use, she was propeller-driven but had no engine, deriving her power from her eight-man crew, posted at cranks along her drive shaft, which they turned on orders from her coxswain-captain. Water was let into ballast tanks to lower her until she was nearly awash; then her two hatches were bolted tight from inside, and as she moved forward the skipper took her down by depressing a pair of horizontal fins, which were also used to level and raise her while in motion. To bring her all the way up, force pumps ejected the water from her tanks, decreasing her specific gravity; or in emergencies her iron keel could be jettisoned in sections by disengaging the bolts that held it on, thus causing her to bob corklike to the surface. A glass port in the forward hatch enabled the steersman to see where he was going while submerged, and interior light was supplied by candles, which also served to warn of the danger of asphyxiation by guttering when the oxygen ran low. Practice dives in Mobile Bay had demonstrated that the *Hunley* could stay down about two hours before coming up for air, and she had proved her effectiveness as an offensive weapon by torpedoing and sinking two flatboats there. Her method of attack was quite as novel as her design. Towing at the end of a 200-foot line a copper cylinder packed with ninety pounds of powder and equipped with a percussion fuze, she would dive as she approached her target, pass completely under it, then elevate a bit and drag the towline across the keel of the enemy ship until the torpdo made contact and exploded, well astern of the submarine, whose crew would be cranking hard for a getaway, still underwater, and a return to port for a new torpedo to use on the next victim. Beauregard looked the strange craft over, had her workings explained to him by Hunley, and predicted an end to the

Yankee blockade as soon as her newly volunteered crew learned to handle her well enough to launch their one-boat offensive against the U. S. Navy.

    Such high hopes were often modified by sudden disappointments, and the *Hunley* was no exception to the general application of the rule. Certain drawbacks were soon as evident here as they had been at Mobile earlier: one being that she was a good deal easier to take down than she was to bring back up, particularly if something went wrong with her machinery, and something often did. She was, in fact — as might have been expected from her combination of primitive means and delicate functions — accident-prone. On August 29, two weeks after her arrival, she was moored to a steamer tied to the Fort Johnson dock, resting her "engine" between dives, when the steamer unexpectedly got underway and pulled her over on her side. Water poured in through the open hatches, front and rear, and she went down so fast that only her skipper and two nimble seamen managed to get out before she hit the bottom. This was a practical demonstration that none of the methods providing for her return to the surface by her own devices would work unless she retained enough air to lift the weight of her iron hull; a started seam or a puncture, inflicted by chance or by enemy action while she was submerged, would mean her end, or at any rate the end of the submariners locked inside her. If this had not been clear before, it certainly was now. Still, there was no difficulty in finding more volunteers to man her, and Hunley himself, as soon as she had been raised and cleared of muck and corpses, petitioned Beauregard to let him take command. He did so on September 22 and began at once a period of intensive training to familiarize his new crew with her quirks. This lasted just over three weeks. On October 15, after making a series of practice dives in the harbor, she "left the wharf at 9.25 A.M. and disappeared at 9.35. As soon as she sank," the official post-mortem continued, "air bubbles were seen to rise to the surface of the water, and from this fact it is supposed the hole at the top of the boat by which the men entered was not properly closed." That was the end of Hunley and all aboard, apparently because someone had been careless. It was also thought to be the end of the vessel that bore his name, for she was nine fathoms down. A diver found her a few days later, however, and she was hauled back up again. Beauregard was on hand when her hatch lids were removed. "The spectacle was indescribably ghastly," he later reported with a shudder of remembrance. "The unfortunate men were contorted into all sorts of horrible attitudes, some clutching candles... others lying in the bottom tightly grappled together, and the blackened faces of all presented the expression of their despair and agony."

    Despite this evidence of the grisly consequences, a third crew promptly volunteered for service under George E. Dixon, an army lieutenant who transferred from an Alabama regiment to the *Hunley* and was also a native of Mobile. Trial runs were renewed in early November, but the method of attack was not the same. Horrified by what he had seen when the unlucky boat was raised the second time, Beauregard had ordered that she was never again to function underwater, and she was equipped accordingly with a spar torpedo like the one her rival *David* had used against the *Ironsides*, ten days before she herself went into her last intentional dive. A surface vessel now like all the rest, except that she was still propelled by muscle power, she continued for the next three months to operate out of her base on Sullivan's Island, sometimes by day, sometimes by night. But conditions were never right for an attack; tide and winds conspired against her, and at times the underpowered craft was in danger of being swept out to sea because of the exhaustion of the men along her crankshaft. Finally though, in the early dusk of February 17, with a near-full moon to steer her by, a low-lying fog to screen her, and a strong-running ebb tide to increase her normal four-knot speed, Dixon maneuvered the *Hunley* out of the harbor and set a course for the Federal fleet, which lay at anchor in the wintry darkness, seven miles away.

At 8.45 the acting master of the 1200-ton screw sloop *Housatonic* — more than two hundred feet in length and mounting a total of nine guns, including an 11-inch rifle — saw what he thought at first was "a plank moving [toward us] in the water" about a hundred yards away. By the time he knew better and ordered "the chain slipped, engine backed, and all hands called to quarters" in an attempt to take evasive action and bring his guns to bear, it was too late; "The torpedo struck forward of the mizzen mast, on the starboard side, in line with the magazine." Still trembling from the shock, the big warship heeled to port and went down stern first. Five of her crew were killed or drowned, but fortunately for the others the water was shallow enough for them to save themselves by climbing the rigging, from which they were plucked by rescuers before the stricken vessel went to pieces.

There were no Confederate witnesses, for there were no Confederate survivors; the *Hunley* had made her first and last attack and had gone down with her victim, either because her hull had been cracked by the force of the explosion, only twenty feet away, or else because she was drawn into the vortex of the sinking *Housatonic*. In any case, searchers found what was left of the sloop and the submarine years later, lying side by side on the sandy bottom, just beyond the bar.

★ ★ ★

Quincy Gillmore had been about as unhappy outside Charleston as Beauregard was inside the place, although for different reasons. Six months of siege, of suffering far greater losses than he inflicted, had gained him nothing more than Morris Island, out on the rim of the harbor, and the chance to heave an occasional long-range shell into the city — a practice which his adversary had predicted would win him "a bad eminence in history." That might be, but what bothered Gillmore most was that it seemed to increase rather than lessen the resolution of the defenders. Besides, the next step was up to the navy, and Dahlgren would not take it. The result was stalemate and frustration, a sharp regret on Gillmore's part that he had come down here in the first place. He wanted to be up and doing; he wanted room for maneuver, a chance to fight an enemy he could see; none of which was available to him here. Then in mid-January a letter from the Commander in Chief relieved his claustrophobia by opening vistas to the south. He was to undertake, without delay, the conquest of Florida.

The letter was not sent through regular channels, but was delivered in person by the President's twenty-five-year-old private secretary John Hay, who arrived wearing a brand-new pair of major's leaves on the shoulders of a brand-new uniform. Moreover, the document he brought with him made it clear that he had been commissioned to play a leading role in the show about to open down the coast. If Gillmore thought it strange at first that the choice for so important a post had been based exclusively on political qualifications — for the young man had had little experience in any other line — he soon perceived, from reading the instructions, that the proposed campaign was intended to be at least as much a political as a military endeavor. "I wish the thing done in the most speedy way possible," Lincoln wrote, "so that, when done, it [will] lie within the range of the late proclamation on the subject." It was the month-old Proclamation of Amnesty and Reconstruction he meant. He already had agents at work in Louisiana and Arkansas, attempting within the framework of its provisions to establish in them the ten-percent governments he maintained would entitle them to representation in Congress, where their gratitude was expected to prove helpful to the Administration, and it had occurred to him that Florida would make a convenient addition to the list. Hay had Unionist friends there who had written to him, he informed his diary and his chief, "asking me to come down ... and be their Representative." Lincoln thought it a fine idea. Useful as the young Hoosier was in his present job, he might be even more so in the House. Accordingly, after commissioning him a major and making sure that he was equipped with enough oath-blanks to accommodate the ten percent of Floridians who presumably were weary of rebellion, he gave him the letter of instructions to pass along to Gillmore and wished him success in his venture into an unfamiliar field. "Great good luck and God's blessing go with you, John," he said.

Arriving in South Carolina, Hay assured Gillmore that it was not the President's intention to disrupt his current operations against Charleston, that all he wanted was "an order directing me to go to Florida and open my books of record for the oaths, as preliminary to future proceedings." He soon found, however, that the general was not touchy on that point. Far from considering Lincoln's project an intrusion, Gillmore saw it as an indorsement and extension of a proposal he himself had made in letters to Stanton and Halleck that same week, unaware that Hay was on the way from Washington. "I have in contemplation the occupation of Florida, on the west bank of the Saint Johns River, at a very early day," he announced, requesting their approval. He had it in mind to extend his coastal holdings a hundred miles inland to the Suwannee River, which he explained would enable him: 1) "To procure an outlet for cotton, timber, lumber, turpentine, and other products"; 2) "To cut off one of the enemy's sources of commissary supplies"; 3) "To obtain recruits for my colored regiments"; and 4) — appended after receiving Lincoln's instructions, which amounted to the approval he was seeking —"To inaugurate measures for the speedy restoration of Florida to her allegiance." In addition to these four "objects and advantages," as he called them, he was also attracted to the venture by the knowledge that the Confederacy had none of its regular troops assigned to the state's defense. The only graybacks there were militia, and Gillmore believed he could walk right over them with a single veteran division from his army lying idle outside Charleston and at Hilton Head, waiting for the navy to take the step it would not take. Now that the President's letter had unleashed him, he was eager to be off, and he fretted because Hay was held up by last-minute administrative details. "There will not be an hour's delay after the major is ready," he informed Lincoln on January 21, and he added: "I have every confidence in the success of the enterprise."

It was another two weeks before the preliminaries had been attended to. Then finally, on February 6, Brigadier General Truman Seymour's division, composed of three brigades of infantry, two regiments of cavalry, and four batteries of artillery — a force of about 8000 in all, mostly Regulars, New Englanders, and Negroes — got aboard twenty transports at Hilton Head and set off down the coast, escorted by two gunboats. Next morning the flotilla steamed into the St Johns estuary and docked unopposed at Jacksonville, which had been reduced to little more than ruins by the two previous Federal occupations and deserted by all but about two dozen of its prewar families. Hay went ashore and set up shop, beginning with a line-up at the guardhouse. He explained to the captive rebels that if they took the prescribed oath they would be given certificates of loyalty and allowed to return home; otherwise they would be sent North to prison camps. "There is to be neither force nor persuasion used in this matter," he told them. "You decide for yourselves." Most signed promptly, about half making their marks, and took their leave. Hay turned next to the civilians, and though they were less eager to signify repentance for their transgressions, he succeeded in getting the signatures of a number whom he described as "men of substance and influence," presumably meaning those who still had something left to lose. Encouraged, he looked forward to lengthening the list as soon as the army extended its occupation and demonstrated that it was here to stay. Meantime he made a $500 investment in Florida real estate, partly because he knew a hard-times bargain when he saw one, but also by way of establishing residence for the political race that would follow close upon his securing the signatures of ten percent of the qualified electors.

He had reason to believe this would not take long. Gillmore and the navy had been as active in their fields of endeavor as Hay had been in his, and they had also been as successful, if not more so; at least at the outset. Steaming on past Jacksonville after debarking most of the force they had escorted down the coast, the two warships trained their guns on Picolata and Palatka, respectively thirty and fifty miles upstream, and put troops ashore to garrison them, thus establishing firm (and, as it turned out, permanent) control of a coastal region twenty to thirty miles in width and seventy miles in length, east from the St Johns River to the Atlantic and south from Fernandina, near the Georgia line, to below Saint Augustine, which had been reoccupied in late December. What was more, while the navy was consolidating these gains, Gillmore had his troops in motion westward, intent on extending the conquest inland all the way to the Suwannee, as he had said he would do when he first announced his plans.

Florida had two railroads, one running southwest from Fernandina, through Gainesville, to Cedar Key on the Gulf of Mexico, the other due west from Jacksonville to Tallahassee. He took the latter as his route of march, the Atlantic & Gulf Central, his primary objective being Lake City, about sixty miles away. Setting out on February 8, the day after his debarkation, by the following morning he had his cavalry in Baldwin, at the crossing of the two railroads and one third of the way to his goal. His infantry marched in next day, still preceded by the troopers, who pressed on ten miles down the line to Barber's and then another ten to Sanderson, only twenty miles from Lake City. But after advancing half that distance, the cavalry commander, Colonel Guy V. Henry, learned on reaching Olustee that rebel militia were massing in sizable numbers for resistance up ahead; so he turned back. It was well for him and his three small regiments that he did, if he had been counting on infantry support in case of trouble; for when he re-entered Sanderson on the 12th he found that Gillmore was withdrawing to Jacksonville, leaving Seymour to backtrack in his wake and hold Baldwin with the major part of his division while he himself returned to Hilton Head to make further arrangements he had not known were needed, until now.

He too had learned of the rebels massing at Lake City to contest a farther blue advance, and this had served to give him pause. However, his main concern was logistics: meaning supplies, primarily food and ammunition, and how to get them forward to the troops as they slogged westward across a sandy waste of stunted oaks, pine trees, and palmettos. He lacked wagons and mules to draw them, having counted on using the railroad, and though he had plenty of boxcars, captured by Henry's fast-riding troopers before they could be withdrawn beyond the Suwannee, the only locomotive he had on hand was one he had brought with him, which had promptly nullified his foresight by breaking down. So he turned back, better than halfway to his goal, not so much in fear of the gray militia up ahead — although they were reported to be numerous — as in anticipation of what would happen to his soldiers once they had eaten up the six-day rations they carried with them on their march through this barren, inland region. Before returning to Hilton Head to correct in person his miscalculation in logistics, he told Seymour to hold Baldwin at all costs, thus to cover Jacksonville in case the enemy moved against him, but otherwise to be content with consolidating rather than extending his occupation of the coastal region east of the St Johns. That was Gillmore's second miscalculation: not taking sufficiently into account the temperament of his chief subordinate, who would assume command while he himself was up the coast.

A forty-year-old Vermont-born West Pointer, Seymour had seen about as much action as any man on either side in the war, including service as an artillery captain at Sumter when the opening shots were fired. Earlier he had been brevetted twice for bravery in Mexico and the Seminole War, and he had risen about as rapidly as he could have wished in the first two years of the contest still in progress, succeeding to the command of a division in the course of the Seven Days, after which had come Second Bull Run, South Mountain, and Antietam. In all these battles, whether his job was staff or line, he had demonstrated ability; yet somehow, while earning an additional three brevets, he had missed distinction. Then had come a transfer to the Carolina coast, and there too he had performed with credit, especially in the taking of Battery Wagner, where he was severely wounded as a result of his practice of exposing himself under fire. Somehow, though, distinction still eluded him at every turn. And now there was this fruitless westward march across the barrens of North Florida, ended in midcareer by a withdrawal and followed by peremptory instructions for him to remain strictly on the defensive in the absence of a superior whose outstanding characteristic seemed to him to be an unwillingness to assume the risks that went with gain and were in fact the handholds to distinction. Gillmore left Jacksonville on February 13; Seymour managed to endure four days of inactivity in his nominal, if temporary, position as commander of the Florida expedition. Then on the fifth day he went over to the offensive.

He did this strictly on his own, ostensibly because of a report that the rebels were about to remove the rails from the Atlantic & Gulf

Central, which he knew would upset Gillmore's plans for a resumption of the advance to the Suwannee. It was not that he was unaware of the risks involved; he was; the question later was whether he had welcomed or ignored them. For example, garrison detachments had reduced his mobile strength to about 5500 effectives, and though he suspected that the Confederates had more troops than that around Lake City, he

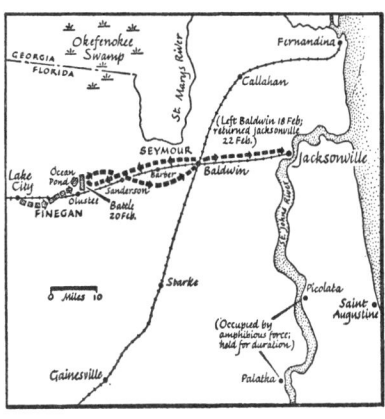

knew they were militia to a man and apt therefore to flinch from contact with anything that came at them in a determined manner, which was precisely what he had in mind. Moreover, he intended to make up for the possible disparity in numbers by seizing the initiative and moving with celerity once he had it. "I wish the thing done in the most speedy way possible," Lincoln had said, and Seymour demonstrated his agreement with this approach when he left Jacksonville on February 18 and cleared Baldwin before nightfall. By sundown of the following day his infantry was beyond Barber's, having covered better than thirty miles of sandy road, and his orders were for the march to be resumed at dawn. For added speed, he advanced in three columns, keeping close on the heels of the cavalry to avoid the delay of having to probe the front or shield the flanks with skirmishers detached from his three infantry brigades. All morning, February 20, he kept his soldiers on the go, slogging through Sanderson and on to Olustee without a rest halt, intent on reaching Lake City before the graybacks had time to get set for the strike. Blown, hungry, and considerably strung out, the three columns converged as they approached Ocean Pond, a swamp just beyond Olustee, around whose southern reaches the road and the railroad passed together along a narrow neck of firm ground with bogs on the left and right. It was here, barely a dozen miles from Lake City and on terrain that was scarcely fit for fighting — at any rate, not the kind of fighting he had in mind — that Seymour first encountered resistance in the form of butternut skirmishers who rose from hiding and took the heads of the three blue columns under fire, then faded back into the palmetto thickets. Recovering as best he could from the surprise, which came all the harder because he had expected to be the inflictor, not the victim, he gave orders for the pursuit to be pressed without delay. It was; but not for long. Within five minutes and two hundred yards, he found himself involved in the battle known thereafter as Olustee or Ocean Pond.

The contest lasted from shortly after noon until about 4 o'clock, not because there was ever much doubt as to the outcome, but simply because that much time was required to make Seymour admit he'd been whipped. In the end, it was his own men who convinced him, although the Confederates, with four guns against his sixteen, had been highly persuasive in this regard from the start. Brigadier General Joseph Finegan, a thirty-nine-year-old Irish-born Floridian, had about the same number of troops as his opponent, just over or under 5500, and though they were as green as their commander, an unblooded prewar lumberman and railroader, they were by contrast rested and forewarned, having moved out of Lake City two days ago to dig in along the near end of the swamp-bound neck of land and there await the arrival of the bluecoats on terrain that would cramp their style and limit their artillery advantage. As a result, the butternut militia had only to stand more or less firm and keep shooting, whereas the attackers were obliged to try to maneuver, which was practically impossible, hemmed in as they were on the left and right by spongy ground and blasted from the front by masses of graybacks who also enjoyed the protection of intrenchments. The fighting consisted mainly of a series of breakdowns and disintegrations which occurred when a number of blue regiments, exposed to such obvious tactical disadvantages, wavered and finally came apart under pressure. A New Hampshire outfit was the first to give way, followed by another of Negro regulars who fled when their colonel was shot down, and total collapse was only forestalled by Seymour's belated permission for the rest to withdraw. They did so in considerable haste and disorder, leaving six of their guns behind them on the field. Early darkness ended the pursuit, which had been delayed by another Negro regiment assigned to rear-guard duty. Casualties totaled 1861 for the Federals, including more than 700 killed or captured, while the Confederates lost 946, with fewer than 100 dead or missing. Seymour had at last achieved distinction, but not at all of the kind for which he yearned, since it resulted from the addition of his name to the list of those commanders, North and South, who suffered the soundest thrashings of the war.

Slogging rearward under cover of darkness, the whipped and bleeding survivors were as bitter as they were footsore. "This moment of grief is too sacred for anger," an officer wrote home. But that was by no means the general reaction, which was not unlike the one displayed on the similar withdrawal from the field of Chickamauga, five months ago tonight. If this retreat was on a smaller scale, as far as concerned the number of troops involved, it was at any rate much longer, and it was harder in still other ways. Without nearly enough ambulances or wagons to accommodate the wounded, crude litters had to be improvised, with results that were not only painful for the men being jolted but also exhausting for the bearers. Still, they made good time: better, indeed, than they had made on the speedy outward march. By moonrise they were at Sanderson, ten miles from the scene of their defeat, and they passed through Barber's before daybreak. The second of these two segments was even grimmer than the first, partly because the marchers were wearier, partly too because they lacked by then the disconcerting spur of pursuit, the rebels having halted far in the rear. Now they had time for comprehending what had happened back there at Olustee, and that had perhaps the grimmest effect of all. "Ten miles we wended or crawled along," a participant afterwards said of the small-hours trek from Sanderson to Barber's, "the wounded filling the night air with lamentations, the crippled horses neighing in pain, and the full moon kissing the cold, clammy lips of the dying." Moreover, there was no halt on the 21st at Baldwin, despite previous instructions for holding that vital crossing at all costs, and by sunup of the following morning the head of the column was in Jacksonville, which it had left four days and a hard hundred miles ago.

Gillmore's dismay, on learning of what had happened in his absence and against his orders, was increased by information that the Confederates had advanced beyond Baldwin and were intrenching a line along McGirt's Creek, midway between that place and Jacksonville. Whether this was in preparation for defense or attack he did not know, though it might well be for the latter, since they were reported to have been heavily reinforced from Georgia. In any case, the question was no longer whether he could advance to the Suwannee, as he had formerly intended, but whether he could hold the coastal strip he had seized within a week of his arrival; Beauregard had outfoxed him again, he admitted to his superiors in Washington. "The enemy have thrown so large a force into Florida," he informed Halleck on February 23, "that I judge it to be inexpedient to do more at the present time than hold the line of the Saint Johns River."

One thing he could and did do, however, and that was to relieve Seymour of the command he had abused. But this was plainly a case of locking the stable after the pony was stolen. Certainly it was no help to Hay, who was finding it much harder now to obtain signatures for his oath-blanks. In fact, many who had signed appeared to regret that they had done so; while others, as he noted in his diary, "refused to sign, on the ground that they were not repentant." It was becoming increasingly clear, with the spread of news of the recent Union defeat, that he and his chief had miscalculated the temper of the people. Florida, the least populous of the Confederate states, had furnished the smallest number of troops for the rebel armies; but that was by no means a fit basis on which to determine her zeal for the secessionist cause, which was indicated far better by the fact that she had given a larger proportion of her eligible men than had any other state. On March 3, within twelve days of the rebel victory at Olustee, Hay frankly confessed: "I am very sure that we cannot now get the President's 10th." This being so, there was little point in his remaining. Nor did he. After a side excursion to Key West

— where he went in hope of picking up a few more signatures, but found instead "a race of thieves and a degeneration of vipers" — he returned somewhat crestfallen to the capital, intending to resume his former duties if his chief would overlook the unhappy events of the past month and take him back.

He found the hostile papers in full bay, charging Lincoln with having "fooled away 2000 men in a sordid attempt to manufacture for himself three additional votes in the approaching Presidential election." Nor did Hay escape their censure as a party to the conspiracy to overawe Florida, not for any true military purpose, but merely to win himself a seat in Congress and deliver a set of committed delegates to the Republican convention. This last, they said, explained the reckless haste that had brought Seymour to defeat; for the convention would be held in June, and the hapless general had been obliged to expose his troops to slaughter in an attempt to carry out his orders to complete the intended conquest of that waste of sand in time for a new government to be formed and delegates to be chosen who would cast their votes for Lincoln's renomination. Returning at the height of the scandal aroused by the failure of his mission, Hay armed himself with extenuating documents for the confrontation with his chief. He expected at least a grilling — for there was enough unpleasant truth in the opposition's charges to make them sting far worse than the usual fabrications — but he was wrong; Lincoln assumed that the young man had done his best in a difficult situation, and did not blame him for the trouble the journalists were making. "There was no special necessity of my presenting my papers," Hay wrote in his diary that night, "as I found he thoroughly understood the state of affairs in Florida and did not seem in the least annoyed by the newspaper falsehoods about the matter."

Others received a different impression of the President's reaction to this latest in the series of attacks designed to expose him as a master of deceit, an unprincipled opportunist, a clod, a tyrant, a bawdy clown, a monster. Earlier that month a White House visitor observed that Lincoln seemed "deeply wounded" by the allegation that he had been willing to pay in blood for votes. As usual, however, even as he was ringed by critics flinging charges at his head, he could see at least one touch of humor in the situation. He told in this connection of a backwoods traveler who got caught one night in a violent storm and who floundered about in the blackness, his sense of direction lost amid blinding zigzags of lightning and deafening peals of thunder, until finally a bolt crashed directly overhead, awesome as the wrath of God, and brought him to his knees, badly frightened. By ordinary not a praying man, he kept his petition brief and to the point. "O Lord," he cried, "if it's all the same to you, give us a little more light and a little less noise!"

★ ★ ★

While Gillmore and Hay, with Seymour's manic assistance, were failing to bring Florida back into the Union under the terms of the Proclamation of Amnesty and Reconstruction, another quasi-military project which had to do with that document, and which likewise had the President's enthusiastic approval, was moving into its final preparatory stages in Virginia. Aimed at nothing so ambitious as the overnight return of the Old Dominion to its former allegiance, this second venture along those lines was an attempt to see that the people there were acquainted at first hand, rather than through the distorting columns of their local papers or the vituperative speeches of their leaders, with the terms of Lincoln's offer; in which case, it was presumed, a good many of them would be persuaded to see the wisdom of acceptance and the folly of delay. Even if the project fell a long way short of accomplishing the most that could be hoped for, it would at least create doubt and provoke division in the enemy ranks, its authors believed, at a time when the struggle was about to enter its most critical phase. Just as the Florida venture mixed war and politics, so was this Virginia expedition designed to combine a military and a propaganda effort. Lincoln had warned his adversaries that he would not leave "any available card unplayed," and this — though it would go considerably further in bloody intent, before it was over, than he had realized when he approved it — was another example of the fact that he meant exactly what he said.

Designed strictly as a cavalry operation, the project had its beginning in the mind of Judson Kilpatrick, who conceived the notion of launching a bold strike at the Confederate capital, sixty miles in Lee's rear, for the triple purpose of crippling and snarling the lines of supply and communication between the Rapidan and the James, disrupting the rebel government by jangling the nerves of the people who functioned at its center, and freeing the Union captives being held there in increasingly large numbers since the breakdown of the system of exchange. Like his purpose, his motivation was threefold: love of action, desire for acclaim, and envy. Averell having recently been applauded for his successful year-end raid into southwest Virginia, the New Jersey cavalryman planned to win far more applause by striking, not with a lone brigade, but with his whole division, and not at some remote objective on the fringes of the map, as Averell had done, but at the very solar plexus of rebellion. Such a blow would outdo all the horseback exploits that had gone before it, including the highly touted "rides" by Stuart in his heyday. Besides, Kilpatrick did not believe the hit-and-run operation would be nearly as risky, or anyhow as difficult, as it sounded. His information was that Richmond was scantly protected by inexperienced home guardsmen who would not be able to offer serious resistance to an approximately equal number of veteran troopers armed with seven-shot repeaters, not to mention the fact that his strength would be more than doubled, once he broke through the rim of the city's defenses, by the liberation and addition of some 5000 bluecoats reported to be at Libby and on Belle Isle. A more difficult problem, just now, was how to go about securing the approval he had to have before he could take off southward on the venture he was sure would bring him fame. He had little caution in his makeup, but at any rate he knew better than to propose his scheme to Pleasonton, who might hog it, or to the overcautious Meade, who would be certain to see it as harebrained and reject it in short order. Instead, he took care to communicate in private with certain persons known to be close to the highest authority of all. That was in late January, and the result was about as prompt as he expected. On February 11 a high-priority telegram clicked off the wire from Washington, addressed to the commander of the Army of the Potomac: "Unless there be strong reasons to the contrary, please send Gen. Kilpatrick to us here, for two or three days. A. Lincoln."

"Us" included Stanton, who shared with his chief a staunch, perhaps an extravagant admiration for military boldness, a quality sadly lacking in the upper echelons of the eastern theater, as they saw it, but personified by the bandy-legged general known to the army as "Kill Cavalry." The latter arrived in the capital next morning — the President's fifty-fifth birthday — and was received in private by the Secretary of War. Stanton liked the proposition even better at first hand than he had by hearsay, seeing in it, in addition to the fruits predicted by its author, the possibility of affording a real boost to morale on the home front when the news went out that Federal horsemen had clattered through the streets of Richmond, striking terror into the hearts of rebel leaders and freeing thousands of blue-clad martyrs from a durance worse than vile. Moreover, having applauded the young brigadier's conception, which was much in line with his own belief as to the manner in which this war should be fought, the Secretary passed along a suggestion from Lincoln that would give the raid an added dimension, and this was that each trooper carry with him a hundred or so copies of the recent amnesty proclamation for distribution along the way. Kilpatrick pronounced this a splendid notion, then presently, the details having been agreed on, returned to the Rapidan, encouraged and flattered by the confidence thus shown by the head of the War Department — who made it clear that he spoke as well for the Commander in Chief — in a twenty-seven-year-old subordinate, less than three years out of West Point. Hard in his wake, orders came to Culpeper directing that his division be reinforced to a strength of about 4000 for the raid he proposed and that he be given all the assistance he required, including diversionary actions by other units, foot and horse.

Meade was not happy about the project, of which he had known nothing until now. Nor was Pleasonton, who recalled the ill-fated Stoneman raid, which had been similar in purpose and conception, but which had accomplished little except "the loss to the government [of] over 7000 horses, besides the equipments and men left on the road." In short, the chief of cavalry said flatly, the expedition was "not feasible at this time." As for the proposed distribution of the President's proclamation, he suggested that this could be done better, and far cheaper, by undercover agents, and he offered "to have it freely circulated [by this method] in any section of Virginia that may be desired." But nothing came of these objections by the New Jersey cavalryman's immediate superiors. In fact, they were received in Washington as further evidence of the timidity which had crippled the eastern army from the outset. The orders were peremptory, Meade was told; Kilpatrick was to be given a free rein.

About the time of Washington's Birthday, which came ten days after Lincoln's, bales of leaflets reprinting the amnesty proclamation arrived for distribution to the raiders, who were to scatter them broadcast on the way to Richmond. There also arrived from Washington, four days later and only two days short of the jump-off date, a twenty-one-year-old colonel who came highly recommended for his "well-known gallantry, intelligence, and energy" — this last despite a wooden leg and a manner described by an admirer as "soft as a cat's." Ulric Dahlgren was his name. He was the admiral's son, but he preferred the cavalry to the navy because he believed the mounted arm would afford him more and better chances for adventure and individual accomplishment. Commissioned a captain at nineteen by Stanton himself before the war was a year old, he had served in rapid succession on the staffs of Sigel, Burnside, Hooker, and Meade, all of whom had found him useful as well as ornamental, and it had been near Boonsboro, during the pursuit of Lee after Gettysburg, that he received the wound that resulted in the amputation. Once he was able to get about on crutches he went down the coast and convalesced aboard his father's flagship outside Charleston; after which he returned to Washington, where he was jumped three ranks to colonel, reportedly the youngest in the army, and fitted for an artificial leg. While there, he learned of the preparations then in progress for the horseback strike about to be launched against the rebel capital, and he went at once to cavalry headquarters near Brandy to appeal to Pleasonton for permission to go along, despite his crippled condition. Pleasonton sent him to Kilpatrick, who not only acceded to his plea, but also gave him the all-important assignment of leading the way across the Rapidan at the head of a special 500-man detachment, with other hazardous tasks to follow in the course of the ride from that river to the James. "If successful," he wrote his father, delighted to be back in the war at all, let alone with such a daredevil role to play, "[the raid] will be the grandest thing on record; and if it fails, many of us will 'go up.' I may be captured or I may be 'tumbled over,' but it is an undertaking that if I were not in I should be ashamed to show my face again." He was especially taken with the notion that he would be riding into the very heart of the rebellion, and he added: "If we do not return, there is no better place to 'give up the ghost.'"

Jump-off was set for an hour before midnight, February 28, and proceeded without a hitch, partly because Lee was pulled off balance by Sedgwick, who had shifted his corps upstream that day, as if for a crossing in that direction, while Kilpatrick was massing his 3585 troopers under cover of the woods in rear of Ely's Ford, twenty miles downriver. At the appointed hour they splashed across, mindful of their instructions to "move with the utmost expedition possible on the shortest route past the enemy's right flank." So well did it go that by dawn the column reached Spotsylvania, fifteen miles beyond the Rapidan, unchallenged; at which point, as had been prearranged, Dahlgren and his 500 veered slightly right, while the main body continued to move straight ahead for Richmond, less than fifty miles away. The plan was for the smaller column to cross the James near Goochland, well upstream, so as to approach the rebel capital from the southwest at the same time Kilpatrick came upon it from the north, thereby causing the home-guard defenders to spread thinner and thus expose themselves to the breakthrough that would result in the clatter of Federal hoofs in the streets of their city and the release of 5000 captives from Libby and Belle Isle. Dahlgren's was the longer ride; he would have to avoid delay to arrive on schedule. Kilpatrick saw him off from Spotsylvania, wished him Godspeed as he disappeared into the misty dawn of leap-year day, then continued on his own route, south-southeast, which would bring him and his 3000 to the northern gates of Richmond, if all went as planned, at the same time the young colonel and his detached 500 came knocking at the western gates.

Speed was the watchword; Kilpatrick rode hard and fast, unopposed and apparently unpursued. This last was due in part to a second diversion, back on the Rapidan line. While Sedgwick was feinting westward, George Custer was shifting his 1500-man cavalry brigade even farther in that direction for a dash southward into Albemarle County, a movement designed to attract still more of Lee's attention away from the heavier column rounding his opposite flank. Custer, like Kilpatrick, had certain peculiarities of aspect ("This officer is one of the funniest-looking beings you ever saw," a colonel on Meade's staff wrote home, "and looks like a circus rider gone mad! He wears a huzzar jacket and tight trousers, of faded black velvet trimmed with tarnished gold lace. His head is decked with a little gray felt hat; high boots and gilt spurs complete the costume, which is enhanced by the general's coiffure, consisting in short, dry, flaxen ringlets!") but these gaudy trappings, coupled with a flamboyant personality and a reputation as a glory-hunter, did not interfere with his effectiveness when sheer courage was what was called for — as it was here, off on his own in Lee's left rear, with the task of drawing as many of Stuart's horsemen after him as possible, away from the main effort to the east. He could scarcely have done a better job, as it turned out. Crossing the river that same Sunday night, some forty miles upstream from Ely's Ford, he threatened Charlottesville next day and returned to the north bank of the Rapidan on Tuesday, March 1, having ridden more than a hundred miles through hostile territory, burned three large grist mills filled with flour and grain, and captured about fifty graybacks and 500 horses, all without the loss of a man and only a few wounded. So well indeed had he carried out his mission, particularly with regard to attracting the rebel cavalry's attention, that he was notified on his return, officially and in writing, of Pleasonton's "entire satisfaction ... and gratification ... at the prompt manner in which the duties assigned to you have been performed."

Before Custer returned to the Union lines Kilpatrick was knocking at the gates of Richmond. Across the North Anna by noon of February 29, he had paused astride the Virginia Central at Beaver Dam Station, midway to his objective, and after setting fire to the depot and other installations, thus to discourage any pursuit by rail once Lee found out that some 4000 blue raiders were menacing the capital in his rear, pressed on to make camp near the South Anna by nightfall. An hour past midnight he roused his sleeping troopers and was off again through the darkness, undeterred by an icy rainstorm or the fact that he had received no answering signal when he sent up rockets to indicate his position to Dahlgren, whose detachment was somewhere off to the west. "No rockets could be seen for any distance on such a night as that," an officer was to note, recalling that the "sharp wind and sleet forced men to close their eyes" as they rode southward, their wet clothes frozen stiff as armor. By daylight they were over the Chickahominy near Ashland, and at 10 o'clock in the morning, having covered sixty miles of road in the past thirty-five hours, they came jogging down the Brook Pike to within sight of Richmond and range of its outer fortifications, five miles from the heart of town. No sooner did they appear than they were taken under fire. Kilpatrick brought up his six guns for counterbattery work and prepared to overrun the defenders, "believing that if they were citizen soldiers" — by which he meant home guardsmen — "I could enter the city." So he reported some weeks later, in the calmness of his tent. One thing that bothered him now, though, was that the boom and clatter of his engagement had drawn no reply from Dahlgren, who should have arrived simultaneously on the far side of the James, there to create the prearranged diversion, but who had either been delayed or gobbled up. Another matter for concern was that the rebels up ahead were doing a highly professional job of defending their position. They were in fact part-time volunteers — government clerks, old men, and boys, considerably fewer in number than the bluecoats to their front, and serving antiquated or worn-out guns long since replaced by new ones in Lee's army — but they handled their pieces with such precision that Kilpatrick began to believe that they had been reinforced by regulars. "They have too many of those damned guns!" he fumed, riding his line amid shellbursts and withholding the order to charge until he could better determine what stood between him and the breakthrough he intended; "they keep opening new ones on us all the time."

It was strange, this sudden transformation in a hell-for-leather commander who up to now had fairly ached to put his troopers inside Richmond. He had worked all the angles to circumvent his immediate superiors, whose timidity he had seen as the main obstacle to an undertaking that simply could not fail once it got past their disapproval, and had ridden a hard sixty miles through hostile country, bristling with aggressiveness and chafing with impatience all the way. Yet now that he had come within plain view of his goal — the goal, for that matter, of every blue-clad soldier in the eastern theater — he declined to risk the last brief sprint, half a mile down the turnpike, then past or through or over "those damned guns," which were all that stood between him and the completion of the mission he had designed with his own particular talents in mind, or anyhow his notion of those talents. It was unquestionably strange, but perhaps it was not as sudden as it seemed; perhaps it had been this way all along, behind the swagger and the blustering impatience. In any case he limited his aggressiveness, here on the outskirts of his objective, to a tentative sparring match, keeping one ear cocked for some indication that Dahlgren and his daredevil 500 were knocking at the gates beyond the James. After six or seven hours of this, the rebel guns had indeed grown in numbers, along with their infantry support, as reinforcements were hustled to the threatened sector from others undisturbed along the defensive rim, and Kilpatrick finally arrived at a decision. "Feeling confident that Dahlgren had failed to cross the river, and that an attempt to enter the city at that point would but end in a bloody failure," he later reported, "I reluctantly withdrew." He fell back northeastward, recrossing the Chickahominy at Meadow Bridge to give his men and horses some badly needed sleep in the sodden fields around Mechanicsville, where Lee had opened his Seven Days offensive, just over twenty months ago.

There had been no fighting here since then, but presently there was. At 10 o'clock, unable to sleep or rest — in part because of the wet and the cold, in part because of his fret at having failed — Kilpatrick remounted his troopers and prepared to launch a night attack down the Mechanicsville road, avoiding the stoutly held pike to the west, in order to achieve a penetration that would last no longer than it took to free the prisoners and come back out again. Before he could get his weary men in line, however, he was himself attacked by rebel horsemen who came at him from the direction of Yellow Tavern, out of the darkness in his rear. Though he managed to beat off this assault, all thoughts of resuming the offensive gave way at once to the problem of survival: especially when he learned, as he soon did, that the attackers were not "citizen soldiers," which were all he had faced till now, but regulars from Wade Hampton's division, who had taken up the belated pursuit from the Rapidan line and then had narrowed the gap between him and them while he was sparring with Richmond's defenders this afternoon. His concern was no longer with the liberation of the prisoners in the city; it was rather how to keep from joining them as a prisoner himself. Once more his decision was to withdraw northeastward, and this he did, effecting a skillful disengagement to make camp at dawn near Bethesda Church, midway between the Chickahominy and the Pamunkey. Here he remained all morning, March 2, fighting off regular and irregular Confederates who were gathering in ever larger numbers all around him in the woods and swamps. He kept hoping to hear from Dahlgren, but he did not. At noon he abandoned his vigil, together with all hope of entering Richmond, and withdrew to make camp at Tunstall's Station, near McClellan's old base at White House. There at last he was joined that night by a captain and 260 men from Dahlgren's detachment. They had a gloomy tale to tell, though they did not know the even gloomier ending, which was occurring at about that same time, some dozen air-line miles to the northeast.

Despite the almost constant rain, which made for heavy going, Dahlgren had set a rapid pace after he and his picked 500 turned off from the main body at Spotsylvania before sunup, leap-year morning. Proceeding south through Fredericks Hall, where he called a midday halt to feed the horses, he crossed the South Anna late that night and rode into Goochland, thirty miles up the James from the rebel capital, as March 1 was dawning. Here he picked up a young Negro named Martin Robinson, a slave from a nearby plantation, who offered to show him a place where the bridgeless river could be forded. The colonel was in excellent spirits, for he had kept to a difficult schedule and was about to get his troopers into position for the final dash that would put them in southside Richmond before noon, just as he had promised Kilpatrick he would do. So he thought; but not for long. Arriving at the intended crossing — Jude's Ford, it was called — he found the river on the boom, swollen by the two-day rain and running too swift to be breasted; whereupon the handsome young colonel, whose manner was said to be "soft as a cat's," showed his claws. Although the guide appeared to be quite as surprised as he himself was at the condition of the ford, Dahlgren suspected treachery, and in his anger at having been thwarted — for it was clear now, if nothing else was, that he could not reach his objective either on time or from the appointed direction — ordered him hanged. This was accomplished with dispatch there by the river, one end of a picket rope being flung across a convenient limb while the other was fastened snugly about the neck of the Negro, whose protests were cut short when he left the ground. Without further delay, and almost before the suspended man had ended his comic-dreadful jig, the blue column was back in motion, trotting eastward down the north bank of the James, its commander watching intently for some sign of a ford shallow enough to be used.

Finding none he paused occasionally to set fire to a grist mill or damage a lock in the left-bank canal, which delayed him still more. It was late afternoon by the time he cleared Short Pump, eight miles from Richmond, and heard the boom of guns in the misty northeast distance. He quickened the pace, but presently he too encountered resistance, with the result that by the time he got close to the city Kilpatrick had withdrawn. So far as Dahlgren could tell, alone in the gathering dusk with rebel militia all around him, his horses sagging with fatigue and a hard rain coming down, the main body had simply vanished. His instructions in such a case — that is, once the raid was over: as it now definitely was, though not at all in the manner Kilpatrick had predicted — called for a return to the Union lines, either by way of Fredericksburg or down the York-James peninsula. He chose the former route, turning off to the north, away from Richmond and across the Chickahominy, well above Meadow Bridge. His troopers had had little sleep in the past three nights, and by now the column had split in two, some 300 of the men becoming separated from the rest in the gloom and confusion. These were the ones — 260 of them, at any rate; about forty were captured or shot from their saddles next day — who joined the main body at Tunstall's the following night. Meanwhile, Dahlgren and the remaining 200 managed to cross the Pamunkey, a few miles north of there, and continued on through the darkness to the Mattaponi, exchanging shots with roving bands of rebels all the way. This stream too they crossed, but they got only a bit farther. Approaching King and Queen Courthouse, just beyond the river, they stumbled into an ambush laid in their path by Fitz Lee's regulars, who had also arrived from the Rapidan by now. Dahlgren, riding point, decided to brazen or bluff his way through; or perhaps he recalled that he had told his father there was no better place to die. "Surrender, you damned rebels," he cried, flourishing his revolver, "or I'll shoot you!" The answering volley unhorsed him with four bullets in his body, and witnesses afterwards testified that before he struck the ground he had already given up what he had called the ghost.

Most of those with him were likewise killed or captured, a number being flushed from hiding next morning by pursuers who put bloodhounds on their trail. Kilpatrick was incensed when he heard of this unchivalrous practice from a dozen of Dahlgren's men who managed to get through to him a few days later at Yorktown, where he ended his withdrawal down the Peninsula, safe within the Union lines. He spoke, in his official report, of the colonel's death as "murder" — a curious charge for a professional to make — but he did not hesitate, in that same document, to blame the dead man for the unhappy outcome of the project he himself had planned and led. "I am satisfied that if Colonel Dahlgren had not failed in crossing the river," he declared, "... I should have entered the rebel capital and released our prisoners." As it was, instead of decreasing the prison population of Richmond, he had increased it by some 300 veteran troopers (his total loss was 340, but a good many of them were killed) and in addition had lost 583 horses in the course of the ride, plus another 480 too broken down to be of any further use when it was over. About the only profit he could point to was the incidental damage inflicted on various installations along the way, together with the claim that "several thousand of the President's amnesty proclamations were scattered throughout the entire country."

In point of fact, a sizable proportion of these last had been unloaded as dead weight, heaved overboard into roadside ditches when the project degenerated into a race for survival, and whatever of propaganda value was derived from the scattering of Lincoln's amnesty offer had been considerably offset by the hard-handed excesses of the blue troopers engaged in an expedition whose most lamented casualty, according to a Richmond editor, was "a boy named Martin, the property of Mr David Meems, of Goochland." Even so, the resentments stirred up in the course of the raid were mild indeed, compared to those that developed on both sides when it was over: particularly in regard to Ulric Dahlgren, whose zeal was even more in evidence after his death than it had been before he toppled from his horse near King and Queen. His body was subjected to various indignities, including the theft of his artificial leg, the clumsy removal of one of his fingers to get at a ring he was wearing, and the scavenging of other of his private possessions, such as his watch, his boots, and even his clothes. News of these atrocities created a stir of outrage in the North, but this in turn was overmatched by the furor that followed in the South upon the publication of certain papers found among his personal effects. These included the draft of an address to his command and a detailed set of instructions for what he called "a desperate undertaking." "We will cross the James River into Richmond," he had written, "destroying the bridges after us and exhorting the released prisoners to destroy and burn the hateful city; and do not allow the rebel leader Davis and his traitorous crew to escape." Thus the proposed address, though there was no evidence that it had been delivered. The instructions were more specific. "The men must keep together and well in hand," he urged, "and once in the city it must be destroyed and Jeff Davis and cabinet killed. Pioneers will go along with combustible material."

To Southerners, when these exhortations to arson and assassination were released in print, it appeared that this amounted to hoisting the black flag, and they called bitterly for emulation of the example set — conveniently forgetting, it would seem, Quantrill's previous excesses out in Kansas. One of the angriest among them was Seddon, who sent copies of the documents to Lee, stating that in his opinion their "diabolical character" required "something more than a mere informal publication in our newspapers. My own inclinations are toward the execution of at least a portion of those captured at the time.... I desire to have the benefit of your views and any suggestions you may make." Lee replied that he too was shocked by the details of this "barbarous and inhuman plot," but that execution of the captured troopers would bring retaliation, and he wanted no part of a hanging-match with the Yankees. Besides, he told the Secretary, "I do not think that reason and reflection would justify such a course. I think it better to do right, even if we suffer in so doing, than to incur the reproach of our consciences and posterity." Instead he sent the inflammatory documents across the lines to Meade, together with a note inquiring "whether the designs and instructions of Colonel Dahlgren, as set forth in these papers... were authorized by the United States Government or by his superior officers, and also whether they have the sanction and approval of those authorities." Meade investigated the matter and replied "that neither the United States Government, myself, nor General Kilpatrick authorized, sanctioned, or approved the burning of the city of Richmond and the killing of Mr Davis and cabinet, nor any other act not required by military necessity and in accordance with the usages of war." He also included, for whatever it was worth, a letter from Kilpatrick, impugning the authenticity of the papers. "But I regret to say," Meade privately informed his wife, "Kilpatrick's reputation, and collateral evidence in my possession, rather go against this theory."

There the matter rested, so far at least as Meade and Lee were concerned. As for Lincoln, he too was willing to let it lie, if it only would, and he did not call, as he had done after the frustration of the first of his two attempts to extend the influence of his amnesty proclamation, for "more light"; there had been quite enough of that by now. Both failures were depressing for him to look back on, especially the second. The Florida expedition had been merely a fiasco, a military embarrassment, but the Kilpatrick raid was that and more, adding as it did a deeper bitterness to a fratricidal struggle which, in all conscience, was bitter enough already. It was as if Lincoln, in attempting to soothe and heal the national wounds, had reached blindly into the medicine chest and mistaken an irritant for a salve. That this had been the effect was shown in part by the reaction of newspapers North and South. Calling hotly for reprisal, the Richmond *Examiner* now saw the conflict as "a war of extermination, of indiscriminate slaughter and plunder," while the New York *Times* exulted in the damage done by the raiders in Virginia and gloated over reports brought back of "the large number of dilapidated and deserted dwellings, the ruined churches with windows out and doors ajar, the abandoned fields and workshops, the neglected plantations." As for the slave Martin Robinson, whose body had been left dangling beside unusable Jude's Ford, he had met "a fate he so richly deserved," according to the *Times*, because he had "dared to trifle with the welfare of his country."

That was what they had come to, South and North, as the war moved toward and into its fourth and bloodiest spring.

✘ 3 ✘

For Grant, the three-month span of comparative idleness that came after the storming of Missionary Ridge was nothing like the one that had followed his earlier triumph at Vicksburg. His manner then had been that of a man not only uncertain of the future, but also doubtful about the present, with time on his hands and no notion of how to use it. Lacking in effect an occupation, what he mainly had been, through that difficult time — after as well as before the New Orleans horseback accident, which had added pain without distraction and immobility without relaxation — was bored. That was by no means the case now. For one thing, there was his vast new department to be inspected, most of which he had had no chance to visit, even briefly, until the Chattanooga siege was lifted. After a well-earned Christmas rest, he went in early January to Knoxville, then up through Cumberland Gap to Barbourville, from there by way of Lexington to Louisville, and finally back down through Nashville to his starting point, with the added satisfaction of having solved a number of supply and security problems all along the route. He had always enjoyed travel, especially when it took him to new places, and what was more the trip presented many of the aspects of a triumphal tour. "All we needed was a leader," a wounded private had told him when he climbed Missionary Ridge in the wake of the men who had carried it, and that was the reaction wherever he went on his swing through East Tennessee and Central Kentucky. "*Hail to the Chief*, both words and air, greeted him at every stopping place," an associate was to recall.

Nor was this enthusiasm by any means limited to those in uniform. Called to St Louis immediately afterwards by the supposedly dangerous illness of one of his children (a false alarm, as it turned out, for the crisis was past when he arrived) he had no sooner checked into the Lindell Hotel — "U.S.Grant, Chattanooga," he signed the register — than he was besieged by admirers with invitations, including one to a banquet tendered in his honor by two hundred leading citizens, determined to outdo in lavishness the affair put on five months ago by their commercial rivals down in Memphis. This he accepted, along with a resolution of thanks from the Common Council. If he was modest in his demeanor at such functions, and brief in his response to speeches of praise, that did not mean that he enjoyed them any less. The fact was, he enjoyed them very much, comparing the treatment accorded him now with the attitude he had encountered in prewar days, a brief five years ago, when he tried his hand at selling real estate in this same city and hardscrabble farming just outside it, and failed at both so thoroughly that he had been reduced to peddling firewood in its streets. This he knew was the way of the world, but he enjoyed the drama of the contrast between then and now, especially here in his wife's home state, where the opinion once had been fairly unanimous, not only that she had married beneath her station, but also that she had saddled herself with a husband who turned out to be a failure in his chosen line of work and a ne'er-do-well in several others.

In addition to these honors done him at first hand, others came from a distance, including three that arrived in rapid order from the seat of government before the year was out. When, amid salutes and illuminations celebrating the Chattanooga triumph, news spread throughout the North that Knoxville too had been delivered, the President coupled his announcement of the victory with a recommendation that the people gather informally in their churches to pay homage to the Almighty "for this great advancement of the national cause," and he followed this next day, December 8, with a personal message to Grant, who passed it along in a general order: "Understanding that your lodgment at Chattanooga and Knoxville is now secure, I wish to tender you, and all under your command, my more than thanks — my profoundest gratitude — for the skill, courage, and perseverance with which you and they, over so great difficulties, have effected that important object. God bless you all." Congress, not to be outdone, passed before Christmas a joint resolution thanking the Illinois general and his men "for their gallantry and good conduct in the battles in which they have been engaged" and providing for "a gold medal to be struck, with suitable emblems, devices, and inscriptions, to be presented to Major General Grant ... in the name of the people of the United States of America." In time the medal was forwarded as directed, bearing on one side a profile of the general, surrounded by a laurel wreath and a galaxy of stars, and on the other a figure of Fame holding a trumpet and a scroll inscribed with the names of his victories. The motto was "Proclaim liberty throughout the Land." Meantime a bill was offered to revive the grade of lieutenant general — previously held only by George Washington and Winfield Scott, the former briefly, the latter merely by brevet — for the purpose of assuring that Grant, for whom alone it was intended, would assume by virtue of that lofty rank the post now occupied by Halleck, who stood above him on the list of major generals. Senator James Doolittle of Wisconsin, for one, was specific in his reasons for supporting the proposal. So far in the war, he declared with an enthusiasm that avoided understatement, Grant had won 17 battles, captured 100,000 prisoners, and taken 500 pieces of artillery; "He has organized victory from the beginning, and I want him in a position where he can organize *final* victory and bring it to our armies and put an end to this rebellion."

Doolittle's colleagues wanted final victory, too, and agreed that the probable way to get it would be to apply the western formula in the East; but a majority shared two objections to the course proposed. One was that Grant was needed in the field, not behind a desk in the capital — even if the desk was that of the general-in-chief — and the other was an ingrained fear of creating a military Grand Lama who might someday develop political ambitions and use the army to further them. As a result, the bill failed to pass.

On the face of it, this seemed no great loss, since Grant by then had already offered the government his solution to the problem of how to win the war, only to have it rejected out of hand. Reverting to the proposal he had made soon after the fall of Vicksburg, he sent Charles Dana to Washington in mid-December to lay before his superiors a plan for holding the line of the Tennessee with a skeleton force while the rest of his troops steamed down the Mississippi to New Orleans, from which point they would move against Mobile and reduce it, then march through Alabama and across Georgia, living off the abundance of the Confederate heartland as they went. Meantime the Virginia army would pin Lee down by taking the offensive, and in this connection he suggested that Meade be replaced by Sherman or Baldy Smith, who could better appreciate the need for co-ordinating the eastern and the western efforts.... Presently Dana wired Grant that he had explained the scheme to Lincoln, Stanton, and Halleck, all three of whom had seen considerable merit in it: aside, that is, from the risk to which it would expose the weakened Union center while the bulk of the troops from there were on the way downriver. That drawback made it sound to them like something devised by McClellan; which plainly would not do. Besides, they wanted no more Chickamaugas, especially none that would be followed up by the victors, who presumably would do just that if they were given the second chance this seemed to offer. In short — except for that part of it favoring Meade's replacement by Smith, which all three chiefs applauded as an excellent idea, despite some misgivings about Baldy's "disposition and personal character" — Grant's proposal was turned down. Dana added, though, that the trio had welcomed his suggestions and had said that they would like to hear more of them, if he had any more of them in mind.

He did indeed. Still with his eye on Mobile, he then proposed a dual offensive against that place and Atlanta, the two drives to be launched simultaneously from New Orleans and Chattanooga, while the eastern army gave up its weary attempt to capture Richmond from the north and landed instead on the North Carolina coast in order to approach the rebel capital from the south, astride its lines of supply and communication. He said nothing more about replacing Meade with

Sherman — probably because he had decided he would need him to lead one of the two western columns — or with Smith, who by now had begun to exercise the talent for contention that had kept him in hot water most of his military life and would in time cause Grant, who once had seemed to think he hung the moon, to refer to him as "a clog." In his reply, which incorporated Lincoln's and Stanton's views as well as his own, Halleck did not mention Baldy either, no doubt assuming that Grant had confirmed their misgivings about the Vermonter's "disposition," but limited himself to an assessment of the strategy involved in the proposal for a double-pronged offensive, East and West. It would not do. Not only did it commit the cardinal sin of attempting two big things at once in each of the two theaters; it also required more troops than were available in either. If attempted, it would expose both Washington and Chattanooga to risks the government simply could not run, and moreover it showed the flawed conception of a commander who made enemy cities his primary objective, rather than enemy armies, as the President had lately been insisting must be done if this war was ever to be won. In Halleck's opinion, Grant would do better to concentrate on the problems at hand in Tennessee and North Georgia, and leave the large-scale thinking to those who were equipped for it. Just as Meade's objective was Lee's army, Grant's was Johnston's, and both were to keep it firmly in mind that neither Washington nor Chattanooga — nor, for that matter, East Tennessee, the region of Lincoln's acutest concern — was to be exposed to even the slightest danger while they attempted to carry out their separate missions of destroying the rebel masses in the field before them.

Sherman had returned by now from Knoxville. Grant informed him that the spring campaign, which would open as soon as the roads were fit for marching, would be southward against Joe Johnston and Atlanta, and every available man in both his and Thomas's armies would be needed for what promised to be the hardest fighting of the war. The redhead was all for it; but first he wanted to put an end to disruptions that had developed in the department he had left to come to Tennessee. In his absence, guerillas had taken to firing at steamboats from the banks of the big river, north and south of Vicksburg, and he did not intend to abide this outrage. "To secure the safety of the navigation of the Mississippi River," he declared, "I would slay millions. On that point I am not only insane, but mad.... I think I see one or two quick blows that will astonish the natives of the South and will convince them that, though to stand behind a big cottonwood and shoot at a passing boat is good sport and safe, it may still reach and kill their friends and families hundreds of miles off. For every bullet shot at a steamboat, I would shoot a thousand 30-pounder Parrotts into even helpless towns on Red, Ouachita, Yazoo, or wherever a boat can float or soldier march." To those who objected to this as war against civilians, he made the point that if rebel snipers could "fire on boats with women and children in them, we can fire and burn towns with women and children." Angry, he grew angrier by the week. Taking dinner at the home of a Union-loyal Nashville matron, for example, he turned on his hostess when she began to upbraid him for the looting his troops had done on the march to Knoxville. "Madam," he replied, "my soldiers have to subsist themselves even if the whole country must be ruined to maintain them. There are two armies here. One is in rebellion against the Union; the other is fighting for the Union. If either must starve to death, I propose it shall not be the army that is loyal." This said, he added in measured tones: "War is cruelty. There is no use trying to reform it. The crueler it is, the sooner it will be over."

His main fear just now was that the guerillas along the Lower Mississippi, emboldened by the example of the snipers, would band together in sufficient strength to attack the reduced garrisons at various river ports and thus undo much that had been accomplished, at a considerable expense of Federal blood and ingenuity, in the past year. It was Sherman's notion — a notion made more urgent by the need for reducing those garrisons still further in order to furnish additional troops for the campaign scheduled to open in North Georgia in late March or early April — to return to Mississippi between now and then, rather than keep his veteran soldiers lying idle in their winter camps, and nip this threat of renewed obstruction in the bud. As he put it in mid-December, after discussing the problem with Grant, "I think in all January and part of February I can do something in this line." He did not propose to waste his energies in running down individual snipers, which would be like trying to rid a swamp of mosquitoes by swatting them one by one, but rather to destroy the economy — the society, even, if need be — that afforded them subsistence. The way to do this, he maintained, was to wreck their production and transportation facilities so thoroughly that they would have nothing left to defend and nothing left to live on if they attempted resistance for its own sake. What was more, the situation there seemed made to order for the execution of such a project. Less than two hundred miles east of Jackson was Selma, Alabama, whose cannon foundry and other manufacturing installations Jefferson Davis had admired on his October visit, and roughly midway between them was Meridian, where three vital railroads intersected and which served as a storage and distribution center, not only for industrial products from the east, but also for grain and cattle from the fertile Black Prairie region just to the north. A rapid march by a sizable force, eastward from Vicksburg, then back again for a total distance of about five hundred miles, could be made within the two available months, he believed, and the smashing of these two major objectives, together with the widespread destruction he intended to accomplish en route, would assure a minimum of trouble for the skeleton command he would leave behind when he came back upriver to rejoin Grant for the drive on Atlanta — which Johnston, incidentally, would be much harder put to defend without the rations and guns now being sent to him from Meridian and Selma. That was what the Ohioan had had in mind when he spoke of "one or two blows that will astonish the natives."

There were, as he saw it, three main problems, each represented by an enemy commander who would have to be dealt with in launching this massive raid, first across the width of Mississippi and then beyond the Tombigbee to a point nearly halfway across Alabama. One was Polk, who had in his camps of instruction at Demopolis, between Meridian and Selma, the equivalent of two divisions with which to oppose him. Another was Johnston, who might send heavy detachments rearward by rail to catch him far from base and swamp him. The third was Forrest, who by now had attracted a considerable number of recruits to the cavalry division he was forming in North Mississippi and could be expected to investigate, in his usual slashing manner, any blue activity within reach. Discussing these problems with Grant, Sherman arrived at answers to all three. As for the first, he would employ no less than four divisions in his invasion column — two from McPherson's corps at Vicksburg and two from Hurlbut's at Memphis, which he would pick up on his way downriver — for a total of 20,000 infantry, plus about 5000 attached cavalry and artillery. That should take care of Polk, who could muster no better than half that many: unless, that is, he was reinforced by Johnston, and Grant agreed to discourage this by having Thomas menace Dalton. Forrest, the remaining concern, was to be attended to by a special force under W. Sooy Smith, recently placed at the head of all the cavalry in the Army of the Tennessee. At the same time the main body started east from Vicksburg, Smith was to set out south from West Tennessee, with instructions to occupy and defeat Forrest on the way to a link-up with Sherman at Meridian, from which point he and his troopers would take the lead on the march to Selma. His superiors saw, of course, that his more or less incidental defeat of Forrest, en route to the initial objective, was a lot to ask; but to make certain that he did not fail they arranged for him to be reinforced to a strength of 7000, roughly twice the number Forrest had in his green command. In any case, having arrived at this solution to the third of the three problems, Grant and his red-haired lieutenant parted company for a time, the latter to enjoy a Christmas leave with his family in Ohio while the former set out, shortly afterward, on the triumphal inspection tour through East Tennessee and Kentucky, followed by what turned out to be a pleasant visit to St Louis, where he was dined and toasted by civic leaders who once had looked askance at him as a poor catch for a Missouri girl.

In Memphis by mid-January, Sherman found Hurlbut busy carrying out instructions he had sent him to prepare two divisions for the trip downriver and the long march that would follow. While there, he also conferred with Smith, stressing the need for promptness and a vigorous celerity if his horsemen, with nearly twice the distance to cover from their starting point at nearby Collierville, were to reach Meridian at the same time as the foot soldiers, who would set out simultaneously from Vicksburg. Something else he stressed as well, which if neglected could bring on a far direr result than being thrown off schedule. This was what he referred to as "the nature of Forrest as a man, and of his peculiar force," a factor he first had learned to take into account at Fallen Timbers, after Shiloh, where his attempt at a pursuit had been brought to a sudden and unceremonious halt by one of the Tennessean's headlong charges, delivered in defiance not only of the odds, but also of the tactics manuals he had never read. "I explained to him," Sherman said afterwards of this conference with his chief of cavalry, "that in his route he was sure to encounter Forrest, who always attacked with a vehemence for which he must be prepared, and that, after he had repelled the first attack, he must in turn assume the most determined offensive, overwhelm him and utterly destroy his whole force." Without scoffing at the danger, Smith exhibited a confidence in the numerical advantage his superior's foresight had assured him for the impending confrontation with the so-called Wizard of the Saddle. Meantime Hurlbut completed his preparations. On the 25th he embarked with his two divisions, and Sherman followed two days later. By February 1 — the date set for Smith to begin his nearly 250-mile ride from Collierville, southeast to Okolona, then down the Mobile & Ohio to Meridian, wrecking and burning as he went — all the appointed elements of the infantry column were on hand at Vicksburg.

Sherman spent another two days making certain that all was in order for the march, which necessarily would be made without a base of supplies, and assessing the latest intelligence from spies beyond the lines. Polk by now had shifted his headquarters westward across the Tombigbee, from Demopolis to Meridian, and had posted his two divisions at Canton and Brandon, respectively under Loring and Sam French, twenty miles north and twelve miles east of Jackson, while his cavalry, under Stephen Lee, patrolled the region between the Pearl and the Big Black. Far from being alarmed by this, the northern commander was pleased to find his adversaries nearer than he had supposed; for they numbered barely half his strength, with 28 guns opposing 67 in the blue column, and the sooner he came to grips with them, the sooner they would be disposed of as a possible deterrent to his eastward progress and the destruction of everything of value in his path. Intending to move light, without tents or baggage even for corps commanders or himself, he had prescribed a minimum of equipment — "The expedition is one of celerity," he said, "and all things must tend to that" — but, even so, the twenty-day supply of such essentials as hardtack, salt, and coffee, together with ammunition and medical stores, required a 1000-wagon train. On February 3, having assured himself that all was as he had required, he passed the order that put his four divisions in motion for the Big Black River, one third of the way to Jackson, which in turn was a third of the way to Meridian, where Smith was to join him for the march on Selma, another hundred miles along the railroad he would follow all the way.

The march was in two columns, a corps in each, and so rapid that by nightfall both were over the river, trains and all, covering mile after eastward mile of ground for which they had fought in May, while headed in the opposite direction. Now as then, the weather was bright, the roads firm, and the soldiers in high spirits. They reached Edwards next day, swung past Champion Hill to end the third day's march at Bolton, and camped near Clinton the fourth night, within a dozen miles of the Mississippi capital. So far, the only resistance they had encountered was from small bands of cavalry; Lee was trying to slow their advance, and thus gain time for the two Confederate divisions to concentrate beyond the Pearl and there dispute a crossing. But Sherman saw through the design. Refusing to be delayed, he brushed the horsemen aside with his guns and kept his veterans slogging with such speed that Lee had no opportunity to destroy the pontoons of a large bridge, thrown across the river just beyond Jackson, before the Federals marched in on February 7. Twice already, in the past nine months, the torch had been put to this unfortunate town; now Sherman re-re-burned it, meantime pressing on for an uncontested crossing of the Pearl. Loring and French were in retreat by then, on opposite sides of the river — the former scuttling northward and the latter to the east, back to the places they had advanced from — having failed to get together in time to challenge the invaders at the only point where the terrain gave them a chance to prevail against the odds. Sherman kept moving. He reached Brandon the following evening — his forty-fourth birthday — and Morton on the 9th. In less than a week, he had not only covered better than half the distance between Vicksburg and Meridian; he had also scattered his opposition so effectively that now there was nothing between him and his initial objective except one badly rattled gray division, in flight from the four blue ones in its rear.

He pressed on, spurred by fear that he would be late for his rendezvous with Smith, who was due to reach Meridian tomorrow, after ten days on the road. The march was single column now, to provide a more compact defense against Lee's still-probing horsemen, and while McPherson paused for a day of destructive work on the railroad around Morton, Hurlbut made such good time that by sundown of the 12th he had passed through Decatur, northeast of Newton Station, and was less than thirty miles from Meridian. Sherman decided to wait there for McPherson, who was expected within a couple of hours. Detaching a regiment from Hurlbut's rear to serve as a guard, he and his staff unsaddled their horses in the yard of a house where an aide had arranged for supper; after which the general lay down on a bed to get some sleep. He was awakened by shouts and shots, and looked out of a window to find butternut cavalry "dashing about in a cloud of dust, firing their pistols." It developed that the colonel of the regiment detached to guard him, mistaking a front-riding group of staff officers for the head of McPherson's column, had considered himself relieved and pushed on eastward in an attempt to overtake his division before dark. When Sherman learned that this was what had happened, he sent an aide to order the regiment back on the double, while he himself prepared to retire with his companions to a corncrib for a blockhouse-style defense. Fortunately, the rebel troopers were giving their attention to some straggler wagons, never suspecting the larger prize within their reach, and before the townspeople could call it to their attention, the red-faced colonel returned on the run and drove them off, delivering the army commander from the gravest personal danger he had experienced since his near-capture at Collierville, four months ago yesterday. Presently McPherson did in fact come up, and Sherman went back to bed for a full night's sleep.

Another two days of marching brought the head of the blue column into Meridian by midafternoon of February 14. Polk had left by rail with the last of his troops that morning, retiring beyond the Tombigbee to Demopolis. After pleading in vain for reinforcements, he had concerned himself with the removal of an estimated $12,000,000 in military property, south to Mobile or east to Selma, together with the rolling stock of the three railroads; so that when Sherman marched in on Valentine's Day he found the warehouses yawning empty and the tracks deserted in all four directions. Furious at the loss, he put the blame on Smith, who should have arrived four days ago, in time to prevent the removal of the spoils, but who had neither come himself nor sent a courier to account for his departure from the schedule he had agreed to, three weeks back, in Memphis. Determined to make the most of the situation as he found it — for though the military property had been hauled away, the facilities were still there, and there was civilian property in abundance — the red-haired Ohioan gave his men a well-earned day of rest, then distributed the tools he had brought along to assure the efficient accomplishment of the object of his raid. "For five days," he subsequently reported, "10,000 men worked hard and with a will in that work of destruction, with axes, crowbars, sledges, clawbars, and with fire, and I have no hesitation in pronouncing the work as well done. Meridian, with its depots, storehouses, arsenal, hospitals, offices, hotels, and cantonments, no longer exists."

While the rest of the soldiers in the two corps were attending to the railroads — Hurlbut north and east of town, McPherson south and west, burning trestles, smashing culverts, and warping rails over bonfires fed by crossties — Sherman kept peering through the smoke for some sign of Smith and his 7000 troopers, who were to lead the march on Selma as soon as the present demolition work was finished. But there was none. "It will be a novel thing in war," he complained testily, between puffs on a cigar, "if infantry has to await the motions of cavalry."

His impatience was due in large part to the disappointing contrast between his present situation, in which the nonarrival of his cavalry left him marking time in Meridian — albeit vigorously, to a tempo set by pounding sledges and crackling flames — and the prospect that had seemed to lie before him, three weeks ago in Memphis, at the time of his conference with the commander of the mounted column. Smith not only had been eager to undertake the assignment, but had shown a ready appreciation of what was required to make it a success. He was to ride southeast to Okolona, visiting such destruction upon the inhabitants of this 100-mile swath across North Mississippi as his schedule would permit, and then turn south along the Mobile & Ohio, scourging the heart of the Black Prairie region with fire and sword, all the way to his projected link-up with the infantry, another 130 miles below, for the combined march eastward across the Tombigbee. As for the tactical danger, the cavalryman declared that the best procedure would be "to pitch into Forrest wherever I find him." He did not say this boastfully, but rather in accordance with his instructions, which advised him to do just that.

Neither a greenhorn nor a braggart, Smith was a West Pointer like his commander and fellow Ohioan, who was ten years his senior, and had risen on ability in the army to which he returned on the outbreak of war, interrupting what had promised to be (and later was) a distinguished career as a civil engineer. Graduating with Sheridan and McPherson, he had commanded a brigade at Shiloh while these other two Ohioans were still low-ranking staffers, and he led a division with such proficiency throughout the Vicksburg campaign that Grant soon afterwards made him his chief of cavalry. What was more, in the case of his present assignment, his confidence in his combat-tested ability as a leader was greatly strengthened by a look at the composition of the force he would be leading. In addition to five regiments he brought with him from Middle Tennessee, he would have at his disposal a Memphis-based division under Ben Grierson, who had ridden to fame over nearly the same route nine months before, and a veteran brigade already ordered to join him from Union City, up near the Kentucky line. Out of this total of better than 12,000 cavalry, he would select the 7000 he was to have in his hard-riding column, armed to a man with breech-loading carbines and accompanied by twenty pieces of artillery, double-teamed for speed. This would give him not only three times as many guns and twice as many troopers as were with Forrest, whose newly recruited division was all that stood between Smith and his objective, but also the largest and best-equipped body of Federal horsemen ever assembled in the western theater. It was small wonder he expressed no doubt that he could accomplish all that was asked of him at the late-January conference.

But Sherman had no sooner gone downriver than Smith learned that the 2000-man brigade from Union City, nearly one third of his intended force, was being delayed by floods and washouts all along the way. "Exceedingly chagrined," he informed the army commander that he thought it "wisest, best, and most promising" to postpone his departure until the brigade's arrival brought his column up to the strength assured him beforehand. He still felt "eager to pitch into [Forrest]," he said, "but I know that it is not your desire to 'send a boy to the mill.' " This was written on February 2, the day after he was supposed to have left Collierville and the day before Sherman left Vicksburg. As it turned out, moreover, the brigade did not reach Memphis until the 8th, and Smith found its horses so worn by their exertions that he felt obliged to give them a two-day rest. Then at last, on February 11 — one day after he was to have reached his initial objective, 230 miles away — he set out. He would "push ahead with all energy," he declared in a follow-up dispatch to Sherman, reporting that his men and their mounts were "in splendid condition" for the rigorous march. "Weather beautiful; roads getting good," he added. In a companion message to Grant, however, he sounded less ebullient. Earlier he had informed the department commander that his troopers were "well in hand, well provided with everything, and eager for the work," but now he confessed that the last-minute delay — already prolonged one day beyond the ten he was to have spent riding southward for the link-up at Meridian — had been "so long and so vexatious that I have worried myself into a state of morbid anxiety, and fear that I will be entirely too late to perform my part of the work."

Even though he was traversing, southeast of Collierville, what one of his lieutenants called a "rough, hopeless, God-forsaken" country, despoiled by nearly two years of contention and hard-handed occupation, his spirits rose in the course of the early stages of the march, partly because the tension of waiting had finally been relieved and partly because his prediction that Forrest would "show fight between the Coldwater and the Tallahatchie" was not borne out. He crossed the former stream near Holly Springs on the 12th and the latter at New Albany two days later — simultaneously, although he did not know it, with Sherman's arrival in Meridian — "without firing a shot." By now the column was badly strung out, however, and he was obliged to call a halt while the rear elements caught up; with the result that he did not reach Okolona until February 18. His schedule required a march rate of about twenty-five miles a day, but in this first week he had not averaged half that, despite the fact that he had encountered no opposition more formidable than a "rabble of State troops" near Pontotoc, which he brushed aside with ease, and had spent little time on the destructive work that was so much a part of his assignment. This last was because, so far, all he had run across that was worth destroying were a few outlying barns and gins. Now that he was astride the M&O, however, the opportunity for such labor was considerably enlarged: so much so, indeed, that from Okolona to West Point, a distance of about thirty miles, his troopers spent more time ripping up track and setting fires than they did in the saddle. "During two days," a brigade commander later wrote, "the sky was red with the flames of burning corn and cotton."

The sky was red with more flames than these; for the blue horsemen — especially those who were off on their own, as stragglers or outriders; "bummers," they would be called a bit later in the conflict — did not neglect the chance to scorch the holdings of secessionists in their path. What was more, a Federal colonel added, slaves on plantations roundabout, "driven wild with the infection, set the torch to mansion houses, stables, cotton gins, and quarters," and "came en masse to join our column, leaving only fire and absolute destruction behind them." Smith, for one, was "deeply pained" to find his command "disgraced by incendiarism of the most shocking kind. I have ordered the first man caught in the act to be shot," he notified Grierson, "and I have offered $500 reward for his detection." As for the Negroes, though he had encouraged them to join him as a means of increasing the disruption of the region and decreasing its future contribution to the Confederate war effort, he now had some 3000 of them on his hands and was finding them a severe encumbrance to his so-called "flying column," just at a time when he seemed likely to have to move his fastest. Despite his relief that Forrest had failed to "show fight" in the early stages of the march, it had begun to occur to him that the Tennessean might be postponing his attack until he reached a position "where he could concentrate a larger force, and where we would be to some extent jaded and farther from home."

By way of confirmation for these fears, a recently captured Indiana trooper managed to escape and rejoin his outfit on February 19, south of Okolona, with information that "Forrest's whole force was reported to be in the vicinity of West Point," barely a dozen miles ahead, and was "said to be 8000 or 9000 strong." Consequently when his lead elements ran into stiffer resistance next morning in that direction, Smith paused for thought. It seemed to him that his adversary, with the unexpected advantage of superior numbers, was laying a trap for him just down the line. He thought about this long and hard, and that evening his adjutant replied to a dispatch from one of his brigade commanders: "The general is very sick tonight."

His information was partly wrong, but his conclusion was entirely right. Though Forrest had a good deal less than half the number of men reported by the slippery Hoosier, he was indeed laying a trap for the blue column moving toward him down the Mobile & Ohio: a trap whose springing, incidentally, would commit his green command to its first concerted action. He had come to Mississippi in mid-November with fewer than 300 veterans from his old brigade, and two weeks later he took them northward, deep into West Tennessee, on a month-long tour of recruiting duty behind the Union lines, from which he returned by New Year's with some 3500 effectives, a sizable drove of hogs and cattle, and forty wagonloads of bacon. As here applied, the term "effectives" was questionable, however, since his recruits were mostly absentees and deserters, men who had skedaddled at least once before and could be expected to do so again at the first chance. "Forrest may cavort about that country as much as he pleases," Sherman had said when he heard what the rebel cavalryman was up to, north of Memphis. "Every conscript they now catch will cost a good man to watch." That this was a quite reasonable assertion no one knew better than the newly promoted major general who had this jumpy, unarmed mass in charge. But he depended on rigorous training and stern discipline — along with a few summary executions, if they were what was needed — to discourage the fulfillment of the Ohioan's prediction; after which would come the fighting that would knit what he now referred to as "my force of raw, undrilled, and undisciplined troops" into a cohesive unit, stamped with the aggressive personality of its leader and filled with a fierce pride in itself and him. With this in mind, he began in early January a program of unrelenting drill, mounted and dismounted, combined with a system of sharp-eyed inspections to assure compliance with his directives. This had been in progress barely a month when he received word at his headquarters, north of Panola, that Sherman was on the march from Vicksburg, 150 miles to the south, evidently intending to strike at Meridian and possibly also at Selma or Mobile. Eight days later, Smith left Collierville, 50 miles to the north, and Forrest made this second column his concern, determined to prevent a junction of the two, though even the smaller one had twice his strength and was infinitely superior in experience and equipment.

While Smith was moving southeast, from Holly Springs to Okolona, Forrest paralleled the blue march by shifting from Panola to Starkville. Outnumbered two to one, he could not risk an all-out attack in open country; nor could he lie in wait for the invaders until he knew where they were headed and what route they would take to get there. They might, for example, cross the Tombigbee east of Tupelo for a link-up with Sherman at Demopolis or Selma, leaving the graybacks crouched in a useless ambush far behind, or they might turn abruptly southwest and make for Jackson, passing in rear of the butternut column hurrying eastward. So Forrest bided his time and awaited developments, keeping his four undersized brigades spread out to counter an advance from any one of several directions. Then on February 19, when Smith began his wrecking descent of the M&O, it was plain that he intended to follow the railroad all the way to Meridian, and Forrest was free to develop a specific plan to stop him. Which he did. Sending one brigade to West Point as a bait to lure the bluecoats on, he ordered the others to take up a position three miles below, in a swampy pocket enclosed on the west and south by Sakatonchee and Oktibbeha creeks and on the east by the Tombigbee. That was the trap. The bait brigade, commanded by Colonel Jeffrey Forrest, the general's twenty-six-year-old brother, fell back next day as ordered, skirmishing lightly to draw the Federals through West Point and into the pocket prepared for their destruction. They followed cautiously, into and just beyond the town; but there they stopped, apparently for the night. Believing that they would come on again next morning, February 21, Forrest continued his preparations to receive them with a double envelopment.

He was wrong. Although there was an advance, which brought on a brief engagement, it soon became evident that this was a mere feint — a rear-guard action, designed to cover a withdrawal. Nearly two thirds of the way to his objective, Smith had given up trying to reach it; had decided, instead, to backtrack. Ahead were swamps and an enemy force reported to be larger than his own, while he was already ten full days behind schedule, still with eighty-odd miles to go and some 3000 homeless Negroes on his hands. "Under the circumstances," he afterwards declared, "I determined not to move my encumbered command into the trap set for me by the rebels."

Forrest, having gained what he called the "bulge," reacted fast. If the Yankees would not come to him, then he would go to them. And this he did, with a vengeance. Being, as he said later, "unwilling they should leave the country without a fight," he ordered his entire command to take up the pursuit of the retreating bluecoats. Moreover, the rearguard skirmish had no sooner begun than he attended to another matter of grave concern: namely, the behavior of his "raw, undrilled, and undisciplined" troopers in their reaction to being shot at, many of them for the first time. As he approached the firing line he met a panic-stricken Confederate stumbling rearward, hatless and gunless, in full flight from his first taste of combat. Forrest dis-

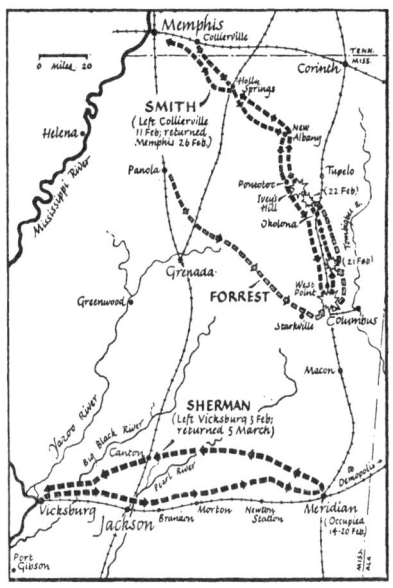

mounted to intercept him, flung him face-down by the roadside, then took up a piece of brush and administered what a startled witness described as "one of the worst thrashings I have ever seen a human being get." This done, he jerked the unfortunate soldier to his feet, faced him about, and gave him a shove that sent him stumbling in the direction of the uproar he had fled from. "Now, God damn you, go back to the front and fight!" he shouted after him. "You might as well be killed there as here, for if you ever run away again you'll not get off so easy." Still raw and undrilled, but by no means undisciplined, the man rejoined his comrades on the firing line, and the story quickly spread, not only through the division — as the general no doubt intended — but also through both armies, until finally it was made the subject of a *Harper's Weekly* illustration titled "Forrest Breaking in a Conscript."

For the next two days he handled Smith in much the same fashion. After driving the rear-guard Federals through West Point, he came upon them again, three miles beyond the town, stoutly posted along a timbered ridge approachable only by a narrow causeway. His solution was to send one regiment galloping wide around the enemy flank, with orders to strike the rear, while the others dismounted to attack in front. Admittedly, this was a lot to ask of green troops, but Forrest employed a method of persuasion quite different from the one he had used a while ago on the panicked conscript. "Come on, boys!" he roared, and led the way, thus setting an example which caused one of his men to recall, years later, that "his immediate presence seemed to inspire everyone with his terrible energy, more like that of a piece of powerful steam machinery than of a human being." So led, they drove the bluecoats from the ridge, then remounted and continued the pursuit until nightfall, when their commander called a halt, midway between West Point and Okolona, in a hastily abandoned bivouac area, stocked not only with rations and forage, but also with wood for the still-burning campfires. While the graybacks bedded down and slept beside the cozy warmth provided by their foes, Smith kept his main body plodding northward and did not stop until well past midnight, within four miles of Okolona. Burdened with captured stock and runaway slaves, and weary as they were from their long march — since sunup, they had covered better than twice the distance they had managed on any one of the other nine days since they left Collierville — his men got a late start next morning. By that time Forrest, who had had his troopers up and on the go by dawn, well rested and unencumbered, had closed the ten-mile gap and was snapping again at the tail and flanks of the blue column.

Smith was learning, as Streight had learned before him, that it could be even more dangerous to run from the Tennessean than it was to stand and fight him. However, instead of turning on him with all he had, he dropped off a couple of regiments just beyond Okolona and a full brigade at Ivey's Hill, five miles farther along on the road to Pontotoc, still intent on saving his train and protecting the Negroes in his charge. After a running fight through the town, hard on the heels of the rear guard, the gray pursuers came upon the first of these two prepared positions and were brought to a halt by fire from the superior Federal weapons. At this point Forrest arrived. "Where is the enemy's whole position?" he asked Colonel Tyree Bell, whose brigade had the lead this morning. "You see it, General," Bell replied, and added: "They are preparing to charge." "Then we will charge them," Forrest said: and did. The result was a blue rout. Five guns were abandoned shortly thereafter by an artillery lieutenant who complained hotly in his report that his battery had been forced off the road and into a ditch by Union troopers who overtook him "in perfect confusion," hallooing: "Go ahead, or we'll be killed!" The chase continued to Ivey's Hill, where the defenders, allowed more time to get set, gave a considerably better account of themselves. Opening ranks to let the fugitives through, they took under well-aimed fire the two brigades advancing toward them across the prairie. At the first volley the commanders of both were shot, one in the hand, the other through the throat. The second of these was Jeffrey Forrest, and though the general reached him immediately after he fell — this youngest of his five brothers, posthumously born and sixteen years his junior, whom he had raised as a son and made into a soldier — he found him dead. He remained bent over him for a minute or two, then rose and ordered his bugler to sound the charge. The fighting that followed was savage and hand-to-hand. Within the next hour, Forrest had two horses killed under him and accounted in person for three enemy soldiers, shot or sabered.

Thus assailed, the Federals once more fell back to try another stand in a position ten miles from Pontotoc; which was also lost, along with another gun, but which at any rate ended the relentless chase that had begun two days ago, nearly fifty miles away, below West Point. "Owing to the broken down and exhausted condition of men and horses, and being almost out of ammunition," Forrest presently reported, "I was compelled to stop pursuit." Smith was unaware of this, however, and kept going even harder than before. Judging the rebel strength by Forrest's aggressiveness, he believed that Stephen Lee had arrived to join the chase, though in point of fact he now had nothing on his trial but the "rabble of state troops" he had brushed aside when he passed this way the week before, headed in the opposite direction. In Pontotoc by midnight, he resumed the march at 3 a.m. and cleared New Albany that afternoon, February 23, destroying in his rear the bridges across the Tallahatchie. All next day he kept moving, unwilling to risk another stand, and rode at last into Collierville on the 25th, having covered in five days the same distance he had required ten days to cover while going south. Not even then did he call a halt, however; he kept going all the following day, through Germantown to Memphis, there ending at last what one brigade commander described as "a weary, disheartened, almost panic-stricken flight, in the greatest disorder and confusion."

His loss in men had not been great (it amounted to 388 in all, including 155 missing, as compared to a total of 144 for his opponent — a disparity which Forrest, as the attacker, could only account for by "the fact that we kept so close to them that the enemy overshot our men") but the cost in horseflesh had been cruel. Smith returned with no more than 2200 riders who could be described as adequately mounted; the other 4800 were either on foot or astride horses no longer fit for service in the field. A corresponding loss in cavalry morale, so lately on the rise in all the Union armies, was indicated by an unhappy colonel's remark that "the expedition filled every man connected with it with a burning shame." Nor was that by any means the worst of it from the northern point of view. The worst was still to come, resulting not so much from Federal losses as from Confederate gains. Practically overnight, by this victory over twice their number — and the capture, in the process, of six guns and several stands of colors — Forrest's green recruits had acquired a considerable measure of that fierce pride which in time would enable their commander to prevail against even longer odds and for much larger stakes. Already he was preparing to go over to the offensive, beginning with a return to West Tennessee and the accomplishment there of a great deal more than the mere enlargement of his now veteran division.

Though Sherman had been doubtful of Smith's competence from the start, deeming him "too mistrustful of himself for a leader against Forrest," this took none of the sting from his censure of his fellow Ohioan for "allowing General Forrest to head him off and defeat him with an inferior force." But that was later, after he learned the gloomy particulars of the cavalry excursion, and in any case he had waited for Smith no longer than it took him to wipe the appointed meeting place off the map. By the time the frazzled horsemen returned to Memphis, Sherman had recrossed the Pearl and gone into bivouac at Canton, north of Jackson, still with no knowledge of what, if anything, had happened to the mounted column, which in fact had begun its retreat from West Point on the day he ended his five-day stay in Meridian and abandoned his proposed advance on Selma.

Not that he considered his own part in the campaign anything less than "successful in the highest degree," both on the outward march and the return, which he made along a different route, twenty-odd miles to the north, so as to avoid the grainless, cowless, hogless trail his twelve brigades of infantry had blazed while slogging eastward. "My movement to Meridian stampeded all Alabama," he informed Halleck three days later, on February 29. "Polk retreated across the Tombigbee and left me to smash things at pleasure, and I think it is well done.... We broke absolutely and effectually a full hundred miles of railroad ... and made a swath of desolation fifty miles broad across the State of Mississippi which the present generation will not forget." After listing his spoils, which included "some 500 prisoners, a good many refugee families, and about ten miles of negroes," he announced that the destruction he had wrought "makes it simply impossible for the enemy to risk anything but light cavalry this side of Pearl River; consequently, I can reduce the garrisons of Memphis, Vicksburg, and Natchez to mere guards, and, in fact, it will set free 15,000 men for other duty. I could have gone on to Mobile or over to Selma," he added, "but without other concurrent operations it would have been unwise." Privately, however, in a companion letter to his wife, he confessed his regret that Smith's nonarrival had prevented him from applying what his foes were calling "the Sherman torch" to Alabama. "As it was," he chuckled, for he always enjoyed a small joke on the clergy, "I scared the bishop out of his senses."

It was Polk he meant, of course, and he was right; the bishop had indeed been frightened, not only for Meridian, Demopolis, and Selma, but also for Mobile, a greater prize than any of those others in his care. His fears for the Confederacy's only remaining Gulf port east of the Mississippi had been enlarged in late January when Farragut — who had just returned from a New York holiday, taken while the *Hartford* was being refitted in the Brooklyn Navy Yard — appeared before the place with a squadron of multigunned warships, evidently intending to launch another of his all-out attacks, not one of which had ever failed with him on hand to see that it was pressed to the required extremity. In point of fact, the admiral was only there to heighten Polk's fears for the loss of the port and to discourage him from drawing reinforcements from its garrison when Sherman began his march. There was no need to attack; he accomplished his purpose merely by his month-long presence, just outside the bay, and gained in the process much valuable information which he would put to substantial use when he came back again, not for a feint or diversion, but in earnest. As a result, when Sherman set out from Vicksburg in early February, Polk was convinced that his goal was Mobile and that what was intended was a combined assault, by land and water, designed to remove that vital port from the list of the South's assets in continuing its struggle to maintain its national existence. Outnumbered two to one, or worse, the bishop called loudly on Richmond for assistance, and Richmond passed his appeal to Johnston, the only possible source for reinforcements in a hurry. Whereupon there was staged in North Georgia a grim comedy involving a balking contest between the two commanders, blue and gray.

Johnson protested for all he was worth. In the first place, he did not believe the proposed reinforcements could reach Polk in time to head off Sherman; and what was more he was convinced that any substantial reduction of his already outnumbered force, which was being required to maintain a position that had "neither intrinsic strength nor strategic advantage," would not only expose Atlanta to capture by the blue mass in his front, but would also be likely to result in the destruction of what would remain of the army charged with its defense. This chilling presentation to the government of a choice between losing one or the other of two of its principal cities had the effect of delaying, though not of forestalling, a peremptory order requiring the immediate detachment of Hardee's corps to Polk for the purpose of covering Mobile. Received on February 16, the order began to be carried out four days later — by coincidence, on the day Sherman began his return march from Meridian — when the three divisions boarded the cars at Dalton for the long ride to Demopolis. Arriving next day they found they were unneeded; Sherman had withdrawn. Polk put them promptly back aboard the cars to rejoin Johnston, who by now was sending up distress signals of his own. His worst fears had been realized; Thomas was advancing. The Union-loyal Virginian had also received peremptory orders, and he too had delayed their execution. Instructed on February 14 to make a "formidable reconnaissance" of

Johnston's position, he took a week to get ready, then started forward from Ringgold on the eighth day, February 22, two days after Hardee departed with the divisions under Cheatham, Walker, and Cleburne. Grant's hope was that Thomas would catch his adversary off balance and thus be able to drive him back from Rocky Face Ridge and beyond Dalton, in order to "get possession of the place and hold it as a step toward a spring campaign."

With three of his seven divisions 350 roundabout miles away, Johnston was something worse than merely off balance when Thomas moved against him. Palmer's corps made the opening thrust at Tunnel Hill. Formerly occupied by Cleburne, this western spur of Rocky Face Ridge was now held only by Wheeler, whose horse artillery raised such a clatter that the bluecoats were discouraged from attacking until the following day, February 24. By then the rebel troopers had fallen back through Buzzard Roost Gap to cover the flanks of the infantry disposed along the ridge. Thomas probed the passes on the 25th, making some progress against the wide-spread defenders — especially at Dug Gap, immediately southwest of Dalton — but when Palmer launched a coordinated assault next morning he found that Hardee's three divisions, having completed their round-trip journey to Demopolis, were in position on the ridge; Cleburne, in fact, was on the flank of the flankers. Accordingly, Thomas withdrew as he had come, returning to Ringgold on the same day Sooy Smith rode back into Memphis and Sherman descended on Canton. His "formidable reconnaissance" had cost him 345 casualties and had failed in its larger purpose of seizing Dalton "as a step toward a spring campaign"; but he, like Farragut outside Mobile, had learned much that would be useful when he returned in earnest. As for Johnston, he was agreeably surprised. He had expected to be thrown into precipitate retreat; whereas his men had not only maintained the integrity of a position which he declared had "little to recommend it," but had inflicted better than twice the 167 casualties they suffered. Even more heartening than the bare tactical result was the contrast between the army's present frame of mind, here on Rocky Face Ridge, and the one that had been evidenced a dozen weeks ago on Missionary Ridge. Unquestionably its spirit had been lifted: perhaps indeed a bit too much, at least in one respect, to suit Old Joe. For in congratulating his troops on their work, he was critical of the artillery officers for having "exhibited a childish eagerness to discharge their pieces."

By now the Confederates had returned to Meridian, or at any rate to the desolation Sherman had created in its place. Speaking in Jackson on his first western visit, just over a year ago, Jefferson Davis had warned that the invaders had it in mind to handle Mississippi "without gloves," and now his words had been borne out; Meridian was an example of what the men he referred to as "worse than vandal hordes" could accomplish when their commander turned them loose with the admonition that "vigorous war ... means universal destruction." In addition to the damage inflicted on the town itself, a total of twenty-four miles of railroad track, extending an average half dozen miles in all four directions, had been demolished, the crossties burned, the rails heated and twisted into what were known as "Sherman neckties." Beyond this circumference of utter destruction, for a distance of nearly fifty miles north and south, not a bridge or a trestle had been left unwrecked on the Mobile & Ohio. Already, in the course of their march from Jackson, the raiders had disposed of fifty-one bridges on the Southern, together with an even larger number of trestles and culverts, and they had extended their work eastward, nine miles beyond the junction, to add three more bridges and five trestles to the tally. Yet, sad as it was to survey the charred remains of what once had passed for prosperity in this nonindustrial region, sadder by far were the people of those counties through which the blue column had slogged on its way to and from the town that now was little more than a scar on the green breast of earth. They had the stunned, unbelieving look of survivors of some terrible natural disaster, such as a five-day hurricane, a tidal wave, or an earthquake: with the underlying difference that their grief had been inflicted by human design and was in fact a deliberate product of a new kind of war, quite unlike the one for which they had bargained three years ago, back in that first glad springtime of secession. It was, moreover, a war that was still in progress, and somehow that was the strangest, most distressful aspect of all. Their deprivation was incidental to the large design. They were faced with the aftermath before the finish.

Polk took no such gloomy view of the prospect. Though he could scarcely deny the all-too-evident validity of Sherman's boast of having "made a swath of desolation fifty miles broad across the State of Mississippi which the present generation will not forget," he did not agree with his adversary's further assertion that the east-central portion of the state could be written off as a factor in the conflict. "I have already taken measures to have all the roads broken up by him rebuilt," the bishop notified Richmond two days after the raiders turned back in the direction they had come from, "and shall press that work vigorously." Press it he did. Summoning to his Demopolis headquarters President Samuel Tate of the Memphis & Charleston Railroad, he put him in general charge of the restoration, with full authority to requisition both property and labor. Tate was a driver. Despite a crippling shortage of rails and spikes — not to mention the inevitable objections of planters to the impressment of such of their Negroes as had not gone off with Smith and Sherman — within twenty-six days he had the Mobile & Ohio back in operation, from Tupelo south to Mobile Bay, along with the Alabama & Mississippi, from Meridian to the Tombigbee. The Southern took longer, mainly because of administrative complications, but within another five weeks it too was open, all the way to the Pearl.

But that was later. At the time he made it, February 28, Sherman's pronouncement: "My movement cleared Mississippi at one swoop, and with the railroad thus destroyed the Confederacy cannot maintain an army save cavalry west of Tombigbee," seemed to him irrefutable. He was back in Vicksburg by then, having come on ahead of the infantry, which he left marking time in Canton, as he said afterwards, "with orders to remain till about the 3d of March" — he was still hoping Sooy Smith would turn up — "and then come into Vicksburg leisurely." Pleased by the added destruction of several miles of the Mississippi Central, north of Jackson — together with 19 locomotives, 28 cars, and 724 carwheels, which helped to ease his disappointment that Polk had managed to save the rolling stock on the other roads within his reach — he proudly announced: "Everything with my command was successful in the highest degree." That this was hardly an overstatement was evidenced by the anguished protests of his opponents and victims, soldiers and civilians, some of whom reported the damage at a larger figure than his own. Stephen Lee, for one, charged the raiders with "burning 10,000 bales of cotton and 2,000,000 bushels of corn and carrying off 8000 slaves, many mounted on stolen mules." He estimated the over-all loss at five million dollars, of which "three fourths was private property," and asked rhetorically: "Was this the warfare of the nineteenth century?" Sherman was not inclined to dispute the statistics, and he had already given his answer to Lee's question. This was indeed the warfare of the nineteenth century, at any rate as he intended to practice it, and he was not only proud of what had been accomplished by this first large-scale application of the methods that had aroused the South Carolinian's moral indignation; he was also looking forward to the time when he could apply those methods elsewhere, perhaps even in the angry young cavalryman's native state, where the provocation had begun.

First though would come Georgia; Mississippi had been something of a warm-up, a practice operation in this regard, just as perhaps Georgia in turn would be a warm-up for the Carolinas. In any case Sherman had composed at Vicksburg, by way of further preparation while waiting to set out across Mississippi, a letter to the assistant adjutant general of his army, most of whose members were in camps around Chattanooga waiting for him to return from his current excursion and lead them against Joe Johnston and Atlanta. Ostensibly addressed to Major R. M. Sawyer, the letter was in fact a warning to the civilians in his southward path, as well as a legalistic justification for military harshness, since it dealt primarily with his intention regarding "the treatment of inhabitants known or suspected to be hostile or 'secesh.'" His policy up to now, he said, had been to leave the question to local commanders of occupation forces, "but [I] am willing to give them the benefit of my acquired knowledge and experience," and though he admitted that it was "almost impossible to lay down rules" for their guidance in such matters, he proceeded to do precisely that, and more.

"In Europe, whence we derive our principles of war, as developed by their histories," he began, "wars are between kings or rulers, through hired armies, and not between peoples. These remain as it were neutral, and sell their produce to whatever army is in possession.... Therefore the rule was, and is, that wars are confined to the armies and should not visit the homes of families or private interests." Little or none of this applied in the present instance, however, any more than it had done in the case of the Irish insurrection against William and Mary, who dispossessed the rebels of their property, sent them forthwith into exile, and gave their lands to Scottish emigrants. The same could be done with justice here, Sherman declared, but he preferred to withhold such measures for a time, on grounds that the guilt was not entirely restricted to the guilty. "For my part," he explained, "I believe this war is the result of false political doctrine, for which we all as a people are responsible ... and I would give all a chance to reflect and when in error to recant. ... I am willing to bear in patience that political nonsense of slave rights, States rights, freedom of conscience, freedom of the press, and such other trash as have deluded the Southern people into war, anarchy, bloodshed, and the foulest crimes that have disgraced any time or any people." He would bear all this in patience, but only for a season; meanwhile he would have the occupation commanders "assemble the inhabitants and explain to them these plain, self-evident propositions, and tell them that it is now for them to say whether they and their children shall inherit the beautiful land which by the accident of nature had fallen to their share." After this, if they persisted in the error of their ways, would come the thunder. "If they want eternal war, well and good; we accept the issue, and will dispossess them and put our friends in their places." Moreover, the longer they delayed recanting, the sterner their fate would be. "Three years ago, by a little reflection and patience, they could have had a hundred years of peace and prosperity, but they preferred war; very well. Last year they could have saved their slaves, but now it is too late. All the powers of earth cannot return to them their slaves, any more than their dead grandfathers. Next year their lands will be taken; for in war we can take them, and rightfully, too, and in another year they may beg in vain for their lives." He warmed as he wrote, assuming the guise of an avenging angel — even the Archangel Michael — to touch on eschatology in the end. "To those who submit to the rightful law and authority, all gentleness and forbearance; but to the petulant and persistent secessionists, why, death is mercy, and the quicker he or she is disposed of the better. Satan and the rebellious saints of Heaven were allowed a continuous existence in hell merely to swell their just punishment. To such as would rebel against a Government so mild and just as ours was in peace, a punishment equal would not be unjust."

A copy went to his senator brother, with the request that it be printed for all to read, along and behind the opposing lines of battle. "It's publication would do no harm," he said, "except to turn the Richmond press against me as the prince of barbarians." Actually he was of the opinion that it would do much good, especially Southward, and he urged his adjutant to see that his views were presented to "some of the better people" of the region already occupied, with the suggestion that they pass them along to friends in whose direction he would be moving in the spring. "Read to them this letter," he wrote, "and let them use it so as to prepare them for my coming."

✘ 4 ✘

Sherman's notion of how the war could be won was definite enough, but whether it would be fought that way — with stepped-up harshness, to and through the finish — depended in no small measure on who would be directing it from the top. This was a presidential election year; the armies might have a new Commander in Chief before the advent of the victory which not even the ebullient Ohioan, in his days of highest feather, predicted would occur within the twelve-month span that lay between his return from Meridian, having demonstrated the effectiveness of his method, and the inauguration of the winner of the November contest at the polls. Moreover, the Republican convention was barely three months off, and though Lincoln had expressed a cautious willingness to stand for re-election — "A second term would be a great honor and a great labor," he had told Elihu Washburne in October, "which together, perhaps, I would not decline if tendered" — whether he would be renominated appeared doubtful. For one thing, recent tradition was against it; none of the other eight Presidents since Andrew Jackson had served beyond a single term. Besides, whatever his popularity with the people, the men who controlled the convention seemed practically unanimous in their conviction that a better candidate could be found. "Not a Senator can be named as favorable to Lincoln's renomination," the Detroit *Free Press* had reported, and the claim went uncontradicted. Nor was this opinion limited to his enemies. David Davis, who had managed his 1860 nomination, and who had been duly rewarded with a seat on the Supreme Court, declared in private: "The politicians in and out of Congress, it is believed, would put Mr Lincoln aside if they dared." Lyman Trumbull, an associate from early days and now a power in the Senate, believed however that it was not so much a question of daring as of tactics. Writing to a constituent back in Illinois, he presented the reasons behind this opposition and suggested that those who held them were merely biding their time between now and early June, when the delegates would convene in Baltimore. "The feeling for Mr Lincoln's re-election *seems* to be very general," he said, "but much of it I discover is only on the surface. You would be surprised, in talking with public men we meet here, to find how few, when you come to get at their real sentiment, are for Mr Lincoln's re-election. There is a distrust and fear that he is too undecided and inefficient to put down the rebellion. You need not be surprised if a reaction sets in before the nomination, in favor of some man supposed to possess more energy and less inclination to trust our brave boys in the hands and under the leadership of generals who have no heart in the war. The opposition to Mr L. may not show itself at all, but if it ever breaks out there will be more of it than now appears."

It broke out sooner than expected, though not from an unpredictable direction, the source of the explosion being Salmon Chase, or at any rate the men around or behind him, who saw in the adverse reaction to the overlenient Amnesty Proclamation an opportunity too fruitful to be neglected. Chase had been sobered by the Cabinet crisis of mid-December, fourteen months ago, but renewed ambition apparently caused him to forget his extreme discomfort at that time. In any case, in an attempt to influence various state conventions soon to be in session, a group of the Secretary's friends banded together and sent out in early February a "strictly private" letter afterwards known as the Pomeroy Circular. So called because it was issued over the signature of the group chairman, Senator Samuel C. Pomeroy of Kansas, a prominent Jacobin and old-line abolitionist, the document charged that "party machinery and official influence are being used to secure the perpetuation of the present Administration," asserted that "those who believe in the interests of the country and of freedom demand a change in favor of vigor and purity," and then went on to present five main points all delegates would do well to bear in mind. The first two were against Lincoln, whose re-election was not only "practically impossible" but also undesirable, since under him "the war may continue to languish" and "the cause of human liberty, and the dignity of the nation, suffer proportionately." The third point found "the 'one-term principle' absolutely essential to the certain safety of our republican institutions." The final two were devoted to Chase, who not only had "more of the qualities needed in a President during the next four years than are combined in any other candidate," but had developed, as well, "a popularity and strength ... unexpected even to his warmest admirers." Finally, each recipient was urged to "render efficient aid by exerting yourself at once to organize your section of the country" and to enter into correspondence with the undersigned chairman "for the purpose either of receiving or imparting information."

Lincoln was told of the "strictly private" circular as soon as it appeared. On February 6, Ward Lamon wrote from New York that a prominent banker there had received in his mail that morning, under the frank of an Ohio congressman, "a most scurrilous and abominable pamphlet about you, your administration, and the succession." Copies arrived from other friends on the lookout, but got no farther than Nicolay's desk; Lincoln would not read them. "I have determined to shut my eyes, so far as possible, to everything of that sort," he explained. "Mr Chase makes a good Secretary, and I shall keep him where he is. If he becomes President, all right. I hope we shall never have a worse man." He knew, of course, of the Ohioan's machinations, which were strengthened by the dispensation of some ten thousand jobs in his department, and he said of his activities as an inside critic, "I suppose he will, like the bluebottle fly, lay his eggs in every rotten spot he can find." But to some who advised that the "perfidious ingrate" be fired he replied: "I am entirely indifferent to his success or failure in these schemes, so long as he does his duty at the head of the Treasury Department." To others he maintained that "the Presidential grub" had much the same effect on the Secretary as a horsefly had on a balky plow horse; he got more work out of him when he was bit. Or perhaps it was even simpler than that. Perhaps Lincoln enjoyed watching the performance Chase gave. It was, after all, pretty much a repeat performance, and he already knew the outcome, agreeing beforehand with Welles, who predicted in his diary that the Pomeroy Circular would be "more dangerous in its recoil than its projectile." His adversaries had bided their time; now he was biding his. A Massachusetts congressman, returning from a visit to the White House at the height of this latest Chase-for-President boom, informed a colleague that Lincoln was only waiting for the Treasury chief to put himself a little more clearly in the wrong. "He thinks that Mr C. will sufficiently soon force the question. In the meantime I think he is wise in waiting till the pear is ripe."

The pear ripened over the weekend of Washington's Birthday. On Saturday, February 20, the *Constitutional Union* printed in full the text of the circular, and when it was picked up on Monday by the *National Intelligencer,* Chase could no longer pretend to be unaware of what his friends were doing in his behalf. Writing to Lincoln that same day, he declared however that he had "had no knowledge of the existence of this letter before I saw it in the *Union.*" Some weeks ago, he went on, "several gentlemen" had called on him "in connection with the approaching election of Chief Magistrate," and though he had not felt that he could forbid them to work as they chose, he had "told them distinctly that I could render them no help, except what might come incidentally from the faithful discharge of public duties, for these must have my whole time"; otherwise, he knew nothing of what had been done by these gentlemen. "I have thought this explanation due to you as well as to myself," he told Lincoln. "If there is anything in my action or position which in your judgment will prejudice the public interest in my charge, I beg you to say so. I do not wish to administer the Treasury Department one day without your entire confidence. For yourself," he continued, appending a sort of amiable tailpiece to his tentative resignation, "I cherish sincere respect and esteem; and, permit me to add, affection. Differences of opinion as to administrative action have not changed these sentiments; nor have they been changed by assaults upon me by persons who profess to spread representations of your views and policy. You are not responsible for acts not your own; nor will you hold me responsible except for what I do or say myself. Great numbers now desire your re-election. Should their wishes be fulfilled by the suffrages of the people, I hope to carry with me into private life the sentiments I now cherish, whole and unimpaired."

He received next day a one-sentence reply, as inconclusive as it was brief. "Yours of yesterday in relation to the paper issued by Senator Pomeroy was duly received; and I write this note merely to say I will answer a little more fully when I can find the leisure to do so. Yours truly, A. Lincoln."

Chase out would be considerably more formidable than Chase in; Lincoln had no intention of accepting a resignation which, by splitting the party, might well lose the Republicans the election, whoever the candidate was. He did wait six full days, however, before he found "the leisure" to compose his promised answer. This may have been done primarily to allow the Ohioan plenty of time to squirm, but it also afforded others a chance to contribute to the squirmer's discomfort by heating up the griddle. When Chase spoke of "assaults upon me by persons who profess to spread representations of your views," it was the Blairs he meant: specifically, Montgomery and Frank. Back in the fall, as principal speaker at a Maryland rally, the Postmaster General had referred to the Jacobins as "co-adjutors of Presidential schemers," making it clear that he had the Treasury head in mind as the chief schemer, and since then he had been castigating his fellow Cabinet member at practically every opportunity. Even so, he was not as harsh in this regard as his brother Frank, the soldier member of the family of whom it was said, "When the Blairs go in for a fight they go in for a funeral." Soon after his corps went into winter quarters near Chattanooga, Frank Blair came to Washington as a Missouri congressman. This had required the surrender of his commission as a major general, but Lincoln had promised to take care of that. He wanted Blair to stand for Speaker of the House, a post at which so stout a fighter could be of even more use to the Administration than on the field of battle, and he agreed that if this did not work out he would restore the commission and Blair could return to his duties as a corps commander under Sherman. But the plan fell through. By the time the Missourian reached the capital in early January, Indiana's Schuyler Colfax, strongly anti-Lincoln in persuasion, had been elected Speaker. Nevertheless, since his corps was still lying idle down in Tennessee, Blair took his seat and stayed on in Washington, alert for a chance to strike at the President's enemies and his own. A chance was not long in coming. On February 5, the day the Pomeroy Circular began to go out across the land, Blair rose in the House to speak in defense of the Administration's policies on amnesty and reconstruction, opposition to which he declared had been "concocted for purposes of defeating the renomination of Mr Lincoln" in order to open the way for "rival aspirants." Everyone knew it was Chase he meant, and three weeks later, on February 27 — four days into the six allowed for squirming — he made the charge specific, along with several others. Referring to the circular, he said of the candidate favored therein: "It is a matter of surprise that a man having the instincts of a gentleman should remain in the Cabinet after the disclosure of such an intrigue against the one to whom he owes his position. [However] I suppose the President is well content that he should stay; for every hour that he remains sinks him in the contempt of every honorable mind." Beyond this, Blair asserted that "a more profligate administration of the Treasury Department never existed under any government," and that investigation would show that "the whole Mississippi Valley is rank and fetid with the frauds and corruptions of its agents... some of [whom] I suppose employ themselves in distributing that 'strictly private' circular which came to light the other day."

Such charges hurt badly. Damage to Chase's reputation was damage to his soul, and though he thought of himself as a scrupulous administrator of the nation's funds, he knew quite well that for political reasons he had made agents of men who could by no means be said to measure up to his own high standards. In any case — perhaps out of pity, for the punishment was heavy — Lincoln ended at least a part of the Secretary's torment, two days later, by declining his resignation. "On consideration," he declared, "I find there is really very little to say. My knowledge of Mr. Pomeroy's letter having been made *public* came to me only the day you wrote; but I had, in spite of myself, known of its *existence* several days before. I have not yet read it, and I think I shall not. I was not shocked or surprised by the appearance of the letter, because I had had knowledge of Mr. Pomeroy's committee, and of secret issues which I supposed came from it, and of secret agents who I supposed were sent out by it, for several weeks." He was saying here that if he could know so much of what was going on behind his back, Chase must have known about it too, despite his fervent denial. However that might be, Lincoln continued, "I have known just as little of these doings as my friends have allowed me to know... and I assure you, as you have assured me, that no assault has been made upon you by my instigation or with my countenance." Then came the close, the answer he had promised: "Whether you shall remain at the head of the Treasury Department is a question which I will not allow myself to consider from any standpoint other than my judgment of the public service, and, in that view, I do not perceive occasion for a change."

Chase was both relieved and pained: relieved to learn that he would remain at his post, which the long wait had taught him to value anew by persuading him that he was about to lose it, and pained because, as he plaintively observed, "there was no response in [the President's] letter to the sentiments of respect and esteem which mine contained." All this was rather beside the original point, however. Welles's prediction as to the "recoil" of the Pomeroy maneuver had already been borne out, its principal effect having been to rally Lincoln's friends to his support. And of these, as events had shown, there were many. By the time of his belated reply to Chase on Leap Year Day, no less than fourteen states, either by formal action of their legislatures or by delegates in convention, had gone on record in favor of a second term for the man in office. Among them were New Hampshire, where the Secretary had been born, Rhode Island, where his new son-in-law was supposedly in political control, and finally — unkindest cut — Ohio. In fact, Chase was advised by men from his home state to disentangle himself from the embarrassment into which his ambition had led him, and this he did in a letter to a Buckeye supporter, requesting that "no further consideration be given my name." He also made it clear, however, that he was only asking this from a sense of duty to the cause, which must not be endangered, even though he was still convinced that "as President I could take care of the Treasury better with the help of a Secretary than I can as Secretary without the help of a President. But our Ohio folks don't want me enough." There was the rub; there was what had given him his quietus. "I no longer have any political side," he presently was saying, "save that of my country, and there are multitudes who like me care little for men but everything for measures."

The upshot of this pose of "honorable disinterestedness," as one of the newspapers reprinting the letter called it, was a general impression that he was merely awaiting a more favorable chance to get back in the running. A member of the Pomeroy group referred to the withdrawal as "a word of declination diplomatically spoken to rouse [our] flagging spirits," and David Davis likened its author to Mr Micawber waiting for something to "turn up." Chase had dreamed too long and too grandly for those who knew him to believe that he had stopped, even though it had been demonstrated conclusively, twice over, that his dreams would not come true. "Mr Chase will subside as a presidential candidate after the nomination is made, not before," the chairman of the Republican National Committee remarked, while the New York *Herald* ventured a comparison out of nature: "The Salmon is a queer fish, very wary, often appearing to avoid the bait just before gulping it down."

Whether Chase continued to dream and scheme made little difference now, though; Lincoln — with the Ohioan's unintentional assistance — had the nomination cinched. The election, however, was quite another matter. Despite the encouragement Republicans could draw from their successes at the polls in the past season, the outcome of the contest in November would depend even more on military than on political events of the next eight months, through spring and summer and into fall. For one thing, the fighting would be expensive both in money and blood, and the voters, as the ones who would do the paying and the bleeding, were unlikely to be satisfied with anything less than continuous victory at such prices. The past year had been highly satisfactory in this regard; Vicksburg and Missionary Ridge, even Gettysburg and Helena, were accomplishments clearly worth their cost. But the new year had started no better than the old year had ended. Sherman's destruction of Meridian could scarcely be said to offset Meade's unhappy stalemate at Mine Run or Seymour's abrupt defeat at Olustee, let alone Kilpatrick's frustration outside Richmond or the drubbing Sooy Smith had suffered at Okolona or the unprofitable demonstration Thomas had attempted against Dalton. A good part of the trouble seemed to proceed from mismanagement at the top, and the critics were likely to hold the top man responsible: especially in light of the fact that he had had a direct hand in a good proportion of these failures, all of which had been undertaken with his permission and some of which had been launched against the judgment of those below him on the military ladder. Now a reckoning time was coming, when the voters would have their say.

Congress, too, would have to face the voters: enough of it, at any rate, for defeat to cost the party now in power its comfortable majority, the loss of which would involve the surrender of committee chairmanships, the say-so in how and by whom the conflict would be pressed, easy access to much the largest pork barrel the nation had ever known, and finally the seizure and distribution of such spoils as would remain, two or three years from now, when the South was brought to its knees and placed at the disposal of the winners of the election this November. With so much at stake, it was no wonder the congressmen were jumpy at the prospect. Moreover, their nervousness was intensified by a presidential order, dated February 1, providing for the draft, on March 10, of "five hundred thousand men to serve for three years or during the war." This call for "500,000 more" — made necessary by the heavy losses in battle this past year, as well as by the pending expiration of the enlistments of those volunteers who had come forward, two and three years ago, with all the fervor Sumter and McClellan had aroused — was graphic evidence of what the campaigns about to open were expected to cost in blood and money, and as such it presented the electorate with a yardstick by which to measure the height and depth of victories and defeats. The former, then, had better be substantial if they were to count for much at the polls, and by the same token the latter had better be minor, especially if they were anything like the recent setbacks, which were so obviously the result of miscalculations at the top and for which the voters could take their revenge by the way they marked their ballots. With this danger in mind, the lawmakers had returned to considering the previously rejected bill providing for a revival of the grade of lieutenant general, which in turn would provide for a man at the top who, by a combination of professional training and proven ability in the field, could operate within a shrinking margin for error that was already too narrow for the amateur who had been in unrestricted control these past three years.

Although Congress had no power to name the officer to whom the promotion would go in the event the bill went through, it was understood that Grant was the only candidate for the honor. Besides, Lincoln would do the naming, and by now the Illinois general was as much his favorite as anyone's. Far from being resentful of what another in his place — Jefferson Davis, for example — would have considered an encroachment by the legislative branch, he welcomed the relief the bill proposed to afford him from a portion of his duties as Commander in Chief. Above all, he was prepared to welcome Grant, who had applied at Donelson, Vicksburg, and Chattanooga the victory formula Lincoln had been seeking all these years. Others had sought it, too, of course, and like him they now believed they had found it in the western commander. So many of them had done so by now, in fact, that they had provoked the only doubts he had about the general's fitness for the post. Like his friend McClernand, Lincoln was thoroughly aware that this war would produce a military hero who eventually would take up residence in the White House, and Grant's appeal in this respect had already reached the stage at which he was being wooed by prominent members of both political parties. They knew a winner when they saw one, and so did Lincoln; and that was the trouble. Involved as he was at the time in disposing of Chase, he was not anxious to promote the interests of a more formidable rival, which was precisely what he would be doing if he brought Grant to Washington as general-in-chief.

Nor was that the only drawback. There might be another even more disqualifying. "When the Presidential grub once gets in a man, it hides well," Lincoln had said of himself, and he thought this might apply as well to Grant, whose generalship would scarcely be improved by the distractive gnawing of the grub. However, when he inquired in that direction about such political aspirations, he was told the general had said in January that he not only was not a candidate for any office, but that as a soldier he believed he had no right to discuss politics at all. Pressed further, he relented so far as to add that, once the war was over, he might indeed run for mayor of Galena — so that, if elected, he could have the sidewalk put in order between his house and the railroad station. Lincoln could appreciate the humor in this (though not the unconscious irony which others would perceive a few years later, when this view of the primary use of political office would be defined as "Grantism") but he was not entirely satisfied. For one thing, that had been several weeks ago, before the would-be kingmakers had begun to fawn on Grant in earnest. Adulation might have turned his head. So Lincoln called in a friend of Grant's and asked him point-blank if the general wanted to be President. The man not only denied this; he produced a letter in which Grant said flatly that he had no political interests whatever. No doubt the statement was similar to one he made about this time in a letter to another friend, in which he declared: "My only desire will be, as it has been, to whip out rebellion in the shortest way possible, and to retain as high a position in the army afterwards as the Administration then in power may think me suitable for." Clearly, if this had been honestly said, it had not been said by a man who nurtured political ambitions. Lincoln's doubts were allayed. If Congress opened the way by passing the bill, he would see that the promotion went to the general for whom it was obviously intended.

Relief in any form would be most welcome, for the strain of frustration these past three years had brought him all too often to the verge of exhaustion and absolute despair. There was, after all, a limit to how many Fredericksburgs and Chancellorsvilles, how many Gettysburgs and Chickamaugas, even how many Olustees and Okolonas a man could survive. Mostly, though, the strain resulted from the difficulty of measuring up to private standards which he defined for a visitor whose petition he turned down, saying: "I desire to so conduct the affairs of this Administration that if, at the end, when I come to lay down the reins of power, I have lost every other friend on earth, I shall at least have one friend left, and that friend shall be deep down inside of me." Public critics he could abide or ignore, even those who called him clod or tyrant, clown or monster — "What's the harm in letting him have his fling?" he remarked of one of the worst of these; "If he did not pitch into me, he would into some poor fellow he might hurt" — but the critic lodged in his own conscience was not so easily lived with or dismissed. Some men appeared to have little trouble muffling that self-critic: not Lincoln, who saw himself "chained here in this Mecca of office-seekers," like Prometheus to his rock, a victim of his own dark-souled nature. "You flaxen men with broad faces are born with cheer, and don't know a cloud from a star," he once told a caller who fit this description; "I am of another temperament." It sometimes seemed to him, moreover, that each recovery from gloom was made at the cost of future resiliency. "Nothing touches the tired spot," he had confessed the year before, and lately he had come back to this expression. Returning from a horseback ride that had seemed to lift his spirits, he was urged by a companion to find more time for rest and relaxation. "Rest?" he said. He shook his head, as if the word was unfamiliar. "I don't know.... I suppose it is good for the body. But the tired part is *inside*, out of reach."

If Grant was the man who could bring this inner weariness some measure of relief, Lincoln was not only willing to call him East to try his hand; he intended to wait no longer, before he did so, than the time required by Congress to pass the necessary legislation.

★ ★ ★

Opposing the Federal war of conquest (for, rebellion or revolution, that was what it would have to come to if the North was going to win) the Confederacy was fighting for survival. This had been, and would continue to be, Davis's principal advantage over his opponent in their respective capacities as leaders of their two nations: that he did not have to persuade his people of the reality of a threat which had been only too apparent ever since the first blue-clad soldier crossed the Potomac, whereas Lincoln was obliged to invoke a danger that was primarily theoretic. In the event that the Union broke in two, democracy might or might not "perish from the earth," but there could be no doubt at all — even before Sherman created, by way of a preview, his recent "swath of desolation" across Mississippi's midriff — about what would happen to the South if its bid for independence failed. However, this was only one face of a coin whose down side bore the inscription *States Rights*. Flip the coin and the advantage passed to Lincoln.

By suspending *habeas corpus*, or by ignoring at will such writs as the courts issued, the northern President kept his left hand free to deal as harshly as he pleased with those who sought to stir up trouble in his rear. It was otherwise with Davis. Denied this resource except in such drastic instances as the insurrection two years ago in East Tennessee, he had to meet this kind of trouble with that hand fettered. Often he had claimed this disadvantage as a virtue, referring by contrast to the North as a land where citizens were imprisoned "in utter defiance of all rights guaranteed by the institutions under which they live." Now though, with the approach of the fourth spring of the war, obstruction and defeatism had swollen to such proportions that conscription could scarcely be enforced or outright traitors prosecuted, so ready were hostile judges to issue writs that kept them beyond the reach of the authorities. Davis was obliged to request of Congress that it permit him to follow procedures he had scorned. "It has been our cherished hope," he declared in a special message on February 3, "that when the great struggle in which we are engaged was past we might exhibit to the world the proud spectacle of a people ... achieving their liberty and independence, after the bloodiest war of modern times, without a single sacrifice of civil right to military necessity. But it can no longer be doubted that the zeal with which the people sprang to arms at the beginning of the contest has, in some parts of the Confederacy, been impaired by the long continuance and magnitude of the struggle.... Discontent, disaffection, and disloyalty are manifested among those who, through the sacrifices of others, have enjoyed quiet and safety at home. Public meetings have been held, in some of which a treasonable design is masked by a pretense of devotion to State sovereignty, and in others is openly avowed.... Secret leagues and associations are being formed. In certain localities, men of no mean position do not hesitate to avow their hostility to our cause and their advocacy of peace on the terms of submission." All this was painful to admit, even in secret session, but Davis foresaw still greater problems unless the trend was checked. "Disappointment and despondency will displace the buoyant fortitude which animates [our brave soldiers] now. Desertion, already a frightful evil, will become the order of the day." He knew how sacred to his hearers the writ was, and he assured them that he would not abuse the license he was asking them to grant him. "Loyal citizens will not feel the danger, and the disloyal must be made to fear it. The very existence of extraordinary powers often renders their exercise unnecessary." In any case, he asserted in conclusion, "to temporize with disloyalty in the midst of war is but to quicken it to the growth of treason. I therefore respectfully recommend that the privilege of the writ of *habeas corpus* be suspended."

After twelve days of acrimonious debate — highlighted by an impassioned protest from the Vice President, who sent word from Georgia that if Davis was given the power he sought, "constitutional liberty will go down, never to rise again on this continent" — Congress agreed, though with profound misgivings, to a six-month suspension of the writ. However, the fight did not end there by any means. Stephens and his cohorts merely fell back to prepared positions, ranged in depth along the borders of their several sovereign states, and there continued their resistance under the banner of States Rights. "Georgians, behold your chains!" an Athens newspaper exhorted in an editorial printed alongside the newly passed regulations, which were appropriately framed in mourning borders. "Freemen of a once proud and happy country, contemplate the last act which rivets your bonds and binds you hand and foot, at the mercy of an unlimited military authority." An Alabama editor demanded the names of those congressmen "who, in secret conclave, obsequiously laid the liberties of this country at the feet of the President," so that they could be defeated if they had the gall to stand for re-election. Henry Foote, having long since warned that he "would call upon the people to rise, sword in hand, to put down the domestic tyrant who thus sought to invade their rights," proceeded to do just that. Nor was this defiance limited to words. Under the leadership of such men, Mississippi and Georgia passed flaming resolutions against the act; Louisiana presently did so, too, and North Carolina soon had a law on its books nullifying the action of the central government. Not even these modifications, crippling as they were to the purpose for which the writ had been suspended, allayed the fears of some that the rights of the states were about to be lost in "consolidation." If such a catastrophe ever came to pass, a Virginian declared, "it would be a kind boon in an overruling Providence to sweep from the earth the soil, along with the people. Better to be a wilderness of waste, than a lasting monument of lost liberty."

A wilderness of waste was what was all too likely to result from this nonrecognition of the fact that the South's whole hope for independence was held up by the bayonets of her soldiers, who in turn required the support of a strong central government if they were to be properly employed — or even, for that matter, clothed and fed — in a years-long conflict so costly in blood and money, at the stage it now had reached, that its demands could only be met by the enactment and rigid enforcement of laws which did in fact, as those who opposed them charged, involve the surrender of basic "rights" hitherto reserved to the states and the individual. Yet this was the one sacrifice the "impossiblists," who valued their rights above their chance at national independence, could not make. "Away with the idea of getting independence first, and looking after liberty afterwards," Stephens had said. "Our liberties, once lost, may be lost forever." "Why, sir," a Georgia congressman exclaimed, "this is a war for the Constitution! It is a *constitutional* war." It was also, and first, a war for survival; but the ultraconservatives, including the fire-eaters who had done so much to bring it on, had been using the weapon of States Rights too long and with too much success, when they were members of the Union, to discard it now that they had seceded. They simply would rather die than drop that cudgel, even when there was no one to use it on but their own people and nothing to strike at except the solidarity that was their one hope for victory over an adversary whose reserves of men and wealth were practically limitless. It was in this inflexibility that the bill came due for having launched a conservative revolution, and apparently it was necessarily so, even though their anomalous devotion to an untimely creed amounted to an irresistible death-wish. But that was precisely their pride. They had inherited it and they would hand it down, inviolate, to the latest generation; or they would pray God "to sweep from the earth the soil, along with the people."

No more than a casual glance at the map sufficed to show the gravity of the military situation they would not relax their civil vigilance to face. Shaded, the Federal gains of the past two years resembled the broad shadow of a bird suspended in flight above the Mississippi Valley, its head hung over Missouri, its tail spread down past New Orleans, and its wings extended from Chesapeake Bay to Texas. What shape the pres-

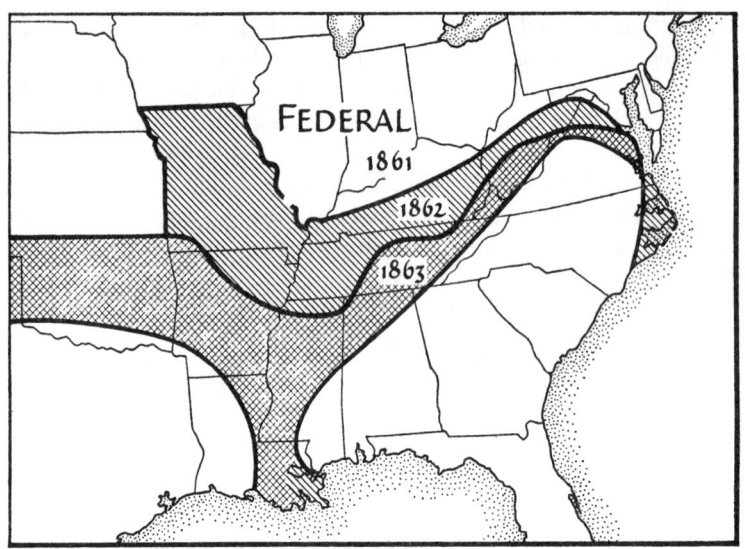

ent year would give this shadow was far from clear to those who lived in its penumbra, but they saw clearly enough that the creature who cast it could not be driven back into the land from which it had emerged; at any rate, not to stay there. R. E. Lee, after two expensive attempts to do just that, admitted as much to Davis in early February. "We are not in a condition, and never have been, in my opinion, to invade the enemy's country with a prospect of permanent benefit," he wrote, although he added that he hoped, by means of a show of force in East Tennessee or Virginia, to "alarm and embarrass him to some extent, and thus prevent his undertaking anything of magnitude against us."

Davis agreed that the South was limited by necessity to the strategic defensive. Indeed, that had been his policy from the start, pursued in the belief that Europe would intervene if the struggle could be protracted. The difference now lay in the object of such protraction. Foreign intervention was obviously never going to come, but he still hoped for intervention of another kind. In the North, a presidential election would be held in November, and he hoped for intervention by a majority of the voters, who then would have their chance to end the bloodshed by replacing Lincoln with a man who stood for peace. Peace, no matter whether it was achieved in the North or the South, in the field or at the polls, meant victory on the terms the Confederate leader had announced at the outset, saying, "All we ask is to be let alone." In the light of this possibility, the South's task was to add to the war weariness of the North; which meant, above all, that the enemy was to be allowed no more spirit-lifting triumphs — especially none like Vicksburg or Missionary Ridge, which had set all the church bells ringing beyond the Potomac and the Ohio — and that whatever was lost, under pressure of the odds, must not only be minor in value, but must also be paid for in casualties so heavy that the gain would be clearly disproportionate to the cost, particularly in the judgment of those who would be casting their ballots in November.

On the face of it — by contrast, that is, with the two preceding years, each of which had included the added burden of launching an invasion that had failed — this did not appear too difficult a task. In the past calendar year, moreover, while the Federal over-all strength was declining from 918,211 to 860,737 men, that of the Confederates increased from 446,622 to 463,181. This was not only the largest number of men the South had had under arms since the war began; it was also nearly 100,000 more than she had had two years ago, on the eve of her greatest triumphs. However, such encouragement as Davis might have derived from a comparison of these New Year's figures, showing the North-South odds reduced to less than two to one, was short-lived. One month later, Lincoln issued his call for "500,000 more."

That was better than ten times the number Lee had on the Rapidan, covering Richmond, or Johnston had around Dalton, covering Atlanta, and since the loss of either of these cities, in addition to being a strategic disaster for the South, would provide the North with a triumph that would be likely to win Lincoln the election, Davis was faced at once with the problem of how to match this call with one of his own. But the hard truth was that nothing like half that many troops — the number required if the current odds were not to be lengthened intolerably for the savage fighting that would open in the spring — could be raised under the present conscription laws, even though these had been strengthened in December by the passage of legislation that modified exemptions, put an end to the hiring of substitutes, and provided for the replacement of able-bodied men, in noncombatant jobs, with veterans who had been incapacitated by wounds or civilians who previously had been passed over for reasons of health. The bottom of the manpower barrel was not only in sight; it had been scraped practically clean to provide the army with every available male within the conscription age-range of eighteen to forty-five. One possibility, unpleasant to contemplate since it would expose the government more than ever to the charge that it was "robbing the cradle and the grave," would be to extend the range in either or both directions. Another possibility, far more fruitful, was suggested by Pat Cleburne; but it was worse than unpleasant, it was unthinkable. In early January the Irish-born former Helena lawyer prepared and read to his fellow generals in the Army of Tennessee a paper in which he examined the sinking fortunes of the Confederacy and proposed to deal simultaneously with what he conceived to be the two main problems blocking the path to independence: the manpower shortage, which was growing worse with every victory or defeat, and slavery, which he saw as a millstone the nation could no longer afford to carry in its effort to stay afloat on the sea of war. In brief, Cleburne's proposal was that the South emancipate its Negroes — thus making a virtue of necessity, since in his opinion slavery was doomed anyhow — and enlist them in its armies. This would "change the race from a dreaded weakness to a [source] of strength," he declared, and added: "We can do this more effectually than the North can now do, for we can give the Negro not only his own freedom, but that of his wife and child, and can secure it to him in his old home." Moreover, he said, such an action "would remove forever all selfish taint from our cause and place independence above every question of property. The very magnitude of the sacrifice itself, such as no nation has ever voluntarily made before, would appall our enemies... and fill our hearts with a pride and singleness of purpose which would clothe us with new strength in battle."

Recovering presently from the shock into which the foreign-born general's views had thrown them, the corps and division commanders were unanimous in their condemnation of the proposal, which they saw as a threat to everything they held dear. "I will not attempt to describe my feelings on being confronted by a project so startling in its character," one wrote in confidence to a friend. He labeled the paper a "monstrous proposition... revolting to Southern sentiment, Southern pride, and Southern honor," and predicted that "if this thing is once openly proposed to the army the total disintegration of that army will follow in a fortnight." Advised by Johnston and the others to proceed no further with the matter, Cleburne did not insist that the paper be forwarded, but another general considered it so "incendiary" in character that he took the trouble to get a copy and send it on to Richmond. There the reaction was much the same, apparently, as the one it had provoked in Dalton. Johnston received, before the month was out, a letter from the Secretary of War, expressing "the earnest conviction of the President that the dissemination or even promulgation of such opinions under the present circumstances of the Confederacy, whether in the army or among the people, can be productive only of discouragement, distraction, and dissension." The army commander was instructed to see to "the suppression, not only of the memorial itself, but likewise of all discussion and controversy respecting or growing out of it." Johnston replied that Cleburne, having observed the manner in which it was received, had already "put away his paper," and that he himself had had "no reason since to suppose that it made any impression." In point of fact, the suppression Richmond called for was so effective that nothing further was heard of the document for more than thirty years, when it finally turned up among the posthumous papers of a staff officer. One possible effect it had, however, and that was on Cleburne himself, or in any case on his career. Although Seddon had assured Johnston that "no doubt or mistrust is for a moment entertained of the patriotic intents of the gallant author of the memorial," and though the Arkansan was considered by many to be the best division commander in either army, South or North, he was never assigned any larger duties than those he had at the time he proposed to emancipate the slaves of the South and enlist them in her struggle for independence.

Davis had not been as shocked by the proposal as Seddon's letter seemed to indicate. For one thing, he agreed with the underlying premise that slavery was doomed, no matter who won or lost the war, and had said as much to his wife. What alarmed him was the reaction, the "distraction and dissension," that would follow the release of what one of its hearers had called "this monstrous proposition." Knowing, as he did, how much more violent than the generals the politicians would be in their denunciation of such views — particularly the large slaveholders among them, such as Howell Cobb, who said flatly: "If slaves will make good soldiers, our whole theory of slavery is wrong" — he foresaw that the result would be calamitous in its effect on the fortunes of the Confederacy, which would be so torn internally by any discussion of the issue that, even though the army could be doubled in size by adoption of the plan, there would be nothing left for that army to defend but discord. Even so, Davis did not completely reject the notion. He kept it — much as Lincoln had kept the Emancipation Proclamation — as an ace in the hole, to be played if all else failed.

Meantime he still was faced with the necessity for matching, at least to some degree, his adversary's call for more additional troops than there were at present in all the southern armies. Left with the alternative of extending conscription, he moved to do so in a message to Congress suggesting 1) that all industrial exemptions be abolished and 2) that the upper and lower age-range limits be raised and reduced, respectively, to fifty and seventeen. The first of these two suggestions kicked up the greater furor. Newspaper editors, who feared (groundlessly, as it turned out) that they would lose their printers if the law was strengthened to this extent, protested that freedom of the press was threatened. For others, the fear was more general. A Virginia congressman, for example, asserted that such legislation would "clothe the President with the powers of an autocrat" and invest him with "prerogatives before which those of Napoleon sink into insignificance," while Foote rose up again in his wrath to declare that "Others may vote to extend this man's power for mischief; I hold in contempt him and his whole tribe of servitors and minions." There were, however, enough of the "tribe" — or, in any case, enough of Foote's colleagues of all persuasions who saw the need for keeping the army up to a strength that would enable it to challenge the blue host that would be advancing with the spring — for the proposed measure to be adopted on February 17, the day Congress adjourned. Word went out at once to the conscription agents of the enlargement of the harvest they would be gleaning. No drawing of lots, no "wheels of fortune," such as were used in the North to select candidates for induction, were required in the South. From this time forward, it was simply the task of the agents to enroll or exempt every white male in the Confederacy between the ages of seventeen and fifty.

Davis's reaction to this granting of his request was mixed. Pleased though he was to have the measure passed, and though he himself had asked for what had been given, he was saddened by the widening of the age-range: not by the raising of the upper limit, which brought it within five years of his own age, but by the reduction of the lower limit, which seemed to him a spending of future hopes. The old and the middle-aged could be spared. The young were another matter. The South would have great need, in the years ahead, of all the talent she could muster — as much, perhaps, if she lost the war, as if she won it — yet there was no telling how much of that talent, still undeveloped at seventeen, would be destroyed and left behind, packed into shallow burial trenches on the fields of battles still unfought. It grieved him that the mill of war, as he remarked, was about to "grind the seed corn of the nation."

While the young and the old were thus being gathered in camps of instruction, where they would be converted into material fit for use in chinking what he once had called "our wall of living breasts," Davis gave his attention to strengthening and replacing the men who would lead them. The appointment in early January of George Davis of North Carolina to succeed Attorney General Watts, who had left Richmond the month before to be inaugurated as governor of Alabama, marked the first change in the Cabinet since Seddon took over the War Department, more than a year ago. Little attention was paid to this, for the post entailed few duties; but the same could not be said of two changes that followed, for they were military, and anything that involved the army was always of consuming interest. Before adjourning, Congress had authorized the President to appoint a sixth full general, thus to allow a freer hand to the commander of the Transmississippi, cut off as he was from either the direction or assistance of the central government. Davis's prompt award of the promotion to Kirby Smith, for whom of course it had been intended, was applauded by everyone, in or out of the army, except Longstreet, whose name headed the list of lieutenant generals, on which Smith's had stood second. "A soldier's honor is his all," Old Peter afterwards protested, "and of that they would rob him and degrade him in the eyes of his troops." Piqued at having thus been overleaped — and unhappy as he was anyhow, because of his late repulse at Knoxville and the disaffection that had spread through his corps in its mountainous camps around Greeneville, seventy miles to the east — his first reaction was that "the occasion seemed to demand resignation." But on second thought he decided that this "would have been unsoldierly conduct. Dispassionate judgment suggested, as the proper rounding of the soldier's life, to stay and go down with faithful comrades of long and arduous service."

Painful though the burning was in Longstreet's ample bosom, it was no more than a pinpoint gleam compared to the fires of resentment lighted by the announcement, a few days later, of the second military change. On February 22, the second anniversary of his inauguration as head of the permanent government, Davis summoned Lee to the capital for another conference. There were matters of strategy to be discussed, and something else as well. The Virginian's former post as advisor to the Commander in Chief had been vacant for more than twenty months; now Davis proposed to name Bragg as his successor. This was certain to surprise and dismay a great many people who saw the North Carolinian as the author of most of their present woes, but Davis believed that Bragg's undeniable shortcomings as a field commander — particularly his tendency to convert drawn battles into defeats by retreating, and victories into stalemates by failing to pursue — were not disqualifications for service in an advisory capacity; whereas his equally undeniable virtues, as an administrator and a strategist — his northward march into Kentucky, for example, undertaken on his own initiative at a time of deepest gloom, had reversed the whole course of the war in the western theater, and he had also proved himself (all too often, some would say) a master in the art of conducting tactical withdrawals — would be of great value to the country. Lee agreed, and the appointment was announced two days later, on February 24: "General Braxton Bragg is assigned to duty at the seat of government, and, under the direction of the President, is charged with the conduct of the military operations in the armies of the Confederacy."

Surprise and dismay, private and public, were indeed the reactions to the terrible-tempered general's elevation, coming as it did only one day short of three months since his rout at Missionary Ridge. "No doubt Bragg can give the President valuable counsel," a War Department diarist observed, but in his opinion Davis — whom he described as being "naturally a little oppugnant" — derived "a secret satisfaction in triumphing thus over popular sentiment, which just at this time is much averse to General Bragg." The sharpest attacks, as might have been expected, were launched by the editors of the Richmond *Whig* and the *Examiner*. Both employed irony in their comments, ignoring the advisory nature of Bragg's assignment by pretending to believe that Davis had given his pet general direct command over Lee and Johnston. "When a man fails in an inferior position," the *Whig* declared, "it is natural and charitable to conclude that the failure is due to the inadequacy of the task to his capabilities, and wise to give him a larger sphere for the proper exertion of his abilities." Pollard of the *Examiner* struck with a heavier hand, though his pen was no less sharp. "The judicious and opportune appointment of General Bragg to the post of commander-in-chief of the Confederate armies will be appreciated," he noted wryly, "as an illustration of that strong common sense which forms the basis of the President's character." He managed to sustain this tone for half a column, then dropped it in midsentence: "This happy announcement should enliven the confidence and enthusiasm reviving among the people like a bucket of water poured on a newly kindled grate."

Davis went his way, as he had done from the beginning. "If we succeed we shall hear nothing of these malcontents," he had told his wife three years ago in Montgomery. "If we do not, then I shall be held accountable by friends as well as foes. I will do my best." That was as much his guiding principle now as ever. He believed that Bragg would serve him and the country well in this new assignment, and so far as he was concerned the decision as to whether to use him ended there. "Opposition in any form can only disturb me inasmuch as it may endanger the public welfare," he had said. For all his aristocratic bearing and his apparent indifference to the barbs flung at him by men like Foote and Pollard, which gave rise to the persistent myth that he was deficient in feeling, he trusted the people far more than he did the politicians and journalists who catered to their weaknesses and fears, and he knew only too well the hardness of their lot in this season of lengthening death lists and spiraling inflation. Ten Confederate dollars would buy a yard of calico or a pound of coffee; bacon was $3.50 a pound, butter $4; eggs were $2 a dozen, chickens $6 a pair. Such prices made for meager living, particularly for city dwellers who had no vegetable gardens to tend or harvest. But even these were fortunate, so far at least as food was concerned, in comparison with the soldiers. The daily ration in the Army of Northern Virginia this winter was four ounces of bacon or salt pork and one pint of unbolted cornmeal, and though a private was free to scrounge what he could in his off hours, including wild onions and dandelion greens, his pay of $11 a month would not go far toward the purchase of supplements, even when they were available, which was seldom. Still, there were those who seemed to make out well enough from time to time: as a hungry infantryman, out on a greens hunt, discovered one day when he came upon a group of commissary officers enjoying an al fresco luncheon in the shade of a clump of trees. He approached the fence surrounding the grove, put his head through the palings, and gazed admiringly at the spread of food. "I say, misters," he called to the diners at last, "did any of you ever hearn tell of the battle of Chance'lorsville?"

This irrepressibility, which sustained him in adversity, this overriding sense of the ridiculous, uncramped even by the pangs of hunger, was as much a part of what made the Confederate soldier "terrible in battle" as was the high-throated yell he gave when he went into a charge or the derisive glee with which he tended to receive one, anticipating a yield of well-shod corpses. Davis counted heavily on this spirit to insure the survival of the armies and the nation through the harder times he knew would begin when the present "mud truce" ended. He was too much a military realist not to take into account the lengthening odds, but he included the imponderables in his calculations. To have done otherwise would have been to admit defeat before it came; which was not at all his way. "I cultivate hope and patience," he said, "and trust to the blunders of our enemy and the gallantry of our troops for ultimate success."

★ ★ ★

In the North, as spring drew nearer and some perspective was afforded for a backward look at the season approaching its end, there was the feeling that such minor reverses as Olustee and Okolona, disappointing though they had been at the time, were no true detractions from the significant victories scored at the outset at Rappahannock Bridge and Chattanooga. These were the pattern-setters, the more valid indications of what was to come when winter relaxed its grip and large-scale fighting was resumed. Along with this, there was also the growing belief that the nation had found in Lincoln, despite his occasional military errors, the leader it needed to see it through what remained of its fiery trial. "The President is a man of convictions," *Harper's Weekly* had declared more than a year ago, combining these two impressions. "He has certain profound persuasions and a very clear purpose. He knows what the war sprang from, and upon what ground a permanent peace can be reared. He is cautious, cool, judicial. [While] he knows that great revolutions do not go backward, he is aware that when certain great steps in their prosecution are once taken, there will be loud outcries and apprehension. But the ninth wave touches the point to which the whole sea will presently rise, although the next wave, and the next, should seem to show a falling off."

What *Harper's* had had in mind at the time was the Emancipation Proclamation, but people rereading this now could see that Missionary Ridge had been just such a ninth wave, lapping far up the military shingle, and though "the next wave, and the next," had shown a falling off, the tide would soon be at the full. Or anyhow they could believe they saw this, and they reacted accordingly. During the current interim of comparative inaction, the home-front war had taken on what would be known in the following decade as a Chautauqua aspect, a revival of the waning lyceum movement, which combined the qualities of the camp meeting and the county fair, yet added a sophistication those old-time activities had lacked. They assembled in churches, halls, and theaters to enjoy in mass the heady atmosphere of pending victory. Primarily, such gatherings were militant in tone — meaning abolitionist, for the antislavery element had always been the militant wing of the party now in power — with the result that those who attended could feel that they were being strengthened and uplifted at the same time they were being entertained. There was, for example, the Hutchinson family: singers who could electrify an audience with their rendition of Whittier's "Hymn of Liberty," sung to the tune of Luther's *Ein' feste Burg ist unser Gott.*

The thought might be muddled, the rhymes atrocious, but the sweetness of the singers' voice and the fervor of their delivery gave the words a power that swept the hearers along as part of the broad surge toward that same freedom for which blue-clad soldiers were giving their lives, beyond the roll of the horizon:

> *What gives the wheat-field blades of steel?*
> *What points the rebel cannon?*
> *What sets the roaring rabble's heel*
> *On the old star-spangled pennon?*
> *What breaks the oath*
> *Of the men o' the South?*
> *What whets the knife*
> *For the Union's life?*
> *Hark to the answer: Slavery!*

Or there was the Boston lecturer Wendell Phillips, who assured a New York audience of its moral superiority over a foe whose only role in life was to block the march of progress. He pictured the young man of the South, "melted in sensuality, whose face was never lighted up by a purpose since his mother looked into his cradle," and declared that for such men "War is gain. They go out of it, and they sink down." Whipped, they would return "to barrooms, to corner groceries, to chopping straw and calling it politics. [Laughter.] You might think they would go back to their professions. They never had any. You might think they would go back to the mechanic arts. They don't know how to open a jackknife. [Great merriment.] There is nowhere for them to go, unless we send them half a million of emancipated blacks to teach them how to plant cotton." His solution to the problem of how to keep the beaten South from relapsing "into a state of society more cruel than war — whose characteristics are private assassination, burning, stabbing, shooting, poisoning" — lifted the North's grim efforts to the height of a crusade: "We have not only an army to conquer. We have a state of mind to annihilate."

Phillips could always fill a hall, but the star attraction this season, all agreed, was the girl orator Anna E. Dickinson, who had begun her career on the eve of her twentieth birthday, when she lost her job at the mint in her native Philadelphia for accusing McClellan of treason at Ball's Bluff. Since then, she had come far, until now she was hailed alternately as the Joan of Arc and the Portia of the Union. Whether she spoke at the Academy of Music in her home city, at New York's Cooper Union, or at the Music Hall in Boston, the house was certain to be packed with those who came to marvel at the contrast between her virginal appearance — "her features well chiseled, her forehead and upper lip of the Greek proportion, her nostrils thin" — and the "torrent of burning, scathing, lightning eloquence," which she released in what the same reviewer called "wonderfully lengthened sentences uttered without break or pause." Hearing Anna was a dramatic experience not easily forgotten, though what you brought away with you was not so much a remembrance of what she had said as it was of the manner in which she had said it: which was how she affected Henry James, apparently, when he came to portray her, more than twenty years later, as Verena Tarrant. Her hatred of Southerners, especially Jefferson Davis, whom she compared to a hyena, was not so all-consuming that none was left for northern Democrats, who were without exception traitors to the cause of human freedom — as, indeed, were all who were not of the most radical persuasion, including such Republicans as Seward, "the Fox of the White House." She loved applause; it thrilled her, and her style became more forward as her listeners responded; so that her addresses were in a sense a form of intercourse, an exchange of emotions, back and forth across the footlights.

Quite different, but curious too in her effect on those who came to hear and see her, was another platform artist, the former slave Sojourner Truth. Tall and gaunt, utterly black, and close to eighty years of age, she made her appearances in a voluminous, floor-length, long-sleeved dress, a crocheted shawl, and the calico turban or headrag that was practically a badge of office for house servants in the South, particularly children's nurses; which was what she had been, before she won her freedom and came North. Battle Creek was now her home, and she journeyed not only through Michigan, but also through Illinois and Indiana and Ohio, including the Copperhead regions of those states, to plead for the extension of freedom to all her race, north as well as south of the Proclamation line. She spoke in a deep, musical voice, with natural grace and simple dignity, and vended as a side line, to help cover her travel expenses, photographs of herself in her speaking costume; "selling the shadow to sustain the substance," she explained. Her most valued possession, despite her illiteracy, was an autograph book containing the signatures of famous men and women she encountered along her way, one of whom would presently be the Great Emancipator himself. "For Aunty Sojourner Truth, A. Lincoln," he wrote, and she gave him one of her photographs, remarking that she sold them for her livelihood, "but this one is for you, without money and without price." She was much admired, though for the most part as an exotic, and was generally welcome wherever she went, although not always. Once in an Indiana town, for instance, when she was introduced to deliver an antislavery address to a large audience, a local Copperhead rose to repeat the rumor that she was a man, disguised in women's clothes, and to suggest that she permit a committee of ladies to examine her in private. She answered the challenge, then and there, by unfastening her dress and showing the crowd her shrunken, hound's-ear breasts. These had fed many black children, she said, but still more white children had nursed at them. By now the Copperheads — who had come to watch her, or his, exposure as a fraud — were filing out of the auditorium, a look of disgust on their faces, and Sojourner Truth shook her breasts at one of them, inquiring after him in her low contralto: "You want to suck?"

Wendell Phillips, Anna Dickinson, Sojourner Truth were only three among the many who were riding the wave of confidence that the worst was over, that the war could have but one ending now, and that it would come as soon as the South could be made to see what already was apparent in the North. Moreover, there had come with this belief a lessening of discord, not only among the people, but also in the conduct of affairs in Washington. "Never since I have been in public life has there been so little excitement in Congress," Sumner wrote on New Year's Day to a friend in England. "The way seems, at last, open. Nobody doubts the result. The assurance of the future gives calmness." This did not mean that the legislators were willing to take chances. Knowing as they did that the public's blame for any failure would be in ratio to the height of its expectations, they were in fact less willing to take chances than they had been at any time before. And it was for this reason that the bill to revive the grade of lieutenant general had itself been revived: to reduce the likelihood of military blunders at the top. "Give us, Sir, a live general!" a Michigan senator exclaimed in the course of the debate. He meant by this a man who would follow a straight path to victory, "and not let us be dragging along under influences such as have presided over the Army of the Potomac for these last many tedious and weary months; an army oscillating alternately between the Rappahannock and the Potomac, defeated today and hardly successful tomorrow, with its commanders changed almost as frequently as the moon changes its face. Sir, for one I am tired of this, and I tell [the] senators here that the country is getting weary of it."

Some proponents were in favor of naming Grant specifically in the bill, while others believed that this would be setting a dangerous precedent. Besides, Fessenden of Maine rose to ask, to whom could the promotion go if not to Grant? and then went on to point out that the honor would be greater if no name was mentioned, since to do so would be to imply that there had been a choice: "When the President says to us, as he will say unquestionably, 'I consider that General Ulysses S. Grant is the man of all others, from his great services, to be placed in this exalted position,' and when we, as we shall unquestionably, unanimously say 'Ay' to that and confirm him, have we not given him a position such as any man living or who ever lived might well be proud of, without putting his name in our bill originally and thus saying to the President, 'Sir, we cannot trust you to act on this matter unless we hint to you that we want such a man appointed'?" Lengthy and thorough the debate was, but there was never much doubt as to the outcome. Introduced on the first day of February, the measure was passed on the last, and the procedure Fessenden had outlined followed swiftly. Receiving the bill on March 1, Lincoln promptly signed it and named Grant for the honor next day. The Senate confirmed the appointment without delay, and on March 3 the general was ordered by telegraph to report at once to Washington, where he would receive his commission directly from the President.

Lincoln had been disappointed too often, over the course of the past three years, for him to allow his hopes to soar too high. He remembered McDowell and McClellan. He remembered Burnside and Hooker. Above all, he remembered Pope, who had also come East with western laurels on his brow. And there at hand, in case memory failed, was Halleck; Old Brains, too, had arrived from that direction, supposedly with a victory formula in his knapsack, and had wound up "a first-rate clerk." Still, after making all proper discounts, it seemed likely to Lincoln that now at last, in this general who had captured two rebel armies and routed a third, he had found the killer-arithmetician he had been seeking from the start.

✗ 5 ✗

Returning to Vicksburg on the last day of February, Sherman took no time out to recuperate from the rigors of the Meridian campaign, for he found there a week-old dispatch from Grant instructing him to cooperate with Banks in order to assure the success of the expedition up the Teche and the Red, which the Massachusetts general and Halleck had designed to accomplish the return of West Louisiana and East Texas to the Union, along with an estimated half million bales of hoarded cotton. Sherman himself was to rejoin Grant at Chattanooga in time to open the spring drive on Atlanta; he would therefore not participate in the Louisiana-Texas venture, save for making a short-term loan of some 10,000 troops to strengthen it; but he decided to confer in person with Banks, before he himself went back to Tennessee, on the logistical details of getting the reinforcements to him somewhere up the Red. Accordingly, he left Vicksburg that same day aboard the fast packet *Diana*, and arrived in New Orleans two days later, on March 2.

He found Banks in high spirits: not only because of the military outlook, which was considered excellent — Franklin had recovered from his early November repulse at Grand Coteau and had three divisions massed at Opelousas, ready to advance — but also because of political developments in accordance with Lincoln's reconstruction policy, whereby a Union-loyal candidate, one Michael Hahn, a native of Bavaria, had been elected governor of Louisiana by the necessary ten percent of the voters on February 22 and was to be inaugurated at New Orleans on March 5. Sherman's logistical problems were settled within two days, the arrangement being that the Vicksburg reinforcements would join Franklin at Alexandria on March 17 for the farther ascent of the Red, but Banks urged his visitor to stay over another two days for Hahn's inauguration, which he assured him would be well worth the delay. A chorus of one thousand voices, accompanied by all the bands of the army, would perform the "Anvil Chorus" in Lafayette Square, while church bells rang and cannon were fired in unison by electrical devices. Sherman declined the invitation. He had already gone on record as opposing such political procedures, and what was more, he said later, "I regarded all such ceremonies as out of place at a time when it seemed to me every hour and every minute were due to the war." His mind on destruction, not reconstruction, he reboarded the *Diana*, and three days later, on March 6, was back in Vicksburg, to which by now the destroyers of Meridian had returned, well rested from their week-long stay in Canton and the additional spoliation they had accomplished at that place.

Remaining in Vicksburg only long enough to pass on to McPherson the details of the arrangement he had made for reinforcing Banks at Alexandria on St Patrick's Day, Sherman set off upriver again the following morning, impatient to rejoin the troops he had left poised near Chattanooga, waiting alongside those under Thomas and Hooker for Grant to give the nod that would start them slogging southward, over or around Joe Johnston, into and through the heart of Georgia. "Prepare them for my coming," he had told his adjutant, in reference to the hapless civilians in his path, and now at last he was on his way. On the second day out, however, the *Diana* was hailed by a southbound packet which, to the Ohioan's surprise, turned out to have one of Grant's staff captains aboard, charged with the delivery of a highly personal letter his chief had written four days ago, on March 4, at Nashville. "Dear Sherman," it read: "The bill reviving the grade of lieutenant general in the army has become a law, and my name has been sent to the Senate for the place. I now receive orders to report to Washington immediately, in person, which indicates either a confirmation or a likelihood of confirmation. I start in the morning to comply with the order, but I shall say very distinctly on my arrival there that I shall accept no appointment which will require me to make that city my headquarters. This, however, is not what I started out to write about.... What I want is to express my thanks to you and McPherson as the men to whom, above all others, I feel indebted for whatever I have had of success. How far your advice and suggestions have been of assistance, you know. How far your execution of whatever has been given you to do entitles you to the reward I am receiving, you cannot know as well as I do. I feel all the gratitude this letter would express, giving it the most flattering construction. The word *you* I use in the plural, intending it for McPherson also," the letter concluded. "I should write to him, and will some day, but starting in the morning I do not know that I will find time just now. Your friend, U. S. Grant."

Sherman vibrated with three conflicting reactions as he read the first three sentences Grant had written: first, delight that his friend was about to be so honored: second, alarm that he had been summoned to the fleshpots of the capital: third, relief that he did not intend to stay there. However, as the boat continued to push its way slowly upriver against the booming current, the third emotion gave way in turn to the second, which came back even stronger than at first. The fact was, though he idolized his friend and superior, he had never really trusted his judgment in matters concerning his career, and though he admired his simplicity of character, seeing it in the quality that perhaps had contributed most to his success, he was forever supposing that it would get him in trouble, especially if he fell into the hands of wily men who would know how to use him for their sordid ends. "Your reputation as a general is now far above that of any man living, and partisans will maneuver for your influence," he had warned him in a letter written during the Christmas visit to Ohio, at a time when the Grant-for-President drums were beginning to rumble. He counseled him earnestly to "Preserve a plain military character and let others maneuver as they will. You will beat them not only in fame, but in doing good in the closing scenes of this war, when somebody must heal and mend up the breaches." Nowhere were the wily more in evidence than in Washington, and the more he thought about it, the more he was convinced that "Grant would not stand the intrigues of the politicians a week," even though he went there with no intention of remaining any longer than it took to get a third star tacked on each shoulder of his weathered blouse. What was more, Sherman had a mystical feeling about the Mississippi River, which he called "the great artery" of America. "I want to live out here and die here also," he wrote to another friend this week, as the *Diana* chugged upstream, "and I don't care if my grave be like De Soto's in its muddy waters." He seemed to fear that if Grant wandered far from the banks of the big river, his reaction would be like that of Antaeus when he lost contact with the earth.

Accordingly, after two days of fretting and fuming, as the boat drew near Memphis on March 10 he dashed off an answer to Grant's "more than kind and characteristic letter," thanking him in McPherson's name and his own, but protesting: "You do yourself injustice and us too much honor in assigning us so large a share of the merits which have led to your high advancement.... At Belmont you manifested your traits, neither of us being near. At Donelson also you illustrated your character; I was not near, and General McPherson [was] in too subordinate a capacity to influence you. Until you had won Donelson, I confess I was almost cowed by the terrible array of anarchical elements that presented themselves at every point; but that victory admitted the ray of light which I have followed ever since.... The chief characteristic in your nature is the simple faith in success you have always manifested, which I can liken to nothing else than the faith a Christian has in his Saviour. This faith gave you victory at Shiloh and Vicksburg. Also, when you have completed your best preparations, you go into battle without hesitation, as at Chattanooga; no doubts, no reserve; and I tell you that it was this that made us act with confidence. I knew wherever I was that you thought of me, and if I got in a tight place you would come — if alive. My only points of doubt were as to your knowledge of grand strategy and of books of science and history, but I confess your common-sense seems to have supplied all this."

Having disposed thus of the disclaimers and the amenities, the volatile redhead passed at once to the main burden of his letter. If Grant stayed East, Sherman almost certainly would be given full charge of the West, and yet, although personally he wanted this above all possible assignments, he was unwilling to secure it at the cost of his friend's ruin, which was what he believed would result from any such arrangement. "Do not stay in Washington," he urged him. "Halleck is better qualified than you are to stand the buffets of intrigue and policy. Come out West; take to yourself the whole Mississippi Valley. Let us make it dead sure, and I tell you the Atlantic slope and Pacific shores will follow its destiny as sure as the limbs of a tree live or die with the main trunk. We have done much; still much remains. . . . For God's sake and your country's sake, come out of Washington! I foretold to General Halleck, before he left Corinth, the inevitable result to him, and I now exhort you to come out West. Here lies the seat of the coming empire, and from the West, when our task is done, we will make short work of Charleston and Richmond and the impoverished coast of the Atlantic."

Within a week he found his warning had been too late. Arriving in Memphis next day he received on March 14 a message from Grant arranging a meeting in Nashville three days later. If Sherman took this as evidence that his chief did not intend to make his headquarters in the East, he soon learned better. In Nashville on the appointed date, invested with the rank of lieutenant general and command of all the armies of the Union, Grant informed him that the Virginia situation required personal attention; he would be returning there to stay, and Sherman would have full charge of the West. However, what with the press of visiting dignitaries, all anxious for a look at a man with three stars on each shoulder, there was so little time for a strategy conference that it was decided the two generals would travel together as far as Cincinnati on Grant's return trip east. That way, it was thought, they could talk on the cars; but the wheels made such a clatter, they finally gave up trying to shout above the racket and fell silent. In Cincinnati they checked into the Burnet House, and there at last, in a private room with a sentry at the door, they spread their maps and got to work.

"Yonder began the campaign," Sherman was to say a quarter century later, standing before the hotel on the occasion of a visit to the Ohio city. "He was to go for Lee and I was to go for Joe Johnston. That was his plan."

List of Maps
Bibliographical Note
Index

LIST OF MAPS

2. Davis, the Long Trip West.
23. Situation: Lee, Burnside.
31. Fredericksburg, 13Dec62.
48. Situation: Prairie Grove.
63. Grant-Sherman, Pemberton.
70. Forrest, Van Dorn Raids.
83. Rosecrans Advances; Bragg.
89. Murfreesboro, 31Dec62.
176. Middle Tennessee Region.
184. Streight Pursued.
193. Vicksburg: Seven Failures.
228. Charleston Harbor.
241. Situation: Lee, Hooker.
246. Kelly's Ford, 17Mar63.
254. Longstreet Southside.
266. Hooker's Envelopment.
288. Chancellorsville, 2May63.
312. Stuart vs Hooker.
313. Lee vs Sedgwick.
322. Situation: Spring 1863.
324. Grant's Bayou Route.
337. Grierson's Raid.
359. Grant Swings East.
362. Converging on Jackson.
373. Champion Hill, 16May63.
381. The Leap at Vicksburg.

392. Banks in the Teche.
409. Vicksburg Besieged.
442. Lee, Hooker: 24Jun63.
462. Lee, Meade: 28Jun63.
476. Gettysburg, 1Jul63.
500. Gettysburg, 2Jul63.
558. Pickett's Charge.
590. Retreat and Pursuit.
604. Helena, 4Jul63.
662. Situation: August 1863.
665. Tullahoma Outflanked.
689. Rosecrans in the Coves.
703. Little Rock, Ft Smith.
714. Chickamauga, 20Sep63.
749. Thomas Stands Fast.
795. Lee, Meade: Oct-Nov63.
807. Grant's Cracker Line.
842. Chattanooga, 23-25Nov63.
874. Mine Run, 26-30Nov63.
903. Olustee, 20Feb64.
931. Meridian, Okolona.
952. Federal Gains 1862-3.
ENDPAPERS.
  Front: Theater of War.
  Back: Vicksburg Campaign.
         Virginia Theater.

Maps drawn by George Annand, of Darien, Connecticut, from originals by the author. All are oriented north.

BIBLIOGRAPHICAL NOTE

In the course of this second of three intended five-year stints, the third of which will bring me to defeat and victory at Appomattox, my debt has grown heavier on both sides of the line where the original material leaves off, but most particularly on the near side of the line. Although the *Official Records,* supplemented by various other utterances by the participants, remain the primary source on which this narrative is based, the hundredth anniversary has enriched the store of comment on that contemporary evidence with biographies, studies of the conflict as a whole, examinations of individual campaigns, and general broodings on the minutiae — all of them, or anyhow nearly all of them, useful to the now dwindling number of writers and readers who, surviving exposure to the glut, continue to make that war their main historical concern. So that, while I agree in essence with Edmund Wilson's observation that "a day of mourning would be more appropriate," the celebration of the Centennial has at least been of considerable use to those engaged, as I am, in the process Robert Penn Warren has referred to as "picking the scab of our fate."

Not that my previous obligations have not continued. They have indeed, and they have been enlarged in the process. Kenneth P. Williams, Douglas Southall Freeman, J. G. Randall, Lloyd Lewis, Stanley F. Horn, Carl Sandburg, Bell I. Wiley, Bruce Catton, T. Harry Williams, Allan Nevins, Robert S. Henry, Jay Monaghan, E. Merton Coulter, Clifford Dowdey, Burton J. Hendrick, Margaret Leech are but a handful among the many to whom I am indebted as guides through the labyrinth. Without them I not only would have missed a great many wonders along the way, I would surely have been lost amid the intricate turnings and the uproar. Moreover, the debt continued to mount as the exploration proceeded: to Hudson Strode, for instance, for the extension of his *Jeffer-*

son Davis at a time when the need was sore, and to Mark Mayo Boatner for his labor-saving *Civil War Dictionary*. Specific accounts of individual campaigns, lately published to expand or replace the more or less classical versions by Bigelow and others, have been of particular help through this relentless stretch of fighting. Edward J. Stackpole's *Chancellorsville*, for example, was used in conjunction with two recent biographies of the hero of that battle, Frank E. Vandiver's *Mighty Stonewall* and Lenoir Chambers' *Stonewall Jackson*. Similarly, for the Vicksburg campaign, there were Earl Schenck Miers's *The Web of Victory* and Peter F. Walker's *Vicksburg, a People at War*, plus biographies of the two commanders, *Pemberton, Defender of Vicksburg* and *Grant Moves South*, by John C. Pemberton and Bruce Catton. For Gettysburg, there were Clifford Dowdey's *Death of a Nation*, Glenn Tucker's *High Tide at Gettysburg*, and George R. Stewart's *Pickett's Charge*. For the battles around Chattanooga, there were Glenn Tucker's *Chickamauga* and Fairfax Downey's *Storming of the Gateway*. James M. Merrill's *The Rebel Shore*, Fletcher Pratt's *Civil War on Western Waters*, and Clarence E. Macartney's *Mr. Lincoln's Admirals* contributed to the naval actions, as Benjamin P. Thomas' and Harold M. Hyman's *Stanton* did to events in Washington. These too were only a few of the most recent among the many, old and new, which I hope to acknowledge in a complete bibliography at the end of the third volume, *Red River to Appomattox*. Other obligations, of a more personal nature, were carried over from the outset: to the John Simon Guggenheim Memorial Foundation, which extended my fellowship beyond the norm: to the National Park Service, whose guides helped me (as they will you) to get to know so many confusing fields: to the William Alexander Percy Memorial Library, in my home town Greenville, Mississippi, which continued its loan of the *Official Records* and other reference works: to Robert D. Loomis of Random House, who managed to keep both his temper and his enthusiasm beyond unmet deadlines: to Memphis friends, who gave me food and whiskey without demanding payment in the form of talk about the war. To all these I am grateful: and to my wife Gwyn Rainer Foote, who bore with me.

Other, less specific obligations were as heavy. The photographs of Mathew Brady, affording as they do a gritty sense of participation — of being in the presence of the uniformed and frock-coated men who fought the battles and did the thinking, such as it was — gave me as much to go on, for example, as anything mentioned above. Further afield, but no less applicable, Richmond Lattimore's translation of the *Iliad* put a Greekless author in close touch with his model. Indeed, to be complete, the list of my debts would have to be practically endless. Proust I believe has taught me more about the organization of material than even Gibbon has done, and Gibbon taught me much; Mark Twain and Faulkner would also have to be included, for they left their sign on

Bibliographical Note

all they touched, and in the course of this exploration of the American scene I often found that they had been there before me. In a quite different sense, I am obligated also to the governors of my native state and the adjoining states of Arkansas and Alabama for helping to lessen my sectional bias by reproducing, in their actions during several of the years that went into the writing of this volume, much that was least admirable in the position my forebears occupied when they stood up to Lincoln. I suppose, or in any case fervently hope, it is true that history never repeats itself, but I know from watching these three gentlemen that it can be terrifying in its approximations, even when the reproduction — deriving, as it does, its scale from the performers — is in miniature.

As for method, it may explain much for me to state that my favorite historian is Tacitus, who dealt mainly with high-placed scoundrels, but that the finest compliment I ever heard paid a historian was tendered by Thomas Hobbes in the foreword to his translation of *The Peloponnesian War*, in which he referred to Thucydides as "one who, though he never digress to read a Lecture, Moral or Political, upon his own Text, nor enter into men's hearts, further than the Actions themselves evidently guide him ... filleth his Narrations with that choice of matter, and ordereth them with that Judgement, and with such perspicuity and efficacy expresseth himself that (as Plutarch saith) he maketh his Auditor a Spectator. For he setteth his Reader in the Assemblies of the People, and in their Senates, at their debating; in the Streets, at their Seditions; and in the Field, at their Battels." There indeed is something worth aiming at, however far short of attainment we fall.

— S.F.

Index

Abington, Virginia, 165
Adams, Charles F., Jr., 233–34
Adams, Daniel W., 734
Aiken, William, 823
Alabama, C.S.S., 125–26, 894
Alabama & Mississippi Railroad, 937
Albatross, U.S.S., 215, 216, 393, 396
Alcorn, James L., 648
Alexander, Edward P., 539–41, 542, 547, 550–51, 552, 577, 586, 710, 838
Alexander's Bridge, Chickamauga, 720, 721, 723
Alexandria, Louisiana, 392, 393, 394, 405, 597
Alpine, Georgia, 692
Anderson, George T., 501, 505
Anderson, J. Patton, 840
Anderson, Richard H., 30, 274, 275, 276, 278, 280, 286, 306, 312, 434, 435, 473, 478, 491, 499, 509, 510, 522, 558, 559, 577
Anderson, William C., 140, 141
Anderson's Crossroads, 761, 803
Angle, The, at Gettysburg, 560–61, 562, 579
Antietam, Battle of, 21
Archer, James J., 467, 468, 469, 470, 473, 536, 577, 579
Arkadelphia, Arkansas, 706, 776
Arkansas, C.S.S., 52, 74, 144, 617
Arkansas, U.S.S., 386
Arkansas Post, 134, 135–36, 138, 192
Arkansas River, 703, 776, 777
Armistead, Lewis, A., 533–34, 536, 549–50, 551, 557, 559, 561–62, 568, 571, 577
Army of Northern Virginia, 5, 25, 95, 237, 241, 249, 251, 255, 300, 306, 316, 431, 443, 446, 497, 498, 525, 578, 641, 659, 695, 708, 787, 793, 878
Army of Tennessee, 6, 7, 8, 18, 64, 175, 670–71, 711, 756, 762, 766, 813, 814–15, 816, 819, 820, 825, 837, 869, 887, 892, 893
Army of the Cumberland, 103, 663, 664, 675–76, 708, 764, 766, 805, 836, 844, 852

Army of the Frontier, 47
Army of the Mississippi, 6, 133
Army of the Ohio, 671, 806
Army of the Potomac, 21, 107, 117–19, 127, 128–29, 131, 132, 232, 250, 255, 300, 315, 431, 446, 447, 451, 452–53, 458, 497, 524, 626, 708, 764, 788, 791, 798, 805, 888–889, 962
Army of the Tennessee, 358–59, 408, 691, 805, 835, 841, 851
Arnold, Matthew, 155
Atlanta, Georgia, 10, 19, 164, 710, 820
Atlanta *Southern Confederacy*, 650
Atlantic, S.S., 782
Atlantic & Gulf Central Railroad, 901, 902–903
Augur, Christopher C., 390, 395, 396, 397, 402
Augusta, Georgia, 19, 710
Averell, William W., 245–47, 315, 888, 907
Avery, Isaac C., 518
Ayres, Romeyn B., 452, 453

Bache, George M., 388–89
Baird, Absalom, 716, 717, 722, 727, 754, 755, 805, 845, 851, 852, 857
Baldwin, Florida, 901, 902, 903, 905
Balloons, observation, 33, 268, 271, 279, 436, 447
Baltimore *Gazette*, 635
Baltimore Pike, Gettysburg, 484, 496, 512, 515, 521, 527, 542, 570
Banks, Nathaniel P., Baton Rouge reoccupied by, 11, 18, 52, 54, 335, 390; Butler relieved by, 54; cotton speculators and, 55, 107; Grant and, 145, 358, 773–74; Halleck and, 399–400, 403, 772, 774, 872; Lincoln and, 626; Mobile operation suggested by, 670–71, 672; at New Orleans, 54–57, 59, 107, 395, 773–74; Port Hudson reduced by, 137, 138, 139, 212, 325, 345, 351, 389–90, 395–404, 596, 597, 600, 614,

[974]   *Index*

Banks, Nathaniel P. (*cont.*)
  615–17, 626; Texas campaign and, 59, 780, 870–72
Banks Ford, 262, 265, 266, 267, 270, 276, 277, 278, 310, 312
Barbourville, Kentucky, 917
Bardstown, Kentucky, 679
Barksdale, William, 26, 27, 28–29, 311, 312, 506, 508–09, 514, 550, 577
Barlow, Francis C., 452, 453, 476, 477, 587
Barnes, James, 452, 453, 503, 507, 517
Bartlett's Mill, Virginia, 875
Bate, William B., 840
Bates, Edward, 110, 630
Baton Rouge, Louisiana, 11, 18, 52, 54, 335, 340, 390, 395
Bayou des Allemands, Louisiana, 53
Bayou La Fourche, Louisiana, 138, 616, 707
Bayou Pierre, Mississippi, 348, 349, 353, 394
Bayou Sara, 394, 395
Beall, William N. R., 401
Beatty, Samuel, 96, 99
Beauregard, Pierre G. T., campaign plans suggested by, 428–29, 817–18; Charleston defended by, 221–24, 231–32, 249, 643, 695, 698–702, 788, 824–25, 895–96, 897, 898; Davis and, 821–24, 878, 886, 896; Florida campaign and, 905; reinforcements from, 347, 361, 442, 586
Bell, John, 831
Bell, Tyree H., 932
Bellbuckle Gap, Tennessee, 666
Benjamin, Judah P., 156, 158, 162–63, 431, 652, 654, 655, 887, 892
Benner's Hill, Gettysburg, 515
Benning, Henry L., 501, 505
Benton, U.S.S., 75–76, 326, 342
Berryville, Virginia, 439, 441
Bethesda Church, Virginia, 913
Bierce, Ambrose, 756
Big Black River, 62, 349, 352, 354, 359, 360, 368, 381; Battle of, 377–78
Birney, David B., 288, 289, 452, 453, 507, 508
Black Hawk, U.S.S., 134, 199, 206
Blair, Francis P., Jr., 76, 332, 333, 358, 370, 371, 374, 375, 421, 424, 830, 943–44
Blair, Montgomery, 110, 943
Blennerhassett's Island, 682
Blockade, federal, 894–95
Blondin, *see* Gravelet, J. F.
Bloodgood, Edward, 177
Blue Wing, packet boat, 134
Blunt, James G., 47–51, 702–03, 706, 707, 776, 779, 780
Bolton, Mississippi, 17, 361, 365, 370, 375
Bonaparte, Louis, *see* Napoleon III
Bond, Frank S., 736
Bond issue, Confederate, 156–57
Boomer, George B., 372, 373
Booth, Edwin, 162
Boston Mountains, 47, 48
Bowen, John S., 346, 348, 349–50, 353, 354, 367, 373, 374, 382, 607, 608, 609, 610

Bradyville, Tennessee, 666, 671
Bragg, Braxton, at Chattanooga, 687, 688, 689–94, 834, 837; at Chickamauga, 711, 712, 713, 715–17, 719, 723, 728–30, 731, 732, 734, 744, 756; commander-in-chief of the Confederate armies, 957–58; commander of Army of Tennessee, 6, 7, 8, 170–71, 669–74; criticism of, 171–74, 669, 812–13; Davis and, 172–74, 670, 814–819, 820–21, 825–26, 868–69; Forrest and, 65, 812–13; Longstreet reinforced by, 837, 839, 862–63; at Lookout Mountain, 805, 811, 840–41, 843–44, 846; at Missionary Ridge, 757–58, 760, 761–62, 813, 848, 850, 852, 853, 856; Morgan's wedding attended by, 84; at Murfreesboro, 18, 19, 80–83, 85, 86, 87, 90, 92–94, 96, 97, 98, 101–02, 168; Pemberton and, 645; Polk and, 171–72; reinforcements for Vicksburg, 9, 424, 677; retreat from Stones River, 124; at Tullahoma, 103, 170, 171–74, 442, 665, 674; Van Dorn and, 340, 346; withdrawal into Georgia, 858, 860, 865, 867–69
Bragg, Mrs. Braxton, 174
Branchville, Georgia, 710
Brandon, Mississippi, 924
Brandy Station, Battle of, 437–38, 787
Brannan, John M., 716, 717, 722, 732, 734, 736, 740, 742, 748, 752, 753, 755, 805
Brashear City, Louisiana, 138, 390, 394, 397, 598, 600, 616
Brazos Santiago, Texas, 871
Bread riots, 163–64, 166
Breckinridge, John C., 86, 92, 96, 98–99, 100, 168–69, 171, 424, 620, 670, 690, 692, 713, 723, 729, 730, 731, 732, 733, 734, 754, 755, 839, 840, 856, 857, 868
Breeze, Kidder R., 332
Brent, Joseph L., 198
Bridgeport, Alabama, 378, 687, 803, 806, 807, 808, 811, 818, 819, 820, 821, 835, 836, 837, 839
Bright, John, 558, 654, 826
Bristoe Station, Virginia, 789, 792–94, 819, 827, 873
Brockenbrough, John M., 536
Brooklyn, U.S.S., 59, 125, 126
Brooks, William T. H., 131
Brough, John, 828
Brown, George, 197–98
Brown, Isaac N., 11, 74, 617
Brown, John, 141, 703
Brown, Joseph E., 649
Browning, Orville H., 112–13, 120
Brownlow, Parson, 633
Brown's Ferry, Alabama, 181, 806–07, 808, 809, 811, 836, 839
Brownson, Orestes A., 108
Brownsville, Texas, 871
Bruinsburg, Mississippi, 344, 347, 356, 357, 381
Buckland Mills, Virginia, 795, 796
Bucklin, McDonough, 149
Buckner, Simon B., 442, 608, 671, 685, 690,

Index [975]

692, 693, 712, 715, 716, 743, 814, 815, 816, 817, 839, 844
Buell, Don Carlos, 79, 80
Buffington, Ohio, 681
Buford, John, 437, 465, 467, 468, 471, 482, 494, 495, 795
Bunker Hill, Virginia, 593
Burnside, Ambrose E., commander of Army of the Ohio, 632-33, 671, 694, 772, 785, 805-06; commander of Army of the Potomac, 5, 9, 117, 119, 262; at Fredericksburg, 20-45, 107; Knoxville taken and held by, 671, 675, 677-78, 684-85, 690, 708, 760, 764, 806, 834, 835, 837, 838-839, 845, 862, 863, 864, 865; Lincoln and, 121-23, 127-28, 130-32, 764; Morgan's raiders and, 683; Mud March, the, 129-130, 146; relieved of Potomac command, 131; Vallandigham arrested by, 633, 634
Bushy Knob, 845, 846
Butler, Andrew, 55
Butler, Benjamin F., 11, 54, 105, 138, 393
Butterfield, Daniel, 250, 267, 270, 279, 280, 289, 524, 525, 542, 590

Cadwallader, Sylvanus, 418-21
Cairo, Illinois, 784
Cairo, U.S.S., 11, 20, 74, 167, 617
Caldwell, John C., 452, 453, 507, 508, 510
Calhoun, John C., 822
Cameron, Simon, 114
Canal project, at Vicksburg, 191-92, 201, 216, 323, 345
Cane Hill, Arkansas, 47, 48, 49, 50
Canton, Mississippi, 378, 934, 93
Caperton's Ferry, Alabama, 687
Carlisle, Pennsylvania, 445, 446, 455, 459, 460, 464, 806
Carondelet, U.S.S., 342
Carr, Eugene A., 347, 370, 371, 377
Carroll, Samuel S., 519
Cashtown, Pennsylvania, 463, 464, 465, 467, 472, 473, 583
Castalian Springs, Tennessee, 8
Castle Pinckney, 222
Catharine Furnace, Virginia, 282, 283, 288, 289, 290, 292, 295, 298, 299, 305
Catskill, U.S.S., 228, 230
Cedar Mountain, 787
Cemetery Hill, Gettysburg, 477-78, 480, 481, 482, 483, 484, 486, 487, 488, 489, 490, 491, 493, 512, 513, 515, 516, 517-20, 524, 526, 545, 547, 554, 556, 565, 830, 833
Cemetery Ridge, Gettysburg, 479, 485, 486, 489, 490, 492, 493, 494, 498, 502, 510-13, 514, 516, 519, 521, 523, 525, 529, 530, 536, 541, 542, 546, 547, 569, 571, 575, 579
Chalmers, James R., 338, 783
Chamberlain, Joshua L., 504
Chambersburg, Pennsylvania, 441, 444, 462, 463, 464, 531, 583, 584
Chambersburg Pike, Gettysburg, 468, 469, 471, 477, 486, 491, 493, 526, 580
Chambliss, John R., 459, 570, 571
Champion Hill, Battle of, 371-75

Chancellorsville, Virginia, 266, 267, 269, 271, 274, 276; Battle of, 278-316, 433, 436
Chandler, Zachariah, 112
"Charge of the Mule Brigade," 810-11
Charleston, South Carolina, 221-23, 230, 231, 428, 643, 648, 695, 696-702, 708, 789, 821-25, 896, 898
Charleston *Courier*, 822
Charleston *Mercury*, 641, 648, 821
Charlotte, North Carolina, 19
Charlottesville, Virginia, 911
Chase, Katherine (Kate), 829
Chase, Salmon P., 109-11, 113-15, 116, 623, 726, 764, 941-46
Chattanooga, Tennessee, 6, 7, 8, 18, 19, 20, 667, 674, 675, 685-86, 687, 688, 725, 747, 748, 757, 759, 760, 761, 763, 764, 766, 768, 782, 785, 803, 804-11, 812, 826, 834, 839, 858, 859, 865, 866, 868
Cheatham, Benjamin F., 88, 92, 101, 171, 692, 713, 717, 722, 729, 733, 816, 817, 840, 846, 868, 893
Chester, Ohio, 681
Chicago *Times*, 634, 639, 832, 881
Chicago *Tribune*, 447, 681
Chickamauga, Tennessee, 782, 786, 818
Chickamauga Creek, 692, 693; Battle of, 694, 711, 712-57, 870
Chickasaw Bluffs, 10, 17, 63, 95, 133, 134, 167; Battle of, 20
Chicora, C.S.S., 223, 224
Chillicothe, U.S.S., 204, 205
Christmas Raid, Morgan's, 84
Churchill, Thomas J., 136
Cincinnati, Ohio, 681, 683
Cincinnati, U.S.S., 135, 388-89
Cincinnati *Commercial*, 217
Clarendon, Arkansas, 702
Clark's Mountain, 873, 875
Clay, Henry, U.S.S., 329
Clayton, Powell, 604
Cleburne, Patrick R., 86, 87, 92, 171, 692, 719, 721, 722, 729, 730, 732, 734, 755, 837, 839, 840, 841, 844, 846, 850-51, 857, 858, 860-61, 867, 953, 954
Clifton, Tennessee, 69
Clifton, U.S.S., 58, 59
Clinton, Mississippi, 366, 367, 368, 369, 371
Cobb, Howell, 167, 955
Cobb, Thomas R. R., 35, 38, 506
Coburn, John, 177
Cochrane, John, 117-18, 131
Coffeeville, Mississippi, 61
Colfax, Schuyler, 943
Collamer, Jacob, 112
Collierville, Tennessee, 783, 923, 933
Colquitt, Peyton H., 734
Colston, E. Raleigh, 286, 294, 295, 297, 306, 307, 311, 434
Columbia, South Carolina, 19
Columbia, Tennessee, 670
Columbus, Kentucky, 65, 72, 784
Columbus, Mississippi, 67
Colvill, William, Jr., 511
Communism, 149

[976]   Index

Communist Manifesto, 149
Conestoga, U.S.S., 74
Conkling, James C., 639, 826
Conscription Act, Confederate, 14, 46, 161; Federal, 151-52, 629, 631, 635-37
Contractors, government, 147-48
Cooksville, Maryland, 459
Cooper, Samuel, 261, 689
Copperheads, 632, 671, 683
Corbell, LaSalle, 259
Cornell University, 151
Corps d'Afrique, 393
Corydon, Indiana, 679-80
Couch, Darius N., 250, 251, 265, 267, 271, 277, 278, 280-81, 300, 303, 304-05, 313, 314, 447
Cowan, Tennessee, 673
Cracker Line, 809, 811, 812, 827, 834, 836, 837
Crawfish Springs, Georgia, 716, 718, 721, 723, 742
Crawford, Samuel W., 452, 453
Crescent City, Louisiana, 53
Crittenden, Thomas L., 81, 82, 85, 89, 90, 91, 97, 99, 168, 666, 667, 668, 671, 672, 687, 688, 692, 693, 694, 713, 715, 716, 720, 726, 727, 731, 735, 736, 746, 763
Crocker, Frederick, 775
Crocker, Marcellus M., 370, 372
Cruft, Charles, 805, 841, 852
Culpeper, Virginia, 437, 440, 594, 765, 787, 788
Culp's Hill, Gettysburg, 477, 484, 486, 488, 491, 493, 494, 511, 512, 515, 516, 517, 521, 523, 524, 527, 528, 542, 544
Cumberland Gap, 7, 684, 685, 862
Cumberland River, 8, 81
Cummings Gap, 807, 809, 811
Cummings Point, South Carolina, 696, 697, 699, 701, 823
Curtin, Governor, 830
Curtis, Henry, 779
Curtis, Samuel R., 140-41, 145
Cushing, Alonzo H., 547, 562
Custer, George A., 571, 796, 910-11

Dahlgren, John A., 695-96, 697, 699-701, 817, 822, 824, 827, 894, 895, 899
Dahlgren, Ulric, 909-10, 911, 912, 913-15, 916
Dalton, Georgia, 860, 861, 865, 868
Dana, Charles A., 218, 326, 327, 328, 343, 363-64, 416, 417, 418, 420, 638-39, 723-724, 745, 747-48, 764, 766-67, 768, 803, 805, 919
Dana, Napoleon Jackson Tecumseh, 871
Dana, Richard, 629
Daniel, Junius, 527
Dargan, Edmund S., 162, 652
David, C.S.S., 824-25, 894
Davidson, John W., 702, 706, 707
Davies, Thomas A., 67
Davis, David, 940, 945
Davis, George, 956
Davis, Jefferson, 3-6, 7, 8-13, 16-17, 142;

Beauregard and, 821-24, 878, 886, 896; Bragg and, 172-74, 814-19, 820, 825-26, 868-69; bread riots and, 164; Chattanooga visited by, 814-19; criticism of, 648-52; *habeas corpus* writ suspended by, 949-50; Jackson (Miss.) speech, 3, 13-16; Johnston and, 6-7, 9-13, 16-17, 886-887, 891-92; Lee and, 6, 430-33, 441-43, 586, 593, 646, 647, 656-59, 708-09, 878, 880, 886-87, 952, 957; Lincoln and, 883-884; Pemberton and, 645-46; proclamation on continuance of the war, 165-67; reaction after Gettysburg and Vicksburg, 642-52; Richmond speech, 103-06; tours of inspection, 6-20, 81, 83, 95, 814-26; Vicksburg campaign and, 346, 354, 355; year-end message to Congress, 879, 883-886
Davis, Jefferson C., 87, 88, 91, 735, 736, 739, 746, 748
Davis, Joseph E., 17, 375-76, 468, 469, 470, 471, 473, 536, 557, 559, 564, 721, 819
Davis, Varina H. (Mrs. Jefferson), 103, 162-63, 642, 891
Decatur, Alabama, 835
Decatur, Mississippi, 925
Decherd, Tennessee, 672, 673, 836
Deer Creek, 208, 211
De Kalb, Baron, U.S.S., 135, 204, 205, 386, 617-18, 669
Demopolis, Alabama, 645, 819
Deshler, James, 136, 734
De Soto, C.S.S., 196
Detroit *Free Press*, 940
De Valls Bluff, Arkansas, 702, 703, 706
Devereux, Arthur, 560-61, 562
Devil's Den, Gettysburg, 496, 498, 499, 501, 502, 504, 505, 509, 513, 523, 529
Dewey, George, 214
Diana, U.S.S., 390, 391
Dickinson, Anna E., 960-61
Diligent, S.S., 417, 418, 419
Dismal Swamp, 258
Disraeli, Benjamin, 655
Dixon, George E., 897-98
Dodge, Grenville M., 180, 181, 186, 835-36
Donaldsville, Louisiana, 53, 138, 599
Doolittle, James, 918-19
Doubleday, Abner, 36, 452, 453, 470, 471, 472, 475, 476, 484, 493, 544, 560, 561, 831
Draft, *see* Conscription Act
Draft riots, 636-37, 707
Dry Valley Road, Chickamauga, 739, 740, 742, 745, 746, 747
Duck River, 19, 102, 665, 672
Dug Gap, 693
Duke, Basil W., 678, 682
Dunnington, John W., 136
Du Pont, Samuel F., 224-31, 232, 256, 428, 695, 822, 824, 894
Dwight, William, 398, 401, 402

Early, Jubal A., 30, 36-37, 285, 309, 310, 311, 312, 434, 435, 436, 439, 440, 445, 461,

Index [977]

464, 465, 472, 475, 480, 487, 488, 514, 516, 517–18, 520, 522, 800, 801, 802, 875
East Tennessee & Virginia Railroad, 709
Ector, Matthew D., 718
Edisto Island, 227
Edwards Station, Mississippi, 359, 360, 367, 370
Elkhorn Tavern, Arkansas, 46, 49, 70
Elk River, 665, 674
Ellet, Alfred W., 195, 215
Ellet, Charles R., 77, 195, 196, 197, 198, 202, 215
Ellet, Charles R., Jr., 195
Ellet, J. A., 215
Elliott, Stephen, 822, 823
Elzey, Arnold, 252, 254–55
Emancipation Proclamation, 111, 120–21, 155, 239, 629, 631, 640, 881, 955, 959
Emmitsburg Road, Gettysburg, 489, 490, 492, 493, 494, 496, 498, 499, 501, 502, 508, 509, 510, 513–14, 521, 536, 552, 556, 557, 559–60, 572, 575
Emory, William H., 390, 391, 394, 395, 397, 403–04, 405, 599
Engels, Friedrich, 149
England, relations with, 154–55, 157–58, 653–56
Era No. 5, C.S.S., 196, 197
Ericsson, John, 225
Erlanger et Cie, 155, 156–57
Essex, U.S.S., 396, 616
Everett, Edward, 827, 831, 833
Ewell, Richard S., commander of Second Army Corps, 434, 435, 787, 789, 800, 801, 802; at Gettysburg, 465, 472, 477, 478, 479, 480, 481, 487, 488, 490, 491, 494, 498, 514–16, 521, 522, 523, 527, 528, 531, 538, 543, 578, 580, 595; in Pennsylvania campaign, 438–39, 441, 443, 445, 446, 455, 456, 458, 460, 461, 463, 464; retreat from Gettysburg, 583, 585, 592
Ewing, Thomas, 703, 705

Fagan, James, 602, 605
Fairfax Court House, Virginia, 457
Fairfax Station, Virginia, 457
Fairfield, Pennsylvania, 583
Farnsworth, Elon J., 572, 573–74
Farragut, David G., 11, 18, 54–55, 62, 212–215, 225, 389, 390, 392, 399, 401, 402, 403, 404, 775, 894, 935
Fayetteville, Arkansas, 47, 49, 50, 51, 139, 140, 444, 600, 673
Ferguson, Milton J., 570
Fernandina, Florida, 901
Fessenden, William Pitt, 108–09, 112, 114, 962
Fillmore, Millard, 831
Finegan, Joseph, 904
Flanagin, Harris, 644
Florence, Alabama, 836
Florida, C.S.S., 126, 894
Florida, conquest of, 899–906
Folly Island, 696
Foote, Andrew H., 695

Foote, Henry S., 161–62, 652, 950, 955, 958
Forbes, John Murray, 109, 826
Foreign relations, 153–58, 653–56, 771–72
Forney, John H., 367, 382, 607
Forrest, Jeffrey E., 930, 932
Forrest, Nathan Bedford, 17, 20, 65–67, 68–69, 71, 72, 81, 95, 175, 177, 179, 181, 182–86, 340, 346, 670, 671, 673–74, 692, 693, 715, 717, 718, 733, 759–60, 812–14, 820, 922, 926–34
Forrest, William, 182
Forster, William E., 654
Fort Baxter, 779
Fort Butler, 599, 616
Fort Curtis, 603–06
Fort De Russy, 393, 396
Fort Fisher, 895
Fort Griffin, 775
Fort Henry, 179, 180
Fort Hindman, 134, 135–36
Fort Huger, 258, 259
Fort Johnson, 897
Fort Loudon, 863
Fort McAllister, 226
Fort Monroe, 253, 586
Fort Moultrie, 222, 228, 229, 230, 701
Fort Pemberton, 203, 204
Fort Sanders, 863, 865
Fort Smith, 702, 706, 707, 776
Fort Sumter, 3, 222, 228, 229, 230, 232, 696, 698, 699–700, 701, 823–24, 825, 895
Fort Wagner, 643
Fort Warren, 633
Foster, John G., 257
Fourteen Mile Creek, 359, 360, 362, 370
Fox, Gustavus V., 200, 207, 225, 231, 341
France, relations with, 153–54, 155–56, 654, 771–72
Franklin, Benjamin, 883
Franklin, William B., 25, 36, 37, 39, 130, 131, 250, 774, 775–76, 870, 871, 963
Frederick, Maryland, 588, 589
Fredericksburg, Virginia, 5, 15, 236–37, 239, 300, 307, 309, 311, 314, 316; Battle of, 20–45, 167, 272, 436
Fremantle, Arthur J. L., 558, 559, 567, 568, 581, 654, 669, 670
French, Samuel G., 252, 255, 256, 258, 259, 261, 425, 791, 801, 923, 924
French, William, 874, 875, 876
Front Royal, Virginia, 439
Fry, Birkett D., 536, 557, 559, 564, 579
Fry, James B., 638

Galveston, Texas, 19, 57–59, 124, 125, 127, 871, 872; Battle of, 20
Gamble, Hamilton R., 140
Gardner, Franklin, 355, 395–96, 399, 400, 402, 404, 596, 597, 600, 614–15
Garesché, Julius P., 91
Garfield, James A., 725–26, 727, 736, 745, 747, 754
Garnett, Richard B., 533, 534, 536, 552, 555, 557, 561, 568, 577

Geary, John W., 453, 485, 493, 494, 516, 809, 810, 848, 849, 852
Genesee, U.S.S., 396
Germanna Ford, Virginia, 874
Getty, George W., 258
Gettysburg, Pennsylvania, 446, 460, 463, 465, 466, 467, 827, 829-33; Battle of, 460, 461, 467-581, 641
Gettysburg Address, Lincoln's, 827, 829-33
Gibbon, John, 36, 270, 281, 289, 300, 308, 309, 311, 312, 482, 485, 486, 496, 511, 512, 519, 524, 525, 541, 543, 544, 560, 562, 831
Gillmore, Quincy A., 696-99, 701, 789, 817, 822, 823-24, 827, 898-902, 905
Gist, States Rights, 713, 717, 734
Glass's Mill, Georgia, 715, 742
Glenn, Eliza, 718, 724
Goldsboro, North Carolina, 253, 254, 257, 259; Battle of, 20
Gordon, John B., 477, 518, 519, 520, 578
Gorgas, Josiah, 642
Gracie, Archibald, Jr., 753-54
Grand Coteau, Louisiana, 871, 872
Grand Gulf, Mississippi, 324, 325, 330, 331, 332, 342, 347, 350, 352, 355, 362
Granger, Gordon, 178, 666, 667, 671, 672, 687, 715, 727, 750-52, 805, 841, 845, 852, 853, 854-55, 857, 866
Grant, Frederick D., 327, 363, 418
Grant, Julia D. (Mrs. U. S.), 327, 363, 417, 785
Grant, Ulysses S., 6, 7, 12, 17, 20, 95, 107; accident suffered by, 774, 780; Chattanooga defended by, 804-11, 812, 826, 834-37, 840, 841-45; commander in the West, 784-85; Halleck and, 61, 62, 137, 144, 145, 188-89, 190, 192, 325, 386, 638, 770-71, 784, 870, 920; Lincoln and, 145, 217, 623-26, 638-39, 771, 773, 918, 947-949, 962-63; McClernand and, 60-62, 64-65, 73, 78, 364, 421-22; at Missionary Ridge, 845-59; Mississippi River campaign, 62-79, 669-74, 780-85; ordered to Washington, 962-63, 966; Pemberton and, 608-12, 613; plans for conduct of the war, 919-20, 922; popularity and honors, 917-18, 922-23; promoted to lieutenant general, 918; promoted to major general, 624, 773; Ringgold Gap campaign, 860-862; Sherman and, 61, 62, 73, 143, 190, 326, 330, 332, 333, 352, 356-57, 365, 377, 380, 385, 415, 421, 424, 614, 836, 841, 920, 922, 964-66; siege of Vicksburg, 379-427, 430, 431, 432, 597, 606-14; Vicksburg campaign, 133, 136-38, 139, 143-47, 186-220, 323-79; whiskey and, 217-18, 219-20, 416-21, 774, 803
Grant, Ulysses S., Jr., 327, 363
Gravelet, J. F., 119
Great Locomotive Chase, 179
Greeley, Horace, 218, 315, 881
Green, Thomas, 58, 597, 598, 599, 616, 871
Greencastle, Pennsylvania, 583, 584
Greene, George S., 517, 520, 524

Gregg, David McM., 437, 494, 570, 571, 572, 795
Gregg, John, 360, 363
Grenada, Mississippi, 62, 770
Grierson, Benjamin H., 334-41, 344, 345, 346, 357, 392, 396, 927
Grindstone Ford, Mississippi, 349, 350
Grover, Cuvier, 390, 391, 396, 397, 402, 616
Guy's Gap, Tennessee, 666, 671
Gwin, William, 75-76

Hagerstown, Maryland, 441, 444, 454, 583, 584
Hahn, Michael, 963
Haines Bluff, Mississippi, 74, 77, 217, 324, 332-33, 344, 354, 378, 379, 380, 381
Halleck, Henry W., Banks and, 399-400, 403, 772, 774, 872; Burnside and, 122, 123-124, 128; Grant and, 61, 62, 137, 144, 145, 188-89, 190, 192, 325, 386, 638, 770-71, 784, 870, 920; Hooker and, 447, 449, 450; Lincoln and, 123-24, 764, 790; Meade and, 589-90, 593-94, 595, 624, 626, 790, 797, 798, 799; personal appearance, 128; Rosecrans and, 79-80, 103, 169, 170, 663, 664, 675, 676, 677, 725, 763; Sherman and, 781, 782
Halstead, Marat, 217
Hamilton, Andrew Jackson, 56-57, 59, 871, 872
Hamilton, Charles S., 61
Hamilton's Crossing, Virginia, 23, 34
Hamlin, Hannibal, 108
Hampton, Wade, 243, 438, 459, 570, 571, 578, 787, 877, 913
Hancock, Winfield Scott, 278, 305, 448, 449, 452, 453, 482, 483-86, 493, 496, 507, 510, 511, 513, 514, 519, 523, 524, 534, 543, 545, 546, 549, 560-61, 575, 576, 791
Hankinson's Ferry, Mississippi, 356
Hanover, Pennsylvania, 459
Hardee, William J., 83, 85, 86, 92, 101, 102, 171, 645, 665, 666, 667, 670, 671, 672, 673, 686, 690, 817, 820, 839, 840, 851, 868, 869, 878, 886, 891
Hardie, James A., 450-52, 458
Harker, Charles G., 741, 749, 856-57
Harmon, John A., 592
Harpers Ferry, Virginia, 272, 451, 594
Harper's Weekly, 118, 147, 341, 931, 959
Harrisburg, Pennsylvania, 445, 456, 459, 463
Harrison (Confederate spy), 462-63
Harrison, Burton N., 815
Hartford, U.S.S., 213, 214, 215, 216, 396, 775, 935
Hartsville, Tennessee, 8; Battle of, 20
Harvard University, 151
Hatch, Edward, 336, 337
Hatteras, U.S.S., 125, 126, 894
Hawks, Wells, 319
Hawthorne, Nathaniel, 152
Hay, John, 152, 831, 899-901, 905-06
Hays, Alexander, 452, 453, 511, 512, 544, 548, 555, 560, 562, 563, 565

Index

Hays, Harry T., 518–20
Hazard, John G., 546
Hazel Grove, Virginia, 288, 289, 292, 298, 299, 300, 303, 304, 306
Hazen, William B., 749
Hazlett, Charles E., 503, 504
Helena, Arkansas, 52, 60, 73, 702, 706; attack on, 601–06
Helm, Ben Hardin, 734
Henry, Guy V., 901, 902
Heroes of America, 651
Herron, Francis J., 47, 48, 49–51, 407, 423, 617–18, 669
Herr Ridge, Gettysburg, 468, 471, 474, 475, 492
Heth, Henry, 306, 307, 311, 434, 435, 465, 467, 468, 469, 470, 472, 473, 478, 491, 501, 530, 535, 536, 578, 592, 792
Hill, Ambrose Powell, at Bristoe Station, 793–94, 800, 819; at Catharine Furnace, 293, 295, 298; at Chancellorsville, 280, 286; at Fredericksburg, 30; at Gettysburg, 467, 472, 473, 475, 476, 478, 479, 489, 491, 498, 509, 510, 513, 514, 522, 523, 529, 531, 578, 580; Jackson and, 301, 319; in Pennsylvania campaign, 439, 440, 441, 443, 444, 449, 456, 463, 464, 465, 467; in Shenandoah campaign, 787, 789, 792, 793–94, 800; promoted lieutenant general, 434, 435; withdrawal from Gettysburg, 583, 585, 592; wounded, 303
Hill, Benjamin H., 161
Hill, Daniel Harvey, Bragg and, 812, 813, 814, 815, 816, 817; at Chickamauga, 690, 691, 692, 693, 694, 713, 715, 716, 717, 723, 728, 729, 732, 733, 734, 756, 757, 762; estimate of Confederate soldier by, 553; Forrest and, 733; at Fredericksburg, 30, 286; at Missionary Ridge, 812, 813, 814, 815, 816, 817; in North Carolina, 239, 252, 254, 257, 258, 259, 435, 817; promoted lieutenant general, 690; relieved of command, 817
Hilton Head, South Carolina, 900, 902
Hindman, Thomas C., 11, 46–52, 139, 142, 690, 692, 712, 716, 723, 737–40, 742, 751, 753, 755, 762, 812, 813
Holden, William W., 650
Holly Springs, Mississippi, 17, 61, 65, 70, 72, 73, 136; Raid on, 20
Holmes, Theophilus H., 11–12, 45–46, 47, 51–52, 59–60, 142, 143, 597, 600–06, 644, 706, 707, 780
Holston River, 677, 838
Holt, John D., 704, 705
Homestead Act of 1862, 151
Honey Springs, Arkansas, 703
Hood, John Bell, at Chancellorsville, 280; at Chickamauga, 710–11, 712, 715, 716, 719, 720, 721, 737, 738, 741; at Fredericksburg, 30; at Gettysburg, 480, 489, 493, 498, 499, 501, 513, 521; Lee and, 237; division commander under Longstreet, 429, 434, 435; in North Carolina, 256, 258, 259, 695; at Petersburg, 261; promoted lieutenant general, 889; Richmond defended by, 240, 252, 255, 889; wounded, 501, 505, 509, 514, 578, 710, 741
Hood's Mill, Maryland, 459
Hooker, Joseph, Burnside and, 130, 131; at Chancellorsville, 269, 271, 276–77, 278–283, 287–91, 293–94, 298–300, 303–06; at Chattanooga, 80, 836, 837, 841, 842, 844, 847, 849, 852, 857, 859, 860, 866; commander of Army of the Potomac, 131, 132–33, 232–36, 261–71, 446–52; commander of Grand Division, 25, 37; at Culpeper, 436–37, 440; at Fort Monroe, 253; at Fredericksburg, 240, 242–44, 245, 309; Halleck and, 447, 449, 450; Lee and, 237–44, 261, 262–71, 273–75, 455; Lincoln and, 232, 234, 235–36, 250–51, 261, 264, 267, 315–16, 447–49, 451, 456, 826; at Lookout Mountain, 847, 848–49; at Marye's Heights, 38, 40–41, 42; nom-de-guerre, 234; reinforcement for Chattanooga, 764, 765, 766, 805, 806, 808, 809–810, 836; relieved of Potomac command, 450–52, 462; Stoneman and, 314–15
Hoover's Gap, Tennessee, 285
Hotchkiss, Jedediah, 285
Housatonic, U.S.S., 223, 224, 898
Houston, Sam, 648
Hovey, Alvin P., 347, 370, 371, 372–73, 374, 375
Howard, Oliver O., at Chancellorsville, 266, 268, 270, 276, 277, 281, 289, 291–92, 296, 297, 298, 300, 305, 313; at Fredericksburg, 315; at Gettysburg, 465, 468, 471, 472, 475, 482, 483, 484, 486, 493, 513, 516, 518, 524, 576; Grant and, 803; Meade and, 591; in Pennsylvania campaign, 448, 453; replaced Sigel, 251; wounded, 251
Humphreys, Andrew A., 40, 452, 453, 508, 511, 590
Hunley, H. L., 896, 897
Hunley, H. L., C.S.S., 896–98
Hunt, Henry J., 28, 495, 496, 509, 541, 545–546, 547, 562, 576
Hurlbut, Stephen A., 67–68, 190, 334, 336, 352, 369, 725, 770, 923, 925, 926
Hutchinson family, 959

Imboden, John B., 463, 489, 580–81, 583, 584–85
Immigrants, 150, 151
Imperial, U.S.S., 617
Indianola, U.S.S., 197, 198–99, 200, 201, 213, 215, 324
Indians, 46–47, 702
Indian Territory, 702, 703, 776
Industrial growth, 150
Inflation, 147–48, 159–60
Ingersoll, Robert G., 66
Ingraham, Duncan, 223
Iron Brigade, 469, 470, 475, 476, 516
Island Ten, 67
Iverson, Alfred, 473, 475
Ivey's Hill, Mississippi, 932

[980]   Index

Jackson, Anna (Mrs. T. J.), 273, 317–18, 319
Jackson, Mary, 163
Jackson, Mississippi, 4, 13, 361, 363–66, 369, 619–22, 669, 924; Battle of, 361–63
Jackson, Thomas Jonathan ("Stonewall"), at Chancellorsville, 271–73, 274, 275, 276, 280, 282–87, 290, 292–98, 300–03; death of, 317–19, 430; fortifications constructed by, 241–42; at Fredericksburg, 22–23, 28, 29, 31, 32–33, 34, 37, 38–39, 44–45, 272; graduate of West Point in 1846, 531; Lee and, 282–87, 303, 306, 311, 316–317, 445, 580, 596; in Shenandoah campaign, 251–52; wounded, 300–03, 306, 311, 316–17
Jackson, Tennessee, 65, 66
Jacksonville, Florida, 900, 902, 903, 905
Jacob's Ford, Virginia, 874
James, Henry, 961
James Island, 698, 699, 700
Jasper, Tennessee, 803
Jefferson City, Missouri, 777
Jenkins, Albert G., 439, 440, 570
Jenkins, Micah, 838, 863, 865
Johnson, Bushrod R., 712, 717, 720, 721, 722, 732, 737, 738–39, 740, 741, 742, 743, 746, 749, 751, 753, 754, 755, 840, 845, 852, 857
Johnson, Edward, 434, 435, 436, 439, 440, 445, 464, 472, 479, 487, 514, 515, 516, 517, 520, 521, 522, 523, 524, 727, 770, 800, 801
Johnson, Herschel V., 649
Johnson, Richard W., 87–88, 91, 644
Johnston, Albert Sidney, 99, 249, 534
Johnston, Joseph E., Beauregard and, 428, 429; Bragg and, 172–74, 677, 816–17, 820; Bragg succeeded by, 886–87, 891–93; criticism of, 622–23, 646–47; Davis and, 6–7, 9–13, 16–17, 646–47, 816, 886–87, 891–92; East Tennessee campaign and, 346; Grant and, 400, 405–06, 407, 408, 409, 410, 421, 424, 614; at Jackson, Mississippi, 358, 366, 368–69, 430; Lee and, 430; Pemberton and, 345, 353, 355–56, 367, 368–69, 378, 379, 387, 400, 412, 413–14, 425, 426–27, 433, 596, 622–23; Port Hudson and, 396, 400, 596; Sherman and, 618, 619, 620, 621, 935, 938
Johnston, Mrs. Joseph E., 7
Johnston, Samuel R., 490, 492
Johnston, William P., 815
Jones, John M., 516
Jones, John Paul, 20
Jones, William E., 438, 463
Jonesboro, Arkansas, 764
Jordan, Thomas, 822, 823
Journal of Commerce, 881
Juárez, Benito, 771
Jude's Ford, Virginia, 913, 917
Julian, George W., 112

Kapital, Das, 149
Kean, Robert G. H., 642
Kearny, Phil, 233

Kelley's Ferry, Tennessee, 807, 811
Kelly, John H., 753–54
Kelly's Ford, Virginia, 245–47, 265, 266, 267, 273, 800, 801–02, 873
Kemper, James L., 533, 552, 555, 557, 559, 561, 568, 577
Keokuk, U.S.S., 228, 230, 231
Kershaw, Joseph B., 506, 712, 713, 723, 737, 740, 741, 742, 749–50, 751, 753
Keystone State, U.S.S., 224
Key West, Florida, 905
Kilpatrick, H. Judson, 437, 494, 569–70, 571, 572–74, 592, 795, 796, 907–16
Kimball, Nathan, 407
Kimble, June, 538, 563–64
King, Preston, 111
Kingsville, South Carolina. 710
Kittoe, Edward D., 784
Knoxville, Tennessee, 7, 671, 675, 677, 685–688, 708, 709, 760, 764, 837, 839, 841, 845, 872, 917, 920; relief of, 862–66
Koch's Plantation, affair at, 616

Lafayette, Alabama, 165
La Fayette, Georgia, 687, 692, 693, 694, 713, 715
Lafayette, U.S.S., 342
La Fayette Road, Chickamauga, 716, 717, 719, 720, 721, 722, 727, 732, 734, 738, 739, 740, 743, 744, 750, 751, 755
La Grange, Georgia, 812, 813, 869
Lake City, Florida, 901, 903, 904
Lamon, Ward H., 830, 831, 832, 941
Lancaster, U.S.S., 215, 216
Lane, Harriet, U.S.S., 58
Lane, James H., 513, 520, 535, 563, 704, 705
Lang, David, 510, 511, 512, 530, 536, 558, 564
Latimer, Joseph W., 515
Lauman, Jacob G., 407, 423, 619–20
Law, Evander McI., 490, 492, 493, 501, 502, 505, 529, 567, 573, 574, 695, 712, 720, 721, 737, 738, 740, 741, 742, 746, 753, 838
Lawler, Michael K., 377
Lawrence, Amos A., 148
Lawrence, Kansas, 703, 704, 708
Lawrence Massacre, 704–05
Lee, Fitzhugh, 244, 245–47, 283, 293, 348, 459, 570, 571, 585, 787, 795, 796, 888
Lee, G. W. Custis, 815, 826
Lee, Robert E., 5, 9, 15, 95; at Chancellorsville, 280–316; Davis and, 6, 430–33, 441–443, 586, 593, 646, 647, 656–59, 708–09, 878, 880, 886–87, 952, 957; at Fredericksburg, 21, 22–24, 26–45; at Gettysburg, 461, 473–81, 486–93, 497–99, 507, 509, 513–14, 520–23, 525–41, 552, 567–69, 576, 578, 579–581; Hooker and, 237–44, 261, 262–71, 273–275; illness, 248–49; Jackson and, 282–87, 306, 311, 316–17, 318; Kilpatrick's raid and, 916; Meade and, 460, 461, 467–581, 641, 794–802; Mine Run campaign, 872–78; northern campaign, 431–33, 436–46, 455–467; reorganization of Army of Northern Virginia by, 434–35; resignation of-

Index [981]

fered by, 656–59; Stuart and, 461, 463; withdrawal from Gettysburg by, 582–96
Lee, Stephen D., ７૯, 923, 933, 938
Lee, William H. F. ("Rooney"), 244, 437, 438, 586
Lee & Gordon's Mill, Georgia, 692, 693, 694, 713, 715, 716, 721, 742
Lee's Hill, Fredericksburg, 31, 33
Leslie's Illustrated, 341
Letcher, John, 163
Lexington, Kentucky, 680, 917
Liberty Gap, Tennessee, 667, 671
Liddell, St. John R., 713, 755
Lincoln, Abraham, Burnside and, 121–23, 127–28, 130–32; Chief Executive, 107–16; Commander in Chief, 116–19, 121–24, 127–33, 140–41; conduct of the war by, 826–28; conquest of Florida and, 899–900, 903, 906; draft enforcement and, 635–38; Emancipation Proclamation and, 120–21, 629, 640, 881, 955, 959; foreign relations, 155, 772; Gettysburg Address, 827, 829–833; Grant and, 145, 217, 364, 623–26, 638–639, 771, 773, 849, 918, 947–49, 962–63; Hooker and, 232, 234, 235–36, 250–51, 264, 267, 315–16, 447–49, 451, 456, 826; illness, 833; Kilpatrick's raid and, 908, 916; leadership recognized, 959; McClernand and, 60–61, 188–89, 422–23; Meade and, 236, 593–94, 595, 623–24, 626–28, 638, 639, 790–91, 797, 798, 799, 827–28; political loyalty to, 628–31, 639; Pomeroy Circular and, 941–46; Proclamation of Amnesty and Reconstruction, 880–89, 899, 907, 941; reconstruction plans, 881–84, 907–908, 915; re-election and, 940–46; Rosecrans and, 169, 663–64, 676–77, 763–65, 767–68; Thanksgiving Proclamation, 627–628, 870; Vallandigham banished by, 633–34; year-end message to Congress, 879–84
Lincoln, Mary Todd, 236, 829, 830
Lincoln, Robert T., 626
Lincoln, Thomas T. ("Tad"), 236–37, 829, 830, 833
Lindsay, William S., 654
Little Rock, Arkansas, 12, 45, 47, 52, 706, 707, 776
Little Round Top, Gettysburg, 479, 484, 490, 493, 494, 496, 499, 501, 502, 503–05, 507, 509, 514, 515, 516, 523, 524, 530, 541, 543, 545, 546, 547, 548, 554, 555, 557, 575
Littletown, Pennsylvania, 459
Livermore, Mary, 218, 219
Lockett, Samuel H., 378, 613
Logan, John A., 360, 370, 372, 373, 609, 612
London *Times*, 154, 653, 656
Longstreet, James, Bragg and, 760–61, 762–763, 814, 816, 817, 821; at Chancellorsville, 436; at Chattanooga, 713, 715, 723, 734, 736–38, 740, 741–44, 752–53, 756, 757, 758, 760–61, 762–63, 814, 816, 817, 821, 834; commander of First Army Corps, 434; at Culpeper, 438, 440, 709; defense of the James region, 240, 251–52, 253–61,

273, 279; at Fredericksburg, 22, 23, 28, 30, 31, 32, 33, 35–36, 37, 41–42, 44, 436; at Gettysburg, 465, 479–80, 485, 488, 489, 490, 491–93, 498, 505, 506, 509, 514, 521, 523, 526, 528–31, 536, 537, 540, 549, 551, 552, 558–59, 566–67, 569, 575, 578, 580, 582, 595; Jackson and, 33, 241–42; Knoxville besieged by, 821, 834, 837–39, 841, 862–66; Lee and, 35–36, 37, 41–42, 436, 536, 537, 595, 709; McLaws sponsored by, 435; in Pennsylvania campaign, 439, 440, 441, 443, 444, 456, 462, 463, 464; Pickett and, 540, 541, 549, 551, 552; plans for conduct of the war, 429, 818; reaction to defeats at Gettysburg and Vicksburg, 641–42; reinforcement for Bragg, 694, 695, 709, 711, 712, 786; retreat from Gettysburg, 583, 585, 592
Lookout Mountain, 686, 687, 692, 715, 759, 760, 766, 804, 806, 807, 809, 812, 836, 840, 846, 847, 849, 861; Battle of, 847–49
Loring, William W., 204, 205, 367, 368, 374, 378, 425, 923, 924
Loudon, Tennessee, 838
Louisville, Kentucky, 765, 784, 785, 917
Louisville, U.S.S., 135, 342
Louisville & Nashville Railroad, 84, 178
Louisville *Courier*, 635
Lowe, Thaddeus S. C., 268, 271, 279, 289, 447
Lowrance, William L. J., 535, 563
Lubbock, Francis R., 644
Luther, Martin, 959
Lynchburg, Virginia, 7
Lynchburg *Virginian*, 649
Lyon, Nathaniel, 49
Lytle, William H., 740, 745

Macon *Telegraph & Intelligencer*, 650
Maffit, James N., 126, 894
Magnolia, U.S.S., 219, 327
Magruder, John B., 18–19, 46, 57–59, 95, 124, 127, 597, 775
Mahone, William, 510, 512, 520
Major, James P., 597, 598, 616
Mallory, Stephen R., 432
Maloney, Patrick, 470
Manchester, Tennessee, 671, 672, 673, 675
Mann, A. Dudley, 157
Marietta, Georgia, 165
Marmaduke, John S., 139–40, 600, 601, 602, 605, 706
Marshall, James K., 536, 559, 564
Marx, Karl, 149
Marye's Heights, Fredericksburg, 33, 34, 38, 39, 236, 266, 307, 308, 309, 311
Maryville, Tennessee, 866
Mason, James M., 156, 157, 653–54, 655–56
Massachusetts Institute of Technology, 151
Massaponax Creek, 22, 23, 30
Maury, Dabney H., 820
Mayo, Joseph, 536, 556, 560, 564
McAfee's Church, Georgia, 750, 751, 752
McArthur, John, 370

McClellan, George B., 5, 21, 24, 57, 119, 121, 123, 431, 531, 791, 826
McClernand, John A., 60–62, 64–65, 73, 78, 107, 133–36, 137, 138, 143–44, 145, 187–89, 190, 216, 218, 324, 326, 331, 335, 338, 342, 344, 345, 347–48, 349, 351, 356, 359–60, 361, 362, 364, 365, 370, 373, 374, 375, 376–77, 380, 381, 383, 384, 385, 386, 408, 421–23
McCook, Alexander McD., 81, 82, 85, 86, 87, 89, 90, 94, 666, 667, 671, 672, 687, 688, 692, 713–15, 726, 727, 731, 735, 736, 739, 746, 752, 763, 766
McCown, John P., 83, 86, 87, 92
McDowell, Irvin, 119
McFarland's Gap, Georgia, 717, 739, 740, 742, 745, 746, 754, 755
McGilvery, Freeman, 546, 547, 555, 557
McGirt's Creek, Florida, 905
McGuire, Hunter, 30., 316, 317, 318, 319
McLaws, Lafayette, 30, 274, 275, 276, 278, 280, 286, 306, 307, 311, 312, 434, 435, 436, 480, 489, 490, 493, 498–99, 505–06, 509, 510, 513, 521, 529, 566–67, 575, 695, 710, 712, 760, 766, 863, 865
McLean, William E., 604, 605
McLemore's Cove, 692, 693, 694, 713, 715, 723, 734, 744, 762, 812
McMinnville, Tennessee, 666, 670, 671, 675, 686, 761
McNeil, John, 601
McPherson, James B., 61, 136, 138, 145, 190, 194, 202, 218–19, 326, 331, 335, 344, 348, 349, 351, 356, 359, 360, 361, 362, 365, 369, 370, 371, 372, 373, 375, 380, 381, 383–85, 423, 609, 624, 773, 925, 926, 964, 965
McPherson's Ridge, Gettysburg, 469, 470, 471, 475, 477, 493
Meade, George G., at Brandy Station, 794–802; Butterfield succeeded by, 250; at Chancellorsville, 277, 278, 281, 300, 303, 305, 313, 315; commander of Army of the Potomac, 450–52, 462, 764, 773, 786, 787, 789–92, 888–89; failure to follow Lee's withdrawal from Gettysburg, 583, 586–92, 593–95; at Fredericksburg, 36, 37, 266, 268–69, 270, 271; at Gettysburg, 462–464, 465–67, 468, 479, 481–82, 483, 485, 486, 487, 492, 493, 494, 495, 496–97, 502, 503, 509, 510, 512, 513, 520, 521, 523–25, 527, 528, 542, 543, 559, 566, 569, 573, 574–575, 580, 583; Halleck and, 589–90, 593–594, 595, 624, 626, 790, 797, 798, 799; Hooker succeeded by, 451; Lincoln and, 236, 593–94, 595, 623–24, 626–28, 638, 639, 790–91, 797, 798, 799, 827–28; Mine Run campaign, 872–78, 888; in Pennsylvania campaign, 448, 451–55, 458; reinforcement for Chattanooga from, 764–65
Meadow Bridge, Virginia, 912
Mechanicsville, Virginia, 912
Meems, David, 915
Memphis, Tennessee, 5, 61, 64, 65, 72, 136, 144, 773, 782, 923
Memphis & Charleston Railroad, 6, 10, 72, 783, 805, 808, 835, 937

Memphis *Evening Bulletin*, 421
Mendenhall, John, 99, 100
Mercedita, U.S.S., 223
Mercer, Hugh, 20
Mercier, Henri, 157, 653
Meredith, Minerva, 163
Meredith, Solomon, 475
Meridian, Mississippi, 819–20, 923, 925–26, 936
Merrimac, C.S.S., 225, 226
Mexico, 771–72
Mexico City, Mexico, 772
Middletown, Pennsylvania, 464, 472, 590
Miles, William R., 401
Milliken's Bend, Mississippi, 75, 133, 135, 326, 329, 345, 352, 406, 414, 421, 597
Milroy, Robert H., 439-40
Mine Run campaign, 872–78
Missionary Ridge, 687, 692, 713, 715, 722, 738, 743, 745, 746, 749, 755, 758, 759, 760, 761, 804, 812, 813, 815–16, 836, 840, 842, 844, 846, 866, 870, 917; Battle of, 845–59
Mississippi, U.S.S., 213, 214, 225
Mississippi Central Railroad, 61, 614, 619, 620, 938
Mississippi River, 9, 15, 617
Mobile, Alabama, 10, 18, 126, 164, 397, 770, 772, 820, 894
Mobile & Ohio Railroad, 336, 338, 923, 928, 929, 930, 937
Mobile *Tribune*, 167
Moccasin Point, 806, 807, 808, 848
Monitor, U.S.S., 125, 225, 226
Monongahela, U.S.S., 213, 214, 396
Monroe Doctrine, 772
Monroe, James, 20
Monroe, Louisiana, 75
Montauk, U.S.S., 226, 228, 230
Montgomery, Alabama, 3, 10, 19, 820
Moon Lake, Mississippi, 202, 203
Moore, Absalom B., 8
Morgan, Calvin, 678, 683
Morgan, Charlton, 678, 682, 683
Morgan, George W., 76, 133, 135
Morgan, John Hunt, 8, 18, 20, 81, 83–84, 95, 175, 179, 671, 678–83, 889–90
Morgan, Mattie Ready (Mrs. John H.), 83–84, 671
Morgan, Richard, 678, 682, 683
Morgan, Thomas, 678, 679
Morgan, William H., 71–72
Morning Light, U.S.S., 127
Morris Island, 228, 643, 696, 697, 698, 699, 700, 701, 702, 898
Morton, Mississippi, 924
Morton, Oliver P., 629, 680
Mosby, John S., 244–45
Mouton, Alfred, 395, 597, 598, 599
Mud March, 129–30, 146, 167, 239
Murfreesboro, Tennessee, 8, 9, 19, 81, 83–84, 85, 124, 664, 665, 761; Battle of, 20, 87–103, 168
Murphy, Robert C., 70, 71
Muscle Shoals, Alabama, 835

Index [983]

Nahant, U.S.S., 228, 229, 230
Nansemond River, 258
Nantucket, U.S.S., 228, 230
Napoleon III, 154, 157, 771, 772-73
Napoleon, Louisiana, 143, 146
Nashville, C.S.S., 220
Nashville, Tennessee, 5, 6, 18, 803, 917, 966
Nashville & Chattanooga Railroad, 81, 83, 178, 665, 673, 808, 835
Nashville & Northwestern Railroad, 67
Natchez, Mississippi, 669, 773
National Union Party, 639, 828
Navy Department, U. S., 225
Negley, James S., 89, 91, 716, 720, 722, 727, 728, 730-31, 732, 735, 746, 749, 805
Negro troops, 393, 406-07, 638, 697, 702, 900, 904
Nelson, William, 88
Neptune, S.S., 57, 58
Neuse River, 9
New Bern, North Carolina, 253, 254, 259
New Carthage, Mississippi, 323, 324, 326, 329, 334, 345
New Iberia, Louisiana, 392
New Ironsides, U.S.S., 227, 228, 229, 230, 231, 824-25, 894, 898
New Orleans, Louisiana, 5, 15, 53, 54, 55, 56, 391, 393, 395, 403-04, 405, 597, 600, 773, 963
New Orleans, Jackson & Great Northern Railroad, 338
New Orleans Crescent, 635
Newton, John, 117-18, 131, 452, 453, 493, 513, 516, 591, 791, 875, 876
New York Herald, 271, 882, 945
New York Times, 44, 107, 481, 881
New York Tribune, 147, 881
New York World, 148, 149, 635, 884
Nicolay, John, 942
Northrop, Lucius B., 162

Oak Hill, Gettysburg, 471, 472, 582
Oates, William C., 501, 502-03, 504, 505, 514, 574
Obion River, 67
Ocean Pond, Battle of, 903-04
Olustee, Florida, 901; Battle of, 903-04, 905
O'Neal, Edward A., 527
Opdyke, Emerson, 749
Opdyke, George, 637
Opelousas, Louisiana, 392, 393
Orange & Alexandria Railroad, 789, 791, 797
Orchard Knob, 845, 846, 847, 849, 851, 853, 854, 855, 857, 866
Ord, Edward O. C., 423, 609, 619, 620
O'Rorke, Patrick H., 504
Osborn, Thomas W., 546, 547, 548, 555
Osterhaus, Peter J., 347, 348, 370, 371, 377, 407, 841, 852
Overall's Creek, 95
Owasco, U.S.S., 58, 59

Paine, Halbert E., 394-95, 396, 397, 402
Palatka, Florida, 901

Palmer, John M., 90, 98, 717, 722, 733, 749, 754, 805, 845
Palmerston, Henry J. T., 154, 155, 157, 656
Palmetto State, C.S.S., 223-24
Pamlico Sound, 256, 259
Parke, John G., 407, 619, 677
Parkersburg, West Virginia, 682
Parker's Crossroads, Tennessee, 68; Battle of, 18
Passaic, U.S.S., 228, 230
Patapsco, U.S.S., 228, 230
Peach Orchard, Gettysburg, 493, 498, 502, 504, 506, 508, 509, 513, 521, 523, 530, 539, 541, 577, 582
Pearl River, 619, 620
Peck, John J., 258, 287
Pelham, John, 34, 37, 247-48
Pelican Island Bar, Texas, 58
Pemberton, John C., Bragg and, 65, 645, 816; at Champion Hill, 371-74; commander of Army of Mississippi, 6, 8-9, 46, 52, 365, 366, 368-69, 371-74, 377; commissioned lieutenant colonel of artillery, 645-46; Davis and, 645, 815; defense of Vicksburg, 78, 331, 344-47, 348, 353-55, 356, 365, 366, 367, 382-83, 387, 405, 408, 411, 412, 413-14, 415, 596; Grant and, 61, 62, 64, 69, 73, 362, 376, 421, 424, 608-09, 610-11; at Grenada, 12, 61, 62; Grierson and, 335, 338, 340; Johnston and, 345, 353, 355-56, 367, 368-69, 378, 379, 387, 400, 412, 413-14, 425, 426-27, 433, 596, 622-23; surrender and evacuation of Vicksburg by, 607-12, 613; Van Dorn and, 70-72, 79, 340
Pender, W. Dorsey, 434, 435, 473, 474, 476, 478, 479, 499, 512-13, 520, 530, 535
Pendleton, Alexander, 318
Pendleton, William N., 434, 435
Pennsylvania Railroad, 765
Perryville, Battle of, 19
Peters, George B., 178
Petersburg, Virginia, 261
Petersburg & Norfolk Railroad, 258
Pettigrew, J. Johnston, 465, 475, 476, 489, 530, 536, 537, 551, 553, 554, 556, 557, 559-60, 562, 563, 564, 578, 579, 593
Pettus, John J., 4, 5, 6, 13, 353, 621
Phelan, James, 5, 6, 13, 15, 70
Philadelphia Evening Journal, 635
Phillips, Wendell, 960, 962
Pickett, George E., defense of Richmond, 252, 255, 695; division commander under Longstreet, 434, 435; at Fredericksburg, 30, 240; at Gettysburg, 489, 490, 497, 522, 523, 526, 529, 530, 531-34, 536-39, 541, 549, 550, 551, 552, 553, 554, 557, 559, 564, 567-68, 579, 580, 595-96; Lee and, 567-68, 595-96; Longstreet and, 540, 541, 549, 551, 552; military background, 531-32; at Petersburg, 261; at Suffolk, 256, 258, 259-260
Pickett's Charge, at Gettysburg, 548-65
Picolata, Florida, 901
Pigeon Mountain, 692, 715

Pin Indians, 47
Pittsburg, U.S.S., 342
Pitzer's Run, Gettysburg, 493, 534
Pleasonton, Alfred, 437, 438, 448, 482, 524, 574–75, 576, 776, 795, 908, 909, 911
Plum Run, Gettysburg, 509, 510, 573, 574
Polk, James K., 108, 602
Polk, Leonidas, 83, 84, 85, 88, 92, 96, 98, 101, 102, 171–72, 665, 667, 670, 671, 672, 673, 686, 691, 692, 693, 713, 715, 716, 728–729, 730, 732, 733, 743, 749, 754, 757, 760, 762, 812, 813, 814, 815, 816, 817, 820, 887, 923, 925, 934–35
Polk, Lucius E., 732–33
Pollard, Edward A., 649, 652, 957, 958
Pomeroy, Samuel C., 941, 943, 944
Pomeroy Circular, 941–44
Pool, David, 140
Pope, John, 119, 235, 268, 725, 786
Porter, David D., 17, 64, 74–75, 77, 78, 134, 135, 136, 143, 146, 195–96, 197, 199–200, 206–10, 211, 215, 217, 225, 324, 327, 329, 330, 341–42, 345, 350–51, 354, 383, 384, 386, 388–89, 393, 396, 406, 597, 613, 614, 617–18, 623, 669, 894
Porter, Fitz-John, 726
Port Gibson, Mississippi, 344, 346, 347, 348, 350, 353, 357; Battle of, 394
Port Hudson, Louisiana, 11, 12, 18, 52, 55, 137, 138, 139, 143, 195, 212, 215, 216, 225, 325, 338, 345, 351, 355, 358, 389, 596, 597, 598, 600, 609, 614–15; siege of, 395–405
Port Royal, Virginia, 22, 23, 29, 224, 227, 231, 256, 825
Posey, Carnot, 510, 512, 793
Potomac River, 585, 590, 592, 594
Potter, Robert B., 407
Powers Hill, Gettysburg, 527, 542, 566
Prairie Grove, Battle of, 11, 20, 49–51
Preble, Edward, 126
Prentiss, Benjamin M., 386, 603, 604, 605, 606, 702, 772
Preston, William, 99, 712, 737, 742, 753, 754, 755, 839
Price, Samuel W., 90–91
Price, Sterling, 142, 143, 601, 602, 605, 706, 707, 776, 780
Pritchett, James M., 605
Proclamation of Amnesty and Reconstruction, 880–86, 899, 907, 941
Profit's Island, 213, 215

Quantrill, William Charles, 140, 141, 703, 704–05, 706, 708, 776, 778–80, 915
Queen of the West, U.S.S., 195, 196, 197, 198–99, 201, 202, 213, 215, 324, 390, 391
Quinby, Isaac F., 205

Raccoon Mountain, 687, 688, 761, 803, 804, 807, 809, 811
Raleigh, North Carolina, 19
Raleigh *Standard*, 650
Raleigh *State Journal*, 650
Ransom, Robert, Jr., 30, 239, 253, 256
Ransom, Thomas E. G., 669

Rapidan River, 787
Rappahannock River, 9, 21, 22, 23, 26, 29, 41, 787
Rappahannock Station, Virginia, 792
Rawlins, John A., 416–17, 419, 420, 422, 611, 773
Raymond, Mississippi, 360, 361
Reagan, John H., 432, 433, 695
Reconstruction, plans for, 880–86, 907–08, 915
Red River, 143, 194, 195, 197, 390, 393, 394
"Red Strings," 651
Reed's Bridge, Chickamauga, 711, 716, 717, 727, 744
Renshaw, William B., 58
Reynolds, John F., 30, 266, 287, 289, 300, 303, 313, 315, 448, 452, 454, 465, 467, 468–469, 481, 482, 576, 691, 716, 720, 722, 734, 735, 736, 738, 740, 741, 754, 755
Reynolds, Joseph J., 668
Reynolds, Thomas C., 644
Rhea's Mills, Arkansas, 50
Rhett, Robert Barnwell, Sr. and Jr., 648, 649, 821, 822, 823
Rice, Samuel A., 604, 605
Richmond, Fredericksburg & Potomac Railroad, 23
Richmond, U.S.S., 213, 214, 396, 404–05
Richmond, Virginia, 9, 19, 158–64, 252, 695, 710, 786, 790–91, 815, 887, 889–91, 907, 908, 910–12, 913, 914, 915, 916
Richmond *Enquirer*, 164
Richmond *Examiner*, 167, 168, 641, 649, 916
Richmond *Sentinel*, 883
Richmond *Whig*, 318, 441, 788
Riggin, John, 420
Ringgold, Georgia, 693, 858, 859, 860–61
Ringgold Bridge, Chickamauga, 760
Ringgold Gap, 861, 867
Rittenhouse, Benjamin F., 546, 547, 555
Roanoke, Virginia, 888
Roanoke Island, 254, 257
Robertson, Beverly H., 438, 463
Robertson, J. B., 501, 505
Robinson, John C., 453
Robinson, Martin, 913, 915, 916–17
Rock Creek, Gettysburg, 516, 527, 528
Rockville, Maryland, 458
Rocky Face Ridge, 861, 867, 936
Rocky Springs, Mississippi, 356, 357, 358
Rodes, Robert E., 286, 294–96, 297, 298, 303, 306, 307, 311, 434, 435, 436, 439, 440, 464, 472, 473, 474, 475, 476, 478, 480, 487, 514, 516, 519, 520, 523, 527, 800, 801, 802
Rodgers, John, 228, 230
Roebuck, John A., 654–55
Rogers, James C., 504–05
Rogersville, Tennessee, 761, 866
Rome, Georgia, 818
Rosecrans, William S., Bragg and, 168, 175, 428, 670, 672–74, 689, 745; Chattanooga occupied and defended by, 685–88, 691–692, 694, 760, 761, 763–64, 766–68, 770, 777, 782, 785, 786; at Chickamauga, 711, 713, 715, 716, 717, 718–19, 723, 724, 725–

Index [985]

727, 728, 730–31, 735–36, 745, 746, 747, 782; commander of Army of the Cumberland, 6, 7, 9, 18, 79–82, 169–70, 428, 663–68, 684, 708; Grant and, 145, 386, 785, 803, 805; Halleck and, 79–80, 103, 169, 170, 663, 664, 675, 676, 677, 725, 763; Lincoln and, 103, 169, 663–64, 676–77, 763–65, 767–68; reinforcement for, 786; relieved of command, 785, 802–03, 819; at Stones River, 85–86, 87, 89, 90–91, 94–95, 96, 97, 102–03, 124; Streight and, 179
Rossville, Georgia, 692, 713, 717, 746, 754, 756, 759, 842, 849, 850, 857
Rossville Gap, 688, 693, 715, 727, 746, 750, 759
Round Forest, Murfreesboro, 91–92, 93, 96, 98
Round Top, Gettysburg, 501, 509, 515, 516, 543, 572, 574, 582
Rousseau, Lovell H., 91
Rowley, William R., 333
Ruffin, Edmund, 648
Russell, John R., 656
Russia, 153

Sabine City, Texas, 775
Sabine Pass, Texas, 127, 775, 788, 870, 871
Sachem, U.S.S., 58, 59
Saint Augustine, Florida, 901
St. Johns River, 901, 905
St. Louis, Missouri, 917, 922
Salem Church, Virginia, 310, 311
Salineville, Ohio, 683
Salomon, Frederick S., 604
Sanders, William P., 677
Sanderson, Florida, 901, 904
Sanson, Emma, 183
Satartia, Mississippi, 417, 418
Savannah, Georgia, 821
Savannah *Republican*, 650
Sawyer, Roswell M., 938
Scales, Alfred M., 535
Schimmelfennig, Alexander, 290, 475, 477, 587
Schofield, John M., 47, 51, 139–42, 702, 705, 725, 772, 776
Schurz, Carl, 290, 395, 452, 453, 471, 475, 476, 484, 809, 810, 811
Scott, Thomas A., 119, 765
Scott, Winfield, 538, 826, 918
Seddon, James A., 173, 174, 252, 347, 354, 356, 366, 425, 429–30, 431, 601, 602, 642, 708, 762, 814, 886, 887, 891, 892, 915–16, 954
Sedgwick, John, 250, 266, 267, 270, 280, 287, 289, 300, 307, 308–09, 311, 312, 315, 317, 448, 452, 453, 485, 486, 494, 496, 497, 527, 576, 588, 788, 791, 801, 875, 876, 910
Selfridge, Thomas O., Jr., 75
Selma, Alabama, 770, 819, 921, 922
Seminary Ridge, Gettysburg, 470, 472, 475, 476, 478, 479, 481, 482, 484, 486, 488, 489, 491, 496, 512, 516, 521, 526, 528, 530, 531, 535, 554, 556, 568, 575, 576, 580, 582, 587
Semmes, Paul J., 506, 507, 509, 577, 894
Semmes, Raphael, 125–26

Seven Pines, Battle of, 7
Sewanee Mountain, 673
Seward, William H., 110, 111–13, 115–16, 117, 120, 157, 629, 630, 764, 830, 961
Seymour, Horatio, 637
Seymour, Truman, 900, 901–05, 906
Shaw, Robert Gould, 697–98
Shelby, Joseph O., 140, 776–78, 779
Shelbyville, Tennessee, 665, 666, 672, 761
Sheridan, Philip H., 87, 88, 91, 92, 177, 721, 724, 735, 739, 746, 748, 805, 852, 855, 856–57, 866
Sherman, John, 146
Sherman, Thomas W., 390, 395, 396, 397–98
Sherman, William T., Bragg and, 840, 844, 846–47; at Bridgeport, 378, 380, 836, 837, 838, 839; canal project, 146–47, 192, 195; at Chattanooga, 836–37, 841, 842, 844, 845, 846–47, 849, 850–51, 852, 857, 859, 860; at Chickasaw Bluffs, 77–78, 95, 133; commander in the West, 966; commander of Army of Tennessee, 785, 805, 806, 835, 841; criticism of, 191; Dana and, 218; death of son, 782–83; at Fort Hindman, 135–36; Grant and, 61, 62, 73, 143, 190, 326, 330, 332, 333, 352, 356–57, 365, 377, 380, 385, 415, 421, 424, 614, 836, 841, 920, 922, 964–66; guerillas and, 920–21; Halleck and, 781, 782; at Hard Times, 352–53; at Helena, 603; at Jackson, 358, 359, 360, 361, 362, 363, 365, 370, 375; Johnston and, 618, 619, 620, 621, 935, 938; march through Northern Mississippi and Alabama, 783–84, 923–40; McClernand and, 326, 385; at Milliken's Bend, 75–76, 78, 133, 326, 352; Porter and, 207, 210–11, 617; promoted permanent brigadier, 624, 773; relief of Chattanooga, 766; relief of Knoxville, 862, 866; Steele Bayou expedition, 207, 210–11, 212; at Vicksburg, 17–18, 61, 62, 63–64, 73, 75–79, 381, 382, 383, 388, 408, 415–16, 423, 424, 617, 618–22, 773; at Young's Point, 331
Sherman, Willy, 782–83
Shields, David, 565
Shreveport, Louisiana, 143, 392
Sibley, Henry H., 58
Sickles, Daniel F., 250, 251, 266, 271, 276, 277, 281, 289, 298, 299, 300, 303, 304, 305, 313, 315, 448, 453, 465, 468, 482, 485, 486, 493, 494–97, 502, 505, 507, 530, 548, 576
Sill, Joshua W., 88
Skinker's Neck, Virginia, 25, 26, 29
Slidell, John, 155, 156, 157, 654, 656
Slidell, Matilda, 155
Slocum, Henry W., 250, 266, 268, 270, 276, 277, 278, 281, 303, 304, 305, 448, 452, 453, 455, 471, 484, 486, 494, 516, 523, 524, 527, 528, 542, 543, 808
Smith, Andrew J., 76, 347, 370, 371, 607, 609
Smith, C. A., 55
Smith, Caleb Blood, 110
Smith, Edmund Kirby, 7, 142–43, 392, 394, 405, 429, 596, 597, 602, 644, 780, 956

Smith, Isaac, U.S.S., 223
Smith, J. B., 104
Smith, James P., 284
Smith, Martin L., 79, 367, 382
Smith, Morgan L., 76
Smith, Watson, 204-05, 206
Smith, William F., 42, 131, 250, 806-09, 837
Smith, William Sooy, 407, 919, 920, 922, 923, 925, 926-34, 936, 938
Snodgrass Hill, Chickamauga, 743
Snyder, S. S., 704
Sons of America, 651
Sons of Liberty, 632
Sorrel, G. Moxley, 259-60
Southern Railroad, 336, 338, 937
Spotsylvania, Virginia, 910
Sprague, William, 829
Springfield, Missouri, 47
Stafford Heights, Fredericksburg, 28, 29, 31, 33, 37, 39
Stannard, George J., 561, 562, 563, 564
Stanton, Edwin M., 60-61, 103, 110, 114, 122, 123, 218, 363-64, 447, 450, 482, 629, 630-31, 634, 637, 638, 653, 675, 747, 763, 764, 765, 766, 767, 768, 784, 785, 803, 805, 828, 908
Star of the West, U.S.S., 204
Steedman, Isaiah G. W., 401, 750, 752, 754, 805
Steele, Frederick, 76, 77, 331, 333, 423, 619, 620, 702, 707, 776, 780
Steele, William, 703, 707, 776
Steinwehr, *see* Von Steinwehr
Stephens, Alexander H., 649, 652-53, 951
Steuart, George H., 516, 517
Stevens, Thaddeus, 631, 829
Stevens Gap, Georgia, 687, 688, 715
Stevenson, Alabama, 803, 835, 836, 840, 848
Stevenson, Carter L., 367, 368, 373, 374, 382, 607
Stevenson's Depot, Virginia, 440
Stewart, Alexander P., 690, 712, 719-21, 724, 734-35, 737, 741, 753, 840, 857
Stoneman, George, 243, 262-64, 268, 281, 288, 300, 314, 315
Stones River, 83, 86, 90, 96, 98, 99, 102, 124
Stonewall Brigade, 516, 533
Stono, C.S.S., 223
Stoughton, Edwin H., 244-45
Streight, Abel D., 179-80, 181-86, 340, 346, 683, 932
Stringer's Ridge, 687
Stuart, James E. B., 30, 32, 34, 247-48, 263, 272, 273-74, 275, 276, 283, 286, 303, 304, 305, 306, 312, 434, 435, 436, 439, 440-41, 445, 456-61, 463, 481, 522, 569-72, 585, 787-88, 789, 795, 796, 806, 820, 875, 888
Submarine, the first, 896-98
Sullivan, Jeremiah C., 66-67, 68-69
Sullivan's Island, 222, 700, 701, 898
Sumner, Charles, 120, 131, 315, 629, 881-82, 962
Sumner, Edwin V., 25, 36, 37, 38, 40, 42, 141, 250

Suwannee River, 901, 902, 903, 905
"Swamp Angel," 698, 699, 701
Swarthmore College, 151
Switzerland, U.S.S., 215-16
Sykes, George, 277, 452, 453, 485, 486, 493, 497, 503, 505, 791, 801, 875, 876
Sykeston, Maryland, 459

Tabernacle Church, Virginia, 276, 277, 307
Taliaferro, William B., 30
Taneytown, Maryland, 465, 466, 468, 481, 482, 486
Taneytown Road, Gettysburg, 494, 512, 515, 521, 523, 542, 575
Tate, Samuel, 937
Taylor, Richard, 46, 52-54, 56, 138, 139, 390-94, 397, 405-06, 414, 421, 597-600, 615-16, 871
Taylor's Ridge, 858, 860
Taylor, Zachary, 53
Teche Bayou, 391, 392, 394, 405, 598
Tennessee & Alabama Railroad, 835
Tennessee & Virginia Railroad, 677, 834, 888
Tennessee River, 65, 685, 686, 688, 708, 747, 759, 806, 809, 836, 840
Texas, 771, 774-76, 870-72
Texas & New Orleans Railroad, 775
Thomas, George H., at Bridgeport, 687, 688; Center Army commander under Rosecrans, 81, 82, 85; at Chattanooga, 785, 804, 805, 806, 808, 809, 834, 836, 840, 841, 842, 843-44, 845, 847, 851, 852-53, 854, 859, 866-67; at Chickamauga, 691, 692, 693, 713, 715, 716, 717, 718, 719, 722, 724, 726, 727-28, 730, 731, 732, 735, 736, 741, 746, 748-52, 754-55, 768; at Crawfish Springs, 716, 718; Grant and, 785, 804, 805, 808, 854; at Hoover's Gap, 666, 667, 668; Lincoln and, 768; at Manchester, 671, 672, 673; at Murfreesboro, 89, 91, 94; at Pond Spring, 713, 715; Rosecrans and, 767; Rosecrans succeeded by, 785
Thomas, Lorenzo, 328, 638, 785
Thomasville, Georgia, 165
Tigress, U.S.S., 133, 136
Tilghman, Lloyd, 203-04, 205, 338, 374
Timrod, Henry, 160
Tod, David, 683
Todd, George, 140
Toombs, Robert A., 167, 648
Torpedo, C.S.S., 653
Trent affair, 155, 656
Trimble, Isaac R., 445, 446, 491, 535, 536, 551, 553, 563, 577
Trumbull, Lyman, 940
Truth, Sojourner, 961-62
Tullahoma, Tennessee, 665, 666, 671, 672, 674, 675, 686
Tunnel Hill, Missionary Ridge, 851, 861, 936
Tunstall's Station, Virginia, 913
Tuscumbia, U.S.S., 342, 384
Tuttle, James M., 333

Index

Tyler, John, 831
Tyler, U.S.S., 333, 603, 605, 606

Union City, Tennessee, 67, 927
United States Ford, 262, 265, 267, 270, 274, 281, 297, 298, 300, 301, 305, 311, 313
University Greys, 562–63
Usher, John Palmer, 110, 830

Vallandigham, Clement L., 107–08, 631, 632, 633–34, 820, 828
Van Buren, Arkansas, 47, 48, 51, 52, 139
Vance, Zebulon B., 648, 649
Van Cleve, Horatio P., 90, 91, 92, 96, 98, 99, 720, 732, 735, 741, 746, 749, 805
Van Dorn, Earl, 12, 17, 18, 46, 49, 70–72, 79, 95, 142, 176, 177, 178, 204, 340, 345, 346
Vassar College, 151
Velocity, U.S.S., 127
Vermilion River, 392
Vick, Newitt, 411
Vicksburg, Mississippi, 6, 8, 9, 10–11, 17–18, 20, 47, 52, 61, 62–63, 73, 75, 77, 78, 79, 137, 146, 186, 345, 351, 353, 355, 359, 365, 367, 379, 596, 771, 773, 780, 782, 938; siege of, 379–427, 964; surrender of, 606–614, 641
Vincent, Strong, 503, 504
Virginia Central Railroad, 266
Von Steinwehr, Adolf, 290, 475, 483, 809, 810

Wade, Benjamin F., 112, 114
Wadsworth, James S., 453, 469, 470, 484, 493, 523, 591
Walden's Ridge, 807, 818, 839
Walker, James A., 516
Walker, John G. (Confederate), 406, 425
Walker, John G. (Federal), 386–87
Walker, Lucius M., 602, 605, 706, 713, 715, 716, 729, 733
Walker, William H. T., 360, 363, 690, 692, 693
Wallace, Lewis (Lew), 51, 386
Walnut Hills, 63, 77, 380
War Department, Confederate, 9, 11, 237, 647
War Department, U. S., 56, 124, 328, 421, 634, 638, 675, 723, 764, 765, 784, 785, 828
Warren, Gouverneur K., 278, 503–04, 514, 523, 524, 548, 576, 791, 792, 793, 875, 876
Warrenton, Georgia, 594, 789, 792
Warrenton, Missouri, 323, 324, 325, 328, 329
Wartrace, Tennessee, 665, 666, 667, 672
Washburn, Cadwallader C., 216–17
Washburne, Elihu B., 203, 216, 219, 416, 940
Washington, D. C., 152–53
Washington, George, 21, 918
Washington, Mary, 21
Watts, Isaac, 318
Watts, Thomas H., 432, 956
Wauhatchie, Tennessee, 807, 808, 809, 810, 821, 849

[987]

Waul, Thomas N., 385
Webb, William H., C.S.S., 196, 197, 198–199, 215
Webster, Daniel, 831
Weed, Stephen H., 503–04
Weed, Thurlow, 829
Weehawken, U.S.S., 228, 230, 894
Weitzel, Godfrey, 138–39, 390, 391, 396, 397, 398, 402, 616
Weldon, North Carolina, 710
Welles, Gideon, 110, 114, 126, 225, 231, 606, 623–24, 626, 695, 696, 895
Welsh, Thomas, 407
Western & Atlantic Railroad, 179, 686
Westfield, U.S.S., 58–59
Westminster, Pennsylvania, 459, 494
Wheat Field, Gettysburg, 506–08, 529
Wheeler, Joseph, 83, 84–85, 175, 177, 178–179, 670, 671, 686, 692, 712–13, 715, 742, 761, 812, 813, 838, 865
White River, 140, 143
Whiting, William H. C., 253–54, 256
Whittier, John G., 959
Wilcox, Cadmus M., 310, 510, 511, 512, 530, 534, 536, 558, 564, 568
Wilder, John T., 668–69, 671, 672, 673, 717, 721, 740, 746, 748
Wilderness, the, 265, 266, 269, 270, 276, 277, 280, 286, 300, 314, 873
Williams, Alpheus S., 452, 453
Williams, J. M., 516, 524
Williamsport, Maryland, 440, 584, 585, 588, 589
Willoughby Run, Gettysburg, 467, 468, 469, 471, 474, 475, 491, 534, 579
Willow Springs, Mississippi, 349
Wills, David, 830
Wilmington, North Carolina, 19, 894
Wilmington & Weldon Railroad, 253
Wilson, Henry, 117, 327
Wilson, James H., 202, 203, 205–06, 348–49, 380, 422
Wilson's Creek, Battle of, 48, 49
Winchester, Tennessee, 673
Winchester, Virginia, 439, 440, 585
Winston Gap, 687, 692
Winter's Gap, 684
Withers, Jones M., 88, 92, 101, 171, 690
Wofford, William T., 506, 530–31
Wood, Thomas J., 90, 731, 735, 738, 739, 745, 749, 805, 844, 852, 857, 866
Worden, John L., 226, 230
Worsham, Johnny, 158, 162, 163
Wright, Ambrose R., 510, 511, 512, 521, 540–41, 550, 566
Wright, Horatio G., 452, 453
Wrightsville, Pennsylvania, 459
Wytheville, Virginia, 7

Yale University, 151
Yalobusha River, 12
Yancey, William L., 161, 648
Yandell, David W., 647
Yates, Richard, 630

Yazoo City, Mississippi, 386, 614, 617, 618
Yazoo Pass, 201, 202–03, 204, 207
Yazoo River, 10, 11, 20, 62, 73, 74, 75, 133, 134, 201, 204, 206, 386, 417, 617

York, Pennsylvania, 459, 460
York Pike, Gettysburg, 570, 571
Yorktown, Virginia, 914
Young's Point, 406, 414, 421

COMPREHENSIVE TABLE OF CONTENTS

Volume One

I.

CHAPTER 1. PROLOGUE—THE OPPONENTS
1. Secession: Davis and Lincoln
2. Sumter; Early Maneuvers
3. Statistics North and South

CHAPTER 2. FIRST BLOOD; NEW CONCEPTIONS
1. Manassas—Southern Triumph
2. Anderson, Frémont, McClellan
3. Scott's Anaconda; the Navy
4. Diplomacy; the Buildup

CHAPTER 3. THE THING GETS UNDER WAY
1. The West: Grant, Fort Henry
2. Donelson—The Loss of Kentucky
3. Gloom; Manassas Evacuation
4. McC Moves to the Peninsula

II.

CHAPTER 4. WAR MEANS FIGHTING...
1. Pea Ridge; Glorieta; Island Ten
2. Halleck-Grant, Jston-Bgard: Shiloh
3. Farragut, Lovell: New Orleans
4. Halleck, Beauregard: Corinth

CHAPTER 5. FIGHTING MEANS KILLING
1. Davis Frets; Lincoln-McClellan
2. Valley Campaign; Seven Pines
3. Lee, McC: The Concentration
4. The Seven Days; Hezekiah

III.

CHAPTER 6. THE SUN SHINES SOUTH
1. Lincoln Reappraisal; Emancipation?
2. Grant, Farragut, Buell
3. Bragg, K. Smith, Breckinridge
4. Lee vs. Pope: Second Manassas

CHAPTER 7. TWO ADVANCES; TWO RETREATS
1. Invasion West: Richmond, Munfordville
2. Lee, McClellan: Sharpsburg
3. The Emancipation Proclamation
4. Corinth-Perryville: Bragg Retreats

CHAPTER 8. LAST, BEST HOPE OF EARTH
1. Lincoln's Late-Fall Disappointments
2. Davis: Lookback and Outlook
3. Lincoln: December Message

Volume Two

I.

CHAPTER 1. THE LONGEST JOURNEY
1. Davis, Westward and Return
2. Goldsboro; Fredericksburg
3. Prairie Grove; Galveston
4. Holly Springs; Walnut Hills
5. Murfreesboro: Bragg Retreats

CHAPTER 2. UNHAPPY NEW YEAR
1. Lincoln; Mud March; Hooker
2. Arkansas Post; Transmiss; Grant
3. Erlanger; Richmond Bread Riot
4. Rosecrans; Johnston; Streit
5. Vicksburg—Seven Failures

CHAPTER 3. DEATH OF A SOLDIER
1. Naval Repulse at Charleston
2. Lee, Hooker; Mosby; Kelly's Ford
3. Suffolk: Longstreet Southside
4. Hooker, Stoneman: The Crossing
5. Chancellorsville; Jackson Dies

II.

CHAPTER 4. THE BELEAGUERED CITY
1. Grant's Plan; the Run; Grierson
2. Eastward, Port Gibson to Jackson
3. Westward, Jackson to Vicksburg
4. Port Hudson; Banks vs. Gardner
5. Vicksburg Siege, Through June

CHAPTER 5. STARS IN THEIR COURSES
1. Lee, Davis; Invasion; Stuart
2. Gettysburg Opens; Meade Arrives
3. Gettysburg, July 2: Longstreet
4. Gettysburg, Third Day: Pickett
5. Cavalry; Lee Plans Withdrawal

CHAPTER 6. UNVEXED TO THE SEA
1. Lee's Retreat; Falling Waters
2. Milliken's Bend; Helena Repulse
3. Vicksburg Falls; Jackson Reburnt
4. Lincoln Exults; N.Y. Draft Riot
5. Davis Declines Lee's Resignation

III.

CHAPTER 7. RIOT AND RESURGENCE
1. Rosecrans; Tullahoma Campaign
2. Morgan Raid; Chattanooga Taken
3. Charleston Seige; Transmississippi
4. Chickamauga—First Day
5. Bragg's Victory Unexploited

CHAPTER 8. THE CENTER GIVES
1. Sabine Pass; Shelby; Grant Hurt
2. Bristoe Station; Buckland Races
3. Grant Opens the Cracker Line
4. Davis, Bragg; Gettysburg Address
5. Missionary Ridge; Bragg Relieved

CHAPTER 9. SPRING CAME ON FOREVER
1. Mine Run; Meade Withdraws
2. Olustee; Kilpatrick Raid
3. Sherman, Meridian; Forrest
4. Lincoln-Davis, a Final Contrast
5. Grant Summoned to Washington

Volume Three

I.

CHAPTER 1. ANOTHER GRAND DESIGN
1. Grant in Washington—His Plan
2. Red River, Camden: Reevaluation
3. Paducah, Fort Pillow; Plymouth
4. Grant Poised; Joe Davis; Lee

CHAPTER 2. THE FORTY DAYS
1. Grant Crosses; the Wilderness
2. Spotsylvania—"All Summer"
3. New Market; Bermuda Hundred
4. North Anna; Cold Harbor; Early

CHAPTER 3. RED CLAY MINUET
1. Dalton to Pine Mountain
2. Brice's; Lincoln; "Alabama"
3. Kennesaw to Chattahoochee
4. Hood Replaces Johnston

II.

CHAPTER 4. WAR IS CRUELTY...
1. Petersburg; Early I; Peace?
2. Hood vs. Sherman; Mobile
   Bay; Memphis Raid; Atlanta Falls
3. Crater; McClellan; Early II
4. Price Raid; "Florida"; Cushing;
   Forrest Raids Mid-Tenn.
5. Hood-Davis; Lincoln Reelected.

CHAPTER 5. YOU CANNOT REFINE IT
1. Petersburg Trenches; Weldon RR
2. March to Sea; Hood, Spring Hill
3. Franklin; Hood Invests Nashville
4. Thomas Attacks; Hood Retreats
5. Savannah Falls; Lincoln Exultant

III.

CHAPTER 6. A TIGHTENING NOOSE
1. Grant; Ft. Fisher; 13th Amendment
2. Confed Shifts; Lee Genl-in-Chief?
3. Blair Received; Hampton Roads
4. Hatcher's Run; Columbia Burned

CHAPTER 7. VICTORY, AND DEFEAT
1. Sheridan, Early; Second Inaugural
2. Goldsboro; Sheridan; City Point
3. Five Forks—Richmond Evacuated
4. Lee, Grant Race for Appomattox

CHAPTER 8. LUCIFER IN STARLIGHT
1. Davis-Johnston; Sumter; Booth
2. Durham; Citronelle; Davis Taken
3. K. Smith; Naval; Fort Monroe
4. Postlude: Reconstruction, Davis

ABOUT THE AUTHOR

SHELBY FOOTE was born in Greenville, Mississippi, and attended school there until he entered the University of North Carolina. During World War II he served in the European theater as a captain of field artillery. He has written five novels: *Tournament, Follow Me Down, Love in a Dry Season, Shiloh* and *Jordan County*. He has been awarded three Guggenheim fellowships. He died in 2005.

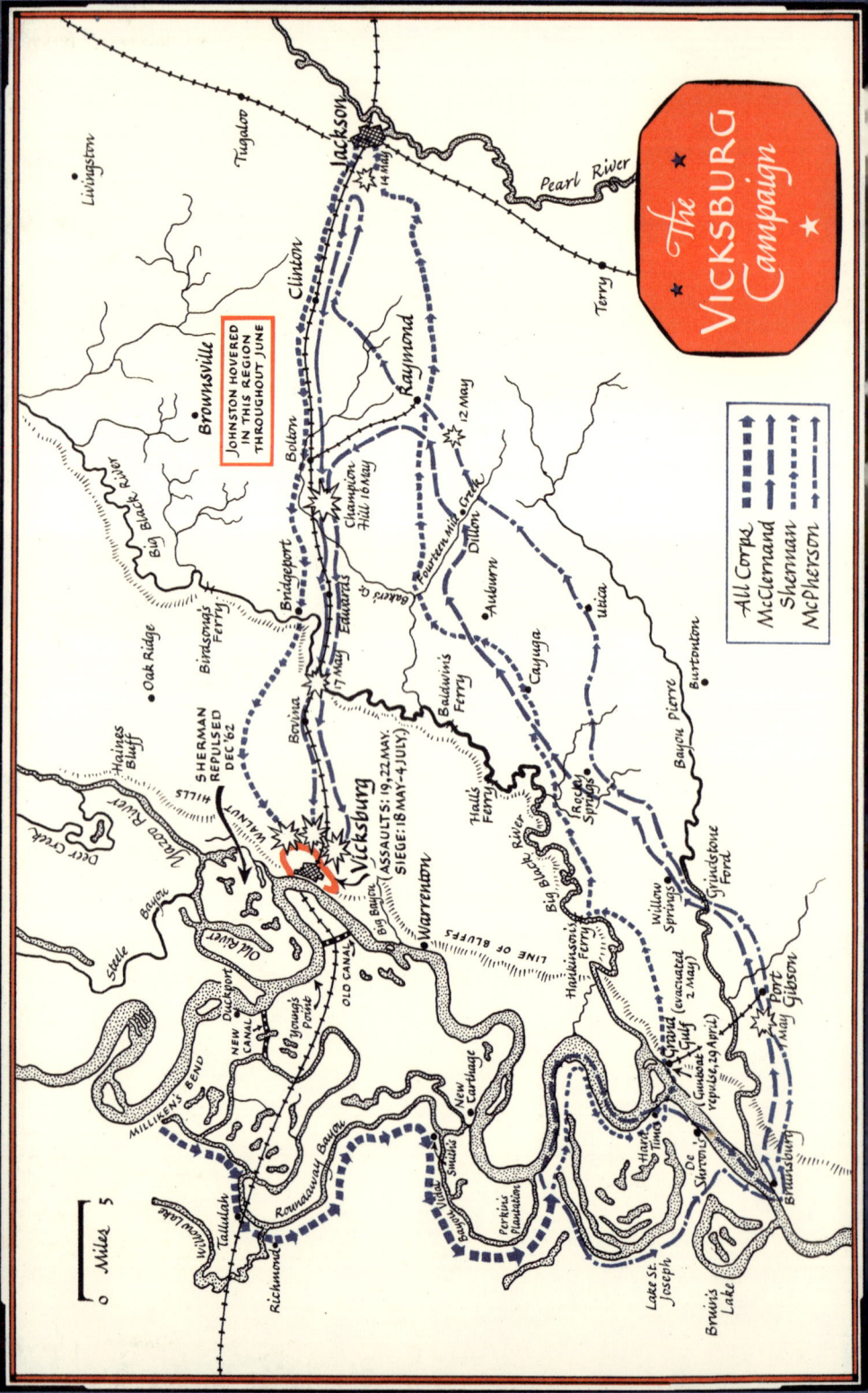

The Civil War
A Narrative

THE
Civil War

A Narrative

---★---

FORT SUMTER *to* PERRYVILLE

---★---

By SHELBY FOOTE

RANDOM HOUSE · NEW YORK

2011 Modern Library Edition

Copyright © 1958 and copyright renewed 1986 by Shelby Foote

All rights reserved.

Published in the United States by Modern Library, an imprint of
The Random House Publishing Group, a division of
Random House, Inc., New York.

MODERN LIBRARY and the TORCHBEARER Design are
registered trademarks of Random House, Inc.

This work was originally published in hardcover in 1958 by
Random House, an imprint of The Random House Publishing Group,
a division of Random House, Inc.

ISBN 978-0-679-64370-8

Printed in China on acid-free paper

www.modernlibrary.com

2 4 6 8 9 7 5 3 1

Case and box photographs: Library of Congress

TABLE OF CONTENTS

★ ✠ ☆

I

1. Prologue — The Opponents ... 3
2. First Blood; New Conceptions ... 73
3. The Thing Gets Under Way ... 168

II

4. War Means Fighting 277
5. Fighting Means Killing ... 392

III

6. The Sun Shines South ... 523
7. Two Advances; Two Retreats ... 650
8. Last, Best Hope of Earth ... 745

List of Maps, Bibliographical Notes, and Index ... 811

CHAPTER

✕ 1 ✕

Prologue – The Opponents

▰ IT WAS A MONDAY IN WASHINGTON, January 21; Jefferson Davis rose from his seat in the Senate. South Carolina had left the Union a month before, followed by Mississippi, Florida, and Alabama, which seceded at the rate of one a day during the second week of the new year. Georgia went out eight days later; Louisiana and Texas were poised to go; few doubted that they would, along with others. For more than a decade there had been intensive discussion as to the legality of secession, but now the argument was no longer academic. A convention had been called for the first week in February, at Montgomery, Alabama, for the purpose of forming a confederacy of the departed states, however many there should be in addition to the five already gone. As a protest against the election of Abraham Lincoln, who had received not a single southern electoral vote, secession was a fact — to be reinforced, if necessary, by the sword. The senator from Mississippi rose. It was high noon. The occasion was momentous and expected; the galleries were crowded, hoop-skirted ladies and men in broadcloth come to hear him say farewell. He was going home.

By now he was one of the acknowledged spokesmen of secession, though it had not always been so. By nature he was a moderate, with a deep devotion to the Union. He had been for compromise so long as he believed compromise was possible; he reserved secession as a last resort. Yet now they were at that stage. In a paper which he had helped to draft and which he had signed and sent as advice to his state in early December, his position had been explicit. "The argument is exhausted," it declared. "All hope of relief in the Union ... is extinguished." At last he was for disunion, with a southern confederacy to follow.

During the twelve days since the secession of Mississippi he had remained in Washington, sick in mind and body, waiting for the news to reach him officially. He hoped he might be arrested as a traitor, thereby gaining a chance to test the right of secession in the federal courts. Now the news had been given him officially the day before, a Sunday, and he stayed to say goodbye. He had never doubted the right of secession. What he doubted was its wisdom. Yet now it was no longer a question even of wisdom; it was a question of necessity — meaning Honor. On the day before Lincoln's election, Davis had struck an organ tone that brought a storm of applause in his home state. "I glory in Mississippi's star!" he cried. "But before I would see it dishonored I would tear it from its place, to be set on the perilous ridge of battle as a sign around which her bravest and best shall meet the harvest home of death."

Thus he had spoken in November, but now in January, rising to say farewell, his manner held more of sadness than defiance. For a long moment after he rose he struck the accustomed preliminary stance of the orators of his day: high-stomached, almost sway-backed, the knuckles of one hand braced against the desk top, the other hand raised behind him with the wrist at the small of his back. He was dressed in neat black broadcloth, cuffless trouser-legs crumpling over his boots, the coat full-skirted with wide lapels, a satin waistcoat framing the stiff white bosom of his shirt, a black silk handkerchief wound stockwise twice around the upturned collar and knotted loosely at the throat. Close-shaven except for the tuft of beard at the jut of the chin, the face was built economically close to the skull, and more than anything it expressed an iron control by the brain within that skull. He had been sick for the past month and he looked it. He looked in fact like a man who had emerged from a long bout with a fever; which was what he was, except that the fever had been a generation back, when he was twenty-seven, and now he was fifty-two. Beneath the high square forehead, etched with the fine criss-cross lines of pain and overwork, the eyes were deep-set, gray and stern, large and lustrous, though one was partly covered by a film, a result of the neuralgia which had racked him all those years. The nose was aquiline, finely shaped, the nostrils broad and delicately chiseled. The cheeks were deeply hollowed beneath the too-high cheekbones and above the wide, determined jaw. His voice was low, with the warmth of the Deep South in it.

"I rise, Mr President, for the purpose of announcing to the Senate that I have satisfactory evidence that the State of Mississippi, by a solemn ordinance of her people in convention assembled, has declared her separation from the United States. Under these circumstances, of course, my functions terminate here. It has seemed to me proper, however, that I should appear in the Senate to announce that fact to my associates, and I will say but very little more."

His voice faltered at the outset, but soon it gathered volume and rang clear — "like a silver trumpet," according to his wife, who sat in the gallery. "Unshed tears were in it," she added, "and a plea for peace permeated every tone." Davis continued:

"It is known to senators who have served with me here, that I have for many years advocated, as an essential attribute of State sovereignty, the right of a State to secede from the Union.... If I had thought that Mississippi was acting without sufficient provocation... I should still, under my theory of government, because of my allegiance to the State of which I am a citizen, have been bound by her action."

He foresaw the founding of a nation, inheritor of the traditions of the American Revolution. "We but tread in the paths of our fathers when we proclaim our independence and take the hazard... not in hostility to others, not to injure any section of the country, not even for our own pecuniary benefit, but from the high and solemn motive of defending and protecting the rights we inherited, and which it is our duty to transmit unshorn to our children." England had been a lion; the Union might turn out to be a bear; in which case, "we will invoke the God of our fathers, who delivered them from the power of the lion, to protect us from the ravages of the bear; and thus, putting our trust in God and in our own firm hearts and strong arms, we will vindicate the right as best we may."

Davis glanced around the chamber, then continued. "I see now around me some with whom I have served long. There have been points of collision; but whatever of offense there has been to me, I leave here. I carry with me no hostile remembrance.... I go hence unencumbered by the remembrance of any injury received, and having discharged the duty of making the only reparation in my power for any injury received." He then spoke the final sentence to which all the rest had served as prologue. "Mr President and Senators, having made the announcement which the occasion seemed to me to require, it remains only for me to bid you a final adieu."

For a moment there was silence. Then came the ovation, the sustained thunder of applause, the flutter of handkerchiefs and hum of comment. Davis shrank from this, however, or at any rate ignored it. As he resumed his seat he lowered his head and covered his face with his hands. Some in the gallery claimed his shoulders shook; he was weeping, they said. It may have been so, though he was not given to public tears. If so, it could have been from more than present tension. His life was crowded with glory, as a soldier, as a suitor, as a statesman; yet the glory was more than balanced by personal sorrow as a man. He had known tears in his time.

He was born in Christian County, Kentucky, within a year and a hundred miles of the man whose election had brought on the present furor. Like that man, he was a log-cabin boy, the youngest of ten children whose grandfather had been born in Philadelphia in 1702, the son of an immigrant Welshman who signed his name with an X. This grandfather moved to Georgia, where he married a widow who bore him one son, Samuel. Samuel raised and led an irregular militia company in the Revolution. After the war he married and moved northwest to south-central Kentucky, where he put up his own log house, farmed six hundred acres of land by the hard agronomy of the time, and supplied himself with children, naming the sons out of the Bible — Joseph, Samuel, Benjamin, and Isaac — until the tenth child, born in early June of 1808, whom he named for the red-headed President then in office, and gave him the middle name Finis in the belief, or perhaps the hope, that he was the last; which he was.

By the time the baby Jefferson was weaned the family was on the move again, south one thousand miles to Bayou Teche, Louisiana, only to find the climate unhealthy and to move again, three hundred miles northeast to Wilkinson County, Mississippi Territory, southeast of Natchez and forty miles from the Mississippi River. Here the patriarch stopped, for he prospered; he did not move again, and here Jefferson spent his early childhood.

The crop now was cotton, and though Samuel Davis had slaves, he was his own overseer, working alongside them in the field. It was a farm, not a plantation; he was a farmer, not a planter. In a region where the leading men were Episcopalians and Federalists, he was a Baptist and a Democrat. Now his older children were coming of age, and at their marriages he gave them what he could, one Negro slave, and that was all. The youngest, called Little Jeff, began his education when he was six. For the next fifteen years he attended one school after another, first a log schoolhouse within walking distance of home, then a Dominican institution in Kentucky, Saint Thomas Aquinas, where he was still called Little Jeff because he was the smallest pupil there. He asked to become a Roman Catholic but the priest told him to wait and learn, which he did, and either forgot or changed his mind. Then, his mother having grown lonesome for her last-born, he came home to the Mississippi schoolhouse where he had started.

He did not like it. One hot fall day he rebelled; he would not go. Very well, his father said, but he could not be idle, and sent him to the field with the work gang. Two days later Jeff was back at his desk. "The heat of the sun and the physical labor, in conjunction with the implied equality with the other cotton pickers, convinced me that school was the lesser evil." Thus he later explained his early decision to work with his head, not his hands. In continuation of this decision, just before his fourteenth birthday he left once more for Kentucky, entering Transylvania University, an excellent school, one of the few in the country to live up to a high-sounding name. Under competent professors he continued his studies in Latin and Greek and mathematics, including trigonometry, and explored the mysteries of sacred and profane history and natural philosophy — meaning chemistry and physics — with surveying and oratory thrown in for good measure. While he was there his father died and his oldest brother, Joseph, twenty-four years his senior, assumed the role of guardian.

Not long before his death, the father had secured for his youngest son an appointment to West Point, signed by the Secretary of War, and thus for the first time the names were linked: Jefferson Davis, John C. Calhoun. Joseph Davis by now had become what his father had never been — a planter, with a planter's views, a planter's way of life. Jefferson inclined toward the University of Virginia, but Joseph persuaded him to give the Academy a try. It was in the tradition for the younger sons of prominent southern families to go there; if at the end of a year he found he did not like it he could transfer. So Davis attended West Point, and found he liked it.

Up to now he had shown no special inclination to study. Alert and affectionate, he was of a mischievous disposition, enjoyed a practical joke, and sought the admiration of his fellows rather more than the esteem of his professors. Now at the Academy he continued along this course, learning something of tavern life in the process. "O Benny Haven's, O!" he sang, linking arms and clinking tankards. He found he liked the military comradeship, the thought of unrequited death on lonely, far-off battlefields:

> *"To our comrades who have fallen, one cup before we go;*
> *They poured their life-blood freely out pro bono publico.*
> *No marble points the stranger to where they rest below;*
> *They lie neglected — far away from Benny Haven's, O!"*

Brought before a court martial for out-of-bounds drinking of "spirituous liquors," he made the defense of a strict constructionist: 1) visiting Benny Haven's was not *officially* prohibited in the regulations, and 2) malt liquors were not "spirituous" in the first place. The defense was successful; he was not dismissed, and he emerged from the scrape a stricter constructionist than ever. He also got to know his fellow cadets. Leonidas Polk was his roommate; Joseph E. Johnston was said to have been his opponent in a fist fight over a girl; along with others, he admired the open manliness of Albert Sidney Johnston, the high-born rectitude of Robert E. Lee.

Davis himself was admired, even liked. Witnesses spoke of his well-shaped head, his self-esteem, his determination and personal mastery. A "florid young fellow," he had "beautiful blue eyes, a graceful figure." In his studies he did less well, receiving his lowest marks in mathematics and deportment, his highest in rhetoric and moral philosophy, including constitutional law. But the highs could not pull up the lows. He stood well below the middle of his class, still a private at the close of his senior year, and graduated in 1828, twenty-third in a class of thirty-four.

As a second lieutenant, U.S. Army, he now began a seven-year adventure, serving in Wisconsin, Iowa, Illinois, Missouri, where he learned to fight Indians, build forts, scout, and lead a simple social existence. He had liked West Point; he found he liked this even better. Soon he proved himself a superior junior officer, quick-witted and resourceful — as when once with a few men he was chased by a band of Indians after scalps; both parties being in canoes, he improvised a sail and drew away. In a winter of deep snow he came down with pneumonia, and though he won that fight as well, his susceptibility to colds and neuralgia dated from then. He was promoted to first lieutenant within four years, and when Black Hawk was captured in 1832, Davis was appointed by his colonel, Zachary Taylor, to escort the prisoner to Jefferson Barracks.

Thus Colonel Taylor, called "Old Rough and Ready," showed his approval of Davis as a soldier. But as a son-in-law, it developed, he wanted no part of him. The lieutenant had met the colonel's daughter, sixteen-year-old Knox Taylor, brown-haired and blue-eyed like himself, though later the color of his own eyes would deepen to gray. Love came quickly, and his letters to her show a man unseen before or after. "By my dreams I have been lately almost crazed, for they were of you," he wrote to her, and also thus: "Kind, dear letter; I have kissed it often and often, and it has driven away mad notions from my brain." The girl accepted his suit, but the father did not; Taylor wanted no soldier son-in-law, apparently especially not this one. Therefore Davis, who had spent the past seven years as a man of action, proposed to challenge the colonel to a duel. Dissuaded from this, he remained a man of action still. He resigned his commission, went straight to Louisville, and married the girl. The wedding was held at the home of an aunt she was visiting. "After the service everybody cried but Davis," a witness remarked, adding that they "thought this most peculiar."

As it turned out, he was reserving his tears. The young couple did not wait to attempt a reconciliation with her father; perhaps they depended on time to accomplish this. Instead they took a steamboat south to Davis Bend, Mississippi, below Vicksburg, where Joseph Davis, the guardian elder brother, had prospered on a plantation called The Hurricane. He presented them with an adjoining 800-acre place and fourteen slaves on credit. Davis put in a cotton crop, but before the harvest time came round they were both down with fever. They were confined to separate rooms, each too sick to be told of the other's condition, though Davis managed to make it to the door of his bride's room in time to see her die. She had been a wife not quite three months, and as she died she sang snatches of "Fairy Bells," a favorite air; she had had it from her mother. Now those tears which he had not shed at the wedding came to scald his eyes. He was too sick to attend the funeral; the doctor believed he would not be long behind her.

The doctor was wrong, though Davis never lost the drawn, gaunt look of a fever convalescent. He returned to the plantation; then, finding it too crowded with recent memories, left for Cuba, thought to be a fine climate and landscape for restoring broken hearts. The sea bathing at least did his health much good, and he returned by way of New York and Washington, renewing acquaintances with old friends now on the rise and gaining some notion of how much he had missed on the frontier. Then he came home to Mississippi. He would be a planter and, at last, a student.

He found a ready tutor awaiting him. Joseph Davis had got a law degree in Kentucky, had set up practice in Natchez, and, prospering, had bought the land which in that section practically amounted to a patent of nobility. By now, in his middle fifties, he was the wealthiest planter in the state, the "leading philosopher" — whatever that meant — and the possessor of the finest library, which he gladly made available to his idolized younger brother. Davis soon had the Constitution by heart and went deeply into *Elliot's Debates*, theories of government as argued by the framers. He read John Locke and Adam Smith, *The Federalist* and the works of Thomas Jefferson. Shakespeare and Swift lent him what an orator might need of cadenced beauty and invective; Byron and Scott were there at hand, along with the best English magazines and the leading American newspapers. He read them all, and discussed them with his brother.

Also there was the plantation; Brierfield, he called it. Here too he worked and learned, making certain innovations in the labor system. The overseer was a Negro, James Pemberton. No slave was ever punished except after a formal trial by an all-Negro jury, Davis only reserving the right to temper the severity of the judgment. James was always James, never Jim; "It is disrespect to give a nickname," Davis said, and the overseer repaid him with frankness, loyalty, and efficiency. Once when something went amiss and the master asked him why, James replied: "I rather think, sir, through my neglect."

Davis gained all this from his decade of seclusion and study; but he gained something else as well. Up to now, his four years at West Point, brief and interrupted as they were, had been the longest period he had spent at any one place in his life. His school years had been various indeed, with instructors ranging from log-cabin teachers to Catholic priests and New England scholars. When a Virginian or a Carolinian spoke of his "country," he meant Virginia or Carolina. It was not so with Davis. Tennessee and Kentucky were as familiar to him as Mississippi; the whole South, as a region, formed his background; he was thirty before he knew a real home in any real sense of the word. Now at last he had this, too, though still with a feeling of being somewhat apart. Like his brother Joseph and his father before him, he was a Democrat, and while this was true of the majority of the people in his state, it was by no means true of the majority in his class, who were Federalists or Whigs.

Then history intervened for him and solved this problem too. Previously the cotton capitalists had thought their interests coincided with the interests of capitalists in general. Now anti-slavery and pro-tariff agitation was beginning to teach them otherwise. In 1844, the year when Davis emerged from seclusion, the upheaval was accomplished. Repudiating Jefferson and Jackson, the Democrats went over to the Whigs, who came to meet them, creating what Calhoun had been after from the start: a solid South. Davis caught the movement at its outset.

Before that, however, in the previous December, his brother produced one more item from the horn of plenty. He had a lawyer friend, W. B. Howell of Natchez, son of an eight-term governor of New Jersey. Howell had married a Kempe of Virginia and moved south to cotton country. Joseph Davis was an intimate of their house; their first son was named for him, and their seventeen-year-old daughter Varina called him Uncle Joe. Now he wrote to the girl's parents, inviting her to visit The Hurricane. She arrived by steamboat during the Christmas season, having just completed an education in the classics. She did not stay at The Hurricane; she stayed at his sister's plantation, fourteen miles away. Presently a horseman arrived with a message. He dismounted to give it to her, lingered briefly, then excused himself and rode off to a political meeting in Vicksburg. That night Varina wrote to her mother, giving her first impression of the horseman.

> Today Uncle Joe sent, by his younger brother (did you know he had one?), an urgent invitation to me to go at once to The Hurricane. I do not know whether this Mr Jefferson Davis is young or old. He looks both at times; but I believe he is old, for from what I hear he is only two years younger than you are. He impresses me as a remarkable kind of man, but of uncertain temper, and has a way of taking for granted that everybody agrees with him when he expresses an opinion, which offends me; yet he is most agreeable and has a peculiarly sweet voice and a winning manner of asserting himself. The fact is, he is the kind of person I should expect to rescue one from a mad dog at any risk, but to insist upon a stoical indifference to the fright afterward. I do not think I shall ever like him as I do his brother Joe. Would you believe it, he is refined and cultivated, and yet he is a Democrat!

This last was the principal difficulty between them. Varina was a Natchez girl, which meant not only that her background was Federalist, but also that she had led a life of gaiety quite unlike the daily round in the malarial bottoms of Davis Bend. The Christmas season was a merry one, however, and Joseph proved an excellent matchmaker, although a rather heavy-handed one. "By Jove, she is as beautiful as Venus!" he told his brother, adding: "As well as good looks, she has a mind that will fit her for any sphere that the man to whom she is married will feel proud to reach." Jefferson agreed, admiring the milk-pale skin, the raven hair, the generous mouth, the slender waist. "She is beautiful and she has a fine mind," he admitted, with some caution at the outset.

In the evenings there were readings from historians and orators, and the brothers marveled at the ease with which the girl pronounced and translated the Latin phrases and quotations that studded the texts. The conquest was nearly complete; there remained only the political difference. In the course of these discussions Varina wore a cameo brooch with a Whig device carved into the stone, a watchdog crouched by a strongbox. Then one day she appeared without it, and Davis knew he had won.

He left The Hurricane in late January, engaged. In February of the following year, 1845, they were married. Davis was thirty-six, Varina half that. They went to New Orleans on the wedding tour, enjoyed a fashionable Creole interlude, and returned after a few weeks to Brierfield.

The house they moved into was a one-story frame twin-wing structure; Davis had planned and built it himself, with the help of James Pemberton. It had charm, but he and his young wife had little time to enjoy it. By then he had emerged from his shell in more ways than one. In 1843 he had run for the state legislature against Sergeant S. Prentiss, famous as an orator, a Whig in an overwhelmingly Whig district. Davis was defeated, though with credit and a growing reputation. The following year, taking time off from courtship, he stumped the state as an elector for James K. Polk. In the year of his marriage, Whigs and Democrats having coalesced, he was elected to Congress as representative-at-large. In Washington, his first act was to introduce a resolution that federal troops be withdrawn from federal forts, their posts to be taken by state recruits. It died in committee, and his congressional career was ended by the outbreak of the Mexican War.

Davis resigned his seat and came home to head a volunteer regiment, the Mississippi Rifles. Under the strict discipline of their West Point colonel, who saw to it that they were armed with a new model rifle, they were the crack outfit of Zachary Taylor's army, fighting bravely at Monterey and saving the day at Buena Vista, where Davis formed them in a V that broke the back of a Mexican cavalry charge and won the battle. He was wounded in the foot, came home on crutches, and at victory banquets in New Orleans and elsewhere heard himself proclaimed a military genius and the hero of the South. Hunched upon his crutches, he responded to such toasts with dignified modesty. Basically his outlook was unchanged. When Polk sent him a commission as a brigadier general of volunteers, Davis returned it promptly, remarking that the President had no authority to make such an appointment, that power inhering in the states alone. Perhaps all these honors were somewhat anticlimactic anyhow, coming as they did after the words General Taylor was supposed to have spoken to him at Buena Vista: "My daughter, sir, was a better judge of men than I was."

Honors fell thickly upon him now. Within sixty days the governor appointed him to the U.S. Senate. At a private banquet tendered before he left, he stood and heard the toasts go round: "Colonel Jeff Davis, the Game Cock of the South!" "Jeff Davis, the President of the Southern Confederacy!" Davis stood there, allowing no change of expression, no flush of emotion on his face. He took this stiffness, this coldness up to Washington and onto the floor of the Senate.

He would not unbend; he would engage in no log-rolling. In a cloakroom exchange, when he stated his case supporting a bill for removing obstructions from the river down near Vicksburg, another senator, who had his pet project too, interrupted to ask, "Will you vote for the Lake appropriations?" Davis responded: "Sir, I make no terms. I accept no compromises. If when I ask for an appropriation, the object shall be shown to be proper and the expenditure constitutional, I defy the gentleman, for his conscience' sake, to vote against it. If it shall appear to him otherwise, then I expect his opposition, and only ask that it shall be directly, fairly, and openly exerted. The case shall be presented on its single merit; on that I wish to stand or fall. I feel, sir, that I am incapable of sectional distinction upon such subjects. I abhor and reject all interested combinations." He would hammer thus at what he thought was wrong, and continue to hammer, icy cold and in measured terms, long after the opposition had been demolished, without considering the thoughts of the other man or the chance that he might be useful to him someday.

He was perhaps the best informed, probably the best educated, and certainly the most intellectual man in the Senate. Yet he too had to take his knocks. Supporting an army pay-increase bill, he remarked in passing that "a common blacksmith or tailor" could not be hired as a military engineer; whereupon Andrew Johnson of Tennessee — formerly a tailor — rose from his desk shouting that "an illegitimate, swaggering, bastard, scrub aristocracy" took much credit to itself, yet in fact had "neither talents nor information." Hot words in a Washington boarding house led to a fist fight between Davis and Henry S. Foote, his fellow senator from Mississippi. An Illinois congressman, W. H. Bissell, said in a speech that Davis' command had been a mile and a half from the blaze of battle at Buena Vista. Davis sent an immediate challenge, and Bissell, having the choice of weapons, named muskets loaded with ball and shot at fifteen paces, then went home, wrote his will, and said he would be ready in the morning. Friends intervening, Bissell explained that he had been referring to another quarter of the field and had not meant to question Davis' personal bravery anyhow; the duel was canceled. Davis made enemies in high places, as for example when he claimed that General Winfield Scott had overcharged $300 in mileage expenses. Scott later delivered himself of a judgment as to Davis: "He is not a cheap Judas. I do not think he would have sold the Saviour for thirty shillings. But for the successorship to Pontius Pilate he would have betrayed Christ and the Apostles and the whole Christian church." Sam Houston of Texas, speaking more briefly, declared that Davis was "ambitious as Lucifer and cold as a lizard."

Out of the rough-and-tumble of debate and acrimony, a more or less accepted part of political life at the time, Davis was winning a position as a leader in the Senate. Successor to Calhoun, he had become the spokesman for southern nationalism, which in those days meant not independence but domination from within the Union. This movement had been given impetus by the Mexican War. Up till then the future of the country pointed north and west, but now the needle trembled and suddenly swung south. The treaty signed at Guadalupe Hidalgo brought into the Union a new southwestern domain, seemingly ripe for slavery and the southern way of life: not only Texas down to the Rio Grande, the original strip of contention, but also the vast sun-cooked area that was to become Arizona, New Mexico, Nevada, Utah, part of Colorado, and California with its new-found gold. Here was room for expansion indeed, with more to follow; for the nationalists looked forward to taking what was left of Mexico, all of Central America south to Panama, and Yucatan and Cuba by annexation. Yet the North, so recently having learned the comfort of the saddle, had no intention of yielding the reins. The South would have to fight for this; and this the South was prepared to do, using States Rights for a spear and the Constitution for a shield. Jefferson Davis, who had formed his troops in a V at Buena Vista and continued the fight with a boot full of blood, took a position, now as then, at the apex of the wedge.

He lost the fight, and lost it quickly — betrayed, as he thought, from within his ranks. The North opposed this dream of southern expansion by opposing the extension of slavery, without which the new southwestern territory would be anything but southern. Attracted by the hope of so much gain, and goaded by the fear of such a loss, Davis and his cohorts adopted more drastic actions, including threats of secession. To give substance to this threat, he called the Nashville Convention of June 1850, and in conjunction with Albert Gallatin Brown of Mississippi, William Lowndes Yancey of Alabama, and Robert Barnwell Rhett of South Carolina, informed the North quite plainly that unless slavery was extended to the territories, the South would leave the Union. It was at this point that Davis was "betrayed," meaning that he discovered that he had outrun his constituents. Henry Clay proposed his Compromise, supported by Daniel Webster, and both houses of Congress gladly accepted it. California came in as a free state and the question of slavery was left to be settled by the various other territories at the time when they should apply for admission into the Union.

What was worse from Davis' point of view, the voters seemed to approve. All over the nation, even in Mississippi, there was rejoicing that disunion and war had been avoided. Davis could scarcely believe it; he must test it at the polls. So he resigned his seat in the Senate and went home to run for governor against Henry S. Foote, the senator with whom he had exchanged first tart remarks and finally blows. Now the issue was clearly drawn, for his opponent was a Unionist Whig of Natchez and had voted consistently against Davis, from the beginning down to the Compromise itself; the voters could make a clear-cut choice before all the world. This they did — repudiating Davis.

It was bad enough to be vanquished as the champion of secession, but to receive defeat at the hands of a man he detested as much as he detested Foote was gall and wormwood. At forty-three, in the hour of his glory and at the height of his prime, he was destroyed; or so he thought. At any rate he was through. He came home to Brierfield to plant cotton.

Then history intervened again, as history always seemed to do for him. This time the muse took the form of Franklin Pierce, who in organizing a cabinet reached down from New Hampshire, all the way to Mississippi, and chose Jefferson Davis as his Secretary of War. They had been fellow officers in Mexico, friends in Congress, and shared a dislike of abolitionists. Whatever his reasons, Pierce chose well. Davis made perhaps the best War Secretary the country ever had, and though it included such capable men as William L. Marcy of New York and Caleb Cushing of Massachusetts, he dominated the cabinet in a time of strain and doubt.

Yet the man who returned to public life in 1853 was somewhat different from the man who had left it in 1851 at the behest of the voters. Rather chastened — though he kept his southern nationalism and clung to the spear of States Rights, the shield of the Constitution — he left the fire-eaters Yancey and Rhett behind him. He was no longer the impetuous champion of secession; he believed now that whatever was to be gained might best be accomplished within the Union. He strengthened the army, renovated the Military Academy, and came out strong for un-Jeffersonian internal improvements, including a Pacific Railway along a southern route through Memphis or Vicksburg, to be financed by a hundred-million-dollar federal appropriation. The Gadsden Purchase was a Davis project, ten million paid for a strip of Mexican soil necessary for the railroad right-of-way. Nor was his old imperialism dead. He still had designs on what was left of Mexico and on Central America, and he shocked the diplomats of Europe with a proclamation of his government's intention to annex Cuba. Above all, he was for the unlimited extension of slavery, with a revival of the slave trade if need be.

Returned to the Senate in 1857, he continued to work along these lines, once more a southern champion, not as a secessionist, but as a believer that the destiny of the nation pointed south. It was a stormy time, and much of the bitterness between the sections came to a head on the floor of the Senate, where northern invective and southern arrogance necessarily met. Here Texas senator Louis T. Wigfall, a duelist of note, would sneer at his northern colleagues as he told them, "The difficulty between you and us, gentlemen, is that you will not send the right sort of people here. Why will you not send either Christians or gentlemen?" Here, too, the anti-slavery Massachusetts senator Charles Sumner had his head broken by Congressman Preston Brooks of South Carolina, who, taking exception to remarks Sumner had made on the floor of the Senate regarding a kinsman, caned him as he sat at his desk. Brooks explained that he attacked him sitting because, Sumner being the larger man, he would have had to shoot him if he had risen, and he did not want to kill him, only maim him. Sumner lay bleeding in the aisle among the gutta-percha fragments of the cane, and his enemies stood by and watched him bleed. Southern sympathizers sent Brooks walking sticks by the dozen, recommending their use on other abolitionists, and through the years of Sumner's convalescence Massachusetts let his desk stand empty as a reproach to southern hotheads, though these were in fact more likely to see the vacant seat as a warning to men like Sumner.

During this three-year furor, which led in the end to the disintegration of the Democratic Party and the resultant election of a Republican President, Davis remained as inflexible as ever. But his arguments now did not progress toward secession. They ended instead against a hard brick wall. He did not even claim to know the answers beyond debate. In 1860, speaking in Boston's Faneuil Hall while he and Mrs Davis were up there vacationing for his health — he was a chronic dyspeptic by now, racked by neuralgia through sleepless nights and losing the sight of one eye — he stated his position as to slavery and southern nationalism, but announced that he remained opposed to secession; he still would not take the logical next step. He was much admired by the people of Massachusetts, many of whom despised the abolitionists as much as he did; but the people of Mississippi hardly knew what to make of him. "Davis is at sea," they said.

Then he looked back, and saw that instead of outrunning his constituents, this time he had let them outrun him. He hurried South, made his harvest-home-of-death speech on the eve of Lincoln's election, and returned to Washington, at last reconverted to secession. South Carolina left the Union, then Mississippi and the others, and opinion no longer mattered. As he said in his farewell, even if he had opposed his state's action, he still would have considered himself "bound."

Having spoken his adieu, he left the crowded chamber and, head lowered, went out into the street. That night Mrs Davis heard him pacing the floor. "May God have us in His holy keeping," she heard him say over and over as he paced, "and grant that before it is too late, peaceful councils may prevail."

Such was Davis' way of saying farewell to his colleagues, speaking out of sadness and regret. It was not the way of others: Robert Toombs of Georgia, for example, whose state had seceded two days before Davis spoke. Two days later Toombs delivered his farewell. "The Union, sir, is dissolved," he told the Senate. A large, slack-mouthed man, he tossed his head in shaggy defiance as he spoke. "You see the glittering bayonet, and you hear the tramp of armed men from yon Capitol to the Rio Grande. It is a sight that gladdens the eye and cheers the hearts of other men ready to second them." In case there were those of the North who would maintain the Union by force: "Come and do it!" Toombs cried. "Georgia is on the war path! We are as ready to fight now as we ever shall be. Treason? Bah!" And with that he stalked out of the chamber, walked up to the Treasury, and demanded his salary due to date, plus mileage back to Georgia.

Thus Toombs. But Davis, having sent his wife home with their three children — Margaret aged six, Jeff three, and the year-old baby named for the guardian elder brother Joseph at Davis Bend — lingered in Washington another week, ill and confined to his bed for most of the time, still hoping he might be arrested as a traitor so as to test his claims in the federal courts, then took the train for Jackson, where Governor J. J. Pettus met him with a commission as major general of volunteers. It was the job Davis wanted. He believed there would be war, and he advised the governor to push the procurement of arms.

"The limit of our purchases should be our power to pay," he said. "We shall need all and many more than we can get."

"General," the governor protested, "you overrate the risk."

"I only wish I did," Davis said.

Awaiting the raising of his army, he went to Brierfield. In Alabama, now in early February, a convention was founding a Southern Confederacy, electing political leaders and formulating a new government. He was content, however, to leave such matters to those who were there. He considered his highest talents to be military and he had the position he wanted, commander of the Mississippi army, with advancement to come along with glory when the issue swung to war.

Then history beckoned again, assuming another of her guises. February 10; he and Mrs Davis were out in the garden, cutting a rose bush in the early blue spring weather, when a messenger approached with a telegram in his hand. Davis read it. In that moment of painful silence he seemed stricken; his face took on a look of calamity. Then he read the message to his wife. It was headed "Montgomery, Alabama," and dated the day before.

> Sir:
> We are directed to inform you that you are this day unanimously elected President of the Provisional Government of the Confederate States of America, and to request you to come to Montgomery immediately. We send also a special messenger. Do not wait for him.
>
> R. Toombs,
> R. Barnwell Rhett...

He spoke of it, Mrs Davis said, "as a man might speak of a sentence of death." Yet he wasted no time. He packed and left next day.

The train made many stops along the line and the people were out to meet him, in sunlight and by the glare of torches. They wanted a look at his face, the thin lips and determined jaw, the hollow cheeks with their jutting bones, the long skull behind the aquiline nose; "a wizard physiognomy," one called it. He brought forth cheers with confident words, but he had something else to say as well — something no one had told them before. He advised them to prepare for the long war that lay ahead. They did not believe him, apparently. Or if they did, they went on cheering anyhow.

He reached Montgomery Sunday night, February 17, and was driven from the station in a carriage, down the long torch-lit avenue to the old Exchange Hotel. The crowd followed through streets that had been decked as for a fair; they flowed until they were packed in a mass about the gallery of the hotel in time to see Davis dismount from the carriage and climb the steps; they cheered as he turned and looked at them. Then suddenly they fell silent. William Lowndes Yancey, short and rather seedy-looking alongside the erect and well-groomed Davis, had raised one hand. They cheered again when he brought it down, gesturing toward the tall man beside him, and said in a voice that rang above the expectant, torch-paled faces of the crowd: "The man and the hour have met."

★ ★ ★

The day that Davis received the summons in the rose garden was Abraham Lincoln's last full day in Springfield, Illinois. He would be leaving tomorrow for Washington and his inauguration, the same day that Davis left for Montgomery and his. During the three months since the election, Springfield had changed from a sleepy, fairly typical western county seat and capital into a bustling, cadging hive of politicians, office seekers, reporters, committees representing "folks back home," and the plain downright curious with time on their hands, many of whom had come for no other reason than to breathe the same air with a man who had his name in all the papers. Some were lodged in railway cars on sidings; boarding houses were feeding double shifts.

All of these people wanted a look at Lincoln, and most of them wanted interviews, which they got. "I can't sleep nights," he was saying. His fingers throbbed from shaking hands and his face ached from smiling. He had leased the two-story family residence, sold the cow and the horse and buggy, and left the dog to be cared for by a neighbor; he and his wife and children were staying now at the Chenery House, where the President-elect himself had roped their trunks and addressed them to "A. Lincoln, The White House, Washington D.C." He was by nature a friendly man but his smile was becoming a grimace. "I am sick of office-holding already," he said on this final day in Illinois.

Change was predominant not only in Springfield; the Union appeared to be coming apart at the seams. Louisiana and Texas had brought the total of seceded states to seven. Banks and business firms were folding; the stock market declined and declined. James Buchanan, badly confused, was doing nothing in these last weeks of office. Having stated in his December message to Congress that while a state had no lawful right to secede, neither had the federal government any right to prevent it, privately he was saying that he was the last President of the United States.

North and South, Union men looked to Lincoln, whose election had been the signal for all this trouble. They wanted words of reassurance, words of threat, anything to slow the present trend, the drift toward chaos. Yet he said nothing. When a Missouri editor asked him for a statement, something he could print to make men listen, Lincoln wrote back: "I could say nothing which I have not already said, and which is in print and accessible to the public.... I am not at liberty to shift my ground; that is out of the question. If I thought a repetition would do any good I would make it. But my judgment is it would do positive harm. The secessionists, *per se* believing they had alarmed me, would clamor all the louder."

People hardly knew what to make of this tall, thin-chested, raw-boned man who spoke with the frontier in his voice, wore a stove-pipe hat as if to emphasize his six-foot four-inch height, and walked with a shambling western slouch, the big feet planted flat at every step, the big hands dangling from wrists that hung down out of the sleeves of his rusty tailcoat. Mr Lincoln, they called him, or Lincoln, never "Abe" as in the campaign literature. The seamed, leathery face was becoming familiar: the mole on the right cheek, the high narrow forehead with the unruly, coarse black shock of hair above it, barely grizzled: the pale gray eyes set deep in bruised sockets, the broad mouth somewhat quizzical with a protruding lower lip, the pointed chin behind its recent growth of scraggly beard, the wry neck — a clown face; a sad face, some observed on closer inspection, perhaps the saddest they had ever seen. It was hard to imagine a man like this in the White House, where Madison and Van Buren had kept court. He had more or less blundered into the Republican nomination, much as his Democratic opponents had blundered into defeat in the election which had followed. It had all come about as a result of linking accidents and crises, and the people, with their accustomed championing of the underdog, the dark horse, had enjoyed it at the time. Yet now that the nation was in truth a house divided, now that war loomed, they were not so sure. Down South, men were hearing speeches that fired their blood. Here it was not so; for there was only silence from Abraham Lincoln. Congressman Horace Maynard, a Tennessee Unionist, believed he knew why. "I imagine that he keeps silence," Maynard said, "for the good and sufficient reason that he has nothing to say."

It was true that he had nothing to say at the time. He was waiting; he was drawing on one of his greatest virtues, patience. Though the Cotton South had gone out solid, the eight northernmost slave states remained loyal. Delaware and Maryland, Virginia and North Carolina, Kentucky and Tennessee, Missouri and Arkansas were banked between the hotheads, north and south, a double buffer, and though Lincoln had not received a single electoral vote from this whole area, he counted on the sound common sense of the people there. What was more — provided he did nothing to alienate the loyalty of the border states — he counted on Union sentiment in the departed states to bring them back into the family.

He had had much practice in just this kind of waiting. One of these days, while he was sitting in his office with a visitor, his son Willie came clattering in to demand a quarter. "I can't let you have a quarter," Lincoln said; "I can only spare five cents." He took five pennies from his pocket and stacked them on a corner of the desk. Willie had not asked for a nickel; he wanted a quarter. He sulked and went away, leaving the pennies on the desk. "He will be back after that in a few minutes," Lincoln told the visitor. "As soon as he finds I will give him no more, he will come and get it." They went on talking. Presently the boy returned, took the pennies from the desk, and quietly left. Patience had worked, where attempts at persuasion might have resulted in a flare-up. So with the departed states; self-interest and family ties might bring them back in time. Meanwhile Lincoln walked as softly as he could.

In this manner he had gotten through three of the four anxious months that lay between the election and inauguration, and on this final afternoon in Springfield he went down to his law office to pick up some books and papers and to say goodbye to his partner, William L. Herndon. Nine years his junior, Herndon was excitable, apt to fling off at a tangent, and Lincoln would calm him, saying, "Billy, you're too rampant." There had been times, too, when the older man had gone about collecting fees to pay the fine when his partner was about to be jailed for disorderly conduct on a spree. Now the two sat in the office, discussing business matters. Then came an awkward silence, which Lincoln broke by asking: "Billy, there's one thing I have for some time wanted you to tell me.... I want you to tell me how many times you have been drunk." Flustered, Herndon stammered, and Lincoln let it pass. This was the closest he ever came to delivering a temperance lecture.

They rose, walked downstairs, and paused on the boardwalk. Lincoln glanced up at the weathered law shingle: LINCOLN & HERNDON. "Let it hang there undisturbed," he said. "Give our clients to understand that the election of a President makes no change in the firm of Lincoln and Herndon. If I live I'm coming back some time, and then we'll go right on practicing law as if nothing ever happened." Again there was an awkward pause. Lincoln put his hand out. "Goodbye," he said, and went off down the street.

Herndon stood and watched him go, the tall, loose-jointed figure with the napless stove-pipe hat, the high-water pantaloons, the ill-fitting tailcoat bulging at the elbows from long wear. This junior partner was one of those who saw the sadness in Lincoln's face. "Melancholy dripped from him as he walked," he was to write. Herndon knew something else as well, something that had not been included in the campaign literature: "That man who thinks that Lincoln sat calmly down and gathered his robes about him, waiting for the people to call him, has a very erroneous knowledge of Lincoln. He was always calculating, and always planning ahead. His ambition was a little engine that knew no rest."

That day, as the sun went down and he returned to the Chenery House for his last sleep in Illinois, there were few who knew this side of him. There were gaps in the story that even Herndon could not fill, and other gaps that no one could fill, ever, though writers were to make him the subject of more biographies and memoirs, more brochures and poems than any other American. On the face of it the facts were simple enough, as he told a journalist who came seeking information about his boyhood years for a campaign biography: "Why, Scripps, it is a great piece of folly to attempt to make anything out of my early life. It can all be condensed into a single sentence, and that sentence you will find in Gray's *Elegy*: 'The short and simple annals of the poor.' "

He was born in the Kentucky wilderness of Daniel Boone, mid-February of 1809, in a one-room dirt-floor cabin put up that same winter by his father, Thomas Lincoln, a thick-chested man of average height, who passed on to Abraham only his coarse black hair and dark complexion. Originally from Virginia, Thomas was a wanderer like the Lincolns before him, who had come down out of New Jersey and Pennsylvania, and though in early manhood he could sign his name when necessary, later he either forgot or else he stopped taking the trouble; he made his X-mark like his wife, born Nancy Hanks.

In after years when Lincoln tried to trace his ancestry he could go no further back than his father's father, also named Abraham, who had been killed from ambush by an Indian. That was on his father's side. On his mother's he discovered only that she had been born out of wedlock to Lucy Hanks who later married a man named Sparrow. Nancy died of the milksick when Abraham was nine, and her body lay in another of those one-room cabins while her husband knocked together a coffin in the yard.

They were in Indiana by then, having come to the big woods after a previous move to Knob Creek, south of Louisville and beside the Cumberland Trail, along which pioneers with many children and few livestock marched northwestward. Thomas Lincoln joined them for the move across the Ohio, and when his wife died took another the following year: Sarah Bush Johnston, a widow with three children. She was called Sally Bush Lincoln now, tall and hard-working, a welcome addition to any frontier family, especially this one, which had been without a woman for almost a year. She brought to Abraham all the love and affection she had given her own. The boy returned it, and in later years, when his memory of Nancy Hanks Lincoln had paled, referred to the one who took her place as "my angel mother," saying: "All that I am I owe to my angel mother."

For one thing, she saw to it that the boy went to school. Previously he had not gone much deeper into learning than his ABC's, and only then at such times as his father felt he could spare him from his chores. Now at intervals he was able to fit in brief weeks of schooling, amounting in all to something under a year. They were "blab" schools, which meant that the pupils studied aloud at their desks and the master judged the extent of their concentration by the volume of their din. Between such periods of formal education he studied at home, ciphering on boards when he had no slate, and shaving them clean with a knife for an eraser. He developed a talent for mimicry, too, mounting a stump when out with a work gang and delivering mock orations and sermons. This earned him the laughter of the men, who would break off work to watch him, but his father disapproved of such interruptions and would speak to him sharply or cuff him off the stump.

He grew tall and angular, with long muscles, so that in his early teens he could grip an ax one-handed at the end of the helve and hold it out, untrembling. Neighbors testified to his skill with this implement, one saying: "He can sink an ax deeper into wood than any man I ever saw," and another: "If you heard him felling trees in a clearing, you would say there was three men at work by the way the trees fell." However, though he did his chores, including work his father hired him out to do, he developed no real liking for manual labor. He would rather be reading what few books he got his hands on: Parson Weems's *Life of Washington*, *Pilgrim's Progress*, *Æsop's Fables*, *Robinson Crusoe*, Grimshaw's *History of the United States*, and *The Kentucky Preceptor*. Sometimes he managed to combine the two, for in plowing he would stop at the end of a row, reading while he gave the horse a breather.

From a flatboat trip one thousand miles downriver to New Orleans, during which he learned to trim a deck and man a sweep, he returned in time for his twenty-first birthday and another family migration, from Indiana out to central Illinois, where he and a cousin hired out to split four thousand rails for their neighbors. Thus he came to manhood, a rail-splitter, wilderness-born and frontier-raised. He was of the West, the new country out beyond the old, a product of a nation fulfilling a manifest destiny. It was in his walk, in his talk and in his character, indelibly. It would be with him wherever he went, along with the knowledge that he had survived in a region where "the Lord spared the fitten and the rest He seen fitten to let die."

He had never had much fondness for his father, and now that he was legally independent he struck out on his own. The family moved once more, deeper into Illinois, but Lincoln did not go with them. He took instead another flatboat trip down to New Orleans, and then came back to another kind of life. This was prairie country, with a rich soil and a future. Lincoln got a job clerking in a New Salem store at fifteen dollars a month plus a bed to sleep in. He defeated the leader of the regional toughs in a wrestling match, and when the leader's friends pitched in, Lincoln backed against a wall and dared them to come at him one by one; whereupon they acknowledged him as their new leader.

This last was rather in line with the life he had led before, but he found something new as well. He attended the New Salem Debating Society, and though at first the charter members snickered at his looks and awkwardness, presently they were admiring the logic and conciseness of his arguments. "All he lacked was culture," one of them said. Lincoln took such encouragement from his success that in the spring of 1832 he announced as a candidate for the state legislature.

The Black Hawk War interrupting his campaign, he enlisted and was elected captain by his fellow volunteers. Discipline was not strong among them; the new commander's first order to one of his men brought the reply, "You go to hell." They saw no action, and Lincoln afterwards joked about his military career, saying that all the blood he lost was to mosquitoes and all his charges were against wildonion beds. When the company's thirty-day enlistment expired he reënlisted for another twenty days as a private, then came home and resumed his campaign for the legislature, two weeks remaining until election day. His first political speech was made at a country auction. Twenty-three years old, he stood on a box, wearing a frayed straw hat, a calico shirt, and pantaloons held up by a single-strap suspender. As he was about to speak, a fight broke out in the crowd. Lincoln stepped down, broke up the fight, then stepped back onto the box.

"Gentlemen and fellow citizens," he said, "I presume you all know who I am: I am humble Abraham Lincoln. I have been solicited by many friends to become a candidate for the legislature. My politics are short and sweet, like the old woman's dance. I am in favor of a national bank. I am in favor of the internal-improvements system and a high protective tariff. These are my sentiments and political principles. If elected, I shall be thankful; if not, it will be all the same."

Election day he ran eighth in a field of thirteen, but he received 277 of the 300 votes in the New Salem precinct.

It was probably then that Lincoln determined to run for the same office next time around. Meanwhile there was a living to earn. He could always split rails and do odd jobs. These he did, and then went into partnership in a grocery store that failed, leaving him a debt beyond a thousand dollars; "the National Debt," he called it ruefully, and worked for years to pay it off. He became village postmaster, sometimes carrying letters in his hat, which became a habit. He studied surveying and worked a while at that. He also began the study of law, reading Blackstone and Chitty, and improved his education with borrowed books. His name was becoming more widely known; he was winning popularity by his great strength and his ability at telling funny stories, but mostly by his force of character. Then in the spring of 1834, when another legislature race came round, he conducted an all-out full-time campaign and was elected.

With borrowed money he bought his first tailor-made suit, paying sixty dollars for it, and left for the first of his four terms in the state law-making body, learning the rough-and-tumble give-and-take of western politics. Two years later he was licensed as an attorney, and soon afterwards moved to Springfield as a partner in a law firm. He said goodbye to the manual labor he had been so good at, yet had never really liked; from now on he would work with his head, as a leader of men. His ambition became what Herndon later called "a little engine."

Springfield was about to be declared the state capital, moved there from Vandalia largely through Lincoln's efforts in the legislature, and here he began to acquire that culture which the New Salem intellectuals had said was "all he lacked." The big, work-splayed hands were losing their horn-hard calluses. He settled down to the law, becoming in time an excellent trial lawyer and a capable stump debater at political rallies, even against such opponents as Stephen A. Douglas, the coming Little Giant. Socially, however, he was slow in getting started. About a month after his arrival he wrote in a letter: "I have been spoken to by but one woman since I've been here, and should not have been by her, if she could have avoided it." He was leery of the ladies, having once remarked, half-jokingly, "A woman is the only thing I am afraid of that I know will not hurt me." Nevertheless, by the time he was elected to his fourth term in the legislature, Lincoln was courting Mary Todd, a visitor from Lexington, Kentucky, and in early November of 1842 he married her.

It was an attraction of opposites, and as such it was stormy. At one point they broke off the engagement; she left Illinois and Lincoln had to go to Kentucky for a reconciliation before she would return to Springfield and marry him in her sister's parlor. If "culture" was what he was after, still, Lincoln again had moved in the proper direction. His wife, the great-granddaughter of a Revolutionary general, had attended a private academy in Lexington, where she learned to speak French, read music after a fashion, paint on china, and dance the sedate figures of the time. At twenty-four she was impulsive and vivacious, short and rather plump, looking especially so alongside her long lean husband, who was thirty-three. Lincoln seemed to take it calmly enough. Five days after the wedding he wrote to a lawyer friend: "Nothing new here, except my marrying, which to me is matter of profound wonder."

Their first child, Robert Todd, called Bob, was born the following year. Three others came in the course of the next decade, all sons: Edward and William and Thomas, called Eddy, Willie, Tad. Eddy died before he was five, and Tad had a cleft palate; he spoke with a lisp. The Lincolns lived a year in rented rooms, then moved into the $1500 white frame house which remained their home. They took their place in Springfield society, and Lincoln worked hard at law, riding the Eighth Judicial Circuit in all kinds of weather, a clean shirt and a change of underwear in his saddlebag, along with books and papers and a yellow flannel nightshirt. Fees averaged about five dollars a case, sometimes paid in groceries, which he was glad to get, since the cost of the house represented something beyond one year's total earnings.

Home life taught him patience, for his wife was high-strung as well as high-born. He called her Mother and met her fits of temper with forbearance, which must have been the last thing she wanted at the time. When her temper got too hot he would walk off to his office and stay until it cooled. Accustomed to Negro house slaves in Kentucky, Mary Lincoln could not get along with Illinois hired girls, who were inclined to answer back. Lincoln did what he could here too, slipping the girls an extra weekly dollar for compensation. Once after a particularly bitter scene between mistress and maid, when Mrs Lincoln had left the room he patted the girl on the shoulder and gave her the same advice he had given himself: "Stay with her, Maria. Stay with her."

His law practice grew; he felt prepared to grow in other directions. Having completed his fourth term in the state legislature, he was ready to move on up the political ladder. He wrote to Whig associates in the district, "Now if you should hear anyone say that Lincoln don't want to go to Congress, I wish you as a personal friend of mine would tell him you have reason to believe he is mistaken. The truth is, I would like to go very much." In the backstage party scramble, however, he lost the nomination in 1842 and again in 1844. It was 1847 before he got to Congress. From a back row on the Whig side of the House he came to know the voices and faces of men he would know better, Ashmun of Massachusetts, Rhett of South Carolina, Smith of Indiana, Toombs and Stephens of Georgia, while a visit to the Senate would show him the elder statesmen Webster and Calhoun, along with newer men of note, such as Cameron of Pennsylvania and Davis of Mississippi.

The Mexican War had ended by then, and though Lincoln voted for whatever army supply bills came before the House, like most Whigs he attacked the motives behind the war, which now was being spoken of, by northern Whigs at least, as "infamous and wicked," an imperialist attempt to extend the slavery realm. This got him into trouble back home, where the Democratic papers began calling him a latter-day Benedict Arnold and the people read and noted all he did as a slur against the volunteers of his state. When Congress convened for his second session, Lincoln was the only Whig from Illinois. It was a hectic session anyhow, with tempers flaring over the question of slavery in the territories. He came home with no chance for reëlection, and did not try. He gave up politics, refusing even a spoils offer of the governorship of Oregon Territory, and returned to the practice of law, once more riding the circuit. Disheartened, he paused now to restore his soul through work and meditation.

Though he did not believe at the outset that it would necessarily ever reach an end — indeed, he believed it would not; otherwise it could never have done for him what it did — this five-year "retreat," coming as it did between his fortieth and his forty-fifth years, 1849 to 1854, was his interlude of greatest growth. Like many, perhaps most, men of genius, Lincoln developed late.

It was a time for study, a time for self-improvement. He went back and drilled his way through the first six books of Euclid, as an exercise to discipline his mind. Not politics but the law was his main interest now. Riding the circuit he talked less and listened more. Together with a new understanding and a deeper reading of Shakespeare and the Bible, this brought him a profounder faith in people, including those who had rejected him and repudiated what he had to offer as a leader. Here, too, he was learning. This was the period in which he was reported to have said, "You can fool some of the people all the time, and all the people some of the time, but you can't fool all the people all the time."

Nonparticipation in public affairs did not mean a loss of interest in them. Lincoln read the papers more carefully now than he had ever done before, learning from them of the deaths of Calhoun, Clay, and Webster, whose passing marked the passing of an era. When the 1850 Compromise — as he and most men believed, including Clay who engineered it shortly before his death — settled the differences that had brought turmoil to the nation and fist fights to the floors of Congress while Lincoln himself was there, he breathed easier. But not for long. The conflict soon was heading up again. *Uncle Tom's Cabin* came from the presses in a stream; southern nationalists were announcing plans for the annexation of Cuba; the case of the slave Dred Scott, suing for his freedom, moved by legal osmosis through the courts; the Whigs seemed lost and the Democrats were splitting. Then Lincoln's old stump opponent, Stephen A. Douglas, who was four years younger than Lincoln but who had suffered no setback in political advancement, filling now his second term in the Senate, brought the crisis to a head.

Scarcely taller than Napoleon, but with all that monarch's driving ambition and belief in a private star, Douglas moved to repeal that part of the Missouri Compromise which served to restrict the extension of slavery. This came as a result of his championing a northern route for the proposed Pacific railway. A southern route was also proposed and Douglas sought to effect a swap, reporting a bill for the organization of two new territories, Kansas and Nebraska, with the provision that the people there should determine for themselves as to the admission or exclusion of slavery, despite the fact that both areas lay well north of the 36°30' line drawn by the Compromise, which had guaranteed that the institution would be kept forever south of there. The Southerners were glad to abandon their New Mexico route for such a gain, provided the repeal was made not only implicit but explicit in the bill. Douglas was somewhat shocked (he brought a certain naivety to even his deepest plots) but soon agreed, and Secretary of War Jefferson Davis persuaded Franklin Pierce to make the bill an Administration issue. "Popular sovereignty," Douglas called it; "Squatter sovereignty," his opponents considered a better name. "It will raise a hell of a storm," Douglas predicted. It did indeed, though the Democrats managed to ram it through by late May of 1854, preparing the ground for Bleeding Kansas and the birth of the Republican Party that same year.

Another effect of the Kansas-Nebraska Bill was that it brought Lincoln out of retirement. It had raised even more of a storm than Douglas predicted, and not only in Congress. For when the senator came home to Illinois he saw through the train window his effigy being burned in courthouse squares, and when he came to explain his case before eight thousand people in Chicago, they jeered him off the rostrum He left, shaking his fist in their faces, and set out to stump the state with a speech that confounded opposition orators and won back many of the voters. Then in early October he came to Springfield, packing the hall of the House of Representatives. After the speech — which had been as successful here as elsewhere in turning the jeers to cheers — the crowd filed out through the lobby and saw Abraham Lincoln standing on the staircase, announcing that he would reply to Douglas the following day and inviting the senator to be present, to answer if he cared.

Next day they were there, close-packed as yesterday; Douglas had a front-row seat. It was hot and Lincoln spoke in shirt sleeves, wearing no collar or tie. His voice was shrill as he began, though presently it settled to lower tones, interrupted from time to time by crackles and thunders of applause. Wet with sweat, his shirt clung to his shoulders and big arms. He had written his speech out beforehand, clarifying in his own mind his position as to slavery, which he saw as the nub of the issue — much to the discomfort of Douglas, who wanted to talk about "popular sovereignty," keeping the issue one of self-government, whereas Lincoln insisted on going beyond, making slavery the main question. Emerging from his long retirement, having restored his soul, he was asking himself and all men certain questions. And now the Lincoln music began to sound.

"The doctrine of self-government is right, absolutely and eternally right; but it has no just application, as here attempted. Or perhaps I should rather say that whether it has such just application depends upon whether a Negro is not or is a man. If he is not a man, why in that case he who is a man may, as a matter of self-government, do just as he pleases with him. But if the Negro is a man, is it not to that extent a total destruction of self-government to say that he too shall not govern himself? When the white man governs himself, that is self-government; but when he governs himself and also governs another man, that is more than self-government; that is despotism. If the Negro is a man, why then my ancient faith teaches me that 'all men are created equal,' and that there can be no moral right in connection with one man's making a slave of another."

He believed that it was a moral wrong; he had not come to believe that it was a legal wrong, though he believed that too would be clarified in time. The words of his mouth came like meditations from his heart: "Slavery is founded in the selfishness of man's nature, opposition to it in his love of justice. These principles are an eternal antagonism, and when brought into collision so fiercely as slavery extension brings them, shocks and throes and convulsions must ceaselessly follow. Repeal the Missouri Compromise, repeal all compromises; repeal the

Declaration of Independence, repeal all past history — you still cannot repeal human nature. It still will be the abundance of man's heart that slavery extension is wrong, and out of the abundance of his heart his mouth will continue to speak."

This, in part, was the speech that caused his name to be recognized throughout the Northwest, though personally he was still but little known outside his state. He repeated it twelve days later in Peoria, where shorthand reporters took it down for their papers, and continued to speak in central Illinois and in Chicago. Winning reëlection to the legislature, he presently had a chance at a seat in the U.S. Senate. His hopes were high and he resigned from the legislature to be eligible, but at the last minute he had to throw his votes to an anti-Nebraska Democrat to defeat the opposition.

Again he had failed, and again he regretted failing. Yet this time he was not despondent. He kept working and waiting. His law practice boomed; he earned a five-thousand-dollar fee on a railroad case, and was retained to assist a high-powered group of big-city lawyers on a patents case in Cincinnati, but when they saw him come to town, wearing his usual rusty clothes and carrying a ball-handled blue cotton umbrella, they would scarcely speak to him. One of the attorneys, Edwin M. Stanton of Pittsburgh, was downright rude; "Where did that long-armed creature come from?" he asked within earshot. Lincoln went his way, taking no apparent umbrage.

Politically he was wary, too, writing to a friend: "Just now I fear to do anything, lest I do wrong." He had good cause for fear, and so had all men through this time of "shocks and throes and convulsions." Popular sovereignty was being tested in Kansas in a manner Douglas had not foreseen. Missouri border ruffians and hired abolitionist gunmen were cutting each other's throats for votes in the coming referendum; the Mormons were resisting federal authority in the West, and while a ruinous financial panic gripped the East, the Know-Nothing Party was sweeping New England with anti-foreigner, anti-Catholic appeals. The Whigs had foundered, the Democrats had split on all those rocks. Like many men just now, Lincoln hardly knew where he stood along party lines.

"I think I am a Whig," he wrote, "but others say there are no Whigs, and that I am an Abolitionist.... I am not a Know-Nothing. That is certain. How could I be? How can anyone who abhors the oppression of Negroes be in favor of degrading classes of white people? Our progress in degeneracy appears to me to be pretty rapid."

He was waiting and looking. And then he found the answer.

It was 1856, a presidential election year. Out of the Nebraska crisis, two years before, the Republican Party had been born, a coalition of foundered Whigs and disaffected northern Democrats, largely abolitionist at the core. They made overtures to Lincoln but he dodged them at the time, not wanting a Radical tag attached to his name. Now, however, seeking to unify the anti-Nebraska elements in Illinois, he came to meet them. As a delegate to the state convention he caught fire and made what may have been the greatest speech of his career, though no one would ever really know, since the heat of his words seemed to burn them from men's memory, and in that conglomerate mass of gaping, howling old-line Whigs and bolted Democrats, Know-Nothings, Free Soilers and Abolitionists, even the shorthand reporters sat enthralled, forgetting to use their pencils. From now on he was a Republican; he would take his chances with the Radical tag.

At the national convention in Philadelphia he received 110 votes on the first ballot for the vice-presidential nomination, yielding them on the second to a New Jersey running mate for John C. Frémont of California. Lincoln had not favored Frémont, but he worked hard for him in the campaign that saw the election of the Democratic nominee James Buchanan, an elderly bachelor whose main advantage lay in the fact that he was the least controversial candidate, having been out of the country as Minister to England during the trying past three years. The Republicans were by no means dispirited at running second. They sniffed victory down the wind, in the race four years from now — provided only that the turmoil and sectional antagonism should continue, which seemed likely.

At this point the United States Supreme Court handed down a decision which appeared to cut the ground from under all their feet. The test case of the slave Dred Scott, suing for freedom on a plea that his master had taken him into a territory where slavery was forbidden by the Missouri Compromise, had at last reached the high court. In filing the majority opinion, Chief Justice Roger B. Taney dismissed Scott's lawyer's claim. A Negro, he said, was not a citizen of the United States, and therefore had no right to sue in a federal court. This was enough to enrage the Abolitionists, who secretly had sponsored the suit. But Taney went even further. The Missouri Compromise itself was void, he declared; Congress had no power over territories except to prepare for their admission to the Union; slaves being private property, Congress had no right to exclude them anywhere. According to this decision, "popular sovereignty" went into the discard, since obviously whatever powers Congress lacked would be lacked by any territorial legislature created by Congress.

The reaction was immediate and uproarious. Secession, formerly the threat of the South, now came as a cry from the North, particularly New England, where secessionist meetings were held in many towns. Douglas, on the other hand, digested the bitter dose as best he could, then announced that the decision was in fact a vindication of his repeal of the Compromise two years before, as well as a confirmation of the principles of popular sovereignty, since slavery, whether legal or not, could never thrive where the people did not welcome it. Lincoln did not mask his disappointment. He believed the decision was erroneous and harmful, but he respected the judgment of the Court and urged his followers to work toward the time when the five-four decision would be reversed. Meanwhile, during the off-year 1857, he prepared to run for the Senate against Douglas, whose third term would expire the following year.

Just then, unexpectedly, Douglas split with the Administration over the adoption of a constitution for Kansas. Threatened with expulsion from his party, he swung over to the Republicans on the issue, bringing many Democrats along with him. The Republicans were surprised and grateful, and it began to look as if Lincoln would be passed over again when nominating time came round. However, they were too accustomed to fighting the Little Giant to break off hostilities now. They nominated Lincoln at the state convention in mid-June. Lincoln was ready, and more than ready. He had not only prepared his acceptance, but now for the first time he read a speech from manuscript, as if to emphasize his knowledge of the need for precision. It was at this point that Lincoln's political destiny and the destiny of the nation became one. The first paragraph once more summed up his thinking and struck the keynote for all that was to follow:

"If we could first know where we are, and whither we are tending, we could better judge what to do, and how to do it. We are now far into the fifth year since a policy was initiated with the avowed object and confident promise of putting an end to slavery agitation. Under the operation of that policy, that agitation has not only not ceased, but has constantly augmented. In my opinion it will not cease until a crisis shall have been reached and passed. 'A house divided against itself cannot stand.' I believe this government cannot endure permanently half slave and half free. I do not expect the Union to be dissolved — I do not expect the house to fall — but I do expect it will cease to be divided. It will become all one thing, or all the other. Either the opponents of slavery will arrest the further spread of it, and place it where the public mind shall be at rest in the belief that it is in the course of ultimate extinction, or its advocates will push it forward till it shall have become alike lawful in all the states, old as well as new, North as well as South."

Seizing upon this as proof of Lincoln's radicalism, and declaring that it proved him not only a proponent of sectional discord but also a reckless prophet of war, Douglas came home and launched an all-out campaign against the Republicans and the Democrats who had not walked out with him. He spoke in Chicago to a crowd that broke into frenzies of cheers, then set out to stump the state, traveling with a retinue of secretaries, stenographers, and influential admirers in a gaily bannered private car placed at his disposal by George B. McClellan, chief engineer of the Illinois Central, who also provided a flatcar mounting a brass cannon to boom the announcement that the Little Giant was coming down the line. Traveling unaccompanied on an ordinary ticket, Lincoln moved in his wake, sometimes on the same train, addressing the crowds attracted by the Douglas panoply. At last he made the arrangement formal, challenging his opponent to a series of debates. Douglas, with nothing to gain, could not refuse. He agreed to meet Lincoln once in each of the seven congressional districts where they had not already spoken.

Thus the colorful Douglas-Lincoln debates got under way, the pudgy, well-tailored Douglas with his scowl, his luxurious mane of hair, gesturing aggressively as his voice wore to a froggy croak, and Lincoln in his claw-hammer coat and straight-leg trousers, tall and earnest, with a shrill voice that reached the outer edges of the crowd, bending his knees while he led up to a point, then straightening them with a jerk, rising to his full height as he made it. Crowds turned out, ten to fifteen thousand strong, thronging the lonesome prairie towns. At Freeport, Lincoln threw Douglas upon the horns of a dilemma, asking: "Can the people of a United States Territory, in any lawful way ... exclude slavery from its limits prior to the formation of a State Constitution?" If Douglas answered No he would offend the free-soil voters of Illinois. If he answered Yes he would make himself unacceptable to the South in the 1860 presidential campaign, toward which his ambition so clearly pointed. He made his choice; Yes, he said, defying both the Supreme Court and the South, and thereby cinched the present election and stored up trouble for the future.

Approaching fifty, Lincoln again took defeat in his stride, turning once more to the practice of law to build up a flattened bank account. He was known throughout the nation now as a result of the cross-state debates. In his mail and in the newspapers there began to appear suggestions that he was presidential timber — to which he replied, sometimes forthrightly: "I must, in candor, say I do not think I am fit for the Presidency," sometimes less forthrightly: "I shall labor faithfully in the ranks, unless, as I think not probable, the judgment of the party shall assign me a different position." Through the long hot summer of 1859, past fifty now, he wrote letters and made speeches and did in general what he could to improve the party strategy, looking toward next year's elections.

Then in mid-October the telegraph clacked a message that drove all such thoughts from men's minds. John Brown, called Osawatomie Brown after a massacre staged in Kansas, had seized the federal arsenal at Harpers Ferry, Virginia, as the first step in leading a slave insurrection. His army counted eighteen men, including five Negroes; "One man and God can overturn the universe," he said. Captured by United States

Marines under Colonel Robert E. Lee, U.S. Army, he was tried in a Virginia court and sentenced to be hanged in early December. He had the backing of several New England Abolitionists; they spent an anxious six weeks while the old fanatic kept their secret, close-mouthed behind his long gray beard. Seated on his coffin while he rode in a wagon to the gallows, he looked out at the hazy Blue Ridge Mountains. "This *is* a beautiful country," he said. "I never had the pleasure of really seeing it before." After the hanging the jailor unfolded a slip of paper Brown had left behind, a prophecy: "I John Brown am now quite certain that the crimes of this guilty land; will never be purged away; but with blood."

This too was added to the issues men were split on; John Brown's soul went marching, a symbol of good or evil, depending on the viewer. Douglas, back in Washington, was quick to claim that such incidents of lawlessness and bloodshed were outgrowths of the House Divided speech, and Lincoln's name was better known than ever. In late February, just past his fifty-first birthday, Lincoln traveled to New York for a speech at Cooper Union. The city audience thought him strange as he stood there, tall and awkward in a new broadcloth suit that hung badly from having been folded in a satchel for the train ride. "Mr Cheerman," he began. Presently, however, the awkwardness was dropped, or else they forgot it. He spoke with calm authority, denying that the Republican Party was either sectional or radical, except as its opponents had made it so. Slavery was the issue, North and South, he said, probing once more for the heart of the matter.

"All they ask, we could readily grant, if we thought slavery right; all we ask, they could as readily grant, if they thought it wrong. Their thinking it right, and our thinking it wrong, is the precise fact upon which depends the whole controversy. Thinking it right, as they do, they are not to blame for desiring its full recognition as being right; but thinking it wrong, as we do, can we yield to them? Can we cast our votes with their view and against our own? In view of our moral, social, and political responsibilities can we do this?" He thought not. "If our sense of duty forbids this, then let us stand by our duty fearlessly and effectively.... Neither let us be slandered from our duty by false accusations against us, nor frightened from it by menaces of destruction to the government nor of dungeons to ourselves. Let us have faith that right makes might, and in that faith let us, to the end, dare to do our duty as we understand it."

That was the peroration, and the listeners surged from their seats to applaud him, waving handkerchiefs and hats as they came forward to wring his hand. Four New York newspapers printed the speech in full next morning, and Lincoln went on into New England, making a series of addresses there before returning to Springfield much enhanced. The time for presidential nominations was drawing close. When a friend asked if he would allow his name to be entered, Lincoln admitted: "The taste *is* in my mouth a little."

Chicago was the scene of the Republican national convention, the result of a political maneuver toward the close of the previous year by one of Lincoln's supporters, who, poker-faced, had suggested the western city as an ideal neutral site, since Illinois would have no candidate of her own. Now in mid-May, however, as the delegates converged upon the raw pine Wigwam put up to accommodate ten thousand in an atmosphere of victory foreseen, they found that Illinois had a candidate indeed, and something beyond the usual favorite son. Alongside such prominent men as William H. Seward of New York, Salmon P. Chase of Ohio, Edward Bates of Missouri, and Simon Cameron of Pennsylvania, Lincoln was comparatively unknown. Yet this had its advantages, since the shorter the public record a candidate presented, the smaller the target he would expose to the mud that was sure to be flung. Each of these men had disadvantages; Seward had spoken too often of the "irrepressible conflict," Chase had been too radical, Bates was tainted by Know-Nothingism, and Cameron was said to be a crook. Besides all this, Lincoln came from the critical Northwest, where the political scale was likely to be tipped.

His managers set up headquarters and got to work behind the scenes, giving commitments, making deals. Then, on the eve of balloting, they received a wire from Springfield: "I authorize no bargains and will be bound by none." "Lincoln aint here and don't know what we have to meet," the managers said, and went on dickering right and left, promising cabinet posts and patronage, printing counterfeit admission tickets to pack the Wigwam nomination morning. The Seward yell was met by the Lincoln yawp. The New Yorker led on the first ballot. On the second there were readjustments as the others jockeyed for position; Lincoln was closing fast. On the third he swept in. The Wigwam vibrated with shouts and cheers, bells and whistles swelling the uproar while the news went out to the nation.

"Just think of such a sucker as me being President," Lincoln had said. Yet in Springfield when his friends came running, those who were not already with him in the newspaper office, they were somewhat taken aback at the new, calm, sure dignity which clothed him now like a garment.

Lincoln himself did not campaign. No presidential candidate ever had, such action being considered incommensurate with the dignity of the office. Nor did two of his three opponents. But Douglas, the only one of the four who seemed to believe that the election might bring war, set forth to stump the country. All four were running on platforms that called for the preservation of the Union. The defeat of

Lincoln depended solely on Douglas, however, since neither of the others could hope to carry the free states. Knowing this, Douglas worked with all his strength. Wherever he went he was met by Lincoln men, including Seward, Chase, and Bates. The Republican campaign for "Honest Abe, the Rail Splitter" was a colorful one, with pole raisings, barbecues, and torchlight parades. Douglas kept fighting. Then in August, when Lincoln supporters carried local elections in Maine and Vermont, and in October when Pennsylvania and Ohio followed suit, Douglas saw what was coming. He told his secretary, "Mr Lincoln is the next President. We must try to save the Union. I will go South."

He did go South in a final attempt to heal the three-way Democratic split, but there men would not listen either. On election day, November 6, though he ran closest to Lincoln in popular votes, he had the fewest electoral votes of all.

That night Lincoln sat in the Springfield telegraph office, watching the tabulations mount to a climax: Bell, 588,879; Breckinridge, 849,781; Douglas, 1,376,957; Lincoln, 1,866,452. The combined votes of his opponents outnumbered his own by almost a million; he would be a minority President, like the indecisive Buchanan now in office. He had carried none of the fifteen southern states, receiving not a single popular ballot in five of them, even from a crank, and no electoral votes at all. Yet he had carried all of the northern states except New Jersey, which he split with Douglas, so that the final electoral vote had a brighter aspect: Lincoln 180, Breckinridge 72, Bell 39, Douglas 12. Even if all the opposing popular votes had been concentrated on a single candidate, he would have received but eleven fewer electoral votes, which still would have left him more than he needed to win. Any way men figured it, North or South, barring assassination or an act of God, Abraham Lincoln would be President of the United States in March.

How many states would remain united was another question. South Carolina had warned that she would secede if Lincoln was elected. Now she did, and within three of the four months that lay between the election and the inauguration, six others followed her out. Lincoln in Springfield gave no assurance that he would seek a compromise or be willing to accept one. "Stand firm," he wrote privately to an Illinois senator. "The tug has to come, and better now than any time hereafter." "Hold firm, as with a chain of steel," he wrote to a friend in the House.

He had troubles enough, right there at home. "No bargains," he had wired his managers at the convention, but they had ignored him out of necessity. Now the claimants hedged him in, swarming into his home and office, plucking at his coat sleeve on the street.

The week before his departure for Washington he made a trip down to Coles County to say goodbye to Sally Bush Lincoln, the step-

Prologue—The Opponents [35]

mother who had done for him all she could. When his father had died there, nine years back, Lincoln had not attended the funeral; but he took time out for this. He kissed her and held her close, then came back to Springfield, closed his office the final day, said goodbye to his partner Herndon, and went to the Chenery House for his last sleep in Illinois.

Next morning dawned cold and drizzly; 8 o'clock was leaving time. Lincoln and his party of fifteen, together with those who had come to say goodbye, assembled in the waiting room of the small brick depot. They felt unaccountably depressed; there was a gloom about the gathering, no laughter and few smiles as people came forward for handshakes and farewells. When the stub, funnel-stack locomotive blew the all-aboard they filed out of the station. The President-elect, and those who were going with him, boarded the single passenger car; those who were staying collected about the back platform, the rain making a steady murmur against the taut cotton or silk of their umbrellas. As he stood at the rail, chin down, Lincoln's look of sadness deepened. Tomorrow he would be fifty-two, one of the youngest men ever to fill the office he had won three months ago. Then he raised his head, and the people were hushed as he looked into their faces.

"My friends," he said quietly, above the murmur of the rain, "no one not in my situation can appreciate my feeling of sadness at this parting. To this place and the kindness of these people I owe everything. Here I have lived for a quarter of a century, and have passed from a young to an old man. Here my children have been born, and one is buried. I now leave, not knowing when, or whether ever, I may return, with a task before me greater than that which rested upon Washington. Without the assistance of that Divine Being who ever attended him, I cannot succeed. With that assistance I cannot fail. Trusting in Him who can go with me and remain with you and be everywhere for good, let us confidently hope that all will yet be well. To His care commending you, as I hope in your prayers you will commend me, I bid you an affectionate farewell."

The train pulled out and the people stood and watched it go, some with tears on their faces. Four years and two months later, still down in Coles County, Sally Bush Lincoln was to say: "I knowed when he went away he wasn't ever coming back alive."

✘ 2 ✘

Throughout the twelve days of his roundabout trip to Washington, traversing five states along an itinerary that called for twenty speeches and an endless series of conferences with prominent men who boarded the train at every station, Lincoln's resolution to keep silent on the vital issues was made more difficult if not impossible. Determined to withhold his plans until the inauguration had given him the authority to act as well as declare, he attempted to say nothing even as he spoke. And in this he was surprisingly successful. He met the crowds with generalities and the dignitaries with jokes — to the confusion and outrage of both. He told the Ohio legislature, "There is nothing going wrong. It is a consoling circumstance that when we look out there is nothing that really hurts anybody. We entertain different views upon political questions, but nobody is suffering anything."

With seven states out of the Union, arsenals and mints seized along with vessels and forts, the Mississippi obstructed, the flag itself fired upon, this man could say there was nothing going wrong. His listeners shrugged and muttered at his ostrich policy. They had come prepared for cheers, and they did cheer him loudly each time he seemed ready to face the issue, as when he warned in New Jersey that if it became necessary "to put the foot down firmly" they must support him. Even so, his appearance was not reassuring to the Easterners. In New York he offended the sensibilities of many by wearing black kid gloves to the opera and letting his big hands dangle over the box rail. Taken in conjunction with the frontier accent and the shambling western gait, it made them wonder what manner of man they had entrusted with their destinies. Hostile papers called him "gorilla" and "baboon," and as caricature the words seemed unpleasantly fitting.

In Philadelphia, raising a flag at Independence Hall, he felt his breath quicken as he drew down on the halyard and saw the bright red and rippling blue of the bunting take the breeze. Turning to the crowd he touched a theme he would return to. "I have often inquired of myself what great principle or idea it was that kept this confederacy so long together. It was not the mere matter of the separation of the colonies from the mother land, but that something in the Declaration giving liberty, not alone to the people of this land, but hope to the world for all future time. It was that which gave promise that in due time the weights should be lifted from the shoulders of all men, and that all should have an equal chance." Men stood and listened with upturned faces, wanting fire for the tinder of their wrath, not ointment for their fears, and the music crept by them. It was not this they had come to hear.

So far Lincoln had seemed merely inadequate, inept, at worst a bumpkin; but now the trip was given a comic-opera finish, in which he was called to play the part not only of a fool but of a coward. Baltimore, the last scheduled stop before Washington, would mark his first entry into a slavery region as President-elect. The city had sent him no welcome message, as all the others had done, and apparently had made no official plans for receiving him or even observing his presence while he passed through. Unofficially, however, according to reports, there awaited him a reception quite different from any he had been given along the way. Bands of toughs, called Blood Tubs, roamed the streets, plotting his abduction or assassination. He would be stabbed or shot, or both; or he would be hustled aboard a boat and taken South, the ransom being southern independence. All this was no more than gossip until the night before the flag-raising ceremony in Philadelphia, when news came from reliable sources that much of it was fact. General Winfield Scott, head of the armed forces, wrote warnings; Senator Seward, slated for Secretary of State, sent his son with documentary evidence; and now came the railroad head with his detective, Allan Pinkerton, whose operatives had joined such Maryland bands, he said, and as members had taken deep and bloody oaths. Such threats and warnings had become familiar over the past three months, but hearing all this Lincoln was disturbed. The last thing he wanted just now was an "incident," least of all one with himself as a corpse to be squabbled over. His friends urged him to cancel the schedule and leave for Washington immediately. Lincoln refused, but agreed that if, after he had spoken at Philadelphia the next morning and at Harrisburg in the afternoon, no Baltimore delegation came to welcome him to that city, he would by-pass it or go through unobserved.

Next afternoon, when no such group had come to meet him, he returned to his hotel, put on an overcoat, stuffed a soft wool hat into his pocket, and went to the railroad station. There he boarded a special car, accompanied only by his friend Ward Hill Lamon, known to be a good man in a fight. As the train pulled out, all telegraph wires out of Harrisburg were cut. When the travelers reached Philadelphia about 10 o'clock that night, Pinkerton was waiting. He put them aboard the Baltimore train; they had berths reserved by a female operative for her "invalid brother" and his companion. At 3.30 in the morning the sleeping-car was drawn through the quiet Baltimore streets to Camden Station. While they waited, Lincoln heard a drunk bawling "Dixie" on the quay. Lamon, with his bulging eyes and sad frontier mustache, sat clutching four pistols and two large knives. At last the car was picked up by a train from the west, and Lincoln stepped onto the Washington platform at 6 o'clock in the morning. "You can't play that on me," a man said, coming forward. Lamon drew back his fist. "Don't strike him!" Lincoln cried, and caught his arm, recognizing Elihu Washburn, an Illinois congressman. They went to Willard's Hotel for breakfast.

Such was the manner in which the new leader entered his capital to take the oath of office. Though the friendly press was embarrassed to explain it, the hostile papers had a field day, using the basic facts of the incident as notes of a theme particularly suited for variations. The overcoat became "a long military cloak," draping the lanky form from heels to eyes, and the wool hat became a Scotch-plaid cap, a sort of tam-o'-shanter. Cartoonists drew "fugitive sketches" showing Lincoln with his hair on end, the elongated figure surrounded by squiggles to show how he quaked as he ran from the threats of the Blood Tubs. "Only an attack of ager," they had his friends explaining. Before long, the Scotch-plaid pattern was transferred from the cap to the cloak, which at last became a garment he had borrowed from his wife, whom he left at the mercy of imaginary assassins. In the North there was shame behind the laughter and the sighs. Elation was high in the South, where people found themselves confirmed in their decision to leave a Union which soon would have such a coward for its leader. Certainly no one could picture Jefferson Davis fleeing from threats to his safety, in a plaid disguise and surrounded by squiggles of fear.

Mrs Lincoln and the children arrived that afternoon, and the family moved into Parlor 6, Willard's finest, which between now and the inauguration became a Little White House. To Parlor 6 came the public figures, resembling their photographs except for a third-dimensional grossness of the flesh, and the office seekers, importunate or demanding, oily or brash, as they had come to Springfield. Here as there, Lincoln could say of the men who had engineered his nomination in Chicago, "They have gambled me all around, bought and sold me a hundred times. I cannot begin to fill all the pledges made in my name."

The card-writing stand in the lobby offered a line of cockades for buttonholes or hatbands, "suitable for all shades of political sentiment," while elsewhere in the rambling structure a Peace Convention was meeting behind closed doors, the delegates mostly old men who talked and fussed, advancing the views of their twenty-one states — six of them from the buffer region, but none from the Cotton South — until at last they gave up and dispersed, having come to nothing. Washington was a southern city, surrounded by slave states, and the military patrolled the streets, drilled and paraded and bivouacked in vacant lots, so that townspeople, waking to the crash of sunrise guns and blare of bugles, threw up their windows and leaned out in nightcaps, thinking the war had begun. Congress was into its closing days, and finally in early March adjourned, having left the incoming President no authority to assemble the militia or call for volunteers, no matter what emergency might arise.

Inauguration day broke fair, but soon a cold wind shook the early flowers and the sky was overcast. Then this too yielded to a change. The wind scoured the clouds away and dropped, so that by noon, when President Buchanan called for Lincoln at Willard's, the sky was clear and summer-blue. Along streets lined with soldiers, including riflemen posted at upper-story windows and cannoneers braced at attention beside their guns, the silver-haired sixty-nine-year-old bachelor and his high-shouldered successor rode in sunshine to the Capitol. From the unfinished dome, disfigured by scaffolds, a derrick extended a skeleton arm. A bronze Freedom lay on the grass, the huge figure of a woman holding a sword in one hand and a wreath in the other, awaiting the dome's completion when she would be hoisted to its summit. In the Senate chamber Buchanan and Lincoln watched the swearing-in of Vice President Hannibal Hamlin of Maine, so dark-skinned that campaign rumors had had him a mulatto; then proceeded to a temporary platform on the east portico, where they gazed out upon a crowd of ten thousand.

Lincoln wore new black clothes, a tall hat, and carried a gold-headed ebony cane. As he rose to deliver the inaugural address, Stephen Douglas leaned forward from among the dignitaries and took the hat, holding it while Lincoln adjusted his spectacles and read from a manuscript he took out of his pocket. A first draft had been written at Springfield; since then, by a process of collaboration, it had been strengthened in places and watered down in others. Now, after months of silence and straddling many issues, he could speak, and his first words were spoken for southern ears.

"I have no purpose, directly or indirectly, to interfere with the institution of slavery in the states where it exists. I believe I have no lawful right to do so, and I have no inclination to do so." However, he denied that there could be any constitutional right to secession. "It is safe to assert that no government proper ever had a provision in its organic law for its own termination.... No state upon its own mere motion can lawfully get out of the Union." Then followed sterner words. "I shall take care, as the Constitution itself expressly enjoins upon me, that the laws of the Union be faithfully executed in all the states. Doing this I deem to be only a simple duty on my part; and I shall perform it, so far as practicable, unless my rightful masters, the American people, shall withhold the requisite means, or in some authoritative manner direct the contrary.... The power confided in me will be used to hold, occupy and possess the property and places belonging to the government, and to collect the duties and imposts."

Having clarified this, he returned to the question of secession, which he considered not only unlawful, but unwise. "Physically speaking, we cannot separate.... A husband and wife may be divorced, and go out of the presence and beyond the reach of each other; but the different parts of our country cannot do this. They cannot but remain face to face, and intercourse, either amicable or hostile, must continue between them." War, too, would be unwise. "Suppose you go to war, you cannot fight always; and when, after much loss on both sides and no gain on either, you cease fighting, the identical old questions as to terms of intercourse are again upon you." The issue lay as in a balance, which they could tip if they chose. "In your hands, my dissatisfied fellow countrymen, and not in mine, is the momentous issue of civil war. The government will not assail you. You can have no conflict without being yourselves the aggressors. You have no oath registered in heaven to destroy the government, while I shall have the most solemn one to 'preserve, protect and defend' it."

He then read the final paragraph, written in collaboration with Seward. "I am loath to close. We are not enemies, but friends. We must not be enemies. Though passion may have strained, it must not break our bonds of affection. The mystic chords of memory, stretching from every battlefield and patriot grave to every living heart and hearthstone all over this broad land, will yet swell the chorus of the Union when again touched, as surely they will be, by the better angels of our nature."

Chief Justice Taney, tall and cave-chested, sepulchral in his flowing robes — "with the face of a galvanized corpse," one witness said — stepped forward and performed the function he had performed eight times already for eight other men. Extending the Bible with trembling hands, he administered the oath of office to Abraham Lincoln as sixteenth President of the United States, and minute guns began to thud their salutes throughout the city.

★ ★ ★

Reactions to this address followed in general the preconceptions of its hearers, who detected what they sought. Extremists at opposite ends found it diabolical or too mild, while the mass of people occupying the center on both sides saw in Lincoln's words a confirmation of all that they were willing to believe. He was conciliatory or cunning, depending on the angle he was seen from. Southerners, comparing it to the inaugural delivered by Jefferson Davis in Montgomery two weeks before, congratulated themselves on the results; for Davis had spoken with the calmness and noncontention of a man describing an established fact, seeking neither approval nor confirmation among his enemies.

Standing on the portico of the Alabama capital, in the heart of the slave country, he did not mention slavery: an omission he had scarcely committed in fifteen years of public speaking. Nor did he waste breath on the possibility of reconciliation with the old government, remarking merely that in the event of any attempt at coercion "the suffering of millions will bear testimony to the folly and wickedness" of those who tried it. He spoke, rather, of agriculture and the tariff, both in Jeffersonian terms, and closed with the calm confidence of his beginning: "It is joyous in the midst of perilous times to look around upon a people united in heart, where one purpose of high resolve animates and actuates the whole, where the sacrifices to be made are not weighed in the balance against honor and right and liberty and equality. Obstacles may retard, but they cannot long prevent the progress of a movement sanctified by its justice and sustained by a virtuous people. Reverently let us invoke the God of our fathers to guide and protect us in our efforts to perpetuate the principles which by His blessing they were able to vindicate, establish, and transmit to their posterity. With the continuance of His favor, ever gratefully acknowledged, we may hopefully look forward to success, to peace, and to prosperity."

He had been chosen over such fire-eaters as Rhett and Yancey, Toombs and Howell Cobb, partly for reasons of compromise, but mainly on grounds that as a moderate he would be more attractive and less alarming to the people of the border states, still hanging back, conservative and easily shocked. Yet whatever their reasons for having chosen him, the people of the Deep South, watching him move among them, his lithe, rather boyish figure trim and erect in a suit of slate-gray homespun, believed they had chosen well. "Have you seen our President?" they asked, and the visitor heard pride in their tone. Charmed by the music of his oratory, the handsomeness of his clear-cut features, the dignity of his manner, they were thankful for the providence of history, which apparently gave every great movement the leader it deserved.

Such doubts as he had he kept to himself, or declared them only to his wife still back at Brierfield, writing to her two days after the inauguration: "The audience was large and brilliant. Upon my weary heart were showered smiles, plaudits, and flowers; but beyond them, I saw troubles and thorns innumerable.... We are without machinery, without means, and threatened by a powerful opposition; but I do not despond, and will not shrink from the task imposed upon me.... As soon as I can call an hour my own, I will look for a house and write you more fully."

Somehow he found both the time and the house, a plain two-story frame dwelling, and Mrs Davis and the children came to join him. "She is as witty as he is wise," one witness said. She was a great help at the levées and the less formal at-homes, having become in their senatorial years a more accomplished political manager than her husband, who had little time for anything but the exactions of his office. The croakers had already begun their chorus, though so far they were mostly limited to disappointed office seekers. Arriving, Mrs Davis had found him careworn, but when she expressed her concern, Davis told her plainly: "If we succeed we shall hear nothing of these malcontents. If we do not, then I shall be held accountable by friends as well as foes. I will do my best."

Rising early, he worked at home until breakfast, then went to his office, where he often stayed past midnight. He had need for all this labor, founding like Washington a new government, a new nation, except that whereas the earlier patriot had worked in a time of peace, with his war for independence safely won, Davis worked in a flurry against time, with possibly a harder war ahead. Like Washington, too, he lived without ostentation or pomp. His office was upstairs in the ugly red brick State House on a downtown corner, "The President" handwritten across a sheet of foolscap pasted to the door. He made himself accessible to all callers, and even at his busiest he was gracious, much as Jefferson had been.

Such aping of the earlier revolutionists was considered by the Confederates not as plagiarism, but simply as a claiming of what was their own, since most of those leaders had been southern in the first place, especially the ones who set the tone, including four of the first five, seven of the first ten, and nine of the first fifteen Presidents. In adopting a national standard, the present revolutionists' initial thought was to take the old flag with them, and the first name proposed for the new nation was The Southern United States of America. Except for certain elucidations, the lack of which had been at the root of the recent trouble, the Confederate Constitution was a replica of the one its framers had learned by heart and guarded as their most precious heritage. "We, the people of the United States," became "We, the people of the Confederate States, each state acting in its sovereign and independent character," and they assembled not "to form a more perfect Union," but "to form a permanent Federal government." There was no provision as to the right of secession. The law-makers explained privately that there was no need for this, such a right being as implicit as the right to revolution, and to have included such a provision would have been to imply its necessity.

One important oversight was corrected, however. Where the founding fathers, living in a less pious age of reason, had omitted any reference to the Deity, the modern preamble invoked "the favor and guidance of Almighty God." Nor were more practical considerations neglected. The President and Vice President were elected to a six-year term, neither of them eligible for reëlection. Congress was forbidden to pass a protective tariff or to appropriate money for internal improvements. Cabinet officers were to be given seats on the floor of Congress. Each law must deal with only one subject, announced in its title, and the President had the right to veto separate items in appropriation bills. Instead of requiring a three-fourths majority, amendments could be ratified by two-thirds of the states. While the newer document expressly prohibited any revival of the slave trade, those chattels referred to in the old one as "persons" now became outright "slaves," and in all territory acquired by the Confederacy, slavery was to be "recognized and protected" by both the federal and territorial governments.

Thus the paperwork foundation had been laid; the Confederacy was a going concern, one of the nations of earth. Whether it would remain so depended in a large part on the events of March and April, following the two inaugurals, particularly as these events affected the sympathies of the eight states in the two- to four-hundred-mile-deep neutral region which lay between the two countries. Davis knew this, of course, and knew as well that it would be the opposition's strategy to maneuver him into striking the first blow. This he was willing to do, provided the provocation to strike it was great enough to gain him the approval of the buffer states and the European powers. Actually, the odds were with him, for the neutral states were slave states, bound to the South by ties of history and kinship, and it was to the interests of the nations of Europe to see a growing competitor split in two. Meanwhile what was needed was patience, which Davis knew was not his dominant virtue, and indeed was hardly a southern virtue at all. Therefore, though his people were united, as he said, by "one purpose of high resolve," he could also speak of his "weary heart" and "troubles and thorns innumerable."

Lincoln up in Washington had most of these troubles, including the problem of holding the border states, and a greater one as well. Having first made up his mind, he must then unite the North before he could move to divide and conquer the South. He had made up his mind; he had stated his position; "The Union is unbroken," he had said. Yet while Europe applauded the forthright manner in which the Confederacy had set itself in motion, Lincoln was confronted with division even among the states that had stayed loyal. New Jersey was talking secession; so was California, which along with Oregon was considering the establishment of a new Pacific nation; so, even, was New York City, which beside being southern in sentiment would have much to gain from independence. While moderates were advising sadly, "Let the erring sisters depart in peace," extremists were violently in favor of the split: "No union with slaveholders! Away with this foul thing! ... The Union was not formed by force, nor can it be maintained by force."

On the other hand, whatever there was of native Union persuasion was sustained by economic considerations. Without the rod of a strong protective tariff, eastern manufacturers would lose their southern markets to the cheaper, largely superior products of England, and this was feared by the workers as well as the owners. The people of the Northwest remained staunchly pro-Union, faced as they were with loss of access to the lower Mississippi, that outlet to the Gulf which they had had for less than fifty years. Then too, following Lincoln's inaugural address, there was a growing belief that separation would solve no problems, but rather would add others of an international character, with the question of domination intensified. In early April the New York *Times* stated the proposition: "If the two sections can no longer live together, they can no longer live apart in quiet till it is determined which is master. No two civilizations ever did, or can, come into contact as the North and South threaten to do, without a trial of strength, in which the weaker goes to the wall.... We must remain master of the occasion and the dominant power on this continent." Reading this, there were men who faced responsibility; they believed they must accept it as members of a generation on trial. "A collision is inevitable," one said.

"Why ought not we test our government instead of leaving it" — meaning the testing — "to our children?"

Walking the midnight corridors of the White House after the day-long din of office seekers and divided counsels, Lincoln knew that his first task was to unite all these discordant elements, and he knew, too, that the most effective way to do this was to await an act of aggression by the South, exerting in the interim just enough pressure to provoke such an action, without exerting enough to justify it. He had good cause to believe that he would not have long to wait. The longer the border states remained neutral, the less they were ashamed of their neutrality in the eyes of their sisters farther south; the Confederates were urged to force the issue. Roger Pryor, a smooth-shaven Virginian with long black hair that brushed his shoulders, a fire-eater irked that his state hung back, was speaking now from a Charleston balcony, advising the South Carolinians how to muster Virginia into their ranks "in less than an hour by Shrewsbury clock: Strike a blow!"

What Pryor had in mind was Fort Sumter, out in Charleston harbor, one of the four Federal forts still flying the Union flag in Confederate territory. Lincoln also had it in mind, along with the other three, all Florida forts: Pickens off Pensacola Bay, Taylor at Key West, and Jefferson in the Dry Tortugas. The crowd was delighted with Pryor's advice. So would Lincoln have been if he had heard him, for by now he saw Sumter as the answer to his need for uniting the North.

The garrison at Fort Sumter had originally occupied the more vulnerable Fort Moultrie on Sullivan's Island, but the night after Christmas, six days after South Carolina seceded, Major Robert Anderson removed his eighty-two men to the stronger fortress three miles out in the harbor. South Carolina protested to Washington, demanding as one nation to another that the troops return to Moultrie. Instead, Buchanan sent an unarmed merchant steamer, the *Star of the West*, with men and supplies to reinforce the fort; but when the Charleston gunners took her under fire, union jack and all, she turned back. That was that. Though they ringed the harbor with guns trained on Sumter and no longer allowed the garrison to buy food at local markets, the Carolinians fired no shot against the fort itself, nor did the Confederate authorities when they took over in March. Buchanan, with his after-me-the-deluge policy, left the situation for his successor to handle as he saw fit, including the question of whether to swallow the insult to the flag. On the day after his inauguration Lincoln received dispatches from Anderson announcing that he had not food enough to last six weeks, which meant that Lincoln had something less than that period of time in which to make up his mind whether to send supplies to the fort or let it go.

During this period, while Lincoln was making up his mind and seemed lost in indecision, there was played in Washington a drama of cross-purposes involving backstairs diplomacy and earnest misrepresentation. Secretary of State William H. Seward, leader of the Republican Party and a man of wide experience in public life, saw the new President as well-meaning but incompetent in such matters, a prairie lawyer fumbling toward disaster, and himself as the Administration's one hope to forestall civil war. He believed that if the pegs that held men's nerves screwed tight could somehow be loosened, or at any rate not screwed still tighter, the crisis would pass; the neutral states would remain loyal, and in time even the seceded states would return to the fold, penitent and convinced by consideration. He did not believe that Sumter should be reinforced or resupplied, since this would be exactly the sort of incident likely to increase the tension to the snapping point.

In this he was supported by most of his fellow cabinet members, for when Lincoln polled them on the issue — "Assuming it to be possible to now provision Fort Sumter, under all the circumstances is it wise to attempt it?" — they voted five-to-two to abandon the fort. The Army, too, had advised against any attempt at reinforcement, estimating that 20,000 troops would be required, a number far beyond its present means. Only the Navy seemed willing to undertake it. Lincoln himself, in spite of his inaugural statement that he would "hold, occupy and possess the property and places belonging to the government," seemed undecided or anyhow did not announce his decision. Seward believed he would come around in time, especially in the light of the odds among his counselors. Meanwhile he, Seward, would do what he could to spare the Southerners any additional provocation.

Three of them were in Washington now, sent there from Montgomery as commissioners to accomplish "the speedy adjustment of all questions growing out of separation, as the respective interests, geographical contiguity, and future welfare of the two nations may render necessary." They had much to offer and much to ask. The Confederate Congress having opened the navigation of the lower Mississippi to the northern states, they expected to secure in return the evacuation of Sumter and the Florida forts, along with much else. Lincoln, however, would not see them. To have done so would have been to give over the constitutional reasoning that what was taking place in Alabama was merely a "rebellion" by private persons, no more entitled to send representatives to the rightful government than any other band of outlaws. Being also an official person, Seward of course could not see them either, no matter how much good he thought would proceed from a face-to-face conciliatory talk. Yet he found a way at least to show them the extent to which he believed the government would go in proving it meant no harm in their direction.

On March 15, the day Lincoln polled his cabinet for its views on Sumter, U.S. Supreme Court Justice John A. Campbell of Alabama, who had not yet gone South, came into Seward's office to urge him to receive the Southerners. The Secretary regretfully declined, then added: "If Jefferson Davis had known the state of things here, he would not have sent those commissioners. The evacuation of Sumter is as much as the Administration can bear."

Justice Campbell was alert at once. Here was Seward, guaranteeing for the government, whose Secretary of State he was, the main concession the commissioners were seeking. To make this even more definite, Campbell remarked that he would write to Davis at once. "And what shall I say to him on the subject of Fort Sumter?"

"You may say to him that before that letter reaches him —— How far is it to Montgomery?"

"Three days."

"You may say to him that before that letter reaches him, the telegraph will have informed him that Sumter will have been evacuated."

Lincoln was still either making up his mind or reinforcing whatever decision he had already made. In this connection he sent three men down to Charleston to observe the situation and report on what they saw. The first two, both southern-born, were Illinois law associates. Both reported reconciliation impossible, and one — the faithful Lamon, who had come through Baltimore on the sleeping-car with Lincoln — went so far as to assure South Carolina's Governor Pickens that Sumter would be evacuated. The third, a high-ranking naval observer who secured an interview with Anderson at the fort, returned to declare that a relief expedition was feasible. Lincoln ordered him to assemble the necessary ships and to stand by for sailing orders; he would use him or not, depending on events. At the same time, in an interview with a member of the Virginia state convention — which had voted against leaving the Union, but remained in session, prepared to vote the other way if the Administration went against the grain of its sense of justice — Lincoln proposed a swap. If the convention would adjourn *sine die*, he would evacuate Sumter. "A state for a fort is no bad business," he said.

Nothing came of this, but at the end of March, when Lincoln again polled the cabinet on the question, the vote was three-to-three, one member being absent. Seward by now had begun to see that he might well have gone too far in his guarantees to the Confederate commissioners. When Justice Campbell returned on April 1 to ask why his promise of two weeks before had not been carried out, Seward replied with the straight-faced solemnity of a man delivering an April Fool pronouncement: "I am satisfied the government will not undertake to supply Fort Sumter without giving notice to Governor Pickens."

"What does this mean?" Campbell asked, taken aback. This was something quite different from the Secretary's former assurances. "Does the President design to supply Sumter?"

"No, I think not," Seward said. "It is a very irksome thing to him to surrender it. His ears are open to everyone, and they fill his head with schemes for its supply. I do not think he will adopt any of them. There is no design to reinforce it."

Campbell reported these developments to the Confederate commissioners, who saw them in a clearer light than Seward himself had done. Restating them in sterner terms, the following day they telegraphed their government in Montgomery: "The war wing presses on the President; he vibrates to that side.... Their form of notice to us may be that of a coward, who gives it when he strikes."

This, or something like this, was what followed; for though Lincoln himself had practiced no deception (at least not toward the Confederates) Seward's well-meant misrepresentations had led exactly to that effect. By now Lincoln was ready. On April 6 he signed an order dispatching the naval expedition to Fort Sumter. Yet Seward was still not quite through. The following day, when Justice Campbell asked him to confirm or deny rumors that such a fleet was about to sail, Seward replied by note: "Faith as to Sumter fully kept. Wait and see." Campbell thought that this applied to the original guarantee, whereas Seward only meant to repeat that there would be no action without warning; and this, too, was taken for deception on the part of the Federal government. For on the day after that, April 8, there appeared before Governor Pickens an envoy who read him the following message: "I am directed by the President of the United States to notify you to expect an attempt will be made to supply Fort Sumter with provisions only, and that if such an attempt be not resisted, no effort to throw in men, arms, or ammunition will be made without further notice, or in case of an attack upon the fort."

Pickens could only forward the communication to the Confederate authorities at Montgomery. Lincoln had maneuvered them into the position of having either to back down on their threats or else to fire the first shot of the war. What was worse, in the eyes of the world, that first shot would be fired for the immediate purpose of keeping food from hungry men.

Davis assembled his cabinet and laid the message before them. Their reactions were varied. Robert Toombs, the fire-eater, was disturbed and said so: "The firing on that fort will inaugurate a civil war greater than any the world has yet seen, and I do not feel competent to advise you." He paced the room, head lowered, hands clasped beneath his coattails. "Mr President, at this time it is suicide, murder, and you will lose us every friend at the North. You will wantonly strike a hornets' nest which extends from mountains to ocean. Legions now quiet will swarm out and sting us to death. It is unnecessary. It puts us in the wrong. It is fatal."

Davis reasoned otherwise, and made his decision accordingly. It was not he who had forced the issue, but Lincoln, and this the world would see and know, along with the deception which had been practiced. Through his Secretary of War he sent the following message to General P. G. T. Beauregard, commanding the defenses at Charleston harbor:

> If you have no doubt as to the authorized character of the agent who communicated to you the intention of the Washington government to supply Fort Sumter by force, you will at once demand its evacuation, and, if this is refused, proceed in such manner as you may determine to reduce it.

Beauregard sent two men out to Sumter in a rowboat flying a flag of truce. They tendered Major Anderson a note demanding evacuation and stipulating the terms of surrender: "All proper facilities will be afforded for the removal of yourself and command, together with company arms and property, and all private property, to any post in the United States which you may select. The flag which you have upheld so long and with so much fortitude, under the most trying circumstances, may be saluted by you on taking it down."

Anderson received it sorrowfully. He was a Kentuckian married to a Georgian, and though he had been the military hero of the North since his exploit in the harbor the night after Christmas, he was torn between his love for the Union and his native state. If Kentucky seceded he would go to Europe, he said, desiring "to become a spectator of the contest, and not an actor." Approaching fifty-six, formerly Beauregard's artillery instructor at West Point, he had made the army his life; so that what he did he did from a sense of duty. The Confederates knew his thoughts, for they had intercepted his reply to Lincoln's dispatch informing him that Sumter would be relieved. "We shall strive to do our duty," he had written, "though I frankly say that my heart is not in the war, which I see is to be thus commenced." Therefore he read Beauregard's note sorrowfully, and sorrowfully replied that it was "a demand with which I regret that my sense of honor, and of my obligations to my government, prevent my compliance." Having written this, however, he remarked as he handed the note to the two aides, "Gentlemen, if you do not batter us to pieces, we shall be starved out in a few days."

Beauregard, hearing this last, telegraphed it immediately to Montgomery. Though he knew that it was only a question of time until the navy relief expedition would arrive to add the weight of its guns to those of the fort, and in spite of the danger that hot-headed South Carolina gunners might take matters in their own hands, Davis was glad to defer the opening shot. The Secretary of War wired back instructions for Beauregard to get Anderson to state a definite time for the surrender. Otherwise, he repeated, "reduce the fort."

It was now past midnight, the morning of April 12; there could be no delay, for advance units of the relief expedition had been sighted off the bar. This time four men went out in the white-flagged boat, empowered by Beauregard to make the decision without further conferences, according to Anderson's answer. He heard their demand and replied that he would evacuate the fort "by noon of the 15th instant" unless he received "controlling instructions from my government, or additional supplies." This last of course, with the relief fleet standing just outside the harbor — though Anderson did not know it had arrived — made the guarantee short-lived at best and therefore unacceptable to the aides, who announced that Beauregard would open fire "in one hour from this time." It was then 3.20 a.m. Anderson, about to test his former gunnery student in a manner neither had foreseen in the West Point classroom, shook the hands of the four men and told them in parting: "If we do not meet again in this world, I hope we may meet in the better one." Without returning to Beauregard's headquarters, they proceeded at once to Cummings Point and gave the order to fire.

One of the four was Roger Pryor, the Virginian who had spoken from a Charleston balcony just two days ago. "Strike a blow!" he had urged the Carolinians. Now when he was offered the honor of firing the first shot, he shook his head, his long hair swaying. "I could not fire the first gun of the war," he said, his voice as husky with emotion as Anderson's had been, back on the wharf at the fort. Another Virginian could and would — white-haired Edmund Ruffin, a farm-paper editor and old-line secessionist, sixty-seven years of age. At 4.30 he pulled a lanyard; the first shot of the war drew a red parabola against the sky and burst with a glare, outlining the dark pentagon of Fort Sumter.

Friday dawned crimson on the water as the siege got under way. Beauregard's forty-seven howitzers and mortars began a bombardment which the citizens of Charleston, together with people who had come from miles around by train and buggy, on horseback and afoot to see the show, watched from rooftops as from grandstand seats at a fireworks display, cheering as the gunnery grew less ragged and more accurate, until at last almost every shot was jarring the fort itself. Anderson had forty guns, but in the casemates which gave his cannoneers protection from the plunging shells of the encircling batteries he could man only flat-trajectory weapons firing nonexplosive shot. Beauregard's gunners got off more than 4000 rounds. As they struck the terreplein and rooted into the turf of the parade, their explosions shook the fort as if by earthquakes. Heated shot started fires, endangering the magazine. Presently the casemates were so filled with smoke that the cannoneers hugged the ground, breathing through wet handkerchiefs. Soon they were down to six guns. The issue was never in doubt; Anderson's was no more than a token resistance. Yet he continued firing, if for no other purpose than to prove that the defenders were still there. The flag was shot from its staff; a sergeant nailed it up again. Once, after a lull —

which at first was thought to be preparatory to surrender — when the Union gunners resumed firing, the Confederates rose from behind their parapets and cheered them. Thus it continued, all through Friday and Friday night and into Saturday. The weary defenders were down to pork and water. Then at last, the conditions of honor satisfied, Anderson agreed to yield under the terms offered two days ago.

So far there had been no casualties on either side. The casualties came later, during the arrangement of the particulars of surrender and finally during the ceremony itself. The first was Roger Pryor, who apparently had recovered from his reluctance and was sent to the fort as one of Beauregard's emissaries. Sitting at a table in the unused hospital while the formal terms were being put to paper, he developed a thirst and poured himself a drink from a bottle which he found at his right hand. When he had tossed it off he read the label, and discovered that it was iodine of potassium. The Federal surgeon took him outside, very pale, his long hair hanging sideways, and laid him on the grass to apply the stomach pump that saved his life.

A second mishap, this time in the Unionist ranks and far more serious, occurred at 4 o'clock Sunday afternoon. While Anderson, in accordance with the capitulation terms, was firing a fifty-gun salute to his flag, an ember fell into some powder. One man was killed in the explosion and five were injured. Private Daniel Hough thus became the first fatality of the war, before a man had fallen in combat. The scorched and shot-torn flag was lowered and given to Anderson, who packed it among his effects — intending, he said, to have it wrapped about him as a winding sheet on his burying day — then marched his men, with flying colors and throbbing drums, to the wharf where they boarded a steamer from the relief expedition which had observed rather than shared their fight, but which at least could perform the service of taking them home once it was over.

As the weary artillerymen passed silently out of the harbor, Confederate soldiers lining the beaches removed their caps in salute. There was no cheering.

★ ★ ★

Lincoln soon had cause to believe he had judged correctly. Sumter did indeed unite and electrify the North. That Sunday, when the news arrived by telegraph of the surrender in Charleston harbor, the White House was besieged by callers anxious to assure the President of their loyalty and support. Among them were senators and congressmen who pledged the resources of their states; their people, they said, would stand by the Union through fire and bloodshed. Among them was Stephen Douglas, who rose from his sickbed, the pallor of death already on his face, "to preserve the Union, maintain the government, and defend the capital." Thus he reported his pledge to the people afterwards, more than a million of whom had voted for him for President, never suspecting that he would be dead by early June. Now in mid-April Lincoln met him with outstretched hands and a smile.

Douglas was one among many throughout the nation. It was a time for oratory and easy promises. Businessmen formerly opposed to war as economically unsound now switched their line. They wanted it, now — as bloody as need be, so long as it was short and vigorous. In Pittsburgh, hangman's nooses dangled from lampposts inscribed "Death to Traitors!" Here as in other northern cities, secession sympathizers were bayed by angry crowds until they waved Union banners from their windows. Down in Knoxville, Tennessee, the loyal newspaper editor William G. Brownlow declared that he would "fight the Secession leaders till Hell froze over, and then fight them on the ice."

That same Sunday, in such a heady atmosphere of elation and indignation, Lincoln assembled his cabinet to frame a proclamation calling on the states for 75,000 militia to serve for ninety days against "combinations too powerful to be suppressed by the ordinary course of judicial proceedings." Technically it was not a declaration of war; only Congress could declare war, and Congress was not in session — a fact for which Lincoln was duly thankful, not wanting to be hampered. Though he called a special session for July 4, he expected to have the situation in hand by then. Meanwhile he proceeded unmolested, having determined in his own mind that extraordinary events called for extraordinary measures. The militia draft was issued the following day, April 15, to all the states and territories except the rebellious seven, apportioning the number of troops to be forwarded by each.

Here too, at first, the reply was thunderous. The northern states quickly oversubscribed their quotas; governor after northern governor wired forthright encouragement, asking only to be informed of the Administration's needs. Then Lincoln met a check. As he raised a pontifical hand, commanding "the persons composing the combinations aforesaid to disperse and retire peacefully to their respective abodes," he was given cause to think that he had perhaps outgeneraled himself. It soon became more or less obvious that, just as Davis had united the North by firing on Sumter, so had Lincoln united the South by issuing this demand for troops to be used against her kinsmen. This was true not only in the cotton states, where whatever remained of Union sentiment now vanished, but also in the states of the all-important buffer region, where Lincoln believed the victory balance hung. Telegram after telegram arrived from governors of the previously neutral states, each one bristling with moral indignation at the enormity of the proclamation, rather as if it had been in fact an invitation to fratricide or incest.

Governor Letcher of Virginia replied that since Lincoln had "chosen to inaugurate civil war," he would be sent no troops from Old

Dominion. "The people of this Commonwealth are freemen, not slaves," Governor Rector answered for Arkansas, "and will defend to the last extremity their honor, lives, and property, against Northern mendacity and usurpation." Governor Ellis of North Carolina declared that his state would "be no party to this wicked violation of the laws of the country and this war upon the liberties of a free people." "Tennessee will furnish not a single man for the purpose of coercion," Governor Harris told Lincoln, "but fifty thousand if necessary for the defense of our rights and those of our Southern brothers."

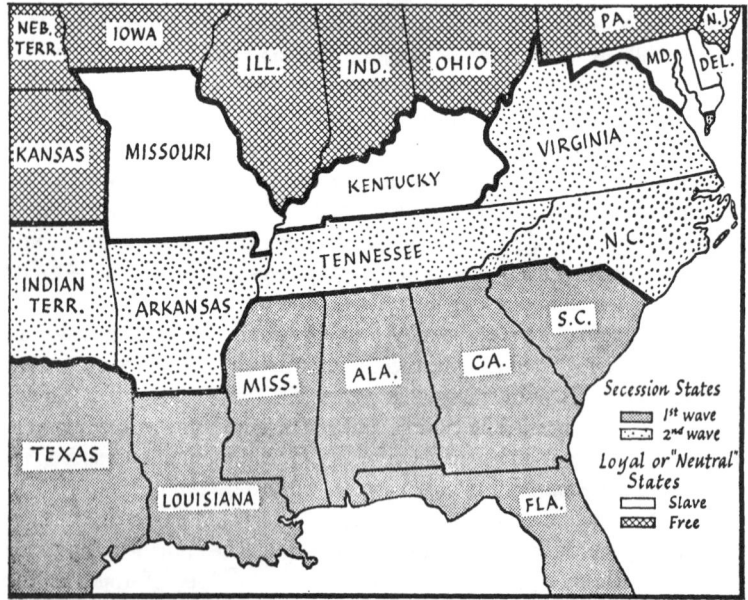

In such hard words did these four governors reply to the call for troops. And their people backed them up. Virginia seceded within two days, followed by the other three, Arkansas and Tennessee and finally North Carolina. East of the Mississippi the area of the Confederacy was doubled, and her flag, which now could claim eleven stars, flew along a boundary that had leapfrogged northward two to four hundred miles, across soil that had been Union.

Four slave states still dangled in the balance, Delaware and Maryland, Kentucky and Missouri. The first two were cautious; Governor Burton of Delaware reported that his state had no militia and therefore could not comply with the call for troops, while Governor Hicks of Maryland replied that he would forward soldiers only for the defense of Washington. Lincoln was somewhat reassured by their cautiousness, which at least indicated that there would be no precipitate action on their part. He could take no such consolation from the othe two wires he received. "I say, emphatically," Governor Magoffin responded, "Kentucky will furnish no troops for the wicked purpose of subduing her sister Southern states." Governor Jackson of Missouri sent the harshest reply of all: "Your requisition is illegal, unconstitutional, revolutionary, inhuman, diabolical, and cannot be complied with."

These were frets with which Lincoln would have to deal through the coming months, particularly the problem of holding onto his native state, Kentucky, with its critical location, its rivers and manpower, its horses and bluegrass cattle. "I think to lose Kentucky is nearly the same as to lose the whole game," he said. "Kentucky gone, we cannot hold Missouri, nor, as I think, Maryland. These all against us, and the job on our hands is too large for us. We would as well consent to separation at once, including the surrender of this capital."

Maryland compassed the District on three sides, while on the fourth, across the Potomac, lay hostile Virginia, whose troops were already on the march, their campfires gleaming on the southern bank. They had seized the arsenal at Harpers Ferry and the Norfolk navy yard, and now the Richmond *Examiner* proclaimed "one wild shout of fierce resolve to capture Washington City, at all and every human hazard. That filthy cage of unclean birds must and will be purified by fire." It seemed possible, even probable. Many of the army's best officers were resigning, going South along with hundreds of civil workers from the various departments.

The day of the proclamation passed, then another, and still another; not a volunteer arrived. The city was defenseless. On April 18, five hundred Pennsylvanians showed up, unarmed, untrained. They had met cold stares in Baltimore, but the troops who arrived next day, the 6th Massachusetts, met something worse. A crowd of southern sympathizers threw bricks and stones and fired into their ranks as they changed trains. They returned the fire, killing twelve citizens and wounding many more, then packed their four dead in ice for shipment north, and came on into Washington, bearing their seventeen wounded on stretchers. Three days later, when a Baltimore committee called on the President to protest the "pollution" of Maryland soil, Lincoln replied that he must have troops to defend the capital. "Our men are not moles, and cannot dig under the earth," he told them. "They are not birds, and cannot fly through the air. There is no way but to march across, and that they must do." So the Baltimore delegation went back and clipped the telegraph lines, tore up railroad tracks, and wrecked the bridges. Washington was cut off from the outside world.

It was now a deserted city, the public buildings barricaded with sandbags and barrels of flour, howitzers frowning from porticoes. The Willard's thousand guests had shrunk to fifty, its corridors as empty as the avenues outside. Many among the few who remained flaunted secession badges, preparing to welcome their southern friends. Virginia's Colonel T. J. Jackson had 8000 men at Harpers Ferry, while Beauregard, the conqueror of Sumter, was reported nearing Alexandria with 15,000 more. If they effected a junction, all Lincoln had to throw in their path was the handful from Pennsylvania and Massachusetts, five companies of the former, a regiment of the latter, quartered in the House of Representatives and the Senate Chamber.

They had arrived on Thursday and Friday. Saturday and Sunday passed, then Monday, and still there was no further sign of the 75,000 Lincoln had called for. "Why don't they come? Why don't they come?" he muttered, pacing his office, peering out through the window. Tuesday brought a little mail, the first in days, and also a few newspapers telling of northern enthusiasm and the dispatching of troops to Washington: Rhode Islanders and New York's 7th Regiment. Lincoln could scarcely credit these reports, and Wednesday when officers and men who had been wounded in the Baltimore fracas called at the White House he thanked them for their presence in the capital, then added: "I don't believe there is any North! The 7th Regiment is a myth; Rhode Island is not known in our geography any longer. You are the only northern realities!"

Then on Thursday, April 25, the piercing shriek of a locomotive broke the noonday stillness of the city. The 7th New York arrived, followed by 1200 Rhode Island militiamen and an equal number from Massachusetts, whose volunteer mechanics had repaired a crippled engine and relaid the torn-up Annapolis track. A route had been opened to the north.

By the end of the month, Washington had 10,000 troops for its defense, with more on the way. Lincoln could breathe easier. An iron hand was laid on Baltimore, securing Maryland to the Union. Major Robert Anderson, the returned hero of Sumter, was promoted to brigadier general and sent to assert the Federal claim to his native Kentucky. Major General John C. Frémont, the California Pathfinder and the Republican Party's first presidential candidate, was sent to perform a like function in Missouri. Before long, Lincoln could even assume the offensive.

Harpers Ferry was recaptured, Arlington Heights and Alexandria occupied. Confederate campfires no longer gleamed across the Potomac; the fires there now were Federal. Fortress Monroe, at the tip of the York-James peninsula, was reinforced, and an attack was launched against western Virginia, across the Ohio. Within another month, so quickly had despair been overcome and mobilization completed, there began to be heard in the North a cry that would grow familiar: "On to Richmond!"

* * *

That city was the southern capital now, moved there from Montgomery toward the end of May at the climax of the fervor following Sumter and the northern call for troops. Vice President Alexander H. Stephens voiced the defiance of the Confederacy, crying: "Lincoln may bring his 75,000 troops against us. We fight for our homes, our fathers and mothers, our wives, brothers, sisters, sons, and daughters! ... We can call out a million of peoples if need be, and when they are cut down we can call another, and still another, until the last man of the South finds a bloody grave."

Davis, with a sidelong glance at Europe and what history might say, reinforced the defensive character of these words in a message to Congress, called into extra session on April 29. Though desirous of peace "at any sacrifice, save that of honor and independence," he said, the South would "meet" — not *wage* — the war now launched by Lincoln. "All we ask is to be let alone," he added. Spoken before the assembly, the words had a defiant ring like those of Stephens. Read off the printed page, however, they sounded somewhat plaintive.

When Congress voted to accept Virginia's invitation to transfer the national capital to Richmond, Davis at first opposed the move. In the event of all-out war, which he expected, the strategic risk would be less disconcerting in the Deep South area, where the revolution had had its birth, than on the frontier, near the jar of battle. Yet when he was overruled by the politicians, who were finding Montgomery uncomfortable and dull, he acceded gracefully, even cheerfully, and made the two-day train trip without ceremony or a special car. He took instead a seat in the rear coach of a regular train and remained unrecognized by his fellow passengers until he was called to their attention by cheers from station platforms along the way.

In Richmond the Virginians, offering something more of pomp, met him at the station with a carriage drawn by four white horses. When a tossed bouquet fell into the street during the ride to the hotel, the President ordered the vehicle stopped, dismounted to pick up the flowers, and handed them to a lady in the carriage before signaling the coachman to drive on. This was noted with approval by the Virginians, already won by the dignified simplicity of his manner, which was tested further at luncheon in the hotel dining room, when a group of ladies stood around the table and fanned him while he ate. Davis proved equal even to this, and afterwards at the Fair Grounds, having gotten through the ordeal of a handshaking ceremony more exhausting than the two-day train ride, he made a short informal speech in which he called his listeners "the last best hope of liberty." "The country relies upon you," he told them. "Upon you rest the hopes of our people; and I have only to say, my friends, that to the last breath of my life I am wholly your own."

Here as in Montgomery — also a city of seven hills; Our Rome,

Virginians called their capital — the people congratulated themselves on having inherited such a President. At St Paul's, the first Sunday after secession, the words of the First Lesson had come with all the force of a prophecy: "I will remove far off from you the northern army, and will drive him into a land barren and desolate... and his stink shall come up, and his ill savour." Now they seemed to have found the man to lead them through its accomplishment. Originally they had had doubts, wondering how a Westerner could head a people so conscious of having furnished the best leaders of the past, but now that they had seen him they were reassured. Daily he rode out to inspect the training camps, sometimes with his staff, more often with a single aide. "Mr Davis rode a beautiful gray horse," a witness wrote of one of these excursions. "His worst enemy will allow that he is a consummate rider, graceful and easy in the saddle."

He devoted most of his energy to organizing an army: work for which his years at West Point and in Mexico, as well as his experience as Pierce's capable Secretary of War, had prepared him well. War was an extension of statecraft, to be resorted to when diplomacy failed its purpose; but Davis took the aphorism one step further, believing that a nation's military policy should logically duplicate its political intentions. Lincoln had more or less maneuvered him into firing the first shot, and while Davis did not regret his action in the case of Sumter, he did not intend to give his opponent another chance to brand him an aggressor in the eyes of history and Europe. "All we ask is to be let alone," he had announced. Therefore, while Lincoln was gathering the resources and manpower of the North in response to the shout, "On to Richmond," Davis chose to meet the challenge by interposing troops where they blocked the more obvious paths of invasion.

All this time, men were being forwarded to Richmond by the states. By mid-July he had three small armies in the Virginia theater: Beauregard, with 23,000 northward beyond the important rail junction at Manassas, facing a Union army of 35,000; Joseph E. Johnston with 11,000 near the Potomac end of the Shenandoah Valley, facing the 14,000 who had retaken Harpers Ferry; and J. B. Magruder, with about 5000 down on the York-James peninsula, facing 15,000 at Fortress Monroe, which the North could reinforce by sea. Outnumbered at every point, with just under 40,000 opposing well over 60,000 troops, the Confederates yet held the interior lines and could thereby move reinforcements from army to army, across any arc of the circle, in much less time than the Federals beyond the long perimeter would require.

Already there had been clashes of arms. Down the Peninsula — at Big Bethel, northwest of Newport News — Major General Benjamin F. Butler attacked one of Magruder's outposts, seven Union regiments against 1400 Confederates. The attackers became confused, firing into one another's ranks until artillery drove them back. Casualties

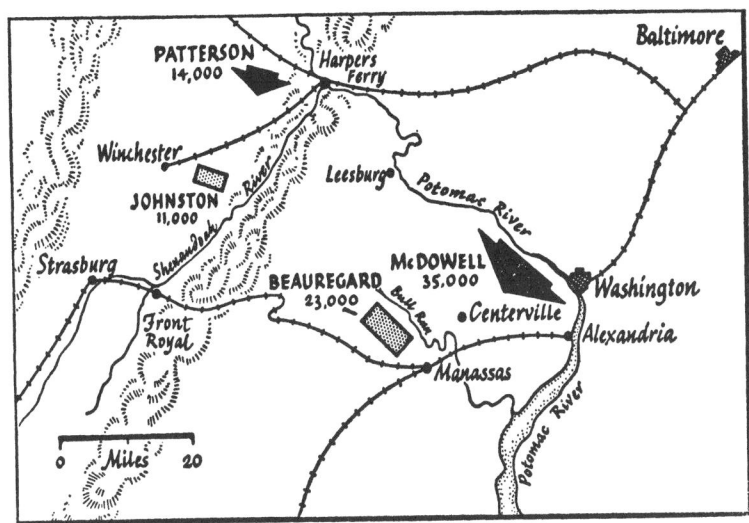

were 76 for the Federals, eight for the Confederates; which, the latter felt, came within a hair of proving their claim that one southern fighting man was worth ten Yankee hirelings. Yet there had been reverses, too. Johnston had abandoned Harpers Ferry in mid-June: a strategic withdrawal, he called it, under pressure from superior numbers. But when the Union commander, Major General Robert Patterson, a sixty-nine-year-old veteran of the War of 1812, crossed the river in early July there was a sharp clash at Falling Waters, casualties being about a dozen on each side, not including fifty Northerners taken prisoner. This too was felt to be a credit to southern arms, considering the odds, even though more of Virginia's "sacred soil" had been yielded to the invader. At the far-off western end of the state the advantage was clearly with the enemy, but this was blamed on bungling and mismanagement of brave troops. All in all, the Confederates were confident and saw far more reasons for pride than despair in the odds. The victories were glorious; the reverses were explicable. Besides, it was said in discussions on the home front, all this was mere jockeying for position, West Pointism, preliminaries leading up to the one big fight that would end the war and establish southern independence for all time.

The first Confederate council of war was held July 14 in the parlor of the Spotswood Hotel, where Davis had temporary quarters. Beauregard, as became the popular conqueror of Sumter, sent an aide down from Manassas to propose a plan of Napoleonic simplicity and brilliance. Reinforced by 20,000 men from Johnston, he would fall upon and shatter the Union army to his front; this accomplished, he would send the reinforcements, plus 10,000 of his own men, back to Johnston, who then could crush the smaller army facing him in the Valley and march through Maryland against Washington from the north, while Beauregard assailed it from the south; together they would dictate peace to Lincoln in the White House. This was opposed by Robert E. Lee, the President's military assistant since the consolidation into the national army of the Virginia forces he had commanded. The handsome Virginian, his dark mustache and hair touched with gray, opposed such an offensive, not only on the obvious grounds that Johnston, already facing long odds in the Valley, had in his whole army barely more than half the number of troops Beauregard was asking to have sent eastward, but also on grounds that the Federal army would retire within its Washington fortifications until it had built up strength enough to sally forth and turn the tables on the Confederates, using Beauregard's own plan against him and Johnston. Davis accepted Lee's judgment, finding that it coincided with his own, and sent the aide back to his chief with instructions to await the Federal advance.

It was not long in coming. On the 17th Beauregard telegraphed that his outposts were under attack; the northern army was on the march. Davis promptly wired Johnston, suggesting that he reinforce Beauregard at Manassas by giving Patterson the slip; which Johnston did, arriving by noon of the 20th with the leading elements of his army while the rest were still en route. The first big battle of the war was about to be fought.

3

Christmas Eve of the year before, William Tecumseh Sherman, superintendent of the Louisiana State Military Academy, was having supper in his quarters with the school's professor of Latin and Greek, a Virginian named Boyd, when a servant entered with an Alexandria newspaper that told of the secession of South Carolina. Sherman was an Ohioan, a West Pointer and a former army officer, forty years old, red-bearded, tall and thin, with sunken temples and a fidgety manner. He had come South because he liked it, as well as for reasons of health, being twenty pounds underweight and possibly consumptive; the room had a smell of niter paper, which he burned for his asthma. Rapidly he read the story beneath the black headline announcing the dissolution of the Union, then tossed it into Boyd's lap and strode up and down the room while the professor read it. Finally he stopped pacing and stood in front of his friend's chair, shaking a bony finger in the Virginian's face as if he had the whole fire-eating South there in the room.

"You people of the South don't know what you are doing," he declared. "This country will be drenched in blood, and God only knows how it will end. It is all folly, madness, a crime against civilization! You people speak so lightly of war; you don't know what you're talking about. War is a terrible thing!" He resumed his pacing, still talking.

"You mistake, too, the people of the North. They are a peaceable people but an earnest people, and they will fight, too. They are not going to let this country be destroyed without a mighty effort to save it.... Besides, where are your men and appliances of war to contend against them? The North can make a steam engine, locomotive or railway car; hardly a yard of cloth or a pair of shoes can you make. You are rushing into war with one of the most powerful, ingeniously mechanical and determined people on earth — right at your doors." Then he delivered a prophecy. "You are bound to fail. Only in your spirit and determination are you prepared for war. In all else you are totally unprepared, with a bad cause to start with. At first you will make headway, but as your limited resources begin to fail, shut out from the markets of Europe as you will be, your cause will begin to wane. If your people will but stop and think, they must see that in the end you will surely fail."

In February he resigned from the academy and came north, stopping off in Washington to see his brother John, a senator, who took him for a visit with the President. It was late March by then; Lincoln was at his busiest, harried by office seekers and conflicting counsels on Sumter. When the senator introduced his brother as a competent witness just arrived from the South, Lincoln said, "Ah. How are they getting along down there?"

"They think they are getting along swimmingly," Sherman told him. "They are preparing for war."

"Oh, well," Lincoln said, "I guess we'll manage to keep house."

Sherman left in disgust. In reply to his brother's plea that he stay and resume his military career, Sherman flung out against him and all politicians: "You have got things in a hell of a fix, and you may get them out as best you can!"

He went to St Louis and accepted a position as head of a streetcar company. However, when Sumter was fired on he returned to Washington, and after refusing a brigadier's commission — saying, to Lincoln's amazement, that he would rather work up to such rank — accepted command of one of the newly organized regiments of regulars. As he came down the White House steps he met a West Point friend and fellow Ohioan, Irvin McDowell, wearing stars on his shoulder straps.

"Hello, Sherman," McDowell said. "What did you ask for?"

"A colonelcy."

"What? You should have asked for a brigadier general's rank. You're just as fit for it as I am."

"I know it," Sherman snapped.

In his anguished tirade on Christmas Eve, comparing the resources of the two regions about to be at war, the waspish Ohio colonel had made a strong case, mostly within the bounds of truth. Yet he could have made a still stronger case, entirely within such bounds, by the use of statistics from the 1860 census. According to this, the southern population was nine million, the northern twenty million, and in the disparity of available manpower for the armies the odds were even longer, rising from better than two-to-one to almost four-to-one. White males between the ages of fifteen and forty numbered 1,140,000 in the South, compared to 4,070,000 in the North: a difference mainly due to the fact that more than three and one-half million out of the total southern population were Negroes. While these of course would contribute to the overall strength, by service as agricultural workers and diggers of intrenchments, their value was about offset by the fact that the North would be open to immigration — particularly from Germany and Ireland, both of which would furnish men in considerable numbers — as well as by the additional fact that the Negroes themselves would constitute a recruitable body for the invaders; 186,017, nearly all of them southern, were to enroll in the northern armies before the finish.

Sherman, however, had underrated the manufacturing capacity of the South. For the past decade the Tredegar Iron Works in Richmond had been building locomotives for domestic and foreign use, as well as projectiles and cannon for the U.S. Navy, and only the previous year a steam fire engine produced for the Russian government had been exhibited in the North before being shipped abroad. All the same, the colonel was mainly right. It was in just this field that the odds were longest. The North had 110,000 manufacturing establishments, the South 18,000 — 1,300,000 industrial workers, compared to 110,000 — Massachusetts alone producing over sixty percent more manufactured goods than the whole Confederacy, Pennsylvania nearly twice as much, and New York more than twice. Only in land area — and only then in a special sense — could the South, with its eleven states, out-statistic the twenty-two states of the North: 780,000 square miles as opposed to 670,000 in the area including Texas and the first tier of states west of the Mississippi. Yet this was a doubtful advantage at best, as might be seen by comparing the railway systems. The South had 9000 miles, the North 22,000, in both cases about a mile of track to every thousand persons. The North, with better than double the mileage in an area somewhat smaller, was obviously better able to move and feed her armies.

Statistically, therefore, Sherman had solid ground for his judgment, "You are bound to fail." Yet wars were seldom begun or even waged according to statistics. Nor were they always won on such a basis. The South had the proud example of the American Revolution, where the odds were even longer against those in rebellion. Now as then, she could reason, the nations of Europe, hungry for produce for their mills, would welcome the establishment of a new, tariff-free market for their goods, as well as the crippling of a growing competitor. And now among the nations offering aid there would be not only France, as in the earlier war for independence, but also the former adversary England, who was most powerful in just those directions where the Confederacy was statistically most weak.

What was more, aside from the likelihood of foreign intervention, there were other advantages not listed in those tables dribbling decimals down the pages. Principal among these, in the southern mind at any rate, was the worth of the individual soldier. The Southerner, being accustomed to command under the plantation system, as well as to the rigors of outdoor living and the use of horse and gun, would obviously make the superior trooper or infantryman or cannoneer. If the North took pride in her million-odd industrial workers, the South could not see it so; "pasty-faced mechanics," she called such, and accounted them a downright liability in any army, jumpy and apt to run from the first danger.

Such beliefs, though in fact they appeared to be borne out in the opening days of the conflict, were mostly prejudices and as such might be discounted by an opponent. There were other considerations, more likely to appeal to a professional soldier such as Sherman. Strategically, the South would fight a defensive war, and to her accordingly would proceed all the advantages of the defensive: advantages which had been increasing in ratio to the improvement of modern weapons, until now it was believed and taught that the attacking force on any given field should outnumber the defenders in a proportion of at least two-to-one; three-to-one, some authorities insisted, when the defenders had had time to prepare, which surely would be the case in the matter at hand. A study of the map would show additional difficulties for the North, particularly in the theater lying between the two capitals, where the rivers ran east and west across the line of march, presenting a series of obstacles to the invader. (In the West it would be otherwise; there the rivers ran north and south for the most part, broad highways for invasion; but few were looking westward in those days.) The northern objective, announced early in the war by the man who would be her leading general, was "unconditional surrender." Against this stern demand, southern soldiers would fight in defense of their homes, with all the fervor and desperation accompanying such a position.

The contrast, of course, would be as true on the home front as in the armies, together with the additional knowledge on both sides that the North could stop fighting at any time, with no loss of independence or personal liberty: whereas the South would lose not only her national existence, but would have to submit, in the course of peace, to any terms the victor might exact under a government that would interpret, and even rewrite, the Constitution in whatever manner seemed most to its advantage. Under such conditions, given the American pride and the American love of liberty and self-government, it seemed certain that the South would fight with all her strength. Whether the North, driven by no such necessities, would exert herself to a similar extent in a war of conquest remained to be seen.

All this, or something like it, must have occurred to Sherman in the months after he left Louisiana for Washington, where he heard Lincoln say with a shrug, "Oh well, I guess we'll manage to keep house." So far had he revised his opinion since that Christmas Eve in his rooms with Professor Boyd, that before the new year was out he informed the Secretary of War that 200,000 troops would be required to put down the rebellion in the Mississippi Valley alone. And it must have gone to convince him even further of a lack of northern awareness and determination when, under suspicion of insanity, he was removed from command of troops for this remark.

★ ★ ★

On the eve of the great battle for which both North and South were now preparing, Lincoln declared in his July message to Congress: "So large an army as the government now has on foot was never before known, without a soldier in it but who has taken his place there of his own free choice. But more than this, there are many single regiments whose members, one and another, possess full practical knowledge of all the arts, sciences, professions, and whatever else, whether useful or elegant, is known to the world; and there is scarcely one from which there could not be selected a President, a Cabinet, a Congress, and perhaps a Court, abundantly competent to administer the government itself. Nor do I say this is not true also in the army of our late friends, now adversaries in this contest."

This estimate of the American volunteer, though pleasant to contemplate before the shock of battle, was discovered to be far beyond the mark, North and South, especially by drill instructors charged with teaching him the manual of arms and parade ground evolutions of the line — in the course of which it often appeared that, far from being the paragon Lincoln discerned, he did not know his left foot from his right, nor his backside from his front. He took cold easily, filling the nighttime barracks and tent camps with the racking uproar of his coughs. He was short-winded and queasy in the stomach, littering the roadsides in the course of conditioning marches, like so many corpses scattered along the way. What was worse, he showed a surprising bewilderment in learning to handle his rifle.

Yet these were but the shortcomings of recruits throughout the world and down the ages, back to the time of the crossbow and the spear. New problems were encountered, peculiar to the two opposing armies. The soldiers of a northern outfit, sleeping for the first time in the open, had their democratic sensibilities offended when their officers rolled themselves in their blankets a few paces apart from the line of enlisted men. On the other hand, accustomed as they were to instances of caste in civilian life, Southerners had no objections to such privileges of rank. The outrage was intensified, however, when a former social relationship was upset, so that an overseer or a storekeeper, say, was placed above a planter in the army hierarchy. "God damn you, I own niggers up the country!" might be the reply to a distasteful order, while officers were sometimes called to account because of the tone in which they gave commands to certain highborn privates.

Such problems were individual, and as such would be solved by time or cease to matter. Even at the outset it was clear to the discerning eye that the two armies were more alike than different. For all the talk of States Rights and the Union, men volunteered for much the same reasons on both sides: in search of glory or excitement, or from fear of being thought afraid, but mostly because it was the thing to do. The one characteristic they shared beyond all others was a lack of preparedness and an ignorance of what they had to face. Arming themselves with bowie knives and bullet-stopping Bibles, they somehow managed at the same time to believe that the war would be bloodless. Though it was in Boston, it might have been in New Orleans or Atlanta that a mother said earnestly to the regimental commander as the volunteers entrained for the journey south: "We look to you, Colonel Gordon, to bring all of these young men back in safety to their homes."

All shared a belief that the war would be short, and some joined in haste, out of fear that it would be over before they got there. Uniforms were at first a matter of personal taste or the availability of materials, resulting in the following exchange:

"Who's that chap?"

"Guess he's the colonel."

"What sort of a way is that for a colonel to rig himself?"

"Morphodite rig, I guess."

"He aint no colonel; he's one of those new brigadier generals that aint got his uniform yet."

"Half general and half minister."

"Well, I said he was a morphodite."

They were not yet cynical; the soldiers of that war earned their cynicism. They were sentimental, and their favorite songs were sad ones that answered some deep-seated need: "The Dew is on the Blossom," "Lorena," "Aura Lea," "The Girl I Left Behind Me," and the tender "Home, Sweet Home." Yet they kept a biting sense of the ridiculous, which they directed against anything pompous. Northern troops, for example, could poke fun at their favorite battle hymn:

> Mary had a little lamb,
> Its fleece was white as snow,
> Shouting the Battle-Cry of Freedom!
> And everywhere that Mary went
> The lamb was sure to go,
> Shouting the Battle-Cry of Freedom!

Some of their other marching songs were briefer, more sardonic, pretending to a roughness which they had not yet acquired:

> Saw my leg off,
> Saw my leg off,
> Saw my leg off
> SHORT!!!

Confederates hardly needed to parody their favorite, "Dixie." The verses were already rollicksome enough:

> Old Missus marry Will de Weaver,
> William was a gay deceiver —
> Look away, look away, look away,
> Dixie land!
> But when he put his arm around 'er
> He smile as fierce as a forty pounder;
> Look away, look away, look away,
> Dixie land!

Northern troops, however, had a stanza of their own for the southern tune:

> I wish I was in Saint Law County,
> Two years up and I had my bounty,
> Away! Look away! Dixie land!

Southern soldiers objected to such onerous details as guard duty; they had joined the army to fight Yankees, not walk a post and miss their sleep. Similarly, Northerners were glad of a chance to move against the Rebels, yet on practice marches they claimed the right to break ranks for berry-picking along the roadside. At this time there was no agreement in either army as to what the war was about, though on both sides there was a general feeling that each was meeting some sort of challenge flung out by the other. They were rather in the position of two men who, having reached that stage of an argument where one has said to the other, "Step outside," find that the subject of dispute has faded into the background while they concern themselves with the actual fight at hand.

Perhaps the best definition of the conflict was given in conversation by a civilian, James M. Mason of Virginia: "I look upon it then, sir, as a war of sentiment and opinion by one form of society against another form of society." No soldier would have argued with this; but few would have found it satisfactory. They wanted something more immediate and less comprehensive. The formulation of some such definition and identification became the problem of opposing statesmen. Meanwhile, perhaps no soldier in either army gave a better answer — one more readily understandable to his fellow soldiers, at any rate — than a ragged Virginia private, pounced on by the Northerners in a retreat. "What are you fighting for anyhow?" his captors asked, looking at him. They were genuinely puzzled, for he obviously owned no slaves and seemingly could have little interest in States Rights or even Independence.

"I'm fighting because you're down here," he said.

Chief among the statesmen seeking a more complex definition men could carry into battle were the two leaders, Davis in Richmond and Lincoln in Washington. At the outset it was the former who had the advantage in this respect, for in the southern mind the present contest was a Second American Revolution, fought for principles no less high, against a tyranny no less harsh. In the Confederate capital stood the white frame church where Patrick Henry had said, "Give me liberty or give me death," and eighty-five years later another Virginian, Colonel T. J. Jackson, commanding at Harpers Ferry, could voice the same thought no less nobly: "What is life without honor? Degradation is worse than death. We must think of the living and of those who are to come after us, and see that by God's blessing we transmit to them the freedom we have ourselves inherited."

The choice, then, lay between honor and degradation. There could be no middle ground. Southerners saw themselves as the guardians of the American tradition, which included the right to revolt, and therefore they launched a Conservative revolution. Davis in his inaugural had said, "Our present condition... illustrates the American idea that government rests upon the consent of the governed.... The declared purpose of the compact of union from which we have withdrawn was 'to establish justice, insure domestic tranquillity, provide for the common defense, promote the general welfare, and secure the blessings of liberty to ourselves and posterity'; and when, in the judgment of the sovereign States now composing this Confederacy, it had been perverted from the purposes for which it was established, a peaceful appeal to the ballot box declared that, so far as they were concerned, the government created by that compact should cease to exist." For him, as for most Southerners, even those who deplored the war that was now upon them, there was no question of seeing the other side of the proposition. There was no other side. Mrs Davis had defined this outlook long ago: "If anyone disagrees with Mr Davis he resents it and ascribes the difference to the perversity of his opponent."

Afterwards in Richmond he repeated, "All we ask is to be let alone," a remark which the Virginia private was to translate into combat terms when he told his captors, "I'm fighting because you're down here." Davis knew as well as Lincoln that after the balance sheet was struck, after the advantages of the preponderance of manpower and matériel had been weighed against the advantages of the strategical defensive, what would decide the contest was the people's will to resist, on the home front as well as on the field of battle. Time after time he declared that the outcome could not be in doubt. Yet now, as he walked the capital streets, to and from the Spotswood and his office, or rode out to the training camps that ringed the seven-hilled city, though his step was lithe on the pavement and his figure erect in the saddle, he was showing the effects of months of strain.

Men looked at him and wondered. They had been of various minds about him all along, both North and South. Back at the outset, when he first was summoned to Montgomery, while the far-north Bangor *Democrat* was calling him "one of the very, very few gigantic minds which adorn the pages of history," old General Winfield Scott, commander-in-chief of all the Union armies, received the news of Davis' election with words of an entirely different nature. Perhaps recalling their squabble over a mileage report, Scott declared: "I am amazed that any man of judgment should hope for the success of any cause in which Jefferson Davis is a leader. There is contamination in his touch."

Lincoln, too, was careworn. A reporter who had known him during the prairie years, visiting the White House now, found "the same fund of humorous anecdote," but not "the old, free, lingering laugh." His face was seamed, eroded by responsibilities and disappointments, fast becoming the ambiguous tragedy mask of the Brady photographs. Loving the Union with what amounted in his own mind to a religious mysticism, he had overrated that feeling in the South; Sumter had cost him more than he had been prepared to pay for uniting the North. Through these months his main concern had been to avoid offending any faction — "My policy is to have no policy," he told his secretary — with the result that he offended all. Yet this was behind him now; Sumter at least had gained him that, and this perhaps was the greatest gain of all. He was free to evolve and follow a policy at last.

Unlike Davis, in doing this he not only did not find a course of action already laid out for him, with his only task being one of giving it the eloquence of words and the dignity of a firm example; he could not even follow a logical development of his own beliefs as he had announced them in the past, but must in fact reverse himself on certain tenets which he had expressed in words that returned to plague him now and in the years to come. At the time of the Mexican War he had spoken plainly for all to hear: "Any people anywhere being inclined and having the power have the right to rise up and shake off the existing government and form a new one that suits them better. This is a most valuable, a most sacred right — a right which we hope and believe is to liberate the world. Nor is this right confined to cases in which the whole people of an existing government may choose to exercise it. Any portion of such people that can may revolutionize and make their own so much of the territory as they inhabit."

He must raze before he could build, and this he was willing to do. Presently some among those who had criticized him for doing nothing began to wail that he did too much. And with good and relevant cause; for now that the issue was unalterably one of arms, Lincoln took unto himself powers far beyond any ever claimed by a Chief Executive. In late April, for security reasons, he authorized simultaneous raids on every telegraph office in the northern states, seizing the originals and copies of all telegrams sent or received during the past year. As a result of this and other measures, sometimes on no stronger evidence than the suspicions of an informer nursing a grudge, men were taken from their homes in the dead of night, thrown into dungeons, and held without explanation or communication with the outside world. Writs of habeas corpus were denied, including those issued by the Supreme Court of the United States. By the same authority, or in the absence of it, he took millions from the treasury and handed them to private individuals, instructing them to act as purchasing agents for procuring the implements of war at home and abroad. In early May, following the call for 75,000 militiamen, still without congressional sanction, he issued a proclamation increasing the regular army by more than 20,000, the navy by 18,000, and authorizing 42,034 three-year volunteers. On Independence Day, when Congress at last convened upon his call, he explained such extraordinary steps in his message to that body: "It became necessary for me to choose whether I should let the government fall into ruin, or whether ... availing myself of the broader powers conferred by the Constitution in cases of insurrection, I would make an effort to save it."

Congress bowed its head and agreed. Though Americans grew pale in prison cells without knowing the charges under which they had been snatched from their homes or places of employment, there were guilty men among the innocent, and a dungeon was as good a place as any for a patriot to serve his country through a time of strain. Meanwhile the arsenals were being stocked and the ranks of the armed forces were being filled. By July 6, within three months of the first shot fired in anger, the Secretary of War could report that 64 volunteer regiments of 900 men each, together with 1200 regulars, were in readiness around Washington. These 60,000, composing not one-fourth of the men then under arms in the North, were prepared to march in all their might against the cockpit of the rebellion whenever the Commander in Chief saw fit to order the advance.

For Lincoln, as for "our late friends, now adversaries" to the south, this was a Second American Revolution; but by a different interpretation. The first had been fought to free the new world from the drag of Europe, and now on the verge of her greatest expansion the drag was being applied again, necessitating a second; the revolution, having been extended, must be secured once more by arms against those who would retard and roll it back. This was a war for democracy, for popular government, not only in a national but also in a universal sense. In that same Europe — though France had sold her revolutionary birthright, first for the starry glitter of one Napoleon, and again for the bourgeois security of a second — other nations were striving toward the freedom goal, and as they strove they looked across the water. Here the birthright had not been sold nor the experiment discontinued; here the struggle still went on, until now it faced the greatest test of all. Lincoln saw his country as the keeper of a trust.

On July 4 he said to Congress: "This is essentially a People's war. On the side of the Union it is a struggle for maintaining in the world that form and substance of government whose leading object is to elevate the condition of man, to lift artificial weights from all shoulders, to clear the paths of laudable pursuit for all, to afford all an unfettered start and a fair chance in the race of life.... Our popular government has often been called an experiment. Two points in it our people have already settled, the successful establishing and the successful administering of it. One still remains — its successful maintenance against a formidable attempt to overthrow it. It is now for them to demonstrate to the world that those who can fairly carry an election can also suppress a rebellion, that ballots are the rightful and peaceful successors of bullets, and that when ballots have fairly and constitutionally decided, there can be no successful appeal except to ballots themselves at succeeding elections. Such will be a great lesson of peace, teaching men that what they cannot take by an election, neither can they take by war — teaching all the folly of being the beginners of a war."

In early May he had said to his young secretary, "For my part I consider the central idea pervading this struggle is the necessity that is upon us of proving that popular government is not an absurdity. We must settle this question now, whether in a free government the minority have the right to break up the government whenever they choose. If we fail it will go far to prove the incapacity of the people to govern themselves." Two months later, addressing Congress, he developed this theme, just as he was to continue to develop it through the coming months and years, walking the White House corridors at night, speaking from balconies and rear platforms to upturned faces, or looking out over new cemeteries created by this war: "The issue embraces more than the fate of these United States. It presents to the whole family of man the question whether...a government of the people, by the same people, can or cannot maintain its territorial integrity against its own domestic foes."

★ ★ ★

These days the military news was mostly good; Lincoln could take pride in the fact that so much had been done so quickly, the armies being strengthened and trained and permanent gains already being made. From northwest Virginia the news was not only good, it was spectacular. Here the contest was between Ohio and Virginia, and the advantage was all with the former. The Federal army had only to cross the Ohio and penetrate the settled river valleys, while the Confederates had to make long marches across the almost trackless Allegheny ridges: 8000 loyal troops against 4000 rebels in an area where the people wanted no part of secession. It was an ideal setting for the emergence of a national hero, and such a hero soon appeared.

At thirty-four, Major General George Brinton McClellan, commanding the Ohio volunteers, had earned both a military and a business reputation in the fifteen years since his graduation near the top of his Academy class, as a distinguished Mexican War soldier, official observer of the Crimean War, designer of the McClellan saddle, superintendent of the Illinois Central, and president of the Ohio & Mississippi Railroad. In late May, directing operations from Cincinnati, he sent troops to Grafton, east of Clarksburg on the B & O, who then marched southward thirty miles against Philippi, where they surprised the Confederates with a night attack, June 3; "the Philippi Races," it was called, for the rebels were demoralized and retreated through rain and darkness to the fastness of the mountains. Then McClellan came up.

"Soldiers!" he announced, in an address struck off on the portable printing press which was part of his camp equipment, "I have heard there was danger here. I have come to place myself at your head and share it with you. I fear now but one thing — that you will not find foemen worthy of your steel."

Seeking such foemen, he pressed the attack. When the southern commander, Brigadier General Robert S. Garnett, retreating up the Tygart Valley, divided his army to defend the passes at Rich Mountain and Laurel Hill, McClellan divided his army, too. Advancing one force to hold Garnett at the latter place, he swung widely to the right with the main body, marching by way of Buckhannon against the rebel detachment on Rich Mountain. Before that place he again divided his forces, sending Brigadier General William S. Rosecrans around by a little-used wagon trail to strike the enemy on the flank. "No prospect of a brilliant victory," he explained, "shall induce me to depart from my intention of gaining success by maneuvering rather than by fighting. I will not throw these raw men of mine into the teeth of artillery and intrenchments if it is possible to avoid it."

Either way, it was brilliant. The flanking column made a rear attack and forced the surrender of the detachment, which in turn rendered Garnett's positon on Laurel Hill untenable; he retreated northward and, having got the remnant of his army across Cheat River, was killed with the rear guard at Carrick's Ford, the first general officer to die in battle on either side. By mid-July the "brief but brilliant campaign," as McClellan called it in his report, was over. He telegraphed Washington: "Our success is complete, and secession is killed in this country." To his troops he issued an address beginning, "Soldiers of the Army of the West! I am more than satisfied with you." It was indeed brilliant, just as the youthful general said, and more; it was Napoleonic. The North had found an answer to the southern Beauregard.

In Lincoln's mind, this western Virginia campaign also served to emphasize a lack of aggressiveness nearer Washington. Patterson had taken Harpers Ferry. Down on the James peninsula Ben Butler at least had shown fight; Big Bethel was better than nothing. But McDowell, with his army of 35,000 around Washington, had demonstrated no such spirit. In late June, responding to a request, he had submitted a plan to General Scott. While Patterson held Johnston fast in the Valley, McDowell proposed "to move against Manassas with a force of thirty thousand of all arms, organized into three columns, with a reserve of ten thousand." Though he warned that his new regiments were "exceedingly raw and the best of them, with few exceptions, not over steady in line," he added that he believed there was every chance of success "if they are well led."

Thus far, nothing had come of this; the old General-in-Chief did not believe in what he called "a little war by piecemeal." Lincoln, however — aware that the time of the three-month volunteers was about to expire before any more than a fraction of them had had a chance to fire a shot at anything in gray — saw in the plan exactly what he had been seeking. At a cabinet meeting, called soon afterwards, General Scott was overruled. McDowell was told to go forward as he proposed.

At first he intended to move on Monday, July 8, but problems of supply and organization delayed him until Tuesday, eight days later, when he issued his march order to the alerted regiments. "The troops will march to the front this afternoon," it began, and included warnings: "The three following things will not be pardonable in any commander: 1st. To come upon a battery or breastwork without a knowledge of its position. 2d. To be surprised. 3d. To fall back. Advance guards, with vedettes well in front and flankers and vigilance, will guard against the first and second."

So they set out, fifty regiments of infantry, ten batteries of field artillery, and one battalion of cavalry, shuffling the hot dust of the Virginia roads. This marching column of approximately 1450 officers and 30,000 men, the largest and finest army on the continent, was led by experienced soldiers and superbly equipped. All five of the division commanders and eight of the eleven brigade commanders were regular army men, and over half of the 55 cannon were rifled. Light marching order was prescribed and Fairfax Courthouse was the immediate march objective, thirteen miles from Arlington, the point of departure. The start had been too late for the army to reach Fairfax that first day, but orders were that it would be cleared by 8 a.m. Wednesday, Centerville being the day's objective, another nine miles down the road and within striking distance of Manassas Junction, where the Confederates were massing.

Perhaps because the warning in the march order had made the leaders meticulous and over-ambush-conscious, and certainly because of the inexperience of the troops, no such schedule could be kept. Accordion-action in the column caused the men to have to trot to keep up, equipment clanking, or stand in the stifling heat while the dust settled; they hooted and complained and fell out from time to time for berry-picking, just as they had done on practice marches. It was all the army could do to reach Fairfax Wednesday night, and at nightfall Thursday the column was just approaching Centerville, 22 miles from the starting point after two and one-half days on the road, stop and go but mostly stop. Then it was found that the men did not have in their haversacks the cooked rations McDowell's order had said "they must have." Friday was spent correcting this and other matters; Saturday was used up by reconnaissance, studying maps and locating approaches to and around the enemy assembled at Manassas. Beauregard thus had been presented with two days of grace, by which time McDowell heard a rumor that Johnston, out in the Valley, had given Patterson the slip and was at hand. He took the news with what calmness he had left, forwarded it to Washington, and set about completing his battle plan. Johnston or no Johnston, the attack was scheduled for first light, Sunday morning.

Lincoln in Washington and Davis in Richmond, one hundred miles apart, now were exposed for the first time to the ordeal of waiting for news of the outcome of a battle in progress between the two capitals. The northern President took it best. When McDowell had asked for a little more time for training, Lincoln told him, "You are green, it is true; but they are green also. You are all green alike." Now that the armies were arrayed and the guns were speaking, Lincoln kept this calmness. The Sunday morning news was reassuring; even old General Scott saw victory in the telegrams from Virginia. Lincoln attended church, came back for lunch and more exultant telegrams, and went for a carriage drive in the late afternoon, believing the battle won.

Davis, being more in the dark, experienced more alarm. Beauregard's wire on the 17th had told him, "The enemy has assailed my outposts in heavy force. I have fallen back on the line of Bull Run, and will make a stand at Mitchell's Ford." He spoke of retiring farther, possibly all the way to the Rappahannock, and closed with a plea for reinforcements for his 29 regiments and 29 guns, only nine of which were rifled. Davis sent what he could, including three regiments and a battery from Fredericksburg, and directed Johnston to move his army to Manassas "if practicable." Johnston's 18 regiments and 20 smooth-bore guns, even if they all arrived in time, would not bring Beauregard up to the reported strength of the Federals, for of the fifty regiments thus assembled to meet the fifty of the enemy, 1700 of the Valley soldiers — the equivalent of two regiments — were down with the measles. Presently, however, it seemed not to matter, or to be no more than a lost academic possibility. For that same Wednesday afternoon in Richmond another telegram arrived from Beauregard: "I believe this proposed movement of General Johnston is too late. Enemy will attack me in force tomorrow morning."

Thursday came and passed, and there was no attack. Then Friday came, and still the wire brought no word of battle. Davis kept busy, forwarding every corporal's guard he could lay hands on. At noon Saturday Johnston reached Manassas with the van of his army, the rest coming along behind as fast as the overworked railroad could transport them. Sunday came and Davis, a soldier himself, could wait no longer. He took a special northbound train.

In mid-afternoon, as it neared the Junction, there were so many signs of a defeat that the conductor would not permit the train to proceed, fearing it would be captured. But Davis was determined to go on. The engine was uncoupled and the President mounted the cab, riding toward the boom of guns and, now, the clatter of musketry. Beyond the Junction he secured a horse and continued north. Fugitives streamed around and past him, the wounded and the ones who had lost nerve. "Go back!" he told them. "Do your duty and you can save the day." Most of the powder-grimed men did not bother to answer the tall, clean civilian riding into the smoky uproar they had just come out of. Others shouted warnings of disaster. The battle had been lost, they cried; the army had been routed. Davis rode on toward the front.

CHAPTER

2

First Blood; New Conceptions

★ ✗ ☆

IRVIN McDOWELL HAD COME A LONG WAY since he said to Sherman on the White House steps in April, "You should have asked for a brigadier general's rank. You're just as fit for it as I am." Now perhaps not even Sherman, still a colonel, commanding a brigade in his fellow Ohioan's army, would have replied as he did then. A West Pointer, in his early forties — he and Beauregard had been classmates — McDowell was six feet tall and heavy-set, with dark brown hair and a grizzled beard worn in the French style. He had attended military school in France and later spent a year's leave of absence there, so that, in addition to wearing a distinctive beard, he was one of the few regular army officers with a first-hand knowledge of the classical tactics texts, mostly French. His manner was modest and friendly in the main, but this was marred from time to time by a tendency to be impulsive and dogmatic in conversation, which offended many people. Some were appalled as well by his gargantuan appetite, one witness telling how he watched in dismay while McDowell, after a full meal, polished off a whole watermelon for dessert and pronounced it "monstrous fine!" He had a strong will along certain lines, as for instance in his belief that alcohol was an evil. Once when his horse fell on him and knocked him out, the surgeon who tried to administer some brandy found his teeth so firmly clamped that they could not be pried apart, and McDowell was proud that, even unconscious, he would not take liquor.

Now, indeed, marching at the head of an army whose fitness for testing under fire he himself had doubted, he had need to clamp his teeth still tighter and call on all his self-control. Since setting out, prodded into motion by a civilian President who discounted the unpreparedness by remarking that the men of both armies were "green alike" — which did not at all take into account that one of them (McDowell's) would be required to execute a tactical march in the presence of the enemy — he had watched his fears come true. While congressmen and other members of Washington society, some of them accompanied by ladies with picnic hampers, harried the column with buggies and gigs, the troops went along with the lark, lending the march the holiday air of an outing. They not only broke ranks for berry-picking; they discarded their packs and "spare" equipment, including their cumbersome cartridge boxes, and ate up the rations intended to carry them through the fighting.

Re-issuing ammunition and food had cost him a day of valuable time, in addition to the one already lost in wretched marching, and now as he spent another day with his army brought up short at Centerville while he explored the roads and fords leading down to and across Bull Run, where the rebels were improving their position, the worst of his fears was rumored to be fact: Johnston had reached Manassas, leaving Patterson holding the bag out in the Valley. As he rose before daylight Sunday morning, having completed his reconnaissance, issued the orders for attack, and eaten his usual oversized supper the night before, it was no wonder he was experiencing the discomfort of an upset digestion. Even McDowell's iron stomach had gone back on him, cramping his midriff with twinges of pain and tightening the tension on his nerves.

Despite the twinges as he waited for the roar of guns to announce that the attack was rolling, there was confidence in his bearing. He felt that his tactical plan, based as it was on careful preparations, was a sound one. A study of the map had shown a battlefield resembling a spraddled X. Bull Run flowed from the northwest to the southeast to form one cross-member; Warrenton Turnpike ran arrow straight, southwest-northeast, to form the other. The stream was steep-banked, dominated by high ground and difficult to cross except at fords above and below a stone bridge spanning the run where the turnpike intersected it. McDowell had planned to attack on the left, that flank affording the best approach to Richmond; but when reconnaissance showed that the fords below the bridge were strongly held by rebel infantry and artillery, he looked to his right. Upstream, out the western arm of the X, he found what he was seeking. Cavalry patrols reported good crossings lightly held in that direction: one at Sudley Springs, all the way out the western arm, and another about halfway out. Both were suitable for wheeled vehicles, the troopers reported, which meant that the main effort, launched by way of these two crossings, could be supported by the superior Federal artillery. Now McDowell had his attack plan, and he committed it to paper.

Of his four divisions, each with about 8000 men, two would demonstrate against the run, while the other two executed a turning movement against the Confederate left flank. The First Division, under

Brigadier General Daniel Tyler, would move "toward the stone bridge... to feint the main attack upon this point." The Fourth Division, under Colonel D. S. Miles, would be held in reserve near Centerville, at the tip of the eastern arm of the X, but one of its brigades would make a "false attack" on Blackburn's Ford, halfway down the eastern leg and midway between Centerville and Manassas. As the Second and Third Divisions, under Colonels David Hunter and S. P. Heintzelman, having made their turning movement and launched their attack, swept down the south bank of the stream, crumpling the Confederate line of battle, they would uncover the bridge and the fords, permitting the First and Fourth Divisions to cross the run and strengthen the main effort with fresh troops. This time there were no admonitions as to what would "not be pardonable"; the troops were to drive right through, with more of savagery than caution. Richmond lay beyond the roll of the southern horizon.

Sound as the plan was, it was also complicated, involving two feints by half the army and a flank attack by the other half, with the main effort to be made at right angles to the line of advance. McDowell knew that much depended on soldierly obedience to orders. Yet his commanders were regulars, and despite their clumsy performance on the long march, he felt that he could count on them for a short one. As a professional soldier he also knew that much would depend on luck, good and bad, but in this connection all he could do was hope for the former and guard against the latter. For one thing, to forestall delay he could order an early start, and this he did. The holding divisions were to leave their camps by 3 a.m. to open the demonstrations at Stone Bridge and Blackburn's Ford, while the turning column was to set out even earlier, at 2 o'clock, in order to clear Sudley Springs by 7 at the latest.

And so it was. The troops lurched into motion on schedule, some having had but very little sleep, others having had no sleep at all, and now again it was stop and go but mostly stop, just as on the other march, except that now there was the added confusion of darkness and bone-deep weariness as they stumbled over logs and roots and were stabbed at by branches in the woods, clanking as they ran to catch up or stood stock-still to breathe the thick dust of the "sacred soil." About 9.30 — two and one-half hours behind schedule — the head of the column reached Sudley Springs, where the men were halted to rest and drink. Away downstream, opposite the stone bridge and the ford, the guns of the other two divisions had been booming with false aggressiveness for more than three hours now.

Beauregard at Manassas, midway between the straddled feet of the X, had no intention of awaiting his classmate's pleasure. When Johnston had joined him Saturday with about half of his 9000 men, the rest being due to arrive in the night, the Creole general's spirits rose. Now that his army was about to be almost equal to the enemy's, he would attack. He made his dispositions accordingly, concentrating his regiments along the eastern leg of the X, from Stone Bridge down to Union Mills Ford, where the crossing would be made in force to envelop the Federal left and crush it while he marched on Centerville.

Thus Beauregard and McDowell, on opposite sides of Bull Run, had more or less identical plans, each intending to execute a turning movement by the right flank to strike his opponent's left. If both had moved according to plan, the two armies might have grappled and spun round and round, like a pair of dancers clutching each other and twirling to the accompaniment of cannon. However, this could only happen if both moved on schedule. And late as McDowell was, Beauregard was later.

In the first place there was trouble on the railroad from Manassas Gap, and though some of Johnston's men had been assigned a share in the forward movement, the remainder of them did not arrive that night. In the second place, the attack order was ambiguous and vague. There was to be an advance across the run, then an advance on Centerville, and though each section of the plan ended: "The order to advance will be given by the commander in chief," it was not clear to the brigade commanders just which advance was meant. They took it to mean the advance on the crossing, whereas Beauregard intended it to mean the second advance, after the crossing had been forced. Accordingly, early Sunday morning at Manassas, while Beauregard listened for the roar of guns, there was only silence from the right.

Then there arrived from Mitchell's Ford, two miles below Stone Bridge, a messenger who reported that the enemy had appeared in strength to the left front of that position; and as if to reinforce this information there came a sound of firing from the vicinity of the bridge. To guard against a crossing, Beauregard sent his reserve brigades, under Brigadier Generals Barnard Bee and T. J. Jackson, to strengthen the few troops he had stationed there, on the left flank of his army. All this time he listened for the boom of cannon to indicate that his attack was underway on the right. From that direction, all he heard was silence; but northward, from the direction of the bridge, the cannonade was swelling to a roar. At 8 o'clock Beauregard left his office at Manassas Junction to establish field headquarters on Lookout Hill, in the rear of Mitchell's Ford.

From there, of course, the roar of guns was louder, coming from both the left and right, Stone Bridge and Blackburn's Ford, but still there were no signs of an advance across the run. By 9 o'clock Beauregard had begun to suspect that the Federal main body was elsewhere, probably on one of his flanks, preparing to surprise him. Just then, as if in substantiation of his fears, a message arrived from a signal officer:

> I see a body of troops crossing Bull Run about two miles above the Stone Bridge. The head of the column is in the woods on this side. The rear of the column is in the woods on the other side. About a half-mile of its length is visible in the open ground between. I can see both infantry and artillery.

Beauregard reacted fast. While a dust cloud floated up from that direction to show the enemy in force, he sent couriers after Bee and Jackson, instructing them to march above the bridge, and ordered Colonel Wade Hampton, just arrived from Richmond with 600 South Carolinians, also to proceed to the exposed flank. When these commands joined the brigade of Colonel N. G. Evans, already posted near the bridge, he would have about 6500 men on the left: barely one-fourth of his army. Still, in spite of a rumor that the mystery column raising its ominous dust cloud might be Patterson, arrived from the Valley with 30,000 men, Beauregard was hoping that somehow the long overdue attack on the enemy left might have smashed through for a counterstroke. Then a message arrived from Brigadier General R. S. Ewell at Union Mills Ford. He had waited all this time for orders; now he was going forward without them. Beauregard despaired. This late, the attack could do no good; it would serve only to make those troops unavailable to help stem whatever success the enemy might achieve on the left. With his army so scattered, it hardly seemed possible to organize any sort of effective resistance. "My heart for a moment failed me," he said later.

Johnston was also there on Lookout Hill, the ranking Confederate, though so far he had left the dispositions in Beauregard's hands, being himself unfamiliar with the terrain. He watched with increasing concern as things went from bad to worse, the dust cloud spreading on the left while Beauregard did what he could to meet the challenge, recalling from across the run the brigades of Ewell, D. R. Jones, and James Longstreet. By 11 o'clock the fury beyond Stone Bridge was approaching crescendo. The tearing clatter of musketry swelled the uproar of the guns, and powdersmoke boiled up dead-white out of the dust. Johnston, chafing under his self-imposed inaction, at last could bear it no longer. "The battle is there," he told Beauregard; "I am going!" And he went.

Beauregard was not far behind him. Remaining only long enough to order Brigadier General T. H. Holmes and Colonel Jubal Early to march their brigades to the left, he overtook Johnston soon after noon, the Virginian having paused to send a couple of unemployed batteries into action, and the two went on together, accompanied by their staffs.

They rode past wounded and frightened men, dazed and blood-stained stragglers from the fight which they could hear but could not see until, climbing a wooded hill, they reached the crest at about 12.30, to find the battle raging below them, a panorama of jetting smoke and furious movement.

A few gray regiments were in action, their muskets flashing pink in the swirl of smoke. Others, shattered by the blue onslaught, were streaming for the rear. Across the line of their retreat a fresh Confederate brigade stood just behind the crest of a ridge adjoining the hill the generals watched from. Their ranks aligned steadily on both sides of a battery whose six guns were firing rapidly into the advancing mass of Federals, these troops had the determined, steadfast appearance of veterans. Otherwise the field had a look of impending disaster.

McDowell at last had got his flanking divisions over the run at Sudley Springs, doubling the column to speed the crossing. It was smartly done, the blue ranks closely packed, water squelching in their shoes after their splash across the creek. But as they emerged from the woods about a mile south of the ford, Colonel Ambrose Burnside's Rhode Islanders heading the advance, they ran into fire from two Confederate regiments drawn up to meet them with two smooth-bore six-pounders barking aggressively on the flank. These were South Carolinians and Louisianians; their commander, Colonel Evans, charged with defending the stone bridge, had soon determined that the cannonade there was no more than a feint. Evans — called "Shanks" because of the thinness of his legs — was an old line soldier, resentful at having been stationed far to the left of where the main effort was intended. When he observed the dust cloud to the northwest, beyond the flank of the army, he saw his opportunity and acted on his own initiative. Leaving a handful to guard the bridge, he marched his thousand men upstream to block the path of 13,000 Federals.

The meeting engagement was sudden and furious, the gray troops having the advantage of firing the first volley. As they were beginning to come apart under pressure, they were joined by the Mississippians, Alabamians and Georgians in the brigade of General Bee, who like Evans had marched without orders toward the point of danger. All the cotton states were represented, presently reinforced by Hampton's Legion, which also came onto the field at a critical time. Then, as the tide turned again, the Federals exerting the pressure of their numbers, in war as in peace the fire-eaters looked to Virginia. On a ridge to their rear — as Johnston and Beauregard had observed, arriving at this moment — Jackson's Virginians were staunchly aligned on their guns.

"There is Jackson standing like a stone wall!" Bee shouted. "Let us determine to die here, and we will conquer."

Jackson too had arrived at a critical moment, but instead of rushing into the melee on the plain, he had formed his troops on the reverse slope of the ridge, protected from artillery and ready for whatever moved against them. When an officer came crying, "General! the day is going against us!" the stern-lipped Jackson calmly replied: "If you think so, sir, you had better not say anything about it." Another reported, "General, they are beating us back!" "Sir, we'll give them the bayonet," Jackson said.

Over the crest and down the hill, high on the western leg of the X, the battle raged around a small frame house where the eighty-year-old widow Judith Henry lay dying. When the Union troops came pounding south from Sudley Springs her invalid sons carried her on a mattress to the shelter of a ravine, but she begged so piteously to be allowed to die in her own bed that they brought her back, and there she had her wish. A shell killed her the instant they laid her down, and her body was riddled with bullets as the house began to flame.

In a dense blue mass, avenging the months of rebel boasting and insults to the flag, the Federal infantry roared to the attack. The advance had cleared the stone bridge now; Tyler's division poured across, adding its weight to the charge. Bee fell, shot as he rallied his men, who leaderless gave back before the cheering ranks of Federal attackers. On they came, their battle flags slanting forward in the sunlight, up the hill and over the crest, where Jackson's men stood sighting down their muskets. For a moment the blue soldiers were outlined black against the sky, and then it was as if the earth exploded in their faces. One volley struck them, then another, and the survivors stumbled back down the slope, where their officers were shouting for them to reform.

By now there were 18,000 Union troops on this quarter of the field. Supported by well-served rifled guns, the men who had been repulsed closed ranks and presently they charged again, up the slope and over the crest where the Virginians were waiting. But it was too late; the crisis had passed. Johnston and Beauregard had come down off the adjoining hill, Beauregard to ride along the battle line, replacing fallen commanders with members of his staff and making at intervals a speech in which, he said, he "sought to infuse into the hearts of my officers and men the confidence and determined spirit of resistance to this wicked invasion of the homes of a free people," while Johnston established a command post to the rear, at a road intersection where troops from the right and reinforcements from the Valley could be rushed to where the issue was in doubt. As fast as they came within reach he spurred them toward the fight on Henry Hill. There, while the battle raged on the forward slope — disintegrated by now into a strung-out, seemingly disconnected series of hand-to-hand skirmishes by knots of men clustered about their shot-ripped flags, each man fighting as if the outcome of the whole battle depended on himself alone — Beauregard used them to strengthen the line along the crest and to extend the left, where McDowell was attempting to envelop the Confederate defense.

The Union commander advanced two batteries of rifled guns, intending to support them with a regiment of New York Fire Zouaves. As these men in baggy trousers were forming off to the right, Colonel J. E. B. Stuart mistook them for an Alabama outfit, similarly clad, which he thought was facing rear, about to retreat. "Don't run, boys; we're here!" he cried, riding toward them at the head of his cavalry regiment. By the time he saw his mistake, it was too late to turn back. So he charged, his troopers slashing at the white turbans of the men in blue and scarlet, who panicked and scattered in gaudy confusion, leaving the eleven guns unsupported, and a Virginia infantry regiment ran forward to deliver at seventy yards a volley that toppled every cannoneer. The guns were out of action.

Back on the crest, having watched all this, the Confederates were cheering. Jackson rode up and down his line. "Steady, men; all's well," he kept saying. Then, as the Federal infantry pushed forward again, he gave his troops instructions: "Hold your fire until they're on you. Then fire and give them the bayonet. And when you charge, yell like furies!"

By now Beauregard had what he had been building toward. Johnston had been feeding him men, including Brigadier General Kirby Smith's brigade from the Valley army, just off the cars from Manassas Gap, and Beauregard had built a solid line along both flanks of Jackson, extending the left westward until it not only met the threat from that direction, but overlapped the Federal right. The general was ready and so were his men, heartened by their recent success and the arrival of reinforcements. About 3.30, as if by signal, the gray line surged forward. "Yell like furies," Jackson had told his soldiers, and now they did. From flank to flank, for the first time in the war, the weird halloo of the rebel yell went up, as if twenty thousand foxhunters were closing on a quarry.

The Federals had watched the rebel line as it thickened and lengthened to their front and on their flank. Now the opposing forces were roughly equal. But the blue troops did not know this; they only knew that the enemy was receiving reinforcements, while they themselves got none. "Where are *our* reserves?" they asked in consternation after the scattering of the zouaves and the loss of their two most effective batteries near the center of the field. Wearied by thirteen hours of marching on dusty roads at night and fighting under a July sun, they began to reason that they had been too thoroughly mismanaged for mere incompetence to account for all the blunders. They were angry and dismayed, and from point to point along the front a strange cry broke out: "Betrayed! We are betrayed! Sold out!" When the long gray line sprang at them, bayonets snapping and glinting in the sun-

First Blood; New Conceptions

light as the shrill, unearthly quaver of the rebel yell came surging down the slope, they faltered. Then they broke. They turned and fled past officers on horseback flailing the smoke with sabers while screaming for them to stand. They ran and they kept on running, many of them throwing down their rifles in order to travel lighter and run faster. "Betrayed! Sold out!" some shouted hoarsely as they fled, explaining — as all men apparently always must — the logic behind their fear.

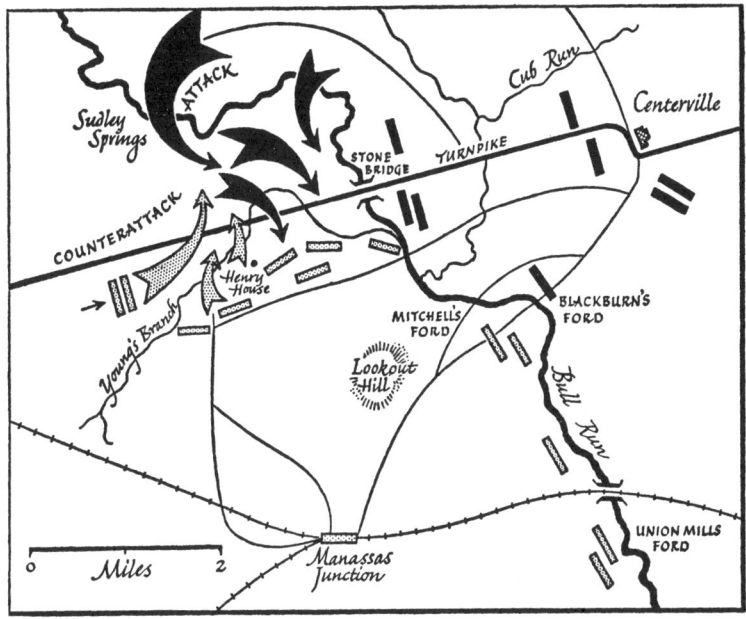

So far the retreat was mainly sullen, with more grim anger than panic in the ranks. It had not yet become a rout, though the Southerners were doing what they could to make it one. Kirby Smith had ridden down the line as his troops came off the cars to form for battle within the sound of guns and the sight of smoke boiling over the northward ridge. "This is the signal, men," he cried, the back of his hand to the bill of his cap; "the watchword is Sumter!" It didn't make much sense but it sounded fine, and the Valley soldiers cheered him riding past. He was wounded as soon as he reached the field; Colonel Arnold Elzey took command. Coming presently into sight of a mass of infantry drawn across the road ahead — whether Union or Confederate none could tell with the naked eye — Elzey halted the column. As he raised his binoculars a breeze stirred the drifting smoke; flags rippled stiffly from their staffs. "Stars and Stripes! Stars and Stripes! Give it to them, boys!" he yelled, and led his regiments forward at a run. Early's brigade had come up, too, their cheers swelling the din on the left as the whole gray line, curving away northeastward along the crest of Henry Hill, came whooping down upon the startled men in blue.

While his flanking column fell back over the run, McDowell did what he could to save the day. Two brigades, withdrawn from the fords below Stone Bridge, along with the one reserve brigade and some regiments just arrived from Alexandria, were combined to form a rally line near Centerville, in hopes that the retreaters from the crushed right flank would fall in here to challenge the Confederate counterattack. But it was no use. Anger was fast giving way to panic as the retreat gathered momentum. These men were bound for the Potomac, along a road that had been traveled prophetically that morning by a regiment of infantry and a battery of field artillery; their enlistments expiring today, they had declined any share in the battle, and deaf alike to pleas and jeers had returned to Washington for discharge. Panic was contagious. Troops from the proposed rally line fell in with the skulkers going past, and now the more or less sullen retreat became a rout, the column once more harried by the carriages and victorias of the junketing politicians who had driven out to see the Union reëstablished. Now, somehow, across the run and down the western leg of that spraddled X, in a roiling cauldron of dust and smoke with fitful, pinkish-yellow stabs of fire mixed in, the carefree lark had been transmuted into something out of a nightmare. "Turn back! Turn back! We are whipped!" the civilians heard the soldiers shout as they came surging up the pike. Darkness spread and the moon came out: a full moon like the one that had flooded the landscape two months ago, when the Grand Army crossed the Potomac to take potshots at an occasional scampering rebel.

Disorderly as the column was, it made good time. In that one night, returning north, McDowell's army covered more distance than it had managed to cover in three days of southward marching the week before.

On the Confederate side there was disorganization, too. It was of a different kind, however, proceeding from the elation of victory rather than from the depression of defeat. The two were strangely alike. Belief that the battle was won produced very much the same effect, as far as concerted action went, as belief that the battle was lost. In either case it was over, and southern leaders could accomplish no more toward organizing pursuit along the turnpike than their northern counterparts could accomplish toward organizing a rally line across it. On the left, above Stone Bridge, the regiments were halted for realignment, all possibility of control being gone; while on the right, where the brigades had forced their way across the fords below the bridge, pursuit was abandoned and the men recalled to the south bank of the run to meet a false alarm of an attack at Union Mills. One brigadier, Longstreet — he had already crossed and recrossed the stream five times that day — was commanded to fall back just as he gave the order for his batteries to open fire on the retreating Federal column. Stuart's cavalry, swinging wide around Sudley Springs, should have been free to accomplish most; but the troopers soon were burdened with so many prisoners picked up along the way that they lost all mobility, and presently they dwindled to a squad. It was the same all along the line. Little could be done to gather the potential fruits of victory.

Even Jefferson Davis, braced for disaster as he rode from Manassas Junction through the backwash of the army, lost some measure of his self-control in the sudden release from anxiety when he emerged to find the Union soldiers fleeing from the charging men in gray. Meeting Colonel Elzey he conferred the first battlefield promotion of the war: "General Elzey, you are the Blücher of the day!" He joined the horseback chase toward Sudley Springs, and everywhere he encountered rejoicing and elation. In the gathering dusk, coming upon a body of men he thought were stragglers, he began a speech to rally them, only to learn that they were Jackson's Virginians, who had done so much to win the battle. Their commander was in a nearby dressing station, having a wounded finger bandaged. "Give me ten thousand men," he was saying, "and I would be in Washington tomorrow."

Davis rather thought so, too. He rode back to see Johnston and Beauregard at the latter's Manassas headquarters. The generals were as elated as their men; but when the President asked what forces were pushing the beaten enemy, they replied that the troops were confused and hungry and needed rest; pursuit had ended for the night. Davis was unwilling to reconcile himself to this, but presently a slow rain came on, turning the dust to mud all over eastern Virginia, and there was no longer even a question of the possibility of pursuit. Out on the field, along the turnpike and the run and in the angles of the X they formed, the drizzle soaked the dead and fell upon the wounded of both armies.

Among them was Major Roberdeau Wheat, commander of the Louisiana Tigers, who had opened the fight alongside Evans above Stone Bridge. He was a lawyer and had been a soldier of fortune, fighting with Carravajal in Mexico, Walker in Nicaragua, and Garibaldi in Sicily; but now a Union bullet had gone through both of his lungs and a surgeon told him he must die.

"I don't feel like dying yet," Wheat said.

The doctor insisted: "There is no instance on record of recovery from such a wound."

"Well, then," the lawyer-soldier replied, "I will put my case on record."

Next morning at breakfast Davis wrote out for Beauregard, subject to the approval of Congress, a promotion to full general. Then he returned to Richmond, where the bodies of General Bee and other leaders killed on yesterday's field were to lie in state, with honor guards and fitting obsequies. In spite of such causes for individual grief, the people in the capital were as elated as the soldiers around Manassas. Here as there, the feeling was that the Yankees had been shown for once and for all. The war was won. Independence was a fact beyond all doubt. Even the casualty lists, the source of their sorrow, reinforced their conviction of superiority to anything the North could bring against them.

The Confederates had lost almost two thousand, but the Union army had lost more than three thousand; 387 were dead in gray, 481 in blue. Only among the wounded were the Northerners outnumbered, 1582 to 1124, and this in itself was interpreted as a credit to the South; what, they asked, could be nobler than for a soldier to bleed for his country? However, they found the principal support for their opinion in the amount of captured equipment and the number of prisoners taken. Fifteen hundred Yankees had thrown down their arms and submitted to being marched away to prison, while in the Confederate ranks only eight were listed as missing, and no one believed that even these had surrendered. Equipment captured during the battle, or garnered from the field when the fighting was over, included 28 artillery pieces, 17 of them rifled, as well as 37 caissons, half a million rounds of small-arms ammunition, 500 muskets, and nine flags.

Later in the week, while southern outpost riders once more gazed across the Potomac at the spires of Washington, the wounded were brought to Richmond to be cared for — including Rob Wheat, who had put his case on record. The ladies turned out with an enthusiasm which sometimes tried the patience of the men. Asked if he wanted his face washed, one replied: "Well, ma'am, it's been washed twenty times already. But go ahead, if you want to." Prisoners came to Richmond, too, where a three-story tobacco warehouse had been hurriedly converted into a military prison. From the sidewalk, citizens tried to bribe the guards for a glimpse at a real live Yankee: especially New York Congressman Alfred Ely, who had strolled too near the scene of battle just as the lines gave way and was discovered trying to hide behind a tree. President Davis sent him two fine white wool blankets to keep him warm in the warehouse prison, and the people in general approved of such chivalry. They felt that they could afford to be magnanimous, now that the war was won.

Lincoln, who had gone out for his Sunday drive believing the battle a Union victory, returned at sundown to find that the Secretary of State had come looking for him, white and shaky, and had left a message that McDowell had been whipped and was falling back. Hurrying to the War Department, he read a telegram confirming the bad news: "General McDowell's army in full retreat through Centerville. The day is lost. Save Washington and the remnants of this army." He returned to the White House and spent the night on a sofa in the cabinet room while bedraggled politicians, with the startled expressions of men emerging from nightmares, brought him eye-witness accounts of the disaster. Next morning, through windows lashed by rain, he watched his soldiers stagger up the streets, many of them so exhausted that they stumbled and slept in yards and on the steps of houses, oblivious to the pelting rain and the women who moved among them offering coffee.

General Scott and others with long faces soon arrived. "Sir, I am the greatest coward in America," Scott told one of them. "I deserve removal because I did not stand up, when my army was not in condition for fighting, and resist it to the last." Lincoln broke in: "Your conversation seems to imply that I forced you to fight this battle." The old general hesitated. He believed this was quite literally true, but he would not be rude. "I have never served a President who has been kinder to me than you have been," he said evasively, leaving Lincoln to draw from this what solace he could.

While Davis was soaring from anxiety to elation and Lincoln was moving in the opposite direction, downhill from elation to anxiety, others around the country and the world were reacting according to their natures. Horace Greeley, who had clamored for invasion, removed the banner "Forward to Richmond!" from the masthead of his New York *Tribune*, and after what he called "my seventh sleepless night — yours, too, doubtless" — wrote to Lincoln: "On every brow sits sullen, scorching, black despair. If it is best for the country and for mankind that we make peace with the rebels at once and on their own terms, do not shrink even from that." Tecumseh Sherman, reassembling his scattered brigade, wrote privately: "Nobody, no man, can save the country. Our men are not good soldiers. They brag, but don't perform, complain sadly if they don't get everything they want, and a march of a few miles uses them up. It will take a long time to overcome these things, and what is in store for us in the future I know not." One English journalist at least believed he could guess what was in store. "So short lived has been the American Union," the London *Times* observed, "that men who saw its rise may live to see its fall."

Allowing for journalistic license, "sullen, scorching, black despair" was scarcely an overstatement. All along the troubled line, from Missouri to the Atlantic, the gloom was lighted at only one point. In western Virginia, scene of the Philippi Races and the rout at Carrick's Ford, there was a commander with a Napoleonic flair who lifted men's hearts and brought cheers. Lincoln looked in that direction, the long sad face grown longer and sadder in the past few hours, and there he believed he found his man of destiny. On that same Monday, while fugitives from Sunday's battle still limped across Long Bridge and slept in the rain, he summoned him by telegraph:

> General George B. McClellan
> Beverly, Virginia:
> Circumstances make your presence here necessary. Charge Rosecrans or some other general with your present department and come hither without delay.

✘ 2 ✘

Lincoln was already dealing with two men of destiny: Robert Anderson, the hero of Sumter, and John Charles Frémont, the California Pathfinder. They were to save Kentucky and Missouri for the Union, both having ties in the states to which they had been sent. Anderson was a Bluegrass native, and Frémont, though Georgia-born, had made important Missouri connections by eloping with the daughter of old Thomas Hart Benton, who lived long enough to be reconciled to the match.

In Kentucky the contest was political, swinging around the problem of the state's declared neutrality. Her sympathies were southern but her interests lay northward, beyond the Ohio, Lincoln having guaranteed the inviolability of her property in slaves. What was more, her desire for peace was reinforced by the knowledge that her "dark and bloody ground," as it was called, would be the scene of bitterest fighting if war came. Therefore, after the furor of Sumter and the departure into Confederate ranks of the eastern border states and Tennessee, the governor and both houses of the legislature announced that Kentucky would defend her borders, north and south, against invaders from either direction, and the people signified their approval in the special congressional election of late June, when nine out of the ten men sent to Washington were Unionists, and again in the August legislature races, which also were overwhelming Union victories.

Meanwhile Kentucky had become a recruiting ground for agents of both armies. The state militia, under Simon Bolivar Buckner, a West Pointer and a wealthy Kentucky aristocrat, was the largest and probably the best-drilled body of nonregular troops in the country. Its 10,000 members were pro-Confederate, but this threat was countered by the Home Guard, swiftly organized under William Nelson, a six-foot five-inch, three-hundred-pound U.S. Navy lieutenant who distributed 10,000 "Lincoln rifles" among men of strong pro-Union beliefs. Whatever caution their political leaders might show, Kentuckians did not stand aside from individual bloodshed; 35,000 would fight for the South before the war was over, while more than twice that many would fight for the

North, including 14,000 of her Negroes. Here the conflict was quite literally "a war of brothers." Senator John J. Crittenden typified the predicament of his state; he who had done so much for peace had two sons who became major generals in the opposing armies. Likewise Henry Clay, that other great compromiser, had three grandsons who fought to preserve the Union and four who enlisted on the other side. All over the state, instances such as these were reproduced and multiplied. Fathers and sons, brothers and cousins were split on issues that split the nation. Kentucky was in truth a house divided. The question was in which direction the house would fall.

Commissioned a brigadier after the public acclaim that greeted him when he landed in New York from Fort Sumter, Anderson was sent west in late August. He had said that his heart was not in the struggle, that if Kentucky seceded he would go to Europe and wait the war out. But now that his native state expressed intentions of holding firm, he determined to take the field. Frail and aged beyond his fifty-six years, he was warned by his physicians that he might break under the stress of active duty: to which, according to a Washington newspaper interview, he replied that "the Union men of Kentucky were calling on him to lead them and that he must and would fall in a most glorious cause."

Out of respect for his state's declared neutrality, and despite his official designation as commander of the Military Department of Kentucky, he established headquarters in Cincinnati, just across the Ohio, and attempted to direct operations from there. He did little, for there was little he could do; which gave the impression that he was biding his time, waiting for the Bluegrass leaders to evolve their own decisions unmolested. Considering their touchy sensibilities — so violently in favor of peace that they were willing to fight for it — this was the best he could possibly have done. It was more, at any rate, than his opponent Leonidas Polk could do.

Polk was a West Pointer who had gone into the ministry and done well. Aged fifty-five at the outbreak of the war, he was Episcopal Bishop of Louisiana. Visiting Richmond in June he dropped by to see his Academy schoolmate Jefferson Davis, and when he emerged from the President's office he held, to his surprise, the commission of a Confederate major general and appointment to the command of troops in the Mississippi Valley. Northerners expressed horror at such sacrilege, but Southerners were delighted with this transfer from the Army of the Lord. Polk himself, considering his new duty temporary, did not resign his bishopric. He felt, he said, "like a man who has dropped his business when his house is on fire, to put it out; for as soon as the war is over I will return to my proper calling."

Just now, however, the bishop-general was alarmed at the development of events in Kentucky, which had gone from bad to worse from the Confederate point of view. Not only was the legislature pro-

Unionist, but in mid-July, feeling that his position was somehow dishonorable or anyhow equivocal, Buckner resigned as head of the militia, which then disbanded, its guns and equipment passing into the hands of the Home Guard. At this rate Kentucky would soon be irretrievably gone. One of the first things Polk did when he arrived at his Memphis headquarters was to order a concentration of Confederate troops at Union City, in northwest Tennessee, prepared to cross the border and occupy Columbus, Kentucky — which Polk saw as the key to the upper Mississippi — whenever some Federal act of aggression made such a movement plausible.

Anderson, marking time in Cincinnati, would give him no such provocation, but Frémont, across the way, was more precipitate. On August 28 he instructed Brigadier General Ulysses S. Grant to take command of "a combined forward movement" and "to occupy Columbus, Ky. as soon as possible." That city's pro-southern citizens had already petitioned the Confederates to march to their defense, and now that he had an excuse Polk moved quickly. Not waiting to deal with an accomplished act of aggression, but hastening to forestall one, he ordered his troops to cross the border. They occupied Columbus on September 4, the day before the Federals were scheduled to arrive. Grant, thus checked, countered by crossing the border and occupying Paducah, strategically located at the junction of the Ohio and the Tennessee. Now both Confederate and Union soldiers, in rapid sequence, had violated Kentucky's declared neutrality.

The reaction, which was immediate, was directed mainly against the Southerners, since they had entered first and could make a less effective show of moral indignation. Anderson left Cincinnati at last, transferring his headquarters to Frankfort, where he appeared before the legislature on September 7 and was given an ovation. Four days later, though it sent no such angry communication to Grant or Frémont, this body issued a formal demand that the Confederacy withdraw its troops. When this injunction was not obeyed, it passed on the 18th an act creating a military force to expel them.

Neutrality was over. Politically, Kentucky had chosen the Union. She had a star in the Confederate flag and a secessionist legislature at Russellville, but these represented hardly anything more than the Kentuckians in the southern army. If she was to be reclaimed, if the northern boundary of the new nation was to reach the natural barrier of the Ohio, it would have to be accomplished by force of arms.

Much of the credit was due Anderson, who had waited. He had spoken of glory on setting out, but there had been little of that for him in his native Kentucky; he had said goodbye to glory in Charleston harbor. And now his physician's prediction came true. His health broke and he was given indefinite sick leave, Sherman replacing him in mid-October. Thus the Union's first man of destiny left the scene. Afterwards brevetted a major general and retired, he spent the war years in New York City, pointed out on the avenue as he took his daily constitutional, still the hero of Sumter, wearing a long military cloak across his shoulders to hide his stars. He read the war news in the papers and took a particular pride in the career of Sherman, who had served under him as a junior lieutenant in the peacetime army; "One of my boys," he called him.

★ ★ ★

Lincoln's second man of destiny was quite different from the first, as indeed he had need to be. In Missouri the secession question had long since passed the political stage. Here there was bloodshed from the outset, and all through the last half of the opening year it was touch and go, a series of furious skirmishes, marches and countermarches by confused commanders, occupations, evacuations, and several full-scale battles. Jesse James studied tactics here, and Mark Twain skedaddled.

Whatever talents Frémont might show, and he was reputed to have many, the ability to wait and do nothing was not one of them. Heading westward on the day of McDowell's defeat on the plains of Manassas, he fell into Missouri's seething cauldron toward the end of July, when he established headquarters in St Louis. Apprised of the situation — disaffection throughout the state, bands of marauders roaming at will, Confederates massed along the southern border — he sent telegrams in all directions, from Washington D.C. out to California, calling for reinforcements. None were forthcoming, but apparently relieved just by the effort of having tried, Frémont settled down at once to making plans for the future.

Something of a mystic, he was a man of action, too, and within the widening circle of his glory he had a magnetism that drew men to him. With the help of such guides as Kit Carson he had explored and mapped the Rocky Mountain passes through which settlers came west. Under his leadership — the Pathfinder, they called him — they broke California loose from Mexico and joined her to the Union, rewarding Frémont by making him one of her first two senators, as well as one of her first millionaires, and subsequently the Republican Party's first presidential nominee. He was in France at the outbreak of war, but he came straight to Washington, where Lincoln made him a major general and sent him westward. His slender yet muscular body evidenced a youthfulness which the touches of gray in his hair and beard only served to emphasize by contrast, as if they represented not so much his forty-eight years, but rather the width of experience and adventure he had packed into them. His features were regular, his glance piercing. There was drama in his gestures, and his voice had overtones of music.

"I have given you carte blanche. You must use your own judgment, and do the best you can," Lincoln had told him, saying goodbye on the portico of the White House. And now in Missouri Frémont took him at his word.

While the news from Manassas dampened Unionist spirits, he continued to exorcise dismay with works and projects. After ordering intrenchments thrown around St Louis to secure it from attack, he occupied and fortified Cape Girardeau, above Cairo, as well as the railheads at Ironton and Rolla and the state capital at Jefferson City. Such actions were mainly defensive, but Frémont had offensive conceptions as well, and of these such occupations were a part. Poring over strategic maps in his headquarters, which he saw as the storm center of events, he looked beyond the present crisis and evolved a master plan for Federal efforts in the West. Whoever controlled the trunk controlled the tree; whoever held the Mississippi Valley, he discerned from his coign of vantage, "would hold the country by the heart." Missouri was only a starting point, elemental but essential to the plan, "of which the great object was the descent of the Mississippi River." With Memphis and Vicksburg lopped off, and finally New Orleans, the Confederacy would wither like a tree with a severed taproot.

Cairo was the key, and having secured it he went ahead. He began construction of 38 mortar boats and two gunboats to scour the rivers, and ordered Grant to seize Columbus, or, as it turned out — since Polk moved first, and thereby won the race and lost Kentucky — Paducah, which served as well. Whatever fit the plan got full attention; whatever did not fit got brushed aside. Some, in fact, found him too vague and exalted for their taste — Grant, for example, who recorded: "He sat in a room in full uniform with his maps before him. When you went in he would point out one line or another in a mysterious manner, never asking you to take a seat. You left without the least idea of what he meant or what he wanted you to do."

It was true that he was difficult to get at. To protect his privacy from obscure brigadiers like Grant while he worked eighteen hours a day in the three-story St Louis mansion which served as headquarters, he had a bodyguard of 300 men, "the very best material Kentucky could afford; average height 5 feet 11½ inches, and measuring 40½ inches around the breast." Resplendent in feathers and loops of the gold braid known locally as "chicken guts," his personal staff included Hungarians and Italians with titles such as "adlatus to the chief" and names that were hardly pronounceable to a Missouri tongue; Emavic, Meizarras, Kalamaneuzze were three among many. The list ran long, causing one of his Confederate opponents to remark as he read it, "There's too much tail to that kite."

Whether he would soar or not, Frémont kept his gaze on far horizons. Down in the southwest corner of the state he had a compact, well-drilled army of 6000, including 1200 regulars and several batteries of artillery. Its commander, Brigadier General Nathaniel Lyon, had been active against rebellion from the start. Back in May, disguised in women's clothes, including a bonnet and veil to hide his red hair and whiskers, he had ridden in an open carriage to reconnoiter a secessionist camp. Afterwards he surrounded the place, forced its surrender under the muzzles of his guns, and marched the would-be Confederates off to prison, shooting down two dozen civilians when a crowd on the streets of St Louis attempted to interfere. By similar forthright action he had saved for the Union the arms in the Federal arsenal there. He was a hard-bitten, capable New Englander, forty-three years old, well acquainted with violence and well adapted for countering that particular brand of it being met with in Missouri. "I was born among the rocks," he once remarked.

So far, however, Lyon had no part in the plan Frémont was spending long hours evolving. In June he had led his troops southwest, intending to secure that section of the state and then move into Arkansas, with Little Rock as his goal. By early August he was beyond Springfield, near the border, but breakdowns along his line of supply had made his army ragged, ill-shod, low on ammunition, and disheartened. Frémont, intent on his master plan, could send no reinforcements. What was worse, the Confederates encamped to Lyon's front around Cowskin Prairie were growing stronger every day. He estimated their strength at 20,000; it was "impractical to advance." On August 4 he reported: "I am under the painful necessity of retreating, and can at most only hope to make my retreat good. I am in too great haste to explain more fully." On the 6th he fell back to a position around Springfield, and the Confederates came on after him, pausing a few miles south before making the final pounce.

They were not as formidable as Lyon thought, and for several reasons. Though they numbered about 12,000 — twice the size of the Union force — for the most part they were miserably equipped and poorly organized, under commanders who were divided in their counsels and ambitions. The majority were Missouri militia led by Sterling Price, a fifty-two-year-old Virginia-born ex-governor who thought so little of West Pointers that he inserted a notice in the papers, indignantly quashing a rumor that he had received a formal military education. His men had neither uniforms nor tents; many had no arms at all, while others had only shotguns or 1812-style flintlocks, and as substitutes for artillery projectiles they had laid in a stock of smooth stones, rusty chains, and iron rods to be shot from their eight antiquated cannon. The remainder, under Ben McCulloch of Tennessee, forty years old and a former Texas Ranger, were somewhat better equipped, being regular Confederate troops.

Price was a major general, McCulloch a brigadier, both veterans of the Mexican War; but the latter, who held his commission directly from Richmond, did not feel that the former should outrank him, and refused to combine the two forces unless the Missourian would yield command. Price, called Old Pap by his men — they asserted that their general had "won more battles in Mexico than McCulloch ever witnessed" — was so anxious to fall upon Lyon that he agreed to the stipulation. As soon as Lyon began his retreat, McCulloch led the combined forces after him. They went into camp along Wilson's Creek, ten miles short of Springfield, where the Federals had halted. McCulloch drew up plans for attack. The movement began on August 9, but was called off because of threatening rain; the troops returned to camp and settled down to sleep, not bothering to put out pickets. At dawn the storm of Lyon's attack exploded in their rear.

The red-haired Federal was also a veteran of Mexico, where he had won promotion for valor, capturing three guns at Cerro Gordo. In the spirit of those days, instead of waiting to receive attack or risking being struck while in motion, he had decided to deliver a blow that would permit him to retreat unmolested. The fact that he was outnumbered two to one — three to one, as he thought — did not discourage this, but rather — in Lyon's eyes, at any rate — demanded it. He felt that his army would do a better job of delivering an attack than of standing to receive one. With his men somewhat heartened by a day's rest and the arrival of shoes from the railhead at Rolla, he distributed the shoes on the afternoon of the 9th and set out south for Springfield. Soon after midnight, the Confederates having averted a meeting engagement by turning back in the face of lowering weather, he had his troops within striking distance of the rebel camp on Wilson's Creek.

He had not minded the rain, and he counted the darkness a positive advantage. Under its cover he disposed his army for one of those complicated envelopments so popular in the early days of the war, when the generals and the soldiers they commanded were least capable of executing them. One column, under Colonel Franz Sigel — two regiments of infantry, two troops of cavalry, and a six-gun battery of artillery — was sent on a wide swing to hit the enemy rear, while Lyon struck in front with the main body, southward down the western bank where most of the rebels lay snug in their blankets. He detached one regiment of regulars — First Infantry, U.S. Army: about as regular as troops could be — sending them beyond the creek to handle whatever Confederates might have pitched their camps on that side.

Sigel set out; Lyon waited in the darkness. Nothing stirred in the rebel camp. As dawn paled the rising ground beyond the creek, the limbs of trees coming black against the sky, there was a sudden spatter of musketry — the skirmishers had opened fire — then the roar and flash of guns like summer lightning on the far horizon: Sigel had come up from the south and was in action, on time and in place. Lyon ordered the main body forward, east and west of the creek, closing the upper jaw of his tactical vise.

First Blood; New Conceptions

Everything was moiling confusion in the camps along the creekbed, guns booming north and south as men came out of their blankets in various stages of undress, tousle-haired, half asleep, and badly frightened. Under the stress of that first panic many fled. Some returned, rather shamefaced. Others ran, and kept on running, right out of the war. Yet those who stood were hard-core men from Arkansas and Louisiana, Texas and Missouri, wanting only to be told what to do. Mc-Culloch and his aides soon established a line of resistance, and these men fell in eagerly. Price had yielded the command, but he was there, too, his white hair streaming in the wind as he rode up and down the line of his rallied Missourians, shouting encouragement. Under such leadership, the Southerners assembled in time to meet the attack from both directions. The battle that followed set the pattern for all such encounters in the West.

Few of the romantic preconceptions as to brilliant maneuver and individual gallantry were realized. Fighting at close quarters because of the short-range Confederate flintlocks and muzzle-loading fowling pieces, a regiment would walk up to the firing line, deliver a volley, then reload and deliver another, continuing this until it dissolved and was replaced by another regiment, which repeated the process, melting away in the heat of that furnace and being in turn replaced. No fighting anywhere ever required greater courage, yet individual gallantry seemed strangely out of place. A plume in a man's hat, for example, accom-

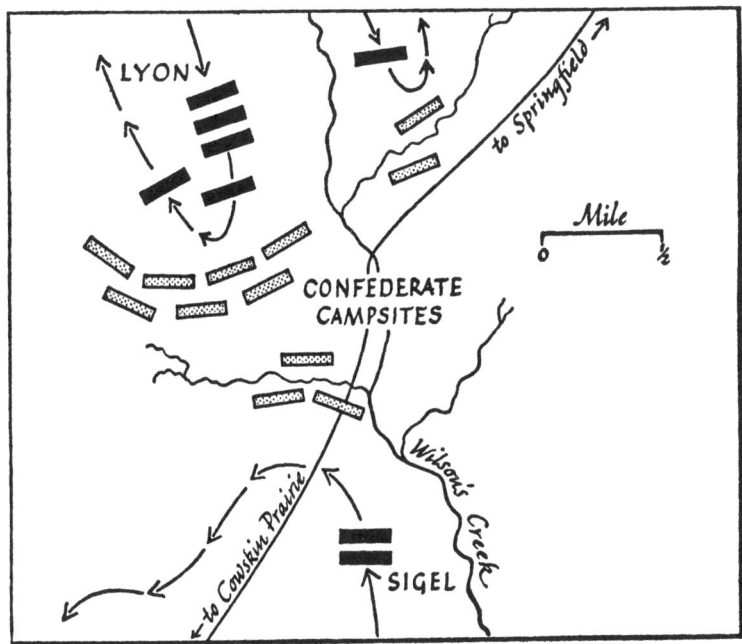

plished nothing except to make him a more conspicuous target. Nor did the rebel yell ring out on the banks of Wilson's Creek. There was little cheering on either side; for a cheer seemed as oddly out of place as a plume. The men went about their deadly business of firing and reloading and melting away in a grim silence broken only by the rattling crash of musketry and the deeper roar of guns, with the screams of the injured sometimes piercing the din. Far from resembling panoplied war, it was more like reciprocal murder.

In such a battle the weight of numbers told. Sigel's surprise attack from the south became a rout almost as soon as he encountered resistance. His men broke, stampeded, and did not stop till they got back to Springfield, having abandoned their colors and all but one of their guns. To the north, Lyon's men were wavering, too. East of the creek the regulars, lacking reinforcements, were blasted off the field. The main body, west of the creek, stood manfully to their work for a while; but presently, the Confederates clustering thicker and thicker to their front, new regiments arriving after their success in dealing with other columns of attack, the Federals began to look back over their shoulders, apprehensive. Lyon rode among them, calling for them to stand firm in the face of gathering resistance. As he sought thus to rally them, a bullet creased his scalp. A second struck his thigh, a third his ankle. His horse was shot and fell dead under him. Stunned, Lyon limped slowly toward the rear, shaking his head. "I fear the day is lost," he said. Presently, though, recovering from the shock and depression, he secured another mount and rode again into the fight, at a place where the troops were about to give way. Swinging his hat he called for them to follow him, and when they rallied he led them forward. Near the point of deepest penetration, a bullet struck his heart and he went down. His men fled, shaken by the loss of their red-bearded leader.

It was Manassas all over again. Once the Federal troops gave way, they did not stand upon the order of their going, but retreated pell-mell to Springfield and then to Rolla, leaving their fallen comrades on the field: Kansas, Missouri, and Iowa farmboys, lying dead in their new shoes, and the brave Lyon, whose body McCulloch forwarded through the lines under a flag of truce, only to recapture it when the Unionists fell back from Springfield, abandoning it in its coffin in the courthouse.

The fighting had been bloody; "the severest battle since Waterloo," one participant called it. Within four hours each side had suffered about 1200 casualties. In one-third the time, and with less than one-third the number of troops involved, more than half as many men had fallen along Wilson's Creek as had fallen along Bull Run. Yet here too, as after that battle three weeks before, on the banks of that other rural stream 800 miles away, one side was about as disorganized by victory as the other was by defeat. Though there was broad open daylight for pursuit, the Confederates could not be put into column to press the retreating Federals. All the same, the battle was taken as further proof, if such was needed, of the obvious superiority of the southern fighting man, and in Missouri as in Virginia there was the feeling that, now that the Yankees had been shown what they were up against, there was no real need for giving chase.

In Richmond, President Davis announced the victory in much the same tone of quiet exultation he had used for the announcement in July. Then, out of respect for Missouri's "neutrality," he ordered McCulloch to return to Arkansas with his Confederate troops, awaiting an invitation from the secessionist legislature soon to assemble in Neosho, Lyon having scattered them from Jefferson City in July. Price and his native militiamen followed slowly as the Federals fell back. The battle was therefore inconclusive in results, since Lyon had been retreating anyhow.

One thing it did, at any rate. It removed Frémont's transfixed gaze from far horizons. The lopping descent of the Mississippi could never be accomplished without Missouri under control. Galvanized by reports of the battle, which indicated that he was in danger of losing his starting-point, he reacted first according to pattern, wiring the Secretary of War for reinforcements: "Let the governor of Ohio be ordered forthwith to send me what disposable force he has; also governors of Illinois, Indiana, and Wisconsin. Order the utmost promptitude." This done — though nothing came of it — he sent five regiments to strengthen the defeated men at Rolla, and declared martial law in St Louis. Other rebel columns were reported to be advancing, however, and all over the northern portion of the state, guerillas were coming out of hiding, emboldened by Confederate successes.

As the month wore on, Frémont realized that something had to be done to stem the tide. The week before the battle, Congress had passed a confiscation act prescribing certain penalties against persons in rebellion. Now Frémont issued a proclamation of his own, with real teeth in it, written in one night and printed for distribution the following morning. Drawing a line from Fort Leavenworth to Cape Girardeau, he directed that any unauthorized person found under arms north of this line would be tried by court martial, the sentence being death before a firing squad. In addition he announced as confiscated the property, real and personal, of all Missourians who should be "proved to have taken an active part with their enemies in the field." Nor was that all. "And their slaves, if any they have," he added, "are hereby declared freemen."

Emancipation: feared or hoped for, the word had been spoken at last. The reaction came from several directions: first from down in the southeast corner of the state, where the Missouri brigadier, M. Jeff Thompson, issued a proclamation of his own. "For every member of the Missouri State Guard, or soldier of our allies the Confederate States, who shall be put to death in pursuance of said order of General Frémont," he avowed, "I will *Hang, Draw* and *Quarter* a minion of said Abraham Lincoln... so help me God!" Throughout the North, on the other hand, antislavery radicals were delighted. They had wanted a proclamation such as Frémont's all along, and now they had a champion who said plainly, "War consists not only in battles, but in well-considered movements which bring the same results." In Kentucky the reaction was otherwise. A Unionist volunteer company threw down its arms on receiving the news, and the legislature balked on the verge of landing the state officially in the Federal camp. Lincoln thus was caught between two fires, having to offend either the abolitionist wing of his own party, which clamored for emancipation, or the loyal men of the border states, who had been promised nonintervention on the slavery question. Three of the latter wired from Louisville: "There is not a day to be lost in disavowing emancipation, or Kentucky is gone over the mill dam."

Lincoln was circumspect, threading his way. He wrote to Frémont "in a spirit of caution, and not of censure," explaining the predicament and requesting that the Pathfinder modify the edict so as to conform to the recent act of Congress. As for the use of firing squads, he reminded the general that the Confederates would retaliate "man for man, indefinitely," and directed that no shootings were to take place without presidential approval. Frémont waited six days, then replied that he would not "change or shade it. It was worth a victory in the field," he earnestly maintained. As Commander in Chief, Lincoln could *order* it modified; otherwise, the proclamation stood.

This letter was entrusted to no ordinary courier, but was taken to Washington by Jessie Benton Frémont, an illustrious father's ambitious daughter, who had been at her husband's elbow all the while. She arrived after two days and nights on the cars, and, despite the late hour at which she checked into Willard's, sent a note to the White House, asking when she might deliver the message. A card was brought: "Now, at once. A. Lincoln." She had not had time to rest or change her clothes, but she went immediately. The President was waiting. "Well?" he said.

She found his manner "hard," she later declared, and when she handed him the letter he smiled "with an expression not agreeable." When she attempted to reinforce her husband's defense of the proclamation, enlarging upon his explanation that the war must be won by more than the force of arms and that Europe would cheer a blow struck at slavery, Lincoln interrupted her lecture by remarking, "You are quite a female politician." At this she lost her temper and reminded Lincoln that the Pathfinder was beyond the ordinary run of soldiers. If the President wanted to "try titles," he would find Frémont a worthy adversary. "He is a man and I am his wife!" she added hotly. Lincoln had not doubted that Frémont was a man, or that Jessie was his wife; but having stirred up this hornets' nest, he mustered what tact he could to try to calm her. It was not enough. She "left in anger," he said afterwards, "flaunting her handkerchief before my face."

Returning westward she traveled in the wake of a letter addressed to her husband in St Louis. Signed "Your Obt Servt A Lincoln," it began: "Yours of the 8th, in answer to mine of the 2d instant, is just received," and remarked that while the President "perceived in general no objection" to the proclamation, he could not allow an Act of Congress to be overridden; therefore he would assume responsibility for revoking so much of Frémont's edict as failed to conform to that Act. "Your answer... expresses the preference on your part that I should make an open order for the modification, which I very cheerfully do." Thus he drew the teeth of the proclamation for the sake of the border Unionists, while for the sake of the abolitionists he explained that this was done, not because of its policy — to which he "perceived in general no objection" — but simply because it was unlawful, interfering as it did with the prerogative of Congress, where the most vociferous of the abolitionists sat.

Such wary action pacified the conservatives, but the antislavery radicals were by no means satisfied. In this first open break within his party Lincoln was assailed on the floor of the Senate, in the press, and from the pulpit. Protests were especially loud among the German emigrants in Missouri — "the St Louis Dutch," their enemies called them — whose devotion to the general was redoubled. Jessie Frémont's threat that her husband might set up for himself and try titles with the President began to seem quite possible.

Meanwhile, alarming reports of a different kind were arriving from the West, where $12,000,000 had gone down the drain for steamboats, fortifications, uniforms, food, and ice for sherry cobblers. Graft and extravagances were charged against the men surrounding Frémont — "a gang of California robbers and scoundrels," the head of a congressional investigating committee called them, adding that while the general refused to confer with men of honor and wisdom, these boodlers "rule, control and direct everything." Lincoln wrote to Major General David Hunter, who had commanded the flanking column at Manassas, saying of Frémont: "He needs to have by his side a man of large experience. Will you not, for me, take that place? Your rank is one grade too high to be ordered to it, but will you not serve the country and oblige me by taking it voluntarily?" Hunter knew well enough what was meant. He also knew an opportunity when he saw one; and he set out at once for St Louis.

There was a need for military wisdom and alertness, for bushwhackers were plundering the state while Price moved northward with his 15,000 militia, their shortage of arms somewhat repaired by 3000 Union rifles picked up after the fight at Wilson's Creek. At Lexington they besieged Mulligan's Irish Guard, 2800 men intrenched on the campus of the Masonic College. Price was low on percussion caps, but when a supply arrived in mid-September he attacked, keeping his casualties down by advancing his men behind water-soaked bales of hemp which they jimmied along as a sort of sliding breastwork. The Irish surrendered, and Price, with 3000 more rifles and a single-handed victory to his credit, issued a call for his fellow Missourians to flock to his standard: "Do I hear your shouts? Is that your war-cry which echoes through the land? Are you coming? Fifty thousand men! Missouri shall move to victory with the tread of a giant. Come on, my brave boys, 50,000 heroic, gallant, unconquerable, Southern men! We await your coming."

Once more Frémont was galvanized. "I am taking the field myself," he telegraphed Washington. "Please notify the President immediately." He assembled five divisions, 38,000 men, and set out after Price. He had not lost sight of his goal, however. "My plan is New Orleans straight," he wrote his wife, October 7 from Tipton, adding: "I think it can be done gloriously."

It might be done gloriously, but not by Frémont; Lincoln had marked him for destruction. Having found that the Pathfinder would not hesitate to embarrass him politically, the President sent observers to investigate his competence in other matters. In addition to the rumors of graft, the Adjutant General and the Secretary of War had both reported the general unfit for his post: an opinion shared by Brigadier General Samuel Curtis in St Louis, who wrote that Frémont lacked "the intelligence, the experience, and the sagacity necessary to his command." Such reports, in themselves, justified removal; but Jessie Frémont's threat, reinforced by warnings from observers — "[Frémont] does not intend to yield his command at your bidding," one flatly declared — made the problem of procedure a difficult one, and Lincoln continued to exercise caution. On October 28 he sent General Curtis two orders for delivery: one relieving Frémont, the other appointing Hunter in his place. Curtis was told to deliver them only on condition that Frémont had not won a battle or was not about to fight one; Lincoln would not risk the clamor that would follow the dismissal of a general on the eve of an engagement or the morrow of a victory.

News of the order had leaked to the press, however, and Frémont, in camp southwest of Springfield, surrounded by his bodyguard and army, was forewarned. Disguised as a farmer with information about the rebels, a captain detailed by Curtis to deliver Lincoln's order got past Frémont's pickets at 5 a.m., November 1. At headquarters he was told that he could not see the general in person but that his information would be passed on. The captain declined, saying he would wait.

He waited hours on end, and then at last was ushered into the presence. Removing the order from the lining of his coat, he handed it to the general. Frémont read it, then frowned. "Sir," he said, trembling with anger, "how did you get admission into my lines?"

There was one chance. A victory would abrogate the order and vindicate his generalship. He placed the disguised captain in arrest to prevent the spread of news of his relief, stirred up the camp, and prepared to fall upon the enemy to his front. But there was no enemy to his front. Undetected, Price had fallen back beyond his reach, recruits and all, and the captain-messenger, having overheard the password, had escaped. Next morning, rounding out one hundred days of glory, Frémont issued a farewell address, beginning: "Soldiers! I regret to leave you," and requesting loyalty to his successor. Then he set out for St Louis to join his wife, who remarked when she received the news of his downfall: "Oh, if my husband had only been more positive! But he never did assert himself enough. That was his greatest fault."

★ ★ ★

While these two men of destiny rose and fell, a third was rising fast, and he kept rising. On the day Frémont received his dismissal, McClellan was appointed to head all the armies of the nation, superseding his old chieftain Winfield Scott. Much had been done in the three months since his arrival, five days after the Bull Run disaster. The army of 50,000 which he then found waiting for him — "a mere collection of regiments cowering on the banks of the Potomac," he called it — had grown to 168,000 well-trained, spirited men, superbly equipped and worshipful of the commander who had accomplished their transformation.

Out in western Virginia when he received the telegram ordering him to "come hither without delay," he rode sixty miles on horseback to the nearest railway station and caught the train for the capital. Given command of the Washington army on the day after his arrival, he found the city "almost in condition to have been taken by a dash of a regiment of cavalry," and himself looked up to from all sides as the deliverer. "I find myself in a new and strange position here," he wrote his wife that evening; "President, cabinet, Gen. Scott, and all deferring to me. By some strange operation of magic I seem to have become the power of the land." With a strong belief in his ability to set things straight, he had gone to work at once. "I see already the main causes of our recent failure," he declared; "I am sure that I can remedy these, and am confident that I can lead these armies of men to victory."

Employing two regiments of regulars as military police — hard-faced men who had stood fast, taking up position after rear-guard position during the Bull Run retreat — he cleared the bars and hotel lobbies of stragglers and shirkers, requiring officers and men alike to show passes authorizing their absence from their outfits. The crests of the hills ringing the city were fortified, the slopes whitened overnight by tent camps that sprang up as the three-year volunteers arrived in answer to Lincoln's call for 400,000 on the morrow of Manassas. Soon the men within the encampments far outnumbered the population of the city they encircled. The clatter of musketry came from the firing ranges, a ragged uproar punctuated by the cries of sergeants on the drill fields: "Your *left!* Your *left!* Now you've *got* it; damn you, *hold* it! *Left!*" Thus McClellan set about restoring order, securing the defenses of the capital as a prelude to the offensive, which he intended to launch as soon as possible. "I shall carry this thing *en grand*," he wrote, "and crush the rebels in one campaign."

Rigid discipline was the order of the day, and the commander himself was on hand to see it inforced. Something new had come into the war; Little Mac, the soldiers called this man who had transformed them from a whipped mob into a hot-blooded army that seemed never to have known the taste of defeat. He brought out the best in them and restored their pride, and they hurrahed whenever he appeared on horseback, which he frequently did, accompanied by his staff, a glittering cavalcade that included two genuine princes of the blood: the Comte de Paris, pretender to the throne of France, and the Duc de Chartres, known respectively to their fellow officers as Captain Parry and Captain Chatters. There was also an American prince among them, John Jacob Astor, who lived in a style that outshone the Europeans, served by his own valet, steward, chef, and female companions whom he took driving four-in-hand, at once the glory and the despair of Washington society.

Yet even in such company as this, of foreign and domestic royalty, McClellan was dominant. The fame that had preceded him was enhanced by his arrival, and unlike Frémont, whose brilliant first impression soon wore thin, McClellan improved with acquaintance. He did not *seem* young; he *was* young, with all the vigor and clear-eyed forcefulness that went with being thirty-four. His eyes were blue, unclouded by suspicion, his glance direct. He wore his dark auburn hair parted far on the left and brushed straight across, adding a certain boyish charm to his air of forthright manliness. Clean-shaven save for a faint goatee and a heavy, rather straggly mustache which hid his mouth except when he threw back his head to laugh, he had strong, regular features that gave cartoonists little to catch hold of. He was of average height, five feet nine and one-half inches, yet was so robust and stockily built — his chest massive, his well-shaped head set firmly on a muscular neck; "a neck such as not one man in ten thousand possesses," an admirer wrote — that he seemed short. The Young Napoleon, journalists had begun to call him, and photographers posed him standing with folded arms, frowning into the lens as if he were dictating terms for the camera's surrender.

Galloping twelve hours a day or poring over paperwork by lamplight, he had in fact the Napoleonic touch. Men looking at him somehow saw themselves as they would have liked to be, and he could therefore draw on their best efforts. He could be firm or he could temper justice. When two regiments mutinied, declaring that their time was up and they were leaving, McClellan handled each in a different way. The ringleaders of one were sent to the Dry Tortugas to serve out their enlistments at hard labor. In the other case he merely took away the regimental colors and kept them in the hall of his headquarters until the mutineers should earn by good behavior the right to have them back, which they presently did. Both regiments soon cheered him to the echo whenever he came riding through their camps.

Within ten days of his arrival he could write, "I have restored order completely." Training now entered a new phase, with emphasis on the development of unit pride, as the men learned to polish equipment to new degrees of brightness and step to parade-ground music. Reviews were staged, the massed columns swinging past reviewing stands, eyes-right, guidons snapping, where the generals and distinguished civilians stood and ladies in hoop skirts watched from under parasols. Then, for climax, McClellan himself rode down the line, his charger Dan Webster setting a pace that made the staff string out behind, the rather desperate faces of the junior officers at the rear affording much amusement to the men in ranks. Yet even they, who had sat up half the night, scrubbing and polishing cloth and leather, could see the purpose behind the panoply and the results that purpose yielded. The young general had an eye for everything. A dingy cartridge box or a special gleam on a pair of shoes could bring a sudden frown or a smile of pride, and the men were disconsolate or happy, depending on which expression flickered across the youthful face. They cheered him riding past, and when he acknowledged the cheers with his jaunty salute, they cheered again. Even the salute was something special. He "gave his cap a little twirl," one witness wrote, "which with his bow and smile seemed to carry a little of personal good fellowship even to the humblest private soldier. If the cheer was repeated he would turn in the saddle and repeat the salute." It was reciprocal. Between them they felt that they were forging the finest army the world had ever seen.

Yet all was not as confident in McClellan's mind as the soldiers judged from his manner on parade. In the small hours of the night, alone in his quarters, musing upon the example of McDowell, whose army had been wrecked on the very plains where the Confederates were still massing under the same victorious commanders, he took counsel of his fears. Soon after his arrival, in the flush of early confidence, he had written: "I flatter myself that Beauregard has gained his last victory." Now he wrote, "I have scarcely slept one moment for the last three nights, knowing well that the enemy intend some movement and fully recognizing our own weakness. If Beauregard does not attack tonight I shall look upon it as a dispensation of Providence. He ought to do it." The dispensation was granted, but that did not keep McClellan from complaining: "I am here in a terrible place. The enemy have from three to four times my force."

Such figures were not guesswork. They came from his chief of intelligence, Allan Pinkerton, the railroad detective who had herded Lincoln through Baltimore on the eve of inauguration, and they were detailed and explicit, based on reports from agents planted behind the rebel lines. Earlier in August, Pinkerton had shown his chief that the forces around Manassas amounted to beyond 100,000 men. This estimate grew steadily as the agents grew more industrious, until by early October, as the days drew in and shadows lengthened, McClellan was reporting: "The enemy have a force on the Potomac not less than 150,000 strong, well drilled and equipped, ably commanded, and strongly intrenched."

What was worse — or was at least more irritating — it seemed to him that he not only had to contend with the threat of overwhelming numbers across the river, but there was a Virginian here in Washington against whom he must also fight his way: Lieutenant General Winfield Scott, second only to the Father of his Country on the list of the nation's military heroes and the first person McClellan had called on to pay his respects when he arrived. Scott had been a great man in his day, six feet four and a quarter inches tall, resplendent in epaulets of solid gold and wearing an aura of victory through two wars. Yet now, as he said himself, "broken down by many particular hurts, besides the general infirmities of age," he could no longer mount a horse and had to be assisted out of his chair before he could rise. When he would indicate troop positions on a wall map, an aide stood by to wield the pointer. "I have become an incumbrance to the Army as well as to myself," he confessed, with pain to his enormous pride.

McClellan's original feelings of veneration and pity ("It made me feel a little strangely when I went into the President's last evening with the old general leaning on me; I could see that many marked the contrast") had turned to resentment and exasperation as Scott continued to get in the way of his plans. Regular army officers commanding companies and battalions of regulars should not be transferred to lead brigades and divisions of volunteers; a hard core of trained regulars, officered by regulars, was needed. Divisions should not even be created; the brigade had been the largest unit in the army he took to Mexico, where he had accomplished maneuvers that now were described in the history books and tactics manuals. Ensconced between McClellan and Lincoln, and between McClellan and the War Department, Scott advanced these views and delayed the reorganization. Worst of all, the old general put little stock in the Pinkerton reports. Regardless of what was set down in black and white, he would not believe the Union army was outnumbered. When McClellan reported his fears for the safety of the capital, Scott protested: "Relying upon our numbers, our forts, and the Potomac River, I am confident in the opposite direction."

"He understands nothing, appreciates nothing," McClellan declared on August 8, and on the 9th: "Gen. Scott is the great obstacle. He will not comprehend the danger. I have to fight my way against him." Five days later he was saying outright, "Gen. Scott is the most dangerous antagonist I have." Plainly, the old general had to go. As McClellan had already told his wife, "The people call upon me to save the country. I must save it, and I cannot respect anything that is in the way." It was not his doing, he wrote. "I was called to it; my previous life seems to have been unwittingly directed to this great end."

With military acumen, he attacked where his adversary was weakest: in his pride. Snubbing him in public and differing with him abruptly in private councils, he goaded him into such trembling fury that the old man requested to be placed on the retired list as soon as possible, "to seek the palliatives of physical pain and exertion." Lincoln felt he could not spare him yet, however, and asked him to stay on, which Scott reluctantly agreed to do. McClellan kept at him, and at last in early October at a War Department meeting Scott turned heavily in his chair, addressing McClellan who lounged in the doorway: "You were called here by my advice. The times require vigilance and activity. I am not active and never shall be again. When I proposed that you should come here to aid, not supersede me, you had my friendship and confidence. You still have my confidence."

A week before, there had been an incident which seemed to support the old man's opinion that the force across the river might not be as powerful as McClellan claimed. About halfway between Washington and Fairfax Courthouse, less than ten miles from the former, was Munson's Hill, the nearest enemy outpost, from which Confederate pickets could look out and see the unfinished dome of the Capitol itself. On the last day of August, on his own responsibility — partly because the rebels had been taking potshots, but mostly because he could no longer abide the impudence of their dominating an area where his men were learning to drill — a New Jersey colonel pushed his regiment forward against the height. This took courage, for the graybacks had a gun up there, black against the skyline. After a few shots and the fall of a few New Jersey boys, though the cannon itself was providently silent, the colonel fell back, with at least the satisfaction of having protested. A month later, September 28, Johnston apparently having decided that the outpost could be captured or destroyed by a more determined push, the Federals woke to find the hill unoccupied. They went up somewhat cautiously, for the gun was still in position and it seemed unlikely that the rebels would abandon ordinance. Then the revelation came. The cannon was not iron but wood, a peeled log painted black, a Quaker gun.

There was general indignation as the newspapers spread word of how McClellan had been tricked, held at bay by the frown of a wooden cannon. Sightseers, riding out to Munson's Hill to be amused and to exercise their wit, could not see what was clear to army Intelligence: that if Johnston hadn't wanted them to think he was equipped with wooden guns he would never have left one in position when he drew back. With the swift, uncluttered logic of civilians, all they could see was the painted log itself, complete with a pair of rickety wagon wheels, and the fact that the Confederates had fallen back unpushed. Mutterings began to be heard against the Young Napoleon, especially among senators and businessmen, who wanted a short quick fight no matter how bloody. The daily bulletin, "All quiet along the Potomac," which had given the war its first indigenous popular song and which had been so reassuring through the weeks of unease that followed defeat, was greeted now with derision.

Then suddenly, as if to reinforce the army's caution, that quiet was shattered by proof that the rebels on the southern bank had something more than wooden ordinance.

In late October, when the leaves were turning and a brisk promise of winter came down the wind, McClellan received word that Johnston was preparing to evacuate Leesburg, up the Potomac about two-thirds of the way to Harpers Ferry. This time he acted. If Old Joe was ready to fall back, Little Mac at least would give him a nudge to hasten his going.

First, though, he must determine if Johnston was really ready to leave. One division was sent up the Virginia shore to investigate, and another, training in Maryland opposite where the Confederates were reported to be sending their baggage to the rear, was told that it might have a share in the reconnaissance. The Union general across the river halted at Dranesville, ten miles short of Leesburg, content to do his observing from there. The commander on the Maryland side, however — Brigadier General Charles P. Stone, who read his instructions as permission to push things — believed that the best way to discover the enemy's strength was to provoke him into showing it. Accordingly, a couple of regiments were put across the Potomac at Edwards Ferry, while others were sent on a night march to complete the envelopment by crossing at Harrison's Island, three miles upstream.

Here the operation was necessarily slow, being made in three small boats with a combined capacity of 25 men. By dawn, one regiment was on the island, looking out across the other half of the river at the wooded Virginia bank. It reared up tall there, over a hundred feet, steep and mean-looking; Ball's Bluff, it was called, and from beyond its rim they heard a nervous popping of musketry, each shot as flat and distinct as a handclap, only more so. They were Massachusetts boys, and they looked at one another, wondering. No one had told them on the drill field or in bivouac that the war might be like this. They continued the crossing, still in groups of 25, herded by their officers, and took a meandering cow path up the bluff toward the hollow-sounding spatter of rifle fire.

At the top, in explanation of the firing — it had a sharper sound up here, less mysterious but considerably more deadly, with the occasional twang of a ricochet mixed in — they found another Massachusetts outfit drawn up in a glade, returning shots that were coming at them from beyond the brush and timber at the far end of the clearing. These men had crossed the river during the night; their colonel, a Boston lawyer, had taken a patrol almost to Leesburg without uncovering the rebel camp; but presently, coming under fire from scouts or pickets, he had drawn back to the glade above the bluff and assembled his troops to meet the threat that seemed to be building up beyond the brush. He and his men were glad to see their sister Bay State regiment arrive as reinforcements from the island, and he sent word to General Stone of what had happened. In reply the general instructed him to hold what he had: Colonel Edward D. Baker was crossing with his Pennsylvania regiment, and would take command when he arrived.

Baker was someone special, not only a colonel but a full-fledged senator, a one-time Illinois lawyer and an intimate friend of Abraham Lincoln, whose second son had been named for him. Veteran of the Mexican War and the California gold rush, in 1860 he had moved to Oregon at the invitation of the people, who promptly elected him to the U.S. Senate. There he became the Administration's chief far-western spokesman, riding in the presidential carriage on inauguration day and introducing Lincoln for the inaugural address. He welcomed the nation's angry reaction to Sumter; "I want sudden, bold, forward, determined war," he told the Senate, and personally raised a Philadelphia regiment. He did not resign his Senate seat, however, and would not accept a major general's commission from his friend the Commander in Chief, since by law this would have required his resignation from Congress. From time to time he would return from the field, appearing in full uniform on the floor of the Senate, where he would unbuckle his sword, lay it across his desktop, and launch an oratorical attack upon those of his fellow lawmakers who appeared to favor any compromise with secession. At fifty he was clean-shaven and handsome, with a high forehead and a fondness for declaiming poetry. "Press where ye see my white plume shine amidst the ranks of war," he quoted as he took the field.

Now on this October 21, coming up the bluff with his Pennsylvanians, he was happy to be where bullets were flying. "I congratulate you, sir, on the prospect of a battle," he told the Massachusetts colonel, shaking hands as he assumed command. In point of fact, it was more than a prospect; he had a battle on his hands already, as he soon found out.

He had managed to get two guns across the river, and now he put them into action, shelling the brush from which the rebel sniping was getting more vicious all the time. Then he went back to the lip of the bluff and, peering down, saw a New York outfit known as the Tammany Regiment toiling up the cow path. This would make a total of four Union regiments on the field. Baker felt confident and expansive. Spotting the colonel at the head of the climbing column, he waved gaily and greeted him with a quotation from "The Lady of the Lake":

> "One blast upon your bugle horn
> Is worth a thousand men."

Reaching the top of the bluff, the New York colonel — a West Pointer and the only professional soldier on a field in charge of lawyers and politicians — was amazed to find Baker so confident and buoyant over a situation in which, to the military eye at any rate, the danger in front was exceeded only by the confusion in the rear. The Confederates, holding high ground beyond the brush and timber where their snipers were picking off men in the glade almost at will, obviously were building up to launching an attack; whereas the Federals, backed up to the rim of a steep drop with an unfordable river one hundred feet below, were doing little more than dodging bullets and listening to their senator-colonel sing out quotations from Walter Scott.

About this time, one of the two guns recoiled sharply and toppled backward off the bluff; the other was already silent, its cannoneers dropped or driven away by snipers. It seemed to the New Yorker that events were moving swiftly toward disaster. Suddenly Baker seemed to realize it, too. He hurried along the wavering line, calling for his soldiers to stand fast. Perhaps he had some counter-movement in mind. If so, no one ever learned it. For just then, by way of climax, he who had called for sudden, bold, forward, determined war received it in the form of a bullet through the brain, which left him not even time for a dying quotation.

The Confederates out in the brush were Mississippians and Virginians, three regiments of the former and one of the latter, brigaded under Shanks Evans, who had marched above the stone bridge at Bull Run to meet McDowell's flank attack head-on. Evans was not here today, but his men had absorbed what he had taught them. Maneuvering on familiar ground, they had allowed the Yankees to penetrate almost to their Leesburg camp, then had taken them under fire and followed them back to the bluff. There, while the Federals drew into a compact mass in the ten-acre glade above the river, with reinforcements coming up to render the mass even more compact and the target plumper, the

Southerners kept up a galling fire, some of them even climbing trees to do so. All this while, two of the four regiments returning from a march to meet the empty threat downriver, their battle line was forming in the timber. There was no hurry. By now they saw clearly that the Yanks were too rattled to organize a charge, and they were enjoying their advantage thoroughly; particularly the Mississippians, who were reminded of turkey-shoots down home. It was late afternoon before the gray line was ready. Then their officers led them forward, and the rebel yell quavered above the crash of snapping brush and trampled saplings.

What followed was pandemonium. Colonel Baker had just fallen, and the troops drawn up to meet the onslaught were demoralized when a group of soldiers carried the colonel's body to the rear. They thought it was the beginning of a retreat. As it turned out, they were right. Remembering the limited capacity of the boats. each man wanted to be in the first wave heading for the Maryland shore and no man wanted to be among the last, with all those screeching fiends in gray concentrating their fire on him. "A kind of shiver ran through the huddled mass upon the brow of the cliff," a Confederate later wrote. Then, as he watched, "it gave way; rushed a few steps; then, in one wild, panic-stricken herd, rolled, leaped, tumbled over the precipice." The descent was steep, with jagged rocks, but they would not wait to take the roundabout cowpath. They leaped and kept on leaping, some still clutching their muskets, and tumbled onto the heads and bayonets of the men below, with resultant screams of pain and terror. Presently, the witness added, "the side of the bluff was worn smooth by the number sliding down."

Some Confederates hesitated in pursuit, horrified at the results of the panic they had just been doing their utmost to create. They shook this off, however, and running to the rim of the bluff they fired into the huddled, leaping rout of blue-clad men as fast as they could manipulate ramrods and triggers. On the narrow bank and in the water — lashed by bullets until the surface boiled "as white as in a great hail storm," one declared — the scene was worse than the one back on the summit. The wounded had been coming down all day, to be ferried across for medical care and safety. Just as two such boatloads were leaving, their comrades came hurtling down the bluff. Making straight for the loaded boats, they filled them till they swamped and went all the way under, and those of the wounded too badly hurt to swim were swept away and drowned. A flatboat Colonel Baker had horsed out of a nearby canal, using it to get his guns across, was scrambled into until it was almost awash. The fugitives set out in this, but presently, live men ducking and dodging and shot men falling heavily on the gunwales, it capsized and thirty or forty were drowned. One skiff remained, a sheet-metal lifeboat, which soon was so riddled by bullets that it sank, and that left none.

It was dusk by now, the pearly gunsmoke turning blue, the pink stabs of muzzle-flashes deepening to scarlet as they stitched the lip of the bluff overhead. Marooned, many of the fugitives surrendered. A few removed their clothes and swam to safety across the bullet-lashed Potomac. Still others discovered a neck-deep ford leading over to Harrison's Island and got away in the darkness.

Confederate casualties were negligible, but Union losses approached 1000 — over 200 shot and more than 700 captured. Prominent men were among them, including a grandson of Paul Revere, a son of Oliver Wendell Holmes, and a nephew of James Russell Lowell. Most prominent of all, however, was the senator from Oregon, Edward D. Baker, called Ned by his friend the President. Back in Washington, Lincoln was at army headquarters while the telegraph clicked off news of the disaster. When the death of Ned Baker came over the wire, Lincoln sat for five minutes, stunned, then made his way unaccompanied through the anteroom, breast heaving, tears streaming down his cheeks. As he stepped out into the street he stumbled, groping blindly, and almost fell. Orderlies and newspapermen jumped to help him, but he recovered his balance and went on alone, leaving them the memory of a weeping President.

Thus Lincoln received the news, with sorrow and tears. Baker's fellow congressmen received it otherwise. Their breasts heaved, too, but with quite different emotions. Men who had squirmed with impatience at the army's over-cautiousness in coming to grips with the rebels now raged against a rashness which had snuffed out one of the Senate's brightest stars. Someone had blundered and blundered badly, and they were out to fix the blame, determined to revenge their martyred colleague. And their rage brought out of this clash on the bluff above the Potomac a new influence, a new force to shape the character of the conflict: the Joint Committee on the Conduct of the War. Senator Ben Wade of Ohio was its chairman, an all-out abolitionist with keen little jet-black eyes and bulldog flews, the upper lip overhanging the lower one at the corners of his mouth, a figure to frighten the disloyal or the inefficient or the merely unlucky. Congress was voting a million dollars a day for war expenses, and now they were out to get their money's worth, in the form of at least a share in its prosecution. "We must stir ourselves," Wade said, "on account of the expense."

Star Chamber-like, the committee's meeting room was in the Capitol basement, and here the military were summoned to answer accusations without being faced by their accusers or even being allowed to learn their names. General Stone was the first. It was Stone who had ordered Baker across the river; whatever had happened there was clearly his fault. He was suspect anyhow. Back in September he had issued general orders admonishing his men "not to incite and encourage insubordination among the colored servants in the neighborhood of the camps." That in itself was enough for Wade; but further investigation turned up

First Blood; New Conceptions

all sorts of things. There had been strange bonfires, mysterious messengers passing between the lines, and much else. Before long it became clear to the committee that Stone had sent those men across the river to get them butchered, probably after prearrangement with the enemy. He was called up, confronted with the evidence, such as it was — but not with the ones who gave it — and when he protested that he was the man who had guarded the capital through the dark week following Sumter ("I could have surrendered Washington," he reminded them) they were unimpressed. He was relieved of his command, placed in a cell at Fort Lafayette in New York harbor, and kept there under lock and key, an example to all who dared the wrath of the joint committee.

All this took time, a matter of months. The man they were really after was McClellan, who had Democratic leanings — it was true he had voted only once, but that once had been for Douglas — in addition to being a "soft war" man, with a concern for rebel property rights, including slaves. Beyond McClellan was Lincoln, who had some of the same attributes, and if they were not precisely after Lincoln's scalp — he had too many votes behind him for that — they intended at least to put some iron in his backbone. Stone was merely an opportunity that popped up, a chance to install the machine and test it, too, even as it was being installed. The trial run had worked out fine, with Stone lodged in a prison cell beyond the help of Lincoln or McClellan. Now they would pass on to bigger things. Ben Wade and his colleagues were out to make this fight a war to the knife, and Stone was their warning to anyone who might think otherwise.

McClellan was aware of this, of course, and was on guard. "I have a set of men to deal with unscrupulous and false," he told his wife. "If possible they will throw whatever blame there is on my shoulders, and I do not intend to be sacrificed by such people." It made him wary, coupled as it was with a belief that he was outnumbered by the enemy to his front. Ball's Bluff had reinforced that belief, and he felt a deep-down sadness.

"There is many a good fellow that wears the shoulder-straps going under the sod before this thing is over," he told Lincoln soon after they received word of Baker's death. Then he added, by way of consolation: "There is no loss too great to be repaired. If I should get knocked on the head, Mr President, you will put another man into my shoes."

"I want you to take care of yourself," Lincoln said.

Presently there was more cause than ever for him to want Little Mac to take care of himself. Within eleven days of the Ball's Bluff fiasco, General Scott having at last broken completely under the pointed snubs and contradictions, McClellan was given command of all the Union armies. The old Virginian's renewed application for retirement was accepted November 1. "Wherever I may spend my little remainder of life," he wrote, "my frequent and latest prayer will be, 'God save the

Union.'" The same day, McClellan was appointed to fill his place, in addition to remaining in command of the Washington army.

Lincoln was worried that the young general might feel overburdened by the increased responsibility. So that evening — while out in Missouri the captain disguised as a farmer was being held incommunicado, having delivered the order relieving Frémont — Lincoln went to McClellan's headquarters to see how he was bearing up.

He found him in high spirits, glad to be out from under the dead weight of General Scott. Lincoln was pleased to find him so, but he wondered whether McClellan was fully aware of how much he was undertaking. After expressing his pleasure that the change had been made, the President added: "I should be perfectly satisfied if I thought this vast increase of responsibility would not embarrass you."

"It is a great relief, sir!" McClellan answered. "I feel as if several tons were taken from my shoulders today. I am now in contact with you and the Secretary. I am not embarrassed by intervention."

"Well," Lincoln said, "draw on me for all the sense I have, and all the information." Still wondering, however, if McClellan was as aware of the weight that had been added as he was of the weight that had been taken away, he returned to the point: "In addition to your present command, the supreme command of the Army will entail a vast labor upon you."

"I can do it all," McClellan told him.

※ 3 ※

After a few hours' sleep the following night, McClellan and his staff got out of their beds at 4 o'clock in the morning, mounted their horses, and, accompanied by a squadron of cavalry, escorted General Scott to the railway station. It was rainy and pitch dark. On the depot platform the gaslight glittered blackly on the officers' rain-suits, so that they seemed clad in lacquered armor.

Touched by this show of respect, as well as by a general order McClellan had issued that day in his praise — "let us do nothing that can cause him to blush for us," it ended; "let no defeat of the army he has so long commanded embitter his last years, but let our victories illuminate the close of a life so grand" — the old warrior was cordial to the man who had made his final weeks in Washington a torment. He sent his regards to the young general's wife and baby, and added that his sensations were "very peculiar" on leaving active duty. Then, the clank of sabers and chink of spur-chains somewhat muffled under the rubberized suits, he received his goodbye salute and boarded the train, which then pulled out.

McClellan returned to his quarters and his bed. Rising for the second time that morning, he found his mind so impressed by the farewell at the depot a few hours ago that he took time to describe it in a letter to his wife. After forwarding Scott's greetings to her and the new baby, he philosophized on what he had seen: "The sight of this morning was a lesson to me which I hope not soon to forget. I saw there the end of a long, active, and industrious life, the end of the career of the first soldier of his nation; and it was a feeble old man scarce able to walk; hardly anyone there to see him off but his successor. Should I ever become vainglorious and ambitious, remind me of that spectacle."

The old soldier had faded away — had gone, in fact, to live for a time at Delmonico's in New York, where he could get his fill of terrapin; "the best food vouchsafed by Providence to man," he called it, admiring a steaming forkful held six inches above his plate. Yet he had left a great deal more behind him than the memory of that final scene from which his young successor drew a moral. In the '40s, commanding in Mexico, he had conducted, on a live-ammunition training ground, a postgraduate course in the art of war for officers who, having fought against Mexicans, would find a broader scope for their talents when they fought against each other in the '60s. Landing at Vera Cruz, outflanking Cerro Gordo, cutting loose from his base in hostile country to reduce Chapultepec and occupy Mexico City, he had established models for operations that would be repeated, time and again, on a larger scale, so that to list the men who received their baptism of fire under his direction was practically to call the roll of army commanders and generals-in-chief, both North and South, in the war that was building toward a climax at the time of his retirement. All this was much, but he had done still more. He had provided a plan for total war: Scott's Anaconda.

As a Virginian, older than the capital he was defending, he believed he knew the temper of the people across the Potomac and the Ohio. Their love for the Union was as deep as his own, he believed, and in time — provided they could be made to feel the dull reality of war against a more powerful opponent, without being pricked in their hot-blooded pride by the bayonets of a penetrating army — they would see the error of their angry choice and renounce the men who had led them into a wilderness, away from the direction in which their devotion and true interests lay. Out of this belief he evolved his plan, though what was called an anaconda might better have been described as a water serpent.

All down the eastern seaboard, from Chesapeake Bay to the Florida Keys, thence along the shores of the Gulf, counter-clockwise from the Keys to Matamoros, he would establish a deep-water naval blockade to wall the Confederacy off from Europe and whatever aid might come from that direction. Meanwhile, down the length of the Mississippi, from Cairo past New Orleans, he would send an army of 60,000 "rough-vigor fellows" backed by gunboats, thus cutting the

Southerners off from the cattle and cereals of Texas, as well as from such foreign help as might be forwarded through the neutral ports of Mexico. Having seized all this he would hold on tight, neither advancing nor yielding ground, and within those constricting coils the South would become in very fact a political and economic wilderness, the awful hug of the serpent producing results which bursting shells and prodding bayonets could never bring about. The flame of rebellion, so difficult to stamp out — as an experienced military leader, Scott was thoroughly aware of all the problems of subduing a hostile and determined people — would die from lack of fuel or be smothered by sheer boredom. Unionist sentiment, unprovoked, would reassert itself. The people would come to their senses and force their hot-headed wrong-minded leaders to sue for peace and readmission to the Union, which they never should have left.

Such was Scott's Anaconda. From the outset, it came in for a considerable measure of ridicule — especially from cartoonists, who confused the metaphor by sketching the old general in a turban, sitting cross-legged as he tried to charm the southern cobra with a flute — as well as violent opposition from such spokesmen as Senator-Colonel Baker, who demanded bold and forward war and would not see that either of these adjectives could be applied to the so-called anaconda plan. Also it was believed to have overrated Unionist sentiment in the South, though whether this was so or not was presently removed to the realm of conjecture; McDowell's march on Manassas, which Scott opposed, applied the goad which the plan would have avoided. It certainly ran against the grain of McClellan's expressed intention to "crush the rebels in one campaign" by an overland march on Richmond. Yet in other respects, of all the plans evolved by many men, right up to the end, it was the first to recognize and utilize the North's tremendous advantage of numbers and material, and it was the first to emphasize the importance of the Mississippi Valley in an over-all view of the war.

Lincoln, at any rate, welcomed it, studied it, and acted on those parts of it which seemed to him most feasible at that stage of the contest. On April 19 — the day the 6th Massachusetts was mobbed in Baltimore and the Friday after the Friday whose dawn saw Sumter under fire in Charleston harbor — he proclaimed a blockade of the southern coast. Proclaiming and enforcing were two different things, however, especially considering the size of the fleet charged with transferring the blockade from dry paper to salt water. At that date the Union navy, scattered over the seven seas, included 42 ships, 555 guns, and 7600 sailors, and though by the end of the year this had been consolidated and increased to 264 ships, 2557 guns, and 22,000 sailors, the magnitude of the task ahead made a navy of almost any size seem small.

The anaconda was required to hug a circumference of about five thousand miles, two-fifths dry land and rivers and the remaining three-fifths shoreline. This 3000-mile coastal portion, belly and crotch of the continent, bisected by the phallic droop of the Florida peninsula, was doubled along much of its length, both in the Atlantic and the Gulf, by intricate mazes of sandbars, lagoons, and outlying islands, which, though less forbidding at first glance than the rocky shores of New England, were obviously at second glance much harder to patrol. Nassau and Havana were less than 700 miles, respectively, from Charleston and New Orleans, while Bermuda was but slightly farther from Wilmington. Such good harbors were few, but each had many entrances and outlets. It would be a slow ship, conned by a clumsy skipper indeed, that could not come and go by the dark of the moon, undetected in making its run to or from the safety of those neutral ports.

Knowing all this, Southerners laughed at the anaconda, much as the northern cartoonists were doing, especially that portion of it covered by the blockade proclamation, and predicted — quite accurately, as it turned out — that when Yankee sailors began patrolling the swampy littoral they would discover that even the mosquitoes had enlisted in the resistance. Besides, there was an economic consideration beyond all this, by which the blockade might be reckoned a positive good from the southern point of view, a reinforcement of one of the most powerful weapons in the Confederate arsenal. Cotton, the raw material of Great Britain's second leading industry, as well as the answer to France's feverish quest for prosperity, was the white gold key that would unlock and swing ajar the door through which foreign intervention would come marching. Remembering the effectiveness of Jefferson's embargo on tobacco, of which the Colonies had not controlled the world supply, the South could expect much greater results from an embargo on cotton, on which she held a world monopoly. Going without tobacco had been unpleasant for Europeans, but they would find it downright impossible to manage without cotton. Unfortunately, there had been a bumper crop the year before; French and English warehouses were bulging with the surplus. But that only lengthened the time factor. When the reserve dwindled and the white stream that fed the jennies and looms and the workers who tended them was shut off, Europe would come knocking at Jefferson Davis' door, offering recognition and the goods of war, the might of the British navy and the use of armies that had blasted Napoleon himself clean off the pages of military history. For all these reasons the South could laugh at and even welcome the proposed blockade, which would strengthen one of her strongest weapons in ratio to its own effectiveness. There was much that was amusing, too, in the contemplation of northern ships patrolling the southern coast to inforce a southern embargo. Few sailors and no ships at all had come over voluntarily to the Confederate side when the nation split in two.

Now, belatedly and paradoxically, they would cross over, under orders from their own Commander in Chief.

At the outset the Confederate government, having almost no regular navy, determined to create an irregular one which would function while the other was being built. The Declaration of Paris, an agreement between the European powers five years back, had defined privateering as illegal; but the United States, remembering the success of independent Yankee vessels against the British merchant marine in the War of 1812 — and not knowing, moreover, when she might be engaged in such a war again — had refused to sign the document. So now the Richmond Congress, recalling such successes, too, authorized the issue of letters of marque to the captains of whatever ships might apply. It was characteristic of the current southern opinion of northern morals that they expected many such applications to come from New England skippers attracted by a chance at easy dollars.

These were not forthcoming, but before long about twenty vessels were on the high seas, privateering in the American tradition. Lincoln declared them outright pirates and announced that the crews would be treated as such when captured, with hanging as the penalty after conviction in the courts. Davis, never the man to decline a challenge of any sort, replied that for every Confederate sailor so hanged he would hang a Union soldier of corresponding rank, chosen by lot from among the thousands of prisoners in the Richmond tobacco warehouse.

Thus it stood, threat countering threat, until presently the world was given what appeared to be a chance to see which President had the courage of his convictions. The privateer *Savannah* was taken in June, its crew lodged in a common jail awaiting trial for piracy. Despite the clamor throughout the North in favor of dancing the defendants at a rope end, when the trial was held the New York jury could not agree on a verdict, and thus the crisis passed. Later in the year, however, when the privateer *Jeff Davis* was taken, the crew brought to trial in Philadelphia, convicted of piracy and sentenced to be hanged, Lincoln showed every sign of going ahead: whereupon Davis reinforced his counterthreat by causing lots to be drawn among the Union prisoners. The short-straw men — including that grandson of Paul Revere, captured at Ball's Bluff — were placed in condemned cells to await the action of Abraham Lincoln in reviewing the sentence of the men condemned to death in the City of Brotherly Love.

Lincoln paused and considered; and having reconsidered, he backed down. Though he thus exposed himself to charges of indecision and cowardice, declining to engage in a hanging match with Jefferson Davis, he saved the lives of Union soldiers and Confederate sailors — Americans both — and thereby saved the nation a blot on its record. North and South, however, many persons saw only that Davis had taken the measure of his opponent.

First Blood; New Conceptions [115]

Whatever apparent moral advantage the Confederates gained from this clash of presidential wills, they soon found their bloodless victory offset by three sudden hammer blows struck by the Federal navy — two on the Atlantic coast and one in the Gulf of Mexico: Cape Hatteras and Port Royal, off North and South Carolina, and Ship Island, near New Orleans.

These objectives were the choice of a joint three-man strategy board composed of Army, Navy, and Coast Survey officers appointed to make "a thorough investigation of the coast and harbors, their access and defenses." The fleet was far too small for the enormous job of patrolling the 189 harbor and river openings along the 3549 miles of shoreline between the Potomac and the Rio Grande, and what there was of it was badly in need of ports of refuge, especially along the stormy South Atlantic. Out of this double necessity the blockade gained a new dimension, one in which the army would have a share. Not only could harbor entrances be patrolled; the harbors themselves might be seized, thus reducing the number of points to be guarded and at the same time freeing ships for duty elsewhere. Now, as the summer of the opening year of the war merged into the drawn-out southern fall, it was the task of the strategy board, with its three-headed knowledge of "the coast and harbors, their access and defenses," to select likely targets for the proposed amphibious operations.

The first was modest in scope but effective in execution. Off North Carolina the wide shallows of Pamlico and Albemarle Sounds, inclosed by a barrier of islands and reefs, afforded an ideal anchorage for raiders and blockade runners. Here if anywhere was the place at which the board should point its finger. Off that stormy cape the sea was frequently too rough for a fleet to be able to keep station. The only way to block it was to take it. At Hatteras Inlet, the break in the barrier, the Confederates had built two forts on opposite sides of the passage, Clark and Hatteras. Whoever held these forts held Pamlico Sound, and on August 26 an expedition of fourteen vessels under Flag Officer Silas H. Stringham sailed from Hampton Roads to take them. Among the ships were four transports carrying 860 men under Ben Butler, who thus was given a chance to redeem his blunders at Big Bethel.

This he did, and easily, for the army had almost nothing to do. Stringham, with superior ordinance, stood just outside the range of the rebel guns and for two days threw shells into the forts at will, suffering no hurt himself. Butler's men, put ashore well north of the forts — 300 of them, anyhow; for the surf staved in the landing-boats by the time that many got ashore — marched down the island, wet and hungry, their ammunition ruined by the surf, and arrived in time to watch their general share with Stringham the honor of receiving the surrender of Fort Hatteras, Fort Clark having run up its white flag the day before. Most of the soldiers and three of the ships were left to hold what had been won, while the rest returned to Fortress Monroe with their 615 prisoners. The navy had taken its first Confederate stronghold, and in doing so had reduced its blockade task.

The second offensive operation, down in the Gulf in mid-September, was even simpler, requiring not even the token assistance of troops. Here the lower delta of the many-mouthed Mississippi posed a problem much like Hatteras, with raiders and blockade runners entering and leaving the great port of New Orleans almost at will. Though the threat of storms was not as constant, a tropical hurricane was something a man had to see to believe, and sandbars lurked as dangerous as reefs. All in all, the strategy board perceived that here, too, the only way to block the port effectively was to seize it. The navy was by no means prepared to undertake such an assignment just yet, but the board believed it was ready to make a beginning. Ship Island, off the Mississippi coast, would provide an excellent station for patrolling the eastern delta outlets and the passes down out of Lake Pontchartrain, as well as an ideal base from which to launch the attack on New Orleans itself, if and when the opportunity came. So the board instructed the navy: Take it. And the navy did, together with its uncompleted fortifications, before the Confederates were prepared to fire a shot in its defense. Thus the Union secured its second foothold along the secession coast.

The third and final operation of the year was far more ambitious than the others, neither of which had given the fleet the large, deep-water harbor it needed in order to maintain a year-round blockade of such busy ports as Wilmington, Charleston, and Savannah. About one-third of the way up the palmetto-studded hundred miles of South Carolina littoral lying between the latter two cities, the strategy board found what it was seeking. Port Royal, the finest natural harbor on the southern coast, would float the navies of the world. Obviously, however, though they had no real need for it themselves, having almost no navy, the Confederates were thoroughly aware of what covetous eyes the Union navy was casting in that direction. If it was to be undertaken, the job must be done in strength, after preparation in great secrecy. Both were provided for; the board took no chances it could avoid. The naval member himself, Captain Samuel F. Du Pont, was appointed to head the expedition of 74 vessels, including transports for a land force of 12,000 men. In late October, sailing under sealed orders, this fleet put out from Hampton Roads, considerable pains having been taken to conceal its destination.

Almost at once, Du Pont was struck a double blow by fate — in the form of Confederate intelligence and the weather. He not only lost the advantages of secrecy; he came close to losing his fleet as well. On the day he put out, the Richmond government alerted its coastal defenses, giving warning that the force had sailed. Three days later, November 1, the defenders of the fleet's objective received a specific telegram: "The enemy's expedition is intended for Port Royal." On the same day, the fleet ran into a gale off Hatteras. The wind approaching hurricane strength, two of the ships went down and the crew of a third had to heave her guns into the sea to keep from foundering. By dawn of the following day, November 2, the fleet was so scattered that Du Pont could sight but one sail from the deck of his flagship, the *Wabash*. He continued southward, however, and in clear weather two days later dropped anchor off the bar at Port Royal. Twenty-five of his ships had rejoined by then, together with reinforcements from the Charleston squadron, and others kept bobbing up along the horizon. He spent another two days replacing the rebel-destroyed channel markers, crossing the bar — a dangerous business for the deep-draft *Wabash* — completing his attack plan, and finally holding a conference at which he outlined for his captains the order of battle. At last he was ready, and at 8 o'clock the following morning, November 7, the attack got under way.

He knew what his wooden ships would encounter. At the entrance to Port Royal Sound the enemy held Fort Beauregard, mounting 20 guns on Bay Point to the north, and Fort Walker, mounting 23 guns on Hilton Head to the south. Less than three miles apart, both of these forts were strongly built, their gunners alerted for a week, awaiting the opportunity Du Pont was about to offer them. Somewhere beyond them, too, was a Confederate flotilla of three tugs, mounting one gun each, and a converted river steamer under Commodore Josiah Tattnall, whom Du Pont knew to be a bold and capable officer, having messed with him in what was already known as "the old navy." The forts were Du Pont's main concern, however, and in attempting their reduction he would have no help from the three brigades of soldiers in the transports. Not only were these landsmen still somewhat green about the gills as a result of their experience off Hatteras, but in that storm, along with much else, they had lost nearly all their landing craft. It was to be a job for the naval force alone. In fact, Du Pont preferred it so. The most he would ask of the army was that it stand by to help pick up the pieces.

To accomplish the double reduction he had evolved a novel plan of attack, an order of battle which divided his fighting force into a main squadron of nine of the heaviest frigates and sloops, ranged in line ahead, and a flanking squadron of five gunboats. They would enter the sound in parallel columns, the lighter squadron ranged to starboard, and pass midway between the forts, receiving and returning the fire of both. At a point about two miles beyond the entrance, the main force was to round by the south and come back west, moving slowly past Fort Walker, maintaining the heaviest possible fire, then round to the north and head back east, slowing again as it passed Fort Beauregard.

The flanking squadron, meanwhile, was to peel off and engage the Confederate flotilla or whatever targets of opportunity the rebels might afford, while the main force kept both forts under fire, widening the elliptical attack so as to bring its guns in closer on every turn.

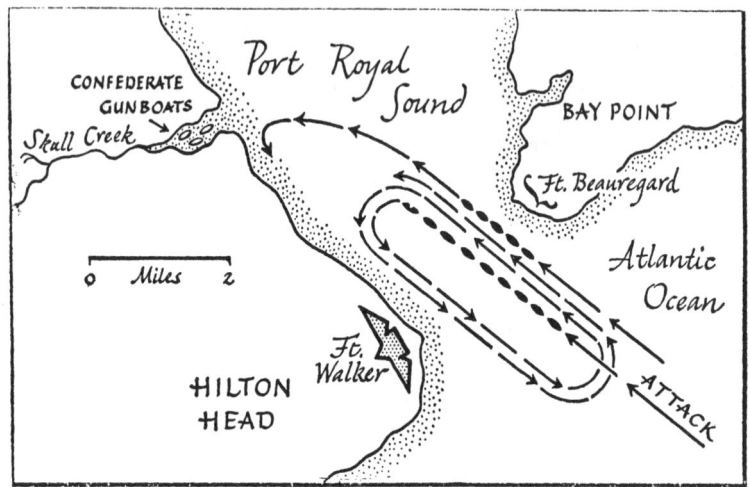

And so it was. At the signal from the commander on the *Wabash*, leading the way across the sunlit water, the fleet steamed forward, two columns in close order. A flash and a roar shot out from Fort Walker, echoed at once by Beauregard. The ships took up the challenge and the fight was on. As they neared the turning point, Tattnall brought his four makeshift warships down the sound, and from a raking position let go several broadsides at the *Wabash* as soon as she came within range. The gunboats gave him their attention then; whereupon the Confederate, with fourteen Union men-of-war to his immediate front, discreetly came about and made a swift, flat-bottomed retreat up Skull Creek, three miles northwest of the fort on Hilton Head. He was out of the fight for good, bottled up by the gunboats, which took station off the creek mouth. According to a Savannah newspaper published five days later, Tattnall dipped his pennant three times in jaunty salute to his old messmate, "regretting his inability to return the highflown compliments of Flag Officer Du Pont in a more satisfactory manner."

By then the Federal captain was busy elsewhere, with little time for compliments, highflown or otherwise. As the main column turned south, beginning its first eastward run, each ship opened with its forward pivot against Fort Walker's northern flank, which Du Pont had learned from reconnaissance was its weakest. The cannon being lodged on the parapet — which, if it increased their range, also increased their vulnerability — several were violently dismounted, others lost their crews, and the gunners, taken thus by enfilade from a direction in which they had not expected to fight, were dismayed. A British correspondent on one of the Union ships saw tall columns of dust spring up from the fort to mark the hits the fleet was scoring, and it looked to him "as if we had suddenly raised from the dust a grove of poplars."

Not that the rebel gunnery had been very effective in the first place. The enemy ships, moving along their elliptical course, with constant changes in speed, range, and deflection, were extremely hard to hit. What was more, the defenders had not wasted their scant powder on anything as unprofitable as target practice, and now that it came to bloody work they found that many of the shells would not fit, the powder was inferior, and the crews became exhausted within an hour of opening fire. All of which, sad as it was in Confederate eyes, was really quite beside the point. Fort Walker — to which Fort Beauregard, across the water, was merely adjunct — had been built to be defended only from dead ahead, against a force moving straight in from the sea. When this became apparent, it became apparent, too, that the fight had been lost from the moment Du Pont conceived his plan of attack. The only conditions left to be satisfied were those of honor.

Erratic or deadly, the firing continued, and as the main squadron steamed slowly past Fort Walker, delivering broadsides at point-blank range, the flanking squadron, maintaining its watch over the mouth of the creek up which Tattnall had retreated, added the weight of its guns to the pressure against the vulnerable northern flank, its shells bowling down the line of metal on the parapet. Assailed from both directions by naval crews who worked with coolness and precision — more guns were dismounted; more men fell — the defenders fired even more wildly. The main squadron completed its first pass, closing upon Fort Beauregard, then swept down and around again, coming within less than 600 yards of the fort on Hilton Head, which had but three guns left in working order by the time the ships completed their second run. The *Wabash* was just rounding to the south, leading the way into a third ellipse, when Du Pont received a message that Fort Walker had been abandoned. At 2.20 a naval landing party raised the Union flag above ramparts that were pocked and battered, strewn with wreckage left by men who would not sweat to keep from bleeding, and then had wound up doing both at once. Army transports now put in. By nightfall, troops had occupied the works. Across the way, Fort Beauregard hauled down its flag at sunset, and early next morning the troops crossed over and occupied it too.

The victory was complete, and by it the Federal navy gained an excellent harbor in the very heart-land of secession. Nor was that all. Within the next three days the victors moved up the rivers and inlets and occupied the colonial towns of Beaufort and Port Royal, bringing under their control some of the finest old plantations in the South and thereby affording an opportunity not to be neglected by their abolitionist brethren, who presently arrived and began conducting uplift experiments among the Negro fieldhands. The battle itself had not been without its romantic aspect, for one of the defenders had been Brigadier General Thomas F. Drayton, C.S.A., whose brother, Captain Percival Drayton, U.S.N., commanded one of the attacking frigates; the South Carolina island for which they fought had been their boyhood home.

Satisfying as all this was to supporters of the Union — the loyal brother having won, Federal guns and Federal notions were now in operation within fifty airline miles of Charleston, where secession had had its birth eleven months before — there emerged from the battle another fact which had, for those who understood its implications, more weight than all the other facts combined, heart-warming and romantic though they were. Against stiffer resistance, this third hammer blow had been even more successful than the other two, and nowhere had the fleet failed to seize any objective assigned by the strategy board. Some standard theories were going to have to be revised: the belief that one gun on land was equal to four on water, for example. Steam had changed all that, removing the restrictions of wind and current, and making possible such maneuvers as Du Pont's expanding ellipse. From now on, apparently, the board had only to select its targets, concentrate the might of the fleet, and blast them into submission. Naval power was going to be a dominant factor in this war.

✗ 4 ✗

Coming as it did in the wake of defeats along Bull Run and Wilson's Creek, near opposite ends of the thousand-mile-long fighting line, this triple victory hammered out by the Federal navy did much to revive the flagging martial spirit of the North. There was no corresponding depression in the South, however, the odds in all three of these naval engagements having been too one-sided to give much cause for doubting the proved superiority of Confederate arms. It had been more or less obvious all along that the enemy could concentrate and strike with superior force at almost any point along the perimeter; that had been one of the conditions accepted by Davis when he chose the strategic defensive. When the pressure elsewhere was relieved, when the advantage shifted so that the South would be doing the concentrating and striking, the world would find out whether the North would be able to hold what it had won. Yet now, since that policy involved the dispersal of force to meet attacks from all directions, as the drawn-out fall wore on and the year was rounding toward a close, Southerners began to discover the price they would have to pay, in the hard cash of lost chances, for the advantages that accrued to the defensive.

In late September, after Hatteras and Ship Island had been lost and a third such operation was probably already into the planning stage, Davis went up to Fairfax Courthouse for a conference with the victors of Manassas. While the blasted oaks on the battlefield to their rear turned red in the fine clear weather of early fall, the men who had won that battle lay idle, watching the blue-clad host to their front grow stronger every day. At this stage, Federal troops were joining at the rate of 40,000 a month — about the total effective strength of Johnston's army. Pinkerton, with his tabulated lists compiled by operatives in Richmond, had misled his employer badly. Yet McClellan had been right in his fears that he might be brought to battle before his soldiers were ready: Beauregard was planning an offensive.

Though volunteering had fallen off to such an extent that the men arriving barely replaced those lost by the expiration of short-term enlistments and a liberal granting of furloughs, and though the army was crippled by a shortage of arms and supplies — food as well as munitions — he believed that the northern army, still in something of a state of shock from the whipping it had taken two months back, had perhaps now merely reached that stage of crystallization at which a smartly administered rap would cause it to fly apart again. In reply to the Federal threat to divide and conquer the South by a descent of the Mississippi, Beauregard wanted to make a sudden thrust across the Potomac and divide the Union, east and west, by seizing the strip of territory lying between Pittsburgh and Lake Erie. When the Yankee army came out from behind its Washington intrenchments he would administer the rap that would accomplish its disintegration, then go about his business of division and conquest. The odds were long, he admitted, but they were shorter than they were likely to be at any time hereafter, especially if the Confederates remained passive and continued to allow the growing enemy host time in which to regain its confidence.

Such was his plan, and as Davis listened to it on the first day of October, closeted with the generals at their Fairfax headquarters, within twenty miles of Washington itself, Beauregard expounding and Johnston nodding approval, he could see its advantages, in spite of its abrogation of his claim that "all we ask is to be let alone." Then came the rub. Beauregard declared that he would undertake the movement with 50,000 men, while Johnston held out for 60,000; which meant that Davis would have the problem of finding 10- to 20,000 reinforcements for the invasion.

The Federal navy, having launched its first two amphibious operations, now was preparing a third, whose objective could only be guessed at. Every general in every department along the Atlantic and the Gulf —

and, what was worse, every governor of every state that touched salt water; which included all but two of the eleven — not only believed that the blow would be struck, but was convinced that it would be aimed straight at him. They were calling loudly for help, and Davis could foresee the clamor that would follow any request that they forward troops to fatten the army now lying idle in northern Virginia. And with good cause; for in practically every case the political clamor would be followed by a military disaster. Down in North Carolina, for example, the loss of Hatteras had exposed New Bern, and the loss of New Bern would mean the loss of the Weldon railroad, the only supply line between Richmond and the South Atlantic states. Without that line the Virginia army not only could not hope to mount an invasion, it could not even be maintained in its present position beyond ten days. On the Gulf the situation was almost as critical. The army being assembled and drilled at Pensacola might be considered available, but the recent seizure of Ship Island had exposed the nation's tender underbelly to assault, and that army was all that stood in a position to blunt the point of such a stab. Wherever Davis looked, the situation was such that to strip one area for the removal of troops to another would be to exchange possible success for probable disaster.

Beauregard urged in vain that the length of the odds was an argument for, not against, the risk; that desperate men must take desperate chances, and that whatever was lost in the interim could be retaken after a victory on northern soil. Davis shook his head. No reinforcements could be sent, he said, without "a total disregard for the safety of other threatened positions."

The Creole could only shrug, while Johnston sat resigned, not being exactly a forward, cut-and-slash sort of commander in the first place. That ended all talk of a fall offensive, either along the Virginia line or elsewhere. For this year at least, the nation was committed to the dispersed defensive, and Davis took the cars back to Richmond.

He had troubles enough to vex him there, what with the day-to-day frets of office, the long nights rendered sleepless by neuralgia, and the fire-eaters shouting angrily that he had no policy that could even hinder, let alone halt, the southward crunch of the gigantic war machine the North was building unmolested. The cabinet he had assembled with such concern for political expediency had already begun to come apart at the seams. The brilliant and unpredictable Toombs, after hesitating to recommend the firing of the opening shot at Sumter, had bridled, once the shot had been fired, at being desk-bound while other men were learning the glad companionship of service in the field. On the day of Manassas, the issue being still in doubt in Richmond, where all that was known was that the guns were booming, he could abide it no longer. He submitted his resignation, as of that day, and left his post as head of the State Department to enter the army as a Georgia brigadier. Within another two months War Secretary Leroy P. Walker had done likewise, though for quite different reasons. Instead of feeling left out or insufficiently employed, the Alabamian had been employed beyond his capabilities, and he knew it. Swamped with work, trussed up in yards of red tape, he too departed for the field, where a man had only the comparatively simple frets of being killed or mangled. They would be missed, especially Toombs, but their going gave Davis a double — or in fact, as he worked it out, a triple — opportunity.

As Attorney General, Judah P. Benjamin was largely wasting his talents, since the Justice Department no more had courts than the Postal Department, in the early months, had stamps. The War Office, which Walker had left in such a snarl, seemed the perfect field for Benjamin's administrative abilities. Accordingly, Davis shifted him there. This still left two vacancies, and in filling them the President corrected another shortcoming. The all-important border states had come into the Confederacy in April, and all this time had been without representation in the cabinet, there having been no vacancy. Now that there were two such, Davis filled them with men of distinction from Virginia and North Carolina: Robert M. T. Hunter of the former and Thomas Bragg of the latter. The Virginian went in as head of the State Department and the North Carolinian was given Benjamin's post as Attorney General. How Davis would get along with them remained to be seen. Like most of the old cabinet members, neither of the new ones had been intimate friends of his in private life before the war; nor were they now.

At any rate he had his family with him, established at last in what was called the White House of the Confederacy, not because it was white (it wasn't; it was gray) but because the President's residence had been called that under the old flag: a handsome, high-ceilinged mansion on the brow of a hill at the eastern end of Clay Street, with a garden to the rear, downhill, shaded by poplars and sycamores and the horse-chestnuts his wife loved. Though the Virginia ladies looked askance and called her "a western belle" behind their fans, Mrs Davis, already heavy with the child she had conceived in Montgomery and would bear in Richmond in December, assumed her social duties with grace and charm. She was a credit to her position and a comfort to her husband. Yet even with her there to minister to his mental and bodily ills, the long hours and the constant strain were telling on his health and on his temper, both highly frangible in the first place.

Twenty years of public life had not thickened his skin against the pricks of criticism, and the past seven months had even thinned it. At times he was like a flayed man in a sandstorm. His wife could overlook the sidelong glances of the FFVs, but to Davis any facial tic of disagreement became at once a frown of disapproval. He had lost none of the gracious manner by which he could charm an opponent into glad agreement, yet now he scorned to employ it, and turned snappishly upon any man who crossed him. Smarting under the goads of office, he fell out with whoever did not yield to him in all things, and any difference was immediately made personal.

It had been thus even in the case of the two generals he had counseled with at Fairfax. Though nothing in their words or manner had shown this at the conference itself — all three being gentlemen and patriots who, in any given situation for which they had had time to steel their tempers, could place the national good above personal bias — Davis had shared a sort of running quarrel-by-courier with both of the ranking heroes of Manassas. Beauregard with his bloodhound eyes and swarthy complexion, his hair brushed forward at the temples, Napoleonic in aspect and conception, eager for glory, Gallic and expansive, and Johnston with his prim, high-colored, wedge-shaped face, his balding head, his gray-shot sideburns and goatee, Virginia-proud, Virginia-genial when he wanted to be, cunctative as Fabius Maximus yet jaunty as a gamecock: these two had known the quick wrath and the withering scorn of the intellectual Davis in dispatches that were alternately hot or icy, but which in either case, when designed to sting, performed that function all too well. Gone was the glad comradeship they had shared on the field of Manassas, born of relief and exultation in that July twilight while the Union flood ran backward up the roads to Washington. Since then, both men had fallen from presidential favor.

Beauregard fell first. The man who had shown much modesty on his arrival at Richmond, with the laurels of Sumter still green on his brow, became a different man entirely when he took up his pen in the seclusion of his tent. After Manassas, talk had grown rife that the President had prevented any pursuit of the routed enemy: so rife, indeed, that Davis took the unusual step of asking his generals to deny the rumor officially. This Beauregard was glad to do, and promptly. But in his report on the battle, which unfortunately got to the newspapers before it reached the presidential desk, he reverted to his original scheme for combining the armies to crush the Union forces in detail — the plan which had been outlined by one of his aides at the first Confederate war council, held at the Spotswood a week before the battle — with the implication that its having been rejected was the reason why the southern army was not in the northern capital now.

Davis would not let this pass. "With much surprise, I found that the newspaper statements were sustained by the text of your report," he wrote, and took the general to task. His last letter to the Louisianian had begun "My dear General" and ended "Very truly, your friend." This one opened with a frigid "Sir" and closed with an ambiguous "Very respectfully, yours &c."

The breach widened as the general's friends took up the cudgel. At last, in early November, Beauregard himself aired the grievance in a letter to the Richmond *Whig*. Headed "within hearing of the enemy's guns," it referred to the "unfortunate controversy now going on," and said in part: "I entreat my friends not to trouble themselves about refuting the slanders and calumnies aimed at me.... If certain minds cannot understand the difference between *patriotism*, the highest civic virtue, and *office-seeking*, the lowest civic occupation, I pity them from the bottom of my heart." However, the reaction was quite different from what he had anticipated. In reference to the "unique" heading, for example, a rival paper asked: "Are we expected to give special credit to the general's lucubrations by reason of a fact certainly not very unusual in military operations?" The public, too, was disenchanted; a star had lost its luster. If Davis himself had chosen the words and directed the actions, the general could not have played more neatly into his hands.

The Creole was unhappy anyhow. He felt cramped, no more than a supernumerary, now that his army was merely a corps in Johnston's command. Practically overnight his dark hair was shot with gray: a phenomenon for which the different factions offered different explanations. Friends said that this was the result of overwork and heavy responsibility. Others attributed it to the blockade, which had cut him off from accustomed shipments of French hair dye. Whatever caused his graying, before the end of the year it was plain that he would have to go. Davis was considering sending him West, where he would find problems of such complexity that even his active mind would be kept busy and there would be ample opportunity for him to exercise his talents, both with the sword and the pen.

Trouble with Johnston had begun even sooner — all the way back in their West Point days, some said, when he and Davis were alleged to have had a fist fight over the favors of Benny Haven's daughter. Johnston won both the fight and the girl, rumor added; which might or might not have been true. At any rate, whatever had gone before, anger flared in considerable heat soon after the last day of August, when Davis forwarded to the Senate the names of five men to be given the rank of full general, lately provided for by law. The Senate confirmed them promptly, and in the order proposed. Adjutant-General Samuel Cooper headed the list, a sixty-six-year-old New Yorker who had married South and crossed over from the old army, in which he had held the same position. Next came Albert Sidney Johnston, still on the way from California after resigning his U.S. commission, a Kentucky-born Texan whom Davis and many others considered the first soldier of the Confederacy. Third was Robert E. Lee, mobilizer and former commander of all the Virginia forces, now campaigning in the

Alleghenies, charged with regaining what had been lost out there. Near the bottom of the list came Joseph E. Johnston himself, followed only by P. G. T. Beauregard, who came fifth.

When notice of these promotions reached Johnston he was outraged in his sense of equity and wounded in his pride. In the old army he had outranked them all, having been appointed Quartermaster-General, with a staff commission as a brigadier, while they were only colonels. He saw no justice in Davis' assumption that seniority for line command must be based exclusively on line service, in which both Lee and the other Johnston had held their commissions. All he saw was that he had been passed over.

Accordingly, while his wrath still smoked, he sat down and wrote a six-page letter of protest addressed to Jefferson Davis as the author of his woes. After expressing his "surprise and mortification," he wrote: "I now and here declare my claims, that notwithstanding these nominations by the President and their confirmation by Congress I still rightfully hold the rank of first general of the Armies of the Southern Confederacy." The order of names on the list, he added, "seeks to tarnish my fair fame as a soldier and a man, earned by more than thirty years of laborious and perilous service. I had but this, the scars of many wounds, all honorably taken in my front and in the front of battle, and my father's Revolutionary sword. It was delivered to me from his venerated hand, without a stain of dishonor. Its blade is still unblemished as when it passed from his hand to mine"; and much else, in much the same vein of outraged virtue. He waited two days before sending it. Then, finding his anger still uncooled, and remaining convinced of the trenchancy of his arguments and the fitness of the words he had used to advance them, he forwarded the letter unrevised.

Davis read it with a wrath that quickly rose to match the sender's. This Virginian, rattling his father's sword between lines that spoke of his "fair fame" and his wounded front, outdid even Beauregard. In composing his reply, however, Davis employed not a foil but a cutlass. Rejecting the nimble parry and riposte of rhetoric and logic, at both of which he was a master, he delivered instead one quick slash of scorn:

> Sir: I have just received and read your letter of the 12th instant. Its language is, as you say, unusual; its arguments and statements utterly one sided, and its insinuations as unfounded as they are unbecoming.
> I am, &c.
>
> Jeff'n Davis.

Knowing Johnston he knew the effect this letter would have. He knew that it would never be forgotten or forgiven and that it must necessarily underlie a relationship involving the fortune, if not the very being, of their new nation. In writing and sending this reply it was therefore as if he deliberately threw off-center a vital gear in a machine which had been delivered into his care and was his whole concern. Yet his reasons, his motivations, were basic. Loving his country he was willing to give it all he owned, including his life; but he would not sacrifice his prerogative or his pride, since in his mind that would have been to sacrifice not only his life but his existence. There was a difference. It was not only that he would not. He could not. Without his prerogative, he would not be President; without his pride, he would not even be Davis.

Men interpreted him as they saw him, and for the most part they considered him argumentative in the extreme, irascible, and a seeker after discord. A Richmond editor later wrote, for all to read, that Davis was "ready for any quarrel with any and everybody, at any time and all times; and the suspicion goes that rather than not have a row on hand with the enemy, he would make one with the best friend he had on earth."

Since Davis seldom chose to explain his actions — such explanations not fitting his conception of the dignity of his office — all too often the editor's charge seemed true. It appeared to be quite literally true in one case which came up about this time. He received from a general in the field a confidential report that a subordinate must be dismissed. This officer was an old friend of Davis', and when he received the presidential order of dismissal he came to Richmond to plead his case before the man who had signed it. "You know me," he said. "How could I ever hold my head up under the implied censure from you, my old friend?" Davis would give him no explanation. Choosing rather to alienate a friend than to betray a confidence, or even infer that there was a confidence he could not betray, he told him: "You have, I believe, your orders. I can suggest nothing but obedience." And neither the friend nor the editor, nor for that matter the parlor gossips in Richmond, ever learned why this was done; nor that Davis came home that evening, suffering from the dyspepsia which was with him a symptom of nervous upset, and went to his room without eating.

In this dark autumn, while Beauregard and Johnston chafed and politicians grew bitter at having to accept disproof of their prediction that the war would be a ninety-day excursion, Davis was disappointed by another general from whom he had expected much. Robert E. Lee's failure, however, came not because he was self-seeking or insubordinate — Lee was never either — but seemingly because he was incompetent in the field. The harshness of this judgment was emphasized by the contrast between what was done and what had been expected.

When Garnett fell in western Virginia and his army scattered before the skillful combinations of McClellan, it became necessary for Davis to send someone out there to put the pieces back together. Lee was the obvious choice. A man of considerable handsomeness and moral grandeur, hero of the Mexican War, he was Virginia's first soldier. Though it was not widely known that he had been tendered command of the U.S. forces before his resignation to go with his state, it was a matter of general knowledge that his rapid mobilization of Virginia's troops had made possible the victory at Manassas. One week after that battle he started west, taking with him the expectations of the President and the southern people.

Federal military successes in the region had reinforced an earlier political maneuver. Back in April, when the Richmond convention voted for secession, the western members crossed the mountains and assembled in Wheeling, where — on grounds that by voting for secession the other members had committed treason and thereby placed themselves outside the law — they drew up a new constitution, elected a new governor, and petitioned Washington for recognition as the lawful government of the state. Lincoln, of course, welcomed them, and presently their representatives were occupying the Virginia seats in Congress and laying the groundwork for the creation of the loyal state of West Virginia. Nothing was more galling to Confederate Virginians than the presence of these men in Washington, and one of the things expected of Lee was that he would abolish the rump government which had sent them there.

Strategically, too, the region was of great importance. Along its far edge ran the Ohio River, which not only was the traditional natural barrier of the new nation, but also flowed down toward the heart of Kentucky. Through its northern counties ran two vital supply lines, the Baltimore & Ohio Railroad and the Chesapeake & Ohio Canal. These severed, Washington would have to find a roundabout route for drawing men and supplies from the West. Still more important, with only a one-hundred-mile neck of land dividing the northward jut of its tiny panhandle from the shores of Lake Erie, it was the best location from which to launch an offensive such as the one proposed by Beauregard at Fairfax. That narrow isthmus also divided the Union, east and west; to seize it would be to split the North in two. When Lee left Richmond, all these opportunities lay before him in the western mountains, and no one went on record then as doubting that he would accomplish everything to which he put his hand.

What the public did not know was that he did not go out there to command but to advise, to coördinate the operations of four small independent "armies" whose commanders included one professional soldier, one scholarly ex-diplomat, and two high-tempered politicians. The campaign was to be conducted seventy miles from the nearest railhead, in an area whose population was largely hostile and whose principal "crop" was mountain laurel, so that supplies had to be brought up over roads made bottomless by rain that seldom slacked. "It rained thirty-*two* days in August," one veteran asserted. The troops were hungry and ragged, cowed by the defeats of the past month, half of them down with measles or mumps and the other half lacking confidence in their leaders. It was here in the mountains that Lee encountered for the first time a new type of animal: the disaffected southern volunteer. "They are worse than children," he declared, "for the latter can be forced."

Nevertheless, with such material and under such conditions, he now tried to work with the first pair in his highly diversified quartet of brigadiers. The soldier, W. W. Loring, who had been there only a week, resented Lee's arrival as a sign that the government did not trust him, and the diplomat, Henry R. Jackson, though willing, was inexperienced; with the result that when Lee attempted to trap the Federals on Cheat Mountain by an involved convergence of five columns from the two commands, the soldier balked, the diplomat blundered, and nothing was accomplished except to warn the Union troops of the movement, which had to be called off. Failing here, Lee looked south, where the two politicians were independently arrayed.

They were John B. Floyd and Henry A. Wise, both one-time governors of Virginia, the latter having occupied that office during the John Brown raid and the former having gone on to become Secretary of War in Buchanan's cabinet. Floyd had shown a tendency to grow flustered under pressure, and Wise had indicated what manner of soldier he was by ordering a battery commander to open fire in woods so thick that he could see no target and could therefore do no execution. "Damn the execution, sir!" Wise replied when the artillerist protested. "It's the *sound* that we want."

These shortcomings were nothing, though, compared to the relationship that Lee discovered existing between the commanders when he arrived. With an eye for past rivalries, and for possible future ones as well, the two ex-governors seemed more intent on destroying each other than they were on injuring the enemy to their front. Wise had raised an independent Legion, and when Floyd, who outranked him, came into the district, he telegraphed Richmond: "I solemnly protest that my force is not safe under his control." Floyd, enjoying the advantages of such rank, countered by offering to swap Wise's Legion for any three regiments of infantry, sight unseen. It was obvious that neither of these generals, intent as they were on mutual destruction — for which Floyd was perhaps the better equipped, having three newspaper editors on his staff — would be anxious, or maybe even willing, to coöperate in any venture which might bring credit to his adversary.

Yet Lee did what he could. He designed another combined operation, this time up the Kanawha Valley, and finally got the two commands in motion: whereupon, at the critical moment, with the enemy before them, the rivals took up separate positions, twelve miles apart, and, each declaring his own position superior, refused to march to join the other. Lee, whose primary reaction to the situation was embarrassment, was spared the ultimate necessity for sternness, however, when a War Department courier arrived with a dispatch instructing Wise to report immediately to Richmond. Wise pondered mutiny, but then, advised by Lee, decided against it and left, muttering imprecations.

With his problem thus reduced at least by half, Lee assembled the forces and took up a strong defensive position, planning destruction for the Federals. He hoped they would attack; if not, then he would launch an attack himself. For three days he waited. On the fourth he found the woods in front of him vacant, the enemy having pulled back out of reach, unobserved. All Lee could do, with winter closing in, was pull back, too. The three-month campaign was over, and he followed Wise to Richmond.

It was over and he had accomplished none of those things the public had expected. He had kept the advancing Federals off the Virginia Central and the Virginia & Tennessee Railroads, but this was generally ignored in the shadow of the darker fact that, with all those bright prospects before him, he had not even fought a battle. A Richmond journalist reviewed the operation thus: "The most remarkable circumstance of this campaign was, that it was conducted by a general who had never fought a battle, who had a pious horror of guerillas, and whose extreme tenderness of blood induced him to depend exclusively upon the resources of strategy to essay the achievement without the cost of life."

Lee had already written his wife, "I am sorry ... that the movements of our armies cannot keep pace with the expectations of the editors.... I know they can arrange things satisfactory to themselves on paper. I wish they could do so in the field." And yet there was justice in the charge. Lee *had* been tender of bloodshed, designing complicated envelopments to avoid it — none of which had worked. Above all, he had shown himself incapable of jamming discipline down insubordinate throats. Besides, the journalist was reflecting general opinion. The public saw Lee now as a theorist, an engineer, a desk soldier, one who must fight by the book if he fought at all, and those who had watched with pride as he set out, expecting satisfaction for their hopes, now prepared looks of scorn for his return.

They did not use them to his face, however. Three months of adversity in the mountains had given him an austerity that would not permit familiarity, not even the familiarity of scorn. At fifty-four he had grown a beard; it came out gray, and people looked at him in awe. But beyond the influence of his presence, they sneered and called him Granny Lee and Evacuating Lee and wondered what use could be made of a soldier who would not fight.

Davis found a use for him as soon as he returned in early November. Having learned in private the details of the campaign — details which the public did not know, since Lee's delicacy, even toward men whose bickering had wrecked his reputation, would not allow him to include them in a report for the record — the President sent him to the South Atlantic coast, where his engineering abilities would be useful in improving the defenses. Hatteras Inlet and Ship Island had been lost, and a third blow seemed about to land. It landed, in fact, the day Lee got there. He arrived just in time to hear the guns at Port Royal and meet the fugitives streaming rearward from that fight. The Virginian could scarcely be blamed for this, yet a South Carolina matron wrote of him in her diary next day: "*Preux chevalier*, booted and bridled and gallant rode he, but so far his bonnie face had only brought us ill luck."

He believed more in work, however, than in luck. Having studied the situation, he strengthened some forts, abandoned others, and redrew the defenses, shifting them back from the sounds and rivers so that the invaders would have to fight beyond range of their gunboats. This called for digging, which Lee ordered done, and this in turn brought a storm of protest. His soldiers, especially the native South Carolinians, found the order doubly onerous. Digging wasn't fit work for a white man, they complained, and a brave man wouldn't hide behind earthworks in the first place. He put them at it anyhow, and as they dug they coined a new name for him: King of Spades.

Granny Lee, Evacuating Lee, the King of Spades, was one of several ranking Confederates who found their loyalty to Davis repaid in kind. Risking, sometimes losing, the affection and confidence of large segments of the people for their sakes, Davis sustained them through adversity and unpopularity, whether the public reaction seemed likely to reach an end or not. Obviously this had its drawbacks. Then and down the years, depending on the critic's estimate of the bolstered individual, it was the quality for which he was at once most highly praised and most deeply blamed. Yet one advantage it clearly had for southern leaders, with a value greatly enhanced by the fact that it was seldom available to their opposite northern numbers: No man, knowing that Davis trusted him and knowing what that trust entailed, ever had to glance back over his shoulder, wondering whether the government — meaning Davis — would support him against the clamor of the disgruntled or sacrifice him on grounds of political expediency. And if this was clear to the generals thus sustained, it was even clearer to the politicians, who knew that Davis would do his duty as he saw it. When legislation which they knew was bad for the country came before them, they did not hesitate to pass the measure if it was popular with the folks back home, knowing that Davis would exercise his veto. (He employed it thirty-nine times in the course of the war, while his opponent used it thrice, and only in one case was it overridden.) Thus in dignified silence he shouldered the blame for men who called him obstinate and argumentative and did their worst to swell the chorus of abuse.

His tenure was no longer merely provisional. On the first Wednesday in November he and Stephens were elected, without opposition, to six-year terms of office. Inauguration ceremonies were scheduled for Washington's birthday, which seemed a fitting date for the formal launching of the permanent government established by the Second American Revolution. That this government *was* permanent, in fact as well as name, Davis had no doubt. "If we husband our means and make a judicious use of our resources," he assured the Provisional Congress at its final session, November 18, "it would be difficult to fix a limit to the period during which we could conduct a war against the adversary whom we now encounter."

For that adversary, whose leader styled the southern revolution a "rebellion" and whose people now were submitting meekly to indignities no American had ever encountered without fight, he expressed contempt. "If instead of being a dissolution of a league, it were indeed a rebellion in which we are engaged, we might find ample vindication for the course we have adopted in the scenes which are now being enacted in the United States. Our people now look with contemptuous astonishment on those with whom they had been so recently associated. They shrink with aversion from the bare idea of renewing such a connection. When they see a President making war without the assent of Congress; when they behold judges threatened because they maintain the writ of *habeas corpus* so sacred to freedom; when they see justice and law trampled under the armed heel of military authority, and upright men and innocent women dragged to distant dungeons upon the mere edict of a despot; when they find all this tolerated and applauded by a people who had been in the full enjoyment of freedom but a few months ago — they believe that there must be some radical incompatibility between such a people and themselves. With such a people we may be content to live at peace, but the separation is final, and for the independence we have asserted we will accept no alternative."

Yet even as he spoke, thus stigmatizing his opponent across the Potomac, Davis was faced with the necessity for emulating his "tyrannous" example. Two days after the first-Wednesday election an insurrection exploded in the loyalist mountain region of East Tennessee. Bridges were burned and armed men assembled to assist the expected advance of a Union army through Cumberland Gap.

Though undeveloped industrially, the area was of considerable economic value as a grain and cattle country, offsetting the one-crop cotton agronomy farther south, and of even greater strategic importance because of the Virginia & Tennessee Railroad running through

Knoxville and Chattanooga, westward to Memphis and the Transmississippi. The insurrection confronted Davis with a problem much like the one that had confronted Lincoln in Maryland immediately after Sumter, and Davis met it with measures even sterner. Troops were sent at once from Memphis and Pensacola. Resistance was quashed and a considerable number of Unionists arrested. Habeas corpus, "so sacred to freedom," went by the board. When the Confederate commander in Knoxville asked what he should do with these men, Davis had the Secretary of War reply that those insurrectionists not actually known to be bridge burners were to be held as prisoners of war. As for the burners themselves, they were "to be tried summarily by drumhead court martial, and, if found guilty, executed on the spot by hanging. It would be well," the Secretary added, "to leave their bodies hanging in the vicinity of the burned bridges."

Five were so hanged, and others were held, including that William G. Brownlow who earlier had said that he would fight secession on the ice in hell. Admittedly the leader of regional resistance, he was editor of the Knoxville *Whig* and formerly had been a Methodist circuit rider; wherefore he was called Parson. An honest, fearless, vociferous man who neither smoked nor drank nor swore, he had courted only one girl in his life "and her I married." Though he was mysteriously absent from home on the night of the burnings, his actual complicity could not be established. He was held in arrest — for a time, at least, until his presence proved embarrassing in the light of Davis' complaint about "upright men ... dragged to distant dungeons" in the North. Again through the Secretary of War, under the theory that it was better for "the most dangerous enemy" to escape than for the honor and good faith of the Confederate government to be "impugned or even suspected," Davis directed that the parson-editor be released to enter the Union lines. Though he was thus denied the chance to recite the speech he had memorized for delivery on the gallows, Brownlow went rejoicing. "Glory to God in the highest," he exclaimed as he crossed over, "and on earth peace, good will toward all men, except a few hell-born and hell-bound rebels in Knoxville."

Under his reek of fire and brimstone there was much that was amusing about Brownlow. But there was nothing laughable about what he represented. Least of all was there anything comical about the situation he and his followers had created in the mountains of Tennessee. Now it had come to this, that Americans danced at rope ends as a consequence of actions proceeding from their political convictions. The harshest irony of all was that they were hanged by the direction of Jefferson Davis, who loved liberty and justice above all things, and who as a grown man, in a time of sickness, halted a reading of the child's story "Babes in the Woods" (it was characteristic that he had never heard it) because he would not endure the horror of the tale. The operation on his high-strung nature of such incidents as these in Tennessee caused him to remark long afterward, concerning his northern opponent's fondness for anecdotes and frontier humor, that he could not "conceive how a man so oppressed with care as Mr Lincoln was could have any relish for such pleasantries."

He was afflicted, however, by troubles both nearer and farther than the stern, unpleasant necessity for jailing, banishing, and hanging insurrectionists in eastern Tennessee. Fire-eaters in Richmond and the Deep South, their claim to the spoils of higher offices denied, their policy of bold aggression rejected, were everywhere disaffected. Vocal in their disaffection, they had now begun to raise a multivoiced outcry like the frantic babble of a miscued chorus. Charging that Davis had "no policy whatever," they represented him as "standing in a corner telling his beads and relying on a miracle to save the country." As caricature, the likeness was not too far-fetched, and the fact that the no-policy charge was true, or nearly true, did not make the barbs of criticism sting one whit the less.

His critics would have had him strip the troops from threatened points and send them marching forthwith against the North, staking everything on one assault. To Davis, this not only seemed inconsistent with his repeated claim that the South was merely defending herself against aggression, it seemed unnecessarily risky. That way the war might be quickly won, as Beauregard had pointed out; but it also might be quickly lost that way. Davis preferred to watch and wait. He believed that time was with him and he planned accordingly, not yet by any means aware that what he was waiting for would require a miracle. At this stage, in Davis' mind at any rate, nothing seemed more likely, more inevitable, than foreign intervention; as had been shown by his first action in attempting to secure it.

Back in the Montgomery days, a month before Sumter, Barnwell Rhett, chairman of the foreign affairs committee, reported a bill to Congress providing for the dispatch of a three-man mission to secure the recognition of the Confederacy by the European powers. Rhett had certain notions as to what these men should do over there, but he could not give instructions to such emissaries; the making of treaties rested with the President, who seemed to believe that nothing more would be needed than a polite call on the various proper statesmen across the water, whereupon those dignitaries would spread their arms to welcome a new sister bringing a dowry of precious cotton into the family of nations. This belief was emphasized by the fact that the man appointed to head the mission was William L. Yancey, the fiercest fire-eater of them all. For fifteen years the southern answer to the most outspoken of northern abolitionists, the Georgia-born Alabamian extended his defense of the "peculiar institution" to include a proposed reopening of the African slave trade — with the result that his name was anathema to every liberal on earth. In selecting Yancey to represent her, it was as if the South said plainly to all Europe: "To get cotton you must swallow slavery."

Nothing in his personality had shown that he would be armed with patience against discouragement or with coolness against rebuff, or indeed that he was in any way suited to a diplomatic post. Discouragement was not expected, however, let alone rebuff. Besides, Yancey having declined the minor cabinet job of Attorney General, the appointment solved the problem of what to do with him. Since that February evening on the gallery of the Exchange Hotel, when he presented "the man and the hour" to the crowd, no fitting use for his talents had been found. Now there was this — though some declared that he was being hustled off the scene as a possible rival before the election of a permanent President came round.

However that might have been, when he and his associates, Pierre A. Rost and A. Dudley Mann, received their instructions from the State Department, something came over Yancey that seemed to come over all fire-eaters when they were abruptly saddled with the responsibility for using more than their lungs and tongues — something akin to the sinking sensation that came over Roger Pryor, for example, when he was offered the honor of firing the first shot of the war. Returning from the conference, Yancey went to Rhett and told him of the instructions. They had agreed at the outset that the power to make commercial treaties was necessary to the success of the mission. However, the commissioners had not been given such power. All they were to do was explain the conflict in terms of the rightness of the southern cause, point out the Confederacy's devotion to low tariffs and free trade, and make a "delicate allusion" to the probable stoppage of cotton shipments if the war continued without European intervention. Hearing this, Rhett shared his friend's dismay. "Then," he told Yancey, "if you will take my advice as your friend, do not accept the appointment. For if you have nothing to propose and nothing to treat about, you must necessarily fail. Demand of the President the powers essential to your mission, or stay at home."

Whatever his qualms and misgivings, Yancey did not take his friend's advice. Sailing on the eve of Sumter, the commissioners reached England in late April to discover that the nation they represented was in the process of being increased from seven states to eleven, doubled in size east of the Mississippi and more than doubled in wealth and population. Soon afterwards, May 3, they secured an interview with Lord John Russell, Secretary of State for Foreign Affairs, who had replied to their request for an audience that he would be pleased to hear them, but that "under present circumstances, I shall have but little to say."

The interview was as one-sided as his lordship predicted. Having heard the envoys out, he replied — without committing his government in the slightest — that the Confederacy's request for recognition would be placed before the Cabinet at an early date. Six days later there was a second, briefer meeting; and that was all. In Paris, Napoleon III was more genial and less forthright, though he did make it clear in the end that, however much he wished to intervene, France could not act without England. So Yancey and Mann, leaving Rost to watch Napoleon, returned to London to try again.

Their hopes were higher now, and with good cause. When Lincoln announced a blockade of the southern coast, Britain — in accordance with international law, since obviously no nation would blockade its own ports — issued in mid-May a proclamation of neutrality, granting the Confederacy the rights of a belligerent, and the other European powers followed suit. That was much, and when more followed, Manassas enhancing the dignity of southern arms, Yancey thought the time was ripe for recognition. Accordingly, another note was sent to Russell, requesting another interview. The reply came back: "Earl Russell presents his compliments to Mr W. L. Yancey, Mr A. Dudley Mann, and would be obliged to them if they would put in writing any communications they wish to make to him."

This was something of a shock; yet they smothered their anger and complied, writing at length and basing their claims for recognition on recent Confederate triumphs. The reply to this was a bare acknowledgment of receipt; which in turn was another shock, for they knew that an English gentleman was never rude except on purpose. Again they swallowed their pride, however, and, Rost having recrossed the channel to lend what weight he could, continued to send letters until early December, when the Foreign Secretary added the last straw: "Lord Russell presents his compliments to Mr Yancey, Mr Rost and Mr Mann. He has had the honour to receive their letters of the 27th and 30th of November, but in the present state of affairs he must decline to enter into any official communication with them."

That broke the camel's back, for Yancey anyhow, whose pride had been subjected to a good deal more than it could bear. He resigned and sailed for home. Arriving he went straight to Rhett, whose advice he had not taken. "You were right, sir," he declared. "I went on a fool's errand."

Davis might continue to comfort despair with hope; Yancey himself had none. "While the war which is waged to take from us the right of self-government can never attain that end," Davis asserted at the final session of the Provisional Congress — knowing the "delicate allusion" would be heard across the Atlantic — "it remains to be seen how far it may work a revolution in the industrial system of the world, which may carry suffering to other lands as well as our own." It did

First Blood; New Conceptions

not remain to be seen as far as Yancey was concerned. He had been there; he had seen already. He put no faith in anything that might happen in those nations whose statesmen had galled his pride.

Speaking in New Orleans in the spring, soon after his return, he told the people outright what he had told Davis earlier in private: "You have no friends in Europe.... The sentiment of Europe is anti-slavery, and that portion of public opinion which forms, and is represented by, the government of Great Britain, is abolition. They will never recognize our independence until our conquering sword hangs dripping over the prostrate heads of the North.... It is an error to say, 'Cotton is King.' It is not. It is a great and influential factor in commerce, but not its dictator. The nations of Europe will never raise the blockade until it suits their interests."

Thus Yancey, who had failed. How much his words were influenced by the fact that he had failed, his pride having been injured in the process, Davis could not know. At any rate, having spoken from the outset scarcely a public word that was not designed for foreign as well as domestic ears, the southern President had banked too heavily on European intervention to turn back now. The pinch of a cotton shortage not yet having been felt, the jennies and looms were running full-speed in England and France, and whether such a pinch, even if it eventually came, would "work a revolution," as Davis remarked in his mid-November speech, "remain[ed] to be seen."

Nor for that matter could he know how much of this initial failure had been due to ineptness. Yancey was many things, including a brilliant orator, but he was obviously no diplomat. Even before the final rebuff, which prompted his departure, Davis had moved to replace him, and the other two commissioners as well. Yancey would be recalled, his talents given a fitter scope, and Mann and Rost "disunited," one being sent to Spain and one to Belgium, their places to be taken at London and Paris by men whose gifts and reputations were more in keeping with the weight of their assignments: James M. Mason and John Slidell, former U.S. senators from Virginia and Louisiana.

The Virginian was the more prominent of the two. Grandson of George Mason of Gunston Hall (framer of the Bill of Rights) and withal an able statesman on his own, at sixty-three he had rather a ferocious aspect, with "burning" eyes and a broad, fleshy nose, a mouth drawn down at the corners, and brown, gray-shot hair bushed out around a large, pale, smooth-shaven face. His name, like Yancey's, was anathema to abolitionists, for he was the author of the Fugitive Slave Law and also of a public letter eulogizing Preston Brooks for caning their common adversary Sumner. Though he had got both his schooling and his wife in Philadelphia, Mason was an ardent secessionist and disapproved in general of things northern. He had been to New England once, to dedicate a monument, and found it quite distasteful. Invited to return, he replied that he would never visit that shore again, "except as an ambassador." Which was what he was now, in effect: on his way to the Court of St James's, however, not to the northern republic.

His companion Slidell was five years older and looked it, with narrowed eyes and a knife-blade nose, his mouth twisted bitterly awry and his pink scalp shining through lank white locks that clamped the upper half of his face like a pair of parentheses. He was New York-born, the son of a candlemaker who had risen, but he had removed to New Orleans as a young man to escape the consequences of debt and a duel with a theatrical manager over the affections of an actress. Importing the methods of Tammany Hall, he prospered in Louisiana politics. Though not without attendant scandal, he won himself a fortune in sugar, a Creole bride, three terms in Congress — one in the House and two in the Senate — and an appointment as Minister to Mexico on the eve of war with that nation, which event prevented his actual service in that capacity. He was aptly named, being noted for his slyness. At the outbreak of hostilities, back in the spring, an English journalist called him "a man of iron will and strong passions, who loves the excitement of combinations and who in his dungeon, or whatever else it may be, would conspire with the mice against the cat rather than not conspire at all." Possessing such qualities, together with the ability to converse in French, New Orleans–style, and also in Spanish, Empress Eugénie's native tongue, Slidell seemed as particularly well suited for the atmosphere of the City of Light as Mason, with his rectitude and cavalier descent, was for London.

Davis and the nation expected much from this second attempt at winning foreign recognition and assistance. By early October the two were in Charleston with their secretaries and Slidell's wife and daughters, awaiting a chance to run the blockade. At first they intended to take the Confederate cruiser *Nashville*, being outfitted there as a commerce raider. That would have been to arrive in a style which the British, as a naval people, could appreciate. Unwilling to wait, however, they booked passage instead an a small private steamer, the *Gordon*, and at 1 o'clock in the morning, October 12, slipped out of the harbor and crossed the bar in a driving rain, bound for Nassau. From there, having found no steamer connection with England, the *Gordon* sailed for St Thomas, a regular port for transatlantic packets. Running low on coal, her captain put into Cárdenas, on the north coast of Cuba, whence the commissioners made their way overland to Havana. November 7 they boarded the British mail steamer *Trent*, which cleared for Southampton that same day. Thus, the blockade having been run without incident, themselves securely quartered on a ship that flew the ensign of the mightiest naval power in the world, the risky leg of the journey was behind them.

So they thought until noon of the following day, when the

Trent, steaming through the Bahama Passage, 240 miles out of Havana, sighted an armed sloop athwart her course at a point where the channel narrowed to fifteen miles. The *Trent* broke out her colors and continued on her way; whereupon the sloop ran up the union jack — and put a shot across her bow. After a second shot, which was closer, the *Trent* stopped engines.

"What do you mean by heaving my vessel to in this way?" the British captain shouted through a trumpet.

For answer the sloop put out two boats, which as they drew nearer were seen to be loaded with sailors, armed marines, and a naval officer who identified himself as he came aboard: Lieutenant D. MacNeill Fairfax of the screw sloop *San Jacinto*, Captain Charles Wilkes, U.S.N., commanding. Having information that Confederate Commissioners James M. Mason and John Slidell were aboard, he demanded the passenger list. At this, Slidell came forward. "I am Mr Slidell. Do you want to see me?" Mason stepped up, too, but no introduction was necessary, he and the lieutenant having met some years ago. (For that matter, Slidell and Captain Wilkes, waiting now aboard the sloop, had been boyhood friends in the old First Ward, back in their New York days, though they had had a falling out before Slidell's departure.) Their identities thus established, together with those of their secretaries, Lieutenant Fairfax informed the British captain, who all this time had scarcely ceased objecting, that he was seizing the four men for return to the United States and trial as traitors. When the captain continued to object — "Pirates! Villains!" some of the passengers were crying; "Throw the damned fellow overboard!" — the lieutenant indicated the *San Jacinto*, whose guns were bearing on the unarmed *Trent*. The captain yielded, still protesting; Mason and Slidell and their secretaries were taken over the side.

"Goodbye, my dear," the Louisianian told his wife on parting. "We shall meet in Paris in sixty days."

The two ships drew apart and continued on their separate courses, northward and northeastward toward their two countries, bearing their respective emotional cargoes of exultation and outrage: cargoes in each case large enough, and fervent enough, to be shared by all the people who, off on those different points of the compass, awaited their arrival all unknowing.

Davis in Richmond was scantly braced for such a smile of fortune. After so many disappointments, he hardly presumed even to hope for such news as this which now was coming his way across the water. Here was a ready-made, bona fide international incident, brought about not by the machinations of cloak-and-dagger agents sent out by the Confederate secret service, but by a responsible northern naval officer who had taken unto himself the interpretation of law on the high seas and who in his rashness had inforced that interpretation against the flag which admittedly ruled those seas.

The news would be no less welcome for being unexpected; Davis was badly in need of encouragement at this point. At the outset he had predicted a long war. Now he was showing the erosive effects of living with the fulfillment of his prediction. He was thinner, almost emaciated; "gaunted" was the southern word. His features were sharper, the cheeks more hollow, the blind left eye with its stone-gray pupil in contrast to the lustrous gleam of the other — a "wizard physiognomy," indeed. The lips were compressed and the square jaw was even more firmly set to express determination, as if this quality might prove contagious to those around him. Under the wide brim of a planter's hat, his face had lost all signs of youth. It had become austere, a symbol; so that a North Carolina soldier, seeing him thus on the street one day, walking unaccompanied as was his custom, stopped him and asked doubtfully, "Sir, mister, be'ent you Jefferson Davis?" And when Davis, employing the careful courtesy which was habitual, admitted his identity: "Sir, that is my name" — "I thought so," the soldier said. "You look so much like a Confederate postage stamp."

* * *

Lincoln, too, was showing the strain, but unlike Davis he found his worries concentrated mostly on one man: Major General George B. McClellan. Since saying that he could "do it all," McClellan had found that "all" involved a great deal more than he had intended or suspected at the time. It included, for instance, the task of pacifying Ben Wade and Zachariah Chandler, members of the joint committee investigating the Ball's Bluff fiasco: men whom the youthful general considered "unscrupulous and false," but who, regardless of what he thought of them, were determined to have a voice in how the war was fought before they would vote the money needed to fight it.

They did not like the way it was being fought at present; or, rather, the way it was not being fought at all. Above Harpers Ferry the Confederates had cut the B & O, one of the main arteries of supply, while down the Potomac they had established batteries denying the capital access to the sea. "For God's sake," Wade cried, infuriated by such effrontery, "at least push back the defiant traitors!" It did no good to explain that such outposts would crumble of their own accord, once the main attack was launched, and that meanwhile, undeterred by incidentals, the proper course was to concentrate on building up the force with which to launch it. The congressmen saw only that the rebels were holding such positions unmolested. Or if McClellan's thesis was true, as to what the rebel reaction would be, they wanted to see it demonstrated. They had had enough of delay.

A Massachusetts Adams declared in August, "We have now gone

through three stages of this great political disease. The first was the cold fit, when it seemed as if nothing would start the country. The second was the hot one, when it seemed almost in the highest continual delirium. The third is the process of waking to the awful reality before it. I do not venture to predict what the next will be."

McClellan had already ventured a prediction: "I shall ... crush the rebels in one campaign." That was still his intention. Yet now, with the war still in the waking stage, all that he was truly sure of was that he did not want this phase to end as the first two had done, at Sumter and Bull Run. In spite of which, to his dismay — with those examples of unpreparedness stark before him — he was being prodded by rash counselors to commit the selfsame errors. Adams had seen the nation struggling for its life as if in the throes of breakbone fever; the war was "this great political disease," attacking the whole organism. But McClellan, who was a soldier, not a politician or a diplomat, could not or would not see that the contest was political as well as military, that the two had merged, that men like Wade and Chandler were as much a part of it as men like Johnston and Beauregard — or McClellan himself, for that matter. Given the time, he believed he could get over or around the enemy intrenched across the Potomac; he could "crush" them. He could never get over or around men like Wade and Chandler, let alone crush them, and he knew it. And knowing it he turned bitter. He turned peevish.

"The people think me all-powerful," he wrote in one of the nightly letters to his wife. "Never was there a greater mistake. I am thwarted and deceived ... at every turn." At first it was the politicians: "I can't tell you how disgusted I am becoming with these wretched politicians." Next it was the Administration itself: "I am becoming daily more disgusted with this Administration — perfectly sick of it. If I could with honor resign I would quit the whole concern tomorrow." "It is sickening in the extreme, and makes me feel heavy at heart, when I see the weakness and unfitness of the poor beings who control the destinies of this great country." "I was obliged to attend a meeting of the cabinet at 8 p.m., and was bored and annoyed. There are some of the greatest geese in the cabinet I have ever seen — enough to tax the patience of Job."

So far, the President was not included in the indictment. McClellan wrote, "I enclose a card just received from 'A. Lincoln'; it shows too much deference to be seen outside." Having come to know Lincoln better, he found he liked him, or at any rate thought him amusing. One day as he was writing he had callers, and when he resumed his letter he wrote, "I have just been interrupted here by the President and Secretary Seward, who had nothing very particular to say, except some stories to tell, which were, as usual, very pertinent, and some pretty good. I never in my life met anyone so full of anecdote as our friend."

It was not all anecdote. One day a division commander came to see the general and found Lincoln with him, poring over a map of Virginia and making operational suggestions, to which McClellan listened respectfully but with obvious amusement. At last the amateur strategist left. Returning from seeing him to the door, McClellan looked back over his shoulder and smiled. "Isn't he a rare bird?" he said.

Lincoln had been boning on the science of war, borrowing military treatises from the Library of Congress and reading them in the small hours of the night. He took a particular pleasure in discussing strategy with his young general-in-chief, who had been so good at such studies himself. McClellan saw no harm in all this. He viewed Lincoln's efforts with that air of amused tolerance reserved by professionals for amateurs, and the visits afforded relaxation from the daily round. Besides, such studies and discussions were leading the President toward a better comprehension of the military problem: especially of the necessity for protecting the commanding general from the interference of politicians.

"I intend to be careful and do as well as possible," McClellan said earnestly one night as they parted after such a conference. "Don't let them hurry me, is all I ask."

"You shall have your own way in the matter, I assure you," Lincoln told him.

Whereupon — as if, having gotten what he wanted in the way of assurance, he could move on now to other things; or perhaps because his tolerance or his capacity for amusement was exhausted — McClellan changed his tone. Now he wrote, "I have not been at home for some three hours, but am concealed at Stanton's to dodge all enemies in the shape of 'browsing' presidents, etc."

The friend affording sanctuary was Edwin M. Stanton, the attorney who had snubbed Lincoln four years ago when the gangling Springfield lawyer came to Chicago to assist in a patents case. Irascible and sharp-tongued, a leading Democrat, Stanton was even more important now. Having served as Attorney General during Buchanan's last four months, he had gone on to become chief legal adviser to the present Secretary of War. His first impression of "that long-armed creature" had not changed, but now at least he took the trouble to exercise his wit at his expense. Du Chaillu, for example, had not needed to go all the way to the Congo in search of the missing link; there was an excellent specimen here in Washington. "The original gorilla," he called Lincoln, and McClellan took up the phrase in letters to his wife. They laughed together at a perspiration splotch on the back of Lincoln's shirt, Stanton remarking that it resembled a map of Africa.

If he noticed this at all, Lincoln took it calmly. He was accustomed to being laughed at, and had even been known to encourage laughter at his own expense. Such friends as he cared about had a deep appreciation of humility, and he could afford to let the others go. Attracted, however, as so many were, by McClellan's forthright air of youthful manliness, he did not want to lose him as a friend. Then one mid-November night he drew the rebuke humility must always draw from pride. He and Seward, accompanied by Lincoln's young secretary John Hay, went over to McClellan's house. When the servant told them the general was attending a wedding but would be back presently, they said they would wait. They had waited about an hour when McClellan returned. The servant told him the President and the Secretary of State were there, but he seemed bemused as he went past the door of the room where they were waiting. They waited another half hour, then once more sent the servant to inform the general that they were there. The answer came — "coolly," Hay recorded — that McClellan had gone to bed.

On the way home, when the secretary broke out angrily against what he called the "insolence of epaulets," Lincoln, though he was saddened by this final indication that he had lost a friend, quietly remarked that this was no time for concern over points of etiquette and personal dignity. "I will hold McClellan's horse if he will only bring us success," he said soon afterward. But Hay observed with satisfaction that from then on, when the President wanted to see McClellan, he summoned him to the White House.

The Young Napoleon had changed. "We shall strike them there," he used to say, gesturing toward the eastern end of the rebel lines at Centerville when he rode out on inspection. After inching some troops forward "by way of getting elbow-room," he gaily told his wife: "The more room I get the more I want, until by and by I suppose I shall be so insatiable as to think I cannot do with less than the whole state of Virginia." He did not talk that way now, or write that way either. That was in the past. Bored, annoyed, disgusted, sick, thwarted and deceived at every turn, he no longer gestured aggressively toward the Centerville-Manassas lines. According to Pinkerton, 90,000 gray-clad soldiers, superbly equipped and thirsty for blood, with one Manassas victory already blazoned on their battleflags, were behind those earthworks praying for McClellan's army to advance and be wrecked, like McDowell's, on those same plains. All that stood between the army and catastrophe was Little Mac, resisting the unscrupulous men who would hurl it into the furnace of combat before the mold had set.

By now, though, more than the frock-coated congressmen were urging him forward against his will. While the clear bright days of autumn declined and the hard roads leading southward were about to dissolve into mud, the public was getting restless, too, wondering at the army's inaction. The soldiers loved and trusted him as much as ever; Our George, they called him still. But to the public he seemed overcautious, like a finicky dandy hesitating to blood a bright new sword, either because he did not want to spoil its glitter, or else because he did not trust its temper. Horace Greeley, the journalistic barometer, had recovered from his fright and recommenced his Forward-to-Richmond chant. Other voices swelled the chorus, while shriller cries came through its pulse to accuse the young commander of vacillation. McClellan was reduced to finding consolation in the approval of his horse, Dan Webster: writing, "He, at least, had full confidence in his master."

Affairs were progressing no better in the West. Politically, though the storm still raged from point to point and fugitive secessionist legislatures were assembling, Missouri and Kentucky had been secured to the Union. Militarily, however, little had been done since Wilson's Creek and Frémont's feverish southward march into the vacuum created by that explosion. Assuming the supreme command on the day the Pathfinder received Lincoln's order deposing him, McClellan promptly reorganized that vast, conglomerate area into two departments.

The first, Frémont's old Department of the West, to which was added that part of Kentucky west of the Cumberland River, was under Henry W. Halleck; while the second, the Department of the Ohio, including the rest of Kentucky and Tennessee, had Don Carlos Buell for commander. Both were responsible to McClellan, but neither was accountable to the other. Each in fact saw the other as his rival for the future command of the whole. And therein lay the seeds of much mischief. Admittedly, ambition and rivalry were the stimuli that made the military organism tick. But in this case, with McClellan racked by problems of his own in Washington, the result was that there was not only little coördination of effort between theaters, East and West; there was also little coöperation between the armies resting flank to flank on opposite banks of the Cumberland.

A major general at forty-six, three years older and one rank higher than his rival, Halleck had the advantage at the outset. Buell was generally considered one of the best officers in the service, particularly as an organizer and disciplinarian; yet Halleck was not only senior in age and grade, he was by far the more distinguished in previous accomplishments. Author of *Elements of Military Art and Science*, a highly respected volume issued fifteen years before, translator of Jomini's *Napoleon*, authority on international law, on which he had published a treatise just before the war began, he was called Old Brains by his fellow officers, not altogether jokingly. In the shadow of all this, even as a result of it, Buell had one not inconsiderable advantage: Halleck had been McClellan's rival for the post of general-in-chief — old Winfield Scott had favored him, for one — and Little Mac, perhaps somewhat influenced by this, considered Buell the superior in practical ability as a soldier in the field. That was arbitrary, though, or anyhow problematical, since the two West Pointers had been promoted equally for gallantry in the Mexican War and had had no such opportunity for distinction since.

In another direction, there was little room for doubt. Both were more impressive in the abstract than prepossessing in the flesh; but here the advantage clearly passed to the junior, if only by default. Of average height, inclined toward fat and flabbiness, Halleck had an unmilitary aspect. Balding, he wore gray mutton-chop side whiskers and looked considerably older than his years. The olive-tinted flesh of his face hung so loosely that it quivered when he moved, particularly his double chin, and he had a strangely repellent habit of crossing his arms on his lower chest to scratch his elbows when he was worried or plunged in thought. In manner he was irritable and sometimes harsh, not inclined to allow for the smaller brains of lesser men. Interviewed, he would hold his head sideways and stare fishily, directing one goggle eye toward a point somewhere beyond his interviewer. This caused one disconcerted officer to remark that conversing with Halleck was like talking to someone over your shoulder.

No one ever said this about Buell. His glance was piercing and direct: too much so, perhaps, for he was even harsher in manner than Halleck. Dark-skinned, with a scraggly, gray-shot beard, close-set eyes, and a hawk-beak nose, Buell maintained an icy reserve, engaged in no small talk, and brooked no difference of opinion from subordinates. Despite his operatic name, Don Carlos, there was nothing flamboyant in his nature. Like McClellan he was an excellent disciplinarian, robust of physique, and a hard, methodical worker round the clock; but he had scarcely a vestige of McClellan's charm, none of his glamor, and therefore none of his popularity, either. He never expressed the least regret at this, however. Apparently he never believed that popularity could be a useful factor in turning farmboys into soldiers. Or if so, not by him; he never sought it.

Instructions given the two commanders on setting out were similar as to policy. Both were told to hold firmly onto all that had been gained in Missouri and Kentucky, meanwhile impressing on the people of the area that the army's purpose was the restoration of the Union, not the abolition of slavery, which was not even incidentally on the agenda. In addition, Halleck was to assemble his troops "on or near the Mississippi, prepared for such ulterior operations as the public interests may demand," while Buell massed for an advance into the loyalist mountain region of eastern Tennessee. The former plan had reference to Frémont's dream of a lopping descent of the Father of Waters. The latter was Lincoln's fondest project. He hoped that Buell would accomplish there what McClellan had accomplished in western Virginia under similar conditions, the people having voted five-to-one against secession back in June. Nothing vexed the President more than the fact that this Union stronghold was in southern hands. "My distress," he wrote, "is that our friends in East Tennessee are being hanged and driven to despair, and even more, I fear, are thinking of taking rebel arms for the sake of personal protection." Besides, he saw great strategic profit in an advance through Cumberland Gap, since taking Knoxville would cut the northernmost east-west Confederate railroad, thus coming between the secessionists and what Lincoln called their "hog and hominy."

Buell, who had helped to frame his own instructions, saw it that way, too, on setting out. Soon after he reached Louisville, however, peering southeast across the barrens in the direction of the Gap, which he saw now as a natural fortress straddled athwart his path, he changed his mind. For him, as for McClellan — whom he addressed as "My dear Friend" in official dispatches — obstacles loomed more starkly at close range. Features that seemed innocuous on a two-dimensional map could dominate a three-dimensional landscape. Even the absence of some feature, whether natural or man-made, could prove ruinous: as for instance a railroad. From his base on the Ohio he observed that there were no railroads by which he could haul supplies to feed and equip an army moving directly upon East Tennessee. He would have to depend on a wagon train, grinding weary distances over wretched roads and vulnerable to raiders throughout its length. The more he looked the more impossible it seemed, until presently he abandoned it altogether.

He did not abandon his offensive plans, however. Buell was nothing if not thorough. Turning his mind's eye westward along a sixty-degree arc, he perceived that Nashville, the Tennessee capital on the Cumberland, a manufacturing center and a transportation nexus, was not only closer than Knoxville, it was even a bit closer than Cumberland Gap. The way led through a land far richer in supplies, with no natural fortress at the end, and best of all there was a railroad all the way. Nashville taken, the Confederates defending East Tennessee would be outflanked; when they fell back he could march in unopposed. This might take a bit longer, but it was surer. As for the Unionists awaiting his advance into the mountains, Buell believed their constancy would "sustain them until the hour of deliverance." Thus he wrote in mid-December, by which time five had already been "sustained" by the necks after drumhead trials for arson.

Before occupying Nashville he would have to cross the Cumberland River, but he did not consider this a drawback. He counted it a positive advantage, since it meant that he could secure the coöperation of Union gunboats on that stream. This in turn meant securing the coöperation of Halleck, and now that his mind had turned that way, Buell went on to essay grand strategy. He proposed nothing less than an all-out concerted drive by both Kentucky armies, with Nashville as the objective: Halleck to advance from the northwest in "two flotilla columns up the Tennessee and the Cumberland," and himself from the northeast, down the railroad. The result would be to penetrate, and thereby outflank, the whole Confederate line; whereupon the Federals could occupy not only East Tennessee, his original objective, but the entire state, along with whatever parts of Kentucky remained in enemy hands. In his enthusiasm, which somewhat resembled the elation of a poet just delivered of an ode, he wrote McClellan of his plan, remarking incidentally that he feared no advance by the rebels at Bowling Green ("I should almost as soon expect to see the Army of the Potomac marching up the road") and closing with a light-hearted request for a few high-ranking officers, "not my seniors," to assist him in carrying out his plan: "If you have any unoccupied brigadiers ... send six or eight, even though they should be no better than marked poles."

Far from being elated, or even amused, McClellan was chagrined and upset by the proposal. He saw the soundness of this substitute plan — which, moreover, had the sort of strategic brilliance he admired — yet he hated to lose the advantages of the first. Invading eastern Tennessee, Buell's army would not only sever one of the arteries supplying the Confederates in northern Virginia; it would also be poised on their flank, and could then be angled forward to maneuver them out of their intrenched position and assist in the taking of Richmond. For this reason, as well as the political ones, McClellan replied that he still considered "a prompt movement on eastern Tennessee imperative," but "if there are causes which render this course impossible," he regretfully allowed, "we must submit to the necessity." All the same, he did not submit without frequent backward glances. By the end of November he was hoping Buell would attempt both movements, one on East Tennessee, "with say 15,000 men," and one on Nashville "with, say, 50,000 men." He added, by way of encouragement, "I will at once take the necessary steps to carry out your views as to the rivers."

This meant that he would urge Halleck to undertake the advance from western Kentucky. When he did so, in a telegram sent December 5, Halleck replied from St Louis the following day: "I assure you, General, this cannot be done with safety at present. Some weeks hence I hope to have a large disposable force for other points; but now, destitute as we are of arms, organization, and discipline, it seems to me madness to remove any of our troops from this State."

In all conscience, McClellan had to admit that Old Brains had his hands full already. Charged with restoring order to the chaos Frémont left — "a system of reckless expenditure and fraud, perhaps unheard of before in the history of the world," his instructions warned him — he had to attend at once to the guerilla bands marauding in his rear, to Price and McCulloch, reported marching against his front, as well as to the enormous task of preparing for the descent of the Mississippi. As if all this was not enough, he was having to deal at the same time with a mentally upset brigadier, red-haired Tecumseh Sherman, who was bombarding headquarters with reports of rebel advances from all directions. "Look well to Jefferson City and the North Missouri Railroad," Sherman would wire; "Price aims at both."

Succeeding Anderson when the Sumter hero's health broke, Sherman earnestly told the Secretary of War that 200,000 troops would be needed to put down the rebellion in the Mississippi Valley alone, and when this "evidence of insanity" was reinforced by other alarming symptoms reported in the papers — a brooding melancholy broken only by intermittent fits of rage and fright — he was relieved of his command. Superseded by Buell, he was sent to serve under Halleck in Missouri, where his fidgety manner and tocsin-shrill dispatches presently served to verify the suspicions which had followed him from Kentucky. He appeared thoroughly demoralized: "stampeded," Halleck called it, but McClellan put it simpler, saying, "Sherman's gone in the head." In hopes that a few weeks' rest would restore his faculties, Halleck gave an indefinite leave of absence to the distraught Ohioan, whose wife then came down and took him home.

Not all of Halleck's personnel problems could be handled so easily. As a sort of counterbalance to the highly nervous Sherman, he had another brigadier who seemed to have no nerves at all. The trouble with U.S. Grant was that, for all Halleck knew, he might have no brains either.

There were indications of such a lack. Grant was a West Pointer and had been commended for bravery in Mexico, but since then his reputation had gone downhill. Stationed out in California, he had had to resign his captain's commission because of an overfondness for the bottle, and in the seven following years he had been signally unsuccessful as a civilian. Commissioned a colonel of Illinois volunteers, he had won promotion to brigadier by a political fluke, his congressman claiming it for him as a due share of the spoils. Since then he had done well enough in a straightforward, soldierly way; he had not panicked under pressure, and best of all he had worked with what he had instead of calling for help in each emergency. Aware of his unsavory past, however, Halleck could never be sure when a relapse might come, exposing the basic instability of Grant's character and leaving the army commander to take the blame for having reposed the nation's trust in such a man.

Despite his seedy appearance (he was five feet eight inches tall and weighed 135 pounds; one eye was set a trifle lower than the other, giving his face a somewhat out-of-balance look; he walked with a round-shouldered slouch, pitching forward on his toes, and paid as scant attention to the grooming of his beard as he did to the cut and condition of his clothes) Grant had proved himself a fighter. But that could have its drawbacks when it included, as it seemed to do in this case, a large element of rashness. Halleck did not want to be embarrassed by Grant, the way Frémont had been embarrassed by the ill-fated Lyon: with whom, for that matter, in spite of his lack of surface fire, the thirty-nine-year-old Illinois brigadier had shown a disturbing degree of kinship. Wilson's Creek had come within three weeks of Bull Run, and had been fought to the same pattern. Then on the eve of Halleck's arrival, within three weeks of Ball's Bluff, came Belmont. Even apart from the balanced chronology, East and West, the resemblance was much too close for comfort.

Though Bishop Polk had won the race for Columbus, Grant had been by no means willing to admit that this gave the Confederates any permanent claim to the place. Within the week, having occupied Paducah, he had written Frémont: "If it were discretionary with me, with a little addition to my present force I would take Columbus." The Pathfinder made no reply to this, but when he took the field at last, marching against the victors of Wilson's Creek, he had his adjutant order Grant to feint against Polk to prevent that general from reinforcing Price. In doing this Grant was to make a show of aggression along both sides of the Mississippi, keeping his troops "constantly moving back and forward... without, however, attacking the enemy." Also in accordance with orders, on November 3 — the day Frémont left Springfield, relieved of command, and Winfield Scott left Washington, retired — Grant sent a column southward, west of the river, to assist in an attempt to bag or destroy a force under M. Jeff Thompson, reported down near the Missouri boot-heel, in the St Francis River area. Two days later a dispatch informed him that Polk was definitely sending reinforcements to Price. Marching "back and forward" not having sufficed to immobilize the bishop, Grant now was ordered to make a demonstration against Columbus itself.

Accordingly, on the 6th he loaded five infantry regiments, supported by two cavalry troops and a six-gun battery, onto four transports — 3114 men in all — and steamed down the river, protected by two gunboats. Nine miles below Cairo, tied up for the night against the eastern bank, he received a report that Polk had ordered a strong column to cut off and destroy the troops Grant had sent to do the same to Thompson. The message arrived at 2 o'clock in the morning, and within the hour Grant made his decision. Instead of a mere demonstration, he would launch a direct, all-out attack on Belmont, the steamboat landing opposite Columbus, where the enemy column was reported to be assembling.

At dawn the downstream approach got under way, the troops experiencing the qualms and elation of facing their first test under fire. Their emotions perhaps would have been less mixed, though probably no less violent, if they had known that none of the conditions their commander assumed existing at or near Columbus was true. Polk had no intention of reinforcing Price, nor was he preparing a column to bag the force that supposed itself to be pursuing Thompson, who for that matter had retired from the field by now. Far from being a staging area, Belmont was only an observation post, a low-lying, three-shack hamlet dominated by the guns on the tall bluff across the river and manned by one regiment of infantry — half of which was on the sick list — one battery of artillery, and a scratch collection of cavalry. Unaware that the drama in which they were taking part was in fact an Intelligence comedy of errors, Grant's men came off their transports at 8 o'clock, three miles above Belmont, their debarkation concealed by a skirt of timber. While the gunboats continued downstream to engage the batteries on the Columbus bluff, the troops formed a line of battle and marched southward toward the landing, skirmishers out. Presently, the guns of the naval engagement booming hollow across the water to their left, they came under heavy musket fire from out in front.

By now there was more to oppose them than one half-sick infantry regiment. Polk, having learned of the attack, had reinforced the Belmont garrison with four regiments under Brigadier General Gideon Pillow, the Tennessean who had preceded him in command. Ferried across the river, they hurried northward from the landing, scorning the protection of previously constructed fortifications, and took position in the path of Grant's advance. It was hard, stand-up fighting, the forces being about equal, five regiments on each side, each force being supported by a battery of light artillery. The Federals had the initiative, however, and also they had Grant, who was something rare in that or any war: a man who could actually learn from experience. Three months before, he had made a similar advance against an enemy position reported held by Colonel Thomas Harris and his command, and as Grant drew closer, mounting the ridge that masked the camp, "my heart kept getting higher and higher until it felt to me as though it was in my throat." He kept his men going, he said, because "I had not the moral courage to halt and consider what to do." Then, topping the rise, he found the camp deserted, the enemy gone. "My heart resumed its place. It occurred to me at once that Harris had been as much afraid of me as I had been of him. This was a view of the question I had never taken before; but I never forgot it afterwards."

He did not forget it now. Leaving five companies near the transports as rear guard, he put the rest in line and pushed straight forward, his six guns barking busily all the while. Under such pressure, the Confederates gave ground stubbornly — until, after about two hours of fighting, the Federals roaring down upon them in the vicinity of the camp, they broke, giving way completely, and took off for the rear in headlong panic. Here, on a narrow mud-flat left by the falling river and protected by a steep low bank, they found shelter from the humming bullets. "Don't land! Don't land!" they called out to reinforcements arriving by boat from Columbus. "We are whipped! Go back!"

They spoke too soon. Grant's men, having overrun the camp, had stopped to loot, and their officers, elated by the rout, "galloped about from one cluster of men to another," according to Grant, "and at every halt delivered a short eulogy upon the Union cause and the achievements of the command." Like the whipped men under the river bank, they thought the battle was over. This was by no means the case, as they presently discovered. Now that their own men were out of the way, the artillerists on the Columbus bluff could bring their guns to bear: particularly one big rifled Whitworth, which began to rake the captured campsite. What was more, the reinforcements arriving by boat ignored the cries, "Don't land! Go back!" and coming up during the lull, formed a line of battle, preparing to attack. Disgusted, Grant ordered the camp set afire to discourage the looters and orators, and did what he could to reassemble his command. Meanwhile other Confederate reinforcements were pouring ashore to the north, between Belmont and the transports. When an aide rode up, exclaiming, "General, we are surrounded!" — "Well," Grant said, "we must cut our way out as we cut our way in."

All this time, Grant's faulty intelligence having made the Federal plans impenetrable, Polk had refused to believe that the action across the river was anything more than a feint to distract his attention from the main effort, which he believed would come from the Kentucky side. Columbus was a prize worth bleeding for, but it made no sense, as far as he could see, for the enemy to launch a serious attack against Belmont, a place not only worthless in its own right, but obviously untenable, even if taken, under the frown of the batteries on the bluff across the river. Therefore, after sending the four regiments at the outset, he had refused to be distracted. Now, though, the attack from the east not having developed and Pillow having been flung back to the landing, Polk sent Brigadier General B. F. Cheatham with three more regiments and crossed the river himself to see how they fared. With 5000 angry, vengeful Confederates on the field, including those who had rallied after cowering under the bank, Grant's elated but disorganized 3000 were going to find it considerably harder to "cut our way out," no matter how bravely the words were spoken, than they had found it to "cut our way in."

In the end, however, that was what they did, though at the cost of abandoning most of their captured material, including four guns, as well as many of the non-walking wounded and one thousand rifles, which the defenders afterwards garnered from the field. Grant had held back no reserves to throw into the battle at critical moments, but he performed more or less as a reserve himself, riding from point to point along his line to direct and animate his troops. Except for one regiment, which was cut off in the fighting and marched upstream to be picked up later, he was the last man aboard the final transport.

The skipper had already pushed off, but looking back he recognized the general on horseback and ran a plank out for him. (Polk saw him, too, though without recognition. From the nearby skirt of timber which had screened the debarkation, the bishop, seeing the horseman, said to his staff, "There is a Yankee; you may try your marksmanship on him if you wish." But no one did.) Grant had already had one mount shot from under him today, and when he chose another he chose well. The horse — which, Grant said, "seemed to take in the situation" — put its forefeet over the lip of the bank, tucked its hind legs under its rump, and "without hesitation or urging," slid down the incline and trotted up the gangplank.

That ended the Battle of Belmont, and though the casualties were about equal — something over 600 on each side, killed, wounded, and captured — it followed in general the pattern of all the battles fought that year, the attackers achieving initial success, the defenders giving way to early panic, until suddenly the roles were reversed and the rebels were left in control of the field, crowing over Yankee cowardice. At Belmont as at Bull Run — and especially as at Ball's Bluff, which it so much resembled, the repulsed troops having narrowly missed annihilation at the end — there were indications of blundering and ineptness. "The victory is complete," Grant asserted in dispatches, but two days after the battle the Chicago *Tribune* editorialized: "The disastrous termination of the Cairo expedition to Columbus is another severe lesson on the management of this contest with the rebels. Our troops have suffered a bad defeat.... The rebels have been elated and emboldened while our troops have been depressed, if not discouraged." The following day, in printing the casualty lists, the editor added: "It may be said of these victims, 'They have fallen, and to what end?'"

To what end, indeed. And now began the talk of Grant the butcher. This was no victory; not a single tactical advantage had been won; he just went out and came back, losing about as many as he killed. Yet certain facts were there for whoever would see them. He had moved instead of waiting for fair weather, had kept his head when things went all against him, and had brought his soldiers back to base with some real fighting experience under their belts. They were having none of the butcher talk. They had watched him alongside them where bullets flew the thickest and had cheered him riding his trick horse up the gangplank, the last man to leave the field. What was more, they knew the expedition had been designed in the first place to save the lives of their friends in the supposedly threatened column out after Thompson, and they knew now that if ever *they* were thought to be so trapped, Grant himself would come to get them out. Best of all, they had met the rebels in a stand-up fight which proved, for one thing, that blue-bellied Yankees were not the only ones who would panic and scatter and take off for defilade, crying, "We are whipped! Go back!"

Appointed to the western command two days after the battle, Halleck, who had been a civilian as well as a soldier, could see both points of view as to Belmont and the general who fought it. However, in spite of his qualms about Grant's rashness and the chances for being embarrassed by it, he was mainly glad to have him. Experienced leaders were all too few in the West. "It is said, General," he told McClellan, "that you have as many regular officers on your personal staff as I have in this whole Department." He had, in fact, hardly an army at all, he protested, "but rather a military rabble," and upon arriving he wired Washington: "Affairs in complete chaos. Troops unpaid; without clothing or arms. Many never properly mustered into service and some utterly demoralized. Hospitals overflowing with sick."

Burdened as he was with such problems — far too little of what he wanted, far too much of what he didn't — it was no wonder that he declined to aid his rival Buell by advancing southeast up the rivers, saying quite plainly: "It seems to me madness." Nor was it any wonder that Buell, similarly laden and thus denied assistance, saw no chance of advancing in any direction, either toward Knoxville, as Lincoln and McClellan kept urging, or toward Nashville, as he himself preferred. Both generals promised results as soon as conditions permitted. Meanwhile they did what they could to improve what they had inherited from Frémont and from Sherman.

To this task they brought their skill as organizers, disciplinarians, and administrators, building a war machine for the West comparable to the one McClellan was forging in the East. Not even their worst enemies denied their considerable talents along these lines, Jefferson Davis remarking before the year's end: "The Federal forces are not hereafter, as heretofore, to be commanded by path-finders and holiday soldiers, but by men of military education and experience in war."

McClellan drew from this what solace he could, knowing it was much. Meanwhile, preparing for the great day if the great day ever came, he continued to drill and train his army, staging large and ever larger reviews, until at last, near Bailey's Crossroads, November 20, he put on the largest one of all.

Seven full divisions — 70,000 riflemen and cannoneers and troopers, equipped to the limit of the nation's purchasing and manufacturing power — swung in cadenced glitter past the reviewing stand, where ladies fluttered handkerchiefs and politicians swelled their chests with pride, covering their hearts with their hats as the colors rippled by. And yet, while the dust settled, while the troops filed off to their encampments and the civilians rode in their carriages back to Washington, there was a feeling that all this panoply, grand and enjoyable as it was, did not make up for the Quaker-gun humiliation of Munson's Hill or erase the shame of Bull Run, which still rankled. Nor, for that matter, did it reopen the Potomac or chase the rebels off the B & O. In fact, looking back on the daylong surge of armed might past the grandstand, the politicians were reinforced in their opinion that so fine an army should be used for something sterner than parading.

The soldiers did not share this let-down feeling and had no sympathy for the protests. Nor did they consider themselves inactive. Loving and trusting Little Mac, inspired by his presence when he rode his charger through their camps, they were content to leave military decisions to his superior judgment. "Marching Along," they sang on their conditioning hikes, back and forth across the "sacred soil" of their Virginia bridgehead:

> *"McClellan's our leader, he's gallant and strong;*
> *For God and our country we are marching along!"*

Prodded by the politicians, who kept pointing out that the weather was fair and the roads still firm, Lincoln hoped that the army would move southward before winter ended all chances for an advance. McClellan apparently having no such plan in mind, the President himself tried his hand at designing a frontal and flank attack on the Confederates at Manassas. This product of midnight fret and study was submitted December 1 to the young general-in-chief, who looked it over and replied ten days later that it was hardly feasible. "They could meet us in front with equal forces nearly," he objected.

Besides, he added as if by afterthought, "I have now my mind turned actively toward another plan of campaign that I do not think at all anticipated by the enemy nor by many of our own people." Thus Lincoln, who apparently was included under the general heading "our own people," received his first inkling of what came to be known as the Urbanna plan.

McClellan had never enjoyed the notion of a head-on tangle with Johnston on those plains where McDowell had gone down. Some day, given the odds, he might chance it; that was what he was building toward. But to attempt it while outnumbered, as he believed his army was, seemed to him downright folly. Then Buell's refusal to advance against and through Knoxville, which would have placed his army on Johnston's flank, in a position to coöperate with the Army of the Potomac, caused McClellan to abandon all intentions of a due south attack, present or future. Poring over headquarters maps he had evolved "another plan of campaign," one moreover enlisting the assistance of the navy, flushed with its three recent victories. He would load his soldiers aboard transports, steam down the Potomac into Chesapeake Bay, then south along the coast to the mouth of the Rappahannock, and up that river a short distance to Urbanna, a landing on the southern bank, less than fifty airline miles from Richmond, his objective. Without the loss of a man, he would have cut his marching distance in half and he would be in the rear of Johnston — who then would be forced to retreat and fight on grounds of McClellan's choosing. The more he thought about it, the better he liked it. It was not only beautifully simple. It was beautifully bloodless.

In the flush of first conception he planned to set out immediately. "I have no intention of putting the army into winter quarters," he declared. "I mean the campaign will be short, sharp, and decisive." But there were numerous details, including the assembling of transports for the 150,000 men he would take along, all of which had to be accomplished in great secrecy if Johnston was to be left holding the bag in northern Virginia. It was enough to overtax the energies of even so expert an organizer as McClellan. Presently he realized that it would probably be spring before he could get the campaign under way. Regretfully he wrote his wife, "I am doing all I can to get ready to move before winter sets in, but it now begins to look as if we were condemned to a winter of inactivity. If it is so," he added, flinching from the protest he knew must follow, "the fault will not be mine: there will be that consolation for my conscience, even if the world at large never knows it."

As if in confirmation, the rains came. The fields were turned to quagmires and the roads were axle deep in mud. At last he had a reason for not advancing which even the politicians could understand. Then, late in the month, he had an even better personal reason. He came down with a cold, which the doctors presently diagnosed as typhoid fever, and was confined to his bed for three weeks, into the new year.

His good friend Stanton, legal light of the War Department, came to his bedside, peering over his spectacles and murmuring, "They are counting on your death, and already are dividing among themselves your military goods and chattels." But when the President called — doing so for the first time since the snub McClellan had given him six weeks back — he was denied admittance. Lincoln was profoundly troubled. Not only was the general sick, but so was his chief of staff, Brigadier General R. B. Marcy, who was also his father-in-law. Subordinates might be able to administer the Army of the Potomac, which obviously was not going into action anyhow, but Lincoln wondered what was happening elsewhere, especially in the West, now that the guiding hand was paralyzed.

On the last day of the year he telegraphed Buell and Halleck, asking if they were acting by mutual arrangement. Buell replied that there were no provisions for concerted action; Halleck replied that he knew nothing of Buell's plans and that he was unable to coöperate in any case. "It is exceedingly discouraging. As everywhere else, nothing can be done," Lincoln wrote on the back of Halleck's letter, and wired for them to get in touch at once. That same day he went to the office of Quartermaster General M. C. Meigs. "General, what shall I do?" he groaned. "The people are impatient; Chase has no money, and tells me he can raise no more; the General of the Army has typhoid fever. The bottom is out of the tub. What shall I do?"

The question was rhetorical: Lincoln already knew what to do, and even how to do it. Midnight study of strategy texts, plus native common sense and conversation with professionals, had increased his understanding of the military problem. In language that was knotty and overpunctuated, showing thereby the extent to which he had labored to evolve it, he said in a letter to Buell at the time: "I state my general idea of this war to be that we have greater numbers, and the enemy has the greater facility of concentrating forces upon points of collision; that we must fail, unless we can find some way of making our advantage an over-match of his; and that this can be done by menacing him with superior forces at different points, at the same time; so that we can safely attack, one, or both, if he makes no change; and if he weakens one to strengthen the other, forbear to attack the strengthened one, but seize, and hold the weakened one, gaining so much."

However, the fact that he knew what to do, and could state it thus in one hard-breathing sentence — the awful hug of the anaconda becoming more awful still as it shifted its coils to exert more pressure where the bones would crack — only rendered more exasperating the fact that "nothing [could] be done." It was a question, Lincoln saw already, of finding the right man to do the job. Already he was looking for a general who would not only believe in his "idea of this war," but would follow it, inexorably, to the end. Meanwhile it was becoming increasingly evident that, for all his gifts, for all his soldiers' love of him, McClellan was not the man.

★ ★ ★

The bottom was not really out of the tub. That was only Lincoln's manner of speaking, designed perhaps to restore some measure of confidence when he got around to comparing the overstatement with the facts. He had known melancholy all his life, and this was one of his ways of working it off — just as sometimes, to clarify in his own mind a relationship with some individual, he would write the man a letter which he never intended to mail; Lincoln was his own psychiatrist. And yet the bottom had been almost out. Riding, or else tossed upon, the seethe and roil of popular opinion during the early weeks of what became known as The Trent Affair, public men on both sides of the ocean lost their heads, and England and the United States came closer to war than they had ever come without war following. Few doubted that it would come. Even fewer, apparently, did not welcome it in the heat of indignation, since in each case national honor seemed at stake. Mason and Slidell had left Havana while the guns of Port Royal and Belmont were booming out accompaniments for victory and repulse. Next day, November 8, while Du Pont's sailors occupied Fort Beauregard and Grant was counting noses back at Cairo, the *Trent* and the *San Jacinto* met in the Bahama Passage, then wore apart, northward and northeastward over a glassy sea, the former having exchanged four passengers for a cargo of outrage explosive enough to blow the bottom out of any tub. In London on the 27th the captain gave the authorities the news.

Immediate and unrestrained, the reaction was in the nature of a shriek; Britannia had been touched where she was tender. "By Captain Wilkes let the Yankee breed be judged," the *Times* declared, and stigmatized both him and it: "Swagger and ferocity, built on a foundation of vulgarity and cowardice, these are his characteristics, and these are the most prominent marks by which his countrymen, generally speaking, are known all over the world." Entering a Cabinet meeting, the eighty-year-old Prime Minister, Lord Palmerston, flung his hat on the table and exploded: "You may stand for this but damned if I will!"

Accordingly, while the cry for war went up all over England, an army of 8000 boarded transports bound for Canada, where fortifications were ordered erected at strategic points along the border, and Royal Navy shipyards were thrown into a bustle of preparation beyond anything since the days when the first Napoleon was mustering all Europe for invasion. Lord John Russell was put to work drafting an ultimatum for presentation to the United States. Its terms were simple: either an abject apology, including surrender of the seized Confederate emissaries, or war.

The republic across the Atlantic had never been one to bow to ultimatums, least of all from its arch-enemy England, and especially not now, with its citizens engaged in a delirium of praise for the latest hero to twist the lion's tail. A week after taking his prisoners aboard, Captain Wilkes had put into Hampton Roads for coal, a tall, clean-shaven regular, romantic in appearance, with becoming streaks of gray in his wavy hair. From there, having informed his superiors of his action, he steamed north again, bound for Boston in accordance with instructions to deliver the rebel envoys at Fort Warren, where a congratulatory telegram awaited him from the Secretary of the Navy: "Your conduct in seizing these public enemies was marked by intelligence, ability, decision, and firmness, and has the emphatic approval of this Department." The Army Secretary was no less enthusiastic. When the news reached the War Department, that dignitary led in the giving of three cheers by a group which included the governor of Massachusetts.

From the press, from the pulpit, from the public at large came praise for the captain's forthright action. Congress rushed through a resolution thanking him for his "brave, adroit, and patriotic conduct in the arrest of the traitors," and voted a gold medal struck in his honor. He was wined and dined and paraded in Boston, and toasts to his boldness were drunk throughout the nation. For the Administration to submit to an ultimatum and apologize for the captain's action would be to disavow that action and repudiate the hero before the eyes of his adoring public. With the nation already split in half and one tremendous conflict already building toward a climax, no one could say for certain what the result would be if the people were forced to choose between their captain-hero and those who let him down.

Thus — as in 1812, with the roles reversed — the two nations were poised for a war that would surely come unless one, or both, backed down: which was plainly impossible, believing as they did the worst of each other. On one side of the water, the British assumed that the impressment had been performed under government sanction, probably in accordance with instructions. On the other, the Americans, already provoked by the granting of belligerency status to the Confederacy, saw only another instance of England's avowing her intention to further the rebellion and assist in the dismemberment of a rival in the scramble for world trade.

As if all this was not enough to make war seem inevitable, the British conception of what had fed the roots of the late outrage was reinforced by the aggressive diplomacy — the announced intention, even — of the American Secretary of State, who was known to favor war with England as a means of reuniting his divided countrymen. He had said so repeatedly, in interviews, in correspondence, and in after-dinner talk. If the North became embroiled with a foreign power, Seward believed, the South would drop its States Rights quarrel and hasten to close ranks against invasion: whereupon, with that war over, the two sections could sit down in a glow of mutual pride at having won it, and reconcile past differences without the need or desire for further bloodshed.

In this he was most likely much mistaken, for the main goal of Confederate diplomacy was to draw England into the conflict on the southern side. And yet he was not entirely wrong — at least so far as regarded human nature. Now that the hope seemed about to be fact, the reaction below the Potomac and the Ohio was not unmixed. Exultation was sobered there by the thought of Americans, under whatever flag, submitting to an old-world ultimatum. "As I read the Northern newspapers, the blood rushes to my head," one diarist wrote. "In the words of the fine fiction writers, my cheek is mantling with shame. Anyhow," she went on to predict, "down they must go to Old England, knuckle on their marrow bones, to keep her on their side — or barely neutral." Right or wrong, however, such was Seward's theory: a foreign war would still domestic strife. And now as if by the bounty of fate, without the slightest effort on his part, Captain Wilkes's action and England's reaction presented him with an all-out chance to test it.

Lincoln himself had his doubts about this theory, not only in general but in particular, as it applied to the case in point. He rather agreed with the southern diarist that there would have to be some knuckling done. "I fear the traitors will prove to be white elephants," he remarked when he received word of the seizure of Mason and Slidell. Unfamiliar with diplomacy, he was feeling his way. When a learned visitor explained to him that his blockade declaration had naturally gained for the Confederacy the rights of a belligerent in all the courts of Europe, since a nation did not blockade its own ports, Lincoln replied: "Yes, that's a fact. I see the point now, but I don't know anything about the Law of Nations and I thought it was all right.... I'm a good enough lawyer in a western law court, I suppose, but we don't practice the Law of Nations out there, and I supposed Seward knew all about it and I left it to him."

He left it to Seward, but he did not let him go unsupervised. It was as if Lincoln said to him, as he had said to Herndon back in Springfield, "Billy, you're too rampant." Seward was called Billy, too — Billy Bowlegs, his enemies dubbed him: a bandy-legged, untidy man with a great deal of personal charm behind the bristling eyebrows, the constant cigar, and the nose of a macaw. Mrs Lincoln detested him outright. "He draws you around his little finger like a skein of thread," she warned her husband. But when other advisers urged that he drop the New Yorker from the cabinet, Lincoln said: "Seward knows that I am his master."

Seward knew no such thing, as yet, but he was learning. Though Lincoln liked him, enjoyed his stories, and respected his political astuteness, from Sumter on he watched him and rode herd on him, toning down his overseas dispatches, which in first draft rather demonstrated his theory that a war with Europe would solve the urgent problems here at home. It was characteristic of Seward that, having styled the coming civil war an "irrepressible conflict," he met it, when it came, with various efforts to repress it. Sumter at least had taught him that Lincoln was more than a prairie bumpkin, for the Secretary informed his wife in early June: "Executive skill and vigor are rare qualities. The President is the best of us, but" — he felt obliged to add — "he needs constant and assiduous coöperation." The *Trent* affair removed this final residue of doubt, and at the same time vindicated Lincoln's decision to keep Seward at his post, despite the clamor of his enemies and the trouble he had made.

Now that the war he thought he wanted was his for the asking — or, indeed, for the not-asking — Seward discovered, perhaps to his profound surprise, that he did not want it at all. He said so, in fact, as soon as the news arrived from Hampton Roads. In the cabinet, while all around them were wild-eyed with praise for the bold captain, only Seward and Montgomery Blair perceived that in turning his quarter-deck into a prize court Wilkes had not only been rash, he had been wrong, and by his illegal action had exposed his country to embarrassment. As Lincoln put it, "We must stick to American principles concerning the rights of neutrals. We fought Great Britain [in 1812] for insisting, by theory and practice, on the right to do precisely what Wilkes has done." Seward agreed. "One war at a time," Lincoln cautioned, and Seward agreed again.

However, these three alone, Lincoln and Seward and the practical-minded Blair, could not breast the popular current running full-tilt against them; they must wait. In his December 1 message to Congress, the President left the affair unmentioned. "Mr Lincoln forgot it!" someone remarked in shocked surprise at his thus ignoring the burning question of the day. The words were passed along, laughter being added to amazement: "Mr Lincoln forgot it!" And then, perceptibly — whether because of the chilling effect of the laughter or because, as in certain diseases, the fever itself had cured the fit — the excitement ebbed.

Cooler heads took over on both sides of the Atlantic. The British began to consider that Captain Wilkes might have acted without orders from his government, and responsible Americans began to see that the Confederate envoys locked up in Fort Warren — where Slidell was being given his chance to "conspire with the mice against the cat" and Mason was abiding by his oath (though in a manner not intended) never to visit that shore again "except as an ambassador" — were accomplishing more toward the fulfillment of their diplomatic mission than they would be doing if they had continued on their way to Europe.

The first official show of reason came from England. Prince Albert, closeted with the Queen in his last illness — he would be dead before the year was out — toned down Russell's ultimatum, modifying its phraseology until the demand for an apology became, in effect, a request for an explanation; so that, instead of finding it "dictatorial or menacing," as he had feared, Seward could pronounce it "courteous and friendly." It was still an ultimatum, requiring an apology for the insult to the British flag, as well as the surrender of the envoys, but at least it opened the door for a reply in the form of something except a declaration of war. That was much. As for the apology — the one thing Seward could not give — verbal additions to the message indicated that a statement to the effect that Wilkes had acted without instructions would render it superfluous, since a nation could hardly be expected to apologize for something it had not done. Seward already had in mind the terms of his reply, but before it could be sent he would have to win the approval of the rest of the cabinet. In the present state of public furor, with even Lincoln feeling that surrender of the captives was "a pretty bitter pill to swallow," nothing less than unanimous action would suffice.

For two days Seward remained shut away in his office, composing a reply to the British demand: a reply intended not only for the eyes of the Minister to whom it was addressed, but also for those of the American man-in-the-street, whose sensibilities were the ones considered most in this explanation of his government's being willing to give up the rebel envoys: so that, though in form and style the document was brilliantly legal, showing Seward at his sparkling best — this was one State Department dispatch Lincoln did not need to doctor — it was not so much designed to stand up under analysis by the Admiralty law lords, as it was to show the writer's countrymen that their leaders were by no means trembling at the roar of the British lion. Having complied with the basic demands of the ultimatum by 1) admitting that Wilkes had acted without orders and 2) offering to deliver the captives whenever and wherever they were wanted, Seward then wrote for his countrymen's eyes, with reasoning that was somewhat specious and language that was at times impertinent, what amounted to an indictment of the British point of view, past and present. In other words, under cover of an apology, he gave the lion's tail a final twist.

Down on the Virginian peninsula that summer, though by the rules of warfare he could not confiscate private property unless it was being used against him, Ben Butler had justified the receiving of slaves into his lines on grounds that their labor for the enemy made them contraband of war. "I'se contraband," they would say, smiling proudly as they crossed the freedom line, and Butler put them to work on his fortifications. Now Seward took a page from the squint-eyed general's book, affirming that the envoys and their secretaries were "contraband," liable to seizure. Wilkes therefore had done right to stop the ship and then to board and search her. His error lay in his leniency; for he should have brought not only the rebel envoys, but also the *Trent* and all her cargo into port for judgment; in which case, Seward was sure, the ship and everything aboard her, including the four Confederates, would have become the lawful property of the United States. However — and here was where the impertinence came in — the Secretary could appreciate his lordship's being taken aback, for in impressing passengers from a merchant vessel Wilkes had followed a British, not an American line of conduct. Seward saw the present ultimatum as an admission of past injuries inflicted by the mistress of the seas, and he congratulated Britannia on having come round to the point of view against which she had fought in 1812: "She could in no other way so effectually disavow any such injury, as we think she does, by assuming now as her own the ground upon which we then stood." Captain Wilkes had been mainly right, but the United States wanted no advantage gained by means of an action which was even partly wrong. Seward was frank to state, however, that if his nation's safety required it he would still detain the captives; but "the effectual check and waning proportions of the existing insurrection, as well as the comparative unimportance of the captured persons themselves, when dispassionately weighed, happily forbid me from resorting to that defense.... The four persons in question are now held in military custody at Fort Warren, in the State of Massachusetts. They will be cheerfully liberated. Your lordship will please indicate a time and place for receiving them."

Doubtless Seward had enjoyed those two days he spent locked away in his office, verbally building a straw man, straw by straw, then verbally demolishing him, handful by handful. When he emerged, however, prepared to receive the applause of his fellow cabinet members, he received instead cold looks and hot objections. They could appreciate the brilliance of his performance, but it did not obscure the fact that they were being asked to yield — which most of them had sworn not to do. It took him, in fact, as long to win their indorsement of the document as he had spent composing it, and the latter two days were far more hectic than the former.

Christmas morning the ministers assembled. When they adjourned that afternoon, to spend what was left of the holiday with their families, there had been no agreement. What Lincoln called "a pretty bitter pill" was for the cabinet, one member said, "downright gall and wormwood." The war was one year old that night, the anniversary of Anderson's removal of his eighty-odd men from Moultrie to Fort Sumter. Next morning the ministers reassembled; the discussion was resumed. It went hard, being asked to go down on their marrow bones against all their oaths and boasts, with only Seward's flimsy curtain of paradox and impertinence to hide them from the public and each other. In the end, however, as one of them wrote, "all yielded to the necessity, and unanimously concurred."

Mason and Slidell were handed over on New Year's Day to continue their roundabout journey, the latter being twenty days late for the appointment he had made with his wife when he told her on parting, "My dear, we shall meet in Paris in sixty days." The public reaction to the outcome of the crisis was considerably less violent than the cabinet members had feared. Though the anti-British press continued to fulminate according to tradition, in general there was a sigh of relief at having to fight only "one war at a time." When Captain Wilkes, still wearing his laurels, was sent about his business, to be supervised more closely in the future, the public did not even feel let down. Poker was not the national game for nothing; the people understood that their leaders had bowed, not to the British, but to expediency.

Only within one group was there despondency that the rebels

had been freed. "Everybody here is satisfied with their surrender," Lincoln heard from a friend in Indiana, "except the secession sympathizers, who are wonderfully hurt at the idea that our national honor is tarnished."

★ ★ ★

On this diplomatic note, which opened shrill, then broke into falsetto, the first year of the conflict reached a close. Politically and militarily speaking, its laurels belonged to those who had established a nation within its span and defended that establishment successfully in battle, meeting and turning back attacks against both flanks of their thousand-mile frontier and staving off an advance against the center. McClellan's gains in western Virginia and the Federal navy's trident amphibious lunge did something to redress the defeats along Bull Run and Wilson's Creek, but when those checks were emphasized, east and west, by the rout at Ball's Bluff and the repulse at Belmont, there was a distinct public impression, North and South, at home and abroad, of failure by the Unionist government to deal with the Confederate bid for independence.

One side called this bid a revolution. The other insisted that it was a rebellion. Whichever it was, it was plainly a fact, and both sides saw clearly now that the contest between northern power and southern élan was not going to be the ninety-day affair they had predicted at the outset.

Realization that this was so had grown until it was unmistakable, at which point violent objections were sounded on both sides by the extremists who had been foremost in predicting that the conflict would be short and decisive. Southerners were all bluster and would not fight if their bluff was called, the abolitionists had declared, and when one fire-eater had offered to wipe up with his handkerchief all the blood that would be shed, a less squeamish colleague had backed him up by offering to drink it. Now that blood had dripped and flowed beyond their power to drink or wipe, they waxed bitterly accusative, North and South, against those who held the reins. Chagrined that the war they had done so much to bring about had been taken out of their hands when it arrived, the two groups still insisted that their prediction had turned out false only because their aims had been betrayed. It could still be rendered valid, they affirmed, provided the war was fought the way they wanted. Each favored an all-out invasion, with fire and sword and the hangman's noose, and each blamed its leader for an obvious lack of vigor in his thinking and in his actions.

"Jeff Davis is conceited, wrong-headed, wranglesome, obstinate — a traitor," Edmund Rhett declared, while back in Springfield the northern President's erstwhile law partner complained that Lincoln was attempting to "squelch out this huge rebellion by popguns filled with rose water. He ought to hang somebody and get up a name for will or decision — for character," Herndon wrote, and added scornfully: "Let him hang some child or woman if he has not the courage to hang a *man*."

Between these two extremes, while the anti-Davis and anti-Lincoln cliques were respectively consolidating their opposition and sharpening their barbs, the mass of men who would do the actual fighting, and the women who would wait for them at home, took what came with a general determination to measure up to what was expected of them. It was their good fortune, or else their misery, to belong to a generation in which every individual would be given a chance to discover and expose his worth, down to the final ounce of strength and nerve. For the most part, therefore, despite the clamor of extremists north and south of the new frontier, each side accepted its leader as a condition of the tournament, and counted itself fortunate to have the man it had and not the other. Seen from opposite banks of the Ohio and the Potomac, both seemed creatures fit for frightening children into quick obedience. On the one hand there was Davis, "ambitious as Lucifer," with his baleful eyes and bloodless mouth, cerebral and lizard-cold, plotting malevolence into the small hours of the night. On the other there was Lincoln, "the original gorilla," with his shambling walk and sooty face, an ignorant rail-splitter catapulted by long-shot politics into an office for which he had neither the experience nor the dignity required.

What they seemed to each other was another matter. Lincoln had recognized his adversary's renowned capabilities from the start, but it was not until well after Sumter — if then — that Davis, like so many of the northern President's own associates, including even his Secretary of State, began to understand that he was having to deal with an opponent not below but beyond the run of men. Their official attitude toward one another gave a certain advantage to the Southerner, since he could arraign his rival before the bar of world opinion, addressing him as a tyrant and "exposing" his duplicity; whereas Lincoln, by refusing to admit that there was any such thing as the Confederate States of America, was obliged to pretend that Davis, too, was nonexistent. However, it was a knife that cut both ways. Lincoln was not only denied the chance to answer charges, he was also relieved of the necessity for replying to a man who wasn't there. Nor was that all. Constitutionally, the Illinois lawyer-politician was better equipped for accepting vilification than the Mississippi planter-statesman was for accepting what amounted to a cut; so that, in their personal duel, the advantages of a cloak of invisibility were canceled, at least in part, by the reaction of the man who had to wear it. Davis wore it, in fact, like an involuntary hair shirt.

Followed by the admiring glances of Richmond ladies in made-over bonnets and men in last year's winter suits, he continued to take his early morning and late evening constitutionals, to and from the office where he spent long hours on administrative details rather than on executive decisions. With the bottom gone out of the slave market and gold already selling at a premium of fifty percent, the croakers were saying that he expended his energies thus to keep from facing the larger issues. But that was to overlook the fact that, rightly or wrongly, those issues had been settled back in the spring, when he committed himself and his nation to the defensive. Now he was pursuing a policy which a later southern-born President would call "watchful waiting" — watching for another northern offensive and waiting for European intervention. His task was to turn back the former and welcome the latter. In the light of Manassas, which set the battle pattern, and the *Trent* affair, which strained British-U.S. relations even further, Davis considered both of these outcomes probable, either of which would validate for all time the existing fact of his country's independence. Waiting had already brought him much, and now that it seemed likely to bring more, he continued to watch and wait, going about his duties as he saw them.

Such duties involved an occasional social function and the daily hour which he reserved for his children. Of these there now were four, Mrs Davis having borne in mid-December the child christened William Howell for her ailing father. They were Davis' chief relaxation, for much as he enjoyed the social amenities, particularly an intimate evening spent with a few close friends, he mostly denied himself that pleasure in these times. He would drop in during his wife's receptions, spend an hour exercising his remarkable memory for names and faces, then dutifully, his invariable charm and courtesy masking whatever boredom he felt, take a cup of tea before retiring to his study and the paperwork that awaited him as a result of his unwillingness to delegate authority.

The lady guests might have their reservations about his wife — she was rather too "intellectual" for their taste; "pleasant, if not wholly genial," one Richmond matron called her — but the men, coming under the sway of those attractions which had drawn her husband, seventeen years and five children ago (Samuel, the first child, died in infancy), did not feel that the breadth of her mind obscured the charm of her person. All were agreed, however, as to the attractiveness of the husband and the dignity he brought to his high office. He was showing the strain, it was true; but that only served to emphasize the wonder at how well he bore up under it, after all. Whatever their opinion as to his policy in adopting a static defensive, they all agreed that as a figurehead for the ship of state he could hardly be improved on.

Ornamentally, Lincoln served less well — though in reply to complaints about his looks his followers could repeat what had been pointed out already: "We didn't get him for ballroom purposes." Even here, however, he was trying. At White House receptions he stood in line and pumped the hands of callers, performing the duty, one witness observed, "like a wood-chopper, at so much a cord." He was learning, too. Though his big hands split through several pairs of kid gloves on such evenings, now at least the gloves were white, not black as at the opera in New York ten months before. He had most of the problems Davis had, and some that Davis did not have. Office seekers still hemmed him in and placed a constant drain on his good humor. Finding him depressed one day, a friend asked in alarm, "What is the matter? Have you bad news from the army?" "No, it isn't the army," Lincoln said with a weary smile. "It is the post office in Brownsville, Missouri."

Unlike his opponent, he had no fixed policy to refer to: not even the negative one of a static defensive, which, whatever its faults, at least had the virtue of offering a position from which to judge almost any combination of events. This lack gave him the flexibility which lay at the core of his greatness, but he had to purchase it dearly in midnight care and day-long fret. Without practical experience on which to base his decisions, he must improvise as he went along, like a doctor developing a cure in the midst of an epidemic. His advisers were competent men in the main, but they were fiercely divided in their counsels; so that, to all his other tasks, Lincoln had added the role of mediator, placing himself as a buffer between factions, to absorb what he could of the violence they directed at each other. What with generals who balked and politicians who champed at the bit, it was no wonder if he sometimes voiced the wish that he were out of it, back home in Illinois. Asked how he enjoyed his office, he told of a tarred and feathered man out West, who, as he was being ridden out of town on a rail, heard one among the crowd call to him, asking how he liked it, high up there on his uncomfortable perch. "If it wasn't for the honor of the thing," the man replied, "I'd sooner walk."

In Richmond and in Washington, one hundred miles apart—the same distance as lay between Fairview and Hodgenville, their birthplaces in Kentucky—Davis and Lincoln toiled their long hours, kept their vigils, and sought solutions to problems that were mostly the same but seemed quite different because they saw them in reverse, from opposite directions. All men were to be weighed in this time, and especially these two. At the far ends of the north-south road connecting the two capitals they strained to see and understand each other, peering as if across a darkling plain. Soon now, that hundred miles of Virginia with its glittering rivers and dusty turnpikes, its fields of grain and rolling pastures, the peace of generations soft upon it like the softness in the voices of its people, would be obscured by the swirl and bank of cannon smoke, stitched by the fitful stabs of muzzle flashes, until at last, lurid as the floor of hell itself, it would seem to have been made for war as deliberately as a chessboard was designed for chess. Even the place-names on the map, which now were merely quaint, would take on the sound of crackling flame and distant thunder, the Biblical,

Indian, Anglo-Saxon names of hamlets and creeks and crossroads, for the most part unimportant in themselves until the day when the armies came together, as often by accident as on purpose, to give the scattered names a permanence and settle what manner of life the future generations were to lead. The road ran straight, a glory road with split-rail fences like firewood ready stacked for the two armies, and many men would travel it wearing Union blue or Confederate gray. Blood had been shed along it once, and would be shed again; how many times?

Neither Lincoln nor Davis knew, but they intended to find out, and soon. The year just past had been in the nature of a prelude, whose close marked only the end of the beginning.

CHAPTER 3

The Thing Gets Under Way

★ ✘ ☆

ALBERT SIDNEY JOHNSTON, THE RANKING Confederate general in the field, was charged with maintaining the integrity of a line that stretched westward more than five hundred miles: from the barrens of eastern Kentucky, through the Bluegrass region, on across the Mississippi, and beyond the kaleidoscopic swirl of conflict in Missouri to Indian territory, where it ended, like a desert stream, as a trickle in dry sand. To accomplish the defense of this western-Europe-sized expanse, penetrated by rivers floating enemy fleets and menaced along its salient points by two Federal armies, each one larger than his own, he had a distinguished reputation, a nobility of looks and character, a high-flown official title — General Commanding the Western Department of the Army of the Confederate States of America — and all too little else. He was a big man, broad-shouldered and deep-chested, over six feet tall and just under two hundred pounds in weight. His wavy dark-brown hair touched with such gray as became his fifty-eight years, the Kentucky-born Texan gave at once an impression of strength and gentleness. No beard disguised his strong, regular features, but a heavy mustache offset somewhat the dominance of brow and width of jaw. Commanding in presence, grave in manner, he wore his dignity with natural charm and was not without the saving grace of humor. It was Johnston, for example, who remarked that there was "too much tail" to Frémont's kite.

In the thirty-five years since his graduation from West Point — where Jefferson Davis, looking up to him from two classes below, as at Transylvania earlier, contracted a severe and lifelong case of hero worship — he had distinguished himself in a colorful career: frontier officer, Texas revolutionist and Secretary of War in Sam Houston's cabinet, gentleman farmer, Mexican War colonel, U.S. Army paymaster, and commander of the famed 2d Cavalry, whose roster carried the names of four future full generals, including himself and R. E. Lee, one lieutenant general, and three major generals, all Confederate, as well as two of the leading Union major generals. Zachary Taylor was reported to have said that Johnston was the finest soldier he ever commanded, and Winfield Scott had called him "a Godsend to the Army and to the country."

While the national storm was heading up, he was a brevet brigadier in command of the Pacific Coast, with headquarters at Fort Alcatraz in San Francisco Bay; but when Texas seceded he declined an offer of high rank in the Union army, tendered his resignation, and led a group of thirty pro-Confederate officers and civilians eastward on horseback across the desert toward his adopted state, dodging Apaches and Federal garrisons on the way. From Galveston he came on to New Orleans, where he was greeted as if an additional army had flocked to the Stars and Bars. His route to Richmond, through a countryside still elated over the six-weeks-old Manassas victory, was blazed with fluttering handkerchiefs and tossed hats, the news of his coming having preceded him all along the line. Davis was waiting, too, and handed him his lofty commission and the accompanying assignment to the far-flung Western Department.

"I hoped and expected that I had others who would prove generals," the southern leader afterwards declared; "but I knew I had *one*, and that was Sidney Johnston." Still later he put it even stronger, calling him "the greatest soldier, the ablest man, civil or military, Confederate or Federal, then living."

This high opinion was shared by the people of the region where the general's orders took him. From Richmond to Nashville, as from New Orleans to Richmond, the journey was one continuous ovation. Yet now that the new year had come in, with its hangover from the heady wine of Manassas and Wilson's Creek, all that seemed far away and long ago — as if it had occurred in another era, a dream world, even, divided from the present by an airtight door which slammed forever shut in mid-September when Johnston arrived and saw for himself, at unmistakable first hand, the magnitude of the task that lay before him and the paucity of the means with which he was expected to accomplish it. Politically the lines were already drawn; Kentucky and Missouri both had stars in the Confederate flag, though it was becoming increasingly clear that Lincoln had mostly won that fight, in spite of secessionist governors and Frémont. The problem now was military, and the line to be drawn lay not along the Ohio River, but along a zigzag course conforming to the mountains and rivers and railroads of Kentucky and the crazy-quilt pattern of Missouri. Such a line would be difficult to defend at best, but with the force at his disposal it was patently impossible. He had something under 50,000 men in all, scarcely amounting to more in effect than a 500-mile-long skirmish line, distributed about equally east and west of the big river that pierced his center.

In the Transmississippi the snarled military situation was aggravated by the rivalry of Price and McCulloch, whose victories had not brought them into accord. Since to elevate one would mean the probable loss of the other, along with many followers, Johnston proposed that the Richmond authorities assign to the region a field commander who would rank them both. Eventually this was done, and soon after the first of the year Major General Earl Van Dorn, West Pointer and Mississippian, a man of considerable fire and reputation, took over the job of welding the two commands into one army. Meanwhile, on his way from Richmond, Johnston stopped off at the far eastern end of his line and ordered Brigadier General Felix Zollicoffer, a former newspaper editor and Tennessee congressman, to take his little army of recruits through Cumberland Gap in order to post them where they could guard the passes giving down upon Knoxville and the Virginia-Tennessee Railroad.

Having provided thus for his flanks, Johnston looked to his center, the critical 150-mile sector extending roughly east-southeast from Columbus, Kentucky, to Nashville. Davis had empowered him to withdraw Polk from Columbus, out of consideration for the state's political sensibilities, or to sustain the occupation. It was not a difficult decision; in fact, Johnston had already made it when he sent Zollicoffer forward. But now he did more. Finding Simon Buckner waiting for him in Nashville — the former head of the Kentucky State Guard was now a private citizen, offering the South his services — Johnston commissioned him a brigadier, assigned him several regiments, and set him in motion for Bowling Green, sixty miles to the north. Far from ordering Polk's withdrawal, the new department commander swung his central sector forward, gate-like, with Columbus as the hinge. The line now extended east-northeast, and within a week of his arrival he had thrown every available armed man northward across the Kentucky border to strengthen it.

It badly needed strengthening. At the outset Johnston had fewer than 20,000 troops to man the long line from the Mississippi to the mountains — 11,000 with Polk, 4000 each with Buckner and Zollicoffer — backed up by a few scattered camps of recruits in Tennessee, some without any weapons at all. But when Johnston appealed for arms and men to the governors of Alabama and Georgia, both were prompt in refusal. "Our own coast is threatened," the former replied, while the latter, if less explanatory, was more emphatic: "It is utterly impossible for me to comply with your request." Not all were so deaf to his pleas, however. More closely threatened, Tennessee coöperated better, putting fifty regiments into the field before the end of the year, and Kentucky volunteers continued to come in, some bringing their long rifles. Four regiments arrived from Mississippi before that state was shut off from him by governmental notification that the area was not properly within the limits of his command. Not that Richmond was unmindful of the danger. It sent what it felt it could afford, including 4650 Enfield rifles brought in by blockade runners, and transferred to the Army of Central Kentucky — so Johnston called it — several of the Confederacy's most distinguished brigadiers.

Georgia-born William J. Hardee, forty-six — not only a West Pointer and one-time commandant of cadets, but also the author of *Rifle and Light Infantry Tactics*, formerly an Academy text and now the official drill and tactics manual of both armies — brought his brigade from northeast Arkansas to Bowling Green, where he took over from Buckner and soon was promoted to major general, as befitted his wider experience and his position as commander of the vital center. Gideon Pillow, who had measured swords with Grant at Belmont, also was shifted eastward to bolster the advance. He too ranked Buckner, and for the present became second in command of the Army of the Center, under Hardee.

Three prominent Kentuckians, all in their forties, also were available for the defense of their state. The oldest was George B. Crittenden, forty-nine, West Pointer and regular army man, son of the senator whose compromise efforts had staved off war for a decade. Commissioned a major general he was sent to the Cumberland Mountains region, with headquarters at Knoxville. Lloyd Tilghman, forty-five, was also a West Pointer and a veteran of the Mexican War, but he had left the army for a career in civil engineering. Johnston soon had him busy designing and building fortifications. The youngest of the three, forty-year-old John C. Breckinridge, was also the most distinguished. Vice President under Buchanan, he had presided over the joint session of Congress which declared Abraham Lincoln elected President, the office for which Breckinridge himself had been runner-up in the electoral college. Since then, he had been elected to the Senate, where his opposition to the Administration's war policy resulted in an order for his arrest. When Buckner first got to Bowling Green, Breckinridge entered his lines as a fugitive. "To defend your birthright and mine," he told his fellow Kentuckians, "I exchange with proud satisfaction a term of six years in the Senate of the United States for the musket of a soldier." Rather than a musket Johnston gave him a brigade, despite his lack of military training.

In addition to these men of rank, all in the vigor of their prime, the army had two cavalrymen who had already contributed exploits to its legend: Captain John Hunt Morgan of Kentucky and Lieutenant Colonel Nathan Bedford Forrest of Tennessee. Though the former had fought in the Mexican War as a youth and later commanded his hometown militia company, neither man had had a military education. The latter, in fact, a Memphis slave dealer and a Mississippi planter, had had little formal schooling of any kind. By the end of the year, however, both had shown an aptitude for war. Morgan, who was thirty-six, took thirteen of his troopers on a reconnaissance completely around Buell's army and returned with thirty-three prisoners. In his first fight, northeast of Bowling Green, the forty-year-old Forrest improvised a double envelopment, combined it with a frontal assault — classic maneuvers which he could not identify by name and of which he had most likely never heard — and scattered the survivors of a larger enemy force. Standing in the stirrups, swinging his sword and roaring "Charge! Charge!" in a voice that rang like brass, the colonel personally accounted for three of the enemy officers, killing two and wounding one; he shot the first, sabered the second, and dislocated the shoulder of a third by knocking him off his horse. Ordinarily, infantrymen had small liking for any trooper, but these two lithe, violent six-footers caught their fancy, and soldiers of all arms predicted brilliant futures for them both — if they lived, which seemed unlikely.

Soon after New Year's the final brigadier arrived from West Virginia at the head of his command. John B. Floyd had had three months in which to recover from the rain-damped campaign under Lee in the Kanawha Valley, where he had been more successful against his Confederate rival, Henry Wise, than against the wily Rosecrans. Ranking Pillow, he now became second in command of the forces under Hardee north of Bowling Green, along the Green and Barren Rivers.

Floyd's brigade completed the order-of-battle with which Johnston was expected to fend off Halleck and Buell, whose combined armies were about twice the size of his own. In the Transmississippi, a weird collection of 20,000 regulars, militiamen, and Indian braves awaited the arrival of Van Dorn to take the offensive against a well-organized command of 30,000 Union troops. East of the river, though Johnston had managed to double the number defending Kentucky, the odds were even longer. Between Columbus and Cumberland Gap, just over 50,000 Confederates opposed just under 90,000 Federals, thus:

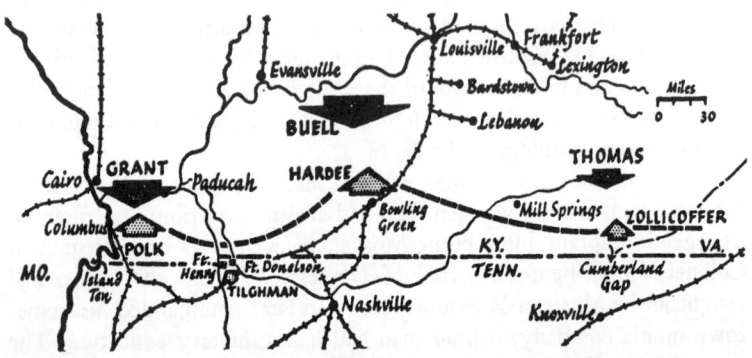

Polk on the left at Columbus had 17,000 men opposing Grant's 20,000 around Cairo; Hardee in the center at Bowling Green had 25,000 opposing Buell's 60,000 southwest of Louisville; Zollicoffer on the right had 4000 in front of Cumberland Gap, opposing 8000 under George Thomas north of Barbourville. Thus Johnston had drawn his line, badly outnumbered at the points of contact and in danger of being swamped by combinations. Fully aware of the risks he ran, he had no choice except to run them, making such use as he could of what he had and resorting to bluff whenever the danger seemed gravest, first at one point, then another. Also, a use had been found for Tilghman, who with 4500 men was stationed where geographical circumstances would give his engineering skill full scope.

The geographic factors were two rivers, the Tennessee and the Cumberland, whose existence threatened catastrophe for Johnston. Running parallel, and piercing as they did the critical center of his line, the two were like a double-barreled shotgun leveled at his heart. Despite the northern direction of their flow, they offered broad twin pathways of invasion for the steam-powered gunboats of the fleet which now controlled their mouths, twelve miles apart on the Ohio. Once into his rear, their paths diverged and they became separate threats, one deeper and the other more immediate, but both dire. Against its current, the Tennessee led down across both borders of the state whose name it bore, and then bent east and north, like a rusty hook plunged into the vitals of the South, touching northeast Mississippi on its way to Muscle Shoals in Alabama, beyond which it swung north, past Chattanooga, and finally on toward Knoxville and its source. The Cumberland, on the other hand, turned eastward soon after it crossed the northern border of Tennessee to curve back into Kentucky, across the front of Cumberland Gap and into the mountains that gave it both its waters and its name. Though the penetration was shallower, the consequences of an invasion along this line were no less stern; for during its dip into Tennessee the river ran past Clarksville and Nashville, the former being the site of the Cumberland Iron Works, second only to Richmond's Tredegar in output, and the latter, besides its importance as a manufacturing center, was the supply base for Johnston's entire army.

Those who were there before him had proposed to meet this two-pronged threat by constructing a fort to guard each river: Fort Henry, on the right bank of the Tennessee, and Fort Donelson on the left bank of the Cumberland. The first problem in each case had been location. Northward in Kentucky the rivers converged briefly to within three miles of each other, which would have allowed the forts to be mutually supporting; but since this was during the period of Bluegrass "neutrality," the chosen sites were necessarily south of the border, where the rivers were twelve miles apart — the same distance as at their mouths, fifty miles downstream — north of the two bridges over which the railroad, running northeast out of Memphis, brought food and munitions for the army. Work on the forts lagged badly from the outset, with much argument among the engineers. Yet enough had been done by the time of Johnston's arrival to cause him to leave them where they were, rather than change their location when he swung his long line outward, gate-like, with Bowling Green as the stop-post and Columbus as the hinge. Consequently, the gate was badly warped, swagged inward to include the forts commanded now by Tilghman, whom Johnston sent to strengthen and complete them.

The concave swag of the Columbus-Bowling Green sector violated the military principle requiring a defending general to operate on an interior line, so that in shifting troops from point to point, along the chord of the arc, he would be moving them a shorter distance than his opponent, outside the arc, would have to do. Between these salients the case was reversed: it was Johnston who was outside the arc, with the greater distance to travel from point to point. However, the textbook disadvantage was offset by the presence of the railroad running along the rear of his line, by which means he could shuttle his troops back and forth with far greater speed than an opponent, lacking such rapid transportation within the arc, could hope to match, despite any difference in distance. What was more, railroad and battle line were mutually supporting. So long as the line was held the road would continue its fast shifting of troops, and so long as the shuttle service went on, the line presumably could be held. The chink in the armor, Johnston knew, was where the railroad bridges spanned the rivers. Gunboats could reduce the trestles to kindling within five minutes of opening fire. They were only as safe as the forts downstream were strong. And that was why he kept urging Tilghman to exert all possible effort to get them finished.

Here as elsewhere, necessity being the mother of invention, Johnston broke or rewrote the rules whenever necessity demanded. Outnumbered severely all along his line, in each sector he improvised defenses which, in event of attack, called for reinforcements from less threatened points. His greatest advantage, indeed almost his only one, was that his army was united under a single leader, whereas the enemy forces were divided. So far, his opponents — Frémont and Anderson, then Hunter and Sherman, and finally Halleck and Buell — had failed to work in concert. What he would do if the latter pair mounted coördinated or even simultaneous offensives, from end to end of the long line or even against several points at once, he did not know and could not know, the odds being what they were. Meanwhile, he used the only means remaining: he used psychological warfare, including the dissemination of propaganda and misinformation. He used it with such skill, in fact, that it kept his shaky line intact throughout the fall and early winter and gave him time to shore it up with all the reinforcements he could find.

Throwing his troops forward he maneuvered them in a threatening manner, always as if on the verge of launching cut-and-slash attacks against the danger points. He announced to all within earshot that he had plenty of arms and plenty of men to use them; that, far from having any fears about being able to hold his ground, he was about to unleash an offensive that would roll to the Ohio, crunching the bones of whatever got in his way. The bluff had worked best against Sherman, who already had the horrors as a result of the insight which had told him just how bloody this war was likely to be. "I am convinced from many facts," he informed headquarters in a dispatch which his opponent might have dictated, "that A. Sidney Johnston is making herculean efforts to strike a great blow in Kentucky; that he designs to move from Bowling Green on Lexington, Louisville, and Cincinnati." Presently Sherman was on sick leave, restoring his Johnston-jangled nerves. If the bluff worked less dramatically on his successor, that was mainly because Buell had a less dramatic personality. At any rate, it caused him to enlarge upon the difficulties that lay between him and East Tennessee, where Lincoln so much wanted him to go. Halleck also felt its effects. They lay at the bottom of his reply that Buell's proposal for a joint advance on Nashville, up the Cumberland, "seems to me madness."

To confuse his enemies Johnston had first to mislead his friends, and this he did. Statements doubling and tripling his actual strength and hinting of an imminent offensive were printed in all the southern papers, in hopes that rival editors north of the defensive line would pick them up and spread them, which they did. Yet psychological warfare was a weapon that could boomerang, returning with a force in direct ratio to the success of its outward flight. While Halleck and Buell were counting themselves fortunate that the Confederates did not storm their lines, readers south of the border were also thoroughly taken in by Johnston, who thus compromised his reputation and risked his countrymen's morale by promising victories he knew he could never deliver with the present force at his command.

In a final effort to get more troops and supplies, on January 9, soon after the arrival of Floyd's brigade, which he had been warned would be the last, Johnston sent a personal messenger with a letter to his friend the President, reëmphasizing the gravity of the western situation. Within a week the messenger returned. He had found Davis in a "disturbed and careworn" frame of mind, but that was nothing compared to the state the Chief Executive was in by the time he had read the letter. "My God!" he cried. "Why did General Johnston send you to me for arms and reinforcements? . . . Where am I to get arms or men?"

The question was rhetorical, but the messenger, who had been primed for it, answered that they might be spared from less immediately threatened points. Davis had heard this suggestion all too often of late, along with the conflicting clamor of governors whose states had Union gunboats off their shores. Petulantly he replied that it could not be done, and remarked in closing the interview, "Tell my friend General Johnston that I can do nothing for him, that he must rely on his own resources."

The slimness of those resources was known to only a handful of men within the limits of strict confidence. Others beyond those limits thought him amply equipped and bountifully supplied, about to launch an offensive. Johnston was therefore in the position of a financier who, to stave off ruin, had overextended his credit with both friends and enemies by putting his name to a sight draft that would come due on presentation. Now that he was in too far to turn back, the President's message reached him like a notice of proceedings in bankruptcy. Kentucky was the only theater in which there had been no major clash of arms. He must have known that reverses were coming, and he must have known, too, that when they came the people would not understand.

They came soon enough. In fact, they came immediately. Coincident with the return of the messenger, Johnston's right caved in, the troops there scattering headlong, demoralized and crying like their foes the year before: "We are betrayed!"

Primarily, though, he lost that wing of his army not because of a Federal advance, as he had feared, but because of Zollicoffer's rashness and military inexperience. After occupying Cumberland Gap, the Tennessean had been ordered to move seventy miles northwest to Mill Springs, on the south bank of the Cumberland River, from which position he could parry an enemy thrust either toward the Gap, where he had posted a guard, or toward Nashville, 150 miles southwest. However, when Crittenden reached Knoxville, assuming command of the region, he learned to his amazement that Zollicoffer had not been content to remain south of the river, but had crossed and set up a camp on the opposite bank. Here at Beech Grove, with a wide unfordable river to his rear, the Tennessean was defying a Union army twice his size and attempting to stir up the doubtfully loyal citizens with proclamations which boldly inquired, "How long will Kentuckians close their eyes to the contemplated ruin of their present structure of society?"

Despite this evidence of literary skill, Crittenden now began to doubt the former editor's military judgment, and at once dispatched a courier, peremptorily ordering him to recross the river. But when he went forward on inspection in early January, to his even greater dismay he found the citizen-soldier's army still on the north bank. Zollicoffer blandly explained that Beech Grove afforded a better campsite; he had stayed where he was, in hopes that they could talk it over when Crittenden arrived. Then too, he explained — to the West Pointer's mounting horror — there were reports that the Yankees were advancing, which made falling back seem a cowardly or at any rate not a manly sort of action.

Investigation proved that the reports were all too true. Not only were the Federals advancing, they had at their head the Union-loyal Virginian George H. Thomas. Whatever his fellow Southerners might think of his "treachery" in not going with his state, they knew him to be an experienced soldier, not the least of his recommendations being that he had been a major in Johnston's 2d Cavalry. Faced with this threat, Crittenden saw that to attempt to withdraw would be to risk being hamstrung while astride the river. So he assumed command and did what he could to brace his troops in their Beech Grove camp for the shock which he believed was imminent.

What came was not the Yankees but a week of pelting rain. Despite its chill discomfort he was thankful, for if it broadened the river to his rear, it also swelled the creeks to his front and transformed into troughs of mud the roads down which the Federals were approaching. "A continuous quagmire," Thomas called them as his army slogged in double column along the opposite watersheds of Fishing Creek, which emptied into the Cumberland just above the Confederate position. Within nine miles of the rebel outposts on the 17th, he went into camp near Logan's Crossroads to rest his men, dry out their equipment, and plan the assault against Beech Grove.

The rain continued all next day, affording Thomas little respite, but presenting Crittenden with what he believed was a chance to exchange probable defeat for possible victory. In its separate camps, the enemy force was still divided by Fishing Creek, which Crittenden figured was swollen now past fording. He would move his army out that night and strike the Union left in a dawn attack. Then, having destroyed or scattered it, he would turn and deal with the other wing, beyond the flooded creek. It was a gamble, even a desperate one, but after a week spent sitting in the rain, awaiting destruction while the river ran deeper and swifter at his back, it was a gamble he was glad to take. Zollicoffer approved as soon as he heard of the plan, and at midnight the two brigades — eight regiments of infantry, plus a six-gun battery and a cavalry battalion — set out on their march through mud and rain to fight the battle variously known as Mill Springs, Fishing Creek, and Logan's Crossroads.

They soon discovered the accuracy of the description the Federal commander had given of the roads. And after a nightmare march through shin-deep mud, with rain coming hard in their faces out of a darkness relieved only by the blinding glare of lightning as they hauled at the wheels of bogged-down cannon and wagons and the heads of foundered horses, they discovered something else about George Thomas. They were launching a surprise attack against a man who could not be surprised, whose emotional make-up apparently excluded that kind of reaction to any event. Imperturbable, phlegmatic, his calm was as unruffled in a crisis as his humor was heavy-handed. Lincoln had hesitated to make the forty-five-year-old Virginian a brigadier, having doubts about his loyalty, but when he questioned Sherman and got the Ohioan's quick assurance that he personally knew Thomas to be loyal, he went ahead and signed the commission. Coming away from the interview with the President, Sherman ran into his friend on the street.

"Tom, you're a brigadier general!" he gaily announced. When Thomas showed no elation at this, Sherman began to have doubts. "Where are you going?" he asked, fearing he might be on his way to the War Department with his resignation, like so many other Virginians.

"I'm going south," Thomas replied glumly.

"My God, Tom," Sherman groaned. "You've put me in an awful position! I've just made myself responsible for your loyalty."

"Give yourself no trouble, Billy," Thomas said. "I'm going south at the head of my troops."

That was where he was going now. After a night and a day and another night spent in bivouac around Logan's Crossroads, straddling Fishing Creek, he sent a cavalry patrol out into the stormy dawn of the 19th to explore the roads leading south toward the Confederate camp. There was a spatter of musketry beyond the curtain of rain, and presently the horsemen reappeared, riding hard back up the puddled road, shouting that they had run into rebel skirmishers in advance of a heavy column. The long roll sounded. Men came stumbling big-eyed out of their tents, clutching weapons and clothes, and formed their regimental lines as if for drill, despite the rain and the fact that it was Sunday. All this while, beyond the steely glitter of the rain, an intermittent banging warned that the pickets were engaged. It sounded more like range-firing than a battle, but then the pickets came running in front of a double bank of men in muddy gray.

Crittenden kept coming. The cavalry clash had cost him the advantage of complete surprise, but he knew his troops were in better shape for an assault than for a retreat back down nine miles of churned-up road. Zollicoffer launched the attack, and at first he met with some success; the Federals recoiled from that first shock. But things went wrong in the Confederate ranks almost from the beginning. The men were cold and hungry, exhausted from their all-night march; the exhilaration of the charge burnt up what little energy they had left. Also, their flintlocks would not fire when wet, and the regiments armed with them had to be sent to the rear. Discouraged by all this, they saw the blue troops massing thick and thicker as Thomas brought up reinforcements from across the creek, whose flood stage Crittenden had mis-estimated.

The crowning blow, however, came when Zollicoffer lost his sense of direction in the rain. Conspicuous in a white rubber coat that made him an ideal target, he rode out between the lines, got turned around, and near-sightedly mistook a Federal colonel for one of his own officers. At this point his luck, which had been running strong, ran out. He was shouting an order when the colonel, a man who recognized an advantage when he saw one, leveled his revolver and put a bullet point-blank into Zollicoffer's breast.

A wail went up from the gray ranks; the Tennessean's men had loved him in spite of his rashness — if not, indeed, because of it. Their strength was mostly spent, and now this loss, occurring in plain view, cracked their spirit. They turned and made for the rear. "Betrayed!" they cried as they brushed past their officers. They ran and they kept on running, their panic infecting the other brigade, which also broke. It was Belmont in reverse, except that the Confederates had no gunboats to fall back on, or transports waiting to bear them away. Thomas replenished his ammunition and set out in pursuit, but his adversaries were well down the Beech Grove road by then. Under cover of darkness they crossed the Cumberland in relays on a rickety sternwheeler, which they burned against the southern bank. In the battle and the evacuation they lost more than 500 men, while the Federals, losing less than half as many, captured 12 guns, 1000 horses and mules, 150 wagons, and half a dozen regimental colors. By the time the pursuers could effect a crossing, there was scarcely anything left to pursue. Retreating through a region which so many of its men called home, Crittenden's army had practically ceased to exist.

Tactically complete as the Confederate defeat had been, it did not turn out to be strategically disastrous. Crossing the Cumberland, Thomas entered a region even more barren than the one he left, and though he put his men on half rations, intending to move on Knoxville, the rain continued and the roads were bottomless. He withdrew, and what was left of Crittenden's army finally called a halt at Chestnut Mound, about sixty miles from Nashville.

The respite was welcome, but it did not erase the fact that the Confederacy had suffered its first drubbing in the field. There had to be an explanation — or, failing that, a scapegoat — and Crittenden was the logical target for accusing fingers. "Betrayed!" the men had cried as they broke and fled. Investigation of what this meant turned up some strange answers, including testimony that the commanding general had been "in an almost beastly state of intoxication" throughout the battle. Remembering that his brother was a Union general, people began to suspect that his heart was not in the cause. There was even a rumor that **one of his messengers had been captured bearing information to Thomas.**

The South had no Joint Committee, such as the North had after the Ball's Bluff fiasco; Crittenden was spared the fate of his Federal counterpart, General Stone, languishing now in a dungeon in New York harbor. But the South had other methods. Eventually a court of inquiry found the Kentuckian innocent of treason but guilty of intoxication. He was reduced to the rank of colonel, and presently he resigned to serve as a civilian on the staff of an obscure brigadier in the Transmississippi, the dustbin of the Confederate army.

That was still in the future, though, and Johnston had nothing to do with it. For the present, he wired Crittenden to regroup his men and offer whatever resistance he could if Thomas came on after him. The western commander had graver worries closer to Bowling Green, where he had set up his headquarters as the best location from which to survey his long, tenuous line. For while Buell was lunging at his right, Halleck was probing his left — particularly at the point of double danger, where the incompleted forts stood guarding the parallel rivers that pierced his front.

It was here that Johnston was most touchy, and with good cause. Arriving in late November, the engineering brigadier Tilghman had reported: "I have completed a thorough examination of Henry and Donelson and do not admire the aspect of things." He wanted more troops, muskets for his unarmed men, and "more heavy guns for both places at once." The report had a gloomy, determined ending: "I feel for the first time discouraged, but will not give up."

Tilghman's gloom was warranted. Neither of the forts was in anything resembling a condition for offering stiff resistance to amphibious attacks. To make matters worse, Fort Henry was located on low ground, dominated by heights across the river and subject to flooding when the river rose. He later declared outright, "The history of military engineering records no parallel to this case."

One solution was to relocate the forts. Another was to fortify the opposite heights. Pondering which was preferable, he did neither. Johnston meanwhile sent him what he could, so that by mid-January Tilghman had 5700 troops: 3400 at Henry and 2300 at Donelson. Then came Buell's lunge and Halleck's probe. Both withdrew, Buell because of the rain and lack of rations, Halleck because he had only intended a feint; but Johnston knew they would be back soon enough. Three days after the Mill Springs rout, announcing the death of Zollicoffer and predicting a Federal strike against the forts, he made a final appeal to the Adjutant General: "The country must now be roused to make the greatest effort that it will be called upon to make during the war. No matter what the sacrifice may be, it must be made, and without loss of time. . . . All the resources of the Confederacy are now needed for the defense of Tennessee."

Now as before, Johnston did what he could with what he had.

He sent Pillow to Clarksville, sixty miles down the railroad, within supporting distance of the forts. Floyd and Buckner were sent with their brigades to Russellville, midway between Pillow and himself, within reach of both. Then, as January wore to a close, he learned to his dismay that Tilghman at Fort Henry was still pondering whether to fortify the high ground across the river. "It is most extraordinary," Johnston exclaimed. "I ordered General Polk four months ago to at once construct those works. And now, with the enemy on us, nothing of importance has been done. It is most extraordinary."

Mastering his alarm as best he could, he wired Tilghman: "Occupy and intrench the heights opposite Fort Henry. Do not lose a moment. Work all night."

★ ★ ★

Johnston was not the only commander alarmed by the success of Buell's lieutenant in East Kentucky. On the day after the battle, still not having heard the news, Henry Halleck returned to his desk after a four-day bout with the measles. During his time in bed he had reconsidered the suggested move against Nashville by means of a two-pronged advance up the Cumberland and the Tennessee. He no longer considered the operation "madness." In fact, he wrote McClellan that Monday morning, such an advance would follow "the great central line of the Western theater of war." However, he was quick to add, the movement should not be launched without a force of at least 60,000 effectives. As for Buell's proposed simultaneous advance upon the Tennessee capital, he considered it neither wise nor necessary. It was "bad strategy," he wrote, "because it requires a double force to accomplish a single object." Halleck wanted a one-man show, with Halleck as the man.

Having dispatched his letter to the General-in-Chief, the convalescent author of the *Elements of Military Art and Science* sat back and scratched his elbows. It was then that the news of Fishing Creek arrived, and the effect was as if a bomb had been exploded under his desk. What Thomas had done for Buell in eastern Kentucky was comparable to what Rosecrans had done for McClellan in western Virginia the year before. McClellan's elevation had followed swiftly after Philippi: so might Buell's after Fishing Creek — especially considering the fact that the advance had opened the way to East Tennessee, which everyone knew was Lincoln's pet concern. In the glare of that bomb-burst, Halleck saw his worst fears outlined stark before him: Buell might get the West.

That changed everything. Before he could consider what to do, however, he must somehow recover from the paralyzing shock which was his first reaction to the news. U. S. Grant returned to Cairo on the same day Halleck got up from the measles; his demonstration to immobilize Polk had not only been successful, it had given him ideas. "A fine reconnaissance," he called it, and requested permission to visit St Louis for a discussion with the commanding general. Halleck by now had the news from East Kentucky. "You have permission to visit headquarters," he replied, as if in a daze, and by Friday Grant was there. He found Halleck vague and noncommittal, still suffering from the shock of his rival's success. Consequently, the interview fell flat. "I was received with so little cordiality," Grant later declared, "that I perhaps stated the object of my visit with less clearness than I might have done, and I had not uttered many sentences before I was cut short as if my plan was preposterous." He returned to Cairo "very much crestfallen."

He was not crestfallen long. On his return he found a dispatch from Brigadier General C. F. Smith, who had demonstrated up the Tennessee while Grant had been pretending to threaten Columbus. Smith was sixty, with a ramrod stiffness, a habit of profanity, and a white walrus mustache. He had been commandant of cadets when Grant was at West Point, but now, as was often the case with old line officers who had stayed in the service, he was outranked by the volunteer commander and came under his authority. His advance had taken him down near the Tennessee line, within three miles of the fort on the east bank of the river, and in his report to Grant he stated flatly, "I think two ironclad gunboats would make short work of Fort Henry."

On his visit with Halleck in St Louis the week before, Grant had proposed a general forward movement. Now here was something specific. Returning to the charge, he promptly wired:

Cairo, January 28
Maj. Gen. H. W. Halleck
Saint Louis, Mo.:
    With permission, I will take Fort Henry on the Tennessee, and establish and hold a large camp there.
U. S. GRANT
Brigadier General.

Halleck was just emerging from his state of shock. Perhaps by now he was even beginning to hear the words Grant had spoken three days ago, before he cut him short. At any rate, he saw that he must accomplish something to counterbalance the success his rival had scored at the opposite end of the line, and on second thought this looked like just the something. A week back, he had told McClellan that the advance up the rivers should not be undertaken by a force of less than 60,000 effectives. Grant had barely one-third that many men, including Smith's. However, leery as Halleck was of the wild man of Belmont, he knew that when Grant said plainly, "I will take Fort Henry," it meant an all-out effort and quick movement by field-hardened troops. There was the risk that Polk might move forward from Columbus, threatening the line of the Ohio while Grant was on his way southward up the Tennessee, but Halleck thought this unlikely, considering the success of the recent feint in that direction.

He was still pondering his decision when a telegram arrived from McClellan, reporting that a rebel deserter had just informed him that Beauregard was leaving Manassas to go to Kentucky with fifteen regiments of Confederate infantry. That resolved Halleck's final doubt. He would strike before Beauregard arrived. Next morning, Thursday the 30th, he wired Grant: "Make your preparations to take and hold Fort Henry. I will send you written instructions by mail."

Fort Henry being in Tennessee, he availed himself of the opportunity to request an enlargement of the area of his command, wiring McClellan: "I respectfully suggest that that state be added to this department." One thing remained to be done: inform Buell. With his campaign launched beyond any possibility of his rival's being able to claim a hand in its inception — but not too late to call on him for help if help was needed — Halleck telegraphed him curtly: "I have ordered an advance of our troops on Fort Henry and Dover. It will be made immediately." Now it was Buell's turn to be shocked at rival progress. "I protest against such prompt proceedings," he wrote McClellan, "as though I had nothing to do but command 'Commence firing' when he starts off."

The written instructions Halleck had promised his lieutenant were short and to the point, giving the latest intelligence on the strength of the fort, repeating McClellan's warning that Beauregard was on the way with reinforcements, and including the sentence, "You will move with the least delay possible." Knowing his man, Halleck knew that such words were as apt to produce results as a yank on the lanyard of a well-primed cannon. Grant's reply, from Paducah during the daylight hours of February 3, was the briefest yet: "Will be off up the Tennessee at 6 o'clock. Command, twenty-three regiments in all." And so it was. In the gathering dusk the transports slipped their moorings. The campaign to take Fort Henry was under way.

In the lead were four ironclad gunboats, unlike any ever seen before on this or any river. They were the invention, the product — and at this stage the property — of James B. Eads, who had built them in one hundred days on an army contract let to him in August, when they were intended, along with three others, to constitute the hard core of the column that would accomplish Frémont's lopping descent of the Mississippi. The Pathfinder was gone now, along with his plan, but the gunboats remained. Designed for river fighting, they were 175 feet long and a bit over 50 feet in the beam. Two and one-half inch overlapping plates of armor were bolted to the bows to give protection from head-on fire, and the sides were sloped at 35° to deflect shots taken broadside. For armament they mounted thirteen guns apiece, three at the bow, two at the stern, and four on each side. Despite the weight of all this metal, they were surprisingly maneuverable and drew only six feet of water: which meant, in river parlance, that they could "run on a heavy dew."

Eads, a native of Indiana and a man of industry, was one of those included in the southern sneer at the North as "a race of pasty-faced mechanics." When he arrived in St Louis to start work on his contract, the trees from which he would hew timbers were still standing in the forests. Within two weeks he had 4000 men at work around the clock, Sundays not excepted. When he ran out of money he used his own, and when that gave out he borrowed more from friends. By the end of November he had launched eight gunboats, a formidable squadron aggregating 5000 tons, with a cruising speed of nine knots an hour and an armament of 107 guns. The government was less prompt in payment, though, than Eads was in delivery. He still had not been reimbursed when the fleet set out for Henry: so that, technically, the ironclads were still his own.

The turtle-back steamers were not a navy project; the admirals left such harebrained notions to the army. For the most part, even the sailors aboard the boats were soldiers, volunteers from Grant's command who had answered a call for river- and seafaring men to transfer for gunboat service. Once the fleet was launched and manned, however, the navy saw its potential and was willing to furnish captains for its quarterdecks. Having made the offer, which was quickly accepted, the admirals did not hold back, but sent some of their most promising officers westward for service on the rivers. None among them was more distinguished, more experienced — or tougher — than the man assigned to flag command.

Commodore Andrew H. Foote was a Connecticut Yankee, a small man with burning eyes, a jutting gray chin-beard, and a long, naked upper lip. A veteran who had fought the Chinese at Canton and chased slavers in the South Atlantic, he was deeply, puritanically religious, and conducted a Bible school for his crew every Sunday, afloat or ashore. Twenty years before, he had had the first temperance ship in the U.S. Navy, and before the present year was out he would realize a lifelong ambition by seeing the alcohol ration abolished throughout the service. At fifty-six he had spent forty years as a career officer fighting the two things he hated most, slavery and whiskey. It was perhaps a quirk of fate to have placed him thus alongside Grant, who could scarcely be said to have shown an aversion for either. But if fate had juxtaposed them so, in hopes that they would strike antagonistic sparks, then fate was disappointed. Foote, like Grant, believed in combined operations, and had joined with him in bombarding Halleck with telegrams urging the undertaking of this one. Army and Navy, the commodore said, "were like blades of shears — united, invincible; separated, almost useless."

So built, so manned and led, the fleet put out in the rainy, early February darkness, southward up the swollen Tennessee: four ironclads and three wooden gunboats escorting nine transports with their cargo of blue-clad soldiers, the first of Grant's two divisions, which together totaled 15,000 men. Having landed the first, the transports would return downriver to bring the second forward; then the two would move together against the fort, the gunboats meanwhile taking it under bombardment. The initial problem was to locate a landing place as near the objective as possible and yet beyond the range of its big guns. One complication was Panther Creek, which flowed westward into the river, a little over three miles north of the fort. A landing north of the creek would mean that the troops would have to cross or go around it. That was undesirable, involving problematical delay. Yet a landing south of the creek might bring the transports under the rebel guns, with resultant havoc and probable disaster. Grant must first determine their range. He did so, characteristically, in the quickest, simplest way: by personal reconnaissance. Halting the fleet in the cold predawn darkness, eight miles short of the fort, he ordered three of the ironclads forward to draw the fire of the guns, and boarded one of them, the *Essex*, to go along and find out for himself.

He found out soon enough. The ironclads steamed past the creek mouth and opened fire within two miles of the fort. The answering shells fell short until a 6-inch rifle came into action, splashing its first shot not only beyond the gunboats, but beyond the mouth of the creek as well. Grant now had the information he wanted; no landing could be made south of the creek without bringing the transports under fire. But then the rifle's gunner made the information even more emphatic by demonstrating the kind of marksmanship the gunboats would encounter in an attack against Fort Henry. Shortening the range, he put the next shot squarely into the *Essex*. Having secured the information they sought, and more, the ironclads turned and went back down the river, the wounded *Essex* bringing up the rear with a 6-inch shell in her steerage and a wiser troop commander on her bridge.

Now that he knew how to do what must be done, Grant went back to get the movement started. The fleet proceeded southward, landing the First division north of the creek, and while the empty transports set out downriver on their hundred-mile round trip to bring the Second division forward, he completed the details of his attack plan. The key to the position, he saw — Belmont having taught him just how briefly troops could hold an objective which came under the plunging fire of enemy guns — was the high ground on the west bank, dominating the low-lying fort across the river. Reconnaissance had drawn no fire from there and Grant had been able to spot no guns through his glasses. But that was inconclusive. Intelligence had warned him that the Confederates were at work there; the batteries might be masked, under orders to hold their fire until a target worth their powder hove in view. Therefore he assigned the Second division the task of seizing the left-bank heights, planting artillery there, while the First division moved against the fort itself, angling around the head of Panther Creek to come in from the east and thus prevent the escape of the garrison in case it tried to retreat from under the fleet bombardment.

How large that garrison was he did not know. There was no way of telling how many reinforcements might have arrived overland from Donelson, twelve miles away, or by rail from Bowling Green or Memphis, since the defenders first learned of the task force moving up the Tennessee. In any case, the right-bank attack would be the main effort, and he detached one brigade from the Second division, which had three, ordering it to land on the eastern bank and support the First division, which had two. One more detachment from the Second division, a rifle company to act as sharpshooters on the warships, and Grant's attack plan was complete. If Fort Henry could be taken by 15,000 men and seven gunboats, he was going to take it.

There were other problems: the fact that the river was mined, for instance, which meant that at any minute any vessel, ironclad or transport, was apt to go sky-high in smoke and flame, the attacking force reduced to that extent by quick subtraction. Contact mines, or "torpedoes" as they were called, were a new and formidable weapon, a fiendish example of rebel ingenuity. Anchored to the river-bottom by cables that held them upright underwater, they were equipped with pronged rods extending upward to just below the surface, ready to trip the detonators on contact. The rising river had reduced their effectiveness, some being submerged by now beyond scraping distance and others floating around loose, torn from their moorings; but there was still a good deal of conjecture and concern about them.

On the afternoon of the 5th, while in conference with Foote and the two division commanders aboard the flagship, Grant got a chance to make a first-hand inspection of one of these new implements of war. A gunboat tied up alongside and her captain sent word that he had fished a torpedo out of the river. He had it there on deck, he said, in case the commodore and the generals wanted to see it. They did indeed want to see it, if only as a diversion. The conference was about finished anyhow; little remained to be done except to await the arrival of the Second division, still being brought in relays from Paducah. Crossing over to the gunboat, the commodore and his aides and the generals and their staffs clustered on the fantail and stood in a semicircle looking down at the torpedo.

It appeared to be quite as dangerous as they had feared. A metal cylinder five feet long and a foot and a half in diameter, the thing was made especially venomous-looking by the pronged rod extending from its head. Grant wanted more than a look, however. He wanted to know how it worked. So the ship's armorer came with his wrenches and chisels, and while he tinkered the interested officers watched. Suddenly, as he was loosening a nut, the device emitted an ominous hissing sound, which seemed to be mounting swiftly toward a climax. The reaction of the watchers was immediate. Some ran, exploding outward from the semicircular cluster, while others threw themselves face-downward on the deck. Rank had no precedent; it was each man for himself.

Foote sprang for the ship's ladder, and Grant, perhaps reasoning that in naval matters the commodore knew best, was right behind him. If he lacked the seaman's agility in climbing a rope ladder, he made up for it with what one witness called "commendable enthusiasm." At the top, the commodore looked back over his shoulder and found Grant closing rapidly upon him. The hissing had stopped. Whatever danger there had been was past. Foote smiled.

"General, why this haste?" he asked, and his words, though calmly spoken, were loud against the silence.

"That the navy may not get ahead of us," Grant replied.

★ ★ ★

Lloyd Tilghman was slim and dark-skinned, with a heavy, carefully barbered mustache and chin-beard, an erect, soldierly bearing, and piercing black eyes intensifying what one observer called "a resolute, intelligent expression of countenance." His resolution had not waned, but after two days of watching the Federal build-up to his front, he was beginning to realize that the fate of the fort was scarcely less predictable than that of a shoe-nail about to be driven by a very large sledge-hammer lustily swung.

His 3400 men were miserably armed with hunting rifles, shotguns, and 1812-style flintlocks, and his cannon were scarcely better. Two out of a shipment cast from what looked like pot-metal had burst in target practice, and several others had been condemned, a British observer pronouncing them less dangerous to the enemy than to the men who served them. Tilghman was threatened, in fact, by more than the gunboats and the blue-clad infantry, and weakened by more than the shortage of serviceable arms. In one week, back in mid-January when the rains came, the river had risen fourteen feet, demonstrating graphically the unwisdom of the engineers who had sited Fort Henry at this particular bend of the Tennessee. Only nine of the fifteen guns bearing riverward remained above water in early February, and now while the river continued to rise, lapping at last at the magazine, it had become a question of which would get there first, flood crest or the Yankees.

In spite of all this, the Kentucky brigadier did not despair when his lookout, peering downriver through the rainy dawn of the 4th, announced the approach of gunboats and behind them the coal-smoke plumes of the transports winding northward out of sight. Determined to fight, he wired Polk for reinforcements from Columbus, and the following day, having turned back the ironclad reconnaissance and seen that the Federals were landing in force, three miles north of the fort, he wired Johnston at Bowling Green: "If you can reinforce strongly and quickly we have a glorious chance to overwhelm the enemy." Accordingly, he sent his troops with their squirrel guns and fowling pieces to man the rifle pits blocking the landward approaches. If no help came, he would fight with what he had.

However, as the day wore on and the transports returned with further relays of northern troops, he began to realize the full length of the odds — particularly on the opposite bank, where the Union brigades were landing and preparing to move against the unfinished, unmanned works on the high ground which dominated the shipwrecked fort on this side. Without losing his resolution to give battle, he saw clearly that whoever stood on this nailhead, under the swing of that sledge, was going to be destroyed; and he saw, too, that, whatever his personal inclination, his military duty was to save what he could of a command whose doom was all but sealed.

At a council of war, called that night in the fort — the enemy build-up continued, seemingly endless, three miles downriver, on both banks — he announced his decision. While a sacrifice garrison manned whatever guns were yet above water, discouraging pursuit, the infantry would be evacuated, marching overland to join the troops at Donelson. Next morning a company of Tennessee artillery, two officers and 54 men, took their posts at the guns, awaiting the attack they knew was coming, while the foot soldiers filed out of the rifle pits and the fort, taking the road eastward.

Tilghman went a certain distance to see them on their way, and then, still resolute, turned back to join the forlorn hope. It was noon by now. As he drew near, the sound of guns came booming across water.

Two-thirds by land, one-third by water, Grant's triple-pronged upriver attack, designed as a simultaneous advance by the two divisions, one along each bank while the gunboats took the middle, was slated to get under way at 11 o'clock, by which time the final relay of troops had arrived from Paducah. Both infantry columns went forward on schedule, but Foote, on his own initiative, held back until almost noon, allowing the landsmen at least a measure of the head start they needed. The rain had stopped; the sun came through, defining the target clearly, and there was even a light breeze to clear away the battle smoke and permit the rapid and accurate fire the commodore expected of his gunners. For almost an hour the crews stood by — converted soldiers and fresh-water sailors bracing themselves for their first all-out action, with "just enough men-of-war's men," as one skipper said, "to leaven the lump with naval discipline" — until the attack pennant was hoisted and the squadron moved upstream, the ironclads steaming four abreast in the lead and the three wooden gunboats bringing up the rear.

"The flagship will, of course, open the fire," Foote had ordered, and at 1700 yards she did so. The others joined the chorus, firing as many of their 54 guns as could be brought to bear on the fort, whose nine gun-crews stood to their pieces and replied at once in kind, loosing what one of the defenders proudly called "as pretty and as simultaneous a 'broadside' as I ever saw flash from the sides of a frigate." This continued. Preceded by "one broad and leaping sheet of flame," as the same defender said, the ironclads deliberately closed the range to 600 yards while the more vulnerable wooden vessels hugged the western bank, adding the weight of their metal to the pressure on the earthworks.

Based as it was on predetermined ranges, fire from the fort was accurate and fast. For a time at least, the Tennessee artillerists seemed to be inflicting the greater damage. Aboard the warships, men were deafened by the din of solid shot pounding and breaking the iron plates and splintering heavy timbers, while shells screamed and whistled in the rigging, bursting, raining fragments. Foote's flagship, the prime target, was struck thirty-two times in the course of the action, two of her guns disabled and her stacks, boats, and after-cabin riddled. The captain of the ironclad on her left, which took thirty hits, said of one shot which he saw strike the flagship, "It had the effect, apparently, of a thunderbolt, ripping her side timbers and scattering the splinters over the vessel. She did not slacken her speed, but moved on as though nothing special had happened." Not so the luckless *Essex*. Patched up from the hurt she had received two days ago, she took another now through her boiler: an unlucky shot which left her powerless in a cloud of escaping steam, with twenty-eight scalded men aboard, some dead and others dying. Out of control, she swung broadside to the current, then careened, leaving a gap in the line of battle, and drifted downstream, out of the fight.

Encouraged by this proof that the turtle-back monsters could be hurt, the defenders cheered and redoubled their efforts. But they had done their worst — in fact, their all: for now there followed a series of accidents and mishaps which abolished whatever chance they had had for victory at the outset. Only two of their guns could really damage the ironclads, the high-velocity 6-inch rifle, which had already proved its effectiveness, and a giant columbiad which made up for its lack of range by the heft of its 128-pound projectile. The rest, low-sited as they were, with their muzzles near the water, could do no more than bounce their 32- and 42-pound shells off the armored prows of the attackers. First to go was the rifle, which burst in firing, disabling not only its own crew, but also those of the flanking pieces. Next, the big columbiad was spiked by a broken priming wire and thus put out of action, despite the efforts of a blacksmith who attempted to repair it under fire. Of the seven cannon left, which could only dent the armor and shiver the timbers of the gunboats, one had to be abandoned for lack of ammunition and two were wrecked almost at once by enemy shells. That left four guns to face the fire of the attackers, the range now being closed, almost point-blank, and even those four were served by skeleton crews, scraped together from among the survivors.

These included Tilghman. The fort commander had returned from seeing the infantry off, and was serving as a cannoneer at one of the four pieces. He had asked the artillerists to hold out for an hour, affording the garrison that much of a head start on its march to Donelson. Now that they had held out two, with the long odds growing longer all the time, the tactical considerations had been satisfied twice over, and those of honor as well. He ordered the flag struck. It was done and the firing ceased.

"That the navy may not get ahead of us," Grant had said, and it was as if he spoke from prescience. In the combined attack, as in the scramble up the ladder, Foote came out on top. The navy fired not only the first shot and the last, but also all the shots between, and suffered all the casualties as well: 12 killed and missing and 27 wounded, compared to the fort's 10 killed and missing and 11 wounded. In fact, the navy's closest rival was not the army, but the river. Another few hours would have put the remaining cannon under water. As it was, the cutter bearing the naval officers to receive the formal surrender pulled right in through the sally port.

Tilghman was waiting for them. He had already earned their respect by his bravery as an opponent, and now, by the dignity of his bearing as a prisoner, he won their sympathy as well. However, his reception of the copy-hungry northern correspondents, who were soon on hand to question him, was less congenial. As a southern gentleman he believed there were only three events in a man's life which warranted the printing of his name without permission: his birth, his marriage, and his death. So that when a Chicago reporter asked him how he spelled his name, he replied in measured terms: "Sir, I do not desire to have my name appear in this matter, in any newspaper connection whatever. If General Grant sees fit to use it in his official dispatches, I have no objection, sir; but I do not wish to have it in the newspapers."

"I merely asked it to mention as one among the prisoners captured," the correspondent said. But the Confederate either did not catch the dig or else ignored it.

"You will oblige me, sir," he repeated, as if this put an end to the matter, "by not giving my name in any newspaper connection whatever."

Grant arrived at 3 o'clock, by which time the Stars and Stripes had been flying over the fort for nearly an hour. His two divisions were still toiling through the mud on opposite banks of the river, one bogged down in the backwater sloughs of Panther Creek and the other slogging toward the empty western heights. Who won the race meant less to him, however, than the winning — and neither meant so much, apparently, as the fact that more remained to be accomplished. He had his mind on the railroad bridge fifteen miles upriver, over which Johnston could speed reinforcements from flank to flank of his line. The three wooden gunboats were dispatched at once to attend to it: which they did in fine style that same day. Nor was that all. Continuing on to Muscle Shoals, the head of navigation, they destroyed or captured six Confederate vessels, including a fast, 280-foot Mississippi steamboat being converted into an ironclad. Intended as an answer to the fleet of the invaders, she became instead a member of that fleet and saw much service.

This 150-mile gunboat thrust, all the way down past Mississippi and into Alabama, was dramatic proof of the fruits resulting from control of the Tennessee. A highway of invasion had been cleared. Yet Grant had his eye on another goal already, another fort on another river a dozen miles from the one he had just taken: as was shown by his wire to the theater commander on the day of his success. "Fort Henry is ours," the dispatch began, and ended with a forecast: "I shall take and destroy Fort Donelson on the 8th and return to Fort Henry."

Halleck passed the word along as promptly to McClellan, repeating Grant's first sentence and adding two of his own: "Fort Henry is ours. The flag of the Union is reëstablished on the soil of Tennessee. It will never be removed."

※ 2 ※

Grant was not alone in his belief that he could "take and destroy" the Cumberland fortress; Albert Sidney Johnston thought so, too. When word of the fall of Henry reached his headquarters at Bowling Green next day, he relayed the news to Richmond, adding that Fort Donelson was "not long tenable." In fact, such was his respect for the promptness and power with which the ironclads had reduced their first objective, he wrote that he expected the second to fall in the same manner, "without the necessity of [the Federals'] employing their land force in coöperation."

All the events he had feared most, and with good cause, had come to pass. Right, left, and center, his long defensive line was coming apart with the suddenness of a shaky split-rail fence in the path of a flood. His right at Mill Springs had been smashed, the survivors scattering deep into Tennessee while Buell inched toward Bowling Green with 40,000 effectives opposing Hardee's 14,000. The loss of Henry and its railroad bridge, with Federal gunboats making havoc up the river to his rear, had split his center from his left, outflanking Columbus and Bowling Green and rendering both untenable. When Donelson fell, as he expected in short order, the gunboats would continue up the Cumberland as they had done up the Tennessee, forcing the fall of Nashville, his main depot of supplies, and cutting off the Army of Central Kentucky from the southern bank.

This left him two choices, both unwelcome. With his communications disrupted and his lines of reinforcement snapped, he could stand and fight against the odds, opposing two converging armies, each one larger than his own. Or he could retreat and save his army while there was time, consolidating south of the river to strike back when the chance came. Whichever he did, one thing was clear: the choice must be made quickly. All those sight-drafts he had signed were coming due at once. The long winter's bluff was over. The uses of psychological warfare were exhausted. He was faced now with the actual bloody thing.

He called at once a council of war to confer with his two ranking generals. One was Hardee, commander of the center, whose prominent forehead seemed to bulge with knowledge left over from what he had packed into the *Tactics*. The other was Beauregard. The hero of Sumter and Manassas had arrived three days ago; but there were no fifteen regiments in his train, only a handful of staff officers. Davis had long since warned that he could spare no more soldiers, and he meant it. But apparently he could spare this one, whom many considered the finest soldier of them all, and by sparing him solve the double problem of removing the Creole's busy pen from the proximity of Richmond and silencing those critics who cried that the President had no thought for the western front.

Beauregard had come to Kentucky believing that Johnston was about to take the offensive with 70,000 men. When he arrived and learned the truth he reacted with a horror akin to that of Crittenden at Zollicoffer's rashness, and like Crittenden he at first proposed an immediate withdrawal. By the time of the council of war, however, he had managed to absorb the shock. His mercurial spirits had risen to such an extent, in fact, that the news of the fall of Henry only increased his belligerency. At the council, held in his hotel room on the afternoon of the 7th — the general was indisposed, down with a cold while convalescing from a throat operation he had undergone just before leaving Virginia — he proposed in a husky voice that Johnston concentrate all his troops at Donelson, defeat Grant at that place, then turn on Buell and send him reeling back to the Ohio.

Johnston shook his head. He could not see it. To give all his attention to Grant would mean abandoning Nashville to Buell, and the loss of that transportation hub, with its accumulation of supplies, would mean the loss of subsistence for his army. Even if that army emerged victorious at Donelson — which was by no means certain, since Grant might well be knocking at the gate already, his invincible ironclads out in front and his numbers doubled by reinforcements from Missouri and Illinois — it would then find Buell astride its communications, possessed of its base, twice its strength, and fresh for fighting. Johnston's army was all that stood between the Federals and the conquest of the Mississippi Valley. To risk its loss was to risk the loss of the Valley, and to lose the Valley, Johnston believed, was to lose the war in the West. It was like the poem about the horseshoe nail: Fort Henry was the nail.

Beauregard at last agreed. Along with Hardee he signed his name approving the document by which Johnston informed Richmond that, Henry having fallen and Donelson being about to fall, the army at Bowling Green would have to retreat behind the Cumberland. For the present at least, Kentucky must be given up.

Preparations for the evacuation began at once. Four days later, with Buell still inching forward, the retrograde movement began. The garrison at Donelson was expected to hold out as long as possible, keeping Grant off Hardee's flank and rear, then slip away, much as Tilghman's infantry had slipped away from Henry, to join the main body around Nashville. Beauregard was up and about by then, helping all he could, but Johnston had a special use for him. Columbus, being outflanked, must also be abandoned. Severed already from headquarters control, it required a high-ranking leader who could exercise independent command. That meant Beauregard. After a final conference with Johnston, who reached Nashville with the van of his army one week after the council of war at Bowling Green, he started for Columbus. His instructions empowered him to give up that place, if in his judgment it was necessary or advisable to do so, then fall back to Island Ten, where the Mississippi swung a lazy S along the Tennessee line, and to Fort Pillow, another sixty airline miles downriver.

Charged with the conduct of a retreat, the Creole's spirits flagged again. His heart was heavy, he wrote to a friend in Virginia; "I am taking the helm when the ship is already on the breakers, and with but few sailors to man it. How it is to be extricated from its present perilous condition, Providence alone can determine."

Southeast of Columbus, the gloom was no less heavy for being fitful. During the week since the fall of its sister fort across the way, the atmosphere at Donelson had been feverish, with a rapid succession of brigadiers hastening preparations for the attack which each believed was imminent.

First had come the fugitives from Henry, shamefaced and angry, with lurid details of the gunboats' might and the host of Federals whose trap they had eluded. Brigadier General Bushrod Johnson assumed command the following day, an Ohio-born West Pointer who had left the army to teach school in Tennessee and, liking it, offered his services when that state seceded. Two days later, on the 9th, Gideon Pillow arrived from Clarksville. Relying on "the courage and fidelity of the brave officers and men under his command," he exhorted them to "drive back the ruthless invaders from our soil and again raise the Confederate flag over Fort Henry.... Our battle cry, 'Liberty or death.'" Simon Buckner marched in from Russellville next day. All this time, John B. Floyd was hovering nearby with his brigade; Johnston had told him to act on his own discretion, and he rather suspected the place of being a trap. By now Pillow had recovered from his notion of launching an offensive, but he wrote: "I will never surrender the position, and with God's help I mean to maintain it." Encouraged by this show of nerve, Floyd arrived on the 13th. Donelson's fourth commander within a week, he got there at daybreak, in time to help repulse the first all-out land attack. Grant's army had come up during the night.

The Federals were apt to find this fort a tougher nut than the one they had cracked the week before. Like Henry, it commanded a bend in the river; but there the resemblance ceased. Far from being in danger of inundation, Donelson's highest guns, a rifled 128-pounder and two 32-pounder carronades, were emplaced on the crown of a hundred-foot bluff. Two-thirds of the way down, a battery mounting a 10-inch columbiad and eight smooth-bore 32-pounders was dug into the bluff's steep northern face. All twelve of these pieces were protected by earthworks, the embrasures narrowed with sandbags. Landward the position was less impregnable, but whatever natural obstacles stood in the path of assault had been strengthened by Confederate engineers.

To the north, flowing into the river where the bluff came sheerly down, Hickman Creek, swollen with backwater, secured the right flank like a bridgeless moat protecting a castle rampart. The fort proper, a rustic sort of stockade affair inclosing several acres of rude log huts, was designed to house the garrison and protect the water batteries from incidental sorties. It could never withstand large-scale attacks such as the one about to be launched, however, and the engineers had met this threat by fortifying the low ridge running generally southeast, parallel to the bend of the river a mile away. Rifle pits were dug along it, the yellow-clay spoil thrown onto logs for breastworks, describing thus a three-mile arc which inclosed the bluff on the north and the county-seat hamlet of Dover on the south, the main supply base. At its weaker and more critical points, as for instance where Indian Creek and the road from Henry pierced its center, chevaux-de-frise were improvised by felling trees so that they lay with their tops outward, the branches interlaced and sharpened to impale attacking troops. All in all, the line was strong and adequately manned. With the arrival of Floyd's brigade there were 28 infantry regiments to defend it: a total of 17,500 men, including the artillery and cavalry, with six light batteries in addition to the big guns bearing riverward.

Floyd had experienced considerable trepidation on coming in, but his success in repulsing attacks against both ends of his line that morning restored his spirits and even sent them soaring. "Our field defenses are good," he wired Johnston. "I think we can sustain ourselves against the land forces." As for his chances against the ironclads, though his batteries turned back a naval reconnaissance that afternoon, he felt less secure. He wired Johnston: "After two hours' cannonade the enemy hauled off their gunboats; will commence probably again."

He was right. Steaming four abreast against his batteries next day, they did indeed commence again. When the squat black bug-shaped vessels opened fire, the cavalry commander Bedford Forrest turned to one of his staff, a former minister. "Parson, for God sake pray!" he cried. "Nothing but God Amighty can save that fort." Floyd emphatically agreed. In fact, in a telegram which he got off to Johnston while the gunboats were bearing down upon him, he defined what he believed were the limits of his resistance: "The fort cannot hold out twenty minutes."

★ ★ ★

Grant had predicted the immediate fall of Donelson to others beside Halleck. On the day the gunboats took Fort Henry he told a reporter from Greeley's *Tribune*, who stopped by headquarters to say goodbye before leaving to file his story in New York: "You had better wait a day or two.... I am going over to capture Fort Donelson tomorrow." This interested the journalist. "How strong is it?" he asked, and Grant replied: "We have not been able to ascertain exactly, but I think we can take it." The reporter would not wait. On the theory that a fort in the hand was worth two in the brush, he made the long trip by river and rail to New York, filed his story — and was back on the banks of the Cumberland before Grant's campaign reached its climax.

The initial delay was caused by a number of things: not the least of which was the fact that on the following day, the 7th, in pursuance of his intention to "take and destroy" the place on the 8th, Grant reconnoitered within a mile of the rifle pits the rebels were digging, and saw for himself the size of the task he was undertaking. To have sent his army forward at once would have meant attacking without the assistance of the gunboats, which would have to make the long trip down the Tennessee and up the Cumberland to Donelson. Besides, the river was still rising, completing the shipwreck of Henry and threatening to recapture from Grant the spoils he had captured from Tilghman, so that his troops, as he reported in explanation, were "kept busily engaged in saving what we have from the rapidly rising waters."

There was danger in delay. Fort Donelson was being reinforced; Johnston might concentrate and crush him. But Grant was never one to give much weight to such considerations, even when they occurred to him. Meanwhile, his army was growing, too. Intent on his chance for command of the West — for which he had already recommended himself in dispatches announcing the capture of Henry and the impending fall of Donelson — Halleck was sending, as he described it, "everything I can rake and scrape together from Missouri." Within a few days Grant was able to add a brigade to each of his two divisions. On second thought, with 10,000 more reinforcements on the way in transports and Foote's ironclads undergoing repairs at Cairo, he believed that he had more to gain from waiting than from haste. So he waited. All the same, in a letter written on the 9th he declared that he would "keep the ball moving as lively as possible." Hearing that Pillow, whose measure he had taken at Belmont, was now in command of the fort, he added: "I hope to give him a tug before you receive this."

By the 11th he was ready to do just that. Unit commanders received that morning a verbal message: "General Grant sends his compliments and requests to see you this afternoon on his boat." That this headquarters boat was called the *New Uncle Sam* was something of a coincidence; "Uncle Sam" had been Grant's Academy nickname, derived from his initials, which in turn were accidental. The congressional appointment had identified him as Ulysses Simpson Grant, when in fact his given name was Hiram Ulysses, but rather than try to untangle the yards of red tape that stood in the way of correction — besides the risk of being nicknamed "Hug" — he let his true name go and took the new one: U. S. Grant. There were accounts of his gallantry under fire in Mexico, and afterwards his colonel had pointed him out on the street with the remark, "There goes a man of fire." However, even for those who had been alongside him at Belmont, these things were not easy to reconcile with the soft-spoken, rather seedy-looking thirty-nine-year-old general who received his brigade and division commanders aboard the steamboat.

Almost as hard to believe, despite the whiskey lines around his eyes, were the stories of his drinking. Eight years ago this spring, the gossip ran, he had had to resign from the army to avoid dismissal for drunkenness. So broke that he had had to borrow travel money from his future Confederate opponent Simon Buckner, he had gone downhill after that. Successively trying hardscrabble farming outside St Louis and real-estate selling inside it, and failing at both, he went to Galena, Illinois, up in the northwest corner of the state, and was clerking in his father's leather goods store — a confirmed failure, with a wife out of a Missouri slave-owning family and two small children — when the war came and gave him a second chance at an army career. He was made a colonel, and then a brigadier. "Be careful, Ulyss," his father wrote when he heard the news of the fluke promotion; "you're a general now; it's a good job, don't lose it."

He was quiet, not from secretiveness (he was not really close-mouthed) but simply because that was his manner, much as another's might be loud. In an army boasting the country's ablest cursers, his strongest expletives were "doggone it" and "by lightning," and even these were sparingly employed. "In dress he was plain, even negligent," one of his officers remarked; yet it was noted — "in partial amendment," the witness added — that "his horse was always a good one and well kept." All his life he had had a way with horses, perhaps because he trusted and understood them. His one outstanding accomplishment at the Academy had been the setting of a high-jump record on a horse no other cadet would ride. There was an unbuttoned informality about him and about the way he did things; but it involved a good deal more of reticence than congeniality, as if his trust and understanding stopped at horses.

The conference aboard the *New Uncle Sam*, for instance, was as casual as the summons that convened it. What the participants mainly came away with was the knowledge that Grant had told them nothing. He had wanted to find out if they were ready to move out, and apparently he believed he could determine this better by listening than by talking or even asking. He sat and smoked his long-stem meerschaum, appearing to get considerable satisfaction from it, and that was all. The council of war ("calling it such by grace," one participant wrote) broke up and the officers dispersed to their various headquarters, where presently they received the written order. Yet even this was vague. Stating only that the march would begin "tomorrow," it gave no starting time and no exact details of attack. "The force of the enemy being so variously reported," it closed, ". . . the necessary orders will be given in the field."

Whatever qualms the troop commanders might be feeling as a result of all this vagueness, the troops themselves, being better accustomed to mystification from above, were in high spirits as the march got under way around mid-morning of Lincoln's birthday. With one quick victory to their credit — in celebration of which, they knew, the folks at home were already ringing church bells — they looked forward to another, even though it did not give promise of being quite so bloodless as the first. Besides, the sun was out and the air was cool and bracing. They were enjoying the first fine weather they had known since boarding the transports at Paducah nine days back.

The column was "light," meaning that there were no wagons for tents or baggage, but the adjective did not apply for the men in ranks, each of whom carried on his person two days' rations and forty rounds of ammunition, in addition to the normal heavy load for winter marching. Glad to be on the move, however burdened, they stepped out smartly, with the usual banter back and forth between the various candidates for the role of company clown. Once clear of the river lowlands, they entered a hilly, scrub-oak country that called for up-and-down marching, with pack straps cutting first one way, then another. Presently, as the sun rose higher and bore down harder, and perhaps as much from sheer elation at being young and on the march as from discomfort, they began to shed whatever they thought they could spare. The roads were littered in their wake with discarded blankets and overcoats and other articles not needed in fair weather.

Grant shared his men's high spirits. He now had under his command over twice as many men as General Scott had employed in the conquest of Mexico: 15,000 in the marching column, 2500 left on call at Henry, available when needed, and another 10,000 aboard the transports, making the roundabout river trip to join the overland column on arrival. Undiscouraged at being already four days past his previous forecast as to the date the fort would fall, in a telegram to Halleck announcing the launching of the movement ("We start this morning ... in heavy force") he essayed another, but with something more of caution as well as ambiguity: "I hope to send you a dispatch from Fort Donelson tomorrow." Whether this meant from in*side* the fort or just in *front* of it, the words would make pleasant reading for the President on his birthday, in case Halleck passed them along (which he did not). But Grant, who perhaps did not even know it was Lincoln's birthday, had his mind on the problem at hand. He must get to the fort before he could take it or even figure how to take it.

He got there a little after noon, the skirmishers coming under sniper fire at the end of the brisk ten-mile hike, and threw his two divisions forward, approaching the spoil-scarred ridge along which the defenders had drawn their curving line of rifle pits. Beyond it, gunfire boomed up off the river: a welcome sound, since it indicated that the navy had arrived and was applying pressure against the Confederate rear. The Second division, led by Grant's old West Point commandant C. F. Smith, turned off to the left and took position opposite the northern half of the rebel arc, while the First, under John A. McClernand, filed off to the right and prepared to invest the southern half, where the ridge curved down past Dover.

McClernand was a special case, with a certain resemblance to the man whose birthday the investment celebrated. An Illinois lawyer-politician, Kentucky-born as well, he had practiced alongside Lincoln in Springfield and on the old Eighth Circuit. From that point on, however, the resemblance was less striking. McClernand was not tall: not much taller, in fact, than Grant: but he *looked* tall, perhaps because of the height of his aspirations. Thin-faced, crowding fifty, with sunken eyes and a long, knife-blade nose, a glistening full black beard and the genial dignity of an accomplished orator, he had exchanged a seat in Congress for the stars of a brigadier. In addition to the usual patriotic motives, he had a firm belief that the road that led to military glory while the war was on would lead as swiftly to political advancement when it ended. Lincoln had already shown how far a prairie lawyer could go in this country, and McClernand, whose eye for the main chance was about as sharp as Lincoln's own, was quite aware that wars had made Presidents before — from Zachary Taylor, through Andrew Jackson, back to Washington himself. He intended to do all he could to emerge from this, the greatest war of them all, as a continuing instance. So far as this made him zealous it was good, but it made him overzealous, too, and quick to snatch at laurels. At Belmont, for example, he was one of those who took time out for a victory speech with the battle half won: a speech which was interrupted by the guns across the river and which, as it turned out, did not celebrate a conquest, but preceded a retreat. He needed watching, and Grant knew it.

What was left of the 12th was devoted to completing the investment. The gunboat firing died away, having provoked no reply from the fort. Grant sent a message requesting the fleet to renew the attack next morning as a "diversion in our favor," and his men settled down for the night. Dawn came filtering through the woods in front of the ridge, showing once more the yellow scars where the Confederates had emplaced their guns and dug their rifle pits. They were still there. Pickets began exchanging shots, an irregular sequence of popping sounds, each emphasizing the silence before and after, while tendrils of pale, low-lying smoke began to writhe in the underbrush. Near the center, Grant listened. Then there was a sudden clatter off to the right, mounting to quick crescendo with the boom and jar of guns mixed in. McClernand had slipped the leash.

His attack, launched against a troublesome battery to his front, was impetuous and headlong. Massed and sent forward at a run, the brigade that made it was caught in a murderous crossfire of artillery and musketry and fell back, also at a run, leaving its dead and wounded to mark the path of advance and retreat. Old soldiers would have let it go at that; but there were few old soldiers on this field. Twice more the Illinois boys went forward, brave and green, and twice more were repulsed. The only result was to lengthen the casualty lists — and perhaps instruct McClernand that a battery might appear to be exposed, yet be protected. The clatter died away almost as suddenly as it had risen. Once more only the pop-popping of the skirmishers' rifles punctuated the stillness.

Presently, in response to Grant's request of the night before, gunboat firing echoed off the river beyond the ridge. To the north, Smith tried his hand at advancing a brigade. At first he was successful, but not for long. The brigade took its objective, only to find itself pinned down by such vicious and heavy sniper fire that it had to be withdrawn. The sun declined and the opposing lines stretched about the same as when it rose. All Grant had really learned from the day's fighting was that the rebels had their backs up and were strong. But he was not discouraged. It was not his way to look much at the gloomy side of things. "I feel every confidence of success," he told Halleck in his final message of the day, "and the best feeling prevails among the men."

The feeling did not prevail for long. At dusk a drizzling rain began to fall. The wind veered clockwise and blew steadily out of the north, turning the rain to sleet and granular snow and tumbling the thermometer to 20° below freezing. On the wind-swept ridge the Confederates shivered in their rifle pits, and in the hollows northern troops huddled together against the cold, cursing the so-called Sunny South and regretting the blankets and overcoats discarded on the march the day before. Some among the wounded froze to death between the lines, locked in rigid agony under the soft down-sift of snow. When dawn came through, luminous and ghostly, the men emerged from their holes to find a wonderland that seemed not made for fighting. The trees wore icy armor, branch and twig, and the countryside was blanketed with white.

Grant was not discomforted by the cold. He spent the night in a big feather bed set up in the warm kitchen of a farmhouse. But he had worries enough to cause him to toss and turn — whether he actually did so or not — without the weather adding more. The gunboat firing of the past two days had had none of the reverberating violence of last week's assault on Henry, and this was due to something beside acoustic difficulties. It was due, rather, to the fact that there was only one gunboat on hand. The others, along with the dozen transports bearing reinforcements, were still somewhere downriver. Their failure to arrive left Grant in the unorthodox position of investing a fortified camp with fewer troops than the enemy had inside it. During the night he sent word back to Henry for the 2500 men left there to be brought forward. That at least would equalize the armies, though it was still a far cry from the three-to-one advantage which the tactics books advised. They arrived at daybreak, and Grant assigned them to Smith, one of whose brigades had been used to strengthen McClernand. Doubtless Grant was glad to see them; but then even more welcome news arrived from the opposite direction. The fleet had come up in the night and was standing by while the transports unloaded reinforcements.

Presently these too arrived, glad to be stretching their legs ashore after their long, cramped tour of the rivers. Grant consolidated them into a Third division and assigned it to Lew Wallace, one of Smith's

The Thing Gets Under Way

brigade commanders, who had been left in charge at Henry and had made the swift, cold march to arrive at dawn. A former Indiana lawyer, the thirty-four-year-old brigadier wore a large fierce black mustache and chin-beard to disguise his youth and his literary ambitions, though so far neither had retarded his climb up the military ladder. Grant put this division into line between the First and Second, side-stepping them right and left to make room, and thickening ranks in the process.

Along that snow-encrusted front, with its ice-clad trees like inverted cutglass chandeliers beneath which men crouched shivering in frost-stiffened garments and blew on their gloveless hands for warmth, he now had three divisions facing the Confederate two, eleven brigades investing seven, 27,500 troops in blue opposing 17,500 in gray. They were not enough, perhaps, to assure a successful all-out assault; he was still only halfway to the prescribed three-to-one advantage, and after yesterday's bloody double repulse he rather doubted the wisdom of trying to storm that fortified line. But now at last the fleet was up, the fleet which had humbled Henry in short order, and that made all the difference. Surely he had enough men to prevent the escape of the rebel garrison when the ironclads started knocking the place to pieces.

Shortly after noon — by which time he had all his soldiers in position, under orders to prevent a breakout — he sent word to the naval commander, requesting an immediate assault by the gunboats. Then he mounted his horse and rode to a point on the high west bank of the Cumberland, beyond the northern end of his line, where he would have a grandstand seat for the show.

Foote would have preferred to wait until he had had time to make a personal reconnaissance, but Grant's request was for an immediate attack and the commodore prepared to give it to him. He had done considerable waiting already, a whole week of it while the armorers were hammering his ironclads back into shape. All this time he had kept busy, supervising the work, replenishing supplies, and requisitioning seafaring men to replace thirty fresh-water sailors who skedaddled to avoid gunboat duty. Nor were spiritual matters neglected. Three days after the Henry bombardment he attended church at Cairo, where, being told that the parson was indisposed, Foote mounted to the pulpit and preached the sermon himself. "Let not your heart be troubled" was his text: "ye believe in God, believe also in me."

Next day, having thus admonished and fortified his crews, he sent one ironclad up the Cumberland — the *Carondelet*, a veteran of Henry — while he waited at Cairo to bring three more: the flagship *St Louis*, another Henry veteran, and the *Pittsburg* and the *Louisville*, replacements for the *Cincinnati*, which remained on guard at the captured fort, and the hard-luck *Essex*, which had been too vitally hurt to share in a second attempt at quick reduction. It took the commodore two more days to complete repairs, replace the runaway sailors, and assemble his revamped flotilla, including two of the long-range wooden gunboats and the twelve transports loaded with infantry reinforcements. Then on the 13th he went forward, southward up the Cumberland in the wake of the *Carondelet,* whose skipper was waiting to report on his two-day action when Foote arrived before midnight at the bend just north of Donelson.

The report had both its good points and its bad, though the former were predominant. On the first day, when the *Carondelet* steamed alone against the fort, firing to signal her presence to Grant, who was just arriving, there was no reply from the batteries on the bluff. The earthworks seemed deserted, their frowning guns untended. All the same, the captain hadn't liked the looks of them; they reminded him, he said later, "of the dismal-looking sepulchers cut into the rocky cliffs near Jerusalem, but far more repulsive." He retired, answered only by echoes booming the sound of his own shots back from the hills, and anchored for the night three miles downstream. It was strange, downright eerie. Next morning, though, in accordance with a request from Grant, who evidently had not known there was only one gunboat at hand, he went forward again, hearing the landward clatter of musketry as McClernand's attack was launched and repulsed.

On this second approach, the *Carondelet* drew fire from every battery on the heights. Under bombardment for two hours, she got off 139 rounds and received only two hits in return. This was poor gunnery on the enemy's part, but one of those hits gave the captain — and, in turn, the commodore — warning of what a gun on that bluff could do to an ironclad on the river below. It was a 128-pound solid shot and it crashed through a broadside casemate into the engine room, where it caromed and ricocheted, ripping at steam pipes and railings, knocking down a dozen men and bounding after the others, as one of the engineers said, "like a wild beast pursuing its prey." Shattering beams and timbers, it filled the air with splinters fine as needles, pricking and stabbing the sailors through their clothes, though in all the grim excitement they were not aware of this until they felt the blood running into their shoes. The *Carondelet* fell back to transfer her wounded and attend to emergency repairs, but when the racket of another land assault broke out at the near end of the line, she came forward again, firing 45 more rounds at the batteries, and then drew off unhit as the clatter died away, signifying that Smith's attack, like McClernand's, had not succeeded.

Aboard the flagship, Foote had the rest of the night and the following morning in which to evaluate this information. Then came the request for an immediate assault. As Grant designed it, the fleet would silence the guns on the bluff, then steam on past the fort and take position opposite Dover, blocking any attempt at retreat across the river while it shelled the rebels out of their rifle pits along the lower ridge; whereupon the army would throw its right wing forward, so that the defenders, cut off from their main base of supplies and barred from retreat in either direction, could then be chewed up by gunfire, front and rear, or simply be outsat until they starved or saw the wisdom of surrender. The commodore would have preferred to have more time for preparation — time in which to give a final honing, as it were, to the naval blade of the amphibious shears — but, for all he knew, Grant had special reasons for haste. Besides, he admired the resolute simplicity of the plan. It was just his style of fighting. Once the water batteries were reduced, it would go like clockwork, and the example of Henry, eight days back, assured him that the hard part would be over in a hurry. He agreed to make the assault at once.

One thing he took time to do, however. Chains, lumber, and bags of coal — "all the hard materials in the vessels," as one skipper said — were laid on the ironclads' upper decks to give additional protection from such plunging shots as the one that had come bounding through the engine room of the *Carondelet*. This done, Foote gave the signal, and at 3 o'clock the fleet moved to the attack, breasting the cold dark water of the river flowing northward between the snowclad hills, where spectators from both armies were assembling for the show. One was Floyd, who took one look at the gunboats bearing down and declared that the fort was doomed. Another was Grant, who said nothing.

They came as they had come at Henry, the ironclads out in front, four abreast, while the brittle-skinned wooden gunboats *Tyler* and *Conestoga* brought up the rear, a thousand yards astern. At a mile and a half the batteries opened fire with their two big guns, churning the water ahead of the line of boats, but Foote did not reply until the range was closed to a mile. Then the flagship opened with her bow guns, echoed at once by the others, darting tongues of flame and steaming steadily forward, under orders to close the range until the batteries were silenced. Muzzles flashing and smoke boiling up as if the bluff itself were ablaze, the Confederates stood to their guns, encouraged by yesterday's success against the *Carondelet*, just as Henry's gunners had been heartened by turning back the *Essex* on the day before their battle. The resemblance did not stop there, however. After the first few long-range shots, as in the fallen fort a week ago, the big 128-pounder rifle on the crest of the bluff — the gun that had scored the only hit in two days of firing — was spiked by its own priming wire, which an excited cannoneer left in the vent while a round was being rammed. This left only the two short-range 32-pounder carronades in the upper battery and the 10-inch columbiad and eight smooth-bore 32-pounders in the lower: one fixed target opposing four in motion, each of which carried more guns between her decks than the bluff had in all, plus the long-range wooden gunboats arching their shells from beyond the smoke-wreathed line of ironclads.

Foote kept coming, firing as he came. At closer range, the *St Louis* and *Pittsburg* in the middle, the *Carondelet* and *Louisville* on the flanks, his vessels were taking hits, the metallic clang of iron on iron echoing from the surrounding hills with the din of a giant forge. But he could also see dirt and sandbags flying from the enemy embrasures as his shots struck home, and he believed he saw men running in panic from the lower battery. The Confederate fire was slackening, he afterwards reported; another fifteen minutes and the bluff would be reduced.

It may have been so, but he would never know. He was not allowed those fifteen minutes. At 500 yards the rebel fire was faster and far more effective, riddling stacks and lifeboats, sheering away flagstaffs and davits, scattering the coal and lumber and scrap iron on the decks. The sloped bulwarks caused the plunging shots to strike not at glancing angles, as had been intended, but perpendicular, and the gunboats shuddered under the blows. Head-on fire was shucking away side armor, one captain said, "as lightning tears the bark from a tree." At a quarter of a mile, just as Foote thought he saw signs of panic among the defenders, a solid shot crashed through the flagship's superstructure, carrying away the wheel, killing the pilot, and wounding the commodore and everyone else in the pilot house except an agile reporter who had come along as acting secretary.

The *St Louis* faltered, having no helm to answer, and went away with the current, out of the fight. Alongside her, the *Pittsburg* had her tiller ropes shot clean away. She too careened off, helmless, taking more hits as she swung. The *Louisville* was the next to go, struck hard between wind and water. Her compartments kept her from sinking while her crew patched up the holes, but then, like her two sister ships, she lost her steering gear and wore off downstream. Left to face the batteries alone, at 200 yards the *Carondelet* came clumsily about, her forward compartments logged with water from the holes punched in her bow, and fell back down the river, firing rapidly and wildly as she went, not so much in hopes of damaging the enemy as in an attempt to hide in the smoke from her own guns.

High on the bluff, the Confederates were elated. In the later stages of the fight they enjoyed comparative immunity, for as the gunboats closed the range they overshot the batteries. Drawing near they presented easier targets, and the cannoneers stood to their pieces, delivering hit after hit and cheering as they did so. "Now, boys," one gunner cried, "see me take a chimney!" He drew a bead, and down went a smokestack. One after another, the squat fire-breathing ironclads were disabled, wallowing helplessly as the current swept them northward, until finally the *Carondelet* made her frantic run for safety, firing indiscriminately to wreathe herself in smoke. The river was deserted; the fight was over quite as suddenly as it started. The flagship had taken 57 hits, the others about as many. Fifty-four sailors were casualties, including eleven dead. In the batteries, on the other hand, though the breastworks had been knocked to pieces, not a man or a gun was lost. The artillerists cheered and tossed their caps and kept on cheering. Fort Henry had shown what the gunboats could do: Fort Donelson had shown what they could not do.

The Confederate commander was as jubilant as his gunners. When the tide of battle turned he recovered his spirits and wired Johnston: "The fort holds out. Three gunboats have retired. Only one firing now." When that one had retired as well, his elation was complete.

It was otherwise with Grant, who saw in the rout of the ironclads a disruption of his plans. Mounting his horse, he rode back to headquarters and reported by wire to Halleck's chief of staff in Cairo: "Appearances indicate now that we will have a protracted siege here." A siege was undesirable, but the rugged terrain and the bloody double repulse already suffered in front of the fortified ridge caused him to "fear the result of an attempt to carry the place by storm with raw troops." Meanwhile, he reported, he was ordering up more ammunition and strengthening the investment for what might be a long-drawn-out affair. Disappointed but not discouraged, he assured the theater commander: "I feel great confidence... in ultimately reducing the place."

★ ★ ★

Glorious as the exploit had been, Floyd's elation was based on more than the repulse of the flotilla. Since the night before, he had had the satisfaction of knowing that he had successfully accomplished the first half of his primary assignment, his reason for being at Donelson in the first place: he had kept Grant's army off Hardee's flank during the retreat from Bowling Green. Johnston was in Nashville with the van, and Hardee was closing fast with the rear, secure from western molestation. Now there remained only the second half of Floyd's assignment: to extract his troops from their present trap for an overland march to join in the defense of the Tennessee capital.

This was obviously no easy task, but he had begun to plan for it at a council of war that morning, when he and his division commanders decided to try for a breakout south of Dover, where a road led south, then east toward Nashville, seventy miles away. Pillow's division would be massed for the assault, while Buckner's pulled back to cover the withdrawal. Troop dispositions had already begun when the ironclads came booming up the river. By the time they had been repulsed, the day was too far gone; Floyd sent orders canceling the attack and calling another council of war. No experienced soldier himself, he wanted more advice from those who were.

The two who were there to give it to him were about as different from each other as any two men in the Confederacy. Pillow was inclined toward the manic. Addicted to breathing fire on the verge of combat, flamboyant in address, he was ever sanguine in expectations and eager for desperate ventures, the more desperate the better. Buckner was gloomy, saturnine. Not much given to seeking out excitement, he was inclined to examine the odds on any gamble, especially when they were as long as they were now. Some of the difference perhaps was due to the fact that Pillow the Tennessean was fighting to save his native state — his country, as he called it — while Buckner the Kentuckian had just seen his abandoned. And their relationship was complicated by the fact that there was bad blood between them, dating from back in the Mexican War, when Buckner had joined not only in the censure of Pillow for laying claim to exploits not his own, but also in the laughter which followed a report that had him digging a trench on the wrong side of a parapet.

Between these two, the confident Pillow and the cautious Buckner, Floyd swung first one way, then another, approaching nervous exhaustion in the process. The indecision he had displayed in West Virginia under Lee was being magnified at Donelson, together with his tendency to grow flustered under pressure. Just now, however, with the rout of the Yankee gunboats to his credit, he was inclined to share his senior general's expectations. Adjourning the council, he announced that the breakout designed for today would be attempted at earliest dawn tomorrow. Even the gloomy Buckner admitted there was no other way to save the army, though he strongly doubted its chances for success.

All night the generals labored, shifting troops for the dawn assault. Pillow massed his division in attack-formation south of Dover, while Buckner stripped the northward ridge of men and guns to cover the withdrawal once the Union right had been rolled back to open the road toward Nashville. Another storm came up in the night, freezing the soldiers thus exposed. Yet this had its advantages; the wind howled down the shouts of command and the snowfall muffled the footsteps of the men and the clang of gunwheels on the frozen ground. No noise betrayed the movement to the Federals, huddled in pairs for warmth and sleep beyond the nearly deserted ridge. As dawn came glimmering through the icy lacework of the underbrush and trees, Pillow sent his regiments forward on schedule, Forrest's cavalry riding and slashing on the flank.

They met stiff resistance, not because the Yankees were expecting this specific attack, but because they were well-disciplined and alert. For better than three hours the issue hung in raging doubt, the points of contact clearly marked by bloodstains on the snow. Running low on ammunition, McClernand's men gave way, fought out, and as they fell back, sidling off to the left and exposing in turn the right flank of Wallace, Pillow saw that he had achieved his objective. The Nashville road was open. He paused to send a telegram to Johnston: "On the honor of a soldier, the day is ours!"

However, having paused he took stock, and it was as if the telegram had used up his last ounce of energy and hope, both of which had formerly seemed boundless. For now a strange thing happened: he and Buckner exchanged roles. Now it was Pillow who was pessimistic, fearing a counterattack against his flank while moving through the gap, and Buckner who was ebullient, declaring that the success should be exploited by ramming the column through. He had brought his soldiers forward to hold the door ajar; he could do it, he said — and in fact he insisted on doing it. When Pillow, standing on seniority, ordered him back to his former position, he refused to go. It was nearing noon by now, and all this time the road was standing open.

While the generals stood there wrangling, Floyd arrived. Smooth-shaven, with a pendulous underlip, he stood between them, looking from one to the other while they appealed to him to settle the dispute. At first he agreed with Buckner and told him to stay where he was, holding the escape hatch ajar. Then Pillow took him aside and he reversed himself, ordering both divisions back into line on the ridge. The morning's fight had gone for nothing, together with the bloodstains on the snow.

Elsewhere along the curving front, practically stripped of Confederate troops for the breakthrough concentration — the sector formerly held by Buckner's whole division, for example, had been left in charge of a single regiment with fewer than 500 men — the lines across the way were strangely silent. To the Southerners, widely spaced along the ridge, this seemed a special dispensation of Providence. Actually, however, the basis for the respite, though unusual, was entirely natural.

Before daylight that morning Grant had received a note from Flag Officer Foote, requesting an interview. The wounded commodore was going back downriver for repairs, both to his worst-hit vessels and to himself, and he wanted to talk with Grant before he left. Grant rode northward to meet him aboard the flagship. Having, he said later, "no idea that there would be any engagement on land unless I brought it on myself," he left explicit orders that his division commanders were not to move from their present positions. Baffled by the wintry trees and ridges, the three-hour uproar of Pillow's assault on the opposite end of the line reached him faintly, if at all. He rode on. Hard-pressed, McClernand was calling for help which Grant's orders prohibited Wallace and Smith from sending, though the former, on his own responsibility, finally sent a brigade which helped to blunt the attack when his own lines were assailed. Grant knew nothing of this until past noon, when, riding back from the gunboat conference, he met a staff captain who informed him, white-faced with alarm, that McClernand's division had been struck and scattered into full retreat. Grant put spurs to his horse.

Speed was impossible on the icy road, however, even for so skillful a horseman as Grant. It was 1 o'clock before he reached the near end of his line, where he found reassurance in the lack of excitement among the troops of Smith's division. Even Wallace's men, already engaged in part, showed fewer signs of panic than the captain who had met him crying havoc. McClernand's, next in sight, were another matter. They had been ousted from their position, taking some rough handling in the process, and they showed it. Now that the rebels had stopped shoving, they stopped running, but as they stood around in leaderless clumps, empty cartridge boxes on display as an excuse for having yielded, they gave little evidence of wanting to regain what they had lost.

There was a report that Confederate prisoners had three days' cooked rations in their haversacks. Some took this as proof that they were prepared for three days of hard fighting, but Grant had a different interpretation. He believed it meant that they were trying to escape, and he believed, further, that they were more demoralized by having failed in a desperate venture than his own men were by a temporary setback. "The one who attacks first now will be victorious," he said to his staff, "and the enemy will have to be in a hurry if he gets ahead of me."

He told McClernand's men, "Fill your cartridge boxes, quick, and get into line. The enemy is trying to escape and he must not be permitted to do so." This worked, he said later, "like a charm. The men only wanted someone to give them a command." To the wounded Foote went a request that the gunboats "make appearance and throw a few shells at long range." He did not expect them to stage a real attack, he added, but he counted on the morale effect, both on his own troops and the enemy's, of hearing naval gunfire from the river. Reasoning also that the rebels must have stripped the ridge to mass for the attack on the south, he rode to the far end of the line and ordered Smith to charge, advising him that he would find only "a very thin line to contend with."

This was what Smith had been waiting for, and for various reasons. His bright blue eyes and oversized snowy mustache standing out in contrast to his high-colored face, he was Regular Army to the shoe-soles, the only man in the western theater, one of his fellow officers said, who "could ride along a line of volunteers in the regulation uniform of a brigadier general, plume, chapeau, epaulets and all, without exciting laughter." Like many old-army men, since that army had been predominantly southern in tone, he was suspected of disloyalty; but

The Thing Gets Under Way

Smith, who had been thrice brevetted for bravery in Mexico, was not disturbed by these suspicions. "They'll take it back after our first battle," he promised. And now, with that first battle in progress, he got his troops into line, gave them orders not to fire until the rebel abatis had been cleared, and led them forward. High on his horse, the sixty-year-old general turned from time to time in the saddle to observe the alignment and gesture with his sword, the bullets of the sharpshooters twittering round him. "I was nearly scared to death," one soldier afterwards said, "but I saw the old man's white mustache over his shoulder, and went on."

They all went on, through the fallen timber and up the ridge, where they drove back the regiment Buckner had left to man the line. All that kept them from storming the fort itself was the arrival of the rest of Buckner's division, which Floyd had ordered back. On the right, McClernand's rallied men hurried the retirement of Pillow, reoccupying the ground they had lost. Wallace took a share in this, shouting as he rode along the line of his division, "You have been wanting a fight; you have got it. Hell's before you!" Two of the battered ironclads reappeared around the bend in answer to Grant's request, lobbing long-range shells to add to the Confederate confusion.

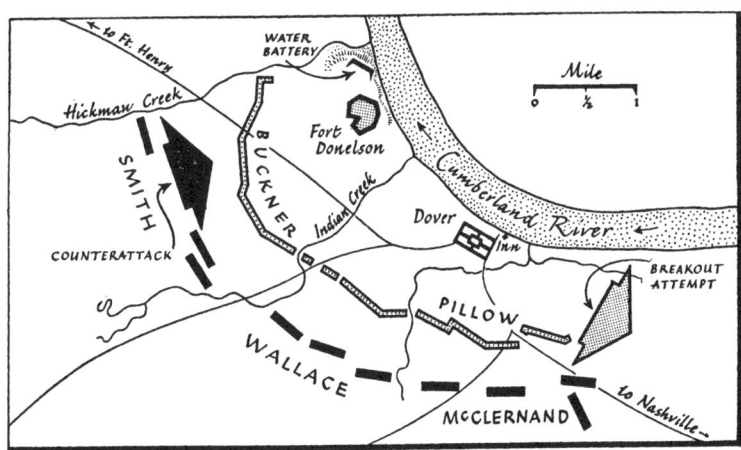

In what remained of the short winter afternoon, since saying, "The one who attacks first now will be victorious," Grant saw his army not only recover from the morning's reverses, but breach the line of rebel intrenchments as well. By daylight there would be Union artillery on the ridge where Smith had forced a lodgment. The fort, the water battery, Dover itself: the whole Confederate position would be under those guns. It was not going to be a siege, after all.

★ ★ ★

This was realized as well by the commanders inside the fort, swinging once more from elation to dejection, as it was by those outside. At the council of war, held late that night in the frame two-story Dover Inn, the prime reaction was consternation. Pillow and Buckner had reverted to their original roles. The former had thrown off his gloom, the latter his ebullience, and each accused the other of having failed to exploit the morning's gains. Pillow declared that he had halted only to send his men back after their equipment; he was ready to cut his way out in earnest, all over again. Buckner said that stopping, for whatever reason, had been fatal; the Federals had restored the line, and his men were too dispirited to make another assault. Floyd was as usual in the middle, looking from one to the other as the recriminations passed him.

This time, though, he sided more with Buckner; Smith's guns were on the ridge by now, waiting for dawn to define the targets. Forrest, who was present in his capacity as cavalry commander, reported that a riverside road was open to the south, though icy backwater stood waist-deep where it crossed a creekbed. However, the army surgeon — who had yet to learn just how tough a creature the Confederate soldier could be, despite his grousing — advised against using the flooded road, predicting that such exposure would be fatal to the troops. Then too, there was a report that Grant had received another 10,000 reinforcements. Floyd already believed his men were outnumbered four-to-one, and as far as he was concerned that settled the matter. Only one course remained: to surrender the command.

Whatever their differences at this final conference, he and Pillow were agreed at least on the question of personal surrender. Neither would have any part of it, and each had his reasons. Floyd had been indicted for malfeasance in office as Secretary of War. The charge had been nol-prossed but it might very well be reopened in a wartime atmosphere. Besides, it was a matter of general belief in the North that he had diverted federal arms and munitions to southern arsenals on the eve of secession. To surrender would be to throw himself on a mercy which he considered nonexistent. Pillow's was a different case, but he was no less determined to avoid captivity. Having sworn that he would never surrender, he intended to keep his oath. He agreed by now as to the necessity for surrender of the army, but like Floyd he refused to be included. His battle cry was "Liberty or death," and he chose liberty.

Buckner felt otherwise. He accepted the facing of possible charges of treason as one of the hazards of waging a revolution. Also, he had done the Federal commander certain personal services, including the loan of money when Grant was on his way home from California in disgrace, and this might have a happy effect when the two sat down together to arrange terms for capitulation. He would surrender the army, and himself as part of it, along with all the others who had fought here and been worsted. The necessary change of commanders was effected in order of rank:

"I turn the command over, sir," Floyd told Pillow.

"I pass it," Pillow told Buckner.

"I assume it," Buckner said. "Give me pen, ink and paper, and send for a bugler."

This colloquy omitted a fourth member of the council. Bedford Forrest rose up in his wrath. "I did not come here for the purpose of surrendering my command," he declared. Buckner agreed that the cavalryman could lead his men out if the movement began before surrender negotiations were under way.

Forrest stamped out into the night, followed by Floyd and Pillow, while Buckner composed his note to Grant: "In consideration of all the circumstances governing the present situation of affairs at this station, I propose to the commanding officer of the Federal forces the appointment of commissioners to agree upon the terms of capitulation of the forces and fort under my command, and in that view suggest an armistice until twelve o'clock today." He signed it, "Very respectfully, your obedient servant."

Buckner's men by no means shared his gloom. Except for the regiment overrun by Smith's division, they had whipped the Yankees on land and water each time they had come to grips. Rested from the previous day's exertions, they expected a renewal of the fight. Consequently, the bugler going forward to sound the parley and the messenger bearing Buckner's note and a white flag of truce had trouble getting through the lines. At last they did, however. The bugle rang out, plaintive in the frosty night, and men of the northern Second division received them and gave them escort back to the division commander. Smith read the note and set out at once through the chill predawn darkness for the farmhouse which was army headquarters.

Grant was snug in his feather bed when Smith came in saying, "There's something for you to read." During the reading the old soldier crossed to the open fire and stroked his mustache while warming his boots and backside. Grant gave a short laugh. "Well, what do you think of it?" he asked. Smith said, "I think, no terms with the traitors, by God!" Grant slipped out of bed and drew on his outer garments. Then he took a sheet of tablet paper and began to write. When he had finished he handed it to Smith, who read it by firelight and pronounced abruptly, "By God, it couldn't be better."

Once more the truce party crossed the lines, headed now in the opposite direction as they picked their way to the Dover Inn, where Buckner was waiting to learn Grant's terms. There had been considerable bustle in their absence. A steamboat had arrived in the night, bringing a final batch of 400 reinforcements who landed thus in time to be surrendered. Floyd commandeered the vessel for the evacuation of his brigade, four regiments from his native Virginia and one from Mississippi, the latter being assigned to guard the landing while the others got aboard. The first two regiments of Virginians had been deposited safely on the other shore; the boat had returned and the second pair were being loaded when word came from Buckner that surrender negotiations had been opened; all who were going must go at once. Floyd hurried aboard with his staff and gave the signal and the steamboat backed away, leaving the Mississippians howling ruefully on the bank.

Pillow had been less fortunate. The best transportation he could find was an abandoned scow, with barely room for himself and his chief of staff, and they were the only two from his command who got away in the night. Forrest, on the other hand, took not only all of his own men, but also a number of infantrymen who swung up behind the troopers, riding double across low stretches where the water was "saddle-skirt deep," as Forrest said. He believed the whole army could have escaped by this route, the venture he had urged at the council of war, only to be overruled. "Not a gun [was] fired at us," he reported. "Not an enemy [was] seen or heard."

Sitting and waiting was the harder task, and it was Buckner's. The first Confederate general to submit a request for surrender terms from an opponent, he knew what condemnation was likely to be heaped upon his head by his own people, who would see only that he had ordered his men to lay down their arms in the face of bloody fighting. Yet he took some consolation, and found much hope, in the fact that those terms would come from an old West Point comrade whom he had befriended in another time of trial, when the tide of fortune was running the other way. The truce messenger returned at last and handed him Grant's reply:

H^d Qrs. Army in the Field
Camp near Donelson, Feby 16th

Gen. S. B. Buckner,
    Confed. Army,
    Sir: Yours of this date proposing Armistice, and appointment of Commissioners, to settle terms of Capitulation is just received. No terms except an unconditional and immediate surrender can be accepted.
    I propose to move immediately upon your works.

I am Sir: very respectfully
Your obt. sevt.
U. S. GRANT
Brig. Gen.

This was not at all what Buckner had expected by way of return for favors past. Neither generous nor chivalrous, even aside from personal obligations, such "terms"—which were, in effect, hardly terms at all—were a far cry from those extended by Beauregard ten months ago at Sumter, back in what already seemed a different war entirely, when Anderson was allowed to salute his flag and march out under arms while the victors lined the beaches and stood uncovered to watch him go. Yet there was nothing Buckner could do about it; Floyd and Pillow had left—which might have been considered good riddance except that the former had taken four-fifths of his brigade, lengthening the odds—and Forrest was gone with his hard-hitting cavalry, which otherwise might have covered a retreat. All that remained was for Buckner to make a formal protest and submit. This he did, informing Grant that the scattering of his own troops, "and the overwhelming forces under your command, compel me, notwithstanding the brilliant success of the Confederate arms yesterday, to accept the ungenerous and unchivalrous terms which you propose."

By now it was broad open daylight. Receiving the message, Grant rode forward, past white flags stuck at intervals along the rebel line, into Dover where he found Lew Wallace already sharing a cornbread-and-coffee breakfast with the Confederates at the inn. He joined the friendly discussion, and when Buckner remarked that if he had been in charge during the fighting, the Federals would not have got up to Donelson as easily as they had done, Grant replied that if such had been the case, "I should not have tried it the way I did." Then he took over the inn as his own headquarters. Before sending Buckner north, however, he sought to make amends by offering his prisoner, who had done the same for him when the degrees of fortune and misfortune were reversed, the use of his purse. The Kentuckian declined it.

The actual surrender was accomplished without formality. One northern correspondent observed a marked difference between rebels from the border states and those from farther south. Moving among them he noted that the former "were not much sorry that the result was as it was," while "those from the Gulf states were sour, not inclined to talk." This only applied to the enlisted men, however. Without exception, he found the officers "spiteful as hornets." By journalistic license, another reporter deduced from what he saw that the common people of the South cared very little which way the war ended, so long as it ended soon.

Sullen or friendly, spiteful or morose, men who had been shooting at each other a few hours ago now mingled on the field for which they had fought. Indeed, the occasion was so informal that some Confederates strolled unchallenged through the lines and got away. Bushrod Johnson, who was among those who made off in this manner, later declared: "I have not learned that a single one who attempted to escape met with any obstacle." Apparently Grant, who at this one stroke had captured more prisoners than all the other Union generals combined, did not particularly care. "It is a much less job to take them than to keep them," he said laconically. As for Pillow, he need not have been in such a hurry to escape, Grant told Buckner. "If I had captured him, I would have turned him loose. I would rather have him in command of you fellows than as a prisoner."

Throughout the North, church bells rang in earnest this Sunday morning, louder even than they had done for Fort Henry, ten days back. Men embraced on the streets and continued to celebrate into the night by the glare of bonfires. The shame of Bull Run was erased. Indeed, some believed they saw in the smashing double victory the end of armed rebellion, the New York *Times* remarking: "After this, it certainly cannot be materially postponed. The monster is already clutched and in his death struggle."

The nation had a new hero: U. S. Grant, who by an accident and a coincidence of initials now became "Unconditional Surrender" Grant. People had his message to Buckner by heart, and they read avidly of his life and looks in the papers: the features stern "as if carved from mahogany," the clear blue eyes (or gray, some said) and aquiline nose, the strong jaw "squarely set, but not sensual." One reporter saw three expressions in his face: "deep thought, extreme determination, and great simplicity and calmness." Another saw significance in the way he wore his high-crowned hat: "He neither puts it on behind his ears, nor draws it over his eyes; much less does he cock it on one side, but sets it straight and very hard on his head." People enjoyed reading of that, and also of the way he "would gaze at anyone who approached him with an inquiring air, followed by a glance of recollection and a grave nod of recognition." On horseback, they read, "he sits firmly in the saddle and looks straight ahead, as if only intent on getting to some particular point." The words "square" and "straight" and "firm" were the ones that appeared most often, and people liked them. Best of all, perhaps, they enjoyed hearing that Grant was "the concentration of all that is American. He talks bad grammar, but talks it naturally, as much as to say, 'I was so brought up, and if I try fine phrases I shall only appear silly.'"

To them the whole campaign was an absolute marvel of generalship, a superb combination of simplicity and drive, in welcome contrast to all that had gone before in the West and was continuing in the East. They did not dissect it in search of flaws, did not consider that Grant had started behind schedule, that men had frozen to death because of a lax discipline which let them throw away coats and blankets in fair weather, that individual attacks had been launched without coördination and been bloodily repulsed, nor that the commanding general had been absent from his post for better than six critical hours while one of his divisions was being mauled, the other two having been barred by his own orders from lending assistance. They saw rather, the sweep and slambang power of a leader who marched on Wednesday, skirmished on

Thursday, imperturbably watched his fleet's repulse on Friday, fought desperately on Saturday, and received the fort's unconditional surrender on Sunday. Undeterred by wretched weather, the advice of the tactics manuals, or the reported strength of the enemy position, he had inflicted about 2000 casualties and suffered about 3000 himself — which was as it should have been, considering his role as the attacker — and now there were something more than 12,000 rebel soldiers, the cream of Confederate volunteers, on their way to northern prison camps to await exchange for as many Union boys, who otherwise would have languished in southern prisons under the coming summer sun. People saw Grant as the author of this deliverance, the embodiment of the offensive spirit, the man who would strike and keep on striking until this war was won. Fifteen years ago, during a lull in the Mexican War, he had written home to the girl he was to marry: "If we have to fight, I would like to do it all at once and then make friends." Apparently he still felt that way about it.

★ ★ ★

Church bells were ringing that Sunday morning in Nashville, too, though not in celebration. The celebration had come the night before, following the release of telegrams from Floyd and Pillow announcing "a victory complete and glorious." Today, instead, they tolled the fall of Donelson, the loss of that whole wing of Johnston's army, and the resultant necessity for abandoning the Tennessee capital.

All morning the remnants of Hardee's 14,000, reduced to less than two-thirds of that by straggling and sickness during the icy retreat from Bowling Green, filed through the city, harrowing the populace with accounts of Buell's bloodthirsty hordes closing fast upon their rear. Thus began a week of panic. Previously the war had seemed a far-off thing, over in Virginia or across the Mississippi or a hundred miles north in Kentucky. They had been too busy, or too confident, to fortify even the river approaches. Now that it was upon them with the abruptness of a pistol shot in a theater, they reacted variously. Some wept in numb despair. Others proposed to burn the city, "that the enemy might have nothing of it but the ashes." Terrified by a rumor that Buell's army and Foote's gunboats would converge upon the city at 3 p.m. to shell it into submission, they milled about, loading their household goods onto carts and wagons. By that time a special train had left for Memphis, with Governor Harris and the state archives aboard. Later that afternoon, the Yankee soldiers and gunboats not having appeared, the mayor informed the crowd in the Public Square that Johnston had promised to make no stand in Nashville. He himself would go out to meet the Federals and surrender the city before they got there, the mayor told the frantic populace. Meanwhile they should calm their fears and stay at home. As a final mollification, he promised to distribute among them all the Confederate provisions that could not be removed by Johnston's army.

This appeal to the greed of the people, while effective, was to have its consequences. Nashville warehouses were bulging with accumulated supplies, and it was Johnston's task — though he had opposed this placing of all the army's eggs in one basket — to save what he could before the Federals got there. Next morning, when Floyd and his brigade (minus the Mississippians) arrived by steamboat, Johnston put him in charge, while he himself continued the retreat with Hardee's men. Floyd took over the railroads, commandeered what few wagons remained, and in general did what he could. The panic had lessened somewhat since the nonarrival of the Federals, but a lurid glare against the northern sky and the clang of firebells in the night caused its resurgence until the people learned that the reflection, which they had feared might be from torches carried by an army of Yankee incendiaries, was from the hulls of two unfinished Confederate gunboats ordered burned in the yards.

Next day Floyd continued his efforts to save the stores. It was unpleasant work, the citizens growing more mutinous every hour — especially after the destruction, over their protest, of their two fine bridges across the Cumberland. Floyd was greatly relieved when Forrest arrived from Donelson on Wednesday, under orders to assist him in the salvaging of government supplies: so relieved, in fact, that next morning he marched his brigade away, and left the task to Forrest and his troopers.

Instructed to stay there one more day, unless Buell arrived sooner, Forrest stayed four. His iron hand snatched order out of chaos. Rifling machinery and other ordnance equipment, rare items in the Confederacy, were sent from the gun foundry to Atlanta. A quarter-million pounds of bacon and hundreds of wagonloads of clothing, flour, and ammunition were hauled to the railroad station for shipment south. The people, seeing this new efficiency and remembering that they had been promised what was left, sought to interfere by gathering in front of the warehouses. Forrest appealed to their patriotism, and when that did not work, ordered his mounted men to lay about with the flat of their sabers, which worked better. One large mob, in front of a warehouse on the Public Square, was dispersed by the use of fire hoses squirting ice-cold muddy water from the river, and as one of the crowd remembered it later, this had "a magical effect."

All day Thursday and Friday and Saturday, Forrest and his troopers worked, on into Sunday morning, when blue pickets appeared on the north bank of the river. Mindful of his instructions to leave Nashville an open city, Forrest fell back through the suburbs, marching to join Johnston and Hardee, who by now were at Murfreesboro, forty miles southeast. The Army of Central Kentucky — or what was left of it, anyhow — would have to find a new name.

The Thing Gets Under Way

Nashville's "Great Panic," as it was called thereafter, had lasted precisely a week, though by way of anticlimax one ignominy remained. True to his promise to the people, the mayor got in a rowboat and crossed the river to deliver the city into the hands of the Yankees before they opened fire with their long-range guns. He found no guns, however, and few soldiers: only half a squad of cavalry and one Ohio captain, who, after some persuasion, agreed to receive the surrender of the city, or at any rate not to attack it. The mayor returned and announced this deliverance to the citizens, who thus were relieved of a measure of their fears — most of which had been groundless in the first place. Buell was still a long way off, toiling down the railroad and the turnpike, repairing washed-out bridges as he came. Grant remained at Donelson, receiving reinforcements. Before the end of the week he had upwards of 30,000 men in four divisions, one of which had been advanced to Clarksville. "Nashville would be an easy conquest," he wrote Halleck's chief of staff, "but I only throw this out as a suggestion.... I am ready for any move the general commanding may order." The general commanding ordered nothing; Grant stayed where he was.

Buell, in fact, did not reach Nashville until Wednesday, though several outfits had come on ahead. A reporter with one of the earliest wrote of what they found. All the stores and most of the better homes were closed; the State House was deserted, the legislators having fled with the governor to Memphis, which had been declared the temporary capital. The correspondent found the door of the leading hotel bolted, and when he rang there was no answer. He kept on ringing, with the persistency of a tired and hungry man within reach of food and a clean bed. At last he was rewarded. A Negro swung the door ajar and stood there smiling broadly. "Massa done gone souf," he said, still grinning.

✘ 3 ✘

Inauguration day broke cold and sullen in Richmond, with a scud of cloud that promised and then delivered rain, first a drizzle, then a steady downpour, hissing and gurgling in the gutters and thrumming against roofs and windowpanes. Davis rose early, as was his custom. Not due at the ceremonies until 11.30, he walked first to his office for an hour of the paperwork which filled so large a share of his existence, then back home. His wife, coming to warn him that the dignitaries were waiting to escort him to the Capitol, found him alone on his knees in the bedroom, praying "for the divine support I need so sorely." That too had been his custom since his first inauguration a year ago, under a cloudless Alabama sky.

The procession formed in the old Virginia Hall of Delegates, then moved out onto Capitol Square where a canopied platform had been set up alongside the equestrian statue of Washington, whose birthday this was. Grouped about the President-elect were cabinet officers, admirals and generals, governors and congressmen, newspaper representatives and members of various benevolent societies. Beside him stood Vice President Stephens, undersized and sickly, huddled in layers of clothes and resembling more than ever a mummified child. Asked once to define true happiness, Stephens had replied without hesitation, "To be warm." He was not happy now, presumably, for a cold rain fell in sheets, blown under the canopy by intermittent gusts of northern wind. When the Right Reverend John Johns, Episcopal Bishop of Virginia, raised his arms to pronounce the invocation, his lawn sleeves hung limp and his heavy satin vestments were splotched with wet. Close-packed, the crowd stood and took its drenching, conscious of being present at a historic occasion. Some held strips of canvas or worn carpet over their heads, but there were enough umbrellas to give the square what one witness called "the effect of an immense mushroom bed." They could hear few of the words above the impact of the rain. They saw Davis take the oath, however, and they knew they had a permanent President at last. When he bent forward to kiss the Book a shout went up. Then they quieted. The drumming of the rain was loud as he turned to address them.

He was thinner and even more austere in appearance, the cheekbones brought into greater prominence and the eyes sunk even deeper in their sockets; "singularly imposing," one witness found him today, albeit with "a pallor painful to look upon." He wore a suit of black for the ceremonies instead of his customary gray, so that to Mrs Davis he seemed "a willing victim going to his funeral pyre." Her thoughts had been directed into such channels by an occurrence on the way. Observing that the carriage moved at a snail's pace, accompanied by a quartet of black-suited Negro footmen wearing white cotton gloves, she asked the coachman, to whom she had left the arrangements, what it meant. He told her, "This, ma'am, is the way we always does in Richmond at funerals and sichlike."

A year ago there had been no talk of funerals; "joyous" was the word Davis had used to describe the atmosphere on the day of his first inaugural. It was not so now. The outlook was as different as the weather. Nor did he assume a falsely joyous manner on this second occasion of taking the oath as President of the Confederacy. After referring to the birthday of the Virginian who looked out from his bronze horse nearby, he once more outlined and defended the course of events which had led to secession, characterizing the North as barbarous and expressing scorn for the "military despotism" which had "our enemies" in its grip. All this was as it had been before, but soon he passed to words that touched the present:

"A million men, it is estimated, are now standing in hostile array and waging war along a frontier of thousands of miles. Battles have been fought, sieges have been conducted, and' although the contest is not ended and the tide for the moment is against us, the final result in our favor is not doubtful. We have had our trials and difficulties. That we are to escape them in the future is not to be hoped. It was to be expected when we entered upon this war that it would expose our people to sacrifices and cost them much, both of money and blood. But the picture has its lights as well as its shadows. This great strife has awakened in the people the highest emotions and qualities of the human soul. It was, perhaps, in the ordination of Providence that we were to be taught the value of our liberties by the price we pay for them. The recollection of this great contest, with all its common traditions of glory, of sacrifice and blood, will be the bond of harmony and enduring affection amongst the people, producing unity in policy, fraternity in sentiment, and just effort in war."

An invocation had opened the proceedings. Now another closed them. Davis lifted his hands and eyes to heaven as he spoke the final words. "My hope is reverently fixed on Him whose favor is ever vouchsafed to the cause which is just. With humble gratitude and adoration, acknowledging the Providence which has so visibly protected the Confederacy during its brief but eventful career, to Thee, O God, I trustingly commit myself and prayerfully invoke Thy blessing on my country and its cause."

Under the spell of that closing prayer, the people dispersed in silence and good order, "as though they had attended divine service," one remarked. Later, however, away from the magic of his voice and presence, they doubted that there was "unity in policy" or "fraternity in sentiment" or "just effort" in the prosecution of the war. Prompted by hostile editors, whose critiques of the address came out in their papers the following day — along with the news from Donelson and Nashville announcing the loss of Kentucky and most of Tennessee — they began to consider not only what he had said, but also what he had not said. He had outlined no future policy for raising the blockade, whose pinch was already being felt, or for overcoming the recent military reverses. Though his words were obviously spoken as much for foreign as for domestic ears, he had not foretold international recognition or the receiving of assistance from abroad. Except in vague and general terms, including the closing appeal to the Almighty, he had announced no single plan for coming to grips with the host of calamities they knew were included in his admission that "the tide for the moment is against us."

The fact that he refrained from explicit mention of these reverses did not mean that the people were unaware of them. They knew all too well that even a bare listing would have doubled the length of his address. Foremost among the disappointments, at least to men who took a long view of the chance for victory, was the failure of Confederate diplomacy. Original computations had shown that, before spring, England would have begun to suffer from the cotton famine which would bring her to her knees. Yet the looms and jennies, spinning away at the surplus bulging the warehouses, had not slowed. Ironically, the shortage there was not in cotton, but in wheat, the result of a crop failure in the British Isles. They were buying it now by the shipload from the North, which had harvested a bumper crop with its new McCormick reapers: another example of what it meant to fight a race of "pasty-faced mechanics."

Back at the outset, Southerners had predicted that the great Northwest — meaning Michigan, Wisconsin, Minnesota, and Iowa, along with northern Illinois and Indiana — would be pro-Confederate because of its need for an outlet to the Gulf of Mexico. Some who lived there had thought so, too. The Detroit *Free Press* had declared at the time: "If troops shall be raised in the North to march against the people of the South, a fire in the rear will be opened against such troops, which will either stop their march altogether or wonderfully accelerate it." But events had not worked out that way at all. The men of Grant's army were mostly from that region, and they had been accelerated, not by any "fire in the rear," but rather by an intense concern that the Union be preserved. Then too, instead of working an economic hardship, as the Southerners had predicted, the war had provided the farmers of the area with a new and profitable market for their wheat. The Northwest had not only stood by the Union; it was growing rich from having done so.

To some, this one among the many was the greatest disappointment of them all. The main hope of redress was that foreign intervention would be won by the new team of professional diplomats, Mason and Slidell, who had made a spectacular entry into the field. Yet here, too, there was disappointment. After serving the South so well from their cells in Boston Harbor, they were proving far less useful now in freedom at their posts. They stepped onto the London railway platform as if into obscurity, unwelcomed and unnoticed save by the late friendly *Times*, which announced their arrival with the following observations: "We sincerely hope that our countrymen will not give these fellows anything in the shape of an ovation. The civility that is due to a foe in distress is all that they can claim. The only reason for their presence in London is to draw us into their own quarrel. The British public has no prejudice in favor of slavery, which these gentlemen represent. What they and their secretaries are to do here passes our experience. They are personally nothing to us. They must not suppose, because we have gone to the verge of a great war to rescue them, that they are precious in our eyes."

Bitter as it was for Mason to see himself and his partner referred to as unprecious "fellows," the reception he received from the Foreign Minister dampened his spirits even more. Ushered into the presence, he was about to present his credentials when his lordship checked him: "That is unnecessary, since our relations are unofficial." Icily polite, but disinclined to enter into any discussion of policy, the most Earl Russell ventured was the hope that Mason would find his visit "agreeable." In parting he did not express the hope that they might meet again. This was the treatment Yancey had broken under, and the Virginian took it scarcely better, reporting: "On the whole it was manifest enough that his personal sympathies were not with us."

Slidell, continuing his voyage across the channel, also encountered conditions which had plagued his predecessor. Unlike Mason, he had no difficulty in securing audiences. He got about as many as he wanted, and Eugénie was obviously charmed — a fact which he reported with some pride — but Napoleon would only repeat what he had said before: France could not act without England. That was the crux of the matter. The Crimean War had been a struggle between West and East, which the West had won, and now in the normal course of events, as demonstrated by history, the victors should have turned upon each other for domination of the whole. Yet it had not worked out that way. There was no such tenuous balance as had obtained at the time of the American Revolution, bringing France to the assistance of the Colonies. On the contrary, the *entente* remained strong, drawing its strength from the weakness of Napoleon, whose shaky finances and doubtful popularity would not allow him to risk bringing all of Europe down on his unprotected back. Slidell could only inform his government of these conditions. It began to seem that, economically and politically — so far at least as Europe was concerned — the South had chosen the wrong decade in which to make her bid for independence.

Like others who took the long view, seeing foreign intervention as the one quick indisputable solution to the Confederacy's being outnumbered and outgunned and outmachined, Davis received this latest news from abroad with whatever grace and patience he could muster. He could wait — though by the hardest. Meantime he had other, more immediate problems here at home, within his own official family: in evidence of which, as even the short-view men could see, the chief post in his cabinet was vacant. The Secretary of State had left in a huff that very week.

At the time when he accepted the appointment, Hunter had announced that he intended to be a responsible and independent official, not just "the clerk of Mr Davis." As Virginia's favorite-son candidate at the Democratic convention of 1860, he had his political dignity to consider. Besides, in the early days of the secession movement, when it was thought that the Old Dominion would be among the first to go, he had been slated for the presidency of the impending Confederacy. Virginia had held back and he had missed it; but there was still the future to keep his eye on, and his dignity to be maintained. The result was a personality clash with Davis, a build-up of bad feeling which reached a climax during a general cabinet discussion of the military situation. When Hunter expressed an opinion on the subject, Davis told him: "Mr Hunter, you are Secretary of State, and when information is wished of that department it will be time for you to speak." The Virginian's resignation was on the presidential desk next morning.

Davis of course accepted it. He made no appointment to fill the post immediately, however. Vacant for a week at the time of the inauguration, it would remain so for three more. The man he had in mind was too deeply embroiled in other matters, filling another cabinet position, to be considered available just yet. And this was one more item which might have been included in any listing of reverses.

As Secretary of War, the rotund, smiling Judah P. Benjamin had been under fire almost since the day of his appointment: not under actual bombardment from the enemy beyond the gates, but rather from the plain citizens and congressmen within, whose ire was aroused by his summary treatment of the nation's military heroes, coming as they did under the jurisdiction of his department. Benjamin had no such notion as Hunter's concerning the duties of his post. As head of the War Department he considered himself quite literally the President's secretary for military affairs, and it did not irk him at all to be tagged "the clerk of Mr Davis." The field of arms was one of the few that had not previously engaged the interest of this myriad-minded man, whereas Davis, a West Pointer and a Mexican War hero, had been the ablest Secretary the Federal War Department ever had. Benjamin's duty, as he saw it — and here the two men's concepts coincided — was to execute the will and, if necessary, defend the actions of his Commander in Chief. Besides, he saw Davis's needs, the desire for warmth behind his iciness, the ache for understanding behind his stiff austerity. Judah Benjamin was one of the few who perceived this, or at any rate one of the few — like Mrs Davis — who acted on it, and in doing so he not only made himself pleasant; in time he also made himself indispensable. That was his reward. He gained the President's gratitude, and with it the unflinching loyalty which Davis always gave in return for loyalty received.

Whatever he lacked in the knowledge of arms as a profession, he brought to his job a considerable facility in the handling of administrative matters. Unlike Walker, who had fumed and stewed in tangles of red tape and never got from under the avalanche of army paperwork, Benjamin would clear his desk with dispatch, then sit back smiling, ready for what came next. What came next, as often as not, was an opportunity for exercising his talent in dialectics. Here his skill was admittedly superior — "uncanny," some called it, and they spoke resentfully; for by the precision of his logic he could lead men where they would not go, making them seem clumsy in the process. In taking up his superior's quarrels with the generals on the Manassas line — which seemed to him one of the duties of his post — he gave full play to his talents in this direction, undeterred by awe for the military mind. That was what had caused Beauregard to reach for his pen in such a frenzy, writing with ill-concealed irony of the pity he felt, "from the bottom of my heart," for any man who could not see "the difference between *patriotism*, the highest civic virtue, and *office-seeking*, the lowest civic occupation." It was Benjamin he meant. But in making the charge the general entered a field where his fellow Louisianian was master; and presently he went West.

Even more vulnerable in this respect, though banishment did not follow so close on the heels of contention, was Joseph E. Johnston. After Johnston's protest at being outranked, and Davis's quick slash in reply, Benjamin took up the cudgel for his chief. Johnston was a careless administrator, and whenever he lapsed in this regard, the Secretary took him to task with a letter that prickled his sensitive pride. Infuriated, the general would reply in kind, only to be brought up short by another missive which proved him even further in the wrong. A later observer wrote that Benjamin treated the Virginian as if he were "an adversary at the bar," but sometimes it was worse; he dealt with him as if he were a prisoner in the dock. Johnston's outraged protests against such treatment did him no more good than Beauregard's had done. Once when the Creole complained to Davis that the Secretary's tone was offensive and that he was being "put into the strait jackets of the law," the President replied: "I do not feel competent to instruct Mr Benjamin in the matter of style. There are few whom the public would probably believe fit for the task." As for the second objection, "You surely do not intend to inform me that your army and yourself are outside the limits of the law. It is my duty to see that the laws are faithfully executed and I cannot recognize the pretensions of anyone that their restraint is too narrow for him."

Exalted thus at the expense of those who attempted to match wits with him, Benjamin continued to maintain order at headquarters and to ride herd on recalcitrants among the military. Then, unexpectedly, he ran full tilt into a man who had no use for dialectics, who stood instead on his own ground and gave the Secretary his first check. T. J. Jackson, called "Stonewall" since Manassas, had been promoted to major general in the fall and assigned to command a division in the Shenandoah Valley, from which strategic location he had proposed that he be reinforced for an all-out invasion of the North. Having just rejected a similar proposal from Beauregard at Centerville, the Administration would send him no reinforcements, but attached to his command the three brigades of W. W. Loring, the one professional in the quartet who had tried the patience and damaged the reputation of R. E. Lee in West Virginia. Told to accomplish what he could with this total force of about 9000, Jackson launched on New Year's Day a movement designed to recover the counties flanking the western rim of the Valley theater.

The first phase of the campaign went as planned. Marching in bitter midwinter weather, Jackson's men harried the B & O Railroad, captured enemy stores, and in general created havoc among the scattered Federal camps. This done, Stonewall stationed Loring's troops at Romney, on the upper Potomac, and took the others back to Winchester, thirty-odd miles eastward, to begin the second phase. Just what that would have been remained a mystery, for Jackson was a most secretive man, agreeing absolutely with Frederick II's remark, "If I thought my coat knew my plans I would take it off and burn it." He did say, however, that he left the attached brigades on outpost duty because his own were better marchers and could move more swiftly toward any threatened point. Loring's volunteers did not subscribe to this. Rather, it was their belief that Stonewall was demented. (They saw various symptoms of this — including the fact that he never took pepper in his food, on grounds that it gave him pains in his left leg.) And so were his men, for that matter, since they had a habit of cheering him on the march. Exposed as they were to the elements and the possible swoop of Federal combinations, Loring and his officers petitioned the War Department to withdraw them from their uncomfortable position. On the next to last day of January, Jackson received the following dispatch signed by Benjamin: "Our news indicates that a movement is being made to cut off General Loring's command. Order him back to Winchester immediately."

Jackson promptly complied with the order. Acknowledging its receipt and reporting its execution, the next day he addressed the War Department: "With such interference in my command I cannot expect to be of much service in the field," wherefore he asked to be returned to his teaching job at V.M.I., or else "I respectfully request that the President will accept my resignation from the army." The letter went through channels to Johnston, who forwarded it regretfully to Richmond. He too had been by-passed, and he told Benjamin: "Let me suggest that, having broken up the dispositions of the military commander, you give whatever other orders may be necessary."

Eventually the trouble was smoothed over and Jackson's resignation returned to him, Governor Letcher and various congressmen exerting all the pressure of their influence, but not before violent recriminations had been heaped on the head of the smiling Secretary, especially by Stonewall's fellow officers. Tom Cobb of Georgia, a brigadier in the Virginia army, stated flatly: "A grander rascal than this Jew Benjamin does not exist in the Confederacy and I am not particular in concealing my opinion of him." Nor were others particular in that respect, their fury being increased when Loring was promoted in mid-

The Thing Gets Under Way

February and taken from under the stern control of Jackson, who had recommended that he be cashiered.

Benjamin kept smiling through it all, though by then the indestructibility of his smile was being tested even further. Previous recriminations had come mainly from army men, outraged at his interfering in tactical matters. Now he was being condemned by the public at large, and for a lack of similar interference.

Down on the North Carolina coast, set one above the other, Albemarle and Pamlico Sounds were divided by a low-lying marshy peninsula. At its eastern tip, where the jut of land approached the narrow sands of the breakwater guarding the coast from the gales that blew so frequently off Hatteras, lay Roanoke Island, the site of Raleigh's "Lost Colony" and birthplace of the first English child born in the Western Hemisphere. Just now, however, this boggy tract had an importance beyond the historic. Pamlico, the lower and larger sound, had fallen to Stringham's gunboats back in August; Albemarle could be taken, too, once the narrows flanking the island had been forced. Loss of the lower sound had given the Federals a year-round anchorage and access to New Bern, principal eastern depot on the vital railroad supply line to Richmond and the armies in Virginia. That was bad enough, though the invaders had not yet exploited it, but loss of the upper sound would expose Norfolk and Gosport Navy Yard to attack

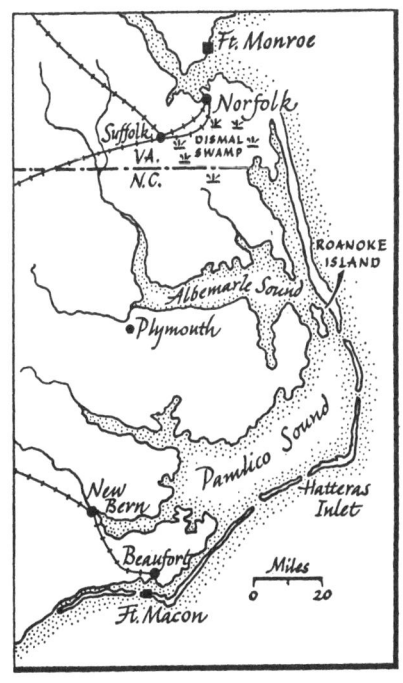

from the rear. This would be worse than bad; it would be tragic, for the Confederates had things going on in the navy yard that would not bear interruption. The focal point for its defense, as anyone could see, was Roanoke Island. Situated north of all four barrier inlets, it was like a loose-fitting cork plugging the neck of a bottle called Albemarle Sound. Nothing that went by water could get in there without going past the cork.

One who saw this clearly was Henry Wise. Still seething from his defeat in West Virginia at the hands of his fellow ex-governor Floyd, he arrived and took command of the island forces in late December. He entered upon his duties with his usual enthusiasm. By the time he was halfway through his first inspection, however, he saw that the cork was not only loose, but also apt to crumble under pressure. Little had been done to block the passes, either by driving pilings or by sinking obstructions in the channel. What was worse, the water batteries were badly sited, clustered up at the northern end of the island as if in expectation of attack from that direction after Norfolk fell, while the southern end, giving down upon Pamlico Sound — which the enemy fleet had held for four months now — was left open to amphibious assault. In the face of this threat Wise had a garrison of about 2500 men, fewer than he believed were necessary to slow, let alone halt, such an attack once the Federals got ashore. Yet he was no defeatist. He got to work, driving pilings and sinking hulks in the channel, and called on the district commander at Norfolk, Major General Benjamin Huger, for additional artillery and ammunition, pile drivers, supplies of every kind, and especially more soldiers. A fifty-six-year-old South Carolina aristocrat, West Pointer and Chief of Ordnance under Scott in Mexico, Huger was placid in manner and deliberate in judgment. He had never inspected the island defenses, but he replied to Wise's requisitions by recommending "hard work and coolness among the troops you have, instead of more men."

Being told to keep cool only lowered Wise's boiling point, which was reached when Flag Officer William F. Lynch, of the Confederate navy, commandeered all his work boats except a single tug, converting them to one-gun gunboats. A "mosquito fleet," Wise dubbed the result in derision, and left for Norfolk to protest in person. When Huger still gave him no satisfaction, he set out for Richmond, where he had influential friends bound to him during years of politics. He would appeal directly to the Secretary of War. This was contrary to Army Regulations, he knew; to go was to risk court martial. But he believed the situation justified irregularity. "Damn the execution, sir!" he had cried in West Virginia; "it's the *sound* that we want." As tactics, this could be applied to more than field artillery.

Arriving January 19 he stayed three days; but he got nowhere with the Secretary. Already Benjamin had replied to his urgent demands for cannon powder by informing him that the Confederacy's "very limited" reserve was being saved for use at more closely threatened points. "At the first indication, however, of an attack on Roanoke Island," he wrote, "a supply will be sent you." Wise replied that there *was* no more closely threatened point and that once the assault had begun it would be too late, but the Secretary had considered the matter closed. Now, face to face with Benjamin in Richmond, the Virginian fared no better in his plea for powder. Nor did he get reinforcements.

When he pointed out that Huger had 13,000 men lying idle around Norfolk, the Secretary, obviously preferring the military judgment of the professionally trained senior to that of the politically appointed subordinate, shrugged and said that he supposed the district commander knew best. He would not interfere.

Wise remained in town, complaining vociferously to his high-placed friends until the 22d, when a dispatch arrived from Commander Lynch announcing symptoms of an enemy build-up and attack: whereupon Benjamin, doubtless glad to be rid of him, issued a peremptory order for the general to go back to his island post. Bad weather and transportation difficulties delayed his return till the end of the month. On the 31st — while Stonewall Jackson was composing his resignation out in the Valley — the distraught Wise, his condition aggravated by the frustration of trying to get someone to realize the weakness of his tactical position, took to his bed with a severe attack of pleurisy.

He was still there a week later when the all-out Federal amphibious assault was launched, just as he had said it would be, against the undefended south end of the island.

In his search for someone who understood the difficulties and dangers of his assignment Wise was cut off from the one person who, next to himself, appreciated them best. The trouble was, the man wore blue and exercised his authority on the other side of the line.

Ambrose Burnside had not gone home with his Rhode Islanders when they were mustered out in early August, two weeks after crossing Bull Run as the fist of the roundhouse right McDowell had swung at Beauregard in an effort to end the war on the plains of Manassas. He had tried civilian life as a businessman a few years back and, failing, hadn't liked it. Now, at thirty-seven, an Indiana-born West Pointer and a veteran of the Mexican War, he accepted promotion to brigadier and stayed on in the service. A tall, rather stout, energetic man with large features and dark-socketed eyes, he made up for his premature baldness with a fantastic set of whiskers describing a double parabola from in front of his ears, down over his chops, and up across his mouth. This was his trademark, a half-ruff of facial hair standing out in dark-brown contrast to his shaven jowls and chin. Affecting the casual in his dress — low-slung holster, loose-fitting knee-length double-breasted jacket, and wide-brimmed bell-crowned soft felt hat — he was something of a pistol-slapper, but likable all the same for his hearty manner and open nature, his forthright, outgoing friendliness. McClellan liked him, at any rate, and called him "Dear Burn" in letters. So that when Burnside approached him in the fall with a plan for the seizure of coastal North Carolina, completing what had been begun at Hatteras Inlet and opening thereby a second front in the Confederate rear, the general-in-chief was attentive and said he would like to see it submitted in writing.

Burnside did so, expanding his original plan, and McClellan liked it even more. He indorsed it, got the Secretary of War to give it top priority, and told the Hoosier general to go ahead, the quicker the better.

The Burnside Expedition, as it was designated, was assembled and ready for action by early January, Annapolis being the staging area for its 13,000 troops and 80 vessels. Grouped into three divisions under brigadiers who had been cadets with their commander at West Point — J. G. Foster, Jesse L. Reno, John G. Park; "three of my most trusted friends," he called them — the men were mostly rock-ribbed New Englanders, "many of whom would be familiar with the coasting trade, and among whom would be found a goodly number of mechanics." The naval components of this task force, under Rear Admiral Louis M. Goldsborough, a big, slack-bodied regular of the type called "barnacles," had no such homogeneity. In addition to twenty light-draft gunboats armed with cannon salvaged from the armories of various navy yards, there was a rickety lot of sixty-odd transports and supply ships, including tugs, ferries, converted barges, and flat-bottomed river steamers: a conglomeration, in short, of whatever could be scraped together by purchasing agents combing northern rivers and harbors for vessels rejected by agents who had come and gone before them. The only characteristic they shared was that they all drew less than eight feet of water, the reported high-tide depth across the bar at Hatteras Inlet.

This was the cause of much grumbling at the outset. Seafaring men among the soldiers took one look at the shallow-draft transports and shook their heads. At the worst, they had volunteered for getting shot at, not drowned — which was what they believed would happen, once those tubs reached open water. Burnside answered the grumbling by taking the smallest, least seaworthy craft of the lot for his headquarters boat. Thus reassured, or anyhow reproached, the troops filed onto the transports, and on the morning of the 9th the flotilla steamed out of the harbor to rendezvous next day off Fort Monroe. On the 11th, clearing Hampton Roads, the skippers broke open their sealed orders and steered south.

The near-mutiny among his sea-going soldiers at the outset was only the first of Burnside's troubles. In fact, the method by which he had quelled the grumbling almost cost him his life the following night, when the fleet ran into a gale off Hatteras. The dinky little headquarters boat got into the trough of the sea and nearly foundered. As he remembered it years later, still somewhat queasy from the experience, everything not securely lashed above-decks was swept overboard, while "men, furniture, and crockery below decks were thrown about in a most promiscuous manner." Eventually, her steersman brought her head-to and she rode the storm out, staggering up and down the mast-high waves to arrive next morning off Hatteras Inlet, the entrance to Pamlico Sound, where an even worse shock awaited him.

The water through there was not eight feet deep, as he had been told, but six: which barred many of his vessels from a share in the expedition as effectively as if they had been sunk by enemy action. Here was where the "goodly number of mechanics, . . . familiar with the coasting trade," stood their commander in good stead. The tide running swift above the swash, they sent several of the larger ships full-speed-ahead to ground on the bar, and held them there with tugs and anchors while the racing current washed the sand from under their bottoms. It was a slow process, bumping them forward length by length; but it worked. By early February a broad eight-foot channel had been cut and the fleet assembled safely in the sound. On the 4th, after a conference with the flag officer, Burnside gave his brigadiers detailed instructions for the landing on Roanoke Island. Another two-day blow delayed it, but on the morning of the 7th, a fine, clear day with sunshine bright on the placid, sapphire water, the fleet steamed forward in attack formation.

Still suffering from the multiple pangs of pleurisy and frustration, Wise had been confined all this time at Nags Head, the Confederate command post on the sandy rim of Albemarle Sound, just opposite the north end of the island. He knew what was coming, and even how, though until now he had not realized the strength of the blow the Federals were aiming. Goldsborough's warships were out in front, mounting a total of 64 guns, eager to take on the seven makeshift rebel vessels, each mounting a single 32-pounder rifle. Behind the Yankee gunboats came the transports, crowded with 13,000 assault troops ready to swarm ashore and try their strength against the island's fewer than 3000 defenders. The mosquito fleet took station in front of the uncompleted line of pilings Wise had started driving across the channel, but when the Federals roared and bore down on them belching smoke and flame from 9-inch guns and 100-pounder rifles, they scurried back through the gap and out of range, leaving the water batteries to take up the defense.

There were two of these, both up toward the northern end of the island, and while the warships took them under fire the transports dropped anchor three miles astern and began unloading troops for the landing at Ashby's Harbor, midway up the island's ten-mile length. The first boats hit the beach at 4 o'clock. All this time the duel between the gunboats and the batteries continued, with more noise than damage on either side. At sundown the mosquito fleet attempted a darting attack that was repulsed about as soon as it began. By midnight all the troops were ashore. The undefended southern half of the island had been secured without the infantry firing a shot. Drenched by a chill rain, they tried to get what sleep they could before the dawn advance, knowing that tomorrow would be tougher.

Down the boggy center of the island, a little more than a mile from the opposite beaches, ran a causeway. Astride this backbone of defense the Confederates had placed a three-gun battery supported by infantry and flanked by quicksand marshes judged impenetrable. To advance along the causeway toward those guns would be like walking up a hardwood alley toward a bowler whose only worry was running out of balls before the advancer ran out of legs. Yet there was no other way, and the men of both armies knew it: Burnside as well as anyone, for he had been briefed for the landing by a twenty-year-old contraband who had run away from his island master the week before and was thoroughly familiar with the dispositions for defense. Instructing Foster to charge straight up the causeway while Reno and Park were probing the boggy flanks, Burnside put all three brigades into line and sent them forward as soon as the light was full.

Right off, the center brigade ran into murderous head-on fire. Bowled over and pinned down, they were hugging the sandy embankment and wondering what came next, when off to the right and left fronts they heard simultaneous whoops of exultation. The flank brigades had made it through the knee-deep ooze and slush of the "impenetrable" marsh. While the rebel cannoneers tried frantically to turn their guns to meet these attacks from opposite and unexpected directions, the men along the causeway jumped up, whooping too, and joined the charge. The battery was quickly overrun.

With the fall of the three-gun battery the island's defenses collapsed of a broken backbone. Burnside's infantry broke into the clear, taking the water batteries in reverse while the fleet continued its bombardment from the channel. By midafternoon the Confederates had retreated as far as they could go. Corralled on the northern tip of the island, their ammunition exhausted, they laid down their arms. Casualties had been relatively light on both sides: 264 for the attackers, 143 for the defenders. The difference came in the fruits of victory; 2675 soldiers and 32 cannon were surrendered, losses which the South could ill afford. Best of all, from the northern point of view, Burnside had won control of North Carolina's inland sea, thereby tightening the blockade one hard twist more, opening a second front in the Virginia army's rear, gaining access to the back door to Norfolk, and arousing the immediate apprehension of every rebel posted within gunshot of salt water. No beach was safe. This newly bred amphibious beast, like some monster out of mythology — half Army, half Navy: an improbable, unholy combination if ever there was one — might come splashing and roaring ashore at any point from here on down.

North and south the news went out and men reacted. In New York, Horace Greeley swung immediately to the manic, celebrating the double conquest of Roanoke Island and Fort Henry even as Grant was knocking at the gates of Donelson: "The cause of the Union now marches on in every section of the country. Every blow tells fearfully against the rebellion. The rebels themselves are panic-stricken, or despondent. It now requires no very far-reaching prophet to predict the end of this struggle."

In Richmond, as elsewhere throughout the Confederacy and among her representatives overseas, the spirits of men were correspondingly grim. As if in confirmation of Greeley's paean in the *Tribune*, letters came from Mason and Slidell. The former wrote from London that "the late reverses... have had an unfortunate effect upon the minds of our friends here." The latter wrote from Paris: "I need not say how unfavorable an influence these defeats, following in such quick succession, have produced in public sentiment. If not soon counterbalanced by some decisive success of our arms, we may not only bid adieu to all hopes of seasonable recognition, but must expect that the declaration of the inefficiency of the blockade, to which I had looked forward with great confidence at no distant day, will be indefinitely postponed."

These were hard lines for Davis on the eve of his inaugural, but he had other reactions to deal with, nearer and far more violent. Norfolk was in turmoil — with good cause. Lynch's mosquito fleet, attempting to make a stand against Goldsborough's gunboats at the mouth of the Pasquotank River, was wrecked in short order, six of the seven vessels being captured, rammed, blown up, or otherwise sunk. Only one made its escape up the river and through the Dismal Swamp Canal to Norfolk, barely forty miles away, bringing wild stories of the destruction it had run from and predicting that Norfolk was next on the monster's list. The consternation which followed this report was hardly calmed by the arrival of Wise, who, convalescent from pleurisy, had made his escape by marching up the breakwater from Nags Head. "Nothing! Nothing!! Nothing!!!" he proclaimed. "That was the disease which brought disaster at Roanoke Island." Thus he shook whatever confidence the citizens had managed to retain in Huger, who was charged with their defense.

The city seethed with rumors of doom, and the panic spread quickly up the James to Richmond. Davis met it as he had met the East Tennessee crisis early that winter. Five days after the inaugural in which he had excoriated Lincoln for doing the same thing, and scorned the northern populace for putting up with it, he suspended the privilege of habeas corpus in the Norfolk area, placing the city under martial law. Two days later, March 1, Richmond itself was gripped by the iron hand.

This action added fuel to the fire already raging in certain breasts. Taking their cue from Wise, who was vociferous in accusation, the people put the blame where he pointed: squarely at the Secretary of War. Benjamin took it as he took everything, blandly. "To do the Secretary justice," one observer wrote, "he bore the universal attack with admirable good nature and sang froid." More than that, "to all appearances, equally secure in his own views and indifferent to public odium, he passed from reverse to reverse with perfectly bland manner and unwearying courtesy."

The principal charge against him was that he had failed, despite repeated pleas, to supply the island defenders with powder for their cannon. He had the best possible answer to this: that there was and had been none to send. But to admit as much would have been to encourage his country's enemies and alienate the Europeans considering recognition and support. The Louisianian kept silent under attack and abuse, and Davis was given further proof of his loyalty and devotion to the cause. However, his very urbanity was more infuriating to his foes than any defense or counterattack he might have made. The Richmond *Examiner* was irked into commenting acidly, "The Administration has now an opportunity of making some reputation; for, nothing being expected of it, of course every success will be clear gain." Plainly, the ultimate sacrifice was called for. Benjamin had to go.

He had to go, but not from the cabinet entirely. That would be a loss which Davis believed the nation could not afford. At any rate *he* could not. And though, as always, he would not attempt to justify or even explain his action — would not say to the hostile editors and fuming politicians, "Let me keep this man; I need him" — he found a way to keep him: a way, however, that infuriated his critics even more.

The post of Secretary of State had been vacant since Hunter left in a huff the month before. Davis had kept it so, with this in mind. Now in mid-March the Permanent Congress, which had convened four days before his inauguration, received for confirmation the name of the man he wanted appointed to fill the vacancy: Judah P. Benjamin of Louisiana, former Attorney General and present Secretary of War. Some in that body called the move audacious. Others called it impudent. Whatever it was, Davis had the devotion of the people and the personal support of a majority of the legislators, and he was willing to risk them both, here and now, to get what he believed both he and the Confederacy needed to win the war and establish independence. And he got it. Despite the gasps of outrage and cries of indignation, Benjamin was quickly confirmed as head of the State Department and thus assured a voice in the nation's councils, a seat at the right hand of Jefferson Davis.

Having angered many congressmen by requiring them to promote the Secretary of War as a reward for what they termed his inefficiency, the President now proceeded to make them happy and proud by placing before them, for confirmation, the name of George Wythe Randolph as Benjamin's successor. Appointment of this forty-four-year-old Richmond lawyer, scion of the proud clan of Randolph, would make amends for the snub given Hunter and restore to the Old

Dominion a rightful place among those closest to the head of government. What was more, Randolph had had varied military experience as a youthful midshipman in the U.S. Navy, as a gentleman ranker in a prewar Richmond militia company, and as artillery commander under Magruder on the peninsula, where in eight months he had risen from captain to colonel, with a promotion to brigadier moving up through channels even now. All this was much, and augured well. But best of all, from the point of view of those who had the privilege of voting his confirmation, he was the grandson of Thomas Jefferson, born at the hilltop shrine of Monticello and dandled on the great Virginian's knee. Blood would tell, as all Southerners knew, and this was the finest blood of all, serving to reëmphasize the ties between the Second American Revolution and the First. The appointment was confirmed at once, enthusiastically and with considerable mutual congratulation among the senators.

Whether the highborn Randolph would bear up better than Hunter had done as a "clerk of Mr Davis" remained to be seen. For the present, at least, the Chief Executive had placated the rising anger of his friends by nominating Randolph, and had foiled his critics by tossing his personal popularity into the balance alongside the hated Benjamin, causing the opposite pan to kick the beam. How long he could continue to win by such methods, standing thus between his favorites and abuse, was another question. Certainly every such victory subtracted from the weight he would exert in any weighing match that followed. What he lost, each time, his critics gained: particularly those who railed against his static defensive policy and his failure to share with the public the grim statistics of the lengthening odds. Down in Georgia, even now, an editor was writing for all to read: "President Davis does not enjoy the confidence of the Southern people. . . . With a cold, icy, iron grasp, [he] has fettered our people, stilled their beating pulses of patriotism, cooled their fiery ardor, imprisoned them in camps and behind entrenchments. He has not told the people what he needed. As a faithful sentinel, he has not told them what of the night."

So far, the Georgian was one among a small minority; but such men were vociferous in their bitterness, and when they stung they stung to hurt. The people read or heard their complaints, printed in columns alongside the news of such reverses as Fort Donelson and Roanoke Island, and they wondered. They did not enjoy being told that they were not trusted by the man in whom their own trust was placed. A South Carolina matron, friendly to Davis and all he stood for, confided scornfully in her diary: "In Columbia I do not know a half-dozen men who would not gaily step into Jeff Davis's shoes with a firm conviction that they would do better in every respect than he does."

There was one glimmer in the military gloom — indeed, a brightness — though it was based not on accomplishment, but on continuing confidence despite the lengthening odds and the late reverses. The gleam in fact proceeded from the region where the gloom was deepest: off in the panic-stricken West, where the left wing of the Confederacy had been crippled. What his wife represented in private life, what Benjamin meant to him in helping to meet the cares of office, Albert Sidney Johnston was to Davis in military matters. He was in plain fact his notion of a hero. They had not been together since mid-September, when the tall, handsome Kentucky-born Texan came to Richmond to receive from Davis his commission and his assignment to command of the Western Department. That had been a happy time, the plaudits of the entire nation ringing in his ears. They had kept on ringing, too, until Grant called his game of bluff on the Tennessee and the Cumberland, and the whole western house of cards went crash.

At the outset the newspapers had expected "results at once brilliant, scientific, and satisfactory" (the diminution of the adjectives was prophetic) but not this: not defeat, with the loss of half his army, all of Kentucky, and a goodly portion of Tennessee including its capital. The uproar outdid anything the nation had known since the defection of Benedict Arnold. Johnston was accused of stupidity and incompetence or worse, for there were the usual post-defeat cries of treason and corruption. Those who had sung his praises loudest such a short while back were loudest now in abuse. The army was demoralized, they shrilled; Johnston must be removed or the cause would fail. New troops being sworn in made it a condition of their enlistment oath that they would not be required to serve under his command.

He took the blame as he had taken the praise. Calm at the storm center, he displayed still the nobility of mind and strength of character which had drawn men to him all his life. Urged by friends to make a public defense, he replied: "I cannot correspond with the people. What the people want is a battle and a victory. That is the best explanation I can make." Retreating again—from Murfreesboro now, all the way to Decatur, Alabama, where he would be south of the Tennessee River and on the Memphis & Charleston Railroad, in a position to coöperate with the forces under Beauregard, retreating south along the Mississippi—he wrote to Davis more explicitly of his reason for keeping his temper: "I observed silence, as it seemed to me the best way to serve the cause and the country." He offered then to yield the command, saying: "The test of merit in my profession is success. It is a hard rule, but I think it right." To concentrate and strike was his present aim, in which case "those who are now declaiming against me will be without an argument."

It was a letter to warm the heart of any superior in distress—which Davis certainly was. He replied: "My confidence in you has never wavered, and I hope the public will soon give me credit for judgment rather than continue to arraign me for obstinacy."

The public might, in time; but for the present the clamor did not die; it grew. Davis stood under an avalanche of letters, protests, and demands for his friend's dismissal. Yet all this time, as he said, he never wavered. When a delegation of Tennessee congressmen called at his office to insist en masse that Johnston be relieved — he was no general, they said scornfully — Davis stood at his desk and heard their demand with an icy silence. When they had spoken, he told them: "If Sidney Johnston is not a general, we had better give up the war, for we have no general," and bowed them out.

★ ★ ★

The other Johnston, back in Virginia, was another matter. There would never be any such letter from him, and Davis knew it: not only because it was not in Joe Johnston's nature to be selfless in a crisis — he had small belief in the efficacy of silence — but also because his problems were quite different. He had no quarrel with the public; the public, like his soldiers, now and always, showed the greatest affection for him. His difficulties were rather with his superiors, the Commander in Chief and the Secretary of War, and with the laws and regulations which Congress passed in an attempt to be what it called helpful, but which Johnston himself considered meddlesome and harmful.

A case in point was the so-called Furlough and Bounty Act, which had been passed in December in an effort to meet the crisis that would arise when the enlistments of the twelve-month volunteers expired in late winter and early spring. Obviously something would have to be done to encourage reënlistments; few men were likely to expose themselves voluntarily to a continuance of the dull life they had been leading all through the Virginia fall and winter. Under the act, all who would sign on for three years — or the duration, in case the end came first — would receive a sixty-day furlough and a fifty-dollar bounty. Further, on their return they would be allowed to transfer to whatever outfit they chose, even into another arm of service, and elect their own field- and company-grade officers once the reorganization was effected. Johnston realized the necessity for some such encouragement, but the only part of this particular act that he approved of was the bounty. The transfer and election privileges he considered ruinous, and the furloughs, if granted in numbers large enough to be effective, would expose the remainder of his army to slaughter at the hands of the Federals, already twice his strength around Manassas and likely to attack at any time. Besides, when he wrote to the War Department, asking how the act was to be applied and what numbers were to be furloughed at any one time, the Secretary replied that he was to go to the "extreme verge of prudence." Now Johnston was a very prudent man; entirely too much so, his critics said. The extreme verge of his prudence was still very prudent indeed. As a result, the act accomplished little except to vex the general charged with its application.

Another, more serious vexation was the loss of experienced officers of rank. He had lost the embittered Beauregard and he had nearly lost Stonewall Jackson as a result of Benjamin's out-of-channels interference. Kirby Smith had returned to duty, healed of his Manassas wound, only to be assigned to deal with the powder-keg East Tennessee situation. Earl Van Dorn, whose dash and brilliance promised much, had been sent to the Transmississippi. These were hard losses, and there were more, in addition to some who were so disgruntled that they threatened to resign. "The Army is crippled and its discipline greatly impaired by a want of general officers," Johnston reported plaintively to Richmond.

These were causes enough for disturbance in any commander, let alone one as irascible and gloomy as Joe Johnston; but coming as they did, at a time when the odds were what he knew them to be in northern Virginia, they filled him with forebodings of disaster. His loss of respect for McClellan's character as a man of war — in letters he now referred to him as "George" or "the redoubtable McC" or even " 'George,' " employing the pointed sarcasm of inverted commas — did not preclude a respect for McClellan's numbers or his ability to forge them into an effective striking force. And not only were the numerical odds forbidding; the situation itself was bad from the southern point of view. Operating behind the screen of the Potomac, the northern host could concentrate and strike at any point from the Blue Ridge Mountains down to Aquia Creek, and thus be on the flank or in the rear of the army around Manassas and Occoquan. All that was holding them back, so far as Johnston could see, was rainy weather and the mud that it produced. Spring was coming, the sudden vernal loveliness of blue skies, new grass, and solid roads. A week of sunshine would remove all the obstacles that stood between McClellan and success, or between Johnston and ruin.

It was at this point, aggravated further by a shortage of arms and powder, that the general was summoned to ride down to Richmond, two days before the inauguration, for a conference on the military situation. Reporting to the President at 10 o'clock that morning, he found the cabinet in session and the discussion already begun. After an exchange of greetings, in which there was no evidence of the lately strained relations, he was asked to state his views as to the disposition of his army. He replied that from its present position along Bull Run and the Potomac it could not block the multiple routes by which McClellan could march against the capital. Unequivocally, he stated that his army must fall back to a position farther south before the roads were dry. Somewhat taken aback, Davis asked to just what line the retreat would be conducted. When Johnston replied that he did not know, being unfamiliar with the country between Richmond and Manassas, Davis was even more alarmed.

As he said later, "That a general should have selected a line which he himself considered untenable, and should not have ascertained the typography of the country in his rear was inexplicable on any other theory than that he had neglected the primary duty of a commander."

For the present, however, he let this pass. If Johnston advised retreat, retreat it had to be, so long as he was in command. Davis had to content himself with trying to get assurances from the general that the army's supplies and equipment, particularly the large-caliber guns along the Potomac and the mountains of subsistence goods now stored in forward depots, would not be abandoned. He did not get it. Johnston merely said that he would do what he could to delay the retreat until the last possible moment, so that the roads would be firm enough to bear the heavy guns and the high-piled wagons. Further than that he would not go. The meeting broke up without any specific date being set for the withdrawal. All that was determined was that the army would move southward to take up a securer line whenever practicable.

Back at his hotel, it was Johnston's turn to be alarmed. He found the lobby buzzing with rumors that the Manassas intrenchments were about to be abandoned. The news had moved swiftly before him, though he had come directly from the conference: with the result that his reluctance to discuss military secrets with civilians, no matter how highly placed, was confirmed. No tactical maneuver was more difficult than a withdrawal from the presence of a superior enemy. Everything depended on secrecy; for to be caught in motion, strung out on the roads, was to invite destruction. Yet here in the lobby of a Richmond hotel, where every pillar might hide a spy, was a flurry of gossip predicting the very movement he was about to undertake. Next day, riding back to Manassas on the cars, his reluctance was reconfirmed and his anger heightened when a friend approached and asked if it was true that the Bull Run line was about to be abandoned. There could be no chance that the man had overheard the news by accident, for he was deaf. Nor did it improve the general's humor when he arrived that afternoon to find his headquarters already abuzz with talk of the impending evacuation.

Two things he determined to do in reaction: 1) to get his army out of there as quickly as he could — if possible, before McClellan had time to act on the leaked information — and 2) to confide no more in civilians, which as far as he was concerned included the Chief Executive. The first was easier said than done, however. Rain fell all the following day, drenching alike the inaugural throng on Capitol Square and the roads of northern Virginia. The army was stalled in a sea of mud, just when Johnston was most anxious to get it moving. Well-mounted cavalry, riding light, could not average two miles an hour along the roads. Four-horse teams could not haul the field artillery guns, and nothing at all could budge the heavier pieces. The general's determination to share none of his plans with the Government did not prevent his expressing his ire and apprehension in dispatches which repeated his former complaints and advanced new ones. "A division of five brigades is without generals," he wrote on the 25th, "and at least half the field officers are absent — generally sick. The accumulation of subsistence stores at Manassas is now a great evil. The Commissary General was requested more than once to suspend these supplies. A very extensive meat-packing establishment at Thoroughfare is also a great incumbrance. The great quantities of personal property in our camps is a still greater one."

He did what he could to hasten his army's departure, but with horses and wagons foundered and mired on the roads, he had to depend solely on the single-track Orange & Alexandria Railroad. Overcrowded, it quickly snarled to a standstill and pitched the general's anguished cries an octave higher. In truth, there was much to vex him, here where ruin stared him in the face. The amount of personal baggage piled along the railroad "was appalling to behold," one witness said. A "trunk had come with every volunteer," Johnston later declared, reporting now that the army, over his protest, "had accumulated a supply of baggage like that of Xerxes' myriads." All this time, while he was struggling to save what he could with so little success, there had been reports of enemy advances, each a confirmation of his fears. Soon after his return from the capital, a Union force had appeared at Harpers Ferry, from which position it could move forward and outflank him on the left. Two weeks later, March 5, he was warned of "unusual activity" on the Maryland shore opposite Dumfries, indicating preparations for attack. This was the movement he feared most, considering it not only the most dangerous, but also the most likely. An advance from there would turn his right and bring the Federals between his army and Richmond.

That did it. He did not intend to let himself get caught like that other Johnston in the West, who lost half his army through delay in pulling back when enemy pressure increased the strain beyond the breaking point. To retreat now meant the loss of much equipment. The heavy guns were still in place along the Potomac; supplies and personal baggage were still piled high along the railroad. But equipment was nothing, compared to the probable loss of men and possible loss of the war itself. Nor was terrain, not even the "sacred soil" of his native state. That same day he issued orders for all his forces east of the Blue Ridge to fall back to the line of the Rappahannock.

Davis in Richmond knew nothing of this. Ever since Johnston's departure he had been urging a delay in the retrograde movement. In fact, when Virginia officials came to him with a plan for mass recruitment to turn back the invaders, Davis took heart and urged the general to hold his ground while the army was brought up to strength for an offensive, which he now referred to as "first policy." March 10, believing that Johnston and his army still held the Manassas intrenchments, he wired: "Further assurance given to me this day that you shall be promptly and adequately reënforced, so as to enable you to maintain your position and resume first policy when the roads will permit."

Johnston was not there to receive it, nor were any of his men. The cavalry rear guard had pulled out that morning, following the southward trail of the army on its way to the Rappahannock, accompanied by its general — who was already contemplating another retreat, from there back to the Rapidan. The one in progress had not gone well. One division, in an advance position, had not been informed of the movement at all, but was left to find its way out as best it could. The heavy guns were left in their emplacements, some of them not even thrown from their carriages. Supplies and equipment, including the trunks the volunteers had brought, went up in smoke. The packing plant at Thoroughfare Gap was put to the torch, along with one million pounds of meat remaining after farmers in the neighborhood had been given all they could haul away. For twenty miles around, all down the greening slopes of Bull Run Mountain, there was a smell of burning bacon, an aroma which the natives would remember through the hungry months ahead.

※ 4 ※

Lincoln's efforts all this time as Commander in Chief, though on the face of it they were exerted in quite the opposite direction and for an entirely different purpose, were much like those of his southern counterpart; for while Davis had been trying to get Johnston to hold his ground, Lincoln had been doing his best to nudge McClellan forward. All through the fall and winter, as far as these two tasks were concerned, Lincoln had failed and Davis had succeeded. Both generals stayed exactly where they were. Yet in the end it was the northern leader who was successful: Johnston fell back and McClellan at last went forward. In both cases, however, on that final day, March 9, the civilian heads were shown to have urged good counsel to generals who now were exposed before the public in a cold unflattering light. Johnston fled where no man pursued, and McClellan encountered none of the bloody opposition he had predicted.

For both civil leaders the time had been long and harrowing, a season of waste and unhappiness for Lincoln no less than for Davis. The burden of action was on the North; the South had only to keep the status quo, which was exactly what she had been doing here in Virginia. If on the northern side the gloom had been relieved by victories East and West — Roanoke Island and Fort Donelson — it had no bright, original, face-to-face East-West triumph such as Manassas or Wilson's Creek to hark back to. Also, for Lincoln, the period of inaction around

Washington had been darkened by personal tragedy, including the death of one of his sons and signs that his wife was losing her mind. For him the year had opened, not with a glimmer as of dawn, but rather with gathering shadows, as of dusk. The army head was down with typhoid; the bottom was out of the tub; "What shall I do?" he groaned in his melancholy.

It was January 10; Quartermaster General M. C. Meigs replied that if the typhoid diagnosis was correct it meant a six-weeks' illness for McClellan, during which time the nation's armies would be leaderless and vulnerable. He suggested that the President call a conference of the ranking officers of the Army of the Potomac, one of whom might have to take over in a crisis. Lincoln liked the advice and called the meeting for that evening. Two generals attended, McDowell and William B. Franklin, along with several cabinet members. Lincoln told them the situation and expressed his desire for an early offensive. If McClellan did not want to use the army, he said, he would like to borrow it for a while.

McDowell replied that he would be willing to try his hand at another advance on Richmond by way of Manassas, while Franklin, who had taken part in that first debacle under McDowell and was moreover in the confidence of McClellan, favored the roundabout salt-water route, approaching the southern capital from the east. On this divided note the conference adjourned. Next night, when they met again, the generals were agreed that the overland method was best, despite the previous failure, because it would require less time for preparation. Pleased with this decision, Lincoln adjourned the second meeting, instructing the generals to go back to their headquarters, work on the plan, and return tomorrow night. They did return, having worked on it all through the day, but the third White House session was brief, since they still had much to do.

The fourth such conference, on the 13th, was the last. McClellan was there — pale and shaky, but very much there. He had gotten wind of what was going on: perhaps from Stanton, who had been visiting him and murmuring, "They are counting on your death": Stanton was adept at this kind of thing, having served in Buchanan's cabinet as an informer for the opposition. Anyhow, McClellan had learned of the meetings and had risen from his sickbed to confront these men who met behind his back. As a result, the atmosphere was strained. According to McClellan, "my unexpected appearance caused very much the effect of a shell in a powder magazine." When Lincoln asked McDowell to outline the plan he had been working on, McDowell gave it nervously and wound up with an apology for offering his opinion in the presence of his chief. "You are entitled to have any opinion you please!" McClellan said, obviously miffed.

During the discussion which followed, while Lincoln kept asking where and when an offensive could be launched, McClellan remained silent. Seward drawled that he didn't much care whether the army whipped the rebels at Manassas or in Richmond itself, so long as it whipped them *some*where. McClellan kept silent. Finally Chase questioned him directly, asking what he intended to do with the army and when he intended to do it. The general replied that he had a perfectly good plan, with a perfectly good schedule of execution, but he would not discuss it in front of civilians unless the President ordered him to do so. He would say, however, that Buell was about to move forward in Kentucky, after which he himself would move. Another awkward silence followed. Presently Lincoln asked him if he "counted upon any particular time." He was not asking him to divulge it, he added hastily; he just wanted to know if he had it in mind. McClellan said he did. "Then I will adjourn this meeting," Lincoln said.

McClellan did not go back to his sickbed. Now that he was up, he stayed up, his youth and stout constitution — he had reached thirty-five in December — permitting him to convalesce on horseback, so to speak. Once more he spent "long days in the saddle and... nights in the office," riding to inspect the camps and returning with a jaunty salute the worshipful cheers of his soldiers. There was something other than cheering in the air, however. For one thing, there was suspicion: which meant that the Joint Committee on the Conduct of the War was interested. Now that he was up where they could get at him, the committeemen summoned the general to appear and be examined.

Ben Wade and Zachariah Chandler — who, along with Andrew Johnson, were the members from the Senate — did most of the questioning. Chandler began it by asking why the army, after five long months of training, was not marching out to meet the enemy. McClellan began explaining that there were only two bridges across to Alexandria, which did not satisfy the requirement that a commander must safeguard his lines of retreat in event that his men were repulsed.

"General McClellan," Chandler interrupted. He spoke with the forthright tone of a man translating complicated matters into simpler terms for laymen. "If I understand you correctly, before you strike at the rebels you want to be sure of plenty of room so you can run in case they strike back."

"Or in case you get scared," Wade put in.

McClellan then went into a rather drawn-out explanation of how wars were fought. Lines of retirement were sometimes as necessary to an army's survival, he said, as lines of communication and supply. The committeemen listened scornfully. It was not this they had called him in to tell them.

"General," Wade said, "you have all the troops you have called for, and if you haven't enough, you shall have more. They are well organized and equipped, and the loyal people of this country expect that you will make a short and decisive campaign. Is it really necessary for you to have more bridges over the Potomac before you move?"

"Not that. Not that exactly," McClellan told him. "But we must bear in mind the necessity of having everything ready in case of a defeat, and keep our lines of retreat open."

After this, they let him go in disgust. When he had gone, Chandler turned to Wade and sneered. "I don't know much about war," he said, "but it seems to me that this is infernal, unmitigated cowardice."

Wade thought so, too, and as chairman he went to see Lincoln about it. McClellan must be discarded, he cried. When the President asked who should be put in his place, Wade snorted: "Anybody!"

"Wade," Lincoln replied sadly, "anybody will do for you, but I must have somebody."

Already that week he had made one replacement in a high place. For months now there had been growing reports of waste and graft in the War Department; of contracts strangely let; of shoddy cloth, tainted pork, spavined horses, and guns that would not shoot; of the Vermont jobber who boasted at Willard's, grinning, "You can sell anything to the government at almost any price you've got the guts to ask."

Simon Cameron was responsible, though there was no evidence that the Secretary had profited personally except in the use of his office to pay off his political debts and strengthen his political position. Lincoln could understand this last, having himself done likewise — in point of fact, that was how Cameron got the job — and he knew, too, that much of the waste and bungling, much of the greed and dishonesty, even, was incident to the enormous task of preparing the unprepared nation for war and increasing the army from 16,000 to better than half a million men in the process. All the same, the Pennsylvanian was unquestionably lax in his conduct of business affairs, and when Lincoln warned him of this, resisting the general outcry for his removal, Cameron made his first really serious mistake. He made it, however, not through any ordinary brand of stupidity — Cameron was a very canny man — but rather through his canniness in trying to safeguard his position in the cabinet by strengthening his position in the public eye and in the minds of the increasingly powerful radicals in Congress. He fell because he did what many men had done before and what others would do in the future, after he himself was off the scene. He underestimated Lincoln.

Despite the example of Frémont, or perhaps because he thought that the furor which had followed Frémont's dismissal would have taught Lincoln a lesson, Cameron reasoned that by ingratiating himself with the Jacobins he would insure himself against any action by the President, who would not dare to antagonize them further by molesting another man who had won their favor. Any attack on slavery was the answer. Emancipation was the issue on which Lincoln was treading softest, since it was the one that cut sharpest along the line dividing the

Administration's supporters and opponents. Accordingly, with the help of his legal adviser Stanton, Cameron drafted and included in his annual Department report a long passage advocating immediate freedom for southern slaves and their induction into the Union army, thereby adding muscle to the arm of the republic and weakening the enemy, who as "rebellious traitors" had forfeited their rights to any property at all, let alone the ownership of fellow human beings. Without consulting the President — though it was usual for such documents to be submitted for approval — the Secretary had the report printed and sent out to the postmasters of all the principal cities for distribution to the press as soon as it was being read to Congress.

So far all was well. Even when Lincoln discovered what had been done and recalled the pamphlet by telegraphic order, for reprinting without the offensive passage, things still went as Cameron had expected. Critics of the President's tread-easy policy, comparing the original with the expurgated report — some copies of course escaped destruction, so that both versions appeared in the papers — were harsh in their attacks, charging Lincoln simultaneously with dictatorship and timidity. The Jacobins reacted as expected by taking the Secretary to their bosoms and pronouncing him "one of us." Other praises came his way, less vigorous perhaps, but no less pleasant. "You have touched the national heart," a friend declared, while another, in a punning mood, wrote that he much preferred the "Simon pure" article in the *Tribune* to the "bogus" report in the *World*. From Paris a member of the consulate, hearing of the dissension in the President's official family, wrote home asking: "Are Cameron and Frémont to be canonized as martyrs?"

Cameron might be canonized, at any rate by the antislavery radicals, but it did not appear that he would be martyred by anyone, least of all by Lincoln, who seemed to have learned a dearly bought lesson in martyring Frémont. The report had been published in mid-December, and now in January he still had made no further reference to the matter. Outwardly the relationship between the two men remained cordial, though Cameron still felt some inward qualms, perhaps because he sensed that Lincoln's measure was not so easily taken. The thing had gone *too* well.

Then on January 11, a Saturday — the date of the second of the three conferences with McDowell and Franklin, none of which Cameron had been urged to attend, despite his position as Secretary of War — he learned that he had been right to feel qualms. He received a brief note in which Lincoln informed him curtly, out of the blue: "I ... propose nominating you to the Senate next Monday as Minister to Russia." Almost literally, he was being banished to Siberia for his sins.

The sins were political, and as a politician he could appreciate the justice of his punishment. He suffered anguish, though, at the manner in which it was inflicted. To be rebuked thus in a brief note, he complained, "meant personal as well as political destruction." So Lincoln, who cared little for the manner of his going, just so he went, agreed that Cameron might antedate a letter of resignation, to which he would reply with a letter of acceptance expressing his "affectionate esteem" and "undiminished confidence" in the Secretary's "ability, patriotism, and fidelity to the public trust." It was done accordingly and Cameron's name was sent to Congress for confirmation as Minister to Russia. There, however, he encountered opposition, not only from members of his own party, the Democrats, but also from some of the radical Republicans who so lately had clustered round him and proclaimed him "one of us." At last the nomination was put through; Cameron was on his way to St Petersburg, having earned not martyrdom and canonization, as some had hoped or feared, but banishment and damage to a reputation already considered shaky. One senator, a former colleague, remarked on his departure: "Ugh! ugh! Send word to the Czar to bring in his things of nights."

In this case Lincoln engaged in no fruitless search for "somebody" to replace him. The somebody was ready and very much at hand: Edwin McMasters Stanton, who as his predecessor's legal adviser had helped to charge and fuse the bomb that blew him out of the War Department and the Cabinet, while Stanton himself was sucked into the resultant vacuum and sat ensconced as successor before all the bits of wreckage had hit the ground. Whether he had proceeded with malice aforethought in this instance was not known; but it was not unthinkable. Stanton had done devious things in his time. A corporation lawyer, he delighted also in taking criminal cases when these were challenging and profitable enough. His fees were large and when one prospective client protested, Stanton asked: "Do you think I would argue the wrong side for less?" For a murder defense he once took as his fee the accused man's only possession, the house he lived in. When he had won the case and was about to convert the mortgage into cash, the man tried to persuade him to hold off, saying that he would be ruined by the foreclosure. "You deserve to be ruined," Stanton told him, "for you were guilty."

And yet there was another side to him, too, offsetting the savagery, the joy he took in fixing a frightened general or petitioner with the baleful glare of his black little near-sighted eyes behind small, thick-lensed, oval spectacles. He was a bundle of contradictions, his father a New Englander, his mother a Virginian. In private, the forty-seven-year-old lawyer sometimes put his face in his hands and wept from the strain, and if his secretary happened in at such a time he would say, "Not now, please. Not now." He was asthmatic, something of a hysteric as well, and he had more than a touch of morbidity in his nature. His bushy hair was thinning at the front, but he made up for this by letting it grow long at the back and sides. His upper lip he kept clean-shaven to expose a surprisingly sensitive mouth — a reminder that he had been considered handsome in his youth — while below his lower lip a broad streak of iron-gray ran down the center of his wide black beard. His body was thick-set, bouncy on short but energetic legs. His voice, which was deep in times of calm, rose to piercing shrillness in excitement. One petitioner, badly shaken by the experience, described a Stanton interview by saying, "He came at me like a tiger."

He came at many people like a tiger, especially at those in his Department who showed less devotion to work than he himself did. Soon after he took office he received from Harpers Ferry an urgent call for heavy guns. He ordered them sent at once. Going by the locked arsenal after hours, he learned that the guns were still there: whereupon he ordered the gates broken open, helped the watchmen drag the guns out, and saw them loaded onto a north-bound train. Next morning the arsenal officer reported that he had not found it convenient to ship the guns the day before; he would get them off this morning, he said. "The guns are now at Harpers Ferry!" Stanton barked. "And you, sir, are no longer in the service of the United States Government."

He would engage in no secret deals. Whoever came to him on business, as for instance seeking a contract, was required to make his request in the sight and hearing of all. Stanton would snap out a Yes or No, then wave him on to make way for the next petitioner. He did not care whose toes he stepped on; "Individuals are nothing," he declared. To a man who came demanding release for a friend locked up on suspicion of treason, Stanton roared: "If I tap that little bell, I can send *you* to a place where you will never hear the dogs bark. And by heaven I'll do it if you say another word!" He brought to the War Department a boundless and bounding energy. "As soon as I can get the machinery of the office working, the rats cleared out, and the rat holes stopped," he told an assistant, "we shall *move*." Lincoln himself was by no means exempt from Stanton's scorn. Asked when he took office, "What will you do?": "Do? . . ." he replied. "I will make Abe Lincoln President of the United States."

The government could use such a man, despite his idiosyncrasies, his sudden judgments and hostile attitude. So could Lincoln use him in his official family, despite the abuse he knew that Stanton had been heaping on him since they first met in Cincinnati, when the big-time lawyer referred to the country one as "that long-armed creature." More recently he had been employing circus epithets; "the original gorilla," he called him, "a low, cunning clown," and "that giraffe." Lincoln knew of some of this, but he still thought he could use him — provided he could handle him. And he believed he could. Stanton's prancing and bouncing, he said, put him in mind of a Methodist preacher out West who got so wrought up in his prayers and exhortations that his congregation was obliged to put bricks in his pockets to hold him down. "We may have to serve Stanton the same way," Lincoln drawled. "But I guess we'll let him jump a while first."

The bricks were applied much sooner than anyone expected. One day the President was busy with a roomful of people and Stanton came hurrying through the doorway, clutching a sheet of paper in his hand. "Mr President," he cried, "this order cannot be signed. I refuse to sign it!" Lincoln told him calmly, "Mr Secretary, I guess that order will have to be signed." In the hush that followed, the two men's eyes met. Then Stanton turned, still with the order in his hand, and went back to his office and signed it.

Whether or not McClellan could handle him, too, was one of the things that remained to be seen. At the outset, the general had good cause to believe that the change in War Department heads would work to his advantage. For on the evening of January 13 — the one on which he rose from his sickbed to confront the men who had been conferring behind his back — Stanton came by his quarters and informed him that his nomination as Secretary of War had gone to the Senate that afternoon. Personally, he went on to say, he considered the job a hardship, but the chance of working in close harness with his friend McClellan persuaded him to undergo the sacrifice involved. If the general would approve he would accept. McClellan did approve; he urged acceptance on those grounds. Two days later the nomination was confirmed. Stanton took the post the following day. And almost immediately, from that January 16 on, McClellan found the doors of the War Department barred to him. The Secretary, suddenly hostile, became at once the Young Napoleon's most outspoken critic. McClellan had been given another lesson in the perfidy of the human animal. One more had been added, at the top, to that "set of men... unscrupulous and false."

What he did not know was that, all this time, Stanton had been working both sides of the street. While his name was up for approval in the Senate, Charles Sumner was saying: "Mr Stanton, within my knowledge, is one of us." Ben Wade thought so, too. And on the day the new Secretary moved into office their opinion was confirmed. After saying that he was going to "make Abe Lincoln President," Stanton added that as the next order of business, "I will force this man McClellan to fight or throw up." Later that same day he said baldly, "This army has got to fight or run away. And while men are striving nobly in the West, the champagne and oysters on the Potomac must be stopped."

Formerly he had run with the fox and hunted with the hounds. Now he was altogether with the latter. On January 20, at his own request, he appeared before the Joint Committee, and after the hearing its members were loud in his praise. "We are delighted with him," Julian of Indiana exclaimed. In the Senate, Fessenden of Maine announced: "He is just the man we want! We agree on every point: the duties of the

Secretary of War, the conduct of the war, the Negro question and everything." In the *Tribune* Horace Greeley hailed him as the man who would know how to deal with "the greatest danger now facing the country — treason in Washington, treason in the army itself, especially the treason which wears the garb of Unionism."

Treason was a much-used word these days. For Greeley to use it three times within a dependent clause was nothing rare. In fact it was indicative. The syllables had a sound that caught men's ears, overtones of enormity that went beyond such scarehead words as rape or arson or incest. Observing this, the radicals had made it their watchword, their cry in the night, expanding its definition in the process.

Many acts were treasonous now which had never been considered so before. Even a lack of action might be treason, according to these critics in long-skirted broadcloth coats. Delay, for instance: all who counseled delay were their special targets, along with those who favored something less than extermination for rebels. Obviously, the way to administer sudden death was to march out within musket range and bang away until the serpent Rebellion squirmed no more. And as a rallying cry this forthright logic was effective. Up till now the Administration's opposition had been no more than an incidental irritant. By mid-January of this second calendar year of the war, however, so many congressmen had discovered the popular value of pointing a trembling finger at "treason" in high places that their conglomerate, harping voice had grown into a force which had to be reckoned with as surely as the Confederates still intrenched around Manassas.

Lincoln the politician understood this perfectly. They were men with power, who knew how to use it ruthlessly, and as such they would have to be dealt with. McClellan the soldier could never see it at all, partly because he operated under the disadvantage of considering himself a gentleman. For him they were willful, evil men, "unscrupulous and false," and as such they should be ignored as beneath contempt, at least by him. He counted on Lincoln to keep them off his back: which Lincoln in fact had promised to do. "I intend to be careful and do as well as possible," McClellan had said. "Don't let them hurry me, is all I ask." And Lincoln had told him, "You shall have your own way in the matter, I assure you." Yet now he seemed to be breaking his promise to McClellan, just as he had broken his word to Frémont, whom he had told: "I have given you carte-blanche. You must use your own judgment, and do the best you can." Frémont had used his judgment, such as it was, and been flung aside. McClellan was discouraged.

That was something else he never understood: Lincoln himself. Some might praise him for being flexible, while others called him slippery, when in truth they were both two words for just one thing. To argue the point was to insist on a distinction that did not exist. Lincoln was out to win the war; and that was all he was out to do, for the present. Unfettered by any need for being or not being a gentleman, he would keep his word to any man only so long as keeping it would help to win the war. If keeping it meant otherwise, he broke it. He kept no promise, anyhow, any longer than the conditions under which it was given obtained. And if any one thing was clear in this time when treason had become a household word, it was that the conditions of three months ago no longer obtained. McClellan would have to go forward or go down.

On January 27, without consulting anyone — least of all McClellan — Lincoln himself composed and issued over his signature, as Commander in Chief of the nation's military forces, General War Order Number 1, in which he announced that a forward movement by all land and naval units would be launched on February 22, to celebrate Washington's Birthday and also, presumably, to disrupt the Confederate inaugural in Richmond. It was not a suggestion, or even a directive. It was a peremptory order, and as such it stated that all commanders afield or afloat would "severally be held to their strict and full responsibilities" for its "prompt execution." Lest there be any misunderstanding as to whether this applied to the general-in-chief and his army around Washington, Lincoln supplemented this with a Special Order four days later, directing that on or before the date announced an expedition would move out from the capital, leaving whatever force would insure the city's safety, and seize a point on the railroad "southwestward of . . . Manassas Junction."

McClellan was aghast. He had counted on the President to keep the hot-eyed amateurs off his back: yet here, by a sudden and seemingly gleeful leap, Lincoln had landed there himself, joining the others in an all-out game of pile-on. Besides, committed as he was to the Urbanna Plan for loading his army on transports, taking it down the Potomac and up the Rappahannock for a landing in Johnston's rear, the last thing he wanted now was any movement that might alarm the enemy at Manassas into scurrying back to safety. So he went to Lincoln and outlined for the first time in some detail the plan which would be spoiled by any immediate "forward" movement. Lincoln did not like it. It would endanger Washington, he said, in case the rebels tried a quick pounce while the Federal army was making its roundabout boat-trip to Urbanna. McClellan then asked if he could submit in writing his objections to the President's plan and his reasons for favoring his own. Lincoln said all right, go ahead. While the general was preparing his brief he received from Lincoln a set of questions, dated February 3: "Does not your plan involve a larger expenditure of time and money than mine? Wherein is a victory more certain by your plan than mine? Would it not be less valuable in that yours would not break a great line of the

The Thing Gets Under Way

enemy's communications, while mine would? In case of disaster, would it not be more difficult to retreat by your plan than mine?"

In asking these questions Lincoln was meeting McClellan on his own ground, and McClellan answered him accordingly, professionally ticking off the flaws in Lincoln's plan and pointing up the strong points of his own. At best, he declared, the former would result in nothing more than a barren and costly victory which would leave still harder battles to be fought all the way to Richmond, each time against an enemy who would have retired to a prepared defensive position, while the Federal supply lines stretched longer and more vulnerable with every doubtful success: whereas the latter, striking at the vitals of the Confederacy, would maneuver Johnston out of his formidable Bull Run intrenchments by requiring him to turn in defense of his capital and give battle wherever McClellan chose to fight him, with control of all Virginia in the balance. Supply lines would run by water, which meant that they would be secure, and in event of the disaster which Lincoln seemed to fear, the army could retreat down the York-James peninsula, an area which afforded plenty of opportunity for maneuver because, "the soil [being] sandy," the roads were "passable at all seasons of the year." Nor was this all. Besides its other advantages, he wrote, his plan had a flexibility which the other lacked entirely. If for some reason Urbanna proved undesirable, the landing could be made at Mobjack Bay or Fortress Monroe, though admittedly this last would be "less brilliant." As for the question as to whether victory was more certain by the roundabout route, the general reminded his chief that "nothing is certain in war." However, he added, "all the chances are in favor of this project." If Lincoln would give him the go-ahead, along with a little more time to get ready, "I regard success as certain by all the chances of war."

There Lincoln had it. In submitting the questions he had said, "If you will give me satisfactory answers ... I shall gladly yield my plan to yours." Now that the Young Napoleon had given them, Lincoln yielded; but not gladly. Though he liked McClellan's plan better now that the general had taken him into his confidence and explained it in detail, he was still worried about what Johnston's army — better than 100,000 men, according to the Pinkerton reports — might do while McClellan's was in transit. Confederates in Washington might win foreign recognition for their government, and with it independence. However, since McClellan had come out so flatly in favor of his own plan and in rejection of the other, Lincoln had no choice except to fire him or sustain him. And that in fact was no choice at all. To fire Little Mac would be to risk demoralizing the Army of the Potomac on the eve of great exertions. All the same, Lincoln did not rescind the order for an advance on the 22d. He merely agreed not to require its execution.

Whereupon the radicals returned to the charge, furious that their demands had gone unheeded. Lincoln held them off as best he could, but they were strident and insistent. "For God's sake, at least push back the defiant traitors!" Wade still cried. Lincoln saw that something had to be done to appease them — perhaps by clearing the lower Potomac of enemy batteries, or else by reopening the B & O supply line west of Harpers Ferry. Either would be at least a sop to throw the growlers. So he went again to McClellan: who explained once more that the rebels along the lower Potomac were just where he wanted them to be when he made his Urbanna landing in their rear, forcing them thus to choose between flight and capture. It would be much better to have them there, he said, than back on the Rappahannock contesting his debarkation. Lincoln was obliged to admit that as logic this had force.

As for the reopening of the B & O, McClellan remarked that he had it in mind already. What he wanted to avoid was another Ball's Bluff or anything resembling the fiasco which had resulted from making a river crossing without a way to get back in event of repulse. He was bringing up from downriver a fleet of canal boats which could be lashed together to bridge the upper Potomac. Across this newfangled but highly practical device he would throw a force for repairing and protecting the railroad, a force that would be exempt from disaster because its line of retreat would be secure. Lincoln liked the notion and was delighted that something at last was about to be done. Then came word from McClellan that the project had had to be abandoned because the boats turned out to be six inches too wide for the lift-locks at Harpers Ferry. Once more Lincoln was cast down, his expectations dashed, and Secretary Chase, a solemn, indeed a pompous man, got off his one joke of the war. The campaign had died, he said, of lockjaw.

Washington's Birthday came and went, and the Army of the Potomac remained in its training camps, still awaiting the day when its commander decided that the time had come for it to throw the roundhouse left designed to knock Virginia out of the war. In the West, meanwhile, Thomas had counterpunched Crittenden clean out of East Kentucky, and Grant had delivered to Sidney Johnston's solar plexus the one-two combination that sent him reeling, all the way from Bowling Green to northern Alabama. Burnside, down in North Carolina, had rabbit-punched Huger and Wise, and even now was following up with a series of successes. Everywhere, boldness had been crowned with success: everywhere, that was, except in Virginia, where boldness was unknown.

Stanton could see the moral plainly enough, and when Greeley came out with an editorial praising the new Secretary and giving him chief credit for the victories — he had been in office exactly a month on the day Fort Donelson fell — Stanton replied with a letter that was printed in the *Tribune*, declining the praise and making a quick backthrust at McClellan in the process: "Much has been said recently of military combinations and 'organizing victory.' I hear such phrases with apprehension. They commenced in infidel France with the Italian campaign, and resulted in Waterloo. Who can organize victory? We owe our recent victories to the spirit of the Lord, that moved our soldiers to rush into battle and filled the hearts of our enemies with terror and dismay. . . . We may well rejoice at the recent victories, for they teach that battles are to be won now, and by us, in the same and only manner that they were ever won by any people, since the days of Joshua — by boldly pursuing and striking the foe. What, under the blessing of Providence, I conceive to be the true organization of victory and military combinations to win this war was declared in a few words by General Grant's message to General Buckner: 'I propose to move immediately upon your works.' "

Lincoln, too, could praise Grant and the Lord for victories in the West, but the news came at a time when there was sickness in the house and, presently, sorrow. Robert was at Harvard; "one of those rare-ripe sort," his father called him once, "that are smarter at about five than ever after." It was Willie, the middle son and his mother's favorite, who was the studious member of the family; Tad, the youngest, could still neither read nor write at the age of nine. Now Willie lay sick with what the doctor said was "bilious fever." He got better, then worse, then suddenly much worse, until one afternoon Lincoln came into the room where one of his secretaries lay half-asleep on a couch. "Well, Nicolay," he said, "my boy is gone. He is actually gone!" And then, as if having spoken the words aloud had brought their reality home to him, he broke into tears and left.

Hard as it was for Lincoln to absorb the shock in this time of strain, the blow was even harder on his wife. All her life she had been ambitious, but in her ambition she had looked forward more to the pleasures than to the trials of being First Lady — only to discover, once the place was hers, that the tribulations far outnumbered the joys. In Richmond, Varina Davis could overlook, or anyhow seem to overlook, being referred to as "a coarse Western woman," which was false. Mary Lincoln could not weather half so well being criticized for "putting on airs," which was true. A fading Kentucky belle, she clung to her gentility, already sorely tried by two decades of marriage with a man who, whatever his political attainments, liked to sit around the house in slippers and shirtsleeves. She punctuated her conversation with "sir" and spent a great deal of money on dresses and bonnets and new furnishings for the antiquated White House. Washington was not what she had expected, its former social grace having largely departed with the southern-mannered hostesses whose positions had been taken over by Republican ladies whose chief virtues were not social.

Yet these disappointments were by no means the worst she had to bear. Her loyalty was undivided, but the same could not be said of her family, which had split badly over the issues that split Kentucky and the nation. A brother and a half-sister stayed with the Union; another brother and three half-brothers went with the South, while three half-sisters were married to Confederates. This division of her family, together with her Bluegrass manner, caused critics to say that she was "two-thirds slavery and the other third secesh." The rumors were enlarged as the war continued. The President's enemies sought to make political capital with a whispering campaign, accusing Mrs Lincoln of specific acts of treason, which at last reached such proportions that the matter was taken up by a congressional investigating committee. One morning her husband came unexpectedly into one of its secret sessions to announce in a sad voice: "I, Abraham Lincoln, President of the United States, appear of my own volition before this committee of the Senate to say that I, of my own knowledge, know that it is untrue that any of my family hold treasonable communication with the enemy."

That removed her from the reach of the committee, but it did not spare her the ridicule being heaped upon her almost daily in the opposition papers, which struck at the husband through the wife. And now, with all this burden on her, to lose her favorite child was altogether more than she could bear. She wept grievously and was often in hysterics. She could neither accept nor reject her sorrow, and between the two she lost her mental balance. Lincoln had Tad, whom he took more and more for his own and even slept with. He had, too, the day-long, sometimes night-long occupation of running the country. She had nothing, not even Lincoln: who did not help matters by leading her one day to a window and pointing to the lunatic asylum as he said, "Mother, do you see that large white building on the hill yonder? Try and control your grief, or it will drive you mad and we may have to send you there."

A distracted wife was one among the many problems Lincoln faced. His main problem was still McClellan. During the weeks since the general first outlined the Urbanna plan, much of what he called its brilliance had worn off, at least for Lincoln, who still had fears that it would expose the capital to capture. Again he told McClellan his doubts, and once more McClellan sought to allay them, this time by proposing to submit the plan to his twelve division commanders for a professional decision. They assembled March 8, many of them hearing details of the plan for the first time. When the vote was taken they favored it, eight to four, and repaired in a body to the White House to announce the result to the President, whose objections thus were effectively spiked again. As he told Stanton, who shared his mistrust, "We can do nothing else than accept their plan and discard all others.... We can't reject it and adopt another without assuming all the responsibility in the case of the failure of the one we adopt."

One thing he could do, and did, that same day. The members of the Joint Committee had called on him the week before with a plan for reorganizing the Army of the Potomac into corps. This, they saw, would not only gain prestige for certain generals who had their favor — McDowell, for example — but would weaken McClellan's authority as general-in-chief, since, as the committeemen saw it, corps commanders would take orders directly from Stanton. Lincoln saw other merits in the plan. For one thing it would simplify the transmission of orders and lessen the burden on the Young Napoleon. Besides, he was anxious to placate Wade and the others wherever he could. When he went to McClellan, however, to urge that it be effected and to get the general's recommendations for the appointments, McClellan told him that he had already thought it over and had decided that it would be best to wait until all the division commanders had been tested in combat before making his recommendations. Once more Lincoln had been shown that he would lose in any face-to-face encounter with the general over military logic. So the following week, when he decided to act on the matter, he did so without consulting McClellan. Later that day, after having reported their vote on the Urbanna plan, the division commanders learned that four of their number had been appointed to corps command: McDowell, E. V. Sumner, S. P. Heintzelman, and E. D. Keyes. Notification came in the form of a paper headed "President's General War Order Number 2."

Whatever elation this document produced in the breasts of the men thus elevated, it came as a terrible shock to McClellan, even though the earlier General War Order's being numbered had indicated that there might well be others. The shock was mainly due to the fact that among the four who were raised to corps command — and would therefore have the principal responsibility, under McClellan himself, for executing the Urbanna plan — three had voted against it in the balloting that morning. The officers he wanted had been held back. Franklin, for instance, who had spoken in favor of the sea route at the conference held while McClellan was in bed with fever, was not appointed, nor were any of the others among his protégés; "gentlemen and Democrats," he called them, who thought of war and politics as he did. He felt himself hobbled at the outset, held in check by a high council of Republicans friendly toward the enemies who were working for his ruin.

If he had ever doubted that they were out to wreck him, any such doubts had been dispelled during the early morning hours of that same busy March 8. He learned of whispered charges, touching his honor as a soldier, and he learned of them from Lincoln himself, who had sent for him to come over to the White House after breakfast. As McClellan told it later, he found the President looking worried; there was "a very ugly matter," Lincoln said, which needed airing. Again he hesitated, and McClellan, seated opposite, suggested that perhaps it would be best to come right out with it. Well, Lincoln said, choosing his words cautiously at first, there was an ugly rumor going round, to the effect that the Urbanna plan "was conceived with the traitorous intent of removing its defenders from Washington, and thus giving over to the enemy the capital and the government, thus left defenseless." He added that the whole thing had a sound and look of treason.

The word was out, and it brought McClellan straight up out of his chair, declaring that he would "permit no one to couple the word treason with my name," and demanding an immediate retraction. No, no, Lincoln said hastily; he did not believe a word of it; he was only repeating what had been told him. Somewhat calmer, McClellan suggested "caution in the use of language," and reëmphasized that he could "permit no doubt to be thrown upon my intentions." Lincoln again apologized, and let the matter go at that. McClellan left to round up his division commanders for a vote that would prove that the proposed campaign was militarily sound, then brought them back to announce their eight-to-four support in Lincoln's presence.

As far as McClellan was concerned, that settled it. He had shown him, once and for all. But then, as soon as he turned his back, War Order 2 came dropping onto his desk, and he was upset all over again. The day had opened with charges of treason and closed with the appointment of unsympathetic officers to head the corps of the army he was about to take into battle. As he saw it, Lincoln had gone over to the scoundrels, bag and baggage; or, in McClellan's words, "the effects of the intrigues by which he had been surrounded became apparent."

He did not see, then or ever, that he had helped to bring all this trouble on himself by not taking Lincoln into his confidence sooner. And if he had seen it, the seeing would not have made the end result any easier to abide; McClellan was never one to find ease in admission of blame. Nor did he see that Lincoln had not called him to the White House merely to insult him by repeating ugly rumors, that what he was really trying to tell him was that Wade and the others were powerful and vindictive men who would hurt him all they could, and with him the cause, if they were not dealt with in some manner that would take some of the pressure off their anger: whereas the Young Napoleon, who had been before them and heard them accuse him of cowardice, was determined to yield them not a single military inch of the solid ground he stood on. Whatever they took from him they must take by force, with Lincoln's help. Already they had taken much, including his trust of Lincoln, and he could see that they were after more, with an excellent chance of getting it.

* * *

Present troubles were grief enough; but as if they were not, there was added, the following morning, news of what had happened at Hampton Roads on the afternoon of that same crowded Saturday, March 8. A single Confederate ten-gun vessel, steaming out of Norfolk on what had been planned as a trial run, made obsolete the navies of the world. Between noon and sunset of that one day, the strange craft — which resembled, some said, "a terrapin with a chimney on its back" — served graphic notice that the proud tall frigates and ships of the line, with their billowing sails and high wooden sides that could flash out hundred-gun salvos, would soon be gone in all their beauty and obsolescence.

She herself had been one of them, once: the 350-ton, forty-gun U.S. steam frigate *Merrimac*, burned and scuttled in her berth when the Union forces abandoned Gosport Navy Yard the previous spring. She sank so quickly her hull and engines were saved from the fire, and Lieutenant John M. Brooke, C.S.N., went to Secretary Mallory with a plan for converting her into a seagoing ironclad, wherewith the tightening Federal blockade might be lifted. Mallory approving, she was plugged, pumped out, and raised, the salt mud swabbed out of her engines and her hull cut down to the water's edge. While some workers were attaching a four-foot iron ram-beak to her prow, others were building amidships a slope-walled structure, 130 feet long and seven feet tall, in which to house her guns, two 6- and two 7-inch rifles and six 9-inch smoothbores, the two lightest pieces being bound at the breech with iron hoops, shrunk on like the tires on wagon wheels, to strengthen them for firing extra-heavy powder charges: another Brooke innovation. Finally, they covered her all over, down to two feet below the waterline, with overlapping plates of two-inch armor rolled from railroad iron at the Tredegar Works in Richmond. She was finished. What she lacked in looks, and she was totally lacking there, she made up for in her ability to give and take a pounding.

However, she had faults more serious than her ugliness: faults which caused head-shakings and predictions that she would be "an enormous metallic burial-case" for her crew. For one, the weight of all that iron made her squat so low in the water, 22 feet, that she had to confine her movements to deep-water channels. Not that she was much at maneuvering in the first place; "unwieldy as Noah's ark," one of her officers called her. Her top speed was five knots, and what with her great length and awkward steering, it took half an hour to turn her in calm water. This was mainly because of her wheezy, antiquated engines, which had been condemned on the *Merrimac*'s last cruise and had scarcely been improved by the fire and the months of immersion. Nevertheless, Mallory and her builders expected great things of her: nothing less, in fact, than the raising of the blockade by the destruction of whatever attempted to enforce it. They renamed her the *Virginia*, recruited a large part of her 300-man crew from the army, and placed her in the charge of Commodore Franklin Buchanan, the sixty-two-year-old "Father of Annapolis," so called because, under the old flag, he had been instrumental in founding the Naval Academy and had served as its first superintendent. Some measure of Mallory's expectations of the *Virginia* was shown by the fact that he had given command of her to the ranking man in the whole Confederate navy.

When she steamed down Elizabeth River on her trial run at noon that Saturday, her inherent faults — low speed, deep draft, and sluggish handling — were immediately apparent. Her guns had not yet been fired, and workmen still swarmed over her superstructure, making last-minute adjustments. But as she came in sight of open water, Buchanan saw across the Roads five warships of the blockade squadron lying at anchor, three off Fort Monroe and two off Newport News. The three were the *Minnesota* and the *Roanoke*, sister ships of the *Merrimac*, and the fifty-gun frigate *St Lawrence*. The two were the *Congress*, another fifty-gun frigate, and the thirty-gun sloop *Cumberland*. It was more than the commodore could resist. He hove-to off Craney Island, sent the workmen ashore, cleared the *Virginia*'s decks for action, and set out north across the Roads with his crew at battle stations. The "trial run" would be just that — all-out.

On the southern shore, from Willoughby Spit to Ragged Island, gray-clad infantry and artillerymen lined the beaches. They saw his intention and tossed their caps, cheering and singing "Dixie." Across the water, from Old Point Comfort westward, men in blue observed it too, but with mixed emotions. They had heard that this strange new thing was being built, and now they saw her coming slowly toward them. To an Indiana volunteer, watching her across five miles of water, she "looked very much like a house submerged to the eaves, borne onward by a flood."

It was washday aboard the Federal warships, sailor clothes drying in the rigging. Yet there was plenty of time in which to get ready for what was coming so slowly at them. The *Congress* and the *Cumberland* cleared for action, and when the *Virginia* came within range, the former gave her a well-aimed broadside: which broke against the sloping iron with no apparent effect at all. Ports closed tight, she came on, biding her time as she closed the range, unperturbed and inexorable. Another salvo struck her, together with shots from the coastal batteries: with no more effect than before. Then her ports came open, swinging deliberately upward on their hinges to expose the muzzles of her guns. Turning, she raked the *Congress* with a starboard broadside and rammed the *Cumberland* at near right-angles just under her fore rigging, punching a hole which one of her officers said would admit "a horse and cart" — except for the iron beak which broke off in her when the Confederate swung clear. The *Cumberland* began to fill, firing as long as a gun remained above water. Called on to surrender, her captain shouted, "Never! I'll sink alongside!"

Presently he did just that, his flag still flying from the mainmast, defiant above the waves after the ship herself struck bottom. Horrified, the captain of the *Congress* slipped his cable and tried to get away before the ironclad could complete its ponderous turn, but ran aground in the attempt. The *Virginia*, held at 200-yard range by her deeper draft, raked the helpless ship from end to end until, her captain dead and her scuppers running red with blood, a lieutenant ran up the white flag of surrender.

Buchanan ceased firing and stood by to take on prisoners, but the coastal batteries redoubled their fire under command of Brigadier General Joseph K. Mansfield, West Point '22. When one of his own officers protested that the enemy had the right to take possession unmolested once the *Congress* struck her flag, the crusty old regular replied, "I know the damned ship has surrendered, but *we* haven't!" Two Confederate lieutenants were killed in this unexpected burst of artillery and musketry, and Buchanan himself was wounded. So were many of the Union sailors on the decks of the surrendered ship — including Buchanan's brother, a lieutenant who had stayed with the old flag and who presently died in the flames on the quarterdeck when the *Virginia* dropped back and retaliated by setting the *Congress* afire with red-hot cannonballs that started fires wherever they struck wood.

By now the three frigates off Old Point Comfort had started west to join the fight. Hugging the northern shore to avoid the rebel guns on Sewell's Point, however, the *Roanoke* and the *St Lawrence* ran aground, and presently the *Minnesota*, left alone to deal with the iron monster, did likewise. It was well for her that it happened so, for the *Virginia*, having finished with the *Congress*, turned to deal with her erstwhile sister ship and found that, the tide being on the ebb, she could not come within effective range. So she drew off across the Roads to unload her wounded, survey her damage, and wait for the flooding of the tide tomorrow morning, when she intended to complete this first day's work by sinking the three grounded frigates.

Her 21 killed and wounded, including Buchanan, were removed, after which the officers surveyed the effects of the fight on the ship herself. The damage, though considerable, was not vital. In spite of having been exposed to the concentrated fire of at least one hundred guns, her armor showed only dents, no cracks, and nothing inside the shell was hurt. Outside was another matter. She had lost her iron beak, and two of her guns had had their muzzles blown off; besides which, one of her crew later wrote, "one anchor, the smoke-stack, and the steam pipes were shot away. Railings, stanchions, boat-davits, everything was swept clean."

All this seemed a small enough price to pay for the victory they had won that afternoon and the one they had prepared for completion tomorrow. Officers and men stayed up on deck, too elated to sleep, and watched the *Congress* burn. She lit up the Roads from across the way and paled the second-quarter moon, which came up early. From time to time, another of her loaded guns went off with a deep reverberant boom, but the big effect did not come until 1 o'clock in the morning, when her magazine blew up. After that, the Confederate crew turned in to get some sleep. Ashore, a Georgia private, writing home of the sea battle he had watched, exulted that the *Virginia* had "invented a new way of destroying the blockade. Instead of raising it, she sinks it. Or I believe she is good at both," he added, "for the one she burned was raised to a pretty considerable height when the magazine exploded."

A telegram reached Washington from Fort Monroe within two hours of the explosion of the *Congress,* informing the War Department that the Confederates' indestructible "floating battery" had sunk two frigates and would sink three more tomorrow before moving against the fortress itself — after which there was no telling what might happen.

Lincoln had his cabinet in session by 6.30, the prevailing gloom being broken only by the Secretary of War, who put on for his colleagues a remarkable display of jangled nerves. The jaunty Seward was glum for once; Chase was petulant; the President himself seemed quite unstrung; but Stanton was unquestionably the star of the piece. According to Welles, who did not like him, he was "inexpressibly ludicrous" with his "wild, frantic talk, action, and rage" as he "sat down and jumped up ... swung his arms, scolded and raved." The *Virginia* would "change the whole character of the war," the lawyer-statesman cried. "She will destroy, *seriatim,* every naval vessel; she will lay all the cities on the seaboard under contribution." He would recall Burnside, abandon Port Royal, and "notify the governors and municipal authorities in the North to take instant measures to protect their harbors." Then, crossing to a window which commanded a long view of the Potomac, he looked out and, trembling visibly, exclaimed: "Not unlikely, we shall have a shell or a cannonball from one of her guns in the White House before we leave this room."

Welles, who recorded with pride that his own "composure was not disturbed," replied that Stanton's fear for his personal safety was unfounded, since the heavily armored vessel would surely draw too much water to permit her passage of Kettle Bottom Shoals; he doubted, in fact, that she would venture outside the Capes. This afforded at least a measure of relief for the assembly. Besides, Welles said, the navy already had an answer to the rebel threat: a seagoing ironclad of its own. *Monitor* was her name. She had left New York on Thursday, and should have reached Hampton Roads last night. "How many guns does she carry?" Stanton asked. Two, the Naval Secretary told him, and Stanton responded with a look which, according to Welles, combined "amazement, contempt, and distress."

The gray-bearded brown-wigged Welles spoke truly. The *Monitor* had arrived the night before. She had not only arrived; she was engaged this Sunday morning, before the cabinet adjourned to pray in church for the miracle which Stanton said was all that could save the eastern seaboard. And in truth it was something like a miracle that she was there at all. Coming south she had run into a storm that broke waves over her, down her blower-pipes and stacks, flooding her hold; pumps were rigged to fight a losing battle — and the wind went down, just as the ship was about to do the same. The fact was, she had not been built to stand much weather. She was built almost exclusively for what she was about to do: engage the former *Merrimac*, rumors of which had been coming north ever since work on the rebel craft began in mid-July.

There was a New York Swede, John Ericsson, who thought he had the answer, but when he went before the naval board with his plan for "an impregnable steam-battery of light draft," the members told him that calculations of her displacement proved the proposed *Monitor* would not float. He persisted, however; "The sea shall ride over her, and she will live in it like a duck," he said; until at last they offered him a contract with a clause providing for refund of all the money if she was not as invulnerable as he claimed. Ericsson took them up on that and got to work. Her keel was laid in October, three months behind the beginning of work on her rival, and she was launched within one hundred days.

As Welles had said, she had only two guns; but they were hard-hitting 11-inch rifles, housed in a revolving turret (another Ericsson invention) which gave them the utility of many times that number, though it caused the vessel to be sneered at as "a tin can on a shingle" or "a cheese-box on a raft." Her armor was nine inches thick in critical locations, and nowhere less than five, which would give her an advantage over her thinner-skinned opponent. The factors that made her truly the David to meet Goliath, however, were her 12-foot draft and her high maneuverability, which would combine her heavy punch with light fast footwork. Her sixty-man crew, men-of-war's men all, had volunteered directly from the fleet, and "a better one no naval commander ever had the honor to command," her captain said. His name was John L. Worden, a forty-four-year-old lieutenant with twenty-eight years in the service. He had been given the assignment — admittedly no plum — after seven months in a rebel prison, the result of having been captured back in April while trying to return from delivering secret messages to the Pensacola squadron. Obviously he was a man for desperate ventures, and perhaps the Department heads believed his months in durance would make him extra-anxious to hit back at the people who had held him. If they thought so, they were right. Nine days after the *Monitor* was commissioned he took her south for Hampton Roads.

Having weathered the storm, Worden rounded Cape Henry near sundown Saturday and heard guns booming twenty miles away. He guessed the cause and cleared for battle. But when he passed the Rip Raps, just before moonrise, and proceeded up the brightly lighted roadstead — each wave-crest a-sparkle with reflections of the flame-wrapped *Congress* — all he saw of the *Virginia* was the damage she had done: one ship sunk, another burning, and three more run ingloriously aground. An account of what had happened quickly told him what to do. Believing the *Virginia* would head first for her next morning, he put the *Monitor* alongside the *Minnesota*, kept his steam up, and waited.

Dawn came and at 7.30 he saw the big rebel ironclad coming straight for his stranded charge: whereupon he lifted anchor, darted out from behind the screening bulk of the frigate, and steamed forward to the attack. The *Monitor's* sudden appearance was as unexpected as if she had dropped from the sky or floated up from the harbor bottom, squarely between the *Virginia* and her intended prize. "I guess she took us for some kind of a water tank," one of the *Monitor* crewmen later said. "You can see surprise in a ship just as you can see it in a man, and there was surprise all over the *Merrimac*."

He was right, or almost right. Instead of a water tank, however, "We thought at first it was a raft on which one of the *Minnesota's* boilers was being taken to shore for repairs," a *Virginia* midshipman testified, "and when suddenly a shot was fired from her turret we imagined an accidental explosion of some kind had taken place on the raft."

This mistake was not for long. Rumors of work-in-progress had been trickling south as well as north, and the *Monitor* was recognized and saluted in her own right with a salvo which broke against her turret with as little effect as the ones that had shattered against the armored flanks of the *Virginia* yesterday, when the superiority of iron over wood was first established. Now it was iron against iron. The *Monitor* promptly returned the fire, swinging her two guns to bear in rapid succession. The fight was on.

It lasted four hours, not including a half-hour midway intermission, and what it mainly showed — in addition to its reinforcement of what one of them had proved the day before: that wooden navies were obsolete — was that neither could sink the other. The *Monitor* took full advantage of her higher speed and maneuverability, of her heavier, more flexible guns, and particularly of her lighter draft, which enabled her to draw off into the shallows for a breather where the other could not pursue. The *Virginia's* supposed advantages, so impressive to the eye, were in fact highly doubtful. Her bigness, for example — the "Colossus of Roads," one northern correspondent dubbed her —

only made her more sluggish and easier to hit, and her eight guns were limited in traverse. The effectiveness of her knockout punch, demonstrated yesterday when she rammed the *Cumberland*, was considerably reduced by the loss of her iron beak. Also, she had come out armed for the destruction of the frigates; her explosive shell shattered easily against an armored target, and she had brought only a few solid rounds to be used as hot shot. Worden's task, on the other hand, was complicated by the need for protecting the grounded *Minnesota*, which the *Virginia* would take under fire if he allowed her to get within range. Then too, his gun crews were disconcerted by whizzing screwheads that flew off the inner ends of the armor bolts and rattled about inside the turret whenever the enemy scored a direct hit.

Buchanan gone, command of the *Virginia* had passed to her executive, Lieutenant Catesby ap R. Jones. He gave the *Monitor* everything he had given the wooden warships yesterday, and more: to no avail. When he tried to ram her, she drew aside like a skillful boxer and pounded him hard as he passed. After a few such exchanges, the crews of his after-guns, deafened by the concussion of 180-pound balls against the cracking railroad iron, were bleeding from their noses and ears. Descending once to the gundeck and observing that some of the pieces were not engaged, Jones shouted: "Why are you not firing, Mr Eggleston?" The gun captain shrugged. "Why, our powder is very precious," he replied, "and after two hours' incessant firing I find that I can do her about as much damage by snapping my thumb at her every two minutes and a half."

At this point the *Monitor* hauled off into shallow water, where she spent fifteen minutes hoisting a new supply of shot and powder to her turret. Left alone, the *Virginia* made one of her drawn-out turns to come as near as possible to the grounded *Minnesota*, whose captain received her with what he called "a broadside which would have blown out of the water any timber-built ship in the world." Unwincing, the ironclad put a rifled bow-gun shell into her and was about to swing broadside, bringing all her guns to bear, when the *Monitor* came steaming out of the shallows and intervened again, Worden having refreshed himself with a stroll on the deck and a general look-round while the fresh supply of ammunition was being made handy for his guns. The two ironclads reëngaged.

Jones by now had decided that if he was going to destroy his foe, it would have to be with something other than his guns. First he tried ramming, despite the absence of his iron beak. But the *Monitor* was too spry for him. The best he could manage was a blunt-prowed, glancing blow that shivered her timbers — "a tremendous thump," one of her officers called it — but did her no real damage. The smaller ship kept circling her opponent, pounding away, one crewman said, "like a cooper with his hammer going round a cask." Doubly frustrated, Jones then determined to try an even more desperate venture, one that would bring his crew's five-to-one numerical advantage to bear. Having taken naval warfare a long stride forward yesterday, today he would take it an even longer one — back to the pistol-and-cutlass days of John Paul Jones. He would board his adversary. Equipping his men with tarpaulins for blinding the *Monitor*'s gun-slits and iron crows for jamming her turret and prying open her hatch, he had them stand by the sally ports while he maneuvered to get within grappling distance. It was a risky plan at best (far riskier than he knew; the Federal gunners were supplied with hand grenades for just such an emergency) yet it might have worked, if he could only have managed to bring the *Virginia* alongside. He could not. Nimble as a skittish horse, the smaller vessel danced away from contact every time.

For two more hours this second act of the long fight continued, and all this time the *Monitor* was pounding her opponent like an anvil, cracking and breaking her armor plate, though not enough to penetrate its two-foot oak and pitch-pine backing. Soon after noon, in a last attempt at boarding — though by now the *Virginia*'s stack was so riddled that her fires could get almost no draft and her speed, already slow, was cut in half — Jones brought his ship within ten yards of the enemy and delivered at that point-blank range a 9-inch shell which exploded against the pilot house, squarely in front of the sight-slit where Worden had taken station to direct the helm and relay fire commands. The concussion cracked the crossbeam and partly lifted the iron lid, exposing the dark interior. Worden was stunned and blinded, ears ringing, beard singed, eyes filled with burning powder; but not too stunned to feel dismay, and not so blind that he did not see the sudden glare of the noonday sky through the break in the overhead armor. "Sheer off!" he cried, and the helmsman put her hard to starboard, running for the shallows.

While the *Monitor* retired to shoal water, and remained there to assess the damage she and her captain had suffered, the *Virginia* steamed ponderously across the deep-water battle scene with the proud air of a wrestler who has just thrown his opponent out of the ring. Presently, however — the ebb tide was running, keeping her out of range of the *Minnesota*, and she had settled considerably as a result of taking water through her seams — she drew off south across the Roads for Norfolk, claiming victory. As she withdrew, the *Monitor* came forward and took her turn at dominating the scene, basing her victory counterclaim on the fact that the *Virginia* did not turn back to continue the fight. This would result in much argument all around, though privately both antagonists admitted the obvious truth: that, tactically, the fight had been a draw. In a stricter sense, the laurels went to the *Monitor* for preventing the *Virginia* from completing her mission of destruction. Yet in the largest sense of all, and equally obvious, both had been victorious — over the wooden navies of the world.

Stretched out on the sofa in his cabin, Worden was "a ghastly sight," according to the executive who went to receive instructions from him upon assuming command. When the captain could speak, lying there with his beard singed, his face bloody, and his eyes tight shut as if to hold the pain in, his first words were a question: "Have I saved the *Minnesota?*"

"Yes," he was told, "and whipped the *Merrimac*."

"Then I don't care what happens to me," he said.

★ ★ ★

As it had a perverse tendency to do in times of crisis, the telegraph line to Washington from Fort Monroe had gone out that Sabbath morning, and it stayed dead till just past 4 that afternoon. During all this long, exasperating time, among all the officials waiting fidgety behind the sound-proof curtain which sealed them off from news of the fight at Hampton Roads, none awaited the outcome with a deeper concern than George McClellan. The campaign he was about to launch depended on the Federal navy's maintaining domination of the bays and coastal rivers north of the James. It required very little imagination — far less, at any rate, than McClellan was blessed or cursed with — to picture what would happen if enemy gunboats — even wooden ones, let alone the frigate-killing *Merrimac-Virginia* — got among his loaded transports on their way down Chesapeake Bay or up the Rappahannock River.

Before news of the ironclad duel reached Washington, however, he received outpost dispatches which shipwrecked the Urbanna plan as completely as the sinking of the *Monitor* would have done: Joe Johnston was gone from the Manassas line. Most of his army was already back on the banks of the Rappahannock, intrenching itself near the very spot McClellan had picked for a beachhead. To land at Urbanna now, he saw, would be to land not in Johnston's rear, but with Johnston in his own.

Despite this abrupt and, so to speak, ill-mannered joggling of the military chessboard after all the pains he had taken to dispose the pieces to his liking, he was none the less relieved when, immediately following the news of Johnston's retrograde maneuver, the wire from Fort Monroe came suddenly alive with jubilant chatter of a victory by stalemate. The rebel ironclad had gone limping back to Norfolk, neutralized. He could breathe. What was more, he saw in this new turn of events an opportunity to put the finishing touch to his army's rigorous eight-month course of training: a practice march, deep into enemy territory — under combat conditions, with full field equipment and carefully worked-out logistics — and then another march right back again, since there was nothing there that he would not gain, automatically and bloodlessly, by going ahead with his roundabout plan for a landing down the coast. Warning orders went out that night, alerting the commanders. Next day the troops were slogging south, well-ordered dark-blue columns probing the muddy North Virginia landscape.

Excellent as this was as a graduation exercise to cap the army's basic training program, it had a bad effect on the public's opinion of Little Mac as the man to whip the rebels. Armchair strategists found in it the answer to the taunting refrain of a current popular song, "What are you waiting for, tardy George?" What he had been waiting for, apparently, was the departure of Johnston's army, which he had not ventured to risk encountering face-to-face. There was truth in this, though it omitted the balancing truth that, however frightened he might have been of Johnston, the thing he had least wanted was for Johnston to be frightened of him — frightened, that was, into pulling back and thus eluding the trap McClellan had spent all these months contriving. Lacking this restricted information, all the public could see was that Tardy George had delayed going forward until he knew there was nothing out there on the southern horizon for him to fear.

The outrage was screwed to a higher pitch when reports came back from newspapermen who had marched with the army through the supposedly impregnable fortifications along the Centerville ridge, where Quaker guns had been left in the embrasures to mock the Yankees. It was Munson's Hill all over again, the correspondents cried; "Our enemies, like the Chinese, have frightened us by the sound of gongs and the wearing of devils' masks." What was more, the smoldering wreckage of the Confederate camps showed conclusively that Johnston's army had been no more than half the size McClellan estimated. "Utterly dispirited, ashamed and humiliated," one reporter wrote, "I return from this visit to the rebel stronghold, feeling that their retreat is *our defeat*." The feeling was general. "It was a contest of inertia," another declared; "our side outsat the other."

These were nonprofessional opinions, which in general the army did not share. Civilians liked their victories bloody: the bloodier the better, so long as the casualty lists did not touch home. Soldiers — except perhaps in retrospect, when they had become civilians, too — preferred them bloodless, as in this case. The Centerville fortifications looked formidable enough to the men who would have had to assault them, peeled log guns or no. Besides, some of them — old-timers now — could contrast this march with the berry-picking jaunt which had ended so disastrously in July.

It went smoothly, with a minimum of stop-and-go. There was no need to fall out of column when everything a man could want was right there in the supply train. They were an army now, and they looked it, in their manner and their dress. There were still a few outlandish Zouave outfits to lend the column sudden garish bursts of color, like mismatched beads on a string, but for the most part they wore the uniform which had lately become standard: light-blue trousers and a tunic of dark blue, with a crisp white edge of collar showing just under the jowls of the men in regiments whose colonels, being dudes or incurable old-army martinets, preferred it so.

Whatever truth there might once have been in the Confederate claim that Southerners made better soldiers, or anyhow started from a better scratch because they came directly from life in the open and were familiar with the use of firearms, applied no longer. After six months of army drill, a factory hand was indistinguishable from a farmer. Individually, the Northerners knew, they were at least as tough as any men the South could bring against them, and probably as a whole they were better drilled — except of course the cavalry, since admittedly it took longer to learn to fork a horse in style. McClellan's men were aware of the changes he had wrought and they were proud of them; but the thing that made them proudest of all was the sight of Little Mac himself. He was up and down the column all that day, glad to be out from under the shadow of the Capitol dome and the sneers of the politicians, not answering ignorant questions or countering even more ignorant proposals, but returning the cheers of his marching men with a jaunty horseback salute.

Presently, crossing Bull Run by Blackburn's Ford, they came onto the scene of last year's smoky, flame-stabbed panorama. It was a sobering sight, for those who had been there then and those who hadn't: the corpse of a battlefield, silent and deserted except perhaps for the ghosts of the fallen. Shell-blasted, the treetops were twisted "in a hundred directions, as though struck by lightning," one correspondent wrote. Manassas Junction lay dead ahead, the embers of it anyhow, at the base of a column of bluish-yellow smoke, and off to the right were the tumbled bricks of Judith Henry's chimney, on the hill where the Stonewall Brigade had met the jubilant attackers, freezing the cheers in their throats, and flung them back; Jeb Stuart's horsemen had come with a thunder of hoofs, hacking away at the heads of the New York Fire Zouaves. All that was left now was wreckage, the charred remains of a locomotive and four freight cars, five hundred staved-in barrels of flour, and fifty-odd barrels of pork and beef "scattered around in the mud." McDowell was there, at the head of his corps, and one of his soldiers wrote that he saw him weeping over the sun-bleached bones of the light-hearted berry-picking men he had led southward under the full moon of July.

McClellan was not weeping. This field held no memories for him, sad or otherwise, except that what had happened here had prompted Lincoln to send for him to head the army he found "cowering on the banks of the Potomac" and later to replace Scott as chief of all the nation's armies. He went to bed that night, proud to have taken without loss the position McDowell had been thrown back from after spilling on it the blood of 1500 men. Next day he was happy still, riding among the bivouacs. But the day that followed was another matter. He woke to find his time had come to weep.

Once more he had turned his back on Lincoln, and once more Lincoln had struck with a War Order. This one, numbered 3, relieved McClellan as general-in-chief and left him commanding only the Department of the Potomac, one of seven in the eastern theater. The worst of it, in damage to his pride, was that he learned of the order, not through military channels, but by a telegram from friends in Washington who read it in the papers: Stanton's office had leaked the order to the press before forwarding it to McClellan in the field. Within one week of learning that his Commander in Chief had listened to charges of treason against him, of being forced to reorganize his army on the eve of committing it to action under corps commanders who had gone on record as being opposed to his military thinking, he was toppled unceremoniously from the highest rung of the professional ladder.

This was hard. Indeed, it might have been the crowning blow, except that later that same day, March 12, he was comforted by a mutual friend whom the President sent with the full text and an explanation of the order. He was relieved of the chief command "until otherwise ordered," it read: which implied that the demotion was temporary. Furthermore, the envoy explained, the order had been issued primarily to allow him to concentrate, without distractions, on the big campaign ahead. McClellan took heart at this and wrote to Lincoln at once, informing him that "I shall work just as cheerfully as before, and that no consideration of self will in any manner interfere with the discharge of my public duties."

So he said, and doubtless believed. He would have been considerably less cheerful, though, if he had known of other things that were happening behind his back, this same week in Washington; "that sink of iniquity," he called it.

Ethan Allen Hitchcock, a sixty-four-year-old Vermonter, West Point graduate and veteran of the Seminole and Mexican Wars, was surprised to receive from the War Department in mid-March a telegram summoning him to Washington. He had been retired from the army since 1855, and never would have entered it in the first place if his parents had not insisted that the grandson and namesake of the Hero of Ticonderoga was obliged to take up arms as a profession. Hitchcock's principal interests were philosophy and mysticism; he considered himself "a scholar rather than a warrior," and had written books on Swedenborg and alchemy and Jesus. His first reaction to the summons that plucked him from retirement was a violent nosebleed. He got aboard a train, however, suffering a second hemorrhage on the way and a third on arrival, each more violent than the one before. Checking into a Washington hotel, he took to the bed in a dazed, unhappy condition.

Presently the Secretary of War was at his bedside. While the old soldier lay too weak to rise and greet him, Stanton told him why he had been sent for. He and Lincoln needed him as a military adviser. The air was thick with treason! ... Before Hitchcock could recover from his alarm at this, the Secretary put a question to him: Would he consider taking McClellan's place as commander of the Army of the Potomac? Hitchcock scarcely knew what to make of this. Next thing he knew, Stanton had him out of bed and on the way to the White House, where Lincoln repeated the Secretary's request. Badly confused, Hitchcock wrote in his diary when he got back to his room that night: "I want no command. I want no department. ... I am uncomfortable." Finally he agreed to accept an appointment as head of the Army Board, made up of War Department bureau chiefs. In effect, this amounted to being the right-hand man of Stanton, who terrified him daily by alternately bullying and cajoling him. He was perhaps the unhappiest man in Washington.

Unsuspecting that the President and the Secretary of War were even now casting about for a replacement for him, McClellan completed his army's graduation exercise by marching it back to its starting point, Fairfax Courthouse, to deliver the baccalaureate address. After congratulating his soldiers on their progress, he announced that their long months of study were behind them; he was about to take them "where you all long to be — the decisive battlefield." In solicitude, he added, "I am to watch over you as a parent over his children; and you know that your general loves you from the depths of his heart. It shall be my care, as it ever has been, to gain success with the least possible loss; but I know that, if necessary, you will willingly follow me to our graves for our righteous cause. ... I shall demand of you great, heroic exertions, rapid and long marches, desperate combats, privations perhaps. We will share all these together; and when this sad war is over we will return to our homes, and feel that we can ask no higher honor than the proud consciousness that we belonged to the Army of the Potomac."

With their cheers ringing in his ears, he turned at once to perfect his plans for a landing down the coast. Urbanna was out, but Mobjack Bay and Fort Monroe were still available. In fact, though he had pronounced these alternatives "less brilliant"— by which he meant that they would not outflank the enemy, neither Johnston to the north nor Magruder to the south — now that he came to examine it intently, Fort Monroe had definite advantages Urbanna had not afforded. For one thing, the beachhead was already established, Old Point Comfort having been held throughout the secession furor despite the loss of Norfolk across the way. For another, during his advance up the York-James peninsula toward Richmond, his flanks would be protected by the navy, which could also assist in the reduction of any strongpoints he encountered within range of its big guns. The more he studied the scheme the better he liked it.

By now, however, he had learned to look back over his shoulder. Lincoln had to be considered: not only considered, but outmaneuvered. Once before, he had accomplished this by calling a conference of his generals and confronting the President with their concerted opinions as to the soundness of a military plan. In that case Lincoln had not dared to override him; nor would he now. So McClellan called his corps commanders together, there at Fairfax, and presented them with his proposal for a landing at Fort Monroe. Having heard him out, the four generals expressed unanimous approval — provided four conditions could be met. These were that the *Merrimac* could be kept out of action, that there were sufficient transportation facilities to take the army down the coast, that the navy could silence certain fortifications on York River, and that enough troops were left behind to give the capital "an entire feeling of security for its safety from menace." They were not in full agreement as to how many men would be needed to accomplish this last condition, but their estimates ran generally to 40,000.

McClellan had them put their approval in writing, that same March 13, then sent McDowell to Washington to present it to Stanton and Lincoln. As soon as McDowell had had time to get there, McClellan received a wire from Stanton. McDowell had shown up with a paper signed by the corps commanders; did McClellan intend for the plan it approved to be taken as his own? McClellan replied that it did. After another interval, allowing time for the Secretary and Lincoln to confer, a second Stanton telegram arrived. Lincoln did not exactly approve; rather, as Stanton phrased it, he "[made] no objection," so long as enough of McClellan's men were left behind to keep Washington and Manassas safe while the army was down the coast. The final paragraph, which made consent explicit, was petulant and sneering: "Move the remainder of the force down the Potomac, choosing a new base at Fortress Monroe, or anywhere between here and there, or, at all events, move such remainder of the army at once in pursuit of the enemy by some route."

Perhaps by now McClellan had learned to abide the tantrums and exasperations of his former friend and sympathizer. At any rate, having won the consent he sought, he could overlook the tone in which it was given. However, that Manassas, too, was to be afforded what the generals called "an entire feeling of security" imposed an additional manpower drain on which he had not counted. He was tempted to give Lincoln another tactics-strategy lecture, proving that the place would be in no danger, and in fact of small importance, once his landing on the Peninsula had drawn Johnston's army farther south to oppose his swoop on Richmond. But there was too much else to do just now; he had no time for arguments and lectures. The transports were being assembled at Alexandria — 113 steamers, 188 schooners, and 88 barges: by far the largest amphibious expedition the hemisphere had ever seen — to take his army down the Virginia coast, with all its equipment and supplies, guns and wagons, food and ammunition, horses and beef cattle, tents and records, all the impedimenta required to feed, clothe, and arm 146,000 men. They were to move in echelons of 10,000, on a schedule designed to complete the shuttle within three weeks. McClellan worked hard and long, giving the loading his personal attention. Within four days of receiving Lincoln's approval, or anyhow what amounted to approval, he stood on an Alexandria wharf and saw the first contingent off on its journey south.

"The worst is over," he wired Stanton. "Rely upon it that I will carry this thing through handsomely."

Such optimistic expressions by the Young Napoleon were usually precursors of disappointment or disaster. Not only was this one no exception, it had in fact a double repercussion, set off in his rear by two men who opposed McClellan as well as each other: Stonewall Jackson, who had done so much to wreck McDowell on Henry Hill, and John Charles Frémont, who had done so much — though with less success — to damage Lincoln in Missouri. The two blows landed in that order, both before the Army of the Potomac had completed its roundabout journey down Chesapeake Bay. The first echelon left Alexandria on March 17, a Monday. Before the week was up, Jackson stabbed hard at the troops McClellan had left behind (in accordance with Lincoln's concern) to block any Confederate drive on Washington through the Shenandoah Valley, that corridor pointed shotgun-like at the Union solar plexus.

When Johnston fell back to the Rappahannock he instructed Jackson to conform by retreating southward up the Valley in event of a Federal push, taking care meanwhile to protect the main army's western flank by guarding the eastern passes of the Blue Ridge. Jackson of course obeyed, but not without a plea that he be allowed at least a chance to hurt the man who pushed him. As he put it, "If we cannot be successful in defeating the enemy should he advance, a kind Providence may enable us to inflict a terrible wound and effect a safe retreat in the event of having to fall back."

Old Blue Light, his soldiers called him; they had seen the fire of battle in his eyes. He read the New Testament in his off-hours, but did his military thinking in accordance with the Old, which advised smiting the enemy, hip and thigh, and assured the assistance of Providence in the infliction of terrible wounds.

At any rate, he soon had the chance he prayed for. When Johnston fell back the Federals came forward, two divisions of them marching up the Valley in coöperation with McClellan's excursion east of the mountains. Jackson, with 4600 men, retreated watchfully before the Federal 17,000, awaiting the answer to his prayers. Then it came. As he fell back through Winchester, spies reported the enemy regiments scattered. A quick slash at the head might confuse the whole column into exposing one or two of its segments to destruction. When he called a meeting of his officers to plan the attack, however, he learned that his wagon train was already miles to the south. Without food or reserve ammunition, his hungry men would have to continue their retreat. Jackson was furious, somehow placing the blame on the assembly of officers. "That is the last council of war I will ever hold!" he vowed. And it was.

The retreat continued through Kernstown, four miles to the south, then another forty miles up the Valley pike, past the slopes of the Massanuttons. All through the retreat Jackson watched and prayed, but for ten days Providence did not smile on him again. Then suddenly it did. On Friday the 21st his cavalry commander reported the enemy pulling back; one division had turned off eastward toward Manassas, and the other was retiring north toward Winchester. Next morning Jackson had his infantry on the road. Twenty-five miles they marched that day and fifteen the next, retracing their steps to reach Kernstown at 2 p.m. Sunday and find the horse artillery already skirmishing with what the cavalry commander said was the Federal rear guard, four regiments left to protect the tail of the column slogging north for Harpers Ferry. Jackson's blue eyes lighted. Here was the chance to inflict that terrible wound.

Certain considerations urged postponement. He had made no detailed personal reconnaissance. His ranks were thinned by 1500 stragglers he had left along the pike in the past two days. Last but not least, this was the Lord's day; Jackson would not even write a letter on a Sunday, or post one that would be in transit then, fearing that Providence might punish the profanation. These were all set aside, however, when weighed against the chances for success. There must be no delay; the sun was already down the sky. Without taking time to brief his commanders, he put his men into attack formation, the Stonewall Brigade in the center, and threw them forward. This was his first full-scale battle on his own, and he intended to make the victory sudden and complete.

It was sudden enough, but it was so far from complete that it was not even a victory. It was a repulse, and a bloody one at that. When the men in gray went forward, the Federals absorbed the shock and held their ground, returning the fire. Quickly it swelled to crescendo as Jackson sent in his reserves. Presently, to his amazement, men began to stumble out of the roar and flash of battle, making for the rear. He rode forward to block the way. "Where are you going, man?" he shouted at one retreater. The soldier explained that he had fired all his cartridges. "Then go back and give them the bayonet!" Jackson cried. But the man ran on, unheeding, one among many. Even the Stonewall Brigade, with its hard core of veterans who had stood fast on Henry Hill, was wavering. Just as it was about to break, its commander Brigadier General Richard Garnett gave the order to retreat. Amazed at what appeared to be his army's disintegration, Jackson seized a drummer boy by the shoulder and dragged him onto a knoll, shouting as he held him: "Beat the rally!" The roll of the drum did nothing to slow the rout; Jackson fell back in the demoralized wake of his soldiers. Fortunately for him, the Federals did not pursue. The Battle of Kernstown, such as it was, was over.

Suffering 700 casualties to the enemy's 590, Jackson's men had done a better job than Jackson himself when it came to estimating Federal strength. That was no mere rear guard they had charged, but a whole 9000-man division. When he learned that he had thus unknowingly reversed the dictum that the attacker must outnumber the defender three-to-one, Jackson did not allow it to temper the sternness of his discipline. Garnett had retreated without orders; peremptorily Jackson relieved him of command and put him in arrest to await court martial for neglect of duty. It did not matter that he had graduated from West Point the year before Jackson came there as a plebe, that he was a member of the proud Tidewater family which had given the Confederacy the first general officer lost in battle, or that his men loved him and resented the harshness that took him from them. It did not even matter that his brigade might have been cut to pieces if he had held it there, outnumbered, outflanked, and out of ammunition, while he went fumbling along the chain of command in search of permission to withdraw. What mattered was that the next officer who found himself in a tight spot would stay there, awaiting higher sanction, before ordering a retreat.

As for accepting any personal blame for this loss of nearly one-fourth of his little army because of ragged marching, faulty reconnaissance, poor intelligence, ill-prepared assault, or disorganized retreat, Jackson could not see it. In fact, he did not seem to understand that he had been defeated. "The Yankees don't seem willing to quit Winchester, General," a young cavalryman said in bivouac that night. Jackson replied, "Winchester is a very pleasant place to stay in, sir." The trooper attempted a further pleasantry: "It was reported that they were retreating, but I guess they were retreating after us." Jackson, who had a limited sense of humor, kept looking into the campfire. "I think I may say I am satisfied, sir," he said.

How far he saw into the future as he said this would remain a question to be pondered down the years, but most likely Old Blue Light would have been still more "satisfied" if he had known the reaction his repulse was producing that night in the enemy camp, even as he warmed his hands at the bivouac fire and refused to admit that what he had suffered was a defeat. His adversary, while congratulating himself on a hard-fought victory, could not believe that Jackson would have dared to attack without expecting reinforcements. Orders went out, recalling to the Valley the division that had left for Manassas two days ago: which meant, in effect, a loss of 8000 men for McClellan, who was charged with leaving a covering force to protect the Junction when the balance of his army sailed. Equally important, if not more so, was the effect on Lincoln, who quarter-faced at the news of the battle, victory or no, and found himself looking once more down the muzzle of the Shenandoah shotgun. The Kernstown explosion seemed to prove that it was loaded.

Whatever it was for Lincoln, news of the battle, coupled with the recall of the division headed eastward, was a thorn in McClellan's side — a hurt which in time might fester and hurt worse. As such, however, it was no sharper than the thorn that stuck him one week later, on the eve of his own departure for Fort Monroe. He had in his army, in Sumner's corps, a division commanded by Louis Blenker, a man of considerable flamboyance. Blenker was a soldier of fortune, a German, and his men were known as Germans, too, this being the current generic term for immigrants of all origins except Ireland. But the fact was, they were almost everything: Algerians, Cossacks, Sepoys, Turks, Croats, Swiss, French Foreign Legionnaires, and a Garibaldi regiment with a Hungarian colonel, one d'Utassy, who had begun his career as a circus rider and was to end it as an inmate of Sing Sing. Blenker affected a red-lined cape and a headquarters tent made of "double folds of bluish material, restful to the eye," where the shout, "*Ordinans numero eins!*" was the signal for the serving of champagne. His soldiers got lager beer and there was a prevailing aroma of sauerkraut around the company messes. All this — the glitter of fire-gilt buttons, the babble of polyglot commands, and the smell of German cooking — was reminiscent of one of Frémont's old Transmississippi outfits. And the fact was, Frémont was doing all he could to get hold of the division even now.

The Pathfinder was back on the road to glory, though it led now, not through Missouri or down the winding course of the Mississippi, but along the western border of Virginia and across the rolling peaks of the Alleghenies. Under pressure from the Jacobins, who had never stopped protesting their favorite's dismissal and urging that he be returned to duty, Lincoln, in the same War Order which removed McClellan from over-all command, plucked Frémont out of retirement and gave him what was called the Mountain Department, specially created for this purpose, along with 25,000 men. Having learned that the former explorer was a poor administrator, he now presented him with this chance to prove himself a fighter. Frémont at once came up with a plan he knew would delight the President. Give him 10,000 additional soldiers, he said, and he would capture Knoxville. What was more, he had a particular 10,000 in mind: Blenker's Germans.

Lincoln pricked up his ears at this offer to accomplish one of his pet war aims, then went down to Alexandria to see if McClellan was willing to give up the division. Far from willing, McClellan urged the Commander in Chief not to weaken the Army of the Potomac at the moment when it was half-embarked on its trip to the gates of Richmond. Lincoln agreed on second thought that it would not do, and returned to Washington. Once more he had gotten nowhere with McClellan face-to-face. Within the week, however, on the final day of March, the general received a presidential note: "This morning I felt constrained to order Blenker's division to Frémont; and I write this to assure you that I did so with great pain, understanding that you would wish it otherwise. If you could know the full pressure of the case I am confident that you would justify it, even beyond a mere acknowledgment that the Commander in Chief may order what he pleases. Yours very truly, A. Lincoln."

The closing phrase had a Stantonian ring, administering a backhand cut that stung; but what alarmed McClellan most was the undeniable evidence that, under political pressure, the nation's leader would swerve into paths which he knew were militarily unwise. How much grief this might hold for the army remained to be seen. For the present, McClellan could only repeat what he had written to his wife three weeks ago, when he learned of War Order 3: "The rascals are after me again. I had been foolish enough to hope that when I went into the field they would give me some rest, but it seems otherwise. Perhaps I should have expected it. If I can get out of this scrape you will never catch me in the power of such a set again."

Now as then, however, he was too busy to protest. Just before embarking next afternoon — All Fools' Day — he sent Lincoln a roster of the troops he was leaving for the protection of the capital. His generals had advised a covering force of 40,000. McClellan listed 77,456, thus: 10,859 at Manassas, 7780 at Warrenton, 35,476 in the Shenandoah Valley, 1350 along the lower Potomac, and 22,000 around Washington proper. This done, he went aboard a steamer, worked in his cabin on last-minute paperwork details till after midnight, then set out for Fort Monroe. McDowell's corps and what was left of Sumner's were to come along behind within the week. Looking back on the journey after landing at Old Point Comfort, he informed his wife, "I did not feel safe until I could see Alexandria behind us."

What was called for now, he saw, was action. He kept busy all that day and the next. "The great battle," he wrote his wife, "will be

(I think) near Richmond, as I have always hoped and thought. I see my way very clearly, and, with my trains once ready, will move rapidly." The following morning, April 4, he put two columns in motion for Yorktown, where the Confederate left was anchored on York River, behind fortifications whose reduction his corps commanders had said would depend on naval coöperation. All went well on the approach march. The day was clear, the sky bright blue, the trees new-green and shiny. Near sundown, exultant, he wired Stanton: "I expect to fight tomorrow."

His spirits were much improved at the prospect, and also perhaps from having observed what he called "a wonderfully cool performance" by three of his soldiers that afternoon. The trio of foragers had chased a sheep within range of the rebel intrenchments, where, ignoring the fire of sharpshooters — but not the fact that they were being watched by McClellan and their comrades while they demonstrated their contempt for the enemy's marksmanship — they calmly killed and skinned the animal before heading back for their own lines. The Confederates then brought a 12-pounder to bear, scoring a near miss. Undaunted, the soldiers halted, picked up the shot, and lugged it along, still warm, for presentation to Little Mac.

"I never saw so cool and gallant a set of men," he declared, seeing in this bright cameo of action a reflection of the spirit of his whole army. "They did not seem to know what fear is."

This gap in their education was about to be filled, however.

CHAPTER

* 4 *

War Means Fighting ...

★ ✕ ☆

 EARL VAN DORN CAME WEST WITH GREAT
expectations. He knew what opportunities awaited a bold commander
there, and his professional boldness had been tested and applauded.
Approaching his prime at forty-one, he was dark-skinned and thin-
faced, with a shaggy mustache, an imperial, and a quick, decisive manner; "Buck," his fellow Confederates called him. Except for his size (he
was five feet five: two inches taller than Napoleon) he was in fact the
very beau sabreur of Southern fable, the Bayard-Lochinvar of maiden
dreams. Not that his distinction was based solely on his looks. He was a
man of action, too — one who knew how to grasp the nettle, danger,
and had done so many times. Appointed to West Point by his great-
uncle Andrew Jackson, he had gone on to collect two brevets and five
wounds as a lieutenant in the Mexican War and in skirmishes with Comanches on the warpath. In the end, he had been rewarded with a captaincy in Sidney Johnston's 2d Cavalry, adding his own particular glitter
to that spangled company.

He was a Mississippian, which simplified his decision when the
South seceded; for him there was little or none of the "agony" of the
border state professionals. Furthermore, as it did for others blessed or
cursed with an ache for adventure, the conflict promised deferment of
middle age and boredom. He came home and was made a brigadier,
second only to Jefferson Davis in command of Mississippi troops, and
then received the command itself, with the rank of major general, when
Davis left for Montgomery. This was much, but not enough. Wanting
action even more than rank, and what he called "immortal renown"
more than either, Van Dorn resigned to accept a colonel's commission
in the Confederate army and assignment to service in Texas. Here he
found at least a part of what he was seeking. At Galveston he assembled
a scratch brigade of volunteers and captured three Federal steamships in

the harbor — including the famous *Star of the West*, which had been fired on, back in January, for attempting relief of Sumter — then marched on Indianola, where he forced the surrender of the only body of U.S. regulars in the state.

For these exploits, characterized by incisiveness and daring, he was tendered a banquet and ball in San Antonio and had his praises sung in all the southern papers, though perhaps the finest compliment paid him was by a northern editor who put a price of $5000 on his head, this being nearly twice the standing offer for the head of Beauregard. In acknowledgment of his services and fame, the government gave him a double promotion and summoned him to Richmond; he was a major general again, this time in command of all the cavalry in Virginia. Even this did not seem commensurate with his abilities, however. Presently, when Davis was in need of a commander for what was to be called Transmississippi Department Number 2, he had to look no farther than his fellow-Mississippian Earl Van Dorn, right there at hand. It was another case, apparently, of History attending to her own.

Within nine days of his mid-January assignment to the West, despite the fact that he was convalescing from a bad fall suffered while attempting a risky ditch jump — he was an excellent horseman; his aide, required by custom to try it too, was injured even worse — Van Dorn established headquarters at Pocahontas, Arkansas, and began a first-hand estimate of the situation. This in itself was quite a task, since the command included all of Missouri and Arkansas, Indian Territory, and Louisiana down to the Red River. But one thing he had determined at the outset: he would go forward, north along the line of the Mississippi, taking cities and whipping Yankee armies as he went. In short, as Van Dorn saw it, the campaign was to be a sort of grand reversal of Frémont's proposed descent of the big river. On the day of his appointment, already packing for the long ride west from Richmond, he had written his wife: "I must have St Louis — then huzza!"

So much he intended; but first, he knew, he must concentrate his scattered troops for striking. Ben McCulloch's army of 8000 was camped in the Boston Mountains south of Fayetteville, the position it had taken after the victory over Lyon at Wilson's Creek. Off in the Territory, moving to join him, was a band of about 2000 pro-Confederate Indians, Creeks and Seminoles, Cherokees, Chickasaws and Choctaws, won over by the persuasions of the lawyer-poet, scholar-duelist, orator-soldier Albert Pike, who led them. Sterling Price's 7000 Missourians, under pressure from a superior Federal army after their late fall and early winter successes in their home state, had fallen back to a position near the scene of their August triumph. Combined, these three totaled something under half the striking force the new commander had envisioned; but 17,000 should be enough to crush the Federals threatening Springfield — after which would come St Louis, "then huzza!" Van

War Means Fighting ... [279]

Dorn planned to unite at Ironton, fight, and then swing north, augmented by the enthusiasts a victory would bring trooping to the colors. Deep in the bleak western woods, he hailed his army with Napoleonic phrases: "Soldiers! Behold your leader! He comes to show you the way to glory and immortal renown.... Awake, young men of Arkansas, and arm! Beautiful maidens of Louisiana, smile not on the craven youth who may linger by your hearth when the rude blast of war is sounding in your ears! Texas chivalry, to arms!"

This might have brought in volunteers, a host bristling with bayonets much as the address itself bristled with exclamation points, though as events turned out there was no time for knowing. By now it was late February, and the pressure of the 12,000-man northern army against Springfield was too great. Price gave way, retreating while his rear guard skirmished to delay the Federals: first across the Arkansas line, then down through Fayetteville, until presently he was with McCulloch in the Boston Mountains, the southernmost reach of the Ozarks. By that time, Pike had come up too; Van Dorn's command was concentrated — not where he had wanted it, however, and not so much by his own efforts as by the enemy's. Then too, except in the actual heat of battle, Price and McCulloch had never really got along, and they did no better now. Both appealed to their leader at Pocahontas to come and resolve their differences in person.

Van Dorn was more than willing. In four days, after sending word for them to stand firm and prepare to attack, he rode two hundred horseback miles through the wintry wilds of Arkansas. Arriving March 3, he was given a salute of forty guns, as befitted his rank, and that night orders went out for the men to prepare three days' cooked rations and gird themselves for a forced march, with combat at its end. The Federals, widely separated in pursuit of Price, were about to be destroyed in detail.

Early next morning the Southerners set out, 17,000 men and sixty guns moving north to retake what had been lost by retrograde: as conglomerate, as motley an army as the sun ever shone on, East or West — though as a matter of fact the sun was not shining now. Snow fell out of an overcast sky and the wind whipped the underbrush and keened in the branches of the winter trees. Price's Missourians led the way, marching homeward again, proud of the campaign they had staged and proud, too, of their 290-pound ex-governor commander, who could be at once so genial and majestic. McCulloch, the dead-shot former Ranger, wearing a dove-gray corduroy jacket, sky-blue trousers, Wellington boots, and a highly polished Maynard rifle slung across one shoulder, rode among his Texans and Arkansans; "Texicans" and "Rackansackers," they were called — hard-bitten men accustomed to life in the open, who boasted that they would storm hell itself if McCulloch gave the order. Off on the flank, in a long thin file, the Five Nations

Indians followed their leader Albert Pike, a big man bearded like Santa Claus except that the beard was not white but a vigorous gray. He rode in a carriage and was dressed in Sioux regalia, buckskin shirt, fringed leggins, and beaded moccasins, while his braves, harking back to their warpath days, wore feathers stuck in their hats and scalping knives in their waistbands, some marching with a musket in one hand and a tomahawk in the other. The knives were for more than show; they intended to use them, having promised their squaws the accustomed trophies of battle.

Van Dorn also rode horse-drawn. He rode, in fact, supine in an ambulance, still feeling the effects of the ditch-jump back in Virginia and down as well with chills and fever as a result of swimming his mare across an icy river two days ago in his haste to join the army and get it moving. The mare was hitched alongside now, available in emergencies, and Price rode alongside too, identifying passing units and ready to relay orders when the time came. The new commander was nothing if not a man of action, bold and forward, sick or well, and the troops he led had caught something of his spirit. Trudging up the road down which they had retreated just the week before, they were in a high good humor despite the norther blowing wet snow in their faces.

The previous afternoon, some dozen miles away on a grassy knoll near Cross Hollows, Arkansas, where his headquarters tent was pitched, the commander of the army that had just cleared southwest Missouri of organized Confederates sat writing a letter home. At fifty-seven, having put on weight, he found that long hours in the saddle wearied him now a good deal more than they had done fifteen years before, when he had abandoned army life for civil engineering. A dish-faced man with a tall forehead and thinning, wavy hair, hazel eyes and a wide, slack-lipped mouth, he drew solace from such periods of relaxation as this, sitting in full uniform, polished boots, epaulets and spurs, enjoying the sounds of camp life in the background and the singing of the birds, while he inscribed to the wife of his bosom letters which he signed, rather ponderously, "yours Saml R. Curtis." A West Pointer like the opponent he did not yet know he was facing, he had commanded an Ohio regiment in the Mexican War, had been chief engineer for the city of St Louis, and had served for the past three years as Republican congressman from Iowa. Of all his accomplishments, however, he was proudest of the current one, performed as a brigadier general of volunteers. Chasing the rebels out of Missouri might not sound like much, compared to Grant's recent unconditional capture of two forts and one whole army in Tennessee, but Curtis felt that it was a substantial achievement. He was saying so in the letter when his writing was interrupted by the sudden far-off rumble of cannon. It came from the south, and he counted forty well-spaced booms: the salute for a major general.

This gave him pause, and with the pause came doubts. His four divisions were rather scattered, two of them twelve miles in his rear and two thrown forward under Franz Sigel, the immigrant mathematics instructor who had shown a talent for retreat at Wilson's Creek. Curtis was a cautious or at any rate a highly methodical person; he liked to allow for contingencies, an engineer's margin for stress and strain, and he could never feel comfortable until he knew he had done so. Back in the fall, inspecting Frémont's pinwheel dispositions, he had reported that the Pathfinder "lacked the intelligence, the experience, and the sagacity necessary to his command." Placing as he did the highest value on all three of these qualities — especially the last, which he himself personified — that was about the worst he could say of a man. Accordingly, when Frémont was removed and Curtis was given the task of driving the rebels out of Missouri — which Frémont had considered more or less incidental to the grand design — he went about it differently. He gave it his full attention, and it went well: too well, in fact, or anyhow too easy. Price fell back and the Federals followed through a deserted region, cabins empty though food was still bubbling in pots on ranges, laundry soaking in lukewarm sudsy water, clocks ticking ominously on mantels, and now this: forty booms from across the wintry landscape, signifying for all to hear that an over-all enemy chieftain had arrived. Curtis thought perhaps he had better consolidate to meet developments that threatened stress and strain.

Next day his fears were reinforced, and indeed confirmed, when scouts — including young Wild Bill Hickok, addicted to gaudy shirts and a mustache whose ends could be knotted behind his head — came riding in with reports that the Confederates were marching north in strength. Convinced and alarmed, Curtis sent word for Sigel to exercise his talent by falling back on Sugar Creek, up near the Missouri line, where he himself would be waiting with the other two divisions. There they would combine and, in turn, await the enemy. It was a good defensive position, with a boggy stream across the front and a high ridge to protect the rear, as both men knew from having come through it the week before, in pursuit of Price. Also, if they hurried, there would be time to fortify. Curtis fell back, as planned, and presently received word that Sigel was coming, skirmishing as he came. Near sundown, March 6, he got there with the grayback cavalry close behind him, hacking at his rear. He strode into the commander's tent, a small, quick-gestured, red-haired man in gold-frame spectacles, each lens scarcely bigger around than a quarter, and announced in broken English that he was hungry. He had lost two regiments, pinched off in the chase as had been feared; otherwise he was whole and hearty, eager for more fighting. Just now, though, he was hungry.

Curtis hardly knew what to make of such a man, but he fed him and took him out for an inspection of the lines. Sigel's two divisions were on the right, the other two having side-stepped to make room for them on the two-mile-long shelf of land overlooking the hollow of Sugar Creek. A mile to their rear was the hamlet of Leetown, a dozen cabins clustered around a store and blacksmith shop, which in turn lay about halfway between the line of battle and the sudden rise of Pea Ridge, rearing abruptly against the northern sky like a backdrop for a theatrical production. Outcropped with granite and feathered with trees along its crest, the ridge extended eastward for two miles, then gave down upon a narrow north-south valley. Through this defile ran the Springfield-Fayetteville road, known locally as the wire road because the telegraph had its southern terminus here in a two-story frame building where the telegrapher lived and took in lodgers overnight; Elkhorn Tavern, it was called, acquiring its name from the giant skull and antlers nailed to the rooftree. The tavern lay to the left rear of the position Curtis had chosen, and the road led down past it, through the intrenchments his troops had been digging all that day, and on across the creek to where the rebel army, filing in, was settling down and kindling campfires in the dusk.

They had brought their weather with them. It was snowing, and their fires twinkled in the gathering moonless darkness, more and more of them as more soldiers filed in from the south to extend the line. Down to 10,500 as a result of Sigel's losses, the Federals were outnumbered and they knew it, watching the long, strung-out necklace of enemy campfires growing longer every hour. Still, they felt reasonably secure behind their new-turned mounds of dirt and logs, white-blanketed under the sift of snow falling softly out of the darkness. They built their own fires higher against the cold, then bedded down for a good night's sleep before the dawn which they believed would light the way for an all-out Confederate lunge across the creek and against their works.

March 7 came in bleak and gray, overcast but somewhat warmer. The snow had stopped; the wind had fallen in the night. As Curtis' men turned out of their bedrolls, peering south through the fog that rose out of the hollow, they saw something they had not expected to see. The plain was empty over there. Last night's rebel campfires were cold ashes, and the men who had kindled and fed them were nowhere in sight.

In the past three days the Confederates had marched better than fifty miles, the wind driving wet snow in their faces all the way. Their rations were gone, consumed on the march, and they were tired and hungry. There had to be a battle now, if only for the sake of capturing enemy supplies.

However, Van Dorn had no intention of sending his weary men against breastworks prepared for their reception. Impetuous though he was, that was not his way. Conferring with his generals, who knew the country well, he decided to send half his troops on a night march, clean around the north side of Pea Ridge, then down the road past Elkhorn Tavern for a dawn attack on the Union left rear. Once this was launched, the other half of his army, having made a coincidental, shorter march to the west end of the ridge, would come down through Leetown to strike the enemy right rear, which by then should be in motion to support the hard-pressed left. In short, it was to be a double envelopment much like the one Nathaniel Lyon had attempted at Wilson's Creek, except that this time the attackers would outnumber the defenders, 17,000 men with sixty guns opposing 10,500 with fifty.

Price's Missourians drew the longer march, beyond the screening ridge. McCulloch and Pike, with their Texans, Arkansans, Louisianians, and Indians, would make the secondary attack. Van Dorn himself, still in his ambulance — the three-day ride through wind and snow had not reduced his fever — would go with the roundabout column, to be on hand for the charge that would open the conflict. Soon after dark the army filed off to the left, leaving its long line of campfires burning to deceive the Federals, and moved northward in column beyond the enemy right flank. In this hare-and-tortoise contest — the youthful, impetuous cavalryman Earl Van Dorn against the aging, methodical engineer Sam Curtis — the hare was off and running.

Puzzled by the disappearance of the rebels from across the creek next morning, Curtis was in the worse-than-tortoise position of not even knowing that a race was being run, let alone that the goal was his own rear. Through the early morning hours, while the sun climbed higher up the sky to melt away the fog and fallen snow, he was left wondering where and why Van Dorn had gone. Then suddenly he knew. Just as they had confirmed his fears about the forty-gun salute he had heard on Monday, so now on Friday his scouts came riding in to solve the mystery of the rebels' disappearance. They were behind Pea Ridge, about to enter the north-south valley that gave down upon his unprotected rear. They had been delayed by obstructions along the road, the scouts reported, but they were coming fast now and in strength. Curtis would have to do one of two things. He could wheel about and meet them here, fighting with his back to his own intrenchments, or he could try to make a run for it. In the latter case, the choice lay between possible and probable destruction. If he tried to get away northward, up the wire road through the defile, the Confederate spearhead would be plunged into the flank of his moving column. If on the other hand he ran southward, through enemy country — retreating *forward*, so to speak — Van Dorn would be across his lines of supply and communication; the rebels would have him bottled in a wintry vacuum.

He chose to meet them. His four divisions were in line, facing south: Sigel's two on the right, led by Peter Osterhaus and Alexander Asboth, the former a German, the latter a Hungarian: then his own two, under Eugene Carr, a vigorous, hard-mannered regular, and an Indiana-born colonel with the improbable name of Jefferson Davis. Curtis ordered them to about-face, the rear thus becoming the front, the left the right, the right the left. Carr was sent at once to meet the threat beyond Elkhorn Tavern. Osterhaus moved up past Leetown to protect

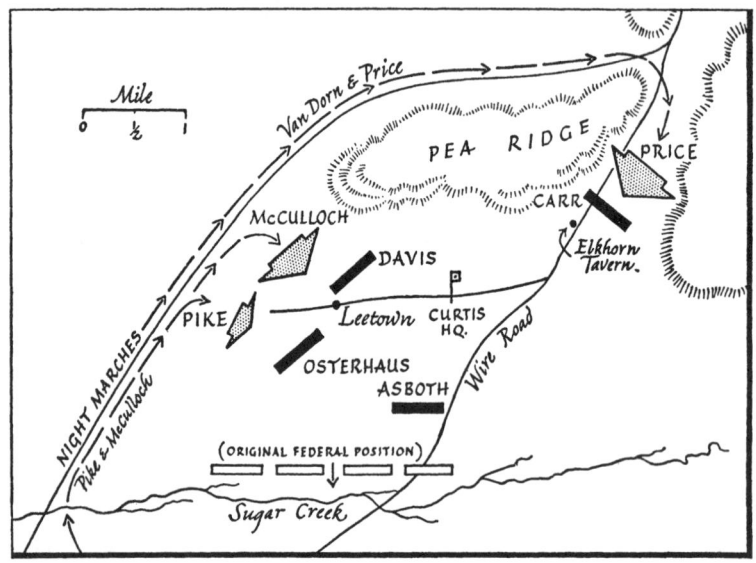

the western flank, and presently on second thought Curtis sent Davis to support him, while Asboth remained under Sigel, in reserve. Curtis had confidence in his commanders. Colonels Osterhaus, Carr, and Davis had had considerable combat experience, the first two at Wilson's Creek and the third from as far back as Fort Sumter, where he had been an artillery lieutenant; Asboth, a brigadier, had been Frémont's chief of staff and a fighter under Kossuth back in Europe. How far beyond the claims of past performance they deserved their leader's confidence was about to be determined. And this was especially true of Carr, who stood where the first blow was about to fall.

At 10.30 it fell, and it fell hard. Tired and hungry after their stumbling all-night march, but keyed up by the order to charge at last, Price's men came crashing through the brush along both sides of the wire road, guns barking aggressively on the flanks and from the rear. Carr had prepared a defense in depth, batteries staggered along the road and a strong line of infantry posted to support the foremost while the other three fired over their heads. Presently, though, they had nothing to support. A well-directed salvo knocked out three of the four guns and blew up two caissons, killing all the cannoneers. Unnerved, the infantry fell back on the second battery, just north of the tavern, where they managed to repulse the first attack, then the second, both of which were piecemeal. Bearded like a Cossack, Carr rode among his soldiers, shouting encouragement. Out front, the brush was boiling with butternut veterans forming for a third assault. This one would come in strength, he knew, and he doubted if his thin line could resist it. He sent a courier galloping back to Curtis with an urgent request for reinforcements.

Curtis had his headquarters on a little knoll just south of a farm road leading from Elkhorn Tavern to Leetown; here the courier found him surrounded by his staff, mounted and resplendent, wearing their best clothes for battle. They were looking toward the left front, their attention drawn by a sudden rattle of musketry and a caterwaul of unearthly, high-pitched yelling. Carr's message had scarcely been delivered when a horseman came riding fast from that direction. Osterhaus had been swamped by a horde of befeathered, screaming men who bore down on him brandishing scalping knives and hatchets. Taken aback — they had bargained for nothing in all the world like this — his troops had broken, abandoning guns and equipment. Davis had moved up; he was holding as best he could, but he needed reinforcements. Appealed to thus by the commanders of both wings at once, Curtis chose to wait before committing his reserve. He sent word for both to hold with what they had. At this point the battle racket swelled to new and separate climaxes, right and left.

In contrast to the gloom that had descended on him — first as a result of his failure to gobble up the scattered Federal units on the march, and then because of the delay of his flanking column as it moved around Pea Ridge in the night, which had thrown him three hours behind schedule and cost him the rich fruits of full surprise — Van Dorn was exultant. Price's men were surging ahead, knocking back whatever stood in their way, and off to the west the rolling crackle of McCulloch's attack told him of success in that quarter as well. The fighting still raged furiously at the near end of the ridge; Carr's second line was thrown back by the all-out third assault, so that presently the Missourians were whooping around the tavern itself and drinking from the horse trough in the yard.

All this took time, however. As the sun slid down the sky, Van Dorn's exultation began to be tempered by concern. His men had had no sleep all night and nothing to eat since the day before, whereas the Federals had had a good night's rest and a hot breakfast. The Confederates still fought grimly, battering now at Carr's third line, drawn south and west of the tavern, but weariness and hunger were sapping their strength; much of the steam had gone out of their attacks. Worse still, there was no longer any sound of serious fighting on the far side of the field, where McCulloch's earlier gains had been announced by the clatter moving south and east to mark his progress. Van Dorn was left wondering until near sundown, when a messenger arrived to explain the silence across the way.

There, as here, the battle had opened on a note of victory. Pike's Indians, delighted at having frightened Osterhaus into hurried retreat, pranced around the cannon the white men had abandoned; "wagon guns," they called them, and took the horse collars from the slaughtered animals to wear about their own necks; "me big Injun, big as horse!" they chanted, dancing so that the trace-chains jingled against the frozen ground. It was a different matter, though, when Pike tried to get them back into line to help McCulloch, who had run into stiffer resistance on the left. They had had enough of that. They wanted to fight from behind rocks or up in trees, not lined up like tenpins, white-man-style, to be struck by the iron bowling balls the wagon guns threw with a terrifying boom and a sudden, choking cloud of smoke. Some stood firm — a dismounted cavalry battalion of mixbloods, for example, under Colonel Stand Watie, a Georgia-born Cherokee — but, in the main, whatever was to be accomplished from now on would have to be done without the help of anything more than a scattering of red men.

Not that McCulloch particularly minded. He was not given to calling on others for help, either back in his Texas Ranger days or now. When his advance was held up by an Illinois outfit which had rallied behind a snake-rail fence at the far end of a field, he brought up an Arkansas regiment, shook out a skirmish line, and took them forward, sunlight glinting on the sharpshooter's rifle he carried for emergencies and sport. The Illinois troops delivered a volley that sent the butternuts scampering back across the field. They re-formed and charged again. Sixty yards short of the tree-lined fence, they came upon a body in sky-blue trousers and a dove-gray corduroy jacket, sprawled in the grass: McCulloch. His rifle was gone, along with a gold pocket watch he had prized, but he still wore the expensive boots he had died in when the bullet found his heart.

Quickly then word spread among the men who had sworn that they would storm hell itself at his command: "McCulloch's dead. They killed McCulloch!" Their reaction to the news was much the same, in effect, as the Indians' reaction to artillery. Whatever they had sworn they would do with McCulloch to lead them, it soon became clear that they would do little without him. To complete the confusion, his successor was killed within the hour, and the third commander was captured while attempting to rally some soldiers who, as it turned out, were Federals. By the time Pike was found and notified — he had been trying vainly, all the while, to reorganize his frightened or jubilant Indians —

the sun was near the landline and there were considerably fewer troops for him to head. Dazed with grief for their lost leader, many had simply wandered off the field, following him in death as they had in life; Osterhaus and Davis, having themselves had enough fighting for one day, had been content to watch them go, unmolested. At sundown Pike assembled what men he could find and set out on a march around the north side of Pea Ridge to join Van Dorn and Price, whose battle still raged near Elkhorn Tavern.

News of his right wing's disintegration reached Van Dorn as one more in a series of disappointments and vexations. Repeated checks and delays, here on the left where Price's men were being held up by less than half their number, had brought him to the verge of desperation. There was another problem, no less grave and quite as vexing. Having left his wagon train on the far side of the battleground, the diminutive commander had discovered an unwelcome military axiom: namely, that when you gain the enemy's rear you also place him in your own, unless you bring it with you. Consequently, in addition to a numbing lack of sleep and food, just as he was doing all he could to launch a final charge that would crush Carr at last and sweep the field before nightfall ended the fighting and gave the Federals a chance to realign their now superior forces, his men were experiencing an ammunition shortage. Desperately he ordered them forward, putting all he had into what he knew would use up the last of daylight, as well as the last of their strength and ammunition. Price was there to help him. Nicked by a bullet, but refusing to retire for medical treatment, he wore his wounded arm in a sling as he rode from point to point to bolster his men's spirits for an all-out climax to the night-long march and day-long battle. At last, between the two of them, they got the Missourians into assault formation and sent them forward, streaming around the tavern and down both sides of the wire road, across which Carr had drawn his third stubborn line of resistance.

The red ball of the sun had come to rest on the horizon; Carr's men could see it over their left shoulders — the direction in which they had been watching all these hours for reinforcements that did not come. Now as before, their batteries were distributed in depth along the road, and now as then the Confederates wrecked them, gun by gun, with a preliminary bombardment. After an ominous lull they saw the rebels coming, yelling and firing as they came, hundreds of them bearing down to complete the wreckage their artillery had begun. As the Federals fell back from their shattered pieces an Iowa cannoneer paused to toss a smoldering quilt across a caisson, then ran hard to catch up with his friends. Still running, he heard a tremendous explosion and looked back in time to see a column of fire and smoke standing tall above the place where he had fuzed the vanished caisson. Stark against the twilight sky, it silhouetted the lazy-seeming rise and fall of blown-off arms and legs and heads and mangled trunks of men who just now had been whooping victoriously around the captured battery position.

Over on his headquarters knoll, Curtis heard and saw it too, and finally — as if that violent column of smoke and flame standing lurid against the twilight on the right, followed after an interval by the boom and rumble as the sound of the explosion echoed off the ridge to the north, had at last brought home to him, like the ultimate shout of despair from a drowning man, at least some measure of the desperation Carr had been trying to communicate ever since Price first struck him, eight hours back — responded. By then the sporadic firing on the left had died away; Osterhaus and Davis reported the rebels gone or going. Van Dorn was tricky, but Curtis felt the danger from that direction had been removed; he could look to the right, where by now the column of fire had turned into a mushrooming pillar of smoke. Asboth, who had remained all this time in reserve to meet disaster in either direction, was sent up the wire road in relief of Carr.

Arriving at 7 he found the firing reduced to a sputter here as well. Torn and weary, Carr's regiments moved back from their fourth position of the day, retiring through the ranks of the division that relieved them. Forward of there, extending right and left of the tavern, half a mile each way, the Confederates were bedding down for the rest they sorely needed, their campfires in the tavern yard illuminating the building up to the bleached skull and antlers on the rooftree. The long day's fight was over.

Curtis rode out for a night inspection of his lines, which at some points were so near the enemy's that the opposing soldiers could overhear each other's groans and laughter. Despite their bone-deep weariness, the men were still too keyed up for sleep. They amused themselves by taunting the rebs across the way, hooting at the replies provoked, and recounting, for mutual admiration, exploits they had performed on the field today. Several could even substantiate their claims. One, for example — an Illinois private, Peter Pelican by name — displayed a gold watch he had taken as a trophy off a rebel he had shot: an officer, he said, in "sky-blue britches" and a dove-colored jacket. Some other quick-thinking scavenger had got the Maynard rifle, much to Pelican's regret, and the Johnnies had come swarming back too soon for him to have time to strip the dead man of his fancy boots.

The Federal commander might have heard this as he made the rounds, along with much else like it; but the truth was, he took little pleasure in small talk, and especially not now. He had too much on his mind. For one thing, he was irked at Sigel, who he considered had undertaken considerably less than his share of the work today, sparing Osterhaus and Asboth while Davis and Carr were doing most of the bleeding. Consequently, when he discovered that the German planned a temporary withdrawal to feed his troops, his temper snapped. "Let Sigel's men hold their lines. Send supper out, not the men in," he said gruffly. And having thus relieved his spleen he returned to his headquarters tent. It was time to decide what to do about tomorrow. Still fully dressed, he lay down on some blankets spread on a pile of straw and sent for his division commanders to join him for a council of war.

It was midnight when they assembled. Sigel spoke first, and he spoke from desperation, proposing his specialty: slashing retreat. The army, he said, must select an escape route and cut its way out in the morning. Osterhaus agreed, and so did Carr, whose command had been fought to a frazzle. He was nursing a wound, as was Asboth, who had been winged by a stray bullet in the dark and also saw no answer but retreat. Davis was silent, but that was his manner — a gloomy man with a long nose and lonesome-looking eyes. Reclined on the blanketed pile of straw, Curtis weighed their counsel. No less deliberate in conference than he had been in combat, he was not going to be stampeded by his own commanders, any more than he had been stampeded by Van Dorn. In his opinion the Confederates had most likely shot their bolt. The threat to his left having been abolished, he could reinforce his right. Thus bolstered, the army could hold its own, he believed, and even perhaps go forward. On this note the council adjourned, and its members, their advice declined, went out into the darkness to consolidate their commands and await the dawn.

The night was cold and windless, so that when dawn came through at last, smoke from yesterday's battle still hung in long folds and tendrils about the fields, draping the hillsides and filling the hollows level-full. The sun rose red, then shone wanly through the haze, like tarnished brass; Van Dorn's dispositions were at once apparent across the way. South and west of Elkhorn Tavern, between the Federals and the sunrise, Price's Missourians held the ground they had won when nightfall closed the fighting. Pike having arrived in the night with his and McCulloch's remnants, the Confederate commander had stationed the Indians along the crest of Pea Ridge, supporting several batteries — stark up there against the sky they looked like stick-men guarding toy guns — while the Texans and Arkansans occupied the fields along its base.

It was a long, concave line, obviously drawn with defense in mind: Curtis had been right. Also right, as it turned out, were the dispositions he had made to meet what dawn revealed. Davis was posted opposite the tavern, with Carr's division in support, still binding up its wounds. The left belonged to Sigel, who had strung out Osterhaus and Asboth to overlap the enemy in the shadow of the ridge. After a drawn-out silence, during which the Unionists enjoyed a hot breakfast and the rebels ate what they could find in the knapsacks of the fallen, Van Dorn opened with his batteries, stirring the smoke that wreathed the Federal line.

The cannonade was perfunctory and had no real aggressive drive behind it. Low as he was on ammunition — his unprotected train had gone off southward, fearing capture — Van Dorn fired his guns, not as a prelude to attack, nor even to signify his readiness to receive one, but merely to see what the Yankees would do. In fact, that was why he had remained in position overnight. It had seemed wrong to retreat after the gains he had made, and for all he knew the dawn might show the Federals gone or ready to surrender. Dawn had shown no such thing. It showed them, rather, in what seemed greater strength than ever: a long, compact line, with batteries glinting dangerously through the coppery haze. Hungry, weary, down to their last rounds of ammunition, Van Dorn's men had done their worst and he knew it. Yet, for all he knew, after yesterday's hard knocks Curtis too might be reduced to his last ounce of powder and resistance, needing no more than a prod to send him scampering. At any rate the Mississippian thought it worth a try.

It soon became apparent that the Federals could take a good deal more prodding than the Southerners could exert. Sensing the weakness behind the cannonade, Curtis sent word to Sigel on the left. Yesterday the German had held back: now let him seize the initiative and go forward if he could. Sigel could and did. With a precision befitting a mathematician, he ordered his infantry to lie down in the muddy fields while he advanced his batteries 250 yards out front and opened fire. He rode among the roaring guns, erect as on parade except when he dismounted to sight an occasional piece himself, then patted the breech and stepped back, as if for applause, to observe the effects of his gunnery. It was accurate. Battery after Confederate battery was shattered along the ridge and on the flat, and when others came up to take their places, they were shattered, too. Sigel's soldiers, many of them German like himself, cheered him wildly as they watched the rebel cannoneers fan backward from the wreckage of their guns. Over on the right, the men of Carr and Davis, watching too, began to understand the pride that lay behind the boast: "I fights mit Sigel."

Van Dorn's artillerymen were not the only ones disconcerted by the deadliness of the Yankee gunnery. His infantry showed signs of wavering, too. Sigel rode back to where his cheering soldiers lay obedient in the mud. Gesturing with his saber, he ordered them to stand up and go forward. They did so, still cheering, in a long, undulating line, like a huge snake moving sideways, the head coiling over the lower slope of the ridge, the center thrusting forward with a lunging, sidewinder motion, the tail following in turn. On it moved, with a series of curious sidewise thrusts, preceded by a scattering of graybacks as it slithered over whatever stood in its broad path. The reserve Union regiments, waiting in ranks, tossed their hats and contorted their faces with screams of pride and pleasure at the sight. Exhilarated, Sigel stood in his stirrups, saber lifted, eyes aglow. "Oh — dot was lofely!" he exclaimed.

Over near the tavern, watching the great snake glide sideways up the ridge, the men with Davis began shouting for a charge on this front too, lest Sigel's troops get all the loot and glory. Curtis was with them. Indeed, he was everywhere this morning; already two of his orderlies had been killed riding with him as he galloped amid shellbursts to inspect his line and strengthen weak spots. All the same, active as he was, he had not put aside his meticulous insistence on precision. Sending for reinforcements, he remained to check their prompt arrival by the second hand on his watch, then was off again through the smoke and whistling fragments of exploding shells. When the men in front of the tavern began yelling for a chance to match the tableau Sigel was staging on the left, Curtis nodded quick assent and rode forward onto a low knoll — he had a fondness for such little elevations, in battle or bivouac — to watch as they advanced.

Close-ranked and determined, they surged past him, cheering. Abruptly then, beyond their charging front, he saw the Confederates give way, retreating before contact, and heard his soldiers whooping as they swarmed around and past Elkhorn Tavern, where the telegrapher's family huddled in the cellar and rebel dead were stacked like cordwood on the porch. The Union right and left wings came together with a shout, driving the gray confusion of scampering men, careening guns, and wild-eyed horses pell-mell up the wire road through the defile, past the position Carr's men had abandoned under pressure from the opening guns, twenty-four hours back.

As quickly as that, almost too sudden for realization, the battle was over — won. Curtis rode down off the knoll, then cantered back and forth along his lines. His aging engineer's brown eyes were shining; all his former stiff restraint was gone. Boyishly he swung his hat and shouted, performing a little horseback dance of triumph as he rode up and down the lines of cheering men. "Victory!" he cried. He kept swinging his hat and shouting. "Victory! Victory!" he cried.

Thus Curtis. But Van Dorn was somewhat in the predicament of having prodded a shot bear, thinking it dead, only to have the creature rear up and come charging at him, snarling. Consequently, his main and in fact his exclusive concern, in the face of this sudden show of teeth and claws, was how to get away unmangled. Horrendous as it was, however, the problem was not with him long. His soldiers solved it for him. Emerging from the north end of the defile, they scattered in every direction except due south, where the prodded bear still roared. All through what was left of the day and into the night (while, a thousand miles to the east, the *Merrimac-Virginia* steamed back from her first sortie, leaving the burning *Congress* to light the scene of wreckage she had left in Hampton Roads) various fragments of his army retreated north and east and west, swinging wide to avoid their late opponents when they turned back south to reach the Boston Mountains. Though unpursued, they took a week to reassemble near Van Buren.

Back at his starting point in the foothills of the Ozarks, Van Dorn counted noses and reported his losses as 1000 killed and wounded, 300 captured. He was by no means willing to admit that the battle had been anything more than a temporary setback. Least of all could it be considered a defeat; "I was not defeated, but only foiled in my intentions," he told Richmond. Still with his main goal in mind, he was ready to try again, this time by marching "boldly and rapidly toward St Louis, between Ironton and the enemy's grand depot at Rolla."

Within another week, March 23, he was heading north with 16,000 effectives when he received a peremptory order to turn east, crossing the river by "the best and most expeditious route," and join the concentration being effected in North Mississippi by Johnston and Beauregard after their long retreat from Kentucky. "Your order received," Van Dorn replied, pleased no doubt at the prospect of exchanging the wilds of Arkansas for the comparative comforts of his native state.

Unlike his opponent, who was as dashing, or as slapdash, on a retreat as in an advance, Curtis had not been satisfied to report his casualties in round figures. That would have been neither respectful to the dead nor indicative of sound administration. Consolidating subordinate reports, which showed that Carr's division had suffered more than the other three combined, he prepared a careful table — killed, 203; wounded, 980; captured or otherwise missing, 201; total, 1384 — and forwarded it to Halleck, declaring that he had "completely routed the whole rebel force, which retired in great confusion, but rather safely, through the deep, impassable defiles."

He did not speculate, as others would surely have done in his place — especially Van Dorn — on what the future might reveal as to the importance of the victory he had won at Elkhorn Tavern, in the shadow of Pea Ridge. That was not his way. Besides, he had no means of knowing that Van Dorn would be called east, beyond the Mississippi, and would not be coming back. He did not claim, as in truth he could have done, that he had secured Missouri to the Union for all time; that guerilla bands might rip and tear her, that raider columns of various strengths might cut swaths of destruction up and down her, but that her star in the Confederate flag, placed there like Kentucky's by a fleeing secessionist legislature, represented nothing more from now on than the exiles who bore arms beneath that banner.

Though he did not deal in military imponderables, other imponderables were another matter: those of nature, for example. Spring had come to upland Arkansas at last, and it put him in mind of the ones he had known in his Ohio boyhood. The day after the battle a warm rain fell, washing away the bloodstains, but as the burial squads went about their work the air was tainted with decay. Curtis moved his headquarters off a ways, once more to enjoy the singing birds as he sat at a camp table, writing home. "Silent and sad" were words he used to describe the present scene of recent conflict. "The vulture and the wolf have now communion, and the dead, friends and foes, sleep in the same lonely grave." So he wrote, this highly practical and methodical engineer. Looking up at the tree-fledged ridge with its gray outcroppings of granite, he added that he hoped it would serve hereafter as a monument to perpetuate the memory of those who had fallen at its base.

★ ★ ★

South and west of Pea Ridge lay Texas, where Van Dorn had first shown dash and won success. North and west of Texas — twice the size of that vast Lone Star expanse — the Territories of Utah and New Mexico stretched on beyond the sunset to the California gold fields and the shores of the Pacific. In the minds of most, this sun-baked half-million-square-mile wasteland with its brackish lakes and its few, thirsty rivers was of less than doubtful value, fit only as a breeding ground of lizards and Apaches. Others knew better: Jefferson Davis, for one. Believing in his Union days that the nation's destiny pointed south and west, he had engineered the Gadsden Purchase and even imported camels in an attempt to solve the sandy transportation problem.

Now in his Confederate days, the nebulous future being translated into terms of the urgent present, his belief was reinforced. Out there beyond the sunset lay the gold fields and the ocean. Control of the former would establish sound financial credit on which the South could draw for securing war supplies abroad, while the opening of Confederate ports along the Pacific Coast would insure their delivery by stretching the tenuous Federal blockade past the snapping point. Satisfying as all this was as a solution to present problems, an even more dazzling prospect still remained. Having forged its independence in the crucible of war, the new nation could then return to the old southern nationalist dream of expansion, acquiring by purchase or conquest the adjoining Mexican states of Chihuahua, Sonora, and Baja California. After these would come others, less near but no less valuable: Cuba, for instance, then Central America, and all that lay between. Van Dorn seizing St Louis as a base for a march through Illinois to subdue the Middle West, Beauregard dictating peace terms in the White House after the Battle of Cleveland or Lake Erie — glorious as these scenes were to contemplate in the mind's eye, they were pale indeed in contrast to the glittering light of victory by way of California.

None of this could be accomplished, however, until safe passage west had been assured at the start by clearing Federal troops from the Territory of New Mexico. The answer to this, as Davis knew, lay in control of the Rio Grande. It was therefore with considerable pleasure, two months after Sumter, that he welcomed to Richmond a forty-four-year-old Louisiana-born West Pointer, Henry H. Sibley, lately Major, U.S. Army. Indeed, from Davis' point of view the caller might have tumbled straight out of heaven into the arms of the Confederacy. He had come to offer his services — preferably for duty in the region where he had been stationed for years, commanding various forts throughout the Southwest and along the Rio Grande. An enterprising officer, he had invented a conical tent modeled after the wigwams of the Sioux, and he had kept busy in other ways out there. What was more, he had a plan. And as he told it — a stocky, wind-burnt man with a big-featured face and a heavy mustache that grew down past the corners of his mouth so that his aggressive chin looked naked as a heel — Davis might have been listening to the echo of his own thoughts on the dazzling possibilities of victory by way of California. Granted the authority, Sibley said, he would raise a force in Texas and set out northward from El Paso, capturing forts along the river all the way to Santa Fe. This done, he would consolidate and turn west, his ranks swollen with volunteers whose watchword would be "On to San Francisco."

Davis liked the sound of it and was more than willing to grant him the authority he asked. Unfortunately, however, that was all he had to offer. The government could spare no arms or munitions; in fact it could spare no equipment at all. The ex-major would have to scrape together what he could find in Texas on his own, then make up the balance out of enemy stores from the forts he took as he marched upriver. No matter how fruitful the project promised to be, it would have to be self-sustaining: Davis made that quite clear at the outset, before granting the authority.

In early July, two weeks before Manassas, Sibley was made a brigadier and assigned to command the Department of New Mexico. Like much of his equipment, the department itself was still in Union hands; but that would be corrected, too, when he had accomplished the first stage of the plan he had outlined in the President's office. Davis wished him Godspeed, and Sibley returned at once to Texas, where he recruited a brigade of three mounted regiments by the end of the year and set out for El Paso, the jump-off point for his campaign to control the Rio Grande.

Two men, David E. Twiggs and John R. Baylor, had accomplished much for him already, before and since his trip to Richmond. Twiggs, a Federal brigadier in command of the Texas Department during the secession furor, had repeatedly asked Washington for instructions through that stormy time. Receiving none, he acted in accordance with a statement he had made: "If an old woman with a broomstick should come with full authority from the state of Texas to demand the public property, I would give it to her." He did just that, surrendering all the troops, forts, and equipment in his charge, not to an old woman, but to a posse of citizens who styled themselves a "committee for public safety." Northern howls of "treason to the flag" went up, and Twiggs, being summarily dismissed from the U.S. army, repaired forthwith to New Orleans, where he was solaced and rewarded with a commission as a Confederate major general.

In time, a portion of this surrendered equipment was inherited by Sibley, who needed it badly. Meanwhile Baylor, his other helper, had kept as busy as the first. Issuing a blanket invitation to whoever would join him on what he announced as a 1000-man "buffalo hunt" in Old Mexico, he showed his commission as a Confederate lieutenant colonel to the 350 volunteers who turned up, swore them in, organized them into a regiment called the Texas Mounted Rifles, and marched them to El Paso in time to receive the surrender of Fort Bliss, across the river from the Mexican hamlet.

Upstream the Rio Grande was divided like the nation, north and south, and Baylor saw in this a chance to accomplish a great deal more. For some time now there had been a movement among New Mexicans to split the territory along the 34th parallel and detach the southern portion as Arizona. Since in general the people of this lower region favored the Confederacy, he decided to go up there and help them, adding thereby a future new state to his new nation. There was one problem. Forty miles upriver from El Paso, just this side of the village of Mesilla, Fort Fillmore blocked the way, its garrison of 700 U.S. regulars commanded by Major Isaac Lynde, a veteran of thirty-four years in the infantry. Undeterred at being thus outnumbered two to one, Baylor spent no time musing on the odds. In mid-July — while Sibley was on the final leg of his round-trip journey to Richmond — the Texan led his Mounted Rifles north.

On the night of the 24th, though the Federals had been warned that he was coming, he camped unmolested within 600 yards of the fort on the opposite bank of the river, then next morning splashed across and occupied Mesilla. When Lynde at last marched out to challenge the invaders, the townspeople, who had greeted Baylor with vivas and hurrahs, climbed a nearby hill to watch the contest. After demanding an immediate surrender, and receiving an immediate refusal, the graybearded major sent one squadron forward in a tentative, head-on charge that was repulsed with four men killed and seven wounded. As a battle it wasn't much; but it was quite enough for Lynde. Abandoning any notion of holding the fort, he fired a few short-falling rounds in the direction of the hill where the ungrateful — and unarmed — men, women, and children were cheering the secessionists, then ordered a retreat northeast to Fort Stanton, 150 sandy miles beyond the Organ Mountains.

Next day, displaying what one of his officers called "a sublimity of majestic indifference," he was taking lunch at San Augustín Springs when he discovered that the empty fort had been no more than a tub to Baylor's whale. The Texan wanted the soldiers, too, and was there at hand, demanding their surrender or a fight. Lynde decided the former would be best. After paroling the 492 officers and men taken here — the other 200-odd had already been picked up as stragglers — Baylor returned to Mesilla and on August 1 issued a proclamation establishing the Confederate Territory of Arizona, with the 34th parallel as its northern boundary and himself as its military governor. Richmond quickly sustained his action, and Congress welcomed the delegate who soon arrived to represent the new far-western territory.

Such, then, was the situation Sibley found awaiting him when he reached Fort Bliss in mid-December with his newly recruited brigade. Between them, in their different ways, Twiggs and Baylor had accomplished much of his project for him already, supplying his men with surrendered equipment and clearing the Rio Grande well beyond the Texas border. Fort Stanton's garrison had withdrawn to Albuquerque, while the Unionists at Fort Thorn, fifty miles above Mesilla, had retreated eighty miles upriver to Fort Craig, which now remained the only prepared defensive position in Federal hands below the boundary parallel. Once it fell, the others to the north should fall like toppled blocks: Albuquerque, Santa Fe, and Fort Union, eastward beyond the foothills of the Sangre de Cristo mountains. At Fort Craig, he knew, 4000 troops were preparing to move against him, with perhaps as many more in support beyond the parallel. He himself had 3700, including Baylor's.

Yet he was no more discouraged by these odds than Baylor had been by longer ones. Three days after New Year's he marched northward, four regiments in a long, mounted column, and within the week he occupied Fort Thorn. The rest of the month was spent developing the situation. Then on February 7 he set out for Fort Craig, where the Federals were massing. His purpose was offensive; he did not intend to surrender the initiative. On the 19th, after a series of probing actions by his scouts, the main body came up and made camp on an open plain across the river from the fort on the west bank. The stage was set for the first major clash to determine who would control the Rio Grande.

That night, when the wind was from the east, Confederate voices could be heard across the water by the troops inside the fort. Colonel Edward R. S. Canby was in command, not only of the fort but also of the whole department, and this was only the latest of his trials since the advent of secession. He had taken over by appointment upon the departure into enemy ranks of the previous commander, W. W. Loring, the one professional in the quartet of prima donnas who brought grief to R. E. Lee in West Virginia. Indiana-born, tall, clean-shaven and soldierly-looking, with mild manners and a big nose that dominated his otherwise surprisingly delicate features, Canby was a year younger than Sibley and had finished at West Point a year behind him. Thrust into command at the outbreak of hostilities, he had about 1000 territorial militia, poorly armed and even more poorly trained, to supplement the scattering of peacetime regulars stationed at the various posts and forts in his department. Supplies were as scarce as distances were vast. Consequently, while Baylor took Fort Bliss and then Fort Fillmore, Canby could do nothing but work with what he had in an attempt to strengthen his defenses, meanwhile sending out repeated calls for volunteers. All this time, Sibley was raising soldiers down in Texas: for what purpose his opponent knew all too well for his mind's ease.

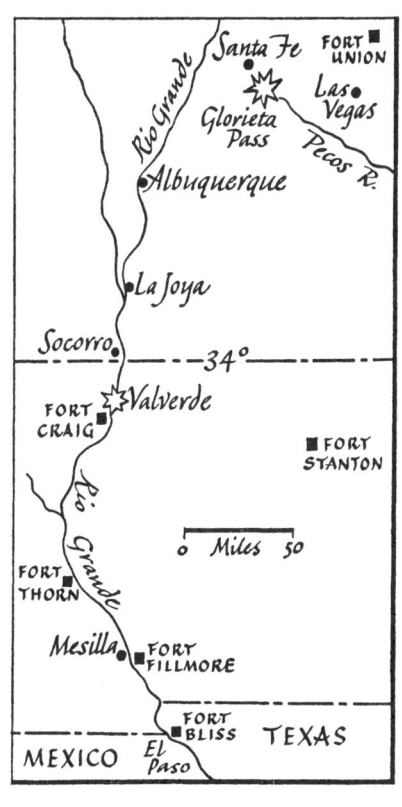

By the end of the year Canby had five regiments, recruited by prominent New Mexicans — Kit Carson was one — and sent them out to bolster such remaining scattered strongpoints as had not been abandoned or surrendered during the build-up.

All through January he continued his preparations to move southward from Fort Craig. Perhaps he might even have done so, in time, if Sibley had not spared him the risk and trouble by moving north against him, arriving February 19 and making camp within earshot of the fort on the opposite bank of the Rio Grande. In expectation of a siege, Canby spent the night making his strong position even stronger, preparing to repulse the attack which he believed would come at dawn. It did not come. Instead, as the light grew, he looked across the river and saw, between him and the rising sun, enemy wagons rolling north: Sibley was bypassing the fort, leaving it — and the Federals inside it — to wither on the vine, while he moved northward into the unprotected region on beyond the parallel, the region whose protection was Canby's primary assignment. What he had seen, out there between him and the rising sun, left the Union commander no choice. He himself would have to attack, to fight without the defensive advantage of the adobe walls he had been strengthening all this time. Accordingly, he sent a regiment up the western bank, under orders to cross the river five miles upstream and charge the rebels, who he believed were moving north across the mesa of Valverde in march column.

In this he was mistaken. Sibley had not intended to go north without at least an attempt to cripple any enemy force he left behind. He was maneuvering for a crossing and an assault against the fort. But now that Canby had obliged him by coming out for a fight in the open, Sibley was appreciative and ready. Crashing through the rust-colored reeds on the eastern bank, then charging up the slope onto the mesa, the Federals found the Texans waiting with double-shotted guns. Cannon and rifle fire broke up the attack in short order, the blue troopers scattering for what little cover they could find. They clung there, under sniper fire through what was left of daylight, and withdrew after dark to report to their commander that the rebels were still there: very much so, in fact. The two-day Battle of Valverde was half over.

For Canby, that first day had begun in error and ended in repulse. Now at least, as dawn of the second came glimmering through, there would be no error in estimating the enemy situation. Sibley was there, outnumbered, and he would attack him. He sent three more regiments up to join the first, with orders to force the crossing in strength and whip the rebels, still drawn up on the mesa within musket range of the river. He had not wanted this kind of fighting; these 4000 men were all he had to protect the whole Southwest. But now that it could no longer be avoided, he was determined to make the work as short and decisive as possible, no matter how bloody.

It was far from short work, but it turned out bloody enough. After losing a good many men at the crossing — they came under a galling fire and the bodies of men and horses floated slowly downstream, bumping along in the shallow water — they managed to get their guns across and with them knock the enemy back into the sandy ridges at the far edge of the mesa. From there, the Texans tried cavalry charges against the flanks and dismounted charges against the center, the sand-polished rowels of their spurs as big and bright as silver dollars. Past midday the charges continued; all were repulsed. Then at 2.45 Canby himself came up from the fort, bringing the remaining regiment. He assumed command just as Colonel Tom Green, on the other side, took over from Sibley, who had become indisposed — from the heat, some said, while others said from whiskey. Whichever it was, it was a Confederate advantage: Green was an all-out fighter. He put his cavalry out front, massing behind them all the dismounted men he could lay hands on, and sent them charging all together against a six-gun battery at the north end of the Federal line. For eight minutes, one participant said, the fighting was "terrific beyond description." By then Green's men were among the guns; the battery officers and cannoneers were dead. When the Texans turned the captured pieces against the line they had so lately been a part of, it broke badly, one Confederate declaring that the Northerners, in their haste to reach the west bank of the river, became "more like a herd of frightened mustangs than men." Once again there was slaughter at the crossing and more bodies floating sluggishly downstream in the blood-stained water.

Green was reassembling his elated troopers, preparing to use what was left of the short hot winter day to butcher or capture what was left of the rattled Federal army before it could reach the fort five miles downstream. He got his men together and was about to charge the enemy drawn up shakily on the opposite bank, when a truce party came forward under a white flag: Canby requested an armistice, time to care for the wounded and bury the dead. His chivalry thus appealed to, Green agreed to the cease fire, and while the defeated New Mexicans retreated under its protection to the adobe fastness of Fort Craig the victorious Texans rifled the knapsacks of the fallen, bolting "Yankee light-bread and other most delicious eatables," washed down with whiskey found in the canteens of the Union dead. Darkness fell; the battle was over. The men poured the sand from their boots and took their rest.

Recovered from his indisposition next morning, Sibley found that Green had left it to him to decide whether to go after the survivors in the fort, bagging the lot, or turn his back on them and continue the march northward. Federal casualties had been 263, Confederate 187, but the victory had been even more decisive as to proof of who would fight and who would panic under pressure. The opening phase of the campaign to seize the Southwest as a base for operations farther west had been accomplished; ahead lay the chief cities of the region, Albuquerque and Santa Fe. As Sibley saw it, such poor soldiers as Canby's were not worth the time that would be spent in completing their destruction. He gave his Texans a full day's rest as a reward for their exertions, then pressed on north without delay.

Within a week, having paused to establish a hospital for his wounded at Socorro, just beyond the boundary parallel, he had covered the hundred-odd miles to Albuquerque. He had good reason for haste. This was desert country, where loss of a canteen or a last handful of crackers could be as fatal as a bullet through the heart, and he had left Valverde with only five days' rations in his train. Fortunately, he had encountered no enemy soldiers on the way; apparently they had heard what had happened to their friends the week before and were falling back from contact. Then, as he came within sight of Albuquerque, he saw something that affected him worse than if he had seen a whole new Federal army drawn up for battle on the outskirts. Three great columns of smoke stood tall and black above the town. Anticipating his arrival, and his hunger, the Union garrison had set fire to their rich depot of supplies when they fell back on Santa Fe that morning.

He moved in unopposed and took the place, scraping together what few provisions he could buy or commandeer in order to continue the movement north. Four days later, March 5, he occupied the capital. Here too he was unopposed; the garrison pulled out on the eve of his arrival. All Sibley and his Texans got of the Santa Fe depot was its ashes.

The burnings had been done under orders from Canby. When he fell back on Fort Craig under cover of the flag of truce on the night of his defeat, he sent couriers to the northward posts with instructions that all public properties, "and particularly provisions," were to be destroyed as soon as the invaders seemed about to come within reach. He knew this country and what it could do to an army without supplies. Having tried stand-up fighting at Valverde, and having lost, he adopted now a "scorched earth" policy, one not difficult to apply in a region where the earth was already scorched enough to burn the sole off a boot in a morning's walk.

Sibley's men were already feeling the pinch. Nor were the discomforts of short rations, threadbare clothes, and sand-leaking boots relieved by any considerable sympathy from the people of Albuquerque or Santa Fe. Expecting cheers and volunteers at the end of their long victory march, the Texans instead had found the atmosphere definitely unfriendly ever since they crossed the parallel. The southern commander's prediction that troops of sympathizers would come marching in to join him, miners and trappers from Utah Territory and beyond, had by no means been fulfilled; in fact, there were rumors that groups there were organizing to join the other side. Sibley was finding that all he won with victory was miles and miles of sand. Still, he had done nearly all of what he set out to do in preparing a base for the conquest of the Far West. Those miles and miles included the Rio Grande and the territorial capital. Except for the stunned remnant of Canby's army, still cowering inside the adobe protection of Fort Craig, all that remained was Fort Union, sixty miles east of Santa Fe, beyond the foothills of the Sangre de Cristo Mountains, so called because their slopes were the color of blood each day at sunset.

Fort Union had been the rallying point for all the garrisons Sibley had flushed from their accustomed posts. By now, he knew, it was held in strength, and he figured he would have to fight to take it.

Preparing to do so, he advanced a picket of 600 men from Santa Fe twenty miles southeast to the mouth of Apache Canyon, which led on to Las Vegas, the new capital, and Fort Union. They were to hold the canyon mouth, preventing any Federal advance, while the rest of the Confederates were being assembled to join them; then they would all go forward together to wipe out the final enemy stronghold. Preparations continued through most of March. Then, on the 26th, the picket got word that a small force — "200 [New] Mexicans and about 200 regulars" — was coming through the canyon for an attack on Santa Fe. It sounded too good to be true, but the Texans were not missing any chance to give the Yankees another drubbing. They mounted up and rode forward, taking two guns along for good measure.

Four miles up the canyon they caught sight of what they had been told to expect: a column of 400 Union troopers riding foolhardily within gun range of a body of seasoned Confederates who had them outnumbered three-to-two. There in the rocky trough of the pass the Texans formed their line for slaughter. Slaughter it was, but not as had been intended. Suddenly, one wrote his wife, Federal infantry "were upon the hills on both sides of us, shooting us down like sheep." They had been sucked into an ambush. As they fell back, startled, they could see up on the overhead ledges enemy sharpshooters "jumping from rock to rock like so many mountain sheep." Losing men at every attempt to take up a new position, they were near panic, not only because of the bullets, but also from sheer astonishment. New Mexicans — "Mexicans," they called them, with all the contempt a Texan could put into the word — had never fought like this. Then they discovered something else, which startled them even more. "Instead of Mexicans and regulars, they were regular demons... in the form of Pike's Peakers, from the Denver City gold mines."

That was what they were, all right, recruits from frontier mining towns; 1st Colorado, they called themselves, 1342 volunteers, with one battery of field guns and another of mountain howitzers. They had made a long cold wet march to reach Fort Union on the same day Sibley pulled into Santa Fe at the end of his long hot dry one. After two weeks of sandy drill in the vicinity of the fort, they felt ready and came looking for a fight. Now they had it, here in Apache Canyon. The Texans had finally rallied and were making a last-ditch stand near the mouth of the canyon. Drawn up in a strong position behind the moat of a dry streambed, they felt ready at last for whatever came. What came was the Federal cavalry. Released from decoy duty, they came riding fast, leaped the arroyo, and landed among the defenders, hacking and shooting. The Texans broke and fled, all but 71 who surrendered, bringing their casualties to 146 in all. The Coloradans had lost a total of 19.

While the Federals withdrew to meet reinforcements from Fort

Union, the Confederate survivors sent out news of the disaster, which brought two regiments hurrying next day to their support. By dawn of the third day, March 28, the main bodies of both armies were moving through the canyon from opposite directions. An hour before noon they met at Glorieta Pass: "a terrible place for an engagement," a northern lieutenant afterward remembered, "a deep gorge, with a narrow wagon-track running along the bottom, the ground rising precipitously on each side, with huge bowlders and clumps of stunted cedars interspersed." Maneuver was impossible. All the two forces could do was scramble for cover and start banging away, the tearing rattle of pistol and rifle fire punctuated cacophonously by the deeper booms of cannon. Neither could advance, yet both knew that to fall back would be even more fatal than to stay there. For five hours the fighting continued in a boiling cloud of rock dust. Then an armistice was called to permit care for the wounded and burial of the dead.

The Texas commander had proposed it, and during the lull he received word of a calamity in his rear. A party of 300 Coloradans, led by a former preacher, had circled around behind the hills and come down upon the Confederate supply train, capturing the guard, burning the 85 provision-laden wagons, and bayoneting the nearly 600 horses and mules. In addition to Yankees, the Texans now would be fighting thirst and starvation. Against those odds they pulled back under cover of the truce and got away, out of the canyon and up the road to Santa Fe. The Federals, who had inflicted 123 casualties at a cost of 86, were all for going after them, up to the gates of the capital itself. But word had come from Canby at Fort Craig. He feared an attack on Fort Union by some roundabout route, perhaps across the eastern plains from the Texas panhandle. They were to hold that final stronghold "at all hazards, and to leave nothing to chance." Grudgingly the Coloradans obeyed, retracing their steps back through the canyon where they had fought and won two battles.

Four days later, April 1 — the day McClellan took ship at Alexandria for his overnight voyage to the Peninsula — Canby left Fort Craig at last, marching north on Sibley's five-weeks-old trail. He was a brigadier general now, promoted as of the day before. On the 8th he arrived before Albuquerque. Sibley was ready for him, having been there all the while with half his army. The two exchanged artillery salvos, and Canby retired beyond the nearby Sandía Mountains, calling for the Fort Union garrison to come out and reinforce him. Sibley likewise sent word for the Glorieta survivors, licking their wounds in Santa Fe, to join him there on the banks of the Rio Grande. Both armies thus were concentrating within one day's march of each other. The great winner-take-all battle of the Southwest, to which all that had gone before would have served as prologue, seemed about to be fought near **Albuquerque**.

It was never fought, either there or elsewhere, and for several reasons — mostly Sibley's. The countryside was too poor to support an invading army without the help of the people living there or supply lines leading back to greener regions, and he had neither. Rather, the inhabitants were unexpectedly hostile, more inclined to cache their scant provisions than to exchange them for Confederate money, which they considered worthless. Sibley's artillery ammunition was nearly exhausted and his wagon train had been destroyed. The recruits he expected had not appeared, or if they had — the Pike's Peakers, for example — they came against him wearing blue, so that the numerical odds were even longer now than they had been at the outset. Perceiving all this, he saw his dream dissolve in the encroaching gloom. There was but one thing left for him to do with his ragged, ill-fed, weary army: get it out of there and back to Texas. He was by no means certain that he could manage this, however, depending as it did on whether he would have the coöperation of his opponent.

He got it in full. Canby, having fought once at Valverde, wanted no more fighting he could possibly avoid. Sibley began his retreat on April 12, crossing the river with his main body to make camp that night, twenty miles south, on the west bank at Los Lunas. Next day, having stayed behind to bury their brass field pieces, for which they had neither shells nor powder, the remainder followed down the east bank to Peralta, nearly opposite. Canby marched in pursuit, his reinforcements having arrived that day from Fort Union. He was not trying to cut the rebels off and then destroy them. The last thing he wanted, in fact, was for them to turn and fight or even stop to catch their breath. What he wanted was for them to leave, the sooner the better; he wanted them out of the territory for whose protection he was responsible. At Peralta, coming upon the smaller Confederate segment, he gave it a nudge. "As we galloped across the bottom toward them they fluttered like birds in a snare," a Coloradan wrote. But that was all. When they scurried across the river, then turned south with the main body to continue the retreat, Canby turned south, too, but he remained on the eastern bank. For two days the retreat continued in this fashion, the two armies marching in plain view of each other, often within cannon range, on opposite banks of the fordable Rio Grande. Canby's men were outraged, shouting for him to send them across the river to slaughter the tatterdemalions who had been so arrogant two months before, when they were headed in the opposite direction. The northern commander was deaf alike to protests and appeals, however passionate. If there was to be any killing done, he would rather let the desert do it for him.

Beginning with the third day, the desert got its chance. When the Federals woke to reveille that morning near La Joya, they could see campfires burning brightly across the river. Dawn showed no signs of life in the camp, however, and after waiting a long while for the

Texans to begin their march Canby sent some scouts across, who returned with news that the camp was abandoned; the rebels had left in the night. Sibley, it appeared, had wanted a battle even less than Canby did. Approaching Socorro, with Fort Craig only a day's march beyond, he had left under cover of darkness in an attempt to shake his pursuers and swung westward on a hundred-mile detour to avoid a clash with whatever troops the fort's commander might have left to garrison it. Canby did not pursue. He knew the country Sibley was taking his men through, out there beyond the narrow valley benches. It was all desert, and he was having no part of it. He marched his troopers leisurely on to the safety and comfort of Fort Craig, arriving April 22. By that time Sibley's Texans were at the midpoint of their detour. Canby was content to leave their disposal to the desert.

It was one of the great marches of all time, and one of the great nightmares ever after for the men who survived it. They had no guide, no road, not even a trail through that barren waste, and they began the ten-day trek with five days' poor rations, including water. What few guns they had brought along were dragged and lowered up- and downhill by the men, who fashioned long rope harnesses for the purpose. For miles the brush and undergrowth were so dense that they had to cut and hack their way through with bowie knives and axes. Skirting the western slopes of the Madelenas, they crossed the Sierra de San Mateo, then staggered down the dry bed of the Palomas River until they reached the Rio Grande again, within sight of which the Texans sent up a shout like the "Thalassa!" of Xenophon's ten thousand. From start to finish, since heading north at the opening of the year, they had suffered a total of 1700 casualties. Something under 500 of these fell or were captured in battle, and of the remaining 1200 who did not get back to Texas, a good part crumpled along the wayside during this last one hundred miles. They reached the river with nothing but their guns and what they carried on their persons. A northern lieutenant, following their trail a year later, reported that he "not infrequently found a piece of a gun-carriage, or part of a harness, or some piece of camp or garrison equipage, with occasionally a white, dry skeleton of a man. At some points it seemed impossible for men to have made their way."

Sibley reached Fort Bliss in early May, with what was left of his command strung out for fifty miles behind him. Here he made his report to the Richmond government, a disillusioned man. He did not mention the California gold fields or the advantages of controlling the Pacific Coast. He confined his observations to the field of his late endeavor, and even these were limited to abuse: "Except for its geographical position, the Territory of New Mexico is not worth a quarter of the blood and treasure expended in its conquest. As a field for military operations it possesses not a single element, except in the multiplicity of its defensible positions. The indispensable element, food, can-

War Means Fighting . . .

not be relied on." Nor did he express any intention of giving the thing another try. The grapes had soured in the desert heat, setting his teeth on edge. "I cannot speak encouragingly for the future," he concluded, "my troops having manifested a dogged, irreconcilable detestation of the country and the people."

The report was dated May 4. Ten days later he assembled the 2000 survivors on the parade ground, all that were left of the 3700 Texans he had taken north from there four months ago. After thanking them for their devotion and self-sacrifice during what he called "this more than difficult campaign," he continued the retreat to San Antonio, where he took leave of them and they disbanded. It was finished. All his high hopes and golden dreams had come to nothing, like the newly founded Territory of Arizona, which had gone out of existence with his departure. Any trouble the Unionists might encounter in the upper Rio Grande Valley from now on would have to come from rattlers and Apaches; the Confederates were out of there for good. As far as New Mexico and the Far West were concerned, the Civil War was over.

★ ★ ★

All this time, while Sibley and Van Dorn were undergoing their defeats and suffering frustration of their plans, Beauregard kept busy doing what he could to shore up the western flank of the long line stretching eastward from the Mississippi River. Loss of Henry and Donelson, along with the troops who were charged with their defense, had irreparably smashed its center, throwing left and right out of concert and endangering the rear. "You must now act as seems best to you," Johnston had told him. "The separation of our armies is for the present complete." He was alone.

Gloomily the Creole left Nashville on February 15. Two days later — the day after Donelson fell — he passed through Corinth, the northeast Mississippi railroad nexus, on his way to inspect Polk's dispositions at Columbus, but his sore throat got sorer from anxiety and exposure, forcing him off the train at Jackson, Tennessee. From a hotel bed he summoned the bishop-general to join him for a conference. Waiting, he was downcast. Now indeed, as he had said, the ship of state was "on the breakers." When Polk arrived Beauregard informed him that Columbus must be abandoned.

The bishop protested. He had spent the past five months strengthening "the Gibraltar of the West" for just such an emergency, he said. But his fellow Louisianian explained that the manpower expense was too great. The 17,000-man garrison must fall back to New Madrid, forty miles downriver near the Tennessee line, where the swampy terrain would require less than half as large a defensive force, freeing the balance to assist in restoring the shattered center. In desperation

Polk then offered to hold Columbus with 5000 men. Beauregard shook his head. It would not do. They would be by-passed and captured at leisure, cut off from assisting in the defense of Memphis, which seemed next on the Federal list of major downriver objectives, or from coöperating with Johnston, who was retreating southwest with Hardee's troops for a possible conjunction. Polk returned to his fortified bluff, as heavy-hearted now as his commander, and set about dismounting his heavy guns and packing his wagons. Orders were orders; he would retreat — but not without every ounce of equipment charged against his name.

Beauregard's new line, covering Memphis and the railroads running spokelike from that hub, extended generally north-northwest along the roadbed of the Mobile & Ohio, from Corinth on the right, through Jackson and Humboldt, Tennessee, to the vicinity of New Madrid on the left. To defend this 150-mile airline stretch he had only such men as would be available from Polk's command when they pulled out of Columbus. As he examined the maps in his sickroom he saw that, despite the renewed advantage of a railroad shuttle from flank to flank of his line, he was worse off, even, than Johnston had been in Kentucky. However, his spirits rose as his health improved, until presently he had recovered his accustomed Napoleonic outlook. Back in Nashville he had seen the problem: "We must defeat the enemy *somewhere*, to give confidence to our friends.... We must give up some minor points, and concentrate our forces, to save the most important ones, or we will lose all of them in succession." To relieve what he called his "profound anxiety," he addressed on the 21st a confidential circular to the governors of Louisiana, Alabama, Mississippi, and Tennessee, unfolding for them a plan that would transmute disaster into glorious success by turning the tables on the Yankees. If the governors would send him reinforcements to bring his strength to 40,000 he would take the offensive forthwith. He would march on Paducah, then on Cairo, and having taken those two points he would lay St Louis itself under siege. This last would involve Van Dorn, across the river. Describing the project and invoking his assistance, the Creole general inquired of the Mississippian: "What say you to this brilliant programme?"

Van Dorn's reply came two weeks later, in the form of a dispatch giving news of his defeat at Elkhorn Tavern. This ruled out any chance of his coöperating in an advance against St Louis, even if the governors east of the river had been able to send the troops requested; which they had not. But Beauregard did not relapse into his former depression. He kept busy, issuing rhetorical addresses to his soldiers and rallying the populace to "resist the cruel invader." In an attempt to repair his shortage of artillery, for example, he broadcast an appeal to the planters of the Mississippi Valley for brass and iron bells to provide metal for casting cannon: "I, your general, intrusted with the command of the army embodied of your sons, your kinsmen, and your neighbors, do now call on you to send your plantation bells to the nearest railroad depot, subject to my order, to be melted into cannon for the defense of your plantations. Who will not cheerfully and promptly send me his bells under such circumstances? Be of good cheer; but time is precious." This produced more poetry in southern periodicals than bells in Confederate foundries, but the general refused to let his spirits be dampened, even by such taunts as the one his appeal provoked in the pro-Union Louisville *Courier:* "The rebels can afford to give up all their church bells, cow bells and dinner bells to Beauregard, for they never go to church now, their cows have all been taken by foraging parties, and they have no dinner to be summoned to."

Polk meanwhile was completing his preparations to evacuate Columbus, working mainly at night to hide his intentions from prying enemy eyes. This was no easy task, involving as it did the repulse of a gunboat reconnaissance on the 23d and the removal of 140 emplaced guns and camp equipment for 17,000 men, but he accomplished it without loss or detection. By March 2, the heaviest guns and 7000 of his soldiers having been sent downriver to New Madrid, he was on his way south with the remainder. Within the week he reached Humboldt, the crossing of the Mobile & Ohio and the Memphis & Louisville Railroads, where he stopped. From here, his 10,000 troops could be hurried to meet whatever developed in any direction, either up where they had just come from, or down at Corinth, or back in Memphis. Little as he approved of retreat in general, the militant churchman had shown a talent for it under necessity.

The detached 7000 saw less cause for gladness on occupying the post assigned them around New Madrid. Rather, it seemed to them on arrival that they had been sent to the swampy back-end of nowhere. After they had been there a while, however, they began to appreciate that the difficulty of the terrain was what made the position especially suitable for defense. Both banks of the river were boggy swamps, impenetrable to marching men; besides which, the Mississippi itself collaborated with the defenders to render its placid-looking, chocolate surface something less than convenient as a highway for invaders. As it approached the Kentucky-Tennessee line, several miles upstream, the river began one of its compass-boxing double twists, like a snake in convulsions, describing an S drawn backwards and tipped on its face, so that two narrow peninsulas lay side by side, the one to the west pointing north, the other south. Off the tip of the former, across the river in Missouri, lay the town of New Madrid, whose three forts, mounting seven guns each, commanded the second bend. At the tip of the other peninsula, nearer the Tennessee bank, was Island Ten — so called because it was the tenth such in the forty winding miles below the mouth of the Ohio — whose 39 guns, including a 16-gun floating battery tied up off the foot of the island, commanded the straight stretch of river leading into the first bend. Beauregard placed much reliance on those 60 guns; they constituted the twin-fluked, left-flank anchor of his tenuous line. The next defensible position was Fort Pillow, another hundred miles downriver. Engineers had been ordered there to constrict the fortifications so that they could be held by 3000 troops instead of the 10,000 for which they had been designed in the palmier days just past. That would take time, however. For the present, as Beauregard saw it, the fall of the batteries at New Madrid and Island Ten "must necessarily be followed immediately by the loss of the whole Mississippi Valley to the mouth of the Mississippi River." His instructions were that they were to be "held at all costs," which in soldier language meant that those guns were worth their weight in blood and must be served accordingly.

Polk thought so too. Forwarding heavy guns and reinforcements, he expressed his hopes and confidence to a colonel whose regiment had been stationed in the area all along: "Your position is a strong one, which you have well studied, and I have no doubt of the vigor and efficiency of your defense. Keep me informed."

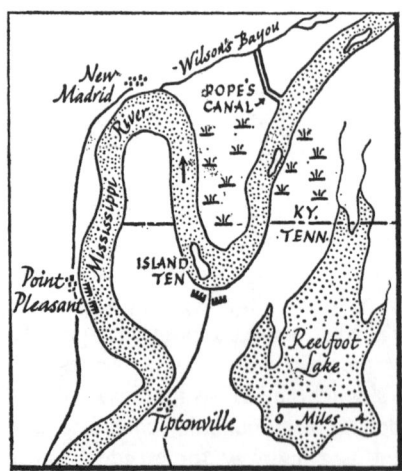

Another who agreed was Commodore Andrew Foote. He agreed, in fact, with both of them: with Beauregard in stressing the importance to the Confederates of their river-line defense, and with Polk in expecting that it would be conducted with vigor and efficiency, taking full account of all the advantages in their favor. The Federal flag officer had had time to think the problem over. After the sudden victory at Henry and the abrupt repulse at Donelson, he had returned to Cairo for badly needed repairs, both to his battered gunboats and to himself. The fall of the forts having delivered the whole Tennessee-Cumberland water system into Union hands, he could now give full attention to the western navy's primary assignment: the clearing of the Father of Waters, all the way to the Gulf.

This would be a much harder job than what had gone before, and the commodore knew it. For one thing, there was the distance. From the mouth of the Ohio to the mouth of the Mississippi was about

500 crow-flight miles, but it was well over twice that far by the twisting course his boats would have to take. A tawny vastness lay before him, winding south beyond the enemy horizon, with various obstacles in and on and around it, natural and man-made. For another, there was the difference in the rivers themselves. The Mississippi ran swifter — and it ran the other way. This meant that he would have to fight downstream, in which case even a slight mishap, such as a fouled rudder or a sudden loss of steam, could lead to destruction or capture. Highly vulnerable except from dead ahead, his ironclads carried little armor back from the prow and none at all at the stern. What was more, experiments conducted on the Mississippi during the refitting showed that they could not maintain station under reverse power, even with the help of anchors, which could get no firm purchase on the river's slimy bottom. If one of them went out of control in a downstream fight, through breakdown or damage to her engine or her steering apparatus, she would not drift rearward to safety — as three out of four had done in the upstream fight just past — but forward, under enemy guns and into enemy hands. Consideration brought doubts. When his brother, a judge in Ohio, reminded him that the public expected "dash and close fighting, something sharp and decisive," Foote replied: "Don't you know that my gunboats are the only protection you have upon your rivers... that without my flotilla everything in your rivers, your cities and your towns would be at the mercy of the enemy? My first duty then is to care for my boats, if I am to protect you." He had not spoken thus before the point-blank assault on Donelson. But now, with the wound in his ankle not yet healed and the sound of breaking armor still loud in his memory of that repulse, the commodore took counsel of his fears.

Despite his qualms, Foote set off downriver before daylight, March 4, prepared to assault the Columbus bluff with all seven of his ironclads. Arriving he found the fortress strangely silent, no stir of life on the ramparts and no metal frowning down from the embrasures. Two officers and thirty men, covered by all the guns of the fleet, made a dash for shore in a tug — and presently returned, more sheepish than exultant, with word that the Union flag had been flying there since yesterday. Out on a scout, four companies of Illinois cavalry had found the place deserted, then trooper-like had settled down and made themselves at home, rooting into the conglomerate litter Polk's men had left behind. Foote went ashore for a look at the fortifications, wrote a formal report on their capture, supervised further repairs to his gunboats — necessary because the armor above the Texas decks was so badly cracked and buckled that the civilian pilots refused to continue downriver until it had been replaced — then finally, on the 17th, set off again for his next objective: Island Ten.

Arriving that day, he moored his flotilla against the Missouri bank, three miles above the head of the fortified island, and began lobbing shells across the low-lying southern tip of the first peninsula. His fire was not very effective at that range, but neither was the enemy's, which was the commodore's main concern in his present frame of mind. In fact he had come prepared for this style of fighting. His seven ironclads were supplemented by eleven strange vessels, compressed hexagons 60 feet long and 25 feet wide, each with a single 13-inch mortar bolted to its deck. Originally there had been doubts as to whether they would stand the recoil, but three of the gunboat captains had settled that by firing the first shot: in spite of which they were still suspected of being about as dangerous at one end of the trajectory as the other. When the piece was loaded, the crew slipped through a door cut in one end of the surrounding seven-foot armored bulwark and stood on tiptoe on the outer deck, hands over ears, mouths agape, knees flexed against the concussion, until it was fired; then they would hurry back inside for the reloading. Foote at least was happy with them, despite the doubts and drawbacks. As soon as he got within range of the island he had them towed to the head of the column and started them firing in the direction of the nearest Confederate batteries, two airline miles away.

Army men, who had been on the scene for two weeks now, anticipating the arrival of the gunboats with their Sunday punch, were much less happy about these new-style naval tactics, so different from what had gone before. At Henry the navy had taken the lead, leaving the landsmen with little to do, and now that the case was more or less reversed, the army howled with resentment. As time went by, the commodore refusing to budge from his upstream station, the howls took on a note of shrill derision. One exasperated colonel, when asked just what the flotilla was accomplishing, replied contemptuously, "Oh, it is still bombarding the state of Tennessee at long range."

None among the soldiers was more critical of the navy than their commander, Brigadier General John Pope. In protesting against caution he stood on solid ground. His notion of the way to fight a war was to locate the enemy and then go after him, preferably point-blank. These tactics were especially valid when operating, as Pope was here, with the advantage of three-to-one numerical odds, and he had proceeded to put them into practice. A forty-year-old West Pointer with a robust physique to match his positive manner, he had brought his four divisions overland down the right bank of the river, arriving March 3, and moved without delay against New Madrid and Point Pleasant, eleven miles below. Within ten days — four days before the navy's tardy arrival — he had captured both places, along with 25 heavy guns and quantities of equipment and supplies, when the defenders retreated to the security of the east bank and the fastness of Island Ten. He would have taken that place, too — he knew exactly how to go about it — except that he could not effect a crossing without protection for his transports. Confederate batteries commanded the river from the opposite bank, and even worse there was a motley collection of makeshift rebel gunboats on patrol. Neither of these deterrents would be much of a problem for even a single ironclad, Pope declared, if Foote would only send it. But this the naval commander would not do. Any attempt to run the gauntlet of the island batteries, he replied, "would result in the sacrifice of the boat, her officers and men, which sacrifice I would not be justified in making."

Pope was more vexed than discouraged. A week after his capture of New Madrid, in recognition of his hard-hitting competence, he had been made a major general. He would keep up the pressure, hoping in time to stiffen the navy's backbone. Meanwhile he had the rebels in a cul-de-sac, backed up against the swamps that lay between Reelfoot Lake and the river. There was no way out for them, and no way in for supplies, except along the road leading south through Tiptonville. Once the Federals were astride the river, the road would be cut; he could bag the lot by quick assault or, at the worst, by siege. All he wanted was a chance to ferry his men across with a fair degree of safety. Suspecting that the navy would never get up nerve enough to run past Island Ten, he began to construct a navy of his own: high-sided barges armored with boiler plate, designed to accommodate field guns. He kept busy in other ways as well, manning the captured heavy guns to strengthen his domination of Madrid Bend and bringing down supplies and reinforcements from upriver. This last took ingenuity, for the right-bank swamps blocked the direct route, but the general had that too. He had his engineers cut a channel (a canal, it was called, 50 feet wide, 9 miles long, and 4½ feet deep — this being the depth at which the flooded trees were sawed off under water) connecting the river, five miles north of the gunboat station, with Wilson's Bayou, which gave down upon New Madrid, thus by-passing the bend commanded by the guns on Island Ten. Shallow-draft transports got through with another whole division, bringing Pope's total strength to 23,000, but not the gunboats, whose bottoms would have been torn out by the stumps. Their only way led down past the cannon-bristled island, which Foote believed would sink in short order whatever came within range.

All but one of the gunboat captains agreed with the flag officer's estimate as to the outcome of a downstream fight or a try at running the batteries. That one was Commander Henry Walke, skipper of the *Carondelet*. For two weeks now the diurnal mortar bombardment had continued, and except for a single boat expedition, which spiked some guns in an abandoned battery on All Fools' Night, all that had been accomplished by the navy was a heavy expenditure of ammunition. A fifty-four-year-old Virginia-born Ohioan and a veteran of all the river engagements from Belmont on, Walke was touched in his pride, and had been so ever since Donelson, when, as last boat out of the fight, he had retreated firing blindly in an attempt to hide in the gunsmoke. It was his belief that the run could be made with a good chance of success, provided it was made in silence and by the dark of the moon. If the rebels did not know he was there, they would not shoot; or if they knew he was there, but could not see him, they would not be likely to hit him. At any rate he was willing to give it a try, and he said so at a conference on the flagship in late March. Foote was pleased to hear that someone thought the run could be made, though he himself was doubtful. The army gibes had begun to sting, and there were reports that the Confederates were building a fleet of giant ironclads at Memphis: he might soon have a downstream fight on his hands, against much longer odds, whether he wanted it or not. He asked Walke if he would be willing to back up his opinion by trying the run in the *Carondelet*. Walke said he would, emphatically. Foote said all right, go ahead. He would not order a man to try what he himself had already said was too risky, but he would approve it on a volunteer basis. Walke began his preparations at once.

 The moon would be new and early-down on the night of April 4, which left him just under a week for getting ready. During this time he piled his decks with planks from a wrecked barge to give protection from plunging shot, coiled surplus chain in vulnerable spots, and wound an 11-inch hawser round and round the pilothouse as high up as the windows. Cordwood barriers were built to inclose the boilers, and a coal barge loaded with bales of hay was lashed to the port side, which caused an observer to remark that the gunboat resembled "a farmer's wagon prepared for market." The only light she carried would be a lantern in the engine room, invisible from outside, and to insure silence the engines were muffled by piping the escape steam through the paddle-wheel housing instead of through the stacks as usual. The one thing Walke was to avoid beyond all others was being captured; fighting upstream in rebel hands, the *Carondelet* might be a match for all her sister ships combined. To guard against this, the crew was armed with cutlasses, pistols, and hand grenades; two dozen volunteer sharp shooters were taken aboard; hot-water hoses were connected to the boilers for the purpose of scalding boarders; and if all else failed, Walke's orders were that she was to be sunk beneath their feet. Through the early evening of April 4 the sickle moon shone brightly, if intermittently, over and under a scud of black clouds racing past. Then came moonset, 10 o'clock; Walke passed the word, "All ready," and the gunboat slipped her moorings. The muffled engines merely throbbed; the gathering clouds had masked the stars. So absolute were the darkness and the silence as the *Carondelet* stood out for New Madrid, the officers on deck asked through the speaking pipes if the engineer was going ahead on her.

It was not so for long. Just as she cleared the line of mortar rafts at the head of the moored column, the storm broke with tropical fury. Vast and vivid streaks of lightning split the sky, so that to one who watched it was as if the gates of hell "were opened and shut every instant, suffering the whole fierce reflection of the infernal lake to flash across the sky." Thunder crashed and rumbled and the rain came down in gulfs. The river ahead was an illuminated highway, with Island Ten looming in ominous silhouette, its drowsy lookouts no doubt startled into wide-eyed action at seeing the Yankee gunboat bearing down on them like something on a brightly lighted stage. Yet apparently not: Walke held his course past the first battery without being fired on — when suddenly, of her own accord, the *Carondelet* signaled her presence to her enemies ashore. Dry soot in her chimneys, normally kept wet by the escape steam, took fire and shot five-foot torches from their crowns, bathing with a yellow glare the upper deck and everything around. That did it. Ashore, there were cries of alarm and an officer shouting, "Elevate! Elevate!" and then the crash of gunfire through the thunder.

Carondelet went with the current, a leadsman knee-deep in muddy foam on her bow to sing out the soundings. The coal barge lashed alongside impeded her speed, but was no less welcome for that, coming as it did between the batteries and their target. Shells shrieked overhead or were heard plunging into the water as the island guns were echoed by others along the Tennessee bank. Wallowing in the wind-whipped waves, still under the crash and flash of thunder and lightning, the little ironclad held her course and took no hits. Clear of the island, she still had the floating battery to pass, but the final six shots from there were misses, like the rest. She had made it. Pulling up to the New Madrid landing, where army cannoneers were giving the navy its due at last by tossing their caps and cheering, Walke proudly took up a speaking trumpet and announced his arrival to those on bank, then turned to his bosun's mate and authorized the sounding of "grog, oh." Against regulations, the main brace then was spliced.

Pope at last had what he had been saying was all he needed, a gunboat south of Island Ten; and presently he had two. Learning of the *Carondelet*'s successful run — she had taken two hits after all, it turned out: one in the coal barge, one in a bale of hay — Foote sent the *Pittsburg* down to repeat the performance on the night of the 6th, which was also dark and stormy. The makeshift rebel flotilla scattered, awed, and the ironclads knocked out the batteries opposite Point Pleasant. Pope put his men on transports and had the gunboats herd them over. The Tiptonville road was cut within an hour of the unopposed landing. All he had to do then was put his hand out; the 7000 Confederates were in it, along with more than a hundred pieces of light and heavy artillery, 7000 small arms, horses and mules by droves, mounds of equipment including tents for 12,000 men, and several boatloads of provisions.

It was all over before the dawn of April 8, accomplished without the loss of a single man in combat. The North had another hero: bluff John Pope. A forthright combination of ingenuity and drive — large-bodied, with stolid eyes and a full beard that spread down over his upper chest, his broad, flat face framed by dark brown hair brushed straight back from the bulging expanse of forehead and falling long at the sides — he commanded confidence by his very presence. Once he saw what he wanted, he went after it on his own, unflinchingly. The military worth of such a man was clear for all to see, including his commander. Halleck wired, exuberant: "I congratulate you and your command on your splendid achievement. It excels in boldness and brilliancy all other operations of the war. It will be memorable in military history and will be admired by future generations. You deserve well of your country."

Thus Halleck rejoiced and Pope basked in well-earned laudation, while their opponent Beauregard experienced quite opposite emotions. Once more on the eve of scoring what he had hoped would be "a beautiful *ten strike*," he was suddenly faced instead with the imminent testing of his prediction that the fall of New Madrid and Island Ten would mean the immediate loss of the whole Mississippi Valley. For him this meant the loss of the war, and he was correspondingly cast down. Midway of the campaign, which was stretching his nerves to the breaking point — one fluke of his left-flank anchor had snapped, and the other seemed about to snap as well — he wrote to a friend in Congress, inquiring distractedly: "Will not heaven open the eyes and senses of our rulers? Where in the world are we going to, if not to destruction?"

※ 2 ※

Good news was doubly welcome in St. Louis, where Halleck had sat desk-bound all this time, scratching his elbows and addressing his goggle-eyed stare in the general direction of the back-area correspondents who came clamoring for information he could not give because he did not have it. The month between the mid-February capture of Fort Donelson and the mid-March fall of New Madrid had been for him a time of strain, one in which he saw his probable advancement placed in precarious balance opposite his probable stagnation. He had come out top man in the end, but the events leading up to that happy termination — as if, perversely, the fates had established a sort of inverse ratio between the success of Federal arms and the rise of Henry Halleck — had contained, for him, far more of anguish than of joy. There was small consolation in realizing later that the fates had been with him all along, that the cause for all that anguish had existed only in his own mind, as a product of fear and suspicion.

His first reaction, the day after the fall of the Cumberland fortress, was to request promotions for Buell, Grant, and C. F. Smith — and advancement for himself. "Give me command of the West," he wired McClellan. "I ask this in return for Forts Henry and Donelson." His second reaction, following hard on the heels of the first, was fear that Grant's victory might sting the Confederates into desperation. Even now perhaps they were massing for a sudden all-or-nothing lunge, northward around Grant's flank. Beauregard's plan for an attack on Paducah and Cairo had not gone beyond the dream stage, but Halleck feared it quite literally, and called urgently for Buell to come help him. Buell replied in effect that he had troubles of his own, and Halleck was even more firmly convinced of the necessity for authority to bend him to his will. "I must have command of the armies of the West," he told McClellan in a second wire, sent three days after the first, which had gone unanswered. "Hesitation and delay are losing us the golden opportunity. Lay this before the President and the Secretary of War. May I assume command? Answer quickly." This time McClellan did answer quickly, but not as his fretful subordinate had hoped. Replying that he believed Buell could handle his own army better from Bowling Green than Halleck could do from St Louis, he declined to lay Old Brains' self-recommendation on the presidential desk.

Perhaps it was what Halleck had expected. At any rate he had already put a second string to his bow, forwarding for Stanton's out-of-channels approval a plan for reorganizing the western department under his command. February 21, the day after McClellan's refusal, Stanton replied that he liked the plan, "but on account of the domestic affliction of the President" — Willie Lincoln had died the day before and was lying in state in the White House — "I have not yet been able to submit it to him." Halleck's hopes took a bound at this. Determined to strike while the iron was hot, he wired back that same day, urging the won-over Secretary to break in on the President's family trouble, whatever it was. "One whole week has been lost already by hesitation and delay," he complained. "There was, and I think there still is, a golden opportunity to strike a fatal blow, but I can't do it unless I can control Buell's army.... There is not a moment to be lost. Give me the authority, and I will be responsible for results." Stanton's reply came the following day, and Halleck's hopes hit bottom with a thud. The Secretary had gotten to Lincoln, but "after full consideration of the subject," he telegraphed, "[the President] does not think any change in the organization of the army or the military departments at present advisable."

Halleck's bow was completely unstrung; there was no one left to appeal to, either in or out of channels. After two days spent absorbing the shock, he replied with what grace he could muster: "If it is thought that the present arrangement is best for the public service, I have nothing to say. I have done my duty in making the suggestions, and I leave it to my superiors to adopt or reject them." For others closer at hand, however, he either had less grace to spare or else it was exhausted. Encountering signs of paperwork confusion down at Cairo that same day, he testily informed his chief of staff: "There is a screw loose in that command. It had better be fixed pretty soon, or the command will hear from me."

That was still his irascible, sore-pawed frame of mind the following week, when his worst fears in regard to Grant appeared to have been realized. At a time when Halleck was most concerned about a possible rebel counterattack, launched with all the fury of desperation, Grant and his 30,000 soldiers — the combat-hardened core of any defense the department commander might have to make — lost touch with headquarters, apparently neglecting to file reports because he was off on a double celebration of victory and promotion. The former alcoholic captain was now a major general, tenth-ranking man in the whole U.S. Army; Lincoln had signed the recommendation on the night of the day the Donelson news reached Washington, and the Senate had promptly confirmed it as of the Unconditional Surrender date. Halleck himself had urged the promotion, but not as warmly as he had urged several others, and he had yet to congratulate Grant personally for the capture of the forts. Other promotions were in the mill, soon to be acted on — Buell and Pope were to be major generals within a week, along with others, including Smith — but Grant would outrank them, which was not at all what Halleck had intended or expected. The fact was, absorbed as he had been in his rivalry with Buell, he was beginning to see that he had raised an even more formidable hero-opponent right there in his own front yard. Donelson having caught the public fancy, the public in its short-sighted way was giving all the credit to the general on the scene, rather than to the commander who had masterminded the campaign from St Louis. Irked by this, he then was confronted with what he considered the crowning instance of Grant's instability. Having won his promotion, the new hero apparently thought himself above the necessity for filing reports as to his whereabouts or condition. Where he was now, Halleck did not know for sure; but there were rumors.

On March 3 McClellan received a dispatch indicating that Halleck's sorely tried patience at last had snapped: "I have had no communication with General Grant for more than a week. He left his command without my authority and went to Nashville. His army seems to be as much demoralized by the victory of Fort Donelson as was that of the Potomac by the defeat of Bull Run. It is hard to censure a successful general immediately after a victory, but I think he richly deserves it. I can get no returns, no reports, no information of any kind from him. Satisfied with his victory, he sits down and enjoys it without any regard to the future. I'm worn-out and tired with this neglect and inefficiency." McClellan, whose eye for a possible rival was quite as sharp as Halleck's own, was sudden in reply: "Generals must observe discipline as well as private soldiers. Do not hesitate to arrest him at once if the good of the service requires it.... You are at liberty to regard this as a positive order if it will smooth your way."

Halleck did not hesitate. The order went by wire to Grant at once: "You will place [Brig.] Gen. C. F. Smith in command of expedition, and remain yourself at Fort Henry. Why do you not obey my orders to report strength and positions of your command?" The question was largely rhetorical; Halleck believed he already knew the answer, and he gave it in a telegram informing McClellan of his action in the matter: "A rumor has just reached me that since the taking of Fort Donelson, General Grant has resumed his former bad habits. If so, it will account for his neglect of my often-repeated orders." To anyone with an ear for army gossip, and McClellan's was highly tuned in that respect, this meant that Grant was off on a bender. "I do not deem it advisable to arrest him at present," Halleck continued, "but have placed General Smith in command of the expedition up the Tennessee. I think Smith will restore order and discipline."

Grant had been guilty of none of these things, and he said so in a telegram to Halleck as soon as he had complied with the instructions to turn over his command: "I am not aware of ever having disobeyed any order from headquarters — certainly never intended such a thing." The communications hiatus was explained by the defection of a telegraph operator who took Grant's dispatches with him, unsent, when he deserted. It was true, Grant said, that he had been to Nashville, but that was because Halleck had told him nothing; he had gone there to meet Buell and work out a plan for coöperation. When Halleck still showed resentment at having been left in the dark, Grant observed that there must be enemies between them, and asked to be relieved from further duty in the department. Halleck refused to agree to this, but continued to bolster his case by forwarding an anonymous letter charging that the property captured at Fort Henry had been questionably handled. His dander really up now, Grant replied: "There is such a disposition to find fault with me that I again ask to be relieved from further duty until I can be placed right in the estimation of those higher in authority."

Suddenly, incredibly, all was sweetness and light at Halleck's end of the wire. "You cannot be relieved from your command," he answered. "There is no good reason for it.... Instead of relieving you, I wish you as soon as your new army is in the field to assume command and lead it on to new victories."

There were a number of reasons behind this sudden change in attitude and disposition, all of which had occurred between the leveling and the withdrawing of the charges against Grant. First, the evacuation of Columbus had relieved Halleck's fears that the Confederates were about to unleash an attack on Cairo or Paducah, and while Curtis was stopping Van Dorn at Elkhorn Tavern, Pope was applying a bear hug on New Madrid. Then, just as he was congratulating himself on these improvements in the tactical situation, a stiff letter came from the Adjutant General, demanding specifications for the vague charges he had been making against his new major general. Trial-by-rumor would not do, the army's head lawyer informed him. "By direction of the President, the Secretary of War desires you to ascertain and report whether General Grant left his command at any time without proper authority, and, if so, for how long; whether he has made to you proper reports and returns of his force; whether he has committed any acts which are unauthorized or not in accordance with military subordination or propriety, and, if so, what." To reply as directed would be to give Grant what he had been seeking, a chance to "be placed right in the estimation of those higher in authority." Besides, Halleck had no specifications to report, only rumors. Instead, he replied that he was "satisfied" Grant had "acted from a praiseworthy although mistaken zeal.... I respectfully recommend that no further notice be taken of it.... All these irregularities have now been remedied."

However, there was something more behind this sudden volte-face, this willingness to bury the hatchet he had been flourishing lately. March 11 — the day after the Adjutant General's call for specifics, and two days before he blandly informed Grant that there was "no good reason" for relieving him — the fond hope for which he had labored in and out of channels all these months was realized. He got the West. His command, which was called the Department of the Mississippi and extended for better than 500 miles eastward, from Kansas to a north-south line through Knoxville, was awarded him by Lincoln in the same War Order that deposed McClellan as general-in-chief and recalled Frémont to active duty. Receiving it that way, out of the blue, after two solid weeks of despair, Halleck was in no mood to quarrel with anyone, not even Grant: in fact, especially not Grant. Beauregard was reported to be intrenching around Corinth, reinforced to a strength of 20,000 men. "If so, he will make a Manassas of it," Halleck said. That meant hard fighting: in which case he wanted his hardest-fighting general in command: and that meant Grant, whatever his instability in other respects. "The power is in your hands," Halleck told him. "Use it, and you will be sustained by all above you."

So Grant got aboard a steamboat at Fort Henry and went up the Tennessee to rejoin his army.

★ ★ ★

Beauregard was at Corinth, and he had been reinforced: Halleck's information was true, as far as it went. But the Creole was not planning a Manassas. He was planning a Cannae, or at least an Austerlitz, and for once (though he did not neglect the accustomed flourish at the outset: "Soldiers: I assume this day the command of the Army of the Mississippi, for the defense of our homes and liberties, and to resist the subjugation, spoliation, and dishonor of our people. Our mothers and wives, our sisters and children, expect us to do our duty even to the sacrifice of our lives.... Our cause is as just and sacred as ever animated men to take up arms, and if we are true to it and to ourselves, with the continued protection of the Almighty, we must and shall triumph") his dream was built on something more than rhetoric and hope.

Recent and looming disasters at last had jarred the Richmond government into action. The fall of Henry and Donelson, followed at once by the loss of Kentucky and Middle Tennessee, now threatened the railroad leading eastward from Memphis, through Corinth and Tuscumbia, to Chattanooga, where it branched south, through Atlanta, to Charleston and Savannah, and north, through Knoxville, to Lynchburg and Richmond. "The vertebrae of the Confederacy," former War Secretary L. P. Walker called it, and rightly; for once this only east-west all-weather supply line was cut, the upper South would be divided — as prone for conquest as a man with a broken backbone. Now when Beauregard cried wolf, as he had done unheeded so often before, the authorities listened. Without Major General Braxton Bragg and the 10,000 soldiers he commanded at Mobile and Pensacola, the southern coast would be wide open to amphibious attack, but under the press of necessity the dispersed defensive was out, no matter the risk; Bragg and his men were ordered north to Corinth. So were Brigadier General Daniel Ruggles and his 5000 from New Orleans, though their departure left the South's chief city without infantry to defend it. By early March they were with Beauregard, absorbed into the Army of the Mississippi. Combined with Polk's 10,000 — so that in point of fact it was they who did the absorbing — they brought the expansive Creole's total strength to 25,000 men.

His spirits were lifted toward elation by this considerable transfusion of troops from his native shore — including one elite New Orleans outfit which carried his name on its roster as an honorary private; "Pierre Gustave Toutant Beauregard!" rang out daily at roll call, like the sudden unfurling of a silken banner; "Absent on duty!" the color-sergeant proudly answered for him. He looked forward to combinations and maneuvers that would be nothing less than Napoleonic in concept and execution. Johnston by now was across the Tennessee, marching westward from Decatur with the remnant of what had been the Army of Kentucky. Floyd's brigade had been sent to

Chattanooga, but Forrest's troopers had caught up with the column, bringing Hardee's total to 15,000. When they arrived there would be 40,000 soldiers around Corinth, exactly the number the impatiently waiting general had said would allow a strike at Cairo and Paducah. Nor was that all. Van Dorn's 15,000, licking their Elkhorn Tavern wounds in Arkansas, had been alerted for an eastward march that would bring them across the Mississippi at Memphis, where they would find boxcars waiting to bring them rapidly down the vital railroad line to Corinth. The total then would soar to 55,000. Any twinge of regret for the 20,000 lost at Donelson and penned up now on Island Ten was quickly assuaged by the thought that, even without them, the Army of the Mississippi would not only be the largest any Confederate had ever commanded, but in fact would be almost twice as large as the combined force that had covered itself and its generals — particularly Beauregard — with glory at Manassas. As he waited now for Johnston he rehearsed in his mind the recommendations he would make for the utilization of this strength.

Scouts had been bringing him full reports of the enemy situation all this time. Grant's army was twenty-odd miles to the north, in camp on the left bank of the Tennessee, awaiting the arrival of Buell's army, which was moving west from Nashville. Even with the addition of Van Dorn and Johnston, the southern army would not be as large as the two northern armies combined, but it would be larger than either on its own. The answer, then — provided the gray-clad reinforcements won the race, which seemed likely, since the Yankees marching overland from Nashville were encountering various obstacles such as burned bridges — was a slashing attack. If Van Dorn and Johnston reached Corinth before Buell reached the Tennessee, the superior Confederate army would pounce on Grant and accomplish his destruction, then fall in turn on Buell and treat him likewise, after which the way to Louisville and St Louis would lie open. Beauregard saw and rehearsed it thus in his mind, complete no doubt with the final surrender ceremonies at the point of deepest penetration, wherever that might be. When Johnston arrived on the 24th at the head of the column which now reached the end of its long retreat from Bowling Green, he considered the race half won.

The tall, handsome Texan, who had set out seven months ago, buoyed up by the confident hopes of the South that he would drive the blue invaders from the soil of his native Kentucky, now came back to Mississippi oppressed by the seething resentment of those who had cheered him loudest then. He took it calmly, the flared mustache and deep-set eyes masking whatever hurt the barbs of criticism gave him. "What the people want is a victory," he had said, and he welcomed Beauregard's proposal — the more so since it coincided with plans he had made on the march — as a chance to give them one. In fact, as a sign of appreciation for all the Louisiana general had done in the trying past few weeks, Johnston made the gesture of offering him command of the army for the coming battle; he himself would act as department commander, he said, with headquarters at Memphis or at nearby Holly Springs. Beauregard's heart gave a leap at this, touching his fiery ambition as it did, but he recognized a gesture when he saw one, and declined. Then the two got down to preparing the army for combat, prescribing rigid training schedules for the soldiers, who being raw needed all the instruction they could possibly absorb, and reorganizing them into four corps: 10,000 under Polk, 16,000 under Bragg, 7000 under Hardee, and 7000 under Breckinridge. (The last was designated as Crittenden's at first, but he was presently removed to suffer demotion for the Fishing Creek debacle.) The 15,000 under Van Dorn would add a substantial fifth corps when they got there, but even without them the army was about as large as the one Grant had in camp on the near bank of the Tennessee, twenty-two miles to the north.

The reinstated Federal commander had been with his army a week by the time Johnston joined Beauregard at Corinth. After the hundred-mile boat ride Grant came ashore at Savannah, a hamlet on the east bank, where C. F. Smith, an old soldier who never neglected the creature comforts, had established headquarters in a fine private mansion overlooking a bend of the Tennessee. One division was at Crump's Landing, three miles upstream on the opposite bank, and as Grant arrived the other five were debarking at Pittsburg Landing, six miles farther south and also on the west side of the river. The site had been recommended by the commander of one of the new divisions; a "magnificent plain for camping and drilling," he called it, "and a military point of great strength."

This was Tecumseh Sherman. He too had been reinstated, Halleck having decided that he was not really insane after all, just highstrung and talkative; besides, he had a brother in the Senate. Grant, for one, thought highly of him. During the Donelson campaign Sherman had worked hard, forwarding reinforcements and supplies and offering to waive his then superior rank for a chance to come up and join the fighting. But the men assigned to him were not so sure, not at the outset anyhow. Red-headed and gaunt, with sunken temples and a grizzled, short-cropped ginger beard, he had a wild expression around his eyes and a hungry look that seemed to have been with him always. "I never saw him but I thought of Lazarus," one declared. His shoulders twitched and his hands were never still, always picking at something, twirling a button or fiddling with his whiskers. They had not fancied getting their first taste of combat under a man who had been sent home such a short while back under suspicion of insanity. Three days before Grant's arrival, though at first their fears were intensified, they learned better. Smith sent them south for a try at breaking the vital Memphis & Charleston Railroad, down across the Mississippi line.

They came off the transports at midnight in a blinding rain. By daylight they were far inland, and still the rain came pouring. Bridges were washed out, so that the cavalry, scouting ahead, lost men and horses, drowned while trying to ford the swollen creeks. Behind them, the Tennessee was rising fast, threatening to cut them off by flooding the bottom they had marched across. At this point, just when things were at their worst, Sherman ordered them back to the transports. It had been a nightmare operation, and probably they had done no earthly good; they were wet, tired, hungry, cold; for the most part they had been thoroughly frightened. But curiously enough, when they were back aboard the transports, drinking hot coffee and snuggling into blankets, they felt fine about the whole thing. They had been down into enemy country, the actual Deep South — a division on its own, looking for trouble: that gave them the feeling of being veterans — and they had seen their commander leading them. Sherman was not the same man at all. He was not nervous; his shoulders did not twitch; he was calm and confident, and when he saw the thing was impossible he did not hesitate to give it up. Whatever else he might be, he certainly was not crazy. They knew that now, and they were willing to follow wherever he led them.

Grant too had changed, the veterans saw when he came up to Pittsburg to inspect them. Mostly it was the aura of fame that had been gathering around him in the month since the news from Donelson first set the church bells ringing. He was Unconditional S. Grant now, and his picture was on the cover of *Harper's Weekly*. There was a hunger for particulars about him, for instance how he "generally stood or walked with his left hand in his trousers pocket, and had in his mouth an unlighted cigar, the end of which he chewed restlessly." The cigar was an example of the change that stemmed from fame. Learning that he had kept one clamped in his teeth that critical afternoon at Donelson, whenever he was not using it like a marshal's baton to point the direction for attack, readers had sent him boxes of them to express their admiration, and since Grant had never been one to waste things, least of all good tobacco, the long-stemmed meerschaum that had given him so much satisfaction in the past was put away while he concentrated on smoking up those crates of gift cigars. One other change he had made on his own. His beard, which formerly had reached down past the second button on his coat, had been clipped short. It seemed to the soldiers, observing him now, a gesture not unlike that of a man rolling up his sleeves in preparation for hard work.

For him, work meant fighting; that was his trade, the only one he had ever been any good at or able to earn a living by, and he wanted to be at it right away. Restrained by Halleck, however — "We must strike no blow until we are strong enough to admit no doubt of the result," the department commander warned — all Grant could do now was prepare for the attack he would launch when Buell got there. Meanwhile the position appeared to him to be about as good as Sherman had reported. A hundred-foot yellow-clay bluff rose abruptly from the narrow shelf of the landing, where steamboats had unloaded peacetime cargoes for Corinth, to a plateau eroded by gullies and covered with second-growth timber except for scattered clearings cut by farmers for orchards and grain fields. It was not quite a "magnificent plain," but it did have points of military strength, the flanks being protected by Lick and Snake Creeks, which emptied into the Tennessee above and below the landing. The area between them, a quadrilateral varying roughly from three to five miles on a side, gave plenty of room for drilling the five divisions camped there and was conveniently crosshatched by a network of wagon trails leading inland and connecting the small farms. But Grant's primary interest was on the main road leading southwest to Corinth, one hard day's march away. That was the one he would take when the time came: meaning Buell. Halleck reported him nearing Waynesboro, forty miles away, but cautioned Grant: "Don't let the enemy draw you into an engagement now. Wait till you are properly fortified and receive orders."

This raised another question; for the position had not been fortified at all. Smith had already expressed an opinion on that. The crusty general had been put to bed with an infected leg, having skinned his shin on the sharp edge of a rowboat seat, but he was quite undaunted. "By God," he said, "I ask nothing better than to have the rebels come out and attack us! We can whip them to hell. Our men suppose we have come here to fight, and if we begin to spade it will make them think we fear the enemy." Grant agreed and left things as they were, despite the warning. The war was on its last legs, he told Halleck, and the enemy too demoralized to constitute a danger: "The temper of the rebel troops is such that there is but little doubt but that Corinth will fall much more easily than Donelson did when we do move. All accounts agree in saying that the great mass of the rank and file are heartily tired."

One man at least did not agree at first, and that was Sherman. Privately he was telling newsmen, "We are in great danger here." But when asked why he did not protest to those in charge, he shrugged; "Oh, they'd call me crazy again." As time went by, however, and no attack developed, he became as complacent as the rest. Before the end of March he wrote gaily to an army friend in Cairo: "I hope we may meet in Memphis. Here we are on its latitude, and you have its longitude. Draw our parallels, and we breakfast at the Gayoso, whither let us God speed, and then rejoice once more at the progress of our cause."

Already there had been cause for rejoicing by some of his

fellow generals, promotions having come through on the 21st for the three who commanded divisions at Donelson. Smith received his in bed — his leg was getting worse instead of better — but McClernand took his step-up with the continuing belief that other advancements were in store, and Lew Wallace was now the youngest major general in the army. Smith's division was placed in charge of W. H. L. Wallace, an Ohio lawyer who had won his stars at Donelson. Two of the three divisions added since were led by brigadiers who had moved to Illinois from the South and stood by the Union when trouble came: Benjamin M. Prentiss, a Virginia-born merchant, and Stephen A. Hurlbut, a lawyer originally from Charleston, South Carolina. Sherman, commanding the remaining green division, had had less combat experience than any of them — none at all, in fact, since that grievous July afternoon on the banks of Bull Run in far-away Virginia, where McClellan, now that April was at hand, was boarding a steamer to go down the coast and join his army for an advance up the James peninsula — but he was the only one of the six who was regular army, and Grant left the tactical arrangements in general to him, commuting daily by steamboat from the Savannah mansion, nine miles away.

Between them, these six commanded eighteen brigades: 74 regiments containing 42,682 soldiers, some raw, some hardened by combat. Green or seasoned, however, they approved to a man of their commander's intention to march down to Corinth, as soon as Buell arrived with 30,000 more, and administer another dose of the medicine they had forced down rebel throats the month before.

Johnston had sixteen brigades, 71 regiments with a total strength of 40,335. But even apart from the day-to-day danger of Buell's reaching Pittsburg Landing with three fourths that many more, the present near-equality in numbers was considerably offset by a contrasting lack of combat experience. Two thirds of Grant's men had been in battle — in fact had been victorious in battle — whereas in Johnston's army, except for Forrest's troopers and the handful Polk had sent to Pillow's aid five months ago at Belmont, few had heard a shot fired in anger, and only Hardee's men had even done much real marching. Bragg referred to the forces around Corinth as "this mob we have, miscalled soldiers," and complained that a good part of them had never done a day's work in their lives. Johnston of course was aware of these shortcomings, but his scouts having kept him well informed he counted much on the element of surprise. He knew what he would find up there: an army camped with its back to a deep river, unfortified, hemmed in by boggy creeks, disposed for comfort, and scattered the peacetime way. Meanwhile, drill and instruction were repairing the Confederate flaws Bragg had pointed out so harshly. He would strike as soon as he felt it possible. The question was, how long would he have before Buell got there or Grant saw the danger and corrected his dispositions or, worse, moved out and beat him to the punch?

Late at night, April 2, a telegram from Bethel, twenty miles north on the M & O, seemed to Beauregard to confirm the last and worst of these fears: Lew Wallace was maneuvering in that direction. Taking this for the beginning of a full-scale attack on Memphis, he forwarded the message to Johnston after writing on the bottom: "Now is the moment to advance, and strike the enemy at Pittsburg Landing." Johnston read it, then crossed the street to confer with Bragg, who had been made chief of staff in addition to his other duties under last week's reorganization. Johnston wanted more time for drilling his army and awaiting the arrival of Van Dorn, but Bragg was insistent in support of Beauregard's indorsement. Whatever this latest development meant, Buell was drawing closer every day. It had to be now or never, he said, and Johnston at last agreed. Ready or unready, Van Dorn or no Van Dorn, they would go up to Pittsburg and attack the Federal army in its camp. Within an hour of the telegram's midnight arrival, orders went out for the four corps commanders to "hold their commands in hand, ready to advance upon the enemy in the morning by 6 a.m. with three days' cooked rations in haversacks, 100 rounds of ammunition for small arms, and 200 rounds for field-pieces."

Early next morning Beauregard's chief of staff got to work, preparing the march instructions from notes the general had made on scraps of paper during the night. As he worked he had at his elbow Napoleon's Waterloo order, using it as a model despite the way that battle had turned out for the one who planned it. Since this would require considerable time — first the writing, then the copying and the distribution — Beauregard called Hardee and Bragg to his room to explain the march routes verbally; their corps would lead the way, and the written instructions could be delivered after they got started. As he spoke he drew a crude map on the top of a camp table, indicating distances and directions.

Two roads ran from Corinth up to Pittsburg. On the map they resembled a strung bow leaned sideways, curved side up, with the two armies at the top and bottom tips. The lower route, through Monterey, was the string; the upper route, through Mickey's, was the bow. Bragg and Breckinridge were to travel the string, Hardee and Polk the bow, in that order. Hardee was to reach Mickey's that night, bivouac, then at 3 a.m. pass on and form for battle in the fields beyond. Polk was to wait while Bragg marched up the road from Monterey and cleared the junction at Mickey's, then follow him into position, clearing the way for Breckinridge in turn. They were to regulate their columns so as not to delay each other, keeping their files well closed and the various elements properly spaced. So much for the march order; the battle order followed.

Beyond Mickey's, within charging distance of the enemy outposts, they were to form for battle in successive lines, Hardee across the front with one brigade from Bragg, who was to form a second line five hundred yards in rear. Polk and Breckinridge were to mass their corps to the left and right, a half-mile behind Bragg, so that when he went forward, following Hardee, Polk could spread out wide in his support, leaving Breckinridge in column as the general reserve. The flanks of the army, with the three lead corps extending individually across the entire front, rested on the creeks that hemmed Grant in. As they advanced, each line would thus support the one in front, and the reserve corps would feed troops from the rear toward those points where resistance turned out stiffest. The attack on the right was intended to move fastest, bearing generally left in a long curve, first along the watershed of Lick Creek and then down the west bank of the Tennessee, so as to sweep the Federals clear of the landing and drive them back against the boggy northward loop of Snake Creek, where they could be destroyed.

Today was Thursday, April 3. According to schedule, the troops would complete the twenty-mile approach march and be deployed for battle no later than midmorning tomorrow. But when the council broke up at 10 o'clock, already four hours past the starting time, and the generals dispersed to get their columns on the road, troops and wagons quickly snarled to a standstill, blocking the streets of Corinth. Polk at last got clear of the jam, but had to wait while Hardee doubled his column and took the lead. By then it was late afternoon, and Polk was held up till after sunset. When he stopped for the night he had covered a scant nine miles. Down on the lower road, Bragg's unwieldy column did no better. Manifestly, the schedule would have to be revised. Beauregard set it forward a whole day, intending now to be deployed in time to strike the Federals early Saturday morning.

But if Thursday had been like a bad dream, Friday was a nightmare. The march, which had seemed so easy to regulate on the flat, uncluttered table-top, turned out to be something quite different on the ground, which was neither flat nor uncluttered — nor, as it turned out, dry. The abrupt, thunderous showers of a Mississippi April broke over the winding column, and soon the wagon and artillery wheels had churned the roads into shin-deep mud. There were halts and unaccountable delays, times when the men had to trot to keep up, and times when they stood endlessly in the rain, waiting for the file ahead to stumble into motion. In their wake, the roadsides were littered with discarded equipment, overcoats and playing cards, bowie knives and Bibles. A more welcome delay was the rest halt given each regiment while its colonel read the commanding general's address, written in Corinth while they were assembling for the march.

> Soldiers of the Army of the Mississippi:
> I have put you in motion to offer battle to the invaders of your country. With the resolution and disciplined valor becoming men fighting, as you are, for all worth living or dying for, you can but march to a decisive victory over the agrarian mercenaries sent to subjugate and despoil you of your liberties, property, and honor. Remember the precious stake involved; remember the dependence of your mothers, your wives, your sisters, and your children on the result; remember the fair, broad, abounding land, the happy homes and the ties that would be desolated by your defeat.
> The eyes and hopes of eight millions of people rest upon you. You are expected to show yourselves worthy of your race and lineage; worthy of the women of the South, whose noble devotion in this war has never been exceeded in any time. With such incentives to brave deeds, and with the trust that God is with us, your generals will lead you confidently to the combat, assured of success.
> A. S. JOHNSTON, General

It was delivered in various styles, ranging from the oratorical, with flourishes, to the matter-of-fact, depending on the previous civil occupation of the reader. The troops cheered wildly or perfunctorily, depending on their degree of weariness and in part on how the address was read, then fell back into column on the muddy roads for more of the stop-and-go marching.

But the one who had it worst that day was Bragg. He too had made a late start out of Corinth, and the head of his oversized column did not reach Monterey, where it should have bivouacked the night before, until near midday. One of his divisions was lost somewhere in the rear, perhaps sidetracked, and he had had no word from Breckinridge at all. As a result, though Hardee and Polk were marching hard to make up for yesterday's wasted time, the latter was held up short of Mickey's, waiting for Bragg to clear the junction, and the former had no sooner got past it than he received a message asking him to call a halt so that Bragg's dragging column could close the expanding gap. Bragg was a tall, gangling man, a West Pointer and a Mexican War hero — "A little more grape, Captain Bragg," Zachary Taylor was supposed to have told him at Buena Vista, as every schoolboy knew (though what he really said was, "Captain, give 'em hell") — a native

North Carolinian, lately a Louisiana sugar planter, in his middle forties but looking ten years older because of chronic stomach trouble and a coarse gray-black beard which emphasized his heaviness of jaw and sternness of aspect; not that the latter needed emphasis, already having been rendered downright ferocious by the thick bushy eyebrows which grew in a continuous line across the bottom of his forehead. It galled him to have to send that message to Hardee, amounting as it did to an admission of being to blame for the delay; for he was a strict disciplinarian, and like most such he was quick to lose his temper when things went wrong.

Still jammed on the roads leading into and out of Mickey's, when they should have been moving into the final position where they would deploy for the attack tomorrow morning, the weary and bedraggled troops were caught that night in the same thunderstorm that attended the *Carondelet* on her run past Island Ten, just over a hundred miles away. All semblance of order dissolved under torrents of rain. When Johnston and Beauregard rode into Mickey's soon after sunrise, expecting to find the army arrayed for combat — they had left Corinth the day before and spent the night at Monterey — the rain had stopped and the sun was shining bright on the flooded fields, but the army was far from arrayed. In fact, most of it had not even arrived. Hardee was approximately in position, but he was waiting for the brigade from Bragg that would complete his line. By the time it got there, the sun was already high in the sky and Beauregard was fuming. He had cause. As they marched forward to file into line, the men began to worry about the dampness of the powder in their rifles; but instead of drawing the charges and reloading, they tested them by snapping the triggers; with the result that, within earshot of the Federal outposts, there was an intermittent banging up and down the columns, as rackety as a sizeable picket clash. Nor was that all. The returning sun having raised their spirits, the men began to tune up their rebel yells and practice marksmanship on birds and rabbits.

For two hours then, with Johnston and Beauregard standing by, Bragg continued to deploy the remainder of his corps — all but the rear division, which still had not arrived. When Johnston asked where it was, the harassed Bragg replied that it was somewhere back there; he was trying to locate it. Johnston waited, his impatience mounting, then took out his watch: 12.30. "This is perfectly puerile! This is not war!" he exclaimed, and set off down the road himself to look for the missing division. He found it wedged behind some of Polk's troops, who had not been willing to yield the right of way. The daylight hours were going fast. By the time Johnston got the road cleared and the last of Bragg's men passed to the front, his watch showed 2 o'clock. Polk's deployment used up another two hours, and Breckinridge, who had come up at last, was still to be brought forward. The shadows were getting longer every minute. It was not until about 4.30, however, that Johnston received the worst shock of all.

Riding forward he came upon a roadside conference between Beauregard and Polk and Bragg. The Creole's big sad bloodhound eyes were rimmed with angry red and his hands were fluttering as he spoke. He was upset: which was understandable, for it was already ten hours past the time when he expected to launch the attack. He favored canceling the whole movement and returning at once to Corinth. In his mind, surprise was everything, and what with the delay piled on the previous postponement, the constant tramping back and forth and the racket the men had been making, all chance for surprise had been forfeited. He knew this, he said, because at one point that afternoon he had heard a drum rolling, but when he sent to have it silenced, the messenger came back and reported that it could not be done; the drum was in the Union camp. Beauregard reasoned that if he could hear enemy drumtaps, there was small doubt that the Federals had heard the random firing and whooping in the Confederate columns. Besides, ten southern troopers had been captured in a cavalry clash the night before; surely by now they had been questioned, and one at least had talked.

"There is no chance for surprise," he ended angrily. "Now they will be intrenched to the eyes."

Johnston heard him out, then turned to Polk, his West Point roommate. The bishop disagreed. His troops were eager for battle; they had left Corinth on the way to a fight, he said in that deep, pulpit voice of his, and if they did not find one they would be as demoralized as if they had been whipped. Bragg said he felt the same way about it. While he was speaking Breckinridge rode up. Surprised that withdrawal was even being considered, he sided with Polk and Bragg, declaring that he would as soon be defeated as retire without a fight. Hardee was the only corps commander not present, but there was no doubt which side he would favor; he was already formed for battle, anxious to go forward. The vote was in, and Johnston made it official. There would be another delay, another postponement, but there would be no turning back.

"Gentlemen, we shall attack at daylight tomorrow," he said.

He told the corps commanders to complete the deployment and have the troops sleep on their arms in line of battle. Beauregard was protesting that Buell most likely had come up by now, bringing the Federal total to 70,000. But that made no difference either: not to Johnston, who had reached what he believed would be his hour of vindication after his long retreat. As he walked off he spoke to one of his staff. "I would fight them if they were a million," he said. "They can present no greater front between those two creeks than we can, and the more men they crowd in there, the worse we can make it for them."

While the army completed its deployment, the troops bedding

down so that when they woke in darkness they would already be in line for the dawn assault, the sun set clear and red beyond the tasseling oaks. There was a great stillness in the blue dusk, and then the stars came out, dimming the pale sickle moon already risen in the daylight sky. Mostly the men slept, for they were weary; but some stayed awake, huddled around fires built in holes in the ground to hide them. In part they stayed awake because of hunger, for it was a Confederate belief that rations carried lighter in the stomach than in a haversack, and they had consumed their three days' rations at the outset. The nearest of them could hear Yankee bugles, faint and far like foxhorns three fields off, sounding out of the dark woods where tomorrow's battle would be fought. "The elephant," veterans called combat, telling recruits the time had come to meet the elephant.

Strictly speaking, Beauregard was right, at least in part. Buell had arrived — that is, he slept that night on the outskirts of Savannah, intending to confer with Grant next morning — but with only one of his divisions, the others being scattered along twenty miles of the road back toward Nashville. They would arrive tomorrow and the next day. Grant, being informed of this, could go to bed that night rejoicing that things had worked out so well at last. He intended to send Buell's men upstream to Hamburg. The road from there to Corinth was a mile shorter than the one leading down from Pittsburg, and the two converged eight miles this side of the objective. Conditions thus were ideal for his intention, which was to attack as soon as Buell's army could be transferred to the west bank for coöperation with his own. Irksome as the delay had been, it had given him time to study the terrain and whip his reinforcements into shape, including even some seasoning clashes with rebel cavalry who ventured up to probe the rim of his camp at Pittsburg Landing.

The men themselves were feeling good by now, too, though at the outset they had had their doubts and discomforts. They had spent a rough first week clearing campsites, a week full of snow and sleet and a damp cold that went through flesh to bone. "The sunny South!" they jeered. All night, down the rows of tents, there was coughing, a racking uproar. Diarrhea was another evil, but they made jokes about that too; "the Tennessee quickstep," they called it, laughing ruefully on sick call when the surgeons advised them to try the application of red-hot pokers. Then suddenly the weather faired, and this was the sunny South indeed; even the rain was warm. By the end of March Grant was reporting, "The health of the troops is materially improving under the influence of a genial sun which has blessed us for a few days past."

He knew because he had been among them, making his daily commuter trip by steamboat from Savannah. Mostly, though, he kept his mind on the future, the offensive he would launch when Buell got there. He left the present — the defensive — largely to Sherman, who had kept busy all this time confirming his commander's high opinion of him. The red-haired Ohioan's green division was the largest in the army, and he had awarded it the position of honor, farthest from the landing. Three miles out, on the Corinth road, his headquarters tent was pitched alongside a rude log Methodist meeting-house called Shiloh Chapel. Two of his brigades were in line to the west of there, extending over toward Owl Creek, which flowed into Snake Creek where it turned northwest, a mile from the river, leaving Owl Creek to protect the army's right flank south of the junction. His third brigade was east of the chapel, and his fourth was on the far side of the position, beyond Prentiss's two brigades, whose camp was in line with his own. The others were three-brigade divisions: McClernand's just in rear of Sherman's, Hurlbut's and W. H. L. Wallace's well back toward the landing, and Lew Wallace's five miles north, beyond Snake Creek. It was not so much a tactical arrangement, designed for mutual support, as it was an arrangement for comfort and convenience, the various positions being selected because of the availability of water or open fields for drilling. In Sherman's mind, as in Grant's, the main concern was getting ready to move out for Corinth as soon as Buell arrived. He had long since got over his original concern, privately admitted, that the army was "in great danger here."

The same could not be said for all his officers. One in particular, the colonel of the 53d Ohio, had sounded the alarm so often that his soldiers were jeered at for belonging to what was called the Long Roll regiment. High-strung and jumpy — like Sherman himself in the old days — he was given to imagining that the whole rebel army was just outside his tent flap. During the past few days his condition had grown worse. Friday, April 4, he lost a picket guard of seven men, gobbled up by grayback cavalry, and when he advanced a company to develop the situation they ran into scattered firing and came back. All day Saturday he was on tenterhooks, communicating his alarm to Sherman. That afternoon he piled on the last straw by sending word to headquarters that a large force of the enemy was moving on the camp. Sherman mounted and rode out to confront him. While the colonel told excitedly of the hordes of rebels out there in the brush, Sherman sat with his mouth clamped down, looking into the empty woods. At last the man stopped talking. Sherman sat glaring down at him, then jerked the reins to turn his horse toward camp. "Take your damned regiment back to Ohio," he said, snapping the words. "Beauregard is not such a fool as to leave his base of operations and attack us in ours. There is no enemy nearer than Corinth."

So he said, adding the final remark to sharpen the sting of the rebuke, though actually he knew better. This was but one of several such clashes, including one the previous evening in which ten rebel prisoners were taken, and just this morning he had notified Grant: "The enemy has cavalry in our front, and I think there are two regiments of infantry and one battery of artillery about 2 miles out. I will send you 10 prisoners of war and a report of last night's affair in a few minutes."

There was a need for frequent reports, for Grant would not be coming up to visit the camps today. He had sprained his ankle during the violent thunderstorm the night before, when his horse slipped and fell on his leg. The soft ground had saved him from serious injury, but his boot had had to be cut off because of the swelling and he was limping painfully on crutches. The first dispatch from Sherman had opened, "All is quiet along my lines," and presently there was another, apparently sent after he got back from administering the stinging rebuke to the Ohio colonel: "I have no doubt that nothing will occur today more than some picket firing. The enemy is saucy, but got the worst of it yesterday, and will not press our pickets far.... I do not apprehend anything like an attack on our position."

The prisoners, if sent, went unquestioned. What could they possibly have to say that would interest a man who had already made up his mind that if he was to have a battle he would have to march his soldiers down to Corinth and provoke it? Sustained in his opinion by reports such as these two from Sherman, Grant refused to be disconcerted by incidentals. Besides, the staff officer who was best at conducting interrogations was at Hamburg, inspecting the campsite selected for Buell's army. No time was to be lost now, for the lead division had arrived at noon, along with a note from Buell: "I shall be in Savannah tomorrow with one, perhaps two, divisions. Can I meet you there?" The note was dated yesterday; "tomorrow" meant today. But Grant either did not observe the heading (another incidental) or else he was in no hurry. "Your dispatch received," he replied. "I will be there to meet you tomorrow." — meaning Sunday.

Ever since his run-in with Halleck, regarding the alleged infrequency of his reports, he had kept the St Louis wire humming. Before he went to bed tonight in the fine big house on the bluff at Savannah, with nothing to fret him but the pain in his swollen ankle, he wrote a letter informing his chief that Buell's lead division had arrived; the other two were close on its heels and would get there tomorrow and the next day. He told him also of yesterday's picket clash. "I immediately went up," he said, "but found all quiet." Then he added: "I have scarcely the faintest idea of an attack (general one) being made upon us, but will be prepared should such a thing take place."

Next morning at breakfast he heard a distant thunder from the south. The guns of Shiloh were jarring the earth.

★ ★ ★

War Means Fighting . . .

Until then, Beauregard had not given up urging a withdrawal. Between dawn and sunup, wearing for luck the jaunty red flat-topped cap he had worn at Manassas, he came to Johnston's overnight camp for a last-minute plea that the attack plan be abandoned. He looked fresh and rested after a sound sleep in his ambulance — his personal tent had been misplaced on the march — but he had lost none of yesterday's conviction that the assault could not succeed. In fact he was more than ever convinced that all chance for surprise was gone. He had heard Federal bands playing marches in the night and there had been bursts of cheering from the direction of the landing. This meant only one thing, he said: Buell had come up, urged forward by the alerted Grant, and now there were 70,000 men in the Union camp, intrenched and expectant, waiting for the Confederates to walk into the trap.

The reply came not from Johnston, who stood with a cup of coffee in his hands, sipping from it as he heard him out, but from the army itself. The Creole was caught in midsentence by a rattle of musketry from dead ahead, a curious ripping sound like tearing canvas. Staff officers looked in that direction, then back at Johnston, who was handing the half-empty cup to an orderly. "The battle has opened, gentlemen," he said. "It is too late to change our dispositions." Beauregard mounted and rode away; the argument was no longer a matter for words. Johnston swung onto his horse and sat there for a long moment, his face quite grave. Then he twitched the reins, and as the big bay thoroughbred began to walk toward the sound of firing, swelling now across the front, the general turned in the saddle and spoke to his staff: "Tonight we will water our horses in the Tennessee River."

The opening shots had been fired ahead of schedule because one of Prentiss's brigade commanders, sleepless and uneasy in the hours before dawn, had sent a three-company reconnaissance out to explore the woods to his front. Encountering a portion of Hardee's skirmish line, which had not yet gone forward, they mistook it for a scouting party and attacked with spirit, driving the skirmishers back on the main body. Repulsed in turn by heavy volleys, they fell back to give the alarm that the enemy was moving in strength against the Federal position. Prentiss thus was warned of what was coming before it got there, and turned his green division out to meet the shock.

Sherman too was warned, but took no heed because the alarm was sounded by the same colonel he had rebuked for crying wolf the day before. A man had stumbled out of a thicket into the Ohio camp, holding a wound and crying, "Get in line! The rebels are coming!" A captain who went to investigate quickly returned shouting, "The rebs are out there thicker than fleas on a dog's back!" But when the colonel sent a courier to inform Sherman, word came back: "You must be badly scared over there."

Presently, though, riding forward with an orderly to where the colonel was shakily getting his men into line, he saw for himself the Confederates advancing across a large field in front, the skirmishers holding their rifles slantwise like quail hunters and the main body massed heavily behind them. The sun, which had risen fast in a cloudless sky — "the sun of Austerlitz," Southerners called it, seeing in this a Napoleonic omen — flashed on their bayonets as they brought their rifles up to fire. "My God, we're attacked!" Sherman cried, convinced at last as the volley crashed and his orderly fell dead beside him. "Hold your position; I'll support you!" he shouted, and spurred away to send up reinforcements. But: "This is no place for us," the colonel wailed, seeing his general head for the rear, and went over and lay face-down behind a fallen tree. His men were wavering, firing erratically at the attackers. When the next enemy volley crashed, the colonel jumped up from behind the tree; "Retreat! Save yourselves!" he cried, and set the example by taking off rearward at a run.

Most of his men went with him, believing they knew a sensible order when they heard one, but enough stayed to give Sherman time to warn the brigades on his other flank to drop their Sunday breakfast preparations and brace themselves for the assault. They formed in haste along the ridge where their tents were pitched, looking out over a valley choked with vines and brambles, and began to fire into the wave of gray that was surging out of the woods on the far side. Green as they were, they held their ground against four successive charges, firing steadily until the fifth swept up the slope, then gave way in tolerable good order to take up a second position farther back. The 6th Mississippi, for one, could testify to the accuracy of their fire; for it started across that valley with 425 men and reached the tented ridge with just over 100; the rest lay dead or wounded among the brambles. So thick they lay, the dead of this and the other four regiments in those charges, that one observer remarked that he could have walked across that valley without touching his feet to the ground; "a pavement of dead men," he called it.

Prentiss was fighting as doggedly on the left, and McClernand had marched to the sound of guns, filling the gap between the two divisions, so that the three were more or less in line, resisting stubbornly. All three were leaking men to the rear, the faint-hearted who sought safety back at the landing under the bluff, but the ones who stayed were determined to yield nothing except under pressure that proved itself irresistible. By the time Sherman's soldiers got settled in their second position, waiting for what came next, they had the feel of being veterans. Whatever came next could not possibly be worse than what had gone before, and having their commander move among them added to their confidence. He had been hit twice already, but gave no sign of even considering leaving the field. The first time was in the hand; he wrapped it in a handkerchief and thrust it into his breast, never taking his eyes off the enemy. The other bullet clipped a shoulder strap, nicking the skin, but that did not seem to bother him much either. When a headquarters aide came riding up to ask how things were going, he found Sherman leaning against a tree, propped on his uninjured hand, watching the skirmishers. "Tell Grant if he has any men to spare I can use them," he said, still narrow-eyed. "If not, I will do the best I can. We are holding them pretty well just now. Pretty well; but it's hot as hell."

By midmorning Grant himself was at his lieutenant's elbow, amid the bursting shells and whistling bullets. Brought to his feet by the rumble of guns from the south, he had left the breakfast table and gone aboard his steamer at the wharf below the mansion, pausing only long enough to send two notes. One was to Buell, canceling their meeting in Savannah, and the other was to Brigadier General William Nelson, whose division had arrived the day before, directing him to "move your entire command to the river opposite Pittsburg." On the way upstream — it was now about 8.30 — he found Lew Wallace waiting for him on the jetty at Crump's. The firing sounded louder; Pittsburg was definitely under attack, but Grant still did not know but what a second attack might be aimed in this direction. Without stopping the boat he called out to Wallace as he went by, "General, get your troops under arms and have them ready to move at a moment's notice." Wallace shouted back that he had already done so. Grant nodded and went on.

When he docked and rode his horse up the bluff from the landing, a crutch strapped to the saddle like a carbine, the tearing rattle of musketry and the steady booming of cannon told him the whole trouble was right here in the three-sided box where his main camp had been established. Wounded men and skulkers were stumbling rearward, seeking defilade, and beyond them the hysterical quaver of the rebel yell came through the crash of gunfire and the deeper-throated shouts of his own soldiers. Grant's first act was to establish a straggler line, including a battery with its guns trained on the road leading out of the uproar. Then he went forward to where W. H. L. Wallace and Hurlbut had formed ranks and by now were sending reinforcements to the hard-pressed divisions on the far edge of the fight. The situation was critical, but Grant kept as calm as he had done at Donelson in a similar predicament. This time, though, he had reserves, and he sent for them at once. A summons went to Lew Wallace, five miles away, instructing him to join the embattled army. Another went to Nelson, presumably already toiling across the boggy stretch of land between Savannah and the river bank opposite Pittsburg, urging him to "hurry up your command as fast as possible."

By 10 o'clock he was up front with Sherman. One of the Ohioan's brigades had disintegrated under fire, but the other two were resisting heavy pressure against their second position, half a mile back from the ridge where their tents were pitched. He said his biggest worry was that his men would run out of ammunition, but Grant assured him that this had been provided for; more was on the way. Satisfied that Sherman could look out for himself, the army commander then visited McClernand, fighting as hard in rear of Shiloh Chapel, and finally Prentiss, whose division had been repulsed by the fury of the initial onslaught, but in falling back across the open field had come upon an eroded wagon trail which wound along the edge of some heavy woods on the far side. They had got down into the shallow natural trench of this sunken road to make a stand, and that was what they were doing when Grant arrived. In fact they were doing a thorough job of it, dropping the Confederates in windrows as they charged across the fields. Approving of this execution, Grant told Prentiss to "maintain that position at all hazards." Prentiss said he would try.

He not only tried, he did maintain that position against repeated headlong charges delivered without apparent concern for loss. Elsewhere, however, conditions were much worse. At noon, when Grant returned to his headquarters near the rim of the bluff, he found the fugitives streaming rearward thicker than ever, through and past the straggler line, white-faced and unmindful of the officers who tried to rally them. Bad news awaited him: Sherman and McClernand had been forced back still farther. Both were retiring sullenly, fighting as they did so, but if either division broke into a rout, the rebels would come whooping down on the landing and the battle would be over. W. H. L. Wallace and Hurlbut had committed all their troops, and nothing had been heard from Lew Wallace, who should have completed his five-mile march before now, nor from Nelson across the river. There was no reserve at hand to block a breakthrough. In desperation Grant sent two staff officers beyond Snake Creek to hurry Wallace along and a third across the Tennessee with a note for Nelson, worded to show the urgent need for haste: "If you will get upon the field, leaving all your baggage on the east bank of the river, it will be a move to our advantage, and possibly save the day to us. The rebel force is estimated at over 100,000 men."

Beauregard had taken over the log church called Shiloh, and from this headquarters he performed for the army commander the service the other Johnston had performed for him at Manassas, exercising control of the rear area and forwarding reinforcements to those points where additional strength was needed. Thus Johnston was left free to move up and down the line of battle, encouraging the troops, and this he did. Some he sought to steady by speaking calmly. "Look along your guns, and fire low," he told them. Others he sought to inspirit with fiercer words: "Men of Arkansas, they say you boast of your prowess with the bowie knife. Today you wield a nobler weapon: the bayonet. Employ it well!" Whichever he did, or whether he did neither, but merely rode among them, tall and handsome on his tall, handsome horse, the men cheered at the sight of their commander exposing himself to the dangers he was requiring them to face. This was indeed his hour of vindication.

His men swept forward, overrunning the enemy's front-line camps and whooping with elation as they took potshots at the backs of fleeing Yankees. Where resistance stiffened, as along the ridge where Sherman's tents were pitched, they matched valor against determination and paid in blood for the resultant gain. Not that there were no instances of flinching at the cost. An Arkansas major reported angrily that a Tennessee regiment in front of his own "broke and ran back, hallooing 'Retreat, retreat,' which being mistaken by our own men for orders of their commander, a retreat was made by them and some confusion ensued." No sooner was this corrected than the same thing happened again, only this time the major had an even more shameful occurrence to report: "They were in such great haste to get behind us that they ran over and trampled in the mud our brave color-bearer." There were other, worse confusions. The Orleans Guard battalion, the elite organization with Beauregard's name on its muster roll, came into battle wearing dress-blue uniforms, which drew the fire of the Confederates they were marching to support. Promptly they returned the volley, and when a horrified staff officer came galloping up to tell them they were shooting at their friends: "I know it," the Creole colonel replied. "But dammit, sir, we fire on everybody who fires on us!"

Such mishaps and mistakes could be corrected or even overlooked by the high command. More serious were the evils resulting from straggling, caused mainly by hunger and curiosity. When some Northerners later denied that they had been surprised at Shiloh, a Texan who had scalded his arm in snatching a joint of meat from a bubbling pot as he charged through one of the Federal camps replied that if Grant's army had not been surprised it certainly had "the most devoted mess crews in the history of warfare." Sunday breakfasts, spread out on tables or still cooking over campfires, were more than the hungry Confederates could resist. Many sat down, then and there, to gorge themselves on white bread and sweet coffee. Others explored the Yankee tents, foraging among the departed soldiers' belongings, including their letters, which they read with interest to find out what northern girls were like. Hundreds, perhaps thousands, were lost thus to their comrades forging ahead, and this also served to blunt the impetus of the attack which in its early stages had rolled headlong over whatever got in its way.

Most serious of all, though, were the flaws that developed when the attack plan was exposed to prolonged strain. Neatly efficient as the thing had looked on paper, it was turning out quite otherwise on the rugged plateau with its underbrush and gullies and its clusters of stubborn blue defenders. Attacking as directed — three corps in line from creek to creek, one behind another, each line feeding its components piecemeal into the line ahead — brigades and regiments and even companies had become so intermingled that unit commanders lost touch with their men and found themselves in charge of strangers who never before had heard the sound of their voices. Coördination was lost. By noon, when the final reserves had been committed, the army was no longer a clockwork aggregation of corps and divisions; it was a frantic mass of keyed-up men crowded into an approximate battle formation to fight a hundred furious skirmishes strung out in a crooked line. Confusing as all this was to those who fought thus to the booming accompaniment of two hundred guns, it was perhaps even more confusing to those who were trying to direct them. And indeed how should they have understood this thing they had been plunged into as if into a cauldron of pure hell? For this was the first great modern battle. It was Wilson's Creek and Manassas rolled together, quadrupled, and compressed into an area smaller than either. From the inside it resembled Armageddon.

Attempting to regain control, the corps commanders divided the front into four sectors, Hardee and Polk on the left, Bragg and Breckinridge on the right. Coördination was lacking, however, and all the attacks were frontal. Besides, compliance with Johnston's original instructions — "Every effort will be made to turn the left flank of the enemy, so as to cut off his line of retreat to the Tennessee River and throw him back on [Snake] Creek, where he will be forced to surrender" — was being frustrated by Prentiss, who stood fast along the sunken road. "It's a hornets' nest in there!" the gray-clad soldiers cried, recoiling from charge after charge against the place. When Sherman and McClernand gave way, taking up successive rearward positions, the Confederate left outstripped the right, which was stalled in front of the Hornets Nest, and thus presented Johnston with the reverse of what he wanted. He rode toward the far right to correct this, carrying in his right hand a small tin cup which he had picked up in a captured camp. Seeing a lieutenant run out of one of the tents with an armload of Yankee souvenirs, Johnston told him sternly: "None of that, sir. We are not here for plunder." Then, observing that he had hurt the young man's feelings, which after all was a poor reward for the gallantry shown in the capture, by way of apology he leaned down without dismounting and took the tin cup off a table. "Let this be my share of the spoils today," he said, and from then on he had used it instead of a sword to direct the battle. He used it so now, his index finger hooked through the loop of the handle, as he rode toward the right where his advance had stalled.

At this end of the battle line, on the far flank of the Hornets Nest, there was a ten-acre peach orchard in full bloom. Hurlbut had a heavy line of infantry posted among the trees, supported by guns whose smoke lazed and swirled up through the branches sheathed in pink, and a bright rain of petals fell fluttering like confetti in the sunlight as bullets clipped the blossoms overhead. Arriving just after one of Breckinridge's brigades had recoiled from a charge against the orchard, Johnston saw that the officers were having trouble getting the troops in line to go forward again. "Men! they are stubborn; we must use the bayonet," he told them. To emphasize his meaning he rode among them and touched the points of their bayonets with the tin cup. "These must do the work," he said. When the line had formed, the soldiers were still hesitant to reënter the smoky uproar. So Johnston did what he had been doing all that morning, all along the line of battle. Riding front and center, he stood in the stirrups, removed his hat, and called back over his shoulder: "I will lead you!" As he touched his spurs to the flanks of his horse, the men surged forward, charging with him into the sheet of flame which blazed to meet them there among the blossoms letting fall their bright pink rain.

This time the charge was not repulsed; Hurlbut's troops gave way, abandoning the orchard to the cheering men in gray. Johnston came riding back, a smile on his lips, his teeth flashing white beneath his mustache. There were rips and tears in his uniform and one bootsole had been cut nearly in half by a minie bullet. He shook his foot so the dangling leather flapped. "They didn't trip me up that time," he said, laughing. His battle blood was up; his eyes were shining. Presently, however, as the general sat watching his soldiers celebrate their capture of the orchard and its guns, Governor Isham Harris of Tennessee, who had volunteered to serve as his aide during the battle, saw him reel in the saddle.

"General — are you hurt?" he cried.

"Yes, and I fear seriously," Johnston said.

None of the rest of his staff was there, the general having sent them off on various missions. Riding with one arm across Johnston's shoulders to prevent his falling, Harris guided the bay into a nearby ravine, where he eased the pale commander to the ground and began unfastening his clothes in an attempt to find the wound. He had no luck until he noticed the right boot full of blood, and then he found it: a neat hole drilled just above the hollow of the knee, marking where the femoral artery had been severed. This called for a knowledge of tourniquets, but the governor knew nothing of such things. The man who knew most about them, Johnston's staff physician, had been ordered by the general to attend to a group of Federal wounded he encountered on his way to the far right. When the doctor protested, Johnston cut him off: "These men were our enemies a moment ago. They are our prisoners now. Take care of them." So Harris alone was left to do what he could to staunch the bright red flow of blood.

He could do little. Brandy might help, he thought, but when he poured some into the hurt man's mouth it ran back out again. Presently a colonel, Johnston's chief of staff, came hurrying into the ravine. But he could do nothing either. He knelt down facing the general. "Johnston, do you know me? Johnston, do you know me?" he kept asking, over and over, nudging the general's shoulder as he spoke.

But Johnston did not know him. Johnston was dead.

It was now about 2.30. When the command passed to Beauregard — who in point of fact had been exercising it all along, in a general way, from his headquarters at Shiloh Chapel — his first order was that news of Johnston's death was to be kept from the men, lest they become disheartened before completing the destruction of the northern army. There would be no let-up; the attack was to continue all along the line, particularly against the Hornets Nest, whose outer flank was threatened now by the Confederates who had flung Hurlbut's men gunless out of the orchard and taken their place. After a lull, which allowed for the shifting of troops to strengthen the blow, the line was ready to go forward. A dozen separate full-scale assaults had been launched against the sunken road, each one over a thickening carpet of dead and wounded. All twelve had failed; but this one would not fail. Pressure alone not having been enough, now pressure was to be combined with blasting. At point-blank range, with Beauregard's approval, Dan Ruggles had massed 62 guns to rake the place with canister and grape.

When those guns opened, clump by clump, then all together, blending their separate crashes into one continuous roar, it was as if the Hornets Nest exploded, inclosing its defenders in a smoky, flame-cracked din of flying clods, splintered trees, uprooted brush, and whirring metal. Elsewhere on the field that morning a wounded soldier, sent to the rear by his company commander, had soon returned, shouting to be heard above the racket: "Captain, give me a gun! This durn fight aint got any rear!" Presently this was quite literally true for Prentiss, who held fast along the sunken road. On the flanks, the men of Hurlbut and W. H. L. Wallace scrambled backward to get from under the crash. The line was bent into a horseshoe. Then Wallace fell, cut down as he tried to rally his men, and they gave way entirely, running headlong. Hurlbut's followed suit. Only Prentiss's troops remained steadfast along the sunken road, flanked and then surrounded. The horseshoe became an iron hoop as the Confederates, pursuing Hurlbut and the remnants of Wallace around both flanks of Prentiss, met in his rear and sealed him off.

He could hear them yelling back there, triumphant, but he fought on, obedient to his strict instructions to "maintain that position at all hazards." The dead lay thick. Every minute they lay thicker. Still he fought. By 5.30 — two long hours after Ruggles' guns began their furious cannonade — further resistance became futile, and Prentiss knew it. He had the cease-fire sounded and surrendered his 2200 survivors, well under half the number he had started with that morning. Sherman and McClernand on the right, and Hurlbut to a lesser degree on the left, had saved their divisions by falling back each time the pressure reached a certain intensity. Prentiss had lost his by standing fast: lost men, guns, colors, and finally the position itself: lost all, in fact, but honor. Yet he had saved far more in saving that. Sherman and McClernand had saved their divisions by retreating, but Prentiss had saved Grant by standing fast.

Beauregard saw it otherwise. During twelve hours of fighting, in addition to much other booty found in the captured camps, his army had taken 23 cannon, exclusive of those surrendered by Prentiss, and flushed the Northerners from every position they had chosen to try for a stand. The Hornets Nest, if the toughest of these, was merely one more in a series of continuing successes. Now that the sunken road lay in rear of the advance, the shortened line could be strengthened for the final go-for-broke assault that would shove what was left of Grant's army over the bluff and into the Tennessee. So he thought, at any rate; until he tried it. On the left, Hardee and Polk were pecking away at Sherman and McClernand, but the attacks were not delivered with spirit or conviction. Too many of their men had died or straggled, and those who stayed were near exhaustion. On the right, where more could be expected in the wake of the recent collapse, Bragg and Breckinridge fared even worse. Their casualties had been about as high and the number of stragglers was even higher; hundreds stayed behind to gawk at the captured thousands, including one real live Yankee general, who came marching out of the Hornets Nest under guard. Two of Bragg's brigades — or the remnants — tried an assault on the left flank of the Federals, who were crowded into a semicircular position along the road that led from the landing to the bridge that spanned Snake Creek. However, it was delivered across a ravine knee-deep in backwater, and when the weary troops emerged on the far side they were met by massed volleys almost as heavy as those that had shattered Prentiss. They ran back, scrambling for cover, and the long day's fight was over.

The sun was down. Beauregard merely made the halt official when he sent couriers riding through the gathering twilight with orders for the attacks to be suspended and the men brought back to rest for the completion of their work tomorrow morning. Much of the Yankee army might escape under cover of darkness, but it could not be helped. The lesson of Manassas was repeated. For green troops, victory could be as destructive of effective organization as defeat, and even more exhausting. As the men withdrew, a patter of rain began to sound. The rumble of heavy guns, fired intermittently from beyond the bluff, was

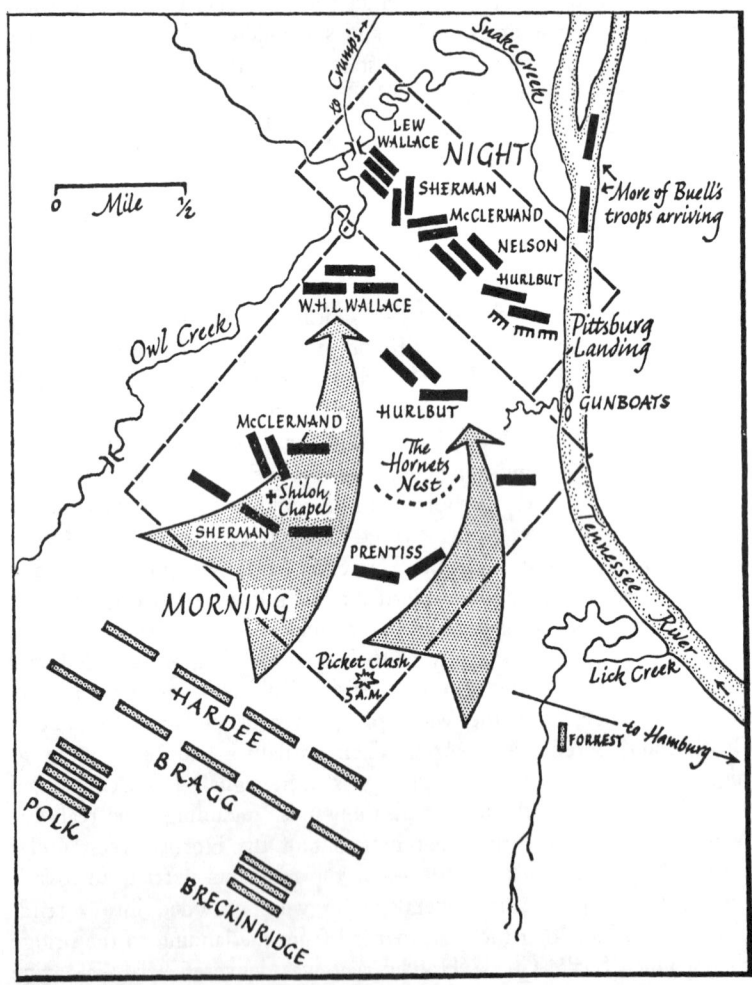

mixed with peals of thunder. Lightning flashed; the rain fell harder. A hundred miles northwest, the *Pittsburg's* crew was thankful for the storm as they prepared to make their run past Island Ten; the *Carondelet* was waiting. Here on the battlefield which took its name from the log church called Shiloh — interpreted by Bible scholars to mean "the place of peace" — those who could found shelter in the Federal camps and had their dreams invaded by the drum of rain on canvas. Others slept in the open, where the rain fell alike on the upturned faces of the dead and of those who slept among them, inured by having seen so much of death that day already, or else just made indifferent by exhaustion.

* * *

Confidence south of the battle line, that when the attack was renewed tomorrow the Federals would be driven into the river, was matched by confidence north of it, at least on the part of the northern commander, that the reverse would rather be the case. Surrounded by his staff Grant sat on horseback just in rear of the guns whose massed volleys had shattered the final rebel assault. His army had been driven two miles backward; one division had surrendered en masse; another had been decimated, its commander killed, and the other three were badly shaken, bled to half their strength. So that when one of the staff officers asked if the prospect did not appear "gloomy," it must have seemed an understatement to the rest; but not to Grant. "Not at all," he said. "They can't force our lines around these batteries tonight. It is too late. Delay counts everything with us. Tomorrow we shall attack them with fresh troops and drive them, of course."

Fresh troops were the answer, and he had them; Buell's men were arriving as he spoke. By morning, 20,000 of them would have climbed the bluff in the wake of Nelson's lead brigade, which had been ferried across from the opposite bank in time to assist in repulsing the attack against the fifty guns assembled on the left. The navy, too, was in support and had a share in wrecking the last assault. Though all the ironclads were at Island Ten, two wooden gunboats were at Pittsburg, anchored where a creek ran out of the last-ditch ravine into the river, and thus were able to throw their shells into the ranks of the Confederates as they charged. Nor was that all. As twilight deepened into dusk, Lew Wallace at last came marching across Snake Creek bridge to station his division on the right flank of the army. He had marched toward what he thought was such a junction as soon as he received Grant's first order, but then had had to countermarch for the river road when he learned that the flank had been thrown back near the landing. Five hours behind schedule, he got jaundiced looks on arrival, but his 6000 soldiers, mostly Donelson veterans, were no less welcome for being late. Combined with Buell's troops and the survivors of the all-day fight, they meant that Grant would go into battle on the second day with more men than he had had at dawn of the first. Then too, well over half of them would be unworn by fighting: whereas the Confederates would not only have been lessened by their casualties, but would most likely not have recovered from the weariness that dropped so many of them in their tracks as soon as the firing stopped.

Grant had another sizeable reserve — 6000 to 12,000 men, depending on various estimates — but he did not include them in his calculations. These were the skulkers, fugitives who took shelter along the river bank while the battle raged on the plateau overhead. Every man on the field had come up this way, debarking from the transports, so that when the going got too rough they remembered that high bluff, reared up one hundred feet tall between the landing and the fighting, and made for it as soon as their minds were more on safety than on honor. Some were trying to cadge rides on the ferries plying back and forth; others, more enterprising, paddled logs and jerry-built rafts in an attempt to reach the safety of the eastern bank. Still others were content to remain where they were, calling out to Buell's men as they came ashore: "We are whipped! Cut to pieces! You'll catch it! *You*'ll see!" Nelson, a six-foot five-inch three-hundred-pound former navy lieutenant, lost his temper at the sight. "They were insensible to shame and sarcasm," he later declared, "for I tried both; and, indignant of such poltroonery, I asked permission to fire on the knaves." However, the colonel who commanded the fuming general's lead brigade was more sickened than angered by the display. "Such looks of terror, such confusion, I never saw before, and do not wish to see again," he recorded in his diary.

Perhaps like the colonel Grant preferred to leave them where they were, out of contact with the men who had stood and fought today or were expected to stand and fight tomorrow. Fear was a highly contagious emotion, and even if threats or cajolery could have herded them back up the bluff, they would most likely run again as soon as the minies began whizzing. Perhaps, too, he saw them as a reproach, a sign that his army had been surprised and routed, at least to this extent, because its commander had left it unintrenched, green men to the front, and had taken so few precautions against an enemy who, according to him, was "heartily tired" of fighting. At any rate he allotted the skulkers no share in his plans for tomorrow. Nor did he return to the fine big house nine miles downriver, or even seek shelter in one of the steamboat cabins. After inspecting his battle line — his four divisions would take the right, Buell's three the left — he wrapped himself in a poncho and lay down under a large oak to get some sleep. The rain had already begun, however, and presently it fell in torrents, dripping through the branches to add to the discomfort of his aching ankle. Unable to sleep, he wandered off to take refuge in a cabin on the bluff. But that would not do either. The surgeons had set up a field hospital there and were hard at work, bloody past the elbows. Driven out by the screams of the wounded and the singing of the bone-saws, Grant returned to his oak and got to sleep at last, despite the rain and whatever twinges he was feeling in his ankle and his conscience.

He had an insomniac counterpart beyond the line of battle. But Bedford Forrest's ankle and conscience were intact; his sleeplessness proceeded from entirely different causes. His regiment had been assigned to guard the Lick Creek fords, but after some hours of hearing the guns he had crossed over on his own initiative and claimed a share in the fighting. It stopped soon after sundown, but not Forrest. Out on a scout, he reached the lip of the bluff, south of the landing, and saw Buell's reinforcements coming ashore. For Forrest this meant just one thing: the Confederates must either stage a night attack or else get off that tableland before the Federals charged them in the morning. Unable to locate Beauregard, he went from camp to camp, telling of what he had seen and urging an attack, but few of the brigadiers even knew where their men were sleeping, and those who did were unwilling to take the responsibility of issuing such an order. At last he found Hardee, who informed him that the instructions already given could not be changed; the cavalryman was to return to his troops and "keep up a strong and vigilant picket line." Forrest stomped off, swearing. "If the enemy comes on us in the morning, we'll be whipped like hell," he said.

Unlocated and uninformed — he slept that night in Sherman's bed, near Shiloh Chapel — Beauregard not only did not suspect that Buell had arrived, he had good reason for thinking that he would not be there at all, having received from a colonel in North Alabama — it was Ben Hardin Helm, one of Lincoln's Confederate brothers-in-law — a telegram informing him that Buell had changed his line of march and now was moving toward Decatur. The Creole went to bed content with what had been done today and confident that Grant's destruction would be completed tomorrow. Before turning in, he sent a wire to Richmond announcing that the army had scored "a complete victory, driving the enemy from every position."

His chief of staff, sharing an improvised bed in the adjoining headquarters tent with the captured Prentiss, was even more ebullient, predicting that the northern army would surrender as soon as the battle was resumed. The distinguished captive, accepting his predicament with such grace as became a former Virginian, did not agree with his host's prognostication; nor was he reticent in protest. "You gentlemen have had your way today," he said, "but it will be very different tomorrow. You'll see. Buell will effect a junction with Grant tonight and we'll turn the tables on you in the morning." No such thing, the Confederate declared, and showed him the telegram from Helm. Prentiss was unimpressed. "You'll see," he said.

Outside in the rain, those who had been too weary to look for shelter, along with those who had looked without success, got what sleep they could, in spite of the 11-inch shells fired two every fifteen minutes by the gunboats. Their fuzes describing red parabolas across the starless velvet of the night, they came down steeply, screaming, to explode among the sleepers and the wounded of both sides; "wash pots" and "lampposts," the awed soldiers called the big projectiles. All night the things continued to fall on schedule. Dawn grayed the east, and presently from the direction of the sunrise came the renewed clatter of musketry, the crack and boom of field artillery. As it swelled quickly to a roar, Prentiss sat bolt upright on the pallet of captured blankets inside Sherman's headquarters tent, grinning at his Confederate bedmate. "There is Buell!" he cried. "Didn't I tell you so?"

★ ★ ★

It was Buell, just as Prentiss said. His other two divisions, under Brigadier Generals Alexander D. McCook and Thomas L. Crittenden — the latter being the brother of the Confederate corps commander who had been relieved on the eve of battle — had come up in the night; he was attacking. Grant's four divisions — one hale and whole, if somewhat shamefaced over its roundabout march the day before, the others variously battered and depleted, but quite willing — took up the fire on the right, and at 7 o'clock the general sent a message to the gunboats. They were to cease their heavy caliber bombardment; the army was going forward.

Grant's orders, sent as soon as he rose at dawn from his sleep beneath the dripping oak, directed his generals to "advance and recapture our original camps." At first it was easy enough. The rebels, having broken contact the night before, were caught off balance and gave ground rapidly, surprised to find the tables turned by unexpected pressure. Wallace, Sherman, and McClernand, with Hurlbut's remnants in reserve, pushed forward to the vicinity of McClernand's camp before they ran into heavy artillery fire and halted, as Sherman said, "patiently waiting for the sound of General Buell's advance." They had not long to wait: Buell's men were taking their baptism of fire in stride. One Indiana colonel, dissatisfied with signs of shakiness when his men encountered resistance — Sherman, who was looking on, referred to it as "the severest musketry fire I ever heard" (which would make it severe indeed, after all he had been through yesterday) — halted them, then and there, and put them briskly through the manual of arms, "which they executed," he later reported, "as if on the parade ground." Considerably steadied, the Hoosiers resumed their advance. By noon, Buell's men had cleared the peach orchard on the left and Grant's were approaching Shiloh Chapel on the right. There the resistance stiffened.

After the initial shock of finding Buell on the field after all, Beauregard recovered a measure of his aplomb and went about the task of preparing his men to receive instead of deliver an attack. This was by no means easy, not only because of the gallant rivalry which urged the two armies of Westerners forward against him, but also because his own troops had scattered badly about the blasted field in their search for food and shelter the night before. Polk, in fact, had misunderstood the retirement order and marched his survivors all the way back to their pre-battle camp on the Corinth road. Improvising as best he could, the Creole assigned Hardee the right, Breckinridge the center, and Bragg the left. When Polk returned, belatedly, he put him in between the last two. It was touch and go, however. Like Johnston, he found it necessary to set a spirited example for his men. Twice he seized the colors of wavering regiments and led them forward. Reproved for rashness by a friend who doubtless recalled what had happened to Johnston yesterday, Beauregard replied: "The order now must be 'Follow,' not 'Go'!"

At one point that afternoon he received a shock that was followed in quick succession by a hopeful surge of elation and a corresponding droop of disappointment. He noticed in some woods along his front a body of troops dressed in what appeared to be shiny white silk uniforms. At first he thought they were Federals who had breached his line, but when he saw that they were firing north, it occurred to him — though he had long since given up the notion that they could possibly arrive on time — that they might be the vanguard of Van Dorn's 15,000 reinforcements, hurried east by rail from Memphis. Certainly there were no such uniforms in the Army of the Mississippi, while there was no telling what outlandish garb the Elkhorn Tavern veterans might wear. Presently, however, a staff officer, sent to investigate, returned with the explanation. They were the general's own Orleans Guard battalion, who had turned their dress blue jackets wrong side out to put an end to being fired on by their friends. Yesterday they had startled the defenders of the Hornets Nest by charging thus with the white silk linings of their coats exposed; "graveyard clothes," the Federals had called them.

The Confederates had their backs up and were holding well along the ridge where Sherman's tents were pitched; today as yesterday Shiloh Chapel was army headquarters. But the men were bone-weary. Clearly they had no chance of defeating the reinforced Federals now applying pressure all along the line, the breaking of a single link of which might prove disastrous to the whole. Not only were they weary: their spirits had flagged at the sudden frown of fortune, the abrupt removal of victory just as it seemed within their grasp. Governor Harris, still a volunteer aide, sensed this feeling of futility in the soldiers. Shortly after 2 o'clock, he expressed his fear of a collapse to the chief of staff, who agreed and went to Beauregard with the question: "General, do you not think our troops are very much in the condition of a lump of sugar thoroughly soaked in water — preserving its original shape, though ready to dissolve? Would it not be judicious to get away with what we have?" Beauregard nodded, looking out over the field of battle. "I intend to withdraw in a few moments," he said calmly.

Couriers soon rode out with orders for the corps commanders to begin the retreat. Breckinridge was posted along the high ground just south of Shiloh Chapel, his line studded with guns which kept up a steady booming as the other corps retired. Executed smoothly and without disorder, the retrograde maneuver had been completed by 4 o'clock, with time allowed for captured goods to be gleaned from the field and loaded into wagons, including five stands of regimental colors and twenty-one flags of the United States. Hardee, Bragg, and Polk marched their men a mile beyond and camped for the night where they had slept on their arms two nights before, in line of battle for Sunday's dawn assault. Breckinridge stayed where he was, prepared to discourage pursuit. But there was none to discourage: Grant's men were content with the recovery of their pillaged camps.

All day there had been intermittent showers, brief but thunderous downpours that drenched the men and then gave way to steamy sunshine. That night, however, the rain came down in earnest. Privates crowded into headquarters tents and stood close-packed as bullets in a cartridge box, having lost their awe of great men. When Breckinridge moved out next morning to join the long Confederate column grinding its way toward Corinth, the roads were quagmires. The wind veered, whistling out of the north along the boughs of roadside trees, and froze the rain to sleet; the countryside was blanketed with white. Hailstones fell as large as partridge eggs, plopping into the mud and rattling into the wagon beds to add to the suffering of the wounded, who, as one of them said, had been "piled in like bags of grain." Beauregard doubled the column all day to encourage and comfort the men, speaking to them much as he would do on a visit to one of their camps a week later, when, seeing a young soldier with a bandaged head, he rode up to him, extended his hand, and said: "My brave friend, were you wounded? Never mind; I trust you will soon be well. Before long we will make the Yankees pay up, interest and all. The day of our glory is near." Cheered by the bystanders, he gave them a bow as he rode away, and that night the boy wrote home: "It is strange Pa how we love that little black Frenchman."

For the present, though, the cheers were mostly perfunctory along that column of jolted, sleet-chilled men. They had had enough of glory for a while. It was not that they felt they had been defeated. They had not. But they had failed in what they had set out to do, and the man who had led them out of Corinth to accomplish the destruction of "agrarian mercenaries" was laid out dead now in a cottage there. All the same, they took much consolation in the thought that they had held their lines until they were ready to leave, and then had done so in good order, unpursued.

They were not entirely unpursued. In the Federal camp the burial details were at work and the surgeons moved about the field, summoned by the anguished cries of mangled soldiers from both armies; but Sherman was not there. Prompted by Grant, he had moved out that morning with one brigade to make a show of pursuit, or at any rate to see that the Confederates did not linger. A show was all it was, however, for when he reached a point on the Corinth road, four miles beyond his camps, he was given a lesson hunters sometimes learned from closing in too quickly on a wounded animal.

The place was called the Fallen Timbers, a half-mile-wide boggy swale where a prewar logging project had been abandoned. The road dipped down, then crested a ridge on the far side, where he could see enemy horsemen grouped in silhouette against the sky. Not knowing their strength or what might lie beyond the ridge, he shook out a regiment of skirmishers, posted cavalry to back them up and guard their flanks, then sent them forward, following with the rest of the brigade in attack formation at an interval of about two hundred yards. The thing was done in strict professional style, according to the book. But the man he was advancing against had never read the book, though he was presently to rewrite it by improvising tactics that would conform to his own notion of what war was all about. "War means fighting," he said. "And fighting means killing." It was Forrest. Breckinridge had assigned him a scratch collection of about 350 Tennessee, Kentucky, Mississippi, and Texas cavalrymen, turning over to him the task of protecting the rear of the retreating column.

As he prepared to defend the ridge, outnumbered five-to-one by the advancing blue brigade, he saw something that caused him to change his mind and his tactics. For as the skirmishers entered the vine-tangled hollow, picking their way around felled trees and stumbling through the brambles, they lost their neat alignment. In fact, they could hardly have been more disorganized if artillery had opened on them there in the swale. Forrest saw his chance. "Charge!" he shouted, and led his horsemen pounding down the slope. Most of the skirmishers had begun to run before he struck them, but those who stood were knocked sprawling by a blast from shotguns and revolvers. Beyond them, the Federal cavalry had panicked, firing their carbines wildly in the air. When they broke too, Forrest kept on after them, still brandishing his saber and crying, "Charge! Charge!" as he plowed into the solid ranks of the brigade drawn up beyond. The trouble was, he was charging by himself; the others, seeing the steady brigade front, had turned back and were already busy gathering up their 43 prisoners. Forrest was one gray uniform, high above a sea of blue. "Kill him! *Kill* the goddam rebel! Knock him off his horse!" It was no easy thing to do; the horse was kicking and plunging and Forrest was hacking and slashing; but one of the soldiers did his best. Reaching far out, he shoved the muzzle of his rifle into the colonel's side and pulled the trigger. The force of the explosion lifted Forrest clear of the saddle, but he regained his seat and sawed the horse around. As he came out of the mass of dark blue uniforms and furious white faces, clearing a path with his saber, he reached down and grabbed one of the soldiers by the collar, swung him onto the crupper of the horse, and galloped back to safety, using the Federal as a shield against the bullets fired after him. Once he was out of range, he flung the hapless fellow off and rode on up the ridge where his men were waiting in open-mouthed amazement.

Sherman was amazed, too, but mostly he was disgusted. As soon as he had gathered up his wounded and buried his dead, he turned back toward Pittsburg Landing. Snug once more in his tent near Shiloh Chapel, he wrote his report of the affair. It concluded: "The check sustained by us at the fallen timbers delayed our advance.... Our troops being fagged out by three days' hard fighting, exposure and privation, I ordered them back to camp, where all now are."

★ ★ ★

The ball now lodged alongside Forrest's spine as he followed the column grinding its way toward Corinth was the last of many to draw blood in the Battle of Shiloh. Union losses were 1754 killed, 8408 wounded, 2885 captured: total, 13,047 — about 2000 of them Buell's. Confederate losses were 1723 killed, 8012 wounded, 959 missing: total, 10,694. Of the 100,000 soldiers engaged in this first great bloody conflict of the war, approximately one out of every four who had gone into battle had been killed, wounded, or captured. Casualties were 24 percent, the same as Waterloo's. Yet Waterloo had settled something, while this one apparently had settled nothing. When it was over the two armies were back where they started, with other Waterloos ahead. In another sense, however, it had settled a great deal. The American volunteer, whichever side he was on in this war, and however green, would fight as fiercely and stand as firmly as the vaunted veterans of Europe.

Now that this last had been proved beyond dispute, the leaders on both sides persuaded themselves that they had known it all along, despite the doubts engendered by Manassas and Wilson's Creek, which dwindled now by contrast to comparatively minor engagements. Looking instead at the butcher's bill — the first of many such, it seemed — they reacted, as always, according to their natures. Beauregard, for example, recovered his high spirits in short order. Two days after the battle he wired Van Dorn, still marking time in Arkansas: "Hurry your forces as rapidly as possible. I believe we can whip them again." He believed what he told the wounded soldier, "The day of our glory is near," and saw no occasion for retracting the announcement of "complete victory" sent to Richmond on the night of the first day. In fact, the further he got from the battle in time, the greater it seemed to him as a continuing demonstration of the superiority of southern arms. Nor did Davis retract the exultant message he sent to Congress in passing the telegram along. He was saddened, however, by other news it contained: namely, the loss of Albert Sidney Johnston. "When he fell," Davis wrote long afterward, "I realized that our strongest pillar had been broken."

Reactions on the other side were also characteristic. Once more Halleck saw his worst fears enlarged before his eyes, and got aboard a St Louis steamboat, bound for Pittsburg Landing, to take charge of the army himself before Grant destroyed it entirely. "Your army is not now in condition to resist an attack," he wired ahead. "It must be made so without delay." Grant tightened his security regulations, as instructed, but he did not seem greatly perturbed by the criticism. Now as always, he was a good deal more concerned with what he would do to the enemy than he was with what the enemy might try to do to him, and in any case he had grown accustomed by now to such reactions from above. The battle losses were another matter, providing some grim arithmetic for study. Total American casualties in all three of the nation's previous wars — the Revolution, the War of 1812, and the Mexican War: 10,623+6765+5885 — were 23,273. Shiloh's totaled 23,741, and most of them were Grant's.

Perhaps this had something to do with his change of mind as to the fighting qualities of his opponents. At any rate, far from thinking them "heartily tired" and ready to chuck the war, he later said quite frankly that, from Shiloh on, "I gave up all idea of saving the Union except by complete conquest."

✗ 3 ✗

While the ironclad gunboats of the western navy were pounding out their victories on the Tennessee, the Cumberland, and the mile-wide Mississippi — past Island Ten, they now were bearing down on undermanned Fort Pillow; Memphis, unbraced for the shock, was next on the list — the wooden ships of the blue-water navy were not idle in the east. Along the coasts of the Atlantic and the Gulf, where the thickened blockade squadrons hugged the remaining harbors and river outlets, the fall and winter amphibious gains had been continued and extended. Three times the *Monitor* had declined the *Merrimac-Virginia*'s challenge to single combat in Hampton Roads; if the rebel vessel wanted trouble, let her make it by trying to interfere with the *Monitor*'s task of protecting the rest of the fleet off Old Point Comfort. This she could not or would not do, and the *Monitor* maintained station in shoal water, content with a stalemate, while elsewhere other Federal warships were stepping up the tempo of Confederate disasters.

By mid-March the month-old Roanoke Island victory had been extended to New Bern and other important points around the North Carolina sounds, including control of the railroad which had carried men and supplies to the armies in Virginia. Simultaneously, down on the Florida coast, Fernandina was seized, followed before the end of the month by the uncontested occupation of Jacksonville and St Augustine. Charleston and Savannah had been threatened all this time by the army-navy build-up at Port Royal. In April, while preparations were under way for a siege of the South Carolina city, an attack was mounted against Fort Pulaski, a stout brick pentagon on Cockspur Island, guarding the mouth of the Savannah River. Heavy guns and mortars knocked it to pieces, breaching the casemates and probing for the powder magazine. After thirty-odd hours of bombardment, the white flag went up and the blue-clad artillerists moved in to accept the surrender. Mostly they were New Englanders, and when a Georgian made the inevitable allusion to wooden nutmegs, a Connecticut man, pointing to a 10-inch solid shot that had pierced the wall, told him: "We don't make them of wood any longer."

Savannah itself was not taken, and indeed there was no need to take it. Sealed off as it was by the guns of Fort Pulaski, it was no more important now, at least from the naval point of view, than any other inland Confederate city which had lost its principal reason for existence. Wilmington, North Carolina, a much tougher proposition, with stronger and less accessible defenses, was presently the only major Atlantic port not captured or besieged by Union soldiers. Here the sleek low ghost-gray blockade-runners made their entrances and exits, usually by the dark of the moon, burning smokeless coal and equipped with telescopic funnels and feathered paddles to hide them from the noses, eyes, and ears of their pursuers. Martial and flippant names they had, the *Let Her Be* and *Let Her Rip*, the *Fox, Leopard, Lynx* and *Dream*, the *Banshee, Secret, Kate* and *Hattie*, the *Beauregard*, the *Stonewall Jackson*, the *Stag* and *Lady Davis*. The risks were great (one out of ten had been caught the year before; this year the odds were one-to-eight) but the profits were even greater. Two trips would pay the purchase price; the third and all that followed were pure gravy, as well as a substantial aid to the southern problem of supply. Last fall, one of the slim speedy vessels had steamed into Savannah with 10,000 Enfield rifles, a million cartridges, two million percussion caps, 400 barrels of powder, and a quantity of cutlasses, revolvers, and other badly needed materials of war. For all their reduction of the number of ports to be guarded, the blockade squadrons had their hands full.

Meanwhile, down along the Gulf, another Federal fleet was

War Means Fighting . . . [353]

scoring corresponding successes to maintain the victory tempo set by its Atlantic rivals. At the mouth of the Florida river whose name it bore, Apalachicola fell in early April, followed in quick succession by the seizure of Pass Christian and Biloxi, on the Mississippi coast. These were bloodless conquests, the defenders having left to fight at Shiloh alongside the main body summoned north from Pensacola, which in turn was taken early the following month. Like Wilmington, Mobile remained — a much tougher proposition; but even before the capture of Pensacola, the Federals had made substantial lodgments on the coast of every southern state except Texas and Alabama.

Satisfying as all these salt-water victories were to the over-all command, the fact remained that, unlike the western navy on its way down the Mississippi, they had merely nibbled at the rim of the rebellion. Except for simplifying the blockade difficulties — which was much — they had accomplished very little, really, even as diversions. The problem, seen fairly clearly now by everyone, from Secretary Welles down to the youngest powder monkey, was conquest: *divide et impera,* pierce and strangle: which had been the occupation of the river gunboats all these months while the blue-water ships were pounding at the beaches. It was time for them, too, to try their hand at conquest by division instead of subtraction.

If the Mississippi could be descended, perhaps it could be ascended as well, so that when the salt- and fresh-water sailors met somewhere upstream like upper and nether millstones, having ground any fugitive elements of the enemy fleet between them, the Confederacy — and the task of its subjugation — would be riven. Much effort and much risk would be involved; the problems were multitudinous, including the fact that the thing would have to be done by wooden ships. But surely it was worth any effort, and almost any risk, considering the prize that awaited success at the very start: New Orleans.

The Crescent City was not only the largest in the South, it was larger by population than any other four combined, and in the peacetime volume of its export trade, as a funnel for the produce of the Mississippi Valley, it ranked among the foremost cities of the world. Its loss would not only depress the South, and correspondingly elate the North; it would indicate plainly to Europe — especially France, where so many of its people had connections of blood and commerce — the inability of the rebels to retain what they had claimed by rebellion. In short, its capture would be a feather, indeed a plume, in the cap of any man who could conceive and execute the plan that would prise this chief jewel from the crown of King Cotton.

One man already had such a plan, along with an absolute ache for such a feather. Commodore David Porter had made naval history as captain of the *Essex* in the War of 1812, and his son David Dixon

Porter, forty-eight years old and recently promoted to commander, was determined to have at least an equal share of glory in this one. What was more, in the case of New Orleans he knew whereof he spoke. Thirty trips in and out of the Passes during a peacetime hitch in the merchant marine had familiarized him with the terrain, and months of blockade duty off the river's four main mouths had given him a chance to talk with oystermen and pilots about recent developments in the city's defenses. He knew the obstacles, natural and man-made, and he believed he knew how to get around or through them. Nor was he one to wait for fame to find him. In late '61 he turned up in Washington to unfold his plan for the approval of the Navy Secretary.

New Orleans itself was a hundred miles upriver, but its principal defense against attack from below was a pair of star-shaped masonry works, Forts Jackson and St Philip, built facing each other on opposite banks of the river, just above a swift-currented bend three fourths of the way down. Formerly part of the U.S. system of permanent defenses, they had been taken over and strengthened by the Confederates. Fort Jackson, on the right bank, was the larger, mounting 74 guns; Fort St Philip, slightly upstream on the east bank, mounted 52. Between them, with a combined garrison of 1100 men and an armament of 126 guns, they dominated a treacherous stretch where approaching ships would have to slow to make the turn. Originally there had been doubt that all this strength would be needed, rivermen having assured the defenders that no deep draft vessel could ever get over the bars that blocked the outlets. However, this had been disproved in early October when the commander of the Gulf Blockade Squadron, finding the task of patrolling the multi-mouthed river well-nigh impossible from outside, sent three heavy warships across the southwest bar and stationed them fifteen miles above, at the juncture called Head of the Passes, a deep-water anchorage two miles long and half as wide, where the river branched to create its lower delta. As long as those sloops and their frowning guns remained there, nothing could get in or out of the Passes; New Orleans would languish worse than ever, her trade being limited to what could be sneaked out by the roundabout route through Lake Pontchartrain and past the vigilant Federals on Ship Island, which had been seized the month before.

Clearly this was intolerable, and the city's defenders prepared to correct it at once. They had a makeshift fleet of four flat-bottomed towboats mounting two guns each, a seven-gun revenue cutter seized from Mexico before the war, under highly improbable charges of piracy, and a Boston-built seagoing tug covered over with boiler plate and equipped with an iron beak and a single 32-pounder trained unmovably dead ahead. Perhaps to offset her ugliness — all that metal caused her to ride so low in the water, she rather resembled a floating eggplant — the authorities had given the ram the proud name *Manassas*.

On the dark night of October 11, moving swiftly with the help of the four-knot current, she led the way downriver for an attack on the three big warships patrolling the Head of the Passes. Surprise was to be the principal advantage; the six-boat flotilla moved with muffled engines and no lights. To help offset the armament odds — 16 guns, of moderate size or smaller, would be opposed by 51, over half of which were 8-inch or larger — tugs brought along three "fire-rafts," long flatboats loaded with highly combustible pine knots and rosin, which would be ignited and sent careening with the current when the time came. The plan was for the *Manassas* to make a ram attack in darkness, then fire a rocket as the signal for the fire rafts to be lit and loosed and the gunboats to come down and join the melee.

The Federals had no lookout stationed, only the normal anchor watches they would have carried in any harbor. The first they knew of an attack was at 3.40 a.m. when a midshipman burst into his captain's cabin crying, "Captain, there's a steamer alongside of us!" On deck, the skipper barely had time to see "an indescribable object" emit a puff of smoke even darker than the night. As Beat-to-Quarters sounded there was a crash; the *Manassas* had struck the 1900-ton flagship *Richmond*, which now began firing indiscriminate broadsides, like bellows of pain, and hoisted three light-signals in rapid succession: ENEMY PRESENT. GET UNDER WAY. ACT AT DISCRETION. All three of the sloops were firing frantically, though none of them could see anything to aim at. The *Manassas* was groping blindly, filled with coal smoke. She had struck a barge lashed alongside the Federal flagship; the force of the blow had knocked her engines loose and a hawser had carried her stacks away, flush with the deck. In time she got the rocket off, however, and presently three distant sparks appeared upriver, growing in size as the rafts flamed higher and drew closer.

Aboard the sloops, delay had only served to increase the panic. PROCEED DOWN SOUTHWEST PASS. CROSS THE BAR, the flagship signaled, and all three went with the current, the sluggish *Richmond* swinging broadside to it, helpless. One got over; the next lodged fast on the bar, stern upriver; then the *Richmond* struck and stuck, still broadside. The fire-rafts had run harmless against bank, but the Confederate gunboats, which up to now had not engaged, took the grounded sloops under fire with their small-caliber long-range Whitworths. Presently the Union flag-officer, Captain John Pope — called "Honest John" to distinguish him from the general who would win fame at Island Ten — was amazed to see the skipper of the other stranded vessel appear on the flagship's quarterdeck, wrapped in a large American flag. He had abandoned ship, bringing his colors with him, after laying and lighting a slow fuze to the powder magazine, intending thus to keep her from falling into the hands of the rebels.

After a long wait for the explosion — which would bring what an observer called "a shower of 1½-ton guns through the decks and bottom of almost any near-by ship" — it finally became evident that the sloop was not going to blow after all. Pope sent the flag-draped captain back to defend her and, if possible, get her afloat; which he subsequently managed to do by heaving most of her guns and ammunition over the side. (It later developed that the seaman charged with lighting the fuze had obeyed orders, but then, not being in sympathy with them, had cut off the sputtering end and tossed it overboard.) By now it was broad open daylight; the Confederates withdrew upstream, satisfied with their morning's work of clearing the Head of the Passes, and Pope made a tour of inspection to assess damages. Except for a small hole punched in the flagship when the *Manassas* struck the coal barge, there were none. Not a man had been hurt, not a hit had been scored; or so he thought until next morning, when he found a 6-pound Whitworth solid lodged in his bureau drawer. Explaining his performance, Honest John reported: "The whole affair came upon me so suddenly that no time was left for reflection." His request that he be relieved of command "on account of ill health" was quickly granted. "I truly feel ashamed for our side," one executive said when the smoke had cleared away.

Porter, on blockade duty outside the Southwest Pass at the time, expressed a stronger opinion. It was, he said, "the most ridiculous affair that ever took place in the American Navy." All the same, it helped in the formulation of his plan by showing what manner of resistance could be expected below New Orleans. In addition to the problem of getting across the bar and past the heavily gunned forts, he knew that the small Confederate flotilla would attempt to make up, in daring and ingenuity, for what it lacked in size. Besides, it might not be so small in time. There were reports of two monster ironclads, larger and faster than any the Federal navy had ever dreamed of, already under construction in the city's shipyards. Then too, there were land batteries at Chalmette, where Andrew Jackson's volunteers had stood behind a barricade of cotton bales and mowed down British regulars fifty years ago. The bars, the forts, the rebel boats, the batteries — these four, plus unknown others: but the greatest of these, as things now stood, was the problem of passing the forts. It was as a solution of this that Porter conceived and submitted his plan for the capture of New Orleans. The rest could be left to a flag-officer who, having done his reflecting beforehand, would not panic in a crisis.

The naval expedition, as Porter saw it, would have at its core a flotilla of twenty mortar vessels, each mounting a ponderous 13-inch mortar supplied with a thousand shells. Screened by intervening trees, they would tie up to bank, just short of the bend, and blanket the forts with high-angle fire while the seagoing sloops and frigates made a run past in the darkness and confusion. The fleet was to mount no fewer than 200 heavy guns, exclusive of the mortars, which would assure it more firepower than the enemy had in his forts and boats combined, with the Chalmette batteries thrown in for good measure. Once past the forts, it could wreck the rebel vessels and batteries by the sheer weight of thrown metal: New Orleans, under the frown of Federal warships, would have to choose between destruction and surrender. Army troops, brought along for the purpose — otherwise the show would be purely Navy — would go ashore to guard against internal revolt and outside attempts at recapture, thus freeing the fleet for other upriver objectives: Baton Rouge, Natchez, Vicksburg, and conjunction with Foote's ironclads steaming south. The Mississippi would be Federal, from Minnesota all the way to the Gulf.

By mid-November Porter was in Washington, submitting his proposal to the Secretary. Welles had small use for the commander personally — he had too much gasconade for the New Englander's taste, and before the war he had associated overmuch with Southerners — but the plan itself, coinciding as it did with some thinking Welles had been doing along this line, won his immediate approval. He took him to see the President, who liked it too. "This should have been done sooner," Lincoln said, and arranged a conference with McClellan, whose coöperation would be needed. McClellan saw merit in the plan, but raised some characteristic objections. In his opinion the expedition would entail a siege by 50,000 troops, for the heavy guns inside the forts would crush the wooden ships like eggshells. Bristling, Welles replied that the navy would do the worrying about the risk to its ships; all he wanted from the army was 10,000 men, to be added to the 5000 which Benjamin Butler, flushed by the recent amphibious victory at Hatteras Inlet, was raising now in Massachusetts for service down on the Gulf. When McClellan replied that he could spare that many — Butler in particular could be spared, along with his known talent for cabal — the conference at once got down to specifics.

Secrecy, a prime element of the plan, would be extremely difficult to maintain because of the necessarily large-scale preparations. However, if the expedition's existence could hardly be hidden, perhaps its destination could. With this in mind, a new blockade squadron would be set up in the West Gulf, coincident with some loose talk about Pensacola, Mobile, Galveston — any place, in fact, except New Orleans. Next a roster of ships was drawn up, with an armament of about 250 guns. The choice of a fleet commander was left to Assistant Secretary G. V. Fox, himself a retired Annapolis man, who conferred with Porter on the matter, combing the list of captains. One after another they were rejected, either for being otherwise employed or else for being too much of the Honest John type. At last they came to David Glasgow Farragut, thirty-seventh on the list. Of Spanish extraction, sixty years old and sitting now as a member of a retirement board at Brooklyn Navy Yard, Farragut was a veteran of more than fifty years' active service, having begun as a nine-year-old acting midshipman aboard the *Essex*, whose captain, Porter's father, had informally adopted him and supervised his baptism of fire in the War of 1812. Here was a possibility. He was known to be stout-hearted and energetic; every year on his birthday he turned a handspring, explaining that he would know he was beginning to age when he found the exercise difficult. The trouble was he was southern born, a native of Knoxville, and southern married — twice in fact, both times to ladies from Norfolk — which raised doubts as to his loyalty and accounted for his present inactive assignment. Porter, on his way to New York to arrange for the purchase and assembly of the mortar flotilla, was instructed to call on his foster brother and sound him out.

The retirement board member was waiting for him, a smooth-shaven, square-built, hale-looking man with hazel eyes and heavy eyebrows, wearing his long side hair brushed across the top of his head to hide his baldness. Porter began by asking what he thought of his former associates now gone South. "Those damned fellows will catch it yet," Farragut replied. Asked if he would accept a command to go and fight "those fellows," he said he would. Porter then badgered him by pretending that the objective would be Norfolk, his wife's birthplace. Farragut jumped up crying, "I will take the command: only don't you trifle with me!"

Summoned to Washington, still without suspecting the purpose, he was questioned next by Fox, who asked — as if for a purely theoretical opinion — if he thought New Orleans could be taken from below. "Yes, emphatically," Farragut told him. "The forts are well down the river; ships could easily run them, and New Orleans itself is undefended. It would depend somewhat on the fleet, however."

"Well," Fox said, "— with such a fleet as, say, two steam frigates, five screw sloops of the cities class, a dozen gunboats, and some mortar vessels to shell the forts from high angle?"

"Why, I would engage to run those batteries with two thirds of such a force...."

"What would you say if appointed to head such an expedition?"

"What would I say?" Farragut cried. He leaped to his feet and began to prowl about the room. Now he understood. The goal was to be New Orleans, which he knew well from years of living in it, and he was to have the flag. "What would I say?" he cried, and broke into exclamations of delight.

So it was settled. He received his orders during the last week of the year and began at once to fit out the eighteen warships assigned to his fleet, including two steam frigates, seven screw sloops, and nine gunboats, all of wood and mounting 243 guns, most heavy. Porter meanwhile had been assembling his mortar flotilla of twenty schooners; the weapons themselves were cast in Pittsburgh, along with 30,000 bomb-shells, while the beds were manufactured in New York. In late January Farragut dropped down to Hampton Roads, Porter coming along behind, and by mid-February reached Key West, where final orders from Welles were broken open: "This most important operation of the war is confined to yourself and your brave associates. ... If successful, you open the way to the sea for the great West, never again to be closed. The rebellion will be riven in the center, and the flag to which you have been so faithful will recover its supremacy in every State."

Convinced by inspection that the way to stop the small-time blockade runners working in and out of the coastal lakes and bayous was to intercept them with vessels adapted to the task, Farragut wrote to the Navy Department asking for some light ships of five-foot draft or less. Since he neglected to say what use would be made of them, Fox thought they were wanted for the upriver attack, which would have meant an unconscionable delay. Dismayed, the Assistant Secretary began to suspect that he had erred in his choice of a fleet commander. Instead of writing to Farragut, however, he wrote to Porter: "I trust that we have made no mistake in our man, but his dispatches are very discouraging. It is not too late to rectify our mistake. You must frankly give me your views. ... I shall have no peace until I hear from you." Porter replied that it was too late for a change, but that he would do what he could to bolster the old man's shaky judgment. "Men of his age in a seafaring life are not fit for important enterprises, they lack the vigor of youth. He talks very much at random at times and rather underrates the difficulties before him without fairly comprehending them. I know what they are, and as he is impressible hope to make him appreciate them also." He added by way of consolation, "I have great hopes of the mortars if all else fails."

Happily unaware of the distrust of his superiors or the condescension of his adoptive brother, Farragut proceeded to Ship Island for refueling and refitting. By mid-March he was off the mouths of the Mississippi, maneuvering for an entrance, which was finally effected by sending Porter's mortars and the gunboats through Pass à l'Outre and taking the heavier frigates and sloops around to Southwest Pass. After much sweat and inch-by-inch careening — back-breaking labor that tried even Farragut's sunny disposition — all got over the bar except the largest, a 50-gun frigate, twenty of whose guns were distributed among the other vessels of the fleet now assembled at Head of the Passes. There the schooners discharged their seagoing spars and made ready for the work they had been built to do.

By mid-April the preparations were complete. Butler's soldiers were at hand: 18,000 of them, so persuasively had the former politician done his recruiting job in New England. The fleet was at anchor two miles below the bend where the mortar schooners had tied up to both banks, the tips of their masts disguised with foliage lest they show above the trees that screened the vessels from the forts. Ranges were quickly established: 2850 yards to Fort Jackson, 3680 to Fort St Philip. Farragut was somewhat doubtful as to the efficacy of the snub-nosed weapons, but Porter declared confidently that two days of mortar bombardment would reduce both forts to rubble. April 18 — Good Friday — he opened fire.

★ ★ ★

Holy Week was gloomy in New Orleans, the more so because of the contrast between the present frame of mind, with danger looming stark in both directions, and the elation felt six months ago at the comic repulse of the sloops from the Head of the Passes, which had seemed to give point to the popular conviction that "Nothing afloat could pass the forts. Nothing that walked could get through our swamps." Since then a great deal had happened, and all of it bad.

For one thing, the blockade had tightened. Roustabouts no longer swarmed on the levee, for there were no cargoes to unload; the wharves lay idle, and warehouses formerly bulging with cotton and sugar and grain yawned hollow; trade having come to a standstill, ready money was so scarce that there was a current joke that an olive-oil label would pass for cash "because it was greasy, smelt bad, and bore an autograph." For another, Foote's gunboats and Pope's soldiers were smashing obstacles so rapidly upriver that the danger seemed even greater from that direction, with neither forts nor swamps to slow them down. In the midst of these discouragements and fears, troops assigned to the city's defense were called north to fight at Shiloh, and all that returned from that repulse were the members of the honor guard with Sidney Johnston's body, following the muffled drums and the empty-saddled warhorse out St Charles Street to fire the prescribed three volleys across his crypt. Now there was this: Yankee ships once more across the bar, but in such strength that no small-scale attack, however ingenious and daring, could hope to budge them. For New Orleans, as for the South at large, the prospect was grim in this season of death and resurrection.

No one responsible for the city's defense was more aware of the danger than the man who was most responsible of all: Mansfield Lovell, a thirty-nine-year-old Maryland-born West Pointer who had resigned as New York Deputy Street Commissioner to join the Confederacy in September. Impressed with the Chapultepec-brevetted artilleryman's record as an administrator, Davis made him a major general and sent him to replace the over-aged Twiggs in New Orleans; which would not only give the city an energetic and efficient commander, but would also call widespread attention to the fact that willingness to fight for the South's ideals was by no means restricted to men of southern background, Lovell having spent most of his civilian years as a New Jersey ironworks executive. The new major general arrived in early October, and was appalled at the unpreparedness. There was plenty of Gallic enthusiasm, but it found release at champagne parties rather than at work. He wrote to Richmond, protesting that the city was "greatly drained of arms, ammunition, clothing, and supplies for other points." Presently it was drained of fighting men as well, leaving him with what he called a "heterogeneous militia" of 3000 short-term volunteers, "armed mostly with shotguns against 9- and 11-inch Dahlgrens."

The Creoles did not resent his criticisms. They found his intensity amusing and his presence ornamental. "A very attractive figure," one pronounced him, "giving the eye, at first glance, a promise of much activity." His horsemanship was especially admirable; they enjoyed watching him ride dragoon-style "with so long a stirrup-leather that he simply stood astride the saddle, as straight as a spear." To add to the effect, he wore a facial ruff of hair much like Burnside's, except that it was light brown and somewhat less flamboyant.

Despite his activity, no one was more surprised when the Union fleet showed its true intention. Not that he had not known it was assembling. Agents had kept him informed of its strength and location; but they had also relayed the loose talk about Mobile and Pensacola, and Lovell believed them — perhaps because he wanted to. What misled him most, though, was the presence of Ben Butler, who at the Democratic convention of 1860 had voted fifty-seven consecutive times for the nomination of Jefferson Davis before switching over to Breckinridge with the majority. "I regard Butler's Ship Island expedition as a harmless menace so far as New Orleans is concerned," Lovell had told Richmond in late February. "A black Republican dynasty will never give an old Breckinridge Democrat like Butler command of any expedition which they had any idea would result in such a glorious success as the capture of New Orleans." Now he knew better; the warships were across the bar, above the Head of the Passes. But the knowledge came too late. He had been looking upriver all this time, where the Foote-Grant Foote-Pope amphibious teams were wrecking whatever stood in their way, ashore or afloat.

Hastening to meet the threat from above — his intelligence reports were quite good from that direction: too good, as it turned out — he had commandeered fourteen paddle-wheel steamers and converted them into one-gun gunboats, plating their outer bulwarks with inch-thick railroad iron to give them mass and rigidity for use as rams. Launched one by one between January and April, they made up the River Defense Fleet under J. E. Montgomery, a river captain, and were independent of Commander J. K. Mitchell, whose miniature flotilla had thrown such a scare into Honest John Pope six months before. Lovell did not like the command arrangement, which left him no real control over either. Besides, the new gunboats were put in the hands of a notoriously independent breed of men; "fourteen Mississippi river captains and pilots will never agree about anything once they get under way," he predicted. As fast as they came off the ways, eight of the boats were sent upriver to challenge the descending Union fleet at Memphis or Fort Pillow, though Lovell managed to hold onto six of them for the immediate protection of New Orleans. They would not amount to much in the way of a deterrent once the heavy-gunned armada below the forts broke into the clear, but anything that would delay or distract the Federal fleet, however briefly — even to the extent of making it pause to brush them aside — might be of enormous value because of something else that was going on inside the city. He had an ace in the hole; two, in fact. The question was whether he would have time to bring them out and play them.

Porter had heard aright in his talks with the pilots and oystermen; the Confederates were at work on two giant ironclads in the city's shipyards, each of them more formidable than the *Merrimac-Virginia*, which had just completed her work of destruction in Hampton Roads against vessels as stout as any in Farragut's fleet. The first, the *Louisiana*, mounting sixteen heavy rifles, had been launched and cased in a double row of T-shaped rails for armor, the inner rails bolted vertically to the bulwarks, the outer ones reversed and driven down the gaps. There had been various delays, including strikes — one lasted three full weeks — because the workers were unwilling to take Confederate bonds for pay, but the main trouble now was her power plant, which had been transferred from a steamboat. While Farragut was crossing the bar, mechanics were trying without success to coax the *Louisiana*'s engines into motion.

The other ironclad, the *Mississippi*, was an even more novel and formidable proposition, at least in prospect. Over 4000 tons in weight, 270 feet long and 58 feet in the beam, drawing only 14 feet and mounting 20 guns, she was a true dreadnought, designed to wear three-inch armor, have an iron snout set over a casing three feet thick, and be propelled by three engines at a speed of 14 knots; all of which would make her the most powerful and fastest warship ever built. The plan for her use was quite in scale with her proportions. She was to clear the Mississippi of enemy vessels, then the Gulf and the Atlantic, after which she would lay the northern coastal cities under levy. Improbable as this program sounded, it was by no means impossible; certainly nothing afloat or under construction could stand in her way. But first she would have to be finished, and she was still a considerable way from that. She had been launched, her timberwork completed, but so far she was armored only below the gun deck, and her vital

50-foot central drive shaft was too big a casting job for any southern rolling mill except the Tredegar in Richmond, which began work on the order in February. It would be weeks, or months, before delivery and installation of the shaft would permit her to move under her own power.

Time, then, was golden. Lovell bought what he could and tried to buy more by calling for the eight departed gunboats to be returned from upriver. This the government would not do, considering them more needed there to stem the rout at Island Ten and make a shield for Memphis; New Orleans would have to resist with what she had. Primarily then — with the Federal fleet already approaching the bend they guarded — that put the burden on Forts Jackson and St Philip, whose strength or vulnerability had become a subject of disagreement among the river men who had been so confident such a short time back. A chain boom, held afloat by cypress logs, spanned the Mississippi just below the forts, so that when the Yankees ran afoul of it or stopped to try and break it, plunging fire from the parapets would blow them out of the water like sitting ducks. So the river men had reckoned; but the March floods — the highest in anyone's memory — brought such a press of uprooted trees and brush against it that the boom gave way, depriving the gunners of their hope for stationary targets. Quickly the break was mended and the obstacle strengthened by adding a line of hulks to buoy it up. Now that it had broken once, however, there was considerable doubt that it would hold against the pressure, which was building up again.

In desperation Lovell ordered the *Louisiana* towed downstream, to be tied up to the east bank just above Fort St Philip. No less than fifty mechanics continued to tinker with her engines, but even if they never got them going she could serve as a floating battery, adding the weight of her bow and starboard guns to those of the forts. Work continued aboard the *Mississippi*, too, on the outside chance that her drive shaft would arrive before the Federals did. It was Holy Week; Ash Wednesday, then Good Friday, and a message arrived from downriver; both forts were under heavy bombardment, receiving two 200-pound mortar shells a minute. Lovell rode down to see for himself how bad it was.

★ ★ ★

It was bad enough, or anyhow it seemed so. At the end of the first day's firing, the citadel and barracks of Fort Jackson were ablaze, rubble and sandbags thrown about and the protective levee cut, letting backwater into the place. "I was obliged to confine the men most rigidly to the casemates," the commandant reported, "or else we should have lost the best part of the garrison." They huddled there, white-faced with alarm, while the world outside seemed turned to flame and thunder. And yet it was by no means as bad as it seemed, being a good deal more spectacular than effective. Casualties were extremely low in both forts, and nothing really vital was hit in either. In fact, when Porter slowed the rate of fire at nightfall to give his weary crews some rest, his own men were rather more shaken up than those at the opposite ends of the looping trajectories. Soon after noon the lead east-bank schooner had taken a solid through her deck and bottom and had to be shifted down the line. What was more, the work itself was heavy, each piece being required to deliver a round every ten minutes, and the strain of absorbing the ear-pounding, bone-jarring concussions was severe. It was as if the bombardiers had spent those hours inside a tolling bell.

Porter had them back at their rapid-fire work by dawn. He had said he would silence the forts by sunset of the second day, and he intended to do it. All day the firing continued, but with less apparent effect than yesterday, the bursting shells having done all the superficial damage there was to do. At dusk the rebel casemate guns were still in action. Porter did not slacken fire. All night it continued; all Easter Day, all Easter night, all Monday; still the guns replied. In 96 hours — twice Porter's original estimate as to the time it would take to reduce them — the forts had absorbed over 13,000 shells, at a cost of only four men killed, fourteen wounded, and seven guns disabled. Porter's crews were near exhaustion, but he would not slacken fire. All Monday night, all Tuesday, Tuesday night, and Wednesday morning it continued; 16,800 shells had been pumped into the forts, which still replied. Then Farragut intervened. He had never placed much reliance on the mortars anyhow.

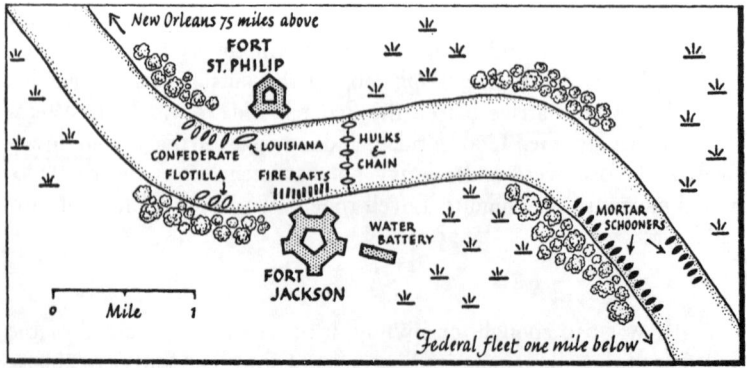

"Look here, David," he said. "We'll demonstrate the practical value of mortar work." He turned to his clerk. "Mr Osbon, get two small flags, a white one and a red one, and go to the mizzen topmast-head and watch the shells fall. If inside the fort, wave the red flag. If outside, wave the white one." In the beginning the fire had been accurate, but the gunners had been numbed into indifference by now; the white flag waved from the masthead far more often than the red. Farragut said calmly, "There's the score. I guess we'll go up the river tonight."

Porter protested, heart and soul. Even if the fleet got past the forts, it would leave them alive in its rear; how would the infantry manage the run in unarmed and unarmored transports? Besides, with the Federal warships gone upriver, what would prevent the surviving enemy gunboats from attacking the mortar flotilla? Farragut replied casually that Butler's men could make a roundabout trip, coming in through the Gulf bayous. As for the threat of rebel survivors, he didn't intend for there to be any; but if there were, then Porter would just have to look out for himself. He called his gig and made the rounds of all his ships, confirming the orders already issued for the run to be made that night. He would "abide by the result," he told them: "conquer or be conquered."

His two biggest worries — how to get across or through the boom and how to deal with fire-rafts — had already been lessened or disposed of. Sunday night two gunboats had gone forward under heavy fire and opened a gap by releasing the chain from one of the hulks. When the defenders responded by sending a fire-raft through the breach, flames leaping a hundred feet in the air, considerable frenzy had ensued, including a collision between two ships whose captains panicked at the threat of being roasted. However, by the time the current had carried the burning mass of pitch and pine harmlessly into the east bank, they knew better how to deal with or avoid them. Farragut had been for running the forts the following night, but a strong north wind had risen to slow him down. It blew through Tuesday; then Wednesday it died and he was ready, having spent the interim preparing his wooden ships for the ordeal. Chains were looped down over the sides to protect the engines and magazines; Jacob's ladders were hung all round, so the carpenters could descend quickly and patch from the outside any holes shot in the hulls. Tubs of water were spotted about, and each ship had a well-drilled fire brigade equipped with grapnels for handling fire-rafts. The outer bulwarks were smeared with mud to hide the ships from the spotters in the forts, but the decks and the breeches of the guns were given a coat of whitewash to provide reflected light for nightwork. As a final touch — one that never failed to provoke a sensation at the pit of every sailor's stomach, no matter how often he had seen it done before — the area around each gun was strewn with sand and ashes, so that when the fight grew hot the guncrews would not slip in their own blood. That was all. Now there was only the waiting, which a gunner aboard the flagship thought the hardest job of all. "One has nothing to do to occupy the mind," he complained. "The mind runs on the great uncertainty about to take place, until it is a relief when the battle opens."

At 2 a.m. — it was Thursday now, the 24th — the hour being, as Farragut said, "propitious" — he had just received a signal that the gateway through the boom was still ajar — two red lanterns appeared at the *Hartford*'s mizzen peak, and the lead division began to move upstream. His original plan had been to lead the attack himself, aboard the flagship, but the senior captains, agreeing that the losses would be heavy, persuaded him that to risk losing the fleet commander at the outset would be to court disaster through confusion. So Farragut had arranged his seventeen warships in three divisions of eight, three, and six vessels, himself at the head of the second. It was a powerful aggregation, heavily gunned, and backed by the fire of the mortars. If the weight of thrown metal was to decide the issue, there could be but one result, for an entire round of projectiles from all the Federal guns would weigh more than ten tons, while one from all the Confederate guns, afloat and ashore, would weigh just three and a half. Farragut and his captains were not aware of these figures, however, or at any rate not the latter. All they knew was what they had been taught: that one gun ashore was worth four afloat. They knew, too, that the forts were built of brick and mortar, while the ships were built of wood. Farragut was confident, even cheerful, but when his clerk declared that he did not expect the fleet to lose beyond a hundred men, the Tennessee-born captain shook his head in doubt. "I wish I could think so," he said.

There were delays as the various sloops and gunboats jockeyed for position, each division moving in line ahead, breasting the broad dark current. Then at 3.40 the rebel lookouts spotted the lead division just as it reached the boom and started through the gap. Now delay was on the other side; the first eight ships were clear of the chain before the forts reacted. But when they did, according to an army man who had come up to watch the show, the effect was tremendous: "Imagine all the earthquakes in the world, and all the thunder and lightnings together in a space of two miles, all going off at once. That would be like it." Flaming brush-piles along the banks and fire-rafts on the river cast an eerie refulgence, pocked with rolling clouds of gunsmoke and the sudden scarlet of exploding shells. At this point the *Hartford*, leading the second division through the gap, made her entrance as if upon a brightly lighted stage.

It seemed to Farragut, high in the mizzen rigging, his feet on the ratlines and his back against the shrouds, "as if the artillery of heaven were playing on earth," but one of his gunners drew a comparison from the opposite direction: "My youthful imagination of hell did not equal the scene about us at this moment." Presently, however, there could be little doubt as to which description was more fitting. Attempting to dodge a fire-raft, the flagship's helmsman ran her into shallow water, directly under the guns of Fort St Philip. Farragut, who had descended to the quarterdeck just before a shellburst cut away most of the rigging where he had been standing, saw a mud flat dead ahead. "Hard a-port!" he shouted. Too late; she ran aground. Fortunately, the casemate gunners, expecting a landing party when they saw the *Hartford*'s bowsprit looming over their heads, deserted their pieces. But the fire-raft, pushed by a tug, changed course and rammed the flank of the grounded sloop, flames curling over the bulwarks and shooting up the rigging.

When Farragut saw his ship afire, his men giving back from the press of heat as the tug held the mass of burning pine firmly against her quarter, he threw up his hands and clasped them over his head in an anguished gesture. "My God, is it to end this way?" he cried. But he soon recovered his composure. Down on the gundeck, his clerk had conceived the notion of rolling some 20-pound shells onto the flaming raft, where they would explode and sink it. As he knelt to unscrew the fuze-caps Farragut saw him and mistook his attitude. "Come, sir, this is no time for prayer," he told him sternly, and called down also to the gunners, still holding back from the licking tongues of flame: "Don't flinch from that fire, boys. There's a hotter fire than that waiting for those who don't do their duty. Give that rascally little tug a shot!"

Then suddenly the worst was over. Catching the old man's spirit, despite the heat, the port crews returned to their guns and gave the tug two shots that hulled and sank her. The clerk got three of the shells uncapped and dropped them onto the blazing raft, which was torn apart by the explosion and went down in a hissing cloud of steam. While the fire brigade got busy with hoses and buckets, extinguishing the flames, the helmsman called for full power astern, and the ship careened off the mud flat, free to continue her course upriver and join in the destruction of the rebel flotilla.

Very little of it was left by now. When the skippers of the dozen Confederate vessels saw the northern warships clear the boom, run the gauntlet of fire from the forts, and head directly for them, apparently unscathed, big guns booming, they reacted with dismay — as well they might; all twelve of them together, with the immobilized *Louisiana* thrown in for good measure though only six of her 16 guns could be brought to bear, could not throw as much metal as a single Federal sloop. They scattered headlong, some for bank, where their crews set them afire and took to the swamps, while others tried for a getaway upriver. Three stayed to accept the challenge, upholding naval tradition by a form of naval suicide.

Two of the three were from the Confederate flotilla: the 7-gun former Mexican revenue cutter, which was reduced to kindling by the converging fire of three Union men-of-war as soon as she came within their range, and the low-riding armored ram *Manassas*, which headed downriver as soon as the guns began to roar and gave one of the heavy sloops an ineffectual glancing bump, firing her Cyclops cannon as she struck. (Aboard the sloop the cry went up, "The ram, the ram!" and the captain saw a rebel officer come out of the iron hatch and run forward along the port gunnel to inspect the damage, if any. Suddenly he whirled with an odd, disjointed motion and tumbled into the water. Hardly able to believe his eyes, the captain called to the leadsman in the chains, asking if he had seen him fall. "Why, yes sir," he said: "I saw him fall overboard. In fact, I helped him; for I hit him alongside the head with my hand-lead.") The *Manassas* backed off and continued downriver, intending to do better with the next one, but took a terrific pounding from the guns of both forts, whose cannoneers mistook her for a disabled Federal vessel. She came about, staggering back upstream, her armor pierced, her engines smashed, and was pounded again by four of the enemy warships. Avoiding a fifth, which charged to run her down, she veered into bank and stuck there, smoke curling from her hatch and punctures. What was left of her crew jumped ashore and scurried to safety while the Union gunboats flailed the brush with canister and grape.

Third to accept the challenge was the unarmored sidewheel steamboat *Governor Moore*, one of two vessels sent by the state of Louisiana to make up a third division of the fleet defending New Orleans. When the firing began she moved upriver, adding rosin to her fires to get up steam before turning to join the fight. As she moved through the darkness she saw the 1300-ton screw steamer *Varuna*, the fastest ship in the Federal fleet, coming hard upstream in pursuit of the fugitive gunboats. The *Moore* carried two guns, one forward and one aft; the *Varuna* carried ten, eight of them 8-inchers; but the former, undetected against a dark backdrop of trees along the bank, had the advantage of surprise. She opened fire at a hundred yards — and missed. Startled, the Federal replied, strewing the steamboat's decks with dead and wounded. The *Moore* was now too close to bring her forward gun to bear, her bow being in the way, but the captain ordered the piece depressed and fired it through his own deck. The first shot was deflected by a hawse pipe, but the second, fired through the hole in the deck and bow, burst against the *Varuna*'s pivot gun, inflicting heavy casualties. The third came as the *Moore* rammed her opponent hard amidships, receiving a broadside in return. She backed off, then fired and rammed again. That did it. The *Varuna* limped toward bank; whereupon one of the fleeing Confederate gunboats, seeing her distress, turned and gave her another bump before she made it. She went down quickly then, leaving her topgallant forecastle above water, crowded with survivors.

The *Moore*'s captain, having his blood up, ordered a downriver course, intending to take on the whole Yankee fleet with one broken-nosed steamboat. The crew seemed willing, what there was left — well over half were dead or dying — but the wounded first lieutenant at the helm had had enough. "Why do this?" he protested. "We have no men left. I'll be damned if I stand here to be murdered." And with that he slapped the wheel hard to starboard, making a run for the west bank. Five Union ships, within range by now, cut loose at her with all their guns; she seemed almost to explode. All told, her crew of 93, mostly infantry detachments and longshoremen, lost 57 killed and 17 wounded. The rest were captured or escaped through the swamps when she struck bank, already ablaze, her colors burning at the peak.

Dawn glimmered and spread through the latter stages of the fighting. When the sun came up at 5 o'clock the Federal ships broke out their flags to greet it and salute their victory. All being safely past the forts except the sunken *Varuna* and three of the lighter gunboats — one had taken a shot in her boiler, losing her head of steam; another had got tangled in the barricade; a third had turned back, badly cut up by the crossfire — Farragut ordered them to anchor, wash down, and take count. Casualties were 37 dead and 149 wounded, nearly twice the clerk's hopeful estimate and more than three times the losses in the forts: 12 dead and 40 wounded. On the other hand, the Confederate flotilla was utterly destroyed, including the fleeing gunboat which had given the *Varuna* a final butt; her skipper burned her at the levee in New Orleans.

Below the boom, Porter's anxiety was relieved as he watched the charred remnants of the rebel fleet come floating down the river. When his demand for immediate surrender of the forts was declined, he put his mortar crews back to work, firing up the remainder of their shells.

New Orleans was in a frenzy of rage and disappointment at the news from downriver. Other cities might accept defeat and endure the aftermath in sullen silence; but not this one. All afternoon and most of the night, while crowds milled in the streets, brandishing knives and pistols and howling for resistance to the end, drays rattled over the cobbles, hauling cotton from the presses for burning on the quays, where crates of rice and hogsheads of molasses were broken open and thrown into the river. This at least won the people's approval; "The damned Yankees shall not have it!" they cried, and the night was hazed with acrid smoke that hid the stars.

They were no less violent next morning when they heard the guns of the enemy fleet make short work of the Chalmette batteries, then come slowly into view around Slaughterhouse Bend as a drizzle of rain began to fall; "silent, grim, and terrible," one among the watchers called the warships, "black with men, heavy with deadly portent." Their great hope had been the ironclads, built and launched in their own yards. One had already gone downriver, powerless, and been by-passed. Now here came the other, the unfinished *Mississippi,* drifting helpless, set afire to keep her from falling into Federal hands. The crowd howled louder than ever at the sight, shouting "Betrayed! Betrayed!" and screaming curses at the Yankee sailors who watched from the decks and yardarms. Aboard the *Hartford,* one old tar grinned broadly back at them as he stood beside a 9-inch Dahlgren, holding the lanyard in one hand and patting the big black bottle-shaped breech with the other. The rain came down harder.

Despite the threats and invective from the quay, Farragut's strength was so obvious that he didn't have to use it. Two officers went ashore and walked unescorted through the hysterical mob to City Hall, where the mayor was waiting for them. Lovell had retreated, leaving New Orleans an open city. However, if the citizens were willing to undergo naval bombardment, he offered to "return with my troops and not leave as long as one brick remained upon another." The offer was declined: as was the navy's demand for an immediate surrender. "This satisfaction you cannot obtain at our hands," the mayor told the two officers. He would not resist, but neither would he yield; if they wanted the city, let them come and take it.

Farragut wanted no pointless violence; he had had enough violence the day before, when, as he told a friend, "I seemed to be breathing flame." Saturday, while negotiations continued, he ordered his captains to assemble their crews at 11 o'clock the following morning and "return thanks to Almighty God for his great goodness and mercy for permitting us to pass through the events of the past two days with so little loss of life and blood. At that hour the Church pennant will be hoisted on every vessel of the fleet, and their crews assembled will, in humiliation and prayer, make their acknowledgments thereof to the Great Disposer of all human events." That would be ceremony enough for him, with or without a formal surrender by the municipal authorities.

The occupation problem still remained, but not for long. Monday the garrisons of Forts Jackson and St Philip — they were "mostly foreign enlistments," the commandant said; "A reaction set in among them," he explained — mutinied, spiked the guns, and forced their officers to surrender. Still powerless, the *Louisiana* was blown up to forestall capture. Butler's 18,000 men ascended the river unopposed and marched into the city on the last day of the month. "In family councils," a resident wrote, "a new domestic art began to be studied — the art of hiding valuables" from looters under the general known thereafter as "Spoons" Butler. One cache he uncovered with particular satisfaction: 418 bronze plantation bells collected there in answer to Beauregard's impassioned pleas for metal. Sent to Boston, they sold for $30,000 to mock the rebels from New England towers and steeples. Other aspects of the occupation were less pleasant for the visitors. Not only was southern hospitality lacking, the people seemed utterly unwilling to accept the consequences of defeat: particularly the women, who responded to northern overtures with downright abuse. Butler knew how to handle that, however. "I propose to make some brilliant examples," he wrote Stanton.

Farragut now was free to continue his trip upriver, and in early May he did so. Baton Rouge fell as easily as New Orleans, once the guns of the fleet were trained on its streets and houses; the state government had fled the week before to Opelousas, which was safely away from the river. Natchez was next, and it too fell without resistance. Then in mid-May came Vicksburg, whose reply to a demand for surrender was something different from the others: "Mississippians don't know, and refuse to learn, how to surrender to an enemy. If Commodore Farragut or Brigadier General Butler can teach them, let them come and try." The ranks were wrong; Butler was a major general, Farragut a captain; but the writer seemed to mean what he was saying. The guns frowned down from the tall bluff — "so elevated that our fire will not be felt by them," Farragut said — and there were reports of 20,000 reinforcements on the way from Jackson. Deciding to label this first attempt a mere reconnaissance, he left garrisons at Baton Rouge and Natchez, and was back in New Orleans before the end of May. Vicksburg was a problem that could wait. In time he intended to "teach them," but just now it needed study.

Welles was angry, hotly demanding to know why the attack against Vicksburg's bluff had not been pressed, but the feeling in the fleet was that enough had been done in one short spring by one upriver thrust. New Orleans was now in northern hands and a second southern capital had fallen — both delivered as outright gifts to the army from the navy. Southerners agreed that it was quite enough, though some found bitter solace in protesting that the thing had been done by mechanical contrivance, with small risk and no gallantry at all. The glory was departing. "This is a most cowardly struggle," a Louisiana woman told her diary. "These people can do nothing without gunboats.... These passive instruments do their fighting for them. It is at best a dastardly way to fight." Then she added, rather wistfully: "We should have had gunboats if the Government had been efficient, wise or earnest."

※ 4 ※

The North had found a new set of western heroes — Farragut, Curtis, Canby, Pope, Ben Butler: all their stars were in ascendance — but some of the former heroes now had tarnished reputations: Grant, for instance. If the news from Donelson had sent him soaring like a rocket in the public's estimation, the news from Shiloh dropped him sparkless like the stick. Cashiered officers, such as the Ohio colonel who cried "Retreat! Save yourselves!" at first sight of the rebels, were spreading tales back home at his expense. He was incompetent; he was lazy; he was a drunk. Correspondents, who had come up late and gathered their information in the rear — "not the best place from which to judge correctly what is going on in front," Grant remarked — were soon in print with stories which not only seemed to verify the rumors of "complete surprise," but also included the casualty lists. Shocking as these were to the whole country, they struck hardest in the Northwest, where most of the dead boys were being mourned.

Hardest hit of all was Ohio, which not only had furnished a large proportion of the corpses, but also was smarting under the charge that several Buckeye regiments had scattered for the rear before firing a shot. Governor David Tod was quick to announce that these men were not cowards; they had been caught off guard as a result of the "criminal negligence" of the high command. By way of securing proof he sent the lieutenant governor down to talk with the soldiers in their camps. They agreed with the governor's view, and the envoy returned to publish in mid-April a blast against "the blundering stupidity and negligence of the general in command." He found, he said, "a general feeling among the most intelligent men that Grant and Prentiss ought to be court-martialed or shot." Grant himself was an Ohioan, but they disclaimed him; he had moved to Illinois.

Nor was Ohio alone in her resentment. Harlan of Iowa rose in Congress to announce that he discerned a pattern of behavior: Grant had blundered at Belmont until he was rescued by Foote's navy, had lost at Donelson until C. F. Smith redeemed him, and had been surprised at Shiloh and saved by Buell. "With such a record," Harlan declared, "those who continue General Grant in active command will in my opinion carry on their skirts the blood of thousands of their slaughtered countrymen."

Eventually the problem landed where the big ones always did: on the shoulders of Abraham Lincoln. Late one night at the White House a Pennsylvania spokesman made a summary of the charges. Grant had been surprised because of his invariable lack of vigilance and because he disregarded Halleck's order to intrench. In addition, he was reported drunk: which might or might not have been true, but in any case he had lost the public's confidence to such an extent that any future blood on his hands would be charged against the officials who sustained him. He had better be dismissed. Lincoln sat there thinking it over, profoundly alone with himself, then said earnestly: "I can't spare this man. He fights."

He was not fighting now, nor was he likely to be fighting any time in the near future. Halleck had seen to that by taking the field himself. As soon as he reached Pittsburg Landing, four days after the battle, he began reorganizing his forces by consolidating Grant's Army of the Tennessee and Buell's Army of the Ohio with Pope's Army of the Mississippi, summoned from Island Ten. When George Thomas, now a major general as a reward for Fishing Creek, arrived with Buell's fifth division — the other four, or parts of them, had come up in time for a share in the fighting — Halleck assigned it to Grant's army and gave Thomas the command in place of Grant, who was appointed assistant commander of the whole, directly under Halleck. That way he could watch him, perhaps use him in an advisory capacity, and above all keep him out of contact with the troops. Having thus disposed of one wild man, he attended to another. McClernand, with his and Lew Wallace's divisions, plus a third from Buell, was given command of the reserve. So organized, Halleck told his reshuffled generals, "we can march forward to new fields of honor and glory, till this wicked rebellion is completely crushed out and peace restored to our country." He was confident, and with good cause. His fifteen divisions included 120,172 men and more than 200 guns.

Thomas and Pope were pleased with the arrangement; but not Buell and McClernand. Buell, whose command was thus reduced to three green divisions while his former lieutenant Thomas had five, all veteran, protested: "You must excuse me for saying that, as it seems to me, you have saved the feelings of others very much to my injury." McClernand, too, was bitter. He saw little chance for "honor and glory," as Halleck put it, let alone advancement, when his army — if it could be called such; actually it was a pool on which the rest would call for reinforcements — did not even have a name. But the saddest of all was Grant. He had no troops at all, or even duties, so far as he could see. When he complained about being kicked upstairs into a supernumerary position, Halleck snapped at him with charges of ingratitude: "For the past three months I have done everything in my power to ward off the attacks which were made upon you. If you believe me your friend you will not require explanations; if not, explanations on my part would be of little avail."

C. F. Smith, who at Donelson had proved himself perhaps the hardest fighter of them all, was not included in the reshuffling because he was still confined to his sickbed in Savannah. After Shiloh, the infected shin got worse; blood poisoning set in. Or perhaps it was simply a violent reaction of the old man's entire organism, outraged at being kept flat on his back within earshot of one of the world's great battles. At any rate, he sickened and was dead before the month was out. Halleck ordered a salute fired for him at every post and aboard every warship in the department. The army would miss him, particularly the volunteers who had followed where he led, alternately cursed and cajoled, but always encouraged by his example. Grant would miss him most of all.

April 28, having completed the reorganization and briefed the four commanders, Halleck sent his Grand Army forward against Beauregard, who was intrenched at Corinth with a force which Halleck estimated at 70,000 men. Buell had the center, Thomas the right, and Pope the left; McClernand brought up the rear. Halleck intended to follow along, though for the present he kept his command post at Pittsburg. The great day had come, but he did not seem happy about it according to a reporter who saw him May Day: "He walks by the hour in front of his quarters, his thumbs in the armpits of his vest, casting quick looks, now to the right, now to the left, evidently not for the purpose of seeing anything or anybody, but staring into vacancy the while." Part of what was fretting him was the thing that had fretted Grant the year before, when he marched for the first time against the enemy and felt his heart "getting higher and higher" until it seemed to be in his throat. What Halleck felt was the presence of the enemy. "The evidences are that Beauregard will fight at Corinth," he wired Washington this same day.

Certain comparisons were unavoidable for a man accustomed to weighing all the odds. In the fight to come it would be Beauregard, who had co-directed the two great battles of the war, versus Halleck, the former lieutenant of engineers, who had never been in combat. True, he had written or translated learned works on tactics; but so had Hardee, waiting for him now beyond the woods. Bragg was there, grim-faced and wrathful, alongside Polk, the transfer from the Army of the Lord, and Breckinridge, an amateur and therefore unpredictable. So was Van Dorn, who had crossed the Mississippi with 17,000 veterans of Pea Ridge, where the diminutive commander had thrown them at Curtis in a savage double envelopment. It had failed because Curtis had kept his head while the guns were roaring. Could Halleck keep his? He wondered. Besides, Van Dorn might have learned enough from that experience to make certain it did not fail a second time.... For Halleck, the woods were filled with more than shadows.

Nevertheless, he put on a brave face when he wired Washington two days later: "I leave here tomorrow morning, and our army will be before Corinth tomorrow night."

Pope was off and running, in accordance with the reputation earned at New Madrid. Advancing seven miles from Hamburg on the 4th, he did not stop until he reached a stream appropriately called Seven Mile Creek, and from there he leapfrogged forward again to another creekline within two miles of Farmington, which in turn was only four miles from Corinth. He reported his position a good one, protected by the stream in front and a bog on his left, but he was worried about his other flank; "I hope Buell's forces will keep pace on our right," he told headquarters. It turned out he was right to worry. Buell was not there. Lagging back, he was warning Halleck: "We have now reached that proximity to the enemy that our movements should be conducted with the greatest caution and combined methods." The last phrase meant siege tactics, and the army commander took his cue from that. "Don't advance your main body at present," he told Pope. "We must wait till Buell gets up."

Buell was back near Monterey, with Thomas conforming on his right. Presently Pope was back there, too: Beauregard made a stab at his front, and he had to withdraw to avoid an attempt to envelop the flank protected by the bog. In fact the whole countryside was fast becoming boggy. Assistant Secretary Thomas Scott, an observer down from the War Department, wired Stanton: "Heavy rains for the past twenty hours. Roads bad. Movement progressing slowly." Gloomily Halleck confirmed the report: "This country is almost a wilderness and very difficult to operate in." Scott attended a high-level conference and passed the word along: Halleck would continue the advance, and "in a few days invest Corinth, then be governed by circumstances." He made no conjecture as to what those circumstances might be, but Stanton could see one thing clearly. Last week's "tomorrow" had stretched to "a few days."

It was more than a few. Every evening the troops dug in: four hours' digging, six hours' sleep, then up at dawn to repel attack. The attack didn't come, not in force at least, but Halleck had every reason to expect one. Rebel deserters were coming in with eye-witness accounts of the arrival of reinforcements for the 70,000 already behind the formidable intrenchments. He took thought of the host available to Beauregard by rail from Fort Pillow, Memphis, Mobile, and intermediary points. No less than 60,000 could be sped there practically overnight, he computed, which would give the defenders a larger army than his own. Taking thought, he grew cautious; he grew apprehensive. "Don't let Pope get too far ahead," he warned, acutely aware by now that he had another wild man on his hands. "It is dangerous and effects no good."

He had cause for caution, especially since the accounts of deserters were confirmed by observers of his own. In mid-May the officer in charge of pickets reported that he had heard trains pulling into Corinth during the night. "Such trains were greeted with immense cheering on arrival," he declared. "The enemy are concentrating a powerful army." Next night it was repeated. A scouting party, working near town, heard more trains arriving "and, after they stopped, marching music from the depot in the direction of the front lines." Intelligence could hardly be more definite, and Halleck found his apprehension shared. Indiana's Governor O. P. Morton, down to see how well his Hoosiers had recovered from the bloody shock of Shiloh, wired Stanton on May 22: "The enemy are in great force at Corinth, and have recently received reinforcements. They evidently intend to make a desperate struggle at that point, and from all I can learn their leaders have utmost confidence in the result.... It is fearful to contemplate the consequences of a defeat at Corinth." Halleck thought it fearful, too: the more so after McClernand capped the climax with a report he had from a doctor friend, captured at Belmont and recently exchanged. The Illinois general, fretting in his back-seat position, was finding "the amount of duty ... very great, indeed exhausting, if not oppressive." Now he crowded into the frame of the big picture by passing along what he heard from the doctor, who had left Memphis on May 15. While there, he had spoken with some former classmates now in the rebel army, who "informed him that on that date the enemy's force at Corinth numbered 146,000." Other details were given, the doctor said, "prospectively increasing their number to 200,000." To palliate the shock of this, he added that "a considerable portion of the force ... consists of new levies, being in large part boys and old men."

Two hundred thousand of anything, even rabbits, could make a considerable impression, however, if they were launched at a man who was unprepared: which was the one thing Halleck was determined not to be. Orders went out for the troops to dig harder and deeper, not only on the flanks, but across the center. They cursed and dug — the rains were over; summer was almost in — sweating in wool uniforms under the Mississippi sun. Only the Shiloh veterans, looking back, saw any sense in all that labor. Apparently all but four of the ranking generals shared their commander's apprehension: Pope, who chafed at restraint, bristling offensively on the left: Thomas, who did not have it in his nature to be quite apprehensive about anything: Sherman, who, happy over a pending promotion, called the movement "a magnificent drill": and Grant. Not even Shiloh had taught him caution to this extent. He suggested once to Halleck that he shift Pope's army from the left to the right, out of the swamps and onto the ridge beyond the opposite flank, then send it bowling directly along the high ground into the heart of Corinth. Halleck gave him a fish-eye stare of unbelief. "I was silenced so quickly," Grant said later, "that I felt that possibly I had suggested an unmilitary movement." He drew back and kept his own counsel. This was not his kind of war.

It was Halleck's kind, and he kept at it, burrowing as he went. An energetic inchworm could have made better time — half a mile a day now, sometimes less — but not without the danger of being swooped on by a hawk: whereas, by Halleck's method, the risk was small, the casualties low, and the progress sure. The soldiers, digging and cursing under the summer sun, might agree with the disgruntled McClernand's definition of the campaign as "the present unhappy drama," but they would be there for roll call when the time came for the bloody work ahead. Besides, nothing could last forever; not even this. By the morning of May 28 — a solid month from the jump-off — all three component armies were within cannon range of Beauregard's intrenchments. After four weeks of marching and digging, Halleck had his troops where he had said they would be "tomorrow." He had reached the second stage, the one in which he had said he would "be governed by circumstances."

★ ★ ★

East and far northeast of Corinth, Halleck had two more divisions, both left behind by Buell when he marched for Pittsburg Landing. The latter, commanded by Brigadier General George W. Morgan, was maneuvering in front of Cumberland Gap, prepared to move in if the Confederates evacuated or weakened the already small defensive force. Morgan had further plans, intending not only to seize the gap, but to penetrate the Knoxville region — a project dear, as everyone knew, to the heart of Abraham Lincoln. However, the place was a natural fortress; Morgan reported it "washed into deep chasms or belly-deep in mud." So long as the rebels stayed there he could do nothing but hover and maneuver. The more substantial threat would have to come from the opposite direction, beyond the gap, and that was where Buell's other division, under Brigadier General Ormsby M. Mitchel, came in.

He was already in North Alabama, deeper into enemy country than any other Federal commander, having occupied Huntsville the day Halleck got to Pittsburg. From there he pushed on and took Bridgeport just as Halleck's army started south. A bright prospect lay before him. Once he had taken Chattanooga, thirty miles away, he would continue his march along the railroad and threaten Knoxville from the rear. This would cause the evacuation of Cumberland Gap, and when Morgan came through, hard on the heels of the defenders, Mitchel would join forces with him and make Lincoln's fondest hope a fact by chasing the scattered rebels clean out of East Tennessee. That was his plan at the outset, and it tied in well with another he had already put in motion, which resulted in what was known thereafter as the Great Locomotive Chase.

James J. Andrews, a Kentucky spy who had gained the trust of Confederates by running quinine through the lines, volunteered to lead a group of 21 Ohio soldiers, dressed like himself in civilian clothes, down into Georgia to burn bridges and blow up tunnels along the Western & Atlantic, the only rail connection between Atlanta and Chattanooga. Andrews and his men infiltrated south and assembled at Marietta, Georgia, where — on April 12, the day after Mitchel took Huntsville — they boarded a northbound train as passengers. During the breakfast halt at

Big Shanty they made off with the locomotive and three boxcars, heading north. The conductor, W. A. Fuller, took the theft as a personal affront and started after them on foot. Commandeering first a handcar, then a switch engine, and finally a regular freight locomotive, along with whatever armed volunteers he encountered along the way, he pressed the would-be saboteurs so closely that they had no time for the destruction they had intended. Overtaken just at the Tennessee line, where they ran out of fuel and water, they took to the woods, but were captured. Eight were hanged as spies, including Andrews; eight escaped while awaiting execution, and the remaining six were exchanged. All received the Congressional Medal of Honor in recognition of their valor "above and beyond the call of duty." Fuller and his associates received a vote of thanks from the Georgia legislature, but no medals. The Confederacy never had any, then or later.

Andrews' failure meant that the rebels could reinforce Chattanooga rapidly by rail. Advancing toward it, Mitchel found other drawbacks to his plan, chief among them being a shortage of supplies. Except for the fact that he could bring food and other necessities along the railroad, he told Washington, "it would be madness to attempt to hold my position a single day." Presently gray raiders were loose in his rear, capturing men and disrupting communications. "As there is no [hope] of an immediate advance upon Chattanooga," he wired Stanton, "I will now contract my line." He remained in North Alabama, doing what he could — mainly destroying railroad bridges which later Union commanders would have to replace — but on the day that Halleck halted within range of the Corinth intrenchments, Mitchel requested a transfer to another theater. "My advance beyond the Tennessee River seems impossible," he said.

Chattanooga was untaken, and though Morgan still hovered north of Cumberland Gap, Knoxville was spared pressure from either direction. Halleck could expect no important strategic diversion on his left as he entered the final stage of his campaign against Corinth.

It turned out, simultaneously, that he could expect none on his right flank either. Farragut turned back from frowning Vicksburg, abandoning for the present his planned ascent of the Mississippi, and the descending fleet of ironclads, steaming south after the fall of Island Ten, received a jolt which gave the Confederates not only a sense of security on the river, but also a heady feeling of elation, long unfamiliar, and a renewal of their confidence in the valor of southern arms.

Midway between New Madrid and Memphis, Fort Pillow was next on the navy's list of downriver objectives, and Foote did not delay. With a burst of his old-time energy, he had the place under mortar bombardment within a week of the fall of Island Ten. The plan was for him to apply pressure from the river, while Pope moved in from the land side, a repetition of his tactics in Missouri. However, when Halleck took the field in person he summoned Pope to Pittsburg Landing, leaving only two regiments to coöperate with the navy. Foote felt let down and depressed. Fort Pillow was a mean-looking place, with the balance of the guns from Columbus dug into its bluff, and he did not think the navy could do the job alone. Downstream there was a Confederate flotilla of unknown strength, perhaps made stronger than his own by the addition of giant ironclads reportedly under construction in the Memphis yards. The commodore was feverish — "much enfeebled," one of his captains wrote — still on crutches from his Donelson wound, which would not heal in this climate, and distressed, as only a brave man could be, by his loss of nerve. In this frame of mind he applied to Welles for shore duty in the North; which was granted with regret.

May 9 he said farewell on the deck of the flagship, crowded with sailors come for a last look at him. He took off his cap and addressed them, saying that he regretted not being able to stay till the war was over; he would remember all they had shared, he said, "with mingled feelings of sorrow and of pride." Supported by two officers, he went down the gangway and onto a transport, where he was placed in a chair on the guards. When the crew of the flagship cheered him he covered his face with a palm-leaf fan to hide the tears which ran down into his beard. As the transport pulled away, they cheered again and tossed their caps in salute. Greatly agitated, Foote rose from the chair and cried in a broken voice across the widening gap of muddy water: "God bless you all, my brave companions! ... I can never forget you. Never, never. You are as gallant and noble men as ever fought in a glorious cause, and I shall remember your merits to my dying day." It was one year off, that dying day, and when the doctors told him it had come he took the news without regret. "Well," he said quietly, "I am glad to be done with guns and war."

His successor, Commodore Charles Henry Davis, a fifty-five-year-old Bostonian with a flowing brown mustache and gray rim whiskers, had been a salt-water sailor up to now, a member of the planning board and chief of staff to Du Pont at Port Royal, but before he had spent a full day in his new command he got a taste of what could happen on the river. His first impression had been one of dullness. Agreeing with Foote that the fleet alone could never take Fort Pillow — though in time, if ordered to do so, he would be willing to try running past it — he kept all but one of the gunboats anchored at Plum Run Bend, five miles above the fort. That one was stationed three miles below the others, protecting the single mortar-boat assigned to keep up a harassing fire by dropping its 13-inch shells at regular intervals into the rebel fortifications. "Every half-hour during the day," a seaman later wrote, "one of these little pills would climb a mile or two into the air, look around a bit at the scenery, and finally descend and disintegrate around the fort, to the great interest and excitement of the occupants." There was little interest and still less excitement at the near end of the trajectory. This had been going on for some weeks now, and as duty it was dull. The seven ironclads took the guard-mount times about, one day a week for each.

While Foote was telling his crew goodbye, J. E. Montgomery, the river captain who had brought the eight River Defense Fleet gunboats up from New Orleans, was holding a council of war at Memphis. The bitter details of what Farragut's blue-water ships had done to the Confederate flotilla above Forts Jackson and St Philip had reached Memphis by now, along with the warning that Farragut himself might not be far behind; he was on his way, and in fact had captured Baton Rouge the day before. Montgomery's captains believed they could do better when the time came, but in any case there was no point in waiting to fight both Federal fleets at once. They voted to go upriver that night and try a surprise attack on the ironclads next morning, May 10.

It was Saturday. The ironclad *Cincinnati* had the duty below, standing guard while *Mortar 10* threw its 200-pound projectiles, one every half-hour as usual, across the wooded neck of land hugged by the final bend above Fort Pillow. The gunboat was not taking the assignment very seriously, however. Steam down, she lay tied to some trees alongside bank, and her crew was busy holystoning the decks for weekly inspection. About 7 o'clock one of the workers gave a startled yell. The others looked and saw eight rebel steamboats rounding the bend, just over a mile away — eight minutes, one of the sailors translated — bearing down, full steam ahead, on the tethered *Cincinnati*. Things moved fast then. While the deck crew slipped her cables, the engineers were throwing oil and anything else inflammable into her furnaces for quick steam. They were too late. The lead vessel, the *General Bragg*, came on, twenty feet tall, her great walking-beam engine driving so hard she had built up a ten-foot billow in front of her bow. The *Cincinnati* delivered a broadside at fifty yards, then managed to swing her bow around and avoid right-angle contact. The blow, though glancing, tore a piece out of her midships six feet deep and twelve feet long, letting a flood into her magazine.

Three miles upstream, around Plum Run Bend, the rest of the fleet knew nothing of the sudden attack until they heard the guns. They too were lazing alongside bank, steam down. By the time they got up pressure enough to maneuver — which they did as soon as possible, the *Mound City* leading the way — they were too late to be of any help to their sister ship below. When the *General Bragg* sheered off, the second ram-gunboat, *Sumter*, struck the *Cincinnati* in the fantail, wrecking her steering gear and punching another hole that let the river in. Next came the *Colonel Lovell*, whose iron prow crashed into the port quarter. Taking water from three directions, the proud *Cincinnati*, the fleet's first flagship and leader of the crushing assault on Henry, rolled first to one side, now the other, then gave a convulsive shudder and went down in water shallow enough to leave her pilot-house above the surface for survivors to cling to, including her captain, who had taken a sharpshooter's bullet through the mouth. It appeared that one of the ironclad monsters could be sunk after all. And having proved it, the attacking flotilla proceeded to re-prove it.

The *Mound City* arrived too late for the *Cincinnati*'s good, and too early for her own. A fourth ram-gunboat, the *General Van Dorn*, met her almost head-on, and punched such a hole in her forward starboard quarter that the *Mound City* barely managed to limp toward bank in time to sink with her nose out of water. Two down and five to go: but when the rest of the ironclads came on the scene, their 9-inch Dahlgrens booming, the river captains decided enough had been done for one day. They drew off downstream, unpursued, to the protection of Fort Pillow's batteries. Montgomery brought up the rear in his jaunty flagship *Little Rebel*.

After a full year of war, afloat and ashore, a contradictory pattern was emerging. In naval actions — with the exception of Fort Donelson — whoever attacked was the winner; while in land actions of any size — again with the same notable exception — it was the other way around. Montgomery was satisfied, however, with the simpler fact that an ironclad could be sent to the bottom. He knew because he had done it twice in a single morning. Returning to a cheering reception at Memphis he informed Beauregard that if the Federal fleet remained at its present strength, "they will never penetrate farther down the Mississippi."

★ ★ ★

The Creole had need of all the assurance and encouragement he could get. With Halleck knocking at its gate, Corinth was one vast groaning camp of sick and injured. Hotels and private residences, stables and churches, stores and even the railroad station were jammed, not only with the wounded back from Shiloh — eight out of ten amputees died, victims of erysipelas, tetanus, and shock — but also with a far greater number incapacitated by a variety of ailments. For lack of sanitary precautions, unknown or at any rate unpracticed, the inadequate water supply was soon contaminated. While dysentery claimed its toll, measles and typhoid fever both reached epidemic proportions. By mid-May, with the arrival of Van Dorn, Beauregard had 18,000 soldiers on the sick list, which left him 51,690 present for duty: well under half the number Halleck was bringing so cautiously against him.

He had done what he could to increase that caution at every opportunity. Many of the "deserters," for example, who had given the Union commander such alarming information as to the strength and intentions of the invaders, had been sent out by Beauregard himself, after intensive coaching on what to say when questioned. Valid prisoners were almost as misleading, for Beauregard had a report spread through the ranks that immediate advances were intended, and interrogated captives passed it on. Nor did the inventive general neglect to organize diversions which he hoped would cause detachments from the army in his front. Two regiments of cavalry were ordered to assemble at Trenton, Tennessee, then dash across western Kentucky for an attack on lightly held Paducah, meanwhile spreading the rumor that they were riding point for Van Dorn's army, which was on its way to seize the mouth of the Tennessee River and thus cut off Halleck's retreat when Beauregard struck him in front with superior numbers. A second, less ambitious cavalry project was intrusted to Captain John H. Morgan, who had shown promise on outpost duty the year before. He was promoted to colonel, given a war bag of $15,000, and sent to Kentucky to raise a regiment for disrupting the Federal rear. Though the former scheme was a failure — Beauregard blamed "the notorious incapacity of the officer in command" — the latter was carried out brilliantly from the outset. These were the gray raiders who caused Ormsby Mitchel to "contract" his line in North Alabama. However, it worked less well on the Corinth front. When Andrew Johnson protested that troops were needed to restrain Tennessee "disloyalists," the War Department referred the matter to Halleck, who refused to be disconcerted. "We are now at the enemy's throat," he replied, "and cannot release our great grasp to pare his toenails."

If Old Brains was to be stopped it would have to be done right here in front of Corinth, and Beauregard did what he could with what he had. His army took position along a ridge in rear of a protective creek, three to six miles out of town, thus occupying a quadrant which extended from the Mobile & Ohio on the north to the Memphis & Charleston Railroad on the east. Polk had the left, Bragg the center, and Hardee the right; Breckinridge and Van Dorn supported the flanks, being posted just in rear of the intersections of the railroads and the ridge. All through what was left of April and most of May, the defenders intrenched as furiously as the attackers, but with the advantage that while their opponents were honeycombing the landscape practically all the way from Monterey, their own digging was done in the same place from day to day. Even before Halleck started forward, the natural strength of the lines along the Corinth ridge had been greatly increased, and as he drew nearer they became quite formidable — especially in appearance. This was what Beauregard wanted: not only to give his men the added protection of solid-packed red earth, but also to free a portion of them for operations beyond the fortified perimeter, in case some segment of the advancing host grew careless and exposed itself, unsupported, to a sudden crippling slash by the gray veterans who had practiced such tactics at Elkhorn Tavern and Shiloh.

Pope was the likeliest to expose himself to such treatment, bristly as he was, and he had not been long in doing so. When he rushed forward in early May and took up an isolated position at Farmington, calling for the other commanders to hurry and catch up, Beauregard planned to destroy him by throwing Bragg at his front and Van Dorn on his flank. "Soldiers, can the result be doubtful?" he asked. "Shall we not drive back into the Tennessee the presumptuous mercenaries collected for our subjugation?" However, the result was worse than doubtful. Bragg hit Pope as planned, and hit him hard, but Van Dorn found the flank terrain quite different from the description in the attack order; Pope scurried back to safety before his flank was even threatened. In late May, when he returned to his old position — this time by more gradual approaches, allowing his fellow commanders to keep pace — Beauregard ordered the same trap sprung. Once more his hopes were high. "I feel like a wolf and will fight Pope like one," Van Dorn declared as he set out. But the results were the same as before, except that this time the Federals did not fall back, neither Pope nor the others alongside him.

The failure of this second attempt to repulse the Union host before it got a close-up hug on his intrenchments confirmed what Beauregard had suspected since mid-May. Outnumbered as he was, he would never be able to hold onto Corinth once the contest became a siege. In fact, if it came to that, he might not be able to hold onto his army. In addition to the water shortage and the lengthening sick-list, there was now a scarcity of food. The arrival of a herd of cattle, driven overland from Texas, had already saved the defenders from starvation, but the herd was dwindling fast. Even if the Yankees failed, disease and hunger would force him out in time. So on May 25 he called a conference of his generals: Bragg, Van Dorn, Polk, Hardee, Breckinridge, and Price. Hardee, as became a student, had prepared a statement of primer-like simplicity: "The situation ... requires that we should attack the enemy at once, or await his attack, or evacuate the place." To attack such numbers, intrenched to their front, "would probably inflict on us and the Confederacy a fatal blow." The only answer, as Hardee saw it, was to fall back down the line of the M & O while there was still a chance to do so unmolested, no matter how slim that chance appeared to be.

Beauregard and the others could do nothing but agree: the more so two days later, when Halleck got his whole Grand Army up within range of the fortified ridge and next morning — May 28 — opened a dawn-to-dusk cannonade, which paused from time to time to allow the infantry to probe for weak spots in the Confederate defenses. Fortunately, none developed; the wily Creole was left free to continue his plans for a withdrawal so secret that few of his officers suspected that one was intended. While the wounded and sick, along with the heavy baggage and camp equipment, were being evacuated by rail, the able-bodied men in the intrenchments were issued three days' cooked rations and told that they were about to launch an all-out attack: with the result that a timorous few — who indeed had cause to be frightened, being conscious of the odds — went over to the enemy with the news. Meanwhile the march details were formulated and rehearsed, the generals being assembled at army headquarters and required to repeat their instructions by rote until all had mastered their parts. No smallest detail was neglected, down to the final arrangements for bewildering the Federal pursuit by removing all the finger boards and mileposts south of Corinth.

Next afternoon, of necessity, the front-line troops were told of the planned deception in time to prepare for it that evening. They responded with enthusiasm, glad to have a share in what promised to be the greatest hoax of the war, and some proved almost as resourceful and inventive as their commander. When they stole out of the intrenchments after nightfall, they left dummy guns in the embrasures and dummy cannoneers to serve them, fashioned by stuffing ragged uniforms with straw. A single band moved up and down the deserted works, pausing at scattered points to play retreat, tattoo, and taps. Campfires were left burning, with a supply of wood alongside each for the drummer boys who stayed behind to stoke them and beat reveille next morning. All night a train of empty cars rattled back and forth along the tracks through Corinth, stopping at frequent intervals to blow its whistle, the signal for a special detail of leather-lunged soldiers to cheer with all their might. The hope was that this would not only cover the incidental sounds of the withdrawal, but would also lead the Federals to believe that the town's defenders were being heavily reinforced.

It worked to perfection. Beauregard would have been delighted if he had had access to the messages flying back and forth in reaction behind the northern lines. At 1.20 in the morning Pope telegraphed Halleck: "The enemy is reinforcing heavily, by trains, in my front and on my left. The cars are running constantly, and the cheering is immense every time they unload in front of me. I have no doubt, from all appearances, that I shall be attacked in heavy force at daylight." He turned his men out and did what he could to brace them for the shock, while Halleck alerted the other commanders. At 4 o'clock, mysteriously, the rattling and the cheering stopped, giving way to a profound silence which was broken at dawn by "a succession of loud explosions." Daylight showed "dense black smoke in clouds," but no sign of the enemy Pope expected to find massed in his front. Picking his way forward he came upon dummy guns and dummy cannoneers, some with broad grins painted on. Otherwise the works were deserted. So, apparently, was the town beyond. He sent back word of the evacuation, adding: "The whole country here seems to be fortified."

Halleck came out to see for himself. He had wanted a victory as bloodless as digging and maneuvering could make it; but not this bloodless, and above all not this empty. Even rebel civilians were scarce, all but two of the local families having departed with Beauregard's army. Seven full weeks of planning and strain, in command of the largest army ever assembled under one field general in the Western Hemisphere, had earned him one badly smashed-up North Mississippi railroad intersection.

In hope that more could yet be done, the order went out: "General Pope, with his reinforcements from the right wing, will proceed to feel the enemy on the left." Happy at being unleashed at last, Pope was hot on the trail with 50,000 men. At first there was little for him to "feel," but he reported joyfully: "The roads for miles are full of stragglers from the enemy, who are coming in in squads. Not less than 10,000 men are thus scattered about, who will come in within a day or two." This was mainly hearsay — like the information from a farmer that Beauregard, in a panic, had told his men to take to the woods and "save themselves as best they could" — but Halleck, anxious for a substantial achievement to put on the wire to Washington, was glad to hear it. Two days later, when Pope reported continuing success — a cavalry dash had destroyed an ammunition train and captured about 200 Confederate wounded — Halleck misunderstood him to mean that his former prediction had been fulfilled, and passed the news along to the War Department that 10,000 prisoners and 15,000 stand of arms had been seized because of the boldness of Pope's pursuit. Duly elated, Stanton replied: "Your glorious dispatch has just been received, and I have sent it into every State. The whole land will soon ring with applause at the achievement of your gallant army and its able and victorious commander."

Adjectivally, this was rather in line with Halleck's own opinion. The day after Corinth fell he informed his troops that they had scored "a victory as brilliant and important as any recorded in history," one that was "more humiliating to [the leaders of the rebellion] and to their cause than if we had entered the place over the dead and mangled bodies of their soldiers." However, this was a good deal more than any of his generals would say: except possibly John Pope. McClernand still considered the campaign an "unhappy drama," and not even Sherman, glad as he was to be out in the open, wearing his new major general's stars, praised it for being anything more than a "drill." Harsher words were left to the newspaper correspondents, who had never admired the elbow-scratching commander anyhow. "General Halleck ... has achieved one of the most barren triumphs of the war," the Chicago *Tribune* asserted. "In fact, it is tantamount to a defeat." The Cincinnati *Commer-*

cial extended this into a flat statement that, by means of his sly withdrawal, "Beauregard [has] achieved another triumph."

These verdicts, these ex post facto condemnations, were delivered before all the testimony was in. Hoax or no, the Confederate retrograde movement was, after all, a retreat; and as such it had its consequences. Fort Pillow, being completely outflanked, was evacuated June 4, along with the supplementary Fort Randolph, fifteen miles below. Now all that stood between the Federal ironclads and Memphis was the eight-boat flotilla which had been resting on its laurels since the affair at Plum Run Bend. Captain Montgomery had said then that the Yankees would "never penetrate farther down" unless their fleet was reinforced; but two days after Pillow and Randolph were abandoned he discovered, in the most shocking way, that it had indeed been reinforced.

Back in March — after years of failing to interest the navy in his theory — an elderly civil engineer named Charles Ellet, Jr., wrote and sent to the War Department a pamphlet applying the formula $f = mv^2$ to demonstrate the superiority of the ram as a naval weapon, particularly in river engagements, which allowed scant room for dodging. Stanton read it and reacted. He sent for the author, made him a colonel, and told him to build as many of the rams as he thought would be needed to knock the rebels off the Mississippi. Ellet got to work at once, purchasing and converting suitable steamers, and joined the ironclad fleet above Fort Pillow on May 25 with nine of the strange-looking craft. They carried neither guns nor armor, since neither had any place in the mass-velocity formula; nor did they have sharp dogtooth prows, which Ellet said would plug a hole as quickly as they punched one. All his dependence was on the two formula-components. Velocity was assured by installing engines designed to yield a top speed of fifteen knots, which would make them the fastest things on the river, and "mass" was attained by packing the bows with lumber and running three solid bulkheads, a foot or more in thickness, down the length of each vessel, so that the impact of the whole rigid unit would be delivered at a single stroke. Engines and boilers were braced for the shock of ramming, and the crews were river men whose courage Ellet tested in various ways, getting rid of many in the process. Perhaps his greatest caution, however, was shown in the selection of his captains. All were Pennsylvanians, like himself, and all were named Ellet. Seven were brothers and nephews of the designer-commander, and the eighth was his nineteen-year-old son.

Anxious to put $f = mv^2$ to work, the thin-faced lank-haired colonel was for going down and pitching into the rebel flotilla as soon as he joined up, but Flag Officer Davis had learned caution at Plum Run Bend. In spite of the fact that both sunken ironclads had been raised from their shallow graves and put back into service, the fleet was still under strength, three of its seven units having returned to Cairo for repairs. No matter, Ellet said; he and his kinsmen were still for immediate action, with or without the ironclads. But Davis continued to refuse the "concurrence" Stanton had told the colonel he would have to have in working with the navy.

The Confederates in Memphis, knowing nothing of all this, had assumed from reports that the new arrivers were some kind of transport. They relied on the guns of Forts Pillow and Randolph; or if the batteries failed to stop the Yankees, there was still the eight-boat flotilla which had given them such a drubbing three weeks back. Moreover, as at New Orleans, the keels of two monster ironclads, the *Arkansas* and the *Tennessee*, had been laid in the city's yards. The former, having been launched and armored up to her maindeck, was floated down to Vicksburg, then towed up the Yazoo River for completion in safety after the fall of Island Ten; but the latter was still on the stocks, awaiting the arrival of her armor. Like the city itself, she would have to take her chances that the enemy would be stopped.

Those chances were considerably thinned by the evacuation of Corinth and the two forts upriver. It now became a question of which would get there first, a sizeable portion of Halleck's Grand Army or the Federal fleet. The citizens hoped it would be the latter, for they had the gunboat flotilla to stand in its way, while there was absolutely nothing at all to stand in the way of the former. They got their wish. At dawn of June 6, two days after Fort Pillow was abandoned, the ironclads showed up, coming round the bend called Paddy's Hen and Chickens, four of them in line abreast just above the city, offering battle to the eight Confederate gunboats. The people turned out in tens of thousands, lining the bluffs for a grandstand seat at what they hoped would be a reënactment of the affair at Plum Run Bend. The first shot was fired at sunup, and they cheered and waved their handkerchiefs as at a tableau when the southern gunboats, mounting 28 light cannon, moved out to meet their squat black bug-shaped northern opponents, mounting 68, mostly heavy.

Ellet had his rams in rear of the ironclad line of battle. When the first shot was fired, he took off his hat and waved it to attract the attention of his brother commanding the ram alongside his own. "Round out and follow me! Now is our chance!" he cried. Both boats sprang forward under full heads of steam and knifed between the ironclads, whose crews gave them a cheer as they went by. Ellet made straight for the *Colonel Lovell*, leader of the Confederate line, and when she swerved at the last minute to avoid a head-on collision, struck her broadside and cut her almost in two. She sank within a few minutes: brief, conclusive proof of the relation between force and mv^2. Meanwhile his brother had accomplished something different. Striking for the *General Price*, which held her course while the *General Beauregard* moved to aid her by converging on the ram, he darted between the two — which then collided in his wake. The *General Price* lost one of her sidewheels, sheared off in the crash, and while she limped toward bank, out of the fight, the ram came about in a long swift curve and rammed the *Beauregard* at the moment the rebel's steam drum was punctured by a shell from one of the ironclads. She struck her colors.

Four of the remaining five did not last much longer, and none ever managed to come to grips with an adversary. Montgomery's *Little Rebel*, the only screw steamer of the lot, took a shell in her machinery, then went staggering into the Arkansas bank, where her crew made off through the woods. The *Jeff Thompson* was set afire by a Federal broadside; the *Sumter* and the *Bragg*, like the flagship, were knocked into bank by the Dahlgrens. The whole engagement lasted no longer than the one at Plum Run Bend, which it avenged. One Confederate was sunk beyond raising; two were burned; four were captured, and in time became part of the fleet they had fought. *Van Dorn*, the only survivor, managed to get enough of a head start in the confusion to make a getaway downriver. Two of the rams gave chase for a while, but then turned back to join the celebration.

The cheering was all on the river, where the rams and ironclads anchored unopposed, not on the bluffs, where the cheers had turned to groans. Smoke had blanketed the water; all the spectators could see was the flash of Union guns and the tall paired stacks of Confederate steamboats riding above the murk. Pair by pair, in rapid order, the crown-top chimneys disappeared. "The deep sympathizing wail which followed each disaster," one who heard it wrote, "went up like a funeral dirge from the assembled multitude, and had an overwhelming pathos." When the sun-dazzled smoke finally cleared away they saw that their flotilla had been not only defeated but abolished, and they turned sadly away to await the occupation which the Corinth retreat had made inevitable anyhow. There still was time to burn the *Tennessee*, sitting armorless on the stocks, and this they did, taking considerable satisfaction in at least making sure that she would never be part of the fleet whose destruction had been the aim of her designers. It was bitter, however, to surrender as they did to a nineteen-year-old medical cadet, Colonel Ellet's son, who landed in a rowboat with three seamen and a folded flag, the stars and stripes, which presently he was hoisting over the post office. Later that day the two regiments Pope had left behind marched in for the formal occupation. Thus was Memphis returned to her old allegiance.

Colonel Ellet himself did not come ashore. The only Federal casualty of the engagement, he had been pinked in the knee by a pistol ball while waving his hat on the hurricane deck of his flagship, directing the ram attack. The wound, though painful, was not considered dangerous; prone on the deck, he continued in command throughout the fight; but infection set in, and he died of it two weeks later, while being taken north aboard one of the rams. Before his death, however, he had the satisfaction of proving his theory in action and of knowing that his genius — in conjunction with the no doubt larger genius of that other civil engineer, James Eads — had cleared the Mississippi down to Vicksburg, whose batteries now would be grist for Davis' and Farragut's upper and nether millstones.

★ ★ ★

At Tupelo, where he called a halt fifty-two miles south of Corinth, Beauregard was infuriated by Halleck's widely circulated dispatch which glorified Pope at the Creole's expense by claiming a large bag of demoralized prisoners and abandoned equipment. He hotly replied, through the columns of newspapers guilty of spreading this libel, that the report "contained as many lies as lines." Far from being a rout, he said, or even a reverse, "the retreat was conducted with great order and precision, doing much credit to the officers and men under my orders, and must be looked upon, in every respect, by the country as equivalent to a brilliant victory."

Not all of his own countrymen agreed with him, any more than Halleck's had agreed with Halleck; but in the Southerner's case the dissenters included the Chief Executive. While the army was falling back, exposing his home state and the river down its western flank to deeper penetration, Davis told his wife: "If Mississippi troops lying in camp, when not retreating under Beauregard, were at home, they would probably keep a section of the river free for our use and closed against Yankee transports." The general had been sent west to help recover territory, not surrender more, and when it became evident after Shiloh that this was not to be accomplished, an intimate of the Davis circle wrote prophetically in her diary in reference to the hero of Sumter and Manassas: "Cock robin is as dead as he ever will be now. What matters it who killed him?"

As if in confirmation, soon after the loss of Memphis and its covering flotilla opened the river south to Vicksburg, the Tupelo commander received from the Adjutant General in Richmond a telegraphic warning that trouble was brewing for him there: "The President has been expecting a communication explaining your last movement. It has not yet arrived." Beauregard replied: "Have had no time to write report. Busy organizing and preparing for battle if pursued.... Retreat was a most brilliant and successful one," he added, maneuvering for solid ground on which to meet objections now that he had begun to see that the hoax might seem less fruitful and amusing from a distance. Next day, June 13, he forwarded a complete report, inclosing a clipping from the Chicago *Tribune* which showed that the enemy, at least, admired his generalship. He ended with a prediction that Halleck would find Corinth "a barren locality, which he must abandon as wholly worthless for his purposes."

If the document lacked his usual verve, there were more reasons than the melancholia resulting from lack of appreciation from above. Though the army's health was improving rapidly in the more salubrious Tupelo surroundings, the general's own was not. He had never entirely recovered from the throat operation he had undergone in Virginia, and the strain of long-odds campaigning had lowered his resistance even more. For months his doctors had been urging him to take a rest. Always he had replied that the military crisis would not permit it. But now that his army was out of contact with the enemy, he thought he might safely go to Bladon Springs, a resort north of Mobile, for a week or ten days of rest and relaxation before returning to take up the reins again. Bragg, the next ranking general, could hold them in his absence; Beauregard considered him fully qualified, having recommended him for the position just after Shiloh. Armed with a certificate of disability from his medical director, he was packing to leave on the 14th when he learned that Bragg had received, clean over his commander's head, a War Department order instructing him to assume command of the Vicksburg defenses.

Angry at having been by-passed, Beauregard wired that Bragg could not be spared. He himself was taking a short sick leave, he said, and was leaving the North Carolinian in charge of the army during his absence. Then, as if suddenly aware that this was the first he had told the authorities of his intended departure, he wrote a letter describing his run-down physical condition, quoting his doctors' insistence that he take a rest, and giving his travel schedule. He did not ask permission to go; he simply told the government he was going. Nor did he send the information by wire. He sent it by regular mail, and was on his way to Bladon Springs before the letter got to Richmond.

Bragg considered his position awkward, knowing the trouble that was brewing, and with Regular Army prudence wired Richmond for instructions as soon as his chief was gone. The reaction was immediate, perhaps because the wire arrived on the same day as news of another consequence of the retreat, the fall of Cumberland Gap. As far as Davis was concerned, the situation at Tupelo spoke for itself: Beauregard was AWOL. Accordingly, a telegram went to Bragg at once, assigning him to permanent command. The Creole first learned of the action from a telegram Bragg sent to intercept him in Mobile. "I envy you, and am almost in despair," Bragg said. Beauregard replied: "I cannot congratulate you, but am happy for the change."

He was not happy; he just said that to cover his anger and disappointment. Four months ago he had come west full of resentment at having been shunted away from the main field of endeavor into a vaster but relatively much less important theater. Since then, he had learned better. The war was to be won or lost as readily here as in the East. What was more, he had come to respect and love the western army, just as it loved and respected him, and he was bitter against the man who had taken it from him as abruptly as if by a pull on the trigger of a pistol already leveled at his head. Replying to a letter of sympathy sent by a friend, he wrote: "If the country be satisfied to have me laid on the shelf by a man who is either demented or a traitor to his high trust — well, let it be so. I require rest and will endeavor meanwhile by study and reflection to fit myself for the darkest hours of our trial, which I foresee are yet to come." Part at least of the study and reflection was devoted to composing other phrases which he considered descriptive of the enemy who had wronged him. "That living specimen of gall and hatred," he called Davis now; " 'that Individual.' "

CHAPTER

× 5 ×

Fighting Means Killing

★ ✗ ☆

☞ DISASTER CAME IN VARIOUS FORMS THIS spring, and it moved to various tempos. In the West it came like fireworks, looming after a noisy rush and casting a lurid glow. Whole states, whole armies fell at once or had large segments broken off by the tread of the invader. Kentucky and Missouri, most of Tennessee, much of Arkansas, North Alabama and North Mississippi were lost in rapid succession, along with 30,000 fighting men, dead or in northern prison camps, and finally New Orleans, Memphis, and the fleets that had been built — or, worse, were being built — to hold the river that ran between them. That was how it reached the West. In the East it came otherwise: not with a gaudy series of eruptions and collapses and attendant pillars of fire, but with a sort of inexorable hover, an inching-forward through mist and gloom, as if it were conserving energy for an even more spectacular climax: the collapse of the national capital, the destruction of the head and front of Government itself. On damp evenings, such as the one that fell on May Day, the grumble of McClellan's guns at Yorktown, faintly audible from Richmond's hills, reached listeners through what seemed to them the twilight of the gods.

Nowhere, east or west, had there been a victory to celebrate since Ball's Bluff in October seven months ago. Foreign intervention, the cure-all formerly assured by early spring because that was when England's cotton reserves were supposed to be exhausted, now seemed further away than ever. "There are symptoms that the Civil War cannot very long be protracted," the once friendly London *Times* was saying. "Let its last embers burn down to the last spark without being trodden out by our feet." Confederates could tell themselves they had known all along that the English had never made a habit of retrieving other people's chestnuts; but additional, less deniable disappointments loomed much nearer. Although the near-exhaustion of the nation's war supplies, especially powder, was kept secret, other effects of the naval blockade were all too well known. After a disastrous attempt at price control was abandoned, the regulated items having simply disappeared from grocery shelves, prices went up with a leap. Meat was 50¢ a pound, butter 75¢, coffee $1.50, and tea $10: all in contrast to cotton, which had fallen to 5¢. Salt — "Lot's wife" in the slang of the day — was scarce after the loss of the Kanawha works, and sugar went completely out of sight with the news of the fall of New Orleans. What was more, all this took place in an atmosphere not only of discouragement, but also of suspicion. Treasonable slogans were being chalked on fences and walls: "Union men to the rescue!" "Now is the time to rally round the Old Flag!" "God bless the Stars and Stripes!" There were whispers of secret and mysterious Union meetings, and one morning a black coffin was found suggestively near the Executive Mansion, a noosed rope coiled on its lid.

Few citizens approved of the coffin threat, but many approved of its implication as to where the blame for their present troubles lay, and so did a number of their elected representatives. The permanent Congress was different from the one that had come to Richmond from Montgomery — not so much in composition, however, as in outlook. Though for the most part they were the same men, reëlected, they served under different circumstances, the bright dawn having given way to clouds. A member who had resigned to enter the army, but who kept in touch with his former colleagues, told his wife, "It seems that things are coming to this pass; to be a patriot you must hate Davis." They took their cue from R. B. Rhett, whose Charleston *Mercury* was saying, "Jefferson Davis now treats all men as if they were idiotic insects." One among them who felt that way was Yancey. Back from his fruitless European mission, he was angrily demanding to know why Virginia had twenty-nine generals and Alabama only four. Another was Tom Cobb, who wrote home that he and his fellows were secretly debating the deposition of Davis. "He would be deposed," Cobb declared, "if the Congress had any more confidence in Stephens than in him."

If they could not get rid of him, they could at least try the next best thing by limiting his powers: especially in the conduct of military affairs. This had been the basis for the virulent attack on Benjamin, who administered the War Department under the close supervision of his chief. Reasoning that a professional soldier would be less pliant, they attempted to oust Benjamin by recommending R. E. Lee for the position. When Davis refused to make the change, on grounds that the law required a civilian at the post, Congress retaliated with an act calling for the appointment of a commanding general who would have full authority to take charge of any army in the field whenever he thought best. Davis vetoed the measure as a violation of his rights as Commander in Chief, but at the same time — it was early March by then — ordered Lee "to duty at the seat of government," where he would be charged with the conduct of military operations "under the direction of the President." Thus Davis frustrated his enemies in Congress. He gained a military secretary — "an orderly sergeant," one newspaper sneered — without sacrificing one jot of his constitutional prerogative. Lee saw well enough what it came to. Returning to Richmond from his work on the South Atlantic coastal defenses, he observed: "I cannot see either advantage or pleasure in my duties. But I will not complain, but do the best I can."

His best was better than might have been expected, considering the limitations of his authority and his early failures in the field. Mainly what he accomplished was done through tactful handling of the President, whose admission that "events have cast on our arms and hopes the gloomiest shadows" Lee now saw at first hand was the mildest possible statement of conditions. Not only was there a crippling shortage of weapons, it now appeared probable that there soon would be a lack of men to shoulder the few they had. The so-called "bounty and furlough law" having proved a failure, except as a disruptive influence, few of the volunteers whose Sumter-inspired one-year enlistments would expire in April seemed willing to forego at least a vacation at home before signing up again, and many were saying quite openly that they were through with army life for good. In the heat of their conviction that they had earned a rest, the already badly outnumbered southern armies seemed likely to melt away just as the northern juggernaut was scheduled to gather speed in the East as in the West. Virginia had already met the problem by providing for a general enrollment in the state militia of all citizens between the ages of eighteen and forty-five, to be used as replacements for the men whose army enlistments expired. Under the influence of Lee, Davis proposed more stringent measures on a larger scale. In a late-March message to Congress he recommended outright conscription, within the same age bracket, throughout the Confederacy — to make sure, he said, that the burden of fighting did not fall "exclusively on the most ardent and patriotic."

Congress debated hotly, then on April 16, after lowering the upper age limit to thirty-five, passed the first national conscription law in American history. They passed it because they knew it was necessary, but they blamed Davis for having made it necessary by adopting the "dispersed defensive," which they said had dampened national enthusiasm. His reply — that "without military stores, without the workshops to create them, without the power to import them, necessity not choice has compelled us to occupy strong positions and everywhere to confront the enemy without reserves" — did nothing to assuage the anger of the States Righters, who saw in conscription a repudiation of the principles for which the war was being fought. Georgia's governor

Joseph E. Brown flatly declared that no "act of the Government of the United States prior to the secession of Georgia struck a blow at constitutional liberty so fell as has been struck by the conscription act." The fire-eaters, already furious at having been denied high offices, renewed their attacks on Davis as a despot. He replied in a letter to a friend, "When everything is at stake and the united power of the South alone can save us, it is sad to know that men can deal in such paltry complaints and tax their ingenuity to slander because they are offended in not getting office.... If we can achieve our independence, the office seekers are welcome to the one I hold."

However, the critics were in full bay now and were not to be turned aside by scorn or reason. Ominously, they pointed out that Napoleon's rise to absolute power had been accomplished by just such an act of conscription. Nothing Davis said or did was above suspicion. Even his turning to the solace of religion — up till now he had never been a formal member of any church — was seen as a possibly sinister action. "The President is thin and haggard," a War Department clerk observed in mid-April, "and it has been whispered that he will immediately be baptised and confirmed. I hope so, because it may place a great gulf between him and the descendant of those who crucified the Saviour. Nevertheless, some of his enemies allege that professions of Christianity have sometimes been the premeditated accompaniments of usurpation. It was so with Cromwell and Richard III."

The descendant referred to, of course, was the clerk's former department chief, Benjamin, now head of the State Department. He was as skillful an administrator as ever, but the problems here were not the kind that could be solved by rapid pigeon-holing. Europe was reacting to the news of Union successes along the line of the Mississippi, and that reaction worked strongly against Confederate recognition. Slidell was beginning to weary of the French emperor's slippery courtesies, which led to nothing above-board or official, and Mason was suffering from the same feeling of affront that had vanquished Yancey. He wrote that he intended to present his next proposal for recognition "as a demand of *right;* and if refused — as I have little doubt it would be — to follow the refusal by a note, that I did not consider it compatible with the dignity of my government, and perhaps with my own self-respect, to remain longer in England." Benjamin's smile faded, for once, as he replied, imploring Mason not to act rashly. His mere presence in London was of enormous value; he must await eventualities.

Fortunately, the Virginian had not acted on his impulse, but his patience was wearing thin, and this was one more worry that had to be passed along to Davis. He had tried to steel his harrowed nerves against the criticisms flung at him from all sides, telling his wife: "I wish I could learn just to let people alone who snap at me — in forbearance and charity to turn away as well from the cats as the snakes."

But it was too much for him. He could approach his work with humility, but not his critics. When they snapped he snapped back. Nor was he highly skilled as an arbitrator; he had too much admiration and sympathy for those who would not yield, whatever their cause, to be effective at reconciling opponents. In fact, this applied to a situation practically in his own back yard. The White House stood on a tall hill, surrounded by other mansions. On the plain below were the houses of the poor, whose sons had formed a gang called the Butcher Cats, sworn to eternal hatred of the Hill Cats, the children of the gentry on the hill. The two gangs had rock fights and occasional gouging matches. After one particularly severe battle, in which his oldest son was involved, Davis walked down the hill to try his hand at arbitration. He made them a speech, referring to the Butcher Cats as future leaders of the nation. One of them replied: "President, we like you. We don't want to hurt any of your boys. But we aint *never* going to be friends with them Hill Cats."

Davis came back up the hill.

Everywhere Lee had been in this war he had arrived to find disaster looming ready-made, and this was no exception. Militarily as well as politically, the mid-March outlook in Virginia was bleak indeed. Federal combinations totaling well over 200,000 men were threatening less than 70,000 Confederates strung out along an arc whose chord extended northwest-southeast through Richmond. At the lower end, Huger held Norfolk with 13,000, threatened from below by Burnside with the same number. Down near the tip of the York-James peninsula, Major General John B. Magruder's 12,000 were intrenched in front of Fort Monroe and its garrison of the same number. Northward, after retreating to their new position at Fredericksburg and along the near bank of the Rapidan, Johnston's 37,000 had been followed as far as Manassas by McClellan, who had 175,000 effectives in and out of the Washington defenses. Both main armies — the Army of Northern Virginia, as Lee now began to style it, and the Army of the Potomac — had detachments in the Shenandoah Valley, where Jackson with 5000 was falling back before Major General Nathaniel P. Banks with twice as many. Finally, at the upper or western end of this long arc, beyond Staunton, a little force of 2800 under Brigadier General Edward Johnson prepared to do what it could to block Frémont's proposed descent of the Alleghenies with McClellan's old army of 12,500, which in time would be doubled, despite McClellan's protests, by accretions from his new one.

Much of this was unknown to Lee — especially enemy strengths, which in general were overestimated; the Confederate spy system was yielding very little information these days — but one thing was quite clear. After leaving a sizeable garrison to hold the Washington intrench-

Fighting Means Killing

ments, McClellan's large main body could slide anywhere along that arc, or rather under cover just beyond it, then bull straight through for Richmond, outnumbering three-to-one — or for that matter ten-to-one, depending on where it struck — any force that stood in its path. Just now its actions were suspicious. After following Johnston's army as far as Manassas, it turned mysteriously back and reëntered the cordon of forts around the northern capital. This seemed to indicate that it was about to start its slide, but before Lee could even begin to try to second-guess its destination, news arrived from the south that upset his already inadequate dispositions: Burnside had taken New Bern. This was a challenge that had to be met, for he was now within sixty miles of Richmond's only direct rail connection with the South Atlantic states. Lee met it in the only way he could: by weakening what was far too weak already. Detaching several regiments from Huger at Norfolk and two brigades from Johnston's right wing at Fredericksburg, he sent them south into North Carolina under Major General Theophilus Holmes, a native of the threatened area.

The following week, March 23, Stonewall Jackson turned on Banks at Kernstown, intending to "inflict a terrible wound" on what he thought was a small segment, but soon retreated, badly cut up himself, when the segment turned out to be a full division. One more defeat was added to the growing list, though the news was less discouraging than it might have been, arriving as it did on the heels of more disturbing information. Just as Lee returned to giving the main danger — McClellan — his main attention, Huger reported by telegraph that more than twenty transports had come down Chesapeake Bay the night before and were disembarking troops at Old Point Comfort, across the way. Soon afterward, this alarming news was confirmed by a wire from Magruder calling urgently for reinforcements. The force confronting him, he said, had risen to 35,000 overnight. Neither general identified the enemy units, but Lee considered their arrival a probable sign that McClellan had started his slide along the arc.

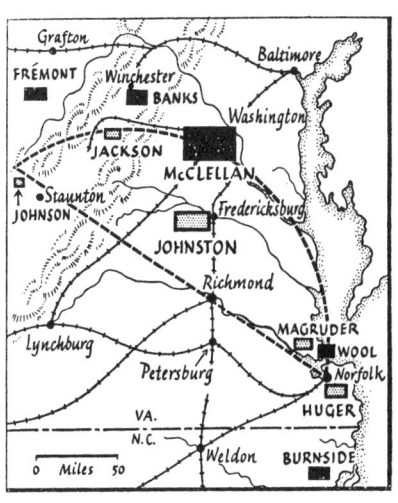

However, even if Lee had been certain of this, he still could not be certain of their goal. They might be on their way to Burnside for operations in North Carolina. They might be mounting an offensive against Norfolk. They might be intended as a diversion to hold Magruder in position while the main body jumped on Johnston. Or they might be the advance of McClellan's whole army, arriving for an all-out drive up the Peninsula. Until he knew which of these possibilities was (or were) at least probable, he would be taking an enormous risk in strengthening the arc at any point by weakening it at another. To lose Norfolk, for example, would be to lose the *Virginia*, which was all that was keeping the Federal gunboats from wrecking Magruder's right flank on their way up the James to bombard Richmond. Or to weaken Johnston's army, already reduced by more than ten percent as a result of detaching the two brigades for Holmes, might be to expose that mainstay of the Confederate defense to utter destruction.

While awaiting further indications, Lee warned Huger and Magruder to be ready for mutual assistance, one to reinforce the other as soon as events showed which was the Federal objective, Norfolk or Yorktown. Meanwhile, the water batteries along the James were strengthened, particularly the ones at Drewry's Bluff, eight miles below Richmond, and the city's scant reserves — two regiments of infantry and some odd squadrons of cavalry — were dispatched to Magruder, who was told to put on as brave a show as possible in the face of the build-up at Fort Monroe. If it became necessary to give ground, he was told to yield it stubbornly, fighting all the way to the gates of the city, sixty miles in his rear. Magruder answered excitedly that a council of war, held the night before, had voted to evacuate Yorktown unless 10,000 reinforcements were sent to him at once. Lee replied that councils of war were always timid in such situations, then repeated his instructions: keep up a bold front and yield nothing except to absolute pressure. He would send him what he could.

Whatever he sent him would have to come from Johnston, who had already expressed his unwillingness to furnish any more troops for other commanders. He would bring his whole army down, if ordered, but he was opposed to piecemeal reinforcement as a violation of sound principles. Concentration, not dispersal, was the answer, he declared. He could spare two more brigades — another ten percent of his original force — but that was all. Lee took them, duly thankful for small favors; sent one to Magruder, salving his anxiety a bit, and one to Holmes, hoping thus to keep Burnside out of the squeeze play; and then proceeded to exercise on the touchy Johnston the same tact and delicacy he was using simultaneously in his dealings with Davis, who was quite as touchy. Lighthorse Harry Lee and Peter Johnston had soldiered together in the First Revolution; now their sons worked together in the Second. During the ten days between March 24, when the arrival of the transports was reported, and April 4, Lee managed by gradual detachment to transfer three of Johnston's six divisions from the Rapidan to the James. By the latter date, the Army of Northern

Virginia — exclusive of Jackson, out in the Valley — had been reduced to 23,000, while Magruder had 31,500 troops either with him or on the way.

They were in capable hands and well employed. If Magruder was high-strung and overimaginative by ordinary standards, it presently developed that these qualities, so doubtful in a military leader, could be positive advantages in an extraordinary situation, such as the one that involved him now. A fifty-two-year-old Virginian, tall and flamboyantly handsome, with a great shock of dark hair, bushy sideburns, and a large but carefully barbered mustache — "Prince John," he had been called in the old army — he spoke with a lisp except when he sang in a clear tenor, as he often did, songs of his own composition. That had been his greatest spare-time pleasure: staging concerts and amateur theatricals, in which he took a leading role, to relieve the tedium of peacetime garrison duty. Now he had a chance to exercise his talents on a larger scale and for a more deadly purpose. Exploiting to the full Lee's admonition to show a brave front to the heavily reinforced enemy, he staged an extravaganza with a cast of thousands, playing as it were to a packed house. He bristled aggressively whenever he imagined a Yankee spyglass trained in his direction, shifting his artillery from point to point along his line and firing noisily at anything in sight. No wheeze was too old for Magruder to employ it. One morning he sent a column along a road that was heavily wooded except for a single gap in plain view of the enemy outposts. All day the gray files swept past in seemingly endless array, an army gathering in thousands among the pines for an offensive. They were no such thing, of course. Like a low-budgeted theatrical director producing the effect with an army of supernumeraries, Magruder was marching a single battalion round and around, past the gap, then around under cover, and past the gap again.

He had the men working as well as parading; the buskin was supplementary to the spade. Utilizing the old British earthworks around Yorktown, moldering since the days of the Revolution, they dug furiously down to the Warwick River, which was dammed near its mouth and at several points upstream to create an intermittent moat in front of the high ground leading southward to the James. This was the first peninsular line, fourteen miles in length: a great deal too long for the number of men available to defend it. Its principal drawback, however, was that the flanks were open to naval bombardment if the Union warships decided to brave the *Virginia* on the right or the additional water battery on the left, across the York at Gloucester Point. Ten miles in his rear, just east of Williamsburg, Magruder was constructing a second defensive line, though in fact it was not so much a line as it was a sort of rally-point in case the first gave way. Here he had two streams to protect his flanks from infantry assault, one flowing north, the other south. On the high ground in the center, just in front of the old colonial capital, he was improvising a bastioned earthwork which he or his officers, after the Thespian custom of sometimes naming a theater for a star, christened Fort Magruder. This second peninsular line had all the drawbacks of the first, plus certain intrinsic weaknesses all its own. Magruder was not a skilled engineer; he admitted it, and even complained about it. But he tried to make up in energy for what he lacked in skill. A dozen small redoubts were scattered about for the fort's protection; fields of fire were cleared by felling trees; additional rifle pits were dug, extending the line behind the tidal creeks. Magruder was doing the best he could.

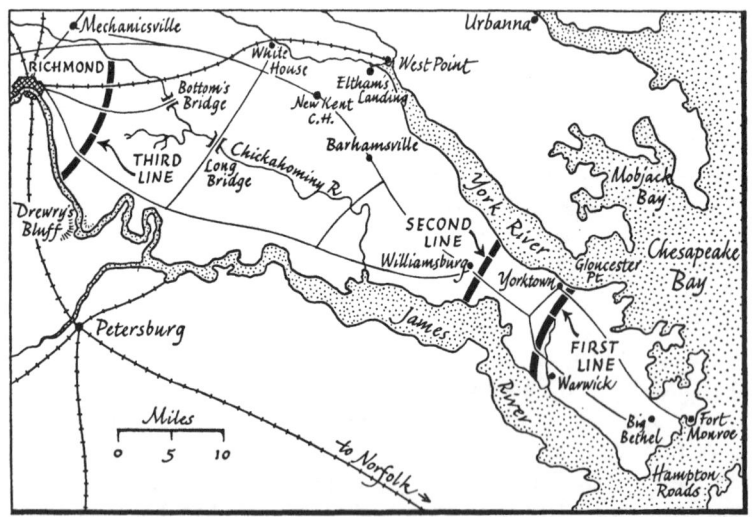

In case that best was not enough — which seemed likely, considering the odds and limitations — Lee had a third line under construction, forty miles behind the second and within ten miles of Richmond. Its right was anchored on the James and its left on the Chickahominy, a boggy stream which also covered a portion of the front with a tributary known as White Oak Swamp. This was the strongest of the three peninsular lines, being immune from naval attack, but Lee did not want to use it until he had to. Resistance below would give him time to bring up whatever troops he could spare from other points and to complete the reorganization now in progress while Congress debated conscription. That was why he was sending all the men he could lay hands on, including half of Johnston's army, down to Yorktown.

For a time he feared that he had guessed wrong. The Federals were strangely inactive at Fort Monroe. Then on April 4 he received word from Jeb Stuart, on outpost duty north of the Rappahannock, that another relay of transports was on its way down the Potomac. Simultaneously, Magruder reported heavy blue columns moving in his direction. These two pieces of evidence were strong, but Lee was still not sure that this was McClellan's main effort. Then five days later, on the heels of the depressing news that Albert Sidney Johnston had fallen at Shiloh, a minister who had escaped from Alexandria gave a detailed account of Unionist activities at that port of embarkation, adding that he personally had seen McClellan himself board one of the steamers for the journey down the coast. For Lee, this was conclusive. He went to Davis with the evidence, and that same day — April 9 — the President ordered Johnston to report at once to Richmond, bringing his two strongest divisions along for duty on the Peninsula.

He arrived on the 12th. Two of his divisions, under Major Generals G. W. Smith and Longstreet, were in his wake; the third, under Major General Ewell, stayed where it was, with instructions to cooperate with Jackson if the necessity arose. Informed that his command now included the Peninsula and Norfolk, Johnston left Richmond that same day for an inspection of the Yorktown and Williamsburg lines. Two mornings later, April 14, he was back again, waiting in the presidential office when Davis arrived for work. The bleakness of his outlook matched the brevity of his absence. Both of Magruder's defensive lines were utterly untenable, he told Davis. Not only were they improperly sited and too long; vulnerable as they were to artillery in front and amphibious landings in the rear, they would most likely prove a trap for any army that tried to hold them. In short, he favored an immediate withdrawal to the third line of defense. Davis, somewhat taken aback at this suggestion that the war be brought forthwith to the gates of Richmond, asked the general to return at 11 a.m. and present his views to Lee and Secretary Randolph. This being the case, Johnston asked that Smith and Longstreet also be invited, thus to preserve the balance. Davis agreed.

When the six men assembled at the specified hour it was evident that the general had chosen his supporters wisely. Longstreet had won considerable renown as a poker player, but had given it up three months ago, on the eve of his forty-first birthday, when his three children died of scarlet fever, all within a week. Grief had given him a stolid and ponderous dignity, augmented by a slight deafness which he could sit behind, when he chose, as behind a wall of sound-proof glass. He chose to sit so now. A large, square-built, hairy man, a native of the Deep South — born in South Carolina, raised in Georgia, and appointed to West Point from Alabama — he left the talking to Smith, who was a year younger but had been trained for disputation as Street Commissioner of New York City. Like Mansfield Lovell, his New York deputy, Smith had joined the Confederacy late, after waiting to see what his native Kentucky would do. Two months after Manassas he made his choice, which Davis applauded by making him a major general and giving him a division under Johnston, who admired him; the two were "Joe" and "G.W." to each other. A big-framed man with a large nose and firm-set lips, a West Pointer and a Mexico veteran, a former assistant professor of engineering at the Academy, Smith had been a civilian for the past eight years and was quite accustomed to attending such high-level councils as this. With Davis' and Johnston's permission, he said, he would like to submit a memorandum he had prepared. Johnston looked it over, then passed it to Davis, who read it aloud.

It was as if the ghost of Beauregard had been transported eastward 700 airline miles from Mississippi. What Smith proposed, in essence, was a withdrawal from Norfolk and the lower Peninsula, a concentration of all available troops, and then a sudden strike, either against McClellan as he came up, or against the northern heartland beyond the Potomac. Smith was convinced that the fast-marching southern army could occupy Philadelphia or New York before McClellan could take Richmond. Johnston, questioned by Randolph, said he agreed — up to a point. He was not anxious to march on New York but he did want to cripple McClellan, and this was the way to do it; Norfolk and Yorktown were untenable anyhow. Randolph, a former navy man, protested that the loss of Gosport Navy Yard would mean the loss of the *Virginia*, which could neither put to sea nor ascend the James, unseaworthy and deep-drafted as she was, as well as the loss of all hope of ever building a real Confederate fleet. Johnston replied that it could not be helped. To attempt to hold positions that could readily be flanked would be to invite the destruction not only of the future navy but also of the present army.

All day the discussion continued, Randolph and Lee against Johnston and Smith, with Longstreet saying little and Davis acting as moderator. At suppertime they recessed for an hour, then reassembled at the Executive Mansion, where the argument continued into the night, apparently without affecting the convictions of any of the six. Then at 1 a.m. Davis adjourned the meeting with the decision to hold both Norfolk and Yorktown by uniting Johnston's and Magruder's armies on the lower Peninsula, under instructions to resist all Federal attempts to advance. Johnston thus was being sent to defend a position which he had declared untenable. He would have been removed, Davis later wrote, except that "he did not ask to be ... and I had no wish to separate him from troops with whom he was so intimately acquainted." Johnston had his reasons, though he did not give them then. "The belief that events on the Peninsula would soon compel the Confederate government to adopt my method of opposing the Federal army," he wrote later, "reconciled me somewhat to the necessity of obeying the President's order."

As the general returned to Yorktown, convinced that things would work out his way in the end, Longstreet's men were marching through Richmond to join him. "The Walking Division," they called themselves, and one of them grumbled: "I suppose that if it was intended to reinforce Savannah, Mobile, or New Orleans with our division, we would be compelled to foot it all the way." But now that they were nearing the end of the march their spirits rose. It was the anniversary of Virginia's secession and the whole city had turned out to greet them with cheers and armloads of early spring flowers. Jonquils, hyacinths, narcissuses, and violets were tossed and caught, looped into wreaths or stuck into rifle muzzles. The drab mud-stained column seemed to burst into bloom as it swung down Main Street, a riot of colors dominated by the bright nodding yellow of the jonquils. Bands played "Dixie" and "The Bonnie Blue Flag," and the men returned the cheers of the crowd along the way. At one window they saw a lady and a pale young man waving handkerchiefs, and one of the bearded veterans shouted: "Come right along, sonny. The lady'll spare ye. Here's a little musket for ye!" The answer came back: "All right, boys. Have you got a leg for me, too?" As he spoke he placed on the window sill the stump of the leg he had lost at Manassas. The battalion made an effective apology. Wheeling spontaneously into line, it halted, presented arms, and rattled the windows of the block with cheering.

Johnston found a quite different spirit around Yorktown, fifty miles below. Magruder and his men were worn out by the strain of the long bluff. Their food was poor and their uniforms in rags. What was more, the enemy had begun to probe the Warwick River line with field artillery. There were night alarms and occasional stampedes, one including a work party of several hundred slaves, who broke for the rear and in their flight swept away part of the infantry support. Whatever his vaunted gallantry in the open field, the southern volunteer did not relish this kind of warfare, huddling under bombardments and waiting to be overrun. One detachment gave way completely under the tension, a member of the relief party reporting that he had found "some of these poor lads ... sobbing in their broken sleep, like a crying child just before it sinks to rest. It was really pathetic. The men actually had to be supported to the ambulances sent down to bring them away."

They had the sympathy of their new commander, who was convinced that they should not have stayed there in the first place. To the War Department the last ten days of April brought word of the fall of New Orleans and the opening of Halleck's campaign against Corinth, as well as a trickle of I-told-you-so dispatches from the lower Peninsula. Johnston declared that Magruder's lines were even more defective than he had supposed when he made his first inspection. "No one but McClellan could have hesitated to attack," he reported on the 22d, and urged that some bridges across the Chickahominy, twenty-odd miles in his rear, should be repaired at once. Two days later he was suggesting that supplies be sent to meet the army on its way to the gates of the city "in the event of our being compelled to fall back from this point." On the 27th he instructed Huger to prepare to evacuate Norfolk. Two days later he wrote to Lee in the plainest language he had yet employed: "The fight for Yorktown, as I said in Richmond, must be one of artillery, in which we cannot win. The result is certain; the time only doubtful.... We must abandon the Peninsula at once."

There they had it; he had been right all along. May Day was a time of gloom in the southern capital. Ball's Bluff seemed far away and long ago.

★ ★ ★

One source of consolation existed, but it was unknown in Richmond, being hidden in the fog of war, far down the James and beyond the enemy lines. Johnston's worries were balanced — more than balanced, at least in number — by the woes of his opponent, which differed as much in quality as they did in multiplicity. The southern commander's fretfulness was based almost exclusively on strictly tactical considerations: the weakness of the Yorktown defenses and the shortage of troops to man them. But McClellan's was the product of a variety of pressures, roughly divisible under three main headings: 1) downright bad luck, 2) Lincoln, and — as always — 3) his own ripe imagination.

The first of a rapid succession of blows, like the preliminary tap of a farrier taking aim, landed the moment he stepped off the steamer at Old Point Comfort. Flag Officer Goldsborough, up from the North Carolina sounds to provide naval support for the movement up the narrow tongue of land, met him with word that the fleet would not be able to assist in reducing the enemy batteries on the York or the James. The navy already had its hands full, he said, patrolling Hampton Roads to neutralize the *Merrimac-Virginia*. One of the primary conditions of success, as stated by the corps commanders on the eve of departure, thus was removed before the campaign had even begun. Fortunately, McClellan had a full day in which to absorb the shock of this. But after that brief respite the blows began to land with trip-hammer rapidity.

On the second day, April 4, as he started his army forward — much gratified by the "wonderfully cool performance" of the trio of foragers who brought him the still-warm 12-pound shot — he made two dreadful discoveries. The first was that his handsome Coastal Survey maps were woefully inaccurate. The roads all ran the wrong way, he complained, and the Warwick River, shown on the maps as an insignificant creek flowing parallel to the James, was in fact a considerable barrier, cutting squarely across his line of march. To add to its effectiveness as an obstacle, the Confederates had dammed it in five places, creating five unwadable lakes and training their heavy artillery on the boggy intervals. McClellan was amazed at the river's location and condition; "[It] grows worse the more you look at it," he wailed.

As he stood gazing forlornly at this waste of wetness in his path, another unexpected development overtook him, also involving water. It began to rain. And from this there grew an even worse disclosure. Those fine sandy roads, recommended as being "passable at all seasons on the year," turned out to be no such thing. What they were was gumbo — and they were apparently bottomless. Guns and wagons bogged past the axles, then sat there, immovably stuck. One officer later testified that he saw a mule go completely out of sight in one of the chunk-holes, "all but the tips of its ears," but added, in the tall-tale tradition, that the mule was a rather small one.

No navy, no fit maps, no transportation: McClellan might well have thought the fates had dealt him all the weal they intended. Writing to his wife of his unenviable position — "the rebels on one side, and the abolitionists and other scoundrels on the other" — he said, "Don't worry about the wretches; they have done nearly their worst, and can't do much more." He was wrong, and before the day was over he would discover just how wrong he was. The people he referred to could do a great deal more. If McClellan did not realize this, Lincoln's two young secretaries knew it quite well already. "Gen McC is in danger," one was telling the other. "Not in front, but in rear."

Returning to army headquarters at the close of that same busy day — his first in bristling proximity to the enemy since the campaign in West Virginia, almost nine months ago — McClellan found the atmosphere of the lantern-hung interior as glum as the twilit landscape of rain-soaked fields and dripping woods through which he had just ridden. Sorrow and anger, despair and incredulity were strangely combined on the faces of his staff. Soon the Young Napoleon was sharing these mixed emotions; for the answer, or answers, lay in a batch of orders and directives just off the wire from Washington. The first was dated yesterday, April 3: Fort Monroe and its garrison of 12,000, placed under McClellan two weeks ago as a staging area and a pool from which to draw replacements, were removed forthwith from his control. Before he could recover from the shock of learning that he had lost not only that number of troops, but also command of his present base of operations, he was handed a second order, more drastic than the first. McDowell's corps of 38,000, still awaiting sailing orders at Alexandria — McClellan intended to bring it down in mass as soon as he decided where to land it, whether on the south bank of the York, for operations against Yorktown, or on the north bank, against Gloucester Point — was detached and withheld as part of the force assigned to provide close-in protection for the capital. This action was given emphasis by a supplementary order creating what was called the Department of the Rappahannock, under McDowell, as well as another new one, called the Department of the Shenandoah, under Banks, whose corps was also declared no longer a part of the Army of the Potomac. McClellan was floored. Even without the loss of Banks, which made no actual change in dispositions, the combined detachments of Blenker, McDowell, and the Fort Monroe garrison — an approximate total of 60,000 fighting men — reduced by well over one third the 156,000 he had said at the outset would be necessary for the success of his Peninsula campaign.

Nor was this all. As he took to his troubled bed that night he had something else to think about: something that seemed to him and his staff conclusive proof that the Administration, disapproving of the campaign in the first place, was determined to assure its failure before the opening shot was fired. A final order, dated yesterday and signed by the Adjutant General for distribution to the governors of all the loyal states, put an end to the recruiting of volunteers throughout the Union. All recruiting offices were closed, the equipment put up for sale to the highest bidders, and all recruiting personnel were reassigned to other duties. In some ways this was the hardest blow of all, or anyhow the most incredible. At a time when the Confederate authorities, sixty miles away in Richmond, were doing all they could to push through the first conscription law in American history — a law which could be expected to swell the ranks of the army facing him — it seemed to McClellan that his Washington superiors, twice that distance in his rear, had not only taken a full one third of his soldiers from him, but then had proceeded to make certain that they could never be replaced. The fact was, on the eve of bloody fighting, Lincoln and Stanton had seen to it that he would not even be able to replace his casualties. So it seemed to McClellan. At any rate, as he went to bed that night he could say, "They have done nearly their worst," and be a good deal closer to the truth.

Next morning, if somewhat daunted by all the knocks he had had to absorb in one short night, he was back at the front, probing the enemy defenses with his three remaining corps. Heintzelman and Keyes, on the right and left, had two divisions each, with a third on the way down Chesapeake Bay for both. Sumner, in the center, had only one; his second was en route, and his third had been Blenker. All three of these brigadiers were hard-shell regulars — Sumner had put in seven of his forty-three years of army service before McClellan was born, and both of the others were thirty-year men or better — but after coming under heavy fire from long-range guns and bogging down in the flooded approaches, all agreed with the Chief Engineer's report that the rebel line was "certainly one of the most extensive known to modern times." If the navy had been there to wreck the batteries on the flanks, or if the weight of McDowell's corps, the largest of the original four, could be added to the pressure the army could exert, things might be different. As it was, however, all felt obliged to agree with Keyes, who later reported bluntly: "No part of [the Yorktown-Warwick River] line, so far discovered, can be taken by assault without an enormous waste of life."

If the Confederate defenses could not be broken by flanking operations, if assault was too doubtful and expensive, only one method remained: a siege. McClellan would do it that way if he had to; he had studied siege tactics at Sebastopol. But he much preferred his original plan, which he now saw was impractical without his original army. As he rode back to headquarters this second night he decided to make a final appeal to Lincoln. Under the heading "Near Yorktown, 7.30 p.m." he outlined for the President the situation as he saw it, neglecting none of the drawbacks, and begged him to "reconsider" the order detaching McDowell. "In my deliberate judgment," he wrote, "the success of our cause will be imperiled by so greatly reducing my force when it is actually under the fire of the enemy and active operations have commenced.... I am now of the opinion that I shall have to fight all the available forces of the rebels not far from here. Do not force me to do so with diminished numbers."

Lincoln's reply, the following day, was a brief warning that delay on the Peninsula would benefit the Confederate defenders more than it would the Federal attackers: "You now have over 100,000 troops with you.... I think you better break the enemy's line from Yorktown to Warwick River at once." McClellan's first reaction, he told his wife, was "to reply that he had better come and do it himself." Instead, he wired on the 7th that, after the three recent detachments, his "entire force for duty" amounted to about 85,000 men, more than a third of whom were still en route from Alexandria. Lincoln took a day to study this, then replied on the 9th at considerable length. He was puzzled, he said, by "a curious mystery." The general's own report showed a total strength of 108,000; "How can the discrepancy of 23,000 be accounted for?"

Beyond this, however, the President's main purpose was to point out to McClellan that more factors were involved in this war than those which might occur to a man with an exclusively military turn of mind. In other words, this was a Civil war. The general was aware of certain pressures in his rear, but Lincoln suggested in a final paragraph that he would gain more from studying those pressures, and maybe finding ways to relieve them, than he would from merely complaining of their presence. It was a highly personal communication, and in it he gave McClellan some highly personal advice:

"Once more let me tell you that it is indispensable to *you* that you strike a blow. *I* am powerless to help this. You will do me the justice to remember I always insisted that going down the bay in search of a field, instead of fighting at or near Manassas, was only shifting and not surmounting a difficulty; that we would find the same enemy and the same or equal intrenchments in either place. The country will not fail to note — is now noting — that the present hesitation to move upon an intrenched enemy is but the story of Manassas repeated. I beg to assure you that I have never written you or spoken to you in greater kindness of feeling than now, nor with a fuller purpose to sustain you, so far as, in my most anxious judgment, I consistently can. But you must act."

That "most anxious judgment" had been under considerable strain ever since McClellan's leading elements started down the coast in transports. Ben Wade and Zachariah Chandler were bombarding Lincoln with protests that the general's treasonable intent was plain at last for any eye to see: The whole campaign had been designed to sidetrack the main Union army by bogging it down in the slews southeast of Richmond, thus clearing the path for a direct rebel sweep on Washington, with little to stand in its way. Stanton not only encouraged the presentation and acceptance of this view, but also enlarged it by assigning additional motives to account for his former intimate's treachery: McClellan was politically ambitious, "more interested in reconstructing the Democratic party than the Army of the Potomac."

Lincoln wondered. He did not believe McClellan was a traitor, but in suggesting that the capital was in danger the Jacobins had touched him where he was tender. "This is a question which the country will not allow me to evade," he said. He could not afford the slightest risk in that direction; too much hung in the balance — including war with England and France as a result of the recognition both would almost certainly give the Confederacy once its army had occupied Washington. Then, as he pondered, an alarm was sounded which seemed to give substance to his fears.

On the day McClellan landed at Old Point Comfort, Brigadier General James Wadsworth, the elderly commander of the Washington defenses and one of the founders of the Republican Party, came to Stanton complaining that his force was inadequate for its task, both in numbers and in training. The Secretary sent his military assistant, the hapless Hitchcock, and Adjutant General Lorenzo Thomas to investigate, and when they confirmed Wadsworth's report that the capital was in danger, Stanton took him triumphantly to Lincoln. McClellan's note of the day before, claiming that he had left 77,456 men behind to give Washington the stipulated "entire feeling of security," was checked for accuracy. Certain discrepancies showed at once, and the harder the three men looked the more they saw. In the first place, by an arithmetical error, the troops at Warrenton had been counted twice. Proposed reinforcements from Maryland, Pennsylvania, and New York had not arrived, though they were listed. Blenker's division, on the way to Frémont, had also been included, on grounds that Banks could interrupt its march if it was needed. All these had to be subtracted. And so for that matter did the two divisions already with Banks in the Valley; Patterson's army, out there in July, had done nothing to protect the capital after the debacle at Bull Run. In fact, by actual count as Lincoln saw it, once McClellan's whole army had gone down the coast, there would be fewer than 29,000 men in all to stand in the way of a direct Confederate drive on Washington: 11,000 less than the general's own corps commanders had said were necessary.

The way to keep this from happening was to stop one corps from going to join McClellan, and that was what Lincoln did, creating in the process the Departments of the Rappahannock and the Shenandoah to give McDowell and Banks their independence. The former would make his headquarters at Falmouth, opposite Fredericksburg, and in time — conditions permitting — march overland to join his former chief in front of Richmond. That way, he would always be in a position to strike the front or flank of any rebel force that tried a direct lunge at Washington, and yet he would still be in on the kill when the time came. Lincoln did not want to hurt McClellan any more than he had to. In fact, on the day after telling him, "You must act," he released McDowell's lead division, under Franklin — a great favorite of McClellan's, who asked in a final desperate plea that this, at least, not be withheld — to proceed by the water route as originally planned. Exuberantly grateful, McClellan wired on April 13: "We shall soon be at them, and I am sure of the result."

Lincoln had heard him say such things before; they were part of what made the Young Napoleon at once so likeable and exasperating. The President knew by now not to put much stock in such expressions, which after all only meant that McClellan was feeling good again. Lincoln himself was not. The past week had been a strain, in some ways harder than the strain which had followed defeat on the plains of Manassas. His sadness had deepened, along with the lines in his face, though he still kept his wry sense of humor. A country editor called at the White House, claiming to have been the first to suggest Lincoln's nomination for President. Lincoln was busy, but when he tried to escape by saying he had to go over to the War Department on business, the editor offered to accompany him. "Come along," Lincoln said. When they got there he told his visitor, "I shall have to see Mr Stanton alone, and you must excuse me." He turned to enter, but then, perhaps considering this too abrupt, turned back and took the editor by the hand. "Goodbye," he said. "I hope you will feel perfectly easy about having nominated me. Don't be troubled about it. I forgive you."

As April wore on and the rains continued, so did the siege preparations; McClellan was hard at work. He had not wanted this kind of campaign, but now that he had it he was enjoying it immensely.

Back in the West Virginia days he had said, "I will not throw these raw men of mine into the teeth of artillery and intrenchments if it is possible to avoid it." He still felt that way about it. "I am to watch over you as a parent over his children," he had told his army the month before, and that was what he was doing. If it was to be a siege, let it be one in the grand manner, with fascines and gabions, zigzag approaches, and much digging and shifting of earth, preparatory to blasting the rebel fortifications clean out of existence. "Do not misunderstand the apparent inaction here," he wired Lincoln on the 23d, concerned lest a civilian fail to appreciate all this labor. "Not a day, not an hour has been lost. Works have been constructed that may almost be called gigantic."

Gigantic was particularly the word for the fifteen ten-gun batteries of 13-inch siege mortars being installed within two miles of Yorktown; on completion, they would be capable of throwing 400 tons of metal daily into the rebel defenses. Six were installed and ready before the end of the month, but McClellan held his fire, preferring to open with all of them at once. Meanwhile he neglected nothing which he thought would add to the final effect. On the 28th he wired Stanton: "Would be glad to have the 30-pounder Parrotts in the works around Washington. Am short of that excellent gun." When Lincoln saw the request, his thin-stretched patience snapped. "Your call for Parrott guns... alarms me," he answered on May Day, "chiefly because it argues indefinite procrastination. Is anything to be done?" McClellan replied that the Parrotts would hasten, not delay, the breaking of the enemy lines; "All is being done that human labor can accomplish." The build-up continued. Then suddenly, May 4, it paid off. The noonday Sabbath quiet of the War Department telegraph office was broken by the brief, jubilant clatter of a message from the Peninsula: "Yorktown is in our possession. Geo. B. McClellan."

That there was more to it than that, in fact a great deal more, became apparent from the messages which followed. McClellan had not "taken" Yorktown; he had received it by default. Joe Johnston had been observing all those large-scale preparations, then had pulled back on the eve of what was to have been the day of his destruction. It was Centerville-Manassas all over again, except this time the guns he left behind were real ones: 56 heavy siege pieces, many with their ammunition still neatly stacked and only three of them damaged. However, he had saved all of his field artillery and given his army a head start toward whatever defensive line he intended to occupy next. McClellan did not mean for him to do so unmolested. He sent the cavalry in pursuit at once, despite a thunderstorm that approached cloudburst proportions, and followed it with the whole army, under Sumner, while he himself remained at Yorktown to launch an amphibious end run up the York, attempting to cut off Johnston's retreat by landing Franklin's division in his rear. The result was a bloody rear-guard action next day in front of

Williamsburg, anticipated and reviewed in two telegrams he sent, the first at 9 a.m. and the last at 9.40 p.m. The former was to Stanton, an announcement of intention: "I shall push the enemy to the wall." The latter was to Franklin, who was coming up by water while McClellan himself hurried overland to where Sumner's guns were growling: "We have now a tangent hit. I arrived in time."

Johnston, whose men were plodding along the single miry road behind their slow-grinding wagon train, had not planned a halt until he crossed the Chickahominy, but the Union infantry was closing fast, unimpeded by wagons, and the cavalry was taking potshots at his rear guard before sundown. So he instructed Longstreet's division to delay the pursuit by holding Fort Magruder long enough to give the rest of the army time to draw off. When Sumner's men came slogging up they were met by a spatter of musketry that stopped them for the night. The fight next day — dignified by time into the Battle of Williamsburg — was confusion from start to finish, with lunges and counterlunges and a great deal of slipping and sliding in the mud. Cannonfire had a metallic ring in the saturated air, and generals on both sides lost their sense of direction in the rain. Sumner kept pushing and probing; Longstreet had to call for help, and Major General D. H. Hill countermarched his whole division and joined the melee. In the end, the Confederates managed to hang on until nightfall, when they fell back and the Federals took possession of Fort Magruder. Both claimed a victory: the latter because they had gained the field, the former because they had delayed the pursuit. The only apparent losers were the casualties: 1703 for the South, 2239 for the North.

Whatever else it amounted to, and that seemed very little, the day-long battle had given the troops of both sides two clear gains at least. The first was that, as soldiers, they were tangibly worth their salt. Despite the confusion and the milling about, which gave the action a superficial resemblance to Bull Run, the men had fought as members of military units, not as panicky individuals. This in itself was a substantial gain, one they knew was beyond value. Training had paid off. But the second was even more appealing. This was a new confidence in their respective commanding generals, in spite of the fact that neither had been present for the fighting.

Johnston was toiling westward through the mud with his main body. Coming upon a deeply mired 12-pound brass Napoleon which a battery lieutenant was about to abandon in obedience to orders that nothing was to be allowed to impede the march, Johnston said: "Let me see what I can do." He dismounted, waded into the bog — high-polished boots, gold braid, and all — and took hold of a muddy spoke. "Now, boys: all together!" he cried, and the gun bounded clear of the chunk-hole. After that, one cannoneer said, "our battery used to swear by Old Joe."

McClellan's performance was no less endearing. Arriving just at the close of the battle, mud-stained from hard riding, his staff strung out behind him trying desperately to keep up, he went from regiment to regiment, congratulating his men for their victory and acknowledging their cheers. Often he paused for a question-and-answer exchange, strophe and antistrophe:

"How do you feel, boys?"

"We feel bully, General!" they cried.

"Do you think anything can stop you from going to Richmond?"

"No! No!" they shouted, all together.

Little Mac would give them his jaunty salute, made even flashier today by the glazed waterproof cover he was wearing on his cap, and be off down the line at a gallop, to halt again in front of another regiment:

"How do you feel, boys?"

"We feel bully, General!"

"Do you think anything can stop you from going to Richmond?"

"No! No!"

Rain-soaked and hungry, but glad to be out of the trenches, the Confederates continued their march toward the Chickahominy. Smith, in the lead, was instructed to halt at Barhamsville, eighteen miles beyond Williamsburg, and guard against a flank attack from the direction of York River while the other three divisions were catching up. He got there on the afternoon of the 6th, just as Franklin's men were coming ashore at Eltham Landing, six miles away, to execute the movement Johnston feared. Informed of this, Johnston ordered Magruder, Longstreet, and Hill to hurry forward. While they were doing so, Smith moved toward Eltham to attack. Deciding that it would be better not to try to stop the Yankees within range of their gunboats, he waited until next morning when they were a couple of miles from the landing, then hit them with Hampton's Legion and a brigade of Texans and Georgians under a 30-year-old West Pointer named John Bell Hood, a prewar junior lieutenant in Sidney Johnston's 2d Cavalry. Franklin's men, deep in unfamiliar country and not knowing how many graybacks might be coming at them, gave ground rapidly until they regained the covering fire of the gunboats.

They had been hit harder than Johnston intended, anxious as he was to avoid the delay another general engagement would have entailed. Later he admonished the blond-bearded six-foot-two-inch Kentucky brigadier: "General Hood, have you given an illustration of the Texas idea of feeling an enemy gently and falling back? What would your Texans have done, sir, if I had ordered them to charge and drive back the enemy?" Hood's blue eyes were somber. He said gravely, "I suppose, General, they would have driven them into the river, and tried to swim out and capture the gunboats."

At any rate Smith was satisfied; Franklin was disposed of, and the wagon train was well along the road. He led his and Magruder's divisions on through New Kent Courthouse and made camp the following night beside the road, nineteen miles from Barhamsville and within easy reach of Bottom's Bridge across the Chickahominy. Five miles downstream, at Long Bridge, the divisions of Hill and Longstreet tried to sleep in a torrent of rain which finally sent them sloshing off in search of higher ground. Whatever their discomfort, Johnston's reaction was primarily a feeling of relief that his 54,000 soldiers had escaped a trap laid by twice their number. Not that he was through retreating. Already he had notified Lee in Richmond: "The want of provision and of any mode of obtaining it here, still more the dearth of forage, makes it impossible to wait to attack [the enemy] while landing. The sight of the ironclad boats makes me apprehensive for Richmond, too, so I move on...."

The Federals were after him, moving slowly, however, along the cut-up roads. Sumner at Williamsburg and Franklin at Eltham Landing had failed to bag the retreating enemy, but McClellan was not discouraged. His men had shown all the dash a commander could ask for, and the rebels were dribbling casualties and equipment as they fled. "My troops are in motion and in magnificent spirits," he informed the War Department. "They have all the air and feelings of veterans. It will do your heart good to see them." The frontal attack, up the middle of the Peninsula, had left the foe no time to get set for another prolonged resistance, and the long end run, despite the savage repulse next day, had "fully served its purpose in clearing our front to the banks of the Chickahominy." In accordance with plans made months ago, when Urbanna was the intended place of debarkation, he set up his base at West Point, the terminus of the 35-mile-long Richmond & York River Railroad. Here the Mattapony and the Pamunkey converged to form the York, which afforded a deep-draft supply line all the way back to Chesapeake Bay. Regiment after regiment, division after division of reinforcements could be landed here, fresh for combat, and McClellan was quick to suggest that this be done. May 8 he wired Stanton: "The time has arrived to bring all the troops in Eastern Virginia into perfect coöperation. I expect to fight another and very severe battle before reaching Richmond and with all the troops the Confederates can bring together.... All the troops on the Rappahannock, and if possible those on the Shenandoah, should take part in the approaching battle. We ought immediately to concentrate everything."

The wire did not have to go all the way to Washington; the Secretary was at Fort Monroe. He had arrived two days ago with Lincoln and Chase, primarily for relaxation and a look-see, but as it turned out was lending a hand in the direction of one of the strangest small-scale campaigns in American military history.

Amazed to find that McClellan had made no provision for the capture of Norfolk, outflanked by the drive up the opposite bank of the James, the President decided to undertake the operation himself, employing the fortress garrison under Major General John E. Wool. Wool was 78, two years older than Winfield Scott, and though he was more active physically than his fellow veteran of the War of 1812 — he could still mount a horse, for instance — he had other infirmities all his own. After twenty-five years as Inspector General, his hands trembled; he repeated things he had said a short while back, and he had to ask his aide if he had put his hat on straight. However, there was no deficiency of the courage he had shown under Anthony Wayne. He said he would gladly undertake the movement his Commander in Chief proposed.

The first trouble came with the navy: Goldsborough thought it would be dangerous to ferry the men across the Roads with the *Merrimac* still on the loose. But Lincoln not only overruled him, he and Chase got in separate tugs and reconnoitered the opposite shore for a suitable landing place. When they returned, however, they found that Wool had already chosen one from the chart and was embarking with the troops who were to seize it. Chase went along, but Lincoln and Stanton stayed behind to maintain a command post at the fort and question various colonels and generals who, the President thought, were to follow in support.

"Where is your command?" he asked one, and got the answer: "I am awaiting orders." To another he said, "Why are you here? Why not on the other side?" and was told: "I am ordered to the fort." Experiencing for the first time some of the vexations likely to plague a field commander, Lincoln lost his temper. He took off his tall hat and slammed it on the floor. "Send me someone who can write," he said, exasperated. When the someone came forward — a colonel on Wool's staff — the President dictated an order for the advance to be pushed and supported.

As things turned out, no push or support was needed. The Confederates had evacuated Norfolk the day before, leaving only a handful of men behind to complete the wrecking of Gosport Navy Yard. Chase and Wool were met just short of the city limits by a municipal delegation, including the mayor, who carried a large bunch of rusty keys and a sheaf of documents which he insisted on reading, down to the final line, before making the final formal gesture of handing over the keys. Unknown to Wool and the Secretary, while the mayor droned on, the rebel demolition crew was completing its work and setting out for Richmond. Then Chase and the general moved in with their troops and took charge, sending word back to Lincoln that his first field campaign had been a complete success, despite vexations.

★ ★ ★

One demolition job remained, and it was done that night. No nation ever owed more to a single ship than the Confederacy owed the *Merrimac-Virginia;* yet, with Norfolk gone, she had not only lost her home, she had lost her occupation. Josiah Tattnall, who had dipped his colors in salute to his old friend Du Pont at Port Royal and had been in command of the ironclad since late March, saw two choices: either to steer her out into the Roads for a suicidal finish, taking as many of the enemy with her as possible when she sank, or else to try and lighten her enough to ascend the James. In point of fact, however, there was really no choice. No matter how fitting the former seemed as a death for a gallant vessel, it obviously would not benefit the country; whereas the latter course would preserve her for future service, a second career. She now drew twenty-three feet as a result of recent additions to her armor, but the pilots assured the commodore that if she could be lightened to eighteen feet before daylight they would take her up to Harrison's Landing or City Point, where she could be put in fighting trim again. Tattnall assembled the crew and told them what had to be done. They gave three cheers and got to work, heaving everything movable over the side except her powder and shot. She had been lightened three feet by midnight — when the pilots announced that a strong west wind had reduced the tide so much that she could not be taken up at all.

The first choice was gone with the second, for the work had exposed two feet of her hull below the shield, and to let in water ballast to settle her again would be to flood her fires and magazines. Now that she could neither run nor fight, a third choice, unconsidered at the outset, was all that remained: to destroy her. Tattnall gave the necessary orders. The *Virginia* was run ashore near Craney Island and set afire. By the light of her burning, the crew set out on their march to Suffolk, where they took the cars for Richmond. There they were ordered to Drewry's Bluff, whose batteries now were all that stood between the Confederate capital and the Federal fleet, including their old adversary the *Monitor.*

Those batteries were of primary concern to Lee, who also had lost a good part of his occupation when Johnston came down and took command on the Peninsula. All through late April and early May, while Johnston was warning that he was about to bring the war to the outskirts of Richmond, Lee had been supervising work on the close-in defenses, of which the installations at Drewry's were a part, and now that Johnston was falling back with all the speed the mud allowed, Lee continued to do what he could to protect his ancestral capital from assault. Called on at a cabinet meeting to say where the next stand could be made if the city had to be abandoned, he made an unaccustomed show of his emotions. It would have to be along the Staunton River, he said calmly, a hundred miles southwest. Then suddenly his eyes brimmed with tears. "But Richmond must not be given up; it shall not be given up!" he exclaimed.

Davis felt much the same way about it. Twice he had ridden down to Drewry's with Lee to inspect the work in progress there, the hulks being sunk alongside pilings driven across the channel and the heavy naval cannon being emplaced on the high bluff. But in spite of hearing that Butler's men, with Farragut on his way up the Mississippi, were sacking and looting Briarfield, he kept an even closer rein on his emotions than did the Virginian who had been nicknamed "The Marble Monument" while they were at the Academy together. Many interpreted this calmness to mean a lack of concern by the Chief Executive, and when he was baptized and confirmed at St Paul's on the 9th, the *Examiner* took him to task for finding time for such ministrations on the day of Norfolk's evacuation. Faced with imminent assault by land and water, the people wanted assurance from Davis that Richmond would be defended, block by block and house by house. A committee called at his office on the morning of May 15, inquiring whether the government shared their determination, but their spokesman was interrupted by a messenger who came to inform the President that the masts of Federal warships had been sighted on the James from the hills of the city. "This manifestly concludes the matter," Davis said, dismissing the committee.

Soon the guns began to roar, clangorous on the hilltops and reverberant in the hollows. They kept it up for three full hours and twenty minutes, rattling Richmond windows from a distance of eight miles. It was deafening; people trembled at the sound. Then suddenly it stopped, and that was worse. With the abrupt descent of silence, they took their hands down from their ears and looked at one another, not knowing which to expect: a messenger announcing that the assault had been repulsed, or the gunboats celebrating a victory by lobbing 11-inch shells into the city. Presently they had the answer.

The attack had been led by two ironclads, the *Monitor* and the *Galena*, supported by two wooden vessels. The latter kept their distance, but the armored ships began the bombardment at a range of 800 yards. The *Monitor* soon retired, unable to elevate her guns enough to reach the batteries on the bluff. The *Galena* stayed and took twenty-eight hits, including eighteen perforations which cost her 13 killed and 11 wounded, before she dropped back down the river with the others, winding lamely out of sight around the bend. The Confederate gunners leaped on the unfinished parapets, cheering and tossing their caps: especially the sailors off the *Virginia*, who at last had scored the triumph that had been beyond their reach at water level.

Richmond had been delivered, at least for a day. But Johnston was still retreating. That same morning he abandoned the middle and lower stretches of the Chickahominy, taking up an intermediary position which he abandoned in turn, two days later, because he found it tactically weak and inadequately supplied with drinking water. What he would do next he would not say, not even to the President. A South Carolinian recalled that before the war Wade Hampton had brought Johnston down there on a bird hunt, but Johnston had not fired a shot all day. "The bird flew too high or too low; the dogs were too far or too near. Things never did suit exactly." It seemed to be that way with him now, but one thing at least was clear. The next withdrawal would have to be beyond the capital. His present left was at Fairfield Race Course, just outside the northeast city limits, and his right was on the near bank of the James, across from Drewry's Bluff. Richmond was beleaguered. At nightfall people saw from her hills the semicircular twinkle of the campfires of the Army of Northern Virginia. Beyond them, a greater refulgence along the eastern and northeastern sky reflected the glow of campfires kindled by McClellan's hundred thousand.

In preparation for what he believed might be the last great battle of the war, the Federal commander had reorganized his army while it was still on the march toward the Chickahominy crossings. Shuffling and reconsolidating while in motion, he created two new corps, one under Fitz-John Porter, the other under Franklin—both of them original pro-McClellan brigadiers—which gave him five corps in all, each with two three-brigade divisions. The order of battle, as reported in mid-May:

SUMNER	HEINTZELMAN	KEYES	PORTER	FRANKLIN
Richardson	Hooker	Couch	Morell	Slocum
Sedgwick	Kearny	Casey	Sykes	Smith

gave him a tightly knit yet highly flexible fighting force of 102,236 front-line soldiers and 300 guns. Another 5000 extra-duty men, including cooks and teamsters, laborers and suchlike, were with the advance, while 21,000 more had been left at various points along the road from Fort Monroe, sick or absent without leave or on garrison duty, to give him an over-all total of 128,864.

McClellan did not consider this a man too many. In fact he was convinced it was not enough. Pinkerton was at work again, questioning prisoners and contrabands and totting up figures he received from his operatives beyond the enemy lines. A month ago, in front of Yorktown, he had said that the Confederates were issuing 119,000 daily rations. Presently this grew to 180,000, reported along with a warning that the figure was probably low, since 200 separate regiments of southern infantry had already been identified on the Peninsula, plus assorted battalions of artillery, cavalry, and combat engineers. One corps commander wrote in his journal that 240,000 rebels were concentrated in front of the northern army. McClellan never believed the figure was quite that high, but he clearly believed it might be. Complaining to the War Department on May 10 that he himself could put barely 70,000 on the firing line, he continued to plead for more: "If I am not reinforced, it is probable that I will be obliged to fight nearly double my numbers, strongly intrenched."

Whatever their strength, the Confederates kept falling back and McClellan continued to follow. By May 15 he had advanced his base another fifteen miles along the railroad, from West Point to the head of navigation on the Pamunkey, which gave him both water and rail facilities for bringing supplies forward. Here was a large southern mansion called the White House, where the nation's first President had courted the Widow Custis, and there was a note attached to the front door. "Northern soldiers who profess to reverence Washington," it read, "forbear to desecrate the home of his first married life, the property of his wife, now owned by her descendants. A Grand-daughter of Mrs Washington." The author of the note was Mrs R. E. Lee. She had already lost one home in the path of war — Arlington, near Alexandria — and McClellan respected her wishes in regard to this one. He pitched his headquarters tents in the yard and set up a permanent supply dump at the landing, but he stationed guards around the house itself to keep out prowlers and souvenir-hunters, and provided an escort with a flag of truce to see the lady through the lines to join her husband.

Glad of this chance to show that the practice of chivalry was not restricted to soldiers dressed in gray, he then enjoyed a brief sojourn among the relics. Even though the house itself was a reconstruction, the sensation of being on the site where Washington had slept and eaten and taken his ease gave the youthful commander a feeling of being borne up and on by the stream of history; he hoped, he said, "that I might serve my country as well as he did." Riding toward the front on May 16, he came to old St Peter's Church, where Washington was married. Here too he stopped, dismounted, and went in. That night he wrote his wife: "As I happened to be there alone for a few minutes, I could not help kneeling at the chancel and praying."

What followed next day was enough to convince an agnostic of the efficacy of prayer. Officially and out of the blue, he heard from Stanton that McDowell was being reinforced by a division already on its way from Banks in the Shenandoah Valley. As soon as it got there, McClellan was told, McDowell would move south to join him in front of Richmond with an additional 40,000 men.

This was the one calamity beyond all others Lee had been seeking for means to avoid. McClellan was a hovering threat — his frontline troops could hear the clocks of Richmond strike the hours — but at least Johnston stood in his path; whereas at present there was nothing between McDowell and Richmond that he could not brush aside with an almost careless gesture, and if Johnston sidled to block him too, the capital's defenses would be stretched beyond the snapping point. The fall of the city would follow as surely as nightfall followed sunset of the day McDowell got there.

For possible deliverance, Lee looked north. Numerically the odds were even longer in Northern Virginia than they were on the Peninsula — three-to-two against Johnston, three-to-one against the troops he had left behind — but Johnston was wedged tight in coffin corner, while northward there was still room for maneuver. If anything, there was too much room. A brigade of 2500 under Brigadier General Charles Field — another of Sidney Johnston's ubiquitous former U.S. Cavalry lieutenants — had been left on the Rappahannock to watch McDowell. Jackson's command, grown by now to about 6000, opposed Banks in the Valley. Ewell's 8500 were posted at Gordonsville, equidistant from both, instructed to be ready to march in support of whichever needed him worse. Beyond Jackson, Edward Johnson with 2800 was observing Frémont's Allegheny preparations. McDowell, with Franklin detached, had 30,000; Banks had 21,000; Frémont had 17,000 and more on the way. Numerically, then — with 68,000 Federals distributed along a perimeter guarded by just under 20,000 Confederates — the outlook was as gloomy there as elsewhere, even gloomier. But Lee saw possibilities through the gloom. If the two largest southern commands, under Jackson and Ewell, could be combined, they might be able to hit one of the three opposing forces hard enough to alarm the Union high command into delaying the advance of all the rest: including McDowell. That is, Lee would stop McDowell not by striking him — he was too strong — but by striking Banks or Frémont, who would call on him for help.

Daring as the conception was, a great deal more than daring would be needed before it could be translated into action. Field, for instance, would have to be reinforced. To leave him where he was, without support from Ewell, would be to invite McDowell to smother him. But when Lee appealed to Johnston to spare the men from the Yorktown intrenchments, Johnston would not hear of it. "To detach troops from this position would be ruin to those left," he said. Once more Lee had to improvise, robbing Peter to pay Paul, and this he did. Burnside's aggressiveness having subsided, he took three brigades from North and South Carolina, 10,000 men in all, and sent them up to Fredericksburg under Brigadier General J. R. Anderson, who combined them with Field's brigade and assumed command by seniority. Ewell could now slide westward toward the Blue Ridge and conjunction with Jackson.

They were a strange pair: so strange, indeed, that perhaps the most daring thing about Lee's plan was that he was willing to trust it to these two to carry out. Dick Ewell was an eccentric, a queer-looking forty-five-year-old bachelor who spoke with a sort of twittering lisp and subsisted on a diet of cracked wheat to palliate the tortures of dyspepsia. With his sharp nose and bald-domed head, which he frequently let droop far toward one shoulder, he reminded many people of a bird — an eagle, some said; others said a woodcock. He was a West Pointer, but a generation of frontier duty, he declared, had taught him all about handling fifty dragoons and driven all other knowledge from his mind. So far, his only appreciable service in the war had been at the Battle of Manassas, where he crossed and recrossed Bull Run, far on the right, and never came to grips with the enemy at all. He had a habit of interjecting odd remarks into everyday conversations: as for instance, "Now why do you suppose President Davis made me a major general anyway?"

Stonewall seemed about as bad. The fame he had won along with his nickname at Manassas had been tarnished by last winter's fruitless Romney expedition, which resulted in much friction with the War Department, as well as by the bloody repulse he had blundered into recently at Kernstown. His abrupt cashiering of Garnett after that fight had caused his officers to think of him distastefully, and quite accurately, as a man who would be quick to throw the book at a subordinate who stepped or wandered out of line. Like Ewell, who was three months his junior in rank and seven years his senior in age, he had adopted a peculiar diet to ease the pains of dyspepsia: raspberries and plain bread and milk, supplemented by lemons — many lemons — though he would take no seasoning in his food: pepper made his left leg ache, he said. Nor was his appearance reassuring. His uniform was a single-breasted threadbare coat he had worn in the Mexican War, a rusty V.M.I. cadet cap, which he wore with the broken visor pulled well down over his weary-looking eyes, and an outsized pair of flop-top cavalry boots. A religious fanatic, he sometimes interrupted his soldiers at their poker and chuck-aluck games by strolling through camp to hand out Sunday School pamphlets. They did not object to this so much, however, as they did to the possible truth of rumors that he imagined himself a southern Joshua and in combat got so carried away by the notion that he lost his mental balance. They feared it might be so with him, for they had seen his pale blue eyes take on a wild unearthly glitter in the gunsmoke; Old Blue Light, they called him. And there was substance for their fears. Just now he was writing his wife that he hoped to make his Valley command "an army of the living God as well as of its country."

Such as they were, they were all Lee had — and strictly speaking he did not even have them. Both were still a part of Johnston's army, subject to Johnston's orders, and Johnston was extremely touchy about out-of-channels interference. Whatever was to be done in Northern Virginia would have to be done with his coöperation, or anyhow his acquiescence, which he seemed likely to withhold in the case of a proposal that violated, as this one did, his cherished principles of "concentration." On the other hand, Lee had Davis to sustain him. Unlike Lincoln, who did not count a soldier as part of the Washington defenses unless he could ride out and touch him in the course of an afternoon's round-trip carriage drive from the White House, Davis could see that a man a hundred miles away might do more to relieve the pressure, or stave off a threat, than if he stood on the capital ramparts. With the President's approval, Lee went ahead, trusting that he and Johnston would not issue conflicting orders — or, in Lee's case, suggestions — to the generals out in the Valley.

April 21 he wrote to Jackson, outlining the situation at Richmond and emphasizing the need for holding McDowell on the Rappahannock line. The key force, as he saw it, was Ewell's, which could be used in one of three ways: either by leaving it where it was, or by reinforcing Field — Anderson was still on the way — or by reinforcing Jackson. Lee preferred the latter, and he was writing to find out whether Stonewall thought it practicable: "If you can use General Ewell's division in an attack on General Banks, and to drive him back, it will prove a great relief to the pressure on Fredericksburg." A letter went to Ewell the same day, stressing the necessity for "a speedy blow." Four days later this emphasis on the necessity for speed was added in another note to Jackson: "The blow, wherever struck, must, to be successful, be sudden and heavy. The troops used must be efficient and light."

Jackson replied that he did indeed think an attack was practicable, either against Banks, who had advanced to Harrisonburg, or against Frémont's lead division, which was threatening Edward Johnson near the village of McDowell, west of Staunton. In fact, now that Ewell was at hand, Jackson had formulated three alternate plans of attack: 1) to reinforce Johnson for a sudden lunge at Frémont, leaving Ewell to watch Banks; 2) to combine with Ewell for a frontal assault on Banks; or 3) to march far down the Valley and strike Banks's rear by swinging around the north end of Massanutton Mountain. For the present, he wrote, he preferred the first; "for, if successful, I would afterward only have Banks to contend with, and in doing this would be reinforced by General Edward Johnson."

That was the last Lee heard from Stonewall for a while, though on May Day Ewell informed him, in a postscript to a report: "He moves toward Staunton and I take his position." Plan One was in the course of execution. Ten days later the silence was broken by a wire from Jackson himself. Routed through Staunton, it was dated the 9th: "God blessed our arms with victory at McDowell yesterday."

In normal times the dispatch would have been received with an exultation to match the sender's, but this was the day the Federals took Norfolk, forcing the *Virginia*'s destruction, and Pensacola toppled.

down on the Gulf. From Mississippi came news that Farragut had followed his occupation of New Orleans by forcing the upriver surrender of Baton Rouge and Natchez, while Halleck's ponderous southward advance inched closer and closer to Corinth. Worse still, from Richmond's point of view, Johnston's army was crossing the Chickahominy, near the end of its muddy retreat up the Peninsula. The government archives were being loaded onto canal boats for shipment to Lynchburg, in anticipation of the fall of the capital; the Treasury's gold reserve was packed aboard a special train with a full head of steam kept in its boiler, ready to whisk it out of the city ahead of the Yankees. President Davis had sent his wife and children to North Carolina, and there was talk that he and the cabinet were soon to follow. The soldiers seemed disheartened by their long retreat, and their general had submitted his resignation in a fit of pique because men under his command on the south side of the James had been ordered about by Lee. "My authority does not extend beyond the troops immediately around me," Johnston wrote. "I request therefore to be relieved of a merely nominal geographical command."

Lee managed to calm Johnston down — "suage him" was the term he generally employed in such cases — but the flare-up seemed likely to occur again whenever the general thought he detected signs of circumvention; which he well might do if he looked out toward the Valley. It was a testy business at best. By now, too, details of Jackson's "victory at McDowell" had shown it to be less spectacular than the brief dispatch had indicated. As at Kernstown, more Confederates than Federals had fallen. In fact, except that the outnumbered enemy had retreated, it hardly seemed a victory at all. Meanwhile, alarming news had come from Ewell: Banks was moving northward down the Valley toward the Manassas Gap Railroad, which could speed his army eastward to reinforce McDowell or McClellan. Apparently Jackson's strategy had soured. His attack on Frémont's van seemed to have had an effect quite opposite from the one he had intended.

Lee did not despair. On May 16, the day after the repulse of the Union gunboats on the James — perhaps as McClellan knelt in prayer at the chancel of St Peter's — he wrote to Stonewall, urging an immediate attack: "Whatever may be Banks' intention, it is very desirable to prevent him from going either to Fredericksburg or the Peninsula.... A successful blow struck at him would delay, if it does not prevent, his moving to either place." A closing sentence opened vistas; Banks was not the only high-ranking Federal the Valley blow was aimed at. "Whatever movement you make against Banks do it speedily, and if successful drive him back toward the Potomac, and create the impression, as far as practicable, that you design threatening that line."

✗ 2 ✗

McDowell, the sharp but limited engagement fought twenty-five miles beyond Staunton on May 8, was in the nature of a prologue to the drama about to be performed in the Shenandoah Valley. Jackson at any rate thought of it as such, and though, like a good actor, he gave it his best effort, all through it he was looking forward to the larger action whose cast and properties — Ewell and Banks, with their two armies, and the mountains and rivers with their gaps and bridges — were already in position, awaiting the entrance of the star who would give them their cues and put them to use. In the wings there were supernumeraries, some of whom did not yet know that they were to be called on stage: McDowell, for example, who by coincidence shared his surname with the furious little battle that served as prologue and signaled the raising of the curtain.

As such it held the seeds of much that followed, and this was especially true of the manner in which Stonewall put his army in motion to reinforce Edward Johnson for the attack on Frémont's van. Staunton lay to the southwest, with Johnson west of there; but Jackson marched southeast, toward Richmond, so that his men, along with whatever Federal scouts and spies might be observing, thought they were on the way to help Joe Johnston stop McClellan. Leaving his cavalry with Ewell, who moved in through Swift Run Gap to take over the job of watching Banks while he was gone, the Valley commander took his 5000 infantry through Brown's Gap, then — apparently in rehearsal for the boggy work awaiting them on the Peninsula — exposed them to a three-day nightmare of floundering through eighteen miles of ankle-deep mud before they struck the Virginia Central Railroad, ten miles short of Charlottesville, and boarded a long string of boxcars, double-headed for speed with two locomotives. When the train jerked into motion the men cheered; for it headed not east, toward Richmond, but west toward Staunton. Sunday, May 4, they got there — to the delight of the townspeople, who had thought they were being left at the mercy of Frémont, whose 3500-man advance under Brigadier General Robert Milroy was already pressing Johnson back. In compensation for the violated Sabbath, Jackson gave his men two days' rest, acquired a new uniform — it was homespun and ill-fitting, but at least it was regulation gray — then marched westward to combine with Johnson for a surprise attack that would outnumber the enemy better than two to one.

Numerically it did not work out that way; nor was it a surprise. Despite Stonewall's roundabout approach and careful picketing of the roads, Federal scouts and spies had informed Milroy of the odds he faced. He fell back to the village of McDowell — a sort of miniature Harpers Ferry, surrounded by heights — and called for help from his fellow brigadier, Robert Schenck, thirty-four miles away at Franklin. Schenck got started before midday of May 7, made a driving all-night march with 1500 men, and arrived next morning, just as Jackson was assembling his 8000 for a downhill charge against Milroy, who was in position on the outskirts of McDowell, firing gamely with the trails of his guns set in trenches to elevate the tubes. Reinforced to 5000, he decided to attack before the Confederates got their artillery on the heights. It was done with spirit, catching Jackson off balance and rocking him on his heels. But Milroy fell back on the town, lacking the strength for anything more than one hard punch, and retreated toward Franklin under cover of darkness, having inflicted 498 casualties at a cost of 256.

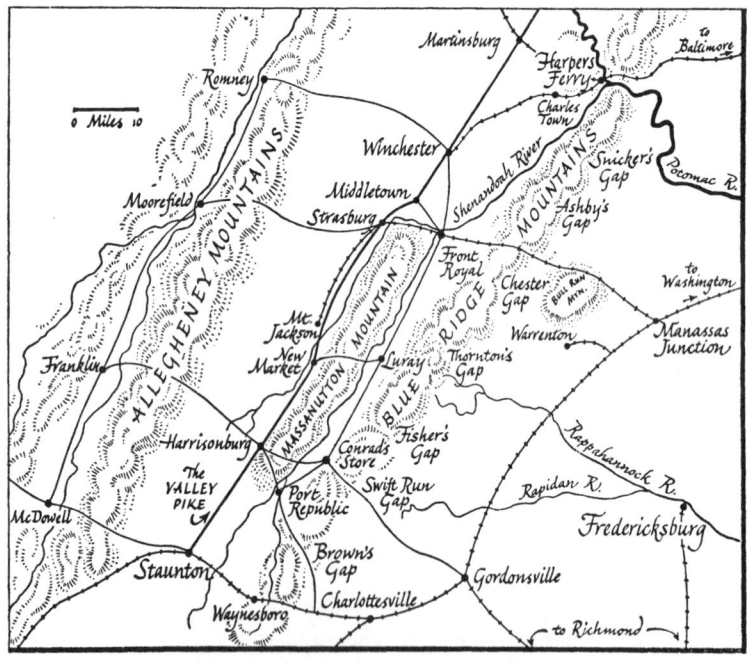

Jackson took up the pursuit next morning and continued it for three days, including another violated Sabbath, but gained nothing from it except some abandoned wagons. Milroy was not only too quick for him; to make matters worse, he set the woods afire along the road, causing the rebels to dance on embers as they groped their way through eye-stinging clouds of smoke. With regretful admiration, Stonewall called a halt near Franklin and issued a congratulatory order, urging his men "to unite with me, this morning, in thanksgiving to Almighty God, for having thus crowned your arms with success." Having done what he came west to do — knock Frémont back from Staunton — he

Fighting Means Killing

now was ready, as he later reported, to "return to the open country of the Shenandoah Valley, hoping, through the blessing of Providence, to defeat Banks before he should receive reinforcements."

It was open only by comparison, but it had opened itself to him. Long and painful hours spent committing its geography to memory with the assistance of mileage charts, listing the distance between any two points in the region, had enabled him to quote from the map as readily as he could quote from Scripture, sight unseen. From Staunton to Winchester, eighty miles, the Valley Turnpike led northeast, cradled by the Blue Ridge and the Alleghenies. Whoever controlled the macadamized pike could move the fastest, particularly in rainy weather; but there were possibilities for maneuver. East of the pike, from Harrisonburg to Strasburg, lay a smoke-colored ridge forty miles long, called Massanutton Mountain, and an alternate road led through the narrow valley just beyond it, connected to the turnpike by roads leading westward from Conrad's Store and Front Royal, around the upper and lower ends of the mountain. Embraced by the twin forks of the Shenandoah, which combined at Front Royal and flowed northward into the Potomac, the ridge could be crossed at only one point, about midway, by a road connecting New Market and Luray. Here was where Jackson fixed his eye, and the harder he looked the more he saw in the way of opportunities. The road net thus inclosing Massanutton resembled an elongated italicized capital *H:*

The crossbar was the key. Whoever held it could move up or down either shank of the H, not only with his own flank protected, but also with an excellent chance of striking the flank of an enemy in motion on the opposite side. Then too, the narrow eastern valley afforded an ideal covered approach for gaining the rear of an army coming southward up the pike, as Banks had done. Afterwards, if necessary, the attacker could make a quick escape by retracing his steps and swinging eastward through the passes of the Blue Ridge while the enemy was trying to get at him by marching around either end of the forty-mile-long mountain.

Ripe as were the opportunities awaiting him back in the Valley, they would never be available to an army that straggled as badly as his had done on the march to Kernstown. Since then, the marching had improved; but not enough. Mindful of Lee's suggestion that the troops must be "efficient and light," Jackson issued on May 13, while his men were clearing their lungs of the smoke they had breathed in pursuit of

Milroy, an order requiring strict discipline on the march. The troops were to fall in at attention, step off in cadence, hold it for two or three hundred yards before shifting to route step, and maintain prescribed intervals thereafter. No one was to leave the column for any reason whatever, except by express permission from an officer. Fifty minutes of each hour they were to march. The other ten were for rest, which preferably was to be taken prone. "A man rests all over when he lies down," Jackson said. He had little patience with frailty; a broken-down man and a straggler were two of a kind to him. As one of his officers remarked, "He classed all who were weak and weary, who fainted by the wayside, as men wanting in patriotism. If a man's face was as white as cotton and his pulse so low you could scarcely feel it, he looked upon him merely as an inefficient soldier and rode off impatiently." The men grumbled, seeing in the order further evidence of their general's crackbrained meticulosity; but, having no choice, they obeyed. In time they even saw sense in it, especially after compliance had transformed them into such rapid marchers that they became known as "foot cavalry."

Having prescribed the exact manner in which it was to be conducted, Stonewall was ready that same day to begin his march back to Staunton and beyond. Whatever its shortcomings as a tactical victory, the Battle of McDowell had earned him certain definite advantages. Despite his losses, he would be returning to the Valley with about 2500 more soldiers than he had had when he left, two weeks ago. Johnson himself would not be coming — he had suffered a bad leg wound in the fight — but his men would, in spite of the fact that it meant leaving Frémont's advance down the Alleghenies unopposed. As far as Jackson was concerned, there was no longer much danger from that direction. He could turn his back on Frémont and walk off, as if dismissing him absolutely from his mind. In bullfight terms — or, for that matter, in veterinary jargon — he had "fixed" him.

For Ewell, back at Conrad's Store, the past two weeks had been "the most unhappy I ever remember.... I never suffered as much with dyspepsia in my life." He had cause. Recently he had learned that one of Banks' two divisions was preparing to march east to join McDowell. According to Johnston's orders, this would require him to follow, but Jackson had left strict instructions for him to stay where he was until the rest of the Valley command returned. Ewell hardly knew what to do; "I have been keeping one eye on Banks, one on Jackson, all the time jogged up from Richmond, until I am sick and worn down." Stonewall — "that enthusiastic fanatic," Ewell called him — was keeping his intentions to himself, limiting his communications mostly to announcements of things past: as for instance a dispatch informing his lieutenant that, with the aid of divine Providence, he had captured much of

Milroy's wagon train. Ewell could find little comfort in this, nor could he fathom the connection. "What has Providence to do with Milroy's wagon train?" he asked, distracted and outdone.

On May 17 the crisis became acute with the arrival of definite information that one of Banks' divisions, under Major General James H. Shields, had already crossed the Blue Ridge, on its way to Fredericksburg. Though Johnston's orders left him no choice except to follow, Ewell saw that to do so would be to give up a rare chance to annihilate Banks, who was pulling his remaining division back down the pike toward Strasburg. Deciding to delay his departure at least long enough for a talk with Jackson, next morning Ewell rode west, beyond Harrisonburg, and met the Valley commander approaching that place at the head of his marching men. Stonewall's eyes flashed at the news of Banks' depletion, but then were clouded with regret that Johnston's orders denied him the chance to take advantage of it. Infected by his enthusiasm, Ewell offered to stay and lend a hand if Jackson would cover him with a letter of instructions. Quickly this was done, and Ewell returned to Conrad's Store, much happier than when he left that morning. Jackson had given him orders to prepare to march, as well as a dazzling glimpse into the secret corners of his mind.

Banks now had 9000 men occupying the three points of a triangle which rested against the northern face of Massanutton Mountain: 1500 at Winchester, his main base of supplies, 1000 at Front Royal, where the vital Manassas Gap Railroad crossed the Shenandoah River, and 6500 at Strasburg, intrenched to block an attack down the Valley pike. As protection against guerilla raids, these dispositions were judicious, but they were something less than that against anything more substantial. Banks was quite aware of this, and as a result had been feeling apprehensive ever since he learned of Ewell's arrival at Conrad's Store. In point of fact, however, he had brought this predicament on himself. A self-made man at forty-six, he had risen rapidly in politics and business. Three times governor of Massachusetts, speaker of the Federal House of Representatives, and president of the Illinois Central Railroad, he was determined to do as well in his new career, which might bring him the largest rewards of all.

On April 28 he had wired the War Department that he was "entirely secure" at Harrisonburg. "The enemy is in no condition for offensive movements," he declared. Two days later, while Jackson was setting out on his roundabout march to Staunton, Banks reported him "bound for Richmond. This is the fact, I have no doubt.... There is nothing to be done in this Valley." There was the rub. He wanted to be where guns were booming and reputations could be gained, not off in an inactive theater, watching the war go by. That night he wired again, suggesting that his corps be sent to join McDowell or McClellan. Satisfied that this would be "the most safe and effective disposition possible," he added: "I pray your favorable consideration. Such order will electrify our force."

Stanton took him at his word — but not to the extent he had intended. After conferring with Lincoln, the Secretary instructed Banks to send (not bring) one (not both) of his divisions beyond the Blue Ridge to McDowell, who would move south to join McClellan's assault on Richmond as soon as the Valley troops arrived to reinforce him. Here, then, was the natural explanation for the seemingly miraculous response to McClellan's prayers at the chancel of St Peter's. As for Banks, his plan for gaining a share of the glory available on the Peninsula had resulted in nothing, so far, but the loss of half his force — and the better half at that, for it was Shields who had whipped Jackson at Kernstown, back in March. Meanwhile, Ewell had come onto the scene, replacing the vanished Stonewall, who was presently making havoc west of Staunton. Banks, growing cautious, drew back to Strasburg and dug in, preparing to fight whatever came at him down the pike.

The electrification he had sought was closer than he knew, and it would not come from Washington. After sending Ewell back to Conrad's Store with instructions to advance two of his three brigades to Luray, Jackson continued his march through Harrisonburg, preceded by a screen of cavalry, and made camp just south of New Market on May 20. Later that day, Ewell's third brigade joined him after a trek around the south end of the mountain. Jackson sat on a rail fence, sucking thoughtfully at a lemon as he watched the troops arrive. Bayonets glinting steely in sunlight, 3000 neat gray uniforms glided past in strict alignment above the cadenced flash of white gaiters. They were Louisianians: Creoles and Irishmen, plus a battalion of New Orleans wharf rats under Roberdeau Wheat, who had put his case on record at Manassas. When they reached their assigned bivouac areas, the commands to halt were given in French — gobble-talk, the Valley soldiers called it, and hooted at the sound. Presently they had more to hoot about. The bands switched to polkas; the men broke ranks, clasped each other about the waist, and began to dance. Stonewall sat and watched in silence, the lemon gleaming yellow in his beard. "Thoughtless fellows for serious work," he said.

Another command crisis was threatening to cost him their services even now. Some hours before, a courier from Ewell had crossed the mountain with a dispatch just received from Johnston, vetoing the proposed attack and ordering him to follow Shields across the Blue Ridge while Jackson stayed behind to observe Banks. This meant that the plan to "drive him back toward the Potomac" would have to be abandoned: Ewell had no choice except to obey, unless the peremptory order was countermanded by higher authority: meaning Davis himself. Jackson moved swiftly, wiring an appeal to Lee in Richmond — "Please answer by telegraph at once," it ended — and instructing Ewell to stay where he was, pending the outcome of the plea for intercession. Now there was the strain of waiting. None of it showed, however, as Stonewall sat on the rail fence pulling thoughtfully at the lemon. When the commander of the Louisianians, Brigadier General Richard Taylor, requested instructions for tomorrow's march, Jackson merely informed him that it would begin at earliest dawn and the newly arrived brigade would head the column. When Taylor asked — not unreasonably, it seemed to him — in which direction they would move, Jackson replied that he would be with him by then to point the way.

He was there before daylight glimmered, and if there was extreme pleasure in his face this morning he had reason: Lee had conferred with Davis and wired back, countermanding Johnston's orders. The march would be north, Jackson told Taylor, and sat his horse beside the pike to watch the gaitered dandies set off down it. His mount was a close-coupled thick-necked ox-eyed creature, taken from the enemy a year ago this month; Little Sorrel was its name, but the men called it "Fancy" in derision. They made a strange pair, the undersized, rather muscle-bound horse and the tall, angular rider with his ill-fitting clothes and his taciturnity. A certain aura was gathering around him, a magnetism definite but impersonal. "No one could love the man for himself," one of his officers wrote home. "He seems to be cut off from his fellow men and to commune with his own spirit only, or with spirits of which we know not." Another put it more briefly, calling him "a one-idea-ed man." Two things he believed in absolutely, "the vigorous use of the bayonet and the blessings of Providence," and he would not be distracted in his efforts to employ them. Lately he had inquired sharply about a missing courier and was told that the boy had just been killed while delivering a message under fire. "Very commendable. Very commendable," Jackson muttered, and went back to the matter at hand.

A mile beyond New Market, just as Taylor's men settled down for the twenty-five-mile march he thought would end with an assault on Banks' main body in its Strasburg intrenchments, the Louisiana brigadier got orders to swing right and take the road across Massanutton — back into the narrow valley he had left the day before. He scarcely knew what to make of this, but presently, hiking through the lofty gap that gave simultaneous breath-taking views of the Blue Ridge and the Alleghenies, he decided that Stonewall was "an unconscious poet" who "desired to give strangers an opportunity to admire the beauties of his Valley." Though his father and his brother-in-law, Zachary Taylor and Jefferson Davis, had been professional soldiers, Taylor himself had attended Yale and Harvard, not West Point. He could not yet see that his arrival had thickened the column which, by now, Banks' scouts would have reported advancing northward on the pike: an illusion that was being continued by the cavalry, which had been left on the west side of the mountain, under orders to keep up the threatening movement, letting no one through or past with information that the infantry had turned off.

It was a hard, leg-throbbing march, steeply uphill, then steeply down, but at its end the two wings of the Army of the Valley were united at Luray. When the cavalry crossed the ridge tomorrow morning Jackson would have 17,000 soldiers concentrated for a strike at Banks' dispersed 9000. Rewarded at last for sticking by a man he swore was crazy, Ewell had absorbed his commander's spirit to such an extent that he spoke with his very accent. "We can get along without anything but food and ammunition," he warned his subordinates; "The road to glory cannot be followed with much baggage." Not only Ewell but a good part of the men in the ranks could appreciate now what Stonewall had wrought, usually to their bewilderment and over their muttered objections. Twenty miles ahead lay Front Royal. Once its 1000-man garrison had been scattered or wiped out, Jackson would be on Banks' flank and astride the Manassas Gap Railroad, blocking his path of retreat across the Blue Ridge. If he stayed to fight, outnumbered worse than two to one, with his back to his Strasburg intrenchments, he would be overwhelmed. Or if he fled northward down the pike toward the Potomac, he might be caught in motion and destroyed. Jackson had the answer to his prayers. Meanwhile — as always — his principal concern was secrecy, and for this he had the covered approach of the Luray Valley, leading directly to Front Royal.

Next day, May 22, while the cavalry was fading back from Strasburg to rejoin the main body, the infantry marched to within ten miles of Front Royal — near enough to get there early the following afternoon, with plenty of daylight left for fighting, yet far enough back to keep from alarming the unsuspecting garrison — then halted for a good night's sleep before the day of battle. Up and on the way by dawn, with Ewell in the lead, Jackson sent his troopers ahead to circle east and west of the town, tearing up sections of railroad track and clipping telegraph wires to prevent the arrival of reinforcements from Strasburg or Manassas and the spreading of alarm in either direction. The odds being what they were, seventeen-to-one, the fight could have only one outcome. But Stonewall wanted more than a lopsided victory that would yield him nothing more than control of an isolated outpost. He wanted to kill or capture every bluecoat in the place.

That was about what it came to, in the end, though for a time the thing was touch and go. Learning that the garrison was the Federal 1st Maryland, Ewell halted his column long enough to pass the Confederate 1st Maryland to the front. They came at a trot, anxious to have at the "homemade Yankees," as they called them. About 2 o'clock they struck the advance picket, drove it back through the streets of Front

Royal, and came upon the main body, drawn up north of town, preparing to resist what its colonel thought was a guerilla raid. He soon found out better, but he continued fighting, determined to hold his ground, whatever the odds. Both forks of the Shenandoah were at his back, crossable only by three narrow bridges, two over the South Fork and one over the North; so that when he saw a body of grayback cavalry riding hard to cut him off, he knew it was no use. Falling back, he won the race for the North Fork bridge, crossed it, and held off the troopers with his two rifled guns while his rear guard set the wooden span afire.

Jackson looked down from the heights south of town and saw the Federals escaping, a compact blue column hurrying north beyond the spiral of smoke from the burning bridge whose flames kept the Confederates from pursuit. "Oh, what an opportunity for artillery! Oh that my guns were here!" he cried, and turning to his staff he shouted, "Order up every rifled gun and every brigade in the army!" It was easier said than done; the guns were far back, and only three of the forty-eight were rifled. But Stonewall did not wait for their arrival. He rode down the hill and beyond the town, where a glad sight awaited him. The skirmishers had beaten out the flames, preserving enough of the damaged span to permit a crossing by horsemen. The general sent about 250 cavalry in pursuit of the Federals, who had disappeared over a ridge. They soon caught up, forcing a stand, and charged. The bluecoats broke, tried another stand, were charged again, and scattered. By now the infantry had caught up. Gleefully the rebel Marylanders beat the bushes, rounding up their late compatriots and neighbors. Out of 1063, the Federals lost 904 killed or captured. Jackson had fewer than 50 casualties, all told. Mostly they were cavalry, shot from their saddles in the two headlong charges that made his victory complete.

When first reports of the disaster reached Strasburg that same Friday, Banks informed Washington that the attack had been made by a rebel force of 5000, which "had been gathering in the mountains, it is said, since Wednesday. Reinforcements should be sent us if possible." Troops would be sent, he was told in reply; "Do not give up the ship before succor can arrive." He had no intention of giving up the ship, but by the following morning his estimate of the enemy strength had risen to "not less than 6000 to 10,000. It is probably Ewell's force, passing through the Shenandoah valley. Jackson is still in our front." He added: "We shall stand firm."

Presently the ugly truth came home. Jackson was not "in our front," nor was Ewell merely "passing through." They were not only united, they were united on Banks' flank: moving, he heard, toward Middletown, which was six miles in his rear, one third of the way to Winchester, his main supply base. Still, Banks was determined not to budge. "I must develop the force of the enemy," he kept saying. When one of his brigade commanders, Colonel G. H. Gordon, who had attended West Point with Jackson, came to reason with him, urging that the proper action would be to fall back in an attempt to save his men and supplies, the former governor said he would not hear of it; he intended to stand firm.

"It is not a retreat," Gordon explained, "but a true military movement to escape from being cut off — to prevent stores and sick from falling into the hands of the enemy."

"By God, sir!" Banks cried hotly, "I will not retreat. We have more to fear from the opinions of our friends than the bayonets of our enemies!"

Gordon now saw what the trouble was: Banks was afraid of being accused of being afraid. The colonel rose. "This, sir, is not a military reason for occupying a false position," he said. He returned to his camp, saw to the packing of his stores and baggage, got the wagons headed for Winchester, and alerted his men for the order he knew was inevitable. At last it came. The army would fall back, Banks informed him.

Jackson spent a good part of the night staring thoughtfully into a campfire, exploring a problem in geometry. At Strasburg and Front Royal, opposite ends of the base of the triangle resting against the northern face of Massanutton, he and Banks were equidistant from the apex at Winchester. By marching fast he could get there first and capture or destroy the Federal supply dump. But Stonewall wanted more than Banks' supplies; he wanted his army, too. There was the nub of the problem. If he set out north in a race for Winchester, Banks might move eastward, across his wake, and get away eastward beyond the Blue Ridge. Or if he marched west, against Strasburg, Banks might flee northward, down the pike, and save both his army and his stores. Morning came before the problem had been solved, but at least it had been explored. The latter being the graver risk, Jackson decided to take the former. With luck — or, as he preferred to express it, "with the assistance of an ever kind Providence" — he might still accomplish both his goals.

Luck or Providence seemed at first to be against him. The weather had turned blustery overnight, and the wind was whipping rain in the men's faces. Slow to fall in, they were even slower in getting started. Before long, the rain turned to hail, plopping into the mud and pelting the marchers. "Press on, men; press on," Jackson urged them, riding alongside. His impatience increased when he received a cavalry report that Banks was blowing up his Strasburg ammunition dump, preparing to evacuate. In hopes of catching the Federals in motion on the pike, he sent a section of artillery, supported by Wheat's Tigers, on a road that branched west to Middletown, seven miles away, while the rest of the army continued slogging north, straining to outstrip the head of the Federal column somewhere short of Winchester, where their paths converged.

Almost nothing went right for the Southerners today, and to lengthen the odds — in spite of his original reluctance, which had given him an even later start than his opponent — Banks was showing a real talent for retreat. His rested men hiked fast on the macadamized pike, while Stonewall's plodded wearily through mud. Twice the Union column was cut, at Middletown and five miles beyond, with resultant slaughter and confusion, but both were basically rear-guard actions, marred by the fact that the hungry Confederates could not be kept from plundering abandoned wagons instead of forging ahead after more, and the cavalry practically disbanded as the troopers set out for their nearby homes with captured horses. Jackson was furious, but neither he nor Taylor, who brought his brigade across country to join the pursuit along the turnpike, could deal with more than a handful at a time, and even these returned to their looting as soon as the generals' backs were turned. They would fight when they had to — as for instance in repulsing a 2000-man cavalry charge, which they did in style, emptying hundreds of saddles — but otherwise they were concerned with nothing they could not stuff in their mouths or pockets.

For all their slackness, the pursuers were gleaning a rich harvest of prisoners and equipment. Too badly outnumbered to turn and fight until he gained a strong defensive position, Banks was sacrificing companies in rear-guard ambuscades and dribbling wagons in his wake like tubs to Jackson's whale. With them he was buying time and distance so successfully that by sunset it was obvious that his main body was winning the race for Winchester, where just such a strong position awaited him. Even Stonewall was obliged to admit it. But he had no intention of allowing his quarry any more time than he could possibly avoid. He pushed his weary brigades through the gathering twilight. "Press on. Press on, men," he kept saying. Impatiently he rode with the handful of cavalry in advance, when suddenly the darkness ahead was stitched with muzzle flashes. The troopers drew rein. "Charge them! Charge them!" Jackson shouted. A second volley crashed ahead; bullets whistled past; the horsemen scattered, leaving the general alone in the middle of the road. "Shameful!" he cried after them in his shrill, womanish voice. "Did you see anybody struck, sir? Did you see anybody struck?" He sat there among the twittering bullets, still complaining. "Surely they need not have run, at least until they were hurt."

Sheepishly the troopers returned, and Jackson sent them forward, following with the infantry. Kernstown lay dead ahead, the scene of blundering in March. Tonight — it was Sunday again by now, as then — there was only a brief skirmish in the darkness. Winchester lay four miles beyond, and he did not intend to allow Banks time to add to the natural strength of the double line of hills south of town. When one officer remarked that his men were "falling by the roadside from fatigue and loss of sleep. Unless they are rested," he complained, "I shall be able to present but a thin line tomorrow," Jackson replied: "Colonel, I yield to no man in sympathy for the gallant men under my command, but I am obliged to sweat them tonight that I may save their blood tomorrow." He pressed on through Kernstown, but eventually saw that the colonel was right. If he kept on at this rate he would arrive with almost no army at all. He called a halt and the men crumpled in their tracks, asleep as soon as their heads touched the ground.

Jackson did not share their rest. He was thinking of the double line of hills ahead, outlining a plan of battle. At 4 o'clock, unable to wait any longer, he had the sleepy men aroused and herded back onto the road. Before the stars had paled he was approaching the high ground south of Winchester. To his relief he saw that Banks had chosen to make his stand on the second ridge, leaving only a few troops on the first. Quickly Stonewall threw out skirmishers, drove the pickets off, and brought up guns to support the assault he would launch as soon as his army filed into position. Banks had his cannon zeroed in, blasting away at the rebel guns while the infantry formed their lines. Jackson saw that the work would be hot, despite his advantage of numbers. Riding back to bring up Taylor, whose Louisianians he planned to use as shock troops, he passed some Virginia regiments coming forward. They had been ordered not to cheer, lest they give away their position, but as Jackson rode by they took off their hats in salute to the man who had driven them, stumbling with fatigue, to where the guns were growling. He removed his battered cap, riding in silence past the uncovered Virginians, and came upon Taylor, whom he greeted with a question:

"General, can your brigade charge a battery?"

"It can try."

"Very good; it must do it then. Move it forward."

Taylor did so. Passing along the ridge the Louisianians came under fire from the Union guns. Shells screamed at them, tearing gaps in their ranks, and the men began to bob and weave. "What the hell are you dodging for?" Taylor yelled. "If there is any more of it, you will be halted under this fire for an hour!" As they snapped back to attention, he felt a hand on his shoulder. He looked around.

"I am afraid you are a wicked fellow," Jackson said, and rode away.

What followed was brief but decisive. Taylor's charge, on the left, was a page out of picture-book war: a long line of men in gray sweeping forward after their commander, who gestured on horseback, pointing the way through shellbursts with his sword. On the opposite flank, Ewell had come into position up the Front Royal road in time to share in the assault. In the center, the Stonewall Brigade surged forward,

Fighting Means Killing

down the first slope and up the second, where 7000 Federals were breaking for the rear at the sight of 16,000 Confederates bearing down on them — or, strictly speaking, up at them — from three different directions. The attackers swept over the second ridge and charged through Winchester, firing after the bluecoats as they ran. Jackson rode among his soldiers, his eyes aglow at the sight.

"Order forward the whole line! The battle's won!" he shouted. All around him, men were kneeling to fire after the scampering Yankees. He snatched off his cap and waved it over his head in exultation. "Very good!" he cried. "Now let's holler!" The men took it up, and the Valley army's first concerted rebel yell rang out so loud it seemed to rock the houses. Stonewall cheered as wildly as the rest. When a staff officer tried to remonstrate with him for thus exposing himself, he paid him no mind except to shout full in his face: "Go back and tell the whole army to press forward to the Potomac!"

The Potomac was thirty-six miles ahead, but distance meant nothing to Jackson so long as an opportunity like the present was spread before his eyes. North of Winchester, all the way to the horizon, Banks' army was scattered in headlong flight, as ripe for the saber this fine May morning as grain for the scythe in July. At Front Royal his artillery had failed him; today it was his cavalry. As he watched the blue fugitives scurry out of musket range, the Valley commander clenched his fists and groaned: "Never was there such a chance for cavalry! Oh that my cavalry were in place!" Attempting to improvise a horseback pursuit, he brought up the nearest batteries, had the teams uncoupled, and mounted the cannoneers. But he soon saw it would not do; the horses were worn out, wobbly from fatigue, and so were the men. The best he could manage was to follow at a snail's pace through the waning Sunday afternoon, picking up what the fleeing enemy dropped.

Added to what had already been gleaned in three days of marching and fighting, the harvest was considerable, entirely aside from the Federal dead, the uncaptured wounded, and the tons of goods that had gone up in smoke. At a cost of 400 casualties — 68 killed, 329 wounded, and 3 missing — Jackson had taken 3030 prisoners, 9300 small arms, two rifled cannon, and such a wealth of quartermaster stores of all descriptions that his opponent was known thereafter as "Commissary" Banks.

Those were only the immediate and material fruits of the opening phase of the campaign. A larger gain — as Lee had foreseen, or at any rate had aimed at — was in its effect on Lincoln, who once more swung round to find the Shenandoah shotgun loaded and leveled at his head. Banks put on a brave face as soon as he got what was left of his army beyond the Potomac. "It is seldom that a river crossing of such magnitude is achieved with greater success," he reported. Though he admitted that "there were never more grateful hearts in the same number of men than when at midday of the 26th we stood on the opposite shore," he denied that his command had "suffered an attack and rout, but had accomplished a premeditated march of nearly 60 miles in the face of the enemy, defeating his plans and giving him battle wherever he was found."

Lincoln was not deceived. Anxious though he was for reassurance, he saw clearly that Banks was in no condition to repulse the rebels if they continued their advance beyond the Potomac. In fact, he had already reacted exactly as Lee had hoped and intended. Shields had reached McDowell, and they had set out to join McClellan in front of Richmond; but on Saturday, as soon as news reached Washington of the disaster at Front Royal, they were halted six miles south of the Rappahannock and ordered to countermarch for operations against Jackson. McDowell replied with "a heavy heart" that he would attempt what the President commanded, though he did not believe the movement would succeed. "I am entirely beyond helping distance of General Banks," he told Lincoln; "no celerity or vigor will avail so far as he is concerned." Nor did he have a high opinion of Lincoln's scheme to use him to recover control of the Valley. "I shall gain nothing for you there, and shall lose much for you here.... I feel that it throws us all back, and from Richmond north we shall have our large masses paralyzed." The Commander in Chief thanked him for his promptness, but rejected his advice. "For you it is a question of legs," he urged as soon as McDowell's men were on the march for the Valley. "Put in all the speed you can."

Lincoln had something more in mind than the relief of pressure on Banks or even the salvation of Washington. He wanted to capture Jackson, bag and baggage. Poring over maps of Northern Virginia, he had evolved a plan whereby he would block the rebel general's retreat and crush him with overwhelming numbers. McDowell's command, advancing on the Valley from the east, was one jaw of the crusher; Frémont's was the other. Concentrated at Franklin, the Pathfinder was thirty miles from Harrisonburg, which was eighty miles in Stonewall's rear. Lincoln wired instructions for him "to move against Jackson at Harrisonburg, and operate against the enemy in such a way as to relieve Banks." He added: "This movement must be made immediately. You will acknowledge the receipt of this order and specify the hour it is received by you." Frémont replied within the hour that he would march at once. "Put the utmost speed into it. Do not lose a minute," Lincoln admonished. And having ordered the combination of two large forces in the presence of the enemy — the movement Napoleon characterized as the most difficult in the art of war — he sat back, like a long-distance chess player, to await results.

Fighting Means Killing [437]

Not that he was not kept busy with other matters growing out of this one. The North was in turmoil. "Intelligence from various quarters leaves no doubt that the enemy in great force are advancing on Washington," Stanton wired the governors of thirteen states, asking them to send him whatever militia they could lay hands on. Three others were told, "Send all the troops forward that you can immediately. Banks is completely routed. The enemy in large force are advancing upon Harpers Ferry." Recruiting offices were reopened. The railroads were taken over to provide speedy transportation for reinforcements before the capital was beleaguered. Rumors spread fast on Monday, so quickly had Sunday's bolt come tumbling. The New York *Herald*, whose morning edition had carried an editorial captioned "Fall of Richmond," replaced it with a report that the whole rebel army was on the march for the Potomac. Harried by congressmen and distraught citizens, Lincoln hoped that his opponent in the Confederate seat of government could be given a hard time, too. To McClellan in front of Richmond went a wire: "Can you get near enough to throw shells into the city?"

The Young Napoleon was scarcely in a mood to throw anything at anybody: except possibly at Lincoln. When he first got the news that McDowell would not be joining him just yet, after all, his first reaction was, "Heaven save a country governed by such counsels!" On second thought, however, he could see at least one benefit proceeding from the panic in the capital: "A scare will do them good, and may bring them to their senses." But the President wired on Sunday that the enemy movement was "general and concerted," not merely a bluff or an act of desperation — "I think the time is near," he wrote, "when you must either attack Richmond or else give up the job and come to the defense of Washington" — McClellan reacted fast. The last thing he wanted in this world was to return to "that sink," within reach of "those hounds." Replying that "the time is very near when I shall attack," he added that he disagreed with Lincoln's appraisal of Confederate strategy: "The object of the movement is probably to prevent reinforcements being sent to me. All the information from balloons, deserters, prisoners, and contrabands agrees in the statement that the mass of the rebel troops are still in the immediate vicinity of Richmond, ready to defend it."

Lincoln knew how to translate "very near" and also how to assess McClellan's estimates as to the strength of an enemy intrenched to his front; he had encountered both before. Just now, though, his attention was distracted. On Tuesday, May 27, he received from Frémont a message that alarmed him: not because of what it said, but because of the heading, which showed that the Pathfinder had moved north instead of east. "I see that you are at Moorefield," Lincoln wired. "You were expressly ordered to march to Harrisonburg. What does this mean?" Frémont replied that it meant the road leading east from

Franklin was "impossible," that he had swung north to pick up food for his men, who otherwise would have starved, and that he was obeying instructions to "relieve Banks" in the best way he saw fit: by marching on Strasburg. "In executing any order received," he declared, "I take it for granted that I am to exercise discretion concerning its literal execution, according to circumstances. If I am to understand that literal obedience to orders is required, please say so."

The reply threw Lincoln into much the same state as when he flung his hat on the floor at Fort Monroe, three weeks ago. Frémont now had seventy miles to march instead of thirty. However, McDowell was closing in fast from the east, and Jackson was still reported near Harpers Ferry. There was plenty of time to cut him off, if the troops marched on schedule. On May 30 Lincoln sent two wires, one to Frémont: "You must be up in the time you promised," the other to McDowell: "The game is before you." Three days later he had Stanton give them both a final warning: "Do not let the enemy escape you."

For once, Jackson — "the game," as Lincoln styled him — was exactly where the Federal high command had him spotted: at Charles Town, with his infantry thrown forward to demonstrate against Harpers Ferry, seven miles away. Though he had known for two days now of the forces moving east and west toward a convergence that would put 35,000 soldiers in his rear, nothing in his manner showed that the information bothered him at all. After setting Monday aside for rest and prayer, in compensation for another violated Sabbath, he had come on by easy marches, driving the enemy not merely "toward the Potomac," as Lee had suggested, but to and beyond it. While the reassembled cavalry was pressing northward down the Valley pike, through Martinsburg and on to the Williamsport crossing, the infantry took the fork that branched northeast to Harpers Ferry. It was all rather anticlimactic, though, even lackadaisical, compared to what had gone before, and on the 28th — the day he was warned of the movement that threatened to cut off his retreat — he ordered his troops to resume the prescribed four hours of daily drill. Howls went up from the ranks at this, but the howls availed the outraged soldiers no more than did the complaints of the staff that the present delay would result in utter ruin. If Jackson was oblivious to the danger in his rear, they certainly were not. Once more they called him crack-brained, and one young officer muttered darkly: *"quem Deus vult perdere, prius dementat."*

There was no middle ground for confidence where Stonewall was concerned; you either trusted him blindly, or you judged him absolutely mad. That was the obverse of his method, never better illustrated than now. It was true that he had already wrung every possible psychological advantage from his present exposed position, which he knew was growing more perilous by the hour, but there were other considerations. He had 2300 unparoled prisoners on his hands, each of whom could be exchanged for a southern soldier now in a northern prison camp, and near Winchester his chief of transportation was assembling a double line of wagons eight miles long, loaded with a wealth of captured goods, including 9000 badly needed rifles, mostly new, and invaluable medical equipment shut off from the Confederacy by blockade. All this took time, but Jackson was determined to give the grinding column of spoils and captives a head start up the Valley turnpike before he attempted to bring his army out of the two-jawed trap about to snap shut in its rear.

On May 30, when the long train started rolling south, there were even more urgent reasons for the army to follow in its wake at once. Intelligence reports placed the advance of McDowell's column within a day's march of Front Royal and Frémont's about the same distance from Strasburg, both of which places were more than forty miles in Jackson's rear. Banks had been reinforced at Williamsport and presumably was about ready to take the field again, tamping the Confederates into the grinder that would be created when Frémont and McDowell met in the shadow of the northern face of Massanutton Mountain. Nothing in Stonewall's manner expressed concern, however, when he emerged from his tent this Friday morning. After receiving a delegation of Charles Town ladies who called to pay their respects, he rode toward Harpers Ferry and watched some desultory skirmishing. When a shower of rain came up, he stretched out under a tree for shelter and presently fell asleep.

He woke to find A. R. Boteler, a Valley congressman who had volunteered for duty on his staff, making a sketch of him. Jackson studied it, then remarked: "Colonel, I have some harder work than this for you to do, and if you'll sit down here now I'll tell you what it is.... I want you to go to Richmond for me; I must have reinforcements. You can explain to them down there what the situation is here." Boteler replied that he would be glad to go, but that he was not sure he understood the situation: whereupon Jackson outlined it for him. "McDowell and Frémont are probably aiming to effect a junction at Strasburg, so as to cut us off from the upper Valley, and are both nearer to it now than we are. Consequently, no time is to be lost. You can say to them in Richmond that I'll send on the prisoners, secure most if not all of the captured property, and with God's blessing will be able to baffle the enemy's plans here with my present force, but that it will have to be increased as soon thereafter as possible." If Boteler thought the general wanted to use those reinforcements merely to help stand off the various columns now converging on him, he was much mistaken — as he discovered from what Stonewall said in closing: "You may tell them, too, that if my command can be gotten up to 40,000 men a movement may be made ... which will soon raise the siege of Richmond and transfer this campaign from the banks of the Potomac to those of the Susquehanna."

* * *

Riding south with all the speed he could manage — by rail to Winchester, by horseback to Staunton, by rail again to Richmond — the congressman-colonel arrived to find that the eastern theater's first major engagement since Manassas, eighty miles away and ten full months ago, had been fought at the city's gates while he was traveling. With his back to the wall and the choice narrowed to resistance or evacuation, Johnston at last had found conditions suitable for attack.

In point of fact, despite his fondness for keeping the tactical situation fluid—in hopes that his opponent would commit some error or be guilty of some oversight and thereby expose a portion of the blue host to destruction—Johnston really had no choice. With McDowell poised for a southward advance, a junction that would give the Federals nearly a three-to-one advantage over the 53,688 Confederates drawn up east of Richmond, not even evacuation would assure the salvation of Johnston's army, which now as always was his main concern: McClellan would still be after him, and with overwhelming numbers. The only thing to do, he saw, was to strike one Mac before the other got there. Besides, the error he had been hoping for seemed already to have been committed. McClellan's five corps were unequally divided, three north and two south of the Chickahominy. Normally a sluggish stream, not even too broad for leaping in the dry months, the river was greatly swollen as a result of the continual spring rains, and thus might serve to isolate the Union wings, preventing their mutual support and giving the Confederates a chance to slash at one or the other with equal or perhaps superior numbers. Johnston would have preferred to attack the weaker south-bank wing, keeping Richmond covered as he did so; but this would not only leave McDowell's line of advance unblocked, it would probably also hasten the junction by provoking a rapid march from Fredericksburg when McClellan yelled for help. By elimination, then, Johnston determined to strike down the north bank, risking uncovering Richmond for the sake of wrecking McClellan's right wing and blocking McDowell's advance at the same time.

He had his plan, a product of necessity; but as usual he took his time, and kept his counsel as he took it. Least of all did he confer with the President, afterwards explaining: "I could not consult him without adopting the course he might advise, so that to ask his advice would have been, in my opinion, to ask him to command for me." The result, with the Federals a rapid two-hour march away, was a terrible strain on Davis. Unable to get the general's assurance that an all-out defense of the city would be attempted, he never knew from day to day which flag might be flying over the Capitol tomorrow. May 22, riding out the

Mechanicsville turnpike with Lee, he found few troops, no fortifications, indeed no preparations of any kind, as he wrote Johnston, for blocking a sudden Union drive "toward if not to Richmond." Two days later Johnston came to town for a conference, but he told his superior nothing except that he intended to be governed by circumstances. To make matters worse, while he was there the Federals seized Mechanicsville, five miles north, just as Davis had predicted. Not only was this an excellent location for a hook-up when McDowell made his three- or four-day march from Fredericksburg, but now there was nothing at all to stand in the way of such an advance, Johnston having instructed Anderson to fall back from the line of the Rappahannock.

Two days later, May 26, while he was reviewing the situation with Lee, the President's anxiety over Johnston's undivulged intentions was so obviously painful that Lee proposed, "Let me go and see him, and defer this discussion until I return." When he was gone a dispatch arrived from Jackson, who broke his silence with an outright shout of joy. "During the past three days," it began, "God has blessed our arms with brilliant success." Banks had been routed and Stonewall was in pursuit, "capturing the fugitives." Whether this would have the intended effect of frightening the Union high command into holding back McDowell remained to be seen, but the news was a tonic for Davis, arriving as it did at the very crisis of his concern. Presently Lee returned, to be heartened by this early yield from the seeds of strategy he had sown in the Valley and to deliver tidings that bore directly on the subject of the President's anxiety. Johnston at last had announced his decision to attack. Intended to crumple McClellan's right wing, which brushed the purlieus of the city, the strike would be made on the 29th.

That was Thursday; today was Monday. Davis braced himself for the three-day wait.

McClellan was quite aware of the danger of straddling what he called "the confounded Chickahominy," but his instructions left him no choice. In the dispatch of the 17th, rewarding his prayers with the announcement that McDowell would be moving south as soon as Shields arrived, Stanton had told McClellan: "He is ordered — keeping himself always in position to save the capital from all possible attack — so to operate as to place his left wing in communication with your right wing, and you are instructed to coöperate, so as to establish this communication as soon as possible, by extending your right wing to the north of Richmond."

That was that, and there was nothing he could do to change it, though he tried. Next day, as if he knew how little an appeal to Stanton would avail him, he wired Secretary Seward: "Indications that the enemy intend fighting at Richmond. Policy seems to be to concentrate everything there. They hold central position, and will seek to meet us while divided. I think we are committing a great military error in having so many independent columns. The great battle should be fought by our troops in mass; then divide if necessary." Three days later, when this had brought no change in his instructions, he wrote to his friend Burnside: "The Government have deliberately placed me in this position. If I win, the greater the glory. If I lose, they will be damned forever, both by God and men."

Consoled by this prediction as to the verdict that would be recorded in history as in heaven, and reassured the following day by a message from Fredericksburg — "Shields will join me today," McDowell wrote, and announced that he would be ready to march on the 24th with 38,000 men and 11,000 animals — McClellan took heart and labored to make the dangerous waiting period as brief as possible. On the scheduled date he sent his cavalry to drive the rebels out of Mechanicsville, thus extending his grasp north of Richmond in accordance with Stanton's instructions. Before the day was over, however, he received a telegram from the President which informed him that he was clutching at emptiness: "In consequence of General Banks' position, I have been compelled to suspend McDowell's movements." Next day, with Banks "broken up into a total rout," Lincoln explained his action by combining a justification with an appeal: "Apprehensions of something like this, and no unwillingness to sustain you, have always been my reason for withholding McDowell from you. Please understand this, and do the best you can with the force you have."

That was what McClellan did. Though he found the order "perfectly sickening," he took comfort at least in the fact that McDowell's southward movement had been "suspended," not revoked, and he worked hard to strengthen his army's position astride the river and to pave the way for the eventual junction on the right as soon as the Fredericksburg command got back from what McDowell himself considered a wild-goose chase. Eleven new bridges, "all long and difficult, with extensive log-way approaches," were erected across the swollen Chickahominy between Mechanicsville and Bottom's Bridge, twelve miles apart. It was an arduous and unending task, for the spans not only had to be constructed, they often had to be replaced; the river, still rising though it was already higher than it had been in twenty years, swept them away about as fast as they were built. While thus providing as best he could for mutual support by the two wings in event that either was attacked, he saw to the improvement of the tactical position of each. Keyes, supported by Heintzelman on the south bank, pushed forward along the Williamsburg road on the 25th and, a mile and a half beyond Seven Pines, constructed a redoubt within five miles of the heart of the enemy capital. Though McClellan could not comply with Lincoln's request next day that he "throw some shells into the city," he could see Richmond's tallest steeples from both extremities of his line, north and south of the river, and hear the public clocks as they struck the quiet hours after midnight.

On the north bank, Porter was farthest out; behind him were Franklin, in close support, and Sumner, who occupied what was called the center of the position, eight miles downstream from Mechanicsville. The latter's corps was theoretically on call as a reserve for either wing, though the rising flood was steadily increasing its pressure on the two bridges he had built for crossing the river in event of an attack on Keyes or Heintzelman. To protect his rear on the north bank, and to shorten McDowell's march from Fredericksburg, McClellan on the 27th had Porter take a reinforced division twelve miles north to Hanover Courthouse, where a Confederate brigade had halted on its fifty-mile retreat from Gordonsville. Porter encountered the rebels about noon, and after a short but sharp engagement drove them headlong, capturing a gun and two regimental supply trains. At a cost of 397 casualties, he inflicted more than 1000, including 730 prisoners, and added greatly to the morale of his corps.

It was handsomely done; McClellan was delighted. The sizeable haul of men and equipment indicated a decline of the enemy's fighting spirit. Lying quiescent all this time in the Richmond intrenchments, despite his reported advantage in numbers, Joe Johnston seemed to lack the nerve for a strike at the divided Federal army. At this rate, the contest would soon degenerate into a siege — a type of warfare at which his young friend George was an expert. "We are getting on splendidly," McClellan wrote his wife before he went to bed that night. "I am quietly clearing out everything that could threaten my rear and communications, providing against the contingency of disaster, and so arranging as to make my whole force available in the approaching battle. The only fear is that Joe's heart may fail him."

That seemed to be about what had happened Thursday morning when, after hurrying through some office work, Davis rode out to observe the scheduled attack, but found the troops lounging at ease in the woods and heard no sound of gunfire anywhere along the line. Johnston had told him nothing of canceling or postponing the battle; Davis was left to wonder and fret until late in the day, when investigation uncovered what had happened.

At a council of war held the previous night for issuing final instructions, something in the nature of a miracle had been announced. Only the day before, Johnston had been given definite information that McDowell was on the march; already six miles south of Fredericksburg, his advance was within thirty miles of Hanover Courthouse, where Porter had been waiting since his midday repulse of the Confederate brigade. But now, at the council held on Wednesday evening, a dispatch from Jeb Stuart announced that McDowell, with nothing at all between him and a junction with McClellan, had halted his men and was countermarching them back toward the Rappahannock. It seemed entirely too good to be true; yet there it was. Johnston breathed a sigh of relief and canceled tomorrow's attack. That was why Davis heard no gunfire when he rode out next morning, expecting to find the battle in full swing.

Johnston did not abandon his intention to wreck one wing of McClellan's divided army, but he was doubly thankful for the delay. For one thing, it gave him additional time, and no matter how he squandered that commodity while backing up, time was something he prized highly whenever he considered moving forward. For another, with McDowell no longer a hovering threat, he could shift the attack to the south bank of the Chickahominy, where the Federals were less numerous and reportedly more open to assault. With this in mind he drew up a plan of battle utilizing three roads that led eastward out of the capital so patly that they might have been surveyed for just this purpose. In the center was the Williamsburg road, paralleling the York River Railroad to the Chickahominy crossing, twelve miles out. On the left was the Nine Mile road, which turned southeast to intersect the railroad at Fair Oaks Station and the Williamsburg road at Seven Pines, halfway to Bottom's Bridge. On the right, branching south from the Williamsburg road about two miles out, was the Charles City road, which reached a junction six miles southeast leading north to Seven Pines and Fair Oaks. Thus all three roads converged upon the objective, where the advance elements of the Federal left wing were intrenched. The attack could be launched with all the confidence of a bowler rolling three balls at once, each one down a groove that had been cut to yield a strike.

A third advantage of the delay was that it brought in reinforcements. R. H. Anderson's command, at the end of its long withdrawal from the line of the Rappahannock, was combined with the brigade that had been thrown out of Hanover Courthouse, thus creating a new division for A. P. Hill, a thirty-seven-year-old Virginia West Pointer just promoted to major general. Another division was on the way from Petersburg under Huger, who had stopped there after evacuating Norfolk. These additions would bring Johnston's total strength to nearly 75,000 men, giving him the largest army yet assembled under the Stars and Bars. What was more, the six divisions were ideally located to fit the plan of battle. A. P. Hill and Magruder, north of Richmond, could maintain their present positions, guarding the upper Chickahominy crossings. Smith and Longstreet were camped in the vicinity of Fairfield Race Course, where the Nine Mile road began; Longstreet would move all the way down it to strike the Union right near Fair Oaks, while Smith halted in reserve, facing left as he did so, to guard the lower river crossings. D. H. Hill was east of the city, well out the Williams-

Fighting Means Killing   [445]

burg road; he would advance and deliver a frontal attack on signal from Huger, who had the longest march, coming up from the south on the Charles City road. The object was to maul Keyes, then maul Heintzelman in turn as he came up, leaving McClellan a single wing to fly on.

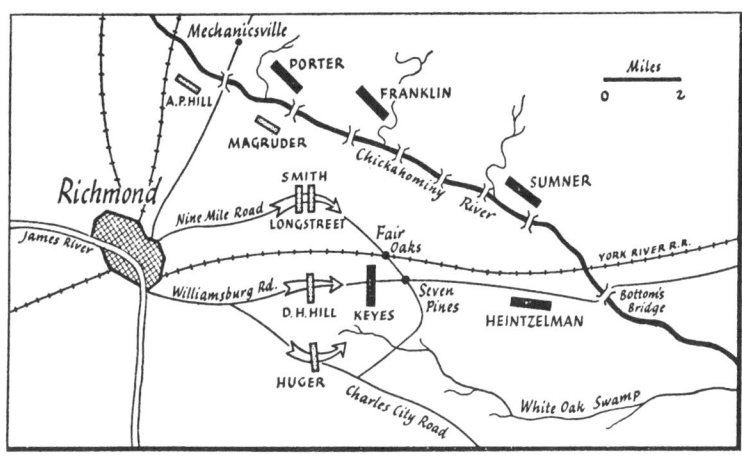

It was a simple matter, as such things went, to direct the attacking divisions to their separate, unobstructed routes. On the evening of May 30, as Johnston did so, a pelting rainstorm broke, mounting quickly to unprecedented violence and continuing far into the night. This would no doubt slow tomorrow's marches on the heavy roads and add to the difficulty of deploying in the sodden fields, but it would also swell the Chickahominy still farther and increase the likelihood that the Federal right wing would be floodbound on the northern bank, cut off from rendering any help to the assailed left wing across the river. Johnston was glad to see the rain come down, and glad to see it continue; this was "Confederate weather" at its best. Some of the instructions to his six division commanders were sent in writing. Others were given orally, in person. In either case, he stipulated that the attack, designed to throw twenty-three of the twenty-seven southern brigades against a single northern corps, was to be launched "early in the morning — as early as practicable," he added, hearing the drumming of the rain.

The most remarkable thing about the ensuing action was that a plan as sound as Johnston's appeared at the outset — so simple and forthright, indeed, as to be practically fool-proof, even for green troops under green commanders — could produce such an utter brouhaha, such a Donnybrook of a battle. Seven Pines, or Fair Oaks as some called it, was unquestionably the worst-conducted large-scale conflict in a war that afforded many rivals for that distinction. What it came to, finally, was a military nightmare: not so much because of the suffering and bloodshed, though there was plenty of both before it was over, but rather because of the confusion, compounded by delay.

Longstreet began it. Since his assigned route, out the Nine Mile road, would put him under Smith, who outranked him, he persuaded Johnston to give him command of the forces on the right. As next-ranking man he was entitled to it, he said, and Johnston genially agreed, on condition that control would revert to him when the troops converged on Seven Pines. Longstreet, thus encouraged, decided to transfer his division to the Williamsburg road, which would give him unhampered freedom from Smith and add to the weight of D. H. Hill's assault on the Union center. He did not inform Johnston of this decision, however, and that was where the trouble first began. Marching south on the outskirts of Richmond, across the mouth of the Nine Mile Road, he held up Smith's lead elements while his six brigades of infantry trudged past with all their guns and wagons.

This in itself amounted to a considerable delay, but Longstreet was by no means through. When Huger prepared to enter the Williamsburg road, which led to his assigned route down the Charles City road, he found Longstreet's 14,000-man division to his front, passing single file over an improvised bridge across a swollen creek. Nor would the officers in charge of the column yield the right of way; first come first served, they said. When Huger protested, Longstreet informed him that he ranked him. They stood there in the morning sunlight, the South Carolina aristocrat and the broad, hairy Georgian, and that was the making of one career and the wrecking of another. Huger accepted the claim as true, though it was not, and bided his time while Longstreet took the lead.

The morning sun climbed up the sky, and now it was Johnston's turn to listen, as Davis had done two days ago, for the boom of guns that remained silent. As he waited with Smith, whose five brigades were in position two miles short of Fair Oaks Station, his anxiety was increased by the fact that he had lost one of his divisions as completely as if it had marched unobserved into quicksand. Nobody at headquarters knew where Longstreet was, nor any of his men, and when a staff officer galloped down the Nine Mile road to find him, he stumbled into the enemy lines and was captured. When at last Longstreet and his troops were found — they were halted beside the Williamsburg road, two miles out of Richmond, while Huger's division filed past to enter the Charles City road — Johnston could only presume that Longstreet had misinterpreted last night's verbal orders. The delay could be ruinous. Everything depended on the action being completed before nightfall; if it went past that, McClellan would bring up reinforcements under cover of darkness and counterattack with superior numbers in the morning. As the sun went past the overhead, Johnston remarked that he wished his

Fighting Means Killing

army was back in its suburban camps and the thing had never begun.

He could no more stop it, however, than he could get it started. All he could do was wait; and the waiting continued. Lee rode out from Richmond, determined not to spend another day like the office-bound day of Manassas. Johnston greeted him courteously, but spared him the details of the mix-up. Presently there came from the southeast an intermittent far-sounding rumble of cannon. It grew until just after 3 o'clock, with ten of the fifteen hours of daylight gone, the rumble was vaguely intensified by a sound that Lee believed was musketry. No, no, Johnston told him; it was only an artillery duel. Lee did not insist, although it seemed to him that the subdued accompaniment was rising in volume. Then at 4 o'clock a note came from Longstreet, informing the army commander that he was heavily engaged in front of Seven Pines and wanted support on his left.

That was the signal Johnston had been awaiting. Ordering Smith's lead division to continue down the Nine Mile road until it struck the Federal right, he spurred ahead to study the situation at first hand. As he rode off, the President rode up; so that some observers later said that the general had left in haste to avoid an irksome meeting.

Davis asked Lee what the musketry meant.

Had he heard it, too? Lee asked.

Unmistakably, Davis said. What was it?

Mostly it was D. H. Hill. He had been in position for six hours, awaiting the signal from Huger as instructed, when at 2 o'clock he ran out of patience and surged forward on his own. (It was just as well; otherwise the wait would have been interminable. Cutting cross-country to take his assigned position on Hill's right, Huger had become involved in the upper reaches of White Oak Swamp. He would remain so all through what was left of this unhappy Saturday, as removed from the battle — except that the guns were roaring within earshot — as if he had been with Jackson out in the Shenandoah Valley.) Hill's attack was no less furious for being unsupported on the flanks. A forty-year-old North Carolinian, a West Point professional turned schoolmaster as a result of ill health, he was a caustic hater of all things northern and an avid critic of whatever displeased him anywhere at all. Dyspeptic as Stonewall Jackson, his brother-in-law, he suffered also from a spinal ailment, which gave him an unmilitary bearing whether mounted or afoot. His friends called him Harvey; that was his middle name. A hungry-looking man with haunted eyes and a close-cropped scraggly beard, he took a fierce delight in combat — especially when it was hand to hand, as now. His assault swept over the advance Federal redoubt, taking eight guns and a brigade camp with all its equipment and supplies. Scarcely pausing to reform his line, he went after the rest of Keyes' corps, which was drawn up to receive him just west of Seven Pines.

Here too the fight was furious, the Federals having the advantage of an abatis previously constructed along the edge of a line of woods, while the Confederates, emerging from a flooded swamp, had to charge unsupported across an open space to reach them. Longstreet's complaint, made presently when he appealed to Johnston for help on the left, that green troops were "as sensitive about the flanks as a virgin," did not apply to Hill's men today. Especially it did not apply to the lead brigade, four regiments from Alabama and one from Mississippi, under Brigadier General Robert E. Rodes. Inexperienced as they were, their only concern was the tactics manual definition of the mission of the infantry in attack: "to close with the enemy and destroy him." Advancing through the swamp, thigh-deep in mud and stagnant water, they propped their wounded against the trunks of trees to keep them from drowning, and came on, yelling as they came. They reached the abatis, pierced it, and drove the bluecoats back again.

It was gallantly done, but at a dreadful cost: Rodes' 2000-man command, for instance, lost 1094 killed, wounded, or drowned. And there were no replacements near at hand. Out of thirteen brigades available to Longstreet here on the right — his six, Hill's four, and Huger's three — less than half went into action. Three of his six he had sent to follow Huger into the ooze of White Oak Swamp, and a fourth he had posted on the left to guard against a surprise attack, in spite of the fact that there was nothing in that direction except the other half of the Confederate army. However, the Federals were forming a new line farther back, perhaps with a counterattack in mind, and he was not so sure. Huger was lost on the right; so might Smith be lost on the left. At any rate, that was when he sent the note to Johnston, appealing for the protection of his virginal left flank.

Smith's division, reinforced by four brigades from Magruder and A. P. Hill, followed the army commander down the Nine Mile road toward Fair Oaks, where the leading elements were formed under his direction for a charge that was intended to strike the exposed right flank of Keyes, whose center was at Seven Pines, less than a mile away. Late as the hour was, Johnston's juggernaut attack plan seemed at last to be rolling toward a repetition of his triumph at Manassas. But not for long. Aimed at Keyes, it struck instead a substantial body of men in muddy blue, who stood and delivered massed volleys that broke up the attack before it could gather speed.

They were strangers to this ground; the mudstains on their uniforms were from the Chickahominy bottoms. It was Sumner's corps, arrived from across the river. Commander of the 1st U.S. Cavalry while Albert Sidney Johnston commanded the 2d — Joe Johnston was his lieutenant-colonel, McClellan one of his captains — Sumner was an old army man with an old army notion that orders were received to be obeyed, not questioned, no matter what obstacles stood in the way of execution. "Bull" Sumner, he was called — in full, "the Bull of the Woods" — because of the loudness of his voice; he had a peacetime custom of removing his false teeth to give commands that carried from end to end of the regiment, above the thunder of hoofs. Alerted soon after midday (Johnston's aide, who had ridden into the Union lines in search of Longstreet, had told his captors nothing; but his presence was suspicious, and the build-up in the woods and swamps out front had been growing more obvious every hour) Sumner assembled his corps on the north bank, near the two bridges he had built for this emergency. Foaming water had buckled them; torn from their pilings, awash knee-deep in the center, they seemed about to go with the flood. When the order to support Keyes arrived and the tall white-haired old man started his soldiers across, an engineer officer protested that the condition of the bridges made a crossing not only unsafe, but impossible. "Impossible?" Sumner roared. "Sir, I tell you I *can* cross! I am ordered!"

Marching toward the sound of firing, he got his men over the swaying bridges and across the muddy bottoms, on to Fair Oaks and the meeting engagement which produced on both sides, in about equal parts, feelings of elation and frustration. If Sumner had kept going he would have struck the flank of Longstreet; if Smith had kept going he would have struck the flank of Keyes. As it was, they struck each other, and the result was a stalemate. Smith could make no headway against Sumner, who was content to hold his ground. Hill, to the south, had shot his bolt, and Keyes was thankful that the issue was not pressed beyond the third line he had drawn while waiting for Heintzelman, who had sent one division forward to help him but did not bring the other up till dusk.

By then the battle was practically over. Seven Pines, the Southerners called it, since that was where they scored their gains; to the Northerners it was Fair Oaks, for much the same reason. The attackers had the advantage in spoils — 10 guns, 6000 rifles, 347 prisoners, and a good deal of miscellaneous equipment from the captured camp — but the price was excessive. 6134 Confederates were dead or wounded: well over a thousand more than the 5031 Federals who had fallen.

These were the end figures, not known or attained until later, but they included one casualty whose fall apparently tipped the balance considerably further in favor of the Yankees. Near Fair Oaks, Johnston watched as the uproar swelled to a climax; then, as it diminished, he rode closer to the battle line, and perceiving that nothing more could be accomplished — the flame-stabbed dusk was merging into twilight — sent couriers to instruct the various commanders to have their men cease firing, sleep on their arms in line of battle, and prepare to renew the contest in the morning. Just then he was hit in the right shoulder by a bullet. As he reeled in the saddle, a shell fragment struck him in the chest and unhorsed him. Two aides carried the unconscious general to a less exposed position and were lifting him onto a stretcher when the President and Lee came riding up. As they dismounted and approached, Johnston opened his eyes and smiled. Davis knelt and took his hand, beginning to express his regret that the general had been hit. This affecting scene was interrupted, however, by Johnston's shock at discovering that he had lost his sword and pistols: the "unblemished" sword of which he had written in protest at being oversloughed by the man who now held his hand and murmured condolences. "I would not lose it for $10,000," he said earnestly. "Will not someone please go back and get it and the pistols for me?" They waited then while a courier went back under fire, found the arms where they had fallen, and returned them to Johnston, who rewarded him by giving him one of the pistols. This done, the stretcher-bearers took up their burden and set off.

Davis and Lee went looking for Smith, who as the next-ranking field commander would now take charge of the uncompleted battle. Presently they found him. But the man they found bore little resemblance to the stern-lipped, confident "G.W." who the month before had urged an all-or-nothing assault on Philadelphia and New York. He had learned of Johnston's misfortune and he counted it as his own. It made him tremble. He looked sick. In fact he *was* sick: not from fear, or anyhow not from any ordinary fear (he was brave as the next man in battle, if not braver) but from the strain of responsibility suddenly loaded on his shoulders. The effect was paralyzing — quite literally — for within two days he would leave the army, suffering from an affliction of the central nervous system. Just now, when Davis asked what his plans were, he replied that he had none. First he would have to discover Longstreet's situation on the right, of which he knew nothing. He might have to withdraw; on the other hand, he might be able to hold his ground.... Davis suggested that he take the latter course. The Federals might fall back in the night; if the Confederates stayed they would gain the moral effect of a victory. Smith said he would if he could.

The best that could be hoped for under present circumstances was that the army would be able to disengage itself tomorrow, without further excessive losses, for a future effort under a new commander. As Davis and Lee rode together up the Nine Mile road, clogged like all the others tonight with wounded and disheartened men who had stumbled and hobbled out of the day-long nightmare of bungled marches and mismanaged fire-fights, one thing at least was clear. The new commander would not be Smith, who had had retreat in the front of his mind before he even knew the situation. The two men rode in silence under a sickle moon: Davis was making his choice. If he hesitated, there was little wonder. His companion was the obvious candidate; but he could easily be by-passed. Davis, knowing better than anyone how well Lee had served in his present advisory capacity, could as logically keep him there as he kept Samuel Cooper at the Adjutant General's post. "Evacuating Lee," the press had called the fifty-five-year-old graybeard, and with cause. Disappointing lofty expectations, he had shown a woeful incapacity to deal with high-strung subordinates in the field — and Johnston's army had perhaps the greatest number of high-strung troop commanders, per square yard, of any army ever assembled. Besides, in the more than thirteen months of war, Lee had never taken part in a general engagement. Today in fact, riding about the field as an observer, he had been under close-up rifle fire for the first time since Chapultepec, nearly fifteen years ago.

Nevertheless, by the time the lights of beleaguered Richmond came in sight Davis had made his decision. In a few words lost to history, but large with fate for the two riders and their country, he informed Lee that he would be given command of the army known thereafter as the Army of Northern Virginia.

★ ★ ★

In a telegram to McClellan, written while the guns were roaring around Seven Pines and Sumner was assembling his corps for its march across the Chickahominy, Lincoln described the geometrical dilemma he had created for the Confederates in the Shenandoah Valley: "A circle whose circumference shall pass through Harpers Ferry, Front Royal, and Strasburg, and whose center shall be a little northeast of Winchester, almost certainly has within it this morning the forces of Jackson, Ewell, and Edward Johnson. Quite certainly they were within it two days ago. Some part of their forces attacked Harpers Ferry at dark last evening and are still in sight this morning. Shields, with McDowell's advance, retook Front Royal at 11 a.m. yesterday ... and saved the bridge. Frémont, from the direction of Moorefield, promises to be at or near Strasburg at 5 p.m. today. Banks, at Williamsport with his old force, and his new force at Harpers Ferry, is directed to coöperate." He added, by way of showing that the picture was brightening all over: "Corinth is certainly in the hands of General Halleck."

The circle was not quite complete, however. There was still the Front Royal-Strasburg gap, and Jackson — who knew as well as Lincoln that for him, as for the blue columns attempting a convergence, the question was one of "legs" — was making for it with all the speed he could coax from his gray marchers. Leaving the Stonewall Brigade to continue the demonstration against Harpers Ferry, he had boarded the train yesterday at Charles Town for a fast ride to Winchester, where the rest of the army was being assembled for the race up the Valley turnpike. Time was running out now and he knew it. Still, nothing in his manner showed distress. Folding his arms on the back of the seat ahead, he rested his face on them and went to sleep. He was wakened by a mounted courier, who flagged the train to a stop and handed him a message through the window. Jackson read it without comment, then tore it up and dropped the pieces on the floor. "Go on, sir, if you please," he told the conductor. He put his head on his arms again, and soon was rocked to sleep by the vibration of the train.

At Winchester, when the other passengers learned the contents of the dispatch that had been delivered en route, they wondered that Stonewall had not blenched. Shields had turned the tables on him. Marching fast from the east through Manassas Gap, the leader of McDowell's advance had surprised the Front Royal garrison, a regiment of Georgians whose colonel fled at the first alarm, leaving his men and $300,000-worth of captured goods to be scooped up by the Yankees. Jackson interviewed the runaway colonel that night — "How many men did you have killed?" "None"; "How many wounded?" "None, sir"; "Do you call that much of a fight?" — and put him in arrest. Fortunately, the senior captain had taken command, burned the supplies, and brought the troops out. But the damage was done, and the implications were ominous. Shields stood squarely across the entrance to the narrow eastern valley with its many avenues of escape through the passes of the Blue Ridge. Stonewall's only remaining line of retreat was up the Valley pike, through Strasburg. At Front Royal, Shields was only eleven miles from there: Jackson, at Winchester with his wagon train and prisoners and the main body of his army, was seventeen. Worst of all, the Stonewall Brigade, still menacing Harpers Ferry, had forty-four miles to go before it reached that mid-point in the narrowing gap where Shields and Frémont would converge. Jackson sent a staff officer to bring up the brigade with all possible speed. "I will stay in Winchester until you get here if I can," he told him, "but if I cannot, and the enemy gets here first, you must bring it around through the mountains."

The army was moving by dawn, May 31: first the wagon train, a double column eight miles long, loaded with captured goods that were literally priceless; then the prisoners, a brigade-sized throng of men in blue, who, having missed the pell-mell northward retreat from here to the Potomac the week before, would march faster under Jackson than they had ever done before: and finally the main body, the "foot cavalry," already looking a little larger than life because of the fame they were beginning to share with their strange captain. By early afternoon they had cleared the town, all but a couple of cavalry regiments left to wait for the Stonewall Brigade. Winchester's seven days of liberation were about over. Ahead lay Strasburg, which they might or might not clear before Lincoln's steel circumference was closed. They did not worry about that, however. They left such worries to Jackson, who knew best how to handle them. The worst it could mean was fighting, and they had fought before. Nor did they worry about the rain, a slow drizzle that gave promise of harder showers to come. In fact, they welcomed it. They had the macadamized pike to march on, while their opponents slogged through mud. "Press on; press on, men," Stonewall urged them.

They pressed on, halting for ten minutes out of every hour, as prescribed, and joking among themselves that Jackson would never allow the train to be captured; he had his reserve supply of lemons in one of the wagons. Presently, sure enough, good news was passed back down the line. The head of the column had entered Strasburg — and found the gap unclosed. To the east and west, the cavalry was skirmishing within earshot, but the infantry saw no sign of bluecoats as they swung into sight of the little town and made camp for the night. Eighteen miles they had marched today, despite the long wait for the wagons and the prisoners to clear the road ahead, and now they had reached the rim of the map-drawn circle. They were into the clear.

Good news came from the rear as well. By midnight the Stonewall Brigade was four miles south of Winchester, the men dropping dog-tired in their tracks after a record-breaking march of thirty-five miles. Next morning they were off again on wobbly legs, cursing their old commander for having left them far in the rear to fight the whole compounded Yankee army. Always he gave them the dirty end of the stick, lest he be accused of favoritism — and now they were to be sacrificed for the sake of this glory-hunter's mad gyrations. So they complained. Approaching Strasburg, however, they heard a spatter of musketry from the west, mixed in with the boom of guns. It was Jackson, fighting to hold the gap ajar for the men of his old brigade. Their hearts were lifted. Once more they sang his praises. "Old Jack knows what he's about! He'll take care of us, you bet!"

It was a strange day, this June 1 Sunday: particularly for Ewell. Except for a feint by one brigade, repulsed the afternoon before, Shields seemed to be resting content with the retaking of Front Royal; but Frémont was hovering dangerously close in the opposite direction, as if he were tensing his muscles for a leap at the west flank of the long column. Ewell was given the task of holding him back while the Stonewall Brigade caught up with the main body, plodding southward up the pike behind the train and the leg-weary captives. He was warned not to bring on a general engagement; all Jackson wanted was a demonstration that would encourage the Pathfinder to hesitate long enough for the Stonewall Brigade to pass through Strasburg. The warning seemed superfluous, however. Contact was established early, but nothing would provoke Frémont into close-up fighting. He stopped as soon as his skirmishers came under fire.

If Frémont was not provoked, Ewell was. "I can't make out what those people are about," he said. "They won't advance, but stay out there in the woods, making a great fuss with their guns." Taylor suggested that he place his brigade on the Federal flank and then see what developed. "Do so," Old Baldy told him; "that may stir them up, and I am sick of this fiddling about." Taylor gained the position he wanted, then walked down Frémont's line of battle until he came under fire from Ewell's other brigades; there he stopped and they came up alongside him. Frémont gave ground, refusing to be provoked into what he evidently thought was rashness. After all that marching, seventy miles in seven days, lashed by rain and pelted by hail as he picked his way over mountain roads, the Pathfinder seemed to want no part of what he had been marching toward. It was strange.

At last, about midafternoon, the Stonewall Brigade passed Strasburg. Ewell broke off the fight, if it could be called that, and followed the main body up the turnpike. Frémont again became aggressive, slashing so savagely at the rear of the moving column that Taylor's men and the cavalry had all they could do to hold them off. Up front, Jackson was having his troubles, too. Twelve miles beyond Strasburg, a portion of the train fell into confusion and presently was overtaken by the lead brigade. The result was turmoil, a seemingly inextricable mix-up of wagons and men and horses. Stonewall came riding up and rebuked the infantry commander:

"Colonel, why do you not get your brigade together, keep it together, and move on?"

"It's impossible, General. I can't do it."

"Don't say it's impossible! Turn your command over to the next officer. If he can't do it, I'll find someone who can, if I have to take him from the ranks."

He got the tangle straightened out and pressed on southward under a scud of angry-looking clouds and jagged streaks of lightning. Soon after sunset the tempest broke. Rain came down in torrents. (Near Strasburg, Frémont called a halt for the night, wiring Lincoln: "Terrible storm of thunder and hail now passing over. Hailstones as large as hens' eggs.") Jackson kept moving, having just received word that he was now involved in another race. McDowell had joined Shields at Front Royal, and had sent him south up the Luray valley to parallel Jackson's advance on the opposite side of Massanutton Mountain. If Shields marched fast he would intercept the rebels as they came around the south end of the ridge; or he might cross it, marching from Luray to New Market, and thus strike the flank of the gray column moving along the turnpike. Either way, Jackson would have to stop and deploy, and Frémont could then catch up and attack his rear, supported perhaps by Banks, who had reëntered Winchester, urged by Lincoln to lend a hand in accomplishing Jackson's destruction.

Once more it was "a question of legs," and Stonewall was duly thankful for the downpour. Even though it bruised his men with phenomenal hailstones, it would deepen the mud in the eastern valley and swell the South Fork of the Shenandoah, which lay between Shields and the mountain. To make certain he did not cross it, Jackson sent a detail to burn the bridges west of Luray. That way, he would have only Frémont to deal with, at least until he passed Harrisonburg. When he finally stopped for the night, the Sabbath was over; he could write a letter to his wife. "[The Federals] endeavored to get in my rear by moving on both flanks of my gallant army," he told her, "but our God has been my guide and saved me from their grasp." And he added, with a tenderness that would have shocked the men he had been driving southward through rain and hail, under sudden forks of lightning: "You must not expect long letters from me in such busy times as these, but always believe your husband never forgets his little darling."

All next day the rain poured down; "our God," as Stonewall called Him, continued to smile on the efforts of the men in gray. Jackson, never one to neglect an advantage, continued to press the march of his reunited army along the all-weather pike. There was an off chance that Shields, within earshot of Frémont's guns as he slogged through the mud in the opposite valley, might somehow have managed to rebuild the Luray bridges and thereby have gained access to the road across the mountain. A staff officer, sent to check on the work of destruction, returned and reported it well done, but Jackson did not rest easy until he entered New Market with the advance and found the mountain road empty.

Meanwhile, far back down the pike, the rear guard was having its hands full. Shields had sent his troopers around through Strasburg to coöperate with Frémont, and they were doing their work with dash and spirit. Several times that day they charged the Confederate rear guard, throwing it into confusion. Late in the afternoon they made their most effective attempt, breaking through the scattered ranks and riding hard up the pike until they struck a Virginia regiment, which had halted to receive them with massed volleys. The result was as if they had ridden into a trip wire. Saddles were emptied and horses went down screaming; all except one of the attackers were killed or captured. That night, reporting the incident to Jackson, the Virginia colonel expressed his regret at having had to deal so harshly with such gallantry. The general heard him out, then asked: "Colonel, why did you say you saw those Federal soldiers fall with regret?" Surprised at Stonewall's inability to appreciate chivalrous instincts, the colonel said that it was because he admired their valor; he hated to have to slaughter such brave men. "No," Jackson said dryly. "Shoot them all. I do not wish them to be brave."

He had in mind the expectation that he would soon be facing them in battle: not a series of piecemeal rear-guard actions, fought to gain time for retreating, but a full-scale conflict into which he would throw every soldier in his army. Having employed defensive tactics to escape the first and second traps at Strasburg and New Market, he now was thinking of ways to assume the offensive in dealing with the third, which he would encounter somewhere beyond Harrisonburg when he rounded the south end of Massanutton. At that point he might be able to turn on one or another of the Federal columns and give it a mauling before the other could come to its relief. He would await developments; meanwhile that was what he had in mind.

Before it could be attempted, however, he would have to give his men a chance to rest. Next day — June 3 — they got it. The North Fork of the Shenandoah intersected the Valley turnpike just above the railroad terminus at Mount Jackson, and as Frémont's advance approached that place, the last gray cavalrymen crossed the bridge and set it afire, leaving their pursuers stranded on the northern bank. Stonewall took advantage of this to give his men a full day's badly needed rest and the wagon train and prisoners a substantial head start toward the Virginia Central, where they could be loaded for shipment by rail to warehouses and prisons down near Richmond. If there seemed to be a considerable risk in this delay, he felt he could afford it. Beyond the mountain, Shields was toiling through the mud; he would be at least a day behind and badly worn by the time he reached Conrad's Store, where he would reënter the tactical picture. On this side, there was the danger that Frémont might bridge the swollen river — he had brought a pontoon train across the Alleghenies for just such an emergency — but Jackson doubted if this could be successful, considering all the water that was trickling down the slopes of all the mountains. It was not. Frémont got his pontoon bridge across, all right, but before he could make much use of it, the North Fork rose twelve feet in four hours. He had to cut it loose from the southern bank to keep it from being swept away and lost in the raging water.

While his men were taking their ease beyond New Market, and leg-weary stragglers were catching up to share in the first hot meals the army had had since leaving Winchester four days ago, Jackson took out his Valley map and resumed his study of geography. As always, the harder he looked the more he saw. Resting against the southern face of Massanutton there was a road-net triangle much like the one at the opposite end, which he had used to discomfort Banks; and as Stonewall pored over the map he began to see possibilities for using this upper triangle in an even more ambitious venture against Shields and Frémont. Its base ran from Harrisonburg to Conrad's Store; its apex was at Port Republic, which lay at the tip of a tongue of land where North and South Rivers joined to form the South Fork of the Shenandoah. A bridge spanned North River, connecting the town with Harrisonburg, nine miles away, but all the other crossings were badly swollen fords. Once the South Fork bridge at Conrad's Store was destroyed, this upper bridge at Port Republic would be Shields' only way of joining Frémont. If Jackson's army got there first, he would be between the two, and therefore able to deal with them one at a time. Defensively, too, the position was a sound one. If Frémont attempted an advance on Staunton, Jackson would be on his flank; or if Shields somehow managed to cross the South Fork and marched toward a junction at Harrisonburg, he could then be served in the same fashion. Or if everything went wrong and disaster loomed, Jackson could make a quick getaway by moving southeast through Brown's Gap, as he had done the month before on his roundabout march to fight the Battle of McDowell. All this was much, but mainly he prized the offensive advantages of the position, which would put his army between Frémont and Shields, with a chance to strike at one or the other; or both.

Resuming the march that afternoon, he dispatched two mounted details to perform two separate but allied tasks: one to burn the bridge at Conrad's Store, the other to establish a signal station on the southernmost peak of Massanutton Mountain. The first would frustrate Shields when he attempted to turn west. The second would observe his reaction. Meanwhile, fed and rested, each man carrying two days' cooked rations and a fresh supply of ammunition on his person, the main body made good time up the turnpike. The rain had slacked to a drizzle, which meant that Frémont would soon be able to recommission his pontoon bridge, but for the present the Valley soldiers enjoyed an unmolested march. After stopping for the night just short of Harrisonburg, they entered that place next morning, June 5, and turned southeast toward Port Republic and the execution of Stonewall's design.

As soon as they left the turnpike they encountered what Shields had had to cope with all along: Napoleon's "fifth element," mud. Presently it became obvious that they were not much better at coping with the stuff than they had been on the nightmare march near here five weeks ago. By nightfall the head of the column was approaching North River, but the tail was no more than a mile from Harrisonburg, while the rest of the army was strung out along the six or seven intervening miles of boggy road. Jackson's wrath was mollified, however, by the return of the detail he had sent to Conrad's Store. They had won the race and done their job. From the signal station, high on Massanutton, came a message that Shields had halted two miles north of the burned bridge, which placed him fourteen muddy miles from Port Republic. Frémont was a good deal farther back. He had crossed North Fork above Mount Jackson, but the cavalry was hacking away at the head of his column, impeding his progress up the pike. Reassured, though still regretful, Stonewall called a halt. The rain had slacked to a mizzle by now; perhaps tomorrow the road would be firmer.

It was. Saturday, after an early start, Ewell's division stopped just beyond the hamlet of Cross Keys, six miles from Harrisonburg, to stand in Frémont's path when he came up. Jackson's plodded another three miles and went into position on the heights above the confluence of the rivers at Port Republic, overlooking the low-lying opposite bank of the South Fork, where the road wound southwest from Conrad's Store; this would be Shields' line of advance, and the guns on the heights would enfilade his column at close range. Neither of the Union forces was yet in sight, however, so the Valley soldiers had time for reading their mail, which had just been forwarded along with the latest newspapers. Elated by their victories, the editors had broken out their blackest type. The Charleston *Mercury* called Stonewall "a true general" and predicted that he would soon be "leading his unconquerable battalions through Maryland into Pennsylvania." By way of contrast, gloomy reports from the northern press were reprinted in adjoining columns, and the Richmond *Whig* combined a mock protest with a backhand swipe at the Administration: "This man Jackson must be suppressed, or else he will change the humane and Christian policy of the war, and demoralize the Government." The men, of course, enjoyed this flood of praise. Jackson, too, had an ache for fame — "an ambition boundless as Cromwell's," Taylor called it, "and as merciless" — but he considered this a spiritual infirmity, unbecoming in a Christian and a deacon of the Presbyterian Church. Also, he was pained that the glory was not ascribed to its true source: God Almighty. Members of his staff observed that from this time on he gave up reading the papers — perhaps for the same reason he had given up drinking whiskey: "Why, sir, because I like the taste of [it], and when I discovered that to be the case I made up my mind to do without [it] altogether."

Included in the packet of mail was a congratulatory letter in the handwriting of the President. Congressman Boteler had delivered Jackson's request for more troops; Davis regretted that none were available. "Were it practicable to send you reinforcements it should be done, and your past success shows how surely you would, with an adequate force, destroy the wicked designs of the invader of our homes and assailer of our political rights." For the present, however, the Chief Executive added, "it is on your skill and daring that reliance is to be placed. The army under your command encourages us to hope for all which men can achieve."

Welcome though the praise was, the letter itself was disappointing. Without substantial reinforcements Jackson knew he could not hope to drive Shields and Frémont from the Valley as he had driven Banks. In fact, unless they came against him in his present strong position — which seemed unlikely, considering their caution; neither was yet in sight — he could scarcely even hope to give them a prod. So he began thinking of alternatives, including the possibility of taking his little army down to the Peninsula for a knockout combination against his old academy classmate, McClellan. Replying that same day (not to Davis, but to Johnston, who he thought was still in charge despite his wound) Stonewall wrote: "Should my command be required at Richmond I can be at Mechum's River Depot, on the Central Railroad, the second day's march, and part of the command can reach there the first day, as the distance is 25 miles. At present," he added, unhappy in the middle of what seemed to be a stalemate, "I do not see that I can do much more than rest my command and devote its time to drilling."

In this he was much mistaken. He could, and indeed would have to, do a great deal more — as he found out next morning in a most emphatic manner. Shields was a politician, having represented both Illinois and Minnesota in the U.S. Senate, but he was also a veteran of the Black Hawk War and a Mexico brigadier. A fifty-six-year-old native of Tyrone County, Ireland, he had proved his fighting ability by whipping Jackson at Kernstown back in March, and now that his opponent's fame had risen he was anxious to prove it again in the same way. From Conrad's Store, where he had paused to let his division catch its breath near the end of its wearing march up the narrow valley, he sent two brigades forward along the right bank of the South Fork to explore the situation at Port Republic. Stonewall was there already and might launch a sudden attack across the river, so Shields sent a message requesting cooperation from Frémont, whose guns he had been hearing intermittently for a week: "If he attempts to force a passage, as my force is not large there yet, I hope you will thunder down on his rear.... I think Jackson is caught this time."

He very nearly was: quite literally. The Valley chieftain had spent the night at Port Republic, saddened by the death of his cavalry commander, Brigadier General Turner Ashby, who had fallen that afternoon in a skirmish just this side of Harrisonburg. Ashby had had his faults, the main one being an inability to keep his troopers on the job when there was loot or applejack within reach, but he had established a reputation for personal bravery that was never outdone by any man in either army. In death the legend was complete; "Charge, men! For God's sake, charge!" he cried as he took the bullet that killed him; now only the glory remained. "As a partisan officer I never knew his superior," Jackson declared. Next morning, June 8, when the chief of staff — a theologian who, conditions permitting, did double duty by preaching Sunday sermons in the camps — inquired if there would be any military operations today, Stonewall told him there would not; "You know I always try to keep the Sabbath if the enemy will let me."

The men put no stock in this at all. Convinced by now that Jackson thought he enjoyed an advantage when fighting on the Lord's day, they believed that he did so every time he got the chance. Statistics seemed to bear them out, and presently this statistical trend was strengthened. As the minister-major went back into the house to compose his sermon and the rest of the staff prepared to ride out for an inspection of the camp on the northward ridge, a rattle of musketry shattered the Sunday-morning stillness and a cavalryman came galloping with alarming news. The Federals had forded South River, scattering the pickets, and were entering the town! "Go back and fight them," Jackson snapped. He mounted and rode hard for the North River bridge, clattering across the long wooden structure just in time. A colonel and a lieutenant who brought up the rear were cut off and captured.

Gaining the heights, which overlooked the town, Jackson ordered his batteries to open fire on the bluecoats in the streets below, and sent two brigades of infantry to clear them out at the point of the bayonet. It was smartly done; the Federals fell back in haste, abandoning a fieldpiece and the prisoners they had taken. Stonewall, peering down from the ridge as his men advanced across the bridge and through the smoke that hung about the houses, dropped the reins on his horse's neck and lifted both hands above his head, palms outward. When the men looked up and saw him stark against the sky, invoking the blessing of the God of battle, they cheered with all their might. The roar of it reached him there on the heights, and the cannoneers swelled the chorus.

As the cheering subsided, the men on the ridge became aware of a new sound: the rumble and boom of cannon, swelling from the direction of Cross Keys. It was Frémont, responding to Shields' request that he "thunder down." Going forward, however, he struck not Jackson's rear but Ewell's front. The first contact, after a preliminary bombardment, was on the Confederate right, where Ewell had posted a Virginia brigade along a low ridge overlooking some fields of early grain. Frémont came on with unaccustomed vigor, a regiment of New Yorkers in the lead, their boots crunching the young stalks of buckwheat. As they started up the slope there was a sudden crash of gunfire from the crest and the air was full of bullets. A second volley thinned the ranks of the survivors as they tried to re-form their shattered line. They fell back, what was left of them. Frémont, reverting to the form he had shown at Strasburg, settled down to long-range fighting with his artillery, which was skillfully handled. Out in the buckwheat the wounded New Yorkers lay under this fire, crying for water. Their cries decreased as the day wore on and Frémont continued his cannonade.

In essence that was all there was to the Battle of Cross Keys.

Ewell, fretting because he could not get the Pathfinder to make another attack, at last pushed forward for more than a mile until he occupied the ground from which the Federals had advanced that morning. There he stopped, having been warned not to put too much space between the two wings of the army. Frémont, with 10,500 infantry effectives, faded back before Ewell's 5000. It was finished. The North had lost 684 men, nearly half of them lying dead of their wounds in the grainfields; the South had lost 288, only 41 of them killed. Jackson's trust in Old Bald Head was confirmed. Except for a quick ride out, to see how things were going, he had let Ewell fight his own battle while he himself remained on the heights above Port Republic. Asked if he did not think there was some danger that Shields would advance to help Frémont, whose guns were within earshot, Stonewall gestured toward his batteries and said grimly: "No, sir; no; he cannot do it! I should tear him to pieces." As he stood there, listening to the sound of Ewell's battle, intoxicated as if by music, he remarked to his ministerial chief of staff: "Major, wouldn't it be a blessed thing if God would give us a glorious victory today?" One who overheard him said that as he spoke he wore the expression "of a child hoping to receive some favor."

But, childlike, having received it, he was by no means satisfied. He wanted more. That night he issued orders for Ewell to leave a reinforced brigade in front of Frémont and march the rest of his division through Port Republic to join the other wing for a combined assault on the Union troops beyond the river. Once Shields was properly broken up, they could both return and fall on Frémont, completing the destruction Ewell had begun today.

The march began at earliest dawn of what was to be a lovely sun-drenched day. Jackson's division came down off the heights, crossed the North River bridge, filed through the town, and forded South River. The Stonewall Brigade was in the lead, under thirty-three-year-old Brigadier General Charles S. Winder, a tall, wavy-haired Maryland West Pointer who, by strict discipline and a resolute bearing under fire, had gained the respect of his men, despite their resentment at losing Garnett. For an hour the advance up the right bank of the South Fork continued. Then at 7 o'clock word came back that Federal pickets had been encountered. Jackson studied the situation briefly, then told Winder to go ahead and drive them. He did not know the enemy strength, but he believed more would be gained by a sudden assault than by a detailed reconnaissance of the position. Besides, Ewell would soon be coming up, and Stonewall wanted to get the thing over with quickly, so as to return and deal with Frémont before the Pathfinder, discovering the weakness of the force to his front, pushed it back into Port Republic and burned the bridge.

Winder went forward, driving hard, but entered a maelstrom of bullets and shells that stopped the charge in its tracks. Once more, as at Kernstown against these same men, Jackson's old brigade had to pay in blood for his rashness. What was worse, by way of indignity — though he did not know it — there were only two small brigades before him, fewer than 3000 soldiers. But they made up in fury and grit for what they lacked in numbers. Their commander, Brigadier General E. B. Tyler, had placed six of his sixteen guns in a lofty charcoal clearing on his left. While the blue infantry held in front, these guns delivered a rapid and accurate fire, enfilading the stalled ranks of the attackers. Winder sent two regiments to flank and charge the battery, but they were met by volleys of grape and flung back with heavy losses. All this time the Stonewall Brigade was being decimated, its ranks plowed by shells from the guns in the coaling.

Jackson was dismayed, seeing his hopes dissolve in the boil and swirl of gunsmoke. Frémont by now must have attacked in response to the uproar, and Ewell was nowhere in sight. It seemed likely that McDowell might be coming up with the rest of his 20,000 troops: in which case there was nothing to do but concentrate everything against him for a decisive battle right here, or else retreat and put a sorry ending to the month-long Valley campaign. Stonewall chose the former course, sending couriers to hasten Ewell's march and inform the holding force at Cross Keys to fall back through Port Republic, burning the North River bridge behind them so that Frémont, at least, would be kept out of the action. Meanwhile, Winder must hang on. His men were wavering, almost out of ammunition, but he held them there, perhaps remembering what had happened to his predecessor after falling back from a similar predicament.

Presently the unaccustomed frown of fortune changed suddenly to a smile. Taylor appeared, riding at the head of his Louisianians; he had marched toward the sound of firing. Jackson greeted him with suppressed emotion, saying calmly: "Delightful excitement." Taylor looked at the hard-pressed front, then off to the right, where smoke was boiling up from the hilltop clearing. If those guns were not silenced soon, he said, the army "might have an indigestion of such fun." Stonewall agreed, and gave him the job.

While Taylor was setting out to perform it, the Valley commander joined Winder, whose men were dropping fast along the front. From his horseback perch Jackson saw enemy skirmishers beginning to creep forward. Quickly he ordered a charge, hoping to shock them into caution until Taylor reached their flank. The Stonewall Brigade gave him what he asked for. Winder's troops advanced, the skirmishers recoiling before them, and took up a new position behind a snake-rail fence. Here they were even worse exposed to the shells that tore along their line. Wavering, they began to leak men to the rear. A gap appeared. Rapidly it widened. Soon the brigade was in full retreat — past

Winder, past Jackson, past whatever tried to stand in their way or slow them down. It was a rout worse than Kernstown.

But fortune's smile was steady. The men of Ewell's brigade, arriving on the left soon after Taylor's men filed off to the right, replaced Winder's and blocked a Federal advance. As they did so, a terrific clatter erupted at the far end of the line. It was Taylor; he had come up through a tangle of laurel and rhododendron. Three charges he made against double-shotted guns, and the third charge took them, though the cannoneers fought hard to the last, swinging rammer-staffs against bayoneted rifles. Then, as the Union commander attempted a left wheel, intending to bring his whole force against Taylor, Ewell's third brigade arrived in time to go forward with the second. Outnumbered three to one, fighting now with both flanks in the air and their strongest battery turned against them, the Federals fell back, firing erratically as they went. For the Confederates it was as if all the pieces of a gigantic jigsaw puzzle had fallen suddenly into place of their own accord. Eyes aglow, Stonewall touched Ewell's arm and pointed: "He who does not see the hand of God in this is *blind*, sir. Blind!"

It was now 11 o'clock; a good eight hours of daylight remained for pursuit. Pursue was easier said than done, however. Tyler's men withdrew in good order, covering the retreat with their ten remaining guns. Jackson had to content himself with gleaning 800 muskets from the field while the cavalry pressed the retreating column, picking up prisoners as they went. Soon the ambulances were at work. When all the wounded Confederates had been gathered, the aid men gave their attention to the Federals. However, this show of mercy was interrupted by Frémont. Free at last to maneuver, he put his guns in position on the heights across the river and, now that the battle was over, began to shell the field. Jackson, much incensed, ordered the ambulances back. Federal casualties for the day were 1018, most of them inflicted during the retreat, including 558 prisoners; Stonewall's were in excess of 800, the heaviest he had suffered.

The battle was over, and with it the campaign. Jackson put his army in motion for Brown's Gap before sundown, following the prisoners and the train, which had been sent ahead that morning. By daylight he was astride the gap, high up the Blue Ridge, well protected against attack from either direction and within a day's march of the railroad leading down to Richmond, which the past month's fighting in the Valley had done so much to save. He intended to observe Shields and Frémont from here, but that turned out to be impossible: Lincoln ordered them withdrawn that same day. Frémont was glad to go — he had "expended [his troops'] last effort in reaching Port Republic," he reported — but not Shields, who said flatly: "I never obeyed an order with such reluctance." Jackson came down off the mountain, sent his cavalry ahead to pick up 200 sick and 200 rifles Frémont abandoned at

Harrisonburg, and recrossed South River, making camp between that stream and Middle River. There was time now for rest, as well as for looking back on what had been accomplished.

"God has been our shield, and to His name be all the glory," he wrote his wife. Not that he had not coöperated. To one of his officers he confided that there were two rules to be applied in securing the fruits which the Lord's favor made available: "Always mystify, mislead, and surprise the enemy, if possible. And when you strike and overcome him, never let up in the pursuit so long as your men have strength to follow; for an army routed, if hotly pursued, becomes panic-stricken, and can then be destroyed by half their number. The other rule is, never fight against heavy odds if by any possible maneuvering you can hurl your own force on only a part, and that the weakest part, of your enemy and crush it. Such tactics will win every time, and a small army may thus destroy a large one in detail, and repeated victory will make it invincible."

Application of these strategic principles, plus of course the blessing of Providence — particularly in the form of such meteorological phenomena as cloudbursts and hailstones large as hen-eggs — had enabled Stonewall, with 17,000 troops, to frustrate the plans of 60,000 Federals whose generals were assigned the exclusive task of accomplishing his destruction. Four pitched battles he had fought, six formal skirmishes, and any number of minor actions. All had been victories, and in all but one of the battles he had outnumbered the enemy in the field, anywhere from two- to seventeen-to-one. The exception was Cross Keys, where his opponent showed so little fight that there was afterwards debate as to whether it should be called a battle or a skirmish. Mostly this had been done by rapid marching. Since March 22, the eve of Kernstown, his troops had covered 646 miles of road in forty-eight marching days. The rewards had been enormous: 3500 prisoners, 10,000 badly needed muskets, nine rifled guns, and quartermaster stores of incalculable value. All these were things he could hold and look at, so to speak. An even larger reward was the knowledge that he had played on the hopes and fears of Lincoln with such effect that 38,000 men — doubtless a first relay, soon to have been followed by others — were kept from joining McClellan in front of Richmond. Instead, the greater part of them were shunted out to the Valley, where, fulfilling their commander's prediction, they "gained nothing" and "lost much."

Beyond these tangibles and intangibles lay a further gain, difficult to assess, which in time might prove to be the most valuable of all. This was the campaign's effect on morale, North and South. Federals and Confederates were about equally fagged when the fighting was over, but there was more to the story than that. There was such a thing as a tradition of victory. There was also such a thing as a tradition of defeat. One provoked an inner elation, *esprit de corps,* the other an inner weariness. Banks, Frémont, and Shields had all three had their commands broken up in varying degrees, and the effect in some cases was long-lasting. The troops Stonewall had defeated at McDowell were known thereafter, by friend and foe, as "Milroy's weary boys," and he had planted in the breasts of Blenker's Germans the seeds of a later disaster. Conversely, "repeated victory" — as Jackson phrased it — had begun to give his own men the feeling of invincibility. Coming as it did, after a long period of discouragement and retreat, it gave a fierceness to their pride in themselves and in their general. He marched their legs off, drove them to and past exhaustion, and showed nothing but contempt for the man who staggered. When they reached the field of battle, spitting cotton and stumbling with fatigue, he flung them into the uproar without pausing to count his losses until he had used up every chance for gain. When it was over and they had won, he gave the credit to God. All they got in return for their sweat and blood was victory. It was enough. Their affection for him, based mainly on amusement at his milder eccentricities, ripened quickly into something that very closely resembled love. Wherever he rode now he was cheered. "Let's make him take his hat off," they would say when they saw him coming. Hungry as they often were, dependent on whatever game they could catch to supplement their rations, they always had the time and energy to cheer him. Hearing a hullabaloo on the far side of camp, they laughed and said to one another: "It's Old Jack, or a rabbit."

✗ 3 ✗

Confederate authorities at the seat of government did what they could to keep the news of Johnston's wound and the subsequent change of commanders out of the papers. Enterprising newsboys sometimes wandered out beyond the fortifications, profitably hawking their journals in the Union camps, and the authorities feared that the enemy might find comfort and encouragement in the news. They were right. "I prefer Lee to Johnston," McClellan declared when he heard of the shift — meaning that he preferred him as an opponent. "The former is too cautious and weak under grave responsibility. Personally brave and energetic to a fault, he yet is wanting in moral firmness when pressed by heavy responsibility, and is likely to be timid and irresolute in action."

He wrote this under the influence of a new surge of confidence and elation. At the time of Fair Oaks, in addition to the depression he felt at hearing that McDowell was being withheld, he had been confined to bed with neuralgia and a recurrent attack of malaria, contracted long ago in Mexico; but he was feeling much better now. Pride in the reports of his army's conduct in that battle — so fierce that eight out of the nine general officers in Keyes' corps had been wounded or had had their horses shot from under them — restored his health and sent his spirits soaring: as was shown in the congratulatory address he issued a few days later. "Soldiers of the Army of the Potomac!" it began. "I have fulfilled at least a part of my promise to you. You are now face to face with the rebels, who are held at bay in front of their capital. The final and decisive battle is at hand. Unless you belie your past history, the result cannot be for a moment doubtful.... Soldiers!" it ended. "I will be with you in this battle and share its dangers with you. Our confidence in each other is now founded on the past. Let us strike a blow which is to restore peace and union to this distracted land. Upon your valor, discipline and mutual confidence the result depends."

The men enjoyed the sound of this, the reference to their valor and the notion that the war was being fought for peace. Some of them had wondered; now they knew. It was being fought to get back home. That knowledge was a gain, and there were others. Having done well in one big battle, they felt they would do better in the next one. They could laugh now at things that had seemed by no means humorous at the time: for instance, the boy going up to the firing line with the fixed stare of a sleepwalker, pale as moonlight, moaning "Oh Lord, dear good Lord," over and over as he went. They had a familiarity with the mechanics of death in battle. Coming up the Peninsula they had passed a rebel graveyard with a sign tacked over the gate: "Come along, Yank. There's room outside to bury you." Since then, many of them had served on burial details, fulfilling the implication, and undertakers were doing a rush business with both the quick and the dead, embalming the latter and accepting advance payments from the former, in return for a guarantee of salvation from a nameless grave in this slough they called the Chicken Hominy. The going price was $20 for a private and up to $100 for an officer, depending on his rank.

Their main consolation was McClellan. He gave the whole thing meaning and lent a glitter to the drabness of their camps. They cheered him as he rode among them; they took their note of confidence from him. Presently, after fretful news from the Shenandoah Valley, they saw his confidence increase. He had just been informed that Lincoln had called off the goose-chase after Jackson and was bringing McDowell back to Fredericksburg, with orders to resume the advance on Richmond as soon as his men recovered from their exertions. Best of all, as a cause for immediate rejoicing, the 9500-man division of Brigadier General George A. McCall — left on the Rappahannock while the rest of the First Corps was crossing the Blue Ridge — had been ordered to join McClellan at once, moving by water to assure the greatest speed. Their transports began to arrive at White House June 11, five days after the march order was issued. As these reinforcements came ashore a dispatch arrived from Stanton: "Be assured, General, that there has never been a moment when my desire has been otherwise than to aid you with my whole heart, mind and strength since the hour we first met.... You have never had and never can have anyone more truly your friend or more anxious to support you."

Next day army headquarters moved to the south bank of the Chickahominy, where three of the five corps now were: Keyes on the left at White Oak Swamp, Heintzelman covering the Williamsburg road in the center, and Sumner on the right, astride the railroad. Porter and Franklin were still on the north bank, the former advanced to Mechanicsville, the latter in support. When McCall arrived he would be assigned to Porter, whose strength would be 27,500 men, and Franklin would join the main body, taking position between Sumner and the river. The army then would present an unbroken front, anchored firmly on the left and extending a strong right arm to meet McDowell, who had wired on June 8: "McCall goes in advance by water. I will be with you in ten days with the remainder by land from Fredericksburg."

McClellan had plenty to do while he waited. The rains had returned with a vengeance, taking the bridges out again, flooding the bottoms, and sweeping away the corduroy approaches. "The whole face of the country is a perfect bog," he informed Washington. "The men are working night and day, up to their waists in water." Lincoln and Stanton kept wanting to know when he would be ready to attack, and he kept stalling them off with a series of loop-holed replies. A week after Fair Oaks he told them: "I shall be in perfect readiness to move forward and take Richmond the moment McCall reaches here and the ground will admit the passage of artillery." Six days later, with McCall on hand and four corps consolidated south of the Chickahominy, he declared: "I shall attack as soon as the weather and the ground will permit." June 18 the rain slacked and he wired: "After tomorrow we shall fight the rebel army as soon as Providence will permit."

It was a tantalizing progression of near-commitments and evasions: first McCall, then the weather, and finally Providence itself: Lincoln and Stanton scarcely knew what to think. McClellan knew, though. He had read rumors that the powers in Washington were engaged in a frenzy of backbiting over the recent fiasco in the Valley. "Alas! poor country that should have such leaders," he groaned, adding: "When I see such insane folly behind me I feel that the final salvation of the country demands the utmost prudence on my part, and that I must not run the slightest risk of disaster, for if anything happened to this army our cause would be lost." He saw his way to victory. According to the Pinkertons, the rebels had the advantage of numbers, but he had the advantage of superior training and equipment. Therefore he would make the contest a siege. Employing "the utmost prudence" to avoid "the slightest risk," he had evolved a formula for victory, ponderous but sure. He kept it from Lincoln and Stanton, who would neither approve nor understand, but he told it gladly to his wife, who would do both: "I will push them in upon Richmond and behind their works. Then I will bring up my heavy guns, shell the city, and carry it by assault."

Whether Lee was "cautious... weak... wanting in moral firmness... timid and irresolute" remained to be seen, but part at least of McClellan's judgment of his opponent had already been confirmed. He was "energetic" — and southern soldiers agreed with the northern commander that it was "to a fault." Reverting to his former role as King of Spades, he had them digging as they had never dug before. Their reaction was the one he had encountered in the Carolinas: that intrenchments were cowardly affairs, and that shoveling dirt wasn't fit work for a white man. Lee's reply was that hard work was "the very means by which McClellan has [been] and is advancing. Why should we leave to him the whole advantage of labor? ... There is nothing so military as labor, and nothing so important to an army as to save the lives of its soldiers." A third complaint, that digging would never drive the Yankees away from the gates of Richmond, he left for time to answer. Meanwhile there were those who, remembering his earnest statement back in May — "Richmond must not be given up; it shall not be given up!" — considered that he might be saving his soldiers' lives for a quite different purpose, entirely aside from the sheer humanity of the thing.

He saw the problem posed for him by his fellow engineer: "McClellan will make this a battle of posts. He will take position from position under cover of his heavy guns and we cannot get at him." What Lee needed in the face of this was time, and he got it. The first ten days of June were solid rain. "You have seen nothing like the roads on the Chicky bottom," he reported thankfully. McClellan's big guns were immobilized unless he brought them forward on the York River Railroad, and Lee moved quickly to block this route by mounting a long-range 32-pounder on a railway truck and running it eastward to outrange the swamp-bound Federal ordnance. This was the birth of the railroad gun, fathered by necessity and Lee.

The men could appreciate this kind of thing, its benefit being immediately apparent. They could appreciate, too, the new administrative efficiency which brought them better rations and an equitable distribution of the clothes and shoes it prised from quartermaster warehouses. There was a rapid improvement of their appearance and, in consequence, their tone. Lee himself was frequently among them, riding the lines to inspect the progress of their work on the intrenchments. Tall, handsome, robust, much younger-looking up close than from a distance, he had a cheerful dignity and could praise them without seeming to court their favor. They began to look forward to his visits, and even take pride in the shovel work they had performed so unwillingly up to now. The change for the better was there for everyone to see, including their old commander, convalescent in Richmond. "No, sir," Johnston said manfully when a friend remarked that his wound was a calamity for the South. "The shot that struck me down is the very best that has been fired for the southern cause yet. For I possess in no degree the confidence of our government, and now they have in my place one who does possess it, and who can accomplish what I never could have done: the concentration of our armies for the defense of the capital of the Confederacy."

This in fact was a main key to Lee's success in the course of his first weeks as head of the army in Virginia. He knew how to get along with Davis. Unlike Johnston, who had kept his intentions from the President as assiduously as if the two had been engaged as opponents in high-stakes poker, Lee sought his advice and kept him informed from day to day, even from hour to hour. One of the first letters he sent from the field was to Davis, describing certain administrative difficulties in one of the commands. "I thought you ought to know it," he wrote. "Our position requires that you should know everything and you must excuse my troubling you." Davis fairly basked in the unfamiliar warmth — and gave, as always, loyalty for loyalty received. Knowing him well, Lee knew that this support would never be revoked. Whatever lay before him, down the months and years, he knew that he would never have to look back over his shoulder as he went. Nor would he, like his opponent, have to step cautiously in anticipation of a fall from having the rug jerked from under him by wires leading back to his capital.

What lay before him now was McClellan, whose "battle of posts" would begin as soon as the weather turned Union and dried the roads. Such a battle could have only one outcome, the odds being what they were. As Lee saw it, he had but two choices: to retreat, abandoning Richmond, or to strike before his opponent got rolling. The former course had possibilities. He could fall back to the mountains, he said, "and if my soldiers will stand by me I will fight those people for years to come." However, it was the latter course he chose. At first he considered a repetition of Johnston's tactics, an attack on the Federal left, but he soon rejected the notion of making a frontal assault against an intrenched and superior enemy who, even if defeated, could retreat in safety down the Peninsula, much as Johnston had retreated up it. The flank beyond the Chickahominy was weaker and more exposed to attack, and once it was crushed or brushed aside, the way would be open for seizure of McClellan's base at White House. Cut off from his food and munitions, the Union commander would be obliged to come out of his intrenchments and fight the Confederates on ground of their choice, astride his lines of supply and communication.

When Lee submitted the plan for presidential approval, Davis raised a question. If McClellan behaved like an engineer, giving all his concern to his line of supply, the thing might work; but what if he assaulted the weakened line in front of Richmond while Lee was mounting the flank attack with troops stripped from the capital defenses? Would that not mean the fall of the city? Lee bridled at the reference to engineers, his own branch of the service as well as McClellan's, but said that he did not believe his opponent would attempt such a desperate venture. Besides, that was why he had put the men to digging: to enable a thin line to withstand an assault by superior numbers. It would not have to be for long. "If you will hold as long as you can at the intrenchments, and then fall back on the detached works around the city, I will be on the enemy's heels before he gets here." So he said, and Davis, after consideration, agreed that the long odds required long chances. He approved the plan of attack.

The first problem, once the plan had been approved, was the securing of reinforcements. No matter how ingenious the tactics, 61,000 Confederates could not hope to drive more than 100,000 Federals from a position they had been strengthening ever since their repulse of the full-scale assault two weeks before. As a problem it was thorny. South Carolina could spare no men at all, Charleston being menaced by an amphibious force assembling at Hilton Head; but Burnside seemed to be resting on his New Bern laurels, so that the rest of Holmes' division could be brought from North Carolina, adding 6500 bayonets to the ranks. Georgia could furnish a single brigade; Lee sent it to Jackson. "We must aid a gallant man if we perish," he said, having already weakened his army for this purpose. Besides, it was in the nature of a loan. Stonewall was to use the troops offensively if the opportunity arose, discouraging the Washington authorities from sending reinforcements to the Peninsula from the Valley or the line of the Rappahannock. Then, when everything was ready for the leap at McClellan, he was to leave his cavalry and his least effective infantry units in their present location, and take the cars for Richmond, adding 18,500 veterans to the column of assault.

This would bring Lee's total strength to 86,000: still about 20,000 short of McClellan's. Total strengths were not as important, however, as critical strengths at the point of vital contact — and that was where Lee proposed to secure the advantage. He would hold the Richmond intrenchments with the combined commands of Magruder, Huger, and Holmes, while those of Longstreet, the two Hills, and Jackson struck the isolated enemy corps on the north bank of the Chickahominy. In round figures, 30,000 men would be facing 75,000 to the east, while 55,000 assaulted 30,000 to the north; or, more roughly speaking, one third of Lee's army would resist three fourths of McClellan's, while the remaining two thirds attacked the remaining one fourth. The risk was great, as Davis said, but not so great as the possibilities for gain. As the

Fighting Means Killing

Federal main body, its right wing crushed, fell back to recover or protect its seized or threatened base, the Confederates would catch it in motion and destroy it, flank and rear. Richmond would be delivered.

No matter how devoutly this consummation was to be wished, a great deal remained to be done before it could begin to be accomplished. Jackson's approach march from the railroad would be along the ridge between the Chickahominy River and Totopotomoy Creek, an affluent of the Pamunkey. Lee knew that McClellan had withdrawn Porter's troops from Hanover Courthouse soon after the junction with McDowell was suspended, but he did not know the present location of Porter's right or the condition of the roads in that direction. Both of these necessary pieces of information could be gathered, along with possibly much else, by a reconnaissance in force. That meant cavalry, and cavalry meant Jeb Stuart. Accordingly, on June 10, Lee sent for him and told him what he wanted.

Stuart was delighted. A brigadier at twenty-nine, square-built, of average height, with china-blue eyes, a bushy cinnamon beard, and flamboyant clothes — thigh-high boots, yellow sash, elbow-length gauntlets, red-lined cape, soft hat with the brim pinned up on one side by a gold star supporting a foot-long ostrich plume — he had had no chance for individual distinction since the charge that scattered the Fire Zouaves at Manassas. He had a thirst for such exploits, both for his own sake and his troopers', whose training he was conducting in accordance with a credo: "If we oppose force to force we cannot win, for their resources are greater than ours. We must substitute *esprit* for numbers. Therefore I strive to inculcate in my men the spirit of the chase." That partly explained the gaudy fox-hunt clothes, and it also explained what he proposed as soon as Lee had finished speaking. Once he was in McClellan's rear, he said, it might be practicable to ride all the way around him.

Lee might have expected something of the sort, for Stuart had been an industrious collector of demerits as an adventurous cadet at the Point while his fellow Virginian was superintendent. At any rate, in the written instructions sent next day while Jeb was happily selecting and assembling 1200 troopers for the ride, the army commander warned him explicitly against rashness: "You will return as soon as the object of your expedition is accomplished, and you must bear constantly in mind, while endeavoring to execute the general purpose of your mission, not to hazard unnecessarily your command or to attempt what your judgment may not approve; but be content to accomplish all the good you can, without feeling it necessary to obtain all that might be desired." These were sobering words, but Stuart was pleased to note that the general called the proposed affair an "expedition," not merely a scout or a raid.

At 2 a.m. on the 12th he passed the word to his unit commanders standing by: "Gentlemen, in ten minutes every man must be in the saddle." Within that time they set out, riding north out of Richmond as if bound for the Shenandoah Valley. Only Stuart, who rode at the head of the column, knew their true destination. His high spirits were heightened by the knowledge that his opposite number, commanding McClellan's cavalry, was Brigadier General Philip St George Cooke, his wife's father, an old-line soldier who, to his son-in-law's discomfort and chagrin, had stayed with the old flag. "He will regret it but once," Jeb said, "and that will be continuously."

The three-day wait, following Stuart's disappearance into the darkness, was a time of strain for Lee and the Army of Northern Virginia. For one thing, the weather turned Union; the roads were drying fast under the influence of a hot spell. For another, there was information that McClellan was receiving reinforcements; McCall's division had come up the York in transports, adding its strength to the preponderance of numbers already enjoyed by the blue army in front of Richmond. Taken together, these two factors indicated that the "battle of posts" was about to begin before Lee could put his own plan into execution. The strain was not considerably relieved by the arrival of a courier, late on the 14th, with the first news from Stuart since he left. Far in the Federal rear, after wrecking a wagon train and capturing more than 300 men and horses, he had decided that it would be safer to continue on his way instead of turning back to cut a path through the disrupted forces gathering in his rear. Accordingly, he had pushed on eastward, then veered south to complete his circuit of the enemy army. But when he reached the Chickahominy, thirty-odd miles below the capital, he found the bridges out and the water too swift and deep for fording. That had been his plight when the courier left him: a swollen river to his front and swarms of hornet-mad Federal horsemen converging on his rear. However, he was confident he would get out all right, he said, if Lee would only make a diversion on the Charles City road to distract the bluecoats while he continued his search for an escape route.

Lee was not given to swearing, or else he would have done so now. At any rate, the day was too far gone for the diversion Stuart requested, and next morning, before the order could be issued, Jeb himself came jingling up to headquarters. His fine clothes were bedraggled and the face above the cinnamon beard showed the effects of two nights in the saddle without sleep, but he was jubilant over his exploit, which he knew was about to be hailed and bewailed in southern and northern papers. Improvising a bridge, he had crossed the Chickahominy with his entire command, guns and all, then ridden up the north bank of the James to report to Lee in person. At a cost of one man, lost in a skirmish two days back, he had brought out 170 prisoners, along with 300 horses and mules, and added considerably to whatever regret his father-in-law had been feeling up to now. Beyond all this, he had also brought out the information Lee had sent him after. McClellan's base was still at White House, and there was no indication that he intended to change it. The roads behind the Federal lines, which the enemy would have to use in bringing his big guns forward, were in even worse shape than those in the Confederate front. And, finally, Porter's right did not extend to the ridge between the Chickahominy and Totopotomoy Creek. In fact, that whole flank was practically "in the air," open to Jackson's turning movement along the ridge.

The moment was at hand. After feeling out the enemy lines that afternoon to determine whether Stuart's ride around McClellan had alarmed the northern commander into weakening his front in order to reinforce his flank beyond the river — it had not — Lee wrote to Jackson next morning, June 16. Five days ago, congratulating Stonewall for the crowning double victory at Cross Keys and Port Republic, he had sent him a warning order, alerting him for the march toward Richmond. Now the instructions to move were made explicit, though in language that was courteous to the point of being deferential: "The present... seems to be favorable for a junction of your army with this. If you agree with me, the sooner you can make arrangements to do so the better. In moving your troops you can let it be understood that it was to pursue the enemy in your front. Dispose those to hold the Valley so as to deceive the enemy, keeping your cavalry well in their front, and at the proper time suddenly descending upon the Pamunkey.... I should like to have the advantage of your views and to be able to confer with you. Will meet you at some point on your approach to the Chickahominy."

With the date of the attack dependent on Jackson's rate of march, there was little for the southern commander to do now except wait, perfecting the details of the north-bank convergence, and hope that his opponent would remain astride the river with his right flank in the air. The strain of waiting was relieved by good news of a battle fought in South Carolina on the day Lee summoned Stonewall from the Valley. The Federals had mounted their offensive against Charleston, landing 6500 troops on James Island, but were met and repulsed at Secessionville by Shanks Evans with less than half as many men. Inflicting 683 casualties at a cost of 204, Evans increased the reputation he had won above the stone bridge at Manassas and on the wooded plateau above Ball's Bluff and was proclaimed the savior of Charleston. Though this minor action scarcely balanced the recent loss of Fort Pillow and Memphis, or the evacuation of Cumberland Gap two days later, it made a welcome addition to the little string of victories won along the twin forks of the Shenandoah River. Lee was encouraged to hope that the tide was turning, at least in the East, and that the blue host in front of Richmond might soon be caught in the undertow and swept away or drowned. "Our enemy is quietly working within his lines, and collecting additional forces to drive us from our capital," he wrote in a private letter June 22, three weeks after taking command. "I hope we shall be able yet to disappoint him, and drive him back to his own country."

Next afternoon the possibility of such a deliverance was considerably enhanced by the arrival of a dusty horseman who came riding out the Nine Mile road to army headquarters. It was Jackson. Stiff from fourteen hours in the saddle, having covered fifty-two miles of road on relays of commandeered horses, he presently was closeted with Lee and the other three division commanders who would share with him the work of destruction across the river. Lee spread a crude map and explained the plan as he had worked it out.

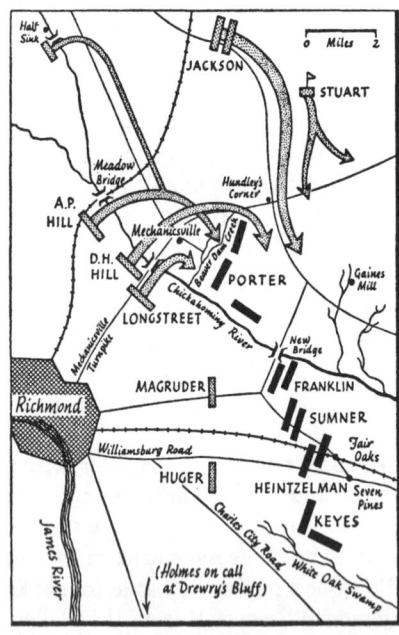

Stonewall, coming down from the north with Stuart's troopers guarding his left, was to clear the head of Beaver Dam Creek, outflanking Porter and forcing him to evacuate his main line of resistance, dug in along the east bank of the stream. That way, there would be no fighting until after the enemy had been flushed from his intrenchments, and by then the other three attack divisions would be on hand, having crossed the Chickahominy as soon as they learned that Jackson was within range. The crossing was to be accomplished in sequence. A. P. Hill would post a brigade at Half Sink, four miles upstream from his position at Meadow Bridge. Informed of Jackson's approach, this brigade would cross to the left bank and move down it, driving Porter's outposts eastward until they uncovered Meadow Bridge, which Hill would cross to advance on Mechanicsville. This in turn would uncover the turnpike bridge, permitting a crossing by D. H. Hill and Longstreet at that point and in that order. The former would move past his namesake's rear and swing wide around Beaver Dam Creek in support of Jackson. The latter would form on A. P. Hill's right for the advance through Porter's abandoned intrenchments. All four commands would then be in line — in echelon, from left to right: Jackson, D. H. Hill, A. P. Hill, and Longstreet — for the sweep down the left bank of the Chickahominy. Once they cleared New

Fighting Means Killing [475]

Bridge, four miles below Mechanicsville, they would be in touch with Magruder and Huger, who would have been maneuvering Prince-Johnstyle all this time to discourage an attack on their thin line by the Federal main body in their front. With contact reëstablished between the two Confederate wings, the danger of such an attack would have passed; as Lee said, they would "be on the enemy's heels" in case he tried it. The advance beyond the river would continue, slashing McClellan's communications and coming between him and his base of supplies at White House.

There were objections. Harvey Hill had expressed the opinion that an attack on the Federal left would be more rewarding; McClellan might respond to the assault on his right by changing his base to the James, beyond reach of the attackers. Lee had pointed out, however, that this would involve the army in the bogs of White Oak Swamp and rob it of the mobility which was its principal asset. Besides, Stuart's reconnaissance had shown that the Union base was still at White House, and Lee did not believe the Federals would attempt to make the shift while under attack. Longstreet, too, had indicated what he thought were disadvantages, the main one being the great natural strength of Porter's position along Beaver Dam Creek. However, this objection would be nullified by Jackson, whose approach would maneuver Porter out of his intrenchments by menacing his rear, and if he fell back to another creekbank stronghold — there were several such in his rear, at more or less regular intervals along the north bank of the Chickahominy — the same tactics could be applied, with the same result. Thus were Hill and Longstreet answered. Stonewall made no comment, being a stranger to the scene, and A. P. Hill, the junior officer present, held his tongue. After the brief discussion, Lee retired to give the quartet of generals a chance to talk his plan over among themselves.

They were young men, all four of them, though they disguised the fact with beards. Longstreet was the oldest, forty-one, A. P. Hill the youngest, thirty-seven; D. H. Hill was forty, Jackson thirty-eight; they had been at West Point together, twenty years ago. Longstreet spoke first, asking Jackson to set the date for the attack, since his was the only command not on the scene. The 25th, Jackson replied without hesitation. Longstreet demurred, advising him to take an extra day to allow for poor roads and possible enemy interference. All right, Jackson said, the 26th. Presently Lee returned and approved their decision. Today was Monday; the attack would be made on Thursday, at the earliest possible hour. He would send them written orders tomorrow.

The council broke up about nightfall. Jackson had spent most of the previous night in the saddle, but he would take no rest until he rejoined his men on the march. Mounting, he rode through the darkness, accompanied as before by a single aide, whom he had instructed to call him Colonel as a precaution against being recognized before he got his army into position to come booming down along McClellan's flank.

While Stonewall clattered north along unfamiliar roads to rejoin the Valley soldiers moving to meet him, McClellan sat alone in his tent, winding up a long day's work by writing to his wife. For various reasons, some definite, some vague, but all disturbing, he felt uneasy. Intelligence reports showed that his army was badly outnumbered, and Stuart's circumferential raid had not only afforded hostile journalists much amusement at the Young Napoleon's expense, it had also emphasized the danger to his extended flank and to his main supply base, both of which lay on the far side of what he still called "the confounded Chickahominy." He had protested, for McDowell's sake as well as his own, against the instructions requiring that general's overland advance and "an extension of my right wing to meet him." Such dispositions, he warned Stanton, "may involve serious hazard to my flank and line of communications and may not suffice to rescue [him] from any peril in which a strong movement of the enemy may involve him."

Nothing having come of this, he was obliged to keep Porter where he was. The danger to his base was another matter, one in which he could act on his own, and that was what he did. On the day Stuart returned to his lines and reported to Lee, McClellan ordered a reconnaissance toward James River, intending to look into the possibility of establishing a new base in that direction. Three days later, June 18, he began sending transports loaded with food and ammunition from White House down the Pamunkey and the York, up the James to Harrison's Landing. Gunboats, stationed there to protect them, would also protect his army in case it was thrown back as a result of an overwhelming asault on its present all-too-vulnerable position astride the Chickahominy. Meanwhile he continued to reconnoiter southward, sending cavalry and topographical engineers beyond White Oak Swamp to study the largely unknown country through which the army would have to pass in order to reach the James.

He had the satisfaction of knowing that he was doing what he could to meet such threats as he could see. However, there were others, vague but real, invisible but felt, against which he could take no action, since all he could feel was their presence, not their shape. He felt them tonight, writing the last lines of the bedtime letter to his wife: "I have a kind of presentiment that tomorrow will bring forth *something — what*, I do not know. We will see when the time arrives."

What tomorrow brought was a rebel deserter who gave his captors information confirming McClellan's presentiment of possible disaster. Picked up by Federal scouts near Hanover Courthouse, the man identified himself as one of Jackson's Valley soldiers; Stonewall now had three divisons, he said, and was moving rapidly south and east for an all-out attack on the Union flank and rear. It would come, he added, on

Fighting Means Killing

June 28: four days away. McClellan alerted Porter and passed the news along to the War Department, asking for "the most exact information you have as to the position and movements of Jackson." Stanton replied next day, June 25, that Jackson's army, with an estimated strength of 40,000, was variously reported at Gordonsville, at Port Republic, at Harrisonburg, and at Luray. He might be moving to join Lee in front of Richmond; other reports had him marching on Washington or Baltimore. Any one of them might be true. All of them might be false. At any rate, the Secretary concluded, the deserter's information "could not safely be disregarded."

McClellan scarcely knew what to believe, though as always he was ready to believe the worst: in which case only the stump of a fuze remained before the explosion. He opened at once with all his artillery, north and south of the river, and sent Heintzelman's corps out the Williamsburg road to readjust its picket lines and test the enemy strength in that direction. The result was a confused and savage fight, the first in a sequence to be known as the Seven Days. He lost 626 men and inflicted 541 casualties on Huger, whose troops finally halted the advance and convinced the attackers that the front had not been weakened in that direction. McClellan's spirits rose with the sound of firing — he shucked off his coat and climbed a tree for a better view of the fighting — but declined again as the firing died away. Though his line south of the river was now within four miles of the enemy capital, he could not clear his mind of the picture of imminent ruin on the opposite flank, drawn by the deserter the day before.

Returning to headquarters at sundown he wired Stanton: "I incline to think that Jackson will attack my right and rear. The rebel force is stated at 200,000.... I regret my great inferiority in numbers, but feel that I am in no way responsible for it, as I have not failed to represent repeatedly the necessity of reinforcements; that this was the decisive point, and that all the available means of the Government should be concentrated here. I will do all that a general can do with the splendid army I have the honor to command, and if it is destroyed by overwhelming numbers, can at least die with it and share its fate. But if the result of the action which will probably occur tomorrow, or within a short time, is a disaster, the responsibility cannot be thrown on my shoulders; it must rest where it belongs."

Riding toward the sound of heaviest firing, Lee had arrived in time to see Huger's men stop Heintzelman's assault before it reached their main line of resistance. The attack had been savage, however, and it had the look of at least the beginning of a major push. A fine rain was falling, the first in a week, but not hard enough to affect the roads, which had dried out considerably during the hot spell: McClellan might be starting his "battle of posts," advancing his infantry to cover the arrival of his siege guns. Or he might have attacked to beat Lee to the punch, having learned somehow that the line to his front had been weakened to mount the offensive against his flank. In either case, the safest thing for the Confederates to do was call off the north-bank assault and concentrate here for a last-ditch defense of the capital.

These things were in Lee's mind as he rode back through the camps where the men of Longstreet and D. H. Hill were cooking three days' rations in preparation for their march to get in position under cover of darkness for the attack across the Chickahominy next morning. He weighed the odds and made his decision, confirming the opinion one of his officers had given lately in answer to doubts expressed by another as to the new commander's capacity for boldness: "His name might be Audacity. He will take more desperate chances, and take them quicker, than any other general in this country, North or South. And you will live to see it, too." The plan would stand; the Richmond lines would be stripped; McClellan's flank would be assaulted, whatever the risk. And as Lee rode to his headquarters, people drawn to the capital hills by the rumble of guns looked out and saw what they took to be an omen. The sun broke through the mist and smoke and a rainbow arched across the vault, broad and clear above the camps of their defenders.

It held and then it faded; they went home. Presently, for those in the northeast suburbs unable to sleep despite the assurance of the spectral omen, there came a muffled sound, as if something enormous was moving on padded feet in the predawn darkness. Hill and Longstreet were in motion, leaving their campfires burning brightly behind them as they marched up the Mechanicsville turnpike and filed into masked positions, where they crouched for the leap across the river as soon as the other Hill's advance uncovered the bridges to their front. By sunup Lee himself had occupied an observation post on the crest of the low ridge overlooking the Chickahominy. The day was clear and pleasant, giving a promise of heat and a good view of the Federal outposts on the opposite bank. The bluecoats took their ease on the porches and in the yards of the houses that made up the crossroads hamlet. Others lolled about their newly dug gun emplacements and under the trees that dotted the landscape. They seemed unworried; but Lee was not. He had received unwelcome news from Jackson, whose foot cavalry was three hours behind schedule as a result of encountering poor roads and hostile opposition.

This last increased the cumulative evidence that McClellan suspected the combination Lee had designed for his destruction. At any moment the uproar of the Union assault feared by Davis might break out along the four-mile line where Magruder, his men spread thin, was attempting to repeat the theatrical performance he had staged with such success at Yorktown, back in April. By 8 o'clock all the units were in position along the near bank of the river, awaiting the sound of Stonewall's guns or a courier informing them that he too was in position. But there was only silence from that direction. A. P. Hill sent a message to the brigade posted upstream at Half Sink: "Wait for Jackson's notification before you move unless I send you other orders." Time wore on. 9 o'clock: 10 o'clock. The three-hour margin was used up, and still the only word from Jackson was a note written an hour ago, informing the commander of Hill's detached brigade that the head of his column was crossing the Virginia Central — six hours behind schedule.

President Davis came riding out and joined the commanding general at his post of observation. Their staffs sat talking, comparing watches. 11 o'clock: Lee might have remembered Cheat Mountain, nine months ago in West Virginia, where he had attempted a similar complex convergence once before, with similar results. High noon. The six-hour margin was used up, and still no sound of gunfire from the north. 1 o'clock: 2 o'clock: 3 o'clock. Where was Jackson?

McClellan knew the answer to that. His scouts had confirmed his suspicions and kept him informed of Stonewall's whereabouts. But he had another question: Why didn't he come on?

After the dramatic and bad-tempered telegram sent at sundown of the day before, he had ridden across the river to check on Porter's dispositions, and finding them judicious — one division posted behind Beaver Dam Creek, the other two thrown forward — had returned in better spirits, despite a touch of neuralgia. "Every possible precaution is being taken," he informed the authorities in Washington before turning in for the night. "If I had another good division I could laugh at Jackson.... Nothing but overwhelming forces can defeat us." This morning he had returned for another look, and once more he had come back reassured. Now, however, as the long hours wore away in silence and the sun climbed up the sky, apprehension began to alternate with hope. At noon he wired Stanton: "All things very quiet on this bank of the Chickahominy. I would prefer more noise."

✗ 4 ✗

If noise was what he wanted, he was about to get it — in full measure — from a man who had plenty of reasons, personal as well as temperamental, for wanting to give it to him. Before the war, A. P. Hill had sued for the hand of Ellen Marcy. The girl was willing, apparently, but her father, a regular army career officer, disapproved; Hill's assets were $10,000, a Virginia background, and a commission as a Coast Survey lieutenant, and Colonel Marcy aimed a good deal higher for his daughter than that. Ellen obeyed her father, whose judgment was rewarded shortly thereafter when George McClellan, already a railroad president at thirty-three, with an annual income amounting to more than the rejected lieutenant's total holdings, made a similar suit and was accepted, thereby assuring the daughter's freedom from possible future want and the father's position, within a year, as chief of staff to the commander of the Army of the Potomac. Hill meanwhile had gone his way and married the beautiful sister of John Hunt Morgan of Kentucky, red-haired like himself and so devoted to her husband that it sometimes required a direct order from the commander of the Army of Northern Virginia to remove her from the lines when a battle was impending. Hill, then, had in fact more cause to feel gratitude than resentment toward the enemy chief of staff and commander for rejecting and supplanting him. However, he was a hard fighter, with a high-strung intensity and a great fondness for the offensive; so that in time McClellan's soldiers, familiar with the history of the tandem courtships, became convinced that the Virginian's combativeness was a highly personal matter, provoked by a burning determination to square a grudge. Once at least, as Hill's graybacks came swarming over the landscape at them, giving that high-throated fiendish yell, one of McClellan's veterans, who had been through this sort of thing before, shook his head fervently and groaned in disgust: "God's sake, Nelly — why didn't you marry him?"

  A narrow-chested man of average height, thin-faced and pale, with flowing hair, a chiseled nose, and cheekbones jutting high above the auburn bush of beard, Hill had a quick, impulsive manner and a taste that ran to the picturesque in clothes. Today, for instance — as always, when fighting was scheduled — he wore a red wool deer-hunter's shirt; his battle shirt, he called it, and his men, knowing the sign, would pass the word, "Little Powell's got on his battle shirt!" More and more, however, as the long hours wore away in front of Meadow Bridge, they began to think he had put it on for nothing. The detached brigade had crossed at Half Sink soon after 10 o'clock, when Jackson sent word that he had reached the railroad. Since then, nothing had been heard from that direction; five hours had passed, and barely that many still remained of daylight. Hill chafed and fretted until he could take no more. At 3 o'clock, "rather than hazard the failure of the whole plan by longer deferring it," as he subsequently reported, "I determined to cross at once."

  From his post on the heights overlooking the river Lee heard a sudden popping of musketry from upstream. As it swelled to a clatter he saw bluecoats trickling eastward from a screen of woods to the northwest, followed presently by the gray line of skirmishers who had flushed them. Then came the main body in heavy columns, their bayonets and regimental colors glinting and gleaming silver and scarlet in the sunlight. The Yankees were falling back on Mechanicsville, where tiny figures on horseback gestured theatrically with sabers, forming a line of battle. East of the village, the darker foliage along Beaver Dam Creek began to leak smoke as the Union artillery took up the challenge. Far to the north, directly on Jackson's expected line of advance, another smoke cloud rose in answer; Stonewall's guns were booming. As Little Powell's men swept eastward, the troops of D. H. Hill and Longstreet advanced from their masked positions along the turnpike and prepared to cross the Chickahominy in support. Late as it was — past 4 now, with the sun already halfway down the sky — the plan was working. All the jigsaw pieces were being jockeyed into their assigned positions to form Lee's pattern of destruction for the invaders of Virginia.

As usual, there were delays. The turnpike bridge had to be repaired before Harvey Hill and Longstreet could go to the assistance of A. P. Hill, who was fighting alone on the north bank, prodding the makeshift Yankee line back through Mechanicsville. Lee sent him word not to press too close to the guns massed along Beaver Dam Creek until support arrived and Jackson had had time to outflank the fortified position. While the repairmen were still at work on the bridge, a cavalcade of civilians, mostly congressmen and cabinet members, clattered across in the wake of President Davis, who was riding as always toward the sound of firing. D. H. Hill and Longstreet followed, and at 5 o'clock Lee came down off the heights and crossed with them.

The plain ahead was dotted with bursting shells and the disjointed rag-doll shapes of fallen men. A. P. Hill had taken the village, and by now there were no armed Federals west of Beaver Dam Creek. But there were plenty of them along it, supporting the guns creating havoc on the plain. Unable to remain out in the open, in clear view of the Union gunners, Hill's men had pushed eastward, against Lee's orders, to find cover along the near bank of the creek. Here they came under infantry fire as well, taking additional losses, but fortunately the artillery was firing a little too high; otherwise they would have been slaughtered. Several attempts to storm the ridge beyond the creek had been bloodily repulsed. The position was far too strong and Porter had too many men up there — almost as many, in fact, as Longstreet and both Hills combined. Everything depended on Jackson, who should have been rounding their flank by now, forcing them to withdraw in order to cover their rear. However, there was no sign of this; the Federals stood firm on the ridge, apparently unconcerned about anything except killing the Confederates to their front. The question still obtained: Where was Stonewall? And now Lee learned for the first time that Little Powell had crossed the Chickahominy with no more knowledge of Jackson's whereabouts than Lee himself had, which was none at all.

To add to his worries, there on the plain where Union shells were knocking men and horses about and wrecking what few guns A. P. Hill had been able to bring within range, Lee saw Davis and his cavalcade, including the Secretaries of State and War, sitting their horses among the shellbursts as they watched the progress of the battle. A single burst might topple them like tenpins any minute. Lee rode over and gave Davis a cold salute. "Mr President, who is all this army and what is it doing here?" Unaccustomed to being addressed in this style, especially by the gentle-mannered Lee, Davis was taken aback. "It is not my army, General," he replied evasively. Lee said icily, "It is certainly not *my* army, Mr President, and this is no place for it." Davis shifted his weight uneasily in the saddle. "Well, General," he replied, "if I withdraw, perhaps they will follow." He lifted his wide-brim planter's hat and rode away, trailing a kite-tail of crestfallen politicians. Once he was out of sight, however, he turned back toward the battle, though he took a path that would not bring him within range of Lee. He did not mind the shells, but he wanted no more encounters such as the one he had just experienced.

This minor problem attended to, Lee returned to the major one at hand: the unequal battle raging along Beaver Dam Creek, where he had not expected to have to fight at all. Jackson's delay seemed to indicate that McClellan, having learned in advance of the attempt to envelop his flank, had intercepted Stonewall's march along the Totopotomoy ridge. Still worse, he might be mounting an overwhelming assault on the thinly held intrenchments in front of Richmond before Lee could get in position to "be on his heels." Immediately, the southern commander sent messages ordering Magruder to hold his lines at all costs and instructing Huger to test McClellan's left with a cavalry demonstration. Daylight was going fast. Until Lee reached New Bridge, two miles beyond the contested ridge, both wings of his army would be fighting in isolation: McClellan well might do to him what he had planned to do to McClellan. If the Federals were not dislodged from Beaver Dam today, they might take the offensive in the morning with reinforcements brought up during the night. In desperation, Lee decided to attempt what he had been opposed to until now. He would storm the ridge beyond the creek.

All of A. P. Hill's men had been committed, but Harvey Hill's were just arriving. Lee ordered the lead brigade to charge on the right, near the river, and flank the Federals off the ridge. They went in with a yell, surging down the slope to the creek, but the high ground across the way exploded in their faces as the Union guns took up the challenge. Shattered, the graycoats fell back over their dead and wounded, losing more men as they went. The sun went down at 7.15 and the small-arms fire continued to pop and sputter along the dusky front. By 9 o'clock it had stopped. The enemy artillery fired blind for another hour, as if in mockery of the attackers. Then it too died away, and

Fighting Means Killing [483]

the cries of the wounded were heard along the creek bank. The Army of Northern Virginia's first battle was over.

It was over and it was lost, primarily because of the absence of the 18,500 troops whose arrival had been intended to unhinge the Federal line along the ridge. The persistent daylong question, Where was Jackson? still obtained. In a way, that was just as well; for in this case, disturbing as the question was, the answer was even more so. Finding his advance expected and contested by enemy cavalry, Stonewall had moved cautiously after crossing the Central Railroad six hours late. At 4.30 that afternoon, after a southward march of seven miles in seven hours — he was now ten hours behind schedule — he reached his objective, Hundley's Corner. From there he could hear the roar of guns along Beaver Dam, three airline miles away. However, with better than three hours of daylight still remaining, he neither marched toward the sound of firing nor sent a courier to inform Lee of his arrival. Instead, he went into bivouac, apparently satisfied that he had reached his assigned position, however late. His men were much fatigued, being unaccustomed to the sandy roads and dripping heat of the lowlands, and so was their commander, who had had a total of ten hours' sleep in the past four nights. If Lee wanted him to fight the Yankees, let him drive them across his front as had been arranged.

While Stonewall's veterans took their rest, A. P. Hill's green troops were fighting and losing their first battle. Lee's ambitious plan for a sweep down the north bank of the river, cutting the enemy off from his base and forcing him to choose between flight and destruction, had begun with a total and bloody repulse that left McClellan a choice of two opportunities, both golden. He could reinforce his right and take the offensive here tomorrow, or he could hold the river crossings and bull straight through for Richmond on the south, depending on which he wanted first, Virginia's army or Virginia's capital. Such was the result of Lee's first battle. Hill's impetuosity and Jackson's lethargy were to blame, but the final responsibility was the army commander's; he had planned the battle and he had been present to direct it. Comparatively speaking, though there was little time for assessment, it had been fought in such a disjointed fashion as to make even Seven Pines seem a masterpiece of precision. Of the 56,000 men supposedly available on this bank of the Chickahominy, Lee had got barely one fourth into action, and even these 14,000 went in piecemeal. Mercifully, the casualty figures were hidden in the darkness and confusion, but time would disclose that the Confederates had lost 1350 soldiers, the Federals 361. In short, it was the worst fiasco either army had staged since Ball's Bluff, back in October, when the figures were approximately reversed.

McClellan was elated. Though he left all the tactical dispositions to Porter, he had recrossed the river in time to watch the battle from start to finish. At 9 o'clock, with the guns still intermittently booming defiance, he wired Stanton: "The firing has nearly ceased.... Victory of today complete and against great odds. I almost begin to think we are invincible."

However, he was by no means ready to take advantage of either of the golden opportunities afforded by Lee's repulse. Believing himself as heavily outnumbered on the left as on the right, he did not consider a shift to the offensive on either bank of the Chickahominy. He was proud in fact to be holding his own, and he restrained his elation somewhere short of rashness. Nor did he consider reinforcing the embattled Porter with troops from Sumner, Heintzelman, Keyes, or Franklin, who reported the rebels unusually active on their front. Convinced as he was that Lee had at least 180,000 men, McClellan saw all sorts of possible combinations being designed for his destruction. The attack on Mechanicsville, for example, might be a feint, intended to distract his attention while troops were massed for overrunning the four-mile line that covered Seven Pines and Fair Oaks. Such considerations weighed him down. In point of fact, his elation and his talk of being invincible were purely tactical, so to speak. Strategically, he was already preparing to retreat.

Ever since the beginning of the action he had been shifting Porter's wagons and heavy equipment to the south bank — "impediments," he called them — in preparation for a withdrawal as soon as the pressure grew too great. Jackson's late-afternoon arrival within striking distance of Porter's flank and rear, though his attitude when he got there was anything but menacing, had the effect Lee had intended. As soon as the Beaver Dam fight was broken off, McClellan instructed Porter to fall back down the Chickahominy, out of reach of Stonewall, who had brought not only his Valley army, but also his Valley reputation with him. After crossing Powhite Creek, three miles in his rear, Porter was to dig in along the east bank of Boatswain Swamp, a stream inclosing a horseshoe-shaped position of great natural strength, just opposite the northern end of the four-mile line beyond the river.

At daybreak Porter carried out the movement with such skill that McClellan, who had already crossed, wired Stanton in delight: "This change of position was beautifully executed under a sharp fire, with but little loss. The troops on the other side are now well in hand, and the whole army so concentrated that it can take advantage of the first mistake made by the enemy."

★ ★ ★

Lee's safest course, after yesterday's repulse, would have been to recross the Chickahominy at Mechanicsville Bridge and concentrate for a defense of his capital by occupying, in all possible strength, the line of intrenchments now thinly held by Huger and Magruder. But he no more considered turning back, apparently, than McClellan had considered moving forward. After sending a staff officer to locate Jackson and instruct him to continue his march eastward beyond the Union flank, Lee ordered a renewal of the assault on the ridge overlooking Beaver Dam, which the bluecoats seemed to be holding as strongly as ever. He intended to force its evacuation by a double turning movement, right and left; but before it could be organized, the Federals pulled back. They were only a rear guard, after all. Lee sent A. P. Hill and Longstreet in direct pursuit, with instructions to attack the enemy wherever they found him, while Harvey Hill swung wide around the left to reinforce Jackson in accordance with the original plan. Though the element of surprise was lost and there were no guarantees against breakdowns such as the one that had occurred the day before, the machine was back in gear at last.

About 9.30 Lee rode forward, doubling Longstreet's column, and mounted the ridge beyond the creek, where burning stores and abandoned equipment showed the haste with which the enemy had departed. Two miles eastward he came upon Jackson and A. P. Hill standing together in a country churchyard. Hill soon left, but Lee dismounted and sat on a cedar stump to confer with Stonewall. The two were a study in contrast, the immaculate Lee and the dusty Jackson, and so were their staffs, who stood behind them, looking each other over. Any advantage the former group had in grooming was more than offset by the knowledge that the latter had worn out their clothes in fighting. Now that D. H. Hill had joined him, Stonewall had fourteen brigades under his command: two more than Longstreet and the other Hill combined. Lee expected the enemy to make a stand at Powhite Creek, just over a mile ahead, and his instructions were for Jackson to continue his march to Cold Harbor, three and a half miles east. There he would be well in rear of the Federals and could cut them off or tear their flank as they came past him, driven by A. P. Hill and Longstreet. Jackson nodded approval, then mounted and rode away.

Lee overtook the head of A. P. Hill's column as it approached Powhite Creek. It was now about noon, and the gravest danger of the original plan was past. Hill's advance had uncovered New Bridge; the two wings of the army were again in contact; Magruder could be reinforced from across the Chickahominy if McClellan lunged for Richmond on that side. Ahead, as Lee had expected, enemy riflemen held the high ground beyond the creek. Determined to force a crossing without delay, Little Powell sent his lead brigade forward unsupported. After a short fire-fight, centered around a brick and timber structure known as Gaines Mill — there was a dam there with a spillway and a sizeable pond above it, placid, shaded by oaks; a cool, unwarlike place of refuge on a hot day in any June but this — the Federals withdrew. Hill's men followed, crossing the creek and occupying the high ground without further opposition. Unlike yesterday, rashness had paid off.

It had been easy: too easy, Lee thought as he mounted the slope and reached the seized position. Then he found out why. Ahead there was a sudden, tearing clatter of musketry, and the men of Hill's lead brigade came stumbling wild-eyed out of the wooded valley into which they had pursued the fleeing bluecoats. "Gentleman, we must rally those men," Lee told his staff, riding forward. Now he knew. Not here along the Powhite as he had expected, but somewhere down in that swale, or just beyond it, the enemy was at bay. While the panicked troops were being rallied — a good many more of them had gone in than had come back out — Hill brought up three additional brigades, and at 2.30, with Longstreet just arriving on the right, sent them forward. Again that sudden clatter erupted, now with the boom of guns mixed in, and again the men came stumbling back, as wild-eyed as before.

Penetrating deeper into the swampy woods, they had come face to face with the death-producing thing itself: three separate lines of Federal infantry, dug one above another into the face of a long, convex hill crowned with guns. McClellan, with his engineer's skill, had chosen a position of enormous strength, moated along its front by a boggy stream called Boatswain Swamp. Rising below Cold Harbor, two miles east of Gaines Mill, it flowed southwest, then turned back east and south around the face of Turkey Hill, affording a clear field of fire for Porter's three successive lines and the batteries massed on the dominant plateau. None of this was shown on the crude map Lee was using, not even Boatswain Swamp; Hill had had to find it for him, groping blind and paying in blood for discouraging information. Now he knew the worst. Yesterday's Union position, overlooking Beaver Dam, had been strong enough to shatter everything he had been able to throw against it; but today's was infinitely stronger. McClellan had found himself a fortress, ready-made.

Lee's hope was that Jackson, threatening the Federal right from the direction of Cold Harbor, would cause Porter to weaken his left by shifting troops to meet him. Until that happened, to continue the assault would be suicidal. In fact, the shaken condition of Hill's men made it doubtful whether they would be able to hold their ground if the enemy counterattacked. Sending word for Longstreet to discourage this with a demonstration on the right, Lee set out for the left to find the answer to yesterday's question, which applied again today: Where was Jackson? On the way, he met Ewell and found out. Harvey Hill had reached Cold Harbor, but Stonewall had been delayed by taking a wrong road. Riding ahead, he had found Hill deploying for attack — precisely what Lee, across the way, was hoping for — and had stopped him; Lee's instructions were for him to strike the Federals after they had been dislodged, not before. To stave off disaster while he digested this bad news, Lee told Ewell to go in on A. P. Hill's left, supporting him, while he himself rode on to talk with Jackson.

Ewell's veterans started forward with a shout. "You need not go in!" Little Powell's troops called out when they saw them coming. "We are whipped; you can't do anything!" The Valley men did not falter. "Get out of our way," they growled as they went by. "We'll show you how to do it." Yelling, they went in on the double. Again there was that uproarious clatter, as if a switch had been tripped, and that triple line of fire ripping back and forth across the face of Turkey Hill, and the roar of guns from the crest. Still on the double, the Valley soldiers came back out again. It was more than they had bargained for, despite the warning, and they were considerably fewer now than when they started forward. Roberdeau Wheat was lying dead in there, along with hundreds of others who had been through Kernstown, Winchester, Cross Keys, and Port Republic. Dick Taylor was not; he had been confined to an ambulance with a mysterious ailment that paralyzed his legs. Missing his firm grip, the gaitered Louisianians broke within sight of the fuming hill and had to be withdrawn. The rest of Ewell's survivors hung on, deep in the swampy woods alongside Hill's, while concentrations of shell and canister flailed the brush around them. Their aim distracted by a constant shower of broken twigs and branches, they kept up a blind long-range fire across Boatswain Swamp.

Riding toward the left, Lee heard a welcome sound from that direction: the popping of muskets and the quaver of the rebel yell. Jackson at last had realized the changed situation and had unleashed Harvey Hill against the Union right, meanwhile sending word to his other division commanders: "This affair must hang in suspense no longer. Sweep the field with the bayonet!" He sounded like himself again, and presently Lee saw him approaching, horse and rider covered with dust, the dingy cadet cap pulled so far down over his face that the bill almost touched the lemon he was sucking.

"Ah, General," Lee said as he rode up, "I am very glad to see you. I had hoped to be with you before." Stonewall jerked his head at the implied rebuke and muttered something indistinguishable in the din. Ewell's attack was reaching its climax; Jackson's division, under Winder, would go in on Ewell's right, filling a widening gap between him and A. P. Hill. "That fire is very heavy," Lee said. "Do you think your men can stand it?" Jackson listened, then replied, raising his voice to be heard above the racket: "They can stand almost anything! They can stand that."

It was now past 5 o'clock, but Lee at last had all of his troops within reach or in position. Far on the right, Longstreet had examined the enemy line with deliberate care and found it too strong to be affected by a feint; only an all-out attack would serve, he said, and he was preparing to deliver one. Lee approved, having reached the same conclusion everywhere along the front. The sun was near the landline; time was running out. At this late hour, no matter what it cost in blood, nothing less than a general assault, all down the line — D. H. Hill and Ewell on the left, Jackson in the center, A. P. Hill and Longstreet on the right — could possibly convert defeat into victory by sweeping the Federals off the face of Turkey Hill and back across the plateau where their massed guns boomed defiance.

Fitz-John Porter was holding his own, and he intended to go on holding it, whatever the rebels brought against him. His three divisions had been reinforced by a fourth from Franklin, sent him by McClellan along with a message expressing his pride in the fighting qualities of the men on the north bank: "Send word to all your troops that their general thanks them for their heroism, and says to them that he is now sure that nothing can resist them. Their conduct and your own have been magnificent, and another name is added to their banners.... I look upon today as decisive of the war. Try to drive the rascals and take some prisoners and guns."

Much of the credit was due to the division on the right. Its members were U.S. regulars to a man, all 6000 of them, and they fought with the same steady determination they had shown at Bull Run, where they had been fewer than 1000. Their commander, now as then, was George Sykes, then a major but now a major general. He was from Delaware, forty years old, and he held his lines today with a special doggedness, knowing the attacks were launched by Harvey Hill, who had been his roommate at West Point. Porter left the defense of that flank to Sykes and gave his main attention to the left and center of his convex line, supporting his two divisions in that direction with the fourth, which came up soon after 4 o'clock. His 35,000 soldiers were outnumbered three to two, but they gained confidence from every repulse they administered to the screaming graybacks who came charging through the swamp just under their rifles. It was shooting-gallery work, with an excitement out of proportion to the danger involved. Meanwhile they were improving their hillside position, piling dirt and logs, stacking rocks and even knapsacks to thicken and raise the breastworks along their triple line. Dead rebels lay in windrows at the base of the slope, but the defenders had suffered comparatively little. Wherever Porter checked — a handsome man with a neatly barbered, lustrous dark-brown beard, clean linen, and a calm, unruffled manner that matched his clothes — he found his men in excellent spirits, elated over their success and ready to continue it as long as he required.

It would not be much longer now; McClellan had made it clear from the start that this was primarily a holding action. The sun was already red beyond the trees along the Chickahominy when a follow-up message arrived from the army commander, setting a definite limit to their stay: "I am ordering up more troops. Do your best to hold your own . . . until dark."

But the blow was about to fall. Except for two brigades that were coming up now in rear of A. P. Hill, Lee had all his men in position along a nearly semicircular three-mile arc. He planned to use these late arrivers for a breakthrough at the point where Little Powell had tried and failed. One of the two was the Texas Brigade, under John B. Hood, which had shown an aptitude for this kind of work at Eltham Landing. Lee rode back, met Hood at the head of the column, and — omitting none of the difficulties the previous attackers had encountered — told him what he wanted.

"This must be done," he said. "Can you break his line?" Hood did not know whether he could or not; but he said he was willing to try. That was enough for Lee. As he turned to ride away he raised his hat. "May God be with you," he said.

Hood formed along the line of departure, a Georgia regiment on the right, Hampton's Legion on the left, and three Texas regiments in the center. Beyond the Legion, the other brigade commander, Colonel E. M. Law, aligned his four regiments, two from Mississippi and one each from Alabama and North Carolina. Longstreet and Jackson had already gone into action on the right and left when these men from the Deep South started forward. The sun was down behind the ridge, twilight gathering in the valley, as Hood and Law passed through the shattered ranks of A. P. Hill and beyond into a clearing, in full view of the blue tiers on the hillside and the batteries massed on the crest, which went into a rapid-fire frenzy at the sight, stabbing the dusk with spits of flame as fast as men could pull triggers and lanyards, then load and pull again. Still the gray-clad attackers came on, through the tempest of iron and lead, not pausing to fire, not even yelling, but moving with long strides down the slope, their rifles at right shoulder lift, closing ranks as they took their losses, which were heavy. If they had looked back they would have seen the ground behind them strewn with their dead and wounded; nearly a thousand had fallen before they reached the near bank of Boatswain Swamp, where they paused to fix bayonets and dress their line. But they did not look back; they looked forward, moving now at the double, across the creek and up the slope on the enemy side, yelling as they came on. Not a shot had been fired by the charging men, but their rifles were now at a carry, the bayonets glinting: twenty yards from the Union line, then ten . . . and the bluecoats scattered in unison, scrabbling uphill and swamping the second line, which joined them in flight, overrunning the third. In the lead, the Texans fired their first volley at a range where every bullet lodged in flesh, then surged over the crest and onto the plateau, where they fired again into a heaving mass of horses and men as the cannoneers tried to limber for a withdrawal. Too late: Hood was out front, tall and blond, gesturing with his sword. Fourteen guns were taken here, while two full regiments from Pennsylvania and New Jersey threw down their arms in surrender, along with other large detachments. Lee now had the breakthrough he had asked for.

Longstreet and Jackson widened the breach in both directions, pumping additional volleys into the wreckage and turning back a desperate cavalry charge, delivered Balaklava-style, which accomplished nothing except the addition of pain-crazed, riderless horses to the turmoil. Ewell, moving forward beyond Jackson, outflanked Sykes and forced him to fall back under pressure from D. H. Hill. Eight more guns were taken and several hundred more prisoners were rounded up in the gathering dusk. However, there was too much confusion and too little daylight for the final concerted push that might have swept the Federals off the sloped plateau and into the boggy flats of the Chickahominy. Besides, in retreat as in resistance, the signs were clear that McClellan's was a very different army from the one that had broken and scattered in the twilight at Manassas; whereas the Confederates, now as then, were too disrupted for pursuit. Not only did Sykes' regulars maintain their reputation by retiring in good order, but as the frightened survivors of the other three divisions broke for the bridges leading south to safety, they met two brigades coming up from Sumner, reinforcements ordered north by McClellan while the battle racket was swelling toward its climax. The fugitives cheered and rallied. Porter saved his reserve artillery and got his soldiers across the river in the darkness, using these fresh troops and the unshaken regulars to cover the withdrawal.

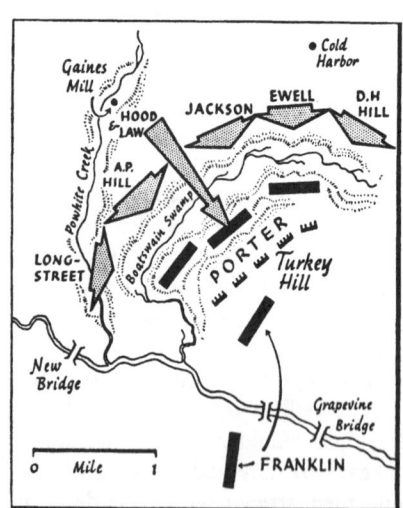

"Profoundly grateful to Almighty God," Lee sent a dispatch informing Davis that the Army of Northern Virginia had won its first victory. Twenty-two guns and more than 2000 prisoners had been taken, together with a great deal of excellent equipment and a clear road leading eastward to the Union base at White House. But it had been accomplished at a fearful price. Lee had lost 8500 fighting men, the bravest and best the South could ever give him; Porter had lost 6837. Numerically, here at the critical point of contact, the odds were growing longer every day. Its right wing drawn in, shaken but uncrushed, McClellan's army was now assembled as a unit for the struggle that lay ahead, while the southern army was still divided.

"We sleep on the field," Lee closed his dispatch to the President, "and shall renew the contest in the morning."

★ ★ ★

McClellan met that night with his corps commanders at Savage Station, a point on the York River Railroad about midway between Fair Oaks and the Chickahominy crossing. They were not there to help him arrive at a decision, but rather to receive instructions for carrying out a decision already reached. Early that afternoon, before Porter had completed his occupation of the position overlooking Boatswain Swamp, McClellan notified Flag Officer Goldsborough of his desire "that you will forthwith instruct the gunboats in the James River to cover the left flank of this army.... I am obliged to fall back." And at 8 o'clock — as the uproar died away beyond the Chickahominy, but before he knew the results of the fighting there — he wired Stanton from his south-bank headquarters: "Have had a terrible contest. Attacked by greatly superior numbers in all directions on this side.... The odds have been immense. We hold our own very nearly."

The decision to retreat — or, as McClellan preferred to express it, the decision to "change his base" — was supported by dispatches he had been receiving all day from troop commanders along the four-mile line that ran from Grapevine Bridge down into the near fringe of White Oak Swamp. Here Prince John Magruder had repeated his Yorktown performance with such remarkable success, marching and countermarching his men, demonstrating noisily and retiring stealthily to threaten or seem to threaten other points along the front, thundering aggressively all the while with his guns — "They have it in mind to advance," Joseph Hooker of Heintzelman's corps reported; "I can be whipped before the reserve will get up" — that all four of the south-bank corps commanders were apprehensive that they were about to be swamped, individually and collectively, by overwhelming numbers. Late in the day, when McClellan asked what additional troops they could spare to help Porter, they replied that they needed all they had in order to hold their ground. In fact, they said, if any more reinforcing was being considered, it had better be done in their direction.

By nightfall, having combined these tactical reports with information received from Pinkerton, McClellan was convinced that Lee was jabbing with his left in preparation for throwing a knockout right. The thing to do, if time permitted, was to step back before it landed; or if not back, then sideways. Porter's withdrawal across the Chickahominy had given the Confederates access to the York River supply line and a clear shot at the left flank of McClellan's moving column if he attempted a retreat back down the Peninsula. The only way to go was south to the James, where his foresight had provided a sanctuary under the guns of the fleet and a landing place for the reinforcements Lincoln would be obliged to send, now that a near-disaster had proved the need for them.

Accordingly, at the Savage Station conference he issued instructions for a withdrawal in that direction. Keyes, being farthest south, would cross White Oak Swamp in the morning, followed by Porter as soon as he completed the retirement now in progress. Together they would guard the flank against an attack below the swamp, while Franklin, Sumner, and Heintzelman held the present lines above it and the Chickahominy crossings to the north, covering the passage of the army train with its 25,000 tons of food, ammunition, and medical supplies. Once the train was across the swamp with its 3600 wagons, 700 ambulances, and a herd of 2500 beeves, the remaining corps would follow, guarding the rear on the way to Harrison's Landing.

It was well conceived, well thought out: McClellan took pride in the foresight and coolness which had enabled him to improvise the details under pressure. He did not consider the movement a retreat. It was a readjustment, a change of base required by a change in conditions. However, once the conference was over and the corps commanders had gone out into the night with their instructions for tomorrow, he began to consider the adverse reaction that might follow: not among his soldiers — they would understand — but among the members of the body politic, the public at large, and especially among the molders of popular opinion: the editors, and later the historians. The record would speak for itself in time. He was confident that it would show how Lincoln and Stanton had thwarted him, diverting his troops when his back was turned and ignoring his pleas for reinforcements, in spite of documentary evidence that he was facing an army twice the size of his own. Meanwhile, though, he was not only in danger of being condemned and ridiculed; about to undertake one of the most difficult maneuvers in the art of war, the transfer of an army from one base to another across a fighting front, he was in danger of being physically destroyed. In that event, the record would indeed have to speak for itself, since he would not be there to supplement it before the bar of judgment. Therefore it had better be supplemented in advance, bolstered so as to present the strongest possible case in the strongest possible language. Shortly after midnight, before retiring to sleep for what he knew would be a grinding day tomorrow, he got off a wire to Stanton.

"I now know the full history of the day," it began. After saying flatly, "I have lost this battle because my force was too small," he got down to cases: "I again repeat that I am not responsible for this, and I say it with the earnestness of a general who feels in his heart the loss of every brave man who has been needlessly sacrificed today.... If, at this instant, I could dispose of 10,000 fresh men, I could gain a victory tomorrow. I know that a few thousand more men would have changed this battle from a defeat to a victory. As it is, the Government must not and cannot hold me responsible for the result." The clincher came at the end: "I feel too earnestly tonight. I have seen too many dead and wounded comrades to feel otherwise than that the Government has not sustained this army. If you do not do so now the game is lost. If I save this army now, I tell you plainly that I owe no thanks to you or to any other persons in Washington. You have done your best to sacrifice this army."

Having thus unburdened his troubled mind, and bolstered the record in the process, he took to his bed. "Of course they will never forgive me for that," he subsequently told his wife. "I knew it when I wrote it; but as I thought it possible that it might be the last I ever wrote, it seemed better to have it exactly true."

Saturday's dawn, June 28, showed Confederate ambulances moving about the field where thousands of wounded soldiers from both armies had suffered through the night. Lee was there before sunrise. Presently couriers began to arrive from Longstreet and Jackson, informing him that Porter had pulled out. They had pushed down toward the Chickahominy without encountering any live Federals except the injured and stragglers, including one of McCall's brigade commanders, Brigadier General John F. Reynolds, who had slept too long in the woods and was captured. The bridges had been burned, they said, and guns were massed on the ridge beyond to challenge any attempt to rebuild them.

Lee did not mind the watchful guns or the wrecked bridges; he had no intention of crossing the river here. However, the original plan for marching in force down the left bank to get astride McClellan's communications could not be followed until he knew for certain in which direction the Federals were retreating — toward White House, toward Williamsburg, or, conceivably, toward the James — or whether, indeed, they might not be massing on the right bank for a drive on Richmond, slicing between the divided wings of the Confederate army to get there. A move in the wrong direction would throw Lee out of position for interfering with either of McClellan's remaining alternatives. Until he knew, he was stymied. For the present all he could do was order Stuart to press on down the left bank, supported by Ewell's division, and cut the railroad at or near Dispatch Station, the advance Union supply base just east of the river. McClellan's reaction to that would tell him much. Meanwhile, there was little to do but attend the wounded, bury the dead, and take such rest as fretfulness would permit.

A sort of wanderlust came over the army in its idleness. Too much had happened too fast these past two days, apparently, for the troops to sit still now. As the sun climbed up the sky, giving promise of much heat, they began to roam the field, singly or in groups, mingling with the burial squads in their search for missing friends and relatives. Even Stonewall was infected. Examining the terrain where Hood and Law had made their breakthrough, the dead still lying thick to mark the path of their assault, he shook his head and exclaimed in admiration: "The men who carried this position were soldiers indeed." Lee too took time to ride in search of his youngest son Robert, an eighteen-year-old cannoneer in a Virginia battery. At first the boy could not be found, but a comrade finally spotted him sleeping under a caisson, unresponsive to the shouts. Prodded with a sponge staff, he came out into the sunlight, grimy and blinking. Lee spoke to him and rode on, and nobody seemed to think it strange that the son of the army commander should be serving in the ranks.

Information began to trickle in. Shortly before midday one of Ewell's brigadiers reported that a man he had sent up a tree with a spy-glass had seen the Federals moving south in heavy columns. As if in confirmation, a widening cloud of dust began to darken the sky beyond the river, rising over the treetops. Then came flashes, followed by the crump and rumble of distant explosions and pillars of smoke standing tall along the horizon. Magazines were being fired; McClellan was unquestionably on the march. But where to? Lee did not know, though presently he learned at least that it was not toward White House. A courier arrived from Stuart. He had cut the railroad at Dispatch Station, encountering only token resistance, and the Federal horsemen, falling back, had burned the Chickahominy trestle. Definitely, then, McClellan was abandoning his base on the Pamunkey.

Three alternatives were left to him: a retreat down the Peninsula, a change of base to the James, or a lunge at Richmond. Without anything resembling definite evidence — any one of the three, for instance, might be preceeded by a movement south — Lee now began to consider the second of these choices the most likely. This belief was arrived at by a process of elimination, rejecting those movements which did not seem to him to be in keeping with the character of his opponent. He did not think McClellan had the boldness to adopt the latter course, nor did he think he would willingly risk the damage to his prestige that would result from adopting the former. If this logic was correct, then he was making for the James: in which case there was a need for haste if Lee was to cut him off before he reached the shelter of his gunboats. But the stakes were too great and the odds too long for a gamble based on logic. Confederate guns, shelling the wooded ridge beyond the Chickahominy, were receiving return fire. The Federals were still there, and as long as that was so, Lee could not afford to risk throwing **three fourths of his army out of position by sending it off on what** might turn out to be an empty chase. Sunset came, then nightfall. The long day was over, and all Lee knew for certain was that McClellan was not reacting as he had expected him to do.

Early Sunday morning two of Longstreet's engineers made a reconnaissance across the river, and soon after sunrise Lee received a message from them which added considerable weight to yesterday's logic. The extensive fortifications covering the key Federal position opposite the mouth of Powhite Creek had been abandoned.

This meant that McClellan had no intention of making a lunge at Richmond. He was retreating, and almost certainly he was retreating in the direction of the James, since neither Stuart nor Ewell had reported any movement toward the lower crossings of the Chickahominy. It was not conclusive evidence; the Federals' nonarrival at Bottom's Bridge or Long Bridge, another five miles downstream, might have been caused by a bungled march or a late start; but it shortened the odds at least enough for Lee to risk a gamble. His original plan had been designed to force the enemy to fall back from in front of Richmond or else come out from behind his intrenchments, where he could be hit. McClellan had obliged by doing both. In doing so, however, he had moved in an unexpected direction and had gained a full day's head start in the process. Lee's problem now was to devise a new plan: one that would take advantage of the opportunities created by the old one, now outmoded, and at the same time overcome the advantage his opponent had made for himself. In brief, Lee wanted a plan by which he could overtake McClellan and destroy him.

Before he could be overtaken, however, he would have to be impeded, and Lee's principal asset in this regard was White Oak Swamp. A sort of miniature Chickahominy, it rose southwest of Seven Pines, in the angle between the Williamsburg and Charles City roads, and flowed in a slow crescent across the Federal line of march, emptying into the parent river midway between Bottom's Bridge and Long Bridge. Scantily spanned and badly swollen, impenetrable along most of its length, the stream disguised its quicksand deadliness behind a mazy screen of vines and creepers, luring the northern commander toward an excellent possibility of destruction. If this army could be caught with its head south and its tail north of this boggy stretch, it might be slaughtered like a hamstrung ox, more or less with impunity. McClellan might or might not be aware of this; Lee was. Before the sun was midmorning high, he had begun to compose and issue orders which, if carried out, would place his troops in position to begin the butchery.

Magruder, moving east along the railroad and the Williamsburg road, was to attack the tail, supported on the left by Jackson, who was to repair and cross Grapevine Bridge with his own and D. H. Hill's divisions. Huger, moving southeast along the Charles City road, was to attack the head, supported on the right by Longstreet, who was to cross New Bridge with his own and A. P. Hill's divisions, marching across Huger's rear to get in position south of the swamp. Meanwhile, on the off chance that McClellan might veer east and try for a getaway down the Peninsula, Ewell was to hold his present position at Bottom's Bridge, supported by Stuart farther down. The assault on the head, below the swamp, could not be made today; Longstreet and Little Powell had fifteen dusty miles to go before they would be in position; their attack would have to be launched on Monday. However, the assault on McClellan's hindquarters could and should be made without delay, since it would impede him further by causing him to have to turn in mid-career and fight a rear-guard action north of White Oak Swamp.

Once more then, with his orders issued, Lee had to wait for the execution of another ambitious convergence. If this one worked, McClellan's oxhide would hang dripping on the Confederacy's barn door before tomorrow's sun went down. Now as before, however, the first move was up to Stonewall — and Magruder.

★ ★ ★

Prince John had been having his troubles all along. In fact, so wholly had he flung himself into the part he was playing — his "method" presaged that of Stanislavsky, who would not be born till the following year, five thousand miles away — his theatrical exertions had been as hard on his own nervous system as on those of the blue-coated spectators out front. This intensity had infected his supporting players, too. Yesterday, for example, one of his brigadiers — fiery, slack-mouthed Robert Toombs, Georgia statesman turned Georgia troop commander — had got so carried away that he converted a demonstration into a full-scale assault on the heavily manned Federal intrenchments. The result, of course, was a bloody repulse and, Magruder believed, a decided increase in the likelihood that the enemy would discover the true weakness behind the ferocious mask. Ever since then, like an actor with the illusion lost and the audience turned irate, he had been expecting to be booed and overrun.

This morning, after dosing himself with medicine in an attempt to ease the pangs of indigestion, he decided to stage an attack. The enemy guns had slacked their fire and then had fallen silent in the fortifications to his immediate left front. Mindful of his instructions to keep pressure on the Union lines, he was determined to develop the situation in strength. However, when he sent word to Lee of his intention, the army commander replied facetiously that a forward movement was indeed in order, but that in storming the works he was to exercise care not to injure Longstreet's two engineers, who had already occupied them. Chagrined, Magruder advanced and was relieved to find it true. Not that there was any lessening of the general tension. Whatever victories had been scored on the far side of the Chickahominy, the peril here on the south bank, now that all five of the Federal corps were united in his front, seemed to him even greater today than yesterday or the day before. Presently, with the arrival of Lee's orders for overhauling and destroying McClellan, Prince John's alarm increased at once to the point of horror and unbelief. Except for the doubtful assistance of that unpredictable eccentric, Stonewall Jackson — who had yet to arrive anywhere on time — it seemed to Magruder that he was being required to assault the whole 100,000-man Yankee army with his one frazzled 13,000-man division.

Lee rode over before midday and explained in person just what it was he wanted. Magruder was to push eastward along the railroad, making contact with Jackson south of Grapevine Bridge, and together they would assail the Union rear. Magruder listened and nodded distractedly; Lee rode on, convinced that his orders were understood. However, Prince John's misgivings were by no means allayed. He got his men into assault formation, straddling the tracks so that Lee's big railway gun protected his center, and started forward. At Fair Oaks, surrounded by piles of smoldering equipment abandoned by the Federals in haste, he came under long-range artillery fire; whereupon he halted and called for help from Huger, who was advancing down the Charles City road. Huger countermarched with two brigades, stayed with him briefly, then went his way, unable to see that he was needed. Magruder went forward again, but with mounting misgivings.

Sure enough, just short of Savage Station, two miles down the track, he came under heavy close-up fire and saw bluecoats clustered thickly in his front, supported by batteries massed in their rear. It was 5 o'clock; Magruder was where Lee wanted him, due south of Grapevine Bridge, in position to press the Federals when Jackson came slamming down on their flank. But now it was his turn to ask the question others had been asking for the past two days: Where was Jackson? There was no sign of him off to the left, no sound of his guns, not even any dust in that direction. Nettled, Prince John went on without him; or anyhow he tried, probing tentatively at the Union line and banging away with the "Land Merrimac."

None of it did any good at all. The Federals repulsed every advance and concentrated so much counterbattery fire on the railway gun that it was forced to backtrack and take shelter in a cut. Night came on, and the cannon kept up their long-range quarrel. Then at 9 o'clock a thunderstorm broke and ended the Battle of Savage Station, in which about 500 men had fallen on each side. Magruder had advanced five miles in the course of the day, but the Federals had not yielded a single unwilling inch. Fighting stubbornly, they had preserved the integrity of their line wherever challenged. More important, they had covered the retreat of the slow-grinding wagon train, which wound southward unmolested. In effect, McClellan had gained another day in his race against time and Lee.

The one person most responsible for this success was not the Union commander or any of his lieutenants, however stubbornly they had fought. Nor was it Magruder, who had fumbled his way forward and then had fought without conviction. It was Jackson, who had not fought at all. Thursday and Friday he had had reasons for failing to strike or threaten the Federal flank on schedule: not good ones, but anyhow reasons. He had been delayed on the march. He had gotten lost. Today, as the sound of Magruder's guns rolled up from the south, he replied to a request for help by saying that he had "other important duties to perform." Presumably this was the repairing of Grapevine Bridge, so listlessly attempted that it turned out to be an all-day job. At any rate, he had kept his men on the north bank of the Chickahominy while Magruder's were fighting and dying at Savage Station.

Consequently, there were some who recalled an early rumor as to how he won his battle name on the field of Manassas. According to this version, Bee had called him Stonewall, not in admiration of his staunchness, but in anger at his refusal to come to his assistance there on the forward slope of Henry Hill. What the South Carolinian had really said, men whispered now about the camps, was: "There stands Jackson — like a damned stone wall!"

Lee now knew the results of the day, and mostly they were worse than disappointing. North of the swamp, where Magruder had faltered and Jackson had stood stock still, the limited attack had probably done more to assist than to impede McClellan's withdrawal. Southward, the situation was not much better. Delayed by a countermarch which had served no purpose, Huger had moved a scant half-dozen miles down the Charles City road and had gone into camp without making contact with the enemy. But even this poor showing put him well in advance of Longstreet and A. P. Hill, who had been stopped by darkness and the thunderstorm, six miles short of tomorrow's objective. Such encouragement as there was came from Stuart, and it was more of a negative than of a positive nature: McClellan had destroyed his base at White House and severed all connections with the Pamunkey and the York.

Thus assured that there was now not even an outside chance that his opponent had it in mind to veer off down the Peninsula, Lee could withdraw Ewell's division from its post at Bottom's Bridge and add its weight to the attempted strike at McClellan's flank and rear. Also, he learned from Richmond, Holmes' division had crossed from Drewry's Bluff, so that it too would be available when — and if — the retreating Federal host was brought to bay.

To effect this end, while thunder pealed and lightning described

Fighting Means Killing

its garish zigzag patterns against the outer darkness where the men of his scattered divisions took such rest as they could manage in the rain-lashed woods and fields, Lee gave his attention to the map, once more studying ways and means to correct a plan that had gone awry. For all its sorry showing today, the army was approximately in position for the destructive work he had assigned it for tomorrow. Three roads led southeast below White Oak Swamp, roughly parallel to each other and perpendicular to the Federal line of retreat: the Charles City road, the Darbytown road, and the New Market road. Huger was on the former, nearest the swamp; Holmes was on the latter, nearest the James; Longstreet and A. P. Hill were in the center. Advancing, all three columns would enter the Long Bridge road, which led east-northeast to the Chickahominy crossing that gave it its name, and encounter McClellan's

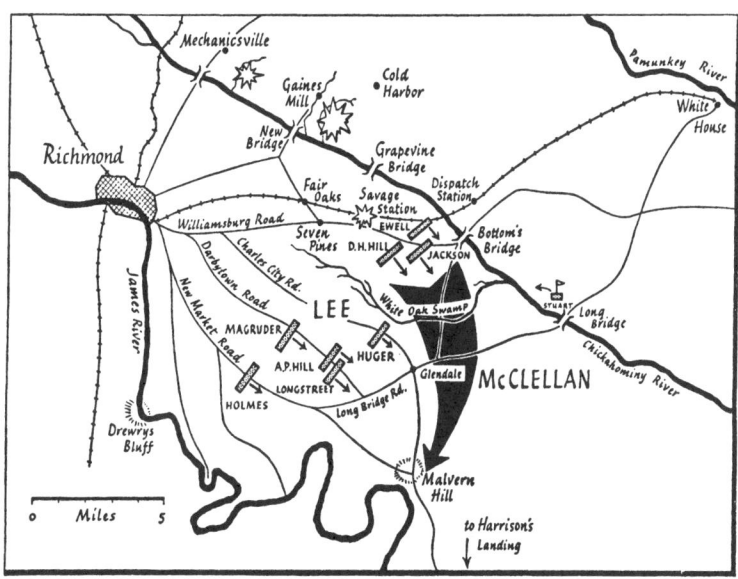

southbound column in the vicinity of Glendale, a crossroads hamlet located at the intersection of the Charles City and the Long Bridge roads. These four divisions, reinforced by Magruder — who would countermarch on the Williamsburg road, then swing south and take position as a general reserve well down the Darbytown road — would constitute the striking force. Its mission was to intercept and assail the head and flank of the enemy column, while Jackson and Harvey Hill, rejoined by Ewell, would continue (or rather, begin) to press the Federal rear, to and beyond White Oak Swamp. Caught in the resultant squeeze, with 45,000 graybacks on his flank and another 25,000 in his rear — so that, observed from above, his predicament somewhat resembled that of a thick-bodied snake pursued by hornets — McClellan would be forced to stop and fight, strung out in the open as he was, thereby affording Lee the best chance so far to destroy him.

His orders written and given to couriers who rode out into the slackening storm, Lee could sleep at last for what he hoped would be a happier tomorrow. Seeking to avoid delay — the main cause of disappointment up to now — he had instructed his troop commanders to move at dawn. Huger, being nearest the enemy, was to signal the opening of the battle by firing his guns as soon as he made contact, whereupon the others were to close in for the destruction according to plan. Unless today's ragged performance was improved, however, that goal would never be attained. Lee knew this, of course, and the knowledge made him edgy: so much so, in fact, that in his concern he rebuked not Jackson — the principal offender — but Magruder, the only one of his generals who had struck a blow in the past two days.

"I regret very much that you have made so little progress today in the pursuit of the enemy," he informed him by courier. "In order to reap the fruits of our victory the pursuit should be most vigorous.... We must lose no more time, or he will escape us entirely."

★ ★ ★

Always, up to now, when McClellan spoke to them of tests and hardships — Yorktown, Williamsburg, Fair Oaks: the victory hill got steeper with every step — the men had cheered him and kept climbing, reinforcing their belief in their commander, Little Mac, with an increasing belief in themselves. Now there was this sterner downhill test.

In some ways, the past four days had been harder on the Federals south of the Chickahominy than on those who were fighting for their lives on the opposite bank. Thursday and Friday there had been a boiling cloud of smoke obscuring the northern sky, and conflicting reports of battles won or lost as the boom and rumble of guns swelled or sank in that direction. Saturday the smoke and noise subsided, then rose again in the afternoon, farther east and of a different intensity, more deliberate than frantic: supply and ammunition dumps were burning and exploding. Also, there was a constant movement of men and wagons across the rear: Porter's troops were over the river, slogging south in the wake of Keyes', who had pulled out on the left. The men of Franklin and Sumner and Heintzelman, left behind, looked at one another and passed the word along: "It's a big skedaddle."

Sunday they themselves had backtracked, fighting a series of rear-guard skirmishes as they moved eastward down the railroad. Then at Savage Station they called a halt and rocked the pursuers back on their heels, "Land Merrimac" and all. It was a victory, and they felt considerably better: especially Sumner, whose battle blood was up. The old man could scarcely believe his ears when he got orders to continue the retrograde movement. "I never leave a victorious field," he sputtered. "Why, if I had 20,000 more men I would crush this rebellion!" When someone finally found a candle, struck a light, and showed him the written order, he still protested. "General McClellan did not know the circumstances when he wrote that note. He did not know that we would fight a battle and gain a victory." Finally, though, he acquiesced; orders were orders. Heintzelman had already left, and Franklin and Sumner followed, crossing White Oak Swamp in the darkness. By 10 o'clock next morning the last man was safely across and the bridge had been burned to discourage pursuit.

It had not been accomplished without losses. A hospital camp of 2500 sick and wounded was abandoned at Savage Station, together with an ample supply of medicines and surgeons who volunteered to stay behind with their charges. At the Chickahominy railroad crossing, loaded ammunition trains were set afire and run full tilt off the wrecked bridge, with spectacular results. Sunday's landscape was smudged with the acrid smoke of burning cloth and leather, relieved from time to time by the more pleasant aroma of coffee and bacon given to the flames instead of to the rebels. The price, in fact, had been heavy; but so was the gain. Whatever else might be in store, McClellan's army was not going to be caught astride the only natural obstacle that lay athwart its line of march to the James.

Monday was Lee's last, best chance for the Cannae he had been seeking all along, and as usual he was early on the scene. The main blow, as he designed it, would be delivered by Longstreet and A. P. Hill just south of Glendale. If successful, this would sever the Union column, interrupt its retreat, and expose its disjointed segments to destruction in detail. But much depended also on the commanders of the various other columns of attack: on Huger, who would open the action on the left: on Jackson, who would force a crossing of White Oak Swamp and press the Federal rear: on Magruder, who would come up in support of the center: and on Holmes, who would advance on the right so as to bring the disorganized bluecoat survivors under his guns as they fled past him, reeling from the effect of the multiple blows.

Since Magruder had the longest march, Lee rode over to Savage Station before sunrise to make certain he understood the orders and started promptly. The first commander he encountered there was not Prince John, however, but Jackson, who had finally repaired Grapevine Bridge and started his men across it before dawn. Both generals dismounted and advanced for a handshake, Lee removing his gauntlet as he came forward. According to a young artillery officer who observed the meeting, Stonewall "appeared worn down to the lowest point of flesh consistent with active service. His hair, skin, eyes and clothes were all one neutral dust tint, and his badges of rank so dulled and tarnished as to be scarcely perceptible." Yesterday's strange lethargy had left him, along with his accustomed reticence. He "began talking in a jerky, impetuous way, meanwhile drawing a diagram on the ground with the toe of his right boot. He traced two sides of a triangle with promptness and decision; then, starting at the end of the second line, began to draw a third projected toward the first. This third line he traced slowly and with hesitation, alternately looking up at Lee's face and down at the diagram, meanwhile talking earnestly." Suddenly, as the third line intersected the first, he stamped his foot, apparently indicating the point at which McClellan would be wrecked beyond repair. "We've got him," he said decisively, and signaled for his horse.

Lee watched him go, that strange man in another of his strange guises, then mounted too and continued his search for Magruder. Presently he found him. After making certain that Prince John understood today's orders as well as Stonewall did, Lee hurried down the Darbytown road to establish army headquarters in rear of the proposed center of the impending battle.

As events turned out, however, there was no need for haste: at any rate, not on his part. Longstreet's men were going forward, supported by Hill's, but it was noon by the time they formed their line near the junction with the Long Bridge road, facing eastward to await the already overdue boom of Huger's guns signaling contact on the left. What came instead was a message: the South Carolinian's progress was "obstructed" — whatever that meant. Lee was left wondering. Southward, Holmes was silent too; nor was there any indication that Jackson was pressing down from the north against the enemy rear. Somewhere out beyond the screening pines and oaks, east of where Lee stood waiting for his lost columns to converge, the Federals were hurrying southward past the point where he had intended to stage his Cannae. He might still stage it — seven hours of daylight still remained — if he could find the answer to certain questions: What had delayed Huger? What had happened to Holmes? And again, as so often before: Where was Jackson?

Huger had the shortest march of all, and what was more he had made an early start. But he went slowly, fearing ambush, for which the terrain was particularly suited. This had been tobacco country in the old days, checkerboard-neat for the most part, but in time the soil had leached out; neglected, it had gone back to second-growth scrub timber, broken here and there by clearings where men still tried to scratch a living from it. The general's natural caution was further increased by the presence of White Oak Swamp, which afforded a covered approach to his left flank. Presently, to make matters worse, word came back that the road ahead was obstructed, the Yankees having chopped down trees that fell across it as they retreated. Instead of leaving his

Fighting Means Killing

artillery behind or trying to clear the fallen timber from his path, Huger ordered a new road cut through the woods, parallel to the old one. Progress was slowed to even more of a snail's pace than before. And while he chopped, Longstreet and Hill, having formed for battle, waited. At 2.30, detecting signs of the enemy ahead, Huger brought up a couple of light fieldpieces and shelled the brush.

Holmes too was involved in a nightmare this day — a far bloodier and noisier one than Huger's contest of axes, though in point of fact the noise was not a very disturbing element for the fifty-seven-year-old North Carolinian, who was deaf. After waiting most of the afternoon at the junction of the New Market and Long Bridge roads, he received word that the bluecoats were streaming in thousands across Malvern Hill, a tall ridge three miles ahead, in the final stage of deliverance from the unsprung trap Lee had contrived for their destruction around Glendale. His 6000 men were too few for a successful infantry attack on the heavy column of Federals, but Holmes decided to do what he could with his artillery to frustrate their escape. Accordingly he rode forward, found a position well within range of the hill, then brought up six rifled pieces, supported by a regiment of infantry, and prepared to open fire.

While the guns were being laid he stepped into a house by the side of the road. Just then a single large-caliber projectile broke with a clap like sudden blue-sky thunder over the heads of his startled men, followed promptly by what one of them called "a perfect shower of shells of tremendous proportion and hideous sound." The result was instantaneous pandemonium. Infantry and artillery alike, the green troops clustered and scattered and milled aimlessly about in search of cover, which was scarce. Some in their greenness took shelter from the ten-inch shells by crouching behind two-inch saplings; others simply knelt in their tracks and clasped their hands, palms down, on the tops of their heads. Placid in the midst of all this uproar — bursting projectiles, screaming men and horses, hoarse and futile shouts of command by rattled captains — Holmes emerged from the roadside house, suspiciously cupping one ear. "I thought I heard firing," he said.

The big shells, called "lamp posts," came from gunboats on James River, which looped northward within half a mile of the Confederate position. Soon Malvern Hill was wreathed in smoke as siege guns on its crest added canister to the weight of metal already falling on Holmes' demoralized soldiers. He pulled them back out of range. It was nearly sunset, and like Huger — whose daylong two-mile march left him a full mile short of contact with the Federal main body hastening south across his front — Holmes had taken no appreciable part in the day's fighting. Nor had Magruder, who came up in rear of Longstreet just as the uproar exploded on the far right, near the James, and was sent in that direction to help stem what sounded like a full-scale counterattack up the River road. Nor had Jackson, with better than one third of the whole army under his command.

After the early morning Savage Station conference with Lee, Stonewall had pushed on down toward White Oak Swamp, gleaning in the woods and fields a bumper harvest of abandoned U.S. equipment and prisoners as he went. This was always a pleasant task for the "wagon hunter," and today it gave him particular satisfaction, affording as it did an outlet for his apparent superabundance of nervous energy. When a companion protested that the captives would be of considerable expense to the government, Jackson shook his head. "It is cheaper to feed them than to fight them," he said. He pressed on, encountering no opposition. There was time, even, to stop and write the usual Monday letter to his wife. "An ever-kind Providence has greatly blessed our efforts," it began. About noon, approaching the sodden jungle of the swamp, he found that the Federals had already crossed it, burning the bridge behind them, and had emplaced their artillery on a commanding southside ridge, supported by heavy columns of infantry. Promptly he brought up his own guns under cover, opened suddenly on the enemy batteries, and saw them displace in frantic haste, abandoning three pieces in their confusion. Delighted, Jackson ordered his cavalry to ford the stream at once, intending for them to harry the fleeing bluecoats, and — in accordance with Lee's instructions — put a crew to work without delay, rebuilding the bridge in order to take up the pursuit with his infantry.

So far it had gone well: Stonewall seemed to have recovered his identity. But now, quite abruptly, it stopped cold. The cavalry, having crossed, was repulsed by the Federal batteries, which had not fled, as had been thought, but had simply moved to a new position, where they outgunned their smooth-bore rivals north of the swamp. Worse still, the ring of the sharpshooter's rifle, accompanied from time to time by the sickening thwack of a bullet striking flesh, drove the bridgebuilders from their work almost as soon as they got started. Worst of all, however, was Jackson's reaction, which was rather as if the mainspring of some tightly wound-up mechanism had suddenly lost its resilience or run down. Formerly alert and energetic, he grew taciturn and drowsy, even sullen. Recalling his troops from exposure to danger, he lay down under a tree and went to sleep.

That was about 3 o'clock. When he woke an hour later — or half-woke, rather, sitting slump-shouldered on a log, the bill of his dingy cadet cap pulled down over his sleep-puffed eyes — he heard sounds of heavy firing from the south. It made little impression on him, though. Nor did the suggestions of his lieutenants, who had been reconnoitering for a way around the impasse while he slept. A cavalry colonel sent word that he had located a useable ford nearby, but Jackson ignored the message. Wade Hampton, commanding an infantry brigade, went off on his own and presently returned to report in person that he had found an excellent downstream crossing that would bring his men in position to strike the unsuspecting Federal flank. Jackson stirred. Could Hampton build a bridge there? Yes, the South Carolinian said, but the noise might alert the enemy. Build the bridge, Jackson told him. Hampton left. Soon he was back, reporting that the work had been done without alarming the Union troops. Stonewall gave no sign that he had heard him. For a long time he sat there on the log, silent, collapsed like a jointed doll whose spinal string had snapped. Then abruptly he rose, still without replying, and walked away.

Hampton's bridge went unused — as did Jackson's third of Lee's army, which remained north of White Oak Swamp, out of touch with the enemy all day. At supper, soon after dark, Stonewall went to sleep with a piece of unchewed biscuit between his teeth. Jarred awake by his own nodding, he looked blankly about, then got up from the table. "Now, gentlemen," he told his staff, "let us at once to bed... and see if tomorrow we cannot do something."

Of all the days in the eventful month since that last night in May when the President tendered him command of the leaderless army as they rode back from the confused and gloomy field of Seven Pines, this final day of June had been for Lee the longest and the saddest. None had promised more at the outset, or yielded less in the end, than this in which better than two thirds of his soldiers were withheld from contact with the fleeing enemy by the inabilities and eccentricities of the commanders of three out of his four intended columns of attack.

Davis was with him, now as then. At 2.30, mistaking the boom of Huger's guns, shelling the brush on the Charles City road, for the prearranged signal that the battle had opened on the left, Lee hurried north on the Long Bridge road in search of Longstreet and found him talking with the President in a little clearing of stunted pines and broomstraw. As Lee rode up, Davis greeted him with a question designed to forestall a repetition of the repulse he had suffered at the Virginian's hands four days ago at Mechanicsville: "Why, General, what are you doing here? You are in too dangerous a position for the commander of the army."

"I'm trying to find out something about the movements and plans of those people," Lee replied. (For him, the Federals were invariably "those people.") Then, attempting to recover the initiative, he added: "But you must excuse me, Mr President, for asking what *you* are doing here, and for suggesting that this is no place for the Commander in Chief of all our armies."

"Oh," Davis told him with a smile, airy but determined, "I am here on the same mission that you are."

Lee had to let it go at that, though presently the danger was considerably heightened. When Longstreet rode away and had some nearby batteries open fire in acknowledgment of what he thought was Huger's signal, the reply came not from the Confederates to the north, but from the Federals to the east. Suddenly the clearing was dotted with bursting shells. Concerned with the peril to Davis and Lee, A. P. Hill came dashing up and addressed them sternly: "This is no place for either of you, and as commander of this part of the field I order you both to the rear!" The two moved off — "We will obey your orders," Davis said — but when they drew rein, still within the zone of fire, red-bearded Little Powell overtook them and spoke with the same mock harshness as before: "Did I not tell you to go away from here, and did you not promise to obey my orders? Why, one shot from that battery over yonder may presently deprive the Confederacy of its President and the Army of Northern Virginia of its commander." Abashed, the two withdrew beyond range of the exploding shells and the explosive Hill.

It was then that Lee received unwelcome news that McClellan was closer to safety than he had supposed. A cavalry commander, patrolling ahead of Holmes on the River road, informed him by courier that the enemy, undamaged and unhindered, was crossing Malvern Hill within gunshot of the James. Lee at once rode down and saw for himself the truth of the report. The bulk of the Union supply train, accompanied by heavy columns of infantry, was making its escape. If the Confederate attack was delayed much longer, it would strike not the enemy flank, but the enemy rear: which meant that the chance for a Cannae would be gone. In fact, it might be gone already. Having approved Holmes' intention to disrupt the retreat as much as possible with his guns, Lee turned back toward Glendale. He still had heard nothing from Jackson, and nothing from Huger except that his route was "obstructed." But time was running out. Concentrated or not, he would throw what he had at the Federal flank before the tail of the blue column cleared the junction near which Hill and Longstreet had been waiting all this time.

Encountering Davis, who reproached him again for rashly exposing himself, Lee replied quite truly — it was, in fact, the crux of the problem, what with the inadequate communications and the lack of an adequate staff — that all he could learn of the situation was what he saw with his own eyes. As he rode northward, the uproar of the naval bombardment exploded behind him. What it meant he did not know, but when he returned to the broomstraw clearing, still under fire from the batteries ahead, he found that Magruder, arriving at last, had been ordered south by Longstreet, who interpreted the heavy-caliber uproar as a counterattack by the Federals near the James. For all Lee knew, that was what it was. Besides, there was no time for recalling Magruder.

If the assault was to be delivered before the bluecoats cleared the junction, it would have to be launched at once by the troops at hand; that is, by the divisions of Longstreet and A. P. Hill. He told them to go forward — which they did. The result was the Battle of Glendale; or Frayser's Farm, it was sometimes called, since much of the hottest fighting occurred on this two-hundred-acre property south of the junction.

Not that it wasn't hot enough all over. In sending two divisions against an enemy force of undetermined strength, Lee's hope was that they would find the Federals strung out on the roads and unprepared. As it turned out, however, he was hoping for a good deal more of an advantage than his opponent was willing to grant. McClellan had disposed his eleven divisions with several eventualities in mind, and in fact was readier for this than for any other. Keyes' two divisions, along with two of Porter's, were already in position on Malvern Hill; two more — one from Sumner and one from Franklin — were on rear-guard duty, observing the quiescent Jackson across White Oak Swamp; Franklin's other division was astride the Charles City road, blocking Huger. The remaining four — Heintzelman's two and one each from Sumner and Porter — were in front of Glendale, ready for whatever came their way. The result was a savage, stand-up fight, beginning two hours before sundown and continuing through twilight into darkness.

Longstreet went in, driving hard and capturing guns in the rush, but presently, encountering stiffer resistance as the blue mass absorbed the blow, called for help. Hill's men charged with a yell on the left and right, their backs to the setting sun. Again the Federals yielded; again they rallied. The fighting now was hand to hand. Bayonets crossed and musket butts cracked skulls. More guns were taken, lost, and retaken as the lines surged back and forth in the dusk, across clearings and through woods. 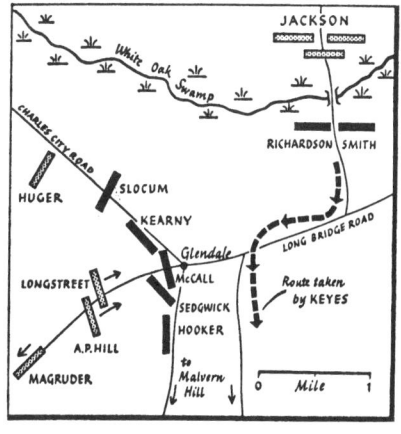 Longstreet remained calm, feeding men into the holocaust and matching his skill against the odds. When a group of jubilant Virginians brought him a captured brigadier, he recognized an old army comrade, George McCall, commander of Porter's third division. About to extend his hand in greeting, he saw that the prisoner was in no mood for the amenities, however, and directed instead that he be taken at once to Richmond as a trophy.

Gradually the battle racket died away in the darkness: the Confederates held the field. Having paid for it with the blood of 3300 men, they received by way of dividend eighteen Yankee guns and one Yankee general. But these were the only substantial results. The real objective — McClellan's supply train and reserve artillery, for which he would have had to turn and fight without the alternative of an orderly retreat — was not obtained, and in fact had been unobtainable since midday, five hours before the battle started. Under cover of night, the Federals continued their withdrawal toward the James.

McClellan himself was there already, having gone aboard the ironclad *Galena* to confer with the gunboat commander and arrange for support while Keyes and Porter were filing into position on Malvern Hill. A telegram from Lincoln, sent two days ago and rerouted through Fortress Monroe, showed something of the official reaction up to the time the White House line was cut. "Save your army at all events," the President urged him. "Will send reinforcements as fast as we can.... If you have had a drawn battle or a repulse it is the price we pay for the enemy not being in Washington.... It is the nature of the case, and neither you nor the Government are to blame."

Though he agreed with no more than half of the final sentence, McClellan was too worn down by exertion and anxiety to press the point just yet. At sundown, proud but gloomy, he replied: "My army has behaved superbly, and have done all that men can do. If none of us escape, we shall at least have done honor to the country. I shall do my best to save the army. Send more gunboats."

★ ★ ★

Tuesday's dawn, July 1, showed the Union lines abandoned around Glendale, and though there was no longer a chance for interception, Lee ordered his army to concentrate for pursuit. He had no real way of knowing what effect the past six days of fighting — and the past five days of falling back — might have had on the Federals. Up to now they had fought stubbornly and hard; but last night's fierce encounter, followed by still another retreat, might have tipped the scale toward panic. If they were in fact demoralized, the slightest tap on this seventh day of combat might cause the blue host to fly apart, like an overstrained machine, and thus expose it to destruction in detail. At any rate, Lee was determined to take advantage of any opening McClellan might afford him for striking a crippling blow.

Magruder was already on hand, having countermarched in the night to relieve the battle-weary men of Hill and Longstreet. The southern commander joined these three while awaiting the arrival of Jackson and Huger, whose advance was unopposed. He bore himself calmly, but it was obviously with considerable effort. The cumulative strain of watching his combinations fail and his plans go awry because of fumbling had upset his digestion and shortened his temper. Longstreet, on the other hand, seemed as confident as ever, if not more so. When a Union surgeon came to request protection and supplies for the wounded he had stayed behind to tend, Longstreet asked him what division he belonged to. McCall's, the doctor said. "Well, McCall is safe in Richmond," Longstreet told him, adding that if it had not been for the Pennsylvanian's stubborn resistance along this road the day before, "we would have captured your whole army. Never mind," he said. "We will do it yet."

Lee said nothing. But Harvey Hill, whom they presently encountered, did not agree with the burly, eupeptic Georgian. One of Hill's chaplains, a native of the region, had given him a description of the terrain ahead. It was well adapted for defense, he said: particularly Malvern Hill, which the bluecoats were reported to have occupied already. "If General McClellan is there in strength, we had better let him alone," the saturnine Hill declared.

"Don't get scared, now that we have got him whipped," Longstreet broke in with a laugh.

Hill made no reply to this. Nor did Lee, who apparently had all he could do to maintain his composure. In this he was not entirely successful, however. When a newly arrived brigadier came up to the group and expressed concern lest McClellan escape, the gray-bearded commander's patience snapped. "Yes, he will get away," Lee said bitterly, "because I cannot have my orders carried out!"

Events coming hard on the heels of this uncharacteristic outburst did not improve the general's disposition. Malvern Hill was less than three miles away, no more than a normal one-hour march, but with seven divisions crowding a single southward road, the result was confusion and delay. (A parallel road, half a mile to the east, which Keyes had taken with his whole corps the previous night, went unused because it was not shown on Lee's crude map.) On top of all this, a mix-up in Magruder's orders sent his division swinging off on a tangent; time was lost before he was missed, and still more before he could be found and put back on the track. It soon developed that today, as on every other of what was to be known as the Seven Days — one gigantic twenty-mile-long conflict, with bewildering intermissions, not for resting, but for groping spastically in the general direction of an enemy who fought so savagely when cornered that the whole thing had been rather like playing blindman's buff with a buzz saw — Lee's army would not be within striking distance of the day's objective until well past noon. In fact, it was 1.30 before six of the eight Confederate divisions — Magruder was still off on his tangent, and Holmes was still licking yesterday's wounds, down on the River road — had filed into position facing the 150-foot height, which bristled with guns parked hub-to-hub to the front and rear of long blue stalwart-looking lines of Federal infantry.

Bad as it looked at first glance from the attacker's point of view, closer inspection of the position McClellan had chosen produced even stronger confirmation of D. H. Hill's long-range opinion that "we had better let him alone." Porter, who was in tactical command, was obviously ready for anything Lee might throw at him there on the undulating plateau, a mile and a half long and half as wide. He and Keyes, with two divisions each, held a line about midway up the slope; Heintzelman was in immediate reserve with two more, while Sumner and Franklin remained on call, in case their four were needed; which seemed unlikely, considering the narrow front, the apparently unassailable flanks, and the direct support of more than one hundred guns. These last were what made the position especially forbidding, and it was on them that Porter seemingly placed his chief reliance. First, in advance of the heavy ranks of infantry on the left and center, fieldpieces were massed in a long crescent so as to sweep the open ground across which the graybacks would have to charge if they were to come within musket range of the defenders. Other batteries were in support, all the way back to the brow of the hill, where siege guns were emplaced. Still farther back, on the James itself, naval gunners stood to their pieces, ready to arch their heavy-caliber shells into the ranks of the attackers.

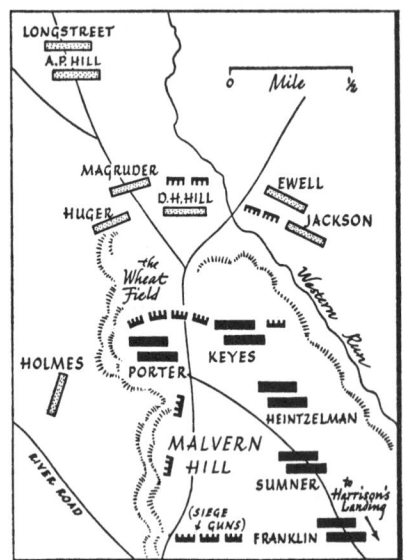

In full view of all those cannon frowning down, attack seemed outright suicide. But this was Lee's last chance to destroy McClellan before he reached the safety of the river, rested and refitted his army under cover of the gunboats, then launched another drive on Richmond, giving the Confederates the bloody task of driving him back again. This first repulse had been hard enough to manage; a second, with the Federal host enlarged by reinforcements and based securely on the James, might be impossible. With this in mind — and also the thought that the stalwart look of the Union troops, near the end of their long retreat, might be no more than a veneer that covered profound despair — Lee ordered his men to take up assault positions while he searched for a way to get at "those people" and administer the rap which he hoped would cause them to come apart at the seams. Huger was on the right, D. H. Hill in the center; Magruder would form between them when he arrived. Jackson and Ewell were on the left. Longstreet and A. P. Hill, still weary from yesterday's fight, were in reserve; Holmes, around on the River road, would coöperate as developments permitted. This arrangement left much to be desired, but it would have to do until a better could be evolved. What that would be Lee did not know until he was on his way to reconnoiter Jackson's front, which seemed to offer the best chance for success.

As he set out, a message came from Longstreet, who reported that he had found a good artillery position on the right, a terraced knoll with a direct line of fire to the Union batteries. From there, he added, he could see on the Confederate left an open field which also afforded an excellent position. If guns were massed at these two points, Longstreet said — forty on the right, say, and twice that many on the left — a converging fire would throw the northern batteries into confusion and open the way for an attack by the southern infantry. Lee saw in this the opportunity he was seeking: a charge in the style of the one across Boatswain's Swamp four days ago, with even greater rewards to follow success. Accordingly, he ordered the guns to occupy the two positions and notified his front-line commanders of the plan. One of Huger's brigades, posted closest to the enemy, would be able to judge best the effect of the bombardment. If it was successful, the brigade would go forward with a yell, which in turn would be the signal for an end-to-end assault by the whole gray line, the object being to close with the blue army and destroy it there on the rolling slopes of Malvern Hill.

It was not going to be easy; it might even be impossible; but as a last chance Lee thought it worth a try. In any case, if the bombardment failed in its purpose, the infantry need not advance. Already they were taking punishment from the siege guns on the brow of the hill as they filed through the wooded and swampy lowlands to get in position for the jump-off. The heavy-caliber fire was deliberate and deadly: as Harvey Hill could testify. While his troops were forming under a rain of metal and splintered branches, the North Carolinian sat at a camp table on the exposed side of a large tree, drafting orders for the attack. When one of his officers urged him at least to put the trunk between him and the roaring guns: "Don't worry about me," Hill said. "Look after the men. I am not going to be killed until my time comes." With that, a shell crashed into the earth alongside him, the concussion lifting the predestinarian from his chair and rolling him over and over on the ground. Hill got up, shook the dirt from his coat, the breast of which had been torn by a splinter of iron, and resumed his seat — on the far side of the tree. This and what followed were perhaps the basis for his later statement that, with Confederate infantry and Yankee artillery, he **believed he could whip any army in the world.**

What followed was a frustrating demonstration that southern gunners were no match for their northern counterparts: not here and now, at any rate. On the right and left, batteries came up piecemeal, no more than twenty guns in all — less than a fifth the number Longstreet had recommended — and piecemeal they were bludgeoned by counter-battery fire. Nowhere in this war would Federal artillerists have a greater advantage, and they did not neglect it. Sometimes concentrating as many as fifty guns on a single rebel battery, they pounded it to pulp and wreckage before changing deflection to repeat the treatment on the next one down the line. Half an hour was all they needed. By 2.30, with the whole Union position still billowing smoke and coughing flame — one six-gun battery near the center, for example, fired 1300 rounds in the course of the afternoon — not a single Confederate piece with a direct line of fire remained in action. What had been intended as a preliminary bombardment, paving the way for the infantry, had been reduced to a bloody farce. If Lee's soldiers were to come to grips with the bluecoats on that gun-jarred slope, they would have to do it some other way than this.

The southern commander resumed his reconnaissance on the left, hoping to find an opening for an attack that would flank the Federals off the hill. Far on the right, Huger's lead brigade was working its way forward. In its front was a large field of wheat, lately gleaned, with sharpshooters lurking behind the gathered sheaves of grain. Little would be gained by taking the wheatfield — on its far side, just beyond musket range, the crescent of guns standing hub to hub could clip the stubble as close as the scythe had lately done — but Huger's men, bitterly conscious that theirs was the only division which had done no real fighting since the opening attack six days ago, were determined to have a share in the bloody work of driving the invaders. Taking their losses, they surged ahead and finally took cover in a gully at the near edge of the wheatfield, well in advance of the rest of the army, while the sharpshooters fell back on their guns. Magruder, arriving about 4 o'clock to assume command of the right, notified Lee that he was on hand at last and that Huger's men had driven the enemy and made a substantial lodgment.

Lee meanwhile had found what he thought might be an opening on the left, and had sent word for the men of Longstreet and A. P. Hill to come forward and exploit it. Weary though they were, they were all he had. Just then, however, as Lee rode back toward the center, the message arrived from Magruder, together with one from the left reporting signs of a Federal withdrawal. That changed everything. This first advantage, if followed up, might throw McClellan's army into panic and open the way for an all-out flank-to-flank assault. Quickly he gave verbal orders, which the messenger took down for delivery to Magruder: "General Lee expects you to advance rapidly. He says it is reported the enemy is getting off. Press forward your whole command."

By now Prince John had had a chance to look into the situation a bit more carefully on the right, and as a result he was feeling considerably less sanguine. However, Lee's three-hour-old order, calling for a general advance if the preliminary bombardment was successful, reached him soon after he arrived. Since it bore no time of dispatch, Magruder assumed that it was current: an assumption presently strengthened by the prompt arrival of the message directing him to "press forward your whole command." That was what he did, and he did it without delay, despite the unpromising aspect which a hasty examination had revealed on this shell-torn quarter of the field. Quickly he formed his men and sent them forward on the right of Huger's lead brigade, which cheered at the sight of this unexpected support, leaped eagerly out of the gully, and joined the charge across the wheatfield. On the far side of the cropped plain, the long crescent of guns began to buck and jump with redoubled fury, licking the stubble with tongues of flame.

After the failure of the preliminary bombardment and the encounter with the shell that had seemed to have his name written on it, D. H. Hill had decided that no large-scale attack would be delivered. All the same, since Lee had never countermanded the tentative order for an advance if Huger's troops raised a yell, he kept his brigade commanders with him, ready to give them time-saving verbal instructions in case the unexpected signal came. Near sundown, just as he was advising them to return to their men and prepare to bed them down for the night, the firing rose suddenly to crescendo on the smoky hill and the sound of cheering broke out on the right. "That must be the general advance!" Hill exclaimed. "Bring up your brigades as soon as possible and join it." Quickly they rejoined their commands and led them forward through the woods. By the time they came out into the open, however, a fair proportion of the troops who had attacked on the right were lying dead or dying in the wheatfield, and the rest were either hugging what little defilade they could find or else were running pell-mell toward the rear. The flaming crescent of Union guns shifted east in time to catch the new arrivers at the start of their advance up the long slope. "It was not war, it was murder," Hill said later.

That was what it was, all right: mass murder. Hill and Magruder and Huger gave it all they had, despite the hurricane of shells, only to see charge after charge break in blood and flow back from the defiant line of guns. Dusk put an end to the fighting — none of it had been hand to hand, and much of it had been done beyond musket range — though the cannon sustained the one-sided argument past dark. By that time, 5590 Confederates had fallen, as compared with less that a third that many Federals, and all for nothing. The Seven Days were over; Lee had failed in his final effort to keep McClellan from reaching the James.

Now that he had examined the ground over which the useless attack had been launched, he saw that it had clearly been foredoomed, and he could not understand how any commander, there on the scene, with all those guns staring down his throat, could not have known better than to undertake it in the first place. So he went looking for Magruder. At Savage Station, two days ago, he had reproached him by messenger; this time he intended to do it in person, or at any rate demand an explanation. At last he found him. "General Magruder, why did you attack?" he said. Prince John had remained silent under the previous rebuke; but this time he had an answer, and he gave it. "In obedience to your orders, twice repeated," he told Lee.

Jackson's men, at the far end of the line of battle, had spent another non-fighting day — their sixth out of the seven. Only the artillery had been engaged on the left. The infantry, moving forward through the swampy underbrush, had not been able to come up in time to take part in the assault, though as Stonewall rode through the gathering dusk he found one of Ewell's brigadiers forming his troops under cover of the woods, their faces reflecting the eerie red flicker of muzzle-flashes out on the slope ahead. Jackson drew rein.

"What are you going to do?" he asked.

"I am going to charge those batteries, sir!"

"I guess you had better not try it," Stonewall told him. "General D. H. Hill has just tried it with his whole division and been repulsed; I guess you had better not try it, sir."

Presently the firing died to a rumble. About 10 o'clock it stopped, and out of the moonless darkness came the agonized cries of the wounded, beyond reach on the uptilted, blood-soaked plain. Jackson lay down on a blanket and went to sleep. Three hours later he was wakened by Ewell and Harvey Hill, who believed that McClellan was preparing to launch a dawn attack and had come to ask if Stonewall wanted them to make any special dispositions to meet it. One sleepy officer, seeing the three men squatting in a circle, thought they resembled a triumvirate of frogs. "No," Jackson said quietly, "I believe he will clear out in the morning."

★ ★ ★

He was right; McClellan did clear out, but not without having to override the protests of several high-ranking subordinates. Even Porter, who was his friend and generally favored all his actions, opposed this one, saying that he believed a determined advance from Malvern Hill would throw Lee into retreat through the streets of his capital. Phil Kearny, the hardest fighter among the brigade commanders — a spike-bearded New Jersey professional whose thirst for combat had not been slaked by the loss of an arm while leading a cavalry charge in Mexico — was the most vociferous of all. When the retirement order reached him at the close of the battle, he rose in the presence of his staff and cried out in anger: "I, Philip Kearny, an old soldier, enter my solemn protest against this order for retreat. We ought instead of retreating to follow up the enemy and take Richmond. And in full view of the responsibility of such a declaration, I say to you all, such an order can only be prompted by cowardice or treason."

McClellan either ignored this protest, or else he never heard it. In any case, his reply to Kearny would have been the same as the one he had made three days ago, when a cavalry colonel suggested a dash on the southern capital while Lee still had most of his men on the north bank of the Chickahominy: "If an army can save this country it will be the Army of the Potomac, and it must be saved for that purpose." He was taking no chances. If Lee would let him alone for the present, he was more than willing to return the favor.

And so it was that the same cavalry colonel found himself and his regiment alone on the hilltop next morning at dawn, with only a skirmish line of infantry left for show, while the rest of the army followed the road to Harrison's Landing. A mizzling rain had fallen before daylight, and mist blotted the lower slope from view. He could see nothing down there, but out of the mist came a babble of cries and wails and groans from the wounded who had managed to live through the night. After a while the sun came out, and when it burned the mist away he saw a thing he would never forget, and never remember except with a shudder. Down there on the lower slope, the bodies of five thousand gray-clad soldiers were woven into a carpet of cold or agonized flesh. "A third of them were dead or dying," he later wrote, "but enough of them were alive and moving to give the field a singular crawling effect."

Disposing his troops in a pretense of strength, the colonel presently agreed with feigned reluctance to an informal truce, and while rebel ambulance details came out of the woods and moved among the sufferers on the hillside, he withdrew under cover of a drenching rain and joined the rear of the retreating column, the van of which was led by the army commander. "My men are completely exhausted," McClellan wired Washington, "and I dread the result if we are attacked today by fresh troops.... I now pray for time. My men have proved themselves the equals of any troops in the world, but they are worn-out.... We have failed to win only because overpowered by superior numbers."

He had not lost: he had "failed to win." Nor had he been outfought: he had been "overpowered." So he said. And if his words were unrealistic, it might be added in extenuation that all the events of the past week had occurred in an atmosphere of unreality. Watching the week-long twenty-mile-wide conflict had been something like watching a small man beat a large one, not by nimble footwork or artful dodging or even boxing skill, but rather by brute force, driving headlong, never relinquishing the offensive, and taking a good deal more punishment than he inflicted. This last was confirmed by the casualty lists, which were beginning to be compiled now that the two armies were out of contact.

Three months ago the news of Shiloh had arrived from the West with a dreadful shock; 23,741 American fighting men had been killed, wounded, or captured in that battle. Now the East's turn had come. The best, and the worst, that could be said of the battle known as the Seven Days was that this grim western figure had been exceeded by more than half; 36,463 was the total. And though in the earlier conflict most of the casualties had been Union, here it was the other way around; 15,849 Federals and 20,614 Confederates were on the list. In killed and wounded, moreover, the advantage increased from almost three to four to better than one to two. Nearly 10,000 Federals had fallen, 1734 killed and 8062 wounded, as opposed to nearly 20,000 Confederates, 3478 and 16,261. However, this preponderance was considerably reduced by the 6053 Federals missing in action; only 875 Confederates were in that category. In the end, since approximately half of the uncaptured wounded would return in time to the ranks of their respective armies, this made the actual loss of fighting men somewhat lower for the Confederates, 8000 of whom would be returning, whereas half of the Federal wounded had been captured, leaving only half of the remainder to return — about 2000 — so that the actual loss in combat strength, after recuperation of the injured, would be 14,000 Federals and 12,500 Confederates.

Knowing as he did that the South could not afford a swapping game on anything like a man-for-man basis of exchange, Lee found little solace in such figures. When Jackson and Longstreet came by headquarters, seeking refuge from the storm while the aid men and the burial squads worked among the wounded and the dead on the rain-swept hillside, he asked Longstreet for his impression of the fighting. "I think you hurt them about as much as they hurt you," the forthright Georgian told him. Lee winced at this, for he knew how badly his army had suffered, and there was a touch of irony in his reply: "Then I am glad we punished them well, at any rate."

Longstreet left. Soon afterward, unexpectedly, President Davis walked in, taking Lee so much by surprise that he omitted the Mister from his salutation. "President," he said, "I am delighted to see you." They shook hands. Across the room, Jackson had risen and was standing at attention beside his chair. Lee saw Davis looking at him. "Why, President, don't you know General Jackson? This is our Stonewall Jackson." They were acquainted, of course, but the relationship had been strained by the Romney controversy, in which the Mississippian had supported

Benjamin and the Virginian had submitted his resignation. The result, in this first meeting since then, was a curious exchange. Observing the Valley general's bristling manner, Davis did not offer his hand. Instead he bowed, and Jackson replied with a rigid salute. Neither of them said anything to the other.

Their last encounter had been under similar circumstances, after the victory at Manassas, and here again the question was how or whether to pursue a driven foe. Stonewall felt the same way about it as he had felt a year ago, but Lee and Davis agreed that the disorganized condition of the southern army precluded any chance to overcome the Federals' substantial head start down the muddy road, which would be under gunboat fire at several points. Asked for his opinion, Jackson said dourly: "They have not all got away if we go immediately after them." Lee shook his head. For the present at least, pursuit would have to be left to the cavalry, which had arrived the night before. The rest of the army would spend what was left of the day attending the wounded, burying the dead, and preparing to resume the chase tomorrow.

For today, then — as well as for a good part of tomorrow, since Harrison's Landing was eight muddy miles from Malvern Hill — Jeb Stuart had McClellan to himself. And the truth was, he preferred it so. Except for an encounter with a gunboat on the Pamunkey, three days ago — he reported with pride that he had repulsed it with a single howitzer, forcing the monster to close its ports and slink off, full-speed-astern; "What do you think of that?" he wrote his wife — outpost duty along the lower Chickahominy had kept his troopers out of the main channel of events during the past momentous week, affording them little chance for a share in the glory of driving the Yankees away from the gates of Richmond. All that was behind them at last, however, and now that they were back in the limelight — stage center, so to speak — their plumed commander intended to make the most of whatever opportunities came his way. Today there were few, the pursuit being mainly a matter of gathering up the stragglers and equipment which the blue host dribbled in its wake on the River road. Night fell before he found what he was seeking.

Next morning, though — July 3; the rain had slacked and stopped in the night; the day was bright and sunny — he came within sight of the answer to his prayers. The northern army had gone into camp beside the James, and Stuart, mounting a low ridge called Evelington Heights, looked down and saw the quarry spread out before him, close-packed and apparently ripe for destruction. McClellan had chosen the position with care. The creeks on his flanks, one of which curved along his front as well, and the gunboats anchored in his rear, their big guns trained across the meadows, gave him excellent protection from attack by infantry. But in failing to occupy Evelington Heights he had left his soldiers open to terrible punishment from the plunging fire of any guns the Confederates might bring up. Stuart saw this at once, and quickly got off a message informing Lee of the opportunity. Unwilling to wait, however, and with no regard for the long odds or concern for the consequences of alerting the Federals to the danger of leaving the dominant ridge unoccupied, he brought up the little howitzer that had peppered a gunboat into retreat four days ago, and at 9 o'clock opened fire on the bluecoats huddled on the mudflats down below.

The effect was instantaneous and spectacular, a moil of startled men and rearing horses thrown abruptly into milling consternation. Stuart was delighted. Informed by Lee that Longstreet, Jackson, and A. P. Hill were on the march to join him, he kept the little fieldpiece barking terrier-like to sustain the confusion until they arrived to compound it. But it was a case of too little too soon. Spotting the trouble at last, the Federals moved to get rid of it by advancing a six-gun battery and a regiment of infantry. Stuart held his position until he was down to his last two rounds, still hoping for the arrival of support. At 2 o'clock, with hostile guns approaching his front and infantry probing around his flanks, he fired his two last shells and pulled back off the ridge. He had done no appreciable damage, but he was pleased that he had found this chance to give McClellan one last prod. Moreover, he wrote home next day, "If the army had been up with me we would have finished his business."

As it was, however, the lead elements of Longstreet's division, moving in front of the other two, did not arrive until sunset, too late to undertake an attack even if the heights had still been naked of guns, which they were not; McClellan had been shown his mistake and had moved to rectify it. Next morning the ridge was crowned with batteries, supported by heavy columns of infantry. Hill and Jackson had come up by then, and Longstreet, who assumed command by seniority, put them in line for an all-out assault, holding his own division in reserve. Lee arrived to find Jackson protesting that his men were too weary and the heights too strong for the attack to be anything but a fiasco. After looking the situation over, Lee was obliged to agree regretfully with Stonewall; the assault was canceled, and the troops went into camp. The campaign was over.

Certain regiments were left on picket duty to observe the enemy, and one among them was stationed in a clump of woods overlooking an open field, beyond which there was another clump of woods where a Federal regiment was posted. All in all, the situation indicated a sudden renewal of bloodshed. This was the Fourth of July, however, and what was more the field was full of ripe blackberries; "so," as one rebel private later remembered, "our boys and the Yanks made a bargain not to fire at each other, and went out in the field, leaving one man on each post with the arms, and gathered berries together and talked over the fight, traded tobacco and coffee and exchanged newspapers as peacefully and kindly as if they had not been engaged for the last seven days in butchering one another."

CHAPTER
× **6** ×

The Sun Shines South

☆ ✄ ☆

⚐ NAPOLEON WAS TAKING THE WATERS AT Vichy when news of the Seven Days reached him in mid-July. Hard on its heels came John Slidell, with an offer of one hundred thousand bales of cotton if France would denounce the Federal blockade. Unable to act alone in the matter, however eager he might be to feed his country's looms, the Emperor — called "Napoleon the Little" to distinguish him from his illustrious uncle — promptly telegraphed his Foreign Minister: "Demandez au gouvernement anglais s'il ne croit pas le moment venu de reconnaître le Sud."

Across the channel the mills were hungry, too, and though Mason was somewhat handicapped by the impracticality of offering an Englishman anything so indelicate as a bribe, the time was propitious from the Confederate point of view. "There is an all but unanimous belief that you *cannot* subject the South to the Union," an influential partisan of Northern interests was informing a friend across the ocean. "I feel quite convinced that unless cotton comes in considerable quantities before the end of the year, the governments of Europe will be knocking at your door." Moreover, even as he wrote, a pro-Confederate member was introducing a motion before Parliament for British-French mediation in the American Civil War, which in effect amounted to recognition of the infant nation as a reward for throwing the blue invader off its doorstep. Fortunately, however — from the Federal point of view — the long vacation was under way, and before the issue could be forced the Cabinet was scattered from Scotland to Germany, in pursuit of grouse and relaxation. Action was deferred.

Distracting as these transatlantic dangers were, or might have been, the truth was Lincoln had more than enough material for full-time worry here at home. Hedged in by cares, blamed alike by critics right and left of the hostile center, he later said of the period under question: "I was as nearly inconsolable as I could be and live." In contrast to the adulation heaped on Davis, whose critics had been muzzled by the apparent vindication of his policies and whose countrymen now hailed him as a second Hezekiah, the northern leader heard himself likened unto Sennacherib, the author and director of a ponderous fiasco. Henry Ward Beecher was saying of him from a pulpit in Brooklyn, "Not a spark of genius has he; not an element for leadership. Not one particle of heroic enthusiasm." Wendell Phillips thought him something worse, and said so from a Boston lecture platform: "He may be honest — nobody cares whether the tortoise is honest or not. He has neither insight, nor prevision, nor decision.... As long as you keep the present turtle at the head of the government, you make a pit with one hand and fill it with the other."

The politicians were in full bay, particularly those of his own party who had been urging, without success, his support of antislavery legislation which he feared would lose him the border states, held to the Union so far by his promise that no such laws would be passed. It also seemed to these Republicans that entirely too many Democrats were seated in high places, specifically in the cabinet and the army; and now their anger was increased by apprehension. About to open their campaigns for reëlection in November, they had counted on battlefield victories to increase their prospects for victory at the polls. Instead, the main eastern army, under the Democrat McClellan — "McNapoleon," they called him — had held back, as if on purpose, and then retreated to the James, complaining within hearing of the voters that the Administration was to blame. Privately, many of the Jacobins agreed with the charge, though for different reasons, the main one being that Lincoln, irresolute by nature, had surrounded himself with weak-spined members of the opposition party. Fessenden of Maine put it plainest: "The simple truth is, there was never such a shambling half-and-half set of incapables collected in one government since the world began."

The people themselves were disconsolate. "Give me a victory and I will give you a poem," James Russell Lowell wrote his publisher; "but I am now clear down in the bottom of the well, where I see the Truth too near to make verses of." Apparently the people shared his gloom. Their present reaction was nothing like the short-lived panic they had staged five weeks ago, when Stonewall Jackson broke through to the line of the Potomac. Nor was it characterized by aroused determination, as in the period following Bull Run the year before. It was in fact strangely apathetic and difficult to measure, even for a man who had spent a lifetime with one hand on the public pulse, matching the tempo of his actions to its beat. Lincoln watched and wondered. One indication was the stock market, which broke badly under the impact of the news from the Peninsula; another was the premium on the gold in the Union dollar, which had stood at three and one-half percent a month ago, but since then had risen to seventeen. He watched and wondered, unable to catch the beat.

In response to McClellan's call for reinforcements on the day of Malvern Hill — "I need 50,000 more men, and with them I will retrieve our fortunes" — Lincoln told him: "Maintain your ground if you can, but save the army at all events, even if you fall back to Fort Monroe. We still have strength enough in the country, and will bring it out." Well, McClellan had "saved the army," and the "strength enough" was there; but Lincoln was uncertain as to how to "bring it out." The present apathy might be a lull before the storm that would be brought on by another call for troops. As he phrased it, "I would publicly appeal to the country for this new force were it not that I fear a general panic and stampede would follow, so hard is it to have a thing understood as it really is."

As usual, he found a way. To call for troops was one thing; to receive them was another. Seward was sent to New York to confer with men of political and financial power, explain the situation, and arrange for the northern governors to "urge" the President to issue a call for volunteers to follow up "the recent successes of the Federal arms." Lest there be any doubt as to whether the Administration intended to fight this war through to a finish, Seward took with him a letter: "I expect to maintain this contest until successful, or till I die, or am conquered, or my term expires, or Congress or the country forsake me.... Yours, very truly, A. Lincoln."

Seventeen governors, plus the president of the Military Board of Kentucky, responded promptly by affixing their signatures to a communication written by Seward, addressed to the Chief Executive, and saying in part: "We respectfully request, if it meets with your entire approval, that you at once call upon the several States for such number of men as may be required ... to garrison and hold all of the numerous cities and military positions that have been captured by our armies, and to speedily crush the rebellion that still exists in several of the Southern States, thus practically restoring to the civilized world our great and good Government." Being thus urged, Lincoln took his cue and in early July — "fully concurring in the wisdom of the views expressed to me in so patriotic a manner" — issued a call for 300,000 volunteers. In fact, so entirely did the request meet with his approval, he followed this first call with another, one month later, for 300,000 more.

Lowell, "clear down in the bottom of the well," had said he could produce no poem unless he received a victory as payment in advance; but lesser talents apparently required a lesser fee. J. S. Gibbons found in this second call a subject fit for his muse, and Stephen Foster set the result to music:

*If you look up all our valleys where the growing harvests shine
You may see our sturdy farmer boys fast forming into line,
And children from their mothers' knees are pulling at the weeds
And learning how to reap and sow against their country's needs,
And a farewell group stands weeping at every cottage door:
We are coming, Father Abraham, three hundred thousand more!*

Reinforcements would be welcome all along the line; there was scarcely a mile of it that did not have some general calling plaintively or angrily for more soldiers. But more soldiers, even half a million of them, would not solve the basic problem, which was one of high command. For four months now, ever since the abrupt relief of McClellan back in March, the overall conduct of the war had been directed by Lincoln and Stanton — a sort of two-headed, four-thumbed amateur — with results just short of disastrous in the theater which had received their main attention. Stonewall Jackson, for example, had frightened Stanton and decoyed Lincoln into breaking up the combinations McClellan had designed for taking Richmond: so that Davis and Lee, professionals both, had been able to turn the tables on the Army of the Potomac, effecting countercombinations that drove it headlong to the James. Part of the fault could be assigned to flaws that developed in subordinate commanders — on the one hand, Frémont's ineptness; on the other, McClellan's lack of aggressive instincts — but most of it lay with the overall direction, which had permitted the enemy to bring pressure on those flaws.

Lincoln could see this now in retrospect, much of it at any rate, and in fact he had begun to suspect it soon after the failure of his chessboard combinations in the Valley. In his distress, before the blow fell on the Peninsula, his mind turned back to Winfield Scott, the one general who had shown thus far that he really knew what war was all about. The old man was in retirement up the Hudson at West Point, too infirm for travel. So on June 23 — a Monday; the first of the Seven Days was two days off — Lincoln boarded a special train and rode north to see him. What they talked about was a secret, and it remained so. But when McClellan wired the War Department on June 27, while Porter was under attack on Turkey Hill: "I will beg that you put some one general in command of the Shenandoah and of all troops in front of Washington for the sake of the country. Secure unity of action and bring the best men forward," Lincoln, who had returned two days before, had already done what he suggested, even before his visit up the Hudson. That is, he had united the troops under one commander. Whether he had brought the best man forward remained to be seen.

John Pope was the man: Halleck had praised him so highly he had lost him. Indeed, for months now the news from that direction had seemed to indicate that the formula for victory, so elusive here on the seaboard, had been discovered by the generals in the West — in which case, as Lincoln and Stanton saw it, the thing to do was bring one of them East and give him a chance to apply it. Grant's record having been tarnished by Shiloh and the subsequent rumors of negligence and whiskey, Pope was the more or less obvious choice, not only because of Island Ten and Halleck's praise of his aggressiveness during the campaign against Corinth, but also because Lincoln, as a prairie lawyer pleading cases in Pope's father's district court, had known him back in Illinois. There were objections. Montgomery Blair, for instance, warned that old Judge Pope "was a flatterer, a deceiver, a liar and a trickster; all the Popes are so." But the President could not see that these were necessarily drawback characteristics in a military man. While admitting the general's "infirmity" when it came to walking the chalk-line of truth, he protested that "a liar might be brave and have skill as an officer." Also, perhaps as a result of a belief in the Westerner's ability to combine effectively the several family traits Blair had warned of, he credited him with "great cunning," a quality Lincoln had learned to prize highly as a result of his brush with Stonewall Jackson in the Valley. So Pope was sent for.

Arriving while Lincoln was up the country seeing Scott, he made at once an excellent impression on Stanton and the members of the Committee on the Conduct of the War, who saw in him the antithesis of McClellan. For one thing, there was nothing of caution about him; he was a talker, and his favorite words were "I" and "forward." (If he had been placed in charge of the West in the early spring, he said, nothing could have stopped his march on New Orleans; by now he would have split the South in two and gone to work on the crippled halves.) For another, he was sound on the slavery question, assuring the committee that he and it saw eye to eye on the matter. Wade and the others were delighted, not only with his opinions, civil as well as military, but also with his appearance, which they found as reassuring as his beliefs. He had shaved his cheeks and his upper lip, retaining a spade-shaped chin beard that bobbed and wagged decisively as he spoke, lending weight and point to his utterances and increasing the overall impression of forcefulness and vigor. Lincoln, when he returned from the visit with Scott, was pleased to see the confidence Pope had managed to invite within so brief a span, and gave him at once his orders and his assignment to the command of an army expressly created for his use.

The Army of Virginia, it was called. Its strength was 56,000 men and its mission was to move in general down the line of the Orange & Alexandria Railroad, just east of the Blue Ridge Mountains, so as to close in on the Confederate capital from the west and north, while McClellan's Army of the Potomac applied pressure from the east; thus Richmond would be crushed in a giant nutcracker, with Pope as the upper jaw. His army was created by consolidating the commands of McDowell, Banks, and Frémont. All three of these generals outranked him — an unusual arrangement, to say the least — but only one of them took official umbrage. This was Frémont: which solved another problem. His protest resignation was accepted, and Lincoln replaced him with Franz Sigel, whose appointment, though it involved a thousand-mile transfer, was considered especially felicitous since so many of the troops involved were of German extraction.

Pope's instructions, issued June 26 as part of the order creating his army, required him to operate so as to protect Washington from "danger or insult" and to "render the most effective aid to relieve General McClellan and capture Richmond." It was a large order, but Pope only laid down one condition: McClellan must be given peremptory orders to attack the minute he heard that Pope was engaged. This was necessary, Pope said, because of the known timidity and irresolution of his partner in the squeeze play.

For the present, however — as he learned all too soon — the stipulation was unnecessary. On the day the Army of Virginia came officially into being, McClellan no longer had any choice in the matter; the Seven Days had opened, and the Army of the Potomac found itself engaged in a tremendous struggle for survival, trying first to fend off Lee's assault down the north bank of the Chickahominy and then to reach the gunboat sanctuary of the James. When news of the attack reached Washington, Pope showed that there were elements of caution in his make-up after all. He advised Lincoln not to let McClellan fall back southward, since this would unhinge the jaws of the nutcracker, but to order him to retire in the direction of the York. That way, Pope said, he could eventually go to his assistance — and vice versa, in case the Army of Virginia ran into similar trouble moving south. But there was nothing Lincoln could do about it, even if he had wanted to; the wires were cut and the Army of the Potomac was already in motion for the James. Pope began to see the handwriting on the wall. It warned him plainly that there was an excellent chance that he would be entirely on his own as he moved down the road that led to Richmond.

Discouraging as this prospect was to the newly arrived commander, a look into the backgrounds of the three groups he was expected to weld into an effective striking force proved equally discouraging, if not more so. Two of the three (Banks' and Sigel's) had traditions of defeat, and the third (McDowell's) had slogged all over northern Virginia, seemingly without profit to anyone, least of all to itself. Unquestionably, even in their own eyes — "Milroy's weary boys" were a case in point — this was the second team, restricted to an occasional scrimmage which served primarily to emphasize its lack of style, while the first team got the cheers and glory on the Peninsula. For all his bluster, Pope saw one thing clearly. However second-rate his material might be in some respects, he had here the makings of a first-class disaster, unless he could somehow restore or establish confidence in the breasts of his down-

The Sun Shines South

hearted charges. Accordingly, as a first step before he took the field, he issued an address "To the Officers and Soldiers of the Army of Virginia," giving them, along with much else in the way of advice, a chance to see what manner of man was about to lead them against the rebel force that had just finished mauling the first team and flinging it back from the goal-post gates of Richmond.

"Let us understand each other," he told them. "I have come to you from the West, where we have always seen the backs of our enemies; from an army whose business it has been to seek the adversary and to beat him when he was found; whose policy has been attack and not defense.... I presume that I have been called here to pursue the same system and to lead you against the enemy. It is my purpose to do so, and that speedily." He supposed they longed for distinction in the jar and shock of battle, and he was prepared to show them how to win it. In any event, he said, "I desire you to dismiss from your minds certain phrases, which I am sorry to find so much in vogue amongst you. I hear constantly of 'taking strong positions and holding them,' of 'lines of retreat,' and of 'bases of supplies.' Let us discard such ideas. The strongest position a soldier should desire to occupy is one from which he can most easily advance against the enemy. Let us study the probable lines of retreat of our opponents, and leave our own to take care of themselves. Let us look before us, and not behind. Success and glory are in the advance, disaster and shame lurk in the rear."

The words had a Stantonian ring, which Pope explained long afterwards by identifying the Secretary himself as their author. At any rate, whoever wrote them, the effect was something other than the one that had been intended: particularly among the men the undersigned general addressed. They found the comparison odious, and they resented the boasting tone in which it was made. "Five Cent Pope," they dubbed their new commander, while old-time regulars recalled a parody that had made the army rounds some years ago, when he issued oversanguine reports of success in boring for artesian water on the bone-dry plains of Texas:

> *Pope told a flattering tale*
> *Which proved to be bravado*
> *About the streams which spout like ale*
> *On the Llano Estacado.*

McClellan's supporters of course resented him, too: Fitz-John Porter for example, who declared that Pope had "written himself down [as] what the military world has long known, an ass.... If the theory he proclaims is practiced you may look for disaster."

Beyond the lines, where the address enjoyed wide circulation, the Confederate reaction combined contempt and amusement. Reports that this new spread-eagle opponent was heading his dispatches "Headquarters in the Saddle" prompted a revival of the old army jibe that he had his headquarters where his hindquarters ought to be.

By the time Pope's flamboyant address was issued in mid-July, Lincoln had been down to the Peninsula and back. Between the two boat-rides, going and coming, he not only made a personal inspection of the Army of the Potomac and questioned its chief and subordinate generals, but he also made up his mind about a matter he had been pondering ever since his visit to Winfield Scott three weeks ago — a command decision, involving this and all the other armies of the Union.

Within two days of his July 1 plea for 50,000 men, with which to "retrieve our fortunes" after the blood-letting of the Seven Days, McClellan doubled the ante; 100,000 would now be needed, he declared. Lincoln replied on the 4th that any such figure "within a month, or even six weeks, is impossible.... Under these circumstances the defensive for the present must be your only care. Save the army — first, where you are, if you can; secondly, by removal, if you must." He added, perhaps ironically: "P.S. If at any time you feel able to take the offensive, you are not restrained from doing so." Once more he was losing patience fast. Sending troops to McClellan, he said, was like trying to shovel fleas across a barnlot; so few seemed to get there. Also, there were alarming rumors as to the condition of the men the general already had. Lincoln decided to see for himself. Boarding a steamer on the night of July 7, he reached Harrison's Landing late the following afternoon and rode out at once with the army commander for a sundown inspection of the camps.

Apparently to his surprise he found the men in good condition and high spirits — though the latter could be accounted for, at least in part, as a reaction to seeing the President on horseback. For one thing, an observer wrote home, there was the imminent danger that his long legs "would become entangled with those of the horse... and both come down together." Occupied as he was in the attempt to control his mount, which seemed equally nervous, he had trouble tipping his tall hat in response to cheers that were redoubled when the difficulty was seen. "That arm with which he drew the rein, in its angles and position resembled the hind leg of a grasshopper — the hand before, the elbow away back over the horse's tail.... But the boys liked him," the soldier-observer added. "In fact his popularity with the army is and has been universal. Most of our rulers and leaders fall into odium, but all have faith in Lincoln. 'When he finds out,' they say, 'it will be stopped.'... God bless the man and give answer to the prayers for guidance I am sure he offers."

If guidance was what he was seeking he could find it right there alongside him, astride Dan Webster. Less than three weeks ago McClellan had requested permission to present his views on the state of military affairs throughout the country; Lincoln had replied that he would be glad to have them — preferably in a letter, he said — if their presentation would not divert too much of the general's time and attention from his immediate duties. So tonight, when they returned to headquarters, McClellan handed the President a letter "covering the whole ground of our national trouble" and setting forth the conditions under which he believed the struggle could be won.

The rebellion, he said, had now "assumed the character of a war," and "as such ... it should be conducted upon the highest principles known to Christian civilization. It should not be a war looking to the subjugation of the people of any State in any event. It should not be at all a war upon population, but against armed forces and political organizations. Neither confiscation of property, political executions of persons, territorial organization of States, or forcible abolition of slavery should be contemplated for a moment." This last was a point he emphasized, since "a declaration of radical views" in this direction would "rapidly disintegrate our present armies." More strictly within the military province, he advised concentration as the guiding rule. "The national force should not be dispersed in expeditions, posts of occupation, and numerous armies, but should be mainly collected into masses, and brought to bear upon the armies of the Confederate States. Those armies thoroughly defeated, the political structure which they support would soon cease to exist," and the southern people, unembittered by depredations, would turn against the willful men who had misled them out of the Union and sue at once for peace and reëntry. So he saw it. However, no matter what "system of policy" was adopted, he strongly urged the appointment of a general-in-chief, "one who possesses your confidence, understands your views, and who is competent to execute your orders." He did not ask that post for himself, he said; but he made it clear that he would not decline the reappointment, since he was "willing to serve you in such position as you may assign me," including this one. In closing he added a final explanation and disclaimer: "I may be on the brink of eternity, and as I hope forgiveness from my Maker I have written this letter with sincerity toward you and from love for my country."

Lincoln took it and read it through, with McClellan standing by. "All right," he said, and put it in his pocket. That was all. Apparently he had not come down here in search of guidance.

What he had come for, it developed, was a look at the present condition of the army and some specific answers to a specific question which he put the following day to the five corps commanders: "If it were desired to get the army away from here, could it be safely effected?" Keyes and Franklin replied that it could and should be done. The other three thought otherwise. "It would be ruinous to the country," Heintzelman said; "We give up the cause if we do it," Sumner said;

"Move the army and ruin the country," Porter said. Once the questioning was over, Lincoln and the generals took a glass of wine together and the President got ready to go back to Washington.

McClellan was upset: particularly by the evidence that the Administration might order him to evacuate the Peninsula. After seeing Lincoln off next morning, he wrote his wife that he feared the President had some "paltry trick" up his sleeve; his manner, he said, "seemed that of a man about to do something of which he was ashamed." For a week the general brooded and delivered himself of judgments. Lincoln was "an old stick, and of pretty poor timber at that," while Stanton was "the most unmitigated scoundrel I ever knew, heard, or read of." He believed he saw which way the wind was blowing: "Their game seems to be to withhold reinforcements, and then to relieve me for not advancing, well knowing that I have not the means to do so." Accordingly, in mid-July he wrote to his friend William H. Aspinwall, asking the New York transportation tycoon to be on the lookout for a job for him.

Lincoln meanwhile had made up his mind to act on the command decision which he had been considering for weeks. All through the previous autumn, old General Scott had held out in Washington for as long as he could, putting up with McClellan's snubs and digs for the sake of Halleck, who was on his way from California. It was Scott's hope that Old Brains would be there to take his place when he retired as general-in-chief. But the way was long and the digs were sharp; the old man gave up before Halleck got there, and McClellan got the job. Since then, the contrast in accomplishments East and West seemed to reinforce Scott's original opinion, which he repeated when the President came to West Point on the eve of the Seven Days. Lincoln saw merit in the recommendation, but he thought he would have a talk with Halleck before he acted on it. Back in Washington in time for the outbreak of the Seven Days, he wired the western commander: "Please tell me, could you make me a flying visit for a consultation without endangering the service in your department?"

Halleck did not want to come, and said so. Even if he did, he added, "I could advise but one thing: to place all the [eastern] forces ... under one head, and hold that head responsible."

Refusal was always provocative for Lincoln; in the course of the war, several men were to learn that the surest way to get something from him was to pretend they did not want it. He almost made up his mind, then and there. Down on the Peninsula, however, the matter was more or less cinched by McClellan himself. His Harrison's Landing letter, an exegesis of the conservative position, was the strongest possible proof that its author was not the kind of man to fight the kind of war Lincoln was rapidly coming to believe the country was going to have to fight if it was going to win. Returning to Washington on the night of July 10, he had Stanton send a wire to Corinth next morning, which left the recipient no choice in the matter: "*Ordered*, that Maj. Gen. Henry W. Halleck be assigned to command the whole land forces of the United States as General-in-Chief, and that he repair to this capital as soon as he can with safety to the positions and operations within the department under his charge."

There were delays; Halleck did not arrive for nearly two weeks, being occupied with the incidentals of transferring his command. The delay was hard on Lincoln; "I am very anxious — almost impatient — to have you here," he wired. Down on the Peninsula, McClellan was spared for nine days the shock of hearing that his old post had gone to a rival. Then he read of it in a newspaper. "In all these things," he wrote his wife, "the President and those around him have acted so as to make the matter as offensive as possible. He has not shown the slightest gentlemanly or friendly feeling, and I cannot regard him as in any respect my friend. I am confident that he would relieve me tomorrow if he dared to do so. His cowardice alone prevents it. I can never regard him with other feelings than those of contempt."

★ ★ ★

This was going to be a harder war from here on out, and Lincoln knew it. He knew it because he was going to make it so. In fact, he was going to make it just as hard as he had to, and he said as much quite frankly to anyone who asked him. Most particularly, despite conflicting advice from McClellan and men like him, it was going to be harder on civilians. Of the four actions which the general had said "should [not] be contemplated for a moment" — 1) confiscation of property, 2) political execution of persons, 3) territorial organization of states, and 4) forcible abolition of slavery — the first and second had already been carried out with governmental sanction, the third was in the legislative works, and the fourth was under urgent consideration.

The second of these was the most obviously harsh, and for that reason should be the most obviously effective in securing obedience to occupation rule. So Benjamin Butler reasoned, at any rate, when he reached New Orleans and found that the national ensign, prematurely raised over the Mint, had been ripped from its staff by the mob. "They have insulted our flag — torn it down with indignity," he notified the War Department. "This outrage will be punished in such manner as in my judgment will caution both the perpetrators and abettors of the act, so that they shall fear the stripes if they do not reverence the stars in our banner." As good as his word, Butler found a man still wearing a tatter of the outraged bunting in his buttonhole, brought him before a drumhead court, and carried out the resultant sentence by hanging him in public from a window of the building where the crime had been committed.

It worked about as well as he had expected. The sight of one man dangling by his neck from the eaves of the Mint sobered the others considerably. Fear, not reverence, was what Butler had wanted, and he got it — at least from the men. The women were another matter. In them he saw no signs of fear, and certainly none of reverence. In fact, they missed no chance to show their contempt for the blue-clad invaders. Passing them on the street, they drew their skirts aside to escape contamination, or else they walked straight ahead, taking their half of the sidewalk out of the middle, and forced oncoming Yankees to step off into the mud. The climax came when one of them, taking careful aim from an upstairs window, emptied a slopjar onto the head of Farragut himself. Butler retaliated with a general order, directing "that hereafter when any female shall, by word, gesture or movement, insult or show contempt for any officer or soldier of the United States, she shall be regarded and held liable to be treated as a woman of the town plying her avocation."

At home and abroad, the reaction was uproarious. Beauregard made Butler's order the subject of one of his own: "Men of the South! shall our mothers, our wives, our daughters and our sisters be thus outraged by the ruffianly soldiers of the North, to whom is given the right to treat, at their pleasure, the ladies of the South as common harlots? Arouse, friends, and drive back from our soil those infamous invaders of our homes and disturbers of our family ties!" Overseas, Lord Palmerston remarked: "Any Englishman must blush to think that such an act has been committed by one belonging to the Anglo-Saxon race." In Richmond, before the year was out, Davis branded Butler a felon, an outlaw, an enemy of mankind, and ordered that in the event of his capture "the officer in command of the capturing force do cause him to be immediately executed by hanging."

Southerners and their blushful friends abroad were not the only ones offended by the cock-eyed general's zeal. Pro-Union men of the region he controlled found that they too came under his strictures, particularly in economic matters such as the seizure of cotton and the freezing of foreign funds, and they were equally vociferous in protest. But Lincoln had little use or sympathy for them. If these riders on the ship of state thought they were "to touch neither a sail nor a pump, but to be merely passengers — deadheads at that — to be carried snug and dry throughout the storm, and safely landed right side up," they were mistaken. He gave them a midsummer warning that the voyage was about to get rougher.

"The true remedy," he said, switching metaphors, "does not lie in rounding the rough angles of the war, but in removing the necessity for war." This they could accomplish, he replied to one protestant, by bringing Louisiana back into the Union. Otherwise, "it is for them to consider whether it is probable I will surrender the government to save them from losing all. If they decline what I suggest, you scarcely need to ask what I will do. What would you do in my position? Would you drop the war where it is? Or would you prosecute it in future with elder-stalk squirts charged with rosewater? Would you deal lighter blows rather than heavier ones? Would you give up the contest, leaving any available means unapplied?" The questions were rhetorical, and he closed by answering them: "I am in no boastful mood. I shall do no more than I can, and I shall do all I can, to save the government, which is my sworn duty as well as my personal inclination. I shall do nothing in malice. What I deal with is too vast for malicious dealing."

Already he had sent an official observer, a Maryland senator, down to New Orleans to look into the situation. But when the senator reported that there was indeed much harshness and irregularity (Butler's brother was getting rich on confiscated cotton, and the general himself had been given the nickname "Spoons," implying considerable deftness in the execution of his duties) as well as much disturbance of the master-slave relationship by the enlistment of Negroes in labor battalions, Lincoln was even more forthright in his statement of conditions and intentions: "The people of Louisiana — all intelligent people everywhere — know full well that I never had a wish to touch the foundations of their society or any right of theirs. With perfect knowledge of this they forced a necessity upon me to send armies among them, and it is their own fault, not mine, that they are annoyed." Here again the remedy was reëntry into the Union. "And might it not be well for them to consider whether they have not already had time enough to do this? If they can conceive of anything worse ... within my power, would they not better be looking out for it? .... I am a patient man, always willing to forgive on the Christian terms of repentance. Still, I must save this Government if possible. What I cannot do, of course, I will not do; but it may as well be understood, once for all, that I shall not surrender this game leaving any available card unplayed."

The unplayed card was emancipation. Mindful, so far, of his inaugural statement: "I have no purpose, directly or indirectly, to interfere with the institution of slavery in the states where it exists. I believe I have no lawful right to do so, and I have no inclination to do so," Lincoln had resisted all efforts to persuade him to repudiate his words. He resisted mainly on practical grounds, considering the probable reaction in the border states; "We should lose more than we should gain," he told one Jacobin delegation. Not only had he refused to issue such a proclamation as they were urging on him, he had revoked three separate pronouncements or proclamations issued by subordinates: one by Frémont, one by Cameron, and recently a third by Hunter in South Carolina. In the instance of the latter revocation, however, he had shown which way his mind was turning in mid-May: "Whether it be competent for me, as Commander in Chief of the army and navy, to declare the slaves of any state or states free, and whether, at any time, in any case, it shall have become a necessity indispensable to the maintenance of the government to exercise such supposed power, are questions which, under my responsibility, I reserve to myself."

This was putting a new face on the matter. What a President had no right or inclination to do in peacetime, Lincoln was saying, might become an indispensable necessity for a wartime Commander in Chief. Besides, he had done some ciphering back in March, and had come up with a simple dollars-and-cents solution to the problem. Figuring the cost of the war at two million dollars a day, and the cost of slaves at four hundred dollars a head, he had found the value of Delaware's 1798 slaves to be less than the cost of half a day of fighting. Extending his computations on this basis, he found that the total value of the 432,622 slaves in the District of Columbia and the four border states — Delaware, Maryland, Kentucky, Missouri — amounted to less than the cost of three months of warfare. Accordingly, he laid these figures before Congress in support of a resolution proposing compensated emancipation. In early April it was adopted, despite the objections of abolitionists who considered it highly immoral to traffic thus in souls; but nothing practical came of it, because the slave-state legislatures would not avail themselves of the offer. Lincoln was saddened by this failure, and on revoking Hunter's proclamation the following month addressed a special plea to the people of the border region: "I do not argue — I beseech you to make arguments for yourselves. You cannot, if you would, be blind to the signs of the times. I beg of you a calm and enlarged consideration of them, ranging, if it may be, far above personal and partisan politics. This proposal makes common cause for a common object, casting no reproaches upon any. It acts not the Pharisee. The change it contemplates would come gently as the dews of heaven, not rending or wrecking anything. Will you not embrace it? So much good has not been done, by one effort, in all past time, as in the providence of God it is now your high privilege to do. May the vast future not have to lament that you have neglected it."

The signs of the times were indeed plain to read; they had in fact the glistening clarity of wet paint, most of them having been posted about the legislative landscape during the current session of Congress. In March, subscribing to the opinion that the Dred Scott decision did not constitute law, the members fulfilled a Republican campaign promise by passing an act prohibiting slavery in all present or future national territories. The following month, the "peculiar institution" was abolished in the District of Columbia, with compensation for the owners and provisions for colonization of the freedmen, which Lincoln considered the best practical solution to the problem. "There has never been in my mind any question upon the subject," he declared as he signed the bill, "except the one of expediency, arising in view of all the circumstances." In May, the United States and Britain agreed by treaty to coöperate in suppressing the slave trade: a diplomatic move that gave much pleasure to the Jacobins, whom Lincoln had been at pains to please whenever he could. For their sake he had proposed that the country give formal recognition to the Negro republics of Haiti and Liberia, which Congress gladly did, and back in February — despite the known leniency of his nature in such matters — he sustained the sentence of execution brought against Nathaniel Gordon of Portland, Maine, the first and only slave trader ever hanged in accordance with Federal law.

Gratifying as all this was, including the hanging, the Jacobins were by no means satisfied. They wanted more, much more, and they never stopped letting Lincoln know it. "The pressure in this direction is still upon me and increasing," he said on July 12 when he called twenty border-state congressmen into his office for a final appeal before next week's adjournment sent them scattering for their homes. He spoke of the continuing attempts by the seceded states to persuade their sister slave communities farther north to join them in revolt — attempts which, incidentally, if successful would deprive these representatives of their jobs. The pull was strong, Lincoln admitted, and he wanted these men to help him weaken it. "You and I know what the lever of their power is. Break that lever before their faces and they can shake you no more forever." Besides, he said, slavery was failing fast already. "If the war continues long ... the institution in your states will be extinguished by mere friction and abrasion.... How much better for you and for your people to take the step which at once shortens the war and secures substantial compensation for that which is sure to be wholly lost in any other event."

They heard him out, and then they shook their heads. The adopted resolution not only seemed to them a violation of State Rights, but they also questioned the constitutional power of Congress to appropriate funds for such a purpose. What was more, they doubted the sincerity of their fellow congressmen; the offer, one of the callers said, "was but the enunciation of a sentiment which could not or was not likely to be reduced to an actual tangible proposition." If Congress really meant it, let the money be put in the President's hands, and then they would consider acceptance. Then too — though this objection went unspoken — the plan entailed payment in government bonds, and though slave property was admittedly precarious and declining fast in value, the national credit was declining even faster. In short, they wanted no part of the offer as things now stood. Respectfully they bowed and took their leave, and Lincoln was left saddened and alone.

Left alone, he would act alone. He knew well enough the arguments against what McClellan, four days before, had called "a declaration of radical views" on the slavery issue: possible loss of the border states, possible loss of large segments of the army through desertion, possible loss of the fall elections. He knew, too, of currents that ran deeper — of Archbishop John Hughes of New York, for example, who had warned in a widely reprinted official declaration: "We, Catholics, and a vast majority of our brave troops in the field, have not the slightest idea of carrying on a war that costs so much blood and treasure just to gratify a clique of Abolitionists in the North." A Westerner, Lincoln knew the rabid division on the subject in the West, where candidates were tagged "charcoal" and "snowflake" in anger and derision, regardless of party. Such considerations, the concrete along with the nebulous, had weight. But he also knew the arguments in favor of positive action. First, it would allay the danger of foreign intervention by engaging the sympathy and arousing the enthusiasm of the rank and file of Europe, against which not even the most avid of the pro-Confederate rulers and ministers would dare to act. Second, whatever it did to the Democrats here at home, it would heal the split in his own party, which was rapidly getting out of hand.

Beyond if not above all these, and entirely aside from his promises to those who claimed to have removed themselves from his authority, there was the question of personal ethics, of whether the considered step was consonant with honor. He had called the nation to arms in support of a single issue, the preservation of the Union; could he now adopt a second — superimpose it, so to speak — without being guilty of chicanery or worse? He believed he could, and he based his persuasion on necessity. "Things had gone on from bad to worse," he later explained, "until I felt that we had reached the end of our rope on the plan of operations we had been pursuing; that we had about played our last card, and must change our tactics or lose the game." The truth was, the war had already outlasted the heady burst of enthusiasm that had flared up after Sumter. What was needed was a new cause, not to supplant, but to supplement the old; and this was it. Having appealed at the outset to reason, he now would appeal to conscience. He would translate the conflict into the terms of a holy war — a crusade — for which Julia Ward Howe had already composed the anthem:

> *In the beauty of the lilies Christ was born across the sea...*
> *As he died to make men holy, let us die to make men free,*
>   *While God is marching on.*

Before the night was over, though the details were still to be worked out, he had completed his decision. He would do it. And next afternoon — much to their surprise, since always before, as one of them said, "he had been prompt and emphatic in denouncing any interference by the general government with the subject" — he spoke of it to two members of his cabinet.

The occasion was a funeral; the Stantons had lost a new-born child, and Lincoln rode to the burial in a carriage with Welles and Seward. According to Welles, the President "dwelt earnestly on the gravity, importance, and delicacy" of the slavery question and the advisability of issuing an emancipation proclamation "in case the rebels did not cease to persist in their war on the government ... of which he saw no evidence." He said he "had about come to the conclusion that it was a military necessity absolutely essential for the salvation of the Union, that we must free the slaves or be ourselves subdued." Asked for their opinions on the matter, both men were at first too taken aback by what Welles called "this new departure" to say anything at all. Seward, recovering first, replied that "his present opinion inclined to the measure as justifiable," but he would rather think the matter through before giving a final answer. Welles said he felt the same way about it. Lincoln let it go at that, though he made it clear that he was "earnest in the conviction that something must be done."

Four days later, July 17, Congress came very close to stealing his thunder. In August of the previous year, this body had passed a Confiscation Act endorsing Butler's contention that the slaves of disloyal masters were "contraband," liable to seizure and eligible for freedom on entering Union lines. Now, in the final hours before adjournment of the current session, a second such Act was passed. Considerably sharper-toothed than the one that had gone before, it provided "That every person who shall hereafter commit the crime of treason against the United States, and shall be adjudged guilty thereof, shall suffer death, and all his slaves, if any, shall be declared and made free." Discretion was left to the courts as to whether a prison term and/or a fine should be substituted in lieu of the death penalty, but no leeway was allowed as to the disposition of a traitor's slaves, who were automatically freed upon his conviction. At first glance, with nearly the whole slave region in rebellion, this appeared to be the very proclamation Lincoln was considering. However, closer reading showed it to be no such thing. No slave was to be freed by it until his master had been convicted of treason in a federal court. There was the rub. Secession — or rebellion, as the Jacobins preferred to call it — might be treason, but no court had ever said so (or ever would say so) no matter what opinion the radicals had on the matter. All the Acts really did was provide a sanctuary for such slaves as crossed the Federal lines: with the result that the U.S. government became, in effect, the greatest slaveholder the world had ever known, not excepting the Pharaohs of Egypt.

Lincoln doubted the legality of the Act; "It is startling to say that Congress can free a slave within a State," he declared in a veto message which he had prepared against its passage. All the same, he signed it as soon as it reached his desk; but in doing so he forwarded the proposed veto message in order to make his objections part of the record when the legislation was tested in the courts. Read in both houses as a prelude to adjournment, the message was greeted with sneers and laughter by the radicals, who took it as an admission that when the chips were down he did not dare to oppose them with anything but words.

In this they were much mistaken, though words were very much a part of what he had in mind. On July 22, to the surprise of all but Welles and Seward, who had been prepared for something of the sort by his remarks in the funeral carriage nine days back, he read to the assembled cabinet an emancipation proclamation which he proposed to issue without delay. Unlike the Confiscation Act, which required that individuals be convicted of treason before their slaves were freed, Lincoln's edict left no burden of proof upon the government. He intended it as a military pronouncement, designed to help win the war, and that was all. He was not concerned with "legality," as such, since he did not deal with individuals as such; all he required was that they live within an area where the authorities, after a specified date, continued to defy the federal government. The object of the war, he repeated, was the preservation of the Union; "And as a fit and necessary military measure for effecting this object, I, as Commander in Chief of the Army and Navy of the United States, do order and declare that on the first day of January, in the year of our Lord one thousand eight hundred and sixty-three, all persons held as slaves within any State or States wherein the constituted authority of the United States shall not then be practically recognized, submitted to, and maintained, shall then, thenceforward, and forever be free."

Reactions varied. Chase and Stanton approved, but wanted it stronger; Bates wanted it as it was; Welles wanted it weaker; Blair and Smith did not want it at all, or at least not before the fall elections. Then Seward spoke, having turned the matter over in his mind. "Mr President," he said, "I approve of the proclamation, but I question the expediency of its issue at this juncture. The depression of the public mind, consequent upon our repeated reverses, is so great that I fear the effect of so important a step. It may be viewed as the last measure of an exhausted government, a cry for help; the government stretching forth its hands to Ethiopia, instead of Ethiopia stretching forth her hands to the government. It will be considered our last *shriek* on the retreat. Now, while I approve the measure, I suggest, sir, that you postpone its issue until you can give it to the country supported by military success, instead of issuing it, as would be the case now, upon the greatest disasters of the war."

Lincoln had not considered this aspect of the question, but now that he did so, he perceived its wisdom and acted in accord with Seward's view. "I put the draft of the proclamation aside," he later told an artist friend, "as you do your sketch for a picture, waiting for a victory." Halleck, the man he counted on to give him one, was on the way at last: would arrive, in fact, tomorrow. Meanwhile, this thunderbolt would keep.

✗ 2 ✗

There was gloom in the West as in the East, but it was of a different nature, proceeding from different causes. Here too the advance had stalled; yet it was precisely in this apparent similarity that the difference obtained. McClellan had been stopped by Lee, but Halleck stopped himself. Curiously enough, or perhaps not curiously at all, the men on the Peninsula who had fought and fallen back, fighting as they went, had developed a fierce pride that burned brighter at the end of their retreat than it had ever burned before; they had fought well and they knew it; whereas Halleck's soldiers felt less elation at the end of their burrowing advance than at the start, not having fought at all. That was the source of a different kind of gloom.

Sherman did not share it, still being happy with the new stars on his shoulders and the sense of having "found" himself in the ordeal of Shiloh. But when he called by army headquarters not long after the fall of Corinth, he heard something that caused him to suspect that his friend Grant was in lower spirits than ever. Halleck happened to remark that Grant had applied for a thirty-day leave; he was going away next morning. Halleck said he did not know why, but Sherman took it to mean that Grant, "chafing under the slights," intended this as a first step in submitting his resignation. Determined to stop him if he could, Sherman rode over and found him sitting in his tent, sorting some letters and tying them into bundles with red tape. Grant said it was true that he was leaving, and when the red-headed general asked him why, he replied: "Sherman, you know. You know I am in the way here. I have stood it as long as I can, and can endure it no longer."

Where was he going? "St Louis," Grant said. Did he have any business there? "Not a bit," Grant said. So Sherman, being then in what he called "high feather," began to argue with him, illustrating Grant's case with his own. Look at him, he said. They had called him crazy as a loon, but he had hung on through Shiloh, and "that single battle had given me new life." Besides, if Grant went away, "events would go right along, and he would be left out; whereas, if he remained, some happy accident might restore him to favor and his true place." This had its effect; Grant promised to wait, or at any rate not to leave without seeing Sherman again or sending him word. Satisfied, Sherman left, and before the week was out received a note from Grant. He had reconsidered; he would stay. Sherman replied that he was glad to hear it; "for you could not be quiet at home for a week when armies were moving."

Armies were moving now, though not in the direction of the Confederates who had fallen back before them. Like a man riding an oversized mettlesome horse, which he feared might take the bit in its teeth and bolt off with him any minute, Halleck kept as close a rein as possible on his 120,000-man army. Even so, the advance had already covered more ground than he had intended. Once he had accomplished what he set out for — in particular, control of a sizeable stretch of the Memphis & Charleston Railroad — he was more than ready to call a halt and consolidate his gains. Four days after the occupation of Corinth, he warned the commander of the pursuit against goading the rebels into rashness. All he wanted, he said, was for them to fall back far enough to be beyond reach of the railroad. And he added: "There is no object in bringing on a battle if this object can be obtained without one. I think by showing a bold front for a day or two the enemy will continue his retreat, which is all that I desire."

Having withheld his army from pursuit, he now proceeded to dismember it. Eastward, westward, even northward he dispersed it: every way, in fact, but southward. On June 9 he instructed Pope — who presently was on his way to Washington, superseded by Rosecrans — to draw back closer to Corinth and take up outpost positions to defend it. And that same day the scattering began: a scattering that divided the Grand Army into four main parts, rather as if the aforementioned timid rider had decided not only to get rid of his mettlesome horse, but to do so by having it drawn and quartered. Buell was ordered east with four divisions to make connection with Ormsby Mitchel, who had encountered so much difficulty in North Alabama; his goal was Chattanooga, which would put him within possible reach of Knoxville or Atlanta. Sherman was sent west; he would garrison Memphis with two divisions, repairing the railroad on the way and doing what he could to restore the wrecked economy by "assur[ing] all country people that they will be permitted to take their cotton freely to market and that the ordinary channels of trade will be immediately reopened." McClernand, with a similar force, was given a similar mission, except that his destination lay fifty miles north at Jackson, Tennessee; he too was to repair the lines of supply and give the "country people" whatever assurance was needed to make them happy. Halleck himself would remain with the force at Corinth, coördinating the efforts of the other three.

His main concern in ordering the dispersal, he told Stanton, was the "sanitary condition" of the men. At present it was good, he said, but the question arose: "Can it be kept so during the summer?" He thought it could, provided he steered clear of a southward advance; for "if we follow the enemy into the swamps of Mississippi there can be no doubt that the army will be disabled by disease." (At least one of the general's wool-clad soldiers agreed with him. After being exposed to what Halleck was now avoiding, an Indiana veteran declared: "You load a man down with a sixty-pound knapsack, his gun and forty rounds of ammunition, a haversack full of hardtack and sow belly, and a three-pint canteen full of water, then start him along this narrow roadway with the mercury up to 100 and the dust so thick you could taste it, and you have done the next thing to killing this man outright.") "And yet," Halleck wrote, "to lie still, doing nothing, will not be satisfactory to the country nor conducive to the health of the army." He had therefore "deemed it best" to do as he had done. There was one drawback, one calculated risk: "This plan is based on the supposition that the enemy will not attempt an active campaign during the summer months. Should he do so ... the present dispositions must be varied to suit the change of circumstances."

One immediate result the shake-up had. George Thomas returned to his old division, which was stationed under Halleck's eye at Corinth, and Grant was restored to the command of his old Army of the Tennessee, which included the divisions under Sherman and McClernand. Receiving permission to establish headquarters at Memphis, he set out on June 21 with a dozen troopers as escort, and after narrowly escaping capture on the way — Confederate horsemen, tipped off that he was coming, missed intercepting him by less than an hour — arrived three days later to find affairs "in rather bad order, secessionists governing much in their own way." He reported that there was even a plot to burn the city, which he thought might "prove partially successful," though he believed that such an action would "operate more against the rebels than ourselves." The main thing he needed, he told Halleck, was more troops.

Old Brains was in no mood just now to give him anything but trouble. By the end of June they had renewed their old-time wrangle. Halleck began it, wiring: "You say 30,000 men are at Shelbyville to attack La Grange. Where is Shelbyville? I can't find it on any map. Don't believe a word about an attack in large force on La Grange or Memphis. Why not send out a strong reconnaissance and ascertain the *facts*? It looks very much like a mere stampede. Floating rumors must never be received as facts.... I mean to make somebody responsible for so gross a negligence." Grant replied: "I did not say 30,000 troops at Shelbyville, but at Abbeville, which is south of Holly Springs, on the road to Grenada." Then he too got his back up. "I heed as little of floating rumors about this city as anyone," he protested. He had asked for more troops, he said, "that I might do effectively what you now ask. Stampeding is not my weakness. On the contrary, I will always execute any order to the best of my ability with the means at hand."

Halleck drew in his horns at this, replying four days later: "I made no insinuation that there had been the slightest neglect on your part.... Nor did I suppose for a moment that you were stampeded; for I know that is not in your nature." Then — as if he had leaned down to stroke Old Rover, only to have Old Rover snap at his hand — he added: "I must confess that I was very much surprised at the tone of your dispatch and the ill-feeling manifested in it, so contrary to your usual style, and especially toward one who has so often befriended you when you were attacked by others."

This was more or less the note on which the other hassle had ended, four months back; Grant was willing to let it go at that. But five days later, July 8, Halleck was at him again: "The Cincinnati *Gazette* contains the substance of your demanding reinforcements and my refusing them. You either have a newspaper correspondent on your staff or your staff is very leaky." Three days later, the Memphis telegraph receiver clacked off a blunt one dozen words from Corinth: "You will immediately repair to this place and report to these headquarters."

Just what have I done now? Grant must have thought. It was not his way to worry, but he apparently had cause. For the past two weeks — and, indeed, before — Halleck had shown all the earmarks of a commander engaged in the old army game of needling an unwanted subordinate enough to keep him edgy and fatten the record against him, but of holding back from the big pounce until something downright ruinous turned up to head the list of charges and specifications. Whether his sin was one of omission or commission, Grant did not know, though he had three full days for wondering while his horse retraced the steps taken three weeks ago with its head in the opposite direction. At last, July 15, the worried general reached Corinth and was face to face with his tormentor. What he was confronted with, however, was not the climax to a series of well-organized reproaches, but rather the accomplishment of the "happy accident" Sherman had persuaded him to wait for. Halleck was ordered to Washington to take over the direction of all the armies, East and West, and Grant was to receive, by seniority, the lion's share of what he left behind. Specifically, this included command of two armies — his own, now under McClernand and Sherman, and Pope's, now under Rosecrans — and of the department embracing North Mississippi, West Tennessee, and Kentucky west of the Cumberland River.

He had what he wanted, but not as he preferred it. The fact was, he disapproved of nearly all that had been done since Halleck's arrival from St Louis, later saying: "For myself I am satisfied Corinth could have been captured in a two days' campaign commenced promptly on the arrival of reinforcements after the battle of Shiloh." Most of all he disapproved of what had been done, or left undone, since Beauregard's sly evacuation of Corinth. With the Mississippi in Union hands, northward above Baton Rouge and southward below Memphis, "the Confederates at the west were narrowed down for all communication with Richmond to the single line of road running east from Vicksburg." That was the true goal now: that city, that stretch of river, that railroad. "To dispossess them of this... would be equal to the amputation of a limb in its weakening effects." As he saw it, "after the capture of Corinth a moveable force of 80,000 men, besides enough to hold all the territory acquired, could have been set in motion for the accomplishment of [this] great campaign for the suppression of the rebellion." Thus Grant, by hindsight. But Halleck could not see it, or else he feared to undertake it, and "the work of depletion commenced."

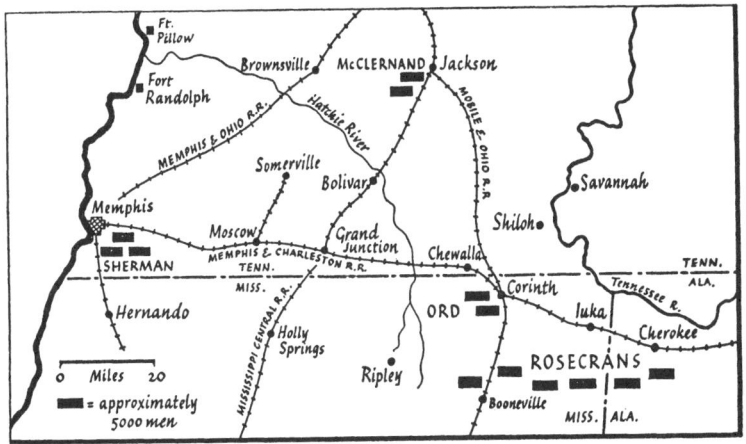

Even so, when he wound up his paperwork and departed for Washington two days later, he left his successor in immediate command of more than the 80,000 troops which Grant afterwards said would have been enough for the taking of Vicksburg that summer. The trouble was, they were far from "moveable," except when they were needed as reinforcements in adjoining departments. Before he had been at his post a week he was ordered to send a division to strengthen Samuel Curtis, who had marched from Northwest Arkansas to Helena, where the St Francis River flowed into the Mississippi, fifty airline miles below Memphis. Still, this left Grant with well over 75,000 effectives. Sherman had 16,000 at Memphis, and McClernand had 10,000 around Jackson. Another 7500 were stationed at Columbus, Cairo, and Paducah, while the rest of the Army of the Tennessee, 12,000 men under Major General E. O. C. Ord — a West Point classmate of Halleck's, just arrived from Virginia — were at Corinth. Rosecrans' Army of the Mississippi, 32,000 strong, was spread along a thirty-five-mile front that extended from south of Corinth to Cherokee, Alabama.

It was a sizeable force, but deep in enemy country as he was, charged with the consolidation of all that had been gained since Donelson and Shiloh, Grant found that its very size increased his major immediate problem: which was how to keep it fed and equipped. Just as the foregoing spring had set records for rainfall, so now the summer was breaking records for drouth, and as a result the Tennessee River was all but worthless as a supply line. So was the Memphis & Charleston Railroad, for the rebels had torn up the track between Chewalla and Grand Junction, and west of there the line had had to be abandoned for lack of rolling stock. All that was left him — except in Memphis, which of course could be supplied by river; the Mississippi never got really thirsty — was the slender thread of the Mobile & Ohio, stretching back to Columbus across more than a hundred miles of guerilla-infested West Tennessee, vulnerable throughout its length to attack by bands of regular and irregular cavalry, equally skilled at burning bridges and wrecking culverts, of which there were many. Tactically, too, the problems were not simple. Principal among them was the presence in North Mississippi of a highly mobile Confederate force, reckoned at 35,000 men, under the command of the resourceful and diabolical Earl Van Dorn, who sooner or later was probably going to succeed in one of his hair-trigger schemes. Its strength was less than half Grant's own, but its advantages were large. Van Dorn, for example, did not have to post a single man on guard in his rear, and best of all — or worst — he could choose the point of attack. He could strike the unconnected extremities, Corinth at one end, Memphis at the other, or he could pierce the lightly held center and knife straight through for Bolivar, Jackson, or Brownsville. What was more, he could choose the time.

Grant did not look forward to the coming months. Committed as he was to the defensive — much as he had been while biding his time before Shiloh — this was still not his kind of war. It was true, he had learned from what had happened then; from now on, he would keep in close touch with his field commanders and see to it that they had their men intrench. But he still did not like it, and he declared long afterwards that these midsummer months had been for him "the most anxious period of the war."

★ ★ ★

Discontent was general — amphibious, so to speak. For the navy, too, the successes of late spring and early summer, up and down the falling river, north and south of Vicksburg, were followed by a hot-weather season of doubts and tribulations. Every victory was accompanied by a setback, and the fruits thereof were bitter, their savor turning to ashes in the mouth. For Flag Officers Farragut and Davis, as for Grant, the midsummer word was *anxious*.

Davis ran into trouble first. As if Plum Run Bend had not been proof enough that his ironclads were vulnerable, it was presently reproved in backwoods Arkansas, and on one of the resurrected victims of that earlier disaster. In the course of his eastward march from Pea Ridge to Helena, Curtis had to cross White River: a task that was complicated by the presence of a Confederate fort at St Charles, sixty miles from the mouth. Given orders to reduce it immediately after his Memphis triumph, Davis assigned the mission to four gunboats and an Indiana regiment which went along in transports. Raised, pumped out, and patched, the *Mound City* had the flag; this was her first outing since her encounter with the *Van Dorn,* back in May. When the flotilla came within sight of the fort, June 17, the Hoosier colonel requested permission to assault by land — there were only just over a hundred rebels in the place — but the naval commander refused to yield or even share the honors. Closing with the flagship, he opened fire at point-blank range: whereupon the fort replied with a 42-pound solid that pierced the *Mound City*'s casemate and went right through her steam drum, scalding to death or drowning 125 out of her crew of 175 men, injuring 25 more, and leaving only 25 unhurt. (It was freakish in more ways than one, including arithmetically; for the round-looking casualty figures were exact.) Helpless, the ironclad went with the current and the other gunboats withdrew, leaving the proposed reduction to the Indianians, who encircled the fort and took it without the loss of a man. Davis had himself another victory, though he had it at far from a bargain price and the credit went to the army.

Farragut's troubles, downriver, were at once less bloody and more personal, and having a slopjar emptied onto his head from a French Quarter window was only the least of them. Five days after congratulating him for his "magnificent execution" and "unparalleled achievements" at New Orleans, Assistant Secretary Fox heard that the Tennessee sailor had abandoned the attempt against Vicksburg. "Impossible!" Fox cried. "Sending the fleet up to meet Commodore Davis was the most important part of the whole expedition. The instructions were positive." Quickly he reiterated them in triplicate, dispatching the original and two copies in three different ships to make certain of delivery: "It is of paramount importance that you go up and clear the river with utmost expedition. Mobile, Pensacola, and, in fact, the whole coast sinks into insignificance compared with this." Two days later he repeated the admonition in a second dispatch, invoking the support of higher authority: "The President requires you to use your utmost exertions (without a moment's delay, and before any other naval operation shall be permitted to interfere) to open the Mississippi and effect a junction with Flag Officer Davis."

On his previous trip upriver, Farragut had explained to Butler why he did not think a limited expedition against Vicksburg should be undertaken: "As they have so large a force of soldiers here, several thousand in and about the town, and the facility of bringing in 20,000 in an hour by railroad from Jackson, altogether, [I] think it would be useless to bombard it, as we could not hold it if we take it." He still felt that way about it; but the orders from Fox, which presently arrived, left him no choice. He put the fleet in order for the 400-mile ascent, taking part of Porter's mortar flotilla with him this time, as well as 3000 men from Butler, and came within sight of Vicksburg's red clay bluff on the same day the *Mound City* took the solid through her boiler. He was back again, and though he still did not like the task before him, he wrote home that he was putting his trust in the Lord: "If it is His pleasure to take me, may He protect my wife and boy from the rigors of a wicked world."

He spent ten days reëxamining the problem and giving the mortars time to establish ranges. Then on the night of June 27 he made his run. Eleven warships were in the 117-gun column: three heavy sloops, two light sloops, and six gunboats. Skippers of the eight smaller vessels were instructed to hug the western bank while the large ones took the middle, the *Richmond* leading because her chase guns were situated best for high-angle fire, then the flagship *Hartford*, and finally the *Brooklyn*, lending a heavy sting to the tail. Two hours after midnight the attack signal was hoisted, and for the next three hours it was New Orleans all over again — except that this time the rebel gunners, high on their 200-foot bluff, were taking little punishment in return. Down on the river, by contrast, everything was smoke and uproar; the *Brooklyn* and two of the gunboats were knocked back, and all of the others were hit repeatedly. Total casualties were 15 killed and 30 wounded. But when daylight came, eight of the ships were beyond the hairpin turn, and Farragut was farther from salt water than he had been since he first left Tennessee to join the navy, more than fifty years before.

Two days later, July 1, Davis brought his gunboats down from Memphis and the two fleets were joined. There was much visiting back and forth, much splicing of the main brace — and with cause. Upper and nether millstones had come together at last, and now there was not even grist between them.

There, precisely, was the trouble; for now that Farragut was up here, there was nothing left for him to do. The day before the bluewater ships steamed past the batteries, Colonel A.W. Ellet, his brother's successor, took two of his rams up the Yazoo River, which emptied into the Mississippi a dozen miles above Vicksburg, to investigate a report that the rebels had three gunboats lurking there. It turned out to be true, one of them being the *Van Dorn*, only survivor of the Memphis rout; but all three were set afire as soon as the rams hove into view, and Ellet came back out again to report that he had destroyed the fag end of Confederate resistance on the western rivers. Then the Gulf squadron made its run and the two fleets rode at anchor, midway between Vicksburg and the mouth of the Yazoo. As far as Farragut could see, however, all the exploit had really yielded was more proof that he could take his ships past fortifications: a fact he had never doubted in the first place. "We have done it," he informed the Department, "and can do it again as often as may be required of us." Just now, though, what he mainly wanted was a breath of salt air in his lungs. Requesting permission from Washington to go back downriver again, he emphasized the point that there were now two fleets biding their time in an area where there was not even work enough for one.

While awaiting an answer he did what he could to keep his sailors busy, including having them fire a high-noon 21-gun salute in celebration of the Fourth. The 3000 soldiers were no problem in this respect. With an ingenuity worthy of Butler himself, their commander Brigadier General Thomas Williams had them digging a canal across the narrow tongue of land dividing the shanks of the hairpin bend in front of Vicksburg. When the river rose, the general said, it would widen the ditch and sluice out a passage for the fleet, beyond the range of the batteries on the bluff. But there was the rub. The river was not rising; it was falling. It was falling so fast, in fact, that Farragut had begun to fear that his deep-draft sea-going fleet would be stranded up here all summer. On July 13 he sent a wire which he hoped would jog the Department into action on his request: "In ten days the river will be too low for the ships to go down. Shall they go down, or remain up the rest of the year?"

One problem more there was, though he did not consider it a matter for real concern, never having had much of an ear for rumor. In addition to the three gunboats whose destruction Ellet had effected when he appeared up the Yazoo, there were whispers that the Confederates were building themselves an ironclad up there. Farragut did not give the rumor much credence. Even if it were true, he said, there was small chance that the rebels would ever be able to use such a craft, bottled up as she was, with two powerful Federal fleets standing guard in the Mississippi, just below the only point of exit. "I do not think she will ever come forth," he reported.

Davis was not so sure. Unlike Farragut, he had Plum Run Bend in his memory, which had taught him what havoc a surprise attack could bring. Determined not to suffer such a reverse again, he ordered three warships up the Yazoo to investigate and take up lookout stations. They left immediately after early breakfast, July 15: the ironclad *Carondelet*, the wooden gunboat *Tyler*, and the steam ram *Queen of the West*.

The rumors were all too true, as Farragut was about to discover. The mystery ship was the *Arkansas*, floated unfinished down the Mississippi and towed up the Yazoo to Greenwood after the fall of Island Ten exposed her to capture in Memphis. Naval Lieutenant Isaac Newton Brown, a forty-five-year-old Kentuckian who had held the same rank as a Vera Cruz veteran in the old navy, which he had entered from

Mississippi nearly thirty years ago, was given command of her in late May, together with orders to "finish and equip that vessel without regard to expenditure of men or money."

He did not realize what a large order this was until he got to Greenwood and saw her. Unfinished was not the word; she was scarcely even begun.

"The vessel was a mere hull, without armor. The engines were apart. Guns without carriages were lying about the deck. A portion of the railroad iron intended as armor was at the bottom of the river, and the other and far greater part was to be sought for in the interior of the country." So he later reported; but now he got to work. After a day spent fishing up the sunken iron, he towed the skeleton *Arkansas* 150 miles downriver to Yazoo City, where the facilities were better, though not much. Scouring the plantations roundabout, he set up fourteen forges on the river bank and kept them going around the clock, rural blacksmiths pounding at the wagonloads of scrap iron brought in from all points of the compass. Two hundred carpenters added to the din, hammering, sawing, swarming over the shield and hull. Perhaps the biggest problem was the construction of carriages for the guns; nothing of the sort had ever been built in Mississippi; but this too was met by letting the contract to "two gentlemen of Jackson," who supplied them from their Canton wagon factory. Other deficiencies could not be overcome, and were let go. Since there was no apparatus for bending the iron around the curve of the vessel's quarter or stern, for example, boiler plate was tacked over these parts — "for appearance' sake," Brown explained. Also, the paint was bad. She was intended to be chocolate brown, the color of the river, but no matter how many coats were applied she kept her original hue, rusty red. Despite all this, the work in the improvised yard went on. Within five weeks, according to one of her lieutenants, "we had a man-of-war (such as she was) from almost nothing."

By July 12 she was as finished as she would ever be. Brown sent the mechanics ashore and dropped down to Sartartia Bar, where, as he later said, "I now gave the executive officer a day to organize and exercise his men." In the crew of about 175, two thirds were from the recently burned gunboats; the rest were infantry volunteers, distributed among the ten guncrews serving weapons of various calibers, three in each broadside, two forward, and two aft. July 14, the descent resumed. Fifteen miles below, at the mouth of the Sunflower River — the guns of the two Union fleets, engaged in target practice out on the Mississippi, were plainly audible from here — it was discovered that steam from the engines and boiler had penetrated the forward magazine. Brown tied up alongside a sawmill clearing, landed the wet powder, and spread it on tarpaulins to dry in the sun. "By constant shaking and turning," he reported, "we got it back to the point of ignition before the sun sank below the trees." Packing what they could of it into the after magazine, the guncrews came back aboard and the *Arkansas* continued on her way, "guns cast loose and men at quarters, expecting every moment to meet the enemy."

At midnight her commander called a rest-halt near Haines Bluff; then at 3 a.m. — July 15 — continued down the river. Information received from Vicksburg put the number of enemy warships at thirty-seven, and Brown intended to be among them by daylight, with every possible advantage of surprise. It was not to be. The twin-screw vessel's engines had a habit of stopping on dead center, one at a time, which would throw her abruptly into bank, despite the rudder, and this was what happened now in the predawn darkness. While the rest of the crew was engaged in getting her off again, a lieutenant went ashore in search of information. He came to a plantation house, but found that the residents had fled at the first sound of a steamer on the river. All that was left was one old Negro woman, and she would tell him nothing, not even the whereabouts of her people. In fact, she would not admit that they had been there in the first place.

"They have but just left," the lieutenant insisted. "The beds are yet warm."

"Don't know 'bout that. And if I did, I wouldn't tell you."

"Do you take me for a Yankee? Don't you see I wear a gray coat?"

"Certain you's a Yankee," the woman said. "Our folks aint got none them gumboats."

It took an hour to get the unwieldy *Arkansas* underweigh again; the lieutenant returned from his profitless excursion with time to spare. Attempting to get back on schedule, Brown called for all the speed the engineers could give him, but it was by no means enough. When daylight filtered through, the ironclad was still in the Yazoo. The sun came up fiery as she entered Old River, a ten-mile lake formed by a cutoff from the Mississippi, and the lookout spotted three Union warships dead ahead, steaming upstream in line abreast, the *Carondelet* in the center, flanked by the *Tyler* and the *Queen of the West*. Brown made a brief speech, ending: "Go to your guns!" Stripped to the waist in the early morning heat, with handkerchiefs bound about their heads to keep the sweat from trickling into their eyes, the guncrews stood to their pieces. The officers, too, had removed their coats, and paced the sanded deck in their undershirts — all but Brown, who remained in full uniform, his short, tawny beard catching the breeze as he stood on the shield, directly over the bow guns, which he ordered not to fire until the action was fully joined, "lest by doing so we should diminish our speed." He and the *Carondelet's* captain, Henry Walke, had been friends in the old navy, messmates on a voyage around the world, and he wanted nothing to delay this first meeting since they had gone their separate ways.

The Federal skippers reacted variously to their first glimpse of the rust-red vessel bearing down on them out of nowhere. The *Queen of the West*, unarmed and with her speed advantage canceled by the current, turned at once and frankly ran. The *Carondelet* and *Tyler* stayed on course, intending to fire their bow guns, then swing round and make a downstream fight with their stern pieces, hoping the noise would bring help from the rest of the fleet. Both fired and missed. By the time they had turned to run for safety, the *Arkansas* was upon them.

She chose the *Carondelet*, the slower of the two, pumping shells into her lightly armored stern, which ate at her vitals and slowed her even more. The return shots glanced off the *Arkansas*' prow, doing no considerable damage except to one seaman who, more curious than prudent, stuck his head out of a gunport for a better view and had it taken off by a bolt from an 8-inch rifle. The headless body fell back on the deck, and a lieutenant, fearing the sight would demoralize the rest of the guncrew, called upon the nearest man to heave it overboard. "Oh, I can't do it, sir! It's my brother," he replied.

Other casualties followed, one among them being Brown himself. Most of the shots from dead ahead struck the inclined shield and were deflected back and upwards, ricocheting, but presently one did not carom high enough and Brown received what he later called "a severe contusion on the head." He thought he was done for until he drew a handful of clotted blood from the wound and failed to find any particles of brain mixed in. He stayed at his post, continuing to direct both the gunnery and the navigation. Just then, however, the *Tyler* dropped back to help the crippled *Carondelet*, her riflemen firing volleys at Brown, the only live target outside the shield. A minie struck him over the left temple, tumbling him down a hatchway and onto the forward guns. When he regained consciousness, the aid men were laying him among the dead and wounded below deck. He promptly got up and returned to his place on the shield.

The *Carondelet* was much closer now, he saw, and so was the mouth of the river. Just as she reached it, and just as he was about to ram her stern, she veered into bank, leaking steam and frantic survivors from all her ports. Brown did not stay to complete her destruction or force her surrender. Instead, he took up pursuit of the *Tyler*, which by now had entered the Mississippi and was doing all she could to overtake the *Queen*. Aboard the fleet, the sailors had heard the firing, but had assumed that the boats were shelling snipers in the woods. Now they saw better, though they still did not understand what they saw. Observing the gunboat returning with a strange red vessel close on her heels, one officer remarked: "There comes the *Tyler* with a prize."

They soon learned better. Within range of the fleet — "a forest of masts and smokestacks," Brown called it; "In every direction, except astern, our eyes rested on enemies" — noting that the army rams were anchored behind the bigger ships, in position to dart out through the intervals, the Confederate skipper told his pilot: "Brady, shave that line of men-of-war as close as you can, so that the rams will not have room to gather headway in coming out to strike us." Brady gave him what he asked for, and the second battle opened.

At its beginning, steam down, guns unloaded, not a single Federal vessel was prepared for action; but this was presently so thoroughly corrected that Brown could later say, "I had the most lively realization of having steamed into a real volcano." Guns were flashing, and as he advanced "the line of fire seemed to grow into a circle constantly closing." Even so, he saw one definite advantage to fighting solo from an interior position, and the *Arkansas* was not neglectful of it, "firing rapidly to every point of the circumference, without the fear of hitting a friend or missing an enemy."

Now, though, she was taking about as much punishment as she gave. The big ocean-going sloops had run their guns out, and the Davis ironclads were firing for all they were worth. The *Arkansas* took hits from all directions. An 11-inch solid broke through her casemate armor and laid a sixteen-man guncrew dead and dying on her deck. A rifle bolt laid out eleven more. Shrapnel quickly gave her stack the look of a nutmeg grater, so that for lack of draft the pressure dropped from 120 pounds to 20, barely enough to turn the engines. The temperature in the fire-room soared to 130°, and the engineers worked fifteen-minute shifts, by the end of which they had to be hauled up, half-roasted, and relieved by men from the guns. Sixty dead and wounded men were in her; her cast-iron snout was broken off; one whole section of plating was ripped from her flank; her boats were shot away and dragging. However, she still was giving as good as she got, or better. Out on the shield, where he had had his spyglass shot from his hands, her captain had never stopped calling orders to the pilot house and guns. A ram broke into the clear at last, driving hard in a final effort to block the way; "Go through him, Brady!" Brown shouted. But one of the bow guns averted the need for a collision by putting a shell through the Federal's boiler. Steam went up like a geyser and the bluejacket crew went overboard.

That was the final round. The *Arkansas* was into the clear, past the outer rim of the volcano. Limping badly, but unpursued, she held her course for Vicksburg, where a crowd had assembled on the bluff to greet her. Soldiers and townspeople alike, they tossed their hats in joy and admiration, but the cheers froze in their throats when they looked down and saw the carnage on her gundeck.

Farragut was infuriated. He had been sleeping late that morning, and when the cannonade erupted he appeared on the *Hartford*'s deck in his nightshirt. However, the flagship's engines were under repair; there was nothing he could do but watch and fire at the strange vessel as it went by. When the action was over he surveyed the wreckage — which was not only considerable, but was largely self-inflicted by cross fire — then returned to his cabin, muttering as he went: "Damnable neglect, or worse, somewhere!"

The more he thought about it, the madder he got. By the time he came back on deck again, fully dressed, he had made up his mind to steam down to Vicksburg with all his ships and attack the *Arkansas* in broad open daylight, hillside batteries and all. His staff managed to dissuade him from this — at least give the fleet captains time to wash the blood from their scuppers, they said — but, even so, the old man would not be put off any longer than nightfall: Porter's mortar schooners, together with the *Brooklyn* and the two laggard gunboats, were still below the city, where the apparently unsinkable rebel ironclad might engage them any minute. He ordered all guns loaded with solid and suspended his heaviest anchor from the tip of the *Hartford*'s port mainyardarm, intending to drop it through the *Arkansas*' deck and bottom when he got alongside her. The Davis gunboats and the Porter mortars would give covering fire, above and below, while he went in and dragged the upstart monster from its lair. Just before sunset he hoisted the familiar pennant for attack, and the fleet moved downriver.

It did not work out at all the way he intended. For one thing, in the ruddy murk between sunset and dusk, the rust-red boat was almost invisible under the red clay bank. The first each skipper saw of her as the ships came past in single file, taking in turn a pounding from the batteries overhead, was the flash of her guns as he crossed her line of fire. By then it was too late to attempt to check up and grapple; all there was time for was one quick broadside in reply, before the current swept him out of range. Aboard the *Arkansas*, dismay at having to fight the day's third battle, tied to bank and with less than half her crew still functional, gave way to elation as the action progressed. One by one, the ships glided past with their towering spars in silhouette against the glow of the western cloudbank, and one by one they took them under fire, as if in a gigantic shooting gallery. But when the *Hartford* stood in close, groping blindly with the anchor swaying pendulous from her yardarm, and they loosed a broadside at her, she thundered back with a tremendous salvo. An 11-inch solid pierced the side of the *Arkansas* just above the waterline, crashed through the engine room, killing and mangling as it went, and lodged in the opposite casemate armor, making what one of her officers called "a bulging protuberance outside." She kept firing until the river stopped sending her targets. Then once more there was silence.

Farragut was where he wanted to be, south of the infernal bluff, and he had made the downstream run with fewer casualties than before — 5 killed, 16 wounded: only a handful more than his adversary had suffered — but he was far from satisfied. He wanted that ram, and he intended to have her, whatever the cost. At daylight he sent an urgent message to Davis, proposing that both fleets go in together at high noon and fight the rebel to a finish. Davis declined the invitation, counseling prudence and self-control. "I have watched eight rams for a month," he replied, "and now find it no hard task to watch one."

He continued to resist the pressure which Farragut kept applying. Five days later, July 21 — the *Arkansas* having ventured out meanwhile on a sortie that was aborted by another engine failure — he agreed to make an attempt next morning with the ironclad *Essex* and the *Queen of the West*. The plan was for the gunboat to shove the rebel vessel hard against bank and hold her there, sitting-duck fashion, so that the ram could butt a hole in her side and send her to the bottom. But this did not work either. Brown had the *Arkansas* moored with her head upstream, and when he saw the *Essex* coming at him he slacked his bow-line and presented his sharp armored prow to the blunt-nosed gunboat, which swerved at the last minute to avoid being sliced in two, taking and giving punishment as she passed. The *Queen*, following close behind, anxious to redeem her performance up the Yazoo the week before, could manage no more than a glancing blow. She worked her way back upstream, rejoining Davis, but the *Essex* went with the current, her engines badly shot up in the melee, and joined the fleet below.

Farragut threw up his hands at this. Fuel was low, and what with the need for keeping up steam in case the *Arkansas* staged another sudden appearance, was getting considerably lower every day. Sanitation was also a problem, as Halleck had foreseen. The swampy Mississippi heat had nearly half of Farragut's sailors on the sick list, along with three quarters of the canal-digging soldiers. The falling river seemed about to make good its threat to strand him up here, out of circulation for the rest of the year. Besides, a message from Welles — sent before the Secretary learned of the rebel ram's emergence — had just arrived: "Go down the river at discretion." That was what Farragut did, and he did it without delay. Starting south on July 26, he dropped the orphaned *Essex* and two of the smaller wooden gunboats off at Baton Rouge, along with Williams' shovel-weary soldiers, and put into New Orleans for repairs that would fit the rest of his salt-water ships for more agreeable blockade duty along the Gulf. Back in his native element at last, able to breathe all the way to the depths of his lungs, he said goodbye to the Mississippi — forever, he hoped.

Davis pulled out northward that same day, transferring his base to Helena, two hundred miles upstream. Vicksburg was delivered, along with a great stretch of the river between Napoleon and Natchez.

Welles was extremely angry when he heard the news. He told Farragut, "It is an absolute necessity that the neglect or apparent neglect of the squadron should be wiped out by the destruction of the *Arkansas*." Nothing came of this as far as Farragut was concerned; he was downstream and he stayed there. But it was an event that rankled in the Secretary's memory ever after — worse than Donelson, worse than Hampton Roads; worse, even, than Head of the Passes or Plum Run Bend. Bitter and chagrined, Welles later wrote: "The most disreputable naval affair of the war was the descent of the steam ram *Arkansas* through both squadrons, until she hauled into the batteries of Vicksburg, and there the two Flag Officers abandoned the place and the ironclad ram, Farragut and his force going down to New Orleans, and Davis proceeding with his flotilla up the river."

On Vicksburg's bluff, conversely, there was rejoicing and there was pride, not only because the naval siege had been raised, but also because of the manner in which the feat had been accomplished. The combined might of two victorious Union fleets had been challenged, sundered, and repulsed by a single homemade ten-gun ironclad, backed by the industry and daring of her builder and commander. Coming as it did, after a season of reverses, this exploit gave the people of the Lower Mississippi Valley a new sense of confidence and elation. They were glad to be alive in a time when such things could happen, and they asked themselves how a nation could ever be conquered when its destiny rested with men like those who served aboard the *Arkansas* under Isaac Newton Brown.

★ ★ ★

In the Transmississippi, too, there was the discomfort of indigestion, proceeding from a difficulty in assimilating all that had been gained.

Sam Curtis was glad to have the Davis rams and gunboats with him: almost as glad as he had been to receive the division from Grant, which reached Helena the week before and brought his total strength to 18,000. This was the largest force he had yet commanded, half again larger than the army with which he had won the Battle of Pea Ridge; but, as he saw it, he had need of every man and gun he could get, ashore or afloat. Looking back on that savage conflict, which involved the repulse of a slashing double envelopment by Price and McCulloch, with Van Dorn hovering wild-eyed in the background and swarms of painted Indians on his flank, he perceived a hundred things that might have spelled defeat if they had gone against instead of for him. It seemed to him now in late July that events were building up to another such encounter, in which the scales — balanced against him, he believed, as they had been in early March — might tip the other way.

For a time it had been otherwise. Through April and May he had occupied a vacuum, so to speak; Van Dorn and Price had crossed the Mississippi and left Arkansas to him. On the final day of May, however, this leisure season ended with the Confederate appointment of Major General Thomas C. Hindman, a Helena lawyer and congressman who had led a division at Shiloh, to command the area including Missouri, Arkansas, Louisiana south to the Red, and Indian Territory. A dapper little man just over five feet tall, addicted to ruffled shirts and patent-leather boots, Hindman — like his predecessor, Earl Van Dorn — made up in activity for what he lacked in size. He had need of all his energy now. The situation on his arrival was about as bad as it could be, the scarcity of volunteers lending support to the postwar tall tale that the entire state of Montana was afterwards populated by rebel fugitives from Elkhorn Tavern; but he went immediately to work, issuing fiery proclamations and enforcing the new conscription law in his native state with troops brought from Texas. Lacking arms and munitions, he set up factories and chemical works to turn them out, operated lead mines and tanyards, and even organized the women of his department into sewing circles to furnish uniforms for all the able-bodied men he could lay hands on. Word of his activity soon spread, and recruits began to trickle in from Missouri, some of whom he sent back home with orders to raise guerilla bands to harass the invader's rear. Before long, Curtis was receiving intelligence reports that put the Confederate strength in midland Arkansas at 25,000 men.

His plan had been to march on Little Rock as soon as his army had recovered from its exertions, thus adding to the southern list of fallen capitals, but the presence of Hindman's newborn army in that direction changed his mind. Instead, after much conferring back and forth with Washington, he moved toward Helena for a possible share in the amphibious descent of the Mississippi. Even that was hard enough. All through June, bridge-burners and irregular cavalrymen, instructed by Hindman to bushwhack Union pickets, destroy all food, and pollute the water "by killing cattle, ripping the carcasses open and throwing them in," harassed his line of march and kept him in almost constant expectation of being swamped by overwhelming numbers. At last he reached the big river — only to find that the descent had been called off; Halleck was busy consolidating his gains. It was just as well, as far as Curtis was concerned. He began to fortify his Helena position, not knowing what all-out mischief Hindman might be plotting in the brush.

Even after the arrival of the division from Memphis and the ironclads from Vicksburg, together with siege guns brought down-river from Birds Point, Columbus, and Fort Pillow, he felt far from easy about his situation. Not only was there danger in front; he now learned of a new danger in his rear. The Missourians who had gone back home with instructions for making trouble were showing a good deal of talent for such work. Brigadier General John M. Schofield, the Federal commander there, reported that he had discovered "a well-devised scheme" for a monster guerilla outbreak involving thirty to fifty thousand men who were assembling now at designated places to await the appointed signal "and, by a sudden *coup de main*, seize the important points in the state, surprise and capture our small detachments guarding railroads, &c., thus securing arms and ammunition, and coöperate with an invading army from Arkansas." He called on Curtis to deal with this invasion force, which had moved into the vacated area around Pea Ridge, while he did his best to deal with the guerillas. "You are aware, General, that I have no force sufficient to drive them back without your assistance," he implored. "Let me ask you to act as quickly as possible."

Curtis could not help him. If it came to the worst, he wasn't even sure he could help himself. He had all sorts of troubles. As a result of trying to encourage trade in cotton, he said, his camp was "infested with Jews, secessionists, and spies." Then too, his health was failing; or, as he put it, "I am not exactly well." At any rate, whatever rebel hosts were gathering in Northwest Arkansas, the last thing he intended was a retracing of his steps on the harried march he had just completed. All he could do was hold what he had, probing occasionally at the country roundabout as the long hot summer wore on toward a close.

Schofield's fears for Missouri were soon fulfilled, though in a less concerted fashion than he had predicted. No less than eighty skirmishes were fought there during July and August, including one that resulted in the capture of Independence by guerillas under Charles Quantrill, who presently was commissioned a Confederate captain as a reward for this exploit. Kansas too was threatened. Jim Lane, the grim Jayhawk chieftain, was raising Negro troops; "Zouaves d'Afrique," they were called, for they drilled in baggy scarlet pantaloons Stanton had purchased, in the emergency, from France. North of there, in the absence of soldiers transferred south and east, the Minnesota Sioux went on the warpath, massacring settlers by the hundreds.

Everywhere Curtis looked he saw trouble, though most of it was fortunately well beyond his reach at Helena. Remaining in the fine big house on a hill overlooking the river — it was Hindman's, or it had been; Curtis had taken it for his headquarters — he improved his fortifications, put his trust in the Mississippi as a supply line, and shook his head disapprovingly at the chaos all around him. "Society is terribly mutilated," he reported.

★ ★ ★

At the opposite end of the western line, Buell was moving eastward; or he had been, anyhow, until he encountered troubles he would gladly have swapped for those of Curtis and Grant combined, with Schofield's thrown in for good measure. As it turned out, he not only had supply and guerilla problems as acute as theirs; presently it became obvious, too, that his was the column that was to receive the main attention of the main Confederate army in the West — beginning with the twin thunderbolts, Morgan and Forrest, who were thrown at him soon after he got started.

In giving him instructions for the eastward move, ten days after the fall of Corinth, Halleck was heeding the repeated suggestion of

The Sun Shines South

Ormsby Mitchel, who for a month had been signaling frantically that he could see the end of the war from where he stood in Northeast Alabama. If he were reinforced, he said, he could march straight into Chattanooga, then turn south and take Atlanta. From there, he added, the way lay open to Richmond's back door, through a region that was "completely unprotected and very much alarmed." Old Brains could see merit in this — and he also saw a possible variation. Knoxville, too, lay beyond that mountain gateway: an objective he knew was dear to the heart of Lincoln, who was anxious to disenthrall the pro-Union citizens of East Tennessee and gain control of the railroad connecting Virginia and North Georgia. Accordingly, Halleck gave Buell his instructions on June 9 for a lateral offensive, the only one of any kind that he intended to launch in the West this summer, simultaneously notifying Washington of the intended movement, and two days later received the expected reply: Lincoln was "greatly delighted."

The extent of the President's delight was shown before the month was out. Alarmed by Lee's assault on McClellan, who was crying for reinforcements as he fell back, the War Department called on the western commander for 25,000 troops to be shifted to the East; but when Halleck replied that to send them would mean that the Chattanooga expedition would have to "be abandoned or at least be diminished," the reaction was immediate and negative, and it came in the form of a telegram from Lincoln himself. This must not be done on any account, he said. "To take and hold the railroad at or east of Cleveland, in East Tennessee, I think fully as important as the taking and holding of Richmond."

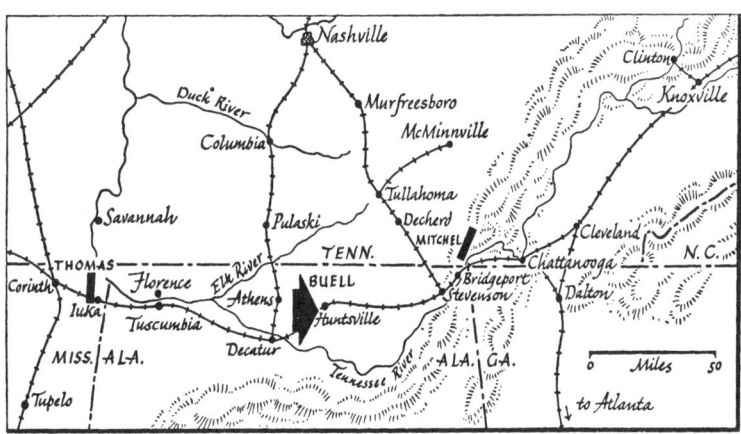

By that time Buell was well on his way. He had by no means reached Cleveland — a junction thirty miles beyond his immediate objective, where the railroad, coming down from Knoxville, branched west to Chattanooga and south to Atlanta — but he had advanced his four divisions to Huntsville, having ferried the Tennessee River at Florence, and had repaired the Memphis & Charleston line as far east as Decatur. He had about 35,000 men in his present column, including cavalry and engineers, and Mitchel was waiting up ahead with 11,000 more. Off to the north, ready to coöperate as soon as Knoxville became the goal, George Morgan occupied Cumberland Gap with a division of 9000, which was also a component of Buell's Army of the Ohio. In addition to these 55,000 troops, Thomas was at Iuka, awaiting orders to march east with his own division of 8000, plus two from Grant, which had been promised in case they were required. Just now, however, Buell did not want them. He was having trouble enough feeding the men he had, and the problem got progressively worse as he moved eastward, lengthening his supply line.

The 300 tons of food and forage needed daily — 3¼ pounds for a man, 26 for a horse, 23 for a mule — were more than the guerilla-harried railroads could supply. Besides a shortage of rolling stock, destruction of the Elk River bridge on the Nashville-Decatur line necessitated a forty-mile wagon haul around the break, and sniper fire was so frequent and effective that ironclad boxcars had to be provided for the protection of the train crews. Buell put his men and animals on half rations, much to the discomfort of both. "We are living from day to day on short supplies and our operations are completely crippled," he complained to the Louisville quartermaster. Ahead, he knew, lay additional problems: the river crossing at Bridgeport, for example. Retiring from in front of Chattanooga the month before, Mitchel had burned the mile-long span, and Buell had no material with which to build another. In an attempt to fill the shortage and make amends, Mitchel ordered all the sawmills between Huntsville and Stevenson put to work supplying lumber for pontoons and a bridge floor, but this too was an occasion for guerilla interference, causing the workers to run away for fear of being murdered on the job or in their beds.

All in all, the prospect was grim. Buell's chief solace was the knowledge that he was doing the best he could with what he had, and his chief hope was that his industry was appreciated by those above him. The latter was dispelled by an alarming and discouraging message from Halleck, July 8. The alarm came first: Bragg's army was reported to be in motion, either against Grant at Memphis or Corinth, or against Buell at Tuscumbia or Chattanooga. "A few days more may reduce these doubts to a certainty, when our troops will operate accordingly," Halleck reported, unruffled. Then came the discouragement: "The President telegraphs that your progress is not satisfactory and that you should move more rapidly. The long time taken by you to reach Chattanooga will enable the enemy to anticipate you by concentrating a large force to meet you. I communicate his views, hoping that your movements hereafter may be so rapid as to remove all cause of complaint, whether well founded or not."

Buell later declared, "I was so astonished at the message that I made no reply until three days afterward." What jogged him then was a six-word dispatch: "I want to hear from you. H. W. Halleck." In reply, Buell reviewed his difficulties, remarking as he did so: "I regret that it is necessary to explain the circumstances which must make my progress seem so slow." As he saw it, the object was not only to reach his goal quickly, but also to be in condition to fight when he got there. "The advance on Chattanooga must be made with the means of acting in force; otherwise it will either fail" — as Mitchel's had done — or else the city would "prove a profitless and transient prize." His arrangements, made in accordance with this, were "being pushed forward as rapidly as possible," and though he quite understood that "these are matters of fact that cannot be gratifying," he added: "The dissatisfaction of the President pains me exceedingly."

Next day Halleck responded with assurances of personal good will. He could see both sides of the question, and he urged Buell to be more tolerant of the amateurs above them. "I can well understand the difficulties you have to encounter and also the impatience at Washington. In the first place they have no conception of the length of our lines of defense and of operations. In the second place the disasters before Richmond have worked them up to boiling heat." At any rate, he assured him, "I will see that your movements are properly explained to the President."

This was helpful in relieving the pain — lately added to by John Morgan, who had led his gray raiders up through Middle Tennessee and was capturing railroad guards, burning bridges, and smashing culverts in Kentucky — but still more comforting to Buell was the fact that his advance was now past Stevenson, where the Nashville & Chattanooga, coming down through Murfreesboro and Tullahoma, joined the Memphis & Charleston, thus affording him an additional rail supply line. Anticipating this, he had work gangs all along the road, repairing the damage done by retreating Confederates, and to make certain that it was not wrecked again, either by raiders or guerillas, he had stationed a brigade at Murfreesboro — two regiments of infantry, a cavalry detachment, and a four-gun battery — ready to move out in either direction at the first sign of trouble. On June 12, the date of Halleck's sympathetic message, Buell was informed that the repairs had been completed. The first trainload of supplies would leave Nashville tomorrow or the next day; he would be able to take his soldiers off half rations and replace their worn-out shoes as soon as it got there.

What got there tomorrow, however, was not a trainload of supplies, but rather an announcement of disaster. In the gray dawn light, Bedford Forrest struck Murfreesboro with three regiments of cavalry, wrecking the railroad at that point and capturing the Federal commander, Brigadier General T. T. Crittenden, together with all his men, guns, and equipment. Stung, Buell reacted fast by hurrying William Nelson's whole division to the scene; but when it got there, the hard-riding Confederate and his captives had disappeared eastward, in the direction of the mountains. Nor was that all. The work gangs had barely completed their repairs when, eight days later, Forrest struck again — this time up near Nashville, where he celebrated the anniversary of Manassas by firing his captured guns within sight of the capitol tower and wrecking the three bridges across Mill Creek. When Nelson's division marched from Murfreesboro to intercept him, he took a side road, camped for the night within earshot of the bluecoats tramping northward on the pike, then once more made his escape into the mountains beyond McMinnville.

Nettled but not disheartened, Buell put his repair gangs back to work. Within a week, practice having increased their skill, they had the line in operation. July 29, the first train pulled into Stevenson from Nashville with 210,000 rations, followed next day by another with a comparable amount. The troops went back on full allowances of food, and Nelson's infantry replaced the shoes they had worn out chasing Forrest's cavalry. This was a help and was duly appreciated; but something more than footgear had been damaged in the process, and there were pains in other regions than the stomach. Morale and pride were involved here, too. Buell's men began to consider that, with the doubtful exception of Shiloh — which was not really their fight, since they only arrived on the second day and even then were only engaged in part — the Army of the Ohio was the only major Federal command that had never fought a pitched battle on its own. The blame for this, as they saw it, rested with Buell, whose military policy was referred to by one of his colonels as that of a dancing master: "By your leave, my dear sir, we will have a fight; that is, if you are sufficiently fortified. No hurry; take your time."

Distasteful as this was to the men, there was something else about their commander that irked them even more. When Ormsby Mitchel's division came through this region, back in May, one soldier wrote happily in his diary: "Our boys find Alabama hams better than Uncle Sam's side meat, and fresh bread better than hard crackers." Buell, on the other hand, not only put them on half rations, but issued and enforced stern orders against foraging, which he believed would discourage southern civilians from returning to their old allegiance. However true this was or wasn't, it seemed to the men that he was less concerned with their hunger pangs than he was with the comfort and welfare of the rebels, who after all were to blame for their being down here in the first place. Also, he was denying them the fun and profit enjoyed by comrades who had come this way before them. For example, in reprisal for guerilla activities, one of Mitchel's brigade commanders, Colonel John Basil

Turchin — formerly Ivan Vasilevich Turchininov, of the Imperial Russian Army — had turned the town of Athens over to his three regiments, saying, "I shut mine eyes for one hour": whereupon the Illinois, Ohio, and Indiana boys took it completely apart, Cossack-style, raping Negro servant girls and stuffing their pockets and haversacks with $50,000 worth of watches, plate, and jewelry. Grudgingly, Buell's men complained that he would never turn them loose like that, despite the fact that, officially, it would apparently do his career far more good than harm. Turchin was court-martialed and dismissed for the Athens debauch, but before the summer was over he was reinstated and promoted to brigadier. Likewise Mitchel, though he was called to Washington in early July to explain illegal cotton transactions made in his department, was promoted to major general and transferred to the mild, sea-scented atmosphere of coastal South Carolina, where unfortunately he died of yellow fever in October.

Actually, though, the trouble with Buell lay deeper. It was not so much what he did as what he was. Other generals shared his views on the subject of foraging, and enforced them quite as sternly: notably McClellan and, at the present stage of the conflict, Sherman. "This demoralizing and disgraceful practice of pillage must cease," the West Tennessee commander admonished his troops in a general order, "else the country will rise on us and justly shoot us down like dogs or wild beasts." In fact, on the face of it, both were harder on offenders than Buell ever was or tried to be. In Sherman's command, for example, the punishment for molesting civilians or stealing was confinement on bread and water, and he sent out patrols with instructions to shoot if foragers tried to escape arrest. But they gave their men something instead. Better situated, they fed better, and they moved among their soldiers in a way that made the individual feel that, outside battle, his comfort and well-being were his general's main concern. Above all, in their different ways, they had a flair for the dramatic. McClellan's men would turn from their first hot meal in days for a chance to cheer him riding past, and Sherman could make a soldier proud for weeks by asking him for a light for his cigar. It was personal, a matter of personality.

Buell was seldom "personal," and never at all in public. In private, he had a parlor trick which he sometimes performed to amaze his guests with the strength of his rather stubby arms and his stocky, close-knit torso. Grasping his hundred-and-forty-pound wife by the waist, he would lift her straight out before him, hold her there with her feet dangling clear of the carpet, then perch her deftly on the mantelpiece. It was a good trick, and it won him the admiration of those who watched him do it. But the soldiers never saw this side of his nature. He was a headquarters general, anyhow. They saw him only briefly as he made his hurried, sour-mouthed inspections, peering at them with his beady eyes and poking his hawk-beak nose into unexpected corners. The good he took for granted; it was the less-good he was looking for, and he seldom failed to find it. As a result, there was an absence of warmth — and an absence, too, of incidents in which men let their food grow cold while they took time out to cheer him riding by or fished in their pockets for a light for his cigar. They were well drilled, beyond question. Three months ago, their professional tone had been such that when Grant's skulkers saw them march ashore at Shiloh they had cried, "Here come the regulars!" Under fire next day, their confident demeanor as they rolled the rebels back had sustained the basic accuracy of this mistake. Since then, however, a great deal had happened, and all of it bad. The inchworm advance on Corinth, with empty earthworks at the end, had been followed by these two belt-tightening months in North Alabama, where they observed with disgust — as if, by a process of unnatural reversion, a butterfly were to have its wings refolded and be stuffed unceremoniously back into its cocoon — their transformation from happy-go-lucky soldiers into ill-fed railroad workers. Out of this had come a loss of former gladness, and a suspicion that they had lost their fighting edge.

This might or might not be the case, but at any rate the signs had been increasing that a test was about to come. Bragg was not only on the move: both Grant and Rosecrans reported him moving eastward, in the direction of Chattanooga. Before Halleck left for Washington in mid-July he released Thomas to Buell's control, bringing his total strength to 46,000, exclusive of the force at Cumberland Gap. Of these, however, 15,000 were needed for guarding Nashville and the railroads, which left him no more than 31,000 for a forward move. For two weeks the advance had been stalled by the lack of a bridge across the Tennessee at Bridgeport; lumber for the pontoons had been cut by now, but there was still a shortage of nails, oakum, and pitch. While waiting for them, Buell was doing his best to build up a forward supply depot from which to feed and equip his men when they crossed the river to close in on the city. He was still at it on the last day of July, when a message reached his Huntsville headquarters from the commander of his advance division, reporting that Bragg himself had arrived in Chattanooga two days ago — apparently in advance of his whole army. "On the same evening two trains came in with soldiers. Railroad agent says he has orders to furnish cars for 30,000 as fast as he can."

Informed of this, Halleck replied that Grant would furnish reinforcements "if you should find the enemy too strong." Six days later, learning that Bragg's troops had not yet come up, he prodded Buell again: "There is great dissatisfaction here [in Washington] at the slow movement of your army toward Chattanooga. It is feared that the enemy will have time to concentrate his entire army against you." Buell wired back: "It is difficult to satisfy impatience, and when it proceeds from anxiety, as I know it does in this case, I am not disposed to complain of it.

My advance has not been rapid, but it could not be more rapid under the circumstances. I know I have not been idle nor indifferent." Next day, August 7, he got down to specifics. The Confederate force in East Tennessee was estimated at 60,000 men, he said; "yet I am prepared to find the reports much more exaggerated than I have supposed, and shall march upon Chattanooga at the earliest possible day, unless I ascertain certainly that the enemy's strength renders it imprudent. If, on the other hand, he should cross the river I shall attack him, and I do not doubt that we shall defeat him." Encouraged, Halleck replied that Grant had been ordered to transfer two divisions to the Army of the Ohio if they were needed; but he cautioned Buell, "Do not ask for them if you can avoid it with safety."

With that, the roof fell in: quite literally. John Morgan had left Kentucky in late July, but now he suddenly reappeared in Middle Tennessee. On August 12 he captured the guard at Gallatin, above Nashville, and wrecked the L & N Railroad by pushing blazing boxcars into the 800-foot tunnel, seven miles north of there, so that the timbers burned and let the dirt cave in. Unplugging it would be a long-term if not an impossible job, and with the Cumberland River too low for shipping, Buell was cut off from his main supply base at Louisville: which meant that his army would have to eat up the rations collected at Stevenson for the intended drive on Chattanooga. Learning next that a Confederate force estimated at 15,000 men had left Knoxville, bound for Nashville and other points in his rear, he called for the two divisions from Grant and on the 16th detached William Nelson to go to Kentucky with a cadre of experienced officers "to organize such troops as could be got together there to reëstablish our communications and operate against Morgan's incursions." Nor was that all; for the pressure came from various directions, including Washington. Two days later, when Halleck threatened to fire him if he did not speed up his operations — "So great is the dissatisfaction here at the apparent want of energy and activity in your district, that I was this morning notified to have you removed. I got the matter delayed till we could hear further of your movements" — Buell replied forthrightly: "I beg that you will not interpose on my behalf. On the contrary, if the dissatisfaction cannot cease on grounds which I think might be supposed if not apparent, I respectfully request that I may be relieved. My position is far too important to be occupied by any officer on sufferance. I have no desire to stand in the way of what may be deemed necessary for the public good."

Either he was past caring or else he recognized a bluff when he saw one. At any rate, whatever satisfaction this gave him, he had only a short time to enjoy it. Next morning, August 19, he learned that Bragg's army was crossing the river in force at Chattanooga. This was the eventuality in which he had said, "I shall attack him"; but now that he was faced with the actual thing, it began to seem to him that his first responsibility was the protection of Nashville, lying exposed in his rear. Accordingly, he shifted his headquarters to Decherd, forty miles northeast on the railroad leading back to the capital. Four days later — by which time Bragg was reported to have crossed the Tennessee with fifty regiments, "well armed and [with] good artillery" — he had made up his mind. Orders went to the commanders of the two divisions on their way from Grant; they were to change direction and "move by forced marches on Nashville." Simultaneously, the officer in charge of the advance depot at Stevenson was told to "expedite the shipment of stores ... in every possible way, and be ready to evacuate the place at a moment's notice." The work of nailing and caulking the floats for the 1400-yard-long span at Bridgeport had been completed two weeks before, and this too was remembered: "Let engineers quietly prepare the pontoons for burning, and when you leave destroy everything that cannot be brought away."

Presently, like the campaign itself, the unused bridge went up in smoke. "Don Carlos won't do; he won't do," one division commander muttered when he received the order to retire. Others protested likewise, but to no avail. Before the end of August the withdrawal was complete, and the Decherd provost marshal, describing himself as "weak, discouraged, and worn out," recorded in his diary: "The whole army is concentrated here, or near here; but nobody knows anything, except that the water is bad, whiskey scarce, dust abundant, and the air loaded with the scent and melody of a thousand mules."

※ 3 ※

Having accomplished Buell's repulse without the firing of a shot on either side — except in his rear, when Forrest and Morgan were on the rampage — Bragg now turned his mind to larger prospects, involving nothing less than the upset and reversal of the entire military situation in the enormous theater lying between the Appalachians and the Mississippi, the Ohio and the Gulf of Mexico.

The actual movement which placed him in a position to accomplish this design had been undertaken as the result of a decision reached on the spur of a moment in late July: specifically, the anniversary of Manassas. Before that, he had spent a month reorganizing and refitting the army he inherited when Beauregard left Tupelo for what he thought would be a ten-day convalescence. It had been no easy job. After the long retreat, the troops were badly in need of almost everything, including rest. What they needed most, however, was discipline; or so Bragg told "the brave men of Shiloh and of Elkhorn" in an address issued on June 27, the date of his official appointment to command the Army of the Mississippi.

"I enter hopefully on my duties," he declared. "But, soldiers, to secure the legitimate results of all your heavy sacrifices which have brought this army together, to infuse that unity and cohesion essential for a resolute resistance to the wicked invasion of our country, and to give to serried ranks force, impetus, and direction for driving the invader beyond our borders, be assured discipline at all times and obedience to the orders of your officers on all points, as a sacred duty, an act of patriotism, is an absolute necessity." Great events were impending. "A few more days of needful preparation and organization and I shall give your banners to the breeze ... with the confident trust that you will gain additional honors to those you have already won on other fields." After much that was turgid, he ended grimly: "But be prepared to undergo privation and labor with cheerfulness and alacrity."

Cheerfulness was by no means a primary characteristic of this sixth among the Confederacy's full generals; dyspepsia and migraine had made him short-tempered and disputatious all his life. In the old army there was a story that in his younger days, as a lieutenant commanding one of several companies at a post where he was also serving as quartermaster, he had submitted a requisition for supplies, then as quartermaster had declined by indorsement to fill it. As company commander he resubmitted the requisition, giving additional reasons for his needs, but as quartermaster he persisted in denial. Having reached this impasse, he referred the matter to the post commandant, who took one look at the correspondence and threw up his hands: "My God, Mr Bragg, you have quarreled with every officer in the army, and now you are quarreling with yourself!" Other stories were less humorous: as for instance that one of his soldiers had attempted to assassinate him not long after the Mexican War by exploding a 12-pound shell under his cot. When the smoke cleared away, the cot was reduced to tatters and kindling, but Bragg himself emerged without a scratch.

He had left the army in 1856 for a civilian career, not in his native North Carolina but as a sugar planter and commissioner of swamp lands in Louisiana. With the coming of the present war — which he believed had been brought on by such ill-advised political measures as the extension of "universal suffrage" — he had sustained his former reputation as a disciplinarian and a fighter by whipping his Gulf Coast command rapidly into a state of efficiency and leading it aggressively at Shiloh. There, he said in his report immediately afterwards, the army had been given "a valuable lesson, by which we should profit — never on a battlefield to lose a moment's time, but leaving the killed, wounded, and spoils to those whose special business it is to care for them, to press on with every available man, giving a panic-stricken and retreating foe no time to rally, and reaping all the benefits of success never complete until every enemy is killed, wounded, or captured."

He was now in a position, with the approval of the authorities in

Richmond, to give this precept large-scale application. After informing him on June 29 that his department had been "extended so as to embrace that part of Louisiana east of the Mississippi, the entire states of Mississippi and Alabama, and the portion of Georgia and Florida west of the Chattahoochee and Apalachicola Rivers," Secretary Randolph not only authorized an offensive, but urged him to "Strike the moment an opportunity offers." That was what Bragg had already told his soldiers he intended to do, as soon as he had completed the reorganization-in-progress. However, this was attended by many difficulties. One problem, beyond the need for restoring (or, Bragg would say, injecting) discipline, was the army's health. The troops had brought their Corinth ailments with them; including the men from the Transmississippi, the July 1 "aggregate present" of 61,561 was reduced to 45,393 by deduction of those who were sick or in arrest or on extra duty. Healthier conditions at Tupelo, plus the absence of strain — the nearest bluecoat was two days off — would restore a good part of these 16,000 soldiers to the ranks. More serious, as Bragg saw it, was the shortage of competent high-ranking officers. Van Dorn was gone, transferred to Vicksburg in mid-June when Davis and Farragut threatened the city from above and below; Breckinridge went with him, taking 6000 troops to oppose a landing by the men from Butler, and Hindman was detached at the same time to raise an army in Arkansas. Polk having been relieved of his corps and named second in command of the whole, Hardee and Price were the only experienced major generals left in direct charge of troops. The rest, Bragg told Richmond, including most of the brigadiers in the sweeping indictment, were "in my judgment unsuited for their responsible positions"; were, in fact, "only incumbrances, and would be better out of the way."

Despite these shortcomings — and despite the fact that the War Department increased his difficulties by not allowing him to consolidate under-strength regiments bled white at Shiloh, then further reduced to skeletons by pestilence at Corinth — he kept his army hard at work, convinced that this was the sovereign remedy for injured health as well as for injured discipline. In compensation for long hours of drill he issued new uniforms and better rations, both of which had an additional salutary effect. New problems were dealt with as they arose, including an upsurge of desertion. He met it harshly. "Almost every day we would hear a discharge of musketry, and knew that some poor trembling wretch had bid farewell to mortal things here below," one soldier afterwards recalled. The effectiveness of such executions was increased, Bragg believed, by lining up the condemned man's former comrades to watch him pay for his crime. It worked; desertion decreased; but at a price. "We were crushed," the same observer added bitterly. "Bragg, so the soldiers thought, was the machine that did it.... He loved to crush the spirit of his men. The more of a hangdog look they had about them the better was General Bragg pleased. Not a single soldier in the whole army ever loved or respected him."

True or false, all this was rather beside the point as far as Bragg was concerned. He was not out after love or respect; he was after results, and he got them. On July 12 he informed the Adjutant General that the time since his last report, forwarded to Richmond when he assumed official command two weeks before, "has been diligently applied to organization, discipline, and instruction, with a very marked improvement. The health and general tone of the troops, too, exhibits results no less gratifying. Our condition for service is good and has reached a culminating point under the defective skeleton organization."

He was ready to strike. The question was, where? In what direction? Grant's army, considerably larger than his own and occupying strong positions under Sherman and Rosecrans at Memphis and Corinth, seemed practically unassailable; besides which, Bragg told Richmond, "A long and disastrous drouth, threatening destruction to the grain crop, continues here and renders any move [into North Mississippi] impracticable for want of water." As for Buell, his lateral advance had been so slow and apparently so uncertain that for a long time the Confederates had found it impossible to determine his objective. It might be Chattanooga — in that case, Bragg had already sent a 3000-man brigade of infantry to reinforce the troops in East Tennessee — or it might be Atlanta, depending on what direction he took after crossing the river at Bridgeport. Whichever it was, Bragg decided in mid-July to give him all the trouble he could by sending two brigades of cavalry, under Colonel Joseph Wheeler and Brigadier General Frank Armstrong, to harass his lines of supply and communication in West Tennessee and North Alabama.

They had excellent models for their work, commanders who had already given cavalry operations — and, indeed the war itself — a new dimension, based on their proof that sizeable bodies of hard-riding men could not only strike and create havoc deep in the enemy's rear, Jeb Stuart-style, but could stay there to strike again and again, spreading the havoc over hundreds of miles and wearing out their would-be pursuers by causing them to converge repeatedly on thin air. By now the whole Confederate West was ringing with praise for Morgan and Forrest: particularly the former, whose exploits had surrounded him with the aura of a legend. A tall, white-faced, handsome, cold-eyed man, soft-spoken and always neatly dressed in conservative but obviously expensive clothes — fine gray broadcloth, fire-gilt buttons, richly polished boots, and spotless linen — he knew the effectiveness of reticence, yet he could be flamboyant on occasion. "Kentuckians!" he exhorted in a broadside struck off at Glasgow and distributed on his sweep through the Bluegrass, "I have come to liberate you from the hands of your oppressors." Calling for volunteer recruits, "fifty thousand of Kentucky's bravest sons," and implying thereby that he would take only the bravest, he broke into verse:

> "*Strike — for your altars and your fires;*
> *Strike for the green graves of your sires,*
> *God, and your native land!*"

He was seldom flamboyant, however, except for a purpose. For example, he carried with him a telegrapher, a wire-tap expert who, though he would sometimes chat waggishly with enemy operators — once he even went so far as to complain directly to Washington, in Morgan's name, about the inferior grade of mules being furnished Buell's army — not only intercepted messages that kept his chief informed of the Federal efforts to surround him, but also sent out false instructions that turned the converging blue columns off his trail. Such devices yielded profits. Leaving Knoxville on July 4 with fewer than 900 men, he made a thousand-mile swing through Middle Tennessee and Kentucky, in the course of which he captured seventeen towns, together with tons of Union supplies, paroled nearly 1200 regular army prisoners, and dispersed about 1500 home-guards, all at a cost of less than 90 casualties, and returned before the end of the month with an additional 300 volunteers picked up along the way. Two weeks later he was back again. Lest it be thought that he was merely a hit-and-run sort of soldier, after wrecking the Gallatin tunnel he turned on his pursuer — Brigadier General R. W. Johnson, a West Pointer and fellow-Kentuckian, whom Buell had assigned the task of intercepting the raiders with an equal force — and whipped him soundly, breaking up his command and capturing the general and his staff.

Forrest was a different sort of man; different in method, that is, if not in results. Recuperating in Memphis from his Fallen Timbers wound — the ball had lodged against his spine and was removed in the field a week later, without the benefit of an anesthetic — he put a recruiting notice in the local paper, calling for "able-bodied men ... with good horse and gun. I wish none but those who desire to be actively engaged.... Come on, boys, if you want a heap of fun and to kill some Yankees." When he returned to Corinth, shortly before the evacuation, Beauregard sent him to Chattanooga with orders to weld the scattered East Tennessee cavalry units into a brigade. He arrived in late June, assembled his men, and, believing active duty the best possible training for a green command, crossed the Tennessee River on July 9 to camp the following night atop Cumberland Mountain, deep in enemy territory. At dawn Sunday, three mornings later and ninety roundabout miles away, civilian hostages held in the Murfreesboro jail — several were under sentence of death, in retaliation for the bushwhacking of Union soldiers on or near their farms — heard what one of them later called "a strange noise like the roar of an approaching storm." It was hoofbeats: Forrest's 1400 troopers were pounding up the turnpike. Two regiments of infantry, one from Michigan, one from Minnesota, each with a section of artillery and cavalry support — their combined strength was about the same as Forrest's, except that he had no guns — were camped on opposite sides of town, with detachments guarding the jail and the courthouse, in which the brigade supplies were stored. Quickly the town was taken, along with the Federal commanding general, and fire-fights broke out on the outskirts, where the blue infantry prepared to defend its camps. Once the hostages had been freed and the captured goods packed for removal along with the prisoners already taken, some of the raiders, believing the alarm had spread to other Union garrisons by now, suggested withdrawal. But Forrest would have none of that. "I didn't come here to make half a job of it," he said, influenced perhaps by the fact that today was his forty-first birthday; "I'm going to have them all."

He got them, too — though he hastened matters somewhat by sending notes to the two commanders in their barricaded camps, demanding "unconditional surrender... or I will have every man put to the sword." He added, by way of extenuation and persuasion: "This demand is made to prevent the effusion of blood," and though like Morgan he was still a colonel, in his signature he promoted himself to "Brigadier General of Cavalry, C.S. Army," doubtless to lend additional weight to the threat. It worked. The two blue colonels surrendered in sequence, and Forrest marched his 1200 prisoners back eastward to McMinnville, where he paroled them and forwarded the captured arms and supplies to Chattanooga — all but the guns; he kept them for use around Nashville the following week, where he gave Nelson the slip after re-wrecking Buell's vital railroad supply line.

"I am happy to see that my two lieutenants, Morgan and Forrest, are doing such good service in Kentucky and Tennessee," Beauregard wrote from Bladon Springs, where he was still in exile. "When I appointed them I thought they would leave their mark wherever they passed." This was said in reply to a letter from Bragg, in which the present army commander told his former chief, "Our cavalry is paving the way for me in Middle Tennessee and Kentucky." The letter was dated July 22. By that time Bragg had decided not only on Buell's intentions, but also on his own. After a forty-day Federal head start, it was to be a race for Chattanooga: with further possibilities as the prize.

Kirby Smith, commanding in East Tennessee, had never had much doubt about Buell's intentions from the outset. Promoted to major general after recovering from being shot through the neck at Manassas, Smith had been given the thorny job of restoring order in the area around Knoxville, and in this he had succeeded remarkably well, considering the extent to which the region was torn by conflicting loyalties and ambitions. But since the fall of Corinth the military situation had grown increasingly ominous; George Morgan occupied Cumberland Gap, an immediate threat to Knoxville itself, and Buell began his eastward advance in the direction of Chattanooga, while Smith himself had less than 15,000 of all arms with which to resist the two-pronged menace. The arrival of the 3000-man brigade from Bragg afforded some relief, but not for long. Learning from northern papers in mid-July that several of Grant's divisions had been released to Buell, he protested to Davis in Richmond: "This brings an overwhelming force that cannot be resisted except by Bragg's coöperation." Four days later, July 19, he reported to the Adjutant General that "Buell with his whole force" had reached Stevenson, thirty miles from Chattanooga, which he was "daily expected to attack." Fortunately, Smith added, Forrest had broken the Union supply line at Murfreesboro. "This may delay General Buell's movement and give General Bragg time to move on Middle Tennessee. The safety of Chattanooga depends upon his coöperation." Next day, not knowing of his opponent's difficulties in procuring pitch and oakum, he made a telegraphic appeal to Bragg himself: "Buell has completed his preparations, is prepared to cross near Bridgeport, and his passage there may be hourly expected. General Morgan's command moving on Knoxville from Cumberland Gap. Your coöperation is much needed. It is your time to strike at Middle Tennessee."

Bragg's reply, sent from Tupelo that same day, was not encouraging. "Confronted here by a largely superior force strongly intrenched" and threatened on the left by Curtis, who would "now be enabled to unite against us," he found it "impossible ... to do more than menace and harass the enemy from this quarter." The land was parched; both armies, Grant's and his own, were living out of wells; so that whichever ventured far from its base in search of the other would die of thirst. "The fact is we are fearfully outnumbered in this department, the enemy having at least two to our one in the field, with a comparatively short line upon which he may concentrate." After this recital of obstacles and woes, he made it clear that Smith would have to shift for himself in East Tennessee, without the hope of further reinforcements.

Then overnight he changed his mind. Next day was the anniversary of Manassas, and he saluted it with a telegram as abruptly brief as the discharge of a starting-gun in the race which it announced:

> Tupelo, Miss., July 21
>
> President Jefferson Davis,
> Richmond, Va.:
>
> Will move immediately to Chattanooga in force and advance from there. Forward movement from here in force is not practicable. Will leave this line well defended.
>
> BRAXTON BRAGG

Next day, in the midst of large-scale preparations for the shift — he was not waiting for specific governmental approval; "Strike the moment an opportunity offers," he had been told three weeks ago — he expanded this somewhat in a second wire to Davis, who he knew must have been startled at being told, without preamble, that the army which was the mainstay of his native Mississippi was being removed forthwith: "Obstacles in front connected with danger to Chattanooga induce a change of base. Fully impressed with great importance of that line, am moving to East Tennessee. Produce rapid offensive from there following the consternation now being produced by our cavalry. Leave this State amply protected by Van Dorn at Vicksburg and Price here."

In a letter to Beauregard that same day — the one in which he wrote, "Our cavalry is paving the way" — he gave a fuller explanation. "As I am changing entirely, under altered circumstances, the plan of operations here," he told his former chief, "I submit to you what I propose and beg your candid criticism, and in view of the cordial and sincere relations we have ever maintained, I trust to your compliance." With Smith "so weak as to give me great uneasiness for the safety of his line," Bragg had had to choose between four alternatives: 1) to remain idle at Tupelo, 2) to attack Grant, 3) to move into Middle Tennessee by crossing the river in Buell's rear and thus disrupt his and Grant's supply lines, or 4) to attack Buell. Of these, the first was unthinkable; the second was impracticable, considering the drouth in North Mississippi and the strength of the fortifications at Memphis and Corinth; the third was unwise and overrisky, since it would invite both Grant and Buell to assault him simultaneously from opposite directions. Therefore he had chosen the fourth, which would not only provide for a combination with Smith, but would also afford possibilities for maneuver and mystification. "By throwing my cavalry forward toward Grand Junction and Tuscumbia" — this referred to Wheeler and Armstrong, who had left three days ago — "the impression is created that I am advancing on both places and [the Federals] are drawing in to meet me. The Memphis & Charleston road has been kept cut, so they have no use of it and have at length given it up. Before they can know my movement I shall be in front of Buell at Chattanooga, and by cutting off his transportation may have him in a tight place.... Thus you have my plan."

As might have been expected — for, though it lacked the language, it had nearly the grandeur of one of the Creole's own — Beauregard gave the plan his fervent approval. "Action, action, and action is what we require," he replied, paraphrasing Danton's "De l'audace, encore l'audace, et toujours de l'audace," and added with a paternalistic glow: "I have no doubt that with anything like equal numbers you will meet with success." By the time these encouraging words reached him, however, Bragg was far from Tupelo. He left on July 24, after notifying the Adjutant General: "Major General Van Dorn, with about 16,000 effectives, will hold the line of the Mississippi. Major General Price, with a similar force, will face the enemy on this frontier, and a sufficient garrison will be left for Mobile and the Gulf. With the balance of the forces, some 35,000 effectives, I hope, in conjunction with Major General Smith, to strike an effective blow through Middle Tennessee, gaining the enemy's rear, cutting off his supplies and dividing his forces, so as to encounter him in detail. In any event much will be accomplished in simply preserving our line and preventing a descent into Georgia, than which no greater disaster could befall us."

His confidence that he would win the race, despite the handicap of a six-week lag — not to mention the sobering example of the hare-and-tortoise fable — was based on an appreciation of railroads as a strategic factor in this war. (For one thing, by bringing Joe Johnston's men down from the Valley, through Manassas Gap, to unload within earshot of the Union guns, they had won the battle whose anniversary had now come round.) Ever since his assumption of command Bragg had kept busy, doing not only all he could to wreck Buell's rail facilities, but also all he could to improve his own, especially in urging the completion of a line connecting Meridian and Selma. In the former effort, by grace of Morgan and Forrest, he had been successful, but in the latter he had failed; the Confederacy, it appeared, could afford neither the effort nor the iron. Consequently, with the Memphis & Charleston wrecked and in Federal hands, the only rail connection between Tupelo and Chattanooga was a roundabout, far-south route through Mobile and Atlanta, involving a journey of 776 miles over no less than half a dozen separate railroads, with through trains prohibited by the water gap across Mobile Bay and the narrow gauge of the Montgomery & West Point road. Nevertheless, the sending of the 3000-man brigade to Smith in late June, as a trial run over this route, had opened Bragg's eyes to the possibilities it afforded for a rapid, large-scale movement. The troops had left Tupelo on June 27, and despite congestion all along the line — conflicting orders from Richmond had put other units simultaneously on the rails — reached Chattanooga on July 3, within a week of the day the movement order had been issued.

Now he was out to repeat or better the performance with ten times as many soldiers, the "effective total" of his four divisions being 31,638 of all arms. Horse-drawn elements, including engineers and wagon trains, as well as cavalry and artillery, would move overland — due east to Rome, then north — but the bulk of the command would go by rail, dispatched from Tupelo a division at a time. For this, though they were made on quite short notice, the preparations were extensive, with the emphasis on discipline, as was always the case when Bragg was in charge. Each man was to be handed seven days' cooked rations as he stepped aboard, thus forestalling any excuse for foraging en route, and unit commanders were cautioned to be especially vigilant at junction

The Sun Shines South

points to prevent the more adventurous from disrupting the schedule by stealing away for a visit to the fleshpots. The first division left on July 23, the second and third immediately thereafter, and the fourth on July 29: by which time the units forwarded from Mobile and other scattered points to clear the line had been in Chattanooga for two full days. They were followed by a week-long procession of jam-packed cars whose engines came puffing around Missionary Ridge and into the city.

In all the bustle and hurry of preparation and departure, and in spite of the number of wires and letters flying back and forth, Bragg had neglected to mention his sudden volte-face to the one person most immediately concerned: Kirby Smith. While changing trains in Montgomery, however, he was handed an intercepted letter the East Tennessee commander had sent from Knoxville on the 24th — the day Bragg left Tupelo — proposing, with what amounted to clairvoyance if not downright telepathy, the very movement now in progress: "Buell's movements and preparations indicate a speedy attack....

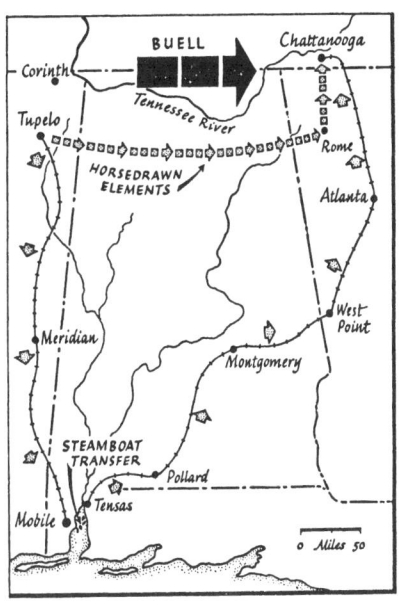

Can you not leave a portion of your forces in observation in Mississippi, and, shifting the main body to this department, take command in person? There is yet time for a brilliant summer campaign; you will have a good and secure base, abundant supplies, the Tennessee can be crossed at any point by the aid of steam and ferry boats, and the campaign opened with every prospect of regaining possession of Middle Tennessee and possibly Kentucky." He added: "I will not only coöperate with you, but will cheerfully place my command under you subject to your orders."

With this in his pocket, a happy omen as well as an affirmation of his strategic judgment, Bragg continued his journey and reached Chattanooga early on the morning of July 30. Informed of his arrival, Smith came down from Knoxville the following day to confer with him on what Bragg called "measures for material support and effective coöperation." Smith had two divisions, one in front of Cumberland Gap, observing the Federals who occupied that point, the other at Chattanooga; their strength was about 9,000 men each, including the brigade that had arrived four weeks ago to thicken the ranks of the slim force confronting Buell. Bragg was reorganizing his still-arriving army into two "wings," one under Polk, the other under Hardee, each with two infantry divisions and a cavalry brigade; their combined strength was 34,000, including the units forwarded in driblets from points along the railroad. His problem was how best to employ these 52,000 men — his and Smith's — against the larger but badly scattered Federal forces to his front and on his flank.

The solution, as communicated to the Adjutant General on August 1, was for Smith to "move at once against General Morgan in front of Cumberland Gap," while Bragg was collecting supplies and awaiting the arrival of his artillery and trains for an advance from Chattanooga. This would require ten days or two weeks, he said. At the end of that time, if Smith had been successful against Morgan, both armies would then combine for a march "into Middle Tennessee with the fairest prospect of cutting off General Buell, should that commander continue in his present position. Should he be reinforced from the west side of the Tennessee River, so as to cope with us, then Van Dorn and Price can strike and clear West Tennessee of any force that can be left to hold it." Furthermore, once Grant and Buell had been disposed of, either by destruction or by being maneuvered into retreat, he considered the time propitious for an invasion of the region to the north. "The feeling in Middle Tennessee and Kentucky is represented by Forrest and Morgan to have become intensely hostile to the enemy, and nothing is wanted but arms and support to bring the people into our ranks, for they have found that neutrality has afforded them no protection."

Returning to Knoxville much encouraged by these developments, Smith informed his wife that he had found his new partner "a grim old fellow" (he himself was thirty-eight; Bragg was forty-five) "but a true soldier." Presently he was further gladdened by the arrival of two brigades detached by Bragg to reinforce him for the offensive, one from Polk and one from Hardee, and being thus strengthened on the eve of his advance he began to see larger prospects looming out beyond the horizon — prospects based in part on a dispatch from John Morgan, who had reported from northern Kentucky in mid-July: "I am here with a force sufficient to hold all the country outside of Lexington and Frankfort. These places are garrisoned chiefly with Home Guards. The bridges between Cincinnati and Lexington have been destroyed. The whole country can be secured, and 25,000 or 30,000 men will join you at once. I have taken eleven cities and towns with very heavy army stores." If one small brigade of cavalry could accomplish all this, Smith reasoned, what might a whole army do? Accordingly, on August 9 he wrote to Bragg that he "understood" the Federals intrenched at Cumberland Gap had "nearly a month's supply of provisions. If this be true the reduction of the place would be a matter of more time than I presume you are willing I should take. As my move direct to Lexington, Ky. would effectually invest [the Gap] and would be attended with other most brilliant results in my judgment, I suggest my being allowed to take that course, if I find the speedy reduction of the Gap an impractical thing."

Bragg too was nurturing hopes in that direction, though not without reservations. He replied next day: "It will be a week yet before I can commence crossing the river, and information I hope to receive will determine which route I shall take, to Nashville or Lexington. My inclination is now for the latter." All the same, Smith's plan to by-pass Cumberland Gap and head straight for North Central Kentucky was more than his partner had bargained for, even though Smith reinforced his proposal by inclosing a letter from John Morgan's lieutenant-colonel, stressing the opinion that flocks of eager volunteers were waiting to double the size of his army as soon as it reached the Bluegrass. Strategically, Bragg approved, but tactically he urged caution: "It would be unadvisable, I think, for you to move far into Kentucky, leaving [George] Morgan in your rear, until I am able to fully engage Buell and his forces on your left. But I do not credit the amount of Morgan's supplies [at Cumberland Gap] and have confidence in his timidity. When once well on the way to his rear you might safely leave but 5000 to his front, and by a flank movement draw the rest to your assistance. He will never advance to escape."

Smith's ebullience was contagious: as was shown in the final sentence of Bragg's letter. "Van Dorn and Price will advance simultaneously with us from Mississippi on West Tennessee, and I trust we may all unite in Ohio."

★ ★ ★

Just now, however, Van Dorn was looking south, not north; he had New Orleans on his mind, not Ohio. The grim determination he had brought to embattled Vicksburg in late June — "Let it be borne in mind by all that the army here is defending the place against occupation. This will be done at all hazards, even though this beautiful and devoted city should be laid in ruin and ashes" — gave way to elation in mid-July when the *Arkansas* made her run through the Yankee sloops and gunboats. "Glorious for the navy, and glorious for her heroic commander, officers, and men," he wired Davis. The iron ram changed everything. "Smokestack riddled; otherwise not materially damaged," he exulted. "Soon be repaired and then, Ho! for New Orleans." Both enemy fleets were still on hand, and across the way the bluecoats were still digging their canal; but Van Dorn no longer saw them as much of a threat. A week later, after two all-out attempts to sink the *Arkansas* under the tall red bluff, he pronounced "the failure so complete that it was almost ridiculous." The same went for the engineering project. "Nothing can be accomplished by the enemy," he told Richmond, "unless they bring overwhelming number of troops. This must be anticipated."

His favorite method of anticipation, now as always, was to seize the offensive; to snatch the ball from his opponent and start running. That was what he had done, or tried to do, in Arkansas back in the early spring, and that was what he decided to do now in his native Mississippi in midsummer. When Davis and Farragut gave up the game, turned their backs on each other and went their separate ways — the former to Helena, the latter to New Orleans after dropping the infantry off at Baton Rouge — Van Dorn ordered Breckinridge to pursue southward with 4000 men and knock the bluecoats off balance in the Louisiana capital before they could get set for a return. If possible, he was to take the city: after which, as Van Dorn saw it, would come much else. Five months ago the byword had been "St Louis, then huzza!" Now it was "Ho! for New Orleans."

Breckinridge wasted no time in getting started. On July 27, the day after the Yankee fleets took off in opposite directions, he put his troops aboard railroad cars and proceeded by way of Jackson to Ponchatoula, Louisiana, where they detrained the following afternoon to prepare for the overland advance on Baton Rouge, sixty miles to the west. On the 30th the march began, but was halted the following morning when reports came in "that the effective force of the enemy was not less than 5000 and that the ground was commanded by three gunboats lying in the river." Down to 3400 men as a result of sickness, Breckinridge wired Van Dorn that he would nonetheless "undertake to capture the garrison if the *Arkansas* could be sent down to clear the river or divert the fire of the gunboats." Promptly the reply came back: The ram would be in front of Baton Rouge at dawn, August 5. Breckinridge made his plans accordingly.

Isaac Brown was not in Vicksburg at the time, having left his shipmates "to sustain without me the lassitude of inaction" while he took a four-day leave in Grenada. If rest and relaxation were what he was after (which was probable; he had had precious little of either in the past two months) he was disappointed in more ways than one. For one thing, he had no sooner arrived than he was taken violently ill and put to bed. For another, while he was in this condition, supposedly unable to lift his head off the pillow, he received a wire from his first lieutenant, informing him that the *Arkansas* was under orders to proceed at once to Baton Rouge, despite the fact that her engines were under major repair and much of her rusty plating had still not been refastened to her battered sides. Brown replied with "a positive order to remain at Vicksburg until I could join him," and had himself carried to the depot, where he boarded the first southbound train. Collapsed on some mail bags, too weak to sit up or even change his position, he rode the 130 miles to

Jackson, where he applied for a special train to take him the rest of the way, only to learn that the *Arkansas* had already gone downriver.

She cast off Sunday evening, August 3, barely thirty hours before she was due at her Tuesday-morning rendezvous with Breckinridge, 300 winding miles below. This called for her best speed: with the result that there were stoppages from overstrain all along the way, each requiring additional make-up speed thereafter, which produced more frequent breakdowns. Caught up in this vicious cycle, her engines had become so cranky by the time she reached the mouth of the Red, 200 miles out of Vicksburg, that her substitute skipper, Lieutenant Henry Stevens, called a council of war to decide whether to continue or turn back. The decision was to press on. At daybreak, August 5, approaching the final bend above Baton Rouge, the crew heard the boom of guns, which told that the land attack was under way. The *Arkansas* herself appeared to sense this; or, as one of her officers put it, "Like a war horse she seemed to scent the battle from afar, and in point of speed outdid anything we had ever before witnessed." Then, just before rounding the bend, they heard a familiar sound: the crack and jar of naval guns mixed in with the bark of field artillery. The ironclad *Essex* and the two Farragut gunboats were adding the weight of their metal to the attempt to fling back the Confederate attackers. Urged on by the knowledge "that our iron sides should be receiving those missiles which now were mowing down our ranks of infantry," Stevens decided to make an immediate ram attack on the *Essex*, sinking her where she lay, then steam below the city to cut off the retreat of the two wooden gunboats, reducing them to kindling at his leisure. Such was his intention: whereupon the starboard engine suddenly quit, and before the helmsman could port her wheel, the ram ran hard aground. The engineers got to work at once with files and chisels, trying to coax the balky engine into motion, but it would obviously be some hours before they could succeed. Meanwhile, the land attack continued. "There lay the enemy in plain view," one of the *Arkansas* lieutenants afterwards wrote, still mortified years later, "and we as helpless as a shear-hulk."

Breckinridge had marched to within ten miles of the place the night before in order to launch his assault on schedule, although by now he was down to 2600 effectives as a result of sickness brought on by the heat and an irregular diet, the rail movement having been made in such haste that commissary supplies and cooking utensils were left behind. "The day before the battle we had nothing to eat but roasting ears," one Kentucky infantryman afterwards recalled, "and these we ate raw because we had not time to stop long enough to roast them. Our command, with the horses, consumed forty acres of green corn one evening; for we stopped only long enough to gather the corn and feed the horses, [and] we then moved forward to take position to make the attack at daylight." His brigade, which had left Vicksburg with 1800 men, was reduced to 580 within two weeks. "Such were the ravages of sickness, exposure, and battle," he declared.

Of these, the last were the least as the thing turned out, in spite of the fact that they found the enemy waiting to receive them. The Federal commander, Thomas Williams, had formed his line closer to the town than some of his regimental camps, contracting it thus because he was down to about the same effective strength as the attackers: not because of exposure or bad food, but because so many of his men had still not recovered from lowland ailments encountered while plying their shovels opposite Vicksburg. However, he had the advantage in artillery, eighteen pieces to eleven, besides the tremendous added power of the gunboats, plowing the ranks of the charging rebels by arching their big projectiles over the capital, where a naval observer directed their fire by signals from the tower of the statehouse. In the face of this, Breckinridge scored considerable early success, forcing the bluecoats back through the suburbs on the right and capturing two guns; but the warships, unopposed by the missing *Arkansas,* more than tipped the balance. By 10 o'clock, having lost the commanders of one of his two divisions and three of his four brigades, he halted to adjust his line. Williams, observing this, ordered a charge to recover what had been yielded, but then was killed by a bullet through his chest — the first Union general to fall in battle since Nathaniel Lyon died much the same way at Wilson's Creek, a year ago next week. Breckinridge held his ground until late afternoon, hoping to renew the attack as soon as the *Arkansas* arrived. When he learned that the ram was lying helpless four miles above town, he left a small force in observation and pulled the main body back to the Comite River, from which he had marched the night before. The Federals did not follow.

Aboard the grounded ram, the engineers were still at work with their files and chisels. Stevens got her afloat by throwing off some railroad iron lying loose on her deck, and by dusk the black gang had her engines back in operation. She started down the four-mile reach, where the Union boats were standing guard, but had gone no more than a hundred yards when the crankpin in the rocking shaft of the starboard engine snapped. A forge was set up on the gundeck, and one of the engineers, a former blacksmith, hammered out a new one. By the time it was finished, dawn was glimmering through and the lookout spotted the *Essex* coming upstream, making a scant two knots against the current. Hurriedly, the new pin was installed; the rust-red *Arkansas* stood out for battle. Stevens intended to make a short run upstream, then turn and launch a ram attack with the added momentum. Before he could start back, however, the port engine suddenly quit and spun the vessel once more into bank. The *Essex* was coming slowly on, firing as she came, and the *Arkansas* was hard aground, able to bring only one of her guns to bear. The situation spoke for itself. Stevens ordered the crew ashore and fired the vessel, tears streaming down his face as he did so. When the flames reached the gundeck, the loaded guns began to explode: so that the *Arkansas* not only kept the *Essex* at a respectful distance during her death throes, but administered her own *coup de grâce* and fired her own salute as she went down. Thus she made a fitting end to her twenty-three-day career.

Brown almost got there in time to see it. Cured of his fever by the news that his ram had gone downriver without him, he got back onto the southbound train and rode to Ponchatoula, where he transferred to horseback and struck out westward for the river, in hope that he could hail the *Arkansas* from bank and somehow manage to board her or at any rate be near enough to watch and cheer her as she fought What he saw instead were exultant Union gunboats steaming back and forth across the muddy water where she had exploded and sunk with her colors flying. Sadly — though he was proud, he later wrote, that her deck "had never been pressed by the foot of an enemy" — he rode back the way he had come and returned to Vicksburg.

Breckinridge shared the pride, but not the sadness, at the outcome of the brief campaign. This reaction was based not on the casualty lists — both sides had lost 84 killed, though the Confederate total of wounded and captured was the larger: 372 to 299 — but on his view of the fighting qualities shown. "In one respect the contrast between the opposing forces was very striking," he declared. "The enemy were well clothed, and their encampments showed the presence of every comfort and even luxury. Our men had little transportation, indifferent food, and no shelter. Half of them had no coats, and hundreds were without either shoes or socks; yet no troops ever behaved with greater gallantry and even reckless audacity. What can make this difference unless it be the sublime courage inspired by a just cause?"

Whether right made might, or might made right — or, indeed, whether either was on the former Vice President's side in this case — was a question open to much debate, then and thereafter. Butler, for one, did not agree with his assessment. According to him, the rebels "took advantage of [the garrison's] sickness from the malaria of the marshes of Vicksburg to make a cowardly attack," which was bloodily repulsed with "more than a thousand killed and wounded." But the Southerner's claim to physical as well as moral victory was considerably strengthened two weeks later when Butler, after congratulating his soldiers for their staunchness — "The Spanish conqueror of Mexico won imperishable renown by landing in that country and burning his transport ships, to cut off all hope of retreat. You, more wise and economical, but with equal providence against retreat, sent yours home" — ordered Baton Rouge abandoned, and dispatched those same transports upriver to bring the endangered troops back to New Orleans.

The flow of what Horace Greeley, back in May, had been calling "A Deluge of Victories" was seemingly reversed, and there was corresponding elation in the South. Next to the capture of a northern capital, what could be better than the recovery of a southern one? More important, tactically speaking, the Federal grip on the Mississippi — so close to strangulation a month ago — had been loosened even further, and to make sure that it was not reapplied Breckinridge had already sent most of his troops to occupy and fortify Port Hudson, a left-bank position of great natural strength. Potentially another Vicksburg, its bluff commanded a sharp bend of the river about midway between Baton Rouge and the mouth of the Red, thus assuring a continuation of commerce with the Transmississippi, including the grainlands of Northwest Louisiana and the cattle-rich plains of Texas.

That was but part of the brightening overall picture. In Virginia, McClellan had been repulsed. Grant was stalled in North Mississippi. Buell had lost the race for Chattanooga. And in all these widespread regions Confederate armies were poised to take the offensive: particularly in East Tennessee, as Breckinridge learned from a letter Bragg sent him immediately after the fight at Baton Rouge. Extending an invitation to the former Bluegrass politician, the terrible-tempered North Carolinian was in a strangely rollicking mood: "My army has promised to make me military governor of Ohio in ninety days (Seward's time for crushing the rebellion), and as they cannot do that without passing your home, I have thought you would like to have an escort to visit your family." He added, in a more serious vein, "Your influence in Kentucky would be equal to an extra division in my army.... If you desire it, and General Van Dorn will consent, you shall come at once. A command is ready for you, and I shall hope to see your eyes beam again at the command 'Forward,' as they did at Shiloh, in the midst of our greatest success."

This was seconded by Hardee, who telegraphed on August 23, five days before the Chattanooga jump-off: "Come here, if possible. I have a splendid division for you to lead into Kentucky."

Breckinridge wired back: "Reserve the division for me."

One prominent Kentuckian already commanded a division under Hardee: Simon Buckner. Exchanged at last, after five months in prison at Fort Warren, he reported in late July to Richmond, where he was promoted to major general and assigned to duty with the army then on its way to Chattanooga. The army commander was glad to have him, not only because of his proved fighting qualities, but also as a recruiting attraction in his native state; spare muskets were being taken along in wagons, ready for transfer to the shoulders of Kentucky volunteers. Bragg was glad, too, to have the approval of the President for the campaign he was about to undertake, though Davis warned him at the outset with a two-edged compliment predicting future strife, off as well as on the field of battle: "You have the misfortune of being regarded as my personal friend, and are pursued, therefore, with malignant censure by men regardless of truth, and whose want of principle to guide their conduct renders them incapable of conceiving that you are trusted because of your known fitness for command and not because of friendly regard. Revolutions develop the high qualities of the good and the great, but they cannot change the nature of the vicious and the selfish."

Kirby Smith — described in the same letter as "one of our ablest and purest officers... [whose] promotions, like your own, have come unsought" — left Knoxville on August 14 to move against his West Point classmate George Morgan at Cumberland Gap. The two brigades received from Bragg had raised his striking force to 21,000 men, well over twice the number holding the gap; but finding, as he had predicted, that Morgan was better prepared to resist a siege than he himself was prepared to maintain one, he left a 9000-man division in front of the mountain stronghold, as Bragg had advised, and with the rest of his army crossed the Cumberlands thirty miles to the southwest at Big Creek Gap. This was no raid, he told Richmond. "My advance is made in the hope of permanently occupying Kentucky. It is a bold move, offering brilliant results, but will be accomplished only with hard fighting, and must be sustained by constant reinforcements." He marched fast, swinging north for Barbourville, which he occupied on August 18. The "constant reinforcements," of course, would have to be in the form of local volunteers; but none were forthcoming here. Six days later, while preparing to resume the march, he notified Bragg: "Thus far the people are universally hostile to our cause. This sentiment extends through the mountain region of Eastern Kentucky. In the bluegrass region I have better expectations and shall soon test their loyalty."

Bragg's own estimate was rosier and a good deal more specific. "Everything is ripe for success," he informed his co-commander. "The country is aroused and expecting us. Buell's forces are much scattered, and from all accounts much demoralized. By rapid movements and vigorous blows we may beat him in detail, or by gaining his rear very much increase his demoralization and break him up." On August 27, the day before the jump-off, he sent word to Sterling Price, holding the line in North Mississippi: "We move from here immediately, later by some days than expected, but in time we hope for a successful campaign. Buell has certainly fallen back from the Memphis & Charleston Railroad and will probably not make a stand this side of Nashville, if there. He is now fortifying that place. General Smith, reinforced by two brigades from this army, has turned Cumberland Gap, and is now marching on Lexington, Ky.... We shall thus have Buell pretty well disposed of. Sherman and Rosecrans we leave to you and Van Dorn, satisfied that you can dispose of them, and we shall confidently expect to meet you on the Ohio and there open the way to Missouri."

Unquestionably — even without the inclusion of Missouri, which was scarcely more than a closing flourish for the benefit of Price — this was an ambitious project. But Bragg was not only ready and willing to undertake its execution; he had already selected a guide, a model. Beauregard and McClellan, along with a cluster of lesser lights, might take Napoleon. Not Bragg. His chosen prototype was a contemporary, a man who in fact was seven years his junior. Back in Tupelo, on the occasion of promising his soldiers to "give your banners to the breeze," he also told them: "Others of your countrymen, under the lead of Jackson and Ewell in the Valley of Virginia, have recently shed imperishable renown on our arms, and shown what a small, obedient, disciplined volunteer army can do." What he intended now, as he stood poised for the jump-off, was a Valley Campaign on a much larger scale, with Smith as Ewell and himself as Stonewall. Like him, he could expect to be badly outnumbered strategically (he had fewer than 30,000 of all arms); yet like him, too, he would translate this disadvantage into "imperishable renown" by means of "rapid movements and vigorous blows." So far, it was true, the only attributes original and copy had in common were dyspepsia and a readiness to stand deserters before a firing squad. However, it was Bragg's intention to extend these similarities into other fields of reaction and endeavor during the trial that lay ahead.

Some measure of this intention, complete with Old Testament overtones, was communicated to his troops in a general order read to them before they left their camps around Chattanooga:

> The enemy is before us, devastating our fair country, imprisoning our old and venerated men (even the ministers of God), insulting our women, and desecrating our altars. It is our proud lot to be assigned the duty of punishing and driving forth these deluded men, led by desperate adventurers and goaded on by Abolition demagogues and demons. Let us but deserve success and an offended Deity will certainly assure it. Should we be opposed, we must fight at any odds and conquer at any sacrifice. Should the foe retire, we must follow him rapidly to his own territory and make him taste the bitters of invasion.
>
> Soldiers, the enemy is before you and your banners are free. It is for you to decide whether our brothers and sisters of Tennessee and Kentucky shall remain bondmen and bondwomen of the Abolition tyrant or be restored to the freedom inherited from their fathers.

Having heard him out, the long files shouldered their muskets and headed north.

※ 4 ※

In Virginia, though the basis for it was obviously a good deal less substantial — westward, the blue glacier had not only ground to a halt, it had even reversed direction, whereas here in the East no more than a pause, a hesitation of the mass, had seemingly been effected; McClellan, after all, was scarcely a dozen miles farther from Richmond than he had been on the eve of the Seven Days, besides being more securely based on the James than he had been while crouched astride the treacherous Chickahominy, and Pope was hovering northward, a considerably graver threat, both in numbers and position, than McDowell had ever been — the elation mounted higher. One reason was that the result, however far it fell short of expectation, had been obtained by actual fighting, not by maneuver or mere Federal acquiescence. Another was the return of confidence in the government: especially in the President, whose vindication now appeared complete.

Less than a week before the launching of the assault that flung the bluecoats back from the capital gates, Tom Cobb had been declaring that he saw in Davis "the embodiment and concentration of cowardly littleness [which] he garnishes over with pharisaical hypocrisy. How can God smile upon us while we have such a man [to] lead us?" Few were asking that question now: God *had* smiled upon them, and a large part of the credit went to the man who by deed as well as title filled the position of Commander in Chief and triumphed over the adversary who occupied that post in the country to the north. The Hezekiah-Sennacherib analogy still held.

As far as the soldiers themselves were concerned, however, the credit went to the general who had been placed at their head in their darkest hour and in one short month, despite their initial resentment, had welded their four disparate components — Johnston's Manassas army and Magruder's frazzled Yorktown brigades, Jackson's Valley command and Huger's unblooded Norfolk division — into a single striking force, the Army of Northern Virginia, which he hurled with cunning and fury at the blue invaders, massed in their thousands within sight and hearing of Richmond's steeples and public clocks, and sent them reeling backwards or sidling crablike to their present mud-flat sanctuary under the muzzles of their gunboats. Granny Lee, Evacuating Lee, the King of Spades, had become for his troops what he would remain: Mars Robert. They watched him as he rode among them, the high-colored face above and behind the iron-gray beard, the active, dark-brown eyes, the broad forehead whose upper half showed unexpectedly dazzling white when he removed his wide-brimmed hat to acknowledge their cheers. Distrust had yielded to enthusiasm, which in turn was giving way to awe.

On horseback, deep-chested and long-waisted, with his big, leonine head set thick-necked on massive shoulders, he looked gigantic. Partly that was the aura. It must have been; for when he dismounted, as he often did, to rest his horse — he had a tender concern for the welfare of all animals, even combat infantrymen, aside from those times when he flung them into the crackling uproar of battle like chaff into a furnace — you saw the slight legs, the narrow hips, and realized, with something of a shock, that he was no larger than many of the men around him, and not as large as some. The same contrast, above and below, was apparent in his extremities; the hands were oversized and muscular, the feet tiny as a woman's. He was in fact just under six feet tall and weighed less than 170 pounds. Quickly, though, you got over the shock (which after all was only the result of comparing flesh and perfection. However he *was* was how you preferred him) and when you saw him thus in the field your inclination was to remove your hat — not to wave it: just to hold it — and stand there looking at him: Mars Robert.

Not everyone offered such adulation, either in or out of the army. Robert Toombs, for one, who had commanded a brigade under Magruder throughout the Peninsula campaign, considered Lee "far below the occasion." The Charleston *Mercury* for another, while it praised the strategy — "projected, as we hear, by General Johnston" — agreed with Toombs as to the tactics: "The blundering manner in which [McClellan] has been allowed to get away, the desultory manner in which he has been pursued by divisions instead of our whole force, enabling him to repulse our attacks, to carry off his artillery, and, finally, to make a fresh stand with an army reinforced are facts, we fear, not very flattering to the generalship of General Lee."

Lee was rather inclined to agree with the former Georgia statesman, as well as with the South Carolina editor, not only because of his inherent modesty, but also because he knew that what they said was largely true. "His great victory did not elate him, so far as one could see," his cannoneer son later recalled. This was not for lack of material success. The booty had been ample: 52 fine Union guns (by coincidence, one for every battery in the Army of the Potomac), 31,000 rifles (which gave some measure of the Federal panic, since half were either dropped by casualties or handed over by captives, while the other half were abandoned by men who preferred to travel light) and 10,000 prisoners, most of them unwounded. All this was duly appreciated, especially the rifled guns and the badly needed small arms, but Lee's essential agreement with Toombs and the *Mercury* was based on a consideration of what had been left undone, as well as of what had been done — on the contrast, in fact, between conception and execution. "Under ordinary circumstances," he said in his report to the Adjutant General, "the Federal army should have been destroyed."

Sound strategy had largely counterbalanced woeful tactics to produce, within limits, a successful campaign. After all, Richmond was no longer even semi-beleaguered. But for the failure, so far as it was a failure beyond those limits, there were three main reasons: 1) poor maps and intelligence, which left the Confederates groping blind, or half blind, all the way from Mechanicsville to Harrison's Landing, inclusively; 2) poor staff work, especially in the transmission of orders, which was the basis for much of the lack of coördination; and 3) the Army of the Potomac, the hard-core staunchness of its infantry and the skill with which its superior artillery was employed. Of these, the last — referred to by one of Lee's own aides as "the character and personality of the men behind the Federal guns" — was clearly the most decisive in preventing the wreckage intended, but it was the first which caused what Harvey Hill summed up in one acid sentence: "Throughout this campaign we attacked just when and where the enemy wished us to attack."

Time and effort, self-application on Lee's part, might correct the first two of these drawbacks; the third would be with him from here on out. Yet there was still another problem — one he would always face with reluctance, though it too would remain. This was the task of assessing the character and performance of his lieutenants. Longstreet and the two Hills, whatever their personal eccentricities, whether headstrong or impetuous or caustic, had emerged from the test of combat with brighter laurels than before. The same could not be said of another trio: Magruder, Holmes, and Huger. Their reasons for failure were varied — overexcitability, deafness, chronic bad luck — but now that Lee had faced the problem, no matter with what reluctance, he was quick to act. He got rid of them. In Magruder's case it was simple; for he had been offered, and had accepted, command of a department in the Transmississippi. Lee wished him Godspeed along with Holmes, who went out there too, being placed in charge of the whole far-western theater. That left Huger; but not for long. He was kicked upstairs to the War Department, as chief inspector of artillery and ordnance.

In the course of replacing these departed leaders and redistributing their twelve brigades — which meant, in effect, a drastic reorganization for the work that lay ahead — Lee dealt with another problem of command: the question of what to do about Jackson, whose poor showing throughout the Seven Days was now the subject of much talk. He was reported to have said that he did not intend for his men to do all the fighting, and when he overheard some of his staff discussing his strange delay above White Oak Swamp while Longstreet was struggling desperately at Glendale, he remarked coldly: "If General Lee had wanted me, he could have sent for me." Lee of course did not join the chorus of critics, nor did he consider shunting Stonewall off to the Transmississippi; but in his regrouping of the army's nine divisions into two "wings" under its two ranking generals, Longstreet and Jackson, the former was assigned twenty-eight brigades, the latter seven. Stonewall thus had only half as many as had been under him during the late campaign, while Old Pete had nearly five times as many as the half dozen with which he had crossed the Chickahominy.

All through this period of refitting and reorganization, of distributing the captured arms and replacing his veterans' flop-soled shoes and tattered jackets, Lee had also kept busy trying to determine the enemy's intentions. It was a complicated problem, involving no less than four Federal armies of various strengths, all unknown. First there was the main force, under McClellan at Harrison's Landing. Then there was Pope's newly consolidated Army of Virginia, assumed to be in the vicinity of Manassas. Either or both might take the offensive at any time. The third was at Fredericksburg, threatening Richmond from the north, much as McDowell had done for months. The fourth was Burnside's, brought up from North Carolina in the emergency, but still kept aboard its transports, anchored mysteriously off Fort Monroe. Both of these last two forces were in positions from which they could move rapidly to combine and join either of the other two: Pope, for an advance against the vital Virginia Central Railroad: or McClellan, for a renewal of his drive on the capital itself. For the present, though both of course were possible, Lee could find out nothing that would indicate which was probable. All he knew for certain was that delay was not to the advantage of the South. Northern determination had stiffened after this defeat, just as it had done the year before, and Lincoln's call for 300,000 volunteers had gone out on the day of Malvern Hill.

In chess terms, Lee's immediate problem was whether to keep his pieces where they were, concentrated to checkmate the king — McClellan — or to disperse them in order to meet an advance by the knights and bishops, off on another quarter of the board. While awaiting developments he withdrew his infantry from the malarial swamps and left the observation of Harrison's Landing to the cavalry, newly gathered into a two-brigade division under Stuart, who was promoted to major general. Simultaneously, by way of discouraging an attack from that direction, he put his engineers to work constructing permanent fortifications. Anchored to the James at Drewry's Bluff and extending north along an arc shielding Richmond, these installations would also permit his present lines to be more thinly held if alternate pressure required dispersion. Once they were completed he would be much better prepared for whatever came.

What came, on July 12, was startling news from the north: Pope had occupied Culpeper that morning. What made this startling was that Culpeper was on the Orange & Alexandria, less than thirty miles above Gordonsville. And Gordonsville was on the Virginia Central, at the northern apex of an exposed bend known as "the Gordonsville loop," which led on westward to Charlottesville and Staunton. This was alternate pressure indeed; for if Pope took Gordonsville he would cut the

Confederate supply line connecting Richmond and the Shenandoah Valley, where a bumper crop of corn and wheat was ripening for the harvest. Lee was obliged to meet this threat, and he did so the following day by sending Jackson with his own and Ewell's divisions — the old Army of the Valley — by rail to Louisa Courthouse, fifteen miles this side of Gordonsville, which he was instructed to occupy if Pope had not already got there in too great strength to be dislodged. The movement was made rapidly by way of Hanover Junction, using eighteen trains of fifteen cars each to transport Stonewall's 10,000 infantry and artillery, while his cavalry and wagons moved by road.

Strategically, this riposte was as sound as it was necessary, but Lee had other compelling reasons for ordering the movement: one being that he had developed a scathing contempt for the leader of the force at which it was aimed. After issuing the bombastic address to his soldiers ("Let us understand each other.... Disaster and shame lurk in the rear") Pope had joined them in the field and had proceeded at once, in a series of formal orders, to give his attention to the civilians in his prospective theater of operations. One directed his army to live off the country and to reimburse only those persons who could prove devotion to the flag he represented. Another prescribed stern measures to be taken in retaliation for guerilla activities. A third provided for the arrest of all male noncombatants within his lines, the expulsion of those who refused to take a loyalty oath, and their prosecution as spies if they returned. Furthermore, any man or woman who remained would be liable to the death penalty for attempting to communicate with the enemy — presumably including a mother who wrote to a son in the southern army. These mandates were not in accordance with Lee's notion of civilized warfare; he was downright contemptuous of the man who ordered their adoption. "The miscreant Pope," he called him, and he said of him: "He ought to be suppressed if possible."

Just now it was not possible, Jackson reported. He had beaten Pope to Gordonsville, arriving there from Louisa on July 19, but the bluecoats around Culpeper were too numerous to be attacked at present. Reinforce him, Stonewall added, and he would gladly undertake all the suppression Lee could ask for. That was what Lee was considering, though the risk was admittedly great. Left with just under 70,000 men — including Holmes' former command, shifted south of the James to cover Petersburg and placed under D. H. Hill with an eye toward possible future operations in his native North Carolina — he knew he was badly outnumbered by McClellan, who moreover was beginning to show signs of activity. Besides, there were those other two armies, at Fredericksburg and off Fort Monroe: Lee still did not know in which direction they might move. Much as he wanted Pope whipped and driven back across the Rappahannock, the odds were long against weakening the capital defenses for that purpose. Nevertheless he decided to take the gamble. On July 27 he ordered A. P. Hill to Gordonsville, where the Light Division would join the Valley Army for a strike at Pope.

His hope was that this combined force would deliver its blow quickly, disposing of Pope with a knockout punch, then return to Richmond in time to help block any assault McClellan might attempt when he learned of its detachment. This would call for rapid, well-coördinated movements and a style of fighting characterized by a minimum of confusion and hesitation: quite the opposite, in fact, of the style Jackson had demonstrated throughout the Seven Days. One reason for his poor showing on the Peninsula, Lee suspected, was his known reluctance to take subordinate commanders into his military confidence. Also, in consideration of Little Powell's sensitive and highly volatile nature — he had already clashed with Longstreet over what he considered a slight to his division in the distribution of honors, and Longstreet had promptly put him in arrest, from which Lee had released him for the present expedition — there was the danger of an explosion when he came into contact with the stern and taciturn Stonewall. Accordingly, Lee wrote Jackson a letter in which he alluded tactfully to the problem. After repeating the injunction, "I want Pope to be suppressed," he concluded: "A. P. Hill you will, I think, find a good officer, with whom you can consult, and by advising with your division commanders as to your movements much trouble will be saved you in arranging details, as they can act more intelligently.... Cache your troops as much as possible till you can strike your blow, and be prepared to return to me when done, if necessary. I will endeavor to keep General McClellan quiet till it is over, if rapidly executed."

Keeping McClellan quiet might well turn out to be a good deal easier said than done. With one third of his army off after Pope, Lee was down to 56,000 men, including two brigades that arrived next day from South Carolina: whereas McClellan was not only half again larger now, he would have twice as many troops as Lee if he were reinforced by Burnside and the brigades at Fredericksburg, which Lee could do absolutely nothing to prevent. Besides, the Young Napoleon had considerable freedom of action. He could stay where he was, a hovering threat; he could steam back up the Potomac to join Pope and the others; he could advance from his present camp against the southern capital, less than twenty airline miles away. In the latter case, two routes were available to him. He could move up the left bank of the James, more or less as before, except that he would be securely based; or he could cross the river, under cover of his gunboats, capture Petersburg, and swarm into Richmond by the back door. All were possibilities to fret the mind of Lee, who so far had been able to find no clew as to which course his adversary favored. "In the prospect before me," he wrote his wife, "I cannot see a single ray of pleasure during this war."

One way to keep McClellan quiet, Lee reasoned paradoxically, or at any rate make him hug his camp while the southern army was divided, might be to stir him up; that is, make him think he was about to be attacked. An infantry feint being impractical, Lee decided on an artillery demonstration. Under cover of darkness, forty-three guns of various calibers were concentrated on the south side of the James at Coggin's Point, opposite Harrison's Landing, and on the last night of July they opened fire on the Federal camp. The result, as in the case of Stuart's popgun bombardment four weeks back, was more spectacular than effective. After some original confusion, the Union artillerists and sailors brought their heavier guns to bear and smothered the Confederate batteries. On August 3, threatened with capture by an amphibious countermovement, they had to be withdrawn. Except for the effect it might have had on McClellan himself, enlarging his natural caution, the demonstration was a failure.

Two days later, by way of recompense, Lee got his first real hint as to the Federal overall strategy. A young Confederate cavalry officer, Captain John S. Mosby, had been captured two weeks before while on his way upstate to find recruits for a partisan command, and had been taken to Fort Monroe to await exchange. As soon as he was released he came to Lee with information he had picked up while imprisoned: Burnside was under orders to take his transports up the Potomac, debark his troops at Aquia Creek, and march them overland to Fredericksburg. If true, this meant considerable danger to Jackson, who was already badly outnumbered by the enemy north of Gordonsville, as well as to the Virginia Central, which led westward to the Valley granary. What was more, it was a strong indication that the enemy's next major effort would be in northern Virginia, where Lee was weakest, not here on the James. He would have moved at least a portion of his force to meet this threat at once, except that on the same day his cavalry reported a heavy force advancing from Harrison's, up the left bank of the river, against Richmond. Apparently it was not McClellan's caution which had been enlarged by the abortive Coggin's Point demonstration, but rather his self-confidence.

Lee marched three divisions out to meet him the following day, August 6, and approaching Malvern Hill near sundown found the Federals drawn up menacingly on the crest. Intending no repetition of last month's headlong, blind attack up the rolling slope, he extended his left, skirmished briskly on the right, and braced his troops for the downhill assault. At nightfall there was every indication that the armies would be locked in battle tomorrow. Instead — as had been more or less the case five weeks ago — dawn showed the hill empty of all but a handful of blue vedettes, who at the first sign of a Confederate advance scampered down the reverse slope to join the main body, already well on its way back to its camp on the James.

This was strange indeed: passing strange. Lee decided that the only explanation for McClellan's sudden advance-and-retreat was that it was intended to cover the movement Mosby had discerned at Fort Monroe. If this was so, and Burnside was headed for Fredericksburg, there still remained the question of what he would do when he got there. He could join Pope directly; he could operate against Richmond from the north; or he could attempt to cut the Virginia Central in Jackson's rear, between Gordonsville and Hanover Junction. The best way to forestall this last — the most immediately dangerous of the three — would be for Jackson to strike Pope, who would then be likely to call on Burnside for support. Until Lee knew whether McClellan intended to renew his advance on Richmond, however, he did not feel that he could further weaken the capital defenses in order to reinforce Jackson; nor did he feel that he should give him peremptory orders to attack, unsupported, without himself knowing the tactical situation at first hand. Accordingly, before the day was over, he did the next best thing. He sat down and wrote Stonewall a long letter in which he made it clear that he relied on his discretion.

After warning him not to count on reinforcements — "If I can send them I will; if I cannot, and you think it proper and advantageous, act without them" — he outlined the dilemma as he saw it and suggested what he believed was the best solution, an immediate thrust at Pope, though he cautioned against rashness: "I would rather you should have easy fighting and heavy victories." It was a warning addressed more to the erstwhile hard-driving hero of the Valley, who smote the enemy hip and thigh, wherever found, than to the sluggard of the Seven Days, who dawdled and withheld his hand from bloodshed. Apparently Lee had put the latter out of his mind. "I must now leave the matter to your reflection and good judgment," he concluded. "Make up your mind what is best to be done under all the circumstances which surround us, and let me hear the result at which you arrive. I will inform you if any change takes place here that bears on the subject."

Mosby was right: Burnside had been ordered to Fredericksburg a week ago, on August 1, nine days after Halleck's arrival in Washington from the West. Having scattered the armies there for an assimilation of what had been won, Old Brains now proposed to unite those of the East for a new beginning. In both cases, however — since the concentration was not to be on the Peninsula, where defeat was recent, but in northern Virginia, where defeat was a full year old — the effect was the same: to shift the Union juggernaut into reverse. McClellan, too, was about to be withdrawn.

Nothing less than a new beginning would put the derailed engine back on the track; or so it seemed to the newly appointed general-in-chief, who had reached the capital in a time of gloom. Flags drooped at half-mast under the press of heat and crape festooned the public buildings in observance of the death of Martin Van Buren, a used-up man. No such honors had marked the passing of the Virginian John Tyler the month before; but that was in a sunnier time, and even in the present instance the crape seemed more an expression of the general mood than grief for a particular man, ex-President or not; Van Buren was already part of ancient history. Halleck, at any rate, wasted little time in speculation on such matters. Instead, after spending a day in Washington, he got aboard a steamer and went straight to what he believed was the source of discontent: the Army of the Potomac, camped now on the mud flats of the James.

In spite of the pride he took in having executed the movement under pressure, and in spite of the fact that Lincoln had been congratulatory and Stanton even fawning, McClellan had been expecting trouble ever since his change of base. The President had wired him "a thousand thanks" after Malvern Hill. "Be assured," he added, "the heroism and skill of yourself and officers and men is, and forever will be, appreciated. If you can hold your present position [at Harrison's] we shall hive the enemy yet." Stanton put it stronger, or anyhow longer. "Be assured," he wrote, "that you shall have the support of this Department as cordially and faithfully as was ever rendered by man to man, and if we should ever live to see each other face to face you will be satisfied that you have never had from me anything but the most confiding integrity." That was larding it pretty thick, but he larded it even thicker in conversation with McClellan's father-in-law, who went to Washington to see him. "General Marcy," he told the chief of staff, with a sudden rush of feeling, "I have from the commencement of our acquaintance up to the present moment been General McClellan's warmest friend. I feel so kind toward him that I would get down on my knees to him if that would serve him. Yes sir," he continued, warming as he spoke. "If it would do him any service I would be willing to lay down naked in the gutter and allow him to stand upon my body for hours."

Stanton lying naked in the gutter was a prospect McClellan could contemplate with pleasure, but he was not deluded into thinking such a scene would ever be staged — except in his mind's eye. He knew well enough that Stanton was working against him, tooth and nail. Nor did Lincoln's assurances carry their former weight: especially after the arrival of John Pope and the Administration's tacit approval of the mandates he issued regarding noncombatants in his theater of operations. That was what really tore it, McClellan wrote his wife. "When you contrast the policy I urged in my letter to the President with that of Congress and of Mr Pope, you can readily agree with me that there can be little natural confidence between the government and myself. We are the antipodes of each other; and it is more than probable that they will take the earliest opportunity to relieve me from command and get me out of sight."

Now here came Halleck, slack-fleshed and goggle-eyed, formerly his subordinate, now his chief, holding the office he himself had lost. It was bitter. Presently, however, after a hasty review of the troops, Halleck calmed McClellan's apprehensions by informing him that he had not come to undermine him or relieve him of command, but to find out what he required in the way of additional men in order to renew the drive on the rebel capital. McClellan brightened and unfolded a map on which he began to indicate, with pride and enthusiasm, a new plan of attack. He would cross the James and capture Petersburg, outflanking the enemy fortifications and severing the southside supply lines, then swing north and enter Richmond by the back door. Halleck shook his head. Too risky, he said, and vetoed the proposal then and there. McClellan, his enthusiasm dampened, proceeded to an estimate of the situation. His effective strength, he said, was 88,665; Lee's was 200,000. Nevertheless, if the government would give him 30,000 reinforcements he would assault the northside intrenchments with "a good chance of success." Halleck frowned. No more than 20,000 were available, and if these would not suffice, he said, the army would have to be withdrawn from the Peninsula to unite with Pope in the vicinity of Washington. Horrified at the notion, McClellan excused himself in order to confer with his corps commanders. Next morning he reported, somewhat gloomily, that he was "willing to try it" with that number. Halleck nodded and got back aboard the steamboat to return to Washington. McClellan's genial spirits rose again. "I think that Halleck will support me and give me the means to take Richmond," he wrote his wife.

Whatever Halleck intended when he left, his final decision was considerably affected by a telegram he found waiting for him when he docked. It was from McClellan; apparently it had been sent almost as soon as Halleck's steamer passed from sight. Confederate reinforcements, he said, were "pouring into Richmond from the South." To meet this new development, and to enable him to deliver "a rapid and heavy blow," he wanted more troops than the 20,000 just agreed on. "Can you not possibly draw 15,000 or 20,000 men from the West to reinforce me temporarily?" he pleaded. "They can return the moment we gain Richmond. Please give weight to this suggestion; I am sure it merits it."

Halleck was amazed, and went to Lincoln with the problem. Lincoln was not amazed at all. In fact, he found the telegram very much in character. If by some magic he could reinforce McClellan with 100,000 troops today, he said, Little Mac would be delighted and would promise to capture Richmond tomorrow; but when tomorrow came he would report the enemy strength at 400,000 and announce that he could not advance until he got another 100,000 reinforcements. Halleck turned this over in his mind, together with another consideration. If Lee was as strong as McClellan said he was — stronger than Pope and McClellan combined — it was folly to keep the Federal armies exposed to destruction in detail. It was in fact imperative to unite them without delay. At last he made his decision, agreeing with Lincoln that McClellan's army would have to be withdrawn. On July 29 he ordered every available steamer in Baltimore harbor to proceed at once to the James, and next day he instructed McClellan to prepare to evacuate his sick and wounded. He did not tell him why; he merely remarked ambiguously that this was being done "in order to enable you to move in any direction." Two days later, Burnside was told to take his transports up the Potomac to Aquia Creek, where the troops would debark for a twelve-mile march to Fredericksburg. McClellan's own orders were sent on August 3: "It is determined to withdraw your army from the Peninsula to Aquia Creek. You will take immediate measures to effect this, covering the movement as best you can."

McClellan was thunderstruck. The order for the removal of his sick had aroused his suspicions five days ago, despite — or perhaps because of — the disclaimer that it would leave him free "to move in any direction," and he had been prompt to register his protest: "Our true policy is to reinforce [this] army by every available means and throw it again upon Richmond. Should it be determined to withdraw it, I shall look upon our cause as lost." Perhaps he thought the weight of this opinion would forestall any such calamity. If so, he now saw how useless it had been. Yet he did not abandon hope; or anyhow he did not stop trying to ward off the blow. At noon on August 4 he knelt figuratively at the feet of Halleck and made a final anguished plea. "Your telegram of last evening is received. I must confess that it has caused me the greatest pain I ever experienced, for I am convinced that the order to withdraw this army to Aquia Creek will prove disastrous to our cause." First he pointed out that it was tactical folly to make "a march of 145 miles to reach a point now only 25 miles distant, and to deprive ourselves entirely of the powerful aid of the gunboats and water transportation. Add to this the certain demoralization of this army which would ensue, and these appear to me sufficient reasons to make it my imperative duty to urge in the strongest terms afforded by our language that this order may be rescinded." Then came the impassioned words to which the rest had served as prologue: "Here, directly in front of this army, is the heart of the rebellion. It is here that all our resources should be collected to strike the blow which will determine the fate of the nation.... It matters not what partial reverses we may meet with elsewhere. Here is the true defense of Washington. It is here, on the banks of the James, that the fate of the Union should be decided."

Halleck replied by wire and by mail. "I must take things as I find them," he said in the letter. "I find the forces divided, and I wish to unite them. Only one feasible plan has been presented for doing this. If you or anyone else had presented a better plan I certainly should have adopted it. But all of your plans require reinforcements, which it is impossible to give you. It is very easy to ask for reinforcements, but it is not so easy to give them when you have no disposable troops at your command." The telegram, being briefer, was more to the point. After saying, "You cannot regret the order of withdrawal more than I did the necessity of giving it," Halleck put an end to the discussion: "It will not be rescinded and you will be expected to execute it with all possible promptness." Next day, August 7 — the date of Lee's letter urging Jackson to consider a strike at Pope — the need for haste was emphasized in a second wire received by the harassed commander at Harrison's Landing. "I must beg of you, General, to hurry along this movement," Halleck told him. "Your reputation as well as mine may be involved in its rapid execution."

Left with neither voice nor choice in the matter, McClellan worked hard to speed the evacuation. But he wrote his wife: "They are committing a fatal error in withdrawing me from here, and the future will show it. I think the result of their machination will be that Pope will be badly thrashed within ten days, and that they will be very glad to turn over the redemption of their affairs to me."

The danger, the crying need for haste as Halleck saw it, was that Lee might take advantage of his interior lines and attack one or the other of the two main Federal forces before the northward shift began, or, worse still, while the movement was in progress. Of the two — Pope on the Rappahannock and McClellan on the James — Old Brains was most concerned about the former. As he put it to McClellan, who was struggling to extract his troops from the malarial Peninsula bottoms, "This delay might not only be fatal to the health of your army, but in the meantime General Pope's forces would be exposed to the heavy blows of the enemy without the slightest hope of assistance from you."

Pope was worried too, although he did not let it show in his manner. Privately he was complaining to Halleck about "the supineness of the Army of the Potomac," which he said "renders it easy for the enemy to reinforce Jackson heavily," and he urged: "Please make McClellan do something." Publicly, however, he showed no symptoms of doubt or trepidation. On August 8, when he transferred his headquarters southward to Culpeper, Halleck wired him uneasily: "Do not advance, so as to expose yourself to any disaster, unless you can better your line of defense, until we can get more troops upon the Rappahannock. ... You must be very cautious." Pope seemed unalarmed; he appeared, in fact, not to have a single cautious bone in his whole body. He intended to hold where he was, despite the risk involved in the knowledge that Stonewall Jackson was before him with a force he estimated at 30,000 men.

Numerically, as of early August, his confidence was well founded. Exclusive of Burnside, whose 12,000 had debarked at Aquia and were now at Falmouth, he had 77,779 soldiers in the Army of Virginia. Even after deducting the troops in the Washington fortifications, along with those in the Shenandoah Valley and beyond, he was left with just over 56,000 in the eight divisions of infantry and two brigades of cavalry comprising the three corps under McDowell, Banks, and Sigel. This was the field force proper, and it seemed ample for the execution of the project he had conceived at the outset. His intention had been to operate southward down the Orange & Alexandria to Gordonsville and beyond, thereby menacing the Virginia Central so that Lee would weaken the Richmond defenses to the point where McClellan could make a successful assault. 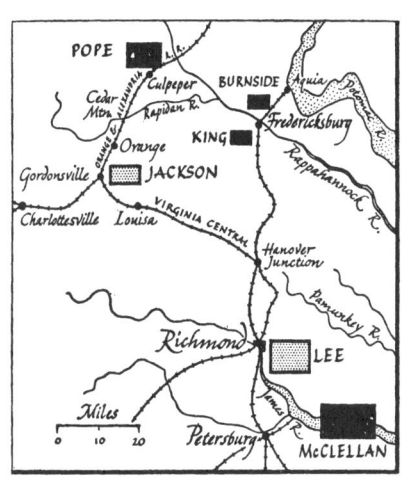 McClellan's pending withdrawal would alter at least a part of this, of course, but Pope still thought the plan a good one: not the least of its advantages being that it had the approval and support of the Administration, since it simultaneously covered Washington. What was more, his assignment — formerly minor, or anyhow secondary — now became major. Instead of setting Richmond up for capture by McClellan, he would take the place himself and be known thereafter as the man who broke the back of the rebellion. That was a thought to warm the heart. He would consolidate his gains, then proceed with his advance, reinforced by such numbers as reached him from the Army of the Potomac.

At present, it was true, his striking force was rather scattered. More than a third of McDowell's corps — 11,000 infantry, with 30 guns and about 500 cavalry — was still at Fredericksburg, under Brigadier General Rufus King, blocking the direct approach to Washington. Now that Burnside had arrived, Pope might have summoned King to join him, but just now he preferred to keep him where he was, menacing Jackson's supply line and playing on Lee's fears for the safety of his capital. Besides, he felt strong enough without him. Banks and Sigel had come eastward through the passes of the Blue Ridge, and though their five divisions had not been consolidated, either with each other or with McDowell's two, Pope still had better than 44,000 troops with which to oppose the estimated 30,000 rebels in his immediate front. The situation was not without its dangers: Halleck kept saying so, at any rate, and old General Wool, transferred from Fort Monroe to Maryland, had warned him at the outset: "Jackson is an enterprising officer. Delays are dangerous." But Pope was not alarmed. If the highly touted Stonewall wanted a fight, at those odds, he would gladly accommodate him.

Banks felt the same way about it, only more so; for while Pope intended to earn a reputation here in the East, Banks was determined to retrieve one. On August 8, therefore, he was pleased to receive at Culpeper an order directing him to march his two divisions south: Jackson had crossed the Rapidan, moving north, and Pope wanted Banks to delay him while the rest of the army was being assembled to give him the battle he seemed to be seeking. Banks did not hesitate. McDowell and Sigel were behind him; King was on the way from Fredericksburg. Next morning, eight hot and dusty miles out of Culpeper, he came under long-range artillery fire from the slopes of a lone peak called Cedar Mountain, and pressing on found rebel infantry disposed in strength about its northern base and in the woods and fields off to the right. After more than two months of brooding over the shocks of May, he was face to face with the old Valley adversary whose soldiers had added insult to injury by giving him the nickname "Commissary" Banks.

He was itching to attack, then and there, but in the face of the known odds — he was down to about 8000 men as a result of multiple detachments, while Jackson was reported to have at least three times that many — he did not feel free to do so on his own responsibility. Then a courier arrived from Culpeper, a staff colonel sent by Pope with a verbal message which seemed to authorize an immediate all-out attack. (The officer's name was Louis Marshall, a Union-loyal Virginian and a nephew of R. E. Lee, who had said of him: "I could forgive [his] fighting against us, but not his joining Pope.") Welcome as the message was, Banks could scarcely believe his ears. In fact, he had it written down and then read back for verification:

> General Banks will move to the front immediately, assume command of all the forces in the front, deploy his skirmishers if the enemy approaches, and attack him immediately as soon as he approaches, and be reinforced from here.

This ambiguous farrago, dictated by Lee's nephew in the name of Pope, was open to conflicting interpretations. It might mean that the attack was to be made with skirmishers only, holding the main body on the defensive until McDowell arrived to even the odds and Sigel came up to stretch them in favor of the Union. On the other hand, it might mean what it said in the words that were quickest to catch the eye: "Attack him immediately as soon as he approaches." That sounded like the army commander who three weeks ago had admonished his generals "to seek the adversary and to beat him when he was found." At any rate, whatever the odds, Banks took him at his word. He put his men in attack formation and sent them forward, on the left and on the right.

Lee's letter of August 7, recommending a swipe at Pope, had not been needed; for while he was writing it Jackson was already putting his 25,000 soldiers in motion to carry out the strategy it suggested. His cavalry having reported the superior enemy forces badly scattered beyond the Rapidan, he hoped to make a rapid march across that stream, pounce on one of the isolated segments, and withdraw Valley-style before Pope could concentrate against him. So far, it had not worked at all that way, however — primarily because another letter of Lee's, while needed, had not been heeded. A. P. Hill was kept as much in the dark as to his chief's intentions as Winder and Ewell had ever been. "I pledge you my word, Doctor," the latter told an inquiring chaplain before the movement got under way, "I do not know whether we march north, south, east or west, or whether we will march at all. General Jackson has simply ordered me to have the division ready to move at dawn. I have been ready ever since, and have no further indication of his plans. That is almost all I ever know of his designs."

Stonewall was still Stonewall, especially when secrecy was involved, and no one — not even Robert E. Lee, of whom he said: "I am willing to follow him blindfolded" — was going to change him. The result, as Lee had feared, was mutual resentment and mistrust. Not only did Jackson not "consult" with his red-haired lieutenant, whose so-called Light Division was as large as the other two combined; he rode him unmercifully for every slight infraction of the rules long since established for the Army of the Valley. Consequently, glad as he had been to get away from Longstreet, Hill began to suspect that he had leaped from the frying pan into the fire. Resentment bred confusion, and confusion mounted quickly toward a climax in the course of the march northward against Pope. Having reached Orange in good order the first day, August 7, Jackson issued instructions for the advance across the Rapidan tomorrow, which would place his army in position for a strike at Culpeper the following day. The order of march would be Ewell, Hill, Winder; so he said; but during the night he changed his mind and told Ewell to take an alternate road. Uninformed of the change, Hill had his men lined up next morning on the outskirts of town, waiting for Ewell to take the lead. That was where Jackson found him. Angry at the delay, he rebuked him and passed Winder to the front. The result was further delay and a miserable showing, complicated by Federal cavalry probing at his wagon train. Ewell made barely eight miles before sundown, Winder about half that, and Hill was less than two miles out of Orange when the army halted for the night. Jackson was furious. So was Hill. Ewell fretted. Winder was down with fever, riding in an ambulance despite his doctor's orders that he leave the field entirely. Several men had died of sunstroke, and the rest took their cue from their commanders, grumbling at the way they had been shuffled about in the dust and heat.

Overnight, Jackson's wrath turned to gloom. The fast-stepping Army of the Valley, formerly such a close-stitched organization, seemed to be coming apart at the seams. Rising next morning to resume the march, he informed Lee: "I am not making much progress.... Today I do not expect much more than to close up [the column] and clear the country around the train of the enemy's cavalry. I fear that the expedition will, in consequence of my tardy movements, be productive of but little good."

Ewell had the lead; Winder was in close support; Hill was marching hard to close the gap. The morning wore on, hot as yesterday. Noon came and went. Presently, up ahead, there was the boom of guns, and word came back to Jackson that the Federals were making a stand, apparently with horse artillery. He rode forward and made a brief reconnaissance. This was piedmont country, rolling, heavily wooded except for scattered fields of grain. The bluecoats did not appear to be present in strength, but there was no real telling: Jackson decided to wait for Hill before advancing. Off to the right was Cedar Mountain, obviously the key to the position. Ewell was told to put his batteries there and his infantry below them, along the northern base; Winder would take position on the left in order to overlap the Yankee line when the signal was given to go forward. There was no hurry. It was now past 2 o'clock and Culpeper was eight miles away: too far, in any event, for an attack to be made on it today. Jackson went onto the porch of a nearby farmhouse and lay down to take a nap.

Meanwhile the artillery duel continued, the Union guns firing accurately and fast. This was clearly something more than a mere delaying action staged by cavalry; there was infantry out there beyond the woods, though in what strength could not be told. Manifestly weak, pale as his shirt — he was in fact in his shirt sleeves — Winder had left his ambulance, ignoring the doctor's protests, put his troops in line, extending the left as instructed, and then had joined his batteries, observing their fire with binoculars and calling out corrections for the gunners. It was now about 4 o'clock. An officer went down alongside him, clipped on the head by a fragment of shell; another was eviscerated by a jagged splinter; a third was struck in the rump by an unexploded ricochet and hurled ten feet, though he suffered only bruises as a result. Then came Winder's turn. Tall and wavy-haired, he kept his post, and as he continued to direct the counterbattery fire, calm and cool-looking in his shirt sleeves, with the binoculars held to his eyes, a shell came screaming at him, crashing through his left arm and tearing off most of the ribs on that side of his chest. He fell straight back and lay full length on the ground, quivering spasmodically.

"General, do you know me?" a staff lieutenant asked, bending over the sufferer in order to be heard above the thunder of the guns.

"Oh yes," Winder said vaguely, and his mind began to wander. The guns were bucking and banging all around him, but he was back at home again in Maryland. In shock, he spoke disconnectedly of his wife and children until a chaplain came and knelt beside him, seeking to turn his thoughts from worldly things.

"General, lift up your head to God."

"I do," Winder said calmly. "I do lift it up to him."

Carried to the rear, he died just at sundown, asking after the welfare of his men, and those who were with him were hard put for a comforting answer. By then the fury of the Union assault had crashed against his lines, which had broken in several places. Jackson's plan for outflanking the enemy on the left had miscarried; it was he who was outflanked in that direction. The sudden crash of musketry, following close on the news that Winder had been mangled by a shell, brought him off the farmhouse porch and into the saddle. He rode hard toward the left, entering a moil of fugitives who had given way in panic when the bluecoats emerged roaring from the cover of the woods. Drawing his sword — a thing no one had ever seen him do before in battle — he brandished it above his head and called out hoarsely: "Rally, brave men, and press forward! Your general will lead you; Jackson will lead you! Follow me!"

This had an immediate effect, for the sight was as startling in its way as the unexpected appearance of the Federals had been. The men halted in their tracks, staring open-mouthed, and then began to rally in response to the cries of their officers, echoing Stonewall, who was finally persuaded to retire out of range of the bullets twittering round him. "Good, good," he said as he turned back, Winder's successor having assured him that the Yankees would be stopped. Whether this promise could have been kept in the face of another assault was another matter, but fortunately by now the battle was moving in the opposite direction: A. P. Hill had arrived with the Light Division. Opening ranks to let the fugitives through, Little Powell's veterans swamped the blue attackers, flung them back on their reserves, and pursued them northward through the gathering twilight. So quickly, after the manner of light fiction, had victory been snatched from the flames of defeat, if not disaster.

Thankful as Jackson was for this deliverance, he was by no means satisfied. Banks had escaped him once before; he did not intend to let him get away again. A full moon was rising, and he ordered the chase continued by its light. Whenever resistance was encountered he passed his guns to the front, shelled the woods, and then resumed the pursuit, gathering shell-dazed prisoners as he went. Four hundred bluecoats were captured in all, bringing the total Federal losses to 2381; Jackson himself had lost 1276. At last, however, receiving word from his cavalry that the enemy had been heavily reinforced, he called a halt within half a dozen miles of Culpeper and passed the word for his men to sleep on their arms in line of battle. He himself rode back toward Cedar Mountain, seeking shelter at roadside houses along the way. At each he was told that he was welcome but that the wounded filled the rooms. Finally he drew rein beside a grassy plot, dismounted stiffly, and lay face down on the turf, wrapped in a borrowed cloak. When a staff officer asked if he wanted something to eat: "No," he groaned, "I want rest: nothing but rest," and was soon asleep.

Sunday, August 10, dawned hot and humid, the quiet broken only by the moans and shrieks of the injured, blue and gray, presently augmented by their piteous cries for water as the sun rose burning, stiffening their wounds. Surgeons and aid men passed among them, and burial details came along behind. The scavengers were active, too, gleaning the field of arms and equipment; as usual, Old Blue Light wanted all he could lay hands on. Thus the morning wore away, and not a shot was fired. Aware that Sigel and McDowell had arrived to give Pope two whole corps and half of a third — King was still on the way from Fredericksburg, where Burnside was on call — Jackson would not deliver a Sabbath attack; but he was prepared to receive one, whatever the odds, so long as there were wounded men to be cared for and spoils to be loaded into his wagons. That afternoon, as always seemed to be the case on the morrow of a battle, the weather broke. There were long peals of thunder, followed by rain. Jackson held his ground, and the various details continued their work into the night.

Next morning a deputation of Federal horsemen came forward under a flag of truce, proposing an armistice for the removal of the wounded. Jackson gladly agreed; for King's arrival that night would give Pope better than twice as many troops as he himself had, and this would afford him additional time in which to prepare for the withdrawal he now knew was necessary. While the soldiers of both armies mingled on the field where they had fought, he finished packing his wagons and got off a message to Lee: "God blessed our arms with another victory." When darkness came he lighted campfires all along his front, stole away southward under cover of their burning, and recrossed the Rapidan, unmolested, unpursued.

Another victory, he called it: not without justification. He had inflicted a thousand more casualties than he suffered, and for two days after the battle he had remained in control of the field. Yet there were other aspects he ignored. Banks had done to him what he had tried to do to Shields at Kernstown, and what was more had done it with considerably greater success, even apart from the initial rout; for in the end it was Stonewall who retreated. But now that the roles were reversed he applied a different set of standards. Privately, according to his chief of staff, he went so far as to refer to Cedar Mountain as "the most successful of his exploits." Few would agree with him in this, however, even among the men in his own army. They had been mishandled and they knew it. Outnumbering the enemy three to one on the field of fight, he had been careless in reconnaissance, allowing his troops to be outflanked while he drowsed on a farmhouse veranda, and had swung into vigorous action only after his left wing had been shattered. Following as it did his sorry performance throughout the Seven Days, the recrossing of the Rapidan gave point to a question now being asked: Had Stonewall lost his touch? "Arrogant" was the word applied by some. Others remarked that his former triumphs had been scored against secondraters out in the Valley, "but when pitted against the best of the Federal commanders he did not appear so well." Then too, there had always been those who considered him crazy — crazy and, so far, lucky. Give him "a month uncontrolled," one correspondent declared, "and he would destroy himself and all under him."

Time perhaps would show who was right, the general or his critics, but for the present at least two other men derived particular satisfaction from the battle and its outcome, despite the fact that they viewed it from opposite directions. One of the two was A. P. Hill. Still fuming because of the undeserved rebuke he had received on the outskirts of Orange the day before, he had marched toward the sound of firing and reached the field to find his tormentor face to face with disaster. After opening his ranks to let the fugitives through — including hundreds from the Stonewall Brigade itself — he had launched the counterattack that saved the day and provided whatever factual basis there was for Jackson's claim to "another victory." Revenge was seldom sweeter; Hill enjoyed it to the full.

The other satisfied observer was John Pope, who celebrated his eastern debut as a fighting man by publishing, for the encouragement of his army, Halleck's personal congratulations "on your hard earned but brilliant success against vastly superior numbers. Your troops have covered themselves with glory." Pope thought so too, now, although at first he had experienced definite twinges of anxiety and doubt. Alarmed by what had happened to Banks as a result of misinterpreting the verbal message garbled by Lee's nephew, he had hastened to assemble his eight divisions (including King's, which arrived Monday evening to give him well over 50,000 men) for a renewal of the contest on the morning after the armistice expired. While Jackson was stealing away in the darkness behind a curtain of blazing campfires, Pope was wiring Halleck: "The enemy has been receiving reinforcements all day.... I think it almost certain that we shall be attacked in the morning, and we shall make the best fight we can." This did not sound much like the belligerent commander who had urged his subordinates to "discard such ideas" as the one of " 'taking strong positions and holding them.' " However, when he found Stonewall gone with the dawn he recovered his former tone and notified Halleck: "The enemy has retreated under cover of the night.... Our cavalry and artillery are in pursuit. I shall follow with the infantry as far as the Rapidan." Now it was Halleck's turn to be alarmed. "Beware of a snare," he quickly replied. "Feigned retreats are secesh tactics."

But he need not have worried; not just yet. Pope was content to follow at a distance, and when he reached the near bank of the Rapidan he stopped as he had said he would do. Presently he fell back toward Culpeper, pausing along the way to publish Halleck's congratulations. He was "delighted and astonished," he told his soldiers, at their "gallant and intrepid conduct." Whatever their reaction to this astonishment might be, he went on to venture a prophecy: "Success and glory are sure to accompany such conduct, and it is safe to predict that Cedar Mountain is only the first in a series of victories which shall make the Army of Virginia famous in the land."

* * *

Lee saw it otherwise. Pleased with Jackson's repulse of Banks, he congratulated him "most heartily on the victory which God has granted you over our enemies" and expressed the hope that it was "but the precursor of others over our foe in that quarter, which will entirely break up and scatter his army." However, the withdrawal to Gordonsville on August 12, despite Stonewall's subsequent double-barreled explanation that it was done "in order to avoid being attacked by the vastly superior force in front of me, and with the hope that by thus falling back General Pope would be induced to follow me until I should be reinforced," not only ended the prospect that his lieutenant would be able to "suppress" Pope and return to Richmond in time to help deal with McClellan; it also re-exposed the Virginia Central. This was as intolerable now as it had been a month ago, and Lee moved promptly to meet the threat the following day by ordering Longstreet to Gordonsville with ten brigades, which reduced by half the army remnant protecting the capital from assault on the east and south. Simultaneously he sent Hood, who now commanded a demi-division composed of his own and Law's brigades, to Hanover Junction in order to block an advance from Fredericksburg; or if Burnside moved westward to join Pope, Hood could parallel his march and join Jackson. Something of a balance was thus maintained in every direction except McClellan's, potentially the most dangerous of them all.

Still, potential was a long way from kinetic: especially where McClellan was concerned. A week ago, when the bluecoats marched up

The Sun Shines South

Malvern Hill and then back down again, Lee had said of him: "I have no idea that he will advance on Richmond now." He took the risk, not thinking it great, and presently found it even smaller than he had supposed. On this same August 13, while Longstreet's men were boarding the cars for their journey out to the piedmont, an English deserter came into the southern lines with a story that part of McClellan's army was being loaded onto transports. Next day this was confirmed by D. H. Hill, whose scouts on the south side of the James reported Fitz-John Porter's corps already gone. That was enough for Lee. Convinced that Pope was about to be reinforced from the Peninsula — though he did not know to what extent — he decided to turn his back on Little Mac and give his undivided close-up personal attention to "the miscreant" on the Rapidan. The time was short. Before he went to bed that night he notified Davis: "Unless I hear from you to the contrary I shall leave for G[ordonsville] at 4 a.m. tomorrow. The troops are accumulating there and I must see that arrangements are made for the field." Tactfully — for he expected to be busy and he understood the man with whom he dealt — he added: "When you do not hear from me, you may feel sure that I do not think it necessary to trouble you. I shall feel obliged to you for any directions you may think proper to give."

In this sequence of events, Halleck's worst fears moved toward realization. The Federal dilemma, as he saw it, was that the rebels might concentrate northward and jump Pope before McClellan completed his roundabout transfer from the James to the Rappahannock. The southern commander had already proved himself an opponent not to be trusted with the initiative; yet that was precisely what he would have so long as the Army of the Potomac was in transit. The contest was in the nature of a race, with the Army of Virginia as the prize to be claimed by whichever of the two superior armies moved the fastest.

Lee was not long in seeing it that way, too, and once he had seen it he acted. In fact — necessity, in this case, being not only the mother of invention, but also first cousin to prescience — he acted before he saw it: first, by detaching Jackson: then by reinforcing him with Hill: finally, by sending Longstreet up to reinforce them both: so that, in a sense, he was already running before he heard the starting gun. And now that he heard it he ran faster. As a result he not only got there first, he got there before McClellan had done much more than lift his knees off the cinders. Yet that was all: Fortune's smile changed abruptly to a frown. Having reached the finish line, Lee found himself unable to break the ribbon he was breasting.

The ribbon was the Rapidan, and Pope was disposed behind it. However, it was not the Union commander who forestalled the intended destruction, but rather a recurrence of the malady which had plagued the Confederates throughout the Seven Days: lack of coördination. Detraining at Gordonsville on August 15, Lee conferred at once with Longstreet and Jackson, who showed him on the map how rare an opportunity lay before him. Nine miles this side of Fredericksburg, the Rapidan and the Rappahannock converged to form the apex of a V laid on its side with the open end to the west. Pope's attitude within the V, and consequently the attitude of the fifty-odd thousand soldiers he had wedged in there between the constricting rivers, was not unlike that of a browsing ram with his attendant flock. Unaware that the butcher was closing in, he had backed himself into a fence corner, apparently in the belief that he and they were safer so.

In this he was considerably mistaken, as Lee was now preparing to demonstrate. Across the open end of the V, at an average distance of twenty miles from the apex, ran the Orange & Alexandria Railroad, leading back to Manassas Junction, the Army of Virginia's main supply base. While the infantry of the Army of Northern Virginia was being concentrated behind Clark's Mountain, masked from observation from across the Rapidan, the cavalry would swing upstream, cross in the darkness, and strike for Rappahannock Station. Destruction of the railroad bridge at that point, severing Pope's supply line and removing his only chance for a dry-shod crossing of the river in his rear, would be the signal for the infantry to emerge from hiding and surge across the fords to its front. Pope's army, caught off balance, would be tamped into the cul-de-sac and mangled.

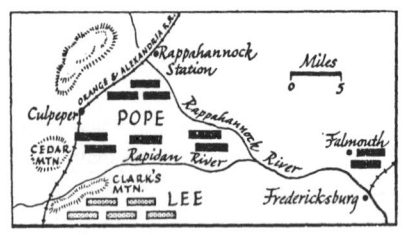

Both wing commanders approved of the plan. Jackson, in fact, was so enthusiastic that he proposed to launch the assault tomorrow. But Longstreet, as on the eve of the Seven Days, and no doubt recalling the Valley general's faulty logistics on that occasion, suggested a one-day wait. Moreover, though he approved of the basic strategy proposed, he thought better results would be obtained by moving around the enemy right, where the army could take up a strong defensive position in the foothills of the Blue Ridge, forcing Pope to attack until, bled white, too fagged to flee, he could be counterattacked and smothered. Lee agreed to the delay — which was necessary anyhow, the cavalry not having arrived — but preferred to assault the enemy left, so as to come between Pope and whatever reinforcements might try to join him, by way of Fredericksburg, either from Washington or the Peninsula. Next day it was so ordered. The army would take up masked positions near the Rapidan on Sunday, August 17, and be prepared to cross at dawn of the following day, on receiving word that the bridge was out at Rappahannock Station.

That was when things started going wrong: particularly in the cavalry. Stuart had two brigades, one under Wade Hampton, left in front of Richmond, the other under Fitzhugh Lee, the army commander's nephew, stationed at Hanover Junction. The latter was to be used in the strike at Rappahannock Station; he was expected Sunday night, and Stuart rode out to meet him east of Clark's Mountain, in rear of Raccoon Ford. Midnight came; there was no sign of him; Jeb and his staff decided to get some sleep on the porch of a roadside house. Just before dawn, hearing hoofbeats in the distance, two officers rode forward to meet what they thought was Lee, but met instead a spatter of carbine fire and came back shouting, "Yankees!" Stuart and the others barely had time to jump for their horses and get away in a hail of bullets, leaving the general's plumed hat, silk-lined cape, and haversack for the blue troopers, who presently withdrew across the river, whooping with delight as they passed the captured finery around. Subsequently it developed that the ford had been left unguarded by Robert Toombs, who, feeling mellow on his return from a small-hours celebration with some friends, had excused the pickets. Placed in arrest for his neglect, he defied regulations by buckling on his sword and making an impassioned speech to his brigade: whereupon he was relieved of command and ordered back to Gordonsville, much to the discomfort of his troops. This did little to ease Stuart's injured pride and nothing at all to recover his lost plumage. Skilled as he was at surprising others, the laughing cavalier was not accustomed to being surprised himself. Nor were matters improved by the infantrymen who greeted him for several days thereafter with the question, "Where's your hat?"

Fitz Lee's nonarrival, which required a one-day postponement of the attack — it was as well; not all the infantry brigades were in position anyhow — was explained by the fact that, his orders having stressed no need for haste, he had marched by way of Louisa to draw rations and ammunition. When this was discovered it caused another one-day postponement, the attack now being set for August 20. Even this second delay seemed just as well: Pope appeared oblivious and docile, and in the interim Lee would have time to bring another division up from Richmond. Before nightfall on the 18th, however, word came to headquarters that the Federals were breaking camp and retiring toward Culpeper. Next morning Lee climbed to a signal station on Clark's Mountain and saw for himself that the report was all too true. The sea of tents had disappeared. Long lines of dark-clothed men and white-topped wagons, toylike in the distance, were winding away from the bivouac areas, trailing serpentine clouds of dust in the direction of the Rappahannock. After watching for a time this final evidence of Pope's escape from the destruction planned for him there between the rivers, Lee put away his binoculars, took a deep breath, and said regretfully to Longstreet, who stood beside him on the mountain top: "General, we little thought that the enemy would turn his back upon us thus early in the campaign."

If there could be no envelopment, at least there could be a pursuit. Lee crossed the Rapidan the following day: only to find himself breasting another ribbon he could not break. This time, too, the ribbon was a river — the Rappahannock — but the failure to cross this second stream was not so much due to a lack of efficiency in his own army as it was to the high efficiency of his opponent's. Pope knew well enough now what dangers had been hanging over his head, for he had captured along with Stuart's plume certain dispatches showing Lee's plan for his destruction, and in spite of his early disparagement of defensive tactics he was displaying a real talent for such work. After pulling out of the suicidal V, he skillfully took position behind its northern arm, and for two full days, four times around the clock, wherever Lee probed for a crossing there were solid ranks of Federals, well supported by artillery, drawn up to receive him on the high left bank of the Rappahannock.

Notified of the situation, Halleck wired: "Stand firm on that line until I can help you. Fight hard, and aid will soon come." Pope replied: "You may rely upon our making a very hard fight in case the enemy advances." Halleck, preferring firmer language, repeated his instructions: "Dispute every inch of ground, and fight like the devil till we can reinforce you. Forty-eight hours more and we can make you strong enough." Encouraged by this pep talk, as well as by his so-far success in preventing a crossing of the river to his front, Pope reassured the wrought-up Washington commander: "There need be no apprehension, as I think no impression can be made on me for some days."

Once more Lee was in disagreement. He not only intended to make what his opponent called an "impression," he knew he had to make one soon or else give up the game. Information from Richmond, added to what he gleaned from northern papers, had convinced him by now that the whole of the Army of the Potomac was on its way to the Rappahannock. Burnside's troops, under Major General Jesse L. Reno, had already joined Pope, bringing his total strength to 70,000 according to Lee's computations, and this figure would in turn be more than doubled when McClellan's men arrived. To oppose this imminent combination, Lee himself had 55,000 of all arms, plus 17,000 still at Richmond. Manifestly, with the odds getting longer every day, whatever was to be done must be done quickly. At any rate, the present stalemate was intolerable. Perhaps one way to break it, Lee reasoned, would be to startle Pope and make him jump by sending Stuart to probe at his rear, particularly the Orange & Alexandria Railroad, which stretched like an exposed nerve back to his base at Manassas. Stuart thought so, too. Ever since the loss of his plume, five days ago near Raccoon Ford, he had been chafing under the jibes and begging Lee to turn him loose. "I intend to make the Yankees pay for that hat," he had written his wife.

He took off on the morning of August 22, crossing the Rappahannock at Waterloo Bridge with 1500 troopers and two guns. His goal was Catlett's Station on the O & A, specifically the bridge over Cedar Run just south of there, and he intended to reach it by passing around the rear of Pope's army, which was drawn up along the east bank of the river north of Rappahannock Station to contest a crossing by Lee's infantry. During a midday halt at Warrenton a young woman informed him that she had wagered a bottle of wine against a Union quartermaster's boast that he would be in Richmond within thirty days. "Take his name and look out for him," Stuart told one of his staff. The column pushed on toward Auburn Mills, rounding the headwaters of Cedar Run, and then proceeded southeastward down the opposite watershed. At sunset a violent storm broke over the troopers' heads. Night came early; "the darkest night I ever knew," Stuart called it; but he pressed on, undetected in the rain and blackness, and within striking distance of Catlett's was rewarded with a piece of luck in the form of a captured orderly, a contraband who, professing his joy at being once more among his "own people," offered to guide them to the private quarters of General Pope himself. Stuart took him up on that. Surrounding the brightly lighted camp, he had the bugler sound the charge, and a thousand yelling horsemen emerged from the outer darkness, swinging sabers and firing revolvers. The startled bluecoats scattered, and the troopers pursued them, spotting targets by the sudden glare of lightning. It was strange. A lightning flash would show the road filled with running men; then the next would show it empty, the runners vanished.

Despite the effectiveness of evasive tactics which appeared to enlist the aid of the supernatural, more than 200 prisoners and about as many horses were rounded up, including a number of staff officers and blooded animals, along with a good deal of miscellaneous loot. From Pope's tent — though the general himself, fortunately or unfortunately, was away on a tour of inspection — the raiders appropriated his personal baggage, a payroll chest stuffed with $350,000 in greenbacks, and a dispatch book containing headquarters copies of all messages sent or received during the past week. The railroad bridge over Cedar Run, however — the prime objective of the raid — resisted all attempts at demolition. Too wet to burn, too tough to chop, it had to be left intact when Stuart pulled out before dawn, returning the way he had come.

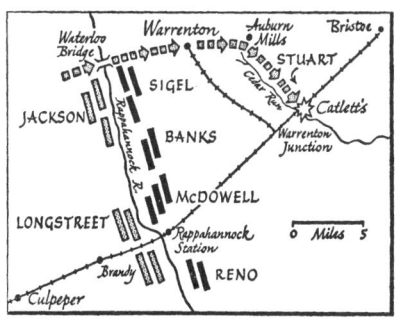

By daylight, one bedraggled trooper remarked, "guns, horses, and men look[ed] as if the whole business had passed through a shower of yellow mud last night." But Stuart's spirits were undampened. At Warrenton he called a halt in front of the young woman's house and had the captured quartermaster brought forward to collect the wagered bottle of wine for drinking in Libby Prison. Fitz Lee was in equally high spirits. Safely back across Waterloo Bridge that afternoon, he hailed an infantry brigadier and said he had something to show him. Stepping behind a large oak, he presently emerged wearing the cockaded hat and blue dress coat of a Federal major general. The infantryman roared with laughter, for the coat was so much too long for the bandy-legged Lee that the hem of it nearly covered his spurs. Stuart laughed hardest of all, and when he saw the name John Pope on the label inside the collar, he extended the joke by composing a dispatch addressed to the former owner: "You have my hat and plume. I have your best coat. I have the honor to propose a cartel for a fair exchange of the prisoners." Although nothing came of this — the coat was sent instead to Richmond, where it was put on display in the State Library — Stuart was quite satisfied. "I have had my revenge out of Pope," he told his wife.

Pope's coat was a prize R. E. Lee could appreciate as well as the next man, not excepting his charade-staging nephew; but more important to him, by far, was the captured dispatch book which reached his headquarters the following morning, August 24. In it he found laid before him, as if he were reading over his adversary's shoulder, a sequent and detailed account of the Federal build-up beyond the Rappahannock. In addition to Reno, whose two divisions had already joined, Pope had other forces close at hand, including one on its way from western Virginia by rail and canal boat. Most urgent, though, was the news that Porter, whose corps was the advance unit of McClellan's army, had debarked at Aquia Creek three days ago and marched next day to Falmouth, which placed him within twenty miles of Pope's left at Kelly's Ford, five miles downstream from Rappahannock Station. He might have joined today — or yesterday, for that matter — along with Heintzelman, whose corps was reported steaming northward close behind him. "Forty-eight hours more and we can make you strong enough," Halleck had wired Pope, and Pope had replied: "There need be no apprehension." That, too, was three days ago, while Porter's men were filing off their transports. The race was considerably nearer its finish than Lee had supposed.

In point of fact, it was over. Pope was already too strong and too securely based for Lee to engage him in a pitched battle with anything like certainty of the outcome. Unless he could maneuver him out of his present position, and by so doing gain the chance to fall on some exposed detachment, Pope would go unscathed. And unless Lee could do this quickly, he could not do it at all; for once McClellan's whole army was on the scene, or even the greater part of it, the odds would be hopeless. Lee, then, had two choices, neither of which included standing still. He could retreat, or he could advance. To retreat would be to give up the piedmont and probably the Shenandoah Valley; the siege of Richmond, lately raised, would be renewed under conditions worse than those which had followed Joe Johnston's retreat. That would not do at all. And yet to advance might also worsen matters, since Pope might retire on Fredericksburg and thereby hasten the concentration Lee was seeking to delay.

The gray-bearded general studied his map, and there he found what he thought might be the answer. Pope's supply line, the Orange & Alexandria Railroad, extended northeastward in his rear, so that to maneuver him in that direction would be to make him increase the distance between his present force and the troops coming ashore at Aquia Creek. Twice already Lee had tried to cut that artery: once with a blow aimed at Rappahannock Station, which had failed because Pope pulled back before it landed, and once more with another aimed at Catlett's, which had failed because the rain soaked the bridge too wet for burning. Now he would try again, still farther up the line. If successful, this would not only provoke a longer retreat by threatening Pope's main base of supplies, miles in his rear, but would also repeat the months-old Valley ruse of seeming to threaten Washington, which had yielded such rich dividends before. In reasoning thus, Lee was not discouraged by his two previous failures; rather, he resolved to profit by them. This time he would swing a heavier blow. Instead of using cavalry, he would use infantry. And he would use it in strength.

Infantry in this case meant Stonewall: not only because his three divisions were on the flank from which the march around Pope's right would most conveniently begin, but also because he knew the country he would be traversing and his men had won their "foot cavalry" fame for long, fast marches such as the one now proposed. Conversely, Longstreet too would be assigned the kind of work he preferred and did best: holding, with his four divisions, the line of the Rappahannock against possible assault by Pope's ten divisions across the way. This was risky in the extreme, both for Jackson and Old Pete. Pope was not only stronger now than both of them combined; he was apt to be heavily reinforced at any time, if indeed he had not been already. Furthermore, in dividing his army Lee was inviting disaster by reversing the basic military principle of concentration in the presence of a superior enemy. Yet he did not plan this out of contempt for Pope (Pope the blusterer, Pope the "miscreant" had handled his army with considerable skill throughout the five days since his escape from the constricting V); he planned it out of necessity. Unable on the one hand to stand still, or on the other to retire — either of which would do no more than postpone ruin and make it all the more ruinous when it inevitably came — Lee perceived that the only way to deal with an opponent he did not feel strong enough to fight was to maneuver him into retreat, and to do that he would have to divide his army. Thus the argument, pro and con, came full circle to one end: He would do it because there was nothing else to do. The very thing which made such a division seem overrash — Pope's numerical superiority — was also its strongest recommendation, according to Lee, who later remarked: "The disparity ... between the contending forces rendered the risks unavoidable."

Today was Sunday. Shortly after noon, having made his decision, he rode to left-wing headquarters at Jeffersonton to give Stonewall his assignment. Jeffersonton was two miles back from the river, where a noisy artillery duel was in progress from opposite banks; Lee spoke above the rumble of the guns. The march would begin tomorrow, he said. Moving upstream for a crossing well above Pope's right, Jackson would then swing northward behind the screen of the Bull Run Mountains, beyond which he would turn southeast through Thoroughfare Gap — the route he had followed thirteen months ago, coming down from the Valley to reach the field where he had won his nickname — for a strike at Pope's supply line, far in his rear. No precise objective was assigned. Anywhere back there along the railroad would do, Lee said, just so Pope was properly alarmed for the safety of his communications, the welfare of his supply base, and perhaps for the security of Washington itself. Lee explained that he did not want a general engagement; he wanted Pope drawn away from the reinforcements being assembled on the lower Rappahannock. Once that was done, the two wings would reunite in the vicinity of Manassas and take advantage of any opening Pope afforded, either through negligence or panic.

Jackson began his preparations at once. After sending a topographical engineer ahead to select the best route around the Bull Run Mountains, he set his camps astir. The march would begin at earliest dawn, "with the utmost promptitude, without knapsacks" — without everything, in fact, except weapons, the ordnance train, and ambulances. Beef on the hoof would serve for food, supplemented by green corn pulled from fields along the way. Ewell would lead, followed by A. P. Hill; Winder's division, now under Brigadier General W. B. Taliaferro, would bring up the rear, with orders to tread on the heels of Hill's men if they lagged. During the night, Longstreet's guns replaced Jackson's along the Rappahannock south of Waterloo Bridge, and Lee, who would be left with 32,000 troops — including Stuart's cavalry, which would join the flanking column the second day — prepared to stage whatever demonstrations would be needed to conceal from Pope the departure of Jackson's 23,000.

What with the moving guns, the messengers coming and going, the night-long activity in the camps, Stonewall himself got little sleep before the dawn of August 25. He rose early, ate a light breakfast, and took a moment, now that the Sabbath was over, to write a brief note to his wife. In it he said nothing of the march that lay ahead; merely that "I have only time to tell you how much I love my little pet dove." Presently he was in the saddle, doubling the column. The men looked up and sideways at him as he passed, the bill of his mangy cadet cap pulled down over his pale eyes. As usual, they did not know where they were going, only that there would most likely be fighting when they got there. Meanwhile, they did the marching and left the thinking to Old Jack. "Close up, men. Close up," he said.

Ten days ago, still down on the Peninsula, preparing for the withdrawal he had unsuccessfully protested, McClellan had warned Halleck: "I don't like Jackson's movements. He will suddenly appear where least expected."

This was not exactly news to Halleck, coming as it did on the heels of Banks' repulse at Cedar Mountain. Besides, Old Brains had other problems on his mind: not the least of which was the situation in the West, where his carefully worked-out tactical dispositions seemed about to come unglued. Kirby Smith left Knoxville that same week, bound for Kentucky, and Bragg had his whole army at Chattanooga, apparently poised for a leap in the same direction. Lincoln was distressed, and so was Halleck. So, presently, was McClellan. Earlier, to encourage haste in the evacuation, Halleck had assured him: "It is my intention that you shall command all the troops in Virginia as soon as we can get them together." McClellan's spirits rose at the prospect. To Burnside, who arrived with further assurances of Halleck's good will, he said as they stood beside the road down which his army was withdrawing to Fort Monroe: "Look at them, Burn. Did you ever see finer men? Oh, I want to see those men beside of Pope's." But there were subsequent delays, chiefly the result of a shortage of transports, and Halleck's cries for haste once more grew strident: so much so, in fact, that McClellan felt obliged to take official exception to what he called his "tone." Privately he protested to his wife that Halleck "did not even behave with common politeness; he is a *bien mauvais sujet* — he is not a gentleman. . . . I fear that I am very mad."

All the same, he made what haste he could. Porter left for Aquia Creek on August 20, and Heintzelman left next day for Alexandria. Both were to join Pope at once, the former by moving up the left bank of the Rappahannock, the latter by moving down the Orange & Alexandria Railroad. But Lee was across the Rapidan by now. "The forces of Burnside and Pope are hard-pressed," Halleck wired, "and require aid as quickly as you can send it. Come yourself as soon as you can." The bitter satisfaction McClellan found in this appeal was expressed in a letter to his wife: "Now they are in trouble they seem to want the 'Quaker,' the 'procrastinator,' the 'coward,' and the 'traitor.' *Bien.*" Two days later, Franklin followed Heintzelman to Alexandria, and Sumner embarked the following day to follow Porter to Aquia Creek. Four of the five corps were gone, leaving Keyes to man the Yorktown defenses: McClellan had answered Halleck's cries for haste. But he no longer put any stock in any promises made him, either by the general in chief or by any other representative of the Administration. In fact, he told his wife as he left Old Point Comfort, August 23, "I take it for granted that my orders will be as disagreeable as it is possible to make them — unless Pope is beaten," he added, "in which case they will want me to save Washington again. Nothing but their fears will induce them to give me any command of importance or to treat me otherwise than with discourtesy."

Sure enough, when he got to Aquia next morning — Sunday — he found that Porter and Heintzelman had already been released to Pope, and when he wired for instructions Halleck replied: "You can either remain at Aquia or come to Alexandria, as you may deem best, so as to direct the landing of your troops." In other words, it didn't matter; the Young Napoleon was merely to serve as an expediter, dispatching the rest of his men to Pope as fast as they came ashore at those two points. He chose Alexandria, presumably to be close at hand for the call he believed would follow the calamity he expected. Monday and Tuesday were doubtful days; Pope's scouts had spotted a column of "well-closed infantry" moving northward, up the far bank of the Rappahannock, and Pope reported Lee's whole army bound for the Shenandoah Valley "by way of Luray and Front Royal." Then Tuesday night the line went dead. All was silent beyond Manassas Junction, where there had been some sort of explosion. . . .

The next five days were smoke and flame; McClellan ran the gamut of emotions. With Porter and Heintzelman committed, he sent Franklin to join them, saying: "Go, and whatever may happen, don't allow it to be said that the Army of the Potomac failed to do its utmost for the country." Sumner followed. "You now have every man . . . within my reach," McClellan told Halleck, requesting that "I may be permitted to go to the scene of battle with my staff, merely to be with my own men, if nothing more. They will fight none the worse for my being with them." Halleck replied, "I cannot answer without seeing the President, as General Pope is in command, by his orders, of the department." When McClellan asked where this left him, the answer came from the War Department: "General McClellan commands that portion of the Army of the Potomac that has not been sent forward to General Pope's command." In all, this amounted to nothing more than his staff and the handful of convalescents at Alexandria. Instead of being removed from command, as he had feared at the outset, he now perceived that his command had been removed from him.

He was left, he told his wife, "flat on my back without any command whatever. . . . I feel too blue and disgusted to write any more now, so I will smoke a cigar and try to get into a better humor." It did no good. Far off, beyond Fairfax, he could hear the rumble of guns from a field where his soldiers were fighting under a man he despised and considered professionally incompetent. Unable to go, yet unable to sit still, doing nothing, he took up his pen. "They have taken all my troops from me! I have even sent off my personal escort and camp guard, and am here with a few orderlies and the aides. I have been listening to the sound of a great battle in the distance. My men engaged in it and I away! I never felt worse in my life."

★ ★ ★

"Let us look before us," Pope had said, "and not behind." In taking advantage of this policy, obligingly announced for all to hear, Jackson not only fulfilled McClellan's prediction that he would "suddenly appear where least expected," but he did so — in accordance with Lee's instructions — by landing squarely and emphatically astride those lines of retreat which Pope had said could be left "to take care of themselves."

In point of fact, however sudden his appearance was to Pope, to his own men it was something else again, coming as it did at the end of two of the longest and hardest days of marching any 23,000 soldiers ever did. At the outset the two views coincided. Like Pope, whose lookouts promptly reported the upstream movement, when they first marched into Monday's dawn they thought they were headed for another bloody game of hide-and-seek out in the Valley. That was fine with them. Rations had been scarce of late, and they recalled the largess of Commissary Banks. They swung on through the dust and heat, a long column of striding men whose uniforms, as one of their number later said, were "of that nondescript hue which time and all weathers give to ruins": Jeffersonton to Amissville, then northward across the river to Orlean, halfway through the first day's march, which would end just short of Salem, a station on the Manassas Gap Railroad. Where they would go from there they did not know. Nor did they seem to care. Approaching that place, with twenty-five leg-aching miles behind them, they forgot their weariness when they saw Jackson standing upon a large stone by the roadside, cap off, watching the sun turn red as it went down beyond the Blue Ridge. But when they cheered him, as was their custom, he made a startled gesture of protest and sent an officer to explain that the noise might give away their presence to the Yankees. So they raised their hats in mute salute as they swung past him, smiling, proud-eyed, silent except for the shuffle of feet in the dust. Flushed with pleasure, for their silence was more eloquent than cheers, Stonewall turned to his staff. "Who could not conquer with such troops as these?" he asked.

Wherever it was they were going, they knew next morning it was not to be the Valley; for at Salem they turned east toward White Plains, then southeast, following the railroad into the sunrise, blood red at first, then fiery in the broad notch of Thoroughfare Gap. That was the critical point. If it was held, there would be fighting and the loss of a large portion of the element of surprise. They quickened the step. Then word came down the column, Ewell to Hill to Taliaferro: the gap was empty, not a Federal in sight. They pressed on, eastward to Hay Market, then south-southeast to Gainesville, where they struck the Warrenton Turnpike, which led east-northeast from Pope's position on the Rappahannock, traversing the scene of last year's triumph on the plains of Manassas, across Bull Run at Stone Bridge, then on to Centerville and Alexandria. Tactically — so far, at least, as it had been kept from the marchers themselves — the secret was more or less out. "Disaster and shame lurk in the rear," Pope had said. Now Jackson lurked there, too.

It became obvious at once, though, that he intended to do a good deal more than simply lurk there. Stuart having arrived with all the cavalry — Lee had released him late the night before; he had ridden hard to catch up by midafternoon, when the head of the infantry column got to Gainesville — Jackson fanned the troopers out to the right, protecting the flank in the direction of the Rappahannock, and pushed on southward across the turnpike. Six miles ahead was Bristoe Station, where the Orange & Alexandria crossed Broad Run; destruction of the bridge there would sever Pope's supply line for days. "Push on, men. Push on," he told the marchers. But this was easier said than done. They were showing the effects of strain, and there was much less talk and horseplay up and down the column. Nearing Bristoe they had covered more than fifty miles, most of it in blazing heat and on secondary roads, with little to eat but green corn and apples along the way. Still, now that the goal was nearly in sight, according to one admiring cavalryman, "the feeling seemed to be a dread with each one that he would give out and not be there to see the fun." Many did give out, especially during this last half-dozen miles. As usual, however, though the column dribbled blown and blistered stragglers in its wake, Stonewall showed no pity for either the fainting or the stalwart, whatever their rank. Just short of Bristoe he dismounted and went onto the porch of a roadside cabin to wait for the column to close. He sat in a split-bottom chair, tilted back against the wall, and fell asleep. Presently a staff officer arrived and shouted him awake: "General Blank failed to put a picket at the crossroads! and the following brigade took the wrong road!" The eyelids lifted; two pale blue chinks appeared in the thin-lipped mask. "Put him under arrest and prefer charges," Jackson snapped. The eyelids dropped and he was back asleep at once.

The lead brigade hit Bristoe just at sunset. Coming forward on the run, the whooping graybacks overpowered the startled guards and were taking charge when they heard the approaching rumble of a northbound train. Hurriedly they threw crossties on the track and began a frantic attempt to unbolt a rail. Too late: the engine was upon them, scattering ties and men, then clattering out of sight in the gathering dusk — doubtless to give warning up the line. Their disappointment was relieved, however, by news that this was the hour when empty supply trains made their run, one after another from Pope's advance depots around Warrenton, back to Manassas and Alexandria. When the next prize came along the raiders were ready. Riflemen lining one flank of the right-of-way gave the locomotive a volley as it thundered past, struck an open switch, and plunged with half its cars down the embankment, where it struck with a gaudy eruption of red coals and hissing steam. Delighted with this effect, the Confederates gathered round and were pointing with elation at a bullet-pocked portrait of Lincoln on the steam dome — the engine was called *The President* — when the whistle of a third train was heard. It rammed into the cars left on the track, creating another rackety tableau of splintered wood and twisted iron: whereupon still a fourth whistle sounded. But while the watchers were getting set to enjoy another eruption of sparks and steam, they heard instead a screech of brakes as the locomotive stopped, then backed rapidly away and out of sight. The raiders cursed the engineer for his vigilance. Now the alarm would be sounded below as well as above the captured station; the fireworks fun was at an end.

Though he had enjoyed all this as much as anyone, now that it was over Jackson wasted no time on regret that it could not have lasted longer. Instead, he put his troops to work at once on the job for which he had brought them here in the first place: destruction of the Broad Run railroad bridge. While this was being done he stood beside a fire, hastily kindled for light, and began to interrogate one of the captured engineers. Across the way, a Federal civilian was laid out on the ground; a middle-aged man — probably a politician, for he had come down from Washington on a visit to Pope's army — he had suffered a broken leg in one of the train wrecks. Hearing who his captors were, and that their commander was just on the opposite side of the campfire, he asked to be lifted, despite the pain, for a look at the famed rebel. When the soldiers obliged, he saw beyond the dancing flames a stoop-shouldered figure in outsized boots and road-colored clothes slouched with a crumpled cadet cap pulled far down over his nose. For half a minute the civilian stared at the plain-looking man his captors assured him was the gallant Stonewall, scourge of the Yankee nation. Then, anticipation having given way to incredulity, which in turn gave way to disillusionment, he said with a groan of profound disgust: "O my God! Lay me down."

Jackson himself knew nothing of this: which was why he never understood the basic implication of the expression used by his soldiers in almost every conceivable situation from now on, whether confronted with an issue of meager rations or a charging Union line: "O my God! Lay me down!" In any case, even if he had heard it, he had no time for laughter. Interrogation of the engineer, along with other captives, had divulged that Pope's main base of supplies, four miles up the line at Manassas, was lightly guarded and wide open to attack. How long it would remain so, now that the alarm had been sounded in both directions, was another matter. Jackson decided to take no chance on being shut off from this richest of all prizes. Leg-weary though the men were, some of them would have to push on through the darkness to Manassas, block the arrival of reinforcements sent by rail from Alexandria, and hold the place until their comrades joined them in the morning. Two of Ewell's regiments drew the duty; or, more strictly speaking, were volunteered for it by their commander, Brigadier General Isaac Trimble. It was Trimble, a sixty-year-old Virginia-born Kentucky-raised Marylander, who had wanted to make a twilight charge up the blasted slope of Malvern Hill the month before; Stonewall had restrained him then, but he remained undaunted; "Before this war is over," he declared as the army started northward, "I intend to be a major general or a corpse." He set off into the night, riding out of Bristoe at the head of his two foot-sore regiments, a burly white-haired West Pointer with a drooping black mustache. On second thought, Jackson sent Stuart and his troopers along to support him. Then the rest of the command bedded down, too weary to worry overmuch about the fact that they were sleeping between an army of 75,000 bluecoats and the capital whose safety was supposedly that army's first concern.

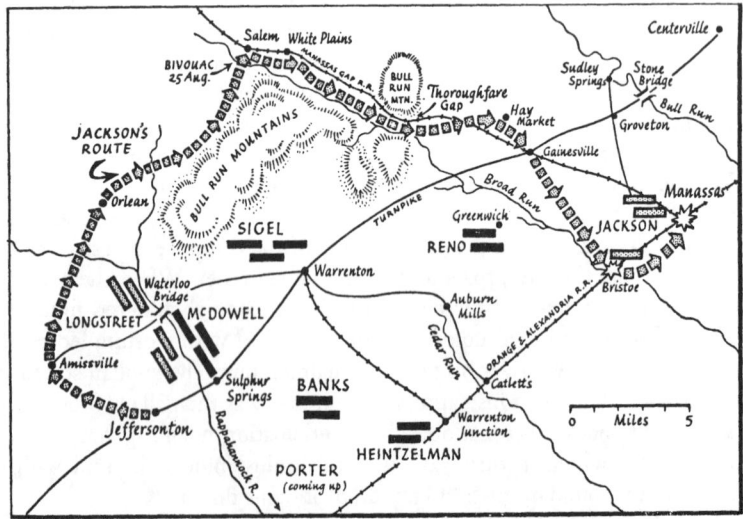

Early next morning, August 27, leaving the rest of Ewell's division to guard the Broad Run crossing in his rear, Jackson moved on Manassas with the troops of Hill and Taliaferro. The sight that awaited them there was past the imagining of Stonewall's famished tatterdemalions. Acres — a square mile, in fact — of supplies of every description were stacked in overwhelming abundance, collected here against the day when the armies of Pope and McClellan combined for another advance on Richmond. Newly constructed warehouses overflowed with rations, quartermaster goods, and ordnance stores. Two spur tracks, half a mile long each, were jammed with more than a hundred brand-new boxcars, similarly freighted. Best of all, from the point of view of the luxury-starved raiders, sutler wagons parked hub-to-hub were packed with every delicacy their vanished owners had thought might tempt a payday soldier's jaded palate. There it all was, spread out before the butternut horde as if the mythical horn of plenty had been upended here, its contents theirs for the taking. So they supposed; but when they broke ranks, surging forward, they found that Jackson, frugal as always, had foreseen their reaction and had moved to forestall it by placing Trimble's men on guard to hold them back. For once, though, he had underrated their aggressive instincts. Veterans of harder fights, with infinitely smaller rewards at the end, they broke through the cordon and fell on the feast of good things. Canteens were filled with molasses, haversacks with coffee; pockets bulged with cigars, jackknives, writing paper, handkerchiefs, and such. However, the chief object of search, amid the embarrassment of riches, was whiskey. This too their commander had foreseen, and by his orders the guards staved in the barrels and shattered the demijohns; whereupon the looters dropped to their hands and knees, scooping and sipping at the pools and rivulets before the liquor soaked into the earth or drained away. Some, more abstemious, were satisfied with loaves of unfamiliar light-bread, which they ate like cake. Others, preferring a still richer diet, found pickled oysters and canned lobster more to their taste, spooning it up with grimy fingers and washing it down with bottles of Rhine wine.

Off to the east, a troublesome Federal battery had been banging away in protest all this while. Jackson sent one of his own to attend to it, but presently word came back that enemy infantry was crossing the Bull Run railroad bridge and forming for attack. Most of Hill's division was moved out quickly to meet the threat, which turned out to be a brigade of four New Jersey regiments sent down by rail from Alexandria under a zealous and badly informed commander, Brigadier General George W. Taylor. His orders were to save the bridge, but he decided to press on to the junction itself and drive away the raiders, whom he mistook for cavalry. The Jerseymen came on in style, green and eager, not knowing that they were up against the largest and probably the hardest-fighting division in Lee's whole army. Jackson opened on them with his guns — prematurely it seemed to Little Powell's men, waiting with cocked rifles for the interrupters of their feast to come within butchering distance. But the bluecoats took their long-range losses and kept coming, bayonets fixed and fire in their eyes.

Then Stonewall did an unfamiliar thing. Admiring their valor, which he knew was based on ignorance — the charge, he said later, "was made with great spirit and determination and under a leader worthy of a better cause" — he called a cease-fire and rode out in front of the guns, waving a handkerchief and shouting for the Federals to surrender and be spared extermination. By way of reply, one attacker took deliberate aim and sent a bullet whistling past him. Cured of his lapse into leniency, Jackson rode back and ordered the fire resumed. By now the Jerseymen were nearer, and this time it was as if they struck a trip-wire. Suddenly demoralized, they turned and scampered, devil-take-the-hindmost. Their losses were surprisingly light, considering the danger to which their rashness had exposed them: 200 captured and 135 killed or wounded, including their commander, who, as he was being carried dying to the rear, appealed to his men to rally "and for God's sake ... prevent another Bull Run."

They paid him no mind; nor did Jackson. Already burdened with more spoils than he could handle — victim, as it were, of the law of diminishing utility — for once he was unconcerned about pursuit. The whole comic-opera affair was over before noon. After burning the railroad bridge to insure against further interruption from that direction, he brought Hill's men back to the junction, where some measure of order had been restored in their absence. It was maintained, at least for a while. While the plunderers were held at bay, the ambulances and ordnance wagons — all the rolling stock he had — were filled with such Federal stores as were most needed, principally medical supplies. Once this was done, the rest were thrown open to the troops, who fell upon them whooping, their appetites whetted by the previous unauthorized foray. Painful as it was to Stonewall, watching the improvident manner in which his scarecrow raiders snatched up one luxurious armload only to cast it aside for another, he was reconciled to the waste by the knowledge that what was rejected would have to be given to the flames. Word had come from Ewell that he was under attack at Bristoe from the opposite direction; Jackson knew the time had come to abandon his exposed position for one in which he could await, with some degree of security, the arrival of Longstreet and reconsolidation of the army under Lee.

By now, of course, Pope had learned the nature of the explosion in his rear. Instead of heading for the Shenandoah Valley, as had been supposed when the signal station reported a well-closed gray column moving north two days ago, Lee had divided his army and sent half of it swinging around the Bull Run Mountains for a strike at Manassas; that half of it was there now, under Jackson. But Pope was not dismayed. Far from it; he was exultant, and with cause. He had forty brigades of infantry on hand, including a dozen of McClellan's, with others on the way. It seemed to him that Lee, who had less than thirty brigades — fourteen in one direction, fifteen in another, more than twenty airline miles apart, with 75,000 Federals on the alert between the two segments — had committed tactical suicide. Hurrying to Bristoe, where Hooker's division of Heintzelman's corps was skirmishing with the enemy, Pope arrived as night was falling and found that the rebels, soundly thrashed according to Hooker, had retreated across Broad Run. Encouraged by today's success, he decided to bring up six more divisions and with them crush Jackson's three before the sun went down tomorrow. A depot of supplies, however vast, seemed a small price to pay for bait when it brought such a catch within his reach.

To Phil Kearny, commanding Heintzelman's other division at Warrenton Junction, went a wire: "At the very earliest blush of dawn push forward ... with all speed to this place.... Jackson, A. P. Hill, and Ewell are in front of us.... I want you here at day-dawn, if possible, and we shall bag the whole crowd. Be prompt and expeditious, and never mind wagon trains or roads till this affair is over." To Reno, at Greenwich with Burnside's two divisions, went another: "March at the earliest dawn of day ... on Manassas Junction. Jackson, Ewell, and A. P. Hill are between Gainesville and that place, and if you are prompt and expeditious we shall bag the whole crowd.... As you value success be off at the earliest blush of dawn." A third wire went to McDowell, whose three divisions were helping to hold the line of the Rappahannock: "Jackson, Ewell, and A. P. Hill are between Gainesville and Manassas Junction. We had a severe fight with them today, driving them back several miles along the railroad. If you will march promptly and rapidly at the earliest dawn of day upon Manassas Junction we shall bag the whole crowd.... Be expeditious, and the day is our own."

Northeastward, exploding ammunition dumps imitated the din of a great battle and the night sky was lurid with the reflection of a square mile of flames: Jackson's graybacks were evidently staging a high revel, oblivious to the destruction being plotted by their adversary, five short miles away. But next morning, after fording Broad Run unopposed and marching past the wreckage at Bristoe Station, when Pope reached Manassas all he found was the charred evidence of what one of his staff colonels called "the recent rebel carnival." The scene was one of waste and desolation. "On the railroad tracks and sidings stood the hot and smoking remains of what had recently been trains of cars laden with ordnance and commissary stores intended for our army. As far as the eye could reach, the plain was covered with boxes, barrels, cans, cooking utensils, saddles, sabers, muskets, and military equipments generally; hard bread and corn pones, meat, salt, and fresh beans, blankets, clothes, shoes, and hats, from brand-new articles, just from the original packages, to the scarcely recognizable exuviae of the rebels, who had made use of the opportunity to renew their toilets." Of the revelers themselves there was no sign. Nor was there agreement among the returning guards and sutlers as to the direction in which they had disappeared. Some said one way, some another. As far as Pope could tell, the earth had swallowed them up.

As things now stood, last night's orders would result in nothing more than a convergence on a vacuum. Presently, however, reports began to come in, pinpointing the gray column first in one place, then another, most of them quite irreconcilable. Pope sifted the conflicting evidence, rejecting this, accepting that, and arrived at the conviction that Stonewall was concentrating his three divisions at Centerville. Revised orders went out accordingly, canceling the convergence on Manassas; Centerville was now the place. If they would still be expeditious, the day would still be Pope's.

His exuberance and zest were undiminished; he kept his mind, if not his eye, on the prize within his reach. But for others under him — particularly the dust-eating soldiers in the ranks, left hungry by the destruction of their commissary stores — the chase, if it could be called such, had already begun to pall. Marched and countermarched since the "earliest blush of dawn" in pursuit of phantoms, they were being mishandled and they knew it. The very terrain was of evil memory. It seemed to them that they were heading for a repetition of last year's debacle on these same rolling plains, under some of these same commanders. McDowell, for example; "I'd rather shoot McDowell than Jackson," men were saying. Now as then, they turned on him, muttering imprecations. Nothing about him escaped suspicion, even his hat, a bamboo-and-canvas affair he had invented to keep his scalp cool in the Virginia heat. They suspected that it was a signaling device, to be used for communicating with the rebels or as an identification to keep him from being shot by mistake. "That basket," they called it, contemptuous not only of the helmet, but also of the general it shaded. "Pope has his headquarters in the saddle, and McDowell his head in a basket."

All through the long hot afternoon of August 28 Pope kept groping, like the "it" in a game of blindman's buff, arms outstretched, fingers spread, combing the landscape for the ubiquitous, elusive rebel force: to no avail. Riding into Centerville at sunset, in advance of most of the twelve divisions he had slogging the dusty roads — all, that is, but the two with Banks, which, being still unrecovered from the shock of Cedar Mountain, had been left behind to guard the army trains — he found that he had ordered another convergence on another vacuum. The graybacks had been there, all right, but they were there no longer. They had vanished. Once more it was as if the earth had swallowed them, except that this time he would have to look for them in darkness, with troops worn down by fourteen hours of fruitless marching. Pope felt the first twinges of dismay. Not because of fear; he was afraid of nothing, not even Stonewall; but because the time allotted for the destruction of Lee's army, wing by isolated wing, was running out. Such fear as he felt was that Jackson would make his escape and rejoin Longstreet, who by now would be moving to meet him.

Pope's dismay was short-lived, however. After nightfall, two dispatches reached him that changed everything and sent his spirits soaring higher than ever. The first informed him that Longstreet's column, after penetrating Thoroughfare Gap, had been driven back to the west side of Bull Run Mountain. This afforded considerable relief, allowing as it did additional time in which to catch the rebel host divided. But the best news of all came just before 10 o'clock. Late that afternoon, marching as ordered toward Centerville, one of McDowell's divisions had found Jackson lurking in the woods beside the Warrenton Turnpike, two miles short of Stone Bridge, and had flushed him. There on the field of last year's battle, Pope wired Halleck, "a severe fight took place, which was terminated by darkness. The enemy was driven back at all points, and thus the affair rests."

Determined not to let it rest there long, he sent peremptory orders to the commanders of his five converging corps for the execution of a plan he improvised, then and there, for the absolute destruction of his just-found adversary. McDowell and Sigel, with 30,000 men, would attack at dawn from the south and west, blocking any possible withdrawal by way of Thoroughfare Gap, while Heintzelman, Porter, and Reno, with another 30,000, would attack from the east: twin hammers whose concerted blows would pound to a pulp the 23,000 butternut marauders, pinned to the anvil by their own commander. Pope's instructions were explicit: "Assault him vigorously at daylight in the morning." Exultant — and with cause; Jackson's 14 gray brigades were about to be mauled simultaneously by 34 in blue, 17 from one direction, 17 from another — he added: "I see no possibility of his escape."

Stoutly conceived though the plan was, and stoutly though he strove to put it into execution, Pope was again the victim of several misconceptions. For one thing, Jackson was not trapped; nor was he trying to "escape." He very much wanted to be where he was, and he very much hoped that Pope could be persuaded to attack him, whatever the odds. In fact, if he could have been at Federal headquarters, with control over the messages coming and going, he scarcely would have changed a line in a single one of them. His luck was in and he knew it — the old Valley luck, by which even his worst errors worked to his advantage. The night march out of Manassas, for example:

When Ewell came up from Bristoe about sunset, having disengaged from the skirmish with Hooker's division across Broad Run, Stonewall gave these late arrivers a chance at the fag end of the feast — "What we got was ... not of a kind to invigorate," one cannoneer grumbled, "consisting as it did of hard-tack, pickled oysters, and canned stuff generally" — then put all three divisions in motion while the rear guard set fire to the picked-over wreckage left behind. What followed, as the troops slogged more or less northward in three columns, looking back over their shoulders at the spreading glow of flames, was one of the worst executed marches in the history of his command. Heavy-stomached, with bulging haversacks and pockets, the men fell by the wayside or crawled under bushes to sleep off their excesses of food and drink. The result was confusion and a great deal of lost time as the fileclosers probed the countryside, rounding them up and persuading them to fall back into column. Taliaferro did best, moving almost due north up the Sudley Springs road to Groveton, the designated point of concentration, where that road intersected the Warrenton Turnpike. Hill did worst; he went all the way to Centerville, then swung west. Ewell, following Hill for a time, crossed Bull Run at Blackburn's Ford, then recrossed it at Stone Bridge, Hill coming along somewhere behind. Morning found the three divisions badly scattered and dangerously exposed; it was midday before they were reunited at Groveton. For this there were various causes — Jackson's sketchy instructions, inefficient guides, the droves of stragglers — but even this blundering performance worked to Stonewall's advantage, providing as it did the basis for the conflicting Federal reports of his whereabouts, which led Pope off on a tangential pursuit.

Whatever blame he deserved for the confusion in all three columns along the way, Jackson had chosen their destination with care and daring. A rapid withdrawal to rejoin Lee beyond the mountains was in order, but it was not Stonewall's way to turn his back on a situation, no matter how risky, so long as possible benefits remained within his reach. Tomorrow or the next day, Longstreet would be coming down through Thoroughfare Gap or up the Warrenton Turnpike. At Groveton, Jackson knew from last year's extended stay in the area, there was an excellent covered position in which to await Old Pete's arrival by either route, and if the pressure grew too great his line of retreat would be reasonably secure. Meanwhile, the Federals — or, as he preferred to express it. "a kind Providence" — might afford him a chance at the infliction of another "terrible wound." About midday, when he finally got his scattered divisions back together, he put the men in position just north of the turnpike, behind a low ridge and under cover of some woods. One soldier later remembered that they were "packed [in there] like herring in a barrel." They stacked arms and lounged about, all 23,000 of them (minus stragglers) snoozing, playing cards, and munching at more of the good things they had in their haversacks by courtesy of Commissary Pope. The bands were silent; the troops were instructed not to shout; but as that same soldier remembered it, there were "no restrictions as to laughing and talking ... and the woods sounded like the hum of a beehive in the warm sunshine."

Jackson himself remained on the ridge, which afforded a clear view of the pike in both directions. When a report arrived that a strong Union column was advancing from Gainesville, he moved Taliaferro and Ewell two miles west and posted them in the woods adjacent to the pike for a surprise attack on the flank of the passing bluecoats. Nothing came of this; the column turned off south toward Manassas before it came abreast. Stonewall was cross and restless, reminding one observer of "an explosive missile, an unlucky spark applied to which would blow you sky high." Lee had told him to avoid a general engagement, but he did not like to see the Federals escape the ambush he had laid. Besides, he knew now that reinforcements from the Peninsula were at Alexandria — better than 30,000 of them, in addition to the two corps already joined. If Pope withdrew in that direction, the combined might of his and McClellan's forces would be too great for a strike at them, even after Lee arrived with Longstreet. So Jackson continued to patrol the ridge, trotting back and forth on his horse, peering up and down the pike. His staff and several brigade and regimental commanders sat their mounts at a respectful distance, not wanting to come near him in his present frame of mind or take a chance on interrupting his prayers that Providence would send another blue column into the trap the first had avoided.

Along toward sunset, his prayers were answered after the flesh. A well-closed Federal column was approaching, trudging hard up the turnpike in the direction of Stone Bridge, flankers out. Jackson rode down off the ridge for a closer look and trotted back and forth, within easy musket range of the bluecoats, who gave him no more attention than a casual rebel cavalryman deserved. Back on the ridge, the officers watched in horror and fascination. "We could almost tell his thoughts by his movements," one declared. "Sometimes he would halt, then trot on briskly, halt again, wheel his horse, and pass again along the [flank] of the marching column." They thought they knew what he would do, and presently he did it. When the head of the blue column drew abreast, he whirled and galloped back toward the group on the ridge. "Here he comes, by God," one shouted. Jackson pulled up, touched his cap, and said calmly: "Bring your men up, gentlemen." At this, they turned and rode fast toward the woods where the infantry was waiting. "The men had been watching their officers with much interest," the same observer remarked, "and when they wheeled and dashed toward them they knew what it meant, and from the woods arose a hoarse roar like that from cages of wild animals at the scent of blood."

The artillery led off. Three batteries emerged from the woods, went into position in the open, and began to slam away at the compact column on the pike. As the cannonade got under way, Taliaferro's men swarmed down the slope, yelling as they came, the battle flags of the Stonewall Brigade gleaming blood-red in the fading light. The result should have been panic, for the bluecoats taken thus unawares were from Rufus King's division — specifically, John Gibbon's brigade of four regiments, three from Wisconsin and one from Indiana — one of the largest but also one of the greenest in Pope's conglomerate command. However, instead of panicking at this abrupt baptism of fire, the Westerners wheeled to meet the attackers and stopped them in their tracks with massed volleys. Gibbon was regular army, loyal to the Union despite the fact that three of his North Carolina brothers went with the Stars and Bars. Supported by two regiments sent forward from Abner Doubleday's brigade, he handled his troops skillfully, holding off Taliaferro, who presently was reinforced by two brigades from Ewell. What ensued, first by the red glare of sunset, then on through dusk and twilight into darkness, with 2800 Federals facing nearly twice as many Confederates, was one of the hardest close-quarter fights of the whole war.

Jackson did not attempt to maneuver. Contrary to his usual practice once the advance had stalled, he was content to let the weight of numbers settle the issue. In point of fact, however, neither the pressure nor the savagery of his veterans settled anything at all. If the Wisconsin and Indiana farm boys were in a hopeless predicament, outnumbered nearly two to one by fighters whose fame was the highest in either army, they did not seem to recognize the odds. Experience had afforded them nothing by way of comparison; for all they knew, combat was supposed to be like this. The opposing lines stood face to face, parade-style, and slugged it out for two solid hours. Gibbon, who at thirty-five had a long career ahead of him, said afterwards that this was the heaviest infantry fire he ever heard, and Taliaferro referred to the engagement as "one of the most terrific conflicts that can be conceived of."

Finally the firing slacked; by 9 o'clock it died away, by mutual consent. The Federals withdrew across the turnpike, unpursued. More than a thousand of them had fallen, well over a third of the number engaged; the 2d Wisconsin, which had gone into the fight 500 strong, came out with 202, having begun tonight to establish the record it would set, before the war was over, by having more of its members killed in combat than any other regiment in the U.S. Army. Gibbon and Doubleday wondered what to do. Their latest orders called for a march on Centerville, but if the two-hour fight proved nothing else, it certainly had proved that the way was blocked in that direction. King was sick in an ambulance; no one knew where McDowell was. (He was in fact lost in the woods, having strayed from the pike in the darkness, and would not himself know where he was till morning.) So Gibbon and Doubleday, conferring with the ailing King, decided that the best thing to do would be to swing on down to Manassas, the original objective, taking such of their wounded along as could be recovered from the field. Grass-green three hours ago, the western soldiers fell back in and set off down the road as veterans. They were known as the Black Hat Brigade, Gibbon having seen to it that they were equipped with nonregulation black felt hats. In time, the rebels too would know them by that name; "Here come them damn black hat fellers!" the gray pickets would yell. But presently they changed it. Within a month they were calling themselves the Iron Brigade.

Few men anywhere were inclined to question their right to call themselves by any name they fancied — least of all Taliaferro's and Ewell's, who had suffered about as heavily as the troops they sought to ambush. The Stonewall Brigade took 635 soldiers into the twilight conflict and came out with 425, a ghost of the proud 3,000-man command that won its *nom de guerre* on nearby Henry Hill the year before and then passed through the glory of the Valley Campaign and the carnage of the Seven Days. Some of its most famous regiments were reduced to the size of a small company; the 27th Virginia, for example, was down to a scant two dozen men by the time the firing stopped. Murderous as these figures were, they told but part of the story, for they included a high percentage of officers of all ranks. The 2d Virginia had only one captain and one lieutenant left with the colors, and others were stripped almost as bare of leaders. Nor were the losses restricted to those of field and company grade. This fight brought down generals, too, including two of the three ranking just under Jackson himself. Taliaferro, who had succeeded Winder less than three weeks ago, was thrice wounded. He kept on his feet till the melee ended, but then, bled white, was carried off the field. His successor, Brigadier General William E. Starke — a former New Orleans cotton man, professionally untrained in arms — had been promoted on the eve of Cedar Mountain and had led a brigade in action for the first time tonight. Now suddenly he found himself in command of the most famous of all Confederate divisions.

The other high-ranking casualty was Ewell. Unable to resist the lure of close-up combat, he had gone forward to direct a charge by the 21st Georgia. As he knelt, squinting under the smoke for a glimpse of the enemy line, several of the Georgians called out proudly: "Here's General Ewell, boys!": whereupon the Federals, hearing the cheering, cut loose with heavy volleys in that direction. The regiment scattered, taking such losses here and elsewhere that it emerged from the battle with only 69 of its 242 men unhurt. Old Bald Head himself was found on the field when the fight was over, unconscious from loss of blood, one knee badly shattered by a minie. The surgeons assessed the damage and pronounced the verdict: amputation. Apparently he was out of the war for good. His successor was Alexander R. Lawton, who had held the rank of brigadier for sixteen months — longer than any other general in the army — apparently because Jackson, who had by-passed him in favor of Winder, did not consider him competent for divisional command. Now, as a result of attrition, his seniority could no longer be denied.

Any fight that cost the Confederacy the services of the profane and eccentric Ewell, along with those of the fast-developing Taliaferro and nearly a thousand other veterans of all ranks, could scarcely be called an unclouded victory, no matter who held the field when the smoke cleared. Moreover, Jackson himself had displayed symptoms of a relapse into tactical lethargy once the thing was under way. Yet if he felt either dismay or dissatisfaction at being thus deprived of two of his three chief lieutenants — all, in fact, but the one he trusted least, the thin-skinned and erratic A. P. Hill — he showed no signs of it, any more than he showed signs of apprehension for what Pope would surely try to do to him tomorrow. He seemed in fact, according to one of his soldiers, "calm as a May morning." What was left of the night he devoted to sleep. Purposely, as if with a shout of Boo! in the game of blindman's buff he was playing, he had attracted Pope's attention, hoping to hold him there by absorbing his attacks until Lee arrived with Longstreet and made possible a shift to the offensive he preferred.

★ ★ ★

Longstreet was nearer than Jackson knew: near enough, even, to have heard the tearing rattle of musketry in the twilight west of Groveton, six miles off, and to wonder at the silence that ensued. For Lee, who was with the approaching column, this was one more enigma to be added to the many that had fretted him since Stonewall marched away, four days ago. The first day had been spent continuing the artillery demonstration along the Rappahannock. That night, after wiring Davis to ask if more troops could be spared from the Richmond defenses, he sent Stuart off with all the cavalry. Next morning, August 26, he continued the cannonade, hoping to keep Pope's attention fixed on his front while Jackson moved around his flank to strike his rear. By midday, however, there were signs that the Federals were beginning to pull back: which might or might not mean that the ruse had been detected. Lee sent for Longstreet. The time had come to reunite the two wings of the army, he said, and he left to him the choice of routes, either up the Warrenton Pike or roundabout through Salem. Old Pete chose the latter. Leaving Major General R. H. Anderson's division, formerly Huger's, to hold the fords and mask the movement, he set out that afternoon with his other three divisions — Hood's, reinforced by Shanks Evans, whose brigade had come up from South Carolina; Brigadier General D. R. Jones', formerly half of Magruder's; and Longstreet's own, now split in two, under Brigadier Generals Cadmus Wilcox and James Kemper. This gave him, in effect, five divisions, each with three brigades; 32,000 men in all.

He made eleven miles before bivouacking near Orlean after nightfall, and by noon of the following day the head of the column had passed through Salem, matching the performance of Stonewall's fabled marchers over these same roads, thirty-six hours ago. That was gratifying indeed. Even more so, however, were two dispatches Lee received before going into bivouac on the outskirts of White Plains. The first was from Jackson, informing him that he had taken Bristoe and Manassas the night before. He was concentrating now at the latter place, he added, squarely in Pope's rear, and saw no evidence, so far, that the Federals were massing against him. The second welcome dispatch, brought by a courier from the opposite direction, was from Davis, replying to Lee's request for reinforcements. They were on the way, the President told him: Wade Hampton's cavalry brigade and two divisions of infantry under Harvey Hill and Major General Lafayette McLaws, the latter having been assigned the other half of Magruder's old command. Howls of protest might ordinarily be expected when his critics learned that the seat of government was being stripped of defenders, Davis said, but "confidence in you overcomes the view which would otherwise be taken of the exposed condition of Richmond, and the troops retained for the defense of the capital are surrendered to you on a new request."

Lee's anxiety, both for the present and the future, was considerably relieved. In addition to the badly needed brigade of cavalry — he had none at all for the screening of Longstreet's column; riding point that morning near Salem, he and his staff had barely avoided capture by a roving Federal squadron — the arrival of the promised ten brigades of infantry would add 17,000 veteran bayonets to his army. That would by no means even the odds Pope and Burnside and McClellan could bring to bear, combined, but it would at any rate reduce them to the vicinity of two to one: 150,000 vs 72,000. If the present odds were less heartening — McClellan, after all, might be with Pope already — in other respects the situation appeared quite promising. Reinforcements on the way, Jackson astride the railroad in Pope's rear, the main Union supply base up in flames: all this was much, besides which it held out interesting possibilities for maneuver. Manassas being just twenty-two miles from White Plains, Longstreet's present bivouac, Lee could reasonably expect to have the two wings of his army reunited by tomorrow night, prepared to undertake the completion of the "suppression" already begun. Before dawn, more good news arrived. Jackson informed him by courier that he was withdrawing from his exposed position at Manassas and would concentrate at Groveton, thus reducing by three full miles the interval between himself and Longstreet.

Refreshed by sleep, Old Pete's veterans swung off into a rising sun that seemed destined to shine today on a reunited Army of Northern Virginia. Only one natural obstacle lay in their path: Thoroughfare Gap. If the Yankees held it in strength there would be the delay of an uphill fight or a roundabout march, either of which would throw the schedule out of kilter. This seemed unlikely, though, since Jackson's couriers had been coming through unhindered, and presently another arrived, bringing further assurance that the pass was open and that his chief had reached Groveton, unmolested and unobserved, and was concentrating his troops in the woods overlooking the turnpike at that place. At 3 o'clock, topping the final rise that brought the gap into view, Longstreet's lead division pushed rapidly forward. Back with the main body, Lee presently heard from up ahead the reverberant clatter of musketry in the gorge. "Its echoes were wonderful," one staff officer later recalled. "A gun fired in its depths gave forth roars fit to bring down the skies."

Lee's reaction was less esthetic, for this of all sounds was the one he least wanted to hear. Then came the message that confirmed his fears: The Federals not only held the pass itself, they also had a reserve line posted on a dominant ridge beyond. John Pope had turned the tables, it seemed. Instead of panicking when he found Stonewall interposed between himself and Washington, the Union commander apparently had seized the initiative and posted his superior force between the two Confederate wings, preparing to crush them in sequence.

This was the darkest possible view. But Longstreet — "that undismayed warrior," his chief of staff afterwards called him, adding that he was "like a rock in steadiness when sometimes in battle the world seemed flying to pieces" — put his troops at once in motion to test the validity of such gloom. While Jones, supported by Kemper, kept up the pressure dead ahead, Hood probed for an opening near at hand and Wilcox set out for Hopewell Gap, three miles north. These dispositions took time. Near sunset, during lulls in the firing here at the pass, Lee heard from the direction of Groveton the mutter of distant musketry, mixed in with the grumble of guns. This was presently blotted out, however, by the stepped-up firing close at hand: Hood's men had found a cleft in the ridge and were on the Federal flank. Promptly the bluecoats retreated, unplugging the gap and withdrawing from the ridge beyond. (They were only a single division, after all, sent by McDowell on his own initiative, shortly before he wandered off and got himself lost in the woods.) Jones and Kemper marched through unopposed, joining Hood on the eastern slope, and the three divisions settled down to await the arrival of Wilcox, who had likewise penetrated Hopewell Gap.

Now that their own guns were silent, they heard again the growl and rumble of those near Groveton, half a dozen miles away. The uproar swelled to climax. Then it sank. At 9 o'clock it stopped. This might mean almost anything; all that was certain was that Jackson had been engaged. Whether he had won or lost — whether, indeed, that wing of the army still existed — they would know tomorrow. Whichever it was, it was over now. After sending a courier to inform Stonewall that the main body was safely through the pass, Lee told Longstreet to bed his men down for a good night's sleep in preparation for a fast march at sunup.

Friday, August 29, Hood's troops took the lead, marching so fast that their commander later reported proudly, "General Longstreet sent me orders, two or three times, to halt, since the army was unable to keep within supporting distance of my forces." There was need for haste. Ahead, the guns were booming again and a great white bank of smoke was piling up against the hot, bright blue, windless sky. Comforting though this was as proof that Jackson's men were still alive and kicking, it also demonstrated Pope's determination to destroy them before reinforcements got there. The Texans pushed on through Hay Market, raising a red cloud of dust with their feet, then down to Gainesville, where they struck the Warrenton Turnpike and swung left, advancing another three miles toward the ground-jarring thunder of guns, until they came upon Stonewall's right flank, above Groveton. It was now about 10 o'clock: Lee's army was reunited. Hood went into position north of the pike, establishing contact, and the other divisions filed into position on his right, extending the line generally southward, across the pike and down toward the Manassas Gap Railroad. From left to right, Longstreet's order of battle was Hood, Kemper, Jones, Wilcox. Anderson, who had masked the withdrawal from the Rappahannock line, was due to arrive by nightfall.

Moving from the scene of last night's bloody encounter, Jackson had placed his three divisions along the grade of an unfinished railroad. Part cut, part fill, it furnished an excellent defensive position, practically a ready-made system of intrenchments, roughly parallel to the turnpike across which Longstreet's line was drawn. When the Valley soldiers heard that their comrades had completed the march from Thoroughfare Gap and were filing into position on the right — "covered with dust so thick," one cavalryman observed, "that all looked as if they had been painted one color" — they rose and cheered them, despite the cannonade, which had scarcely slacked since sunup. Presently, though, they had more to worry about than bursting shells. The blue infantry was swarming to the attack.

The Federal chieftain's plans for a simultaneous double blow at both of Stonewall's flanks had gone astray, Porter having been delayed by darkness and two of the missing McDowell's three divisions having fallen back on Manassas after their twilight fights at Groveton and the Gap. "God damn McDowell, he's never where I want him," Pope was saying, angry but undaunted. He sent staff officers to locate them and hurry them along. Meanwhile, Sigel, Reno, and Heintzelman were at hand, and he flung them forward, still convinced that Jackson was trying to escape. One after another, they surged across the open fields, breaking in waves against the embankment where Stonewall's bayonets glittered. The closest they came to success was on the rebel left, where some woods afforded a covered approach. This was on Little Powell's front, the extreme flank of which was held by Brigadier General Maxcy Gregg's South Carolinians. Kearny's division struck hard here, effecting a lodgment astride the ramp and pressing down on the end of the line as if to roll it up. On a rocky knoll, here on the far-east margin of the conflict, Rebs and Yanks fought hand to hand. Bayonets crossed; rifle butts cracked skulls. A bachelor lawyer, somewhat deaf, Gregg strode up and down, brandishing an old Revolutionary scimitar and calling for a rally. "Let us die here, my men. Let us die here," he said. Many did die, something over 600 in all, but the knoll was held. The Federals withdrew.

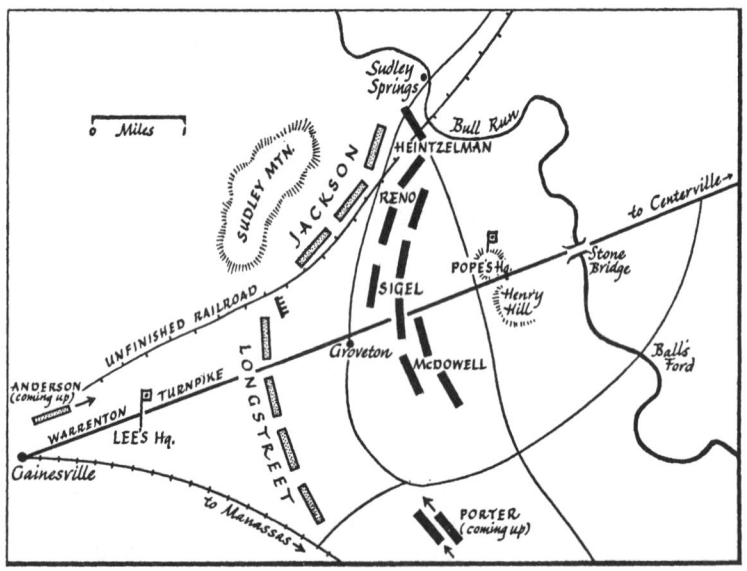

Hill did not think it would be for long. He sent word to Jackson that he would do his best, but that he doubted whether his men could withstand another such assault. Jackson sent the courier back with a sharp message: "Tell him if they attack him again he must beat them!" Riding toward the left to see for himself, he met the red-haired Hill coming to speak to him in person. "General, your men have done nobly," Jackson told him. "If you are attacked again, you will beat the enemy back." At this, the clatter broke out again in the woods on the left. "Here it comes," Hill said. As he turned his horse and rode back into the uproar, Jackson called after him: "I'll expect you to beat them!" The clatter rose to climax, then subsided. A messenger came galloping out of the smoke and pulled up alongside Jackson: "General Hill presents his respects and says the attack of the enemy was repulsed." Jackson smiled. "Tell him I knew he would do it," he said.

That was how it went, touch and go, all along his line all afternoon. Pope paid no mind to Longstreet, being unaware that he was even on the field: which, indeed, might practically as well have been the case, so far as relief of the pressure on Jackson was concerned, except for some batteries in brisk action on a ridge to Hood's left where the lines were hinged, like widespread jaws gaping east-southeast. Lee was quick to suggest that Old Pete swing the lower jaw forward and upward in order to engage the bluecoats and absorb some of the single-minded pressure they were applying to the weary men along the unfinished railroad. But Longstreet demurred. He never liked to go piecemeal into battle unprepared; Anderson was not yet up, and he had not had time enough for a thorough study of the ground. Besides, Stuart reported a force of undetermined strength gathering on the right; this, too, would have to be investigated. Regretfully Lee agreed to a delay. Longstreet left on a personal reconnaissance, then presently returned. He did not like the look of things. More Federals were coming up from the south, he said, in position to stab at his flank if he moved east. If they would venture squarely into the jaws, he would gladly clamp and chew them with gusto; but for the present he saw little profit, and much risk, in advancing.

Jackson rode up, dusty and worn. The two generals greeted him, and in reply to his statement that his line was hard pressed Lee turned to Longstreet. "Hadn't we better move our line forward?" he suggested.

"I think not," Longstreet said. "We had better wait until we hear more from Stuart about the force he has reported moving against us from Manassas."

A step-up in the firing toward the east caused Jackson to ride off in that direction. Federal dead and wounded were heaped along the forward slope where the Confederates, drawing their beads under cover of the cuts and fills, had dropped them. Charge after charge was repulsed all down the line, but this was accomplished at a high cost to the badly outnumbered defenders: especially when the fighting was conducted at close quarters, as it often was today. In Starke's division, on the right, not a single brigade was under a general officer, and one was led by a major. In Lawton's, when bull-voiced old Ike Trimble was hit and carried from the field, command of his brigade passed for a time to a captain. For the survivors, fighting their battle unrelieved and unsupported, this was the longest of all days. One remembered, years afterward, how he spent the infrequent lulls "praying that the great red sun, blazing and motionless overhead, would go down." He added, looking back: "For the first time in my life I understood what was meant by 'Joshua's sun standing still on Gibeon,' for it would not go down."

At last, however, as it approached the landline, Lee suggested for the third time that Longstreet attack. But Longstreet still demurred.

Stuart had identified the hovering bluecoats as Porter's corps, two veteran divisions. Besides, Old Pete had a new objection: There was too little daylight left. The best thing to do, he said, would be to make a forced reconnaissance at dusk; then, if an opening was discovered, the whole army could exploit it at dawn tomorrow. Once more Lee deferred to Longstreet, who assigned the task to Hood.

The Texans moved out at sunset, advancing up the Warrenton Turnpike, "the light of battle in our eyes — I reckon," one recalled — "and fear of it in our hearts — I know." They collided in the dusk with King's division, returning from Manassas, in a fight so confused that one Union major was captured when he tried to rally a regiment that turned out to be the 2d Mississippi. Hood held his ground, driving the weary Federals back, but when he reported to Lee and Longstreet after dark, he recommended that his troops be withdrawn to their original position. Nor did he think that an attack next morning would succeed in that direction; the enemy position was too strong, he said. Thus Longstreet's daylong judgment was apparently confirmed. Lee gave Hood permission to withdraw, which he did, encountering in the darkness the men of Anderson's division, just arrived from Thoroughfare Gap, and thus prevented them from stumbling blindly into the Union lines.

The long day's fight was over. Out across the night-shrouded fields and in the woods behind the corpse-strewn embankment, the groans of the wounded were incessant. "Water! For God's sake, water!" men were crying. Jackson's medical director, reporting the heavy casualties to his chief, said proudly: "General, this day has been won by nothing but stark and stern fighting." Stonewall shook his head. "No," he said. "It has been won by nothing but the blessing and protection of Providence."

Dawn found Pope in excellent spirits. His headquarters were on a little knoll in the northeast quadrant formed by the intersection of the Manassas-Sudley road with the Warrenton Turnpike, and as he stood there in the growing light, burly and expansive, smoking a cigar and chatting informally with his staff and those commanders who found time to ride over for a visit, the gruffness which was habitual — one of his aides referred to it as "infusing some of his western energy into the caravan" — seemed merely a form of bantering this morning, pleased as he was with the overall success of his efforts to keep Stonewall from escaping. He had cast his net and the foe was entangled; now all that remained, apparently, was the agreeable task of hauling him in, hand over hand.

By no means had all gone to suit him yesterday. The attacks, though pressed with vigor, had been delivered somewhat piecemeal. Most irksome of all, Fitz-John Porter had declined to advance against

Jackson's right flank, claiming that Longstreet barred the way with something like three times as many men as he himself had. Pope did not believe this for an instant. At 4.30 he repeated his orders for Porter to "press forward into action at once on the enemy's flank, and, if possible, on his rear." Porter balked, still insisting that he had more than half of the rebel army to his front, and darkness fell before Pope could budge him. Disappointed, the Federal commander moved the sluggish Porter around to the main line, paralleling the turnpike, and prepared for an all-out assault at dawn, when he wired Halleck a summary of his achievements: "We fought a terrific battle here yesterday ... which lasted with continuous fury from daybreak until dark, by which time the enemy was driven from the field, which we now occupy. Our troops are too much exhausted yet to push matters, but I shall do so in the course of the morning.... The enemy is still in our front, but badly used up. We have lost not less than 8000 men killed and wounded, but from the appearance of the field the enemy lost at least two to one. He stood strictly on the defensive, and every assault was made by ourselves. Our troops behaved splendidly. The battle was fought on the identical battlefield of Bull Run, which greatly increased the enthusiasm of our men." In midparagraph he added, "The news just reaches me from the front that the enemy is retreating toward the mountains. I go forward at once to see."

He did go forward, onto the knoll at any rate, and what he saw encouraged him still more. Where bayonets had glittered yesterday along the bed of the unfinished railroad, the goal of so many charges that had broken in blood along its base, today there was stillness and apparent vacancy. Only a few gray riflemen contested the sniping from Federal outposts. Combined with the knowledge of Hood's withdrawal down the turnpike after midnight, this intelligence led Pope to believe that Jackson had pulled out, leaving only a skeleton force to discourage the blue pursuit. Still, anxious though he was to garner the utmost fruits of victory, Pope curbed his tendency toward rashness. In the end, he knew, more would be gained if the chase was conducted in a well-coördinated fashion than if he took off half-cocked and overeager. While he stood there on the headquarters knoll, wreathed in cigar smoke as he chatted with his staff, orders went out prescribing the dispositions for pursuit. McDowell would be in general charge of the two-pronged advance. Porter's corps and two divisions from McDowell's would move directly down the pike; Heintzelman's corps, supported by McDowell's other division, would move up the Hay Market road. With Stonewall's getaway thus contested in both directions, troop commanders were expressly instructed to "press him vigorously during the whole day."

All this took time, but Pope felt he could afford it now that he had a full-scale victory under his belt. Careful preparations, with strict attention to details, would pay dividends in the long run, when the rebels were brought to bay and the mopping-up began. Noon came and went. A heavy silence lay over the heat-shimmered field, broken from time to time by sputters of fire exchanged by the men on outpost. At 2 o'clock, informed that all was in order at last, Pope gave the signal and the pursuit got under way.

Deliberate though these preparations were, the pursuit itself — or anyhow what Pope conceived as such — was probably the briefest of the war. Jackson was by no means retreating; he had merely withdrawn his troops for some unmolested and hard-earned rest in the woods along the base of Sudley Mountain just in his rear, leaving a thin line to man the works and give the alarm in case the Yankees showed signs of advancing. He doubted that they would do so, after their failures yesterday, but he was perfectly willing to meet them if they tried it. Longstreet — who was very much on hand with all five of his divisions, no matter what evidence Pope had received (or deduced) in denial of the fact — was more than willing; he was downright eager. In fact, now that Porter's corps had been shifted from its threatening position off his flank, he desired nothing in all the world quite so much as that the Federals would launch a full-scale attack across his front, though he too doubted that Fortune's smile could ever be that broad.

Lee, who doubted it most of all, began to be concerned that Pope would get away unsuppressed, having suffered only such punishment as Jackson had managed to inflict while receiving his headlong charges the day before. As the long morning wore away, marked by nothing more eventful than the occasional growl of a battery or the isolated sputter of an argument between pickets, Lee took the opportunity to catch up on his correspondence. "My desire," he wrote the President, "has been to avoid a general engagement, being the weaker force, and by maneuvering to relieve the portion of the country referred to." By this he meant the region along the Rappahannock, whose relief had been accomplished by forcing Pope's retreat on Manassas. Now his mind turned to the possibilities at hand. If Pope would not attack, then he would have to be "maneuvered." About noon, while Lee was working on a plan for moving again around his opponent's right, crossing Bull Run above Sudley Springs in order to threaten his rear, Stuart came to headquarters with an interesting report. He had sent a man up a large walnut tree, Jeb said, and the man had spotted the bluecoats massing in three heavy lines along Jackson's front. Quickly Lee sent couriers to warn of the danger. Jackson alerted his troops but kept them in the woods. He had been observing the Federal activity for some time, but, concluding that nothing would come of it, had remarked to the colonel commanding the Stonewall Brigade: "Well, it looks as if there will be no fight today...."

Shortly before 3 o'clock he found out just how wrong he was. Suddenly, without even the warning preamble of an artillery bombardment, the blue infantry came roaring at him in three separate waves, stretching left and right as far as the eye could see. Buglers along the unfinished railroad gobbled staccato warnings, and the startled troops came running out of the woods to man the line. This was far worse than yesterday. Not only were the attacking forces much heavier; they seemed much more determined, individually and in mass, not to be denied a lodgment. Immediately Jackson began to receive urgent requests for reinforcements all along the front. One officer rode up to report that his brigade commander had been shot down and the survivors were badly shaken. They needed help.

"What brigade, sir?" Jackson asked, not having caught the name.

"The Stonewall Brigade."

"Go back," Jackson told him. "Give my compliments to them, and tell the Stonewall Brigade to maintain her reputation."

For the present, reduced though it was to a ghost of its former self, the brigade managed to do as its old commander asked; but how long it would be able to continue to do so, under the strain, was another question. Rifle barrels grew too hot to handle, and at several points the defenders exhausted their ammunition. At one such critical location, the enemy having penetrated to within ten yards of the embankment, the graybacks beat them back with rocks. All along the two-mile front, the situation was desperate; no sooner was the pressure relieved in one spot than it increased again in another. Broken, then restored, Hill's line wavered like a shaken rope. He was down to his last ounce of strength, he reported, and still the bluecoats came against him, too thick and fast for killing to do more than slow them down. Whereupon Jackson, who had no reserves to send in response to Hill's plea for reinforcements, did something he had never done before. Outnumbered three to one by the attackers, whose bullets he was opposing with flung stones, he appealed to Lee to send him help from Longstreet.

In the Federal ranks there was also a measure of consternation, especially at the brevity of what they had been assured was a "pursuit." Recovering from the shock of this discovery, however, the men fought with redoubled fury, as if glad of a chance to take their resentment of Pope out on the rebels. As usual, McDowell came in for his share of their bitterness — as witness the following exchange between a gray-haired officer and a wounded noncom limping rearward out of the fight:

"Sergeant, how does the battle go?"

"We're holding our own; but McDowell has charge of the left."

"Then God save the left!"

For the better part of an hour they came on, running hunched as if into a high wind, charging shoulder to shoulder across fields where long tendrils and sheets of gunsmoke writhed and billowed, sulphurous and "tinged with a hot coppery hue by the rays of the declining sun." One among them was to remember it so, along with the accompanying distraction of rebel shells "continually screeching over our heads or plowing the gravelly surface with an ugly rasping whirr that makes one's flesh creep." Still they came on. Time after time, they faltered within reach of the flame-stitched crest of the embankment, then time after time came on again, stumbling over the huddled blue forms that marked the limits of their previous advances. They battered thus at Jackson's line as if at a locked gate, beyond which they could see the cool green fields of peace. Determined to swing it ajar or knock it flat, they struck it again and again, flesh against metal, and feeling it tremble and crack at the hinges and hasp, they battered harder.

Longstreet stood on the ridge where his and Jackson's lines were hinged. This not only gave him a panoramic view of the action, it also afforded an excellent position for massing the eighteen guns of a reserve artillery battalion which had arrived at dawn. The batteries were sighted so that they commanded, up to a distance of about 2000 yards to the east and northeast, the open ground across which the Federals were advancing. For the better part of an hour the cannoneers had watched hungrily while the blue waves were breaking against Stonewall's right and center, perpendicular to and well within range of their guns. This was the answer to an artillerist's prayer, but Old Pete was in no hurry. He was saving this for a Sunday punch, to be delivered when the time was right and the final Union reserves had been committed. Then it came: Jackson's appeal for assistance, forwarded by Lee with the recommendation that a division of troops be sent. "Certainly," Longstreet said. He spoke calmly, suppressing the excitement he and all around him felt as they gazed along the troughs and crests of the blue waves rolling northward under the muzzles of his guns. "But before the division can reach him, the attack will be broken by artillery."

So it was. When Longstreet turned at last and gave the signal that unleashed them, the gunners leaped to their pieces and let fly, bowling their shots along the serried rows of Federals who up to now had been unaware of the danger to their flank. The effect was instantaneous. Torn and blasted by this fire, the second and third lines milled aimlessly, bewildered, then retreated in disorder: whereupon the first-line soldiers, looking back over their shoulders to find their supports in flight, also began to waver and give ground. This was that trembling instant when the battle scales of Fortune signal change, one balance pan beginning to rise as the other sinks.

Down on the flat, just after remarking calmly to one of his staff as he watched a line of wagons pass to the front, "I observe that some of those mules are without shoes; I wish you would see to it that all of the animals are shod at once," Lee heard the uproar and divined its meaning. Without a change of expression, he sent word to Longstreet that if he saw any better way to relieve the pressure on Jackson than by sending troops, he should adopt it. Headquarters wigwagged a signal station on the left: "Do you still want reinforcements?" When the answer came back, "No. The enemy are giving way," Lee knew the time had come to accomplish Pope's suppression by launching an all-out counterstroke to compound the blue confusion. An order went at once to Longstreet, directing him to go forward with every man in his command. It was not needed; Old Pete was already in motion, bearing down on the moil of Federals out on the plain. A similar order went to Jackson, together with a warning: "General Longstreet is advancing. Look out for and protect his left flank." But this also was unnecessary. When Stonewall's men saw the bluecoats waver on their front, they too started forward. Right and left, as the widespread jaws began to close, the weird halloo of the rebel yell rang out.

Porter's corps was on the exposed flank, under the general direction of McDowell, and Porter, who had been expressing dark forebodings all along — "I hope Mac is at work, and we will soon get ordered out of this," he had written Burnside the night before — had taken the precaution of stationing two New York regiments, the only volunteer outfits in Sykes' division of regulars, on his left as a shield against disaster. Facing west along the base of a little knoll on which a six-gun battery was posted, these New Yorkers caught the brunt of Longstreet's assault, led by Hood. One regiment, thrown forward as a skirmish line, was quickly overrun. The other — Zouaves, nattily dressed in white spats, tasseled fezzes, short blue jackets, and baggy scarlet trousers — stood on the slope itself, holding firm while the battery flailed the attackers, then finally limbered and got away, permitting the New Yorkers to retire. They did this at a terrible cost, however. Out of 490 present when the assault began, 124 were dead and 223 had been wounded by the time it was over: which amounted to the largest percentage of men killed in any Federal regiment in any single battle of the war. Next morning, one of Hood's men became strangely homesick at the sight of the dead Zouaves strewn about in their gaudy clothes. According to him, they gave the western slope of the little knoll "the appearance of a Texas hillside when carpeted in the spring by wild flowers of many hues and tints."

The respite bought with their blood, however brief, had given Pope time to bring up reinforcements from the right, and they too offered what resistance they could to the long gray line surging eastward along both sides of the pike. This was undulating country, with easy ridges at right angles to the advance, so that to one defender it seemed that the Confederates, silhouetted against the great red ball of the setting sun, "came on like demons emerging from the earth." There was delay as Longstreet's left became exposed to enfilading fire from some batteries on Jackson's right, but when these were silenced the advance swept on, tilted battle flags gleaming in the sunset. On Henry Hill, where Stonewall had won his nickname thirteen months ago, Sykes' regulars stood alongside the Pennsylvanians of Reynolds' division — he had been exchanged since his capture near Gaines Mill — and hurled back the disjointed rebel attacks that continued on through twilight into darkness.

There was panic, but it was not of the kind that had characterized the retreat from this same field the year before. The regulars were staunch, now as then, but there was by no means the same difference, in that respect, between them and the volunteers. Sigel's Germans and the men with Reno also managed to form knots of resistance, while the rest withdrew across Stone Bridge in a drizzle of rain. McDowell, seeing the Iron Brigade hold firm along a critical ridge, put Gibbon in charge of the rear guard and gave him instructions to blow up the bridge when his Westerners had crossed over.

After McDowell left, Phil Kearny rode up, empty sleeve flapping, spike whiskers bristling with anger at the sudden reverse the army had suffered. "I suppose you appreciate the condition of affairs here, sir," he cried. "It's another Bull Run, sir. It's another Bull Run!" When Gibbon said he hoped it was not as bad as that, Kearny snapped: "Perhaps not. Reno is keeping up the fight. He is not stampeded; I am not stampeded; you are not stampeded. That is about all, sir. My God, that's about all!"

Two miles west of there, near Groveton, Lee was composing a dispatch to be telegraphed to Richmond for release by the President:

> This army today achieved on the plains of Manassas a signal victory over combined forces of Generals McClellan and Pope.... We mourn the loss of our gallant dead in every conflict, yet our gratitude to Almighty God for his mercies rises higher and higher each day. To Him and to the valor of our troops a nation's gratitude is due.

His losses were 1481 killed, 7627 wounded, 89 missing; Pope's were 1724 killed, 8372 wounded, 5958 missing. Lee reported the capture of 7000 prisoners, exclusive of 2000 wounded left by Pope on the field, along with 30 guns and 20,000 small arms, numerous colors, and a vast amount of stores in addition to those consumed or destroyed by Jackson at Manassas Junction two days back.

Nor was that all. A larger triumph was reflected in the contrast between the present overall military situation, here in the East, and that which had existed when Lee assumed command three months ago. McClellan had stood within sight of the spires of Richmond; Jackson had been in flight up the Shenandoah Valley, pursued by superior enemy combinations; West Virginia had been completely in Federal hands, as well as most of coastal North Carolina, with invasion strongly threatened from both directions. Now Richmond had not only been delivered, but the Union host was in full retreat on Washington, with the dome of the Capitol practically in view and government clerks being mustered for a last-ditch defense of the city; the Valley was rapidly being scoured of the blue remnants left behind when Pope assembled his army to cross the Rappahannock; West Virginia was almost cleared of Federals, and the North Carolina coast was safe. Except for the garrisons at Fort Monroe and Norfolk, the only bluecoats within a hundred miles of the southern capital were prisoners of war and men now busy setting fire to U.S. stores and equipment at Aquia Creek, just north of Fredericksburg, preparing for a hasty evacuation.

Nor was that all, either. Beyond all this, there was the transformation effected within the ranks of the Army of Northern Virginia itself: a lifting of morale, based on a knowledge of the growth of its fighting skill. Gone were the clumsy combinations of the Seven Days, the piecemeal attacks launched headlong against positions of the enemy's own choice. Here in the gallant rivalry of Manassas, where Longstreet's soldiers vied with Jackson's for the "suppression" of an opponent they despised, the victory formula had apparently been found; Lee's orders had been carried out instinctively, in some cases even before they were delivered. Tonight at army headquarters, which had been set up in an open field with a campfire of boards to read dispatches by, there was rejoicing and an air of mutual congratulation as officer after officer arrived to report new incidents of triumph. Lee — who had told his wife a month ago, "In the prospect before me I cannot see a single ray of pleasure during this war" — stood in the firelight, gray and handsome, impeccably uniformed, welcoming subordinates with the accustomed grace of a Virginia host.

"General, here is someone who wants to speak to you," a staff captain said.

Lee turned and saw a smoke-grimed cannoneer standing before him, still with a sponge staff in one hand. "Well, my man, what can I do for you?"

"Why, General, don't you know me?" Robert wailed.

There was laughter at this, a further lifting of spirits as troop commanders continued to report of the day's successes. Hood rode up, weary but still elated over what he called "the most beautiful battle scene I have ever beheld." When Lee, adopting the bantering tone he often used in addressing the blond young man, asked what had become of the enemy, Hood replied that his Texans had driven them "almost at a double-quick" across Bull Run. He added that it had been a wonderful sight to see the Confederate battle flags "dancing after the Federals as they ran in full retreat." Lee dropped his jesting manner and said gravely, "God forbid I should ever live to see our colors moving in the opposite direction."

While Lee was at Groveton, composing the dispatch to Davis, Pope was at Centerville, composing one to Halleck. All things being considered, the two were by no means as different as might have been expected.

> We have had a terrific battle again today.... Under all the circumstances, both horses and men having been two days without food, and the enemy greatly outnumbering us, I thought it best to draw back to this place at dark. The movement has been made in perfect order and without loss. The troops are in good heart, and marched off the field without the least hurry or confusion.... Do not be uneasy. We will hold our own here.... P.S. We have lost nothing; neither guns nor wagons.

Of the several inaccuracies here involved (one being the comparison of forces; Lee had had 50,000 men engaged, while Pope had had 60,000 — exclusive of Banks, who was guarding his trains) the greatest, perhaps, was the one in which he declared that his troops were "in good heart." It was true that, after the first wild scramble for an exit, they had steadied and retired in column, under cover of the rear-guard action on Henry Hill; but their spirits were in fact so far from being high that they could scarcely have been lower. If Pope did not know the extent of his defeat, his men did. They agreed with the verdict later handed down by one of their corps historians, that Pope "had been kicked, cuffed, hustled about, knocked down, run over, and trodden upon as rarely happens in the history of war. His communications had been cut; his headquarters pillaged; a corps had marched into his rear, and had encamped at its ease upon the railroad by which he received his supplies; he had been beaten or foiled in every attempt he had made to 'bag' those defiant intruders; and, in the end, he was glad to find a refuge in the intrenchments of Washington, whence he had sallied forth, six weeks before, breathing out threatenings and slaughter."

They agreed with this in all its harshness, but just now what they mainly were was sullen. They had fought well and they knew it. Defeat had come, not because they were outfought, but because they were outgeneraled — or misgeneraled. As one of their number put it, "All knew and felt that as soldiers we had not had a fair chance." The fault, they believed, was Pope's; he had "acted like a dunderpate." And McDowell's; he had revived their suspicions by repeating his past performance on this field. "General McDowell was viewed as a traitor by a large majority of the officers and men," one diarist wrote, adding: "Thousands of soldiers firmly believed that their lives would be purposely wasted if they obeyed his orders in the time of the conflict." The story was told that one of his regiments had stepped gingerly up to the firing line, loosed a random volley, then turned and made for the rear, the men shouting over their shoulders as they ran: "You can't play it on us!" Slogging tonight through the drizzle of rain, they saw him sitting his horse beside the pike, identifiable in the murk because of the outlandish silhouette of his canvas helmet. One Massachusetts private nudged another, pointing, and said darkly: "How guilty he looks, with that basket on his head!"

Pope, too, came in for his share of abuse. "Open sneering at General Pope was heard on all sides," one veteran observed. Another, passing the luckless commander by the roadside, hailed him with a quote from Horace Greeley: "Go west, young man! Go west!" Perhaps this had something to do with changing his mind as to the state of his men's hearts. At any rate, when morning came — Sunday, August 31 — he wired Halleck: "Our troops are... much used-up and worn-out," and he spoke of giving the enemy "as desperate a fight as I can force our men to stand up to." Franklin's corps had come up the night before, in time to establish a straggler line in front of Centerville; Sumner too was at hand, giving Pope 20,000 fresh troops with which to oppose the rebels. But his confidence was ebbing. He told Halleck, "I should like to know whether you feel secure about Washington should this army be destroyed. I shall fight it as long as a man will stand up to the work. You must judge what is to be done, having in view the safety of the capital."

No sooner had he sent this, however, than a reply to last night's rosy message bucked him up again. "My Dear General: You have done nobly," Halleck wired. "Don't yield another inch if you can avoid it." Pope thanked him for this "considerate commendation" and passed along the encouraging news that "Ewell is killed. Jackson is badly wounded.... The plan of the enemy will undoubtedly be to turn my flank. If he does so he will have his hands full." Meanwhile, Franklin's soldiers mocked and taunted the bedraggled Army of Virginia, jeering along the straggler line at its "new route" to Richmond. Overnight, Pope's confidence took another sickening drop. Three hours after sunrise, September 1, he got off another long dispatch to Halleck. After a bold beginning — "All was quiet yesterday and so far this morning. My men are resting; they need it much.... I shall attack again tomorrow if I can; the next day certainly" — he passed at once to darker matters: "I think it my duty to call your attention to the unsoldierly and dangerous conduct of many brigade and some division commanders of the forces sent here from the Peninsula. Every word and act and intention is discouraging, and calculated to break down the spirits of the men and produce disaster." In the light of this, he closed with a recommendation that ran counter to the intention expressed at the outset: "My advice to you — I give it with freedom, as I know you will not misunderstand it — is that, in view of any satisfactory results, you draw back this army to the intrenchments in front of Washington, and set to work in that secure place to reorganize and rearrange it. You may avoid great disaster by doing so."

While waiting to see what would come of this, he found that Jackson (who was no more wounded than Ewell was dead) was in the act of fulfilling his prediction that Lee would try to turn his flank. Stonewall's men had crossed Bull Run at Sudley Springs, then moved north to the Little River Turnpike, which led southeast to Fairfax Courthouse, eight miles in the Union rear. Pope pulled the troops of Phil Kearny and Brigadier General I. I. Stevens, who commanded Burnside's other division under Reno, out of their muddy camps and sent them slogging northward to intercept the rebel column. They did so, late that afternoon. There beside the pike, around a mansion called Chantilly, a wild fight took place during a thunderstorm so violent that it drowned the roar of cannon. Jackson's march had been slow; consequently he was in a grim and savage humor. In the rain-lashed confusion, when one of his colonels requested that his men be withdrawn because their cartridges were too wet to ignite, the reply came back: "My compliments to Colonel Blank, and tell him the enemy's ammunition is just as wet as his."

This spirit was matched on the Federal side by Kearny, who dashed from point to point, his empty sleeve flapping as he rode with the reins clamped in his teeth in order to have his one arm free to gesture with his saber, hoicking his troops up to the firing line and holding them there by showing no more concern for bullets than he did for raindrops. His prescription for success in leading men in battle was a simple one; "You must never be afraid of anything," he had told a young lieutenant two days ago. Stevens followed his example, and between them they made Stonewall call a halt. The firing continued into early darkness, when on A. P. Hill's front the men were surprised to see a Union general come riding full-tilt toward them, suddenly illuminated by a flash of lightning. They called on him to surrender, but he whirled his mount, leaning forward onto its withers with his arm around its neck, and tried to gallop away in the confusion. They fired a volley that unhorsed him, and when they went out to pick him up they found that he was dead, lying one-armed in the mud, the back of his coat and the seat of his trousers torn by bullets. They brought his body into their lines. "Poor Kearny," Hill said, looking down at him. "He deserved a better death than that."

Stevens too was dead by now, shot while leading a charge, and the Federals fell back down the pike and through the woods. They did so more from being disheartened by the loss of their leaders, however, than from being pressed; Jackson did not pursue. Thus ended the Battle of Chantilly, a rain-swept drama with off-stage thunder, vivid flashes of lightning, and an epilogue supplied next morning by Lee, who sent Kearny's body forward under a flag of truce, "thinking that the possession of his remains may be a consolation to his family."

Pope by then was back at Fairfax, within twenty miles of Washington, having received from Halleck the instructions he had sought: "You will bring your forces as best you can within or near the line of fortification." As the army retreated — "by squads, companies, and broken parts of regiments and brigades," according to one enlisted diarist — its commander lost the final vestige of his former boldness. "The straggling is awful in the regiments from the Peninsula," he complained to Halleck. "Unless something can be done to restore tone to this army it will melt away before you know it." This was a new and different Pope, a Pope not unlike a sawdust doll with most of its stuffing leaked away. A surgeon who looked through a headquarters window the previous evening saw him so: "He sat with his chair tipped back against the wall, his hands clasped behind his head, which bent forward, his chin touching his breast — seeming to pay no attention to the generals as they arrived, but to be wholly wrapped in his own gloomy reflections." The doctor wrote long afterward, and being a kind-hearted man, who had dealt with much misery in his life, he added: "I pitied him then. I pity him now."

It was perhaps the only pity felt for him by anyone in the whole long weary column slogging its way eastward. Last night's thunderstorm had deepened the mud along the pike, and overhead a scud of clouds obscured the sun, which shed an eerie yellow light upon the sodden fields. In a way, though, the weather was fitting, matching as it did the mood of the retreat. "Everyone you met had an unwashed, sleepy, downcast aspect," one officer observed, "and looked as if he would like to hide his head somewhere from all the world." Now that the immediate danger was past, a still worse reaction of sullenness had set in among the troops, whose mistrust of Pope quite balanced his expressed mistrust of them. As one colonel put it, "No salutary fear kept them in the ranks, and many gave way to the temptation to take a rest. ... There was everywhere along the road the greatest confusion. Infantry and cavalry, artillery and wagons, all hurried on pell mell, in the midst of rallying cries of officers and calls and oaths of the men."

Banks had come up from Bristoe Station, bringing the army's wagons with him though he had been obliged to put the torch to all the locomotives and freight cars loaded with stores and munitions from Warrenton and other points below the wreckage of Broad Run bridge. His corps, having seen no fighting since Cedar Mountain, was assigned the rear guard duty, which consisted mainly of prodding frazzled stragglers back into motion and gathering up abandoned equipment littered along the roadside. At the head of the column — miles away, for the various units were badly strung out, clotted in places and gapped in others as a result of accordion action — rode Pope and McDowell, attended by their staffs and followed closely by the lead division, formerly King's but now under Brigadier General John P. Hatch, who had succeeded the ailing King. That afternoon the sun came out, but it did little to revive the downcast marchers: least of all Hatch, who had more cause for gloom than most. He had commanded a cavalry brigade, that being the arm of service he preferred, until Pope relieved him for inefficiency and transferred him to the infantry. So Hatch had this to brood over, in addition to the events of the past few days. Then suddenly, up ahead, he saw something that made him forget his and the army's troubles.

Off to one side loomed Munson's Hill, which Joe Johnston had held with a dummy gun last winter. From its crown, Hatch knew, you could see the dome of the Capitol. But what engaged his attention just now was a small group of horsemen coming down the road toward Pope and McDowell: particularly the man in front, who rode a large black horse and wore a vivid yellow sash about his waist. Hatch thought there was something familiar about the trim and dapper way he sat his charger. Then, as the man reined to a halt in front of the two generals, returning their salutes with one of his own which "seemed to carry a little of personal good fellowship to even the humblest private soldier," Hatch knew the unbelievable was true; it was Little Mac. He spurred ahead in time to hear McClellan tell Pope and McDowell he had been authorized to take command of the army. Off to the left rear just then there was a sudden thumping of artillery, dim in the distance. What was that? McClellan asked. Pope said it was probably an attack on Sumner, whose corps was guarding the flank in that direction. Then he inquired if there would be any objection if he and McDowell rode on toward Washington. None at all, McClellan replied; but as for himself, he was riding toward the sound of gunfire.

Before the two could resume their journey, Hatch took advantage of the chance to revenge the wrong he believed had been done when his cavalry brigade was taken from him the month before. Trotting back to the head of his infantry column, within easy hearing distance of Pope and McDowell, he shouted: "Boys, McClellan is in command of the army again! Three cheers!" The result, after an instant of shock while the words sank in, was pandemonium. Caps and knapsacks went sailing high in the air, and men who a moment ago had been too weary and dispirited to do anything more than plant one leaden foot in front of the other were cheering themselves hoarse, capering about, and slapping each other joyfully on the back. "From an extreme sadness," one Massachusetts volunteer recalled, "we passed in a twinkling to a delirium of delight. A deliverer had come." This was the reaction all down the column as the news traveled back along its length, pausing at the gaps between units, then being taken up again, moving westward like a spark along a ten-mile train of powder.

Such demonstrations were not restricted to green troops, volunteers likely to leap at every rumor. Sykes' regulars, for example, were far back toward the rear and did not learn of the change till after nightfall. They were taking a rest-halt, boiling coffee in a roadside field, when an officer on picket duty saw by starlight the familiar figure astride Dan Webster coming down the pike. "Colonel! Colonel!" he hollered, loud enough to be heard all over the area, "General McClellan is here!" Within seconds every man was on his feet and cheering, raising what one of them called "such a hurrah as the Army of the Potomac had never heard before. Shout upon shout went out into the stillness of the night; and as it was taken up along the road and repeated by regiment, brigade, division and corps, we could hear the roar dying away in the distance. The effect of this man's presence upon the Army of the Potomac — in sunshine or rain, in darkness or in daylight, in victory or defeat — was electrical." Hard put for words to account for the delirium thus provoked, he could only add that it was "too wonderful to make it worth while attempting to give a reason for it."

Nor was the enthusiasm limited to veterans of Little Mac's own army, men who had fought under him before. When Gibbon announced the new commander's arrival to the survivors of the Iron Brigade, they too reacted with unrestrained delight, tossing their hats and breaking ranks to jig and whoop, just as the Peninsula boys were doing. Later that night, Gibbon remembered afterward, "the weary, fagged men went into camp cheerful and happy, to talk over their rough experience of the past three weeks and speculate as to what was ahead."

It was Lincoln's doing, his alone, and he had done it against the will of a majority of his advisers. Chase believed that the time had come, beyond all doubt, when "either the government or McClellan must go down," and Stanton had prepared and was soliciting cabinet signatures for an ultimatum demanding "the immediate removal of George B. McClellan from any command in the armies of the United States." When Welles protested that such a document showed little consideration for their chief, the War Secretary bristled and said coldly: "I know of no particular obligation I am under to the President. He called me to a difficult position and imposed on me labors and responsibilities which no man could carry." Already he had secured four signatures — his own, Chase's, Bates', and Smith's — and was working hard for more (Welles and Blair were obdurate, and Seward was still out of town) when, on the morning of this same September 2, he came fuming into the room where his colleagues were waiting for Lincoln to arrive and open the meeting. It was a time of strain. Reports of Pope's defeat had caused Stanton to call out the government clerks, order the contents of the arsenal shipped to New York, and forbid the retail sale of spirituous liquors in the city. Now came the climactic blow as he announced, in a choked voice, the rumor that McClellan had been appointed to conduct the defense of Washington.

The effect was stunning: a sort of reversal of what would happen later that day along the blue column plodding east from Fairfax. Just as Chase was declaring that, if true, this would "prove a national calamity," Lincoln came in and confirmed the rumor. That was why he was late for the meeting, he explained. He and Halleck had just come from seeing McClellan and ordering him to assume command of the armies roundabout the capital. Stanton broke in, trembling as he spoke: "No order to that effect has been issued from the War Department." Lincoln turned and faced him. "The order is mine," he said, "and I will be responsible for it to the country."

Four nights ago he had gone to bed confident that the army had won a great victory on the plains of Manassas: a triumph which, according to Pope, would be enlarged when he took up the pursuit of Jackson's fleeing remnant. Overnight, however, word arrived that it was Pope who was in retreat, not Stonewall, and Lincoln came into his secretary's room next morning, long-faced and discouraged. "Well, John, we are whipped again, I am afraid," he said. All day the news got worse as details of the fiasco trickled through the screen of confusion. Halleck was a weak prop to lean on; Lincoln by now had observed that his general in chief was "little more than... a first-rate clerk." What was worse, he was apt to break down under pressure; which was presently what happened. Before the night was over, Old Brains appealed to McClellan at Alexandria: "I beg of you to assist me in this crisis with your ability and experience. I am utterly tired out."

Lincoln's mind was also turning in Little Mac's direction, although not without reluctance. Unquestionably, it appeared to him, McClellan had acted badly in regard to Pope. One of his subordinates had even been quoted as saying publicly, "I don't care for John Pope a pinch of owl dung." It seemed to Lincoln that they had wanted Pope to fail, no matter what it cost in the blood of northern soldiers. McClellan, when appealed to for counsel, had advised the President to concentrate all the reserves in the capital intrenchments and "leave Pope to get out of his scrape" as best he could. To Lincoln this seemed particularly callous, if not crazy; his mistrust of the Young Napoleon was increased. But early Tuesday morning, when Pope warned that "unless something can be done to restore tone to this army it will melt away before you know it," he did what he knew he had to do. "We must use what tools we have," he told his secretary. "There is no man in the army who can man these fortifications and lick these troops of ours into shape half as well as [McClellan].... If he can't fight himself, he excels in making others ready to fight."

So he went to him and told him to return to the army whose wounded were already beginning to pour into the city. And that afternoon, despite the howls of the cabinet — Stanton was squelched, but Chase was sputtering, "I cannot but feel that giving command to McClellan is equivalent to giving Washington to the rebels" — Lincoln had Halleck issue the formal order: "Major General McClellan will have command of the fortifications of Washington and of all the troops for the defense of the capital." This left Pope to be disposed of, which was done three days later. "The Armies of the Potomac and Virginia being consolidated," he was told by dispatch, "you will report for orders to the Secretary of War." Reporting as ordered, he found himself assigned to duty against the Sioux, who had lately risen in Minnesota. From his headquarters in St Paul, where he was settled before the month was out, Pope protested vehemently against the injustice of being "banished to a remote and unimportant command." But there he stayed, for the duration.

CHAPTER

7

Two Advances; Two Retreats

★ ✗ ☆

ON THE DAY LEE WRECKED POPE ON THE plains of Manassas, driving him headlong across Bull Run to begin his scamper for the Washington intrenchments, Kirby Smith accomplished in Kentucky the nearest thing to a Cannae ever scored by any general, North or South, in the course of the whole war. This slashing blow, the first struck in the two-pronged offensive Bragg had designed to recover for the Confederacy all that had been lost by his predecessors, was delivered in accordance with Smith's precept, announced at the outset, that "brilliant results... will be accomplished only with hard fighting."

Accordingly, on August 25, after a week's rest at Barbourville, he had resumed his northward march. There were 21,000 men in his four divisions, but the largest of these — 9000-strong; the others had about 4000 each — remained in front of Cumberland Gap, observing the 9000 Federals who held it, while the rest continued their advance toward the Bluegrass. Meanwhile this was still the barrens, which meant that water was scarce, the going rough, and people in general unfriendly. This last might well have been based on fear, however, for the appearance of the marchers, whether they came as "liberators" or "invaders," struck at least one citizen as anything but prepossessing: "[They were] ragged, greasy, and dirty, and some barefoot, and looked more like the bipeds of pandemonium than beings of this earth.... They surrounded our wells like the locusts of Egypt and struggled with each other for the water as if perishing with thirst, and they thronged our kitchen doors and windows, begging for bread like hungry wolves.... They tore the loaves and pies into fragments and devoured them. Some even threatened to shoot others if they did not divide with them." ("Notwithstanding such a motley crew," the alarmed observer added with relief, "they abstained from any violence or depredation and appeared exceedingly grateful.") As a supplement to what could be cadged in this manner, they gathered apples and roasting ears from roadside orchards and fields, eating them raw on the march with liberal sprinklings of salt, a large supply of which had been procured at Barbourville. Spirits were high and there was much joking, up and down the column. CSA, they said, stood for "Corn, Salt, and Apples."

No matter how much horseplay went on within the column itself, passing through London on the 27th the men continued to obey their commander's insistence upon "the most perfect decorum of conduct toward the citizens and their property." Two days later, by way of reward for good behavior, they climbed Big Hill, the northern rim of the barrens, and saw spread out before them, like the promised land of old, the lush and lovely region called the Bluegrass. Years afterward, Smith would remember it as it was today, "a long rolling landscape, mellowing under the early autumn rays," and would add that when it "burst upon our sight we were astonished and enchanted." However, there was little time for undisturbed enjoyment of the Pisgah view. Up ahead, near the hamlet of Rogersville, seven miles short of Richmond, the principal settlement this side of the Kentucky River, the cavalry encountered resistance and was driven back upon the infantry. This was a sundown affair, soon ended by darkness. Although he did not know the enemy strength, Smith was not displeased at this development; for it indicated that the Federals would make a stand here in the open, rather than along the natural line of defense afforded by the bluffs of the river eight miles beyond Richmond. Earlier that week he had written Bragg that he would "fight everything that presents itself," and now, having issued instructions for his men to sleep on their arms in line of battle, he prepared to do just that at dawn. After more than a hundred miles of marching, they were about to be required to prove their right to be where they were and — if they won — to penetrate farther into what Smith would call the "long rolling landscape."

The bluecoats slept in line of battle, too, and there were about 7000 of them. They were under William Nelson, whom Buell had sent north two weeks ago, a month after his promotion to major general, to take charge of the defense of his native Kentucky. "The credit of the selection will be mine," Buell had told him. "The honor of success will be yours." Nelson was of a sanguine nature — "ardent, loud-mouthed, and violent," a fellow officer called him — but by now, having completed a tour of inspection of what he had to work with, he was not so sure that either credit or success, let alone honor, was very likely to come his way as a result of the contest he saw looming. Kirby Smith was closing on him with an army of 12,000 hardened veterans, while his own, hastily organized into two small divisions under two ex-civilian brigadiers, was composed almost entirely of green recruits hurried forward by the governors of Ohio and Indiana in response to an urgent call from Washington. Their periods of service ranged in general from three weeks to three days, and for all his arrogant manner, his six feet five inches of height and his three hundred pounds of weight, Nelson was considerably worried as to what they would do when they heard the first shot fired in their direction.

He was not long in finding out. At 2.30 in the morning, August 30, a courier knocked at his bedroom door in Lexington and informed him that the Confederates had come over Big Hill the previous afternoon, approaching Richmond, but that his two brigadiers — Mahlon Manson and Charles Cruft — were on the alert and had intercepted the gray column before it reached the town. This was not at all what Nelson wanted to hear, for he was doubtful that his green men could be maneuvered in open combat, and had intended for them to be pulled back to a better defensive position. Apprehensive, he got dressed and rode forward to see for himself, hearing gunfire as soon as he crossed the Kentucky River. It was well past noon by the time he got to Richmond, however, since he was obliged to travel the byroads to avoid being picked up by rebel horsemen. Arriving at last he found the troops, as he later declared, "in a disorganized retreat or rather rout." With the assistance of Manson and Cruft he got what was left of his army into line on the edge of town, partly under cover of the rock walls and tombstones of a cemetery. Once the rallied men were in position, he walked up and down the firing line, exposing his huge bulk to enemy marksmen and talking all the while to encourage his nervous recruits. "If they can't hit me they can't hit anything!" he roared as he strode back and forth amid the twittering bullets.

In this he was mistaken, as he presently found out. They hit him twice, in fact, both flesh wounds, no less painful for being superficial. But what hurt him worst, apparently, was the conduct of his men, who refused to be encouraged by his example. "Our troops stood about three rounds," he afterwards reported, "when, struck by a panic, they fled in utter disorder. I was left with my staff almost alone." He made his escape, considerably hampered by a bullet in his thigh. So did Cruft; but not Manson, who was pinned under his fallen horse and captured.

Nelson listed his casualties as 206 killed, 844 wounded, 4303 captured or missing.

Smith's were 78 killed, 372 wounded, 1 missing out of the approximately 7000 he too had had engaged. After the initial decision to give battle he had left the tactical details to the commander of his lead division, Brigadier General Patrick R. Cleburne, who had charge of the two brigades sent by Bragg from Chattanooga. Cleburne was Irish — about as Irish in fact as possible, having been born in County Cork on St Patrick's Day, thirty-four years ago. As a youth he had done a hitch in the British army, rising to the rank of corporal, then had emigrated to Helena, Arkansas, where he studied and practiced law with the same diligence he applied to his other two prime absorptions, pistol marksmanship and chess. When the war broke out he was elected captain of the local volunteer company, the Yell Rifles. By the time of Shiloh he had attained his present rank and led his brigade of Tennesseans, Mississippians, and Arkansans with conspicuous skill and gallantry through that fight. Today in Kentucky he did likewise, keeping up a slow fire with his guns until the situation was developed, then launching an attack which broke the first of the three lines the bluecoats managed to form between then and sundown. Cleburne himself was not on hand for the breaking of the others, nor for the rounding up of the fugitives in the twilight. While speaking to a wounded colonel, he was struck in the left cheek by a bullet that knocked his teeth out on that side before emerging from his mouth — "which," as one who was with him said, "fortunately happened to be open" — and forced his retirement, speechless, from the field. But the continued application of his tactics against the subsequent two rallies produced the same results, together with the capture of about 4000 prisoners, the entire Union wagon train, substantial army stores, 10,000 small arms, and 9 guns.

"Tomorrow being Sunday," Smith announced in his congratulatory order, "the general desires that the troops shall assemble and, under their several chaplains, shall return thanks to Almighty God, to whose mercy and goodness these victories are due." The day was also spent attending the wounded, burying the dead, and paroling the host of prisoners, after which preparations were made for continuing the advance. September 1, unopposed — three fourths of Nelson's army had been shot or captured; the rest were fugitives, hiding out in the woods and cornfields — the gray marchers crossed the Kentucky River and made camp on the northern bank. Next day they entered Lexington, where large numbers of townspeople turned out to greet them with smiles and cheers, including a delegation of ladies who presented Smith with a flag they had embroidered in his honor. September 3 his troopers rode into Frankfort, to find the governor and the legislature fled to Louisville. Having no suitable Confederate ensign with them, the graybacks raised the colors of the 1st Louisiana Cavalry over the state house. Another southern capital had returned to what the victors called its true allegiance.

Lexington had been the goal announced by Smith when he left Knoxville, and there he made his headquarters throughout September, in virtual control of Central Kentucky, while waiting for Bragg to join or send for him. Back at Cumberland Gap, after holding out through a month of siege, the Federals under George Morgan blew up their magazine, set fire to a warehouse containing 6000 small arms, and made their escape across the barrens, via Manchester and Booneville, to Greenup on the Ohio River, eluding pursuers all two hundred miles of the way. This was a disappointment to Smith, who had counted on capturing his West Point classmate, but at least it permitted his other division to join him at Lexington. Meanwhile he had not been idle. In addition to occupying Frankfort, Cynthiana, Georgetown, and Paris, he sent sizeable detachments of cavalry and infantry to demonstrate against Louisville and Cincinnati, both of which were thrown into turmoil. Summoned to command the defense of the latter city, Lew Wallace decreed martial law, ordered all business activities suspended, and impressed citizens to resume work on the fortifications begun the year before at Covington and Newport, on the opposite bank of the Ohio. "To arms!" the Cincinnati *Gazette* urged its readers. "The time for playing war has passed. The enemy is now approaching our doors!"

Smith was not so much concerned with the reaction of the people of Ohio, however, as he was with the reaction of the people of Kentucky. So far, this had been most gratifying, he informed the Adjutant General on September 6. "It would be impossible for me to exaggerate the enthusiasm of the people here on the entry of our troops. They evidently regarded us as deliverers from oppression and have continued in every way to prove to us that the heart of Kentucky is with the South in this struggle.... If Bragg occupies Buell we can have nothing to oppose us but raw levies, and by the blessing of God will always dispose of them as we did on the memorable August 30."

His purpose in seeming to threaten Cincinnati, he added, was "in order to give the people of Kentucky time to organize," and by way of encouragement he broadcast assurances to the citizens in the form of proclamations:

> Let no one make you believe we come as invaders, to coerce your will or to exercise control over your soil. Far from it.... We come to test the truth of what we believe to be a foul aspersion, that Kentuckians willingly join the attempt to subjugate us and to deprive us of our prosperity, our liberty, and our dearest rights.... Are we deceived? Can you treat us as enemies? Our hearts answer, "No!"

★ ★ ★

Bragg too was in Kentucky by now, and he too was issuing proclamations assuring the people that he had come, not to bind them, but to assist them in striking off their chains:

> Kentuckians, I have entered your State with the Confederate Army of the West, and offer you an opportunity to free yourselves from the tyranny of a despotic ruler. We come not as conquerors or as despoilers, but to restore to you the liberties of which you have been deprived by a cruel and relentless foe. We come to guarantee to all the sanctity of their homes and altars, to punish with a rod of iron the despoilers of your peace, and to avenge the cowardly insults to your women.... Will you remain indifferent to our call, or will you rather vindicate the fair fame of your once free and envied State? We believe that you will, and that the memory of your gallant dead who fell at Shiloh, their faces turned homeward, will rouse you to a manly effort for yourselves and posterity.
> Kentuckians, we have come with joyous hopes. Let us not depart in sorrow, as we shall if we find you wedded in your choice to your present lot. If you prefer Federal rule, show it by your frowns and we shall return whence we came. If you choose rather to come within the folds of our brotherhood, then cheer us with the smiles of your women and lend your willing hands to secure you in your heritage of liberty.

Dated September 14 at Glasgow, which he had reached the day before, the proclamation was issued during a two-day rest halt, the first he had made in the course of the more than one hundred and fifty miles his army had covered since leaving Chattanooga, seventeen days ago. Despite their exertions, the men were in excellent spirits. Marching over Walden's Ridge, then up the lovely Sequatchie Valley to Pikeville, where they swung east across the Cumberland Plateau — thus passing around Buell's left wing at Decherd — they enjoyed the scenery, the bracing air of the uplands, and the friendly offerings of buttermilk and fried chicken by country people all along the way.

Bragg was happy, too, and with cause. Strategically, as events disclosed, the movement had been as sound as it was rapid. He had predicted that Buell would "recede to Nashville before giving us battle," and now his scouts reported that this was just what Buell was doing, as fast as he could: which meant that North Alabama and Chattanooga, along with much of Middle Tennessee, had already been relieved without the firing of a shot. To cap the climax, when he drew near Sparta on September 5, halfway across Tennessee, he received a dispatch from Kirby Smith reporting the destruction of Nelson's army and urging him "to move into Kentucky and, effecting a junction with my command and holding Buell's communications, to give battle to him with superior forces and with certainty of success." Then and there, by way of celebration, Bragg issued a congratulatory address to his soldiers, informing them of Smith's lopsided victory and Buell's hasty withdrawal: "Comrades, our campaign opens most auspiciously and promises complete success.... The enemy is in full retreat, with consternation and demoralization devastating his ranks. To secure the full fruits of this condition we must press on vigorously and unceasingly."

Press on they did, and vigorously, for Bragg had now decided on his goal. Finally abandoning any intention to launch an assault on Nashville, where Buell was concentrating his forces and improving the fortifications, he marched hard for Glasgow. Eight days later he arrived and, calling a halt, issued the proclamation announcing his "joyous hopes" that the people of Kentucky would assist him in "punish[ing] with a rod of iron the despoilers of your peace." He was exactly where he wanted to be: squarely between Buell and Kirby Smith, whom he could summon to join him. Or if he chose, he could move on to the Bluegrass and the Ohio, combining there with Smith to capture Louisville or Cincinnati, both of which were nearer to him now than they were to Buell.

On the day Bragg issued his proclamation at Glasgow, where his four divisions were taking a hard-earned rest, Buell entered Bowling Green, thirty-five miles to the west. He had five divisions with him and three more back at Nashville under Thomas, who was serving as his second-in-command through the present crisis. His total strength, including a division just arrived from Grant, was 56,000: exactly twice Bragg's, though Buell did not know this, having lately estimated it at 60,000, not including the troops with Kirby Smith.

The past two weeks had been for him in the nature of a nightmare. So much had happened so fast, and nearly all of it unpleasant. Having transferred his headquarters in rapid succession from Stevenson to Decherd to McMinnville, he shifted them once again to Murfreesboro on the day Bragg set out north from Chattanooga. He did this, he told Thomas, by way of preparation for the offensive: "Once concentrated, we may move against the enemy wherever he puts himself if we are strong enough." This sentence, as a later observer remarked, had "an escape clause at both ends," and Buell was not long in giving more weight to them than to the words that lay between. Two days later, while Bragg was passing around his left and Smith was wrecking Nelson up at Richmond, he notified Andrew Johnson, the military governor of Tennessee: "These facts make it plain that I should fall back on Nashville, and I am preparing to do so. I have resisted the reasons which lead to the necessity until it would be criminal to delay any longer."

He arrived September 2 to find the capitol barricaded with cotton

Two Advances; Two Retreats   [657]

bales and bristling with cannon. Inside, Governor Johnson defied the
rebels, declaring heatedly that he would defend the citadel with his
heart's blood and never be taken alive. Encouraged by this, as well as
by the arrival of 10,000 men from Grant, Buell wired Halleck: "I
believe Nashville can be held and Kentucky rescued. What I have will
be sufficient here with the defenses that are being prepared, and I
propose to move with the remainder of the army against the enemy
in Kentucky." Two nights ago, swamped by troubles resulting from
Nelson's and Pope's simultaneous defeats, Old Brains had thrown up
his hands and complained to McClellan that he was "utterly tired out."
By now, though, he had recovered enough to send a one-sentence reply
to Buell's wire. "Go where you please," he told him, "provided you will
find the enemy and fight him."

Buell went nowhere until September 7. Warned then that Bragg was headed for Bowling Green, where a large supply of provisions had been stored for the campaign which had already gone up in smoke, he set out for that point with five of his eight divisions, leaving Thomas to hold Nashville with the others in case the gray invaders doubled back. A week later he got there, only to find that Bragg was at Glasgow, which not only placed him nearer Louisville than the Federals were, but also enabled him to call on Smith for reinforcements. In danger of being attacked (as he thought) by superior numbers, Buell wired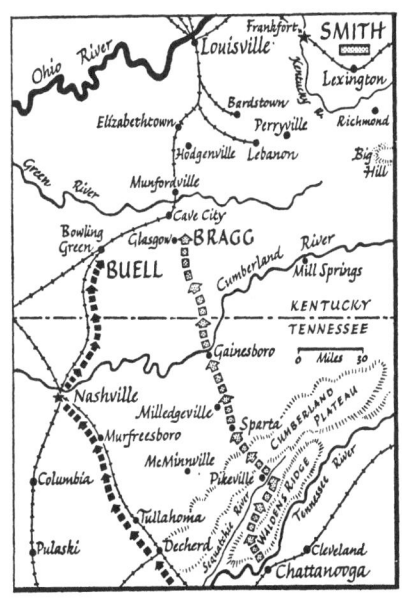
for Thomas to hurry north with two divisions, explaining the grounds
on which he thus was willing to risk the Tennessee capital: "If Bragg's
army is defeated Nashville is safe; if not, it is lost." Another wire went
to Halleck. He was "not insensible to the difficulty and embarrassment
of the position," Buell declared, and he further assured the harassed
general in chief: "I arrived here today ... and shall commence to move
against Bragg's force on the 16th."

The day before the one on which Buell had said he would
"commence to move," Bragg himself was in motion with his whole

army. He moved, however, not toward Buell's main body at Bowling Green, but toward the Green River, twenty miles north, where a 4000-man Federal detachment held a fort on the south bank, opposite Munfordville, guarding the L & N railroad crossing at that point. His original intention had been to hold his ground at Glasgow, receiving attack if Buell turned east, or to lunge forward and strike his flank if he pushed on toward Louisville. What changed his mind was what he later called an "unauthorized and injudicious" action, precipitated two days before by Brigadier General James R. Chalmers.

Chalmers, whose infantry brigade was on outpost and reconnaissance duty at Cave City, ten miles northwest of Glasgow, had made contact on the 13th with one of Kirby Smith's far-ranging cavalry regiments, the colonel of which had sent him word of what he called a rare opportunity. His troopers had cut the railroad north of Munfordville, isolating the south-bank garrison, but his request for its capitulation had been sharply refused. Would Chalmers move up and add the weight of his brigade to the demand? Chalmers would indeed. A youthful and ardent Mississippian, one of the authentic Shiloh heroes, he put his troops in motion at once, without bothering to notify Bragg at Glasgow. Arriving at daylight next morning, he launched an attack on the fort, then drew back and sent a note complimenting the bluecoats on their "gallant defense," pointing out the hopelessness of their position, with Bragg's whole army "a short distance in my rear," and demanding an unconditional surrender "to avoid further bloodshed." The reply, signed by Colonel J. T. Wilder, 17th Indiana Volunteers, was brief and to the point: "Thank you for your compliments. If you wish to avoid further bloodshed keep out of the range of my guns."

Concluding from this that the Hoosier colonel had better be left alone, Chalmers gathered up his dead and wounded — which amounted to exactly four times as many as Wilder's: 288, as compared to 72 — and withdrew. Back at Cave City next morning he reported the affair to Bragg, expressing "fear that I may have incurred censure at headquarters by my action in this matter." He was right. Bragg was furious that this first show of combat should be a blot on the record of a campaign which had already yielded such rich fruits without the firing of a shot. Accordingly, being as he said "unwilling to allow the impression of a disaster to rest on the minds of my men," he prepared at once to erase it. All four divisions started that same day for Munfordville.

He was taking no chances. Hardee's wing moved through Cave City that evening, making the direct approach, while Polk's crossed the river a few miles above and circled around to the rear, occupying positions on the bluffs overlooking the fort on the opposite bank. By mid-afternoon, September 16, the investment was complete. After firing a few rounds to establish ranges, Bragg sent a note informing the Federal commander that he was surrounded by an overwhelming force and repeating the two-day-old demand for an unconditional surrender to avoid "the terrible consequences of an assault." When Wilder asked for proof that such a host was really at hand, Bragg replied: "The only evidence I can give you of my ability to make good my assertion of the presence of a sufficient force to compel your surrender, beyond the statement that it now exceeds 20,000, will be the use of it.... You are allowed one hour in which to make known your decision."

Wilder was in something of a quandary. A former Indiana industrialist, he had been thirteen months in service, but nothing so far in his experience had taught him how much credence to give the claims that accompanied such demands for capitulation. Finally he arrived at an unorthodox solution. Knowing that Simon Buckner commanded a division on this side of the river, and knowing moreover that Buckner was a man of honor, he went to him under a flag of truce and asked his advice — as one gentleman to another. If resistance was hopeless, he said, he did not want to sacrifice his men; but neither did he want to be stampeded into surrendering because of his lack of experience in such matters. What should he do? Buckner, taken aback, declined to advise him. Wars were not fought that way, he said. He offered, however, to conduct him on a tour of the position and let him see for himself the odds against him. The colonel took him up on that, despite the fact that it was now past midnight and the truce had expired two hours ago. After counting 46 guns in position on the south bank alone, Wilder was convinced. "I believe I'll surrender," he said sadly.

It was arranged without further delay; Bragg subsequently listed the capture of 4267 prisoners, 10 guns, 5000 rifles, "and a proportionate quantity of ammunition, horses, mules, and military stores." While the bluecoats were being paroled — officers retaining their side arms and the men marching out, as Wilder proudly reported, "with all the honors of war, drums beating and colors flying" — Bragg wired the Adjutant General: "My junction with Kirby Smith is complete. Buell still at Bowling Green."

He had cause for elation. Already astride the Green River, halfway across Kentucky, the western prong of his two-pronged offensive had scored a victory as rich in spoils as the one the eastern prong had scored against Nelson, eighteen days ago at Richmond. In an order issued at Munfordville that same morning, he congratulated his soldiers "on the crowning success of their extraordinary campaign which this day has witnessed," and he told the Adjutant General: "My admiration of and love for my army cannot be expressed. To its patient toil and admirable discipline am I indebted for all the success which has attended this perilous undertaking."

This last sounded more like McClellan than it did like Bragg, and less like Jackson than it did like either: the Jackson of the Valley, that is, whom Bragg had announced as his prototype. And now that he had begun to sound like Little Mac, the terrible-tempered Bragg began to imitate his manner. After telling his men, "A powerful foe is assembling in our front and we must prepare to strike him a sudden and decisive blow," when Buell moved forward to Cave City, still waiting for Thomas to join him, Bragg left Polk's wing north of the Green and maneuvered Buckner's division across Buell's front, attempting to provoke him into attacking the south-bank intrenchments much as Chalmers had done, to his sorrow, five days back. But when Buell refused to be provoked, Bragg pulled Hardee's troops across the river and resumed his northward march, leaving Buell in his rear.

He had his reasons, and gave them later in his report: "With my effective force present, reduced . . . to half that of the enemy, I could not prudently afford to attack him there in his selected position. Should I pursue him farther toward Bowling Green he might fall back to that place and behind his fortifications. Reduced at the end of four days to three days' rations, and in a hostile country, utterly destitute of supplies, a serious engagement brought on anywhere in that direction could not fail (whatever its results) to materially cripple me. The loss of a battle would be eminently disastrous. . . . We were therefore compelled to give up the object and seek for subsistence."

So he said. But it seemed to others in his army that there was more to it than this; that the trouble, in fact, was personal; that it lay not within the situation which involved a shortage of rations and a surplus of bluecoats, but somewhere down deep inside Bragg himself. For all the audacity of his conception, for all his boldness through the preliminaries, once the critical instant was at hand he simply could not screw his nerves up to the sticking point. It was strange, this sudden abandonment of Stonewall as his model. It was as if a lesser poet should set out to imitate Shakespeare or Milton. With luck and skill, he might ape the manner, the superficial arrangement of words and even sentences; but the Shakespearian or Miltonic essence would be missing. And so it was with Bragg. He lacked the essence. Earlier he had said that the enemy was to be broken up and beaten in detail, Jackson-style, "by rapid movements and vigorous blows." Now this precept was revised. As he left Munfordville he told a colonel on his staff: "This campaign must be won by marching, not fighting."

When Thomas came up on the 20th, Buell pushed forward and found the rebels gone. Convinced that they were headed for Louisville, he followed at a respectful distance, fearing an ambush but hoping to strike their rear while they were engaged with the troops William Nelson was assembling for the defense of the city. To his surprise, how-

Two Advances; Two Retreats

ever, less than twenty miles beyond the river Bragg swung east through Hodgenville, over Muldraugh's Hill and across the Rolling Fork to Bardstown, leaving his opponent a clear path to Louisville. Gratefully Buell took it.

He was not the only one who was grateful. Nelson, his flesh wounds healing rapidly since the removal of the bullet from his thigh, had been preparing feverishly, and with a good deal of apprehension based on previous experience, to resist the assault he expected Bragg to launch at his second collection of recruits. When he learned that the gray column had turned off through Lincoln's birthplace he drew his first easy breath since the early-morning knocking at his bedroom door, almost four weeks ago, first warned him that Kirby Smith's invaders had come over Big Hill and were nearing Richmond. The arrival, September 24, of Buell's advance division — 12,000 veterans and half a dozen batteries of artillery — produced a surge of confidence within his shaggy breast. He wired department headquarters, Cincinnati: "Louisville is now safe. We can destroy Bragg with whatever force he may bring against us. God and liberty."

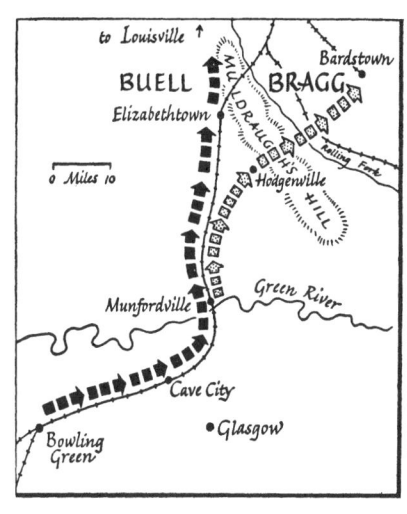

✗ 2 ✗

As Pope's frazzled army faded eastward up the pike toward Washington, and as Lee's — no less frazzled, but considerably lighter-hearted — poked among the wreckage in search of hardtack, the problem for them both was: What next? For the former, the battered and misused conglomeration of troops now under McClellan, who had ridden out to meet them, the question was answered by necessity. They would defend their capital. But for the victors, confronted as usual with a variety of choices, the problem was more complex. Lee's solution, reached before his men's clothes were dry from the rain-lashed skirmish at Chantilly, resulted — two weeks later, and by coincidence on the same date as Wilder's surrender to Bragg at Munfordville — in the bloodiest single day of the whole war.

The solution, arrived at by a narrowing of choices, was invasion.

He could not attack the Washington defenses, manned as they were by McClellan's army, already superior in numbers to his own and about to be strengthened, as he heard, by 60,000 replacements newly arrived in response to Lincoln's July call for "300,000 more." Nor could he keep his hungry soldiers in position where they were. The northern counties had been stripped of grain as if by locusts, and his wagon train was inadequate to import enough to feed the horses, let alone the troops. A third alternative would be to fall back into the Valley or south of the Rappahannock. But this not only would be to give up much that had been gained; it would permit a renewal of pressure on the Virginia Central — and eventually on Richmond. By elimination, then, the march would be northward, across the Potomac.

Not that there were no practical arguments against taking such a step. After much strenuous marching on meager rations, the men were bone-weary and Lee knew it. What was more, he wrote Davis on September 3, "The army is not properly equipped for an invasion of an enemy's territory. It lacks much of the material of war, is feeble in transportation, the animals being much reduced, and the men are poorly provided with clothes, and in thousands of instances are destitute of shoes.... What occasions me the most concern is the fear of getting out of ammunition." Nevertheless, in Lee's mind the advantages far outweighed the drawbacks. Two successful campaigns within two months, on Virginia soil and against superior numbers, had won for the Confederacy the admiration of the world. A third, launched beyond the Potomac in conjunction with Bragg's two-pronged advance beyond the Cumberland, might win for her the foreign recognition which Davis had known from the start was the one best assurance that this second Revolution, like the first, would be successful. Besides, Maryland was a sister state, not enemy territory. Thousands of her sons were in the Virginia army, and it was believed that thousands more would join the colors once they were planted on her soil. In any event, invasion would draw off the northern armies and permit the Old Dominion farmers, now that the harvest was at hand, to gather their crops unmolested. The one thing Lee could not do was nothing; or as he put it, "We cannot afford to be idle, and though weaker than our opponents in men and military equipments, must endeavor to harass them if we cannot destroy them." Next day, having convinced himself — and hoping, by the usual kid-gloves treatment, to have convinced the President — he wired Davis that he was "fully persuaded of the benefit that will result from an expedition into Maryland, and I shall proceed to make the movement at once, unless you should signify your disapprobation."

Without waiting for a reply — indeed, without allowing time for one — he put the army in motion that same day for White's Ferry, twenty miles south of Frederick, the immediate objective. Approaching the ford on September 6 and 7, the men removed their shoes, those who had them, rolled up their trouser legs, and splashed across the shallows into Maryland. One cavalryman considered it "a magnificent sight as the long column... stretched across this beautiful Potomac. The evening sun slanted upon its clear placid waters and burnished them with gold, while the arms of the soldiers glittered and blazed in its radiance." There were for him, in the course of the war, "few moments... of excitement more intense, or exhilaration more delightful, than when we ascended the opposite bank to the familiar but now strangely thrilling music of *Maryland, My Maryland*."

Not everyone was so impressed, however, with the beauty of the occasion. A boy who stood on that opposite bank and watched the vermin-infested scarecrows come thronging past him, hairy and sun-baked, with nothing bright about them but their weapons and their teeth, was impressed by them in much the same way as the Kentucky civilian, this same week, had been impressed by their western counterparts. They made him think of wolves. "They were the dirtiest men I ever saw," he afterwards recalled, "a most ragged, lean, and hungry set of wolves." Accustomed to the Federals he had seen marching in compact formations and neat blue uniforms, he added: "Yet there was a dash about them that the northern men lacked. They rode like circus riders. Many of them were from the far South and spoke a dialect I could scarcely understand. They were profane beyond belief and talked incessantly."

Their individuality, which produced the cackling laughter, the endless chatter, and the circus-rider gyrations, was part of what made them "terrible in battle," as the phrase went. But in the present instance it also produced hampering effects: one being that Lee had considerably fewer men in Maryland than he had counted on when he made his decision to move north. Hampton's cavalry brigade, the reserve artillery, and three divisions of infantry under D. H. Hill, Major General Lafayette McLaws, and Brigadier General John G. Walker — 20,000 troops in all — had been forwarded from Richmond and had joined the army on its march to the Potomac. After the deduction of his Manassas casualties, this should have given Lee a total strength of 66,000. The truth was, he had barely more than 50,000 men in Maryland; which meant that close to 15,000 were absent without leave. Some few held back because of conscientious objections to invasion, but most were stragglers, laggards broken down in body or skulkers broken down in spirit. They would be missed along the thin gray line of battle, invalids and cowards alike, though their defection gave the survivors an added sense of pride and resolution. "None but heroes are left," one wrote home.

Hard-core veterans though they were, they were subject to various ills. Diarrhea was one, the result of subsisting on green corn; "the Confederate disease," it was coming to be called, and the sufferers, trotting white-faced to catch up with the column, joked ruefully about it, offering to bet that they "could hit a dime at seven yards." Another was sore feet; a fourth of the army limped shoeless on the stony Maryland roads. In addition to these ailments, mostly but by no means entirely confined to the ranks, a series of accidents had crippled the army's three ranking generals, beginning with Lee himself. Clad in rubber overalls and a poncho, he had been standing beside his horse on the rainy last day of August when a sudden cry, "Yankee cavalry!" startled the animal. Lee reached for the bridle, tripped in his clumsy clothes, and caught himself on his hands as he fell forward, with the result that a small bone was broken in one and the other was badly sprained. Both were put in splints, and Lee, unable to handle a mount, entered Maryland riding in an ambulance. Longstreet too was somewhat incapacitated by a raw blister on his heel; he crossed the river wearing a carpet slipper on his injured foot. Marylanders thus were robbed of the chance to see these two at their robust and energetic best. The third high-ranking casualty was Jackson. Ox-eyed Little Sorrel having been missing for two weeks, the gift of a sinewy gray mare from a group of Confederate sympathizers was welcome on the day he crossed the Potomac. Next morning, however, when he mounted and gave her the reins she did not move. He touched her with his spur: whereupon she reared, lost her balance, and toppled backward. Stunned, Jackson lay in the dust for half an hour, fussed over by surgeons who feared for a spinal injury, then was transferred, like Lee, to an ambulance.

These were partial incapacitations. Two others involving men of rank were unfortunately total, at least for the time being. The charges against Bob Toombs had been dropped in time for him to share in the final hour of victory at Manassas, but no sooner was the battle won than his place in arrest was taken by a general whose services the army could less afford to lose. When Shanks Evans laid claim to some ambulances Hood's Texans had captured, Hood, although outranked, refused to give them up. Evans referred the matter to the wing commander, who ruled in his favor, and when Hood still declined to yield, Longstreet ordered him back to Culpeper to await trial for insubordination. Lee intervened to the extent of allowing Hood to remain with his division, though not to exercise command.

By then the trouble between A. P. Hill and Jackson had come to a head, with the result that another of the army's hardest fighters was in arrest. On the march to the Potomac, Little Powell's division straggled badly. As far as Stonewall could see, Hill was doing little to correct this. What was more, he broke regulations by not calling rest-halts at the specified times. Finally Jackson himself halted one brigade: whereupon the red-bearded general came storming back down the column, asking by whose orders the troops were being delayed. The brigadier indicated Stonewall, who sat his horse beside the road. Hill unbuckled his sword and held it out to Jackson. "If you are going to give the orders, you have no need of me," he declared, trembling with rage. Stonewall did not take it. "Consider yourself under arrest for neglect of duty," he said coldly. "You're not fit to be a general," Hill snapped, and turned away.

With his army thus short of equipment and presenting its worst appearance, himself and his two chief lieutenants distracted by injuries, and two of his best division commanders in arrest, Lee busied himself and his staff with the composition, in accordance with instructions received from Davis, of a proclamation addressed "To the People of Maryland":

> The people of the Confederate States... have seen with profound indignation their sister State deprived of every right and reduced to the condition of a conquered province.... [We] have long wished to aid you in throwing off this foreign yoke, to enable you again to enjoy the inalienable rights of freemen.... We know no enemies among you, and will protect all, of every opinion. It is for you to decide your destiny freely and without constraint... and while the Southern people will rejoice to welcome you to your natural position among them, they will only welcome you when you come of your own free will.

Having thus complied with the President's recommendations, he made some of his own concerning another matter. The time had come, it seemed to him, in view of the present military situation, for the Confederacy to make a peace proposal to the North, based of course on permanent separation. "Such a proposition, coming from us at this time, could in no way be regarded as suing for peace," he wrote Davis; "but, being made when it is in our power to inflict injury upon our adversary, would show conclusively to the world that our sole object is the establishment of our independence and the attainment of an honorable peace. The rejection of this offer would prove to the country that the responsibility of the continuance of the war does not rest upon us, but that the party in power in the United States elect to prosecute it for reasons of their own." This he thought might have an effect upon the pending congressional elections in the North, enabling the voters "to determine... whether they will support those who favor a prolongation of the war, or those who wish to bring it to a termination, which can but be productive of good to both parties without affecting the honor of either."

This was perhaps more opportune than he suspected, especially with regard to the effect it might have on foreign opinion, if Davis would act on the advice and Lee could give him time in which to do so. Napoleon III had been friendly all along; but now, stimulated by the offer of one hundred thousand bales of badly needed cotton, as well as by concern for the success of certain machinations already in progress south of the Texas border, he was downright eager. Across the English Channel, meanwhile, the news of Pope's defeat and Lee's entry into Maryland caused Lord Palmerston to write Earl Russell: "The Federals ... got a very complete smashing.... Even Washington or Baltimore may fall into the hands of the Confederates. If this should happen, would it not be time for us to consider whether in such a state of things England and France might not address the contending parties and recommend an arrangement on the basis of separation?" The Foreign Minister replied: "I agree with you that the time is come for offering mediation to the United States Government, with a view to recognition of the independence of the Confederates. I agree further that, in case of failure, we ought ourselves to recognize the Southern States as an independent State." Presently the Prime Minister wrote again: "It is evident that a great conflict is taking place to the northwest of Washington, and its issue may have a great effect on the state of affairs. If the Federals sustain a grave defeat, they may be at once ready for mediation, and the iron should be struck while it is hot. If, on the other hand, they should have the best of it, we may wait a while and see what may follow."

What followed was in a large part up to Lee and his tatterdemalion army, and having given his attention to the question of peace, he turned his mind once more to thoughts of war — in particular to the problem of securing his lines of communication and supply. Once he moved westward, beyond the Catoctins and the trans-Potomac prolongation of the Blue Ridge, these would extend southward up the Shenandoah Valley, through Martinsburg and Winchester. He had expected the Federals to evacuate those places when they found him in their rear, and in the latter case they had done so; but the former still was occupied in strength, as was Harpers Ferry, sixteen miles away. Lee felt obliged to detach part of his army to reduce them before continuing his advance. When he broached this to Longstreet, however, Old Pete argued forcefully against such a division of strength in the enemy's own back yard. Jackson, on the other hand — recovered by now from his fall the day before — was delighted at the prospect, remarking somewhat wistfully that of late he had been entirely too neglectful of his friends in the Valley. Lee thought so, too. Dividing the army had worked wonders against Pope; now he would attempt it against McClellan, whose return to command had been announced in the northern papers. Despite Longstreet's objections, Lee began to work out a plan, not only for removing the threat to his supply line, but also for capturing the bluecoats who made it.

The result was Special Orders 191, which called for another of those ambitious simultaneous convergences by widely separated columns upon an assigned objective; in short, a maneuver not unlike the one that had failed, a year ago this week, against Cheat Mountain. In this case, however, since the capture of the Federals could be effected only by cutting off all their avenues of escape, the complication was unavoidable. The basis for it was geography. Low-lying Harpers Ferry, more trap than fortress, was dominated by heights that frowned down from three directions: Bolivar Heights to the west, Maryland Heights across the Potomac, and Loudoun Heights across the Shenandoah. With this in mind, Lee designed a convergence that would occupy all three. Jackson, who had been in command of the Ferry the year before and therefore knew it well, would be in general charge of the operation in its final stage. He would move with his three divisions through Boonsboro to the vicinity of Williamsport, where he would cross the Potomac and descend on Martinsburg, capturing the garrison there or driving it eastward to Harpers Ferry, where he would occupy Bolivar Heights. McLaws, with his own and Anderson's divisions, would move southwest and take position on Maryland Heights. Walker would move south with his two-brigade division, cross the Potomac below Point of Rocks, and occupy Loudoun Heights. The result, with all those guns bearing down on the compact mass of bluecoats, should be something like shooting fish in a rain barrel. Longstreet meanwhile would move westward, beyond the mountains, and occupy Boonsboro with his other four divisions, supported by D. H. Hill. The order was dated September 9; all movements would begin the following morning, with the convergence scheduled for the 12th.

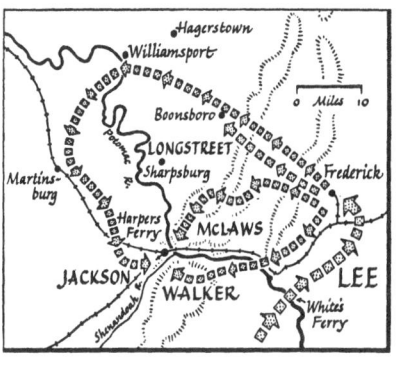

After the capitulation, which was expected to be accomplished that same day, or the next day at the latest, Jackson, McLaws, and Walker would rejoin the main body at Boonsboro for a continuation of the campaign through Maryland and into Pennsylvania.

Distribution of the order, which was quite full and gave in detail the disposition of Lee's whole army for the next four days, was to the commanders of the various columns as well as to the commanders of those divisions whose normal assignments were affected. Longstreet took one look at it and, realizing the danger if it should fall into unfriendly hands, committed it to memory; after which he tore it up and chewed the pieces into pulp. Jackson, too, hugged it close. Observing, however, that Harvey Hill, who had been attached to his wing for the river crossing, was now assigned to Longstreet, he decided that the best way to let his brother-in-law know that he was aware of the transfer would be to send him a copy of the order. With his usual regard for secrecy, Stonewall himself made the transcript in his spidery handwriting and dispatched it under seal. Hill studied it, then put it carefully away. When the copy arrived from Lee's adjutant, one of Hill's staff officers decided to keep it for a souvenir, but meanwhile used it as a wrapper for three cigars which he carried in his pocket.

Lee knew nothing of this duplication, nor of the menial use to which an important army order was being put. He was doing all he could, however, to make certain that nothing went astray in the intended convergence, as unfortunately had happened every time such a maneuver had been attempted in the past. One precaution he took was to have a personal interview with each of the generals in charge: with Longstreet, who would guard the trains while the others were gone, and with Jackson, McLaws, and Walker, who would be on their own throughout the expedition. In the latter's case this was particularly apt; for Walker, a forty-year-old regular army Missourian, had just come up from the James with his small division — formerly a part of Holmes', in which he had commanded a brigade during the Seven Days — and was therefore unfamiliar with what had since become the army's operational procedure. Lee went over the plan with him, indicating details on the map with his crippled hands. When this was done, he spoke of what he intended to do once his forces were reunited north of the Potomac. If Walker, with his "Show Me" background, had been inclined to suspect that much of the recent praise for the Virginian's audacity was overdone, that doubt was ended now. The sweep and daring of the prospect Lee exposed, speaking quietly here in the fly-buzzed stillness of his tent, widened Walker's eyes and fairly took his breath away.

Sixty airline miles beyond Hagerstown lay Harrisburg, Pennsylvania, where the Pennsylvania Railroad crossed the Susquehanna River. "That is the objective point of the campaign," Lee explained. Destruction of the bridge there, supplementing the previous seizure of the B & O crossing at Harpers Ferry and the wrecking of the Monocacy aqueduct of the Chesapeake & Ohio Canal — this last would be done by Walker, in accordance with instructions already given him, on the way to Point of Rocks — would isolate the Federal East from the Federal West, preventing the arrival of reinforcements for McClellan except by the slow and circuitous Great Lakes route. "After that," Lee concluded, "I can turn my attention to Philadelphia, Baltimore, or Washington, as may seem best for our interests." The war would be over — won.

Observing Walker's astonishment, Lee said: "You doubtless regard it hazardous to leave McClellan practically on my line of communication, and to march into the heart of the enemy's country?" When the Missourian said he did indeed, Lee asked him: "Are you acquainted with General McClellan?" Walker replied that he had seen little of him since the Mexican War. "He is an able general," Lee said, "but a very cautious one. His enemies among his own people think him too much so. His army is in a very demoralized and chaotic condition, and will not be prepared for offensive operations (or he will not think it so) for three or four weeks. Before that time I hope to be on the Susquehanna."

★ ★ ★

This judgment contained several errors of degree as to the Federal potential, but in none of them was Lee more mistaken than in his estimate of the present condition of the Army of the Potomac, which in fact was less "chaotic" than his own, at least so far as its physical well-being was concerned. Nor was it "demoralized." McClellan was back, along with regular rations, a sense of direction, and a general sweeping up of croakers such as had followed the previous Bull Run fiasco which had brought him on the scene the year before. All this had been the source of much rejoicing, but there were others, no less heartening for being negative. Pope and McDowell, whom the men considered the authors of their woe, were gone — the former to pack his bags for the long ride to Minnesota, the latter to await the outcome of a formal hearing he had demanded in order to clear himself of all the charges brought by rumor — and so was Banks, a sort of junior-grade villain in their eyes, to assume command of the Washington defenses after McClellan marched the field force out the National Road to challenge the invaders up in Maryland.

That too was heartening. After four solid weeks of retreating, some from the malarial bottoms of the Peninsula, some from the blasted fields that bordered the dusty rivers of northern Virginia, and some from both — followed always by eyes that watched from roadside windows, hostile and mocking — not only were they moving forward, against the enemy, but they were doing it through a region that was friendly. "Fine marching weather; a land flowing with milk and honey; a general tone of Union sentiment among the people, who, being little cursed by slavery, had not lost their loyalty; scenery, not grand but picturesque," one young abolition-minded captain wrote, "all contributed to make the march delightful." A Maine veteran recorded that, "like the Israelites of old, we looked upon the land and it was good."

Best of all was Frederick, which they entered after the rebels had withdrawn beyond the Catoctins. "Hundreds of Union banners floated from the roofs and windows," one bluecoat recalled, "and in many a threshold stood the ladies and children of the family, offering food and water to the passing troops, or with tiny flags waving a welcome to their deliverers." Army rations went uneaten, "so sumptuous was the fare of cakes, pies, fruits, milk, dainty biscuit and loaves." A Wisconsin diarist apparently spoke for the whole army in conferring the accolade: "Of all the memories of the war, none are more pleasant than those of our sojourn in the goodly city of Frederick."

Presently it developed that there was more here for soldiers than an abundance of smiles and tasty food. For two of them, at any rate — three, in fact, if Private B. W. Mitchell and Sergeant J. M. Bloss, Company E, 27th Indiana, decided to share the third with a friend — there were cigars. Or so it seemed at the outset. Saturday morning, September 13, the Hoosier regiment was crossing an open field, a recent Confederate camp site near Frederick, when the men got orders to stack arms and take a break. Soon afterwards Mitchell and Bloss were lounging on the grass, taking it easy, when the former noticed a long thick envelope lying nearby. He picked it up and found the three cigars inside, wrapped in a sheet of official-looking paper. While Bloss was hunting for a match, Mitchell examined the document. "Headquarters, Army of Northern Virginia, Special Orders 191," it was headed. At the bottom was written, "By command of General R. E. Lee: R. H. Chilton, Assistant Adjutant-General." In between, eight paragraphs bristled with names and place-names: Jackson, Martinsburg, Harpers Ferry; Longstreet, Boonsboro; McLaws, Maryland Heights; Walker, Loudoun Heights. Mitchell showed it to Bloss, and together they took it to the company commander, who conducted them to regimental headquarters, where the colonel examined the handwritten sheet, along with the three cigars — as if they too might have some hidden significance — and left at once for division headquarters, taking all the evidence with him. Mitchell and Bloss returned to their company area and lay down again on the grass, perhaps by now regretting that they had not smoked the lost cigars before taking the rebel paper to the captain. As it turned out, they had sacrificed most of their rest-halt, too; for, according to Bloss, "In about three-quarters of an hour we noticed orderlies and staff officers flying in all directions."

McClellan's first considered reaction, after the leap his heart took at his first sight of the document which dispelled in a flash the fog of war and pinpointed the several components of Lee's scattered army, was that it must be spurious, a rebel trick. It was just too good to be true. But a staff officer who had known Chilton before the war identified the writing as unquestionably his. This meant that the order was valid beyond doubt: which in turn meant that McClellan's army, once it crossed the unoccupied Catoctins just ahead, would be closer to the two halves of Lee's army than those halves were to each other. What was more, one of those halves was itself divided into unequal thirds, the segments disposed on naked hilltops on the opposite banks of unfordable rivers. The thing to do, quite obviously, was to descend at once on Boonsboro, where the nearest half was concentrated, overwhelm it, and then turn on the other, destroying it segment by segment. The war would be over — won. At any rate that was how McClellan saw it. Standing there with the documentary thunderbolt in his hand, he said to one of his brigadiers: "Here is a paper with which if I cannot whip Bobby Lee I will be willing to go home."

Partly his elation was a manic reaction to the depression he had been feeling throughout most of the eleven days since Halleck's order, issued in confirmation of Lincoln's verbal instructions, gave him "command of the fortifications of Washington and of all the troops for [its] defense." This had not been supplemented or broadened since. What he did beyond its limitations he did on his own — including the march into Maryland to interpose his army between Lee's and the capital whose defense was his responsibility. Consequently, as he said later, he felt that he was functioning "with a halter around my neck.... If the Army of the Potomac had been defeated and I had survived I would, no doubt, have been tried for assuming authority without orders." What the Jacobins wanted, he knew, was his dismissal in disgrace, and he had long since given up the notion that the President would support him in every eventuality. In fact, knowing nothing of Lincoln's defiance of a majority of the cabinet for his sake, he no longer trusted the President to stand for long between him and the political clamor for his removal; and he was right. Back at the White House, after telling Hay, "McClellan is working like a beaver. He seems to be aroused to doing something after the snubbing he got last week," Lincoln added thoughtfully: "I am of the opinion that this public feeling against him will make it expedient to take important command from him ... but he is too useful just now to sacrifice."

All this while, moreover, Halleck had been giving distractive twitches to the telegraphic lines attached to the halter. Though Banks had three whole corps with which to man the capital fortifications — Heintzelman's, Sigel's, and Porter's, which, together with the regular garrison, gave him a total defensive force of 72,500 men — the general in chief swung first one way, then another, alternately tugging or nudging, urging caution or headlong haste. Four days ago he had wired: "It may be the enemy's object to draw off the mass of our forces, and then attempt to attack us from the Virginia side of the Potomac. Think of this." Two days later he was calmer: "I think the main force of the enemy is in your front. More troops can be spared from here." Today, however, his fears were back, full strength: "Until you know more certainly the enemy forces south of the Potomac you are wrong in thus uncovering the capital." McClellan, his natural caution thus enlarged and played on—he estimated Lee's army at 120,000 men, half again larger than his own — pushed gingerly northwestward up the National Road, which led from Washington to Frederick, forty miles, then on through Hagerstown and Wheeling, out to Ohio.

He averaged about six miles a day, despite the fact that he had reorganized his army into two-corps "wings" in order to march by parallel roads rather than in a single column, which would have left the tail near Washington while the head was approaching Frederick. The right wing, assigned to Burnside, included his own corps, still under Reno, and McDowell's, now under Hooker, who had already won the nickname "Fighting Joe." The center wing was Sumner's and included his own and Banks' old corps, now under the senior division commander, Brigadier General Alpheus Williams. The left wing, Franklin's, included his own corps and the one division so far arrived from Keyes', still down at Yorktown. Porter's corps, which was released to McClellan on the 12th, the day his advance units reached Frederick, was the reserve. Including the troops arrived from West Virginia and thirty-five new regiments distributed throughout the army since its retreat from Manassas, McClellan had seventeen veteran divisions, with an average of eight brigades in each of his seven corps; or 88,000 men in all. Yet he believed himself outnumbered, and he could not forget that the army he faced — that scarecrow multitude of lean, vociferous, hairy men who reminded even noncombatants of wolves — had two great recent victories to its credit, while his own had just emerged from the confusion and shame of one of the worst drubbings any American army had ever suffered. Nor could he dismiss from his mind the thought of what another defeat would mean, both to himself and to his country. Despised by the leaders of the party in power, mistrusted by Lincoln, badgered by Halleck, he advanced with something of the manner of a man walking on slippery ice through a darkness filled with wolves.

It was at Frederick, that "goodly city," that the gloom began to lift. "I can't describe to you for want of time the enthusiastic reception we met with yesterday in Frederick," he wrote his wife next morning. "I was nearly overwhelmed and pulled to pieces. I enclose with this a little flag that some enthusiastic lady thrust into or upon Dan's bridle. As to flowers — they came in crowds! In truth, I was seldom more affected.... Men, women, and children crowded around us, weeping, shouting, and praying." Then, near midday, his fears were abolished and his hopes were crowned. "Now I know what to do," he exclaimed when he read Special Orders 191, and one of the first things he did was share his joy with Lincoln in a wire sent at noon. In his elation he had the sound of a man who could not stop talking:

"I have the whole rebel force in front of me, but am confident, and no time shall be lost. I have a difficult task to perform, but with God's blessing will accomplish it. I think Lee has made a gross mistake, and that he will be severely punished for it. The army is in motion as rapidly as possible. I hope for a great success if the plans of the rebels remain unchanged. We have possession of Catoctin. I have all the plans of the rebels, and will catch them in their own trap if my men are equal to the emergency. I now feel that I can count on them as of old.... My respects to Mrs. Lincoln. Received most enthusiastically by the ladies. Will send you trophies."

He said he would lose no time, and five days ago he had told Halleck, "As soon as I find out where to strike, I will be after them without an hour's delay." But that did not mean he would be precipitate. In fact, now that the once-in-a-lifetime opportunity was at hand, its very magnitude made him determined not to muff it as a result of careless haste. Besides, despite its fullness in regard to the location of the Confederate detachments, the order gave him no information as to their various strengths. For all he knew, Longstreet and Hill had almost any conceivable number of men at Boonsboro, and the nature of the terrain between there and Frederick afforded them excellent positions from which to fight a delaying action while the other half of their army shook itself together and rejoined them — or, worse still, moved northward against his flank. He already had the Catoctins, as he said, but beyond them reared South Mountain, the lofty extension of the Blue Ridge. The National Road crossed this range at Turner's Gap, with Boonsboro just beyond, while six miles south lay Crampton's Gap, pierced by a road leading down to Harpers Ferry from Buckeystown, where Franklin's left wing was posted, six miles south of Frederick. These roads and gaps gave McClellan the answer to his problem. He would force Turner's Gap and descend on Boonsboro with his right and center wings, smashing Longstreet and Hill, while Franklin marched through Crampton's Gap and down to Maryland Heights, where he would strike the rear of Anderson and McLaws, capturing or brushing their men off the mountaintop and thereby opening the back door for the escape of the 12,000 Federals cooped up in Harpers Ferry. That way, too, the flank of the main body would be protected against an attack from the south, in case resistance delayed the forcing of the upper gap.

By late afternoon his plans were complete, and at 6.20 he sent Franklin his instructions. After explaining the situation at some length, he told him: "You will move at daybreak in the morning.... Having gained the pass"— Crampton's Gap —"your duty will be first to cut off, destroy, or capture McLaws' command and relieve [Harpers

Ferry]." After saying, "My general idea is to cut the enemy in two and beat him in detail," he concluded: "I ask of you, at this important moment, all your intellect and the utmost activity that a general can exercise." Intellect and activity were desirable; haste, apparently, was not. Just as he did not ask it of himself, so he did not ask it of Franklin. Lee's disjointed army lay before him, and the best way to pick up the pieces — as he saw it — was deliberately, without fumbling. The army would get a good night's sleep, then start out fresh and rested "at daybreak in the morning."

And so it was. At sunrise, Franklin's 18,000 — who should indeed have been rested; they had seen no combat since the Seven Days, and not a great deal of it then except for the division that reinforced Porter at Gaines Mill — pushed westward out of Buckeystown, heading for the lower gap, a dozen miles away. The other two wings, 70,000 men under Sumner and Burnside, with Porter bringing up the rear, moved down the western slope of the Catoctins, then across the seven-mile-wide valley toward Turner's Gap, a 400-foot notch in the 1300-foot wall of the mountain, where a fire fight was in progress. They moved in three heavy columns, along and on both sides of the National Road, and to one of the marchers, down in the valley, each of these columns resembled "a monstrous, crawling, blue-black snake, miles long, quilled with the silver slant of muskets at a 'shoulder,' its sluggish tail writhing slowly up over the distant eastern ridge, its bruised head weltering in the roar and smoke upon the crest above, where was being fought the battle of South Mountain."

McClellan was there beside the pike, astride Dan Webster, the central figure in the vast tableau being staged in this natural amphitheater, and the men cheered themselves hoarse at the sight of him. It seemed to one Massachusetts veteran that "an intermission had been declared in order that a reception might be tendered to the general in chief. A great crowd continually surrounded him, and the most extravagant demonstrations were indulged in. Hundreds even hugged the horse's legs and caressed his head and mane." This was perhaps the Young Napoleon's finest hour, aware as he was of all those thousands of pairs of worshipful eyes looking at him, watching for a gesture, and the New England soldier was pleased to note that McClellan did not fail to supply it: "While the troops were thus surging by, the general continually pointed with his finger to the gap in the mountain through which our path lay."

* * *

Harvey Hill was watching him, too, or anyhow he was looking in that direction. Seeing from the notch of Turner's Gap, which he had been ordered to hold with his five-brigade division, the serpentine approach of those four Union corps across the valley — twelve divisions

Two Advances; Two Retreats [675]

with a total of thirty-two infantry brigades, not including one corps which was still beyond the Catoctins — he said later that "the Hebrew poet whose idea of the awe-inspiring is expressed by the phrase, 'terrible as an army with banners,' [doubtless] had his view from the top of a mountain." He experienced mixed emotions at the sight. Although it was, as he observed, "a grand and glorious spectacle, and it was impossible to look at it without admiration," he added that he had never "experienced a feeling of greater *loneliness*. It seemed as though we were deserted by 'all the world and the rest of mankind.'"

Despite the odds, all too apparent to anyone here on the mountaintop, he had one real advantage in addition to the highly defensible nature of the terrain, and this was that he could see the Federals but they could not see him. Consequently, McClellan knew little of Hill's strength, or lack of it, and nothing at all of his loneliness. He thought that Longstreet, in accordance with Special Orders 191, was there too; whereas he was in fact at Hagerstown, a dozen miles away. Lee had sent him there from Boonsboro, three days ago, to head off a blue column erroneously reported to be advancing from Pennsylvania. After protesting against this further division of force — "General," he said in a bantering tone which only partly covered his real concern, "I wish we could stand still and let the damned Yankees come to us" — Longstreet marched his three divisions northward through the heat and dust. As a result, while McClellan back in Frederick was saying that he intended "to cut the enemy in two," Lee had already obliged him by cutting himself in five:

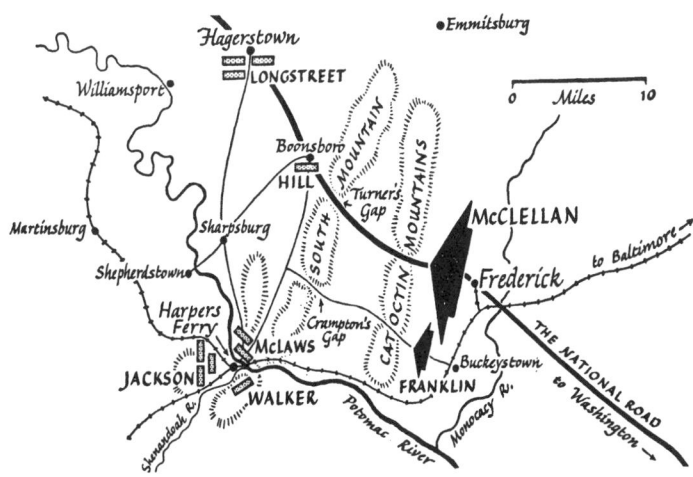

It was puzzling, this manifest lack of caution on McClellan's part, until late that night a message from Stuart explained the Young Napoleon's apparent change of character. A Maryland citizen of southern sympathies had happened to be at Federal headquarters when the lost order arrived, and he had ridden west at once, beyond the Union outposts, to give the news to Stuart, who passed it promptly on to Lee. So now Lee knew McClellan knew his precarious situation, and now that he knew he knew he moved to counteract the disadvantage as best he could. He sent for Longstreet and told him to march at daybreak in support of Hill, whose defense of Turner's Gap would keep the Federal main body from circling around South Mountain to relieve the Harpers Ferry garrison by descending on McLaws. Longstreet protested. The march would have his men so blown that they would be in no shape for fighting when they got there, he said, and he urged instead that he and Hill unite at Sharpsburg, twelve miles south of Hagerstown and half that far from Boonsboro; there, near the Potomac, they could organize a position for defense while awaiting the arrival of the rest of the army, or else cross in safety to Virginia in case the troops from Harpers Ferry could not join them in time to meet McClellan's attack. Lee overruled him, however, and Longstreet left to get some sleep. After sending word to McLaws of the danger to his rear and stressing "the necessity of expediting your operations as much as possible," Lee received a note from Longstreet repeating his argument against opposing the Federals at South Mountain. Later the Georgian explained that he had not thought the note would alter Lee's decision, but that the sending of it "relieved my mind and gave me some rest." What effect it had on Lee's rest he did not say. At any rate, he received no reply, and the march for Turner's Gap began at dawn.

As usual, once he got them into motion, Longstreet's veterans marched hard and fast, trailing a long dust cloud in the heat. Shortly after noon they came within earshot of the battle Hill was waging on the mountain. The pace quickened on the upgrade. About 3 o'clock, nearing the crest, Lee pulled off to the side of the road to watch the troops swing past him. Though his hands were still in splints, which made for awkward management of the reins, he was mounted; he could abide the ambulance no longer. Presently the Texas brigade approached. "Hood! Hood!" they yelled when they saw Lee by the roadside. For two weeks Hood had been in arrest, but now that they were going into battle they wanted him at their head. "Give us Hood!" they yelled. Lee raised his hat. "You shall have him, gentlemen," he said.

When the tail of the column came abreast he beckoned to the tall young man with the tawny beard and told him: "General, here I am just on the eve of entering into battle, and with one of my best officers under arrest. If you will merely say that you regret this occurrence"— referring to the clash with Evans over the captured ambulances — "I will release you and restore you to the command of your division." Hood shook his head regretfully and replied that he "could not consistently do so." Lee urged him again, but Hood again declined. "Well," Lee said at last, "I will suspend your arrest till the impending battle is decided." Beaming, Hood saluted and rode off. Presently, from up ahead, loud shouts and cheers told Lee that the Texans had their commander back again.

It was well that they did, for they had need of every man they could muster, whatever his rank. Hill had been fighting his Thermopylae since early morning, and events had shown that the gap was by no means as defensible as it had seemed at first glance. High ridges dominated the notch from both sides, and there were other passes north and south, so that he had had to spread his small force thin in order to meet attacks against them all. Coming up just as Hill was about to be overwhelmed — one brigade had broken badly when its commander Brigadier General Samuel Garland was killed, and others were reduced to fighting Indian-style, scattered among the rocks and trees — Longstreet counterattacked on the left and right and managed to stabilize the situation until darkness ended the battle. McClellan had had about 30,000 men engaged, Lee about half that many. Losses were approximately 1800 killed and wounded on each side, with an additional 800 Confederates taken captive. Among the dead was Jesse Reno, shot from his saddle just after sundown while making a horseback inspection of his corps. Lieutenant Colonel Rutherford B. Hayes of the 23d Ohio, fifteen years away from the Presidency, was wounded. Sergeant William McKinley, another future President from that regiment, was unhurt; the bullet that would get him was almost forty years away.

For Lee it was a night of anxiety. He had saved his trains and perhaps delayed a showdown by holding McClellan east of the mountain, but he had done this at a cost of nearly 3000 of his hard-core veterans. What was more, he knew he could do it no longer: Hill and Longstreet both reported that the gap could not be held past daylight, and defeat here on the mountain would mean annihilation. The only thing to do, Lee saw, was to adopt the plan Old Pete had favored so argumentatively the night before. Gone were his hopes for an invasion of Pennsylvania, the destruction of the Susquehanna bridge, the descent on Philadelphia, Baltimore, or the Union capital. Gone too was his hope of relieving Maryland of what he called her foreign yoke. Outnumbered worse than four to one, this half of the army — which in fact was barely more than a third: fourteen brigades out of the total forty — would have to retreat across the Potomac, and the other half would have to abandon its delayed convergence on Harpers Ferry. For Jackson and Walker this would not be difficult, but McLaws was already in the gravest danger. Soon after nightfall Lee sent him a message admitting defeat: "The day has gone against us and this army will go by Sharpsburg and cross the river. It is necessary for you to abandon your position tonight." McLaws of course would not be able to do this over the Ferry bridge, which was held by the Federal garrison; he would have to cross the Potomac farther upstream. Lee urged him, however, to do this somewhere short of Shepherdstown, which was just in rear of Sharpsburg. He wanted that ford clear for his own command, which would be retreating with McClellan's victorious army hard on its heels.

The evacuation began with Hill, followed by Longstreet; the cavalry brought up the rear. Obliged to abandon his dead and many of his wounded there on the mountain where they had fallen, Lee did not announce that he intended to withdraw across the Potomac, nor did he tell the others that he had instructed McLaws to abandon Maryland Heights. But news that arrived while the retreat was just getting under way confirmed the wisdom, indeed the necessity, of his decision. Crampton's Gap, six miles south, had been lost by the troopers sent to defend it: which not only meant that the Federals were pouring through, directly in rear of McLaws, but also that they were closer to Sharpsburg than Hill and Longstreet were. Unable to count any longer on McClellan's accustomed caution and hesitation, Lee saw that the march would have to be hard and fast, encumbered though he was with all his trains, if he was to get there first. Whereupon, with the situation thus at its worst and his army in graver danger of piecemeal annihilation than ever, Lee displayed for the first time a side to his nature that would become more evident down the years. He was not only no less audacious in retreat than in advance, but he was also considerably more pugnacious, like an old gray wolf wanting nothing more than half a chance to turn on whoever or whatever tried to crowd him as he fell back. And presently he got it.

It came in the form of a message from Jackson, to whom Lee had been sending couriers with information of the latest developments. "Through God's blessing," Stonewall had written at 8.15 p.m. from Bolivar Heights, "the advance, which commenced this evening, has been successful thus far, and I look to Him for complete success tomorrow.... Your dispatch respecting the movements of the enemy and the importance of concentration has been received." To Lee this represented a chance to retrieve the situation. By the shortest route, Harpers Ferry was only a dozen miles from Sharpsburg. If the place fell tomorrow, that would mean that a part at least of the besieging force could join him north of the Potomac tomorrow night; for when Jackson said that instructions had been "received," he meant that they would be obeyed. McLaws, too, might give the Federals the slip and march northwest without crossing the river. Accordingly, while Hill and Longstreet pushed on westward unpursued, Lee sent couriers galloping southward through the darkness. Unless the Army of the Potomac got into position for an all-out attack on Sharpsburg tomorrow — which seemed doubtful, despite McClellan's recent transformation; for one thing, there would be no more lost orders — the Army of Northern Virginia would not return to native ground without the shedding of a good deal more blood, Union and Confederate, than had been shed on South Mountain.

McLaws was a methodical man, not given to indulging what little imagination he had, and in this case — his present dangers being what they were, with McClellan's left wing coming down on his rear through Crampton's Gap — that was preferable. A forty-one-year-old Georgian, rather burly, with a bushy head of hair and a beard to match, he had been four months a major general, yet except for commanding two brigades under Magruder during the Seven Days had seen no previous service with Lee's army. Now he had ten brigades, his own four and Anderson's six, and he had been given the most critical assignment in the convergence on Harpers Ferry. Maryland Heights was the dominant one of the three. If the place was to be made untenable, it would be his guns that would do most to make it so.

His march from Frederick had been deliberate: so much so that he was a day late in approaching his objective, after which he spent another day brushing Federal detachments off the hilltop and a night cutting a road in order to manhandle his guns up the side of the mountain. At last, two days late, he got them into position on the morning of September 14 and opened wigwag communications with Jackson and Walker, across the way. Northward, up the long ridge of South Mountain, D. H. Hill's daylong battle rumbled and muttered; but McLaws, having posted three brigades in that direction to protect his rear, kept his mind on the business of getting his high-perched guns laid in time to open a plunging fire on the Ferry whenever Stonewall, who was a day late and still completing his dispositions, gave the signal. During the afternoon a much nearer racket broke out northward, but whatever qualms McLaws felt at the evidence that his rear guard was under attack were eased by Stuart, who had ridden down from Turner's Gap. The bluecoats in front of Crampton's Gap did not amount to more than a brigade, he said, and McLaws turned back to his guns. Presently, though, as the noise swelled louder, he rode in that direction to see for himself — and arrived to find that he had a first-class panic on his hands. Right, left, and center, his troops had given way and were fleeing in disorder. That was no blue brigade pouring through the abandoned gap, they told him. It was McClellan's entire left wing, a reinforced corps.

Fortunately they had given a good account of themselves before they broke: good enough, at any rate, to instill a measure of caution in their pursuers. McLaws had time to rally the fugitives and bring three more brigades down off the heights, forming a line across the valley less than two miles south of the lost gap. The day was far gone by then, the valley filled with shadows, and Franklin did not press the issue. McClellan had told him to "cut off, destroy, or capture McLaws' command," and apparently he figured that the seizure of Crampton's Gap had fulfilled the first of these alternatives. Also, now that he was in McLaws' rear, he had the worry of knowing that the Confederate main body was in *his*. Anyhow he decided not to be hasty; he had his men bed down for the night in line of battle.

Next morning, as he was about to proceed with his advance, the rebels just ahead began to cheer. One curious bluecoat sprang up on a stone wall and called across to them:

"What the hell are you fellows cheering for?"

"Because Harpers Ferry is gone up, God damn you!"

"I thought that was it," the Federal said, and he jumped back down again.

McLaws had stood fast and Jackson had kept the promise sent by courier to Lee twelve hours before. One hour of plunging fire from the surrounding heights smothered the batteries below. Soon afterwards the white flag went up. Except for two regiments of cavalry that had escaped under cover of darkness — across the Potomac, then northward up the same road old John Brown had come south on, three years ago next month — the whole garrison surrendered, including the men who had marched in from Martinsburg. "Our Heavenly Father blesses us exceedingly," Jackson wrote his wife, enumerating his gains: 12,520 prisoners, 13,000 small arms, 73 cannon, and a goodly haul of quartermaster stores.

According to a northern reporter's O-my-God lay-me-down reaction to his first sight of Stonewall and his men, they had great need of the latter — especially the general himself. "He was dressed in the coarsest kind of homespun, seedy and dirty at that; wore an old hat which any northern beggar would consider an insult to have offered him, and in general appearance was in no respect to be distinguished from the mongrel, bare-footed crew who follow his fortunes. I had heard much of the decayed appearance of the rebel soldiers, but such a looking crowd! Ireland in her worst straits could present no parallel, and yet they glory in their shame." The captive Federals (except perhaps the Irish among them) could scarcely argue with this, but they drew a different conclusion. "Boys, he isn't much for looks," one declared, inspecting Jackson, "but if we'd had him we wouldn't have been caught in this trap."

Pleased as he was, the Valley commander took little time for gloating. "Ah," he said to a jubilant companion as they stood looking at the booty, "this is all very well, Major, but we have yet much hard work before us." Though he was unaware of the lost order — "I thought I knew McClellan," he remarked, "but this movement of his puzzles me" — he was aware that Lee was being pressed, and he was eager to move to his support. Five of the six divisions started for Sharpsburg that afternoon and night. The sixth was A. P. Hill's. Like Hood, once combat was at hand, he had burned to pass from the rear to the front of his division on the march to Harpers Ferry, but like Hood he would not compromise his honor with an expression of regret. He simply requested, through a member of the staff, to be released from arrest for the duration of the fighting, after which he would report himself in arrest again. Jackson not only assented; he gave him a prominent part in the operation, and afterwards left him in charge of the place while he himself rode off in the wake of a message he had sent Lee that morning soon after he saw the white flag go up:

> Through God's blessing, Harpers Ferry and its garrison are to be surrendered. As Hill's troops have borne the heaviest part of the engagement, he will be left in command until the prisoners and public property shall be disposed of, unless you direct otherwise. The other forces can move off this evening so soon as they get their rations.

"That is indeed good news," Lee said when it reached him at Sharpsburg about noon. "Let it be announced to the troops."

★ ★ ★

McClellan's soldiers were feeling good, and so was their commander. For the first time since Williamsburg, back in early May, they were following up a battle with an advance, and as they went forward, past clumps of fallen rebels, they began to observe that their opponents were by no means the supermen they had seemed at times; were in fact, as one New York volunteer recorded, "undersized men mostly... with sallow, hatchet faces, and clad in 'butternut,' a color running all the way from a deep, coffee brown up to the whitish brown of ordinary dust." He even found himself feeling sorry for them. "As I looked down on the poor, pinched faces, worn with marching and scant fare, all enmity died out. There was no 'secession' in those rigid forms, nor in those fixed eyes staring blankly at the sky."

They left them where they lay and pushed on down the western slope, following McClellan, whose enthusiasm not even the fall of Harpers Ferry could dampen. Though this deprived him of 12,000 reinforcements which he thought he needed badly, it also vindicated the judgment he had shown in vainly urging the general in chief to order the post evacuated before Jackson rimmed the heights with guns. Moreover, though Old Brains could take no credit for it, his blunder had resulted in the dispersion of Lee's army, and this in turn had made possible yesterday's victory at South Mountain, as well as the larger triumph which now seemed to be within McClellan's grasp. Elated, he passed on this morning to Halleck "perfectly reliable [information] that the enemy is making for Shepherdstown in a perfect panic," and that "Lee last night stated publicly that he must admit they had been shockingly whipped." To old General Scott, in retirement at West Point, went a telegram announcing "a signal victory" and informing him that his fellow Virginian and former protégé had been soundly trounced: "R. E. Lee in command. The rebels routed, and retreating in disorder." Both reactions were encouraging. "Bravo, my dear general! Twice more and it's done," Scott answered, while Lincoln himself replied to the earlier wire: "God bless you and all with you. Destroy the rebel army if possible."

That was precisely what McClellan intended to do, if possible, and that afternoon, five miles southeast of Boonsboro — the scene of another triumphal entry and departure — he came upon a line of hills overlooking a shallow, mile-wide valley through which a rust-brown creek meandered south from its source in Pennsylvania; Antietam Creek, it was called. Beyond it, somewhat lower than the ridge on which he stood with his staff while his army filed in and spread out north and south along the line of hills outcropped with limestone, rose another ridge that masked the town of Sharpsburg, all but its spires and rooftops, and the Potomac, which followed a tortuous southward course, dividing Maryland and Virginia, another mile or so away. What interested him just now, though, was the ridge itself. There were Confederates on it, and Confederate guns, and one reason that they interested him was that they took him under fire. He sent his staff back out of range, dissolving the gaudy clot of horsemen who had drawn the fire in the first place, and went on with his study of the terrain.

A mile to the right of the point where the cluster of spires and gables showed above the ridge, and facing the road that led northward along it to Hagerstown, a squat, whitewashed building was set at the forward edge of a grove of trees wearing their full late-summer foliage; the autumnal equinox was still a week away. The sunlit brick structure, dazzling white against its leafy backdrop, was a church, but it was a Dunker church and therefore had no steeple; the Dunkers believed that steeples represented vanity, and they were as much opposed to vanity as they were to war, including the one that was about to move into their churchyard. On the near side of the road, somewhat farther to the right, was another grove of trees, parklike on the crown of the ridge, and between the two was a forty-acre field of dark green corn, man-tall and ripening for the harvest.

McClellan put his glasses back in their case and retired to do some thinking. Lee had chosen his army's position with care, disposing it along the high ground overlooking the shallow valley so that its flanks were anchored at opposite ends of the four-mile bend of the Potomac. That was his strength; but McClellan thought it might also be his weakness. Once Lee was dislodged from that ridge, with only a single ford in his rear, he might be caught in the coils of the river and cut to pieces. The problem was how to dislodge him, strong as he was. McClellan estimated yesterday's rebel casualties at 15,000 men, but that still left Lee with more than 100,000 according to Mc-Clellan, whose total strength — including Franklin, still hovering north of Harpers Ferry — was 87,164. Fortunately, however, there was no hurry; not just yet. The army was still filing in, hot and dusty from its march, and anyhow the day was already too far gone for an attack to succeed before darkness provided cover for a rebel getaway. He decided to work the thing out overnight. Meanwhile the troops could get a hot meal and a good night's rest by way of preparation for whatever bloody work he designed for them to do tomorrow.

Tomorrow came, September 16, but such bloody work as it brought was done by long-range shells from batteries on those ridges east and west of the mile-wide valley with its lazy little copper-colored creek. Wanting another good look at the terrain before completing his attack plan, McClellan rose early and went to the observation post where his staff had set up headquarters. Off to the right of the Boonsboro road and half a mile north of the center of the position, it was an excellent location, just beyond reach of the rebel guns, and there was plenty of equipment there for studying the enemy dispositions, including high-power telescopes strapped to the heads of stakes driven solidly into the ground. Unfortunately, however, these could not penetrate the thick mist that overhung the field until midmorning. By then the sun had burned enough of it away for McClellan to see that the Confederates had made some changes, shifting guns at various points along their line. The time consumed in noting these was well spent, he felt, for he wanted to eliminate snags and thus leave as little to chance as he possibly could. When the blow fell he wanted it to be heavy. Noon came and went, and on both sides men lay drowsing under the press of heat while the cannoneers continued their intermittent argument, jarring the ground and disrupting an occasional card game. By 2 o'clock McClellan had his attack plan: not for today — today, like yesterday, was too far gone — but for tomorrow.

It was based essentially on the presence of three stone bridges that spanned the creek on the left, center, and right. The one on the left was closest to Sharpsburg and the enemy line; in fact it was barely more than its own length away from the latter, since the western ridge came down sharply here, overlooking the bridge and whoever tried to use it. The center bridge, crossed by the Boonsboro road a mile above the first, had some of the same drawbacks, being under observation from the ridge beyond, as well as some of its own growing out of the fact that it debouched onto an uphill plain that was swept by guns clustered thickly along the rebel center. The upper bridge, a mile and a half above the second, had none of these disadvantages, being well out of range of the batteries across the way. What was more, an upstream crossing would permit an unmolested march to a position astride the Hagerstown road, well north of Lee's left flank, and a southward attack from that direction, if successful, would accomplish exactly what McClellan most desired. It would bowl the Confederates off their ridge and — in conjunction with attacks across the other two bridges, launched when the first was under way with all its attendant confusion — expose them to utter destruction.

In essence that was McClellan's plan, the outgrowth of much poring over the landscape and the map, and now that it had been formulated, all that remained — short, that is, of the execution itself — was for him to assign the various corps their various tasks in the over-all scheme for accomplishing Lee's downfall. Scrapping the previous organization into "wings," he decided that Fighting Joe Hooker was the man to lead the attack down the Hagerstown road, supported by Brigadier General J. K. F. Mansfield, who had arrived from Washington the day before to take over Banks' corps from Williams. Sumner, too, would come down from that direction, bringing a total of three corps, half of the whole army, to bear on Lee's left flank. If that did not break him, Franklin too could be thrown in there — he had been summoned from Maryland Heights and was expected to arrive tomorrow morning — raising the preponderance to two thirds. Burnside, back in command of his own corps after the death of Reno, was given the job of forcing the lower bridge and launching the direct assault on Sharpsburg, after which he would seize the Shepherdstown ford and thus prevent the escape of even a remnant of the shattered rebel force. Porter, astride the Boonsboro road, in rear of the center bridge, would serve a double function. As the army reserve, his corps could be used to repulse any counterattack Lee might launch in desperation, or it could be committed to give added impetus at whatever point seemed most critical, once success was fully in sight. Or else he could force the middle bridge for an uphill charge that would pierce Lee's center and chop him in two; whereupon Porter could wheel left or right to assist either Burnside or Hooker in wiping out whichever half of the rebel army survived the amputation.

The battle would open at daylight tomorrow, but McClellan — after taking his staff on a fast two-mile ride along his outpost line, drawing fire all the way from the guns across the creek, which permitted his own superior batteries, emplaced along the eastern ridge, to spot and pound them heavily — decided to use what was left of today in getting his men into position to launch the opening attack. Accordingly, about 4 o'clock that afternoon, Hooker's corps began its upstream crossing, the general leading the way on a high-stepping big white charger. The crossing itself was well beyond range of the rebel guns, but the line of march led near the grove of trees northeast of the Dunker Church, with the result that as the flank of the column went past that point it struck sparks, like a file being raked across a grindstone. Hooker drew off; he wanted those woods, but not just yet; and made camp for the night in line of battle astride the Hagerstown road, less than a mile beyond the Confederate left-flank outposts. Poised to strike as soon as there was light enough for him to aim the blow, he was exactly where McClellan wanted him.

So were the others, or anyhow they soon would be. Mansfield was crossing now in the darkness, to be followed by Sumner; Franklin was on the way. Porter was bivouacked in an open field, protected by defilade, just across the Boonsboro road from army headquarters. Farthest south, Burnside had massed his troops in rear of the triple-arched stone bridge which after tomorrow would bear his name. The night was gloomy, with a slow drizzle of rain and occasional sputters of musketry when the outpost men got nervous. For security reasons, the high command had forbidden fires. This was not so bad in itself — for all its dampness, the night was fairly warm — except that it kept the soldiers from boiling water. All along that dark, four-mile arc of blue-clad men, many of whom were going to die tomorrow, those who could not sleep chewed unhappily on dry handfuls of ground coffee.

The sun had burned the mist away that morning, but it could not disperse the mental fog which hid from McClellan, whose eye was glued to a telescope even then across the way, the fact that Lee at the time had less than one fifth as many troops as his opponent gave him credit for. He had in fact, along and behind the Sharpsburg ridge, barely 18,000 soldiers under D. H. Hill and Longstreet — fewer than were in Sumner's corps alone — until Jackson arrived at noon with three thin divisions, his own and Ewell's, under Brigadier General J. R. Jones and Lawton, and Walker's, which had crossed the Shenandoah to join him on the march from Harpers Ferry the night before. This brought the total to 26,000 and lowered the odds to three to one. McLaws and Anderson, still on the march, would not arrive before nightfall, and A. P. Hill was still at the Ferry; he might well not arrive at all. Even if he did, so heavy had the straggling been, together with the losses at South Mountain, Lee would not be able to count on putting more than 40,000 men into his line of battle, including the cavalry and artillery, and would still face odds worse than two to one.

Aware of this, Walker expected to find Lee anxious and careworn when he joined him on the outskirts of Sharpsburg, just after noon on the 16th. "Anxious enough, no doubt, he was," Walker observed; "but there was nothing in his look or manner to indicate it. On the contrary, he was calm, dignified, and even cheerful. If he had had a well-equipped army of a hundred thousand veterans at his back, he could not have appeared more composed and confident."

His confidence was doubly based: first, on the troops themselves, the hard-core men who had proved their battle prowess at Manassas and their hardiness by surviving the stony Maryland marches; and, second, on the advantages of the position he had established here on the ridge behind Antietam Creek. "We will make our stand on those hills," he had said as he came within sight of them at dawn of the day before. Unwilling to end his ambitious invasion campaign with the repulse just suffered at South Mountain, he crossed the shallow valley and spread his army north and south along the low western ridge. Longstreet took the right, blocking the near approach, from Sharpsburg down to the heights overlooking the lower bridge; Hill the center, posting his men along a sunken lane that crooked across the northeast quadrant formed by the intersection of the Boonsboro and Hagerstown roads; and Hood the left, occupying the woods beyond the Dunker Church. Next day, when Jackson and Walker came up, Lee sent the former to take charge of the left, joining Hood with his two divisions, while Walker extended Longstreet's right in order to guard the lower fords of the Antietam.

The long odds were somewhat offset by the fact that he would have the interior line, with a good road well below the crest for shifting troops to threatened points along the ridge. In addition, he had the advantage of knowing that McClellan could not swing around his flanks, securely anchored as they were near the Potomac in both directions. This last, however, was also the source of some concern. Just as the river afforded the enemy no room for maneuver in his rear, so too it would afford him none in case his army was flung back off the ridge, and what was more there was only a single ford, a mile below the former site of the Shepherdstown bridge, which had been destroyed. He did not expect to be dislodged, but he did take the precaution of covering the ford, from the Virginia side, with such guns as could be spared from the reserve under Brigadier General W. N. Pendleton, his chief of artillery. That completed his preparations. Until McLaws and Anderson came up, Jackson's, Hill's, and Longstreet's 26,000 were all the troops he would have for opposing the blue host whose officers were examining his dispositions from the higher ground across the valley and whose superior guns had already begun the pounding that would make this field "artillery hell" for Confederate cannoneers. "Put them all in, every gun you have, long range and short range," Longstreet said to his battery commanders, but Lee had already cautioned them not to waste their limited ammunition in duels with the heavier Federal pieces. Save it for the infantry, he told them.

Hooker's upstream crossing, and the resultant brush with the Texans in the woods beyond the Dunker Church, gave Lee fair warning that tomorrow's first blow would be aimed at Jackson and Hood. This was not without its comforting aspect, for the men who stood in its path not only were the ones who had held the unfinished railroad against repeated assaults by Pope, but were also the ones who had led the charge that wrecked him; perhaps they would serve Hooker the same way. However, the odds were even longer now, and as night came down Lee's apprehension increased. He had heard nothing from McLaws and Anderson, without whom he had no reserves with which to plug a break in his line or follow up a Federal repulse. Improvising as best he could, he ordered Stuart out beyond the left, hoping that he would find a position there from which to harass the flank of the attacking column or possibly launch a distracting counterstroke. He also sent a courier to A. P. Hill, seventeen miles away at Harpers Ferry, urging him to join the army with all possible speed. Whether this would get him there in time for a share in tomorrow's battle was highly doubtful, but at least Lee knew that Hill would make the effort.

As Lee was about to retire for the night, conscious that he had drawn his final card in the high-stakes game of showdown he was about to play with McClellan, Hood came to report that his men were near exhaustion, having received only half a ration of beef in the past three days. He requested that they be withdrawn from the line to get some rest and fry some dough and bacon. Distressed though Lee was to hear that his shock brigades were enfeebled, he was obliged to admit that he had no others to put in their place. He told him to see Jackson, and while Lee turned in, the rain murmurous on the canvas, Hood left to do just that.

He found him asleep under a large tree whose exposed roots made a pillow for his head. Hood nudged him awake, and when Stonewall sat up, blinking, told him what he wanted. Jackson had already rearranged his line, shifting troops around to the north and west to meet the attack he knew would come at dawn against those two stretches of woodland and the cornfield in between, but he agreed to spread them thinner in order to give Hood's hungry soldiers a chance to cook their rations, provided they were kept close at hand, ready to come running when he called. Hood agreed, and about midnight his two brigades filed southward to kindle their cookfires in the Dunker churchyard.

Presently a great stillness settled down, broken from time to time by picket firing, the individual shots coming sharp as handclaps through the mist and drizzle. All along the Sharpsburg ridge, while their opposite numbers munched ground coffee in the encircling darkness, men who could not sleep took out their pipes and smoked and thought about tomorrow.

* * *

It came in gray, with a pearly mist that shrouded the fields and woodlands, and it came with a crash of musketry, backed by the deeper roar of cannonfire that mounted in volume and intensity until it was continuous, jarring the earth beneath the feet of the attackers and defenders. Hooker bore down, his three divisions in line abreast, driving the rebel pickets southward onto the high ground where the road, flanked by what now was called the East Wood and the West Wood, ran past the squat white block of the Dunker Church. That was his immediate objective, barely a thousand yards away, though he was already taking heavy losses. Noting the glint of bayonets and the boil of smoke from the forty-acre cornfield, he called a halt while six of his batteries came up and began to flail the standing grain with shell and canister, their three dozen fieldpieces joined presently by heavier long-range guns pouring in a crossfire from the ridge beyond the creek. Haversacks and splintered muskets began to leap up through the dust and smoke, along with the broad-leafed stalks of corn and the dismembered heads and limbs of men. Hooker said later that "every stalk in the northern and greater part of the field was cut as closely as could have been done with a knife."

Yet when he got his batteries quieted and started his soldiers forward again, the fire seemed no less heavy. Entering the woods on the left and right, and approaching the shattered cornfield in the center, they ran into blinding sheets of flame and the air was quivering with bullets. "Men, I cannot say fell; they were knocked out of ranks by the dozen," one survivor wrote. Still they came on, their battle flags swooping and fluttering, falling and then caught up again. The red flags of the Confederates staggered backward, and still the bluecoats came on, driving them through the blasted corn and through the early morning woods, until at last they broke and fled, their ranks too thin to rally. The Dunker Church lay dead ahead. But just as the Federals saw it within their reach, a butternut column emerged from the woods beyond it and bore down on them, yelling. At point-blank range, the rebels pulled up short, delivered a volley which one receiver said "was like a scythe running through our line," and then came on again, the sunlight glinting and snapping on their bayonets.

It was Hood; Jackson had called for him while his men were preparing their first hot meal in days, and perhaps that had something to do with the violence of their assault. Leaving the half-cooked food in their skillets, they formed ranks and charged the bluecoats who were responsible. Their attack was necessarily unsupported, for Jackson's and

Two Advances; Two Retreats   [689]

Ewell's divisions were shattered. J. R. Jones had been stunned by a shell that exploded directly above his head, and Starke, who resumed command, received three wounds, all mortal, within minutes; command of the Stonewall Division passed to a colonel. Lawton was down, badly wounded, and in his three brigades only two of the fifteen regimental commanders were still on their feet. But Hood took no account of this,

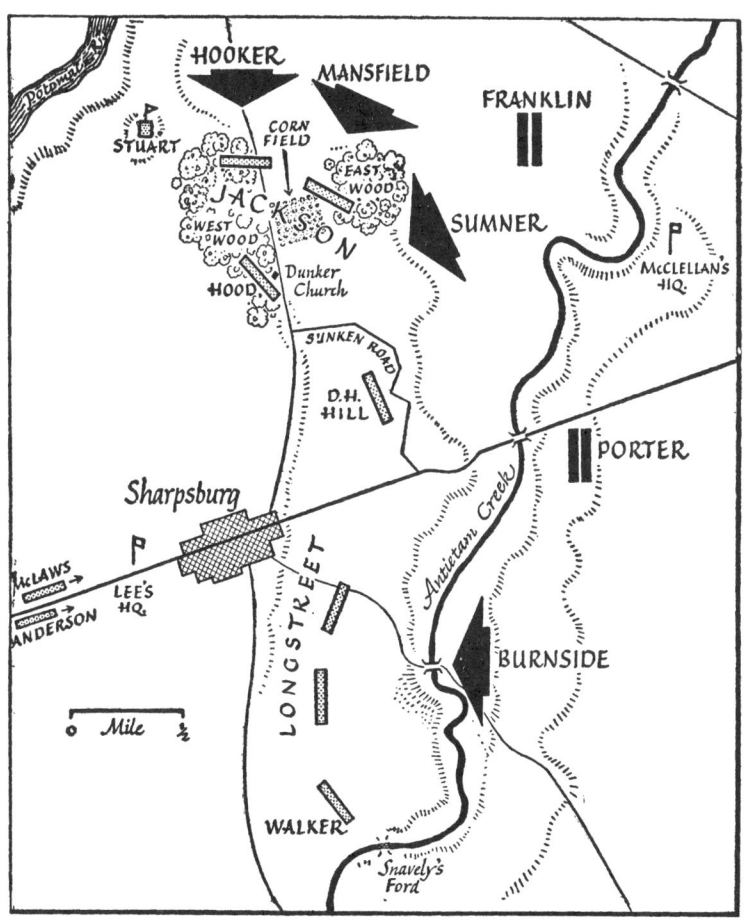

nor did his men. Intent on vengeance, they struck the Federals north of the Dunker Church and drove them back through the cornfield, whooping and jeering, calling for them to stand and fight. They did so at the far edge of the field, forming behind their guns, and there the two lines engaged. With only 2400 men in his two brigades, Hood knew that he would not be able to hold on long in the face of those guns, but he was determined to do what he could. When a staff officer arrived to inquire after the situation, Hood said grimly: "Tell General Jackson unless I get reinforcements I must be forced back, but I am going on while I can."

His chances of going on just now were better than he knew; for though the uproar had not slacked perceptibly, Hooker had already shot his bolt. Assailed in front by the demoniacal Texans, on the right by Early's brigade moving east from its position in support of Stuart, whose guns had been tearing the flank of the blue column all along, and on the left by two brigades from D. H. Hill, he was forced back to the line from which he had launched his dawn assault, two hours ago. With 2500 of his men shot down and at least that many more in headlong flight, he was through and he knew it. As he retreated through the shambles of the cornfield, he sent word to Mansfield that he was to bring up his corps and try his hand at completing the destruction so expensively begun.

Mansfield was altogether willing. So far in the war, though he had been in charge of the bloodless occupation of Suffolk, the only real action he had seen was with the coastal batteries that took the *Merrimac* under fire at Hampton Roads. Now he had two divisions of Valley and Manassas veterans, most of them unborn at the time of his West Point graduation forty years before. He liked them and they liked him, even on short aquaintance. "A calm and dignified old gentleman," one called him, while another noted with approval that he had "a proud, martial air and was full of military ardor." This last perhaps was a result of his habit of removing his hat as he rode among them, letting his long white hair and beard stream in the wind. As a performance it was effective, and he did it again this morning, evoking cheers from his troops as they moved forward in response to Hooker's call.

"That's right, boys — cheer!" he cried. "We're going to whip them today!" Doubling the column, he kept waving his hat and repeating his words to regiment after regiment: "Boys, we're going to lick them today!"

They almost did, but not while he was with them. As they approached the East Wood, deploying for action, Hooker rode up on his white horse. "The enemy are breaking through my lines!" he shouted above the roar of guns. "You must hold this wood!" Taken aback, Mansfield watched him gallop off; he had thought Hooker was driving the graybacks handsomely and that his own corps had been summoned to complete the victory. By now his lead regiments had reached a rail fence at the near edge of a field just short of the woods, and he saw to his horror that they had spread along it and were shooting at figures that moved in the shadows of the trees. "You are firing at our own men!" he cried. As soon as he got them stopped he leaped his horse over the fence, intending to ride ahead and see for himself. "Those are rebels,

General!" a soldier yelled. Mansfield pulled up, leaning forward to peer into the shadows. "Yes — you're right," he said, and as he spoke his words were confirmed by a volley that came crashing out of the woods, crippling his horse. He dismounted and walked back to the fence, but as he tried to climb over it, moving with the terrific deliberation of an old man among young ones, a bullet struck him in the stomach. He went down, groaning. Three veterans, who saw in the wounded general a one-way ticket out of chaos, took him up and lugged him back to an aid station, where a flustered surgeon half-strangled him with a jolt of whiskey, and presently he died.

Williams resumed command of the corps and sent both divisions forward, swinging one to the right so that its advance swept through the cornfield. Hood's survivors were knocked back, yielding ground and losing a stand of colors for the first time in their brief, furious history. On the bluecoats came, a Massachusetts colonel waving the captured Texas flag. They followed the route Hooker's men had taken an hour ago — and, like them, were stopped within reach of the Dunker Church by a two-brigade counterstroke. Jackson had called for reinforcements at the height of the first attack, and Lee had sent Walker's division from the right flank to the left, taking a chance that the Federals would not storm the lower Antietam crossings. These two North Carolina brigades arrived too late to contest the first penetration, but they got there in time to meet the second at its climax. Like Hooker's, Mansfield's men were stopped. However, they did not fall back. They stayed where they were, and Williams sent word to headquarters that if he could be reinforced he would have the battle won.

Reinforcements were already on the way — three divisions of them under Sumner, whose corps was the largest in the army — but they came by a different route: not down the Hagerstown road or parallel to it, but in at an angle through the lower fringes of the East Wood, which had been cleared of all but dead or dying rebels. So far, the close-up fighting had been left to troops formerly under Pope; now McClellan's own were coming in, led by the man who had saved the day at Fair Oaks. Dragoon-style, Sumner rode at the head of his lead division, leaving the others to come along behind. As he emerged from the woods he saw to his right the wreckage of the cornfield and up ahead the Dunker Church, dazzling white through rifts in the smoke boiling up from the line which Mansfield's men were struggling to hold against Walker's counterstroke. As Sumner saw it, the thing to do was get there fast, before that line gave way. With what his corps historian later called "ill-regulated ardor," he kept the lead division in march formation, three brigades close-packed in as many files, moving southwest across the open stretch of ground between the East Wood and the church. It was then that he was struck, two thirds of the way back down the column and squarely on the flank, with results that were sudden and altogether murderous. Too tightly wedged to maneuver as a unit, or even dodge as individuals, men fell in windrows, the long files writhing like wounded snakes. More than two thousand of them were shot down within a quarter of an hour. "My God, we must get out of this!" Sumner cried. His soldiers thought so, too, scrambling frantically for the rear as the graybacks charged.

It was McLaws. When his and Anderson's divisions finally reached Sharpsburg about 7 o'clock that morning — incredibly, they had been delayed at the outset because the paroled Federals, impatient to get home from Harpers Ferry, had clogged the bridge leading northward across the Potomac to the foot of Maryland Heights — more time was lost in a search for Lee, who was away from headquarters inspecting his right and center while Hooker was hammering at his left. When they found him, nearly an hour later, he sent Anderson to reinforce Hill, and McLaws to reinforce Jackson, who by then was receiving the full force of Mansfield's attack. This too had been stopped by the time McLaws got there, but just as he came over the ridge he saw Sumner's lead division emerge from the East Wood, driving straight for the Dunker Church with its flank exposed. He struck it, wrecked it, and took up the pursuit with his four brigades, joined on the left by Walker and Early, who threw Williams into retreat as well. Hooker by now was one of the nearly 7000 casualties the Federals had suffered at this end of the field; he rode northward out of the fight, dripping blood from a wounded foot, and his men followed, along with Mansfield's and Sumner's, to reform beyond the line of guns from which they had taken off at dawn. In rapid sequence, two whole corps and part of a third — six divisions containing 31,000 men — had been shattered and repulsed.

Jackson's losses had been comparable — probably in excess of 5000, which represented a larger percentage of casualties than he had inflicted — but he was strangely elated. Looking out over the shambles of the cornfield, which had just changed hands for the fourth time that morning and which by now was so thickly carpeted with dead men that one witness claimed you could walk in any direction across it and never touch the ground, his pale blue eyes had a fervent light to them. "God has been very kind to us this day," he said. For the first time since daylight glimmered across the eastern ridge his lines were free of pressure, and so was he himself. Sitting his horse in the yard of the Dunker Church, he ate a peach while his medical director submitted a preliminary casualty report. Stonewall made no comment, except to remark between bites that it was heavy, but when the surgeon expressed the fear that the survivors were too badly shaken to withstand another assault he shook his head, apparently unconcerned, and pointed in the direction of the bluecoats, huddled behind their line of guns a mile to the north. "Dr McGuire, they have done their worst," he said.

He was right, so far as concerned the left; the Federals there had done their worst and best. But Sharpsburg was, in effect, three battles piled one on top of another, and just as the first had ended with the repulse of Sumner's lead division, so did the second open with the repulse of the other two. Recovering his balance in the midst of disaster, the old man rode back through the woods in search of the rest of his corps, which was missing. One division he found had failed to cross the creek on schedule, while the other had lost contact and veered south, coming upon an eroded country lane from which a zigzag line of graybacks loosed a close-up volley that shattered the lead brigade and sent the others scrambling back. The third division, coming up at last, received the same reception and gave ground, but presently rallied and formed a line on which the second rallied, too. And thus, no sooner was Jackson's battle over, than Hill's got under way.

Here along the center the Confederates occupied what amounted to an intrenched position, the only one on the field. For the lane was not only worn below the level of the ground, affording them a considerable measure of protection, but it also ran between snake-rail fences, and they had dismantled the outer fence to make a substantial breastworks of the rails. What was more, the crest of the ridge was just over a hundred yards forward and uphill, so that the bluecoats could not see what they had to face until they were practically upon it, within easy musket range and outlined target-sharp against the eastern sky. This was unnerving, to say the least, and to make matters worse — psychologically, at any rate — the rebels jeered and hooted at the dark-clothed attackers coming over the rise, silhouetted against the glare of sunlight. "Go away, you black devils! Go home!" they yelled as they loosed their volleys. They felt confident and secure, and so did Hill: for a time at least. But as the Federals continued to press their attack with increasing persistency and numbers — Sumner had more than 12,000 men in his remaining two divisions, while Hill himself had less than 7,000, even after Anderson's arrival — the issue began to grow doubtful. Then presently, as a result of two unforeseen mishaps, it grew worse than doubtful. It grew impossible.

The first of these was that Anderson was severely wounded and carried from the field, command of his division passing to the senior brigadier, long-haired Roger Pryor, who by now had proved that his reluctance to fire the first shot at Fort Sumter had not proceeded from a lack of nerve, but whose talents were still primarily oratorical. From that time on, the division no longer functioned as a unit, and in fact went out of existence except as a loose collection of regiments and companies, each one fighting on its own as it saw fit. Which perhaps was just as well, in the end; for that was what happened to Hill's division, too, though its commander emerged unscathed from the experience of having three horses shot from under him in rapid succession.

This second disintegration was a result of the second mishap, which occurred when the brigade on the left, receiving the order to "refuse" its threatened flank, misunderstood the command and pulled out altogether; whereupon the opposing Federals hurried forward, occupied the abandoned portion of the line, and began to lay down an enfilading fire which gave the sunken road the name it bore thereafter: Bloody Lane. What had been a sheltered position, one from which to hoot at charging Yankees and shoot them down when they were so unmissably close that their faces filled the gunsight, became a trap. Quite suddenly, as if they had tumbled headlong by the hundreds out of the sky, dead men filled whole stretches of the road to overflowing. Horrified, unit by unit from left to right, the survivors broke for the rear, and now it was the Yankees doing the hooting and the shooting.

Faced with the abrupt disintegration of the isolated center, the exploitation of which would mean the end of Lee's army, Hill did what he could to rally the fugitives streaming back across the ridge, and though few of them had a mind for anything but their present dash for safety, he managed to scrape together a straggler line along the outskirts of Sharpsburg. While these men were delivering a sporadic fire against the bluecoats, who were massing along the sunken road, apparently preparing to continue their advance, Hill sent an urgent call for guns and reinforcements. There were none of the latter to send him; the right had been stripped and the left had been fought to exhaustion. But Longstreet had seen the trouble and was already sending every cannon he could lay hands on. He had not wanted to fight this battle in the first place — or for that matter, the odds being what they were, any battle in which there was so little to gain and so very much to lose — but now that it was unavoidably under way, he gave it everything he had. Limping about in carpet slippers and gesturing with an unlighted cigar, he ordered gun crew after gun crew to put their pieces in action along the ridge where Hill was forming his thin new line. As fast as these guns came into the open, the powerful Union batteries took them under fire from across the way, exploding caissons and mangling cannoneers. Observing one section of guns whose fire was weak because there were too few survivors to serve them properly, Old Pete dismounted his staff and improvised two high-ranking gun crews, himself holding their horses and correcting the ranges while they fired.

Hill meanwhile had been watching the bluecoats down in the sunken road. He believed they were about to attack him. Such an attack would surely be successful, weak as he was, and the only way he knew to delay it was to attack them first. However, when he called along his line for volunteers, there was no answer until presently one man said he would go if Hill would lead. Quickly taking him up on that, Hill seized a rifle and started forward with a shout, joined by about two hundred others who were persuaded by his example. The attack was brief; in fact, it was repulsed almost as soon as it began; but Hill believed it served its purpose. Here opposite the denuded Confederate center, the Federals stayed where they were for the rest of the day. According to Hill, this was either because he had frightened them into immobility or else it was an outright miracle.

It was neither, unless it was something of both. What it really was was Sumner — and McClellan. Franklin had come up by now, and though he had left one division on Maryland Heights, he still brought more than 8000 soldiers onto the field. One brigade had shared in the fight on the right, and now he wanted to use the other five in an assault on the gray line beyond the sunken road. But Sumner stopped him. The old man's corps had lost 5100 men today, more than Hooker's and Mansfield's combined; apparently he had seen enough of killing north of the Dunker Church and here in front of Bloody Lane. The thirty-nine-year-old Franklin tried to argue, but Sumner, who not only outranked him but was also nearly twice his age, kept insisting that the army was on the verge of disintegration and that another repulse would mean catastrophe. Presently a courier arrived from McClellan, bringing a suggestion that the attack be pressed by both commands if possible. Sumner — to whom, except for his long, pointed nose, old age had given the glaring look of a death's head — turned on him and cried hotly: "Go back, young man, and tell General McClellan I have no command! Tell him my command, Banks' command, and Hooker's command are all cut up and demoralized. Tell him General Franklin has the only organized command on this part of the field!"

When McClellan received this message he came down off the hill and crossed the creek to see for himself the situation in the center. Sumner and Franklin presented their arguments, and now that he had a close-up view of the carnage, McClellan sided with the senior. He told them both to hold what had been won; then he rode back across the creek. It was now about 2 o'clock, and the second battle, which like the first had lasted about four hours, was over. The third was about to begin.

In a broader sense, it had already been going on for as long as the other two combined. That is, the opponents had been exchanging shots across the lower reaches of the creek since dawn. But, so far, all that had come of this was the maiming of a few hundred soldiers, most of them in blue. Despite McClellan's repeated orders — including one sent at 9 o'clock, directing that the crossing be effected "at all hazards" — not a man out of the nearly 14,000 enrolled in Burnside's four divisions had reached the west bank of the Antietam by the time the sun swung past the overhead. "McClellan appears to think I am not trying my best to carry this bridge," the ruff-whiskered general said testily to a staff colonel his friend the army commander sent to prod him. "You are the third or fourth one who has been to me this morning with similar orders."

As he spoke he sat his horse beside a battery on a hilltop, looking down at the narrow, triple-arched stone span below. He watched it with a fascination amounting to downright prescience, as if he knew already that it was to bear his name and be in fact his chief monument, no matter what ornate shafts of marble or bronze a grateful nation might raise elsewhere in his honor. So complete was his absorption by the bridge itself, he apparently never considered testing the depth of the water that flowed sluggishly beneath it. If he had, he would have discovered that the little copper-colored stream, less than fifty feet in width, could have been waded at almost any point without wetting the armpits of the shortest man in his corps. However, except for sending one division downstream in search of a local guide to point out a ford that was rumored to exist in that direction, he remained intent on effecting a dry-shod crossing.

Admittedly this was no easy matter. The road came up from the southeast, paralleling the creek for a couple of hundred yards, and then turned sharply west across the bridge, where it swung north again to curve around the heights on the opposite bank. Just now those heights were occupied by rebels — many of them highly skilled as marksmen, though at that range skill was practically superfluous — which meant that whoever exposed himself along that road, in the shadow of those heights, was likely to catch a faceful of bullets. Nevertheless, this was the only route Burnside could see, and he kept sending men along it, regiment by regiment, intermittently all morning, with predictable results.

Observing from across the way the ease with which this lower threat was being contested, Lee all this time had been stripping his right of troops in order to strengthen his hard-pressed left and center. By noon he was down to an irreducible skeleton force; so that presently, when he learned that Hill had lost the sunken road and was calling in desperation for reinforcements, he had none to send him. Like Hill in this extremity, knowing that he probably could not withstand an assault, he decided that his only recourse was to deliver one — preferably on the left, which had been free of heavy pressure for two hours. Accordingly, he sent word for Jackson to attack the Federal right, if possible, swinging it back against the river. Stonewall was delighted at the prospect, and set out at once to reconnoiter the ground in that direction. "We'll drive McClellan into the Potomac," he said fervently. Back at Sharpsburg, meanwhile, Lee was doing what little he could to make this possible. When the captain of a shattered Virginia battery reported with his few surviving men, he instructed him to join Jackson for the proposed diversion. One of the smoke-grimed cannoneers spoke up: "General, are you going to send us in again?" Lee saw then that it was Robert. "Yes, my son," he told him. "You all must do what you can to help drive these people back." The battery left, heading northward; but no such attack was delivered. Reconnoitering, Stonewall found the Union flank securely anchored to the east bank of the river and well protected by massed artillery. He had to abandon his hopes for a counterstroke. "It is a great pity," he said regretfully. "We should have driven McClellan into the Potomac."

By the time Lee learned that the proposed attack could not be delivered, that no diversion to relieve the pressure against the sagging center would be made, the urgent need for it had passed. Hill's thin line — along which, in accordance with his instructions now that his feeble two-hundred-man charge had been repulsed, the colorbearers flourished their tattered battle flags, hiding his weakness behind gestures of defiance — went unchallenged by the bluecoats massed along the sunken road. But Lee was not allowed even a breathing space in which to enjoy the relaxation of tension. Catastrophe, it seemed, was still with him; had in fact merely withdrawn in order to loom up elsewhere. Immediately on the heels of the news that the Federal advance had stalled in front of the center, word came from the right that the contingency most feared had come to pass. Burnside was across the bridge at last.

Robert Toombs was in command there, holding the heights with three slim Georgia regiments against four Federal divisions. Lately, just as previously he had wearied of his cabinet post, he had been feeling disenchanted with the military life. Exasperated, now as then, by the obtuseness of those around him, he had decided to resign his commission, but not before he had distinguished himself in some great battle. "The day after such an event," he wrote his wife, "I will retire if I live through it." Such an event was now at hand, and he had been in his glory all that morning, successfully challenging with 550 men the advance of more than twenty times their number. At 1 o'clock, after seven hours of fitful and ineffectual probing, Burnside at last sent two regiments pounding straight downhill for the bridge, avoiding the suicidal two-hundred-yard gauntlet-run along the creek bank. They got across in a rush, joined presently by others, until the west-bank strength had increased to a full division at that point. Meanwhile the downstream division had finally located the ford and splashed across it, the men scarcely wetting their legs above the knees. About to be swamped from the front and flank, Toombs reported the double crossing and received permission to avoid capture by withdrawing from the heights. He did so in good order, proud of himself and his weary handful of fellow Georgians, whom he put in line along the rearward ridge. There on the outskirts of Sharpsburg with the rest of Longstreet's troops — not over 2500 in all, so ruthlessly had Lee thinned their ranks in his need for reinforcements on the left and center — they prepared to resist the advance of Burnside's four divisions.

What came just then, however, was a lull. After forming ranks for a forward push, the commander of the lead blue division found that his men had burnt up most of their ammunition banging away all morning at the snipers on the heights. Informed of this, Burnside decided to replace them with another division instead of taking time to bring up cartridges. This too took time though. It was nearly 3 o'clock before the new division started forward. Off to the left, after crossing the ford and floundering in the bottoms, the other division at last recovered its sense of direction and joined the attack. Few though the rebels seemed to be, they were laying down a mass of fire out of all proportion to their numbers. A New York soldier, whose regiment was pinned down by what he termed "the hiss of bullets and the hurtle of grapeshot," later recalled that "there burst forth from it the most vehement, terrible swearing I have ever heard." When the order came to rise and charge, he observed another phenomenon: "The mental strain was so great that I saw at that moment the singular effect mentioned, I think, in the life of Goethe on a similar occasion — the whole landscape for an instant turned slightly red."

Across this reddened landscape they came charging, presenting a two-division front that overlapped the Confederate flank and piled up against the center. Down at his headquarters, beyond the town (the lull had been welcome, but he could only use it to rest his men, not to bring up others; he had no others, and would have none until — and if — A. P. Hill arrived from Harpers Ferry) Lee heard the uproar drawing nearer across the eastern hills, and presently the evidences of Federal success were visual as well. The Sharpsburg streets were crowded with fugitives, their demoralization increased by shells that burst against the walls and roofs of houses, startling flocks of pigeons into bewildered flight, round and round in the smoke. Blue flags began to appear at various points along the ridge above. The men who bore them had advanced almost a mile beyond the bridge; another mile would put them astride the Shepherdstown road, which led west to the only crossing of the Potomac.

Observing a column moving up from the southeast along the ridge line, Lee called to an artillery lieutenant on the way to the front with a section of guns: "What troops are those?" The lieutenant offered him his telescope. "Can't use it," Lee said, holding up a bandaged hand. The lieutenant trained and focused the telescope. "They are flying the United States flag," he reported. Lee pointed to the right, where another distant column was approaching from the southwest, nearly perpendicular to the first, and repeated the question. The lieutenant swung the glass in that direction, peered intently, and announced: "They are flying the Virginia and Confederate flags." Lee suppressed his elation, although the words fulfilled his one hope for deliverance from defeat. "It is A. P. Hill from Harpers Ferry," he said calmly.

It was indeed. Receiving Lee's summons at 6.30 that morning, Little Powell had left one brigade to complete the work at the Ferry, and put the other five on the road within the hour. Seventeen roundabout miles away, the crash and rumble of gunfire spurred him on — particularly when he drew near enough for the sound to be intensified by the clatter of musketry. Forgotten were Stonewall's march regulations, which called for periodic rest-halts; Hill's main concern was to get to Sharpsburg fast, however bedraggled, not to get there after sundown with a column that arrived well-closed and too late for a share in the fighting. Jacket off because of the heat, he rode in his bright red battle shirt alongside the panting troops, prodding laggards with the point of his saber. Beyond this, he had no dealings with stragglers, but left them winded by the roadside, depending on them to catch up in time if they could. Not many could, apparently; for he began the march with about 5000 men, and ended it with barely 3000. But with these, as was his custom, he struck hard.

In his path, here on the Federal left, was an outsized Connecticut regiment, 900-strong. That was a good many more soldiers than Hill had in any one of his brigades, but they were grass green, three weeks in service, and already considerably shaken by what they had seen of their first battle. To add to their confusion, a large proportion of the rebels bearing down on them wore new blue uniforms captured at Harpers Ferry. The first thing they received by way of positive identification was a close-up volley that dropped about four hundred of them and broke and scattered the rest. A Rhode Island outfit, coming up just then, was likewise confused, as were two Ohio regiments which arrived to find bluecoats fleeing from bluecoats and held their fire until they too were knocked sprawling. With that, the Union left gave way in a backward surge, pursued by Hill, whose men came after it, screaming their rebel yell. The panic spread northward to the outskirts of Sharpsburg, where several blue companies, meeting little resistance, had already entered the eastern streets of the town; Burnside's whole line came unpinned, and presently the retreat was general. Toombs' Georgians, along with the rest of Longstreet's men, took up the pursuit and chased the Northerners back onto the heights they had spent the morning trying to seize.

And now in the sunset, here on the right, as previously on the left and along the center, the conflict ended; except that this time it was for good. Twilight came down and the landscape was dotted with burning haystacks, set afire by bursting shells. For a time the cries of wounded men of both armies came from these; they had crawled up into the hay for shelter, but now, bled too weak to crawl back out again, were roasted. Lee's line was intact along the Sharpsburg ridge. McClellan had failed to break it; or, breaking it, had failed in all three cases, left and center and right, to supply the extra push that would keep it broken.

★ ★ ★

There were those in the Federal ranks who had been urging him to do just that all afternoon. Nor did he lack the means. The greater part of four divisions — two under Franklin, two under Porter: no less than 20,000 men, a solid fourth of his effective force — had stood idle while the battle raged through climax after climax, each of which offered McClellan the chance to wreck his adversary. But he could not dismiss the notion that somewhere behind that opposite ridge, or off beyond the flanks, Lee was massing enormous reserves for a knockout blow. The very thinness of the gray line, which was advanced as an argument for assaulting it, seemed to him to prove that the balance of those more than 100,000 rebels were being withheld for some such purpose, and when it came he wanted to have something with which to meet it.

"At this critical juncture," he afterwards reported, "I should have had a narrow view of the condition of the country had I been willing to hazard another battle with less than an absolute assurance of success. At that moment — Virginia lost, Washington menaced, Maryland invaded — the national cause could afford no risks of defeat. Lee's army might then have marched as it pleased on Washington, Baltimore, Philadelphia, or New York . . . and nowhere east of the Alleghenies was there another organized force able to arrest its march."

It never occurred to him, apparently, to look at the reverse of the coin: to consider that Lee's army, like his own, was the only organized force that blocked the path to its capital. But it did occur to Sykes, who appealed to him, late in the day and in the presence of Porter, to be allowed to strike at the rebel center with his regulars. Part of one of his brigades had been up close to the western ridge, serving as a link between Sumner's left and Burnside's right, and its officers had seen that D. H. Hill was about to buckle — indeed, had buckled already, if someone would only take advantage of the fact. Let him launch an attack against that point, Sykes said, supported by Porter's other division and one from Franklin, and he would cut Lee's line in two, thereby exposing the severed halves to destruction.

At first McClellan seemed about to approve; but in the moment of hesitation he looked at Porter, and Porter slowly shook his head. "Remember, General," one witness later quoted him as saying, "I command the last reserve of the last army of the republic." That cinched it.

The attack was not made. Porter and Franklin, who between them lost only 548 of today's more than 12,000 casualties, remained in reserve.

As night came down, the two armies disengaged, and when the torches of the haystack pyres went out, darkness filled the valley of the Antietam, broken only by the lanterns of the medics combing the woods and cornfields for the injured who were near enough to be brought within the lines. Lee remained at his headquarters, west of Sharpsburg, greeting his generals as they rode up. Jackson, the two Hills, McLaws and Walker, Hood and Early, all had heavy losses to report. The gray commander spoke with each, but he seemed unshaken by the fact that more than a fourth of his army lay dead or wounded on the field. Nor did he mention the word that was in all their minds: retreat. "Where is Longstreet?" he asked, after he had talked with all the others. Presently Old Pete arrived, still limping in carpet slippers and still chewing on the unlighted cigar; he had stopped in the town to help some ladies whose house was on fire. Lee stepped forward to greet him. "Ah," he said, placing his crippled hands on the burly Georgian's shoulders. "Here is Longstreet. Here is my old warhorse."

This last report was as gloomy as the others. The army was bled white and near exhaustion, with all its divisions on the firing line. Aside from a trickle of stragglers coming in, Lee's only reserve, and in fact the only reserve in all northern Virginia, was the one brigade A. P. Hill had left to complete the salvage work at Harpers Ferry. All the generals here informally assembled were agreed that another day like today would drive the surviving remnant headlong into the Potomac. All, that is, but Lee. When he had heard his lieutenants out, he told them to return to their men, make such tactical readjustments as would strengthen their defenses, and see that rations were cooked and distributed along the present line of battle. If McClellan wanted another fight, he would give him one tomorrow.

McClellan, it seemed, wanted no such thing. Despite an early morning telegram to Halleck: "The battle will probably be renewed today. Send all the troops you can by the most expeditious route," and a letter in which he told his wife: "[Yesterday's battle] was a success, but whether a decided victory depends on what occurs today," he soon took stock and found the portents far from favorable. Reno and Mansfield were dead, along with eight other general officers; Hooker was out of action, wounded; Sumner was despondent; Burnside was even doubtful whether his troops could hold the little they had gained the day before. After what he called "a careful and anxious survey of the condition of my command, and my knowledge of the enemy's force and position," McClellan decided to wait for reinforcements, including two divisions on the way from Maryland Heights and Frederick. As a result, the armies lay face to face all day, like sated lions, and between them, there on the slopes of Sharpsburg ridge and in the valley of the Antietam, the dead began to fester in the heat and the cries of the wounded faded to a mewling.

There were a great many of both, the effluvium of this bloodiest day of the war. Nearly 11,000 Confederates and more than 12,000 Federals had fallen along that ridge and in that valley, including a total on both sides of about 5000 dead. Losses at South Mountain raised these doleful numbers to 13,609 and 14,756 respectively, the latter being increased to 27,276 by the surrender of the Harpers Ferry garrison. Lee had suffered only half as many casualties as he had inflicted in the course of the campaign; but even this was more than he could afford. "Where is your division?" someone asked Hood at the close of the battle, and Hood replied, "Dead on the field." After entering the fight with 854 men, the Texas brigade came out with less than three hundred, and these figures were approximated in other veteran units, particularly in Jackson's command. The troops Lee lost were the best he had — the best he could ever hope to have in the long war that lay ahead, now that his try for an early ending by invasion had been turned back.

Orders for the retirement were issued that afternoon, and at nightfall, in accordance with those orders, fires were kindled along the ridge to curtain the retreat across the Potomac. Longstreet went first, forming in support of Pendleton's guns on the opposite bank. Two brigades of cavalry followed, then moved upstream, prepared to recross and harry the enemy flank in case the withdrawal was contested. Walker's division was the last to cross. At sunup, as Walker followed the tail of his column into the waist-deep water of the ford, he saw Lee sitting his gray horse in midstream. Apparently he had been there all night. When Walker reported all of his troops safely across the river except some wagonloads of wounded and a battery of artillery, which were close at hand, Lee showed for the first time the strain he had been under. "Thank God," he said.

That was in fact the general reaction, though in most cases it was expressed with considerably less reverence. Crossing northward two weeks ago, the bands had played "My Maryland" and the men had gaily swelled the chorus; but now, as one of the round-trip marchers remarked, "all was quiet on that point. Occasionally some fellow would strike up that tune, and you would then hear the echo, 'Damn my Maryland.'" Another recorded his belief that "the confounded Yankees" could shoot straighter on their home ground. Nor was this aversion restricted to the ranks. "I have heard but one feeling expressed about [Maryland]," one brigadier informed his wife, "and that is a regret at our having gone there." A youthful major on Lee's own staff wrote home to his sister: "Don't let any of your friends sing 'My Maryland' — not 'My Western Maryland' anyhow."

Presently there was apparent cause for greater regret than ever.

Leaving Pendleton with forty-four guns and two slim brigades of infantry to discourage pursuit by holding the Shepherdstown ford, Lee moved the rest of his army into bivouac on the hills back from the river, then lay down under an apple tree to get some badly needed sleep himself. Not long after midnight he woke to find Pendleton bending over him. The former Episcopal rector was shaken and bewildered, and as he spoke Lee found out why. McClellan had brought up his heavy guns for counterbattery work, Pendleton explained, and then at the height of the bombardment had suddenly thrown Porter's corps across the Potomac, driving off the six hundred rear-guard infantry and the startled cannoneers. All the guns of the Confederate reserve artillery had been captured.

"*All?*" Lee said, brought upright.

"Yes, General, I fear all."

Unwilling to attempt a counterattack in the dark with his weary troops, Lee decided to wait for daylight. But when Jackson heard the news he was too upset to wait for anything. He had A. P. Hill's men turn out at once and put them in motion for the ford, arriving soon after sunrise to find that things were by no means as bad as the artillery chief had reported. A subordinate had brought off all but four of the guns, and only a portion of Porter's two divisions had crossed the river. "With the blessing of Providence," Stonewall informed Lee, "they will soon be driven back." They were. Hill launched another of his savage attacks: one of those in which, as he reported, "each man felt that the fate of the army was centered in himself." Something over 250 Federals were shot or drowned in their rush to regain the Maryland bank, and when it was over, all who remained in Virginia were captives. Hill drew back to rejoin the main body, unpursued.

What at first had been taken for a disaster turned out in the end to be a tonic — a sort of upbeat coda, after the crash and thunder of what had gone before. The army moved on to Martinsburg, where by September 22 enough stragglers had returned to bring its infantry strength to 36,418. A week later, with all ten divisions — or at any rate what was left of them — resting between Mill Creek and Lick River, Lee wrote Davis: "History records but few examples of a greater amount of labor and fighting than has been done by this army during the present campaign.... There is nothing to report, but I desire to keep you always advised of the condition of the army, its proceedings, and prospects."

He had occupied his present position near Winchester, he told the President, "in order to be prepared for any flank movement the enemy might attempt." It soon developed, however, that he had no grounds for worry on that score. McClellan was not contemplating a flank movement. In point of fact, despite renewed pressure from Washington, McClellan was not contemplating any immediate movement at all.

After completing the grisly and unaccustomed work of cleaning up the battlefield, he reoccupied Harpers Ferry with Sumner's corps and spread the others along the north bank of the Potomac, guarding the fords. The main problem just now, as he saw it, was the old one he had always been so good at: reorganizing, drilling, and resupplying his 93,149 effectives. Lee's strength — precisely tabulated at 97,445 — forbade an advance, even if the Federal army had been in any condition to make one, which McClellan did not believe to be the case.

As he went about the familiar task of preparing his men for what lay ahead, he looked back with increasing pride on what had gone before. Originally he had been guarded in his pronouncements as to the outcome of the battle on the 17th. "The general result was in our favor," he wrote his wife next morning; "that is to say, we gained a great deal of ground and held it." But now that he had had time to consider the overall picture, he said, "I feel that I have done all that can be asked in twice saving the country." He felt, too, "that this last short campaign is a sufficient legacy for our child, so far as honor is concerned." And he added, rather wistfully: "Those in whose judgment I rely tell me that I fought the battle splendidly and that it is a masterpiece of art."

❌ 3 ❌

For Lincoln it was something less, and also something more. The battle had been fought on a Wednesday. At noon Monday, September 22, he assembled at the White House all the members of his cabinet, and after reading them an excerpt from a collection of humorous sketches by Artemus Ward, got down to the business at hand. "When the rebel army was at Frederick," he told them, "I determined, as soon as it should be driven out of Maryland, to issue a proclamation of emancipation, such as I thought most likely to be useful. I said nothing to anyone; but I made the promise to myself and" — hesitating slightly — "to my Maker. The rebel army is now driven out, and I am going to fulfill that promise." And with that he began to read from a manuscript which was the second draft of the document he had laid aside, two months ago today, on Seward's advice that to have issued it then would have been to give it the sound of "our last *shriek* on the retreat" down the Peninsula. Second Bull Run had been even worse, particularly from this point of view. But now had come Antietam, and though it was scarcely a "masterpiece," or even a clear-cut victory, Lincoln thought it would serve as the occasion for his purpose.

It was highly characteristic, and even fitting, that he opened this solemn conclave with a reading of the slapstick monologue, "High Handed Outrage at Utica," not only because he himself enjoyed it, along with most of his ministers — all except Stanton, who sat glumly through the dialect performance, and Chase, who maintained his reputation for never laughing at anything at all — but also because it was in line with the delaying tactics and the attitude he had adopted toward the question during these past two months. With the first draft of the proclamation tucked away in his desk, only awaiting a favorable turn of military events to launch it upon an unsuspecting world, he had seemed to talk against such a measure to the very people who came urging its promulgation. Presumably he did this in order to judge their reaction, as well as to prevent a diminution of the thunderclap effect which he foresaw. At any rate, he had not even hesitated to use sarcasm, particularly against the most earnest of these callers.

One day, for example, a Quaker woman came to request an audience, and Lincoln said curtly: "I will hear the Friend." She told him she had been sent by the Lord to inform him that he was the minister appointed to do the work of abolishing slavery. Then she fell silent. "Has the Friend finished?" Lincoln asked. She said she had, and he replied: "I have neither the time nor disposition to enter into discussion with the Friend, and end this occasion by suggesting for her consideration the question whether, if it be true that the Lord has appointed me to do the work she has indicated, it is not probable he would have communicated knowledge of the fact to me as well as to her?"

Similarly, on the day before the Battle of South Mountain, when a delegation of Chicago ministers called to urge presidential action on the matter, he inquired: "What good would a proclamation of emancipation from me do, especially as we are now situated? I do not want to issue a document that the whole world will see must necessarily be inoperative, like the Pope's bull against the comet. Would my word free the slaves, when I cannot even enforce the Constitution in the rebel states? Is there a single court or magistrate or individual that would be influenced by it there? ... I will mention another thing, though it meet only your scorn and contempt. There are fifty thousand bayonets in the Union armies from the border slave states. It would be a serious matter if, in consequence of a proclamation such as you desire, they should go over to the rebels." In parting, however, he dropped a hint. "Do not misunderstand me because I have mentioned these objections. They indicate the difficulties that have thus far prevented action in some such way as you desire. I have not decided against a proclamation of liberty to the slaves, but hold the matter under advisement. ... I can assure you that the subject is on my mind, by day and night, more than any other. Whatever shall appear to be God's will, I will do."

Sadly the Illinois ministers filed out; but one, encouraged by the closing words, remained behind to register a plea in that direction. "What you have said to us, Mr President, compels me to say to you in reply, that it is a message to you from our Divine Master, through me, commanding you, sir, to open the doors of bondage that the slaves may go free." Lincoln gave him a long look, not unlike the one he had given the Quaker woman. "That may be, sir," he admitted, "for I have studied this question by night and by day, for weeks and for months. But if it is, as you say, a message from your Divine Master, is it not odd that the only channel he could send it by was the roundabout route by way of that awful wicked city of Chicago?"

These remarks were in any case supplementary to those he had made already in reply to Horace Greeley, who published in the August 20 *Tribune* an open letter to the President, titled "The Prayer of Twenty Millions," in which he charged at some length that Lincoln had been "strangely and disastrously remiss in the discharge of your official and imperative duty." The first such duty, as Greeley saw it, was to announce to the army, the nation, and the world that this war was primarily a struggle to put an end to slavery. Lincoln, having heard that the New Yorker was preparing to attack him, had asked a mutual friend, "What is he wrathy about? Why does he not come down here and have a talk with me?" The friend replied that Greeley had said he would not allow the President of the United States to act as advisory editor of the *Tribune*. "I have no such desire," Lincoln said. "I certainly have enough on my hands to satisfy any man's ambition." But now that the journalist had aired his grievance publicly, Lincoln answered two days later with a public letter of his own, headed "Executive Mansion" and addressed to Greeley:

> As to the policy I "seem to be pursuing," as you say, I have not meant to leave anyone in doubt.
> I would save the Union. I would save it the shortest way under the Constitution. The sooner the national authority can be restored, the nearer the Union will be "the Union as it was." If there be those who would not save the Union unless they could at the same time save slavery, I do not agree with them. If there be those who would not save the Union unless they could at the same time destroy slavery, I do not agree with them. My paramount object in this struggle is to save the Union, and is not either to save or destroy slavery. If I could save the Union without freeing any slave, I would do it; and if I could save it by freeing all the slaves, I would do it; and if I could save it by freeing some and leaving others alone, I would also do that. What I do about slavery and the colored race, I do because I believe it helps to save the Union; and what I forbear, I forbear because I do not believe it would help to save the Union. I shall do less whenever I shall believe what I am doing hurts the cause, and I shall do more whenever I shall believe doing more will help the cause. I shall try to correct errors when shown to be errors, and I shall adopt new views so fast as they shall appear to be true views.
> I have here stated my purpose according to my view of official duty; and I intend no modification of my oft-expressed personal wish that all men everywhere could be free.

And having thus to some extent forestalled his anticipated critics — particularly the conservatives, whose arguments he advanced as his own while pointing out the expediency of acting counter to them — he read to the cabinet this latest draft of what he called a Preliminary Emancipation Proclamation. Two opening paragraphs emphasized that the paper was being issued by him as Commander in Chief, upon military necessity; that reunion, not abolition, was still the primary object of the war; that compensated emancipation was still his goal for loyal owners, and that voluntary colonization of freedmen, "upon this continent or elsewhere," would still be encouraged. In the third paragraph he got down to the core of the edict, declaring "That on the first day of January, in the year of our Lord one thousand eight hundred and sixty-three, all persons held as slaves within any State or designated part of a State the people whereof shall then be in rebellion against the United States, shall be then, thenceforward, and forever free." He closed, after quoting from congressional measures prohibiting the return of fugitive slaves to disloyal masters, with the promise that, on restoration of the Union, he would recommend that loyal citizens of all areas "be compensated for all losses by acts of the United States, including the loss of slaves."

In this form, after adopting some minor emendations suggested by Seward and Chase, Lincoln gave the document to the world next morning. *Return to the Union within one hundred days,* he was telling the rebels, *and you can keep your slaves — or anyhow be compensated for them, when and if (as I propose) the law takes them away. Otherwise, if you lose the war, you lose your human property as well.* It was in essence counterrevolutionary, a military edict prompted by expediency. Whoever attacked him for it, whatever the point of contention, would have to attack him on his own ground.

This the South was quick to do. Recalling his inaugural statement, "I have no purpose, directly or indirectly, to interfere with the institution of slavery in the states where it exists. I believe I have no lawful right to do so, and I have no inclination to do so," southern spokesmen cried that Lincoln at last had dropped the mask. They quoted with outright horror a passage from the very core of the proclamation which seemed to them to incite the slaves to riot and massacre: "The Executive Government of the United States, including the military and naval authority thereof ... will do no act or acts to repress such persons, or any of them, in any efforts they may make for their actual freedom." What was this, they asked, if not an invitation to the Negroes to murder them in their beds? Bestial, they called Lincoln, for here he had touched the quick of their deepest fear, and the Richmond *Examiner* charged that the proclamation was "an act of malice towards the master, rather than one of mercy to the slave." Abroad, the London *Spectator* reinforced this view of the author's cynicism: "The principle is not that a human being cannot justly own another, but that he cannot own him unless he is loyal to the United States." Jefferson Davis, while he deplored that such a paper could be issued by the head of a government of which he himself had once been part, declared that it would inspire the South to new determination; for "a restitution of the Union has been rendered forever impossible by the adoption of a measure which ... neither admits of retraction nor can coexist with union."

In the North, too, there were critics, some of whom protested that the proclamation went too far, while others claimed that it did not go far enough. Some, in fact, maintained that it went nowhere, since it proclaimed freedom only for those unfortunates now firmly under Confederate control. One such critic was the New York *World*, whose editor pointed out that "the President has purposely made the proclamation inoperative in all places where we have gained a military footing which makes the slaves accessible. He has proclaimed emancipation only where he has notoriously no power to execute it." Not only were the loyal or semiloyal slave states of Delaware and Maryland, Kentucky and Missouri omitted from the terms to be applied, but so was the whole rebel state of Tennessee, as well as those parts of Virginia and Louisiana under Federal occupation. This was a matter of considerable alarm to the abolitionists. For if emancipation was not to be extended to those regions a hundred days from now, they asked, when would it ever be extended to them? What manner of document was this anyhow?

Yet these objections were raised only by those who read it critically. Most people did not read it so. They took it for more than it was, or anyhow for more than it said; the container was greater than the thing contained, and Lincoln became at once what he would remain for them, "the man who freed the slaves." He would go down to posterity, not primarily as the Preserver of the Republic — which he was — but as the Great Emancipator, which he was not. "A poor *document*, but a mighty *act*," the governor of Massachusetts privately called the proclamation, and Lincoln himself said of it in a letter to Vice-President Hamlin, six days later: "The time for its effect southward has not come; but northward the effect should be instantaneous." Whatever truth there was in Davis' claim that it would further unite the South in opposition, Lincoln knew that it had already done much to heal the split in his own party; which was not the least of his reasons for having released it.

Seward understood such things. Asked by a friend why the cabinet had done "so useless and mischievous a thing as to issue the proclamation," he told a story. Up in New York State, he said, when the news came that the Revolutionary War had been won and American independence at last established, an old patriot could not rest until he had put up a liberty pole. When his neighbors asked him why he had gone to so much trouble — wasn't he just as free without it? — the patriot replied, "What is liberty without a pole?" So it was with the present case, Seward remarked between puffs on his cigar: "What is war without a proclamation?"

Something more it had done, or was doing, which was also included in Lincoln's calculations. Abroad, as at home, a bedrock impact had been felt. In London, like the pro-Confederate *Spectator*, the *Times* might call the proclamation "A very sad document," which the South would "answer with a hiss of scorn"; a distinguished Member of Parliament might refer to it as "a hideous outburst of weak yet demoniacal spite" and "the most unparalleled last card ever played by a reckless gambler"; Earl Russell himself might point out to his colleagues that it was "of a very strange nature" and contained "no declaration of a principle adverse to slavery." Yet behind these organs of opinion, below these men of influence, stood the people. In their minds, now that Lincoln had spoken out — regardless of what he actually said or left unsaid — support for the South was support for slavery, and they would not have it so. From this point on, the editors might favor and the heads of state might ponder ways and means of extending recognition to the Confederacy, but to do this they would have to run counter to the feelings and demands of the mass of their subscribers and electors. Not even the nearly half-million textile workers already idle as a result of the first pinch of the cotton famine were willing to have the blockade broken on such terms. And the same was true in France. With this one blow — though few could see it yet: least of all the leader most concerned — Lincoln had shattered the main pillar of what had been the southern President's chief hope from the start. Europe would not be coming into this war.

Another change the document had wrought, though this one was uncalculated, occurring within the man himself. Sixteen years ago, back in Illinois, when an election opponent charged that he was an infidel, Lincoln refuted it with an open letter to the voters; but this was mainly a denial that he was a "scoffer," and not even then did he make any claim to being truly religious. Herndon, who saw him almost daily through that period, as well as before and after, later declared that he had never heard his partner mention the name of Jesus "but to confute the idea that he was the Christ." The fact remains that in a time when even professional soldiers called upon God in their battle reports, Lincoln seemed not to be a praying man and he never joined a church. Concerned as he had always been with logic, he had not yet reached a stage of being able to believe in what he could not comprehend. But now, in this second autumn of the war, a change began to show. In late September, when an elderly Quaker woman came to the White House to thank him for having issued the Emancipation Proclamation, Lincoln replied in a tone quite different from the one with which he had addressed her fellow Quaker the month before.

"I am glad of this interview," he told her, "and glad to know that I have your sympathy and prayers. We are indeed going through a great trial — a fiery trial. In the very responsible position in which I happen to be placed, being a humble instrument in the hands of our Heavenly Father, as I am, and as we all are, to work out his great purposes, I have desired that all my works and acts may be according to his will; and that it might be so, I have sought his aid. But if, after endeavoring to do my best in the light which he affords me, I find my efforts fail, I must believe that for some purpose unknown to me, he wills it otherwise. If I had had my way, this war would never have been commenced. If I had been allowed my way, this war would have been ended before this. But we find it still continues, and we must believe that he permits it for some wise purpose of his own, mysterious and unknown to us; and though with our limited understandings we may not be able to comprehend it, yet we cannot but believe that he who made the world still governs it."

This was a theme that would bear developing. In the proclamation itself he had omitted any reference to the Deity, and it was at the suggestion of Chase that he invoked, in the body of a later draft, "the gracious favor of Almighty God." But now, out of the midnight trials of his spirit, out of his concern for a race in bondage, out of his knowledge of the death of men in battle, something new had come to birth in Lincoln, and through him into the war. After this, as Davis said, there could be no turning back; Lincoln had sounded forth a trumpet that would never call retreat. And having sounded it, he turned in these final days of September to the inscrutable theme he had touched when he thanked the second Quaker woman for her prayers. His secretary found on the presidential desk a sheet of paper containing a single paragraph, a "Meditation on the Divine Will," which Lincoln had written with no thought of publication. Hay copied and preserved it:

> The will of God prevails. In great contests each party claims to act in accordance with the will of God. Both may be, and one must be, wrong. God cannot be for and against the same thing at the same time. In the present civil war it is quite possible that God's purpose is something different from the purpose of either party; and yet the human instrumentalities, working just as they do, are of the best adaptation to effect his purpose. I am almost ready to say that this is probably true; that God wills this contest, and wills that it shall not end yet. By his mere great power on the minds of the now contestants, he could have either saved or destroyed the Union without a human contest. Yet the contest began. And, having begun, he could give the final victory to either side any day. Yet the contest proceeds.

✕ 4 ✕

Whatever else it was or might become, whatever reactions it produced within the minds and hearts of men — including Lincoln's — the proclamation was first of all a military measure; which meant that, so far, its force was merely potential. Its application dependent on the armies of the Union, its effect would be in direct ratio to their success, 1) in driving back the Confederate invaders, and 2) in resuming the southward movement whose flow had been reversed, east and west, by the advances of Lee and Bragg into Maryland and Kentucky. The nearer of these two penetrating spearheads had been encysted and repelled by McClellan, and for this Lincoln was grateful, though he would have preferred something more in the way of pursuit than an ineffectual bloodying of the waters at Shepherdstown ford. Even this, however, was better than what he saw when he looked westward in the direction of his native state. The other spearhead was not only still deeply embedded in the vitals of Kentucky, but to Lincoln's acute distress it seemed likely to remain so. After winning by default the race for Louisville, Buell appeared to be concerned only with taking time to catch his breath; with the result that, near the end of September, Lincoln's thin-stretched patience snapped. He ordered Buell's removal from command.

His distress no doubt would have been less acute if he had known that, with or without pressure from Buell, Bragg was already considering a withdrawal. At the outset the North Carolinian had announced that he would make the "Abolition demagogues and demons... taste the bitters of invasion," but now he found his own teeth set on edge. From Bardstown, which he had reached three days before, he reported to Richmond on September 25 that his troops were resting from "the long, arduous, and exhausting march" over Muldraugh's Hill. "It is a source of deep regret that this move was necessary," he declared, "as it has enabled Buell to reach Louisville, where a very large force is now concentrated." Then he got down to the bedrock cause of his discontent: "I regret to say we are sadly disappointed at the want of action by our friends in Kentucky. We have so far received no accession to this army. General Smith has secured about a brigade — not half our losses by casualties of different kinds. We have 15,000 stand of arms and no one to use them. Unless a change occurs soon we must abandon the garden spot of Kentucky to its cupidity. The love of ease and fear of pecuniary loss are the fruitful sources of this evil."

In saying this he took his cue from Smith, who — though privately he admitted, "I can understand their fears and hesitancy; they have so much to lose" — had written him from Lexington the week before: "The Kentuckians are slow and backward in rallying to our standard. Their hearts are evidently with us, but their blue-grass and fat cattle are against us." The day after Bragg reached Bardstown — with Buell still moving northward, more or less across his flank and rear — Smith told him that he regarded "the defeat of Buell before he effects a junction with the force at Louisville as a military necessity, for Buell's army has always been the great bugbear to these people, and until [it is] defeated we cannot hope for much addition to our ranks." In other words, before the citizens would risk their lives and property in open support of the Confederates, they wanted to be assured that they would *stay* there. But to Bragg it seemed that this was putting the cart before the horse. He later explained his reluctance in a letter to his wife: "Why should I stay with my handful of brave Southern men to fight for cowards who skulked about in the dark to say to us, 'We are with you. Only whip these fellows out of our country and let us see you can protect us, and we will join you'?"

And so for a time the two Confederate commanders, both flushed with recent victories, remained precisely where they were, Smith at Lexington and Bragg at Bardstown, fifty airline miles apart, gathering supplies and issuing recruiting appeals which largely went unanswered. The former kept urging the latter to pounce on Buell, claiming that he could whip him unassisted, while he himself continued to load his wagons and round up herds of cattle. Bragg was unwilling to move on Louisville alone, and yet he was also unwilling to ask Smith to abandon the heart of the Bluegrass region by moving westward to join him. Between the two, they had arrived at a sort of impasse of indecision, behind which both were intent on the fruitful harvest they were gleaning against the day when they would retrace their steps across the barrens. What had been announced as a full-scale offensive, designed to establish and maintain the northern boundary of the Confederacy along the Ohio River, had degenerated into a giant raid.

This did not mean that Bragg abandoned all his hopes. Unwilling though he was to risk a pitched battle while Buell hugged the Louisville intrenchments, he thought there still might be a bloodless way to encourage prospective bluegrass volunteers by replacing the Unionist state government, which had fled its capital, with one that was friendly to the South. Moreover, he had the means at hand. In November of the previous year, an irregular convention had met at Russellville to declare the independence of Kentucky, establish a provisional government, and petition the Confederacy for admission. All this it did, and was accepted; Kentucky had representatives in the Confederate Congress and a star in the Confederate flag. Presently, however, when Albert Sidney Johnston's long line came unhinged at Donelson, the men who followed that star were in exile — including Provisional Governor George W. Johnson, who fell at Shiloh and was succeeded by the lieutenant governor, Richard Hawes. Hawes was now on his way north from Chattanooga, and it was Bragg's intention to inaugurate him at Frankfort. With a pro-Confederate occupying the governor's chair in the capitol, supported by a *de facto* government of Confederate sympathies, the entire political outlook would be changed; or so Bragg thought. At any rate, he considered it so thoroughly worth the effort that he decided to see it done himself, lending his personal dignity to the occasion.

Accordingly, leaving Polk in charge of the army around Bardstown, he set out for Lexington on September 28 to confer with Smith before proceeding to Frankfort. Joined by Hawes and his party two days later at Danville, he wrote Polk: "The country and the people grow better as we get into the one and arouse the other." October 1, he reached Lexington, where he arranged for Smith to move his whole army up to Frankfort for the inaugural ceremonies, two or three days later. By now, however, though he still expected much from the current political maneuver, his reaction to what he had seen during his ride through the Bluegrass was mixed. "Enthusiasm is unbounded, but recruiting at a discount," he wired Polk. "Even the women are giving reasons why individuals cannot go."

Bragg was not the only army commander displaying symptoms of discouragement at this stage of the far-flung campaign. A Cincinnati journalist, watching Buell ride north through Elizabethtown at the head of his retrograding column on September 24, was unfavorably impressed: "His dress was that of a brigadier instead of a major general. He wore a shabby straw hat, dusty coat, and had neither belt, sash or sword about him.... Though accompanied by his staff, he was not engaged in conversation with any of them, but rode silently and slowly along, noticing nothing that transpired around him.... Buell is, certainly, the most reserved, distant and unsociable of all the generals in the army. He never has a word of cheer for his men or his officers, and in turn his subordinates care little for him save to obey his orders, as machinery works in response to the bidding of the mechanic." The reporter believed that this lack of cheer and sociability on the part of the commander was the cause of the army's present gloom. McClellan, for example, had "an unaccountable something, that keeps this machinery constantly oiled and easy-running; but Buell's unsympathetic nature makes it 'squeak' like the drag wheels of a wagon."

More than the past was fretting Buell; more, even, than the present. After the lost opportunities down along the Tennessee River, after the long hot weary trudge back north to the Ohio, he was confronted with the prospect of having to fight two opponents who, inured by and rested from their recent victories, could now combine to move against him. Nor was this all. Near the end of his 250-mile withdrawal — aware that his superiors were hostile, ready to let fall the Damoclean sword of dismissal, and that his subordinates were edgy, ready to leap at his own and each other's throats — he was also suffering forebodings: forebodings which were presently borne out all too abruptly. Passing through Elizabethtown, he reached Louisville next day. Within another three days he had his whole army there. On the day after that, September 29, in the midst of a general reorganization, he was struck two knee-buckling blows, both of which fell before he had even had time to digest his breakfast.

The first was that, in a time when aggressiveness was at a considerable premium, he lost William Nelson, the most aggressive of his several major generals. He lost him because the Indiana brigadier Jefferson Davis, home from the Transmississippi on a sick leave, had come down to Louisville to assist Nelson in preparing to hold the city against Smith. Nelson was overbearing, Davis touchy; the result was a personality clash, at the climax of which the former ordered the latter out of his department. Davis went, but presently he returned, bringing the governor of Indiana with him. This was Oliver P. Morton, who also had a bone to pick with Nelson over his alleged mishandling of Hoosier volunteers during the fiasco staged at Richmond a month ago tomorrow. They accosted him in the lobby of the Galt House, Buell's Louisville headquarters, just after early breakfast. In the flare-up that ensued, Davis demanded satisfaction for last week's rudeness, and when Nelson called him an "insolent puppy," flipped a wadded calling-card in his face; whereupon Nelson laid the back of a ham-sized hand across his jaw. Davis fell back, and the burly Kentuckian turned on Morton, asking if he too had come there to insult him. Morton said he had not. Nelson started up the staircase, heading for Buell's room on the second floor. "Did you hear that damned insolent scoundrel insult me, sir?" he demanded of an acquaintance coming down. "I suppose he don't know me, sir. I'll teach him a lesson, sir." He went on up the stairs, then down the hall, and just as he reached the door of Buell's room he heard someone behind him call his name. Turning, he saw Davis standing at the head of the stairs with a pistol in his hand.

Davis had not come armed to the encounter, but after staggering back from the slap he had gone around the lobby asking bystanders for a weapon. At last he came to a certain Captain Gibson. "I always carry the article," Gibson said, producing a pistol from under his coat. Davis took it, and as he started up the stairs Gibson called after him, "It's a tranter trigger. Work light." So when Nelson turned from Buell's door and started toward him, Davis knew what to do. "Not another step farther!" he cried; and then, at a range of about eight feet, shot the big man in the chest. Nelson stopped, turned back toward Buell's door, but fell before he got there. "Send for a clergyman; I wish to be baptized," he told the men who came running at the sound of the shot. Gathering around him, they managed to lift the 300-pound giant onto a bed in a nearby room. "I have been basely murdered," he said. Half an hour later he was dead.

Buell had Davis placed in arrest, intending to try him for murder, but before he could appoint a court or even prepare to conduct an investigation — indeed, before Nelson's blood had time to dry on the rug outside his door — he found that he no longer had any authority in the matter. The second blow had landed. Halleck's order for Buell's removal, issued at Lincoln's insistence, was delivered by special courier that morning. The courier, a colonel aide of Halleck's, acting under instructions similar to the ones given in Frémont's case the year before — that is, the order was not to be delivered if Buell had fought or was about to fight a battle — had left Washington on the 24th, before Lincoln or Halleck knew the outcome of the race for Louisville. Three days later, learning that Buell had reached the Ohio ahead of Bragg, Halleck wired the colonel: "Await further orders before acting." But it was too late. At noon of the 29th the reply came back: "The dispatches are delivered. I think it is fortunate that I obeyed instructions. Much dissatisfaction with General Buell." On its heels came a wire from Buell himself: "I have received your orders... and in further obedience... I shall repair to Indianapolis."

The government thus was put in the position of having sacked the man who, in some quarters at least, was being hailed as the savior of Louisville and his home state of Ohio. The reaction was prompt. Three congressmen and a senator from the region wired that the double catastrophe of Nelson's death and Buell's supersession had produced "great regret and something of dismay.... In our judgment the removal of General Buell will do great injury to the service in Kentucky." However, the courier had carried not one message, but three: a brief note informing Buell that he was relieved, a War Department order appointing George Thomas to succeed him, and a letter warning the new commander that the general-in-chief expected "energetic operations." Thomas answered without delay: "General Buell's preparations have been completed to move against the enemy, and I therefore respectfully ask that he may be retained in command. My position is very embarrassing." Halleck replied: "You may consider the order as suspended until I can lay your dispatch before the Government and get instructions." This was a way out, and Lincoln took it; the order changing commanders was suspended, "by order of the President." Whatever doubt there was that Buell would be willing to turn the other cheek and expose himself to another buffeting was removed by the acknowledgment he sent the following day: "Out of sense of public duty I shall continue to discharge the duties of my command to the best of my ability until otherwise ordered."

That was the last day of September. By then he had completed the reorganization, incorporating the green men with the seasoned men — seasoned, that is, by marching, if not by fighting; his army still had never fought a battle on its own — for a total of better than 75,000 effectives. This was half again more than were with Bragg and Smith, he knew, but he was also aware that, except for the few recruits they had managed to attract in the Bluegrass, their troops were veterans to a man, whereas no less than a third of his own had barely progressed beyond the manual of arms. Whatever qualms proceeded from this, on the first day of October he moved out. Too busy to concern himself with Nelson's slayer or spare the officers for a court to try him, he recommended that Halleck appoint a commission to look into the case. But nothing came of this, not even the filing of charges. Later that month a Louisville grand jury indicted Davis for manslaughter, but nothing came of this either; he was admitted to bail and released. Presently he was back on duty, having acquired a reputation as a man whom it was advisable not to provoke.

Buell had ten divisions, nine of them distributed equally among three corps led by major generals, with Thomas as second in command of the whole. The march was southeast, out of Louisville toward Bardstown, and the army made it in three columns, a corps in each, commanded (left to right) by Alexander McCook, T. L. Crittenden, and Charles Gilbert. Bragg was in that direction, Smith at Frankfort. Buell figured his chances were good if he could keep them divided and thus encounter them one at a time; less good — in fact, not good at all — if he had to face them both at once. So he feinted toward the latter place with a division detached from McCook, supported by the large 15,000-man tenth division, composed almost entirely of recruits under Brigadier General Ebenezer Dumont. That way, Buell would not only cover Louisville; but also, by confusing his opponents as to his true objective, he might keep them from combining against him in the battle he was seeking at last. After four months of building and repairing roads and railroads, tediously advancing and hastily backtracking, enduring constant prodding from above, he was about to fight.

★ ★ ★

Down in Mississippi all this while, Van Dorn and Price had been pursuing separate courses, neither of which had produced anything substantial even in the way of a diversion. Not only were they independent of each other; Van Dorn was also independent of Bragg, and now that he (and Isaac Brown) had accomplished the salvation of Vicksburg, the diminutive Mississippian had larger things in mind than keeping Grant amused along the lower Tennessee border while Bragg got all the glory in Kentucky. After the loss of the *Arkansas* and Breckinridge's repulse at Baton Rouge, Van Dorn had abandoned his "Ho! for New Orleans" notion and shifted his gaze upriver, reverting to his earlier slogan: "St Louis, then huzza!" His plan was to swing through West Tennessee, skirting Memphis to pounce on Paducah, from which point he would move "wherever circumstances might dictate." So when Price, mindful of Bragg's instructions to harry the Federals in

North Mississippi, called on his former chief for aid, Van Dorn replied that he would rather have Price join *him*. Price declined. Nettled, Van Dorn invoked his seniority and appealed directly to the Secretary of War: "I ought to have command of the movements of Price, that there may be concert of action.... Bragg is out of reach; I refer to you." Davis himself wired back: "Your rank makes you the commander, and such I supposed were the instructions of General Bragg."

Van Dorn had what he wanted. But Price had already moved on his own, striking for Iuka, twenty-odd miles down the Memphis & Charleston Railroad from Corinth, the fortified eastern anchor of Grant's contracted line. September 14, as Price's nearly 15,000 troops approached, the badly outnumbered Union garrison retreated in haste, leaving a quantity of confiscated cotton and army stores behind. Price burned the one and appropriated the other. It was now his intention to march on Middle Tennessee, to which Bragg informed him the Federals were retiring; but finding that this was not entirely the case — that Grant, though he had sent three of his five left-flank divisions to Buell, still had the other two near Iuka under Rosecrans — he hesitated to leave such a substantial force in his rear. While he was pondering this dilemma and distributing the captured stores, the problem was solved by the arrival of a courier from Van Dorn's headquarters at Holly Springs, sixty miles west of Corinth, informing Price that the President had authorized his fellow Mississippian to order a junction of the two armies, under his command, for whatever "concert of action" he had in mind.

The Missourian's intention was to stay in Iuka until he heard from Van Dorn just what it was he wanted him to do; then he would move out, more or less at his leisure, in whatever direction Van Dorn advised in order to combine the two commands for a resumption of the offensive. However, this was overlooking Grant's plans in the matter — and Grant intended not only to interrupt Price's leisure, but also to destroy him. In fact, he said later, "It looked to me that, if Price would remain in Iuka until we could get there, his annihilation was inevitable."

By "we" he meant himself and Rosecrans, whose two divisions contained about 9000 effectives, and he also meant Ord, who would advance from Corinth with another two divisions, leaving a strong garrison to man the fortifications in case Van Dorn pushed east from Holly Springs for an assault while he was gone. Price had 15,000 men; Rosecrans and Ord had 17,000 between them. This in itself was by no means enough of a preponderance to assure the annihilation Grant expected, but he had designed a tactical convergence to accomplish that result. Ord would swing north and descend on Iuka from that direction, while Rosecrans came up from the south. Once Price had his attention thoroughly fixed on the former, the latter would fall on his rear; so that the rebels, demoralized and cut off from all avenues of escape, would have to choose between death and capitulation. Advised of the plan, both of Grant's subordinate commanders were as optimistic as their chief, though Rosecrans warned: "Price is an old woodpecker," meaning that he would be hard to take by surprise.

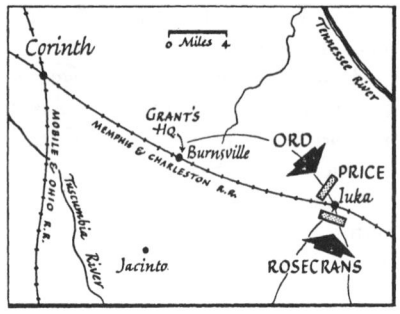

Accordingly, on September 17 (while Lee, with his back to the Potomac, was defending Sharpsburg against McClellan, and Wilder, with his back to the Green, was surrendering Munfordville to Bragg) Ord moved twelve miles down the Memphis & Charleston to Burnsville, where Grant established headquarters, having instructed Rosecrans to concentrate at Jacinto, eight miles south. From these two points, the four divisions were to push on to within striking distance of Iuka the following day in order to deliver their sequential north-south attacks soon after dawn of the 19th. But that was not to be. Rosecrans reported that one of his divisions had been so badly delayed that he could not be in position before midafternoon of the appointed day. Ord moved up on schedule, however, establishing contact with the Confederate cavalry outposts, and Grant used the waiting time to engage in a bit of psychological warfare.

Last night he had received from the telegraph superintendent at Cairo a dispatch concerning the Battle of Antietam. According to this gentleman, the news was very good indeed: "Both sides engaged until 4 p.m. at which time Hooker gained position, flanked rebels, and threw them into disorder. Longstreet and his entire division prisoners. General Hill killed. Entire rebel army of Virginia destroyed, Burnside having reoccupied Harpers Ferry and cut off retreat.... Latest advices say entire rebel army must be captured or killed, as Potomac is rising and our forces pressing the enemy continually." Grant sent the message forward to Ord, who passed it on to the Confederates this morning under a flag of truce. "I think this battle decides the war finally," he explained in a covering note, "and that upon being satisfied of its truth General Price or whoever commands here will avoid useless bloodshed and lay down his arms. There is not the slightest doubt of the truth of the dispatch in my hand." The reply was prompt. Formally employing the third person, Price said flatly that he did not believe the report was true, but "that if the facts were as stated in those dispatches they would only move him and his soldiers to greater exertions in behalf of their country, and that neither he nor they will ever lay down their arms — as humanely suggested by General Ord — until the independence of the Confederate States shall have been acknowledged by the United States."

Psychological warfare having failed to produce the desired result, Grant told Ord to go ahead with the opening phase, diverting Price's attention northward, though he warned: "[Rosecrans] is behind where we expected. Do not be too rapid in your advance... unless it should be found that the enemy are evacuating." Ord moved forward, encountering light resistance, but since there still was no word that the southward escape route was blocked, Grant told him to halt within four miles of the town "and there await sounds of an engagement between Rosecrans and the enemy before engaging the latter." Ord did so, and the afternoon wore on. About 6 o'clock he received a message written two hours before by the commander of his lead division: "For the last twenty minutes there has been a dense smoke arising from the direction of Iuka. I conclude that the enemy are evacuating and destroying the stores." Ord pushed forward tentatively, but still hearing no sound of conflict from the south, halted his troops in line of battle, and there they remained through twilight into darkness, a northwest wind blowing hard against their backs. His total loss for the day, in both divisions, was 1 man wounded.

The smoke had been beyond, not in the town, and it came from Price's guns, not his stores. Just as Grant had intended, the "old woodpecker" had concentrated northward against Ord; but about 2 o'clock, learning that another Union column was approaching from the south, he shifted one brigade in that direction and presently followed it with another. Soon afterwards, since Ord seemed disinclined to press the issue, he called for a third. Before it got there, the fight with Rosecrans had begun. Seeing the lead blue division waver, Price ordered a charge that drove the Federals back on their supports and captured nine of their guns. Upwind, Ord heard nothing. Grant, in fact, did not suspect that his other column was at hand until next morning, when he received a note Rosecrans had written the night before. Headed "Two miles south of Iuka," it reported that he had "met the enemy in force just above this point.... The ground is horrid, unknown to us, and no room for development.... Push on into them until we can have time to do something." The convergence, though delayed, had worked exactly as Grant planned it; but instead of producing a victory, as expected, had resulted in a repulse which, though it cost him nine guns and nearly 800 soldiers, gained him nothing.

An ill wind had blown no good, but now at least he knew he had both of his columns in position north and south of the town, ready to put the squeeze on Price, who was boxed in. Or so Grant thought when he told Ord at 8.35 that morning, "Get your troops up and attack as soon as possible." Ord did so, banging away with his guns as he advanced, and so did Rosecrans: only to find that they were converging on emptiness. Price — whose wagons had been packed for the move before the Federals appeared — had evacuated Iuka during the night, taking a southeast road which Rosecrans left unguarded. At Grant's insistence, the latter took up the pursuit, hoping at least to recapture the stores being hauled away, but abandoned it when he ran into an ambush eight miles out. All Grant's strategic pains had netted him was an empty town and the task of burying the dead of both armies. Rosecrans had lost 790 men, Price 535, and the latter had gotten away with all his spoils.

Ord meanwhile was hurrying back west by rail, in case Van Dorn had left Holly Springs and crossed the Hatchie River for a leap at Corinth. The prospect of this held no dismay for Rosecrans. In fact, he welcomed it. Whatever blunders he had committed against Price, he looked forward to a contest with Van Dorn. They had been classmates, West Point '56; he had finished fourth from the top, the Southerner fourth from the bottom, and Rosecrans was eager to extend this proof of his superiority beyond the academic. Back at Jacinto that night, he wired Grant: "If you can let me know that there is a good opportunity to cross the railroad and march on Holly Springs to cut off the forces of Buck Van Dorn I will be in readiness to take everything. If we could get them across the Hatchie they would be clean up the spout."

He was about to be accommodated in his desire for a bloody reunion east of the Hatchie, although not in the manner he imagined, since it would involve a change of roles. Instead of the hunter, he would be the hunted.

Van Dorn had set aside the elaborate scheme for a march on Paducah, which would expose both of his flanks to attack by superior numbers, and had decided to precede it with a much simpler, though in its way no less daring, operation. He was planning a direct assault on Corinth. That place, he saw now, was the linchpin of the Federal defenses in North Mississippi. Once it was cracked and unseated, he could move at will on Memphis or he could revert to his earlier plan for a march on St Louis, gobbling up blue detachments as he went. "We may take them in detail if they are not wary," he explained in a dispatch that reached Price the day before the Battle of Iuka; "but once combined we will make a successful campaign, clear out West Tennessee, and then ——"

His new plan, outlined in this and other messages written after Price's hairbreadth escape from Iuka with the aid of a friendly wind, was for their two commands to unite at Ripley, just west of the Hatchie, then move north, up that bank of the river, as if against Bolivar. However, this would only be a feint, serving to immobilize Grant's reserve force under Hurlbut at that point. When they reached the Memphis &

Charleston at Pocahontas, they would turn sharp right and drive for Corinth, twenty miles away, blocking the path of reinforcements from the northwest and striking before Rosecrans had time to bring in troops from the east for its defense. Combined, Van Dorn and Price had 22,000 men, while in Corinth, the former explained, there were no more than 15,000, the rest — about 8000 — being posted out toward Burnsville and Jacinto, guarding against attack from that direction. These odds, he said, gave him "a reasonable hope of success" in driving the defenders from their guns and intrenchments and capturing the lot, together with the supplies being collected for an advance.

Price, who had been associated with the Mississippian in a similar venture against Curtis seven months before in the wilds of Arkansas — with results barely short of disastrous — was not so sure; but at any rate, after eight weeks of being hamstrung by conflicting orders and exposed to ridicule, he was glad to be doing *some*thing. Back in his home state, the 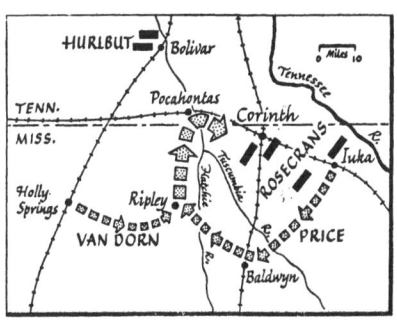 290-pound Missourian had been nicknamed "Old Skedad" by Unionist editors, one of whom remarked that "as a racer he has seen few equals for his weight." To cap the climax, rumors had been spread that he was a West Pointer. After these and other such vexations (although the educational slander was promptly refuted by a friendly correspondent who assured the public that Price "owes his success to practical good sense and hard fighting. He never attended a military school in his life") he was glad of a chance to move against the enemy, even though Van Dorn himself, sanguine as he was by nature, characterized their "hope of success" as no more than "reasonable."

Accordingly, both commands reached Ripley on September 28: Van Dorn's one division under Mansfield Lovell — who, like his chief, was out to redeem misfortune, New Orleans bulking even larger in this respect than Elkhorn Tavern — and Price's two under Brigadier Generals Dabney Maury and Louis Hébert. Lovell began the northward march that afternoon, followed by Maury and Hébert the next morning. They had fifty miles to go, thirty up to Pocahontas, then twenty down to Corinth, all along a single narrow road through densely wooded country, bone-dry after the summer-long drouth. The final lap would be the hardest, not only because it called for speed and accurate timing to achieve concerted action and surprise, but also because, after they crossed the Hatchie, there would be no water until they reached Corinth, where they would have to fight for it and win or else go thirsty. Nevertheless, according to Van Dorn, "the troops were in fine spirits, and the whole Army of West Tennessee" — so he called it, anticipating the movement which would follow victory — "seemed eager to emulate the armies of the Potomac and of Kentucky." Like their leaders, the soldiers were out to undo past reverses. Van Dorn himself reported: "No army ever marched to battle with prouder steps, more hopeful countenances, or with more courage."

October 1 the van approached Pocahontas and, ending the feint at Bolivar, swung east. Encountering cavalry here and infantry the following day at Chewalla, ten miles short of Corinth, Van Dorn knew that whatever the element of secrecy could accomplish was behind him. From here on in, Rosecrans was forewarned. The Confederates pressed on, skirmishing as they advanced, and next morning, October 3, two miles short of their objective, came upon a heavy line of Federal infantry occupying the intrenchments Beauregard — and, incidentally, Van Dorn himself — had dug along the crescent ridge to hold off Halleck, back in May. Unlike Halleck, the Mississippian put his troops into assault formation and sent them forward without delay: Lovell on the right, astride the Memphis & Charleston, and Maury and Hébert beyond him, reaching over to the Mobile & Ohio, so that as they moved east and south the three divisions would converge on the crossing. Whooping, the graybacks started up the ridge after the bluecoats firing down at them from the crest, and that was the beginning of what turned out to be a two-day battle which was one of the most violent of the war.

The reason it stretched to two days, despite its having been designed as a slashing attack that would crumple in a matter of hours whatever stood in its path, was that Rosecrans was not only braced for the shock but actually outnumbered his assailants. For the wrong reasons, he had done the right things; and what was more he had done them mostly on his own. Grant, following the post-Donelson pattern — the Shiloh pattern, too, for that matter — had gone off to St Louis to confer with Curtis about the possibility of bringing reinforcements across the river from Helena, and, failing in this, had not returned to his headquarters at Jackson, Tennessee, until Van Dorn and Price had already begun their northward march out of Ripley. Supposing — as Van Dorn intended for him to suppose — that the rebels were moving against Hurlbut at Bolivar, Rosecrans reacted in a fashion which his opponent had not foreseen. That is, he called in his troops from Burnsville and Jacinto, two full divisions of them, and prepared to go to Hurlbut's assistance; so that when the Confederates swung east at Pocahontas, ending their feint and driving hard in his direction, the Corinth commander was ready for them. Instead of catching 15,000 Federals unaware, Van Dorn and his 22,000 were moving against an army which had not only been consolidated, but also in fact outnumbered his own by more than a thousand men.

Two Advances; Two Retreats

As if this was not advantage enough, Rosecrans had his four divisions posted behind a formidable double line of intrenchments. Three were thrust forward along the northward ridge, where Beauregard had done their digging for them, and one was held in reserve to man the works recently constructed along the northern and western perimeter of the town itself. Van Dorn and Price struck hard. Advancing with thirsty desperation, the Confederates threw the defenders off the outer ridge soon after midday, taking several pieces of artillery in the process. But the Federals were stubborn. Yielding each to only the heaviest pressure, they took up four separate positions between the two fortified lines. The sun was near the land line and the attackers were near exhaustion by the time they came within musket range of the gun-bristled outskirts of Corinth. Regretfully, while his men dispersed to draw water from the captured Union wells, Van Dorn deferred the coup de grâce — or anyhow what he conceived as such — till morning.

Losses on both sides had been heavy. Rosecrans (though he was later to claim, like Van Dorn, that another hour of daylight would have meant victory on the first day of battle) was thankful for the respite. That morning, with the graybacks bearing down on him, he had complained to Grant at Jackson: "Our men did not act or fight well." Now, though, he felt better. "If they fight us tomorrow," he wired Grant half an hour before midnight, "I think we shall whip them." Then, bethinking himself of the unpredictable nature of his classmate Buck Van Dorn, he added: "If they go to attack you we shall advance upon them."

Van Dorn, however, was through with trickery, double envelopments and the like — at least for the present. His blood was up; it was Rosecrans he was after, and he was after him in the harshest, most straightforward way imaginable. Today he would depend not on deception to complete the destruction begun the day before, but on the rapid point-blank fire of his guns and the naked valor of his infantry. Before dawn, October 4, his artillery opened on the Federal inner line, which was prompt in reply. "It was grand," one Union brigadier declared. "The different calibers, metals, shapes, and distances of the guns caused the sounds to resemble the chimes of old Rome when all her bells rang out." This continued until after sunrise, when a long lull succeeded the uproar, punctuated by sharpshooters banging away at whatever showed a head. Rosecrans was curious but cautious, wondering what was afoot out there beyond the screen of trees. "Feel them," he told one regimental commander, "but don't get into their fingers." "I'll feel them!" the colonel said, and led a sally. Entering the woods, the regiment was received with a crash of musketry and fell back, badly cut up, its colonel having been shot through the neck and captured. All that Rosecrans learned from this was that Van Dorn was still there, in strength.

Shortly after 10 o'clock he received even more emphatic proof that this was the case; for at that hour Van Dorn launched his all-or-

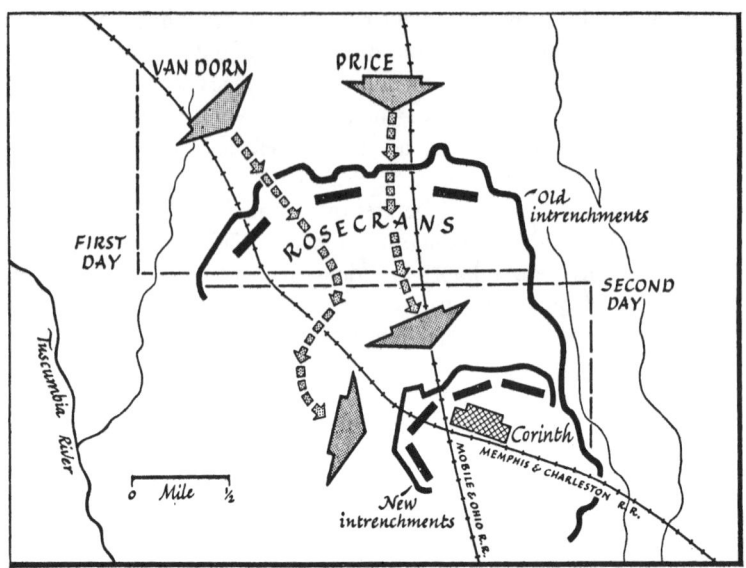

nothing assault. Price's two divisions began it, surging forward in echelon, to be met with a blast of cannonfire. The left elements suffered a sudden and bloody repulse, but three regiments in the center achieved a breakthrough when the Union cannoneers fell back from their guns in a panic that spread to the supporting infantry. Yelling men in butternut burst into the streets of Corinth, driving snipers out of houses by firing through the windows, swept past Rosecrans' deserted headquarters and on to the depot beyond the railroad crossing. At that point, however, finding their advance unsupported and the Federals standing firm, they turned and fought their way back out again. On the far right, pinned down by heavy fire from a ridge to its immediate front, Lovell's division gained no ground at all. The day was hot, 94° in the shade; panting and thirsty, the attackers hugged what cover they could find. From time to time they would rise and charge, urged on by their officers, but after the original short-lived penetration they had no luck at all. The bluecoats stood firm. "Our lines melted under their fire like snow in thaw," one Confederate afterwards recalled. Perhaps the hardest fighting of the day occurred in front of Battery Robinette, just north of the Memphis & Charleston Railroad, a three-gun redan protected by a five-foot ditch which overflowed with dead and dying Texans and Arkansans within two hours. By then it was noon and Van Dorn knew his long-shot gamble had failed. "Exhausted from loss of sleep, wearied from hard marching and fighting, companies and regiments without officers," he later reported, "our troops — let no one censure them — gave way. The day was lost."

How lost it was he would not know until he counted the casualties he had suffered, and weighed them against the number he had inflicted: 4233 Confederates, as compared to 2520 Federals, with well over one third of the former listed as "missing." Price wept as he watched his thinned ranks withdraw, the men's faces sullen with the knowledge that hard fighting had won them nothing more than the right to stitch the name of another defeat on their battle flags. By 1 o'clock they were in full retreat — unpursued. Instead of pressing their rear, Rosecrans was riding along his battered line to deny in person a rumor that he had been slain. "Old Rosy," his men called him, a red-faced man in his middle forties, with the profile of a Roman orator. At Battery Robinette he drew rein, dismounted, bared his head, and told his soldiers, most of whom were Ohioans like himself: "I stand in the presence of brave men, and I take my hat off to you." Van Dorn meanwhile had stopped for the night at Chewalla, from which he had launched his first attack the day before. Next morning, finding the Hatchie crossing blocked by 8000 fresh troops sent down from Bolivar, he fought a holding action in which about 600 men fell on each side, then turned back south and crossed by a road leading west out of Corinth, which Rosecrans — as at Iuka — had left open. Stung into vigor, Old Rosy at last took up the pursuit, complaining bitterly when Grant called him off. Van Dorn returned to Holly Springs by way of Ripley, accompanied by Price.

The brief, vicious campaign was over. What had been intended as a third prong in the South's late-summer early-fall offensive had snapped off short as soon as it was launched. Including the holding action on the Hatchie, it had gained the Confederacy nothing except the infliction of just over 3000 casualties on the Federals in North Mississippi, and for this Van Dorn had paid with nearly 5000 of his own. A cry went up that the nation could no longer afford to pay in blood for the failure of his thick-skulled fights and harebrained maneuvers. Nor were the protests limited in reference to his military judgment. The man himself was under fire. "He is regarded as the source of all our woes," a senator from his native state complained, "and disaster, it is prophesied, will attend us so long as he is connected with this army. The atmosphere is dense with horrid narratives of his negligence, whoring, and drunkenness, for the truth of which I cannot vouch; but it is so fastened in the public belief that an acquittal by a court-martial of angels would not relieve him of the charge." These and other allegations — specifically, that he had been drunk on duty at Corinth, that he had neglected his wounded on the retreat, and that he had failed to provide himself with a map of the country — resulted in a court of inquiry, called for by the accused himself. The court, by a unanimous decision, cleared him of all blame, adding that the charges "are not only not proved, but they are disproved."

Thus were Van Dorn's critics officially answered and rebuked. However, the best answer, although unofficial, had already been made for him on the field of battle itself, shortly after his departure. Near Battery Robinette, having bared his head "in the presence of brave men," Rosecrans came upon an Arkansas lieutenant, shot through the foot and propped against a tree. He offered him a drink of water. "Thank you, General; one of your men just gave me some," the Confederate replied. When the Federal commander, glancing around at the heaped and scattered corpses in their butternut rags, remarked that there had been "pretty hot fighting here," the rebel Westerner agreed. "Yes, General, you licked us good," he said. "But we gave you the best we had in the ranch."

★ ★ ★

The best they had was not enough; but even if it had served the Mississippi general's purpose, it would have been of small help to Bragg, three hundred airline miles northeastward in Kentucky. At the same hour of the same day that Van Dorn broke off the fight at Corinth and retreated — 1 p.m. October 4 — the boom of Union guns lobbing shells into the outskirts of Frankfort disrupted the inaugural ceremonies and ended in midsentence the address being delivered by Confederate Governor Hawes, who had been sworn in at high noon and whose *de facto* tenure of office thus was brief.

Despite a shortage of cavalry for outpost work and scouting — Forrest had been sent back to Middle Tennessee to raise another new brigade, and John Morgan was off chasing his Federal namesake across the barrens — Bragg was not entirely surprised at this development. Nor was he in any sense dismayed. In fact, having been forewarned, he had expressed the hope that Buell would attempt just such a maneuver. Informed two days before, October 2, that a blue column was moving east from Louisville toward Shelbyville and Frankfort, he passed the word along to Polk, whom he had left in command of the four divisions around Bardstown while he himself joined Kirby Smith to attend the inauguration at the capital. "It may be a reconnaissance," he added, "but should it be a real attack we have them.... With Smith in front and our gallant army on the flank I see no hope for Buell if he is rash enough to come out. I only fear it is not true.... Hold yourself informed by scouts toward Shelbyville, and if you discover a heavy force that has moved on Frankfort strike without further orders." A few hours later, more positive evidence was at hand, and Bragg followed this first message with a second: "The enemy is certainly advancing on Frankfort. Put your whole available force in motion ... and strike him in flank and rear. If we can combine our movements he is certainly lost."

Couriers taking these messages to Bardstown — Pennsylvania's Stephen Foster's Old Kentucky Home — passed en route a courier bringing a dispatch Polk had written that same morning. He too was being advanced on, he declared: not by a single Federal column, but by three, all moving southeast out of Louisville on as many different roads.

His original instructions, in the event that he was menaced by a superior force, had been to fall back eastward. Accordingly, he told Bragg, "I shall keep the enemy well under observation, and my action shall be governed by the circumstances which shall be developed. If an opportunity presents itself I will strike. If it shall be clearly inexpedient to do that I will, according to your suggestion, fall back on Harrodsburg and Danville on the roads indicated by you, with a view to a concentration [of both armies]." Pointedly, he observed in closing: "It seems to me we are too much scattered."

Next morning, October 3, having received Bragg's two messages of the day before, instructing him to strike the flank and rear of the column moving against Frankfort, he replied: "The last twenty-four hours have developed a condition of things on my front and left flank which I shadowed forth in my last note to you, which makes compliance with this order not only eminently inexpedient but impractical. I have called a conference of wing and division commanders to whom I have submitted the matter, and find that they unanimously indorse my views of what is demanded. I shall therefore pursue a different course, assured that when facts are submitted to you you will justify my decision." Reverting to his original instructions to fall back eastward, he added: "The head of my column will move this evening."

Bragg concurred: at least for the time being. Receiving Polk's dispatch at Frankfort during the early hours of inauguration day, he replied: "Concentrate your force in front of Harrodsburg.... Smith's whole force is concentrating here and we will strike the enemy just as soon as we can concentrate." Mindful of the effect the retrograde movement might have on the troops, he admonished the bishop-general: "Keep the men in heart by assuring them it is not a retreat, but a concentration for a fight. We can and must defeat them." Near midday he followed this with further assurance: "We shall put our governor in power soon and then I propose to seek the enemy." Just then, however, the ceremony was interrupted by the boom of guns. The enemy, it appeared, had sought *him*. So Bragg tacked a postscript on the message: "1.30 p.m. Enemy in heavy force advancing on us; only 12 miles out. Shall destroy bridges and retire on Harrodsburg for concentration and then strike. Reach that point as soon as possible."

Throughout the greater part of this exchange, despite the sudden and apparently unpremeditated changes of decision and direction — which came full circle and brought him back to the start before the finish — Bragg had given an effective imitation of a man who not only knew where he was going, but also knew what he was going to do when he got there; "concentrate" and "strike" were the predominant verbs, especially the former. But the truth was, he was badly confused, whether he knew it or not. Buell's feint toward Frankfort, led by Brigadier General Joshua Sill's division and supported by the oversized division of green men under Dumont, succeeded admirably: Bragg, being directly confronted, considered this the major Federal effort and, discounting Polk's specific warning to the contrary, underrated the strength of the three-corps column moving down toward Bardstown.

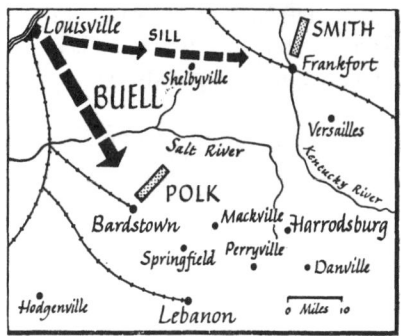

Not that Buell himself had no problems. Though his army was large — 55,000 soldiers in one column, 22,000 in the other; the former alone was larger than Bragg's and Smith's, even if they had been combined, which they had not — size also had its drawbacks, particularly on the march, as he was rapidly finding out. Besides, at least one third of this 77,000-man collection were recruits, so-called Squirrel Hunters, rallied to the call of startled governors who had suddenly found the war approaching their Ohio River doorsteps. A gloomy-minded general, and Buell was certainly that, would be inclined to suppose that such troops had established their all-time pattern of behavior at the Battle of Richmond, five short weeks ago: in which case, panic being highly contagious in combat, they were likely to prove more of a liability than an asset. Nor was this inexperience limited to the ranks. The corps commanders themselves, raised to their present positions during the hasty reorganization at Louisville the week before, were doubtful quantities at best, untested by the pressure of command responsibility in battle. Crittenden had dignity, but according to a correspondent who knew and respected him, his talents were mainly those of a country lawyer. In his favor was a fervid devotion to the Union, no doubt intensified by the fact that his brother had chosen the opposite side. McCook, on the other hand, was "an overgrown schoolboy" according to the same reporter. Barely thirty-one, he had a rollicking manner and was something of a wag, and as such he irritated more often than he cheered. By all odds, however, the strangest of the three, at least in the method by which he had arrived at his present eminence, was Gilbert. A regular army captain of infantry, he had happened to be in Louisville when Bragg started north, and the department commander at Cincinnati, alarmed and badly in need of professional help, issued the order: "Captain C. C. Gilbert, First Infantry, U.S. Army, is hereby appointed a major general of volunteers, subject to the approval of the President of the United States." Lincoln in time appointed him a brigadier, subject to confirmation by Congress — which decided after some debate that he was only a captain after all. For the present, though, he was apparently a bona fide major general, and as such he received the corps command to which his rank entitled him.

These, then, were the troops with which Buell was expected to fling Bragg's and Smith's veterans out of Kentucky, and these were the ranking officers on whom he depended for execution of his orders. In partial compensation, there was Thomas; but Old Pap, as he was coming to be called, had never been one to offer unsolicited advice. Officially designated as second in command of the whole army, for the present he was riding with Crittenden's column as a sort of super corps commander. This arrangement not only placed Buell's most competent subordinate in a superfluous position and beyond his immediate reach, but what was more it led in time to trouble.

The Confederates having evacuated Bardstown on the 4th, the Federals entered or by-passed the place that evening and slogged on down the dusty roads toward Mackville, Springfield, and Lebanon, encountering only rebel horsemen who faded back whenever contact was established. This was satisfactory, but there was a disturbing lack of coördination between the three columns with which Buell was groping for Bragg as if with widespread fingers. On the left, McCook wrote Thomas, who was with Crittenden on the right, twenty miles away: "Please keep me advised of your movements, so that I can coöperate. I am in blissful ignorance." Another lack was more immediately painful, at least to the marchers themselves. One Illinois volunteer later recalled that after the summer-long drouth, which had stretched into fall, creeks and even rivers were "either totally dry or shrunken into little, heated, tired-looking threads of water, brackish and disagreeable to taste and smell." Brackish or not, water was much on the men's minds, as well as on the minds of their commanders. Pushing on through Springfield, Buell ordered a concentration near Perryville on the 7th. There was water there — in Doctor's Creek, a tributary of Chaplin River, which in turn was a tributary of the Salt. There were also rebels there, or so he heard, in strength. After four hard months of marching hundreds of miles, sneered and sniped at by the authorities much of the time, the Army of the Ohio was about to come to grips with the gray-clad authors of its woes.

They did come to grips that evening, or nearly to grips — part of them at any rate. McCook, coming down through Mackville, was delayed by a bad road and went into camp eight miles short of his objective. Crittenden, coming up from Lebanon, was delayed by a detour Thomas authorized him to make in search of water; he too had to stop for the night, ten miles short of the designated point of concentration. Only Gilbert's central column, trudging east from Springfield by the direct route, reached the field on schedule. His troops marched in near sundown, tired and thirsty, but found Doctor's Creek defended by snipers on a ridge across the way. Sorely in need of the water standing in pools along the creek bed, the bluecoats launched a vigorous downhill attack. Repulsed, they fell back toward the sunset, re-formed, and tried again, this time by the light of a full moon rising beyond the ridge where enemy riflemen lay concealed to catch them in their sights. Again they were repulsed. Exhausted by these added exertions, and thirstier than ever, they made a dry camp in the woods, tantalized by the thought of water gleaming silver in the moonlight just ahead.

It was an inauspicious beginning. What was more, Buell himself was indisposed, having been lamed and badly shaken up as a result of being thrown by a fractious horse that afternoon. But he was not discouraged. He had suffered and sweltered too much and too long, all through the long summer into fall, to be anything but relieved by the thought that he had Bragg's whole army at last within reach of the widespread fingers now being clenched into a fist. The feint at Frankfort having served its purpose, Sill was on the way south to rejoin McCook, who himself had only a short way left to come. Off to the southwest, Crittenden too was within easy marching distance. To make certain that his army was concentrated without further delay, Buell had his chief of staff send a message to Thomas, urging him to be on the road by 3 a.m. Bragg had been brought to bay at Perryville, he told him, adding: "We expect to attack and carry the place tomorrow."

Buell's estimate of the enemy situation, particularly in regard to the strength of the force which had denied his men a drink from Doctor's Creek, was considerably mistaken. Bragg's whole army was not there on the opposite ridge; only a part of it was — so far only half, in fact — which in turn was the result of a mistake in the opposite direction. Still confused by the feint at Frankfort, Bragg assumed that only a part of Buell's army was approaching Perryville. And thus was achieved a curious balance of error: Buell thought he was facing Bragg's whole army, whereas it was only a part, and Bragg thought he was facing only a part of Buell's army, whereas it was (or soon would be) the whole. This compound misconception not only accounted for much of the confusion that ensued, but it was also the result of much confusion in the immediate past.

At Harrodsburg that morning Bragg had issued a confidential circular, calling for a concentration of both armies near Versailles, south of Frankfort, west of Lexington, and east of the Kentucky River. Polk was to move his two divisions there at once, joining Kirby Smith, while Hardee followed, delaying the enemy column as he fell back. It was all quite carefully worked out; each commander was told just what to do. But no sooner was it completed than Bragg received a dispatch Polk had written late the night before, reporting that he had told Hardee "to ascertain, if possible, the strength of the enemy which may be covered by his advance. I cannot think it large." Polk meant by this that he did not think the Federal covering force, or advance guard, was large; but Bragg took him to mean the main body. Accordingly, he decided to have Hardee give the enemy column a rap that would slow it down and afford him the leisure he needed to cross the Salt and Kentucky Rivers and effect the concentration. Polk was instructed to have one of his divisions continue its march to join Smith beyond the river, but to return to Perryville with the other in order to reinforce Hardee for this purpose. "Give the enemy battle immediately," Bragg wrote. "Rout him, and then move to our support at Versailles."

This was written at sundown, just as the Federals began their fight for the water west of Perryville. A copy of it reached Hardee, together with the confidential circular, just after the second repulse. The *Tactics* author read them both, and while he approved of the circular, finding it militarily sound, he was horrified by the instructions given Polk to divide his wing and precipitate a battle in which Bragg would employ only three of the four divisions of one of the armies moving toward a proper concentration. So horrified was Hardee, in fact, by this violation of the principles he had outlined in his book on infantry tactics, that he retired at once to his tent and wrote the commanding general a personal letter of advice:

> Permit me, from the friendly relations so long existing between us, to write you plainly. Do not scatter your forces. There is one rule in our profession which should never be forgotten; it is to throw the masses of your troops on the fractions of the enemy. The movement last proposed will divide your army and each may be defeated, whereas by keeping them united success is certain. If it be your policy to strike the enemy at Versailles, take your whole force with you and make the blow effective; if, on the contrary, you should decide to strike the army in front of me, first let that be done with a force which will make success certain. Strike with your whole strength first to the right then to the left. I could not sleep quietly tonight without giving expression to these views. Whatever you decide to do will meet my hearty co-operation.

He signed it, "Your sincere friend," then added a postscript: "If you wish my opinion, it is that in view of the position of your depots you ought to strike this force first," and gave it to an officer courier for immediate delivery.

Three hours would suffice to bring an answer, but there was none: except that Polk arrived in the night with one division, which in itself was a sort of negative answer, and assumed command by virtue of his rank. The Confederate over-all strength was 16,000 men. What the Federal strength was, neither Polk nor Hardee knew, though they suspected that it was considerably larger than their own. At earliest dawn, while they were discussing whether to attack as Bragg had ordered, Buell solved the problem for them by attacking first.

Once more it was a dash for water, and this time it succeeded. Where other units had failed the night before, Brigadier General Philip H. Sheridan, commanding a division under Gilbert, went forward with one of his brigades in the gray twilight before sunrise, October 8, and seized not only a stretch of the creek itself, with several of its precious pools of water, but also the dominant heights beyond, throwing the rebel snipers back and posting his own men along the ridge to prevent their return. A thirty-one-year-old bandy-legged Ohioan with heavy, crescent-shaped eyebrows, cropped hair, and a head as round as a pot, he looked more like a Mongolian than like the Irishman he was. Less than ten years out of West Point, he had received his star two weeks ago and had been a division commander just nine days, previous to which time he had been a commissary captain under Halleck for six months until by a fluke he secured a promotion to colonel and command of a Michigan cavalry regiment which he led with such dash, in pursuit of Beauregard after the Corinth evacuation, that in late July five of his superiors, including Rosecrans, recommended his promotion with the indorsement: "He is worth his weight in gold."

Now in Kentucky, having received his star, he was out to prove the validity of their claim, as well as his right to further advancement. Other inducements there were, too. The son of immigrant parents — born in County Cavan, some said, or en route in mid-Atlantic, according to others, though Sheridan himself denied this: not only because he was strenuously American and preferred to think of himself as having sprung from native soil, but also because he learned in time that no person who drew his first breath outside its limits could ever become President of the United States — he had an intense dislike of Southerners, particularly those with aristocratic pretensions, and had suffered a year's suspension from the Academy for threatening with a bayonet a Virginia upperclassman whose tone he found offensive on the drill field. He was a man in a hurry. In addition to other provocations, real or imaginary, he felt that the South owed him repayment, preferably in blood, for the year he had lost; and this morning he began to collect in earnest. However, the fury of his attack across Doctor's Creek was apparently about as alarming to his own corps commander as it had been to the Confederates. Gilbert kept wigwagging messages forward, imploring the young enthusiast not to bring on a general engagement contrary to Buell's wishes. Sheridan, who was up where he could see what was going on, later wrote that he "replied to each message that I was not bringing on an engagement, but that the enemy evidently intended to do so, and that I believed I should shortly be attacked."

Attacked as he predicted, he brought up his other brigades and held his ground; after which a long lull ensued. Gilbert, taking heart at this, sent the other two divisions forward to take position along the ridge and astride the Springfield road, which crossed it on the way to Perryville, just under two miles ahead. This done, he went to report his success to army headquarters, three miles back down the road. He got there about 12.30 to find that McCook had just arrived. Much to Buell's relief, his two divisions were filing in on the Mackville road to take position on Gilbert's left, separated from it by a quarter-mile-wide valley cradling a bend of Doctor's Creek. Within another half hour, more good news was received: Crittenden too was at hand, entering by the Lebanon road and preparing to move northward up the ridge beyond the creek, taking position on Gilbert's right and thus extending the line of battle.

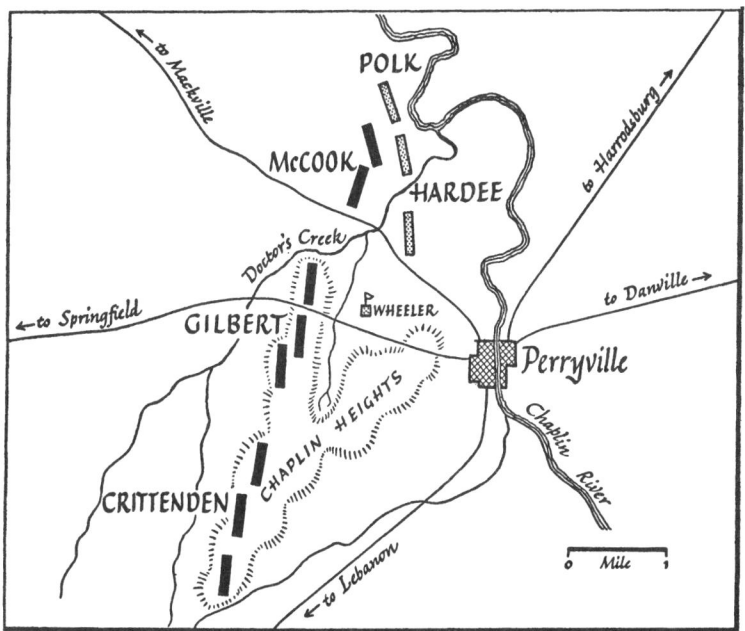

During these early afternoon hours everything was falling into place, as if the pieces of an enormous jigsaw puzzle had suddenly interlocked of their own accord: a common enough phenomenon, but one that never failed to exhilarate and amaze. Except for Sill's division, which was on the way from Frankfort, and the green division under Dumont, which was continuing the feint, Buell at last had all his troops collected. Eight divisions, with an over-all strength of 55,000 men, were posted along a six-mile front. His latest information was that Hardee was definitely at Perryville with two divisions. What else might be there he did not know, but for the present all was suspiciously quiet in that direction. At any rate, the Federal fist was clenched and ready to strike.

This time, though, it was Buell's turn to be beaten to the punch — with results a good deal more costly than the loss of a few spare pools of brackish water. What would be lost now was blood.

Bragg had waited at Harrodsburg through the early morning hours, cocking an ear to catch the steady roar of guns ten miles southwest, which would signify that the attack he had ordered was under way; but, hearing nothing, had ridden down to Perryville to see for himself the reason for delay. Arriving about 10 o'clock, he found Polk reconnoitering the high ground near the confluence of Doctor's Creek and Chaplin River. The three divisions were in line: from right to left, Buckner, Patton Anderson, and Cheatham, the latter posted near the town itself, while Wheeler's cavalry was off to the south, making a show of strength in that direction. Except for the occasional pop of an outpost rifle, a heavy silence overhung the field. Confronted by Bragg, who wanted to know why his orders to "give the enemy battle immediately" had not been carried out, Polk explained that he was convinced that most of Buell's entire army was gathering in his front. What was more, the Yankees had struck first. Consequently, he had called another council of war, and "in view of the great disparity of our forces," he and Hardee had decided "to adopt the defensive-offensive, to await the movements of the enemy, and to be guided by events as they were developed." In short, he "did not regard [last night's] letter of instructions as a peremptory order to attack at all hazards, but that... I should carry the instructions into execution as judiciously and promptly as a willing mind and sound discretion would allow."

So he said, then and later. However, he added that he had observed signs of activity here on the Federal left and had decided to switch Cheatham's division to this flank in order to guard against being overlapped in this direction. If Bragg approved, he would convert this into an offensive as soon as the men were in position. Bragg did approve, emphatically, and Polk began to make his dispositions accordingly, massing Cheatham's and Buckner's divisions under cover of the woods beyond the confluence of the creek and river. They would be supported by two brigades from Anderson, whose remaining two brigades would make a simultaneous holding attack to the south and west, thereby discouraging any weakening of the enemy right to bolster the left when it was assailed. By 1 o'clock, apparently without Federal detection of what was going on behind the screen of trees, the butternut troops were in assault formation, supported rank on rank by heavy concentrations of artillery. Soon afterward, Polk passed the word for both divisions to move forward.

The attack could scarcely have come at a more propitious time: propitious for the Confederates, that is. The bluecoats Polk had spotted late that morning on the Federal left were members of McCook's advance elements, reconnoitering for occupation of the position by his two divisions shortly after noon. While they were filing in, McCook himself rode back to report to Buell at army headquarters, having explained to the commander of his lead division, Brigadier General J. S. Jackson, that he was to form a line of battle along the near bank of Chaplin River. Jackson was glad to hear this, for his men were thirsty after their dusty march. So was his senior brigade commander, Brigadier General William Terrill, whom he told to advance his skirmishers to the river bank as soon as he had his troops in attack formation. "I'll do it, and that's my water," Terrill said. He was a Union-loyal Virginian. In fact, he was the former cadet Sheridan had lunged at with a bayonet, ten years ago at the Academy. Since then, they had shaken hands and agreed to forget their grievance. Sheridan was thankful ever afterwards that they had staged this reconciliation; for Terrill was dead within an hour of his arrival on the field.

Cheatham and Buckner struck with tremendous force and all the added impact of surprise, emerging suddenly from the drowsy-looking woods in a roaring charge. Terrill's men were mostly green, and being taken thus while they were advancing toward their baptism of fire, they heard in the rebel yell the fulfillment of their dry-mouthed apprehensions. Jackson, who was with them when the blow fell, was killed by one of the first volleys. They wavered, then broke completely when a bullet cut down Terrill. Behind them, the other deploying brigades were also taken unawares. Some of the men fled at once under the shock. Others stood and fought, sometimes hand to hand. Steadily, though, they were thrown back, the massed Confederate batteries knocking down the stone walls and fences behind which the retreating Federals had sought refuge. A mile or more they were driven, losing fifteen guns in the process. By the time McCook returned from the rear he found his two divisions near demoralization and utter ruin staring him in the face. In this extremity he called across the way for help from Gilbert.

That general also had his hands full, however. Or anyhow he thought so. He had repulsed Anderson's attack down the south bank of the creek, but he did not know how soon another would be launched or in what strength. Sheridan, from his advanced position on the left, could look across the intervening valley and see the graybacks sweeping westward, driving McCook's troops before them. All he could do for the present was turn his guns in that direction, heaving shells into the flank of the gray columns as they crossed his line of fire. This threw them into considerable confusion and encouraged Gilbert to detach first one brigade, then another, to go to McCook's assistance. When they had left, he counterattacked with his right-flank brigade and drove Anderson back on Perryville, capturing a fifteen-wagon ammunition train. But this was late in the day. Having advanced so far, the brigade commander put his batteries in position west of the town and, firing his shells across the rooftops, engaged some rebel guns on the opposite side until darkness put an end to the duel and relieved the terror of the civilians, who had crouched in their cellars and heard the projectiles arching overhead with a flutter as of wings.

Such was Gilbert's contribution, and such was the contribution of his 20,000 men, who faced barely 2500 Confederates while McCook and his 12,500 were being mauled by nearly equal numbers, just beyond easy musket range on the left. Crittenden, on the right with 22,500 men, contributed even less; in fact he contributed nothing at all, being bluffed into immobility by Joe Wheeler's 1200 horsemen and two guns. Thus it was that 16,000 rebels could successfully challenge 55,000 bluecoats, not more than half of whom were seriously engaged. In partial extenuation, because of unusual atmospheric and topographical factors reminiscent of Grant's experience with the ill wind at Iuka, the clatter of musketry did not carry far today; so that in this respect the six-mile-long scene of action (or nonaction) was compartmented, each sector being sealed off from the others as if by soundproof walls. One Union staff officer, riding the field, later made the incredible statement that "at one bound my horse carried me from stillness into the uproar of battle." Partially, too, this explained the lack of over-all control which should have remedied the drawback of temporary deafness. Buell, nursing yesterday's bruises back at headquarters, not only did not know what had hit him today; it was after 4 o'clock before he even knew he had been struck.

By that time the battle was more than two hours old, and the Confederates too had been thrown into considerable confusion. This was accomplished partly by Sheridan's gunners, bowling shells across the narrow valley to crush the flank of the advancing files, toppling men like tenpins — including Pat Cleburne, who had recovered from the face wound he had suffered at Richmond in time to receive a leg wound here when his horse was shot from under him by one of the fast-firing guns across the way — and partly by the disorganization incident to the rapid advance itself. Units had intermingled, not only gray and gray, but also blue and gray, as some stood fast and others retreated. On both sides there was much anguished crying of *"Friends! You are firing into friends!"* However, this too was not without its advantages to the attackers: particularly in one instance. When the commander of one of the brigades Gilbert had sent to reinforce McCook approached an imposing-looking officer to ask for instructions as to the posting of his troops — "I have come to your assistance with my brigade!" the Federal shouted above the uproar — the gentleman calmly sitting his horse in the midst of carnage turned out to be Polk, who was wearing a dark-gray uniform. Polk asked the designation of the newly arrived command, and upon being told raised his eyebrows in surprise. For all his churchly faith in miracles, he could scarcely believe his ears. "There must be some mistake about this," he said. "You are my prisoner."

Fighting without its commander, the brigade gave an excellent account of itself. Joined presently by the other brigade sent over from the center, it did much to stiffen the resistance being offered by the remnants of McCook's two divisions. Sundown came before the rebels could complete the rout begun four hours ago, and now in the dusk it was Polk's turn to play a befuddled role in another comic incident of confused identity. He saw in the fading light a body of men whom he took to be Confederates firing obliquely into the flank of one of his engaged brigades. "Dear me," he said to himself. "This is very sad and must be stopped." None of his staff being with him at the time, he rode over to attend to the matter in person. When he came up to the erring commander and demanded in angry tones what he meant by shooting his own friends, the colonel replied with surprise:

"I don't think there can be any mistake about it. I am sure they are the enemy."

"Enemy!" Polk exclaimed, taken aback by this apparent insubordination. "Why, I have only just left them myself. Cease firing, sir! What is your name, sir?"

"Colonel Shryock, of the 87th Indiana," the Federal said. "And pray, sir, who are you?"

The bishop-general, learning thus for the first time that the man was a Yankee and that he was in rear of a whole regiment of Yankees, determined to brazen out the situation by taking further advantage of the fact that his dark-gray blouse looked blue-black in the twilight. He rode closer and shook his fist in the colonel's face, shouting angrily: "I'll soon show you who I am, sir! Cease firing, sir, at once!" Then he turned his horse and, calling in an authoritative manner for the bluecoats to cease firing, slowly rode back toward his own lines. He was afraid to ride fast, he later explained, because haste might give his identity away; yet "at the same time I experienced a disagreeable sensation, like screwing up my back, and calculated how many bullets would be between my shoulders every moment."

Screened at last by a small copse, he put the spurs to his horse and galloped back to the proper side of the irregular firing line. But the fighting was practically over by now. Two of his brigades had been withdrawn to meet Gilbert's threat to the left rear, ending all chance for a farther advance, even if Bragg had been willing to risk a night engagement. Presently even the guns east and west of Perryville ceased their high-angle quarrel across the rooftops.... Buell had fought his first battle, and fought it badly, having been assaulted and outdone by an army less than a third the size of his own. More than 7600 men had fallen: 4211 Federals, 3396 Confederates. The former had had 845 killed, 2851 wounded, and 515 captured or missing, while the latter had lost 510, 2635, and 251 in those same categories. Buell consoled himself for this disparity by predicting that the conflict would "stand conspicuous for its severity in the history of the rebellion." Bragg agreed, later reporting that "for the time engaged, it was the severest and most desperately contested engagement within my knowledge."

The moon being only just past the full, the night was nearly as bright as day, and there were those in the Union army who were in favor of launching an immediate full-scale counterattack. Buell himself had tried to get such a movement under way on the right as soon as he discovered he had a battle on his hands; but the messenger, who set out at 4.15 with a verbal order for Thomas to have Crittenden move forward, got lost in the tricky bottoms of Doctor's Creek and did not find him till past sunset. Thomas, who was convinced that the rebels were in heavy strength to his front, sent back word that it was too late for an attack today, but that he would "advance in the morning with the first sound of action on the left." Dissatisfied with this dependence on his shattered left, which he knew was in no condition for more fighting, Buell replied that Thomas was to tell Crittenden "to press his command forward as much as possible [tonight] and be prepared to attack at daylight in the morning." The Virginian then rode back to army headquarters, where Buell repeated these instructions after midnight. Thomas passed them along to Crittenden at 1.30: "Have your different divisions ready to attack at daylight. Issue orders at once." Crittenden replied: "I am all ready. My post will be to the rear of the center of the line."

Morning came, October 9, but with it there came to headquarters no sound of conflict on the right. Buell waited, then waited some more. At 8 o'clock, three hours past dawn, he had his chief of staff send Crittenden the message: "Have you commenced the advance? What delays your attack?" Crittenden replied that he had received no orders to attack; he had been told, rather, to have his troops "ready to attack," and that was precisely what he had done. If they wanted him to go forward, let them say so. Exasperated, Buell told him to get moving, and he did. But Bragg was gone.

★ ★ ★

The Confederates had pulled out after midnight. Convinced at last that he had most of Buell's army to his front, and moreover having accomplished what he had intended when he told Polk to "rout him" and thus gain time for a concentration to the east, Bragg ordered a prompt junction with Kirby Smith, whom he instructed to move forward from Versailles to Harrodsburg for that purpose. Two miles short of the latter place, having crossed the Salt and burned the bridges behind him, Polk halted and formed a line of battle in the rain, the long drouth apparently having been broken by the booming of heavy guns the day before. Receiving word from Wheeler, who had charge of the rear-guard cavalry, that the Federals had not ventured beyond Perryville today, Polk rode with Chaplain C. T. Quintard — afterwards a bishop like himself — to an Episcopal church in Harrodsburg, where the Tennessee chaplain donned his surplice and stole and entered the sanctuary. While Polk knelt at the altar, Quintard read the litany and pronounced the benediction, accompanied by the murmur of rain against the stained-glass windows. Overcome by emotion as he contrasted the peace of the present interlude with what he had seen yesterday in one of the great battles of that fratricidal war, the gray-clad bishop bowed his head and wept.

Kirby Smith arrived next morning, several hours before Buell at last came up. Bragg now had all his available troops consolidated, and that night the two armies lay face to face outside the town, each waiting to see what the other was going to do. "Fifty thousand effectives" was Buell's estimate of the Confederate strength, and though he himself had sixty thousand — including Sill, who had promised to join him "*without fail* tomorrow, I think" — he could not forget that Bragg, with less than a third his present number of men, had wrecked one wing of the Federal army when it had been nearly as large as it was now. So Buell did nothing, waiting for Bragg to show his hand. And Bragg did nothing either.

"For God's sake, General," Smith exclaimed, "let us fight Buell here."

"I will do it, sir," Bragg replied.

But he did not. Whatever it was that had come over him three weeks ago at Munfordville, when he stood aside while Buell passed around his flank and on to Louisville, came over him again. What was more, disheartening news from North Mississippi informed him that Van Dorn and Price had failed at Corinth, just as Lee had failed in Maryland; Bragg's was the only one of the three intended invasion barbs still stuck in the enemy's hide. Besides, unable to see that he had much to gain from a victory — whereas a defeat might cost him not only the bountiful supply of goods and foodstuffs he had collected, but also his army — he had already decided to withdraw. As he put it in the letter to his wife, "With the whole southwest thus in the enemy's possession, my crime would have been unpardonable had I kept my noble little army to be ice-bound in a northern clime, without tents or shoes, and obliged to forage daily for bread, etc."

Evincing what one observer called "a perplexity and vacillation which had now become simply appalling to Smith, to Hardee, and to Polk," Bragg ordered a retreat toward Bryantsville that night. At dawn, when Buell found the southern army gone again, he could scarcely believe that it was not maneuvering for a better position in which to fight the battle which he, and indeed practically everyone else in both armies except Bragg, believed was about to be fought. He followed warily through Harrodsburg, waiting for Bragg to make a stand or else come flailing back at him, guns booming. Beyond Dick's (or Dix) River, the

Confederates again formed line of battle near Camp Dick Robinson, but Buell once more found the position too strong for him to risk attacking it. For a full day Bragg stayed there; then on the following day, October 13, when Buell sidled around toward the south, threatening his line of retreat, he got under way in earnest for Cumberland Gap. As long ago as September 29, anticipating withdrawal from Kentucky ten days before the Battle of Perryville, he had ordered 100,000 rations collected there, as well as another 200,000 at London, half way between the present position of his army and the gap.

The retreat — though Bragg did not call it that; he called it a withdrawal, the successful completion of a giant raid — was in two columns, Polk and Hardee marching by way of Lancaster and Crab Orchard, Kirby Smith by way of Big Hill, accompanying the heavy-laden trains. It was, as a later observer remarked, "a dismal but picturesque affair." Cavalry fanned out front and rear and flankwards to protect the enormous droves of hogs, sheep, and beef cattle, herded by cowboys recruited from Texas regiments. Conspicuous among the motley aggregation of vehicles in the creaking train, which included carriages, omnibuses, and stagecoaches pressed into service to remove the mountain of supplies, were the 400 bright new wagons, each with "US" stenciled on its canvas, which had been captured nearby from Nelson in late August. Approaching Big Hill from the opposite direction, Smith was feeling none of the elation he had experienced then, with victory still before him, not behind. "My command from loss of sleep for five nights, is completely exhausted," he reported during the early morning hours of October 14. "The straggling has been unusually great. The rear of the column will not reach here before daybreak. I have no hope of saving the whole of my train, as I shall be obliged to double teams in going up Big Hill, and will necessarily be delayed there two or three days."

His near-despair was based on an overrating of Buell, who he thought would press him hard, and an underrating of his own troops, particularly those in the rear guard under Wheeler. These horsemen fought no less than twenty-six separate engagements during the first five days and nights of the march — one for each year of their youthful colonel's life — beating off Federal attempts to hack at the long, slow-moving line of wagons. By dawn of the second day, however, Smith's gloom had deepened. Still at Big Hill, he notified Bragg: "I have little hope of saving any of the train, and fear much of the artillery will be lost." But here again he was unduly pessimistic. While Stevenson's division held a line beyond range of the hill, Heth's men lined the difficult slope from foot to summit and, as one of them later wrote, when "starved and tired mules faltered and fell, seized the wagons and lifted them by sheer force over the worst places." All day, all night, until noon of the following day, October 16, "the trains, in one unbroken stream, continued to pour over Big Hill, and then the troops followed." Smith felt considerably better now, having broken into the clear. Even the fact that this was hostile country had its advantages, since it encouraged stragglers to keep up. Beyond Mount Vernon next day at Big Rockcastle River, he appealed to Polk, who had already crossed: "Cannot we unite and end this disastrous retreat by a glorious victory?"

But even if Bragg had been willing — which he was not — it was too late. Hearing from Nashville this same day that a Confederate force was "rapidly concentrating" against that place, Buell broke contact just beyond London, abandoned the pursuit, and turned west. "I have no apprehension," the Nashville commander had assured him; but Buell more than made up for this lack. He was apprehensive not only for the safety of the Tennessee capital but also for the safety of his army, which by now had entered the barrens. He wired Halleck: "The enemy has been driven into the heart of this desert and must go on, for he cannot exist in it. For the same reason we cannot pursue in it with any hope of overtaking him, for while he is moving back on his supplies and as he goes consuming what the country affords we must bring ours forward.... I deem it useless and inexpedient to continue the pursuit, but propose to direct the main force under my command rapidly upon Nashville, which General Negley reported to me as already being invested by a considerable force and toward which I have no doubt Bragg will move the main part of his army."

In thus abandoning the pursuit, which in the end might have taken him into East Tennessee — the one region Lincoln most wanted "delivered" — Buell knew that he was fanning the wrath of his superiors, who had removed him from command once already and had restored him only under political pressure after his successor had declined the post. Anticipating what would follow, he told Halleck: "While I shall proceed with these dispositions, deeming them to be proper for the public interest, it is but meet that I should say that the present time is perhaps as convenient as any for making any change that may be thought proper in the command of this army." And having thus invited his dismissal, he said of the army he had led: "It has not accomplished all that I had hoped or all that faction might demand; yet, composed as it is, one half of perfectly new troops, it has defeated a powerful and thoroughly disciplined army in one battle and has driven it away baffled and dispirited at least, and as much demoralized as an army can be under such discipline as Bragg maintains over all troops that he commands."

Bragg would have appreciated the closing compliment, dealing as it did with the quality on which he placed the strongest emphasis, but just now he was satisfied with being allowed to continue his withdrawal unmolested. He pressed on through Barbourville, leaving Kirby Smith to bring up the rear. That general, much disgusted, formally resumed command of the Department of East Tennessee on October 20, as soon as he reached Flat Lick, Kentucky. Approaching Cumberland Gap two days later, he was astounded and enraged to receive from Bragg, already in Knoxville, orders for him to leave 3000 men at that strategic point and prepare the remainder for another joint incursion — this time into Middle Tennessee. His troops were "worn down," he replied, "much in want of shoes, clothing, and blankets," and reduced by straggling to about 6000 effectives. "Having resumed the command of my department," he added pointedly, "I am directly responsible to the Government for the condition and safety of my army." It was in effect a bill of divorcement. He wanted no more joint campaigns, not with Bragg at any rate, and doubtless he was relieved to find the North Carolinian gone from Knoxville when he himself arrived October 24, so weary and discouraged that he slipped into town under cover of darkness in order to avoid a public reception planned in his honor. The main thing he wanted now was rest, which he hoped would enable him to forget the final lap of his seventy-day round-trip journey through Central Kentucky.

No such rousing welcome had been planned for Bragg, whose problem on his return was the avoidance, not of praise, but of blame amounting to downright condemnation. Though he had never courted or apparently even desired popularity, much preferring to be respected for the sternness of his discipline rather than admired for the warmth of his nature — of which, in truth, he had little — this opprobrium, heaped on the shoulders of the man who had conceived and led the most successful offensive so far launched by a Confederate commander outside the strict national limits, seemed to him as unfair as it was unrealistic. Where Lee had failed, for example, he (Bragg) had succeeded, not only with a smaller army against longer odds, but with far fewer casualties and far greater material results; yet Lee was praised and he was blamed. In his final report of the campaign, submitted some months later, though he avoided comparisons, he attempted to refute his critics point by point. Whatever there was of failure, or shortcoming, he assigned to the backwardness of the expected Kentucky volunteers, who by their lack of native patriotism — so he called or thought of it — had forced him to travel the long road back to Tennessee with 20,000 unused muskets in his wagons. Nor was he reticent in summing up his gains:

> Though compelled to yield to largely superior numbers and fortuitous circumstances a portion of the valuable territory from which we had driven the enemy, the fruits of the campaign were very large and have had a most important bearing upon our subsequent military operations here and elsewhere. With a force enabling us at no time to put more than 40,000 men of all arms and in all places in battle, we had redeemed North Alabama and Middle Tennessee and recovered possession of Cumberland Gap, the gateway to the heart of the Confederacy. We had killed, wounded, and captured

no less than 25,000 of the enemy; taken over 30 pieces of artillery, 17,000 small-arms, some 2,000,000 cartridges for the same; destroyed some hundreds of wagons and brought off several hundreds more with their teams and harness complete; replaced our jaded horses by a fine mount; lived two months upon supplies wrested from the enemy's possession; secured material to clothe the army, and finally secured subsistence from the redeemed country to support not only the army but also a large force of the Confederacy to the present time.

Though some of this was actually understated, it made no real impression on his critics. They were not so much concerned with what he had done, which admittedly was considerable, as they were with what he had not done. In fact, their complaints in this respect were so immediately vociferous that on October 23, the day after he reached Knoxville, Bragg was summoned to Richmond by a wire from the Adjutant General, who informed him: "The President desires... that you will lose no time in coming here." Amid rumors that he was about to be relieved, he caught an eastbound train the following morning, thus avoiding a meeting with Kirby Smith, who arrived that night.

Whatever weight Davis and Cooper might attach to Bragg's claims in determining whether to sustain or fire him, Lincoln and Halleck apparently were inclined not only to accept them at face value, but also to deduct them from what little credit his opponent had left in their direction. Receiving Buell's dispatch of October 17, wherein he announced that he was abandoning the pursuit to return to Nashville, the general-in-chief replied next morning: "The great object to be attained is to drive the enemy from Kentucky and East Tennessee. If we cannot do it now we need never to hope for it." This was followed by another wire, in which Halleck brought Lincoln's logic to bear by indirect quotation, reinforcing the protest he had made the day before: "The capture of East Tennessee should be the main object of your campaign. You say it is the heart of the enemy's resources; make it the heart of yours. Your army can live there if the enemy's can.... I am directed by the President to say to you that your army must enter East Tennessee this fall, and that it ought to move there while the roads are passable.... He does not understand why we cannot march as the enemy marches, live as he lives, and fight as he fights, unless we admit the inferiority of our troops and of our generals."

Logic was a knife that could cut both ways, however, and prewar service in the Adjutant General's office had made Buell familiar with its use. He replied October 20 with a long, closely reasoned exegesis on the difficulties of what was being required of him. But that was not what Lincoln and Halleck wanted to hear. Besides, as an indication of his progress, the sequential headings on his telegrams — Mount Vernon,

Crab Orchard, Danville — spoke a clearer language than their contents. Despite his former suggestion that "the present time is perhaps as convenient as any for making any change that may be thought proper," Buell's military life line was running out much faster than he thought. Previously, after being relieved, he had been restored to command partly as a result of political pressure in his favor; but such pressure as was being exerted now was in the opposite direction. His old enemy Governor Morton, for example, was wiring Lincoln: "The butchery of our troops at Perryville was terrible.... Nothing but success, speedy and decided, will save our cause from utter destruction. In the Northwest distrust and despair are seizing upon the hearts of the people." Armed with this, and presently reinforced by similar expressions of displeasure from Yates of Illinois and Tod of Ohio, Halleck told Buell on October 22: "It is the wish of the Government that your army proceed to and occupy East Tennessee with all possible dispatch. It leaves to you the selection of the roads upon which to move to that object.... Neither the Government nor the country can endure these repeated delays. Both require a prompt and immediate movement toward the accomplishment of the great object in view — the holding of East Tennessee."

Buell now had his orders, the first specific ones he had received. But before he could put them into execution (and on the same day Bragg left Knoxville, bound for Richmond) the following was delivered:

> Washington, October 24
>
> Maj. Gen. D. C. Buell, *Commanding, &c.:*
>
> General: The President directs that on the presentation of this order you will turn over your command to Maj. Gen. W. S. Rosecrans, and repair to Indianapolis, Ind., reporting from that place to the Adjutant General of the Army for further orders.
>
> Very respectfully, your obedient servant,
>
> H. W. HALLECK
> *General-in-Chief.*

Last, Best Hope of Earth

⚔ BUELL WAS NOT THE FIRST NOR WAS HE the last of the blue-clad puppets whose strings had been cut, or would be cut, in what turned out to be a season of dismissals. Others had been or were about to be packed away in their boxes, mute, their occupations gone like Othello's and themselves removed, like him, from "the big wars, That make ambition virtue." Halleck, from his position near the vital center, had forecast the political weather at the outset, back in August, when he told a friend: "I can hardly describe to you the feeling of disappointment here in the want of activity," and added: "The Government seems determined to apply the guillotine to all unsuccessful generals. It seems rather hard to do this where the general is not in fault, but perhaps with us now, as in the French Revolution, some harsh measures are required."

The ax was descending. Pope's head rolled before Buell's; McDowell, too — though admittedly he was more sinned against than sinning — was gone, complaining wistfully as he went: "I did not ask to be relieved. I only asked for a court." Even the navy, barnacle-encrusted during the nearly fifty peacetime years since the War of 1812, had stretched some necks beneath the blade. Down on the Gulf, glad to be breathing salt air after the Vicksburg-*Arkansas* fiasco, Farragut gave his late-summer and early-fall attention to the Texas coast, where the blockaders worked without the advantage of a lodgment on the mainland. With this in mind, he sent out three expeditions in as many months. The first attacked Corpus Christi in mid-August but, having no occupation troops, withdrew after giving the place a pounding. Next month the second expedition went up Sabine Pass, wrecked the railroad bridge and the fort at Sabine City, captured a pair of rebel steamers, and retired again to the bay. The third was more ambitious, being aimed at Galveston. It was also more successful. Two regular gunboats and two converted ferries hit the port on October 5, drove the Confederates out with a few well-aimed salvos, then landed a token force of 260 men commanded by a colonel; after which, by a tacit understanding, the warships patrolling the bay refrained from further shelling on condition that the rebels would not move artillery into Galveston over the two-mile-long bridge connecting the island town with the mainland. Alabama was now the only southern state with an unoccupied coast, and Farragut had redeemed, at least in part, his midsummer performance up the Mississippi.

Gratifying as this redemption was to Secretary Welles — whom Lincoln dubbed "Father Neptune" and sometimes "Noah" — it also called attention to the contrast between the Tennessee sailor's make-up and that of his former upriver partner, the Boston Brahmin Charles H. Davis, who had run into little but trouble since he replaced Foote as flotilla commander on the upper Mississippi, back in May. He was, as one of his officers said, "a most charming and lovable man," author of two esoteric books, and a member of the commission which had planned the strikes at Hatteras and Port Royal, but it was becoming increasingly apparent that he lacked what Farragut had and what Foote had had before him: a hard-driving, bulldog, cut-and-slash aggressiveness, a preference for action at close quarters, and a burning sense of personal insult at the slightest advantage gained by an opponent at his expense. Since it was this quality, or combination of qualities, which would be needed for the work that lay ahead on the big river, Welles decided Captain Davis had to go. In mid-October he acted. Davis was eased upstairs to the Bureau of Navigation, where he would find work better suited to his intellectual capacities.

There was little that was surprising in this removal. What was surprising was the Secretary's choice of a successor: David Dixon Porter. Porter was only a junior commander, so that to give him the job Welles had to disappoint and outrage more than eighty senior officers. Besides, there were personal drawbacks. Like his brother Dirty Bill, Porter was not above claiming other men's glory as his own; he would stretch or varnish the truth to serve his purpose; he would undermine a superior; he would promise a good deal more than he could deliver — all of which he had done at New Orleans, and then had gone on to do them again at Vicksburg. Yet he had virtues, too, of the sort which Othello said proceeded from ambition in "the big wars." Like Lincoln in his pre-Manassas judgment of John Pope, Welles apparently believed that "a liar might [yet] be brave and have skill as an officer." Weighing the virtues against the vices, the gray-bearded brown-wigged naval head confided in his diary: "Porter is but a Commander. He has, however, stirring and positive qualities, is fertile in resources, has great energy, excessive and sometimes not overscrupulous ambition; is impressed with and boastful of his own powers, given to exaggeration in relation to himself — a Porter infirmity — is not generous to older and superior living officers, whom he is too ready to traduce, but is kind and patronizing to favorites who are juniors; is given to cliquism, but is brave and daring like all his family. He has not the conscientious and high moral qualities of Foote to organize the flotilla, and is not considered by some of our best naval men a fortunate officer. His selection will be unsatisfactory to many, but his field of operations is peculiar, and a young and active officer is required for the duty to which he is assigned."

Having decided that the credits overbalanced the debits, in weight if not in number, Welles called Porter into his office and informed him that he was being sent as an acting rear admiral to take charge of the navy on the western waters. The order was dated October 9; Porter, who had come north on leave, hoping to cure a touch of fever he had contracted in the region to which his chief was now returning him, accepted both the assignment and the promotion as no more than his due. Six days later he was in Cairo, where he assumed command of the 125 vessels comprising the Mississippi Squadron, together with 1300 officers, only twenty-five of whom had been in the old navy, and approximately 10,000 sailors. What he would do with these boats and officers and men — and whether Welles would be sustained by circumstance in his choice of a man whose character he doubted — remained to be seen.

At any rate, Buell and Davis had been brought down. And now as October wore toward a close, giving occasion in the East for a mocking revival of "All Quiet Along the Potomac," Lincoln was after larger game. In fact he was after the top-ranking man in the whole U.S. Army: George B. McClellan. The other two had been wing shots — targets of opportunity, so to speak — but this one he was stalking with care, intending to catch him on the sit.

According to some observers this should not be difficult, since that was the Young Napoleon's accustomed attitude. The managing editor of the New York *Tribune*, for example, had written privately in late September, a week after the Battle of Antietam, that one of his reporters had just returned from the army, "and his notion is that it is to be quiet along the Potomac for some time to come. George, whom Providence helps according to his nature, has got himself on one side of a ditch, which Providence had already made for him, with the enemy on the other, and has no idea of moving. Wooden-head at Washington will never think of sending a force through the mountains to attack Lee in the rear, so the two armies will watch each other for nobody knows how many weeks, and we shall have the poetry of war with pickets drinking from the same stream, holding friendly converse and sending newspapers across by various ingenious contrivances." In other words, this Indian summer, with its firm roads and its fair skies tinged with woodsmoke, was to be wasted, militarily, like the last one, in getting ready for a movement which bad weather would postpone. Whether the country would stand for another such winter of apparent inactivity Lincoln did not know. But he himself could not; nor did he intend to.

On the first day of October, without sending word that he was coming, he boarded a train and rode out to Western Maryland to see the general and his army. McClellan, however, got word that he was on the way and met him at Harpers Ferry. Pleased to find that the President had brought no politicians with him, "merely some western officers," McClellan wrote his wife: "His ostensible purpose is to see the troops and the battlefield; I incline to think that the real purpose of his visit is to push me into a premature advance into Virginia. I may be mistaken, but think not."

He was not mistaken. That was precisely why Lincoln had come; "I went up to the field to try to get [McClellan] to move," he said later. But as usual when he was face to face with Little Mac, discussing military matters, he got nowhere. Apparently he did not really try very hard; the primary inertia was too great. When he urged an advance, McClellan went into an explanation of shortages and drawbacks, and Lincoln dropped the subject. According to the general, "He more than once assured me that he was fully satisfied with my whole course from the beginning; that the only fault he could possibly find was that I was perhaps too prone to be sure that everything was ready before acting, but that my actions were all right when I started." Later they sat on a hillside, Lincoln with his long legs drawn up so that his knees were almost under his chin, and McClellan afterwards wrote that Lincoln told him: "General, you have saved the country. You must remain in command and carry us through to the end." When McClellan said that this would be impossible — "The influences at Washington will be too strong for you, Mr President. I will not be allowed the required time for preparation" — Lincoln replied: "General, I pledge myself to stand between you and harm."

It was a three-day visit, and much of the time was spent reviewing the troops. The President "looked pale," according to one veteran who saw him, while another remarked that as he "rode around every battalion [he] seemed much worn and distressed and to be looking for those who were gone." Doubtless he was thinking of the fallen, but he was also thinking of the men he saw — and of what they represented. A Union surgeon noted that Lincoln was "well received" by the soldiers, "but by no means so enthusiastically as General McClellan." Lincoln did not mind this much. What he minded was the thought that this gave rise to. "The Army of the Potomac is my army as much as any army ever belonged to the man that created it," McClellan told a member of his staff about this time. "We have grown together and fought together. We are wedded and should not be separated." The army felt that way, too, and Lincoln knew it. He also knew that if the soldiers felt it strongly enough, mutiny would follow any order for the general's removal from command. This was much on his mind during the visit, and resulted in a curious scene. Just before dawn of the second morning, he woke O. M. Hatch, an Illinois friend. "Come, Hatch," he said, "I want you to take a walk with me." Together they climbed to a hilltop overlooking the camps, and as sunrise lighted the valley where the troops lay waiting for reveille, Lincoln made an abstracted gesture, indicating the tented plain below. "Hatch, Hatch," he said in a husky voice, barely above a whisper. "What is all this?" His companion was confused. "Why, Mr Lincoln, this is the Army of the Potomac," he replied. Lincoln shook his head. "No, Hatch, no. This is General McClellan's bodyguard."

He returned to Washington, October 4. Two days later Halleck astonished McClellan with a telegraphic dispatch: "The President directs that you cross the Potomac and give battle to the enemy or drive him south. Your army must move now while the roads are good. ... I am directed to add that the Secretary of War and the General-in-Chief concur with the President in these instructions." McClellan replied that he was "pushing everything as rapidly as possible in order to get ready for the advance." Beyond this bare acknowledgment, however, the only sign he gave that he had received the directive was a step-up in the submission of requisitions for more supplies of every description. He wanted shoes, hospital tents, and horses: especially horses, the need for which was presently emphasized by Jeb Stuart, who once more covered himself with glory at the Young Napoleon's expense.

Under instructions from Lee to scout the Federal dispositions — and, if possible, destroy the railroad bridge over the Conococheague near Chambersburg, which would limit McClellan's rail supply facilities to the B & O — Stuart crossed the Potomac above Martinsburg at early dawn, October 10. He had with him 1800 horsemen and four guns. By noon he was across the Pennsylvania line, approaching Mercersburg. Soon after dark, the lights of Chambersburg were in view. Demanding and receiving the surrender of the place, he appointed Wade Hampton "Military Governor," quite as if he intended to stay there all fall, and bivouacked that night in the streets of the town. There were two disappointments. A bank official had escaped with all the cash in the vault, and the Conococheague bridge, being built of iron, proved indestructible. However, there were material compensations, including the capture and parole of 280 bluecoats, the opportunity to spend Confederate money in well-stocked Pennsylvania stores, and the impressment of more than a thousand excellent horses. Many of these last were draft animals of Norman and Belgian stock, and it was fortunate that they were seized in harness, since no southern quartermaster could furnish collars large enough for the big-necked creatures soon to be hauling rebel guns and wagons. Their former owners, never having seen an actual secessionist, were under the impression that Stuart's troopers were Federal soldiers, sent to harass farmers suspected of disloyalty, and many of them protested indignantly as the raiders led their heavy-footed animals away: "I'm just as good a Union man as any of you!"

Jeb's men had come nearly forty miles to reach their assigned objective, stirring up a hive of enemy cavalry in the process, and now the problem was how to get them back. Stuart met it as he had done before. When the column formed outside Chambersburg next morning, he led it, not southwest in the direction he had come from, but due east. Though he would have to ride more than twice as far to reach the Potomac by this route, it gave him the advantage of being unexpected along the way. The gray-jackets whooped at this evidence that they were about to repeat their Peninsula performance by staging another "Ride Around McClellan." Eastward they rode, beyond the Blue Ridge, on through Cashtown, where they stopped to feed the horses, then turned south, avoiding the college town of Gettysburg, eight miles off. Late that afternoon they recrossed the Pennsylvania line and entered Emmitsburg; beyond which, riding in darkness now and frequently changing to captured horses to spare their own, they forded the Monocacy. Some fought sleep by dismounting to walk a mile or so from time to time. Others slumped in their saddles and frankly slept, their snores droning loud above the hoofclops.

Word of the raid had spread to Washington by now. "Not a man should be permitted to return to Virginia," Halleck wired McClellan, who replied: "I have given every order necessary to insure the capture or destruction of those forces, and I hope we may be able to teach them a lesson they will not soon forget." But that was not to be. Sunday morning, October 12, near the mouth of the Monocacy — where Lee had crossed with his whole army, marching north the month before — Stuart broke through a weak link in the cordon, splashed across the Potomac, and regained the safety of the Confederate lines. He had two men missing, victims most likely of commandeered Yankee whiskey, and a handful slightly wounded. That seemed to him a small price to pay for the nearly three hundred bluecoats paroled at Chambersburg and the thirty-odd public officials brought back as hostages to secure the release or considerate treatment of Southerners now in Union hands. More than a quarter of a million dollars in public and railroad property had been destroyed, and in exchange for about sixty lame or worn-out animals abandoned along the way, the gray troopers had brought 1200 horses back from Pennsylvania for service under the Stars and Bars. Most satisfactory of all — at least to Stuart, who thus once more had justified his plume — was the knowledge that all this had been accomplished in the immediate presence of more than 100,000 enemy soldiers whose commander, midway through the raid, had announced his intention to "teach [the rebels] a lesson" by effecting their capture or destruction.

Instead it was McClellan who had been taught a lesson, though whether he would profit from it was doubtful; apparently he had failed to absorb much from the same lesson when it was first administered, four months ago on the Peninsula. Now as then, he was the object of much derision, North and South — only this time Lincoln himself led the chorus. He was aboard a steamer, returning from a troop review at Alexandria, when someone asked him: "Mr President, what about McClellan?" Without looking up, Lincoln drew a circle on the deck with the ferrule of his umbrella. "When I was a boy we used to play a game," he said, " 'Three Times Round, and Out.' Stuart has been round him twice. If he goes around him once more, gentlemen, McClellan will be out."

A new and biting note of mockery was coming into the President's references to the commander of the Army of the Potomac. Formerly this had been restricted mainly to comments on Little Mac's political suggestions — as when the governor of Massachusetts asked what Lincoln was going to reply to some advice McClellan had offered on a civil matter; "Nothing," Lincoln said. "But it made me think of the man whose horse kicked up and stuck his foot through the stirrup. He said to the horse, 'If you are going to get on I'll get off.' " Thus he had dealt with McClellan the would-be statesman, reserving his respect for McClellan the soldier. Now this too was fading. On the day after Stuart got back from his raid, Lincoln sent the circumnavigated Young Napoleon a long letter full of advice, in effect a lecture on strategy and tactics. "You remember my speaking to you of what I called your over-cautiousness. Are you not over-cautious when you assume that you cannot do what the enemy is constantly doing? Should you not claim to be at least his equal in prowess, and act upon the claim? ... Exclusive of the water-line, you are now nearer Richmond than the enemy is by the route you can and he must take. Why can you not reach there before him, unless you admit that he is more than your equal on the march? ... I would press closely to him, fight him if a favorable opportunity should present, and at least try to beat him to Richmond on the inside track. I say 'try'; if we never try, we shall never succeed." That was the main thing, as Lincoln saw it: Beat him. A stalemate would not serve. Even a repulse was not enough. "We should not so operate as to merely drive him away. As we must beat him somewhere or fail finally, we can do it, if at all, easier near to us than far away. If we cannot beat the enemy where he now is, we never can, he being again within the intrenchments of Richmond. ... It is all easy if our troops march as well as the enemy, and it is unmanly to say they cannot do it." He added: "This letter is in no sense an order."

Thus Lincoln. But McClellan apparently had as little respect for Lincoln the would-be strategist as Lincoln had for McClellan the would-be statesman. October's perfect weather went sliding by, and the army hugged its camps while its commander, despite his own chief quartermaster's protest that "no army was ever more perfectly supplied than this one has been as a general rule," continued to call for more and more supplies. He also wanted more soldiers, believing himself outnumbered, though his strength report of October 20 listed 133,433 men "present for duty," with an "aggregate present" of 159,860. Next day Halleck wired him: "Telegraph when you will move, and on what lines you propose to march." McClellan replied that he was nearly ready, but when he followed this with an urgent request for more horses, claiming that the ones he had were broken down by arduous service and weakened by foot-and-mouth disease, Lincoln lost his temper. "I have just read your dispatch about sore-tongued and fatigued horses," he wired on October 25. "Will you pardon me for asking what the horses of your army have done since the battle of Antietam that fatigues anything?"

McClellan was upset. "It was one of those little flings that I can't get used to when they are not merited," he wrote his wife, and he protested at some length to Lincoln the following day, defending his troopers and announcing that the long-awaited movement of his army across the Potomac had begun. Mollified, the President replied that he had "intended no injustice to any, and if I have done any I deeply regret it. To be told, after more than five weeks' total inaction of the army ... that the cavalry horses were too much fatigued to move, presents a cheerless, almost hopeless, prospect for the future, and it may have forced something of impatience in my dispatch." McClellan had an apology, such as it was, yet his gloom was unrelieved. Through it he saw plainly what was coming. When one of his corps commanders indicated a spot on the map where he thought the next great battle would be fought, he nodded agreement but added sadly: "I may not have command of the army much longer. Lincoln is down on me."

Lincoln was indeed down on him. Though he wired that he was "glad to believe you are crossing," privately he was saying that he was tired of trying to "bore with an auger too dull to take hold." However, he had a final secret test in mind. Lee's army, drawn up around Winchester, was farther from Richmond than McClellan's, which was crossing the Potomac below Harpers Ferry; "His route is the arc of a circle, while yours is the chord," Lincoln had said in the tactics lecture, two weeks before. If, in spite of this disadvantage, the Confederate commander managed to interpose his troops between the advancing Federals and his capital, McClellan would be out. So Lincoln decided, and kept his decision to himself, watching and waiting. He waited long. It took the blue host nine days to cross the river and begin its southward creep, east of the Blue Ridge, toward a concentration around Warrenton. By that time, Lee — unmolested — had shifted half his army to Culpeper, squarely across the Federal line of march. McClellan had failed the test, and Lincoln's mind was made up. He would remove him.

Fearing that this was about to happen, old Francis Blair pled against it with all the persuasion learned in a lifetime spent advising Presidents. McClellan was the Union's one best hope for preservation, he declared. Lincoln disagreed. "I said I would remove him if he let Lee's army get away from him, and I must do so. He has got the slows, Mr Blair."

He would remove him: but not just yet. November 4 was the first Tuesday in the month, which meant that it was election day in most of the northern states, and therefore not a propitious time for disturbing voters who were disturbed enough already. Even Chase, who vied with Stanton in the intensity of his desire to see McClellan ousted, admitted privately that it was inexpedient to fire the general on the eve of the congressional elections, lest the Administration's motives be misconstrued as a sop to the radicals. There was a widespread conviction among conservatives that the Preliminary Emancipation Proclamation had been sop enough in that direction. Political unrest found its basis there, together with objection to arbitrary arrests and the general lack of satisfaction with the prosecution of the war itself, which seemed to have stalled on every front. Nor was this dissatisfaction limited to moderates and conservatives. Iowa Senator J. W. Grimes, a loyal Republican whose constituents had voted heavily for Lincoln in 1860, was saying flatly: "We are going to destruction as fast as imbecility, corruption, and the wheels of time can carry us." Lyman Trumbull of Lincoln's home state was complaining bitterly of a "lack of affirmative, positive action and business talent in the cabinet," while to Governor Andrew of Massachusetts it seemed that "the President has never yet seemed quite sure that we [are] in a war at all."

Such remarks were straws in the wind, down which Democrats sniffed victory in November. And in many instances they got it. New York, Pennsylvania, Ohio, Indiana — all of which had gone solidly Republican in the election held two years ago — sent Democratic delegations to the House of Representatives. So did Illinois, where Lincoln's good friend Leonard Swett went down in defeat to John T. Stuart, the President's former law partner, who thus made one among the nine Democrats elected as opposed to five Republicans. New Jersey, which had split its vote before, now went solidly Democratic; Wisconsin, on the other hand, now split her six-man delegation down the middle. Although the number of Democratic congressmen increased from 44 to 75 as a result of this election, the Republicans would remain the majority party because they managed to carry three widely scattered regions:

New England, the Border States, and the Far West. Such comfort as Lincoln found in this was considerably soured, however, by the fact that most observers saw in the individual defeats a rebuke of the party leader and a rejection of his policies on the conduct of the war. The friendly New York *Times* ran the election story under the heading, "Vote of Want of Confidence," and in Lincoln's own home state the Salem *Advocate* declared: "We saw the President of the United States stretching forth his hand and seizing the reins of government with almost absolute power, and yet the people submitted. On the 4th day of November, 1862, the people arose in their might, they uttered their voice, like the sound of many waters, and tyranny, corruption and maladministration trembled."

Lincoln took it philosophically, though he found it hard to do so, remarking that he felt like the boy who stubbed his toe on the way to see his girl; he was too big to cry, he said, and it hurt too much to laugh. One thing it did, at any rate, however it came out. It cleared the way for action on McClellan. November 5, before the election tabulations were complete, Lincoln had the orders for his removal drawn up. The following evening they were given to Brigadier General C. P. Buckingham, the so-called "confidential assistant adjutant-general to the Secretary of War," who left with them next morning, November 7, aboard a special train bound for McClellan's headquarters at Rectortown, near Manassas Gap. The first snowfall of winter was whitening the North Virginia landscape and the car in which he rode was drafty; but Buckingham did not wonder that an officer with so much rank as his was being exposed to such discomfort and employed as a sort of overdressed messenger boy, Stanton having explained that McClellan might refuse to relinquish command of his army if the order was presented to him by a man with anything less than stars on his shoulders. Even with them, the Secretary had added darkly, there was a strong possibility of some such mutinous action on the part of the commander of the Army of the Potomac. He advised the brigadier to make his arrival unannounced, thus gaining the military advantage of a surprise attack.

It was still snowing at 11 o'clock that night. McClellan sat alone in his tent, ending the day as usual with a letter to his wife, who was busy getting settled in their new home at Trenton, New Jersey. Nothing in his manner showed that the proposed surprise had failed; but it had. He knew that Buckingham had arrived early that evening, and he knew what his arrival probably meant. Whatever there was of real surprise lay in the fact that, instead of coming directly from the depot to army headquarters here at Rectortown, the War Department emissary had ridden down to Salem, five miles south, where Burnside's corps was posted. Presently, however, this too was explained. A knock came at the tent pole, and when McClellan looked up from his letter, calling for whoever it was to enter, the canvas flap lifted and there stood Buckingham and Burnside, snow collected on the crowns and brims of their hats and sifted into the folds of their greatcoats. Behind his facial ruff of dark brown whiskers — also lightly powdered with snow, so that it resembled a badly printed trademark — "Dear Burn" looked both embarrassed and distressed.

McClellan knew what that meant, too, but for the present he gave no sign of this. He invited the visitors in, quite as if for an informal midnight chat, and for a time he and Buckingham exchanged pleasantries, Burnside sitting glumly by, looking rather as if he had been struck a hard blow on the head. Finally, though, the staff brigadier remarked that he had come to deliver some papers; and with that he passed them over. There were two of them, both dated November 5. Lincoln having authorized Halleck, "in [his] discretion, to issue an order [removing McClellan] forthwith, or so soon as he may deem proper," the general-in-chief had deemed it proper to act without delay:

> Major General McClellan, *Commanding, &c.:*
> General: On receipt of the order of the President, sent herewith, you will immediately turn over your command to Major General Burnside, and repair to Trenton, N.J., reporting, on your arrival at that place, by telegraph, for further orders.
> Very respectfully, your obedient servant.

The second was from the Adjutant General's office, and was a direct quotation of the first sentence of Lincoln's message to Halleck:

> By direction of the President of the United States, it is ordered that Major General McClellan be relieved from the command of the Army of the Potomac, and that Major General Burnside take the command of that army.
> By order of the Secretary of War.

Neither of the orders being really any stronger than the other, it appeared that the Young Napoleon's superiors considered two blows likelier to floor him than just one. However that might have been, he kept his balance under the double impact. He read both sheets, then said with a smile and in the same pleasant tone as before: "Well, Burnside, I turn the command over to you." Close to tears, the Indiana-born Rhode Islander implored McClellan to stay with him for a day or two while he began to get accustomed to handling the reins. He had not wanted this job; had, in fact, refused it twice already, pleading incompetence, and once again this evening when Buckingham first came to Salem — that was why they had arrived so late; he had spent two hours arguing against his appointment — but Buckingham had reminded him that this was no request, it was a double-barreled order; he had no choice. Besides, the staff brigadier had added, if Burnside declined the command it would go to Hooker. That decided it; he had accepted, and all he asked now was that Little Mac stay with him for a couple of days to help him get settled in the driver's seat. McClellan agreed, and the two generals went back out into the snowy night.

Alone again, the deposed commander took up his pen and returned to his letter: "Another interruption — this time more important. It was in the shape of Burnside, accompanied by Gen. Buckingham. . . . Alas for my poor country! I know in my inmost heart she never had a truer servant." He did not say, as he had said before, that this was a temporary step-down, that he would be recalled when things went as wrong for Burnside as they had gone for Pope. He was through and he knew it. But he added: "Do not be at all worried — I am not. I have done the best I could for my country; to the last I have done my duty as I understand it. That I must have made many mistakes I cannot deny. I do not see any great blunders; but no one can judge of himself. Our consolation must be that we have tried to do what was right."

All that really remained to be done was say goodbye to the army whose affection for him was, in the end, his most enduring monument. Next day, when the order for his removal was published, the reaction combined disbelief and horror, both of which gave way to rage, which in turn was tempered by sadness. The various corps, drawn up for a farewell exchange of salutes, broke ranks as they had done before at his approach. Now as before, they crowded around him, touched his boots, and stroked the flanks of his horse, only this time the tears were produced by sorrow, not by jubilation. Nor had all the anger been drained off. "Send him back! Send him back!" they cried in his wake, as if their shouts could be heard in the capital, fifty miles away. The Irish brigade cast its colors in the dust for him to ride over; "but, of course," one observer wrote, "he made them take them up again." The same man heard a general say he "wished to God that McClellan would put himself at the head of the army and throw the infernal scoundrels at Washington into the Potomac." Another yelled: "Lead us to Washington, General — we'll follow you!" Burnside shared the prevailing gloom, still so badly choked up that when one division commander, having voiced his regrets to McClellan, turned to him and offered congratulations, the new army head could hardly speak. "Couch, don't say a word about it," he implored.

McClellan accepted this adulation with as much satisfaction as ever, possibly more, but he remained strangely calm in the midst of it and did nothing to encourage the various expressions of resentment. "The officers and men feel terribly about the change," he wrote his wife on the second night after receiving the order for his removal. "I learn today that the men are very sullen and have lost their good spirits entirely." This was putting it mildly indeed; but the truth was, he had lost much of his former flamboyance. Even his written farewell to his soldiers was comparatively restrained. "In you I have never found doubt or coldness," he told them, and he added: "We shall ever be comrades in supporting the Constitution of our country and the nationality of its people."

That was all; or almost all. November 11 he took his final leave of them, riding down to Warrenton Junction, where a train was waiting to carry him away. After receiving the salute of a 2000-man detachment stationed here, he boarded the train and took his seat. But before the engineer could obey the highball, the troops broke ranks, surrounded the car, then uncoupled it and ran it back, yelling threats against the Administration and insisting that McClellan should not leave. "One word, one look of encouragement, the lifting of a finger," one witness later declared, "would have been a signal for a revolt against lawful authority, the consequences of which no man can measure." Instead, McClellan stepped onto the front platform and delivered a short address to the men, who had fallen silent as soon as he appeared. "Stand by General Burnside as you have stood by me, and all will be well," he said. Calmed, the soldiers recoupled the car and the train pulled out, followed by "one long and mournful huzza [as the men] bade farewell to their late commander." His route led through the capital, but he had already told his wife: "I shall not stop in Washington longer than for the next train, and will not go to see anybody."

In their tears, in their passionate demonstrations of affection for this man who moved them in a way no other general ever had or ever would, it was as if the soldiers had sensed a larger meaning in the impending separation; it was as if they knew they were saying goodbye to something more than just one stocky brown-haired man astride a tall black horse. It was, indeed, as if they were saying goodbye to their youth — which, in a sense, they were. Or it might also have been prescience, intimations of mortality, intimations of suffering down the years. There had been Pope, and now it appeared that there would be others more or less like him. Knowing what that meant, they might well have been weeping for their own lot, as well as for McClellan's. "My army," he had called them from the start, and it was true. He had made them into what they were, and whatever they accomplished he would accomplish too, in part, even though he would no longer be at their head.

That was no doubt his greatest satisfaction; but there were others, no less welcome for being delayed. Five years after the guns had cooled and were parked in town squares and on courthouse lawns, with sparrows building nests in their muzzles, he received what was perhaps his finest professional compliment, and received it from the man who had occupied the best of all possible positions from which to formulate a judgment. Asked then who was the ablest Federal general he had opposed throughout the war, Robert E. Lee replied without hesitation: "McClellan, by all odds."

★ ★ ★

McClellan was gone, and others were gone with him: Fitz-John Porter, for example, who was relieved from command by authority of the same message Lincoln had sent Halleck on November 5, relieving Little Mac. His corps went to Hooker, whose own had been severely cut up at Antietam, and Porter himself was brought back to Washington to face charges for having failed to obey Pope's order for an attack on the Confederate right "at or near Manassas, in the State of Virginia, on or about the 29th day of August, 1862." The court having convicted him, Lincoln ordered that he be "cashiered and dismissed from the service... and forever disqualified from holding any office of trust or profit under the Government of the United States." Winged thus by a stray pellet from the blast that felled his chief, Porter had to wait long for vindication. It came at last, officially, nearly a quarter of a century later, when Congress in 1886 commissioned him a regular-army colonel, to rank from 1861, and permitted him to retire immediately thereafter, without back pay but with honor.

One other major figure was to go, though not entirely: Benjamin Butler was too useful a man, and too powerful a politician, to be assigned to limbo alongside Buell and McClellan. Like them he was a Democrat, but he was blatantly so — with the result that what had been for them a disadvantage was for him a downright blessing. So long as he occupied a high position in the army, the Administration could not be accused of conducting a strictly Republican war, whereas his dismissal would have exactly the reverse effect. Butler of course was aware of this advantage, and operated accordingly. What was more, he was efficient, particularly as an administrator. Yet for all his ingenuity in dealing with the problems attending the occupation of New Orleans (he had not only succeeded in making the Creoles "fear the stripes" in his flag, he had also brought them some of the sanitary benefits of Lowell, Massachusetts, including an intensive flushing-out of their sewers and an equally intensive regulation of their morals) the squint-eyed general had not fulfilled his early promise as a terror to the rebels in the field. Of late, in fact, he had entirely neglected that side of military life, even having gone so far as to pull his troops out of Baton Rouge in order to avoid a return engagement with the Confederates who had attacked the place in early August. Obviously he would not do for the bloody work Lincoln now saw would have to be done if the war was ever to end. However, the disposition of Butler was no large problem. His talents were so manifold that he would be about as useful in one place as another. He could be shifted.

Fortunately for Lincoln's purpose he had a replacement there at hand, in the form of the commander of the Washington defenses. Banks, like Butler, was a Massachusetts politician, so that to exchange them, one for another, would not upset the voters of their region. Besides, Banks was resourceful, energetic, and pugnacious: a combination of qualities all too rare of late, in more places than New Orleans. In short, he was just the kind of man Lincoln thought he wanted for the job he had in mind. It was true that wherever he had fought he had been whipped, sometimes rather spectacularly, but this had not been the result of any unwillingness to fight; quite the reverse — and generally it had been against Stonewall Jackson, whom he would be unlikely to encounter down in Louisiana or up the Mississippi. That was where Lincoln intended to send him. On November 8, the day after Buckingham left for Rectortown with the orders placing Burnside in command of the Army of the Potomac, Lincoln had the Adjutant General issue an order assigning Banks "to the command of the Department of the Gulf, including the State of Texas," and the following day he had Halleck write the new commander a letter of instructions, explaining the purpose — or, more strictly speaking, purposes — for which he was being transferred so far south.

Vicksburg and Mobile were to be his primary objectives, and he was to have the coöperation of the navy in effecting their reduction. "The President regards the opening of the Mississippi River as the first and most important of all our military and naval operations," he was told, "and it is hoped that you will not lose a moment in accomplishing it." Following this, Halleck continued — quite as if the thing had been done already with a flourish of the pen — Banks was to move eastward from Vicksburg to Jackson, "and thus cut off all connection by rail between Northern Mississippi ... and Atlanta ... the chief military depot of the rebel armies in the West." This done, he would return approximately to his starting point in order to "ascend with a naval and military force the Red River as far as it is navigable, and thus open an outlet for the sugar and cotton of Northern Louisiana." Not even then did Halleck allow him time for a breather. "It is also suggested that, having Red River in our possession, it would form the best base for operations in Texas." There at last he closed with the assurance, "These instructions are not intended to tie your hands or to hamper your operations in the slightest degree ... and I need not assure you, general, that the Government has unlimited confidence not only in your judgment and discretion, but also in your energy and military promptness."

Although this was clearly one of the largest tasks ever assigned a commander in all the history of warfare — and unquestionably the most difficult ever assigned a nonprofessional who, after eighteen months in the field and a major share in three campaigns, lacked so much as a single tactical victory to his credit — Banks shared Halleck's "unlimited confidence" that the thing could be done and that he was the man to do it. Summoned to Washington and informed that he would be given 20,000 reinforcements to accompany him on the coastal voyage to New Orleans — one expeditionary force would sail from New York, the other from Hampton Roads — the New Englander was delighted. "Everything is favorable for my purpose," he had replied to an earlier warning order. "I shall obtain troops at once, and be ready for movement as early as you wish.... Requisitions will be made and forwarded by mail. No material delay will occur, unless for want of transports." Now, having conferred in person with Lincoln and Halleck as to the details of the multi-faceted project, he was more enthusiastic than ever. There was "much to do," he said as he departed for New York, but he would "lose no time."

Lincoln was delighted, too: not only by the prospect of seeing so much accomplished, but also by the unfamiliar experience of having sat face to face with a commander who recognized the worth of time and the military fruits that haste could gather. Moreover, it augured well for larger matters. For all the vastness of the project thus assigned to Banks, the main value of his operations would be diversionary, serving 1) to drain off rebel front-line troops by threatening their rear, and 2) to distract the enemy high command from concentrating against the Federal main effort, about to be exerted against their front. After a hundred thousand casualties and a year and a half of successes, near-successes, and sickening failures — the last, as Lincoln saw them, being mainly due to the vacillation and nonaggressiveness of generals like Buell and McClellan, who, desiring combat less than they feared defeat, believed in preparation more than they believed in movement — a victory pattern had emerged. Three southern cities were the three main northern objectives. Richmond, Chattanooga, and Vicksburg were the brain, heart, and bowels of the rebellion. A successful blow struck any one of the three might well prove fatal, in time, to the corpus as a whole; but *three* successful blows, struck simultaneously, would produce immediate results. Whatever movement followed then, on the part of the creature named Rebellion, would be no more than death throes and the setting in of rigor mortis.

Immediate results being what he was after, Lincoln had assigned these three main objectives to the commanders of the three main armies of the Union: Burnside, Rosecrans, and Grant. He himself had chosen the first and second, and he had sustained the third against strident demands for his dismissal, saying of him: "I can't spare this man. He fights." He believed he could say it of the other two as well. Whatever shortcomings they might develop under pressure (Grant's, for instance, was said to be whiskey; hearing which, the President was supposed to have asked what brand he drank, intending to send a barrel each to all his other generals) it seemed unlikely that a distaste for combat was going to be the flaw in any case. All three had fought, and fought hard: Burnside at Roanoke Island and Antietam, Rosecrans in West Virginia and at Corinth, Grant at Belmont, Donelson, and Shiloh — which was practically to call the roll of all the victories the army could lay claim to, east of the Mississippi, even by stretching the point in an instance or two or three. So had Banks fought hard, and though admittedly it had been with less success, Lincoln believed that the war had reached a stage where hard fighting, sustained by the superior resources of the nation, would create its own success. At any rate, that was what he was asking for now: hard fighting. And with this in mind, as Commander in Chief, he had placed his major armies under leaders he considered most likely to give it to him without delay.

So he thought, this melancholy man with his incurable optimism: only to find that what his high hopes mainly afforded him — once more, alas — was another occasion for exploring the gap that yawned between conception and execution. One by one, two by two, and finally all four together, his hand-picked generals failed his expectations as to haste. And, paradoxically, he discovered that the reason for delay, in all four cases, was just those superior resources which he had thought assured them victory.

Banks was first, the most enthusiastic of the lot. He had scarcely been gone from the capital a week before the President saw a monster requisition the Massachusetts general submitted, calling for mountains of supplies and thousands of horses to haul them through the jungles of the Lower South. Horses were a sore subject with Lincoln just now, anyhow, and when he was assured by the chief quartermaster that the requisition could not "be filled and got off within an hour short of two months," he wrote Banks a letter in which anger vied with sorrow for predominance. "I have just been overwhelmed and confounded," he declared, and continued: "My dear general, this expanding and piling up of impedimenta has been so far almost our ruin, and will be our final ruin if it is not abandoned.... When you parted with me you had no such ideas in your mind. I know you had not, or you could not have expected to be off so soon as you said. You must get back to something like the plan you had then or your expedition is a failure before you start. You must be off before Congress meets. You would be better off anywhere, and especially where you are going, for not having a thousand wagons doing nothing but hauling forage to feed the animals that draw them, and taking at least 2000 men to care for the wagons and animals, who otherwise might be 2000 good soldiers." In closing he added a further admonition: "Now, dear general, do not think this is an ill-natured letter; it is the very reverse. The simple publication of this requisition would ruin you."

As usual in cases where the offense presaged delay, Banks had what he considered a reasonable explanation. Two days later, November 24, he replied that the request for supplies "was drawn up by an officer who did not fully comprehend my instructions, and inadvertently approved by me without sufficient examination." In other words, he had signed without looking. "My purpose has not been changed since I left Washington," he assured Lincoln, "and I have waited [for] nothing not absolutely necessary." Apparently, though, a great many items fell in that category; for the waiting continued. Banks kept saying he would be off any day now, but the disillusioned President had doubts. And his doubts were valid. Banks' purpose might not have changed, but his schedule had. November went out; December came in; Banks remained at his New York starting point. Finally, on December 4, he sailed for Fort Monroe. How long he would stay there before continuing on to New Orleans, Lincoln did not know.

Anyhow, he had a good deal more on his mind by then. Troubles of a similar nature, involving delay, but derived from a different and even more unexpected source, were looming in the West: specifically in Grant's department, and even more specifically in U. S. Grant himself. After the ill-wind fiasco at Iuka and the bloody repulse of the rebels at Corinth, which he had missed, Grant had been sounding oddly unlike himself. When Halleck, after the latter fight, asked why he did not press the defeated and retreating foe — "Why order a return of our troops? Why not ... pursue the enemy into Mississippi, supporting your army on the country?" — Grant replied that an army could not "subsist itself on the country except in forage.... Disaster would follow in the end." This did not sound like the Grant of old, who never spoke of disaster except with the intention of inflicting it, and presently he was sounding even less so, calling urgently for reinforcements in expectation of having to fight another battle. This fall, in fact, his aggressive instincts mostly seemed reserved for the Jews in his department. "Refuse all permits to come south of Jackson for the present," he wired Hurlbut at that place, adding: "The Israelites especially should be kept out." He instructed his railroad superintendent to "give orders to all conductors on the road that no Jews are to be permitted to travel on the railroad southward from any point. They may go north and be encouraged in it; but they are such an intolerable nuisance that the department must be purged of them."

Lincoln would not have admired this talk of purges, not only because it ran counter to his personal belief in the equality of men before the law (whether the law was military or civil) but also because it could be applied to a father or mother on the way to visit a soldier son; for there were, of course, Jewish soldiers in all the nation's armies — even Grant's. In time this would be called to his attention, but for the present Lincoln was disturbed enough at the general's tone in regard to the pursuit of a beaten foe. One explanation was given by Rosecrans in a private letter to Halleck, written on the day before he was ordered north to replace Buell. He complained of "the spirit of mischief among the mousing politicians on Grant's staff," spoke of Grant becoming "sour and reticent," and asked to be "relieved from duty here." When a fighter Lincoln respected as much as he did Rosecrans asked for a transfer, apparently all was not well in the area he wished himself away from. Also — as always — there was talk that Grant had reverted to his old fondness for the bottle. Doubtless, too, Lincoln heard gossip similar to what a Chicago reporter heard from his fellow passengers as he rode south about this time on a train bound for Memphis. Officers and men returning from leaves and furloughs declared that Grant "never did amount to anything, and never would. He had been kicked out of the United States Army once, and would be again. He was nothing but a drunken, wooden-headed tanner, that would not trouble the country very long. &c. &c."

Whatever his past successes, Vicksburg was too important a prize for its capture to hinge entirely on the problematic advance of a man who was the subject of so many ugly rumors and whose character, even aside from the truth or falseness of such talk, seemed to have undergone a discouraging reversal. At any rate, Lincoln in this case had provided not one but two extra strings for the bow that was to be bent in that direction. While Banks was moving upriver against the place, supported by warships from Farragut's fleet, and Grant was marching overland down the Mississippi Central from Grand Junction, a third force was to descend the river from southern Illinois, its mission being to coöperate with Porter's ironclad flotilla for an attack on the stronghold which Jefferson Davis had called "the Gibraltar of the West." This third force was irregular and highly secret in nature, its purpose known only to three men: Lincoln, Stanton, and its commander, John McClernand. They had created it — out of the whole cloth, so to speak. McClernand had come north on leave in late September, saying privately that he was "tired of furnishing brains" for Grant's army, and had appealed to his friend the President to "let one volunteer officer try his abilities." In accordance with the plan he submitted, Stanton gave him on October 21 a confidential order authorizing him "to proceed to the States of Indiana, Illinois, and Iowa, and to organize the troops remaining in those States and to be raised by volunteering or draft ... to the end that, when a sufficient force not required by the operations of General Grant's command shall be raised, an expedition may be organized under General McClernand's command against Vicksburg ... to clear the Mississippi River and open navigation to New Orleans." A presidential indorsement further authorized him to show this confidential document "to Governors, and even others, when in his discretion he believes so doing to be indispensable to the progress of the expedition."

Armed with this order, which he saw as placing his star in the ascendant — his ambition had not been lessened by the singeing he took at Donelson while seeking the bubble reputation at the cannon's mouth — McClernand left for his home state in late October, there to begin assembling the force which he believed would put him not only in

Vicksburg but also in the White House. Even the first of these steps would take time, however; and time, he knew, was the foe of secrecy. Sure enough, by early November Grant began hearing what he called "mysterious rumors of McClernand's command." Glad as he had been to get rid of his fellow Illinoisan, he did not want him back in his department at the head of a rival army. When Halleck — whom the three lawyers had also not let in on their secret — informed him that Memphis would "be made the depot of a joint military and naval expedition on Vicksburg," Grant took alarm and wired back: "Am I to understand that I lie still here while an expedition is fitted out from Memphis, or do you want me to push as far south as possible? Am I to have Sherman move subject to my orders, or is he and his forces reserved for some special service?" Halleck replied blandly: "You have command of all troops sent to your department, and have permission to fight the enemy where you please."

That was enough for Grant. Receiving Halleck's go-ahead message near Grand Junction on November 11, he had cavalry in Holly Springs two days later. He followed at once with the infantry, established a supply base there, and continued his advance down the Mississippi Central. By December 1 his cavalry was across the Hatchie, the rebels fading back. Still Grant followed. Within another week he had occupied Oxford, fifty miles beyond his starting point, setting up a command post in the courthouse and repairing the railroad in his rear.... Whatever else McClernand's behind-the-scenes maneuver might accomplish in the end, it had effected at least one thing before it even got beyond the plans-and-training stage: Grant's mind had emerged from the tunnel it had entered after Shiloh. He was himself again, or anyhow he appeared to be, and this in itself was encouraging to Lincoln. However, he could also see that in North Mississippi, as elsewhere along the thousand-mile front, the fine autumn weather had mostly gone to waste, so far as offensive operations were concerned. Grant was still 150 airline miles from Vicksburg, and neither Banks nor McClernand had even begun to move.

Here in the East, delay was especially discouraging for being close at hand; Lincoln's torture, as a result, was not unlike that of Tantalus, who saw the surface of the pool recede each time he bent to drink. In this case, too, he was soon obliged to suspect that he had made an error in personal judgment, no matter how well founded that judgment had seemed at the time he acted on it. In addition to native combativeness, demonstrated on independent service, Burnside had other qualities which had caused Lincoln to overrule his twice-repeated protest that he was not competent to command the Army of the Potomac, despite the fact that his rank entitled him to the post. Less than three years older than McClellan, he had been his friend before and during the war and had taken no part in the bickering that surrounded him.

It was Lincoln's hope that this would ease the blow and soften the reaction when "McClellan's bodyguard" got the news that its hero had been replaced. Also, Burnside had no political opinions: a lack that might have been expected to spare him the mistrust and enmity of the Jacobins who had hounded his predecessor. Both calculations, one regarding the army, the other Congress, appeared to have been valid at the outset. For a time, they even worked; or else they seemed to. But the President was not long in finding out that both had been something less than inclusive. According to one general in a group who came to congratulate Burnside on his promotion, he thanked them "and then, with that transparent sincerity which made everyone believe what he said, he added that he knew he was not fit for so big a command, but he would do his best." The witness remarked: "One could not help feeling a certain tenderness for the man. But when a moment later the generals talked among themselves, it was no wonder that several shook their heads and asked how we could have confidence in the fitness of our leader if he had no such confidence in himself?" Such in part was the reaction in the army he was about to lead into battle. As for the radicals in Congress, it soon became apparent that an absence of politics was by no means a recommendation in their eyes. They had no objection to politics, per se; they merely insisted that the politics be Republican. All they really knew of Burnside was that he was the acknowledged friend of the man whose ruin they were proud to have helped accomplish, and they were prepared to do as much for him in turn, if on closer acquaintance it appeared that he deserved it.

Such objections were mainly personal, however, and Lincoln did not share them, or if he did he thought them incidental. His main concern was with Burnside as a strategist, a seeker after battle: which was where his doubts came in. Aware that the President wanted immediate action, and had in fact removed his predecessor for not giving it to him, the new commander immediately prepared a plan which he submitted for approval. Not liking the army's present location — which seemed to him uncomfortably similar to the one John Pope had occupied before he came to grief — Burnside had the notion of converting the advance just east of the Blue Ridge into a feint, under cover of which he would "accumulate a four or five days' supply for the men and animals; then make a rapid move of the whole force to Fredericksburg, with a view to a movement upon Richmond from that point." This was the so-called "covering approach" which Lincoln had always favored, since it protected Washington. But in this case he thought the plan defective, in that it made the southern capital the primary Federal objective, not Lee's army, which in fact it seemed that Burnside was attempting to avoid. Halleck felt that way about it, too, and on November 12 went down to Warrenton for a talk with the lush-whiskered general, who argued forcefully in favor of the change of base.

Still doubtful, Halleck returned to Washington and reported the discussion to the President. Lincoln too was unconvinced, but he was so pleased at the prospect of early action — here in the East, if nowhere else — that he agreed to let Burnside go ahead — or, more strictly speaking, sideways, then ahead — provided he moved fast. Halleck passed the word to Warrenton on the 14th: "The President has just assented to your plan. He thinks that it will succeed, if you move very rapidly; otherwise not."

Burnside did move rapidly, "very rapidly." Despite the tremendous supply problems which went with having an "aggregate present" of approximately 250,000 officers and men for whose welfare he was responsible — 150,441 in the field force proper, 98,738 in the capital defenses — the fact was, he had turned out to be an excellent administrator. On the day he received Lincoln's qualified assent to an eastward shift, he regrouped his seven corps into Right, Left, and Center "Grand Divisions" of two corps each, respectively under Sumner, Franklin, and Hooker, leaving the seventh in "independent reserve" under Sigel. With his army thus reorganized for deft handling, he took up the march for Falmouth the following day, November 15. Sumner went first, followed on subsequent days by Franklin, Hooker, and the cavalry. Moving down the north bank of the Rappahannock, which thus covered the exposed flank of the column, the Right Grand Division arrived on the 17th and the others came along behind on schedule. Burnside himself reached Falmouth on the 19th, just in advance of the rear-guard elements. Proudly he wired Washington: "Sumner's two corps now occupy all the commanding positions opposite Fredericksburg.... The enemy do not seem to be in force." So far, indeed, except for an occasional gray cavalry vedette across the way, the only sign of resistance had come from a single rebel battery on the heights beyond the historic south-bank town, and it had been smothered promptly by counterbattery fire. Lincoln had asked for speed, and Burnside had given it to him. He seemed about to give him all else he had asked for, too — hard fighting — for he added: "As soon as the pontoon trains arrive, the bridge will be built and the command moved over."

But there was the rub. Burnside had left the sending of the pontoons to Halleck, who in turn had left it to a subordinate, and somewhere along the chain of command the word "rush" had been dropped from the requisition. The army waited a week, during which a three-day rain swelled the fords and turned the roads into troughs of mud. Still the pontoons did not come. On the eighth day they got there; but so by then had something else; something not nearly so welcome. "Had the pontoon bridge arrived even on the 19th or 20th, the army could have crossed with trifling opposition," Burnside notified Halleck on the 22d. "But now the opposite side of the river is occupied by a large rebel force under General Longstreet, with batteries ready to be placed in position to operate against the working parties building the bridge and the troops in crossing." Vexed that his forty-mile change of base, executed with such efficiency and speed that it had given him the jump on his wily opponent, had gained him nothing by way of surprise in the end, he said flatly: "I deem it my duty to lay these facts before you, and to say that I cannot make the promise of probable success with the faith that I did when I supposed that all the parts of the plan would be carried out.... The President said that the movement, in order to be successful, must be made quickly, and I thought the same."

Lincoln was distressed: not only because of the delay, which he had predicted would be fatal to the success of the campaign, but also because the new commander, in the face of all those guns across the river, seemed to believe it was part of his duty to expose his army to annihilation by way of payment for other men's mistakes. November 25, the day the first relay of pontoons reached Falmouth, the President wired: "If I should be in a boat off Aquia Creek at dark tomorrow (Wednesday) evening, could you, without inconvenience, meet me and pass an hour or two with me?" He made the trip, saw Burnside and the situation — which he characterized by understatement as "somewhat risky" — then returned to Washington, worked out a supplementary plan of his own, and sent for the general to come up and discuss it with him and Halleck. As he saw it, the enemy should be confused by diversionary attacks, one upstream from Fredericksburg, the other on the lower Pamunkey, each to be delivered by a force of about 25,000 men and the latter to be supported by the fleet. Both generals rejected the plan, however, on grounds that it would require too much time for preparation. So Lincoln, with his argument stressing haste thus turned against him, had to content himself with telling Burnside to go back to his army and use his own judgment as to when and where he would launch an assault across the Rappahannock.

Burnside returned to Falmouth on the next to last day of November. His notion was to strike where Lee would least expect it, and the more he thought about the problem, the more it seemed to him that this would be at Fredericksburg itself, where Lee was strongest. Accordingly, he began to mass his 113,000 effectives — Sigel having been posted near Manassas — along and behind the north-bank heights, overlooking the streets of the Rappahannock town whose citizens had already been given notice to evacuate their homes. November was gone by then, however. In the East as in the West, to Lincoln's sorrow, there had been no fall offensive, only a seemingly endless preparation for one which had not come off.

Between these two East-West extremes, the trouble in Middle Tennessee, while similar to the trouble in Virginia and North Mississippi, was in its way even more exasperating. Burnside and Grant at least regretted the delay and expressed a willingness to end it, but

Rosecrans not only would not say that he regretted it, he declared flatly that he would not obey a direct order to end it until he personally was convinced that his hard-marched army was ready for action, down to the final shoenail in the final pair of shoes. This came as a shock to Lincoln, who had expected Old Rosy's positivism to take a different form. He would have been less surprised, no doubt, if he had known Grant's reaction when that general learned in late October that his then subordinate was leaving. "I was delighted," he later wrote, adding: "I found that I could not make him do as I wished, and had determined to relieve him from duty that very day."

Whatever reasons lay behind Rosecrans' reluctance to move forward, they could not have proceeded from any vagueness in his instructions, which were covered in a letter Halleck sent him along with his appointment as Buell's successor: "The great objects to be kept in view in your operations in the field are: First, to drive the enemy from Kentucky and Middle Tennessee; second, to take and hold East Tennessee, cutting the line of railroad at Chattanooga, Cleveland, or Athens, so as to destroy the connection of the valley of Virginia with Georgia and the other Southern States. It is hoped that by prompt and rapid movements a considerable part of this may be accomplished before the roads become impassable from the winter rains." After emphasizing "the importance of moving light and rapidly, and also the necessity of procuring as many of your supplies as possible in the country passed over," the general-in-chief concluded on an even sterner note: "I need not urge upon you the necessity of giving active employment to your forces. Neither the country nor the Government will much longer put up with the inactivity of some of our armies and generals."

There he had it, schedule and all; even the name of the army was changed, so that what had been called the Army of the Ohio was now the Army of the Cumberland, signifying the progress made, as well as the progress looked forward to. He knew well enough that Buell had been relieved because the authorities in Washington lacked confidence in his inclination or ability to get these missions accomplished in a hurry. That, too — in addition to the reluctance shown in declining the same appointment a month before — was why Thomas had been passed over in order to give the job to Rosecrans, whom they apparently considered the man to get it done. As a sign of this confidence, Halleck at once agreed to let him do what he had been unwilling to grant Buell. That is, he allowed him to return to Nashville with the army, agreeing at last with Buell's old contention that this was the best starting point for an advance on Chattanooga. Having won this concession, Rosecrans moved into the fortified Tennessee capital, and while butternut cavalry under Morgan and Forrest tore up tracks in his rear and slashed at his front, he set about reorganizing his command, more or less in the manner of Burnside, into Right, Left, and Center "Wings" of four divisions each.

Gilbert having faded back into the obscurity he came out of, these went respectively to McCook, Crittenden, and Thomas. The mid-November effective strength of the army was 74,555 men — as large or larger, it was thought, than the enemy force at Murfreesboro, thirty-odd miles southeast — but Rosecrans still had not advanced beyond the outskirts of Nashville. He was hoping, he said, for a sudden rise of the Tennessee River to cut off the rebels' retreat; in which case, as he put it, "I shall throw myself on their right flank and endeavor to make an end of them." For the present, however, he confided, "I am trying to lull them into security, that I do not intend soon to move, until I can get the [rail]road fully opened and throw in a couple of millions of rations here."

The Confederates might be lulled by his apparent inactivity, but his own superiors were not. Alarmed by this casual reference to "a couple of millions of rations" — followed as it was by urgent requisitions for "revolving rifles," back pay, "an iron pontoon train long enough to cross the Tennessee," and much else — Halleck told him sternly on November 27: "I must warn you against this piling up of impediments. Take a lesson from the enemy. Move light." The Tennessee commander protested that he was asking for nothing that was not "indispensable to an effectual and steady advance, which is the only one that will avail us anything worth the cost." By now it was December, and Rosecrans had begun to sound more like Buell than Buell himself had done. Halleck lost his temper, wiring curtly: "The President is very impatient.... Twice have I been asked to designate someone else to command your army. If you remain one more week in Nashville, I cannot prevent your removal." Rosecrans, unintimidated, bristled back at him: "Your dispatch received. I reply in few but earnest words. I have lost no time. Everything I have done was necessary, absolutely so; and has been done as rapidly as possible.... If the Government which ordered me here confides in my judgment, it may rely on my continuing to do what I have been trying to do — that is, my whole duty. If my superiors have lost confidence in me, they had better at once put someone in my place and let the future test the propriety of the change. I have but one word to add, which is, that I need no other stimulus to make me do my duty than the knowledge of what it is. To threats of removal or the like I must be permitted to say that I am insensible."

Now Lincoln knew the worst. With autumn gone and winter at hand, not a single one of the three major blows he had hoped for and designed had been struck. Right, left, and center, for all he knew — and he had observed signs of this with his own eyes, down on the Rappahannock — all that had been accomplished in each of these three critical theaters was a fair-weather setting of the stage for a foul-weather disaster. Halleck was saying of him during this first week in December: "You can hardly conceive his great anxiety," and Lincoln himself had told a friend the week before: "I certainly have been dissatisfied with the slowness of Buell and McClellan; but before I relieved them I had great fears I should not find successors to them who would do better; and I am sorry to add that I have seen little since to relieve those fears."

★ ★ ★

These words were written in a letter to Carl Schurz, a young German emigrant whom the Republican central committee had sent to Illinois four years ago to speak in Lincoln's behalf during the senatorial race against Douglas. Grateful for this and later, more successful work, Lincoln appointed him Minister to Spain in 1861, and when Schurz resigned to come home and fight, the President made him a brigadier under Frémont in the Alleghenies. After the fall election returns were in, he wrote Lincoln his belief that they were "a most serious reproof to the Administration" for placing the nation's armies in "the hands of its enemies," meaning Democrats. "What Republican has ever had a fair chance in this war?" Schurz asked, apparently leaving his own case out of account, and urged: "Let us be commanded by generals whose heart is in the war." Lincoln thought this over and replied: "I have just received and read your letter of [November] 20th. The purport of it is that we lost the late elections and the Administration is failing because the war is unsuccessful, and that I must not flatter myself that I am not justly to blame for it. I certainly know that if the war fails, the Administration fails, and that I will be blamed for it, whether I deserve it or not. And I ought to be blamed if I could do better. You think I could do better; therefore you blame me already. I think I could not do better; therefore I blame you for blaming me." Having thus disposed of the matter of blame, he passed on to the matter of hearts. "I understand you now to be willing to accept the help of men who are not Republicans, provided they have 'heart in it.' Agreed. I want no others. But who is to be the judge of hearts, or of 'heart in it'? If I must discard my own judgment and take yours, I must also take that of others; and by the time I should reject all I should be advised to reject, I should have none left, Republicans or others — not even yourself. For be assured, my dear sir, there are men who have 'heart in it' that think you are performing your part as poorly as you think I am performing mine.... I wish to disparage no one, certainly not those who sympathize with me; but I must say I need success more than I need sympathy, and that I have not seen the so much greater evidence of getting success from my sympathizers than from those who are denounced as the contrary."

He closed with a suggestion that the citizen soldier come to see him soon at the White House: which Schurz did, arriving early one morning, and was taken at once to an upstairs room where he found the President sitting before an open fire, his feet in large Morocco slippers.

Told to pull up a chair, he did so: whereupon Lincoln brought his hand down with a slap on Schurz's knee. "Now tell me, young man, whether you really think that I am as poor a fellow as you have made me out in your letter." He was smiling, but Schurz could not keep from stammering as he tried to apologize. This made the tall man laugh aloud, and again he slapped his visitor's knee. "Didn't I give it to you hard in my letter? Didn't I? But it didn't hurt, did it? I did not mean to, and therefore I wanted you to come so quickly." Still laughing, he added: "Well, I guess we understand one another now, and it's all right." They talked for the better part of an hour, and as Schurz rose to leave he asked whether he should keep on writing letters to the President. "Why, certainly," Lincoln told him. "Write me whenever the spirit moves you."

It was Schurz's belief that the visit had done Lincoln good, and unquestionably it had. Busy as he was with the details of office, not all of which were directly connected with the war, he had all too few occasions for relaxation, let alone laughter, the elixir he had always used against his natural melancholia. Out in Minnesota, for example, John Pope had been more successful against the marauding Sioux than he had against Lee and Jackson. He had defeated Chief Little Crow in battle and brought the surviving braves before a military court which sentenced 303 of them to be hanged. Reviewing the list, Lincoln reduced to thirty-eight the number slated for immediate execution and ordered the rest held, "taking care that they neither escape nor are subjected to any unlawful violence." This was of course only one distraction among many, the most troublesome being the host of importunate callers, all of whom wanted some special favor from him. Sometimes he lost patience, as when he told a soldier who came seeking his intervention in a routine army matter: "Now, my man, go away. I cannot attend to all these details. I could as easily bail out the Potomac with a spoon!" But mostly he was patient and receptive. He put them at ease, heard their complaints, and did what he could to help them. When a friend remarked, "You will wear yourself out," he shook his head and replied with a sad smile: "They don't want much; they get but little, and I must see them."

One place of refuge he had, the war telegraph office, and one companion whose demands on his time apparently brought him nothing but pleasure, Tad. Often he would combine the two, taking his son there with him during the off-hours, when the place was quiet, with only a single operator on duty. He would sit at a desk, reading the accumulated flimsies, while the nine-year-old went to sleep on his lap or rummaged around in search of mischief, which he seldom failed to find. John Hay once remarked that Tad "had a very bad opinion of books, and no opinion of discipline." The former was mainly his father's fault. "Let him run," Lincoln said. "There's time enough yet for him to learn his letters and get poky." So was the latter; for since the death of Willie, eight months before, this youngest child had been overindulged by way of double compensation. "I want to give him all the toys I did not have," Lincoln explained, "and all the toys I would have given the boy who went away." Nor would he allow his son to be corrected. Once when they were at the telegraph office Tad wandered into the adjoining room, where he found the combination of black ink and white marble-topped tables quite irresistible. Presently the operator, whose name was Madison Buell, saw what was being done. Indignant at the ruin, he seized the dabbler by the collar and marched him out to his father, pointing through the open door at the irreparable outrage. Lincoln reacted promptly. Rising, he took the boy in his arms, unmindful of the hands still dripping ink. "Come, Tad," he said; "Buell is abusing you," and left.

In these and other ways he sought relaxation during this season which had opened with reverses and closed before the big machine could overcome the primary inertia which had gripped it when it stalled. Such large-scale battles as had been fought — Antietam, Corinth, Perryville — had been set down as Union victories; but they had been near things at best — particularly the first and the last, which the rebels also claimed — and what was more, all three had been intrinsically defensive; which would not do. It would do for the insurgents, whose task was merely to defend their region against what they called aggression, but not for the loyalists, whose goal could be nothing short of conquest. Besides, the defensive encouraged the fulfillment of Lincoln's two worst fears: utter war-weariness at home, and recognition for the Confederacy abroad. Other developments might prolong the war, but these two could lose it, and he had taken their avoidance as his personal responsibility. During the period just past, he had sought to prevent the first by appealing directly to the people for confidence in his Administration, and to forestall the second by issuing the Preliminary Emancipation Proclamation. How well he had done in both cases he did not know; it was perhaps too soon to tell, though here too the signs were not encouraging. Some said the fall elections were a rejection of the former, while the latter had been greeted in some quarters — including England, so far as could be judged from the public prints — with derision.

He would wait and see, improvising to meet what might arise. Meanwhile, the armies were getting into position at last for another major effort — and, incidentally, fulfilling the *Tribune* reporter's prediction about "the poetry of war." Down on the Rappahannock, for example, another of Greeley's men overheard the following exchange between two pickets on opposite banks:

"Hallo, Secesh!"

"Hallo, Yank."

"What was the matter with your battery Tuesday night?"

"You made it too hot. Your shots drove the cannoneers away, and they haven't stopped running yet. We infantry men had to come out and withdraw the guns."

"You infantry men will run, too, one of these fine mornings."

The Confederate picket let this pass, as if to say it might be so, and responded instead with a question:

"When are you coming over, bluecoat?"

"When we get ready, butternut."

"What do you want?"

"Want Fredericksburg."

"Don't you wish you may get it!"

✗ 2 ✗

As if in accordance with the respective limitations of their available resources — which of course applied to men as well as to the food they ate, the powder they burned, and the shoes and clothes and horses they wore out — while Lincoln was getting rid of experienced commanders, Davis was making use of those he had. Yet this difference in outlook and action was not merely the result of any established ratio between profligacy and frugality, affordable on the one hand and strictly necessary on the other; it was, rather, an outgrowth of the inherent difference in their natures. Lincoln, as he said, was more in need of success than he was in need of sympathy. And while this was also true of Davis, he placed such value on the latter quality — apparently for its own sake — that its demands for reciprocal loyalty, whatever shortcomings there might be in regard to the former, were for him too strong to be denied.

Braxton Bragg and R. E. Lee were cases in point. Ever since the western general began his retreat from Harrodsburg, Davis had been receiving complaints of dissension in the ranks of the Army of Kentucky, along with insistent demands that its commander be removed: in spite of which (if not, indeed, because of them; for such agitations often seemed to strengthen instead of weaken Davis' will) the summons Bragg found waiting for him in Knoxville had not been sent with any notion of effecting his dismissal, but rather with the intention of giving him the chance to present in person his side of the reported controversy. When he got to Richmond, October 25, the President received him with a smile and a congratulatory handshake. On the face of it, both were certainly deserved: the first because it was not Davis' way to dissolve a friendship or condemn any man on the basis of hearsay evidence, and the second because, of the three offensives designed to push Confederate arms beyond the acknowledged borders of secession, only Bragg's had been even moderately successful. In fact, "moderately" was putting it all too mildly. Whatever else had been left undone, a campaign which relieved the pressure on Chattanooga and recovered for the Confederacy all of northwest Alabama, as well as eastern and south-central Tennessee, including Cumberland Gap — not to mention the fact that its two columns had inflicted just under 14,000 battle casualties while suffering just over 4000, and had returned with an enormous train of badly needed supplies and captured matériel, including more than thirty Union guns — could scarcely be called anything less than substantial in its results. What was more, Bragg had conceived and, in conjunction with Kirby Smith, executed the whole thing, not only without prodding from above, but also without the government's advance permission or even knowledge. Initiative such as that was all too rare. Davis heard him out, and though he did not enjoy hearing his old friend and classmate Bishop Polk accused of bumbling and disloyalty, sustained him. Bragg was told to rejoin his army, which meanwhile was moving rapidly by rail, via Stevenson, Alabama, from Knoxville to Tullahoma and Murfreesboro, where it would threaten Nashville and block a Federal advance from that direction.

Polk was summoned to the capital as soon as Bragg had left it. Invited to present his side of the controversy, the bishop came armed with documents — messages from Bragg to him, messages from him to Bragg, and affidavits provided by fellow subordinates, similarly disaffected — which he believed would protect his reputation and destroy his adversary's, or at any rate neutralize the poison lately poured into the presidential ear. "If you choose to rip up the Kentucky campaign you can tear Bragg into tatters," Hardee told him. However, Davis urged him to put them away, appealing to his patriotism as well as his churchman's capacity for forgiveness, and the bishop agreed to go back and do his Christian best along those lines. By way of compensation, the President handed him his promotion to lieutenant general, a new rank lately authorized by Congress at the same time it legalized the previously informal division of the armies into "wings" and corps. That was gratifying. Equally so was the news that his friend Hardee's name appeared immediately below his own on the seven-man list of generals so honored.

Above them both — next to the very top, in fact — was Kirby Smith, who thus was rewarded for his independent accomplishments in Kentucky, even though he had written to the War Department soon after his return, complaining acidly of Bragg's direction of the campaign during its later stages and requesting transfer to Mobile or elsewhere, anywhere, if staying where he was would require further coöperation with that general. Davis himself replied to this on October 29. He agreed that the campaign had been "a bitter disappointment" in some respects, but he also felt that events should not be judged by "knowledge acquired after they transpired." Besides, having talked at length with Bragg that week, he could assure Smith that "he spoke of you in the most complimentary terms, and does not seem to imagine your dissatisfaction." Davis admitted some other commanders might "excite more enthusiasm" than the dyspeptic North Carolinian, but he doubted that they would be "equally useful" to the country. In motion now for Middle Tennessee, Bragg would need reinforcements in order to parry the Federal counterthrust from Nashville. Where were they to be procured if not from Smith? He asked that, and then concluded: "When you wrote your wounds were fresh, your lame and exhausted troops were before you. I hope time may have mollified your pain and that future operations may restore the confidence essential to cheerfulness and security in campaign."

That was enough for Smith, whose admiration for Davis was such that, if the President requested it, he would not only coöperate with Bragg, he would even serve under him if it was absolutely necessary. Grateful, Davis sent for him to come to Richmond in early November. Smith went and, like Polk, gave the President his personal assurance that his rancor had been laid by — as indeed it had. A week later he sent Bragg his strongest division, Stevenson's, and neither Smith nor any member of his staff permitted himself a public word of criticism of the leader of the Kentucky campaign for the balance of the war. Returning to Knoxville by way of Lynchburg (where he had convalesced from his Manassas wound and married the young lady who had nursed him) he had an unexpected encounter during a change of trains. "I saw Gen. Bragg," he wrote his wife; "everyone prognosticated a stormy meeting. I told him what I had written to Mr. Davis, but he spoke kindly to me & in the highest terms of praise and admiration of 'my personal character and soldierly qualities.' I was astonished but believe he is honest & means well."

Breckinridge was already with Bragg: in fact, had preceded the army to its present location. Following the repulse at Baton Rouge, after wiring Hardee to "reserve the division for me," he had reached Knoxville in early October with about 2500 men. Reinforced by an equal number of exchanged prisoners, he had been about to start northward in order to share in the "liberation" of his native Bluegrass, when he received word that Bragg was on the way back and wanted him to proceed instead to Murfreesboro, where he was to dispose his troops "for the defense of Middle Tennessee or an attack on Nashville." He got there October 28, joining Forrest, who had been deviling the Federals by way of breaking in his newly recruited "critter companies." Bragg's 30,000 veterans arrived under Polk and Hardee ten days later, and when Stevenson's 9000-man division marched in from Knoxville shortly afterward, the army totaled 44,000 infantry and artillery effectives, plus about 4000 organic cavalry under Wheeler. This was by no means as large a force as Rosecrans was assembling within the Nashville intrenchments, but Bragg did not despair of whipping him when he emerged. Returning from Richmond with assurances of the President's confidence, he set about the familiar task of drilling his troops and stiffening the discipline which Buell had admired. Meanwhile, he turned Forrest and Morgan loose on Rosecrans, front and rear. "Harass him in every conceivable way in your power," he told them. And they did, thus fulfilling the anticipation announced in general orders, November 20: "Much is expected by the army and its commander from the operations of these active and ever-successful leaders."

Nor were the infantry neglected in their commander's announcement of his hopes. Having posted Stevenson's division in front of Manchester, Hardee's corps at Shelbyville, and Polk's at Murfreesboro — the latter now including Breckinridge, so that Polk had three and Hardee two divisions — Bragg announced in the same general order that the army had a new name: "The foregoing dispositions are in anticipation of the great struggle which must soon settle the question of supremacy in Middle Tennessee. The enemy in heavy force is before us, with a determination, no doubt, to redeem the fruitful country we have wrested from him. With the remembrance of Richmond, Munfordville, and Perryville so fresh in our minds, let us make a name for the now Army of Tennessee as enviable as those enjoyed by the armies of Kentucky and the Mississippi."

Presumably this was the best that could be done in that direction: Davis had sustained the army commander and persuaded his irate subordinates to lay aside their personal and official differences in order to concentrate on the defense of the vital center in Tennessee. South and west of there, however, the problem was not one of persuading delicate gears to mesh, but rather one of filling the near vacuum created by the bloody repulse Van Dorn and Price had suffered in front of Corinth. Vicksburg was obviously about to become the target for a renewed endeavor by Federal combinations. What these would be, Davis did not know, but whatever they were, they posed a problem that would have to be met before they got there. He met it obliquely, so to speak, by turning initially to a second problem, seven hundred miles away, whose solution automatically provided him with a solution to the first.

This was the problem of Charleston, where the trouble was also an outgrowth of dissension. John Pemberton, in command there, had been a classmate of Bragg's and had several of that general's less fortunate characteristics, including an abruptness of manner which, taken in conjunction with his northern birth, had earned him a personal unpopularity rivaling the North Carolinian's. Indeed, not being restricted to the army, it surpassed it. He was "wanting in polish," according to one Confederate observer, "and was too positive and domineering ... to suit the sensitive and polite people among whom he had been thrown." As a result, he had not been long in incurring the displeasure of Governor Pickens and the enmity of the Rhetts, along with that of other Charlestonians of influence, who by now were clamoring for his removal. They wanted their first hero back: meaning Beauregard. It was a more or less familiar cry to Davis, for others were also calling for the Creole, still restoring his "shattered health" at Bladon Springs. In mid-September two Louisiana congressmen brought to the President's office a petition signed by themselves and fifty-seven fellow members, requesting the general's return to command of the army that had been taken from him. Davis read the document aloud, including the signatures, then sent for the official correspondence relating to Beauregard's removal for being absent without leave. This too he read aloud, as proof of justice in his action on the case, and closed the interview by saying: "If the whole world were to ask me to restore General Beauregard to the command which I have already given to General Bragg, I would refuse it."

In any case, he had decided by then to use him in the opposite direction: meaning Charleston. Orders had been drawn up in late August, appointing Beauregard to command the Department of South Carolina and Georgia, with headquarters in Charleston. Whether he would accept the back-area appointment, which amounted in effect to a demotion, was not known. Yet there should have been little doubt; for the choice, after all, lay between limited action and *in*action. "*Nil desperandum* is my motto," he had declared, chafing in idleness earlier that month, "and I feel confident that ere long the glorious sun of Southern liberty will appear more radiant than ever from the clouds which obscure its brilliant disk." He wanted a share in scouring those clouds away. Receiving the orders in early September, he told a friend: "If the country is willing I should be put on the shelf thro' interested motives, I will submit until our future reverses will compel the Govt to put me on duty. I scorn its motives and present action." He wired acceptance, took the cars at Mobile on September 11, and received a tumultuous welcome on the 15th when he returned to the city whose harbor had been the scene of his first glory.

This not only freed the embittered Charlestonians of Pemberton; it also freed Pemberton for the larger duty Davis had in mind for him, along with a promotion as seventh man on the seven-man list of new lieutenant generals. Slender and sharp-faced, the forty-eight-year-old Pennsylvanian had been pro-Southern all his adult life, choosing southern cadets as his West Point friends and later marrying a girl from Old Point Comfort. He was, indeed, an out-and-out States Righter, and it was generally known in army circles that in making his choice of sides in the present conflict, despite the fact that two of his brothers had joined a Philadelphia cavalry troop, he had declined a Federal colonelcy in order to accept a commission as a Confederate lieutenant colonel and assignment to Norfolk, where he had been charged with organizing

Virginia's cavalry and artillery. Efficiency at that assignment had won him a brigadier's stars and transfer to Charleston, where his ability as an administrator — whatever his shortcomings when it came to social converse — had won him another promotion and eventually still another, along with another transfer, in connection with the larger duty Davis had in mind. This was for Pemberton to take charge of a department created October 1, consisting of the whole state of Mississippi and that part of Louisiana east of the Mississippi River. Instructed to "consider the successful defense of those States" — one already invaded from the north, the other already invaded from the south — "as the first and chief object of your command," he was told to proceed at once to his new post: which he did. Arriving October 14, he established department headquarters at Jackson, Mississippi.

There were, as usual, objections. Mainly these came from men over whose heads he had been advanced in his rush up the ladder of rank, including Van Dorn and Lovell, here in his own department, as well as others back in the theater he had come from; "officers who," as one of them protested, "had already distinguished themselves and given unquestioned evidence of capacity, efficiency, and other soldierly qualities." By this last, the disgruntled observer meant combat — for Pemberton had seen none since the Mexican War. Also, it was felt that he lacked the flexibility of mind necessary to independent command of a region under pressure from various directions. But the fact was, Davis had already taken this into consideration. Pemberton's main job would be to keep a bulldog grip on Vicksburg and Port Hudson, denying free use of the Mississippi to the Federals and keeping the stretch of river between those two bastions open as a Confederate supply line connecting its opposite banks. Inflexibility in the performance of such a job — even tactical and strategic near-sightedness, of which the new commander was also accused by those who had known him in the East — might turn out to be a positive virtue when he was confronted, as surely he would be, by combinations which well might cause a more "flexible" man to fly to pieces. So Davis reasoned, at any rate, when he assigned the Northerner to defend his home state. And at least one Vicksburg editor agreed, declaring that Pemberton's arrival at last demonstrated that the far-off Richmond government had not "failed to appreciate the vast importance of preserving this important region" and that Mississippians were no longer "to be put off and imposed upon with one-horse generals."

Whatever their resentment of his rapid rise, his northern birth, his lack of exposure to gunfire, and his uncongenial manner, Pemberton's by-passed fellow officers — even Van Dorn, whose ruffled feathers Davis smoothed by explaining that the appointment had been made, not to overslough him, but to unburden him of paperwork and other backarea concerns, in order to free him for the offensive action which he so much preferred — would doubtless have been less envious if they had been able to compare the magnitude of the new commander's "first and chief object" with the means which he had inherited for effecting it. He had fewer than 50,000 troops of all arms in his entire department: 24,000 under Van Dorn and Price — disaffected Transmississippians for the most part, anxious to get back across the river for the close-up protection of their homes — and another 24,000 mainly comprising the permanent garrisons of Vicksburg and Port Hudson. Even without knowledge of the three-pronged Federal build-up now in progress north and south of these two critical points (a combined force of more than 100,000 men, supported by the guns of two fleets) it was obvious that the difficulties of the assignment would be exceeded only by the clamor which would follow if he failed, whatever the odds.

Here too, however, Davis had done what he could and as he thought best. Having sustained Bragg, installed Pemberton, and incidentally disposed of Beauregard, he found it in a way a relief to give his attention to the army closest to the capital: for its troubles, although manifold, were at least of a different nature. Though Lee's invasion had been less profitable than Bragg's, and his repulse far bloodier, no one could accuse him of unwillingness to exploit any opening the enemy afforded, regardless of the numerical odds or the tactical risks of annihilation. As a result, such disaffection as arose was not directed against him, either by his army or by the public it protected, but against Congress, which bridled at passing certain measures Lee suggested for the recruitment of new men, the establishment of proper supply facilities for the benefit of the men he had — including the more than 10,000 who now were marching barefoot in the snow — and the authority to tighten discipline.

The President supported Lee in the controversy and wrote him of the scorn he felt for their opponents, who were reacting simultaneously to rumors that the enemy was about to advance on Richmond from Suffolk: "The feverish anxiety to invade the North has been relieved by the counter-irritant of apprehension for the safety of the capital in the absence of the army, so long criticised for a 'want of dash,' and the class who so vociferously urged a forward movement, in which they were not personally involved, would now be most pleased to welcome the return of that army. I hope their fears are as poor counselors as was their presumption." He assured the Virginian, "I am alike happy in the confidence felt in your ability, and your superiority to outside clamor, when the uninformed assume to direct the movements of armies in the field." Lee replied characteristically: "I wish I felt that I deserved the confidence you express in me. I am only conscious of an earnest desire to advance the interests of the country and of my inability to accomplish my wishes."

Davis left the field work to Lee, while he himself took up the fight with Congress throughout its stormy second session, which extended from mid-August to mid-October. Two of the general's recommendations resulted in much violent debate: 1) that a permanent court martial be appointed, with authority to inflict the death penalty in an attempt to reduce straggling and desertion, and 2) that the Conscription Act be extended to include all able-bodied men between the ages of eighteen and forty-five. The first of these suggestions was not only not acceptable to the law-makers, it led to vigorous inquiries as to whether such powers had not been overexercised already. But it was the second which provoked the greatest furor, especially after Davis gave it presidential support. Yancey was particularly vitriolic, shouting that if he had to have a dictator, he wanted it to be Lincoln, "not a Confederate." Joe Brown of Georgia thought so, too, declaring that the people had "much more to apprehend from military despotism than from subjection by the enemy." A Texas senator added point to the assertion, as here applied, by recalling that it had been conscription which "enabled [Napoleon] to put a diadem on his head." Davis met these charges with a bitterness matching that of the men who made them; and in the end he won the fight. Conscription was extended, but not without the estrangement of former loyal friends whose loss he could ill afford. As always, he was willing to pay the price, though it was becoming increasingly steep in obedience to the law of diminishing utility.

At any rate the measure helped secure for Lee the men he badly needed, and while Davis engaged these wranglers in the army's rear, the bluecoats to its front were obligingly idle, affording time for rest, recruitment, and reorganization of its shattered ranks. The need for these was obvious at a glance. Recrossing the Potomac, only fourteen of the forty brigades had been led by brigadiers, and many of them had dwindled until they were smaller than a standard regiment. Yet the return of stragglers and convalescents, along with the influx of conscripts, more than repaired the shortage in the course of the five-week respite the Federals allowed. By October 10, Lee's strength had risen to 64,273 of all arms, and within another ten days — on which date McClellan reported 133,433 present for duty in the Army of the Potomac — he had 68,033, or better than half as many as his opponent. High spirits, too, were restored. Pride in their great defensive fight at Sharpsburg, when the odds had been even longer, and presently their jubilation over Stuart's second "Ride Around McClellan," solidified into a conviction that the Army of Northern Virginia was more than a match for whatever came against it, even if the Yankees continued to fight as well as they had fought in Maryland. Shortages of equipment there still were, especially of shoes and clothes, but these were accepted as rather the norm and relatively unimportant. A British army observer, visiting Lee at the time, expressed surprise at the condition of the trousers of the men in Hood's division, the rents and tatters being especially apparent after the first files had passed in review. "Never mind the raggedness, Colonel," Lee said quietly. "The enemy never sees the backs of my Texans."

He spoke, the colonel observed, "as a man proud of his country and confident of ultimate success." However, this was for the southern commander a time of personal sorrow. Soon after October 20 he heard from his wife of the death on that date of the second of his three daughters. She was twenty-three years old and had been named for his mother, born Ann Carter. He turned to some official correspondence, seeking thus to hide his grief, but presently an aide came into the tent and found him weeping. "I cannot express the anguish I feel at the death of my sweet Annie," he wrote home.

Work was still the best remedy, he believed, and fortunately there was plenty to occupy him. The previously informal corps arrangement was made official in early November with the promotion of Longstreet and Jackson, respectively first and fifth on the list of lieutenant generals. By that time, moreover, the Federals had crossed the river which gave their army its name, and Lee had divided his own in order to cover their alternate routes of approach, shifting Old Pete down to Culpeper while Stonewall remained in the lower Valley, eager to pounce through one of the Blue Ridge gaps and onto the enemy flank. But this was not Pope; this was McClellan. He maneuvered skillfully, keeping the gaps well plugged as he advanced against the divided Confederates. Then suddenly, inexplicably, he stopped. For two days Lee was left wondering: until November 10, that is, when he learned that Little Mac had been relieved. The southern reaction was not unmixed. Some believed that the Federals would be demoralized by McClellan's removal, while others found assurance in the conviction that his successor would be more likely to commit some blunder which would expose the blue host to destruction. Lee, however, expressed regret at the departure of a familiar and respected adversary. "We always understood each other so well," he said wryly. "I fear they may continue to make these changes till they find someone whom I don't understand."

When Burnside shifted east in mid-November, Lee's first plan was to occupy the line of the North Anna, twenty-five miles south of the Rappahannock. From there he would draw the bluecoats into the intervening wintry swamps and woodlands, then move forward and outflank them in order to slash at them from astride their line of retreat. If successful, this would have been to stage a Sedan eight years ahead of the historical schedule; Jackson, for one, was very much in favor of it. If on the other hand the Confederates contested the Rappahannock crossing, where the position afforded little depth for maneuver and was dominated by the north-bank heights, it was Stonewall's opinion that they would "whip the enemy, but gain no fruits of victory." However, Lee did not want to give up the previously unmolested territory and expose the vital railroad to destruction; so while Burnside balked at Falmouth, awaiting the delayed pontoons, the southern commander moved Longstreet onto the heights in rear of Fredericksburg. This suited Old Pete fine; for the position offered all the defensive advantages he most admired, if only "the damned Yankees" could be persuaded to "come to us."

Apparently they were coming, here or somewhere near here, but they were taking their time about it. ("When are you coming over, bluecoat?" "When we get ready, butternut.") For ten days Lee left the vigil to Longstreet, withholding Jackson for a flank attack if Burnside crossed upstream. Then, as the indications grew that a crossing would be attempted here, he sent for Stonewall, whose troops began to file into position alongside Longstreet's on the first day of December. By that time the army had grown to 70,000 infantry and artillery, plus 7000 cavalry, and its spirit was higher than ever, despite the fact that one man in every six was barefoot. They now bore with patience, one officer remarked, "what they once would have regarded as beyond human endurance." Even a four-inch snowfall on the night of December 5, followed by bitter cold weather, failed to lower their morale. Rather, they organized brigade-sized snowball battles, during which their colonels put them through the evolutions of the line, and thus kept in practice while waiting for the Yankees to cross the river flowing slate gray between its cake-icing banks.

Lee shared their hardships and their confidence. Sometimes, though, alone in his tent, he was oppressed by sorrow for the daughter who had died six weeks ago. "In the quiet hours of the night, when there is nothing to lighten the full weight of my grief," he wrote home, "I feel as if I should be overwhelmed. I have always counted, if God should spare me a few days after this Civil War has ended, that I should have her with me, but year after year my hopes go out, and I must be resigned." Mainly his consolation was his army. Though he told his wife, "I tremble for my country when I hear of confidence expressed in me. I know too well my weakness, and that our only hope is in God," his admiration for the men he led was almost without bounds. "I am glad you derive satisfaction from the operations of the army," he replied to a congratulatory letter from his brother. "I acknowledge nothing can surpass the valor and endurance of our troops, yet while so much remains to be done, I feel as if nothing had been accomplished. But we must endure to the end, and if our people are true to themselves and our soldiers continue to discard all thoughts of self and to press nobly forward in defense alone of their country and their rights, I have no fear of the result. We may be annihilated, but we cannot be conquered. No sooner is one [Federal] army scattered than another rises up. This snatches from us the fruits of victory and covers the battlefield with our dead. Yet what have we to live for if not victorious?"

It was this spirit which made Lee's army "terrible in battle," and it was in this spirit that he and his men awaited Burnside's crossing of the Rappahannock.

★ ★ ★

Off in the Transmississippi, the sixth of the new lieutenant generals, Theophilus Holmes, had established headquarters at Little Rock and from there was surveying a situation which was perhaps as confusing for him as the one near Malvern Hill, where he had cupped a deaf ear in the midst of a heavy bombardment and declared that he thought he "heard firing." If he was similarly bewildered it was no wonder, considering the contrast between the geographical vastness of his command and the slimness of his resources. In addition to Texas and Missouri, the two largest states of the old Union, he was theoretically responsible for holding or reclaiming Arkansas, Indian Territory, West Louisiana, and New Mexico, in all of which combined he had fewer than 50,000 men, including guerillas. These last were sometimes as much trouble to him as they were to the enemy, especially as an administrative concern, and even the so-called "regulars" were generally well beyond his reach, being loosely connected with headquarters, if at all, by lines of supply and communication which could only be characterized as primitive, telegraph wire being quite as rare as railroad iron. By late October, after three months of pondering the odds, he had begun to consider not only the probability of total defeat, but also the line of conduct he and his men would follow in the wake of that disaster. In this he showed that, whatever his physical shortcomings and infirmities, his spirit was undamaged. "We hate you with a cordial hatred," he told an Indiana colonel who came to Little Rock bearing messages under a flag of truce. "You may conquer us and parcel out our lands among your soldiers, but you must remember that one incident of history: to wit, that of all the Russians who settled in Poland not one died a natural death."

Moreover, his three department commanders — John Magruder, Richard Taylor, and Thomas Hindman, respectively in charge of Texas, West Louisiana, and Arkansas — shared his resolution, but not his gloom. All three were working, even now, on plans for the recovery of all that had been lost. Prince John for example, as flamboyant in the Lone Star State as ever he had been in the Old Dominion, was improvising behind the scenes a two-boat cotton-clad navy with which he intended to steam down Buffalo Bayou and retake Galveston, the only Federal-held point in his department. Taylor's ambition was longer-ranged — as well it had to be; New Orleans was occupied by something more than ten times as many soldiers and sailors as he had in his whole command —

but he had hopes for the eventual recapture of the South's first city, along with the lower reaches of the Father of Waters itself. Meanwhile, having recovered from the mysterious paralysis which had gripped his legs on the eve of the Seven Days, thus preventing any addition to the reputation he had won under Jackson in the Valley, he was working hard with what little he had in the way of men and guns, seeking first to establish dispersed strong-points with which to forestall a further penetration by the gunboats and the probing Union columns, after which he intended to swing over to the offensive and reclaim what had been lost to amphibious combinations heretofore considered too powerful to resist with any substantial hope of success.

Of the three, so far, it was Hindman who had accomplished most, however, and against the longest odds. Operating in a region which had been stripped of troops when Van Dorn crossed the Mississippi back in April, he yet had managed to raise and equip an army of 16,000 men, and with them he had already begun to launch an offensive against Schofield, who had about the same number for the protection of the Missouri border. By late August, Hindman was across it; or anyhow a third of his soldiers were, and he was preparing to join them with the rest. Skirting Helena, where 15,000 Federals were intrenched — they now were under Brigadier General Frederick Steele, Curtis having moved on to St Louis and command of the department, belatedly rewarded for his Pea Ridge victory — the Confederate advance occupied Newtonia, beyond Neosho and southwest of Springfield. All through September they stayed there, 2500 Missouri cavalry under Colonel J. O. Shelby and about 3000 Indians and guerillas, called in to assist in holding the place until Hindman arrived with the other two thirds of his hastily improvised army. Shelby was a graduate of the prewar Kansas border conflict, a stocky, heavily bearded man approaching his thirty-second birthday. Called "Jo" for his initials, just as Stuart was called "Jeb," and wearing like him an ostrich plume attached to the upturned brim of a soft felt hat, he was a veteran of nearby Wilson's Creek and of Elkhorn Tavern, forty miles to the south. With him out front, and the stone walls of the town to fight behind, the garrison was more than a match for a 4000-man column Schofield sent to retake Newtonia on the last day of September. The Confederates broke the point of the counterthrust and drove the bluecoats north. However, learning three days later (October 3: Van Dorn and Price were moving against Corinth) that the Federals had been reinforced to thrice their former strength, they fell back next day in the direction of the Boston Mountains, Shelby skillfully covering the retreat with a succession of slashing attacks and quick withdrawals.

Hindman was not discouraged by this turn of events. In fact, he saw in it certain advantages. Schofield should be easier to whip if he advanced into Arkansas, lengthening his lines of supply — and lengthening, too, the distance he would have to backtrack through the wintry woods in order to regain the comparative security of Missouri. Under such disadvantages, a simple repulse might be transformed into a disaster. At any rate, Hindman intended to do all he could to bring about that result. But as he prepared to move forward in early November, consolidating the segments of his army, he received news that was discouraging indeed. It came from Holmes, who had just received in Little Rock a dispatch from Richmond, dated October 27 and signed by the Secretary of War: "Coöperation between General Pemberton and yourself is indispensable to the preservation of our connection with your department. We regard this as an object of first importance, and when necessary you can cross the Mississippi with such part of your forces as you may select, and by virtue of your rank direct the combined operations on the eastern bank."

This meant, in effect, that Hindman's offensive would have to be abandoned. And when it was followed in mid-November by a specific request from the Adjutant General ("Vicksburg is threatened and requires to be reinforced. Can you send troops from your command — say 10,000 — to operate either opposite to Vicksburg or to cross the river?") Holmes perceived that it meant the abandonment, not only of his hopes for regaining Missouri, but also of his hopes for hanging onto Arkansas. "I could not get to Vicksburg in less than two weeks," he protested. "There is nothing to subsist on between here and there, and [Steele's] army at Helena would come to Little Rock before I reached Vicksburg."

However, he need not have worried. He was not going anywhere. Nor was Hindman's offensive to be interrupted: at any rate not by anyone in Richmond, and least of all by Thomas Jefferson's grandson George Randolph. Presently it became fairly clear that the original dispatch sent by that official, though couched in the form of a military directive, was in effect an act of political suicide, whereby the Confederacy lost the third of its several Secretaries of War.

Joe Johnston was one of the first to get inside news of the impending disruption in the President's official family, and what was more he got it at first hand. His Seven Pines wound had proved troublous, resulting in what the doctors called "an obstinate adhesion of the lungs to the side, and a constant tendency to pleurisy," for which the prescribed treatments were "bleedings, blisterings, and depletions of the system." All three were stringently applied: in spite of which, having sufficiently recovered by early November to begin taking horseback exercise — "My other occupation," he told a friend, "is blistering myself, to which habit hasn't yet reconciled me" — the general called at the War Department on the 12th of that month to report himself fit for duty. Closeted with the Secretary, he learned that the government intended to send him West, where his assignment would be to coördinate the efforts of Bragg and Pemberton for the defense of Tennessee and Mississippi. Perceiving that each was not only too weak to reinforce the other, but also most likely too weak to handle what was coming at him — particularly the latter, since the Federals were certain to make Vicksburg their prime objective in the offensive they were clearly about to launch — Johnston at once suggested that the best solution would be to bring additional troops from the Transmississippi to assist in the eastbank defense of the big river.

Randolph replied that he had reached the same decision, more than two weeks ago, and read to his fellow Virginian the dispatch he had sent Holmes. When he had finished, he smiled rather strangely and took up another document, which he also read aloud. It was dated today and signed by Jefferson Davis: "I regret to notice that in your letter to General Holmes of October 27, a copy of which is before me, you suggest the propriety of his crossing the Mississippi and assuming command on the east side of the river. His presence on the west side is not less necessary now than heretofore, and will probably soon be more so. The coöperation designed by me was in co-intelligent action on both sides of the river of such detachment of troops as circumstances might require and warrant. The withdrawal of the commander from the Trans-Mississippi Department for temporary duty elsewhere would have a disastrous effect, and was not contemplated by me."

Johnston recognized the tone, having received such directives himself. He knew, too, what response this son of Thomas Jefferson's oldest daughter was likely to make to such a letter. The question was, what had made him so deliberately provoke it? Yet Johnston knew the answer here as well. Eight months of service as "the clerk of Mr Davis," sometimes learning of vital military decisions only after they had been made and acted on, had brought home to Randolph the truth of one observer's remark "that the real war lord of the South resided in the executive mansion." The message to Holmes, sent without previous consultation with the Commander in Chief, was in the nature of a gesture of self-assertion, desperate but necessary to the preservation of his self-respect. And now he accepted the consequences. Two days later, having added an indorsement to the offending document sent by Davis — "Inclose a copy of this letter to General Holmes, and inform the President that it has been done, and that [Holmes] has been directed to consider it as part of his instructions" — he submitted his formal resignation.

This had been neither intended nor expected by Davis, who up to now had been highly pleased with Randolph as a member of his cabinet. Except for two particulars, he had not even disapproved of the Secretary's decision to bring troops across the river to assist in the defense of Vicksburg. In fact, he himself ordered this done that same week, when he had the Adjutant General send Holmes the request for 10,000 men to be used for this very purpose. What he objected to, most strenuously, were the two particulars: 1) that Holmes himself was advised to cross, which would leave his department headless, and 2) that the thing had been done behind his back, without his knowledge. It was this last which disturbed him most. As Commander in Chief he saw himself as chief engineer of the whole vast machine; if adjustments were made without his knowledge, a wreck was almost certain. In this case, however, receiving the tart letter of resignation, he sought to prevent a break by suggesting a personal interview at which he and the Virginian could discuss their differences. Randolph declined, and Davis would bend no further. "As you thus without notice and in terms excluding inquiry retired," he replied, "nothing remains but to give you this formal notice of the acceptance of your resignation."

G. W. Smith, recovered from the collapse he had suffered when Johnston's fall left him in charge of the confused and confusing field of Seven Pines, had been serving as commander of the Richmond defenses ever since Lee and his army departed to deal with Pope, back in August. Now Davis found a further use for the former New York Street Commissioner by assigning him to serve as head of the War Department during the three-day interim, which he himself spent in search of a permanent — if the word could be used properly in reference to a position which, so far, had been so impermanent — replacement for Randolph, who retired at once to private life and subsequently "refugeed" in Europe with his family.

Once more the Old Dominion had been left without a representative among the President's chief advisers, and once more Davis solved the problem, this time by appointing James A. Seddon to be Secretary of War. A Richmond lawyer who had served two terms as U.S. Congressman from the district, a former occupant of the present Confederate White House, and a descendant of James River grandees, Seddon ranked about as high in the complicated Virginia caste system as even Randolph did, with the result that his selection was a source of considerable satisfaction to those who had become accustomed to looking down their noses at what they called "the middle-class atmosphere" of official Richmond. Moreover, he had a reputation as a scholar and a philosopher, though what service this would be to him in his new position was unknown; he had had no previous military experience whatever. Nor was his appearance reassuring. "Gaunt and emaciated," one observer called him, "with long straggling hair, mingled gray and black." He was forty-seven, but looked much older, perhaps because of chronic neuralgia, which racked him nearly as badly as it racked Davis. He looked, in fact, according to the same diarist, "like a dead man galvanized into muscular animation. His eyes are sunken and his features have the hue of a man who has been in his grave a full month."

At any rate, whatever his lack of the kind of training which would have cautioned him to guard his flanks and rear, it soon became apparent that he did not intend to expose himself to attack from above, as his predecessor had done. Johnston went to him on November 22, the new Secretary's first full day in office, and renewed his suggestion that troops be ordered east from the Transmississippi. Seddon listened sympathetically. But when Johnston received his orders two days later, assigning him to the region lying between the Blue Ridge Mountains and the Mississippi River, he was surprised to find that they contained no reference to troops not already within those limits. "The suggestion was not adopted or noticed," he afterwards recorded dryly.

Davis had a higher opinion of Johnston's abilities at this stage than the Virginian probably suspected. "I wish he were able to take the field," the President had told Mrs Davis during the general's convalescence. "Despite the critics, who know military affairs by instinct, he is a good soldier, never brags of what he did do, and could at this time render most valuable service." In no way, indeed, could the Commander in Chief have demonstrated this confidence more fully than by assigning him, as soon as he was fairly up and about, to what was called "plenary command" of the heartland of the Confederacy, an area embracing all of Tennessee, Mississippi, and Alabama, together with parts of North Carolina, Florida, and Georgia, including the main regional supply base at Atlanta. Moreover, he placed on him no restrictions within that geographical expanse, either as to his movements or the location of his headquarters, which he was instructed to establish "at Chattanooga, or such other place as in his judgment will best secure facilities for ready communication with the troops within the limits of his command, and will repair in person to any part of said command wherever his presence may, for the time, be necessary or desirable."

These instructions embodied a new concept of the function of departmental command, which in turn had been prompted by the example of R. E. Lee in his conduct of the defense of his native state. Lee's achievements here in Virginia, before as well as after he had been given field command, were in a large part the result of a successful coördination of the efforts of separate forces, either through simultaneous actions at divergent points — as when Jackson took the offensive in the Valley, threatening Washington to play on Lincoln's fears, while Johnston delayed McClellan's advance up the Peninsula — or through rapid concentration against a common point, as when all available forces were brought together for the attack which opened the Seven Days and accomplished the deliverance of Richmond. Subsequent repetition of this strategy, with a similar coördination of effort, had brought about the "suppression" of Pope and opened the way for invasion of the North, removing the war to that extent beyond the Confederate border.

Now it was Davis' hope that such methods, which had won for southern arms the admiration of the world and for Lee a place among history's great captains, would result in similar achievements in the West and give to the commander there a seat alongside Lee in Valhalla.

Choice of Johnston for the post was prompted by more than the fact that he was entitled to it by rank. Not only did Davis consider him a "good soldier" who could "render most valuable service," but the Virginian had also been asked for already by two of the three generals who would be his chief subordinates. During their recent visits to the capital, Bragg and Kirby Smith had both expressed an eagerness to have him over them, and doubtless Pemberton would be equally delighted to have the benefit of his advice, along with whatever reinforcements would become available in times of crisis as a result of the shuttle service the new theater commander was expected to establish between his several departments. How well he would do — whether he was potentially another Lee, and whether Bragg and Pemberton would serve him as well as Longstreet and Jackson had served the eastern commander — remained to be seen. So far, however, the resemblance had been anything but striking. His first reaction, expressed in a letter sent to the Adjutant General on the day he received the appointment, was a protest that his forces were "greatly inferior in number to those of the enemy opposed to them, while in the Trans-Mississippi Department our army is very much larger than that of the United States." He also complained of the presence of the Tennessee River, "a formidable obstacle" which divided his two main armies, and found it highly irregular that his department commanders — by an arrangement which Davis had designed "to avoid delay" — would be in direct correspondence with the War Department. This combination of drawbacks and irregularities, discerned by him before he even left Richmond, had already led him to suspect what he later stated flatly: "that my command was a nominal one merely, and useless."

Depressed by these several misgivings, he began at once to make arrangements for his journey west, and five days later he was off, accompanied by his wife and a new staff. In the interim, however, he found time to attend a farewell breakfast given in his honor and also in the hope that it would effect a reconciliation between two of his political friends, Senators Foote and Yancey, who had quarreled despite the common bond of their detestation of Davis. Under the healing influence of their admiration for Johnston, along with that of a bountiful meal accompanied by champagne, the two statesmen forgot their differences. Presently Yancey called for fresh glasses and proposed a toast. "Gentlemen, let us drink to the only man who can save the Confederacy. General Joseph E. Johnston!" All applauded, drank their wine, and took their seats: whereupon the guest of honor rose, glass in hand, and responded. "Mr Yancey," he said firmly, "the man you describe is now in the field — in the person of General Robert E. Lee. I will drink to his health." Not to be outdone, the silver-tongued Yancey rose and countered: "I can only reply to you, sir, as the Speaker of the House of Burgesses did to General Washington: 'Your modesty is only equaled by your valor.'" Again the celebrants applauded and drank the balding general's health. But he remained taciturn and preoccupied, as if his mind was already engaged by the frets he knew awaited him in the West.

In the course of the five-day trip to Chattanooga, delayed by no less than three railroad accidents, Johnston was much wearied, despite the ministrations of his wife and the cheers from station platforms along the way. Early on the morning of December 4 he got there. After resting briefly, he issued an order formally accepting his new responsibilities, although his gloom was unrelieved. "Nobody ever assumed a command under more unfavorable circumstances," he wrote to a friend in Richmond that same day.

* * *

Johnston's gloom, though it was not shared by the people in general, East or West — nor, for that matter, by those who cheered him from station platforms as he traveled from one to the other — was nonetheless reflected in the value of their dollar. After holding at 1.5 through August, it fell in October to 2, in November to 2.9, and by December it had dropped to 3. Statistics were dreary at best, however, except perhaps for those who dealt in money as a commodity. It was in terms of what the stuff would buy, shoved coin by coin across a counter or laid down bill by badly printed bill, that the meaning of such quotations really struck home. Now with winter hard upon the upper South, coal was $9 a handcartload and wood $16 a cord. Bacon was 75¢ a pound, sugar five cents higher. Butter was $1.25 and coffee twice that. To the despair of Richmond housewives, laundry soap was 75¢ a cake, flour $16 a barrel, and potatoes $6 a bushel.

For those of an analytical turn of mind, accustomed to looking behind effects for causes, it was more or less clear that the cause behind this particular close-to-home effect was the failure of the Confederacy's one concerted effort at invasion, East and West. Yet even here their reaction contained a good deal more of pride than of regret. "It was to be expected," Davis had told them, back at the outset, "... that [this war] would expose our people to sacrifices and cost them much, both of money and blood.... It was, perhaps, in the ordination of Providence that we were to be taught the value of our liberties by the price we pay for them." In the light of this, Bragg's thousand-mile hegira through Kentucky and Lee's bloody defense of the Sharpsburg ridge became for their countrymen, not occasions for despair, but instances for the promotion of the growth of national pride and the evocation of applause from those who watched from afar. "Whatever may be the fate of the new nationality," the London *Times* was saying, "in its subsequent claims to the respect of mankind it will assuredly begin its career with a reputation for genius and valour which the most famous nations might envy."

Such public praise was welcome, as were certain private remarks from that same quarter. Thomas Carlyle, for example — though he pleased neither side with a reference to the American war as the burning out of a dirty chimney, a conflagration which could be regarded only with satisfaction by neighbors too long plagued by soot — amused and gladdened Southerners by subsequently professing his impatience with people who were "cutting each other's throats, because one half of them prefer hiring their servants for life, and the other by the hour." Most gratifying of all, however, were the observations colorfully expressed in the course of a banquet speech made at Newcastle, October 7, by Chancellor of the Exchequer William E. Gladstone. Professing the kindliest feeling toward the people of the North — "They are our kin. They were ... our customers, and we hope they will be our customers again" — he denied that the British government had "any interest in the disruption of the Union." But he also declared, with particular emphasis: "There is no doubt that Jefferson Davis and other leaders of the South have made an army. They are making, it appears, a navy. And they have made what is more than either; they have made a nation." This was greeted with applause and cheers. "Hear, hear!" the diners cried. When they subsided, Gladstone added: "We may anticipate with certainty the success of the Southern States so far as regards their separation from the North."

Coming as it did from the third-ranking member of the Cabinet, the statement was assumed to reflect the views of the Government: which it did, except that Palmerston and Russell considered it precipitate and unpropitious: which it was, the Prime Minister having recently advised the Foreign Secretary that he thought it best to "wait awhile and see what may follow" Lee's retreat from Maryland. What had followed was the Preliminary Emancipation Proclamation, and though this document was greeted with sneers on the one hand and confusion on the other, it too provided an occasion for more waiting. Gladstone's outburst caused an immediate drop in the price of cotton, which apparently would soon be plentiful as a result of the lifting of the blockade, as well as an increase of activity by Members of Parliament sympathetic to the North. On October 22, two weeks after the Newcastle speech, Palmerston wrote Russell: "We must continue to be mere lookers-on till the war shall have taken a more decided turn."

On that same day, the French Emperor granted Slidell an audience at St Cloud during which he let the Confederate minister understand that he considered the time ripe for joint mediation by France,

England, and Russia. "My own preference is for a proposition of an armistice of six months," he said. "This would put a stop to the effusion of blood, and hostilities would probably never be resumed. We can urge it on the high grounds of humanity and the interest of the whole civilized world. If it be refused by the North, it will afford good reason for recognition, and perhaps for more active intervention." Eight days later, as good as his word — and with his eye still fixed on the promised hundred thousand bales of cotton — he addressed, through his Minister of Foreign Affairs, a dispatch to his ambassadors at St Petersburg and London, proposing that the three governments "exert their influence at Washington, as well as with the Confederates, to obtain an armistice." Russia's answer was emphatic: "In our opinion, what ought specially to be avoided [is] the appearance of any pressure whatsoever of a nature to wound public opinion in the United States and to excite susceptibilities very easily aroused at the bare idea of foreign intervention." England's was scarcely less so, Russell declining for the reason "that there is no ground at the present moment to hope that the Federal government would accept the proposal suggested, and a refusal from Washington at the present time would prevent any speedy renewal of the offer."

Napoleon, then, was as far as ever from those hundred thousand bales, and so was the Confederacy from recognition by the powers of Europe. England was to blame; for France could act without Russia, but not without England; England swung the balance. And yet, admittedly, Southerners already had much to be thankful for, if not from the British government, then at least from British individuals: particularly the owners of and workers in shipyards up the Mersey. Gladstone's remark that the Confederates "are making, it appears, a navy" was based on solid ground — ground which, indeed, was of his own countrymen's making. In late July, a powerful new screw steamer known mysteriously as the *290* had steamed down from Liverpool, supposedly on a trial run, but headed instead for the open sea and a rendezvous off the Azores, where she took on provisions, coal, and guns, struck her English colors in favor of the Stars and Bars, swore in a crew, and exchanged her numerical designation for a name: the *Alabama*. She was the second to follow this course. Four months before, another such vessel, called the *Oreto*, had accomplished this same metamorphosis from merchantman to raider, and already she was at work as the Confederate cruiser *Florida*, her mission being the high-seas destruction of Federal commerce. Commanded by Captain J. N. Maffit, she was to take thirty-four prizes before her career ended two years later; but it was the *Alabama* which did most in this direction, provoking a rise of more than 900 percent in U.S. marine insurance and the transfer of over seven hundred Union merchant ships to British registry. Also, she gave the South another hero in the person of her skipper, Captain Raphael Semmes, a fifty-three-year-old Maryland-born Alabamian, known to his crew — mostly foreigners off the docks of Liverpool, whom he referred to as "a precious set of rascals" — as "Old Beeswax" because of the care he gave his long black needle-sharp mustachios.

He had had considerable experience at this kind of work as captain of the *Sumter*, the first of the rebel raiders. A commander in the old navy, ensconced in comfort as head of the Lighthouse Board in Washington, he had gone south in February of the year before and offered his services to the new government in Montgomery. Secretary Mallory sent him back north on a purchasing expedition, and when he returned informed him that the Confederacy had acquired a small propeller steamer of 500 tons. She was tied up to a New Orleans wharf, he added, awaiting a chance to slip past the Federal blockaders in order to undertake disruption of the sea lanes. "Mr Secretary, give me that ship," Semmes said. "I think I can make her answer the purpose." Mallory gave him what he asked for, along with general instructions: "On reaching the high seas you are to do the enemy's commerce the greatest injury in the shortest time. Choose your own cruising grounds. Burn, sink, and destroy, and be guided always by the laws of the nations and of humanity." That was in mid-April; Semmes made his escape from the mouth of the Mississippi on the last day of June, and took his first prize four days later. In the course of the next seven months he took seventeen more barks, brigantines, and schooners, which he captured, burned, or ransomed in the Gulf and the Atlantic. Bottled up in Gibraltar from January to April, he sold the *Sumter*, discharged her crew, and took passage for Southampton. Late in May he left for Nassau, intending to board a blockade runner there and get back home. If the navy had another ship for him, he would take it; if not, he planned to transfer to the army. What awaited him at Nassau, however, were instructions for him to return to England and assume secret command of the *290-Alabama*.

He took over, officially, off the island of Terceira on August 24, when the cruiser was formally commissioned. Having named the *Florida* for his native state, Mallory had named this second English-built warship for the state in which the Confederacy itself was born. Bark-rigged, with handsome, rakish lines, she was 235 feet in length, 32 feet in the beam, and displaced a thousand tons. Her armament was eight guns, three 32-pounders on each broadside and two pivot guns on the center line, one a 7-inch rifle and the other an 8-inch smoothbore. Two 300-horsepower engines gave her a speed of ten knots on steam alone, but with the help of her sails and a friendly wind she could make nearly fifteen, which approached top speed for sea-going ships of the time. When traveling under sail alone — as she often would, to conserve fuel; the 275 tons of coal in her bunkers were barely enough for eighteen days of steaming at moderate speed — her two-bladed screw could be triced up into a propeller well, clear of the water, and thus afford no drag. To her crew of 24 gray-clad officers and 120 men, she was a beautiful thing on her commissioning day. Her brass was bright; her decks were clean and fragrant; her taunt-hauled rigging gleamed with newness. To Semmes himself she seemed "a bride with the orange wreath about her brows, ready to be led to the altar."

Led instead on her shakedown cruise, she took her first prize twelve days later, the whaling schooner *Ocmulgee* of Edgartown, Massachusetts, caught with her sails furled, a dead whale moored alongside, and her crew busy stripping blubber. Brimming with sperm oil, she was valued at $50,000 and made a spectacular conflagration. Semmes took her crew aboard the *Alabama*, released them next day within sight of land, their whaleboats loaded to the gunnels with all they had managed to salvage before their ship was burned, and continued his search for other prizes. Before September was over he had taken ten. In October he took eleven. By early December he had raised the total to twenty-six, removing from each its chronometer, which he added to the others in his collection, including the eighteen transferred from the *Sumter*, and wound them regularly by way of counting tally.

By now his fame, or infamy, was established. To Northerners, despite the invariable courtesy and consideration he showed his temporary captives, he was a bloodthirsty pirate, an "Algerine corsair." To his crew, often vexed that he allowed no individual pillage, he seemed no such thing. In time, despite the strangeness of his manner, including the fact that he seldom spoke to anyone, and the tightness of his discipline — "Democracies may do very well for the land," he once explained, "but monarchies, and pretty absolute monarchies at that, are the only successful governments for the sea" — the officers and men of the *Alabama* paid him not only his due of absolute obedience, but also the homage of genuine affection. It was not a question of patriotism. Few of the officers and none of the men were even Americans, let alone Southerners; they were mostly English, Welsh, and Irish, with a scattering of French, Italian, Spanish, and Russian sailors among them. Their allegiance was to him and the *Alabama*. They liked to watch his gray eyes glint blue when he sighted a prize off on the bulge of the horizon, and they approved of his Catholic devoutness, knowing that he began and ended each day on his knees before the little shrine in his cabin.

Blurred by distance, to his countrymen he was something less — and also something more. He was, in fact, a member of that growing band of heroes who, as the *Alabama* began her career with the burning of the *Ocmulgee*, seemed about to make good the impossible claims and threats with which the fire-eaters had prefaced the reality of war. Lee was crossing the Potomac, Bragg was on the march for Kentucky, and Kirby Smith was in Lexington; Semmes was therefore proof that the South could take the offensive at sea as well as on land. Moreover, though those others had been turned back, he kept on, taking prizes which he burned or sank or, if it was impractical to remove their crews and passengers to safety, released on "ransom bond." This last, sometimes resorted to when the cruiser was crowded to capacity with captives, was an agreement between Semmes and the master of the vessel, whereby the latter pledged the owner to pay a stipulated amount "unto the President of the Confederate States of America ... within thirty days after the conclusion of the present war." It was, in effect, a bet that the South would win, and as such it did much to increase the pride of Southerners in their lawyer-raider, who thus expressed before the eyes of the world their confidence in the outcome of their struggle for independence.

Another cause for pride in southern arms derived from an older source: in fact, from the oldest source of all. Though Lee and Bragg and Kirby Smith had returned from their expeditions, disappointing the hopes that had gone with them, Beauregard — the original hero, back on the scene of his original triumph — had not been long in justifying the cheers with which Charlestonians had greeted his return. October 22, five weeks after his arrival, a Federal attempt to cut the Charleston & Savannah Railroad at Pocotaligo, midway between those two coastal cities, was foiled when 4500 bluecoats under Ormsby Mitchel — within eight days of sudden death from yellow fever — were thrown back to their landing boats by half as many rebels. Casualties were 340 and 163, respectively. "Railroad uninjured," Beauregard wired Richmond. "Abolitionists left dead and wounded on the field. Our cavalry in hot pursuit." Old Bory was himself again.

★ ★ ★

Slight though they were — by comparison, that is, with the resounding double failure, East and West, of the Confederacy's first concerted attempt at all-out invasion — these late fall and early winter successes, afloat and ashore, did much to sustain or restore the confidence of the southern people. Besides, they could tell themselves, the strategic offensive was for extra: a device to be employed from time to time, not so much with the intention of keeping the graybacks north of the Potomac or the Cumberland, but rather of establishing an interlude for harvesting the crops in forward areas and thereby gaining a breathing spell in which the natives could enjoy at least a temporary freedom from the oppressive presence of the bluecoats. It was the strategic defensive that counted; it was this they had been pledged to by their President when he told the world, "All we ask is to be let alone." And in this — considering the odds — they had been singularly successful: especially in the East, where three full-scale attempts at invasion had been smashed and a fourth halted dead in its tracks when its commander was retired for the second time. In the West, too, there was occasion for rejoicing and self-congratulation. After a long season of reverses, a series of collapses under inexorable pressure, the front of the principal sector had been advanced a hundred and fifty miles, from North Mississippi to Middle Tennessee; on the Mississippi itself, the upper and lower Union fleets, conjoined triumphantly above Vicksburg, had been sundered and sent their separate ways by a single homemade ironclad; while across the river, in Arkansas, an army created seemingly out of thin air was on the march for Missouri.

All this was much, enough indeed to satisfy the hungriest of seekers after glory, and the thought of such accomplishments went far toward offsetting the pain of earlier reverses. However, to ease the ache was not to cure the ailment; the effect of the worst of the early reverses still remained. Norfolk was lost, and with it the one hope for the home construction of a Confederate deep-sea navy. So — continuing clockwise, down and around the coast — were the North Carolina sounds, Port Royal and Fort Pulaski, Brunswick and Fernandina, Jacksonville and St Augustine, Apalachicola and Pensacola, Biloxi and Pass Christian, Ship Island and Galveston. All these were tangent hits, mainly painful to southern pride (and to southern pocketbooks, augmenting as they did the effectiveness of the Federal blockade) but there were others that hurt worse, being vital. Nashville was gone, and so were New Orleans and Memphis. At the time of their loss, people had told themselves that these cities would be recovered, along with the outlying points around the littoral, once the pressure in front had been relieved. Apparently, though, that had been mere whistling in the dark. Four times now the pressure had eased up: after First Manassas, Wilson's Creek, the evacuation of Corinth, and Second Manassas: yet in all four instances the southern commanders who tried to take advantage of the respite gained were either repulsed when they moved forward or else they fell back eventually of their own accord. In fact, of the four advances which had followed these events — Johnston's into northern Virginia, Price's into northern Missouri, Bragg's into Kentucky, and Lee's into Maryland — all but Bragg's had wound up south of the point from which they had been launched. It was small wonder then, at this stage, that Southerners discounted the advantages of the offensive, considering how little had been gained from three of these four attempts and how much had been lost by two others, Shiloh and Baton Rouge, even though both were generally referred to as tactical victories and were prime sources of the glory, which, so far, had been the South's chief gain from twenty months of war.

Yet glory was a flimsy diet at best, containing far more of what Southerners called "suption" than of substance. No one realized this better than Davis, who had had an overplus of glory down the years and who, familiar with it as he was, knew how little real sustenance it afforded. Moreover, as a professional soldier, in touch with every department of the army he commanded, he not only recognized the odds his country faced in its struggle for independence; he saw that they were lengthening with every passing month as the North's tremendous potential was converted into actuality. In that sense, not only was time against him; even success was against him, for each northern reverse brought on a quickening of the tempo of conversion. And yet, paradoxically, it was time for which he was fighting. Time alone could bring into being, in the North, the discouragement — the sheer boredom, even — which was the South's chief hope for victory if foreign intervention failed to materialize, as now seemed likely.

Meanwhile, there were the odds to face, and Davis faced them. He did not know what future combinations were being designed for the Confederacy's destruction, but he knew they would be heavy when they came. Here in the East, Lee could be trusted to cope with whatever forces the Union high command might conceive to be his match. Likewise in the Transmississippi, though the outlook was far from bright, Hindman's improvisations, Magruder's theatrical ingenuity, and Taylor's hard-working common sense gave promise of achieving at least a balance. It was in the West — that region between the Blue Ridge and the Mississippi, where Federal troops had scored their most substantial gains — that the Commander in Chief perceived the gravest danger. Whether Johnston would prove himself another Lee, coördinating the

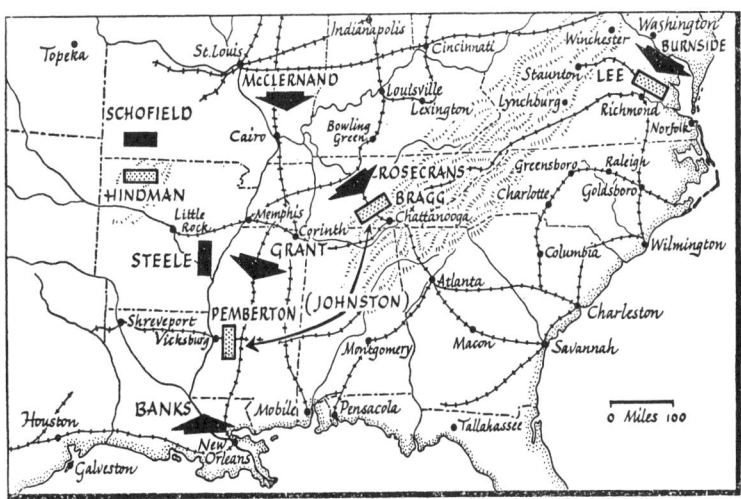

efforts of his separate armies in order to frustrate those of his opponents, remained to be seen. So far, though, the signs had not been promising. A gloom had descended on the gamecock general, who seemed more intent on acquiring troops from outside his department than on setting up a system for the mutual support of those within it. Also, there were continuing rumors of dissension in Bragg's army. All this seemed to indicate a need for intervention, or at any rate a personal inspection, by the man who had designed the new command arrangement in the first place. Davis had not been more than a day's trip from Richmond since his arrival in late May of the year before, but now in early December he packed his bags for the long ride to Chattanooga and Vicksburg. Thus he would not only see at first hand the nature of the problems in the region which was his home; he would also provide an answer to those critics who complained that the authorities in the capital had no concern for what went on outside the eastern theater.

One drawback this had, and for Davis it was of the kind that could never be taken lightly. The trip would mean another separation from the family he had missed so much while they were in North Carolina for the summer. "I go into the nursery as a bird may go to the robbed nest," he had written his wife in June, and he added: "My ease, my health, my property, my life I can give to the cause of my country. The heroism which could lay my wife and children on any sacrificial altar is not mine." For all the busyness and anxiety of those days and nights when McClellan's campfires rimmed the east, the White House had seemed to him an empty thing without the laughter of his sons and the companionship of the woman who was his only confidante. "I have no attraction to draw me from my office now," he wrote, "and home is no longer a locality."

In September they returned, to his great joy. Mrs Davis found him thinner, the failing eye gone blinder and the lines grooved deeper in his face. "I have no political wish beyond the success of our cause," he had written her, "no personal desire but to be relieved from further connection with office. Opposition in any form can only disturb me inasmuch as it may endanger the public welfare." But the critics were in full bay again as the fall wore on, including his own Vice President, and it was clear to his wife that he was indeed disturbed. At the outset, back in Montgomery, he had spoken of "a people united in heart, where one purpose of high resolve animates and actuates the whole." Lately this evaluation had been considerably modified. "Revolutions develop the high qualities of the good and the great," he wrote, "but they cannot change the nature of the vicious and the selfish." He had this to live with now, this change of outlook, this reassessment of his fellow man: with the result that he was more troubled by neuralgia than ever, and more in need of his wife's ministrations. Present dangers, front and rear, had given even pretended dangers an increased reality and had added to his sympathy for all sufferers everywhere, including those in the world of light fiction. One day, for example, when he was confined to bed with a cloth over his eyes and forehead, she tried to relieve the monotony by reading to him from a current melodramatic novel. He was so quiet she thought he was asleep, but she did not stop for fear of waking him.

As she approached the climax of the story, wherein the bad man had the heroine in his power and was advancing on her for some evil purpose, Mrs Davis heard a voice exclaim: "The infernal villain!" and looking around saw her husband sitting bolt upright in bed, with both fists clenched.

Whether this was the result of too much imagination, or too little, was a question which would linger down the years. But some there were, already, who believed that nothing except short-sightedness could hide the eventual outcome of the long-odds struggle from anyone willing to examine the facts disclosed in the course of this opening half of the second year of conflict. Senator Herschel V. Johnson of Georgia, Stephen Douglas's running-mate in the 1860 election and now a prominent member of the Confederate Congress, replied to a question from a friend in late October: "You ask me if I have confidence in the success of the Southern Confederacy? I pray for success but I do not expect success.... The enemy in due time will penetrate the heart of the Confederacy ... & the hearts of our people will quake & their spirits will yield to the force of overpowering numbers." He saw the outcome clearly, and he found it unavoidable. "The enemy is superior to us in everything but courage, & therefore it is quite certain, if the war is to go on until exhaustion overtake the one side or the other side, that we shall be the first to be exhausted."

Whether or not this would be the case — whether the South, fighting for such anachronisms as slavery and self-government, could sustain the conflict past the breaking point of northern determination — Davis did not know. Much of what his dead friend Albert Sidney Johnston had called "the fair, broad, abounding land" had already fallen to the invaders. How much more would fall, or whether the rising blue tide could be stemmed, was dependent on the gray-clad men in the southern ranks and the spirit with which they followed their star-crossed battle flags. Just now that spirit was at its height. "We may be annihilated," the first soldier of them all had said, "but we cannot be conquered." Davis thought so, too, though he offered no easy solutions in support of his belief. Now in December, as he prepared to leave on his journey to the troubled western theater, he could only repeat what he had told his wife in May: "I cultivate hope and patience, and trust to the blunders of our enemy and the gallantry of our troops for ultimate success."

※ 3 ※

"Our cause, we love to think, is specially God's," the Connecticut theologian Horace Bushnell told his Hartford congregation. "Every drum-beat is a hymn; the cannon thunder God; the electric silence, darting victory along the wires, is the inaudible greeting of God's favoring word." His belief that the evil was all on the other side was based on a conviction that war had come because willful men beyond the Potomac had laid rude hands on the tabernacle of the law. "Law... is grounded in right, [and] right is a moral idea, at whose summit stands God, as the everlasting vindicator." Thus the logic came full circle: "We associate God and religion with all we are fighting for, and we are not satisfied with any mere human atheistic way of speaking as to means, or measures, or battles, or victories, or the great deeds to win them."

The assertion that this was a holy war — in fact, a crusade — was by no means restricted to those who made it from a pulpit. "Vindicating the majesty of an insulted Government, by extirpating all *rebels*, and fumigating their nests with the brimstone of unmitigated Hell, I conceive to be the holy purpose of our further efforts," a Massachusetts colonel wrote home to his governor from Beaufort, South Carolina, and being within fifty airline miles of the very birthplace of rebellion, he added: "I hope I shall...do something...in 'The Great Fumigation,' before the sulphur gives out." Just what it was that he proposed to do, with regard to those he called "our Southern brethren," he had announced while waiting at Annapolis for the ship that brought him down the coast. "Do we fight them to avenge...insult? No! The thing we seek is *permanent* dominion. And what instance is there of permanent dominion without changing, revolutionizing, absorbing, the institutions, life, and manners of the conquered peoples?...They think we mean to take their *Slaves*. Bah! We must take their *ports*, their *mines*, their *water power*, the very *soil* they plough, and develop them by the hands of our *artisan* armies....We are to be a regenerating, colonizing power, or we are to be whipped. Schoolmasters, with howitzers, must instruct our Southern brethren that they are a set of d----d fools in everything that relates to...modern civilization.... *This army must not come back*. Settlement, migration must put the seal on battle, or we gain nothing."

Tecumseh Sherman, biding his time in Memphis — where sharp-eyed men with itchy palms had followed in the wake of advancing armies, much as refuse along the right-of-way was sucked into the rearward vacuum of a speeding locomotive — threw the blame in another direction. "The cause of the war is not alone in the nigger," he told his wife, "but in the mercenary spirit of our countrymen.... Cincinnati furnishes more contraband goods than Charleston, and has done more to prolong the war than the State of South Carolina. Not a merchant there but would sell salt, bacon, powder and lead, if they can make money by it." So the volatile red-haired general wrote, finding his former nerve-jangled opinion reinforced by the difficulties since encountered all along the fighting front. "If the North design to conquer the South, we must begin at Kentucky and reconquer the country from there as we did from the Indians. It was this conviction then as plainly as now that made men think I was insane. A good many flatterers now want to make me a prophet."

Prophet or not, he could speak like one in an early October letter to his senator brother: "I rather think you now agree with me that this is no common war.... You must now see that I was right in not seeking prominence at the outstart. I knew and know yet that the northern people have to unlearn all their experience of the past thirty years and be born again before they will see the truth." None of it had been easy thus far, nor was it going to be any easier in the future. The prow of the ship might pierce the wave, yet once it was clear of the vessel's stern the wave was whole again: "Though our armies pass across and through the land, the war closes in behind and leaves the same enemy behind. ... I don't see the end," he concluded, "or the beginning of the end, but suppose we must prevail and persist or perish." He saw only one solution, an outgrowth of the statement to his wife that the Federal armies would have to "reconquer the country ... as we did from the Indians." What was required from here on was harshness. "We cannot change the hearts of the people of the South," he told his friend and superior Grant: "but we can make war so terrible that they will realize the fact that however brave and gallant and devoted to their country, still they are mortal and should exhaust all peaceful remedies before they fly to war."

For Lincoln, too, it was a question of "prevail and persist or perish." For him, moreover, there was the added problem of coördinating the efforts — and, if possible, reconciling the views — of these three random extremists, together with those of more than twenty million other individuals along and behind the firing line. The best way to accomplish this, he knew, was to unite them under a leader whose competence they believed in and whose views they would adopt as their own, even when those views came into conflict with their preconceptions. In facing this task, he started not from scratch, but from somewhere well behind it. "The President is an honest, plain, shrewd magistrate," *Harper's Weekly* had told its readers a year ago this December. "He is not a brilliant orator; he is not a great leader. He views his office as strictly an executive one, and wishes to cast responsibility, as much as possible, upon Congress." This tallied with the view of Attorney General Edward Bates, who wrote in his diary after attending a cabinet meeting held at about the same time, "The President is an excellent man, and in the main wise, but he lacks will and purpose, and I greatly fear he has not the power to command."

Since then, a good many high-placed men — including Bates, who had seen Cameron banished and the bricks applied to Stanton — had had occasion to learn better: though not all. The poet Whittier, for example, saw victory only through a haze of *ifs*. "The worst of the *ifs* is the one concerning Lincoln," he privately declared. "I am much afraid that a domestic cat will not answer when one wants a Bengal tiger." His fellow poet William Cullen Bryant agreed. "The people after their gigantic preparation and sacrifice have looked for an adequate return, and looked in vain," he editorialized in the New York *Evening Post*. "They have seen armies unused in the field perish in pestilential swamps. They have seen their money wasted in long winter encampments, or frittered away on fruitless expeditions along the coast. They have seen a huge debt roll up, yet no prospect of greater military results." Wendell Phillips, bitter as ever, continued to aim an indignant finger at the White House. "The North has poured out its blood and money like water; it has leveled every fence of constitutional privilege," he declaimed, "and Abraham Lincoln sits today a more unlimited despot than the world knows this side of China. What does he render for this unbounded confidence? Show us something," he cried in the direction he was pointing, "or I tell you that within two years the indignant reaction of the people will hurl the Cabinet in contempt from their seats."

Confronted with such judgments handed down by public men, who thus came between him and his purpose of unification, Lincoln kept his temper and his poise. If he failed in his attempts to win these critics over by means of personal discussion, face to face in his office — "What is he wrathy about? Why does he not come down here and have a talk with me?" — he went beyond them to the people. Sometimes he did so in cold print, as in the case of his answer to Greeley's "Prayer of Twenty Millions," but generally he proceeded in a manner that was strangely intimate in its effect, acting on a larger stage the role he had played in Illinois. In Washington, as in Springfield, he received all comers, and for the most part he received them with a sympathy which, by their own admission, equaled or exceeded their deserving. He shook their hands at frequent public receptions held in the White House, which was his home and yet belonged to them; he attended the theater, a form of relaxation which kept him still within their view; he drove or rode, almost daily, through the spokelike streets of the hive-dense city, returning the looks and salutes of men and women and children along the way. Thousands touched him, heard him, saw him at close range, and scarcely one in all those thousands ever forgot the sight of that tall figure, made still taller by the stovepipe hat, and the homely drape of the shawl across the shoulders. Never forgotten, because it was unforgettable, the impression remained, incredible and enduring, imperishable in its singularity — and, finally, dear.

Millions who did not see him saw his picture, and this too was a part of the effect. Widely broadcast as it was — the result of recent developments in photography and the process of reproduction — his had become, within two crowded years, the most familiar face in American history. At first sight this might appear to be a liability. The Paris correspondent of the *New York Times*, for example, sent home a paragraph titled "Lincoln's Phiz in Europe," in which he suggested the wisdom of declaring an embargo on portraits of the President, at least so far as France was concerned: "The person represented in these pictures looks so much like a man condemned to the gallows, that large numbers of them have been imposed on the people here by the shopkeepers as Dumollard, the famous murderer of servant girls, lately guillotined near Lyons. Such a face is enough to ruin the best of causes. ... People read the name inscribed under it with astonishment, or rather bewilderment, for the thing appears more like a hoax than a reality." Yet here, too, something worked in his favor. It was as if, having so far overshot the mark of ugliness, the face was not to be judged by ordinary standards. You saw it not so much for what it was, as for what it held. Suffering was in it; so were understanding, kindliness, and determination. "None of us to our dying day can forget that countenance," an infantryman wrote on the occasion of a presidential visit to the army. "Concentrated in that one great, strong, yet tender face, the agony of the life and death struggle of the hour was revealed as we had never seen it before. With a new understanding, we knew why we were soldiers."

Herein lay the explanation for much that otherwise could not be understood — by Jefferson Davis, for one, who had expressed "contemptuous astonishment" at seeing his late compatriots submit to what he called "the mere edict of a despot." They did not see their submission in that light. "I know very well that many others might... do better than I can," Lincoln had told the cabinet in September, "and if I were satisfied that the public confidence was more fully possessed by any one of them than by me, and knew of any constitutional way he could be put in my place, he should have it. I would gladly yield it to him. But ... I do not know that, all things considered, any other person has more [of the confidence of the people]; and, however this may be, there is no way in which I can have any other man put where I am. I am here. I must do the best I can, and bear the responsibility of taking the course which I feel I ought to take." Though these words were spoken in private, their import carried over: with the result that such power as he seized — and it was much, far more in fact than any President had ever had before, in peace or war — was surrendered by the people in confidence that the power was not being seized for its own sake, or even for Lincoln's sake, but rather for the sake of preserving the Union. They gave him the power, along with the responsibility, glad to have a strong hand on the reins.

This fear of weakness had been the source of their gravest doubt through the opening year of conflict, as well as the subject of the editors' most frequent complaint — Lincoln was lacking in "will and purpose." Now they knew that their fears had been misplaced. A Kentucky visitor, turning to leave the White House, asked the President what cheering news he could take home to friends. By way of reply, Lincoln told him a story about a chess expert who had never met his match until he tried his hand against a machine called the Automaton Chess Player, and was beaten three times running. Astonished, the defeated expert got up from his chair and walked slowly around and around the machine, examining it minutely as he went. At last he stopped and leveled an accusing finger in its direction. "There's a man in there!" he cried. Lincoln paused, then made his point: "Tell my friends there is a man in here."

Something else he was, as well — a literary craftsman — though so far this had gone unrecognized, unnoticed, and for the most part would remain so until critics across the Atlantic, unembarrassed by proximity, called attention to the fact. Indeed, complaints had been registered that he wrote "like a half-educated lawyer" with little or no appreciation for the cadenced beauties latent in the English language, awaiting the summons of the artist who knew how to call them up. That there was such a thing as the American language, available for literary purposes, had scarcely begun to be suspected by the more genteel, except as it had been employed by writers of low dialog bits, which mainly served to emphasize its limitations. Lincoln's jogtrot prose, compacted of words and phrases still with the bark on, had no music their ears were attuned to; it crept by them. However, an ambiguity had been sensed. Remarking "the two-fold working of the two-fold nature of the man," one caller at least had observed the contrast between "Lincoln the Westerner, slightly humorous but thoroughly practical and sagacious," and "Lincoln the President and statesman ... seen in those abstract and serious eyes, which seemed withdrawn to an inner sanctuary of thought, sitting in judgment on the scene and feeling its far reach into the future."

Here was a clew; but it went uninvestigated. Apparently it was miracle enough that a prairie lawyer had become President, without pressing matters further to see that he had also become a stylist. In fact, so natural and unlabored had his utterance seemed, that when people were told they had an artist in the White House, their reaction was akin to that of the man in Molière who discovered that all his life he had been speaking prose. "I am here. I must do the best I can," Lincoln had said, and that best included this. Natural perhaps it was; unlabored it was not. Long nights he toiled in his workshop, the "inner sanctuary" from which he reached out to the future, and here indeed was the best clew of all. For he worked with the dedication of the true artist, who, whatever his sense of superiority in other relationships, preserves his humility in this one. He knew, as a later observer remarked, "the dangers that lurk in iotas." There were days when callers, whatever their importance, were turned away with the explanation that the President was at work: which meant writing.

A series of such days came in November, and the occasion was the preparation of a message to Congress, which would convene December 1. Lincoln saw already what would later become obvious, but was by no means obvious yet: that the war had ended one phase and was about to enter another. This message was intended to signal that event, bidding farewell to the old phase and setting a course for the new. Basically it was dedicatory, for there was need for dedication. The fury of Perryville, the blood that had stained the Antietam and sluiced the ridge in front of Sharpsburg, had reëmphasized the fact disclosed on a smaller scale at First Bull Run and Wilson's Creek, then augmented at Shiloh and the Seven Days, that both armies were capable of inflicting and withstanding terrible wounds. Though it was incredible that the ratio of increase would be maintained, there would be other Shilohs, other Sharpsburgs, other terrors. Men in their thousands now alive would presently be dead; homes so far untouched by sorrow would know tears; new widows and new orphans, some as yet unmarried or unborn, would be made — all, as Lincoln saw it, that the nation might continue and that men now in bondage might have freedom. In issuing the Preliminary Emancipation Proclamation he had made certain that there would be no peace except by conquest. He had weighed the odds and made his choice, foreseeing the South's reaction. "A restitution of the Union has been rendered forever impossible," Davis said. Lincoln had known he would say it; the fact was, he had been saying it all along. What he meant, and what Lincoln knew he meant, was that the issue was one which could only be settled by arms, and that the war was therefore a war for survival — survival of the South, as Davis saw it: survival of the Union, as Lincoln saw it — with the added paradox that, while neither of the two leaders believed victory for his side meant extinction for the other, each insisted that the reverse was true.

On the face of it, Davis had rather the better of his opponent in this contention, since the immediate and admitted result of a southern defeat would be that the South would go out of existence as a nation, however well it might survive in the sense that Lincoln intended to convey. The threat of national extinction was a sharper goad than any the northern leader could apply in attempting the unification he saw was necessary; therefore he determined to try for something other than sharpness. It was here that his particular talent, though so far it had gone unrecognized in general, could most effectively be brought to bear. As he had done against Douglas in the old days, so now in his long-range contest with Davis he shifted the argument onto a higher plane. Douglas had wanted to talk about "popular sovereignty," the right of the people of a region to decide for themselves the laws and customs under which they would live, but Lincoln had made slavery the issue, to the Little Giant's unavoidable discomfort. Similarly, in the present debate, while Davis spoke of self-government, Lincoln — without ever dropping the pretense that Davis was invisible, was in fact not there at all — appealed to "the mystic chords of memory" and "the chorus of the Union," then presently moved on to slavery and freedom, which Davis could no more avoid than Douglas had been able to do. Lincoln tarred them both with the same brush, doing it so effectively in the present case that the tar would never wear off, and managed also to redefine the Davis concept of self-government as destructive of world democracy, which was shown to depend on survival of the Union with the South as part of the whole. In thus discounting the claims of his opponent, he rallied not only his own people behind him, but also those of other lands where freedom was cherished as a possession or a goal, and thus assured nonintervention. Davis in time, like other men before and since, found what it meant to become involved with an adversary whose various talents included those of a craftsman in the use of words.

A case in point was this December message. It was a long one, nearly fifty thousand words, and it covered a host of subjects, all of them connected directly or indirectly with the war. "Fellow-Citizens of the Senate and House of Representatives," it opened. "Since your last annual assembling another year of health and bountiful harvest has passed, and while it has not pleased the Almighty to bless us with a return of peace, we can but press on, guided by the best light he gives us, trusting that in his own good time and wise way all will yet be well.... The civil war, which has so radically changed, for the moment, the occupations and habits of the American people, has necessarily disturbed the social condition and affected very deeply the prosperity of the nations with which we have carried on a commerce that has been steadily increasing throughout a period of half a century. It has at the same time excited political ambitions and apprehensions which have produced a profound agitation throughout the civilized world.... We have attempted no propagandism and acknowledged no revolution; but we have left to every nation the exclusive conduct and management of its own affairs. Our struggle has been, of course, contemplated by foreign nations with reference less to its own merits than to its supposed and often exaggerated effects and consequences resulting to those nations themselves. Nevertheless, complaint on the part of this government, even if it were just, would certainly be unwise."

After this rather mild and dry beginning, he passed at once — or the clerk did, for Lincoln did not deliver the message in person — to matters drier still. A new commercial treaty had been arranged with the Sultan of Turkey, while similar arrangements with Liberia and Haiti were pending. Financially, he was pleased to report, the country was quite sound. Treasury receipts for the July-through-June fiscal year were $583,885,247.06, and disbursements totaling $570,841,700.25 had left a balance of $13,043,546.81 to be carried over. Restlessness among the frontier tribes perhaps indicated that the Indian system needed to be remodeled. The Pacific Railway was being pushed toward completion. A Department of Agriculture had been established.... The clerk droned on, advising the squirming congressmen that these details "will claim your most diligent consideration," though this could hardly have been easy, comprising as they did nearly half of the long document. By now, the assembled politicians were nearly as restless as the red men on the frontier. Presently, however, approaching its mid-point, the message changed its tone.

"A nation may be said to consist of its territory, its people, and its laws. The territory is the only part which is of certain durability. 'One generation passeth away, and another generation cometh: but the earth abideth forever.' It is of the first importance to duly consider and estimate this ever-enduring part. That portion of the earth's surface which is owned and inhabited by the people of the United States is well adapted to be the home of one national family, and it is not well adapted for two or more.... There is no line, straight or crooked, suitable for a national boundary upon which to divide. Trace through, from east to west, upon the line between the free and slave country, and we shall find a little more than one-third of its length are rivers, easy to be crossed, and populated, or soon to be populated, thickly upon both sides; while nearly all its remaining length are merely surveyors' lines, over which people may walk back and forth without any consciousness of their presence."

Such an argument might have been advanced in support of the unification of Europe or the annexation of Canada, but presently the listeners saw what Lincoln was getting at. He was talking to the inhabitants of the region to which he himself was native, "the great interior region, bounded east by the Alleghenies, north by the British dominions, west by the Rocky Mountains, and south by the line along which the culture of corn and cotton meets.... Ascertain from the statistics the small proportion of the region which has as yet been brought into cultivation, and also the large and rapidly increasing amount of its products, and we shall be overwhelmed with the magnitude of the prospect presented. And yet this region has no seacoast, touches no ocean anywhere. As part of the nation, its people now find, and may forever find, their way to Europe by New York, to South America and Africa by New Orleans, and to Asia by San Francisco.... These outlets, east, west, and south, are indispensable to the well-being of the people inhabiting, and to inhabit, this vast interior region. Which of the three may be the best is no proper question. All are better than either, and all of right belong to that people and to their successors forever. True to themselves, they will not ask where a line of separation shall be, but will vow rather that there shall be no such line." After a pause, he added: "Our national strife springs not from our permanent part, not from the land we inhabit, not from our national homestead.... Our strife pertains to ourselves — to the passing generations of men; and it can without convulsion be hushed forever with the passing of one generation."

This brought him at last to what he considered the nub of the issue. "Without slavery the rebellion could never have existed; without slavery it could not continue." So far, he had not mentioned the Preliminary Emancipation Proclamation except to note that it had been issued; nor did he return to it now. What he returned to, instead, was his old plan for compensated emancipation, the one way he saw for bringing the war to an end "without convulsion." His plan, as expanded here, would leave to each state the choice of when to act on the matter, "now, or at the end of the century, or at any intermediary time." The federal government was to have no voice in the action, but it would bear the total expense by issuing long-term bonds as payment to loyal masters. To those critics who would complain that the expense was too heavy, Lincoln replied beforehand that it was cheaper to pay in bonds than in blood, as the country was doing now. Besides, even in dollars and cents the cost would be less. "Certainly it is not so easy to pay something as it is to pay nothing; but it is easier to pay a large sum than it is to pay a larger one. And it is easier to pay any sum when we are able, than it is to pay it before we are able. The war requires large sums, and requires them at once. The aggregate sum necessary for compensated emancipation of course would be large. But it would require no ready cash, nor the bonds even, any faster than the emancipation progresses. This might not, and probably would not, come before the end of the thirty-seven years."

At this point, apparently — at any rate, somewhere along the line — the President had done some ciphering. By 1900, he predicted, "we shall probably have 100,000,000 of people to share the burden, instead of 31,000,000 as now." This was no wild guess on Lincoln's part; or as he put it, "I do not state this inconsiderately. At the same ratio of increase which we have maintained, on an average, from our first national census of 1790 until that of 1860, we should in 1900 have a population of 103,208,415. And why may we not continue that ratio far beyond that period? Our abundant room — our broad national homestead — is our ample resource." The past seventy years had shown an average decennial increase of 34.6 percent. Applying this to the coming seventy years, he calculated the 1930 population at 251,680,914. "And we will reach this, too," he added, "if we do not ourselves relinquish the chance by the folly and evils of disunion, or by long and exhausting war springing from the only great element of national discord among us."

Descending from these rather giddy mathematical heights, Lincoln continued his plea for gradual emancipation, not only for the sake of the people here represented, but also for the sake of the Negroes, whom it would spare "the vagrant destitution which must largely attend immediate emancipation in localities where their numbers are very great." Whatever objections might be raised, he wanted one thing kept in mind: "If there ever could be a proper time for mere catch arguments, that time surely is not now. In times like the present, men should utter nothing for which they would not willingly be responsible through time and in eternity." And having thus admonished the assembly, after forcing it to accompany him on an excursion into the field of applied mathematics, he thought perhaps some note of apology — if not of retraction — was in order. "I do not forget the gravity which should characterize a paper addressed to the Congress of the nation by the Chief Magistrate of the nation. Nor do I forget that some of you are my seniors, nor that many of you have more experience than I in the conduct of public affairs. Yet I trust that in view of the great responsibility resting upon me, you will perceive no want of respect to yourselves in any undue earnestness I may seem to display." Apparently, however, this was intended not only to make amends for what had gone before, but also to brace them for what was to come. Nor was it long in coming. Hard on the heels of this apology for "undue earnestness," he threw a cluster of knotty, rhetorical questions full in their faces:

"Is it doubted, then, that the plan I propose, if adopted, would shorten the war, and thus lessen its expenditure of money and of blood? Is it doubted that it would restore the national authority and national prosperity, and perpetuate both indefinitely? Is it doubted that we here — Congress and Executive — can secure its adoption? Will not the good people respond to a united and earnest appeal from us? Can we, can they, by any other means so certainly or so speedily assure these vital objects? We can succeed only by concert. It is not 'Can any of us imagine better?' but 'Can we all do better?' Object whatsoever is possible, still the question recurs, 'Can we do better?'"

As the long message approached its end, Lincoln asked that question: "Can we do better?" Oratory was not enough. "The North responds ... sufficiently in breath," he had said of the reaction to the September proclamation; "but breath alone kills no rebels." He knew as well as Sherman the need for the nation to be "born again," and he would also have agreed with the New England major who this month wrote home that he sometimes felt like changing the old soldier's prayer into "O God, if there be a God, save my country, if my country is worth saving." A majority of 100,000 voters in Lincoln's own state, fearing the backwash of liberated slaves that would result from Grant's advance, had approved in November the adoption of a new article into the Illinois constitution prohibiting the immigration of Negroes into the state. He knew, too, the reaction of most of the lawmakers to the proposal he was now advancing — including that of Senator Orville Browning, his fellow

Illinoisan and confidant, who would write in his diary of his friend's plea when he went home tonight: "It surprised me by its singular reticence in regard to the war, and some other subjects which I expected discussed, and by the hallucination the President seems to be laboring under that Congress can suppress the rebellion by adopting his plan of compensated emancipation." Yet according to Lincoln it was not he, but they, who were hallucinated and enthralled, and he told them so as the long message wore on toward a close: "The dogmas of the quiet past are inadequate to the stormy present. The occasion is piled high with difficulty, and we must rise with the occasion. As our case is new, so we must think anew and act anew. We must disenthrall ourselves, and then we shall save our country."

Then came the end, the turn of a page that opened a new chapter. And now, through the droning voice of the clerk, the Lincoln music sounded in what would someday be known as its full glory: "Fellow-citizens, we cannot escape history. We of this Congress and this Administration will be remembered in spite of ourselves. No personal significance or insignificance can spare one or another of us. The fiery trial through which we pass will light us down, in honor or dishonor, to the latest generation. We say we are for the Union. The world will not forget that we say this. We know how to save the Union. The world knows we do know how to save it. We — even we here — hold the power and bear the responsibility. In giving freedom to the slave, we assure freedom to the free — honorable alike in what we give and what we preserve. We shall nobly save or meanly lose the last, best hope of earth. Other means may succeed; this could not fail. The way is plain, peaceful, generous, just — a way which, if followed, the world will forever applaud, and God must forever bless."

List of Maps
Bibliographical Note
Index

LIST OF MAPS

- 52. The Waves of Secession.
- 57. Situation: Virginia, mid-July.
- 81. Manassas, 21Jul61.
- 93. Wilson's Creek, 10Aug61.
- 118. Port Royal, 7Nov61.
- 172. Johnston's Long Kentucky Line.
- 209. Fort Donelson, 14-16Feb62.
- 225. Roanoke Island and the Sounds.
- 284. Elkhorn Tavern, 7-8Mar62.
- 297. The Rio Grande.
- 308. New Madrid, Island Ten.
- 326. Johnston's Advance.
- 342. Shiloh, 6-7Apr62.
- 364. Forts Jackson and St Philip.
- 397. East Virginia, Arc and Chord.
- 400. The Peninsula: Three Lines.
- 424. The Shenandoah Valley.
- 445. Seven Pines, 31May62.
- 458. Cross Keys, Port Republic.
- 474. Lee's Intended Convergence.
- 490. Gaines Mill, 27Jun62.
- 499. McClellan Shifts, Pursued.
- 507. Glendale, 30Jun62.
- 510. Malvern Hill, 1Jul62.
- 545. Grant's Dispositions.
- 559. Region of Buell's Advance.
- 575. Bragg Shifts to Chattanooga.
- 597. Situation: Virginia, August.
- 606. Pope in the V.
- 609. Stuart's Raid on Catlett's.
- 618. Jackson Swings Around Pope.
- 632. Second Manassas, 29-30Aug62.
- 652. Kirby Smith's Advance.
- 657. Bragg's Advance.
- 661. Bragg, Buell Go Their Ways.
- 667. Convergence on Harpers Ferry.
- 675. McClellan's Advance.
- 689. Sharpsburg, 17Sep62.
- 718. Iuka, 19Sep62.
- 721. Van Dorn's Advance.
- 724. Corinth, 3-4Oct62.
- 728. Buell's Advance.
- 733. Perryville, 8Oct62.
- 797. Situation: December 1862.

ENDPAPERS.

Front: Theater of War.
Back: Virginia Theater.

Maps drawn by George Annand, of Darien, Connecticut, from originals by the author. All are oriented north.

BIBLIOGRAPHICAL NOTE

Many books by many men, predominantly military experts or professional historians, went into the making of this one book by one man who is neither, and of these the most useful, as well as the largest, were the 128-volume *War of the Rebellion: a Compilation of the Official Records of the Union and Confederate Armies* and the 30-volume *Official Records of the Union and Confederate Navies in the War of the Rebellion,* issued by the government in 1880-1901 and 1897-1927 respectively. There you hear the live men speak — there and in their diaries and letters, their newspapers and periodicals — although not always as they spoke in later life, when they got around to writing their memoirs, regimental histories, and a host of articles such as the ones collected in four large volumes and published in 1887 under the title *Battles and Leaders of the Civil War.* Early or late, taken in conjunction with the diplomatic correspondence and the congressional transcripts, these complete the first-hand testimony by soldiers and civilians, some of high rank, some of low rank, some of no rank at all. The evidence is in. All else is speculation or sifting, an attempt to reconcile differences and bring order out of multiplicity by sorting the fruits that have poured from this horn of plenty.

Biographies of the participants and studies of the war itself, in part or as a whole, make up the secondary sources. These are not only interesting and rewarding in their own right, filling in and deepening the over-all impression, but they also serve as a guide through the labyrinth. I found them invaluable on both counts: so much so, indeed, that while this narrative is based throughout on the original material referred to above, my obligations are equally heavy on this side of the line where it leaves off. The present is the first of three intended volumes — *Fort Sumter to Perryville, Fredericksburg to Meridian, Red River to Appomattox* — and though the last will include a complete bibliography, I want to state here at the outset my chief debts, particularly to those works still available in bookstores. These include the following biographies, of and by the following men: of Lee by Douglas Southall Freeman, Scribner's, 1934-35: of McClellan by Warren W. Hassler, LSU Press, 1957: of Beauregard by T. Harry Williams, LSU Press, 1954: of Sherman by Lloyd Lewis, Harcourt, Brace, 1932: of Joe Johnston by G. E. Govan and J. W. Livingood, Bobbs-Merrill, 1956: of Sheridan by Richard O'Connor, Bobbs-Merrill, 1953: of Jackson by Burke Davis, Rinehart, 1954: of Kirby Smith by Joseph H. Parks, LSU Press, 1954: of Davis by William E. Dodd, Jacobs, 1907, and Hudson Strode, Harcourt, Brace, 1955: of Lincoln by Carl Sandburg, Harcourt, Brace, 1939; J. G. Randall, Dodd, Meade, 1945-55; and Benjamin P. Thomas, Knopf, 1952.

Among the more general works, my chief debts are to the following: *Lincoln Finds a General* by Kenneth P. Williams, Macmillan, 1949-56: *Lee's Lieutenants* by Douglas Southall Freeman, Scribner's, 1942-44: *The Army of Tennessee* by Stanley F. Horn, Bobbs-Merrill, 1941: *Civil War on the Western Border* by Jay Monaghan, Little, Brown, 1955: *Mr. Lincoln's Army* and *This Hallowed Ground* by Bruce Catton, Doubleday, 1951 and 1956: *Guns on the Western Waters* by H. Allen Gosnell, LSU Press, 1949: *Lincoln and His Generals* by T. Harry Williams, Knopf, 1952: *Statesmen of the Lost Cause* and *Lincoln's War Cabinet* by Burton J. Hendrick, Little, Brown, 1939 and 1946: *The North Reports the Civil War* by J. Cutler Andrews, University of Pittsburgh Press, 1955: *The Railroads of the Confederacy* by Robert C. Black, UNC Press, 1952: *The Life of Johnny Reb* and *The Life of Billy Yank* by Bell Irvin Wiley, Bobbs-Merrill, 1943 and 1952: *Reveille in Washington* by Margaret Leech, Harper, 1941: *The Beleaguered City* by Alfred Hoyt Bill, Knopf, 1946: *Experiment in Rebellion* by Clifford Dowdey, Doubleday, 1946: *The Civil War and Reconstruction* by J. G. Randall, Heath, 1937: *The Story of the Confederacy* by Robert S. Henry, Bobbs-Merrill, 1931: *The American Civil War* by Carl Russell Fish, Longmans, Green, 1937: *The Confederate States of America* by E. Merton Coulter, LSU Press, 1950. There were others but these were the main ones, and to each I owe much.

Other obligations, of a more personal nature, I also incurred during the five years that went into the writing of this first volume: to the John Simon Guggenheim Memorial Foundation, for an extended fellowship which made possible the buying of books and bread: to the superintendents, historians, and guides of the National Park Service, for unfailing industry and courtesy in helping me to get the look and feel of the various battlefields: to Robert N. Linscott and Robert D. Loomis of Random House, for combining enthusiasm and patience: to Mrs. O. B. Crittenden of the William Alexander Percy Memorial Library, Greenville, Mississippi, for the continuing loan of that institution's set of the *Official Records.* To all these I am grateful, as well as to friends in Memphis who had the out-of-hours grace to refrain from mentioning the Civil War.

A word I suppose is in order as to the use I made of these materials, original and secondary, not only because it is customary but also because it appears to be necessary, at least in certain eyes. One of the best of the latter-day authorities, in the course of his carefully documented exegesis, cautions against accepting the testimony of Lew Wallace as to what took place at a council of war preceding the march on Donelson. "Recollections of events long past are always to be suspected," he explains, "and especially when set down by a writer of fiction." Wallace then was doubly suspect. He had waited, and he had written *The Fair God* and *Ben-Hur.* He was a novelist.

Well, I am a novelist, and what is more I agree with D. H. Lawrence's estimate of the novel as "the one bright book of life." I might also agree with the professor quoted above, but only by considering each witness on his merit, his devotion as a writer to what should be his main concern. The point I would make is that the novelist and the historian are seeking the same thing: the truth — not a different truth: the same truth — only they reach it, or try to reach it, by different routes. Whether the event took place in a world now gone to dust, preserved by documents and evaluated by scholarship, or in the imagination, preserved by memory and distilled by the creative process, they both want to tell us *how it was:* to re-create it, by their separate methods, and make it live again in the world around them.

This has been my aim, as well, only I have combined the two. Accepting the historian's standards without his paraphernalia, I have employed the novelist's methods without his license. Instead of inventing characters and incidents, I searched them out — and having found them, I took them as they were. Nothing is included here, either within or outside quotation marks, without the authority of documentary evidence which I consider sound. Although I have left out footnotes, believing that they would detract from the book's narrative quality by intermittently shattering the illusion that the observer is not so much reading a book as sharing an experience, I have thought it proper to employ the three dots of elision to signify the omission of interior matter from quotations. In all respects, the book is as accurate as care and hard work could make it. Partly I have done this for my own satisfaction; for in writing a history, I would no more be false to a fact dug out of a valid document than I would be false to a "fact" dug out of my head in writing a novel. Also, I have tried for accuracy because I have never known a modern historical instance where the truth was not superior to distortion, by any standard and in every way. Wherever the choice lay between soundness and "color," soundness had it every time. Many problems were encountered in the course of all this study, but lack of color in the original materials was never one of them. In fact, there was the rub. Such heartbreak as was here involved came not from trying to decide what to include, but rather from trying to decide what to omit, and in the end the omissions far outnumbered the inclusions.

One word more perhaps will not be out of place. I am a Mississippian. Though the veterans I knew are all dead now, down to the final home guard drummer boy of my childhood, the remembrance of them is still with me. However, being nearly as far removed from them in time as most of them were removed from combat when they died, I hope I have recovered the respect they had for their opponents until Reconstruction lessened and finally killed it. Biased is the last thing I would be; I yield to no one in my admiration for heroism and ability, no matter which side of the line a man was born or fought on when the war broke out, fourscore and seventeen years ago. If pride in the resistance my forebears made against the odds has leaned me to any degree in their direction, I hope it will be seen to amount to no more, in the end, than the average American's normal sympathy for the underdog in a fight.

—S.F.

Index

Abolitionists,
  and cotton capitalists, 10
  and emancipation, 538
    proclamation, 708
  and John Brown, 32
  in Kansas, 28
Adams [Henry], 140
Alabama, 78, 170, 250, 306, 353, 357, 377–378, 392, 759
Alabama, S.S., 791–795
Albemarle Sound, 115, 225, 229
Albuquerque, 296, 300
Alexandria, 54, 82, 616
Amissville, 615
Anaconda, Scott's, 111–113
Anderson, J. R., 419, 421
Anderson, Richard H.,
  injury, 693
  and Johnston, 441, 444
  and Lee, 667, 673, 685, 692
  and Longstreet's order of battle, 628, 631
Anderson, Robert
  brevetted major general, 89
  in Cincinnati, 88
  and Fort Sumter, 44, 48–50, 86, 89, 212–213
  at Frankfort, 88
  in Kentucky, 54, 87–89
  promotion to brigadier general, 87
  retired, 89
Andrews, James J., 377–378
Antietam, 682, 704, 718, 760, 772, 805
  battle, 685–700
  See also Sharpsburg
Apalachicola, 353, 796
Aquia Creek, 595–596, 641, 767
Arizona, 13, 294–296, 305
Arkansas, 19, 52, 72, 289, 337, 392, 568, 578–579, 653, 783–785
Arkansas, S.S., 387, 549, 556, 577, 580–581
Arlington Heights, 54
Armstrong, Frank, 569

Army, U.S.
  Coastal survey, 115, 404
  See also specific battles and generals
Asboth, Alexander, 284, 288–289
Ashby, Turner, 459
Ashby's Harbor, 229
Aspinwall, William H., 532

Baker, Edward D.
  at Ball's Bluff, 105
  on Scott's Anaconda, 112
Ball's Bluff, 104–108, 114, 148, 152, 392, 473
Baltimore and Ohio Railroad, 68, 128, 140, 668
Banks, Nathaniel Prentiss
  Army of Virginia, 527–528
  at Cedar Mountain, 601–603, 613, 622
  at Culpeper, 398
  Department of Gulf, 759
  Department of Shenandoah, 406
  versus Ewell, 431
  and Gordon, 432
  and Halleck, 671, 759–760
  at Harpers Ferry, 451
  versus Jackson, 396–397, 419, 431–432, 441–442, 465, 598, 601–603, 759
  and Lincoln, 437, 461–462, 760
  and Pope, 527–528, 597–598, 645
  protection against guerilla raids, 427
  race for Winchester, 433
  removal from McClellan's command, 406
  in Shenandoah Valley, 396, 398, 439–442, 601–603, 613, 622
  at Strasburg, 428
  and Sumner, 695
  support by Farragut's fleet, 763
  talent for retreat, 433
  Washington defense assigned to, 669
  at Williamsport, 439, 451
Banshee, blockade runner, 352
Barbourville, 650
Bardstown, 711–712, 727–729

[818]   *Index*

Bates, Edward, and Lincoln, 33–34
  on emancipation, 540
  evaluation of, 801
Baton Rouge, 371, 422, 796
Battles
  See also specific
  Antietam. *See* Sharpsburg
  Ball's Bluff, 104–108
  Baton Rouge, 579–580
  Belmont, 149–152
  Big Bethel, 56–57
  Bull Run. *See* First Manassas; Second Manassas
  Carrick's Ford, 70
  Cedar Mountain, 599–604
  Chantilly, 644–645
  Corinth, 720–726
  Cross Keys, 460–464
  Drewry's Bluff, 416
  Elkhorn Tavern, 284–291
  Eltham Landing, 412–413
  Fair Oaks. *See* Seven Pines
  Falling Waters, 56–57
  First Manassas, 71–72, 77–86
  Fishing Creek. *See* Mill Springs
  Fort Donelson, 194–209
  Fort Henry, 183–191
  Fort Pulaski, 352
  Fort Sumter, 44–50
  Frayser's Farm. *See* Glendale
  Front Royal, 435–438
  Gaines Mill, 485–491
  Glendale, 505–508
  Glorieta Pass, 302
  Hanover Courthouse, 443
  Harpers Ferry, 679–680
  Head of the Passes, 355–356
  Island Ten, 313–314
  Iuka, 717–720
  Kernstown, 270–271
  Lexington, Mo., 98
  Logan's Crossroads. *See* Mill Springs
  McDowell, 421–423
  Malvern Hill, 508–514, 525
  Mechanicsville, 481–483
  Memphis, 387–388
  Mill Springs, 177–180
  Munfordville, 658–659
  New Orleans: Forts Jackson and St Philip, 366–369
  Pea Ridge. *See* Elkhorn Tavern
  Perryville, 733–738
  Philippi, 69
  Plum Run Bend, 380–381
  Pocotaligo, 795
  Port Republic, 461–463
  Port Royal, 116–120
  Rich Mountain, 69–70
  Richmond, Ky., 651–653
  Roanoke Island, 225–230
  St Charles, Ark., 547
  Savage Station, 496–498
  Secessionville, 473
  Second Manassas, 621–627
  Seven Days, 508–514, 516
  Seven Pines, 446–449
  Sharpsburg, 688–702
  Shepherdstown ford, 703–704
  Shiloh, 340–348, 350
  South Mountain, 674–677
  Williamsburg, 411
  Wilson's Creek, 91–95
  Winchester, 434–435
Baylor, John R.
  capture of Forts, Bliss, 295
  and Fillmore, 297
  establishment of Confederate territory of Arizona, 294–296
Bay Point, 117
Beauregard, Fort, 117–119
Beauregard, Pierre Gustave Toutant
  Army of Mississippi, 319
  and Bee, 76, 78–79, 84
  bells collected for, 306–307
  confiscated by Butler, 370–371
  on Benjamin, 223
  and Bragg, 325, 329, 390, 566, 573
  and Breckinridge, 321, 325, 339–342, 347–348, 374
  versus Buell, 345–346, 375
  at Bull Run, 76
  on Butler's general order, 534
  at Centerville, 223
  command passed to, at Johnston's death, 340
  at Corinth, 305, 319, 374–376, 381, 386, 722
  and Cumberland Gap fall, 390
  and Dan Ruggles, 319, 341–342
  and Davis, 58, 124–125, 389–390
  defenses at Charleston harbor, 47–50, 777
  Department of South Carolina and Georgia, 777, 779
  and Ewell, 77
  and fall of New Madrid and Island Ten, 308, 314
  versus Halleck, 374–375
  and Hardee, 321, 325, 347
  headquarters, 76, 340
  at Hornets Nest, 340–341
  and Jackson, T. J., 76
  and Johnston, A. S., 192–193, 320–321, 328–329, 336–337
  and Johnston, J., 58, 75, 77, 79, 83, 122, 236
  at Lookout Hill, 76
  and McDowell, 73, 76
  at Manassas, 56–58, 71, 75–76, 320
  versus Mitchel, 795
  on Morgan and Forrest, 571
  at Nashville, 305
  and Orleans Guard battalion, 337, 347
  at Pocotaligo, 795
  and Polk, 305–306, 329
  promotion to full general, 83, 126
  relieved of command, 390–391
  recalled to duty, 777
  retreat, 193, 234, 292, 348, 386

Index

on roadbed of Mobile & Ohio, 306
versus Sheridan, 732
at Shiloh, 340-343, 345-346, 348
standing offer for head of, 278
at Sumter, 48-50, 54, 212-213
and Van Dorn, 350, 374, 722
Beauregard, S.S., blockade runner, 352
Beaver Dam Creek, 481-483
Bee, Barnard, 76, 78-79, 84
Beecher, Henry Ward, 524
Bell, John, 34
Belmont, Battle of, 149-152
Benjamin, Judah Philip
  and Loring's petition, 224-225
  Secretary of State, 232-233
  Secretary of War, 123, 222-225
  and Roanoke Island disaster, 231-233
Benton, Thomas Hart, 86
Big Bethel, 56-57, 70, 115
Big Hill, Kentucky, 651, 740
Biloxi, Mississippi, 353, 796
Bissell, W. H., 12
Blackburn's Ford, 75, 265
Black Hat Brigade, 627
Blair, Francis, 753
Blair, Montgomery
  on Lincoln's emancipation proclamation, 540
  warning on Pope, 527
Blenker, Louis, 272-273, 406, 408
Bliss, Fort, 295-297
Blockade, Federal naval. *See* Anaconda
Blood Tubs, 37-38
Bloody Lane, 694-695
Bloss, J. M., 670
Boatswain Swamp, 489, 511
Bolivar, 722
  Heights, 667
Booneville, 654
Boteler, A. R., 439
Bottom's Bridge, 443-445
Bragg, Braxton
  at Bardstown, 711-712, 727-729
  and Beauregard, 325, 329, 390, 566, 573
  and Breckinridge, 338, 341, 582, 775
  and Buckner's division, 660
  versus Buell, 564-566, 569, 573, 660, 711-712, 727-729, 738-743
  and Chalmers, 658, 660
  at Chattanooga, 564-566, 571, 613, 653
    plan for, 572-573
  at Corinth, 325, 327, 568
  and Davis, 572, 582-583, 773-774, 789, 797-798
  Davis and Cooper versus Lincoln and Halleck in evaluation, 743
  deployment of troops, 327-330
  at Frankfort, 726-727
  at Glasgow, 656-657
  and Hardee, 568, 575, 731, 739-740, 744, 776
  at Harrodsburg, 730-731
  and Polk at Perryville, 734-738
  and Jackson, 584, 660

and Johnston, 329
in Kentucky, 655-656, 796
in Knoxville, 742-743
movement toward Green River, 658
at Munfordville, 658
at Murfreesboro, 776
and Pemberton, 776-777
at Perryville, 730, 737-743
and Polk, 575, 660, 726, 776
versus Pope, 383
and Price, 568, 583, 716-717
proclamation to people, 655-656
relationship with troops, 566-569, 797-798
  general order read to, 584
sent to Nashville, 774
at Shelbyville, 776
at Shiloh, 342, 348, 568
and Smith, 572, 575, 584, 653, 711-712, 728, 738-743, 773-775
at Snake Creek, 341
summons to Richmond, 743
and Army of Tennessee, 773-776
Wilder's capture, 659, 661
Bragg, S.S., 388
Bragg, Thomas, 123
Breckinridge, John Cabell
  and *Arkansas*, 578-580
  and Baton Rouge, 578
  and Beauregard, 321, 325 339-342, 347-348, 374
  and Bragg, 338, 341, 582, 775
  versus Grant, 347-348
  versus Halleck, 374
  at Hornets Nest, 339-342
  and Johnston, 171, 329, 338-339
  and Port Hudson, 581-582
  presidential candidate, 34
  at Shiloh, 342, 347-348
  transferred to Vicksburg, 568
  versus Williams, 580
Bridgeport, 377
Bristoe Station, 616
Broad Run railroad bridge, 617
Brooke, John M., 255
Brooklyn, S.S., 548
Brooks, Preston, 15, 137
Brown, Albert Gallatin, 13-14
Brown, Isaac Newton, 549, 578
  and *S.S. Arkansas*, 551-556, 581
Brown, John, 31-32
Brown, Joseph E., 395, 780
Brownlow, William G., 133
Brown's Gap, 457
Brunswick, 796
Bryant, William Cullen, 802
Buchanan, Franklin, 256-258
Buchanan, James, 29
  and Fort Sumter, 44
  and secession, 18
Buck. *See* Van Dorn, Earl
Buckhannon, 69
Buckingham, C. P., 754
Buckner, Simon Bolivar
  and censure of Pillow, 206

Buckner, Simon Bolivar (*cont.*)
  at Donelson, 205-209
  at Dover Inn, 210
  exchanged after imprisonment, 582
  and Floyd, 205-207, 210
  at Fort Henry, 194
  and Grant, 196, 210-213
  and Johnston, 180
  at Perryville, versus Terrill, 735
  promotion to major general, 582
  in state militia, 86, 88
  and Wilder's surrender, 659
Buell, Don Carlos
  Army of Ohio, 560
  at Bardstown, 716
  versus Beauregard, 345-346, 375
  at Bowling Green, 172, 656-657
  versus Bragg, 564-566, 569, 573, 660, 711-712, 727-729, 738-743
  and Chattanooga, 564, 572
  at Decherd, 566
  feint toward Frankfort, 727-728
  versus Forrest, 345-346, 571
  and Governor Johnson, 656-657
  and Grant, 317, 335, 343, 346, 656, 736
  guerilla problems, 558-559
  and Halleck, 144, 155-156, 180-181, 183, 316-316, 372-374, 542, 558, 657, 715, 741-745
  versus Hardee, 172, 192
  at Huntsville, 564
  versus Johnston, 174-175, 180
  and Lincoln, 145-146, 155-156, 711, 715, 743-744, 760
  and McClellan, 147, 241, 315
  Memphis & Charleston line repair, 560
  and Morgan's wrecking of railroad, 565
  at Murfreesboro, 656-657
  at Nashville, 564-566, 656-657
  and Nelson, 651, 657, 714-716
  at Perryville, 729-730, 733, 737
  and Pittsburg Landing, 377
  plan for Tennessee conquest, 146-147
  promotion to major general, 316
  race for Chattanooga, 582
  refusal to advance through Knoxville, 154
  relationship with troops, 563-564, 713
  and Savannah, 330
  at Shiloh, 343, 346
  suspension order suspended, 715
  and Thomas, 716, 729
  thrown from horse, 730
  troops, 558-559
    reorganization, 711-712
    strength, 656, 711-712, 728, 733
Bull Run, 74, 120, 154, 265, 316-317, 524, 616, 644, 650
  See also First Manassas; Second Manassas
Bull Sumner. *See* Sumner
Burnside, Ambrose
  at Antietam, 695-700, 760
  corps regrouped, 766
  Expedition, 228
  near-mutiny, 228
  and Fredericksburg, 592, 595, 597, 765-766
  and Goldsborough, 228-229
  and Halleck, 592
  headquarters, 228, 588
  versus Huger and Wise, 250
  and Lincoln, 760, 765-766
  and McClellan, 227-228, 672-674, 685, 695-701, 755-757
  men from Rhode Island, 78
  at New Bern, 397, 470
  at Norfolk, 396
  and Parke, 228, 230
  promotion to brigadier general, 227
  at Roanoke Island, 229-230, 760
  and Reno, 608
  at Salem, 754
  at Sharpsburg, 696-700
Burton, William, and Lincoln's militia request, 52
Bushnell, Horace, 799-800
Butler, Benjamin
  and Baton Rouge, 581
  at Big Bethel, 70, 115
  and Farragut, 359, 547
  and Fort Clark, 115
  and Hatteras, 115, 357
  at Head of Passes, 359
  on the James peninsula, 70
  and looting, 370, 416
  and Negroes, 161, 535, 539
  at New Orleans, occupation, 533-538, 758
  new western hero, 371

Calhoun, John C., 7, 25-26
California, 13-14, 43, 293-294
Cameron, Simon, 25
  and Lincoln, 33, 801
  appointment as Minister to Russia, 243-244
  Secretary of War, 242-243, 535
Campbell, John A., 45-47
Canby, Edward R. S.
  colonel, appointment, 296-297
  at Fort Craig, 300-302, 304
  new western hero, 371
  at Peralta, 303
  promotion to brigadier general, 302
  at Santa Fe, 297
  "scorched earth" policy, 300
  versus Sibley, 297, 303
  at Valverde, 300, 303
Carlyle, Thomas, 791
Carondelet, S.S., 201-205, 312-313, 342
  and Brown's *Arkansas*, 551-553
Carr, Eugene, and Curtis, 284, 288-290
Carrick's Ford, 70
Carson, Kit, 89, 297
Cedar Mountain, 598
  battle of, 599-604
Centerville, 71, 75-76, 223, 264, 616, 622
  See also Manassas

Index

Chalmers, James R., 658, 660
Chandler, Zachariah
  on Joint Committee on Conduct of War, 140, 241
  on McClellan, 408
Chantilly, Battle of, 644-645
Charleston, 113, 116, 473, 776-778
  Mercury, comments on war, 458, 586
Chase, Salmon Portland
  and Fort Monroe, 413
  and Lincoln, 33, 241, 540
  and news of *Virginia*, 258
  and Stanton, on McClellan's removal, 753
Chattanooga, 320, 564-566, 571-573, 613, 653, 655, 797-798
Chatters, Captain (Duc de Chartres), 100
Cheat Mountain, 667
Cheatham, B. F., 151, 735
Chesapeake and Ohio Canal, 128
Chewalla, 722
Chickahominy, 410-412, 417, 442, 471-494, 500-501
Chilton, R. H., 670-671
Cincinnati, 68, 654
  Commercial, 385
  Gazette, 544, 654
Clark, Fort, 115-116
Clay, Henry, 14, 26, 87
Cleburne, Patrick Ronayne
  Captain of Yell Rifles, 653
  at Perryville, 736
  personal injury, 653, 736
  promotion to brigadier general, 653
  at Shiloh, 653
Cobb, Thomas, 224, 393, 585
Cockspur Island, 352
Colonel Lovell, S.S., 380-381, 387
Colorado, 13, 301
"Colossus of Roads." See *S.S. Virginia*
Columbus, 151, 172
  bluff, 309
Compromise of 1850, and Clay, 14, 26
Conestoga, S.S., 203
Confederacy
  See also Davis, Jefferson; and specific persons and places
  advantages of defensive, 61, 95
  bid for foreign aid, 134-136, 220-221, 395, 523, 791-792
  and cotton, 60-61, 113, 137
  capital moved, 55
  Congress, permanent, 393
  conscription, 406
  disorganization by victory, 94
  dollar values, 393, 790
  foundation and structure, 42
  Justice Department, 123
  purpose of compact of union, 65
  rights of belligerent, grant, 136
  substitutes for ammunition, 91
  spy system, 396-397
  welcome of Scott's Anaconda, 113-114
Confiscation Act, 539-540

Congress, SS., 256-258, 260
Conrad's Store, 425, 456-457
Conscription, 394, 406
  and Curtis, 557
  and Lee, 396-400, 780
Cooke, Philip St George, 471-472
Cooper, Samuel, 125, 451
Corinth, 305, 319, 325, 327, 374-376, 381-386, 568, 720-726, 760, 772, 796
Corpus Christi, 745
Covington, fortification, 654
Cowskin Prairie, 91
Craig, Fort, 296
Crittenden, George Bibb, 171
  at Fishing Creek, 176-177, 321
  versus Thomas, 177, 250
  and Zollicoffer, 177-180, 192
Crittenden, John Jordan, 87, 171
Crittenden, Thomas Leonidas, 171
  and Buell, 716
  and Grant taking Shiloh, 346
  at Perryville, 736
  and Rosecrans, 769
Crittenden, Thomas Theodore, 562
Cross Keys, Battle of, 460-464
Cruft, Charles, 652
Cuba, 26, 293
Culpeper, 596-602
Cumberland, Army of, 768
Cumberland Gap, 132, 390, 473, 654
Cumberland Iron Works, 173
Cumberland, S.S., 256-258, 261
Curtis, Samuel R.
  brigadier general of volunteers, 280
  at Elkhorn Tavern, 285-292, 318
  and Frémont, 98, 281
  and Grant, 722
  at Helena, 545, 557
  new western hero, 371
  and Pea Ridge, 545-547, 556-557, 784
  and Sigel, 281, 290-291
  versus Van Dorn, 280, 291, 318
  at Wilson's Creek, 284
Cushing, Caleb, 14

Davis, Charles Henry
  assigned to Bureau of Navigation, 746
  and Farragut, 548
  Flag Officer, 386, 546
  successor to Foote, 379, 746
  victory at St Charles, 547
Davis, Jefferson
  See also specific battle, and specific commander
  addresses by, 15, 40-41, 55
  for annexation of Cuba, 15
  announcement of Mississippi's secession, 3-5
  and Benjamin, 223, 232-233
  and Butcher Cats, versus Hill Cats, 396
  and California, 294
  challenge to Bissell, 12
  childhood, 5-7
  children of, 16, 165

[822] Index

Davis, Jefferson (*cont.*)
  and confidence of people, 121-122, 124-127, 233, 395-396, 585
  and congress, provisional, 132, 394-395, 780
  on conscription, 394-395
  and Cooper, 743
  defeat by Prentiss, 11
  as Democrat, 10
  education, 6-8
  election to Congress, 11, 25
    resignation and return, 14-15
  exercise of veto, 131
  first council of war, 56-57
  at first Manassas, 71, 83
    conference with victors, 121
  and Foote in politics, 12, 14
  on Fort Sumter, 45-47, 51
  Gadsden Purchase engineered by, 14-15, 293
  health, 8, 11, 15, 122, 127, 140, 251
  and Knox Taylor, 8
  and Lincoln, 16, 56
    Emancipation Proclamation, 708
    maneuver into firing the first shot, 56
    on privateering, 114
    understanding of, 164
  Mississippi Rifles, 11
  Nashville Convention, 13
  Norfolk's evacuation, 416
  organization of army, 56
  and overseer, of plantation, 9
  as president, 17, 165
    inauguration, 18, 40-41, 217-218
    six-year term, 132
  and Randolph, 232-233, 786-787
  reception, by Virginians, 55
  and recruitment, 238
  and religion, 395
  and Scott, 13, 66
  and secession, 3, 14-15
  as second Hezekiah, 524
  second lieutenant, U.S. Army, 8
  in Senate, 3-5, 12
  and slavery, 15
  spokesman for southern nationalism, 13-14
  statement of southern position, 65
  successor to Calhoun, 13
  suspension of habeas corpus in Norfolk, 231
  War Department, 14, 26, 482
    and Wise, recall, 130
  watch of battles, 479, 481-482, 506, 578
Davis, Jefferson, Indiana brigadier, 741-716
Davis, Joseph, 7-9
Davis, Varina Howell, 10, 123, 165, 251, 798-799
Decherd, 655-656
Declaration of Paris, 114
Delaware, 19, 708
Democratic Party
  congressmen increase, 753
  disintegration of, 15
  and Whigs, 10
Department of Agriculture, 807
Dismal Swamp Canal, 231
Doctor's Creek, 729
Donelson, Fort, 174, 191, 194-209, 305-306, 314, 319
Doubleday, Abner, 626-627
Douglas, Stephen A., 26
  and Dred Scott decision, 29
  in Illinois, 30-31
  and Lincoln, 23, 27, 30-31, 33-34
  pledge to preserve Union, 50
Dover Inn, 194, 210
Drayton, Percival, 120
Drayton, Thomas F., 120
Dream, blockade runner, 352
Dred Scott Decision, 26, 29, 536
Drewry's Bluff, 398, 415, 416, 588
Duc de Chartres, (Captain Chatters), 100
Dumont, Ebenezer, 716, 727-728
Dunker Church, 685-695
Du Pont, Samuel F.
  appointed head of blockade fleet, 116-117
  occupied Fort Beauregard, 157

Eads, James B., 183-184, 389
Early, Jubal, 77, 81, 690
Edwards Ferry, 104
Elk River bridge, 560
Elkhorn Tavern, 282, 285, 287
Ellet, A. W., 548
Ellet, Charles, 386-389
Ellis, John W., reply to Lincoln's demand for troops, 52
Ely, Alfred, 84
Elzey, Arnold, 81, 83
Emancipation
  and Cameron, 242-243
  and foreign intervention, 538, 709
  and Frémont, 95-96, 535
  and Hunter, 535-536
  and Lincoln, 705-709
    and political unrest, 753-754
    pressure for, 242-243, 537
    proposal for compensated, 536, 808, 810
    reactions to first proposal, 540-541
  Proclamation, 704-710
England
  and Confederate bid for aid, 135-137, 220-221
  merchantmen's response, 792-795
  and Confederate recognition, 666
  London *Times*, 157, 220, 392, 791
  Prince Albert, and Russell's ultimatum, 160
  proclamation of neutrality, 136
  and slave trade, 537
  Trent Affair, 156-157
Essex, S.S., 189, 201, 203, 554-556, 580
Europe
  See also specific country
  anti-slavery, and abolition, 137

Index

and Confederate recognition, 395, 666
and Emancipation Proclamation, 538, 709
interests of, and split of U.S., 43
interpretation of law on high seas, 139
Evans, N. G.
  Ball's Bluff, 106–107
  and Beauregard, 77–78
  and Hood, 664
  at Secessionville, 473
Evelington Heights, 517–518
Ewell, Richard Stoddert
  versus Banks, 431
  and Beauregard, 77
  at Boatswain Swamp, 487
  at Bottom's Bridge, 496, 498
  at Broad Run, 618, 623–624
  at Conrad's Store, 426
  at Cross Keys, 457, 462–463
  at Dunker Church, 689
  false rumor of death, 643–644
  versus Frémont, 453–454, 457, 461
  at Front Royal, 430
  at Groveton, 624
  and Hill, 487, 616, 624
  versus Hooker's division, 623
  injury, and amputation, 627
  and Jackson, 419, 426, 428, 431–432, 453–454, 462–464, 621–627
  divisions under, 685, 689
  and Lincoln's plan in Shenandoah Valley, 451
  versus McDowell, 419, 421
  at Manassas, 621, 625, 627
  march to Culpeper, 599–600
  promotion to major general, 401, 420
  on Rappahannock line, 421
  versus Sykes under pressure from D. H. Hill, 490
  at Thoroughfare Gap, 616
  on Turkey Hill, 488
  at Union Mills Ford, 77

Fair Oaks, 444, 500
See also Seven Pines
Fairfax, D. MacNeill, 139
Falling Waters, 56–57
Falmouth, 597, 766–767
Farmington, 374
Farragut, David Glasgow
  at Baton Rouge, 422, 555
  versus Brown and his *Arkansas*, 553–556, 745–746
  at Corpus Christi, 745
  and Fort Jackson, 363–369
  and Fort Pillow, 378, 380
  at Fort St Philip, 363–369
  Galveston, 745–746
  at Head of the Passes, 359
  at Natchez, 422
  and New Orleans, 357–358, 370, 422, 534, 547, 578
  new western hero, 371
  and Porter, 363–369
  Sabine City, 745

support of Banks, 763
turned back from Vicksburg, 378, 546–547, 745–746
"Father of Annapolis." *See* Buchanan, F.
"Father Neptune." *See* Welles
Fernandina, 352, 796
Fessenden, William Pitt, 246, 524
Field, Charles, 419
Fighting Joe. *See* Hooker
Fillmore, Fort, 295, 297
First Manassas, 71–72, 77–86, 805
  battle plan, 56–57, 165
  casualty lists, 83–84
Fishing Creek, 177–180
Florida, 3, 113, 352
Floyd, John Buchanan
  and Buckner, 205–207, 210
  at Fort Donelson, 194–195, 203, 211–212
  indictment for malfeasance, 210
  and Johnston, 181
  and Lee in Kanawha Valley, 129–130, 272
  and Nashville, 205–207, 216
  and Pillow, 205–207, 210
  sent to Chattanooga, 320
  versus Wise, defeat in West Virginia, 225–226
Foote, Andrew Hull
  at Columbus bluff, 309
  at Donelson, 201–205, 207–208, 308
  and Grant, 184–185, 201–205, 207–208
  at Fort Henry, 186–191, 308, 310
  injury, 208, 379
  at Island Ten, 309
  and New Orleans defense, 360
Foote, Henry S., 14
  and Yancey, 789
Forrest, Nathan Bedford
  at Bowling Green, 171–172
  versus Buell, 345–346, 571
  at Donelson, 206, 211–212
  at Fallen Timbers, 350
  and Floyd at Dover Inn, 210
  and Lick Creek fords, 345
  at Murfreesboro, 562, 570–572
  at Nashville, 216, 562
  receipt of unconditional surrender, 571
  sent back to Middle Tennessee, 726
  sent to Chattanooga, 570
  versus Sherman, 350
  troopers, 320, 324
Fort. *See* specific name
Foster, J. G., 228, 230
Foster, Stephen, 525
Fox, G. V., and Farragut, 357–359, 547
Fox, blockade runner, 352
France
  and Confederate bid for aid, 135–137
  and Slidell, 395, 791–792
  and Confederate recognition, 666
  on Emancipation Proclamation, 709
  and Great Britain's Industry, 113
  and New Orleans, 353

## [824]	Index

Frankfort, 653–654, 712–713, 726
Franklin, William Buel
  at Battle of Glendale, 507
  and Battle of Seven Pines, 444–451
  at Bloody Lane, 695
  and Burnside, 766
  at Centerville, 643
  at Eltham, 412–413
  versus Huger, 507
  and Lincoln, 240–242, 531
  and McClellan, 240–242, 253, 409, 614, 673–674, 685, 695
  versus McLaws, 679–680
  on Malvern Hill, 510
  and Mechanicsville, 443, 467
  and Pope, 613–614, 643
  and Sharpsburg battles, 700
  Slocum, and Smith, 417
  and Sumner, 695
  in wake of Keyes at Savage Station, 500
  at White Oak Swamp, 501
Frayser's Farm, 505–508
Frederick, 670, 672–673
Fredericksburg, 443, 467, 588, 592, 595, 765–766
Frémont, John Charles
  advance at Mount Jackson, 456–457
  and Anderson, versus Johnston, 174
  chaos left by, 147
  and charges of graft, 97
  at Cross Keys, 460–461
  and Curtis, 98, 281
  for descent of Mississippi, gunboats built for, 183
  dismissal, 242, 528
    reinstatement and command of Mountain Department, 272–273, 318
  on emancipation, 95–96, 535
  versus Ewell, 453–454, 457, 461
  and Grant, 90
  and Halleck's command, 145
  versus Jackson, 454–457, 463
  and Jackson's repeated victories, 465
  left Springfield, 149
  and Lincoln, 89–90, 242, 247, 269, 272–273, 435–438, 463, 535
  in Missouri, 54, 89–90, 269
  at Moorefield, 437
  near Strasburg, 439, 454
  occupation Paducah, 149
  offensive conceptions of Mississippi River, 90
  and Pope's Army of Virginia, 527
  presidential candidate, 29
  versus Price, 98
  proclamation, 95–97
  and Shields convergence, 452
  versus Taylor, 454
Frémont, Jessie Benton, 96–98
Front Royal, 425, 431, 451
  battle, 435–438
Fugitive Slave Law, 137
Fuller, W. A., 378
Furlough and Bounty Act, 235–236, 394

Gadsden Purchase, 14–15, 293
Gainesville, 616
Galena, S.S., 416
Galveston, 277–278, 745–746, 796
Garland, Samuel, 677
Garnett, Richard, 271
Garnett, Robert S., 69–70, 127, 461
General Beauregard, S.S., 387
General Bragg, S.S., 380–381
General Price, S.S., 387–388
General Van Dorn, S.S., 380–381
Georgia, 3, 78, 170, 412
Gibbons, James Sloan, 525
Gibbon, John, and Iron Brigade, 626–627, 647
Gilbert, Charles C.
  and Buell, 716, 728–730
  at Doctor's Creek, 729–730
  and McCook at Perryville, 735–736
  and Rosecrans, 769
Gladstone, William E., 791
Glasgow, 655
Glendale, 507
Glorieta Pass, 302
Goldsborough, Louis M.
  and Burnside Expedition, 228–231
  gunboats in the James River, 491
  and Lincoln, 414
Gordon, George Henry, 432
Gordon, Nathaniel, 537
Gordonsville, 443, 588
Gosport Navy Yard, 255, 414
Governor Moore, S.S., 368
Grant, Ulysses S.
  at Battle of Belmont, 149–153, 760
  and Buckner, 196, 211–213
  versus Bragg, 569
  and Buell, 317, 335, 343, 346, 656, 736
  at Cairo, 157, 181
  characteristics, 762–763
  colonel of Illinois volunteers, 148
  at Columbus, 151, 172
  and Curtis, 722
  at Donelson, 195–209, 213–214, 372, 760
    plan for, 202–203
    reinforcements, 217
  and Foote, 183–191, 201–205, 207–208, 308, 310
  and formation of Third division, 200–201
  at Fort Henry, 183–191, 308, 310
  and Frémont, 90
  and Halleck, 148, 153, 181–183, 196, 316–318, 351, 372, 543–545, 764
  versus Harris, 150
  headquarters, 330
  New Uncle Sam, 196
  and Iuka, 717, 736
  versus Johnston, 191, 250
  and Lincoln, 251, 316, 376, 760, 762–763
  and McClernand, 199, 207, 326, 334, 346, 544
  name changed, 196
  nickname, "Uncle Sam," 196
  in North Mississippi, 582

Index

[825]

occupation of Paducah, 88
and Ord, 718–720
at Panther Creek, 191
versus Pillow, 171, 196
and Pittsburg attack, 335
versus Polk, 149–152, 172, 544
prewar army career, 196–197
versus Price, 717–720
promotion to brigadier general, 148
promotion to major general, 316
psychological warfare, 718–719
and Rosecrans, 717–720, 763, 768
at Savannah, 321
and Sherman, 148, 321, 324, 326, 331, 334–336, 346, 541–542
at Shiloh, 338–343, 351, 372, 527, 760
and Smith, 182, 374
and Tennessee, 191, 217, 320, 330, 543–544
"Unconditional Surrender," 214, 280, 322
Great Britain. *See* England
Greeley, Horace (New York *Tribune*)
and capture of Donelson, 195
and Emancipation Proclamation, 706
Forward-to-Richmond chant, 144
on Halleck, 385, 389
and Manassas retreat, 85
on poetry of war, 772–773
"Prayer of Twenty Millions," 802
on Roanoke Island conquest, after Fort Henry, 230–231
on Stanton, 247, 250–251
Gregg, David McMurtrie Maxcy, 632
Grimes, J. W., 706, 753
Guerilla warfare, 95, 427, 558–559, 562
Gulf Blockade Squadron, 354

Haiti, formal recognition of, 537
Halleck, Henry Wager
See *also* specific battles and commanders
and advance on Chattanooga, 768–769
author of "Elements of Military Art and Science," 181
and Banks, 671, 759–760
versus Beauregard, 374–375
and Buell, 144, 155–156, 180–181, 183, 315–316, 372–374, 542, 558, 657, 715, 741–745
and Burnside, 592–593
and Cedar Mountain, 603
at Corinth, 374, 378, 403
Department of Mississippi, 318
Department of the West, 144, 315
effects of Johnston's psychological warfare, 175
and Grant, 148, 153, 181–183, 196, 315–318, 322–323, 351, 372–373, 543–546, 764
and Lincoln, 318, 533, 544, 594, 648, 715, 743–744, 755
and McClellan, 182–183, 594–596, 613, 622, 749–750, 755
made general-in-chief, 533, 544, 755
measles, 181

Memphis & Charleston Railroad, control, 542
and news of Fishing Creek, 181
at Pittsburg Landing, 373
and Pope, 314, 526, 603, 608, 643, 645
relationship with troops, 181, 315, 316, 541
reorganization of armies, 315, 592
and Rosecrans, 768–769
Hamlin, Hannibal, 39
Hampton, Wade, 77
cavalry brigade in Maryland, 663
Chambersburg's military governor, 749
and Johnston, 417
Legion, 78
and Stuart's brigade, 607
Hampton Roads, 255–263, 404
Hanks, Nancy, 21
Hardee, William J.
author of "Rifle and Light Infantry Tactics," 171
and Beauregard, 321, 325, 347
at Bowling Green, 171–172, 205, 215
and Bragg, 568, 575, 731, 739–740, 744, 776
and Breckinridge, 582
brigades sent to Smith, 576
versus Buell, 172, 192
at Corinth, 320
to Pittsburg, 325
deployment of troops, 327–330
and Floyd, 272
and Johnston, 193, 216, 324
move through Cave City, 658
at Murfreesboro, 216
at Nashville, 215
and Polk, 338, 341, 774
promotion to lieutenant general, 774
promotion to major general, 171
versus Sherman and McClernand, 341
at Shiloh, 342, 348
transfer from Transmississippi, 172
Harlan, James
charges against Grant, 372
Harpers Ferry, 53–54, 70, 250, 451, 666–667, 680, 681, 692, 702
Harper's Weekly, 322, 801
Harris, Isham, 52, 215, 339, 347
Harris, Thomas, 150
Harrisonburg, 425, 456
Harrison's Landing, 588
Harrodsburg, 730–731
Hartford, S.S., 366–367, 370, 548, 553–556
Hatch, John P., 646
Hatch, O. M., 749
Hatteras, Fort, 115–116, 121
Hatteras Inlet, 115, 131, 229
Hattie, blockade runner, 352
Hawes, Richard, 712–713
Hay, John, 771
Hay Market, 616
Hayes, Rutherford B., 677
Head of Passes, 354–355
Health problems, military
diarrhea, 330, 664

Health problem, military (cont.)
  dysentery, 381
  erysipelas, 381
  malaria, 465, 581
  measles, 72, 181, 381
  tetanus, 381
  typhoid fever, 155, 381
  yellow fever, 563
Hébert, Louis, 721
Heintzelman, Samuel Peter
  for Alexandria, 613
  appointed to corps command, 253
  and Banks to man capital fortifications, 671
  at Battle of Glendale, 507
  and Battle of Seven Pines, 444-451
  and Hooker, 491
    and Kearny, 417
  and McClellan, 406-408, 614
  and McDowell's plan, 75
  on Malvern Hill, 510
  and Mechanicsville, 443
  at Savage Station, 500
  versus Jackson's escape, 631, 635-636
  versus Johnston, 445
  at White Oak Swamp, 467, 501
  on Williamsburg road, 467
Henry, Fort, 174, 180, 183-191, 193-194, 230, 305, 319
Henry, Judith, 79, 265
Herndon, William L., 20, 164
Heth, Henry, 740
Hickman Creek, 194
Hickok, Wild Bill, 281
Hicks, Thomas H., reply to Lincoln's militia request, 52
Hill, Ambrose Powell
  at Beaver Dam, 485
  at Boatswain Swamp, 486-487
  crossed Chickahominy, 481
  and Davis, 506
  delay in reaching Stuart, 518
  and Ellen Marcy, 479
  at Glendale, 507
  at Harpers Ferry, 685
    from, to Sharpsburg, 698-700
  and Jackson, 485, 599-600, 632, 664-665
  and Kearny's death, 644
  and Lee, 474-475, 481-483, 506, 696
  and Longstreet, 485, 496, 508-512
  at Malvern Hill, 512
  and Morgan, 480
  promotion to major general, 444
  and Richmond, 470
  after Savage Station, 496, 498
  in Seven Days, 508-512
  at Seven Pines, 444-451
  at Shepherdstown ford, attack on Porter, 703
  on Turkey Hill, 488
Hill, Daniel Harvey
  at Beaver Dam, 481, 485
  at Bloody Lane, 693-695
  from Charles City Road, 445
  at Cold Harbor, 486
  at Dunker Church, 690
  and Ewell, and Taliaferro, 616
  after Harpers Ferry, 681
  and Huger, 445
  and Jackson, 482, 485, 599-600, 681
  and Keyes corps, 447-448
  and Lee, 474-475, 487, 495, 510-513, 667-668, 678, 695-700
  at Long Bridge, 413
  and Longstreet, 478, 694
  at Malvern Hill, 509-514
  at Mechanicsville turnpike, 478
  and Petersburg, 589
  and Pope's attack, 637
  and Richmond intrenchments, 470
  Seven Days, 510-513
  at Seven Pines, 446-449
  at Sharpsburg, 693-699, 702
  on South Mountain, 679
  and Special Orders 191, 668
  at Thoroughfare Gap, 616
  on Turkey Hill, 488
  at Turner's Gap, 674-678
  and Williamsburg, 411
Hill, Henry, 640
Hilton Head, 117, 119
Hindman, Thomas Carmichael
  appointment, major general, 556
  in Arkansas, 568, 785
  and Davis, 797
  and Holmes, 783-785
Hitchcock, Ethan Allen, 266-267, 408
Holmes, Theophilus H.
  versus Burnside, 397
  and Davis, 786-787
  and Drewry's Bluff, 498
  headquarters at Little Rock, 783
  and Lee's reorganization, 587
  near Malvern Hill, 503
  at Manassas, 77
  on New Market road, 499
  order to defend Vicksburg, 785
  and Randolph, 785-787
  and Richmond, 470
Holmes, Oliver Wendell, 108
Hood, John Bell
  arrest, 676
  at Eltham Landing, 412-413
  and Evans, 664
  Hopewell Gap penetration, 630
  and Jackson at Dunker Church, 682-695
  versus King's division, 634
  and Law, at Boatswain Swamp, 489
  and Longstreet, 631, 639
  Warrenton Turnpike, 634
Hooker, Joseph
  and Burnside, 766
  at Dunker Church, 682-695
    injury, 692, 701
  and Heintzelman, 491
    and Kearney, 417
  versus Jackson, 621
  and McClellan, 672, 682-695

Index

and Mansfield, 684, 690-691
receipt of Porter's troops, 758
Hopewell Gap, 628-631
Hornets Nest, 338-341
Hough, Daniel, 50
Houston, Sam, 13
Howe, Julia Ward, 538
Howell, W. B., 10
Huger, Benjamin
  on Charles City road, 446, 499
  and disaster of Roanoke Island, 231
  and evacuation of Norfolk, 444, 446
  and Lee, 475, 495, 587
  on Malvern Hill, 510
  in North Carolina, versus Burnside, 250
  reports troops at Old Point Comfort, 397
  and Richmond, 470
  and Savage Station, 498
  and Seven Pines, 444-451, 477
  transferred to War Department, 587
  and White Oak Swamp, 447, 502
  and Wise, 226
Hughes, Archbishop John, 538
Hunter, David
  and emancipation, 535-536
  and Frémont, 97
  and McDowell Plan, 75
  and Sherman versus Johnston, 174
Hunter, Robert Mercer Taliaferro
  appointment, 98
  and Davis, 221-222
  head of State Department, 123
  resignation, 221-222
Hurlbut, Stephen A., 324
  at Bolivar, 722
  and Grant, 335-336
  at Hornets Nest, 340
  versus Johnston, 326, 339
  at Shiloh, 331, 342

Illinois, 29, 753
Illinois Central Railroad, 69
Indiana, 626, 658, 737, 753
Indian Creek, 194
Iron Brigade, 627
Island Ten, 307-308, 311, 342-343, 363, 378-379
Iuka, 717-720, 762

Jackson, Claiborne F., reply to Lincoln's militia request, 53-54
Jackson, Andrew, 83, 199
Jackson, Fort, 354, 363-364, 370
Jackson, Henry R., 129
Jackson, J. S., 735
Jackson, Thomas Jonathan
  advance across Rapidan, 599
  at Antietam, 686-692, 696-700
  and A. P. Hill, 485, 599-600, 632, 664-665
  and Ashby, 459
  versus Banks, 396-397, 419, 431-432, 441-442, 465, 598, 601-603, 759
  at base of Sudley Mountain, 636, 644

[827]

Battle of Chantilly, 644
Battle of McDowell, 426, 457
and Beauregard, 76
and Beaver Dam Creek, 474
and Bee, naming of Stonewall, 498
and Boatswain Swamp, 489
at Bolivar Heights, 678
Brown's Gap, 457
and Bull Run, 616, 644
on Cedar Mountain, 601-603, 759
Charleston *Mercury* on, 458
at Charles Town, 438
and Conrad's Store, 456-457, 525
at Cross Keys, 473
and Davis, 458, 516-517, 788
destruction of Broad Run railroad bridge, 617
at Dunker Church, 688-695
and Ewell, 419, 426, 428, 431-432, 453-454, 462-464, 499, 621-628, 685, 689
versus Frémont, 422-424, 454, 456, 463
and Front Royal, 434, 451-452
and Garnett, 271, 420
at Glendale, 507
at Groveton, 624, 630
and Harpers Ferry, 64-65, 452, 680-681
and Harvey Hill, 482, 485, 599-600, 681
on Henry Hill, 269
and Hood, 686-687
injury, 664
and Johnston, 269
and Kernstown, 270-271, 397, 420, 428, 434
and Lee, 435-436, 473-475, 481, 495, 501, 587-588, 592, 599, 604-606, 633-634, 665-668, 696-700
Lincoln's plan for capture, 436
and Little River Turnpike, 644
and Longstreet, 638
  positions near the Rapidan, 606
and Loring, 224
versus McClellan's troops, 269, 524-526
versus McDowell, 269, 421
McLaws' reinforcement, 691-692
at Malvern Hill, 514
at Manassas, 78, 223, 618-620
march between Chickahominy and Totopotomoy Creek, 471
versus Milroy, 424
at New Market, 455
at North River, 460-462
and Orange and Alexandria Railroad, 612-613
and Pendleton's rescue, 703
versus Pope, 589, 637
at Port Republic, 463, 473
promotion to major general, 223
repairing of Grapevine Bridge, 498
resignation and return, 224-225
retreat across Rapidan, 602
and Richmond, 439, 470
Romney expedition, 420
at Savage Station, 498
in Shenandoah Valley, 419

Jackson, Thomas Jonathan (*cont.*)
  command of division, 223
  and Lincoln's plan, 451
  and unparoled prisoners, 439
  at Shepherdstown ford, 703
  versus Shields, 428, 452, 456
  and Strasburg, 434, 452-455
  and Stuart, 474, 518
  versus Sumner, 691-692
  supported by Wheat's Tigers, 432
  and Taliaferro, 618, 628
  and Taylor, 433-434
  on Turkey Hill, 488
  Walker's division with, versus Williams, 691
  and White Oak Swamp, 504, 507, 587
  and Winchester, 433-434, 452-453
  and Winder, 462, 601
Jacksonville, 352, 796
James, Jesse, 89
James River, 398
Jeff Davis, S.S., privateer, 114
Jeff Thompson, S.S. and Ellet's rams, 388
Jefferson City, 90
Jefferson, Fort, 44
Johns, Right Reverend John, 218
Joint Committee, on the Conduct of the War, 108
  investigating Ball's Bluff fiasco, 140
  and McClellan, 241-242
    plan for reorganizing Army of Potomac, 253
Jones, Catesby ap Roger, 261-263
Jones, D. R., 77
  at Dunker Church, 689
  given Ewell's division, 685
  Hopewell Gap penetration, 630
Johnson, Andrew, 12
  and Buell, 656, 657
  on Joint Committee on Conduct of War, 241
Johnson, Bushrod, 194, 213
Johnson, Edward, 396, 419, 451
Johnson, Herschel V., 799
Johnson, R. W., 570
Johnston, Albert Sidney, 7
  appeal for arms and men, 170-171, 180
  Army of Central Kentucky, 171
  and Beauregard, 192-193, 320-321, 328-329, 336-337
  and Bowling Green, 180, 250, 320
  and Bragg, 325, 328-329, 338
  and Breckinridge, 329, 338
  charge, and capture of Hurlbut's stand, 339
  at Columbus-Bowling Green sector, 174
  commissioned general in Confederate Army, 125
  at Corinth, 320-325, 327
  and Davis, 168, 175-176, 234-235, 351, 799
  death, 339-340, 351, 401
  at Fort Donelson, 192-195, 215, 712
  and Hardee, 192, 216, 306, 338
  at Hornets Nest, 338-340
  in Kentucky, 168, 181, 193, 292, 306, 319
  line on Cumberland River, 173
  at Mickey's, 328
  at Murfreesboro, 216, 234
  in Nashville, 205, 215-216
  and Polk, 329, 338
  at Shiloh, 336-340
  and Transmississippi, 168-181
  use of psychological warfare, 174-175, 192
Johnston, George W., 712
Johnston, Joseph Eggleston, 7
  accusations of, after Roanoke Island disaster, 234-235
  and Battle of Seven Pines, 444-451
  and Beauregard, 58, 75, 77, 79, 83, 121, 236
  and Benjamin, 223-225, 235
  and Chickahominy, 410-411, 416, 444
  choice for post in West, 789-790
  conference on Richmond's defense, 236-237
  and Davis, 124-127, 223, 235-236, 440, 443, 786-789, 797
  Foote and Yancey, 789
  and Fort Magruder, 411
  and Hampton, 417
  at Harpers Ferry, 56-57
  on Henry Hill, 79
  and Hill, 412
  and Holmes, 398
  inclusion of Peninsula and Norfolk command, 401
  injury, 426, 449-450, 785
  and Jackson, 224-225
  and Longstreet, 411-412
  on Lookout Hill, 77, 79
  versus McClellan, 236, 263-264
  and Magruder, 398, 403, 412-413
  at Manassas, 58, 75-83, 121, 237-238, 396
  in northern Virginia, 796
  ordered to Richmond, 401
  versus Patterson, 70
  and Randolph, 785-786
  and rank of full general, 126
  retreat to Rappahannock, 238-239
  and Seven Pines, 445-447, 449-450, 785
  Shenandoah Valley, 56, 70-71
  and Williamsburg, 411
  wooden cannon trick on Munson's Hill, 103-104
  and Yorktown, 401-404, 410

Kanawha Valley, 129-130, 272
Kansas, 30
Kansas-Nebraska Bill, 26
Kate, blockade runner, 352
Kearny, Philip
  death, 644
  on Henry Hill, 640
  and Hooker, under Heintzelman, 417
  near Manassas, 632
  opposition to McClellan's leaving Malvern Hill, 514

Index

[829]

and Pope, 644
at Warrenton Junction, 621
Kemper, James L.
Hopewell Gap penetration, 630
and Longstreet's order of Battle, 631
Kentucky, 19, 86-88, 96, 144, 169-171, 392, 650-654, 708
Army of Central Kentucky, 171
Kernstown, 270-271, 397, 420, 428, 434
Keyes, E. D.
appointed to corps command, 253
at Battle of Glendale, 507
and Battle of Seven Pines, 444-451
Couch and Casey, 417
versus Jackson, 466
versus Johnston, 445
and Lincoln, 531
and McClellan, 406-408
on Malvern Hill, 508
and Mechanicsville, 443
and Sumner, 449
supported by Heintzelman, 442, 449
for Yorktown defenses, 614
King, Rufus
follows troops, in ambulance, 626
at Fredericksburg, 597
and Pope, 602
returning from Manassas, 634
King of Spades. *See* Lee
Know-Nothing Party, 28, 29
Knoxville, 742-743
Knoxville and Virginia-Tennessee Railroad, 170

Lady Davis, blockade runner, 352
Lamon, Ward Hill, 37
Lane, Jim, "Zouaves d'Afrique," 558
Laurel Hill, 68-69
Law, E. M., 489
Lawton, Alexander
given Ewell's division, 627, 685
injury at Dunker Church, 689
Lee, Fitzhugh, 607, 610
Lee, Mrs. Robert E., 418
Lee, Robert Edward, 7
administrative efficiency, 468
and Anderson, 692
at Antietam, 686, 696-700
artillery demonstration for McClellan, 591
versus Banks, 604
after Battle of Savage Station, 498
Battle of Seven Days, 517
at Beaver Dam, 485
and Bloody Lane, 696
at Boatswain Swamp, 489
versus Burnside, 781-783
capture of John Brown, 32
on Cheat Mountain, 129
and Chickahominy, 478, 528
and conscription, 396-400, 780
versus Cooke, 471
at Cross Keys, 473
and Davis, 58, 127-131, 416, 444, 451, 469,
479-482, 505-506, 517, 578, 662-663, 779-780, 788, 797
and Charleston *Mercury*, 586
and death of daughter, 781
at Drewry's Bluff, 416, 417, 588
Federal command offered to, 128
first campaign, 129-131
at Front Royal, 435-436
at Glendale, 503
at Gordonsville, 604-606
at Groveton, 640, 642
versus Halleck, 605
versus Heintzelman's assault, 477
and Hill, 485, 590, 605, 696
and Hood, 489, 604, 664, 676-677
and Huger, 397-398, 477
injury to hands, 664
and Johnston, 168-169, 397, 420, 447
in Kanawha Valley, 129-130
and Longstreet, 402-403, 448, 474-475, 481, 487-488, 587-588, 604, 606, 633-634, 666-667, 678, 702
and Loring, 223-224, 297
versus McClellan, 469, 495-496, 503, 559, 591-592, 605, 666-667, 718, 752
on McClellan's ability, 468, 757
versus McDowell, 419
and Magruder, 398, 500
and Manassas, 517, 640, 650
in Maryland, 191, 662-667, 796
in Northern Virginia, 420-421, 451
plans of attack, 399-400, 421, 451, 474-475, 481, 587-588, 606, 702
versus Pope, 589-590, 599, 610, 637, 650, 666
and nephew Marshall, 598
at Port Republic, 473
railroad gun, 468
rank of full general, 125
repercussions of Seven Days, 586
and Richmond, 402-403, 470-471, 474-475
at Seven Pines, 447-450
at Sharpsburg, 683-700, 718
at Shepherdstown ford, 703
and son Robert, 494, 641, 697
Special Orders 191 issued, 667
copy found and delivered to McClellan, 670-671, 676
and Stuart, 471, 676, 749-751
suggestion for peace proposal to North, 665-666
versus Union armies. *See* individual generals
in Valhalla, and Johnston in West, 789
and Virginia Central and Virginia & Tennessee Railroads, 130
and West Virginia campaign, 128, 223-224
at White Oak Swamp, 496
at White's Ferry, 662-663
and Wilder's surrender to Bragg, 661
at Winchester, 752
and Yorktown, 402
Leopard, blockade runner, 352

Let Her Be, blockade runner, 352
Let Her Rip, blockade runner, 352
Letcher, John
  and Jackson's resignation refused, 224
  and Lincoln's demand for troops, 51–52
Lexington, 98, 653–654
Liberia, formal recognition, 537
Lincoln, Abraham
  See also specific battle and specific commander
  and advisors, 647–649
  and Andrew, Governor of Massachusetts, 753
  and anti-Nebraska elements, 29
  assembly in Wheeling, 128
  and Bates, 33, 540, 801
  on Butler's orders, 534–535
  call for volunteers and troops, 52, 67, 100, 662
  and Cameron, 242–244
    appointment as Minister to Russia, 243
  and Carl Schurz, 770–771
  and Chase, at Norfolk, 414
  childhood, 20–22
  and Congress, 62, 67, 806–810
    Confiscation Act, 539–540
    declaration of war, 51
    and Dred Scott decision, 536
  and Davis, 16, 56, 164, 708
    burden of action, 239
    on privateering, 114
  on doctrine of self government, 27
  and Douglas, 23, 31, 33
  education and early life, 21–26
  and Emancipation Proclamation, 704–710
    criticisms, 706–707, 708–710
    and pressure for, 96–97, 535–537, 705, 709–710
  exercise of veto, 132
  field campaign, 412–413
  figures, on war costs versus cost of slaves, 536
  and Fort Sumter, 44–47, 66
  general war orders, 253–254, 266
  and Goldsborough, 414
  on Gordon, 537
  and government of people, 68–69
  and Hatch, 749
  and Illinois legislature, 22–23
  and Illinois ministers, 705–706
  inauguration, 17, 38–40
  inspection of camps, 22, 72, 530, 767
  and Joint Committee on Conduct of War, 109
  and Kansas-Nebraska Bill, 26–27
  law practice, 23, 28
  and Mary Todd Lincoln, 24, 251–252
  military career, 22–23
  New Salem Debating Society, 22
  at news of Baker's death, 108
  and news of *Virginia*, 258
  and people's confidence, 524, 753–754, 801–804
  personal tragedy, 240
  popularity with army, 530, 748
  proposal for formal recognition to the Negro republics, 537
  and Republican Party, 29
  pre-election politics, 753–754
  and Sally Bush Lincoln, 34
  and Scott's Anaconda, 111–113
  and seizure of Mason and Slidell, 156–159
  and Seward, 156–159, 525, 539
  speeches, 27, 30, 32, 35–36, 39, 62, 67–69, 806–810
  and Stanton, 242–247, 414, 428, 467, 492–493, 526, 763
  and Tad Lincoln, 771–772
  threats to safety, 38
  on war, 61–66, 157, 242
    issues, 39–40, 534–535
    versus keeping word, 247–248
  at White House receptions, 165–166
  Wigwam nomination, 33
  and writs of habeas corpus denial, 67, 132
  as a writer, 804
Lincoln, Edward, 24
Lincoln, Mary Todd, 24, 251–252
Lincoln, Robert Todd, 24
Lincoln, Sarah Bush Johnston (Sally Bush), 21, 34
Lincoln, Thomas (Tad), 24, 66, 771–772
Lincoln, William, 24
"Little Mac." *See* McClellan
Logan's Crossroads, 177–180
London. *See* England
Long Roll Regiment, 331
Longstreet, James, 77
  at Antietam, 686
  assault on two New York regiments, 639
  and Boatswain Swamp, 486, 489
  on Bull Run Mountain, 623
  and Chickahominy, 470
  command of forces, 446
  at Fredericksburg, 766–767
  at Glendale, 478, 507, 587
  at Hagerstown, 675
  and Hill, 478
  and Hood, 664
  at Hopewell Gap, 628–631
  injured foot, 664
  and Jackson, 606, 612, 634, 638
  and Lee, 402–403, 448, 474–475, 481, 487–488, 587–588, 604, 606, 633–634, 666–667, 678, 702
  at Long Bridge, 413
  versus McClellan, 486
  on Malvern Hill, 512
  at Manassas, 86
  at Manassas Gap Railroad, 631–634
  versus Porter, 634, 636
  and Rapidan, 606
  on Rappahannock south of Waterloo Bridge, 612
  and Richmond, 446
  after Savage Station, 498
  and Seven Pines, 444–451
  and Stuart, 518

Index [831]

on Turkey Hill, 488
march for Turner's Gap, 676
moved to Gordonsville, 604
and Union surgeon's request of protection, 509
and Walker, 686
Loring, W. W., 297
and Jackson, 224-225
and Lee, in West Virginia, 223-224
promotion to general, 224-225
Louisiana, 3, 18, 78, 306, 708
Louisiana, S.S., 362-363, 367, 370
Louisville, 654, 660-661
Courier, 307
Louisville-Nashville Railroad, 565
Louisville, S.S., 201, 204
Lovell, Mansfield
  at Corinth, 722-726
  and New Orleans, 360-362
  retreat, 370
  and Van Dorn at Ripley, 721
Lowell, James Russell, 108, 524
Lynch, William F., 226, 231
Lynde, Isaac, 295-296
Lynx, blockade runner, 352
Lyon, Nathaniel, 91
  at Wilson's Creek, 92-95, 283, 580

McCall, George B., 466, 507
McClellan, George B.
  after Antietam, 747-753
  losses, 701-702
  Army of the Potomac, 396, 466, 490, 595, 614, 646
    base at White House, Virginia, 418, 466, 469, 473, 498
    changed to James, 517, 527-528, 585, 593
    transfer to Rappahannock, 596, 605, 608
  at Bailey's Crossroads, 153-154
  and Beaver Dam, 479
  and Bloody Lane, 695
  at Boatswain Swamp, 486
  and Buckingham, 754
  and Buell, 147, 241, 315
  and Burnside, 227-228, 672-674, 685, 695-701, 755-757
  and Chickahominy, 467
  command of all Union armies, 109, 614, 646
    order to relinquish, 754-757
  versus Confederates. *See* individual generals
  on confiscation of property, 109, 533, 563
  crossing Potomac below Harpers Ferry, 752
  and Ellen Marcy McClellen, 179-180
  on forcible abolition of slavery, 531
  formulas for victory, 268, 409-410, 467, 673
  and Fort Henry, 182-183
  and Fort Monroe, 268-269, 405
  and Franklin, 240-242, 253, 409, 614, 673-674, 685, 695
  and Frederick, 672-673
  at Fredericksburg, 467, 588
  and Goldsborough, Flag Officer, 404
  and Halleck, 182-183, 594-596, 613, 622, 749-750, 755
  and Harpers Ferry, 681, 704, 748
  and Harrison's Landing, 515, 588
  and Heintzelman, 477, 614
  and Hill, 480
  and ironclad *Galena*, 508
  and Joint Committee on Conduct of War, 109
  Lee's Special Orders 191 found and given to, 670-671
  and Lincoln, 86, 141-143, 155, 239-242, 246-255, 265-266, 272, 407, 437, 451, 464, 508, 531, 533, 593-594, 613, 671, 748, 760
    test set for removal, 752-753
  and McDowell, 407, 442, 465
  and malaria, 465
  and Malvern Hill, 506, 514
  and Manassas, 640
  and Mansfield, 685
  and Marcy, 593
  at Mechanicsville, 442
  North's answer to Beauregard, 70
  at Old Point Comfort, 408
  and Pamunkey, 418, 494
  on political execution of persons, 533
  and Pope, 596, 614, 640, 661
  and Porter, 476, 479, 483, 758
  at Rectortown, 754-757
  relationship with troops, 266, 318, 563-564, 713, 755
  and Richmond, 437, 464-467, 526
  at Savage Station, 491, 501
  and Secretary Seward, 441
  and Scott, 99-103, 110, 144, 265-266, 682
  and Seven Days, 508-514, 528
  at Sharpsburg, 683-700
  and Shenandoah Valley, 451, 466
  on South Mountain, 681-682
    and McLaws, 679-680
  and Stanton, 246, 268-269, 467, 476-477, 492-493, 593-594
  and Sumner, 695
  and Stuart's circumferential raid, 476, 517, 749-750, 780
  on territorial organization of states, 531
  typhoid fever, 155
  Urbanna Plan, 154, 248-250, 252-254
    in Virginia, 582
  at Yorktown, 392, 407, 410
McClernand, John A.
  at Belmont, 199
  at Donelson, 198-199, 202, 206-207
  and Grant, 199, 207, 326, 334, 346, 544
  and Halleck, 372-374, 376, 542
  and Lincoln, 763-764
  at Owl Creek, 331
  promotion, 324
  and Sherman, 341, 385

McClernand, John A. (*cont.*)
  and Shiloh, 336, 342, 346
McCook, Alexander McDowell
  and Buell, 716, 728
  and Gilbert, 735-736
  at Perryville, 733-735
  and Rosecrans, 769
  at Shiloh, 346
  and Thomas with Crittenden toward Springfield, 729
McCulloch, Ben
  in Boston Mountains, 278
  death, 286-287
  and Price, 279
  in Van Dorn's double envelopment, 283
  versus Buell, 147
  at Wilson's Creek, 91-95, 278
    Lyon's body forwarded by, 94
McDowell, Fort, 421-423, 426, 457, 465
McDowell, Irvin, 59
  appointed to corps command, 253, 527
  and Beauregard, 73, 76
  and Bull Run, 74
  and Centerville, 71, 75-76
  Department of Rappahannock, 405, 444, 621
  versus Ewell, 419, 421
  at Falmouth, 409
  and Fredericksburg, 443, 466
  and Front Royal, 439, 454
  and Fort Monroe proposal, 268
  and Harrisburg, 436
  and Hopewell Gap, 630
  versus Jackson, 436, 623, 635
  and Lincoln, 428, 436
  and McClellan, 240-242, 266, 268, 585, 672
  at Manassas, 71, 74-75, 82, 112, 265, 266, 631
  and Pope, 528, 597, 602, 623, 637
  and Porter's troops, 639
  and protection of capital, 405
  and Richmond, 418
  and Scott, 112
  in Shenandoah Valley, 418, 423
  and Shields, 454
  at Sudley Springs, 78
  viewed as a traitor, 642-643, 669, 745
  at Warrenton Turnpike, 623
  withheld from McClellan, 442
McKinley, William, 677
McLaws, Lafayette
  and Anderson's divisions, at Sharpsburg, 692
  and Lee, 663, 667, 676, 677, 685
  at Maryland Heights, 678-680

Madrid Bend, 311
Maffit, Captain J. N., 792
Magoffin, Beriah, reply to Lincoln's militia request, 53
Magruder, Fort, 400, 411
Magruder, John Bankhead
  and Davis, 797

Department of Transmississippi, 587
at Fort Monroe, 396
and Grapevine Bridge, 491, 497
and Hill, 508
and Holmes, in charge of Texas, 783
and Huger, 497
and Lee, 398, 401, 475, 485, 495, 497, 502, 587
and Longstreet, 496, 506, 508
on Malvern Hill, 512-513
at Old Point Comfort, 397
and Richmond intrenchments, 470
at Savage Station, 497-500
and Seven Pines, 444-451
and Toombs, 496
and White Oak Swamp, 491
on Williamsburg road, 499
York-James peninsula, 56
at Yorktown, 399-400
Mallory, Stephen Russell, 255
Malvern Hill, 525
  battle, 508-514
Manassas
  See also First Manassas; Second Manassas
  casualties, 83-84, 640, 663
  and Davis, 72, 121
  versus Lincoln, 239
  first council of war, 57
  health problems, 72
  railroad junction, 71-72, 76, 265, 615, 621
  reactions to battles, 169, 350, 471, 473, 796
Manassas, S.S., 354-355, 368
Mann, A. Dudley, 135-137
Mansfield, Joseph K., 257, 684-685
  death, 701
  at Dunker Church, 689-691
  loss of men, 695
Manson, Mahlon, 652
"The Marble Monument." *See* Lee
Marcy, Ellen, 479
Marcy, William L., 14, 593
Maryland, 19, 53-54, 708
Maryland Heights, 667, 678-680
Mason, James M.
  author of Fugitive Slave Law, 137
  and Confederate bid for foreign intervention, 220-221, 231, 523
  definition of conflict, 64
  secessionist, 137
  sent to Court of St James, 138, 157, 395, 523
  and Trent Affair, 139, 162
Massachusetts, 15, 53, 105
Massanutton Mountain, 425, 454, 457
Maury, Dabney, 721
Maynard, Horace, 19
Mechanicsville, 441-442, 480-481, 484
Meigs, M. C., 156, 240
Memphis, 351, 363, 381, 388, 392, 796
  and Nashville's "Great Panic," 215, 217
Memphis and Charleston Railroad, 546, 561, 573, 720-722
Memphis and Louisville Railroad, 307
Merrimac, S. S. See Virginia, S. S.

Index [833]

Mesilla, 295
Mickey's, 327–330
Miles, D. S., 75
Mill Springs, 177–180
Milroy, Robert
   at McDowell, 465
   versus Jackson, 423–424
Minnesota, S. S., 256–257, 260–263
Mississippi, 11, 14–17, 78, 171, 306–309, 319, 334, 653
   and secession, 3, 16
Mississippi Railroad, 69
Mississippi River, and Scott's Anaconda, 111–112
Mississippi, S. S., 362, 370
Missouri, 19, 91–97, 144, 169, 279, 289, 558–559, 708, 796
Missouri Compromise, 26–27
   and the Dred Scott decision, 29
Mitchel, Ormsby, 559
   versus Beauregard, 795
   and Buell, 560
   died of yellow fever, 563
   and guerillas, 562
   and Halleck's division of Grand Army, 542
   at Huntsville, 377
   at Pocotaligo, 795
   in North Alabama, 377–378
Mitchell, B. W., 670
Mitchell, J. K., 361–362
Mitchell's Ford, 72, 76
Mobile, 353, 357, 759
Mobile and Ohio Railroad, 307, 546
Monitor, S.S., 258–263, 351, 415–416
Monroe, Fort, 54, 228, 268–269, 398, 400, 406, 413
Montgomery, J. E.
   and Captain Semmes, 793
   flagship *Little Rebel*, 381, 388
   at Fort Pillow, 380
   at Plum Run Bend, 386
Moore, S.S., 368–369
Morgan, George W.
   at Cumberland Gap, 377, 560, 572, 654
Morgan, John Hunt, 726
   capturing railroad guards, 561, 565
   Johnson's capture, 570
   in northern Kentucky, 576
   reconnaissance around Buell's army, 171–172
   wrecking of Gallatin tunnel, 570
Mortar 10, S.S., 380–381
Morton, O. P., 375
Mosby, John S., 591
Mound City, S.S., 380–381, 547
Munfordville, 659, 661
Munson's Hill, 103–104, 154, 646
Murfreesboro, 561, 570, 656–657
Muscle Shoals, 173

Napoleon III, 523, 666
Nashville, 146, 192–193, 796
   "Great Panic," 215–217

Nashville and Chattanooga Railroad, 561, 564
Natchez, 371, 422
Navy, U.S.
   See also specific person or ship
   Coastal Survey, 115
   inaccuracy, 404
   Declaration of Paris, 114
   first Confederate stronghold taken, 115–116
   personnel increase, 67
   and Scott's Anaconda, 112–113
Nebraska, 26
Nelson, William, 562
   and Buell, 660–661, 714–716
   and Grant, 335, 343
   injury, 652
   Kentucky Home Guard, 86
   and Pittsburg, 335
   at Rogersville, 653
   at Shiloh, 342–343
   shot by Jefferson Davis, Indiana brigadier, 714–716
   and Smith, 656
   troops, too green to fight, 651–652
New Bern, 122, 352
New England, 29, 113
New Jersey, 43, 753
New Madrid, 307, 310, 314
New Market, 425
New Mexico, 13, 26, 293, 304–305
New Orleans, 113, 354, 360–361, 369–371, 403, 422, 796
New Uncle Sam, S.S., 196–197
New York, 43, 54, 80, 265, 525, 639–640, 753
   Herald, 435–438
   Times, 214, 754, 803
   Tribune, 85, 747
   World, 708
New York Fire Zouaves, 80, 265, 471
Newport, Ohio, 654
Newport News, 56
Nevada, 13
Nine Mile road, 444
"Noah." *See* Welles
Norfolk, 414, 421, 796
Norfolk, Virginia
   under martial law, 231–233
North Carolina, 19, 52, 225–230, 641, 796
North Fork, 456
North River, 456, 460–462

Ohio, 372, 753
   Army of Ohio, 560
   changed to Army of Cumberland, 768
Ohio and Mississippi Railroad, 68
Ohio and Virginia Railroad, 68
Ohio River, 173, 308–309
"Old Bald Head." *See* Ewell
"Old Blue Light." *See* Jackson
"Old Brains." *See* Halleck
"Old Jack." *See* Jackson
"Old Pap." *See* Thomas

[834]

Index

"Old Pete." *See* Longstreet
"Old Rosy." *See* Rosecrans
"Old Skedad." *See* Price
Orange and Alexandria Railroad, 238, 588, 611
Ord, E. O. C.
   at Burnsville, 718–720
   and Corinth, 545
   and Grant near Iuka, 717
Oregon, 43
Oreto, S. S., 792
Orlean, 615
Orleans Guard Battalion, 337, 347
Osterhaus, Peter, 284–285, 288–289

Pacific Railway, 14–15, 26, 807
Paddy's Hen and Chickens, 387
Palmerston, Lord, 157, 534, 666, 791
Pamlico Sound, 115, 225, 229
Pamunkey, 473, 498
Panther Creek, 185
Paris, Kentucky, 654
Park, John G., 228, 230
Parry, Captain (Comte de Paris), 100
Pass à l'Outre, 359
Pass Christian, 353, 796
"Pathfinder." *See* Frémont, J. C.
Patterson, Robert, 409
   at Falling Waters, 56–57
   and Harpers Ferry, 70
Pea Ridge, 282–291, 556, 784
Peace Convention, 38
Pelican, Peter, 228
Pemberton, John
   at Charleston, 776–778
   and Johnston, 789
   promotion by Davis, 777–778
Pendleton, W. N., 686, 703
Pennsylvania, 53–54, 753
Pensacola, 353, 357, 421, 796
Perryville, 729–730, 772, 805
   battle, 733–738
Pettus, J. J., 16
Philips, Wendell, 524
Pickens, Fort, 44
Pickens, Francis W.
   and John Pemberton, 777
   report on Fort Sumter, 46
Pierce, Franklin, 14, 26
Pike, Albert
   army against Springfield, 279
   battle near Elkhorn Tavern, 287
   at Fort Union, 301
   Indian leader, 280, 286
   and McCulloch, 289
   and Van Dorn, 283, 287
Pillow, Fort, 351, 379, 386–387, 473
Pillow, Gideon
   at Belmont, 150, 170
   and Buckner, 205–207
   at Donelson, 194, 209
      escape with chief-of-staff, 212
   and Floyd at Dover Inn, 216

   at Fort Henry, 194
   versus Grant, 171, 196
   and Hardee, 171
   and Johnston, 181
   and opening of Nashville road, 207
Pinkerton, Allan, 37, 102, 143, 467, 491
Pittsburg, S.S., 201, 204, 342
Pittsburgh, 335, 343
Plum Run Bend, 379, 386
Pocahontas, 720–722
Pocotaligo, 795
Point Pleasant, 310
Polk, James K., 11
Polk, Leonidas, 7
   at Bardstown, 713, 726–727
   and Beauregard, 321, 325, 347, 374
   and Bragg, 575, 658, 660, 713, 730–731, 740–743, 774, 776
   brigades sent to Smith, 576
   in Columbus, 149, 172, 307
   commissioned major general and assigned, 87–88
   and Corinth, 325, 347, 374
   and Davis, 774
   deployment of troops, 327–330
   and Frémont, 90
   versus Gilbert, 737
   versus Grant, 149–152, 172, 544
   versus Halleck, 181–182
   and Hardee, 338, 341, 774
   at Humboldt, 307
   and Johnston, 324, 329
   at New Madrid, 307
   at Perryville, retreat after, 740–743
   and Price, 150
   promotion to lieutenant general, 774
   and Quintard in Episcopal church in Harrodsburg, 738–739
   reinforced Belmont garrison, 150
   at Shiloh, 342
   at Union City, 88
Pope, John, 526
   Administration approval of mandates, 593
   Army of Virginia, 527, 588
   and Banks, 527–528, 597–598, 645
   versus Bragg, 383
   at Bull Run, 650
   on Cedar Mountain, 603
   at Centerville, 616, 622, 642
   and Committee on Conduct of War, 527
   at Culpeper, 588, 596, 607
   defeat, reasons for, 642
   at Fairfax, 645
   and Foote, 311, 361
   and Halleck, 314, 372–374, 379, 526, 603, 608, 635, 642–643, 645
   and Heintzelman, 613–614, 623
   versus Hill, 599
   at Island Ten, 311
   versus Jackson, 599, 619–620, 631
   versus Lee, 608, 610–611
   and Lincoln, 746
   and McClellan, 529, 619
   and McDowell, 528, 597, 602, 623, 637, 646

and Manassas, 620, 635-636
in Minnesota, 649, 771
at New Madrid, 310-311, 318
and New Orleans defense, 360
new western hero, 371
at Point Pleasant, 310
and Porter, 529
promotion to major general, 311, 316
on the Rappahannock, 596, 608
relationship with troops, 643
removal from command, 669
retreat to Washington, 645-646, 661
and Stanton, 527
and Stuart, 607-609
summoned to Pittsburg Landing, 379
superseded by Rosecrans, 542
supply line, 611, 619
and Van Dorn, 383
and Wool, 598
Pope, John ("Honest John"), 355-356
Port Republic, 456-457, 463
Port Royal, 352, 796
 battle, 116-120
Porter, Bill, 746
Porter, David Dixon, 353
 Captain Davis' successor, 746-747
 and Farragut, 358, 359
 at Fort Jackson, 364
  and Fort St Philip, 364
 and Lincoln, 357
 mortar flotilla, 358-359
 and New Orleans plan, 354-357
 and Welles, 357, 746
Porter, Fitz-John, 417
 and Aquia Creek, 613
 and Battle of Seven Pines, 444-451
 at Boatswain Swamp, 484, 491
 and Chickahominy, 490-492
 at Hanover Courthouse, 443, 471
 versus Jackson, 473, 481, 634-636
 and Lincoln, 532
 and McClellan, 357, 479, 483, 614, 672, 674
  for Hooker's support, 685
 on Malvern Hill, 507-508, 510
 and Mechanicsville, 443, 467
 and Morell, 417
 and Pope, 614, 623
 reinforced Franklin's men, 488
 relieved from command, 758
 at Savage Station, 500
 and Sharpsburg battles, 700
 at Shepherdstown ford, 703
 and Sykes, 417
 and York River, 491-492
Potomac, Army of. *See* McClellan
Preliminary Emancipation Proclamation, 753, 791, 805
Prentiss, Benjamin M., 324
 capture of, 345
 and Grant, 326, 334, 336, 341
 versus Hardee, 33
 at Hornets Nest, 338-340
 at Shiloh, 331-342

Price, Sterling
 versus Buell, 147
 at Corinth, 776, 784
 versus Curtis, 721
 escape from Iuka, 717-720
 versus Grant and Ord, 717-720
 and McCulloch, 279
  rivalry, and Johnston, 170
 major general, 91, 93
 in Mississippi, 556, 583
 in Missouri, 279, 796
 at Tupelo, 573
 and Van Dorn, 283, 289, 721
 and Wilson's Creek, 91-95, 97-98, 721
"Prince John." *See* Magruder
Pryor, Roger
 advice to South Carolinians, 44
 command of Anderson's troops, 693
 and firing first shot of war, 49, 135
 life saved by Federal surgeon, 50
 one of Beauregard's emissaries, 50
Pulaski, Fort, 352, 796

Quantrill, Charles, 558
Queen, S. S., 549
Queen of the West, S. S., 551-556
Quintard, C. T., 738-739

Railroads, 68-69, 72, 76, 319, 352, 444, 501, 559, 615
 See also specific line
Randolph, Fort, 386
Randolph, George Wythe, 232-233, 785-787
Rapidan, 239, 608
Rappahannock, 238-239, 606-608
 Department of, 409
Rector, Henry M., reply to Lincoln's demand for troops, 52
Reno, Jesse L.
 and Burnside, 228, 230
 at Greenwich, 621
 and McClellan, 672
 killed in Maryland, 677, 701
 in Pope's revised plan, 623, 631
Republican Party
 birth of, 26
 versus Democratic, in Congress, 753-754
 and emancipation, 97, 708
 Lincoln nomination, 30
Reynolds, John F., 493
Rhett, R. Barnwell, 17
 chairman of Confederate foreign affairs committee, 134
 Charleston *Mercury* on, 393
 election to Congress, 25
 for extension of slavery, 13-14
 and John Pemberton, 777
Rhode Island, 54, 78
Richardson, Israel B.
 under Sumner, 417
Richmond, 55, 114
 Examiner, on Benjamin, 232
 Whig, on Jackson, 458
Richmond, S.S., 355, 548

Rio Grande, 294, 296, 304-305
River Defense Fleet, 361
Roanoke, S. S., 256-257
Roanoke Island, 239, 352, 760
  battle, 225-230
Rosecrans, William S., 69
  army of the Mississippi, 545
  Buell's command turned over to, 744
  and Corinth, 545, 569, 760
  and Grant, 717-720, 763, 768
  and Halleck, for advance on Chattanooga, 768-769
  in Kanawha Valley, 272
  and Lincoln, 760
  versus Price, 719-720
  reorganization of command, 768-769
  versus Van Dorn, 722-726
  in West Virginia, 181, 760
Rodes, Robert E., 448
Rogersville, 651-653
Rolla, 90, 94-95
Rost, Pierre A., 135-137
Ruffin, Edmund, 49
Ruggles, Daniel, 319, 340-341
Russell, John Francis Stanley (Earl)
  and Confederate bid for aid from England, 135-137, 157, 221
  on emancipation proclamation, 709
  Lord Palmerston's letter to, 666

Sabine Pass, 745
St Augustine, 352, 796
St Philip, Fort, 354, 363-364, 370
St Lawrence, S. S., 256-257
St Louis, 90, 95
St Louis, S. S., 201, 204
Salem, 615
  Advocate, 754
San Jacinto, sloop, 139, 157
Santa Fe, 296, 300
Savage Station, 496-498
Savannah, 116, 352
Savannah, S. S., 114
Schofield, John M.
  and guerilla outbreak, 557-558
  versus Hindman, 784
Schurz, Carl, 770-771
Scott, Dred, 26, 29
Scott, Winfield, 37
  Anaconda, 111-113
  Halleck's recommendation by, 532
  and Jefferson Davis, 13, 66
  and Lincoln, 85, 99, 111-113, 526, 532
  and McClellan, 99-103, 110, 144, 265, 266, 682
  and McDowell, 70, 112
  in Mexico, 111, 198
  retirement, 109, 111
Secession, 3, 14-15, 18, 50-52
Secessionville, 473
Second American Revolution, 65, 68, 132
Second Manassas, 616, 632, 650, 663, 704
  battle, 621-627
Secret, blockade runner, 352

Seddon, James A., 787-788
Sedgwick, John, and Sumner, 417
Semmes, Captain Raphael, 792-795
Seven Days, 528, 805
  battles, 509-514, 516
Seven Mile Creek, 374
Seven Pines, 444, 500
  battle, 446-449
Seward, William H.
  on emancipation proclamation, 708-709
    postponement asked, 540-541
  favor of war with England, 158
  on Fort Sumter evacuation, 46
  leader of Republican Party, 45
  and Lincoln, 33, 241
  and news of *Virginia*, 258
  Secretary of State, 158
  Senator, 37
  sent to New York, 525
  on Trent Affair, 161
"Shanks." *See* Evans
Sharpsburg, 702, 805
  battle, 685-700
Shelby, J. O., 784
Shelbyville, 776
Shenandoah Valley, 396, 398, 406, 409, 435-442, 454, 456, 473, 601-603, 613, 622
  See also specfic incidents
Shepherdstown, 686
  battle, 703-704
Sheridan, Philip H.
  and Gilbert at Doctor's Creek, 732
  at Perryville and Cleburne's injury, 736
  promotion to general, 732
Sherman, William Tecumseh, 85
  Anderson replacement, 88, 148
  battle injuries, 334-335
  command of regiment of regulars, 59
  at Corinth, 323
  foraging views, 563
  and Grant, 148, 321, 324, 326, 331, 334-336, 346, 541-542, 544
  and Halleck, 148, 542
  versus Johnston's psychological warfare, 174-175
  and Lincoln, 178
  as Louisiana State Military Academy superintendent, 58
  and McClernand, 341, 385
  at Memphis, 322, 545, 569, 800-801
  relationship with troops, 563-564
  reports of rebel advances, 148
  at Shiloh battlefield, 331-333, 336, 342, 346
  superseded by Buell, 148
  suspicion of insanity, 62, 321
  turned back toward Pittsburg Landing, 350
Shields, James
  and Conrad's store, 456, 459
  and Frémont, 452, 455, 459
  at Front Royal, 451-452
  versus Jackson, 428, 452, 459, 465
  at Kernstown, 428, 459

Index [837]

Lincoln's withdrawal order after Port Republic, 463
and McDowell, 451
on Massanutton Mountain, 454
troopers through Strasburg, 455
Shiloh, 350, 516, 796, 805
  battle, 340-348, 350
  casualties, 350-351
Shiloh Chapel, 331, 347
Ship Island, 121, 131, 354, 796
Sibley, Henry H.
  base for conquest of Far West, 300
  and Canby at West Point, 297
  at Fort Bliss, 296, 303-305
  at Fort Craig, 296
  at Fort Thorn, 296
  at Fort Union, 300-302
  retreat to San Antonio, 304-305
  and Rio Grande, 294-296, 302
  at Santa Fe, 297, 301
  and Van Dorn, 305
Sigel, Franz
  and Banks, 671
  and Curtis, 284, 289-290
  and Davis, Indiana brigadier, 288
  Frémont's replacement, 528
  versus Jackson, 631
  and Lyon, 92
  and Pope, 528
  at Wilson's Creek, 92-94, 281
Sill, Joshua, and Buell, 727-728, 733
Skull Creek, 118
Slaughterhouse Bend, 369
Slidell, John
  and Confederate bid for aid, in France, 138, 231, 395, 523, 791-792
  with Mason, reception in London, 220, 221
  and Trent Affair, 139, 162
Smith, Charles Ferguson, 182
  attack on Memphis & Charleston Railroad, 322
  at Donelson, 198, 373
  and Grant, 182, 198
  Halleck's request for advancement for, 315
  headquarters at Savannah, 321
  injured, 323
  and death, 373-374
  promotion to major general, 316, 324
Smith, G. W., 401-402
Smith, Kirby
  Barbourville occupied, 583
  at Bardstown, 728
  at Barhamsville, 412
  and Battle of Seven Pines, 444-451
  at Big Creek Gap, 583
  at Big Hill, 740
  at Big Rockcastle River, 741
  and Bragg, 572, 575, 584, 653, 711-712, 728, 738-743, 773-775
  and Cumberland Gap, 575-576, 583
  and Davis, 572, 773-775, 789
  divisions at Chattanooga, 575

Frankfort occupation, 653-654
  and Grant, 207-209
  injured, 81
  and Johnston, 450, 789
  in Kentucky, 576-577, 583, 613, 650-654
  at Manassas, 80
  versus Morgan, 583
  versus Nelson, 651
  and Polk, 741
  promotion to lieutenant general, 774
  promotion to major general, 571
  resumed command of Department of East Tennessee, 741
  at Rogersville, 651-653
  withdrawal after Perryville, 738-743
Snake Creek, 341
South Carolina, 3, 16, 34, 58, 78
South Mountain, 674, 677, 679
  losses at, 702
South River, 460
Southern United States of America, 16, 42
"Spoons." *See* Butler
Springfield, 91, 94, 279, 282, 729
Stag, blockade runner, 352
Stanton, Edwin McMasters, 28
  appointment as Secretary of War, 244-245
  and Banks, 428
  and Bates, 647
  before Joint Committee, 246-247
  in Buchanan's cabinet, 240
  and Cameron, 243
  and Chase, 647
  and Emancipation Proclamation, 540
  Fort Monroe, 413
  Grant's praise, 251
  Greeley's praise, 250-251
  and Halleck, 375
  and Hitchcock, 266-267
  and Lincoln, 142, 266-267, 428, 438, 763
  and McClernand, 763
  and McDowell, 428
  and Marcy, 155, 593
  and news of *Virginia*, 258
  and Smith, 647
Stanton, Fort, 296
Star of the West, S. S., 278
Steele, Frederick, 784
Stephens, Alexander H., 25, 55, 132, 218
Stevens, Henry, 579
Stevens, I. I., 644
Stevenson, 656, 740, 774
Stevenson's division, 775, 776
Stone, Charles P., 104-105
  and Joint Committee, 109, 180
Stone Bridge, 75-76, 82
"Stonewall." *See* Jackson, T. J.
Stonewall Brigade, 452-454, 637
Stonewall Jackson, blockade runner, 352
Strasburg, 425, 453, 454
Stringha'n, Silas H., 115, 225
Stuart, James Ewell Brown
  after Battle of Savage Station, 498
  at Chambersburg, 749-750

[838]   Index

Stuart, James Ewell Brown (*cont.*)
  at Chickahominy, 472
  versus Cooke, 471
  and Davis, 628
  dispatches and plume lost, 607–608
  and Early, and Dunker Church, 690
  east of Clark's Mountain, 607
  on Evelington Heights, 517–518
  at Gainesville, 616
  at Harrison Landing, 588
  and Jackson, 616
  and Lee, 400–401, 417
  versus McClellan, 476, 517, 749–750, 780
  on McDowell, 443–444
  and McLaws, 679
  at Manassas, 83, 471
  versus New York Fire Zouaves, 80, 265, 471
  versus Pope, 609, 618
  promoted to major general, 588
  and railroad wrecking, 472, 493–494
  "Ride Around McClellan," 749–750, 780
Stuart, John T., 753
Sudley Springs, 75, 79
Sumner, Charles, 15, 246
Sumner, Edwin Vose
  appointed corps commander, 253
  to Aquia Creek, 613
  and Banks, 695
  at Battle of Glendale, 507
  and Battle of Seven Pines, 444–451
  at Bloody Lane, 695
  and Burnside, 766
  command of first U.S. Cavalry, 448–449
  at Dunker Church, 695
  in front of Centerville and Pope, 643
  Harpers Ferry reoccupation, 704
  and Lincoln, 531
  on Malvern Hill, 510
  and Mansfield's men, 691–692
  and Mechanicsville, 443
  Richardson, and Sedgwick, 417
  at Savage Station, 500
  versus Walker, 691–692
  at White Oak Swamp, 501
  at Williamsburg, 413
  at Yorktown, 410
Sumter, Fort, 44–50
Sumter, S. S., 388
Swett, Leonard, 753
Sykes, George
  division of regulars, 639–640, 647
  and Hill, A. P., 490
  and Hill, D. Harvey, 488

Tattnall, Josiah, 117, 415
Taylor, Richard
  and Davis, 797
  and Ewell, 453–454, 463
  versus Frémont, 453–454
  and Holmes, 783
  and Jackson, 433, 458
  paralysis, and Seven Days, 487
    recovery, 784
  at Strasburg, 453–454
Taylor, Zachary, 8, 11
Tennessee, 19, 52, 132–134, 170, 306, 319, 392, 708
  Armies of, 543, 653, 772, 776
Tennessee, S.S., 387–388
Tennessee River, 173, 326, 338, 546
  contact mines, 187–188
Terrill, William, 735
Texas, 3, 13, 18, 293–301, 412
Thomas, George Henry
  appointed assistant commander, 373
  at Beech Grove, 177
  and Buell, 564, 660, 715–716, 738
  camp near Logan's Crossroads, 177
  command, in place of Grant, 373
  at Corinth, 543
  versus Crittenden, 188–190, 250, 738–739
  at Cumberland Gap, 172
  at Fishing Creek, 177–181
  and Halleck, 372–374, 543
  in Kentucky, 250, 729
  at Logan's Crossroads and Mill Springs, 177–180
  and Nashville defense, 657
  at Perryville, 738
  promotion to brigadier general, 178
  promotion to major general, 373
  and Rosecrans, 768–769
  versus Zollicoffer, 172, 177–180
Thomas, Lorenzo, 408
Thompson, M. Jeff, 95, 149
Thorn, Fort, 296
Thoroughfare Gap, 238–239, 616, 631
Tilghman, Lloyd
  evacuation of Fort Henry, 187–188
    taken prisoner, 190
  fortification of forts, 171, 174, 180–181
Tod, David, 372
Todd, Mary, 24
Toombs, Robert, 16–17
  Confederate Secretary of State, 122
  and Fort Sumter, 47
  election to Congress, 25
  on generalship of General Lee, 586
  and Gordonsville, 607
  joining army, 123
  at Manassas, 664
  and Seven Days, 496
  at Sharpsburg, 697–698
Transmississippi, 168–181, 556
Treason
  acts now considered as, 247
  and Secession—or rebellion, 539
  slogans, 393
Tredegar Iron Works, 173, 255
Trent Affair, 156–157, 165
Trimble, Isaac, 618, 633
Trumbull, Lyman, 753
Turchin, John Basil, 562–563
Turkey Hill, 487, 490–491
Turner's Gap, 674
Twain, Mark, 89
Twiggs, David E., 294–295

Index

Tygart Valley, 68
Tyler, Daniel, 75, 79
Tyler, E. B., 461
Tyler, John, 593
Tyler, S. S., 203, 549-553

Uncle Tom's Cabin, 26
Union Mills Ford, 76
Union, Fort, 296, 300
United States Supreme Court, Dred Scott decision, 29
Urbanna Plan, 155, 248-250, 252-254, 263
See also McClellan
Utah, 13, 293

Van Buren, Martin, 593
Van Dorn, Earl, 280
   army against Springfield, 279
   and Beauregard, 350, 374, 722
   captaincy in A. S. Johnston's 2d Cavalry, 277
   Carr's second line thrown back, 285-287
   and Confederate expansion, 293
   at Corinth, 320, 720, 722-726, 776, 784
   versus Curtis, 288, 291, 292, 318
   and Davis, 288
      on Pemberton's promotion, 778-779
   at Elkhorn Tavern, 290-292, 306, 318
   versus Grant, 722
   versus Halleck, 374, 722
   headquarters at Pocahontas, Arkansas, 278
   and help from Arkansas, 577
   and Jefferson Davis, brigadier, 277
   major general, 170
      command of all cavalry in Virginia, 278
   and McCulloch, 170, 285
   in Mississippi, 546, 556, 784
   order to Breckinridge, 578
   versus Pope, 383
   and Price, 170, 285, 716-717, 721-726
   price on head by northern editor, 278
   reassembly of troops near Van Buren, 291-292
   at Ripley, 721
   versus Rosecrans, 722-726
   sent to Transmississippi, 235-236
   and Vicksburg, 568, 573, 716
Van Dorn, S. S., 388
Varuna, S. S., 368-369
Vicksburg, 371, 581, 759, 776, 787, 797-798
Virginia, 19, 52, 56, 78, 238, 394, 403, 708
   Army of, 527, 588, 604-606
      Northern, 396-399, 585, 606, 641
   creation of West Virginia, 128
Virginia, S. S., 255-263, 268, 291, 402, 404, 415-416
Virginia Central Railroad, 423, 456
Virginia and Tennessee Railroad, 132-133

Wabash, S. S., 117-119
Wade, Benjamin Franklin
   on Joint Committee on Conduct of War, 231-242
   chairman, 108, 140
   and McClellan, 408

   and Pope, 527
   on Stanton, 246
Wadsworth, James, 408
Walke, Henry, 311-313, 551
Walker, Fort, 117-119
Walker, John G.
   given Ewell's division, 685
   and Lee, 663, 667-669, 702
   on outskirts of Sharpsburg, 685-686
   and Longstreet at Antietam, 686
Walker, Leroy P.
   joining army, 123
   War Secretary, resignation as, 123
"The Walking Division," 403
Wallace, Lewis
   brigade sent to McClernand, 207-208
   and Buckner, 213
   Cincinnati defense, martial law decreed, 654
   at Dover Inn, 213
   and Grant, 213, 326, 335, 346
   and Nelson, 335
   promotions, 324
   at Shiloh, 342, 346
   at Snake Creek bridge, 343
   Third division assigned to, 200-201
Wallace, W. H. L.
   and Grant, 326, 335-336
   at Hornets Nest, 340
   at Owl Creek, 331
   at Shiloh, 342
   Smith's division in charge of, 324
Warrenton Turnpike, 74, 408, 616
Warwick River, 404-405
Washburn, Elihu, 37
Watie, Stand, 286
Webster, Daniel, 14, 25-26
Weldon railroad, 122
Welles, Gideon, 353
   and Farragut, 555-556, 746
   on Lincoln's Emancipation Proclamation, 540
   and Porter, 357, 746-747
   and Stanton, 258-259
West Virginia, 70, 128, 641, 760
Western and Atlantic Railroad, 377-378
Wheat, Roberdeau, 83-84, 428, 487
   death, 487
Wheeler, Joseph
   and Bragg, 738, 740
   and Perryville, 736, 738, 740
   versus Crittenden, 736
   in West Tennessee, 569
Whigs, 11, 28, 29
White Oak Swamp, 447, 501
White Plains, 615
Wigfall, Louis T., 15
Wilcox, Cadmus, 628-631
Wilder, J. T., 658-661, 718
Wilkes, Charles, 139, 157
Williams, Alpheus, 672, 691-692
Williams, Thomas, 549, 580
Williamsburg, 444, 500
   battle, 411

Wilmington, 113, 116, 352
Wilson's Bayou, 311
Wilson's Creek, 120, 149, 169, 239, 284, 288-289, 796, 805
  battle, 91-95
Winchester, 451-453
Winder, Charles S.
  and Ewell, 463
  and A. P. Hill, 487
  march to Culpeper, 599
  death, 600
  versus Tyler, 461-462
Wisconsin, 626, 753
Wise, Henry A.
  and Benjamin, 226-227
  versus Floyd, defeat in West Virginia, 225-226
  in Kanawha Valley, 129-130, 272
  and Lee, 129-130
  and Lynch's commandeering of boats, 226
  at Nags Head, 229
  in North Carolina, versus Burnside, 250
  and Roanoke Island, 225-230

Wool, John E., 414, 598
Worden, John L., and *Monitor*, 259-263

Yancey, William Lowndes
  of Alabama, for extension of slavery, 13-14
  and Confederate bid for European aid, 134-137
  and Davis, 17, 393, 780
  and Foote, 789
  and Rhett, 135
Yell Rifles, 653
York River Railroad, 444
Yorktown, 398, 500
"Young Napoleon." *See* McClellan

Zollicoffer, Felix, 170
  at Beech Grove, 176-177
  and Crittenden, 177-180
  death, 179
  occupation of Cumberland Gap, 172, 176-177

COMPREHENSIVE TABLE OF CONTENTS

Volume One

I.

CHAPTER 1. PROLOGUE–THE OPPONENTS
1. Secession: Davis and Lincoln
2. Sumter; Early Maneuvers
3. Statistics North and South

CHAPTER 2. FIRST BLOOD; NEW CONCEPTIONS
1. Manassas—Southern Triumph
2. Anderson, Frémont, McClellan
3. Scott's Anaconda; the Navy
4. Diplomacy; the Buildup

CHAPTER 3. THE THING GETS UNDER WAY
1. The West: Grant, Fort Henry
2. Donelson—The Loss of Kentucky
3. Gloom; Manassas Evacuation
4. McC Moves to the Peninsula

II.

CHAPTER 4. WAR MEANS FIGHTING...
1. Pea Ridge; Glorieta; Island Ten
2. Halleck-Grant, Jston-Bgard: Shiloh
3. Farragut, Lovell: New Orleans
4. Halleck, Beauregard: Corinth

CHAPTER 5. FIGHTING MEANS KILLING
1. Davis Frets; Lincoln-McClellan
2. Valley Campaign; Seven Pines
3. Lee, McC: The Concentration
4. The Seven Days; Hezekiah

III.

CHAPTER 6. THE SUN SHINES SOUTH
1. Lincoln Reappraisal; Emancipation?
2. Grant, Farragut, Buell
3. Bragg, K. Smith, Breckinridge
4. Lee vs. Pope: Second Manassas

CHAPTER 7. TWO ADVANCES; TWO RETREATS
1. Invasion West: Richmond, Munfordville
2. Lee, McClellan: Sharpsburg
3. The Emancipation Proclamation
4. Corinth-Perryville: Bragg Retreats

CHAPTER 8. LAST, BEST HOPE OF EARTH
1. Lincoln's Late-Fall Disappointments
2. Davis: Lookback and Outlook
3. Lincoln: December Message

Volume Two

I.

CHAPTER 1. THE LONGEST JOURNEY
1. Davis, Westward and Return
2. Goldsboro; Fredericksburg
3. Prairie Grove; Galveston
4. Holly Springs; Walnut Hills
5. Murfreesboro: Bragg Retreats

CHAPTER 2. UNHAPPY NEW YEAR
1. Lincoln; Mud March; Hooker
2. Arkansas Post; Transmiss; Grant
3. Erlanger; Richmond Bread Riot
4. Rosecrans; Johnston; Streit
5. Vicksburg—Seven Failures

CHAPTER 3. DEATH OF A SOLDIER
1. Naval Repulse at Charleston
2. Lee, Hooker; Mosby; Kelly's Ford
3. Suffolk: Longstreet Southside
4. Hooker, Stoneman: The Crossing
5. Chancellorsville; Jackson Dies

II.

CHAPTER 4. THE BELEAGUERED CITY
1. Grant's Plan; the Run; Grierson
2. Eastward, Port Gibson to Jackson
3. Westward, Jackson to Vicksburg
4. Port Hudson; Banks vs. Gardner
5. Vicksburg Siege, Through June

CHAPTER 5. STARS IN THEIR COURSES
1. Lee, Davis; Invasion; Stuart
2. Gettysburg Opens; Meade Arrives
3. Gettysburg, July 2: Longstreet
4. Gettysburg, Third Day: Pickett
5. Cavalry; Lee Plans Withdrawal

CHAPTER 6. UNVEXED TO THE SEA
1. Lee's Retreat; Falling Waters
2. Milliken's Bend; Helena Repulse
3. Vicksburg Falls; Jackson Reburnt
4. Lincoln Exults; N.Y. Draft Riot
5. Davis Declines Lee's Resignation

III.

CHAPTER 7. RIOT AND RESURGENCE
1. Rosecrans; Tullahoma Campaign
2. Morgan Raid; Chattanooga Taken
3. Charleston Seige; Transmississippi
4. Chickamauga—First Day
5. Bragg's Victory Unexploited

CHAPTER 8. THE CENTER GIVES
1. Sabine Pass; Shelby; Grant Hurt
2. Bristoe Station; Buckland Races
3. Grant Opens the Cracker Line
4. Davis, Bragg; Gettysburg Address
5. Missionary Ridge; Bragg Relieved

CHAPTER 9. SPRING CAME ON FOREVER
1. Mine Run; Meade Withdraws
2. Olustee; Kilpatrick Raid
3. Sherman, Meridian; Forrest
4. Lincoln-Davis, a Final Contrast
5. Grant Summoned to Washington

Volume Three

I.

CHAPTER 1. ANOTHER GRAND DESIGN
1. Grant in Washington—His Plan
2. Red River, Camden: Reevaluation
3. Paducah, Fort Pillow; Plymouth
4. Grant Poised; Joe Davis; Lee

CHAPTER 2. THE FORTY DAYS
1. Grant Crosses; the Wilderness
2. Spotsylvania—"All Summer"
3. New Market; Bermuda Hundred
4. North Anna; Cold Harbor; Early

CHAPTER 3. RED CLAY MINUET
1. Dalton to Pine Mountain
2. Brice's; Lincoln; "Alabama"
3. Kennesaw to Chattahoochee
4. Hood Replaces Johnston

II.

CHAPTER 4. WAR IS CRUELTY...
1. Petersburg; Early I; Peace?
2. Hood vs. Sherman; Mobile Bay; Memphis Raid; Atlanta Falls
3. Crater; McClellan; Early II
4. Price Raid; "Florida"; Cushing; Forrest Raids Mid-Tenn.
5. Hood-Davis; Lincoln Reelected.

CHAPTER 5. YOU CANNOT REFINE IT
1. Petersburg Trenches; Weldon RR
2. March to Sea; Hood, Spring Hill
3. Franklin; Hood Invests Nashville
4. Thomas Attacks; Hood Retreats
5. Savannah Falls; Lincoln Exultant

III.

CHAPTER 6. A TIGHTENING NOOSE
1. Grant; Ft. Fisher; 13th Amendment
2. Confed Shifts; Lee Genl-in-Chief?
3. Blair Received; Hampton Roads
4. Hatcher's Run; Columbia Burned

CHAPTER 7. VICTORY, AND DEFEAT
1. Sheridan, Early; Second Inaugural
2. Goldsboro; Sheridan; City Point
3. Five Forks—Richmond Evacuated
4. Lee, Grant Race for Appomattox

CHAPTER 8. LUCIFER IN STARLIGHT
1. Davis-Johnston; Sumter; Booth
2. Durham; Citronelle; Davis Taken
3. K. Smith; Naval; Fort Monroe
4. Postlude: Reconstruction, Davis

ABOUT THE AUTHOR

SHELBY FOOTE was born in Greenville, Mississippi, and attended school there until he entered the University of North Carolina. During World War II he served in the European theater as a captain of field artillery. He has written five novels: *Tournament, Follow Me Down, Love in a Dry Season, Shiloh* and *Jordan County*. He has been awarded three Guggenheim fellowships. He died in 2005.

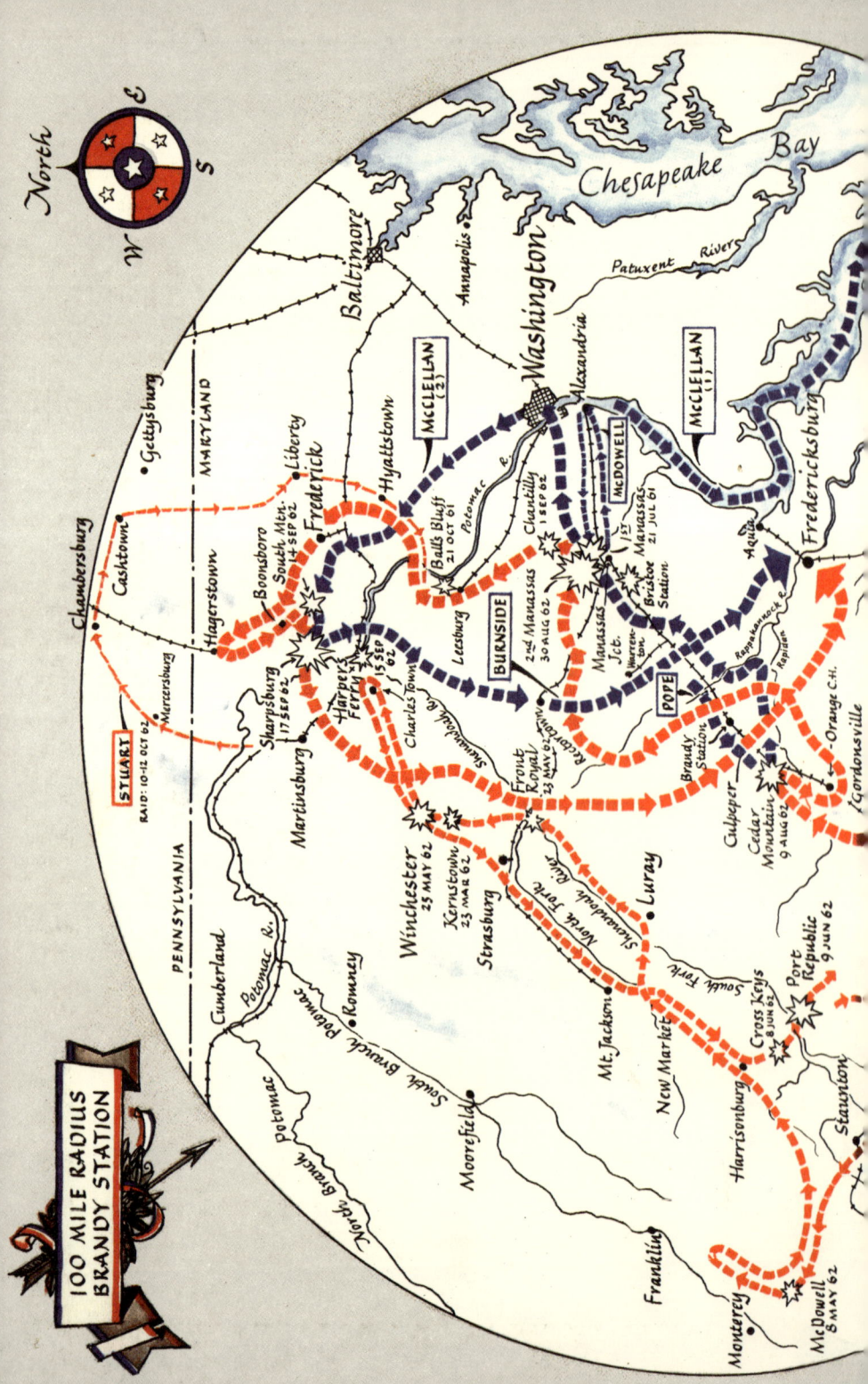

AMERICAN HOMER

AMERICAN HOMER

REFLECTIONS ON SHELBY FOOTE AND

HIS CLASSIC *THE CIVIL WAR: A NARRATIVE*

Edited by Jon Meacham

THE MODERN LIBRARY

NEW YORK

Copyright © 2011 by Jon Meacham

All rights reserved.

Published in the United States by Modern Library, an imprint of
The Random House Publishing Group, a division
of Random House, Inc., New York.

MODERN LIBRARY and the TORCHBEARER Design are
registered trademarks of Random House, Inc.

"Foote and Lincoln" by Michael Beschloss, copyright © 2011
by Michael Beschloss. Reprinted by permission of the author.
"History and Memory: A Critique of the Foote Vision" by Annette Gordon-Reed,
copyright © 2011 by Annette Gordon-Reed. Reprinted by permission of the author.
"A Reader's Appreciation" by Don Graham, copyright © 2011 by Don Graham.
Reprinted by permission of the author.
"Editing Shelby Foote" by Bob Loomis, copyright © 2011 by Bob Loomis.
Reprinted by permission of the author.
"The War in the Southern Mind" by John M. McCardell, Jr., copyright © 2011
by John M. McCardell, Jr. Reprinted by permission of the author.
"The Greenville Factor" by Julia Reed, copyright © 2011 by Julia Reed.
Reprinted by permission of the author.
"Art, War, and Shelby Foote" by Jay Tolson, copyright © 1996 by Jay Tolson.
Originally published in the Winter 1996 issue of *Double Take* magazine,
published by the Center for Documentary Studies at Duke University.
Reprinted by permission of the author.

Grateful acknowledgment is made to W. W. Norton & Company, Inc.,
for permission to reprint excerpts from *The Correspondence of Shelby Foote and
Walker Percy* by Jay Tolson, copyright © 1997 by Jay Tolson, copyright © 1997
by Mary Bernice Townsend, copyright © 1997 by Shelby Foote.
Used by permission of W. W. Norton & Company, Inc.

ISBN 978-0-679-64370-8

Printed in China on acid-free paper

www.modernlibrary.com

2 4 6 8 9 7 5 3 1

Contents

An American Master by Jon Meacham	3
Foote and Lincoln by Michael Beschloss	10
Art, War, and Shelby Foote by Jay Tolson	14
The Voice of Authority by Jon Meacham	37
Editing Shelby Foote by Bob Loomis	42
A Reader's Appreciation by Don Graham	47
The War in the Southern Mind by John M. McCardell, Jr.	50
History and Memory: A Critique of the Foote Vision by Annette Gordon-Reed	60
Foote and the Problem of Race by Michael Eric Dyson	67
The Greenville Factor by Julia Reed	73
Correspondences of Shelby Foote and Walker Percy	82

American Homer

AN AMERICAN MASTER

by Jon Meacham

It was supposed to be a brief assignment—eighteen months or so, tops. In 1954, with the centennial of the Civil War approaching, Bennett Cerf, the president of Random House, wrote the novelist Shelby Foote to propose a "short history" of the conflict. In midsummer the author traveled from his home in Memphis to meet with the publisher in New York, and the two quickly came to terms. The target was 200,000 words; the advance, four hundred dollars. The plan was to get the book done fast and return to writing novels. "Fiction is hard work," Foote recalled thinking; "history I figured, well, there's not much to that."

He was then thirty-seven. By the time he finished the third volume of his *The Civil War: A Narrative*, he would be fifty-six. In a notable case of literary understatement, Foote later observed, "It expanded as I wrote"—ultimately to just over 1,500,000 words, or, as Foote said, "a third of a million longer than Gibbon's *Decline & Fall*, which took about the same length of time to write." The war had come alive in his imagination—he heard the hoofbeats and smelled the gunpowder and felt the anguish and the anxiety of

Lincoln and Davis and the hundreds of thousands of unknown soldiers. "Don't underrate it as a thing that can claim a man's whole waking mind for years on end," Foote said of the war.

It surely claimed his. Now, on the occasion of the 150th anniversary of the beginning of the war, the Modern Library is republishing Foote's masterpiece, and this small accompanying volume collects a number of perspectives on author and subject. The story of Foote's *The Civil War* is one of the great literary tales of the twentieth century, and his rendering of a nineteenth-century saga remains as fresh and as compelling to twenty-first-century readers as it was when it first emerged from his mind, written in longhand in his house in West Tennessee. "The further I go in my studies, the more amazed I am," he told Walker Percy in 1956. "What a war! Everything we are or will be goes right back to that period. It decided once and for all which way we were going, and we've gone."

Ralph Waldo Emerson once said that there is "properly no history; only biography," and to reread Foote is to see how the greatest historians are those who recognize that the past, like the present, is shaped by the vices and the virtues of flawed, flesh-and-blood individuals, from presidents to foot soldiers. He said so explicitly: "The whole thing is wonderfully human.... In that furnace (the War) they were shown up, every one, for what they were."

Born on Friday, November 17, 1916, in Greenville, Mississippi, Shelby Dade Foote, Jr., grew up in a relatively cosmopolitan atmosphere—or at least cosmopolitan by the standards of the midcentury American South. Foote's mother was Jewish in a time and place where Jews were broadly accepted in the social and cultural circles of certain Southern cities. Greenville was one of them (Foote later remarked that there were more Jews in the Greenville Country Club than there were Baptists). His father was the son of a lost Delta fortune, and one suspects that Foote's tragic view of the world likely came in part from the saga of the Foote clan.

Shelby Jr.'s great-great-great-grandfather had bad luck back in Virginia, losing valuable tobacco land in Prince William County, and later generations gambled away the family's sprawling Mississippi Delta plantations. Loss, then, was something young Shelby understood in his bones: it was an intrinsic element of his ancestry, the central fact of his paternal history.

His forebears fought for the Confederacy and engaged in the grim politics of Reconstruction Mississippi, but the defining influence in Foote's youth—and thus in his life—came less from tales of Southern sentimentality and more from talk of literature, art, and philosophy in the house of William Alexander Percy, scion of a Delta dynasty and uncle of Walker. Will Percy was a planter-poet who took Walker and his brother LeRoy in after their father's death, and Mr. Will, as he was known, asked young Shelby to come over to help entertain his young kinsmen when they arrived from Athens, Georgia.

The Percy salon fundamentally shaped Foote, who decided to become a novelist. His early books, particularly 1951's *Love in a Dry Season*, were good but achieved little commercial success. He also had an expensive tendency to go through wives, creating obligations for alimony and child support. On the occasion of his third marriage, Foote said, "I cannot function outside the married state, no matter how much I'm galled inside it. (Nothing special about that. I think it's true of most people: women as well as men.)"

A literary man by training and inclination (he dropped out of the University of North Carolina at Chapel Hill), Foote was one of the great readers of his age. Proust, Hemingway, Homer, the Russians—nothing of note seems to have escaped him. It was this immersion in the most enduring works of imaginative literature that informed his rendering of the Civil War. "The *Iliad* is the great model for any war book, history or novel," he said.

Like Homer, Foote focused on two things: the clash of arms and the lives of the warriors. The grand issues of politics and diplomacy, of economics and culture, mattered less to Foote than re-creating the reality of battle. "The idea is to strike fire," he said, "prodding the reader much as combat quickened the pulses of the people at the time." Critics took Foote to task for this single-minded focus, but he believed in his approach, and stuck to it. "I think the superiority of southern writers lies in our driving interest in just... two things, the story and the people." In a way, Foote is one of the little-noted pioneers of the New Journalism, the movement to bring fictional technique to nonfiction subjects, elevating journalism, history, and biography to the level of literature.

He also saw himself working in a broader tradition than that of many mainstream historians. "My hope was that if I wrote well enough about what you would have seen with your own eyes, you yourself would see how those things, the politics and economics, entered in," he said. "I quite deliberately left those things out. My job was to put it all in perspective, to give it shape. Look at Flaubert: He didn't criticize Emma Bovary as a terrible woman; he didn't judge her; he just put down what happened."

Time has vindicated his view. There are other books about other parts of the war—great books. No other volumes, however, put the reader in the horror and the haze so effectively and so memorably. It was hard but rewarding work. "The battle scenes are lit by a strange, lurid light.... I have never enjoyed writing so much as I do this writing," he said. "It goes dreadful slow; sometimes I feel like I'm trying to bail out the Mississippi with a teacup; but I like it, I like it." He grew obsessive in his study in Memphis: "All I want is to work on my book, a great wide sea of words."

He visited the battlefields in season, walking them at the same time of year as the soldiers had walked them. "For one thing, it's teaching me to love my country—especially the South, but all the rest as well. I'm learning so many things: geography, for instance. I never saw this country before now—the rivers and mountains, the watersheds and valleys." The books are as much a biography of the land and the elements as they are of the men who fought the war: it is the accumulation of such atmospheric detail that lends the trilogy much of its vivid novelistic feel.

Foote undertook his narrative of what he would later call "the cross-roads of our being" in the years in which the civil rights movement forced the South to confront the war's worst legacy: segregation. He began work in the months after the first *Brown v. Board of Education* decision came down, published his second volume in the year of the March on Washington, and completed the trilogy as the struggles over affirmative action were taking shape.

Foote was no liberal on issues of race, but he was more fair-minded than many of his contemporaries in the South. His admiration of Nathan Bedford Forrest's military genius, for instance, transcended his sense of outrage at Forrest's politics, including the general's founding of the Ku Klux Klan. To Foote, the Confederacy's defeat was in a way foreordained, but more for material reasons than moral ones: "You just can't whip 23,000,000 people with 9,000,000—especially when nearly half of the latter number are slaves."

Yet Foote knew evil when he saw it. In a bibliographical note composed for the second volume in 1963, he wrote: "I am obligated to the governors of my native state and the adjoining states of Arkansas and Alabama for helping to lessen my sectional bias by reproducing, in their actions during several of the years that went into the writing of this volume, much that was least admirable in the position my forebears occupied when they stood up to Lincoln." Ross Barnett, Orval Faubus, and George Wallace were fighting battles that should have been settled on the side of justice. "I feel death all in the air in Memphis, and I'm beginning to hate the one thing I really ever loved—the South," Foote told Percy. In the note at the conclusion of the second volume, he added: "I suppose, or in any case fervently hope, it is true that history never repeats itself, but I know from watching these three gentlemen [Barnett, Faubus, and Wallace] that it can be terrifying in its approximations."

In the summer of 1973, recuperating from a head cold and fascinated by the Watergate hearings on television, Foote neared the conclusion. "There's a strange sort of twilight over all this part of the book, a murkiness as if the rebels were slogging along the floor of hell, stomachs all knotted with hunger and knees about unjointed from fatigue." He told Percy of a small but telling moment on the eve of Appomattox: "Yanks threw down one scarecrow retreater, yelling: 'Surrender! We got you!' He dropped his rifle, raised his hands. 'Yes,' he said, 'and a hell of a git you got.' There was never an army so thoroughly whipped, short of annihilation."

Shelby Foote, two days before his seventy-fifth birthday. The Tuileries, Paris, November 15, 1991.
Huger Foote

William Faulkner was Foote's literary idol, and Walker Percy was the friend of his heart, but it was Robert Penn Warren who, with a single telephone call, may have done the most to elevate Foote to his present status as the American bard of war. Ken Burns, a young documentary filmmaker, had told Warren, whom he knew from an earlier work on Huey Long (Warren's Willie Stark in *All the King's Men*), that he was thinking about a project on the Civil War. At dinnertime one evening, Burns's phone rang, and it was Warren. Warren's suggestion: You have to talk to Shelby Foote. Thus began an enormously influential collaboration. Burns's epic PBS film, which debuted in 1990, relied heavily on Foote's voice. Celebrity followed almost instantly. By the time of Foote's death in Memphis in 2005, he was one of the most iconic of American writers.

At the end of the drafting of the third and final volume, in July 1974, twenty years to the season after Foote first went to New York to talk over the project, Walker Percy finished reading the proofs and sat down to write his friend. "Dear Shelby," he said, "Yes, it's as good as you think. It has a fine understated epic quality, a slow measured period, and a sustained noncommittal, almost laconic, tone of the narrator. I've no doubt it will survive; might even be read in the ruins." It might indeed.

Foote and Lincoln

by Michael Beschloss

Renderings of Abraham Lincoln through the decades often show a sneaking resemblance to their creators. Carl Sandburg's version of the sixteenth president, for example, is animated by the soul of a rustic poet. The Harvard historian David Herbert Donald's Lincoln is professorial and self-effacing. Thus it is not surprising that the Lincoln who walks through the pages of this classic shows many of the qualities that the author no doubt saw in the people of his Mississippi boyhood. They appear in Foote's novels. Some of them he must have perceived in himself. Like a dog who hears a whistle audible only to other canines, Foote is alert to Lincoln's sporadic cold-bloodedness and his willingness to try tawdry tactical maneuvers, as well as the growth of his powerful moral vision and literary prowess, which helped him both in steeling the Union side to win the war and in paving the way for the reunion of North and South.

Foote was hardly brought up a member of the Lincoln fan club. As he once recalled, he was taught "reams of obscene doggerel" about Lincoln by his parents and grandparents, and was raised on the idea that "the South, founded on the highest ideals," was "never guilty of the slightest stain or smudge." Until the end of his life, Foote remained certain that, had he been alive in 1861, he would have fought for the Confederacy. After taking on this great work on the "bloody mess" of the War between the States, he was bemused when he told General Nathan Bedford Forrest's granddaughter on the telephone that he had come to consider Lincoln and Forrest the two "authentic geniuses" of the struggle and she replied, without a speck of irony, "You know, we never thought much of Mr. Lincoln in my family."

Foote's Southern heritage certainly made him conscious of the hagiographical excesses that afflicted much of what was written about Lincoln during the first century after his death, turning Lincoln into "a sort of TV image of himself, with a ghost alongside." Nor might a Northern writer have aspired, as Foote did, to interweave Lincoln's tale with that of Jefferson Davis. As the careful reader of this narrative will find, Foote wanted to describe some of the less explored features of the ghost. He wanted "to know him as he was, rather than as he has come to be." His verdict: "Christ, what a man."

Foote does not neglect the qualities in Lincoln cited by the Lincoln haters of the 1860s. He writes that Lincoln's "ruthlessness," although "long apparent to his foes," was "an element of his political genius that was to receive small recognition from posthumous friends who were safe beyond his reach." He later remarked that Lincoln had come to be "known as the Great Emancipator, the man of infinite tenderness," yet "the records show that he approved the execution of 267 men during the crisis of the war." By contrast, Jefferson Davis "never approved the execution of a single man."

As a boy, Foote had been predictably told much about Lincoln the tyrant. As an adult, he imagined what Lincoln would have done in 1957 had he been president when the Arkansas governor, Orval Faubus, blocked the integration of Little Rock High

School: "Faubus would never have known what would have happened to him. Lincoln would have chopped his legs off." Foote enjoys how Lincoln concealed his toughness. He writes that "nothing pleased Lincoln more than to have an opponent think he was an idealist. It was like swiping somebody with a razor and then telling them to shake their head." He has little use for the legend of Honest Abe, writing that "unfettered by any need for being or not being a gentleman, he would keep his word to any man only so long as keeping it would help to win the war."

While vouching for the presence of the brutal and dishonest Lincoln, Foote is also willing to conclude that such rough means almost consistently served a deepening maturity and moral purpose. He writes that "out of the midnight trials of his spirit, out of his concern for a race in bondage, out of his knowledge of the death of men in battle, something new had come to birth in Lincoln, and through him into the war." To Foote, Lincoln swung the truncheon but was still "as compassionate as everybody thought he was.... His eyes were red with weeping about some of the things that happened." Foote finds the flexibility in Lincoln at the "core of his greatness, but he had to purchase it dearly in midnight care and day-long fret." No stranger to depression himself, Foote detects "the deep melancholy that was so much a part of his complex nature."

Foote came to feel that "there's never been a man function the way Lincoln did." He marveled at how quickly Lincoln mastered an office of which he knew almost nothing, and felt that Lincoln's "particular talent" was to shift "the arguments onto a higher plane." In Foote's construct, the "slightly humorous" Lincoln, "thoroughly practical and sagacious," alternates with the statesman "seen in those abstract and serious eyes, which seemed withdrawn to an inner sanctuary of thought, sitting in judgment on the scene and feeling its far reach into the future."

A lesser wordsmith than Foote could not have been so effective in describing how Lincoln's increasing talent as "a craftsman in the use of words," his "music," empowered that moral leadership. Foote shows how he used and developed his literary abilities into a vital force that united his "political destiny and the destiny of the nation." No doubt describing himself as well as Lincoln, he writes of a man who "worked with the dedication of the true artist, who, whatever his sense of superiority in other relationships, preserves his humility in this one."

During his period of composition, Abraham Lincoln was a vibrant presence in Foote's own life. Nearing the end of his work, he wrote his friend Walker Percy, "I killed Lincoln last week—Saturday, at noon," and worried that the last seventy pages of his book would be "strange" without him—"like *Hamlet* with Hamlet left out." (But it was "on to Andy Johnson, who looks to me as if he's headed for impeachment.") So much did Foote identify with Lincoln that, like his hero, he refused to smile when people asked to photograph him.

In literary terms, American leaders move from politics to history to art. During the first stage of examination, they cannot be separated from their politics. During the second, we can stand back and view the leader with greater dispassion. But in the third, the writer of aspiration and talent uses materials assembled during the earlier stages to create a full-blooded portrait that, though rooted in fact, might rival the imperishable characters of fiction. Shelby Foote's three-volume work is not a biography of Abraham Lincoln, but the intermittent portrait in this book makes one regret that he never tried to write one.

ART, WAR, AND SHELBY FOOTE

by Jay Tolson

Although he will go down in the annals of American letters for his three-volume history, *The Civil War: A Narrative,* Shelby Foote would have you know that he is, above all, a novelist, a votary at the shrine of what D. H. Lawrence called the "one bright book of life." So there is no small irony in the way Foote entered the national limelight in the fall of 1990. The vehicle, as almost any TV-owning American knows, was Ken Burns's award-winning PBS documentary *The Civil War,* in which Foote appeared as one of several commentators but gradually became something more, a sort of bardic figure who seemed able to call forth actual lived moments of the war. To say that Foote captivated the viewing audience is an understatement. "He was oral bourbon," remarked one enthusiast, a Southern clergyman. But Southerners were not the only Americans held rapt by his commentary. Even before the series had ended, people from all over the country besieged Foote

---

Excerpted from an article first published in DoubleTake *magazine (Winter 1996), Center for Documentary Studies at Duke University*

with letters and phone calls, questioning him about everything from the order of battle at Gettysburg to his marital status. (One such caller, disappointed to learn that Foote was married, followed up with an even more pointed question: "But are you *happily* married?")...

For all that, Foote sees his role as a modest one. "My big contribution was to make Ken see the wisdom of doing the Vicksburg campaign before the Gettysburg campaign and not to play down Vicksburg. I got him to see the balance between the western and the eastern campaigns. That's important when you talk about Gettysburg, because some people think it was something that Lee hit upon almost overnight."

If Foote understates his influence on Burns's work, he doesn't minimize the film's impact on his own life. "My private life was completely changed," he says. We are sitting in his study on a warm June morning, Foote worrying a pipe while we talk and sip coffee. "That phone over there was ringing its head off, but I refused to have my number taken out of the book." The phone rings twice that morning, and both times it is callers with questions about the war—this, almost four years since the film's first airing. Three years earlier, when I had visited Foote on other business, it had been almost impossible to get a word in between calls.

Then, as now, the jangling intrusions seemed to violate the monastic calm and order of Foote's study, a room in every way reflective of the man, his habits, and his interests. "Those shelves behind you I had specially built and beveled so they wouldn't sag under the weight of the books," he says proudly. The room—the scriptorium, it could be called—is truly a world apart, even from the larger, somewhat otherworldly house. It has a high, vaulted ceiling with open beams and whitewashed plaster walls and is dominated by a large fireplace. The furnishings include a double bed, a small typing table, two large swivel chairs, and, extending along most of one wall, a custom-made oak desk, where Foote writes his first drafts in careful longhand. Above the desk is a long pin board where Foote affixes notes when he is working, and over the pin board are more bookshelves containing various editions of Foote's works as well as bound manuscript volumes of the final handwritten versions, meticulously penned in his distinctive script. (It is modeled, he tells me, after the Gothic script he was introduced to in college German classes, but it is very much his own style—elegant, precise, even finicky.) Arranged on the shelves are many of the books that Foote considers "sacred"— Stendahl, Flaubert, Gogol, Mann, Joyce, Dostoyevsky, the Bible, Shakespeare—as well as a number of source and reference books, including *The Oxford Companion to American History, Personal Memoirs of U. S. Grant,* Mencken's *American Language, Grove's Dictionary of Music and Musicians,* and John A. Wyeth's *Life of General Nathan Bedford Forrest.*

If rooms have themes, this one's is "War and Art," and its most striking emblem is an M1 rifle mounted directly on a reproduction of Picasso's *Guernica,* itself flanked by two of Foote's own hand-drawn maps of Civil War campaigns. Around the fireplace are yet more war-related items—among them a very good reproduction of a rebel cap, a French cavalry bugle, and a helmet from World War II days, the Fifth Division red diamond emblem brightly embossed on its front. Just in front of the fireplace, hanging on a long wire from the ceiling, are two large model airplanes, a German Fokker triplane and a British SE-5, suspended in perpetual dogfight. But art is the ubiquitous counterpoint: a large drawing of three small-town Southern rustics by Carroll Cloar, a local artist, hangs over the bed, and next to it is a picture of Marcel Proust, the writer who stands at the top of Foote's literary pantheon (and whose entire *Remembrance of Things Past* Foote has read nine times since he was given the set at age seventeen). Wherever books are not crammed into the specially built shelves, there are records and CDs of mostly classical music.

This is the room where Foote has spent most days and nights since he and his wife, Gwyn, moved into the house in 1966. Close to nine of the twenty years that went into the writing of *The Civil War: A Narrative* were passed here, amid a clutter of at least three hundred more war-related books, stacks of note cards, and photographs of officers, politicians, and foot soldiers posted on every available inch of wall space. It was here, also, riding the beneficent high that came with completing his twenty-year labor, that Foote wrote his sixth novel, *September September*, a work remarkable for its portrayal of a black Memphis couple thrown into turmoil when their son is kidnapped by a trio of white ne'er-do-wells from the Mississippi Delta. And finally, it was here that Foote came up against his nemesis for the second time in his life: the block that has kept him from completing his intended magnum opus, *Two Gates to the City*, a family epic set in the Mississippi Delta. "It defeated me," Foote says laconically, "twice."

Because of that setback, Foote was not altogether put out by the attention he began to receive in the fall of 1990. In fact, he welcomed it—or at least much of it. Keeping his phone number listed and responding to most callers' queries, he also made a valiant effort to answer his mail. "After appearing on the tube, I'd receive two armloads of mail every day. There'd be a lot of requests for autographs, which I'd throw away—after removing the return postage. But there would always be five or six good letters that I felt obliged to respond to. After about six weeks of that nonsense, I realized I was becoming nothing but a damn answerer of letters. Then I remembered what Grant said when a friend asked him if he was still getting big stacks of mail. 'Not nearly so many as when I used to respond.' So I gave up answering."

Never a money-driven man and fortunate that his third wife came into a comfortable inheritance, Foote remains astonished by the documentary's effect on his income. Although *The Civil War* had been a steady seller over the years, his earnings tripled in 1990 and shot up to almost three-quarters of a million dollars in 1991, thanks both to hefty royalties and speaking fees. The former might have been even heftier if Foote's publisher, Random House, had heeded his early warnings. "I asked them to print up a few more copies of *The Civil War*, but they didn't listen. They couldn't even begin to meet the demand that first Christmas season after the show came on. I guess writers don't know a damn thing about publishing, but they sure know more than publishers and editors do."

Foote doesn't grieve over the missed opportunity. Apart from one extravagance, the purchase of a BMW, he lives a simple life and, in fact, has given a generous portion of his earnings to the library in his hometown of Greenville, Mississippi. Still, Foote would never say that the money and the recognition were unappreciated. Among the awards and honorary degrees that came his way after the show aired, he took keenest satisfaction from his induction into the American Academy of Arts and Letters in May of 1994. "It was Alfred Kazin who called to tell me I had been elected to the Academy, and I said, very ungraciously I'm afraid, 'I've been waiting twenty years to hear that.' I think he was astounded by my bad manners. And then I said, 'But I'm pleased to accept, because I know how pleased it would have made Walker [Percy].' Walker had tried during most of those years to get me in the Academy but couldn't do it. So I was reproaching them twice, you see, in one lick."

Foote laughs at the episode, but there is an undercurrent of rancor. The delayed Academy election hasn't been the only thing that has rankled over the years. He tells how he had fully expected to win the big literary prizes when the third volume of his one-and-a-half-million-word history was completed in 1974. But one by one the prizes were announced—the Pulitzer, the National Book Award, the Bancroft—and each went to somebody else. "I should have been prepared for it, because in 1929 three books appeared, *The Sound and the Fury*, *A Farewell to Arms*, and *Look Homeward, Angel*, and they gave the Pulitzer to Julia M. Peterkin for *Scarlet Sister Mary*. When you look at it more carefully, you see that there was no way any one of those three could win."

Foote, one senses, is a man long accustomed to disappointments. The first—and no doubt the deepest—was the death of his father, Shelby Dade Foote, when Shelby Dade Jr. was five. The year was 1922, and the family had just moved to Mobile, Alabama, Mr. Foote having received a promotion, the last in a series that had taken him up the ranks of the Armour meatpacking company. His rapid rise from shipping clerk to general manager of Southern operations had been all the more remarkable in light of the dissolute life that he had led as a young man, the overindulged scion of a once-wealthy Delta planter. But things had changed when he married Lillian Rosenstock in 1915. Lillian was the second of three daughters of Morris Rosenstock, a Viennese Jew who had made his way to Washington County, Mississippi, married the daughter of a plantation owner for whom he worked as a bookkeeper, and become a wealthy landowner himself. Patient, supportive, and wise, Lillian had made a good man of Shelby Foote, Sr., and also, according to his son, who was born November 17, 1916, a good and gentle father.

Mr. Foote's untimely death resulted from a bacterial infection that today would easily be subdued by antibiotics. The day Mr. Foote died, a Mr. Watts from the Armour company took young Shelby to a park near the hospital. There they sat in swings and Mr. Watts told him that his father "had gone away," a euphemism that even the five-year-old boy found too weaselly. "Does that mean he's dead?" Foote asked. "When he said yes," Foote recalls, "I had this feeling of absolute responsibility—that I had to be the man of the family—and so I said, 'Who will get the money?' "

There wasn't much money as it turned out, apart from a small life insurance settlement. So when the family moved back to Greenville, they lived in the house of Lillian's sister and brother-in-law, Maude and Mick Moyse, while Lillian helped run a gift shop and studied typing and the Pittman method of shorthand. When Foote finished the third grade, his mother took a secretarial job with Armour and Company in Pensacola, Florida. "I was a latchkey kid from fourth through sixth grade, but I liked it. In fact, I can't see anything but good in having been on my own. It taught me self-reliance." As they did in Greenville, Shelby and his mother attended a Reform synagogue, and Foote did so well in Sunday school classes that at age eleven he won a special prize, a fine edition of Dickens's *David Copperfield*, a book that made a profound impression. "I had read lots of children's books, but I had never read a really serious book. It was such a revelation to discover a world more real than the world I lived in. I knew David better than I knew anybody, including myself."

When the Footes moved back to Greenville in 1927 so that Lillian could help take care of her ailing father, Shelby was all but set in his ways. Bright, bookish, independent, he could also be brash, mischievous, and occasionally reckless. Once, while showing off with a pistol he had inherited from his father, he accidentally shot and killed his neighbors' dog—much to the horror of the neighbors, who feared they might be next. Foote had a rebellious streak, and some Greenvillians thought his mother spoiled him, but the only son sees matters somewhat differently: "My mother was strict, but the remarkable thing is that she never hurt my feelings, and God knows she had all sorts of occasions to tell me how bad I was. What she wanted was for me to be happy in whatever I chose to do. For a time, I thought I wanted to be an architect, and she would encourage me with my drawing—just as much as she would later, with my writing." This comes across, as Foote says it, with the force of great conviction, and one can guess why. The inner fortitude and confidence Foote needed for the lonely pursuit of elusive literary goals owe much to Lillian's wise and forgiving love.

Foote counts himself almost as fortunate for having spent so many of his early years in one of the most unusual towns in the South. Greenville, Mississippi, was a river town and a Delta town, heir to a history of floods, plague, war, and Reconstruction, and populated by a rich mix of peoples, including African Americans (who made up more than half of the fifteen thousand inhabitants in Foote's day), Chinese, Italians, Jews, and the usual assortment of Anglo-Saxons. And it was at least as unusual for its cultural vigor as it was for its diverse citizenry. In the 1930s, Ellery Sedgwick, the editor of the *Atlantic*, told the Greenville author David Cohn that Greenville had produced more writers for a town its size than any other in the world, and considering some of the town's products from that time and slightly later—Cohn, Hodding Carter, William Alexander Percy and his cousin Walker, Josephine Haxton, Charles Bell, Ben Wasson, and Foote himself—the claim doesn't seem overstated.

In many ways, Greenville's Jewish community set the town's unusually vigorous tone. They sponsored the arts, hosted the informal salons, and helped support one of the strongest public school systems in the nation. Political as well as cultural leaders, they were assimilated in the upper levels of Greenville society. "There were more Jews than Baptists in the Greenville Country Club," Foote explains. In this remarkably tolerant and progressive town—progressive, that is, up to but never straying beyond a paternalistic concern for the securely segregated black population—people got along amiably and knew almost everybody.

In Greenville, the future writer acquired what he would later consider the most important element of his work—a sense of place and history, the essential "platform," as he calls it, of a rich fictional world. Washington County would become the Jordan County of his fiction; Greenville, his Bristol. Among the family histories he drew on to stock his fiction was that of his father's family, particularly the colorful story of Huger Foote, who had come to the Delta a decade after the Civil War to manage four plantations owned by his father, Hezekiah. It was Huger's story, his amassing and subsequent loss of a large fortune, and his reputation as a card player and trapshoot artist, that would provide the raw material for Foote's apprentice novel, *Tournament*. A greatly transformed Morris Rosenstock would also appear in that novel, cast as a tragic figure whose fear of a financial scandal drives him to suicide.

Another family in Greenville, the Percys, proved to be a decisive influence on Foote's life. Senator LeRoy Percy, the son of a Civil War hero, was already something of a legend when Foote and his mother returned to Greenville. The former U.S. senator had led the resistance to the Ku Klux Klan and was one of the people responsible for Greenville's growth and prosperity. He and his wife died in 1929, but their only surviving son, William Alexander Percy, a published poet, a decorated war veteran, and a lawyer, took over his father's role as a community leader. And in the summer of 1930, Foote was pulled directly into the Percy orbit when Will Percy approached him at the country club and told him that three of his kinsmen were coming to spend the summer, two of them Foote's age, and that he hoped Foote would come to the house and help them enjoy their stay. Foote was only too happy to do so and quickly became friends with all three boys, Phinizy, Roy, and particularly the oldest, Walker.

It was not an easy time for the Percy boys—their father had committed suicide the summer before—but Shelby and Walker busied themselves with their common interests, reading and building model airplanes and generally "helling about" the Delta. When the Percy boys and their mother decided to accept "Uncle Will's" invitation to remain in his house, Foote became something close to a fourth brother, and like the Percy boys, he fell under Uncle Will's spell. As busy as he was, Will Percy always made time for them, reading aloud from his favorite poets or introducing the boys to his favorite composers. Most important, he gave them free run of a remarkable house, visited regularly by poets, novelists, politicians, and just about every touring journalist and sociologist engaged in making sense of the South.

A year behind Walker Percy in school (later two, when Foote was forced to repeat his senior year), Foote shadowed his slightly older peer in a number of ways. Like Percy, Foote wrote for the school newspaper, the *Pica* (he was its editor in chief in 1935, when it tied for first place among the nation's high school newspapers). Like Percy, he too would attend the University of North Carolina at Chapel Hill—but only after a struggle. Foote's trouble with authority figures brought him into repeated scrapes with his high school principal, E. J. Leuckenbach. Leuckenbach not only suspended Foote on several occasions but went so far as to expel him when one of his teachers alleged that he had made improper advances. It turned out that the allegations were false (the teacher had suffered from a mental breakdown), and Foote was reinstated, but Leuckenbach did not relent in his vendetta. The next year, Leuckenbach caught him in the *Pica* room during PE period reading Joyce's *Ulysses*—a "dirty book," Leuckenbach declared. Unfazed, Foote informed the principal that the Supreme Court itself had ruled that the book was not obscene. Leuckenbach was not one to be mocked. When Foote applied to Chapel Hill, the principal sent the admissions office a letter saying that under no circumstance should they accept him. The rejection came as a shock, but Foote was undaunted. The next fall, he showed up at the registrar's office and begged the university officials to give him a chance, which they reluctantly did. That wouldn't be the last time Foote would thumb his nose at the principal: Leuckenbach would appear in Foote's novella *Child by Fever* as the absurd figure of Professor Rosenback, nicknamed Frozen Back because of his way of walking "with a stiff Prussian carriage as if he were pacing off the distance between barriers for a duel."

After just two months at Chapel Hill, Foote realized that he had no interest in earning a degree. From then on, he ignored all classes that failed to interest him, even those that were required. "I'd drop in on all kinds of history and English classes, and you couldn't get me out of the library—nine floors of stacks, where I prowled around pretending to be a graduate student." Besides following his own curriculum, Foote became a regular contributor to the *Carolina Magazine,* producing fiction that bore markings of his idol William Faulkner as well as his own later work. The editors of the magazine took everything he gave them, except for a story whose treatment of miscegenation proved too daring for the time. Prolific as he was, Foote did not think of himself as a writer. Writers, in his view, occupied another realm, and when in his sophomore year he happened to see the gigantic figure of Thomas Wolfe coming up the stairs of the library toward him, he was too awed to speak or nod.

Foote did, however, have a sense of himself as an outsider. It was partly chosen and partly thrust upon him, the gift and burden of his Jewish grandfather's heritage. Even in Greenville, that most tolerant of towns, he had learned that there were, as he put it, "certain disadvantages to being Jewish." His father's mother urged him to become an Episcopalian, and he would do so during the war. If he had any uncertainties about the "disadvantages" as a younger man, Chapel Hill provided clarification. The Sigma Alpha Epsilon fraternity, to which his friends Walker and Roy Percy belonged, blackballed him because of his religion, and the fraternity that accepted him, Alpha Tau Omega, grew less friendly when it learned from a Greenville alumnus that he was not a Christian. "My standing wasn't very good anyway," Foote says. "I had a reputation for saying the blessing somewhat irreverently. The president of the fraternity—the Worthy Master—came to me near the end of my freshman year and asked, 'How do you feel about Jesus?' I said, 'I'm all for him. He interests me very much. My problem is with his father.' " Later, the Worthy Master asked him how he felt about being an ATO, and Foote admitted that he was not sure whether he should return the following year. "Well, don't bother," the president informed him. "We've decided we don't want you as a brother." It suited Foote just fine to live in a boardinghouse his sophomore year, but such experiences left him chastened and possibly contributed to views about race that most of his white friends considered scandalous. On a bus trip to New York in 1937, Foote suggested to Walker Percy that segregation might one day have to be dismantled. His friend, who would later become an avid integrationist himself, was shocked: "How can you, a white Southerner, say such a thing?"

Foote left Chapel Hill at the end of his second year and took a string of jobs back in Greenville—construction work on a nearby bridge and proofreading at Hodding Carter's *Delta Star* (later the *Delta-Democrat Times*)—while he began work on his first novel, *Tournament*. Betty Carter, whose tireless work on the business and advertising fronts helped keep her husband's paper solvent, remembers Foote as a free spirit. "You'd look up at work sometimes, and he'd be gone, nowhere to be found. Then two days later, he'd show up and tell you he'd gone to New Orleans to listen to jazz. 'Shelby,' I'd say to him, 'you don't listen to jazz, you dance to it.' Turns out he was right, I later realized."

Foote, meanwhile, was working diligently on a novel whose hybrid style blended elements of Wolfe, Faulkner, Joyce, and Proust. By early 1939, he had a manuscript of *Tournament* ready and sent it to Alfred A. Knopf, Will Percy's publisher. An editor there was impressed by the twenty-three-year-old writer's gifts but concluded that the book wouldn't sell—perhaps because of the uncompromising bleakness of its vision. He urged Foote to put the book aside and work on something a little more marketable, but Foote by then had other things on his mind. Closely following Hitler's progress, he had joined the Mississippi National Guard in 1939, and the next year his division, the Thirty-first "Dixie" Division, was mobilized for national service.

Foote's war years would end with another disappointment, but the military experience proved invaluable to the future war historian. "Just knowing Close Order Drill and the Manual of Arms is a huge help when you're writing about the army," Foote says. Not surprisingly, he approached military life in a bookish way. "I was fascinated by Napoleon and read everything I could about him. I also had Freeman's *Lee* with me all the way through the war. I began to understand war and campaigns."

But even while his fascination with military matters grew, Foote ran into his old problem with authority. Selected for Officer Candidate School, he came out with his lieutenant bars and soon was promoted to captain. In 1943 he was sent to Northern Ireland to command Battery A of the Fiftieth Field Artillery of the Fifth Division, slated for the eventual invasion of occupied Europe. "A battery commander had four 105 Howitzers, about 130 men, and about fourteen trucks, and that suited me just fine." The men liked their commander, whose affection for them was obvious—perhaps too much so for his own good. One day the brigade chief of staff, a lieutenant colonel, showed up to inspect Foote's unit and began to berate one of Foote's men for not polishing his boots. The soldier explained that rain had dulled them, but the colonel called him a liar. Foote, hearing this, was furious and ordered his superior to apologize. The colonel, a West Pointer, did so, but Foote could see the anger in his eyes. "From then on he and his friends were gunning for me."

It didn't take them long to get their man. Foote had met and fallen in love with a Protestant woman named Tess Lavery, the daughter of a Belfast busman, who happened to live almost exactly fifty-two miles from Foote's encampment. Technically, the limit on passes was fifty miles, but the rule was winked at, particularly since Foote's encampment was a little farther from the city than the others in the brigade. After one of Foote's weekends in Belfast, however, his newly made enemies seized upon the technicality. He was court-martialed for falsifying an official document and summarily discharged from the army just months before D-Day. "It destroyed me," Foote says. "I couldn't even go home. I went to New York and got a job working the night desk for AP. But I felt that I had missed the big event of my lifetime, and I felt terrible that I wasn't with my men."

Tess Lavery came to New York and the two were married. Walker Percy, then between tuberculosis sanatoriums and teaching at Columbia's College of Physicians and Surgeons, stood as

Shelby Foote, Greenville, 1949. *Franke Keating*

his best man. But domesticity and a desk job wouldn't do when the war was still on. So in January 1945, Foote enlisted in the Marines and went through basic training and combat intelligence training. Assigned to a unit bound for the Pacific theater, he reached the West Coast just as Japan surrendered. Having missed combat twice, Foote returned to Greenville with his bride and took up residence in Allen Court Apartments, where he would live until he moved to Memphis in late 1953.

Life in Greenville moved at a convivial small-town tempo. Foote wrote ads for the local radio station, WJPR, while Tess worked as a clerk at a department store. Much of his free time Foote passed among a circle of friends that included Kenneth Haxton, a businessman and composer, and his then-wife Josephine; Ben Wasson, the literary editor of the *Delta-Democrat Times;* and Walker Percy, who was living in Greenville while trying to determine what to do next now that medicine no longer seemed an option. Outwardly, it was a pleasant enough life, but things were going badly at home. Foote's marriage, shaky to begin with, ended abruptly in 1946.

Perhaps because he now had more time to himself, Foote returned to the *Tournament* manuscript and found parts of it that looked respectable. Extracting an episode, Foote gave it to Ben Wasson, who sold it to the *Saturday Evening Post* for $750. Another, longer submission to the same magazine—a story that eventually became "Ride Out" in the novel *Jordan County*—brought an even larger check for $1,500. Feeling confident, Foote sent in a third and even longer story, but this time the manuscript was returned with a note "informing me and Ben that the *Post* did not publish stories containing implications of incest."

Making the best of the rejection, Foote decided to bid farewell to magazines and work on something longer—on what turned out to be the novel *Shiloh*. Meanwhile, New York literary agents had gotten wind of the new Greenville talent, and one of them, Jacques Chambrun, invited Foote to come to New York to talk. Foote did, and was introduced to the editors of *Dial*, who liked the manuscript but told Foote—echoing the earlier advice from Knopf—that it would not sell. They wondered what he was working on next, and Foote summarized the plot of *Tournament*, for which they promptly paid a $1,500 advance. Foote returned to Greenville and in three months reworked the novel, "removing," as he later explained, "nearly all the Joyce, most of the Wolfe, and some of the Faulkner. What Proust I encountered I either left in or enlarged on."

At the end of 1948, with his first novel ready for publication, Foote married Marguerite (Peggy) Dessommes, the daughter of a Memphis physician. "She was bright and charming," Josephine Haxton says, even while hinting at what might have been a cause of friction between Foote and his second wife. "Peggy made a trip home to Memphis and her friends up there asked her what she'd been reading in Greenville. She told them Thomas Mann, and they asked who that was. 'Thank God,' Peggy said, 'I'm home at last.' " Peggy might also have required more pampering than Foote was able to provide. "She seemed to sleep a lot," Betty Carter recollects.

The marriage lasted only four years, but those years produced a daughter, Margaret, and an outpouring of fiction. Foote's third-written but second-published novel, *Follow Me Down,* based on a murder and trial that took place in Greenville in 1941, appeared in 1950. And his fourth and possibly best novel, *Love in a Dry Season,* came out in 1951. *Shiloh,* a fictionalized account of the Civil War battle, made its belated appearance in 1952.

But even at its best, the writing life proved hard. Reviewers were not uniformly enchanted by Foote's work. Some faulted his bleak view of humanity, while others complained of "immorality." Modest sales following such reviews did not augur an easy living. But Foote received praise and encouragement from the people who meant most to him, including William Faulkner. Foote had first read Faulkner's work in 1932 and had met the man himself in 1938, stopping by the writer's house, Rowan Oak, while on a road trip to Tennessee with Walker Percy. Eventually, he established a cordial friendship with his literary idol, had a dinner or two at Rowan Oak, and once led Faulkner on a tour of Shiloh. (Perhaps the most memorable thing about their trip was Faulkner's ability to track down a bootlegger and a bottle of whiskey in the town of Corinth on a blue-law Sunday.) Faulkner, for his part, came to admire Foote's work, even though, after reading *Tournament,* he told friends that he would like Foote more if he sounded less like Faulkner and more like Foote. *Follow Me Down* earned higher marks from the master. "It's good," Faulkner told Foote, before adding, "Do better on the next one." His praise for *Shiloh,* however, was unequivocal. He rated it even higher than Stephen Crane's *Red Badge of Courage.*

Faulkner was not the only person to suggest that Foote's work suffered from his influence, but far too much has been made of the charge over the years. Though Foote's prose has its rococo moments, it is more restrained than Faulkner's, the sentences less loopy and the diction more precise. Foote built his fictional landscape out of his patch of Mississippi in some of the same ways that Faulkner built his, but their respective patches—the Delta and the hill country—were very different indeed. Washington County was a place of sharp social contrasts, from high planter culture to a quite cosmopolitan urban scene; it also contained great economic extremes, with wealthy planters, professionals, and merchants at one end and landless sharecroppers at the other. While Faulkner's social landscape had similar extremes, they were tempered by a large yeoman class of independent small farmers, a group far less present in Delta society and in Foote's fiction. Lacking this stability of the middle, Foote's world comes across as even more precariously modern than Faulkner's. One finds in the former little of the nobility of spirit that flickers through Faulkner's stories and novels—and even less regard for the faded claims of honor and virtue.

Foote, like many writers, has always voiced discomfort with talk about the meaning of his novels. As he told his friend Walker Percy, with whom he engaged in a lifelong debate about the means and ends of art, his foremost goal was "to teach people how to *see*. I want to impart a 'quality of vision.' " But if there is a recurrent theme of his work, it may be that life in the modern world is a gamble, a test of chance, a tournament, in which most people lose and are forced to adapt to defeat, sometimes in the most bizarre ways. If the tortured accommodation to Fortune's fatal turn is a characteristic of Southern fiction in general, where defeat and the Lost Cause are built into cultural memory, it is even more prominently a part of the Delta imagination. Inhabiting a vast floodplain, Delta people have long played the biggest crap game of all, gambling their lives and prosperity on the hope that the waters of the periodically swollen Mississippi will not breach the levees and leave the region a vast lake—as happened in 1927, the summer Foote and his mother moved back to Greenville. Such facts of geography inevitably shape a view of the world.

While Foote's austere literary vision may have kept him from achieving great commercial success, his literary confidence was brimming during the early postwar years. In a letter to Walker Percy written on December 22, 1950, while Foote was deep in the middle of *Love in a Dry Season,* the author practically crowed over his achievement:

> Something happened to me this week. I approached work sluggishly Monday morning and all of a sudden something took me by the hair: I had to hold back to keep from covering reams of paper with gouts of words. By yesterday afternoon (Thursday) I had produced 5000 of the best words I ever wrote.... I am beginning to feel a part of what comes from being in the American tradition.

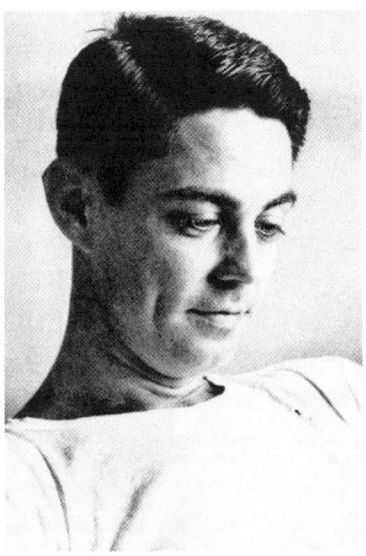

Shelby Foote, Greenville, 1951. *Franke Keating*

On such heights it was difficult to remain. After finishing *Love in a Dry Season* and seeing *Shiloh* into print, Foote embarked on what he hoped would be his epic of the Delta, *Two Gates to the City*, and for several months in 1951 and early 1952 things went promisingly. But then disaster: his second marriage blew up, Peggy took their daughter and moved back to Memphis, and by the end of 1952 Foote was involved in further romantic woes and unable to write. In a note to Percy, he unloaded his despair: "I'm done with it for now, all right. 1952 was pure nightmare, and here comes 1953. Peace be with us" (December 26, 1952).

But 1953 only brought more frustrations and his own move to Memphis, where he settled on the bluffs overlooking the Mississippi River in a neighborhood inhabited mainly by middle-class blacks. There he salvaged parts of his big novel for a more modest book, *Jordan County*, which Foote called a novel but which was, in truth, more a cycle of stories linked by common geography. Then came perhaps the biggest turn of fate. Bennett Cerf at Random House asked Foote if he would be interested in writing a short history of the Civil War for the centennial. Foote accepted but soon discovered that he couldn't make it short. In fact, he saw that it would have to be something massive, and he presented Cerf with an outline of a three-volume narrative history. More surprising than his counterproposal, perhaps, was Cerf's decision to accept it. The next twenty years consisted of rarely interrupted labor on the history. Along the way, Foote took time out for a film script commissioned by Stanley Kubrick (but never produced); a stint at Arena Stage in Washington, D.C., where, as a Ford Foundation fellow, he adapted a story from *Jordan County* for the stage; a year in Gulf Shores, Alabama, where he incurred the wrath of local Klansmen by criticizing segregationists and sporting a Lyndon Johnson sticker on the bumper of his car; and a depressingly unproductive half year of teaching at Hollins College. ("How anybody can teach and write is a mystery to me," Foote says. "I couldn't get anything done with all that talking.") Most important, two years after starting the trilogy, Foote married Gwyn Rainer, a woman of uncommon intelligence and striking good looks. This time the marriage took, and a son, Huger Lee Foote II, was born in 1961. Gwyn Foote, independent in her ways, knew how to live with a man possessed.

And possessed Foote had to be in order to bring off so large an undertaking—and to do so without the help of so much as a secretary or a research assistant. Besides the endless reading, the extensive travel to important battlefields (partially subsidized by three Guggenheim grants), and the tremendous intellectual labor of synthesis, Foote never lost sight of his primary intention: to shape a narrative that would allow contemporary readers to experience the drama of the Civil War, to see it through its characters roundly presented. If Foote held himself to high historical standards, he held himself to even higher literary ones: the *Iliad* in Richmond Lattimore's translation "put a Greekless author in close touch with his model," Foote himself acknowledged.

What was the value of Foote's abandoning fiction for twenty years of historical writing? It might seem a silly question, considering the masterpiece those years yielded. And there was little doubt that it was a masterpiece. Even though the big prizes eluded him at the completion of the trilogy—perhaps because literati and historians were baffled by a work that fell between their respective fields—critics, middle- and high-brow alike, saw they had a great work before them. What the eminent scholar of Southern letters Louis D. Rubin, Jr., said of the book—"It seems very unlikely to me that it will ever be superseded"—was more or less echoed by *Newsweek*, which declared that no further histories of the war would need to be written. ("That's wrong, of course," Foote says when I bring this up. "Every generation has to do its version of that war. There will always be different ways of seeing it. The Vietnam War has to change the way the future will see the Civil War, for example.")

It could be argued—and has been, by Foote himself among

others—that *The Civil War* was not really an abandonment of what he had been working toward in his fiction. Twenty years ago, the critic George Garrett wrote that Foote's history was not "a turning away from one form to another; rather it is the rarer example of a mature artist adapting and assimilating all of his skills and applying these to a different sort of problem." In fact, it was not entirely a "different sort of problem." If Foote's vision in his fiction is often uncharitable, it is because he sees a society deficient in love, fellow feeling, imagination, bravery, and self-sacrifice: in short, a society ruled increasingly by "me-firstism" and the main chance. The countervailing forces—faith, community, and tradition—have been eroded by the usual pressures of modernity, aggravated by the special burden of the South, its lamentations over the Lost Cause, and its related inability to confront, much less correct, the legacy of slavery. The grip of the past is felt like a cold, fatal hand in Foote's fictional world.

But in *The Civil War,* Foote sought to return to the defining moment in the South's and the larger national past, when Americans were compelled to resolve their differences—and the contradiction within the American Creed—through force of arms. The tragedies of the war were many, including the failure of its success—that is, as Foote explains, the nation's failure to do anything to help the newly liberated people to become productive, self-sufficient citizens: "They just set them free, four million or more, and didn't do a damn thing to help them make their lives, despite the piddling efforts of the Freedmen's Bureaus." But the other tragedy is that the horrible, destructive war brought out much that was noble and self-sacrificing in people on both sides, something that would have never been seen outside so mortal a conflict, and it was this tragedy, the demonstration of greatness amid waste, that Foote sought to dramatize and make visible in his narrative history.

"I want everybody everywhere to read it so they can learn to love their country," Foote told Percy when he finished the trilogy.

How well he succeeded can be measured not only by the work's effect on its many readers but also by how much it tempered Foote's own view of the world. *September September*, the only novel he has completed since he finished his history, has its dark side, but it is ultimately an affirmative novel, nowhere more obviously than in its depiction of the rebirth of a moribund marriage. The union of Eben and Martha Kinship, the black middle-class Memphians at the center of the novel, seems fated for slow death until Eben stands up for what he believes, doing what he thinks should be done to recover his son from the kidnappers rather than deferring to the strategy of his overbearing father-in-law. Such a vision of renewal was, in Foote's case, hard and truly earned.

George Garrett was also shrewd about what Foote risked in attempting to write a historical narrative of such epic proportions: "Even assuming the good fortune of living to complete his

Shelby Foote with his wife, Gwyn, in Paris, April 1985. *Huger Foote*

marathon enterprise and doing it tolerably well, the odds were strong, if not overwhelming, that in a time of instant attention and instant oblivion, he would find himself and his work cheerfully forgotten. And to a degree that has happened, though there have been a few critics through the years who have preserved the memory of his reputation and accomplishments."

The reasons for Foote's relative neglect—at least up until Burns's documentary—also have much to do with literary fashion. For if the problem Foote applied himself to in his history was not so different from what he was up to in his earlier, fictional labors, it was strikingly different from the dominant literary preoccupations of our time: that is, the depiction of an individual consciousness caught in the web of the present moment. Foote's fiction—and particularly the narrative voices he developed in his fiction—had set him on the path toward an even more ambitious engagement with history, with a large sweep of time, and with the great Proustian theme of time's effect on consciousness.

Foote's work is all about voice, which is a way of both seeing and telling things. That voice—disillusioned yet forgiving, humorous and sometimes savage—is not simply engaged with time but comes close to being the voice of time itself. We hear it no less clearly in *The Civil War* than we do in Foote's greatest fictional moments. Reading *The Civil War,* one is always aware of the narrator—no less, in fact, than viewers were aware of Foote himself when he appeared in Burns's documentary. In both, one hears a voice shaped by a particular experience of the first two-thirds of the twentieth century— years that include two world wars, a great depression, and a social struggle that addressed the contradictions that the previous century's war had left unresolved—telling about an event in the more distant past that continues to affect him, and us, to this day. The strands of time and consciousness are tightly wound in the man, artfully braided in his work. It is their union that gives Foote such powers of enchantment, and his authority.

THE VOICE OF AUTHORITY

by Jon Meacham

Foote's truly popular fame came late. On the evening of Sunday, September 23, 1990, the filmmaker Ken Burns debuted his epic nine-part series *The Civil War*. In it Foote served, as Burns notes in the following interview with Jon Meacham, as a kind of "force field"—a commentator so powerful that his visage and voice linger down the decades.

MEACHAM: When did you first become aware of Shelby Foote?

BURNS: It was Christmas 1984, and I was in Michigan with my family. I had just finished reading a novel about Gettysburg—*The Killer Angels*, by Michael Shaara—and I came out of my bedroom into the living room and told my father, "I know what my next project is going to be." "What's that?" he asked. "The Civil War," I said. "What part of the Civil War?" he asked. "All of it," I said, and he basically waved his hand in the air, as if to say, "There goes my crazy son again." But I meant it. I was hooked.

And so I started reading everything—Bruce Catton in particular. One evening, Robert Penn Warren in Connecticut—he had just helped me on a film I had made about Huey Long—called me, interrupting dinner. I had told him awhile back I was thinking about the Civil War. In that amazing, smoky Kentucky accent, Red said down the phone, in almost a chant, "Thinkin' about the Civil War... Thinkin' about the Civil War... Thinkin' about the Civil War." Then he said, "Well, if you're thinkin' about the Civil War, you've got to talk to Shelby Foote."

That was the beginning. I got the books, and I realized almost immediately that here was our Gibbon, our Macauley. I called Shelby in Memphis—his number was listed then, and later, even when he was so famous the phone would ring in the middle of the night with someone wanting to argue about Bull Run—and asked if I could come down.

He spoke of the war in human terms. He knew everything—not just the battles and the strategy and the tactics and the politics, but what the soldiers ate, and wore, and felt. He knew what the weather was like on each battlefield on the day of the clash, knew what was in bloom and how the light played in that particular season, because he walked those fields on the precise date the fighting had taken place. For him history was totally tactile, totally human.

In our film, he gave us a human dimension and a Southern dimension without a Southern bias. On that first trip, we went from Memphis to Shiloh—stopping, of course, for the best barbecue, Shelby claimed, in West Tennessee; he was always doing that, making great claims for barbecue or catfish—and the moment we walked onto the field it was as if a maestro had taken over a symphony orchestra that had been invisible and silent until that moment. He could make us see Nathan Bedford Forrest, make us feel the rush of battle.

You would ask him a question like "How was the war going for the South in 1864?" and while a lot of historians would have given you a fairly dry, big-picture answer, Shelby would say, "Well, you see, they had this thing they called 'sloosh,' a mix of bacon grease and cornmeal batter that soldiers would roll into a snakelike thing and cook over a campfire with a bayonet or ramrod. And they ate a lot of sloosh." It was that kind of detail that made Shelby so important to us. I remember asking him about U. S. Grant, and he said Grant had what they called "four o'clock in the morning" courage. By which he meant that you could wake him up at four in the morning and tell him that the enemy had turned his right flank, and he'd be as cool as a cucumber, make a decision, and be at peace with it.

MEACHAM: Do you remember the moment of filming when Foote called the war the "cross-roads of our being"? It's a line of Foote's that I remember so clearly and quote a good deal. I had never heard a better description of the war, and I had been hearing about the war my whole life.

BURNS: It was amazing, wasn't it? That remark is from the first film in the series, in the opening. It is Shelby's first on-camera bite, and it really set the stage for everything that followed. It came early in our interviewing, too, on an early roll of film. One of the things about Shelby in our work was how he really became a force field that prevented anyone else—and this is not to take away from any of the great people who worked with us as well—from moving in the same orbit with him.

MEACHAM: So is the lesson that it takes a great novelist to write great history? Or at least great historians need to have novelistic skills?

BURNS: It would seem so, wouldn't it? That and bourbon, which I loved to drink with Shelby, until I quit.

MEACHAM: Foote was writing in the most difficult years of the civil rights movement. To what extent do you think his narrative reflected the unfinished business of the war—business that took us an additional century to settle?

BURNS: Jim Crow was, I think, a huge, huge presence for Shelby. And he saw it in complex terms, as a kind of moderate Southerner, not in caricatures. He was like Red Warren and C. Vann Woodward—Southerners who knew the right thing to do, but who also understood why things were the way they were. Someone once said that slavery lay coiled like a snake under the table at the Constitutional Convention, and that's true.

MEACHAM: What was your relationship with Foote like after the film?

BURNS: We kept drinking [laughs]. We talked three or four times a year, and I would see him in Memphis. Once, when his royalties check came in from Random House after the film had driven sales of the trilogy far, far beyond what they had been before, the phone rang. It was Shelby, and he drawled in that voice of his, "Ken, you made me a millionaire."

He would tell me about all the proposals of marriage that materialized once the film was broadcast—he was touched, but passed, being happily married.

When I think of him, I think of those beautiful pages of his text, written in a virtual calligraphy. Or his remark—so true—that "God is the greatest dramatist." Shelby was thinking of how no novelist—and surely no historian—would ever have imagined such an end for Lincoln. There the president was, finally victorious, taking a night off. Taking a night off to go to the theater. Only Shelby would think of that as the work of a providential dramatist, but he was right.

Once—I think it was in Jackson, Mississippi—I walked up to

Shelby's friend Walker Percy. Percy had that great brow and that great shock of white hair—a formidable figure. I asked him, "Mr. Percy, why do so many great writers come from the South?"

Percy stood up at his full height, threw back his shoulders, and said, "Because we lost."

In most of history, the story of the past is written by the victors, but Southerners wrote our history—Southerners like Shelby who felt the tragedy of it all, the blood and the sacrifice and the human toll from Ford's Theatre to Grant's tent to Forrest's Critter Company. That was his story, and ours.

Editing Shelby Foote

by Bob Loomis

In the early 1950s, Bennett Cerf sent a letter to Shelby Foote asking him if he would consider writing a one-volume narrative history of the Civil War. At that point, Shelby had written five novels, but those books promised a unique knowledge of and affinity for the war and its times. Shelby liked the idea immediately. He thought it would be a good break before beginning the future novels he had planned.

By 1956, however, Shelby began to realize what a daunting project he had taken on. He wrote us that he did not see how he could finish the book he now wanted to produce in one volume. He thought it would take at least three volumes and, of course, many more years to complete. He said he would understand if we could not go along with that and he would be happy to pay us back the advance. Thank God Bennett immediately saw the merit in Shelby's new ambition for the book, and we drew up a new contract.

Shelby was a disciplined worker, writing every day until about four-thirty in the afternoon. He wrote all of the million and a half words in longhand—with a special wide-tipped pen and India ink on unruled paper (he once told me that he thought he had bought up the last supply of India ink in the United States). The result looked like a medieval manuscript. He then had that first marvelous-looking manuscript typed, made a few small corrections and additions, and sent it in to Random House.

He had read widely, of course, in the literature, but he primarily plowed the treasures in the 128-volume *War of the Rebellion,* which was a compilation of the official records of the Union and the Confederate armies. He also kept by his side the thirty-volume official records of the Union and Confederate navies. Each manuscript was complete with maps, all drawn by Shelby himself. I thought they were good enough to be published as they were, but we had them redone by an exacting calligrapher by the name of George Annand. The full-color endpaper maps were particularly marvelous, showing the sweep and movement of the armies and navies of both sides over many months, all on one page.

On the walls of Shelby's workroom in Memphis were dozens and dozens of portraits of the men he was writing about. They became his constant companions over the years. Without question they contributed to the book's depth and intimacy.

That first volume, *Fort Sumter to Perryville,* was like nothing else I had ever seen. It was incredibly precise in its presentation—and I should add here, of course, that Shelby was incapable of writing a bad sentence. It was also a narrative both magnificent and authoritative. Uniquely, it had no footnotes or chapter notes, or even a bibliography.

Shelby took such extraordinary care with this text that when the manuscript for volume two, *Fredericksburg to Meridian,* came in, I suggested that it be put through directly to the printer without copyediting it—except to mark it up for style. This is a most important stage for a manuscript, in which style, capitalization, internal contradictions, repetitions, and redundancies are all flagged. There was a throwing up of hands in the copyediting department,

Handwritten manuscript page in India Ink.

of course—no one had ever done that before—but we did go ahead and set it "as is" and sure enough there were no problems at all when the galleys came in. We did the same thing for volume three, *Red River to Appomattox,* as well. To my personal knowledge, we never had to make any corrections in future printings.

> *for Bob Loomis, at Random:*

Late afternoon of a raw, gusty day in early spring — March 8, a Tuesday, 1864 — the desk clerk at Willard's Hotel, just down Pennsylvania Avenue from the White House, glanced up to find an officer accompanied by a boy of thirteen facing him across the polished oak of the registration counter and inquiring whether he could get a room. "A short, round-shouldered man in a very tarnished major general's uniform," he seemed to a bystanding witness to have "no gait, no station, no manner," to present instead, with his ill-fitting jacket cut full in the skirt and his high-crowned hat set level on his head, a conglomerate, somewhat threadbare, not quite down-at-heels impression of "rough, light-brown whiskers, a blue eye, and a rather scrubby look withal ... as if he was out of office and on half pay; with nothing to do but hang round the entry of Willard's, cigar in mouth." Discerning so much of this as he chose, together perhaps with the bystander's added observation that the applicant had "rather the look of a man who did, or once did, take a little too much to drink," the clerk was no more awed by the stranger's rank than he was attracted by his aspect. This was, after all, Willard's, the best known hostelry in Washington. There had been by now close to five hundred Union generals, and of these the majority, particularly among those with what was defined as "station," had checked in and out of here in the past three wartime years. In the course of its recent and rapid growth, under the management of a pair of Vermont brothers who gave it their name along with their concern, it had swallowed whole, together with much other adjacent real estate, a former Presbyterian church; the President-elect himself had stayed here throughout the ten days preceding **his** inauguration, making of its Parlor 6 a "little White House," and it was here, one dawn two years ago in one of its upper rooms, that Julia Ward Howe had written her "Battle Hymn of the Republic," the anthem for the crusade the new President had begun to design as soon as he took office. Still, bright or tarnished, stars were stars; a certain respect was owed, if not to the man who wore them, then in any case to the rank they signified; the clerk replied at last that he would give him what he had, a small top-floor room, if that would do. It would, the other said, and when the register was given its practiced half-circle twirl he signed without delay. The desk clerk turned it back again, still maintaining the accustomed condescending air he was about to lose in shock when he read what the weathered applicant had written: "U.S.Grant & Son — Galena, Illinois."

> — *Opening paragraph,*
> *Volume III, The Civil War.*
> *Shelby Foote : September*
> *1965.*

Opening paragraph from *Red River to Appomattox*, typed after initially being handwritten, 1965.

I mentioned that there were no sources or bibliography, which took some getting used to. Shelby, however, finally wrote a two-and-a-half page note at the end of volume three in which he listed some of the books he found most useful to him.

Inexplicably—and shamefully—Shelby never received a

Pulitzer Prize or a National Book Award. It has occurred to me more than once that perhaps the reason was that *The Civil War* did not have the paraphernalia deemed necessary for most history books of that period. Shelby was also an outsider, remember, not an academic or a professional historian. But he had accomplished something far greater than any of the other writers about the war in re-creating and making it live again in the world around us. In his note at the end of volume three, he quoted Chaucer when he said, "Farewell my book and my devotion."

It was indeed a devotion and it took four times longer to finish than the war itself.

A Reader's Appreciaton

by Don Graham

More than thirty years ago, my brother gave me Shelby Foote's *The Civil War* as a gift. He said a learned friend had told him it was the best book on the war.

I decided I would dip into it and began, as Jefferson Davis resigned from the Senate. To my astonishment, I found myself reading on and on, enthralled, all the way to the end.

The book was amazing enough that I knew I would return to it. And last year I did, in a different format. Wherever I drove, Grover Gardner's voice reading the whole of *The Civil War* accompanied me. It is just as good the second time through.

I am not a "Civil War buff" and am certainly not learned. Instead, I am lucky; lucky to have encountered this great book at a time when I could read it all.

This is a reader's book, not a scholar's. There are no footnotes and not even a complete bibliography. There is only the story.

In his note at the end of the last volume, Foote refers in passing to *The Civil War* as "this iliad." He was probably being self-deprecating but the analogy is not a bad one.

Over the centuries, many great things, and many bad ones, have been done in America and by Americans. The Civil War dwarfs them all. For four years, millions of men, ancestors to many of us, roamed up and down the southeastern quarter of the United States in a war that decided the fate of the country. There was slaughter on a scale unimaginable until then: political, racial, and economic.

Foote published his first volume in 1958; he was, as they say, a man of his time. Slavery plays a role in the book, but slaves do not appear much. Nathan Bedford Forrest is lionized for his military exploits; his postwar role as an early member of the Ku Klux Klan and perhaps its leader is ignored.

Foote understands the importance of politics: the book begins with Jefferson Davis leaving the Senate and ends with Davis's death in 1889. His last postwar chapters may be his best of all. Lincoln's and Davis's cabinets and Congresses are (of course) important actors in the story, though not its heroes.

Most of this long book takes place in army camps and battlefields (and on a few ships as well). Our Homer knows where to focus, and quickly reminds us that we have met obscure brigade and division commanders before: at New Market, General Franz Sigel longs for "his first victory since Pea Ridge, out in Arkansas more than two years ago." As Lieutenant General John B. Hood relieves General Joseph E. Johnston before Atlanta, the younger man's body recites part of his career: "Gettysburg had cost him the use of his left arm, paralyzed by a fragment of bursting shell as he charged the Devil's Den, and at Chickamauga his right leg had been amputated so close to the hip that from then on he had to be strapped to ride a horse."

Reading this story will remind you of the utter unpredictability of events. The victorious army suffered defeat after humiliating defeat; no one in any camp saw much hope for Lincoln in early 1863, as the war dragged into its third year, nor in mid-1864 as he faced his reelection.

As the war becomes larger, so does the book. Perhaps Foote is self-consciously Homeric: Oliver O. Howard is always "the one-armed general" and Ben Butler is "cock-eyed"; how often is Sherman "the red-haired Ohioan"? His cavalry men are "hard-handed," his artillery pieces "high-sighted."

But real heroes walk out of these pages, greater because the reader has marched with them through all the misery that preceded their elevated moments. Foote's Lincoln is monumental; if his Lee reflects too much the idolatry of his soldiers, his Grant and Sherman are brilliant characters, so complete that when Sherman turns down (in effect) the presidency—perhaps the only American other than Washington to do so—the reader understands and may even sigh in relief.

Enter this book at your peril. Foote took twenty years writing it. To read it takes weeks or months; bestsellers will pile up on your table as you toil through obscure battlefields in Arkansas or Florida. But you may finish it feeling that for all its obvious faults, this is the greatest telling of our greatest story, perhaps the single best work of American history.

THE WAR IN THE SOUTHERN MIND

by John M. McCardell, Jr.

Memory believes before knowing remembers. Believes longer than recollects, longer than knowing even wonders.
—WILLIAM FAULKNER

Words matter. Shelby Foote, native Southerner, calls it *The Civil War*. But among many of his fellow white Southerners in times past, it was "the war between the states" or "the war for Southern independence" or even "the war of Northern aggression." It might also be called, but seldom is, "the war for emancipation" or "the war to end slavery." That is certainly how many black Southerners remembered it. But for most of the first hundred years after Appomattox, the voice of black Southerners on the subject was muted. By any name, as James McPherson notes, it is "the war that will not go away."

Memory also matters, and how this war has been remembered—and how the remembering has established principles of inclusion and exclusion in the narrative—has a long and troubled history. David Blight has recounted well how the choice facing the country in 1865 led to fundamental decisions about remembering—and forgetting. The road from Appomattox forked to lead to two different destinations. One fork led to Reconstruction, and along its bumpy, hazardous path lay social justice, economic progress, and political equality for those who had been enslaved. The other led to reconciliation, a route straighter and smoother that sought to bring the seceded states as quickly as possible back into the Union.

The price of reconciliation, Blight writes, was Reconstruction; the price of Reconstruction, reconciliation. It was one or the other. It could not be both. After a brief reconnoitering of the distance and risks of the journey to Reconstruction, the country, North and South, chose the shorter, easier, path. Within a generation, the white South, which lost the war, had won the peace. The nightmare of segregation, disenfranchisement, a place of seemingly permanent social and economic inferiority for African Americans became the ugly underside of the dream of speedy and complete sectional reconciliation. And so it remained for almost a century.

One cannot begin to understand the place of the Civil War in the (white) Southern imagination without first comprehending the context in which that imagination could be exercised and expressed. Reconciliation had clear ground rules. There would be no discussing the war's causes, no rehashing of the arguments for and against slavery, no more John Browns or Simon Legrees, no more debates over the equality of the white and black races. Writers, politicians, educators, and public officials who accepted the deal had less to discuss, but had the freedom to explore what was left, what remained permissible, far more deeply.

And so began a cascade of reminiscences. Memoirs, unit histories, intense debates over strategy and tactics, reminded Northerners and Southerners that valor came clad in both blue and gray. Veterans' organizations kept battlefield memories alive. Reunions of old Union and Confederate soldiers, even as they dwindled in numbers year by year, served as vivid reminders of bravery and courage, abundant on both sides.

Implicit, occasionally explicit, in this understanding was that the stronger, not necessarily the better, side had prevailed in the war. Beginning with General Robert E. Lee's farewell message to the Army of Northern Virginia, "overwhelming numbers and resources" explained the war's outcome. Soon after, Virginia historian Edward A. Pollard coined the term "Lost Cause" in his 1866 history of the war. By the mid-1870s, owing to the concerted efforts of a group of Virginia ex-Confederates, a "Lost Cause" mythology had emerged, with Lee as the "marble man," the noble leader, who led a doomed effort against a destructive Yankee war machine. Moreover, as this view took hold, Lee's army and the eastern campaigns dominated the military narrative, with the war in the West little more than a sideshow.

With tales of military heroics came nostalgia, not just for the adventures of days gone by but for the simpler lives led before the war. In particular, as Americans coped with the wrenching changes of the Gilded Age, an imagined Old South compelled. This was the South of Joel Chandler Harris's Uncle Remus and Thomas Nelson Page's Marse Chan, characters who spoke in dialect and who made clear that in the old times, civility, order, graciousness—traits seemingly absent in modern American life—had flourished. Harris and Page were too young to fight during the war, barely remembered the plantation regime, and yet waxed poetic about days now gone. The loyal retainer Sam, in Page's "Marse Chan," put it best: "Dem wuz good ole times, marster—de bes' Sam ever see! Dey wuz, in fac'! Niggers didn' hed nothin' 't all to do—jes' hed to 'ten' to de feedin' an' cleanin' de hosses, an' doin' what de marster tell 'em to do; an' when dey wuz sick, dey had things sont 'em out de house, an' de same doctor come to see 'em whar 'ten' to de white folks when dey wuz po'ly. Dyar warn' no trouble nor nothin'." These stories appeared in major national periodicals. Readers couldn't get enough.

Such was reconciliation and the consensus that reinforced it: white Northerners and Southerners more alike than different; gallantry on both sides, Union and Confederate; new social arrangements that retained the best of the old and under the control of white Southerners who understood best how to keep order.

By the time of the fiftieth anniversary observances in 1911–15, this reconciliationist view had clearly triumphed. Speaking at the commemoration of the battle of Gettysburg in 1913, President Woodrow Wilson, a professional historian and the first Southerner in the White House since before the war, remarked: "How wholesome and healing the peace has been! We have found one another again as brothers and comrades in arms, enemies no longer, generous friends rather, our battles long past, the quarrel forgotten, except that we shall not forget the splendid valor, the manly devotion of the men then arrayed against one another, now grasping hands and smiling into each other's eyes." A bitter war had become a "quarrel." The only black faces present at Gettysburg in 1913 belonged to cooks, stewards, janitors.

With the appearance of the landmark film *Birth of a Nation* in 1915, the "Southern" version of the Civil War reached a national audience. Producer D. W. Griffith's epic, complete with footnoted tableaux and dazzling special effects, and including an endorsement by President Wilson, played before large crowds. All the familiar themes were present: dear friends on opposing sides; devastation of the plantation society led by abolitionist politicians and their ignorant, rapacious black allies; and the restoration of order by the Ku Klux Klan.

A fifteen-year-old girl left an Atlanta theater mesmerized by what she had just seen. Young Margaret Mitchell tried first to tell the story she had just witnessed in a play, entitled *The Traitor.* By the mid-1920s she was hard at work on *Gone with the Wind.* Later she would acknowledge the influence of the film, as well as the novel, Thomas Dixon's *The Clansman,* on which the film had been based.

When the film version of *Gone with the Wind* premiered in 1939, in the opening scene, with a haunting rendition of "Dixie" being hummed in the background, viewers read these prefatory lines:

> There was a land of Cavaliers and Cotton Fields called the Old South. Here in this pretty world Gallantry took its last bow. Here was the last ever to be seen of Knights and their Ladies Fair, of Master and of Slave. Look for it only in books, for it is no more than a dream remembered, a Civilization gone with the wind...

Yet by 1939, the remembered war as handed down by the participant generation and solidified by Page, Harris, Griffith, and others of the successor generation had begun to be reconsidered. Inspired by the words of the Irish poet William Butler Yeats—"Out of the quarrel with others we make rhetoric; out of the quarrel with ourselves, poetry"—Allen Tate observed that, in the 1920s, Southerners "looked around and saw for the first time since about 1830 that the Yankees were not to blame for everything." A new generation of Southern writers, in Tate's words, took the "southern legend of defeat and heroic frustration" and converted it "into a universal myth of the human condition." In the work of Tate, Andrew Lytle, Donald Davidson, John Crowe Ransom, Robert Penn Warren, and especially William Faulkner, the South's quarrel with itself imparted a far more profound and complex meaning to the experience of civil war. "Sin and love and fear," wrote Faulkner, "are just sounds that people who never sinned nor loved nor feared have for what they never had and cannot have until they forgot the words...."

From rhetoric to poetry—and profound insight: slavery as America's, not just the South's, original sin; secession as banishment from the garden; good works providing no absolution; death in battle the beginning of redemption; and still the "quarrel with ourselves." Or, as Faulkner would put it, "the human heart in conflict with itself."

It remained the war that would not go away, and a war that still went on. Perhaps it might yet turn out differently. Again Faulkner:

For every Southern boy fourteen years old, not once but whenever he wants it, there is the instant when it's still not yet two o'clock on that July afternoon in 1863, the brigades are in position behind the rail fence, the guns are laid and ready in the woods and the furled flags are already loosened to break out and Pickett himself with his long oiled ringlets and his hat in one hand probably and his sword in the other looking up the hill waiting for Longstreet to give the word and it's all in the balance, it hasn't happened yet, it hasn't even begun yet, it not only hasn't begun yet but there is still time for it not to begin against that position and those circumstances which made more men than Garnett and Kemper and Armistead and Wilcox look grave yet it's going to begin, we all know that, we have come too far with too much at stake and that moment doesn't need even a fourteen-year-old boy to think This time. Maybe this time with all this much to lose and all this much to gain: Pennsylvania, Maryland, the world, the golden dome of Washington itself to crown with desperate and unbelievable victory the desperate gamble, the cast made two years ago....

Meanwhile, by mid-century, the long road to reconciliation found itself intersecting, once again, with the road not taken in 1865, the road to Reconstruction. The landmark *Brown v. Board of Education* in 1954, the year Shelby Foote started his work on *The Civil War: A Narrative*, began the slow and painful process of ending Jim Crow. September 1957 brought both the confrontation in Little Rock over the integration of Central High School and the creation of a commission to plan the centennial commemoration of the Civil War.

Ulysses S. Grant III, grandson of the great general, accepted the chairmanship of the commission. The influence of Southern commissioners, and thus the choice of the reconciliationist theme, became clear in Grant's view that "the war did not divide us. Rather it united us." Continuing, he outlined how the observance would be conducted: "Battles will be reenacted, many on a huge scale. Colorful ceremonies will be held—there will be memorials, parades, new historical markers, and a great many special ceremonies." The old ground rules seemed hardly to have changed.

But the Civil War centennial was a disaster almost from the start. Black commissioners, denied lodging at a Charleston hotel during the commemoration of the firing on Fort Sumter in April 1961, forcefully reminded Americans that the war had causes and also legacies. Coinciding with the Freedom Rides across the South in 1961, the beginning of the centennial marked its end. After a heavily commercialized reenactment of the battle of Bull Run in July 1961, General Grant resigned, and the pageantry, for the most part, came to an end.

Instead, and with no real planning, the country found itself reenacting the centennial of Reconstruction. Only this time, the legislation had teeth, and the descendants of slaves demanded their full civil rights.

The irony did not escape one of the most astute of Southern historians, C. Vann Woodward, who published in 1968 a collection of essays entitled *The Burden of Southern History*. Woodward perceptively noted that among Americans, only those in the states of the old Confederacy had inherited the legacy of military defeat, occupation by an invading force, and social reconstruction. How ironic, then, that the wisdom that might have been imparted by these unique experiences seemed utterly lacking among most white Southerners.

In the years since, Americans not once but twice have elected presidents from the South and in 2008 elected an African American. White Southerners have for the most part accepted, even embraced, the new order. Such erstwhile segregationists as Strom Thurmond of South Carolina and George Wallace of Alabama admitted their errors and received not only forgiveness but votes from black Southerners.

Yet the Confederate legacy remains an unsettled, and unsettling, question. Its symbols evoke emotional, sometimes irrational, responses. So do its heroes. Its history is increasingly relegated to battlefields. Its dead still slumber in the dark and bloody ground. Yet the Lost Cause still lives. "The citizen-soldiers who fought for the Confederacy personified the best qualities of America," proclaims the homepage of the Sons of Confederate Veterans. "The preservation of liberty and freedom was the motivating factor in the South's decision to fight the Second American Revolution. The tenacity with which Confederate soldiers fought underscored their belief in the rights guaranteed by the Constitution." And, the page concludes, "the memory and reputation of the Confederate soldier, as well as the motives for his suffering and sacrifice, are being consciously distorted by some in an attempt to alter history. Unless the descendants of Southern soldiers resist those efforts, a unique part of our nation's cultural heritage will cease to exist."

On the other hand, an African American city councilman in Richmond, Virginia, contends, "Any public support of any Confederate memorial on public property violates the rights of those who were once victimized by slavery."

Perhaps, then, as the Civil War sesquicentennial looms, a new edition of Foote's *The Civil War* is especially timely. Readers will find, in a beautifully composed narrative, a story in many ways shaped by the old rules. The emphases are clearly on battles and leaders and whites. The story begins and ends with Jefferson Davis—"Lucifer," as Andrew Johnson called him—and views the Confederate president, in all his complexity, sympathetically. Bravery and courage abound on both sides. Not much is made of fundamental causes. Foote acknowledges his "sympathy for the underdog." There is little here a white Southern readership would find objectionable.

But there is also much that violates, or, rather, transcends, the old rules. "Until the government and the courts were ready to take the Constitution at its word," Foote writes, ex-slaves would find themselves "in a caste system of 'race etiquette' as rigid as any [they] had known in formal bondage." (III, 1045) Reconciliation and reconstruction were indeed mutually exclusive. Moreover, Foote's treatment of the war itself quite consciously attaches greater importance to the war in the West. The subtitles of each volume contain improbable pairings: *Fort Sumter to Perryville, Fredericksburg to Meridian, Red River to Appomattox*. Foote makes explicit his purpose to challenge the view "that the War was fought in Virginia, while elsewhere—in an admittedly large but rather empty region known as 'the West'—a sort of running skirmish wobbled back and forth, presumably as a way for its participants, faceless men with unfamiliar names, to pass the time while waiting for the issue to be settled in the East." (III, 1064–65)

This formulation matters because so much of what shaped the white South's memory of the war drew upon a sense of Southern nationality. Though Confederates may have thought they were forming a nation by writing a constitution in Montgomery in February 1861, Foote notes that, for Americans North and South, nationality was a result of the war, not a cause. The subject/verb agreement changed from "the United States are" to "the United States is." Yet the western South may have grasped the idea of nationality earlier on. "When a Virginian or a Carolinian spoke of his 'country,'" Foote writes, "he meant Virginia or Carolina. It was not so with Davis. Tennessee and Kentucky were as familiar to him as Mississippi; the whole South, as a region, formed his background." (I, 9)

And of course it is this "solid South," whose history began not in 1607 or 1776 or 1860 but rather in 1865, that became the breeding ground for Southern memory of "the cause," white, Confederate, honorable, valorous, and lost. One might hope that the republication of *The Civil War* could allow the South's "quarrel with itself" to resume. One could then in turn hope that commemorations of the sesquicentennial can find room for three narratives—Union, Confederate, and African American—and not just two.

For the South that continues to live in memory, like the Confederate experience itself, represents a critical part of the national story. As Stephen Vincent Benet writes in the closing lines of his epic poem *John Brown's Body*, the Confederacy represents "the America we have not been... the passion that is dead, the pomp we never knew." And perhaps the reader of Foote's eloquent trilogy might, upon reaching the end of volume three, take Benet's concluding admonition agreeably:

> *So, when the crowd gives tongue*
> *And prophets, old or young,*
> *Bawl out their strange despair*
> *Or fall in worship there,*
> *Let them applaud the image or condemn*
> *But keep your distance and your soul from them....*
> *And while the prophets shudder or adore*
> *Before the flame, hoping it will give ear,*
> *If you at last must have a word to say,*
> *Say neither, in their way,*
> *"It is a deadly magic and accursed,"*
> *Nor "It is blest," but only "It is here."*

HISTORY AND MEMORY:
A CRITIQUE OF THE FOOTE VISION

by Annette Gordon-Reed

Shelby Foote's massive and hugely popular *The Civil War: A Narrative* is, perhaps, an American novelist's most ambitious attempt at writing history. Foote, who wrote fiction and poetry, was defiant in his belief that he was qualified to take on the task of telling the story of the monumental struggle between North and South that preserved the Union, brought chattel slavery to an end, and put the United States on the path to becoming a great nation. "There is," Foote once said during an interview, "no great difference between writing novels and writing history," because both novelists and historians deal with facts. The only difference he saw was the source of these facts: while the novelist deals "with facts that come out of [his or her head] or most likely out of…memory," historians work "with facts that [come] out of documents." Facts alone, he hastened to add, were not enough to make a good history. Quoting John Keats, Foote proclaimed his credo about the nature of history writing and getting at historical truths: "A fact is not a truth until you love it."

It is a wonderful phrase, as one would expect from Keats. But it needs, as academic historians would say, some "unpacking." What is a fact until it reaches the stage of being loved? What if some people love the fact and others do not? What are the implications of loving a fact so much that it becomes a truth, particularly when one is dealing with a subject matter as raw and continuing as the American Civil War, which had slavery, white supremacy, and violence all in the mix? The language of affect and emotion are critical, for as Robert Penn Warren noted, "the Civil War is our *felt* history." Americans have debated and grappled with the war's meaning from its end in 1865 until today. So much is tied up in the discussion: the legacy of slavery, white supremacy, sectional cultural differences that still persist to this day. Foote's intervention into the conversation, his great trilogy, has had a profound effect upon the contours of that discussion. But there are other, much more important things about the process of discerning and writing the facts of history than love, and Foote's invocation of the line goes to the heart of the major problem with this flawed masterpiece.

No one can doubt that Foote did the basic work of a historian in preparing these volumes, although one Civil War historian, Gary Gallagher, has said that "his research did not approach what would be considered an acceptable standard among contemporary scholars, who typically spend a great deal of time combing through unpublished manuscripts." Foote did, Gallagher notes, pore over "the 128 thick volumes of the Official Record and the extensive memoir literature" and made extensive use of secondary material, though that material "would be described as quite dated today." Even after those criticisms, Gallagher believed that Foote "did his best to write evocatively and accurately" and "succeeded to an impressive degree" regarding details of various military campaigns.

That goes to the history side of Foote's explication of the difference between his role as a historian and his role as a novelist. He used documents to discern facts and, apparently, had come to love them enough to present them as truth. But what about the novelist in him—how did that aspect of his persona help shape *The Civil War: A Narrative* beyond giving him the capacity to craft a very well written piece of history, which this most certainly is?

One keys in on one part of Foote's description of how novelists put together facts for their work, "out of memory." There has been much literature on the fraught relationship between memory and history in writings about slavery, the Civil War, and the aftermath of war, namely, Reconstruction. Historian David W. Blight explained the problem:

> History is what trained historians do, a reasoned reconstruction of the past rooted in research; it tends to be critical and skeptical of human motive and action, and therefore more secular than what people commonly call memory. History can be read by or belong to everyone; it is more relative, contingent on place, chronology, and scale. If history is shared and secular, memory is often treated as a sacred set of absolute meanings and stories, possessed as the heritage or identity of a community. Memory is often owned; history is interpreted. Memory is passed down through the generations; history is revised. Memory often coalesces in objects, sites, and monuments; history seeks to understand contexts in all their complexity.... In an essay about the slave trade and the problem of memory, Bernard Bailyn aptly stated memory's appeal: "Its relation to the past is an embrace...ultimately emotional, not intellectual."

In a very real sense, Foote's conception of the Civil War—his approach, his understanding of the facts of that contest—bears the very strong mark of memory as opposed to history. It is the novelist in him, working from memory, that presents the reader with the basic takeaway from the book, a takeaway that draws heavily from the romance of the so-called "Lost Cause" mythology—the South gallantly fighting a just war to preserve states' rights (disputing that the right at issue was the right to keep slaves and extend slavery into the West), against an overwhelmingly powerful, mechanistic, and coldhearted society that lacked the panache of their Southern white counterparts. There is a vast amount of documents in these volumes, to be sure, but Foote's love of his home state, Mississippi, and the memories of that war which grew up among many white Southern males of his generation, are what power the narrative. It is that love, that emotion, not intellect, that is at the core of Foote's presentation. Those memories gave him the facts that he loved enough to call truths.

Take, for example, the way Foote handles the conflict between the races in these volumes. It is not just that he talks very little about the racial implications involved in racially based slavery, the war, and emancipation. Although the discussions are not very extensive, what is more problematic is the way he discusses these matters. He pays attention to race, but he does so in the old-world, genteel white Southern way—that is to say, in a very patronizing manner. "The South" is basically about the white race, and blacks are akin to resident aliens in the place. Foote makes it plain that given his Mississippi roots, he would have fought for the Confederacy, even though not every white person in Mississippi was a Confederate; some supported the Union. In this, Foote resembles another writer from his home state, William Faulkner, who in the midst of the civil rights movement said that although "the Negro" deserved his rights and should have them, he would shoot "Negroes in the street" before he would allow outsiders to tell white Mississippians how to live their lives. One can know what is right, but still fight on the side of wrong when racial solidarity comes into the mix.

Foote's trilogy was also written during the civil rights era. He was much aware of what he could and could not say and was careful to talk about white supremacy as a negative thing. But there is a difference between taking note of a particular reality, on the one hand, and actually understanding that reality and having it form the basis of one's worldview and how one analyzes situations, on the other. He does not seem to know, or was unwilling to recognize, white supremacy when it was present. Take Foote's admiration (love?) for the notorious Nathan Bedford Forrest, who after the war was instrumental in setting up the Ku Klux Klan. Foote pronounced Abraham Lincoln and Nathan Bedford Forrest the two greatest geniuses the war produced. There is no question that Forrest was a creative and effective general, but his men and, thus, he were also involved in the Fort Pillow massacre, in which after a horrific battle a number of black soldiers were killed after they had surrendered. One member of Forrest's garrison described in a letter home how "the poor deluded negroes [sic] would run up to our men, fall upon their knees and with uplifted hands scream for mercy, but were ordered to their feet and shot down." Foote puts the term "massacre" in quotes. How does he absolve his hero Forrest of any responsibility? Well, General William T. Sherman did an investigation and decided that nothing had happened that warranted any type of retaliation by Union troops or reprimand for the soldiers involved. But earlier in the volume, Foote notes Sherman's deep hostility toward black troops. He did not want them in his army. When it was pointed out that "a Negro" was "as good as a white man" at stopping "a bullet," he replied, "Yes; and a sandbag is better." Why would anyone think that such a man would care much if unarmed black soldiers were shot down? Sherman's action, or inaction, simply cannot be taken as proof that Forrest's men did not massacre black soldiers with his acquiescence.

And then there is Foote's statement about the ultimate end of the Civil War: the abolition of slavery. Because he became famous as a talking head on Ken Burns's magisterial PBS series *The Civil War,* Foote became much sought after by members of the news media. It is through these interviews that one gets a true picture of Foote's ideology and way of thinking about the war, the South, and race in a way that sheds light on his treatment of these topics in these volumes.

> This country has two great sins on its very soul. One is slavery, which we'll never get out of our history and our conscience and everything else, the marrow of our bones. The other one is emancipation. They told four million people, "You are free. Hit the road." Two-thirds of them couldn't read or write. Very few of them had trades except farming.... I'm not saying emancipation is a sin, for God's sakes [he actually did before he realized how that must have sounded], and I'm not saying there shouldn't have been emancipation, but it should have been an emancipation that brought those people into society without all those handicaps on their heads.

There is little doubt that Foote thought he was being humane in his understanding of what happened during the aftermath of the conflict that he spent twenty years writing about, although he could barely conceal his contempt for the men called "Radical" Republicans, who wanted to transform the racial order in the South. They were "Jacobins" in Foote's eyes. And when they appear in the narrative, one expects to hear sinister organ music while they, after twirling their mustaches, tie the innocent white South to the metaphorical railroad track as the engine of "Negro suffrage" barrels down on the fair maiden. This is the stuff of Foote's historical memory, his understanding, born of his allegiance to the cultural ideal that he grew up with and that formed his worldview. It was a memory impervious to time and evidence. When Foote made these pronouncements, the scholarly consensus on what had happened in Reconstruction had moved well beyond the "white-man-didn't-have-any-rights-under–the-specter-of-Negro rule" horror show adhered to by the so-called Dunning School of Reconstruction during the first half of the twentieth century.

Note who is cited as the source of the problem in Foote's quote: it is the ignorant blacks who were freed without education. It is not the white Southerners who unleashed a torrent of violence against the freedmen, and who fought tooth and nail against land reform that would have given blacks—who were indeed farmers—land to till and provided them with the kind of independence that citizens of the time longed for. It was white Southerners who passed the black codes and vigorously opposed any effort to give blacks the franchise. Foote knew these things happened and he referred to some of them in his writings. The implication in this passage, however, is that blacks were not ready for freedom, not that the white South uniformly rejected any move to recognize blacks' equal humanity. The former slaves themselves were the problem with emancipation.

So, what are we to make of this, finally? Foote's work will likely remain pivotal to many Americans' understanding of the Civil War, even though, as one critic put it when writing about *The Civil War: A Narrative,* "there has, perhaps, never been a history, even a popular history, so devoid of ideas or economic forces." It is a good account of the military campaigns of the war, a serviceable account of the politics of war, but not at all a good account of the social and cultural forces surrounding the conflagration—slavery and white supremacy—that has helped make us who we are today.

FOOTE AND THE PROBLEM OF RACE

by Michael Eric Dyson

Let's be honest: Shelby Foote's view that Lincoln injected slavery as an issue into the Civil War to gain tactical advantage over the South is just too close for comfort to the idea that all that bloodshed was more about states' rights than whether we should continue to shackle black humanity. Foote's Civil War trilogy unabashedly tilted toward the Confederacy and can be read as a monumental brief in behalf of the Southern view of the Late Unpleasantness. There's little denying that Foote's pedigree as a son of the South shaped his views of the war, but to his credit, he plumbed the depths of both sides of the struggle with equal parts literary art and anthropological observation. That's why he could conclude that the war produced two authentic geniuses: Abraham Lincoln and Nathan Bedford Forrest, a military wizard and allegedly later the Grand Wizard of the Ku Klux Klan. What may be most telling about Foote is his honesty about the evolving racial views that inevitably colored his interpretation of history.

As a young man, Foote was mentored by his best friend Walker Percy's adopted father, the writer William Alexander Percy, known to Foote as "Mr. Will." While once visiting the elder Percy, Foote answered the door and was greeted by a well-dressed black man looking for Foote's mentor. "Mr. Will, there's a nigger out here to see you," Foote said matter-of-factly. "I had not meant anything by it, just a Mississippi boy talking." Percy corrected Foote with the sort of indirect reprimand that shines in the Southern art of the noble implicit. Percy fixed his young charge with a hard stare and simply said, "Tell Dr. So-and-So to come right in." No big lecture, no harsh words, just a respect of title that recognized his fellow human being's dignity and achievement.

But the severe political limits of the noble implicit were painfully apparent. Foote recalls that Percy agreed once to introduce Langston Hughes at a black church gathering in Mississippi and was mortified at Hughes's "radical" demand for equal rights. Foote lets on that of course Hughes was no radical but that he sounded like one to a man like Percy, who believed that black folk shouldn't so much demand their rights as earn them. (Though Percy might be hard-pressed to explain exactly how whites earned the right to deny black folk their rights, and how whites could insist with a straight face that blacks could only have restored to them what should have never been denied them by proving they were equal to a humanity that whites had obviously failed to show. It was more than begging the question; it begged the system. But that was Hughes's great offense: he tore at the fabric of the noble implicit and wove into its place a forthright imperative for equal treatment that composes the vulgar explicit of the black freedom movement.) But it was Foote the unconscious and inadvertent, even genial racist—another term for a Mississippi boy talking, which meant that it was racial business as usual, just how things were, no harm to blacks intended beyond what the "natural" order of things did to them—who later insisted that a "man is not supposed to have to prove he's equal in this country. That was one of the flaws in it."

A growing sense of black equality wore on Foote and gave him a bigger appreciation for black art and black humanity. Foote heaped praise on jazz despite its alleged technical inferiority to European classical music. (Foote said, "The jazz musician... could not read music. His technique was marvelous, but it was by nature an inferior technique. He could not play that instrument the way a man in a symphony orchestra can play it.") Foote's evolving views didn't make him any less cantankerous about the pretensions of the black bourgeoisie. Foote admitted that most of the black folk he had known had "either been servants or doctors, none of them in the middle." The warped perception of black life at the extremes feeds stereotypes and ignorance about just how complicated and oddly enmeshed black life is despite the climb to higher station. The stubborn fact of racist culture is the insistence that the doctor is no different than the servant, a conclusion that, in other circumstances, might be celebrated as the revelation of enlightened people. As it stands, it expresses the blinding force of brute bigotry.

Even as Foote congratulated himself for overcoming his ignorance, he forgave himself his aversion to the black bourgeoisie because they did little more than imitate white folk. Coming from renowned sociologist E. Franklin Frazier, such a criticism is a withering indictment, not because Frazier is black, but because he turned a lifetime habit of observing black life into admittedly controversial science. Foote worked backward: his art fueled his desire to know more—his novel *September, September* involves the kidnapping of a black boy in Memphis, Tennessee. That's not a bad motive at all for learning more about what you know little of, but Foote's episodic and selective interactions with black life hampered the same kind of intuitive appreciation for intricacy and nuance that breathed throughout his Civil War trilogy.

If Foote didn't much like the black bourgeoisie, he didn't cotton to the black bottom any better. (Not that Foote liked poor whites any better: he socked it hard to the "yahoos" who lynched black folk in Southern towns, although he claimed they were poor proxies for the resistance to integration by the "decent" white folk, and he agreed with Mark Twain that the main reason for lynching was—not race hatred, or the desire to spread terror, or the yen for the complete subordination of black life to white rule—but boredom.) Foote lamented the missed chance of his white Southern ancestors during Reconstruction to handle their "Negro problem" and resented the burden of having it passed down to his generation: "They held the Negro down and left him for us to deal with when he finally busted out." Busting out for the Negro, in Foote's view, consisted of rape and mugging; he says that "when you can't do anything else," such crime is "a perfectly natural thing to do," although the hope is that the Negro will eventually become more civilized. "I'm glad that they've been let up, but certainly there's a price to be paid." Foote simply doesn't want that civilizing process to resemble too much of what passes for vapid white culture. It's a hard place for blacks to be in: they've got to avoid the incivility of their rise from forced savagery while avoiding the vacuous vices of Caucasian society.

Foote was quite honest about the supposed, and questionable, advantage of Southern whites knowing blacks far better than their Northern colleagues. "I've always heard Southerners say how well they know Negroes because they've lived around them all their lives. Well, I sometimes think I and most Southerners know less about Negroes than anybody else on the face of the Earth." That's both a frank admission and a reason for grief if its author can't find a way to repent of his ignorance to tell the truth of how crucial black bodies and minds were to the biggest narrative in American life: the intricately intertwined story of the Civil War and race. Foote believes, like a lot of Southerners believe, that slavery was a ruse Lincoln foisted upon the war's interpretation to make things go his way.

That might be true, but the bigger truth is that the Civil War was always about race—its denials, its privileges, its opportunities, its bitter contradictions, its bloody rights and rites. At his best, Foote understood that facts can never be equated with truth; he just didn't understand how such a distinction might be related to his denial of the intimate kinship between the blood of brothers spilled on fields of battle and the question of full citizenship for enslaved blacks who toiled in fields of forced labor. Foote used the example of how much might be missed about John Kennedy by future historians who would fail to "get any true view of John Kennedy and what he meant to us at the time he was alive, because the facts don't support what we felt."

> What we felt about Kennedy cannot be expressed with facts. It was a feeling and that is going to be very difficult for future generations. They may be able to quote what some of us had to say about him, but that is not enough either. It was a feeling that has to be communicated and some future historian is—in the course of writing the history of the United States—going to get to the Kennedy years and just be plumb mystified.

If it's not the case that Foote was plumb mystified by race and the Civil War, he was at least trumped by the racial traditions from which he sprang and from which he derived his sense of history, one that steadfastly denied the place of race from the start in the War between the States. Much later Foote could even understand the consternation of black folk around the Confederate flag while concluding they hadn't got it right. After denouncing the "knotheads down home—the Ku Kluxers and the rest of them," Foote said: "I know that flag really pains black people. It was used against them in a dastardly way, and they hate it. And I understand their hating it. But they are wrong."

When it comes to the Civil War, Foote rose to poetry to describe the intramural tragedies that stabbed the American breast. He knew the facts of chattel slavery and the realities of subjugation. But he missed the truth of just how entangled with the

American soul was the greatest war we fought to clarify our national destiny. And one of the reasons we know that is because he was so open and honest about the struggles he endured, and the beliefs he held, around race in America.

When Bobby Kennedy said in the early sixties that he would have gone to the Mississippi Delta to work "for the Negro" if he hadn't gone into politics, that shamed Foote into a recognition that, had it been applied to his trilogy, may have made a substantive difference in his telling of the story.

> And it hurt me to think that I had turned my back on something that Bobby Kennedy had been willing to devote his whole life to. You grow up in a thing and you're not inclined to see the evil as clearly as you would if you were visiting that place. It seems so much a part and parcel of the life, especially when it contributes to your comfort, as it did to mine. The race question is the big thing.

Race *is* the big thing, and Foote's acknowledgment of its role in national life should be the starting place for assessing any history of the country's greatest war to make itself all that it promised to be.

The Greenville Factor

by Julia Reed

Whenever Shelby Foote was asked why so many writers hailed from his hometown of Greenville, Mississippi—and he was asked a lot—he always said pretty much the same thing he told Dick Cavett in 1979: "If Will Percy had grown up and lived in Greenwood, it would have been Greenwood where the writers come from."

Will Percy was William Alexander Percy, poet, lawyer, and author of *Lanterns on the Levee,* an elegiac and literary look back at the semi-feudal world that he—and Foote—were born into. The only son of Senator LeRoy Percy, one of the Mississippi Delta's most influential planters, Percy was also the adoptive father of his three much younger cousins, LeRoy, Phinizy, and Walker Percy, who became Shelby Foote's lifelong best friend. To Walker and his brothers, Percy was "Uncle Will"; to Foote and most of the rest of the town, black or white, he was "Mr. Will." By the time the teenage Foote got to know him well, Percy had already graduated from the University of the South and Harvard Law (where he also taught), traveled the world and lived in Japan, earned the French

Croix de Guerre for his service in World War I, and headed Washington County's Flood Relief Committee after the devastating Great Flood of 1927. In between, he'd written four volumes of poetry. Foote was dazzled by Percy's library, which contained "literally thousands of books," and by his visitors, who included Carl Sandburg, Stephen Vincent Benet, and Vachel Lindsay, among other authors on its shelves.

"His was an example of a cultured house, in a sense of having books and music, and the master of the house having been a well-traveled man in Europe and Asia and South America," Foote once told an interviewer. "It was a window through which you could see the world. No—it was even more than that. It was as if some of that other world had been brought into this little town."

To be sure, Percy brought a heightened worldliness to the thriving "little town," but by the time Foote was born, in 1916, Greenville, like much of the Mississippi Delta, had long been a cosmopolitan world apart from the rest of Mississippi and even most of the South. "The Delta," as it is simply known, is actually the diamond-shaped alluvial floodplain of the Yazoo and Mississippi rivers and home to some of the richest farmland in the world. Greenville, situated on the highest point of the Mississippi between Memphis and Vicksburg, was—geographically and figuratively—at its center, serving as the business and cultural hub for surrounding plantations, including the Percys' Tralake and the Foote family's Mount Holly.

Until 1825, when the first white settlers arrived, the Delta had been an oft-flooded tangle of primeval swamp and hardwood forest, all but untouched for thousands of years by anyone except mound-dwelling Indians. From the beginning, it was the domain of what Greenville author (and Percy protégé) David Cohn referred to as "pioneers with means," substantial planters from other parts of the South where the land was already beginning to tap out, who were also necessarily adventurers and gamblers at heart—willing to risk their slaves and their fortunes hacking through a mosquito-infested jungle to get at the sandy loam that became known as Delta Gold.

By 1830, the population had grown to 1,976, of which 1,184 were slaves. Just thirty-one years later, when war broke out, the Deltans were determined to protect their newly carved-out fiefdom, and Greenville was the home of a particularly energetic band of snipers who fired at Union gunboats as they made their way down the river. Sherman singled out the town in orders to "let the planters and inhabitants see and feel that they will be held accountable for the acts of guerrillas and Confederates who sojourn in their county." And at one point, more than 2,000 troops overran the area, seizing slaves and livestock. Still, the community would have largely been spared after the fall of Vicksburg had it not been for a recalcitrant sniper who fired on a gunboat, causing Union forces to return and burn down all but two of Greenville's structures.

It was rebuilt on land donated by a wealthy female landowner, and by the turn of the century—in stunning contrast to the rest of the state and most of the South itself—both the city and the region had fully recovered from the deprivations of war, emancipation, and Reconstruction. The cotton kingdom was booming—but it was a boom possible only with a large and willing workforce. Though Foote once correctly told an interviewer, "The condition of the Negro when I was a boy was not very much above slavery," the planters' rule was marked by an eminently practical paternalism, and the Delta was absent the more virulent forms of racism that marked the surrounding piney woods and clay hills. (Foote himself almost proudly told an interviewer that his hometown had been the site of only one lynching.) Without blacks in the fields, after all, the economy would completely implode. Between 1900 and 1930, the black population increased by 50 percent. Washington County, where Greenville is county seat, had a population of roughly 54,000 people, of which 40,000 were black.

Both of Foote's grandfathers were part of the so-called Delta aristocracy, but also of two of the more notable private boom-and-bust dramas that marked the period. His paternal grandfather, Huger Foote, arrived in the Delta from eastern Mississippi in 1870 to manage one of his own family's plantations, Mount Holly, which he later inherited. Like a lot of Delta scions, his son was brought up to do little but hunt and fish and socialize: "My father never thought he would have to do a thing in this world," Foote said. When Huger Foote abruptly lost everything, he moved into town and spent his last days playing poker at the Elks Club. His son, meanwhile, married Shelby's mother, was forced to go to work, and died when Shelby was a young boy, leaving him to be raised by a female coterie that included a group of aunts and his mother, who became a legal secretary.

Foote's maternal grandfather, a Viennese-born Jew named Morris Rosenstock, arrived in Greenville in the 1880s, became business manager of a plantation in nearby Avon, and married the owner's prettiest daughter. Rosenstock lost his own fortune in the 1921 market crash, but not before being part of one of the more odious schemes of the planter class. Consistently consumed by the fear of a black exodus that would destroy their universe, a group including LeRoy Percy imported labor from southern Italy and Sicily to an Arkansas plantation called Sunnyside, just across the river from Greenville. Conditions were abysmal and the Italians were forced to work off their transport, opening up the planters to charges of peonage. In the end, the indictment was squashed—the president, Teddy Roosevelt, knew Percy from his days in the Senate and had gone hunting on land owned by Huger Foote, where he famously did not shoot a bear.

"The Delta was a place where credit was easy and the crashes hard," Foote told an interviewer. "My grandfathers were approximate millionaires at one time in their lives, and both had scarcely enough money to dig the hole to bury them in." The easy nature—and consequences—of boom and bust among the landed gentry was the predominant theme in four of Foote's novels, with

Jordan County standing in for Washington County and the town of Bristol for Greenville. But it was a theme of individual land and loss—ironically, given his life's work, Foote said there was little talk, or even thought, of the war when he was growing up. For one thing, of course, not much had changed. For another, unlike such shrines to the antebellum South as Charleston or Savannah or Natchez, the Delta's prewar history had been brief in the extreme. Also, the loose nature of its economy attracted a more diverse population to the port community of Greenville, especially. "The first thing you have to understand is that all this business about moonlight, magnolias, and Anglo-Saxon bloodlines has to go out the window," Foote once explained. "The Delta is a great melting pot."

Foote's grandfather was only one of a thriving group of prominent Jews in Greenville who came from Austria, Poland, and Russia. Percy may have brought the culture of "that other world" into town, but men like Morris Rosenstock served as more concrete reminders. ("I was perfectly aware that there was a world outside," Foote said, "because my grandfather came from that world." When Greenville was incorporated after the war, the first elected mayor was Jewish, as were the owners of the first businesses to open. The first school was the Jewish-founded nonsectarian German and English School, which served the entire white community, and in 1887, a Delta diarist named Harry Ball described the "largest public ball we ever had," with more than two hundred people in attendance at the local Jewish club. Foote often marveled over the fact that the country club in Greenwood, less than fifty miles to the east, excluded Jews, while the one in Greenville numbered Jews among its founders.

There was also a sizable Syrian population, which, like most of the Jews, had arrived as traveling salesmen, as well as an enormous influx of Chinese, whose "influence," Foote said, "was considerable." Arriving in the area as itinerant railroad workers, they drew the line at picking cotton and chose instead to open businesses catering to poor blacks. Foote recalled "at least fifty Chinese groceries" in his youth. Such was the size of the Chinese population that they were placed in their own school system—separate from both black and white—until 1948. (Foote noted drily that the year after they were allowed to integrate, "they had a Chinese valedictorian in the graduating class.")

Greenville's racial diversity and religious tolerance (in addition to primarily Presbyterians, Episcopalians, and Jews, there was a Catholic congregation that included William Alexander and Percy's mother) made it easy for the Percys to enlist the aid of the community in keeping the Ku Klux Klan at bay. In 1922, when the candidate of LeRoy and Will Percy defeated the Klan's candidate for sheriff (thus effectively shutting out the Klan for the duration), Leroy provided four kegs of whiskey for a huge celebration. "There were few inhibitions and no social distinctions," his son wrote of the bash. "The banker's wife hobnobbed with the hot tamale man, the lawyer's careened with the bootlegger."

The mix often mirrored the mix at Percy's own house, a salon-like haven that Walker Percy's biographer Jay Tolson called "the most interesting house in Mississippi, if not the entire South." For his time—and place—Percy was considered progressive, receiving blacks at home and conferring on black men the title of "Mr." When Langston Hughes came to town to give a speech, Percy introduced him, showing him the respect of a fellow poet, prompting Hughes to call Percy one of "less than half a dozen Southern gentlemen" he'd met on his tour (though Foote reported that Percy found the content of Hughes's talk bordering on revolutionary). Other visitors were less problematic. The psychiatrist Harry Stack Sullivan stayed with Percy while in the area to study the "race problem"; the New York sculptor Malvina Hoffman, whom Percy commissioned to do a sculpture for his father's grave, was a frequent guest. David Cohn, scion of a prominent Greenville Jewish merchant family, came home from New Orleans for the weekend and ended up staying in Percy's house almost two years, writing a book. "Uncle Will's," Tolson wrote, "was a mandatory stop on the itinerary of poets, novelists, journalists, and any other notables touring the region."

Foote himself was a fixture in the house from the time he was fourteen, when the Percy boys first arrived after their father's suicide and "Uncle Will" thought Foote might be a suitable companion. Foote and Walker Percy had a front-row seat for all the action at the Percy house, but Percy's influence on Foote went far deeper. He was, Foote said, a "great teacher," in that "he could read you a poem by Keats that, by the time he finished reading it, made you want to run home and be with Keats by yourself. He communicated his love of the thing that you accepted as valid and wanted to possess for yourself." More fundamentally, Percy "was an example of a man who had written and published books, and you not only believed it could be done, you *saw* it could be done."

In high school, Foote became editor of Greenville High's newspaper (where Walker wrote the gossip column) and fiddled with poetry. "So I suppose I had some literary pretensions," he said. "But it didn't interfere with my life before then or even at that time. I've always been glad I enjoyed dances and helling around the Delta." He followed his friend Walker to the University of North Carolina but never graduated, preferring to create his own curricula, and four years later returned home to write the first version of *Tournament,* based on his paternal grandfather, and to take a job on the *Delta Star,* a new paper in town that had been started while he was away. Will Percy and David Cohn had persuaded Hodding Carter, a crusading young Louisiana editor who had taken on Huey Long, to move to Greenville, staked by a group of citizens whom Percy had convinced to be backers. In Mississippi, Carter's targets included the Klan-loving Senator Bilbo, who called Carter a "a mongrelizer and lymoculous liar" and urged Greenvillians to rise up and "skin" him. Carter was gratified to find that his fellow citizens not only didn't skin him, "they didn't ostracize me or promise economic retribution." His continued editorials in support of racial and religious tolerance would go on to win him the Pulitzer Prize.

At the paper, Foote covered the Lions Club, ran the poetry column, and served as a proofreader, where he was known as a joker. (In a story on the wedding of young LeRoy Percy, Walker's brother, a line describing the bridesmaids' gowns of "pink lice" miraculously survived; another day the weather was "cloudy with shitting winds.") After a stint in the service (where he was court-martialed for mouthing off to a superior after going AWOL in Ireland to see the woman who would become his first wife), he came back to Greenville to work for the paper (now called the *Delta Democrat-Times*) and to rewrite *Tournament*, which an editor at Knopf had told him was too experimental.

An episode from the novel was published as a slim book titled *The Merchant of Bristol* by the local Levee Press (whose founders included Carter and Foote's high school friend Kenneth Haxton), and *Tournament* was published in its entirety in 1949 by Dial Press. It sold 750 copies in Greenville alone and its success inspired him to press on with *Follow Me Down* (1950), *Love in a Dry Season* (1951), and *Jordan County*, a group of interrelated stories subtitled *A Landscape in Narrative* (1954). Describing *Jordan County*, Foote said it "has place for its hero and time for its plot ... the land itself is the main character. And you go backwards through time to find out what made it what it is."

Shiloh, the novel that led to the Civil War trilogy, was also published during this period (1952), but it was to the Delta—"the land itself"—and Greenville that Foote always planned to return as a novelist. His great unfinished work, one he'd planned and outlined since the forties, was "Two Gates to the City," a family novel set in Jordan County and spanning the period from just after the Civil War to the 1940s. As early as 1952, he sent Walker Percy a "skeleton outline of my work-in-progress," which he called "absolutely the most stupendous book since The Brothers," referring to *The Brothers Karamazov*, a favorite of both men. After he finished the trilogy, he repeatedly mentions "settling down" to tackle "the big job" to Percy, describing an upcoming trip from Memphis to Greenville in 1978 to get himself reacquainted with the landscape, and at one point, he and his third wife, Gwen, toyed with the idea of buying his grandfather's old place, the enormous Italianate brick house at Mount Holly. But "Two Gates"—as well as the purchase of the old house—was not to be. The Delta, apparently, was a tougher nut to crack than even the Civil War.

Correspondences of Shelby Foote and Walker Percy

Foote to Percy

January 31, 1955
697 Arkansas Street
Memphis

Dear Walker,
   ...All I want is to work at my book, a great wide sea of words with a redoubled necessity for precision. If I dont watch it every instant, it bolts off with me, degenerates into detail, conversation and discussion. Every item is worth pages and pages: just finished a hundred on the opening maneuvers in the West: Grant and Sidney Johnston. What Ive done so far is about one-fourth again longer than FOLLOW ME DOWN, and I havent even got to Shiloh, the first big battle. 1st Manassas and Ft Donelson, Wilson's

Excerpts from The Correspondence of Shelby Foote and Walker Percy, *edited by Jay Tolson (New York: W. W. Norton, 1996)*

Creek and Ball's Bluff, Belmont and Logan's X-road, Ive done, along with events leading up to them & Sumter. So far, R E Lee is a failure: failed in W Va, failed again on the South Atlantic coast: Granny Lee, they call him, The King of Spades. Forrest is an interprising Lt-Col. McClellan and Joe Johnston are top dogs.

April 13, 1955
Memphis

Dear Walker,
 ...Have been working hard and steady—about 80,000 words into the thing, approximately one-fifth, and going strong. I think maybe I'm writing a great book; but thats nothing: I always think so.... I would enjoy talking the war with you, though it could be you wouldnt enjoy listening. Dont underrate it as a thing that can claim a man's whole waking mind for years on end. For one thing, it's teaching me to love my country—especially the South, but all the rest as well. I'm learning so many things: geography, for instance. I never saw this country before now—the rivers and mountains, the watersheds and valleys.

November 8, 1955

Dear Walker,
 ...Right now, through a study of one of the world's most horrible wars, I am coming to an understanding of the beauty of goodness—not for me; I cant attain it; but as a power in the world brought to bear by men like Lee and Grant—& Forrest. Grant's simplicity is his goodness, Forrest's strength, and Lee's purity and devotion to duty. Any other period of history would have served I reckon, but this three-year (or whatever) period is doing for me what similar "retirements" have done for many: Dostoevsky's Siberia, Grant's Galena, Lincoln's Eighth Circuit, Davis' Briarfield—Proust's cork-lined room.

June 30, 1956
697 Arkansas Street
Memphis

Dear Walker,
 ...I'm happy to be back at my History. Ive been having a great read at the Greeks—especially Homer and Aeschylus, who seem to me infinitely superior to the rest (except maybe Pindar, whom I like almost as well). The Illiad is the great model for any war book, history or novel....

August 8, 1956
697 Arkansas Street
Memphis

Dear Walker,
 ...I inclose the opening five pages of my history, to show you something of the method. The battle scenes are lit by a strange, lurid light, and the long analytical sections (analytical in a new sense; not explanation, but demonstration—the problems are not so much analyzed as just shown, together with their effect on the men who tried to solve them, principally Lincoln and Davis). I have never enjoyed writing so much as I do this writing. It goes dreadful slow; sometimes I feel like I'm trying to bail out the Mississippi with a teacup; but I like it, I like it.

November 29, 1956
697 Arkansas Street
Memphis

Dear Walker,
 Forgive the lapse, the long hiatus. All thats happened to me is I have been engaged in the hardest, or at least the most tedious, occupation of my writing life. That doesnt mean I dont enjoy it; I do

indeed. What I have to do is learn everything possible from all possible sources about a certain phase or campaign, then digest it so that it's clear in my own mind, then reproduce it even clearer than it has been to me until I actually began writing about it. (The right words will invariably do that, if theyre arranged so as to bring out the essential meaning and drama. Drama *is* meaning, just as character is action, provided it is clear.) Just now I'm on something I think would interest you: the New Mexico campaign, a wild and little known action, fought for control of a few thirsty rivers, with ownership of California in the offing. Christ, what a lost opportunity! Davis saw it, too; but he couldnt do more than he did. You just cant whip 23,000,000 people with 9,000,000—especially when nearly half of the latter number are slaves.... The further I go in my studies, the more amazed I am. What a war! Everything we are or will be goes right back to that period. It decided for once and for all which way we were going, and we've gone.

January 19, 1970
542 E. Parkway S.
Memphis

Dear Pecan Pete,

There went Christmas; good riddance. Happy New Year too.... Ive been spending the past three weeks trying to get over the interruption, and now am finally back on pulse, crossing the Chattahoochee with Sherman and getting ready to send a bullet straight up James Birdseye McPherson's ass. A good lodgment.... Yank soldier coming down to Chattahoochee, where early arrivers were burning houses along the bank, told comrade: "Charley, I believe Sherman has set the river on fire." Rebel prisoner, seeing Federal host that covered the landscape: "Sherman ought to get up on a high hill and command, 'Attention! Kingdoms by the right wheel!'" George Thomas, burly Virginian, heavy set, with bulb-flat eyes and bulgy forehead, stolid and without smalltalk; newsman declared that a look at his face "made one feel as if he were gazing into the mouth of a cannon; and the cannon said nothing." Cavalry brigadier reported he found a factory manufacturing Confed uniforms at Roswell under the French flag, owner claiming immunity because he was a French national. "Such nonsense cannot deceive me," Sherman told Halleck; "I take it a neutral is no better than one of our own citizens." He sent word to the cavalryman: "Should you, under the impulse of natural anger, natural at contemplating such perfidy, hang the wretch, I approve the act beforehand." Good Nazi thinking; good Nuremburg document—along with one he sent a couple of months later to another subordinate at Calhoun, Ga.: "Cannot you send over about Fairmount and Adairsville, burn ten or twelve houses of known secessionists, kill a few at random and let them know it will be repeated every time a train is fired on from Resaca to Kingston?" After the war, he was hard put to understand why former Southern friends wouldnt speak to him on the street. He claimed he wanted to reduce bloodshed by shortening the war; and did. Red-headed Sherman. I have a scene of him taking a bath in the Chattahoochee, talking with a teamster on bank; beard bristly and grizzled, face freckled, liver spots on backs of hands, pubic hair pink in sunlight. Cant use any of it; I made it up. Wait, sweet Christ, till I get back to novels!

October 9, 1971

Dear Walker,
 ... My stretch of good hard work continues. I tell you, that R. E. Lee is a *bear*. He wanted Grant's ass so bad he stayed in a tremble all through the last year of the war. I'm with Ben Butler now; got a plan for blowing up Fort Fisher (near Wilmington) with a steamer packed to the gunwales with 350 tons of black powder.

He tried it. Nothing. Next day a Confederate cannoneer wrote home: "It was awful! It woke up everyone in the fort."

June 19, 1972
542 E. Parkway S.
Memphis

Dear Walker,
...I'm onto the swift downslope of my narrative; only about 100,000 words left to do—out of 1,300,000, which makes it seem very little indeed. Ai! It scares me pissless; first, to finish it, be without it; second, to turn to new work and get my hand in, all over again. Thats terrifying. I do know, though, I can never really stop without turning into a monster, at home and abroad, railing at friends and quaking at foes; a poor halfass unworking writer, carrying his own little corner of hell around with him wherever he goes and sharing it with everyone within reach.

Good for you for rereading C&P. While you are at it, go to the short novels and give The Eternal Husband another run-through. He writes much like you in that one.

We have no plans whatever. Which suits me fine. I like hot weather and plan to stay here and work right on through Appomattox and Durham Station, Citronelle and Galveston, then beyond them through the death of Davis in 1889, an epilog in which he watches the country get Vietnamized, what time it wasnt being raped by U.S. Grant and Jim Fisk.

July 6, 1972

Dear Walker,
...I'm truly excited about this stage of the book, a gray twilight shot through with lightning flashes, and the poor goddam ragged Confederates fighting on parched corn and Nassau bacon, and

Sherman ripping up Georgia and the Carolinas with nothing but old men and boys in his path, and Jefferson Davis mumbling "We'll whip them yet" and almost believing it, and Sheridan (that bastard) going around grinding one fist in the other palm and hissing "Smash em up!" It's much of it highly unreal. Gotterdammerung; a rehearsal for later glories, such as Viet Nam, and future leaders, such as Nixon and what's his name—McGovern. Thank God I dont plan on going deeply into Reconstruction and the Gilded Age, though I do intend a postscript chapter, Lucifer in Starlight, about Davis's postwar life up to his New Orleans death in 1889. Some epilog. His dying words were "I cant take it"—meaning a dose of medicine. The hell he couldnt.

Percy to Foote

Wednesday [spring 1973]

Dear Shelby,
 ... But I write to say this: when you write the last sentence of the Narrative, send me a copy on a postcard and we'll meet you and Gwyn wherever you say, Vicksburg, Jackson, here, Gulf Shores, and I'll buy you a bottle of champaigne.

Foote to Percy

May 13, 1973
542 E. Parkway S.
Memphis

Dear Walker,
 ... Thanks too for offering to meet me at any midpoint when I wind up Vol III. The midpoint is right here in Memphis and I'll

give you all the needed warning. We have an imperial of Mouton-Rothschild (1959) resting for the occasion and want to have a dinner party for about a dozen people—probably sometime around New Year's. Will count on your being here for two-three days to help me celebrate reaching the end of my 20-year road. I may blow my brains out by way of a finale....

Evacuated Richmond yesterday: Jeff Davis on the road. Lee strung out. Grant yelling, "Git em." And Sheridan doing it. And Lincoln about to get shot. First was Old John Brown; now there's J. W. Booth—two madmen, one to start it, another to wind it up. Then Davis: Lucifer in Starlight.

July 10, 1973
542 E. Parkway S.
Memphis

Dear Walker,
...I'm working like a fiend, cooking Bobby Lee's goose but good. He sure looks good in those last scenes. Grant in some ways looks even better—for the first time in his life. Got overawed into goodness I expect.
See you Tuesday:
Shelby

December 11, 1973
542 E. Parkway S.
Memphis

Dear Walker,
I killed Lincoln last week—Saturday, at noon. While I was doing it (he had his chest arched up, holding his last breath to let it out) some halfassed doctor came to the door with vols I and II under his arm, wanting me to autograph them for his son for Xmas. I was in such a state of shock, I not only let him in; I even

signed the goddam books, a thing I seldom do. Then I turned back and killed him and had Stanton say, "Now he belongs to the ages." A strange feeling, though. I have another 70-odd pages to go, and I have a fear theyll be like *Hamlet* with Hamlet left out. Christ, what a man. It's been a great thing getting to know him as he was, rather than as he has come to be—a sort of TV image of himself, with a ghost alongside.

PERCY TO FOOTE

June 12, 1974

Dear Shelby—
 ...It's a noble work. I'm still staggered by the size of the achievement.
 I am still bothered by the prominence of Lucifer. [Jefferson Davis]. It is after all a history of the Civil War, not the Confederacy, yet you've made the hero of your narrative of a *military* event the *civilian* leader of the losing side.
 O.K., I'm not picking—otherwise it is *The Iliad*.

FOOTE TO PERCY

July 3, 1974

Dear Walker,
 Herewith the last chapter of Volume III—the final 100 pages. Keep these as long as you like, then send them back the cheapest way. I'm curious to know whether these pages can conceivably be as good as they seem to me, and dont know anyone else whose judgment I respect enough to give a hoot whether they like them or not. Let me know in your spare time.

Percy to Foote

July 7, 1974

Dear Shelby—
Yes, it's as good as you think. It has a fine understated epic quality, a slow measured period, and a sustained noncommittal, almost laconic, tone of the narrator. I've no doubt it will survive; might even be read in the ruins.
2 demurrers, 1 about English, the other about ideology:
The paragraph on p. 1042, a very important paragraph, is seriously ambiguous. It is not clear whether the "sense of nationhood" you mention means in USA with solid South, or the USA for northern vets and SS for Southerners, or both. Finally, it appears you mean both. Sumpin wrong.
Most of the last 40 pp. goes to Davis. O.K., but it seems a departure from the almost icy neutrality of the narrator up to now (you can't tell whether he's from Ala or Ohio—maybe the latter considering his treatment of Sherman), then the rather partisan finale on Davis. Is this how you want it? (maybe this is Percy anti-Dorsey sentiment).
—W—

P.S. I'll return the galleys when Bunt [Percy's wife] finishes too.

Foote to Percy

July 11, 1974
542 E. Parkway S.
Memphis

Dear Walker,
Glad you liked the last chapter. It brought the total to 1,500,000-plus words: a third of a million longer than Gibbon's

Decline & Fall, which took about the same length of time to write. Funny; I thought those old boys wrote a lot faster than we do, not being much concerned about mot juste and suchlike.

The ambiguity of that "nationhood" paragraph was not only intentional, it was intended to be so in just the way it struck you, just the way you describe your reaction: "It is not clear whether the 'sense of nationhood' you mention means the USA with Solid South, or the USA for northern vets and SS for Southerners, or both. Finally it appears you mean both." Just so—a gradual dawning, a gradual realization that it is both I mean. If of course it didnt work in its end effect, thats something else entirely; "sumpin wrong" indeed. Ambiguity is a dangerous thing to fool around with, but a useful device all the same.

As for the closeout narrowing-down on Davis, I think if you go back youll see that it balances the antebellum biography that opens Vol I, no more sympathetic and with the same narrow-focussed point of view. There, though, it was offset by the antebellum biography of Lincoln, and originally I intended to do two things I dropped at the end—one, a contrapuntal treatment of L's funeral, the train winding north and west while Davis fled southward; the other, an account of the growth of L's postwar reputation, interwoven with Davis's postwar life at Beauvoir. But once I had written Lincoln's death scene in such detail, once he had drawn that last long breath, I found I couldnt come back to him; it would be wrong for him to be anything but *gone* once the doctor put those half-dollars on his eyes—except, that is, the two closing touches: when the thieves attempt to steal his body for ransom, then when I re-quote him on the war as "philosophy to learn wisdom from," a final touch of the Lincoln music Davis couldnt match or even catch. I may have done wrong to drop my early plan for coming back to him, thereby offsetting the total concentration on Davis, but I dont think so. He's gone, man, gone—"like a turkey through the cawn," as Leadbelly says. Sometimes (and often they are the best of times) writing has to be done by instinct, and this was one of them. You get these instinctive reactions, and if you dont trust them youre not going with your talent....

Anyhow all goes well with me. I'm just wondering who in hell is going to pay $60 for a three-volume set of books about a war as useless and ugly in its way as Viet Nam was. Hoo!

August 2, 1974
542 E. Parkway S.
Memphis

Dear Walker,

...It's hard to explain how extraordinarily good I feel about my book; little things in it, I mean, that others will scarcely notice or just rush by in the reading—like the expression on Jeb Stuart's face when they jogged him off in an ambulance with a bullet through his liver; or Lee with dysentery, tossed about on his cot and crying out of Grant, "If I could just get one more pull at him!" Or Forrest at Brice's Crossroads. "Hit 'em on the ee-end," he told a brigade commander. Or Mary Lincoln at L's bedside, saying: "Send for Tad. He will speak to Tad, he loves him so."... So many things, and all of them seem to me so extraordinarily *good*. It's quite different from any reaction I ever had to a novel, I guess because I didnt make it up. I want everybody everywhere to read it so they can learn to love their country.

December 7, 1974
542 E. Parkway S.
Memphis

Dear Walker,

...A real geewhiz review by Louis Rubin in last week's New Republic, and Random tells me there's an all-stops-out one by John Barkham (syndicated chap) making the rounds of some 300-odd newspapers. I havent seen it yet but they tell me he makes me out to be an American Gibbon. Several of them have done that—no doubt on clew from me in the bibliographical note; but I'd much rather be known as an American Foote. Still, I'm a long way from looking any gifthorse in the mouth. Right now I'm involved in the tearing business of waiting around to find out whether I'll be rich or poor.

Percy to Foote

May 1, 1975

Dear Shelby,

… The Narrative looks immortal: almost too good; time will tell. I think what will make it survive is control and purity and economy of the writing, which you don't even notice at first, and which I reckon Thucydides and those other chaps had.

About the Contributors

MICHAEL BESCHLOSS is an award-winning historian and the author of eight books, including the acclaimed *New York Times* bestseller *The Conquerors: Roosevelt, Truman and the Destruction of Hitler's Germany, 1941–1945.*

KEN BURNS has been making award-winning documentary films for more than thirty years. His series about the Civil War, which has been honored with more than forty major film and television awards—including two Emmy Awards and two Grammy Awards, among dozens of others—heavily featured Shelby Foote.

MICHAEL ERIC DYSON, named by *Ebony* as one of the hundred most influential black Americans, is the author of sixteen books, including *Holler If You Hear Me, Is Bill Cosby Right?,* and *I May Not Get There With You: The True Martin Luther King, Jr.* He is currently University Professor of Sociology at Georgetown University. He lives in Washington, D.C.

ANNETTE GORDON-REED is a professor of history and professor of law at Harvard University, and the Carol K. Pforzheimer Professor at the Radcliffe Institute for Advanced Studies at Harvard.

DONALD E. GRAHAM is chairman of the board of The Washington Post Company.

BOB LOOMIS has been an editor at Random House for over fifty years. He was the editor of Shelby Foote's *The Civil War.*

JOHN M. MCCARDELL, JR., is vice-chancellor and president as well as professor of history at Sewanee: The University of the South. He is president emeritus and professor of history emeritus at Middlebury College, where he served as a faculty member from 1976 to 2010, and as president from 1991 to 2004. He earned an AB degree from Washington and Lee University, and a PhD from Harvard. He is the author of *The Idea of a Southern Nation,* winner of Allan Nevins Prize; co-editor of *A Master's Dues: Essays in Honor of David Herbert Donald;* and co-editor of *In the Cause of Liberty.* McCardell is a board member of the American Civil War Center at Historic Tredegar in Richmond, Virginia.

JON MEACHAM is executive vice president and executive editor at Random House. He is the author of the *New York Times* bestsellers *Franklin and Winston: An Intimate Portrait of an Epic Friendship; American Gospel: God, the Founding Fathers, and the Making of a Nation;* and *American Lion: Andrew Jackson in the White House,* which was awarded the 2009 Pulitzer Prize.

JULIA REED was born in Greenville, Mississippi. She is contributing editor at *Garden & Gun* and the author of three books, including *Queen of the Turtle Derby and Other Southern Phenomena* and *The House on First Street: My New Orleans Story.*

JAY TOLSON is currently the news director of Radio Free Europe/Radio Liberty in Prague. He is the author of *Pilgrim in the Ruins: A Life of Walker Percy* and editor of *The Correspondence of Shelby Foote & Walker Percy.*